CU00661107

2020

To Ma,
Happy Birthday
Love,
Timbles

Collins

ULTIMATE
SCRABBLE
BRAND Crossword Game
DICTIONARY
& WORD LIST

S

1

Published by Collins
An imprint of HarperCollins Publishers
Westerhill Road
Bishopbriggs
Glasgow G64 2QT

Fourth Edition 2019

10 9 8 7 6 5 4 3 2 1

© HarperCollins Publishers 2009, 2012, 2015, 2019

ISBN 978-0-00-832028-7

Collins® is a registered trademark of
HarperCollins Publishers Limited

SCRABBLE™ and associated trademarks and
trade dress are owned by, and used under
licence from, J. W. Spear & Sons Limited, a
subsidiary of Mattel, Inc. © 2019 Mattel, Inc.
All Rights Reserved.

www.harpercollins.co.uk/scrabble

Typeset by Davidson Publishing Solutions

Printed and bound at Replika Press Pvt. Ltd.

The contents of this publication are believed
correct at the time of printing. Nevertheless
the Publisher can accept no responsibility
for errors or omissions, changes in the detail
given or for any expense or loss thereby
caused.

HarperCollins does not warrant that any
website mentioned in this title will be
provided uninterrupted, that any website will
be error free, that defects will be corrected,
or that the website or the server that makes
it available are free of viruses or bugs. For full
terms and conditions please refer to the site
terms provided on the website.

A catalogue record for this book is available
from the British Library.

If you would like to comment on any aspect
of this book, please contact us at the given
address or online.
E-mail: puzzles@harpercollins.co.uk
 facebook.com/collinsdictionary
 @collinsdict

Scrabble Consultants
Darryl Francis
David Sutton

Editors
Robert Groves
Andrew Holmes
Helen Newstead
Mary O'Neill

Computing Support
Claire Dimeo
Agnieszka Urbanowicz

For the Publisher
Gerry Breslin
Kerry Ferguson

Contents

Introduction

This book is the most comprehensive Scrabble reference, comprising the game's complete word list together with definitions for words of up to nine letters. As such, this book is an invaluable tool for any competitive or club player, as well as the ultimate authority for settling disputes between those who play with their friends and family.

A staggering 279,496 words are listed in this book – representing an exhaustive list of every valid play in Scrabble. The book is divided into two sections: Section 1 contains every word of between two and nine letters, with either a definition or a cross reference to a defined root word at each entry, while Section 2 contains words of ten to fifteen letters, without definitions. In any Scrabble game, most words will be between two and nine letters, with longer words being formed only very rarely. Therefore, while this book lists every word that could conceivably be played on the Scrabble board, the main focus is on words that players are likely to have the opportunity to form from the seven letters on their rack and the words that are placed on the board during the game.

Section 1 thus allows every Scrabble player, whether a beginner or veteran, access to the definitions of all the most useful words in Scrabble, enabling them to learn words by meaning rather than simply as combinations of letters. For many players definitions are the key to remembering words, and to using them in Scrabble, and the ability to check meanings, inflections, and variant spellings will add interest to most social games.

Definitions in Section 1 are succinct and practical. In many cases, only a single definition is given, and in general only those parts of speech necessary for existing inflections are included. Cross-referred words include noun plurals, verb inflections, the comparative and superlative forms of adjectives, and variant spellings. Adjectives formed with obvious suffixes, such as -like and -less, are often cross-referred to the root word when the meaning is easily deduced.

Section 2 contains all of the longer words permissible in Scrabble, from ten to fifteen letters in length. Most of these words will only rarely appear on the board, due to their length, which is why definitions are not provided. The main function of this section of the book is to act as an indisputable authority when such longer words are played. Players may also wish to explore ways in which they can 'build' on words on the board by consulting Section 2. By exploring the ways in which shorter words can be combined with common suffixes such as -man, -woman, -like, -less, -ness and -lessness, and prefixes such as non-, un-, over- and under-, the keen Scrabble player can add an extra dimension to his or her game.

There is also a supplementary section, *Improving Your Scrabble Game*, in the centre of this book. This section includes expert advice on the best words for using up the **J**, **Q**, **X** and **Z** tiles, tips to help you outwit your opponent, and advice on how to achieve higher scores.

Unlike a conventional dictionary, every word in each section is listed in strict alphabetical order, regardless of the relationship between words. Thus there may be several, or many, words between the singular form of a noun and its plural. This strict alphabetization allows rapid checking of words – which is particularly important during Scrabble tournaments.

Collins would like to give warm thanks to Darryl Francis and David Sutton for their enormous contribution to the word list in this dictionary. They worked tirelessly with the editorial team to get this right. Any errors – and all the definitions in this book – are the responsibility of the Publisher.

Disclaimer
This dictionary and word list includes all playable Scrabble words, and no word is excluded on the grounds of religion, gender, race, or for any reason other than that it is an invalid word form for the game of Scrabble. The presence or exclusion of any word does not in any way represent the views of the Publisher, HarperCollins.

Using the Ultimate Scrabble Dictionary and Word List

Section 1 of this book includes all playable words of two to nine letters in length, in one straight alphabetical list. These words are either defined or cross-referred. Cross-referred words include noun plurals, verb inflections, the comparative and superlative forms of adjectives, and variant spellings. Adjectives formed with obvious suffixes such as *-like* and *-less* are often also cross-referred to the root word.

In *Collins Ultimate Scrabble Dictionary and Word List*, only a single definition is given for each part of speech, and in general only those parts of speech necessary for existing inflections are included. Definitions are based on those of the *Collins English Dictionary*, complete and unabridged, but have been shortened to make them more concise. Some definitions have been specifically written for this product.

Word order	*Collins Ultimate Scrabble Dictionary and Word List* is in strict alphabetical order.
Main entry words	printed in bold capitals, eg: **AA**
Accents	as English language Scrabble tiles are not accented, no accents are shown.
Parts of speech	shown in italics as an abbreviation, eg: **AA** *n*

when more than one part of speech is given, the change of part of speech is shown after an arrow, eg:

ABANDON *vb* desert or leave
▷ *n* lack of inhibition

the abbreviated parts of speech are:

adj	adjective
adv	adverb
conj	conjunction
interj	interjection
n	noun
pl n	plural noun
prep	preposition
pron	pronoun
vb	verb

Definitions	definitions are succinct, with abbreviations sometimes used:

Brit	British
eg	for example
esp	especially
orig	originally
Scot	Scottish
sing	singular
usu	usually
E	East or eastern
N	North or northern
S	South or southern
W	West or western

Cross-references	noun plurals, verb inflections, comparatives and superlatives, and derivatives are cross-referred to their root form, eg:

ABASH *vb* cause to feel ill at ease
ABASHES > ABASH
ABASHING > ABASH
ABASHLESS > ABASH
ABASHMENT > ABASH

Variant forms	variant forms and synonyms are cross-referred to the most commonly used form of a word, eg:

CAFTAN *same as* > KAFTAN

noun plurals, verb inflections, comparatives and superlatives, and derivatives of the variant form are all cross-referred to the root form of that particular variant, eg:

CAFTAN *same as* > KAFTAN
CAFTANS > CAFTAN

Phrases	when a word is most commonly used in a phrase, the phrase is given in italics and defined, eg:

BANGALORE as in *bangalore torpedo*
explosive device in a long metal tube

Offensive terms	*Collins Ultimate Scrabble Dictionary and Word List* includes words which may be deemed rude or offensive.

Other Scrabble Resources

Associations

World English-Language Scrabble Players Association (WESPA) – www.wespa.org

The WESPA website also provides access to resources for national associations, tournament organizers, players and youth players.

Association of British Scrabble Players (ABSP) – www.absp.org.uk

The ABSP website includes details of UK Scrabble clubs and UK tournaments.

North American Scrabble Players Association (NASPA) – www.scrabbleplayers.org

The NASPA website contains numerous word lists and lists of further Scrabble resources.

Mindsports Academy – www.mindsportsacademy.com

Facebook

Several Scrabble groups, including:

World English-Language Scrabble Players Association

Scrabble International

Scrabble Snippetz

Collins Scrabble Players

Mindsports Academy

Interactive Scrabble games

Internet Scrabble Club (ISC) – www.isc.ro

Mobile phone – Real Networks

Sky Interactive – Sky TV platform

iTouch / iPhone / Android / iPad – Electronic Arts (EA)

Collins Scrabble App

Download the Collins Official SCRABBLE™ app from the App Store.

Perfect for adjudication, solving and training.

Collins Scrabble online

www.collinsdictionary.com/scrabble

Tools and tips, plus *Collins Scrabble Word Finder*, giving instant access to all official playable Scrabble words and scores.

SECTION 1:

Words between 2 and 9 letters in length

Aa

AA n volcanic rock

AAH vb exclaim in pleasure

AAHED > AAH

AAHING > AAH

AAHS > AAH

AAL n Asian shrub or tree

AALII n bushy shrub

AALIIS > AALII

AALS > AAL

AARDVARK n S African anteater with long ears and snout

AARDVARKS > AARDVARK

AARDWOLF n nocturnal mammal

AARGH same as > ARGH

AARRGH same as > ARGH

AARRGHH same as > ARGH

AARTI n Hindu ceremony

AARTIS > AARTI

AAS > AA

AASVOGEL n South African bird of prey

AASVOGELS > AASVOGEL

AB n abdominal muscle

ABA n type of Syrian cloth

ABAC n mathematical diagram

ABACA n species of banana

ABACAS > ABACA

ABACI > ABACUS

ABACK adv towards the back; backwards

ABACS > ABAC

ABACTINAL adj situated away from the mouth

ABACTOR n cattle thief

ABACTORS > ABACTOR

ABACUS n mathematical instrument

ABACUSES > ABACUS

ABAFT adv by the rear of (a ship) ▷ adj closer to the stern

ABAKA n abaca

ABAKAS > ABAKA

ABALONE n edible sea creature

ABALONES > ABALONE

ABAMP same as > ABAMPERE

ABAMPERE n cgs unit of current

ABAMPERES > ABAMPERE

ABAMPS > ABAMP

ABAND vb abandon

ABANDED > ABAND

ABANDING > ABAND

ABANDON vb desert or leave ▷ n lack of inhibition

ABANDONED adj deserted

ABANDONEE n person to whom something is relinquished

ABANDONER > ABANDON

ABANDONS > ABANDON

ABANDS > ABAND

ABAPICAL adj away from or opposite the apex

ABAS > ABA

ABASE vb humiliate or degrade (oneself)

ABASED > ABASE

ABASEDLY > ABASE

ABASEMENT > ABASE

ABASER > ABASE

ABASERS > ABASE

ABASES > ABASE

ABASH vb cause to feel ill at ease

ABASHED adj embarrassed and ashamed

ABASHEDLY > ABASHED

ABASHES > ABASH

ABASHING > ABASH

ABASHLESS > ABASH

ABASHMENT > ABASH

ABASIA n disorder affecting ability to walk

ABASIAS > ABASIA

ABASING > ABASE

ABASK adv in pleasant warmth

ABATABLE > ABATE

ABATE vb make or become less strong

ABATED > ABATE

ABATEMENT n diminution or alleviation

ABATER > ABATE

ABATERS > ABATE

ABATES > ABATE

ABATING > ABATE

ABATIS n rampart of felled trees

ABATISES > ABATIS

ABATOR n person who effects an abatement

ABATORS > ABATOR

ABATTIS same as > ABATIS

ABATTISES > ABATTIS

ABATTOIR n place where animals are killed for food

ABATTOIRS > ABATTOIR

ABATTU adj dejected

ABATURE n trail left by hunted stag

ABATURES > ABATURE

ABAXIAL adj facing away from the axis

ABAXILE adj away from the axis

ABAYA n Arab outer garment

ABAYAS > ABAYA

ABB n yarn used in weaving

ABBA n Coptic bishop

ABBACIES > ABBACY

ABBACY n office of abbot or abbess

ABBAS > ABBA

ABBATIAL adj relating to abbot, abbess, or abbey

ABBE n French abbot

ABBED adj displaying strong abdominal muscles

ABBES > ABBE

ABBESS n nun in charge of a convent

ABBESSES > ABBESS

ABBEY n dwelling place of monks or nuns

ABBEYS > ABBEY

ABBOT n head of an abbey of monks

ABBOTCIES > ABBOT

ABBOTCY > ABBOT

ABBOTS > ABBOT

ABBOTSHIP > ABBOT

ABBS > ABB

ABCEE n alphabet

ABCEES > ABCEE

ABCOULOMB n unit of electric charge

ABDABS n highly nervous state

ABDICABLE > ABDICATE

ABDICANT n one who abdicates

ABDICANTS > ABDICANT

ABDICATE vb give up a responsibility

ABDICATED > ABDICATE

ABDICATES > ABDICATE

ABDICATOR > ABDICATE

ABDOMEN n part of the body

ABDOMENS > ABDOMEN

ABDOMINA > ABDOMEN

ABDOMINAL > ABDOMEN

ABDUCE vb abduct

ABDUCED > ABDUCE

ABDUCENS n as in abducens nerve cranial nerve

ABDUCENT adj (of a muscle) abducting

ABDUCES > ABDUCE

ABDUCING > ABDUCE

ABDUCT vb carry off, kidnap

ABDUCTED > ABDUCT

ABDUCTEE > ABDUCT

ABDUCTEES > ABDUCT

ABDUCTING > ABDUCT

ABDUCTION n act of taking someone away

ABDUCTOR > ABDUCT

ABDUCTORS > ABDUCT

ABDUCTS > ABDUCT

ABEAM adj at right angles to a ship

ABEAR vb bear or behave

ABEARING > ABEAR

ABEARS > ABEAR

ABED adv in bed

ABEGGING adj in the act of begging

ABEIGH adv aloof

ABELE n white poplar tree

ABELES > ABELE

ABELIA n garden plant with pink or white flowers

ABELIAN > ABELIA

ABELIAS > ABELIA

ABELMOSK n tropical plant

ABELMOSKS > ABELMOSK

ABER n estuary

ABERNETHY n crisp unleavened biscuit

ABERRANCE > ABERRANT

ABERRANCY > ABERRANT

ABERRANT adj showing aberration ▷ n person whose behaviour is aberrant

ABERRANTS > ABERRANT

ABERRATE vb deviate from what is normal

ABERRATED > ABERRATE

ABERRATES > ABERRATE

ABERS > ABER

ABESSIVE n grammatical case indicating absence

ABESSIVES > ABESSIVE

ABET vb help in wrongdoing

ABETMENT > ABET

ABETMENTS > ABET

ABETS > ABET

ABETTAL > ABET

ABETTALS > ABET

ABETTED > ABET

ABETTER > ABET

ABETTERS > ABET

ABETTING > ABET

ABETTOR > ABET

ABETTORS > ABET

ABEYANCE n state of being suspended

ABEYANCES > ABEYANCE

ABEYANCY n abeyance

ABEYANT > ABEYANCE

ABFARAD n unit of capacitance

ABFARADS > ABFARAD

ABHENRIES > ABHENRY

ABHENRY n unit of inductance

ABHENRYS > ABHENRY

ABHOR vb detest utterly

ABHORRED > ABHOR

ABHORRENT adj hateful, loathsome

ABHORRER > ABHOR

ABHORRERS > ABHOR
ABHORRING > ABHOR
ABHORS > ABHOR
ABID > ABIDE
ABIDANCE > ABIDE
ABIDANCES > ABIDE
ABIDDEN > ABIDE
ABIDE *vb* endure, put up with
ABIDED > ABIDE
ABIDER > ABIDE
ABIDERS > ABIDE
ABIDES > ABIDE
ABIDING *adj* lasting ▷ *n* action of one who abides
ABIDINGLY > ABIDING
ABIDINGS > ABIDING
ABIES *n* fir tree
ABIETES > ABIES
ABIETIC *adj* as in *abietic acid* yellowish powder
ABIGAIL *n* maid for a lady
ABIGAILS > ABIGAIL
ABILITIES > ABILITY
ABILITY *n* competence, power
ABIOGENIC *adj* abiogenetic
ABIOSES > ABIOSIS
ABIOSIS *n* absence of life
ABIOTIC > ABIOSIS
ABITUR *n* German examination
ABITURS > ABITUR
ABJECT *adj* utterly miserable ▷ *vb* throw down
ABJECTED > ABJECT
ABJECTING > ABJECT
ABJECTION > ABJECT
ABJECTLY > ABJECT
ABJECTS > ABJECT
ABJOINT *vb* cut off
ABJOINTED > ABJOINT
ABJOINTS > ABJOINT
ABJURE *vb* deny or renounce on oath
ABJURED > ABJURE
ABJURER > ABJURE
ABJURERS > ABJURE
ABJURES > ABJURE
ABJURING > ABJURE
ABLATE *vb* remove by ablation
ABLATED > ABLATE
ABLATES > ABLATE
ABLATING > ABLATE
ABLATION *n* removal of an organ
ABLATIONS > ABLATION
ABLATIVAL > ABLATIVE
ABLATIVE *n* case of nouns ▷ *adj* relating to the ablative case
ABLATIVES > ABLATIVE
ABLATOR *n* heat shield of a space craft
ABLATORS > ABLATOR
ABLAUT *n* vowel gradation
ABLAUTS > ABLAUT
ABLAZE *adj* burning fiercely ▷ *adv* on fire
ABLE *adj* capable, competent ▷ *vb* enable
ABLED *adj* having physical powers
ABLEGATE *n* papal envoy
ABLEGATES > ABLEGATE

ABLEISM *n* discrimination against disabled people
ABLEISMS > ABLEISM
ABLEIST > ABLEISM
ABLEISTS > ABLEISM
ABLER > ABLE
ABLES > ABLE
ABLEST > ABLE
ABLET *n* freshwater fish
ABLETS > ABLET
ABLING > ABLE
ABLINGS *adv* possibly
ABLINS *adv* Scots word meaning perhaps
ABLOOM *adj* in flower
ABLOW *adj* blooming
ABLUENT *n* substance used for cleansing
ABLUENTS > ABLUENT
ABLUSH *adj* blushing
ABLUTED *adj* washed thoroughly
ABLUTION *n* ritual washing of a priest's hands
ABLUTIONS > ABLUTION
ABLY *adv* competently or skilfully
ABMHO *n* unit of electrical conductance
ABMHOS > ABMHO
ABNEGATE *vb* deny to oneself
ABNEGATED > ABNEGATE
ABNEGATES > ABNEGATE
ABNEGATOR > ABNEGATE
ABNORMAL *adj* not normal or usual ▷ *n* abnormal person or thing
ABNORMALS > ABNORMAL
ABNORMITY > ABNORMAL
ABNORMOUS > ABNORMAL
ABO *n* offensive word for an Aborigine
ABOARD *adv* onto a vehicle ▷ *adj* onto a vehicle
ABODE *n* home, dwelling ▷ *vb* forebode
ABODED > ABODE
ABODEMENT > ABODE
ABODES > ABODE
ABODING > ABODE
ABOHM *n* unit of resistance
ABOHMS > ABOHM
ABOIDEAU *n* dyke with sluicegate
ABOIDEAUS > ABOIDEAU
ABOIDEAUX > ABOIDEAU
ABOIL *adj* boiling
ABOITEAU *same as* **>** ABOIDEAU
ABOITEAUS > ABOITEAU
ABOITEAUX > ABOITEAU
ABOLISH *vb* do away with
ABOLISHED > ABOLISH
ABOLISHER > ABOLISH
ABOLISHES > ABOLISH
ABOLITION *n* act of abolishing
ABOLLA *n* Roman cloak
ABOLLAE > ABOLLA
ABOLLAS > ABOLLA
ABOMA *n* South American snake
ABOMAS > ABOMA
ABOMASA > ABOMASUM
ABOMASAL > ABOMASUM

ABOMASI > ABOMASUS
ABOMASUM *n* compartment of a stomach
ABOMASUS *n* abomasum
ABOMINATE *vb* dislike intensely **ABONDANCE** *same as* **>** ABUNDANCE
ABOON *Scots word for* **>** ABOVE
ABORAL *adj* away from the mouth
ABORALLY > ABORAL
ABORD *vb* accost
ABORDED > ABORD
ABORDING > ABORD
ABORDS > ABORD
ABORE > ABEAR
ABORIGEN *n* aborigine
ABORIGENS > ABORIGEN
ABORIGIN *n* aborigine
ABORIGINE *n* original inhabitant
ABORIGINS > ABORIGIN
ABORNE *adj* Shakespearean form of auburn
ABORNING > ABEAR
ABORT *vb* terminate ▷ *n* termination or failure
ABORTED > ABORT
ABORTEE *n* woman having an abortion
ABORTEES > ABORTEE
ABORTER > ABORT
ABORTERS > ABORT
ABORTING > ABORT
ABORTION *n* operation to end a pregnancy
ABORTIONS > ABORTION
ABORTIVE *adj* unsuccessful
ABORTS > ABORT
ABORTUARY *n* place where abortions are performed
ABORTUS *n* aborted fetus
ABORTUSES > ABORTUS
ABOS > ABO
ABOUGHT > ABY
ABOULIA *same as* **>** ABULIA
ABOULIAS > ABOULIA
ABOULIC > ABOULIA
ABOUND *vb* be plentiful
ABOUNDED > ABOUND
ABOUNDING > ABOUND
ABOUNDS > ABOUND
ABOUT *adv* nearly, approximately
ABOUTS *prep* about
ABOVE *adv* higher (than) ▷ *n* something that is above
ABOVES > ABOVE
ABRACHIA *n* condition of having no arms
ABRACHIAS > ABRACHIA
ABRADABLE > ABRADE
ABRADANT > ABRADE
ABRADANTS > ABRADE
ABRADE *vb* wear down by friction
ABRADED > ABRADE
ABRADER > ABRADE
ABRADERS > ABRADE
ABRADES > ABRADE
ABRADING > ABRADE
ABRAID *vb* awake
ABRAIDED > ABRAID
ABRAIDING > ABRAID
ABRAIDS > ABRAID
ABRAM *adj* auburn

ABRASAX *same as* **>** ABRAXAS
ABRASAXES > ABRASAX
ABRASION *n* scraped area on the skin
ABRASIONS > ABRASION
ABRASIVE *adj* harsh and unpleasant ▷ *n* substance for cleaning
ABRASIVES > ABRASIVE
ABRAXAS *n* ancient charm composed of Greek letters
ABRAXASES > ABRAXAS
ABRAY *vb* awake
ABRAYED > ABRAY
ABRAYING > ABRAY
ABRAYS > ABRAY
ABRAZO *n* embrace
ABRAZOS > ABRAZO
ABREACT *vb* alleviate through abreaction
ABREACTED > ABREACT
ABREACTS > ABREACT
ABREAST *adj* side by side
ABREGE *n* abridgment
ABREGES > ABREGE
ABRI *n* shelter or place of refuge, esp in wartime
ABRICOCK *n* apricot
ABRICOCKS > ABRICOCK
ABRIDGE *vb* shorten by using fewer words
ABRIDGED > ABRIDGE
ABRIDGER > ABRIDGE
ABRIDGERS > ABRIDGE
ABRIDGES > ABRIDGE
ABRIDGING > ABRIDGE
ABRIM *adj* full to the brim
ABRIN *n* poisonous compound
ABRINS > ABRIN
ABRIS > ABRI
ABROACH *adj* (of a cask, barrel, etc) tapped
ABROAD *adv* in a foreign country ▷ *adj* in general circulation ▷ *n* foreign place
ABROADS > ABROAD
ABROGABLE *adj* able to be abrogated
ABROGATE *vb* cancel (a law or agreement) formally
ABROGATED > ABROGATE
ABROGATES > ABROGATE
ABROGATOR > ABROGATE
ABROOKE *vb* bear or tolerate
ABROOKED > ABROOKE
ABROOKES > ABROOKE
ABROOKING > ABROOKE
ABROSIA *n* condition involving refusal to eat
ABROSIAS > ABROSIA
ABRUPT *adj* sudden, unexpected ▷ *n* abyss
ABRUPTER > ABRUPT
ABRUPTEST > ABRUPT
ABRUPTION *n* breaking off of a part
ABRUPTLY > ABRUPT
ABRUPTS > ABRUPT
ABS > AB
ABSCESS *n* inflamed swelling ▷ *vb* form a swelling
ABSCESSED > ABSCESS
ABSCESSES > ABSCESS
ABSCIND *vb* cut off
ABSCINDED > ABSCIND

ABSCINDS > ABSCIND
ABSCISE vb separate or be separated by abscission
ABSCISED > ABSCISE
ABSCISES > ABSCISE
ABSCISIC adj as in abscisic acid type of acid
ABSCISIN n plant hormone
ABSCISING > ABSCISE
ABSCISINS > ABSCISIN
ABSCISS same as > ABSCISSA
ABSCISSA n cutting off
ABSCISSAE > ABSCISSA
ABSCISSAS > ABSCISSA
ABSCISSE same as > ABSCISSA
ABSCISSES > ABSCISSE
ABSCISSIN n plant hormone
ABSCOND vb leave secretly
ABSCONDED > ABSCOND
ABSCONDER > ABSCOND
ABSCONDS > ABSCOND
ABSEIL vb go down by a rope ⊳ n instance of abseiling
ABSEILED > ABSEIL
ABSEILER n person who abseils
ABSEILERS > ABSEILER
ABSEILING > ABSEIL
ABSEILS > ABSEIL
ABSENCE n being away
ABSENCES > ABSENCE
ABSENT adj not present ⊳ vb stay away
ABSENTED > ABSENT
ABSENTEE n person who is not present
ABSENTEES > ABSENTEE
ABSENTER > ABSENT
ABSENTERS > ABSENT
ABSENTING > ABSENT
ABSENTLY adv in an absent-minded manner
ABSENTS > ABSENT
ABSEY n alphabet
ABSEYS > ABSEY
ABSINTH same as > ABSINTHE
ABSINTHE n liqueur
ABSINTHES > ABSINTHE
ABSINTHS > ABSINTH
ABSIT n leave from college
ABSITS > ABSIT
ABSOLUTE adj complete, perfect ⊳ n something absolute
ABSOLUTER > ABSOLUTE
ABSOLUTES > ABSOLUTE
ABSOLVE vb declare to be free from sin
ABSOLVED > ABSOLVE
ABSOLVENT n something that absolves
ABSOLVER > ABSOLVE
ABSOLVERS > ABSOLVE
ABSOLVES > ABSOLVE
ABSOLVING > ABSOLVE
ABSONANT adj unnatural and unreasonable
ABSORB vb soak up (a liquid)
ABSORBANT n absorbent substance
ABSORBATE n absorbed substance

ABSORBED adj engrossed
ABSORBENT adj able to absorb liquid ⊳ n substance that absorbs
ABSORBER n thing that absorbs
ABSORBERS > ABSORBER
ABSORBING adj occupying one's attention
ABSORBS > ABSORB
ABSTAIN vb choose not to do something
ABSTAINED > ABSTAIN
ABSTAINER > ABSTAIN
ABSTAINS > ABSTAIN
ABSTERGE vb cleanse
ABSTERGED > ABSTERGE
ABSTERGES > ABSTERGE
ABSTINENT adj refraining from a certain activity
ABSTRACT adj existing as an idea ⊳ n summary ⊳ vb summarize
ABSTRACTS > ABSTRACT
ABSTRICT vb release
ABSTRICTS > ABSTRICT
ABSTRUSE adj not easy to understand
ABSTRUSER > ABSTRUSE
ABSURD adj incongruous or ridiculous ⊳ n conception of the world
ABSURDER > ABSURD
ABSURDEST > ABSURD
ABSURDISM n belief that life is meaningless
ABSURDIST > ABSURDISM
ABSURDITY > ABSURD
ABSURDLY > ABSURD
ABSURDS > ABSURD
ABTHANE n ancient Scottish church territory
ABTHANES > ABTHANE
ABUBBLE adj bubbling
ABUILDING adj being built
ABULIA n pathological inability to take decisions
ABULIAS > ABULIA
ABULIC > ABULIA
ABUNA n male head of Ethiopian family
ABUNAS > ABUNA
ABUNDANCE n copious supply
ABUNDANCY n abundance
ABUNDANT adj plentiful
ABUNE Scots word for > ABOVE
ABURST adj bursting
ABUSABLE > ABUSE
ABUSAGE n wrong use
ABUSAGES > ABUSAGE
ABUSE vb use wrongly ⊳ n prolonged ill-treatment
ABUSED > ABUSE
ABUSER > ABUSE
ABUSERS > ABUSE
ABUSES > ABUSE
ABUSING > ABUSE
ABUSION n wrong use or deception
ABUSIONS > ABUSION
ABUSIVE adj rude or insulting
ABUSIVELY > ABUSIVE
ABUT vb be next to or touching
ABUTILON n shrub

ABUTILONS > ABUTILON
ABUTMENT n construction supporting the end of a bridge
ABUTMENTS > ABUTMENT
ABUTS > ABUT
ABUTTAL same as > ABUTMENT
ABUTTALS > ABUTTAL
ABUTTED > ABUT
ABUTTER n owner of adjoining property
ABUTTERS > ABUTTER
ABUTTING > ABUT
ABUZZ adj noisy, busy with activity etc
ABVOLT n unit of potential difference in the electromagnetic system
ABVOLTS > ABVOLT
ABWATT n unit of power
ABWATTS > ABWATT
ABY vb pay the penalty for
ABYE same as > ABY
ABYEING > ABYE
ABYES > ABYE
ABYING > ABY
ABYS > ABY
ABYSM archaic word for > ABYSS
ABYSMAL adj extremely bad, awful
ABYSMALLY > ABYSMAL
ABYSMS > ABYSM
ABYSS n very deep hole or chasm
ABYSSAL adj of the ocean depths
ABYSSES > ABYSS
ACACIA n tree or shrub
ACACIAS > ACACIA
ACADEME n place of learning
ACADEMES > ACADEME
ACADEMIA n academic world
ACADEMIAS > ACADEMIA
ACADEMIC adj of a university ⊳ n lecturer at a university
ACADEMICS > ACADEMIC
ACADEMIES > ACADEMY
ACADEMISM n adherence to rules
ACADEMIST > ACADEMY
ACADEMY n society for arts or sciences
ACAI n berry
ACAIS > ACAI
ACAJOU n type of mahogany
ACAJOUS > ACAJOU
ACALCULIA n inability to make calculations
ACALEPH n invertebrate
ACALEPHAE > ACALEPHE
ACALEPHAN > ACALEPH
ACALEPHE n acaleph
ACALEPHES > ACALEPHE
ACALEPHS > ACALEPH
ACANTH n acanthus
ACANTHA n thorn or prickle
ACANTHAE > ACANTHA
ACANTHAS > ACANTHA
ACANTHI > ACANTHUS
ACANTHIN n organic chemical
ACANTHINE adj of or resembling an acanthus

ACANTHINS > ACANTHIN
ACANTHOID adj resembling a spine
ACANTHOUS adj of an acanthus
ACANTHS > ACANTH
ACANTHUS n prickly plant
ACAPNIA n lack of carbon dioxide
ACAPNIAS > ACAPNIA
ACARBOSE n diabetes medicine
ACARBOSES > ACARBOSE
ACARI > ACARUS
ACARIAN > ACARUS
ACARIASES > ACARIASIS
ACARIASIS n infestation of hair
ACARICIDE n any drug for killing acarids
ACARID n small arachnid ⊳ adj of these arachnids
ACARIDAN same as > ACARID
ACARIDANS > ACARIDAN
ACARIDEAN > ACARID
ACARIDIAN > ACARID
ACARIDS > ACARID
ACARINE n acarid
ACARINES > ACARINE
ACAROID adj resembling a mite
ACAROLOGY n study of mites and ticks
ACARPOUS adj producing no fruit
ACARUS n type of mite
ACATER n buyer of provisions
ACATERS > ACATER
ACATES n provisions
ACATHISIA same as > AKATHISIA
ACATOUR n buyer of provisions
ACATOURS > ACATOUR
ACAUDAL adj having no tail
ACAUDATE same as > ACAUDAL
ACAULINE adj having no stem
ACAULOSE same as > ACAULINE
ACAULOUS adj having a short stem
ACCA n academic
ACCABLE adj dejected or beaten
ACCAS > ACCA
ACCEDE vb consent or agree (to)
ACCEDED > ACCEDE
ACCEDENCE > ACCEDE
ACCEDER > ACCEDE
ACCEDERS > ACCEDE
ACCEDES > ACCEDE
ACCEDING > ACCEDE
ACCEND vb set alight
ACCENDED > ACCEND
ACCENDING > ACCEND
ACCENDS > ACCEND
ACCENSION > ACCEND
ACCENT n style of pronunciation ⊳ vb place emphasis on
ACCENTED > ACCENT
ACCENTING > ACCENT

a

ACCENTOR n songbird

ACCENTORS > ACCENTOR

ACCENTS > ACCENT

ACCENTUAL adj of accents

ACCEPT vb receive willingly

ACCEPTANT adj receiving willingly

ACCEPTED adj generally approved

ACCEPTEE n person who has been accepted

ACCEPTEES > ACCEPTEE

ACCEPTER > ACCEPT

ACCEPTERS > ACCEPT

ACCEPTING > ACCEPT

ACCEPTIVE adj ready to accept

ACCEPTOR n person signing a bill of exchange

ACCEPTORS > ACCEPTOR

ACCEPTS > ACCEPT

ACCESS n right to approach ▷ vb obtain data

ACCESSARY same as > ACCESSORY

ACCESSED > ACCESS

ACCESSES > ACCESS

ACCESSING > ACCESS

ACCESSION n taking up a position ▷ vb make a record

ACCESSORY n supplementary part ▷ adj supplementary

ACCIDENCE n inflectional morphology

ACCIDENT n mishap, often causing injury

ACCIDENTS > ACCIDENT

ACCIDIA same as > ACCIDIE

ACCIDIAS > ACCIDIA

ACCIDIE n spiritual sloth

ACCIDIES > ACCIDIE

ACCINGE vb put a belt around

ACCINGED > ACCINGE

ACCINGES > ACCINGE

ACCINGING > ACCINGE

ACCIPITER n hawk

ACCITE vb summon

ACCITED > ACCITE

ACCITES > ACCITE

ACCITING > ACCITE

ACCLAIM vb applaud, praise ▷ n enthusiastic approval

ACCLAIMED > ACCLAIM

ACCLAIMER > ACCLAIM

ACCLAIMS > ACCLAIM

ACCLIMATE vb adapt to a new climate

ACCLIVITY n upward slope

ACCLIVOUS > ACCLIVITY

ACCLOY vb choke or clog

ACCLOYED > ACCLOY

ACCLOYING > ACCLOY

ACCLOYS > ACCLOY

ACCOAST vb accost

ACCOASTED > ACCOAST

ACCOASTS > ACCOAST

ACCOIED > ACCOY

ACCOIL n welcome ▷ vb gather together

ACCOILS > ACCOIL

ACCOLADE n award ▷ vb give an award

ACCOLADED > ACCOLADE

ACCOLADES > ACCOLADE

ACCOMPANY vb go along with

ACCOMPT vb account

ACCOMPTED > ACCOMPT

ACCOMPTS > ACCOMPT

ACCORAGE vb encourage

ACCORAGED > ACCORAGE

ACCORAGES > ACCORAGE

ACCORD n agreement, harmony ▷ vb fit in with

ACCORDANT adj in conformity or harmony

ACCORDED > ACCORD

ACCORDER > ACCORD

ACCORDERS > ACCORD

ACCORDING adj in proportion

ACCORDION n portable instrument

ACCORDS > ACCORD

ACCOST vb approach and speak to ▷ n greeting

ACCOSTED > ACCOST

ACCOSTING > ACCOST

ACCOSTS > ACCOST

ACCOUNT n report, description ▷ vb judge to be

ACCOUNTED > ACCOUNT

ACCOUNTS > ACCOUNT

ACCOURAGE vb encourage

ACCOURT vb entertain

ACCOURTED > ACCOURT

ACCOURTS > ACCOURT

ACCOUTER same as > ACCOUTRE

ACCOUTERS > ACCOUTER

ACCOUTRE vb provide with equipment

ACCOUTRED > ACCOUTRE

ACCOUTRES > ACCOUTRE

ACCOY vb soothe

ACCOYED > ACCOY

ACCOYING > ACCOY

ACCOYLD vb past tense of accoil

ACCOYS > ACCOY

ACCREDIT vb give official recognition to

ACCREDITS > ACCREDIT

ACCRETE vb grow together

ACCRETED > ACCRETE

ACCRETES > ACCRETE

ACCRETING > ACCRETE

ACCRETION n gradual growth

ACCRETIVE > ACCRETION

ACCREW vb accrue

ACCREWED > ACCREW

ACCREWING > ACCREW

ACCREWS > ACCREW

ACCROIDES n red alcohol-soluble resin

ACCRUABLE > ACCRUE

ACCRUAL n act of accruing

ACCRUALS > ACCRUAL

ACCRUE vb increase gradually

ACCRUED > ACCRUE

ACCRUES > ACCRUE

ACCRUING > ACCRUE

ACCUMBENT adj lying against

ACCURACY n representation of truth

ACCURATE adj exact, correct

ACCURSE vb curse

ACCURSED adj under a curse

ACCURSES > ACCURSE

ACCURSING > ACCURSE

ACCURST same as > ACCURSED

ACCUSABLE > ACCUSE

ACCUSABLY > ACCUSE

ACCUSAL n accusation

ACCUSALS > ACCUSAL

ACCUSANT n person who accuses

ACCUSANTS > ACCUSANT

ACCUSE vb charge with wrongdoing

ACCUSED n person accused of a crime

ACCUSER > ACCUSE

ACCUSERS > ACCUSE

ACCUSES > ACCUSE

ACCUSING > ACCUSE

ACCUSTOM vb make used to

ACCUSTOMS > ACCUSTOM

ACE n playing card with one symbol on it ▷ adj excellent ▷ vb serve an ace in racquet sports

ACED > ACE

ACEDIA same as > ACCIDIE

ACEDIAS > ACEDIA

ACELDAMA n place with ill feeling

ACELDAMAS > ACELDAMA

ACELLULAR adj not made up of or containing cells

ACENTRIC adj without a centre ▷ n acentric chromosome or fragment

ACENTRICS > ACENTRIC

ACEPHALIC adj having no head or one that is reduced and indistinct, as certain insect larvae

ACEQUIA n irrigation ditch

ACEQUIAS > ACEQUIA

ACER n type of tree

ACERATE same as > ACERATED

ACERATED adj having sharp points

ACERB adj bitter

ACERBATE vb embitter or exasperate

ACERBATED > ACERBATE

ACERBATES > ACERBATE

ACERBER > ACERB

ACERBEST > ACERB

ACERBIC adj harsh or bitter

ACERBITY n bitter speech or temper

ACEROLA n cherry-like fruit

ACEROLAS > ACEROLA

ACEROSE adj shaped like a needle

ACEROUS same as > ACEROSE

ACERS > ACER

ACERVATE adj growing in heaps or clusters

ACERVULI > ACERVULUS

ACERVULUS n spore-producing part of plant

ACES > ACE

ACESCENCE > ACESCENT

ACESCENCY > ACESCENT

ACESCENT adj slightly sour or turning sour ▷ n something that is turning sour

ACESCENTS > ACESCENT

ACETA > ACETUM

ACETABULA n deep cuplike cavities on the side of the hipbones that receive the head of the thighbone

ACETAL n colourless liquid

ACETALS > ACETAL

ACETAMID same as > ACETAMIDE

ACETAMIDE n white or colourless soluble deliquescent crystalline compound

ACETAMIDS > ACETAMID

ACETATE n salt or ester of acetic acid

ACETATED adj combined with acetic acid

ACETATES > ACETATE

ACETIC adj of or involving vinegar

ACETIFIED > ACETIFY

ACETIFIER > ACETIFY

ACETIFIES > ACETIFY

ACETIFY vb become vinegar

ACETIN n type of acetate

ACETINS > ACETIN

ACETONE n colourless liquid used as a solvent

ACETONES > ACETONE

ACETONIC > ACETONE

ACETOSE same as > ACETOUS

ACETOUS adj containing acetic acid

ACETOXYL n medicine used to treat acne

ACETOXYLS > ACETOXYL

ACETUM n solution that has dilute acetic acid as solvent

ACETYL n type of monovalent radical

ACETYLATE vb introduce an acetyl group into (a chemical compound)

ACETYLENE n colourless flammable gas used in welding metals

ACETYLIC > ACETYL

ACETYLIDE n any of a class of carbides in which the carbon is present as a diatomic divalent ion

ACETYLS > ACETYL

ACH interj Scots expression of surprise

ACHAENIA > ACHAENIUM

ACHAENIUM n achene

ACHAGE n pain

ACHAGES > ACHAGE

ACHALASIA n failure of the cardiac sphincter of the oesophagus to relax, resulting in difficulty in swallowing

ACHAR n spicy pickle made from mango

ACHARNE adj furiously violent

ACHARS > ACHAR

ACHARYA n religious teacher and spiritual guide

ACHARYAS > ACHARYA

ACHATES same as > ACATES

ACHE n dull continuous pain ▷ vb be in or cause continuous dull pain

ACHED > ACHE
ACHENE n type of fruit
ACHENES > ACHENE
ACHENIA > ACHENIUM
ACHENIAL > ACHENE
ACHENIUM n achene
ACHENIUMS > ACHENIUM
ACHES > ACHE
ACHIER > ACHY
ACHIEST > ACHY
ACHIEVE vb gain by hard work or ability
ACHIEVED > ACHIEVE
ACHIEVER > ACHIEVE
ACHIEVERS > ACHIEVE
ACHIEVES > ACHIEVE
ACHIEVING > ACHIEVE
ACHILLEA n type of plant with white, yellow, or purple flowers, often grown in gardens
ACHILLEAS > ACHILLEA
ACHIMENES n tropical plant of the S America with showy red, blue, or white tubular flowers
ACHINESS > ACHY
ACHING > ACHE
ACHINGLY > ACHE
ACHINGS > ACHE
ACHIOTE n annatto
ACHIOTES > ACHIOTE
ACHIRAL adj of a tuber producing arrowroot
ACHKAN n man's coat in India
ACHKANS > ACHKAN
ACHOLIA n bile condition
ACHOLIAS > ACHOLIA
ACHOO n sound of a sneeze
ACHOOS > ACHOO
ACHROMAT n lens designed to bring light of two wavelengths to the same focal point
ACHROMATS > ACHROMAT
ACHROMIC adj colourless
ACHROMOUS same as **>** ACHROMIC
ACHY adj affected by a continuous dull pain
ACICLOVIR same as **>** ACYCLOVIR
ACICULA n needle-shaped part
ACICULAE > ACICULA
ACICULAR > ACICULA
ACICULAS > ACICULA
ACICULATE adj having aciculae
ACICULUM n bristle that supports the appendages of some polychaetes
ACICULUMS > ACICULUM
ACID n corrosive compound that combines with a base to form a salt ▷ adj containing acid
ACIDEMIA n abnormally high level of acid in blood
ACIDEMIAS > ACIDEMIA
ACIDER > ACID
ACIDEST > ACID
ACIDHEAD n person who uses LSD
ACIDHEADS > ACIDHEAD
ACIDIC adj containing acid
ACIDIER > ACIDY

ACIDIEST > ACIDY
ACIDIFIED > ACIDIFY
ACIDIFIER > ACIDIFY
ACIDIFIES > ACIDIFY
ACIDIFY vb convert into acid
ACIDITIES > ACIDITY
ACIDITY n quality of being acid
ACIDLY > ACID
ACIDNESS > ACID
ACIDOPHIL adj (of cells or cell contents) easily stained by acid dyes ▷ n acidophil organism
ACIDOSES > ACIDOSIS
ACIDOSIS n abnormal increase in the acidity of the blood and bodily fluids
ACIDOTIC > ACIDOSIS
ACIDS > ACID
ACIDULATE vb make slightly acid or sour
ACIDULENT same as **>** ACIDULOUS
ACIDULOUS adj rather sour
ACIDURIA n abnormally high level of acid in urine
ACIDURIAS > ACIDURIA
ACIDY adj resembling or containing acid
ACIERAGE n iron-plating of metal
ACIERAGES > ACIERAGE
ACIERATE vb change (iron) into steel
ACIERATED > ACIERATE
ACIERATES > ACIERATE
ACIFORM adj shaped like a needle
ACINAR adj of small sacs
ACING > ACE
ACINI > ACINUS
ACINIC > ACINUS
ACINIFORM adj shaped like a bunch of grapes
ACINOSE > ACINUS
ACINOUS > ACINUS
ACINUS n parts of a gland
ACKEE n tropical tree
ACKEES > ACKEE
ACKER same as **>** ACCA
ACKERS > ACKER
ACKNEW > ACKNOW
ACKNOW vb recognize
ACKNOWING > ACKNOW
ACKNOWN > ACKNOW
ACKNOWNE adj aware
ACKNOWS > ACKNOW
ACLINIC adj unbending
ACMATIC adj highest or ultimate
ACME n highest point of achievement or excellence
ACMES > ACME
ACMIC same as **>** ACMATIC
ACMITE n chemical with pyramid-shaped crystals
ACMITES > ACMITE
ACNE n pimply skin disease
ACNED adj marked by acne
ACNES > ACNE
ACNODAL > ACNODE
ACNODE n mathematical term
ACNODES > ACNODE
ACOCK adv cocked

ACOELOUS adj not having a stomach
ACOEMETI n order of monks
ACOLD adj feeling cold
ACOLUTHIC adj of an afterimage
ACOLYTE n follower or attendant
ACOLYTES > ACOLYTE
ACOLYTH n acolyte
ACOLYTHS > ACOLYTH
ACONITE n poisonous plant with hoodlike flowers
ACONITES > ACONITE
ACONITIC > ACONITE
ACONITINE n poison made from aconite
ACONITUM same as **>** ACONITE
ACONITUMS > ACONITUM
ACORN n nut of the oak tree
ACORNED adj covered with acorns
ACORNS > ACORN
ACOSMISM n belief that no world exists outside the mind
ACOSMISMS > ACOSMISM
ACOSMIST > ACOSMISM
ACOSMISTS > ACOSMISM
ACOUCHI n South American rodent with a white-tipped tail
ACOUCHIES > ACOUCHY
ACOUCHIS > ACOUCHI
ACOUCHY same as **>** ACOUCHI
ACOUSTIC adj of sound and hearing
ACOUSTICS n science of sounds
ACQUAINT vb make familiar, inform
ACQUAINTS > ACQUAINT
ACQUEST n something acquired
ACQUESTS > ACQUEST
ACQUIESCE vb agree to what someone wants
ACQUIGHT vb acquit
ACQUIGHTS > ACQUIGHT
ACQUIRAL > ACQUIRE
ACQUIRALS > ACQUIRE
ACQUIRE vb gain, get
ACQUIRED > ACQUIRE
ACQUIREE n one who acquires
ACQUIREES > ACQUIREE
ACQUIRER > ACQUIRE
ACQUIRERS > ACQUIRE
ACQUIRES > ACQUIRE
ACQUIRING > ACQUIRE
ACQUIS n as in acquis communautaire European Union laws
ACQUIST n acquisition
ACQUISTS > ACQUIST
ACQUIT vb pronounce (someone) innocent
ACQUITE vb acquit
ACQUITES > ACQUITE
ACQUITING > ACQUITE
ACQUITS > ACQUIT
ACQUITTAL n deliverance and release of a person appearing before a court on a charge of crime, as by a finding of not guilty

ACQUITTED > ACQUIT
ACQUITTER > ACQUIT
ACRASIA n lack of willpower
ACRASIAS > ACRASIA
ACRASIN n chemical
ACRASINS > ACRASIN
ACRATIC > ACRASIA
ACRAWL adv crawling
ACRE n measure of land, 4840 square yards (4046.86 square metres)
ACREAGE n land area in acres ▷ adj of or relating to a large allotment of land, esp in a rural area
ACREAGES > ACREAGE
ACRED adj having acres of land
ACRES > ACRE
ACRID adj pungent, bitter
ACRIDER > ACRID
ACRIDEST > ACRID
ACRIDIN n acridine
ACRIDINE n colourless crystalline solid
ACRIDINES > ACRIDINE
ACRIDINS > ACRIDIN
ACRIDITY > ACRID
ACRIDLY > ACRID
ACRIDNESS > ACRID
ACRIMONY n bitterness and resentment felt about something
ACRITARCH n type of fossil
ACRITICAL adj not critical
ACRO n event where acrobatic skiing moves are performed to music
ACROBAT n person skilled in gymnastic feats requiring agility and balance
ACROBATIC > ACROBAT
ACROBATS > ACROBAT
ACRODONT adj (of reptile teeth) fused at the base to the jawbones ▷ n acrodont reptile
ACRODONTS > ACRODONT
ACRODROME adj (of the veins of a leaf) running parallel to the edges of the leaf and fusing at the tip
ACROGEN n flowerless plant
ACROGENIC > ACROGEN
ACROGENS > ACROGEN
ACROLECT n most correct form of language
ACROLECTS > ACROLECT
ACROLEIN n colourless or yellowish flammable poisonous pungent liquid
ACROLEINS > ACROLEIN
ACROLITH n wooden sculpture with the head, hands, and feet in stone
ACROLITHS > ACROLITH
ACROMIA > ACROMION
ACROMIAL > ACROMION
ACROMION n outermost edge of the spine of the shoulder blade
ACRONIC adj acronical
ACRONICAL adj occurring at sunset
ACRONYCAL same as **>** ACRONICAL

ACRONYM n word formed from the initial letters of other words, such as NASA

ACRONYMIC > ACRONYM

ACRONYMS > ACRONYM

ACROPETAL adj (of leaves and flowers) produced in order from the base upwards so that the youngest are at the apex

ACROPHOBE n person afraid of heights

ACROPHONY n use of symbols to represent sounds

ACROPOLIS n citadel of an ancient Greek city

ACROS > ACRO

ACROSOMAL > ACROSOME

ACROSOME n structure in reproductive cell

ACROSOMES > ACROSOME

ACROSPIRE n first shoot developing from the plumule of a germinating grain seed

ACROSS adv from side to side (of)

ACROSTIC n lines of writing in which the first or last letters of each line spell a word or saying

ACROSTICS > ACROSTIC

ACROTER n plinth

ACROTERIA n acroters

ACROTERS > ACROTER

ACROTIC adj of a surface

ACROTISM n absence of pulse

ACROTISMS > ACROTISM

ACRYLATE n chemical compound in plastics and resins

ACRYLATES > ACRYLATE

ACRYLIC adj (synthetic fibre, paint, etc) made from acrylic acid ▷ n man-made fibre used for clothes and blankets

ACRYLICS > ACRYLIC

ACRYLYL n type of monovalent group

ACRYLYLS > ACRYLYL

ACT n thing done ▷ vb do something

ACTA pl n minutes of meeting

ACTABLE > ACT

ACTANT n grammatical term

ACTANTS > ACTANT

ACTED > ACT

ACTIN n protein

ACTINAL adj part of a jellyfish

ACTINALLY > ACTINAL

ACTING n art of an actor ▷ adj temporarily performing the duties of

ACTINGS > ACTING

ACTINIA n type of sea anemone

ACTINIAE > ACTINIA

ACTINIAN n sea anemone

ACTINIANS > ACTINIAN

ACTINIAS > ACTINIA

ACTINIC adj (of radiation) producing a photochemical effect

ACTINIDE n member of the actinide series

ACTINIDES > ACTINIDE

ACTINISM > ACTINIC

ACTINISMS > ACTINIC

ACTINIUM n radioactive chemical element

ACTINIUMS > ACTINIUM

ACTINOID adj having a radiate form, as a sea anemone or starfish ▷ n member of the actinide series

ACTINOIDS > ACTINOID

ACTINON same as > ACTINIDE

ACTINONS > ACTINON

ACTINOPOD n type of single-celled invertebrate

ACTINS > ACTIN

ACTION n process of doing something ▷ vb put into effect

ACTIONED > ACTION

ACTIONER n film with a fast-moving plot, usually containing scenes of violence

ACTIONERS > ACTIONER

ACTIONING > ACTION

ACTIONIST n activist

ACTIONS > ACTION

ACTIVATE vb make active

ACTIVATED > ACTIVATE

ACTIVATES > ACTIVATE

ACTIVATOR > ACTIVATE

ACTIVE adj moving, working ▷ n active form of a verb

ACTIVELY > ACTIVE

ACTIVES > ACTIVE

ACTIVISE same as > ACTIVIZE

ACTIVISED > ACTIVISE

ACTIVISES > ACTIVISE

ACTIVISM n taking direct or militant action to achieve a political or social end

ACTIVISMS > ACTIVISM

ACTIVIST > ACTIVISM

ACTIVISTS > ACTIVISM

ACTIVITY n state of being active

ACTIVIZE vb make active

ACTIVIZED > ACTIVIZE

ACTIVIZES > ACTIVIZE

ACTON n jacket

ACTONS > ACTON

ACTOR n person who acts in a play, film, etc

ACTORISH > ACTOR

ACTORLIER > ACTORLY

ACTORLY adj characteristic of an actor

ACTORS > ACTOR

ACTRESS n woman who acts in a play, film, broadcast, etc

ACTRESSES > ACTRESS

ACTRESSY adj exaggerated and affected in manner

ACTS > ACT

ACTUAL adj existing in reality

ACTUALISE same as > ACTUALIZE

ACTUALIST n person dealing in hard fact

ACTUALITE n humorous word for truth

ACTUALITY n reality

ACTUALIZE vb make actual or real

ACTUALLY adv really, indeed

ACTUALS pl n commercial commodities that can be bought and used

ACTUARIAL > ACTUARY

ACTUARIES > ACTUARY

ACTUARY n statistician who calculates insurance risks

ACTUATE vb start up (a device)

ACTUATED > ACTUATE

ACTUATES > ACTUATE

ACTUATING > ACTUATE

ACTUATION > ACTUATE

ACTUATOR > ACTUATE

ACTUATORS > ACTUATE

ACTURE n action

ACTURES > ACTURE

ACUATE adj sharply pointed ▷ vb sharpen

ACUATED > ACUATE

ACUATES > ACUATE

ACUATING > ACUATE

ACUITIES > ACUITY

ACUITY n keenness of vision or thought

ACULEATE adj cutting ▷ n insect, such as a bee, with a sting

ACULEATED same as > ACULEATE

ACULEATES > ACULEATE

ACULEI > ACULEUS

ACULEUS n prickle or spine, such as the thorn of a rose

ACUMEN n ability to make good judgments

ACUMENS > ACUMEN

ACUMINATE adj narrowing to a sharp point, as some types of leaf ▷ vb make pointed or sharp

ACUMINOUS > ACUMEN

ACUPOINT n points on the body stimulated with acupuncture or acupressure

ACUPOINTS > ACUPOINT

ACUSHLA n Irish endearment

ACUSHLAS > ACUSHLA

ACUTANCE n physical rather than subjective measure of the sharpness of a photographic image

ACUTANCES > ACUTANCE

ACUTE adj severe ▷ n accent over a letter to indicate the quality or length of its sound, as over e in café

ACUTELY > ACUTE

ACUTENESS > ACUTE

ACUTER > ACUTE

ACUTES > ACUTE

ACUTEST > ACUTE

ACYCLIC adj not cyclic

ACYCLOVIR n antiviral drug

ACYL n member of the monovalent group of atoms RCO-

ACYLATE vb add acyl group to

ACYLATED > ACYLATE

ACYLATES > ACYLATE

ACYLATING > ACYLATE

ACYLATION n introduction into a chemical compound of an acyl group

ACYLOIN n organic chemical compound

ACYLOINS > ACYLOIN

ACYLS > ACYL

AD n advertisement

ADAGE n wise saying, proverb

ADAGES > ADAGE

ADAGIAL > ADAGE

ADAGIO adv (to be played) slowly and gracefully ▷ n movement or piece to be performed slowly

ADAGIOS > ADAGIO

ADAMANCE n being adamant

ADAMANCES > ADAMANCE

ADAMANCY n being adamant

ADAMANT adj unshakable in determination or purpose ▷ n any extremely hard or apparently unbreakable substance

ADAMANTLY > ADAMANT

ADAMANTS > ADAMANT

ADAMSITE n yellow poisonous crystalline solid that readily sublimes

ADAMSITES > ADAMSITE

ADAPT vb alter for new use or new conditions

ADAPTABLE > ADAPT

ADAPTED > ADAPT

ADAPTER same as > ADAPTOR

ADAPTERS > ADAPTER

ADAPTING > ADAPT

ADAPTION n adaptation

ADAPTIONS > ADAPTION

ADAPTIVE > ADAPT

ADAPTOGEN n any of various natural substances used in herbal medicine to normalize and regulate the systems of the body

ADAPTOR n device for connecting several electrical appliances to a single socket

ADAPTORS > ADAPTOR

ADAPTS > ADAPT

ADAW vb subdue

ADAWED > ADAW

ADAWING > ADAW

ADAWS > ADAW

ADAXIAL adj facing the axis

ADAYS adv daily

ADBOT n spyware that collects information about a person to display targeted adverts

ADBOTS > ADBOT

ADD vb combine (numbers or quantities)

ADDABLE > ADD

ADDAX n antelope

ADDAXES > ADDAX

ADDEBTED adj indebted

ADDED > ADD

ADDEDLY > ADD

ADDEEM vb adjudge

ADDEEMED > ADDEEM

ADDEEMING > ADDEEM

ADDEEMS > ADDEEM

ADDEND n any of a set of numbers that is to be added

ADDENDA > ADDENDUM
ADDENDS > ADDEND
ADDENDUM *n* addition
ADDENDUMS > ADDENDUM
ADDER *n* small poisonous snake
ADDERBEAD *n* type of prehistoric ornamental bead
ADDERS > ADDER
ADDERWORT *n* plant of the dock family
ADDIBLE *adj* addable
ADDICT *n* person who is unable to stop doing or taking something ▷ *vb* cause (someone or oneself) to become dependent (on something)
ADDICTED > ADDICT
ADDICTING > ADDICT
ADDICTION *n* condition of being abnormally dependent on some habit
ADDICTIVE *adj* causing addiction
ADDICTS > ADDICT
ADDIES > ADDY
ADDING *n* act or instance of addition ▷ *adj* of, for, or relating to addition
ADDINGS > ADDING
ADDIO *interj* farewell ▷ *n* cry of addio
ADDIOS > ADDIO
ADDITION *n* adding
ADDITIONS > ADDITION
ADDITIVE *n* something added, esp to a foodstuff, to improve it or prevent deterioration ▷ *adj* characterized or produced by addition
ADDITIVES > ADDITIVE
ADDITORY *adj* adding to something
ADDLE *vb* become muddled ▷ *adj* indicating a muddled state
ADDLED > ADDLE
ADDLEMENT > ADDLE
ADDLES > ADDLE
ADDLING > ADDLE
ADDOOM *vb* adjudge
ADDOOMED > ADDOOM
ADDOOMING > ADDOOM
ADDOOMS > ADDOOM
ADDORSED *adj* back to back
ADDRESS *n* place where a person lives ▷ *vb* mark the destination, as on an envelope
ADDRESSED > ADDRESS
ADDRESSEE *n* person addressed
ADDRESSER > ADDRESS
ADDRESSES > ADDRESS
ADDRESSOR > ADDRESS
ADDREST > ADDRESS
ADDS > ADD
ADDUCE *vb* mention something as evidence or proof
ADDUCED > ADDUCE
ADDUCENT > ADDUCE
ADDUCER > ADDUCE
ADDUCERS > ADDUCE
ADDUCES > ADDUCE

ADDUCIBLE > ADDUCE
ADDUCING > ADDUCE
ADDUCT *vb* draw towards medial axis ▷ *n* compound
ADDUCTED > ADDUCT
ADDUCTING > ADDUCT
ADDUCTION > ADDUCT
ADDUCTIVE > ADDUCE
ADDUCTOR *n* muscle that adducts
ADDUCTORS > ADDUCTOR
ADDUCTS > ADDUCT
ADDY *n* e-mail address
ADEEM *vb* cancel
ADEEMED > ADEEM
ADEEMING > ADEEM
ADEEMS > ADEEM
ADELGID *n* type of small sap-feeding insect
ADELGIDS > ADELGID
ADEMPTION *n* failure of a specific legacy, as by a testator disposing of the subject matter in their lifetime
ADENINE *n* chemical
ADENINES > ADENINE
ADENITIS *n* inflammation of a gland or lymph node
ADENOID *adj* of or resembling a gland
ADENOIDAL *adj* having a nasal voice caused by swollen adenoids
ADENOIDS *pl n* tissue at the back of the throat
ADENOMA *n* tumour occurring in glandular tissue
ADENOMAS > ADENOMA
ADENOMATA > ADENOMA
ADENOSES > ADENOSIS
ADENOSINE *n* nucleoside formed by the condensation of adenine and ribose
ADENOSIS *n* disease of glands
ADENYL *n* enzyme
ADENYLATE *n* type of enzyme
ADENYLIC *adj* as in *adenylic acid* nucleotide consisting of adenine, ribose or deoxyribose, and a phosphate group
ADENYLS > ADENYL
ADEPT *n* very skilful (person) ▷ *adj* proficient in something requiring skill
ADEPTER > ADEPT
ADEPTEST > ADEPT
ADEPTLY > ADEPT
ADEPTNESS > ADEPT
ADEPTS > ADEPT
ADEQUACY > ADEQUATE
ADEQUATE *adj* sufficient, enough
ADERMIN *n* vitamin
ADERMINS > ADERMIN
ADESPOTA *n* anonymous writings
ADESSIVE *n* grammatical case denoting place
ADESSIVES > ADESSIVE
ADHAN *n* call to prayer
ADHANS > ADHAN
ADHARMA *n* wickedness
ADHARMAS > ADHARMA

ADHERABLE > ADHERE
ADHERE *vb* stick (to)
ADHERED > ADHERE
ADHERENCE > ADHERE
ADHEREND *n* something attached by adhesive
ADHERENDS > ADHEREND
ADHERENT *n* devotee, follower ▷ *adj* sticking or attached
ADHERENTS > ADHERENT
ADHERER > ADHERE
ADHERERS > ADHERE
ADHERES > ADHERE
ADHERING > ADHERE
ADHESION *n* sticking (to)
ADHESIONS > ADHESION
ADHESIVE *n* substance used to stick things together ▷ *adj* able to stick to things
ADHESIVES > ADHESIVE
ADHIBIT *vb* administer or apply
ADHIBITED > ADHIBIT
ADHIBITS > ADHIBIT
ADHOCRACY *n* management that responds to urgent problems rather than planning to avoid them
ADIABATIC *adj* (of a thermodynamic process) taking place without loss or gain of heat ▷ *n* curve or surface on a graph representing the changes in two or more characteristics (such as pressure and volume) of a system undergoing an adiabatic process
ADIAPHORA *n* matters of indifference
ADIEU *n* goodbye
ADIEUS > ADIEU
ADIEUX > ADIEU
ADIOS *sentence substitute* Spanish for goodbye ▷ *n* goodbye
ADIOSES > ADIOS
ADIPIC *adj* as in *adipic acid* crystalline solid used in the preparation of nylon
ADIPOCERE *n* waxlike substance formed during decomposition
ADIPOCYTE *n* fat cell that accumulates and stores fats
ADIPOSE *adj* of or containing fat ▷ *n* animal fat
ADIPOSES > ADIPOSIS
ADIPOSIS *n* obesity
ADIPOSITY > ADIPOSE
ADIPOUS *adj* made of fat
ADIPSIA *n* complete lack of thirst
ADIPSIAS > ADIPSIA
ADIT *n* shaft into a mine, for access or drainage
ADITS > ADIT
ADJACENCE > ADJACENT
ADJACENCY > ADJACENT
ADJACENT *adj* near or next (to) ▷ *n* side lying between a specified angle and a right angle in a right-angled triangle
ADJACENTS > ADJACENT

ADJECTIVE *n* word that adds information about a noun or pronoun ▷ *adj* additional or dependent
ADJIGO *n* SW Australian yam plant with edible tubers
ADJIGOS > ADJIGO
ADJOIN *vb* be next to
ADJOINED > ADJOIN
ADJOINING *adj* being in contact
ADJOINS > ADJOIN
ADJOINT *n* type of mathematical matrix
ADJOINTS > ADJOINT
ADJOURN *vb* close (a court) at the end of a session
ADJOURNED > ADJOURN
ADJOURNS > ADJOURN
ADJUDGE *vb* declare (to be)
ADJUDGED > ADJUDGE
ADJUDGES > ADJUDGE
ADJUDGING > ADJUDGE
ADJUNCT *n* something incidental added to something else
ADJUNCTLY > ADJUNCT
ADJUNCTS > ADJUNCT
ADJURE *vb* command (to do)
ADJURED > ADJURE
ADJURER > ADJURE
ADJURERS > ADJURE
ADJURES > ADJURE
ADJURING > ADJURE
ADJUROR > ADJURE
ADJURORS > ADJURE
ADJUST *vb* adapt to new conditions
ADJUSTED > ADJUST
ADJUSTER > ADJUST
ADJUSTERS > ADJUST
ADJUSTING > ADJUST
ADJUSTIVE > ADJUST
ADJUSTOR > ADJUST
ADJUSTORS > ADJUST
ADJUSTS > ADJUST
ADJUTAGE *n* nozzle
ADJUTAGES > ADJUTAGE
ADJUTANCY > ADJUTANT
ADJUTANT *n* army officer in charge of routine administration
ADJUTANTS > ADJUTANT
ADJUVANCY > ADJUVANT
ADJUVANT *adj* aiding or assisting ▷ *n* something that aids or assists
ADJUVANTS > ADJUVANT
ADLAND *n* advertising industry and the people who work in it
ADLANDS > ADLAND
ADMAN *n* man who works in advertising
ADMASS *n* mass advertising
ADMASSES > ADMASS
ADMEASURE *vb* measure out (land, etc) as a share
ADMEN > ADMAN
ADMIN *n* administration
ADMINICLE *n* something contributing to prove a point without itself being complete proof
ADMINS > ADMIN
ADMIRABLE *adj* deserving or inspiring admiration

ADMIRABLY > ADMIRABLE

ADMIRAL n highest naval rank

ADMIRALS > ADMIRAL

ADMIRALTY n office or jurisdiction of an admiral

ADMIRANCE n admiration

ADMIRE vb regard with esteem and approval

ADMIRED > ADMIRE

ADMIRER > ADMIRE

ADMIRERS > ADMIRE

ADMIRES > ADMIRE

ADMIRING > ADMIRE

ADMISSION n permission to enter

ADMISSIVE > ADMISSION

ADMIT vb confess, acknowledge

ADMITS > ADMIT

ADMITTED > ADMIT

ADMITTEE n one who admits

ADMITTEES > ADMITTEE

ADMITTER > ADMIT

ADMITTERS > ADMIT

ADMITTING > ADMIT

ADMIX vb mix or blend

ADMIXED > ADMIX

ADMIXES > ADMIX

ADMIXING > ADMIX

ADMIXT > ADMIX

ADMIXTURE n mixture

ADMONISH vb reprove sternly

ADMONITOR > ADMONISH

ADNASCENT adj growing with something else

ADNATE adj growing closely attached to an adjacent part or organ

ADNATION > ADNATE

ADNATIONS > ADNATE

ADNEXA pl n organs adjoining the uterus

ADNEXAL > ADNEXA

ADNOMINAL n word modifying a noun ▷ adj of or relating to an adnoun

ADNOUN n adjective used as a noun

ADNOUNS > ADNOUN

ADO n fuss, trouble

ADOBE n sun-dried brick

ADOBELIKE > ADOBE

ADOBES > ADOBE

ADOBO n Philippine dish

ADOBOS > ADOBO

ADONIS n beautiful young man

ADONISE vb adorn

ADONISED > ADONISE

ADONISES > ADONISE

ADONISING > ADONISE

ADONIZE vb adorn

ADONIZED > ADONIZE

ADONIZES > ADONIZE

ADONIZING > ADONIZE

ADOORS adv at the door

ADOPT vb take (someone else's child) as one's own

ADOPTABLE > ADOPT

ADOPTED adj having been adopted

ADOPTEE n one who has been adopted

ADOPTEES > ADOPTEE

ADOPTER n person who adopts

ADOPTERS > ADOPTER

ADOPTING > ADOPT

ADOPTION > ADOPT

ADOPTIONS > ADOPT

ADOPTIOUS adj adopted

ADOPTIVE adj related by adoption

ADOPTS > ADOPT

ADORABLE adj very attractive

ADORABLY > ADORABLE

ADORATION n deep love or esteem

ADORE vb love intensely

ADORED > ADORE

ADORER > ADORE

ADORERS > ADORE

ADORES > ADORE

ADORING adj displaying intense love

ADORINGLY > ADORING

ADORKABLE adj charmingly unfashionable

ADORN vb decorate, embellish

ADORNED > ADORN

ADORNER > ADORN

ADORNERS > ADORN

ADORNING > ADORN

ADORNMENT > ADORN

ADORNS > ADORN

ADOS > ADO

ADOWN adv down

ADOZE adv asleep

ADPRESS vb press together

ADPRESSED > ADPRESS

ADPRESSES > ADPRESS

ADRAD adj afraid

ADRATE n price or tariff that businesses pay to advertise

ADRATES > ADRATE

ADREAD vb dread

ADREADED > ADREAD

ADREADING > ADREAD

ADREADS > ADREAD

ADRED adj filled with dread

ADRENAL adj near the kidneys ▷ n adrenal gland

ADRENALIN n hormone secreted by the adrenal glands in response to stress

ADRENALLY > ADRENAL

ADRENALS > ADRENAL

ADRIFT adv drifting

ADROIT adj quick and skilful

ADROITER > ADROIT

ADROITEST > ADROIT

ADROITLY > ADROIT

ADRY adj dry

ADS > AD

ADSCRIPT n serf

ADSCRIPTS > ADSCRIPT

ADSORB vb condense to form a thin film

ADSORBATE n substance that has been or is to be adsorbed on a surface

ADSORBED > ADSORB

ADSORBENT adj capable of adsorption ▷ n material, such as activated charcoal, on which adsorption can occur

ADSORBER > ADSORB

ADSORBERS > ADSORB

ADSORBING > ADSORB

ADSORBS > ADSORB

ADSPEAK n kind of language or jargon used in advertising or in advertisements

ADSPEAKS > ADSPEAK

ADSUKI same as > ADZUKI

ADSUKIS > ADSUKI

ADSUM sentence substitute I am present

ADUKI same as > ADZUKI

ADUKIS > ADUKI

ADULARIA n white or colourless glassy variety of orthoclase

ADULARIAS > ADULARIA

ADULATE vb flatter or praise obsequiously

ADULATED > ADULATE

ADULATES > ADULATE

ADULATING > ADULATE

ADULATION n uncritical admiration

ADULATOR > ADULATE

ADULATORS > ADULATE

ADULATORY adj expressing praise, esp obsequiously

ADULT adj fully grown, mature ▷ n adult person or animal

ADULTERER n person who has committed adultery

ADULTERY n sexual unfaithfulness of a spouse

ADULTHOOD > ADULT

ADULTLIKE > ADULT

ADULTLY > ADULT

ADULTNESS > ADULT

ADULTRESS n US word for a female adulterer

ADULTS > ADULT

ADUMBRAL adj shadowy

ADUMBRATE vb outline

ADUNC adj hooked

ADUNCATE adj hooked

ADUNCATED adj hooked

ADUNCITY n quality of being hooked

ADUNCOUS adj hooked

ADUST vb dry up or darken by heat

ADUSTED > ADUST

ADUSTING > ADUST

ADUSTS > ADUST

ADVANCE vb go or bring forward ▷ n forward movement ▷ adj done or happening before an event

ADVANCED adj at a late stage in development

ADVANCER > ADVANCE

ADVANCERS > ADVANCE

ADVANCES > ADVANCE

ADVANCING > ADVANCE

ADVANTAGE n more favourable position or state

ADVECT vb move horizontally in air

ADVECTED > ADVECT

ADVECTING > ADVECT

ADVECTION n transferring of heat in a horizontal stream of gas

ADVECTIVE > ADVECTION

ADVECTS > ADVECT

ADVENE vb add as extra

ADVENED > ADVENE

ADVENES > ADVENE

ADVENING > ADVENE

ADVENT n arrival

ADVENTIVE adj (of a species) introduced to a new area and not yet established there ▷ n such a plant or animal

ADVENTS > ADVENT

ADVENTURE n exciting and risky undertaking or exploit ▷ vb take a risk or put at risk

ADVERB n word that adds information about a verb, adjective, or other adverb

ADVERBIAL n word or group of words with the grammatical role of an adverb ▷ adj of or relating to an adverb

ADVERBS > ADVERB

ADVERSARY n opponent or enemy

ADVERSE adj unfavourable

ADVERSELY > ADVERSE

ADVERSER > ADVERSE

ADVERSEST > ADVERSE

ADVERSITY n very difficult or hard circumstances

ADVERT n advertisement ▷ vb draw attention (to)

ADVERTED > ADVERT

ADVERTENT adj heedful

ADVERTING > ADVERT

ADVERTISE vb present or praise (goods or services) to the public in order to encourage sales

ADVERTIZE same as > ADVERTISE

ADVERTS > ADVERT

ADVEW vb look at

ADVEWED > ADVEW

ADVEWING > ADVEW

ADVEWS > ADVEW

ADVICE n recommendation as to what to do

ADVICEFUL > ADVICE

ADVICES > ADVICE

ADVISABLE adj prudent, sensible

ADVISABLY > ADVISABLE

ADVISE vb offer advice to

ADVISED adj considered, thought-out

ADVISEDLY > ADVISED

ADVISEE n person receiving advice

ADVISEES > ADVISEE

ADVISER n person who offers advice, eg on careers to students or school pupils

ADVISERS > ADVISER

ADVISES > ADVISE

ADVISING > ADVISE

ADVISINGS > ADVISE

ADVISOR same as > ADVISER

ADVISORS > ADVISOR

ADVISORY adj giving advice ▷ n statement giving advice or a warning

ADVOCAAT n liqueur with a raw egg base

ADVOCAATS > ADVOCAAT

ADVOCACY n active support of a cause or course of action

ADVOCATE vb propose or recommend ▷ n person who publicly supports a cause
ADVOCATED > ADVOCATE
ADVOCATES > ADVOCATE
ADVOCATOR n person who advocates
ADVOUTRER n adulterer
ADVOUTRY n adultery
ADVOWSON n right of presentation to a vacant benefice
ADVOWSONS > ADVOWSON
ADWARD vb award
ADWARDED > ADWARD
ADWARDING > ADWARD
ADWARDS > ADWARD
ADWARE n computer software
ADWARES > ADWARE
ADWOMAN n woman working in advertising
ADWOMEN > ADWOMAN
ADYNAMIA n loss of vital power or strength, esp as the result of illness
ADYNAMIAS > ADYNAMIA
ADYNAMIC > ADYNAMIA
ADYTA > ADYTUM
ADYTUM n sacred place in ancient temples
ADZ same as > ADZE
ADZE n woodworking tool ▷ vb use an adze
ADZED > ADZE
ADZELIKE adj like an adze
ADZES > ADZE
ADZING > ADZE
ADZUKI n type of plant
ADZUKIS > ADZUKI
AE determiner one
AECIA > AECIUM
AECIAL > AECIUM
AECIDIA > AECIDIUM
AECIDIAL > AECIDIUM
AECIDIUM same as > AECIUM
AECIUM n area of some fungi
AEDES n type of mosquito which transmits yellow fever and dengue
AEDICULE n door or a window framed by columns and a pediment
AEDICULES > AEDICULE
AEDILE n magistrate of ancient Rome
AEDILES > AEDILE
AEDINE adj of a species of mosquito
AEFALD adj single
AEFAULD adj single
AEGIRINE n green mineral
AEGIRINES > AEGIRINE
AEGIRITE n green mineral
AEGIRITES > AEGIRITE
AEGIS n sponsorship, protection
AEGISES > AEGIS
AEGLOGUE n eclogue
AEGLOGUES > AEGLOGUE
AEGROTAT n certificate allowing a candidate to pass an examination missed through illness
AEGROTATS > AEGROTAT
AEMULE vb emulate

AEMULED > AEMULE
AEMULES > AEMULE
AEMULING > AEMULE
AENEOUS adj brass-coloured or greenish-gold
AENEUS n aquarium fish
AENEUSES > AENEUS
AEOLIAN adj of or relating to the wind
AEOLIPILE n device illustrating the reactive forces of a gas jet: usually a spherical vessel mounted so as to rotate and equipped with angled exit pipes from which steam within it escapes
AEOLIPYLE same as > AEOLIPILE
AEON n immeasurably long period of time
AEONIAN adj everlasting
AEONIC > AEON
AEONS > AEON
AEPYORNIS n type of large extinct flightless bird whose remains have been found in Madagascar
AEQUORIN n type of protein
AEQUORINS > AEQUORIN
AERADIO n radio system for pilots
AERADIOS > AERADIO
AERATE vb put gas into (a liquid), as when making a fizzy drink
AERATED > AERATE
AERATES > AERATE
AERATING > AERATE
AERATION > AERATE
AERATIONS > AERATE
AERATOR > AERATE
AERATORS > AERATE
AERIAL adj in, from, or operating in the air ▷ n metal pole, wire, etc, for receiving or transmitting radio or TV signals
AERIALIST n trapeze artist or tightrope walker
AERIALITY > AERIAL
AERIALLY > AERIAL
AERIALS > AERIAL
AERIE a variant spelling (esp US) of > EYRIE
AERIED adj in a very high place
AERIER > AERY
AERIES > AERIE
AERIEST > AERY
AERIFIED > AERIFY
AERIFIES > AERIFY
AERIFORM adj having the form of air
AERIFY vb change or cause to change into a gas
AERIFYING > AERIFY
AERILY > AERY
AERO n aerodynamic vehicle or component
AEROBAT n person who does stunt flying
AEROBATIC adj pertaining to stunt flying
AEROBATS > AEROBAT
AEROBE n organism that requires oxygen to survive

AEROBES > AEROBE
AEROBIA > AEROBIUM
AEROBIC adj designed for or relating to aerobics
AEROBICS n exercises designed to increase the amount of oxygen in the blood
AEROBIONT n organism needing oxygen to live
AEROBIUM same as > AEROBE
AEROBOMB n bomb dropped from aircraft
AEROBOMBS > AEROBOMB
AEROBOT n unmanned aircraft used esp in space exploration
AEROBOTS > AEROBOT
AEROBRAKE vb use airbrakes to slow aircraft
AEROBUS n monorail suspended by an overhead cable
AEROBUSES > AEROBUS
AERODART n metal arrow dropped from an aircraft as a weapon
AERODARTS > AERODART
AERODROME n small airport
AERODUCT n air duct
AERODUCTS > AERODUCT
AERODYNE n aircraft that derives its lift from aerodynamic forces
AERODYNES > AERODYNE
AEROFOIL n part of an aircraft, such as the wing, designed to give lift
AEROFOILS > AEROFOIL
AEROGEL n colloid
AEROGELS > AEROGEL
AEROGRAM n airmail letter on a single sheet of paper that seals to form an envelope
AEROGRAMS > AEROGRAM
AEROGRAPH n airborne instrument recording meteorological conditions
AEROLITE n stony meteorite consisting of silicate minerals
AEROLITES > AEROLITE
AEROLITH n meteorite
AEROLITHS > AEROLITH
AEROLITIC > AEROLITE
AEROLOGIC > AEROLOGY
AEROLOGY n study of the atmosphere, particularly its upper layers
AEROMANCY n using weather observation to foretell the future
AEROMETER n instrument for determining the mass or density of a gas, esp air
AEROMETRY n branch of physics concerned with the mechanical properties of gases, esp air
AEROMOTOR n aircraft engine
AERONAUT n person who flies in a lighter-than-air craft, esp the pilot or navigator
AERONAUTS > AERONAUT

AERONOMER n scientist studying atmosphere
AERONOMIC > AERONOMY
AERONOMY n science of the earth's upper atmosphere
AEROPAUSE n region of the upper atmosphere above which aircraft cannot fly
AEROPHAGY n spasmodic swallowing of air
AEROPHOBE n person suffering from aerophobia
AEROPHONE n wind instrument
AEROPHORE n device for playing a wind instrument
AEROPHYTE another name for > EPIPHYTE
AEROPLANE n powered flying vehicle with fixed wings
AEROPULSE n type of jet engine
AEROS > AERO
AEROSAT n communications satellite
AEROSATS > AEROSAT
AEROSCOPE n device for observing the atmosphere
AEROSHELL n parachute used to slow spacecraft
AEROSOL n pressurized can from which a substance can be dispensed as a fine spray
AEROSOLS > AEROSOL
AEROSPACE n earth's atmosphere and space beyond ▷ adj of rockets or space vehicles
AEROSPIKE n type of rocket engine
AEROSTAT n lighter-than-air craft, such as a balloon
AEROSTATS > AEROSTAT
AEROTAXES > AEROTAXIS
AEROTAXIS n movement away from or towards oxygen
AEROTONE n bath incorporating air jets for massage
AEROTONES > AEROTONE
AEROTRAIN n train driven by a jet engine
AERUGO (esp of old bronze) another name for > VERDIGRIS
AERUGOS > AERUGO
AERY adj lofty, insubstantial, or visionary
AESC n rune
AESCES > AESC
AESCULIN n chemical in horse-chestnut bark
AESCULINS > AESCULIN
AESIR pl n Norse gods
AESTHESES > AESTHESIS
AESTHESIA n normal ability to experience sensation, perception, or sensitivity
AESTHESIS variant of > ESTHESIS
AESTHETE n person who has or affects an extravagant love of art
AESTHETES > AESTHETE

AESTHETIC *adj* relating to the appreciation of art and beauty ▷ *n* principle or set of principles relating to the appreciation of art and beauty

AESTIVAL *adj* of or occurring in summer

AESTIVATE *vb* pass the summer

AETATIS *adj* at the age of

AETHER *same as* > ETHER

AETHEREAL *a variant spelling of* > ETHEREAL

AETHERIC > AETHER

AETHERS > AETHER

AETIOLOGY *n* philosophy or study of causation

AFALD *adj* single

AFAR *adv* at, from, or to a great distance ▷ *n* great distance

AFARA *n* African tree

AFARAS > AFARA

AFARS > AFAR

AFAWLD *adj* single

AFEAR *vb* frighten

AFEARD *an archaic or dialect word for* > AFRAID

AFEARED *same as* > AFEARD

AFEARING > AFEAR

AFEARS > AFEAR

AFEBRILE *adj* without fever

AFF *adv* off

AFFABLE *adj* friendly and easy to talk to

AFFABLY > AFFABLE

AFFAIR *n* event or happening

AFFAIRE *n* love affair

AFFAIRES > AFFAIRE

AFFAIRS *pl n* personal or business interests

AFFEAR *vb* frighten

AFFEARD > AFFEAR

AFFEARE *vb* frighten

AFFEARED > AFFEAR

AFFEARES > AFFEARE

AFFEARING > AFFEAR

AFFEARS > AFFEAR

AFFECT *vb* act on, influence ▷ *n* emotion associated with an idea or set of ideas

AFFECTED *adj* displaying affectation

AFFECTER > AFFECT

AFFECTERS > AFFECT

AFFECTING *adj* arousing feelings of pity

AFFECTION *n* fondness or love

AFFECTIVE *adj* relating to affects

AFFECTS > AFFECT

AFFEER *vb* assess

AFFEERED > AFFEER

AFFEERING > AFFEER

AFFEERS > AFFEER

AFFERENT *adj* directing inwards to a body part, esp the brain or spinal cord ▷ *n* nerve that conveys impulses towards an organ of the body

AFFERENTS > AFFERENT

AFFIANCE *vb* bind (a person or oneself) in a promise of marriage ▷ *n* solemn pledge, esp a marriage contract

AFFIANCED > AFFIANCE

AFFIANCES > AFFIANCE

AFFIANT *n* person who makes an affidavit

AFFIANTS > AFFIANT

AFFICHE *n* poster

AFFICHES > AFFICHE

AFFIDAVIT *n* written statement made on oath

AFFIED > AFFY

AFFIES > AFFY

AFFILIATE *vb* (of a group) link up with a larger group ▷ *n* person or organization that is affiliated with another

AFFINAL > AFFINE

AFFINE *adj* involving transformations which preserve collinearity ▷ *n* relation by marriage

AFFINED *adj* closely related

AFFINELY > AFFINE

AFFINES > AFFINE

AFFINITY *n* close connection or liking

AFFIRM *vb* declare to be true

AFFIRMANT > AFFIRM

AFFIRMED > AFFIRM

AFFIRMER > AFFIRM

AFFIRMERS > AFFIRM

AFFIRMING > AFFIRM

AFFIRMS > AFFIRM

AFFIX *vb* attach or fasten ▷ *n* word or syllable added to a word to change its meaning

AFFIXABLE > AFFIRM

AFFIXAL > AFFIX

AFFIXED > AFFIX

AFFIXER > AFFIX

AFFIXERS > AFFIX

AFFIXES > AFFIX

AFFIXIAL > AFFIX

AFFIXING > AFFIX

AFFIXMENT > AFFIX

AFFIXTURE > AFFIX

AFFLATED *adj* inspired

AFFLATION *n* inspiration

AFFLATUS *n* supposed divine inspiration, esp in poetry

AFFLICT *vb* give pain or grief to

AFFLICTED > AFFLICT

AFFLICTER *n* one who afflicts

AFFLICTS > AFFLICT

AFFLUENCE *n* wealth

AFFLUENCY *n* affluence

AFFLUENT *adj* having plenty of money ▷ *n* tributary stream

AFFLUENTS > AFFLUENT

AFFLUENZA *n* guilt or lack of motivation experienced by people who have made or inherited large amounts of money

AFFLUX *n* flowing towards a point

AFFLUXES > AFFLUX

AFFLUXION *n* flow towards something

AFFOGATO *n* dessert made by pouring espresso over ice cream

AFFOGATOS > AFFOGATO

AFFOORD *vb* consent

AFFOORDED > AFFOORD

AFFOORDS > AFFOORD

AFFORCE *vb* strengthen

AFFORCED > AFFORCE

AFFORCES > AFFORCE

AFFORCING > AFFORCE

AFFORD *vb* have enough money to buy

AFFORDED > AFFORD

AFFORDING > AFFORD

AFFORDS > AFFORD

AFFOREST *vb* plant trees on

AFFORESTS > AFFOREST

AFFRAP *vb* strike

AFFRAPPED > AFFRAP

AFFRAPS > AFFRAP

AFFRAY *n* noisy fight, brawl ▷ *vb* frighten

AFFRAYED > AFFRAY

AFFRAYER > AFFRAY

AFFRAYERS > AFFRAY

AFFRAYING > AFFRAY

AFFRAYS > AFFRAY

AFFRENDED *adj* brought back into friendship

AFFRET *n* furious attack

AFFRETS > AFFRET

AFFRICATE *n* composite speech sound consisting of a stop and a fricative articulated at the same point

AFFRIGHT *vb* frighten ▷ *n* sudden terror

AFFRIGHTS > AFFRIGHT

AFFRONT *n* insult ▷ *vb* hurt someone's pride or dignity

AFFRONTE *adj* facing

AFFRONTED > AFFRONT

AFFRONTEE *adj* facing

AFFRONTS > AFFRONT

AFFUSION *n* baptizing of a person by pouring water onto his or her head

AFFUSIONS > AFFUSION

AFFY *vb* trust

AFFYDE > AFFY

AFFYING > AFFY

AFGHAN *n* type of blanket

AFGHANI *n* monetary unit of Afghanistan

AFGHANIS > AFGHANI

AFGHANS > AFGHAN

AFIELD *adj* away from one's usual surroundings or home

AFIRE *adj* on fire

AFLAJ > FALAJ

AFLAME *adj* burning

AFLATOXIN *n* toxin produced by a fungus growing on peanuts, maize, etc, which causes liver disease (esp cancer) in humans

AFLOAT *adj* floating ▷ *adv* floating

AFLUTTER *adv* in or into a nervous or excited state

AFOCAL *adj* relating to a method for transferring an image without bringing it into focus

AFOOT *adj* happening, in operation ▷ *adv* happening

AFORE *adv* before

AFOREHAND *adv* beforehand

AFORESAID *adj* referred to previously

AFORETIME *adv* formerly

AFOUL *adj* in or into a state of difficulty, confusion, or conflict (with)

AFRAID *adj* frightened

AFREET *n* powerful evil demon or giant monster

AFREETS > AFREET

AFRESH *adv* again, anew

AFRIT *same as* > AFREET

AFRITS > AFRIT

AFRO *n* bush-like frizzy hairstyle

AFRONT *adv* in front

AFROS > AFRO

AFT *adv* at or towards the rear of a ship or aircraft ▷ *adj* at or towards the rear of a ship or aircraft

AFTER *adv* at a later time

AFTERBODY *n* any discarded part that continues to trail a satellite, rocket, etc, in orbit

AFTERBURN *n* burning of calories after exercise

AFTERCARE *n* support given to a person discharged from a hospital or prison

AFTERCLAP *n* unexpected consequence

AFTERDAMP *n* poisonous gas formed after the explosion of firedamp in a coal mine

AFTERDECK *n* unprotected deck behind the bridge of a ship

AFTEREYE *vb* gaze at someone or something that has passed

AFTEREYED > AFTEREYE

AFTEREYES > AFTEREYE

AFTERGAME *n* second game that follows another

AFTERGLOW *n* glow left after a source of light has gone

AFTERHEAT *n* heat generated in a nuclear reactor after it has been shut down, produced by residual radioactivity in the fuel elements

AFTERINGS *n* last of the milk drawn in milking

AFTERLIFE *n* life after death

AFTERMAST *n* mast nearest the stern of a ship

AFTERMATH *n* results of an event considered together

AFTERMOST *adj* closer or closest to the rear or (in a vessel) the stern

AFTERNOON *n* time between noon and evening

AFTERPAIN *n* pain that comes after a while

AFTERPEAK *n* space behind the aftermost bulkhead, often used for storage

AFTERS *n* sweet course of a meal

AFTERSHOW *n* party held after a public performance of a play or film

AFTERSUN n moisturizing lotion applied to the skin to soothe the sunburn and avoid peeling

AFTERSUNS > AFTERSUN

AFTERTAX adj after tax has been paid

AFTERTIME n later period

AFTERWARD adv after an earlier event or time

AFTERWORD n epilogue or postscript in a book, etc

AFTMOST adj furthest towards rear

AFTOSA n foot-and-mouth disease

AFTOSAS > AFTOSA

AG n agriculture

AGA n title of respect

AGACANT adj irritating

AGACANTE adj irritating

AGACERIE n coquetry

AGACERIES > AGACERIE

AGAIN adv once more

AGAINST prep in opposition or contrast to

AGALACTIA n absence or failure of secretion of milk

AGALLOCH another name for > EAGLEWOOD

AGALLOCHS > AGALLOCH

AGALWOOD n eaglewood

AGALWOODS > AGALWOOD

AGAMA n small lizard

AGAMAS > AGAMA

AGAMETE n reproductive cell

AGAMETES > AGAMETE

AGAMI n South American bird

AGAMIC adj asexual

AGAMID same as > AGAMA

AGAMIDS > AGAMID

AGAMIS > AGAMI

AGAMOGONY n asexual reproduction in protozoans that is characterized by multiple fission

AGAMOID n lizard of the agamid type

AGAMOIDS > AGAMOID

AGAMONT another name for > SCHIZONT

AGAMONTS > AGAMONT

AGAMOUS adj without sex

AGAPAE > AGAPE

AGAPAI > AGAPE

AGAPE adj (of the mouth) wide open ▷ n love feast among the early Christians

AGAPEIC > AGAPE

AGAPES > AGAPE

AGAR n jelly-like substance obtained from seaweed and used as a thickener in food

AGARIC n type of fungus

AGARICS > AGARIC

AGAROSE n gel used in chemistry

AGAROSES > AGAROSE

AGARS > AGAR

AGARWOOD n aromatic wood of an Asian tree

AGARWOODS > AGARWOOD

AGAS > AGA

AGAST adj aghast ▷ vb terrify or be terrified

AGASTED > AGAST

AGASTING > AGAST

AGASTS > AGAST

AGATE n semiprecious form of quartz with striped colouring ▷ adv on the way

AGATES > AGATE

AGATEWARE n ceramic ware made to resemble agate or marble

AGATISE same as > AGATIZE

AGATISED > AGATISE

AGATISES > AGATISE

AGATISING > AGATISE

AGATIZE vb turn into agate

AGATIZED > AGATIZE

AGATIZES > AGATIZE

AGATIZING > AGATIZE

AGATOID adj like agate

AGAVE n tropical plant

AGAVES > AGAVE

AGAZE adj gazing at something

AGAZED adj amazed

AGE n length of time a person or thing has existed ▷ vb make or grow old

AGED adj old

AGEDLY > AGED

AGEDNESS > AGED

AGEE adj awry, crooked, or ajar ▷ adv awry

AGEING n fact or process of growing old ▷ adj becoming or appearing older

AGEINGS > AGEING

AGEISM n discrimination against people on the grounds of age

AGEISMS > AGEISM

AGEIST > AGEISM

AGEISTS > AGEISM

AGELAST n someone who never laughs

AGELASTIC > AGELAST

AGELASTS > AGELAST

AGELESS adj apparently never growing old

AGELESSLY > AGELESS

AGELONG adj lasting for a very long time

AGEMATE n person the same age as another person

AGEMATES > AGEMATE

AGEN archaic form of > AGAIN

AGENCIES > AGENCY

AGENCY n organization providing a service

AGENDA n list of things to be dealt with, esp at a meeting

AGENDAS > AGENDA

AGENDER adj of a person who does not identify with a gender

AGENDUM same as > AGENDA

AGENDUMS > AGENDUM

AGENE n chemical used to whiten flour

AGENES > AGENE

AGENESES > AGENESIS

AGENESIA n imperfect development

AGENESIAS > AGENESIA

AGENESIS n (of an animal or plant) imperfect development

AGENETIC > AGENESIS

AGENISE same as > AGENIZE

AGENISED > AGENISE

AGENISES > AGENISE

AGENISING > AGENISE

AGENIZE vb whiten using agene

AGENIZED > AGENIZE

AGENIZES > AGENIZE

AGENIZING > AGENIZE

AGENT n person acting on behalf of another ▷ vb act as an agent

AGENTED > AGENT

AGENTIAL > AGENT

AGENTING > AGENT

AGENTINGS > AGENT

AGENTIVAL adj of the performer of an action

AGENTIVE adj denoting a case of noun etc indicating the agent described by the verb ▷ n agentive case

AGENTIVES > AGENTIVE

AGENTRIES > AGENTRY

AGENTRY n acting as agent

AGENTS > AGENT

AGER n something that ages

AGERATUM n tropical American plant with thick clusters of purplish-blue flowers

AGERATUMS > AGERATUM

AGERS > AGER

AGES > AGE

AGEUSIA n lack of the sense of taste

AGEUSIAS > AGEUSIA

AGFLATION n inflation due to a rise in the demand for and price of agricultural products

AGGADA n explanation in Jewish literature

AGGADAH same as > AGGADA

AGGADAHS > AGGADAH

AGGADAS > AGGADA

AGGADIC adj of aggada

AGGADOT > AGGADA

AGGADOTH > AGGADA

AGGER n rampart

AGGERS adj aggressive

AGGIE n American agricultural student

AGGIES > AGGIE

AGGRACE vb add grace to

AGGRACED > AGGRACE

AGGRACES > AGGRACE

AGGRACING > AGGRACE

AGGRADE vb build up by the deposition of sediment

AGGRADED > AGGRADE

AGGRADES > AGGRADE

AGGRADING > AGGRADE

AGGRATE vb gratify

AGGRATED > AGGRATE

AGGRATES > AGGRATE

AGGRATING > AGGRATE

AGGRAVATE vb make worse

AGGREGATE n total ▷ adj gathered into a mass ▷ vb combine into a whole

AGGRESS vb attack first or begin a quarrel

AGGRESSED > AGGRESS

AGGRESSES > AGGRESS

AGGRESSOR n person or body that engages in aggressive behaviour

AGGRI adj of African beads

AGGRIEVE vb grieve

AGGRIEVED adj upset and angry

AGGRIEVES > AGGRIEVE

AGGRO n aggressive behaviour

AGGROS > AGGRO

AGGRY adj of African beads

AGHA same as > AGA

AGHAS > AGHA

AGHAST adj overcome with amazement or horror

AGILA n eaglewood

AGILAS > AGILA

AGILE adj nimble, quick-moving

AGILELY > AGILE

AGILENESS > AGILE

AGILER > AGILE

AGILEST > AGILE

AGILITIES > AGILE

AGILITY > AGILE

AGIN prep against, opposed to

AGING same as > AGEING

AGINGS > AGING

AGINNER n someone who is against something

AGINNERS > AGINNER

AGIO n difference between the nominal and actual values of a currency

AGIOS > AGIO

AGIOTAGE n business of exchanging currencies

AGIOTAGES > AGIOTAGE

AGISM same as > AGEISM

AGISMS > AGISM

AGIST vb care for and feed (cattle or horses) for payment

AGISTED > AGIST

AGISTER n person who grazes cattle for money

AGISTERS > AGISTER

AGISTING > AGIST

AGISTMENT > AGEISM

AGISTOR n person who grazes cattle for money

AGISTORS > AGISTOR

AGISTS > AGIST

AGITA n acid indigestion

AGITABLE > AGITATE

AGITANS adj as in paralysis agitans Parkinson's disease

AGITAS > AGITA

AGITATE vb disturb or excite

AGITATED > AGITATE

AGITATES > AGITATE

AGITATING > AGITATE

AGITATION n state of excitement, disturbance, or worry

AGITATIVE > AGITATE

AGITATO adv (to be performed) in an agitated manner

AGITATOR n person who agitates for or against a cause, etc

AGITATORS > AGITATOR

AGITPOP n use of pop music to promote political propaganda

AGITPOPS > AGITPOP

AGITPROP n political agitation and propaganda

AGITPROPS > AGITPROP

AGLARE adj glaring

AGLEAM adj glowing

AGLEE same as > AGLEY

AGLET n metal tag

AGLETS > AGLET

AGLEY adj awry

AGLIMMER adj glimmering

AGLITTER adj sparkling, glittering

AGLOO same as > AGLU

AGLOOS > AGLOO

AGLOSSAL > AGLOSSIA

AGLOSSATE > AGLOSSIA

AGLOSSIA n congenital absence of the tongue

AGLOSSIAS > AGLOSSIA

AGLOW adj glowing

AGLU n breathing hole made in ice by a seal

AGLUS > AGLU

AGLY Scots word for > WRONG

AGLYCON n chemical compound

AGLYCONE same as > AGLYCON

AGLYCONES > AGLYCONE

AGLYCONS > AGLYCON

AGMA n symbol used to represent a velar nasal consonant

AGMAS > AGMA

AGMINATE adj gathered or clustered together

AGNAIL another name for > HANGNAIL

AGNAILS > AGNAIL

AGNAME n name additional to first name and surname

AGNAMED adj having an agname

AGNAMES > AGNAME

AGNATE adj related through a common male ancestor ▷ n descendant by male links from a common male ancestor

AGNATES > AGNATE

AGNATHAN n type of jawless eel-like aquatic vertebrate

AGNATHANS > AGNATHAN

AGNATHOUS adj (esp of lampreys and hagfishes) lacking jaws

AGNATIC > AGNATE

AGNATICAL > AGNATE

AGNATION > AGNATE

AGNATIONS > AGNATE

AGNISE vb acknowledge

AGNISED > AGNISE

AGNISES > AGNISE

AGNISING > AGNISE

AGNIZE vb acknowledge

AGNIZED > AGNIZE

AGNIZES > AGNIZE

AGNIZING > AGNIZE

AGNOLOTTI n small pasta shapes stuffed with fillings

AGNOMEN n name used by ancient Romans

AGNOMENS > AGNOMEN

AGNOMINA > AGNOMEN

AGNOMINAL > AGNOMEN

AGNOSIA n loss of power to recognize familiar objects

AGNOSIAS > AGNOSIA

AGNOSIC > AGNOSIA

AGNOSTIC n person who believes that it is impossible to know whether God exists ▷ adj of agnostics

AGNOSTICS > AGNOSTIC

AGO adv in the past

AGOG adj eager or curious

AGOGE n ancient Greek melodic form

AGOGES > AGOGE

AGOGIC n musical accent

AGOGICS > AGOGIC

AGOING adj moving

AGON n ancient Greek festival

AGONAL adj of agony

AGONE an archaic word for > AGO

AGONES > AGON

AGONIC adj forming no angle

AGONIES > AGONY

AGONISE same as > AGONIZE

AGONISED > AGONISE

AGONISES > AGONISE

AGONISING > AGONISE

AGONISM n struggle between opposing forces

AGONISMS > AGONISM

AGONIST n any muscle that is opposed in action by another muscle

AGONISTES n person suffering inner struggle

AGONISTIC adj striving for effect

AGONISTS > AGONIST

AGONIZE vb worry greatly

AGONIZED > AGONIZE

AGONIZES > AGONIZE

AGONIZING > AGONIZE

AGONS > AGON

AGONY n extreme physical or mental pain

AGOOD adv seriously or earnestly

AGORA n place of assembly in ancient Greece

AGORAE > AGORA

AGORAS > AGORA

AGOROT pl n Israeli coins

AGOROTH same as > AGOROT

AGOUTA n Haitian rodent

AGOUTAS > AGOUTA

AGOUTI n rodent

AGOUTIES > AGOUTI

AGOUTIS > AGOUTI

AGOUTY n agouti

AGRAFE same as > AGRAFFE

AGRAFES > AGRAFE

AGRAFFE n loop and hook fastening

AGRAFFES > AGRAFFE

AGRAPHA > AGRAPHON

AGRAPHIA n loss of the ability to write, resulting from a brain lesion

AGRAPHIAS > AGRAPHIA

AGRAPHIC > AGRAPHIA

AGRAPHON n saying of Jesus not in Gospels

AGRARIAN adj of land or agriculture ▷ n person who

favours the redistribution of landed property

AGRARIANS > AGRARIAN

AGRASTE > AGGRACE

AGRAVIC adj of zero gravity

AGREE vb be of the same opinion

AGREEABLE adj pleasant and enjoyable

AGREEABLY > AGREEABLE

AGREED adj determined by common consent

AGREEING > AGREE

AGREEMENT n agreeing

AGREES > AGREE

AGREGE n winner in examination for university teaching post

AGREGES > AGREGE

AGREMENS n amenities

AGREMENT n diplomatic approval of a country

AGREMENTS n amenities

AGRESTAL adj (of uncultivated plants such as weeds) growing on cultivated land

AGRESTIAL adj agrestal

AGRESTIC adj rural

AGRIA n appearance of pustules

AGRIAS > AGRIA

AGRIMONY n yellow-flowered plant with bitter-tasting fruits

AGRIN adv grinning ▷ n type of protein

AGRINS > AGRIN

AGRIOLOGY n study of primitive peoples

AGRISE vb fill with fear

AGRISED > AGRISE

AGRISES > AGRISE

AGRISING > AGRISE

AGRIZE vb fill with fear

AGRIZED > AGRIZE

AGRIZES > AGRIZE

AGRIZING > AGRIZE

AGRO n student of agriculture

AGRODOLCE n Italian sweet-and-sour sauce

AGROLOGIC > AGROLOGY

AGROLOGY n scientific study of soils and their potential productivity

AGRONOMIC > AGRONOMY

AGRONOMY n science of soil management and crop production

AGROS > AGRO

AGROUND adv onto the bottom of shallow water ▷ adj on the ground or bottom, as in shallow water

AGRYPNIA n inability to sleep

AGRYPNIAS > AGRYPNIA

AGRYZE vb fill with fear

AGRYZED > AGRYZE

AGRYZES > AGRYZE

AGRYZING > AGRYZE

AGS > AG

AGTERSKOT n final payment to a farmer for crops

AGUACATE n avocado

AGUACATES > AGUACATE

AGUE n periodic fever with shivering

AGUED adj suffering from fever

AGUELIKE > AGUE

AGUES > AGUE

AGUEWEED n N American plant with clusters of pale blue-violet or white flowers

AGUEWEEDS > AGUEWEED

AGUISE vb dress

AGUISED > AGUISE

AGUISES > AGUISE

AGUISH > AGUE

AGUISHLY > AGUE

AGUISING > AGUISE

AGUIZE vb dress

AGUIZED > AGUIZE

AGUIZES > AGUIZE

AGUIZING > AGUIZE

AGUNA n (in Jewish law) woman whose husband will not grant her a divorce

AGUNAH same as > AGUNA

AGUNOT > AGUNA

AGUNOTH > AGUNA

AGUTI n agouti

AGUTIS > AGUTI

AGYRIA n brain disease

AGYRIAS > AGYRIA

AH interj exclamation expressing surprise, joy etc ▷ vb say ah

AHA interj exclamation of triumph or surprise

AHCHOO interj sound made by someone sneezing

AHEAD adv in front

AHEAP adv in a heap

AHED > AH

AHEIGHT adv at height

AHEM interj clearing of the throat in order to attract attention

AHEMERAL adj not constituting a full 24-hour day

AHENT adv behind

AHI n yellowfin tuna

AHIGH adv at height

AHIMSA n the law of reverence for every form of life

AHIMSAS > AHIMSA

AHIND adv behind

AHING > AH

AHINT adv behind

AHIS > AHI

AHISTORIC adj not related to history; not historical

AHOLD adv holding

AHOLDS > AHOLD

AHORSE adv on horseback

AHOY interj hail used to call a ship

AHS > AH

AHULL adv with sails furled

AHUNGERED adj very hungry

AHUNGRY adj very hungry

AHURU n type of small pink cod of SW Pacific waters

AHURUHURU same as > AHURU

AHURUS > AHURU

AI n shaggy-coated slow-moving animal of South America

AIA n female servant in E Asia

AIAS > AIA

AIBLINS Scots word for > PERHAPS

AID n assistance or support ▷ vb help financially or in other ways

AIDA n cotton fabric with a natural mesh

AIDANCE n help

AIDANCES > AIDANCE

AIDANT adj helping ▷ n helper

AIDANTS > AIDANT

AIDAS > AIDA

AIDE n assistant

AIDED > AID

AIDER > AID

AIDERS > AID

AIDES > AIDE

AIDFUL adj helpful

AIDING > AID

AIDLESS adj without help

AIDMAN n military medical assistant

AIDMEN > AIDMAN

AIDOI adj of the genitals

AIDOS Greek word for > SHAME

AIDS > AID

AIERIES > AIERY

AIERY n eyrie

AIGA n Māori word for family

AIGAS > AIGA

AIGHT adv all right

AIGLET same as > AGLET

AIGLETS > AIGLET

AIGRET same as > AIGRETTE

AIGRETS > AIGRET

AIGRETTE n long plume worn on hats or as a headdress, esp one of long egret feathers

AIGRETTES > AIGRETTE

AIGUILLE n rock mass or mountain peak shaped like a needle

AIGUILLES > AIGUILLE

AIKIDO n Japanese self-defence

AIKIDOS > AIKIDO

AIKONA interj South African expression meaning no

AIL vb trouble, afflict

AILANTHIC > AILANTHUS

AILANTHUS n type of deciduous tree with small greenish flowers and winged fruits, planted in Europe and N America

AILANTO n Asian tree

AILANTOS > AILANTO

AILED > AIL

AILERON n movable flap on an aircraft wing which controls rolling

AILERONS > AILERON

AILETTE n shoulder armour

AILETTES > AILETTE

AILING adj sickly

AILMENT n illness

AILMENTS > AILMENT

AILS > AIL

AIM vb point (a weapon or missile) or direct (a blow or remark) at a target ▷ n aiming

AIMED > AIM

AIMER > AIM

AIMERS > AIM

AIMFUL adj with purpose or intention

AIMFULLY > AIMFUL

AIMING > AIM

AIMLESS adj having no purpose

AIMLESSLY > AIMLESS

AIMS > AIM

AIN variant of > AYIN

AINE adj French word for elder (male)

AINEE adj French word for elder (female)

AINGA n Māori word for village

AINGAS > AINGA

AINS > AIN

AINSELL n Scots word meaning own self

AINSELLS > AINSELL

AIOLI n garlic mayonnaise

AIOLIS > AIOLI

AIR n mixture of gases forming the earth's atmosphere ▷ vb make known publicly

AIRBAG n safety device in a car

AIRBAGS > AIRBAG

AIRBALL n missed shot in basketball ▷ vb throw an airball

AIRBALLED > AIRBALL

AIRBALLS > AIRBALL

AIRBASE n centre from which military aircraft operate

AIRBASES > AIRBASE

AIRBOARD n inflatable body board

AIRBOARDS > AIRBOARD

AIRBOAT n boat

AIRBOATS > AIRBOAT

AIRBORNE adj carried by air

AIRBOUND adj heading into the air

AIRBRICK n brick with holes in it, put into the wall of a building for ventilation

AIRBRICKS > AIRBRICK

AIRBRUSH n atomizer that sprays paint by compressed air ▷ vb paint using an airbrush

AIRBURST n explosion of a bomb, shell, etc, in the air ▷ vb (of a bomb, shell, etc) to explode in the air

AIRBURSTS > AIRBURST

AIRBUS n commercial passenger aircraft

AIRBUSES > AIRBUS

AIRBUSSES > AIRBUS

AIRCHECK n recording of a radio broadcast

AIRCHECKS > AIRCHECK

AIRCOACH n bus travelling to and from an airport

AIRCON n air conditioner

AIRCONS > AIRCON

AIRCRAFT n any machine that flies, such as an aeroplane

AIRCREW n crew of an aircraft

AIRCREWS > AIRCREW

AIRDATE n date of a programme broadcast

AIRDATES > AIRDATE

AIRDRAWN adj imaginary

AIRDROME same as > AERODROME

AIRDROMES > AIRDROME

AIRDROP n delivery of supplies by parachute ▷ vb deliver (supplies, etc) by an airdrop

AIRDROPS > AIRDROP

AIRED > AIR

AIRER n device on which clothes are hung to dry

AIRERS > AIRER

AIREST > AIR

AIRFARE n money for an aircraft ticket

AIRFARES > AIRFARE

AIRFIELD n place where aircraft can land and take off

AIRFIELDS > AIRFIELD

AIRFLOW n flow of air past a moving object

AIRFLOWS > AIRFLOW

AIRFOIL same as > AEROFOIL

AIRFOILS > AIRFOIL

AIRFRAME n body of an aircraft, excluding its engines

AIRFRAMES > AIRFRAME

AIRGAP n gap between parts in an electrical machine

AIRGAPS > AIRGAP

AIRGLOW n faint light in the night sky

AIRGLOWS > AIRGLOW

AIRGRAPH n photographic reduction of a letter for sending airmail

AIRGRAPHS > AIRGRAPH

AIRGUN n gun fired by compressed air

AIRGUNS > AIRGUN

AIRHEAD n stupid person

AIRHEADED > AIRHEAD

AIRHEADS > AIRHEAD

AIRHOLE n hole that allows the passage of air

AIRHOLES > AIRHOLE

AIRIER > AIRY

AIRIEST > AIRY

AIRILY adv in a light-hearted and casual manner

AIRINESS n quality or condition of being fresh, light, or breezy

AIRING n exposure to air for drying or ventilation

AIRINGS > AIRING

AIRLESS adj stuffy

AIRLIFT n transport of troops or cargo by aircraft when other routes are blocked ▷ vb transport by airlift

AIRLIFTED > AIRLIFT

AIRLIFTS > AIRLIFT

AIRLIKE > AIR

AIRLINE n company providing scheduled flights for passengers and cargo

AIRLINER n large passenger aircraft

AIRLINERS > AIRLINER

AIRLINES > AIRLINE

AIRLOCK n air bubble blocking the flow of liquid in a pipe

AIRLOCKS > AIRLOCK

AIRMAIL n system of sending mail by aircraft ▷ adj of, used for, or concerned with airmail ▷ vb send by airmail

AIRMAILED > AIRMAIL

AIRMAILS > AIRMAIL

AIRMAN n member of an air force

AIRMEN > AIRMAN

AIRMOBILE adj using aircraft as transport

AIRN Scots word for > IRON

AIRNED > AIRN

AIRNING > AIRN

AIRNS > AIRN

AIRPARK n car park at airport

AIRPARKS > AIRPARK

AIRPLANE same as > AEROPLANE

AIRPLANES > AIRPLANE

AIRPLAY n broadcast performances of a record on radio

AIRPLAYS > AIRPLAY

AIRPORT n airfield for civilian aircraft, with facilities for aircraft maintenance and passengers

AIRPORTS > AIRPORT

AIRPOST n system of delivering mail by air

AIRPOSTS > AIRPOST

AIRPOWER n strength of a nation's air force

AIRPOWERS > AIRPOWER

AIRPROOF vb make something airtight

AIRPROOFS > AIRPROOF

AIRPROX n near collision involving aircraft

AIRPROXES > AIRPROX

AIRS pl n manners put on to impress people

AIRSCAPE n picture or view of sky

AIRSCAPES > AIRSCAPE

AIRSCREW n aircraft propeller

AIRSCREWS > AIRSCREW

AIRSHAFT n shaft for ventilation

AIRSHAFTS > AIRSHAFT

AIRSHED n air over a particular geographical area

AIRSHEDS > AIRSHED

AIRSHIP n lighter-than-air self-propelled aircraft

AIRSHIPS > AIRSHIP

AIRSHOT n shot that misses the ball completely

AIRSHOTS > AIRSHOT

AIRSHOW n occasion when an air base is open to the public

AIRSHOWS > AIRSHOW

a

AIRSICK adj nauseated from travelling in an aircraft
AIRSIDE n part of an airport nearest the aircraft
AIRSIDES > AIRSIDE
AIRSOME adj cold
AIRSPACE n atmosphere above a country, regarded as its territory
AIRSPACES > AIRSPACE
AIRSPEED n speed of an aircraft relative to the air in which it moves
AIRSPEEDS > AIRSPEED
AIRSTOP n helicopter landing-place
AIRSTOPS > AIRSTOP
AIRSTREAM n wind, esp at a high altitude
AIRSTRIKE n attack by military aircraft
AIRSTRIP n cleared area where aircraft can take off and land
AIRSTRIPS > AIRSTRIP
AIRT n point of the compass ▷ vb direct
AIRTED > AIRT
AIRTH same as > AIRT
AIRTHED > AIRTH
AIRTHING > AIRTH
AIRTHS > AIRTH
AIRTIGHT adj sealed so that air cannot enter
AIRTIME n time period on radio and TV
AIRTIMES > AIRTIME
AIRTING > AIRT
AIRTRAM n cable car
AIRTRAMS > AIRTRAM
AIRTS > AIRT
AIRVAC n evacuation by air ambulance
AIRVACS > AIRVAC
AIRWARD adj into air
AIRWARDS adv into air
AIRWAVE n radio wave used in radio and television broadcasting
AIRWAVES > AIRWAVE
AIRWAY n air route used regularly by aircraft
AIRWAYS > AIRWAY
AIRWISE adv towards the air
AIRWOMAN > AIRMAN
AIRWOMEN > AIRMAN
AIRWORTHY adj (of aircraft) fit to fly
AIRY adj well-ventilated
AIS > AI
AISLE n passageway separating seating areas, rows of shelves, etc
AISLED > AISLE
AISLELESS > AISLE
AISLES > AISLE
AISLEWAY n aisle
AISLEWAYS > AISLEWAY
AISLING Irish word for > DREAM
AISLINGS > AISLING
AIT n islet, esp in a river
AITCH n letter h or the sound represented by it
AITCHBONE n cut of beef from the rump bone

AITCHES > AITCH
AITS > AIT
AITU n half-human half-divine being
AITUS > AITU
AIVER n working horse
AIVERS > AIVER
AIYEE interj expressing alarm
AIZLE n Scots word for hot ashes
AIZLES > AIZLE
AJAR adv (of a door) partly open ▷ adj not in harmony
AJEE same as > AGEE
AJI n type of spicy pepper
AJIES > AJI
AJIS > AJI
AJIVA n Jainist term for non-living thing
AJIVAS > AJIVA
AJOWAN n plant related to caraway
AJOWANS > AJOWAN
AJUGA n garden plant
AJUGAS > AJUGA
AJUTAGE n nozzle
AJUTAGES > AJUTAGE
AJWAN n plant related to caraway
AJWANS > AJWAN
AKA n type of New Zealand vine
AKARYOTE n cell without a nucleus
AKARYOTES > AKARYOTE
AKARYOTIC > AKARYOTE
AKAS > AKA
AKATEA n New Zealand vine with white flowers
AKATEAS > AKATEA
AKATHISIA n inability to sit still because of uncontrollable movement caused by reaction to drugs
AKE vb old spelling of ache
AKEAKE n New Zealand tree
AKEAKES > AKEAKE
AKEBIA n E Asian climbing plant
AKEBIAS > AKEBIA
AKED > AKE
AKEDAH n binding of Isaac in Bible
AKEDAHS > AKEDAH
AKEE same as > ACKEE
AKEES > AKEE
AKELA n adult leader of a pack of Cub Scouts
AKELAS > AKELA
AKENE same as > ACHENE
AKENES > AKENE
AKENIAL > ACHENE
AKES > AKE
AKHARA n (in India) gymnasium
AKHARAS > AKHARA
AKIMBO adj as in with arms akimbo with hands on hips and elbows projecting outwards
AKIN adj related by blood
AKINESES > AKINESIS
AKINESIA n loss of power to move
AKINESIAS > AKINESIA

AKINESIS same as > AKINESIA
AKINETIC > AKINESIA
AKING > AKE
AKIRAHO n small New Zealand shrub with white flowers
AKIRAHOS > AKIRAHO
AKITA n large dog
AKITAS > AKITA
AKKAS slang word for > MONEY
AKOLUTHOS n leader of Byzantine Varangian Guard
AKRASIA n weakness of will
AKRASIAS > AKRASIA
AKRATIC > AKRASIA
AKVAVIT same as > AQUAVIT
AKVAVITS > AKVAVIT
AL same as > AAL
ALA n winglike structure
ALAAP n part of raga in Indian music
ALAAPS > ALAAP
ALABAMINE old name for > ASTATINE
ALABASTER n soft white translucent stone ▷ adj of or resembling alabaster
ALACHLOR n type of herbicide
ALACHLORS > ALACHLOR
ALACK archaic or poetic word for > ALAS
ALACKADAY same as > ALACK
ALACRITY n speed, eagerness
ALAE > ALA
ALAIMENT old spelling of > ALLAYMENT
ALAIMENTS > ALAIMENT
ALALAGMOI > ALALAGMOS
ALALAGMOS n ancient Greek war cry
ALALIA n complete inability to speak
ALALIAS > ALALIA
ALAMEDA n public walk lined with trees
ALAMEDAS > ALAMEDA
ALAMO n poplar tree
ALAMODE n soft light silk used for shawls and dresses, esp in the 19th century
ALAMODES > ALAMODE
ALAMORT adj exhausted and downcast
ALAMOS > ALAMO
ALAN n member of ancient European nomadic people
ALAND vb come onto land
ALANDS > ALAND
ALANE Scots word for > ALONE
ALANG n type of grass in Malaysia
ALANGS > ALANG
ALANIN n alanine
ALANINE n chemical
ALANINES > ALANINE
ALANINS > ALANIN
ALANNAH interj term of endearment ▷ n cry of alannah
ALANNAHS > ALANNAH
ALANS > ALAN

ALANT n flowering plant used in herbal medicine
ALANTS > ALANT
ALANYL n chemical found in proteins
ALANYLS > ALANYL
ALAP n Indian vocal music without words
ALAPA n part of raga in Indian music
ALAPAS > ALAPA
ALAPS > ALAP
ALAR adj relating to, resembling, or having wings or alae
ALARM n sudden fear caused by awareness of danger ▷ vb fill with fear
ALARMABLE > ALARM
ALARMED > ALARM
ALARMEDLY > ALARM
ALARMING > ALARM
ALARMISM > ALARMIST
ALARMISMS > ALARMIST
ALARMIST n person who alarms others needlessly ▷ adj causing needless alarm
ALARMISTS > ALARMIST
ALARMS > ALARM
ALARUM n alarm, esp a call to arms ▷ vb raise the alarm
ALARUMED > ALARUM
ALARUMING > ALARUM
ALARUMS > ALARUM
ALARY adj of, relating to, or shaped like wings
ALAS adv unfortunately, regrettably
ALASKA n dessert made of cake and ice cream
ALASKAS > ALASKA
ALASTOR n avenging demon
ALASTORS > ALASTOR
ALASTRIM n form of smallpox
ALASTRIMS > ALASTRIM
ALATE adj having wings or winglike extensions ▷ n winged insect
ALATED adj having wings
ALATES > ALATE
ALATION n state of having wings
ALATIONS > ALATION
ALAY vb allay
ALAYED > ALAY
ALAYING > ALAY
ALAYS > ALAY
ALB n long white robe worn by a Christian priest
ALBA n song of lament
ALBACORE n tuna found in warm seas, eaten for food
ALBACORES > ALBACORE
ALBARELLI > ALBARELLO
ALBARELLO n storage jar
ALBAS > ALBA
ALBATA n variety of German silver consisting of nickel, copper, and zinc
ALBATAS > ALBATA
ALBATROSS n large sea bird with very long wings
ALBE old word for > ALBEIT
ALBEDO n ratio of the intensity of light
ALBEDOES > ALBEDO

ALBEDOS > ALBEDO
ALBEE archaic form of > ALBEIT
ALBEIT conj even though
ALBERGHI > ALBERGO
ALBERGO n Italian word for inn
ALBERT n watch chain
ALBERTITE n black solid variety of bitumen that has a conchoidal fracture and occurs in veins in oil-bearing strata
ALBERTS > ALBERT
ALBESCENT adj shading into, growing, or becoming white
ALBESPINE old name for > HAWTHORN
ALBESPYNE old name for > HAWTHORN
ALBICORE n species of tuna
ALBICORES > ALBICORE
ALBINAL > ALBINO
ALBINESS n female albino
ALBINIC > ALBINO
ALBINISM > ALBINO
ALBINISMS > ALBINO
ALBINO n person or animal with white skin and hair and pink eyes
ALBINOISM > ALBINO
ALBINOS > ALBINO
ALBINOTIC > ALBINO
ALBITE n type of mineral
ALBITES > ALBITE
ALBITIC > ALBITE
ALBITICAL > ALBITE
ALBITISE same as > ALBITIZE
ALBITISED > ALBITISE
ALBITISES > ALBITISE
ALBITIZE vb turn into albite
ALBITIZED > ALBITIZE
ALBITIZES > ALBITIZE
ALBIZIA n mimosa
ALBIZIAS > ALBIZIA
ALBIZZIA n mimosa
ALBIZZIAS > ALBIZZIA
ALBRICIAS interj expression of joy
ALBS > ALB
ALBUGO n opacity of the cornea
ALBUGOS > ALBUGO
ALBUM n book with blank pages for keeping photographs or stamps in
ALBUMEN same as > ALBUMIN
ALBUMENS > ALBUMEN
ALBUMIN n protein found in blood plasma, egg white, milk, and muscle
ALBUMINS > ALBUMIN
ALBUMOSE the US name for > PROTEOSE
ALBUMOSES > ALBUMOSE
ALBUMS > ALBUM
ALBURNOUS > ALBURNUM
ALBURNUM former name for > SAPWOOD
ALBURNUMS > ALBURNUM
ALBUTEROL n drug used to treat lung diseases
ALCADE same as > ALCALDE

ALCADES > ALCADE
ALCAHEST same as > ALKAHEST
ALCAHESTS > ALCAHEST
ALCAIC n verse consisting of strophes with four tetrametric lines
ALCAICS > ALCAIC
ALCAIDE n commander of a fortress or castle
ALCAIDES > ALCAIDE
ALCALDE n (in Spain and Spanish America) the mayor or chief magistrate in a town
ALCALDES > ALCALDE
ALCARRAZA n Spanish water container
ALCATRAS n pelican
ALCAYDE n alcaide
ALCAYDES > ALCAYDE
ALCAZAR n Moorish palace or fortress
ALCAZARS > ALCAZAR
ALCHEMIC > ALCHEMY
ALCHEMIES > ALCHEMY
ALCHEMISE same as > ALCHEMIZE
ALCHEMIST n person who practises alchemy
ALCHEMIZE vb alter (an element, metal, etc) by alchemy
ALCHEMY n medieval form of chemistry
ALCHERA n mythical Golden Age
ALCHERAS > ALCHERA
ALCHYMIES > ALCHYMY
ALCHYMY old spelling of > ALCHEMY
ALCID n bird of the auk family
ALCIDINE adj relating to a family of sea birds including the auks, guillemots, and puffins
ALCIDS > ALCID
ALCO same as > ALKO
ALCOHOL n colourless flammable liquid present in intoxicating drinks
ALCOHOLIC adj of alcohol ▷ n person addicted to alcohol
ALCOHOLS > ALCOHOL
ALCOLOCK n breath-alcohol ignition-interlock device
ALCOLOCKS > ALCOLOCK
ALCOOL n form of pure grain spirit distilled in Quebec
ALCOOLS > ALCOOL
ALCOPOP n alcoholic drink that tastes like a soft drink
ALCOPOPS > ALCOPOP
ALCORZA n Spanish sweet
ALCORZAS > ALCORZA
ALCOS > ALCO
ALCOVE n recess in the wall of a room
ALCOVED adj with or in an alcove
ALCOVES > ALCOVE
ALDEA n Spanish village
ALDEAS > ALDEA
ALDEHYDE n one of a group of chemical compounds derived from alcohol by oxidation

ALDEHYDES > ALDEHYDE
ALDEHYDIC > ALDEHYDE
ALDER n tree related to the birch
ALDERFLY n insect with large broad-based hind wings, which produces aquatic larvae
ALDERMAN n formerly, senior member of a local council
ALDERMEN > ALDERMAN
ALDERN adj made of alder wood
ALDERS > ALDER
ALDICARB n crystalline compound used as a pesticide
ALDICARBS > ALDICARB
ALDOL n colourless or yellowish oily liquid
ALDOLASE n enzyme present in the body
ALDOLASES > ALDOLASE
ALDOLS > ALDOL
ALDOSE n type of sugar
ALDOSES > ALDOSE
ALDOXIME n oxime formed by reaction between hydroxylamine and an aldehyde
ALDOXIMES > ALDOXIME
ALDRIN n brown to white poisonous crystalline solid
ALDRINS > ALDRIN
ALE n kind of beer
ALEATORIC same as > ALEATORY
ALEATORY adj dependent on chance
ALEBENCH n bench at alehouse
ALEC same as > ALECK
ALECITHAL adj (of an ovum) having little or no yolk
ALECK n irritatingly oversmart person
ALECKS > ALECK
ALECOST another name for > COSTMARY
ALECOSTS > ALECOST
ALECS > ALEC
ALECTRYON n type of tree found in Australasia, SE Asia, and Micronesia
ALEE adj on or towards the lee
ALEF n first letter of Hebrew alphabet
ALEFS > ALEF
ALEFT adv at or to left
ALEGAR n malt vinegar
ALEGARS > ALEGAR
ALEGGE vb alleviate
ALEGGED > ALEGGE
ALEGGES > ALEGGE
ALEGGING > ALEGGE
ALEHOUSE n public house
ALEHOUSES > ALEHOUSE
ALEMBIC n anything that distils
ALEMBICS > ALEMBIC
ALEMBROTH n mercury compound in alchemy
ALENCON n elaborate lace worked on a hexagonal mesh
ALENCONS > ALENCON

ALENGTH adv at length
ALEPH n first letter in the Hebrew alphabet
ALEPHS > ALEPH
ALEPINE n type of cloth
ALEPINES > ALEPINE
ALERCE n wood of the sandarac tree
ALERCES > ALERCE
ALERION n eagle in heraldry
ALERIONS > ALERION
ALERT adj watchful, attentive ▷ n warning of danger ▷ vb warn of danger
ALERTED > ALERT
ALERTER > ALERT
ALERTEST > ALERT
ALERTING > ALERT
ALERTLY > ALERT
ALERTNESS > ALERT
ALERTS > ALERT
ALES > ALE
ALETHIC adj of philosophical concepts
ALEURON n outer layer of seeds
ALEURONE same as > ALEURON
ALEURONES > ALEURONE
ALEURONIC > ALEURON
ALEURONS > ALEURON
ALEVIN n young fish, esp a young salmon or trout
ALEVINS > ALEVIN
ALEW n cry to call hunting hounds
ALEWASHED adj showing effects of beer drinking
ALEWIFE n North American fish
ALEWIVES > ALEWIFE
ALEWS > ALEW
ALEXANDER n cocktail made with creme de cacao
ALEXIA n disorder of the central nervous system
ALEXIAS > ALEXIA
ALEXIC > ALEXIA
ALEXIN n protein in blood serum
ALEXINE same as > ALEXIN
ALEXINES > ALEXINE
ALEXINIC > ALEXIN
ALEXINS > ALEXIN
ALEYE vb allay
ALEYED > ALEYE
ALEYES > ALEYE
ALEYING > ALEYE
ALF n uncultivated Australian
ALFA n type of grass
ALFAKI same as > ALFAQUI
ALFAKIS > ALFAKI
ALFALFA n kind of plant used to feed livestock
ALFALFAS > ALFALFA
ALFAQUI n expert in Muslim law
ALFAQUIN same as > ALFAQUI
ALFAQUINS > ALFAQUIN
ALFAQUIS > ALFAQUI
ALFAS > ALFA
ALFERECES > ALFEREZ
ALFEREZ n Spanish standard-bearer

a

ALFILARIA n plant with finely divided leaves and small pink or purplish flowers

ALFILERIA same as > ALFILARIA

ALFORJA n saddlebag made of leather or canvas

ALFORJAS > ALFORJA

ALFREDO adj cooked with a cheese and egg sauce

ALFRESCO adj in the open air ▷ adv in the open air

ALFS > ALF

ALGA n multicellular organism

ALGAE > ALGA

ALGAECIDE n substance for killing algae

ALGAL > ALGA

ALGAROBA same as > ALGARROBA

ALGAROBAS > ALGAROBA

ALGARROBA n edible pod of these trees

ALGARROBO n carob

ALGAS > ALGA

ALGATE adv anyway

ALGATES adv anyway

ALGEBRA n branch of mathematics using symbols to represent numbers

ALGEBRAIC adj of or relating to algebra

ALGEBRAS > ALGEBRA

ALGERINE n soft striped woollen cloth

ALGERINES > ALGERINE

ALGESES > ALGESIS

ALGESIA n capacity to feel pain

ALGESIAS > ALGESIA

ALGESIC > ALGESIA

ALGESIS n feeling of pain

ALGETIC > ALGESIA

ALGICIDAL > ALGICIDE

ALGICIDE n any substance that kills algae

ALGICIDES > ALGICIDE

ALGID adj chilly or cold

ALGIDITY > ALGID

ALGIDNESS > ALGID

ALGIN n seaweed solution

ALGINATE n salt or ester of alginic acid

ALGINATES > ALGINATE

ALGINIC adj as in alginic acid powdery substance extracted from kelp

ALGINS > ALGIN

ALGOID adj resembling or relating to algae

ALGOLOGY n branch of biology concerned with the study of algae

ALGOMETER n instrument for measuring sensitivity to pressure or to pain

ALGOMETRY > ALGOMETER

ALGOR n chill

ALGORISM n Arabic or decimal system of counting

ALGORISMS > ALGORISM

ALGORITHM n logical arithmetical or computational procedure for solving a problem

ALGORS > ALGOR

ALGUACIL n Spanish law officer

ALGUACILS > ALGUACIL

ALGUAZIL n Spanish law officer

ALGUAZILS > ALGUAZIL

ALGUM n type of wood mentioned in Bible

ALGUMS > ALGUM

ALIAS adv also known as ▷ n false name ▷ vb give or assume an alias

ALIASED > ALIAS

ALIASES > ALIAS

ALIASING n error in a vision or sound signal

ALIASINGS > ALIASING

ALIBI n plea of being somewhere else when a crime was committed ▷ vb provide someone with an alibi

ALIBIED > ALIBI

ALIBIES > ALIBI

ALIBIING > ALIBI

ALIBIS > ALIBI

ALIBLE adj nourishing

ALICANT n wine from Alicante in Spain

ALICANTS > ALICANT

ALICYCLIC adj (of an organic compound) having aliphatic properties, in spite of the presence of a ring of carbon atoms

ALIDAD same as > ALIDADE

ALIDADE n surveying instrument

ALIDADES > ALIDADE

ALIDADS > ALIDAD

ALIEN adj foreign ▷ n foreigner ▷ vb transfer (property, etc) to another

ALIENABLE adj able to be transferred to another owner

ALIENAGE > ALIEN

ALIENAGES > ALIEN

ALIENATE vb cause to become hostile

ALIENATED > ALIENATE

ALIENATES > ALIENATE

ALIENATOR > ALIENATE

ALIENED > ALIEN

ALIENEE n person to whom a transfer of property is made

ALIENEES > ALIENEE

ALIENER > ALIEN

ALIENERS > ALIEN

ALIENING > ALIEN

ALIENISM n old term for the study of mental illness

ALIENISMS > ALIENISM

ALIENIST n old term for psychiatrist specializing in the legal aspects of mental illness

ALIENISTS > ALIENIST

ALIENLY > ALIEN

ALIENNESS > ALIEN

ALIENOR n person who transfers property to another

ALIENORS > ALIENOR

ALIENS > ALIEN

ALIF n first letter of Arabic alphabet

ALIFORM adj wing-shaped

ALIFS > ALIF

ALIGARTA n alligator

ALIGARTAS > ALIGARTA

ALIGHT vb step out of (a vehicle) ▷ adj on fire ▷ adv on fire

ALIGHTED > ALIGHT

ALIGHTING > ALIGHT

ALIGHTS > ALIGHT

ALIGN vb bring (a person or group) into agreement with the policy of another

ALIGNED > ALIGN

ALIGNER > ALIGN

ALIGNERS > ALIGN

ALIGNING > ALIGN

ALIGNMENT n arrangement in a straight line

ALIGNS > ALIGN

ALIKE adj like, similar ▷ adv in the same way

ALIKENESS > ALIKE

ALIMENT n something that nourishes the body ▷ vb support or sustain

ALIMENTAL > ALIMENT

ALIMENTED > ALIMENT

ALIMENTS > ALIMENT

ALIMONIED adj provided with alimony

ALIMONIES > ALIMONY

ALIMONY n allowance paid under a court order to a separated or divorced spouse

ALINE a rare spelling of > ALIGN

ALINED > ALINE

ALINEMENT > ALINE

ALINER > ALINE

ALINERS > ALINE

ALINES > ALINE

ALINING > ALINE

ALIPED n bat-like creature ▷ adj having digits connected by a membrane

ALIPEDS > ALIPED

ALIPHATIC adj (of an organic compound) having an open chain structure

ALIQUANT adj denoting or belonging to a number that is not an exact divisor of a given number

ALIQUOT adj of or denoting an exact divisor of a number ▷ n exact divisor

ALIQUOTS > ALIQUOT

ALISMA n marsh plant

ALISMAS > ALISMA

ALISON same as > ALYSSUM

ALISONS > ALISON

ALIST adj leaning over

ALIT rare past tense and past participle of > ALIGHT

ALITERACY > ALITERATE

ALITERATE n person who is able to read but disinclined to do so ▷ adj of or relating to aliterates

ALIUNDE adj from a source under consideration

ALIVE adj living, in existence

ALIVENESS > ALIVE

ALIYA same as > ALIYAH

ALIYAH n immigration to the Holy Land

ALIYAHS > ALIYAH

ALIYAS > ALIYA

ALIYOS n remission of sin in Jewish faith

ALTYOT > ALIYAH

ALIYOTH > ALIYAH

ALIZARI n madder plant from Middle East

ALIZARIN n brownish-yellow powder or orange-red crystalline solid

ALIZARINE n alizarin

ALIZARINS > ALIZARIN

ALIZARIS > ALIZARI

ALKAHEST n hypothetical universal solvent sought by alchemists

ALKAHESTS > ALKAHEST

ALKALI n substance which combines with acid and neutralizes it to form a salt

ALKALIC adj geological term

ALKALIES > ALKALI

ALKALIFY vb make or become alkaline

ALKALIN adj alkaline

ALKALINE adj having the properties of or containing an alkali

ALKALIS > ALKALI

ALKALISE same as > ALKALIZE

ALKALISED > ALKALISE

ALKALISER > ALKALISE

ALKALISES > ALKALISE

ALKALIZE vb make alkaline

ALKALIZED > ALKALIZE

ALKALIZER > ALKALIZE

ALKALIZES > ALKALIZE

ALKALOID n any of a group of organic compounds containing nitrogen

ALKALOIDS > ALKALOID

ALKALOSES > ALKALOSIS

ALKALOSIS n abnormal increase in the alkalinity of the blood and extracellular fluids

ALKALOTIC > ALKALOSIS

ALKANE n saturated hydrocarbon

ALKANES > ALKANE

ALKANET n European plant whose roots yield a red dye

ALKANETS > ALKANET

ALKANNIN same as > ALKANET

ALKANNINS > ALKANNIN

ALKENE n unsaturated hydrocarbon

ALKENES > ALKENE

ALKIE same as > ALKY

ALKIES > ALKY

ALKINE n alkyne

ALKINES > ALKINE

ALKO n slang word for alcoholic

ALKOS > ALKO

ALKOXIDE n chemical compound containing oxygen

ALKOXIDES > ALKOXIDE

ALKOXY adj of a type of chemical compound containing oxygen

ALKY n slang word for alcoholic

ALKYD n synthetic resin

ALKYDS > ALKYD

ALKYL n type of monovalent radical

ALKYLATE vb add alkyl group to a compound

ALKYLATED > ALKYLATE

ALKYLATES > ALKYLATE

ALKYLIC > ALKYL

ALKYLS > ALKYL

ALKYNE n any unsaturated aliphatic hydrocarbon

ALKYNES > ALKYNE

ALL adj whole quantity or number (of) ▷ adv wholly, entirely ▷ n entire being, effort, or property

ALLANITE n rare black or brown mineral

ALLANITES > ALLANITE

ALLANTOIC > ALLANTOIS

ALLANTOID adj relating to or resembling the allantois

ALLANTOIN n chemical used in cosmetics

ALLANTOIS n membranous sac growing out of the ventral surface of the hind gut of embryonic reptiles, birds, and mammals. It combines with the chorion to form the mammalian placenta

ALLATIVE n word in grammatical case denoting movement towards

ALLATIVES > ALLATIVE

ALLAY vb reduce (fear or anger)

ALLAYED > ALLAY

ALLAYER > ALLAY

ALLAYERS > ALLAY

ALLAYING > ALLAY

ALLAYINGS > ALLAY

ALLAYMENT n mitigation

ALLAYS > ALLAY

ALLCOMERS n everyone who comes

ALLEDGE vb allege

ALLEDGED > ALLEDGE

ALLEDGES > ALLEDGE

ALLEDGING > ALLEDGE

ALLEE n avenue

ALLEES > ALLEE

ALLEGE vb state without proof

ALLEGED adj stated but not proved

ALLEGEDLY adv reportedly

ALLEGER > ALLEGE

ALLEGERS > ALLEGE

ALLEGES > ALLEGE

ALLEGGE vb alleviate

ALLEGGED > ALLEGGE

ALLEGGES > ALLEGGE

ALLEGGING > ALLEGGE

ALLEGIANT n loyalty

ALLEGING > ALLEGE

ALLEGORIC adj used in, containing, or characteristic of allegory

ALLEGORY n story with an underlying meaning as well as the literal one

ALLEGRO adv (to be played) in a brisk lively manner ▷ n piece or passage to be

performed in a brisk lively manner

ALLEGROS > ALLEGRO

ALLEL n form of gene

ALLELE n variant form of a gene

ALLELES > ALLELE

ALLELIC > ALLELE

ALLELISM > ALLELE

ALLELISMS > ALLELE

ALLELS > ALLEL

ALLELUIA n song of praise to God

ALLELUIAH interj alleluia

ALLELUIAS > ALLELUIA

ALLEMANDE n first movement of the classical suite, composed in a moderate tempo in a time signature of four-four

ALLENARLY adv solely

ALLERGEN n substance capable of causing an allergic reaction

ALLERGENS > ALLERGEN

ALLERGIC adj having or caused by an allergy ▷ n person suffering from an allergy

ALLERGICS > ALLERGIC

ALLERGIES > ALLERGY

ALLERGIN n allergen

ALLERGINS > ALLERGIN

ALLERGIST n physician skilled in the diagnosis and treatment of diseases or conditions caused by allergy

ALLERGY n extreme sensitivity to a substance, which causes the body to react to it

ALLERION n eagle in heraldry

ALLERIONS > ALLERION

ALLETHRIN n clear viscous amber-coloured liquid

ALLEVIANT n medical treatment that reduces pain but does not cure the underlying problem

ALLEVIATE vb lessen (pain or suffering)

ALLEY n narrow street or path

ALLEYCAT n homeless cat that roams in back streets

ALLEYCATS > ALLEYCAT

ALLEYED adj having alleys

ALLEYS > ALLEY

ALLEYWAY n narrow passage with buildings or walls on both sides

ALLEYWAYS > ALLEYWAY

ALLHEAL n plant with reputed healing powers

ALLHEALS > ALLHEAL

ALLIABLE adj able to form an alliance

ALLIAK n Inuit sledge

ALLIAKS > ALLIAK

ALLIANCE n state of being allied

ALLIANCES > ALLIANCE

ALLICE n species of fish

ALLICES > ALLICE

ALLICHOLY n melancholy

ALLICIN n chemical found in garlic

ALLICINS > ALLICIN

ALLIED adj joined, as by treaty, agreement, or marriage

ALLIES > ALLY

ALLIGARTA n alligator

ALLIGATE vb join together

ALLIGATED > ALLIGATE

ALLIGATES > ALLIGATE

ALLIGATOR n reptile of the crocodile family, found in the southern US and China

ALLIS n species of fish

ALLISES > ALLIS

ALLIUM n type of plant

ALLIUMS > ALLIUM

ALLNESS n being all

ALLNESSES > ALLNESS

ALLNIGHT adj lasting all night

ALLOBAR n form of element

ALLOBARS > ALLOBAR

ALLOCABLE > ALLOCATE

ALLOCARPY n production of fruit through cross-fertilization

ALLOCATE vb assign to someone or for a particular purpose

ALLOCATED > ALLOCATE

ALLOCATES > ALLOCATE

ALLOCATOR > ALLOCATE

ALLOD same as > ALLODIUM

ALLODIA > ALLODIUM

ALLODIAL adj (of land) held as an allodium

ALLODIUM n lands held free from rent or services due to an overlord

ALLODIUMS > ALLODIUM

ALLODS > ALLOD

ALLODYNIA n pain caused by a normally painless stimulus

ALLOGAMY n cross-fertilization in flowering plants

ALLOGENIC adj having different genes

ALLOGRAFT n tissue graft from a donor genetically unrelated to the recipient

ALLOGRAPH n document written by a person who is not a party to it

ALLOMERIC adj of similar crystalline structure

ALLOMETRY n study of the growth of part of an organism in relation to the growth of the entire organism

ALLOMONE n chemical substance secreted by certain animals

ALLOMONES > ALLOMONE

ALLOMORPH n any of the phonological representations of a single morpheme

ALLONGE n paper extension to bill of exchange ▷ vb (in fencing) lunge

ALLONGED > ALLONGE

ALLONGES > ALLONGE

ALLONGING > ALLONGE

ALLONS interj French word meaning let's go

ALLONYM n name assumed by a person

ALLONYMS > ALLONYM

ALLOPATH n person who practises or is skilled in allopathy

ALLOPATHS > ALLOPATH

ALLOPATHY n orthodox method of treating disease, by using drugs that produce an effect opposite to the effect of the disease being treated

ALLOPATRY n condition of taking place or existing in areas that are geographically separated from one another

ALLOPHANE n variously coloured amorphous mineral consisting of hydrated aluminium silicate and occurring in cracks in some sedimentary rocks

ALLOPHONE n any of several speech sounds that are regarded as contextual or environmental variants of the same phoneme

ALLOPLASM n part of the cytoplasm that is specialized to form cilia, flagella, and similar structures

ALLOSAUR n any large carnivorous bipedal dinosaur common in North America in late Jurassic times

ALLOSAURS > ALLOSAUR

ALLOSTERY n condition of an enzyme in which the structure and activity of the enzyme are modified by the binding of a metabolic molecule

ALLOT vb assign as a share or for a particular purpose

ALLOTMENT n distribution

ALLOTROPE n any of two or more physical forms in which an element can exist

ALLOTROPY n existence of an element in two or more physical forms

ALLOTS > ALLOT

ALLOTTED > ALLOT

ALLOTTEE n person to whom something is allotted

ALLOTTEES > ALLOTTEE

ALLOTTER n person who allots

ALLOTTERS > ALLOTTER

ALLOTTERY n something allotted

ALLOTTING > ALLOT

ALLOTYPE n type of specimen that differs from the original type

ALLOTYPES > ALLOTYPE

ALLOTYPIC > ALLOTYPE

ALLOTYPY n existence of allotypes

ALLOVER n fabric completely covered with a pattern

ALLOVERS > ALLOVER

ALLOW vb permit

ALLOWABLE adj permissible

ALLOWABLY > ALLOWABLE

ALLOWANCE n amount of money given at regular intervals

ALLOWED > ALLOW

ALLOWEDLY adv by general admission or agreement

ALLOWING > ALLOW

ALLOWS > ALLOW

ALLOXAN n chemical found in uric acid

ALLOXANS > ALLOXAN

ALLOY n mixture of two or more metals ▷ vb mix (metals)

ALLOYED > ALLOY

ALLOYING > ALLOY

ALLOYS > ALLOY

ALLOZYME n different form of an enzyme

ALLOZYMES > ALLOZYME

ALLS > ALL

ALLSEED n type of plant

ALLSEEDS > ALLSEED

ALLSORTS pl n assorted sweets

ALLSPICE n spice made from the berries of a tropical American tree

ALLSPICES > ALLSPICE

ALLUDE vb refer indirectly to

ALLUDED > ALLUDE

ALLUDES > ALLUDE

ALLUDING > ALLUDE

ALLURE n attractiveness ▷ vb entice or attract

ALLURED > ALLURE

ALLURER > ALLURE

ALLURERS > ALLURE

ALLURES > ALLURE

ALLURING adj extremely attractive

ALLUSION n indirect reference

ALLUSIONS > ALLUSION

ALLUSIVE adj containing or full of allusions

ALLUVIA > ALLUVIUM

ALLUVIAL adj of or relating to alluvium ▷ n soil consisting of alluvium

ALLUVIALS > ALLUVIAL

ALLUVION n wash of the sea or of a river

ALLUVIONS > ALLUVION

ALLUVIUM n fertile soil deposited by flowing water

ALLUVIUMS > ALLUVIUM

ALLY vb unite or be united, esp formally, as by treaty, confederation, or marriage ▷ n country, person, or group allied with another

ALLYING > ALLY

ALLYL n type of monovalent hydrocarbon

ALLYLIC > ALLYL

ALLYLS > ALLYL

ALLYOU pron all of you

ALMA same as > ALMAH

ALMAGEST n medieval treatise concerning alchemy or astrology

ALMAGESTS > ALMAGEST

ALMAH n Egyptian dancing girl

ALMAHS > ALMAH

ALMAIN n German dance

ALMAINS > ALMAIN

ALMANAC n yearly calendar with detailed information on anniversaries, phases of the moon, etc

ALMANACK same as > ALMANAC

ALMANACKS > ALMANACK

ALMANACS > ALMANAC

ALMANDINE n deep violet-red garnet

ALMANDITE n form of garnet

ALMAS > ALMA

ALME same as > ALMEH

ALMEH n Egyptian dancing girl

ALMEHS > ALMEH

ALMEMAR n area in a synagogue

ALMEMARS > ALMEMAR

ALMERIES > ALMERY

ALMERY n cupboard for church vessels

ALMES > ALME

ALMIGHTY adj all-powerful ▷ adv extremely

ALMIRAH n cupboard

ALMIRAHS > ALMIRAH

ALMNER n almoner

ALMNERS > ALMNER

ALMOND n edible oval-shaped nut which grows on a small tree

ALMONDIER > ALMONDY

ALMONDITE n violet-red garnet

ALMONDS > ALMOND

ALMONDY adj containing or resembling almond

ALMONER n formerly, a hospital social worker

ALMONERS > ALMONER

ALMONRIES > ALMONRY

ALMONRY n house of an almoner, usually the place where alms were given

ALMOST adv very nearly

ALMOUS Scots word for > ALMS

ALMS pl n gifts to the poor

ALMSGIVER n one who gives alms

ALMSHOUSE n (formerly) a house, financed by charity, which offered accommodation to the poor

ALMSMAN n person who gives or receives alms

ALMSMEN > ALMSMAN

ALMSWOMAN n woman who gives or receives alms

ALMSWOMEN > ALMSWOMAN

ALMUCE n fur-lined hood or cape

ALMUCES > ALMUCE

ALMUD n Spanish unit of measure

ALMUDE same as > ALMUD

ALMUDES > ALMUDE

ALMUDS > ALMUD

ALMUG n type of wood mentioned in Bible

ALMUGS > ALMUG

ALNAGE n measurement in ells

ALNAGER n inspector of cloth

ALNAGERS > ALNAGER

ALNAGES > ALNAGE

ALNICO n alloy including iron, nickel, and cobalt

ALNICOS > ALNICO

ALOCASIA n type of tropical plant

ALOCASIAS > ALOCASIA

ALOD n feudal estate with no superior

ALODIA > ALODIUM

ALODIAL > ALODIUM

ALODIUM same as > ALLODIUM

ALODIUMS > ALODIUM

ALODS > ALOD

ALOE n plant with fleshy spiny leaves

ALOED adj containing aloes

ALOES another name for > EAGLEWOOD

ALOESWOOD n aromatic wood of an Asian tree

ALOETIC > ALOE

ALOETICS > ALOE

ALOFT adv in the air ▷ adj in or into a high or higher place

ALOGIA n inability to speak

ALOGIAS > ALOGIA

ALOGICAL adj without logic

ALOHA a Hawaiian word for > HELLO

ALOHAS > ALOHA

ALOIN n crystalline compound

ALOINS > ALOIN

ALONE adv without anyone or anything else

ALONELY > ALONE

ALONENESS > ALONE

ALONG adv forward

ALONGSIDE adv beside (something)

ALONGST adv along

ALOO n (in Indian cookery) potato

ALOOF adj distant or haughty in manner

ALOOFLY > ALOOF

ALOOFNESS > ALOOF

ALOOS > ALOO

ALOPECIA n loss of hair

ALOPECIAS > ALOPECIA

ALOPECIC > ALOPECIA

ALOPECOID n fox-like animal

ALOUD adv in an audible voice ▷ adj in a normal voice

ALOW adj in or into the lower rigging of a vessel, near the deck

ALOWE Scots word for > ABLAZE

ALP n high mountain

ALPACA n Peruvian llama

ALPACAS > ALPACA

ALPACCA same as > ALPACA

ALPACCAS > ALPACCA

ALPARGATA n Spanish sandal

ALPEEN n Irish cudgel

ALPEENS > ALPEEN

ALPENGLOW n reddish light on the summits of snow-covered mountain peaks at sunset or sunrise

ALPENHORN same as > ALPHORN

ALPHA n first letter in the Greek alphabet

ALPHABET n set of letters used in writing a language

ALPHABETS > ALPHABET

ALPHAS > ALPHA

ALPHASORT vb arrange in alphabetical order

ALPHATEST vb subject (an experimental product such as computer software) to an initial test

ALPHORN n wind instrument

ALPHORNS > ALPHORN

ALPHOSIS n absence of skin pigmentation, as in albinism

ALPHYL n univalent radical

ALPHYLS > ALPHYL

ALPINE adj of high mountains ▷ n mountain plant

ALPINELY > ALPINE

ALPINES > ALPINE

ALPINISM > ALPINIST

ALPINISMS > ALPINIST

ALPINIST n mountain climber

ALPINISTS > ALPINIST

ALPS > ALP

ALREADY adv before the present time

ALRIGHT adj all right

ALS > AL

ALSIKE n clover native to Europe and Asia

ALSIKES > ALSIKE

ALSO adv in addition, too

ALSOON same as > ALSOONE

ALSOONE adv as soon

ALT n octave directly above the treble staff

ALTAR n table used for Communion in Christian churches

ALTARAGE n donations placed on altar for priest

ALTARAGES > ALTARAGE

ALTARS > ALTAR

ALTARWISE adv in the position of an altar

ALTER vb make or become different

ALTERABLE > ALTER

ALTERABLY > ALTER

ALTERANT n alternative

ALTERANTS > ALTERANT

ALTERCATE vb argue, esp heatedly

ALTERED > ALTER

ALTERER > ALTER

ALTERERS > ALTER

ALTERING > ALTER

ALTERITY n quality of being different

ALTERN adj alternate

ALTERNANT adj alternating

ALTERNAT n practice of deciding precedence by lot

ALTERNATE vb (cause to) occur by turns ▷ adj occurring by turns ▷ n person who substitutes for another in their absence

ALTERNATS > ALTERNAT

ALTERNE n neighbouring but different plant group
ALTERNES > ALTERNE
ALTERS > ALTER
ALTESSE n French word for highness
ALTESSES > ALTESSE
ALTEZA n Spanish word for highness
ALTEZAS > ALTEZA
ALTEZZA n Italian word for highness
ALTEZZAS > ALTEZZA
ALTHAEA n type of plant
ALTHAEAS > ALTHAEA
ALTHEA same as > ALTHAEA
ALTHEAS > ALTHEA
ALTHO conj short form of although
ALTHORN n valved brass musical instrument
ALTHORNS > ALTHORN
ALTHOUGH conj despite the fact that; even though
ALTIGRAPH n instrument that measures altitude
ALTIMETER n instrument that measures altitude
ALTIMETRY n science of measuring altitudes, as with an altimeter
ALTIPLANO n high plateau
ALTISSIMO adj (of music) very high in pitch ▷ n as in in altissimo the octave commencing an octave above the treble clef
ALTITUDE n height above sea level
ALTITUDES > ALTITUDE
ALTO n (singer with) the highest adult male voice ▷ adj denoting an instrument, singer, or voice with this range
ALTOIST n person who plays the alto saxophone
ALTOISTS > ALTOIST
ALTOS > ALTO
ALTRICES pl n altricial birds
ALTRICIAL adj (of the young of some species of birds after hatching) naked, blind, and dependent on the parents for food ▷ n altricial bird, such as a pigeon
ALTRUISM n unselfish concern for the welfare of others
ALTRUISMS > ALTRUISM
ALTRUIST > ALTRUISM
ALTRUISTS > ALTRUISM
ALTS > ALT
ALU same as > ALOO
ALUDEL n pear-shaped vessel
ALUDELS > ALUDEL
ALULA n tuft of feathers
ALULAE > ALULA
ALULAR > ALULA
ALULAS > ALULA
ALUM n double sulphate of aluminium and potassium
ALUMIN same as > ALUMINA
ALUMINA n aluminium oxide
ALUMINAS > ALUMINA

ALUMINATE n salt of the ortho or meta acid forms of aluminium hydroxide
ALUMINE n French word for alumina
ALUMINES > ALUMINE
ALUMINIC adj of aluminium
ALUMINIDE n type of aluminium compound
ALUMINISE same as > ALUMINIZE
ALUMINIUM n light silvery-white metal that does not rust
ALUMINIZE vb cover with aluminium
ALUMINOUS adj resembling aluminium
ALUMINS > ALUMIN
ALUMINUM same as > ALUMINIUM
ALUMINUMS > ALUMINUM
ALUMISH adj like alum
ALUMIUM old name for > ALUMINIUM
ALUMIUMS > ALUMIUM
ALUMNA n female graduate of a school, college, etc
ALUMNAE > ALUMNA
ALUMNI > ALUMNUS
ALUMNUS n graduate of a college
ALUMROOT n North American plant
ALUMROOTS > ALUMROOT
ALUMS > ALUM
ALUMSTONE same as > ALUNITE
ALUNITE n white, grey, or reddish mineral
ALUNITES > ALUNITE
ALURE n area behind battlements
ALURES > ALURE
ALUS > ALU
ALVAR n area of exposed limestone
ALVARS > ALVAR
ALVEARIES > ALVEARY
ALVEARY n beehive
ALVEATED adj with vaults like beehive
ALVEOLAR adj articulated with the alveoli ▷ n alveolar consonant
ALVEOLARS > ALVEOLAR
ALVEOLATE adj having many alveoli
ALVEOLE n alveolus
ALVEOLES > ALVEOLE
ALVEOLI > ALVEOLUS
ALVEOLUS n sockets in which the roots of teeth are embedded
ALVINE adj of or relating to the intestines or belly
ALWAY same as > ALWAYS
ALWAYS adv at all times
ALYSSUM n garden plant with small yellow or white flowers
ALYSSUMS > ALYSSUM
AM vb form of the present tense of be
AMA n vessel for water
AMABILE adj sweet
AMADAVAT same as > AVADAVAT

AMADAVATS > AMADAVAT
AMADODA pl n grown men
AMADOU n spongy substance made from fungi
AMADOUS > AMADOU
AMAH n (in the East, formerly) a nurse or maidservant
AMAHS > AMAH
AMAIN adv with great strength, speed, or haste
AMAKHOSI > INKHOSI
AMAKOSI > INKHOSI
AMALGAM n blend or combination
AMALGAMS > AMALGAM
AMANDINE n protein found in almonds
AMANDINES > AMANDINE
AMANDLA n political slogan calling for power to the Black population
AMANDLAS > AMANDLA
AMANITA n type of fungus
AMANITAS > AMANITA
AMANITIN n poison from amanita
AMANITINS > AMANITIN
AMARACUS n marjoram
AMARANT n amaranth
AMARANTH n imaginary flower that never fades
AMARANTHS > AMARANTH
AMARANTIN n protein
AMARANTS > AMARANT
AMARELLE n variety of sour cherry that has pale red fruit and colourless juice
AMARELLES > AMARELLE
AMARETTI > AMARETTO
AMARETTO n Italian liqueur with a flavour of almonds
AMARETTOS > AMARETTO
AMARNA adj pertaining to the reign of the Pharaoh Akhenaton
AMARONE n strong dry red Italian wine
AMARONES > AMARONE
AMARYLLID n plant of the amaryllis family
AMARYLLIS n lily-like plant with large red, pink, or white flowers
AMAS > AMA
AMASS vb collect or accumulate
AMASSABLE > AMASS
AMASSED > AMASS
AMASSER > AMASS
AMASSERS > AMASS
AMASSES > AMASS
AMASSING > AMASS
AMASSMENT > AMASS
AMATE vb match
AMATED > AMATE
AMATES > AMATE
AMATEUR n person who engages in a sport or activity as a pastime rather than as a profession ▷ adj not professional
AMATEURS > AMATEUR
AMATING > AMATE
AMATION n lovemaking
AMATIONS > AMATION
AMATIVE a rare word for > AMOROUS

AMATIVELY > AMATIVE
AMATOL n explosive mixture
AMATOLS > AMATOL
AMATORIAL same as > AMATORY
AMATORIAN > AMATORY
AMATORY adj relating to love
AMAUROSES > AMAUROSIS
AMAUROSIS n blindness, esp when occurring without observable damage to the eye
AMAUROTIC > AMAUROSIS
AMAUT n hooded coat worn by Inuit women
AMAUTI same as > AMAUT
AMAUTIK same as > AMAUT
AMAUTIKS > AMAUTIK
AMAUTIS > AMAUTI
AMAUTS > AMAUT
AMAZE vb surprise greatly, astound
AMAZED > AMAZE
AMAZEDLY > AMAZE
AMAZEMENT n incredulity or great astonishment
AMAZES > AMAZE
AMAZING adj causing wonder or astonishment
AMAZINGLY > AMAZING
AMAZON n any tall, strong, or aggressive woman
AMAZONIAN > AMAZON
AMAZONITE n green variety of microcline used as a gemstone
AMAZONS > AMAZON
AMBACH same as > AMBATCH
AMBACHES > AMBACH
AMBAGE n ambiguity
AMBAGES > AMBAGE
AMBAGIOUS > AMBAGE
AMBAN n Chinese official
AMBANS > AMBAN
AMBARI same as > AMBARY
AMBARIES > AMBARY
AMBARIS > AMBARI
AMBARY n tropical Asian plant that yields a fibre similar to jute
AMBASSAGE n embassy
AMBASSIES > AMBASSY
AMBASSY n embassy
AMBATCH n tree or shrub
AMBATCHES > AMBATCH
AMBEER n saliva coloured by tobacco juice
AMBEERS > AMBEER
AMBER n clear yellowish fossil resin ▷ adj brownish-yellow
AMBERED adj fixed in amber
AMBERGRIS n waxy substance secreted by the sperm whale, used in making perfumes
AMBERIER > AMBERY
AMBERIES > AMBERY
AMBERIEST > AMBERY
AMBERINA n type of glassware
AMBERINAS > AMBERINA
AMBERITE n powder like amber
AMBERITES > AMBERITE
AMBERJACK n type of large fish with golden markings

a

when young, found in Atlantic waters

AMBEROID n synthetic amber

AMBEROIDS > AMBEROID

AMBEROUS adj like amber

AMBERS > AMBER

AMBERY adj like amber ▷ n cupboard for church vessels

AMBIANCE same as > AMBIENCE

AMBIANCES > AMBIANCE

AMBIENCE n atmosphere of a place

AMBIENCES > AMBIENCE

AMBIENT adj surrounding ▷ n ambient music

AMBIENTS > AMBIENT

AMBIGUITY n possibility of interpreting an expression in more than one way

AMBIGUOUS adj having more than one possible meaning

AMBIPOLAR adj (of plasmas and semiconductors) involving both positive and negative charge carriers

AMBIT n limits or boundary

AMBITION n desire for success

AMBITIONS > AMBITION

AMBITIOUS adj having a strong desire for success

AMBITS > AMBIT

AMBITTY adj crystalline and brittle

AMBIVERT n person who is intermediate between an extrovert and an introvert

AMBIVERTS > AMBIVERT

AMBLE vb walk at a leisurely pace ▷ n leisurely walk or pace

AMBLED > AMBLE

AMBLER > AMBLE

AMBLERS > AMBLE

AMBLES > AMBLE

AMBLING n walking at a leisurely pace

AMBLINGS > AMBLING

AMBLYOPIA n impaired vision with no discernible damage to the eye or optic nerve

AMBLYOPIC > AMBLYOPIA

AMBO n early Christian pulpit

AMBOINA same as > AMBOYNA

AMBOINAS > AMBOINA

AMBONES > AMBO

AMBOS > AMBO

AMBOYNA n mottled curly-grained wood

AMBOYNAS > AMBOYNA

AMBRIES > AMBRY

AMBROID same as > AMBEROID

AMBROIDS > AMBROID

AMBROSIA n anything delightful to taste or smell

AMBROSIAL > AMBROSIA

AMBROSIAN > AMBROSIA

AMBROSIAS > AMBROSIA

AMBROTYPE n early type of glass negative that could be made to appear as a positive by backing it with black varnish or paper

AMBRY n cupboard in the wall of a church

AMBSACE n double ace, the lowest throw at dice

AMBSACES > AMBSACE

AMBULACRA n radial bands on the ventral surface of echinoderms, such as the starfish and sea urchin, on which the tube feet are situated

AMBULANCE n motor vehicle designed to carry sick or injured people

AMBULANT adj moving about from place to place

AMBULANTS > AMBULANT

AMBULATE vb wander about or move from one place to another

AMBULATED > AMBULATE

AMBULATES > AMBULATE

AMBULATOR n person who walks

AMBULETTE n motor vehicle designed for transporting ill or disabled people

AMBUSCADE n ambush ▷ vb ambush or lie in ambush

AMBUSCADO n ambuscade

AMBUSH n act of waiting in a concealed position to make a surprise attack ▷ vb attack from a concealed position

AMBUSHED > AMBUSH

AMBUSHER > AMBUSH

AMBUSHERS > AMBUSH

AMBUSHES > AMBUSH

AMBUSHING > AMBUSH

AME n soul

AMEARST old form of > AMERCE

AMEBA same as > AMOEBA

AMEBAE > AMEBA

AMEBAN > AMEBA

AMEBAS > AMEBA

AMEBEAN same as > AMOEBEAN

AMEBIASES > AMEBIASIS

AMEBIASIS n disease caused by amoeba

AMEBIC > AMEBA

AMEBOCYTE n any cell having properties similar to an amoeba, such as shape, mobility, and ability to engulf particles

AMEBOID same as > AMOEBOID

AMEER n (formerly) the ruler of Afghanistan

AMEERATE n country ruled by an ameer

AMEERATES > AMEERATE

AMEERS > AMEER

AMEIOSES > AMEIOSIS

AMEIOSIS n absence of pairing of chromosomes during meiosis

AMELCORN n variety of wheat

AMELCORNS > AMELCORN

AMELIA n congenital absence of arms or legs

AMELIAS > AMELIA

AMEN n term used at the end of a prayer or religious statement ▷ vb say amen

AMENABLE adj likely or willing to cooperate

AMENABLY > AMENABLE

AMENAGE vb tame

AMENAGED > AMENAGE

AMENAGES > AMENAGE

AMENAGING > AMENAGE

AMENAUNCE n person's bearing

AMEND vb make small changes

AMENDABLE > AMEND

AMENDE n public apology

AMENDED > AMEND

AMENDER > AMEND

AMENDERS > AMEND

AMENDES > AMENDE

AMENDING > AMEND

AMENDMENT n improvement or correction

AMENDS n recompense for injury, insult, etc

AMENE adj pleasant

AMENED > AMEN

AMENING > AMEN

AMENITIES > AMENITY

AMENITY n useful or enjoyable feature

AMENS > AMEN

AMENT n catkin

AMENTA > AMENTUM

AMENTAL > AMENTUM

AMENTIA n old word for congenital mental disability

AMENTIAS > AMENTIA

AMENTS > AMENT

AMENTUM same as > AMENT

AMERCE vb punish by a fine

AMERCED > AMERCE

AMERCER > AMERCE

AMERCERS > AMERCE

AMERCES > AMERCE

AMERCING > AMERCE

AMERICIUM n white metallic element artificially produced from plutonium

AMES > AME

AMESACE same as > AMBSACE

AMESACES > AMESACE

AMETHYST n bluish-violet variety of quartz used as a gemstone ▷ adj purple or violet

AMETHYSTS > AMETHYST

AMETROPIA n loss of ability to focus images on the retina, caused by an imperfection in the refractive function of the eye

AMETROPIC > AMETROPIA

AMI n male friend

AMIA n species of fish

AMIABLE adj friendly, pleasant-natured

AMIABLY > AMIABLE

AMIANTHUS n any of the fine silky varieties of asbestos

AMIANTUS n amianthus

AMIAS > AMIA

AMICABLE adj friendly

AMICABLY > AMICABLE

AMICE n item of clothing

AMICES > AMICE

AMICI > AMICUS

AMICUS n Latin for friend

AMID prep in the middle of, among ▷ n amide

AMIDASE n enzyme

AMIDASES > AMIDASE

AMIDE n type of organic compound

AMIDES > AMIDE

AMIDIC > AMIDE

AMIDIN n form of starch

AMIDINE n crystalline compound

AMIDINES > AMIDINE

AMIDINS > AMIDIN

AMIDMOST adv in the middle

AMIDO adj containing amide

AMIDOGEN n chemical compound derived from ammonia

AMIDOGENS > AMIDOGEN

AMIDOL n chemical used in developing photographs

AMIDOLS > AMIDOL

AMIDONE n pain-killing drug

AMIDONES > AMIDONE

AMIDS same as > AMID

AMIDSHIP adj in the middle of a ship

AMIDSHIPS adv at or towards the middle of a ship ▷ adj at, near, or towards the centre of a vessel

AMIDST same as > AMID

AMIE n female friend

AMIES > AMIE

AMIGA n Spanish female friend

AMIGAS > AMIGA

AMIGO n friend

AMIGOS > AMIGO

AMILDAR n manager in India

AMILDARS > AMILDAR

AMIN same as > AMINE

AMINE n chemical

AMINES > AMINE

AMINIC > AMINE

AMINITIES > AMINITY

AMINITY n amenity

AMINO n type of organic compound present in amino acids

AMINOS > AMINO

AMINS > AMIN

AMIR n (formerly) the ruler of Afghanistan

AMIRATE > AMIR

AMIRATES > AMIR

AMIRS > AMIR

AMIS archaic form of > AMICE

AMISES > AMIS

AMISS adv wrongly, badly ▷ adj wrong, faulty ▷ n evil deed

AMISSES > AMISS

AMISSIBLE adj likely to be lost

AMISSING adj missing

AMITIES > AMITY

AMITOSES > AMITOSIS

AMITOSIS n unusual form of cell division

AMITOTIC > AMITOSIS

AMITROLE n pesticide

AMITROLES > AMITROLE

AMITY n friendship

AMLA n species of Indian tree

AMLAS > AMLA

AMMAN same as > AMTMAN

AMMANS > AMMAN
AMMETER n instrument for measuring electric current
AMMETERS > AMMETER
AMMINE n chemical compound
AMMINES > AMMINE
AMMINO adj containing ammonia molecules
AMMIRAL old word for **>** ADMIRAL
AMMIRALS > AMMIRAL
AMMO n ammunition ·
AMMOCETE n ammocoete
AMMOCETES > AMMOCETE
AMMOCOETE n larva of primitive jawless vertebrates, such as the lamprey, that lives buried in mud and feeds on microorganisms
AMMOLITE n fossilized ammonite shell
AMMOLITES > AMMOLITE
AMMON n Asian wild sheep
AMMONAL n explosive
AMMONALS > AMMONAL
AMMONATE same as **>** AMMINE
AMMONATES > AMMONATE
AMMONIA n strong-smelling alkaline gas containing hydrogen and nitrogen
AMMONIAC n strong-smelling gum resin obtained from the stems of a N Asian plant
AMMONIACS > AMMONIAC
AMMONIAS > AMMONIA
AMMONIATE vb unite or treat with ammonia
AMMONIC adj of ammonia
AMMONICAL > AMMONIC
AMMONIFY vb treat or impregnate with ammonia or a compound of ammonia
AMMONITE n fossilized spiral shell of an extinct sea creature
AMMONITES > AMMONITE
AMMONITIC > AMMONITE
AMMONIUM n type of monovalent chemical group
AMMONIUMS > AMMONIUM
AMMONO adj using ammonia
AMMONOID n type of fossil
AMMONOIDS > AMMONOID
AMMONS > AMMON
AMMOS > AMMO
AMNESIA n loss of memory
AMNESIAC > AMNESIA
AMNESIACS > AMNESIA
AMNESIAS > AMNESIA
AMNESIC > AMNESIA
AMNESICS > AMNESIA
AMNESTIC adj relating to amnesia
AMNESTIED > AMNESTY
AMNESTIES > AMNESTY
AMNESTY n general pardon for offences against a government ▷ vb overlook or forget (an offence)
AMNIA > AMNION
AMNIC adj relating to amnion
AMNIO n amniocentesis

AMNION n innermost of two membranes enclosing an embryo
AMNIONIC > AMNION
AMNIONS > AMNION
AMNIOS > AMNIO
AMNIOTE n group of animals
AMNIOTES > AMNIOTE
AMNIOTIC adj of or relating to the amnion
AMNIOTOMY n breaking of the membrane surrounding a fetus to induce labour
AMOEBA n microscopic single-celled animal able to change its shape
AMOEBAE > AMOEBA
AMOEBAEAN adj of or relating to lines of verse dialogue that answer each other alternately
AMOEBAN > AMOEBA
AMOEBAS > AMOEBA
AMOEBEAN same as **>** AMOEBAEAN
AMOEBIC > AMOEBA
AMOEBOID adj of, related to, or resembling amoebae
AMOK n frenzied state
AMOKS > AMOK
AMOKURA n type of sea bird
AMOKURAS > AMOKURA
AMOLE n American plant
AMOLES > AMOLE
AMOMUM n plant of ginger family
AMOMUMS > AMOMUM
AMONG prep in the midst of
AMONGST same as **>** AMONG
AMOOVE vb stir someone's emotions
AMOOVED > AMOOVE
AMOOVES > AMOOVE
AMOOVING > AMOOVE
AMORAL adj without moral standards
AMORALISM > AMORAL
AMORALIST > AMORAL
AMORALITY > AMORAL
AMORALLY > AMORAL
AMORANCE n condition of being in love
AMORANCES > AMORANCE
AMORANT > AMORANCE
AMORCE n small percussion cap
AMORCES > AMORCE
AMORET n sweetheart
AMORETS > AMORET
AMORETTI > AMORETTO
AMORETTO n (esp in painting) a small chubby naked boy representing a cupid
AMORETTOS > AMORETTO
AMORINI > AMORINO
AMORINO same as **>** AMORETTO
AMORISM > AMORIST
AMORISMS > AMORIST
AMORIST n lover or a writer about love
AMORISTIC > AMORIST
AMORISTS > AMORIST
AMORNINGS adv each morning
AMOROSA n lover

AMOROSAS > AMOROSA
AMOROSITY n quality of being amorous
AMOROSO adv (to be played) lovingly ▷ n sherry
AMOROSOS > AMOROSO
AMOROUS adj feeling, showing, or relating to love
AMOROUSLY > AMOROUS
AMORPHISM > AMORPHOUS
AMORPHOUS adj without distinct shape
AMORT adj in low spirits
AMORTISE same as **>** AMORTIZE
AMORTISED > AMORTISE
AMORTISES > AMORTISE
AMORTIZE vb pay off (a debt) gradually by periodic transfers to a sinking fund
AMORTIZED > AMORTIZE
AMORTIZES > AMORTIZE
AMOSITE n form of asbestos
AMOSITES > AMOSITE
AMOTION n act of removing
AMOTIONS > AMOTION
AMOUNT n extent or quantity ▷ vb be equal to or add up to
AMOUNTED > AMOUNT
AMOUNTING > AMOUNT
AMOUNTS > AMOUNT
AMOUR n love affair
AMOURETTE n minor love affair
AMOURS > AMOUR
AMOVE vb stir someone's emotions
AMOVED > AMOVE
AMOVES > AMOVE
AMOVING > AMOVE
AMOWT same as **>** AMAUT
AMOWTS > AMOWT
AMP n ampere ▷ vb excite or become excited
AMPACITY n ampere capacity of a conductor
AMPASSIES > AMPASSY
AMPASSY n ampersand
AMPED > AMP
AMPERAGE n strength of an electric current measured in amperes
AMPERAGES > AMPERAGE
AMPERE n basic unit of electric current
AMPERES > AMPERE
AMPERSAND n character (&), meaning and
AMPERZAND n ampersand
AMPHIBIA n class of amphibians
AMPHIBIAN n type of animal that lives on land but breeds in water
AMPHIBOLE n any of a large group of minerals consisting of the silicates of calcium, iron, magnesium, sodium, and aluminium
AMPHIBOLY n ambiguity of expression, esp where due to a grammatical construction
AMPHIGORY n piece of nonsensical writing in verse or, less commonly, prose
AMPHIOXI > AMPHIOXUS

AMPHIOXUS another name for the **>** LANCELET
AMPHIPATH adj of or relating to a molecule that possesses both hydrophobic and hydrophilic elements
AMPHIPOD n type of marine or freshwater crustacean with a flat body
AMPHIPODS > AMPHIPOD
AMPHOLYTE n electrolyte that can be acid or base
AMPHORA n two-handled ancient Greek or Roman jar
AMPHORAE > AMPHORA
AMPHORAL > AMPHORA
AMPHORAS > AMPHORA
AMPHORIC adj resembling the sound of blowing into a bottle
AMPING > AMP
AMPLE adj more than sufficient
AMPLENESS > AMPLE
AMPLER > AMPLE
AMPLEST > AMPLE
AMPLEXUS n mating in amphibians
AMPLIDYNE n magnetic amplifier
AMPLIFIED > AMPLIFY
AMPLIFIER n device used to amplify a current or sound signal
AMPLIFIES > AMPLIFY
AMPLIFY vb increase the strength of (a current or sound signal)
AMPLITUDE n greatness of extent
AMPLOSOME n stocky body type
AMPLY adv fully or generously
AMPOULE n small sealed glass vessel
AMPOULES > AMPOULE
AMPS > AMP
AMPUL n ampoule
AMPULE same as **>** AMPOULE
AMPULES > AMPULE
AMPULLA n dilated end part of certain tubes in the body
AMPULLAE > AMPULLA
AMPULLAR > AMPULLA
AMPULLARY > AMPULLA .
AMPULS > AMPUL
AMPUTATE vb cut off (a limb or part of a limb) for medical reasons
AMPUTATED > AMPUTATE
AMPUTATES > AMPUTATE
AMPUTATOR > AMPUTATE
AMPUTEE n person who has had a limb amputated
AMPUTEES > AMPUTEE
AMREETA same as **>** AMRITA
AMREETAS > AMREETA
AMRIT n liquid used in the Amrit Ceremony
AMRITA n ambrosia of the gods that bestows immortality
AMRITAS > AMRITA
AMRITS > AMRIT
AMSINCKIA n Californian herb

AMTMAN n magistrate in parts of Europe
AMTMANS > AMTMAN
AMTRAC n amphibious tracked vehicle
AMTRACK same as > AMTRAC
AMTRACKS > AMTRACK
AMTRACS > AMTRAC
AMTRAK same as > AMTRAC
AMTRAKS > AMTRAK
AMU n unit of mass
AMUCK same as > AMOK
AMUCKS > AMUCK
AMULET n something carried or worn as a protection against evil
AMULETIC > AMULET
AMULETS > AMULET
AMUS > AMU
AMUSABLE adj capable of being amused
AMUSE vb cause to laugh or smile
AMUSEABLE same as > AMUSABLE
AMUSED > AMUSE
AMUSEDLY > AMUSE
AMUSEMENT n state of being amused
AMUSER > AMUSE
AMUSERS > AMUSE
AMUSES > AMUSE
AMUSETTE n type of light cannon
AMUSETTES > AMUSETTE
AMUSIA n inability to recognize musical tones
AMUSIAS > AMUSIA
AMUSIC > AMUSIA
AMUSING adj mildly entertaining
AMUSINGLY > AMUSING
AMUSIVE adj deceptive
AMYGDAL n almond
AMYGDALA n almond-shaped part, such as a tonsil or a lobe of the cerebellum
AMYGDALAE > AMYGDALA
AMYGDALE n small hole in volcanic rock filled with minerals
AMYGDALES > AMYGDALE
AMYGDALIN n white soluble bitter-tasting crystalline glycoside extracted from bitter almonds
AMYGDALS > AMYGDAL
AMYGDULE same as > AMYGDALE
AMYGDULES > AMYGDULE
AMYL n chemical compound
AMYLASE n enzyme
AMYLASES > AMYLASE
AMYLENE another name (no longer in technical usage) for > PENTENE
AMYLENES > AMYLENE
AMYLIC adj of or derived from amyl
AMYLOGEN n soluble part of starch
AMYLOGENS > AMYLOGEN
AMYLOID n complex protein ▷ adj starchlike
AMYLOIDAL > AMYLOID
AMYLOIDS > AMYLOID

AMYLOPSIN n enzyme of the pancreatic juice that converts starch into sugar
AMYLOSE n type of chemical
AMYLOSES > AMYLOSE
AMYLS > AMYL
AMYLUM another name for > STARCH
AMYLUMS > AMYLUM
AMYOTONIA another name for > MYOTONIA
AMYTAL n as in sodium amytal type of sedative
AMYTALS > AMYTAL
AN adj form of a used before vowels ▷ n additional condition
ANA adv in equal quantities ▷ n collection of reminiscences
ANABAENA n type of freshwater alga
ANABAENAS > ANABAENA
ANABANTID n type of spiny-finned fish of the family which includes the fighting fish, climbing perch, and gourami
ANABAS n type of fish
ANABASES > ANABASIS
ANABASIS n military expedition to the interior of a country
ANABATIC adj (of air currents) rising upwards, esp up slopes
ANABIOSES > ANABIOSIS
ANABIOSIS n ability to return to life after apparent death
ANABIOTIC > ANABIOSIS
ANABLEPS n type of tropical freshwater fish with eyes adapted for seeing both in air and water
ANABOLIC adj of or relating to anabolism
ANABOLISM n metabolic process in which body tissues are synthesized from food
ANABOLITE n product of anabolism
ANABRANCH n stream that leaves a river and enters it again further downstream
ANACHARIS n water plant
ANACLINAL adj (of valleys and similar formations) progressing in a direction opposite to the dip of the surrounding rock strata
ANACLISES > ANACLITIC
ANACLISIS > ANACLITIC
ANACLITIC adj of or relating to relationships that are characterized by the strong dependence of one person on others or another
ANACONDA n large S American snake
ANACONDAS > ANACONDA
ANACRUSES > ANACRUSIS
ANACRUSIS n one or more unstressed syllables at the beginning of a line of verse
ANADEM n garland for the head
ANADEMS > ANADEM

ANAEMIA n deficiency in the number of red blood cells
ANAEMIAS > ANAEMIA
ANAEMIC adj having anaemia
ANAEROBE n organism that does not require oxygen
ANAEROBES > ANAEROBE
ANAEROBIA same as > ANAEROBES
ANAEROBIC adj not requiring oxygen
ANAGEN n phase of hair growth
ANAGENS > ANAGEN
ANAGLYPH n type of stereoscopic picture
ANAGLYPHS > ANAGLYPH
ANAGLYPHY > ANAGLYPH
ANAGOGE n allegorical interpretation
ANAGOGES > ANAGOGE
ANAGOGIC > ANAGOGE
ANAGOGIES > ANAGOGY
ANAGOGY same as > ANAGOGE
ANAGRAM n word or phrase made by rearranging the letters of another word or phrase
ANAGRAMS > ANAGRAM
ANAL adj of the anus
ANALCIME same as > ANALCITE
ANALCIMES > ANALCIME
ANALCIMIC > ANALCIME
ANALCITE n white, grey, or colourless zeolite mineral
ANALCITES > ANALCITE
ANALECTA same as > ANALECTS
ANALECTIC > ANALECTS
ANALECTS pl n selected literary passages from one or more works
ANALEMMA n scale shaped like a figure of eight
ANALEMMAS > ANALEMMA
ANALEPTIC adj (of a drug, etc) stimulating the central nervous system ▷ n any drug, such as doxapram, that stimulates the central nervous system
ANALGESIA n absence of pain
ANALGESIC adj (drug) relieving pain ▷ n drug that relieves pain
ANALGETIC n painkilling drug
ANALGIA same as > ANALGESIA
ANALGIAS > ANALGIA
ANALITIES > ANALITY
ANALITY n quality of being psychologically anal
ANALLY > ANAL
ANALOG same as > ANALOGUE
ANALOGA > ANALOGON
ANALOGIC > ANALOGY
ANALOGIES > ANALOGY
ANALOGISE same as > ANALOGIZE
ANALOGISM > ANALOGIZE
ANALOGIST > ANALOGY
ANALOGIZE vb use analogy

ANALOGON n analogue
ANALOGONS > ANALOGON
ANALOGOUS adj similar in some respects
ANALOGS > ANALOG
ANALOGUE n something that is similar in some respects to something else ▷ adj displaying information by means of a dial
ANALOGUES > ANALOGUE
ANALOGY n similarity in some respects
ANALYSAND n any person who is undergoing psychoanalysis
ANALYSE vb make an analysis of (something)
ANALYSED > ANALYSE
ANALYSER > ANALYSE
ANALYSERS > ANALYSE
ANALYSES > ANALYSIS
ANALYSING > ANALYSE
ANALYSIS n separation of a whole into its parts for study and interpretation
ANALYST n person skilled in analysis
ANALYSTS > ANALYST
ANALYTE n substance that is being analysed
ANALYTES > ANALYTE
ANALYTIC adj relating to analysis ▷ n analytical logic
ANALYTICS > ANALYTIC
ANALYZE same as > ANALYSE
ANALYZED > ANALYZE
ANALYZER > ANALYZE
ANALYZERS > ANALYZE
ANALYZES > ANALYZE
ANALYZING > ANALYZE
ANAMNESES > ANAMNESIS
ANAMNESIS n ability to recall past events
ANAMNIOTE n any vertebrate animal, such as a fish or amphibian, that lacks an amnion, chorion, and allantois during embryonic development
ANAN interj expression of failure to understand
ANANA n pineapple
ANANAS n plant related to the pineapple
ANANASES > ANANAS
ANANDA n Buddhist principle of extreme happiness
ANANDAS > ANANDA
ANANDROUS adj (of flowers) having no stamens
ANANKE n unalterable necessity
ANANKES > ANANKE
ANANTHOUS adj (of higher plants) having no flowers
ANAPAEST n metrical foot of three syllables, the first two short, the last long
ANAPAESTS > ANAPAEST
ANAPEST same as > ANAPAEST
ANAPESTIC > ANAPEST
ANAPESTS > ANAPEST
ANAPHASE n third stage of mitosis

ANAPHASES > ANAPHASE

ANAPHASIC > ANAPHASE

ANAPHOR n word referring back to a previous word

ANAPHORA n use of a word that has the same reference as a word used previously

ANAPHORAL > ANAPHORA

ANAPHORAS > ANAPHORA

ANAPHORIC adj of or relating to anaphorism

ANAPHORS > ANAPHOR

ANAPLASIA n reversion of plant or animal cells to a simpler less differentiated form

ANAPLASTY n plastic surgery

ANAPTYXES > ANAPTYXIS

ANAPTYXIS n insertion of a short vowel between consonants in order to make a word more easily pronounceable

ANARCH n instigator or personification of anarchy

ANARCHAL > ANARCHY

ANARCHIAL > ANARCHY

ANARCHIC > ANARCHY

ANARCHIES > ANARCHY

ANARCHISE vb make anarchic

ANARCHISM n doctrine advocating the abolition of government

ANARCHIST n person who advocates the abolition of government

ANARCHIZE vb make anarchic

ANARCHS > ANARCH

ANARCHY n lawlessness and disorder

ANARTHRIA n loss of the ability to speak coherently

ANARTHRIC > ANARTHRIA

ANAS > ANA

ANASARCA n accumulation of fluid within subcutaneous connective tissue

ANASARCAS > ANASARCA

ANASTASES > ANASTASIS

ANASTASIS n Christ's harrowing of hell

ANASTATIC > ANASTASIS

ANATA n Buddhist belief

ANATAS > ANATA

ANATASE n rare blue or black mineral

ANATASES > ANATASE

ANATEXES > ANATEXIS

ANATEXIS n partial melting of rocks

ANATHEMA n detested person or thing

ANATHEMAS > ANATHEMA

ANATMAN same as > ANATA

ANATMANS > ANATMAN

ANATOMIC > ANATOMY

ANATOMIES > ANATOMY

ANATOMISE same as > ANATOMIZE

ANATOMIST n expert in anatomy

ANATOMIZE vb dissect (an animal or plant)

ANATOMY n science of the structure of the body

ANATOXIN n bacterial toxin used in inoculation

ANATOXINS > ANATOXIN

ANATROPY n plant ovule inverted by a bending of the stalk

ANATTA n annatto

ANATTAS > ANATTA

ANATTO same as > ANNATTO

ANATTOS > ANATTO

ANAXIAL adj asymmetrical

ANBURIES > ANBURY

ANBURY n soft spongy tumour occurring in horses and oxen

ANCE dialect form of > ONCE

ANCESTOR n person from whom one is descended

ANCESTORS > ANCESTOR

ANCESTRAL adj of or inherited from ancestors ▷ n relation that holds between x and y if there is a chain of instances of a given relation leading from x to y

ANCESTRY n lineage or descent

ANCHO n chili pepper

ANCHOR n heavy hooked device to fasten a ship to the sea bottom ▷ vb fasten with or as if with an anchor

ANCHORAGE n place where boats can be anchored

ANCHORED > ANCHOR

ANCHORESS > ANCHORITE

ANCHORET n anchorite

ANCHORETS > ANCHORET

ANCHORING > ANCHOR

ANCHORITE n religious recluse

ANCHORMAN n broadcaster in a central studio who links up and presents items from outside camera units and other studios

ANCHORMEN > ANCHORMAN

ANCHORS pl n brakes of a motor vehicle

ANCHOS > ANCHO

ANCHOVETA n type of small anchovy of the American Pacific, used as bait by tuna fishermen

ANCHOVIES > ANCHOVY

ANCHOVY n small strong-tasting fish

ANCHUSA n Eurasian plant

ANCHUSAS > ANCHUSA

ANCHUSIN same as > ALKANET

ANCHUSINS > ANCHUSIN

ANCHYLOSE same as > ANKYLOSE

ANCIENT adj dating from very long ago ▷ n member of a civilized nation in the ancient world, esp a Greek, Roman, or Hebrew

ANCIENTER > ANCIENT

ANCIENTLY adv in ancient times

ANCIENTRY n quality of being ancient

ANCIENTS > ANCIENT

ANCILE n mythical Roman shield

ANCILIA > ANCILE

ANCILLA n Latin word for servant

ANCILLAE > ANCILLA

ANCILLARY adj supporting the main work of an organization ▷ n subsidiary or auxiliary thing or person

ANCILLAS > ANCILLA

ANCIPITAL adj flattened and having two edges

ANCLE old spelling of > ANKLE

ANCLES > ANCLE

ANCOME n inflammation

ANCOMES > ANCOME

ANCON n projecting bracket

ANCONAL > ANCON

ANCONE same as > ANCON

ANCONEAL > ANCON

ANCONES > ANCONE

ANCONOID > ANCON

ANCORA adv Italian for encore

ANCRESS n female anchorite

ANCRESSES > ANCRESS

AND n additional matter or problem

ANDANTE adv (to be played) moderately slowly ▷ n passage or piece to be performed moderately slowly

ANDANTES > ANDANTE

ANDANTINI > ANDANTINO

ANDANTINO adv slightly faster or slower than andante ▷ n passage or piece to be performed in this way

ANDESINE n feldspar mineral of the plagioclase series

ANDESINES > ANDESINE

ANDESITE n fine-grained tan or grey volcanic rock

ANDESITES > ANDESITE

ANDESITIC > ANDESITE

ANDESYTE n andesite

ANDESYTES > ANDESYTE

ANDIRON n iron stand for supporting logs in a fireplace

ANDIRONS > ANDIRON

ANDOUILLE n spicy smoked pork sausage with a blackish skin

ANDRADITE n yellow, green, or brownish-black garnet

ANDRO n type of hormone

ANDROECIA n stamens of flowering plants collectively

ANDROGEN n type of steroid

ANDROGENS > ANDROGEN

ANDROGYNE n person having both male and female characteristics

ANDROGYNY n condition of having male and female characteristics

ANDROID n robot resembling a human ▷ adj resembling a human being

ANDROIDS > ANDROID

ANDROLOGY n branch of medicine concerned with diseases and conditions specific to men

ANDROMEDA n type of shrub

ANDROS > ANDRO

ANDS > AND

ANDVILE old form of > ANVIL

ANDVILES > ANDVILE

ANE Scots word for > ONE

ANEAR adv nearly ▷ vb approach

ANEARED > ANEAR

ANEARING > ANEAR

ANEARS > ANEAR

ANEATH Scots word for > BENEATH

ANECDOTA pl n unpublished writings

ANECDOTAL adj containing or consisting exclusively of anecdotes rather than connected discourse or research conducted under controlled conditions

ANECDOTE n short amusing account of an incident

ANECDOTES > ANECDOTE

ANECDOTIC > ANECDOTE

ANECDYSES > ANECDYSIS

ANECDYSIS n period between moults in arthropods

ANECHOIC adj having a low degree of reverberation of sound

ANELACE same as > ANLACE

ANELACES > ANELACE

ANELASTIC adj not elastic

ANELE vb anoint, esp to give extreme unction to

ANELED > ANELE

ANELES > ANELE

ANELING > ANELE

ANELLI pl n pasta shaped like small rings

ANEMIA n anaemia

ANEMIAS > ANEMIA

ANEMIC same as > ANAEMIC

ANEMOGRAM n record produced by anemograph

ANEMOLOGY n study of winds

ANEMONE n plant with white, purple, or red flowers

ANEMONES > ANEMONE

ANEMOSES > ANEMOSIS

ANEMOSIS n cracking in timber caused by wind affecting growing tree

ANENST dialect word for > AGAINST

ANENT prep lying against

ANERGIA n anergy

ANERGIAS > ANERGIA

ANERGIC > ANERGY

ANERGIES > ANERGY

ANERGY n lack of energy

ANERLY Scots word for > ONLY

ANEROID adj not containing a liquid ▷ n barometer that does not contain liquid

ANEROIDS > ANEROID

ANES > ANE

ANESTRA > ANESTRUM

ANESTRI > ANESTRUS

ANESTROUS > ANESTRUS

ANESTRUM n anestrus

ANESTRUS same as > ANOESTRUS

ANETHOL n substance derived from oil of anise

ANETHOLE n white water-soluble crystalline substance with a liquorice-like odour

ANETHOLES > ANETHOLE

ANETHOLS > ANETHOL

ANETIC adj medically soothing

ANEUPLOID adj (of polyploid cells or organisms) having a chromosome number that is not an exact multiple of the haploid number ▷ n cell or individual of this type

ANEURIN a less common name for > THIAMINE

ANEURINS > ANEURIN

ANEURISM same as > ANEURYSM

ANEURISMS > ANEURISM

ANEURYSM n permanent swelling of a blood vessel

ANEURYSMS > ANEURYSM

ANEW adv once more

ANGA n part in Indian music

ANGAKOK n Inuit shaman

ANGAKOKS > ANGAKOK

ANGARIA n species of shellfish

ANGARIAS > ANGARIA

ANGARIES > ANGARY

ANGARY n right to use the property of a neutral state during a war

ANGAS > ANGA

ANGASHORE n miserable person given to complaining

ANGEKKOK n Inuit shaman

ANGEKKOKS > ANGEKKOK

ANGEKOK n Inuit shaman

ANGEKOKS > ANGEKOK

ANGEL n spiritual being believed to be an attendant or messenger of God ▷ vb provide financial support for

ANGELED > ANGEL

ANGELFISH n South American aquarium fish with large fins

ANGELHOOD n state of being an angel

ANGELIC adj very kind, pure, or beautiful

ANGELICA n aromatic plant

ANGELICAL same as > ANGELIC

ANGELICAS > ANGELICA

ANGELING > ANGEL

ANGELS > ANGEL

ANGELUS n series of prayers

ANGELUSES > ANGELUS

ANGER n fierce displeasure or extreme annoyance ▷ vb make (someone) angry

ANGERED > ANGER

ANGERING > ANGER

ANGERLESS > ANGER

ANGERLY adv old form of angrily

ANGERS > ANGER

ANGICO n South American tree

ANGICOS > ANGICO

ANGINA n heart disorder causing sudden severe chest pains

ANGINAL > ANGINA

ANGINAS > ANGINA

ANGINOSE > ANGINA

ANGINOUS > ANGINA

ANGIOGRAM n X-ray picture obtained by angiography

ANGIOLOGY n branch of medical science concerned with the blood vessels and the lymphatic system

ANGIOMA n tumour consisting of a mass of blood vessels or lymphatic vessels

ANGIOMAS > ANGIOMA

ANGIOMATA > ANGIOMA

ANGISHORE same as > ANGASHORE

ANGKLUNG n Asian musical instrument

ANGKLUNGS > ANGKLUNG

ANGLE n space between or shape formed by two lines or surfaces that meet ▷ vb bend or place (something) at an angle

ANGLED > ANGLE

ANGLEDUG n earthworm

ANGLEDUGS > ANGLEDUG

ANGLEPOD n American wild flower

ANGLEPODS > ANGLEPOD

ANGLER n person who fishes with a hook and line

ANGLERS > ANGLER

ANGLES > ANGLE

ANGLESITE n white or grey secondary mineral

ANGLEWISE > ANGLE

ANGLEWORM n earthworm used as bait by anglers

ANGLICE adv in English

ANGLICISE same as > ANGLICIZE

ANGLICISM n word, phrase, or idiom peculiar to the English language, esp as spoken in England

ANGLICIST n expert in or student of English literature or language

ANGLICIZE vb make or become English in outlook, form, etc

ANGLIFIED > ANGLIFY

ANGLIFIES > ANGLIFY

ANGLIFY same as > ANGLICIZE

ANGLING n art or sport of fishing with a hook and line

ANGLINGS > ANGLING

ANGLIST same as > ANGLICIST

ANGLISTS > ANGLIST

ANGLO n White inhabitant of the US not of Latin extraction

ANGLOPHIL n person having admiration for England or the English

ANGLOS > ANGLO

ANGOLA same as > ANGORA

ANGOPHORA n Australian tree related to the eucalyptus

ANGORA n variety of goat, cat, or rabbit with long silky hair

ANGORAS > ANGORA

ANGOSTURA n bitter aromatic bark

ANGRIER > ANGRY

ANGRIES > ANGRY

ANGRIEST > ANGRY

ANGRILY > ANGRY

ANGRINESS > ANGRY

ANGRY adj full of anger ▷ n angry person

ANGST n feeling of anxiety

ANGSTIER > ANGSTY

ANGSTIEST > ANGSTY

ANGSTROM n unit of length used to measure wavelengths

ANGSTROMS > ANGSTROM

ANGSTS > ANGST

ANGSTY adj displaying angst

ANGUIFORM adj shaped like a snake

ANGUINE adj of, relating to, or similar to a snake

ANGUIPED adj having snakes for legs ▷ n mythological Persian creature with snakes for legs

ANGUIPEDE n Persian mythological creature

ANGUIPEDS > ANGUIPED

ANGUISH n great mental pain ▷ vb afflict or be afflicted with anguish

ANGUISHED adj feeling or showing great mental pain

ANGUISHES > ANGUISH

ANGULAR adj (of a person) lean and bony

ANGULARLY > ANGULAR

ANGULATE adj having angles or an angular shape ▷ vb make or become angular

ANGULATED > ANGULATE

ANGULATES > ANGULATE

ANGULOSE same as > ANGULOUS

ANGULOUS adj having angles

ANHEDONIA n inability to feel pleasure

ANHEDONIC > ANHEDONIA

ANHEDRAL n downward inclination of an aircraft wing in relation to the lateral axis

ANHEDRALS > ANHEDRAL

ANHINGA n type of bird

ANHINGAS > ANHINGA

ANHUNGRED adj very hungry

ANHYDRASE n enzyme that catalyzes the removal of water

ANHYDRIDE n substance that combines with water to form an acid

ANHYDRITE n colourless or greyish-white mineral found in sedimentary rocks

ANHYDROUS adj containing no water

ANI n tropical bird

ANICCA n Buddhism belief

ANICCAS > ANICCA

ANICONIC adj (of images of deities, symbols, etc) not portrayed in a human or animal form

ANICONISM > ANICONIC

ANICONIST > ANICONIC

ANICUT n dam in India

ANICUTS > ANICUT

ANIDROSES > ANIDROSIS

ANIDROSIS n absence of sweating

ANIGH adv near

ANIGHT adv at night

ANIL n West Indian shrub

ANILE adj of or like a feeble old woman

ANILIN n aniline

ANILINE n colourless oily liquid

ANILINES > ANILINE

ANILINGUS n oral stimulation of anus

ANILINS > ANILIN

ANILITIES > ANILE

ANILITY > ANILE

ANILS > ANIL

ANIMA n feminine principle as present in the male unconscious

ANIMACIES > ANIMACY

ANIMACY n state of being animate

ANIMAL n living creature capable of voluntary motion, esp one other than a human being ▷ adj of animals

ANIMALIAN > ANIMAL

ANIMALIC > ANIMAL

ANIMALIER n painter or sculptor of animal subjects, esp a member of a group of early 19th-century French sculptors who specialized in realistic figures of animals, usually in bronze

ANIMALISE same as > ANIMALIZE

ANIMALISM n preoccupation with physical matters

ANIMALIST > ANIMALISM

ANIMALITY n animal instincts of human beings

ANIMALIZE vb make (a person) brutal or sensual

ANIMALLY adv physically

ANIMALS > ANIMAL

ANIMAS > ANIMA

ANIMATE vb give life to ▷ adj having life

ANIMATED adj interesting and lively

ANIMATELY > ANIMATE

ANIMATER same as > ANIMATOR

ANIMATERS > ANIMATER

ANIMATES > ANIMATE

ANIMATEUR n active promoter of an artistic endeavour

ANIMATI > ANIMATO

ANIMATIC n animated film sequence

ANIMATICS > ANIMATIC

ANIMATING > ANIMATE

ANIMATION n technique of making cartoon films

ANIMATISM n belief that inanimate objects have consciousness

ANIMATIST > ANIMATISM

ANIMATO n piece of music performed in a lively manner

ANIMATOR n person who makes animated cartoons

ANIMATORS > ANIMATOR

ANIMATOS > ANIMATO

ANIME n type of Japanese animation

ANIMES > ANIME

ANIMI > ANIMUS

ANIMIS > ANIMI

ANIMISM n belief that natural objects possess souls

ANIMISMS > ANIMISM

ANIMIST > ANIMISM

ANIMISTIC > ANIMISM

ANIMISTS > ANIMISM

ANIMOSITY n hostility, hatred

ANIMUS n hatred, animosity

ANIMUSES > ANIMUS

ANION n ion with negative charge

ANIONIC > ANION

ANIONS > ANION

ANIRIDIA n absence of the iris, due to a congenital condition or an injury

ANIRIDIAS > ANIRIDIA

ANIRIDIC > ANIRIDIA

ANIS > ANI

ANISE n plant with liquorice-flavoured seeds

ANISEED n liquorice-flavoured seeds of the anise plant

ANISEEDS > ANISEED

ANISES > ANISE

ANISETTE n liquorice-flavoured liqueur made from aniseed

ANISETTES > ANISETTE

ANISIC > ANISE

ANISOGAMY n type of reproduction in which the gametes are dissimilar

ANISOLE n colourless pleasant-smelling liquid used as a solvent

ANISOLES > ANISOLE

ANKER n old liquid measure for wine

ANKERITE n greyish to brown mineral that resembles dolomite

ANKERITES > ANKERITE

ANKERS > ANKER

ANKH n ancient Egyptian symbol

ANKHS > ANKH

ANKLE n joint between the foot and leg ▷ vb move

ANKLEBONE the nontechnical name for > TALUS

ANKLED > ANKLE

ANKLES > ANKLE

ANKLET n ornamental chain worn round the ankle

ANKLETS > ANKLET

ANKLING > ANKLE

ANKLONG n Asian musical instrument

ANKLONGS > ANKLONG

ANKLUNG n Asian musical instrument

ANKLUNGS > ANKLUNG

ANKUS n stick used, esp in India, for goading elephants

ANKUSES > ANKUS

ANKUSH n Indian weapon

ANKUSHES > ANKUSH

ANKYLOSE vb (of bones in a joint, etc) to fuse or stiffen by ankylosis

ANKYLOSED > ANKYLOSE

ANKYLOSES > ANKYLOSE

ANKYLOSIS n abnormal immobility of a joint, caused by a fibrous growth

ANKYLOTIC > ANKYLOSIS

ANLACE n medieval short dagger with a broad tapering blade

ANLACES > ANLACE

ANLAGE n organ or part in the earliest stage of development

ANLAGEN > ANLAGE

ANLAGES > ANLAGE

ANLAS same as > ANLACE

ANLASES > ANLAS

ANN n old Scots word for a widow's pension

ANNA n former Indian coin worth one sixteenth of a rupee

ANNAL n recorded events of one year

ANNALISE vb record in annals

ANNALISED > ANNALISE

ANNALISES > ANNALISE

ANNALIST > ANNAL

ANNALISTS > ANNAL

ANNALIZE vb record in annals

ANNALIZED > ANNALIZE

ANNALIZES > ANNALIZE

ANNALS > ANNAL

ANNAS > ANNA

ANNAT n old Scots word for a widow's pension

ANNATES pl n money paid to the Pope

ANNATS > ANNAT

ANNATTA n annatto

ANNATTAS > ANNATTA

ANNATTO n tropical tree

ANNATTOS > ANNATTO

ANNEAL vb toughen by heating and slow cooling ▷ n act of annealing

ANNEALED > ANNEAL

ANNEALER > ANNEAL

ANNEALERS > ANNEAL

ANNEALING > ANNEAL

ANNEALS > ANNEAL

ANNECTENT adj connecting

ANNELID n type of worm with a segmented body

ANNELIDAN > ANNELID

ANNELIDS > ANNELID

ANNEX vb seize (territory)

ANNEXABLE > ANNEX

ANNEXE n extension to a building

ANNEXED > ANNEX

ANNEXES > ANNEXE

ANNEXING > ANNEX

ANNEXION n old form of annexation

ANNEXIONS > ANNEXION

ANNEXMENT > ANNEX

ANNEXURE n something that is added

ANNEXURES > ANNEXURE

ANNICUT n dam in India

ANNICUTS > ANNICUT

ANNO adv Latin for in the year

ANNONA n American tree or shrub

ANNONAS > ANNONA

ANNOTATE vb add notes to (a written work)

ANNOTATED > ANNOTATE

ANNOTATES > ANNOTATE

ANNOTATOR > ANNOTATE

ANNOUNCE vb make known publicly

ANNOUNCED > ANNOUNCE

ANNOUNCER n person who introduces radio or television programmes

ANNOUNCES > ANNOUNCE

ANNOY vb irritate or displease

ANNOYANCE n feeling of being annoyed

ANNOYED > ANNOY

ANNOYER > ANNOY

ANNOYERS > ANNOY

ANNOYING adj causing irritation or displeasure

ANNOYS > ANNOY

ANNS > ANN

ANNUAL adj happening once a year ▷ n plant that completes its life cycle in a year

ANNUALISE same as > ANNUALIZE

ANNUALIZE vb calculate (a rate) for or as if for a year

ANNUALLY > ANNUAL

ANNUALS > ANNUAL

ANNUITANT n person in receipt of or entitled to an annuity

ANNUITIES > ANNUITY

ANNUITISE same as > ANNUITIZE

ANNUITIZE vb convert a lump sum to a series of payments

ANNUITY n fixed sum paid every year

ANNUL vb declare (something, esp a marriage) invalid

ANNULAR adj ring-shaped ▷ n ring finger

ANNULARLY > ANNULAR

ANNULARS > ANNULAR

ANNULATE adj having, composed of, or marked with rings ▷ n annelid

ANNULATED > ANNULATE

ANNULATES > ANNULATE

ANNULET n moulding in the form of a ring

ANNULETS > ANNULET

ANNULI > ANNULUS

ANNULLED > ANNUL

ANNULLING > ANNUL

ANNULMENT n formal declaration that a contract or marriage is invalid

ANNULOSE adj having a body formed of a series of rings

ANNULS > ANNUL

ANNULUS n area between two concentric circles

ANNULUSES > ANNULUS

ANOA n type of small cattle

ANOAS > ANOA

ANOBIID n any type of beetle

ANOBIIDS > ANOBIID

ANODAL > ANODE

ANODALLY > ANODE

ANODE n positive electrode in a battery, valve, etc

ANODES > ANODE

ANODIC > ANODE

ANODISE same as > ANODIZE

ANODISED > ANODISE

ANODISER same as > ANODIZER

ANODISERS > ANODISER

ANODISES > ANODISE

ANODISING > ANODISE

ANODIZE vb coat (metal) with a protective oxide film by electrolysis

ANODIZED > ANODIZE

ANODIZER n something that anodizes

ANODIZERS > ANODIZER

ANODIZES > ANODIZE

ANODIZING > ANODIZE

ANODONTIA n congenital absence of teeth

ANODYNE n something that relieves pain or distress ▷ adj relieving pain or distress

ANODYNES > ANODYNE

ANODYNIC > ANODYNE

ANOESES > ANOESIS

ANOESIS n feeling without understanding

ANOESTRA > ANOESTRUS

ANOESTRI > ANOESTRUS

ANOESTRUM same as > ANOESTRUS

ANOESTRUS n period between two periods of oestrus in many mammals

ANOETIC > ANOESIS

ANOINT vb smear with oil as a sign of consecration

ANOINTED > ANOINT

ANOINTER > ANOINT

ANOINTERS > ANOINT

ANOINTING n act of anointing

ANOINTS > ANOINT

ANOLE n type of lizard

ANOLES > ANOLE

ANOLYTE n part of electrolyte around anode

ANOLYTES > ANOLYTE

ANOMALIES > ANOMALY

ANOMALOUS adj different from the normal or usual order or type

ANOMALY n something that deviates from the normal, irregularity

ANOMIC > ANOMIE

ANOMIE n lack of social or moral standards

ANOMIES > ANOMIE

ANOMY same as > ANOMIE

ANON adv in a short time, soon

ANONYM n anonymous person or publication

ANONYMA n main vessel in the arterial network

ANONYMAS > ANONYMA

ANONYMISE same as > ANONYMIZE

ANONYMITY > ANONYMOUS

ANONYMIZE vb organize in a way that preserves anonymity

ANONYMOUS *adj* by someone whose name is unknown or withheld

ANONYMS > ANONYM

ANOOPSIA *n* squint in which the eye turns upwards

ANOOPSIAS > ANOOPSIA

ANOPHELES *n* type of mosquito which transmits the malaria parasite to humans

ANOPIA *n* inability to see

ANOPIAS > ANOPIA

ANOPSIA *n* squint in which the eye turns upwards

ANOPSIAS > ANOPSIA

ANORAK *n* light waterproof hooded jacket

ANORAKS > ANORAK

ANORECTAL *adj* of the anus and rectum

ANORECTIC > ANOREXIA

ANORETIC *n* anorectic

ANORETICS > ANORETIC

ANOREXIA *n* psychological disorder characterized by fear of becoming fat and refusal to eat

ANOREXIAS > ANOREXIA

ANOREXIC > ANOREXIA

ANOREXICS > ANOREXIA

ANOREXIES > ANOREXY

ANOREXY *old name for* > ANOREXIA

ANORTHIC *another word for* > TRICLINIC

ANORTHITE *n* white to greyish-white or reddish-white mineral

ANOSMATIC > ANOSMIA

ANOSMIA *n* loss of the sense of smell

ANOSMIAS > ANOSMIA

ANOSMIC > ANOSMIA

ANOTHER *adj* one more

ANOUGH *adj* enough

ANOUROUS *adj* having no tail

ANOVULANT *n* drug preventing ovulation

ANOVULAR *adj* without ovulation

ANOW *adj* old form of enough

ANOXAEMIA *n* deficiency in the amount of oxygen in the arterial blood

ANOXAEMIC > ANOXAEMIA

ANOXEMIA *same as* > ANOXAEMIA

ANOXEMIAS > ANOXEMIA

ANOXEMIC > ANOXEMIA

ANOXIA *n* lack or absence of oxygen

ANOXIAS > ANOXIA

ANOXIC > ANOXIA

ANS *pl n* as in *ifs and ans* things that might have happened, but which did not

ANSA *n* either end of Saturn's rings

ANSAE > ANSA

ANSAPHONE *n* telephone answering machine

ANSATE *adj* having a handle or handle-like part

ANSATED *adj* ansate

ANSATZ *n* (in mathematics) assumption made to help solve a problem

ANSATZES > ANSATZ

ANSERINE *adj* of or resembling a goose ▷ *n* chemical compound

ANSERINES > ANSERINE

ANSEROUS *same as* > ANSERINE

ANSWER *n* reply to a question, request, letter, etc ▷ *vb* give an answer (to)

ANSWERED > ANSWER

ANSWERER > ANSWER

ANSWERERS > ANSWER

ANSWERING > ANSWER

ANSWERS > ANSWER

ANT *n* small insect living in highly organized colonies

ANTA *n* pilaster

ANTACID *n* substance that counteracts acidity ▷ *adj* having the properties of this substance

ANTACIDS > ANTACID

ANTAE > ANTA

ANTALGIC *n* pain-relieving drug

ANTALGICS > ANTALGIC

ANTALKALI *n* substance that neutralizes alkalis

ANTAR *old word for* > CAVE

ANTARA *n* South American panpipes

ANTARAS > ANTARA

ANTARCTIC *adj* relating to Antarctica

ANTARS > ANTAR

ANTAS > ANTA

ANTBEAR *n* aardvark

ANTBEARS > ANTBEAR

ANTBIRD *n* South American bird

ANTBIRDS > ANTBIRD

ANTE *n* player's stake in poker ▷ *vb* place (one's stake) in poker

ANTEATER *n* mammal which feeds on ants by means of a long snout

ANTEATERS > ANTEATER

ANTECEDE *vb* go before, as in time, order, etc

ANTECEDED > ANTECEDE

ANTECEDES > ANTECEDE

ANTECHOIR *n* part of a church in front of the choir, usually enclosed by screens, tombs, etc

ANTED > ANTE

ANTEDATE *vb* precede in time ▷ *n* earlier date

ANTEDATED > ANTEDATE

ANTEDATES > ANTEDATE

ANTEED > ANTE

ANTEFIX *n* carved ornament

ANTEFIXA > ANTEFIX

ANTEFIXAE > ANTEFIX

ANTEFIXAL > ANTEFIX

ANTEFIXES > ANTEFIX

ANTEING > ANTE

ANTELOPE *n* deerlike mammal with long legs and horns

ANTELOPES > ANTELOPE

ANTELUCAN *adj* before daylight

ANTENATAL *adj* during pregnancy, before birth ▷ *n* examination during pregnancy

ANTENATI *pl n* people born before certain date

ANTENNA *n* insect's feeler

ANTENNAE > ANTENNA

ANTENNAL > ANTENNA

ANTENNARY > ANTENNA

ANTENNAS > ANTENNA

ANTENNULE *n* one of a pair of small mobile appendages on the heads of crustaceans in front of the antennae, usually having a sensory function

ANTEPAST *n* appetizer

ANTEPASTS > ANTEPAST

ANTERIOR *adj* the front

ANTEROOM *n* small room leading into a larger one, often used as a waiting room

ANTEROOMS > ANTEROOM

ANTES > ANTE

ANTETYPE *n* earlier form

ANTETYPES > ANTETYPE

ANTEVERT *vb* displace (an organ or part) by tilting it forward

ANTEVERTS > ANTEVERT

ANTHELIA > ANTHELION

ANTHELION *n* faint halo sometimes seen in polar or high altitude regions around the shadow of an object cast onto a thick cloud bank or fog

ANTHELIX *n* prominent curved fold of cartilage just inside the outer rim of the external ear

ANTHEM *n* song of loyalty, esp to a country ▷ *vb* provide with an anthem

ANTHEMED > ANTHEM

ANTHEMIA > ANTHEMION

ANTHEMIC > ANTHEM

ANTHEMING > ANTHEM

ANTHEMION *n* floral design, used esp in ancient Greek and Roman architecture and decoration, usually consisting of honeysuckle, lotus, or palmette leaf motifs

ANTHEMIS *n* genus of herbs of Mediterranean and SW Asia

ANTHEMS > ANTHEM

ANTHER *n* part of a flower's stamen containing pollen

ANTHERAL > ANTHER

ANTHERID *n* antheridium

ANTHERIDS > ANTHERID

ANTHERS > ANTHER

ANTHESES > ANTHESIS

ANTHESIS *n* time when a flower begins reproductive cycle

ANTHILL *n* mound near an ants' nest

ANTHILLS > ANTHILL

ANTHOCARP *n* fruit developing from many flowers

ANTHOCYAN *n* any of a class of water-soluble glycosidic pigments

ANTHODIA > ANTHODIUM

ANTHODIUM *another name for* > CAPITULUM

ANTHOID *adj* resembling a flower

ANTHOLOGY *n* collection of poems or other literary pieces by various authors

ANTHOTAXY *n* arrangement of flowers on a stem or parts on a flower

ANTHOZOAN *n* type of marine invertebrate with a body in the form of a polyp, such as corals, sea anemones, and sea pens

ANTHOZOIC > ANTHOZOAN

ANTHRACES > ANTHRAX

ANTHRACIC *adj* of anthrax

ANTHRAX *n* dangerous disease of cattle and sheep, communicable to humans

ANTHRAXES > ANTHRAX

ANTHRO *n* short for anthropology

ANTHROPIC *adj* of or relating to human beings

ANTHROS > ANTHRO

ANTHURIUM *n* tropical American plant cultivated as a house plant for its showy foliage and flowers

ANTI *adj* opposed (to) ▷ *n* opponent of a party, policy, or attitude

ANTIABUSE *adj* designed to prevent abuse

ANTIACNE *adj* inhibiting the development of acne

ANTIAGING *adj* resisting the effects of ageing

ANTIAIR *adj* countering attack by aircraft or missile

ANTIALIEN *adj* designed to prevent foreign animal or plant species from becoming established

ANTIAR *another name for* > UPAS

ANTIARIN *n* poison derived from antiar

ANTIARINS > ANTIARIN

ANTIARMOR *adj* designed or equipped to combat armoured vehicles

ANTIARS > ANTIAR

ANTIATOM *n* atom composed of antiparticles

ANTIATOMS > ANTIATOM

ANTIAUXIN *n* substance acting against auxin

ANTIBIAS *adj* countering bias

ANTIBLACK *adj* hostile to Black people

ANTIBODY *n* protein produced in the blood, which destroys bacteria

ANTIBOSS *adj* acting against bosses

ANTIBUG *adj* acting against computer bugs

ANTIBUSER *n* person who opposes the policy of transporting students to faraway schools to achieve racial balance

ANTIC n actor in a ludicrous or grotesque part ▷ adj fantastic

ANTICAL adj position of plant parts

ANTICALLY > ANTICAL

ANTICAR n opposed to cars

ANTICHLOR n substance used to remove chlorine from a material after bleaching or to neutralize the chlorine present

ANTICISE same as > ANTICIZE

ANTICISED > ANTICISE

ANTICISES > ANTICISE

ANTICITY adj opposed to cities

ANTICIVIC adj opposed to citizenship

ANTICIZE vb play absurdly

ANTICIZED > ANTICIZE

ANTICIZES > ANTICIZE

ANTICK vb perform antics

ANTICKE archaic form of > ANTIQUE

ANTICKED > ANTICK

ANTICKES > ANTICKE

ANTICKING > ANTICK

ANTICKS > ANTICK

ANTICLINE n fold of rock raised up into a broad arch so that the strata slope down on both sides

ANTICLING adj acting against clinging

ANTICLY adv grotesquely

ANTICODON n element of RNA

ANTICOLD adj preventing or fighting the common cold

ANTICOUS adj on the part of a flower furthest from the stem

ANTICRACK adj protecting a computer against unauthorized access

ANTICRIME adj preventing or fighting crime

ANTICS pl n absurd acts or postures

ANTICULT n organization that is opposed to religious cults

ANTICULTS > ANTICULT

ANTIDORA > ANTIDORON

ANTIDORON n consecrated bread

ANTIDOTAL > ANTIDOTE

ANTIDOTE n substance that counteracts a poison ▷ vb counteract with an antidote

ANTIDOTED > ANTIDOTE

ANTIDOTES > ANTIDOTE

ANTIDRAFT adj opposed to conscription

ANTIDRUG adj intended to discourage illegal drug use

ANTIDUNE n type of sand hill or inclined bedding plane

ANTIDUNES > ANTIDUNE

ANTIELITE adj opposed to elitism

ANTIENT old spelling of > ANCIENT

ANTIENTS > ANTIENT

ANTIFA n antifascist organization

ANTIFAS > ANTIFA

ANTIFAT adj acting to remove or prevent fat

ANTIFLU adj acting against influenza

ANTIFOAM adj allowing gas to escape rather than form foam

ANTIFOG adj preventing the buildup of moisture on a surface

ANTIFRAUD adj acting against fraud

ANTIFUR adj opposed to the wearing of fur garments

ANTIGANG adj designed to restrict the activities of criminal gangs

ANTIGAY adj hostile to homosexuals

ANTIGEN n substance causing the blood to produce antibodies

ANTIGENE n antigen

ANTIGENES > ANTIGENE

ANTIGENIC > ANTIGEN

ANTIGENS > ANTIGEN

ANTIGLARE adj cutting down glare

ANTIGRAFT adj designed to reduce corruption

ANTIGUN adj opposed to the possession of guns

ANTIHELIX same as > ANTHELIX

ANTIHERO n central character in a book, film, etc, who lacks the traditional heroic virtues

ANTIHUMAN adj inhuman

ANTIJAM adj preventing jamming

ANTIKING n rival to an established king

ANTIKINGS > ANTIKING

ANTIKNOCK n substance added to motor fuel to reduce knocking in the engine caused by too rapid combustion

ANTILABOR adj opposed to labor interests

ANTILEAK adj preventing leaks

ANTILEFT adj opposed to the left wing in politics

ANTILIFE adj opposed to living in harmony with the natural order

ANTILIFER > ANTILIFE

ANTILOCK adj designed to prevent overbraking

ANTILOG n number whose logarithm to a given base is a given number

ANTILOGS > ANTILOG

ANTILOGY n contradiction in terms

ANTIMACHO adj opposed to macho attitudes

ANTIMALE adj opposed to men

ANTIMAN adj opposed to men ▷ n offensive term for a homosexual man

ANTIMASK n interlude in a masque

ANTIMASKS > ANTIMASK

ANTIMEN > ANTIMAN

ANTIMERE n body part or organ that mirrors a similar structure on the other side

ANTIMERES > ANTIMERE

ANTIMERIC > ANTIMERE

ANTIMINE adj designed to counteract landmines

ANTIMONIC adj of or containing antimony in the pentavalent state

ANTIMONY n brittle silvery-white metallic element

ANTIMONYL n the monovalent group SbO-

ANTIMUON n antiparticle of a muon

ANTIMUONS > ANTIMUON

ANTIMUSIC n music intended to overthrow traditional conventions and expectations

ANTIMYCIN n antibiotic drug

ANTING n rubbing of ants by birds on their feathers

ANTINGS > ANTING

ANTINODAL > ANTINODE

ANTINODE n point of amplitude of displacement of opposite value to a node

ANTINODES > ANTINODE

ANTINOISE n sound generated so that it is out of phase with a noise, such as that made by an engine, in order to reduce the noise level by interference

ANTINOME n opposite

ANTINOMES > ANTINOME

ANTINOMIC > ANTINOMY

ANTINOMY n contradiction between two laws or principles that are reasonable in themselves

ANTINOVEL n type of prose fiction in which conventional elements of the novel are rejected

ANTINUKE same as > ANTINUKER

ANTINUKER n person who is opposed to nuclear weapons or energy

ANTINUKES > ANTINUKE

ANTIPAPAL adj opposed to the pope

ANTIPARTY adj opposed to a political party

ANTIPASTI > ANTIPASTO

ANTIPASTO n appetizer in an Italian meal

ANTIPATHY n dislike, hostility

ANTIPHON n hymn sung in alternate parts by two groups of singers

ANTIPHONS > ANTIPHON

ANTIPHONY n antiphonal singing of a musical composition by two choirs

ANTIPILL adj (of a material) not forming pills

ANTIPODAL adj of or relating to diametrically opposite points on the earth's surface

ANTIPODE n exact or direct opposite

ANTIPODES pl n any two places diametrically opposite one another on the earth's surface

ANTIPOLAR > ANTIPOLE

ANTIPOLE n opposite pole

ANTIPOLES > ANTIPOLE

ANTIPOPE n pope set up in opposition to the one chosen by church laws

ANTIPOPES > ANTIPOPE

ANTIPORN adj opposed to pornography

ANTIPOT adj opposed to illegal use of marijuana

ANTIPRESS adj hostile to the news media

ANTIPYIC n drug acting against suppuration

ANTIPYICS > ANTIPYIC

ANTIQUARK n antiparticle of a quark

ANTIQUARY n student or collector of antiques or ancient works of art

ANTIQUATE vb make obsolete or old-fashioned

ANTIQUE n object of an earlier period, valued for its beauty, workmanship, or age ▷ adj made in an earlier period ▷ vb give an antique appearance to

ANTIQUED > ANTIQUE

ANTIQUELY > ANTIQUE

ANTIQUER n collector of antiques

ANTIQUERS > ANTIQUER

ANTIQUES > ANTIQUE

ANTIQUEY adj having the appearance of an antique

ANTIQUIER > ANTIQUEY

ANTIQUING > ANTIQUE

ANTIQUITY n great age

ANTIRADAR adj preventing detection by radar

ANTIRAPE adj protecting against rape

ANTIRED adj of a particular colour of antiquark

ANTIRIOT adj designed for the control of crowds

ANTIROCK adj designed to prevent a vehicle from rocking

ANTIROLL adj designed to prevent a vehicle from tilting

ANTIROYAL adj opposed to the monarchy

ANTIRUST adj (of a product or procedure) effective against rust ▷ n substance or device that prevents rust

ANTIRUSTS > ANTIRUST

ANTIS > ANTI

ANTISAG adj preventing sagging

ANTISCIAN n person living on other side of equator

ANTISENSE adj acting in opposite way to RNA

ANTISERA > ANTISERUM

ANTISERUM n blood serum containing antibodies used to treat or provide immunity to a disease

a

ANTISEX adj opposed to sexual activity

ANTISHAKE adj (in photography) intended to reduce blurring caused by movement ▷ n antishake technology

ANTISHARK adj protecting against sharks

ANTISHIP adj designed for attacking ships

ANTISHOCK n one of a pair of walking poles designed to reduce stress on the knees

ANTISKID adj intended to prevent skidding

ANTISLEEP adj acting to prevent sleep

ANTISLIP adj acting to prevent slipping

ANTISMOG adj reducing smog

ANTISMOKE adj preventing smoke

ANTISMUT adj opposed to obscene material

ANTISNOB n person opposed to snobbery

ANTISNOBS > ANTISNOB

ANTISOLAR adj opposite to the sun

ANTISPAM adj intended to prevent spam

ANTISPAST n group of four syllables in poetic metre

ANTISTAT n substance preventing static electricity

ANTISTATE adj opposed to state authority

ANTISTATS > ANTISTAT

ANTISTICK adj preventing things from sticking to a surface

ANTISTORY n story without a plot

ANTISTYLE n style that rejects traditional aesthetics

ANTITANK adj (of weapons) designed to destroy military tanks

ANTITAX adj opposed to taxation

ANTITHEFT adj (of a device, campaign, system, etc) designed to prevent theft

ANTITHET n example of antithesis

ANTITHETS > ANTITHET

ANTITOXIC > ANTITOXIN

ANTITOXIN n (serum containing) an antibody that acts against a toxin

ANTITRADE n wind blowing in the opposite direction to a trade wind

ANTITRAGI n cartilaginous projections of the external ear opposite the tragus

ANTITRUST adj (of laws) opposing business monopolies ▷ n regulating or opposing trusts, monopolies, cartels, or similar organizations, esp in order to prevent unfair competition

ANTITUMOR n drug which acts against tumours

ANTITYPAL > ANTITYPE

ANTITYPE n something foreshadowed by a type or symbol

ANTITYPES > ANTITYPE

ANTITYPIC > ANTITYPE

ANTIULCER adj used to treat ulcers

ANTIUNION adj opposed to union

ANTIURBAN adj opposed to city life

ANTIVAX adj opposed to vaccination

ANTIVAXER n person opposed to vaccination

ANTIVENIN n antitoxin that counteracts a specific venom, esp snake venom

ANTIVENOM n venom antidote

ANTIVIRAL adj inhibiting the growth of viruses ▷ n any antiviral drug: used to treat diseases caused by viruses, such as herpes infections and AIDS

ANTIVIRUS adj relating to software designed to protect computer files from viruses ▷ n such a piece of software

ANTIWAR adj opposed to war

ANTIWEAR adj preventing wear

ANTIWEED adj killing or preventing weeds

ANTIWHITE adj hostile to White people

ANTIWOMAN adj hostile to women

ANTIWORLD n hypothetical or supposed world or universe composed of antimatter

ANTLER n branched horn of a male deer

ANTLERED adj having antlers

ANTLERS > ANTLER

ANTLIA n butterfly proboscis

ANTLIAE > ANTLIA

ANTLIATE adj relating to antlia

ANTLIKE adj of or like an ant or ants

ANTLION n type of insect resembling a dragonfly

ANTLIONS > ANTLION

ANTONYM n word that means the opposite of another

ANTONYMIC > ANTONYM

ANTONYMS > ANTONYM

ANTONYMY n use of antonyms

ANTPITTA n S American bird whose diet consists mainly of ants

ANTPITTAS > ANTPITTA

ANTRA > ANTRUM

ANTRAL > ANTRUM

ANTRE n cavern or cave

ANTRES > ANTRE

ANTRORSE adj directed or pointing upwards or forwards

ANTRUM n natural cavity, esp in a bone

ANTRUMS > ANTRUM

ANTS > ANT

ANTSIER > ANTSY

ANTSIEST > ANTSY

ANTSINESS > ANTSY

ANTSY adj restless, nervous, and impatient

ANTWACKIE adj old-fashioned

ANUCLEATE adj without a nucleus

ANURA pl n order of animals that comprises frogs and toads

ANURAL adj without a tail

ANURAN n type of amphibian

ANURANS > ANURAN

ANURESES > ANURESIS

ANURESIS n inability to urinate

ANURETIC > ANURESIS

ANURIA n result of a kidney disorder

ANURIAS > ANURIA

ANURIC > ANURIA

ANUROUS adj lacking a tail

ANUS n opening at the end of the alimentary canal, through which faeces are discharged

ANUSES > ANUS

ANVIL n heavy iron block on which metals are hammered into particular shapes ▷ vb forge on an anvil

ANVILED > ANVIL

ANVILING > ANVIL

ANVILLED > ANVIL

ANVILLING > ANVIL

ANVILS > ANVIL

ANVILTOP n type of cloud formation

ANVILTOPS > ANVILTOP

ANXIETIES > ANXIETY

ANXIETY n state of being anxious

ANXIOUS adj worried and tense

ANXIOUSLY > ANXIOUS

ANY adj one or some, no matter which ▷ adv at all

ANYBODIES > ANYBODY

ANYBODY n any person at random

ANYHOW adv anyway

ANYMORE adv at present

ANYON n (in mathematics) projective representation of a Lie group

ANYONE pron any person ▷ n any person at random

ANYONES > ANYONE

ANYONS > ANYON

ANYPLACE adv in, at, or to any unspecified place

ANYROAD a northern English dialect word for **>** ANYWAY

ANYTHING pron any object, event, or action whatever ▷ n any thing at random

ANYTHINGS > ANYTHING

ANYTIME adv at any time

ANYWAY adv at any rate, nevertheless

ANYWAYS nonstandard word for **>** ANYWAY

ANYWHEN adv at any time

ANYWHERE adv in, at, or to any place

ANYWHERES nonstandard word for **>** ANYWHERE

ANYWISE adv in any way or manner

ANZIANI pl n Italian word for councillors

AORIST n tense of the verb in classical Greek

AORISTIC > AORIST

AORISTS > AORIST

AORTA n main artery of the body, carrying oxygen-rich blood from the heart

AORTAE > AORTA

AORTAL > AORTA

AORTAS > AORTA

AORTIC > AORTA

AORTITIS n inflammation of the aorta

AOUDAD n wild mountain sheep

AOUDADS > AOUDAD

APACE adv swiftly

APACHE n Parisian gangster or ruffian

APACHES > APACHE

APADANA n ancient Persian palace hall

APADANAS > APADANA

APAGE interj Greek word meaning go away

APAGOGE n reduction to absurdity

APAGOGES > APAGOGE

APAGOGIC > APAGOGE

APAID > APAY

APANAGE same as **>** APPANAGE

APANAGED adj having apanage

APANAGES > APANAGE

APAREJO n kind of packsaddle made of stuffed leather cushions

APAREJOS > APAREJO

APART adv to pieces or in pieces

APARTHEID n former official government policy of racial segregation in S Africa

APARTMENT n room in a building

APARTNESS > APART

APATETIC adj of or relating to coloration that disguises and protects an animal

APATHATON old word for **>** EPITHET

APATHETIC adj having or showing little or no emotion

APATHIES > APATHY

APATHY n lack of interest or enthusiasm

APATITE n pale green to purple mineral, found in igneous rocks

APATITES > APATITE

APATOSAUR n long-necked dinosaur

APAY vb old word meaning satisfy

APAYD > APAY

APAYING > APAY

APAYS > APAY

APE *n* tailless monkey such as the chimpanzee or gorilla ▷ *vb* imitate

APEAK *adj* in a vertical or almost vertical position

APED > APE

APEDOM *n* state of being an ape

APEDOMS > APEDOM

APEEK *adv* nautical word meaning vertically

APEHOOD *n* state of being ape

APEHOODS > APEHOOD

APELIKE > APE

APEMAN *n* primate thought to have been the forerunner of humans

APEMEN > APEMAN

APEPSIA *n* digestive disorder

APEPSIAS > APEPSIA

APEPSIES > APEPSY

APEPSY *n* apepsia

APER *n* person who apes

APERCU *n* outline

APERCUS > APERCU

APERIENT *adj* having a mild laxative effect ▷ *n* mild laxative

APERIENTS > APERIENT

APERIES > APERY

APERIODIC *adj* not periodic

APERITIF *n* alcoholic drink taken before a meal

APERITIFS > APERITIF

APERITIVE *n* laxative

APERS > APER

APERT *adj* open

APERTNESS > APERT

APERTURAL > APERTURE

APERTURE *n* opening or hole

APERTURED *adj* having an aperture

APERTURES > APERTURE

APERY *n* imitative behaviour

APES > APE

APESHIT *adj* vulgar slang word meaning crazy or furious

APETALIES > APETALOUS

APETALOUS *adj* (of flowering plants) having no petals

APETALY > APETALOUS

APEX *n* highest point

APEXES > APEX

APGAR *n* as in *apgar score* system for determining the condition of an infant at birth

APHAGIA *n* refusal or inability to swallow

APHAGIAS > APHAGIA

APHAKIA *n* absence of the lens of an eye

APHAKIAS > APHAKIA

APHANITE *n* type of fine-grained rock, such as basalt

APHANITES > APHANITE

APHANITIC > APHANITE

APHASIA *n* disorder of the central nervous system

APHASIAC > APHASIA

APHASIACS > APHASIA

APHASIAS > APHASIA

APHASIC > APHASIA

APHASICS > APHASIA

APHELIA > APHELION

APHELIAN > APHELION

APHELION *n* point of a planet's orbit that is farthest from the sun

APHELIONS > APHELION

APHERESES > APHERESIS

APHERESIS *n* omission of a letter or syllable at the beginning of a word

APHERETIC > APHERESIS

APHESES > APHESIS

APHESIS *n* gradual disappearance of an unstressed vowel at the beginning of a word

APHETIC > APHESIS

APHETISE *vb* lose a vowel at the beginning of a word

APHETISED > APHETISE

APHETISES > APHETISE

APHETIZE *vb* lose a vowel at the beginning of a word

APHETIZED > APHETIZE

APHETIZES > APHETIZE

APHICIDE *n* substance for killing aphids

APHICIDES > APHICIDE

APHID *n* small insect which sucks the sap from plants

APHIDES > APHIS

APHIDIAN > APHID

APHIDIANS > APHID

APHIDIOUS > APHID

APHIDS > APHID

APHIS *n* type of aphid such as the blackfly

APHOLATE *n* type of pesticide

APHOLATES > APHOLATE

APHONIA *n* loss of the voice caused by damage to the vocal tract

APHONIAS > APHONIA

APHONIC *adj* affected with aphonia ▷ *n* person affected with aphonia

APHONICS > APHONIC

APHONIES > APHONY

APHONOUS > APHONIA

APHONY *same as* > APHONIA

APHORISE *same as* > APHORIZE

APHORISED > APHORISE

APHORISER > APHORISE

APHORISES > APHORISE

APHORISM *n* short clever saying expressing a general truth

APHORISMS > APHORISM

APHORIST > APHORISM

APHORISTS > APHORISM

APHORIZE *vb* write or speak in aphorisms

APHORIZED > APHORIZE

APHORIZER > APHORIZE

APHORIZES > APHORIZE

APHOTIC *adj* characterized by or growing in the absence of light

APHRODITE *n* North American butterfly

APHTHA *n* small ulceration

APHTHAE > APHTHA

APHTHOUS > APHTHA

APHYLLIES > APHYLLOUS

APHYLLOUS *adj* (of plants) having no leaves

APHYLLY > APHYLLOUS

APIACEOUS *adj* parsley-like

APIAN *adj* of, relating to, or resembling bees

APIARIAN *adj* of or relating to the breeding and care of bees ▷ *n* apiarist

APIARIANS > APIARIAN

APIARIES > APIARY

APIARIST *n* beekeeper

APIARISTS > APIARIST

APIARY *n* place where bees are kept

APICAL *adj* of, at, or being an apex ▷ *n* sound made with the tip of the tongue

APICALLY > APICAL

APICALS > APICAL

APICES *plural of* > APEX

APICIAN *adj* of fine or dainty food

APICULATE *adj* (of leaves) ending in a short sharp point

APICULI > APICULUS

APICULUS *n* short sharp point

APIECE *adv* each

APIEZON *adj* as in *apiezon oil* oil left by distillation

APIMANIA *n* extreme enthusiasm for bees

APIMANIAS > APIMANIA

APING > APE

APIOL *n* substance derived from parsley seeds

APIOLOGY *n* study of bees

APIOLS > APIOL

APISH *adj* stupid or foolish

APISHLY > APISH

APISHNESS > APISH

APISM *n* behaviour like an ape

APISMS > APISM

APIVOROUS *adj* eating bees

APLANAT *n* aplanatic lens

APLANATIC *adj* (of a lens or mirror) free from spherical aberration

APLANATS > APLANAT

APLANETIC *adj* (esp of some algal and fungal spores) nonmotile or lacking a motile stage

APLASIA *n* congenital absence of an organ

APLASIAS > APLASIA

APLASTIC *adj* relating to or characterized by aplasia

APLENTY *adv* in plenty

APLITE *n* type of igneous rock

APLITES > APLITE

APLITIC > APLITE

APLOMB *n* calm self-possession

APLOMBS > APLOMB

APLUSTRE *n* stern ornament on an ancient Greek ship

APLUSTRES > APLUSTRE

APNEA *same as* > APNOEA

APNEAL > APNEA

APNEAS > APNEA

APNEIC > APNEA

APNEUSES > APNEUSIS

APNEUSIS *n* gasping inhalation followed by short exhalation

APNEUSTIC *adj* of or relating to apneusis

APNOEA *n* temporary inability to breathe

APNOEAL > APNOEA

APNOEAS > APNOEA

APNOEIC > APNOEA

APO *n* type of protein

APOAPSES > APOAPSIS

APOAPSIS *n* point in an orbit furthest from the object orbited

APOCARP *n* apocarpous gynoecium or fruit

APOCARPS > APOCARP

APOCARPY *n* presence of many carpels

APOCOPATE *vb* omit the final sound or sounds of (a word)

APOCOPE *n* omission of the final sound or sounds of a word

APOCOPES > APOCOPE

APOCOPIC > APOCOPE

APOCRINE *adj* denoting a type of glandular secretion

APOCRYPHA *n* writings or statements of uncertain authority

APOD *n* animal without feet

APODAL *adj* (of snakes, eels, etc) without feet

APODE *n* animal without feet

APODES > APODE

APODICTIC *adj* unquestionably true by virtue of demonstration

APODOSES > APODOSIS

APODOSIS *n* consequent of a conditional statement

APODOUS *same as* > APODAL

APODS > APOD

APOENZYME *n* protein component that together with a coenzyme forms an enzyme

APOGAEIC > APOGEE

APOGAMIC > APOGAMY

APOGAMIES > APOGAMY

APOGAMOUS > APOGAMY

APOGAMY *n* type of reproduction in some ferns

APOGEAL > APOGEE

APOGEAN > APOGEE

APOGEE *n* point of moon's orbit

APOGEES > APOGEE

APOGEIC > APOGEE

APOGRAPH *n* exact copy

APOGRAPHS > APOGRAPH

APOLLO *n* strikingly handsome youth

APOLLOS > APOLLO

APOLOG *same as* > APOLOGUE

APOLOGAL > APOLOGUE

APOLOGIA *n* formal written defence of a cause

APOLOGIAE > APOLOGIA

APOLOGIAS > APOLOGIA

APOLOGIES > APOLOGY

APOLOGISE *same as* > APOLOGIZE

APOLOGIST n person who formally defends a cause

APOLOGIZE vb make an apology

APOLOGS > APOLOG

APOLOGUE n allegory or moral fable

APOLOGUES > APOLOGUE

APOLOGY n expression of regret for wrongdoing

APOLUNE n point in a lunar orbit

APOLUNES > APOLUNE

APOMICT n organism, esp a plant, produced by apomixis

APOMICTIC > APOMIXIS

APOMICTS > APOMICT

APOMIXES > APOMIXIS

APOMIXIS n type of asexual reproduction

APOOP adv on the poop deck

APOPHASES > APOPHASIS

APOPHASIS n device of mentioning a subject by stating that it will not be mentioned

APOPHATIC adj of theology that says God is indescribable

APOPHENIA n tendency to see patterns in random things

APOPHONY n change in the quality of vowels

APOPHYGE n outward curve at each end of the shaft of a column, adjoining the base or capital

APOPHYGES > APOPHYGE

APOPHYSES > APOPHYSIS

APOPHYSIS n process, outgrowth, or swelling from part of an animal or plant

APOPLAST n nonprotoplasmic component of a plant

APOPLASTS > APOPLAST

APOPLEX vb afflict with apoplexy

APOPLEXED > APOPLEX

APOPLEXES > APOPLEX

APOPLEXY n stroke

APOPTOSES > APOPTOSIS

APOPTOSIS n programmed death of some of an organism's cells as part of its natural growth and development

APOPTOTIC > APOPTOSIS

APORETIC > APORIA

APORIA n doubt, real or professed, about what to do or say

APORIAS > APORIA

APORT adj on or towards the port side

APOS > APO

APOSITIA n unwillingness to eat

APOSITIAS > APOSITIA

APOSITIC > APOSITIA

APOSPORIC > APOSPORY

APOSPORY n development of the gametophyte from the sporophyte without the formation of spores

APOSTACY same as > APOSTASY

APOSTASY n abandonment of one's religious faith or other belief

APOSTATE n person who has abandoned his or her religion, political party, or cause ▷ adj guilty of apostasy

APOSTATES > APOSTATE

APOSTATIC > APOSTATE

APOSTIL n marginal note

APOSTILLE n apostil

APOSTILS > APOSTIL

APOSTLE n one of the twelve disciples chosen by Christ to preach His gospel

APOSTLES > APOSTLE

APOSTOLIC adj of or relating to the Apostles or their teachings

APOTHECE n obsolete word for shop

APOTHECES > APOTHECE

APOTHECIA n cup-shaped structures that contain the asci in lichens

APOTHEGM n short cryptic remark containing some general or generally accepted truth; maxim

APOTHEGMS > APOTHEGM

APOTHEM n geometrical term

APOTHEMS > APOTHEM

APOZEM n medicine dissolved in water

APOZEMS > APOZEM

APP n application program

APPAID > APPAY

APPAIR vb old form of impair

APPAIRED > APPAIR

APPAIRING > APPAIR

APPAIRS > APPAIR

APPAL vb dismay, terrify

APPALL same as > APPAL

APPALLED > APPALL

APPALLING adj dreadful, terrible

APPALLS > APPALL

APPALOOSA n North American horse breed

APPALS > APPAL

APPALTI > APPALTO

APPALTO n Italian word for contact

APPANAGE n land granted by a king for the support of a younger son

APPANAGED adj having appanage

APPANAGES > APPANAGE

APPARAT n Communist Party organization

APPARATS > APPARAT

APPARATUS n equipment for a particular purpose

APPAREL n clothing ▷ vb clothe, adorn, etc

APPARELED > APPAREL

APPARELS > APPAREL

APPARENCY old word for > APPARENT

APPARENT adj readily seen, obvious ▷ n heir apparent

APPARENTS > APPARENT

APPARITOR n officer who summons witnesses and

executes the orders of an ecclesiastical and (formerly) a civil court

APPAY old word for > SATISFY

APPAYD > APPAY

APPAYING > APPAY

APPAYS > APPAY

APPEACH old word for > ACCUSE

APPEACHED > APPEACH

APPEACHES > APPEACH

APPEAL vb make an earnest request ▷ n earnest request

APPEALED > APPEAL

APPEALER > APPEAL

APPEALERS > APPEAL

APPEALING adj attractive or pleasing

APPEALS > APPEAL

APPEAR vb become visible or present

APPEARED > APPEAR

APPEARER > APPEAR

APPEARERS > APPEAR

APPEARING > APPEAR

APPEARS > APPEAR

APPEASE vb pacify (a person) by yielding to his or her demands

APPEASED > APPEASE

APPEASER > APPEASE

APPEASERS > APPEASE

APPEASES > APPEASE

APPEASING > APPEASE

APPEL n stamp of the foot, used to warn of one's intent to attack

APPELLANT n person who makes an appeal to a higher court

APPELLATE adj of appeals

APPELLEE n person who is accused or appealed against

APPELLEES > APPELLEE

APPELLOR n person initiating a law case

APPELLORS > APPELLOR

APPELS > APPEL

APPEND vb join on, add

APPENDAGE n thing joined on or added

APPENDANT adj attached, affixed, or added ▷ n person or thing attached or added

APPENDED > APPEND

APPENDENT same as > APPENDANT

APPENDING > APPEND

APPENDIX n separate additional material at the end of a book

APPENDS > APPEND

APPERIL old word for > PERIL

APPERILL old word for > PERIL

APPERILLS > APPERILL

APPERILS > APPERIL

APPERTAIN vb belong to

APPESTAT n part of the brain that regulates hunger and satiety

APPESTATS > APPESTAT

APPETENCE n craving or desire

APPETENCY same as > APPETENCE

APPETENT adj eager

APPETIBLE adj old word meaning desirable

APPETISE vb stimulate the appetite

APPETISED > APPETISE

APPETISER same as > APPETIZER

APPETISES > APPETISE

APPETITE n desire for food or drink

APPETITES > APPETITE

APPETIZE vb stimulate the appetite

APPETIZED > APPETIZE

APPETIZER n thing eaten or drunk to stimulate the appetite

APPETIZES > APPETIZE

APPLAUD vb show approval of by clapping one's hands

APPLAUDED > APPLAUD

APPLAUDER > APPLAUD

APPLAUDS > APPLAUD

APPLAUSE n approval shown by clapping one's hands

APPLAUSES > APPLAUSE

APPLE n round firm fleshy fruit that grows on trees

APPLECART n cart used to carry apples

APPLEJACK n brandy made from apples

APPLES > APPLE

APPLET n computing program

APPLETINI n apple-flavoured alcoholic cocktail

APPLETS > APPLET

APPLEY adj resembling or tasting like an apple

APPLIABLE adj applicable

APPLIANCE n device with a specific function

APPLICANT n person who applies for something

APPLICATE adj applied practicably

APPLIED adj (of a skill, science, etc) put to practical use

APPLIER > APPLY

APPLIERS > APPLY

APPLIES > APPLY

APPLIEST > APPLEY

APPLIQUE n decoration or trimming of one material sewn or otherwise fixed onto another ▷ vb sew or fix (a decoration) on as an appliqué

APPLIQUED > APPLIQUE

APPLIQUES > APPLIQUE

APPLY vb make a formal request

APPLYING > APPLY

APPOINT vb assign to a job or position

APPOINTED > APPOINT

APPOINTEE n person who is appointed

APPOINTER > APPOINT

APPOINTOR n person to whom a power to nominate persons to take property is given by deed or will

APPOINTS > APPOINT

APPORT n production of objects at a seance

APPORTION vb divide out in shares

APPORTS > APPORT

APPOSABLE adj capable of being apposed or brought into apposition

APPOSE vb place side by side or near to each other

APPOSED > APPOSE

APPOSER > APPOSE

APPOSERS > APPOSE

APPOSES > APPOSE

APPOSING > APPOSE

APPOSITE adj suitable, apt

APPRAISAL n assessment of the worth or quality of a person or thing

APPRAISE vb estimate the value or quality of

APPRAISED > APPRAISE

APPRAISEE n person being appraised

APPRAISER > APPRAISE

APPRAISES > APPRAISE

APPREHEND vb arrest and take into custody

APPRESS vb press together

APPRESSED > APPRESS

APPRESSES > APPRESS

APPRISE vb make aware (of)

APPRISED > APPRISE

APPRISER > APPRISE

APPRISERS > APPRISE

APPRISES > APPRISE

APPRISING > APPRISE

APPRIZE same as
> APPRISE

APPRIZED > APPRIZE

APPRIZER > APPRIZE

APPRIZERS > APPRIZE

APPRIZES > APPRIZE

APPRIZING > APPRIZE

APPRO n approval

APPROACH vb come near or nearer (to) ▷ n approaching or means of approaching

APPROBATE vb accept as valid

APPROOF old word for
> TRIAL

APPROOFS > APPROOF

APPROS > APPRO

APPROVAL n consent

APPROVALS > APPROVAL

APPROVE vb consider good or right

APPROVED > APPROVE

APPROVER > APPROVE

APPROVERS > APPROVE

APPROVES > APPROVE

APPROVING > APPROVE

APPS > APP

APPUI n support

APPUIED > APPUY

APPUIS > APPUI

APPULSE n close approach of two celestial bodies

APPULSES > APPULSE

APPULSIVE > APPULSE

APPUY vb support

APPUYED > APPUY

APPUYING > APPUY

APPUYS > APPUY

APRACTIC > APRAXIA

APRAXIA n disorder of the central nervous system

APRAXIAS > APRAXIA

APRAXIC > APRAXIA

APRES prep French word for after

APRICATE vb bask in sun

APRICATED > APRICATE

APRICATES > APRICATE

APRICOCK old word for
> APRICOT

APRICOCKS > APRICOCK

APRICOT n yellowish-orange juicy fruit like a small peach ▷ adj yellowish-orange

APRICOTS > APRICOT

APRIORISM n philosophical doctrine that there may be genuine knowledge independent of experience

APRIORIST > APRIORISM

APRIORITY n condition of being innate in the mind

APRON n garment worn over the front of the body to protect the clothes ▷ vb equip with an apron

APRONED > APRON

APRONFUL n amount held in an apron

APRONFULS > APRONFUL

APRONING > APRON

APRONLIKE > APRON

APRONS > APRON

APROPOS adv appropriate(ly)

APROTIC adj (of solvents) neither accepting nor donating hydrogen ions

APSARAS n Hindu water sprite

APSARASES > APSARAS

APSE n arched or domed recess, esp in a church

APSES > APSE

APSIDAL > APSIS

APSIDES > APSIS

APSIDIOLE n small arch

APSIS n points in the elliptical orbit of a planet or satellite

APSO n Tibetan terrier

APSOS > APSO

APT adj having a specified tendency ▷ vb be fitting

APTAMER n artificially created DNA or RNA molecule

APTAMERS > APTAMER

APTED > APT

APTER > APT

APTERAL adj (esp of a classical temple) not having columns at the sides

APTERIA > APTERIUM

APTERISM > APTEROUS

APTERISMS > APTEROUS

APTERIUM n bare patch on the skin of a bird

APTEROUS adj (of insects) without wings, as silverfish and springtails

APTERYX n kiwi (the bird)

APTERYXES > APTERYX

APTEST > APT

APTING > APT

APTITUDE n natural ability

APTITUDES > APTITUDE

APTLY > APT

APTNESS > APT

APTNESSES > APT

APTOTE n noun without inflections

APTOTES > APTOTE

APTOTIC > APTOTE

APTS > APT

APYRASE n enzyme

APYRASES > APYRASE

APYRETIC > APYREXIA

APYREXIA n absence of fever

APYREXIAS > APYREXIA

AQUA n water

AQUABATIC adj of gymnastic feats in water

AQUABOARD n board used to ride on water

AQUACADE same as
> AQUASHOW

AQUACADES > AQUACADE

AQUADROME n venue for water sports

AQUAE > AQUA

AQUAFABA n vegan substitute for egg whites

AQUAFABAS > AQUAFABA

AQUAFARM vb cultivate fish or shellfish

AQUAFARMS > AQUAFARM

AQUAFER n aquifer

AQUAFERS > AQUAFER

AQUAFIT n type of aerobic exercise done in water

AQUAFITS > AQUAFIT

AQUALUNG n mouthpiece attached to air cylinders, worn for underwater swimming

AQUALUNGS > AQUALUNG

AQUANAUT n person who lives and works underwater

AQUANAUTS > AQUANAUT

AQUAPHOBE n person afraid of water

AQUAPLANE n board on which a person stands to be towed by a motorboat ▷ vb ride on an aquaplane

AQUAPORIN n any one of a group of proteins in cell membranes that allow the passage of water across the membrane

AQUARELLE n method of watercolour painting in transparent washes

AQUARIA > AQUARIUM

AQUARIAL > AQUARIUM

AQUARIAN n person who keeps an aquarium

AQUARIANS > AQUARIAN

AQUARIIST same as
> AQUARIST

AQUARIST n curator of an aquarium

AQUARISTS > AQUARIST

AQUARIUM n tank in which fish and other underwater creatures are kept

AQUARIUMS > AQUARIUM

AQUAROBIC adj pertaining to exercises performed standing up in a swimming pool

AQUAS > AQUA

AQUASCAPE n extensive view of a body of water seen from one place

AQUASHOW n exhibition of swimming and diving, often accompanied by music

AQUASHOWS > AQUASHOW

AQUATIC adj living in or near water ▷ n marine or freshwater animal or plant

AQUATICS pl n water sports

AQUATINT n print like a watercolour, produced by etching copper ▷ vb etch (a block, etc) in aquatint

AQUATINTA n aquatint

AQUATINTS > AQUATINT

AQUATONE n fitness exercise in water

AQUATONES > AQUATONE

AQUAVIT n grain- or potato-based spirit

AQUAVITS > AQUAVIT

AQUEDUCT n structure carrying water across a valley or river

AQUEDUCTS > AQUEDUCT

AQUEOUS adj of, like, or containing water

AQUEOUSLY > AQUEOUS

AQUIFER n deposit of rock containing water used to supply wells

AQUIFERS > AQUIFER

AQUILEGIA another name for
> COLUMBINE

AQUILINE adj (of a nose) curved like an eagle's beak

AQUILON n name for the north wind

AQUILONS > AQUILON

AQUIVER adv quivering

AR n letter R

ARAARA another name for
> TREVALLY

ARAARAS > ARAARA

ARABA n Asian carriage

ARABAS > ARABA

ARABESK same as
> ARABESQUE

ARABESKS > ARABESK

ARABESQUE n ballet position in which one leg is raised behind and the arms are extended ▷ adj designating, of, or decorated in this style

ARABIC adj as in gum arabic gum exuded by certain acacia trees

ARABICA n high-quality coffee bean

ARABICAS > ARABICA

ARABICISE same as
> ARABICIZE

ARABICIZE vb make or become Arabic

ARABILITY n suitability of land for growing crops

ARABIN n essence of gum arabic

ARABINOSE n pentose sugar in plant gums

ARABINS > ARABIN

ARABIS n type of plant

ARABISE vb make or become Arab

ARABISED > ARABISE
ARABISES > ARABISE
ARABISING > ARABISE
ARABIZE *vb* make or become Arab
ARABIZED > ARABIZE
ARABIZES > ARABIZE
ARABIZING > ARABIZE
ARABLE *adj* suitable for growing crops on ▷ *n* arable land or farming
ARABLES > ARABLE
ARACEOUS *same as* **>** AROID
ARACHIS *n* Brazilian plant
ARACHISES > ARACHIS
ARACHNID *n* eight-legged invertebrate, such as a spider, scorpion, tick, or mite
ARACHNIDS > ARACHNID
ARACHNOID *n* middle of the three membranes that cover the brain and spinal cord ▷ *adj* of or relating to the middle of the three meninges
ARAGONITE *n* generally white or grey mineral, found in sedimentary rocks
ARAHUANA *n* tropical freshwater fish
ARAHUANAS > ARAHUANA
ARAISE *vb* old form of raise
ARAISED > ARAISE
ARAISES > ARAISE
ARAISING > ARAISE
ARAK *same as* **>** ARRACK
ARAKS > ARAK
ARALIA *n* type of plant
ARALIAS > ARALIA
ARAME *n* Japanese edible seaweed
ARAMES > ARAME
ARAMID *n* synthetic fibre
ARAMIDS > ARAMID
ARANCINI *pl n* fried rice balls with a savoury filling
ARANEID *n* member of the spider family
ARANEIDAN > ARANEID
ARANEIDS > ARANEID
ARANEOUS *adj* like a spider's web
ARAPAIMA *n* very large primitive freshwater teleost fish that occurs in tropical S America
ARAPAIMAS > ARAPAIMA
ARAPONGA *n* South American bird with a bell-like call
ARAPONGAS > ARAPONGA
ARAPUNGA *n* South American bird with a bell-like call
ARAPUNGAS > ARAPUNGA
ARAR *n* African tree
ARAROBA *n* Brazilian leguminous tree
ARAROBAS > ARAROBA
ARARS > ARAR
ARAUCARIA *n* type of coniferous tree of S America, Australia, and Polynesia, such as the monkey puzzle and bunya-bunya
ARAWANA *n* tropical freshwater fish

ARAWANAS > ARAWANA
ARAYSE *vb* old form of raise
ARAYSED > ARAYSE
ARAYSES > ARAYSE
ARAYSING > ARAYSE
ARB *short for* **>** ARBITRAGE
ARBA *n* Asian carriage
ARBALEST *n* large medieval crossbow, usually cocked by mechanical means
ARBALESTS > ARBALEST
ARBALIST *same as* **>** ARBALEST
ARBALISTS > ARBALIST
ARBAS > ARBA
ARBELEST *n* arbalest
ARBELESTS > ARBELEST
ARBITER *n* person empowered to judge in a dispute
ARBITERS > ARBITER
ARBITRAGE *n* purchase of currencies, securities, or commodities in one market for immediate resale in others in order to profit from unequal prices
ARBITRAL *adj* of or relating to arbitration
ARBITRARY *adj* based on personal choice or chance, rather than reason
ARBITRATE *vb* settle (a dispute) by arbitration
ARBITRESS *n* female arbitrator
ARBITRIUM *n* power to decide
ARBLAST *n* arbalest
ARBLASTER > ARBLAST
ARBLASTS > ARBLAST
ARBOR *n* revolving shaft or axle in a machine
ARBOREAL *adj* of or living in trees
ARBORED *adj* having arbors
ARBOREOUS *adj* thickly wooded
ARBORES > ARBOR
ARBORET *n* old name for an area planted with shrubs
ARBORETA > ARBORETUM
ARBORETS > ARBORET
ARBORETUM *n* place where rare trees or shrubs are cultivated
ARBORIO *n* as in *arborio rice* variety of round-grain rice used for making risotto
ARBORIOS > ARBORIO
ARBORISE *same as* **>** ARBORIZE
ARBORISED > ARBORISE
ARBORISES > ARBORISE
ARBORIST *n* specialist in the cultivation of trees
ARBORISTS > ARBORIST
ARBORIZE *vb* give or take on a treelike branched appearance
ARBORIZED > ARBORIZE
ARBORIZES > ARBORIZE
ARBOROUS *adj* of trees
ARBORS > ARBOR
ARBOUR *n* glade sheltered by trees
ARBOURED *adj* having arbours

ARBOURS > ARBOUR
ARBOVIRAL > ARBOVIRUS
ARBOVIRUS *n* any one of a group of viruses that cause such diseases as encephalitis and dengue and are transmitted to humans by arthropods, esp insects and ticks
ARBS > ARB
ARBUSCLE *n* small tree
ARBUSCLES > ARBUSCLE
ARBUTE old name for **>** ARBUTUS
ARBUTEAN > ARBUTUS
ARBUTES > ARBUTE
ARBUTUS *n* evergreen shrub with strawberry-like berries
ARBUTUSES > ARBUTUS
ARC *n* part of a circle or other curve ▷ *vb* form an arc
ARCADE *n* covered passageway lined with shops ▷ *vb* provide with an arcade
ARCADED > ARCADE
ARCADES > ARCADE
ARCADIA *n* traditional idealized rural setting
ARCADIAN *n* person who leads a rural life
ARCADIANS > ARCADIAN
ARCADIAS > ARCADIA
ARCADING > ARCADE
ARCADINGS > ARCADE
ARCANA *n* either of the two divisions of a pack of tarot cards
ARCANAS > ARCANA
ARCANE *adj* mysterious and secret
ARCANELY > ARCANE
ARCANIST *n* person with secret knowledge
ARCANISTS > ARCANIST
ARCANUM *n* profound secret or mystery known only to initiates
ARCANUMS > ARCANUM
ARCATURE *n* small-scale arcade
ARCATURES > ARCATURE
ARCCOSINE *n* trigonometric function
ARCED > ARC
ARCH *n* curved structure supporting a bridge or roof ▷ *vb* (cause to) form an arch ▷ *adj* superior, knowing
ARCHAEA *n* order of prokaryotic microorganisms
ARCHAEAL *same as* **>** ARCHAEAN
ARCHAEAN *n* type of microorganism
ARCHAEANS > ARCHAEAN
ARCHAEI > ARCHAEUS
ARCHAEON *same as* **>** ARCHAEAN
ARCHAEUS *n* spirit believed to inhabit a living thing
ARCHAIC *adj* ancient
ARCHAICAL *same as* **>** ARCHAIC
ARCHAISE *same as* **>** ARCHAIZE
ARCHAISED > ARCHAISE
ARCHAISER > ARCHAISE

ARCHAISES > ARCHAISE
ARCHAISM *n* archaic word or phrase
ARCHAISMS > ARCHAISM
ARCHAIST > ARCHAISM
ARCHAISTS > ARCHAISM
ARCHAIZE *vb* give an archaic appearance or character to, as by the use of archaisms
ARCHAIZED > ARCHAIZE
ARCHAIZER > ARCHAIZE
ARCHAIZES > ARCHAIZE
ARCHANGEL *n* chief angel
ARCHDRUID *n* chief or principal druid
ARCHDUCAL *adj* of or relating to an archduke, archduchess, or archduchy
ARCHDUCHY *n* territory of an archduke or archduchess
ARCHDUKE *n* duke of specially high rank
ARCHDUKES > ARCHDUKE
ARCHEAN *same as* **>** ARCHAEAN
ARCHED *adj* provided with or spanned by an arch or arches
ARCHEI > ARCHEUS
ARCHENEMY *n* chief enemy
ARCHER *n* person who shoots with a bow and arrow
ARCHERESS *n* female archer
ARCHERIES > ARCHERY
ARCHERS > ARCHER
ARCHERY *n* art or sport of shooting with a bow and arrow
ARCHES > ARCH
ARCHEST > ARCH
ARCHETYPE *n* perfect specimen
ARCHEUS *n* spirit believed to inhabit a living thing
ARCHFIEND *n* the chief of fiends or devils
ARCHFOE *n* chief enemy
ARCHFOES > ARCHFOE
ARCHFOOL *n* very foolish person
ARCHFOOLS > ARCHFOOL
ARCHI > ARCO
ARCHICARP *n* female reproductive structure in ascomycetous fungi that consists of a cell or hypha and develops into the ascogonium
ARCHIL *a variant spelling of* **>** ORCHIL
ARCHILOWE *n* treat given in return
ARCHILS > ARCHIL
ARCHIMAGE *n* great magician or wizard
ARCHINE *n* Russian unit of length equal to about 71 cm
ARCHINES > ARCHINE
ARCHING *n* arched part
ARCHINGS > ARCH
ARCHITECT *n* person qualified to design and supervise the construction of buildings
ARCHITYPE *n* primitive original from which others derive
ARCHIVAL > ARCHIVE

ARCHIVE n collection of records or documents ▷ vb store (documents, data, etc) in an archive or other repository

ARCHIVED > ARCHIVE

ARCHIVES > ARCHIVE

ARCHIVING > ARCHIVE

ARCHIVIST n person in charge of archives

ARCHIVOLT n moulding around an arch, sometimes decorated

ARCHLET n small arch

ARCHLETS > ARCHLET

ARCHLIKE adj like an arch

ARCHLUTE n old bass lute

ARCHLUTES > ARCHLUTE

ARCHLY > ARCH

ARCHNESS > ARCH

ARCHOLOGY n study of the origins of things

ARCHON n (in ancient Athens) one of the nine chief magistrates

ARCHONS > ARCHON

ARCHONTIC > ARCHON

ARCHOSAUR n early type of dinosaur

ARCHRIVAL n chief rival

ARCHSTONE n wedge-shaped stone forming the curved part of an arch

ARCHWAY n passageway under an arch

ARCHWAYS > ARCHWAY

ARCHWISE adv like an arch

ARCIFORM adj shaped like an arch

ARCING n formation of an arc

ARCINGS > ARCING

ARCKED > ARC

ARCKING n formation of an arc

ARCKINGS > ARCKING

ARCMIN n 1/60 of a degree of an angle

ARCMINS > ARCMIN

ARCMINUTE n unit of angular measurement, 1/60 of a degree

ARCO adv musical direction meaning with bow ▷ n bow of a stringed instrument

ARCOGRAPH n instrument used for drawing arcs without using a central point

ARCOLOGY n architecture blending buildings with the natural environment

ARCOS > ARCO

ARCS > ARC

ARCSEC n 1/3600 of a degree of an angle

ARCSECOND n unit used in astronomy

ARCSECS > ARCSEC

ARCSINE n trigonometrical function

ARCSINES > ARCSINE

ARCTIC adj very cold ▷ n high waterproof overshoe with buckles

ARCTICS > ARCTIC

ARCTIID n type of moth

ARCTIIDS > ARCTIID

ARCTOID adj like a bear

ARCTOPHIL n arctophile

ARCUATE adj shaped or bent like an arc or bow

ARCUATED same as > ARCUATE

ARCUATELY > ARCUATE

ARCUATION n use of arches or vaults in buildings

ARCUS n circle around the cornea of the eye

ARCUSES > ARCUS

ARD n primitive plough

ARDEB n unit of dry measure

ARDEBS > ARDEB

ARDENCIES > ARDENT

ARDENCY > ARDENT

ARDENT adj passionate

ARDENTLY > ARDENT

ARDOR same as > ARDOUR

ARDORS > ARDOR

ARDOUR n passion

ARDOURS > ARDOUR

ARDRI n Irish high king

ARDRIGH n Irish high king

ARDRIGHS > ARDRIGH

ARDRIS > ARDRI

ARDS > ARD

ARDUOUS adj hard to accomplish, strenuous

ARDUOUSLY > ARDUOUS

ARE n unit of measure, 100 square metres ▷ vb form of the present tense of be

AREA n part or region

AREACH vb old form of reach

AREACHED > AREACH

AREACHES > AREACH

AREACHING > AREACH

AREAD vb old word meaning declare

AREADING > AREAD

AREADS > AREAD

AREAE > AREA

AREAL > AREA

AREALLY > AREA

AREAR n old form of arrear

AREARS > AREAR

AREAS > AREA

AREAWAY n passageway

AREAWAYS > AREAWAY

ARECA n type of palm tree

ARECAS > ARECA

ARECOLINE n drug derived from betel nut

ARED > AREAD

AREDD > AREAD

AREDE vb old word meaning declare

AREDES > AREDE

AREDING > AREDE

AREFIED > AREFY

AREFIES > AREFY

AREFY vb dry up

AREFYING > AREFY

AREG a plural of > ERG

AREIC adj relating to area

ARENA n seated enclosure for sports events

ARENAS > ARENA

ARENATION n use of hot sand as a medical poultice

ARENE n aromatic hydrocarbon

ARENES > ARENE

ARENITE n any arenaceous rock

ARENITES > ARENITE

ARENITIC > ARENITE

ARENOSE adj sandy

ARENOUS adj sandy

AREOLA n small circular area

AREOLAE > AREOLA

AREOLAR > AREOLA

AREOLAS > AREOLA

AREOLATE > AREOLA

AREOLATED adj areolate

AREOLE n space outlined on a surface

AREOLES > AREOLE

AREOLOGY n study of the planet Mars

AREOMETER n instrument for measuring the density of liquids

AREOMETRY n use of an araeometer

AREOSTYLE n building with widely spaced columns

AREPA n Colombian cornmeal cake

AREPAS > AREPA

ARERE adv old word meaning backwards

ARES > ARE

ARET vb old word meaning entrust

ARETE n sharp ridge separating two glacial valleys

ARETES > ARETE

ARETHUSA n N American orchid

ARETHUSAS > ARETHUSA

ARETS > ARET

ARETT vb old word meaning entrust

ARETTED > ARETT

ARETTING > ARETT

ARETTS > ARETT

AREW adv old word meaning in a row

ARF n barking sound

ARFS > ARF

ARGAL same as > ARGALI

ARGALA n Indian stork

ARGALAS > ARGALA

ARGALI n wild sheep

ARGALIS > ARGALI

ARGALS > ARGAL

ARGAN n Moroccan tree

ARGAND n lamp with a hollow circular wick

ARGANDS > ARGAND

ARGANS > ARGAN

ARGEMONE n prickly poppy

ARGEMONES > ARGEMONE

ARGENT n silver

ARGENTAL adj of or containing silver

ARGENTIC adj of or containing silver in the divalent or trivalent state

ARGENTINE adj of, relating to, or resembling silver ▷ n type of small silver fish

ARGENTITE n dark grey mineral

ARGENTOUS adj of or containing silver in the monovalent state

ARGENTS > ARGENT

ARGENTUM an obsolete name for > SILVER

ARGENTUMS > ARGENTUM

ARGH interj cry of pain

ARGHAN n agave plant

ARGHANS > ARGHAN

ARGIL n clay, esp potters' clay

ARGILLITE n any argillaceous rock, esp a hardened mudstone

ARGILS > ARGIL

ARGINASE n type of enzyme

ARGINASES > ARGINASE

ARGININE n essential amino acid

ARGININES > ARGININE

ARGLE vb quarrel

ARGLED > ARGLE

ARGLES > ARGLE

ARGLING > ARGLE

ARGOL n chemical compound

ARGOLS > ARGOL

ARGON n inert gas found in the air

ARGONAUT n paper nautilus

ARGONAUTS > ARGONAUT

ARGONON n inert gas

ARGONONS > ARGONON

ARGONS > ARGON

ARGOSIES > ARGOSY

ARGOSY n large merchant ship

ARGOT n slang or jargon

ARGOTIC > ARGOT

ARGOTS > ARGOT

ARGUABLE adj capable of being disputed

ARGUABLY adv it can be argued that

ARGUE vb try to prove by giving reasons

ARGUED > ARGUE

ARGUER > ARGUE

ARGUERS > ARGUE

ARGUES > ARGUE

ARGUFIED > ARGUFY

ARGUFIER > ARGUFY

ARGUFIERS > ARGUFY

ARGUFIES > ARGUFY

ARGUFY vb argue or quarrel, esp over something trivial

ARGUFYING > ARGUFY

ARGUING > ARGUE

ARGULI > ARGULUS

ARGULUS n parasite on fish

ARGUMENT n quarrel

ARGUMENTA n appeals to reason

ARGUMENTS > ARGUMENT

ARGUS n any of various brown butterflies

ARGUSES > ARGUS

ARGUTE adj shrill or keen

ARGUTELY > ARGUTE

ARGYLE adj with a diamond-shaped pattern ▷ n sock with this pattern

ARGYLES > ARGYLE

ARGYLL n sock with diamond pattern

ARGYLLS > ARGYLL

ARGYRIA n staining of skin by exposure to silver

ARGYRIAS > ARGYRIA

ARGYRITE n mineral containing silver sulphide

ARGYRITES > ARGYRITE

ARHAT n Buddhist who has achieved enlightenment

ARHATS > ARHAT

ARHATSHIP > ARHAT

ARHYTHMIA n irregular heartbeat

ARHYTHMIC > ARHYTHMIA

ARIA n elaborate song for solo voice, esp one from an opera

ARIARIES > ARIARY

ARIARY n currency of Madagascar

ARIAS > ARIA

ARID adj parched, dry

ARIDER > ARID

ARIDEST > ARID

ARIDITIES > ARID

ARIDITY > ARID

ARIDLY > ARID

ARIDNESS > ARID

ARIEL n type of Arabian gazelle

ARIELS > ARIEL

ARIETTA n short aria

ARIETTAS > ARIETTA

ARIETTE same as > ARIETTA

ARIETTES > ARIETTE

ARIGHT adv rightly

ARIKI n first-born male or female in a notable family

ARIKIS > ARIKI

ARIL n appendage on certain seeds

ARILED adj having an aril

ARILLARY adj having an aril

ARILLATE > ARILLATED

ARILLATED adj having an aril

ARILLI > ARILLUS

ARILLODE n structure in certain seeds

ARILLODES > ARILLODE

ARILLOID adj of or like an aril

ARILLUS n aril

ARILS > ARIL

ARIOSE adj songlike

ARIOSI > ARIOSO

ARIOSO n recitative with the lyrical quality of an aria

ARIOSOS > ARIOSO

ARIOT adv riotously

ARIPPLE adv in ripples

ARIS n Cockney slang for buttocks

ARISE vb come about

ARISEN > ARISE

ARISES > ARISE

ARISH n field that has been mown

ARISHES > ARISH

ARISING > ARISE

ARISTA n stiff bristle

ARISTAE > ARISTA

ARISTAS > ARISTA

ARISTATE > ARISTA

ARISTO n aristocrat

ARISTOS > ARISTO

ARISTOTLE n bottle

ARK n boat built by Noah, which survived the Flood ▷ vb place in an ark

ARKED > ARK

ARKING > ARK

ARKITE n passenger in ark

ARKITES > ARKITE

ARKOSE n type of sandstone

ARKOSES > ARKOSE

ARKOSIC > ARKOSE

ARKS > ARK

ARLE vb make a down payment

ARLED > ARLE

ARLES > ARLE

ARLING > ARLE

ARM n limbs from the shoulder to the wrist ▷ vb supply with weapons

ARMADA n large number of warships

ARMADAS > ARMADA

ARMADILLO n small S American mammal covered in strong bony plates

ARMAGNAC n dry brown brandy

ARMAGNACS > ARMAGNAC

ARMAMENT n military weapons

ARMAMENTS > ARMAMENT

ARMATURE n revolving structure in an electric motor or generator

ARMATURED > ARMATURE

ARMATURES > ARMATURE

ARMBAND n band worn on the arm

ARMBANDS > ARMBAND

ARMCHAIR n upholstered chair with side supports for the arms ▷ adj taking no active part

ARMCHAIRS > ARMCHAIR

ARMED adj equipped with or supported by arms, armour, etc

ARMER > ARM

ARMERIA n generic name for the plant thrift

ARMERIAS > ARMERIA

ARMERS > ARM

ARMET n close-fitting medieval visored helmet with a neck guard

ARMETS > ARMET

ARMFUL n as much as can be held in the arms

ARMFULS > ARMFUL

ARMGAUNT adj word in Shakespeare of uncertain meaning

ARMGUARD n covering to protect the arm

ARMGUARDS > ARMGUARD

ARMHOLE n opening in a garment through which the arm passes

ARMHOLES > ARMHOLE

ARMIES > ARMY

ARMIGER n person entitled to bear heraldic arms

ARMIGERAL > ARMIGER

ARMIGERO n armiger

ARMIGEROS > ARMIGERO

ARMIGERS > ARMIGER

ARMIL n bracelet

ARMILLA n bracelet

ARMILLAE > ARMILLA

ARMILLARY adj of or relating to bracelets

ARMILLAS > ARMILLA

ARMILS > ARMIL

ARMING n act of taking arms or providing with arms

ARMINGS > ARMING

ARMISTICE n agreed suspension of fighting

ARMLESS > ARM

ARMLET n band worn round the arm

ARMLETS > ARMLET

ARMLIKE > ARM

ARMLOAD n amount carried in the arms

ARMLOADS > ARMLOAD

ARMLOCK vb grip someone's arms

ARMLOCKED > ARMLOCK

ARMLOCKS > ARMLOCK

ARMOIRE n large cabinet

ARMOIRES > ARMOIRE

ARMONICA n glass harmonica

ARMONICAS > ARMONICA

ARMOR same as > ARMOUR

ARMORED same as > ARMOURED

ARMORER same as > ARMOURER

ARMORERS > ARMORER

ARMORIAL adj of or relating to heraldry or heraldic arms ▷ n book of coats of arms

ARMORIALS > ARMORIAL

ARMORIES > ARMORY

ARMORING > ARMOR

ARMORIST n heraldry expert

ARMORISTS > ARMORIST

ARMORLESS > ARMOR

ARMORS > ARMOR

ARMORY same as > ARMOURY

ARMOUR n metal clothing formerly worn to protect the body in battle ▷ vb equip or cover with armour

ARMOURED adj having a protective covering

ARMOURER n maker, repairer, or keeper of arms or armour

ARMOURERS > ARMOURER

ARMOURIES > ARMOURY

ARMOURING > ARMOUR

ARMOURS > ARMOUR

ARMOURY n place where weapons are stored

ARMOZEEN n material used for clerical gowns

ARMOZEENS > ARMOZEEN

ARMOZINE n material used for clerical gowns

ARMOZINES > ARMOZINE

ARMPIT n hollow under the arm at the shoulder

ARMPITS > ARMPIT

ARMREST n part of a chair or sofa that supports the arm

ARMRESTS > ARMREST

ARMS > ARM

ARMSFUL > ARMFUL

ARMURE n silk or wool fabric with a small cobbled pattern

ARMURES > ARMURE

ARMY n military land forces of a nation

ARMYWORM n caterpillar of a widely distributed noctuid moth

ARMYWORMS > ARMYWORM

ARNA n Indian water buffalo

ARNAS > ARNA

ARNATTO n annatto

ARNATTOS > ARNATTO

ARNICA n temperate or Arctic plant

ARNICAS > ARNICA

ARNOTTO n annatto

ARNOTTOS > ARNOTTO

ARNUT n plant with edible tubers

ARNUTS > ARNUT

AROBA n Asian carriage

AROBAS > AROBA

AROHA n love, compassion, or affection

AROHAS > AROHA

AROID n type of plant

AROIDS > AROID

AROINT vb drive away

AROINTED > AROINT

AROINTING > AROINT

AROINTS > AROINT

AROLLA n European pine tree

AROLLAS > AROLLA

AROMA n pleasant smell

AROMAS > AROMA

AROMATASE n enzyme involved in the production of oestrogen

AROMATIC adj having a distinctive pleasant smell ▷ n something, such as a plant or drug, that gives off a fragrant smell

AROMATICS > AROMATIC

AROMATISE same as > AROMATIZE

AROMATIZE vb make aromatic

AROSE > ARISE

AROUND adv on all sides (of)

AROUSABLE > AROUSE

AROUSAL > AROUSE

AROUSALS > AROUSE

AROUSE vb stimulate, make active

AROUSED > AROUSE

AROUSER > AROUSE

AROUSERS > AROUSE

AROUSES > AROUSE

AROUSING > AROUSE

AROW adv in a row

AROWANA n tropical freshwater fish

AROWANAS > AROWANA

AROYNT vb old word meaning to drive away

AROYNTED > AROYNT

AROYNTING > AROYNT

AROYNTS > AROYNT

ARPA n website concerned with structure of the internet

ARPAS > ARPA

ARPEGGIO n notes of a chord played or sung in quick succession

ARPEGGIOS > ARPEGGIO

ARPEN n old French measure of land

ARPENS > ARPEN

ARPENT n former French unit of length

ARPENTS > ARPENT

ARPILLERA n Peruvian wall-hanging

ARQUEBUS n portable long-barrelled gun dating from the 15th century
ARRACACHA n S American plant
ARRACK n alcoholic drink distilled from grain or rice
ARRACKS > ARRACK
ARRAH interj Irish exclamation
ARRAIGN vb bring (a prisoner) before a court to answer a charge
ARRAIGNED > ARRAIGN
ARRAIGNER > ARRAIGN
ARRAIGNS > ARRAIGN
ARRANGE vb plan
ARRANGED > ARRANGE
ARRANGER > ARRANGE
ARRANGERS > ARRANGE
ARRANGES > ARRANGE
ARRANGING > ARRANGE
ARRANT adj utter, downright
ARRANTLY > ARRANT
ARRAS n tapestry wall-hanging
ARRASED adj having an arras
ARRASENE n material used in embroidery
ARRASENES > ARRASENE
ARRASES > ARRAS
ARRAUGHT > AREACH
ARRAY n impressive display or collection ▷ vb arrange in order
ARRAYAL > ARRAY
ARRAYALS > ARRAY
ARRAYED > ARRAY
ARRAYER > ARRAY
ARRAYERS > ARRAY
ARRAYING > ARRAY
ARRAYMENT n act of arraying
ARRAYS > ARRAY
ARREAR n singular of arrears
ARREARAGE same as > ARREARS
ARREARS pl n money owed
ARRECT adj pricked up
ARREEDE vb old word meaning declare
ARREEDES > ARREEDE
ARREEDING > ARREEDE
ARREST vb take (a person) into custody ▷ n act of taking a person into custody
ARRESTANT n substance that stops a chemical reaction
ARRESTED > ARREST
ARRESTEE n arrested person
ARRESTEES > ARRESTEE
ARRESTER n person who arrests
ARRESTERS > ARRESTER
ARRESTING adj attracting attention, striking
ARRESTIVE adj making something stop
ARRESTOR n person or thing that arrests
ARRESTORS > ARRESTOR
ARRESTS > ARREST
ARRET n judicial decision
ARRETS > ARRET
ARRHIZAL adj without roots

ARRIAGE n Scottish feudal service
ARRIAGES > ARRIAGE
ARRIBA interj exclamation of pleasure or approval
ARRIDE vb old word meaning gratify
ARRIDED > ARRIDE
ARRIDES > ARRIDE
ARRIDING > ARRIDE
ARRIERE adj French word meaning old-fashioned
ARRIERO n Spanish word for mule driver
ARRIEROS > ARRIERO
ARRIS n sharp edge at the meeting of two surfaces
ARRISES > ARRIS
ARRISH n corn stubble
ARRISHES > ARRISH
ARRIVAL n arriving
ARRIVALS > ARRIVAL
ARRIVANCE n old word meaning people who have arrived
ARRIVANCY n arrivance
ARRIVE vb reach a place or destination
ARRIVED > ARRIVE
ARRIVER > ARRIVE
ARRIVERS > ARRIVE
ARRIVES > ARRIVE
ARRIVING > ARRIVE
ARRIVISME n unscrupulous ambition
ARRIVISTE n person who is unscrupulously ambitious
ARROBA n unit of weight in Spanish-speaking countries
ARROBAS > ARROBA
ARROCES > ARROZ
ARROGANCE > ARROGANT
ARROGANCY > ARROGANT
ARROGANT adj proud and overbearing
ARROGATE vb claim or seize without justification
ARROGATED > ARROGATE
ARROGATES > ARROGATE
ARROGATOR > ARROGATE
ARROW n pointed shaft shot from a bow
ARROWED adj having an arrow pattern
ARROWHEAD n pointed tip of an arrow
ARROWIER > ARROWY
ARROWIEST > ARROWY
ARROWING > ARROW
ARROWLESS > ARROW
ARROWLIKE > ARROW
ARROWROOT n nutritious starch obtained from the root of a W Indian plant
ARROWS > ARROW
ARROWWOOD n any of various trees or shrubs, esp certain viburnums, having long straight tough stems formerly used by Native Americans to make arrows
ARROWWORM n type of small marine invertebrate with an elongated transparent body
ARROWY adj like an arrow
ARROYO n usually dry stream bed

ARROYOS > ARROYO
ARROZ n Spanish word for rice, used in name of various dishes
ARROZES > ARROZ
ARS > AR
ARSE n vulgar slang word for the buttocks or anus ▷ vb play the fool
ARSED > ARSE
ARSEHOLE n vulgar slang word for the anus
ARSEHOLED adj vulgar slang word for very drunk
ARSEHOLES > ARSEHOLE
ARSENAL n place where arms and ammunition are made or stored
ARSENALS > ARSENAL
ARSENATE n salt or ester of arsenic acid
ARSENATES > ARSENATE
ARSENIATE n arsenate
ARSENIC n toxic grey element ▷ adj of or containing arsenic
ARSENICAL adj of or containing arsenic ▷ n drug or insecticide containing arsenic
ARSENICS > ARSENIC
ARSENIDE n compound in which arsenic is the most electronegative element
ARSENIDES > ARSENIDE
ARSENIOUS adj of or containing arsenic in the trivalent state
ARSENITE n salt or ester of arsenous acid
ARSENITES > ARSENITE
ARSENO adj containing arsenic
ARSENOUS same as > ARSENIOUS
ARSES > ARSIS
ARSEY adj slang word meaning aggressive or irritable
ARSHEEN n old measure of length in Russia
ARSHEENS > ARSHEEN
ARSHIN n old measure of length in Russia
ARSHINE n old measure of length in Russia
ARSHINES > ARSHINE
ARSHINS > ARSHIN
ARSIER > ARSY
ARSIEST > ARSY
ARSINE n colourless poisonous gas
ARSINES > ARSINE
ARSING > ARSE
ARSINO adj containing arsine
ARSIS n long or stressed syllable in a metrical foot
ARSON n crime of intentionally setting property on fire
ARSONIST > ARSON
ARSONISTS > ARSON
ARSONITE n person committing arson
ARSONITES > ARSONITE
ARSONOUS adj of arson
ARSONS > ARSON

ARSY same as > ARSEY
ART n creation of works of beauty, esp paintings or sculpture
ARTAL a plural of > ROTL
ARTEFACT n something made by human beings
ARTEFACTS > ARTEFACT
ARTEL n cooperative union
ARTELS > ARTEL
ARTEMISIA n type of herbaceous plant of the N hemisphere, such as mugwort, sagebrush, and wormwood
ARTERIAL adj of an artery ▷ n major road
ARTERIALS > ARTERIAL
ARTERIES > ARTERY
ARTERIOLE n any of the small subdivisions of an artery that form thin-walled vessels ending in capillaries
ARTERITIS n inflammation of an artery
ARTERY n one of the tubes carrying blood from the heart
ARTESIAN adj as in artesian well sunken well receiving water from a higher altitude
ARTFUL adj cunning, wily
ARTFULLY > ARTFUL
ARTHOUSE n cinema which shows artistic films
ARTHOUSES > ARTHOUSE
ARTHRITIC > ARTHRITIS
ARTHRITIS n painful inflammation of a joint or joints
ARTHRODIA n joint
ARTHROPOD n animal, such as a spider or insect, with jointed limbs and a segmented body
ARTHROSES > ARTHROSIS
ARTHROSIS n disease of joint
ARTI n ritual performed in homes and temples
ARTIC n articulated vehicle
ARTICHOKE n flower head of a thistle-like plant, cooked as a vegetable
ARTICLE n written piece in a magazine or newspaper ▷ vb bind by a written contract
ARTICLED > ARTICLE
ARTICLES > ARTICLE
ARTICLING > ARTICLE
ARTICS > ARTIC
ARTICULAR adj of or relating to joints
ARTIER > ARTY
ARTIES > ARTY
ARTIEST > ARTY
ARTIFACT same as > ARTEFACT
ARTIFACTS > ARTIFACT
ARTIFICE n clever trick
ARTIFICER n craftsman or craftswoman
ARTIFICES > ARTIFICE
ARTIGI n kind of hooded coat worn in Canada
ARTIGIS > ARTIGI**

ARTILLERY n large-calibre guns

ARTILY > ARTY

ARTINESS > ARTY

ARTIS > ARTI

ARTISAN n skilled worker, craftsman or craftswoman

ARTISANAL > ARTISAN

ARTISANS > ARTISAN

ARTIST n person who produces works of art, esp paintings or sculpture

ARTISTE n professional entertainer such as a singer or dancer

ARTISTES > ARTISTE

ARTISTIC adj of or characteristic of art or artists

ARTISTRY n artistic skill

ARTISTS > ARTIST

ARTLESS adj free from deceit or cunning

ARTLESSLY > ARTLESS

ARTMAKER n person who creates art

ARTMAKERS > ARTMAKER

ARTMAKING n process of making art

ARTS > ART

ARTSIE n arts student

ARTSIER > ARTSY

ARTSIES > ARTSY

ARTSIEST > ARTSY

ARTSINESS > ARTSY

ARTSMAN old word for **>** CRAFTSMAN

ARTSMEN > ARTSMAN

ARTSY adj interested in the arts ▷ n person interested in the arts

ARTWORK n all the photographs and illustrations in a publication

ARTWORKS > ARTWORK

ARTY adj having an affected interest in art ▷ n person interested in art

ARUANA n tropical freshwater fish

ARUANAS > ARUANA

ARUGOLA n salad plant

ARUGOLAS > ARUGOLA

ARUGULA another name for **>** ROCKET

ARUGULAS > ARUGULA

ARUHE n edible root of a fern

ARUHES > ARUHE

ARUM n type of plant

ARUMS > ARUM

ARUSPEX variant spelling of **>** HARUSPEX

ARUSPICES > ARUSPEX

ARVAL adj of ploughed land

ARVEE n short for recreational vehicle (RV)

ARVEES > ARVEE

ARVICOLE n water rat

ARVICOLES > ARVICOLE

ARVO n afternoon

ARVOS > ARVO

ARY dialect form of **>** ANY

ARYBALLOS n ancient Greek flask

ARYL n an aromatic group

ARYLS > ARYL

ARYTENOID adj denoting either of two small cartilages

of the larynx that are attached to the vocal cords ▷ n arytenoid cartilage or muscle

ARYTHMIA n any variation

ARYTHMIAS > ARYTHMIA

ARYTHMIC > ARYTHMIA

AS adv used to indicate amount or extent in comparisons ▷ n ancient Roman unit of weight

ASAFETIDA n bitter resin with an unpleasant onion-like smell

ASANA n any of various postures in yoga

ASANAS > ASANA

ASAR > AS

ASARUM n dried strong-scented root

ASARUMS > ASARUM

ASBESTIC > ASBESTOS

ASBESTINE > ASBESTOS

ASBESTOS n fibrous mineral which does not burn

ASBESTOUS > ASBESTOS

ASBESTUS n asbestos

ASCARED adj afraid

ASCARID n type of parasitic nematode

ASCARIDES > ASCARID

ASCARIDS > ASCARID

ASCARIS n ascarid

ASCARISES > ASCARIS

ASCAUNT adv old word meaning slantwise

ASCEND vb go or move up

ASCENDANT adj dominant or influential

ASCENDED > ASCEND

ASCENDENT same as **>** ASCENDANT

ASCENDER n part of some lower-case letters that extends above the body of the letter

ASCENDERS > ASCENDER

ASCENDEUR n metal grip that is threaded on a rope and can be alternately tightened and slackened as an aid to climbing the rope: used attached to slings for the feet and waist

ASCENDING adj moving upwards

ASCENDS > ASCEND

ASCENSION n act of ascending

ASCENSIVE adj moving upwards

ASCENT n act of ascending

ASCENTS > ASCENT

ASCERTAIN vb find out definitely

ASCESES > ASCESIS

ASCESIS n exercise of self-discipline

ASCETIC adj abstaining from worldly pleasures and comforts ▷ n person who abstains from worldly comforts and pleasures

ASCETICAL adj ascetic

ASCETICS > ASCETIC

ASCI > ASCUS

ASCIAN n person living in the tropics

ASCIANS > ASCIAN

ASCIDIA > ASCIDIUM

ASCIDIAN n type of minute marine invertebrate, such as the sea squirt

ASCIDIANS > ASCIDIAN

ASCIDIATE > ASCIDIUM

ASCIDIUM n part of a plant that is shaped like a pitcher

ASCITES n accumulation of serous fluid in the peritoneal cavity

ASCITIC > ASCITES

ASCITICAL > ASCITES

ASCLEPIAD n Greek verse form

ASCLEPIAS n type of plant often grown as a garden or greenhouse plant for its showy orange-scarlet or purple flowers

ASCOCARP n (in some ascomycetous fungi) a globular structure containing the asci

ASCOCARPS > ASCOCARP

ASCOGONIA n female reproductive bodies in some fungi

ASCON n type of sponge having an oval shape and a thin body wall

ASCONCE adv old form of askance

ASCONOID adj like an ascon

ASCONS > ASCON

ASCORBATE n salt of ascorbic acid

ASCORBIC adj as in ascorbic acid vitamin present in citrus fruits, tomatoes, and green vegetables

ASCOSPORE n one of the spores (usually eight in number) that are produced in an ascus

ASCOT n type of cravat

ASCOTS > ASCOT

ASCRIBE vb attribute, as to a particular origin

ASCRIBED > ASCRIBE

ASCRIBES > ASCRIBE

ASCRIBING > ASCRIBE

ASCUS n saclike structure in fungi

ASDIC an early form of **>** SONAR

ASDICS > ASDIC

ASEA adv towards the sea

ASEISMIC adj denoting a region free of earthquakes

ASEITIES > ASEITY

ASEITY n existence derived from itself, having no other source

ASEMANTIC adj not semantic

ASEPALOUS adj (of a plant or flower) having no sepals

ASEPSES > ASEPSIS

ASEPSIS n aseptic condition

ASEPTATE adj not divided into cells or sections by septa

ASEPTIC adj free from harmful bacteria ▷ n aseptic substance

ASEPTICS > ASEPTIC

ASEXUAL adj without biological sex

ASEXUALLY > ASEXUAL

ASH n powdery substance left when something is burnt ▷ vb reduce to ashes

ASHAKE adv shaking

ASHAME vb make ashamed

ASHAMED adj feeling shame

ASHAMEDLY > ASHAMED

ASHAMES > ASHAME

ASHAMING > ASHAME

ASHCAKE n cornmeal bread

ASHCAKES > ASHCAKE

ASHCAN n large metal dustbin

ASHCANS > ASHCAN

ASHED > ASH

ASHEN adj pale with shock

ASHERIES > ASHERY

ASHERY n place where ashes are made

ASHES > ASH

ASHET n shallow oval dish or large plate

ASHETS > ASHET

ASHFALL n dropping of ash from a volcano

ASHFALLS > ASHFALL

ASHIER > ASHY

ASHIEST > ASHY

ASHINE adv old word meaning shining

ASHINESS > ASHY

ASHING > ASH

ASHIVER adv shivering

ASHKEY n winged fruit of the ash

ASHKEYS > ASHKEY

ASHLAR n block of hewn stone ▷ vb build with ashlars

ASHLARED > ASHLAR

ASHLARING > ASHLAR

ASHLARS > ASHLAR

ASHLER same as **>** ASHLAR

ASHLERED > ASHLER

ASHLERING > ASHLER

ASHLERS > ASHLER

ASHLESS > ASH

ASHMAN n man who shovels ashes

ASHMEN > ASHMAN

ASHORE adv towards or on land ▷ adj on land, having come from the water

ASHPAN n pan or tray to catch ashes

ASHPANS > ASHPAN

ASHPLANT n walking stick made from an ash sapling

ASHPLANTS > ASHPLANT

ASHRAF > SHERIF

ASHRAM n religious retreat where a Hindu holy man lives

ASHRAMA n stage in Hindu spiritual life

ASHRAMAS > ASHRAMA

ASHRAMITE n person living in an ashram

ASHRAMS > ASHRAM

ASHTANGA n type of yoga

ASHTANGAS > ASHTANGA

ASHTRAY n receptacle for tobacco ash and cigarette butts

ASHTRAYS > ASHTRAY

ASHY adj pale greyish

ASIAGO n type of cheese
ASIAGOS > ASIAGO
ASIDE adv one side ▷ n remark not meant to be heard by everyone present
ASIDES > ASIDE
ASINICO n old Spanish word for fool
ASINICOS > ASINICO
ASININE adj stupid, idiotic
ASININELY > ASININE
ASININITY > ASININE
ASK vb say (something) in a form that requires an answer
ASKANCE adv with an oblique glance ▷ vb turn aside
ASKANCED > ASKANCE
ASKANCES > ASKANCE
ASKANCING > ASKANCE
ASKANT same as > ASKANCE
ASKANTED > ASKANT
ASKANTING > ASKANT
ASKANTS > ASKANT
ASKARI n (in East Africa) a soldier or policeman or policewoman
ASKARIS > ASKARI
ASKED > ASK
ASKER > ASK
ASKERS > ASK
ASKESES > ASKESIS
ASKESIS n practice of self-discipline
ASKEW adj one side, crooked
ASKEWNESS > ASKEW
ASKING > ASK
ASKINGS > ASK
ASKLENT Scots word for > ASLANT
ASKOI > ASKOS
ASKOS n ancient Greek vase
ASKS > ASK
ASLAKE vb slake
ASLAKED > ASLAKE
ASLAKES > ASLAKE
ASLAKING > ASLAKE
ASLANT adv at a slant (to), slanting (across)
ASLEEP adj sleeping
ASLOPE adj sloping
ASLOSH adj awash
ASMEAR adj smeared
ASMOULDER adv old word meaning smouldering
ASOCIAL n person who avoids social contact
ASOCIALS > ASOCIAL
ASP n small poisonous snake
ASPARAGUS n plant whose shoots are cooked as a vegetable
ASPARKLE adv sparkling
ASPARTAME n artificial sweetener
ASPARTATE n enzyme found in blood
ASPARTIC adj as in aspartic acid nonessential amino acid that is a component of proteins
ASPECT n feature or element ▷ vb look at
ASPECTED > ASPECT
ASPECTING > ASPECT
ASPECTS > ASPECT

ASPECTUAL adj of or relating to grammatical aspect
ASPEN n kind of poplar tree ▷ adj trembling
ASPENS > ASPEN
ASPER n former Turkish monetary unit
ASPERATE adj (of plant parts) having a rough surface due to a covering of short stiff hairs ▷ vb make rough
ASPERATED > ASPERATE
ASPERATES > ASPERATE
ASPERGE vb sprinkle
ASPERGED > ASPERGE
ASPERGER > ASPERGE
ASPERGERS > ASPERGE
ASPERGES > ASPERGE
ASPERGILL n perforated instrument used to sprinkle holy water
ASPERGING > ASPERGE
ASPERITY n roughness of temper
ASPERMIA n failure to form or emit semen
ASPERMIAS > ASPERMIA
ASPEROUS same as > ASPERATE
ASPERS > ASPER
ASPERSE vb spread false rumours about
ASPERSED > ASPERSE
ASPERSER > ASPERSE
ASPERSERS > ASPERSE
ASPERSES > ASPERSE
ASPERSING > ASPERSE
ASPERSION n disparaging or malicious remark
ASPERSIVE > ASPERSE
ASPERSOIR n sprinkler for holy water
ASPERSOR > ASPERSE
ASPERSORS > ASPERSE
ASPERSORY n sprinkler for holy water
ASPHALT n black hard tar-like substance used for road surfaces etc ▷ vb cover with asphalt
ASPHALTED > ASPHALT
ASPHALTER n person who lays asphalt
ASPHALTIC > ASPHALT
ASPHALTS > ASPHALT
ASPHALTUM n asphalt
ASPHERIC adj not spherical ▷ n lens that is not completely spherical
ASPHERICS > ASPHERIC
ASPHODEL n plant with clusters of yellow or white flowers
ASPHODELS > ASPHODEL
ASPHYXIA n suffocation
ASPHYXIAL > ASPHYXIA
ASPHYXIAS > ASPHYXIA
ASPHYXIED > ASPHYXY
ASPHYXIES > ASPHYXY
ASPHYXY vb smother, suffocate
ASPIC n savoury jelly used to coat meat, eggs, fish, etc
ASPICK old word for > ASP
ASPICKS > ASPICK
ASPICS > ASPIC

ASPIDIA > ASPIDIUM
ASPIDIOID > ASPIDIUM
ASPIDIUM n variety of fern
ASPIE n potentially offensive term for person with Asperger's syndrome
ASPIES > ASPIE
ASPINE old word for > ASPEN
ASPINES > ASPINE
ASPIRANT n person who aspires ▷ adj aspiring or striving
ASPIRANTS > ASPIRANT
ASPIRATA n rough stop
ASPIRATAE > ASPIRATA
ASPIRATE vb pronounce with an h sound ▷ n h sound ▷ adj (of a stop) pronounced with a forceful and audible expulsion of breath
ASPIRATED > ASPIRATE
ASPIRATES > ASPIRATE
ASPIRATOR n device for removing fluids from a body cavity by suction
ASPIRE vb yearn (for), hope (to do or be)
ASPIRED > ASPIRE
ASPIRER > ASPIRE
ASPIRERS > ASPIRE
ASPIRES > ASPIRE
ASPIRIN n drug used to relieve pain and fever
ASPIRING > ASPIRE
ASPIRINS > ASPIRIN
ASPIS n horned viper
ASPISES > ASPIS
ASPISH adj like an asp
ASPLENIUM n type of fern
ASPORT vb old word meaning take away
ASPORTED > ASPORT
ASPORTING > ASPORT
ASPORTS > ASPORT
ASPOUT adv spouting
ASPRAWL adv sprawling
ASPREAD adv spreading
ASPRO n associate professor at an academic institution
ASPROS > ASPRO
ASPROUT adv sprouting
ASPS > ASP
ASQUAT adv squatting
ASQUINT adj with a glance from the corner of the eye
ASRAMA n stage in Hindu spiritual life
ASRAMAS > ASRAMA
ASS n donkey
ASSAGAI same as > ASSEGAI
ASSAGAIED > ASSAGAI
ASSAGAIS > ASSAGAI
ASSAI adv (usually preceded by a musical direction) very ▷ n Brazilian palm tree
ASSAIL vb attack violently
ASSAILANT n person who attacks another, either physically or verbally
ASSAILED > ASSAIL
ASSAILER > ASSAIL
ASSAILERS > ASSAIL
ASSAILING > ASSAIL
ASSAILS > ASSAIL
ASSAIS > ASSAI
ASSAM n (in Malaysia) tamarind as used in cooking

ASSAMS > ASSAM
ASSART vb clear ground for cultivation
ASSARTED > ASSART
ASSARTING > ASSART
ASSARTS > ASSART
ASSASSIN n person who murders a prominent person
ASSASSINS > ASSASSIN
ASSAULT n violent attack ▷ vb attack violently
ASSAULTED > ASSAULT
ASSAULTER > ASSAULT
ASSAULTS > ASSAULT
ASSAY n analysis of a substance ▷ vb make such an analysis
ASSAYABLE > ASSAY
ASSAYED > ASSAY
ASSAYER > ASSAY
ASSAYERS > ASSAY
ASSAYING > ASSAY
ASSAYINGS > ASSAY
ASSAYS > ASSAY
ASSEGAAI same as > ASSEGAAI
ASSEGAAIS > ASSEGAAI
ASSEGAI n slender spear used in S Africa ▷ vb spear with an assegai
ASSEGAIED > ASSEGAI
ASSEGAIS > ASSEGAI
ASSEMBLE vb collect or congregate
ASSEMBLED > ASSEMBLE
ASSEMBLER n person or thing that assembles
ASSEMBLES > ASSEMBLE
ASSEMBLY n assembled group
ASSENT n agreement or consent ▷ vb agree or consent
ASSENTED > ASSENT
ASSENTER n person supporting another's nomination
ASSENTERS > ASSENTER
ASSENTING > ASSENT
ASSENTIVE > ASSENT
ASSENTOR n voter legally required to endorse the nomination of a candidate
ASSENTORS > ASSENTOR
ASSENTS > ASSENT
ASSERT vb declare forcefully
ASSERTED > ASSERT
ASSERTER > ASSERT
ASSERTERS > ASSERT
ASSERTING > ASSERT
ASSERTION n positive statement, usu made without evidence
ASSERTIVE adj confident and direct in dealing with others
ASSERTOR > ASSERT
ASSERTORS > ASSERT
ASSERTORY adj making affirmation
ASSERTS > ASSERT
ASSES > ASS
ASSESS vb judge the worth or importance of
ASSESSED > ASSESS
ASSESSES > ASSESS
ASSESSING > ASSESS

ASSESSOR n person who values property for taxation or insurance purposes

ASSESSORS > ASSESSOR

ASSET n valuable or useful person or thing

ASSETLESS > ASSET

ASSETS > ASSET

ASSEVER vb old form of asseverate

ASSEVERED > ASSEVER

ASSEVERS > ASSEVER

ASSEZ adv (as part of a musical direction) fairly

ASSHOLE same as > ARSEHOLE

ASSHOLES > ASSHOLE

ASSIDUITY n constant and close application

ASSIDUOUS adj hard-working

ASSIEGE vb old form of besiege

ASSIEGED > ASSIEGE

ASSIEGES > ASSIEGE

ASSIEGING > ASSIEGE

ASSIENTO n former slave trade treaty between Britain and Spain

ASSIENTOS > ASSIENTO

ASSIGN vb appoint (someone) to a job or task ▷ n person to whom property is assigned

ASSIGNAT n paper money issued in France by the Constituent Assembly in 1789

ASSIGNATS > ASSIGNAT

ASSIGNED > ASSIGN

ASSIGNEE n person to whom some right, interest, or property is transferred

ASSIGNEES > ASSIGNEE

ASSIGNER > ASSIGN

ASSIGNERS > ASSIGN

ASSIGNING > ASSIGN

ASSIGNOR n person who transfers or assigns property

ASSIGNORS > ASSIGNOR

ASSIGNS > ASSIGN

ASSIST vb give help or support ▷ n pass by a player which enables another player to score a goal

ASSISTANT n helper ▷ adj junior or deputy

ASSISTED > ASSIST

ASSISTER > ASSIST

ASSISTERS > ASSIST

ASSISTING > ASSIST

ASSISTIVE adj providing a means of reducing a physical impairment

ASSISTOR > ASSIST

ASSISTORS > ASSIST

ASSISTS > ASSIST

ASSIZE n sitting of a legislative assembly

ASSIZED > ASSIZE

ASSIZER n weights and measures official

ASSIZERS > ASSIZER

ASSIZES > ASSIZE

ASSIZING > ASSIZE

ASSLIKE > ASS

ASSOCIATE vb connect in the mind ▷ n partner in

business ▷ adj having partial rights or subordinate status

ASSOIL vb absolve

ASSOILED > ASSOIL

ASSOILING > ASSOIL

ASSOILS > ASSOIL

ASSOILZIE vb old Scots word meaning absolve

ASSONANCE n rhyming of vowel sounds but not consonants

ASSONANT > ASSONANCE

ASSONANTS > ASSONANCE

ASSONATE vb show assonance

ASSONATED > ASSONATE

ASSONATES > ASSONATE

ASSORT vb arrange or distribute equally

ASSORTED adj consisting of various types mixed together

ASSORTER > ASSORT

ASSORTERS > ASSORT

ASSORTING > ASSORT

ASSORTIVE > ASSORT

ASSORTS > ASSORT

ASSOT vb old word meaning make infatuated

ASSOTS > ASSOT

ASSOTT vb besot

ASSOTTED > ASSOT

ASSOTTING > ASSOT

ASSUAGE vb relieve (pain, grief, thirst, etc)

ASSUAGED > ASSUAGE

ASSUAGER > ASSUAGE

ASSUAGERS > ASSUAGE

ASSUAGES > ASSUAGE

ASSUAGING > ASSUAGE

ASSUASIVE > ASSUAGE

ASSUETUDE n state of being accustomed

ASSUMABLE > ASSUME

ASSUMABLY > ASSUME

ASSUME vb take to be true without proof

ASSUMED adj false

ASSUMEDLY > ASSUME

ASSUMER > ASSUME

ASSUMERS > ASSUME

ASSUMES > ASSUME

ASSUMING adj expecting too much ▷ n action of one who assumes

ASSUMINGS > ASSUMING

ASSUMPSIT n (before 1875) an action to recover damages for breach of an express or implied contract or agreement that was not under seal

ASSURABLE > ASSURE

ASSURANCE n assuring or being assured

ASSURE vb promise or guarantee

ASSURED adj confident ▷ n beneficiary under a life assurance policy

ASSUREDLY > ASSURED

ASSUREDS > ASSURED

ASSURER > ASSURE

ASSURERS > ASSURE

ASSURES > ASSURE

ASSURGENT adj (of leaves, stems, etc) curving or growing upwards

ASSURING > ASSURE

ASSUROR > ASSURE

ASSURORS > ASSURE

ASSWAGE old spelling of > ASSUAGE

ASSWAGED > ASSWAGE

ASSWAGES > ASSWAGE

ASSWAGING > ASSWAGE

ASSWIPE n vulgar word for a contemptible person

ASSWIPES > ASSWIPE

ASTABLE adj not stable

ASTANGA same as > ASHTANGA

ASTANGAS > ASTANGA

ASTARE adv staring

ASTART old word for > START

ASTARTED > ASTART

ASTARTING > ASTART

ASTARTS > ASTART

ASTASIA n inability to stand

ASTASIAS > ASTASIA

ASTATIC adj not static

ASTATIDE n binary compound of astatine with a more electropositive element

ASTATIDES > ASTATIDE

ASTATINE n radioactive nonmetallic element

ASTATINES > ASTATINE

ASTATKI n fuel derived from petroleum

ASTATKIS > ASTATKI

ASTEISM n use of irony

ASTEISMS > ASTEISM

ASTELIC > ASTELY

ASTELIES > ASTELY

ASTELY n lack of central cylinder in plants

ASTER n plant with daisy-like flowers

ASTERIA n gemstone with starlike light effect

ASTERIAS > ASTERIA

ASTERID n variety of flowering plant

ASTERIDS > ASTERID

ASTERISK n star-shaped symbol (*) used in printing or writing to indicate a footnote, etc ▷ vb mark with an asterisk

ASTERISKS > ASTERISK

ASTERISM n three asterisks arranged in a triangle to draw attention to the text that follows

ASTERISMS > ASTERISM

ASTERN adv at or towards the stern of a ship ▷ adj at or towards the stern of a ship

ASTERNAL adj not connected or joined to the sternum

ASTEROID n any of the small planets that orbit the sun between Mars and Jupiter ▷ adj of, relating to, or belonging to the class Asteroidea

ASTEROIDS > ASTEROID

ASTERS > ASTER

ASTERT vb start

ASTERTED > ASTERT

ASTERTING > ASTERT

ASTERTS > ASTERT

ASTHANGA n type of yoga

ASTHANGAS > ASTHANGA

ASTHENIA n abnormal loss of strength

ASTHENIAS > ASTHENIA

ASTHENIC adj of, relating to, or having asthenia ▷ n person having long limbs and a small trunk

ASTHENICS > ASTHENIC

ASTHENIES > ASTHENY

ASTHENY same as > ASTHENIA

ASTHMA n illness causing difficulty in breathing

ASTHMAS > ASTHMA

ASTHMATIC adj of, relating to, or having asthma ▷ n person who has asthma

ASTHORE n Irish endearment

ASTHORES > ASTHORE

ASTICHOUS adj not arranged in rows

ASTIGMIA n defect of a lens resulting in the formation of distorted images

ASTIGMIAS > ASTIGMIA

ASTILBE n type of plant

ASTILBES > ASTILBE

ASTIR adj out of bed

ASTOMATAL adj having no stomata

ASTOMOUS adj having no mouth

ASTONE same as > ASTONISH

ASTONED > ASTONE

ASTONES > ASTONE

ASTONIED adj stunned

ASTONIES > ASTONY

ASTONING > ASTONE

ASTONISH vb surprise greatly

ASTONY same as > ASTONISH

ASTONYING > ASTONY

ASTOOP adv stooping

ASTOUND vb overwhelm with amazement

ASTOUNDED > ASTOUND

ASTOUNDS > ASTOUND

ASTRACHAN same as > ASTRAKHAN

ASTRADDLE adj with a leg on either side of something

ASTRAGAL n small convex moulding, usually with a semicircular cross section

ASTRAGALI n bones of the ankles that articulate with the leg bones to form ankle joints

ASTRAGALS > ASTRAGAL

ASTRAKHAN n dark curly fleece of lambs from Astrakhan in Russia

ASTRAL adj of stars ▷ n oil lamp

ASTRALLY > ASTRAL

ASTRALS > ASTRAL

ASTRAND adv on shore

ASTRANTIA n flowering plant

ASTRAY adv off the right path

ASTRICT vb bind, confine, or constrict

ASTRICTED > ASTRICT
ASTRICTS > ASTRICT
ASTRIDE adv with a leg on either side (of) ▷ adj with a leg on either side
ASTRINGE vb cause contraction
ASTRINGED > ASTRINGE
ASTRINGER n person who keeps goshawks
ASTRINGES > ASTRINGE
ASTROCYTE n any of the star-shaped cells in the tissue supporting the brain and spinal cord (neuroglia)
ASTRODOME n transparent dome on the top of an aircraft, through which observations can be made, esp of the stars
ASTROFELL n plant in Spenser's poetry
ASTROID n hypocycloid having four cusps
ASTROIDS > ASTROID
ASTROLABE n instrument formerly used to measure the altitude of stars and planets
ASTROLOGY n study of the alleged influence of the stars, planets, and moon on human affairs
ASTRONAUT n person trained for travelling in space
ASTRONOMY n scientific study of heavenly bodies
ASTROPHEL n plant in Spenser's poetry
ASTRUT adv old word meaning in a protruding way
ASTUCIOUS adj old form of astute
ASTUCITY n quality of being astute
ASTUN vb old form of astonish
ASTUNNED > ASTUN
ASTUNNING > ASTUN
ASTUNS > ASTUN
ASTUTE adj perceptive or shrewd
ASTUTELY > ASTUTE
ASTUTER > ASTUTE
ASTUTEST > ASTUTE
ASTYLAR adj without columns or pilasters
ASUDDEN adv old form of suddenly
ASUNDER adv into parts or pieces ▷ adj into parts or pieces
ASURA n demon in Hindu mythology
ASURAS > ASURA
ASWARM adj filled, esp with moving things
ASWAY adv swaying
ASWIM adv floating
ASWING adv swinging
ASWIRL adv swirling
ASWOON adv swooning
ASYLA > ASYLUM
ASYLEE n person who is granted asylum
ASYLEES > ASYLEE
ASYLLABIC adj not functioning in the manner of a syllable

ASYLUM n refuge or sanctuary
ASYLUMS > ASYLUM
ASYMMETRY n lack of symmetry
ASYMPTOTE n straight line closely approached but never met by a curve
ASYNAPSES > ASYNAPSIS
ASYNAPSIS n failure of pairing of chromosomes at meiosis
ASYNDETA > ASYNDETON
ASYNDETIC adj (of a catalogue or index) without cross references
ASYNDETON n omission of a conjunction between the parts of a sentence
ASYNERGIA n lack of coordination between muscles or parts, as occurs in cerebellar disease
ASYNERGY same as **>** ASYNERGIA
ASYSTOLE n absence of heartbeat
ASYSTOLES > ASYSTOLE
ASYSTOLIC > ASYSTOLE
AT n Laotian monetary unit worth one hundredth of a kip
ATAATA n grazing marine gastropod
ATAATAS > ATAATA
ATABAL n N African drum
ATABALS > ATABAL
ATABEG n Turkish ruler
ATABEGS > ATABEG
ATABEK n Turkish ruler
ATABEKS > ATABEK
ATABRIN n drug formerly used for treating malaria
ATABRINE same as **>** ATABRIN
ATABRINES > ATABRINE
ATABRINS > ATABRIN
ATACAMITE n mineral containing copper
ATACTIC adj attribute of a polymer
ATAGHAN a variant of **>** YATAGHAN
ATAGHANS > ATAGHAN
ATALAYA n watchtower in Spain
ATALAYAS > ATALAYA
ATAMAN n elected leader of the Cossacks
ATAMANS > ATAMAN
ATAMASCO n N American lily
ATAMASCOS > ATAMASCO
ATAP n palm tree of S Asia
ATAPS > ATAP
ATARACTIC adj able to calm or tranquillize ▷ n ataractic drug
ATARAXIA n calmness or peace of mind
ATARAXIAS > ATARAXIA
ATARAXIC same as **>** ATARACTIC
ATARAXICS > ATARAXIC
ATARAXIES > ATARAXY
ATARAXY same as **>** ATARAXIA
ATAVIC > ATAVISM

ATAVISM n recurrence of a trait present in distant ancestors
ATAVISMS > ATAVISM
ATAVIST > ATAVISM
ATAVISTIC adj of or relating to reversion to a former or more primitive type
ATAVISTS > ATAVISM
ATAXIA n lack of muscular coordination
ATAXIAS > ATAXIA
ATAXIC > ATAXIA
ATAXICS > ATAXIA
ATAXIES > ATAXY
ATAXY same as **>** ATAXIA
ATCHIEVE same as **>** ACHIEVE
ATCHIEVED > ATCHIEVE
ATCHIEVES > ATCHIEVE
ATE > EAT
ATEBRIN n drug formerly used to treat malaria
ATEBRINS > ATEBRIN
ATECHNIC adj without technical ability ▷ n person with no technical ability
ATECHNICS > ATECHNIC
ATELIC adj of action without end
ATELIER n workshop, artist's studio
ATELIERS > ATELIER
ATEMOYA n tropical fruit tree
ATEMOYAS > ATEMOYA
ATEMPORAL adj not governed by time
ATENOLOL n type of beta-blocker
ATENOLOLS > ATENOLOL
ATES n shop selling confectionery
ATHAME n witch's ceremonial knife
ATHAMES > ATHAME
ATHANASY n absence of death
ATHANOR n alchemist's furnace
ATHANORS > ATHANOR
ATHEISE vb speak atheistically
ATHEISED > ATHEISE
ATHEISES > ATHEISE
ATHEISING > ATHEISE
ATHEISM n belief that there is no God
ATHEISMS > ATHEISM
ATHEIST > ATHEISM
ATHEISTIC > ATHEISM
ATHEISTS > ATHEISM
ATHEIZE vb speak atheistically
ATHEIZED > ATHEIZE
ATHEIZES > ATHEIZE
ATHEIZING > ATHEIZE
ATHELING n (in Anglo-Saxon England) a prince of any of the royal dynasties
ATHELINGS > ATHELING
ATHEMATIC adj not based on themes
ATHENAEUM n institution for the promotion of learning
ATHENEUM same as **>** ATHENAEUM

ATHENEUMS > ATHENEUM
ATHEOLOGY n opposition to theology
ATHEOUS adj without a belief in god
ATHERINE n small fish
ATHERINES > ATHERINE
ATHEROMA n fatty deposit on or within an artery
ATHEROMAS > ATHEROMA
ATHETESES > ATHETESIS
ATHETESIS n dismissal of a text as not genuine
ATHETISE vb reject as not genuine
ATHETISED > ATHETISE
ATHETISES > ATHETISE
ATHETIZE vb reject as not genuine
ATHETIZED > ATHETIZE
ATHETIZES > ATHETIZE
ATHETOID > ATHETOSIS
ATHETOSES > ATHETOSIS
ATHETOSIC > ATHETOSIS
ATHETOSIS n condition characterized by uncontrolled rhythmic writhing movement, esp of fingers, hands, head, and tongue, caused by cerebral lesion
ATHETOTIC > ATHETOSIS
ATHIRST adj having an eager desire
ATHLETA same as **>** ATHLETE
ATHLETAS > ATHLETA
ATHLETE n person trained in or good at athletics
ATHLETES > ATHLETE
ATHLETIC adj physically fit or strong
ATHLETICS n track and field events
ATHODYD another name for **>** RAMJET
ATHODYDS > ATHODYD
ATHRILL adv feeling thrills
ATHROB adv throbbing
ATHROCYTE n cell able to store matter
ATHWART adv transversely
ATIGI n type of parka worn by the Inuit in Canada
ATIGIS > ATIGI
ATILT adj in a tilted or inclined position
ATIMIES > ATIMY
ATIMY n loss of honour
ATINGLE adv tingling
ATISHOO n sound of a sneeze
ATISHOOS > ATISHOO
ATLANTES > ATLAS
ATLAS n book of maps
ATLASES > ATLAS
ATLATL n Native American throwing stick
ATLATLS > ATLATL
ATMA same as **>** ATMAN
ATMAN n personal soul or self
ATMANS > ATMAN
ATMAS > ATMA
ATMOLOGY n study of aqueous vapour
ATMOLYSE vb separate gases by filtering

ATMOLYSED > ATMOLYSE
ATMOLYSES > ATMOLYSIS
ATMOLYSIS *n* method of separating gases that depends on their differential rates of diffusion through a porous substance
ATMOLYZE *vb* separate gases by filtering
ATMOLYZED > ATMOLYZE
ATMOLYZES > ATMOLYZE
ATMOMETER *n* instrument for measuring the rate of evaporation of water into the atmosphere
ATMOMETRY > ATMOMETER
ATMOS *n* (short for) atmosphere
ATMOSES > ATMOS
ATOC *n* skunk
ATOCIA *n* inability to have children
ATOCIAS > ATOCIA
ATOCS > ATOC
ATOK *n* skunk
ATOKAL *adj* having no children
ATOKE *n* part of a worm
ATOKES > ATOKE
ATOKOUS *adj* having no children
ATOKS > ATOK
ATOLL *n* ring-shaped coral reef enclosing a lagoon
ATOLLS > ATOLL
ATOM *n* smallest unit of matter which can take part in a chemical reaction
ATOMIC *adj* of or using atomic bombs or atomic energy
ATOMICAL > ATOMIC
ATOMICITY *n* state of being made up of atoms
ATOMICS *n* science of atoms
ATOMIES > ATOMY
ATOMISE *same as*
> ATOMIZE
ATOMISED > ATOMISE
ATOMISER *same as*
> ATOMIZER
ATOMISERS > ATOMISER
ATOMISES > ATOMISE
ATOMISING > ATOMISE
ATOMISM *n* ancient philosophical theory
ATOMISMS > ATOMISM
ATOMIST > ATOMISM
ATOMISTIC > ATOMISM
ATOMISTS > ATOMISM
ATOMIZE *vb* reduce to atoms or small particles
ATOMIZED > ATOMIZE
ATOMIZER *n* device for discharging a liquid in a fine spray
ATOMIZERS > ATOMIZER
ATOMIZES > ATOMIZE
ATOMIZING > ATOMIZE
ATOMS > ATOM
ATOMY *n* atom or minute particle
ATONABLE > ATONE
ATONAL *adj* (of music) not written in an established key
ATONALISM > ATONAL
ATONALIST > ATONAL

ATONALITY *n* absence of or disregard for an established musical key in a composition
ATONALLY > ATONAL
ATONE *vb* make amends (for sin or wrongdoing)
ATONEABLE > ATONE
ATONED > ATONE
ATONEMENT *n* something done to make amends for wrongdoing
ATONER > ATONE
ATONERS > ATONE
ATONES > ATONE
ATONIA *n* lack of normal muscle tone
ATONIAS > ATONIA
ATONIC *adj* carrying no stress ▷ *n* unaccented or unstressed syllable
ATONICITY > ATONIC
ATONICS > ATONIC
ATONIES > ATONY
ATONING > ATONE
ATONINGLY > ATONE
ATONY *n* lack of normal tone or tension, as in muscles
ATOP *adv* on top
ATOPIC *adj* of or relating to hypersensitivity to certain allergens
ATOPIES > ATOPY
ATOPY *n* tendency to be hypersensitive to certain allergens
ATRAMENT *n* old word meaning black liquid
ATRAMENTS > ATRAMENT
ATRAZINE *n* white crystalline compound
ATRAZINES > ATRAZINE
ATREMBLE *adv* trembling
ATRESIA *n* absence of or unnatural narrowing of a body channel
ATRESIAS > ATRESIA
ATRESIC > ATRESIA
ATRETIC > ATRESIA
ATRIA > ATRIUM
ATRIAL > ATRIUM
ATRIP *adj* (of an anchor) no longer caught on the bottom
ATRIUM *n* upper chamber of either half of the heart
ATRIUMS > ATRIUM
ATROCIOUS *adj* extremely cruel or wicked
ATROCITY *n* wickedness
ATROPHIA *n* wasting disease
ATROPHIAS > ATROPHIA
ATROPHIC > ATROPHY
ATROPHIED > ATROPHY
ATROPHIES > ATROPHY
ATROPHY *n* wasting away of an organ or part ▷ *vb* (cause to) waste away
ATROPIA *n* atropine
ATROPIAS > ATROPIA
ATROPIN *same as*
> ATROPINE
ATROPINE *n* poisonous alkaloid obtained from deadly nightshade
ATROPINES > ATROPINE
ATROPINS > ATROPIN
ATROPISM *n* condition caused by using belladonna

ATROPISMS > ATROPISM
ATROPOUS *adj* growing straight
ATS > AT
ATT *n* old Siamese coin
ATTABOY *sentence substitute* expression of approval or exhortation
ATTABOYS > ATTABOY
ATTACH *vb* join, fasten, or connect
ATTACHE *n* specialist attached to a diplomatic mission
ATTACHED *adj* fond of
ATTACHER > ATTACH
ATTACHERS > ATTACH
ATTACHES > ATTACH
ATTACHING > ATTACH
ATTACK *vb* launch a physical assault (against) ▷ *n* act of attacking
ATTACKED > ATTACK
ATTACKER > ATTACK
ATTACKERS > ATTACK
ATTACKING > ATTACK
ATTACKMAN *n* attacking player in sport
ATTACKMEN > ATTACKMAN
ATTACKS > ATTACK
ATTAGIRL *humorous feminine version of* > ATTABOY
ATTAIN *vb* achieve or accomplish (a task or aim)
ATTAINDER *n* (formerly) the extinction of a person's civil rights resulting from a sentence of death or outlawry on conviction for treason or felony
ATTAINED > ATTAIN
ATTAINER > ATTAIN
ATTAINERS > ATTAIN
ATTAINING > ATTAIN
ATTAINS > ATTAIN
ATTAINT *vb* pass judgment of death ▷ *n* dishonour
ATTAINTED > ATTAINT
ATTAINTS > ATTAINT
ATTAP *n* palm tree of South Asia
ATTAPS > ATTAP
ATTAR *n* fragrant oil made from roses
ATTARS > ATTAR
ATTASK *old word for*
> CRITICIZE
ATTASKED > ATTASK
ATTASKING > ATTASK
ATTASKS > ATTASK
ATTASKT > ATTASK
ATTEMPER *vb* modify by blending
ATTEMPERS > ATTEMPER
ATTEMPT *vb* try, make an effort ▷ *n* effort or endeavour
ATTEMPTED > ATTEMPT
ATTEMPTER > ATTEMPT
ATTEMPTS > ATTEMPT
ATTEND *vb* be present at
ATTENDANT *n* person who assists, guides, or provides a service ▷ *adj* accompanying
ATTENDED > ATTEND
ATTENDEE *n* person who is present at a specified event

ATTENDEES > ATTENDEE
ATTENDER > ATTEND
ATTENDERS > ATTEND
ATTENDING > ATTEND
ATTENDS > ATTEND
ATTENT *old word for*
> ATTENTION
ATTENTAT *n* attempt
ATTENTATS > ATTENTAT
ATTENTION *n* concentrated direction of the mind
ATTENTIVE *adj* giving attention
ATTENTS > ATTENT
ATTENUANT *adj* causing dilution or thinness, esp of the blood ▷ *n* attenuant drug or agent
ATTENUATE *vb* weaken or become weak ▷ *adj* diluted, weakened, slender, or reduced
ATTERCOP *n* spider
ATTERCOPS > ATTERCOP
ATTEST *vb* affirm the truth of, be proof of
ATTESTANT > ATTEST
ATTESTED *adj* (of cattle) certified to be free from a disease, such as tuberculosis
ATTESTER > ATTEST
ATTESTERS > ATTEST
ATTESTING > ATTEST
ATTESTOR > ATTEST
ATTESTORS > ATTEST
ATTESTS > ATTEST
ATTIC *n* space or room within the roof of a house
ATTICISE *same as*
> ATTICIZE
ATTICISED > ATTICISE
ATTICISES > ATTICISE
ATTICISM *n* elegant, simple, and clear expression
ATTICISMS > ATTICISM
ATTICIST > ATTICISM
ATTICISTS > ATTICISM
ATTICIZE *vb* conform or adapt to the norms of Attica
ATTICIZED > ATTICIZE
ATTICIZES > ATTICIZE
ATTICS > ATTIC
ATTIRE *n* fine or formal clothes ▷ *vb* dress, esp in fine elegant clothes
ATTIRED > ATTIRE
ATTIRES > ATTIRE
ATTIRING > ATTIRE
ATTIRINGS > ATTIRE
ATTITUDE *n* way of thinking and behaving
ATTITUDES > ATTITUDE
ATTOLASER *n* high-power laser capable of producing pulses with a duration measured in attoseconds
ATTOLLENS *adj* (of muscle) used to lift
ATTOLLENT *adj* muscle used in lifting
ATTOMETER *same as*
> ATTOMETRE
ATTOMETRE *n* ten to the power of minus eighteen metres
ATTONCE *adv* old word for at once

ATTONE vb old word meaning appease
ATTONED > ATTONE
ATTONES > ATTONE
ATTONING > ATTONE
ATTORN vb acknowledge a new owner of land as one's landlord
ATTORNED > ATTORN
ATTORNEY n person legally appointed to act for another
ATTORNEYS > ATTORNEY
ATTORNING > ATTORN
ATTORNS > ATTORN
ATTOTESLA n ten to the power of minus eighteen teslas
ATTRACT vb arouse the interest or admiration of
ATTRACTED > ATTRACT
ATTRACTER > ATTRACT
ATTRACTOR > ATTRACT
ATTRACTS > ATTRACT
ATTRAHENS adj (of muscle) drawing towards
ATTRAHENT adj something that attracts
ATTRAP vb adorn
ATTRAPPED > ATTRAP
ATTRAPS > ATTRAP
ATTRIBUTE vb regard as belonging to or produced by ▷ n quality or feature representative of a person or thing
ATTRIST vb old word meaning to sadden
ATTRISTED > ATTRIST
ATTRISTS > ATTRIST
ATTRIT vb wear down or dispose of gradually
ATTRITE vb wear down
ATTRITED > ATTRITE
ATTRITES > ATTRITE
ATTRITING > ATTRITE
ATTRITION n constant wearing down to weaken or destroy
ATTRITIVE > ATTRITION
ATTRITS > ATTRIT
ATTRITTED > ATTRIT
ATTUENT adj carrying out attuition
ATTUITE vb perceive by attuition
ATTUITED > ATTUITE
ATTUITES > ATTUITE
ATTUITING > ATTUITE
ATTUITION n way of mentally perceiving something
ATTUITIVE > ATTUITION
ATTUNE vb adjust or accustom (a person or thing)
ATTUNED > ATTUNE
ATTUNES > ATTUNE
ATTUNING > ATTUNE
ATUA n spirit or demon
ATUAS > ATUA
ATWAIN adv old word meaning into two parts
ATWEEL Scots word for > WELL
ATWEEN an archaic or Scots word for > BETWEEN
ATWITTER adv twittering
ATWIXT old word for > BETWEEN

ATYPIC adj not typical
ATYPICAL adj not typical
AUA n yellow-eye mullet
AUAS > AUA
AUBADE n song or poem greeting the dawn
AUBADES > AUBADE
AUBERGE n inn or tavern
AUBERGES > AUBERGE
AUBERGINE n dark purple tropical fruit, cooked and eaten as a vegetable
AUBRETIA same as > AUBRIETIA
AUBRETIAS > AUBRETIA
AUBRIETA same as > AUBRIETIA
AUBRIETAS > AUBRIETA
AUBRIETIA n trailing plant with purple flowers
AUBURN adj (of hair) reddish-brown ▷ n moderate reddish-brown colour
AUBURNS > AUBURN
AUCEPS n old word meaning person who catches hawks
AUCEPSES > AUCEPS
AUCTION n public sale in which articles are sold to the highest bidder ▷ vb sell by auction
AUCTIONED > AUCTION
AUCTIONS > AUCTION
AUCTORIAL adj of or relating to an author
AUCUBA n Japanese laurel
AUCUBAS > AUCUBA
AUDACIOUS adj recklessly bold or daring
AUDACITY > AUDACIOUS
AUDAD n wild African sheep
AUDADS > AUDAD
AUDIAL adj of sound
AUDIBLE adj loud enough to be heard ▷ n audible change of tactics in American football ▷ vb call an audible
AUDIBLED > AUDIBLE
AUDIBLES > AUDIBLE
AUDIBLING > AUDIBLE
AUDIBLY > AUDIBLE
AUDIENCE n group of spectators or listeners
AUDIENCES > AUDIENCE
AUDIENCIA n court in South America
AUDIENT n person who hears
AUDIENTS > AUDIENT
AUDILE n person with a faculty for auditory imagery ▷ adj of or relating to such a person
AUDILES > AUDILE
AUDING n practice of listening to try to understand
AUDINGS > AUDING
AUDIO adj of sound or hearing ▷ n sound
AUDIOBOOK n recorded reading of a book
AUDIOGRAM n graphic record of the acuity of hearing of a person obtained by means of an audiometer
AUDIOLOGY n scientific study of hearing, often

including the treatment of persons with hearing defects
AUDIOPHIL n audiophile
AUDIOS > AUDIO
AUDIOTAPE n (esp formerly) tape for recording sound
AUDIPHONE n type of hearing aid consisting of a diaphragm that, when placed against the upper teeth, conveys sound vibrations to the inner ear
AUDISM n prejudice against deaf people
AUDISMS > AUDISM
AUDIST n person prejudiced against deaf people
AUDISTS > AUDIST
AUDIT n official examination of business accounts ▷ vb examine (business accounts) officially
AUDITABLE > AUDIT
AUDITED > AUDIT
AUDITEE n one who is audited
AUDITEES > AUDITEE
AUDITING n act of auditing
AUDITINGS > AUDITING
AUDITION n test of a performer's ability for a particular role or job ▷ vb test or be tested in an audition
AUDITIONS > AUDITION
AUDITIVE n person who learns primarily by listening
AUDITIVES > AUDITIVE
AUDITOR n person qualified to audit accounts
AUDITORIA n areas of concert halls, theatres, schools, etc, in which audiences sit
AUDITORS > AUDITOR
AUDITORY adj of or relating to hearing
AUDITRESS n female auditor
AUDITS > AUDIT
AUE interj Māori exclamation
AUF old word for > OAF
AUFGABE n word used in psychology to mean task
AUFGABES > AUFGABE
AUFS > AUF
AUGEND n number to which a number is added
AUGENDS > AUGEND
AUGER n tool for boring holes
AUGERS > AUGER
AUGH interj expressing frustration
AUGHT adv in any least part ▷ n less common word for nought
AUGHTS > AUGHT
AUGITE n black or greenish-black mineral
AUGITES > AUGITE
AUGITIC > AUGITE
AUGMENT vb increase or enlarge ▷ n vowel prefix forming a past tense
AUGMENTED > AUGMENT
AUGMENTER > AUGMENT
AUGMENTOR > AUGMENT

AUGMENTS > AUGMENT
AUGUR vb be a sign of (future events) ▷ n religious official who interpreted omens
AUGURAL > AUGUR
AUGURED > AUGUR
AUGURER old word for > AUGUR
AUGURERS > AUGURER
AUGURIES > AUGURY
AUGURING > AUGUR
AUGURS > AUGUR
AUGURSHIP > AUGUR
AUGURY n foretelling of the future
AUGUST adj dignified and imposing ▷ n auguste
AUGUSTE n type of circus clown
AUGUSTER > AUGUST
AUGUSTES > AUGUSTE
AUGUSTEST > AUGUST
AUGUSTLY > AUGUST
AUGUSTS > AUGUST
AUK n sea bird with short wings
AUKLET n type of small auk
AUKLETS > AUKLET
AUKS > AUK
AULA n hall
AULARIAN n Oxford University student belonging to a hall
AULARIANS > AULARIAN
AULAS > AULA
AULD a Scots word for > OLD
AULDER > AULD
AULDEST > AULD
AULIC adj relating to a royal court
AULNAGE n measurement in ells
AULNAGER n inspector of cloth
AULNAGERS > AULNAGER
AULNAGES > AULNAGE
AULOI > AULOS
AULOS n ancient Greek pipe
AUMAIL old word for > ENAMEL
AUMAILED > AUMAIL
AUMAILING > AUMAIL
AUMAILS > AUMAIL
AUMBRIES > AUMBRY
AUMBRY same as > AMBRY
AUMIL n manager in India
AUMILS > AUMIL
AUNE n old French measure of length
AUNES > AUNE
AUNT n father's or mother's sister
AUNTER old word for > ADVENTURE
AUNTERS > AUNTER
AUNTHOOD > AUNT
AUNTHOODS > AUNT
AUNTIE n aunt
AUNTIES > AUNTIE
AUNTLIER > AUNTLY
AUNTLIEST > AUNTLY
AUNTLIKE > AUNT
AUNTLY adj of or like an aunt
AUNTS > AUNT
AUNTY same as > AUNTIE

AURA n distinctive air or quality of a person or thing
AURAE > AURA
AURAL adj of or using the ears or hearing
AURALITY > AURAL
AURALLY > AURAL
AURAR plural of > EYRIR
AURAS > AURA
AURATE n salt of auric acid
AURATED adj combined with auric acid
AURATES > AURATE
AUREATE adj covered with gold, gilded
AUREATELY > AUREATE
AUREI > AUREUS
AUREITIES > AUREITY
AUREITY n attributes of gold
AURELIA n large jellyfish
AURELIAN n person who studies butterflies and moths
AURELIANS > AURELIAN
AURELIAS > AURELIA
AUREOLA same as > AUREOLE
AUREOLAE > AUREOLA
AUREOLAS > AUREOLA
AUREOLE n halo ▷ vb encircle
AUREOLED > AUREOLE
AUREOLES > AUREOLE
AUREOLING > AUREOLE
AURES > AURIS
AUREUS n gold coin of the Roman Empire
AURIC adj of or containing gold in the trivalent state
AURICLE n upper chamber of the heart
AURICLED > AURICLE
AURICLES > AURICLE
AURICULA n alpine primrose with leaves shaped like a bear's ear
AURICULAE > AURICULA
AURICULAR adj of, relating to, or received by the sense or organs of hearing ▷ n auricular feather
AURICULAS > AURICULA
AURIFIED > AURIFY
AURIFIES > AURIFY
AURIFORM adj shaped like an ear
AURIFY vb turn into gold
AURIFYING > AURIFY
AURIS n medical word for ear
AURISCOPE n medical instrument for examining the external ear
AURIST n former name for an audiologist
AURISTS > AURIST
AUROCHS n recently extinct European wild ox
AUROCHSES > AUROCHS
AURORA n bands of light seen in the sky
AURORAE > AURORA
AURORAL > AURORA
AURORALLY > AURORA
AURORAS > AURORA
AUROREAN adj of dawn

AUROUS adj of or containing gold, esp in the monovalent state
AURUM n gold
AURUMS > AURUM
AUSFORM vb temper steel
AUSFORMED > AUSFORM
AUSFORMS > AUSFORM
AUSLANDER n German word meaning foreigner
AUSPEX same as > AUGUR
AUSPICATE vb inaugurate with a ceremony intended to bring good fortune
AUSPICE n patronage or guidance
AUSPICES > AUSPICE
AUSTENITE n solid solution of carbon in face-centred-cubic gamma iron, usually existing above 723°C
AUSTERE adj stern or severe
AUSTERELY > AUSTERE
AUSTERER > AUSTERE
AUSTEREST > AUSTERE
AUSTERITY n state of being austere
AUSTRAL adj southern ▷ n former monetary unit of Argentina
AUSTRALES > AUSTRAL
AUSTRALIS adj Australian
AUSTRALS > AUSTRAL
AUSUBO n tropical tree
AUSUBOS > AUSUBO
AUTACOID n any natural internal secretion, esp that exerts an effect similar to a drug
AUTACOIDS > AUTACOID
AUTARCH n absolute ruler
AUTARCHIC > AUTARCHY
AUTARCHS > AUTARCH
AUTARCHY n absolute power or autocracy
AUTARKIC > AUTARKY
AUTARKIES > AUTARKY
AUTARKIST > AUTARKY
AUTARKY n policy of economic self-sufficiency
AUTECIOUS adj (of parasites, esp the rust fungi) completing the entire life cycle on a single species of host
AUTECISM > AUTECIOUS
AUTECISMS > AUTECIOUS
AUTEUR n director
AUTEURISM > AUTEUR
AUTEURIST > AUTEUR
AUTEURS > AUTEUR
AUTHENTIC adj known to be real, genuine
AUTHOR n writer of a book etc ▷ vb write or originate
AUTHORED > AUTHOR
AUTHORESS n female author
AUTHORIAL > AUTHOR
AUTHORING n creation of documents, esp multimedia documents
AUTHORISE same as > AUTHORIZE
AUTHORISH > AUTHOR
AUTHORISM n condition of being author

AUTHORITY n power to command or control others
AUTHORIZE vb give authority to
AUTIIORS > AUTHOR
AUTISM n disorder characterized by lack of response to people and difficulty in communicating with them
AUTISMS > AUTISM
AUTIST n autistic person
AUTISTIC > AUTISM
AUTISTICS > AUTISM
AUTISTS > AUTIST
AUTO n automobile ▷ vb travel in an automobile
AUTOBAHN n German motorway
AUTOBAHNS > AUTOBAHN
AUTOBANK n automated teller machine
AUTOBANKS > AUTOBANK
AUTOBODY n body of a motor vehicle
AUTOBUS n motor bus
AUTOBUSES > AUTOBUS
AUTOCADE another name for > MOTORCADE
AUTOCADES > AUTOCADE
AUTOCAR n motor car
AUTOCARP n fruit produced through self-fertilization
AUTOCARPS > AUTOCARP
AUTOCARS > AUTOCAR
AUTOCIDAL adj (of insect pest control) effected by the introduction of sterile or genetically altered individuals into the wild population
AUTOCLAVE n apparatus for sterilizing objects by steam under pressure ▷ vb put in or subject to the action of an autoclave
AUTOCOID n hormone
AUTOCOIDS > AUTOCOID
AUTOCRACY n government by an autocrat
AUTOCRAT n ruler with absolute authority
AUTOCRATS > AUTOCRAT
AUTOCRIME n crime of stealing a car
AUTOCRINE adj relating to self-stimulation through production of a factor and its receptor
AUTOCROSS n motor-racing over a rough course
AUTOCUE n electronic television prompting device
AUTOCUES > AUTOCUE
AUTOCUTIE n young and attractive but inexperienced female television presenter
AUTOCYCLE n bicycle powered or assisted by a small engine
AUTODIAL vb dial a telephone number automatically
AUTODIALS > AUTODIAL
AUTODROME n track for motor racing
AUTODYNE adj using the same elements and valves as

oscillator and detector ▷ n autodyne circuit
AUTODYNES > AUTODYNE
AUTOECISM n (of a parasite) completion of an entire life cycle on a single species of host
AUTOED > AUTO
AUTOFLARE n automatic landing system in aircraft
AUTOFOCUS n camera system in which the lens is focused automatically
AUTOGAMIC > AUTOGAMY
AUTOGAMY n self-fertilization in flowering plants
AUTOGENIC adj produced from within
AUTOGENY n hypothetical process by which living organisms first arose on earth from nonliving matter
AUTOGIRO n self-propelled aircraft resembling a helicopter but with an unpowered rotor
AUTOGIROS > AUTOGIRO
AUTOGRAFT n tissue graft obtained from one part of a patient's body for use on another part
AUTOGRAPH n handwritten signature of a (famous) person ▷ vb write one's signature on or in
AUTOGUIDE n traffic information transmission system
AUTOGYRO same as > AUTOGIRO
AUTOGYROS > AUTOGYRO
AUTOHARP n zither-like musical instrument
AUTOHARPS > AUTOHARP
AUTOICOUS adj (of plants, esp mosses) having male and female reproductive organs on the same plant
AUTOING > AUTO
AUTOLATRY n self-worship
AUTOLOAD vb load automatically
AUTOLOADS > AUTOLOAD
AUTOLOGY n study of oneself
AUTOLYSE vb undergo or cause to undergo autolysis
AUTOLYSED > AUTOLYSE
AUTOLYSES > AUTOLYSE
AUTOLYSIN n any agent that produces autolysis
AUTOLYSIS n destruction of cells and tissues of an organism by enzymes produced by the cells themselves
AUTOLYTIC > AUTOLYSIS
AUTOLYZE same as > AUTOLYSE
AUTOLYZED > AUTOLYZE
AUTOLYZES > AUTOLYZE
AUTOMAGIC adj done with such ease and speed that it seems like magic
AUTOMAKER n car manufacturer
AUTOMAN n car manufacturer

AUTOMAT n vending machine

AUTOMATA > AUTOMATON

AUTOMATE vb make (a manufacturing process) automatic

AUTOMATED > AUTOMATE

AUTOMATES > AUTOMATE

AUTOMATIC adj (of a device) operating mechanically by itself ▷ n self-loading firearm

AUTOMATON n robot

AUTOMATS > AUTOMAT

AUTOMEN > AUTOMAN

AUTOMETER n small device inserted in a photocopier to enable the process of copying to begin and to record the number of copies made

AUTONOMIC adj occurring involuntarily or spontaneously

AUTONOMY n self-government

AUTONYM n writing published under the real name of an author

AUTONYMS > AUTONYM

AUTOPEN n mechanical device used to produce imitation signatures

AUTOPENS > AUTOPEN

AUTOPHAGY n consumption of one's own tissue

AUTOPHOBY n reluctance to refer to oneself

AUTOPHONY n medical diagnosis by listening to vibration of one's own voice in patient

AUTOPHYTE n autotrophic plant, such as any green plant

AUTOPILOT n automatic pilot

AUTOPISTA n Spanish motorway

AUTOPOINT n point-to-point race in cars

AUTOPSIA n autopsy

AUTOPSIAS > AUTOPSIA

AUTOPSIC > AUTOPSY

AUTOPSIED > AUTOPSY

AUTOPSIES > AUTOPSY

AUTOPSIST > AUTOPSY

AUTOPSY n examination of a body to determine the cause of death

AUTOPTIC > AUTOPSY

AUTOPUT n motorway in the former Yugoslavia

AUTOPUTS > AUTOPUT

AUTOREPLY n email facility for sending automatic replies

AUTOROUTE n French motorway

AUTOS > AUTO

AUTOSAVE n computer facility for automatically saving data ▷ vb save (computer data) automatically

AUTOSAVED > AUTOSAVE

AUTOSAVES > AUTOSAVE

AUTOSCOPY n hallucination in which one sees oneself

AUTOSOMAL > AUTOSOME

AUTOSOME n type of chromosome

AUTOSOMES > AUTOSOME

AUTOSPORE n nonmotile algal spore that develops adult characteristics before being released

AUTOSPORT n sport of motor racing

AUTOTELIC adj justifying itself

AUTOTEST n motor race in which standard cars are driven round a circuit

AUTOTESTS > AUTOTEST

AUTOTIMER n device for turning a system on and off automatically at times predetermined by advance setting

AUTOTOMIC > AUTOTOMY

AUTOTOMY n casting off by an animal of a part of its body, to facilitate escape when attacked

AUTOTOXIC > AUTOTOXIN

AUTOTOXIN n any poison or toxin formed in the organism upon which it acts

AUTOTROPH n organism capable of manufacturing complex organic nutritive compounds from simple inorganic sources

AUTOTUNE n software that changes a recording of a vocal track

AUTOTUNES > AUTOTUNE

AUTOTYPE n photographic process for producing prints in black and white, using a carbon pigment ▷ vb process using autotype

AUTOTYPED > AUTOTYPE

AUTOTYPES > AUTOTYPE

AUTOTYPIC > AUTOTYPE

AUTOTYPY > AUTOTYPE

AUTOVAC n vacuum pump in a car petrol tank

AUTOVACS > AUTOVAC

AUTUMN n season between summer and winter

AUTUMNAL adj of, occurring in, or characteristic of autumn

AUTUMNIER > AUTUMNY

AUTUMNS > AUTUMN

AUTUMNY adj like autumn

AUTUNITE n yellowish fluorescent radioactive mineral

AUTUNITES > AUTUNITE

AUXESES > AUXESIS

AUXESIS n increase in cell size without division

AUXETIC n something that promotes growth

AUXETICS > AUXETIC

AUXILIAR old word for **>** AUXILIARY

AUXILIARS > AUXILIAR

AUXILIARY adj secondary or supplementary ▷ n person or thing that supplements or supports

AUXIN n plant hormone that promotes growth

AUXINIC > AUXIN

AUXINS > AUXIN

AUXOCYTE n any cell undergoing meiosis

AUXOCYTES > AUXOCYTE

AUXOMETER n instrument for measuring magnification

AUXOSPORE n diatom cell before its silicaceous cell wall is formed

AUXOTONIC adj (of muscle contraction) occurring against increasing force

AUXOTROPH n mutant strain of microorganism having nutritional requirements additional to those of the normal organism

AVA adv at all ▷ n Polynesian shrub

AVADAVAT n Asian weaverbird with usu red plumage, often kept as a cagebird

AVADAVATS > AVADAVAT

AVAIL vb be of use or advantage (to) ▷ n use or advantage

AVAILABLE adj obtainable or accessible

AVAILABLY > AVAILABLE

AVAILE old word for **>** LOWER

AVAILED > AVAIL

AVAILES > AVAILE

AVAILFUL old word for **>** USEFUL

AVAILING > AVAIL

AVAILS > AVAIL

AVAL adj of a grandparent

AVALANCHE n mass of snow or ice falling down a mountain ▷ vb come down overwhelmingly (upon)

AVALE old word for **>** LOWER

AVALED > AVALE

AVALEMENT n skiing technique where the knees are kept flexible

AVALES > AVALE

AVALING > AVALE

AVANT prep before

AVANTI interj forward!

AVANTIST n proponent of the avant-garde

AVANTISTS > AVANTIST

AVARICE n greed for wealth

AVARICES > AVARICE

AVAS > AVA

AVASCULAR adj (of certain tissues, such as cartilage) lacking blood vessels

AVAST sentence substitute stop! cease!

AVATAR n appearance of a god in animal or human form

AVATARS > AVATAR

AVAUNT sentence substitute go away! depart! ▷ vb go away; depart

AVAUNTED > AVAUNT

AVAUNTING > AVAUNT

AVAUNTS > AVAUNT

AVE n expression of welcome or farewell

AVEL a variant of **>** OVEL

AVELLAN adj of hazelnuts

AVELLANE same as **>** AVELLAN

AVELS > AVEL

AVENGE vb take revenge in retaliation for (harm done) or on behalf of (a person harmed)

AVENGED > AVENGE

AVENGEFUL > AVENGE

AVENGER > AVENGE

AVENGERS > AVENGE

AVENGES > AVENGE

AVENGING > AVENGE

AVENIR n future

AVENIRS > AVENIR

AVENS n any of several temperate or Arctic rosaceous plants

AVENSES > AVENS

AVENTAIL n front flap of a helmet

AVENTAILE n aventail

AVENTAILS > AVENTAIL

AVENTRE old word for **>** THRUST

AVENTRED > AVENTRE

AVENTRES > AVENTRE

AVENTRING > AVENTRE

AVENTURE old form of **>** ADVENTURE

AVENTURES > AVENTURE

AVENTURIN n dark-coloured glass, usually green or brown, spangled with fine particles of gold, copper, or some other metal

AVENUE n wide street

AVENUES > AVENUE

AVER vb state to be true

AVERAGE n typical or normal amount or quality ▷ adj usual or typical ▷ vb calculate the average of

AVERAGED > AVERAGE

AVERAGELY > AVERAGE

AVERAGER n average adjuster

AVERAGERS > AVERAGER

AVERAGES > AVERAGE

AVERAGING > AVERAGE

AVERMENT > AVER

AVERMENTS > AVER

AVERRABLE > AVER

AVERRED > AVER

AVERRING > AVER

AVERS > AVER

AVERSE adj disinclined or unwilling

AVERSELY > AVERSE

AVERSION n strong dislike

AVERSIONS > AVERSION

AVERSIVE n tool or technique intended to repel animals etc

AVERSIVES > AVERSIVE

AVERT vb turn away

AVERTABLE > AVERT

AVERTED > AVERT

AVERTEDLY > AVERT

AVERTER > AVERT

AVERTERS > AVERT

AVERTIBLE > AVERT

AVERTING > AVERT

AVERTS > AVERT

AVES > AVE

AVGAS n aviation fuel

AVGASES > AVGAS

AVGASSES > AVGAS

AVIAN adj of or like a bird ▷ n bird

a

AVIANISE *same as* > AVIANIZE

AVIANISED > AVIANISE

AVIANISES > AVIANISE

AVIANIZE *vb* modify microorganisms in a chicken embryo

AVIANIZED > AVIANIZE

AVIANIZES > AVIANIZE

AVIANS > AVIAN

AVIARIES > AVIARY

AVIARIST *n* person who keeps an aviary

AVIARISTS > AVIARIST

AVIARY *n* large cage or enclosure for birds

AVIATE *vb* pilot or fly in an aircraft

AVIATED > AVIATE

AVIATES > AVIATE

AVIATIC *adj* pertaining to aviation

AVIATING > AVIATE

AVIATION *n* art of flying aircraft

AVIATIONS > AVIATION

AVIATOR *n* pilot of an aircraft

AVIATORS > AVIATOR

AVIATRESS > AVIATOR

AVIATRICE > AVIATOR

AVIATRIX > AVIATOR

AVICULAR *adj* of small birds

AVID *adj* keen or enthusiastic

AVIDER > AVID

AVIDEST > AVID

AVIDIN *n* protein found in egg-white

AVIDINS > AVIDIN

AVIDITIES > AVIDITY

AVIDITY *n* quality or state of being avid

AVIDLY > AVID

AVIDNESS > AVID

AVIETTE *n* aeroplane driven by human strength

AVIETTES > AVIETTE

AVIFAUNA *n* all the birds in a particular region

AVIFAUNAE > AVIFAUNA

AVIFAUNAL > AVIFAUNA

AVIFAUNAS > AVIFAUNA

AVIFORM *adj* like a bird

AVIGATOR *another word for* > AVIATOR

AVIGATORS > AVIGATOR

AVINE *adj* of birds

AVION *n* aeroplane

AVIONIC > AVIONICS

AVIONICS *n* science and technology of electronics applied to aeronautics and astronautics

AVIONS > AVION

AVIRULENT *adj* (esp of bacteria) not virulent

AVISANDUM *n* consideration of a law case by a judge

AVISE *old word for* > ADVISE

AVISED > AVISE

AVISEMENT > AVISE

AVISES > AVISE

AVISING > AVISE

AVISO *n* boat carrying messages

AVISOS > AVISO

AVITAL *adj* of a grandfather

AVIZANDUM *n* judge's or court's decision to consider a case privately before giving judgment

AVIZE *old word for* > ADVISE

AVIZED > AVIZE

AVIZEFULL > AVIZE

AVIZES > AVIZE

AVIZING > AVIZE

AVO *n* Macao currency unit

AVOCADO *n* pear-shaped tropical fruit with a leathery green skin and yellowish-green flesh

AVOCADOES > AVOCADO

AVOCADOS > AVOCADO

AVOCATION *n* occupation

AVOCET *n* long-legged wading bird

AVOCETS > AVOCET

AVODIRE *n* African tree

AVODIRES > AVODIRE

AVOID *vb* prevent from happening

AVOIDABLE > AVOID

AVOIDABLY > AVOID

AVOIDANCE *n* act of keeping away from or preventing from happening

AVOIDANT *adj* (of behaviour) demonstrating a tendency to avoid intimacy or interaction with others

AVOIDED > AVOID

AVOIDER > AVOID

AVOIDERS > AVOID

AVOIDING > AVOID

AVOIDS > AVOID

AVOISION *n* nonpayment of tax

AVOISIONS > AVOISION

AVOPARCIN *n* type of antibiotic

AVOS > AVO

AVOSET *n* avocet

AVOSETS > AVOSET

AVOUCH *vb* vouch for

AVOUCHED > AVOUCH

AVOUCHER > AVOUCH

AVOUCHERS > AVOUCH

AVOUCHES > AVOUCH

AVOUCHING > AVOUCH

AVOURE *old word for* > AVOWAL

AVOURES > AVOURE

AVOUTERER *old word for* > ADULTERER

AVOUTRER *old word for* > ADULTERER

AVOUTRERS > AVOUTRER

AVOUTRIES > AVOUTRY

AVOUTRY *old word for* > ADULTERY

AVOW *vb* state or affirm

AVOWABLE > AVOW

AVOWABLY > AVOW

AVOWAL > AVOW

AVOWALS > AVOW

AVOWED *adj* openly declared

AVOWEDLY > AVOWED

AVOWER > AVOW

AVOWERS > AVOW

AVOWING > AVOW

AVOWRIES > AVOWRY

AVOWRY *old word for* > AVOWAL

AVOWS > AVOW

AVOYER *n* former Swiss magistrate

AVOYERS > AVOYER

AVRUGA *n* herring roe

AVRUGAS > AVRUGA

AVULSE *vb* take away by force

AVULSED > AVULSE

AVULSES > AVULSE

AVULSING > AVULSE

AVULSION *n* forcible tearing away of a bodily structure or part

AVULSIONS > AVULSION

AVUNCULAR *adj* (of a man) friendly, helpful, and caring towards someone younger

AVYZE *old word for* > ADVISE

AVYZED > AVYZE

AVYZES > AVYZE

AVYZING > AVYZE

AW *variant of* > ALL

AWA *adv* away

AWAIT *vb* wait for

AWAITED > AWAIT

AWAITER > AWAIT

AWAITERS > AWAIT

AWAITING > AWAIT

AWAITS > AWAIT

AWAKE *vb* emerge or rouse from sleep ▷ *adj* not sleeping

AWAKED > AWAKE

AWAKEN *vb* awake

AWAKENED > AWAKEN

AWAKENER > AWAKEN

AWAKENERS > AWAKEN

AWAKENING *n* start of a feeling or awareness in someone

AWAKENS > AWAKEN

AWAKES > AWAKE

AWAKING *n* emergence from sleep

AWAKINGS > AWAKING

AWANTING *adj* missing

AWARD *vb* give (something, such as a prize) formally ▷ *n* something awarded, such as a prize

AWARDABLE > AWARD

AWARDED > AWARD

AWARDEE > AWARD

AWARDEES > AWARD

AWARDER > AWARD

AWARDERS > AWARD

AWARDING > AWARD

AWARDS > AWARD

AWARE *adj* having knowledge, informed

AWARENESS > AWARE

AWARER > AWARE

AWAREST > AWARE

AWARN *vb* old form of warn

AWARNED > AWARN

AWARNING > AWARN

AWARNS > AWARN

AWASH *adv* washed over by water ▷ *adj* washed over by water

AWATCH *adv* watching

AWATO *n* New Zealand caterpillar

AWATOS > AWATO

AWAVE *adv* in waves

AWAY *adv* from a place ▷ *adj* not present ▷ *n* game played or won at an opponent's ground

AWAYDAY *n* day trip taken for pleasure

AWAYDAYS > AWAYDAY

AWAYES *old word for* > AWAY

AWAYNESS > AWAY

AWAYS > AWAY

AWDL *n* traditional Welsh poem

AWDLS > AWDL

AWE *n* wonder and respect mixed with dread ▷ *vb* fill with awe

AWEARIED *old word for* > WEARY

AWEARY *old form of* > WEARY

AWEATHER *adj* towards the weather

AWED > AWE

AWEE *adv* for a short time

AWEEL *interj* Scots word meaning well

AWEIGH *adj* (of an anchor) no longer hooked onto the bottom

AWEING > AWE

AWELESS > AWE

AWES > AWE

AWESOME *adj* inspiring awe

AWESOMELY > AWESOME

AWESTRIKE *vb* inspire great awe in

AWESTRUCK *adj* filled with awe

AWETO *n* New Zealand caterpillar

AWETOS > AWETO

AWFUL *adj* very bad or unpleasant ▷ *adv* very

AWFULLER > AWFUL

AWFULLEST > AWFUL

AWFULLY *adv* in an unpleasant way

AWFULNESS > AWFUL

AWFY *adv* (Scots) awfully, extremely

AWHAPE *old word for* > AMAZE

AWHAPED > AWHAPE

AWHAPES > AWHAPE

AWHAPING > AWHAPE

AWHATO *n* New Zealand caterpillar

AWHATOS > AWHATO

AWHEEL *adv* on wheels

AWHEELS *same as* > AWHEEL

AWHETO *n* New Zealand caterpillar

AWHETOS > AWHETO

AWHILE *adv* for a brief time

AWHIRL *adv* whirling

AWING > AWE

AWK *n* type of programming language

AWKS > AWK

AWKWARD *adj* clumsy or ungainly

AWKWARDER > AWKWARD

AWKWARDLY > AWKWARD

AWL *n* pointed tool for piercing wood, leather, etc

AWLBIRD *n* woodpecker

AWLBIRDS > AWLBIRD

AWLESS > AWE

AWLS > AWL

AWLWORT *n* type of aquatic plant

AWLWORTS > AWLWORT

AWMOUS *Scots word for* > ALMS

AWMRIE n cupboard for church vessels

AWMRIES > AWMRIE

AWMRY n cupboard for church vessels

AWN n bristles on grasses

AWNED > AWN

AWNER n machine for removing awns

AWNERS > AWNER

AWNIER > AWNY

AWNIEST > AWNY

AWNING n canvas roof supported by a frame to give protection against the weather

AWNINGED adj sheltered with awning

AWNINGS > AWNING

AWNLESS > AWN

AWNS > AWN

AWNY adj having awns

AWOKE > AWAKE

AWOKEN > AWAKE

AWOL n person who is absent without leave

AWOLS > AWOL

AWORK adv old word meaning at work

AWRACK adv in wrecked condition

AWRONG adv old word meaning wrongly

AWRY adj with a twist to one side, askew

AWSOME adj old form of awesome

AX same as > AXE

AXAL adj of an axis

AXE n tool with a sharp blade for felling trees or chopping wood ▷ vb dismiss (employees), restrict (expenditure), or terminate (a project)

AXEBIRD n nightjar

AXEBIRDS > AXEBIRD

AXED > AXE

AXEL n ice-skating movement

AXELIKE adj like an axe in form

AXELS > AXEL

AXEMAN n man who wields an axe, esp to cut down trees

AXEMEN > AXEMAN

AXENIC adj (of a biological culture) free from other microorganisms

AXES > AXIS

AXIAL adj forming or of an axis

AXIALITY > AXIAL

AXIALLY > AXIAL

AXIL n angle where the stalk of a leaf joins a stem

AXILE adj of, relating to, or attached to the axis

AXILEMMA same as > AXOLEMMA

AXILEMMAS > AXILEMMA

AXILLA n area under a bird's wing

AXILLAE > AXILLA

AXILLAR same as

> AXILLARY

AXILLARS > AXILLAR

AXILLARY adj of, relating to, or near the armpit ▷ n one of the feathers growing from the axilla of a bird's wing

AXILLAS > AXILLA

AXILS > AXIL

AXING > AXE

AXINITE n crystalline substance

AXINITES > AXINITE

AXIOLOGY n theory of values, moral or aesthetic

AXIOM n generally accepted principle

AXIOMATIC adj containing axioms

AXIOMS > AXIOM

AXION n type of hypothetical elementary particle

AXIONS > AXION

AXIS n imaginary line round which a body can rotate

AXISED adj having an axis

AXISES > AXIS

AXITE n type of gunpowder

AXITES > AXITE

AXLE n shaft on which a wheel or pair of wheels turns

AXLED adj having an axle

AXLES > AXLE

AXLETREE n bar fixed across the underpart of a wagon or carriage

AXLETREES > AXLETREE

AXLIKE > AX

AXMAN same as > AXEMAN

AXMEN > AXMAN

AXOID n type of curve

AXOIDS > AXOID

AXOLEMMA n membrane that encloses the axon of a nerve cell

AXOLEMMAS > AXOLEMMA

AXOLOTL n aquatic salamander of central America

AXOLOTLS > AXOLOTL

AXON n threadlike extension of a nerve cell

AXONAL > AXON

AXONE same as > AXON

AXONEMAL > AXONEME

AXONEME n part of cell consisting of proteins

AXONEMES > AXONEME

AXONES > AXONE

AXONIC > AXON

AXONS > AXON

AXOPLASM n part of cell

AXOPLASMS > AXOPLASM

AXSEED n crown vetch

AXSEEDS > AXSEED

AY adv ever ▷ n expression of agreement

AYAH n Indian or Malay maidservant or nursemaid in former British Empire

AYAHS > AYAH

AYAHUASCA n type of Brazilian plant

AYAHUASCO n South American vine

AYATOLLAH n Islamic religious leader in Iran

AYAYA n type of Inuit singing

AYAYAS > AYAYA

AYE n affirmative vote or voter ▷ adv always

AYELP adv yelping

AYENBITE old word for > REMORSE

AYENBITES > AYENBITE

AYES > AYE

AYGRE old word for > EAGER

AYIN n 16th letter in the Hebrew alphabet

AYINS > AYIN

AYONT adv beyond

AYRE old word for > AIR

AYRES > AYRE

AYRIE old word for > EYRIE

AYRIES > AYRIE

AYS > AY

AYU n small Japanese fish

AYURVEDA n ancient medical treatise on the art of healing and prolonging life

AYURVEDAS > AYURVEDA

AYURVEDIC > AYURVEDA

AYUS > AYU

AYWORD n old word meaning byword

AYWORDS > AYWORD

AZALEA n garden shrub grown for its showy flowers

AZALEAS > AZALEA

AZAN n call to prayer

AZANS > AZAN

AZEDARACH n astringent bark of the chinaberry tree, formerly used as an emetic and cathartic

AZEOTROPE n mixture of liquids that boils at a constant temperature, at a given pressure, without a change in composition

AZEOTROPY > AZEOTROPE

AZERTY n European version of keyboard

AZIDE n type of chemical compound

AZIDES > AZIDE

AZIDO adj containing an azide

AZIMUTH n arc of the sky between the zenith and the horizon

AZIMUTHAL > AZIMUTH

AZIMUTHS > AZIMUTH

AZINE n organic compound

AZINES > AZINE

AZIONE n musical drama

AZIONES > AZIONE

AZLON n fibre made from protein

AZLONS > AZLON

AZO adj of the divalent group -N:N-

AZOIC adj without life

AZOLE n organic compound

AZOLES > AZOLE

AZOLLA n tropical water fern

AZOLLAS > AZOLLA

AZON n type of drawing paper

AZONAL adj not divided into zones

AZONIC adj not confined to a zone

AZONS > AZON

AZOTAEMIA a less common name for > URAEMIA

AZOTAEMIC > AZOTAEMIA

AZOTE an obsolete name for > NITROGEN

AZOTED > AZOTE

AZOTEMIA same as > AZOTAEMIA

AZOTEMIAS > AZOTEMIA

AZOTEMIC > AZOTAEMIA

AZOTES > AZOTE

AZOTH n panacea postulated by Paracelsus

AZOTHS > AZOTH

AZOTIC adj of, containing, or concerned with nitrogen

AZOTISE same as > AZOTIZE

AZOTISED > AZOTISE

AZOTISES > AZOTISE

AZOTISING > AZOTISE

AZOTIZE vb combine or treat with nitrogen or a nitrogen compound

AZOTIZED > AZOTIZE

AZOTIZES > AZOTIZE

AZOTIZING > AZOTIZE

AZOTOUS adj containing nitrogen

AZOTURIA n presence of excess nitrogen in urine

AZOTURIAS > AZOTURIA

AZUKI same as > ADZUKI

AZUKIS > AZUKI

AZULEJO n Spanish porcelain tile

AZULEJOS > AZULEJO

AZURE n (of) the colour of a clear blue sky ▷ adj deep blue

AZUREAN adj azure

AZURES > AZURE

AZURIES > AZURY

AZURINE n blue dye

AZURINES > AZURINE

AZURITE n azure-blue mineral associated with copper deposits

AZURITES > AZURITE

AZURN old word for > AZURE

AZURY adj bluish ▷ n bluish colour

AZYGIES > AZYGY

AZYGOS n biological structure not in a pair

AZYGOSES > AZYGOS

AZYGOUS adj developing or occurring singly

AZYGOUSLY > AZYGOUS

AZYGY n state of not being joined in a pair

AZYM n unleavened bread

AZYME same as > AZYM

AZYMES > AZYME

AZYMITE n member of a church using unleavened bread in the Eucharist

AZYMITES > AZYMITE

AZYMOUS adj unleavened

AZYMS > AZYM

Bb

BA n symbol for the soul in Ancient Egyptian religion

BAA vb the characteristic bleating sound of a sheep ▷ n cry made by a sheep

BAAED > BAA

BAAING > BAA

BAAINGS > BAA

BAAL n any false god or idol

BAALEBOS n master of the house

BAALIM > BAAL

BAALISM > BAAL

BAALISMS > BAAL

BAALS > BAAL

BAAS South African word for > BOSS

BAASES > BAAS

BAASKAAP same as > BAASKAP

BAASKAAPS > BAASKAAP

BAASKAP n (in South Africa) control by Whites of non-Whites

BAASKAPS > BAASKAP

BAASSKAP same as > BAASKAP

BAASSKAPS > BAASSKAP

BABA n small cake of leavened dough

BABACO n greenish-yellow egg-shaped fruit

BABACOOTE n large lemur

BABACOS > BABACO

BABACU n type of Brazilian palm tree

BABACUS > BABACU

BABALAS adj South African word for drunk

BABAS > BABA

BABASSU n Brazilian palm tree with hard edible nuts

BABASSUS > BABASSU

BABBELAS same as > BABALAS

BABBITRY same as > BABBITT

BABBITT vb line (a bearing) or face (a surface) with a similar soft alloy

BABBITTED > BABBITT

BABBITTRY n narrow-minded materialism

BABBITTS > BABBITT

BABBLE vb talk excitedly or foolishly ▷ n muddled or foolish speech

BABBLED > BABBLE

BABBLER n person who babbles

BABBLERS > BABBLER

BABBLES > BABBLE

BABBLIER > BABBLE

BABBLIEST > BABBLE

BABBLING > BABBLE

BABBLINGS > BABBLE

BABBLY > BABBLE

BABE n baby

BABEL n confused mixture of noises or voices

BABELDOM > BABEL

BABELDOMS > BABEL

BABELISH > BABEL

BABELISM > BABEL

BABELISMS > BABEL

BABELS > BABEL

BABES > BABE

BABESIA n parasite causing infection in cattle

BABESIAE > BABESIA

BABESIAS > BABESIA

BABICHE n thongs or lacings of rawhide

BABICHES > BABICHE

BABIED > BABY

BABIER > BABY

BABIES > BABY

BABIEST > BABY

BABIRUSA n Indonesian wild pig with an almost hairless skin and huge curved canine teeth

BABIRUSAS > BABIRUSA

BABIRUSSA same as > BABIRUSA

BABKA n cake

BABKAS > BABKA

BABLAH n type of acacia

BABLAHS > BABLAH

BABOO same as > BABU

BABOOL n type of acacia

BABOOLS > BABOOL

BABOON n large monkey with a pointed face and a long tail

BABOONERY n uncouth behaviour

BABOONISH adj uncouth

BABOONS > BABOON

BABOOS > BABOO

BABOOSH same as > BABOUCHE

BABOOSHES > BABOOSH

BABOUCHE n Middle-Eastern slipper

BABOUCHES > BABOUCHE

BABU n title or form of address used in India

BABUCHE same as > BABOUCHE

BABUCHES > BABUCHE

BABUDOM > BABU

BABUDOMS > BABU

BABUISM > BABU

BABUISMS > BABU

BABUL n N African and Indian tree with small yellow flowers

BABULS > BABUL

BABUS > BABU

BABUSHKA n headscarf tied under the chin, worn by Russian peasant women

BABUSHKAS > BABUSHKA

BABY n very young child or animal ▷ adj comparatively small of its type ▷ vb treat as a baby

BABYCCINO n drink of frothy milk with a chocolate topping, esp for young children

BABYCINO same as > BABYCCINO

BABYCINOS > BABYCINO

BABYDADDY n father of a child, who is not the current partner of the child's mother

BABYDOLL n woman's short nightdress

BABYDOLLS > BABYDOLL

BABYFOOD n puréed food for babies

BABYFOODS > BABYFOOD

BABYHOOD > BABY

BABYHOODS > BABY

BABYING > BABY

BABYISH > BABY

BABYISHLY > BABY

BABYLIKE adj like a baby

BABYMOON n early period of new parenthood

BABYMOONS > BABYMOON

BABYPROOF adj safe for babies to handle ▷ vb make babyproof

BABYSAT > BABYSIT

BABYSIT vb look after a child in its parents' absence

BABYSITS > BABYSIT

BAC n baccalaureate

BACALAO n dried salt cod

BACALAOS > BACALAO

BACALHAU same as > BACALAO

BACALHAUS > BACALHAU

BACCA n berry

BACCAE > BACCA

BACCALA same as > BACALAO

BACCALAS > BACCALA

BACCARA same as > BACCARAT

BACCARAS > BACCARA

BACCARAT n card game involving gambling

BACCARATS > BACCARAT

BACCARE same as > BACKARE

BACCAS > BACCA

BACCATE adj like a berry in form, texture, etc

BACCATED > BACCATE

BACCHANAL n follower of Bacchus ▷ adj of or relating to Bacchus

BACCHANT n priest or votary of Bacchus

BACCHANTE n priestess or female votary of Bacchus

BACCHANTS > BACCHANT

BACCHIAC > BACCHIUS

BACCHIAN same as > BACCHIC

BACCHIC adj riotously jovial

BACCHII > BACCHIUS

BACCHIUS n metrical foot of one short syllable followed by two long ones

BACCIES > BACCY

BACCIFORM adj shaped like a berry

BACCO n tobacco

BACCOES > BACCO

BACCOS > BACCO

BACCY n tobacco

BACH same as > BATCH

BACHA n Indian English word for young child

BACHARACH n German wine

BACHAS > BACHA

BACHATA n type of dance music originating in the Dominican Republic

BACHATAS > BACHATA

BACHCHA n Indian English word for young child

BACHCHAS > BACHCHA

BACHED > BACH

BACHELOR n unmarried man

BACHELORS > BACHELOR

BACHES > BACH

BACHING > BACH

BACHS > BACH

BACILLAR same as > BACILLARY

BACILLARY adj of or caused by bacilli

BACILLI > BACILLUS

BACILLUS n rod-shaped bacterium

BACK n rear part of the human body, from the neck to the pelvis ▷ vb (cause to) move backwards ▷ adj situated behind ▷ adv at, to, or towards the rear

b

BACKACHE n ache or pain in one's back
BACKACHES > BACKACHE
BACKACTER n mechanical excavator
BACKARE interj instruction to keep one's distance; back off
BACKBAND n back support
BACKBANDS > BACKBAND
BACKBAR n area behind a bar where bottles are stored
BACKBARS > BACKBAR
BACKBEAT n beat in music not usually accented
BACKBEATS > BACKBEAT
BACKBENCH n lower-ranking seats in Parliament
BACKBEND n gymnastic exercise in which the trunk is bent backwards until the hands touch the floor
BACKBENDS > BACKBEND
BACKBIT > BACKBITE
BACKBITE vb talk spitefully about an absent person
BACKBITER > BACKBITE
BACKBITES > BACKBITE
BACKBLOCK n singular of backblock: bush or remote farming area
BACKBOARD n board that is placed behind something to form or support its back
BACKBOND n legal document
BACKBONDS > BACKBOND
BACKBONE n spinal column
BACKBONED. > BACKBONE
BACKBONES > BACKBONE
BACKBURN vb clear an area of bush by creating a fire ▷ n act or result of backburning
BACKBURNS > BACKBURN
BACKCAST n backward casting of fishing rod ▷ vb cast a fishing rod backwards
BACKCASTS > BACKCAST
BACKCHAT n impudent replies
BACKCHATS > BACKCHAT
BACKCHECK vb (in ice hockey) return from attack to defence
BACKCLOTH n painted curtain at the back of a stage set
BACKCOMB vb comb (the hair) towards the roots to give more bulk to a hairstyle
BACKCOMBS > BACKCOMB
BACKCOURT n part of the court between the service line and the baseline
BACKCROSS vb mate (a hybrid of the first generation) with one of its parents ▷ n offspring so produced
BACKDATE vb make (a document) effective from a date earlier than its completion
BACKDATED > BACKDATE
BACKDATES > BACKDATE
BACKDOOR adj secret, underhand, or obtained through influence

BACKDOWN n abandonment of an earlier claim
BACKDOWNS > BACKDOWN
BACKDRAFT n reverse movement of air
BACKDROP vb provide a backdrop to (something)
BACKDROPS > BACKDROP
BACKDROPT > BACKDROP
BACKED adj having a back or backing
BACKER n person who gives financial support
BACKERS > BACKER
BACKET n shallow box
BACKETS > BACKET
BACKFALL n fall onto the back
BACKFALLS > BACKFALL
BACKFAT n layer of fat in animals between the skin and muscle
BACKFATS > BACKFAT
BACKFIELD n quarterback and running backs in a team
BACKFILE n archives of a newspaper or magazine
BACKFILES > BACKFILE
BACKFILL vb refill an excavated trench, esp (in archaeology) at the end of an investigation ▷ n soil used to do this
BACKFILLS > BACKFILL
BACKFIRE vb (of a plan) fail to have the desired effect ▷ n (in an engine) explosion of unburnt gases in the exhaust system
BACKFIRED > BACKFIRE
BACKFIRES > BACKFIRE
BACKFISCH n young girl
BACKFIT vb overhaul nuclear power plant
BACKFITS > BACKFIT
BACKFLIP n backwards somersault
BACKFLIPS > BACKFLIP
BACKFLOW n reverse flow
BACKFLOWS > BACKFLOW
BACKHAND n stroke played with the back of the hand facing the direction of the stroke ▷ adv with a backhand stroke ▷ vb play (a shot) backhand
BACKHANDS > BACKHAND
BACKHAUL vb transmit data
BACKHAULS > BACKHAUL
BACKHOE n digger ▷ vb dig with a backhoe
BACKHOED > BACKHOE
BACKHOES > BACKHOE
BACKHOUSE n toilet
BACKIE n ride on the back of someone's bicycle
BACKIES > BACKIE
BACKING n support
BACKINGS > BACKING
BACKLAND n undeveloped land behind a property
BACKLANDS > BACKLAND
BACKLASH n sudden and adverse reaction ▷ vb create a sudden and adverse reaction
BACKLESS adj (of a dress) low-cut at the back

BACKLIFT n backward movement of bat
BACKLIFTS > BACKLIFT
BACKLIGHT vb illuminate (something) from behind
BACKLINE n defensive players in a sports team as a unit
BACKLINER n defender in ice hockey
BACKLINES > BACKLINE
BACKLIST n publisher's previously published books that are still available ▷ vb put on a backlist
BACKLISTS > BACKLIST
BACKLIT adj illuminated from behind
BACKLOAD n load for lorry on return journey ▷ vb load a lorry for a return journey
BACKLOADS > BACKLOAD
BACKLOG n accumulation of things to be dealt with
BACKLOGS > BACKLOG
BACKLOT n area outside a film or television studio used for outdoor filming
BACKLOTS > BACKLOT
BACKMOST adj furthest back
BACKOUT n instance of withdrawing (from an agreement, etc)
BACKOUTS > BACKOUT
BACKPACK n large pack carried on the back ▷ vb go hiking with a backpack
BACKPACKS > BACKPACK
BACKPEDAL vb retract or modify a previous opinion, principle, etc
BACKPIECE n tattoo on the back
BACKPLANE n type of circuit board in a computer
BACKPLATE n plate of armour which guards the back
BACKRA n White person
BACKRAS > BACKRA
BACKREST n support for the back of something
BACKRESTS > BACKREST
BACKRONYM n contrived acronym using the initial letters of an existing word
BACKROOM n place where research or planning is done, esp secret research in wartime
BACKROOMS > BACKROOM
BACKRUSH n seaward return of wave
BACKS > BACK
BACKSAW n small handsaw
BACKSAWS > BACKSAW
BACKSEAT n seat at the back, esp of a vehicle
BACKSEATS > BACKSEAT
BACKSET n reversal ▷ vb attack from the rear
BACKSETS > BACKSET
BACKSEY n sirloin
BACKSEYS > BACKSEY
BACKSHISH same as > BAKSHEESH
BACKSHORE n area of beach above high tide mark

BACKSIDE n buttocks
BACKSIDES > BACKSIDE
BACKSIGHT n sight of a rifle nearer the stock
BACKSLAP vb demonstrate effusive joviality
BACKSLAPS > BACKSLAP
BACKSLASH n slash which slopes to the left (\)
BACKSLID > BACKSLIDE
BACKSLIDE vb relapse into former bad habits
BACKSPACE vb move a typewriter carriage or computer cursor backwards ▷ n typewriter key that effects such a movements
BACKSPEER same as > BACKSPEIR
BACKSPEIR vb interrogate
BACKSPIN n backward spin given to a ball to reduce its speed at impact
BACKSPINS > BACKSPIN
BACKSPLIT n house with a higher storey at the rear
BACKSTAB vb attack deceitfully
BACKSTABS > BACKSTAB
BACKSTAGE adj behind the stage in a theatre ▷ adv behind the stage in a theatre ▷ n area behind the stage in a theatre
BACKSTAIR adj underhand
BACKSTALL n backward flight of a kite ▷ vb execute a backstall with a kite
BACKSTAMP n mark stamped on the back of an envelope ▷ vb mark with a backstamp
BACKSTAY n stay leading aft from the upper part of a mast to the deck or stern
BACKSTAYS > BACKSTAY
BACKSTOP n screen or fence to prevent balls leaving the playing area ▷ vb provide with backing or support
BACKSTOPS > BACKSTOP
BACKSTORY n events assumed before a story begins
BACKSTRAP n cut of meat from the back of an animal
BACKSWEPT adj slanting backwards
BACKSWING n backward movement of a bat, etc
BACKSWORD n broad-bladed sword
BACKTALK n argumentative discourse
BACKTALKS > BACKTALK
BACKTRACK vb return by the same route by which one has come
BACKUP n support or reinforcement
BACKUPS > BACKUP
BACKVELD n (in South Africa) remote sparsely populated area
BACKVELDS > BACKVELD
BACKWALL n rear wall
BACKWALLS > BACKWALL

b

BACKWARD same as
> BACKWARDS
BACKWARDS adv towards
the rear
BACKWASH n water washed
backwards by the motion of
a boat ▷ vb remove oil from
(combed wool)
BACKWATER n isolated or
backward place or condition
▷ vb reverse the direction of a
boat, esp to push the oars of
a rowing boat
BACKWIND vb direct airflow
into the back of a sail
BACKWINDS > BACKWIND
BACKWOOD > BACKWOODS
BACKWOODS pl n remote
sparsely populated area
BACKWORD n act or an
instance of failing to keep a
promise or commitment
BACKWORDS > BACKWORD
BACKWORK n work carried
out under the ground
BACKWORKS > BACKWORK
BACKWRAP n back support
BACKWRAPS > BACKWRAP
BACKYARD n yard at the
back of a house, etc
BACKYARDS > BACKYARD
BACLAVA same as
> BAKLAVA
BACLAVAS > BACLAVA
BACLOFEN n drug used to
treat stroke victims
BACLOFENS > BACLOFEN
BACON n salted or smoked
pig meat
BACONER n pig that weighs
between 83 and 101 kg, from
which bacon is cut
BACONERS > BACONER
BACONS > BACON
BACRONYM same as
> BACKRONYM
BACRONYMS > BACRONYM
BACS > BAC
BACTERIA pl n large group
of microorganisms
BACTERIAL > BACTERIA
BACTERIAN > BACTERIA
BACTERIAS > BACTERIA
BACTERIC > BACTERIA
BACTERIN n vaccine
prepared from bacteria
BACTERINS > BACTERIN
BACTERISE same as
> BACTERIZE
BACTERIUM n single
bacteria
BACTERIZE vb subject to
bacterial action
BACTEROID n type of
rodlike bacterium occurring
in the gut of humans and
animals
BACULA > BACULUM
BACULINE adj relating to
flogging
BACULITE n fossil
BACULITES > BACULITE
BACULUM n bony support in
the penis of certain
mammals
BACULUMS > BACULUM
BAD adj not good ▷ n
unfortunate or unpleasant

events collectively ▷ adv
badly
BADASS n tough or
aggressive person ▷ adj
tough or aggressive
BADASSED > BADASS
BADASSES > BADASS
BADDER > BAD
BADDEST > BAD
BADDIE n bad character in a
story, film, etc, esp an
opponent of the hero
BADDIES > BADDIE
BADDISH > BAD
BADDY same as > BADDIE
BADE > BID
BADGE n emblem worn to
show membership, rank, etc
▷ vb put a badge on
BADGED > BADGE
BADGELESS > BADGE
BADGER n nocturnal
burrowing mammal ▷ vb
pester or harass
BADGERED > BADGER
BADGERING > BADGER
BADGERLY adj resembling
a badger
BADGERS > BADGER
BADGES > BADGE
BADGING > BADGE
BADINAGE n playful and
witty conversation ▷ vb
engage in badinage
BADINAGED > BADINAGE
BADINAGES > BADINAGE
BADINERIE n name given
in the 18th century to a type
of quick, light movement in a
suite
BADIOUS adj chestnut;
brownish-red
BADLAND > BADLANDS
BADLANDS pl n any deeply
eroded barren area
BADLY adv poorly
BADMAN n hired gunman,
outlaw, or criminal
BADMASH n evil-doer ▷ adj
naughty or bad
BADMASHES > BADMASH
BADMEN > BADMAN
BADMINTON n game played
with rackets and a
shuttlecock, which is hit
back and forth over a high
net
BADMOUTH vb speak
unfavourably about
(someone or something)
BADMOUTHS > BADMOUTH
BADNESS > BAD
BADNESSES > BAD
BADS > BAD
BADWARE n software
designed to harm a
computer system
BADWARES > BADWARE
BAE n sweetheart or lover
BAEL n type of spiny Indian
tree
BAELS > BAEL
BAES > BAE
BAETYL n magical meteoric
stone
BAETYLS > BAETYL
BAFF vb strike ground with a
golf club

BAFFED > BAFF
BAFFIES pl n slippers
BAFFING > BAFF
BAFFLE vb perplex or puzzle
▷ n device to limit or regulate
the flow of fluid, light, or
sound
BAFFLED > BAFFLE
BAFFLEGAB n insincere
speech
BAFFLER > BAFFLE
BAFFLERS > BAFFLE
BAFFLES > BAFFLE
BAFFLING adj impossible to
understand
BAFFS > BAFF
BAFFY n obsolete golf club
BAFT n coarse fabric
BAFTS > BAFT
BAG n flexible container with
an opening at one end ▷ vb
put into a bag
BAGARRE n brawl
BAGARRES > BAGARRE
BAGASS same as > BAGASSE
BAGASSE n pulp of sugar
cane or similar plants
BAGASSES > BAGASSE
BAGATELLE n something of
little value
BAGEL n hard ring-shaped
bread roll ▷ vb win a tennis
set by six games to love
BAGELED > BAGEL
BAGELING > BAGEL
BAGELLED > BAGEL
BAGELLING > BAGEL
BAGELS > BAGEL
BAGFUL n amount (of
something) that can be held
in a bag
BAGFULS > BAGFUL
BAGGAGE n suitcases packed
for a journey
BAGGAGES > BAGGAGE
BAGGED > BAG
BAGGER n person who packs
groceries
BAGGERS > BAGGER
BAGGIE n plastic bag
BAGGIER > BAGGY
BAGGIES > BAGGIE
BAGGIEST > BAGGY
BAGGILY > BAGGY
BAGGINESS > BAGGY
BAGGING n act of putting in
a bag
BAGGINGS > BAGGING
BAGGIT n salmon which has
not yet spawned
BAGGITS > BAGGIT
BAGGY adj hanging loosely
BAGH n (in India and
Pakistan) a garden
BAGHOUSE n dust-filtering
chamber
BAGHOUSES > BAGHOUSE
BAGHS > BAGH
BAGIE n turnip
BAGIES > BAGIE
BAGLESS adj (esp of a
vacuum cleaner) not
containing a bag
BAGLIKE > BAG
BAGMAN n travelling
salesman
BAGMEN > BAGMAN

BAGNETTE variant of
> BAGUETTE
BAGNETTES > BAGNETTE
BAGNIO n bathing-house
BAGNIOS > BAGNIO
BAGPIPE vb play the
bagpipes
BAGPIPED > BAGPIPE
BAGPIPER > BAGPIPES
BAGPIPERS > BAGPIPES
BAGPIPES pl n musical wind
instrument with reed pipes
and an inflatable bag
BAGPIPING > BAGPIPE
BAGS > BAG
BAGSFUL > BAGFUL
BAGUET same as
> BAGUETTE
BAGUETS > BAGUET
BAGUETTE n narrow French
stick loaf
BAGUETTES > BAGUETTE
BAGUIO n hurricane
BAGUIOS > BAGUIO
BAGWASH n laundry that
washes clothes without
drying or pressing them
BAGWASHES > BAGWASH
BAGWIG n 18th-century wig
with hair pushed back into a
bag
BAGWIGS > BAGWIG
BAGWORM n type of moth
BAGWORMS > BAGWORM
BAH interj expression of
contempt or disgust
BAHADA same as > BAJADA
BAHADAS > BAHADA
BAHADUR n title formerly
conferred by the British on
distinguished Indians
BAHADURS > BAHADUR
BAHOOKIE n Scottish
informal word for the
buttocks
BAHOOKIES > BAHOOKIE
BAHT n standard monetary
unit of Thailand, divided into
100 satang
BAHTS > BAHT
BAHU n (in India)
daughter-in-law
BAHUS > BAHU
BAHUT n decorative cabinet
BAHUTS > BAHUT
BAHUVRIHI n class of
compound words consisting
of two elements the first of
which is a specific feature of
the second
BAIDAR same as
> BAIDARKA
BAIDARKA n narrow
hunting boat
BAIDARKAS > BAIDARKA
BAIDARS > BAIDAR
BAIGNOIRE n low-level
theatre box
BAIL n money deposited
with a court as security for a
person's reappearance ▷ vb
pay bail for (a person)
BAILABLE adj eligible for
release on bail
BAILBOND n document
guaranteeing a prisoner
released on bail will attend
court

b

BAILBONDS > BAILBOND
BAILED > BAIL
BAILEE n person to whom the possession of goods is transferred under a bailment
BAILEES > BAILEE
BAILER > BAIL
BAILERS > BAIL
BAILEY n outermost wall or court of a castle
BAILEYS > BAILEY
BAILIE n (in Scotland) a municipal magistrate
BAILIES > BAILIE
BAILIFF n sheriff's officer who serves writs and summonses
BAILIFFS > BAILIFF
BAILING > BAIL
BAILIWICK n area a person is interested in or operates in
BAILLI n magistrate
BAILLIAGE n magistrate's area of authority
BAILLIE variant of > BAILIE
BAILLIES > BAILLIE
BAILLIS > BAILLI
BAILMENT n contractual delivery of goods in trust to a person for a specific purpose
BAILMENTS > BAILMENT
BAILOR n owner of goods entrusted to another under a bailment
BAILORS > BAILOR
BAILOUT n instance of helping (a person, organization, etc) out of a predicament
BAILOUTS > BAILOUT
BAILS > BAIL
BAILSMAN n one standing bail for another
BAILSMEN > BAILSMAN
BAININ n Irish collarless jacket made of white wool
BAININS > BAININ
BAINITE n mixture of iron and iron carbide found in incompletely hardened steels
BAINITES > BAINITE
BAIRN n child
BAIRNISH > BAIRN
BAIRNLIER > BAIRN
BAIRNLIKE > BAIRN
BAIRNLY > BAIRN
BAIRNS > BAIRN
BAISA n small unit of currency in Oman
BAISAS > BAISA
BAISEMAIN n kissing of the hand
BAIT n piece of food on a hook or in a trap to attract fish or animals ▷ vb put a piece of food on or in (a hook or trap)
BAITED > BAIT
BAITER > BAIT
BAITERS > BAIT
BAITFISH n small fish used as bait
BAITH adj both
BAITING n act of placing bait

BAITINGS > BAITING
BAITS > BAIT
BAIZA n Omani unit of currency
BAIZAS > BAIZA
BAIZE n woollen fabric used to cover billiard and card tables ▷ vb line or cover with such fabric
BAIZED > BAIZE
BAIZES > BAIZE
BAIZING > BAIZE
BAJADA n sloping surface formed from rock deposits
BAJADAS > BAJADA
BAJAN n freshman at Aberdeen University
BAJANS > BAJAN
BAJILLION n extremely large but unspecified number, quantity, or amount
BAJRA n Indian millet
BAJRAS > BAJRA
BAJREE variant of > BAJRA
BAJREES > BAJREE
BAJRI variant of > BAJRA
BAJRIS > BAJRI
BAJU n Malay jacket
BAJUS > BAJU
BAKE vb cook by dry heat as in an oven ▷ n party at which the main dish is baked
BAKEAPPLE n cloudberry
BAKEBOARD n board for bread-making
BAKED > BAKE
BAKEHOUSE same as > BAKERY
BAKELITE n tradename for a class of resin
BAKELITES > BAKELITE
BAKEMEAT n pie
BAKEMEATS > BAKEMEAT
BAKEN > BAKE
BAKEOFF n baking competition
BAKEOFFS > BAKEOFF
BAKER n person whose business is to make or sell bread, cakes, etc
BAKERIES > BAKERY
BAKERS > BAKER
BAKERY n place where bread, cakes, etc are baked or sold
BAKES > BAKE
BAKESHOP n bakery
BAKESHOPS > BAKESHOP
BAKESTONE n flat stone in an oven
BAKEWARE n dishes for baking
BAKEWARES > BAKEWARE
BAKGAT adj fine, excellent, marvellous
BAKHSHISH same as > BAKSHEESH
BAKING n process of cooking bread, cakes, etc ▷ adj (esp of weather) very hot and dry
BAKINGS > BAKING
BAKKIE n small truck
BAKKIES > BAKKIE
BAKLAVA n rich pastry of Middle Eastern origin
BAKLAVAS > BAKLAVA

BAKLAWA same as > BAKLAVA
BAKLAWAS > BAKLAWA
BAKRA n (in the Caribbean) White person, esp one from Britain ▷ adj (of people) White, esp British
BAKRAS > BAKRA
BAKSHEESH n (in some Eastern countries) money given as a tip ▷ vb give such money to (a person)
BAKSHISH same as > BAKSHEESH
BAL n balmoral
BALACLAVA n close-fitting woollen hood that covers the ears and neck, as originally worn by soldiers in the Crimean War
BALADIN n dancer
BALADINE n female dancer
BALADINES > BALADINE
BALADINS > BALADIN
BALAFON n type of W African xylophone
BALAFONS > BALAFON
BALALAIKA n guitar-like musical instrument with a triangular body
BALANCE n stability of mind or body ▷ vb weigh in a balance
BALANCED adj having weight equally distributed
BALANCER n person or thing that balances
BALANCERS > BALANCER
BALANCES > BALANCE
BALANCING > BALANCE
BALANITIS n inflammation of the glans penis
BALAS n red variety of spinel, used as a gemstone
BALASES > BALAS
BALATA n tropical American tree yielding a latex-like sap
BALATAS > BALATA
BALAYAGE vb highlight hair by painting dye onto sections
BALAYAGED > BALAYAGE
BALAYAGES > BALAYAGE
BALBOA n standard currency unit of Panama
BALBOAS > BALBOA
BALCONET n small balcony
BALCONETS > BALCONET
BALCONIED > BALCONY
BALCONIES > BALCONY
BALCONY n platform on the outside of a building with a rail along the outer edge
BALD adj having little or no hair on the scalp ▷ vb make bald
BALDACHIN n richly ornamented silk and gold brocade
BALDAQUIN same as > BALDACHIN
BALDED > BALD
BALDER > BALD
BALDEST > BALD
BALDFACED same as > BALD
BALDHEAD n person without dreadlocks
BALDHEADS > BALDHEAD

BALDICOOT another name for > COOT
BALDIE same as > BALDY
BALDIER > BALDY
BALDIES > BALDIE
BALDIEST > BALDY
BALDING adj becoming bald
BALDISH > BALD
BALDLY > BALD
BALDMONEY another name for > SPIGNEL
BALDNESS > BALD
BALDPATE n type of duck
BALDPATED > BALDPATE
BALDPATES > BALDPATE
BALDRIC n wide silk sash or leather belt worn across the body
BALDRICK same as > BALDRIC
BALDRICKS > BALDRICK
BALDRICS > BALDRIC
BALDS > BALD
BALDY adj bald ▷ n bald person
BALE same as > BAIL
BALECTION same as > BOLECTION
BALED > BALE
BALEEN n whalebone
BALEENS > BALEEN
BALEFIRE n bonfire
BALEFIRES > BALEFIRE
BALEFUL adj vindictive or menacing
BALEFULLY > BALEFUL
BALER > BAIL
BALERS > BAIL
BALES > BALE
BALING n act of baling
BALINGS > BALING
BALISAUR n badger-like animal
BALISAURS > BALISAUR
BALISE n electronic beacon used on a railway
BALISES > BALISE
BALISTA same as > BALLISTA
BALISTAE > BALISTA
BALISTAS > BALISTA
BALK vb stop short, esp suddenly or unexpectedly ▷ n roughly squared heavy timber beam
BALKANISE variant of > BALKANIZE
BALKANIZE vb divide (a territory) into small warring states
BALKED > BALK
BALKER > BALK
BALKERS > BALK
BALKIER > BALKY
BALKIEST > BALKY
BALKILY > BALKY
BALKINESS > BALKY
BALKING > BALK
BALKINGLY > BALK
BALKINGS > BALKING
BALKLINE n line delimiting the balk area on a snooker table
BALKLINES > BALKLINE
BALKS > BALK
BALKY adj inclined to stop abruptly and unexpectedly

BALL *n* round or nearly round object, esp one used in games ▷ *vb* form into a ball

BALLABILE *n* part of ballet where all dancers perform

BALLABILI > BALLABILE

BALLAD *n* narrative poem or song ▷ *vb* sing or write a ballad

BALLADE *n* verse form

BALLADED > BALLAD

BALLADEER *n* singer of ballads ▷ *vb* perform as a balladeer

BALLADES > BALLADE

BALLADIC > BALLAD

BALLADIN *same as* > BALADIN

BALLADINE *same as* > BALADINE

BALLADING > BALLAD

BALLADINS > BALLADIN

BALLADIST > BALLAD

BALLADRY *n* ballad poetry or songs

BALLADS > BALLAD

BALLAN *n* species of fish

BALLANS > BALLAN

BALLANT *vb* write a ballad

BALLANTED > BALLANT

BALLANTS > BALLANT

BALLAST *n* substance used to stabilize a ship when it is not carrying cargo ▷ *vb* give stability to

BALLASTED > BALLAST

BALLASTER > BALLAST

BALLASTS > BALLAST

BALLAT *vb* write a ballad

BALLATED > BALLAT

BALLATING > BALLAT

BALLATS > BALLAT

BALLBOY *n* boy who retrieves balls during a tennis, football, etc, match

BALLBOYS > BALLBOY

BALLCLAY *n* clay suitable for ceramics

BALLCLAYS > BALLCLAY

BALLCOCK *n* device for regulating the flow of a liquid into a tank

BALLCOCKS > BALLCOCK

BALLED > BALL

BALLER *n* ball-game player

BALLERINA *n* female ballet dancer

BALLERINE > BALLERINA

BALLERS > BALLER

BALLET *n* classical style of expressive dancing based on conventional steps ▷ *vb* sing ballads

BALLETED > BALLET

BALLETIC > BALLET

BALLETING > BALLET

BALLETS > BALLET

BALLFIELD *n* baseball field

BALLGAME *n* any game played with a ball

BALLGAMES > BALLGAME

BALLGIRL *n* girl who retrieves balls during a tennis, football, etc, match

BALLGIRLS > BALLGIRL

BALLGOWN *n* long formal dress

BALLGOWNS > BALLGOWN

BALLHAWK *n* skilled basketball player ▷ *vb* act as a ballhawk

BALLHAWKS > BALLHAWK

BALLIER > BALLY

BALLIES > BALLY

BALLIEST > BALLY

BALLING *n* formation of a ball

BALLINGS > BALLING

BALLISTA *n* ancient catapult for hurling stones, etc

BALLISTAE > BALLISTA

BALLISTAS > BALLISTA

BALLISTIC *adj* of or relating to ballistics

BALLIUM *same as* > BAILEY

BALLIUMS > BALLIUM

BALLOCKS *same as* > BOLLOCKS

BALLON *n* light, graceful quality

BALLONET *n* air or gas compartment in a nonrigid airship

BALLONETS > BALLONET

BALLONNE *n* bouncing step

BALLONNES > BALLONNE

BALLONS > BALLON

BALLOON *n* inflatable rubber bag used as a plaything or decoration ▷ *vb* fly in a balloon

BALLOONED > BALLOON

BALLOONS > BALLOON

BALLOT *n* method of voting ▷ *vb* vote or ask for a vote from

BALLOTED > BALLOT

BALLOTEE > BALLOT

BALLOTEES > BALLOT

BALLOTER > BALLOT

BALLOTERS > BALLOT

BALLOTING *n* act of balloting

BALLOTINI *n* small glass beads

BALLOTS > BALLOT

BALLOW *n* heavy club

BALLOWS > BALLOW

BALLPARK *n* stadium used for baseball games

BALLPARKS > BALLPARK

BALLPEEN *adj* as in *ballpeen hammer* type of hammer

BALLPOINT *n* pen with a tiny ball bearing as a writing point

BALLROOM *n* large hall for dancing

BALLROOMS > BALLROOM

BALLS *n* plural of ball ▷ *vb* vulgar slang word meaning muddle or botch

BALLSED > BALLS

BALLSES > BALLS

BALLSIER > BALLSY

BALLSIEST > BALLSY

BALLSING > BALLS

BALLSY *adj* slang word meaning courageous and spirited

BALLUP *n* vulgar slang word for something botched or muddled

BALLUPS > BALLUP

BALLUTE *n* inflatable balloon parachute

BALLUTES > BALLUTE

BALLY *adj* euphemism for bloody ▷ *n* exaggerated fuss

BALLYARD *n* baseball ground

BALLYARDS > BALLYARD

BALLYHOO *n* exaggerated fuss ▷ *vb* advertise or publicize by sensational or blatant methods

BALLYHOOS > BALLYHOO

BALLYRAG *same as* > BULLYRAG

BALLYRAGS > BALLYRAG

BALM *n* aromatic substance used for healing and soothing ▷ *vb* apply balm to

BALMACAAN *n* man's knee-length loose flaring overcoat with raglan sleeves

BALMED > BALM

BALMIER > BALMY

BALMIEST > BALMY

BALMILY > BALMY

BALMINESS > BALMY

BALMING > BALM

BALMLIKE > BALM

BALMORAL *n* laced walking shoe

BALMORALS > BALMORAL

BALMS > BALM

BALMY *adj* (of weather) mild and pleasant

BALNEAL *adj* of or relating to baths or bathing

BALNEARY *same as* > BALNEAL

BALONEY *n* foolish talk; nonsense

BALONEYS > BALONEY

BALOO *n* bear

BALOOS > BALOO

BALS > BAL

BALSA *n* very light wood from a tropical American tree

BALSAM *n* type of fragrant balm ▷ *vb* embalm

BALSAMED > BALSAM

BALSAMIC > BALSAM

BALSAMIER > BALSAMY

BALSAMING > BALSAM

BALSAMS > BALSAM

BALSAMY *adj* sweet-smelling

BALSAS > BALSA

BALSAWOOD *same as* > BALSA

BALTHASAR *same as* > BALTHAZAR

BALTHAZAR *n* wine bottle holding the equivalent of sixteen normal bottles

BALTI *n* spicy Indian dish served in a metal dish

BALTIC *adj* very cold

BALTIS > BALTI

BALU *same as* > BALOO

BALUN *n* electrical device

BALUNS > BALUN

BALUS > BALU

BALUSTER *n* set of posts supporting a rail ▷ *adj* (of a shape) swelling at the base and rising in a concave curve to a narrow stem or neck

BALUSTERS > BALUSTER

BALZARINE *n* light fabric

BAM *vb* cheat

BAMBI *n* born-again middle-aged biker

BAMBINI > BAMBINO

BAMBINO *n* young child, esp an Italian one

BAMBINOS > BAMBINO

BAMBIS > BAMBI

BAMBOO *n* tall treelike tropical grass with hollow stems

BAMBOOS > BAMBOO

BAMBOOZLE *vb* cheat or mislead

BAMMED > BAM

BAMMER > BAM

BAMMERS > BAM

BAMMING > BAM

BAMPOT *n* fool

BAMPOTS > BAMPOT

BAMS > BAM

BAN *vb* prohibit or forbid officially ▷ *n* unit of currency in Romania and Moldova

BANAK *n* type of Central American tree

BANAKS > BANAK

BANAL *adj* ordinary and unoriginal

BANALER > BANAL

BANALEST > BANAL

BANALISE > BANAL

BANALISED > BANAL

BANALISES > BANAL

BANALITY > BANAL

BANALIZE > BANAL

BANALIZED > BANAL

BANALIZES > BANAL

BANALLY > BANAL

BANANA *n* yellow crescent-shaped fruit

BANANAS *adj* crazy

BANAUSIAN > BANAUSIC

BANAUSIC *adj* merely mechanical

BANC *n* as in *in banc* sitting as a full court

BANCO *n* call made in gambling games

BANCOS > BANCO

BANCS > BANC

BAND *n* group of musicians playing together ▷ *vb* unite

BANDA *n* African thatched hut

BANDAGE *n* piece of material used to cover a wound or wrap an injured limb ▷ *vb* cover with a bandage

BANDAGED > BANDAGE

BANDAGER > BANDAGE

BANDAGERS > BANDAGE

BANDAGES > BANDAGE

BANDAGING *n* act of bandaging

BANDAID *adj* (of a solution or remedy) temporary

BANDALORE *n* old-fashioned type of yo-yo

BANDANA *same as* > BANDANNA

BANDANAS > BANDANA

BANDANNA *n* large brightly coloured handkerchief or neckerchief

b

BANDANNAS > BANDANNA
BANDAR n species of monkey
BANDARI n Indian English word for female monkey
BANDARIS > BANDARI
BANDARS > BANDAR
BANDAS > BANDA
BANDBOX n lightweight usually cylindrical box for hats
BANDBOXES > BANDBOX
BANDBRAKE n type of brake
BANDEAU n narrow ribbon worn round the head
BANDEAUS > BANDEAU
BANDEAUX > BANDEAU
BANDED > BAND
BANDEIRA n 17th-century Portuguese slave-hunting expedition in Brazil
BANDEIRAS > BANDEIRA
BANDELET n moulding round top of column
BANDELETS > BANDELET
BANDELIER same as > BANDOLEER
BANDER > BAND
BANDEROL same as > BANDEROLE
BANDEROLE n narrow flag usually with forked ends
BANDEROLS > BANDEROL
BANDERS > BAND
BANDFISH n Mediterranean fish with an elongated body
BANDH n (in India) a general strike
BANDHS > BANDH
BANDICOOT n ratlike Australian marsupial
BANDIED > BANDY
BANDIER > BANDY
BANDIES > BANDY
BANDIEST > BANDY
BANDINESS > BANDY
BANDING n practice of grouping schoolchildren according to ability
BANDINGS > BANDING
BANDIT n robber, esp a member of an armed gang
BANDITO n Mexican bandit
BANDITOS > BANDITO
BANDITRY > BANDIT
BANDITS > BANDIT
BANDITTI > BANDIT
BANDITTIS > BANDIT
BANDLIKE adj like a band
BANDMATE n fellow member of band
BANDMATES > BANDMATE
BANDOBAST same as > BANDOBUST
BANDOBUST n (in India and Pakistan) an arrangement
BANDOG n ferocious dog
BANDOGS > BANDOG
BANDOLEER same as > BANDOLIER
BANDOLEON same as > BANDONEON
BANDOLERO n highwayman
BANDOLIER n shoulder belt for holding cartridges
BANDOLINE n glutinous hair dressing, used (esp formerly) to keep the hair in place

BANDONEON n type of square concertina, esp used in Argentina
BANDONION same as > BANDONEON
BANDOOK same as > BUNDOOK
BANDOOKS > BANDOOK
BANDORA same as > BANDORE
BANDORAS > BANDORA
BANDORE n 16th-century musical instrument
BANDORES > BANDORE
BANDPASS n range of frequencies transmitted through a bandpass filter
BANDROL same as > BANDEROLE
BANDROLS > BANDROL
BANDS > BAND
BANDSAW n power saw with continuous blade ▷ vb cut with a bandsaw
BANDSAWED > BANDSAW
BANDSAWS > BANDSAW
BANDSHELL n bandstand concave at back
BANDSMAN n player in a musical band
BANDSMEN > BANDSMAN
BANDSTAND n roofed outdoor platform for a band
BANDSTER n binder of wheat sheaves
BANDSTERS > BANDSTER
BANDURA n type of lute
BANDURAS > BANDURA
BANDURIST n bandura player
BANDWAGON n type of wagon
BANDWIDTH n range of frequencies within a given waveband used for a particular transmission
BANDY adj having legs curved outwards at the knees ▷ vb exchange (words) in a heated manner
BANDYING > BANDY
BANDYINGS > BANDY
BANDYMAN n carriage or cart
BANDYMEN > BANDYMAN
BANE n person or thing that causes misery or distress ▷ vb cause harm or distress to (someone)
BANEBERRY n type of plant with small white flowers and red or white poisonous berries
BANED > BANE
BANEFUL adj destructive, poisonous, or fatal
BANEFULLY > BANEFUL
BANES > BANE
BANG vb make a short explosive noise
BANGALAY n Australian tree valued for its hard red wood
BANGALAYS > BANGALAY
BANGALORE adj as in bangalore torpedo explosive device in a long metal tube, used to blow gaps in barbed-wire barriers

BANGALOW n Australian palm tree native to New South Wales and Queensland
BANGALOWS > BANGALOW
BANGBELLY n dense cake with sweet and savoury ingredients
BANGED > BANG
BANGER n old decrepit car
BANGERS > BANGER
BANGING > BANG
BANGKOK n type of straw hat
BANGKOKS > BANGKOK
BANGLE n bracelet worn round the arm or the ankle
BANGLED > BANGLE
BANGLES > BANGLE
BANGS > BANG
BANGSRING same as > BANXRING
BANGSTER n ruffian
BANGSTERS > BANGSTER
BANGTAIL n horse's tail cut straight across but not through the bone
BANGTAILS > BANGTAIL
BANI > BAN
BANIA same as > BANYAN
BANIAN same as > BANYAN
BANIANS > BANIAN
BANIAS > BANIA
BANING > BANE
BANISH vb send (someone) into exile
BANISHED > BANISH
BANISHER > BANISH
BANISHERS > BANISH
BANISHES > BANISH
BANISHING > BANISH
BANISTER same as > BANNISTER
BANISTERS pl n railing supported by posts on a staircase
BANJAX vb ruin; destroy
BANJAXED > BANJAX
BANJAXES > BANJAX
BANJAXING > BANJAX
BANJO n guitar-like musical instrument with a circular body
BANJOES > BANJO
BANJOIST > BANJO
BANJOISTS > BANJO
BANJOLELE n musical instrument with a neck like a ukulele and a body like a banjo
BANJOS > BANJO
BANJULELE n small banjo
BANK n institution offering services such as the safekeeping and lending of money ▷ vb deposit (cash or cheques) in a bank
BANKABLE adj likely to ensure financial success
BANKBOOK n record of deposits, withdrawals, and interest held by depositors at certain banks
BANKBOOKS > BANKBOOK
BANKCARD n card guaranteeing payment of cheque
BANKCARDS > BANKCARD

BANKED > BANK
BANKER n manager or owner of a bank
BANKERLY adj like a banker
BANKERS > BANKER
BANKET n gold-bearing conglomerate found in South Africa
BANKETS > BANKET
BANKING > BANK
BANKINGS > BANKING
BANKIT same as > BANQUETTE
BANKITS > BANKIT
BANKNOTE n piece of paper money
BANKNOTES > BANKNOTE
BANKROLL n roll of currency notes ▷ vb provide the capital for
BANKROLLS > BANKROLL
BANKRUPT n person declared by a court to be unable to pay his or her debts ▷ adj financially ruined ▷ vb make bankrupt
BANKRUPTS > BANKRUPT
BANKS > BANK
BANKSIA n Australian evergreen tree or shrub
BANKSIAS > BANKSIA
BANKSIDE n riverside
BANKSIDES > BANKSIDE
BANKSMAN n crane driver's helper
BANKSMEN > BANKSMAN
BANKSTER n banker whose illegal practices have been exposed
BANKSTERS > BANKSTER
BANLIEUE n suburb of a city
BANLIEUES > BANLIEUE
BANNABLE > BAN
BANNED > BAN
BANNER n long strip of cloth displaying a slogan, advertisement, etc ▷ vb (of a newspaper headline) to display (a story) prominently ▷ adj outstandingly successful
BANNERALL same as > BANDEROLE
BANNERED > BANNER
BANNERET n small banner
BANNERETS > BANNERET
BANNERING > BANNER
BANNEROL same as > BANDEROLE
BANNEROLS > BANNEROL
BANNERS > BANNER
BANNET n bonnet
BANNETS > BANNET
BANNING n act of banning
BANNINGS > BANNING
BANNISTER same as > BANISTERS
BANNOCK n round flat cake made from oatmeal or barley
BANNOCKS > BANNOCK
BANNS pl n public declaration, esp in a church, of an intended marriage
BANOFFEE n filling for a pie, consisting of toffee and banana
BANOFFEES > BANOFFEE

b

BANOFFI same as
> BANOFFEE
BANOFFIS > BANOFFI
BANQUET n elaborate formal dinner ▷ vb hold or take part in a banquet
BANQUETED > BANQUET
BANQUETER > BANQUET
BANQUETS > BANQUET
BANQUETTE n upholstered bench
BANS same as > BANNS
BANSELA same as
> BONSELA
BANSELAS > BANSELA
BANSHEE n (in Irish folklore) female spirit whose wailing warns of a coming death
BANSHEES > BANSHEE
BANSHIE same as
> BANSHEE
BANSHIES > BANSHIE
BANT n string ▷ vb tie with string
BANTAM n small breed of chicken
BANTAMS > BANTAM
BANTED > BANT
BANTENG n wild ox
BANTENGS > BANTENG
BANTER vb tease jokingly ▷ n teasing or joking conversation
BANTERED > BANTER
BANTERER > BANTER
BANTERERS > BANTER
BANTERING > BANTER
BANTERS > BANTER
BANTIES > BANTY
BANTING > BANT
BANTINGS > BANT
BANTLING n young child
BANTLINGS > BANTLING
BANTS > BANT
BANTU n offensive name for a person who speaks a Bantu language
BANTUS > BANTU
BANTY n bantam
BANXRING n tree-shrew
BANXRINGS > BANXRING
BANYA n traditional Russian steam bath
BANYAN n Indian tree
BANYANS > BANYAN
BANYAS > BANYA
BANZAI interj patriotic cheer, battle cry, or salutation
BANZAIS > BANZAI
BAO n steamed dumpling
BAOBAB n African tree with a thick trunk and angular branches
BAOBABS > BAOBAB
BAOS > BAO
BAP n large soft bread roll
BAPS > BAP
BAPTISE same as
> BAPTIZE
BAPTISED > BAPTISE
BAPTISER > BAPTISE
BAPTISERS > BAPTISE
BAPTISES > BAPTISE
BAPTISIA n species of wild flower
BAPTISIAS > BAPTISIA

BAPTISING > BAPTISE
BAPTISM n Christian religious ceremony
BAPTISMAL > BAPTISM
BAPTISMS > BAPTISM
BAPTIST n one who baptizes
BAPTISTRY n part of a Christian church in which baptisms are carried out
BAPTISTS > BAPTIST
BAPTIZE vb perform baptism on
BAPTIZED > BAPTIZE
BAPTIZER > BAPTIZE
BAPTIZERS > BAPTIZE
BAPTIZES > BAPTIZE
BAPTIZING > BAPTIZE
BAPU n spiritual father
BAPUS > BAPU
BAR n rigid usually straight length of metal, wood, etc, longer than it is wide or thick ▷ vb fasten or secure with a bar
BARACAN same as
> BARRACAN
BARACANS > BARACAN
BARACHOIS n (in the Atlantic Provinces of Canada) a shallow lagoon formed by a sand bar
BARAGOUIN n incomprehensible language
BARASINGA n type of deer
BARATHEA n fabric made of silk and wool or cotton and rayon, used esp for coats
BARATHEAS > BARATHEA
BARATHRUM n abyss
BARAZA n place where public meetings are held
BARAZAS > BARAZA
BARB n cutting remark ▷ vb provide with a barb or barbs
BARBAL adj of a beard
BARBARIAN n member of a primitive or uncivilized people ▷ adj uncivilized or brutal
BARBARIC adj cruel or brutal
BARBARISE same as
> BARBARIZE
BARBARISM n condition of being backward or ignorant
BARBARITY n state of being barbaric or barbarous
BARBARIZE vb make or become barbarous
BARBAROUS adj uncivilized
BARBASCO n S American plant
BARBASCOS > BARBASCO
BARBASTEL n insectivorous forest bat
BARBATE adj having tufts of long hairs
BARBATED > BARBATE
BARBE n Waldensian missionary
BARBECUE n grill on which food is cooked over hot charcoal, usu outdoors ▷ vb cook (food) on a barbecue
BARBECUED > BARBECUE
BARBECUER > BARBECUE
BARBECUES > BARBECUE

BARBED > BARB
BARBEL n long thin growth that hangs from the jaws of certain fishes, such as the carp
BARBELL n long metal rod to which heavy discs are attached at each end for weightlifting
BARBELLS > BARBELL
BARBELS > BARBEL
BARBEQUE same as
> BARBECUE
BARBEQUED > BARBEQUE
BARBEQUES > BARBEQUE
BARBER n person who cuts men's hair and shaves beards ▷ vb cut the hair of
BARBERED > BARBER
BARBERING > BARBER
BARBERRY n shrub with orange or red berries
BARBERS > BARBER
BARBES > BARBE
BARBET n type of small tropical bird
BARBETS > BARBET
BARBETTE n earthen platform inside a parapet
BARBETTES > BARBETTE
BARBICAN n walled defence to protect a gate or drawbridge of a fortification
BARBICANS > BARBICAN
BARBICEL n minute hook on the barbule of a feather
BARBICELS > BARBICEL
BARBIE short for
> BARBECUE
BARBIES > BARBIE
BARBING > BARB
BARBITAL same as
> BARBITONE
BARBITALS > BARBITAL
BARBITONE n long-acting barbiturate used medicinally, usually in the form of the sodium salt, as a sedative or hypnotic
BARBLESS > BARB
BARBOLA n creation of small models of flowers, etc from plastic paste
BARBOLAS > BARBOLA
BARBOT same as > BURBOT
BARBOTINE n clay used in making decorated pottery
BARBOTS > BARBOT
BARBOTTE same as > BURBOT
BARBOTTES > BARBOTTE
BARBS > BARB
BARBULE n very small barb
BARBULES > BARBULE
BARBUT n open-faced helmet
BARBUTS > BARBUT
BARBWIRE n barbed wire
BARBWIRES > BARBWIRE
BARBY same as > BARBECUE
BARCA n boat
BARCAROLE n Venetian boat song
BARCAS > BARCA
BARCHAN n crescent-shaped shifting sand dune
BARCHANE same as
> BARCHAN

BARCHANES > BARCHANE
BARCHANS > BARCHAN
BARCODE n machine-readable code printed on goods
BARCODED adj having a barcode
BARCODES > BARCODE
BARD n poet ▷ vb place a piece of pork fat on
BARDASH n kept boy in a homosexual relationship
BARDASHES > BARDASH
BARDE same as > BARD
BARDED > BARDE
BARDES > BARDE
BARDIC > BARD
BARDIE n type of Australian grub
BARDIER > BARD
BARDIES > BARDIE
BARDIEST > BARD
BARDING > BARD
BARDISM > BARD
BARDISMS > BARD
BARDLING n inferior poet
BARDLINGS > BARDLING
BARDO n (in Tibetan Buddhism) the state of the soul between its death and its rebirth
BARDOS > BARDO
BARDS > BARD
BARDSHIP > BARD
BARDSHIPS > BARD
BARDY > BARD
BARE adj unclothed, naked ▷ vb uncover
BAREBACK adv (of horse-riding) without a saddle ▷ vb ride bareback
BAREBACKS > BAREBACK
BAREBOAT n boat chartered without crew, provisions, etc
BAREBOATS > BAREBOAT
BAREBONE n computer casing containing bare essentials
BAREBONED adj short of resources
BAREBONES > BAREBONE
BARED > BARE
BAREFACED adj shameless or obvious
BAREFIT same as
> BAREFOOT
BAREFOOT adv with the feet uncovered
BAREGE n light silky gauze fabric made of wool ▷ adj made of such a fabric
BAREGES > BAREGE
BAREGINE n curative ingredient in thermal waters
BAREGINES > BAREGINE
BAREHAND vb handle with bare hands
BAREHANDS > BAREHAND
BAREHEAD adv with head uncovered
BARELAND adj as in bareland croft refers to a croft with no croft house
BARELY adv only just
BARENESS > BARE
BARER > BARE
BARES > BARE

BARESARK another word for > BERSERK

BARESARKS > BARESARK

BAREST > BARE

BARF vb vomit ▷ n act of vomiting

BARFED > BARF

BARFI n type of Indian dessert

BARFING > BARF

BARFIS > BARFI

BARFLIES > BARFLY

BARFLY n person who frequents bars

BARFS > BARF

BARFUL adj presenting difficulties

BARGAIN n agreement establishing what each party will give, receive, or perform in a transaction ▷ vb negotiate the terms of an agreement

BARGAINED > BARGAIN

BARGAINER > BARGAIN

BARGAINS > BARGAIN

BARGANDER same as > BERGANDER

BARGE n flat-bottomed boat used to transport freight ▷ vb push violently

BARGED > BARGE

BARGEE n person in charge of a barge

BARGEES > BARGEE

BARGEESE > BARGOOSE

BARGELIKE adj like a barge

BARGELLO n zigzag tapestry stitch

BARGELLOS > BARGELLO

BARGEMAN same as > BARGEE

BARGEMEN > BARGEMAN

BARGEPOLE n long pole used to propel a barge

BARGES > BARGE

BARGEST same as > BARGHEST

BARGESTS > BARGEST

BARGHEST n mythical goblin in the shape of a dog

BARGHESTS > BARGHEST

BARGING > BARGE

BARGOON Canadian word for > BARGAIN

BARGOONS > BARGOON

BARGOOSE n type of goose; sheldrake

BARGUEST same as > BARGHEST

BARGUESTS > BARGUEST

BARHOP vb visit several bars in succession

BARHOPPED > BARHOP

BARHOPS > BARHOP

BARIATRIC adj of the treatment of obesity

BARIC adj of or containing barium

BARILLA n impure mixture of sodium carbonate and sodium sulphate

BARILLAS > BARILLA

BARING > BARE

BARISH adj quite thinly covered

BARISTA n person who makes and sells coffee in a coffee bar

BARISTAS > BARISTA

BARITE n colourless or white mineral

BARITES > BARITE

BARITONAL > BARITONE

BARITONE n (singer with) the second lowest adult male voice ▷ adj relating to or denoting a baritone

BARITONES > BARITONE

BARIUM n soft white metallic element

BARIUMS > BARIUM

BARK vb (of a dog) make its typical loud abrupt cry

BARKAN same as > BARCHAN

BARKANS > BARKAN

BARKED > BARK

BARKEEP n barkeeper

BARKEEPER another name (esp US) for > BARTENDER

BARKEEPS > BARKEEP

BARKEN vb become dry with a bark-like outer layer

BARKENED > BARKEN

BARKENING > BARKEN

BARKENS > BARKEN

BARKER n person at a fairground who calls loudly to passers-by in order to attract customers

BARKERS > BARKER

BARKHAN same as > BARCHAN

BARKHANS > BARKHAN

BARKIER > BARKY

BARKIEST > BARKY

BARKING adj mad

BARKLESS > BARK

BARKLIKE adj like a dog's bark

BARKS > BARK

BARKY adj having the texture or appearance of bark

BARLEDUC n French preserve made of currants

BARLEDUCS > BARLEDUC

BARLESS > BAR

BARLEY n tall grasslike plant cultivated for grain ▷ sentence substitute cry for truce or respite from the rules of a game

BARLEYS > BARLEY

BARLOW n type of strong knife

BARLOWS > BARLOW

BARM n yeasty froth on fermenting malt liquors

BARMAID n woman who serves in a pub

BARMAIDS > BARMAID

BARMAN same as > BARTENDER

BARMBRACK n loaf of bread with currants in it

BARMEN > BARMAN

BARMIE same as > BARMY

BARMIER > BARMY

BARMIEST > BARMY

BARMILY > BARMY

BARMINESS > BARMY

BARMKIN n protective wall around castle

BARMKINS > BARMKIN

BARMPOT n foolish or deranged person

BARMPOTS > BARMPOT

BARMS > BARM

BARMY adj insane

BARN n large building on a farm used for storing grain ▷ vb keep in a barn

BARNACLE n shellfish that lives attached to rocks, ship bottoms, etc

BARNACLED > BARNACLE

BARNACLES > BARNACLE

BARNBOARD n softwood board for building barns

BARNBRACK same as > BARMBRACK

BARNED > BARN

BARNET n hair

BARNETS > BARNET

BARNEY n noisy fight or argument ▷ vb argue or quarrel

BARNEYED > BARNEY

BARNEYING > BARNEY

BARNEYS > BARNEY

BARNIER > BARNY

BARNIEST > BARNY

BARNING > BARN

BARNLIKE > BARN

BARNS > BARN

BARNSTORM vb tour rural districts putting on shows or making speeches in a political campaign

BARNWOOD n aged and weathered boards, esp those salvaged from dismantled barns

BARNWOODS > BARNWOOD

BARNY adj reminiscent of a barn

BARNYARD n yard adjoining a barn

BARNYARDS > BARNYARD

BAROCCO same as > BAROQUE

BAROCCOS > BAROCCO

BAROCK same as > BAROQUE

BAROCKS > BAROCK

BAROGRAM n record of atmospheric pressure traced by a barograph or similar instrument

BAROGRAMS > BAROGRAM

BAROGRAPH n barometer that automatically keeps a record of changes in atmospheric pressure

BAROLO n red Italian wine

BAROLOS > BAROLO

BAROMETER n instrument for measuring atmospheric pressure

BAROMETRY > BAROMETER

BAROMETZ n fern whose woolly rhizomes resemble a lamb

BARON n member of the lowest rank of nobility

BARONAGE n barons collectively

BARONAGES > BARONAGE

BARONESS n woman holding the rank of baron

BARONET n commoner who holds the lowest hereditary British title

BARONETCY n rank, position, or patent of a baronet

BARONETS > BARONET

BARONG n broad-bladed cleaver-like knife used in the Philippines

BARONGS > BARONG

BARONIAL adj of, relating to, or befitting a baron or barons

BARONIES > BARONY

BARONNE n baroness

BARONNES > BARONNE

BARONS > BARON

BARONY n domain or rank of a baron

BAROPHILE n living organism that grows best in conditions of high atmospheric pressure

BAROQUE n style of art, architecture, or music ▷ adj ornate in style

BAROQUELY > BAROQUE

BAROQUES > BAROQUE

BAROSAUR n large dinosaur

BAROSAURS > BAROSAUR

BAROSCOPE n any instrument for measuring atmospheric pressure, esp a manometer with one side open to the atmosphere

BAROSTAT n device for maintaining constant pressure, such as one used in an aircraft cabin

BAROSTATS > BAROSTAT

BAROTITIS n inflammation of the ear caused by a change in air pressure

BAROUCHE n type of horse-drawn carriage

BAROUCHES > BAROUCHE

BARP n hillock or bank of stones

BARPERSON n person who serves in a pub: used esp in advertisements

BARPS > BARP

BARQUE n sailing ship, esp one with three masts

BARQUES > BARQUE

BARQUETTE n boat-shaped pastry shell

BARRA n barramundi

BARRABLE > BAR

BARRACAN n thick, strong fabric

BARRACANS > BARRACAN

BARRACE n record of teams entering a sports contest

BARRACES > BARRACE

BARRACK vb criticize loudly or shout against (a team or speaker)

BARRACKED > BARRACK

BARRACKER > BARRACK

BARRACKS pl n building used to accommodate military personnel

BARRACOON n (formerly) a temporary place of confinement for slaves or convicts, esp those awaiting transportation

BARRACUDA n tropical sea fish

b

BARRAGE n continuous delivery of questions, complaints, etc ▷ vb attack or confront with a barrage

BARRAGED > BARRAGE

BARRAGES > BARRAGE

BARRAGING > BARRAGE

BARRANCA n ravine or precipice

BARRANCAS > BARRANCA

BARRANCO same as > BARRANCA

BARRANCOS > BARRANCO

BARRAS > BARRA

BARRASWAY n shallow lagoon by a sandbar

BARRAT n fraudulent dealings ▷ vb quarrel

BARRATED > BARRAT

BARRATER same as > BARRATOR

BARRATERS > BARRATER

BARRATING > BARRAT

BARRATOR n person guilty of barratry

BARRATORS > BARRATOR

BARRATRY n (formerly) the vexatious stirring up of quarrels or bringing of lawsuits

BARRATS > BARRAT

BARRE n rail at hip height used for ballet practice ▷ vb execute guitar chords by laying the index finger over some or all of the strings ▷ adv by using the barre

BARRED > BAR

BARREED > BARRE

BARREFULL same as > BARFUL

BARREING > BARRE

BARREL n cylindrical container with rounded sides and flat ends ▷ vb put in a barrel

BARRELAGE > BARREL

BARRELED > BARREL

BARRELFUL same as > BARREL

BARRELING > BARREL

BARRELLED > BARREL

BARRELS > BARREL

BARREN adj (of a woman or female animal) incapable of producing offspring

BARRENER > BARREN

BARRENEST > BARREN

BARRENLY > BARREN

BARRENS pl n (in North America) a stretch of land that is sparsely vegetated

BARRES > BARRE

BARRET n small flat cap resembling a biretta

BARRETOR n quarrelsome person

BARRETORS > BARRETOR

BARRETRY same as > BARRATRY

BARRETS > BARRET

BARRETTE n clasp or pin for holding hair in place

BARRETTER same as > BARRETOR

BARRETTES > BARRETTE

BARRICADE n barrier, esp one erected hastily for

defence ▷ vb erect a barricade across (an entrance)

BARRICADO same as > BARRICADE

BARRICO n small container for liquids

BARRICOES > BARRICO

BARRICOS > BARRICO

BARRIE adj very good

BARRIER n anything that prevents access, progress, or union ▷ vb create or form a barrier

BARRIERED > BARRIER

BARRIERS > BARRIER

BARRIES > BARRY

BARRIEST > BARRY

BARRING > BAR

BARRINGS > BAR

BARRIO n Spanish-speaking quarter in a town or city, esp in the US

BARRIOS > BARRIO

BARRIQUE n wine barrel made of oak

BARRIQUES > BARRIQUE

BARRISTER n lawyer qualified to plead in a higher court

BARRO adj embarrassing

BARROOM n room or building where alcoholic drinks are served over a counter

BARROOMS > BARROOM

BARROW n wheelbarrow

BARROWFUL same as > BARROW

BARROWS > BARROW

BARRULET n narrow band across heraldic shield

BARRULETS > BARRULET

BARRY n mistake or blunder

BARS > BAR

BARSTOOL n high stool in bar

BARSTOOLS > BARSTOOL

BARTEND vb serve drinks from a bar

BARTENDED > BARTEND

BARTENDER n person who serves in a bar

BARTENDS > BARTEND

BARTER vb trade (goods) in exchange for other goods ▷ n trade by the exchange of goods

BARTERED > BARTER

BARTERER > BARTER

BARTERERS > BARTER

BARTERING > BARTER

BARTERS > BARTER

BARTISAN same as > BARTIZAN

BARTISANS > BARTISAN

BARTIZAN n small turret projecting from a wall, parapet, or tower

BARTIZANS > BARTIZAN

BARTON n farmyard

BARTONS > BARTON

BARTSIA n type of semiparasitic plant

BARTSIAS > BARTSIA

BARWARE n glasses, etc used in a bar

BARWARES > BARWARE

BARWOOD n red wood from small African tree

BARWOODS > BARWOOD

BARYE n unit of pressure

BARYES > BARYE

BARYON n elementary particle that has a mass greater than or equal to that of the proton

BARYONIC adj of or relating to a baryon

BARYONS > BARYON

BARYTA same as > BARITE

BARYTAS > BARYTA

BARYTE same as > BARITE

BARYTES > BARYTE

BARYTIC > BARYTA

BARYTON n bass viol with sympathetic strings as well as its six main strings

BARYTONE adj having the last syllable unaccented ▷ n word in which the last syllable is unaccented

BARYTONES > BARYTONE

BARYTONS > BARYTON

BAS > BA

BASAL adj of, at, or constituting a base

BASALLY > BASAL

BASALT n dark volcanic rock

BASALTES n unglazed black stoneware

BASALTIC > BASALT

BASALTINE adj resembling basalt ▷ n black or greenish-black mineral of the pyroxene group

BASALTS > BASALT

BASAN n sheepskin tanned in bark

BASANITE n black basaltic rock

BASANITES > BASANITE

BASANS > BASAN

BASANT n Pakistani spring festival

BASANTS > BASANT

BASCINET same as > BASINET

BASCINETS > BASCINET

BASCULE n drawbridge that operates by a counterbalanced weight

BASCULES > BASCULE

BASE n bottom or supporting part of anything ▷ vb use as a basis (for) ▷ adj dishonourable or immoral

BASEBALL n type of team ball game

BASEBALLS > BASEBALL

BASEBAND n transmission technique using a narrow range of frequencies

BASEBANDS > BASEBAND

BASEBOARD n board functioning as the base of anything

BASEBORN adj born of humble parents

BASED > BASE

BASEEJ pl n Iranian volunteer militia

BASEHEAD n habitual user of freebased cocaine

BASEHEADS > BASEHEAD

BASELARD n short sword

BASELARDS > BASELARD

BASELESS adj not based on fact

BASELINE n value or starting point on an imaginary scale with which other things are compared

BASELINER n tennis player who plays most of his or her shots from the back of the court

BASELINES > BASELINE

BASELOAD n constant part of an electrical power supply

BASELOADS > BASELOAD

BASELY > BASE

BASEMAN n fielder positioned near a base

BASEMEN > BASEMAN

BASEMENT n partly or wholly underground storey of a building

BASEMENTS > BASEMENT

BASEN Spenserian spelling of > BASIN

BASENESS > BASE

BASENJI n small breed of dog

BASENJIS > BASENJI

BASEPATH n diamond-shaped path between bases on a baseball field

BASEPATHS > BASEPATH

BASEPLATE n flat supporting plate or frame

BASER > BASE

BASES > BASIS

BASEST > BASE

BASH vb hit violently or forcefully ▷ n heavy blow

BASHAW n important or pompous person

BASHAWISM > BASHAW

BASHAWS > BASHAW

BASHED > BASH

BASHER > BASH

BASHERS > BASH

BASHES > BASH

BASHFUL adj shy or modest

BASHFULLY > BASHFUL

BASHING > BASH

BASHINGS > BASH

BASHLESS adj not ashamed

BASHLIK n Caucasian hood

BASHLIKS > BASHLIK

BASHLYK same as > BASHLIK

BASHLYKS > BASHLYK

BASHMENT same as > DANCEHALL

BASHMENTS > BASHMENT

BASHO n grand tournament in sumo wrestling

BASHTAG n (on Twitter) hashtag used for abusive comments

BASHTAGS > BASHTAG

BASIC adj of or forming a base or basis ▷ n fundamental principle, fact, etc

BASICALLY adv in a fundamental or elementary manner

BASICITY n state of being a base

b

BASICS > BASIC
BASIDIA > BASIDIUM
BASIDIAL > BASIDIUM
BASIDIUM *n* spore-forming structure in fungi
BASIFIED > BASIFY
BASIFIER > BASIFY
BASIFIERS > BASIFY
BASIFIES > BASIFY
BASIFIXED *adj* (of an anther) attached to the filament by its base
BASIFUGAL *a less common word for >* ACROPETAL
BASIFY *vb* make basic
BASIFYING > BASIFY
BASIJ *same as >* BASEEJ
BASIL *n* aromatic herb used in cooking
BASILAR *adj* of or situated at a base
BASILARY *same as* > BASILAR
BASILECT *n* debased dialect
BASILECTS > BASILECT
BASILIC > BASILICA
BASILICA *n* rectangular church with a rounded end and two aisles
BASILICAE > BASILICA
BASILICAL > BASILICA
BASILICAN > BASILICA
BASILICAS > BASILICA
BASILICON *n* healing ointment
BASILISK *n* legendary serpent said to kill by its breath or glance
BASILISKS > BASILISK
BASILS > BASIL
BASIN *n* round open container
BASINAL > BASIN
BASINED > BASIN
BASINET *n* close-fitting medieval helmet of light steel usually with a visor
BASINETS > BASINET
BASINFUL *n* amount a basin will hold
BASINFULS > BASINFUL
BASING > BASE
BASINLIKE > BASIN
BASINS > BASIN
BASION *n* (in anatomy) midpoint on the forward border of the foramen magnum
BASIONS > BASION
BASIPETAL *adj* (of leaves and flowers) produced in order from the apex downwards so that the youngest are at the base
BASIS *n* fundamental principles etc from which something is started or developed
BASK *vb* lie in or be exposed to something, esp pleasant warmth
BASKED > BASK
BASKET *n* container made of interwoven strips of wood or cane
BASKETFUL *n* as much as a basket will hold

BASKETRY *n* art or practice of making baskets
BASKETS > BASKET
BASKING > BASK
BASKS > BASK
BASMATI *n* variety of long-grain rice with slender aromatic grains
BASMATIS > BASMATI
BASNET *same as >* BASINET
BASNETS > BASNET
BASOCHE *n* society of medieval French lawyers who performed comic plays
BASOCHES > BASOCHE
BASON *same as >* BASIN
BASONS > BASON
BASOPHIL *adj* (of cells or cell contents) easily stained by basic dyes ▷ *n* basophil cell, esp a leucocyte
BASOPHILE *same as* > BASOPHIL
BASOPHILS > BASOPHIL
BASQUE *n* tight-fitting bodice for women
BASQUED > BASQUE
BASQUES > BASQUE
BASQUINE *n* tight-fitting bodice
BASQUINES > BASQUINE
BASS *n* (singer with) the lowest adult male voice ▷ *adj* relating to or denoting a bass ▷ *vb* speak or sing in a low pitch
BASSE *same as >* BASS
BASSED > BASS
BASSER *n* someone who plays bass guitar or double bass
BASSERS > BASSER
BASSES > BASS
BASSEST > BASS
BASSET *n* breed of hound ▷ *vb* (of rock) protrude through earth's surface
BASSETED > BASSET
BASSETING > BASSET
BASSETS > BASSET
BASSETT *same as >* BASSET
BASSETTED > BASSETT
BASSETTS > BASSETT
BASSI > BASSO
BASSIER > BASSY
BASSIEST > BASSY
BASSINET *n* wickerwork or wooden cradle or pram, usually hooded
BASSINETS > BASSINET
BASSING > BASS
BASSIST *n* player of a double bass, esp in a jazz band
BASSISTS > BASSIST
BASSLINE *n* (in jazz, rock, and pop music) part played by the bass guitar
BASSLINES > BASSLINE
BASSLY > BASS
BASSNESS > BASS
BASSO *n* singer with a bass voice
BASSOON *n* low-pitched woodwind instrument
BASSOONS > BASSOON
BASSOS > BASSO

BASSWOOD *n* N American linden tree
BASSWOODS > BASSWOOD
BASSY *adj* manifesting strong bass tones
BAST *n* fibrous material used for making rope, matting, etc
BASTA *interj* enough; stop
BASTARD *n* offensive term for an obnoxious or despicable person ▷ *adj* offensive term meaning illegitimate by birth
BASTARDLY *adj* like a bastard
BASTARDRY *n* malicious or cruel behaviour
BASTARDS > BASTARD
BASTARDY *n* condition of being a bastard
BASTE *vb* moisten (meat) during cooking with hot fat
BASTED > BASTE
BASTER > BASTE
BASTERS > BASTE
BASTES > BASTE
BASTI *n* (in India) a slum inhabited by poor people
BASTIDE *n* small isolated house in France
BASTIDES > BASTIDE
BASTILE *same as* > BASTILLE
BASTILES > BASTILE
BASTILLE *n* prison
BASTILLES > BASTILLE
BASTINADE *same as* > BASTINADO
BASTINADO *n* punishment or torture by beating on the soles of the feet with a stick ▷ *vb* beat (a person) in this way
BASTING *n* loose temporary stitches
BASTINGS > BASTING
BASTION *n* projecting part of a fortification
BASTIONED > BASTION
BASTIONS > BASTION
BASTIS > BASTI
BASTLE *n* fortified house
BASTLES > BASTLE
BASTO *n* ace of clubs in certain card games
BASTOS > BASTO
BASTS > BAST
BASUCO *n* illegal cocaine-based drug
BASUCOS > BASUCO
BAT *n* any of various types of club used to hit the ball in certain sports ▷ *vb* strike with or as if with a bat
BATABLE > BAT
BATARD *n* canoe made of birchbark
BATARDS > BATARD
BATATA *n* sweet potato
BATATAS > BATATA
BATAVIA *n* variety of lettuce with smooth pale green leaves
BATAVIAS > BATAVIA
BATBOY *n* boy who works at baseball games
BATBOYS > BATBOY

BATCH *n* group of people or things dealt with at the same time ▷ *vb* group (items) for efficient processing
BATCHED > BATCH
BATCHER > BATCH
BATCHERS > BATCH
BATCHES > BATCH
BATCHING > BATCH
BATCHINGS > BATCH
BATE *vb* (of hawks) to jump violently from a perch or the falconer's fist
BATEAU *n* light flat-bottomed boat used on rivers in Canada and the northern US
BATEAUX > BATEAU
BATED > BATE
BATELESS > BATE
BATELEUR *n* African bird of prey with a short tail and long wings
BATELEURS > BATELEUR
BATEMENT *n* reduction
BATEMENTS > BATEMENT
BATES > BATE
BATFISH *n* type of angler fish with a flattened scaleless body
BATFISHES > BATFISH
BATFOWL *vb* catch birds by temporarily blinding them with light
BATFOWLED > BATFOWL
BATFOWLER > BATFOWL
BATFOWLS > BATFOWL
BATGIRL *n* girl who works at baseball games
BATGIRLS > BATGIRL
BATH *n* large container in which to wash the body ▷ *vb* wash in a bath
BATHCUBE *n* cube of soluble scented material for use in a bath
BATHCUBES > BATHCUBE
BATHE *vb* swim in open water for pleasure
BATHED > BATHE
BATHER > BATHE
BATHERS *pl n* swimming costume
BATHES > BATHE
BATHETIC *adj* containing or displaying bathos
BATHHOUSE *n* building containing baths, esp for public use
BATHING *n* act of bathing
BATHINGS > BATHING
BATHLESS > BATH
BATHMAT *n* mat to stand on after a bath
BATHMATS > BATHMAT
BATHMIC > BATHMISM
BATHMISM *n* growth-force
BATHMISMS > BATHMISM
BATHOLITE *same as* > BATHOLITH
BATHOLITH *n* very large irregular-shaped mass of igneous rock, esp granite, formed from an intrusion of magma at great depth, esp one exposed after erosion of less resistant overlying rocks

BATHORSE *n* officer's packhorse

BATHORSES > BATHORSE

BATHOS *n* sudden change from a serious subject to a trivial one

BATHOSES > BATHOS

BATHROBE *n* loose-fitting garment for wear before or after a bath or swimming

BATHROBES > BATHROBE

BATHROOM *n* room with a bath, sink, and usu a toilet

BATHROOMS > BATHROOM

BATHS > BATH

BATHTUB *n* bath, esp one not permanently fixed

BATHTUBS > BATHTUB

BATHWATER *n* used or unused water in a bathtub

BATHYAL *adj* relating to an ocean depth of between 200 and 2000 metres

BATHYBIUS *n* gelatinous substance on seabed

BATHYLITE *same as* > BATHOLITH

BATHYLITH *same as* > BATHOLITH

BATIK *n* process of printing fabric using wax to cover areas not to be dyed ▷ *vb* treat material with this process

BATIKED > BATIK

BATIKING > BATIK

BATIKS > BATIK

BATING > BATE

BATISTE *n* fine plain-weave cotton fabric: used esp for shirts and dresses

BATISTES > BATISTE

BATLER *n* flat piece of wood for beating clothes, etc before washing

BATLERS > BATLER

BATLET *same as* > BATLER

BATLETS > BATLET

BATLIKE > BAT

BATMAN *n* officer's servant in the armed forces

BATMEN > BATMAN

BATOLOGY *n* study of brambles

BATON *n* thin stick used by the conductor of an orchestra ▷ *vb* carry or wave a baton

BATONED > BATON

BATONING > BATON

BATONNIER *n* president of a Bar Association in Quebec

BATONS > BATON

BATOON *same as* > BATON

BATOONED > BATOON

BATOONING > BATOON

BATOONS > BATOON

BATRACHIA *n* group of amphibians including frogs and toads

BATS > BAT

BATSHIT *adj* slang word for eccentric or crazy

BATSMAN *n* person who bats or specializes in batting

BATSMEN > BATSMAN

BATSWING *adj* in the form of the wing of a bat

BATSWOMAN > BATSMAN

BATSWOMEN > BATSMAN

BATT *same as* > BAT

BATTA *n* soldier's allowance

BATTALIA *n* arrangement of army prepared for battle

BATTALIAS > BATTALIA

BATTALION *n* army unit consisting of three or more companies

BATTAS > BATTA

BATTEAU *same as* > BATEAU

BATTEAUX > BATTEAU

BATTED > BAT

BATTEL *vb* make fertile

BATTELED > BATTEL

BATTELER > BATTEL

BATTELERS > BATTEL

BATTELING > BATTEL

BATTELLED > BATTEL

BATTELS > BATTEL

BATTEMENT *n* extension of one leg forwards, sideways, or backwards, either once or repeatedly

BATTEN *n* strip of wood fixed to something, esp to hold it in place ▷ *vb* strengthen or fasten with battens

BATTENED > BATTEN

BATTENER > BATTEN

BATTENERS > BATTEN

BATTENING > BATTEN

BATTENS > BATTEN

BATTER *vb* hit repeatedly ▷ *n* mixture of flour, eggs, and milk, used in cooking

BATTERED *adj* subjected to persistent physical violence

BATTERER *n* person who batters someone

BATTERERS > BATTERER

BATTERIE *n* movement in ballet involving the legs beating together

BATTERIES > BATTERY

BATTERING *n* act or practice of battering someone

BATTERO *n* heavy club

BATTEROS > BATTERO

BATTERS > BATTER

BATTERY *n* device that produces electricity in a torch, radio, etc ▷ *adj* kept in series of cages for intensive rearing

BATTIER > BATTY

BATTIES > BATTY

BATTIEST > BATTY

BATTIK *same as* > BATIK

BATTIKS > BATTIK

BATTILL *vb* fatten an animal

BATTILLED > BATTILL

BATTILLS > BATTILL

BATTILY *adv* in an eccentric or crazy manner

BATTINESS > BATTY

BATTING *n* act of hitting with a bat

BATTINGS > BATTING

BATTLE *n* fight between large armed forces ▷ *vb* struggle

BATTLEAX *same as* > BATTLEAXE

BATTLEAXE *n* kind of axe formerly used in battle

BATTLEBUS *n* coach that transports politicians and their advisers round the country during an election campaign

BATTLED > BATTLE

BATTLER > BATTLE

BATTLERS > BATTLE

BATTLES > BATTLE

BATTLING > BATTLE

BATTOLOGY *n* unnecessary repetition of words

BATTS > BATT

BATTU *adj* (in ballet) involving a beating movement

BATTUE *n* beating of woodland or cover to force game to flee in the direction of hunters

BATTUES > BATTUE

BATTUTA *n* (in music) a beat

BATTUTAS > BATTUTA

BATTUTO *n* (in Italian cookery) selection of chopped herbs

BATTUTOS > BATTUTO

BATTY *adj* eccentric or crazy ▷ *n* person's bottom

BATWING *adj* shaped like the wings of a bat, as a black tie, collar, etc

BATWOMAN *n* female servant in any of the armed forces

BATWOMEN > BATWOMAN

BAUBEE *same as* > BAWBEE

BAUBEES > BAUBEE

BAUBLE *n* trinket of little value

BAUBLES > BAUBLE

BAUBLING > BAUBLE

BAUCHLE *vb* shuffle along

BAUCHLED > BAUCHLE

BAUCHLES > BAUCHLE

BAUCHLING > BAUCHLE

BAUD *n* unit used to measure the speed of transmission of electronic data

BAUDEKIN *old variant of* > BALDACHIN

BAUDEKINS > BAUDEKIN

BAUDRIC *same as* > BALDRIC

BAUDRICK *same as* > BALDRIC

BAUDRICKE *same as* > BALDRIC

BAUDRICKS > BAUDRICK

BAUDRICS > BAUDRIC

BAUDRONS *n* name for a cat

BAUDS > BAUD

BAUERA *n* small evergreen Australian shrub

BAUERAS > BAUERA

BAUHINIA *n* type of climbing or shrubby plant

BAUHINIAS > BAUHINIA

BAUK *same as* > BALK

BAUKED > BAUK

BAUKING > BAUK

BAUKS > BAUK

BAULK *same as* > BALK

BAULKED > BAULK

BAULKER > BAULK

BAULKERS > BAULK

BAULKIER > BAULKY

BAULKIEST > BAULKY

BAULKILY > BAULKY

BAULKING > BAULK

BAULKLINE *n* line across a pool table behind which the cue ball is placed at start of a game

BAULKS > BAULK

BAULKY *same as* > BALKY

BAUR *n* humorous anecdote; joke

BAURS > BAUR

BAUSOND *adj* (of animal) dappled with white spots

BAUXITE *n* claylike substance that is the chief source of aluminium

BAUXITES > BAUXITE

BAUXITIC > BAUXITE

BAVARDAGE *n* chattering

BAVAROIS *n* cold dessert consisting of a rich custard set with gelatine

BAVIN *n* bundle of brushwood or firewood ▷ *vb* bind (brushwood or firewood) into bavins

BAVINED > BAVIN

BAVINING > BAVIN

BAVINS > BAVIN

BAWBEE *n* former Scottish silver coin

BAWBEES > BAWBEE

BAWBLE *same as* > BAUBLE

BAWBLES > BAWBLE

BAWCOCK *n* fine fellow

BAWCOCKS > BAWCOCK

BAWD *n* person who runs a brothel, esp a woman

BAWDIER > BAWDY

BAWDIES > BAWDY

BAWDIEST > BAWDY

BAWDILY > BAWDY

BAWDINESS > BAWDY

BAWDKIN *same as* > BALDACHIN

BAWDKINS > BAWDKIN

BAWDRIC *n* heavy belt to support sword

BAWDRICS > BAWDRIC

BAWDRIES > BAWDRY

BAWDRY *n* obscene talk or language

BAWDS > BAWD

BAWDY *adj* (of writing etc) containing humorous references to sex ▷ *n* obscenity or eroticism, esp in writing or drama

BAWK *n* type of Atlantic seabird

BAWKS > BAWK

BAWL *vb* shout or weep noisily ▷ *n* loud shout or cry

BAWLED > BAWL

BAWLER > BAWL

BAWLERS > BAWL

BAWLEY *n* small fishing boat

BAWLEYS > BAWLEY

BAWLING > BAWL

BAWLINGS > BAWL

BAWLS > BAWL

BAWN *n* fortified enclosure

BAWNEEN *same as* > BAININ

BAWNEENS > BAWNEEN

BAWNS > BAWN

b

BAWR same as > BAUR

BAWRS > BAWR

BAWSUNT adj black and white in colour

BAWTIE n name for a dog

BAWTIES > BAWTIE

BAWTY same as > BAWTIE

BAXTER old variant of > BAKER

BAXTERS > BAXTER

BAY n wide semicircular indentation of a shoreline ▷ vb howl in deep tones ▷ adj (esp of horses) of a reddish brown colour

BAYADEER same as > BAYADERE

BAYADEERS > BAYADEER

BAYADERE n dancing girl, esp one serving in a Hindu temple ▷ adj (of fabric, etc) having horizontal stripes

BAYADERES > BAYADERE

BAYAMO n Cuban strong wind

BAYAMOS > BAYAMO

BAYARD n bay horse

BAYARDS > BAYARD

BAYBERRY n tropical American tree that yields an oil used in making bay rum

BAYE vb bathe

BAYED > BAY

BAYER > BAY

BAYES > BAYE

BAYEST > BAY

BAYFRONT n shoreline of a bay

BAYFRONTS > BAYFRONT

BAYING > BAY

BAYLE n barrier

BAYLES > BAYLE

BAYMAN n fisherman

BAYMEN > BAYMAN

BAYNODDY n person who fishes in a bay

BAYONET n sharp blade that can be fixed to the end of a rifle ▷ vb stab with a bayonet

BAYONETED > BAYONET

BAYONETS > BAYONET

BAYOU n (in the southern US) a sluggish marshy tributary of a lake or river

BAYOUS > BAYOU

BAYS > BAY

BAYSIDE n shore of a bay

BAYSIDES > BAYSIDE

BAYT same as > BATE

BAYTED > BAYT

BAYTING > BAYT

BAYTS > BAYT

BAYWOOD n light soft wood of a tropical American mahogany tree

BAYWOODS > BAYWOOD

BAYWOP n (in Newfoundland) derogatory term for a person from outport communities

BAYWOPS > BAYWOP

BAYYAN n Islamic declaration

BAYYANS > BAYYAN

BAZAAR n sale in aid of charity

BAZAARS > BAZAAR

BAZAR same as > BAZAAR

BAZARS > BAZAR

BAZAZZ same as > PIZZAZZ

BAZAZZES > BAZAZZ

BAZILLION same as > GAZILLION

BAZOO a US slang word for > MOUTH

BAZOOKA n portable rocket launcher that fires an armour-piercing projectile

BAZOOKAS > BAZOOKA

BAZOOM n woman's breast

BAZOOMS > BAZOOM

BAZOOS > BAZOO

BAZOUKI same as > BOUZOUKI

BAZOUKIS > BAZOUKI

BAZZ vb throw (an object)

BAZZAZZ same as > PIZZAZZ

BAZZAZZES > BAZZAZZ

BAZZED > BAZZ

BAZZES > BAZZ

BAZZING > BAZZ

BDELLIUM n African or W Asian tree that yields a gum resin

BDELLIUMS > BDELLIUM

BE vb exist or live

BEACH n area of sand or pebbles on a shore ▷ vb run or haul (a boat) onto a beach

BEACHBALL n light ball for playing on beach

BEACHBOY n male lifeguard on beach

BEACHBOYS > BEACHBOY

BEACHCOMB vb collect objects, seashells, etc on seashore

BEACHED > BEACH

BEACHES > BEACH

BEACHGOER n person who goes to the beach

BEACHHEAD n beach captured by an attacking army on which troops can be landed

BEACHIER > BEACHY

BEACHIEST > BEACHY

BEACHING > BEACH

BEACHSIDE adj situated near a beach

BEACHWEAR n clothes suitable for the beach

BEACHY adj with gentle sandy slopes

BEACON n fire or light on a hill or tower, used as a warning ▷ vb guide or warn

BEACONED > BEACON

BEACONING > BEACON

BEACONS > BEACON

BEAD n small piece of plastic, wood, etc, pierced for threading ▷ vb decorate with beads

BEADBLAST n jet of small glass beads blown from a nozzle under air or steam pressure ▷ vb clean or treat (a surface) with a beadblast

BEADED > BEAD

BEADER n person making things with beads

BEADERS > BEADER

BEADHOUSE n chapel

BEADIER > BEADY

BEADIEST > BEADY

BEADILY > BEADY

BEADINESS > BEADY

BEADING n strip of moulding used for edging furniture

BEADINGS > BEADING

BEADLE n (formerly) a minor parish official who acted as an usher

BEADLEDOM n petty officialdom

BEADLES > BEADLE

BEADLIKE > BEAD

BEADMAN same as > BEADSMAN

BEADMEN > BEADMAN

BEADROLL n list of persons for whom prayers are to be offered

BEADROLLS > BEADROLL

BEADS > BEAD

BEADSMAN n person who prays for another's soul, esp one paid or fed for doing so

BEADSMEN > BEADSMAN

BEADWORK same as > BEADING

BEADWORKS > BEADWORK

BEADY adj small, round, and glittering

BEAGLE n small hound with short legs and drooping ears ▷ vb hunt with beagles, normally on foot

BEAGLED > BEAGLE

BEAGLER n person who hunts with beagles

BEAGLERS > BEAGLER

BEAGLES > BEAGLE

BEAGLING > BEAGLE

BEAGLINGS > BEAGLE

BEAK n projecting horny jaws of a bird

BEAKED > BEAK

BEAKER n large drinking cup

BEAKERFUL n amount of liquid in a full beaker

BEAKERS > BEAKER

BEAKIER > BEAK

BEAKIEST > BEAK

BEAKLESS > BEAK

BEAKLIKE > BEAK

BEAKS > BEAK

BEAKY > BEAK

BEAL n infected sore

BEALING n infected sore

BEALINGS > BEALING

BEALS > BEAL

BEAM n broad smile ▷ vb smile broadly

BEAMED > BEAM

BEAMER n full-pitched ball bowled at the batsman's head

BEAMERS > BEAMER

BEAMIER > BEAM

BEAMIEST > BEAM

BEAMILY > BEAM

BEAMINESS > BEAM

BEAMING > BEAM

BEAMINGLY > BEAM

BEAMINGS > BEAM

BEAMISH adj smiling

BEAMISHLY > BEAMISH

BEAMLESS > BEAM

BEAMLET n small beam

BEAMLETS > BEAMLET

BEAMLIKE > BEAM

BEAMS > BEAM

BEAMY > BEAM

BEAN n seed or pod of various plants, eaten as a vegetable or used to make coffee etc ▷ vb strike on the head

BEANBAG n small cloth bag filled with dried beans and thrown in games

BEANBAGS > BEANBAG

BEANBALL n baseball intended to hit batter's head

BEANBALLS > BEANBALL

BEANED > BEAN

BEANERIES > BEANERY

BEANERY n cheap restaurant

BEANFEAST n any festive or merry occasion

BEANIE n close-fitting woollen hat

BEANIES > BEANIE

BEANING > BEAN

BEANLIKE > BEAN

BEANO n celebration or party

BEANOS > BEANO

BEANPOLE n pole used to support bean plants

BEANPOLES > BEANPOLE

BEANS > BEAN

BEANSTALK n stem of a bean plant

BEANY same as > BEANIE

BEAR vb support or hold up (something) ▷ vb lower the price of (a security) ▷ n type of omnivorous mammal

BEARABLE adj endurable

BEARABLY > BEARABLE

BEARBERRY n type of shrub

BEARBINE n type of bindweed

BEARBINES > BEARBINE

BEARCAT n lesser panda

BEARCATS > BEARCAT

BEARD n hair growing on the lower parts of a person's face ▷ vb oppose boldly

BEARDED > BEARD

BEARDIE n another name for bearded loach

BEARDIER > BEARDY

BEARDIES > BEARDIE

BEARDIEST > BEARDY

BEARDING > BEARD

BEARDLESS adj without a beard

BEARDLIKE adj like a beard

BEARDS > BEARD

BEARDY adj having a beard

BEARE same as > BEAR

BEARED > BEAR

BEARER n person who carries, presents, or upholds something

BEARERS > BEARER

BEARES > BEARE

BEARGRASS n North American plant

BEARHUG n wrestling hold in which the arms are locked tightly round an opponent's chest and arms ▷ vb hold an opponent in a bearhug

b

BEARHUGS > BEARHUG
BEARING > BEAR
BEARINGS > BEAR
BEARISH adj like a bear
BEARISHLY > BEARISH
BEARLIKE > BEAR
BEARNAISE n rich sauce
BEARPAW n paw of a bear
BEARPAWS > BEARPAW
BEARS > BEAR
BEARSKIN n tall fur helmet worn by some British soldiers
BEARSKINS > BEARSKIN
BEARWARD n bear keeper
BEARWARDS > BEARWARD
BEARWOOD another name for > CASCARA
BEARWOODS > BEARWOOD
BEAST n large wild animal ▷ vb torture someone using excessive physical exercise
BEASTED > BEAST
BEASTHOOD > BEAST
BEASTIE n small animal
BEASTIES > BEASTIE
BEASTILY same as > BESTIALLY
BEASTING > BEAST
BEASTINGS same as > BEESTINGS
BEASTLIER > BEASTLY
BEASTLIKE > BEAST
BEASTLY adj unpleasant or disagreeable ▷ adv extremely
BEASTS > BEAST
BEAT vb strike with a series of violent blows ▷ n stroke or blow ▷ adj totally exhausted
BEATABLE > BEAT
BEATBOX n drum machine simulated by a human voice ▷ vb simulate a drum machine with a human voice
BEATBOXED > BEATBOX
BEATBOXER n person who practices beatboxing
BEATBOXES > BEATBOX
BEATDOWN n heavy defeat
BEATDOWNS > BEATDOWN
BEATEN > BEAT
BEATER n device used for beating
BEATERS > BEATER
BEATH vb dry; heat
BEATHED > BEATH
BEATHING > BEATH
BEATHS > BEATH
BEATIER > BEATY
BEATIEST > BEATY
BEATIFIC adj displaying great happiness
BEATIFIED > BEATIFY
BEATIFIES > BEATIFY
BEATIFY vb take first step towards making (a dead person) a saint
BEATING > BEAT
BEATINGS > BEAT
BEATITUDE n any of the blessings on the poor, meek, etc, in the Sermon on the Mount
BEATLESS > BEAT
BEATNIK n young person in the late 1950s who rebelled against conventional attitudes etc

BEATNIKS > BEATNIK
BEATS > BEAT
BEATY adj (of music) having a strong rhythm
BEAU n boyfriend or admirer
BEAUCOUP n large amount
BEAUCOUPS > BEAUCOUP
BEAUFET same as > BUFFET
BEAUFETS > BEAUFET
BEAUFFET same as > BUFFET
BEAUFFETS > BEAUFFET
BEAUFIN same as > BIFFIN
BEAUFINS > BEAUFIN
BEAUISH adj vain and showy
BEAUS > BEAU
BEAUT n person or thing that is outstanding or distinctive ▷ adj good or excellent ▷ interj exclamation of joy or pleasure
BEAUTEOUS adj beautiful
BEAUTER > BEAUT
BEAUTEST > BEAUT
BEAUTIED > BEAUTY
BEAUTIES > BEAUTY
BEAUTIFUL adj very attractive to look at
BEAUTIFY vb make beautiful
BEAUTS > BEAUT
BEAUTY n combination of all the qualities of a person or thing that delight the senses and mind ▷ interj expression of approval or agreement ▷ vb make beautiful
BEAUTYING > BEAUTY
BEAUX > BEAU
BEAUXITE same as > BAUXITE
BEAUXITES > BEAUXITE
BEAVER n amphibious rodent with a big flat tail ▷ vb work steadily or assiduously
BEAVERED > BEAVER
BEAVERIES > BEAVERY
BEAVERING > BEAVER
BEAVERS > BEAVER
BEAVERY n place for keeping beavers
BEBEERINE n alkaloid, resembling quinine, obtained from the bark of the greenheart and other plants
BEBEERU n tropical American tree
BEBEERUS > BEBEERU
BEBLOOD vb stain with blood
BEBLOODED > BEBLOOD
BEBLOODS > BEBLOOD
BEBOP same as > BOP
BEBOPPED > BEBOP
BEBOPPER > BEBOP
BEBOPPERS > BEBOP
BEBOPPING > BEBOP
BEBOPS > BEBOP
BEBUNG n vibrato effect on clavichord
BEBUNGS > BEBUNG
BECALL vb use insulting words about someone
BECALLED > BECALL
BECALLING > BECALL
BECALLS > BECALL

BECALM vb make calm
BECALMED adj (of a sailing ship) motionless through lack of wind
BECALMING > BECALM
BECALMS > BECALM
BECAME > BECOME
BECAP vb put cap on
BECAPPED > BECAP
BECAPPING > BECAP
BECAPS > BECAP
BECARPET vb lay carpet on
BECARPETS > BECARPET
BECASSE n woodcock
BECASSES > BECASSE
BECAUSE conj on account of the fact that; on account of being; since
BECCACCIA n woodcock
BECCAFICO n European songbird, eaten as a delicacy in Italy and other countries
BECHALK vb mark with chalk
BECHALKED > BECHALK
BECHALKS > BECHALK
BECHAMEL n thick white sauce flavoured with onion and seasoning
BECHAMELS > BECHAMEL
BECHANCE vb happen (to)
BECHANCED > BECHANCE
BECHANCES > BECHANCE
BECHARM vb delight
BECHARMED > BECHARM
BECHARMS > BECHARM
BECK n stream ▷ vb attract someone's attention by nodding or gesturing
BECKE same as > BEAK
BECKED > BECK
BECKES > BECKE
BECKET n clevis forming part of one end of a sheave
BECKETS > BECKET
BECKING > BECK
BECKON vb summon with a gesture ▷ n summoning gesture
BECKONED > BECKON
BECKONER > BECKON
BECKONERS > BECKON
BECKONING > BECKON
BECKONS > BECKON
BECKS > BECK
BECLAMOR vb clamour excessively
BECLAMORS > BECLAMOR
BECLAMOUR vb make a clamour
BECLASP vb embrace
BECLASPED > BECLASP
BECLASPS > BECLASP
BECLOAK vb dress in cloak
BECLOAKED > BECLOAK
BECLOAKS > BECLOAK
BECLOG vb put clogs on
BECLOGGED > BECLOG
BECLOGS > BECLOG
BECLOTHE vb put clothes on
BECLOTHED > BECLOTHE
BECLOTHES > BECLOTHE
BECLOUD vb cover or obscure with a cloud
BECLOUDED > BECLOUD
BECLOUDS > BECLOUD

BECLOWN vb clown around
BECLOWNED > BECLOWN
BECLOWNS > BECLOWN
BECOME vb come to be
BECOMES > BECOME
BECOMING adj attractive or pleasing ▷ n any process of change
BECOMINGS > BECOMING
BECOWARD vb make cowardly
BECOWARDS > BECOWARD
BECQUEREL n SI unit of radioactivity
BECRAWL vb crawl all over
BECRAWLED > BECRAWL
BECRAWLS > BECRAWL
BECRIME vb make someone guilty of a crime
BECRIMED > BECRIME
BECRIMES > BECRIME
BECRIMING > BECRIME
BECROWD vb crowd with something
BECROWDED > BECROWD
BECROWDS > BECROWD
BECRUST vb cover with crust
BECRUSTED > BECRUST
BECRUSTS > BECRUST
BECUDGEL vb arm with cudgel
BECUDGELS > BECUDGEL
BECURL vb curl
BECURLED > BECURL
BECURLING > BECURL
BECURLS > BECURL
BECURSE vb curse
BECURSED > BECURSE
BECURSES > BECURSE
BECURSING > BECURSE
BECURST > BECURSE
BED n piece of furniture on which to sleep ▷ vb plant in a bed
BEDABBLE vb dabble; moisten
BEDABBLED > BEDABBLE
BEDABBLES > BEDABBLE
BEDAD interj by God (oath)
BEDAGGLE vb soil by trailing through dirt
BEDAGGLED > BEDAGGLE
BEDAGGLES > BEDAGGLE
BEDAMN vb damn
BEDAMNED > BEDAMN
BEDAMNING > BEDAMN
BEDAMNS > BEDAMN
BEDARKEN vb make dark
BEDARKENS > BEDARKEN
BEDASH vb sprinkle with liquid
BEDASHED > BEDASH
BEDASHES > BEDASH
BEDASHING > BEDASH
BEDAUB vb smear with something sticky or dirty
BEDAUBED > BEDAUB
BEDAUBING > BEDAUB
BEDAUBS > BEDAUB
BEDAWIN same as > BEDOUIN
BEDAWINS > BEDAWIN
BEDAZE vb daze
BEDAZED > BEDAZE
BEDAZES > BEDAZE
BEDAZING > BEDAZE

b

BEDAZZLE *vb* dazzle or confuse, as with brilliance

BEDAZZLED > BEDAZZLE

BEDAZZLES > BEDAZZLE

BEDBATH *n* washing of a sick person in bed

BEDBATHS > BEDBATH

BEDBOARD *n* base of bed

BEDBOARDS > BEDBOARD

BEDBUG *n* small blood-sucking wingless insect that infests dirty houses

BEDBUGS > BEDBUG

BEDCHAIR *n* adjustable chair to support invalid in bed

BEDCHAIRS > BEDCHAIR

BEDCOVER *n* cover for bed

BEDCOVERS > BEDCOVER

BEDDABLE *adj* sexually attractive

BEDDED > BED

BEDDER *n* (at some universities) college servant employed to keep students' rooms in order

BEDDERS > BEDDER

BEDDING > BED

BEDDINGS > BED

BEDE *n* prayer

BEDEAFEN *vb* deafen

BEDEAFENS > BEDEAFEN

BEDECK *vb* cover with decorations

BEDECKED > BEDECK

BEDECKING > BEDECK

BEDECKS > BEDECK

BEDEGUAR *n* growth found on rosebushes

BEDEGUARS > BEDEGUAR

BEDEHOUSE *same as* > BEADHOUSE

BEDEL *archaic spelling of* > BEADLE

BEDELL *same as* > BEADLE

BEDELLS > BEDELL

BEDELS > BEDEL

BEDELSHIP > BEDEL

BEDEMAN *same as* > BEADSMAN

BEDEMEN > BEDEMAN

BEDERAL *same as* > BEDRAL

BEDERALS > BEDERAL

BEDES > BEDE

BEDESMAN *same as* > BEADSMAN

BEDESMEN > BEDESMAN

BEDEVIL *vb* harass, confuse, or torment

BEDEVILED > BEDEVIL

BEDEVILS > BEDEVIL

BEDEW *vb* wet or cover with or as if with drops of dew

BEDEWED > BEDEW

BEDEWING > BEDEW

BEDEWS > BEDEW

BEDFAST *an archaic word for* > BEDRIDDEN

BEDFELLOW *n* temporary associate

BEDFRAME *n* framework of bed

BEDFRAMES > BEDFRAME

BEDGOWN *n* night dress

BEDGOWNS > BEDGOWN

BEDHEAD *n* untidy state of hair, esp caused by sleeping

BEDHEADS > BEDHEAD

BEDIAPER *vb* put a nappy on

BEDIAPERS > BEDIAPER

BEDIDE > BEDYE

BEDIGHT *vb* array or adorn ▷ *adj* adorned or bedecked

BEDIGHTED > BEDIGHT

BEDIGHTS > BEDIGHT

BEDIM *vb* make dim or obscure

BEDIMMED > BEDIM

BEDIMMING > BEDIM

BEDIMPLE *vb* form dimples in

BEDIMPLED > BEDIMPLE

BEDIMPLES > BEDIMPLE

BEDIMS > BEDIM

BEDIRTIED > BEDIRTY

BEDIRTIES > BEDIRTY

BEDIRTY *vb* make dirty

BEDIZEN *vb* dress or decorate gaudily or tastelessly

BEDIZENED > BEDIZEN

BEDIZENS > BEDIZEN

BEDLAM *n* noisy confused situation

BEDLAMER *n* young harp seal

BEDLAMERS > BEDLAMER

BEDLAMISM > BEDLAM

BEDLAMITE *n* lunatic

BEDLAMP *n* bedside light

BEDLAMPS > BEDLAMP

BEDLAMS > BEDLAM

BEDLESS > BED

BEDLIKE *adj* like a bed

BEDLINER *n* lining for the bed of a truck

BEDLINERS > BEDLINER

BEDMAKER *n* person who makes beds

BEDMAKERS > BEDMAKER

BEDMATE *n* person who shares a bed

BEDMATES > BEDMATE

BEDOTTED *adj* scattered; strewn

BEDOUIN *n* member of any of the nomadic tribes of Arabs

BEDOUINS > BEDOUIN

BEDPAN *n* shallow bowl used as a toilet by bedridden people

BEDPANS > BEDPAN

BEDPLATE *n* heavy metal platform or frame to which an engine or machine is attached

BEDPLATES > BEDPLATE

BEDPOST *n* vertical support on a bedstead

BEDPOSTS > BEDPOST

BEDQUILT *n* padded bed cover

BEDQUILTS > BEDQUILT

BEDRAGGLE *vb* make (hair, clothing, etc) limp, untidy, or dirty, as with rain or mud

BEDRAIL *n* rail along the side of a bed connecting the headboard with the footboard

BEDRAILS > BEDRAIL

BEDRAL *n* minor church official

BEDRALS > BEDRAL

BEDRAPE *vb* adorn

BEDRAPED > BEDRAPE

BEDRAPES > BEDRAPE

BEDRAPING > BEDRAPE

BEDRENCH *vb* drench

BEDREST *n* rest in bed, eg to recover from illness

BEDRESTS > BEDREST

BEDRID *same as* > BEDRIDDEN

BEDRIDDEN *adj* confined to bed because of illness or old age

BEDRIGHT *n* rights expected in the marital bed

BEDRIGHTS > BEDRIGHT

BEDRITE *same as* > BEDRIGHT

BEDRITES > BEDRITE

BEDRIVEL *vb* drivel around

BEDRIVELS > BEDRIVEL

BEDROCK *n* solid rock beneath the surface soil

BEDROCKS > BEDROCK

BEDROLL *n* portable roll of bedding

BEDROLLS > BEDROLL

BEDROOM *n* room used for sleeping

BEDROOMED *adj* containing specified number of bedrooms

BEDROOMS > BEDROOM

BEDROP *vb* drop on

BEDROPPED > BEDROP

BEDROPS > BEDROP

BEDROPT > BEDROP

BEDRUG *vb* drug excessively

BEDRUGGED > BEDRUG

BEDRUGS > BEDRUG

BEDS > BED

BEDSHEET *n* sheet for bed

BEDSHEETS > BEDSHEET

BEDSIDE *n* area beside a bed ▷ *adj* placed at or near the side of the bed

BEDSIDES > BEDSIDE

BEDSIT *n* furnished sitting room with a bed

BEDSITS > BEDSIT

BEDSITTER *same as* > BEDSIT

BEDSKIRT *n* drapery round the edge of a bed

BEDSKIRTS > BEDSKIRT

BEDSOCK *n* sock worn in bed

BEDSOCKS > BEDSOCK

BEDSONIA *n* bacterium causing diseases such as trachoma

BEDSONIAS > BEDSONIA

BEDSORE *n* ulcer on the skin, caused by a lengthy period of lying in bed due to illness

BEDSORES > BEDSORE

BEDSPREAD *n* top cover on a bed

BEDSPRING *vb* spring supporting mattress on bed

BEDSTAND *n* bedside table

BEDSTANDS > BEDSTAND

BEDSTEAD *n* framework of a bed

BEDSTEADS > BEDSTEAD

BEDSTRAW *n* plant with small white or yellow flowers

BEDSTRAWS > BEDSTRAW

BEDTICK *n* case containing stuffing in mattress

BEDTICKS > BEDTICK

BEDTIME *n* time when one usually goes to bed

BEDTIMES > BEDTIME

BEDU *adj* relating to beduins

BEDUCK *vb* duck under water

BEDUCKED > BEDUCK

BEDUCKING > BEDUCK

BEDUCKS > BEDUCK

BEDUIN *variant of* > BEDOUIN

BEDUINS > BEDUIN

BEDUMB *vb* make dumb

BEDUMBED > BEDUMB

BEDUMBING > BEDUMB

BEDUMBS > BEDUMB

BEDUNCE *vb* cause to look or feel foolish

BEDUNCED > BEDUNCE

BEDUNCES > BEDUNCE

BEDUNCING > BEDUNCE

BEDUNG *vb* spread with dung

BEDUNGED > BEDUNG

BEDUNGING > BEDUNG

BEDUNGS > BEDUNG

BEDUST *vb* cover with dust

BEDUSTED > BEDUST

BEDUSTING > BEDUST

BEDUSTS > BEDUST

BEDWARD *adj* towards bed

BEDWARDS *adv* towards bed

BEDWARF *vb* hamper growth of

BEDWARFED > BEDWARF

BEDWARFS > BEDWARF

BEDWARMER *n* metal pan containing hot coals, formerly used to warm a bed

BEDWETTER *n* person who urinates in bed

BEDYDE > BEDYE

BEDYE *vb* dye

BEDYED > BEDYE

BEDYEING > BEDYE

BEDYES > BEDYE

BEE *n* insect that makes wax and honey

BEEBEE *n* air rifle

BEEBEES > BEEBEE

BEEBREAD *n* mixture of pollen and nectar prepared by worker bees and fed to the larvae

BEEBREADS > BEEBREAD

BEECH *n* tree with a smooth greyish bark

BEECHEN > BEECH

BEECHES > BEECH

BEECHIER > BEECH

BEECHIEST > BEECH

BEECHMAST *n* nuts of beech tree

BEECHNUT *n* small brown triangular edible nut of the beech tree

BEECHNUTS > BEECHNUT

BEECHWOOD *n* wood of beech tree

BEECHY > BEECH

BEEDI *n* Indian cigarette

BEEDIE *same as* > BEEDI

BEEDIES > BEEDIE

BEEF *n* flesh of a cow, bull, or ox ▷ *vb* complain

BEEFALO n cross between cow and buffalo
BEEFALOES > BEEFALO
BEEFALOS > BEEFALO
BEEFCAKE n muscular man as displayed in photographs
BEEFCAKES > BEEFCAKE
BEEFEATER n yeoman warder at the Tower of London
BEEFED > BEEF
BEEFIER > BEEFY
BEEFIEST > BEEFY
BEEFILY > BEEFY
BEEFINESS > BEEFY
BEEFING > BEEF
BEEFLESS > BEEF
BEEFS > BEEF
BEEFSTEAK n piece of beef that can be grilled, fried, etc, cut from any lean part of the animal
BEEFWOOD n any of various trees that produce very hard wood
BEEFWOODS > BEEFWOOD
BEEFY adj like beef
BEEGAH same as > BIGHA
BEEGAHS > BEEGAH
BEEHIVE n structure in which bees live
BEEHIVED adj (esp of a hairstyle) shaped like a beehive
BEEHIVES > BEEHIVE
BEEKEEPER n person who keeps bees for their honey
BEELIKE > BEE
BEELINE n most direct route between two places ▷ vb make a beeline for (something)
BEELINED > BEELINE
BEELINES > BEELINE
BEELINING > BEELINE
BEEN vb past participle of be
BEENAH n understanding; insight
BEENAHS > BEENAH
BEENTO n person who has resided in Britain ▷ adj of, relating to, or characteristic of such a person
BEENTOS > BEENTO
BEEP n high-pitched sound, like that of a car horn ▷ vb (cause to) make this noise
BEEPED > BEEP
BEEPER > BEEP
BEEPERS > BEEP
BEEPING > BEEP
BEEPS > BEEP
BEER n alcoholic drink brewed from malt and hops
BEERAGE n brewing industry
BEERAGES > BEERAGE
BEERFEST n beer festival
BEERFESTS > BEERFEST
BEERHALL n large public room where beer is consumed
BEERHALLS > BEERHALL
BEERIER > BEERY
BEERIEST > BEERY
BEERILY > BEERY
BEERINESS > BEERY

BEERMAT n small mat put under a glass of beer
BEERMATS > BEERMAT
BEERNUT n coated peanut eaten as a snack
BEERNUTS > BEERNUT
BEERS > BEER
BEERSIES pl n (NZ) beers
BEERY adj smelling or tasting of beer
BEES > BEE
BEESOME same as > BISSON
BEESTING adj as in beesting lips of lips, pouting
BEESTINGS n first milk secreted by a cow or similar animal immediately after giving birth
BEESTUNG adj as in beestung lips of lips, pouting
BEESWAX n wax secreted by bees, used in polishes etc ▷ vb polish with such wax
BEESWAXED > BEESWAX
BEESWAXES > BEESWAX
BEESWING n light filmy crust that forms in port wine
BEESWINGS > BEESWING
BEET n plant with an edible root and leaves ▷ vb improve or make better
BEETED > BEET
BEETFLIES > BEETFLY
BEETFLY n type of fly which is a common pest of beets and mangel-wurzels
BEETING > BEET
BEETLE n insect with a hard wing cover on its back ▷ vb scuttle or scurry
BEETLED > BEETLE
BEETLER n one who operates a beetling machine
BEETLERS > BEETLER
BEETLES > BEETLE
BEETLING > BEETLE
BEETROOT n type of beet plant with a dark red root
BEETROOTS > BEETROOT
BEETS > BEET
BEEVES > BEEF
BEEYARD n place where bees are kept
BEEYARDS > BEEYARD
BEEZER n person or chap ▷ adj excellent
BEEZERS > BEEZER
BEFALL vb happen to (someone)
BEFALLEN > BEFALL
BEFALLING > BEFALL
BEFALLS > BEFALL
BEFANA n Italian gift-bearing good fairy
BEFANAS > BEFANA
BEFELD archaic past participle of > BEFALL
BEFELL > BEFALL
BEFFANA same as > BEFANA
BEFFANAS > BEFFANA
BEFINGER vb mark by handling
BEFINGERS > BEFINGER
BEFINNED adj with fins
BEFIT vb be appropriate or suitable for
BEFITS > BEFIT

BEFITTED > BEFIT
BEFITTING > BEFIT
BEFLAG vb decorate with flags
BEFLAGGED > BEFLAG
BEFLAGS > BEFLAG
BEFLEA vb infest with fleas
BEFLEAED > BEFLEA
BEFLEAING > BEFLEA
BEFLEAS > BEFLEA
BEFLECK vb fleck
BEFLECKED > BEFLECK
BEFLECKS > BEFLECK
BEFLOWER vb decorate with flowers
BEFLOWERS > BEFLOWER
BEFLUM vb fool; deceive
BEFLUMMED > BEFLUM
BEFLUMS > BEFLUM
BEFOAM vb cover with foam
BEFOAMED > BEFOAM
BEFOAMING > BEFOAM
BEFOAMS > BEFOAM
BEFOG vb surround with fog
BEFOGGED > BEFOG
BEFOGGING > BEFOG
BEFOGS > BEFOG
BEFOOL vb make a fool of
BEFOOLED > BEFOOL
BEFOOLING > BEFOOL
BEFOOLS > BEFOOL
BEFORE adv indicating something earlier in time, in front of, or preferred to ▷ prep preceding in space or time
BEFORTUNE vb happen to
BEFOUL vb make dirty or foul
BEFOULED > BEFOUL
BEFOULER > BEFOUL
BEFOULERS > BEFOUL
BEFOULING > BEFOUL
BEFOULS > BEFOUL
BEFRET vb fret about something
BEFRETS > BEFRET
BEFRETTED > BEFRET
BEFRIEND vb become friends with
BEFRIENDS > BEFRIEND
BEFRINGE vb decorate with fringe
BEFRINGED > BEFRINGE
BEFRINGES > BEFRINGE
BEFUDDLE vb confuse, muddle, or perplex
BEFUDDLED > BEFUDDLE
BEFUDDLES > BEFUDDLE
BEG vb solicit (money, food, etc), esp in the street
BEGAD interj emphatic exclamation
BEGALL vb make sore by rubbing
BEGALLED > BEGALL
BEGALLING > BEGALL
BEGALLS > BEGALL
BEGAN > BEGIN
BEGAR n compulsory labour
BEGARS > BEGAR
BEGAT archaic past tense of > BEGET
BEGAZE vb gaze about or around
BEGAZED > BEGAZE
BEGAZES > BEGAZE

BEGAZING > BEGAZE
BEGEM vb decorate with gems
BEGEMMED > BEGEM
BEGEMMING > BEGEM
BEGEMS > BEGEM
BEGET vb cause or create
BEGETS > BEGET
BEGETTER > BEGET
BEGETTERS > BEGET
BEGETTING > BEGET
BEGGAR n person who begs, esp one who lives by begging ▷ vb be beyond the resources of
BEGGARDOM > BEGGAR
BEGGARED > BEGGAR
BEGGARIES > BEGGARY
BEGGARING > BEGGAR
BEGGARLY adj meanly inadequate
BEGGARS > BEGGAR
BEGGARY n extreme poverty or need
BEGGED > BEG
BEGGING > BEG
BEGGINGLY > BEG
BEGGINGS > BEG
BEGHARD n member of a 13th century Christian brotherhood
BEGHARDS > BEGHARD
BEGIFT vb give gift or gifts to
BEGIFTED > BEGIFT
BEGIFTING > BEGIFT
BEGIFTS > BEGIFT
BEGILD vb gild
BEGILDED > BEGILD
BEGILDING > BEGILD
BEGILDS > BEGILD
BEGILT > BEGILD
BEGIN vb start
BEGINNE same as > BEGINNING
BEGINNER n person who has just started learning to do something
BEGINNERS > BEGINNER
BEGINNES > BEGINNE
BEGINNING n start
BEGINS > BEGIN
BEGIRD vb surround
BEGIRDED > BEGIRD
BEGIRDING > BEGIRD
BEGIRDLE vb surround with girdle
BEGIRDLED > BEGIRDLE
BEGIRDLES > BEGIRDLE
BEGIRDS > BEGIRD
BEGIRT > BEGIRD
BEGLAD vb make glad
BEGLADDED > BEGLAD
BEGLADS > BEGLAD
BEGLAMOR same as > BEGLAMOUR
BEGLAMORS > BEGLAMOR
BEGLAMOUR vb glamourize
BEGLERBEG n governor in the Ottoman empire
BEGLOOM vb make gloomy
BEGLOOMED > BEGLOOM
BEGLOOMS > BEGLOOM
BEGNAW vb gnaw at
BEGNAWED > BEGNAW
BEGNAWING > BEGNAW

b

BEGNAWS > BEGNAW
BEGO vb harass; beset
BEGOES > BEGO
BEGOGGLED adj wearing goggles
BEGOING > BEGO
BEGONE > BEGO
BEGONIA n tropical plant with waxy flowers
BEGONIAS > BEGONIA
BEGORAH same as **> BEGORRA**
BEGORED adj smeared with gore
BEGORRA interj emphatic exclamation, regarded as a characteristic utterance of Irish people
BEGORRAH same as **> BEGORRA**
BEGOT > BEGET
BEGOTTEN > BEGET
BEGRIM same as **>** BEGRIME
BEGRIME vb make dirty
BEGRIMED > BEGRIME
BEGRIMES > BEGRIME
BEGRIMING > BEGRIME
BEGRIMMED > BEGRIM
BEGRIMS > BEGRIM
BEGROAN vb groan at
BEGROANED > BEGROAN
BEGROANS > BEGROAN
BEGRUDGE vb envy (someone) the possession of something
BEGRUDGED > BEGRUDGE
BEGRUDGER > BEGRUDGE
BEGRUDGES > BEGRUDGE
BEGS > BEG
BEGUILE vb cheat or mislead
BEGUILED > BEGUILE
BEGUILER > BEGUILE
BEGUILERS > BEGUILE
BEGUILES > BEGUILE
BEGUILING adj charming, often in a deceptive way
BEGUIN another name for **>** BEGHARD
BEGUINAGE n convent for members of beguine sisterhood
BEGUINE n S American dance
BEGUINES > BEGUINE
BEGUINS > BEGUIN
BEGULF vb overwhelm
BEGULFED > BEGULF
BEGULFING > BEGULF
BEGULFS > BEGULF
BEGUM n Muslim woman of high rank
BEGUMS > BEGUM
BEGUN > BEGIN
BEGUNK vb delude; trick
BEGUNKED > BEGUNK
BEGUNKING > BEGUNK
BEGUNKS > BEGUNK
BEHALF n interest, part, benefit, or respect
BEHALVES > BEHALF
BEHAPPEN vb befall
BEHAPPENS > BEHAPPEN
BEHATTED adj wearing a hat
BEHAVE vb act or function in a particular way
BEHAVED > BEHAVE

BEHAVER > BEHAVE
BEHAVERS > BEHAVE
BEHAVES > BEHAVE
BEHAVING > BEHAVE
BEHAVIOR same as **> BEHAVIOUR**
BEHAVIORS > BEHAVIOR
BEHAVIOUR n manner of behaving
BEHEAD vb remove the head from
BEHEADAL > BEHEAD
BEHEADALS > BEHEAD
BEHEADED > BEHEAD
BEHEADER > BEHEAD
BEHEADERS > BEHEAD
BEHEADING > BEHEAD
BEHEADS > BEHEAD
BEHELD > BEHOLD
BEHEMOTH n huge person or thing
BEHEMOTHS > BEHEMOTH
BEHEST n order or earnest request
BEHESTS > BEHEST
BEHIGHT vb entrust
BEHIGHTED > BEHIGHT
BEHIGHTS > BEHIGHT
BEHIND adv indicating position to the rear, lateness, responsibility, etc ▷ n buttocks ▷ prep in or to a position further back than ▷ adj in a position further back
BEHINDS > BEHIND
BEHOLD vb look (at)
BEHOLDEN adj indebted or obliged
BEHOLDER > BEHOLD
BEHOLDERS > BEHOLD
BEHOLDING > BEHOLD
BEHOLDS > BEHOLD
BEHOOF n advantage or profit
BEHOOFS > BEHOOF
BEHOOVE same as **>** BEHOVE
BEHOOVED > BEHOOVE
BEHOOVES > BEHOOVE
BEHOOVING > BEHOOVE
BEHOTE same as **>** BEHIGHT
BEHOTES > BEHOTE
BEHOTING > BEHOTE
BEHOVE vb be necessary or fitting for
BEHOVED > BEHOVE
BEHOVEFUL adj useful; of benefit
BEHOVELY adj useful
BEHOVES > BEHOVE
BEHOVING > BEHOVE
BEHOWL vb howl at
BEHOWLED > BEHOWL
BEHOWLING > BEHOWL
BEHOWLS > BEHOWL
BEIGE adj pale brown ▷ n very light brown
BEIGEL same as **>** BAGEL
BEIGELS > BEIGEL
BEIGER > BEIGE
BEIGES > BEIGE
BEIGEST > BEIGE
BEIGIER > BEIGE
BEIGIEST > BEIGE
BEIGNE variant of **>** BEIGNET

BEIGNES > BEIGNE
BEIGNET n square deep-fried pastry served hot and sprinkled with icing sugar
BEIGNETS > BEIGNET
BEIGY > BEIGE
BEIN adj financially comfortable ▷ vb fill
BEINED > BEIN
BEING > BE
BEINGLESS > BE
BEINGNESS > BE
BEINGS > BEING
BEINING > BEIN
BEINKED adj daubed with ink
BEINNESS > BEIN
BEINS > BEIN
BEJABBERS same as **> BEJABERS**
BEJABERS interj by Jesus!
BEJADE vb jade; tire
BEJADED > BEJADE
BEJADES > BEJADE
BEJADING > BEJADE
BEJANT same as **>** BAJAN
BEJANTS > BEJANT
BEJASUS same as **> BEJESUS**
BEJASUSES > BEJASUS
BEJEEBERS same as **> BEJABERS**
BEJEEZUS same as **> BEJESUS**
BEJESUIT vb convert to Jesuitism
BEJESUITS > BEJESUIT
BEJESUS interj exclamation of surprise ▷ n as in the bejesus mild expletive
BEJESUSES > BEJESUS
BEJEWEL vb decorate with or as if with jewels
BEJEWELED > BEJEWEL
BEJEWELS > BEJEWEL
BEJUMBLE vb jumble up
BEJUMBLED > BEJUMBLE
BEJUMBLES > BEJUMBLE
BEKAH n half shekel
BEKAHS > BEKAH
BEKISS vb smother with kisses
BEKISSED > BEKISS
BEKISSES > BEKISS
BEKISSING > BEKISS
BEKNAVE vb treat as a knave
BEKNAVED > BEKNAVE
BEKNAVES > BEKNAVE
BEKNAVING > BEKNAVE
BEKNIGHT vb esteem
BEKNIGHTS > BEKNIGHT
BEKNOT vb tie a knot or knots in
BEKNOTS > BEKNOT
BEKNOTTED > BEKNOT
BEKNOWN adj known about
BEL n unit for comparing two power levels or measuring the intensity of a sound
BELABOR same as **> BELABOUR**
BELABORED > BELABOR
BELABORS > BELABOR
BELABOUR vb attack verbally or physically
BELABOURS > BELABOUR

BELACE vb decorate with lace
BELACED > BELACE
BELACES > BELACE
BELACING > BELACE
BELADIED > BELADY
BELADIES > BELADY
BELADY vb call a lady
BELADYING > BELADY
BELAH n Australian tree which yields a useful timber
BELAHS > BELAH
BELAMIES > BELAMY
BELAMOUR n beloved person
BELAMOURE n loved one
BELAMOURS > BELAMOUR
BELAMY n close friend
BELAR same as **>** BELAH
BELARS > BELAR
BELATE vb cause to be late
BELATED adj late or too late
BELATEDLY > BELATED
BELATES > BELATE
BELATING > BELATE
BELAUD vb praise highly
BELAUDED > BELAUD
BELAUDING > BELAUD
BELAUDS > BELAUD
BELAY vb secure a line to a pin or cleat ▷ n attachment (of a climber) to a mountain
BELAYED > BELAY
BELAYER > BELAY
BELAYERS > BELAY
BELAYING > BELAY
BELAYS > BELAY
BELCH vb expel wind from the stomach noisily through the mouth ▷ n act of belching
BELCHED > BELCH
BELCHER > BELCH
BELCHERS > BELCH
BELCHES > BELCH
BELCHING > BELCH
BELDAM n old woman, esp an ugly or malicious one
BELDAME same as **>** BELDAM
BELDAMES > BELDAME
BELDAMS > BELDAM
BELEAGUER vb trouble persistently
BELEAP vb leap over
BELEAPED > BELEAP
BELEAPING > BELEAP
BELEAPS > BELEAP
BELEAPT > BELEAP
BELEE vb put on sheltered side
BELEED > BELEE
BELEEING > BELEE
BELEES > BELEE
BELEMNITE n type of extinct marine mollusc related to the cuttlefish
BELEMNOID adj shaped like a dart
BELFRIED adj with a belfry
BELFRIES > BELFRY
BELFRY n part of a tower where bells are hung
BELGA n former Belgian monetary unit worth five francs
BELGARD n kind gaze
BELGARDS > BELGARD

BELGAS > BELGA

BELGICISM n word used by Belgians when speaking French or Dutch

BELIE vb show to be untrue

BELIED > BELIE

BELIEF n faith or confidence

BELIEFS > BELIEF

BELIER > BELIE

BELIERS > BELIE

BELIES > BELIE

BELIEVE vb accept as true or real

BELIEVED > BELIEVE

BELIEVER > BELIEVE

BELIEVERS > BELIEVE

BELIEVES > BELIEVE

BELIEVING > BELIEVE

BELIKE adv perhaps

BELIQUOR vb cause to be drunk

BELIQUORS > BELIQUOR

BELITTLE vb treat as having little value or importance

BELITTLED > BELITTLE

BELITTLER > BELITTLE

BELITTLES > BELITTLE

BELIVE adv speedily

BELL n hollow cup-shaped instrument that emits a ringing sound when struck ▷ vb utter (such a sound)

BELLBIND n bindweed-type climber

BELLBINDS > BELLBIND

BELLBIRD n Australasian bird with bell-like call

BELLBIRDS > BELLBIRD

BELLBOY n man or boy employed to carry luggage and answer calls for service

BELLBOYS > BELLBOY

BELLBUOY n buoy with a bell

BELLBUOYS > BELLBUOY

BELLCAST adj relating to a style of roof with a bell shape

BELLCOTE n small roofed structure for bell

BELLCOTES > BELLCOTE

BELLE n beautiful woman, esp the most attractive woman at a function

BELLED > BELL

BELLEEK n kind of thin fragile porcelain with a lustrous glaze

BELLEEKS > BELLEEK

BELLES > BELLE

BELLETER n person who makes bells

BELLETERS > BELLETER

BELLHOP same as > BELLBOY

BELLHOPS > BELLHOP

BELLIBONE n beautiful and good woman

BELLICOSE adj warlike and aggressive

BELLIED > BELLY

BELLIES > BELLY

BELLING > BELL

BELLINGS > BELL

BELLINI n Prosecco and peach cocktail

BELLINIS > BELLINI

BELLMAN n man who rings a bell, esp (formerly) a town crier

BELLMEN > BELLMAN

BELLOCK vb shout

BELLOCKED > BELLOCK

BELLOCKS > BELLOCK

BELLOW vb make a low deep cry like that of a bull ▷ n loud deep roar

BELLOWED > BELLOW

BELLOWER > BELLOW

BELLOWERS > BELLOW

BELLOWING n act of bellowing

BELLOWS pl n instrument for pumping a stream of air into something

BELLPULL n handle, rope, or cord pulled to operate a doorbell or servant's bell

BELLPULLS > BELLPULL

BELLS > BELL

BELLWORT n N American plant with slender bell-shaped yellow flowers

BELLWORTS > BELLWORT

BELLY n part of the body of a vertebrate which contains the intestines ▷ vb (cause to) swell out

BELLYACHE n pain in the abdomen ▷ vb complain repeatedly

BELLYBAND n strap around the belly of a draught animal, holding the shafts of a vehicle

BELLYBOAT n type of life jacket

BELLYFLOP vb perform a dive into water in which the body lands horizontally

BELLYFUL n more than one can tolerate

BELLYFULS > BELLYFUL

BELLYING > BELLY

BELLYINGS > BELLY

BELLYLIKE > BELLY

BELOMANCY n art of divination using arrows

BELON n type of oyster

BELONG vb be the property of

BELONGED > BELONG

BELONGER n native-born Caribbean

BELONGERS > BELONGER

BELONGING n secure relationship

BELONGS > BELONG

BELONS > BELON

BELOVE vb love

BELOVED adj dearly loved ▷ n person dearly loved

BELOVEDS > BELOVED

BELOVES > BELOVE

BELOVING > BELOVE

BELOW adv at or to a position lower than, under ▷ prep at or to a position lower than

BELOWS same as > BELLOWS

BELS > BEL

BELT n band of cloth, leather, etc, worn usu around the waist ▷ vb fasten with a belt

BELTED > BELT

BELTER n outstanding person or event

BELTERS > BELTER

BELTING n material used to make a bell or belts ▷ adj excellent

BELTINGS > BELTING

BELTLESS > BELT

BELTLIKE adj like a belt

BELTLINE n line separating car's windows from main body

BELTLINES > BELTLINE

BELTMAN n (formerly) a member of a beach life-saving team

BELTMEN > BELTMAN

BELTS > BELT

BELTWAY n people and institutions located in the area bounded by the Washington Beltway

BELTWAYS > BELTWAY

BELUGA n large white sturgeon

BELUGAS > BELUGA

BELVEDERE n building designed and situated to look out on pleasant scenery

BELYING > BELIE

BEMA n speaker's platform in the assembly in ancient Athens

BEMAD vb cause to become mad

BEMADAM vb call a person madam

BEMADAMED > BEMADAM

BEMADAMS > BEMADAM

BEMADDED > BEMAD

BEMADDEN vb cause to become mad

BEMADDENS > BEMADDEN

BEMADDING > BEMAD

BEMADS > BEMAD

BEMAS > BEMA

BEMATA > BEMA

BEMAUL vb maul

BEMAULED > BEMAUL

BEMAULING > BEMAUL

BEMAULS > BEMAUL

BEMAZED adj amazed

BEMBEX n type of wasp

BEMBEXES > BEMBEX

BEMBIX same as > BEMBEX

BEMBIXES > BEMBIX

BEMEAN a less common word for > DEMEAN

BEMEANED > BEMEAN

BEMEANING > BEMEAN

BEMEANS > BEMEAN

BEMEANT > BEMEAN

BEMEDAL vb decorate with medals

BEMEDALED > BEMEDAL

BEMEDALS > BEMEDAL

BEMETE vb measure

BEMETED > BEMETE

BEMETES > BEMETE

BEMETING > BEMETE

BEMINGLE vb mingle

BEMINGLED > BEMINGLE

BEMINGLES > BEMINGLE

BEMIRE vb soil with or as if with mire

BEMIRED > BEMIRE

BEMIRES > BEMIRE

BEMIRING > BEMIRE

BEMIST vb cloud with mist

BEMISTED > BEMIST

BEMISTING > BEMIST

BEMISTS > BEMIST

BEMIX vb mix thoroughly

BEMIXED > BEMIX

BEMIXES > BEMIX

BEMIXING > BEMIX

BEMIXT > BEMIX

BEMOAN vb express sorrow or dissatisfaction about

BEMOANED > BEMOAN

BEMOANER > BEMOAN

BEMOANERS > BEMOAN

BEMOANING > BEMOAN

BEMOANS > BEMOAN

BEMOCK vb mock

BEMOCKED > BEMOCK

BEMOCKING > BEMOCK

BEMOCKS > BEMOCK

BEMOIL vb soil with mud

BEMOILED > BEMOIL

BEMOILING > BEMOIL

BEMOILS > BEMOIL

BEMONSTER vb treat as monster

BEMOUTH vb endow with a mouth

BEMOUTHED > BEMOUTH

BEMOUTHS > BEMOUTH

BEMUD vb cover with mud

BEMUDDED > BEMUD

BEMUDDING > BEMUD

BEMUDDLE vb confound

BEMUDDLED > BEMUDDLE

BEMUDDLES > BEMUDDLE

BEMUDS > BEMUD

BEMUFFLE vb muffle up

BEMUFFLED > BEMUFFLE

BEMUFFLES > BEMUFFLE

BEMURMUR vb murmur at

BEMURMURS > BEMURMUR

BEMUSE vb confuse

BEMUSED adj puzzled or confused

BEMUSEDLY > BEMUSED

BEMUSES > BEMUSE

BEMUSING > BEMUSE

BEMUZZLE vb put muzzle on

BEMUZZLED > BEMUZZLE

BEMUZZLES > BEMUZZLE

BEN n mountain peak ▷ adv in ▷ adj inner

BENADRYL n tradename of an antihistamine drug used in sleeping tablets

BENADRYLS > BENADRYL

BENAME an archaic word for > NAME

BENAMED > BENAME

BENAMES > BENAME

BENAMING > BENAME

BENCH n long seat ▷ vb put a person on a bench

BENCHED > BENCH

BENCHER n member of the governing body of one of the Inns of Court

BENCHERS > BENCHER

BENCHES > BENCH

BENCHIER > BENCHY

BENCHIEST > BENCHY

BENCHING > BENCH

BENCHLAND n level ground at foot of mountains

BENCHLESS > BENCH

BENCHMARK n criterion by which to measure something ▷ vb measure or test against a benchmark

BENCHTOP adj for use at bench ▷ n flat surface area

BENCHTOPS > BENCHTOP

BENCHY adj (of a hillside) hollowed out in benches

BEND vb (cause to) form a curve ▷ n curved part

BENDABLE > BEND

BENDAY vb (printing) reproduce using Benday technique

BENDAYED > BENDAY

BENDAYING > BENDAY

BENDAYS > BENDAY

BENDED > BEND

BENDEE same as > BENDY

BENDEES > BENDEE

BENDER n makeshift shelter

BENDERS > BENDER

BENDIER > BENDY

BENDIEST > BENDY

BENDINESS n state of being bendy

BENDING n curving action

BENDINGLY > BEND

BENDINGS > BENDING

BENDLET n narrow diagonal stripe on heraldic shield

BENDLETS > BENDLET

BENDS > BEND

BENDWAYS same as > BENDWISE

BENDWISE adv diagonally

BENDY adj flexible or pliable ▷ n okra

BENDYS > BENDY

BENE n blessing

BENEATH prep below ▷ adv below

BENEDICK n recently married man

BENEDICKS > BENEDICK

BENEDICT n newly married man

BENEDICTS > BENEDICT

BENEDIGHT adj blessed

BENEFACT vb be benefactor to

BENEFACTS > BENEFACT

BENEFIC adj rare word for beneficent

BENEFICE n church office providing its holder with an income ▷ vb provide with a benefice

BENEFICED > BENEFICE

BENEFICES > BENEFICE

BENEFIT n something that improves or promotes ▷ vb do or receive good

BENEFITED > BENEFIT

BENEFITER > BENEFIT

BENEFITS > BENEFIT

BENEMPT a past participle of > BENAME

BENEMPTED > BENEMPT

BENES > BENE

BENET vb trap (something) in a net

BENETS > BENET

BENETTED > BENET

BENETTING > BENET

BENGA n type of Kenyan popular music featuring guitars

BENGALINE n heavy corded fabric, esp silk with woollen or cotton cord

BENGAS > BENGA

BENI n sesame plant

BENIGHT vb shroud in darkness

BENIGHTED adj ignorant or uncultured

BENIGHTEN same as > BENIGHT

BENIGHTER > BENIGHT

BENIGHTS > BENIGHT

BENIGN adj showing kindliness

BENIGNANT adj kind or gracious

BENIGNER > BENIGN

BENIGNEST > BENIGN

BENIGNITY n kindliness

BENIGNLY > BENIGN

BENIS > BENI

BENISEED n sesame

BENISEEDS > BENISEED

BENISON n blessing, esp a spoken one

BENISONS > BENISON

BENITIER n basin for holy water

BENITIERS > BENITIER

BENJ another word for > BHANG

BENJAMIN same as > BENZOIN

BENJAMINS > BENJAMIN

BENJES > BENJ

BENNE another name for > SESAME

BENNES > BENNE

BENNET n Eurasian and N African plant with yellow flowers

BENNETS > BENNET

BENNI n sesame

BENNIES > BENNY

BENNIS > BENNI

BENNY n US word for a man's overcoat

BENOMYL n fungicide

BENOMYLS > BENOMYL

BENS > BEN

BENT adj not straight ▷ n personal inclination, propensity, or aptitude

BENTGRASS n variety of grass

BENTHAL > BENTHOS

BENTHIC > BENTHOS

BENTHOAL > BENTHOS

BENTHON same as > BENTHOS

BENTHONIC > BENTHOS

BENTHONS > BENTHON

BENTHOS n animals and plants living at the bottom of a sea or lake

BENTHOSES > BENTHOS

BENTIER > BENTY

BENTIEST > BENTY

BENTO n thin lightweight box used in Japanese cuisine

BENTONITE n valuable clay, formed by the decomposition of volcanic ash, that swells as

it absorbs water: used as a filler in the building, paper, and pharmaceutical industries

BENTOS > BENTO

BENTS > BENT

BENTWOOD n wood bent in moulds, used mainly for furniture ▷ adj made from such wood

BENTWOODS > BENTWOOD

BENTY adj covered with bentgrass

BENUMB vb make numb or powerless

BENUMBED > BENUMB

BENUMBING > BENUMB

BENUMBS > BENUMB

BENZAL n transparent crystalline substance

BENZALS > BENZAL

BENZENE n flammable poisonous liquid used as a solvent, insecticide, etc

BENZENES > BENZENE

BENZENOID adj similar to benzene

BENZIDIN same as > BENZIDINE

BENZIDINE n grey or reddish poisonous crystalline powder

BENZIDINS > BENZIDIN

BENZIL n yellow compound radical

BENZILS > BENZIL

BENZIN same as > BENZINE

BENZINE n volatile liquid used as a solvent

BENZINES > BENZINE

BENZINS > BENZIN

BENZOATE n any salt or ester of benzoic acid

BENZOATES > BENZOATE

BENZOIC adj of, containing, or derived from benzoic acid or benzoin

BENZOIN n gum resin used in ointments, perfume, etc

BENZOINS > BENZOIN

BENZOL n crude form of benzene

BENZOLE same as > BENZOL

BENZOLES > BENZOLE

BENZOLINE n unpurified benzene

BENZOLS > BENZOL

BENZOYL n type of monovalent radical

BENZOYLS > BENZOYL

BENZYL n molecular fragment of certain alcohols and solvents

BENZYLIC > BENZYL

BENZYLS > BENZYL

BEPAINT vb dye; paint

BEPAINTED > BEPAINT

BEPAINTS > BEPAINT

BEPAT vb pat

BEPATCHED adj mended with or covered in patches

BEPATS > BEPAT

BEPATTED > BEPAT

BEPATTING > BEPAT

BEPEARL vb decorate with pearls

BEPEARLED > BEPEARL

BEPEARLS > BEPEARL

BEPELT vb pelt energetically

BEPELTED > BEPELT

BEPELTING > BEPELT

BEPELTS > BEPELT

BEPEPPER vb shower with small missiles

BEPEPPERS > BEPEPPER

BEPESTER vb pester persistently

BEPESTERS > BEPESTER

BEPIMPLE vb form pimples on

BEPIMPLED > BEPIMPLE

BEPIMPLES > BEPIMPLE

BEPITIED > BEPITY

BEPITIES > BEPITY

BEPITY vb feel great pity for

BEPITYING > BEPITY

BEPLASTER vb cover in thick plaster

BEPLUMED adj decorated with feathers

BEPOMMEL vb beat vigorously

BEPOMMELS > BEPOMMEL

BEPOWDER vb cover with powder

BEPOWDERS > BEPOWDER

BEPRAISE vb praise highly

BEPRAISED > BEPRAISE

BEPRAISES > BEPRAISE

BEPROSE vb (of poetry) reduce to prose

BEPROSED > BEPROSE

BEPROSES > BEPROSE

BEPROSING > BEPROSE

BEPUFF vb puff up

BEPUFFED > BEPUFF

BEPUFFING > BEPUFF

BEPUFFS > BEPUFF

BEQUEATH vb dispose of (property) as in a will

BEQUEATHS > BEQUEATH

BEQUEST n legal gift of money or property by someone who has died

BEQUESTS > BEQUEST

BERAKE vb rake thoroughly

BERAKED > BERAKE

BERAKES > BERAKE

BERAKING > BERAKE

BERASCAL vb accuse of being rascal

BERASCALS > BERASCAL

BERATE vb scold harshly

BERATED > BERATE

BERATES > BERATE

BERATING > BERATE

BERAY vb soil; defile

BERAYED > BERAY

BERAYING > BERAY

BERAYS > BERAY

BERBER same as > BERBERE

BERBERE n hot-tasting Ethiopian paste

BERBERES > BERBERE

BERBERIN same as > BERBERINE

BERBERINE n yellow bitter-tasting alkaloid obtained from barberry

BERBERINS > BERBERIN

BERBERIS n shrub with red berries

BERBERS > BERBER

b

BERBICE n as in berbice chair large armchair with long arms that can be folded inwards to act as leg rests

BERCEAU n arched trellis for climbing plants

BERCEAUX > BERCEAU

BERCEUSE n lullaby

BERCEUSES > BERCEUSE

BERDACHE n Native American transvestite

BERDACHES > BERDACHE

BERDASH same as > BERDACHE

BERDASHES > BERDASH

BERE n barley

BEREAVE vb deprive (of) something or someone valued, esp through death

BEREAVED adj having recently lost a close friend or relative through death

BEREAVEN > BEREAVE

BEREAVER > BEREAVE

BEREAVERS > BEREAVE

BEREAVES > BEREAVE

BEREAVING > BEREAVE

BEREFT adj deprived

BERES > BERE

BERET n round flat close-fitting brimless cap

BERETS > BERET

BERETTA n type of pistol

BERETTAS > BERETTA

BERG n iceberg

BERGALL n fish of the wrasse family

BERGALLS > BERGALL

BERGAMA n type of Turkish rug

BERGAMAS > BERGAMA

BERGAMASK n person from Bergamo

BERGAMOT n small Asian tree, the fruit of which yields an oil used in perfumery

BERGAMOTS > BERGAMOT

BERGANDER n species of duck

BERGEN n large rucksack with a capacity of over 50 litres

BERGENIA n evergreen ground-covering plant

BERGENIAS > BERGENIA

BERGENS > BERGEN

BERGERE n type of French armchair

BERGERES > BERGERE

BERGFALL n avalanche

BERGFALLS > BERGFALL

BERGHAAN same as > BERGMEHL

BERGHAANS > BERGHAAN

BERGMEHL n light powdery variety of calcite

BERGMEHLS > BERGMEHL

BERGOMASK same as > BERGAMASK

BERGS > BERG

BERGYLT n large northern marine food fish

BERGYLTS > BERGYLT

BERHYME vb mention in poetry

BERHYMED > BERHYME

BERHYMES > BERHYME

BERHYMING > BERHYME

BERIBERI n disease caused by dietary deficiency of thiamine

BERIBERIS > BERIBERI

BERIMBAU n Brazilian single-stringed bowed instrument, used to accompany capoeira

BERIMBAUS > BERIMBAU

BERIME same as > BERHYME

BERIMED > BERIME

BERIMES > BERIME

BERIMING > BERIME

BERINGED adj wearing a ring or rings

BERK n stupid person

BERKELIUM n radioactive element

BERKO adj berserk

BERKS > BERK

BERLEY n bait scattered on water to attract fish ▷ vb scatter (bait) on water

BERLEYED > BERLEY

BERLEYING > BERLEY

BERLEYS > BERLEY

BERLIN n fine wool yarn used for tapestry work, etc

BERLINE same as > BERLIN

BERLINES > BERLINE

BERLINS > BERLIN

BERM n narrow grass strip between the road and the footpath in a residential area ▷ vb create a berm

BERME same as > BERM

BERMED > BERM

BERMES > BERME

BERMING > BERM

BERMS > BERM

BERMUDAS pl n close-fitting shorts that come down to the knees

BERNICLE n barnacle goose

BERNICLES > BERNICLE

BEROB vb rob

BEROBBED > BEROB

BEROBBING > BEROB

BEROBED adj wearing a robe

BEROBS > BEROB

BEROUGED adj wearing rouge

BERRET same as > BERET

BERRETS > BERRET

BERRETTA same as > BIRETTA

BERRETTAS > BERRETTA

BERRIED > BERRY

BERRIES > BERRY

BERRIGAN n Australian tree with hanging branches

BERRIGANS > BERRIGAN

BERRY n small soft stoneless fruit ▷ vb bear or produce berries

BERRYING > BERRY

BERRYINGS > BERRY

BERRYLESS > BERRY

BERRYLIKE > BERRY

BERSEEM n Mediterranean clover grown as a forage crop and to improve the soil

BERSEEMS > BERSEEM

BERSERK adj frenziedly violent or destructive ▷ n fearsome Norse warrior

BERSERKER same as > BERSERK

BERSERKLY > BERSERK

BERSERKS > BERSERK

BERTH n bunk in a ship or train ▷ vb dock (a ship)

BERTHA n wide deep capelike collar, often of lace, usually to cover up a low neckline

BERTHAGE n place for mooring boats

BERTHAGES > BERTHAGE

BERTHAS > BERTHA

BERTHE n type of lace collar

BERTHED > BERTH

BERTHES > BERTHE

BERTHING n act of berthing

BERTHINGS > BERTHING

BERTHS > BERTH

BERYL n hard transparent mineral

BERYLINE > BERYL

BERYLLIA n beryllium oxide

BERYLLIAS > BERYLLIA

BERYLLIUM n toxic silvery-white metallic element

BERYLS > BERYL

BES variant of > BETH

BESAINT vb give saint status to

BESAINTED > BESAINT

BESAINTS > BESAINT

BESANG > BESING

BESAT > BESIT

BESAW > BESEE

BESCATTER vb strew

BESCORCH vb scorch badly

BESCOUR vb scour thoroughly

BESCOURED > BESCOUR

BESCOURS > BESCOUR

BESCRAWL vb cover with scrawls

BESCRAWLS > BESCRAWL

BESCREEN vb conceal with screen

BESCREENS > BESCREEN

BESEE vb provide for; mind

BESEECH vb ask earnestly

BESEECHED > BESEECH

BESEECHER > BESEECH

BESEECHES > BESEECH

BESEEING > BESEE

BESEEKE archaic form of > BESEECH

BESEEKES > BESEEKE

BESEEKING > BESEEKE

BESEEM vb be suitable for

BESEEMED > BESEEM

BESEEMING > BESEEM

BESEEMLY adj becoming; suitable

BESEEMS > BESEEM

BESEEN > BESEE

BESEES > BESEE

BESES > BES

BESET vb trouble or harass constantly

BESETMENT > BESET

BESETS > BESET

BESETTER > BESET

BESETTERS > BESET

BESETTING adj tempting, harassing, or assailing

BESHADOW vb darken with shadow

BESHADOWS > BESHADOW

BESHAME vb cause to feel shame

BESHAMED > BESHAME

BESHAMES > BESHAME

BESHAMING > BESHAME

BESHINE vb illuminate

BESHINES > BESHINE

BESHINING > BESHINE

BESHIVER vb shatter

BESHIVERS > BESHIVER

BESHONE > BESHINE

BESHOUT vb shout about

BESHOUTED > BESHOUT

BESHOUTS > BESHOUT

BESHREW vb wish evil on

BESHREWED > BESHREW

BESHREWS > BESHREW

BESHROUD vb cover with a shroud

BESHROUDS > BESHROUD

BESIDE prep at, by, or to the side of

BESIDES prep in addition ▷ adv in addition

BESIEGE vb surround with military forces

BESIEGED > BESIEGE

BESIEGER > BESIEGE

BESIEGERS > BESIEGE

BESIEGES > BESIEGE

BESIEGING > BESIEGE

BESIGH vb sigh for

BESIGHED > BESIGH

BESIGHING > BESIGH

BESIGHS > BESIGH

BESING vb sing about joyfully

BESINGING > BESING

BESINGS > BESING

BESIT vb suit; fit

BESITS > BESIT

BESITTING > BESIT

BESLAVE vb treat as slave

BESLAVED > BESLAVE

BESLAVER vb fawn over

BESLAVERS > BESLAVER

BESLAVES > BESLAVE

BESLAVING > BESLAVE

BESLIME vb cover with slime

BESLIMED > BESLIME

BESLIMES > BESLIME

BESLIMING > BESLIME

BESLOBBER vb slobber over

BESLUBBER same as > BESLOBBER

BESMEAR vb smear over

BESMEARED > BESMEAR

BESMEARER > BESMEAR

BESMEARS > BESMEAR

BESMILE vb smile on

BESMILED > BESMILE

BESMILES > BESMILE

BESMILING > BESMILE

BESMIRCH vb tarnish (someone's name or reputation)

BESMOKE vb blacken with smoke

BESMOKED > BESMOKE

BESMOKES > BESMOKE

BESMOKING > BESMOKE

BESMOOTH vb smooth

BESMOOTHS > BESMOOTH
BESMUDGE vb blacken
BESMUDGED > BESMUDGE
BESMUDGES > BESMUDGE
BESMUT vb blacken with smut
BESMUTCH same as > BESMIRCH
BESMUTS > BESMUT
BESMUTTED > BESMUT
BESNOW vb cover with snow
BESNOWED > BESNOW
BESNOWING > BESNOW
BESNOWS > BESNOW
BESOGNIO n worthless person
BESOGNIOS > BESOGNIO
BESOIN n need
BESOINS > BESOIN
BESOM n broom made of twigs ▷ vb sweep with a besom
BESOMED > BESOM
BESOMING > BESOM
BESOMS > BESOM
BESONIAN same as > BEZONIAN
BESONIANS > BESONIAN
BESOOTHE vb soothe
BESOOTHED > BESOOTHE
BESOOTHES > BESOOTHE
BESORT vb fit
BESORTED > BESORT
BESORTING > BESORT
BESORTS > BESORT
BESOT vb make stupid or muddled
BESOTS > BESOT
BESOTTED adj infatuated
BESOTTING > BESOT
BESOUGHT > BESEECH
BESOULED adj having a soul
BESPAKE > BESPEAK
BESPANGLE vb cover or adorn with or as if with spangles
BESPAT > BESPIT
BESPATE > BESPIT
BESPATTER vb splash, eg with dirty water
BESPEAK vb indicate or suggest
BESPEAKS > BESPEAK
BESPECKLE vb mark with speckles
BESPED > BESPEED
BESPEED vb get on with (doing something)
BESPEEDS > BESPEED
BESPICE vb flavour with spices
BESPICED > BESPICE
BESPICES > BESPICE
BESPICING > BESPICE
BESPIT vb cover with spittle
BESPITS > BESPIT
BESPOKE adj (esp of a suit) made to the customer's specifications
BESPOKEN > BESPEAK
BESPORT vb amuse oneself
BESPORTED > BESPORT
BESPORTS > BESPORT
BESPOT vb mark with spots
BESPOTS > BESPOT
BESPOTTED > BESPOT

BESPOUSE vb marry
BESPOUSED > BESPOUSE
BESPOUSES > BESPOUSE
BESPOUT vb speak pretentiously
BESPOUTED > BESPOUT
BESPOUTS > BESPOUT
BESPREAD vb cover (a surface) with something
BESPREADS > BESPREAD
BESPRENT adj sprinkled over
BEST adj most excellent of a particular group etc ▷ adv in a manner surpassing all others ▷ n utmost effort ▷ vb defeat
BESTAD Spenserian form of > BESTEAD
BESTADDE Spenserian form of > BESTEAD
BESTAIN vb stain
BESTAINED > BESTAIN
BESTAINS > BESTAIN
BESTAR vb decorate with stars
BESTARRED > BESTAR
BESTARS > BESTAR
BESTEAD vb serve; assist ▷ adj beset (by)
BESTEADED > BESTEAD
BESTEADS > BESTEAD
BESTED > BEST
BESTEST adj best
BESTI Indian English word for > SHAME
BESTIAL adj brutal or savage
BESTIALLY > BESTIAL
BESTIALS > BESTIAL
BESTIARY n medieval collection of descriptions of animals
BESTICK vb cover with sharp points
BESTICKS > BESTICK
BESTIE n best friend
BESTIES > BESTIE
BESTILL vb cause to be still
BESTILLED > BESTILL
BESTILLS > BESTILL
BESTING > BEST
BESTIR vb cause (oneself) to become active
BESTIRRED > BESTIR
BESTIRS > BESTIR
BESTIS > BESTI
BESTORM vb assault
BESTORMED > BESTORM
BESTORMS > BESTORM
BESTOW vb present (a gift) or confer (an honour)
BESTOWAL > BESTOW
BESTOWALS > BESTOW
BESTOWED > BESTOW
BESTOWER > BESTOW
BESTOWERS > BESTOW
BESTOWING > BESTOW
BESTOWS > BESTOW
BESTREAK vb streak
BESTREAKS > BESTREAK
BESTREW vb scatter or lie scattered over (a surface)
BESTREWED > BESTREW
BESTREWN > BESTREW
BESTREWS > BESTREW
BESTRID > BESTRIDE

BESTRIDE vb have or put a leg on either side of
BESTRIDES > BESTRIDE
BESTRODE > BESTRIDE
BESTROW same as > BESTREW
BESTROWED > BESTROW
BESTROWN > BESTROW
BESTROWS > BESTROW
BESTS > BEST
BESTUCK > BESTICK
BESTUD vb set with, or as with studs
BESTUDDED > BESTUD
BESTUDS > BESTUD
BESUITED adj wearing a suit
BESUNG > BESING
BESWARM vb swarm over
BESWARMED > BESWARM
BESWARMS > BESWARM
BET n wager between two parties predicting different outcomes of an event ▷ vb predict
BETA n second letter in the Greek alphabet, a consonant, transliterated as b
BETACISM vb type of speech impediment
BETACISMS > BETACISM
BETAINE n sweet-tasting alkaloid that occurs in the sugar beet
BETAINES > BETAINE
BETAKE vb as in betake oneself go
BETAKEN > BETAKE
BETAKES > BETAKE
BETAKING > BETAKE
BETAS > BETA
BETATOPIC adj (of atoms) differing in proton number by one, theoretically as a result of emission of a beta particle
BETATRON n type of particle accelerator for producing high-energy beams of electrons
BETATRONS > BETATRON
BETATTER vb make ragged
BETATTERS > BETATTER
BETAXED adj burdened with taxes
BETCHA interj bet you
BETE same as > BEET
BETED > BETE
BETEEM vb accord
BETEEME same as > BETEEM
BETEEMED > BETEEM
BETEEMES > BETEEME
BETEEMING > BETEEM
BETEEMS > BETEEM
BETEL n Asian climbing plant, the leaves and nuts of which can be chewed
BETELNUT n seed of the betel palm
BETELNUTS > BETELNUT
BETELS > BETEL
BETES > BETE
BETH n second letter of the Hebrew alphabet, transliterated as b
BETHANK vb thank

BETHANKED > BETHANK
BETHANKIT n grace spoken before meal
BETHANKS > BETHANK
BETHEL n seaman's chapel
BETHELS > BETHEL
BETHESDA n church building of certain Christian denominations
BETHESDAS > BETHESDA
BETHINK vb cause (oneself) to consider or meditate
BETHINKS > BETHINK
BETHORN vb cover with thorns
BETHORNED > BETHORN
BETHORNS > BETHORN
BETHOUGHT > BETHINK
BETHRALL vb make a slave of
BETHRALLS > BETHRALL
BETHS > BETH
BETHUMB vb (of books) wear by handling
BETHUMBED > BETHUMB
BETHUMBS > BETHUMB
BETHUMP vb thump hard
BETHUMPED > BETHUMP
BETHUMPS > BETHUMP
BETHWACK vb strike hard with flat object
BETHWACKS > BETHWACK
BETID > BETIDE
BETIDE vb happen (to)
BETIDED > BETIDE
BETIDES > BETIDE
BETIDING > BETIDE
BETIGHT > BETIDE
BETIME vb befall
BETIMED > BETIME
BETIMES > BETIME
BETIMING > BETIME
BETING > BETE
BETISE n folly or lack of perception
BETISES > BETISE
BETITLE vb give title to
BETITLED > BETITLE
BETITLES > BETITLE
BETITLING > BETITLE
BETOIL vb tire through hard work
BETOILED > BETOIL
BETOILING > BETOIL
BETOILS > BETOIL
BETOKEN vb indicate or signify
BETOKENED > BETOKEN
BETOKENS > BETOKEN
BETON n concrete
BETONIES > BETONY
BETONS > BETON
BETONY n North American plant
BETOOK > BETAKE
BETOSS vb toss about
BETOSSED > BETOSS
BETOSSES > BETOSS
BETOSSING > BETOSS
BETRAY vb hand over or expose (one's nation, friend, etc) treacherously to an enemy
BETRAYAL > BETRAY
BETRAYALS > BETRAY
BETRAYED > BETRAY

BETRAYER > BETRAY
BETRAYERS > BETRAY
BETRAYING > BETRAY
BETRAYS > BETRAY
BETREAD vb tread over
BETREADS > BETREAD
BETRIM vb decorate
BETRIMMED > BETRIM
BETRIMS > BETRIM
BETROD > BETREAD
BETRODDEN > BETREAD
BETROTH vb promise to marry or to give in marriage
BETROTHAL n engagement to be married
BETROTHED adj engaged to be married ▷ n person to whom one is engaged
BETROTHS > BETROTH
BETS > BET
BETTA n fighting fish
BETTAS > BETTA
BETTED > BET
BETTER adj more excellent than others ▷ adv in a more excellent manner ▷ vb improve upon
BETTERED > BETTER
BETTERING > BETTER
BETTERS > BETTER
BETTIES > BETTY
BETTING > BET
BETTINGS > BET
BETTONG n short-nosed rat kangaroo
BETTONGS > BETTONG
BETTOR n person who bets
BETTORS > BETTOR
BETTY n type of short crowbar
BETUMBLED adj thrown into disorder
BETWEEN adv indicating position in the middle, alternatives, etc ▷ prep at a point intermediate to two other points in space, time, etc
BETWEENS > BETWEEN
BETWIXT adv between
BEUNCLED adj having many uncles
BEURRE n butter
BEURRES > BEURRE
BEVATRON n proton synchrotron at the University of California
BEVATRONS > BEVATRON
BEVEL n slanting edge ▷ vb slope
BEVELED > BEVEL
BEVELER > BEVEL
BEVELERS > BEVEL
BEVELING > BEVEL
BEVELLED > BEVEL
BEVELLER > BEVEL
BEVELLERS > BEVEL
BEVELLING > BEVEL
BEVELMENT > BEVEL
BEVELS > BEVEL
BEVER n snack ▷ vb have a snack
BEVERAGE n drink
BEVERAGES > BEVERAGE
BEVERED > BEVER
BEVERING > BEVER
BEVERS > BEVER

BEVIES > BEVY
BEVOMIT vb vomit over
BEVOMITED > BEVOMIT
BEVOMITS > BEVOMIT
BEVOR n armour protecting lower part of face
BEVORS > BEVOR
BEVUE n careless error
BEVUES > BEVUE
BEVVIED > BEVVY
BEVVIES > BEVVY
BEVVY n alcoholic drink ▷ vb drink alcohol
BEVVYING > BEVVY
BEVY n flock or group
BEWAIL vb express great sorrow over
BEWAILED > BEWAIL
BEWAILER > BEWAIL
BEWAILERS > BEWAIL
BEWAILING > BEWAIL
BEWAILS > BEWAIL
BEWARE vb be on one's guard (against)
BEWARED > BEWARE
BEWARES > BEWARE
BEWARING > BEWARE
BEWEARIED > BEWEARY
BEWEARIES > BEWEARY
BEWEARY vb cause to be weary
BEWEEP vb express grief through weeping
BEWEEPING > BEWEEP
BEWEEPS > BEWEEP
BEWENT > BEGO
BEWEPT > BEWEEP
BEWET vb make wet
BEWETS > BEWET
BEWETTED > BEWET
BEWETTING > BEWET
BEWHORE vb treat as a whore
BEWHORED > BEWHORE
BEWHORES > BEWHORE
BEWHORING > BEWHORE
BEWIG vb adorn with a wig
BEWIGGED > BEWIG
BEWIGGING > BEWIG
BEWIGS > BEWIG
BEWILDER vb confuse utterly
BEWILDERS > BEWILDER
BEWINGED adj having wings
BEWITCH vb attract and fascinate
BEWITCHED > BEWITCH
BEWITCHER > BEWITCH
BEWITCHES > BEWITCH
BEWORM vb fill with worms
BEWORMED > BEWORM
BEWORMING > BEWORM
BEWORMS > BEWORM
BEWORRIED > BEWORRY
BEWORRIES > BEWORRY
BEWORRY vb beset with worry
BEWRAP vb wrap up
BEWRAPPED > BEWRAP
BEWRAPS > BEWRAP
BEWRAPT > BEWRAP
BEWRAY an obsolete word for > BETRAY
BEWRAYED > BEWRAY
BEWRAYER > BEWRAY
BEWRAYERS > BEWRAY
BEWRAYING > BEWRAY

BEWRAYS > BEWRAY
BEY n title in the Ottoman Empire
BEYLIC n province ruled over by a bey
BEYLICS > BEYLIC
BEYLIK same as > BEYLIC
BEYLIKS > BEYLIK
BEYOND prep at or to a point on the other side of ▷ adv at or to the far side of something ▷ n unknown, esp life after death
BEYONDS > BEYOND
BEYS > BEY
BEZ n part of deer's horn
BEZANT n medieval Byzantine gold coin
BEZANTS > BEZANT
BEZAZZ another word for > PIZZAZZ
BEZAZZES > BEZAZZ
BEZEL n sloping edge of a cutting tool
BEZELLESS adj without a bezel
BEZELS > BEZEL
BEZES > BEZ
BEZIL archaic word for > ALCOHOLIC
BEZILS > BEZIL
BEZIQUE n card game for two or more players
BEZIQUES > BEZIQUE
BEZOAR n hard mass, such as a stone or hairball, in the stomach and intestines of animals
BEZOARDIC adj relating to bezoar
BEZOARS > BEZOAR
BEZONIAN n knave or rascal
BEZONIANS > BEZONIAN
BEZZANT same as > BEZANT
BEZZANTS > BEZZANT
BEZZAZZ same as > BEZAZZ
BEZZAZZES > BEZZAZZ
BEZZIE n best friend
BEZZIES > BEZZIE
BEZZLE vb waste (money)
BEZZLED > BEZZLE
BEZZLES > BEZZLE
BEZZLING > BEZZLE
BEZZY same as > BEZZIE
BHAGEE same as > BHAJI
BHAGEES > BHAGEE
BHAI n Indian form of address for a man
BHAIS > BHAI
BHAJAN n singing of devotional songs and hymns
BHAJANS > BHAJAN
BHAJEE same as > BHAJI
BHAJEES > BHAJEE
BHAJI n Indian deep-fried savoury of chopped vegetables in spiced batter
BHAJIA > BHAJI
BHAJIS > BHAJI
BHAKTA n Hindu term for devotee of God
BHAKTAS > BHAKTA
BHAKTI n loving devotion to God leading to nirvana
BHAKTIS > BHAKTI
BHANG n preparation of Indian hemp

BHANGRA n Punjabi folk music combined with elements of Western pop music
BHANGRAS > BHANGRA
BHANGS > BHANG
BHARAL n wild Himalayan sheep
BHARALS > BHARAL
BHAT n currency of Thailand
BHATS > BHAT
BHAVAN n (in India) a large house or building
BHAVANS > BHAVAN
BHAWAN same as > BHAVAN
BHAWANS > BHAWAN
BHEESTIE same as > BHISHTI
BHEESTIES > BHEESTY
BHEESTY same as > BHISHTI
BHEL same as > BAEL
BHELPURI n Indian dish of puffed rice and vegetables
BHELPURIS > BHELPURI
BHELS > BHEL
BHIKHU n fully ordained Buddhist monk
BHIKHUS > BHIKHU
BHIKKHUNI n fully ordained Buddhist nun
BHINDI same as > BINDHI
BHINDIS > BHINDI
BHISHTI n (formerly in India) a water-carrier
BHISHTIS > BHISHTI
BHISTEE same as > BHISHTI
BHISTEES > BHISTEE
BHISTI same as > BHISHTI
BHISTIE same as > BHISHTI
BHISTIES > BHISTIE
BHISTIS > BHISTI
BHOONA same as > BHUNA
BHOONAS > BHOONA
BHOOT same as > BHUT
BHOOTS > BHOOT
BHUNA n Indian sauce
BHUNAS > BHUNA
BHUT n Hindu term for type of ghost
BHUTS > BHUT
BI short for > BISEXUAL
BIACETYL n liquid with strong odour
BIACETYLS > BIACETYL
BIACH n slang term for a subordinate or inferior person
BIACHES > BIACH
BIALI same as > BIALY
BIALIES > BIALY
BIALIS > BIALI
BIALY n type of bagel
BIALYS > BIALY
BIANNUAL adj occurring twice a year ▷ n something that happens biannually
BIANNUALS > BIANNUAL
BIAS n mental tendency, esp prejudice ▷ vb cause to have a bias ▷ adj slanting obliquely ▷ adv obliquely
BIASED > BIAS
BIASEDLY > BIAS
BIASES > BIAS

BIASING > BIAS

BIASINGS > BIAS

BIASNESS > BIAS

BIASSED same as > BIASED

BIASSEDLY same as > BIASEDLY

BIASSES same as > BIASES

BIASSING same as > BIASING

BIATCH same as > BIACH

BIATCHES > BIATCH

BIATHLETE n athlete taking part in biathlon

BIATHLON n contest combining skiing with rifle shooting

BIATHLONS > BIATHLON

BIAXAL same as > BIAXIAL

BIAXIAL adj (esp of a crystal) having two axes

BIAXIALLY > BIAXIAL

BIB vb drink

BIBACIOUS adj tending to drink to excess

BIBASIC adj with two bases

BIBATION n drinking to excess

BIBATIONS > BIBATION

BIBB n wooden support on a mast for the trestletrees

BIBBED > BIB

BIBBER n drinker

BIBBERIES > BIBBERY

BIBBERS > BIBBER

BIBBERY n drinking to excess

BIBBING n act of bibbing

BIBBINGS > BIBBING

BIBBLE n pebble

BIBBLES > BIBBLE

BIBBS > BIBB

BIBCOCK n tap with a nozzle bent downwards

BIBCOCKS > BIBCOCK

BIBE n (in Newfoundland folklore) spirit whose wailing warns of a coming death

BIBELOT n attractive or curious trinket

BIBELOTS > BIBELOT

BIBES > BIBE

BIBFUL n as in spill a bibful divulge secrets

BIBFULS > BIBFUL

BIBIMBAP n Korean rice dish

BIBIMBAPS > BIBIMBAP

BIBLE n any book containing the sacred writings of a religion

BIBLES > BIBLE

BIBLESS > BIB

BIBLICAL adj of, occurring in, or referring to the Bible

BIBLICISM n bible-learning

BIBLICIST > BIBLICISM

BIBLIKE > BIB

BIBLIOTIC n study of books

BIBLIST same as > BIBLICIST

BIBLISTS > BIBLIST

BIBS > BIB

BIBULOUS adj addicted to alcohol

BICAMERAL adj (of a legislature) consisting of two chambers

BICARB n bicarbonate of soda

BICARBS > BICARB

BICAUDAL adj having two tails

BICCIES > BICCY

BICCY n biscuit

BICE n medium blue colour

BICENTRIC adj having two centres

BICEP same as > BICEPS

BICEPS n muscle with two origins, esp the muscle that flexes the forearm

BICEPSES > BICEPS

BICES > BICE

BICHIR n African freshwater fish with an elongated body

BICHIRS > BICHIR

BICHORD adj having two strings for each note

BICHROME adj having two colours

BICIPITAL adj having two heads

BICKER vb argue over petty matters ▷ n petty squabble

BICKERED > BICKER

BICKERER > BICKER

BICKERERS > BICKER

BICKERING > BICKER

BICKERS > BICKER

BICKIE short for > BISCUIT

BICKIES > BICKIE

BICOASTAL adj relating to both the east and west coasts of the US

BICOLOR same as > BICOLOUR

BICOLORED same as > BICOLOUR

BICOLORS > BICOLOR

BICOLOUR adj two-coloured

BICOLOURS > BICOLOUR

BICONCAVE adj (of a lens) having concave faces on both sides

BICONVEX adj (of a lens) having convex faces on both sides

BICORN adj having two horns or hornlike parts

BICORNATE same as > BICORN

BICORNE same as > BICORN

BICORNES > BICORNE

BICORNS > BICORN

BICRON n billionth part of a metre

BICRONS > BICRON

BICURIOUS adj showing an interest in bisexuality

BICUSPID adj having two points ▷ n bicuspid tooth

BICUSPIDS > BICUSPID

BICYCLE n vehicle with two wheels, one behind the other, pedalled by the rider ▷ vb ride a bicycle

BICYCLED > BICYCLE

BICYCLER > BICYCLE

BICYCLERS > BICYCLE

BICYCLES > BICYCLE

BICYCLIC adj of, forming, or formed by two circles, cycles, etc

BICYCLING > BICYCLE

BICYCLIST > BICYCLE

BID vb offer (an amount) in attempting to buy something ▷ n offer of a specified amount, as at an auction

BIDARKA same as > BAIDARKA

BIDARKAS > BIDARKA

BIDARKEE same as > BIDARKA

BIDARKEES > BIDARKEE

BIDDABLE adj obedient

BIDDABLY > BIDDABLE

BIDDEN > BID

BIDDER > BID

BIDDERS > BID

BIDDIES > BIDDY

BIDDING > BID

BIDDINGS > BID

BIDDY n woman, esp an old gossipy one

BIDE vb stay or continue

BIDED > BIDE

BIDENT n instrument with two prongs

BIDENTAL n sacred place where lightning has struck

BIDENTALS > BIDENTAL

BIDENTATE > BIDENT

BIDENTS > BIDENT

BIDER > BIDE

BIDERS > BIDE

BIDES > BIDE

BIDET n low basin for washing the genital area

BIDETS > BIDET

BIDI same as > BEEDI

BIDING > BIDE

BIDINGS > BIDE

BIDIS > BIDI

BIDON n oil drum

BIDONS > BIDON

BIDS > BID

BIELD n shelter ▷ vb shelter or take shelter

BIELDED > BIELD

BIELDIER > BIELDY

BIELDIEST > BIELDY

BIELDING > BIELD

BIELDS > BIELD

BIELDY adj sheltered

BIEN adv well

BIENNALE n event occurring every two years

BIENNALES > BIENNALE

BIENNIA > BIENNIUM

BIENNIAL adj occurring every two years ▷ n plant that completes its life cycle in two years

BIENNIALS > BIENNIAL

BIENNIUM n period of two years

BIENNIUMS > BIENNIUM

BIER n stand on which a body or coffin rests before burial

BIERS > BIER

BIERWURST n type of sausage

BIESTINGS same as > BEESTINGS

BIFACE n prehistoric stone tool

BIFACES > BIFACE

BIFACIAL adj having two faces or surfaces

BIFARIOUS adj having parts arranged in two rows on either side of a central axis

BIFF n blow with the fist ▷ vb give (someone) such a blow

BIFFED > BIFF

BIFFER n someone, such as a sportsperson, who has a reputation for hitting hard

BIFFERS > BIFFER

BIFFIES > BIFFY

BIFFIN n variety of red cooking apple

BIFFING > BIFF

BIFFINS > BIFFIN

BIFFO n fighting or aggressive behaviour ▷ adj aggressive

BIFFOS > BIFFO

BIFFS > BIFF

BIFFY n outdoor toilet

BIFID adj divided into two by a cleft in the middle

BIFIDA > BIFIDUM

BIFIDITY > BIFID

BIFIDLY > BIFID

BIFIDUM n type of bacterium

BIFIDUMS > BIFIDUM

BIFIDUS n bacterium of the human digestive system

BIFIDUSES > BIFIDUS

BIFILAR adj having two parallel threads, as in the suspension of certain measuring instruments

BIFILARLY > BIFILAR

BIFLEX adj bent or flexed in two places

BIFOCAL adj having two different focuses

BIFOCALED adj wearing bifocals

BIFOCALS pl n spectacles with lenses permitting near and distant vision

BIFOLD n something folded in two places

BIFOLDS > BIFOLD

BIFOLIATE adj having only two leaves

BIFORATE adj having two openings, pores, or perforations

BIFORKED adj two-pronged

BIFORM adj having or combining the characteristics of two forms, as a centaur

BIFORMED same as > BIFORM

BIFTAH same as > BIFTER

BIFTAHS > BIFTAH

BIFTER n cigarette

BIFTERS > BIFTER

BIFURCATE vb fork into two branches ▷ adj forked into two branches

BIG adj of considerable size, height, number, or capacity ▷ adv on a grand scale ▷ vb build

BIGA n chariot drawn by two horses
BIGAE > BIGA
BIGAMIES > BIGAMY
BIGAMIST > BIGAMY
BIGAMISTS > BIGAMY
BIGAMOUS > BIGAMY
BIGAMY n crime of marrying a person while still legally married to someone else
BIGARADE n Seville orange
BIGARADES > BIGARADE
BIGAROON same as > BIGARREAU
BIGAROONS > BIGAROON
BIGARREAU n any of several heart-shaped varieties of sweet cherry that have firm flesh
BIGEMINAL adj double; twinned
BIGEMINY n heart complaint
BIGENER n hybrid between individuals of different genera
BIGENERIC adj (of a hybrid plant) derived from parents of two different genera
BIGENERS > BIGENER
BIGEYE n type of red marine fish
BIGEYES > BIGEYE
BIGFEET > BIGFOOT
BIGFOOT n yeti ▷ vb throw one's weight around
BIGFOOTED > BIGFOOT
BIGFOOTS > BIGFOOT
BIGG n type of barley
BIGGED > BIG
BIGGER > BIG
BIGGEST > BIG
BIGGETIER > BIGGETY
BIGGETY adj conceited
BIGGIE n something big or important
BIGGIES > BIGGIE
BIGGIN n plain close-fitting cap
BIGGING > BIG
BIGGINGS > BIG
BIGGINS > BIGGIN
BIGGISH > BIG
BIGGITIER > BIGGITY
BIGGITY adj conceited
BIGGON same as > BIGGIN
BIGGONS > BIGGON
BIGGS > BIGG
BIGGY same as > BIGGIE
BIGHA n in India, unit for measuring land
BIGHAS > BIGHA
BIGHEAD n conceited person
BIGHEADED > BIGHEAD
BIGHEADS > BIGHEAD
BIGHORN n large wild mountain sheep
BIGHORNS > BIGHORN
BIGHT n long curved shoreline ▷ vb fasten or bind with a bight
BIGHTED > BIGHT
BIGHTING > BIGHT
BIGHTS > BIGHT
BIGLY > BIG
BIGMOUTH n noisy, indiscreet, or boastful person

BIGMOUTHS > BIGMOUTH
BIGNESS > BIG
BIGNESSES > BIG
BIGNONIA n tropical American climbing shrub
BIGNONIAS > BIGNONIA
BIGOS n Polish stew
BIGOSES > BIGOS
BIGOT n person who is intolerant, esp regarding religion or race
BIGOTED > BIGOT
BIGOTEDLY > BIGOT
BIGOTRIES > BIGOTRY
BIGOTRY n attitudes, behaviour, or way of thinking of a bigot
BIGOTS > BIGOT
BIGS > BIG
BIGSTICK adj of or relating to irresistible military strength
BIGTIME adj important
BIGUANIDE n any of a class of compounds some of which are used in the treatment of certain forms of diabetes
BIGUINE same as > BEGUINE
BIGUINES > BIGUINE
BIGWIG n important person
BIGWIGS > BIGWIG
BIHOURLY adj occurring every two hours
BIJECTION n mathematical function or mapping that is both an injection and a surjection and therefore has an inverse
BIJECTIVE adj (of a function, relation, etc) associating two sets in such a way that every member of each set is uniquely paired with a member of the other
BIJOU adj (of a house) small but elegant ▷ n something small and delicately worked
BIJOUS > BIJOU
BIJOUX > BIJOU
BIJUGATE adj (of compound leaves) having two pairs of leaflets
BIJUGOUS same as > BIJUGATE
BIJURAL adj relating to two coexisting legal systems
BIJWONER same as > BYWONER
BIJWONERS > BIJWONER
BIKE same as > BICYCLE
BIKED > BIKE
BIKER n person who rides a motorcycle
BIKERS > BIKER
BIKES > BIKE
BIKEWAY n cycle lane
BIKEWAYS > BIKEWAY
BIKIE n member of a motorcycle gang
BIKIES > BIKIE
BIKING > BIKE
BIKINGS > BIKE
BIKINI n woman's brief two-piece swimming costume
BIKINIED > BIKINI

BIKINIS > BIKINI
BIKKIE slang word for > BISCUIT
BIKKIES > BIKKIE
BILABIAL adj of, relating to, or denoting a speech sound articulated using both lips ▷ n bilabial speech sound
BILABIALS > BILABIAL
BILABIATE adj divided into two lips
BILANDER n small two-masted cargo ship
BILANDERS > BILANDER
BILATERAL adj affecting or undertaken by two parties
BILAYER n part of cell membrane
BILAYERS > BILAYER
BILBERRY n bluish-black edible berry
BILBIES > BILBY
BILBO n (formerly) a sword with a marked temper and elasticity
BILBOA same as > BILBO
BILBOAS > BILBOA
BILBOES > BILBO
BILBOS > BILBO
BILBY n Australian marsupial with long pointed ears and grey fur
BILE n bitter yellow fluid secreted by the liver ▷ vb boil
BILECTION same as > BOLECTION
BILED > BILE
BILES > BILE
BILESTONE another name for > GALLSTONE
BILEVEL n hairstyle with two different lengths
BILEVELS > BILEVEL
BILGE n nonsense ▷ vb (of a vessel) to take in water at the bilge
BILGED > BILGE
BILGES > BILGE
BILGIER > BILGE
BILGIEST > BILGE
BILGING > BILGE
BILGY > BILGE
BILHARZIA n disease caused by infestation of the body with blood flukes
BILIAN n type of tree used for its wood
BILIANS > BILIAN
BILIARIES > BILIARY
BILIARY adj of bile, the ducts that convey bile, or the gall bladder ▷ n disease found in dogs
BILIMBI n type of fruit-bearing tree
BILIMBING same as > BILIMBI
BILIMBIS > BILIMBI
BILINEAR adj of or referring to two lines
BILING > BILE
BILINGUAL adj involving or using two languages ▷ n bilingual person
BILIOUS adj sick, nauseous
BILIOUSLY > BILIOUS

BILIRUBIN n orange-yellow pigment in the bile
BILITERAL adj relating to two letters
BILK vb cheat, esp by not paying ▷ n swindle or cheat
BILKED > BILK
BILKER > BILK
BILKERS > BILK
BILKING > BILK
BILKS > BILK
BILL n money owed for goods or services supplied ▷ vb send or present an account for payment to (a person)
BILLABLE adj that can be charged to a client
BILLABONG n stagnant pool in an intermittent stream
BILLBOARD n large outdoor board for displaying advertisements
BILLBOOK n business record of bills received, paid, etc
BILLBOOKS > BILLBOOK
BILLBUG n type of weevil
BILLBUGS > BILLBUG
BILLED > BILL
BILLER n stem of a plant
BILLERS > BILLER
BILLET vb assign a lodging to (a soldier) ▷ n accommodation for a soldier in civil lodgings
BILLETED > BILLET
BILLETEE > BILLET
BILLETEES > BILLET
BILLETER > BILLET
BILLETERS > BILLET
BILLETING n act of billeting
BILLETS > BILLET
BILLFISH n type of fish with elongated jaws, such as the spearfish and marlin
BILLFOLD n small folding case, usually of leather, for holding paper money, documents, etc
BILLFOLDS > BILLFOLD
BILLHEAD n printed form for making out bills
BILLHEADS > BILLHEAD
BILLHOOK n tool with a hooked blade, used for chopping etc
BILLHOOKS > BILLHOOK
BILLIARD n (modifier) of or relating to billiards
BILLIARDS n game played on a table with balls and a cue
BILLIE same as > BILLY
BILLIES > BILLY
BILLING n prominence given in programmes, advertisements, etc, to performers or acts
BILLINGS > BILLING
BILLION n one thousand million ▷ determiner amounting to a billion
BILLIONS > BILLION
BILLIONTH > BILLION
BILLMAN n person who uses a billhook

b

BILLMEN > BILLMAN
BILLON n alloy consisting of gold or silver and a base metal
BILLONS > BILLON
BILLOW n large sea wave ▷ vb rise up or swell out
BILLOWED > BILLOW
BILLOWIER > BILLOWY
BILLOWING > BILLOW
BILLOWS > BILLOW
BILLOWY adj full of or forming billows
BILLS > BILL
BILLY n metal can or pot for cooking on a camp fire
BILLYBOY n type of river barge
BILLYBOYS > BILLYBOY
BILLYCAN same as > BILLY
BILLYCANS > BILLYCAN
BILLYCOCK n any of several round-crowned brimmed hats of felt, such as the bowler
BILLYO n as in like billyo phrase used to emphasize or intensify something
BILLYOH same as > BILLYO
BILLYOHS > BILLYOH
BILLYOS > BILLYO
BILOBAR same as > BILOBATE
BILOBATE adj divided into or having two lobes
BILOBATED same as > BILOBATE
BILOBED same as > BILOBATE
BILOBULAR adj having two lobules
BILOCULAR adj divided into two chambers or cavities
BILSTED n American gum tree
BILSTEDS > BILSTED
BILTONG n strips of dried meat
BILTONGS > BILTONG
BIMA same as > BEMA
BIMAH same as > BEMA
BIMAHS > BIMAH
BIMANAL same as > BIMANOUS
BIMANOUS adj having two hands as opposed to four feet
BIMANUAL adj using or requiring both hands
BIMAS > BIMA
BIMBASHI n Turkish military official
BIMBASHIS > BIMBASHI
BIMBETTE n derogatory term for an attractive but empty-headed young woman
BIMBETTES > BIMBETTE
BIMBLE n as in bimble box type of dense Australian tree
BIMBO n derogatory term for an attractive but empty-headed young person
BIMBOES > BIMBO
BIMBOS > BIMBO
BIMENSAL adj occurring every two months

BIMESTER n period of two months
BIMESTERS > BIMESTER
BIMETAL n material made from two sheets of metal
BIMETALS > BIMETAL
BIMETHYL another word for > ETHANE
BIMETHYLS > BIMETHYL
BIMINI n type of awning for a yacht
BIMINIS > BIMINI
BIMODAL adj having two modes
BIMONTHLY adj every two months ▷ adv every two months ▷ n periodical published every two months
BIMORPH n assembly of piezoelectric crystals
BIMORPHS > BIMORPH
BIN n container for rubbish or for storing grain, coal, etc ▷ vb put in a rubbish bin
BINAL adj twofold
BINARIES > BINARY
BINARISM n state of being binary
BINARISMS > BINARISM
BINARY adj composed of, relating to, or involving two ▷ n something composed of two parts or things
BINATE adj occurring in two parts or in pairs
BINATELY > BINATE
BINAURAL adj relating to, having, or hearing with both ears
BIND vb make secure with or as if with a rope ▷ n annoying situation
BINDABLE > BIND
BINDER n firm cover for holding loose sheets of paper together
BINDERIES > BINDERY
BINDERS > BINDER
BINDERY n bookbindery
BINDHI same as > BINDI
BINDHIS > BINDHI
BINDI n decorative dot worn in the middle of the forehead, esp by Hindu women
BINDING > BIND
BINDINGLY > BIND
BINDINGS > BIND
BINDIS > BINDI
BINDLE n small packet
BINDLES > BINDLE
BINDS > BIND
BINDWEED n plant that twines around a support
BINDWEEDS > BINDWEED
BINE n climbing or twining stem of various plants
BINER n clip used by climbers
BINERS > BINER
BINERVATE adj having two nerves
BINES > BINE
BING n heap or pile, esp of spoil from a mine
BINGE n bout of excessive indulgence ▷ vb indulge in a binge

BINGEABLE adj easy to consume in large quantities
BINGED > BINGE
BINGEING n act of indulging in a binge
BINGEINGS > BINGEING
BINGER > BINGE
BINGERS > BINGER
BINGES > BINGE
BINGHI n Australian offensive slang for an Aboriginal person
BINGHIS > BINGHI
BINGIES > BINGY
BINGING n act of indulging in a binge
BINGINGS > BINGING
BINGLE n minor crash or upset, as in a car or on a surfboard ▷ vb layer (hair)
BINGLED > BINGLE
BINGLES > BINGLE
BINGLING > BINGLE
BINGO n gambling game ▷ sentence substitute cry by the winner of a game of bingo ▷ vb (in Scrabble) play all seven of one's tiles in a single turn
BINGOED > BINGO
BINGOES > BINGO
BINGOING > BINGO
BINGOS > BINGO
BINGS > BING
BINGY Australian slang for > STOMACH
BINIOU n small high-pitched Breton bagpipe
BINIOUS > BINIOU
BINIT n (computing) early form of bit
BINITS > BINIT
BINK n ledge
BINKS > BINK
BINMAN another name for > DUSTMAN
BINMEN > BINMAN
BINNACLE n box holding a ship's compass
BINNACLES > BINNACLE
BINNED > BIN
BINNING > BIN
BINOCLE n binocular-style telescope
BINOCLES > BINOCLE
BINOCS > BINOCULAR
BINOCULAR adj involving both eyes
BINOMIAL adj consisting of two terms ▷ n mathematical expression consisting of two terms, such as $3x + 2y$
BINOMIALS > BINOMIAL
BINOMINAL adj of or denoting the binomial nomenclature ▷ n two-part taxonomic name
BINOVULAR adj relating to or derived from two different ova
BINS > BIN
BINT n derogatory term for a girl
BINTS > BINT
BINTURONG n arboreal SE Asian mammal with long shaggy black hair

BINUCLEAR adj having two nuclei
BIO short for > BIOGRAPHY
BIOACTIVE adj able to interact with living system
BIOASSAY n method of determining the effect of a change to substance ▷ vb subject to a bioassay
BIOASSAYS > BIOASSAY
BIOBANK n large store of human samples for medical research
BIOBANKS > BIOBANK
BIOBLAST same as > BIOPLAST
BIOBLASTS > BIOBLAST
BIOCENOSE adj living together in mutual dependence
BIOCHEMIC adj of or relating to chemical compounds, reactions, etc, occurring in living organisms
BIOCHIP n small glass or silicon plate containing an array of biochemical molecules or structures
BIOCHIPS > BIOCHIP
BIOCIDAL > BIOCIDE
BIOCIDE n substance used to destroy living things
BIOCIDES > BIOCIDE
BIOCLEAN adj free from harmful bacteria
BIOCYCLE n cycling of chemicals through the biosphere
BIOCYCLES > BIOCYCLE
BIODATA n information regarding an individual's education and work history
BIODIESEL n biofuel intended for use in diesel engines
BIODOT n temperature-sensitive device stuck to the skin in order to monitor stress
BIODOTS > BIODOT
BIOENERGY n energy derived from organic matter
BIOETHIC > BIOETHICS
BIOETHICS n study of ethical problems arising from biological research and its applications in such fields as organ transplantation, genetic engineering, or artificial insemination
BIOFACT n item of biological information
BIOFACTS > BIOFACT
BIOFIBERS same as > BIOFIBRES
BIOFIBRES pl n vegetable, animal, or mineral fibres existing in nature which are used by humans
BIOFILM n thin layer of living organisms
BIOFILMS > BIOFILM
BIOFOULER n animal that obstructs or pollutes the environment
BIOFUEL n gaseous, liquid, or solid substance of biological origin used as a

fuel ▷ vb fuel (a vehicle, etc) using biofuel

BIOFUELED adj running on biofuel

BIOFUELS > BIOFUEL

BIOG short form of > BIOGRAPHY

BIOGAS n gaseous fuel produced by the fermentation of organic waste

BIOGASES > BIOGAS

BIOGASSES > BIOGAS

BIOGEN n hypothetical protein

BIOGENIC adj originating from a living organism

BIOGENIES > BIOGENY

BIOGENOUS > BIOGENY

BIOGENS > BIOGEN

BIOGENY n principle that a living organism must originate from a parent form similar to itself

BIOGRAPH vb write biography of

BIOGRAPHS > BIOGRAPH

BIOGRAPHY n account of a person's life by another person

BIOGS > BIOG

BIOHACKER n person who engages in biohacking

BIOHAZARD n material of biological origin that is hazardous to humans

BIOHERM n mound of material laid down by sedentary marine organisms

BIOHERMS > BIOHERM

BIOLOGIC adj of or relating to biology ▷ n drug that is derived from a living organism

BIOLOGICS > BIOLOGIC

BIOLOGIES > BIOLOGY

BIOLOGISM n explaining human behaviour through biology

BIOLOGIST > BIOLOGY

BIOLOGY n study of living organisms

BIOLYSES > BIOLYSIS

BIOLYSIS n death and dissolution of a living organism

BIOLYTIC > BIOLYSIS

BIOMARKER n substance, physiological characteristic, gene, etc that indicates, or may indicate, the presence of disease, a physiological abnormality, or a psychological condition

BIOMASS n total number of living organisms in a given area

BIOMASSES > BIOMASS

BIOME n major ecological community

BIOMES > BIOME

BIOMETER n device for measuring natural radiation

BIOMETERS > BIOMETER

BIOMETRIC adj of any automated system using physiological or behavioural traits as a means of identification

BIOMETRY n analysis of biological data

BIOMINING n using plants, etc to collect precious metals for extraction

BIOMORPH n form or pattern resembling living thing

BIOMORPHS > BIOMORPH

BIONIC adj having a part of the body that is operated electronically

BIONICS n study of biological functions to create electronic versions

BIONOMIC > BIONOMICS

BIONOMICS a less common name for > ECOLOGY

BIONOMIES > BIONOMY

BIONOMIST > BIONOMICS

BIONOMY n laws of life

BIONT n living thing

BIONTIC > BIONT

BIONTS > BIONT

BIOPARENT n biological parent

BIOPHILIA n innate love for the natural world, supposed to be felt universally by humankind

BIOPHOR n hypothetical material particle

BIOPHORE same as > BIOPHOR

BIOPHORES > BIOPHORE

BIOPHORS > BIOPHOR

BIOPIC n film based on the life of a famous person

BIOPICS > BIOPIC

BIOPIRACY n use of wild plants by international companies to develop medicines, without recompensing the countries from which they are taken

BIOPIRATE > BIOPIRACY

BIOPLASM n living matter

BIOPLASMS > BIOPLASM

BIOPLAST n very small unit of bioplasm

BIOPLASTS > BIOPLAST

BIOPLAY n play based on the life of a famous person

BIOPLAYS > BIOPLAY

BIOPSIC > BIOPSY

BIOPSIED > BIOPSY

BIOPSIES > BIOPSY

BIOPSY n examination of tissue from a living body ▷ vb perform a biopsy on

BIOPSYING > BIOPSY

BIOPTIC > BIOPSY

BIOREGION n area in which climate and environment are consistent

BIORHYTHM n complex recurring pattern of physiological states, believed to affect physical, emotional, and mental states

BIOS > BIO

BIOSAFETY n precautions taken to control the cultivation and distribution of genetically modified crops and products

BIOSCOPE n kind of early film projector

BIOSCOPES > BIOSCOPE

BIOSCOPY n examination of a body to determine whether it is alive

BIOSENSOR n device used to monitor living systems

BIOSOCIAL adj relating to the interaction of biological and social elements

BIOSOLID n residue from treated sewage

BIOSOLIDS > BIOSOLID

BIOSPHERE n part of the earth's surface and atmosphere inhabited by living things

BIOSTABLE adj resistant to the effects of microorganisms

BIOSTATIC adj of or relating to the branch of biology that deals with the structure of organisms in relation to their function

BIOSTROME n rock layer consisting of a deposit of organic material, such as fossils

BIOTA n plant and animal life of a particular region or period

BIOTAS > BIOTA

BIOTECH n biotechnology

BIOTECHS > BIOTECH

BIOTERROR n use of biological weapons by terrorists

BIOTIC adj of or relating to living organisms ▷ n living organism

BIOTICAL same as > BIOTIC

BIOTICS > BIOTIC

BIOTIN n vitamin of the B complex, abundant in egg yolk and liver

BIOTINS > BIOTIN

BIOTITE n black or dark green mineral of the mica group

BIOTITES > BIOTITE

BIOTITIC > BIOTITE

BIOTOPE n small area that supports its own distinctive community

BIOTOPES > BIOTOPE

BIOTOXIN n toxic substance produced by a living organism

BIOTOXINS > BIOTOXIN

BIOTRON n climate-control chamber

BIOTRONS > BIOTRON

BIOTROPH n parasitic organism, esp a fungus

BIOTROPHS > BIOTROPH

BIOTURBED adj stirred by organisms

BIOTYPE n group of genetically identical plants within a species, produced by apomixis

BIOTYPES > BIOTYPE

BIOTYPIC > BIOTYPE

BIOVULAR adj (of twins) from two separate eggs

BIOWASTE n organic or biodegradable waste

BIOWASTES > BIOWASTE

BIOWEAPON n living organism or a toxic product manufactured from it, used to kill or incapacitate

BIPACK n obsolete filming process

BIPACKS > BIPACK

BIPAROUS adj producing offspring in pairs

BIPARTED adj divided into two parts

BIPARTITE adj consisting of two parts

BIPARTY adj involving two parties

BIPED n animal with two feet ▷ adj having two feet

BIPEDAL adj having two feet

BIPEDALLY > BIPEDAL

BIPEDS > BIPED

BIPHASIC adj having two phases

BIPHENYL n white or colourless crystalline solid used as a heat-transfer agent

BIPHENYLS > BIPHENYL

BIPINNATE adj (of pinnate leaves) having the leaflets themselves divided into smaller leaflets

BIPLANE n aeroplane with two sets of wings, one above the other

BIPLANES > BIPLANE

BIPOD n two-legged support or stand

BIPODS > BIPOD

BIPOLAR adj having two poles

BIPRISM n prism having a highly obtuse angle to facilitate beam splitting

BIPRISMS > BIPRISM

BIPYRAMID n geometrical form consisting of two pyramids with a common polygonal base

BIRACIAL adj for, representing, or including members of two races

BIRADIAL adj showing both bilateral and radial symmetry, as certain sea anemones

BIRADICAL n molecule with two centres

BIRAMOSE same as > BIRAMOUS

BIRAMOUS adj divided into two parts, as the appendages of crustaceans

BIRCH n tree with thin peeling bark ▷ vb flog with a birch

BIRCHBARK n as in birchbark biting Native Canadian craft in which designs are bitten onto bark from birch trees

BIRCHED > BIRCH

BIRCHEN > BIRCH

BIRCHES > BIRCH

BIRCHING n act of birching

BIRCHINGS > BIRCHING

BIRCHIR same as > BICHIR

BIRCHIRS > BIRCHIR

BIRCHWOOD n wood of the birch tree

b

BIRD *n* creature with feathers and wings, most types of which can fly ▷ *vb* hunt for birds

BIRDBATH *n* small basin or trough for birds to bathe in, usually in a garden

BIRDBATHS > BIRDBATH

BIRDBRAIN *n* stupid person

BIRDCAGE *n* wire or wicker cage in which captive birds are kept

BIRDCAGES > BIRDCAGE

BIRDCALL *n* characteristic call or song of a bird

BIRDCALLS > BIRDCALL

BIRDDOG *n* dog used or trained to retrieve game birds

BIRDDOGS > BIRDDOG

BIRDED > BIRD

BIRDER *n* birdwatcher

BIRDERS > BIRDER

BIRDFARM *n* place where birds are kept

BIRDFARMS > BIRDFARM

BIRDFEED *n* food for birds

BIRDFEEDS > BIRDFEED

BIRDHOUSE *n* small shelter or box for birds to nest in

BIRDIE *n* score of one stroke under par for a hole ▷ *vb* play (a hole) in one stroke under par

BIRDIED > BIRDIE

BIRDIEING > BIRDIE

BIRDIES > BIRDIE

BIRDING > BIRD

BIRDINGS > BIRD

BIRDLIFE *n* birds collectively

BIRDLIFES > BIRDLIFE

BIRDLIKE > BIRD

BIRDLIME *n* sticky substance smeared on twigs to catch small birds ▷ *vb* smear (twigs) with birdlime to catch (small birds)

BIRDLIMED > BIRDLIME

BIRDLIMES > BIRDLIME

BIRDMAN *n* man concerned with birds, such as a fowler or ornithologist

BIRDMEN > BIRDMAN

BIRDS > BIRD

BIRDSEED *n* mixture of various kinds of seeds for feeding cage birds

BIRDSEEDS > BIRDSEED

BIRDSEYE *n* type of primrose

BIRDSEYES > BIRDSEYE

BIRDSFOOT *n* type of plant with pods shaped like a bird's foot

BIRDSHOT *n* small pellets designed for shooting birds

BIRDSHOTS > BIRDSHOT

BIRDSONG *n* musical call of a bird or birds

BIRDSONGS > BIRDSONG

BIRDWATCH *vb* watch birds

BIRDWING *n* type of butterfly

BIRDWINGS > BIRDWING

BIREME *n* ancient galley having two banks of oars

BIREMES > BIREME

BIRETTA *n* stiff square cap worn by the Catholic clergy

BIRETTAS > BIRETTA

BIRIANI *same as* > BIRYANI

BIRIANIS > BIRIANI

BIRIYANI *same as* > BIRIANI

BIRIYANIS > BIRIYANI

BIRK *n* birch tree ▷ *adj* consisting or made of birch

BIRKEN *adj* relating to the birch tree

BIRKIE *n* spirited or lively person ▷ *adj* lively

BIRKIER > BIRKIE

BIRKIES > BIRKIE

BIRKIEST > BIRKIE

BIRKS > BIRK

BIRL *same as* > BURL

BIRLE *same as* > BURL

BIRLED > BIRL

BIRLER > BIRL

BIRLERS > BIRL

BIRLES > BIRLE

BIRLIEMAN *n* judge dealing with local law

BIRLIEMEN > BIRLIEMAN

BIRLING > BIRL

BIRLINGS > BIRL

BIRLINN *n* small Scottish book

BIRLINNS > BIRLINN

BIRLS > BIRL

BIRO *n* tradename of a kind of ballpoint pen

BIROS > BIRO

BIRR *vb* make or cause to make a whirring sound ▷ *n* whirring sound

BIRRED > BIRR

BIRRETTA *same as* > BIRETTA

BIRRETTAS > BIRRETTA

BIRRING > BIRR

BIRROTCH *n* Ethiopian monetary unit

BIRRS > BIRR

BIRSE *n* bristle ▷ *vb* bruise

BIRSED > BIRSE

BIRSES > BIRSE

BIRSIER > BIRSY

BIRSIEST > BIRSY

BIRSING > BIRSE

BIRSLE *vb* roast

BIRSLED > BIRSLE

BIRSLES > BIRSLE

BIRSLING > BIRSLE

BIRSY *adj* bristly

BIRTH *n* process of bearing young ▷ *vb* give birth to

BIRTHDATE *n* date on which a person was born

BIRTHDAY *n* anniversary of the day of one's birth

BIRTHDAYS > BIRTHDAY

BIRTHDOM *n* birthright

BIRTHDOMS > BIRTHDOM

BIRTHED > BIRTH

BIRTHER *n* person who believes Barack Obama was not born in the USA

BIRTHERS > BIRTHER

BIRTHING > BIRTH

BIRTHINGS > BIRTH

BIRTHMARK *n* blemish on the skin formed before birth

BIRTHNAME *n* name person was born with

BIRTHRATE *n* ratio of live births in a specified area, group, etc, to the population of that area, etc, usually expressed per 1000 population per year

BIRTHROOT *n* N American plant whose roots were formerly used by Native Americans as an aid in childbirth

BIRTHS > BIRTH

BIRTHWORT *n* type of climbing plant once believed to ease childbirth

BIRYANI *n* Indian rice-based dish

BIRYANIS > BIRYANI

BIS *adv* twice ▷ *sentence substitute* encore! again!

BISCACHA *same as* > VISCACHA

BISCACHAS > BISCACHA

BISCOTTI > BISCOTTO

BISCOTTO *n* small Italian biscuit

BISCUIT *n* small flat dry sweet or plain cake ▷ *adj* pale brown

BISCUITS > BISCUIT

BISCUITY *adj* reminiscent of biscuit

BISE *n* cold dry northerly wind

BISECT *vb* divide into two equal parts

BISECTED > BISECT

BISECTING > BISECT

BISECTION > BISECT

BISECTOR *n* straight line or plane that bisects an angle

BISECTORS > BISECTOR

BISECTRIX *n* bisector of the angle between the optic axes of a crystal

BISECTS > BISECT

BISERIAL *adj* in two rows

BISERIATE *adj* (of plant parts, such as petals) arranged in two whorls, cycles, rows, or series

BISERRATE *adj* (of leaf margins, etc) having serrations that are themselves serrate

BISES > BISE

BISEXUAL *adj* sexually attracted to both men and women ▷ *n* bisexual person

BISEXUALS > BISEXUAL

BISH *n* mistake

BISHES > BISH

BISHOP *n* clergyman or clergywoman who governs a diocese ▷ *vb* make a bishop

BISHOPDOM *n* jurisdiction of bishop

BISHOPED > BISHOP

BISHOPESS > BISHOP

BISHOPING > BISHOP

BISHOPRIC *n* diocese or office of a bishop

BISHOPS > BISHOP

BISK *a less common spelling of* > BISQUE

BISKS > BISK

BISMAR *n* type of weighing scale

BISMARCK *n* type of pastry

BISMARCKS > BISMARCK

BISMARS > BISMAR

BISMILLAH *interj* in the name of Allah, a preface to all except one of the surahs of the Koran, used by Muslims as a blessing before eating or some other action

BISMUTH *n* pinkish-white metallic element

BISMUTHAL > BISMUTH

BISMUTHIC *adj* of or containing bismuth in the pentavalent state

BISMUTHS > BISMUTH

BISNAGA *n* type of cactus

BISNAGAS > BISNAGA

BISOM *same as* > BESOM

BISOMS > BISOM

BISON *same as* > BUFFALO

BISONS > BISON

BISONTINE *adj* relating to bison

BISPHENOL *n* synthetic organic compound used to make plastics and resins

BISQUE *n* thick rich soup made from shellfish

BISQUES > BISQUE

BISSON *adj* blind ▷ *vb* cause to be blind

BISSONED > BISSON

BISSONING > BISSON

BISSONS > BISSON

BIST *a form of the second person singular of* > BE

BISTABLE *adj* (of an electronic system) having two stable states ▷ *n* bistable system

BISTABLES > BISTABLE

BISTATE *adj* involving two states

BISTER *same as* > BISTRE

BISTERED > BISTER

BISTERS > BISTER

BISTORT *n* Eurasian plant with a spike of small pink flowers

BISTORTS > BISTORT

BISTOURY *n* long surgical knife with a narrow blade

BISTRE *n* water-soluble pigment

BISTRED > BISTRE

BISTRES > BISTRE

BISTRO *n* small restaurant

BISTROIC > BISTRO

BISTROS > BISTRO

BISULCATE *adj* marked by two grooves

BISULFATE *n* bisulphate

BISULFIDE *n* bisulphide

BISULFITE *n* bisulphite

BIT *n* small piece, portion, or quantity

BITABLE > BITE

BITCH *n* female dog, fox, or wolf ▷ *vb* complain or grumble

BITCHED > BITCH

b

BITCHEN same as
> BITCHING
BITCHERY n spiteful talk
BITCHES > BITCH
BITCHFEST n malicious
and spiteful discussion of
people, events, etc
BITCHIER > BITCHY
BITCHIEST > BITCHY
BITCHILY > BITCHY
BITCHING adj wonderful or
excellent
BITCHY adj spiteful or
malicious
BITCOIN n type of digital
currency
BITCOINS > BITCOIN
BITE vb grip, tear, or
puncture the skin, as with
the teeth or jaws ▷ n act of
biting
BITEABLE > BITE
BITEPLATE n device used
by dentists
BITER > BITE
BITERS > BITE
BITES > BITE
BITESIZE adj small enough
to put in the mouth whole
BITEWING n dental X-ray film
BITEWINGS > BITEWING
BITING > BITE
BITINGLY > BITE
BITINGS > BITE
BITLESS adj without a bit
BITMAP n picture created by
colour or shading on a visual
display unit ▷ vb create a
bitmap of
BITMAPPED > BITMAP
BITMAPS > BITMAP
BITO n African and Asian tree
BITONAL adj consisting of
black and white tones
BITOS > BITO
BITOU n as in bitou bush type
of sprawling woody shrub
BITRATE n rate of data
processing
BITRATES > BITRATE
BITS > BIT
BITSER n mongrel dog
BITSERS > BITSER
BITSIER > BITSY
BITSIEST > BITSY
BITSTOCK n handle or stock
of a tool into which a drilling
bit is fixed
BITSTOCKS > BITSTOCK
BITSTREAM n sequence of
digital data
BITSY adj very small
BITT n strong post on the
deck of a ship for securing
lines ▷ vb secure (a line) by
means of a bitt
BITTACLE same as
> BINNACLE
BITTACLES > BITTACLE
BITTE interj you're welcome
BITTED > BITT
BITTEN > BITE
BITTER adj having a sharp
unpleasant taste ▷ n beer
with a slightly bitter taste
▷ adv very ▷ vb make or
become bitter

BITTERED > BITTER
BITTERER > BITTER
BITTEREST > BITTER
BITTERING > BITTER
BITTERISH > BITTER
BITTERLY > BITTER
BITTERN n wading marsh
bird with a booming call
BITTERNS > BITTERN
BITTERNUT n E North
American hickory tree with
thin-shelled nuts and bitter
kernels
BITTERS pl n bitter-tasting
spirits flavoured with plant
extracts
BITTIE n small piece
BITTIER > BITTY
BITTIES > BITTIE
BITTIEST > BITTY
BITTILY adv in a disjointed
way
BITTINESS > BITTY
BITTING > BITT
BITTINGS > BITT
BITTOCK n small amount
BITTOCKS > BITTOCK
BITTOR n bittern
BITTORS > BITTOR
BITTOUR same as > BITTOR
BITTOURS > BITTOUR
BITTS > BITT
BITTUR same as > BITTOR
BITTURS > BITTUR
BITTY adj lacking unity,
disjointed
BITUMED adj covered with
bitumen
BITUMEN n black sticky
substance obtained from tar
or petrol
BITUMENS > BITUMEN
BITURBO n engine with two
turbochargers
BITURBOS > BITURBO
BITWISE adj relating to an
operator in a programming
language that manipulates
bits
BIUNIQUE adj relating to a
one-to-one correspondence
BIVALENCE n semantic
principle that there are
exactly two truth values, so
that every meaningful
statement is either true or
false
BIVALENCY > BIVALENT
BIVALENT adj associated
together in pairs ▷ n
structure consisting of two
homologous chromosomes
BIVALENTS > BIVALENT
BIVALVATE same as
> BIVALVE
BIVALVE adj (of a marine
mollusc) with two hinged
segments to its shell ▷ n sea
creature with a shell
consisting of two hinged
valves
BIVALVED > BIVALVE
BIVALVES > BIVALVE
BIVARIANT same as
> BIVARIATE
BIVARIATE adj (of a
distribution) involving two
random variables, not

necessarily independent of
one another
BIVIA > BIVIUM
BIVINYL another word for
> BUTADIENE
BIVINYLS > BIVINYL
BIVIOUS adj offering a
choice of two different ways
BIVIUM n parting of ways
BIVOUAC n temporary camp
in the open air ▷ vb camp in a
bivouac
BIVOUACKS > BIVOUAC
BIVOUACS > BIVOUAC
BIVVIED > BIVVY
BIVVIES > BIVVY
BIVVY n small tent or shelter
▷ vb camp in a bivouac
BIVVYING > BIVVY
BIWEEKLY adv every two
weeks ▷ n periodical
published every two weeks
BIYEARLY adv every two
years
BIZ n business
BIZARRE adj odd or unusual
▷ n bizarre thing
BIZARRELY > BIZARRE
BIZARRES > BIZARRE
BIZARRO n bizarre person
BIZARROS > BIZARRO
BIZAZZ same as > PIZAZZ
BIZAZZES > BIZAZZ
BIZCACHA same as
> VISCACHA
BIZCACHAS > BIZCACHA
BIZE n dry, cold wind in
France
BIZES > BIZE
BIZJET n small jet plane
used by businesspeople
BIZJETS > BIZJET
BIZNAGA same as
> BISNAGA
BIZNAGAS > BIZNAGA
BIZONAL > BIZONE
BIZONE n place comprising
two zones
BIZONES > BIZONE
BIZZAZZ n combination of
energy and style
BIZZAZZES > BIZZAZZ
BIZZES > BIZ
BIZZIES > BIZZY
BIZZO n empty and
irrelevant talk or ideas
BIZZOS > BIZZO
BIZZY n policeman or
policewoman
BLAB vb reveal (secrets)
indiscreetly
BLABBED > BLAB
BLABBER vb talk without
thinking ▷ n person who
blabs
BLABBERED > BLABBER
BLABBERS > BLABBER
BLABBIER > BLABBY
BLABBIEST > BLABBY
BLABBING > BLAB
BLABBINGS > BLAB
BLABBY adj talking too
much; indiscreet
BLABS > BLAB
BLACK adj of the darkest
colour, like coal ▷ n darkest
colour ▷ vb make black

BLACKBALL vb exclude
from a group ▷ n hard boiled
sweet with black-and-white
stripes
BLACKBAND n type of iron
ore
BLACKBIRD n common
European thrush ▷ vb
(formerly) to kidnap and sell
into slavery
BLACKBODY n hypothetical
body that would be capable
of absorbing all the
electromagnetic radiation
falling on it
BLACKBOY n grass tree
BLACKBOYS > BLACKBOY
BLACKBUCK n Indian
antelope, the male of which
has spiral horns, a dark back,
and a white belly
BLACKBUTT n Australian
eucalyptus tree with hard
wood used as timber
BLACKCAP n brownish-grey
warbler, the male of which
has a black crown
BLACKCAPS > BLACKCAP
BLACKCOCK n male of the
black grouse
BLACKDAMP n air that is low
in oxygen content and high
in carbon dioxide as a result
of an explosion in a mine
BLACKED > BLACK
BLACKEN vb make or
become black
BLACKENED > BLACKEN
BLACKENER > BLACKEN
BLACKENS > BLACKEN
BLACKER > BLACK
BLACKEST > BLACK
BLACKFACE n performer
made up to imitate a Black
person
BLACKFIN n type of tuna
BLACKFINS > BLACKFIN
BLACKFISH n small dark
Australian estuary fish
BLACKFLY n type of black
aphid that infests beans,
sugar beet, and other plants
BLACKGAME n large
N European grouse
BLACKGUM n US tree
BLACKGUMS > BLACKGUM
BLACKHEAD n black-tipped
plug of fatty matter clogging
a skin pore
BLACKING n preparation for
giving a black finish to shoes,
metals, etc
BLACKINGS > BLACKING
BLACKISH > BLACK
BLACKJACK n pontoon or a
similar card game ▷ vb hit
with or as if with a kind of
truncheon
BLACKLAND n dark soil
BLACKLEAD n graphite ▷ vb
colour with blacklead
BLACKLEG n person who
continues to work during a
strike ▷ vb refuse to join a
strike
BLACKLEGS > BLACKLEG
BLACKLIST n list of people
or organizations considered

untrustworthy etc ▷ *vb* put on a blacklist

BLACKLY > BLACK

BLACKMAIL *n* act of attempting to extort money by threats ▷ *vb* (attempt to) obtain money by blackmail

BLACKNESS > BLACK

BLACKOUT *n* extinguishing of all light as a precaution against an air attack

BLACKOUTS > BLACKOUT

BLACKPOLL *n* N American warbler, the male of which has a black-and-white head

BLACKS > BLACK

BLACKSPOT *n* as in *accident blackspot* spot where many accidents occur

BLACKTAIL *n* variety of mule deer having a black tail

BLACKTIP *n* shark of coastal tropical waters

BLACKTIPS > BLACKTIP

BLACKTOP *n* bituminous mixture used for paving

BLACKTOPS > BLACKTOP

BLACKWASH *n* wash for colouring a surface black

BLACKWOOD *n* tall Australian acacia tree which yields highly valued black timber

BLAD *same as* > BLAUD

BLADDED > BLAD

BLADDER *n* sac in the body where urine is held

BLADDERED *adj* intoxicated

BLADDERS > BLADDER

BLADDERY *adj* like a bladder

BLADDING > BLAD

BLADE *n* cutting edge of a weapon or tool

BLADED > BLADE

BLADELESS > BLADE

BLADELIKE > BLADE

BLADER *n* person skating with in-line skates

BLADERS > BLADER

BLADES > BLADE

BLADEWORK *n* rowing technique

BLADIER > BLADY

BLADIEST > BLADY

BLADING *n* act or instance of skating with in-line skates

BLADINGS > BLADING

BLADS > BLAD

BLADY *adj* as in *blady grass* coarse leafy Australasian grass

BLAE *adj* bluish-grey

BLAEBERRY *another name for* > BILBERRY

BLAER > BLAE

BLAES *n* hardened clay or shale

BLAEST > BLAE

BLAFF *n* West Indian stew ▷ *vb* make a barking noise

BLAFFED > BLAFF

BLAFFING > BLAFF

BLAFFS > BLAFF

BLAG *vb* obtain by wheedling or cadging ▷ *n* robbery, esp with violence

BLAGGED > BLAG

BLAGGER > BLAG

BLAGGERS > BLAG

BLAGGING > BLAG

BLAGGINGS > BLAG

BLAGS > BLAG

BLAGUE *n* pretentious but empty talk

BLAGUER > BLAGUE

BLAGUERS > BLAGUE

BLAGUES > BLAGUE

BLAGUEUR *n* bluffer

BLAGUEURS > BLAGUEUR

BLAH *n* worthless or silly talk ▷ *adj* uninteresting ▷ *vb* talk nonsense or boringly

BLAHED > BLAH

BLAHER > BLAH

BLAHEST > BLAH

BLAHING > BLAH

BLAHS > BLAH

BLAIN *n* blister, blotch, or sore on the skin

BLAINS > BLAIN

BLAISE *same as* > BLAES

BLAIZE *same as* > BLAES

BLAM *n* representation of the sound of a bullet being fired ▷ *vb* make the noise of a bullet being fired

BLAMABLE > BLAME

BLAMABLY > BLAME

BLAME *vb* consider (someone) responsible ▷ *n* responsibility for something that is wrong

BLAMEABLE > BLAME

BLAMEABLY > BLAME

BLAMED *euphemistic word for* > DAMNED

BLAMEFUL *adj* deserving blame

BLAMELESS *adj* free from blame

BLAMER > BLAME

BLAMERS > BLAME

BLAMES > BLAME

BLAMING > BLAME

BLAMMED > BLAM

BLAMMING > BLAM

BLAMS > BLAM

BLANCH *vb* become white or pale

BLANCHED > BLANCH

BLANCHER > BLANCH

BLANCHERS > BLANCH

BLANCHES > BLANCH

BLANCHING > BLANCH

BLANCO *n* whitening substance ▷ *vb* whiten (something) with blanco

BLANCOED > BLANCO

BLANCOING > BLANCO

BLANCOS > BLANCO

BLAND *adj* dull and uninteresting ▷ *vb* as in *bland out* become bland

BLANDED > BLAND

BLANDER > BLAND

BLANDEST > BLAND

BLANDING > BLAND

BLANDISH *vb* persuade by mild flattery

BLANDLY > BLAND

BLANDNESS > BLAND

BLANDS > BLAND

BLANK *adj* not written on ▷ *n* empty space ▷ *vb* cross out, blot, or obscure

BLANKED > BLANK

BLANKER > BLANK

BLANKEST > BLANK

BLANKET *n* large thick cloth used as covering for a bed ▷ *adj* applying to a wide group of people, situations, conditions, etc ▷ *vb* cover as with a blanket

BLANKETED > BLANKET

BLANKETS > BLANKET

BLANKETY *n* euphemism for any taboo word

BLANKIE *n* child's security blanket

BLANKIES > BLANKIE

BLANKING > BLANK

BLANKINGS > BLANK

BLANKLY > BLANK

BLANKNESS > BLANK

BLANKS > BLANK

BLANKY *same as* > BLANKIE

BLANQUET *n* variety of pear

BLANQUETS > BLANQUET

BLARE *vb* sound loudly and harshly ▷ *n* loud harsh noise

BLARED > BLARE

BLARES > BLARE

BLARING > BLARE

BLARNEY *n* flattering talk ▷ *vb* cajole with flattery

BLARNEYED > BLARNEY

BLARNEYS > BLARNEY

BLART *vb* sound loudly and harshly

BLARTED > BLART

BLARTING > BLART

BLARTS > BLART

BLASE *adj* indifferent or bored through familiarity

BLASH *n* splash ▷ *vb* splash (something) with liquid

BLASHED > BLASH

BLASHES > BLASH

BLASHIER > BLASHY

BLASHIEST > BLASHY

BLASHING > BLASH

BLASHY *adj* windy and rainy

BLASPHEME *vb* speak disrespectfully of (God or sacred things)

BLASPHEMY *n* behaviour or language that shows disrespect for God or sacred things

BLAST *n* explosion ▷ *vb* blow up (a rock etc) with explosives ▷ *interj* expression of annoyance

BLASTED *adv* extreme or extremely ▷ *adj* blighted or withered

BLASTEMA *n* mass of animal cells that will regenerate a lost organ or tissue

BLASTEMAL > BLASTEMA

BLASTEMAS > BLASTEMA

BLASTEMIC > BLASTEMA

BLASTER > BLAST

BLASTERS > BLAST

BLASTHOLE *n* hole containing an explosive

BLASTIE *n* ugly creature

BLASTIER > BLASTY

BLASTIES > BLASTIE

BLASTIEST > BLASTY

BLASTING *n* distortion of sound caused by overloading certain components of a radio system

BLASTINGS > BLASTING

BLASTMENT *n* something that frustrates one's plans

BLASTOFF *n* launching of a rocket

BLASTOFFS > BLASTOFF

BLASTOID *n* extinct echinoderm found in fossil form

BLASTOIDS > BLASTOID

BLASTOMA *n* tumour composed of embryonic tissue that has not yet developed a specialized function

BLASTOMAS > BLASTOMA

BLASTOPOR *n* opening of the archenteron in the gastrula

BLASTS > BLAST

BLASTULA *n* early form of an animal embryo

BLASTULAE > BLASTULA

BLASTULAR > BLASTULA

BLASTULAS > BLASTULA

BLASTY *adj* gusty

BLAT *vb* cry out or bleat like a sheep

BLATANCY > BLATANT

BLATANT *adj* glaringly obvious

BLATANTLY > BLATANT

BLATE *adj* shy; ill at ease ▷ *vb* babble (something)

BLATED > BLATE

BLATER > BLATE

BLATES > BLATE

BLATEST > BLATE

BLATHER *vb* speak foolishly ▷ *n* foolish talk

BLATHERED > BLATHER

BLATHERER > BLATHER

BLATHERS > BLATHER

BLATING > BLATE

BLATS > BLAT

BLATT *n* newspaper

BLATTANT *same as* > BLATANT

BLATTED > BLAT

BLATTER *vb* prattle

BLATTERED > BLATTER

BLATTERS > BLATTER

BLATTING > BLAT

BLATTS > BLATT

BLAUBOK *n* South African antelope

BLAUBOKS > BLAUBOK

BLAUD *vb* slap

BLAUDED > BLAUD

BLAUDING > BLAUD

BLAUDS > BLAUD

BLAW *vb* blow

BLAWED > BLAW

BLAWING > BLAW

BLAWN > BLAW

BLAWORT *n* harebell

BLAWORTS > BLAWORT

BLAWS > BLAW

BLAY *n* small river fish

BLAYS > BLAY

b

BLAZAR n type of active galaxy

BLAZARS > BLAZAR

BLAZE n strong fire or flame ▷ vb burn or shine brightly

BLAZED > BLAZE

BLAZER n lightweight jacket, often in the colours of a school etc

BLAZERED > BLAZER

BLAZERS > BLAZER

BLAZES pl n hell

BLAZING > BLAZE

BLAZINGLY > BLAZING

BLAZON vb proclaim publicly ▷ n coat of arms

BLAZONED > BLAZON

BLAZONER > BLAZON

BLAZONERS > BLAZON

BLAZONING > BLAZON

BLAZONRY n art or process of describing heraldic arms in proper form

BLAZONS > BLAZON

BLEACH vb make or become white or colourless ▷ n bleaching agent

BLEACHED > BLEACH

BLEACHER > BLEACH

BLEACHERS pl n tier of seats in a sports stadium, etc, that are unroofed and inexpensive

BLEACHERY n place where bleaching is carried out

BLEACHES > BLEACH

BLEACHING > BLEACH

BLEAK adj exposed and barren ▷ n type of fish found in slow-flowing rivers

BLEAKER > BLEAK

BLEAKEST > BLEAK

BLEAKISH > BLEAK

BLEAKLY > BLEAK

BLEAKNESS > BLEAK

BLEAKS > BLEAK

BLEAKY same as > BLEAK

BLEAR vb make (eyes or sight) dim with or as if with tears ▷ adj bleary

BLEARED > BLEAR

BLEARER > BLEAR

BLEAREST > BLEAR

BLEAREYED adj with eyes blurred, as with old age or after waking

BLEARIER > BLEARY

BLEARIEST > BLEARY

BLEARILY > BLEARY

BLEARING > BLEAR

BLEARS > BLEAR

BLEARY adj with eyes dimmed, as by tears or tiredness

BLEAT vb (of a sheep, goat, or calf) utter its plaintive cry ▷ n cry of sheep, goats, and calves

BLEATED > BLEAT

BLEATER > BLEAT

BLEATERS > BLEAT

BLEATING > BLEAT

BLEATINGS > BLEAT

BLEATS > BLEAT

BLEB n fluid-filled blister on the skin

BLEBBIER > BLEB

BLEBBIEST > BLEB

BLEBBING n formation of bleb

BLEBBINGS > BLEBBING

BLEBBY > BLEB

BLEBS > BLEB

BLECH interj expressing disgust

BLED > BLEED

BLEE n complexion; hue

BLEED vb lose or emit blood

BLEEDER n despicable person

BLEEDERS > BLEEDER

BLEEDING > BLEED

BLEEDINGS > BLEED

BLEEDS > BLEED

BLEEP n high-pitched signal or beep ▷ vb make such a noise

BLEEPED > BLEEP

BLEEPER n small portable radio receiver that makes a bleeping signal

BLEEPERS > BLEEPER

BLEEPING > BLEEP

BLEEPS > BLEEP

BLEES > BLEE

BLELLUM n babbler; blusterer

BLELLUMS > BLELLUM

BLEMISH n defect or stain ▷ vb spoil or tarnish

BLEMISHED > BLEMISH

BLEMISHER > BLEMISH

BLEMISHES > BLEMISH

BLENCH vb shy away, as in fear

BLENCHED > BLENCH

BLENCHER > BLENCH

BLENCHERS > BLENCH

BLENCHES > BLENCH

BLENCHING > BLENCH

BLEND vb mix or mingle (components or ingredients) ▷ n mixture

BLENDABLE adj capable of being blended

BLENDE n mineral consisting mainly of zinc sulphide

BLENDED > BLEND

BLENDER n electrical appliance for puréeing vegetables etc

BLENDERS > BLENDER

BLENDES > BLENDE

BLENDING > BLEND

BLENDINGS > BLEND

BLENDS > BLEND

BLENNIES > BLENNY

BLENNIOID n type of small, mainly marine spiny-finned fish with an elongated body, such as the blennies, butterfish, and gunnel

BLENNY n small fish with a tapering scaleless body

BLENT a past participle of > BLEND

BLEOMYCIN n drug used to treat cancer

BLERT n foolish person

BLERTS > BLERT

BLESBOK n S African antelope

BLESBOKS > BLESBOK

BLESBUCK same as > BLESBOK

BLESBUCKS > BLESBUCK

BLESS vb make holy by means of a religious rite

BLESSED adj made holy

BLESSEDER > BLESS

BLESSEDLY > BLESS

BLESSER > BLESS

BLESSERS > BLESS

BLESSES > BLESS

BLESSING > BLESS

BLESSINGS > BLESS

BLEST > BLESS

BLET n state of decay in certain fruits, due to overripening ▷ vb go soft

BLETHER same as > BLATHER

BLETHERED > BLETHER

BLETHERER > BLETHER

BLETHERS > BLETHER

BLETS > BLET

BLETTED > BLET

BLETTING > BLET

BLEUATRE adj blueish

BLEW > BLOW

BLEWART same as > BLAWORT

BLEWARTS > BLEWART

BLEWIT same as > BLEWITS

BLEWITS n type of edible fungus with a pale brown cap and a bluish stalk

BLEWITSES > BLEWITS

BLEY same as > BLAY

BLEYS > BLEY

BLIGHT n person or thing that spoils or prevents growth ▷ vb cause to suffer a blight

BLIGHTED > BLIGHT

BLIGHTER n irritating person

BLIGHTERS > BLIGHTER

BLIGHTIES > BLIGHTY

BLIGHTING > BLIGHT

BLIGHTS > BLIGHT

BLIGHTY n home country; home leave

BLIKSEM interj South African expression of surprise

BLIMBING same as > BILIMBI

BLIMBINGS > BLIMBING

BLIMEY interj exclamation of surprise or annoyance

BLIMP n small airship ▷ vb swell out

BLIMPED > BLIMP

BLIMPERY n complacent or reactionary behaviour

BLIMPING > BLIMP

BLIMPISH adj complacent and reactionary

BLIMPS > BLIMP

BLIMY same as > BLIMEY

BLIN Scots word for > BLIND

BLIND adj unable to see ▷ vb deprive of sight ▷ n covering for a window

BLINDAGE n (esp formerly) a protective screen or structure, as over a trench

BLINDAGES > BLINDAGE

BLINDED > BLIND

BLINDER n outstanding performance

BLINDERS > BLINDER

BLINDEST > BLIND

BLINDFISH n any of various small fishes, esp the cavefish, that have rudimentary or functionless eyes and occur in subterranean streams

BLINDFOLD vb prevent (a person) from seeing by covering the eyes ▷ n piece of cloth used to cover the eyes ▷ adv with the eyes covered by a cloth

BLINDGUT same as > CAECUM

BLINDGUTS > BLINDGUT

BLINDING n sand or grit spread over a road surface to fill up cracks ▷ adj making one blind or as if blind

BLINDINGS > BLINDING

BLINDLESS > BLIND

BLINDLY > BLIND

BLINDNESS > BLIND

BLINDS > BLIND

BLINDSIDE vb take (someone) by surprise

BLINDWORM same as > SLOWWORM

BLING adj flashy ▷ n ostentatious jewellery ▷ vb make ostentatious or flashy

BLINGED > BLING

BLINGER > BLING

BLINGEST > BLING

BLINGIER > BLINGY

BLINGIEST > BLINGY

BLINGING adj flashy and expensive

BLINGLISH n spoken English mixed with Black slang

BLINGS > BLING

BLINGY same as > BLING

BLINI pl n Russian pancakes made of buckwheat flour and yeast

BLINIS same as > BLINI

BLINK vb close and immediately reopen (the eyes) ▷ n act of blinking

BLINKARD n something that twinkles

BLINKARDS > BLINKARD

BLINKED > BLINK

BLINKER vb provide (a horse) with blinkers ▷ n flashing light for sending messages

BLINKERED adj considering only a narrow point of view

BLINKERS same as > BLINKER

BLINKING adv extreme or extremely

BLINKS > BLINK

BLINNED > BLIN

BLINNING > BLIN

BLINS > BLIN

BLINTZ n thin pancake folded over a filling usually of apple, cream cheese, or meat

BLINTZE same as > BLINTZ

BLINTZES > BLINTZE

BLINY same as > BLINI

BLIP n spot of light on a radar screen indicating the position of an object ▷ vb produce such a noise

BLIPPED > BLIP
BLIPPING > BLIP
BLIPS > BLIP
BLIPVERT n very short television advertisement
BLIPVERTS > BLIPVERT
BLISS n perfect happiness ▷ vb make or become perfectly happy
BLISSED > BLISS
BLISSES > BLISS
BLISSFUL adj serenely joyful or glad
BLISSING > BLISS
BLISSLESS > BLISS
BLIST archaic form of > BLESSED
BLISTER n small bubble on the skin ▷ vb (cause to) have blisters
BLISTERED > BLISTER
BLISTERS > BLISTER
BLISTERY > BLISTER
BLIT vb move (a block of data) in a computer's memory
BLITE n type of herb
BLITES > BLITE
BLITHE adj casual and indifferent
BLITHEFUL same as > BLITHE
BLITHELY > BLITHE
BLITHER same as > BLETHER
BLITHERED > BLITHER
BLITHERS > BLITHER
BLITHEST > BLITHE
BLITS > BLIT
BLITTED > BLIT
BLITTER n circuit that transfers large amounts of data within a computer's memory
BLITTERS > BLITTER
BLITTING > BLIT
BLITZ n violent and sustained attack by aircraft ▷ vb attack suddenly and intensively
BLITZED > BLITZ
BLITZER > BLITZ
BLITZERS > BLITZ
BLITZES > BLITZ
BLITZING > BLITZ
BLIVE same as > BELIVE
BLIZZARD n blinding storm of wind and snow ▷ vb (of weather) be stormy with wind and snow
BLIZZARDS > BLIZZARD
BLIZZARDY adj like a blizzard
BLOAT vb cause to swell, as with liquid or air ▷ n abnormal distention of the abdomen in cattle, sheep, etc
BLOATED adj swollen, as with a liquid, air, or wind
BLOATER n salted smoked herring
BLOATERS > BLOATER
BLOATING > BLOAT
BLOATINGS > BLOAT
BLOATS > BLOAT
BLOATWARE n software with more features than necessary

BLOB n soft mass or drop ▷ vb put blobs, as of ink or paint, on
BLOBBED > BLOB
BLOBBIER > BLOB
BLOBBIEST > BLOB
BLOBBING > BLOB
BLOBBY > BLOB
BLOBS > BLOB
BLOC n people or countries combined by a common interest
BLOCK n large solid piece of wood, stone, etc ▷ vb obstruct or impede by introducing an obstacle
BLOCKABLE > BLOCK
BLOCKADE n sealing off of a place to prevent the passage of goods ▷ vb impose a blockade on
BLOCKADED > BLOCKADE
BLOCKADER > BLOCKADE
BLOCKADES > BLOCKADE
BLOCKAGE n act of blocking or state of being blocked
BLOCKAGES > BLOCKAGE
BLOCKBUST vb (try to) bring about the sale of property at a bargain price by stirring up fears of racial change in an area
BLOCKED > BLOCK
BLOCKER n person or thing that blocks
BLOCKERS > BLOCKER
BLOCKHEAD n stupid person
BLOCKHOLE n lines marked near stumps on cricket pitch
BLOCKIE n owner of a small property, esp a farm
BLOCKIER > BLOCKY
BLOCKIES > BLOCKIE
BLOCKIEST > BLOCKY
BLOCKING n interruption of anode current in a valve
BLOCKINGS > BLOCKING
BLOCKISH adj lacking vivacity or imagination
BLOCKS > BLOCK
BLOCKSHIP n ship used to block a river or channel and prevent its being used
BLOCKWORK n wall-building style
BLOCKY adj like a block, esp in shape and solidity
BLOCS > BLOC
BLOG n journal written on-line and accessible to users of the internet ▷ vb write a blog
BLOGGABLE adj interesting enough to be a topic for a blog
BLOGGED > BLOG
BLOGGER > BLOG
BLOGGERS > BLOG
BLOGGIER > BLOGGY
BLOGGIEST > BLOGGY
BLOGGING > BLOG
BLOGGINGS > BLOG
BLOGGY adj characteristic of a blog
BLOGPOST n single posting made as part of a blog
BLOGPOSTS > BLOGPOST
BLOGRING n group of blogs joined in a ring

BLOGRINGS > BLOGRING
BLOGROLL n list of blogs
BLOGROLLS > BLOGROLL
BLOGS > BLOG
BLOKART n single-seat three-wheeled vehicle propelled by the wind
BLOKARTS > BLOKART
BLOKE n man
BLOKEDOM n state of being a bloke
BLOKEDOMS > BLOKEDOM
BLOKEISH adj denoting or exhibiting the characteristics believed typical of an ordinary man
BLOKES > BLOKE
BLOKEY same as > BLOKEISH
BLOKIER > BLOKEY
BLOKIEST > BLOKEY
BLOKISH same as > BLOKEISH
BLONCKET adj blue-grey
BLOND adj (of men's hair) of a light colour ▷ n person, esp a man, having light-coloured hair and skin
BLONDE n fair-haired (person) ▷ adj (of hair) fair
BLONDER > BLONDE
BLONDES > BLONDE
BLONDEST > BLONDE
BLONDINE vb dye hair blonde
BLONDINED > BLONDINE
BLONDINES > BLONDINE
BLONDING n act or an instance of dyeing hair blonde
BLONDINGS > BLONDING
BLONDISH > BLOND
BLONDNESS > BLOND
BLONDS > BLOND
BLOOD n red fluid that flows around the body ▷ vb initiate (a person) to war or hunting
BLOODBATH n massacre
BLOODED adj (of horses, cattle, etc) of good breeding
BLOODFIN n silvery red-finned S American freshwater fish, popular in aquariums
BLOODFINS > BLOODFIN
BLOODIED > BLOODY
BLOODIER > BLOODY
BLOODIES > BLOODY
BLOODIEST > BLOODY
BLOODILY > BLOODY
BLOODING > BLOOD
BLOODINGS > BLOOD
BLOODLESS adj without blood or bloodshed
BLOODLIKE > BLOOD
BLOODLINE n all the members of a family group over generations, esp regarding characteristics common to that group
BLOODLUST n desire to see bloodshed
BLOODRED adj having a deep red colour
BLOODROOT n N American plant with a single whitish flower and a fleshy red root that yields a red dye

BLOODS > BLOOD
BLOODSHED n slaughter or killing
BLOODSHOT adj (of an eye) inflamed
BLOODWOOD n any of several species of Australian eucalyptus that exude a red sap
BLOODWORM n red wormlike aquatic larva of the midge
BLOODWORT n plant with red dye in roots
BLOODY adj covered with blood ▷ adv extreme or extremely ▷ vb stain with blood
BLOODYING > BLOODY
BLOOEY adj out of order; faulty
BLOOIE same as > BLOOEY
BLOOK n book published on a blog
BLOOKS > BLOOK
BLOOM n blossom on a flowering plant ▷ vb (of flowers) open
BLOOMED adj (of a lens) coated to reduce light lost by reflection
BLOOMER n stupid mistake
BLOOMERS pl n woman's baggy underwear
BLOOMERY n place in which malleable iron is produced directly from iron ore
BLOOMIER > BLOOMY
BLOOMIEST > BLOOMY
BLOOMING n act of blooming
BLOOMINGS > BLOOMING
BLOOMLESS > BLOOM
BLOOMS > BLOOM
BLOOMY adj having a fine whitish coating on the surface
BLOOP vb (baseball) hit a ball into air beyond infield
BLOOPED > BLOOP
BLOOPER n stupid mistake
BLOOPERS > BLOOPER
BLOOPIER > BLOOPY
BLOOPIEST > BLOOPY
BLOOPING > BLOOP
BLOOPS > BLOOP
BLOOPY adj (in baseball) relating to a ball hit into the air beyond the infield
BLOOSME archaic form of > BLOSSOM
BLOOSMED > BLOOSME
BLOOSMES > BLOOSME
BLOOSMING > BLOOSME
BLOOTERED adj Scots word meaning drunk
BLOQUISTE n supporter of autonomy for Quebec
BLORE n strong blast of wind
BLORES > BLORE
BLOSSOM n flowers of a plant ▷ vb (of plants) flower
BLOSSOMED > BLOSSOM
BLOSSOMS > BLOSSOM
BLOSSOMY adj full of blossoms
BLOT n spot or stain ▷ vb cause a blemish in or on

b

BLOTCH n discoloured area or stain ▷ vb become or cause to become marked by such discoloration

BLOTCHED > BLOTCH

BLOTCHES > BLOTCH

BLOTCHIER > BLOTCHY

BLOTCHILY > BLOTCHY

BLOTCHING > BLOTCH

BLOTCHY adj covered in or marked by blotches

BLOTLESS > BLOT

BLOTS > BLOT

BLOTTED > BLOT

BLOTTER n sheet of blotting paper

BLOTTERS > BLOTTER

BLOTTIER > BLOTTY

BLOTTIEST > BLOTTY

BLOTTING n blot analysis

BLOTTINGS > BLOTTING

BLOTTO adj extremely drunk

BLOTTY adj covered in blots

BLOUBOK same as > BLAUBOK

BLOUBOKS > BLOUBOK

BLOUSE n woman's shirtlike garment ▷ vb hang or cause to hang in full loose folds

BLOUSED > BLOUSE

BLOUSES > BLOUSE

BLOUSIER > BLOUSY

BLOUSIEST > BLOUSY

BLOUSILY > BLOUSY

BLOUSING > BLOUSE

BLOUSON n short loose jacket with a tight waist

BLOUSONS > BLOUSON

BLOUSY adj loose; blouse-like

BLOVIATE vb discourse at length

BLOVIATED > BLOVIATE

BLOVIATES > BLOVIATE

BLOW vb (of air, the wind, etc) move ▷ n hard hit

BLOWBACK n gases escaping to the rear

BLOWBACKS > BLOWBACK

BLOWBALL n dandelion seed head

BLOWBALLS > BLOWBALL

BLOWBY n leakage of gas past the piston of an engine at maximum pressure

BLOWBYS > BLOWBY

BLOWDART n dart from a blowpipe

BLOWDARTS > BLOWDART

BLOWDOWN n accidental burst of a cooling pipe in a nuclear reactor

BLOWDOWNS > BLOWDOWN

BLOWED > BLOW

BLOWER n mechanical device, such as a fan, that blows

BLOWERS > BLOWER

BLOWFISH a popular name for > PUFFER

BLOWFLIES > BLOWFLY

BLOWFLY n fly that lays its eggs in meat

BLOWGUN same as > BLOWPIPE

BLOWGUNS > BLOWGUN

BLOWHARD n boastful person ▷ adj blustering or boastful

BLOWHARDS > BLOWHARD

BLOWHOLE n nostril of a whale

BLOWHOLES > BLOWHOLE

BLOWIE n bluebottle

BLOWIER > BLOWY

BLOWIES > BLOWIE

BLOWIEST > BLOWY

BLOWINESS > BLOWY

BLOWING n moving of air

BLOWINGS > BLOWING

BLOWJOB vulgar slang term for > FELLATIO

BLOWJOBS > BLOWJOB

BLOWKART n land vehicle with a sail

BLOWKARTS > BLOWKART

BLOWLAMP another name for > BLOWTORCH

BLOWLAMPS > BLOWLAMP

BLOWN > BLOW

BLOWOFF n discharge of a surplus fluid

BLOWOFFS > BLOWOFF

BLOWOUT n sudden loss of air in a tyre

BLOWOUTS > BLOWOUT

BLOWPIPE n long tube from which darts etc are shot by blowing

BLOWPIPES > BLOWPIPE

BLOWS > BLOW

BLOWSE n large, red-faced woman

BLOWSED same as > BLOWSY

BLOWSES > BLOWSE

BLOWSIER > BLOWSY

BLOWSIEST > BLOWSY

BLOWSILY > BLOWSY

BLOWSY adj fat, untidy, and red-faced

BLOWTORCH n small burner producing a very hot flame

BLOWTUBE n tube for blowing air or oxygen into a flame to intensify its heat

BLOWTUBES > BLOWTUBE

BLOWUP n fit of temper

BLOWUPS > BLOWUP

BLOWY adj windy

BLOWZE variant of > BLOWSE

BLOWZED same as > BLOWSY

BLOWZES > BLOWZE

BLOWZIER > BLOWZY

BLOWZIEST > BLOWZY

BLOWZILY > BLOWZY

BLOWZY same as > BLOWSY

BLUB a slang word for > BLUBBER

BLUBBED > BLUB

BLUBBER vb sob without restraint ▷ adj swollen or fleshy ▷ n fat of whales, seals, etc

BLUBBERED > BLUBBER

BLUBBERER > BLUBBER

BLUBBERS > BLUBBER

BLUBBERY adj of, containing, or like blubber

BLUBBING > BLUB

BLUBS > BLUB

BLUCHER n high shoe with laces over the tongue

BLUCHERS > BLUCHER

BLUD n slang term for a friend

BLUDE Scots form of > BLOOD

BLUDES > BLUDE

BLUDGE vb evade work ▷ n easy task

BLUDGED > BLUDGE

BLUDGEON n short thick club ▷ vb hit with a bludgeon

BLUDGEONS > BLUDGEON

BLUDGER n person who scrounges

BLUDGERS > BLUDGER

BLUDGES > BLUDGE

BLUDGING > BLUDGE

BLUDIE Scots form of > BLOODY

BLUDIER > BLUDIE

BLUDIEST > BLUDIE

BLUDS > BLUD

BLUDY same as > BLUDIE

BLUE n colour of a clear unclouded sky ▷ adj of the colour blue ▷ vb make or become blue

BLUEBACK n type of salmon

BLUEBACKS > BLUEBACK

BLUEBALL n type of European herb

BLUEBALLS > BLUEBALL

BLUEBEARD n any man who murders his wife or wives

BLUEBEAT n type of West Indian pop music of the 1960s

BLUEBEATS > BLUEBEAT

BLUEBELL n flower with blue bell-shaped flowers

BLUEBELLS > BLUEBELL

BLUEBERRY n very small blackish edible fruit that grows on a North American shrub

BLUEBILL another name for > SCAUP

BLUEBILLS > BLUEBILL

BLUEBIRD n North American songbird with a blue plumage

BLUEBIRDS > BLUEBIRD

BLUEBLOOD n royal or aristocratic person

BLUEBOOK n (in Britain) a government publication, usually the report of a commission

BLUEBOOKS > BLUEBOOK

BLUEBUCK same as > BLAUBOK

BLUEBUCKS > BLUEBUCK

BLUEBUSH n blue-grey herbaceous Australian shrub

BLUECAP another name for > BLUETIT

BLUECAPS > BLUECAP

BLUECOAT n person who wears blue uniform

BLUECOATS > BLUECOAT

BLUECURLS n North American plant

BLUED > BLUE

BLUEFIN another name for > TUNNY

BLUEFINS > BLUEFIN

BLUEFISH n type of bluish marine food and game fish

BLUEGILL n common N American sunfish, an important freshwater food and game fish

BLUEGILLS > BLUEGILL

BLUEGOWN n in past, pauper, recipient of blue gown on king's birthday

BLUEGOWNS > BLUEGOWN

BLUEGRASS n any of several North American bluish-green grasses

BLUEGUM n widely cultivated Australian tree

BLUEGUMS > BLUEGUM

BLUEHEAD n type of fish

BLUEHEADS > BLUEHEAD

BLUEING > BLUE

BLUEINGS > BLUE

BLUEISH same as > BLUISH

BLUEJACK n type of oak tree

BLUEJACKS > BLUEJACK

BLUEJAY n N American jay

BLUEJAYS > BLUEJAY

BLUEJEANS n blue denim jeans

BLUELINE n blue-toned photographic proof

BLUELINER n machine for making blueprints

BLUELINES > BLUELINE

BLUELY > BLUE

BLUEMOUTH n type of deepwater fish

BLUENESS > BLUE

BLUENOSE n puritanical or prudish person

BLUENOSED > BLUENOSE

BLUENOSES > BLUENOSE

BLUEPOINT n type of small oyster

BLUEPRINT n photographic print of a plan ▷ vb make a blueprint of (a plan)

BLUER > BLUE

BLUES pl n type of music

BLUESHIFT n shift in the spectral lines of a stellar spectrum

BLUESIER > BLUES

BLUESIEST > BLUES

BLUESMAN n blues musician

BLUESMEN > BLUESMAN

BLUEST > BLUE

BLUESTEM n type of tall grass

BLUESTEMS > BLUESTEM

BLUESTONE n blue-grey sandstone containing much clay, used for building and paving

BLUESY > BLUES

BLUET n N American plant with small four-petalled blue flowers

BLUETICK n fast-running dog

BLUETICKS > BLUETICK

BLUETIT n small European bird

BLUETITS > BLUETIT

BLUETS > BLUET

BLUETTE n short, brilliant piece of music

BLUETTES > BLUETTE

BLUEWEED n Eurasian weed with blue flowers and pink buds

b

BLUEWEEDS > BLUEWEED
BLUEWING n type of duck
BLUEWINGS > BLUEWING
BLUEWOOD n type of Mexican shrub
BLUEWOODS > BLUEWOOD
BLUEY adj bluish ▷ n informal Australian word meaning blanket
BLUEYS > BLUEY
BLUFF vb pretend to be confident in order to influence (someone) ▷ n act of bluffing ▷ adj good-naturedly frank and hearty
BLUFFABLE > BLUFF
BLUFFED > BLUFF
BLUFFER > BLUFF
BLUFFERS > BLUFF
BLUFFEST > BLUFF
BLUFFING > BLUFF
BLUFFLY > BLUFF
BLUFFNESS > BLUFF
BLUFFS > BLUFF
BLUGGIER > BLUGGY
BLUGGIEST > BLUGGY
BLUGGY same as > BLOODY
BLUID Scots word for > BLOOD
BLUIDIER > BLUID
BLUIDIEST > BLUID
BLUIDS > BLUID
BLUIDY > BLUID
BLUIER > BLUEY
BLUIEST > BLUEY
BLUING > BLUE
BLUINGS > BLUE
BLUISH adj slightly blue
BLUME Scots word for > BLOOM
BLUMED > BLUME
BLUMES > BLUME
BLUMING > BLUME
BLUNDER n clumsy mistake ▷ vb make a blunder
BLUNDERED > BLUNDER
BLUNDERER > BLUNDER
BLUNDERS > BLUNDER
BLUNGE vb mix clay with water
BLUNGED > BLUNGE
BLUNGER n large vat in which the contents are mixed by rotating arms
BLUNGERS > BLUNGER
BLUNGES > BLUNGE
BLUNGING > BLUNGE
BLUNK vb ruin; botch
BLUNKED > BLUNK
BLUNKER > BLUNK
BLUNKERS > BLUNK
BLUNKING > BLUNK
BLUNKS > BLUNK
BLUNT adj not having a sharp edge or point ▷ vb make less sharp
BLUNTED > BLUNT
BLUNTER > BLUNT
BLUNTEST > BLUNT
BLUNTHEAD n frequent user of marijuana
BLUNTING > BLUNT
BLUNTISH > BLUNT
BLUNTLY > BLUNT
BLUNTNESS > BLUNT
BLUNTS > BLUNT
BLUR vb make or become vague or less distinct ▷ n

something vague, hazy, or indistinct
BLURB n promotional description, as on the jacket of a book ▷ vb describe or recommend in a blurb
BLURBED > BLURB
BLURBING > BLURB
BLURBIST n writer of blurbs
BLURBISTS > BLURBIST
BLURBS > BLURB
BLURRED > BLUR
BLURREDLY > BLUR
BLURRIER > BLUR
BLURRIEST > BLUR
BLURRILY > BLUR
BLURRING > BLUR
BLURRY > BLUR
BLURS > BLUR
BLURT vb utter suddenly and involuntarily
BLURTED > BLURT
BLURTER > BLURT
BLURTERS > BLURT
BLURTING > BLURT
BLURTINGS > BLURT
BLURTS > BLURT
BLUSH vb become red in the face, esp from embarrassment or shame ▷ n reddening of the face
BLUSHED > BLUSH
BLUSHER n cosmetic for giving the cheeks a rosy colour
BLUSHERS > BLUSHER
BLUSHES > BLUSH
BLUSHET n modest young woman
BLUSHETS > BLUSHET
BLUSHFUL > BLUSH
BLUSHING > BLUSH
BLUSHINGS > BLUSH
BLUSHLESS > BLUSH
BLUSTER vb speak loudly or in a bullying way ▷ n empty threats or protests
BLUSTERED > BLUSTER
BLUSTERER > BLUSTER
BLUSTERS > BLUSTER
BLUSTERY adj (of wind) noisy or gusty
BLUSTROUS adj inclined to bluster
BLUTWURST n blood sausage
BLYPE n piece of skin peeled off after sunburn
BLYPES > BLYPE
BO interj exclamation uttered to startle or surprise someone ▷ n fellow, buddy
BOA n large nonvenomous snake
BOAB short for > BAOBAB
BOABS > BOAB
BOAK same as > BOKE
BOAKED > BOAK
BOAKING > BOAK
BOAKS > BOAK
BOAR n uncastrated male pig
BOARD n long flat piece of sawn timber ▷ vb go aboard (a train, aeroplane, etc)
BOARDABLE > BOARD
BOARDED > BOARD

BOARDER n person who pays rent for accommodation in someone else's home
BOARDERS > BOARDER
BOARDIES pl n board shorts
BOARDING n act of embarking on an aircraft, train, ship, etc
BOARDINGS > BOARDING
BOARDLIKE > BOARD
BOARDMAN n man who carries a sandwich board
BOARDMEN > BOARDMAN
BOARDROOM n room where the board of a company meets
BOARDS > BOARD
BOARDWALK n promenade, esp along a beach, usually made of planks
BOARFISH n type of spiny-finned marine fish with a compressed body, a long snout, and large eyes
BOARHOUND n dog used to hunt boar
BOARISH adj coarse, cruel, or sensual
BOARISHLY > BOARISH
BOARS > BOAR
BOART same as > BORT
BOARTS > BOART
BOAS > BOA
BOAST vb speak too proudly about one's talents etc ▷ n bragging statement
BOASTED > BOAST
BOASTER > BOAST
BOASTERS > BOAST
BOASTFUL adj tending to boast
BOASTING > BOAST
BOASTINGS > BOAST
BOASTLESS > BOAST
BOASTS > BOAST
BOAT n small vehicle for travelling across water ▷ vb travel in a boat
BOATABLE adj able to be carried by boat
BOATBILL n nocturnal tropical American wading bird with a broad flattened bill
BOATBILLS > BOATBILL
BOATED > BOAT
BOATEL n waterside hotel catering for boating people
BOATELS > BOATEL
BOATER n flat straw hat
BOATERS > BOATER
BOATFUL > BOAT
BOATFULS > BOAT
BOATHOOK n hooked pole used for fending off other vessels or obstacles
BOATHOOKS > BOATHOOK
BOATHOUSE n shelter by the edge of a river, lake, etc, for housing boats
BOATIE n boating enthusiast
BOATIES > BOATIE
BOATING n rowing, sailing, or cruising in boats as a form of recreation
BOATINGS > BOATING

BOATLIFT n evacuation by boat
BOATLIFTS > BOATLIFT
BOATLIKE > BOAT
BOATLOAD n amount of cargo or number of people held by a boat or ship
BOATLOADS > BOATLOAD
BOATMAN n man who works on, hires out, or repairs boats
BOATMEN > BOATMAN
BOATNECK n wide open neck on garment
BOATNECKS > BOATNECK
BOATPORT n enclosure for boats
BOATPORTS > BOATPORT
BOATS > BOAT
BOATSMAN same as > BOATMAN
BOATSMEN > BOATSMAN
BOATSWAIN n petty officer on a merchant ship or a warrant officer on a warship who is responsible for the maintenance of the ship and its equipment
BOATTAIL n type of blackbird
BOATTAILS > BOATTAIL
BOATYARD n place where boats are kept, repaired, etc
BOATYARDS > BOATYARD
BOB vb move or cause to move up and down repeatedly ▷ n short abrupt movement, as of the head
BOBA n type of Chinese tea
BOBAC same as > BOBAK
BOBACS > BOBAC
BOBAK n type of marmot
BOBAKS > BOBAK
BOBAS > BOBA
BOBBED > BOB
BOBBEJAAN n baboon
BOBBER n type of float for fishing
BOBBERIES > BOBBERY
BOBBERS > BOBBER
BOBBERY n mixed pack of hunting dogs ▷ adj noisy or excitable
BOBBIES > BOBBY
BOBBIN n reel on which thread is wound
BOBBINET n netted fabric of hexagonal mesh, made on a lace machine
BOBBINETS > BOBBINET
BOBBING > BOB
BOBBINS > BOBBIN
BOBBISH adj cheery
BOBBITT vb sever the penis of
BOBBITTED > BOBBITT
BOBBITTS > BOBBITT
BOBBLE n small ball of material, usu for decoration ▷ vb (of a ball) to bounce erratically because of an uneven playing surface
BOBBLED > BOBBLE
BOBBLES > BOBBLE
BOBBLIER > BOBBLY
BOBBLIEST > BOBBLY
BOBBLING > BOBBLE
BOBBLY adj (of fabric) covered in small balls; worn

BOBBY *n* policeman or policewoman

BOBBYSOCK *n* ankle-length sock worn esp by teenage girls

BOBBYSOX *pl n* bobbysocks

BOBCAT *n* N American feline

BOBCATS > BOBCAT

BOBECHE *n* candle drip-catcher

BOBECHES > BOBECHE

BOBFLOAT *n* small buoyant float, usually consisting of a quill stuck through a piece of cork

BOBFLOATS > BOBFLOAT

BOBLET *n* two-person bobsleigh

BOBLETS > BOBLET

BOBO *n* rich person who holds bohemian values

BOBOL *n* type of fraud ▷ *vb* commit a bobol

BOBOLINK *n* American songbird

BOBOLINKS > BOBOLINK

BOBOLLED > BOBOL

BOBOLLING > BOBOL

BOBOLS > BOBOL

BOBOS > BOBO

BOBOTIE *n* dish of curried mince

BOBOTIES > BOBOTIE

BOBOWLER *n* large moth

BOBOWLERS > BOBOWLER

BOBS > BOB

BOBSKATE *n* child's skate with two parallel blades

BOBSKATES > BOBSKATE

BOBSLED *same as* > BOBSLEIGH

BOBSLEDS > BOBSLED

BOBSLEIGH *n* sledge for racing down an icy track ▷ *vb* ride on a bobsleigh

BOBSTAY *n* stay between a bowsprit and the stem of a vessel

BOBSTAYS > BOBSTAY

BOBTAIL *n* docked tail ▷ *adj* having the tail cut short ▷ *vb* dock the tail of

BOBTAILED > BOBTAIL

BOBTAILS > BOBTAIL

BOBWEIGHT *n* balance weight

BOBWHEEL *n* poetic device

BOBWHEELS > BOBWHEEL

BOBWHITE *n* brown N American quail

BOBWHITES > BOBWHITE

BOBWIG *n* type of short wig

BOBWIGS > BOBWIG

BOCACCIO *n* edible American fish

BOCACCIOS > BOCACCIO

BOCAGE *n* wooded countryside characteristic of northern France

BOCAGES > BOCAGE

BOCCA *n* mouth

BOCCAS > BOCCA

BOCCE *same as* > BOCCIE

BOCCES > BOCCE

BOCCI *same as* > BOCCIE

BOCCIA *same as* > BOCCIE

BOCCIAS > BOCCIA

BOCCIE *n* Italian version of bowls

BOCCIES > BOCCIE

BOCCIS > BOCCI

BOCHE *n* derogatory slang for a German soldier

BOCHES > BOCHE

BOCK *a variant spelling of* > BOKE

BOCKED > BOCK

BOCKEDY *adj* (of a structure, piece of furniture, etc) unsteady

BOCKING > BOCK

BOCKS > BOCK

BOCONCINI *pl n* small pieces of mozzarella

BOD *n* person

BODACH *n* old man

BODACHS > BODACH

BODACIOUS *adj* impressive or remarkable

BODDLE *same as* > BODLE

BODDLES > BODDLE

BODE *vb* portend or presage

BODED > BODE

BODEFUL *adj* portentous

BODEGA *n* shop in a Spanish-speaking country that sells wine

BODEGAS > BODEGA

BODEGUERO *n* wine seller or grocer

BODEMENT > BODE

BODEMENTS > BODE

BODES > BODE

BODGE *vb* make a mess of

BODGED > BODGE

BODGER *adj* worthless or second-rate

BODGERS > BODGER

BODGES > BODGE

BODGIE *n* unruly or uncouth young man, esp in the 1950s ▷ *adj* inferior

BODGIER > BODGIE

BODGIES > BODGIE

BODGIEST > BODGIE

BODGING > BODGE

BODHI *n* as in *bodhi tree* holy tree of Buddhists

BODHIS > BODHI

BODHRAN *n* shallow one-sided drum popular in Irish and Scottish folk music

BODHRANS > BODHRAN

BODICE *n* upper part of a dress

BODICES > BODICE

BODIED > BODY

BODIES > BODY

BODIKIN *n* little body

BODIKINS > BODIKIN

BODILESS *adj* having no body or substance

BODILY *adj* relating to the body ▷ *adv* by taking hold of the body

BODING > BODE

BODINGLY > BODE

BODINGS > BODE

BODKIN *n* blunt large-eyed needle

BODKINS > BODKIN

BODLE *n* small obsolete Scottish coin

BODLES > BODLE

BODRAG *n* enemy attack

BODRAGS > BODRAG

BODS > BOD

BODY *n* entire physical structure of an animal or human ▷ *vb* give form to

BODYBOARD *n* surfboard that is shorter and blunter than the standard board and on which the surfer lies rather than stands

BODYBUILD *vb* build up the muscles with exercises

BODYBUILT > BODYBUILD

BODYCHECK *n* obstruction of another player ▷ *vb* deliver a bodycheck to (an opponent)

BODYGUARD *n* person or group of people employed to protect someone

BODYING > BODY

BODYLINE *n* (in cricket) fast bowling aimed at the batsman's body

BODYLINES > BODYLINE

BODYMAN *n* person who repairs car bodies

BODYMEN > BODYMAN

BODYSHELL *n* external shell of a motor vehicle

BODYSIDE *n* side of a body of a vehicle

BODYSIDES > BODYSIDE

BODYSUIT *n* one-piece undergarment for a baby

BODYSUITS > BODYSUIT

BODYSURF *vb* ride a wave by lying on it without a surfboard

BODYSURFS > BODYSURF

BODYWASH *n* liquid soap for use in the shower or bath

BODYWORK *n* outer shell of a motor vehicle

BODYWORKS > BODYWORK

BOEHMITE *n* type of grey, red, or brown mineral

BOEHMITES > BOEHMITE

BOEP *n* South African word for a big belly

BOEPS > BOEP

BOERBUL *n* crossbred mastiff used esp as a watchdog

BOERBULL *same as* > BOERBUL

BOERBULLS > BOERBULL

BOERBULS > BOERBUL

BOEREWORS *n* spiced sausage

BOERTJIE *South African word for* > FRIEND

BOERTJIES > BOERTJIE

BOET *n* brother

BOETS > BOET

BOEUF *n* as in *boeuf bourguignon* type of beef casserole

BOEUFS > BOEUF

BOFF *n* boffin ▷ *vb* hit

BOFFED > BOFF

BOFFIN *n* scientist or expert

BOFFING > BOFF

BOFFINIER > BOFFINY

BOFFINS > BOFFIN

BOFFINY *adj* like a boffin

BOFFO *n* boffin

BOFFOLA *n* great success

BOFFOLAS > BOFFOLA

BOFFOS > BOFFO

BOFFS > BOFF

BOG *n* wet spongy ground ▷ *vb* mire or delay

BOGAN *n* youth who dresses and behaves rebelliously

BOGANS > BOGAN

BOGART *vb* monopolize or keep to oneself selfishly

BOGARTED > BOGART

BOGARTING > BOGART

BOGARTS > BOGART

BOGBEAN *same as* > BUCKBEAN

BOGBEANS > BOGBEAN

BOGEY *n* evil or mischievous spirit ▷ *vb* play (a hole) in one stroke over par

BOGEYED > BOGEY

BOGEYING > BOGEY

BOGEYISM *n* demonization

BOGEYISMS > BOGEYISM

BOGEYMAN *n* frightening person, real or imaginary, used as a threat, esp to children

BOGEYMEN > BOGEYMAN

BOGEYS > BOGEY

BOGGARD *same as* > BOGGART

BOGGARDS > BOGGARD

BOGGART *n* ghost or poltergeist **BOGGARTS** > BOGGART

BOGGED > BOG

BOGGER *n* lavatory

BOGGERS > BOGGER

BOGGIER > BOG

BOGGIEST > BOG

BOGGINESS > BOG

BOGGING > BOG

BOGGISH > BOG

BOGGLE *vb* be surprised, confused, or alarmed

BOGGLED > BOGGLE

BOGGLER > BOGGLE

BOGGLERS > BOGGLE

BOGGLES > BOGGLE

BOGGLING > BOGGLE

BOGGY > BOG

BOGHEAD *adj* relating to variety of coal from which paraffin can be derived

BOGHOLE *n* natural hole of wet spongy ground

BOGHOLES > BOGHOLE

BOGIE *same as* > BOGEY

BOGIED > BOGIE

BOGIEING > BOGIE

BOGIES > BOGIE

BOGLAND *n* area of wetland

BOGLANDS > BOGLAND

BOGLE *n* rhythmic dance performed to ragga music ▷ *vb* perform such a dance

BOGLED > BOGLE

BOGLES > BOGLE

BOGLING > BOGLE

BOGMAN *n* body of a person found preserved in a peat bog

BOGMEN > BOGMAN

BOGOAK *n* oak or other wood found preserved in peat bogs; bogwood

BOGOAKS > BOGOAK

BOGONG n large nocturnal Australian moth

BOGONGS > BOGONG

BOGS > BOG

BOGUE n type of Mediterranean fish

BOGUES > BOGUE

BOGUS adj not genuine

BOGUSLY > BOGUS

BOGUSNESS > BOGUS

BOGWOOD same as > BOGOAK

BOGWOODS > BOGWOOD

BOGY same as > BOGEY

BOGYISM same as > BOGEYISM

BOGYISMS > BOGYISM

BOGYMAN same as > BOGEYMAN

BOGYMEN > BOGYMAN

BOH same as > BO

BOHEA n black Chinese tea

BOHEAS > BOHEA

BOHEMIA n area frequented by unconventional (esp creative) people

BOHEMIAN adj unconventional in lifestyle or appearance ▷ n person, esp an artist or writer, who lives an unconventional life

BOHEMIANS > BOHEMIAN

BOHEMIAS > BOHEMIA

BOHO short for > BOHEMIAN

BOHOS > BOHO

BOHRIUM n element artificially produced in minute quantities

BOHRIUMS > BOHRIUM

BOHS > BOH

BOHUNK n derogatory name for a labourer from east or central Europe

BOHUNKS > BOHUNK

BOI n lesbian who dresses like a boy

BOIL vb change from a liquid to a vapour so quickly that bubbles are formed ▷ n state or action of boiling

BOILABLE > BOIL

BOILED > BOIL

BOILER n piece of equipment which provides hot water

BOILERIES > BOILERY

BOILERMAN n man who looks after boilers

BOILERMEN > BOILERMAN

BOILERS > BOILER

BOILERY n place where water is boiled to extract salt

BOILING adj very hot ▷ n sweet

BOILINGLY > BOILING

BOILINGS > BOILING

BOILOFF n quantity of liquefied gases lost in evaporation

BOILOFFS > BOILOFF

BOILOVER n surprising result in a sporting event, esp in a horse race

BOILOVERS > BOILOVER

BOILS > BOIL

BOING vb rebound making a noise

BOINGED > BOING

BOINGING > BOING

BOINGS > BOING

BOINK same as > BOING

BOINKED > BOINK

BOINKING > BOINK

BOINKS > BOINK

BOIS > BOI

BOISERIE n finely crafted wood-carving

BOISERIES > BOISERIE

BOITE n artist's portfolio

BOITES > BOITE

BOK n S African antelope

BOKE vb retch or vomit ▷ n retch

BOKED > BOKE

BOKEH n blurred area of an image

BOKEHS > BOKEH

BOKES > BOKE

BOKING > BOKE

BOKKEN n wooden practice sword in kendo

BOKKENS > BOKKEN

BOKO slang word for > NOSE

BOKOS > BOKO

BOKS > BOK

BOLA n missile used by gauchos and Indians of South America

BOLAR adj relating to clay

BOLAS same as > BOLA

BOLASES > BOLAS

BOLD adj confident and fearless ▷ n boldface ▷ vb be or make bold

BOLDED > BOLD

BOLDEN vb make bold

BOLDENED > BOLDEN

BOLDENING > BOLDEN

BOLDENS > BOLDEN

BOLDER > BOLD

BOLDEST > BOLD

BOLDFACE n weight of type characterized by thick heavy lines ▷ vb print in boldface

BOLDFACED > BOLDFACE

BOLDFACES > BOLDFACE

BOLDING > BOLD

BOLDLY > BOLD

BOLDNESS > BOLD

BOLDS > BOLD

BOLE n tree trunk

BOLECTION n stepped moulding covering and projecting beyond the joint between two members having surfaces at different levels

BOLERO n (music for) traditional Spanish dance

BOLEROS > BOLERO

BOLES > BOLE

BOLETE same as > BOLETUS

BOLETES > BOLETE

BOLETI > BOLETUS

BOLETUS n type of fungus

BOLETUSES > BOLETUS

BOLIDE n large exceptionally bright meteor that often explodes

BOLIDES > BOLIDE

BOLINE n (in Wicca) a knife

BOLINES > BOLINE

BOLIVAR n standard monetary unit of Venezuela, equal to 100 céntimos

BOLIVARES > BOLIVAR

BOLIVARS > BOLIVAR

BOLIVIA n type of woollen fabric

BOLIVIANO n (until 1963 and from 1987) the standard monetary unit of Bolivia, equal to 100 centavos

BOLIVIAS > BOLIVIA

BOLIX same as > BOLLOCKS

BOLIXED > BOLIX

BOLIXES > BOLIX

BOLIXING > BOLIX

BOLL n rounded seed capsule of cotton, flax, etc ▷ vb form into a boll

BOLLARD n short thick post used to prevent the passage of motor vehicles

BOLLARDS > BOLLARD

BOLLED > BOLL

BOLLEN > BOLL

BOLLETRIE n type of W Indian tree

BOLLING > BOLL

BOLLIX same as > BOLLOCKS

BOLLIXED > BOLLIX

BOLLIXES > BOLLIX

BOLLIXING > BOLLIX

BOLLOCK vb vulgar slang word meaning rebuke severely

BOLLOCKED > BOLLOCK

BOLLOCKS pl n vulgar word for the testicles ▷ interj exclamation of annoyance, disbelief, etc ▷ vb rebuke severely

BOLLOX same as > BOLLOCKS

BOLLOXED > BOLLOX

BOLLOXES > BOLLOX

BOLLOXING > BOLLOX

BOLLS > BOLL

BOLLWORM n any of various moth caterpillars that feed on and destroy cotton bolls

BOLLWORMS > BOLLWORM

BOLO n large single-edged knife, originating in the Philippines

BOLOGNA n type of sausage

BOLOGNAS > BOLOGNA

BOLOGNESE n Italian meat and tomato sauce

BOLOGRAPH n record made by a bolometer

BOLOMETER n sensitive instrument for measuring radiant energy by the increase in the resistance of an electrical conductor

BOLOMETRY > BOLOMETER

BOLONEY a variant spelling of > BALONEY

BOLONEYS > BOLONEY

BOLOS > BOLO

BOLSHEVIK n any political radical

BOLSHIE adj difficult or rebellious ▷ n any political radical

BOLSHIER > BOLSHIE

BOLSHIES > BOLSHIE

BOLSHIEST > BOLSHIE

BOLSHY same as > BOLSHIE

BOLSON n desert valley surrounded by mountains, with a shallow lake at the centre

BOLSONS > BOLSON

BOLSTER vb support or strengthen ▷ n long narrow pillow

BOLSTERED > BOLSTER

BOLSTERER > BOLSTER

BOLSTERS > BOLSTER

BOLT n sliding metal bar for fastening a door etc ▷ vb run away suddenly

BOLTED > BOLT

BOLTER > BOLT

BOLTERS > BOLT

BOLTHEAD n glass receptacle used in chemistry

BOLTHEADS > BOLTHEAD

BOLTHOLE n place of escape from danger

BOLTHOLES > BOLTHOLE

BOLTING > BOLT

BOLTINGS > BOLT

BOLTLESS > BOLT

BOLTLIKE > BOLT

BOLTONIA n N American plant with daisy-like flowers with white, violet, or pinkish rays

BOLTONIAS > BOLTONIA

BOLTROPE n rope sewn to the foot or luff of a sail to strengthen it

BOLTROPES > BOLTROPE

BOLTS > BOLT

BOLUS same as > BOLE

BOLUSES > BOLUS

BOMA n enclosure set up to protect a camp, herd of animals, etc

BOMAS > BOMA

BOMB n container fitted with explosive material ▷ vb attack with bombs

BOMBABLE > BOMB

BOMBARD vb attack with heavy gunfire or bombs ▷ n ancient type of cannon that threw stone balls

BOMBARDE n alto wind instrument similar to the oboe

BOMBARDED > BOMBARD

BOMBARDER > BOMBARD

BOMBARDES > BOMBARDE

BOMBARDON n brass instrument of the tuba type, similar to a sousaphone

BOMBARDS > BOMBARD

BOMBASINE same as > BOMBAZINE

BOMBAST n pompous language ▷ vb speak pompous language

BOMBASTED > BOMBAST

BOMBASTER > BOMBAST

BOMBASTIC > BOMBAST

BOMBASTS > BOMBAST

BOMBAX n type of S American tree

BOMBAXES > BOMBAX

BOMBAZINE n twill fabric, usually of silk and worsted,

b

formerly worn dyed black for mourning

BOMBE n dessert of ice cream lined or filled with custard, cake crumbs, etc ▷ adj (of furniture) having a projecting swollen shape

BOMBED > BOMB

BOMBER n aircraft that drops bombs

BOMBERS > BOMBER

BOMBES > BOMBE

BOMBESIN n hormone found in brain

BOMBESINS > BOMBESIN

BOMBILATE same as > BOMBINATE

BOMBINATE vb make a buzzing noise

BOMBING > BOMB

BOMBINGS > BOMB

BOMBLET n small bomb

BOMBLETS > BOMBLET

BOMBLOAD n quantity of bombs carried at one time

BOMBLOADS > BOMBLOAD

BOMBO same as > BUMBO

BOMBORA n submerged reef

BOMBORAS > BOMBORA

BOMBOS > BOMBO

BOMBPROOF adj able to withstand the impact of a bomb

BOMBS > BOMB

BOMBSHELL n shocking or unwelcome surprise

BOMBSIGHT n mechanical or electronic device in an aircraft for aiming bombs

BOMBSITE n area where the buildings have been destroyed by bombs

BOMBSITES > BOMBSITE

BOMBYCID n type of moth of the silkworm family

BOMBYCIDS > BOMBYCID

BOMBYCOID adj of or like bombycids

BOMBYX n type of moth

BOMBYXES > BOMBYX

BOMMIE n outcrop of coral reef

BOMMIES > BOMMIE

BON adj good

BONA pl n goods

BONACI n type of fish

BONACIS > BONACI

BONAMANI > BONAMANO

BONAMANO n gratuity

BONAMIA n parasite

BONAMIAS > BONAMIA

BONANZA n sudden good luck or wealth

BONANZAS > BONANZA

BONASSUS same as > BONASUS

BONASUS n European bison

BONASUSES > BONASUS

BONBON n sweet

BONBONS > BONBON

BONCE n head

BONCES > BONCE

BOND n something that binds, fastens or holds together ▷ vb bind

BONDABLE > BOND

BONDAGE n slavery

BONDAGER > BONDAGE

BONDAGERS > BONDAGE

BONDAGES > BONDAGE

BONDED adj consisting of, secured by, or operating under a bond or bonds

BONDER same as > BONDSTONE

BONDERS > BONDER

BONDING n process by which individuals become emotionally attached to one another

BONDINGS > BONDING

BONDLESS > BOND

BONDMAID n unmarried female serf or slave

BONDMAIDS > BONDMAID

BONDMAN same as > BONDSMAN

BONDMEN > BONDMAN

BONDS > BOND

BONDSMAN n person bound by bond to act as surety for another

BONDSMEN > BONDSMAN

BONDSTONE n long stone or brick laid in a wall as a header

BONDUC n type of North American tree

BONDUCS > BONDUC

BONDWOMAN n female slave

BONDWOMEN > BONDWOMAN

BONE n any of the hard parts in the body that form the skeleton ▷ vb remove the bones from (meat for cooking etc)

BONEBED n site where dinosaur fossils are found

BONEBEDS > BONEBED

BONEBLACK n black residue from the destructive distillation of bones, containing about 10 per cent carbon and 80 per cent calcium phosphate, used as a decolorizing agent and pigment

BONED > BONE

BONEFISH n type of silvery marine game fish occurring in warm shallow waters

BONEHEAD n stupid or obstinate person

BONEHEADS > BONEHEAD

BONELESS > BONE

BONELIKE adj like bone

BONEMEAL n product of dried and ground animal bones, used as a fertilizer or in stock feeds

BONEMEALS > BONEMEAL

BONER n blunder

BONERS > BONER

BONES > BONE

BONESET n N American plant with flat clusters of small white flowers

BONESETS > BONESET

BONETIRED adj completely exhausted

BONEY same as > BONY

BONEYARD an informal name for a > CEMETERY

BONEYARDS > BONEYARD

BONEYER > BONEY

BONEYEST > BONEY

BONFIRE n large outdoor fire

BONFIRES > BONFIRE

BONG n deep reverberating sound, as of a large bell ▷ vb make a deep reverberating sound

BONGED > BONG

BONGING > BONG

BONGO n small drum played with the fingers

BONGOES > BONGO

BONGOIST n bongo player

BONGOISTS > BONGOIST

BONGOS > BONGO

BONGRACE n shade for face

BONGRACES > BONGRACE

BONGS > BONG

BONHAM n piglet

BONHAMS > BONHAM

BONHOMIE n cheerful friendliness

BONHOMIES > BONHOMIE

BONHOMMIE same as > BONHOMIE

BONHOMOUS adj exhibiting bonhomie

BONIATO n sweet potato

BONIATOS > BONIATO

BONIBELL same as > BONNIBELL

BONIBELLS > BONIBELL

BONIE same as > BONNY

BONIER > BONY

BONIEST > BONY

BONIFACE n pub landlord

BONIFACES > BONIFACE

BONILASSE n attractive young woman

BONINESS > BONY

BONING > BONE

BONINGS > BONE

BONISM n doctrine that the world is good, although not the best of all possible worlds

BONISMS > BONISM

BONIST > BONISM

BONISTS > BONISM

BONITA slang term for > HEROIN

BONITAS > BONITA

BONITO n small tuna-like marine food fish

BONITOES > BONITO

BONITOS > BONITO

BONJOUR interj hello

BONK vb hit

BONKED > BONK

BONKERS adj crazy

BONKING > BONK

BONKINGS > BONK

BONKS > BONK

BONNE n housemaid or female servant

BONNES > BONNE

BONNET n metal cover over a vehicle's engine ▷ vb place a bonnet on

BONNETED > BONNET

BONNETING > BONNET

BONNETS > BONNET

BONNIBELL n beautiful girl

BONNIE same as > BONNY

BONNIER > BONNY

BONNIES > BONNY

BONNIEST > BONNY

BONNILY > BONNY

BONNINESS > BONNY

BONNOCK n thick oatmeal cake

BONNOCKS > BONNOCK

BONNY adj beautiful ▷ adv agreeably or well ▷ n beautiful person

BONOBO n type of anthropoid ape of central W Africa

BONOBOS > BONOBO

BONSAI n ornamental miniature tree or shrub

BONSELA n small gift of money

BONSELAS > BONSELA

BONSELLA same as > BONSELA

BONSELLAS > BONSELLA

BONSOIR interj good evening

BONSPELL same as > BONSPIEL

BONSPELLS > BONSPELL

BONSPIEL n curling match

BONSPIELS > BONSPIEL

BONTBOK n antelope found in S Africa

BONTBOKS > BONTBOK

BONTEBOK n S African antelope

BONTEBOKS > BONTEBOK

BONUS n something given, paid, or received above what is due or expected ▷ vb (in Scrabble) play all seven of one's tiles in a single turn

BONUSED > BONUS

BONUSES > BONUS

BONUSING n (in Scrabble) act of playing all seven of one's tiles in a single turn

BONUSINGS > BONUSING

BONUSSED > BONUS

BONUSSES > BONUS

BONUSSING > BONUS

BONXIE n great skua

BONXIES > BONXIE

BONY adj having many bones

BONZA same as > BONZER

BONZE n Chinese or Japanese Buddhist priest or monk

BONZER adj excellent

BONZES > BONZE

BOO interj shout of disapproval ▷ vb shout 'boo' to show disapproval

BOOAI same as > BOOHAI

BOOAIS > BOOAI

BOOAY same as > BOOHAI

BOOAYS > BOOAY

BOOB n foolish mistake ▷ vb make a foolish mistake ▷ adj of poor quality, similar to that provided in prison

BOOBED > BOOB

BOOBHEAD n repeat offender in a prison

BOOBHEADS > BOOBHEAD

BOOBIALLA n type of tree or shrub

BOOBIE same as > BOOBY

BOOBIES > BOOBY

BOOBING > BOOB

BOOBIRD n person who boos

BOOBIRDS > BOOBIRD

BOOBISH adj doltish

b

BOOBOISIE *n* group of people considered as stupid

BOOBOO *n* blunder

BOOBOOK *n* small spotted Australian brown owl

BOOBOOKS > BOOBOOK

BOOBOOS > BOOBOO

BOOBS > BOOB

BOOBY *n* foolish person

BOOBYISH > BOOBY

BOOBYISM > BOOBY

BOOBYISMS > BOOBY

BOOCOO *same as*
> BEAUCOUP

BOOCOOS > BOOCOO

BOODIE *n* type of kangaroo

BOODIED > BOODY

BOODIES > BOODY

BOODLE *n* money or valuables that are counterfeit or used as a bribe *▷ vb* give or receive money corruptly or illegally

BOODLED > BOODLE

BOODLER > BOODLE

BOODLERS > BOODLE

BOODLES > BOODLE

BOODLING > BOODLE

BOODY *vb* sulk

BOODYING > BOODY

BOOED > BOO

BOOFHEAD *n* stupid person

BOOFHEADS > BOOFHEAD

BOOFIER > BOOFY

BOOFIEST > BOOFY

BOOFY *adj* muscular and strong but stupid

BOOGALOO *n* type of dance performed to rock and roll music *▷ vb* dance a boogaloo

BOOGALOOS > BOOGALOO

BOOGER *n* dried mucus from the nose

BOOGERMAN *American form of*
> BOGEYMAN

BOOGERMEN > BOOGERMAN

BOOGERS > BOOGER

BOOGEY *same as* **>** BOOGIE

BOOGEYED > BOOGEY

BOOGEYING > BOOGEY

BOOGEYMAN *same as*
> BOGEYMAN

BOOGEYMEN > BOOGEYMAN

BOOGEYS > BOOGEY

BOOGIE *vb* dance to fast pop music *▷ n* session of dancing to pop music

BOOGIED > BOOGIE

BOOGIEING > BOOGIE

BOOGIEMAN *same as*
> BOGEYMAN

BOOGIEMEN > BOOGIEMAN

BOOGIES > BOOGIE

BOOGY *same as* **>** BOOGIE

BOOGYING > BOOGY

BOOGYMAN *same as*
> BOGEYMAN

BOOGYMEN > BOOGYMAN

BOOH *same as* **>** BOO

BOOHAI *n* as in *up the boohai* thoroughly lost

BOOHAIS > BOOHAI

BOOHED > BOOH

BOOHING > BOOH

BOOHOO *vb* sob or pretend to sob noisily *▷ n* distressed or pretended sobbing

BOOHOOED > BOOHOO

BOOHOOING > BOOHOO

BOOHOOS > BOOHOO

BOOHS > BOOH

BOOING *n* act of booing

BOOINGS > BOOING

BOOJUM *n* American tree

BOOJUMS > BOOJUM

BOOK *n* number of pages bound together between covers *▷ vb* reserve (a place, passage, etc) in advance

BOOKABLE > BOOK

BOOKBAG *n* bag for books

BOOKBAGS > BOOKBAG

BOOKCASE *n* piece of furniture containing shelves for books

BOOKCASES > BOOKCASE

BOOKED > BOOK

BOOKEND *n* one of a pair of supports for holding books upright *▷ vb* occur or be located on either side (of something)

BOOKENDED > BOOKEND

BOOKENDS > BOOKEND

BOOKER > BOOK

BOOKERS > BOOK

BOOKFUL > BOOK

BOOKFULS > BOOK

BOOKIE *short for*
> BOOKMAKER

BOOKIER > BOOKY

BOOKIES > BOOKIE

BOOKIEST > BOOKY

BOOKING *n* reservation, as of a table or seat

BOOKINGS > BOOKING

BOOKISH *adj* fond of reading

BOOKISHLY
> BOOKISH **BOOKLAND** *n* common land given to private owner

BOOKLANDS > BOOKLAND

BOOKLESS > BOOK

BOOKLET *n* thin book with paper covers

BOOKLETS > BOOKLET

BOOKLICE > BOOKLOUSE

BOOKLIGHT *n* small light that can be clipped onto a book for reading by

BOOKLIKE *adj* like a book

BOOKLORE *n* knowledge or beliefs gleaned from books

BOOKLORES > BOOKLORE

BOOKLOUSE *n* wingless insect that feeds on bookbinding paste, etc

BOOKMAKER *n* person whose occupation is taking bets

BOOKMAN *n* learned person

BOOKMARK *n* address for a website stored on a computer so that the user can easily return to the site *▷ vb* identify and store (a website) so that one can return to it quickly and easily

BOOKMARKS > BOOKMARK

BOOKMEN > BOOKMAN

BOOKOO *same as* **>** BOOCOO

BOOKOOS > BOOKOO

BOOKPLATE *n* label bearing the owner's name and an individual design or coat of arms, pasted into a book

BOOKRACK *n* rack for holding books

BOOKRACKS > BOOKRACK

BOOKREST *n* stand for supporting open book

BOOKRESTS > BOOKREST

BOOKS > BOOK

BOOKSHELF *n* shelf for books

BOOKSHOP *n* shop where books are sold

BOOKSHOPS > BOOKSHOP

BOOKSIE *same as* **>** BOOKSY

BOOKSIER > BOOKSY

BOOKSIEST > BOOKSY

BOOKSTALL *n* stall or stand where periodicals, newspapers, or books are sold

BOOKSTAND *n* support for open book

BOOKSTORE *same as*
> BOOKSHOP

BOOKSY *adj* inclined to be bookish or literary

BOOKWORK *n* academic study

BOOKWORKS > BOOKWORK

BOOKWORM *n* person devoted to reading

BOOKWORMS > BOOKWORM

BOOKY *adj* bookish

BOOL *n* bowling ball *▷ vb* play bowls

BOOLED > BOOL

BOOLING > BOOL

BOOLS > BOOL

BOOM *vb* make a loud deep echoing sound *▷ n* loud deep echoing sound

BOOMBOX *n* portable stereo system

BOOMBOXES > BOOMBOX

BOOMBURB *n* large suburb that is growing quickly

BOOMBURBS > BOOMBURB

BOOMED > BOOM

BOOMER *n* large male kangaroo

BOOMERANG *n* curved wooden missile which can be made to return to the thrower *▷ vb* (of a plan) recoil unexpectedly

BOOMERS > BOOMER

BOOMIER > BOOMY

BOOMIEST > BOOMY

BOOMING > BOOM

BOOMINGLY > BOOM

BOOMINGS > BOOM

BOOMKIN *n* short boom projecting from the deck of a ship

BOOMKINS > BOOMKIN

BOOMLET *n* small boom in business, birth rate, etc

BOOMLETS > BOOMLET

BOOMS > BOOM

BOOMSLANG *n* large greenish venomous tree-living snake of southern Africa

BOOMSTICK *n* (in logging) any of the larger logs chained together to create a floating boom

BOOMTOWN *n* town that is enjoying sudden prosperity or has grown rapidly

BOOMTOWNS > BOOMTOWN

BOOMY *adj* characterized by heavy bass sound

BOON *n* something useful, helpful, or beneficial *▷ adj* useful, helpful, or beneficial

BOONDOCK *adj* of or relating to the boondocks

BOONDOCKS *n* remote rural area

BOONER *n* derogatory term for a young working-class person from Canberra

BOONERS > BOONER

BOONEST > BOON

BOONG *n* offensive term for a Black person

BOONGA *n* offensive term for a Pacific Islander

BOONGARY *n* tree kangaroo of NE Queensland, Australia

BOONGAS > BOONGA

BOONGS > BOONG

BOONIES *short form of*
> BOONDOCKS

BOONLESS > BOON

BOONS > BOON

BOOR *n* rude or insensitive person

BOORD *obsolete spelling of*
> BOARD

BOORDE *obsolete spelling of*
> BOARD

BOORDES > BOORDE

BOORDS > BOORD

BOORISH *adj* ill-mannered, clumsy, or insensitive

BOORISHLY > BOORISH

BOORKA *same as* **>** BURKA

BOORKAS > BOORKA

BOORS > BOOR

BOORTREE *same as*
> BOURTREE

BOORTREES > BOORTREE

BOOS > BOO

BOOSE *same as* **>** BOOZE

BOOSED > BOOSE

BOOSES > BOOSE

BOOSHIT *adj* slang word for very good

BOOSING > BOOSE

BOOST *n* encouragement or help *▷ vb* improve

BOOSTED > BOOST

BOOSTER *n* small additional injection of a vaccine

BOOSTERS > BOOSTER

BOOSTING > BOOST

BOOSTS > BOOST

BOOT *n* outer covering for the foot that extends above the ankle *▷ vb* kick

BOOTABLE > BOOT

BOOTBLACK *another word for*
> SHOEBLACK

BOOTCUT *adj* (of trousers) slightly flared at the bottom of the legs

BOOTED *adj* wearing boots

BOOTEE *n* baby's soft shoe

BOOTEES > BOOTEE

BOOTERIES > BOOTERY

BOOTERY *n* shop where boots and shoes are sold

BOOTH *n* small partly enclosed cubicle

BOOTHOSE *n* stocking worn with boots

BOOTHS > BOOTH

BOOTIE *n* Royal Marine

BOOTIES > BOOTY

BOOTIKIN *n* small boot

BOOTIKINS > BOOTIKIN

BOOTING > BOOT

BOOTJACK *n* device that grips the heel of a boot to enable the foot to be withdrawn easily

BOOTJACKS > BOOTJACK

BOOTLACE *n* strong lace for fastening a boot

BOOTLACES > BOOTLACE

BOOTLAST *n* foot shape placed in boots or shoes to keep their shape

BOOTLASTS > BOOTLAST

BOOTLEG *adj* produced, distributed, or sold illicitly ▷ *vb* make, carry, or sell (illicit goods) ▷ *n* something made or sold illicitly

BOOTLEGS > BOOTLEG

BOOTLESS *adj* of little or no use

BOOTLICK *vb* seek favour by servile or ingratiating behaviour

BOOTLICKS > BOOTLICK

BOOTMAKER *n* person who makes boots and shoes

BOOTS > BOOT

BOOTSTRAP *n* leather or fabric loop on the back or side of a boot

BOOTY *n* valuable articles obtained as plunder

BOOZE *n* alcoholic drink ▷ *vb* drink alcohol, esp in excess

BOOZED > BOOZE

BOOZER *n* person who is fond of drinking

BOOZERS > BOOZER

BOOZES > BOOZE

BOOZEY *same as* > BOOZY

BOOZIER > BOOZY

BOOZIEST > BOOZY

BOOZILY > BOOZY

BOOZINESS > BOOZY

BOOZING > BOOZE

BOOZINGS > BOOZE

BOOZY *adj* inclined to or involving excessive drinking of alcohol

BOP *vb* dance to pop music ▷ *n* form of jazz with complex rhythms and harmonies

BOPEEP *n* quick look; peek

BOPEEPS > BOPEEP

BOPPED > BOP

BOPPER > BOP

BOPPERS > BOP

BOPPIER > BOPPY

BOPPIEST > BOPPY

BOPPING > BOP

BOPPISH *same as* > BOPPY

BOPPY *adj* resembling or suggesting bebop

BOPS > BOP

BOR *n* neighbour

BORA *n* Aboriginal ceremony

BORACES > BORAX

BORACHIO *n* pig's skin wine carrier

BORACHIOS > BORACHIO

BORACIC *same as* > BORIC

BORACITE *n* white mineral that forms salt deposits of magnesium borate

BORACITES > BORACITE

BORAGE *n* Mediterranean plant with star-shaped blue flowers

BORAGES > BORAGE

BORAK *n* rubbish

BORAKS > BORAK

BORAL *n* type of fine powder

BORALS > BORAL

BORANE *n* any compound of boron and hydrogen

BORANES > BORANE

BORAS > BORA

BORATE *n* salt or ester of boric acid ▷ *vb* treat with borax, boric acid, or borate

BORATED > BORATE

BORATES > BORATE

BORATING > BORATE

BORAX *n* soluble white mineral occurring in alkaline soils and salt deposits

BORAXES > BORAX

BORAZON *n* extremely hard form of boron nitride

BORAZONS > BORAZON

BORD *obsolete spelling of* > BOARD

BORDAR *n* smallholder who held cottage in return for menial work

BORDARS > BORDAR

BORDE *obsolete spelling of* > BOARD

BORDEAUX *adj* any of several wines produced around Bordeaux

BORDEL *same as* > BORDELLO

BORDELLO *n* brothel

BORDELLOS > BORDELLO

BORDELS > BORDEL

BORDER *n* dividing line between political or geographical regions ▷ *vb* provide with a border

BORDEREAU *n* memorandum or invoice prepared for a company by an underwriter, containing a list of reinsured risks

BORDERED > BORDER

BORDERER *n* person who lives in a border area, esp the border between England and Scotland

BORDERERS > BORDERER

BORDERING > BORDER

BORDERS > BORDER

BORDES > BORDE

BORDS > BORD

BORDURE *n* outer edge of a shield, esp when decorated distinctively

BORDURES > BORDURE

BORE *vb* make (someone) weary by being dull

BOREAL *adj* of or relating to the north or the north wind

BOREALIS *adj* as in *aurora borealis* lights seen around the North Pole

BOREAS *n* name for the north wind

BOREASES > BOREAS

BORECOLE *another name for* > KALE

BORECOLES > BORECOLE

BORED > BORE

BOREDOM *n* state of being bored

BOREDOMS > BOREDOM

BOREE *same as* > MYALL

BOREEN *n* country lane or narrow road

BOREENS > BOREEN

BOREES > BOREE

BOREHOLE *n* hole driven into the ground to obtain geological information, release water, etc

BOREHOLES > BOREHOLE

BOREL *adj* unlearned ▷ *n* boring tool

BORELS > BOREL

BORER *n* machine or hand tool for boring holes

BORERS > BORER

BORES > BORE

BORESCOPE *n* long narrow device for inspection of, eg, bore

BORESOME *adj* boring

BORGHETTO *n* settlement outside city walls

BORGO *n* small attractive medieval village

BORGOS > BORGO

BORIC *adj* of or containing boron

BORIDE *n* compound in which boron is the most electronegative element

BORIDES > BORIDE

BORING *n* act or process of making or enlarging a hole ▷ *adj* dull

BORINGLY > BORING

BORINGS > BORING

BORK *vb* dismiss from a job unfairly

BORKED > BORK

BORKING *n* act of incorrectly configuring a device

BORKINGS > BORKING

BORKS > BORK

BORLOTTI *pl n* as in *borlotti bean* variety of kidney bean

BORM *vb* smear with paint, oil, etc

BORMED > BORM

BORMING > BORM

BORMS > BORM

BORN *adj* possessing certain qualities from birth

BORNA *n* as in *borna disease* viral disease found in mammals, esp horses

BORNE > BEAR

BORNEOL *n* white solid terpene alcohol

BORNEOLS > BORNEOL

BORNITE *n* type of mineral

BORNITES > BORNITE

BORNITIC > BORNITE

BORNYL *n* as in *bornyl alcohol* white solid alcohol from a Malaysian tree

BORNYLS > BORNYL

BORON *n* element used in hardening steel

BORONIA *n* Australian aromatic flowering shrub

BORONIAS > BORONIA

BORONIC > BORON

BORONS > BORON

BOROUGH *n* town or district with its own council

BOROUGHS > BOROUGH

BORREL *adj* ignorant

BORRELIA *n* type of bacterium

BORRELIAS > BORRELIA

BORRELL *same as* > BORREL

BORROW *vb* obtain (something) temporarily

BORROWED > BORROW

BORROWER > BORROW

BORROWERS > BORROW

BORROWING > BORROW

BORROWS > BORROW

BORS > BOR

BORSCH *same as* > BORSCHT

BORSCHES > BORSCH

BORSCHT *n* Russian soup based on beetroot

BORSCHTS > BORSCHT

BORSHCH *same as* > BORSCHT

BORSHCHES > BORSHCH

BORSHT *same as* > BORSCHT

BORSHTS > BORSHT

BORSIC *n* composite material used in aviation

BORSICS > BORSIC

BORSTAL *n* (formerly in Britain) prison for young criminals

BORSTALL *same as* > BORSTAL

BORSTALLS > BORSTALL

BORSTALS > BORSTAL

BORT *n* inferior grade of diamond used for cutting and drilling

BORTIER > BORT

BORTIEST > BORT

BORTS > BORT

BORTSCH *same as* > BORSCHT

BORTSCHES > BORTSCH

BORTY > BORT

BORTZ *same as* > BORT

BORTZES > BORTZ

BORZOI *n* tall dog with a long silky coat

BORZOIS > BORZOI

BOS > BO

BOSBERAAD *n* meeting in an isolated venue to break a political deadlock

BOSBOK *same as* > BUSHBUCK

BOSBOKS > BOSBOK

BOSCAGE *n* mass of trees and shrubs

BOSCAGES > BOSCAGE

BOSCHBOK *same as* > BUSHBUCK

BOSCHBOKS > BOSCHBOK

BOSCHE *same as* > BOCHE

BOSCHES > BOSCHE

b

BOSCHVARK same as
> BUSHPIG
BOSCHVELD same as
> BUSHVELD
BOSH n empty talk, nonsense
BOSHBOK same as
> BUSHBUCK
BOSHBOKS > BOSHBOK
BOSHES > BOSH
BOSHTA same as > BOSHTER
BOSHTER adj excellent
BOSHVARK same as
> BOSCHVARK
BOSHVARKS > BOSHVARK
BOSIE n (in cricket) another
term for googly
BOSIES > BOSIE
BOSK n small wood of bushes
and small trees
BOSKAGE same as
> BOSCAGE
BOSKAGES > BOSKAGE
BOSKER adj excellent
BOSKET n clump of small
trees or bushes
BOSKETS > BOSKET
BOSKIER > BOSKY
BOSKIEST > BOSKY
BOSKINESS > BOSKY
BOSKS > BOSK
BOSKY adj containing or
consisting of bushes or
thickets
BOSOM n chest of a person
▷ adj very dear ▷ vb embrace
BOSOMED > BOSOM
BOSOMIER > BOSOMY
BOSOMIEST > BOSOMY
BOSOMING > BOSOM
BOSOMS > BOSOM
BOSOMY adj (of a woman)
having large breasts
BOSON n type of elementary
particle
BOSONIC > BOSON
BOSONS > BOSON
BOSQUE same as > BOSK
BOSQUES > BOSQUE
BOSQUET same as > BOSKET
BOSQUETS > BOSQUET
BOSS n raised knob or stud
▷ vb employ, supervise, or be
in charge of ▷ adj excellent
BOSSBOY n Black African
foreman of a gang of workers
BOSSBOYS > BOSSBOY
BOSSDOM n bosses
collectively
BOSSDOMS > BOSSDOM
BOSSED > BOSS
BOSSER > BOSS
BOSSES > BOSS
BOSSEST > BOSS
BOSSET n either of the
rudimentary antlers found in
young deer
BOSSETS > BOSSET
BOSSIER > BOSSY
BOSSIES > BOSSY
BOSSIEST > BOSSY
BOSSILY > BOSSY
BOSSINESS > BOSSY
BOSSING n act of shaping
malleable metal
BOSSINGS > BOSSING
BOSSISM n domination of
political organizations by
bosses

BOSSISMS > BOSSISM
BOSSY same as > BOSS
BOSTANGI n imperial
Turkish guard
BOSTANGIS > BOSTANGI
BOSTHOON n boor
BOSTHOONS > BOSTHOON
BOSTON n card game for
four, played with two packs
BOSTONS > BOSTON
BOSTRYX n phenomenon in
which flowers develop on
one side only
BOSTRYXES > BOSTRYX
BOSUN same as
> BOATSWAIN
BOSUNS > BOSUN
BOT vb scrounge
BOTA n leather container
BOTANIC same as
> BOTANICAL
BOTANICA n botany
BOTANICAL adj of or
relating to botany or plants
▷ n any drug or pesticide that
is made from parts of a plant
BOTANICAS > BOTANICA
BOTANICS > BOTANIC
BOTANIES > BOTANY
BOTANISE same as
> BOTANIZE
BOTANISED > BOTANISE
BOTANISER > BOTANISE
BOTANISES > BOTANISE
BOTANIST > BOTANY
BOTANISTS > BOTANY
BOTANIZE vb collect or
study plants
BOTANIZED > BOTANIZE
BOTANIZER > BOTANIZE
BOTANIZES > BOTANIZE
BOTANY n study of plants
BOTARGO n relish consisting
of the roe of mullet or tuna,
salted and pressed into rolls
BOTARGOES > BOTARGO
BOTARGOS > BOTARGO
BOTAS > BOTA
BOTCH vb spoil through
clumsiness ▷ n badly done
piece of work or repair
BOTCHED > BOTCH
BOTCHEDLY > BOTCH
BOTCHER > BOTCH
BOTCHERS > BOTCH
BOTCHERY n instance of
botching
BOTCHES > BOTCH
BOTCHIER > BOTCHY
BOTCHIEST > BOTCHY
BOTCHILY > BOTCHY
BOTCHING > BOTCH
BOTCHINGS > BOTCH
BOTCHY adj clumsily done or
made
BOTE n compensation given
for injury or damage to
property
BOTEL same as > BOATEL
BOTELS > BOTEL
BOTES > BOTE
BOTFLIES > BOTFLY
BOTFLY n type of
stout-bodied hairy fly
BOTH pron two considered
together ▷ adj two
considered together
▷ determiner two

BOTHAN n unlicensed
drinking house
BOTHANS > BOTHAN
BOTHER vb take the time or
trouble ▷ n trouble, fuss, or
difficulty ▷ interj
exclamation of slight
annoyance
BOTHERED > BOTHER
BOTHERING > BOTHER
BOTHERS > BOTHER
BOTHIE same as > BOTHY
BOTHIES > BOTHY
BOTHOLE n hole made by the
larva of the botfly
BOTHOLES > BOTHOLE
BOTHRIA > BOTHRIUM
BOTHRIUM n groove-shaped
sucker on tapeworm
BOTHRIUMS > BOTHRIUM
BOTHY n hut used for
temporary shelter
BOTHYMAN n man who lives
in bothy
BOTHYMEN > BOTHYMAN
BOTNET n network of
infected computers
BOTNETS > BOTNET
BOTONE adj having lobes at
the ends
BOTONEE same as > BOTONE
BOTONNEE same as
> BOTONE
BOTOXED adj indicating
someone who has had Botox
treatment
BOTRYOID adj shaped like a
bunch of grapes
BOTRYOSE same as
> BOTRYOID
BOTRYTIS n type of fungus
which causes plant diseases
BOTS n digestive disease of
horses and some other
animals
BOTT same as > BOT
BOTTARGA same as
> BOTARGO
BOTTARGAS > BOTTARGA
BOTTE n thrust or hit
BOTTED > BOT
BOTTEGA n workshop;
studio
BOTTEGAS > BOTTEGA
BOTTES > BOTTE
BOTTIES > BOTTY
BOTTINE n light boot for
women or children
BOTTINES > BOTTINE
BOTTING > BOT
BOTTLE n container for
holding liquids ▷ vb put in a
bottle
BOTTLED > BOTTLE
BOTTLEFUL same as
> BOTTLE
BOTTLER n exceptional
person or thing
BOTTLERS > BOTTLER
BOTTLES > BOTTLE
BOTTLING > BOTTLE
BOTTLINGS > BOTTLE
BOTTOM n lowest, deepest,
or farthest removed part of a
thing ▷ adj lowest or last
▷ vb provide with a bottom
BOTTOMED > BOTTOM

BOTTOMER n pit worker
BOTTOMERS > BOTTOMER
BOTTOMING n lowest level
of foundation material for a
road or other structure
BOTTOMRY n loan in which a
ship's owner pledges the ship
as security
BOTTOMS > BOTTOM
BOTTOMSET adj as in
bottomset bed fine sediment
deposited at the front of a
growing delta
BOTTONY same as > BOTONE
BOTTS > BOTT
BOTTY n diminutive for
bottom
BOTULIN n potent toxin
which causes botulism
BOTULINAL > BOTULIN
BOTULINS > BOTULIN
BOTULINUM n botulin-
secreting bacterium
BOTULINUS n type of
bacterium whose toxins
(botulins) cause botulism
BOTULISM n severe food
poisoning
BOTULISMS > BOTULISM
BOUBOU n long flowing
garment
BOUBOUS > BOUBOU
BOUCHE n notch cut in top
corner of shield
BOUCHEE n small pastry
case filled with a savoury
mixture
BOUCHEES > BOUCHEE
BOUCHES > BOUCHE
BOUCLE n looped yarn giving
a knobbly effect ▷ adj of or
designating such a yarn or
fabric
BOUCLEE n support for a cue
in billiards using the hand
BOUCLEES > BOUCLEE
BOUCLES > BOUCLE
BOUDERIE n sulkiness
BOUDERIES > BOUDERIE
BOUDIN n French version of
a black pudding
BOUDINS > BOUDIN
BOUDOIR n woman's
bedroom or private sitting
room
BOUDOIRS > BOUDOIR
BOUFFANT adj (of a
hairstyle) having extra
height through
backcombing ▷ n bouffant
hair style
BOUFFANTS > BOUFFANT
BOUFFE n type of light or
satirical opera common in
France during the 19th
century
BOUFFES > BOUFFE
BOUGE vb move
BOUGED > BOUGE
BOUGES > BOUGE
BOUGET n budget
BOUGETS > BOUGET
BOUGH n large branch of a
tree
BOUGHED > BOUGH
BOUGHLESS > BOUGH
BOUGHPOT n container for
displaying boughs

BOUGHPOTS > BOUGHPOT
BOUGHS > BOUGH
BOUGHT n curve
BOUGHTEN archaic past participle of > BUY
BOUGHTS > BOUGHT
BOUGIE n medical instrument
BOUGIES > BOUGIE
BOUGING > BOUGE
BOUILLI n stew
BOUILLIS > BOUILLI
BOUILLON n thin clear broth or stock
BOUILLONS > BOUILLON
BOUK n bulk; volume
BOUKS > BOUK
BOULDER n large rounded rock ▷ vb convert into boulders
BOULDERED > BOULDER
BOULDERER > BOULDER
BOULDERS > BOULDER
BOULDERY adj covered in boulders
BOULE same as > BOULLE
BOULES n game popular in France
BOULEVARD n wide, usu tree-lined, street
BOULLE adj relating to a type of marquetry much used on French furniture from the 17th century ▷ n something ornamented with such marquetry
BOULLES > BOULLE
BOULT same as > BOLT
BOULTED > BOULT
BOULTER > BOULT
BOULTERS > BOLT
BOULTING > BOULT
BOULTINGS > BOULT
BOULTS > BOULT
BOUN vb prepare to go out
BOUNCE vb (of a ball etc) rebound from an impact ▷ n act of rebounding
BOUNCED > BOUNCE
BOUNCER n person employed at a nightclub etc to remove unwanted people
BOUNCERS > BOUNCER
BOUNCES > BOUNCE
BOUNCIER > BOUNCY
BOUNCIEST > BOUNCY
BOUNCILY > BOUNCY
BOUNCING adj vigorous and robust
BOUNCY adj lively, exuberant, or self-confident
BOUND vb jump suddenly ▷ n sudden jump ▷ adj certain
BOUNDABLE > BIND
BOUNDARY n dividing line that indicates the farthest limit
BOUNDED adj (of a set) having a bound
BOUNDEN adj morally obligatory
BOUNDER n morally reprehensible person
BOUNDERS > BOUNDER
BOUNDING > BOUND
BOUNDLESS adj unlimited
BOUNDNESS > BIND

BOUNDS pl n limit
BOUNED > BOUN
BOUNING > BOUN
BOUNS > BOUN
BOUNTEOUS adj giving freely
BOUNTIED > BOUNTY
BOUNTIES > BOUNTY
BOUNTIFUL adj plentiful
BOUNTREE another name for > BOURTREE
BOUNTREES > BOUNTREE
BOUNTY n generosity
BOUNTYHED n generosity
BOUQUET n bunch of flowers
BOUQUETS > BOUQUET
BOURASQUE n violent storm
BOURBON n whiskey made from maize
BOURBONS > BOURBON
BOURD n prank ▷ vb jest or joke
BOURDED > BOURD
BOURDER n prankster
BOURDERS > BOURDER
BOURDING > BOURD
BOURDON n 16-foot organ stop of the stopped diapason type
BOURDONS > BOURDON
BOURDS > BOURD
BOURG n French market town, esp one beside a castle
BOURGEOIS n middle-class (person) ▷ adj characteristic of or comprising the middle class
BOURGEON same as > BURGEON
BOURGEONS > BOURGEON
BOURGS > BOURG
BOURKHA same as > BURKA
BOURKHAS > BOURKHA
BOURLAW same as > BYRLAW
BOURLAWS > BOURLAW
BOURN n (in S Britain) stream
BOURNE same as > BOURN
BOURNES > BOURNE
BOURNS > BOURN
BOURREE n traditional French dance in fast duple time
BOURREES > BOURREE
BOURRIDE n Mediterranean fish soup
BOURRIDES > BOURRIDE
BOURSE n stock exchange of continental Europe, esp Paris
BOURSES > BOURSE
BOURSIER n stock-exchange worker
BOURSIERS > BOURSIER
BOURSIN n tradename of a smooth white creamy cheese, often flavoured with garlic
BOURSINS > BOURSIN
BOURTREE n elder tree
BOURTREES > BOURTREE
BOUSE vb raise or haul with a tackle
BOUSED > BOUSE
BOUSES > BOUSE
BOUSIER > BOUSY
BOUSIEST > BOUSY
BOUSING > BOUSE
BOUSOUKI same as > BOUZOUKI

BOUSOUKIA > BOUSOUKI
BOUSOUKIS > BOUSOUKI
BOUSY adj drunken; boozy
BOUT n period of activity or illness
BOUTADE n outburst
BOUTADES > BOUTADE
BOUTIQUE n small clothes shop
BOUTIQUES > BOUTIQUE
BOUTIQUEY adj typical of boutiques
BOUTON n knob-shaped contact between nerve fibres
BOUTONNE adj reserved or inhibited
BOUTONNEE same as > BOUTONNE
BOUTONS > BOUTON
BOUTS > BOUT
BOUVARDIA n flowering plant
BOUVIER n large powerful dog
BOUVIERS > BOUVIER
BOUZOUKI n Greek stringed musical instrument
BOUZOUKIA > BOUZOUKI
BOUZOUKIS > BOUZOUKI
BOVATE n obsolete measure of land
BOVATES > BOVATE
BOVID n type of ruminant
BOVIDS > BOVID
BOVINE n domesticated bovine mammal
BOVINELY > BOVINE
BOVINES > BOVINE
BOVINITY > BOVINE
BOVVER n rowdiness, esp caused by gangs of teenage youths
BOVVERS > BOVVER
BOW vb lower (one's head) or bend (one's knee or body) as a sign of respect or shame ▷ n movement made when bowing
BOWAT n lamp
BOWATS > BOWAT
BOWBENT adj bent; bow-like
BOWED adj lowered, bent forward, or curved
BOWEL n intestine, esp the large intestine ▷ vb remove the bowels
BOWELED > BOWEL
BOWELING > BOWEL
BOWELLED > BOWEL
BOWELLESS > BOWEL
BOWELLING > BOWEL
BOWELS > BOWEL
BOWER n shady leafy shelter ▷ vb surround as with a bower
BOWERBIRD n songbird of Australia and New Guinea, the males of which build bower-like display grounds to attract females
BOWERED > BOWER
BOWERIES > BOWERY
BOWERING > BOWER
BOWERS > BOWER
BOWERY n farm
BOWES poetic plural form of > BOUGH

BOWET same as > BOWAT
BOWETS > BOWET
BOWFIN n N American freshwater fish
BOWFINS > BOWFIN
BOWFRONT adj having a front that curves outwards
BOWGET obsolete variant of > BUDGET
BOWGETS > BOWGET
BOWHEAD n type of large-mouthed Arctic whale
BOWHEADS > BOWHEAD
BOWHUNT vb hunt using a bow and arrows
BOWHUNTED > BOWHUNT
BOWHUNTER n person hunting with bow and arrows
BOWHUNTS > BOWHUNT
BOWIE n as in bowie knife type of hunting knife
BOWING n musical technique
BOWINGLY > BOWING
BOWINGS > BOWING
BOWKNOT n decorative knot usually having two loops and two loose ends
BOWKNOTS > BOWKNOT
BOWL n round container with an open top ▷ vb roll smoothly along the ground
BOWLDER same as > BOULDER
BOWLDERS > BOWLDER
BOWLED > BOWL
BOWLEG n leg curving outwards like a bow between the ankle and the thigh
BOWLEGGED adj having legs that curve outwards like a bow
BOWLEGS > BOWLEG
BOWLER n player who sends (a ball) towards the batsman
BOWLERS > BOWLER
BOWLESS > BOW
BOWLFUL same as > BOWL
BOWLFULS > BOWLFUL
BOWLIKE > BOW
BOWLINE n line used to keep the sail taut against the wind
BOWLINES > BOWLINE
BOWLING n game in which bowls are rolled at a group of pins
BOWLINGS > BOWLING
BOWLLIKE > BOWL
BOWLS n game involving biased wooden bowls and a small bowl (the jack)
BOWMAN n archer
BOWMEN > BOWMAN
BOWNE same as > BOUN
BOWNED > BOWNE
BOWNES > BOWNE
BOWNING > BOWNE
BOWPOT same as > BOUGHPOT
BOWPOTS > BOWPOT
BOWR n muscle
BOWRS > BOWR
BOWS > BOW
BOWSAW n saw with a thin blade in a bow-shaped frame
BOWSAWS > BOWSAW

b

BOWSE same as > BOUSE

BOWSED > BOWSE

BOWSER n tanker containing fuel for aircraft, military vehicles, etc

BOWSERS > BOWSER

BOWSES > BOWSE

BOWSEY same as > BOWSIE

BOWSEYS > BOWSEY

BOWSHOT n distance an arrow travels from the bow

BOWSHOTS > BOWSHOT

BOWSIE n low-class, mean or obstreperous person

BOWSIES > BOWSIE

BOWSING > BOWSE

BOWSMAN n man who hunts using a bow and arrows

BOWSMEN > BOWSMAN

BOWSPRIT n spar projecting from the bow of a sailing ship

BOWSPRITS > BOWSPRIT

BOWSTRING n string of an archer's bow

BOWSTRUNG > BOWSTRING

BOWWOOD n tree of the mulberry family, native to south-central US

BOWWOODS > BOWWOOD

BOWWOW n imitation of the bark of a dog ▷ vb make a noise like a dog

BOWWOWED > BOWWOW

BOWWOWING > BOWWOW

BOWWOWS > BOWWOW

BOWYANG n band worn round trouser leg below knee

BOWYANGS > BOWYANG

BOWYER n person who makes or sells archery bows

BOWYERS > BOWYER

BOX n container with a firm flat base and sides ▷ vb put into a box

BOXBALL n street ball game

BOXBALLS > BOXBALL

BOXBERRY n fruit of the partridgeberry or wintergreen

BOXBOARD n tough paperboard made from wood and wastepaper pulp: used for making boxes, etc

BOXBOARDS > BOXBOARD

BOXCAR n closed railway freight van

BOXCARS > BOXCAR

BOXED > BOX

BOXEN adj made of boxwood

BOXER n person who participates in the sport of boxing

BOXERCISE n system of sustained exercises combining boxing movements with aerobic activities

BOXERS > BOXER

BOXES > BOX

BOXFISH another name for > TRUNKFISH

BOXFISHES > BOXFISH

BOXFUL same as > BOX

BOXFULS > BOXFUL

BOXHAUL vb method for bringing a square-rigged ship onto a new tack

BOXHAULED > BOXHAUL

BOXHAULS > BOXHAUL

BOXIER > BOXY

BOXIEST > BOXY

BOXILY > BOXY

BOXINESS > BOXY

BOXING n sport of fighting with the fists

BOXINGS > BOXING

BOXKEEPER n person responsible for theatre boxes

BOXLA n type of lacrosse played indoors

BOXLAS > BOXLA

BOXLIKE > BOX

BOXPLOT n (in statistics) type of graph

BOXPLOTS > BOXPLOT

BOXROOM n small room in which boxes, cases, etc may be stored

BOXROOMS > BOXROOM

BOXTHORN n matrimony vine

BOXTHORNS > BOXTHORN

BOXTIES > BOXTY

BOXTY n type of Irish potato pancake

BOXWALLAH n derogatory Indian term for a salesperson

BOXWOOD n hard yellow wood of the box tree, used to make tool handles, etc

BOXWOODS > BOXWOOD

BOXY adj squarish or chunky

BOY n male child ▷ vb act the part of a boy in a play

BOYAR n member of an old order of Russian nobility

BOYARD same as > BOYAR

BOYARDS > BOYARD

BOYARISM > BOYAR

BOYARISMS > BOYAR

BOYARS > BOYAR

BOYAU n connecting trench

BOYAUX > BOYAU

BOYCHICK same as > BOYCHIK

BOYCHICKS > BOYCHICK

BOYCHIK n young boy

BOYCHIKS > BOYCHIK

BOYCOTT vb refuse to deal with (an organization or country) ▷ n instance of boycotting

BOYCOTTED > BOYCOTT

BOYCOTTER > BOYCOTT

BOYCOTTS > BOYCOTT

BOYED > BOY

BOYF n boyfriend

BOYFRIEND n male friend with whom a person is romantically involved

BOYFS > BOYF

BOYG n troll-like mythical creature

BOYGS > BOYG

BOYHOOD n state or time of being a boy

BOYHOODS > BOYHOOD

BOYING > BOY

BOYISH adj of or like a boy in looks, behaviour, or character

BOYISHLY > BOYISH

BOYKIE n chap or fellow

BOYKIES > BOYKIE

BOYLA n Australian Aboriginal word for magician

BOYLAS > BOYLA

BOYO n boy or young man: often used in direct address

BOYOS > BOYO

BOYS > BOY

BOYSHORTS pl n women's underpants resembling close-fitting shorts

BOYSIER > BOYSY

BOYSIEST > BOYSY

BOYSY adj suited to or typical of boys or young men

BOZO n man, esp a stupid one

BOZOS > BOZO

BOZZETTI > BOZZETTO

BOZZETTO n small sketch of planned work

BRA same as > BRASSIERE

BRAAI vb grill or roast (meat) over open coals

BRAAIED > BRAAI

BRAAIING > BRAAI

BRAAIS > BRAAI

BRAATA n small portion added to a purchase to encourage the customer to return

BRAATAS same as > BRAATA

BRAATASES > BRAATAS

BRABBLE rare word for > SQUABBLE

BRABBLED > BRABBLE

BRABBLER > BRABBLE

BRABBLERS > BRABBLE

BRABBLES > BRABBLE

BRABBLING > BRABBLE

BRACCATE adj (of birds) having feathered legs

BRACCIA > BRACCIO

BRACCIO n former unit of measurement; length of man's arm

BRACE n object fastened to something to straighten or support it ▷ vb steady or prepare (oneself) for something unpleasant

BRACED > BRACE

BRACELET n ornamental chain or band for the wrist

BRACELETS pl n handcuffs

BRACER n person or thing that braces

BRACERO n Mexican World War II labourer

BRACEROS > BRACERO

BRACERS > BRACER

BRACES pl n pair of straps worn over the shoulders for holding up the trousers

BRACH n female dog

BRACHAH n blessing

BRACHAHS > BRACHAH

BRACHES > BRACH

BRACHET same as > BRACH

BRACHETS > BRACHET

BRACHIA > BRACHIUM

BRACHIAL adj of or relating to the arm or to an armlike part or structure ▷ n brachial part or structure

BRACHIALS > BRACHIAL

BRACHIATE adj having widely divergent paired branches ▷ vb (of some arboreal apes and monkeys) swing by the arms from one hold to the next

BRACHIUM n arm, esp the upper part

BRACHIUMS > BRACHIUM

BRACHOT > BRACHAH

BRACHS > BRACH

BRACING adj refreshing and invigorating ▷ n system of braces used to strengthen or support

BRACINGLY > BRACING

BRACINGS > BRACING

BRACIOLA n Italian meat roulade

BRACIOLAS > BRACIOLA

BRACIOLE > BRACIOLA

BRACIOLES > BRACIOLE

BRACK same as > BARMBRACK

BRACKEN n large fern

BRACKENS > BRACKEN

BRACKET n pair of characters used to enclose a section of writing ▷ vb put in brackets

BRACKETED > BRACKET

BRACKETS > BRACKET

BRACKISH adj (of water) slightly salty

BRACKS > BRACK

BRACONID n type of fly with parasitic larva

BRACONIDS > BRACONID

BRACT n leaf at the base of a flower

BRACTEAL > BRACT

BRACTEATE adj (of a plant) having bracts ▷ n fine decorated dish or plate of precious metal

BRACTED > BRACT

BRACTEOLE n secondary bract subtending a flower within an inflorescence

BRACTLESS > BRACT

BRACTLET variant of > BRACTEOLE

BRACTLETS > BRACTLET

BRACTS > BRACT

BRAD n small tapered nail with a small head

BRADAWL n small boring tool

BRADAWLS > BRADAWL

BRADDED > BRAD

BRADDING > BRAD

BRADOON same as > BRIDOON

BRADOONS > BRADOON

BRADS > BRAD

BRAE n hill or slope

BRAEHEID n summit of a hill or slope

BRAEHEIDS > BRAEHEID

BRAES > BRAE

BRAG vb speak arrogantly and boastfully ▷ n boastful talk or behaviour ▷ adj boastful

BRAGGART n person who boasts loudly ▷ adj boastful

BRAGGARTS > BRAGGART

BRAGGED > BRAG

BRAGGER > BRAG

BRAGGERS > BRAG

BRAGGEST > BRAG

BRAGGIER > BRAGGY
BRAGGIEST > BRAGGY
BRAGGING > BRAG
BRAGGINGS > BRAG
BRAGGY *adj* boastful
BRAGLY > BRAG
BRAGS > BRAG
BRAHMA *n* breed of domestic fowl
BRAHMAN *n* member of highest Hindu caste
BRAHMANI *n* woman of the highest Hindu caste
BRAHMANIS > BRAHMANI
BRAHMANS > BRAHMAN
BRAHMAS > BRAHMA
BRAHMIN *same as* > BRAHMAN
BRAHMINS > BRAHMIN
BRAID *vb* interweave (hair, thread, etc) ▷ *n* length of hair etc that has been braided ▷ *adj* broad ▷ *adv* broadly
BRAIDE *adj* given to deceit
BRAIDED *adj* flowing in several shallow interconnected channels
BRAIDER > BRAID
BRAIDERS > BRAID
BRAIDEST > BRAID
BRAIDING *n* braids collectively
BRAIDINGS > BRAIDING
BRAIDS > BRAID
BRAIL *n* one of several lines fastened to a fore-and-aft sail to aid in furling it ▷ *vb* furl (a fore-and-aft sail) using brails
BRAILED > BRAIL
BRAILING > BRAIL
BRAILLE *n* system of writing for the blind ▷ *vb* print or write using this method
BRAILLED > BRAILLE
BRAILLER *n* device for producing text in braille
BRAILLERS > BRAILLER
BRAILLES > BRAILLE
BRAILLING > BRAILLE
BRAILLIST *n* braille transcriber
BRAILS > BRAIL
BRAIN *n* soft mass of nervous tissue in the head ▷ *vb* hit (someone) hard on the head
BRAINBOX *n* skull
BRAINCASE *n* part of cranium that covers brain
BRAINDEAD *adj* having suffered irreversible stoppage of breathing due to brain damage
BRAINED > BRAIN
BRAINFART *n* slang word for an idea expressed without much previous thought
BRAINFOOD *n* food containing nutrients that promote brain function
BRAINIAC *n* highly intelligent person
BRAINIACS > BRAINIAC
BRAINIER > BRAINY

BRAINIEST > BRAINY
BRAINILY > BRAINY
BRAINING > BRAIN
BRAINISH *adj* impulsive
BRAINLESS *adj* stupid
BRAINPAN *n* skull
BRAINPANS > BRAINPAN
BRAINS > BRAIN
BRAINSICK *adj* relating to or caused by insanity
BRAINSTEM *n* stalklike part of the brain consisting of the medulla oblongata, the midbrain, and the pons Varolii
BRAINWASH *vb* cause (a person) to alter his or her beliefs, esp by methods based on isolation, sleeplessness, etc
BRAINWAVE *n* sudden idea
BRAINWORK *n* work done with the brain
BRAINY *adj* clever
BRAIRD *vb* appear as shoots
BRAIRDED > BRAIRD
BRAIRDING > BRAIRD
BRAIRDS > BRAIRD
BRAISE *vb* cook slowly in a covered pan with a little liquid
BRAISED > BRAISE
BRAISES > BRAISE
BRAISING > BRAISE
BRAIZE *n* sea bream
BRAIZES > BRAIZE
BRAK *n* crossbred dog ▷ *adj* (of water) slightly salty
BRAKE *n* device for slowing a vehicle ▷ *vb* apply a brake
BRAKEAGE > BRAKE
BRAKEAGES > BRAKE
BRAKED > BRAKE
BRAKELESS > BRAKE
BRAKEMAN *n* crew member of a goods or passenger train
BRAKEMEN > BRAKEMAN
BRAKES > BRAKE
BRAKESMAN *n* pithead winch operator
BRAKESMEN > BRAKESMAN
BRAKIER > BRAKY
BRAKIEST > BRAKY
BRAKING *n* act of braking
BRAKINGS > BRAKING
BRAKS > BRAK
BRAKY *adj* brambly
BRALESS > BRA
BRAMBLE *n* Scots word for blackberry ▷ *vb* pick blackberries
BRAMBLED > BRAMBLE
BRAMBLES > BRAMBLE
BRAMBLIER > BRAMBLE
BRAMBLING *n* Eurasian finch with a speckled head and back and, in the male, a reddish brown breast and darker wings and tail
BRAMBLY > BRAMBLE
BRAME *n* powerful feeling of emotion
BRAMES > BRAME
BRAN *n* husks of cereal grain ▷ *vb* clean with water in which bran has been boiled

BRANCARD *n* couch on shafts, carried between two horses
BRANCARDS > BRANCARD
BRANCH *n* secondary stem of a tree ▷ *vb* (of stems, roots, etc) divide, then develop in different directions
BRANCHED > BRANCH
BRANCHER *n* young bird learning to fly
BRANCHERS > BRANCHER
BRANCHERY *n* branches
BRANCHES > BRANCH
BRANCHIA *n* gill in aquatic animals
BRANCHIAE > BRANCHIA
BRANCHIAL *adj* of or relating to the gills of an aquatic animal, esp a fish
BRANCHIER > BRANCH
BRANCHING > BRANCH
BRANCHLET *n* small branch
BRANCHY > BRANCH
BRAND *n* particular product ▷ *vb* mark with a brand
BRANDADE *n* French puréed fish dish
BRANDADES > BRANDADE
BRANDED *adj* identifiable as being the product of a particular company
BRANDER > BRAND
BRANDERED > BRAND
BRANDERS > BRAND
BRANDIED > BRANDY
BRANDIES > BRANDY
BRANDING > BRAND
BRANDINGS > BRAND
BRANDISE *n* three-legged metal stand for cooking pots
BRANDISES > BRANDISE
BRANDISH *vb* wave (a weapon etc) in a threatening way ▷ *n* threatening or defiant flourish
BRANDLESS > BRAND
BRANDLING *n* type of small red earthworm found in manure and used as bait by anglers
BRANDRETH *n* framework of bars used for cooking meat over fire
BRANDS > BRAND
BRANDY *n* alcoholic spirit distilled from wine ▷ *vb* give brandy to
BRANDYING > BRANDY
BRANE *n* hypothetical component of string theory
BRANES > BRANE
BRANGLE *vb* quarrel noisily
BRANGLED > BRANGLE
BRANGLES > BRANGLE
BRANGLING > BRANGLE
BRANK *vb* walk with swaggering gait
BRANKED > BRANK
BRANKIER > BRANKY
BRANKIEST > BRANKY
BRANKING > BRANK
BRANKS *pl n* (formerly) iron bridle used to restrain scolding women
BRANKY *adj* ostentatious

BRANLE *n* old French country dance performed in a linked circle
BRANLES > BRANLE
BRANNED > BRAN
BRANNER *n* person or machine that treats metal with bran
BRANNERS > BRANNER
BRANNIER > BRANNY
BRANNIEST > BRANNY
BRANNIGAN *n* noisy quarrel
BRANNING > BRAN
BRANNY *adj* having the appearance or texture of bran
BRANS > BRAN
BRANSLE *another word for* > BRANTLE
BRANSLES > BRANSLE
BRANT *n* type of small goose
BRANTAIL *n* singing bird with red tail
BRANTAILS > BRANTAIL
BRANTLE *n* French country dance
BRANTLES > BRANTLE
BRANTS > BRANT
BRAP *interj* exclamation used to imitate a burst of gunfire
BRAS *archaic form of* > BRASS
BRASCO *n* lavatory
BRASCOS > BRASCO
BRASERO *n* metal grid for burning coals
BRASEROS > BRASERO
BRASES > BRAS
BRASH *adj* offensively loud, showy, or self-confident ▷ *n* loose rubbish, such as broken rock, hedge clippings, etc ▷ *vb* assault
BRASHED > BRASH
BRASHER > BRASH
BRASHES > BRASH
BRASHEST > BRASH
BRASHIER > BRASHY
BRASHIEST > BRASHY
BRASHING > BRASH
BRASHLY > BRASH
BRASHNESS > BRASH
BRASHY *adj* loosely fragmented
BRASIER *same as* > BRAZIER
BRASIERS > BRASIER
BRASIL *same as* > BRAZIL
BRASILEIN *same as* > BRAZILEIN
BRASILIN *same as* > BRAZILIN
BRASILINS > BRASILIN
BRASILS > BRASIL
BRASS *n* alloy of copper and zinc ▷ *vb* make irritated or annoyed
BRASSAGE *n* amount charged by government for making coins
BRASSAGES > BRASSAGE
BRASSARD *n* identifying armband or badge
BRASSARDS > BRASSARD
BRASSART *same as* > BRASSARD
BRASSARTS > BRASSART
BRASSED > BRASS

b

BRASSERIE n restaurant serving drinks and cheap meals
BRASSES > BRASS
BRASSET same as > BRASSART
BRASSETS > BRASSET
BRASSICA n any plant of the cabbage and turnip family
BRASSICAS > BRASSICA
BRASSIE n former name for a golf club
BRASSIER > BRASSY
BRASSIERE n bra
BRASSIES > BRASSIE
BRASSIEST > BRASSY
BRASSILY > BRASSY
BRASSING > BRASS
BRASSISH > BRASS
BRASSWARE n items made of brass
BRASSY vb showy and vulgar
BRAST same as > BURST
BRASTING > BRAST
BRASTS > BRAST
BRAT n unruly child
BRATCHET n hunting dog
BRATCHETS > BRATCHET
BRATLING n small badly behaved child
BRATLINGS > BRATLING
BRATPACK n group of precocious and successful young actors, writers, etc
BRATPACKS > BRATPACK
BRATS > BRAT
BRATTICE n partition of wood or treated cloth used to control ventilation in a mine ▷ vb fit with a brattice
BRATTICED > BRATTICE
BRATTICES > BRATTICE
BRATTIER > BRAT
BRATTIEST > BRAT
BRATTISH same as > BRATTICE
BRATTLE vb make a rattling sound
BRATTLED > BRATTLE
BRATTLES > BRATTLE
BRATTLING > BRATTLE
BRATTY > BRAT
BRATWURST n type of small pork sausage
BRAUNCH old variant of > BRANCH
BRAUNCHED > BRAUNCH
BRAUNCHES > BRAUNCH
BRAUNITE n brown or black mineral
BRAUNITES > BRAUNITE
BRAVA n professional assassin
BRAVADO n showy display of self-confidence ▷ vb behave with bravado
BRAVADOED > BRAVADO
BRAVADOES > BRAVADO
BRAVADOS > BRAVADO
BRAVAS > BRAVA
BRAVE adj having or showing courage, resolution, and daring ▷ n Native American warrior ▷ vb confront with resolution or courage
BRAVED > BRAVE

BRAVELY > BRAVE
BRAVENESS > BRAVE
BRAVER > BRAVE
BRAVERIES > BRAVE
BRAVERS > BRAVE
BRAVERY > BRAVE
BRAVES > BRAVE
BRAVEST > BRAVE
BRAVI > BRAVO
BRAVING > BRAVE
BRAVO interj well done! ▷ n cry of 'bravo' ▷ vb cry or shout 'bravo'
BRAVOED > BRAVO
BRAVOES > BRAVO
BRAVOING > BRAVO
BRAVOS > BRAVO
BRAVURA n display of boldness or daring
BRAVURAS > BRAVURA
BRAVURE > BRAVURA
BRAW adj fine or excellent, esp in appearance or dress
BRAWER > BRAW
BRAWEST > BRAW
BRAWL n noisy fight ▷ vb fight noisily
BRAWLED > BRAWL
BRAWLER > BRAWL
BRAWLERS > BRAWL
BRAWLIE adj in good health
BRAWLIER > BRAWLIE
BRAWLIEST > BRAWLIE
BRAWLING > BRAWL
BRAWLINGS > BRAWL
BRAWLS > BRAWL
BRAWLY > BRAW
BRAWN n physical strength
BRAWNED > BRAWN
BRAWNIER > BRAWNY
BRAWNIEST > BRAWNY
BRAWNILY > BRAWNY
BRAWNS > BRAWN
BRAWNY adj muscular and strong
BRAWS pl n fine apparel
BRAXIES > BRAXY
BRAXY n acute and usually fatal bacterial disease of sheep
BRAY vb (of a donkey) utter its loud harsh sound ▷ n donkey's loud harsh sound
BRAYED > BRAY
BRAYER > BRAY
BRAYERS > BRAY
BRAYING > BRAY
BRAYS > BRAY
BRAZA n Spanish unit of measurement
BRAZAS > BRAZA
BRAZE vb join (two metal surfaces) with brass ▷ n high-melting solder or alloy used in brazing
BRAZED > BRAZE
BRAZELESS > BRAZE
BRAZEN adj shameless and bold ▷ vb face and overcome boldly or shamelessly
BRAZENED > BRAZEN
BRAZENING > BRAZEN
BRAZENLY > BRAZEN
BRAZENRY adj audacity
BRAZENS > BRAZEN
BRAZER > BRAZE

BRAZERS > BRAZE
BRAZES > BRAZE
BRAZIER n portable container for burning charcoal or coal
BRAZIERS > BRAZIER
BRAZIERY > BRAZIER
BRAZIL n red wood used for cabinetwork
BRAZILEIN n red crystalline solid
BRAZILIN n pale yellow soluble crystalline solid
BRAZILINS > BRAZILIN
BRAZILS > BRAZIL
BRAZING > BRAZE
BREACH n breaking of a promise, obligation, etc ▷ vb break (a promise, law, etc)
BREACHED > BREACH
BREACHER > BREACH
BREACHERS > BREACH
BREACHES > BREACH
BREACHING > BREACH
BREAD n food made by baking a mixture of flour and water or milk ▷ vb cover (food) with breadcrumbs before cooking
BREADBIN n container for bread
BREADBINS > BREADBIN
BREADBOX n airtight container for bread, cakes, etc
BREADED > BREAD
BREADHEAD n person solely concerned with money
BREADIER > BREADY
BREADIEST > BREADY
BREADING > BREAD
BREADLESS > BREAD
BREADLIKE adj like bread
BREADLINE n queue of people waiting for free food given as charity
BREADNUT n type of Central American and Caribbean tree
BREADNUTS > BREADNUT
BREADROOM n place where bread is kept on ship
BREADROOT n central N American leguminous plant with an edible starchy root
BREADS > BREAD
BREADTH n extent of something from side to side
BREADTHS > BREADTH
BREADY adj having the appearance or texture of bread
BREAK vb separate into pieces ▷ n act of breaking
BREAKABLE adj capable of being broken ▷ n fragile easily broken article
BREAKAGE n act or result of breaking
BREAKAGES > BREAKAGE
BREAKAWAY n dissenting group who have left a larger unit ▷ adj dissenting ▷ vb leave hastily or escape
BREAKBACK adj backbreaking; arduous
BREAKBEAT n type of electronic dance music

BREAKBONE adj as in breakbone fever dengue
BREAKDOWN n act or instance of breaking down
BREAKER n large wave
BREAKERS > BREAKER
BREAKEVEN n the level of commercial activity at which the total cost and total revenue of a business enterprise are equal
BREAKFAST n first meal of the day ▷ vb eat breakfast
BREAKING > BREAK
BREAKINGS > BRACKEN
BREAKNECK adj fast and dangerous
BREAKOFF n act or an instance of breaking off or stopping
BREAKOFFS > BREAKOFF
BREAKOUT n escape, esp from prison or confinement
BREAKOUTS > BREAKOUT
BREAKS > BREAK
BREAKTIME n period of rest or recreation, esp at school
BREAKUP n separation or disintegration
BREAKUPS > BREAKUP
BREAKWALL n breakwater
BREAM n Eurasian freshwater fish ▷ vb clean debris (from the bottom of a vessel)
BREAMED > BREAM
BREAMING > BREAM
BREAMS > BREAM
BREARE same as > BRIER
BREARES > BREARE
BREASKIT same as > BRISKET
BREASKITS > BREASKIT
BREAST n either of the milk-secreting glands on a woman's chest ▷ vb reach the summit of
BREASTED > BREAST
BREASTFED adj fed at mother's breast
BREASTING > BREAST
BREASTPIN n brooch worn on the breast
BREASTS > BREAST
BREATH n taking in and letting out of air during breathing
BREATHE vb take in oxygen and give out carbon dioxide
BREATHED adj denoting a speech sound in which the vocal cords do not vibrate
BREATHER n short rest
BREATHERS > BREATHER
BREATHES > BREATHE
BREATHFUL > BREATH
BREATHIER > BREATHY
BREATHILY > BREATHY
BREATHING n passage of air into and out of the lungs to supply the body with oxygen
BREATHS > BREATH
BREATHY adj (of the speaking voice) accompanied by an audible emission of breath
BRECCIA n type of rock
BRECCIAL > BRECCIA

BRECCIAS > BRECCIA
BRECCIATE > BRECCIA
BRECHAM n straw horse-collar
BRECHAMS > BRECHAM
BRECHAN same as > BRECHAM
BRECHANS > BRECHAN
BRED n person who lives in a small remote place
BREDE archaic spelling of > BRAID
BREDED > BREDE
BREDES > BREDE
BREDIE n meat and vegetable stew
BREDIES > BREDIE
BREDING > BREDE
BREDREN same as > BRETHREN
BREDRENS > BREDREN
BREDRIN same as > BRETHREN
BREDRINS > BREDRIN
BREDS > BRED
BREE n broth, stock, or juice
BREECH n lower part ▷ vb fit (a gun) with a breech
BREECHED > BREECH
BREECHES pl n trousers extending to just below the knee
BREECHING n strap of a harness that passes behind a horse's haunches
BREED vb produce new or improved strains of (domestic animals or plants) ▷ n group of animals etc within a species that have certain clearly defined characteristics
BREEDER n person who breeds plants or animals
BREEDERS > BREEDER
BREEDING > BREED
BREEDINGS > BREED
BREEDS > BREED
BREEKS pl n trousers
BREEM same as > BREME
BREENGE vb lunge forward ▷ n violent movement
BREENGED > BREENGE
BREENGES > BREENGE
BREENGING > BREENGE
BREER another word for > BRAIRD
BREERED > BREER
BREERING > BREER
BREERS > BREER
BREES > BREE
BREESE same as > BREEZE
BREESES > BREESE
BREEST same as > BREAST
BREESTS > BREEST
BREEZE n gentle wind ▷ vb move quickly or casually
BREEZED > BREEZE
BREEZES > BREEZE
BREEZEWAY n roofed passageway connecting two buildings, sometimes with the sides enclosed
BREEZIER > BREEZY
BREEZIEST > BREEZY
BREEZILY > BREEZY
BREEZING > BREEZE

BREEZY adj windy
BREGMA n point on the top of the skull
BREGMAS > BREGMA
BREGMATA > BREGMA
BREGMATE > BREGMA
BREGMATIC > BREGMA
BREHON n (formerly) judge in Ireland
BREHONS > BREHON
BREI vb speak with a uvular r, esp in Afrikaans
BREID n bread
BREIDS > BREID
BREIING > BREI
BREINGE same as > BREENGE
BREINGED > BREINGE
BREINGES > BREINGE
BREINGING > BREINGE
BREIS > BREI
BREIST Scot word for > BREAST
BREISTS > BREIST
BREKKIE same as > BREKKY
BREKKIES > BREKKY
BREKKY slang word for > BREAKFAST
BRELOQUE n charm attached to watch chain
BRELOQUES > BRELOQUE
BREME adj well-known
BREN n type of machine gun ▷ vb burn
BRENNE vb burn
BRENNES > BRENNE
BRENNING > BREN
BRENS > BREN
BRENT n type of goose ▷ adj steep
BRENTER > BRENT
BRENTEST > BRENT
BRENTS > BRENT
BRER n brother: usually prefixed to a name
BRERE same as > BRIER
BRERES > BRERE
BRERS > BRER
BRESAOLA n (in Italian cookery) air-dried, salted beef
BRESAOLAS > BRESAOLA
BRETASCHE another word for > BRATTICE
BRETESSE another word for > BRATTICE
BRETESSES > BRETESSE
BRETHREN > BROTHER
BRETON n hat with an upturned brim and a rounded crown
BRETONS > BRETON
BRETTICE same as > BRATTICE
BRETTICED > BRETTICE
BRETTICES > BRETTICE
BREVE n accent placed over a vowel to indicate shortness
BREVES > BREVE
BREVET n document entitling a commissioned officer to hold temporarily a higher military rank ▷ vb promote by brevet
BREVETCY > BREVET
BREVETE adj patented
BREVETED > BREVET

BREVETING > BREVET
BREVETS > BREVET
BREVETTED > BREVET
BREVIARY n book of prayers to be recited daily by a Roman Catholic priest
BREVIATE n summary
BREVIATES > BREVIATE
BREVIER n (formerly) size of printer's type approximately equal to 8 point
BREVIERS > BREVIER
BREVIS same as > BREWIS
BREVISES > BREVIS
BREVITIES > BREVITY
BREVITY n shortness
BREW vb make (beer etc) by steeping, boiling, and fermentation ▷ n beverage produced by brewing
BREWAGE n product of brewing
BREWAGES > BREWAGE
BREWED > BREW
BREWER > BREW
BREWERIES > BREWERY
BREWERS > BREW
BREWERY n place where beer, etc is brewed
BREWHOUSE n brewery
BREWING n quantity of a beverage brewed at one time
BREWINGS > BREWING
BREWIS n bread soaked in broth, gravy, etc
BREWISES > BREWIS
BREWPUB n pub that incorporates a brewery on its premises
BREWPUBS > BREWPUB
BREWS > BREW
BREWSKI n beer
BREWSKIES > BREWSKI
BREWSKIS > BREWSKI
BREWSTER n person, particularly a woman, who brews
BREWSTERS > BREWSTER
BREY same as > BREI
BREYED > BREY
BREYING > BREY
BREYS > BREY
BRIAR n S European shrub with a hard woody root (briarroot)
BRIARD n medium-sized dog
BRIARDS > BRIARD
BRIARED > BRIAR
BRIARIER > BRIARY
BRIARIEST > BRIARY
BRIARROOT n hard woody root of the briar, used for making tobacco pipes
BRIARS > BRIAR
BRIARWOOD same as > BRIARROOT
BRIARY adj resembling or containing briar
BRIBABLE > BRIBE
BRIBE vb offer or give something to someone to gain favour, influence, etc ▷ n something given or offered as a bribe
BRIBEABLE > BRIBE
BRIBED > BRIBE
BRIBEE n one who is bribed

BRIBEES > BRIBEE
BRIBER > BRIBE
BRIBERIES > BRIBERY
BRIBERS > BRIBE
BRIBERY n process of giving or taking bribes
BRIBES > BRIBE
BRIBING > BRIBE
BRICABRAC n miscellaneous small objects, esp furniture and curios, kept because they are ornamental or rare
BRICHT Scot word for > BRIGHT
BRICHTER > BRICHT
BRICHTEST > BRICHT
BRICK n (rectangular block of) baked clay used in building ▷ vb build, enclose, or fill with bricks
BRICKBAT n blunt criticism
BRICKBATS > BRICKBAT
BRICKCLAY n clay for making bricks
BRICKED > BRICK
BRICKEN adj made of brick
BRICKIE n bricklayer
BRICKIER > BRICKY
BRICKIES > BRICKIE
BRICKIEST > BRICKY
BRICKING > BRICK
BRICKINGS > BRICK
BRICKKILN n kiln for making bricks
BRICKLE variant of > BRITTLE
BRICKLES > BRICKLE
BRICKLIKE > BRICK
BRICKS > BRICK
BRICKWALL same as > BRICOLE
BRICKWORK n structure, such as a wall, built of bricks
BRICKY vb resembling brick
BRICKYARD n place in which bricks are made, stored, or sold
BRICOLAGE n jumbled effect produced by the close proximity of buildings from different periods and in different architectural styles
BRICOLE n billiards shot
BRICOLES > BRICOLE
BRICOLEUR n person who practises bricolage
BRIDAL adj of a bride or a wedding ▷ n wedding or wedding feast
BRIDALLY > BRIDAL
BRIDALS > BRIDAL
BRIDE n woman who has just been or is about to be married ▷ vb act as a bride
BRIDECAKE n wedding cake
BRIDED > BRIDE
BRIDEMAID n old form of bridesmaid
BRIDEMAN n bridegroom's attendant
BRIDEMEN > BRIDEMAN
BRIDES > BRIDE
BRIDESMAN same as > BRIDEMAN
BRIDESMEN > BRIDESMAN

b

BRIDEWELL n house of correction

BRIDGABLE > BRIDGE

BRIDGE n structure for crossing a river etc ▷ vb build a bridge over (something)

BRIDGED > BRIDGE

BRIDGES > BRIDGE

BRIDGING n timber struts fixed between floor or roof joists

BRIDGINGS > BRIDGING

BRIDIE n semicircular pie containing meat and onions

BRIDIES > BRIDIE

BRIDING > BRIDE

BRIDLE n headgear for controlling a horse ▷ vb show anger or indignation

BRIDLED > BRIDLE

BRIDLER > BRIDLE

BRIDLERS > BRIDLE

BRIDLES > BRIDLE

BRIDLEWAY n path for riding horses

BRIDLING > BRIDLE

BRIDOON n horse's bit: small snaffle used in double bridles

BRIDOONS > BRIDOON

BRIE same as > BREE

BRIEF adj short in duration ▷ n condensed statement or written synopsis ▷ vb give information and instructions to (a person)

BRIEFCASE n small flat case for carrying papers, books, etc

BRIEFED > BRIEF

BRIEFER > BRIEF

BRIEFERS > BRIEF

BRIEFEST > BRIEF

BRIEFING n meeting for giving out detailed information or instructions

BRIEFINGS > BRIEFING

BRIEFLESS adj (said of a barrister) without clients

BRIEFLY > BRIEF

BRIEFNESS > BRIEF

BRIEFS pl n men's or women's underpants without legs

BRIER same as > BRIAR

BRIERED > BRIER

BRIERIER > BRIER

BRIERIEST > BRIER

BRIERROOT same as > BRIARROOT

BRIERS > BRIER

BRIERWOOD same as > BRIARROOT

BRIERY > BRIER

BRIES > BRIE

BRIG n two-masted square-rigged ship

BRIGADE n army unit smaller than a division ▷ vb organize into a brigade

BRIGADED > BRIGADE

BRIGADES > BRIGADE

BRIGADIER n high-ranking army officer

BRIGADING > BRIGADE

BRIGALOW n type of acacia tree

BRIGALOWS > BRIGALOW

BRIGAND n bandit

BRIGANDRY > BRIGAND

BRIGANDS > BRIGAND

BRIGHT adj emitting or reflecting much light ▷ adv brightly

BRIGHTEN vb make or become bright or brighter

BRIGHTENS > BRIGHTEN

BRIGHTER > BRIGHT

BRIGHTEST > BRIGHT

BRIGHTISH > BRIGHT

BRIGHTLY > BRIGHT

BRIGHTS pl n high beam of the headlights of a motor vehicle

BRIGS > BRIG

BRIGUE vb solicit

BRIGUED > BRIGUE

BRIGUES > BRIGUE

BRIGUING > BRIGUE

BRIGUINGS > BRIGUE

BRIK n Tunisian pastry

BRIKI same as > CEZVE

BRIKIS > BRIKI

BRIKS > BRIK

BRILL n type of European flatfish popular as a food fish ▷ adj brilliant

BRILLER > BRILL

BRILLEST > BRILL

BRILLIANT adj shining with light ▷ n popular circular cut for diamonds and other gemstones in the form of two many-faceted pyramids (the top one truncated) joined at their bases

BRILLO n tradename for a type of scouring pad impregnated with a detergent

BRILLOS > BRILLO

BRILLS > BRILL

BRIM n upper rim of a vessel ▷ vb fill or be full to the brim

BRIMFUL adj completely filled with

BRIMFULL same as > BRIMFUL

BRIMFULLY > BRIMFUL

BRIMING n phosphorescence of sea

BRIMINGS > BRIMING

BRIMLESS > BRIM

BRIMMED > BRIM

BRIMMER n vessel, such as a glass or bowl, filled to the brim

BRIMMERS > BRIMMER

BRIMMING > BRIM

BRIMS > BRIM

BRIMSTONE n sulphur

BRIMSTONY adj like brimstone

BRIN n thread of silk from silkworm

BRINDED adj streaky or patchy

BRINDISI n song sung in celebration

BRINDISIS > BRINDISI

BRINDLE n brindled animal

BRINDLED adj brown or grey streaked with a darker colour

BRINDLES > BRINDLE

BRINE n salt water ▷ vb soak in or treat with brine

BRINED > BRINE

BRINELESS > BRINE

BRINER > BRINE

BRINERS > BRINE

BRINES > BRINE

BRING vb carry, convey, or take to a designated place or person

BRINGDOWN n comedown

BRINGER > BRING

BRINGERS > BRING

BRINGING > BRING

BRINGINGS > BRING

BRINGS > BRING

BRINIER > BRINY

BRINIES > BRINY

BRINIEST > BRINY

BRININESS > BRINY

BRINING > BRINE

BRINISH > BRINE

BRINJAL n dark purple tropical fruit, cooked and eaten as a vegetable

BRINJALS > BRINJAL

BRINJARRY n grain trader

BRINK n edge of a steep place

BRINKMAN n one who goes in for brinkmanship

BRINKMEN > BRINKMAN

BRINKS > BRINK

BRINNIES > BRINNY

BRINNY n stone, esp when thrown

BRINS > BRIN

BRINY adj very salty ▷ n sea

BRIO n liveliness

BRIOCHE n soft roll or loaf made from a very light yeast dough, sometimes mixed with currants

BRIOCHES > BRIOCHE

BRIOLETTE n pear-shaped gem cut with long triangular facets

BRIONIES > BRIONY

BRIONY same as > BRYONY

BRIOS > BRIO

BRIQUET same as > BRIQUETTE

BRIQUETS > BRIQUET

BRIQUETTE n block of compressed coal dust ▷ vb make into the form of a brick or bricks

BRIS n ritual circumcision of male babies

BRISANCE n shattering effect or power of an explosion or explosive

BRISANCES > BRISANCE

BRISANT > BRISANCE

BRISE n type of jump

BRISES > BRIS

BRISK adj lively and quick ▷ vb enliven

BRISKED > BRISK

BRISKEN vb make or become more lively or brisk

BRISKENED > BRISKEN

BRISKENS > BRISKEN

BRISKER > BRISK

BRISKEST > BRISK

BRISKET n beef from the breast of a cow

BRISKETS > BRISKET

BRISKIER > BRISKY

BRISKIEST > BRISKY

BRISKING > BRISK

BRISKISH > BRISK

BRISKLY > BRISK

BRISKNESS > BRISK

BRISKS > BRISK

BRISKY another word for > BRISK

BRISLING same as > SPRAT

BRISLINGS > BRISLING

BRISS same as > BRIS

BRISSES > BRIS

BRISTLE n short stiff hair ▷ vb (cause to) stand up like bristles

BRISTLED > BRISTLE

BRISTLES > BRISTLE

BRISTLIER > BRISTLE

BRISTLING > BRISTLE

BRISTLY > BRISTLE

BRISTOL n as in bristol board type of heavy cardboard

BRISTOLS pl n vulgar word for a woman's breasts

BRISURE n mark of cadency in heraldry

BRISURES > BRISURE

BRIT n young of a herring, sprat, or similar fish

BRITANNIA n coin bearing figure of Britannia

BRITCHES same as > BREECHES

BRITH same as > BRIS

BRITHS > BRITH

BRITS > BRIT

BRITSCHKA n light open carriage

BRITSKA same as > BRITZKA

BRITSKAS > BRITSKA

BRITT n young herring or sprat

BRITTANIA variant spelling of > BRITANNIA

BRITTLE adj hard but easily broken ▷ vb make brittle ▷ n crunchy sweet made with treacle and nuts

BRITTLED > BRITTLE

BRITTLELY > BRITTLE

BRITTLER > BRITTLE

BRITTLES > BRITTLE

BRITTLEST > BRITTLE

BRITTLING > BRITTLE

BRITTLY > BRITTLE

BRITTS > BRITT

BRITZKA n long horse-drawn carriage

BRITZKAS > BRITZKA

BRITZSKA same as > BRITZKA

BRITZSKAS > BRITZKA

BRIZE same as > BREEZE

BRIZES > BRIZE

BRO n family member

BROACH vb introduce (a topic) for discussion ▷ n spit for roasting meat

BROACHED > BROACH

BROACHER > BROACH

BROACHERS > BROACH

BROACHES > BROACH

b

BROACHING > BROACH

BROAD adj having great breadth or width ▷ n broad part of something

BROADAX same as > BROADAXE

BROADAXE n broad-bladed axe

BROADAXES > BROADAXE

BROADBAND n telecommunication transmission technique using a wide range of frequencies

BROADBEAN n variety of bean

BROADBILL n tropical African and Asian bird with bright plumage and a short wide bill

BROADBRIM n broad-brimmed hat, esp one worn by the Quakers in the 17th century

BROADCAST n programme or announcement on radio or television ▷ vb transmit (a programme or announcement) on radio or television ▷ adj dispersed over a wide area ▷ adv far and wide

BROADEN vb make or become broad or broader

BROADENED > BROADEN

BROADENER > BROADEN

BROADENS > BROADEN

BROADER > BROAD

BROADEST > BROAD

BROADISH > BROAD

BROADLEAF n any tobacco plant having broad leaves, used esp in making cigars

BROADLINE n company dealing in large volumes of cheap products

BROADLOOM n a carpet woven on a wide loom

BROADLY > BROAD

BROADNESS > BROAD

BROADS > BROAD

BROADSIDE n strong verbal or written attack ▷ adv with a broader side facing an object

BROADTAIL n highly valued black wavy fur obtained from the skins of newly born karakul lambs

BROADWAY n wide road

BROADWAYS > BROADWAY

BROADWISE adv rare form of breadthwise

BROAST vb cook by broiling and roasting

BROASTED > BROAST

BROASTING > BROAST

BROASTS > BROAST

BROCADE n rich fabric woven with a raised design ▷ vb weave with such a design

BROCADED > BROCADE

BROCADES > BROCADE

BROCADING > BROCADE

BROCAGE another word for > BROKERAGE

BROCAGES > BROCAGE

BROCARD n basic principle of civil law

BROCARDS > BROCARD

BROCATEL n heavy upholstery brocade

BROCATELS > BROCATEL

BROCCOLI n type of cabbage with greenish flower heads

BROCCOLIS > BROCCOLI

BROCH n (in Scotland) a circular dry-stone tower large enough to serve as a fortified home

BROCHAN n type of thin porridge

BROCHANS > BROCHAN

BROCHE adj woven with a raised design, as brocade

BROCHED > BROCHE

BROCHES > BROCHE

BROCHETTE n skewer used for holding pieces of meat or vegetables while grilling

BROCHING > BROCHE

BROCHO same as > BRACHAH

BROCHOS > BROCHO

BROCHS > BROCH

BROCHURE n booklet that contains information about a product or service

BROCHURES > BROCHURE

BROCK n badger

BROCKAGE same as > BROKERAGE

BROCKAGES > BROCKAGE

BROCKED adj having different colours

BROCKET n small tropical American deer with small unbranched antlers

BROCKETS > BROCKET

BROCKIT same as > BROCKED

BROCKRAM another word for > BRECCIA

BROCKRAMS > BROCKRAM

BROCKS > BROCK

BROCOLI same as > BROCCOLI

BROCOLIS > BROCOLI

BROD vb prod

BRODDED > BROD

BRODDING > BROD

BRODDLE vb poke or pierce (something)

BRODDLED > BRODDLE

BRODDLES > BRODDLE

BRODDLING > BRODDLE

BRODEKIN another word for > BUSKIN

BRODEKINS > BRODEKIN

BRODKIN same as > BRODEKIN

BRODKINS > BRODKIN

BRODS > BROD

BROEKIES pl n underpants

BROG vb prick with an awl

BROGAN n heavy laced, usually ankle-high, work boot

BROGANS > BROGAN

BROGGED > BROG

BROGGING > BROG

BROGH same as > BROCH

BROGHS > BROGH

BROGS > BROG

BROGUE n gentle accent

BROGUEISH > BROGUE

BROGUERY > BROGUE

BROGUES > BROGUE

BROGUISH > BROGUE

BROIDER archaic word for > EMBROIDER

BROIDERED > BROIDER

BROIDERER > BROIDER

BROIDERS > BROIDER

BROIDERY n old form of embroidery

BROIL vb cook by direct heat under a grill ▷ n process of broiling

BROILED > BROIL

BROILER n young tender chicken for roasting

BROILERS > BROILER

BROILING > BROIL

BROILS > BROIL

BROKAGE another word for > BROKERAGE

BROKAGES > BROKAGE

BROKE vb negotiate or deal

BROKED > BROKE

BROKEN > BREAK

BROKENLY > BREAK

BROKER n agent who buys or sells goods, securities, etc ▷ vb act as a broker (in)

BROKERAGE n commission charged by a broker

BROKERED > BROKER

BROKERIES > BROKERY

BROKERING > BROKER

BROKERS > BROKER

BROKERY n work done by a broker

BROKES > BROKE

BROKING > BROKE

BROKINGS > BROKE

BROLGA n large grey Australian crane with a trumpeting call

BROLGAS > BROLGA

BROLLIES > BROLLY

BROLLY n umbrella

BROMAL n synthetic liquid formerly used medicinally

BROMALS > BROMAL

BROMANCE n close friendship between two men

BROMANCES > BROMANCE

BROMANTIC adj pertaining to or indicating a bromance

BROMATE same as > BROMINATE

BROMATED > BROMATE

BROMATES > BROMATE

BROMATING > BROMATE

BROME n type of grass

BROMELAIN n enzyme in pineapples

BROMELIA n type of plant

BROMELIAD n tropical American plant with a rosette of fleshy leaves

BROMELIAS > BROMELIA

BROMELIN n protein-digesting enzyme found in pineapple

BROMELINS > BROMELIN

BROMEOSIN another name for > EOSIN

BROMES > BROME

BROMIC adj of or containing bromine in the trivalent or pentavalent state

BROMID same as > BROMIDE

BROMIDE n chemical compound used in medicine and photography

BROMIDES > BROMIDE

BROMIDIC adj ordinary

BROMIDS > BROMID

BROMIN same as > BROMINE

BROMINATE vb treat or react with bromine

BROMINE n dark red liquid element that gives off a pungent vapour

BROMINES > BROMINE

BROMINISM same as > BROMISM

BROMINS > BROMIN

BROMISE same as > BROMIZE

BROMISED > BROMISE

BROMISES > BROMISE

BROMISING > BROMIZE

BROMISM n bromine poisoning

BROMISMS > BROMISM

BROMIZE vb treat with bromine

BROMIZED > BROMIZE

BROMIZES > BROMIZE

BROMIZING > BROMIZE

BROMMER n S African word for bluebottle

BROMMERS > BROMMER

BROMO n something that contains bromide

BROMOFORM n heavy colourless liquid substance with a sweetish taste

BROMOS > BROMO

BRONC same as > BRONCO

BRONCHI > BRONCHUS

BRONCHIA pl n bronchial tubes

BRONCHIAL adj of the bronchi

BRONCHIUM n medium-sized bronchial tube

BRONCHO same as > BRONCO

BRONCHOS > BRONCHO

BRONCHUS n either of the two branches of the windpipe

BRONCO n (in the US) wild or partially tamed pony

BRONCOS > BRONCO

BRONCS > BRONC

BROND n old form of brand

BRONDE adj in a shade between blonde and brunette ▷ n woman with bronde hair

BRONDER > BRONDE

BRONDES > BRONDE

BRONDEST > BRONDE

BRONDS > BROND

BRONDYRON n sword

BRONZE n alloy of copper and tin ▷ adj made of, or coloured like, bronze ▷ vb (esp of the skin) make or become brown

BRONZED > BRONZE

BRONZEN adj made of or the colour of bronze

b

BRONZER n cosmetic applied to the skin to simulate a sun tan

BRONZERS > BRONZER

BRONZES > BRONZE

BRONZIER > BRONZE

BRONZIEST > BRONZE

BRONZIFY vb cause to become colour of bronze

BRONZING n blue pigment

BRONZINGS > BRONZING

BRONZITE n type of orthopyroxene often having a metallic or pearly sheen

BRONZITES > BRONZITE

BRONZY > BRONZE

BROO n brow of hill

BROOCH n ornament with a pin, worn fastened to clothes ▷ vb decorate with a brooch

BROOCHED > BROOCH

BROOCHES > BROOCH

BROOCHING > BROOCH

BROOD n number of birds produced at one hatching ▷ vb (of a bird) sit on or hatch eggs

BROODED > BROOD

BROODER n structure used for rearing young chickens or other fowl

BROODERS > BROODER

BROODIER > BROODY

BROODIEST > BROODY

BROODILY > BROODY

BROODING > BROOD

BROODINGS > BROOD

BROODLESS > BROOD

BROODMARE n mare for breeding

BROODS > BROOD

BROODY adj moody and sullen

BROOK n small stream ▷ vb bear or tolerate

BROOKABLE > BROOK

BROOKED > BROOK

BROOKIE n brook trout

BROOKIES > BROOKIE

BROOKING > BROOK

BROOKITE n reddish-brown to black mineral

BROOKITES > BROOKITE

BROOKLET n small brook

BROOKLETS > BROOKLET

BROOKLIKE > BROOK

BROOKLIME n type of blue-flowered trailing plant of N America, Europe or Asia, which grows in moist places

BROOKS > BROOK

BROOKWEED n type of white-flowered plant of Europe or North America, growing in moist places

BROOL n low roar

BROOLS > BROOL

BROOM n long-handled sweeping brush ▷ vb sweep with a broom

BROOMBALL n type of ice hockey played with broom

BROOMCORN n variety of sorghum, the long stiff flower stalks of which can be used to make brooms

BROOMED > BROOM

BROOMIER > BROOMY

BROOMIEST > BROOMY

BROOMING > BROOM

BROOMRAPE n type of plant which grows as brownish small-flowered leafless parasites on the roots of other plants

BROOMS > BROOM

BROOMY adj covered with growth of broom

BROOS > BROO

BROOSE n race at country wedding

BROOSES > BROOSE

BROS > BRO

BROSE n oatmeal or pease porridge, sometimes with butter or fat added

BROSES > BROSE

BROSIER > BROSY

BROSIEST > BROSY

BROSY adj smeared with porridge

BROTH n soup, usu containing vegetables

BROTHA n informal term for an African-American man

BROTHAS > BROTHA

BROTHEL n house where people pay to have sex with sex workers

BROTHELS > BROTHEL

BROTHER n boy or man with the same parents as another person ▷ interj exclamation of amazement, disgust, surprise, disappointment, etc ▷ vb treat someone like a brother

BROTHERED > BROTHER

BROTHERLY adj of or like a brother, esp in showing loyalty and affection ▷ adv in a brotherly way

BROTHERS > BROTHER

BROTHIER > BROTHY

BROTHIEST > BROTHY

BROTHS > BROTH

BROTHY adj having appearance or texture of broth

BROUGH same as **>** BROCH

BROUGHAM n horse-drawn closed carriage with a raised open driver's seat in front

BROUGHAMS > BROUGHAM

BROUGHS > BROUGH

BROUGHT > BRING

BROUGHTA same as **>** BRAATA

BROUGHTAS same as **>** BRAATA

BROUHAHA n loud confused noise

BROUHAHAS > BROUHAHA

BROUZE same as **>** BROOSE

BROUZES > BROUZE

BROW n part of the face (from the eyes to the hairline)

BROWALLIA n flowering plant

BROWBAND n strap of a horse's bridle that goes across the forehead

BROWBANDS > BROWBAND

BROWBEAT vb frighten (someone) with threats

BROWBEATS > BROWBEAT

BROWBONE n bone of the brow

BROWBONES > BROWBONE

BROWED adj having a brow

BROWLESS > BROW

BROWN n colour of earth or wood ▷ adj (of bread) made from wheatmeal or wholemeal flour ▷ vb make or become brown

BROWNED > BROWN

BROWNER n brown object

BROWNERS > BROWNER

BROWNEST > BROWN

BROWNIE n small square nutty chocolate cake

BROWNIER > BROWN

BROWNIES > BROWNIE

BROWNIEST > BROWN

BROWNING n substance used to darken gravies

BROWNINGS > BROWNING

BROWNISH > BROWN

BROWNNESS > BROWN

BROWNNOSE vb be abjectly subservient

BROWNOUT n dimming or reduction in the use of electric lights in a city

BROWNOUTS > BROWNOUT

BROWNS > BROWN

BROWNTAIL adj as in browntail moth kind of moth

BROWNY > BROWN

BROWRIDGE n ridge of bone over eyes

BROWS > BROW

BROWSABLE > BROWSE

BROWSE vb look through in a casual manner ▷ n instance of browsing

BROWSED > BROWSE

BROWSER n software package that enables a user to read hypertext, esp on the internet

BROWSERS > BROWSER

BROWSES > BROWSE

BROWSIER > BROWSE

BROWSIEST > BROWSE

BROWSING > BROWSE

BROWSINGS > BROWSE

BROWST n brewing (of ale, tea)

BROWSTS > BROWST

BROWSY > BROWSE

BRR same as **>** BRRR

BRRR interj used to suggest shivering

BRU South African word for **>** FRIEND

BRUCELLA n type of bacterium

BRUCELLAE > BRUCELLA

BRUCELLAS > BRUCELLA

BRUCHID n type of beetle

BRUCHIDS > BRUCHID

BRUCIN same as **>** BRUCINE

BRUCINE n bitter poisonous alkaloid resembling strychnine

BRUCINES > BRUCINE

BRUCINS > BRUCIN

BRUCITE n white translucent mineral

BRUCITES > BRUCITE

BRUCKLE adj brittle

BRUGH n large house

BRUGHS > BRUGH

BRUHAHA same as **>** BROUHAHA

BRUHAHAS > BRUHAHA

BRUILZIE same as **>** BRULZIE

BRUILZIES > BRUILZIE

BRUIN n name for a bear, used in children's tales, fables, etc

BRUINS > BRUIN

BRUISE n discoloured area on the skin caused by an injury ▷ vb cause a bruise on

BRUISED > BRUISE

BRUISER n strong tough person

BRUISERS > BRUISER

BRUISES > BRUISE

BRUISING adj causing bruises, as by a blow ▷ n bruise or bruises

BRUISINGS > BRUISING

BRUIT vb report ▷ n abnormal sound heard within the body

BRUITED > BRUIT

BRUITER > BRUIT

BRUITERS > BRUIT

BRUITING > BRUIT

BRUITS > BRUIT

BRULE n archaic short word for a person of mixed Canadian Indian and White ancestry

BRULES > BRULE

BRULOT n coffee-based alcoholic drink, served flaming

BRULOTS > BRULOT

BRULYIE same as **>** BRULZIE

BRULYIES > BRULYIE

BRULZIE n noisy dispute

BRULZIES > BRULZIE

BRUMAL adj of, characteristic of, or relating to winter

BRUMBIES > BRUMBY

BRUMBY n wild horse

BRUME n heavy mist or fog

BRUMES > BRUME

BRUMMAGEM n something that is cheap and flashy, esp imitation jewellery

BRUMMER same as **>** BROMMER

BRUMMERS > BRUMMER

BRUMOUS > BRUME

BRUNCH n breakfast and lunch combined ▷ vb eat brunch

BRUNCHED > BRUNCH

BRUNCHER > BRUNCH

BRUNCHERS > BRUNCH

BRUNCHES > BRUNCH

BRUNCHING > BRUNCH

BRUNET n boy or man with dark brown hair

BRUNETS > BRUNET

BRUNETTE n girl or woman with dark brown hair

BRUNETTES > BRUNETTE

BRUNG > BRING

BRUNIZEM n prairie soil

BRUNIZEMS > BRUNIZEM

BRUNT n main force or shock of a blow, attack, etc ▷ vb suffer the main force or shock of a blow, attack, etc
BRUNTED > BRUNT
BRUNTING > BRUNT
BRUNTS > BRUNT
BRUS > BRU
BRUSH n device made of bristles, wires, etc ▷ vb clean, scrub, or paint with a brush
BRUSHABLE adj able to be brushed
BRUSHBACK n (baseball) ball intended to hit the batter
BRUSHED adj treated with a brushing process
BRUSHER > BRUSH
BRUSHERS > BRUSH
BRUSHES > BRUSH
BRUSHFIRE n fire in bushes and scrub
BRUSHIER > BRUSHY
BRUSHIEST > BRUSHY
BRUSHING > BRUSH
BRUSHINGS > BRUSH
BRUSHLAND n land characterized by patchy shrubs
BRUSHLESS > BRUSH
BRUSHLIKE > BRUSH
BRUSHMARK n indented lines sometimes left by the bristles of a brush on a painted surface
BRUSHOFF n abrupt dismissal or rejection
BRUSHOFFS > BRUSHOFF
BRUSHUP n the act or an instance of tidying one's appearance
BRUSHUPS > BRUSHUP
BRUSHWOOD n cut or broken-off tree branches and twigs
BRUSHWORK n characteristic manner of applying paint with a brush
BRUSHY adj like a brush
BRUSK same as > BRUSQUE
BRUSKER > BRUSK
BRUSKEST > BRUSK
BRUSQUE adj blunt or curt in manner or speech
BRUSQUELY > BRUSQUE
BRUSQUER > BRUSQUE
BRUSQUEST > BRUSQUE
BRUSSELS adj as in brussels sprout small cabbage-like vegetable
BRUSSEN adj bold
BRUST same as > BURST
BRUSTING > BRUST
BRUSTS > BRUST
BRUT adj (of champagne or sparkling wine) very dry ▷ n very dry champagne
BRUTAL adj cruel and vicious
BRUTALISE same as > BRUTALIZE
BRUTALISM n austere architectural style of the 1950s on, characterized by the use of exposed concrete and angular shapes
BRUTALIST > BRUTALISM

BRUTALITY > BRUTAL
BRUTALIZE vb make or become brutal
BRUTALLY > BRUTAL
BRUTE n brutal person ▷ adj wholly instinctive or physical, like an animal
BRUTED > BRUTE
BRUTELIKE > BRUTE
BRUTELY > BRUTE
BRUTENESS > BRUTE
BRUTER n diamond cutter
BRUTERS > BRUTER
BRUTES > BRUTE
BRUTEST > BRUTE
BRUTIFIED > BRUTIFY
BRUTIFIES > BRUTIFY
BRUTIFY less common word for > BRUTALIZE
BRUTING n diamond cutting
BRUTINGS > BRUTING
BRUTISH adj of or like an animal
BRUTISHLY > BRUTISH
BRUTISM n stupidity; vulgarity
BRUTISMS > BRUTISM
BRUTS > BRUT
BRUX vb grind one's teeth
BRUXED > BRUX
BRUXES > BRUX
BRUXING > BRUX
BRUXISM n habit of grinding the teeth, esp unconsciously
BRUXISMS > BRUXISM
BRYOLOGY n branch of botany concerned with the study of bryophytes
BRYONIES > BRYONY
BRYONY n wild climbing hedge plant
BRYOPHYTE n type of plant such as mosses, liverworts, or hornworts, which has stems and leaves but lacks roots and reproduces by spores
BRYOZOAN n type of aquatic invertebrate which forms colonies of polyps
BRYOZOANS > BRYOZOAN
BUAT same as > BOWAT
BUATS > BUAT
BUAZE n fibrous African plant
BUAZES > BUAZE
BUB n youngster
BUBA another name for > YAWS
BUBAL n any of various antelopes
BUBALE n large antelope
BUBALES > BUBALE
BUBALINE adj (of antelopes) related to or resembling the bubal
BUBALIS same as > BUBAL
BUBALISES > BUBALIS
BUBALS > BUBAL
BUBAS > BUBA
BUBBA n ordinary American person
BUBBAS > BUBBA
BUBBE n Yiddish word for grandmother
BUBBES > BUBBE
BUBBIE same as > BUBBE
BUBBIES > BUBBY

BUBBLE n ball of air in a liquid or solid ▷ vb form bubbles
BUBBLED > BUBBLE
BUBBLEGUM n type of chewing gum that can be blown into large bubbles
BUBBLER n drinking fountain
BUBBLERS > BUBBLER
BUBBLES > BUBBLE
BUBBLIER > BUBBLY
BUBBLIES > BUBBLY
BUBBLIEST > BUBBLY
BUBBLING > BUBBLE
BUBBLY adj excited and lively ▷ n champagne
BUBBY n old word for woman's breast
BUBINGA n reddish-brown wood from African tree
BUBINGAS > BUBINGA
BUBKES n very small amount
BUBKIS n nothing
BUBO n inflammation and swelling of a lymph node, esp in the armpit or groin
BUBOED > BUBO
BUBOES > BUBO
BUBONIC > BUBO
BUBS > BUB
BUBU same as > BOUBOU
BUBUKLE n red spot on skin
BUBUKLES > BUBUKLE
BUBUS > BUBU
BUCARDO n type of Spanish mountain goat, recently extinct
BUCARDOS > BUCARDO
BUCATINI pl n pasta in the shape of long tubes
BUCCAL adj of or relating to the cheek
BUCCALLY > BUCCAL
BUCCANEER n pirate ▷ vb be or act like a buccaneer
BUCCANIER same as > BUCCANEER
BUCCINA n curved Roman horn
BUCCINAS > BUCCINA
BUCELLAS n type of Portuguese white wine
BUCENTAUR n state barge of Venice from which the doge and other officials dropped a ring into the sea on Ascension Day to symbolize the ceremonial marriage of the state with the Adriatic
BUCHU n S African shrub whose leaves are used as an antiseptic and diuretic
BUCHUS > BUCHU
BUCK n male of the goat, hare, kangaroo, rabbit, and reindeer ▷ vb (of a horse etc) jump with legs stiff and back arched
BUCKAROO n cowboy
BUCKAROOS > BUCKAROO
BUCKAYRO same as > BUCKAROO
BUCKAYROS > BUCKAYRO
BUCKBEAN n type of marsh plant with white or pink flowers
BUCKBEANS > BUCKBEAN

BUCKBOARD n open four-wheeled horse-drawn carriage with the seat attached to a flexible board between the front and rear axles
BUCKBRUSH n American shrub
BUCKED > BUCK
BUCKEEN n (in Ireland) poor young man who aspires to the habits and dress of the wealthy
BUCKEENS > BUCKEEN
BUCKER > BUCK
BUCKEROO same as > BUCKAROO
BUCKEROOS > BUCKEROO
BUCKERS > BUCK
BUCKET n open-topped roughly cylindrical container ▷ vb rain heavily
BUCKETED > BUCKET
BUCKETFUL n amount that a bucket is able to hold
BUCKETING > BUCKET
BUCKETS > BUCKET
BUCKEYE n N American tree with erect clusters of white or red flowers and prickly fruits
BUCKEYES > BUCKEYE
BUCKHORN n horn from a buck, used for knife handles, etc
BUCKHORNS > BUCKHORN
BUCKHOUND n hound, smaller than a staghound, used for hunting the smaller breeds of deer, esp fallow deer
BUCKIE n whelk or its shell
BUCKIES > BUCKIE
BUCKING > BUCK
BUCKINGS > BUCK
BUCKISH > BUCK
BUCKISHLY > BUCK
BUCKLE n clasp for fastening a belt or strap ▷ vb fasten or be fastened with a buckle
BUCKLED > BUCKLE
BUCKLER n small round shield worn on the forearm ▷ vb defend
BUCKLERED > BUCKLER
BUCKLERS > BUCKLER
BUCKLES > BUCKLE
BUCKLING another name for > BLOATER
BUCKLINGS > BUCKLING
BUCKO n lively young fellow: often a term of address
BUCKOES > BUCKO
BUCKOS > BUCKO
BUCKRA n (used contemptuously by Black people, esp in the US) White person
BUCKRAKE n large rake attached to tractor
BUCKRAKES > BUCKRAKE
BUCKRAM n cotton or linen cloth stiffened with size, etc ▷ vb stiffen with buckram
BUCKRAMED > BUCKRAM
BUCKRAMS > BUCKRAM
BUCKRAS > BUCKRA
BUCKS > BUCK

BUCKSAW *n* woodcutting saw

BUCKSAWS > BUCKSAW

BUCKSHEE *adj* free

BUCKSHEES > BUCKSHEE

BUCKSHISH *n* tip, present or gift

BUCKSHOT *n* large lead pellets used for shooting game

BUCKSHOTS > BUCKSHOT

BUCKSKIN *n* skin of a male deer *> adj* greyish-yellow

BUCKSKINS *pl n* (in the US and Canada) breeches, shoes, or a suit of buckskin

BUCKSOM *same as >* BUXOM

BUCKTAIL *n* in fishing, fly with appearance of minnow

BUCKTAILS > BUCKTAIL

BUCKTEETH > BUCKTOOTH

BUCKTHORN *n* thorny shrub whose berries were formerly used as a purgative

BUCKTOOTH *n* projecting upper front tooth

BUCKU *same as >* BUCHU

BUCKUS > BUCKU

BUCKWHEAT *n* small black grain used for making flour

BUCKYBALL *n* ball-like polyhedral carbon molecule of the type found in buckminsterfullerene and other fullerenes

BUCKYTUBE *n* tube of carbon atoms structurally similar to buckminsterfullerene

BUCOLIC *adj* of the countryside or country life *> n* pastoral poem

BUCOLICAL > BUCOLIC

BUCOLICS > BUCOLIC

BUD *n* swelling on a plant that develops into a leaf or flower *> vb* produce buds

BUDA *n* derogatory Indian English word for an old man

BUDAS > BUDA

BUDDED > BUD

BUDDER > BUD

BUDDERS > BUD

BUDDHA *n* person who has achieved a state of perfect enlightenment

BUDDHAS > BUDDHA

BUDDIED > BUDDY

BUDDIER > BUDDY

BUDDIES > BUDDY

BUDDIEST > BUDDY

BUDDING > BUD

BUDDINGS > BUD

BUDDLE *n* sloping trough in which ore is washed *> vb* wash (ore) in a buddle

BUDDLED > BUDDLE

BUDDLEIA *n* shrub with long spikes of purple flowers

BUDDLEIAS > BUDDLEIA

BUDDLES > BUDDLE

BUDDLING > BUDDLE

BUDDY *n* friend *> vb* act as a friend to *> adj* friendly

BUDDYING > BUDDY

BUDGE *vb* move slightly *> n* lambskin dressed for the fur to be worn on the outer side

BUDGED > BUDGE

BUDGER > BUDGE

BUDGEREE *adj* good

BUDGERO *same as >* BUDGEROW

BUDGEROS > BUDGERO

BUDGEROW *n* barge used on the Ganges

BUDGEROWS > BUDGEROW

BUDGERS > BUDGE

BUDGES > BUDGE

BUDGET *n* financial plan for a period of time *> vb* plan the expenditure of (money or time) *> adj* cheap

BUDGETARY > BUDGET

BUDGETED > BUDGET

BUDGETEER *n* one who prepares a budget

BUDGETER > BUDGET

BUDGETERS > BUDGET

BUDGETING *n* act of budgeting

BUDGETS > BUDGET

BUDGIE *n* short form of budgerigar

BUDGIES > BUDGIE

BUDGING > BUDGE

BUDI *n* derogatory Indian English word an for old woman

BUDIS > BUDI

BUDLESS > BUD

BUDLIKE > BUD

BUDMASH *same as >* BADMASH

BUDMASHES > BUDMASH

BUDO *n* combat and spirit in martial arts

BUDOS > BUDO

BUDS > BUD

BUDTENDER *n* person working in a shop where cannabis is sold

BUDWOOD *n* branch with buds that is used for grafting

BUDWOODS > BUDWOOD

BUDWORM *n* pest that eats tree leaves and buds

BUDWORMS > BUDWORM

BUFF *n* soft flexible undyed leather *> adj* dull yellowish-brown *> vb* clean or polish with soft material

BUFFA *n* female comic part in an opera

BUFFABLE > BUFF

BUFFALO *n* member of the cattle tribe *> vb* confuse

BUFFALOED > BUFFALO

BUFFALOES > BUFFALO

BUFFALOS > BUFFALO

BUFFAS > BUFFA

BUFFE > BUFFO

BUFFED > BUFF

BUFFEL *adj* as in *buffel grass* grass used for pasture in Africa, India, and Australia

BUFFER *vb* protect from shock

BUFFERED > BUFFER

BUFFERING *n* act of buffering

BUFFERS > BUFFER

BUFFEST > BUFF

BUFFET *n* counter where drinks and snacks are served *> vb* knock against or about

BUFFETED > BUFFET

BUFFETER > BUFFET

BUFFETERS > BUFFET

BUFFETING *n* response of an aircraft structure to buffet, esp an irregular oscillation of the tail

BUFFETS > BUFFET

BUFFI > BUFFO

BUFFIER > BUFFY

BUFFIEST > BUFFY

BUFFING *n* act of polishing

BUFFINGS > BUFFING

BUFFO *n* (in Italian opera of the 18th century) comic part, esp one for a bass

BUFFOON *n* clown or fool

BUFFOONS > BUFFOON

BUFFOS > BUFFO

BUFFS > BUFF

BUFFY *adj* having appearance or texture of buff

BUFO *n* type of toad

BUFOS > BUFO

BUFOTALIN *n* principal poisonous substance in the skin and saliva of the common European toad

BUFTIE *n* offensive term for a homosexual man

BUFTIES > BUFTIE

BUFTY *same as >* BUFTIE

BUG *n* insect *> vb* irritate

BUGABOO *n* imaginary source of fear

BUGABOOS > BUGABOO

BUGBANE *n* European plant whose flowers are reputed to repel insects

BUGBANES > BUGBANE

BUGBEAR *n* thing that causes obsessive anxiety

BUGBEARS > BUGBEAR

BUGEYE *n* oyster-dredging boat

BUGEYES > BUGEYE

BUGGAN *n* evil spirit

BUGGANE *same as >* BUGGAN

BUGGANES > BUGGANE

BUGGANS > BUGGAN

BUGGED > BUG

BUGGER *n* vulgar slang word for an unpleasant or difficult person or thing *> vb* tire *> interj* exclamation of annoyance or disappointment

BUGGERED > BUGGER

BUGGERIES > BUGGERY

BUGGERING > BUGGER

BUGGERS > BUGGER

BUGGERY *n* old term for anal intercourse

BUGGIER > BUGGY

BUGGIES > BUGGY

BUGGIEST > BUGGY

BUGGIN *same as >* BUGGAN

BUGGINESS > BUGGY

BUGGING > BUG

BUGGINGS > BUG

BUGGINS > BUGGIN

BUGGY *n* light horse-drawn carriage *> adj* infested with bugs

BUGHOUSE *n* offensive name for a psychiatric hospital *> adj* offensive word for insane

BUGHOUSES > BUGHOUSE

BUGLE *n* instrument like a small trumpet *> vb* play or sound (on) a bugle

BUGLED > BUGLE

BUGLER > BUGLE

BUGLERS > BUGLE

BUGLES > BUGLE

BUGLET *n* small bugle

BUGLETS > BUGLET

BUGLEWEED *same as >* BUGLE

BUGLING > BUGLE

BUGLOSS *n* hairy Eurasian plant with clusters of blue flowers

BUGLOSSES > BUGLOSS

BUGONG *same as >* BOGONG

BUGONGS > BUGONG

BUGOUT *n* act of running away

BUGOUTS > BUGOUT

BUGS > BUG

BUGSEED *n* form of tumbleweed

BUGSEEDS > BUGSEED

BUGSHA *same as >* BUQSHA

BUGSHAS > BUGSHA

BUGWORT *another name for >* BUGBANE

BUGWORTS > BUGWORT

BUHL *same as >* BOULLE

BUHLS > BUHL

BUHLWORK *n* woodwork with decorative inlay

BUHLWORKS > BUHLWORK

BUHR *same as >* BURR

BUHRS > BUHR

BUHRSTONE *n* hard tough rock containing silica, fossils, and cavities, formerly used as a grindstone

BUHUND *n* type of Norwegian dog

BUHUNDS > BUHUND

BUIBUI *n* black cloth worn as a shawl by Muslim women

BUIBUIS > BUIBUI

BUIK *same as >* BOOK

BUIKS > BUIK

BUILD *vb* make, construct, or form by joining parts or materials *> n* shape of the body

BUILDABLE *adj* suitable for building on

BUILDDOWN *n* planned reduction

BUILDED > BUILD

BUILDER *n* person who constructs houses and other buildings

BUILDERS > BUILDER

BUILDING > BUILD

BUILDINGS > BUILD

BUILDOUT *n* expansion, development, or growth

BUILDOUTS > BUILDOUT

BUILDS > BUILD

BUILDUP *n* gradual approach to a climax or critical point

BUILDUPS > BUILDUP

BUILT > BUILD

BUIRDLIER > BUIRDLY

BUIRDLY *adj* well-built

BUIST *vb* brand sheep with identification mark

b

BUISTED > BUIST
BUISTING > BUIST
BUISTS > BUIST
BUKE same as > BOOK
BUKES > BUKE
BUKKAKE n Japanese noodle dish
BUKKAKES > BUKKAKE
BUKSHEE n person in charge of paying wages
BUKSHEES > BUKSHEE
BUKSHI same as > BUKSHEE
BUKSHIS > BUKSHI
BULB n onion-shaped root which grows into a flower or plant ▷ vb form into the shape of a bulb
BULBAR adj of or relating to a bulb, esp the medulla oblongata
BULBED > BULB
BULBEL same as > BULBIL
BULBELS > BULBEL
BULBIL n small bulblike organ growing on plants such as the onion and tiger lily
BULBILS > BULBIL
BULBING > BULB
BULBLET n small bulb at base of main bulb
BULBLETS > BULBLET
BULBOSITY > BULBOUS
BULBOUS adj round and fat
BULBOUSLY > BULBOUS
BULBS > BULB
BULBUL n songbird of tropical Africa and Asia
BULBULS > BULBUL
BULGAR same as > BULGUR
BULGARS > BULGAR
BULGE n swelling on a normally flat surface ▷ vb swell outwards
BULGED > BULGE
BULGER > BULGE
BULGERS > BULGE
BULGES > BULGE
BULGHUR same as > BULGUR
BULGHURS > BULGHUR
BULGIER > BULGE
BULGIEST > BULGE
BULGINE same as > BULLGINE
BULGINES > BULGINE
BULGINESS > BULGE
BULGING adj curving outwards
BULGINGLY > BULGY
BULGUR n kind of dried cracked wheat
BULGURS > BULGUR
BULGY > BULGE
BULIMIA n eating disorder
BULIMIAC n person who has bulimia
BULIMIACS > BULIMIAC
BULIMIAS > BULIMIA
BULIMIC > BULIMIA
BULIMICS > BULIMIA
BULIMIES > BULIMY
BULIMUS n terrestrial mollusc
BULIMUSES > BULIMIA
BULIMY same as > BULIMIA
BULK n volume, size, or magnitude of something

▷ vb cohere or cause to cohere in a mass
BULKAGE > BULK
BULKAGES > BULK
BULKED > BULK
BULKER n ship that carries bulk cargo
BULKERS > BULKER
BULKHEAD n partition in a ship or aeroplane
BULKHEADS > BULKHEAD
BULKIER > BULKY
BULKIEST > BULKY
BULKILY > BULKY
BULKINESS > BULKY
BULKING n expansion of excavated material to a greater volume
BULKINGS > BULKING
BULKS > BULK
BULKY adj very large and massive, esp so as to be unwieldy
BULL n male bovine animal ▷ vb raise the price of (a security)
BULLA n leaden seal affixed to a papal bull
BULLACE n small Eurasian tree of which the damson is the cultivated form
BULLACES > BULLACE
BULLAE > BULLA
BULLARIES > BULLARY
BULLARY n boilery for preparing salt
BULLATE adj puckered or blistered in appearance
BULLBARS pl n large protective metal grille on the front of some vehicles
BULLBAT another name for > NIGHTHAWK
BULLBATS > BULLBAT
BULLBRIER n prickly American vine
BULLCOOK n casual or odd job worker in a camp
BULLCOOKS > BULLCOOK
BULLDIKE same as > BULLDYKE
BULLDIKES > BULLDIKE
BULLDOG n thickset dog with a broad head and a muscular body
BULLDOGS > BULLDOG
BULLDOZE vb demolish or flatten with a bulldozer
BULLDOZED > BULLDOZE
BULLDOZER n powerful tractor for moving earth
BULLDOZES > BULLDOZE
BULLDUST n fine dust
BULLDUSTS > BULLDUST
BULLDYKE n offensive word for a mannish lesbian
BULLDYKES > BULLDYKE
BULLED > BULL
BULLER vb make bubbling sound
BULLERED > BULLER
BULLERING > BULLER
BULLERS > BULLER
BULLET n small piece of metal fired from a gun ▷ vb move extremely quickly
BULLETED > BULLET

BULLETIN n short official report or announcement ▷ vb make known by bulletin
BULLETING > BULLET
BULLETINS > BULLETIN
BULLFTRIE n W Indian fruit tree
BULLETS > BULLET
BULLEY n fishing boat with two masts
BULLEYS > BULLEY
BULLFIGHT n public show in which a matador kills a bull
BULLFINCH n common European songbird
BULLFROG n large American frog with a deep croak
BULLFROGS > BULLFROG
BULLGINE n steam locomotive
BULLGINES > BULLGINE
BULLHEAD n type of small northern mainly marine fish
BULLHEADS > BULLHEAD
BULLHORN n portable loudspeaker having a built-in amplifier and microphone
BULLHORNS > BULLHORN
BULLIED > BULLY
BULLIER > BULLY
BULLIES > BULLY
BULLIEST > BULLY
BULLING n act of raising the price of a security
BULLINGS > BULLING
BULLION n gold or silver in the form of bars
BULLIONS > BULLION
BULLISH adj like a bull
BULLISHLY > BULLISH
BULLNECK n enlarged neck
BULLNECKS > BULLNECK
BULLNOSE n rounded exterior angle, as where two walls meet
BULLNOSED adj having a rounded end
BULLNOSES > BULLNOSE
BULLOCK n young bull ▷ vb work hard and long
BULLOCKED > BULLOCK
BULLOCKS > BULLOCK
BULLOCKY n driver of a team of bullocks ▷ adj resembling a bullock
BULLOSA adj as in epidermolysis bullosa type of genetic skin disorder
BULLOUS adj blistered
BULLPEN n large cell where prisoners are confined together temporarily
BULLPENS > BULLPEN
BULLPOUT n type of fish
BULLPOUTS > BULLPOUT
BULLRING n arena for staging bullfights
BULLRINGS > BULLRING
BULLRUSH same as > BULRUSH
BULLS > BULL
BULLSEYE n central disc of a target
BULLSEYES > BULLSEYE
BULLSHAT > BULLSHIT

BULLSHIT n vulgar word for exaggerated or foolish talk ▷ vb talk bullshit to
BULLSHITS > BULLSHIT
BULLSHOT n cocktail of vodka and beef stock
BULLSHOTS > BULLSHOT
BULLSNAKE n American burrowing snake
BULLWADDY n N Australian tree which grows in dense thickets
BULLWEED n knapweed
BULLWEEDS > BULLWEED
BULLWHACK vb flog with short whip
BULLWHIP n long tapering heavy whip, esp one of plaited rawhide ▷ vb whip with a bullwhip
BULLWHIPS > BULLWHIP
BULLY n person who repeatedly intimidates another person ▷ vb repeatedly intimidate another person ▷ adj dashing
BULLYBOY n ruffian or tough, esp a hired one
BULLYBOYS > BULLYBOY
BULLYCIDE n suicide as a result of bullying
BULLYING n act of threatening another person
BULLYINGS > BULLYING
BULLYISM > BULLY
BULLYISMS > BULLY
BULLYRAG vb bully, esp by means of cruel practical jokes
BULLYRAGS > BULLYRAG
BULNBULN another name for > LYREBIRD
BULNBULNS > BULNBULN
BULRUSH n tall stiff reed
BULRUSHES > BULRUSH
BULRUSHY adj full of bulrushes
BULSE n purse or bag for diamonds
BULSES > BULSE
BULWADDEE same as > BULLWADDY
BULWADDY same as > BULLWADDY
BULWARK n wall used as a fortification ▷ vb defend or fortify with or as if with a bulwark
BULWARKED > BULWARK
BULWARKS > BULWARK
BUM n loafer or idler ▷ vb get by begging ▷ adj of poor quality
BUMALO same as > BUMMALO
BUMALOTI same as > BUMMALOTI
BUMALOTIS > BUMALOTI
BUMBAG n small bag attached to a belt and worn round the waist
BUMBAGS > BUMBAG
BUMBAZE vb confuse; bewilder
BUMBAZED > BUMBAZE
BUMBAZES > BUMBAZE
BUMBAZING > BUMBAZE

b

BUMBLE *vb* speak, do, or move in a clumsy way ▷ *n* blunder or botch

BUMBLEBEE *n* large hairy bee

BUMBLED > BUMBLE

BUMBLEDOM *n* self-importance in a minor office

BUMBLER > BUMBLE

BUMBLERS > BUMBLE

BUMBLES > BUMBLE

BUMBLING > BUMBLE

BUMBLINGS > BUMBLE

BUMBO *n* African tree

BUMBOAT *n* any small boat used for ferrying goods to a ship at anchor or at a mooring

BUMBOATS > BUMBOAT

BUMBOS > BUMBO

BUMBOY *n* offensive term for a young male homosexual

BUMBOYS > BUMBOY

BUMELIA *n* thorny shrub

BUMELIAS > BUMELIA

BUMF *n* official documents or forms

BUMFLUFF *n* soft and fluffy growth of hair on the chin of an adolescent

BUMFLUFFS > BUMFLUFF

BUMFS > BUMF

BUMFUCK *n* taboo slang for a remote or insignificant place

BUMFUCKS > BUMFUCK

BUMFUZZLE *vb* confuse

BUMKIN *same as* > BUMPKIN

BUMKINS > BUMKIN

BUMMALO *n* Bombay duck

BUMMALOS > BUMMALO

BUMMALOTI *another word for* > BUMMALO

BUMMAREE *n* dealer at Billingsgate fish market

BUMMAREES > BUMMAREE

BUMMED > BUM

BUMMEL *n* stroll

BUMMELS > STROLL

BUMMER *n* unpleasant or disappointing experience

BUMMERS > BUMMER

BUMMEST > BUM

BUMMING > BUM

BUMMLE *Scots variant of* > BUMBLE

BUMMLED > BUMMLE

BUMMLES > BUMMLE

BUMMLING > BUMMLE

BUMMOCK *n* submerged mass of ice projecting downwards

BUMMOCKS > BUMMOCK

BUMP *vb* knock or strike with a jolt ▷ *n* dull thud from an impact or collision

BUMPED > BUMP

BUMPER *n* bar on the front and back of a vehicle ▷ *adj* unusually large or abundant ▷ *vb* toast with a full drinking glass

BUMPERED > BUMPER

BUMPERING > BUMPER

BUMPERS > BUMPER

BUMPH *same as* > BUMF

BUMPHS > BUMPH

BUMPIER > BUMPY

BUMPIEST > BUMPY

BUMPILY > BUMPY

BUMPINESS > BUMPY

BUMPING > BUMP

BUMPINGS > BUMP

BUMPKIN *n* awkward simple country person

BUMPKINLY *adj* like a bumpkin

BUMPKINS > BUMPKIN

BUMPOLOGY *n* humorous word for phrenology

BUMPS > BUMP

BUMPTIOUS *adj* offensively self-assertive

BUMPY *adj* having an uneven surface

BUMS > BUM

BUMSTER *adj* (of trousers) cut very low at the hips

BUMSTERS *pl n* trousers cut very low at the hips

BUMSUCKER *n* toady

BUMWAD *n* type of sketching paper

BUMWADS > BUMWAD

BUN *n* small sweet bread roll or cake

BUNA *n* synthetic rubber

BUNAS > BUNA

BUNBURIED > BUNBURY

BUNBURIES > BUNBURY

BUNBURY *vb* make up a story to avoid an unwanted engagement

BUNCE *n* windfall; boom ▷ *vb* charge someone too much money

BUNCED > BUNCE

BUNCES > BUNCE

BUNCH *n* number of things growing, fastened, or grouped together ▷ *vb* group or be grouped together in a bunch

BUNCHED > BUNCH

BUNCHER *n* person who groups things together

BUNCHERS > BUNCHER

BUNCHES *pl n* hair tied into two sections

BUNCHIER > BUNCHY

BUNCHIEST > BUNCHY

BUNCHILY > BUNCHY

BUNCHING > BUNCH

BUNCHINGS > BUNCH

BUNCHY *adj* composed of or resembling bunches

BUNCING > BUNCE

BUNCO *n* swindle, esp one by confidence tricksters ▷ *vb* swindle

BUNCOED > BUNCO

BUNCOES > BUNCO

BUNCOING > BUNCO

BUNCOMBE *same as* > BUNKUM

BUNCOMBES > BUNCOMBE

BUNCOS > BUNCO

BUND *n* (in Germany) confederation ▷ *vb* form into an embankment

BUNDE > BUND

BUNDED > BUND

BUNDH *same as* > BANDH

BUNDHS > BUNDH

BUNDIED > BUNDY

BUNDIES > BUNDY

BUNDING > BUND

BUNDIST > BUND

BUNDISTS > BUND

BUNDLE *n* number of things gathered loosely together ▷ *vb* cause to go roughly or unceremoniously

BUNDLED > BUNDLE

BUNDLER > BUNDLE

BUNDLERS > BUNDLE

BUNDLES > BUNDLE

BUNDLING > BUNDLE

BUNDLINGS > BUNDLE

BUNDOBUST *same as* > BANDOBUST

BUNDOOK *n* rifle

BUNDOOKS > BUNDOOK

BUNDS > BUND

BUNDT *n* type of sweet cake

BUNDTS > BUNDT

BUNDU *n* largely uninhabited wild region far from towns

BUNDUS > BUNDU

BUNDWALL *n* concrete or earth wall surrounding a storage tank

BUNDWALLS > BUNDWALL

BUNDY *n* time clock at work ▷ *vb* register arrival or departure from work on a time clock

BUNDYING > BUNDY

BUNFIGHT *n* tea party

BUNFIGHTS > BUNFIGHT

BUNG *n* stopper for a cask etc ▷ *vb* close with a bung

BUNGALOID *n* bungalow-type house

BUNGALOW *n* one-storey house

BUNGALOWS > BUNGALOW

BUNGED > BUNG

BUNGEE *n* strong elastic cable

BUNGEES > BUNGEE

BUNGER *n* firework

BUNGERS > BUNGER

BUNGEY *same as* > BUNGEE

BUNGEYS > BUNGEY

BUNGHOLE *n* hole in a cask or barrel through which liquid can be drained

BUNGHOLES > BUNGHOLE

BUNGIE *same as* > BUNGEE

BUNGIES > BUNGIE

BUNGING > BUNG

BUNGLE *vb* spoil through incompetence ▷ *n* blunder or muddle

BUNGLED > BUNGLE

BUNGLER > BUNGLE

BUNGLERS > BUNGLE

BUNGLES > BUNGLE

BUNGLING > BUNGLE

BUNGLINGS > BUNGLE

BUNGS > BUNG

BUNGWALL *n* Australian fern with an edible rhizome

BUNGWALLS > BUNGWALL

BUNGY *same as* > BUNGEE

BUNHEAD *n* ballerina

BUNHEADS > BUNHEAD

BUNIA *same as* > BUNNIA

BUNIAS > BUNIA

BUNION *n* inflamed swelling on the big toe

BUNIONS > BUNION

BUNJE *same as* > BUNGEE

BUNJEE *same as* > BUNGEE

BUNJEES > BUNJEE

BUNJES > BUNJE

BUNJIE *same as* > BUNGEE

BUNJIES > BUNJIE

BUNJY *same as* > BUNGEE

BUNK *n* narrow shelflike bed ▷ *vb* prepare to sleep

BUNKED > BUNK

BUNKER *n* sand-filled hollow forming an obstacle on a golf course ▷ *vb* drive (the ball) into a bunker

BUNKERED > BUNKER

BUNKERING > BUNKER

BUNKERS > BUNKER

BUNKHOUSE *n* (in the US and Canada) building containing the sleeping quarters of workers on a ranch

BUNKIE *n* short for bunkhouse

BUNKIES > BUNKIE

BUNKING > BUNK

BUNKMATE *n* person who sleeps in the same quarters as another

BUNKMATES > BUNKMATE

BUNKO *same as* > BUNCO

BUNKOED > BUNKO

BUNKOING > BUNKO

BUNKOS > BUNKO

BUNKS > BUNK

BUNKUM *n* nonsense

BUNKUMS > BUNKUM

BUNN *same as* > BUN

BUNNET *same as* > BONNET

BUNNETS > BUNNET

BUNNIA *n* Hindu shopkeeper

BUNNIAS > BUNNIA

BUNNIES > BUNNY

BUNNS > BUNN

BUNNY *n* child's word for a rabbit

BUNODONT *adj* (of the teeth of certain mammals) having cusps that are separate and rounded

BUNRAKU *n* Japanese puppet theatre

BUNRAKUS > BUNRAKU

BUNS > BUN

BUNSEN *n* as in *bunsen burner* gas burner used in scientific labs

BUNSENS > BUNSEN

BUNT *vb* (of an animal) butt (something) with the head or horns ▷ *n* act or an instance of bunting

BUNTAL *n* straw obtained from leaves of the talipot palm

BUNTALS > BUNTAL

BUNTED > BUNT

BUNTER *n* batter who deliberately taps ball lightly

BUNTERS > BUNTER

BUNTIER > BUNT

BUNTIEST > BUNT

BUNTING *n* decorative flags

BUNTINGS > BUNTING

BUNTLINE *n* one of several lines fastened to the foot of a square sail

SECTION 1: Words between 2 and 9 letters in length

b

BUNTLINES > BUNTLINE

BUNTS > BUNT

BUNTY > BUNT

BUNYA n tall dome-shaped Australian coniferous tree

BUNYAS > BUNYA

BUNYIP n legendary monster said to live in swamps and lakes

BUNYIPS > BUNYIP

BUOY n floating marker anchored in the sea ▷ vb prevent from sinking

BUOYAGE n system of buoys

BUOYAGES > BUOYAGE

BUOYANCE same as > BUOYANCY

BUOYANCES > BUOYANCE

BUOYANCY n ability to float in a liquid or to rise in a fluid

BUOYANT adj able to float

BUOYANTLY > BUOYANT

BUOYED > BUOY

BUOYING > BUOY

BUOYS > BUOY

BUPKES same as > BUBKES

BUPKIS same as > BUBKIS

BUPKUS same as > BUBKES

BUPLEVER n type of plant

BUPLEVERS > BUPLEVER

BUPPIE n affluent young Black person

BUPPIES > BUPPIE

BUPPY variant of > BUPPIE

BUPRESTID n type of mainly tropical beetle, the adults of which are brilliantly coloured

BUPROPION n antidepressant drug used to help people stop smoking

BUQSHA n former Yemeni coin

BUQSHAS > BUQSHA

BUR same as > BURR

BURA same as > BURAN

BURAN n blizzard, with the wind blowing from the north and reaching gale force

BURANS > BURAN

BURAS > BURA

BURB n suburb

BURBLE vb make a bubbling sound ▷ n bubbling or gurgling sound

BURBLED > BURBLE

BURBLER > BURBLE

BURBLERS > BURBLE

BURBLES > BURBLE

BURBLIER > BURBLY

BURBLIEST > BURBLY

BURBLING > BURBLE

BURBLINGS > BURBLE

BURBLY adj burbling

BURBOT n freshwater fish of the cod family that has barbels around its mouth

BURBOTS > BURBOT

BURBS > BURB

BURD Scots form of > BIRD

BURDASH n fringed sash worn over coat

BURDASHES > BURDASH

BURDEN n heavy load ▷ vb put a burden on

BURDENED > BURDEN

BURDENER > BURDEN

BURDENERS > BURDEN

BURDENING > BURDEN

BURDENOUS > BURDEN

BURDENS > BURDEN

BURDIE Scots form of > BIRDIE

BURDIES > BURDIE

BURDIZZO n surgical instrument

BURDIZZOS > BURDIZZO

BURDOCK n weed with prickly burrs

BURDOCKS > BURDOCK

BURDS > BURD

BUREAU n office that provides a service

BUREAUS > BUREAU

BUREAUX > BUREAU

BURET same as > BURETTE

BURETS > BURET

BURETTE n glass tube for dispensing known volumes of fluids

BURETTES > BURETTE

BURFI same as > BARFI

BURFIS > BURFI

BURG n fortified town

BURGAGE n type of tenure of land or tenement in a town or city

BURGAGES > BURGAGE

BURGANET same as > BURGONET

BURGANETS > BURGANET

BURGEE n triangular or swallow-tailed flag flown from the mast of a merchant ship

BURGEES > BURGEE

BURGEON vb develop or grow rapidly ▷ n bud of a plant

BURGEONED > BURGEON

BURGEONS > BURGEON

BURGER n hamburger

BURGERS > BURGER

BURGESS n (in England) citizen of a borough

BURGESSES > BURGESS

BURGH n Scottish borough

BURGHAL > BURGH

BURGHER n citizen

BURGHERS > BURGHER

BURGHS > BURGH

BURGHUL same as > BULGUR

BURGHULS > BURGHUL

BURGLAR n person who enters a building to commit a crime, esp theft ▷ vb burgle

BURGLARED > BURGLAR

BURGLARS > BURGLAR

BURGLARY n crime of entering a building as a trespasser to commit theft or another offence

BURGLE vb break into (a house, shop, etc)

BURGLED > BURGLE

BURGLES > BURGLE

BURGLING > BURGLE

BURGONET n light 16th-century helmet, usually made of steel, with hinged cheekpieces

BURGONETS > BURGONET

BURGOO n porridge

BURGOOS > BURGOO

BURGOUT same as > BURGOO

BURGOUTS > BURGOUT

BURGRAVE n military governor of a German town or castle, esp in the 12th and 13th centuries

BURGRAVES > BURGRAVE

BURGS > BURG

BURGUNDY adj dark-purplish red

BURHEL same as > BHARAL

BURHELS > BURHEL

BURIAL n burying of a dead body

BURIALS > BURIAL

BURIED > BURY

BURIER n person or thing that buries

BURIERS > BURIER

BURIES > BURY

BURIN n steel chisel used for engraving metal, wood, or marble

BURINIST > BURIN

BURINISTS > BURIN

BURINS > BURIN

BURITI n type of palm tree

BURITIS > BURITI

BURK same as > BERK

BURKA same as > BURQA

BURKAS > BURKA

BURKE vb suppress or silence

BURKED > BURKE

BURKER > BURKE

BURKERS > BURKE

BURKES > BURKE

BURKHA n all-enveloping garment worn by some Muslim women

BURKHAS > BURKHA

BURKING > BURKE

BURKINI n swimming costume covering the whole body apart from the face, hands, and feet

BURKINIS > BURKINI

BURKITE n murderer

BURKITES > BURKITE

BURKS > BURK

BURL n small knot or lump in wool ▷ vb remove the burls from (cloth)

BURLADERO n safe area for bull-fighter in bull ring

BURLAP n coarse fabric woven from jute, hemp, or the like

BURLAPS > BURLAP

BURLED > BURL

BURLER > BURL

BURLERS > BURL

BURLESK same as > BURLESQUE

BURLESKS > BURLESK

BURLESQUE n artistic work which satirizes a subject by caricature ▷ adj of or characteristic of a burlesque ▷ vb represent or imitate (a person or thing) in a ludicrous way

BURLETTA n type of comic opera

BURLETTAS > BURLETTA

BURLEY same as > BERLEY

BURLEYCUE same as > BURLESQUE

BURLEYED > BURLEY

BURLEYING > BURLEY

BURLEYS > BURLEY

BURLIER > BURLY

BURLIEST > BURLY

BURLIKE adj like a bur

BURLILY > BURLY

BURLINESS > BURLY

BURLING > BURL

BURLS > BURL

BURLY adj (of a person) broad and strong

BURN vb be or set on fire ▷ n injury or mark caused by fire or exposure to heat

BURNABLE > BURN

BURNABLES > BURN

BURNED > BURN

BURNER n part of a stove or lamp that produces the flame

BURNERS > BURNER

BURNET n type of rose

BURNETS > BURNET

BURNIE n sideburn

BURNIES > BURNIE

BURNING > BURN

BURNINGLY > BURN

BURNINGS > BURN

BURNISH vb make smooth and shiny by rubbing ▷ n shiny finish

BURNISHED > BURNISH

BURNISHER > BURNISH

BURNISHES > BURNISH

BURNOOSE same as > BURNOUS

BURNOOSED > BURNOUS

BURNOOSES > BURNOOSE

BURNOUS n long circular cloak with a hood, worn esp by Arabs

BURNOUSE same as > BURNOUS

BURNOUSED > BURNOUS

BURNOUSES > BURNOUSE

BURNOUT n failure of a mechanical device from excessive heating

BURNOUTS > BURNOUT

BURNS > BURN

BURNSIDE n land along side of burn

BURNSIDES > BURNSIDE

BURNT > BURN

BUROO n informal Scottish or Irish name for an unemployment benefit office

BUROOS > BUROO

BURP n belch ▷ vb belch

BURPED > BURP

BURPEE n type of physical exercise movement

BURPEES > BURPEE

BURPING > BURP

BURPS > BURP

BURQA n garment worn by some Muslim women in public

BURQAS > BURQA

BURQUINI n swimming costume covering the whole body apart from the face, hands, and feet

BURQUINIS > BURQUINI

BURR n small rotary file ▷ vb form a rough edge on (a workpiece)

BURRAMYS *n* very rare Australian mountain pigmy possum

BURRATA *n* type of Italian cheese

BURRATAS > BURRATA

BURRAWANG *n* Australian plant with fernlike leaves and an edible nut

BURRED > BURR

BURREL *same as* **>** BHARAL

BURRELL *variant of* **>** BHARAL

BURRELLS > BURRELL

BURRELS > BURREL

BURRER *n* person who removes burrs

BURRERS > BURRER

BURRFISH *n* type of fish with sharp spines

BURRHEL *same as* **>** BHARAL

BURRHELS > BURRHEL

BURRIER > BURRY

BURRIEST > BURRY

BURRING > BURR

BURRITO *n* tortilla folded over a filling of minced beef, chicken, cheese, or beans

BURRITOS > BURRITO

BURRO *n* donkey, esp one used as a pack animal

BURROS > BURRO

BURROW *n* hole dug in the ground by a rabbit etc ▷ *vb* dig holes in the ground

BURROWED > BURROW

BURROWER > BURROW

BURROWERS > BURROW

BURROWING > BURROW

BURROWS > BURROW

BURRS > BURR

BURRSTONE *same as* **>** BUHRSTONE

BURRY *adj* full of or covered in burs

BURS > BUR

BURSA *n* small fluid-filled sac that reduces friction between movable parts of the body

BURSAE > BURSA

BURSAL > BURSA

BURSAR *n* treasurer of a school, college, or university

BURSARIAL *adj* of, relating to, or paid by a bursar or bursary

BURSARIES > BURSARY

BURSARS > BURSAR

BURSARY *n* scholarship

BURSAS > BURSA

BURSATE > BURSA

BURSE *n* flat case used at Mass as a container for the corporal

BURSEED *n* type of plant

BURSEEDS > BURSEED

BURSERA *adj* of a type of gum tree

BURSES > BURSE

BURSICON *n* hormone produced by the insect brain

BURSICONS > BURSICON

BURSIFORM *adj* shaped like a pouch or sac

BURSITIS *n* inflammation of a bursa, esp one in the shoulder joint

BURST *vb* break or cause to break open or apart suddenly and noisily ▷ *n* sudden breaking open or apart ▷ *adj* broken apart

BURSTED > BURST

BURSTEN > BURST

BURSTER > BURST

BURSTERS > BURST

BURSTIER > BURSTY

BURSTIEST > BURSTY

BURSTING > BURST

BURSTONE *same as* **>** BUHRSTONE

BURSTONES > BURSTONE

BURSTS > BURST

BURSTY *adj* occurring or happening in sudden bursts; irregular

BURTHEN *archaic word for* **>** BURDEN

BURTHENED > BURTHEN

BURTHENS > BURTHEN

BURTON *n* type of hoisting tackle

BURTONS > BURTON

BURWEED *n* any of various plants that bear burs, such as the burdock

BURWEEDS > BURWEED

BURY *vb* place in a grave

BURYING > BURY

BUS *n* large motor vehicle for carrying passengers between stops ▷ *vb* travel by bus

BUSBAR *n* electrical conductor

BUSBARS > BUSBAR

BUSBIES > BUSBY

BUSBOY *n* waiter's assistant

BUSBOYS > BUSBOY

BUSBY *n* tall fur hat worn by some soldiers

BUSED > BUS

BUSERA *n* Ugandan alcoholic drink made from millet

BUSERAS > BUSERA

BUSES > BUS

BUSGIRL *n* waiter's assistant

BUSGIRLS > BUSGIRL

BUSH *n* dense woody plant, smaller than a tree ▷ *vb* fit a bush to (a casing or bearing)

BUSHBABY *n* small African tree-living mammal with large eyes

BUSHBUCK *n* small nocturnal spiral-horned antelope of Africa

BUSHBUCKS > BUSHBUCK

BUSHCRAFT *n* ability and experience in matters concerned with living in the bush

BUSHED *adj* extremely tired

BUSHEL *n* obsolete unit of measure equal to 8 gallons ▷ *vb* alter or mend (a garment)

BUSHELED > BUSHEL

BUSHELER > BUSHEL

BUSHELERS > BUSHEL

BUSHELFUL *n* amount equivalent to a bushel

BUSHELING > BUSHEL

BUSHELLED > BUSHEL

BUSHELLER > BUSHEL

BUSHELMAN > BUSHEL

BUSHELMEN > BUSHEL

BUSHELS > BUSHEL

BUSHER > BUSH

BUSHERS > BUSH

BUSHES > BUSH

BUSHFIRE *n* uncontrolled fire in the bush

BUSHFIRES > BUSHFIRE

BUSHFLIES > BUSHFLY

BUSHFLY *n* small black Australian fly

BUSHGOAT *n* S African antelope

BUSHGOATS > BUSHGOAT

BUSHIDO *n* feudal code of the Japanese samurai

BUSHIDOS > BUSHIDO

BUSHIE *same as* **>** BUSHY

BUSHIER > BUSHY

BUSHIES > BUSHY

BUSHIEST > BUSHY

BUSHILY > BUSHY

BUSHINESS > BUSHY

BUSHING *same as* **>** BUSH

BUSHINGS > BUSHING

BUSHLAND *n* land characterized by natural vegetation

BUSHLANDS > BUSHLAND

BUSHLESS > BUSH

BUSHLIKE > BUSH

BUSHLOT *n* small wooded area of land

BUSHLOTS > BUSHLOT

BUSHMAN *n* person who lives or travels in the bush

BUSHMEAT *n* meat taken from any animal native to African forests

BUSHMEATS > BUSHMEAT

BUSHMEN > BUSHMAN

BUSHPIG *n* wild brown or black forest pig of tropical Africa and Madagascar

BUSHPIGS > BUSHPIG

BUSHTIT *n* small grey active North American songbird

BUSHTITS > BUSHTIT

BUSHVELD *n* bushy countryside

BUSHVELDS > BUSHVELD

BUSHWA *n* nonsense

BUSHWAH *same as* **>** BUSHWA

BUSHWAHS > BUSHWAH

BUSHWALK *vb* hike through bushland

BUSHWALKS > BUSHWALK

BUSHWAS > BUSHWA

BUSHWHACK *vb* ambush

BUSHWOMAN > BUSHMAN

BUSHWOMEN > BUSHMAN

BUSHY *adj* (of hair) thick and shaggy ▷ *n* person who lives in the bush

BUSIED > BUSY

BUSIER > BUSY

BUSIES > BUSY

BUSIEST > BUSY

BUSILY *adv* in a busy manner

BUSINESS *n* purchase and sale of goods and services

BUSINESSY *adj* of, relating to, typical of, or suitable for

the world of commercial or industrial business

BUSING *n* act of transporting by bus from one area to another

BUSINGS > BUSING

BUSK *vb* act as a busker ▷ *n* strip of whalebone, wood, steel, etc, inserted into the front of a corset

BUSKED > BUSK

BUSKER > BUSK

BUSKERS > BUSK

BUSKET *n* bouquet

BUSKETS > BUSKET

BUSKIN *n* (formerly) sandal-like covering

BUSKINED *adj* relating to tragedy

BUSKING > BUSK

BUSKINGS > BUSK

BUSKINS > BUSKIN

BUSKS > BUSK

BUSKY *same as* **>** BOSKY

BUSLOAD *n* number of people bus carries

BUSLOADS > BUSLOAD

BUSMAN *n* person who drives a bus

BUSMEN > BUSMAN

BUSS *archaic or dialect word for* **>** KISS

BUSSED > BUS

BUSSES > BUS

BUSSING *n* act of transporting by bus from one area to another

BUSSINGS > BUSSING

BUSSU *n* type of palm tree

BUSSUS > BUSSU

BUST *n* chest of a human being ▷ *adj* broken ▷ *vb* burst or break

BUSTARD *n* type of bird

BUSTARDS > BUSTARD

BUSTED > BUST

BUSTEE *same as* **>** BASTI

BUSTEES > BUSTEE

BUSTER *n* person or thing destroying something as specified

BUSTERS > BUSTER

BUSTI *same as* **>** BASTI

BUSTIC *n* type of small American tree

BUSTICATE *vb* break

BUSTICS > BUSTIC

BUSTIER *n* close-fitting strapless women's top

BUSTIERS > BUSTIER

BUSTIEST > BUSTY

BUSTINESS > BUSTY

BUSTING > BUST

BUSTINGS > BUST

BUSTIS > BUSTI

BUSTLE *vb* hurry with a show of activity or energy ▷ *n* energetic and noisy activity

BUSTLED > BUSTLE

BUSTLER > BUSTLE

BUSTLERS > BUSTLE

BUSTLES > BUSTLE

BUSTLINE *n* shape or size of woman's bust

BUSTLINES > BUSTLINE

BUSTLING > BUSTLE

b

BUSTS > BUST
BUSTY adj (of a woman) having a prominent bust
BUSULFAN n drug used to treat cancer
BUSULFANS > BUSULFAN
BUSUUTI n garment worn by Ugandan women
BUSUUTIS > BUSUUTI
BUSY adj actively employed ▷ vb keep (someone, esp oneself) busy
BUSYBODY n meddlesome or nosy person
BUSYING > BUSY
BUSYNESS > BUSY
BUSYWORK n unproductive work
BUSYWORKS > BUSYWORK
BUT prep except ▷ adv only ▷ n outer room of a two-roomed cottage: usually the kitchen
BUTADIENE n colourless easily liquefiable flammable gas
BUTANE n gas used for fuel
BUTANES > BUTANE
BUTANOIC adj as in butanoic acid kind of acid
BUTANOL n colourless substance
BUTANOLS > BUTANOL
BUTANONE n colourless soluble flammable liquid used mainly as a solvent for resins
BUTANONES > BUTANONE
BUTCH adj markedly or aggressively masculine ▷ n strong, rugged man
BUTCHER n person who slaughters animals or sells their meat ▷ vb kill and prepare (animals) for meat
BUTCHERED > BUTCHER
BUTCHERER > BUTCHER
BUTCHERLY adj like a butcher
BUTCHERS > BUTCHER
BUTCHERY n senseless slaughter
BUTCHES > BUTCH
BUTCHEST > BUTCH
BUTCHING n dialect word for butchering
BUTCHINGS > BUTCH
BUTCHNESS > BUTCH
BUTE n drug used illegally to dope horses
BUTENE n pungent colourless gas
BUTENES > BUTENE
BUTEO n type of American hawk
BUTEONINE adj of hawks
BUTEOS > BUTEO
BUTES > BUTE
BUTLE vb act as butler
BUTLED > BUTLE
BUTLER n chief male servant ▷ vb act as a butler
BUTLERAGE > BUTLER
BUTLERED > BUTLER
BUTLERIES > BUTLERY
BUTLERING > BUTLER
BUTLERS > BUTLER

BUTLERY n butler's room
BUTLES > BUTLE
BUTLING > BUTLE
BUTMENT same as > ABUTMENT
BUTMENTS > BUTMENT
BUTOH n style of contemporary Japanese dance
BUTOHS > BUTOH
BUTS > BUT
BUTSUDAN n (in Buddhism) small household altar
BUTSUDANS > BUTSUDAN
BUTT n thicker or blunt end of something, such as the end of the stock of a rifle ▷ vb strike or push with the head or horns
BUTTALS n abuttal
BUTTE n isolated steep flat-topped hill
BUTTED > BUTT
BUTTER n edible fatty yellow solid made form cream ▷ vb put butter on
BUTTERBUR n Eurasian plant with fragrant whitish or purple flowers and woolly stems
BUTTERCUP n small yellow flower
BUTTERED > BUTTER
BUTTERFAT n fatty substance of milk from which butter is made, consisting of a mixture of glycerides, mainly butyrin, olein, and palmitin
BUTTERFLY n insect with brightly coloured wings
BUTTERIER > BUTTERY
BUTTERIES > BUTTERY
BUTTERINE n artificial butter made partly from milk
BUTTERING > BUTTER
BUTTERNUT n E North American walnut tree
BUTTERS > BUTTER
BUTTERY n (in some universities) room in which food and drink are sold to students ▷ adj containing, like, or coated with butter
BUTTES > BUTTE
BUTTHEAD n stupid person
BUTTHEADS > BUTTHEAD
BUTTIES > BUTTY
BUTTING > BUTT
BUTTINSKI same as > BUTTINSKY
BUTTINSKY n busybody
BUTTLE vb act as butler
BUTTLED > BUTTLE
BUTTLES > BUTTLE
BUTTLING > BUTTLE
BUTTOCK n either of the two fleshy masses that form the human rump ▷ vb perform a kind of wrestling manoeuvre on a person
BUTTOCKED > BUTTOCK
BUTTOCKS > BUTTOCK
BUTTON n small disc or knob sewn to clothing ▷ vb fasten with buttons
BUTTONED > BUTTON
BUTTONER > BUTTON

BUTTONERS > BUTTON
BUTTONIER > BUTTONY
BUTTONING > BUTTON
BUTTONS n page boy
BUTTONY adj having a lot of buttons
BUTTRESS n structure to support a wall ▷ vb support with, or as if with, a buttress
BUTTS > BUTT
BUTTSTOCK n part of gun
BUTTY n sandwich
BUTTYMAN n coalmine worker
BUTTYMEN > BUTTYMAN
BUTUT n Gambian monetary unit worth one hundredth of a dalasi
BUTUTS > BUTUT
BUTYL n substituent group of a certain carbon compound
BUTYLATE vb introduce butyl into (compound)
BUTYLATED > BUTYLATE
BUTYLATES > BUTYLATE
BUTYLENE same as > BUTENE
BUTYLENES > BUTYLENE
BUTYLS > BUTYL
BUTYRAL n type of resin
BUTYRALS > BUTYRAL
BUTYRATE n any salt or ester of butyric acid
BUTYRATES > BUTYRATE
BUTYRIC adj as in butyric acid type of acid
BUTYRIN n colourless liquid found in butter
BUTYRINS > BUTYRIN
BUTYROUS adj butyraceous
BUTYRYL n radical of butyric acid
BUTYRYLS > BUTYRYL
BUVETTE n roadside café
BUVETTES > BUVETTE
BUXOM adj (of a woman) healthily plump
BUXOMER > BUXOM
BUXOMEST > BUXOM
BUXOMLY > BUXOM
BUXOMNESS > BUXOM
BUY vb acquire by paying money for ▷ n thing acquired through payment
BUYABLE > BUY
BUYABLES > BUY
BUYBACK n repurchase by a company of some or all of its shares from an early investor
BUYBACKS > BUYBACK
BUYER n customer
BUYERS > BUYER
BUYING n as in panic buying the buying up of large quantities of something feared to be scarce
BUYINGS > BUYING
BUYOFF n purchase
BUYOFFS > BUYOFF
BUYOUT n purchase of a company
BUYOUTS > BUYOUT
BUYS > BUY
BUZKASHI n team sport played in Afghanistan
BUZKASHIS > BUZKASHI

BUZUKI same as > BOUZOUKI
BUZUKIA > BUZUKI
BUZUKIS > BUZUKI
BUZZ n rapidly vibrating humming sound ▷ vb make a humming sound
BUZZARD n bird of prey of the hawk family
BUZZARDS > BUZZARD
BUZZBAIT n fishing lure with small blades that stir the water
BUZZBAITS > BUZZBAIT
BUZZCUT n very short haircut
BUZZCUTS > BUZZCUT
BUZZED > BUZZ
BUZZER n electronic device that produces a buzzing sound as a signal
BUZZERS > BUZZER
BUZZES > BUZZ
BUZZIER > BUZZY
BUZZIEST > BUZZY
BUZZING > BUZZ
BUZZINGLY > BUZZ
BUZZINGS > BUZZ
BUZZKILL n someone or something that spoils the enjoyment of others
BUZZKILLS > BUZZKILL
BUZZSAW n power-operated circular saw
BUZZSAWS > BUZZSAW
BUZZWIG n bushy wig
BUZZWIGS > BUZZWIG
BUZZWORD n vogue word in a certain community or among a particular group
BUZZWORDS > BUZZWORD
BUZZY adj making a buzzing sound
BWANA n (in E Africa) master, often used as a respectful form of address
BWANAS > BWANA
BWAZI same as > BUAZE
BWAZIS > BWAZI
BY prep indicating agent, nearness, movement past, etc ▷ adv near ▷ n pass to the next round
BYCATCH n unwanted fish and sea animals caught along with the desired kind
BYCATCHES > BYCATCH
BYCOKET n former Italian high-crowned hat
BYCOKETS > BYCOKET
BYDE same as > BIDE
BYDED > BYDE
BYDES > BYDE
BYDING > BYDE
BYE n situation where a player or team wins a round by having no opponent ▷ interj goodbye ▷ sentence substitute goodbye
BYELAW n rule made by a local authority
BYELAWS > BYELAW
BYES > BYE
BYGONE adj past ▷ n article from a former time
BYGONES > BYGONE
BYKE n wasp's nest ▷ vb swarm

BYKED > BYKE
BYKES > BYKE
BYKING > BYKE
BYLANDER same as > BILANDER
BYLANDERS > BYLANDER
BYLANE n side lane or alley off a road
BYLANES > BYLANE
BYLAW n rule made by a local authority
BYLAWS > BYLAW
BYLINE n line under the title of a newspaper or magazine article giving the author's name ▷ vb give a byline to
BYLINED > BYLINE
BYLINER > BYLINE
BYLINERS > BYLINE
BYLINES > BYLINE
BYLINING > BYLINE
BYLIVE same as > BELIVE
BYNAME n nickname
BYNAMES > BYNAME
BYNEMPT archaic past participle of > BENAME
BYPASS n main road built to avoid a city ▷ vb go round or avoid

BYPASSED > BYPASS
BYPASSES > BYPASS
BYPASSING > BYPASS
BYPAST > BYPASS
BYPATH n little-used path or track, esp in the country
BYPATHS > BYPATH
BYPLACE n private place
BYPLACES > BYPLACE
BYPLAY n secondary action or talking carried on apart while the main action proceeds
BYPLAYS > BYPLAY
BYPRODUCT n secondary product
BYRE n shelter for cows
BYREMAN n man who works in byre
BYREMEN > BYREMAN
BYRES > BYRE
BYREWOMAN n woman who works in a byre
BYREWOMEN > BYREWOMAN
BYRL same as > BIRL
BYRLADY interj short for By Our Lady
BYRLAKIN interj By Our Ladykin

BYRLAW same as > BYLAW
BYRLAWS > BYRLAW
BYRLED > BYRL
BYRLING > BYRL
BYRLS > BYRL
BYRNIE n archaic word for coat of mail
BYRNIES > BYRNIE
BYROAD n secondary or side road
BYROADS > BYROAD
BYROOM n private room
BYROOMS > BYROOM
BYS > BY
BYSSAL adj of mollusc's byssus
BYSSI > BYSSUS
BYSSINE adj made from flax
BYSSOID adj consisting of fine fibres
BYSSUS n mass of threads that attaches an animal to a hard surface
BYSSUSES > BYSSUS
BYSTANDER n person present but not involved
BYSTREET n obscure or secondary street

BYSTREETS > BYSTREET
BYTALK n trivial conversation
BYTALKS > BYTALK
BYTE n group of bits processed as one unit of data
BYTES > BYTE
BYTOWNITE n rare mineral
BYWAY n minor road
BYWAYS > BYWAY
BYWONER n poor tenant-farmer
BYWONERS > BYWONER
BYWORD n person or thing regarded as a perfect example of something
BYWORDS > BYWORD
BYWORK n work done outside usual working hours
BYWORKS > BYWORK
BYZANT same as > BEZANT
BYZANTINE adj of, characteristic of, or relating to Byzantium or the Byzantine Empire
BYZANTS > BYZANT

b

Cc

CAA *a Scot word for* > CALL
CAAED > CAA
CAAING > CAA
CAAS > CAA
CAATINGA *n* Brazilian semi-arid scrub forest
CAATINGAS > CAATINGA
CAB *n* taxi ▷ *vb* take a taxi
CABA *same as* > CABAS
CABAL *n* small group of political plotters ▷ *vb* form a cabal
CABALA *a variant spelling of* > KABBALAH
CABALAS > CABALA
CABALETTA *n* final section of an aria
CABALETTE > CABALETTA
CABALISM > CABALA
CABALISMS > CABALA
CABALIST > CABALA
CABALISTS > CABALA
CABALLED > CABAL
CABALLER > CABAL
CABALLERO *n* Spanish gentleman
CABALLERS > CABAL
CABALLINE *adj* pertaining to a horse
CABALLING > CABAL
CABALS > CABAL
CABANA *n* tent used as a dressing room by the sea
CABANAS > CABANA
CABARET *n* dancing and singing show in a nightclub
CABARETS > CABARET
CABAS *n* small bag
CABBAGE *n* vegetable with a large head of green leaves ▷ *vb* steal
CABBAGED > CABBAGE
CABBAGES > CABBAGE
CABBAGEY > CABBAGE
CABBAGIER > CABBAGY
CABBAGING > CABBAGE
CABBAGY *adj* resembling cabbage
CABBALA *a variant spelling of* > KABBALAH
CABBALAH *same as* > CABBALA
CABBALAHS > CABBALA
CABBALAS > CABBALA
CABBALISM > CABBALA
CABBALIST > CABBALA
CABBED > CAB
CABBIE *n* taxi driver
CABBIES > CABBIE
CABBING > CAB
CABBY *same as* > CABBIE
CABDRIVER *n* taxi-driver

CABER *n* tree trunk tossed in competition at Highland games
CABERNET *n* type of grape, or the red wine made from it
CABERNETS > CABERNET
CABERS > CABER
CABESTRO *n* halter made from horsehair
CABESTROS > CABESTRO
CABEZON *n* large fish
CABEZONE *same as* > CABEZON
CABEZONES > CABEZON
CABEZONS > CABEZON
CABILDO *n* Spanish municipal council
CABILDOS > CABILDO
CABIN *n* compartment in a ship or aircraft ▷ *vb* confine in a small space
CABINED > CABIN
CABINET *n* piece of furniture with drawers or shelves
CABINETRY *n* cabinetmaking
CABINETS > CABINET
CABINING > CABIN
CABINMATE *n* sharer of cabin
CABINS > CABIN
CABLE *n* strong thick rope; a wire or bundle of wires that conduct electricity ▷ *vb* (esp formerly) send (someone) a message by cable
CABLECAST *n* broadcast on cable
CABLED > CABLE
CABLEGRAM *n* message sent by cable
CABLER *n* cable broadcasting company
CABLERS > CABLER
CABLES > CABLE
CABLET *n* small cable
CABLETS > CABLET
CABLEWAY *n* transport system involving cars, buckets, etc, suspended on cables
CABLEWAYS > CABLEWAY
CABLING > CABLE
CABLINGS > CABLE
CABMAN *n* driver of a cab
CABMEN > CABMAN
CABOB *vb* roast on a skewer
CABOBBED > CABOB
CABOBBING > CABOB
CABOBS > CABOB
CABOC *n* type of Scottish cheese

CABOCEER *n* indigenous African appointed to deal with European slave traders
CABOCEERS > CABOCEER
CABOCHED *adj* in heraldry, with the face exposed, but neck concealed
CABOCHON *n* smooth domed gem, polished but unfaceted
CABOCHONS > CABOCHON
CABOCS > CABOC
CABOMBA *n* type of aquatic plant
CABOMBAS > CABOMBA
CABOODLE *n* lot, bunch, or group
CABOODLES > CABOODLE
CABOOSE *n* guard's van on a train
CABOOSES > CABOOSE
CABOSHED *same as* > CABOCHED
CABOTAGE *n* coastal navigation or shipping, esp within the borders of one country
CABOTAGES > CABOTAGE
CABOVER *n* truck or lorry in which the cab is over the engine
CABOVERS > CABOVER
CABRE *adj* heraldic term designating an animal rearing
CABRESTA *variant of* > CABESTRO
CABRESTAS > CABRESTA
CABRESTO *variant of* > CABESTRO
CABRESTOS > CABRESTO
CABRETTA *n* soft leather obtained from the skins of certain South American or African sheep
CABRETTAS > CABRETTA
CABRIE *n* pronghorn antelope
CABRIES > CABRIE
CABRILLA *n* type of food fish occurring in warm seas around Florida and the Caribbean
CABRILLAS > CABRILLA
CABRIO *short for* > CABRIOLET
CABRIOLE *n* type of furniture leg featuring a tapering curve
CABRIOLES > CABRIOLE
CABRIOLET *n* small horse-drawn carriage with a folding hood
CABRIOS > CABRIO

CABRIT *n* pronghorn antelope
CABRITS > CABRIT
CABS > CAB
CABSTAND *n* taxi-rank
CABSTANDS > CABSTAND
CACA *n* heroin
CACAFOGO *same as* > CACAFUEGO
CACAFOGOS > CACAFUEGO
CACAFUEGO *n* spitfire
CACAO *same as* > COCOA
CACAOS > CACAO
CACAS > CACA
CACHACA *n* white Brazilian rum made from sugar cane
CACHACAS > CACHACA
CACHAEMIA *n* poisoned condition of the blood
CACHAEMIC > CACHAEMIA
CACHALOT *n* sperm whale
CACHALOTS > CACHALOT
CACHE *n* hidden store of weapons or treasure ▷ *vb* store in a cache
CACHECTIC > CACHEXIA
CACHED > CACHE
CACHEPOT *n* ornamental container for a flowerpot
CACHEPOTS > CACHEPOT
CACHES > CACHE
CACHET *n* prestige, distinction ▷ *vb* apply a commemorative design to an envelope, as a first-day cover
CACHETED > CACHET
CACHETING > CACHET
CACHETS > CACHET
CACHEXIA *n* generally weakened condition of body or mind
CACHEXIAS > CACHEXIA
CACHEXIC > CACHEXIA
CACHEXIES > CACHEXIA
CACHEXY *same as* > CACHEXIA
CACHING > CACHE
CACHOLONG *n* type of opal
CACHOLOT *same as* > CACHALOT
CACHOLOTS > CACHALOT
CACHOU *same as* > CATECHU
CACHOUS > CACHOU
CACHUCHA *n* graceful Spanish solo dance in triple time
CACHUCHAS > CACHUCHA
CACIQUE *n* Native American chief in a Spanish-speaking region
CACIQUES > CACIQUE

CACIQUISM n (esp in Spanish America) government by local political bosses

CACK n slang word for nonsense ▷ vb slang word for defecate

CACKED > CACK

CACKIER > CACKY

CACKIEST > CACKY

CACKING > CACK

CACKLE vb laugh shrilly ▷ n cackling noise

CACKLED > CACKLE

CACKLER > CACKLE

CACKLERS > CACKLE

CACKLES > CACKLE

CACKLING > CACKLE

CACKS > CACK

CACKY adj dirty or worthless

CACODEMON n evil spirit or. devil

CACODOXY n heterodoxy

CACODYL n oily poisonous liquid with a strong garlic smell

CACODYLIC > CACODYL

CACODYLS > CACODYL

CACOEPIES > CACOEPY

CACOEPY n bad or mistaken pronunciation

CACOETHES n uncontrollable urge or desire, esp for something harmful

CACOETHIC > CACOETHES

CACOGENIC adj reducing the quality of a race

CACOLET n seat fitted to the back of a mule

CACOLETS > CACOLET

CACOLOGY n bad choice of words

CACOMIXL n carnivorous mammal

CACOMIXLE same as > CACOMIXL

CACOMIXLS > CACOMIXL

CACONYM n erroneous name

CACONYMS > CACONYM

CACONYMY > CACONYM

CACOON n large seed of the sword-bean

CACOONS > CACOON

CACOPHONY n harsh discordant sound

CACOTOPIA n dystopia, the opposite of utopia

CACTI > CACTUS

CACTIFORM adj cactus-like

CACTOID adj resembling a cactus

CACTUS n fleshy desert plant with spines but no leaves

CACTUSES > CACTUS

CACUMEN n apex

CACUMENS > CACUMEN

CACUMINA > CACUMEN

CACUMINAL adj relating to or denoting a consonant articulated with the tip of the tongue turned back towards the hard palate ▷ n consonant articulated in this manner

CAD n dishonourable man

CADAGA n eucalyptus tree

CADAGAS > CADAGA

CADAGI same as > CADAGA

CADAGIS > CADAGI

CADASTER n register of ownership, boundaries, and value of property

CADASTERS > CADASTER

CADASTRAL > CADASTER

CADASTRE same as > CADASTER

CADASTRES > CADASTER

CADAVER n corpse

CADAVERIC > CADAVER

CADAVERS > CADAVER

CADDICE same as > CADDIS

CADDICES > CADDICE

CADDIE n person who carries a golfer's clubs ▷ vb act as a caddie

CADDIED > CADDIE

CADDIES > CADDIE

CADDIS n type of coarse woollen yarn, braid, or fabric

CADDISED adj trimmed with a type of ribbon

CADDISES > CADDIS

CADDISFLY n small fly

CADDISH > CAD

CADDISHLY > CAD

CADDY same as > CADDIE

CADDYING > CADDIE

CADDYSS same as > CADDIS

CADDYSSES > CADDIS

CADE n juniper tree ▷ adj (of a young animal) left by its mother and reared by humans

CADEAU n present

CADEAUX > CADEAU

CADEE old form of > CADET

CADEES > CADEE

CADELLE n type of beetle that feeds on flour, grain, and other stored foods

CADELLES > CADELLE

CADENCE n rise and fall in the pitch of the voice ▷ vb modulate musically

CADENCED > CADENCE

CADENCES > CADENCE

CADENCIES > CADENCY

CADENCING > CADENCE

CADENCY same as > CADENCE

CADENT adj having cadence

CADENTIAL > CADENT

CADENZA n complex solo passage in a piece of music

CADENZAS > CADENZA

CADES > CADE

CADET n young person training for the armed forces or police

CADETS > CADET

CADETSHIP > CADET

CADGE vb get (something) by taking advantage of someone's generosity

CADGED > CADGE

CADGER n person who cadges

CADGERS > CADGER

CADGES > CADGE

CADGIER > CADGY

CADGIEST > CADGY

CADGING > CADGE

CADGY adj cheerful

CADI n judge in a Muslim community

CADIE n messenger

CADIES > CADIE

CADIS > CADI

CADMIC > CADMIUM

CADMIUM n bluish-white metallic element used in alloys

CADMIUMS > CADMIUM

CADRANS n instrument used in gem cutting

CADRANSES > CADRANS

CADRE n group of people trained to form the core of a political or military unit

CADRES > CADRE

CADS > CAD

CADUAC n windfall

CADUACS > CADUAC

CADUCEAN > CADUCEUS

CADUCEI > CADUCEUS

CADUCEUS n mythical staff carried by Hermes (Mercury)

CADUCITY n perishableness

CADUCOUS adj (of parts of a plant or animal) shed during the life of the organism

CAECA > CAECUM

CAECAL > CAECUM

CAECALLY > CAECUM

CAECILIAN n type of tropical limbless amphibian resembling an earthworm

CAECITIS n inflammation of the caecum

CAECUM n pouch at the beginning of the large intestine

CAEOMA n aecium in some rust fungi that has no surrounding membrane

CAEOMAS > CAEOMA

CAERULE same as > CERULE

CAERULEAN same as > CERULEAN

CAESAR n any emperor, autocrat, dictator, or other powerful ruler

CAESAREAN n surgical incision through the abdominal and uterine walls in order to deliver a baby

CAESARIAN variant spelling of > CAESAREAN

CAESARISM n imperialism

CAESARS > CAESAR

CAESE interj Shakespearean interjection

CAESIOUS adj having a waxy bluish-grey coating

CAESIUM n silvery-white metallic element used in photocells

CAESIUMS > CAESIUM

CAESTUS same as > CESTUS

CAESTUSES > CAESTUS

CAESURA n pause in a line of verse

CAESURAE > CAESURA

CAESURAL > CAESURA

CAESURAS > CAESURA

CAESURIC > CAESURA

CAF n short for cafeteria

CAFARD n feeling of severe depression

CAFARDS > CAFARD

CAFE n small or inexpensive restaurant serving light refreshments

CAFES > CAFE

CAFETERIA n self-service restaurant

CAFETIERE n kind of coffeepot in which boiling water is poured onto ground coffee and a plunger fitted with a metal filter is pressed down, forcing the grounds to the bottom

CAFETORIA variant of > CAFETERIA

CAFF n café

CAFFEIN same as > CAFFEINE

CAFFEINE n stimulant found in tea and coffee

CAFFEINES > CAFFEINE

CAFFEINIC adj of or containing caffeine

CAFFEINS > CAFFEIN

CAFFEISM n addiction to caffeine

CAFFEISMS > CAFFEISM

CAFFILA n caravan train

CAFFILAS > CAFFILA

CAFFS > CAFF

CAFILA same as > CAFFILA

CAFILAS > CAFILA

CAFS > CAF

CAFTAN same as > KAFTAN

CAFTANED adj wearing caftan

CAFTANS > CAFTAN

CAG same as > CAGOULE

CAGANER n figure of a squatting defecating person

CAGANERS > CAGANER

CAGE n enclosure of bars or wires, for keeping animals or birds ▷ vb confine in a cage

CAGED > CAGE

CAGEFUL n amount which fills a cage to capacity

CAGEFULS > CAGEFUL

CAGELIKE > CAGE

CAGELING n bird kept in a cage

CAGELINGS > CAGELING

CAGER n basketball player

CAGERS > CAGER

CAGES > CAGE

CAGEWORK n something constructed as if from the bars of a cage

CAGEWORKS > CAGEWORK

CAGEY adj reluctant to go into details

CAGEYNESS > CAGEY

CAGIER > CAGEY

CAGIEST > CAGEY

CAGILY > CAGEY

CAGINESS > CAGY

CAGING > CAGE

CAGMAG adj done shoddily ▷ vb chat idly

CAGMAGGED > CAGMAG

CAGMAGS > CAGMAG

CAGOT n member of a class of French outcasts

CAGOTS > CAGOT

CAGOUL same as > CAGOULE

CAGOULE n lightweight hooded waterproof jacket

C

CAGOULES > CAGOULE
CAGOULS > CAGOUL
CAGS > CAG
CAGY same as > CAGEY
CAGYNESS > CAGY
CAHIER n notebook
CAHIERS > CAHIER
CAHOOT n partnership
CAHOOTS > CAHOOT
CAHOUN n type of S American palm tree
CAHOUNS > CAHOUN
CAHOW n Bermuda petrel
CAHOWS > CAHOW
CAID n Moroccan district administrator
CAIDS > CAID
CAILLACH same as > CAILLEACH
CAILLACHS > CAILLACH
CAILLE n quail
CAILLEACH n old woman
CAILLES > CAILLE
CAILLIACH same as > CAILLEACH
CAIMAC same as > CAIMACAM
CAIMACAM n Turkish governor of a sanjak
CAIMACAMS > CAIMACAM
CAIMACS > CAIMAC
CAIMAN same as > CAYMAN
CAIMANS > CAIMAN
CAIN n (in Scotland and Ireland) payment in kind
CAINS > CAIN
CAIQUE n long narrow light rowing skiff used in the Bosporus
CAIQUES > CAIQUE
CAIRD n travelling tinker
CAIRDS > CAIRD
CAIRN n mound of stones erected as a memorial or marker
CAIRNED adj marked by a cairn
CAIRNGORM n yellow or brownish quartz gemstone
CAIRNIER > CAIRNY
CAIRNIEST > CAIRNY
CAIRNS > CAIRN
CAIRNY adj covered with cairns
CAISSON n watertight enclosure pumped dry to enable construction work to be done
CAISSONS > CAISSON
CAITIFF n cowardly or base person ▷ adj cowardly
CAITIFFS > CAITIFF
CAITIVE n captive
CAITIVES > CAITIVE
CAJAPUT same as > CAJUPUT
CAJAPUTS > CAJAPUT
CAJEPUT same as > CAJUPUT
CAJEPUTS > CAJEPUT
CAJOLE vb persuade by flattery
CAJOLED > CAJOLE
CAJOLER > CAJOLE
CAJOLERS > CAJOLE
CAJOLERY > CAJOLE
CAJOLES > CAJOLE

CAJOLING > CAJOLE
CAJON n Peruvian wooden box used as a drum
CAJONES > CAJON
CAJUN n music of the Cajun people
CAJUPUT n small tree or shrub
CAJUPUTS > CAJUPUT
CAKE n sweet food baked from a mixture of flour, eggs, etc ▷ vb form into a hardened mass or crust
CAKEAGE n charge in a restaurant for serving cake brought in from outside
CAKEAGES > CAKEAGE
CAKEBOX n box for a cake
CAKEBOXES > CAKEBOX
CAKED > CAKE
CAKEHOLE n slang word for mouth
CAKEHOLES > CAKEHOLE
CAKES > CAKE
CAKEWALK n dance based on a march with the prize of a cake for the best performers ▷ vb perform the cakewalk
CAKEWALKS > CAKEWALK
CAKEY > CAKE
CAKIER > CAKE
CAKIEST > CAKE
CAKINESS > CAKE
CAKING > CAKE
CAKINGS > CAKE
CAKY > CAKE
CAL n short for calorie
CALABASH n type of large round gourd
CALABAZA n variety of squash
CALABAZAS > CALABAZA
CALABOGUS n mixed drink containing rum, spruce beer, and molasses
CALABOOSE n prison
CALABRESE n kind of green sprouting broccoli
CALADIUM n type of tropical plant
CALADIUMS > CALADIUM
CALALOO same as > CALALU
CALALOOS > CALALOO
CALALU n edible leaves of various plants
CALALUS > CALALU
CALAMANCO n glossy woollen fabric woven with a checked design that shows on one side only
CALAMANSI n hybrid citrus fruit from the Philippines
CALAMAR n any member of the squid family
CALAMARI n squid cooked for eating, esp cut into rings and fried in batter
CALAMARIS > CALAMARI
CALAMARS > CALAMAR
CALAMARY variant of > CALAMARI
CALAMATA same as > KALAMATA
CALAMATAS > CALAMATA
CALAMI > CALAMUS
CALAMINE n pink powder consisting chiefly of zinc

oxide, used in skin lotions and ointments ▷ vb apply calamine
CALAMINED > CALAMINE
CALAMINES > CALAMINE
CALAMINT n aromatic Eurasian plant with clusters of purple or pink flowers
CALAMINTS > CALAMINT
CALAMITE n type of extinct treelike plant related to the horsetails
CALAMITES > CALAMITE
CALAMITY n disaster
CALAMUS n tropical Asian palm
CALAMUSES > CALAMUS
CALANDO adv (to be performed) with gradually decreasing tone and speed
CALANDRIA n cylindrical vessel through which vertical tubes pass, esp one forming part of an evaporator, heat exchanger, or nuclear reactor
CALANTHE n type of orchid
CALANTHES > CALANTHE
CALASH n horse-drawn carriage with low wheels and a folding top
CALASHES > CALASH
CALATHEA n S American plant often grown as a greenhouse or house plant for its variegated leaves
CALATHEAS > CALATHEA
CALATHI > CALATHUS
CALATHOS same as > CALATHUS
CALATHUS n vase-shaped basket represented in ancient Greek art, used as a symbol of fruitfulness
CALAVANCE n type of pulse
CALCANEA > CALCANEUM
CALCANEAL > CALCANEUS
CALCANEAN > CALCANEUS
CALCANEI > CALCANEUS
CALCANEUM same as > CALCANEUS
CALCANEUS n largest tarsal bone, forming the heel in human beings
CALCAR n spur or spurlike process
CALCARATE > CALCAR
CALCARIA > CALCAR
CALCARINE > CALCAR
CALCARS > CALCAR
CALCEATE vb to shoe
CALCEATED > CALCEATE
CALCEATES > CALCEATE
CALCED adj wearing shoes
CALCEDONY n microcrystalline often greyish form of quartz with crystals arranged in parallel fibres: a gemstone
CALCES > CALX
CALCIC adj of, containing, or concerned with lime or calcium
CALCICOLE n any plant that thrives in lime-rich soils
CALCIFIC adj forming or causing to form lime or chalk
CALCIFIED > CALCIFY
CALCIFIES > CALCIFY

CALCIFUGE n any plant that thrives in acid soils but not in lime-rich soils
CALCIFY vb harden by the depositing of calcium salts
CALCIMINE n white or pale tinted wash for walls ▷ vb cover with calcimine
CALCINE vb oxidize (a substance) by heating
CALCINED > CALCINE
CALCINES > CALCINE
CALCINING > CALCINE
CALCITE n colourless or white form of calcium carbonate
CALCITES > CALCITE
CALCITIC > CALCITE
CALCIUM n silvery-white metallic element
CALCIUMS > CALCIUM
CALCRETE another name for > CALICHE
CALCRETES > CALCRETE
CALCSPAR another name for > CALCITE
CALCSPARS > CALCSPAR
CALCTUFA another name for > TUFA
CALCTUFAS > CALCTUFA
CALCTUFF another name for > TUFA
CALCTUFFS > CALCTUFF
CALCULAR adj relating to calculus
CALCULARY adj relating to stone
CALCULATE vb solve or find out by a mathematical procedure or by reasoning
CALCULI > CALCULUS
CALCULOSE adj relating to calculi
CALCULOUS adj of or suffering from a stonelike accretion of minerals and salts found in ducts or hollow organs of the body
CALCULUS n branch of mathematics dealing with infinitesimal changes to a variable number or quantity
CALDARIA > CALDARIUM
CALDARIUM n (in ancient Rome) a room for taking hot baths
CALDERA n large basin-shaped crater at the top of a volcano
CALDERAS > CALDERA
CALDRON same as > CAULDRON
CALDRONS > CALDRON
CALECHE a variant of > CALASH
CALECHES > CALECHE
CALEFIED > CALEFY
CALEFIES > CALEFY
CALEFY vb make warm
CALEFYING > CALEFY
CALEMBOUR n pun
CALENDAL > CALENDS
CALENDAR n chart showing a year divided up into months, weeks, and days ▷ vb enter in a calendar
CALENDARS > CALENDAR

CALENDER n machine in which paper or cloth is smoothed by passing it between rollers ▷ vb smooth in such a machine

CALENDERS > CALENDER

CALENDRER > CALENDER

CALENDRIC > CALENDAR

CALENDRY n place where calendering is carried out

CALENDS pl n first day of each month in the ancient Roman calendar

CALENDULA n marigold

CALENTURE n mild fever of tropical climates, similar in its symptoms to sunstroke

CALESA n horse-drawn buggy

CALESAS > CALESA

CALESCENT adj increasing in heat

CALF n young cow, bull, elephant, whale, or seal

CALFDOZER n small bulldozer

CALFHOOD n state of being a calf

CALFHOODS > CALFHOOD

CALFLESS > CALF

CALFLICK another word for > COWLICK

CALFLICKS > CALFLICK

CALFLIKE > CALF

CALFS > CALF

CALFSKIN n fine leather made from the skin of a calf

CALFSKINS > CALFSKIN

CALIATOUR n red sandalwood

CALIBER same as > CALIBRE

CALIBERED > CALIBER

CALIBERS > CALIBER

CALIBRATE vb mark the scale or check the accuracy of (a measuring instrument)

CALIBRE n person's ability or worth

CALIBRED > CALIBRE

CALIBRES > CALIBRE

CALICES > CALIX

CALICHE n bed of sand or clay in arid regions

CALICHES > CALICHE

CALICLE same as > CALYCLE

CALICLES > CALICLE

CALICO n white cotton fabric

CALICOES > CALICO

CALICOS > CALICO

CALICULAR > CALYCLE

CALID adj warm

CALIDITY > CALID

CALIF same as > CALIPH

CALIFATE same as > CALIPHATE

CALIFATES > CALIFATE

CALIFONT n gas water heater

CALIFONTS > CALIFONT

CALIFS > CALIF

CALIGO n speck on the cornea causing poor vision

CALIGOES > CALIGO

CALIGOS > CALIGO

CALIMA n Saharan dust-storm

CALIMAS > CALIMA

CALIMOCHO n Spanish cocktail consisting of cola and red wine

CALIOLOGY n the study of birds' nests

CALIPASH n greenish glutinous edible part of the turtle

CALIPEE n edible part of the turtle found next to the lower shell

CALIPEES > CALIPEE

CALIPER same as > CALLIPER

CALIPERED > CALLIPER

CALIPERS > CALIPER

CALIPH n Muslim ruler

CALIPHAL > CALIPH

CALIPHATE n office, jurisdiction, or reign of a caliph

CALIPHS > CALIPH

CALISAYA n bark of a type of tropical tree from which quinine is extracted

CALISAYAS > CALISAYA

CALIVER n type of musket

CALIVERS > CALIVER

CALIX n cup

CALIXES > CALIX

CALK same as > CAULK

CALKED > CALK

CALKER > CALK

CALKERS > CALK

CALKIN same as > CALK

CALKING > CALK

CALKINGS > CALK

CALKINS > CALKIN

CALKS > CALK

CALL vb name ▷ n cry, shout

CALLA n S African plant with a white funnel-shaped spathe enclosing a yellow spadix

CALLABLE adj (of a security) subject to redemption before maturity

CALLAIDES > CALLAIS

CALLAIS n type of green stone

CALLALOO n leafy green vegetable

CALLALOOS > CALLALOO

CALLALOU n crabmeat soup

CALLALOUS > CALLALOU

CALLAN same as > CALLANT

CALLANS > CALLAN

CALLANT n youth

CALLANTS > CALLANT

CALLAS > CALLA

CALLBACK n telephone call made in response to an earlier call

CALLBACKS > CALLBACK

CALLBOARD n notice board listing opportunities for performers

CALLBOY n person who notifies actors when it is time to go on stage

CALLBOYS > CALLBOY

CALLED > CALL

CALLEE n computer function being used

CALLEES > CALLEE

CALLER n person or thing that calls, esp a person who makes a brief visit ▷ adj (of food, esp fish) fresh

CALLERS > CALLER

CALLET n scold

CALLETS > CALLET

CALLID adj cunning

CALLIDITY > CALLID

CALLIGRAM n poem in which words are positioned so as to create a visual image of the subject on the page

CALLING n vocation, profession

CALLINGS > CALLING

CALLIOPE n steam organ

CALLIOPES > CALLIOPE

CALLIPASH same as > CALIPASH

CALLIPEE same as > CALIPEE

CALLIPEES > CALLIPEE

CALLIPER n metal splint for supporting the leg ▷ vb measure the dimensions of (an object) with callipers

CALLIPERS > CALLIPER

CALLOP n edible Australian freshwater fish

CALLOPS > CALLOP

CALLOSE n carbohydrate found in plants

CALLOSES > CALLOSE

CALLOSITY same as > CALLUS

CALLOUS adj showing no concern for other people's feelings ▷ vb make or become callous

CALLOUSED > CALLOUS

CALLOUSES > CALLOUS

CALLOUSLY > CALLOUS

CALLOUT n inset text within a printed article

CALLOUTS > CALLOUT

CALLOW adj young and inexperienced ▷ n someone young and inexperienced

CALLOWER > CALLOW

CALLOWEST > CALLOW

CALLOWLY adj in a manner suggesting immaturity or inexperience

CALLOWS > CALLOW

CALLS > CALL

CALLTIME n time available for making calls on a mobile phone

CALLTIMES > CALLTIME

CALLUNA n type of heather

CALLUNAS > CALLUNA

CALLUS n area of thick hardened skin ▷ vb produce or cause to produce a callus

CALLUSED > CALLUS

CALLUSES > CALLUS

CALLUSING > CALLUS

CALM adj not agitated or excited ▷ n peaceful state ▷ vb make or become calm

CALMANT n sedative

CALMANTS > CALMANT

CALMATIVE adj (of a remedy or agent) sedative ▷ n sedative remedy or drug

CALMED > CALM

CALMER > CALM

CALMEST > CALM

CALMIER > CALMY

CALMIEST > CALMY

CALMING > CALM

CALMINGLY > CALM

CALMINGS > CALM

CALMLY > CALM

CALMNESS > CALM

CALMS > CALM

CALMSTANE same as > CAMSTONE

CALMSTONE same as > CAMSTONE

CALMY adj tranquil

CALO n military servant

CALOMEL n colourless tasteless powder

CALOMELS > CALOMEL

CALORIC adj of heat or calories ▷ n hypothetical fluid formerly postulated as the embodiment of heat

CALORICS > CALORIC

CALORIE n unit of measurement for the energy value of food

CALORIES > CALORIE

CALORIFIC adj of calories or heat

CALORISE same as > CALORIZE

CALORISED > CALORISE

CALORISES > CALORISE

CALORIST n believer in caloric theory

CALORISTS > CALORIST

CALORIZE vb coat (a ferrous metal) by spraying with aluminium powder and then heating

CALORIZED > CALORIZE

CALORIZES > CALORIZE

CALORY same as > CALORIE

CALOS > CALO

CALOTTE n skullcap worn by Roman Catholic clergy

CALOTTES > CALOTTE

CALOTYPE n early photographic process

CALOTYPES > CALOTYPE

CALOYER n monk of the Greek Orthodox Church, esp of the Basilian Order

CALOYERS > CALOYER

CALP n type of limestone

CALPA n Hindu unit of time

CALPAC n large black brimless hat

CALPACK same as > CALPAC

CALPACKS > CALPACK

CALPACS > CALPAC

CALPAIN n type of enzyme

CALPAINS > CALPAIN

CALPAS > CALPA

CALPS > CALP

CALQUE same as > CAULK

CALQUED > CALQUE

CALQUES > CALQUE

CALQUING > CALQUE

CALS > CAL

CALTHA n marsh marigold

CALTHAS > CALTHA

CALTHROP same as > CALTROP

CALTHROPS > CALTROP

c

CALTRAP same as
> CALTROP

CALTRAPS > CALTRAP

CALTROP n floating Asian
plant

CALTROPS > CALTROP

CALUMBA n Mozambiquan
root used for medicinal
purposes

CALUMBAS > CALUMBA

CALUMET n peace pipe

CALUMETS > CALUMET

CALUMNIED > CALUMNY

CALUMNIES > CALUMNY

CALUMNY n false or
malicious statement ▷ vb
make a false or malicious
statement about (a person)

CALUTRON n device used for
the separation of isotopes

CALUTRONS > CALUTRON

CALVADOS n type of apple
brandy

CALVARIA n top part of the
skull of vertebrates

CALVARIAE > CALVARIA

CALVARIAL > CALVARIUM

CALVARIAN > CALVARIUM

CALVARIAS > CALVARIA

CALVARIES > CALVARY

CALVARIUM same as
> CALVARIA

CALVARY n representation
of Christ's crucifixion

CALVE vb give birth to a calf

CALVED > CALVE

CALVER vb prepare fish for
cooking

CALVERED > CALVER

CALVERING > CALVER

CALVERS > CALVER

CALVES > CALF

CALVING > CALVE

CALVITIES n baldness

CALX n powdery metallic
oxide formed when an ore or
mineral is roasted

CALXES > CALX

CALYCATE > CALYX

CALYCEAL adj resembling a
calyx

CALYCES > CALYX

CALYCINAL same as
> CALYCINE

CALYCINE adj relating to,
belonging to, or resembling a
calyx

CALYCLE n cup-shaped
structure, as in the coral
skeleton

CALYCLED > CALYCLE

CALYCLES > CALYCLE

CALYCOID adj resembling a
calyx

CALYCULAR > CALYCLE

CALYCULE n bracts
surrounding the base of the
calyx

CALYCULES > CALYCULE

CALYCULI > CALYCULUS

CALYCULUS same as
> CALYCLE

CALYPSO n West Indian
song with improvised topical
lyrics

CALYPSOES > CALYPSO

CALYPSOS > CALYPSO

CALYPTER n alula

CALYPTERA same as
> CALYPTRA

CALYPTERS > CALYPTER

CALYPTRA n membranous
hood covering the
spore-bearing capsule of
mosses and liverworts

CALYPTRAS > CALYPTRA

CALYX n outer leaves that
protect a flower bud

CALYXES > CALYX

CALZONE n folded pizza
filled with cheese, tomatoes,
etc

CALZONES > CALZONE

CALZONI > CALZONE

CAM n device that converts a
circular motion to a
to-and-fro motion ▷ vb
furnish (a machine) with a
cam

CAMA n hybrid offspring of a
camel and a llama

CAMAIEU n cameo

CAMAIEUX > CAMAIEU

CAMAIL n covering of chain
mail

CAMAILED > CAMAIL

CAMAILS > CAMAIL

CAMAN n wooden stick used
to hit the ball in shinty

CAMANACHD n shinty

CAMANS > CAMAN

CAMARILLA n group of
confidential advisers, esp
formerly, to the Spanish
kings

CAMARON n shrimp

CAMARONS > CAMARON

CAMAS same as > CAMASS

CAMASES > CAMAS

CAMASH same as > CAMASS

CAMASHES > CAMASH

CAMASS n type of North
American plant

CAMASSES > CAMASS

CAMBER n slight upward
curve to the centre of a
surface ▷ vb form or be
formed with a surface that
curves upwards to its centre

CAMBERED > CAMBER

CAMBERING > CAMBER

CAMBERS > CAMBER

CAMBIA > CAMBIUM

CAMBIAL > CAMBIUM

CAMBIFORM > CAMBIUM

CAMBISM > CAMBIST

CAMBISMS > CAMBIST

CAMBIST n dealer or expert
in foreign exchange

CAMBISTRY > CAMBIST

CAMBISTS > CAMBIST

CAMBIUM n meristem that
increases the girth of stems
and roots

CAMBIUMS > CAMBIUM

CAMBOGE n type of gum
resin

CAMBOGES > CAMBOGE

CAMBOGIA another name for
> GAMBOGE

CAMBOGIAS > CAMBOGIA

CAMBOOSE n cabin built as
living quarters for a gang of
lumber workers

CAMBOOSES > CAMBOOSE

CAMBREL a variant of
> GAMBREL

CAMBRELS > CAMBREL

CAMBRIC n fine white linen
fabric

CAMBRICS > CAMBRIC

CAMCORD vb film with a
camcorder

CAMCORDED > CAMCORD

CAMCORDER n combined
portable video camera and
recorder

CAMCORDS > CAMCORD

CAME > COME

CAMEL n humped mammal

CAMELBACK n type of
locomotive

CAMELEER n camel-driver

CAMELEERS > CAMELEER

CAMELEON same as
> CHAMELEON

CAMELEONS > CAMELEON

CAMELHAIR n hair of camel

CAMELIA same as
> CAMELLIA

CAMELIAS > CAMELIA

CAMELID adj of or relating to
camels ▷ n any animal of the
camel family

CAMELIDS > CAMELID

CAMELINE n material made
from camel hair

CAMELINES > CAMELINE

CAMELISH > CAMEL

CAMELLIA n evergreen
ornamental shrub with
white, pink, or red flowers

CAMELLIAS > CAMELLIA

CAMELLIKE > CAMEL

CAMELOID n member of the
camel family

CAMELOIDS > CAMELOID

CAMELOT n supposedly
idyllic period or age

CAMELOTS > CAMELOT

CAMELRIES > CAMELRY

CAMELRY n troops mounted
on camels

CAMELS > CAMEL

CAMEO n brooch or ring with
a profile head carved in relief
▷ vb appear in a brief role

CAMEOED > CAMEO

CAMEOING > CAMEO

CAMEOS > CAMEO

CAMERA n apparatus used
for taking still or moving
images

CAMERAE > CAMERA

CAMERAL adj of or relating to
a judicial or legislative
chamber

CAMERAMAN n man who
operates a camera for
television or cinema

CAMERAMEN > CAMERAMAN

CAMERAS > CAMERA

CAMERATED adj vaulted

CAMES pl n pieces of lead
used in lattice windows

CAMESE same as > CAMISE

CAMESES > CAMESE

CAMI n camisole

CAMION n lorry or, esp
formerly, a large dray

CAMIONS > CAMION

CAMIS n light robe

CAMISA n smock

CAMISADE same as
> CAMISADO

CAMISADES > CAMISADE

CAMISADO n (formerly) an
attack made under cover of
darkness

CAMISADOS > CAMISADO

CAMISAS > CAMISA

CAMISE n loose light shirt,
smock, or tunic originally
worn in the Middle Ages

CAMISES > CAMISE

CAMISIA n surplice

CAMISIAS > CAMISIA

CAMISOLE n woman's
bodice-like garment

CAMISOLES > CAMISOLE

CAMLET n tough waterproof
cloth

CAMLETS > CAMLET

CAMMED > CAM

CAMMIE n webcam award

CAMMIES > CAMMIE

CAMMING > CAM

CAMO n short for camouflage

CAMOGIE n form of hurling
played by women

CAMOGIES > CAMOGIE

CAMOMILE n aromatic
plant, used to make herbal
tea

CAMOMILES > CAMOMILE

CAMOODI a Caribbean name
for > ANACONDA

CAMOODIS > CAMOODI

CAMORRA n secret criminal
group

CAMORRAS > CAMORRA

CAMORRIST > CAMORRA

CAMOS > CAMO

CAMOTE n type of sweet
potato

CAMOTES > CAMOTE

CAMOUFLET n type of bomb
used in a siege to collapse an
enemy's tunnel

CAMP vb stay in a camp ▷ adj
consciously artificial ▷ n
(place for) temporary
lodgings consisting of tents,
huts, or cabins

CAMPAGNA same as
> CHAMPAIGN

CAMPAGNAS > CAMPAGNA

CAMPAGNE > CAMPAGNA

CAMPAIGN n series of
coordinated activities
designed to achieve a goal
▷ vb take part in a campaign

CAMPAIGNS > CAMPAIGN

CAMPANA n bell or bell shape

CAMPANAS > CAMPANA

CAMPANERO n South
American bellbird

CAMPANILE n bell tower,
usu one not attached to
another building

CAMPANILI > CAMPANILE

CAMPANIST n expert on
bells

CAMPANULA n plant with
blue or white bell-shaped
flowers

CAMPCRAFT n skills required
when camping

CAMPEACHY *adj* as in *campeachy wood* kind of wood

CAMPEADOR *n* champion; term applied especially to El Cid

CAMPED > CAMP

CAMPER *n* person who lives or temporarily stays in a tent, cabin, etc

CAMPERIES > CAMPERY

CAMPERS > CAMPER

CAMPERY *n* campness

CAMPESINO *n* Latin American rural peasant

CAMPEST > CAMP

CAMPFIRE *n* outdoor fire in a camp

CAMPFIRES > CAMPFIRE

CAMPHANE *n* one of the terpene hydrocarbons

CAMPHANES > CAMPHANE

CAMPHENE *n* colourless crystalline insoluble terpene

CAMPHENES > CAMPHENE

CAMPHINE *n* type of solvent

CAMPHINES > CAMPHINE

CAMPHIRE *an archaic name for* > HENNA

CAMPHIRES > CAMPHIRE

CAMPHOL *another word for* > BORNEOL

CAMPHOLS > CAMPHOL

CAMPHONE *n* combined mobile phone and digital camera

CAMPHONES > CAMPHONE

CAMPHOR *n* aromatic crystalline substance

CAMPHORIC > CAMPHOR

CAMPHORS > CAMPHOR

CAMPI > CAMPO

CAMPIER > CAMPY

CAMPIEST > CAMPY

CAMPILY > CAMPY

CAMPINESS > CAMPY

CAMPING > CAMP

CAMPINGS > CAMP

CAMPION *n* red, pink, or white wild flower

CAMPIONS > CAMPION

CAMPLE *vb* argue

CAMPLED > CAMPLE

CAMPLES > CAMPLE

CAMPLING > CAMPLE

CAMPLY > CAMP

CAMPNESS > CAMP

CAMPO *n* level or undulating savanna country

CAMPODEID *n* member of the Campodea genus of bristle-tails

CAMPONG *n* in Malaysia, a village

CAMPONGS > CAMPONG

CAMPOREE *n* local meeting or assembly of Scouts

CAMPOREES > CAMPOREE

CAMPOS > CAMPO

CAMPOUT *n* camping trip

CAMPOUTS > CAMPOUT

CAMPS > CAMP

CAMPSHIRT *n* short-sleeved shirt

CAMPSITE *n* area on which holiday makers may pitch a tent

CAMPSITES > CAMPSITE

CAMPSTOOL *n* folding stool

CAMPUS *n* grounds of a university or college ⊳ *vb* restrict a student to campus, as a punishment

CAMPUSED > CAMPUS

CAMPUSES > CAMPUS

CAMPUSING > CAMPUS

CAMPY *adj* consciously artificial

CAMS > CAM

CAMSHAFT *n* part of an engine consisting of a rod to which cams are fixed

CAMSHAFTS > CAMSHAFT

CAMSHO *adj* crooked

CAMSHOCH *same as* > CAMSHO

CAMSTAIRY *adj* perverse

CAMSTANE *same as* > CAMSTONE

CAMSTANES > CAMSTONE

CAMSTEARY *same as* > CAMSTAIRY

CAMSTONE *n* limestone used for whitening stone doorsteps

CAMSTONES > CAMSTONE

CAMUS *n* type of loose robe

CAMUSES > CAMUS

CAMWHORE *vb* perform sexual acts in front of a webcam for money

CAMWHORED > CAMWHORE

CAMWHORES > CAMWHORE

CAMWOOD *n* W African leguminous tree

CAMWOODS > CAMWOOD

CAN *vb* be able to ⊳ *vb* put (food etc) into a can ⊳ *n* metal container for food or liquids

CANADA *n* canada goose

CANADAS > CANADA

CANAIGRE *n* southern US dock, the root of which yields a substance used in tanning

CANAIGRES > CANAIGRE

CANAILLE *n* masses or rabble

CANAILLES > CANAILLE

CANAKIN *same as* > CANNIKIN

CANAKINS > CANAKIN

CANAL *n* artificial waterway ⊳ *vb* dig a canal through

CANALBOAT *n* boat made for canals

CANALED > CANAL

CANALING > CANAL

CANALISE *same as* > CANALIZE

CANALISED > CANALIZE

CANALISES > CANALIZE

CANALIZE *vb* give direction to

CANALIZED > CANALIZE

CANALIZES > CANALIZE

CANALLED > CANAL

CANALLER *n* canal boat worker

CANALLERS > CANALLER

CANALLING > CANAL

CANALS > CANAL

CANAPE *n* small piece of bread or toast with a savoury topping

CANAPES > CANAPE

CANARD *n* false report

CANARDS > CANARD

CANARIED > CANARY

CANARIES > CANARY

CANARY *n* small yellow songbird often kept as a pet ⊳ *vb* perform a dance called the canary

CANARYING > CANARY

CANASTA *n* card game like rummy, played with two packs

CANASTAS > CANASTA

CANASTER *n* coarsely broken dried tobacco leaves

CANASTERS > CANASTER

CANBANK *n* container for receiving cans for recycling

CANBANKS > CANBANK

CANCAN *n* lively high-kicking dance performed by a female group

CANCANS > CANCAN

CANCEL *vb* stop (something that has been arranged) from taking place ⊳ *n* new leaf or section of a book replacing a defective one

CANCELBOT *n* computer program that deletes unwanted mailings to internet usergroups

CANCELED > CANCEL

CANCELEER *vb* (of a hawk) to turn in flight when a stoop fails, in order to re-attempt it

CANCELER > CANCEL

CANCELERS > CANCEL

CANCELIER *a variant of* > CANCELEER

CANCELING > CANCEL

CANCELLED > CANCEL

CANCELLER > CANCEL

CANCELLI *pl n* any lattice-like structures

CANCELS > CANCEL

CANCER *n* serious disease resulting from a malignant growth or tumour

CANCERATE *vb* become cancerous

CANCERED *adj* affected by cancer

CANCEROUS > CANCER

CANCERS > CANCER

CANCHA *n* toasted maize

CANCHAS > CANCHA

CANCRINE *adj* crab-like

CANCROID *adj* resembling a cancerous growth ⊳ *n* skin cancer, esp one of only moderate malignancy

CANCROIDS > CANCROID

CANDELA *n* unit of luminous intensity

CANDELAS > CANDELA

CANDENT *adj* emitting light as a result of being heated to a high temperature

CANDID *adj* honest and straightforward ⊳ *n* unposed photograph

CANDIDA *n* yeastlike parasitic fungus

CANDIDACY > CANDIDATE

CANDIDAL > CANDIDA

CANDIDAS > CANDIDA

CANDIDATE *n* person seeking a job or position

CANDIDER > CANDID

CANDIDEST > CANDID

CANDIDLY > CANDID

CANDIDS > CANDID

CANDIE *n* South Indian unit of weight

CANDIED *adj* coated with sugar

CANDIES > CANDY

CANDIRU *n* parasitic freshwater catfish of the Amazon region

CANDIRUS > CANDIRU

CANDLE *n* stick of wax enclosing a wick, burned to produce light ⊳ *vb* test by holding up to a candle

CANDLED > CANDLE

CANDLELIT *adj* lit by the light of candles

CANDLENUT *n* tropical Asian and Polynesian tree

CANDLEPIN *n* bowling pin, as used in skittles, tenpin bowling, candlepins, etc

CANDLER > CANDLE

CANDLERS > CANDLE

CANDLES > CANDLE

CANDLING > CANDLE

CANDOCK *n* type of water lily, or horsetail

CANDOCKS > CANDOCK

CANDOR *same as* > CANDOUR

CANDORS > CANDOR

CANDOUR *n* honesty and straightforwardness

CANDOURS > CANDOUR

CANDY *n* sweet or sweets ⊳ *vb* make sweet

CANDYGRAM *n* message accompanied by sweets

CANDYING > CANDY

CANDYMAN *n* itinerant seller of toffee

CANDYMEN > CANDYMAN

CANDYTUFT *n* garden plant with clusters of white, pink, or purple flowers

CANE *n* stem of the bamboo or similar plant ⊳ *vb* beat with a cane

CANEBRAKE *n* thicket of canes

CANED > CANE

CANEFRUIT *n* fruit, like the raspberry, which grows on woody-stemmed plants

CANEGRUB *n* Australian grub that feeds on sugarcane

CANEGRUBS > CANEGRUB

CANEH *n* Hebrew unit of length

CANEHS > CANEH

CANELLA *n* fragrant cinnamon-like inner bark of a W Indian tree, used as a spice and in medicine

CANELLAS > CANELLA

CANELLINI *n* white kidney bean

CANEPHOR *n* sculpted figure carrying a basket on its head

CANEPHORA *same as* > CANEPHOR

CANEPHORE *same as* > CANEPHOR

CANEPHORS > CANEPHOR

CANER > CANE

CANERS > CANE

CANES > CANE

CANESCENT adj white or greyish due to the presence of numerous short white hairs

CANEWARE n type of unglazed stoneware

CANEWARES > CANEWARE

CANFIELD n gambling game adapted from a type of patience

CANFIELDS > CANFIELD

CANFUL n amount a can will hold

CANFULS > CANFUL

CANG same as > CANGUE

CANGLE vb wrangle

CANGLED > CANGLE

CANGLES > CANGLE

CANGLING > CANGLE

CANGS > CANG

CANGUE n (formerly in China) a wooden collar worn as a punishment

CANGUES > CANGUE

CANICULAR adj of or relating to the star Sirius or its rising

CANID n animal of the dog family

CANIDS > CANID

CANIER > CANY

CANIEST > CANY

CANIKIN same as > CANNIKIN

CANIKINS > CANIKIN

CANINE adj of or like a dog ▷ n sharp pointed tooth between the incisors and the molars

CANINES > CANINE

CANING n beating with a cane as a punishment

CANINGS > CANING

CANINITY > CANINE

CANISTEL n Caribbean fruit

CANISTELS > CANISTEL

CANISTER n metal container ▷ vb put into canisters

CANISTERS > CANISTER

CANITIES n grey hair

CANKER n ulceration, ulcerous disease ▷ vb infect or become infected with or as if with canker

CANKERED > CANKER

CANKERIER > CANKERY

CANKERING > CANKER

CANKEROUS adj having cankers

CANKERS > CANKER

CANKERY adj like a canker

CANKLE n thickened ankle on an overweight person

CANKLES > CANKLE

CANN vb direct a ship's steering

CANNA n type of tropical plant

CANNABIC > CANNABIS

CANNABIN n greenish-black poisonous resin obtained from the Indian hemp plant

CANNABINS > CANNABIN

CANNABIS n Asian plant with tough fibres

CANNACH n cotton grass

CANNACHS > CANNACH

CANNAE vb can not

CANNAS > CANNA

CANNED > CAN

CANNEL n type of dull coal

CANNELON n type of meat loaf

CANNELONI pl n pasta in the shape of tubes, which are usually stuffed

CANNELONS > CANNELON

CANNELS > CANNEL

CANNELURE n groove or fluting, esp one around the cylindrical part of a bullet

CANNER n person or organization whose job is to can foods

CANNERIES > CANNERY

CANNERS > CANNER

CANNERY n factory where food is canned

CANNIBAL n person who eats human flesh

CANNIBALS > CANNIBAL

CANNIE same as > CANNY

CANNIER > CANNY

CANNIEST > CANNY

CANNIKIN n small can, esp one used as a drinking vessel

CANNIKINS > CANNIKIN

CANNILY > CANNY

CANNINESS > CANNY

CANNING n act of putting food in a can

CANNINGS > CANNING

CANNISTER same as > CANISTER

CANNOLI n Sicilian pudding of pasta shells filled with sweetened ricotta

CANNOLIS > CANNOLI

CANNON n gun of large calibre ▷ vb collide (with)

CANNONADE n continuous heavy gunfire ▷ vb attack (a target) with cannon

CANNONED > CANNON

CANNONEER n (formerly) a soldier who served and fired a cannon

CANNONIER same as > CANNONEER

CANNONING > CANNON

CANNONRY n volley of artillery fire

CANNONS > CANNON

CANNOT vb can not

CANNS > CANN

CANNULA n narrow tube for insertion into a bodily cavity

CANNULAE > CANNULA

CANNULAR adj shaped like a cannula

CANNULAS > CANNULA

CANNULATE vb insert a cannula into ▷ adj shaped like a cannula

CANNY adj shrewd, cautious ▷ adv quite

CANOE n light narrow open boat propelled by a paddle or paddles ▷ vb use a canoe

CANOEABLE > CANOE

CANOED > CANOE

CANOEING > CANOE

CANOEINGS > CANOE

CANOEIST > CANOE

CANOEISTS > CANOE

CANOEMAN n man who canoes

CANOEMEN > CANOEMAN

CANOER > CANOE

CANOERS > CANOE

CANOES > CANOE

CANOEWOOD n type of tree

CANOLA n cooking oil extracted from a variety of rapeseed

CANOLAS > CANOLA

CANON n priest serving in a cathedral

CANONESS n woman belonging to any one of several religious orders

CANONIC same as > CANONICAL

CANONICAL adj conforming with canon law

CANONISE same as > CANONIZE

CANONISED > CANONISE

CANONISER > CANONISE

CANONISES > CANONISE

CANONIST n specialist in canon law

CANONISTS > CANONIST

CANONIZE vb declare (a person) officially to be a saint

CANONIZED > CANONIZE

CANONIZER > CANONIZE

CANONIZES > CANONIZE

CANONRIES > CANONRY

CANONRY n office, benefice, or status of a canon

CANONS > CANON

CANOODLE vb kiss and cuddle

CANOODLED > CANOODLE

CANOODLER > CANOODLE

CANOODLES > CANOODLE

CANOPIC adj of ancient Egyptian vase

CANOPIED > CANOPY

CANOPIES > CANOPY

CANOPY n covering above a bed, door, etc ▷ vb cover with or as if with a canopy

CANOPYING > CANOPY

CANOROUS adj tuneful

CANS > CAN

CANSFUL > CANFUL

CANSO n love song

CANSOS > CANSO

CANST vb form of 'can' used with the pronoun thou or its relative form

CANSTICK n candlestick

CANSTICKS > CANSTICK

CANT n insincere talk ▷ vb use cant ▷ adj oblique

CANTABANK n itinerant singer

CANTABILE adv flowing and melodious ▷ n piece or passage performed in this way

CANTAL n French cheese

CANTALA n tropical American plant, the agave

CANTALAS > CANTALA

CANTALOUP n type of melon

CANTALS > CANTAL

CANTAR variant form of > KANTAR

CANTARS > CANTAR

CANTATA n musical work consisting of arias, duets, and choruses

CANTATAS > CANTATA

CANTATE n 98th psalm sung as a nonmetrical hymn

CANTATES > CANTATE

CANTDOG same as > CANTHOOK

CANTDOGS > CANTDOG

CANTED > CANT

CANTEEN n restaurant attached to a workplace or school

CANTEENS > CANTEEN

CANTER vb move at gait between trot and gallop

CANTERED > CANTER

CANTERING > CANTER

CANTERS > CANTER

CANTEST > CANT

CANTHAL > CANTHUS

CANTHARI > CANTHARUS

CANTHARID n type of beetle with a soft elongated body

CANTHARIS n type of soldier beetle

CANTHARUS n large two-handled pottery cup

CANTHI > CANTHUS

CANTHIC adj relating to the canthus

CANTHITIS n inflammation of canthus

CANTHOOK n wooden pole with a hook used for handling logs

CANTHOOKS > CANTHOOK

CANTHUS n inner or outer corner or angle of the eye

CANTIC > CANT

CANTICLE n short hymn with words from the Bible

CANTICLES > CANTICLE

CANTICO vb dance as part of an act of worship

CANTICOED > CANTICO

CANTICOS > CANTICO

CANTICOY same as > CANTICO

CANTICOYS > CANTICOY

CANTICUM n canticle

CANTICUMS > CANTICUM

CANTIER > CANTY

CANTIEST > CANTY

CANTILENA n smooth flowing style in the writing of vocal music

CANTILY > CANTY

CANTINA n bar or wine shop, esp in a Spanish-speaking country

CANTINAS > CANTINA

CANTINESS > CANTY

CANTING > CANT

CANTINGLY > CANT

CANTINGS > CANT

CANTION n song

CANTIONS > CANTION

CANTLE n back part of a saddle that slopes upwards ▷ vb set up, or stand, on high

C

CANTLED > CANTLE

CANTLES > CANTLE

CANTLET n piece

CANTLETS > CANTLET

CANTLING > CANTLE

CANTO same as **>** CANTUS

CANTON n political division of a country, esp Switzerland ▷ vb divide into cantons

CANTONAL > CANTON

CANTONED > CANTON

CANTONING > CANTON

CANTONISE vb divide into cantons

CANTONIZE same as **>** CANTONISE

CANTONS > CANTON

CANTOR n man employed to lead services in a synagogue

CANTORIAL adj of or relating to a precentor

CANTORIS adj (in antiphonal music) to be sung by the cantorial side of a choir

CANTORS > CANTOR

CANTOS > CANTO

CANTRAIP n witch's spell or charm

CANTRAIPS > CANTRAIP

CANTRAP same as **>** CANTRAIP

CANTRAPS > CANTRAP

CANTRED n district comprising a hundred villages

CANTREDS > CANTRED

CANTREF same as **>** CANTRED

CANTREFS > CANTREF

CANTRIP n magic spell ▷ adj (of an effect) produced by black magic

CANTRIPS > CANTRIP

CANTS > CANT

CANTUS n medieval form of church singing

CANTUSES > CANTUS

CANTY adj lively

CANULA same as **>** CANNULA

CANULAE > CANULA

CANULAR adj shaped like a cannula

CANULAS > CANULA

CANULATE same as **>** CANNULATE

CANULATED > CANULATE

CANULATES > CANULATE

CANVAS n heavy coarse cloth ▷ vb cover with, or be applied to, canvas

CANVASED > CANVAS

CANVASER > CANVAS

CANVASERS > CANVAS

CANVASES > CANVAS

CANVASING > CANVAS

CANVASS vb try to get votes or support (from) ▷ n canvassing

CANVASSED > CANVASS

CANVASSER > CANVASS

CANVASSES > CANVASS

CANY adj cane-like

CANYON n deep narrow valley

CANYONEER n canyon explorer

CANYONING n sport of going down a canyon river by any of various means

CANYONS > CANYON

CANZONA n type of 16th- or 17th-century contrapuntal music

CANZONAS > CANZONA

CANZONE n Provençal or Italian lyric, often in praise of love or beauty

CANZONES > CANZONE

CANZONET n short, cheery, or lively Italian song

CANZONETS > CANZONET

CANZONI > CANZONE

CAP n soft close-fitting covering for the head ▷ vb cover or top with something

CAPA n type of Spanish cloak

CAPABLE adj having the ability (for)

CAPABLER > CAPABLE

CAPABLEST > CAPABLE

CAPABLY > CAPABLE

CAPACIOUS adj roomy

CAPACITOR n device for storing electrical charge

CAPACITY n ability to contain, absorb, or hold ▷ adj of the maximum amount or number possible

CAPARISON n decorated covering for a horse or other animal, esp (formerly) for a warhorse ▷ vb put a caparison on

CAPAS > CAPA

CAPCOM n flight controller who communicates with the crew of a spacecraft

CAPCOMS > CAPCOM

CAPE n short cloak ▷ vb cut and remove the hide of an animal

CAPED > CAPE

CAPEESH same as **>** CAPISCE

CAPELAN another word for **>** CAPELIN

CAPELANS > CAPELAN

CAPELET n small cape

CAPELETS > CAPELET

CAPELIKE adj like a cape

CAPELIN n type of small marine food fish

CAPELINE n cap-shaped bandage to cover the head or an amputation stump

CAPELINES > CAPELINE

CAPELINS > CAPELIN

CAPELLET n wen-like swelling on a horse

CAPELLETS > CAPELLET

CAPELLINE same as **>** CAPELINE

CAPELLINI n type of pasta

CAPER n high-spirited prank ▷ vb skip about

CAPERED > CAPER

CAPERER > CAPER

CAPERERS > CAPER

CAPERING > CAPER

CAPERS pl n pickled flower buds of a Mediterranean shrub used in sauces

CAPES > CAPE

CAPESKIN n soft leather obtained from the skins of a type of lamb or sheep having hairlike wool ▷ adj made of this leather

CAPESKINS > CAPESKIN

CAPEWORK n use of the cape by the matador in bullfighting

CAPEWORKS > CAPEWORK

CAPEX n capital expenditure

CAPEXES > CAPEX

CAPFUL n quantity held by a (usually bottle) cap

CAPFULS > CAPFUL

CAPH n letter of the Hebrew alphabet

CAPHS > CAPH

CAPI > CAPO

CAPIAS n (formerly) a writ directing the arrest of a named person

CAPIASES > CAPIAS

CAPICHE interj do you understand?

CAPICOLLA n Italian cut of pork

CAPICOLLO same as **>** CAPICOLLA

CAPILLARY n very fine blood vessel ▷ adj (of a tube) having a fine bore

CAPING > CAPE

CAPISCE interj expression meaning do you understand?

CAPISH interj do you understand?

CAPITA > CAPUT

CAPITAL n chief city of a country ▷ adj involving or punishable by death

CAPITALLY adv in an excellent manner

CAPITALS > CAPITAL

CAPITAN another name for **>** HOGFISH

CAPITANI > CAPITANO

CAPITANO n chief; captain

CAPITANOS > CAPITANO

CAPITANS > CAPITAN

CAPITATE n largest of the bones of the human wrist

CAPITATED adj having fixed upper limit

CAPITATES > CAPITATE

CAPITAYN n captain

CAPITAYNS > CAPITAYN

CAPITELLA n plural form of singular: capitellum, an enlarged knoblike structure at the end of a bone that forms an articulation with another bone

CAPITOL n (in America) building housing the state legislature

CAPITOLS > CAPITOL

CAPITULA > CAPITULUM

CAPITULAR adj of or associated with a cathedral chapter ▷ n member of a cathedral chapter

CAPITULUM n racemose inflorescence in the form of a disc of sessile flowers, the youngest at the centre. It occurs in the daisy and related plants

CAPIZ n bivalve shell of a mollusc

CAPIZES > CAPIZ

CAPLE n horse

CAPLES > CAPLE

CAPLESS > CAP

CAPLET n medicinal tablet, usually oval in shape, coated in a soluble substance

CAPLETS > CAPLET

CAPLIKE adj like a cap

CAPLIN same as **>** CAPELIN

CAPLINS > CAPLIN

CAPMAKER > CAP

CAPMAKERS > CAP

CAPO n device used to raise the pitch of a stringed instrument

CAPOCCHIA n fool

CAPOEIRA n Brazilian combination of martial art and dance

CAPOEIRAS > CAPOEIRA

CAPON n cock fowl fattened for eating

CAPONATA n Sicilian antipasto relish

CAPONATAS > CAPONATA

CAPONIER n covered passageway built across a ditch as a military defence

CAPONIERE same as **>** CAPONIER

CAPONIERS > CAPONIER

CAPONISE same as **>** CAPONIZE

CAPONISED > CAPONISE

CAPONISES > CAPONISE

CAPONIZE vb make (a cock) into a capon

CAPONIZED > CAPONIZE

CAPONIZES > CAPONIZE

CAPONS > CAPON

CAPORAL n strong coarse dark tobacco

CAPORALS > CAPORAL

CAPOS > CAPO

CAPOT n winning of all the tricks by one player ▷ vb score a capot (against)

CAPOTASTO same as **>** CAPO

CAPOTE n long cloak or soldier's coat, usually with a hood

CAPOTES > CAPOTE

CAPOTS > CAPOT

CAPOTTED > CAPOT

CAPOTTING > CAPOT

CAPOUCH same as **>** CAPUCHE

CAPOUCHES > CAPOUCH

CAPPED > CAP

CAPPER > CAP

CAPPERS > CAP

CAPPING > CAP

CAPPINGS > CAP

CAPRATE n any salt of capric acid

CAPRATES > CAPRATE

CAPRESE n salad of mozzarella, basil, and tomatoes

CAPRESES > CAPRESE

CAPRI adj as in capri pants women's tight-fitting trousers

CAPRIC adj (of a type of acid) smelling of goats

CAPRICCI > CAPRICCIO

CAPRICCIO n lively piece composed freely and without adhering to the rules for any specific musical form

CAPRICE same as > CAPRICCIO

CAPRICES > CAPRICE

CAPRID n any member of the goat family

CAPRIDS > CAPRID

CAPRIFIED > CAPRIFY

CAPRIFIES > CAPRIFY

CAPRIFIG n wild variety of fig of S Europe and SW Asia

CAPRIFIGS > CAPRIFIG

CAPRIFOIL variant of > CAPRIFOLE

CAPRIFOLE n honeysuckle

CAPRIFORM adj goatlike

CAPRIFY vb induce figs to ripen

CAPRINE adj of or resembling a goat

CAPRIOLE n upward but not forward leap made by a horse ▷ vb perform a capriole

CAPRIOLED > CAPRIOLE

CAPRIOLES > CAPRIOLE

CAPRIS pl n women's tight fitting trousers

CAPROATE n any salt of caproic acid

CAPROATES > CAPROATE

CAPROCK n layer of rock that overlies a salt dome

CAPROCKS > CAPROCK

CAPROIC adj. as in caproic acid oily acid found in milk

CAPRYLATE n any salt of caprylic acid

CAPRYLIC variant of > CAPRIC

CAPS > CAP

CAPSAICIN n colourless crystalline bitter alkaloid

CAPSICIN n liquid or resin extracted from capsicum

CAPSICINS > CAPSICIN

CAPSICUM n kind of pepper used as a vegetable or as a spice

CAPSICUMS > CAPSICUM

CAPSID n outer protein coat of a mature virus

CAPSIDAL > CAPSID

CAPSIDS > CAPSID

CAPSIZAL > CAPSIZE

CAPSIZALS > CAPSIZE

CAPSIZE vb (of a boat) overturn accidentally

CAPSIZED > CAPSIZE

CAPSIZES > CAPSIZE

CAPSIZING > CAPSIZE

CAPSOMER n one of the units making up a viral capsid

CAPSOMERE n any of the protein units that together form the capsid of a virus

CAPSOMERS > CAPSOMER

CAPSTAN n rotating cylinder round which a ship's rope is wound

CAPSTANS > CAPSTAN

CAPSTONE n one of a set of slabs on the top of a wall, building, etc

CAPSTONES > CAPSTONE

CAPSULAR adj relating to a capsule

CAPSULARY same as > CAPSULAR

CAPSULATE adj within or formed into a capsule

CAPSULE n soluble gelatine case containing a dose of medicine ▷ adj very concise ▷ vb contain within a capsule

CAPSULED > CAPSULE

CAPSULES > CAPSULE

CAPSULING > CAPSULE

CAPSULISE same as > CAPSULIZE

CAPSULIZE vb state (information) in a highly condensed form

CAPTAIN n commander of a ship or civil aircraft ▷ vb be captain of

CAPTAINCY > CAPTAIN

CAPTAINED > CAPTAIN

CAPTAINRY n condition or skill of being a captain

CAPTAINS > CAPTAIN

CAPTAN n type of fungicide

CAPTANS > CAPTAN

CAPTCHA n test in which the user of a website has to decipher a distorted image

CAPTCHAS > CAPTCHA

CAPTION n title or explanation accompanying an illustration ▷ vb provide with a caption

CAPTIONED > CAPTION

CAPTIONS > CAPTION

CAPTIOUS adj tending to make trivial criticisms

CAPTIVATE vb attract and hold the attention of

CAPTIVE n person kept in confinement ▷ adj kept in confinement ▷ vb take prisoner

CAPTIVED > CAPTIVE

CAPTIVES > CAPTIVE

CAPTIVING > CAPTIVE

CAPTIVITY n state of being kept in confinement

CAPTOPRIL n drug used to treat high blood pressure and congestive heart failure

CAPTOR n person who captures a person or animal

CAPTORS > CAPTOR

CAPTURE vb take by force ▷ n capturing

CAPTURED > CAPTURE

CAPTURER > CAPTURE

CAPTURERS > CAPTURE

CAPTURES > CAPTURE

CAPTURING > CAPTURE

CAPUCCIO n hood

CAPUCCIOS > CAPUCCIO

CAPUCHE n large hood or cowl, esp that worn by Capuchin friars

CAPUCHED adj hooded

CAPUCHES > CAPUCHE

CAPUCHIN n S American monkey with thick hair on the top of its head

CAPUCHINS > CAPUCHIN

CAPUERA variant of > CAPOEIRA

CAPUERAS > CAPUERA

CAPUL same as > CAPLE

CAPULS > CAPUL

CAPUT n main or most prominent part of an organ or structure

CAPYBARA n very large S American rodent

CAPYBARAS > CAPYBARA

CAR n motor vehicle designed to carry a small number of people

CARABAO n water buffalo

CARABAOS > CARABAO

CARABID n type of beetle

CARABIDS > CARABID

CARABIN same as > CARBINE

CARABINE same as > CARBINE

CARABINER a variant spelling of > KARABINER

CARABINES > CARABINE

CARABINS > CARABIN

CARACAL n lynx with reddish fur, which inhabits deserts of N Africa and S Asia

CARACALS > CARACAL

CARACARA n carrion-eating bird of S North, Central, and S America

CARACARAS > CARACARA

CARACK same as > CARRACK

CARACKS > CARACK

CARACOL same as > CARACOLE

CARACOLE n half turn to the right or left ▷ vb execute a half turn to the right or left

CARACOLED > CARACOLE

CARACOLER > CARACOLE

CARACOLES > CARACOLE

CARACOLS > CARACOL

CARACT n sign or symbol

CARACTS > CARACT

CARACUL n fur from the skins of newly born lambs of the karakul sheep

CARACULS > CARACUL

CARAFE n glass bottle

CARAFES > CARAFE

CARAGANA n pea tree

CARAGANAS > CARAGANA

CARAGEEN same as > CARRAGEEN

CARAGEENS > CARAGEEN

CARAMBA interj Spanish interjection similar to 'wow!'

CARAMBOLA n yellow edible star-shaped fruit that grows on a Brazilian tree

CARAMBOLE vb make a carom or carambola (shot in billiards)

CARAMEL n chewy sweet made from sugar and milk ▷ vb turn into caramel

CARAMELS > CARAMEL

CARANGID n type of marine fish

CARANGIDS > CARANGID

CARANGOID same as > CARANGID

CARANNA n gumlike substance

CARANNAS > CARANNA

CARAP n crabwood

CARAPACE n hard upper shell of tortoises and crustaceans

CARAPACED adj having carapace

CARAPACES > CARAPACE

CARAPAX n carapace

CARAPAXES > CARAPAX

CARAPS > CARAP

CARASSOW same as > CURASSOW

CARASSOWS > CARASSOW

CARAT n unit of weight of precious stones

CARATE n tropical disease

CARATES > CARATE

CARATS > CARAT

CARAUNA same as > CARANNA

CARAUNAS > CARAUNA

CARAVAN n large enclosed vehicle for living in ▷ vb travel or have a holiday in a caravan

CARAVANCE same as > CALAVANCE

CARAVANED > CARAVAN

CARAVANER n person who holidays in a caravan

CARAVANS > CARAVAN

CARAVEL n two-or three-masted sailing ship

CARAVELLE variant of > CARAVEL

CARAVELS > CARAVEL

CARAWAY n plant whose seeds are used as a spice

CARAWAYS > CARAWAY

CARB n carbohydrate

CARBACHOL n cholinergic agent

CARBAMATE n salt or ester of carbamic acid

CARBAMIC adj as in carbamic acid hypothetical compound known only in carbamate salts

CARBAMIDE another name for > UREA

CARBAMINO adj relating to the compound produced when carbon dioxide reacts with an amino group

CARBAMOYL same as > CARBAMYL

CARBAMYL n radical from carbamic acid

CARBAMYLS > CARBAMYL

CARBANION n negatively charged organic ion in which most of the negative charge is localized on a carbon atom

CARBARN n streetcar depot

CARBARNS > CARBARN

CARBARYL n organic compound of the carbamate group

CARBARYLS > CARBARYL

CARBAZOLE n colourless insoluble solid obtained from coal tar

CARBEEN n Australian eucalyptus tree

CARBEENS > CARBEEN

CARBENE n type of divalent free radical

CARBENES > CARBENE
CARBIDE n compound of carbon with a metal
CARBIDES > CARBIDE
CARBIDOPA n drug used to treat symptoms of Parkinson's disease
CARBIES > CARBY
CARBINE n light automatic rifle
CARBINEER n (formerly) a soldier equipped with a carbine
CARBINES > CARBINE
CARBINIER same as > CARBINEER
CARBINOL same as > METHANOL
CARBINOLS > CARBINOL
CARBO n carbohydrate
CARBOLIC adj as in carbolic acid phenol, when it is used as a disinfectant
CARBOLICS > CARBOLIC
CARBOLISE same as > CARBOLIZE
CARBOLIZE another word for > PHENOLATE
CARBON n nonmetallic element
CARBONADE n stew of beef and onions cooked in beer
CARBONADO n piece of meat, fish, etc, scored and grilled ▷ vb score and grill (meat, fish, etc)
CARBONARA n pasta sauce containing cream, bacon and cheese
CARBONATE n salt or ester of carbonic acid ▷ vb form or turn into a carbonate
CARBONIC adj containing carbon
CARBONISE same as > CARBONIZE
CARBONIUM n as in carbonium ion type of positively charged organic ion
CARBONIZE vb turn into carbon as a result of heating
CARBONOUS > CARBON
CARBONS > CARBON
CARBONYL n the divalent group =CO
CARBONYLS > CARBONYL
CARBORA n former name for the koala
CARBORAS > CARBORA
CARBORNE adj travelling by car
CARBOS > CARBO
CARBOXYL adj as in carboxyl group functional group in organic acids
CARBOXYLS > CARBOXYL
CARBOY n large bottle with a protective casing
CARBOYED > CARBOY
CARBOYS > CARBOY
CARBS > CARB
CARBUNCLE n inflamed boil
CARBURATE same as > CARBURET
CARBURET vb combine with carbon
CARBURETS > CARBURET

CARBURISE same as > CARBONIZE
CARBURIZE same as > CARBONIZE
CARBY n short for carburettor
CARCAJOU a North American name for > WOLVERINE
CARCAJOUS > CARCAJOU
CARCAKE n (formerly, in Scotland) a cake traditionally made for Shrove Tuesday
CARCAKES > CARCAKE
CARCANET n jewelled collar or necklace
CARCANETS > CARCANET
CARCASE same as > CARCASS
CARCASED > CARCASE
CARCASES > CARCASE
CARCASING > CARCASE
CARCASS n dead body of an animal ▷ vb make a carcass of
CARCASSED > CARCASS
CARCASSES > CARCASS
CARCEL n French unit of light
CARCELS > CARCEL
CARCERAL adj relating to prison
CARCINOID n small serotonin-secreting tumour
CARCINOMA n malignant tumour
CARD n piece of thick stiff paper or cardboard ▷ vb comb out fibres of wool or cotton before spinning
CARDAMINE n bittercress
CARDAMOM n spice obtained from the seeds of a tropical plant
CARDAMOMS > CARDAMOM
CARDAMON same as > CARDAMOM
CARDAMONS > CARDAMON
CARDAMUM same as > CARDAMOM
CARDAMUMS > CARDAMUM
CARDAN n as in cardan joint type of universal joint
CARDBOARD n thin stiff board made from paper pulp ▷ adj without substance
CARDCASE n small case for holding business cards
CARDCASES > CARDCASE
CARDECU n old French coin (a quarter of a crown)
CARDECUE same as > CARDECU
CARDECUES > CARDECUE
CARDECUS > CARDECU
CARDED > CARD
CARDER > CARD
CARDERS > CARD
CARDI n cardigan
CARDIA n lower oesophageal sphincter
CARDIAC adj of the heart ▷ n person with a heart disorder
CARDIACAL > CARDIAC
CARDIACS > CARDIAC
CARDIAE > CARDIA
CARDIALGY n pain in or near the heart

CARDIAS > CARDIA
CARDIE short for > CARDIGAN
CARDIES > CARDIE
CARDIGAN n knitted jacket
CARDIGANS > CARDIGAN
CARDINAL n high-ranking clergyman or clergywoman of the RC Church ▷ adj fundamentally important
CARDINALS > CARDINAL
CARDING > CARD
CARDINGS > CARD
CARDIO adj exercising heart ▷ n cardiovascular exercise
CARDIOID n heart-shaped curve
CARDIOIDS > CARDIOID
CARDIOS > CARDIO
CARDIS > CARDI
CARDITIC > CARDITIS
CARDITIS n inflammation of the heart
CARDON n variety of cactus
CARDONS > CARDON
CARDOON n thistle-like S European plant
CARDOONS > CARDOON
CARDPHONE n public telephone operated by the insertion of a phonecard instead of coins
CARDPUNCH n device for putting data from a CPU onto punched cards
CARDS > CARD
CARDSHARP n professional card player who cheats
CARDUUS n thistle
CARDUUSES > CARDUUS
CARDY same as > CARDIE
CARE vb be concerned ▷ n careful attention, caution
CARED > CARE
CAREEN vb tilt over to one side
CAREENAGE > CAREEN
CAREENED > CAREEN
CAREENER > CAREEN
CAREENERS > CAREEN
CAREENING > CAREEN
CAREENS > CAREEN
CAREER n series of jobs that a person has through their life ▷ vb rush in an uncontrolled way ▷ adj having chosen to dedicate his or her life to a particular occupation
CAREERED > CAREER
CAREERER > CAREER
CAREERERS > CAREER
CAREERING > CAREER
CAREERISM > CAREERIST
CAREERIST n person who seeks advancement by any possible means
CAREERS > CAREER
CAREFREE adj without worry or responsibility
CAREFUL adj cautious in attitude or action
CAREFULLY > CAREFUL
CAREGIVER same as > CARER
CARELESS adj done or acting with insufficient attention

CARELINE n telephone service set up by a company or other organization
CARELINES > CARELINE
CAREME n period of Lent
CAREMES > CAREME
CARER n person who looks after someone who is ill or old, often a relative
CARERS > CARER
CARES > CARE
CARESS n gentle affectionate touch or embrace ▷ vb touch gently and affectionately
CARESSED > CARESS
CARESSER > CARESS
CARESSERS > CARESS
CARESSES > CARESS
CARESSING > CARESS
CARESSIVE adj caressing
CARET n proofreading symbol
CARETAKE vb work as a caretaker
CARETAKEN > CARETAKE
CARETAKER n person employed to look after a place ▷ adj performing the duties of an office temporarily
CARETAKES > CARETAKE
CARETOOK > CARETAKE
CARETS > CARET
CAREWARE n computer software licensed in exchange for a donation to charity
CAREWARES > CAREWARE
CAREWORN adj showing signs of worry
CAREX n any member of the sedge family
CARFARE n fare that a passenger is charged for a ride on a bus, etc
CARFARES > CARFARE
CARFAX n place where principal roads or streets intersect
CARFAXES > CARFAX
CARFOX same as > CARFAX
CARFOXES > CARFOX
CARFUFFLE a variant spelling of > KERFUFFLE
CARFUL n maximum number of people a car will hold
CARFULS > CARFUL
CARGEESE > CARGOOSE
CARGO n goods carried by a ship, aircraft, etc ▷ vb load
CARGOED > CARGO
CARGOES > CARGO
CARGOING > CARGO
CARGOOSE n crested grebe
CARGOS > CARGO
CARHOP n waiter or waitress at a drive-in restaurant ▷ vb work as a carhop
CARHOPPED > CARHOP
CARHOPS > CARHOP
CARIACOU n type of deer
CARIACOUS > CARIACOU
CARIAMA another word for > SERIEMA
CARIAMAS > CARIAMA

CARIBE n piranha
CARIBES > CARIBE
CARIBOO same as > CARIBOU
CARIBOOS > CARIBOO
CARIBOU n large N American reindeer
CARIBOUS > CARIBOU
CARICES > CAREX
CARIED adj (of teeth) decayed
CARIERE obsolete word for > CAREER
CARIERES > CARIERE
CARIES n tooth decay
CARILLON n set of bells played by keyboard or mechanically ▷ vb play a carillon
CARILLONS > CARILLON
CARINA n keel-like part or ridge
CARINAE > CARINA
CARINAL adj keel-like
CARINAS > CARINA
CARINATE adj having a keel or ridge
CARINATED same as > CARINATE
CARING adj feeling or showing care and compassion for other people ▷ n practice or profession of providing social or medical care
CARINGLY > CARING
CARINGS > CARING
CARIOCA n Brazilian dance similar to the samba
CARIOCAS > CARIOCA
CARIOLE n small open two-wheeled horse-drawn vehicle
CARIOLES > CARIOLE
CARIOSE same as > CARIOUS
CARIOSITY > CARIOUS
CARIOUS adj (of teeth or bone) affected with caries
CARITAS n divine love; charity
CARITASES > CARITAS
CARITATES > CARITAS
CARJACK vb attack (a car driver) to rob them or to steal the car
CARJACKED > CARJACK
CARJACKER > CARJACK
CARJACKS > CARJACK
CARJACOU variation of > CARIACOU
CARJACOUS > CARJACOU
CARK vb break down
CARKED > CARK
CARKING > CARK
CARKS > CARK
CARL another word for > CHURL
CARLE same as > CARL
CARLES > CARLE
CARLESS > CAR
CARLIN same as > CARLING
CARLINE same as > CARLING
CARLINES > CARLINE
CARLING n fore-and-aft beam in a vessel

CARLINGS > CARLING
CARLINS > CARLIN
CARLISH adj churlish
CARLOAD n amount that can be carried by a car
CARLOADS > CARLOAD
CARLOCK n type of Russian isinglass
CARLOCKS > CARLOCK
CARLOT n boor
CARLOTS > CARLOT
CARLS > CARL
CARMAKER n car manufacturing company
CARMAKERS > CARMAKER
CARMAN n man who drives a car or cart
CARMELITE n member of an order of mendicant friars
CARMEN > CARMAN
CARMINE adj vivid red ▷ n vivid red colour, sometimes with a purplish tinge
CARMINES > CARMINE
CARN n cairn
CARNAGE n extensive slaughter of people
CARNAGES > CARNAGE
CARNAHUBA same as > CARNAUBA
CARNAL adj of a physical or sensual nature ▷ vb act in a carnal manner
CARNALISE vb make carnal
CARNALISM > CARNALISE
CARNALIST > CARNALISE
CARNALITY > CARNAL
CARNALIZE same as > CARNALISE
CARNALLED > CARNAL
CARNALLY > CARNAL
CARNALS > CARNAL
CARNAROLI n variety of short-grain rice used for risotto
CARNATION n cultivated plant with fragrant white, pink, or red flowers
CARNAUBA n Brazilian fan palm tree
CARNAUBAS > CARNAUBA
CARNELIAN n reddish-yellow gemstone
CARNEOUS adj fleshy
CARNET n type of customs licence
CARNETS > CARNET
CARNEY same as > CARNY
CARNEYED > CARNEY
CARNEYING > CARNEY
CARNEYS > CARNEY
CARNIE same as > CARNY
CARNIED > CARNY
CARNIER > CARNY
CARNIES > CARNY
CARNIEST > CARNY
CARNIFEX n executioner
CARNIFIED > CARNIFY
CARNIFIES > CARNIFY
CARNIFY vb be altered so as to resemble skeletal muscle
CARNITINE n type of white betaine
CARNIVAL n festive period with processions, music, and dancing in the street
CARNIVALS > CARNIVAL

CARNIVORA n members of a group of carnivorous mammals
CARNIVORE n meat-eating animal
CARNIVORY n state of being carnivore
CARNOSAUR n meat-eating dinosaur
CARNOSE adj fleshy
CARNOSITY n fleshy protrusion
CARNOTITE n radioactive yellow mineral
CARNS > CARN
CARNY vb coax or cajole or act in a wheedling manner ▷ n person who works in a carnival ▷ adj sly
CARNYING > CARNY
CARNYX n bronze Celtic war trumpet
CARNYXES > CARNYX
CAROACH same as > CAROCHE
CAROACHES > CAROACH
CAROB n pod of a Mediterranean tree, used as a chocolate substitute
CAROBS > CAROB
CAROCH same as > CAROCHE
CAROCHE n stately ceremonial carriage used in the 16th and 17th centuries
CAROCHES > CAROCHE
CAROL n joyful Christmas hymn ▷ vb sing carols
CAROLED > CAROL
CAROLER > CAROL
CAROLERS > CAROL
CAROLI > CAROLUS
CAROLING > CAROL
CAROLINGS > CAROL
CAROLLED > CAROL
CAROLLER > CAROL
CAROLLERS > CAROL
CAROLLING > CAROL
CAROLS > CAROL
CAROLUS n any of several coins struck in the reign of a king called Charles
CAROLUSES > CAROLUS
CAROM n shot in which the cue ball is caused to contact one object ball after another ▷ vb carambole
CAROMED > CAROM
CAROMEL vb turn into caramel
CAROMELS > CAROMEL
CAROMING > CAROM
CAROMS > CAROM
CARON n inverted circumflex
CARONS > CARON
CAROTENE n orange-red hydrocarbons found in many plants
CAROTENES > CAROTENE
CAROTID n either of the two arteries supplying blood to the head ▷ adj of either of these arteries
CAROTIDAL > CAROTID
CAROTIDS > CAROTID
CAROTIN same as > CAROTENE
CAROTINS > CAROTIN

CAROUSAL n merry drinking party
CAROUSALS > CAROUSAL
CAROUSE vb have a merry drinking party
CAROUSED > CAROUSE
CAROUSEL n revolving conveyor belt for luggage or photographic slides
CAROUSELS > CAROUSEL
CAROUSER > CAROUSE
CAROUSERS > CAROUSE
CAROUSES > CAROUSE
CAROUSING > CAROUSE
CARP n large freshwater fish ▷ vb complain, find fault
CARPACCIO n Italian dish of thin slices of raw meat or fish
CARPAL n wrist bone
CARPALE same as > CARPAL
CARPALES > CARPALE
CARPALIA > CARPAL
CARPALS > CARPAL
CARPED > CARP
CARPEL n female reproductive organ of a flowering plant
CARPELS > CARPEL
CARPENTER n person who makes or repairs wooden structures ▷ vb do the work of a carpenter
CARPENTRY n skill or work of a carpenter
CARPER > CARP
CARPERS > CARP
CARPET n heavy fabric for covering floors ▷ vb cover with a carpet
CARPETBAG n travelling bag made of carpeting
CARPETED > CARPET
CARPETING n carpet material or carpets in general
CARPETS > CARPET
CARPHONE n (formerly) phone designed for use in a car
CARPHONES > CARPHONE
CARPI > CARPUS
CARPING adj tending to make petty complaints ▷ n petty complaint
CARPINGLY > CARPING
CARPINGS > CARPING
CARPLIKE adj like a carp
CARPOLOGY n branch of botany concerned with the study of fruits and seeds
CARPOOL vb share the use of a single car to travel to work or school
CARPOOLED > CARPOOL
CARPOOLER > CARPOOL
CARPOOLS > CARPOOL
CARPORT n shelter for a car, consisting of a roof supported by posts
CARPORTS > CARPORT
CARPS > CARP
CARPUS n set of eight bones of the wrist
CARR n area of bog or fen in which scrub has become established
CARRACK n galleon used as a merchantman

CARRACKS > CARRACK

CARRACT *same as* **>** CARRACK

CARRACTS > CARRACT

CARRAGEEN *n* edible red seaweed of North America and N Europe

CARRAT *same as* **>** CARAT

CARRATS > CARRAT

CARRAWAY *same as* **>** CARRACK

CARRAWAYS > CARRAWAY

CARRECT *same as* **>** CARRACK

CARRECTS > CARRECT

CARREFOUR *n* public square, esp one at the intersection of several roads

CARREL *n* small individual study room or private desk

CARRELL *same as* **>** CARREL

CARRELLS > CARRELL

CARRELS > CARREL

CARRIAGE *n* one of the sections of a train for passengers

CARRIAGES > CARRIAGE

CARRICK *n* as in *carrick bend* type of knot

CARRIED > CARRY

CARRIER *n* person or thing that carries something

CARRIERS > CARRIER

CARRIES > CARRY

CARRIOLE *same as* **>** CARIOLE

CARRIOLES > CARRIOLE

CARRION *n* dead and rotting flesh

CARRIONS > CARRION

CARRITCH *n* catechism

CARROCH *variant of* **>** CAROCHE

CARROCHES > CAROM

CARROM *same as* **>** CAROM

CARROMED > CARROM

CARROMING > CARROM

CARROMS > CARROM

CARRON *n* as in *carron oil* ointment of limewater and linseed oil

CARRONADE *n* obsolete naval gun of short barrel and large bore

CARROT *n* long tapering orange root vegetable

CARROTIER > CARROTY

CARROTIN *n* carotene

CARROTINS > CARROTIN

CARROTS > CARROT

CARROTTOP *n* facetious term for a person with red hair

CARROTY *adj* (of hair) reddish-orange

CARROUSEL *a variant spelling of* **>** CAROUSEL

CARRS > CARR

CARRY *vb* take from one place to another

CARRYALL *n* light four-wheeled horse-drawn carriage usually designed to carry four passengers

CARRYALLS > CARRYALL

CARRYBACK *n* amount carried back in accounting

CARRYCOT *n* light portable bed for a baby, with handles and a hood

CARRYCOTS > CARRYCOT

CARRYING > CARRY

CARRYON *n* fuss or commotion

CARRYONS > CARRYON

CARRYOUT *n* hot cooked food bought in a shop for consumption elsewhere

CARRYOUTS > CARRYOUT

CARRYOVER *n* sum or balance carried forward in accounting

CARRYTALE *n* gossip

CARS > CAR

CARSE *n* riverside area of flat fertile alluvium

CARSES > CARSE

CARSEY *slang word for* **>** TOILET

CARSEYS > CARSEY

CARSHARE *same as* **>** CARPOOL

CARSHARED > CARSHARE

CARSHARES > CARSHARE

CARSICK *adj* nauseated from riding in a car

CARSPIEL *n* curling match which has a car as a prize

CARSPIELS > CARSPIEL

CART *n* open two-wheeled horse-drawn vehicle ▷ *vb* carry, usu with some effort

CARTA *n* charter

CARTABLE > CART

CARTAGE *n* process or cost of carting

CARTAGES > CARTAGE

CARTAS > CARTA

CARTE *n* fencing position

CARTED > CART

CARTEL *n* association of competing firms formed to fix prices

CARTELISE *same as* **>** CARTELIZE

CARTELISM > CARTEL

CARTELIST > CARTEL

CARTELIZE *vb* form or be formed into a cartel

CARTELS > CARTEL

CARTER > CART

CARTERS > CART

CARTES > CARTE

CARTFUL *n* amount a cart can hold

CARTFULS > CARTFUL

CARTHORSE *n* large heavily built horse

CARTILAGE *n* strong flexible tissue forming part of the skeleton

CARTING > CART

CARTLOAD *n* amount a cart can hold

CARTLOADS > CARTLOAD

CARTOGRAM *n* map showing statistical information in diagrammatic form

CARTOLOGY *n* theory of mapmaking

CARTON *n* container made of cardboard or waxed paper ▷ *vb* enclose (goods) in a carton

CARTONAGE *n* material from which mummy masks and coffins were made

CARTONED > CARTON

CARTONING > CARTON

CARTONS > CARTON

CARTOON *n* humorous or satirical drawing ▷ *vb* depict in a cartoon

CARTOONED > CARTOON

CARTOONS > CARTOON

CARTOONY *adj* of or like a cartoon

CARTOP *adj* designed to be transported on top of a vehicle

CARTOPPER *n* anything designed to be transported on top of a vehicle

CARTOUCH *same as* **>** CARTOUCHE

CARTOUCHE *n* ornamental tablet or panel in the form of a scroll

CARTRIDGE *n* casing containing an explosive charge and bullet for a gun

CARTROAD *n* road for carts to drive on

CARTROADS > CARTROAD

CARTS > CART

CARTULARY *n* collection of charters or records, esp relating to the title to an estate or monastery

CARTWAY *n* way by which carts travel

CARTWAYS > CARTWAY

CARTWHEEL *n* sideways somersault supported by the hands with legs outstretched ▷ *vb* perform a cartwheel movement

CARUCAGE *n* tax due on a carucate

CARUCAGES > CARUCAGE

CARUCATE *n* area of land an oxen team could plough in a year

CARUCATES > CARUCATE

CARUNCLE *n* fleshy outgrowth on the heads of certain birds, such as a cock's comb

CARUNCLES > CARUNCLE

CARVACROL *n* aromatic phenol found in oregano

CARVE *vb* cut to form an object

CARVED > CARVE

CARVEL *same as* **>** CARAVEL

CARVELS > CARVEL

CARVEN *an archaic or literary past participle of* **>** CARVE

CARVER *n* carving knife

CARVERIES > CARVERY

CARVERS > CARVER

CARVERY *n* restaurant where customers pay a set price for unrestricted helpings

CARVES > CARVE

CARVIES > CARVY

CARVING *n* figure or design produced by carving stone or wood

CARVINGS > CARVING

CARVY *n* caraway seed

CARWASH *n* drive-through structure containing automated equipment for washing cars

CARWASHES > CARWASH

CARYATIC > CARYATID

CARYATID *n* supporting column in the shape of a female figure

CARYATIDS > CARYATID

CARYOPSES > CARYOPSIS

CARYOPSIS *n* dry seedlike fruit having the pericarp fused to the seed coat of the single seed: produced by the grasses

CARYOTIN *variant of* **>** KARYOTIN

CARYOTINS > CARYOTIN

CASA *n* house

CASABA *n* kind of winter muskmelon

CASABAS > CASABA

CASAS > CASA

CASAVA *same as* **>** CASSAVA

CASAVAS > CASAVA

CASBAH *n* citadel of a N African city

CASBAHS > CASBAH

CASCABEL *n* knoblike protrusion on a type of cannon

CASCABELS > CASCABEL

CASCABLE *same as* **>** CASCABEL

CASCABLES > CASCABLE

CASCADE *n* waterfall ▷ *vb* flow or fall in a cascade

CASCADED > CASCADE

CASCADES > CASCADE

CASCADING > CASCADE

CASCADURA *n* Trinidadian fish

CASCARA *n* bark of a N American shrub, used as a laxative

CASCARAS > CASCARA

CASCHROM *n* wooden hand-plough

CASCHROMS > CASCHROM

CASCO *n* Argentinian homestead

CASCOS > CASCO

CASE *n* instance, example ▷ *vb* inspect (a building) with the intention of burgling it

CASEASE *n* proteolytic enzyme

CASEASES > CASEASE

CASEATE *vb* undergo caseation

CASEATED > CASEATE

CASEATES > CASEATE

CASEATING > CASEATE

CASEATION *n* formation of cheese from casein during the coagulation of milk

CASEBOOK *n* book in which records of legal or medical cases are kept

CASEBOOKS > CASEBOOK

CASEBOUND *another word for* **>** HARDBACK

CASED > CASE

CASEFIED > CASEFY

CASEFIES > CASEFY

CASEFY *vb* make or become similar to cheese

C

CASEFYING > CASEFY

CASEIC adj relating to cheese

CASEIN n phosphoprotein forming the basis of cheese

CASEINATE n protein found in milk

CASEINS > CASEIN

CASELAW n law established by previous cases

CASELAWS > CASELAW

CASELOAD n number of cases that a worker deals with at any one time

CASELOADS > CASELOAD

CASEMAKER n in bookbinding, machine that makes stiff covers for hardbacks

CASEMAN n in printing, a person who sets and corrects type

CASEMATE n armoured compartment in a ship or fortification in which guns are mounted

CASEMATED > CASEMATE

CASEMATES > CASEMATE

CASEMEN > CASEMAN

CASEMENT n window that is hinged on one side

CASEMENTS > CASEMENT

CASEMIX n mix or type of patients treated by a hospital or medical unit

CASEMIXES > CASEMIX

CASEOSE n peptide produced by the peptic digestion of casein

CASEOSES > CASEOSE

CASEOUS adj of or like cheese

CASERN n (formerly) a billet or accommodation for soldiers in a town

CASERNE same as > CASERN

CASERNES > CASERNE

CASERNS > CASERN

CASES > CASE

CASETTE variant of > CASSETTE

CASETTES > CASETTE

CASEVAC vb evacuate (a casualty) from a combat zone, usu by air

CASEVACED > CASEVAC

CASEVACS > CASEVAC

CASEWORK n social work based on close study

CASEWORKS > CASEWORK

CASEWORM n caddis worm

CASEWORMS > CASEWORM

CASH n banknotes and coins ▷ adj of, for, or paid in cash ▷ vb obtain cash for

CASHABLE > CASH

CASHAW n winter squash

CASHAWS > CASHAW

CASHBACK n discount offered in return for immediate payment

CASHBACKS > CASHBACK

CASHBOOK n journal in which cash receipts and payments are recorded

CASHBOOKS > CASHBOOK

CASHBOX n box for holding cash

CASHBOXES > CASHBOX

CASHED > CASH

CASHES > CASH

CASHEW n edible kidney-shaped nut

CASHEWS > CASHEW

CASHIER n person responsible for handling cash in a bank, shop, etc ▷ vb dismiss with dishonour from the armed forces

CASHIERED > CASHIER

CASHIERER > CASHIER

CASHIERS > CASHIER

CASHING > CASH

CASHLESS adj using credit cards or electronic money transfers instead of coins or banknotes

CASHMERE n fine soft wool obtained from goats

CASHMERES > CASHMERE

CASHOO n catechu

CASHOOS > CASHOO

CASHPOINT n cash dispenser

CASHSPIEL n curling match with cash prizes

CASIMERE same as > CASSIMERE

CASIMERES > CASIMERE

CASIMIRE variant of > CASSIMERE

CASIMIRES > CASIMIRE

CASING n protective case, covering

CASINGS > CASING

CASINI > CASINO

CASINO n public building or room where gambling games are played

CASINOS > CASINO

CASITA n small house

CASITAS > CASITA

CASK n large barrel ▷ vb put into a cask

CASKED > CASK

CASKET n small box for valuables ▷ vb put into a casket

CASKETED > CASKET

CASKETING > CASKET

CASKETS > CASKET

CASKIER > CASKY

CASKIEST > CASKY

CASKING > CASK

CASKS > CASK

CASKSTAND n frame on which a cask rests

CASKY adj (of wine) having a musty smell due to resting too long in the cask

CASPASE n type of enzyme

CASPASES > CASPASE

CASQUE n helmet or a helmet-like process or structure

CASQUED > CASQUE

CASQUES > CASQUE

CASSABA same as > CASABA

CASSABAS > CASSABA

CASSAREEP n juice of the bitter cassava root, boiled down to a syrup and used as a flavouring, esp in West Indian cookery

CASSATA n ice cream usually containing nuts and candied fruit

CASSATAS > CASSATA

CASSATION n (esp in France) annulment, as of a judicial decision by a higher court

CASSAVA n starch obtained from the roots of a tropical American plant, used to make tapioca

CASSAVAS > CASSAVA

CASSENA same as > CASSINA

CASSENAS > CASSENA

CASSENE same as > CASSINA

CASSENES > CASSENE

CASSEROLE n covered dish in which food is cooked slowly, usu in an oven ▷ vb cook in a casserole

CASSETTE n (formerly) plastic container for magnetic tape

CASSETTES > CASSETTE

CASSIA n tropical plant whose pods yield a mild laxative

CASSIAS > CASSIA

CASSIE n type of thorny shrub

CASSIES > CASSIE

CASSIMERE n woollen suiting cloth of plain or twill weave

CASSINA n American tree

CASSINAS > CASSINA

CASSINE same as > CASSINA

CASSINES > CASSINE

CASSINGLE n (formerly) cassette single

CASSINO n card game for two to four players

CASSINOS > CASSINO

CASSIOPE n type of evergreen shrub

CASSIOPES > CASSIOPE

CASSIS n blackcurrant cordial

CASSISES > CASSIS

CASSOCK n long tunic, usu black, worn by priests

CASSOCKED > CASSOCK

CASSOCKS > CASSOCK

CASSONADE n raw sugar

CASSONE n highly decorated Italian dowry chest

CASSONES > CASSONE

CASSOULET n stew originating from France, made from haricot beans and goose, duck, pork, etc

CASSOWARY n large flightless bird of Australia and New Guinea

CASSPIR n armoured military vehicle

CASSPIRS > CASSPIR

CAST n actors in a play or film collectively ▷ vb select (an actor) to play a part in a play or film

CASTABLE adj able to be cast

CASTANET > CASTANETS

CASTANETS pl n musical instrument, used by Spanish dancers, consisting of curved pieces of hollow wood clicked together in the hand

CASTAWAY n shipwrecked person ▷ adj shipwrecked or put adrift ▷ vb cause (a ship, person, etc) to be shipwrecked or abandoned

CASTAWAYS > CASTAWAY

CASTE n any of the hereditary classes into which Hindu society is divided

CASTED adj having a caste

CASTEISM n belief in, and adherence to, the caste system

CASTEISMS > CASTEISM

CASTELESS adj having no caste

CASTELLA > CASTELLUM

CASTELLAN n keeper or governor of a castle

CASTELLUM n fort

CASTER n person or thing that casts

CASTERED adj having casters

CASTERS > CASTER

CASTES > CASTE

CASTIGATE vb reprimand severely

CASTING > CAST

CASTINGS > CAST

CASTLE n large fortified building ▷ vb (in chess) make a move involving king and rook

CASTLED adj like a castle in construction

CASTLES > CASTLE

CASTLING n (in chess) act of castling

CASTLINGS > CASTLING

CASTOCK n kale stalk

CASTOCKS > CASTOCK

CASTOFF n person or thing that has been discarded or abandoned

CASTOFFS > CASTOFF

CASTOR same as > CASTER

CASTOREUM n oil secreted from the beaver, used as bait by trappers

CASTORIES > CASTORY

CASTORS > CASTOR

CASTORY n dye derived from beaver pelts

CASTRAL adj relating to camps

CASTRATE vb remove the testicles of

CASTRATED > CASTRATE

CASTRATER > CASTRATE

CASTRATES > CASTRATE

CASTRATI > CASTRATO

CASTRATO n male singer who retains a soprano or alto voice

CASTRATOR > CASTRATE

CASTRATOS > CASTRATO

CASTS > CAST

CASUAL adj careless, nonchalant ▷ n occasional worker

CASUALISE vb make (a regular employee) into a casual worker

CASUALISM > CASUALISE
CASUALIZE *same as* **>** CASUALISE
CASUALLY > CASUAL
CASUALS > CASUAL
CASUALTY *n* person killed or injured in an accident or war
CASUARINA *n* Australian tree with jointed green branches
CASUIST *n* person who attempts to resolve moral dilemmas
CASUISTIC > CASUIST
CASUISTRY *n* reasoning that is misleading or oversubtle
CASUISTS > CASUIST
CASUS *n* event
CAT *n* small domesticated furry mammal ▷ *vb* flog with a cat-'o-nine-tails
CATABASES > CATABASIS
CATABASIS *n* descent or downward movement
CATABATIC > CATABASIS
CATABOLIC *adj* of a metabolic process in which complex molecules are broken down into simple ones with the release of energy
CATACLASM *n* breaking down
CATACLYSM *n* violent upheaval
CATACOMB *n* underground burial place
CATACOMBS > CATACOMB
CATAFALCO *n* temporary raised platform on which a body lies in state before or during a funeral
CATAGEN *n* phase of hair growth
CATAGENS > CATAGEN
CATALASE *n* enzyme that catalyses the decomposition of hydrogen peroxide
CATALASES > CATALASE
CATALATIC *adj* relating to catalase
CATALEPSY *n* trancelike state in which the body is rigid
CATALEXES > CATALEXIS
CATALEXIS *n* the state of lacking a syllable in the last foot of a line of poetry
CATALO *same as* **>** CATTALO
CATALOES > CATALO
CATALOG *same as* **>** CATALOGUE
CATALOGED > CATALOGUE
CATALOGER > CATALOGUE
CATALOGIC > CATALOG
CATALOGNE *n* type of weaving
CATALOGS > CATALOG
CATALOGUE *n* book containing details of items for sale ▷ *vb* enter (an item) in a catalogue
CATALOS > CATALO
CATALPA *n* tree of N America and Asia with bell-shaped whitish flowers
CATALPAS > CATALPA

CATALYSE *vb* speed up (a chemical reaction) by a catalyst
CATALYSED > CATALYSE
CATALYSER > CATALYSE
CATALYSES > CATALYSIS
CATALYSIS *n* acceleration of a chemical reaction by the action of a catalyst
CATALYST *n* substance that speeds up a chemical reaction without itself changing
CATALYSTS > CATALYST
CATALYTIC *adj* of or relating to catalysis
CATALYZE *same as* **>** CATALYSE
CATALYZED > CATALYZE
CATALYZER > CATALYZE
CATALYZES > CATALYZE
CATAMARAN *n* boat with twin parallel hulls
CATAMENIA *another word for* **>** MENSES
CATAMITE *n* boy kept as a homosexual partner
CATAMITES > CATAMITE
CATAMOUNT *n* any of various medium-sized felines, such as the puma or lynx
CATAPAN *n* governor in the Byzantine Empire
CATAPANS > CATAPAN
CATAPHOR *n* word that refers to or stands for another word used later
CATAPHORA *n* use of a word such as a pronoun that has the same reference as a word used subsequently in the same discourse
CATAPHORS > CATAPHOR
CATAPHYLL *n* simplified form of plant leaf, such as a scale leaf or cotyledon
CATAPLASM *another name for* **>** POULTICE
CATAPLEXY *n* sudden temporary paralysis, brought on by severe shock
CATAPULT *n* Y-shaped device with a loop of elastic, used by children for firing stones ▷ *vb* shoot forwards or upwards violently
CATAPULTS > CATAPULT
CATARACT *n* eye disease in which the lens becomes opaque
CATARACTS > CATARACT
CATARHINE *n* ape with nostrils close together
CATARRH *n* excessive mucus in the nose and throat, during or following a cold
CATARRHAL > CATARRH
CATARRHS > CATARRH
CATASTA *n* platform on which slaves were presented for sale
CATASTAS > CATASTA
CATATONIA *n* form of schizophrenia characterized by stupor, with outbreaks of excitement
CATATONIC > CATATONIA
CATATONY *another word for* **>** CATATONIA

CATAWBA *n* type of red North American grape
CATAWBAS > CATAWBA
CATBIRD *n* North American songbird
CATBIRDS > CATBIRD
CATBOAT *n* sailing vessel
CATBOATS > CATBOAT
CATBRIAR *same as* **>** CATBRIER
CATBRIARS *same as* **>** CATBRIERS
CATBRIER *n* greenbrier
CATBRIERS > CATBRIER
CATCALL *n* derisive whistle or cry ▷ *vb* utter such a call (at)
CATCALLED > CATCALL
CATCALLER > CATCALL
CATCALLS > CATCALL
CATCH *vb* seize, capture ▷ *n* device for fastening a door, window, etc
CATCHABLE > CATCH
CATCHALL *n* something designed to cover a variety of situations
CATCHALLS > CATCHALL
CATCHCRY *n* well-known much-used phrase, perhaps associated with a particular group
CATCHED *rarely used past tense of* **>** CATCH
CATCHEN *archaic form of* **>** CATCH
CATCHER *n* person or thing that catches, esp in a game or sport
CATCHERS > CATCHER
CATCHES > CATCH
CATCHFLY *n* type of plant with sticky calyxes and stems on which insects are trapped
CATCHIER > CATCHY
CATCHIEST > CATCHY
CATCHILY *adv* in a pleasant or catchy way
CATCHING > CATCH
CATCHINGS > CATCH
CATCHLINE *n* political or advertising slogan
CATCHMENT *n* structure in which water is collected
CATCHPOLE *n* (in medieval England) a sheriff's officer who arrested debtors
CATCHPOLL *same as* **>** CATCHPOLE
CATCHT *same as* **>** CATCHED
CATCHUP *a variant spelling (esp US) of* **>** KETCHUP
CATCHUPS > CATCHUP
CATCHWEED *n* goosegrass
CATCHWORD *n* well-known and frequently used phrase
CATCHY *adj* (of a tune) pleasant and easily remembered
CATCLAW *n* type of shrub; black bead
CATCLAWS > CATCLAW
CATCON *n* catalytic converter
CATCONS > CATCON
CATE *n* delicacy

CATECHIN *n* soluble yellow solid substance found in mahogany wood
CATECHINS > CATECHIN
CATECHISE *same as* **>** CATECHIZE
CATECHISM *n* instruction on the doctrine of a Christian Church in a series of questions and answers
CATECHIST > CATECHIZE
CATECHIZE *vb* instruct by using a catechism
CATECHOL *n* colourless crystalline phenol found in resins and lignins
CATECHOLS > CATECHOL
CATECHU *n* astringent resinous substance
CATECHUS > CATECHU
CATEGORIC *adj* unqualified
CATEGORY *n* class, group
CATELOG *obsolete word for* **>** CATALOGUE
CATELOGS > CATELOG
CATENA *n* connected series, esp of patristic comments on the Bible
CATENAE > CATENA
CATENANE *n* type of chemical compound
CATENANES > CATENANE
CATENARY *n* curve assumed by a heavy uniform flexible cord hanging freely from two points ▷ *adj* of, resembling, relating to, or constructed using a catenary or suspended chain
CATENAS > CATENA
CATENATE *vb* arrange or be arranged in a series of chains or rings
CATENATED > CATENATE
CATENATES > CATENATE
CATENOID *n* geometrical surface generated by rotating a catenary about its axis
CATENOIDS > CATENOID
CATER *vb* provide what is needed or wanted, esp food or services
CATERAN *n* (formerly) a member of a band of brigands in the Scottish highlands
CATERANS > CATERAN
CATERED > CATER
CATERER *n* person whose job is to provide food for social events
CATERERS > CATERER
CATERESS *n* female caterer
CATERING *n* supplying of food for a social event
CATERINGS > CATERING
CATERS > CATER
CATERWAUL *n* wail, yowl ▷ *vb* make a yowling noise like a cat
CATES *pl n* choice dainty food
CATFACE *n* deformity of the surface of a tree trunk, caused by fire or disease
CATFACES > CATFACE

CATFACING n disorder that affects tomatoes, causing scarring of the fruit

CATFALL n line used as a tackle for hoisting an anchor to the cathead

CATFALLS > CATFALL

CATFIGHT n fight, especially between two women

CATFIGHTS > CATFIGHT

CATFISH vb create a false identity online to lure someone into a relationship

CATFISHED > CATFISH

CATFISHES > CATFISH

CATFLAP n small flap in a door to let a cat go through

CATFLAPS > CATFLAP

CATFOOD n food for cats

CATFOODS > CATFOOD

CATGUT n strong cord used to string musical instruments and sports rackets

CATGUTS > CATGUT

CATHARISE vb purify

CATHARIZE same as > CATHARISE

CATHARSES > CATHARSIS

CATHARSIS n relief of strong suppressed emotions

CATHARTIC adj causing catharsis ⊳ n drug that causes catharsis

CATHEAD n fitting at the bow of a vessel for securing the anchor when raised

CATHEADS > CATHEAD

CATHECT vb invest mental or emotional energy in

CATHECTED > CATHECT

CATHECTIC adj of or relating to cathexis

CATHECTS > CATHECT

CATHEDRA n bishop's throne

CATHEDRAE > CATHEDRA

CATHEDRAL n principal church of a diocese

CATHEDRAS > CATHEDRA

CATHEPSIN n proteolytic enzyme responsible for the autolysis of cells after death

CATHEPTIC > CATHEPSIN

CATHETER n tube inserted into a body cavity to drain fluid

CATHETERS > CATHETER

CATHETUS n straight line or radius perpendicular to another line or radius

CATHEXES > CATHEXIS

CATHEXIS n concentration of psychic energy on a single goal

CATHINONE n synthetic alkaloid compound found in certain stimulants

CATHISMA n short hymn used as a response

CATHISMAS > CATHISMA

CATHODAL > CATHODE

CATHODE n negative electrode, by which electrons leave a circuit

CATHODES > CATHODE

CATHODIC > CATHODE

CATHOLE n hole in a ship through which ropes are passed

CATHOLES > CATHOLE

CATHOLIC adj (of tastes or interests) covering a wide range ⊳ n member of the Roman Catholic Church

CATHOLICS > CATHOLIC

CATHOLYTE same as > CATOLYTE

CATHOOD n state of being a cat

CATHOODS > CATHOOD

CATHOUSE a slang word for > BROTHEL

CATHOUSES > CATHOUSE

CATION n positively charged ion

CATIONIC > CATION

CATIONS > CATION

CATJANG n tropical shrub

CATJANGS > CATJANG

CATKIN n drooping flower spike of certain trees

CATKINATE adj like catkin

CATKINS > CATKIN

CATLIKE > CAT

CATLIN same as > CATLING

CATLING n long double-edged surgical knife for amputations

CATLINGS > CATLING

CATLINITE n type of red-brown clay

CATLINS > CATLIN

CATMINT n Eurasian plant with scented leaves that attract cats

CATMINTS > CATMINT

CATNAP vb doze ⊳ n short sleep or doze

CATNAPER > CATNAP

CATNAPERS > CATNAP

CATNAPPED > CATNAP

CATNAPPER > CATNAP

CATNAPS > CATNAP

CATNEP same as > CATMINT

CATNEPS > CATNEP

CATNIP same as > CATMINT

CATNIPS > CATNIP

CATOLYTE n part of the electrolyte that surrounds the cathode in an electrolytic cell

CATOLYTES > CATOLYTE

CATOPTRIC adj relating to reflection

CATRIGGED adj rigged like a catboat

CATS > CAT

CATSKIN n skin or fur of a cat

CATSKINS > CATSKIN

CATSPAW n person used by another as a tool

CATSPAWS > CATSPAW

CATSUIT n one-piece usually close-fitting trouser suit

CATSUITS > CATSUIT

CATSUP a variant (esp US) of > KETCHUP

CATSUPS > CATSUP

CATTABU n cross between common cattle and zebu

CATTABUS > CATTABU

CATTAIL n reed mace

CATTAILS > CATTAIL

CATTALO n hardy breed of cattle

CATTALOES > CATTALO

CATTALOS > CATTALO

CATTED > CAT

CATTERIES > CATTERY

CATTERY n place where cats are bred or looked after

CATTIE same as > CATTY

CATTIER > CATTY

CATTIES > CATTY

CATTIEST > CATTY

CATTILY > CATTY

CATTINESS > CATTY

CATTING > CAT

CATTISH > CAT

CATTISHLY > CAT

CATTLE pl n domesticated cows and bulls

CATTLEMAN n person who breeds, rears, or tends cattle

CATTLEMEN > CATTLEMAN

CATTLEYA n tropical American orchid cultivated for its purplish-pink or white showy flowers

CATTLEYAS > CATTLEYA

CATTY adj spiteful ⊳ n unit of weight, used esp in China

CATWALK n narrow pathway or platform

CATWALKS > CATWALK

CATWORKS n machinery on a drilling platform

CATWORM n type of carnivorous worm

CATWORMS > CATWORM

CAUCHEMAR n nightmare

CAUCUS n local committee or faction of a political party ⊳ vb hold a caucus

CAUCUSED > CAUCUS

CAUCUSES > CAUCUS

CAUCUSING > CAUCUS

CAUCUSSED > CAUCUS

CAUCUSSES > CAUCUS

CAUDA n tail of an animal

CAUDAD adv towards the tail or posterior part

CAUDAE > CAUDA

CAUDAL adj at or near an animal's tail

CAUDALLY > CAUDAL

CAUDATE adj having a tail or a tail-like appendage ⊳ n lizard-like amphibian

CAUDATED same as > CAUDATE

CAUDATES > CAUDATE

CAUDATION > CAUDATE

CAUDEX n thickened persistent stem base of some herbaceous perennial plants

CAUDEXES > CAUDEX

CAUDICES > CAUDEX

CAUDICLE n stalk to which an orchid's pollen masses are attached

CAUDICLES > CAUDICLE

CAUDILLO n (in Spanish-speaking countries) a military or political leader

CAUDILLOS > CAUDILLO

CAUDLE n hot spiced wine drink made with gruel, formerly used medicinally ⊳ vb make such a drink

CAUDLED > CAUDLE

CAUDLES > CAUDLE

CAUDLING > CAUDLE

CAUDRON Spenserian spelling of > CAULDRON

CAUDRONS > CAUDRON

CAUF n cage for holding live fish in the water

CAUGHT > CATCH

CAUK n type of barite

CAUKER n one who caulks

CAUKERS > CAUKER

CAUKS > CAUK

CAUL n membrane sometimes covering a child's head at birth

CAULD a Scot word for > COLD

CAULDER > CAULD

CAULDEST > CAULD

CAULDRIFE adj susceptible to cold

CAULDRON n large pot used for boiling

CAULDRONS > CAULDRON

CAULDS > CAULD

CAULES > CAULIS

CAULICLE n small stalk or stem

CAULICLES > CAULICLE

CAULICULI n plural form of singular cauliculus: another word for caulicle

CAULIFORM adj resembling a caulis

CAULINARY another word for > CAULINE

CAULINE adj relating to or growing from a plant stem

CAULIS n main stem of a plant

CAULK vb fill in (cracks) with paste etc

CAULKED > CAULK

CAULKER > CAULK

CAULKERS > CAULK

CAULKING > CAULK

CAULKINGS > CAULK

CAULKS > CAULK

CAULOME n plant's stem structure, considered as a whole

CAULOMES > CAULOME

CAULS > CAUL

CAUM same as > CAM

CAUMED > CAUM

CAUMING > CAUM

CAUMS > CAUM

CAUMSTANE same as > CAMSTONE

CAUMSTONE same as > CAMSTONE

CAUP n type of quaich

CAUPS > CAUP

CAURI n former coin of Guinea

CAURIS > CAURI

CAUSA n reason or cause

CAUSABLE > CAUSE

CAUSAE > CAUSE

CAUSAL adj of or being a cause ⊳ n something that suggests a cause

CAUSALGIA n burning sensation along the course of a peripheral nerve together with local changes in the appearance of the skin

CAUSALGIC > CAUSALGIA

CAUSALITY n relationship of cause and effect

CAUSALLY > CAUSAL

CAUSALS > CAUSAL

CAUSATION n relationship of cause and effect

CAUSATIVE adj producing an effect ▷ n causative form or class of verbs

CAUSE n something that produces a particular effect ▷ vb be the cause of

CAUSED > CAUSE

CAUSELESS > CAUSE

CAUSEN old infinitive of > CAUSE

CAUSER > CAUSE

CAUSERIE n informal talk or conversational piece of writing

CAUSERIES > CAUSERIE

CAUSERS > CAUSER

CAUSES > CAUSE

CAUSEWAY n raised path or road across water or marshland

CAUSEWAYS > CAUSEWAY

CAUSEY n cobbled street ▷ vb cobble

CAUSEYED > CAUSEY

CAUSEYS > CAUSEY

CAUSING > CAUSE

CAUSTIC adj capable of burning by chemical action ▷ n caustic substance

CAUSTICAL > CAUSTIC

CAUSTICS > CAUSTIC

CAUTEL n craftiness

CAUTELOUS > CAUTEL

CAUTELS > CAUTEL

CAUTER n cauterizing instrument

CAUTERANT same as > CAUTERY

CAUTERIES > CAUTERY

CAUTERISE same as > CAUTERIZE

CAUTERISM > CAUTERIZE

CAUTERIZE vb burn (a wound) with heat or a caustic agent to prevent infection

CAUTERS > CAUTER

CAUTERY n coagulation of blood or destruction of body tissue by cauterizing

CAUTION n care, esp in the face of danger ▷ vb warn, advise

CAUTIONED > CAUTION

CAUTIONER > CAUTION

CAUTIONRY n in Scots law, standing surety

CAUTIONS > CAUTION

CAUTIOUS adj showing caution

CAUVES > CAUF

CAVA n Spanish sparkling wine

CAVALCADE n procession of people on horseback or in cars

CAVALERO n cavalier

CAVALEROS > CAVALERO

CAVALETTI n bars supported on low stands used in dressage and horse jumping

CAVALIER adj showing haughty disregard ▷ n gallant gentleman

CAVALIERS > CAVALIER

CAVALLA n type of tropical fish

CAVALLAS > CAVALLA

CAVALLIES > CAVALLY

CAVALLY same as > CAVALLA

CAVALRIES > CAVALRY

CAVALRY n part of the army

CAVAS > CAVA

CAVASS n Turkish armed police officer

CAVASSES > CAVASS

CAVATINA n solo song resembling a simple aria

CAVATINAS > CAVATINA

CAVATINE > CAVATINA

CAVE n hollow in the side of a hill or cliff ▷ vb hollow out

CAVEAT n warning ▷ vb introduce a caveat

CAVEATED > CAVEAT

CAVEATING > CAVEAT

CAVEATOR n person who enters a caveat

CAVEATORS > CAVEATOR

CAVEATS > CAVEAT

CAVED > CAVE

CAVEFISH n small N American freshwater fish

CAVEL n drawing of lots among miners for an easy and profitable place at the coalface

CAVELIKE adj resembling a cave

CAVELS > CAVEL

CAVEMAN n prehistoric cave dweller

CAVEMEN > CAVEMAN

CAVENDISH n tobacco that has been sweetened and pressed into moulds to form bars

CAVEOLA n pit in a cell membrane

CAVEOLAE > CAVEOLA

CAVEOLAR > CAVEOLA

CAVER > CAVE

CAVERN n large cave ▷ vb shut in or as if in a cavern

CAVERNED > CAVERN

CAVERNING > CAVERN

CAVERNOUS adj like a cavern in vastness, depth, or hollowness

CAVERNS > CAVERN

CAVERS > CAVER

CAVES > CAVE

CAVESSON n kind of hard noseband, used (esp formerly) in breaking a horse in

CAVESSONS > CAVESSON

CAVETTI > CAVETTO

CAVETTO n concave moulding, shaped to a quarter circle in cross section

CAVETTOS > CAVETTO

CAVIAR n salted sturgeon roe, regarded as a delicacy

CAVIARE same as > CAVIAR

CAVIARES > CAVIARE

CAVIARIE same as > CAVIAR

CAVIARIES > CAVIARIE

CAVIARS > CAVIAR

CAVICORN adj (of sheep, goats, etc) having hollow horns as distinct from the solid antlers of deer ▷ n sheep, goat, etc with hollow horns

CAVICORNS > CAVICORN

CAVIE n hen coop

CAVIER same as > CAVIAR

CAVIERS > CAVIER

CAVIES > CAVY

CAVIL vb make petty objections ▷ n petty objection

CAVILED > CAVIL

CAVILER > CAVIL

CAVILERS > CAVIL

CAVILING > CAVIL

CAVILLED > CAVIL

CAVILLER > CAVIL

CAVILLERS > CAVIL

CAVILLING > CAVIL

CAVILS > CAVIL

CAVING n sport of exploring caves

CAVINGS > CAVING

CAVITARY adj containing cavities

CAVITATE vb form cavities or bubbles

CAVITATED > CAVITATE

CAVITATES > CAVITATE

CAVITIED > CAVITY

CAVITIES > CAVITY

CAVITY n hollow space

CAVORT vb skip about

CAVORTED > CAVORT

CAVORTER > CAVORT

CAVORTERS > CAVORT

CAVORTING > CAVORT

CAVORTS > CAVORT

CAVY n type of small rodent

CAW n cry of a crow, rook, or raven ▷ vb make this cry

CAWED > CAW

CAWING > CAW

CAWINGS > CAW

CAWK same as > CAUK

CAWKER n metal projection on a horse's shoe to prevent slipping

CAWKERS > CAWKER

CAWKS > CAWK

CAWS > CAW

CAXON n type of wig

CAXONS > CAXON

CAY n low island or bank composed of sand and coral fragments

CAYENNE n very hot condiment

CAYENNED adj seasoned with cayenne

CAYENNES > CAYENNE

CAYMAN n S American reptile similar to an alligator

CAYMANS > CAYMAN

CAYS > CAY

CAYUSE n small pony used by Native Americans

CAYUSES > CAYUSE

CAZ short for > CASUAL

CAZH adj casual

CAZIQUE same as > CACIQUE

CAZIQUES > CAZIQUE

CEANOTHUS n N American shrub grown for its ornamental, often blue, flower clusters

CEAS same as > CAESE

CEASE vb bring or come to an end

CEASED > CEASE

CEASEFIRE n temporary truce

CEASELESS adj without stopping

CEASES > CEASE

CEASING > CEASE

CEASINGS > CEASE

CEAZE obsolete spelling of > SEIZE

CEAZED > CEAZE

CEAZES > CEAZE

CEAZING > CEAZE

CEBADILLA same as > SABADILLA

CEBID n any member of the Cebidae family of New World monkeys

CEBIDS > CEBID

CEBOID same as > CEBID

CEBOIDS > CEBOID

CECA > CECUM

CECAL > CECUM

CECALLY > CECUM

CECILS pl n fried meatballs

CECITIES > CECITY

CECITIS n inflammation of the c(a)ecum

CECITISES > CECITIS

CECITY n rare word for blindness

CECROPIA n large North American moth

CECROPIAS > CECROPIA

CECROPIN n antimicrobial peptide originally derived from the cecropia moth

CECROPINS > CECROPIN

CECUM same as > CAECUM

CEDAR n evergreen coniferous tree ▷ adj made of the wood of a cedar tree

CEDARBIRD n type of waxwing

CEDARED adj covered with cedars

CEDARIER > CEDARY

CEDARIEST > CEDARY

CEDARN adj relating to cedar

CEDARS > CEDAR

CEDARWOOD n wood of any of the cedar trees

CEDARY adj like cedar

CEDE vb surrender (territory or legal rights)

CEDED > CEDE

CEDER > CEDE

CEDERS > CEDE

CEDES > CEDE

CEDI n standard monetary unit of Ghana, divided into 100 pesewas

CEDILLA n character placed under a c in some languages

CEDILLAS > CEDILLA

c

CEDING > CEDE

CEDIS > CEDI

CEDRATE n citron

CEDRATES > CEDRATE

CEDRINE adj relating to cedar

CEDULA n form of identification in Spanish-speaking countries

CEDULAS > CEDULA

CEE n third letter of the alphabet

CEES > CEE

CEIBA n type of tropical tree

CEIBAS > CEIBA

CEIL vb line (a ceiling) with plaster, boarding, etc

CEILED > CEIL

CEILER > CEIL

CEILERS > CEIL

CEILI variant spelling of > CEILIDH

CEILIDH n social gathering for singing and dancing

CEILIDHS > CEILIDH

CEILING n inner upper surface of a room ▷ vb make a ceiling

CEILINGED > CEILING

CEILINGS > CEILING

CEILIS > CEILI

CEILS > CEIL

CEINTURE n belt

CEINTURES > CEINTURE

CEL short for > CELLULOID

CELADON n type of porcelain having a greyish-green glaze: mainly Chinese

CELADONS > CELADON

CELANDINE n wild plant with yellow flowers

CELEB n celebrity

CELEBRANT n person who performs a religious ceremony

CELEBRATE vb hold festivities to mark (a happy event, anniversary, etc)

CELEBRITY n famous person

CELEBS > CELEB

CELECOXIB n type of anti-inflammatory drug

CELERIAC n variety of celery with a large turnip-like root

CELERIACS > CELERIAC

CELERIES > CELERY

CELERITY n swiftness

CELERY n vegetable with long green crisp edible stalks

CELESTA n instrument like a small piano

CELESTAS > CELESTA

CELESTE same as > CELESTA

CELESTES > CELESTE

CELESTIAL adj heavenly, divine

CELESTINE same as > CELESTITE

CELESTITE n white, red, or blue mineral

CELIAC same as > COELIAC

CELIACS > CELIAC

CELIBACY > CELIBATE

CELIBATE adj unmarried, esp because of a religious vow ▷ n celibate person

CELIBATES > CELIBATE

CELIBATIC adj celibate

CELL n smallest unit of an organism that is able to function independently

CELLA n inner room of a classical temple

CELLAE > CELLA

CELLAR n underground room for storage ▷ vb store in a cellar

CELLARAGE n area of a cellar

CELLARED > CELLAR

CELLARER n monastic official responsible for food, drink, etc

CELLARERS > CELLARER

CELLARET n case, cabinet, or sideboard with compartments for holding wine bottles

CELLARETS > CELLARET

CELLARING > CELLAR

CELLARIST same as > CELLARER

CELLARMAN n person in charge of a cellar

CELLARMEN > CELLARMAN

CELLAROUS adj relating to a cellar

CELLARS > CELLAR

CELLARWAY n way into cellar

CELLBLOCK n group of prison cells

CELLED adj cellular

CELLI > CELLO

CELLING n formation of cells

CELLINGS > CELLING

CELLIST > CELLO

CELLISTS > CELLO

CELLMATE n person with whom a prisoner shares a prison cell

CELLMATES > CELLMATE

CELLO n large low-pitched instrument of the violin family

CELLOIDIN n nitrocellulose compound

CELLOS > CELLO

CELLOSE n disaccharide obtained by the hydrolysis of cellulose by cellulase

CELLOSES > CELLOSE

CELLPHONE n portable telephone operated by cellular radio

CELLS > CELL

CELLULAR adj of or consisting of cells ▷ n cellular phone

CELLULARS > CELLULAR

CELLULASE n any enzyme that converts cellulose to the disaccharide cellobiose

CELLULE n very small cell

CELLULES > CELLULE

CELLULITE n fat deposits under the skin alleged to resist dieting

CELLULOID n kind of plastic used to make toys and, formerly, photographic film

CELLULOSE n main constituent of plant cell walls, used in making paper, plastics, etc

CELLULOUS > CELLULOSE

CELOM same as > COELOM

CELOMATA > CELOM

CELOMIC > CELOM

CELOMS > CELOM

CELOSIA same as > COCKSCOMB

CELOSIAS > CELOSIA

CELOTEX n tradename for a type of insulation board

CELOTEXES > CELOTEX

CELS > CEL

CELSITUDE n loftiness

CELT n stone or metal axelike instrument with a bevelled edge

CELTS > CELT

CEMBALI > CEMBALO

CEMBALIST > CEMBALO

CEMBALO n harpsichord

CEMBALOS > CEMBALO

CEMBRA n Swiss pine

CEMBRAS > CEMBRA

CEMENT n powder mixed with water and sand to make mortar or concrete ▷ vb join, bind, or cover with cement

CEMENTA > CEMENTUM

CEMENTED > CEMENT

CEMENTER > CEMENT

CEMENTERS > CEMENT

CEMENTING > CEMENT

CEMENTITE n hard brittle compound of iron and carbon

CEMENTS > CEMENT

CEMENTUM n thin bonelike tissue that covers the dentine in the root of a tooth

CEMENTUMS > CEMENTUM

CEMETERY n place where dead people are buried

CEMITARE obsolete spelling of > SCIMITAR

CEMITARES > CEMITARE

CENACLE n supper room, esp one on an upper floor

CENACLES > CENACLE

CENDRE adj ash-blond

CENOBITE same as > COENOBITE

CENOBITES > CENOBITE

CENOBITIC > CENOBITE

CENOTAPH n monument honouring soldiers who died in a war

CENOTAPHS > CENOTAPH

CENOTE n natural well formed by the collapse of an overlying limestone crust

CENOTES > CENOTE

CENOZOIC adj of or relating to the most recent geological era

CENS n type of annual property rent

CENSE vb burn incense near or before (an altar, shrine, etc)

CENSED > CENSE

CENSER n container for burning incense

CENSERS > CENSER

CENSES > CENSE

CENSING > CENSE

CENSOR n person authorized to prohibit anything considered obscene or objectionable ▷ vb ban or cut parts of (a film, book, etc)

CENSORED > CENSOR

CENSORIAL > CENSOR

CENSORIAN > CENSOR

CENSORING > CENSOR

CENSORS > CENSOR

CENSUAL > CENSUS

CENSURE n severe disapproval ▷ vb criticize severely

CENSURED > CENSURE

CENSURER > CENSURE

CENSURERS > CENSURE

CENSURES > CENSURE

CENSURING > CENSURE

CENSUS n official count of a population ▷ vb conduct a census

CENSUSED > CENSUS

CENSUSES > CENSUS

CENSUSING > CENSUS

CENT n hundredth part of a monetary unit such as the dollar or euro

CENTAGE n rate per hundred

CENTAGES > CENTAGE

CENTAI > CENTAS

CENTAL n unit of weight equal to 100 pounds (45.3 kilograms)

CENTALS > CENTAL

CENTARE same as > CENTIARE

CENTARES > CENTARE

CENTAS n monetary unit of Lithuania

CENTAUR n mythical creature

CENTAUREA n type of plant of the genus which includes the cornflower and knapweed

CENTAURIC adj integrating mind and body

CENTAURS > CENTAUR

CENTAURY n plant with purplish-pink flowers

CENTAVO n monetary unit in many Latin American countries

CENTAVOS > CENTAVO

CENTENARY n 100th anniversary or its celebration ▷ adj of or relating to a period of 100 years

CENTENIER n in Jersey, a local police officer

CENTER same as > CENTRE

CENTERED > CENTER

CENTERING same as > CENTRING

CENTERS > CENTER

CENTESES > CENTESIS

CENTESIMI > CENTESIMO

CENTESIMO n former monetary unit of Italy, San Marino, and the Vatican City worth one hundredth of a lira

CENTESIS n surgical puncturing of part of the body with a hollow needle, to extract fluid

CENTIARE n unit of area equal to one square metre

CENTIARES > CENTIARE

CENTIGRAM n one hundredth of a gram

CENTILE n (in statistics) another word for percentile

CENTILES > CENTILE

CENTIME n monetary unit worth one hundredth of a franc

CENTIMES > CENTIME

CENTIMO n monetary unit of Costa Rica, Paraguay, Peru, and Venezuela

CENTIMOS > CENTIMO

CENTINEL obsolete variant of > SENTINEL

CENTINELL obsolete variant of > SENTINEL

CENTINELS > CENTINEL

CENTIPEDE n small wormlike creature with many legs

CENTNER n unit of weight equivalent to 100 pounds (45.3 kilograms)

CENTNERS > CENTNER

CENTO n piece of writing composed of quotations from other authors

CENTOIST n one who composes centos

CENTOISTS > CENTOIST

CENTONATE adj having many patches ▷ n Gregorian chant comprised of a patchwork of texts and melodies

CENTONEL obsolete variant of > SENTINEL

CENTONELL obsolete variant of > SENTINEL

CENTONELS > CENTONEL

CENTONES > CENTO

CENTONIST same as > CENTOIST

CENTOS > CENTO

CENTRA > CENTRUM

CENTRAL adj of, at, or forming the centre ▷ n workplace serving as a telecommunications facility

CENTRALER > CENTRAL

CENTRALLY > CENTRAL

CENTRALS > CENTRAL

CENTRE n middle point or part ▷ vb put in the centre of something

CENTRED adj mentally and emotionally confident, focused, and well-balanced

CENTREING same as > CENTRING

CENTREMAN n ice hockey player occupying a central position

CENTREMEN > CENTREMAN

CENTRES > CENTRE

CENTRIC adj being central or having a centre

CENTRICAL same as > CENTRIC

CENTRIES > CENTRY

CENTRING n temporary structure used to support an arch during construction

CENTRINGS > CENTRING

CENTRIOLE n either of two rodlike bodies in most animal cells that form the poles of the spindle during mitosis

CENTRISM > CENTRIST

CENTRISMS > CENTRIST

CENTRIST n person favouring political moderation

CENTRISTS > CENTRIST

CENTRODE n locus produced by plotting the course of two bodies in relative motion

CENTRODES > CENTRODE

CENTROID n centre of mass of an object of uniform density, esp of a geometric figure

CENTROIDS > CENTROID

CENTRUM n main part or body of a vertebra

CENTRUMS > CENTRUM

CENTRY obsolete variant of > SENTRY

CENTS > CENT

CENTU n former Lithuanian money unit

CENTUM adj denoting or belonging to certain Indo-European languages ▷ n hundred

CENTUMS > CENTUM

CENTUMVIR n one of the Roman judges who sat in civil cases

CENTUPLE n one hundredfold

CENTUPLED > CENTUPLE

CENTUPLES > CENTUPLE

CENTURIAL adj of or relating to a Roman century

CENTURIES > CENTURY

CENTURION n (in ancient Rome) officer commanding 100 men

CENTURY n period of 100 years

CEORL n freeman of the lowest class in Anglo-Saxon England

CEORLISH > CEORL

CEORLS > CEORL

CEP another name for > PORCINO

CEPACEOUS adj having an onion-like smell or taste

CEPAGE n grape variety or type of wine

CEPAGES > CEPAGE

CEPE another spelling of > CEP

CEPES > CEPE

CEPHALAD adv towards the head or anterior part

CEPHALATE adj possessing a head

CEPHALIC adj of or relating to the head ▷ n remedy for pains in the head

CEPHALICS > CEPHALIC

CEPHALIN n phospholipid, similar to lecithin, that occurs in the nerve tissue and brain

CEPHALINS > CEPHALIN

CEPHALOUS adj with a head

CEPHEID n type of variable star with a regular cycle of variations in luminosity

CEPHEIDS > CEPHEID

CEPS > CEP

CERACEOUS adj waxlike or waxy

CERAMAL same as > CERMET

CERAMALS > CERAMAL

CERAMIC n hard brittle material ▷ adj made of ceramic

CERAMICS n art of producing ceramic objects

CERAMIDE n class of compounds used as moisturizers

CERAMIDES > CERAMIDE

CERAMIST > CERAMICS

CERAMISTS > CERAMICS

CERASIN n meta-arabinic acid

CERASINS > CERASIN

CERASTES n type of venomous snake, esp the horned viper

CERASTIUM n mouse-eared chickweed

CERATE n hard ointment or medicated paste

CERATED adj (of certain birds, such as the falcon) having a cere

CERATES > CERATE

CERATIN same as > KERATIN

CERATINS > CERATIN

CERATITIS same as > KERATITIS

CERATODUS n type of extinct lungfish common in Cretaceous and Triassic times

CERATOID adj having the shape or texture of animal horn

CERBEREAN adj of or resembling Cerberus, the three-headed dog that guarded the entrance to Hades in Greek mythology

CERBERIAN same as > CERBEREAN

CERCAL adj of or relating to a tail

CERCARIA n one of the larval forms of trematode worms

CERCARIAE > CERCARIA

CERCARIAL > CERCARIA

CERCARIAN > CERCARIA

CERCARIAS > CERCARIA

CERCI > CERCUS

CERCIS n type of tree or shrub

CERCISES > CERCIS

CERCLAGE n treatment of a malfunctioning cervix by means of a suture in early pregnancy

CERCLAGES > CERCLAGE

CERCOPID n froghopper or spittlebug

CERCOPIDS > CERCOPID

CERCUS n one of a pair of sensory appendages on some insects and other arthropods

CERE n soft waxy swelling at the base of the upper beak of a parrot ▷ vb wrap in a cerecloth

CEREAL n grass plant with edible grain, such as oat or wheat

CEREALIST n expert in cereals

CEREALS > CEREAL

CEREBELLA n plural of singular cerebellum: one of the major divisions of the vertebrate brain

CEREBRA > CEREBRUM

CEREBRAL same as > CACUMINAL

CEREBRALS > CEREBRAL

CEREBRATE vb use the mind

CEREBRIC > CEREBRUM

CEREBROID > CEREBRUM

CEREBRUM n main part of the brain

CEREBRUMS > CEREBRUM

CERECLOTH n waxed waterproof cloth of a kind formerly used as a shroud

CERED > CERE

CEREMENT n any burial clothes

CEREMENTS > CEREMENT

CEREMONY n formal act or ritual

CEREOUS adj waxlike

CERES > CERE

CERESIN n white wax extracted from ozocerite

CERESINE same as > CERESIN

CERESINES > CERESINE

CERESINS > CERESIN

CEREUS n type of tropical American cactus

CEREUSES > CEREUS

CERGE n large altar candle

CERGES > CERGE

CERIA n ceric oxide

CERIAS > CERIA

CERIC adj of or containing cerium in the tetravalent state

CERING > CERE

CERIPH same as > SERIF

CERIPHS > CERIPH

CERISE adj cherry-red ▷ n moderate to dark red colour

CERISES > CERISE

CERITE n hydrous silicate of cerium

CERITES > CERITE

CERIUM n steel-grey metallic element

CERIUMS > CERIUM

CERMET n material consisting of a metal matrix with ceramic particles disseminated through it

CERMETS > CERMET

CERNE obsolete variant of > ENCIRCLE

CERNED > CERNE

CERNES > CERNE

CERNING > CERNE

CERNUOUS adj (of some flowers or buds) drooping

CERO n type of large food fish

CEROC n dance combining many styles, including jive and salsa

CEROCS > CEROC

CEROGRAPH n writing on wax

c

CEROMANCY n divination by interpreting significance of shapes formed when melted wax is dropped into water

CEROON n hide-covered bale

CEROONS > CEROON

CEROS > CERO

CEROTIC adj as in cerotic acid white insoluble odourless wax

CEROTYPE n process for preparing a printing plate

CEROTYPES > CEROTYPE

CEROUS adj of or containing cerium in the trivalent state

CERRADO n vast area of tropical savanna in Brazil

CERRADOS > CERRADO

CERRIAL adj relating to the cerris

CERRIS n Turkey oak

CERRISES > CERRIS

CERT n certainty

CERTAIN adj positive and confident

CERTAINER > CERTAIN

CERTAINLY adv without doubt ▷ sentence substitute by all means

CERTAINTY n state of being sure

CERTES adv with certainty

CERTIE n as in by my certie assuredly

CERTIFIED > CERTIFY

CERTIFIER > CERTIFY

CERTIFIES > CERTIFY

CERTIFY vb confirm, attest to

CERTITUDE n confidence, certainty

CERTS > CERT

CERTY n as in by my certy assuredly

CERULE adj sky-blue

CERULEAN n deep blue colour

CERULEANS > CERULEAN

CERULEIN n type of dyestuff

CERULEINS > CERULEIN

CERULEOUS adj sky-blue

CERUMEN n wax secreted by glands in the external ear

CERUMENS > CERUMEN

CERUSE n white lead

CERUSES > CERUSE

CERUSITE same as > CERUSSITE

CERUSITES > CERUSITE

CERUSSITE n usually white mineral, found in veins

CERVELAS n French garlicky pork sausage

CERVELAT n smoked sausage made from pork and beef

CERVELATS > CERVELAT

CERVEZA n Spanish word for beer

CERVEZAS > CERVEZA

CERVICAL adj of or relating to the neck or cervix

CERVICES > CERVIX

CERVICUM n flexible region between the prothorax and head in insects

CERVICUMS > CERVICUM

CERVID n type of ruminant mammal characterized by the presence of antlers

CERVIDS > CERVID

CERVINE adj resembling or relating to a deer

CERVIX n narrow entrance of the womb

CERVIXES > CERVIX

CESAREAN variant of > CAESAREAN

CESAREANS > CESAREAN

CESAREVNA n wife of a Russian tsar's eldest son

CESARIAN US variant of > CAESAREAN

CESARIANS > CESARIAN

CESIOUS same as > CAESIOUS

CESIUM same as > CAESIUM

CESIUMS > CESIUM

CESPITOSE adj growing in dense tufts

CESS n any of several special taxes, such as a land tax in Scotland ▷ vb tax or assess for taxation

CESSATION n ceasing

CESSE obsolete variant of > CEASE

CESSED > CESS

CESSER n coming to an end of a term interest or annuity

CESSERS > CESSER

CESSES > CESS

CESSING > CESS

CESSION n ceding

CESSIONS > CESSION

CESSPIT same as > CESSPOOL

CESSPITS > CESSPIT

CESSPOOL n covered tank or pit for collecting and storing sewage or waste water

CESSPOOLS > CESSPOOL

CESTA n in jai alai, the basket used to throw and catch the pelota

CESTAS > CESTA

CESTI > CESTUS

CESTODE n type of parasitic flatworm such as the tapeworms

CESTODES > CESTODE

CESTOI > CESTOS

CESTOID adj (esp of tapeworms and similar animals) ribbon-like in form ▷ n ribbon-like worm

CESTOIDS > CESTOID

CESTOS same as > CESTUS

CESTOSES > CESTOS

CESTUI n legal term to designate a person

CESTUIS > CESTUI

CESTUS n girdle of Aphrodite

CESTUSES > CESTUS

CESURA a variant spelling of > CAESURA

CESURAE > CESURA

CESURAL > CESURA

CESURAS > CESURA

CESURE same as > CAESURA

CESURES > CESURE

CETACEAN n fish-shaped sea mammal such as a whale or dolphin ▷ adj relating to these mammals

CETACEANS > CETACEAN

CETACEOUS same as > CETACEAN

CETANE n colourless liquid hydrocarbon, used as a solvent

CETANES > CETANE

CETE n group of badgers

CETERACH n scale-fern

CETERACHS > CETERACH

CETES > CETE

CETOLOGY n branch of zoology concerned with the study of whales (cetaceans)

CETRIMIDE n quaternary ammonium compound used as a detergent

CETUXIMAB n monoclonal antibody used to treat cancer

CETYL n univalent alcohol radical

CETYLS > CETYL

CETYWALL n valerian

CETYWALLS > CETYWALL

CEVADILLA same as > SABADILLA

CEVAPCICI n sausages made with beef and paprika

CEVICHE n Peruvian seafood dish

CEVICHES > CEVICHE

CEVITAMIC adj as in cevitamic acid ascorbic (acid)

CEYLANITE same as > CEYLONITE

CEYLONITE n pleonaste

CEZVE n small metal pot for brewing coffee

CEZVES > CEZVE

CH pron obsolete form of I

CHA n tea

CHABAZITE n pink, white, or colourless zeolite mineral

CHABLIS n dry white French wine

CHABOUK n type of whip

CHABOUKS > CHABOUK

CHABUK same as > CHABOUK

CHABUKS > CHABUK

CHACE obsolete variant of > CHASE

CHACED > CHACE

CHACES > CHACE

CHACHKA n cheap trinket

CHACHKAS > CHACHKA

CHACING > CHACE

CHACK vb bite

CHACKED > CHACK

CHACKING > CHACK

CHACKS > CHACK

CHACMA n type of baboon with coarse greyish hair, living in S and E Africa

CHACMAS > CHACMA

CHACO same as > SHAKO

CHACOES > CHACO

CHACONINE n toxic substance found in potatoes

CHACONNE n musical form consisting of a set of variations on a repeated melodic bass line

CHACONNES > CHACONNE

CHACOS > CHACO

CHAD n small pieces removed during the punching of holes in punch cards, printer paper, etc

CHADAR same as > CHUDDAR

CHADARIM > CHEDER

CHADARS > CHADAR

CHADDAR same as > CHUDDAR

CHADDARS > CHADDAR

CHADDOR same as > CHUDDAR

CHADDORS > CHADDOR

CHADLESS adj (of a keypunch) not producing chads

CHADO n Japanese tea ceremony

CHADOR same as > CHUDDAR

CHADORS > CHADOR

CHADOS > CHADO

CHADRI n shroud which covers the body from head to foot

CHADS > CHAD

CHAEBOL n large, usually family-owned, business group in South Korea

CHAEBOLS > CHAEBOL

CHAETA n the chitinous bristles on the body of annelids

CHAETAE > CHAETA

CHAETAL > CHAETA

CHAETODON n butterfly fish

CHAETOPOD n type of annelid worm

CHAFE vb make sore or worn by rubbing

CHAFED > CHAFE

CHAFER n large beetle

CHAFERS > CHAFER

CHAFES > CHAFE

CHAFF n grain husks ▷ vb tease good-naturedly

CHAFFED > CHAFF

CHAFFER vb haggle

CHAFFERED > CHAFFER

CHAFFERER > CHAFFER

CHAFFERS > CHAFFER

CHAFFERY n bargaining

CHAFFIER > CHAFF

CHAFFIEST > CHAFF

CHAFFINCH n small European songbird

CHAFFING > CHAFF

CHAFFINGS > CHAFF

CHAFFRON same as > CHAMFRON

CHAFFRONS > CHAFFRON

CHAFFS > CHAFF

CHAFFY > CHAFF

CHAFING > CHAFE

CHAFT n jaw

CHAFTS > CHAFT

CHAGAN n Mongolian royal or imperial title

CHAGANS > CHAGAN

CHAGRIN n annoyance and disappointment ▷ vb embarrass and annoy

CHAGRINED > CHAGRIN

CHAGRINS > CHAGRIN

CHAI n tea, esp as made in India with added spices

CHAIN n flexible length of connected metal links ▷ vb restrict or fasten with or as if with a chain

CHAINE adj (of a dance turn) producing a full rotation for every two steps taken ▷ *vb* produce a full rotation for every two steps taken

CHAINED > CHAIN

CHAINER *n* person who chains

CHAINERS > CHAINER

CHAINES > CHAINE

CHAINFALL *n* type of hoist

CHAINING > CHAIN

CHAINLESS *adj* having no chain

CHAINLET *n* small chain

CHAINLETS > CHAINLET

CHAINMAN *n* person who does the chaining in a survey

CHAINMEN > CHAINMAN

CHAINS > CHAIN

CHAINSAW *n* motor-driven saw with teeth linked in a continuous loop ▷ *vb* operate a chainsaw

CHAINSAWS > CHAINSAW

CHAINSHOT *n* cannon shot of two balls joined by a chain

CHAINWORK *n* work linked or looped in the manner of a chain

CHAIR *n* seat with a back, for one person ▷ *vb* preside over (a meeting)

CHAIRBACK *n* back part of a chair

CHAIRDAYS *n* old age

CHAIRED > CHAIR

CHAIRING > CHAIR

CHAIRLIFT *n* series of chairs suspended from a moving cable for carrying people up a slope

CHAIRMAN *n* person in charge of a company's board of directors or a meeting ▷ *vb* act as chairman of

CHAIRMANS > CHAIRMAN

CHAIRMEN > CHAIRMAN

CHAIRS > CHAIR

CHAIS > CHAI

CHAISE *n* light horse-drawn carriage

CHAISES > CHAISE

CHAKALAKA *n* relish made from tomatoes, onions, and spices

CHAKRA *n* (in yoga) any of the seven major energy centres in the body

CHAKRAS > CHAKRA

CHAL *n* in Romany, person or fellow

CHALAH *same as* > CHALLAH

CHALAHS > CHALAH

CHALAN *vb* (in India) to cause an accused person to appear before a magistrate ▷ *n* invoice, pass, or voucher

CHALANED > CHALAN

CHALANING > CHALAN

CHALANNED *same as* > CHALANED

CHALANS > CHALAN

CHALAZA *n* one of a pair of spiral threads holding the yolk of a bird's egg in position

CHALAZAE > CHALAZA

CHALAZAL > CHALAZA

CHALAZAS > CHALAZA

CHALAZIA > CHALAZION

CHALAZION *n* small cyst on the eyelid resulting from chronic inflammation of a meibomian gland

CHALCID *n* type of tiny insect

CHALCIDS > CHALCID

CHALCOGEN *n* any of the elements oxygen, sulphur, selenium, tellurium, or polonium, of group 6A of the periodic table

CHALDER *n* former Scottish dry measure

CHALDERS > CHALDER

CHALDRON *n* unit of capacity equal to 36 bushels

CHALDRONS > CHALDRON

CHALEH *same as* > CHALLAH

CHALEHS > CHALEH

CHALET *n* kind of Swiss wooden house with a steeply sloping roof

CHALETS > CHALET

CHALICE *n* large goblet

CHALICED *adj* (of plants) having cup-shaped flowers

CHALICES > CHALICE

CHALK *n* soft white rock consisting of calcium carbonate ▷ *vb* draw or mark with chalk

CHALKED > CHALK

CHALKFACE *n* work or art of teaching in a school

CHALKIER > CHALK

CHALKIEST > CHALK

CHALKING > CHALK

CHALKLAND *n* land largely composed of chalk

CHALKLIKE > CHALK

CHALKMARK *n* as in *walk the chalkmark* straight line drawn with chalk, used as a sobriety test

CHALKPIT *n* quarry for chalk

CHALKPITS > CHALKPIT

CHALKS > CHALK

CHALKY > CHALK

CHALLA *same as* > CHALLAH

CHALLAH *n* type of bread

CHALLAHS > CHALLAH

CHALLAN *same as* > CHALAN

CHALLANS > CHALLAN

CHALLAS > CHALLA

CHALLENGE *n* demanding or stimulating situation ▷ *vb* issue a challenge to

CHALLIE *same as* > CHALLIS

CHALLIES > CHALLIE

CHALLIS *n* lightweight plain-weave fabric

CHALLISES > CHALLIS

CHALLOT > CHALLAH

CHALLOTH > CHALLAH

CHALLY *same as* > CHALLIS

CHALONE *n* any internal secretion that inhibits a physiological process or function

CHALONES > CHALONE

CHALONIC > CHALONE

CHALOT > CHALAH

CHALOTH > CHALAH

CHALS > CHAL

CHALUMEAU *n* early type of reed instrument, precursor of the clarinet

CHALUPA *n* Mexican dish

CHALUPAS > CHALUPA

CHALUTZ *n* member of an organization of immigrants to Israeli agricultural settlements

CHALUTZES > CHALUTZ

CHALUTZIM > CHALUTZ

CHALYBEAN *adj* (of steel) of superior quality

CHALYBITE *another name for* > SIDERITE

CHAM *an archaic word for* > KHAN

CHAMADE *n* (formerly) a signal by drum or trumpet inviting an enemy to a parley

CHAMADES > CHAMADE

CHAMBER *n* hall used for formal meetings ▷ *vb* act lasciviously

CHAMBERED > CHAMBER

CHAMBERER *n* lascivious person

CHAMBERS *pl n* judge's room for hearing private cases not taken in open court

CHAMBRAY *n* smooth light fabric of cotton, linen, etc, with white weft and a coloured warp

CHAMBRAYS > CHAMBRAY

CHAMBRE *adj* (of wine) at room temperature

CHAMELEON *n* small lizard that changes colour to blend in with its surroundings

CHAMELOT *same as* > CAMLET

CHAMELOTS > CHAMELOT

CHAMETZ *n* leavened food which may not be eaten during Passover

CHAMETZES > CHAMETZ

CHAMFER *same as* > CHASE

CHAMFERED > CHAMFER

CHAMFERER > CHAMFER

CHAMFERS > CHAMFER

CHAMFRAIN *same as* > CHAMFRON

CHAMFRON *n* piece of armour for a horse's head

CHAMFRONS > CHAMFRON

CHAMISA *n* American shrub

CHAMISAL *n* place overgrown with chamiso

CHAMISALS > CHAMISAL

CHAMISAS > CHAMISA

CHAMISE *same as* > CHAMISO

CHAMISES > CHAMISE

CHAMISO *n* four-wing saltbush

CHAMISOS > CHAMISO

CHAMLET *same as* > CAMLET

CHAMLETS > CHAMLET

CHAMMIED > CHAMMY

CHAMMIES > CHAMMY

CHAMMY *same as* > CHAMOIS

CHAMMYING > CHAMMY

CHAMOIS *n* small mountain antelope or a piece of leather from its skin, used for polishing ▷ *vb* polish with a chamois

CHAMOISED > CHAMOIS

CHAMOISES > CHAMOIS

CHAMOIX *same as* > CHAMOIS

CHAMOMILE *same as* > CAMOMILE

CHAMP *vb* chew noisily

CHAMPAC *n* type of tree

CHAMPACA *same as* > CHAMPAC

CHAMPACAS > CHAMPACA

CHAMPACS > CHAMPAC

CHAMPAGNE *n* sparkling white French wine ▷ *adj* denoting a luxurious lifestyle

CHAMPAIGN *n* expanse of open level or gently undulating country

CHAMPAK *same as* > CHAMPAC

CHAMPAKS > CHAMPAK

CHAMPART *n* granting of land to a person for a portion of the crops

CHAMPARTS > CHAMPART

CHAMPAS *n* champagne

CHAMPED > CHAMP

CHAMPER > CHAMP

CHAMPERS *n* champagne

CHAMPERTY *n* (formerly) an illegal bargain between a party to litigation and an outsider whereby the latter agrees to pay for the action and thereby share in any proceeds recovered

CHAMPIER > CHAMPY

CHAMPIEST > CHAMPY

CHAMPING > CHAMP

CHAMPION *n* overall winner of a competition ▷ *vb* support ▷ *adj* excellent ▷ *adv* very well

CHAMPIONS > CHAMPION

CHAMPLEVE *adj* of or relating to a process of enamelling by which grooves are cut into a metal base and filled with enamel colours ▷ *n* object enamelled by this process

CHAMPS > CHAMP

CHAMPY *adj* (of earth) churned up (by cattle, for example)

CHAMS > CHAM

CHANA *n* (in Indian cookery) chickpeas

CHANAS > CHANA

CHANCE *n* likelihood, probability ▷ *vb* risk, hazard

CHANCED > CHANCE

CHANCEFUL > CHANCE

CHANCEL *n* part of a church containing the altar and choir

CHANCELS > CHANCEL

CHANCER *n* unscrupulous or dishonest opportunist

CHANCERS > CHANCER

CHANCERY *n* Lord Chancellor's court, now a division of the High Court of Justice

CHANCES > CHANCE

CHANCEY *same as* > CHANCY

CHANCIER > CHANCY

CHANCIEST > CHANCY

CHANCILY > CHANCY
CHANCING > CHANCE
CHANCRE n small hard growth
CHANCRES > CHANCRE
CHANCROID n soft ulcer caused by a bacterial infection ▷ adj relating to or resembling a chancroid or chancre
CHANCROUS > CHANCRE
CHANCY adj uncertain, risky
CHANDELLE n abrupt climbing turn almost to the point of stalling, in which an aircraft's momentum is used to increase its rate of climb ▷ vb carry out a chandelle
CHANDLER n dealer, esp in ships' supplies
CHANDLERS > CHANDLER
CHANDLERY n business, warehouse, or merchandise of a chandler
CHANFRON same as **>** CHAMFRON
CHANFRONS > CHANFRON
CHANG n loud discordant noise
CHANGA interj in Indian English, an expression of approval or agreement
CHANGE n becoming different ▷ vb make or become different
CHANGED > CHANGE
CHANGEFUL adj often changing
CHANGER > CHANGE
CHANGERS > CHANGE
CHANGES > CHANGE
CHANGEUP n type of baseball pitch
CHANGEUPS > CHANGEUP
CHANGING > CHANGE
CHANGS > CHANG
CHANK n shell of several types of sea conch, used to make bracelets
CHANKS > CHANK
CHANNEL n band of broadcasting frequencies ▷ vb direct or convey through a channel
CHANNELED > CHANNEL
CHANNELER > CHANNEL
CHANNELS > CHANNEL
CHANNER n gravel
CHANNERS > CHANNER
CHANOYO a variant of **>** CHADO
CHANOYOS > CHANOYO
CHANOYU same as **>** CHADO
CHANOYUS > CHANOYU
CHANSON n song
CHANSONS > CHANSON
CHANT vb utter or sing (a slogan or psalm) ▷ n rhythmic or repetitious slogan
CHANTABLE > CHANT
CHANTAGE n blackmail
CHANTAGES > CHANTAGE
CHANTED > CHANT
CHANTER n (on bagpipes) pipe on which the melody is played
CHANTERS > CHANTER

CHANTEUSE n female singer, esp in a nightclub or cabaret
CHANTEY the usual US spelling of **>** SHANTY
CHANTEYS > CHANTEY
CHANTIE n chamber pot
CHANTIES > CHANTY
CHANTILLY n as in chantilly lace delicate ornamental lace
CHANTING > CHANT
CHANTINGS > CHANTING
CHANTOR same as **>** CHANTER
CHANTORS > CHANTOR
CHANTRESS n female chanter
CHANTRIES > CHANTRY
CHANTRY n endowment for the singing of Masses for the founder
CHANTS > CHANT
CHANTY same as **>** SHANTY
CHANUKIAH a variant spelling of **>** HANUKIAH
CHAO n Vietnamese rice porridge
CHAOLOGY n study of chaos theory
CHAORDIC adj combining elements of chaos and order
CHAOS n complete disorder or confusion
CHAOSES > CHAOS
CHAOTIC > CHAOS
CHAP n man or boy ▷ vb (of the skin) to make or become raw and cracked, esp by exposure to cold
CHAPARRAL n (in the southwestern US) a dense growth of shrubs and trees, esp evergreen oaks
CHAPATI n (in Indian cookery) flat thin unleavened bread
CHAPATIES > CHAPATI
CHAPATIS > CHAPATI
CHAPATTI same as **>** CHAPATI
CHAPATTIS > CHAPATTI
CHAPBOOK n book of popular ballads, stories, etc, formerly sold by chapmen or pedlars
CHAPBOOKS > CHAPBOOK
CHAPE n metal tip or trimming for a scabbard
CHAPEAU n hat
CHAPEAUS > CHAPEAU
CHAPEAUX > CHAPEAU
CHAPEL n place of worship with its own altar, within a church
CHAPELESS > CHAPE
CHAPELRY n district legally assigned to and served by an Anglican chapel
CHAPELS > CHAPEL
CHAPERON n older or married woman who supervises a young unmarried woman ▷ vb act as a chaperon to
CHAPERONE same as **>** CHAPERON
CHAPERONS > CHAPERON
CHAPES > CHAPE

CHAPESS n woman
CHAPESSES > CHAPESS
CHAPITER same as **>** CAPITAL
CHAPITERS > CHAPITER
CHAPKA same as **>** CZAPKA
CHAPKAS > CHAPKA
CHAPLAIN n clergyman or clergywoman attached to a chapel, military body, or institution
CHAPLAINS > CHAPLAIN
CHAPLESS adj lacking a lower jaw
CHAPLET n garland for the head ▷ vb create a garland
CHAPLETED > CHAPLET
CHAPLETS > CHAPLET
CHAPMAN n travelling pedlar
CHAPMEN > CHAPMAN
CHAPPAL n one of a pair of sandals, usually of leather, worn in India
CHAPPALS > CHAPPAL
CHAPPATI same as **>** CHAPATI
CHAPPATIS > CHAPPATI
CHAPPED > CHAP
CHAPPESS same as **>** CHAPESS
CHAPPIE n man or boy
CHAPPIER > CHAPPY
CHAPPIES > CHAPPIE
CHAPPIEST > CHAPPY
CHAPPING > CHAP
CHAPPY adj (of skin) chapped
CHAPRASSI n in India, during the British Empire, an office messenger
CHAPS > CHAP
CHAPSTICK n cylinder of a substance for preventing or soothing chapped lips
CHAPT adj chapped
CHAPTER n division of a book ▷ vb divide into chapters
CHAPTERAL > CHAPTER
CHAPTERED > CHAPTER
CHAPTERS > CHAPTER
CHAPTREL n capital of a pillar supporting an arch
CHAPTRELS > CHAPTREL
CHAQUETA n South American cowboy jacket
CHAQUETAS > CHAQUETA
CHAR vb blacken by partial burning ▷ n charwoman
CHARA n type of green freshwater algae
CHARABANC n coach for sightseeing
CHARACID same as **>** CHARACIN
CHARACIDS > CHARACIN
CHARACIN n type of small carnivorous freshwater fish of Central and S America and Africa
CHARACINS > CHARACIN
CHARACT n distinctive mark
CHARACTER n combination of qualities distinguishing a person, group, or place
CHARACTS > CHARACT
CHARADE n absurd pretence

CHARADES n game in which teams act out each syllable of a word or phrase
CHARANGA n type of orchestra used in performing traditional Cuban music
CHARANGAS > CHARANGA
CHARANGO n Andean ten-stringed mandolin
CHARANGOS > CHARANGO
CHARAS another name for **>** HASHISH
CHARASES > CHARAS
CHARBROIL vb grill over charcoal
CHARCOAL n black substance formed by partially burning wood ▷ adj very dark grey ▷ vb write, draw, or blacken with charcoal
CHARCOALS > CHARCOAL
CHARCOALY adj like charcoal
CHARD n variety of beet
CHARDS > CHARD
CHARE same as **>** CHAR
CHARED > CHARE
CHARES > CHARE
CHARET obsolete variant of **>** CHARIOT
CHARETS > CHARET
CHARETTE n public brainstorming session
CHARETTES > CHARETTE
CHARGE vb ask as a price ▷ n price charged
CHARGED > CHARGE
CHARGEFUL adj expensive
CHARGER n device for charging an accumulator
CHARGERS > CHARGER
CHARGES > CHARGE
CHARGING n act of charging
CHARGINGS > CHARGING
CHARGRILL vb grill over charcoal
CHARIDEE n jocular spelling of charity, as pronounced in a mid-Atlantic accent
CHARIDEES > CHARIDEE
CHARIER > CHARY
CHARIEST > CHARY
CHARILY adv cautiously
CHARINESS n state of being chary
CHARING > CHARE
CHARIOT n two-wheeled horse-drawn vehicle ▷ vb ride in a chariot
CHARIOTED > CHARIOT
CHARIOTS > CHARIOT
CHARISM same as **>** CHARISMA
CHARISMA n person's power to attract or influence people
CHARISMAS > CHARISMA
CHARISMS > CHARISM
CHARITIES > CHARITY
CHARITY n organization that gives help, such as money or food, to those in need
CHARIVARI n discordant mock serenade to newlyweds, made with pans, kettles, etc ▷ vb make such a serenade

CHARK vb char
CHARKA same as > CHARKHA
CHARKAS > CHARKA
CHARKED > CHARK
CHARKHA n (in India) a spinning wheel, esp for cotton
CHARKHAS > CHARKHA
CHARKING > CHARK
CHARKS > CHARK
CHARLADY same as > CHARWOMAN
CHARLATAN n person who claims expertise that he or she does not have
CHARLEY n as in charley horse muscle stiffness after strenuous exercise
CHARLEYS > CHARLEY
CHARLIE n fool
CHARLIER n as in charlier shoe special light horseshoe
CHARLIES > CHARLIE
CHARLOCK n weed with hairy leaves and yellow flowers
CHARLOCKS > CHARLOCK
CHARLOTTE n dessert made with fruit and bread or cake crumbs
CHARM n attractive quality ▷ vb attract, delight
CHARMED adj delighted or fascinated
CHARMER n attractive person
CHARMERS > CHARMER
CHARMEUSE n trademark for a lightweight fabric with a satin-like finish
CHARMFUL adj highly charming or enchanting
CHARMING adj attractive
CHARMLESS adj devoid of charm
CHARMONIA pl n elementary particles containing an antiquark and a charm quark
CHARMS > CHARM
CHARNECO n type of sweet wine
CHARNECOS > CHARNECO
CHARNEL adj ghastly ▷ n ghastly thing
CHARNELS > CHARNEL
CHAROSET n dish eaten at Passover
CHAROSETH same as > CHAROSET
CHAROSETS > CHAROSET
CHARPAI same as > CHARPOY
CHARPAIS > CHARPAI
CHARPIE n lint pieces used to make surgical dressings
CHARPIES > CHARPIE
CHARPOY n type of bedstead
CHARPOYS > CHARPOY
CHARQUI n meat, esp beef, cut into strips and dried
CHARQUID > CHARQUI
CHARQUIS > CHARQUI
CHARR same as > CHAR
CHARREADA n Mexican display of skills similar to a rodeo
CHARRED > CHAR

CHARRIER > CHARRY
CHARRIEST > CHARRY
CHARRING > CHAR
CHARRO n Mexican cowboy
CHARROS > CHARRO
CHARRS > CHARR
CHARRY adj of or relating to charcoal
CHARS > CHAR
CHART n graph, table, or diagram showing information ▷ vb plot the course of
CHARTA n charter
CHARTABLE > CHART
CHARTAS > CHARTA
CHARTED > CHART
CHARTER n document granting or demanding certain rights ▷ vb hire by charter
CHARTERED adj officially qualified to practise a profession
CHARTERER > CHARTER
CHARTERS > CHARTER
CHARTING > CHART
CHARTISM n historical reform movement in Britain
CHARTISMS > CHARTISM
CHARTIST n supporter of chartism
CHARTISTS > CHARTIST
CHARTLESS adj not mapped
CHARTS > CHART
CHARVER n derogatory term for a young woman
CHARVERS > CHARVER
CHARWOMAN n woman whose job is to clean other people's homes
CHARWOMEN > CHARWOMAN
CHARY adj wary, careful
CHAS > CHA
CHASE vb run after quickly in order to catch or drive away ▷ n chasing, pursuit
CHASEABLE > CHASE
CHASED > CHASE
CHASEPORT n porthole through which a chase gun is fired
CHASER > CHASE
CHASERS > CHASER
CHASES > CHASE
CHASING > CHASE
CHASINGS > CHASE
CHASM n deep crack in the earth ▷ vb create a chasm
CHASMAL > CHASM
CHASMED > CHASM
CHASMIC > CHASM
CHASMIER > CHASMY
CHASMIEST > CHASMY
CHASMS > CHASM
CHASMY adj full of chasms
CHASSE n one of a series of gliding steps in ballet ▷ vb perform either of these steps
CHASSED > CHASSE
CHASSEED > CHASSE
CHASSEING > CHASSE
CHASSEPOT n breech-loading bolt-action rifle formerly used by the French Army
CHASSES > CHASSE

CHASSEUR n member of a unit specially trained and equipped for swift deployment ▷ adj designating or cooked in a sauce consisting of white wine and mushrooms
CHASSEURS > CHASSEUR
CHASSIS n frame, wheels, and mechanical parts of a vehicle
CHASTE adj pure and modest
CHASTELY > CHASTE
CHASTEN vb subdue by criticism
CHASTENED > CHASTEN
CHASTENER > CHASTEN
CHASTENS > CHASTEN
CHASTER > CHASTE
CHASTEST > CHASTE
CHASTISE vb scold severely
CHASTISED > CHASTISE
CHASTISER > CHASTISE
CHASTISES > CHASTISE
CHASTITY n state of being chaste
CHASUBLE n long sleeveless robe worn by a priest when celebrating Mass
CHASUBLES > CHASUBLE
CHAT n informal conversation ▷ vb have an informal conversation
CHATBOT n computer program that simulates conversation with human users over the internet
CHATBOTS > CHATBOT
CHATCHKA variant of > TCHOTCHKE
CHATCHKAS > CHATCHKA
CHATCHKE same as > TCHOTCHKE
CHATCHKES > CHATCHKE
CHATEAU n French castle
CHATEAUS > CHATEAU
CHATEAUX > CHATEAU
CHATELAIN same as > CASTELLAN
CHATLINE n telephone service enabling callers to join in general conversation with each other
CHATLINES > CHATLINE
CHATON n in jewellery, a stone with a reflective metal foil backing
CHATONS > CHATON
CHATOYANT adj having changeable lustre ▷ n gemstone with a changeable lustre
CHATROOM n site on the internet where users have group discussions by e-mail
CHATROOMS > CHATROOM
CHATS > CHAT
CHATTA n umbrella
CHATTAS > CHATTA
CHATTED > CHAT
CHATTEL n item of movable personal property
CHATTELS > CHATTEL
CHATTER vb speak quickly and continuously about unimportant things ▷ n idle talk
CHATTERED > CHATTER

CHATTERER same as > COTINGA
CHATTERS > CHATTER
CHATTERY adj tending to chatter
CHATTI n (in India) earthenware pot
CHATTIER > CHATTY
CHATTIES > CHATTY
CHATTIEST > CHATTY
CHATTILY > CHATTY
CHATTING > CHAT
CHATTIS > CHATTI
CHATTY adj (of a person) fond of friendly, informal conversation ▷ n (in India) earthenware pot
CHAUFE obsolete variant of > CHAFE
CHAUFED > CHAUFE
CHAUFER same as > CHAUFFER
CHAUFERS > CHAUFER
CHAUFES > CHAUFE
CHAUFF obsolete variant of > CHAFE
CHAUFFED > CHAUFF
CHAUFFER n small portable heater or stove
CHAUFFERS > CHAUFFER
CHAUFFEUR n person employed to drive a car for someone ▷ vb act as driver for (someone)
CHAUFFING > CHAUFF
CHAUFFS > CHAUFF
CHAUFING > CHAUFE
CHAUMER n chamber
CHAUMERS > CHAUMER
CHAUNCE archaic variant of > CHANCE
CHAUNCED > CHAUNCE
CHAUNCES > CHAUNCE
CHAUNCING > CHAUNCE
CHAUNGE archaic variant of > CHANGE
CHAUNGED > CHAUNGE
CHAUNGES > CHAUNGE
CHAUNGING > CHAUNGE
CHAUNT a less common variant of > CHANT
CHAUNTED > CHAUNT
CHAUNTER > CHAUNT
CHAUNTERS > CHAUNT
CHAUNTING > CHAUNT
CHAUNTRY same as > CHANTRY
CHAUNTS > CHAUNT
CHAUSSES n tight-fitting medieval garment covering the feet and legs, usually made of chain mail
CHAUSSURE n any type of footwear
CHAUVIN n chauvinist
CHAUVINS > CHAUVIN
CHAV n insulting word for a young working-class person who wears casual sports clothes
CHAVE vb old dialect term for "I have"
CHAVENDER n chub
CHAVETTE n insulting word for a young working-class woman who wears casual sports clothes

C

CHAVETTES > CHAVETTE
CHAVISH > CHAV
CHAVS > CHAV
CHAVVIER > CHAVVY
CHAVVIEST > CHAVVY
CHAVVY adj relating to or like a chav
CHAW vb chew (tobacco), esp without swallowing it ▷ n something chewed, esp a plug of tobacco
CHAWBACON n bumpkin
CHAWDRON n entrails
CHAWDRONS > CHAWDRON
CHAWED > CHAW
CHAWER > CHAW
CHAWERS > CHAW
CHAWING > CHAW
CHAWK n jackdaw
CHAWKS > CHAWK
CHAWS > CHAW
CHAY n plant of the madder family
CHAYA same as > CHAY
CHAYAS > CHAYA
CHAYOTE n tropical climbing plant
CHAYOTES > CHAYOTE
CHAYROOT n root of the chay plant
CHAYROOTS > CHAYROOT
CHAYS > CHAY
CHAZAN same as > CANTOR
CHAZANIM > CHAZAN
CHAZANS > CHAZAN
CHAZZAN variant of > CHAZAN
CHAZZANIM > CHAZZAN
CHAZZANS > CHAZZAN
CHAZZEN same as > CHAZZAN
CHAZZENIM > CHAZZEN
CHAZZENS > CHAZZEN
CHE pron dialectal form meaning 'I'
CHEAP adj costing relatively little ▷ adv at very little cost ▷ n bargain ▷ vb take the cheapest option
CHEAPED > CHEAP
CHEAPEN vb lower the reputation of
CHEAPENED > CHEAPEN
CHEAPENER > CHEAPEN
CHEAPENS > CHEAPEN
CHEAPER > CHEAP
CHEAPEST > CHEAP
CHEAPIE n something inexpensive
CHEAPIES > CHEAPIE
CHEAPING > CHEAP
CHEAPISH > CHEAP
CHEAPJACK n person who sells cheap and shoddy goods ▷ adj shoddy or inferior
CHEAPLY > CHEAP
CHEAPNESS > CHEAP
CHEAPO n very cheap and possibly shoddy thing
CHEAPOS > CHEAPO
CHEAPS > CHEAP
CHEAPSHOT n abusive remark
CHEAPY same as > CHEAPIE
CHEAT vb act dishonestly to gain profit or advantage ▷ n person who cheats

CHEATABLE > CHEAT
CHEATED > CHEAT
CHEATER > CHEAT
CHEATERS > CHEAT
CHEATERY n cheating
CHEATING > CHEAT
CHEATINGS > CHEAT
CHEATS > CHEAT
CHEBEC n type of boat
CHEBECS > CHEBEC
CHECHAKO same as > CHEECHAKO
CHECHAKOS > CHECHAKO
CHECHAQUO same as > CHEECHAKO
CHECHIA n Berber skullcap
CHECHIAS > CHECHIA
CHECK vb examine or investigate ▷ n control designed to ensure accuracy
CHECKABLE > CHECK
CHECKBOOK n American word for chequebook
CHECKBOX n small clickable box on a computer screen
CHECKED > CHECK
CHECKER same as > CHEQUER
CHECKERED same as > CHEQUERED
CHECKERS n game for two players using a checkerboard and small pieces
CHECKIER > CHECKY
CHECKIEST > CHECKY
CHECKING n act of checking
CHECKINGS > CHECKING
CHECKLESS adj without check or restraint
CHECKLIST vb check items, facts, etc, against those in a list used for verification
CHECKMARK vb make a mark of approval or verification
CHECKMATE n winning position in which an opponent's king is under attack and unable to escape ▷ vb place the king of (one's opponent) in checkmate ▷ interj call made when placing an opponent's king in checkmate
CHECKOFF n paying of an employee's union dues straight from their salary
CHECKOFFS > CHECKOFF
CHECKOUT n counter in a supermarket, where customers pay
CHECKOUTS > CHECKOUT
CHECKRAIL another word for > GUARDRAIL
CHECKREIN n bearing rein
CHECKROOM n place at a railway station, airport, etc, where luggage may be left for a small charge with an attendant for safekeeping
CHECKROW n row of plants, esp corn ▷ vb plant in checkrows
CHECKROWS > CHECKROW
CHECKS > CHECK
CHECKSTOP n roadside area where drivers are randomly breath-tested

CHECKSUM n digit attached to the end of a message to verify data
CHECKSUMS > CHECKSUM
CHECKUP n thorough medical examination
CHECKUPS > CHECKUP
CHECKY adj having squares of alternating tinctures or furs
CHEDARIM same as > CHADARIM
CHEDDAR n type of smooth hard yellow or whitish cheese
CHEDDARS > CHEDDAR
CHEDDARY adj like cheddar cheese
CHEDDITE n type of explosive
CHEDDITES > CHEDDITE
CHEDER n Jewish religious education
CHEDERS > CHEDER
CHEDITE same as > CHEDDITE
CHEDITES > CHEDITE
CHEECHAKO n local name for a newcomer to Alaska
CHEEK n either side of the face below the eye ▷ vb speak impudently to
CHEEKBONE n bone at the top of the cheek, just below the eye
CHEEKED > CHEEK
CHEEKFUL n quantity that can be held in a cheek
CHEEKFULS > CHEEKFUL
CHEEKIER > CHEEKY
CHEEKIEST > CHEEKY
CHEEKILY > CHEEKY
CHEEKING > CHEEK
CHEEKLESS > CHEEK
CHEEKS > CHEEK
CHEEKY adj impudent, disrespectful
CHEEP n young bird's high-pitched cry ▷ vb utter a cheep
CHEEPED > CHEEP
CHEEPER > CHEEP
CHEEPERS > CHEEP
CHEEPING > CHEEP
CHEEPS > CHEEP
CHEER vb applaud or encourage with shouts ▷ n shout of applause or encouragement
CHEERED > CHEER
CHEERER > CHEER
CHEERERS > CHEER
CHEERFUL adj having a happy disposition
CHEERIER > CHEERY
CHEERIEST > CHEERY
CHEERILY > CHEERY
CHEERING n act of cheering
CHEERINGS > CHEERING
CHEERIO interj goodbye ▷ n small red cocktail sausage ▷ sentence substitute farewell greeting
CHEERIOS > CHEERIO
CHEERLEAD vb lead a crowd in formal cheers at sports events

CHEERLED > CHEERLEAD
CHEERLESS adj dreary, gloomy
CHEERLY adv cheerfully
CHEERO same as > CHEERIO
CHEEROS > CHEERO
CHEERS interj drinking toast ▷ sentence substitute drinking toast
CHEERY adj cheerful
CHEESE n food made from coagulated milk curd ▷ vb stop
CHEESED > CHEESE
CHEESES > CHEESE
CHEESEVAT n in cheese-making, vat in which curds are formed and cut
CHEESIER > CHEESY
CHEESIEST > CHEESY
CHEESILY > CHEESY
CHEESING > CHEESE
CHEESY adj like cheese
CHEETAH n large fast-running spotted African wild cat
CHEETAHS > CHEETAH
CHEEWINK same as > CHEWINK
CHEEWINKS > CHEEWINK
CHEF n cook in a restaurant ▷ vb work as a chef
CHEFDOM n state or condition of being a chef
CHEFDOMS > CHEFDOM
CHEFED > CHEF
CHEFFED > CHEF
CHEFFIER > CHEFFY
CHEFFIEST > CHEFFY
CHEFFING > CHEF
CHEFFY adj relating to or characteristic of chefs
CHEFING > CHEF
CHEFS > CHEF
CHEGOE same as > CHIGGER
CHEGOES > CHEGOE
CHEILITIS n inflammation of the lip(s)
CHEKA n secret police set up in Russia in 1917
CHEKAS > CHEKA
CHEKIST n member of the cheka
CHEKISTS > CHEKIST
CHELA n disciple of a religious teacher
CHELAE > CHELA
CHELAS > CHELA
CHELASHIP > CHELA
CHELATE n coordination compound ▷ adj of or possessing chelae ▷ vb form a chelate
CHELATED > CHELATE
CHELATES > CHELATE
CHELATING > CHELATE
CHELATION n process by which a chelate is formed
CHELATOR > CHELATE
CHELATORS > CHELATE
CHELICERA n one of a pair of appendages on the head of spiders and other arachnids: often modified as food-catching claws
CHELIFORM adj shaped like a chela

CHELIPED n (on a arthropod) either of two legs which each carry a claw

CHELIPEDS > CHELIPED

CHELLUP n noise

CHELLUPS > CHELLUP

CHELOID a variant spelling of > KELOID

CHELOIDAL > CHELOID

CHELOIDS > CHELOID

CHELONE n hardy N American plant

CHELONES > CHELONE

CHELONIAN n type of reptile such as the tortoises and turtles, in which most of the body is enclosed in a protective bony capsule

CHELP vb (esp of women or children) to chatter or speak out of turn

CHELPED > CHELP

CHELPING > CHELP

CHELPS > CHELP

CHEM n chemistry

CHEMIC vb bleach ▷ n chemist

CHEMICAL n substance used in or resulting from a reaction involving changes to atoms or molecules ▷ adj of chemistry or chemicals

CHEMICALS > CHEMICAL

CHEMICKED > CHEMIC

CHEMICS > CHEMIC

CHEMISE n woman's loose-fitting slip

CHEMISES > CHEMISE

CHEMISM n chemical action

CHEMISMS > CHEMISM

CHEMISORB vb take up (a substance) by chemisorption

CHEMIST n shop selling medicines and cosmetics

CHEMISTRY n science of the composition, properties, and reactions of substances

CHEMISTS > CHEMIST

CHEMITYPE n process by which a relief impression is obtained from an engraving

CHEMITYPY > CHEMITYPE

CHEMMIES > CHEMMY

CHEMMY n gambling card game

CHEMO n short form of chemotherapy

CHEMOKINE n type of protein

CHEMOS > CHEMO

CHEMOSORB same as > CHEMISORB

CHEMOSTAT n apparatus for growing bacterial cultures at a constant rate by controlling the supply of nutrient medium

CHEMPADUK n Malaysian evergreen tree

CHEMS > CHEM

CHEMSEX n sex while on drugs

CHEMSEXES > CHEMSEX

CHEMTRAIL n supposed vapour trail containing toxic chemicals

CHEMURGIC > CHEMURGY

CHEMURGY n branch of chemistry

CHENAR n oriental plane tree

CHENARS > CHENAR

CHENET another word for > GENIP

CHENETS > CHENET

CHENILLE n (fabric of) thick tufty yarn

CHENILLES > CHENILLE

CHENIX n ancient measure, slightly more than a quart

CHENIXES > CHENIX

CHENOPOD n plant of the beetroot family

CHENOPODS > CHENOPOD

CHEONGSAM n straight dress, usually of silk or cotton, with a stand-up collar and a slit in one side of the skirt, worn by Chinese women

CHEQUE n written order to one's bank to pay money from one's account

CHEQUER n piece used in Chinese chequers ▷ vb make irregular in colour or character

CHEQUERED adj marked by varied fortunes

CHEQUERS n game of draughts

CHEQUES > CHEQUE

CHEQUIER > CHEQUY

CHEQUIEST > CHEQUY

CHEQUING adj as in chequing account (in Canada) account against which cheques can be drawn

CHEQUY same as > CHECKY

CHER adj dear or expensive

CHERALITE n rare phosphate-silicate of thorium and calcium

CHERE feminine variant of > CHER

CHERIMOYA n large tropical fruit with cream-coloured flesh

CHERISH vb cling to (an idea or feeling)

CHERISHED > CHERISH

CHERISHER > CHERISH

CHERISHES > CHERISH

CHERMOULA n type of marinade used in N African cookery

CHERNOZEM n black soil, rich in humus and carbonates, in cool or temperate semiarid regions, as the grasslands of Russia

CHEROOT n cigar with both ends cut flat

CHEROOTS > CHEROOT

CHERRIED > CHERRY

CHERRIER > CHERRY

CHERRIES > CHERRY

CHERRIEST > CHERRY

CHERRY n small red or black fruit with a stone ▷ adj deep red ▷ vb cheer

CHERRYING > CHERRY

CHERT n microcrystalline form of silica

CHERTIER > CHERT

CHERTIEST > CHERT

CHERTS > CHERT

CHERTY > CHERT

CHERUB n angel, often represented as a winged child

CHERUBIC > CHERUB

CHERUBIM > CHERUB

CHERUBIMS > CHERUB

CHERUBIN n cherub ▷ adj cherubic

CHERUBINS > CHERUBIN

CHERUBS > CHERUB

CHERUP same as > CHIRRUP

CHERUPED > CHERUP

CHERUPING > CHERUP

CHERUPS > CHERUP

CHERVIL n aniseed-flavoured herb

CHERVILS > CHERVIL

CHESHIRE n breed of American pig

CHESHIRES > CHESHIRE

CHESIL n gravel or shingle

CHESILS > CHESIL

CHESNUT rare variant of > CHESTNUT

CHESNUTS > CHESNUT

CHESS n board game for two players

CHESSEL n mould used in cheese-making

CHESSELS > CHESSEL

CHESSES > CHESS

CHESSMAN n piece used in chess

CHESSMEN > CHESSMAN

CHEST n front of the body, from neck to waist ▷ vb hit with the chest, as with a ball in football

CHESTED > CHEST

CHESTFUL n amount a chest will hold

CHESTFULS > CHESTFUL

CHESTIER > CHESTY

CHESTIEST > CHESTY

CHESTILY > CHESTY

CHESTING > CHEST

CHESTNUT n reddish-brown edible nut ▷ adj (of hair or a horse) reddish-brown

CHESTNUTS > CHESTNUT

CHESTS > CHEST

CHESTY adj symptomatic of chest disease

CHETAH same as > CHEETAH

CHETAHS > CHETAH

CHETH same as > HETH

CHETHS > CHETH

CHETNIK n member of a Serbian nationalist paramilitary group

CHETNIKS > CHETNIK

CHETRUM n monetary unit in Bhutan

CHETRUMS > CHETRUM

CHEVAL n as in cheval glass full-length mirror that can swivel

CHEVALET n bridge of a stringed musical instrument

CHEVALETS > CHEVALET

CHEVALIER n member of the French Legion of Honour

CHEVELURE n nebulous part of the tail of a comet

CHEVEN n chub

CHEVENS > CHEVEN

CHEVEREL n kid or goatskin leather

CHEVERELS > CHEVEREL

CHEVERIL same as > CHEVEREL

CHEVERILS > CHEVERIL

CHEVERON same as > CHEVRON

CHEVERONS > CHEVERON

CHEVERYE same as > CHIEFERY

CHEVERYES > CHEVERYE

CHEVET n semicircular or polygonal east end of a church

CHEVETS > CHEVET

CHEVIED > CHEVY

CHEVIES > CHEVY

CHEVILLE n peg of a stringed musical instrument

CHEVILLES > CHEVILLE

CHEVIN same as > CHEVEN

CHEVINS > CHEVIN

CHEVIOT n type of British sheep reared for its wool

CHEVIOTS > CHEVIOT

CHEVRE n any cheese made from goats' milk

CHEVRES > CHEVRE

CHEVRET n type of goats' cheese

CHEVRETS > CHEVRET

CHEVRETTE n skin of a young goat

CHEVRON n V-shaped pattern ▷ vb make a chevron

CHEVRONED > CHEVRON

CHEVRONS > CHEVRON

CHEVRONY adj in heraldry, bearing chevrons

CHEVROTIN n soft goat's cheese

CHEVY same as > CHIVY

CHEVYING > CHEVY

CHEW vb grind (food) between the teeth ▷ n act of chewing

CHEWABLE > CHEW

CHEWED > CHEW

CHEWER > CHEW

CHEWERS > CHEW

CHEWET n type of meat pie

CHEWETS > CHEWET

CHEWIE n chewing gum

CHEWIER > CHEWY

CHEWIES > CHEWY

CHEWIEST > CHEWY

CHEWINESS > CHEWY

CHEWING > CHEW

CHEWINK n towhee

CHEWINKS > CHEWINK

CHEWS > CHEW

CHEWY adj requiring a lot of chewing ▷ n dog's rubber toy

CHEZ prep at the home of

CHHERTUM same as > CHETRUM

CHI n 22nd letter of the Greek alphabet

CHIA n plant of the mint family

CHIACK vb tease or banter ▷ n good-humoured banter

CHIACKED > CHIACK

CHIACKING > CHIACK

CHIACKS > CHIACK

CHIANTI n dry red Italian wine

CHIANTIS > CHIANTI

C

C

CHIAO n Chinese coin equal to one tenth of one yuan
CHIAOS > CHIAO
CHIAREZZA n (in music) clarity
CHIAREZZE > CHIAREZZA
CHIAS > CHIA
CHIASM same as **>** CHIASMA
CHIASMA n biological term
CHIASMAL > CHIASMA
CHIASMAS > CHIASMA
CHIASMATA > CHIASMA
CHIASMI > CHIASMUS
CHIASMIC > CHIASMUS
CHIASMS > CHIASM
CHIASMUS n reversal of the order of words in the second of two parallel phrases
CHIASTIC > CHIASMUS
CHIAUS same as **>** CHOUSE
CHIAUSED > CHIAUS
CHIAUSES > CHIAUS
CHIAUSING > CHIAUS
CHIB vb in Scots English, stab or slash with a sharp weapon ▷ n sharp weapon
CHIBBED > CHIB
CHIBBING > CHIB
CHIBOL n spring onion
CHIBOLS > CHIBOL
CHIBOUK n Turkish tobacco pipe with an extremely long stem
CHIBOUKS > CHIBOUK
CHIBOUQUE same as **>** CHIBOUK
CHIBS > CHIB
CHIC adj stylish, elegant ▷ n stylishness, elegance
CHICA n Spanish young girl
CHICALOTE n type of poppy of the southwestern US and Mexico with prickly leaves and white or yellow flowers
CHICANA n female chicano
CHICANAS > CHICANA
CHICANE n obstacle in a motor-racing circuit ▷ vb deceive or trick by chicanery
CHICANED > CHICANE
CHICANER > CHICANE
CHICANERS > CHICANE
CHICANERY n trickery, deception
CHICANES > CHICANE
CHICANING > CHICANE
CHICANO n American citizen of Mexican origin
CHICANOS > CHICANO
CHICAS > CHICA
CHICCORY a variant spelling of **>** CHICORY
CHICER > CHIC
CHICEST > CHIC
CHICH another word for **>** CHICKPEA
CHICHA n Andean drink made from fermented maize
CHICHAS > CHICHA
CHICHES > CHICH
CHICHI adj affectedly pretty or stylish ▷ n quality of being affectedly pretty or stylish
CHICHIER > CHICHI
CHICHIEST > CHICHI
CHICHIS > CHICHI
CHICK n baby bird

CHICKADEE n small North American songbird
CHICKAREE n American red squirrel
CHICKEE n open-sided, thatched building on stilts
CHICKEES > CHICKEE
CHICKEN n domestic fowl ▷ adj cowardly ▷ vb lose one's nerve
CHICKENED > CHICKEN
CHICKENS > CHICKEN
CHICKLING n small chick
CHICKORY same as **>** CHICORY
CHICKPEA n edible yellow pealike seed
CHICKPEAS > CHICKPEA
CHICKS > CHICK
CHICKWEED n weed with small white flowers
CHICLE n gumlike substance obtained from the sapodilla
CHICLES > CHICLE
CHICLY > CHIC
CHICNESS > CHIC
CHICO n spiny chenopodiaceous shrub
CHICON same as **>** CHICORY
CHICONS > CHICON
CHICORIES > CHICORY
CHICORY n plant whose leaves are used in salads
CHICOS > CHICO
CHICOT n dead tree
CHICOTS > CHICOT
CHICS > CHIC
CHID > CHIDE
CHIDDEN > CHIDE
CHIDE vb rebuke, scold
CHIDED > CHIDE
CHIDER > CHIDE
CHIDERS > CHIDE
CHIDES > CHIDE
CHIDING > CHIDE
CHIDINGLY > CHIDE
CHIDINGS > CHIDE
CHIDLINGS n intestines of a pig prepared as a dish
CHIEF n head of a group of people ▷ adj most important
CHIEFDOM n any tribal social group led by a chief
CHIEFDOMS > CHIEFDOM
CHIEFER > CHIEF
CHIEFERY n lands belonging to a chief
CHIEFESS n female chief
CHIEFEST > CHIEF
CHIEFLESS adj lacking a chief
CHIEFLING n petty chief
CHIEFLY adv especially ▷ adj of or relating to a chief or chieftain
CHIEFRIES > CHIEFRY
CHIEFRY same as **>** CHIEFERY
CHIEFS > CHIEF
CHIEFSHIP n state of being a chief
CHIEFTAIN n leader of a tribe
CHIEL n young man
CHIELD same as **>** CHIEL
CHIELDS > CHIELD

CHIELS > CHIEL
CHIFFON n fine see-through fabric ▷ adj made of chiffon
CHIFFONS > CHIFFON
CHIFFONY adj like chiffon
CHIGETAI n variety of the Asiatic wild ass of Mongolia
CHIGETAIS > CHIGETAI
CHIGGA n derogatory word for a young working-class Tasmanian
CHIGGAS > CHIGGA
CHIGGER n parasitic larva of various mites
CHIGGERS > CHIGGER
CHIGNON n knot of hair pinned up at the back of the head ▷ vb make a chignon
CHIGNONED > CHIGNON
CHIGNONS > CHIGNON
CHIGOE same as **>** CHIGGER
CHIGOES > CHIGOE
CHIGRE same as **>** CHIGGER
CHIGRES > CHIGRE
CHIHUAHUA n tiny short-haired dog
CHIK n slatted blind
CHIKARA n Indian seven-stringed musical instrument
CHIKARAS > CHIKARA
CHIKHOR same as **>** CHUKAR
CHIKHORS > CHIKHOR
CHIKOR same as **>** CHUKAR
CHIKORS > CHIKOR
CHIKS > CHIK
CHILBLAIN n inflammation of the fingers or toes, caused by exposure to cold
CHILD n young human being, boy or girl ▷ vb give birth
CHILDBED n condition of giving birth to a child
CHILDBEDS > CHILDBED
CHILDCARE n care provided for children without homes (or with a seriously disturbed home life) by a local authority
CHILDE n young man of noble birth
CHILDED > CHILD
CHILDER dialect variant of **>** CHILDREN
CHILDES > CHILDE
CHILDHOOD n time or condition of being a child
CHILDING > CHILD
CHILDISH adj immature, silly
CHILDLESS > CHILD
CHILDLIER > CHILD
CHILDLIKE adj innocent, trustful
CHILDLY > CHILD
CHILDNESS n nature of a child
CHILDREN > CHILD
CHILDS > CHILD
CHILE a variant spelling of **>** CHILLI
CHILES > CHILE
CHILI same as **>** CHILLI
CHILIAD n group of one thousand
CHILIADAL > CHILIAD

CHILIADIC > CHILIAD
CHILIADS > CHILIAD
CHILIAGON n thousand-sided polygon
CHILIARCH n commander of a thousand men
CHILIASM n belief in the Second Coming of Christ
CHILIASMS > CHILIASM
CHILIAST > CHILIASM
CHILIASTS > CHILIASM
CHILIDOG n hot dog served with chilli sauce
CHILIDOGS > CHILIDOG
CHILIES > CHILI
CHILIS > CHILI
CHILL n feverish cold ▷ vb make (something) cool or cold ▷ adj unpleasantly cold
CHILLADA n spicy Mexican dish made of fried vegetables and pulses
CHILLADAS > CHILLADA
CHILLAX vb take rest or recreation, as from work
CHILLAXED > CHILLAX
CHILLAXES > CHILLAX
CHILLED > CHILL
CHILLER n cooling or refrigerating device
CHILLERS > CHILLER
CHILLEST > CHILL
CHILLI n small red or green hot-tasting capsicum pod, used in cooking
CHILLIER > CHILLY
CHILLIES > CHILLI
CHILLIEST > CHILLY
CHILLILY > CHILLY
CHILLING > CHILL
CHILLINGS > CHILL
CHILLIS > CHILLI
CHILLNESS > CHILL
CHILLS > CHILL
CHILLUM n short pipe used for smoking
CHILLUMS > CHILLUM
CHILLY adj moderately cold
CHILOPOD n type of arthropod of the class which includes the centipedes
CHILOPODS > CHILOPOD
CHILTEPIN n variety of chilli pepper
CHIMAERA same as **>** CHIMERA
CHIMAERAS > CHIMAERA
CHIMAERIC > CHIMAERA
CHIMAR same as **>** CHIMERE
CHIMARS > CHIMAR
CHIMB same as **>** CHIME
CHIMBLEY same as **>** CHIMNEY
CHIMBLEYS > CHIMBLEY
CHIMBLIES > CHIMBLY
CHIMBLY same as **>** CHIMNEY
CHIMBS > CHIMB
CHIME n musical ringing sound of a bell or clock ▷ vb make a musical ringing sound
CHIMED > CHIME
CHIMENEA n freestanding outdoor fireplace
CHIMENEAS > CHIMENEA
CHIMER > CHIME

CHIMERA *n* unrealistic hope or idea

CHIMERAS > CHIMERA

CHIMERE *n* gown worn by bishops

CHIMERES > CHIMERE

CHIMERIC *same as* **>** CHIMERA

CHIMERID *n* fish of the genus Chimaera

CHIMERIDS > CHIMERID

CHIMERISM *n* medical condition in which a person possesses two genetically distinct sets of cells

CHIMERS > CHIME

CHIMES > CHIME

CHIMINEA *n* free-standing outdoor fireplace with a rounded body

CHIMINEAS > CHIMINEA

CHIMING > CHIME

CHIMLA *same as* **>** CHIMNEY

CHIMLAS > CHIMLA

CHIMLEY *same as* **>** CHIMNEY

CHIMLEYS > CHIMLEY

CHIMNEY *n* hollow vertical structure for carrying away smoke from a fire ▷ *vb* climb two vertical, parallel, chimney-like rock faces

CHIMNEYED > CHIMNEY

CHIMNEYS > CHIMNEY

CHIMO *interj* Inuit greeting and toast

CHIMP *n* chimpanzee

CHIMPS > CHIMP

CHIN *n* part of the face below the mouth ▷ *vb* hit someone in the chin

CHINA *n* fine earthenware or porcelain

CHINAMAN *n* type of ball bowled in cricket

CHINAMEN > CHINAMAN

CHINAMPA *n* in Mesoamerican agriculture, an artificially created island used for growing crops

CHINAMPAS > CHINAMPA

CHINAR *same as* **>** CHENAR

CHINAROOT *n* bristly greenbrier

CHINARS > CHINAR

CHINAS > CHINA

CHINAWARE *n* articles made of china, esp those made for domestic use

CHINBONE *n* front part of the mandible which forms the chin

CHINBONES > CHINBONE

CHINCAPIN *n* dwarf chestnut tree

CHINCH *n* (S US) bedbug ▷ *vb* be frugal or miserly

CHINCHED > CHINCH

CHINCHES > CHINCH

CHINCHIER > CHINCHY

CHINCHING > CHINCH

CHINCHY *adj* tightfisted

CHINCOUGH *n* whooping cough

CHINDIT *n* Allied soldier fighting behind the Japanese lines in Burma during World War II

CHINDITS > CHINDIT

CHINE *same as* **>** CHIME

CHINED > CHINE

CHINES > CHINE

CHINESE *adj* of or relating to China

CHING *n* high-pitched ring or chime

CHINGS > CHING

CHINING > CHINE

CHINK *n* small narrow opening ▷ *vb* make a light ringing sound

CHINKAPIN *same as* **>** CHINCAPIN

CHINKARA *n* Indian gazelle

CHINKARAS > CHINKARA

CHINKED > CHINK

CHINKIE *n* offensive term for a (takeaway) meal of Chinese food

CHINKIER > CHINK

CHINKIES > CHINKIE

CHINKIEST > CHINK

CHINKING > CHINK

CHINKS > CHINK

CHINKY > CHINK

CHINLESS *adj* having a receding chin

CHINNED > CHIN

CHINNING > CHIN

CHINO *n* durable cotton twill cloth

CHINOIS *n* conical sieve

CHINOISES > CHINOIS

CHINONE *n* benzoquinone

CHINONES > CHINONE

CHINOOK *n* wind found in the Rocky Mountains

CHINOOKS > CHINOOK

CHINOS *pl n* trousers made of a kind of hard-wearing cotton

CHINOVNIK *n* Russian official or bureaucrat

CHINS > CHIN

CHINSE *vb* fill the seams of a boat

CHINSED > CHINSE

CHINSES > CHINSE

CHINSING > CHINSE

CHINSTRAP *n* strap on a helmet which fastens under the chin

CHINTS *obsolete variant of* **>** CHINTZ

CHINTSES > CHINTS

CHINTZ *n* printed cotton fabric with a glazed finish

CHINTZES > CHINTZ

CHINTZIER > CHINTZY

CHINTZILY *adv* gaudily

CHINTZY *adj* of or covered with chintz

CHINWAG *n* chat

CHINWAGS > CHINWAG

CHIP *n* strip of potato, fried in deep fat ▷ *vb* break small pieces from

CHIPBOARD *n* thin board made of compressed wood particles

CHIPMAKER *n* maker of microchips

CHIPMUCK *another word for* **>** CHIPMUNK

CHIPMUCKS > CHIPMUCK

CHIPMUNK *n* small squirrel-like N American rodent with a striped back

CHIPMUNKS > CHIPMUNK

CHIPOCHIA *same as* **>** CAPOCCHIA

CHIPOLATA *n* small sausage

CHIPOTLE *n* dried chilli pepper

CHIPOTLES > CHIPOTLE

CHIPPABLE > CHIP

CHIPPED > CHIP

CHIPPER *vb* chirp or chatter ▷ *adj* cheerful, lively

CHIPPERED > CHIPPER

CHIPPERER > CHIPPER

CHIPPERS > CHIPPER

CHIPPIE *same as* **>** CHIPPY

CHIPPIER > CHIPPY

CHIPPIES > CHIPPY

CHIPPIEST > CHIPPY

CHIPPING > CHIP

CHIPPINGS > CHIP

CHIPPY *n* fish-and-chip shop ▷ *adj* resentful or oversensitive about being perceived as inferior

CHIPS > CHIP

CHIPSET *n* highly integrated circuit on the motherboard of a computer

CHIPSETS > CHIPSET

CHIRAGRA *n* gout occurring in the hands

CHIRAGRAS > CHIRAGRA

CHIRAGRIC > CHIRAGRA

CHIRAL > CHIRALITY

CHIRALITY *n* configuration or handedness (left or right) of an asymmetric, optically active chemical compound

CHIRIMOYA *same as* **>** CHERIMOYA

CHIRK *vb* creak, like a door ▷ *adj* spritely; high-spirited

CHIRKED > CHIRK

CHIRKER > CHIRK

CHIRKEST > CHIRK

CHIRKING > CHIRK

CHIRKS > CHIRK

CHIRL *vb* warble

CHIRLED > CHIRL

CHIRLING > CHIRL

CHIRLS > CHIRL

CHIRM *n* chirping of birds ▷ *vb* (esp of a bird) to chirp

CHIRMED > CHIRM

CHIRMING > CHIRM

CHIRMS > CHIRM

CHIRO *n* informal name for chiropractor

CHIROLOGY *n* palmistry

CHIRONOMY *n* art of hand movement in oratory or theatrical performance

CHIROPODY *n* treatment of the feet, esp the treatment of corns, verrucas, etc

CHIROPTER *n* type of bat

CHIROS > CHIRO

CHIRP *vb* (of a bird or insect) make a short high-pitched sound ▷ *n* chirping sound

CHIRPED > CHIRP

CHIRPER > CHIRP

CHIRPERS > CHIRP

CHIRPIER > CHIRPY

CHIRPIEST > CHIRPY

CHIRPILY > CHIRPY

CHIRPING *n* act of chirping

CHIRPINGS > CHIRPING

CHIRPS > CHIRP

CHIRPY *adj* lively and cheerful

CHIRR *vb* (esp of certain insects, such as crickets) to make a shrill trilled sound ▷ *n* sound of chirring

CHIRRE *same as* **>** CHIRR

CHIRRED > CHIRR

CHIRREN *pl n* dialect form of children

CHIRRES > CHIRRE

CHIRRING > CHIRR

CHIRRS > CHIRR

CHIRRUP *vb* (of some birds) to chirp repeatedly ▷ *n* chirruping sound

CHIRRUPED > CHIRRUP

CHIRRUPER > CHIRRUP

CHIRRUPS > CHIRRUP

CHIRRUPY *adj* making chirping sounds

CHIRT *vb* squirt

CHIRTED > CHIRT

CHIRTING > CHIRT

CHIRTS > CHIRT

CHIRU *n* Tibetan antelope

CHIRUS > CHIRU

CHIS > CHI

CHISEL *n* metal tool with a sharp end for shaping wood or stone ▷ *vb* carve or form with a chisel

CHISELED *same as* **>** CHISELLED

CHISELER > CHISEL

CHISELERS > CHISEL

CHISELING > CHISEL

CHISELLED *adj* finely or sharply formed

CHISELLER *n* person who uses a chisel

CHISELS > CHISEL

CHIT *n* short official note, such as a receipt ▷ *vb* sprout

CHITAL *n* type of deer

CHITALS > CHITAL

CHITCHAT *n* chat, gossip ▷ *vb* gossip

CHITCHATS > CHITCHAT

CHITIN *n* outer layer of the bodies of arthropods

CHITINOID > CHITIN

CHITINOUS > CHITIN

CHITINS > CHITIN

CHITLIN *n* pig intestine cooked and served as a dish

CHITLING > CHITLINGS

CHITLINGS *same as* **>** CHIDLINGS

CHITLINS > CHITLIN

CHITON *n* (in ancient Greece and Rome) a loose woollen tunic

CHITONS > CHITON

CHITOSAN *n* polysaccharide derived from chitin

CHITOSANS > CHITOSAN

CHITS > CHIT

CHITTED > CHIT

CHITTER *vb* twitter or chirp

CHITTERED > CHITTER

c

CHITTERS > CHITTER
CHITTIER > CHITTY
CHTTTIES > CHITTY
CHITTIEST > CHITT
CHITTING > CHIT
CHITTY adj childish ▷ vb
sprout
CHIV n knife ▷ vb stab
(someone)
CHIVALRIC > CHIVALRY
CHIVALRY n courteous
behaviour, esp by men
towards women
CHIVAREE n charivari ▷ vb
perform a chivaree
CHIVAREED > CHIVAREE
CHIVAREES > CHIVAREE
CHIVARI same as
> CHARIVARI
CHIVARIED > CHIVARI
CHIVARIES > CHIVARI
CHIVE n small Eurasian
plant ▷ vb file or cut off
CHIVED > CHIVE
CHIVES same as > CHIVE
CHIVIED > CHIVY
CHIVIES > CHIVY
CHIVING > CHIVE
CHIVS > CHIV
CHIVVED > CHIV
CHIVVIED > CHIVVY
CHIVVIES > CHIVVY
CHIVVING > CHIV
CHIVVY same as > CHIVY
CHIVVYING > CHIVVY
CHIVY vb harass or nag ▷ n
hunt
CHIVYING > CHIVY
CHIWEENIE n cross
between a chihuahua and a
dachshund
CHIYOGAMI n type of highly
decorated Japanese craft
paper
CHIZ n cheat ▷ vb cheat
CHIZZ same as > CHIZ
CHIZZED > CHIZ
CHIZZES > CHIZ
CHIZZING > CHIZ
CHLAMYDES > CHLAMYS
CHLAMYDIA n type of
bacteria
CHLAMYS n woollen cloak
worn by ancient Greek
soldiers
CHLAMYSES > CHLAMYS
CHLOASMA n patches of
darker colour on a person's
skin
CHLOASMAS > CHLOASMA
CHLORACNE n disfiguring
skin disease that results from
contact with or ingestion or
inhalation of certain
chlorinated aromatic
hydrocarbons
CHLORAL n colourless oily
liquid with a pungent odour
CHLORALS > CHLORAL
CHLORATE n type of
chemical salt
CHLORATES > CHLORATE
CHLORDAN same as
> CHLORDANE
CHLORDANE n white
insoluble toxic solid
CHLORDANS > CHLORDAN

CHLORELLA n type of
microscopic unicellular
green alga, some species of
which are used in the
preparation of human food
CHLORIC adj of or
containing chlorine in the
pentavalent state
CHLORID n type of chlorine
compound
CHLORIDE n compound of
chlorine and another
substance
CHLORIDES > CHLORIDE
CHLORIDIC > CHLORIDE
CHLORIDS > CHLORID
CHLORIN same as
> CHLORINE
CHLORINE n strong-
smelling greenish-yellow
gaseous element, used to
disinfect water
CHLORINES > CHLORINE
CHLORINS > CHLORIN
CHLORITE n any of a group
of green soft secondary
minerals
CHLORITES > CHLORITE
CHLORITIC > CHLORITE
CHLOROSES > CHLOROSIS
CHLOROSIS n disorder,
formerly common in
adolescent girls,
characterized by pale
greenish-yellow skin,
weakness, and palpitation
and caused by insufficient
iron in the body
CHLOROTIC > CHLOROSIS
CHLOROUS adj of or
containing chlorine in the
trivalent state
CHOANA n posterior nasal
aperture
CHOANAE > CHOANA
CHOBDAR n in India and
Nepal, king's macebearer or
attendant
CHOBDARS > CHOBDAR
CHOC short form of
> CHOCOLATE
CHOCCIER > CHOCCY
CHOCCIES > CHOCCY
CHOCCIEST > CHOCCY
CHOCCY n chocolate ▷ adj
made of, tasting of, smelling
of, or resembling chocolate
CHOCHO same as > CHAYOTE
CHOCHOS > CHOCHO
CHOCK n block or wedge used
to prevent a heavy object
from moving ▷ vb secure by
a chock ▷ adv as closely or
tightly as possible
CHOCKED > CHOCK
CHOCKER adj full up
CHOCKERS adj Australian
term meaning full up, packed
CHOCKFUL adj filled to
capacity
CHOCKFULL variant of
> CHOCKFUL
CHOCKIE n chocolate ▷ adj
like chocolate
CHOCKIER > CHOCKIE
CHOCKIES > CHOCKIE
CHOCKIEST > CHOCKIE
CHOCKING > CHOCK

CHOCKO same as > CHOCO
CHOCKOS > CHOCKO
CHOCKS > CHOCK
CHOCKY n chocolate ▷ adj
like chocolate
CHOCO n member of the
Australian army
CHOCOLATE n sweet food
made from cacao seeds ▷ adj
dark brown
CHOCOLATY > CHOCOLATE
CHOCOS > CHOCO
CHOCS > CHOC
CHOCTAW n movement in
ice-skating
CHOCTAWS > CHOCTAW
CHODE > CHIDE
CHOENIX same as > CHENIX
CHOENIXES > CHOENIX
CHOG n core of a piece of fruit
CHOGS > CHOG
CHOICE n choosing ▷ adj of
high quality
CHOICEFUL adj fickle
CHOICELY > CHOICE
CHOICER > CHOICE
CHOICES > CHOICE
CHOICEST > CHOICE
CHOIL n end of a knife blade
next to the handle
CHOILS > CHOIL
CHOIR n organized group of
singers, esp in church ▷ vb
sing in chorus
CHOIRBOY n boy who sings
in a church choir
CHOIRBOYS > CHOIRBOY
CHOIRED > CHOIR
CHOIRGIRL n girl who sings
in a choir
CHOIRING > CHOIR
CHOIRLIKE > CHOIR
CHOIRMAN n man who sings
in a choir
CHOIRMEN > CHOIRMAN
CHOIRS > CHOIR
CHOKE vb hinder or stop the
breathing of (a person) by
strangling or smothering ▷ n
device found in a petrol
engine
CHOKEABLE > CHOKE
CHOKEBORE n shotgun bore
that becomes narrower
towards the muzzle so that
the shot is not scattered
CHOKECOIL n type of
electronic inductor
CHOKED adj disappointed or
angry
CHOKEDAMP another word for
> BLACKDAMP
CHOKEHOLD n act of holding
a person's neck across the
windpipe, esp from behind
CHOKER n tight-fitting
necklace
CHOKERMAN n person who
attaches cables to logs
CHOKERMEN > CHOKERMAN
CHOKERS > CHOKER
CHOKES > CHOKE
CHOKEY n slang word for
prison ▷ adj involving,
caused by, or causing
choking
CHOKEYS > CHOKEY

CHOKIDAR n in India, a
gatekeeper
CHOKIDARS > CHOKIDAR
CHOKIER > CHOKEY
CHOKIES > CHOKY
CHOKIEST > CHOKEY
CHOKING > CHOKE
CHOKINGLY > CHOKE
CHOKO n pear-shaped fruit of
a tropical American vine,
eaten as a vegetable
CHOKOS > CHOKO
CHOKRA n in India, a boy or
young man
CHOKRAS > CHOKRA
CHOKRI n in India, a girl or
young woman
CHOKRIS > CHOKRI
CHOKY same as > CHOKEY
CHOLA n Hispanic girl
CHOLAEMIA n toxic medical
condition indicated by the
presence of bile in the blood
CHOLAEMIC > CHOLAEMIA
CHOLAS > CHOLA
CHOLATE n salt of cholic acid
CHOLATES > CHOLATE
CHOLECYST n gall bladder
CHOLELITH n gallstone
CHOLEMIA same as
> CHOLAEMIA
CHOLEMIAS > CHOLEMIA
CHOLENT n meal prepared
on Friday and left to cook
until eaten for Sabbath lunch
CHOLENTS > CHOLENT
CHOLER n bad temper
CHOLERA n serious
infectious disease
CHOLERAIC > CHOLERA
CHOLERAS > CHOLERA
CHOLERIC adj bad-
tempered
CHOLEROID > CHOLERA
CHOLERS > CHOLER
CHOLI n short-sleeved
bodice, as worn by Indian
women
CHOLIAMB n imperfect
iambic trimeter, with a
spondee as the last foot
CHOLIAMBS > CHOLIAMB
CHOLIC adj as in cholic acid
crystalline acid found in bile
CHOLINE n colourless
viscous soluble alkaline
substance present in animal
tissues
CHOLINES > CHOLINE
CHOLIS > CHOLI
CHOLLA n type of spiny
cactus
CHOLLAS > CHOLLA
CHOLLERS pl n jowls or
cheeks
CHOLO n chicano gangster
CHOLOS > CHOLO
CHOLTRIES > CHOLTRY
CHOLTRY n caravanserai
CHOMETZ same as
> CHAMETZ
CHOMETZES > CHOMETZ
CHOMMIE n (in informal
South African English) friend
CHOMMIES > CHOMMIE
CHOMP vb chew noisily ▷ n
act or sound of chewing in
this manner

CHOMPED > CHOMP
CHOMPER > CHOMP
CHOMPERS > CHOMP
CHOMPING > CHOMP
CHOMPS > CHOMP
CHON n North and South Korean monetary unit
CHONDRAL adj of or relating to cartilage
CHONDRE another word for > CHONDRULE
CHONDRES > CHONDRE
CHONDRI > CHONDRUS
CHONDRIFY vb become or convert into cartilage
CHONDRIN n resilient translucent bluish-white substance that forms the matrix of cartilage
CHONDRINS > CHONDRIN
CHONDRITE n stony meteorite consisting mainly of silicate minerals in the form of chondrules
CHONDROID adj resembling cartilage
CHONDROMA n benign cartilaginous growth or neoplasm
CHONDRULE n one of the small spherical masses of mainly silicate minerals present in chondrites
CHONDRUS n cartilage
CHONS > CHON
CHOOF vb go away
CHOOFED > CHOOF
CHOOFING > CHOOF
CHOOFS > CHOOF
CHOOK n hen or chicken ▷ vb make the sound of a hen of chicken
CHOOKED > CHOOK
CHOOKIE same as > CHOOK
CHOOKIES > CHOOKIE
CHOOKING > CHOOK
CHOOKS > CHOOK
CHOOM n Englishman
CHOOMS > CHOOM
CHOON n slang term for music that one likes
CHOONS > CHOON
CHOOSE vb select from a number of alternatives
CHOOSER > CHOOSE
CHOOSERS > CHOOSE
CHOOSES > CHOOSE
CHOOSEY same as > CHOOSY
CHOOSIER > CHOOSY
CHOOSIEST > CHOOSY
CHOOSILY adv in a fussy or choosy way
CHOOSING > CHOOSE
CHOOSY adj fussy, hard to please
CHOP vb cut with a blow from an axe or knife ▷ n cutting or sharp blow
CHOPHOUSE n restaurant specializing in steaks, grills, chops, etc
CHOPIN same as > CHOPINE
CHOPINE n sandal-like shoe popular in the 18th century
CHOPINES > CHOPINE
CHOPINS > CHOPIN

CHOPLOGIC n person who uses excessively subtle or involved logic
CHOPPED > CHOP
CHOPPER n helicopter ▷ vb travel by helicopter
CHOPPERED > CHOPPER
CHOPPERS > CHOPPER
CHOPPIER > CHOPPY
CHOPPIEST > CHOPPY
CHOPPILY > CHOPPY
CHOPPING > CHOP
CHOPPINGS > CHOP
CHOPPY adj (of the sea) fairly rough
CHOPS > CHOP
CHOPSOCKY n genre of martial arts film
CHOPSTICK n one of a pair of thin sticks used as eating utensils
CHORAGI > CHORAGUS
CHORAGIC > CHORAGUS
CHORAGUS n leader of a chorus
CHORAL adj of a choir
CHORALE n slow stately hymn tune
CHORALES > CHORALE
CHORALIST n singer or composer of chorals
CHORALLY > CHORAL
CHORALS > CHORAL
CHORD n straight line joining two points on a curve ▷ vb provide (a melodic line) with chords
CHORDA n in anatomy, a cord
CHORDAE > CHORDA
CHORDAL > CHORD
CHORDATE n type of animal which includes the vertebrates
CHORDATES > CHORDATE
CHORDED > CHORD
CHORDEE n unusual bending downwards of the penis
CHORDEES > CHORDEE
CHORDING n distribution of chords throughout a piece of harmony
CHORDINGS > CHORDING
CHORDLIKE adj like a chord
CHORDS > CHORD
CHORDWISE adv in the direction of an aerofoil chord ▷ adj moving in this direction
CHORE n routine task ▷ vb carry out chores
CHOREA n disorder of the nervous system
CHOREAL > CHOREA
CHOREAS > CHOREA
CHOREATIC > CHOREA
CHOREBOY n boy who does chores
CHOREBOYS > CHOREBOY
CHORED > CHORE
CHOREE n trochee
CHOREES > CHOREE
CHOREGI > CHOREGUS
CHOREGIC > CHOREGUS
CHOREGUS n in ancient Greece, the producer and financier of a dramatist's works
CHOREIC > CHOREA

CHOREMAN n handyman
CHOREMEN > CHOREMAN
CHOREOID adj resembling chorea
CHORES > CHORE
CHOREUS same as > CHOREE
CHOREUSES > CHOREUS
CHORIA > CHORION
CHORIAL > CHORION
CHORIAMB n metrical foot used in classical verse
CHORIAMBI > CHORIAMB
CHORIAMBS > CHORIAMB
CHORIC adj in the manner of a chorus
CHORINE n chorus girl
CHORINES > CHORINE
CHORING > CHORE
CHORIOID same as > CHOROID
CHORIOIDS > CHORIOID
CHORION n outer membrane forming a sac around an embryo
CHORIONIC > CHORION
CHORIONS > CHORION
CHORISES > CHORISIS
CHORISIS n multiplication of leaves etc by branching or splitting
CHORISM > CHORISIS
CHORISMS > CHORISIS
CHORIST n choir member
CHORISTER n singer in a choir
CHORISTS > CHORIST
CHORIZO n kind of highly seasoned pork sausage of Spain or Mexico
CHORIZONT n person who challenges the authorship of a work
CHORIZOS > CHORIZO
CHOROID adj resembling the chorion, esp in being vascular ▷ n vascular membrane of the eyeball
CHOROIDAL > CHOROID
CHOROIDS > CHOROID
CHOROLOGY n study of the causal relations between geographical phenomena occurring within a particular region
CHORRIE n dilapidated old car
CHORRIES > CHORRIE
CHORTEN n Buddhist shrine
CHORTENS > CHORTEN
CHORTLE vb chuckle in amusement ▷ n amused chuckle
CHORTLED > CHORTLE
CHORTLER > CHORTLE
CHORTLERS > CHORTLE
CHORTLES > CHORTLE
CHORTLING > CHORTLE
CHORUS n large choir ▷ vb sing or say together
CHORUSED > CHORUS
CHORUSES > CHORUS
CHORUSING > CHORUS
CHORUSSED > CHORUS
CHORUSSES > CHORUS
CHOSE n item of property
CHOSEN > CHOOSE
CHOSES > CHOSE

CHOTA adj (in British Empire Indian usage) small
CHOTT a variant spelling of > SHOTT
CHOTTS > CHOTT
CHOU n type of cabbage
CHOUGH n large black Eurasian and N African bird of the crow family
CHOUGHS > CHOUGH
CHOULTRY same as > CHOLTRY
CHOUNTER same as > CHUNTER
CHOUNTERS > CHOUNTER
CHOUSE vb cheat
CHOUSED > CHOUSE
CHOUSER > CHOUSE
CHOUSERS > CHOUSE
CHOUSES > CHOUSE
CHOUSH n Turkish messenger
CHOUSHES > CHOUSH
CHOUSING > CHOUSE
CHOUT n blackmail
CHOUTS > CHOUT
CHOUX > CHOU
CHOW n thick-coated dog with a curled tail, orig from China ▷ vb eat
CHOWCHOW same as > CHOW
CHOWCHOWS > CHOWCHOW
CHOWDER n thick soup containing clams or fish ▷ vb make a chowder of
CHOWDERED > CHOWDER
CHOWDERS > CHOWDER
CHOWDOWN n act of eating a lot of food
CHOWDOWNS > CHOWDOWN
CHOWED > CHOW
CHOWHOUND n person who loves eating
CHOWING > CHOW
CHOWK n marketplace or market area
CHOWKIDAR same as > CHOKIDAR
CHOWKS > CHOWK
CHOWRI n fly-whisk
CHOWRIES > CHOWRI
CHOWRIS > CHOWRI
CHOWRY same as > CHOWRI
CHOWS > CHOW
CHOWSE same as > CHOUSE
CHOWSED > CHOWSE
CHOWSES > CHOWSE
CHOWSING > CHOWSE
CHOWTIME n mealtime
CHOWTIMES > CHOWTIME
CHRESARD n amount of water present in the soil that is available to plants
CHRESARDS > CHRESARD
CHRISM n consecrated oil used for anointing in some churches
CHRISMA > CHRISMON
CHRISMAL n chrism container
CHRISMALS > CHRISMAL
CHRISMON n monogram and symbol of Christ's name
CHRISMONS > CHRISMON
CHRISMS > CHRISM
CHRISOM same as > CHRISM
CHRISOMS > CHRISOM

C

CHRISTEN vb baptize

CHRISTENS > CHRISTEN

CHRISTIAN adj exhibiting kindness or goodness

CHRISTIE same as > CHRISTY

CHRISTIES > CHRISTIE

CHRISTOM same as > CHRISOM

CHRISTOMS > CHRISTOM

CHRISTY n skiing turn for stopping or changing direction quickly

CHROMA n attribute of a colour

CHROMAKEY n (in colour television) a special effect in which a coloured background can be eliminated and a different background substituted

CHROMAS > CHROMA

CHROMATE n any salt or ester of chromic acid

CHROMATES > CHROMATE

CHROMATIC adj of colour or colours

CHROMATID n either of the two strands into which a chromosome divides during mitosis. They separate to form daughter chromosomes at anaphase

CHROMATIN n part of the nucleus of a cell that forms the chromosomes and can easily be dyed

CHROME n anything plated with chromium ▷ vb plate with chromium ▷ adj of or having the appearance of chrome

CHROMED > CHROME

CHROMEL n nickel-based alloy

CHROMELS > CHROMEL

CHROMENE n chemical compound

CHROMENES > CHROMENE

CHROMES > CHROME

CHROMIC adj of or containing chromium in the trivalent state

CHROMIDE n any member of the cichlid family of fish

CHROMIDES > CHROMIDE

CHROMIDIA n chromatins in cell cytoplasm

CHROMIER > CHROME

CHROMIEST > CHROMY

CHROMING > CHROME

CHROMINGS > CHROME

CHROMISE same as > CHROMIZE

CHROMISED > CHROMISE

CHROMISES > CHROMISE

CHROMITE n brownish-black mineral which is the only commercial source of chromium

CHROMITES > CHROMITE

CHROMIUM n grey metallic element used in steel alloys and for electroplating

CHROMIUMS > CHROMIUM

CHROMIZE vb chrome-plate

CHROMIZED > CHROMIZE

CHROMIZES > CHROMIZE

CHROMO n picture produced by lithography

CHROMOGEN n compound that forms coloured compounds on oxidation

CHROMOLY n type of steel alloy

CHROMOLYS > CHROMOLY

CHROMOS > CHROMO

CHROMOUS adj of or containing chromium in the divalent state

CHROMY > CHROME

CHROMYL n type of divalent radical

CHROMYLS > CHROMYL

CHRONAXIE n minimum time required for excitation of a nerve or muscle when the stimulus is double the minimum (threshold) necessary to elicit a basic response

CHRONAXY same as > CHRONAXIE

CHRONIC adj (of an illness) lasting a long time ▷ n chronically ill patient

CHRONICAL > CHRONIC

CHRONICLE n record of events in order of occurrence ▷ vb record in or as if in a chronicle

CHRONICS > CHRONIC

CHRONON n unit of time

CHRONONS > CHRONON

CHRYSALID adj of or relating to a chrysalis

CHRYSALIS n insect in the stage between larva and adult, when it is in a cocoon

CHRYSANTH n chrysanthemum

CHTHONIAN adj of or relating to the underworld

CHTHONIC same as > CHTHONIAN

CHUB n European freshwater fish of the carp family

CHUBASCO n in Mexico, a hurricane

CHUBASCOS > CHUBASCO

CHUBBIER > CHUBBY

CHUBBIEST > CHUBBY

CHUBBILY > CHUBBY

CHUBBY adj plump and round

CHUBS > CHUB

CHUCK vb throw ▷ n cut of beef from the neck to the shoulder

CHUCKED > CHUCK

CHUCKER n person who throws something

CHUCKERS > CHUCKER

CHUCKHOLE n pothole

CHUCKIE n small stone

CHUCKIES > CHUCKIE

CHUCKING > CHUCK

CHUCKLE vb laugh softly ▷ n soft laugh

CHUCKLED > CHUCKLE

CHUCKLER > CHUCKLE

CHUCKLERS > CHUCKLE

CHUCKLES > CHUCKLE

CHUCKLING > CHUCKLE

CHUCKS > CHUCK

CHUCKY same as > CHUCKIE

CHUDDAH same as > CHUDDAR

CHUDDAHS > CHUDDAH

CHUDDAR n large shawl or veil

CHUDDARS > CHUDDAR

CHUDDER same as > CHUDDAR

CHUDDERS > CHUDDER

CHUDDIES pl n underpants

CHUDDY n chewing gum

CHUFA n type of sedge

CHUFAS > CHUFA

CHUFF vb (of a steam engine) move while making a puffing sound ▷ n puffing sound of or as if of a steam engine ▷ adj boorish

CHUFFED adj very pleased

CHUFFER > CHUFF

CHUFFEST > CHUFF

CHUFFIER > CHUFFY

CHUFFIEST > CHUFFY

CHUFFING > CHUFF

CHUFFS > CHUFF

CHUFFY adj boorish and surly

CHUG n short dull sound like the noise of an engine ▷ vb operate or move with this sound

CHUGALUG vb gulp down a drink in one go

CHUGALUGS > CHUGALUG

CHUGGED > CHUG

CHUGGER > CHUG

CHUGGERS > CHUG

CHUGGING n act of drinking a liquid quickly

CHUGGINGS > CHUGGING

CHUGS > CHUG

CHUKAR n common Indian partridge

CHUKARS > CHUKAR

CHUKKA n period of play in polo

CHUKKAR same as > CHUKKA

CHUKKARS > CHUKKAR

CHUKKAS > CHUKKA

CHUKKER same as > CHUKKA

CHUKKERS > CHUKKER

CHUKOR same as > CHUKAR

CHUKORS > CHUKOR

CHUM n close friend ▷ vb be or become an intimate friend (of)

CHUMASH n printed book containing one of the Five Books of Moses

CHUMASHES > CHUMASH

CHUMASHIM > CHUMASH

CHUMLEY same as > CHIMNEY

CHUMLEYS > CHUMLEY

CHUMMAGE n formerly, fee paid by a prisoner for sole occupancy of a cell

CHUMMAGES > CHUMMAGE

CHUMMED > CHUM

CHUMMIER > CHUMMY

CHUMMIES > CHUMMY

CHUMMIEST > CHUMMY

CHUMMILY > CHUMMY

CHUMMING > CHUM

CHUMMY adj friendly ▷ n chum

CHUMP n stupid person ▷ vb chew noisily

CHUMPED > CHUMP

CHUMPING n collecting wood for bonfires on Guy Fawkes Day

CHUMPINGS > CHUMPING

CHUMPS > CHUMP

CHUMS > CHUM

CHUMSHIP n friendship

CHUMSHIPS > CHUMSHIP

CHUNDER vb slang word for vomit ▷ n slang word for vomit

CHUNDERED > CHUNDER

CHUNDERS > CHUNDER

CHUNK n thick solid piece ▷ vb break up into chunks

CHUNKED > CHUNK

CHUNKIER > CHUNKY

CHUNKIEST > CHUNKY

CHUNKILY > CHUNKY

CHUNKING n mnemonic technique involving grouping together of a number of items

CHUNKINGS > CHUNKING

CHUNKS > CHUNK

CHUNKY adj (of a person) broad and heavy

CHUNNEL n rail tunnel linking England and France

CHUNNELS > CHUNNEL

CHUNNER same as > CHUNTER

CHUNNERED > CHUNNER

CHUNNERS > CHUNNER

CHUNTER vb mutter or grumble incessantly in a meaningless fashion

CHUNTERED > CHUNTER

CHUNTERS > CHUNTER

CHUPATI same as > CHUPATTI

CHUPATIS > CHUPATI

CHUPATTI variant spelling of > CHAPATI

CHUPATTIS > CHUPATTI

CHUPATTY same as > CHUPATTI

CHUPPA variant of > CHUPPAH

CHUPPAH n canopy under which a marriage is performed

CHUPPAHS > CHUPPAH

CHUPPAS > CHUPPA

CHUPPOT > CHUPPAH

CHUPPOTH > CHUPPAH

CHUPRASSY same as > CHAPRASSI

CHUR interj expression of agreement

CHURCH n building for public Christian worship ▷ vb bring someone to church for special ceremonies

CHURCHED > CHURCH

CHURCHES > CHURCH

CHURCHIER > CHURCHY

CHURCHING > CHURCH

CHURCHISM n adherence to the principles of an established church

CHURCHLY adj appropriate to, associated with, or suggestive of church life and customs

CHURCHMAN n clergyman

CHURCHMEN > CHURCHMAN

CHURCHWAY n way or road that leads to a church

CHURCHY adj like a church, church service, etc

CHURIDAR n as in churidar pyjamas long tight-fitting trousers, worn by Indian men and women

CHURIDARS > CHURIDAR

CHURINGA n sacred amulet of the native Australians

CHURINGAS > CHURINGA

CHURL n surly ill-bred person

CHURLISH adj surly and rude

CHURLS > CHURL

CHURN n machine in which cream is shaken to make butter ▷ vb stir (cream) vigorously to make butter

CHURNED > CHURN

CHURNER > CHURN

CHURNERS > CHURN

CHURNING n quantity of butter churned at any one time

CHURNINGS > CHURNING

CHURNMILK n buttermilk

CHURNS > CHURN

CHURR same as > CHIRR

CHURRED > CHURR

CHURRING > CHURR

CHURRO n Spanish dough stick snack

CHURROS > CHURRO

CHURRS > CHURR

CHURRUS n hemp resin

CHURRUSES > CHURRUS

CHUSE obsolete variant of > CHOOSE

CHUSED > CHUSE

CHUSES > CHUSE

CHUSING > CHUSE

CHUT interj expression of surprise or annoyance ▷ n such an expression

CHUTE n steep slope down which things may be slid ▷ vb descend by a chute

CHUTED > CHUTE

CHUTES > CHUTE

CHUTING > CHUTE

CHUTIST > CHUTE

CHUTISTS > CHUTE

CHUTNEE same as > CHUTNEY

CHUTNEES > CHUTNEE

CHUTNEY n pickle made from fruit, vinegar, spices, and sugar

CHUTNEYS > CHUTNEY

CHUTS > CHUT

CHUTZPA same as > CHUTZPAH

CHUTZPAH n unashamed self-confidence

CHUTZPAHS > CHUTZPAH

CHUTZPAS > CHUTZPA

CHYACK same as > CHIACK

CHYACKED > CHYACK

CHYACKING > CHYACK

CHYACKS > CHYACK

CHYLDE archaic word for > CHILD

CHYLE n milky fluid formed in the small intestine during digestion

CHYLES > CHYLE

CHYLIFIED > CHYLIFY

CHYLIFIES > CHYLIFY

CHYLIFY vb be turned into chyle

CHYLOUS > CHYLE

CHYLURIA n presence of chyle in urine

CHYLURIAS > CHYLURIA

CHYME n partially digested food that leaves the stomach

CHYMES > CHYME

CHYMIC same as > CHEMIC

CHYMICS > CHYMIC

CHYMIFIED > CHYMIFY

CHYMIFIES > CHYMIFY

CHYMIFY vb form into chyme

CHYMIST same as > CHEMIST

CHYMISTRY same as > CHEMISTRY

CHYMISTS > CHYMIST

CHYMOSIN another name for > RENNIN

CHYMOSINS > CHYMOSIN

CHYMOUS > CHYME

CHYND adj chined

CHYPRE n perfume made from sandalwood

CHYPRES > CHYPRE

CHYRON n caption superimposed on a TV screen

CHYRONS > CHYRON

CHYTRID n variety of fungus

CHYTRIDS > CHYTRID

CIABATTA n type of bread made with olive oil

CIABATTAS > CIABATTA

CIABATTE > CIABATTA

CIAO an informal word for > HELLO

CIBATION n feeding

CIBATIONS > CIBATION

CIBOL same as > CHIBOL

CIBOLS > CIBOL

CIBORIA > CIBORIUM

CIBORIUM n goblet-shaped lidded vessel used to hold consecrated wafers in Holy Communion

CIBORIUMS > CIBORIUM

CIBOULE same as > CHIBOL

CIBOULES > CIBOULE

CICADA n large insect that makes a high-pitched drone

CICADAE > CICADA

CICADAS > CICADA

CICALA same as > CICADA

CICALAS > CICALA

CICALE > CICALA

CICATRICE n scar

CICATRISE same as > CICATRIZE

CICATRIX n scar

CICATRIZE vb (of a wound or defect in tissue) to close or be closed by scar formation

CICELIES > CICELY

CICELY n type of plant

CICERO n measure for type that is somewhat larger than the pica

CICERONE n person who guides and informs sightseers ▷ vb act as a cicerone

CICERONED > CICERONE

CICERONES > CICERONE

CICERONI > CICERONE

CICEROS > CICERO

CICHLID n type of tropical freshwater fish popular in aquariums

CICHLIDAE n cichlids

CICHLIDS > CICHLID

CICHLOID > CICHLID

CICINNUS n scorpioid cyme

CICISBEI > CICISBEO

CICISBEO n escort or lover of a married woman, esp in 18th-century Italy

CICISBEOS > CICISBEO

CICLATON n rich material of silk and gold

CICLATONS > CICLATON

CICLATOUN same as > CICLATON

CICOREE same as > CHICORY

CICOREES > CICOREE

CICUTA n spotted hemlock

CICUTAS > CICUTA

CICUTINE same as > CONIINE

CICUTINES > CICUTINE

CID n leader

CIDARIS n sea urchin

CIDARISES > CIDARIS

CIDE Shakespearean variant of > DECIDE

CIDED > CIDE

CIDER n alcoholic drink made from fermented apple juice

CIDERIER > CIDERY

CIDERIEST > CIDERY

CIDERKIN n weak type of cider

CIDERKINS > CIDERKIN

CIDERS > CIDER

CIDERY adj like cider

CIDES > CIDE

CIDING > CIDE

CIDS > CID

CIEL same as > CEIL

CIELED > CIEL

CIELING same as > CEILING

CIELINGS > CIEL

CIELS > CIEL

CIERGE same as > CERGE

CIERGES > CIERGE

CIG same as > CIGARETTE

CIGAR n roll of cured tobacco leaves for smoking

CIGARET same as > CIGARETTE

CIGARETS > CIGARET

CIGARETTE n thin roll of shredded tobacco in thin paper, for smoking

CIGARILLO n small cigar often only slightly larger than a cigarette

CIGARLIKE > CIGAR

CIGARS > CIGAR

CIGGIE same as > CIGARETTE

CIGGIES > CIGGIE

CIGGY same as > CIGARETTE

CIGS > CIG

CIGUATERA n food poisoning caused by a toxin in seafood

CILANTRO same as > CORIANDER

CILANTROS > CILANTRO

CILIA > CILIUM

CILIARY adj of or relating to cilia

CILIATE n type of protozoan

CILIATED > CILIATE

CILIATELY > CILIATE

CILIATES > CILIATE

CILIATION > CILIATE

CILICE n haircloth fabric or garment

CILICES > CILICE

CILICIOUS adj made of hair

CILIOLATE adj covered with minute hairs, as some plants

CILIUM n short thread projecting from a cell that causes movement

CILL a variant spelling (used in the building industry) for > SILL

CILLS > CILL

CIMAR same as > CYMAR

CIMARS > CIMAR

CIMBALOM n type of dulcimer, esp of Hungary

CIMBALOMS > CIMBALOM

CIMELIA pl n (especially, ecclesiastical) treasures

CIMEX n type of heteropterous insect, esp the bedbug

CIMICES > CIMEX

CIMIER n crest of a helmet

CIMIERS > CIMIER

CIMINITE n type of igneous rock

CIMINITES > CIMINITE

CIMMERIAN adj very dark or gloomy

CIMOLITE n clayey, whitish mineral

CIMOLITES > CIMOLITE

CINCH n easy task ▷ vb fasten a girth around (a horse)

CINCHED > CINCH

CINCHES > CINCH

CINCHING > CINCH

CINCHINGS > CINCH

CINCHONA same as > CALISAYA

CINCHONAS > CINCHONA

CINCHONIC > CINCHONA

CINCINNUS same as > CICINNUS

CINCT adj encircled

CINCTURE n something, such as a belt or girdle, that goes around another thing ▷ vb encircle

CINCTURED > CINCTURE

CINCTURES > CINCTURE

CINDER n piece of material that will not burn, left after burning coal ▷ vb burn to cinders

CINDERED > CINDER

CINDERIER > CINDERY

CINDERING > CINDER
CINDEROUS > CINDER
CINDERS > CINDER
CINDERY adj covered in cinders
CINE n as in cine camera camera able to film moving pictures
CINEAST same as > CINEASTE
CINEASTE n enthusiast for films
CINEASTES > CINEASTE
CINEASTS > CINEAST
CINEMA n place for showing films
CINEMAS > CINEMA
CINEMATIC > CINEMA
CINEOL n colourless oily liquid with a camphor-like odour and a spicy taste
CINEOLE same as > CINEOL
CINEOLES > CINEOLE
CINEOLS > CINEOL
CINEPHILE n film enthusiast
CINEPLEX n large cinema complex
CINERAMIC adj relating to a cinematic process producing widescreen images
CINERARIA n garden plant with daisy-like flowers
CINERARY adj of (someone's) ashes
CINERATOR same as > CREMATOR
CINEREA n grey matter of the brain and nervous system
CINEREAL adj ashy
CINEREAS > CINEREA
CINEREOUS adj of a greyish colour
CINERIN n either of two organic compounds used as insecticides
CINERINS > CINERIN
CINES > CINE
CINGULA > CINGULUM
CINGULAR adj ring-shaped
CINGULATE > CINGULUM
CINGULUM n girdle-like part of certain structures
CINNABAR n heavy red mineral containing mercury
CINNABARS > CINNABAR
CINNAMIC > CINNAMON
CINNAMON n spice obtained from the bark of an Asian tree
CINNAMONS > CINNAMON
CINNAMONY adj like cinnamon
CINNAMYL n univalent radical of cinnamic compounds
CINNAMYLS > CINNAMYL
CINQ n number five
CINQS > CINQ
CINQUAIN n stanza of five lines
CINQUAINS > CINQUAIN
CINQUE n number five in cards, dice, etc
CINQUES > CINQUE
CION same as > SCION
CIONS > CION

CIOPPINO n Italian rich fish stew
CIOPPINOS > CIOPPINO
CIPAILLE n type of pie traditional in Quebec
CIPAILLES > CIPAILLE
CIPHER n system of secret writing ▷ vb put (a message) into secret writing
CIPHERED > CIPHER
CIPHERER > CIPHER
CIPHERERS > CIPHER
CIPHERING > CIPHER
CIPHERS > CIPHER
CIPHONIES > CIPHONY
CIPHONY n ciphered telephony
CIPOLIN n Italian marble with alternating white and green streaks
CIPOLINS > CIPOLIN
CIPOLLINO same as > CIPOLIN
CIPPI > CIPPUS
CIPPUS n pillar bearing an inscription
CIRCA prep approximately, about
CIRCADIAN adj of biological processes that occur regularly at 24-hour intervals
CIRCAR n in India, part of a province
CIRCARS > CIRCAR
CIRCINATE adj (of part of a plant, such as a young fern) coiled so that the tip is at the centre
CIRCITER prep around, about
CIRCLE n perfectly round geometric figure, line, or shape ▷ vb move in a circle (round)
CIRCLED > CIRCLE
CIRCLER > CIRCLE
CIRCLERS > CIRCLE
CIRCLES > CIRCLE
CIRCLET n circular ornament worn on the head
CIRCLETS > CIRCLET
CIRCLING > CIRCLE
CIRCLINGS > CIRCLE
CIRCLIP n type of fastener
CIRCLIPS > CIRCLIP
CIRCS pl n circumstances
CIRCUIT n complete route or course, esp a circular one ▷ vb make or travel in a circuit around (something)
CIRCUITAL > CIRCUIT
CIRCUITED > CIRCUIT
CIRCUITRY n electrical circuit(s)
CIRCUITS > CIRCUIT
CIRCUITY n (of speech, reasoning, etc) a roundabout or devious quality
CIRCULAR adj in the shape of a circle ▷ n letter for general distribution
CIRCULARS > CIRCULAR
CIRCULATE vb send, go, or pass from place to place or person to person
CIRCUS n travelling company of acrobats, clowns, performing animals, etc

CIRCUSES > CIRCUS
CIRCUSIER > CIRCUSY
CIRCUSSY adj like a circus
CIRCUSY adj like a circus
CIRE adj (of fabric) treated with a heat or wax process to make it smooth ▷ n such a surface on a fabric
CIRES > CIRE
CIRL n bird belonging to the bunting family
CIRLS > CIRL
CIRQUE n steep-sided semicircular hollow found in mountainous areas
CIRQUES > CIRQUE
CIRRATE adj bearing or resembling cirri
CIRRHOSED > CIRRHOSIS
CIRRHOSES > CIRRHOSIS
CIRRHOSIS n serious liver disease
CIRRHOTIC > CIRRHOSIS
CIRRI > CIRRUS
CIRRIFORM adj cirrus-like
CIRRIPED same as > CIRRIPEDE
CIRRIPEDE n type of marine crustacean of the subclass including the barnacles
CIRRIPEDS > CIRRIPED
CIRROSE same as > CIRRATE
CIRROUS same as > CIRRATE
CIRRUS n high wispy cloud
CIRRUSES > CIRRUS
CIRSOID adj resembling a varix
CIS adj having two groups of atoms on the same side of a double bond
CISALPINE adj on this (the southern) side of the Alps, as viewed from Rome
CISCO n whitefish, esp the lake herring of cold deep lakes of North America
CISCOES > CISCO
CISCOS > CISCO
CISELEUR n person who is expert in ciselure
CISELEURS > CISELEUR
CISELURE n art or process of chasing metal
CISELURES > CISELURE
CISGENDER adj having an assigned birth gender and gender identity that are the same
CISLUNAR adj of or relating to the space between the earth and the moon
CISPADANE adj on this (the southern) side of the River Po, as viewed from Rome
CISPLATIN n cytotoxic drug used in the treatment of tumours
CISSIER > CISSY
CISSIES > CISSY
CISSIEST > CISSY
CISSIFIED another word for > SISSY
CISSING n appearance of pinholes, craters, etc, in paintwork

CISSINGS > CISSING
CISSOID n type of geometric curve
CISSOIDS > CISSOID
CISSUS n type of climbing plant
CISSUSES > CISSUS
CISSY same as > SISSY
CIST n wooden box for holding ritual objects used in ancient Rome and Greece
CISTED > CIST
CISTERN n water tank, esp one that holds water for flushing a toilet
CISTERNA n sac or partially closed space containing body fluid, esp lymph or cerebrospinal fluid
CISTERNAE > CISTERNA
CISTERNAL > CISTERN
CISTERNS > CISTERN
CISTIC adj cist-like
CISTRON n section of a chromosome that encodes a single polypeptide chain
CISTRONIC > CISTRON
CISTRONS > CISTRON
CISTS > CIST
CISTUS n type of plant
CISTUSES > CISTUS
CISTVAEN n pre-Christian stone coffin or burial chamber
CISTVAENS > CISTVAEN
CIT n pejorative term for a town dweller
CITABLE > CITE
CITADEL n fortress in a city
CITADELS > CITADEL
CITAL n court summons
CITALS > CITAL
CITATION n commendation for bravery
CITATIONS > CITATION
CITATOR n legal publication
CITATORS > CITATOR
CITATORY > CITATION
CITE vb quote, refer to
CITEABLE > CITE
CITED > CITE
CITER > CITE
CITERS > CITE
CITES > CITE
CITESS n female cit
CITESSES > CITESS
CITHARA n ancient stringed musical instrument
CITHARAS > CITHARA
CITHARIST n player of the cithara
CITHER same as > CITTERN
CITHERN same as > CITTERN
CITHERNS > CITHERN
CITHERS > CITHER
CITHREN same as > CITHARA
CITHRENS > CITHREN
CITIED adj having cities
CITIES > CITY
CITIFIED > CITIFY
CITIFIES > CITIFY
CITIFY vb cause to conform to or adopt the customs, habits, or dress of city people
CITIFYING > CITIFY

CITIGRADE *adj* relating to (fast-moving) wolf spiders

CITING > CITE

CITIZEN *n* native or naturalized member of a state or nation

CITIZENLY *adj* like a citizen

CITIZENRY *n* citizens collectively

CITIZENS > CITIZEN

CITO *adv* swiftly

CITOLA *n* type of medieval stringed instrument

CITOLAS > CITOLA

CITOLE *a rare word for* > CITTERN

CITOLES > CITOLE

CITRAL *n* volatile liquid with a lemon-like odour

CITRALS > CITRAL

CITRANGE *n* type of acidic and aromatic orange

CITRANGES > CITRANGE

CITRATE *n* any salt or ester of citric acid

CITRATED *adj* treated with a citrate

CITRATES > CITRATE

CITREOUS *adj* of a greenish-yellow colour

CITRIC *adj* of or derived from citrus fruits or citric acid

CITRIN *n* vitamin P

CITRINE *n* brownish-yellow variety of quartz: a gemstone

CITRINES > CITRINE

CITRININ *n* type of mycotoxin

CITRININS > CITRININ

CITRINS > CITRIN

CITRON *n* lemon-like fruit of a small Asian tree

CITRONS > CITRON

CITROUS *same as* > CITRUS

CITRUS *n* type of tropical or subtropical tree or shrub

CITRUSES > CITRUS

CITRUSIER > CITRUSY

CITRUSSY *adj* having or resembling the taste or colour of a citrus fruit

CITRUSY *same as* > CITRUSSY

CITS > CIT

CITTERN *n* medieval stringed instrument

CITTERNS > CITTERN

CITY *n* large or important town

CITYFIED > CITYFY

CITYFIES > CITYFY

CITYFY *same as* > CITIFY

CITYFYING > CITYFY

CITYSCAPE *n* urban landscape

CITYWARD *adv* towards a city

CITYWIDE *adj* occurring throughout a city

CIVE *same as* > CHIVE

CIVES > CIVE

CIVET *n* spotted catlike African mammal

CIVETLIKE > CIVET

CIVETS > CIVET

CIVIC *adj* of a city or citizens

CIVICALLY > CIVIC

CIVICISM *n* principle of civil government

CIVICISMS > CIVICISM

CIVICS *n* study of the rights and responsibilities of citizenship

CIVIE *same as* > CIVVY

CIVIES > CIVIE

CIVIL *adj* relating to the citizens of a state

CIVILIAN *adj* not belonging to the armed forces ▷ *n* person who is not a member of the armed forces or police

CIVILIANS > CIVILIAN

CIVILISE *same as* > CIVILIZE

CIVILISED *same as* > CIVILIZED

CIVILISER > CIVILISE

CIVILISES > CIVILISE

CIVILIST *n* civilian

CIVILISTS > CIVILIST

CIVILITY *n* polite or courteous behaviour

CIVILIZE *vb* refine or educate (a person)

CIVILIZED *adj* having a high state of culture and social development

CIVILIZER > CIVILIZE

CIVILIZES > CIVILIZE

CIVILLY > CIVIL

CIVILNESS > CIVIL

CIVILS *n* civil engineering

CIVISM *n* good citizenship

CIVISMS > CIVISM

CIVVIES > CIVVY

CIVVY *n* civilian

CIZERS *archaic spelling of* > SCISSORS

CLABBER *vb* cover with mud

CLABBERED > CLABBER

CLABBERS > CLABBER

CLACH *n* stone ▷ *vb* kill by stoning

CLACHAN *n* small village

CLACHANS > CLACHAN

CLACHED > CLACH

CLACHES > CLACH

CLACHING > CLACH

CLACHS > CLACH

CLACK *n* sound made by two hard objects striking each other ▷ *vb* make this sound

CLACKBOX *n* casing enclosing a clack

CLACKDISH *n* formerly, a dish carried by a beggar

CLACKED > CLACK

CLACKER *n* object that makes a clacking sound

CLACKERS > CLACKER

CLACKING > CLACK

CLACKS > CLACK

CLAD *vb* bond a metal to (another metal), esp to form a protective coat

CLADDAGH *n* Irish ring

CLADDAGHS > CLADDAGH

CLADDED *adj* covered with cladding

CLADDER > CLAD

CLADDERS > CLAD

CLADDIE *another name for* > KORARI

CLADDIES > CLADDIE

CLADDING > CLAD

CLADDINGS > CLOTHE

CLADE *n* group of organisms sharing a common ancestor

CLADES > CLADE

CLADISM > CLADIST

CLADISMS > CLADIST

CLADIST *n* proponent of cladistics

CLADISTIC > CLADIST

CLADISTS > CLADIST

CLADODE *n* stem resembling and functioning as a leaf

CLADODES > CLADODE

CLADODIAL > CLADODE

CLADOGRAM *n* treelike diagram illustrating the development of a clade

CLADS > CLAD

CLAES *Scots word for* > CLOTHES

CLAFOUTI *same as* > CLAFOUTIS

CLAFOUTIS *n* French baked pudding

CLAG *n* sticky mud ▷ *vb* stick, as mud

CLAGGED > CLAG

CLAGGIER > CLAGGY

CLAGGIEST > CLAGGY

CLAGGING > CLAG

CLAGGY *adj* stickily clinging, as mud

CLAGS > CLAG

CLAIM *vb* assert as a fact ▷ *n* assertion that something is true

CLAIMABLE > CLAIM

CLAIMANT *n* person who makes a claim

CLAIMANTS > CLAIMANT

CLAIMED > CLAIM

CLAIMER > CLAIM

CLAIMERS > CLAIM

CLAIMING > CLAIM

CLAIMS > CLAIM

CLAM *n* edible shellfish with a hinged shell ▷ *vb* gather clams

CLAMANCY *n* urgency

CLAMANT *adj* noisy

CLAMANTLY > CLAMANT

CLAMBAKE *n* picnic, often by the sea, at which clams, etc, are baked

CLAMBAKES > CLAMBAKE

CLAMBE *old variant of* > CLIMB

CLAMBER *vb* climb awkwardly ▷ *n* climb performed in this manner

CLAMBERED > CLAMBER

CLAMBERER > CLAMBER

CLAMBERS > CLAMBER

CLAME *archaic variant of* > CLAIM

CLAMES > CLAME

CLAMLIKE > CLAM

CLAMMED > CLAM

CLAMMER *n* person who gathers clams

CLAMMERS > CLAMMER

CLAMMIER > CLAMMY

CLAMMIEST > CLAMMY

CLAMMILY > CLAMMY

CLAMMING > CLAM

CLAMMY *adj* unpleasantly moist and sticky

CLAMOR *same as* > CLAMOUR

CLAMORED > CLAMOR

CLAMORER > CLAMOR

CLAMORERS > CLAMOR

CLAMORING > CLAMOR

CLAMOROUS > CLAMOR

CLAMORS > CLAMOR

CLAMOUR *n* loud protest ▷ *vb* make a loud noise or outcry

CLAMOURED > CLAMOUR

CLAMOURER > CLAMOUR

CLAMOURS > CLAMOUR

CLAMP *n* tool with movable jaws for holding things together tightly ▷ *vb* fasten with a clamp

CLAMPDOWN *n* sudden restrictive measure

CLAMPED > CLAMP

CLAMPER *n* spiked metal frame fastened to the sole of a shoe ▷ *vb* tread heavily

CLAMPERED > CLAMPER

CLAMPERS > CLAMPER

CLAMPING *n* act of clamping

CLAMPINGS > CLAMPING

CLAMPS > CLAMP

CLAMS > CLAM

CLAMSHELL *n* dredging bucket that is hinged like the shell of a clam

CLAMWORM *the US name for the* > RAGWORM

CLAMWORMS > CLAMWORM

CLAN *n* group of families with a common ancestor

CLANG *vb* make a loud ringing metallic sound ▷ *n* ringing metallic sound

CLANGBOX *n* device fitted to a jet-engine to change the direction of thrust

CLANGED > CLANG

CLANGER *n* obvious mistake

CLANGERS > CLANGER

CLANGING > CLANG

CLANGINGS > CLANG

CLANGOR *same as* > CLANGOUR

CLANGORED > CLANGOR

CLANGORS > CLANGOR

CLANGOUR *n* loud continuous clanging sound ▷ *vb* make or produce a loud resonant noise

CLANGOURS > CLANGOUR

CLANGS > CLANG

CLANK *n* harsh metallic sound ▷ *vb* make such a sound

CLANKED > CLANK

CLANKIER > CLANKY

CLANKIEST > CLANKY

CLANKING > CLANK

CLANKINGS > CLANK

CLANKS > CLANK

CLANKY *adj* making clanking sounds

CLANNISH *adj* (of a group) tending to exclude outsiders

CLANS > CLAN

CLANSHIP *n* association of families under the leadership of a chieftain

CLANSHIPS > CLANSHIP

CLANSMAN n man belonging to a clan
CLANSMEN > CLANSMAN
CLAP vb applaud by hitting the palms of one's hands sharply together ▷ n act or sound of clapping
CLAPBOARD n long thin timber board with one edge thicker than the other, used esp in the US and Canada in wood-frame construction by lapping each board over the one below ▷ vb cover with such boards
CLAPBREAD n type of cake made from oatmeal
CLAPDISH same as > CLACKDISH
CLAPNET n net that can be closed instantly by pulling a string
CLAPNETS > CLAPNET
CLAPPED > CLAP
CLAPPER n piece of metal inside a bell ▷ vb make a sound like a clapper
CLAPPERED > CLAPPER
CLAPPERS > CLAPPER
CLAPPING > CLAP
CLAPPINGS > CLAP
CLAPS > CLAP
CLAPT > CLAP
CLAPTRAP n foolish or pretentious talk
CLAPTRAPS > CLAPTRAP
CLAQUE n group of people hired to applaud
CLAQUER same as > CLAQUEUR
CLAQUERS > CLAQUER
CLAQUES > CLAQUE
CLAQUEUR n member of a claque
CLAQUEURS > CLAQUEUR
CLARAIN n one of the four major lithotypes of banded coal
CLARAINS > CLARAIN
CLARENCE n closed four-wheeled horse-drawn carriage, having a glass front
CLARENCES > CLARENCE
CLARENDON n style of boldface roman type
CLARET n dry red wine from Bordeaux ▷ adj purplish-red ▷ vb drink claret
CLARETED > CLARET
CLARETING > CLARET
CLARETS > CLARET
CLARIES > CLARY
CLARIFIED > CLARIFY
CLARIFIER > CLARIFY
CLARIFIES > CLARIFY
CLARIFY vb make (a matter) clear and unambiguous
CLARINET n keyed woodwind instrument with a single reed
CLARINETS > CLARINET
CLARINI > CLARINO
CLARINO adj relating to a high passage for the trumpet in 18th-century music ▷ n high register of the trumpet
CLARINOS > CLARINO

CLARION n obsolete high-pitched trumpet ▷ adj clear and ringing ▷ vb proclaim loudly
CLARIONED > CLARION
CLARIONET same as > CLARINET
CLARIONS > CLARION
CLARITIES > CLARITY
CLARITY n clearness
CLARKIA n N American plant cultivated for its red, purple, or pink flowers
CLARKIAS > CLARKIA
CLARO n mild light-coloured cigar
CLAROES > CLARO
CLAROS > CLARO
CLARSACH n Celtic harp of Scotland and Ireland
CLARSACHS > CLARSACH
CLART vb to dirty
CLARTED > CLART
CLARTHEAD n slow-witted or stupid person
CLARTIER > CLARTY
CLARTIEST > CLARTY
CLARTING > CLART
CLARTS pl n lumps of mud, esp on shoes
CLARTY adj dirty, esp covered in mud
CLARY n European plant with aromatic leaves and blue flowers
CLASH vb come into conflict ▷ n fight, argument
CLASHED > CLASH
CLASHER > CLASH
CLASHERS > CLASH
CLASHES > CLASH
CLASHING > CLASH
CLASHINGS > CLASH
CLASP n device for fastening things ▷ vb grasp or embrace firmly
CLASPED > CLASP
CLASPER > CLASP
CLASPERS > CLASPER
CLASPING > CLASP
CLASPINGS > CLASP
CLASPS > CLASP
CLASPT old inflection of > CLASP
CLASS n group of people sharing a similar social position ▷ vb place in a class
CLASSABLE > CLASS
CLASSED > CLASS
CLASSER > CLASS
CLASSERS > CLASS
CLASSES > CLASSIS
CLASSIBLE adj able to be classed
CLASSIC adj being a typical example of something ▷ n author, artist, or work of art of recognized excellence
CLASSICAL adj of or in a restrained conservative style
CLASSICO adj (of Italian wines) coming from the centre of a specific wine-growing region
CLASSICS > CLASSIC
CLASSIER > CLASSY
CLASSIEST > CLASSY

CLASSIFIC adj relating to classification
CLASSIFY vb divide into groups with similar characteristics
CLASSILY > CLASSY
CLASSING > CLASS
CLASSINGS > CLASS
CLASSIS n governing body of elders or pastors
CLASSISM n belief that people from certain social or economic classes are superior to others
CLASSISMS > CLASSISM
CLASSIST > CLASSISM
CLASSISTS > CLASSISM
CLASSLESS adj not belonging to a class
CLASSMAN n graduate of Oxford University with a classed honours degree
CLASSMATE n friend or contemporary in the same class of a school
CLASSMEN > CLASSMAN
CLASSON n elementary atomic particle
CLASSONS > CLASSON
CLASSROOM n room in a school where lessons take place
CLASSWORK n school work done in class
CLASSY adj stylish and elegant
CLAST n fragment of a clastic rock
CLASTIC adj composed of fragments ▷ n clast
CLASTICS > CLASTIC
CLASTS > CLAST
CLAT n irksome or troublesome task ▷ vb scrape
CLATCH vb move making a squelching sound
CLATCHED > CLATCH
CLATCHES > CLATCH
CLATCHING > CLATCH
CLATHRATE adj resembling a net or lattice ▷ n solid compound in which molecules of one substance are physically trapped in the crystal lattice of another
CLATS > CLAT
CLATTED > CLAT
CLATTER n rattling noise ▷ vb make a rattling noise, as when hard objects hit each other
CLATTERED > CLATTER
CLATTERER > CLATTER
CLATTERS > CLATTER
CLATTERY adj making a clattering sound
CLATTING > CLAT
CLAUCHT vb seize by force
CLAUCHTED > CLAUCHT
CLAUCHTS > CLAUCHT
CLAUGHT same as > CLAUCHT
CLAUGHTED > CLAUGHT
CLAUGHTS > CLAUGHT
CLAUSAL > CLAUSE
CLAUSE n section of a legal document

CLAUSES > CLAUSE
CLAUSTRA > CLAUSTRUM
CLAUSTRAL same as > CLOISTRAL
CLAUSTRUM n thin layer of grey matter in the brain
CLAUSULA n type of cadence in polyphony
CLAUSULAE > CLAUSULA
CLAUSULAR > CLAUSE
CLAUT same as > CLAT
CLAUTED > CLAUT
CLAUTING > CLAUT
CLAUTS > CLAUT
CLAVATE adj shaped like a club with the thicker end uppermost
CLAVATED same as > CLAVATE
CLAVATELY > CLAVATE
CLAVATION > CLAVATE
CLAVE n one of a pair of hardwood sticks struck together to make a hollow sound
CLAVECIN n harpsichord
CLAVECINS > CLAVECIN
CLAVER vb talk idly ▷ n idle talk
CLAVERED > CLAVER
CLAVERING > CLAVER
CLAVERS > CLAVER
CLAVES > CLAVE
CLAVI > CLAVUS
CLAVICLE n bone connecting the shoulder blade to the breastbone
CLAVICLES > CLAVICLE
CLAVICORN n type of beetle such as the ladybirds, characterized by club-shaped antennae
CLAVICULA n clavicle
CLAVIE n tar-barrel traditionally set alight in Moray in Scotland on Hogmanay
CLAVIER n any keyboard instrument
CLAVIERS > CLAVIER
CLAVIES > CLAVIE
CLAVIFORM same as > CLAVATE
CLAVIGER n key- or club-bearer
CLAVIGERS > CLAVIGER
CLAVIS n key
CLAVULATE adj club-shaped
CLAVUS n corn on the toe
CLAW n sharp hooked nail of a bird or beast ▷ vb tear with claws or nails
CLAWBACK n recovery of a sum of money
CLAWBACKS > CLAWBACK
CLAWED > CLAW
CLAWER > CLAW
CLAWERS > CLAW
CLAWING > CLAW
CLAWLESS > CLAW
CLAWLIKE adj resembling a claw or claws
CLAWS > CLAW
CLAXON same as > KLAXON
CLAXONS > CLAXON

CLAY n fine-grained earth used to make bricks and pottery ▷ vb cover or mix with clay

CLAYBANK n dull brownish-orange colour

CLAYBANKS > CLAYBANK

CLAYED > CLAY

CLAYEY > CLAY

CLAYIER > CLAYEY

CLAYIEST > CLAYEY

CLAYING > CLAY

CLAYISH > CLAY

CLAYLIKE > CLAY

CLAYMORE n large two-edged sword formerly used by Scottish Highlanders

CLAYMORES > CLAYMORE

CLAYPAN n layer of stiff impervious clay situated just below the surface of the ground

CLAYPANS > CLAYPAN

CLAYS > CLAY

CLAYSTONE n compact very fine-grained rock consisting of consolidated clay particles

CLAYTONIA n low-growing N American succulent plant

CLAYWARE n pottery

CLAYWARES > CLAYWARE

CLEAN adj free from dirt or impurities ▷ vb make (something) free from dirt ▷ adv completely

CLEANABLE > CLEAN

CLEANED > CLEAN

CLEANER n person or thing that removes dirt

CLEANERS > CLEANER

CLEANEST > CLEAN

CLEANING n act of cleaning something

CLEANINGS > CLEANING

CLEANISH adj quite clean

CLEANLIER > CLEANLY

CLEANLILY > CLEANLY

CLEANLY adv easily or smoothly ▷ adj habitually clean or neat

CLEANNESS > CLEAN

CLEANOUT n act or instance of cleaning (something) out

CLEANOUTS > CLEANOUT

CLEANS > CLEAN

CLEANSE vb make clean

CLEANSED > CLEANSE

CLEANSER n cleansing agent, such as a detergent

CLEANSERS > CLEANSER

CLEANSES > CLEANSE

CLEANSING > CLEANSE

CLEANSKIN n unbranded animal

CLEANTECH n clean technology

CLEANUP n process of cleaning up or eliminating something

CLEANUPS > CLEANUP

CLEAR adj free from doubt or confusion ▷ adv in a clear or distinct manner ▷ vb make or become clear

CLEARABLE > CLEAR

CLEARAGE n clearance

CLEARAGES > CLEARAGE

CLEARANCE n clearing

CLEARCOLE n type of size containing whiting ▷ vb paint (a wall) with this size

CLEARCUT n act of felling all trees in area

CLEARCUTS > CLEARCUT

CLEARED > CLEAR

CLEARER > CLEAR

CLEARERS > CLEAR

CLEAREST > CLEAR

CLEAREYED adj having good judgment

CLEARING n treeless area in a wood

CLEARINGS > CLEARING

CLEARLY adv in a clear, distinct, or obvious manner

CLEARNESS > CLEAR

CLEAROUT n act or instance of removing (things or material)

CLEAROUTS > CLEAROUT

CLEARS > CLEAR

CLEARSKIN same as > CLEANSKIN

CLEARWAY n stretch of road on which motorists may stop in an emergency

CLEARWAYS > CLEARWAY

CLEARWEED n plant like nettle

CLEARWING n type of moth

CLEAT n wedge ▷ vb supply or support with a cleat or cleats

CLEATED > CLEAT

CLEATING > CLEAT

CLEATS > CLEAT

CLEAVABLE > CLEAVE

CLEAVAGE n division or split

CLEAVAGES > CLEAVAGE

CLEAVE vb split apart ▷ n split

CLEAVED > CLEAVE

CLEAVER n butcher's heavy knife with a square blade

CLEAVERS n plant with small white flowers and sticky fruits

CLEAVES > CLEAVE

CLEAVING > CLEAVE

CLEAVINGS > CLEAVE

CLECHE adj (in heraldry) voided so that only a narrow border is visible

CLECK vb (of birds) to hatch ▷ n piece of gossip

CLECKED > CLECK

CLECKIER > CLECK

CLECKIEST > CLECK

CLECKING > CLECK

CLECKINGS > CLECK

CLECKS > CLECK

CLECKY > CLECK

CLEEK n large hook, such as one used to land fish ▷ vb seize

CLEEKED > CLEEK

CLEEKING > CLEEK

CLEEKIT > CLEEK

CLEEKS > CLEEK

CLEEP same as > CLEPE

CLEEPED > CLEEP

CLEEPING > CLEEP

CLEEPS > CLEEP

CLEEVE n cliff

CLEEVES > CLEEVE

CLEF n symbol at the beginning of a stave to show the pitch

CLEFS > CLEF

CLEFT vb split ▷ n opening

CLEFTED > CLEFT

CLEFTING > CLEFT

CLEFTS > CLEFT

CLEG another name for a > HORSEFLY

CLEGS > CLEG

CLEIDOIC adj as in cleidoic egg egg of birds and insects

CLEIK same as > CLEEK

CLEIKS > CLEIK

CLEITHRAL adj covered with a roof

CLEM vb be hungry or cause to be hungry

CLEMATIS n climbing plant with large colourful flowers

CLEMENCY n kind or lenient treatment

CLEMENT adj (of weather) mild

CLEMENTLY > CLEMENT

CLEMMED > CLEM

CLEMMING > CLEM

CLEMS > CLEM

CLENCH vb close or squeeze (one's teeth or fist) tightly ▷ n firm grasp or grip

CLENCHED > CLENCH

CLENCHER > CLENCH

CLENCHERS > CLENCH

CLENCHES > CLENCH

CLENCHING > CLENCH

CLEOME n type of herbaceous or shrubby plant

CLEOMES > CLEOME

CLEOPATRA n type of yellow butterfly, the male of which has its wings flushed with orange

CLEPE vb call by the name of

CLEPED > CLEPE

CLEPES > CLEPE

CLEPING > CLEPE

CLEPSYDRA n ancient device for measuring time by the flow of water or mercury through a small aperture

CLEPT > CLEPE

CLERGIES > CLERGY

CLERGY n priests and ministers as a group

CLERGYMAN n member of the clergy

CLERGYMEN > CLERGYMAN

CLERIC n member of the clergy

CLERICAL adj of clerks or office work

CLERICALS pl n distinctive dress of a clergyman or clergywoman

CLERICATE n clerical post

CLERICITY n condition of being a clergyman or clergywoman

CLERICS > CLERIC

CLERID n beetle that preys on other insects

CLERIDS > CLERID

CLERIHEW n form of comic or satiric verse

CLERIHEWS > CLERIHEW

CLERISIES > CLERISY

CLERISY n learned or educated people

CLERK n employee who keeps records, files, and accounts ▷ vb work as a clerk

CLERKDOM > CLERK

CLERKDOMS > CLERK

CLERKED > CLERK

CLERKESS n female office clerk

CLERKING > CLERK

CLERKISH > CLERK

CLERKLIER > CLERKLY

CLERKLIKE adj acting in a scholarly manner

CLERKLING n young or inexperienced clerk

CLERKLY adj of or like a clerk ▷ adv in the manner of a clerk

CLERKS > CLERK

CLERKSHIP > CLERK

CLERUCH n settler in a cleruchy

CLERUCHIA same as > CLERUCHY

CLERUCHS > CLERUCH

CLERUCHY n type of colony of ancient Athens

CLEUCH same as > CLOUGH

CLEUCHS > CLEUCH

CLEUGH same as > CLOUGH

CLEUGHS > CLEUGH

CLEVE same as > CLEEVE

CLEVEITE n crystalline variety of the mineral uraninite

CLEVEITES > CLEVEITE

CLEVER adj intelligent, quick at learning

CLEVERER > CLEVER

CLEVEREST > CLEVER

CLEVERISH > CLEVER

CLEVERLY > CLEVER

CLEVES > CLEVE

CLEVIS n type of fastening used in agriculture

CLEVISES > CLEVIS

CLEW n ball of thread, yarn, or twine ▷ vb coil or roll into a ball

CLEWED > CLEW

CLEWING > CLEW

CLEWS > CLEW

CLIANTHUS n Australian or NZ plant with slender scarlet flowers

CLICHE n expression or idea that is no longer effective because of overuse ▷ vb use a cliché (in speech or writing)

CLICHED > CLICHE

CLICHEED > CLICHE

CLICHES > CLICHE

CLICK n short sharp sound ▷ vb make this sound

CLICKABLE adj (of a website) having links that can be accessed by clicking a computer mouse

CLICKBAIT n hyperlink that entices one to click through to a new website

CLICKED > CLICK

CLICKER > CLICK

CLICKERS > CLICK
CLICKET vb make a click
CLICKETED > CLICKET
CLICKETS > CLICKET
CLICKING > CLICK
CLICKINGS > CLICK
CLICKLESS > CLICK
CLICKS > CLICK
CLICKWRAP adj (of agreement) consented to by user clicking computer button
CLIED > CLY
CLIENT n person who uses the services of a professional person or company
CLIENTAGE same as > CLIENTELE
CLIENTAL > CLIENT
CLIENTELE n clients collectively
CLIENTS > CLIENT
CLIES > CLY
CLIFF n steep rock face, esp along the sea shore ▷ vb scale a cliff
CLIFFED > CLIFF
CLIFFHANG vb (of a serial or film) to end on a note of suspense
CLIFFHUNG > CLIFFHANG
CLIFFIER > CLIFF
CLIFFIEST > CLIFF
CLIFFLIKE > CLIFF
CLIFFS > CLIFF
CLIFFSIDE n side of a cliff
CLIFFTOP n top of a cliff
CLIFFTOPS > CLIFFTOP
CLIFFY > CLIFF
CLIFT same as > CLIFF
CLIFTED > CLIFT
CLIFTIER > CLIFT
CLIFTIEST > CLIFT
CLIFTS > CLIFT
CLIFTY > CLIFT
CLIMACTIC adj consisting of, involving, or causing a climax
CLIMATAL > CLIMATE
CLIMATE n typical weather conditions of an area ▷ vb acclimatize
CLIMATED > CLIMATE
CLIMATES > CLIMATE
CLIMATIC > CLIMATE
CLIMATING > CLIMATE
CLIMATISE vb in Australia, adapt or become accustomed to a new climate or environment
CLIMATIZE same as > CLIMATISE
CLIMATURE n clime
CLIMAX n most intense point of an experience, series of events, or story ▷ vb reach a climax
CLIMAXED > CLIMAX
CLIMAXES > CLIMAX
CLIMAXING > CLIMAX
CLIMB vb go up, ascend ▷ n climbing
CLIMBABLE > CLIMB
CLIMBDOWN n act of backing down from opinion
CLIMBED > CLIMB
CLIMBER n person or thing that climbs

CLIMBERS > CLIMBER
CLIMBING > CLIMB
CLIMBINGS > CLIMB
CLIMBS > CLIMB
CLIME n place or its climate
CLIMES > CLIME
CLINAL > CLINE
CLINALLY > CLINE
CLINAMEN n bias
CLINAMENS > CLINAMEN
CLINCH vb settle (an argument or agreement) decisively ▷ n movement in which one competitor holds on to the other to avoid punches
CLINCHED > CLINCH
CLINCHER n something decisive
CLINCHERS > CLINCHER
CLINCHES > CLINCH
CLINCHING > CLINCH
CLINE n variation within a species
CLINES > CLINE
CLING vb hold tightly or stick closely ▷ n tendency of cotton fibres in a sample to stick to each other
CLINGED > CLING
CLINGER > CLING
CLINGERS > CLING
CLINGFILM n thin polythene material for wrapping food
CLINGFISH n type of small marine fish with a flattened elongated body and a sucking disc beneath the head for clinging to rocks, etc
CLINGIER > CLING
CLINGIEST > CLING
CLINGING > CLING
CLINGS > CLING
CLINGWRAP same as > CLINGFILM
CLINGY > CLING
CLINIC n building where outpatients receive medical treatment or advice
CLINICAL adj of a clinic
CLINICIAN n physician, psychiatrist, etc, who specializes in clinical work as opposed to one engaged in laboratory or experimental studies
CLINICS > CLINIC
CLINIQUE same as > CLINIC
CLINIQUES > CLINIC
CLINK n light sharp metallic sound ▷ vb make a light sharp metallic sound
CLINKED > CLINK
CLINKER n fused coal left over in a fire or furnace ▷ vb form clinker during burning
CLINKERED > CLINKER
CLINKERS > CLINKER
CLINKING > CLINK
CLINKS > CLINK
CLINOAXES > CLINOAXIS
CLINOAXIS n in a monoclinic crystal, the lateral axis which forms an oblique angle with the vertical axis

CLINOSTAT n apparatus for studying tropisms in plants, usually a rotating disc to which the plant is attached so that it receives an equal stimulus on all sides
CLINQUANT adj glittering, esp with tinsel ▷ n tinsel or imitation gold leaf
CLINT n section of a limestone pavement separated from others by fissures
CLINTONIA n type of temperate plant with white, greenish-yellow, or purplish flowers, broad ribbed leaves, and blue berries
CLINTS > CLINT
CLIOMETRY n study of economic history using statistics and computer analysis
CLIP vb cut with shears or scissors ▷ n short extract of a film
CLIPART n large collection of simple drawings stored in a computer
CLIPARTS > CLIPART
CLIPBOARD n portable writing board with a clip at the top for holding paper
CLIPE same as > CLYPE
CLIPED > CLIPE
CLIPES > CLIPE
CLIPING > CLIPE
CLIPPABLE > CLIP
CLIPPED > CLIP
CLIPPER n fast commercial sailing ship
CLIPPERS pl n tool for clipping
CLIPPIE n bus conductress
CLIPPIES > CLIPPIE
CLIPPING > CLIP
CLIPPINGS > CLIP
CLIPS > CLIP
CLIPSHEAR n earwig
CLIPSHEET n sheet of paper with text printed on one side only
CLIPT old inflection of > CLIP
CLIQUE n small exclusive group ▷ vb form a clique
CLIQUED > CLIQUE
CLIQUES > CLIQUE
CLIQUEY adj exclusive, confined to a small group
CLIQUIER > CLIQUEY
CLIQUIEST > CLIQUEY
CLIQUING > CLIQUE
CLIQUISH > CLIQUE
CLIQUISM n small exclusive group
CLIQUISMS > CLIQUE
CLIQUY same as > CLIQUEY
CLIT same as > CLITORIS
CLITELLA > CLITELLUM
CLITELLAR > CLITELLUM
CLITELLUM n thickened saddle-like region of epidermis in earthworms and leeches
CLITHRAL same as > CLEITHRAL
CLITIC adj (of a word) incapable of being stressed ▷ n clitic word

CLITICISE same as > CLITICIZE
CLITICIZE vb pronounce as part of following or preceding word
CLITICS > CLITIC
CLITORAL > CLITORIS
CLITORIC > CLITORIS
CLITORIS n small sensitive organ at the front of the vulva
CLITS > CLIT
CLITTER vb make a shrill noise
CLITTERED > CLITTER
CLITTERS > CLITTER
CLIVERS same as > CLEAVERS
CLIVIA n plant belonging to the Amaryllid family
CLIVIAS > CLIVIA
CLOACA n body cavity in most animals
CLOACAE > CLOACA
CLOACAL > CLOACA
CLOACAS > CLOACA
CLOACINAL > CLOACA
CLOACITIS n inflammation of the cloaca in birds, including domestic fowl, and other animals with a common opening of the urinary and gastrointestinal tracts
CLOAK n loose sleeveless outer garment ▷ vb cover or conceal
CLOAKED > CLOAK
CLOAKING > CLOAK
CLOAKROOM n room where coats may be left temporarily
CLOAKS > CLOAK
CLOAM adj made of clay or earthenware ▷ n clay or earthenware pots, dishes, etc, collectively
CLOAMS > CLOAM
CLOBBER vb hit ▷ n belongings, esp clothes
CLOBBERED > CLOBBER
CLOBBERS > CLOBBER
CLOCHARD n tramp
CLOCHARDS > CLOCHARD
CLOCHE n cover to protect young plants
CLOCHES > CLOCHE
CLOCK n instrument for showing the time ▷ vb record (time) with a stopwatch
CLOCKED > CLOCK
CLOCKER > CLOCK
CLOCKERS > CLOCK
CLOCKFACE n face of a clock
CLOCKING > CLOCK
CLOCKINGS > CLOCK
CLOCKLIKE > CLOCK
CLOCKS > CLOCK
CLOCKWISE adj in the direction in which the hands of a clock rotate
CLOCKWORK n mechanism similar to the kind in a clock, used in wind-up toys
CLOD n lump of earth ▷ vb pelt with clods
CLODDED > CLOD

CLODDIER > CLOD
CLODDIEST > CLOD
CLODDING > CLOD
CLODDISH > CLOD
CLODDY > CLOD
CLODLY > CLOD
CLODPATE n dull or stupid person
CLODPATED adj stupid
CLODPATES > CLODPATE
CLODPOLE same as > CLODPATE
CLODPOLES > CLODPOLE
CLODPOLL same as > CLODPATE
CLODPOLLS > CLODPOLL
CLODS > CLOD
CLOFF n cleft of a tree
CLOFFS > CLOFF
CLOG vb obstruct ▷ n wooden or wooden-soled shoe
CLOGDANCE n dance performed in clogs
CLOGGED > CLOG
CLOGGER n clogmaker
CLOGGERS > CLOGGER
CLOGGIER > CLOG
CLOGGIEST > CLOG
CLOGGILY > CLOG
CLOGGING > CLOG
CLOGGINGS > CLOG
CLOGGY > CLOG
CLOGMAKER n maker of clogs
CLOGS > CLOG
CLOISON n partition
CLOISONNE n design made by filling in a wire outline with coloured enamel ▷ adj of, relating to, or made by cloisonné
CLOISONS > CLOISON
CLOISTER n covered pillared arcade, usu in a monastery ▷ vb confine or seclude in or as if in a monastery
CLOISTERS > CLOISTER
CLOISTRAL adj of, like, or characteristic of a cloister
CLOKE same as > CLOAK
CLOKED > CLOKE
CLOKES > CLOKE
CLOKING > CLOKE
CLOMB a past tense and past participle of > CLIMB
CLOMP same as > CLUMP
CLOMPED > CLOMP
CLOMPING > CLOMP
CLOMPS > CLOMP
CLON same as > CLONE
CLONAL > CLONE
CLONALLY > CLONE
CLONE n animal or plant produced artificially from the cells of another animal or plant ▷ vb produce as a clone
CLONED > CLONE
CLONER > CLONE
CLONERS > CLONE
CLONES > CLONE
CLONIC > CLONUS
CLONICITY > CLONUS
CLONIDINE n anti-hypertensive drug
CLONING > CLONE

CLONINGS > CLONE
CLONISM n series of clonic spasms
CLONISMS > CLONISM
CLONK vb make a loud dull thud ▷ n loud thud
CLONKED > CLONK
CLONKIER > CLONKY
CLONKIEST > CLONKY
CLONKING > CLONK
CLONKS > CLONK
CLONKY same as > CLUNKY
CLONS > CLON
CLONUS n type of convulsion
CLONUSES > CLONUS
CLOOP n sound made when a cork is drawn from a bottle
CLOOPS > CLOOP
CLOOT n hoof
CLOOTIE adj as in clootie dumpling kind of dumpling
CLOOTS > CLOOT
CLOP vb make a sound as of a horse's hooves ▷ n sound of this nature
CLOPPED > CLOP
CLOPPING > CLOP
CLOPS > CLOP
CLOQUE n fabric with an embossed surface
CLOQUES > CLOQUE
CLOSABLE > CLOSE
CLOSE vb shut ▷ n end, conclusion ▷ adj near ▷ adv closely, tightly
CLOSEABLE > CLOSE
CLOSED > CLOSE
CLOSEDOWN n closure or stoppage of operations
CLOSEHEAD n entrance to a close
CLOSELY > CLOSE
CLOSENESS > CLOSE
CLOSEOUT n termination of an account on which the margin is exhausted
CLOSEOUTS > CLOSEOUT
CLOSER > CLOSE
CLOSERS > CLOSE
CLOSES > CLOSE
CLOSEST > CLOSE
CLOSET n cupboard ▷ adj private, secret ▷ vb shut (oneself) away in private
CLOSETED > CLOSET
CLOSETFUL n quantity that may be contained in a closet
CLOSETING > CLOSET
CLOSETS > CLOSET
CLOSEUP n photo taken close to subject
CLOSEUPS > CLOSEUP
CLOSING > CLOSE
CLOSINGS > CLOSE
CLOSURE n closing ▷ vb (in a deliberative body) to end (debate) by closure
CLOSURED > CLOSURE
CLOSURES > CLOSURE
CLOSURING > CLOSURE
CLOT n soft thick lump formed from liquid ▷ vb form soft thick lumps
CLOTBUR n burdock
CLOTBURS > CLOTBUR
CLOTE n burdock
CLOTES > CLOTE

CLOTH n (piece of) woven fabric
CLOTHE vb put clothes on
CLOTHED > CLOTHE
CLOTHES pl n garments
CLOTHIER n maker or seller of clothes or cloth
CLOTHIERS > CLOTHIER
CLOTHING > CLOTHE
CLOTHINGS > CLOTHE
CLOTHLIKE > CLOTH
CLOTHS > CLOTH
CLOTPOLL same as > CLODPOLL
CLOTPOLLS > CLOTPOLL
CLOTS > CLOT
CLOTTED > CLOT
CLOTTER vb to clot
CLOTTERED > CLOTTER
CLOTTERS > CLOTTER
CLOTTIER > CLOTTY
CLOTTIEST > CLOTTY
CLOTTING > CLOT
CLOTTINGS > CLOT
CLOTTISH > CLOT
CLOTTY adj full of clots
CLOTURE n closure in the US Senate ▷ vb end (debate) in the US Senate by cloture
CLOTURED > CLOTURE
CLOTURES > CLOTURE
CLOTURING > CLOTURE
CLOU n crux; focus
CLOUD n mass of condensed water vapour floating in the sky ▷ vb become cloudy
CLOUDAGE n mass of clouds
CLOUDAGES > CLOUDAGE
CLOUDED > CLOUD
CLOUDIER > CLOUDY
CLOUDIEST > CLOUDY
CLOUDILY > CLOUDY
CLOUDING > CLOUD
CLOUDINGS > CLOUD
CLOUDLAND n realm or fantasy or impractical notions
CLOUDLESS > CLOUD
CLOUDLET n small cloud
CLOUDLETS > CLOUDLET
CLOUDLIKE > CLOUD
CLOUDS > CLOUD
CLOUDTOWN n cloudland
CLOUDY adj having a lot of clouds
CLOUGH n gorge or narrow ravine
CLOUGHS > CLOUGH
CLOUR vb to thump or dent
CLOURED > CLOUR
CLOURING > CLOUR
CLOURS > CLOUR
CLOUS > CLOU
CLOUT n hard blow ▷ vb hit hard
CLOUTED > CLOUT
CLOUTER > CLOUT
CLOUTERLY adj clumsy
CLOUTERS > CLOUT
CLOUTING > CLOUT
CLOUTS > CLOUT
CLOVE n tropical evergreen myrtaceous tree
CLOVEN > CLEAVE
CLOVER n plant with three-lobed leaves

CLOVERED adj covered with clover
CLOVERIER > CLOVERY
CLOVERS > CLOVER
CLOVERY adj like clover
CLOVES > CLOVE
CLOVIS n as in clovis point flint projectile dating from the 10th millennium BC
CLOW n clove ▷ vb rake with a fork
CLOWDER n collective term for a group of cats
CLOWDERS > CLOWDER
CLOWED > CLOW
CLOWING > CLOW
CLOWN n comic entertainer in a circus ▷ vb behave foolishly
CLOWNED > CLOWN
CLOWNERY > CLOWN
CLOWNFISH n small, brightly coloured tropical fish
CLOWNING > CLOWN
CLOWNINGS > CLOWN
CLOWNISH > CLOWN
CLOWNS > CLOWN
CLOWS > CLOW
CLOY vb cause weariness through an excess of something initially pleasurable
CLOYE vb to claw
CLOYED > CLOY
CLOYES > CLOYE
CLOYING adj sickeningly sweet
CLOYINGLY > CLOYING
CLOYLESS adj not cloying
CLOYMENT n satiety
CLOYMENTS > CLOYMENT
CLOYS > CLOY
CLOYSOME adj cloying
CLOZAPINE n drug used to treat mental illness
CLOZE adj as in cloze test test of the ability to understand text
CLOZES > CLOZE
CLUB n association of people with common interests ▷ vb hit with a club
CLUBABLE same as > CLUBBABLE
CLUBBABLE adj suitable to be a member of a club
CLUBBED > CLUB
CLUBBER n person who regularly frequents nightclubs
CLUBBERS > CLUBBER
CLUBBIER > CLUBBY
CLUBBIEST > CLUBBY
CLUBBILY > CLUBBY
CLUBBING > CLUB
CLUBBINGS > CLUB
CLUBBISH adj clubby
CLUBBISM n advantage gained through membership of a club or clubs
CLUBBISMS > CLUBBISM
CLUBBIST > CLUBBISM
CLUBBISTS > CLUBBISM
CLUBBY adj sociable, esp effusively so
CLUBFACE n face of golf club

CLUBFACES > CLUBFACE
CLUBFEET > CLUBFOOT
CLUBFOOT n congenital deformity of the foot
CLUBHAND n congenital deformity of the hand
CLUBHANDS > CLUBHAND
CLUBHAUL vb force (a sailing vessel) onto a new tack, esp in an emergency
CLUBHAULS > CLUBHAUL
CLUBHEAD n head of golf club
CLUBHEADS > CLUBHEAD
CLUBHOUSE n premises of a sports or other club, esp a golf club
CLUBLAND n area of London which contains most of the famous clubs
CLUBLANDS > CLUBLAND
CLUBLIKE adj like a club
CLUBMAN n man who is an enthusiastic member of a club or clubs
CLUBMATE n friend or contemporary in the same club
CLUBMATES > CLUBMATE
CLUBMEN > CLUBMAN
CLUBMOSS n type of green moss-like plant
CLUBROOM n room in which a club meets
CLUBROOMS > CLUBROOM
CLUBROOT n disease of cabbages
CLUBROOTS > CLUBROOT
CLUBRUSH n any rush of the genus Scirpus
CLUBS > CLUB
CLUBWOMAN n woman who is an enthusiastic member of a club or clubs
CLUBWOMEN > CLUBWOMAN
CLUCK n low clicking noise made by a hen ▷ vb make this noise
CLUCKED > CLUCK
CLUCKER n chicken
CLUCKERS > CLUCKER
CLUCKIER > CLUCKY
CLUCKIEST > CLUCKY
CLUCKING > CLUCK
CLUCKS > CLUCK
CLUCKY adj wishing to have a baby
CLUDGIE n toilet
CLUDGIES > CLUDGIE
CLUE n something that helps to solve a mystery or puzzle ▷ vb help solve a mystery or puzzle
CLUED > CLUE
CLUEING > CLUE
CLUELESS adj stupid
CLUES > CLUE
CLUEY adj (Australian) well-informed and adroit
CLUIER > CLUEY
CLUIEST > CLUEY
CLUING > CLUE
CLUMBER n type of thickset spaniel
CLUMBERS > CLUMBER
CLUMP n small group of things or people ▷ vb walk heavily

CLUMPED > CLUMP
CLUMPER vb walk heavily
CLUMPERED > CLUMPER
CLUMPERS > CLUMP
CLUMPET n large chunk of floating ice
CLUMPETS > CLUMPET
CLUMPIER > CLUMP
CLUMPIEST > CLUMP
CLUMPING > CLUMP
CLUMPISH > CLUMP
CLUMPLIKE > CLUMP
CLUMPS > CLUMP
CLUMPY > CLUMP
CLUMSIER > CLUMSY
CLUMSIEST > CLUMSY
CLUMSILY > CLUMSY
CLUMSY adj lacking skill or physical coordination
CLUNCH n hardened clay
CLUNCHES > CLUNCH
CLUNG > CLING
CLUNK n dull metallic sound ▷ vb make such a sound
CLUNKED > CLUNK
CLUNKER n dilapidated old car or other machine
CLUNKERS > CLUNKER
CLUNKIER > CLUNKY
CLUNKIEST > CLUNKY
CLUNKING > CLUNK
CLUNKS > CLUNK
CLUNKY adj making a clunking noise
CLUPEID n type of fish
CLUPEIDS > CLUPEID
CLUPEOID n type of soft-finned fish
CLUPEOIDS > CLUPEOID
CLUSIA n tree of the tropical American genus Clusia
CLUSIAS > CLUSIA
CLUSTER n small close group ▷ vb gather in clusters
CLUSTERED > CLUSTER
CLUSTERS > CLUSTER
CLUSTERY adj full of clusters
CLUTCH vb grasp tightly ▷ n mechanical device
CLUTCHED > CLUTCH
CLUTCHES > CLUTCH
CLUTCHIER > CLUTCHY
CLUTCHING > CLUTCH
CLUTCHY adj (of a person) tending to cling
CLUTTER vb scatter objects about (a place) untidily ▷ n untidy mess
CLUTTERED > CLUTTER
CLUTTERS > CLUTTER
CLUTTERY adj full of clutter
CLY vb steal or seize
CLYING > CLY
CLYPE vb tell tales ▷ n person who tells tales
CLYPEAL > CLYPEUS
CLYPEATE > CLYPEUS
CLYPED > CLYPE
CLYPEI > CLYPEUS
CLYPES > CLYPE
CLYPEUS n cuticular plate on the head of some insects
CLYPING > CLYPE
CLYSTER a former name for an > ENEMA

CLYSTERS > CLYSTER
CNEMIAL > CNEMIS
CNEMIDES > CNEMIS
CNEMIS n shin or tibia
CNIDA n stinging organ in jellyfish
CNIDAE > CNIDA
CNIDARIAN n type of invertebrate of the phylum which comprises the coelenterates
COACH n long-distance bus ▷ vb train, teach
COACHABLE adj capable of being coached
COACHDOG n Dalmatian dog
COACHDOGS > COACHDOG
COACHED > COACH
COACHEE n person who receives training from a coach
COACHEES > COACHEE
COACHER > COACH
COACHERS > COACH
COACHES > COACH
COACHIER > COACHY
COACHIES > COACHY
COACHIEST > COACHY
COACHING > COACH
COACHINGS > COACH
COACHLINE n decorative line on the bodywork of a vehicle
COACHLOAD n quantity that a coach can carry
COACHMAN n driver of a horse-drawn coach or carriage
COACHMEN > COACHMAN
COACHROOF n raised part of yacht cabin roof
COACHWHIP n whipsnake
COACHWOOD n Australian tree yielding light aromatic wood used for furniture etc
COACHWORK n body of a car
COACHY n coachman ▷ adj resembling or pertaining to a coach
COACT vb act together
COACTED > COACT
COACTING > COACT
COACTION n any relationship between organisms within a community
COACTIONS > COACTION
COACTIVE > COACTION
COACTOR > COACT
COACTORS > COACT
COACTS > COACT
COADAPTED adj adapted to one another
COADIES > COADY
COADJUTOR n bishop appointed as assistant to a diocesan bishop
COADMIRE vb admire together
COADMIRED > COADMIRE
COADMIRES > COADMIRE
COADMIT vb admit together
COADMITS > COADMIT
COADUNATE same as > CONNATE
COADY n sauce made from molasses

COAEVAL n contemporary
COAEVALS > COAEVAL
COAGENCY n joint agency
COAGENT > COAGENCY
COAGENTS > COAGENCY
COAGULA > COAGULUM
COAGULANT n substance causing coagulation
COAGULASE n any enzyme that causes coagulation of blood
COAGULATE vb change from a liquid to a semisolid mass ▷ n solid or semisolid substance produced by coagulation
COAGULUM n any coagulated mass
COAGULUMS > COAGULUM
COAITA n spider monkey
COAITAS > COAITA
COAL n black rock consisting mainly of carbon, used as fuel ▷ vb take in, or turn into coal
COALA same as > KOALA
COALAS > COALA
COALBALL n in coal, nodule containing petrified plant or animal remains
COALBALLS > COALBALL
COALBIN n bin for holding coal
COALBINS > COALBIN
COALBOX n box for holding coal
COALBOXES > COALBOX
COALDUST n dust from coal
COALDUSTS > COALDUST
COALED > COAL
COALER n ship, train, etc, used to carry or supply coal
COALERS > COALER
COALESCE vb come together, merge
COALESCED > COALESCE
COALESCES > COALESCE
COALFACE n exposed seam of coal in a mine
COALFACES > COALFACE
COALFIELD n area with coal under the ground
COALFISH n type of dark-coloured food fish occurring in northern seas
COALHOLE n small coal cellar
COALHOLES > COALHOLE
COALHOUSE n shed or building for storing coal
COALIER > COAL
COALIEST > COAL
COALIFIED > COALIFY
COALIFIES > COALIFY
COALIFY vb turn into coal
COALING > COAL
COALISE vb form a coalition
COALISED > COALISE
COALISES > COALISE
COALISING > COALISE
COALITION n temporary alliance, esp between political parties
COALIZE same as > COALISE
COALIZED > COALIZE
COALIZES > COALIZE

COALIZING > COALIZE
COALLESS adj without coal
COALMAN n man who delivers coal
COALMEN > COALMAN
COALMINE n mine from which coal is extracted
COALMINER > COALMINE
COALMINES > COALMINE
COALPIT n pit from which coal is extracted
COALPITS > COALPIT
COALS > COAL
COALSACK n dark nebula near the constellation Cygnus
COALSACKS > COALSACK
COALSHED n shed in which coal is stored
COALSHEDS > COALSHED
COALY > COAL
COALYARD n yard in which coal is stored
COALYARDS > COALYARD
COAMING n raised frame round a ship's hatchway for keeping out water
COAMINGS > COAMING
COANCHOR vb co-present a TV programme
COANCHORS > COANCHOR
COANNEX vb annex with something else
COANNEXED > COANNEX
COANNEXES > COANNEX
COAPPEAR vb appear jointly
COAPPEARS > COAPPEAR
COAPT vb secure
COAPTED > COAPT
COAPTING > COAPT
COAPTS > COAPT
COARB n spiritual successor
COARBS > COARB
COARCTATE adj (of a pupa) enclosed in a hard barrel-shaped case (puparium), as in the housefly ▷ vb (esp of the aorta) to become narrower
COARSE adj rough in texture
COARSELY > COARSE
COARSEN vb make or become coarse
COARSENED > COARSEN
COARSENS > COARSEN
COARSER > COARSE
COARSEST > COARSE
COARSISH > COARSE
COASSIST vb assist jointly
COASSISTS > COASSIST
COASSUME vb assume jointly
COASSUMED > COASSUME
COASSUMES > COASSUME
COAST n place where the land meets the sea ▷ vb move by momentum, without the use of power
COASTAL > COAST
COASTALLY > COAST
COASTED > COAST
COASTER n small mat placed under a glass
COASTERS > COASTER
COASTING > COAST
COASTINGS > COAST
COASTLAND n land fringing a coast

COASTLINE n outline of a coast
COASTS > COAST
COASTWARD adv towards the coast
COASTWISE adv along the coast
COAT n outer garment with long sleeves ▷ vb cover with a layer
COATDRESS n garment that can be worn as a coat or a dress
COATE same as > QUOTE
COATED adj covered with an outer layer, film, etc
COATEE n short coat, esp for a baby
COATEES > COATEE
COATER n machine that applies a coating to something
COATERS > COATER
COATES > COATE
COATI n type of omnivorous mammal
COATING n covering layer
COATINGS > COATING
COATIS > COATI
COATLESS adj without a coat
COATLIKE adj like a coat
COATRACK n rack for hanging coats on
COATRACKS > COATRACK
COATROOM n cloakroom
COATROOMS > COATROOM
COATS > COAT
COATSTAND n stand for hanging coats on
COATTAIL n long tapering tail at the back of a man's tailored coat
COATTAILS > COATTAIL
COATTEND vb attend jointly
COATTENDS > COATTEND
COATTEST vb attest jointly
COATTESTS > COATTEST
COAUTHOR n person who shares the writing of a book, article, etc, with another ▷ vb be the joint author of (a book, article, etc)
COAUTHORS > COAUTHOR
COAX vb persuade gently
COAXAL same as > COAXIAL
COAXED > COAX
COAXER > COAX
COAXERS > COAX
COAXES > COAX
COAXIAL adj (of a cable) transmitting by means of two concentric conductors separated by an insulator
COAXIALLY > COAXIAL
COAXING n act of coaxing
COAXINGLY > COAX
COAXINGS > COAXING
COB n stalk of an ear of maize ▷ vb beat
COBAEA n tropical climbing shrub
COBAEAS > COBAEA
COBALAMIN n vitamin B12
COBALT n brittle silvery-white metallic element

COBALTIC adj of or containing cobalt, esp in the trivalent state
COBALTINE same as > COBALTITE
COBALTITE n rare silvery-white mineral
COBALTOUS adj of or containing cobalt in the divalent state
COBALTS > COBALT
COBB same as > COB
COBBED > COB
COBBER n friend
COBBERS > COBBER
COBBIER > COBBY
COBBIEST > COBBY
COBBING > COB
COBBLE n cobblestone ▷ vb pave (a road) with cobblestones
COBBLED > COBBLE
COBBLER n shoe mender
COBBLERS > COBBLER
COBBLERY n shoemaking or shoemending
COBBLES > COBBLE
COBBLING > COBBLE
COBBLINGS > COBBLE
COBBS > COBB
COBBY adj short and stocky
COBIA n large dark-striped game fish
COBIAS > COBIA
COBLE n small single-masted flat-bottomed fishing boat
COBLES > COBLE
COBLOAF n round loaf of bread
COBLOAVES > COBLOAF
COBNUT another name for > HAZELNUT
COBNUTS > COBNUT
COBRA n venomous hooded snake of Asia and Africa
COBRAS > COBRA
COBRIC > COBRA
COBRIFORM adj cobra-like
COBS > COB
COBURG n rounded loaf with a cross cut on the top
COBURGS > COBURG
COBWEB n spider's web
COBWEBBED > COBWEB
COBWEBBY > COBWEB
COBWEBS > COBWEB
COBZA n Romanian lute
COBZAS > COBZA
COCA n S American shrub
COCAIN same as > COCAINE
COCAINE n drug used illegally as a narcotic and as an anaesthetic
COCAINES > COCAINE
COCAINISE same as > COCAINIZE
COCAINISM n use of cocaine
COCAINIST n cocaine addict
COCAINIZE vb anaesthetize with cocaine
COCAINS > COCAIN
COCAPTAIN vb to captain jointly
COCAS > COCA

COCCAL > COCCUS
COCCI > COCCUS
COCCIC > COCCUS
COCCID n type of homopterous insect
COCCIDIA > COCCIDIUM
COCCIDIAN same as > COCCIDIUM
COCCIDIUM n any parasitic protozoan of the order Coccidia
COCCIDS > COCCID
COCCO n taro
COCCOID > COCCUS
COCCOIDAL > COCCUS
COCCOIDS > COCCUS
COCCOLITE n variety of pyroxene
COCCOLITH n any of the round calcareous plates in chalk formations: formed the outer layer of unicellular plankton
COCCOS > COCCO
COCCOUS > COCCUS
COCCUS n any spherical or nearly spherical bacterium
COCCYGEAL > COCCYX
COCCYGES > COCCYX
COCCYGIAN > COCCYX
COCCYX n bone at the base of the spinal column
COCCYXES > COCCYX
COCH obsolete variant of > COACH
COCHAIR vb chair jointly
COCHAIRED > COCHAIR
COCHAIRS > COCHAIR
COCHES > COCH
COCHIN n large breed of domestic fowl
COCHINEAL n red dye obtained from a Mexican insect, used for food colouring
COCHINS > COCHIN
COCHLEA n spiral tube in the internal ear
COCHLEAE > COCHLEA
COCHLEAR adj of or relating to the cochlea ▷ n spoonful
COCHLEARE variant of > COCHLEAR
COCHLEARS > COCHLEAR
COCHLEAS > COCHLEA
COCHLEATE adj shaped like a snail's shell
COCINERA n in Mexico, a female cook
COCINERAS > COCINERA
COCK n male bird, esp of domestic fowl ▷ vb draw back (the hammer of a gun) to firing position
COCKADE n feather or rosette worn on a hat as a badge
COCKADED > COCKADE
COCKADES > COCKADE
COCKAMAMY adj ridiculous or nonsensical
COCKAPOO n cross between a cocker spaniel and a poodle
COCKAPOOS > COCKAPOO
COCKATEEL same as > COCKATIEL

c

COCKATIEL n crested Australian parrot with a greyish-brown and yellow plumage

COCKATOO n crested parrot of Australia or the East Indies

COCKATOOS > COCKATOO

COCKBILL vb tilt up one end of

COCKBILLS > COCKBILL

COCKBIRD n male bird

COCKBIRDS > COCKBIRD

COCKBOAT n any small boat

COCKBOATS > COCKBOAT

COCKCROW n daybreak

COCKCROWS > COCKCROW

COCKED > COCK

COCKER n devotee of cockfighting ▷ vb pamper or spoil by indulgence

COCKERED > COCKER

COCKEREL n young domestic cock

COCKERELS > COCKEREL

COCKERING > COCKER

COCKERS > COCKER

COCKET n document issued by a customs officer

COCKETS > COCKET

COCKEYE n eye affected with strabismus or one that squints

COCKEYED adj crooked, askew

COCKEYES > COCKEYE

COCKFIGHT n fight between two gamecocks fitted with sharp metal spurs

COCKHORSE n rocking horse

COCKIER > COCKY

COCKIES > COCKY

COCKIEST > COCKY

COCKILY > COCKY

COCKINESS n conceited self-assurance

COCKING > COCK

COCKISH adj wanton

COCKLE n edible shellfish ▷ vb fish for cockles

COCKLEBUR n type of coarse weed with spiny burs

COCKLED > COCKLE

COCKLEERT a Southwest English dialect variant of > COCKCROW

COCKLEMAN n man who collects cockles

COCKLEMEN > COCKLEMAN

COCKLER n person employed to gather cockles

COCKLERS > COCKLER

COCKLES > COCKLE

COCKLIKE adj resembling a cock

COCKLING > COCKLE

COCKLINGS > COCKLING

COCKLOFT n small loft, garret, or attic

COCKLOFTS > COCKLOFT

COCKMATCH n cockfight

COCKNEY n native of London, esp of its East End ▷ adj characteristic of cockneys or their dialect

COCKNEYFY vb cause (one's speech, manners, etc) to fit the stereotyped idea of a cockney

COCKNEYS > COCKNEY

COCKNIFY same as > COCKNEYFY

COCKPIT n pilot's compartment in an aircraft

COCKPITS > COCKPIT

COCKROACH n beetle-like insect which is a household pest

COCKS > COCK

COCKSCOMB n comb of a domestic cock

COCKSFOOT n type of Eurasian grass, cultivated as a pasture grass in N America and S Africa

COCKSHIES > COCKSHY

COCKSHOT another name for > COCKSHY

COCKSHOTS > COCKSHOT

COCKSHUT n dusk

COCKSHUTS > COCKSHUT

COCKSHY n target aimed at in throwing games

COCKSIER > COCKSY

COCKSIEST > COCKSY

COCKSMAN n man reputed to be sexually accomplished

COCKSMEN > COCKSMAN

COCKSPUR n spur on the leg of a cock

COCKSPURS > COCKSPUR

COCKSURE adj overconfident, arrogant

COCKSWAIN same as > COXSWAIN

COCKSY adj cocky

COCKTAIL n mixed alcoholic drink

COCKTAILS > COCKTAIL

COCKUP n something done badly ▷ vb ruin or spoil

COCKUPS > COCKUP

COCKY adj conceited and overconfident ▷ n farmer whose farm is regarded as small or of little account

COCO n coconut palm

COCOA n powder made from the seed of the cacao tree

COCOANUT same as > COCONUT

COCOANUTS > COCONUT

COCOAS > COCOA

COCOBOLA n type of rosewood

COCOBOLAS > COCOBOLA

COCOBOLO same as > COCOBOLA

COCOBOLOS > COCOBOLO

COCOMAT n mat made from coconut fibre

COCOMATS > COCOMAT

COCONUT n large hard fruit of a type of palm tree

COCONUTS > COCONUT

COCONUTTY adj tasting of coconut

COCOON n silky protective covering of a silkworm ▷ vb wrap up tightly for protection

COCOONED > COCOON

COCOONER n person who retreats to a secure family environment

COCOONERS > COCOONER

COCOONERY n place where silkworms feed and make cocoons

COCOONING > COCOON

COCOONS > COCOON

COCOPAN n (in South Africa) a small wagon running on narrow-gauge railway lines used in mines

COCOPANS > COCOPAN

COCOPLUM n tropical shrub or its fruit

COCOPLUMS > COCOPLUM

COCOS > COCO

COCOTTE n small fireproof dish in which individual portions of food are cooked

COCOTTES > COCOTTE

COCOUNSEL vb to counsel jointly

COCOYAM n food plant of West Africa with edible underground stem

COCOYAMS > COCOYAM

COCOZELLE n variety of squash

COCREATE vb create jointly

COCREATED > COCREATE

COCREATES > COCREATE

COCREATOR > COCREATE

COCTILE adj made by exposing to heat

COCTION n boiling

COCTIONS > COCTION

COCULTURE vb to culture together

COCURATE vb curate jointly

COCURATED > COCURATE

COCURATES > COCURATE

COCURATOR n joint curator

COCUSWOOD n wood from a tropical American leguminous tree, used for inlaying, musical instruments, etc

COD n large food fish of the North Atlantic ▷ adj having the character of an imitation or parody ▷ vb make fun of

CODA n final part of a musical composition

CODABLE adj capable of being coded

CODAS > CODA

CODDED > COD

CODDER n cod fisherman or fishing boat

CODDERS > CODDER

CODDING > COD

CODDLE vb pamper, overprotect ▷ n stew made from ham and bacon scraps

CODDLED > CODDLE

CODDLER > CODDLE

CODDLERS > CODDLE

CODDLES > CODDLE

CODDLING > CODDLE

CODE n system by which messages can be communicated secretly or briefly ▷ vb put into code

CODEBOOK n book containing the means to decipher a code

CODEBOOKS > CODEBOOK

CODEBTOR n fellow debtor

CODEBTORS > CODEBTOR

CODEC n set of electrical equipment

CODECS > CODEC

CODED > CODE

CODEIA n codeine

CODEIAS > CODEIA

CODEIN same as > CODEINE

CODEINA obsolete variant of > CODEINE

CODEINAS > CODEINA

CODEINE n drug used as a painkiller

CODEINES > CODEINE

CODEINS > CODEIN

CODELESS adj lacking a code

CODEN n identification code assigned to a publication

CODENAME same as > CODEWORD

CODENAMES > CODEWORD

CODENS > CODEN

CODER n person or thing that codes

CODERIVE vb derive jointly

CODERIVED > CODERIVE

CODERIVES > CODERIVE

CODERS > CODER

CODES > CODE

CODESIGN vb design jointly

CODESIGNS > CODESIGN

CODETTA n short coda

CODETTAS > CODETTA

CODEVELOP vb to develop jointly

CODEWORD n (esp in military use) a word used to identify a classified plan, operation, etc

CODEWORDS > CODEWORD

CODEX n volume of manuscripts of an ancient text

CODEXES > CODEX

CODFISH n cod

CODFISHES > CODFISH

CODGER n old man

CODGERS > CODGER

CODICES > CODEX

CODICIL n addition to a will

CODICILS > CODICIL

CODIFIED > CODIFY

CODIFIER > CODIFY

CODIFIERS > CODIFY

CODIFIES > CODIFY

CODIFY vb organize (rules or procedures) systematically

CODIFYING > CODIFY

CODILLA n coarse tow of hemp and flax

CODILLAS > CODILLA

CODILLE n in the card game ombre, term indicating that the game is won

CODILLES > CODILLE

CODING > CODE

CODINGS > CODE

CODIRECT vb direct jointly

CODIRECTS > CODIRECT

CODIST n codifier

CODISTS > CODIST

CODLIN same as > CODLING

CODLING n young cod

CODLINGS > CODLING

CODLINS > CODLIN

CODOLOGY n art or practice of bluffing or deception

CODOMAIN n set of values that a function is allowed to take

CODOMAINS > CODOMAIN

CODON n part of a DNA molecule

CODONS > CODON

CODPIECE n bag covering the male genitals, attached to the breeches

CODPIECES > CODPIECE

CODRIVE vb take alternate turns driving a car with another person

CODRIVEN > CODRIVE

CODRIVER n one of two drivers who take turns to drive a car

CODRIVERS > CODRIVER

CODRIVES > CODRIVE

CODRIVING > CODRIVE

CODROVE > CODRIVE

CODS > COD

COECILIAN n tropical limbless amphibian resembling an earthworm

COED adj educating boys and girls together ▷ n school or college that educates boys and girls together

COEDIT vb edit (a book, newspaper, etc) jointly

COEDITED > COEDIT

COEDITING > COEDIT

COEDITOR > COEDIT

COEDITORS > COEDIT

COEDITS > COEDIT

COEDS > COED

COEFFECT n secondary effect

COEFFECTS > COEFFECT

COEHORN n type of small artillery mortar

COEHORNS > COEHORN

COELIAC adj of or relating to the abdomen ▷ n person who has coeliac disease

COELIACS > COELIAC

COELOM n body cavity of many multicellular animals

COELOMATA n animals possessing a coelom

COELOMATE adj possessing a coelom

COELOME same as > COELOM

COELOMES > COELOME

COELOMIC > COELOM

COELOMS > COELOM

COELOSTAT n astronomical instrument consisting of a plane mirror mounted parallel to the earth's axis and rotated about this axis once every two days so that light from a celestial body, esp the sun, is reflected onto a second mirror, which reflects the beam into a telescope

COEMBODY vb embody jointly

COEMPLOY vb employ together

COEMPLOYS > COEMPLOY

COEMPT vb buy up something in its entirety

COEMPTED > COEMPT

COEMPTING > COEMPT

COEMPTION n buying up of the complete supply of a commodity

COEMPTS > COEMPT

COENACLE same as > CENACLE

COENACLES > COENACLE

COENACT vb enact jointly

COENACTED > COENACT

COENACTS > COENACT

COENAMOR vb enamour jointly

COENAMORS > COENAMOR

COENAMOUR vb enamour jointly

COENDURE vb endure together

COENDURED > COENDURE

COENDURES > COENDURE

COENOBIA > COENOBIUM

COENOBITE n member of a religious order in a monastic community

COENOBIUM n monastery or convent

COENOCYTE n mass of protoplasm containing many nuclei and enclosed by a cell wall: occurs in many fungi and some algae

COENOSARC n system of protoplasmic branches connecting the polyps of colonial organisms such as corals

COENURE variant form of > COENURUS

COENURES > COENURE

COENURI > COENURUS

COENURUS n encysted larval form of a type of tapeworm with many encapsulated heads

COENZYME n type of nonprotein organic molecule

COENZYMES > COENZYME

COEQUAL n equal ▷ adj of the same rank, rank, etc

COEQUALLY > COEQUAL

COEQUALS > COEQUAL

COEQUATE vb equate together

COEQUATED > COEQUATE

COEQUATES > COEQUATE

COERCE vb compel, force

COERCED > COERCE

COERCER > COERCE

COERCERS > COERCE

COERCES > COERCE

COERCIBLE > COERCE

COERCIBLY > COERCE

COERCING > COERCE

COERCION n act or power of coercing

COERCIONS > COERCION

COERCIVE > COERCE

COERECT vb erect together

COERECTED > COERECT

COERECTS > COERECT

COESITE n polymorph of silicon dioxide

COESITES > COESITE

COETERNAL adj existing together eternally

COEVAL n contemporary ▷ adj contemporary

COEVALITY > COEVAL

COEVALLY > COEVAL

COEVALS > COEVAL

COEVOLVE vb evolve together

COEVOLVED > COEVOLVE

COEVOLVES > COEVOLVE

COEXERT vb exert together

COEXERTED > COEXERT

COEXERTS > COEXERT

COEXIST vb exist together, esp peacefully despite differences

COEXISTED > COEXIST

COEXISTS > COEXIST

COEXTEND vb extend or cause to extend equally in space or time

COEXTENDS > COEXTEND

COFACTOR n type of nonprotein substance

COFACTORS > COFACTOR

COFEATURE vb to feature together

COFF vb buy

COFFED > COFF

COFFEE n drink made from the roasted and ground seeds of a tropical shrub ▷ adj medium-brown

COFFEEPOT n pot in which coffee is brewed or served

COFFEES > COFFEE

COFFER n chest, esp for storing valuables ▷ vb store

COFFERDAM n watertight enclosure pumped dry to enable construction work to be done

COFFERED > COFFER

COFFERING > COFFERDAM

COFFERS > COFFER

COFFIN n box in which a corpse is buried or cremated ▷ vb place in or as in a coffin

COFFINED > COFFIN

COFFING > COFF

COFFINING > COFFIN

COFFINITE n uranium-bearing silicate mineral

COFFINS > COFFIN

COFFLE n (esp formerly) line of slaves, beasts, etc, fastened together ▷ vb fasten together in a coffle

COFFLED > COFFLE

COFFLES > COFFLE

COFFLING > COFFLE

COFFRET n small coffer

COFFRETS > COFFRET

COFFS > COFF

COFINANCE vb to finance jointly

COFIRING n combustion of two different types of fuel at the same time

COFIRINGS > COFIRING

COFOUND vb found jointly

COFOUNDED > COFOUND

COFOUNDER > COFOUND

COFOUNDS > COFOUND

COFT > COFF

COG n one of the teeth on the rim of a gearwheel ▷ vb roll (cast-steel ingots) to convert them into blooms

COGENCE > COGENT

COGENCES > COGENT

COGENCIES > COGENT

COGENCY > COGENT

COGENER n thing of the same kind

COGENERS > COGENER

COGENT adj forcefully convincing

COGENTLY > COGENT

COGGED > COG

COGGER n deceiver

COGGERS > COGGER

COGGIE n quaich or drinking cup

COGGIES > COGGIE

COGGING > COG

COGGINGS > COG

COGGLE vb wobble or rock

COGGLED > COGGLE

COGGLES > COGGLE

COGGLIER > COGGLE

COGGLIEST > COGGLE

COGGLING > COGGLE

COGGLY > COGGLE

COGIE same as > COGGIE

COGIES > COGIE

COGITABLE adj conceivable

COGITATE vb think deeply about

COGITATED > COGITATE

COGITATES > COGITATE

COGITATOR > COGITATE

COGITO n philosophical theory

COGITOS > COGITO

COGNAC n French brandy

COGNACS > COGNAC

COGNATE adj derived from a common original form ▷ n cognate word or language

COGNATELY > COGNATE

COGNATES > COGNATE

COGNATION > COGNATE

COGNISANT same as > COGNIZANT

COGNISE same as > COGNIZE

COGNISED > COGNISE

COGNISER > COGNISE

COGNISERS > COGNISE

COGNISES > COGNISE

COGNISING > COGNISE

COGNITION n act or experience of knowing or acquiring knowledge

COGNITIVE adj of or relating to cognition

COGNIZANT adj aware

COGNIZE vb perceive, become aware of, or know

COGNIZED > COGNIZE

COGNIZER > COGNIZE

COGNIZERS > COGNIZE

COGNIZES > COGNIZE

COGNIZING > COGNIZE

COGNOMEN n nickname

COGNOMENS > COGNOMEN

COGNOMINA > COGNOMEN

COGNOSCE vb in Scots law, to give judgment upon

COGNOSCED > COGNOSCE

COGNOSCES > COGNOSCE

COGNOVIT n in law, a defendant's confession that the case against him or her is just

COGNOVITS > COGNOVIT

C

c

COGON n type of coarse tropical grass used for thatching

COGONS > COGON

COGS > COG

COGUE n wooden pail or drinking vessel

COGUES > COGUE

COGWAY n rack railway

COGWAYS > COGWAY

COGWHEEL same as > GEARWHEEL

COGWHEELS > COGWHEEL

COHAB n cohabitor

COHABIT vb live together as spouses without being married

COHABITED > COHABIT

COHABITEE > COHABIT

COHABITER > COHABIT

COHABITOR n one who cohabits

COHABITS > COHABIT

COHABS > COHAB

COHEAD vb head jointly

COHEADED > COHEAD

COHEADING > COHEAD

COHEADS > COHEAD

COHEIR n person who inherits jointly with others

COHEIRESS > COHEIR

COHEIRS > COHEIR

COHEN same as > KOHEN

COHENS > COHEN

COHERE vb hold or stick together

COHERED > COHERE

COHERENCE n logical or natural connection or consistency

COHERENCY same as > COHERENCE

COHERENT adj logical and consistent

COHERER n electrical component

COHERERS > COHERER

COHERES > COHERE

COHERING > COHERE

COHERITOR n coheir

COHESIBLE adj capable of cohesion

COHESION n sticking together

COHESIONS > COHESION

COHESIVE adj sticking together to form a whole

COHIBIT vb restrain

COHIBITED > COHIBIT

COHIBITS > COHIBIT

COHO n type of Pacific salmon

COHOBATE vb redistil (a distillate, esp by allowing it to mingle with the remaining matter

COHOBATED > COHOBATE

COHOBATES > COHOBATE

COHOE same as > COHO

COHOES > COHO

COHOG n quahog, an edible clam

COHOGS > COHOG

COHOLDER n joint holder

COHOLDERS > COHOLDER

COHORN same as > COEHORN

COHORNS > COHORN

COHORT n band of associates

COHORTS > COHORT

COHOS > COHO

COHOSH n type of North American plant

COHOSHES > COHOSH

COHOST vb host jointly

COHOSTED > COHOST

COHOSTESS vb (of a woman) to host jointly

COHOSTING > COHOST

COHOSTS > COHOST

COHOUSING n type of housing with some shared facilities

COHUNE n tropical feather palm

COHUNES > COHUNE

COHYPONYM n word which is one of multiple hyponyms of another word

COIF vb arrange the hair of ▷ n close-fitting cap worn in the Middle Ages

COIFED adj wearing a coif

COIFFE vb coiffure

COIFFED > COIF

COIFFES > COIFFE

COIFFEUR n hairdresser

COIFFEURS > COIFFEUR

COIFFEUSE > COIFFEUR

COIFFING > COIF

COIFFURE n hairstyle ▷ vb dress or arrange (the hair)

COIFFURED > COIFFURE

COIFFURES > COIFFURE

COIFING > COIF

COIFS > COIF

COIGN vb wedge ▷ n quoin

COIGNE same as > COIGN

COIGNED > COIGN

COIGNES > COIGNE

COIGNING > COIGN

COIGNS > COIGN

COIL vb wind in loops ▷ n something coiled

COILED > COIL

COILER > COIL

COILERS > COIL

COILING > COIL

COILS > COIL

COIN n piece of metal money ▷ vb invent (a word or phrase)

COINABLE > COIN

COINAGE n coins collectively

COINAGES > COINAGE

COINCIDE vb happen at the same time

COINCIDED > COINCIDE

COINCIDES > COINCIDE

COINED > COIN

COINER > COIN

COINERS > COIN

COINFECT vb infect at same time as other infection

COINFECTS > COINFECT

COINFER vb infer jointly

COINFERS > COINFER

COINHERE vb inhere together

COINHERED > COINHERE

COINHERES > COINHERE

COINING > COIN

COININGS > COIN

COINMATE n fellow inmate

COINMATES > COINMATE

COINOP adj (of a machine) operated by putting a coin in a slot

COINS > COIN

COINSURE vb insure jointly

COINSURED > COINSURE

COINSURER > COINSURE

COINSURES > COINSURE

COINTER vb inter together

COINTERS > COINTER

COINTREAU n tradename for a French orange liqueur

COINVENT vb invent jointly

COINVENTS > COINVENT

COINVEST vb invest jointly

COINVESTS > COINVEST

COIR n coconut fibre, used for matting

COIRS > COIR

COISTREL n knave

COISTRELS > COISTREL

COISTRIL same as > COISTREL

COISTRILS > COISTRIL

COIT n buttocks

COITAL > COITUS

COITALLY > COITUS

COITION same as > COITUS

COITIONAL > COITION

COITIONS > COITION

COITS > COIT

COITUS n sexual intercourse

COITUSES > COITUS

COJOIN vb conjoin

COJOINED > COJOIN

COJOINING > COJOIN

COJOINS > COJOIN

COJONES pl n manly courage

COKE n solid fuel left after gas has been distilled from coal ▷ vb become or convert into coke

COKED > COKE

COKEHEAD n cocaine addict

COKEHEADS > COKEHEAD

COKELIKE > COKE

COKERNUT same as > COCONUT

COKERNUTS > COKERNUT

COKES n fool

COKESES > COKES

COKIER > COKY

COKIEST > COKY

COKING n act of coking

COKINGS > COKING

COKULORIS n palette with irregular holes, placed between lighting and camera to prevent glare

COKY adj like coke

COL n high mountain pass

COLA n dark brown fizzy soft drink

COLANDER n perforated bowl for straining or rinsing foods

COLANDERS > COLANDER

COLAS > COLA

COLBIES > COLBY

COLBY n type of mild-tasting hard cheese

COLBYS > COLBY

COLCANNON n dish, originating in Ireland, of potatoes and cabbage or other greens boiled and mashed together

COLCHICA > COLCHICUM

COLCHICUM n type of Eurasian liliaceous plant, such as the autumn crocus

COLCOTHAR n finely powdered form of ferric oxide produced by heating ferric sulphate and used as a pigment and as jewellers' rouge

COLD adj lacking heat ▷ n lack of heat

COLDBLOOD n any heavy draught-horse

COLDCOCK vb knock to the ground

COLDCOCKS > COLDCOCK

COLDER > COLD

COLDEST > COLD

COLDHOUSE n unheated greenhouse

COLDIE n cold can or bottle of beer

COLDIES > COLDIE

COLDISH > COLD

COLDLY > COLD

COLDNESS > COLD

COLDS > COLD

COLE same as > CABBAGE

COLEAD vb lead together

COLEADER > COLEAD

COLEADERS > COLEAD

COLEADING > COLEAD

COLEADS > COLEAD

COLECTOMY n surgical removal of part or all of the colon

COLED > COLEAD

COLEOPTER n aircraft that has an annular wing with the fuselage and engine on the centre line

COLES > COLE

COLESEED n seeds or plants of the cole

COLESEEDS > COLESEED

COLESLAW n salad dish of shredded raw cabbage in a dressing

COLESLAWS > COLESLAW

COLESSEE n joint lessee

COLESSEES > COLESSEE

COLESSOR n joint lessor

COLESSORS > COLESSOR

COLETIT n coal tit

COLETITS > COLETIT

COLEUS n Old World plant

COLEUSES > COLEUS

COLEWORT same as > CABBAGE

COLEWORTS > CABBAGE

COLEY same as > COALFISH

COLEYS > COLEY

COLIBRI n hummingbird

COLIBRIS > COLIBRI

COLIC n severe pains in the stomach and bowels

COLICIN n bactericidal protein

COLICINE n antibacterial protein

COLICINES > COLICINE

COLICINS > COLICIN

COLICKIER > COLICKY

COLICKY adj relating to or suffering from colic

C

COLICROOT *n* N American plant with tubular white or yellow flowers and a bitter root formerly used to relieve colic

COLICS > COLIC

COLICWEED *n* type of plant such as the squirrel corn and Dutchman's-breeches

COLIES > COLY

COLIFORM *n* type of bacteria of the intestinal tract

COLIFORMS > COLIFORM

COLIN *n* quail

COLINEAR *same as* > COLLINEAR

COLINS > COLIN

COLIPHAGE *n* bacteriophage

COLISEUM *n* large building, such as a stadium or theatre, used for entertainments, sports, etc

COLISEUMS > COLISEUM

COLISTIN *n* polymyxin antibiotic

COLISTINS > COLISTIN

COLITIC > COLITIS

COLITIS *n* inflammation of the colon

COLITISES > COLITIS

COLL *vb* embrace

COLLAB *n* collaboration

COLLABS > COLLAB

COLLAGE *n* type of art form ▷ *vb* make a collage

COLLAGED > COLLAGE

COLLAGEN *n* protein found in cartilage and bone that yields gelatine when boiled

COLLAGENS > COLLAGEN

COLLAGES > COLLAGE

COLLAGING > COLLAGE

COLLAGIST > COLLAGE

COLLAPSAR *n* collapsed star, either a white dwarf, neutron star, or black hole

COLLAPSE *vb* fall down suddenly ▷ *n* collapsing

COLLAPSED > COLLAPSE

COLLAPSES > COLLAPSE

COLLAR *n* part of a garment round the neck ▷ *vb* seize, arrest

COLLARD *n* variety of the cabbage with a crown of edible leaves

COLLARDS > COLLARD

COLLARED > COLLAR

COLLARET *n* small collar

COLLARETS > COLLARET

COLLARING > COLLAR

COLLARS > COLLAR

COLLATE *vb* gather together, examine, and put in order

COLLATED > COLLATE

COLLATES > COLLATE

COLLATING > COLLATE

COLLATION *n* collating

COLLATIVE *adj* involving collation

COLLATOR *n* person or machine that collates texts or manuscripts

COLLATORS > COLLATOR

COLLEAGUE *n* fellow worker, esp in a profession

COLLECT *vb* gather together ▷ *n* short prayer

COLLECTED *adj* calm and controlled

COLLECTOR *n* person who collects objects as a hobby

COLLECTS > COLLECT

COLLED > COLL

COLLEEN *n* girl

COLLEENS > COLLEEN

COLLEGE *n* place of higher education

COLLEGER *n* member of a college

COLLEGERS > COLLEGER

COLLEGES > COLLEGE

COLLEGIA > COLLEGIUM

COLLEGIAL *adj* of or relating to a college

COLLEGIAN *n* member of a college

COLLEGIUM *n* (in the former Soviet Union) a board in charge of a department

COLLET *n* (in a jewellery setting) a band or coronet-shaped claw that holds an individual stone ▷ *vb* mount in a collet

COLLETED > COLLET

COLLETING > COLLET

COLLETS > COLLET

COLLICULI *n* plural form of singular colliculus: small elevation, as on the surface of the optic lobe of the brain

COLLIDE *vb* crash together violently

COLLIDED > COLLIDE

COLLIDER *n* particle accelerator in which beams of particles are made to collide

COLLIDERS > COLLIDER

COLLIDES > COLLIDE

COLLIDING > COLLIDE

COLLIE *n* silky-haired sheepdog

COLLIED > COLLY

COLLIER *n* coal miner

COLLIERS > COLLIER

COLLIERY *n* coal mine

COLLIES > COLLY

COLLIGATE *vb* connect or link together

COLLIMATE *vb* adjust the line of sight of (an optical instrument)

COLLINEAR *adj* lying on the same straight line

COLLING *n* embrace

COLLINGS > COLLING

COLLINS *n* type of cocktail

COLLINSES > COLLINS

COLLINSIA *n* N American plant with blue, white, or purple flowers

COLLISION *n* violent crash between moving objects

COLLOCATE *vb* (of words) occur together regularly

COLLODION *n* colourless or yellow syrupy liquid that consists of a solution of pyroxylin in ether and alcohol

COLLODIUM *same as* > COLLODION

COLLOGUE *vb* confer confidentially

COLLOGUED > COLLOGUE

COLLOGUES > COLLOGUE

COLLOID *n* suspension of particles in a solution ▷ *adj* relating to the gluelike material found in certain degenerating tissues

COLLOIDAL *adj* of, denoting, or having the character of a colloid

COLLOIDS > COLLOID

COLLOP *n* small slice of meat

COLLOPS > COLLOP

COLLOQUE *vb* converse

COLLOQUED > COLLOQUE

COLLOQUES > COLLOQUE

COLLOQUIA *n* plural form of singular colloquium: informal gathering

COLLOQUY *n* conversation or conference

COLLOTYPE *n* method of lithographic printing from a flat surface of hardened gelatine: used mainly for fine-detail reproduction in monochrome or colour

COLLOTYPY > COLLOTYPE

COLLS > COLL

COLLUDE *vb* act in collusion

COLLUDED > COLLUDE

COLLUDER > COLLUDE

COLLUDERS > COLLUDE

COLLUDES > COLLUDE

COLLUDING > COLLUDE

COLLUSION *n* secret or illegal cooperation

COLLUSIVE > COLLUSION

COLLUVIA > COLLUVIUM

COLLUVIAL > COLLUVIUM

COLLUVIES *n* offscourings

COLLUVIUM *n* mixture of rock fragments from the bases of cliffs

COLLY *n* soot or grime, such as coal dust ▷ *vb* begrime

COLLYING > COLLY

COLLYRIA > COLLYRIUM

COLLYRIUM *a technical name for an* > EYEWASH

COLOBI > COLOBUS

COLOBID *n* type of African monkey

COLOBIDS > COLOBID

COLOBOMA *n* structural defect of the eye, esp in the choroid, retina, or iris

COLOBOMAS > COLOBOMA

COLOBUS *n* type of Old World monkey

COLOBUSES > COLOBUS

COLOCATE *vb* locate together

COLOCATED > COLOCATE

COLOCATES > COLOCATE

COLOCYNTH *n* type of Mediterranean and Asian climbing plant with bitter-tasting fruit

COLOG *n* logarithm of the reciprocal of a number

COLOGNE *n* mild perfume

COLOGNED > COLOGNE

COLOGNES > COLOGNE

COLOGS > COLOG

COLOMBARD *n* type of grape

COLON *n* punctuation mark (:)

COLONE *variant of* > COLON

COLONEL *n* senior commissioned army or air-force officer

COLONELCY > COLONEL

COLONELS > COLONEL

COLONES > COLONE

COLONI > COLONUS

COLONIAL *n* inhabitant of a colony ▷ *adj* of or inhabiting a colony or colonies

COLONIALS > COLONIAL

COLONIC *adj* of or relating to the colon ▷ *n* irrigation of the colon

COLONICS > COLONIC

COLONIES > COLONY

COLONISE *same as* > COLONIZE

COLONISED > COLONISE

COLONISER > COLONISE

COLONISES > COLONISE

COLONIST *n* settler in a colony

COLONISTS > COLONIST

COLONITIS *same as* > COLITIS

COLONIZE *vb* make into a colony

COLONIZED > COLONIZE

COLONIZER > COLONIZE

COLONIZES > COLONIZE

COLONNADE *n* row of columns

COLONS > COLON

COLONUS *n* ancient Roman farmer

COLONY *n* people who settle in a new country but remain ruled by their homeland

COLOPHON *n* publisher's symbol on a book

COLOPHONS > COLOPHON

COLOPHONY *another name for* > ROSIN

COLOR *same as* > COLOUR

COLORABLE > COLOR

COLORABLY > COLOR

COLORADO *adj* (of a cigar) of middling colour and strength

COLORANT *n* any substance that imparts colour, such as a pigment, dye, or ink

COLORANTS > COLORANT

COLORBRED *adj* (of animals) bred for their colour

COLORCAST *vb* broadcast in colour

COLORED *same as* > COLOURED

COLOREDS > COLORED

COLORER > COLOR

COLORERS > COLOR

COLORFAST *adj* variant of colourfast: (of a fabric) having a colour that does not run when washed

COLORFUL > COLOR

COLORIER > COLORY

COLORIEST > COLORY

COLORIFIC *adj* producing, imparting, or relating to colour

COLORING > COLOUR

SECTION 1: Words between 2 and 9 letters in length

c

COLORINGS > COLOUR

COLORISE same as > COLOURIZE

COLORISED > COLORISE

COLORISER > COLORISE

COLORISES > COLORISE

COLORISM > COLOR

COLORISMS > COLOR

COLORIST > COLOR

COLORISTS > COLOR

COLORIZE same as > COLOURIZE

COLORIZED > COLORIZE

COLORIZER > COLORIZE

COLORIZES > COLORIZE

COLORLESS > COLOR

COLORMAN same as > COLOURMAN

COLORMEN > COLORMAN

COLORS > COLOR

COLORWASH n cheap form of distemper ▷ vb paint with this

COLORWAY variant of > COLOURWAY

COLORWAYS > COLORWAY

COLORY adj full of color

COLOSSAL adj very large

COLOSSEUM same as > COLISEUM

COLOSSI > COLOSSUS

COLOSSUS n huge statue

COLOSTOMY n operation to form an opening from the colon onto the surface of the body, for emptying the bowel

COLOSTRAL > COLOSTRUM

COLOSTRIC > COLOSTRUM

COLOSTRUM n thin milky secretion that precedes lactation

COLOTOMY n colonic incision

COLOUR n appearance of things as a result of reflecting light ▷ vb apply colour to

COLOURANT same as > COLORANT

COLOURED adj having colour ▷ n person who is not white

COLOUREDS > COLOURED

COLOURER > COLOUR

COLOURERS > COLOUR

COLOURFUL adj with bright or varied colours

COLOURIER > COLOURY

COLOURING n application of colour

COLOURISE same as > COLOURIZE

COLOURISM n discrimination in which people are judged on the basis of their skin colour

COLOURIST n person who uses colour, esp an artist

COLOURIZE vb add colour electronically to (an old black-and-white film)

COLOURMAN n person who deals in paints

COLOURMEN > COLOURMAN

COLOURS > COLOUR

COLOURWAY n one of several different combinations of colours in which a given pattern is printed on fabrics, wallpapers, etc

COLOURY adj possessing colour

COLPITIS another name for > VAGINITIS

COLPOTOMY n surgical incision into the wall of the vagina

COLS > COL

COLT n young male horse ▷ vb to fool

COLTAN n metallic ore

COLTANS > COLTAN

COLTED > COLT

COLTER same as > COULTER

COLTERS > COLTER

COLTHOOD n state of being a colt

COLTHOODS > COLTHOOD

COLTING > COLT

COLTISH adj inexperienced

COLTISHLY > COLTISH

COLTS > COLT

COLTSFOOT n weed with yellow flowers and heart-shaped leaves

COLTWOOD n plant mentioned in Spenser's Faerie Queene

COLTWOODS > COLTWOOD

COLUBRIAD n epic poem about a snake

COLUBRID n type of snake such as the grass snake and whip snakes

COLUBRIDS > COLUBRID

COLUBRINE adj of or resembling a snake

COLUGO n flying lemur

COLUGOS > COLUGO

COLUMBARY n dovecote

COLUMBATE n niobate

COLUMBIC another word for > NIOBIC

COLUMBINE n garden flower with five petals ▷ adj of, relating to, or resembling a dove

COLUMBITE n black mineral occurring in coarse granite

COLUMBIUM the former name of > NIOBIUM

COLUMBOUS another word for > NIOBOUS

COLUMEL n in botany, the central column in a capsule

COLUMELLA n central part of the spore-producing body of some fungi and mosses

COLUMELS > COLUMEL

COLUMN n pillar ▷ vb create a column

COLUMNAL n part of the stem of a crinoid

COLUMNALS > COLUMNAL

COLUMNAR > COLUMN

COLUMNEA n flowering plant

COLUMNEAS > COLUMNEA

COLUMNED > COLUMN

COLUMNIST n journalist who writes a regular feature in a newspaper

COLUMNS > COLUMN

COLURE n either of two great circles on the celestial sphere

COLURES > COLURE

COLY n S African arboreal bird

COLZA n Eurasian plant with bright yellow flowers

COLZAS > COLZA

COMA n state of deep unconsciousness

COMADE > COMAKE

COMAE > COMA

COMAKE vb make together

COMAKER > COMAKE

COMAKERS > COMAKE

COMAKES > COMAKE

COMAKING > COMAKE

COMAL > COMA

COMANAGE vb manage jointly

COMANAGED > COMANAGE

COMANAGER > COMANAGE

COMANAGES > COMANAGE

COMARB same as > COARB

COMARBS > COMARB

COMART n covenant

COMARTS > COMART

COMAS > COMA

COMATE adj having tufts of hair ▷ n companion

COMATES > COMATE

COMATIC > COMA

COMATIK variant of > KOMATIK

COMATIKS > COMATIK

COMATOSE adj in a coma

COMATULA same as > COMATULID

COMATULAE > COMATULID

COMATULID n any of a group of crinoid echinoderms, including the feather stars, in which the adults are free-swimming

COMB n toothed implement for arranging the hair ▷ vb use a comb on

COMBAT vb fight, struggle ▷ n fight or struggle

COMBATANT n fighter ▷ adj fighting

COMBATED > COMBAT

COMBATER > COMBAT

COMBATERS > COMBAT

COMBATING > COMBAT

COMBATIVE adj eager or ready to fight, argue, etc

COMBATS > COMBAT

COMBATTED > COMBAT

COMBE same as > COMB

COMBED > COMB

COMBER n long curling wave

COMBERS > COMBER

COMBES > COMBE

COMBI n combination boiler

COMBIER > COMBY

COMBIES > COMBY

COMBIEST > COMBY

COMBINATE adj betrothed

COMBINE vb join together ▷ n association of people or firms for a common purpose

COMBINED n competitive event consisting of two skiing competitions

COMBINEDS > COMBINE

COMBINER > COMBINE

COMBINERS > COMBINE

COMBINES > COMBINE

COMBING > COMBINE

COMBINGS pl n loose hair or fibres removed by combing, esp from animals

COMBINING > COMBINE

COMBIS > COMBI

COMBLE n apex; zenith

COMBLES > COMBLE

COMBLESS adj without a comb

COMBLIKE adj resembling a comb

COMBO n small group of jazz musicians

COMBOS > COMBO

COMBOVER n hairstyle in which thinning hair is combed over the scalp

COMBOVERS > COMBOVER

COMBRETUM n any tree or shrub belonging to the genus Combretum

COMBS > COMB

COMBUST vb burn

COMBUSTED > COMBUST

COMBUSTOR n combustion system of a jet engine or ramjet, comprising the combustion chamber, the fuel injection apparatus, and the igniter

COMBUSTS > COMBUST

COMBWISE adv in the manner of a comb

COMBY adj comb-like ▷ n combination boiler

COME vb move towards a place, arrive

COMEBACK n return to a former position ▷ vb return, esp to the memory

COMEBACKS > COMEBACK

COMEDDLE vb mix

COMEDDLED > COMEDDLE

COMEDDLES > COMEDDLE

COMEDIAN n entertainer who tells jokes

COMEDIANS > COMEDIAN

COMEDIC adj of or relating to comedy

COMEDIES > COMEDY

COMEDIST n writer of comedies

COMEDISTS > COMEDIST

COMEDO the technical name for > BLACKHEAD

COMEDONES > COMEDO

COMEDOS > COMEDO

COMEDOWN n decline in status ▷ vb come to a place regarded as lower

COMEDOWNS > COMEDOWN

COMEDY n humorous play, film, or programme

COMELIER > COMELY

COMELIEST > COMELY

COMELILY > COMELY

COMELY adj nice-looking

COMEMBER n fellow member

COMEMBERS > COMEMBER

COMEOVER n person who has come from Britain to the Isle of Man to settle

COMEOVERS > COMEOVER

COMER n person who comes

COMERS > COMER

COMES > COME

COMET n heavenly body with a long luminous tail

COMETARY > COMET

COMETH > COME

COMETHER n coaxing; allure

COMETHERS > COMETHER

COMETIC > COMET

COMETS > COMET

COMFIER > COMFY

COMFIEST > COMFY

COMFILY adv in a manner suggestive of or promoting comfort

COMFINESS > COMFY

COMFIT n sugar-coated sweet

COMFITS > COMFIT

COMFITURE n confiture

COMFORT n physical ease or wellbeing ▷ vb soothe, console

COMFORTED > COMFORT

COMFORTER n person or thing that comforts

COMFORTS > COMFORT

COMFREY n tall plant with bell-shaped flowers

COMFREYS > COMFREY

COMFY adj comfortable

COMIC adj humorous, funny ▷ n comedian

COMICAL adj amusing

COMICALLY > COMICAL

COMICE n kind of pear

COMICES > COMICE

COMICS > COMIC

COMING > COME

COMINGLE same as > COMMINGLE

COMINGLED > COMMINGLE

COMINGLES > COMINGLE

COMINGS > COME

COMIQUE n comic actor

COMIQUES > COMIQUE

COMITADJI n Balkan guerrilla fighter

COMITAL adj relating to a count or earl

COMITATUS n leader's retinue

COMITIA n ancient Roman assembly

COMITIAL > COMITIA

COMITIAS > COMITIA

COMITIES > COMITY

COMITY n friendly politeness, esp between different countries

COMIX n comic books in general

COMM n as in comm badge small wearable badge-shaped radio transmitter and receiver

COMMA n punctuation mark (,)

COMMAND vb order ▷ n authoritative instruction that something must be done

COMMANDED > COMMAND

COMMANDER n military officer in command of a group or operation

COMMANDO n (member of) a military unit trained for swift raids in enemy territory

COMMANDOS > COMMANDO

COMMANDS > COMMAND

COMMAS > COMMA

COMMATA > COMMA

COMMENCE vb begin

COMMENCED > COMMENCE

COMMENCER > COMMENCE

COMMENCES > COMMENCE

COMMEND vb praise

COMMENDAM n temporary holding of an ecclesiastical benefice

COMMENDED > COMMEND

COMMENDER > COMMEND

COMMENDS > COMMEND

COMMENSAL adj (of two different species of plant or animal) living in close association, such that one species benefits without harming the other ▷ n commensal plant or animal

COMMENT n remark ▷ vb make a comment

COMMENTED > COMMENT

COMMENTER > COMMENT

COMMENTOR > COMMENT

COMMENTS > COMMENT

COMMER same as > COMER

COMMERCE n buying and selling, trade ▷ vb to trade

COMMERCED > COMMERCE

COMMERCES > COMMERCE

COMMERE n female compere

COMMERES > COMMERE

COMMERGE vb merge together

COMMERGED > COMMERGE

COMMERGES > COMMERGE

COMMERS > COMMER

COMMIE adj communist

COMMIES > COMMIE

COMMINATE vb to anathematise

COMMINGLE vb mix or be mixed

COMMINUTE vb break (a bone) into several small fragments

COMMIS n apprentice waiter or chef ▷ adj (of a waiter or chef) apprentice

COMMISH n commissioner

COMMISHES > COMMISH

COMMISSAR n (formerly) official responsible for political education in Communist countries

COMMIT vb perform (a crime or error)

COMMITS > COMMIT

COMMITTAL n act of committing or pledging

COMMITTED > COMMIT

COMMITTEE n group of people appointed to perform a specified service or function

COMMITTER > COMMIT

COMMIX a rare word for > MIX

COMMIXED > COMMIX

COMMIXES > COMMIX

COMMIXING > COMMIX

COMMIXT > COMMIX

COMMO short for > COMMUNIST

COMMODE n seat with a hinged flap concealing a chamber pot

COMMODES > COMMODE

COMMODIFY vb to make into a commodity

COMMODITY n something that can be bought or sold

COMMODO same as > COMODO

COMMODORE n senior commissioned officer in the navy

COMMON adj occurring often ▷ n area of grassy land belonging to a community ▷ vb sit at table with strangers

COMMONAGE n use of something, esp a pasture, in common with others

COMMONED > COMMON

COMMONER n person who does not belong to the nobility

COMMONERS > COMMONER

COMMONEST > COMMON

COMMONEY n playing marble of a common sort

COMMONEYS > COMMONEY

COMMONING > COMMON

COMMONLY adv usually

COMMONS n people not of noble birth viewed as forming a political order

COMMORANT n resident

COMMOS > COMMO

COMMOT n in medieval Wales, a division of land

COMMOTE same as > COMMOT

COMMOTES > COMMOTE

COMMOTION n noisy disturbance

COMMOTS > COMMOT

COMMOVE vb disturb

COMMOVED > COMMOVE

COMMOVES > COMMOVE

COMMOVING > COMMOVE

COMMS pl n communications

COMMUNAL adj shared

COMMUNARD n member of a commune

COMMUNE n group of people who live together and share everything ▷ vb feel very close (to)

COMMUNED > COMMUNE

COMMUNER > COMMUNE

COMMUNERS > COMMUNE

COMMUNES > COMMUNE

COMMUNING > COMMUNE

COMMUNION n sharing of thoughts or feelings

COMMUNISE same as > COMMUNIZE

COMMUNISM n belief that all property and means of production should be shared by the community

COMMUNIST n supporter of any form of communism ▷ adj of, characterized by, favouring, or relating to communism

COMMUNITY n all the people living in one district

COMMUNIZE vb make (property) public

COMMUTATE vb reverse the direction of (an electric current)

COMMUTE vb travel daily to and from work ▷ n journey made by commuting

COMMUTED > COMMUTE

COMMUTER n person who commutes to and from work

COMMUTERS > COMMUTER

COMMUTES > COMMUTE

COMMUTING n act of commuting

COMMUTUAL adj mutual

COMMY same as > COMMIE

COMODO adv (to be performed) at a convenient relaxed speed

COMONOMER n monomer that, with another, constitutes a copolymer

COMORBID adj (of illness) happening at same time as other illness

COMOSE another word for > COMATE

COMOUS adj hairy

COMP n person who sets and corrects type ▷ vb set or correct type

COMPACT adj closely packed ▷ n small flat case containing a mirror and face powder ▷ vb pack closely together

COMPACTED > COMPACT

COMPACTER > COMPACT

COMPACTLY > COMPACT

COMPACTOR n machine which compresses waste material for easier disposal

COMPACTS > COMPACT

COMPADRE n masculine friend

COMPADRES > COMPADRE

COMPAGE obsolete form of > COMPAGES

COMPAGES n structure or framework

COMPAND vb (of a transmitter signal) to compress before, and expand after, transmission

COMPANDED > COMPAND

COMPANDER n system for improving the signal-to-noise ratio of a signal at a transmitter or recorder by first compressing the volume range of the signal and then restoring it to its original amplitude level at the receiving or reproducing apparatus

COMPANDOR same as > COMPANDER

COMPANDS > COMPAND

COMPANIED > COMPANY

COMPANIES > COMPANY

COMPANING > COMPANY

COMPANION n person who associates with or accompanies someone ▷ vb accompany or be a companion to

COMPANY n business organization ▷ vb associate or keep company with someone

COMPARE vb examine (things) and point out the resemblances or differences

COMPARED > COMPARE

COMPARER > COMPARE

COMPARERS > COMPARE

COMPARES > COMPARE

COMPARING > COMPARE

COMPART vb divide into parts

COMPARTED > COMPART

COMPARTS > COMPART

COMPAS n rhythm in flamenco

COMPASS n instrument for showing direction ▷ vb encircle or surround

COMPASSED > COMPASS

COMPASSES > COMPASS

COMPAST adj rounded

COMPEAR vb in Scots law, to appear in court

COMPEARED > COMPEAR

COMPEARS > COMPEAR

COMPED > COMP

COMPEER n person of equal rank, status, or ability ▷ vb to equal

COMPEERED > COMPEER

COMPEERS > COMPEER

COMPEL vb force (to be or do)

COMPELLED > COMPEL

COMPELLER > COMPEL

COMPELS > COMPEL

COMPEND n compendium

COMPENDIA n plural form of singular compendium: book containing a collection of useful hints

COMPENDS > COMPEND

COMPER n person who regularly enters competitions

COMPERE n person who presents a stage, radio, or television show ▷ vb be the compere of

COMPERED > COMPERE

COMPERES > COMPERE

COMPERING > COMPERE

COMPERS > COMPER

COMPESCE vb curb

COMPESCED > COMPESCE

COMPESCES > COMPESCE

COMPETE vb try to win or achieve (a prize, profit, etc)

COMPETED > COMPETE

COMPETENT adj having the skill or knowledge to do something well

COMPETES > COMPETE

COMPETING > COMPETE

COMPILE vb collect and arrange (information), esp to make a book

COMPILED > COMPILE

COMPILER n person who compiles information

COMPILERS > COMPILER

COMPILES > COMPILE

COMPILING > COMPILE

COMPING n act of comping

COMPINGS > COMPING

COMPITAL adj pertaining to crossroads

COMPLAIN vb express resentment or displeasure

COMPLAINS > COMPLAIN

COMPLAINT n complaining

COMPLEAT an archaic spelling of > COMPLETE

COMPLEATS > COMPLEAT

COMPLECT vb interweave or entwine

COMPLECTS > COMPLECT

COMPLETE adj thorough, absolute ▷ vb finish

COMPLETED > COMPLETE

COMPLETER > COMPLETE

COMPLETES > COMPLETE

COMPLEX adj made up of parts ▷ n whole made up of parts ▷ vb form a complex

COMPLEXED > COMPLEX

COMPLEXER > COMPLEX

COMPLEXES > COMPLEX

COMPLEXLY > COMPLEX

COMPLEXUS n complex

COMPLIANT adj complying, obliging, or yielding

COMPLICE n associate or accomplice

COMPLICES > COMPLICE

COMPLICIT adj involved in a crime or questionable act

COMPLIED > COMPLY

COMPLIER > COMPLY

COMPLIERS > COMPLY

COMPLIES > COMPLY

COMPLIN same as > COMPLINE

COMPLINE n last service of the day in the Roman Catholic Church

COMPLINES > COMPLINE

COMPLINS > COMPLIN

COMPLISH vb accomplish

COMPLOT n plot or conspiracy ▷ vb plot together

COMPLOTS > COMPLOT

COMPLUVIA n plural form of singular compluvium: an unroofed space over the atrium in a Roman house, though which rain fell and was collected

COMPLY vb act in accordance (with)

COMPLYING > COMPLY

COMPO n mixture of materials, such as mortar, plaster, etc ▷ adj intended to last for several days

COMPONE same as > COMPONY

COMPONENT adj (being) part of a whole ▷ n constituent part or feature of a whole

COMPONY adj made up of alternating metal and colour, colour and fur, or fur and metal

COMPORT vb behave (oneself) in a specified way

COMPORTED > COMPORT

COMPORTS > COMPORT

COMPOS > COMPO

COMPOSE vb put together

COMPOSED adj calm

COMPOSER n person who writes music

COMPOSERS > COMPOSER

COMPOSES > COMPOSE

COMPOSING > COMPOSE

COMPOSITE adj made up of separate parts ▷ n something composed of separate parts ▷ vb merge related motions from local branches of (a political party, trade union, etc) so as to produce a manageable number of proposals for discussion at national level

COMPOST n decayed plants used as a fertilizer ▷ vb make (vegetable matter) into compost

COMPOSTED > COMPOST

COMPOSTER n bin or other container used to turn garden waste into compost

COMPOSTS > COMPOST

COMPOSURE n calmness

COMPOT same as > COMPOTE

COMPOTE n fruit stewed with sugar

COMPOTES > COMPOTE

COMPOTIER n dish for holding compote

COMPOTS > COMPOT

COMPOUND adj (thing, esp chemical) made up of two or more combined parts or elements ▷ vb combine or make by combining ▷ n fenced enclosure containing buildings

COMPOUNDS > COMPOUND

COMPRADOR n (formerly in China and some other Asian countries) a native agent of a foreign enterprise

COMPRESS vb squeeze together ▷ n pad applied to stop bleeding or cool inflammation

COMPRINT vb print jointly

COMPRINTS > COMPRINT

COMPRISAL > COMPRISE

COMPRISE vb be made up of or make up

COMPRISED > COMPRISE

COMPRISES > COMPRISE

COMPRIZE same as > COMPRISE

COMPRIZED > COMPRIZE

COMPRIZES > COMPRIZE

COMPS > COMP

COMPT obsolete variant of > COUNT

COMPTABLE n countable

COMPTED > COMPT

COMPTER n formerly, a prison

COMPTERS > COMPTER

COMPTIBLE same as > COMPTABLE

COMPTING > COMPT

COMPTROLL obsolete variant of > CONTROL

COMPTS > COMPT

COMPULSE vb compel

COMPULSED > COMPULSE

COMPULSES > COMPULSE

COMPUTANT n calculator

COMPUTE vb calculate, esp using a computer ▷ n calculation

COMPUTED > COMPUTE

COMPUTER n electronic machine that stores and processes data

COMPUTERS > COMPUTER

COMPUTES > COMPUTE

COMPUTING n activity of using computers and writing programs for them ▷ adj of or relating to computers

COMPUTIST n one who computes

COMRADE n fellow member of a union or socialist political party

COMRADELY adj like a comrade

COMRADERY n comradeship

COMRADES > COMRADE

COMS pl n one-piece woollen undergarment with long sleeves and legs

COMSAT n communications satellite

COMSATS > COMSAT

COMSYMP n disparaging term for a person sympathetic to communism

COMSYMPS > COMSYMP

COMTE n European noble

COMTES > COMTE

COMUS n wild party

COMUSES > COMUS

CON vb deceive, swindle ▷ n convict ▷ prep with

CONACRE n farming land let for a season or for eleven months ▷ vb let conacre

CONACRED > CONACRE

CONACRES > CONACRE

CONACRING > CONACRE

CONARIA > CONARIUM

CONARIAL > CONARIUM

CONARIUM n pineal gland

CONATION n psychological element that tends towards activity or change

CONATIONS > CONATION

CONATIVE adj aspect of some verbs indicating the effort of the agent in performing the verb

CONATUS n effort or striving of natural impulse

CONCAUSE n shared cause

CONCAUSES > CONCAUSE

CONCAVE adj curving inwards ▷ vb make concave

CONCAVED > CONCAVE

CONCAVELY > CONCAVE

CONCAVES > CONCAVE

CONCAVING > CONCAVE

CONCAVITY n state or quality of being concave

CONCEAL vb cover and hide

CONCEALED > CONCEAL

CONCEALER > CONCEAL

CONCEALS > CONCEAL

CONCEDE vb admit to be true

CONCEDED > CONCEDE

CONCEDER > CONCEDE

CONCEDERS > CONCEDE

CONCEDES > CONCEDE

CONCEDING > CONCEDE

CONCEDO interj I allow; I concede (a point)

CONCEIT n too high an opinion of oneself ▷ vb like or be able to bear (something, such as food or drink)

CONCEITED adj having an excessively high opinion of oneself

CONCEITS > CONCEIT

CONCEITY adj full of conceit

CONCEIVE vb imagine, think

CONCEIVED > CONCEIVE

CONCEIVER > CONCEIVE

CONCEIVES > CONCEIVE
CONCENT n concord, as of sounds, voices, etc
CONCENTER same as **> CONCENTRE**
CONCENTRE vb converge or cause to converge on a common centre
CONCENTS > CONCENT
CONCENTUS n vocal harmony
CONCEPT n abstract or general idea
CONCEPTI > CONCEPTUS
CONCEPTS > CONCEPT
CONCEPTUS n any product of conception, including the embryo, foetus and surrounding tissue
CONCERN n anxiety, worry ▷ vb worry (someone)
CONCERNED adj interested, involved
CONCERNS > CONCERN
CONCERT n musical entertainment
CONCERTED adj done together
CONCERTI > CONCERTO
CONCERTO n large-scale composition for a solo instrument and orchestra
CONCERTOS > CONCERTO
CONCERTS > CONCERT
CONCETTI > CONCETTO
CONCETTO n conceit, ingenious thought
CONCH same as **>** CONCHA
CONCHA n any bodily organ or part resembling a shell in shape
CONCHAE > CONCHA
CONCHAL > CONCHA
CONCHAS > CONCHA
CONCHATE adj shell-shaped
CONCHE n machine used to make chocolate ▷ vb use a conche
CONCHED > CONCHE
CONCHES > CONCHE
CONCHIE n conscientious objector
CONCHIES > CONCHIE
CONCHING > CONCHE
CONCHITIS n inflammation of the outer ear
CONCHO n American metal ornament
CONCHOID n type of plane curve
CONCHOIDS > CONCHOID
CONCHOS > CONCHO
CONCHS > CONCH
CONCHY same as **>** CONCHIE
CONCIERGE n (in France) caretaker in a block of flats
CONCILIAR adj of, from, or by means of a council, esp an ecclesiastical one
CONCISE adj brief and to the point ▷ vb mutilate
CONCISED > CONCISE
CONCISELY > CONCISE
CONCISER > CONCISE
CONCISES > CONCISE
CONCISEST > CONCISE
CONCISING > CONCISE

CONCISION n quality of being concise
CONCLAVE n secret meeting
CONCLAVES > CONCLAVE
CONCLUDE vb decide by reasoning
CONCLUDED > CONCLUDE
CONCLUDER > CONCLUDE
CONCLUDES > CONCLUDE
CONCOCT vb make up (a story or plan)
CONCOCTED > CONCOCT
CONCOCTER > CONCOCT
CONCOCTOR > CONCOCT
CONCOCTS > CONCOCT
CONCOLOR adj of a single colour
CONCORD n state of peaceful agreement, harmony ▷ vb agree
CONCORDAL > CONCORD
CONCORDAT n pact or treaty
CONCORDED > CONCORD
CONCORDS > CONCORD
CONCOURS n contest
CONCOURSE n large open public place where people can gather
CONCREATE vb to create at the same time
CONCRETE n mixture of cement, sand, stone, and water, used in building ▷ vb cover with concrete ▷ adj made of concrete
CONCRETED > CONCRETE
CONCRETES > CONCRETE
CONCREW vb grow together
CONCREWED > CONCREW
CONCREWS > CONCREW
CONCUBINE n woman living in a man's house but not married to him and kept for his sexual pleasure
CONCUPIES > CONCUPY
CONCUPY n concupiscence
CONCUR vb agree
CONCURRED > CONCUR
CONCURS > CONCUR
CONCUSS vb injure (the brain) by a fall or blow
CONCUSSED > CONCUSS
CONCUSSES > CONCUSS
CONCYCLIC adj (of a set of geometric points) lying on a common circle
COND old inflection of **>** CON
CONDEMN vb express disapproval of
CONDEMNED > CONDEMN
CONDEMNER > CONDEMN
CONDEMNOR > CONDEMN
CONDEMNS > CONDEMN
CONDENSE vb make shorter
CONDENSED adj (of printers' type) narrower than usual for a particular height
CONDENSER same as **> CAPACITOR**
CONDENSES > CONDENSE
CONDER n person who directs the steering of a vessel
CONDERS > CONDER
CONDIDDLE vb to steal
CONDIE n culvert; tunnel
CONDIES > CONDIE

CONDIGN adj (esp of a punishment) fitting
CONDIGNLY > CONDIGN
CONDIMENT n seasoning for food, such as salt or pepper
CONDITION n particular state of being ▷ vb train or influence to behave in a particular way
CONDO n condominium
CONDOES > CONDO
CONDOLE vb express sympathy with someone in grief, pain, etc
CONDOLED > CONDOLE
CONDOLENT adj expressing sympathy with someone in grief
CONDOLER > CONDOLE
CONDOLERS > CONDOLE
CONDOLES > CONDOLE
CONDOLING > CONDOLE
CONDOM n contraceptive
CONDOMS > CONDOM
CONDONE vb overlook or forgive (wrongdoing)
CONDONED > CONDONE
CONDONER > CONDONE
CONDONERS > CONDONE
CONDONES > CONDONE
CONDONING > CONDONE
CONDOR n large vulture of S America
CONDORES > CONDOR
CONDORS > CONDOR
CONDOS > CONDO
CONDUCE vb lead or contribute (to a result)
CONDUCED > CONDUCE
CONDUCER > CONDUCE
CONDUCERS > CONDUCE
CONDUCES > CONDUCE
CONDUCING > CONDUCE
CONDUCIVE adj likely to lead (to)
CONDUCT n management of an activity ▷ vb carry out (a task)
CONDUCTED > CONDUCT
CONDUCTI > CONDUCTUS
CONDUCTOR n person who conducts musicians
CONDUCTS > CONDUCT
CONDUCTUS n medieval liturgical composition
CONDUIT n channel or tube for fluid or cables
CONDUITS > CONDUIT
CONDYLAR > CONDYLE
CONDYLE n rounded projection on the articulating end of a bone
CONDYLES > CONDYLE
CONDYLOID adj of or resembling a condyle
CONDYLOMA n skin tumour
CONE n object with a circular base, tapering to a point ▷ vb shape like a cone or part of a cone
CONED > CONE
CONELESS adj not bearing cones
CONELIKE adj like a cone
CONELRAD n US defence and information system for use in the event of air attack

CONELRADS > CONELRAD
CONENOSE n bloodsucking bug of the genus Triatoma
CONENOSES > CONENOSE
CONEPATE same as **> CONEPATL**
CONEPATES > CONEPATE
CONEPATL n skunk
CONEPATLS > CONEPATL
CONES > CONE
CONEY same as **>** CONY
CONEYS > CONEY
CONF n online forum
CONFAB n conversation ▷ vb converse
CONFABBED > CONFAB
CONFABS > CONFAB
CONFECT vb prepare by combining ingredients
CONFECTED > CONFECT
CONFECTS > CONFECT
CONFER vb discuss together
CONFEREE n person who takes part in a conference
CONFEREES > CONFEREE
CONFERRAL > CONFER
CONFERRED > CONFER
CONFERREE same as **> CONFEREE**
CONFERRER > CONFER
CONFERS > CONFER
CONFERVA n type of threadlike green alga typically occurring in fresh water
CONFERVAE > CONFERVA
CONFERVAL > CONFERVA
CONFERVAS > CONFERVA
CONFESS vb admit (a fault or crime)
CONFESSED > CONFESS
CONFESSES > CONFESS
CONFESSOR n priest who hears confessions
CONFEST adj admitted
CONFESTLY adv confessedly
CONFETTI n small pieces of coloured paper thrown at weddings
CONFETTO n sweetmeat
CONFIDANT n person confided in
CONFIDE vb tell someone (a secret)
CONFIDED > CONFIDE
CONFIDENT adj sure, esp of oneself
CONFIDER > CONFIDE
CONFIDERS > CONFIDE
CONFIDES > CONFIDE
CONFIDING adj trusting
CONFIGURE vb to design or set up
CONFINE vb keep within bounds ▷ n limit
CONFINED adj enclosed or restricted
CONFINER > CONFINE
CONFINERS > CONFINE
CONFINES > CONFINE
CONFINING > CONFINE
CONFIRM vb prove to be true
CONFIRMED adj firmly established in a habit or condition
CONFIRMEE n person to whom a confirmation is made

C

SECTION 1: Words between 2 and 9 letters in length

c

CONFIRMER > CONFIRM
CONFIRMOR n person who makes a confirmation
CONFIRMS > CONFIRM
CONFISEUR n confectioner
CONFIT n preserve
CONFITEOR n Catholic prayer asking for forgiveness
CONFITS > CONFIT
CONFITURE n confection, preserve of fruit, etc
CONFIX vb fasten
CONFIXED > CONFIX
CONFIXES > CONFIX
CONFIXING > CONFIX
CONFLATE vb combine or blend into a whole
CONFLATED > CONFLATE
CONFLATES > CONFLATE
CONFLICT n disagreement ▷ vb be incompatible
CONFLICTS > CONFLICT
CONFLUENT adj flowing together or merging ▷ n stream that flows into another, usually of approximately equal size
CONFLUX n merging or following together, especially of rivers
CONFLUXES > CONFLUX
CONFOCAL adj having a common focus or common foci
CONFORM vb comply with accepted standards or customs
CONFORMAL adj (of a transformation) preserving the angles of the depicted surface
CONFORMED > CONFORM
CONFORMER > CONFORM
CONFORMS > CONFORM
CONFOUND vb astound, bewilder
CONFOUNDS > CONFOUND
CONFRERE n colleague
CONFRERES > CONFRERE
CONFRERIE n brotherhood
CONFRONT vb come face to face with
CONFRONTE adj in heraldry, (of two animals) face to face
CONFRONTS > CONFRONT
CONFS > CONF
CONFUSE vb mix up
CONFUSED adj lacking a clear understanding of something
CONFUSES > CONFUSE
CONFUSING adj causing bewilderment
CONFUSION n mistaking one person or thing for another
CONFUTE vb prove wrong
CONFUTED > CONFUTE
CONFUTER > CONFUTE
CONFUTERS > CONFUTE
CONFUTES > CONFUTE
CONFUTING > CONFUTE
CONGA n dance performed by a number of people in single file ▷ vb dance the conga
CONGAED > CONGA
CONGAING > CONGA

CONGAS > CONGA
CONGE n permission to depart or dismissal, esp when formal ▷ vb take one's leave
CONGEAL vb (of a liquid) become thick and sticky
CONGEALED > CONGEAL
CONGEALER > CONGEAL
CONGEALS > CONGEAL
CONGED > CONGE
CONGEE same as > CONGE
CONGEED > CONGEE
CONGEEING > CONGEE
CONGEES > CONGEE
CONGEING > CONGE
CONGENER n member of a class, group, or other category, esp any animal of a specified genus
CONGENERS > CONGENER
CONGENIAL adj pleasant, agreeable
CONGENIC adj (of inbred animal cells) genetically identical except for a single gene locus
CONGER n large sea eel
CONGERIES n collection of objects or ideas
CONGERS > CONGER
CONGES > CONGE
CONGEST vb crowd or become crowded to excess
CONGESTED adj crowded to excess
CONGESTS > CONGEST
CONGIARY n Roman emperor's gift to the people or soldiers
CONGII > CONGIUS
CONGIUS n unit of liquid measure equal to 1 imperial gallon
CONGLOBE vb gather into a globe or ball
CONGLOBED > CONGLOBE
CONGLOBES > CONGLOBE
CONGO same as > CONGOU
CONGOES > CONGO
CONGOS > CONGO
CONGOU n kind of black tea from China
CONGOUS > CONGOU
CONGRATS sentence substitute congratulations
CONGREE vb agree
CONGREED > CONGREE
CONGREES > CONGREE
CONGREET vb (of two or more people) to greet one another
CONGREETS > CONGREET
CONGRESS n formal meeting for discussion
CONGRUE vb agree
CONGRUED > CONGRUE
CONGRUENT adj similar, corresponding
CONGRUES > CONGRUE
CONGRUING > CONGRUE
CONGRUITY > CONGRUOUS
CONGRUOUS adj appropriate or in keeping
CONI > CONUS
CONIA same as > CONIINE
CONIAS > CONIA

CONIC adj having the shape of a cone
CONICAL adj cone-shaped
CONICALLY > CONIC
CONICINE same as > CONIINE
CONICINES > CONICINE
CONICITY > CONICAL
CONICS n branch of geometry
CONIDIA > CONIDIUM
CONIDIAL > CONIDIUM
CONIDIAN > CONIDIUM
CONIDIUM n asexual spore formed at the tip of a specialized filament in certain types of fungi
CONIES > CONY
CONIFER n cone-bearing tree, such as the fir or pine
CONIFERS > CONIFER
CONIFORM adj cone-shaped
CONIINE n colourless poisonous soluble liquid alkaloid found in hemlock
CONIINES > CONIINE
CONIMA n gum resin from the conium hemlock tree
CONIMAS > CONIMA
CONIN same as > CONIINE
CONINE same as > CONIINE
CONINES > CONIINE
CONING > CONE
CONINS > CONIN
CONIOLOGY a variant spelling of > KONIOLOGY
CONIOSES > CONIOSIS
CONIOSIS n any disease or condition caused by dust inhalation
CONIUM n N temperate umbelliferous plant, esp hemlock
CONIUMS > CONIUM
CONJECT vb conjecture
CONJECTED > CONJECT
CONJECTS > CONJECT
CONJEE n gruel of boiled rice and water ▷ vb prepare as, or in, a conjee
CONJEED > CONJEE
CONJEEING > CONJEE
CONJEES > CONJEE
CONJOIN vb join or become joined
CONJOINED > CONJOIN
CONJOINER > CONJOIN
CONJOINS > CONJOIN
CONJOINT adj united, joint, or associated
CONJUGAL adj of marriage
CONJUGANT n either of a pair of organisms or gametes undergoing conjugation
CONJUGATE vb inflect (a verb) systematically
CONJUNCT adj joined ▷ n one of the propositions or formulas in a conjunction
CONJUNCTS > CONJUNCT
CONJUNTO n style of Mexican music
CONJUNTOS > CONJUNTO
CONJURE vb perform tricks that appear to be magic
CONJURED > CONJURE
CONJURER same as > CONJUROR

CONJURERS > CONJUROR
CONJURES > CONJURE
CONJURIES > CONJURY
CONJURING n performance of tricks that appear to defy natural laws ▷ adj denoting or relating to such tricks or entertainment
CONJUROR n person who performs magic tricks for people's entertainment
CONJURORS > CONJUROR
CONJURY n magic
CONK n nose ▷ vb strike (someone) on the head or nose
CONKED > CONK
CONKER n nut of the horse chestnut
CONKERS n game played with conkers tied on strings
CONKIER > CONKY
CONKIEST > CONKY
CONKING > CONK
CONKOUT n time when a machine stops working
CONKOUTS > CONKOUT
CONKS > CONK
CONKY adj affected by the timber disease, conk
CONLANG n artificially constructed language
CONLANGER n person who creates a conlang
CONLANGS > CONLANG
CONMAN n person who uses confidence tricks to swindle or defraud
CONMEN > CONMAN
CONN same as > CON
CONNATE adj existing in a person or thing from birth
CONNATELY > CONNATE
CONNATION n joining of similar parts or organs
CONNATURE n sharing a common nature or character
CONNE same as > CON
CONNECT vb join together
CONNECTED adj joined or linked together
CONNECTER > CONNECT
CONNECTOR > CONNECT
CONNECTS > CONNECT
CONNED > CON
CONNER same as > CONDER
CONNERS > CONNER
CONNES > CONNE
CONNEXION n act or state of connecting
CONNEXIVE adj connective
CONNIE n tram or bus conductor
CONNIES > CONNIE
CONNING > CON
CONNINGS > CON
CONNIVE vb allow (wrongdoing) by ignoring it
CONNIVED > CONNIVE
CONNIVENT adj (of parts of plants and animals) touching without being fused, as some petals, insect wings, etc
CONNIVER > CONNIVE
CONNIVERS > CONNIVE
CONNIVERY n act of conniving

CONNIVES > CONNIVE

CONNIVING n act or instance of allowing (wrongdoing) by ignoring it

CONNOR n type of saltwater fish

CONNORS > CONNOR

CONNOTATE vb to connote

CONNOTE vb imply or suggest

CONNOTED > CONNOTE

CONNOTES > CONNOTE

CONNOTING > CONNOTE

CONNOTIVE adj act or state of connecting

CONNS > CONN

CONNUBIAL adj of marriage

CONODONT n toothlike fossil derived from an eel-like animal

CONODONTS > CONODONT

CONOID n geometric surface ▷ adj conical, cone-shaped

CONOIDAL same as > CONOID

CONOIDIC > CONOID

CONOIDS > CONOID

CONOMINEE n joint nominee

CONQUER vb defeat

CONQUERED > CONQUER

CONQUERER variant of > CONQUEROR

CONQUEROR > CONQUER

CONQUERS > CONQUER

CONQUEST n conquering

CONQUESTS > CONQUEST

CONQUIAN same as > COONCAN

CONQUIANS > COONCAN

CONS > CON

CONSCIENT adj conscious

CONSCIOUS adj alert and awake ▷ n conscious part of the mind

CONSCRIBE vb to enrol compulsorily

CONSCRIPT n person enrolled for compulsory military service ▷ vb enrol (someone) for compulsory military service

CONSEIL n advice

CONSEILS > CONSEIL

CONSENSUS n general agreement

CONSENT n agreement, permission ▷ vb permit, agree to

CONSENTED > CONSENT

CONSENTER > CONSENT

CONSENTS > CONSENT

CONSERVE vb protect from harm, decay, or loss ▷ n jam containing large pieces of fruit

CONSERVED > CONSERVE

CONSERVER > CONSERVE

CONSERVES > CONSERVE

CONSIDER vb regard as

CONSIDERS > CONSIDER

CONSIGN vb put somewhere

CONSIGNED > CONSIGN

CONSIGNEE n person, agent, organization, etc, to which merchandise is consigned

CONSIGNER same as > CONSIGNOR

CONSIGNOR n person, enterprise, etc, that consigns goods

CONSIGNS > CONSIGN

CONSIST vb be composed (of)

CONSISTED > CONSIST

CONSISTS > CONSIST

CONSOCIES n natural community with a single dominant species

CONSOL n consolidated annuity, a British government bond

CONSOLATE vb to console

CONSOLE vb comfort in distress ▷ n panel of controls for electronic equipment

CONSOLED > CONSOLE

CONSOLER > CONSOLE

CONSOLERS > CONSOLE

CONSOLES > CONSOLE

CONSOLING > CONSOLE

CONSOLS pl n irredeemable British government securities

CONSOLUTE adj (of two or more liquids) mutually soluble in all proportions

CONSOMME n thin clear meat soup

CONSOMMES > CONSOMME

CONSONANT n speech sound made by partially or completely blocking the breath stream ▷ adj agreeing (with)

CONSONOUS adj harmonious

CONSORT vb keep company (with) ▷ n spouse of a monarch

CONSORTED > CONSORT

CONSORTER > CONSORT

CONSORTIA n plural form of singular consortium: association of financiers, companies etc

CONSORTS > CONSORT

CONSPIRE vb plan a crime together in secret

CONSPIRED > CONSPIRE

CONSPIRER > CONSPIRE

CONSPIRES > CONSPIRE

CONSPUE vb spit on with contempt

CONSPUED > CONSPUE

CONSPUES > CONSPUE

CONSPUING > CONSPUE

CONSTABLE n police officer of the lowest rank

CONSTANCY n quality of having a resolute mind, purpose, or affection

CONSTANT adj continuous ▷ n unvarying quantity

CONSTANTS > CONSTANT

CONSTATE vb affirm

CONSTATED > CONSTATE

CONSTATES > CONSTATE

CONSTER obsolete variant of > CONSTRUE

CONSTERED > CONSTRUE

CONSTERS > CONSTER

CONSTRAIN vb compel, force

CONSTRICT vb make narrower by squeezing

CONSTRUAL n act of construing

CONSTRUCT vb build or put together ▷ n complex idea resulting from the combination of simpler ideas

CONSTRUE vb interpret ▷ n something that is construed, such as a piece of translation

CONSTRUED > CONSTRUE

CONSTRUER > CONSTRUE

CONSTRUES > CONSTRUE

CONSUL n official representing a state in a foreign country

CONSULAGE n duty paid by merchants for a consul's protection of their goods while abroad

CONSULAR n anyone of consular rank

CONSULARS > CONSULAR

CONSULATE n workplace or position of a consul

CONSULS > CONSUL

CONSULT vb go to for advice or information

CONSULTA n official planning meeting

CONSULTAS > CONSULTA

CONSULTED > CONSULT

CONSULTEE n person who is consulted

CONSULTER > CONSULT

CONSULTOR > CONSULT

CONSULTS > CONSULT

CONSUME vb eat or drink

CONSUMED > CONSUME

CONSUMER n person who buys goods or uses services

CONSUMERS > CONSUMER

CONSUMES > CONSUME

CONSUMING > CONSUME

CONSUMPT n quantity used up; consumption

CONSUMPTS > CONSUMPT

CONTACT n communicating ▷ vb get in touch with ▷ interj (formerly) call made by the pilot to indicate the engine is ready for starting

CONTACTED > CONTACT

CONTACTEE n person contacted by aliens

CONTACTOR n type of switch for repeatedly opening and closing an electric circuit. Its operation can be mechanical, electromagnetic, or pneumatic

CONTACTS > CONTACT

CONTADINA n female Italian farmer

CONTADINE > CONTADINA

CONTADINI > CONTADINO

CONTADINO n Italian farmer

CONTAGIA > CONTAGIUM

CONTAGION n passing on of disease by contact

CONTAGIUM n specific virus or other direct cause of any infectious disease

CONTAIN vb hold or be capable of holding

CONTAINED > CONTAIN

CONTAINER n object used to hold or store things in

CONTAINS > CONTAIN

CONTANGO n postponement of payment for and delivery of stock ▷ vb arrange such a postponement of payment

CONTANGOS > CONTANGO

CONTE n tale or short story, esp of adventure

CONTECK n contention

CONTECKS > CONTECK

CONTEMN vb regard with contempt

CONTEMNED > CONTEMN

CONTEMNER > CONTEMN

CONTEMNOR > CONTEMN

CONTEMNS > CONTEMN

CONTEMPER vb to modify

CONTEMPO adj contemporary

CONTEMPT n dislike and disregard

CONTEMPTS > CONTEMPT

CONTEND vb deal with

CONTENDED > CONTEND

CONTENDER > CONTEND

CONTENDS > CONTEND

CONTENT n meaning or substance of a piece of writing ▷ adj satisfied with things as they are ▷ vb make (someone) content

CONTENTED adj satisfied with one's situation or life

CONTENTLY > CONTENT

CONTENTS > CONTENT

CONTES > CONTE

CONTESSA n Italian countess

CONTESSAS > CONTESSA

CONTEST n competition or struggle ▷ vb dispute, object to

CONTESTED > CONTEST

CONTESTER > CONTEST

CONTESTS > CONTEST

CONTEXT n circumstances of an event or fact

CONTEXTS > CONTEXT

CONTICENT adj silent

CONTINENT n one of the earth's large masses of land ▷ adj able to control one's bladder and bowels

CONTINUA > CONTINUUM

CONTINUAL adj constant

CONTINUE vb (cause to) remain in a condition or place

CONTINUED > CONTINUE

CONTINUER > CONTINUE

CONTINUES > CONTINUE

CONTINUO n continuous bass part, usu played on a keyboard instrument

CONTINUOS > CONTINUO

CONTINUUM n continuous series

CONTLINE n space between the bilges of stowed casks

CONTLINES > CONTLINE

CONTO n former Portuguese monetary unit worth 1000 escudos

CONTORNI > CONTORNO

CONTORNO n in Italy, side dish of salad or vegetables

CONTORNOS > CONTORNO

c

CONTORT vb twist out of shape

CONTORTED adj twisted out of shape

CONTORTS > CONTORT

CONTOS > CONTO

CONTOUR n outline ▷ vb shape so as to form or follow the contour of something

CONTOURED > CONTOUR

CONTOURS > CONTOUR

CONTRA n counter-argument

CONTRACT n (document setting out) a formal agreement ▷ vb make a formal agreement (to do something)

CONTRACTS > CONTRACT

CONTRAIL n aeroplane's vapour trail

CONTRAILS > CONTRAIL

CONTRAIR adj contrary

CONTRALTI > CONTRALTO

CONTRALTO n (singer with) the lowest female voice ▷ adj of or denoting a contralto

CONTRARY n complete opposite ▷ adj opposed, completely different ▷ adv in opposition

CONTRAS > CONTRA

CONTRAST n obvious difference ▷ vb compare in order to show differences

CONTRASTS > CONTRAST

CONTRASTY adj (of a photograph or subject) having sharp gradations in tone, esp between light and dark areas

CONTRAT old form of > CONTRACT

CONTRATE adj (of gears) having teeth set at a right angle to the axis

CONTRATS > CONTRAT

CONTRIST vb make sad

CONTRISTS > CONTRIST

CONTRITE adj sorry and apologetic

CONTRIVE vb make happen

CONTRIVED adj planned or artificial

CONTRIVER > CONTRIVE

CONTRIVES > CONTRIVE

CONTROL n power to direct something ▷ vb have power over

CONTROLE adj officially registered

CONTROLS > CONTROL

CONTROUL obsolete variant of > CONTROL

CONTROULS > CONTROUL

CONTUMACY n obstinate disobedience

CONTUMELY n scornful or insulting treatment

CONTUND vb pummel

CONTUNDED > CONTUND

CONTUNDS > CONTUND

CONTUSE vb injure (the body) without breaking the skin

CONTUSED > CONTUSE

CONTUSES > CONTUSE

CONTUSING > CONTUSE

CONTUSION n bruise

CONTUSIVE > CONTUSE

CONUNDRUM n riddle

CONURBAN adj relating to an urban region

CONURBIA n conurbations considered collectively

CONURBIAS > CONURBIA

CONURE n small American parrot

CONURES > CONURE

CONUS n any of several cone-shaped structures

CONVECT vb circulate hot air by convection

CONVECTED > CONVECT

CONVECTOR n heater that gives out hot air

CONVECTS > CONVECT

CONVENE vb gather or summon for a formal meeting

CONVENED > CONVENE

CONVENER n person who calls a meeting

CONVENERS > CONVENER

CONVENES > CONVENE

CONVENING n act of convening

CONVENOR same as > CONVENER

CONVENORS > CONVENOR

CONVENT n building where nuns live ▷ vb summon

CONVENTED > CONVENT

CONVENTS > CONVENT

CONVERGE vb meet or join

CONVERGED > CONVERGE

CONVERGES > CONVERGE

CONVERSE vb have a conversation ▷ n opposite or contrary ▷ adj reversed or opposite

CONVERSED > CONVERSE

CONVERSER > CONVERSE

CONVERSES > CONVERSE

CONVERSO n medieval Spanish Jew converting to Catholicism

CONVERSOS > CONVERSO

CONVERT vb change in form, character, or function ▷ n person who has converted to a different belief or religion

CONVERTED > CONVERT

CONVERTER n person or thing that converts

CONVERTOR same as > CONVERTER

CONVERTS > CONVERT

CONVEX adj curving outwards ▷ vb make convex

CONVEXED > CONVEX

CONVEXES > CONVEX

CONVEXING > CONVEX

CONVEXITY n state or quality of being convex

CONVEXLY > CONVEX

CONVEY vb communicate (information)

CONVEYAL n act or means of conveying

CONVEYALS > CONVEYAL

CONVEYED > CONVEY

CONVEYER same as > CONVEYOR

CONVEYERS > CONVEYER

CONVEYING > CONVEY

CONVEYOR n person or thing that conveys

CONVEYORS > CONVEYOR

CONVEYS > CONVEY

CONVICT vb declare guilty ▷ n person serving a prison sentence ▷ adj convicted

CONVICTED > CONVICT

CONVICTS > CONVICT

CONVINCE vb persuade by argument or evidence

CONVINCED > CONVINCE

CONVINCER > CONVINCE

CONVINCES > CONVINCE

CONVIVE vb feast together

CONVIVED > CONVIVE

CONVIVES > CONVIVE

CONVIVIAL adj sociable, lively

CONVIVING > CONVIVE

CONVO n conversation

CONVOCATE vb call together

CONVOKE vb call together

CONVOKED > CONVOKE

CONVOKER > CONVOKE

CONVOKERS > CONVOKE

CONVOKES > CONVOKE

CONVOKING > CONVOKE

CONVOLUTE vb form into a twisted, coiled, or rolled shape ▷ adj rolled longitudinally upon itself

CONVOLVE vb wind or roll together

CONVOLVED > CONVOLVE

CONVOLVES > CONVOLVE

CONVOS > CONVO

CONVOY n group of vehicles or ships travelling together ▷ vb escort while in transit

CONVOYED > CONVOY

CONVOYING > CONVOY

CONVOYS > CONVOY

CONVULSE vb (of part of the body) undergo violent spasms

CONVULSED > CONVULSE

CONVULSES > CONVULSE

CONWOMAN n woman who uses confidence tricks to swindle or defraud

CONWOMEN > CONWOMAN

CONY n rabbit

COO vb (of a dove or pigeon) make a soft murmuring sound ▷ n sound of cooing ▷ interj exclamation of surprise, awe, etc

COOCH n vulgar word for the vagina

COOCHES > COOCH

COOCOO old spelling of > CUCKOO

COOED > COO

COOEE interj call to attract attention ▷ vb utter this call ▷ n calling distance

COOEED > COOEE

COOEEING > COOEE

COOEES > COOEE

COOER > COO

COOERS > COO

COOEY same as > COOEE

COOEYED > COOEY

COOEYING > COOEY

COOEYS > COOEY

COOF n simpleton

COOFS > COOF

COOING > COO

COOINGLY > COO

COOINGS > COO

COOK vb prepare (food) by heating ▷ n person who cooks food

COOKABLE adj able to be cooked ▷ n something that can be cooked

COOKABLES > COOKABLE

COOKBOOK n book containing recipes and instructions for cooking

COOKBOOKS > COOKBOOK

COOKED > COOK

COOKER n apparatus for cooking heated by gas or electricity

COOKERIES > COOKERY

COOKERS > COOKER

COOKERY n art of cooking

COOKEY same as > COOKIE

COOKEYS > COOKEY

COOKHOUSE n place for cooking, esp a camp kitchen

COOKIE n biscuit

COOKIES > COOKIE

COOKING > COOK

COOKINGS > COOK

COOKLESS adj devoid of a cook

COOKMAID n maid who assists a cook

COOKMAIDS > COOKMAID

COOKOFF n cookery competition

COOKOFFS > COOKOFF

COOKOUT n party where a meal is cooked and eaten out of doors

COOKOUTS > COOKOUT

COOKROOM n room in which food is cooked

COOKROOMS > COOKROOM

COOKS > COOK

COOKSHACK n makeshift building in which food is cooked

COOKSHOP n shop that sells cookery equipment

COOKSHOPS > COOKSHOP

COOKSTOVE n stove for cooking

COOKTOP n flat unit for cooking in saucepans or the top part of a stove

COOKTOPS > COOKTOP

COOKWARE n cooking utensils

COOKWARES > COOKWARE

COOKY same as > COOKIE

COOL adj moderately cold ▷ vb make or become cool ▷ n coolness

COOLABAH n Australian tree that grows along rivers, with smooth bark and long narrow leaves

COOLABAHS > COOLABAH

COOLAMON n shallow dish of wood or bark, used for carrying water

COOLAMONS > COOLAMON

COOLANT n fluid used to cool machinery while it is working

SECTION 1: Words between 2 and 9 letters in length

C

COOLANTS > COOLANT

COOLDOWN n gentle stretching exercises after strenuous activity

COOLDOWNS > COOLDOWN

COOLED > COOL

COOLER n container for making or keeping things cool

COOLERS > COOLER

COOLEST > COOL

COOLHOUSE n greenhouse in which a cool temperature is maintained

COOLIBAH same as **>** COOLABAH

COOLIBAHS > COOLIBAH

COOLIBAR same as **>** COOLABAH

COOLIBARS > COOLIBAR

COOLIE n offensive term for an unskilled Oriental labourer

COOLIES > COOLIE

COOLING n as in regenerative cooling method of cooling rocket combustion chambers

COOLINGLY > COOL

COOLINGS > COOLING

COOLISH > COOL

COOLIST n person who does not believe in global warming

COOLISTS > COOLIST

COOLLY > COOL

COOLNESS > COOL

COOLS > COOL

COOLTH n coolness

COOLTHS > COOLTH

COOLY same as **>** COOLIE

COOM n waste material **▷** vb blacken

COOMB n short valley or deep hollow

COOMBE same as **>** COOMB

COOMBES > COOMBE

COOMBS > COOMB

COOMED > COOM

COOMIER > COOMY

COOMIEST > COOMY

COOMING > COOM

COOMS > COOM

COOMY adj grimy

COON n raccoon

COONCAN n card game for two players, similar to rummy

COONCANS > COONCAN

COONDOG n dog trained to hunt raccoons

COONDOGS > COONDOG

COONHOUND n dog for hunting raccoons

COONS > COON

COONSHIT n offensive term for a contemptible person

COONSHITS > COONSHIT

COONSKIN n pelt of a raccoon

COONSKINS > COONSKIN

COONTIE n evergreen plant of S Florida

COONTIES > COONTIE

COONTY same as **>** COONTIE

COOP n cage or pen for poultry **▷** vb confine in a restricted area

COOPED > COOP

COOPER n person who makes or repairs barrels **▷** vb make or mend (barrels, casks, etc)

COOPERAGE n craft, place of work, or products of a cooper

COOPERATE vb work or act together

COOPERED > COOPER

COOPERIES > COOPERY

COOPERING > COOPER

COOPERS > COOPER

COOPERY same as **>** COOPERAGE

COOPING > COOP

COOPS > COOP

COOPT vb add (someone) to a group by the agreement of the existing members

COOPTED > COOPT

COOPTING > COOPT

COOPTION > COOPT

COOPTIONS > COOPT

COOPTS > COOPT

COORDINAL adj (of animals or plants) belonging to the same order

COORIE same as **>** COURIE

COORIED > COORIE

COORIEING > COORIE

COORIES > COORIE

COOS > COO

COOSEN same as **>** COZEN

COOSENED > COOSEN

COOSENING > COOSEN

COOSENS > COOSEN

COOSER n stallion

COOSERS > COOSER

COOSIN same as **>** COZEN

COOSINED > COOSIN

COOSINING > COOSIN

COOSINS > COOSIN

COOST Scots form of **>** CAST

COOT n small black water bird

COOTCH n hiding place **▷** vb hide

COOTCHED > COOTCH

COOTCHES > COOTCH

COOTCHING > COOTCH

COOTER n type of freshwater turtle

COOTERS > COOTER

COOTIE n body louse

COOTIES > COOTIE

COOTIKIN n gaiter

COOTIKINS > COOTIKIN

COOTS > COOT

COOZE n vulgar word for the female genitals

COOZES > COOZE

COP same as **>** COPPER

COPACETIC adj very good

COPAIBA n resin obtained from certain tropical trees

COPAIBAS > COPAIBA

COPAIVA same as **>** COPAIBA

COPAIVAS > COPAIVA

COPAL n resin used in varnishes

COPALM n aromatic resin

COPALMS > COPALM

COPALS > COPAL

COPARCENY n form of joint ownership of property

COPARENT n fellow parent

COPARENTS > COPARENT

COPARTNER n partner or associate

COPASETIC same as **>** COPACETIC

COPASTOR n fellow pastor

COPASTORS > COPASTOR

COPATAINE adj (of a hat) high-crowned

COPATRIOT n fellow patriot

COPATRON n fellow patron

COPATRONS > COPATRON

COPAY n amount payable for treatment by person with medical insurance

COPAYMENT n fee paid for medical insurance

COPAYS > COPAY

COPE vb deal successfully (with) **▷** n large ceremonial cloak worn by some Christian priests

COPECK same as **>** KOPECK

COPECKS > COPECK

COPED > COPE

COPEMATE n partner

COPEMATES > COPEMATE

COPEN n shade of blue

COPENS > COPEN

COPEPOD n type of minute crustacean

COPEPODS > COPEPOD

COPER n horse-dealer **▷** vb smuggle liquor to deep-sea fishermen

COPERED > COPER

COPERING > COPER

COPERS > COPER

COPES > COPE

COPESETIC same as **>** COPACETIC

COPESTONE same as **>** CAPSTONE

COPIABLE adj able to be copied

COPIED > COPY

COPIER n machine that copies

COPIERS > COPIER

COPIES > COPY

COPIHUE n Chilean bellflower

COPIHUES > COPIHUE

COPILOT n second pilot of an aircraft **▷** vb act as a copilot

COPILOTED > COPILOT

COPILOTS > COPILOT

COPING n sloping top row of a wall

COPINGS > COPING

COPIOUS adj abundant, plentiful

COPIOUSLY > COPIOUS

COPITA n tulip-shaped sherry glass

COPITAS > COPITA

COPLANAR adj lying in the same plane

COPLOT vb plot together

COPLOTS > COPLOT

COPLOTTED > COPLOT

COPOLYMER n chemical compound of high molecular weight formed by uniting the molecules of two or more

different compounds (monomers)

COPOUT n act of avoiding responsibility

COPOUTS > COPOUT

COPPED > COP

COPPER n soft reddish-brown metal **▷** adj reddish-brown **▷** vb coat or cover with copper

COPPERAH same as **>** COPRA

COPPERAHS > COPPERAH

COPPERAS n ferrous sulphate

COPPERED > COPPER

COPPERIER > COPPERY

COPPERING > COPPER

COPPERISH adj copper-like

COPPERS > COPPER

COPPERY adj like copper

COPPICE n small group of trees growing close together **▷** vb trim back (trees or bushes) to form a coppice

COPPICED > COPPICE

COPPICES > COPPICE

COPPICING > COPPICE

COPPIES > COPPY

COPPIN n ball of thread

COPPING > COP

COPPINS > COPPIN

COPPLE n hill rising to a point

COPPLES > COPPLE

COPPRA same as **>** COPRA

COPPRAS > COPPRA

COPPY n small wooden stool

COPRA n dried oil-yielding kernel of the coconut

COPRAEMIA n type of poisoning caused by faecal matter entering the bloodstream

COPRAEMIC adj relating to or causing copraemia

COPRAH same as **>** COPRA

COPRAHS > COPRAH

COPRAS > COPRA

COPREMIA same as **>** COPRAEMIA

COPREMIAS > COPRAEMIA

COPREMIC same as **>** COPRAEMIC

COPRESENT vb to present jointly

COPRINCE n fellow prince

COPRINCES > COPRINCE

COPRODUCE vb to produce jointly

COPRODUCT n joint product

COPROLITE n rounded stony nodule thought to be fossilized faeces

COPROLITH n hard stony mass of dried faeces

COPROLOGY n preoccupation with excrement

COPROSMA n Australasian shrub sometimes planted for ornament

COPROSMAS > COPROSMA

COPROZOIC adj (of animals) living in dung

COPS > COP

COPSE same as **>** COPPICE

COPSED > COPSE

COPSES > COPSE
COPSEWOOD n brushwood
COPSHOP n police station
COPSHOPS > COPSHOP
COPSIER > COPSY
COPSIEST > COPSY
COPSING > COPSE
COPSY adj having copses
COPTER n helicopter
COPTERS > COPTER
COPUBLISH vb to publish jointly
COPULA n verb used to link the subject and complement of a sentence
COPULAE > COPULA
COPULAR > COPULA
COPULAS > COPULA
COPULATE vb have sexual intercourse
COPULATED > COPULATE
COPULATES > COPULATE
COPURIFY vb purify together
COPY n thing made to look exactly like another ▷ vb make a copy of
COPYABLE > COPY
COPYBOOK n book of specimens for imitation
COPYBOOKS > COPYBOOK
COPYBOY n formerly, in journalism, boy who carried copy and ran errands
COPYBOYS > COPYBOY
COPYCAT n person who imitates or copies someone ▷ vb imitate with great attention to detail
COPYCATS > COPYCAT
COPYDESK n desk where newspaper copy is edited
COPYDESKS > COPYDESK
COPYEDIT vb prepare text for printing by styling, correcting, etc
COPYEDITS > COPYEDIT
COPYFIGHT n legal battle over the use of a copyright
COPYGIRL n female copyboy
COPYGIRLS > COPYGIRL
COPYGRAPH n process for copying type
COPYHOLD n tenure less than freehold of land in England evidenced by a copy of the Court roll
COPYHOLDS > COPYHOLD
COPYING n act of copying
COPYINGS > COPYING
COPYISM n slavish copying
COPYISMS > COPYISM
COPYIST n person who makes written copies
COPYISTS > COPYIST
COPYLEFT n permission to use something free of charge ▷ vb use copyright law to make (work, esp software) free to use
COPYLEFTS > COPYLEFT
COPYREAD vb subedit
COPYREADS > COPYREAD
COPYRIGHT n exclusive legal right to reproduce and control a book, work of art,

etc ▷ vb take out a copyright on ▷ adj protected by copyright
COPYTAKER n (esp in a newspaper office) a person employed to type reports as journalists dictate them over the telephone
COQUET vb behave flirtatiously
COQUETRY n flirtation
COQUETS > COQUET
COQUETTE n woman who flirts
COQUETTED > COQUET
COQUETTES > COQUETTE
COQUI n type of tree-dwelling frog
COQUILLA n type of South American nut
COQUILLAS > COQUILLA
COQUILLE n any dish, esp seafood, served in a scallop shell
COQUILLES > COQUILLE
COQUINA n soft limestone
COQUINAS > COQUINA
COQUIS > COQUI
COQUITO n Chilean palm tree yielding edible nuts and a syrup
COQUITOS > COQUITO
COR interj exclamation of surprise, amazement, or admiration ▷ n Hebrew measure of dry weight
CORACLE n small round boat of wicker covered with skins
CORACLES > CORACLE
CORACOID n paired ventral bone of the pectoral girdle in vertebrates
CORACOIDS > CORACOID
CORAGGIO interj exhortation to hold one's nerve
CORAL n hard substance formed from the skeletons of very small sea animals ▷ adj orange-pink
CORALLA > CORALLUM
CORALLINE n type of red alga impregnated with calcium carbonate
CORALLITE n skeleton of a coral polyp
CORALLOID same as > CORALLINE
CORALLUM n skeleton of any zoophyte
CORALROOT n N temperate leafless orchid with small yellow-green or purple flowers and branched roots resembling coral
CORALS > CORAL
CORALWORT n coralroot or toothwort
CORAM prep before, in the presence of
CORAMINE n type of stimulant
CORAMINES > CORAMINE
CORANACH same as > CORONACH
CORANACHS > CORANACH
CORANTO same as > COURANTE

CORANTOES > CORANTO
CORANTOS > CORANTO
CORBAN n gift to God
CORBANS > CORBAN
CORBE obsolete variant of > CORBEL
CORBEAU n blackish green colour
CORBEAUS > CORBEAU
CORBEIL n carved ornament in the form of a basket of fruit, flowers, etc
CORBEILLE same as > CORBEIL
CORBEILS > CORBEIL
CORBEL n stone or timber support sticking out of a wall ▷ vb lay (a stone or brick) so that it forms a corbel
CORBELED > CORBEL
CORBELING n set of corbels stepped outwards, one above another
CORBELLED > CORBEL
CORBELS > CORBEL
CORBES > CORBE
CORBICULA n pollen basket
CORBIE n raven or crow
CORBIES > CORBIE
CORBINA n type of North American whiting
CORBINAS > CORBINA
CORBY same as > CORBIE
CORCASS n in Ireland, marshland
CORCASSES > CORCASS
CORD n thin rope or thick string ▷ adj (of fabric) ribbed ▷ vb bind or furnish with a cord or cords
CORDAGE n lines and rigging of a vessel
CORDAGES > CORDAGE
CORDATE adj heart-shaped
CORDATELY > CORDATE
CORDED adj tied or fastened with cord
CORDELLE vb to tow
CORDELLED > CORDELLE
CORDELLES > CORDELLE
CORDER > CORD
CORDERS > CORD
CORDGRASS n type of coarse grass
CORDIAL adj warm and friendly ▷ n drink with a fruit base
CORDIALLY > CORDIAL
CORDIALS > CORDIAL
CORDIFORM adj heart-shaped
CORDINER n shoemaker
CORDINERS > CORDINER
CORDING > CORD
CORDINGS > CORD
CORDITE n explosive used in guns and bombs
CORDITES > CORDITE
CORDLESS adj powered by an internal battery rather than a power cable
CORDLIKE > CORD
CORDOBA n standard monetary unit of Nicaragua
CORDOBAS > CORDOBA
CORDON n chain of police, soldiers, etc, guarding an

area ▷ vb put or form a cordon (around)
CORDONED > CORDON
CORDONING > CORDON
CORDONNET n type of thread
CORDONS > CORDON
CORDOTOMY n method of pain relief in which nerves are cut
CORDOVAN n fine leather made principally from horsehide
CORDOVANS > CORDOVAN
CORDS pl n trousers made of corduroy
CORDUROY n cotton fabric with a velvety ribbed surface
CORDUROYS pl n trousers made of corduroy
CORDWAIN an archaic name for > CORDOVAN
CORDWAINS > CORDWAIN
CORDWOOD n wood that has been cut into lengths of four feet so that it can be stacked in cords
CORDWOODS > CORDWOOD
CORDYLINE n any tree of the genus Cordyline
CORE n central part of certain fruits, containing the seeds ▷ vb remove the core from
CORED > CORE
COREDEEM vb redeem together
COREDEEMS > COREDEEM
COREGENT n joint regent
COREGENTS > COREGENT
COREIGN vb reign jointly
COREIGNS > COREIGN
CORELATE same as > CORRELATE
CORELATED > CORELATE
CORELATES > CORELATE
CORELESS > CORE
CORELLA n white Australian cockatoo
CORELLAS > CORELLA
COREMIA > COREMIUM
COREMIUM n spore-producing organ of certain fungi
COREOPSIS n American and tropical African plant cultivated for its yellow, brown, or yellow-and-red daisy-like flowers
CORER > CORE
CORERS > CORE
CORES > CORE
COREY n vulgar word for the penis
COREYS > COREY
CORF n wagon or basket used formerly in mines
CORFHOUSE n shed used for curing salmon and storing nets
CORGI n short-legged sturdy dog
CORGIS > CORGI
CORIA > CORIUM
CORIANDER n plant grown for its aromatic seeds and leaves
CORIES > CORY
CORING > CORE

C

CORIOUS adj leathery

CORIUM n deep inner layer of the skin

CORIUMS > CORIUM

CORIVAL same as > CORRIVAL

CORIVALRY > CORIVAL

CORIVALS > CORIVAL

CORIXID n type of water bug

CORIXIDS > CORIXID

CORK n thick light bark of a Mediterranean oak ▷ vb seal with a cork ▷ adj made of cork

CORKAGE n restaurant's charge for serving wine bought elsewhere

CORKAGES > CORKAGE

CORKBOARD n thin slab made of granules of cork, used as a floor or wall finish and as an insulator

CORKBORER n tool for cutting a hole in a stopper to insert a glass tube

CORKED adj (of wine) spoiled through having a decayed cork

CORKER n splendid or outstanding person or thing

CORKERS > CORKER

CORKIER > CORKY

CORKIEST > CORKY

CORKINESS > CORKY

CORKING adj excellent

CORKIR n lichen from which red or purple dye is made

CORKIRS > CORKIR

CORKLIKE > CORK

CORKS > CORK

CORKSCREW n spiral metal tool for pulling corks from bottles ▷ adj like a corkscrew in shape ▷ vb move in a spiral or zigzag course

CORKTREE n type of evergreen oak tree

CORKTREES > CORKTREE

CORKWING n type of greenish or bluish European fish

CORKWINGS > CORKWING

CORKWOOD n type of small tree of the southeastern US, with very lightweight porous wood

CORKWOODS > CORKWOOD

CORKY same as > CORKED

CORM n bulblike underground stem of certain plants

CORMEL n new small corm arising from the base of a fully developed one

CORMELS > CORMEL

CORMIDIA > CORMIDIUM

CORMIDIUM n collection of polyps in a siphonophore

CORMLET n small corm

CORMLETS > CORMLET

CORMLIKE adj resembling a corm

CORMOID adj like a corm

CORMORANT n large dark-coloured long-necked sea bird

CORMOUS > CORM

CORMS > CORM

CORMUS n corm

CORMUSES > CORMUS

CORN n cereal plant such as wheat or oats ▷ vb feed (animals) with corn, esp oats

CORNACRE same as > CONACRE

CORNACRES > CORNACRE

CORNAGE n rent fixed according to the number of horned cattle pastured

CORNAGES > CORNAGE

CORNBALL n person given to mawkish or unsophisticated behaviour

CORNBALLS > CORNBALL

CORNBORER n larva of the pyralid moth

CORNBRAID vb braid hair in cornrows

CORNBRASH n type of limestone which produces good soil for growing corn

CORNBREAD n bread made from maize meal

CORNCAKE n kind of cornmeal flatbread

CORNCAKES > CORNCAKE

CORNCOB n core of an ear of maize, to which the kernels are attached

CORNCOBS > CORNCOB

CORNCRAKE n brown Eurasian bird with a harsh cry

CORNCRIB n ventilated building for the storage of unhusked maize

CORNCRIBS > CORNCRIB

CORNEA n transparent membrane covering the eyeball

CORNEAE > CORNEA

CORNEAL > CORNEA

CORNEAS > CORNEA

CORNED adj preserved in salt or brine

CORNEITIS n inflammation of cornea

CORNEL n type of plant such as the dogwood and dwarf cornel

CORNELIAN same as > CARNELIAN

CORNELS > CORNEL

CORNEMUSE n French bagpipe

CORNEOUS adj horny

CORNER n area or angle where two converging lines or surfaces meet ▷ vb force into a difficult or inescapable position

CORNERED > CORNER

CORNERING n act of cornering

CORNERMAN n in baseball, first baseman

CORNERMEN > CORNERMAN

CORNERS > CORNER

CORNET n former cavalry officer

CORNETCY n commission or rank of a cornet

CORNETIST n person who plays the cornet

CORNETS > CORNET

CORNETT n musical instrument

CORNETTI > CORNETTO

CORNETTO same as > CORNETT

CORNETTOS > CORNETTO

CORNETTS > CORNETT

CORNFED adj fed on corn

CORNFIELD n field planted with cereal crops

CORNFLAG n gladiolus

CORNFLAGS > CORNFLAG

CORNFLAKE n singular form of plural cornflakes: toasted flakes made from cornmeal, sold as a breakfast cereal

CORNFLIES > CORNFLY

CORNFLOUR n fine maize flour

CORNFLY n small fly

CORNHUSK n outer protective covering of an ear of maize

CORNHUSKS > CORNHUSK

CORNI > CORNO

CORNICE n decorative moulding round the top of a wall ▷ vb furnish or decorate with or as if with a cornice

CORNICED > CORNICE

CORNICES > CORNICE

CORNICHE n coastal road, esp one built into the face of a cliff

CORNICHES > CORNICHE

CORNICHON n type of small gherkin

CORNICING n act of cornicing

CORNICLE n wax-secreting organ on an aphid's abdomen

CORNICLES > CORNICLE

CORNICULA n plural form of singular corniculum: small horn

CORNIER > CORNY

CORNIEST > CORNY

CORNIFIC adj producing horns

CORNIFIED > CORNIFY

CORNIFIES > CORNIFY

CORNIFORM adj horn-shaped

CORNIFY vb turn soft tissue hard

CORNILY > CORNY

CORNINESS > CORNY

CORNING > CORN

CORNIST n horn-player

CORNISTS > CORNIST

CORNLAND n land suitable for growing corn or grain

CORNLANDS > CORNLAND

CORNLOFT n loft for storing corn

CORNLOFTS > CORNLOFT

CORNMEAL n meal made from maize

CORNMEALS > CORNMEAL

CORNMILL n flour mill

CORNMILLS > CORNMILL

CORNMOTH n moth whose larvae feed on grain

CORNMOTHS > CORNMOTH

CORNO n French horn

CORNOPEAN n cornet (the brass musical instrument)

CORNPIPE n musical instrument made from a stalk of corn etc

CORNPIPES > CORNPIPE

CORNPONE n American corn bread

CORNPONES > CORNPONE

CORNRENT n rent for land that is paid in corn

CORNRENTS > CORNRENT

CORNROW n hairstyle in which the hair is plaited in close parallel rows ▷ vb style the hair in a cornrow

CORNROWED > CORNROW

CORNROWS > CORNROW

CORNS > CORN

CORNSILK n threads on an ear of maize

CORNSILKS > CORNSILK

CORNSTALK n stalk or stem of corn

CORNSTONE n mottled green and red limestone

CORNU n part or structure resembling a horn or having a hornlike pattern

CORNUA > CORNU

CORNUAL > CORNU

CORNUS n any member of the genus Cornus, such as dogwood

CORNUSES > CORNUS

CORNUTE adj having or resembling cornua ▷ vb make a cuckold of

CORNUTED same as > CORNUTE

CORNUTES > CORNUTE

CORNUTING > CORNUTE

CORNUTO n cuckold

CORNUTOS > CORNUTO

CORNWORM n cornmoth larva

CORNWORMS > CORNWORM

CORNY adj unoriginal or excessively sentimental

COROCORE same as > COROCORO

COROCORES > COROCORE

COROCORO n South Asian vessel fitted with outriggers

COROCOROS > COROCORO

CORODIES > CORODY

CORODY n feudal law

COROLLA n petals of a flower collectively

COROLLARY n idea, fact, or proposition which is the natural result of something else ▷ adj consequent or resultant

COROLLAS > COROLLA

COROLLATE adj having a corolla

COROLLINE adj relating to a corolla

CORONA n ring of light round the moon or sun

CORONACH n dirge or lamentation for the dead

CORONACHS > CORONACH

CORONAE > CORONA

CORONAL n circlet for the head ▷ adj of or relating to a corona or coronal

CORONALLY > CORONAL

CORONALS > CORONAL

CORONARY adj of the arteries surrounding the heart ▷ n coronary thrombosis
CORONAS > CORONA
CORONATE vb to crown
CORONATED > CORONATE
CORONATES > CORONATE
CORONEL n iron head of a tilting spear
CORONELS > CORONEL
CORONER n official responsible for the investigation of deaths
CORONERS > CORONER
CORONET n small crown
CORONETED adj wearing a coronet
CORONETS > CORONET
CORONIAL adj relating to a coroner
CORONIS n symbol used in Greek writing
CORONISES > CORONIS
CORONIUM n highly ionized iron and nickel seen as a green line in the solar coronal spectrum
CORONIUMS > CORONIUM
CORONOID adj crown-shaped
COROTATE vb rotate together
COROTATED > COROTATE
COROTATES > COROTATE
COROZO n tropical American palm whose seeds yield a useful oil
COROZOS > COROZO
CORPORA > CORPUS
CORPORAL n noncommissioned officer in an army ▷ adj of the body
CORPORALE same as **>** CORPORAL
CORPORALS > CORPORAL
CORPORAS n communion cloth
CORPORATE adj of business corporations
CORPOREAL adj physical or tangible
CORPORIFY vb to embody
CORPOSANT n Saint Elmo's fire
CORPS n military unit with a specific function
CORPSE n dead body ▷ vb laugh or cause to laugh involuntarily or inopportunely while on stage
CORPSED > CORPSE
CORPSES > CORPSE
CORPSING > CORPSE
CORPSMAN n medical orderly or stretcher-bearer
CORPSMEN > CORPSMAN
CORPULENT adj fat or plump
CORPUS n collection of writings, esp by a single author
CORPUSCLE n red or white blood cell
CORPUSES > CORPUS
CORRADE vb erode by the abrasive action of rock particles

CORRADED > CORRADE
CORRADES > CORRADE
CORRADING > CORRADE
CORRAL n enclosure for cattle or horses ▷ vb put in a corral
CORRALLED > CORRAL
CORRALS > CORRAL
CORRASION n erosion of rocks caused by fragments transported over them by water, wind, or ice
CORRASIVE > CORRASION
CORREA n Australian evergreen shrub with large showy tubular flowers
CORREAS > CORREA
CORRECT adj free from error, true ▷ vb put right
CORRECTED > CORRECT
CORRECTER > CORRECT
CORRECTLY > CORRECT
CORRECTOR > CORRECT
CORRECTS > CORRECT
CORRELATE vb place or be placed in a mutual relationship ▷ n either of two things mutually related ▷ adj having a mutual, complementary, or reciprocal relationship
CORRETTO n espresso containing alcohol
CORRETTOS > CORRETTO
CORRIDA the Spanish word for **>** BULLFIGHT
CORRIDAS > CORRIDA
CORRIDOR n passage in a building or train
CORRIDORS > CORRIDOR
CORRIE same as **>** CIRQUE
CORRIES > CORRIE
CORRIGENT n corrective
CORRIVAL a rare word for **>** RIVAL
CORRIVALS > CORRIVAL
CORRODANT > CORRODE
CORRODE vb eat or be eaten away by chemical action or rust
CORRODED > CORRODE
CORRODENT > CORRODE
CORRODER > CORRODE
CORRODERS > CORRODE
CORRODES > CORRODE
CORRODIES > CORRODY
CORRODING > CORRODE
CORRODY same as **>** CORODY
CORROSION n process by which something, esp a metal, is corroded
CORROSIVE adj (esp of acids or alkalis) capable of destroying solid materials ▷ n corrosive substance, such as a strong acid or alkali
CORRUGATE vb fold into alternate grooves and ridges ▷ adj folded into furrows and ridges
CORRUPT adj open to or involving bribery ▷ vb make corrupt
CORRUPTED > CORRUPT
CORRUPTER > CORRUPT
CORRUPTLY > CORRUPT
CORRUPTOR > CORRUPT

CORRUPTS > CORRUPT
CORS > COR
CORSAC n type of fox of central Asia
CORSACS > CORSAC
CORSAGE n small bouquet worn on the bodice of a dress
CORSAGES > CORSAGE
CORSAIR n pirate
CORSAIRS > CORSAIR
CORSE n corpse
CORSELET n one-piece undergarment combining a corset and bra
CORSELETS > CORSELET
CORSES > CORSE
CORSET n women's undergarment ▷ vb dress or enclose in, or as in, a corset
CORSETED > CORSET
CORSETIER n corset-maker
CORSETING > CORSET
CORSETRY n making of or dealing in corsets
CORSETS > CORSET
CORSEY n pavement or pathway
CORSEYS > CORSEY
CORSITE n type of rock
CORSITES > CORSITE
CORSIVE n corrodent
CORSIVES > CORSIVE
CORSLET same as **>** CORSELET
CORSLETED > CORSLET
CORSLETS > CORSLET
CORSNED n ordeal to discover innocence or guilt
CORSNEDS > CORSNED
CORSO n promenade
CORSOS > CORSO
CORTEGE n funeral procession
CORTEGES > CORTEGE
CORTEX n outer layer of the brain or other internal organ
CORTEXES > CORTEX
CORTICAL > CORTEX
CORTICATE adj (of plants, seeds, etc) having a bark, husk, or rind
CORTICES > CORTEX
CORTICOID n steroid hormone
CORTICOSE adj consisting of or like bark
CORTILE n open, internal courtyard
CORTILI > CORTILE
CORTIN n adrenal cortex extract
CORTINA n weblike part of certain mushrooms
CORTINAS > CORTINA
CORTINS > CORTIN
CORTISOL n principal glucocorticoid secreted by the adrenal cortex
CORTISOLS > CORTISOL
CORTISONE n steroid hormone used to treat various diseases
CORULER n joint ruler
CORULERS > CORULER
CORUNDUM n hard mineral used as an abrasive
CORUNDUMS > CORUNDUM

CORUSCANT adj giving off flashes of light
CORUSCATE vb sparkle
CORVEE n day's unpaid labour owed by a feudal vassal to their lord
CORVEES > CORVEE
CORVES > CORF
CORVET same as **>** CURVET
CORVETED > CORVET
CORVETING > CORVET
CORVETS > CORVET
CORVETTE n lightly armed escort warship ▷ vb participate in social activities with fellow Corvette car enthusiasts
CORVETTED > CORVETTE
CORVETTES > CORVETTE
CORVID n any member of the crow family
CORVIDS > CORVID
CORVINA same as **>** CORBINA
CORVINAS > CORVINA
CORVINE adj of, relating to, or resembling a crow
CORVUS n type of ancient hook
CORVUSES > CORVUS
CORY n catfish belonging to the South American Corydoras genus
CORYBANT n wild attendant of the goddess Cybele
CORYBANTS > CORYBANT
CORYDALIS n N temperate plant with finely lobed leaves and spurred yellow or pinkish flowers
CORYLUS n hazel genus
CORYLUSES > CORYLUS
CORYMB n flat-topped flower cluster
CORYMBED > CORYMB
CORYMBOSE > CORYMB
CORYMBOUS > CORYMB
CORYMBS > CORYMB
CORYPHAEI n plural form of singular coryphaeus: leader of the chorus
CORYPHE n coryphaeus
CORYPHEE n leading dancer of a corps de ballet
CORYPHEES > CORYPHEE
CORYPHENE n any fish of the genus Coryphaena
CORYPHES > CORYPHE
CORYZA n acute inflammation in the nose
CORYZAL > CORYZA
CORYZAS > CORYZA
COS same as **>** COSINE
COSCRIPT vb script jointly
COSCRIPTS > COSCRIPT
COSE vb get cosy
COSEC same as **>** COSECANT
COSECANT n ratio of the hypotenuse to the opposite side in a right-angled triangle
COSECANTS > COSECANT
COSECH n hyperbolic cosecant
COSECHS > COSECH
COSECS > COSEC
COSED > COSE**

C

COSEISMAL adj of or designating points at which earthquake waves are felt at the same time ▷ n such a line on a map

COSEISMIC same as > COSEISMAL

COSES > COSE

COSET n mathematical set

COSETS > COSET

COSEY n tea cosy

COSEYS > COSEY

COSH n heavy blunt weapon ▷ vb hit with a cosh

COSHED > COSH

COSHER vb pamper or coddle

COSHERED > COSHER

COSHERER > COSHER

COSHERERS > COSHER

COSHERIES > COSHERY

COSHERING > COSHER

COSHERS > COSHER

COSHERY n Irish chief's right to lodge at their tenants' houses

COSHES > COSH

COSHING > COSH

COSIE same as > COSY

COSIED > COSY

COSIER n cobbler

COSIERS > COSIER

COSIES > COSY

COSIEST > COSY

COSIGN vb sign jointly

COSIGNED > COSIGN

COSIGNER > COSIGN

COSIGNERS > COSIGN

COSIGNING > COSIGN

COSIGNS > COSIGN

COSILY > COSY

COSINE n trigonometric function

COSINES > COSINE

COSINESS > COSY

COSING > COSE

COSMEA n plant of the genus Cosmos

COSMEAS > COSMEA

COSMESES > COSMESIS

COSMESIS n aesthetic covering on a prosthesis to make it look more natural

COSMETIC n preparation used to improve the appearance of a person's skin ▷ adj improving the appearance only

COSMETICS > COSMETIC

COSMIC adj of the whole universe

COSMICAL same as > COSMIC

COSMID n segment of DNA

COSMIDS > COSMID

COSMIN same as > COSMINE

COSMINE n substance resembling dentine

COSMINES > COSMINE

COSMINS > COSMIN

COSMISM n Russian cultural and philosophical movement

COSMISMS > COSMISM

COSMIST > COSMISM

COSMISTS > COSMISM

COSMOCRAT n ruler of the world

COSMOGENY same as > COSMOGONY

COSMOGONY n study of the origin of the universe

COSMOID adj having two inner bony layers and a cosmine outer layer

COSMOLINE n type of petroleum jelly ▷ vb to apply cosmoline to

COSMOLOGY n study of the origin and nature of the universe

COSMONAUT n Russian name for an astronaut

COSMORAMA n lifelike display, using mirrors and lenses, which shows reflections of various views of parts of the world

COSMOS n universe

COSMOSES > COSMOS

COSMOTRON n large type of particle accelerator

COSPHERED adj sharing the same sphere

COSPLAY n recreational activity in which people interact while dressed as fictional characters

COSPLAYS > COSPLAY

COSPONSOR vb to sponsor jointly

COSS another name for > KOS

COSSACK n Slavonic warrior-peasant

COSSACKS > COSSACK

COSSES > COSS

COSSET vb pamper ▷ n any pet animal, esp a lamb

COSSETED > COSSET

COSSETING > COSSET

COSSETS > COSSET

COSSETTED adj pampered, spoilt

COSSIE n informal name for a swimming costume

COSSIES > COSSIE

COST n amount of money, time, labour, etc, required for something ▷ vb have as its cost

COSTA n riblike part, such as the midrib of a plant leaf

COSTAE > COSTA

COSTAL n strengthening rib of an insect's wing

COSTALGIA n pain in the ribs

COSTALLY > COSTAL

COSTALS > COSTAL

COSTAR n actor who shares the billing with another ▷ vb share the billing with another actor

COSTARD n English variety of apple tree

COSTARDS > COSTARD

COSTARRED > COSTAR

COSTARS > COSTAR

COSTATE adj having ribs

COSTATED same as > COSTATE

COSTE vb draw near

COSTEAN vb mine for lodes

COSTEANED > COSTEAN

COSTEANS > COSTEAN

COSTED > COST

COSTER n person who sells fruit, vegetables etc from a barrow

COSTERS > COSTER

COSTES > COSTE

COSTING n as in marginal costing method of cost accounting

COSTINGS > COSTING

COSTIVE adj having or causing constipation

COSTIVELY > COSTIVE

COSTLESS > COST

COSTLIER > COSTLY

COSTLIEST > COSTLY

COSTLY adj expensive

COSTMARY n herbaceous Asian plant

COSTOTOMY n surgical incision into a rib

COSTREL n flask, usually of earthenware or leather

COSTRELS > COSTREL

COSTS > COST

COSTUME n style of dress of a particular place or time, or for a particular activity ▷ vb provide with a costume

COSTUMED > COSTUME

COSTUMER same as > COSTUMIER

COSTUMERS > COSTUMIER

COSTUMERY n collective term for costumes

COSTUMES > COSTUME

COSTUMEY adj (stage) costume-like; unrealistic

COSTUMIER n maker or seller of costumes

COSTUMING n act of providing (someone) with a costume

COSTUS n Himalayan herb with an aromatic root

COSTUSES > COSTUS

COSY adj warm and snug ▷ n cover for keeping things warm ▷ vb make oneself snug and warm

COSYING > COSY

COT n baby's bed with high sides ▷ vb entangle or become entangled

COTAN same as > COTANGENT

COTANGENT n (in trigonometry) the ratio of the length of the adjacent side to that of the opposite side in a right-angled triangle

COTANS > COTAN

COTE same as > COT

COTEAU n hillside

COTEAUS > COTEAU

COTEAUX > COTEAU

COTED > COTE

COTELETTE n cutlet

COTELINE n kind of muslin

COTELINES > COTELINE

COTENANCY > COTENANT

COTENANT n person who holds property jointly or in common with others

COTENANTS > COTENANT

COTERIE n exclusive group, clique

COTERIES > COTERIE

COTES > COTE

COTH n hyperbolic cotangent

COTHS > COTH

COTHURN same as > COTHURNUS

COTHURNAL > COTHURNUS

COTHURNI > COTHURNUS

COTHURNS > COTHURN

COTHURNUS n buskin worn in ancient Greek tragedy

COTICULAR adj relating to whetstones

COTIDAL adj (of a line on a tidal chart) joining points at which high tide occurs simultaneously

COTIJA n salty Mexican cheese

COTIJAS > COTIJA

COTILLION n French formation dance of the 18th century

COTILLON same as > COTILLION

COTILLONS > COTILLON

COTING > COTE

COTINGA n tropical bird

COTINGAS > COTINGA

COTININE n substance used to indicate presence of nicotine

COTININES > COTININE

COTISE same as > COTTISE

COTISED > COTISE

COTISES > COTISE

COTISING > COTISE

COTLAND n grounds that belong to a cotter

COTLANDS > COTLAND

COTQUEAN n coarse woman

COTQUEANS > COTQUEAN

COTRUSTEE n fellow trustee

COTS > COT

COTT same as > COT

COTTA n short form of surplice

COTTABUS n ancient Greek game involving throwing wine into a vessel

COTTAE > COTTA

COTTAGE n small house in the country ▷ vb engage in homosexual activity in a public lavatory

COTTAGED > COTTAGE

COTTAGER n person who lives in a cottage

COTTAGERS > COTTAGER

COTTAGES > COTTAGE

COTTAGEY adj resembling a cottage

COTTAGIER > COTTAGEY

COTTAGING n homosexual activity between men in a public lavatory

COTTAR n cottage-dwelling peasant

COTTARS > COTTAR

COTTAS > COTTA

COTTED > COT

COTTER n pin or wedge used to secure machine parts ▷ vb secure (two parts) with a cotter

COTTERED > COTTER

COTTERING > COTTER

COTTERS > COTTER

COTTID n type of fish typically with a large head, tapering body, and spiny fins

COTTIDS > COTTID

COTTIER *same as* > COTTER

COTTIERS > COTTIER

COTTING > COT

COTTISE *n* type of heraldic decoration ▷ *vb* (in heraldry) decorate with a cottise

COTTISED > COTTISE

COTTISES > COTTISE

COTTISING > COTTISE

COTTOID *adj* resembling a fish of the genus Cottus

COTTON *n* white downy fibre covering the seeds of a tropical plant ▷ *vb* take a liking

COTTONADE *n* coarse fabric of cotton or mixed fibres, used for work clothes, etc

COTTONED > COTTON

COTTONIER > COTTONY

COTTONING > COTTON

COTTONS > COTTON

COTTONY *adj* like cotton

COTTOWN *Scots variant of* > COTTON

COTTOWNS > COTTOWN

COTTS > COTT

COTTUS *n* type of fish with four yellowish knobs on its head

COTTUSES > COTTUS

COTURNIX *n* variety of quail

COTWAL *n* Indian police officer

COTWALS > COTWAL

COTYLAE > COTYLE

COTYLE *n* cuplike cavity

COTYLEDON *n* first leaf of a plant embryo

COTYLES > COTYLE

COTYLOID *adj* shaped like a cup ▷ *n* small bone forming part of the acetabular cavity in some mammals

COTYLOIDS > COTYLOID

COTYPE *n* type specimen in biological study

COTYPES > COTYPE

COUCAL *n* type of ground-living bird of Africa, S Asia, and Australia, with long strong legs

COUCALS > COUCAL

COUCH *n* piece of upholstered furniture for seating more than one person ▷ *vb* express in a particular way

COUCHANT *adj* in a lying position

COUCHE *adj* in heraldry (of a shield), tilted

COUCHED > COUCH

COUCHEE *n* reception held late at night

COUCHEES > COUCHEE

COUCHER > COUCH

COUCHERS > COUCH

COUCHES > COUCH

COUCHETTE *n* bed converted from seats on a train or ship

COUCHING *n* method of embroidery

COUCHINGS > COUCHING

COUDE *adj* relating to the construction of a reflecting telescope ▷ *n* type of reflecting telescope

COUDES > COUDE

COUGAN *n* drunk and rowdy person

COUGANS > COUGAN

COUGAR *n* puma

COUGARS > COUGAR

COUGH *vb* expel air from the lungs abruptly and noisily ▷ *n* act or sound of coughing

COUGHED > COUGH

COUGHER > COUGH

COUGHERS > COUGH

COUGHING > COUGH

COUGHINGS > COUGH

COUGHS > COUGH

COUGUAR *same as* > COUGAR

COUGUARS > COUGUAR

COULD > CAN

COULDEST *same as* > COULDST

COULDST *vb* form of 'could' used with the pronoun *thou* or its relative form

COULEE *n* flow of molten lava

COULEES > COULEE

COULIBIAC *n* Russian fish pie

COULIS *n* thin purée of vegetables or fruit

COULISSE *n* timber grooved to take a sliding panel

COULISSES > COULISSE

COULOIR *n* deep gully on a mountain side, esp in the French Alps

COULOIRS > COULOIR

COULOMB *n* SI unit of electric charge

COULOMBIC > COULOMB

COULOMBS > COULOMB

COULTER *n* blade at the front of a ploughshare

COULTERS > COULTER

COUMARIC > COUMARIN

COUMARIN *n* white vanilla-scented crystalline ester

COUMARINS > COUMARIN

COUMARONE *n* colourless insoluble aromatic liquid obtained from coal tar and used in the manufacture of synthetic resins

COUMAROU *n* tonka bean tree, or its seed

COUMAROUS > COUMAROU

COUNCIL *n* group meeting for discussion or consultation ▷ *adj* of or by a council

COUNCILOR *n* member of a council

COUNCILS > COUNCIL

COUNSEL *n* advice or guidance ▷ *vb* give guidance to

COUNSELED > COUNSEL

COUNSELEE *n* one who is counselled

COUNSELOR *n* person who gives counsel

COUNSELS > COUNSEL

COUNT *vb* say numbers in order ▷ *n* counting

COUNTABLE *adj* capable of being counted

COUNTABLY > COUNTABLE

COUNTBACK *n* system of deciding the winner of a tied competition by comparing earlier points or scores

COUNTDOWN *n* counting backwards to zero of the seconds before an event ▷ *vb* count numbers backwards towards zero, esp in timing such a critical operation

COUNTED > COUNT

COUNTER *n* long flat surface in a bank or shop ▷ *vb* oppose, retaliate against ▷ *adv* in the opposite direction

COUNTERED > COUNTER

COUNTERS > COUNTER

COUNTESS *n* woman holding the rank of count or earl

COUNTIAN *n* dweller in a given county

COUNTIANS > COUNTIAN

COUNTIES > COUNTY

COUNTING *n* act or instance of saying numbers in order

COUNTINGS > COUNTING

COUNTLESS *adj* too many to count

COUNTLINE *n* (in confectionery marketing) a chocolate-based bar

COUNTRIES > COUNTRY

COUNTROL *obsolete variant of* > CONTROL

COUNTROLS > CONTROL

COUNTRY *n* nation

COUNTS > COUNT

COUNTSHIP > COUNT

COUNTY *n* (in some countries) division of a country ▷ *adj* upper-class

COUP *n* successful action ▷ *vb* turn or fall over

COUPE *n* sports car with two doors and a sloping fixed roof

COUPED > COUP

COUPEE *n* dance movement

COUPEES > COUPEE

COUPER *n* dealer

COUPERS > COUPER

COUPES > COUPE

COUPING > COUP

COUPLE *n* two people who are married or romantically involved ▷ *vb* connect, associate

COUPLED > COUPLE

COUPLEDOM *n* state of living as a couple, esp when regarded as being interested in each other to the exclusion of the outside world

COUPLER *n* mechanical device

COUPLERS > COUPLER

COUPLES > COUPLE

COUPLET *n* two consecutive lines of verse

COUPLETS > COUPLET

COUPLING *n* device for connecting things, such as railway carriages

COUPLINGS > COUPLING

COUPON *n* piece of paper entitling the holder to a discount or gift

COUPONING *n* in marketing, distribution or redemption of promotional coupons

COUPONS > COUPON

COUPS > COUP

COUPURE *n* entrenchment made by besieged forces behind a breach

COUPURES > COUPURE

COUR *obsolete variant of* > COVER

COURAGE *n* ability to face danger or pain without fear

COURAGES > COURAGE

COURANT *n* courante ▷ *adj* (of an animal) running

COURANTE *n* old dance in quick triple time

COURANTES > COURANTE

COURANTO *same as* > COURANTE

COURANTOS > COURANTO

COURANTS > COURANT

COURB *vb* to bend

COURBARIL *n* tropical American tree whose wood is a useful timber and whose gum is a source of copal

COURBED > COURB

COURBETTE *same as* > CURVET

COURBING > COURB

COURBS > COURB

COURD *obsolete variant of* > COVERED

COURE *obsolete variant of* > COVER

COURED > COURE

COURES > COURE

COURGETTE *n* type of small vegetable marrow

COURIE *vb* nestle or snuggle

COURIED > COURIE

COURIEING > COURIE

COURIER *n* person employed to look after holiday-makers ▷ *vb* send (a parcel, letter, etc) by courier

COURIERED > COURIER

COURIERS > COURIER

COURIES > COURIE

COURING > COUR

COURLAN *another name for* > LIMPKIN

COURLANS > COURLAN

COURS > COUR

COURSE *n* series of lessons or medical treatment ▷ *vb* (of liquid) run swiftly

COURSED > COURSE

COURSER *n* swift horse

COURSERS > COURSER

COURSES *another word for* > MENSES

COURSING *n* hunting with hounds trained to hunt game by sight

COURSINGS > COURSING

COURT *n* body which decides legal cases ▷ *vb* try to gain the love of

COURTED > COURT

COURTEOUS *adj* polite

COURTER *n* suitor

COURTERS > COURTER

COURTESAN *n* mistress or high-class prostitute**

COURTESY n politeness, good manners

COURTEZAN same as > COURTESAN

COURTIER n attendant at a royal court

COURTIERS > COURTIER

COURTING > COURT

COURTINGS > COURT

COURTLET n small court

COURTLETS > COURTLET

COURTLIER > COURTLY

COURTLIKE adj courtly

COURTLING n fawning courtier

COURTLY adj ceremoniously polite

COURTROOM n room in which the sittings of a law court are held

COURTS > COURT

COURTSHIP n courting of an intended spouse or mate

COURTSIDE n in sport, area closest to the court

COURTYARD n paved space enclosed by buildings or walls

COUSCOUS n type of semolina used in North African cookery

COUSIN n child of one's uncle or aunt

COUSINAGE n kinship

COUSINLY > COUSIN

COUSINRY n collective term for cousins

COUSINS > COUSIN

COUTA n traditional Australian sailing boat

COUTAS > COUTA

COUTEAU n large two-edged knife used formerly as a weapon

COUTEAUX > COUTEAU

COUTER n armour designed to protect the elbow

COUTERS > COUTER

COUTH adj refined ▷ n refinement

COUTHER > COUTH

COUTHEST > COUTH

COUTHIE adj sociable

COUTHIER > COUTHIE

COUTHIEST > COUTHIE

COUTHS > COUTH

COUTHY same as > COUTHIE

COUTIL n type of tightly woven twill cloth

COUTILLE same as > COUTIL

COUTILLES > COUTILLE

COUTILS > COUTIL

COUTURE n high-fashion designing and dressmaking ▷ adj relating to high fashion design and dress-making

COUTURES > COUTURE

COUTURIER n person who designs women's fashion clothes

COUVADE n custom in certain cultures relating to childbirth

COUVADES > COUVADE

COUVERT another word for > COVER

COUVERTS > COUVERT

COUZIN n South African word for a friend

COUZINS > COUZIN

COVALENCE same as > COVALENCY

COVALENCY n ability to form a bond in which two atoms share a pair of electrons

COVALENT > COVALENCY

COVARIANT n variant that varies leaving certain mathematical relationships it has with another variant (its covariant) unchanged

COVARIATE n statistical variable

COVARIED > COVARY

COVARIES > COVARY

COVARY vb vary together maintaining a certain mathematical relationship

COVARYING > COVARY

COVE n small bay or inlet ▷ vb form an architectural cove in

COVED > COVE

COVELET n small cove

COVELETS > COVELET

COVELLINE same as > COVELLITE

COVELLITE n indigo copper (blue sulphide of copper)

COVEN n meeting of witches

COVENANT n contract ▷ vb agree by a covenant

COVENANTS > COVENANT

COVENS > COVEN

COVENT same as > CONVENT

COVENTS > COVENT

COVER vb place something over, to protect or conceal ▷ n anything that covers

COVERABLE > COVER

COVERAGE n amount or extent covered

COVERAGES > COVERAGE

COVERALL n thing that covers something entirely

COVERALLS > COVERALL

COVERED > COVER

COVERER > COVER

COVERERS > COVER

COVERING another word for > COVER

COVERINGS > COVERING

COVERLESS > COVER

COVERLET n bed cover

COVERLETS > COVERLET

COVERLID same as > COVERLET

COVERLIDS > COVERLID

COVERS > COVER

COVERSED adj as in coversed sine obsolete function in trigonometry

COVERSINE n function in trigonometry

COVERSLIP n very thin piece of glass placed over a specimen on a glass slide

COVERT adj concealed, secret ▷ n thicket giving shelter to game birds or animals

COVERTER > COVERT

COVERTEST > COVERT

COVERTLY > COVERT

COVERTS > COVERT

COVERTURE n condition or status of a married woman considered as being under the protection and influence of her husband

COVERUP n concealment of a mistake, crime, etc

COVERUPS > COVERUP

COVES > COVE

COVET vb long to possess (what belongs to someone else)

COVETABLE > COVET

COVETED > COVET

COVETER > COVET

COVETERS > COVET

COVETING > COVET

COVETISE n covetousness

COVETISES > COVETISE

COVETOUS adj jealously longing to possess something

COVETS > COVET

COVEY n small flock of grouse or partridge

COVEYS > COVEY

COVIN n conspiracy between two or more persons

COVINE n conspiracy between people to injure someone else

COVINES > COVINE

COVING same as > COVE

COVINGS > COVING

COVINOUS adj deceitful

COVINS > COVIN

COVYNE same as > COVIN

COVYNES > COVYNE

COW n mature female of certain mammals ▷ vb intimidate, subdue

COWABUNGA interj expression of enthusiasm or delight

COWAGE n tropical climbing plant

COWAGES > COWAGE

COWAL n shallow lake or swampy depression supporting vegetation

COWALS > COWAL

COWAN n drystone waller

COWANS > COWAN

COWARD n person who lacks courage ▷ vb show (someone) up to be a coward

COWARDED > COWARD

COWARDICE n lack of courage

COWARDING > COWARD

COWARDLY adj of or characteristic of a coward

COWARDRY n cowardice

COWARDS > COWARD

COWBANE n poisonous marsh plant

COWBANES > COWBANE

COWBELL n bell hung around a cow's neck

COWBELLS > COWBELL

COWBERRY n evergreen shrub of N temperate and Arctic regions

COWBIND n any of various bryony plants, esp the white bryony

COWBINDS > COWBIND

COWBIRD n American oriole with a dark plumage and short bill

COWBIRDS > COWBIRD

COWBOY n (in the US) ranch worker who herds and tends cattle ▷ vb work or behave as a cowboy

COWBOYED > COWBOY

COWBOYING n act of working or behaving as a cowboy

COWBOYS > COWBOY

COWED > COW

COWEDLY > COW

COWER vb cringe in fear

COWERED > COWER

COWERING > COWER

COWERS > COWER

COWFEEDER n dairyman

COWFISH n type of trunkfish with hornlike spines over the eyes

COWFISHES > COWFISH

COWFLAP n cow dung

COWFLAPS > COWFLAP

COWFLOP n foxglove

COWFLOPS > COWFLOP

COWGIRL n female cowboy

COWGIRLS > COWGIRL

COWGRASS n red clover

COWHAGE same as > COWAGE

COWHAGES > COWHAGE

COWHAND same as > COWBOY

COWHANDS > COWHAND

COWHEARD same as > COWHERD

COWHEARDS > COWHEARD

COWHEEL n heel of a cow, used as cooking ingredient

COWHEELS > COWHEEL

COWHERB n European plant with clusters of pink flowers

COWHERBS > COWHERB

COWHERD n person employed to tend cattle

COWHERDS > COWHERD

COWHIDE n hide of a cow ▷ vb lash with a cowhide whip

COWHIDED > COWHIDE

COWHIDES > COWHIDE

COWHIDING > COWHIDE

COWHOUSE n byre

COWHOUSES > COWHOUSE

COWIER > COWY

COWIEST > COWY

COWING > COW

COWINNER n joint winner

COWINNERS > COWINNER

COWISH adj cowardly ▷ n N American plant with an edible root

COWISHES > COWISH

COWITCH another name for > COWAGE

COWITCHES > COWITCH

COWK vb retch or feel nauseated

COWKED > COWK

COWKING > COWK

COWKS > COWK

COWL same as > COWLING

COWLED adj wearing a cowl

COWLICK n tuft of hair over the forehead

COWLICKS > COWLICK
COWLIKE adj like a cow
COWLING n cover on an engine
COWLINGS > COWLING
COWLS > COWL
COWLSTAFF n pole, used by two people, for carrying a vessel
COWMAN n man who owns cattle
COWMEN > COWMAN
COWORKER n fellow worker
COWORKERS > COWORKER
COWP same as > COUP
COWPAT n pool of cow dung
COWPATS > COWPAT
COWPEA n type of tropical climbing plant
COWPEAS > COWPEA
COWPED > COWP
COWPIE n cowpat
COWPIES > COWPIE
COWPING > COWP
COWPLOP n cow dung
COWPLOPS > COWPLOP
COWPOKE n cowboy
COWPOKES > COWPOKE
COWPOX n disease of cows
COWPOXES > COWPOX
COWPS > COWP
COWPUNK n music that combines country music and punk
COWPUNKS > COWPUNK
COWRIE n brightly marked sea shell
COWRIES > COWRIE
COWRITE vb write jointly
COWRITER > COWRITE
COWRITERS > COWRITE
COWRITES > COWRITE
COWRITING > COWRITE
COWRITTEN > COWRITE
COWROTE > COWRITE
COWRY same as > COWRIE
COWS > COW
COWSHED n byre
COWSHEDS > COWSHED
COWSKIN same as > COWHIDE
COWSKINS > COWSKIN
COWSLIP n small yellow wild European flower
COWSLIPS > COWSLIP
COWTOWN n rural town in a cattle-raising area
COWTOWNS > COWTOWN
COWTREE n South American tree that produces latex
COWTREES > COWTREE
COWY adj cowlike
COX n coxswain ▷ vb act as cox of (a boat)
COXA n technical name for the hipbone or hip joint
COXAE > COXA
COXAL > COXA
COXALGIA n pain in the hip joint
COXALGIAS > COXALGIA
COXALGIC > COXALGIA
COXALGIES > COXALGIA
COXALGY same as > COXALGIA
COXCOMB same as > COCKSCOMB

COXCOMBIC > COXCOMB
COXCOMBRY n conceited arrogance or foppishness
COXCOMBS > COXCOMB
COXED > COX
COXES > COX
COXIB n anti-inflammatory drug
COXIBS > COXIB
COXIER > COXY
COXIEST > COXY
COXINESS > COXY
COXING > COX
COXITIDES > COXITIS
COXITIS n inflammation of the hip joint
COXLESS > COX
COXSACKIE adj as in coxsackie virus type of virus
COXSWAIN n person who steers a rowing boat
COXSWAINS > COXSWAIN
COXY adj cocky
COY adj affectedly shy or modest ▷ vb caress
COYAU n type of steep roof
COYAUS > COYAU
COYDOG n cross between a coyote and a dog
COYDOGS > COYDOG
COYED > COY
COYER > COY
COYEST > COY
COYING > COY
COYISH > COY
COYISHLY > COY
COYLY > COY
COYNESS > COY
COYNESSES > COY
COYOTE n prairie wolf of N America
COYOTES > COYOTE
COYOTILLO n thorny poisonous shrub of Mexico and the southwestern US
COYPOU same as > COYPU
COYPOUS > COYPOU
COYPU n beaver-like aquatic rodent
COYPUS > COYPU
COYS > COY
COYSTREL same as > COISTREL
COYSTRELS > COYSTREL
COYSTRIL same as > COISTREL
COYSTRILS > COYSTRIL
COZ archaic word for > COUSIN
COZE vb to chat
COZED > COZE
COZEN vb cheat, trick
COZENAGE > COZEN
COZENAGES > COZEN
COZENED > COZEN
COZENER > COZEN
COZENERS > COZEN
COZENING > COZEN
COZENS > COZEN
COZES > COZE
COZEY n tea cosy
COZEYS > COZEY
COZIE same as > COZEY
COZIED > COZY
COZIER n cobbler
COZIERS > COZIER
COZIES > COZY

COZIEST > COZY
COZILY > COZY
COZINESS > COZY
COZING > COZE
COZY same as > COSY
COZYING > COZY
COZZES > COZ
COZZIE n swimming costume
COZZIES > COZZIE
CRAAL n enclosure for livestock ▷ vb enclose in a craal
CRAALED > CRAAL
CRAALING > CRAAL
CRAALS > CRAAL
CRAB n edible shellfish with ten legs, the first pair modified into pincers ▷ vb catch crabs
CRABAPPLE n tree bearing small sour apple-like fruit
CRABBED > CRAB
CRABBEDLY > CRAB
CRABBER n crab fisherman
CRABBERS > CRABBER
CRABBIER > CRABBY
CRABBIEST > CRABBY
CRABBILY > CRABBY
CRABBING > CRAB
CRABBIT adj Scots word meaning bad-tempered
CRABBY adj bad-tempered
CRABEATER n species of seal
CRABGRASS n type of coarse weedy grass
CRABLIKE adj resembling a crab
CRABMEAT n edible flesh of a crab
CRABMEATS > CRABMEAT
CRABS > CRAB
CRABSTICK n stick, cane, or cudgel made of crabapple wood
CRABWISE adv (of motion) sideways
CRABWOOD n tropical American tree
CRABWOODS > CRABWOOD
CRACHACH pl n (in Wales) elitists
CRACK vb break or split partially ▷ n sudden sharp noise ▷ adj first-rate, excellent
CRACKA n US derogatory word for a poor White person
CRACKAS > CRACKA
CRACKBACK n in American football, illegal blocking of an opponent
CRACKDOWN n severe disciplinary measures
CRACKED adj damaged by cracking
CRACKER n thin dry biscuit
CRACKERS adj insane
CRACKET n low stool, often one with three legs
CRACKETS > CRACKET
CRACKHEAD n person addicted to the drug crack
CRACKIE n small mongrel dog
CRACKIER > CRACKY

CRACKIES > CRACKY
CRACKIEST > CRACKY
CRACKING adj very fast
CRACKINGS > CRACKING
CRACKJAW adj difficult to pronounce ▷ n word or phrase that is difficult to pronounce
CRACKJAWS > CRACKJAW
CRACKLE vb make small sharp popping noises ▷ n crackling sound
CRACKLED > CRACKLE
CRACKLES > CRACKLE
CRACKLIER > CRACKLY
CRACKLING n crackle
CRACKLY adj making a cracking sound
CRACKNEL n type of hard plain biscuit
CRACKNELS > CRACKNEL
CRACKPOT adj eccentric ▷ n eccentric person
CRACKPOTS > CRACKPOT
CRACKS > CRACK
CRACKSMAN n burglar, esp a safe-breaker
CRACKSMEN > CRACKSMAN
CRACKUP n collapse
CRACKUPS > CRACKUP
CRACKY adj full of cracks ▷ n something that is full of cracks
CRACOWE n medieval shoe with a sharply pointed toe
CRACOWES > CRACOWE
CRADLE n baby's bed on rockers ▷ vb hold gently as if in a cradle
CRADLED > CRADLE
CRADLER > CRADLE
CRADLERS > CRADLE
CRADLES > CRADLE
CRADLING n framework of iron or wood, esp as used in the construction of a ceiling
CRADLINGS > CRADLING
CRAFT n occupation requiring skill with the hands ▷ vb make skilfully
CRAFTED > CRAFT
CRAFTER n person doing craftwork
CRAFTERS > CRAFTER
CRAFTIER > CRAFTY
CRAFTIEST > CRAFTY
CRAFTILY > CRAFTY
CRAFTING > CRAFT
CRAFTLESS adj guileless
CRAFTS > CRAFT
CRAFTSMAN n skilled worker
CRAFTSMEN > CRAFTSMAN
CRAFTWORK n handicraft
CRAFTY adj skilled in deception
CRAG n steep rugged rock
CRAGFAST adj stranded on a crag
CRAGGED same as > CRAGGY
CRAGGER n member of a carbon reduction action group
CRAGGERS > CRAGGER
CRAGGIER > CRAGGY
CRAGGIEST > CRAGGY
CRAGGILY > CRAGGY

CRAGGY adj having many crags
CRAGS > CRAG
CRAGSMAN n rock climber
CRAGSMEN > CRAGSMAN
CRAIC n Irish word meaning fun
CRAICS > CRAIC
CRAIG a Scot word for **>** CRAG
CRAIGS > CRAIG
CRAKE n bird of the rail family, such as the corncrake ▷ vb to boast
CRAKED > CRAKE
CRAKES > CRAKE
CRAKING > CRAKE
CRAM vb force into too small a space ▷ n act or condition of cramming
CRAMBE n any plant of the genus Crambe
CRAMBES > CRAMBE
CRAMBO n word game
CRAMBOES > CRAMBO
CRAMBOS > CRAMBO
CRAME n merchant's booth or stall
CRAMES > CRAME
CRAMESIES > CRAMESY
CRAMESY same as **>** CRAMOISY
CRAMFULL adj very full
CRAMMABLE adj able to be crammed or filled
CRAMMED > CRAM
CRAMMER n person or school that prepares pupils for an examination
CRAMMERS > CRAMMER
CRAMMING n act of cramming
CRAMMINGS > CRAMMING
CRAMOISIE same as **>** CRAMOISY
CRAMOISY adj of a crimson colour ▷ n crimson cloth
CRAMP n painful muscular contraction ▷ vb affect with a cramp
CRAMPBARK n guelder rose
CRAMPED adj closed in
CRAMPER n spiked metal plate used as a brace for the feet in throwing the stone
CRAMPERS > CRAMPER
CRAMPET n cramp iron
CRAMPETS > CRAMPET
CRAMPFISH n electric ray
CRAMPIER > CRAMPY
CRAMPIEST > CRAMPY
CRAMPING > CRAMP
CRAMPIT same as **>** CRAMPET
CRAMPITS > CRAMPIT
CRAMPON n spiked plate strapped to a boot for climbing on ice ▷ vb climb using crampons
CRAMPONED > CRAMPON
CRAMPOON same as **>** CRAMPON
CRAMPOONS > CRAMPOON
CRAMPS > CRAMP
CRAMPY adj affected with cramp
CRAMS > CRAM

CRAN n unit of capacity used for measuring fresh herring, equal to 37.5 gallons
CRANACHAN n Scottish dessert made with oatmeal, cream, and whisky
CRANAGE n use of a crane
CRANAGES > CRANAGE
CRANAPPLE adj (of juice) blended from cranberries and apples
CRANBERRY n sour edible red berry
CRANCH vb to crunch
CRANCHED > CRANCH
CRANCHES > CRANCH
CRANCHING > CRANCH
CRANE n machine for lifting and moving heavy weights ▷ vb stretch (one's neck) to see something
CRANED > CRANE
CRANEFLY n fly with long legs, slender wings, and a narrow body
CRANELIKE adj like a crane
CRANES > CRANE
CRANIA > CRANIUM
CRANIAL adj of or relating to the skull
CRANIALLY > CRANIAL
CRANIATE adj having a skull or cranium ▷ n vertebrate
CRANIATES > CRANIATE
CRANING > CRANE
CRANIUM n skull
CRANIUMS > CRANIUM
CRANK n arm projecting at right angles from a shaft ▷ vb turn with a crank ▷ adj (of a sailing vessel) easily keeled over by the wind
CRANKBAIT n fishing lure shaped so that it stays under water
CRANKCASE n metal case that encloses the crankshaft in an internal-combustion engine
CRANKED > CRANK
CRANKER > CRANK
CRANKEST > CRANK
CRANKIER > CRANKY
CRANKIEST > CRANK
CRANKILY > CRANKY
CRANKING > CRANK
CRANKISH adj somewhat eccentric or bad-tempered
CRANKLE vb bend or wind
CRANKLED > CRANKLE
CRANKLES > CRANKLE
CRANKLING > CRANKLE
CRANKLY adj vigorously
CRANKNESS n (of a vessel) liability to capsize
CRANKOUS adj fretful
CRANKPIN n short cylindrical pin in a crankshaft, to which the connecting rod is attached
CRANKPINS > CRANKPIN
CRANKS > CRANK
CRANKY same as **>** CRANKISH
CRANNIED > CRANNY
CRANNIES > CRANNY
CRANNOG n ancient Celtic lake or bog dwelling

CRANNOGE same as **>** CRANNOG
CRANNOGES > CRANNOGE
CRANNOGS > CRANNOG
CRANNY n narrow opening ▷ vb become full of crannies
CRANNYING > CRANNY
CRANREUCH n hoarfrost
CRANS > CRAN
CRANTS n garland carried in front of a maiden's bier
CRANTSES > CRANTS
CRAP n slang word for rubbish, nonsense ▷ vb defecate
CRAPAUD n frog or toad
CRAPAUDS > CRAPAUD
CRAPE same as **>** CREPE
CRAPED > CRAPE
CRAPELIKE > CRAPE
CRAPES > CRAPE
CRAPIER > CRAPE
CRAPIEST > CRAPE
CRAPING > CRAPE
CRAPLE same as **>** GRAPPLE
CRAPLES > CRAPLE
CRAPOLA n slang word for rubbish, nonsense
CRAPOLAS > CRAPOLA
CRAPPED > CRAP
CRAPPER n toilet
CRAPPERS > CRAPPER
CRAPPIE n N American freshwater fish
CRAPPIER > CRAPPY
CRAPPIES > CRAPPIE
CRAPPIEST > CRAPPY
CRAPPING > CRAP
CRAPPY adj slang word for worthless, of poor quality
CRAPS pl n game using two dice ▷ vb past tense of crap
CRAPSHOOT n dice game
CRAPULENT adj given to or resulting from excessive eating or drinking
CRAPULOUS same as **>** CRAPULENT
CRAPY > CRAPE
CRARE n type of trading vessel
CRARES > CRARE
CRASES > CRASIS
CRASH n collision involving a vehicle or vehicles ▷ vb (cause to) collide violently with a vehicle, a stationary object, or the ground ▷ adj requiring or using great effort in order to achieve results quickly
CRASHED > CRASH
CRASHER > CRASH
CRASHERS > CRASH
CRASHES > CRASH
CRASHING adj extreme
CRASHPAD n place to sleep or live temporarily
CRASHPADS > CRASHPAD
CRASIS n fusion or contraction of two adjacent vowels into one
CRASS adj stupid and insensitive
CRASSER > CRASS
CRASSEST > CRASS
CRASSLY > CRASS

CRASSNESS > CRASS
CRATCH n rack for holding fodder for cattle, etc
CRATCHES > CRATCH
CRATE n large wooden container for packing goods ▷ vb put in a crate
CRATED > CRATE
CRATEFUL > CRATE
CRATEFULS > CRATE
CRATER n bowl-shaped opening at the top of a volcano ▷ vb make or form craters
CRATERED > CRATER
CRATERING > CRATER
CRATERLET n small crater
CRATEROUS > CRATER
CRATERS > CRATER
CRATES > CRATE
CRATHUR same as **>** CRATUR
CRATHURS > CRATHUR
CRATING > CRATE
CRATON n stable part of the earth's continental crust
CRATONIC > CRATON
CRATONS > CRATON
CRATUR n whisky or whiskey
CRATURS > CRATUR
CRAUNCH same as **>** CRUNCH
CRAUNCHED > CRAUNCH
CRAUNCHES > CRAUNCH
CRAUNCHY > CRAUNCH
CRAVAT n man's scarf worn like a tie ▷ vb wear a cravat
CRAVATE same as **>** CRAVAT
CRAVATES > CRAVATE
CRAVATS > CRAVAT
CRAVATTED > CRAVAT
CRAVE vb desire intensely
CRAVED > CRAVE
CRAVEN adj cowardly ▷ n coward ▷ vb make cowardly
CRAVENED > CRAVEN
CRAVENER > CRAVEN
CRAVENEST > CRAVEN
CRAVENING > CRAVEN
CRAVENLY > CRAVEN
CRAVENS > CRAVEN
CRAVER > CRAVE
CRAVERS > CRAVE
CRAVES > CRAVE
CRAVING n intense desire or longing
CRAVINGS > CRAVING
CRAW n pouchlike part of a bird's oesophagus
CRAWDAD n crayfish
CRAWDADDY n crayfish
CRAWDADS > CRAWDAD
CRAWFISH same as **>** CRAYFISH
CRAWL vb move on one's hands and knees ▷ n crawling motion or pace
CRAWLED > CRAWL
CRAWLER n servile flatterer
CRAWLERS > CRAWLER
CRAWLIER > CRAWLY
CRAWLIEST > CRAWLY
CRAWLING n defect in freshly applied paint or varnish characterized by bare patches and ridging
CRAWLINGS > CRAWLING
CRAWLS > CRAWL

C

c

CRAWLWAY n in a mine, low passageway that can only be negotiated by crawling
CRAWLWAYS > CRAWLWAY
CRAWLY adj feeling like creatures are crawling on one's skin
CRAWS > CRAW
CRAY n crayfish ▷ adj crazy
CRAYER same as > CRARE
CRAYERS > CRAYER
CRAYEST > CRAY
CRAYFISH n edible shellfish like a lobster
CRAYON n stick or pencil of coloured wax or clay ▷ vb draw or colour with a crayon
CRAYONED > CRAYON
CRAYONER > CRAYON
CRAYONERS > CRAYON
CRAYONING > CRAYON
CRAYONIST > CRAYON
CRAYONS > CRAYON
CRAYS > CRAY
CRAYTHUR variant of > CRATUR
CRAYTHURS > CRAYTHUR
CRAZE n short-lived fashion or enthusiasm ▷ vb make mad
CRAZED adj wild and uncontrolled
CRAZES > CRAZE
CRAZIER > CRAZY
CRAZIES > CRAZY
CRAZIEST > CRAZY
CRAZILY > CRAZY
CRAZINESS > CRAZY
CRAZING n act of crazing
CRAZINGS > CRAZING
CRAZY adj ridiculous ▷ n crazy person
CRAZYWEED n locoweed
CREACH same as > CREAGH
CREACHS > CREACH
CREAGH n foray
CREAGHS > CREAGH
CREAK n harsh squeaking sound ▷ vb make or move with a harsh squeaking sound
CREAKED > CREAK
CREAKIER > CREAK
CREAKIEST > CREAK
CREAKILY > CREAK
CREAKING > CREAK
CREAKS > CREAK
CREAKY > CREAK
CREAM n fatty part of milk ▷ vb beat to a creamy consistency
CREAMCUPS n Californian plant with small cream-coloured or yellow flowers on long stalks
CREAMED > CREAM
CREAMER n powdered milk substitute for use in coffee
CREAMERS > CREAMER
CREAMERY n place where dairy products are made or sold
CREAMIER > CREAMY
CREAMIEST > CREAMY
CREAMILY > CREAMY
CREAMING > CREAM

CREAMLAID adj (of laid paper) cream-coloured and of a ribbed appearance
CREAMLIKE > CREAM
CREAMPUFF n puff pastry filled with cream
CREAMS > CREAM
CREAMWARE n type of earthenware with a deep cream body developed about 1720 and widely produced
CREAMWOVE adj (of wove paper) cream-coloured and even-surfaced
CREAMY adj resembling cream in colour, taste, or consistency
CREANCE n long light cord used in falconry
CREANCES > CREANCE
CREANT adj formative
CREASE n line made by folding or pressing ▷ vb crush or line
CREASED > CREASE
CREASER > CREASE
CREASERS > CREASE
CREASES > CREASE
CREASIER > CREASE
CREASIEST > CREASE
CREASING > CREASE
CREASOTE same as > CREOSOTE
CREASOTED > CREASOTE
CREASOTES > CREASOTE
CREASY > CREASE
CREATABLE > CREATE
CREATE vb make, cause to exist
CREATED > CREATE
CREATES > CREATE
CREATIC adj relating to flesh or meat
CREATIN same as > CREATINE
CREATINE n metabolite involved in biochemical reactions
CREATINES > CREATINE
CREATING > CREATE
CREATINS > CREATIN
CREATION n creating or being created
CREATIONS > CREATION
CREATIVE adj imaginative or inventive ▷ n person who is creative professionally
CREATIVES > CREATIVE
CREATOR n person who creates
CREATORS > CREATOR
CREATRESS > CREATOR
CREATRIX > CREATOR
CREATURAL > CREATURE
CREATURE n animal, person, or other being
CREATURES > CREATURE
CRECHE n place where small children are looked after
CRECHES > CRECHE
CRED n short for credibility
CREDAL > CREED
CREDENCE n belief in the truth or accuracy of a statement
CREDENCES > CREDENCE
CREDENDA > CREDENDUM

CREDENDUM n article of faith
CREDENT adj believing or believable
CREDENZA n type of small sideboard
CREDENZAS > CREDENZA
CREDIBLE adj believable
CREDIBLY > CREDIBLE
CREDIT n system of allowing customers to receive goods and pay later ▷ vb enter as a credit in an account
CREDITED > CREDIT
CREDITING > CREDIT
CREDITOR n person to whom money is owed
CREDITORS > CREDITOR
CREDITS pl n list of people responsible for the production of a film, programme, or record
CREDO n creed
CREDOS > CREDO
CREDS > CRED
CREDULITY n willingness to believe something on little evidence
CREDULOUS adj too willing to believe
CREE vb soften grain by boiling or soaking
CREED n statement or system of (Christian) beliefs or principles
CREEDAL > CREED
CREEDS > CREED
CREEING > CREE
CREEK n narrow inlet or bay
CREEKIER > CREEKY
CREEKIEST > CREEKY
CREEKS > CREEK
CREEKSIDE n side of a creek
CREEKY adj abounding in creeks
CREEL n wicker basket used by anglers ▷ vb to fish using creels
CREELED > CREEL
CREELING > CREEL
CREELS > CREEL
CREEP vb move quietly and cautiously ▷ n creeping movement
CREEPAGE n imperceptible movement
CREEPAGES > CREEPAGE
CREEPED > CREEP
CREEPER n creeping plant ▷ vb train a plant to creep
CREEPERED > CREEPER
CREEPERS > CREEPER
CREEPIE n low stool
CREEPIER > CREEPY
CREEPIES > CREEPIE
CREEPIEST > CREEPY
CREEPILY > CREEPY
CREEPING > CREEP
CREEPMICE n plural form of singular creepmouse: a term of endearment
CREEPS > CREEP
CREEPY adj causing a feeling of fear or disgust
CREES > CREE
CREESE same as > KRIS

CREESED > CREESE
CREESES > CREESE
CREESH vb lubricate
CREESHED > CREESH
CREESHES > CREESH
CREESHIER > CREESHY
CREESHING > CREESH
CREESHY adj greasy
CREESING > CREESE
CREM n crematorium
CREMAINS pl n cremated remains of a body
CREMANT adj (of wine) moderately sparkling
CREMASTER n muscle which raises and lowers the scrotum
CREMATE vb burn (a corpse) to ash
CREMATED > CREMATE
CREMATES > CREMATE
CREMATING > CREMATE
CREMATION > CREMATE
CREMATOR n furnace for cremating corpses
CREMATORS > CREMATOR
CREMATORY adj of or relating to cremation or crematoriums
CREME n cream
CREMES > CREME
CREMINI n variety of mushroom
CREMINIS > CREMINI
CREMOCARP n any fruit, such as anise or fennel, consisting of two united carpels
CREMONA same as > CROMORNA
CREMONAS > CREMONA
CREMOR n cream
CREMORNE n penis
CREMORNES > CREMORNE
CREMORS > CREMOR
CREMOSIN adj crimson
CREMS > CREM
CREMSIN same as > CREMOSIN
CRENA n cleft or notch
CRENAS > CRENA
CRENATE adj having a scalloped margin, as certain leaves
CRENATED same as > CRENATE
CRENATELY > CRENATE
CRENATION n any of the rounded teeth or the notches between them on a crenate structure
CRENATURE same as > CRENATION
CRENEL n opening formed in the top of a wall having slanting sides ▷ vb crenellate
CRENELATE vb supply with battlements
CRENELED > CRENEL
CRENELING > CRENEL
CRENELLE same as > CRENEL
CRENELLED > CRENEL
CRENELLES > CRENELLE
CRENELS > CRENEL
CRENSHAW n variety of melon

CRENSHAWS > CRENSHAW
CRENULATE adj having a margin very finely notched with rounded projections, as certain leaves
CREODONT n type of extinct Tertiary mammal, the ancestor of modern carnivores
CREODONTS > CREODONT
CREOLE n language developed from a mixture of languages ▷ adj of or relating to a creole
CREOLES > CREOLE
CREOLIAN n Creole
CREOLIANS > CREOLIAN
CREOLISE vb (of a pidgin language) to become the native language of a speech community
CREOLISED same as > CREOLIZED
CREOLISES > CREOLISE
CREOLIST n student of creole languages
CREOLISTS > CREOLIST
CREOLIZE same as > CREOLISE
CREOLIZED adj (of a language) incorporating a considerable range of features from one or more unrelated languages, as the result of contact between language communities
CREOLIZES > CREOLIZE
CREOPHAGY n act of eating meat
CREOSOL n insoluble oily liquid
CREOSOLS > CREOSOL
CREOSOTE n dark oily liquid made from coal tar and used for preserving wood ▷ vb treat with creosote
CREOSOTED > CREOSOTE
CREOSOTES > CREOSOTE
CREOSOTIC > CREOSOTE
CREPANCE n injury to a horse's hind leg caused by being struck by the shoe of the other hind foot
CREPANCES > CREPANCE
CREPE n fabric or rubber with a crinkled texture ▷ vb crimp or frizz
CREPED > CREPE
CREPELIKE adj like crepe
CREPERIE n eating establishment that specializes in pancakes
CREPERIES > CREPERIE
CREPES > CREPE
CREPEY same as > CREPY
CREPIER > CREPY
CREPIEST > CREPY
CREPINESS > CREPY
CREPING > CREPE
CREPITANT > CREPITATE
CREPITATE vb make a rattling or crackling sound
CREPITUS n crackling chest sound heard in pneumonia and other lung diseases
CREPOLINE n light silk material used in dressmaking
CREPON n thin material made of fine wool and/or silk

CREPONS > CREPON
CREPS pl n slang term for training shoes
CREPT > CREEP
CREPUSCLE n twilight
CREPY adj (esp of the skin) having a dry wrinkled appearance like crepe
CRESCENDI > CRESCENDO
CRESCENDO n gradual increase in loudness, esp in music ▷ adv gradually getting louder ▷ vb increase in loudness or force
CRESCENT n (curved shape of) the moon as seen in its first or last quarter ▷ adj crescent-shaped
CRESCENTS > CRESCENT
CRESCIVE adj increasing
CRESOL n aromatic compound
CRESOLS > CRESOL
CRESS n plant with strong-tasting leaves, used in salads
CRESSES > CRESS
CRESSET n metal basket mounted on a pole
CRESSETS > CRESSET
CRESSIER > CRESSY
CRESSIEST > CRESSY
CRESSY > CRESS
CREST n top of a mountain, hill, or wave ▷ vb come to or be at the top of
CRESTA adj as in cresta run high-speed tobogganing down a steep narrow passage
CRESTAL > CRYSTAL
CRESTALS > CRESTAL
CRESTED > CREST
CRESTING same as > CREST
CRESTINGS > CREST
CRESTLESS > CREST
CRESTON n hogback
CRESTONS > CRESTON
CRESTS > CREST
CRESYL n tolyl
CRESYLIC adj of, concerned with, or containing creosote or cresol
CRESYLS > CRESYL
CRETIC n metrical foot
CRETICS > CRETIC
CRETIN n insulting term for a stupid person
CRETINISE vb make (someone) a cretin
CRETINISM n old-fashioned word for a condition arising from a deficiency of thyroid hormone
CRETINIZE same as > CRETINISE
CRETINOID > CRETIN
CRETINOUS > CRETIN
CRETINS > CRETIN
CRETISM n lying
CRETISMS > CRETISM
CRETONNE n heavy printed cotton fabric used in furnishings
CRETONNES > CRETONNE
CRETONS pl n spread made from pork fat and onions

CREUTZER n former copper and silver coin of Germany or Austria
CREUTZERS > CREUTZER
CREVALLE n any fish of the family Carangidae
CREVALLES > CREVALLE
CREVASSE n deep open crack in a glacier ▷ vb make a break or fissure in (a dyke, wall, etc)
CREVASSED > CREVASSE
CREVASSES > CREVASSE
CREVETTE n shrimp
CREVETTES > CREVETTE
CREVICE n narrow crack or gap in rock
CREVICED > CREVICE
CREVICES > CREVICE
CREW n people who work on a ship or aircraft ▷ vb serve as a crew member (on)
CREWCUT n very short haircut
CREWCUTS > CREWCUT
CREWE n type of pot
CREWED > CREW
CREWEL n fine worsted yarn used in embroidery ▷ vb embroider in crewel
CREWELIST > CREWEL
CREWELLED > CREWEL
CREWELS > CREWEL
CREWES > CREWE
CREWING > CREW
CREWLESS adj lacking a crew
CREWMAN n member of a ship's crew
CREWMATE n colleague on the crew of a boat or ship
CREWMATES > CREWMATE
CREWMEN > CREWMAN
CREWNECK n plain round neckline in sweaters
CREWNECKS > CREWNECK
CREWS > CREW
CRIA n baby llama, alpaca, or vicuna
CRIANT adj garish
CRIAS > CRIA
CRIB n piece of writing stolen from elsewhere ▷ vb copy (someone's work) dishonestly
CRIBBAGE n card game for two to four players
CRIBBAGES > CRIBBAGE
CRIBBED > CRIB
CRIBBER > CRIB
CRIBBERS > CRIB
CRIBBING > CRIB
CRIBBINGS > CRIB
CRIBBLE vb to sift
CRIBBLED > CRIBBLE
CRIBBLES > CRIBBLE
CRIBBLING > CRIBBLE
CRIBELLA > CRIBELLUM
CRIBELLAR > CRIBELLUM
CRIBELLUM n sievelike spinning organ in certain spiders that occurs between the spinnerets
CRIBLE adj dotted ▷ n method of engraving with holes or dots
CRIBLES > CRIBLE

CRIBRATE adj sievelike
CRIBROSE adj pierced with holes
CRIBROUS same as > CRIBROSE
CRIBS > CRIB
CRIBWORK same as > CRIB
CRIBWORKS > CRIBWORK
CRICETID n any member of the family Cricetidae, such as the hamster and vole
CRICETIDS > CRICETID
CRICK n muscle spasm or cramp in the back or neck ▷ vb cause a crick in
CRICKED > CRICK
CRICKET n outdoor sport ▷ vb play cricket
CRICKETED > CRICKET
CRICKETER > CRICKET
CRICKETS > CRICKET
CRICKEY same as > CRIKEY
CRICKING > CRICK
CRICKS > CRICK
CRICKY same as > CRIKEY
CRICOID adj of or relating to part of the larynx ▷ n this cartilage
CRICOIDS > CRICOID
CRIED > CRY
CRIER n (formerly) official who made public announcements
CRIERS > CRIER
CRIES > CRY
CRIKEY interj expression of surprise
CRIM short for > CRIMINAL
CRIME n unlawful act ▷ vb charge with a crime
CRIMED > CRIME
CRIMEFUL adj criminal
CRIMELESS adj innocent
CRIMEN n crime
CRIMES > CRIME
CRIMEWAVE n period of increased criminal activity
CRIMINA > CRIMEN
CRIMINAL n person guilty of a crime ▷ adj of crime
CRIMINALS > CRIMINAL
CRIMINATE vb charge with a crime
CRIMINE interj expression of surprise
CRIMING > CRIME
CRIMINI same as > CRIMINE
CRIMINIS n as in particeps criminis accomplice in crime
CRIMINOUS adj criminal
CRIMINY interj cry of surprise
CRIMMER a variant spelling of > KRIMMER
CRIMMERS > CRIMMER
CRIMP vb fold or press into ridges ▷ n act or result of crimping
CRIMPED > CRIMP
CRIMPER > CRIMP
CRIMPERS > CRIMP
CRIMPIER > CRIMP
CRIMPIEST > CRIMP
CRIMPING > CRIMP
CRIMPLE vb crumple, wrinkle, or curl

C

c

CRIMPLED > CRIMPLE
CRIMPLES > CRIMPLE
CRIMPLING > CRIMPLE
CRIMPS > CRIMP
CRIMPY > CRIMP
CRIMS > CRIM
CRIMSON *adj* deep purplish-red ▷ *n* deep or vivid red colour ▷ *vb* make or become crimson
CRIMSONED > CRIMSON
CRIMSONS > CRIMSON
CRINAL *adj* relating to the hair
CRINATE *adj* having hair
CRINATED *same as* > CRINATE
CRINE *vb* to shrivel
CRINED > CRINE
CRINES > CRINE
CRINGE *vb* flinch in fear ▷ *n* act of cringing
CRINGED > CRINGE
CRINGER > CRINGE
CRINGERS > CRINGE
CRINGES > CRINGE
CRINGEY *adj* causing the urge to cringe
CRINGIER > CRINGEY
CRINGIEST > CRINGEY
CRINGING > CRINGE
CRINGINGS > CRINGE
CRINGLE *n* eye at the edge of a sail
CRINGLES > CRINGLE
CRINGY *same as* > CRINGEY
CRINING > CRINE
CRINITE *adj* covered with soft hairs or tufts ▷ *n* sedimentary rock
CRINITES > CRINITE
CRINKLE *n* wrinkle, crease, or fold ▷ *vb* become slightly creased or folded
CRINKLED > CRINKLE
CRINKLES > CRINKLE
CRINKLIER > CRINKLY
CRINKLIES > CRINKLY
CRINKLING > CRINKLE
CRINKLY *adj* wrinkled ▷ *n* derogatory term for an old person
CRINOID *n* type of primitive echinoderm
CRINOIDAL > CRINOID
CRINOIDS > CRINOID
CRINOLINE *n* hooped petticoat
CRINOSE *adj* hairy
CRINUM *n* type of mostly tropical plant
CRINUMS > CRINUM
CRIOLLO *n* native or inhabitant of Latin America of European descent ▷ *adj* of, relating to, or characteristic of a criollo or criollos
CRIOLLOS > CRIOLLO
CRIOS *n* multicoloured woven woollen belt
CRIOSES > CRIOS
CRIP *n* offensive word for a person who is lame or disabled
CRIPE *variant of* > CRIPES
CRIPES *interj* expression of surprise

CRIPPLE *n* offensive word for a person who is lame or disabled ▷ *vb* make lame or disabled
CRIPPLED > CRIPPLE
CRIPPLER > CRIPPLE
CRIPPLERS > CRIPPLE
CRIPPLES > CRIPPLE
CRIPPLING *adj* damaging or injurious
CRIPS > CRIP
CRIS *variant of* > KRIS
CRISE *n* crisis
CRISES > CRISIS
CRISIC *adj* relating to a crisis
CRISIS *n* crucial stage, turning point
CRISP *adj* fresh and firm ▷ *n* very thin slice of potato fried till crunchy ▷ *vb* make or become crisp
CRISPATE *adj* having a curled or waved appearance
CRISPATED *same as* > CRISPATE
CRISPED *same as* > CRISPATE
CRISPEN *vb* make crisp
CRISPENED > CRISPEN
CRISPENS > CRISPEN
CRISPER *n* compartment in a refrigerator
CRISPERS > CRISPER
CRISPEST > CRISP
CRISPHEAD *n* variety of lettuce
CRISPIER > CRISPY
CRISPIES *pl n* as in *rice crispies* puffed grains of rice, eaten esp as breakfast cereal
CRISPIEST > CRISPY
CRISPILY > CRISPY
CRISPIN *n* cobbler
CRISPING > CRISP
CRISPINS > CRISPIN
CRISPLY > CRISP
CRISPNESS > CRISP
CRISPS > CRISP
CRISPY *adj* hard and crunchy
CRISSA > CRISSUM
CRISSAL > CRISSUM
CRISSUM *n* area or feathers surrounding the cloaca of a bird
CRISTA *n* structure resembling a ridge or crest
CRISTAE > CRISTA
CRISTATE *adj* having a crest
CRISTATED *same as* > CRISTATE
CRIT *abbreviation of* > CRITICISM
CRITERIA > CRITERION
CRITERIAL > CRITERION
CRITERION *n* standard of judgment
CRITERIUM *n* type of bicycle race, involving many laps of a short course
CRITH *n* unit of weight for gases
CRITHS > CRITH
CRITIC *n* professional judge of any of the arts
CRITICAL *adj* very important or dangerous

CRITICISE *same as* > CRITICIZE
CRITICISM *n* fault-finding
CRITICIZE *vb* find fault with
CRITICS > CRITIC
CRITIQUE *n* critical essay ▷ *vb* review critically
CRITIQUED > CRITIQUE
CRITIQUES > CRITIQUE
CRITS > CRIT
CRITTER *a dialect word for* > CREATURE
CRITTERS > CRITTER
CRITTUR *same as* > CRITTER
CRITTURS > CRITTUR
CRIVENS *interj* expression of surprise
CRIVVENS *same as* > CRIVENS
CROAK *vb* (of a frog or crow) give a low hoarse cry ▷ *n* low hoarse sound
CROAKED > CROAK
CROAKER *n* animal, bird, etc, that croaks
CROAKERS > CROAKER
CROAKIER > CROAK
CROAKIEST > CROAK
CROAKILY > CROAK
CROAKING > CROAK
CROAKINGS > CROAK
CROAKS > CROAK
CROAKY > CROAK
CROC *short for* > CROCODILE
CROCEATE *adj* saffron-coloured
CROCEIN *n* any one of a group of red or orange acid azo dyes
CROCEINE *same as* > CROCEIN
CROCEINES > CROCEIN
CROCEINS > CROCEIN
CROCEOUS *adj* saffron-coloured
CROCHE *n* knob at the top of a deer's horn
CROCHES > CROCHE
CROCHET *vb* make by looping and intertwining yarn with a hooked needle ▷ *n* work made in this way
CROCHETED > CROCHET
CROCHETER > CROCHET
CROCHETS > CROCHET
CROCI > CROCUS
CROCINE *adj* relating to the crocus
CROCK *n* earthenware pot or jar ▷ *vb* become or cause to become weak or disabled
CROCKED *adj* injured
CROCKERY *n* dishes
CROCKET *n* carved ornament in the form of a curled leaf or cusp
CROCKETED > CROCKET
CROCKETS > CROCKET
CROCKING > CROCK
CROCKPOT *n* tradename for a brand of slow cooker
CROCKPOTS > CROCKPOT
CROCKS > CROCK
CROCODILE *n* large amphibious tropical reptile

CROCOITE *n* rare orange secondary mineral
CROCOITES > CROCOITE
CROCOSMIA *n* type of S African plant
CROCS > CROC
CROCUS *n* flowering plant
CROCUSES > CROCUS
CROFT *n* small farm worked by one family in Scotland ▷ *vb* farm land as a croft
CROFTED > CROFT
CROFTER *n* owner or tenant of a small farm, esp in Scotland or northern England
CROFTERS > CROFTER
CROFTING *n* system or occupation of working land in crofts
CROFTINGS > CROFTING
CROFTS > CROFT
CROG *vb* ride on a bicycle as a passenger
CROGGED > CROG
CROGGIES > CROGGY
CROGGING > CROG
CROGGY *n* ride on a bicycle as a passenger
CROGS > CROG
CROISSANT *n* rich flaky crescent-shaped roll
CROJIK *n* triangular sail
CROJIKS > CROJIK
CROKINOLE *n* board game popular in Canada in which players flick wooden discs
CROMACK *same as* > CRUMMOCK
CROMACKS > CROMACK
CROMB *same as* > CROME
CROMBEC *n* African Old World warbler with colourful plumage
CROMBECS > CROMBEC
CROMBED > CROMB
CROMBING > CROMB
CROMBS > CROMB
CROME *n* hook ▷ *vb* use a crome
CROMED > CROME
CROMES > CROME
CROMING > CROME
CROMLECH *n* circle of prehistoric standing stones
CROMLECHS > CROMLECH
CROMORNA *n* one of the reed stops in an organ
CROMORNAS > CROMORNA
CROMORNE *variant of* > CROMORNA
CROMORNES > CROMORNE
CRON *n* computer application that schedules tasks chronologically
CRONE *n* witchlike old woman
CRONES > CRONE
CRONET *n* hair which grows over the top of a horse's hoof
CRONETS > CRONET
CRONIES > CRONY
CRONISH > CRONE
CRONK *adj* unfit
CRONKER > CRONK
CRONKEST > CRONK
CRONS > CRON

CRONY n close friend
CRONYISM n appointing friends to high-level posts
CRONYISMS > CRONYISM
CROODLE vb nestle close
CROODLED > CROODLE
CROODLES > CROODLE
CROODLING > CROODLE
CROOK n dishonest person ▷ vb bend or curve ▷ adj informal Australian word meaning ill
CROOKBACK a rare word for > HUNCHBACK
CROOKED adj bent or twisted
CROOKEDER > CROOKED
CROOKEDLY > CROOKED
CROOKER > CROOK
CROOKERY n illegal or dishonest activity
CROOKEST > CROOK
CROOKING > CROOK
CROOKNECK n any type of summer squash
CROOKS > CROOK
CROOL vb spoil
CROOLED > CROOL
CROOLING > CROOL
CROOLS > CROOL
CROON vb sing, hum, or speak in a soft low tone ▷ n soft low singing or humming
CROONED > CROON
CROONER > CROON
CROONERS > CROON
CROONIER > CROONY
CROONIEST > CROONY
CROONING > CROON
CROONINGS > CROON
CROONS > CROON
CROONY adj singing like a crooner
CROOVE n animal enclosure
CROOVES > CROOVE
CROP n cultivated plant ▷ vb cut very short
CROPBOUND n poultry disease causing a pendulous crop
CROPFUL n quantity that can be held in the craw
CROPFULL adj satiated ▷ n amount that a crop can take
CROPFULLS > CROPFULL
CROPFULS > CROPFUL
CROPLAND n land on which crops are grown
CROPLANDS > CROPLAND
CROPLESS adj without crops
CROPPED > CROP
CROPPER n person who cultivates or harvests a crop
CROPPERS > CROPPER
CROPPIE same as > CROPPY
CROPPIES > CROPPY
CROPPING > CROP
CROPPINGS > CROP
CROPPY n rebel in the Irish rising of 1798
CROPS > CROP
CROPSICK adj sick from excessive food or drink
CROQUANTE n crisp nut-filled chocolate or cake
CROQUET n game played on a lawn in which balls are hit

through hoops ▷ vb drive away a ball by hitting one's own when the two are in contact
CROQUETED > CROQUET
CROQUETS > CROQUET
CROQUETTE n fried cake of potato, meat, or fish
CROQUIS n rough sketch
CRORE n (in Indian English) ten million
CROREPATI n (in India) person whose assets are at least 10 million rupees
CRORES > CRORE
CROSIER n staff carried by bishops as a symbol of pastoral office ▷ vb bear or carry such a staff
CROSIERED > CROSIER
CROSIERS > CROSIER
CROSS vb move or go across (something) ▷ n structure, symbol, or mark of two intersecting lines ▷ adj angry, annoyed
CROSSABLE adj capable of being crossed
CROSSARM n in mining, horizontal bar on which a drill is mounted
CROSSARMS > CROSSARM
CROSSBAND vb to set the grain of layers of wood at right angles to one another
CROSSBAR n horizontal bar across goalposts or on a bicycle ▷ vb provide with crossbars
CROSSBARS > CROSSBAR
CROSSBEAM n beam that spans from one support to another
CROSSBILL n finch that has a bill with crossed tips
CROSSBIT > CROSSBITE
CROSSBITE vb to trick
CROSSBOW n weapon consisting of a bow fixed across a wooden stock
CROSSBOWS > CROSSBOW
CROSSBRED adj bred from two different types of animal or plant ▷ n crossbred plant or animal, esp an animal resulting from a cross between two pure breeds
CROSSBUCK n US roadsign used at railroad crossings
CROSSCUT vb cut across ▷ adj cut across ▷ n transverse cut or course
CROSSCUTS > CROSSCUT
CROSSE n light staff used in playing lacrosse
CROSSED > CROSS
CROSSER > CROSS
CROSSERS > CROSS
CROSSES > CROSS
CROSSEST > CROSS
CROSSETTE n in architecture, return in a corner of the architrave of a window or door
CROSSFALL n camber of a road
CROSSFIRE n gunfire crossing another line of fire

CROSSFISH n starfish
CROSSHAIR n one of two fine wires that cross in the focal plane of a gunsight or other optical instrument, used to define the line of sight
CROSSHEAD n subsection or paragraph heading printed within the body of the text
CROSSING n place where a street may be crossed safely
CROSSINGS > CROSSING
CROSSISH > CROSS
CROSSJACK n square sail on a ship's mizzenmast
CROSSLET n cross having a smaller cross near the end of each arm
CROSSLETS > CROSSLET
CROSSLIKE adj like a cross
CROSSLY > CROSS
CROSSNESS > CROSS
CROSSOVER n place at which a crossing is made ▷ adj (of music, fashion, art, etc) combining two distinct styles
CROSSPLY adj having layers of fabric with cords running diagonally
CROSSROAD n road that crosses another road
CROSSRUFF n alternate trumping of each other's leads by two partners, or by declarer and dummy ▷ vb trump alternately in two hands of a partnership
CROSSTALK n rapid or witty talk
CROSSTIE n railway sleeper
CROSSTIED adj tied with ropes going across
CROSSTIES > CROSSTIE
CROSSTOWN adj going across town
CROSSTREE n either of a pair of wooden or metal braces on the head of a mast to support the topmast, etc
CROSSWALK n place marked where pedestrians may cross a road
CROSSWAY same as > CROSSROAD
CROSSWAYS same as > CROSSWISE
CROSSWIND n wind that blows at right angles to the direction of travel
CROSSWIRE n either of the two lines that cross in a gunsight
CROSSWISE adv across ▷ adj across
CROSSWORD n puzzle in which the solver deduces words suggested by clues and writes them into a grid
CROSSWORT n herbaceous Eurasian plant with pale yellow flowers and whorls of hairy leaves
CROST > CROSS
CROSTATA n type of fruit tart
CROSTATAS > CROSTATA
CROSTINI > CROSTINO

CROSTINIS > CROSTINO
CROSTINO n piece of toasted bread served with a savoury topping
CROTAL n any of various lichens used in dyeing wool
CROTALA > CROTALUM
CROTALE n type of small cymbal
CROTALES > CROTALE
CROTALINE adj relating to rattlesnakes
CROTALISM n poisoning due to ingestion of plants of the genus Crotalaria
CROTALS > CROTAL
CROTALUM n ancient castanet-like percussion instrument
CROTCH n part of the body between the tops of the legs
CROTCHED > CROTCH
CROTCHES > CROTCH
CROTCHET n musical note half the length of a minim
CROTCHETS > CROTCHET
CROTCHETY adj bad-tempered
CROTON n type of shrub or tree, the seeds of which yield croton oil
CROTONBUG n species of cockroach
CROTONIC adj as in crotonic acid type of colourless acid
CROTONS > CROTON
CROTTLE same as > CROTAL
CROTTLES > CROTTLE
CROUCH vb bend low with the legs and body close ▷ n this position
CROUCHED > CROUCH
CROUCHES > CROUCH
CROUCHING > CROUCH
CROUP n throat disease of children, with a cough ▷ vb have croup
CROUPADE n leap by a horse, pulling the hind legs towards the belly
CROUPADES > CROUPADE
CROUPE same as > CROUP
CROUPED > CROUP
CROUPER obsolete variant of > CRUPPER
CROUPERS > CROUPER
CROUPES > CROUPE
CROUPIER n person who collects bets and pays out winnings at a gambling table in a casino
CROUPIERS > CROUPIER
CROUPIEST > CROUP
CROUPILY > CROUP
CROUPING > CROUP
CROUPON n type of highly polished flexible leather
CROUPONS > CROUPON
CROUPOUS > CROUP
CROUPS > CROUP
CROUPY > CROUP
CROUSE adj lively, confident, or saucy
CROUSELY > CROUSE
CROUSTADE n pastry case in which food is served
CROUT n sauerkraut

c

CROUTE n small round of toasted bread on which a savoury mixture is served
CROUTES > CROUTE
CROUTON n small piece of fried or toasted bread served in soup
CROUTONS > CROUTON
CROUTS > CROUT
CROW n large black bird with a harsh call ▷ vb (of a cock) make a shrill squawking sound
CROWBAIT n worn-out horse
CROWBAITS > CROWBAIT
CROWBAR n iron bar used as a lever ▷ vb use a crowbar to lever (something)
CROWBARS > CROWBAR
CROWBERRY n low-growing N temperate evergreen shrub with small purplish flowers and black berry-like fruit
CROWBOOT n type of Inuit boot made of fur and leather
CROWBOOTS > CROWBOOT
CROWD n large group of people or things ▷ vb gather together in large numbers
CROWDED > CROWD
CROWDEDLY > CROWD
CROWDER > CROWD
CROWDERS > CROWD
CROWDFUND vb fund a project via a large number of small donations
CROWDIE n porridge of meal and water
CROWDIES > CROWDIE
CROWDING > CROWD
CROWDS > CROWD
CROWDY same as > CROWDIE
CROWEA n Australian shrub with pink flowers
CROWEAS > CROWEA
CROWED > CROW
CROWER > CROW
CROWERS > CROW
CROWFEET > CROWFOOT
CROWFOOT n type of plant
CROWFOOTS > CROWFOOT
CROWING n act of crowing
CROWINGLY > CROW
CROWINGS > CROW
CROWLIKE adj like a crow
CROWN n monarch's headdress of gold and jewels ▷ vb put a crown on the head of (someone) to proclaim him or her monarch
CROWNED > CROWN
CROWNER n promotional label
CROWNERS > CROWNER
CROWNET n coronet
CROWNETS > CROWNET
CROWNING n coronation
CROWNINGS > CROWNING
CROWNLAND n large administrative division of the former empire of Austria-Hungary
CROWNLESS > CROWN
CROWNLET n small crown
CROWNLETS > CROWNLET

CROWNLIKE adj like a crown
CROWNS > CROWN
CROWNWORK n manufacture of artificial crowns for teeth
CROWS > CROW
CROWSFEET > CROWSFOOT
CROWSFOOT n wrinkle at side of eye
CROWSTEP n set of steps to the top of a gable on a building
CROWSTEPS > CROWSTEP
CROZE n recess cut at the end of a barrel or cask to receive the head
CROZER n machine which cuts grooves in cask staves
CROZERS > CROZER
CROZES > CROZE
CROZIER same as > CROSIER
CROZIERS > CROZIER
CROZZLED adj blackened or burnt at the edges
CRU n (in France) a vineyard, group of vineyards, or wine-producing region
CRUBEEN n pig's trotter
CRUBEENS > CRUBEEN
CRUCES > CRUX
CRUCIAL adj very important
CRUCIALLY > CRUCIAL
CRUCIAN n European fish
CRUCIANS > CRUCIAN
CRUCIATE adj shaped or arranged like a cross ▷ n cruciate ligament
CRUCIATES > CRUCIATE
CRUCIBLE n pot in which metals are melted
CRUCIBLES > CRUCIBLE
CRUCIFER n type of plant with four petals arranged like a cross
CRUCIFERS > CRUCIFER
CRUCIFIED > CRUCIFY
CRUCIFIER > CRUCIFY
CRUCIFIES > CRUCIFY
CRUCIFIX n model of Christ on the Cross
CRUCIFORM adj cross-shaped ▷ n geometric curve, shaped like a cross, that has four similar branches asymptotic to two mutually perpendicular pairs of lines
CRUCIFY vb put to death by fastening to a cross
CRUCK n wooden timber supporting the end of certain roofs
CRUCKS > CRUCK
CRUD n sticky or encrusted substance ▷ interj expression of disgust, disappointment, etc ▷ vb cover with a sticky or encrusted substance
CRUDDED > CRUD
CRUDDIER > CRUDDY
CRUDDIEST > CRUDDY
CRUDDING > CRUD
CRUDDLE vb curdle
CRUDDLED > CRUDDLE
CRUDDLES > CRUDDLE
CRUDDLING > CRUDDLE
CRUDDY adj dirty or unpleasant

CRUDE adj rough and simple ▷ n crude oil
CRUDELY > CRUDE
CRUDENESS > CRUDE
CRUDER > CRUDE
CRUDES > CRUDE
CRUDEST > CRUDE
CRUDIER > CRUDY
CRUDIEST > CRUDY
CRUDITES pl n selection of raw vegetables often served with a variety of dips before a meal
CRUDITIES > CRUDE
CRUDITY > CRUDE
CRUDO n sliced raw seafood
CRUDOS > CRUDO
CRUDS > CRUD
CRUDY adj raw
CRUE obsolete variant of > CREW
CRUEL adj delighting in others' pain
CRUELER > CRUEL
CRUELEST > CRUEL
CRUELLER > CRUEL
CRUELLEST > CRUEL
CRUELLS same as > CRUELS
CRUELLY > CRUEL
CRUELNESS > CRUEL
CRUELS n disease of cattle and sheep
CRUELTIES > CRUELTY
CRUELTY n deliberate infliction of pain or suffering
CRUES > CRUE
CRUET n small container for salt, pepper, etc, at table
CRUETS > CRUET
CRUFT n redundant technical hardware
CRUFTS > CRUFT
CRUISE n sea trip for pleasure ▷ vb sail from place to place for pleasure
CRUISED > CRUISE
CRUISER n fast warship
CRUISERS > CRUISER
CRUISES > CRUISE
CRUISEWAY n canal used for recreational purposes
CRUISEY same as > CRUISY
CRUISIE same as > CRUIZIE
CRUISIER > CRUISY
CRUISIES > CRUISIE
CRUISIEST > CRUISY
CRUISING > CRUISE
CRUISINGS > CRUISE
CRUISY adj relaxed or easy-going
CRUIVE n animal enclosure
CRUIVES > CRUIVE
CRUIZIE n oil lamp
CRUIZIES > CRUIZIE
CRULLER n light sweet ring-shaped cake, fried in deep fat
CRULLERS > CRULLER
CRUMB n small fragment of bread or other dry food ▷ vb prepare or cover (food) with breadcrumbs ▷ adj (esp of pie crusts) made with a mixture of biscuit crumbs, sugar, etc
CRUMBED > CRUMB

CRUMBER > CRUMB
CRUMBERS > CRUMB
CRUMBIER > CRUMBY
CRUMBIEST > CRUMBY
CRUMBING > CRUMB
CRUMBLE vb break into fragments ▷ n pudding of stewed fruit with a crumbly topping
CRUMBLED > CRUMBLE
CRUMBLES > CRUMBLE
CRUMBLIER > CRUMBLY
CRUMBLIES pl n derogatory term for elderly people
CRUMBLING > CRUMBLE
CRUMBLY adj easily crumbled or crumbling
CRUMBS interj expression of dismay or surprise
CRUMBUM n rogue
CRUMBUMS > CRUMBUM
CRUMBY adj full of crumbs
CRUMEN n deer's larmier or tear-pit
CRUMENAL n purse
CRUMENALS > CRUMENAL
CRUMENS > CRUMEN
CRUMHORN n medieval woodwind instrument of bass pitch
CRUMHORNS > CRUMHORN
CRUMMACK same as > CRUMMOCK
CRUMMACKS > CRUMMACK
CRUMMIE n cow with a crumpled horn
CRUMMIER > CRUMMY
CRUMMIES > CRUMMY
CRUMMIEST > CRUMMY
CRUMMILY adv in a manner suggestive of or indicating poor quality
CRUMMOCK n stick with a crooked head
CRUMMOCKS > CRUMMOCK
CRUMMY adj of poor quality ▷ n lorry that carries loggers to work from their camp
CRUMP vb thud or explode with a loud dull sound ▷ n crunching, thudding, or exploding noise ▷ adj crooked
CRUMPED > CRUMP
CRUMPER > CRUMP
CRUMPEST > CRUMP
CRUMPET n round soft yeast cake, eaten buttered
CRUMPETS > CRUMPET
CRUMPIER > CRUMPY
CRUMPIEST > CRUMPY
CRUMPING > CRUMP
CRUMPLE vb crush, crease ▷ n untidy crease or wrinkle
CRUMPLED > CRUMPLE
CRUMPLES > CRUMPLE
CRUMPLIER > CRUMPLE
CRUMPLING > CRUMPLE
CRUMPLY > CRUMPLE
CRUMPS > CRUMP
CRUMPY adj crisp
CRUNCH vb bite or chew with a noisy crushing sound ▷ n crunching sound
CRUNCHED > CRUNCH
CRUNCHER > CRUNCH
CRUNCHERS > CRUNCH

CRUNCHES > CRUNCH
CRUNCHIE n derogatory word for an Afrikaner
CRUNCHIER > CRUNCH
CRUNCHIES > CRUNCHIE
CRUNCHILY > CRUNCH
CRUNCHING > CRUNCH
CRUNCHY > CRUNCH
CRUNK n form of hip-hop music originating in the Southern US
CRUNKED adj excited or intoxicated
CRUNKLE Scots variant of > CRINKLE
CRUNKLED > CRUNKLE
CRUNKLES > CRUNKLE
CRUNKLING > CRUNKLE
CRUNKS > CRUNK
CRUNODAL > CRUNODE
CRUNODE n mathematical term
CRUNODES > CRUNODE
CRUOR n blood clot
CRUORES > CRUOR
CRUORS > CRUOR
CRUPPER n strap that passes from the back of a saddle under a horse's tail
CRUPPERS > CRUPPER
CRURA > CRUS
CRURAL adj of or relating to the leg or thigh
CRUS n leg, esp from the knee to the foot
CRUSADE n medieval Christian war to recover the Holy Land from the Muslims ▷ vb take part in a crusade
CRUSADED > CRUSADE
CRUSADER > CRUSADE
CRUSADERS > CRUSADE
CRUSADES > CRUSADE
CRUSADING > CRUSADE
CRUSADO n former gold or silver coin of Portugal
CRUSADOES > CRUSADO
CRUSADOS > CRUSADO
CRUSE n small earthenware jug or pot
CRUSES > CRUSE
CRUSET n goldsmith's crucible
CRUSETS > CRUSET
CRUSH vb compress so as to injure, break, or crumple ▷ n dense crowd
CRUSHABLE > CRUSH
CRUSHED > CRUSH
CRUSHER > CRUSH
CRUSHERS > CRUSH
CRUSHES > CRUSH
CRUSHING n act or instance of compressing so as to injure or break
CRUSHINGS > CRUSHING
CRUSIAN variant of > CRUCIAN
CRUSIANS > CRUSIAN
CRUSIE same as > CRUIZIE
CRUSIES > CRUSIE
CRUSILY adj (in heraldry) strewn with crosses
CRUST n hard outer part of something, esp bread ▷ vb cover with or form a crust
CRUSTA n hard outer layer

CRUSTACEA n members of the Crustacea class of arthropods including the lobster
CRUSTAE > CRUSTA
CRUSTAL adj of or relating to the earth's crust
CRUSTAS > CRUSTA
CRUSTATE adj covered with a crust
CRUSTATED same as > CRUSTATE
CRUSTED > CRUST
CRUSTIER > CRUSTY
CRUSTIES > CRUSTY
CRUSTIEST > CRUSTY
CRUSTILY > CRUSTY
CRUSTING > CRUST
CRUSTLESS adj lacking a crust
CRUSTLIKE adj like a crust
CRUSTOSE adj having a crustlike appearance
CRUSTS > CRUST
CRUSTY adj having a crust ▷ n scruffy type of punk or hippy whose lifestyle involves travelling and squatting
CRUSY same as > CRUIZIE
CRUTCH n long sticklike support with a rest for the armpit ▷ vb support or sustain (a person or thing) as with a crutch
CRUTCHED > CRUTCH
CRUTCHES > CRUTCH
CRUTCHING > CRUTCH
CRUVE same as > CRUIVE
CRUVES > CRUVE
CRUX n crucial or decisive point
CRUXES > CRUX
CRUZADO same as > CRUSADO
CRUZADOES > CRUZADO
CRUZADOS > CRUZADO
CRUZEIRO n former monetary unit of Brazil, replaced by the cruzeiro real
CRUZEIROS > CRUZEIRO
CRUZIE same as > CRUIZIE
CRUZIES > CRUZIE
CRWTH n ancient stringed instrument of Celtic origin
CRWTHS > CRWTH
CRY vb shed tears ▷ n fit of weeping
CRYBABIES > CRYBABY
CRYBABY n person, esp a child, who cries too readily
CRYER same as > CRIER
CRYERS > CRYER
CRYING > CRY
CRYINGLY > CRY
CRYINGS > CRY
CRYOBANK n place for storing genetic material at low temperature
CRYOBANKS > CRYOBANK
CRYOCABLE n highly conducting electrical cable cooled with a refrigerant such as liquid nitrogen
CRYOGEN n substance used to produce low temperatures

CRYOGENIC adj of the branch of physics concerned with the production of very low temperatures
CRYOGENS > CRYOGEN
CRYOGENY n cryogenic science
CRYOLITE n white or colourless mineral
CRYOLITES > CRYOLITE
CRYOMETER n thermometer for measuring low temperatures
CRYOMETRY > CRYOMETER
CRYONIC adj relating to or involving cryonics
CRYONICS n practice of freezing a human corpse in the hope of restoring it to life in the future
CRYOPHYTE n organism, esp an alga or moss, that grows on snow or ice
CRYOPROBE n supercooled instrument used in surgery
CRYOSCOPE n any instrument used to determine the freezing point of a substance
CRYOSCOPY n determination of freezing points, esp for the determination of molecular weights by measuring the lowering of the freezing point of a solvent when a known quantity of solute is added
CRYOSTAT n apparatus for maintaining a constant low temperature
CRYOSTATS > CRYOSTAT
CRYOTRON n switch working at the temperature of liquid helium
CRYOTRONS > CRYOTRON
CRYPT n vault under a church, esp one used as a burial place
CRYPTADIA n things to be kept hidden
CRYPTAL > CRYPT
CRYPTIC adj obscure in meaning, secret
CRYPTICAL same as > CRYPTIC
CRYPTO n person who is a secret member of an organization or sect
CRYPTOGAM n plant that reproduces by spores not seeds
CRYPTON n krypton
CRYPTONS > CRYPTON
CRYPTONYM n code name
CRYPTOS > CRYPTO
CRYPTS > CRYPT
CRYSTAL n symmetrically shaped solid formed naturally ▷ adj bright and clear
CRYSTALS > CRYSTAL
CSARDAS n type of Hungarian folk dance
CSARDASES > CSARDAS
CTENE n locomotor organ found in ctenophores (or comb jellies)

CTENES > CTENE
CTENIDIA > CTENIDIUM
CTENIDIUM n one of the comblike respiratory gills of molluscs
CTENIFORM adj comblike
CTENOID adj toothed like a comb, as the scales of perches
CUADRILLA n matador's assistants in a bullfight
CUATRO n four-stringed guitar
CUATROS > CUATRO
CUB n young wild animal such as a bear or fox ▷ adj young or inexperienced ▷ vb give birth to cubs
CUBAGE same as > CUBATURE
CUBAGES > CUBAGE
CUBANE n rare octahedral hydrocarbon
CUBANELLE n variety of pepper
CUBANES > CUBANE
CUBATURE n determination of the cubic contents of something
CUBATURES > CUBATURE
CUBBED > CUB
CUBBIER > CUBBY
CUBBIES > CUBBY
CUBBIEST > CUBBY
CUBBING > CUB
CUBBINGS > CUB
CUBBISH > CUB
CUBBISHLY > CUB
CUBBY n cubbyhole ▷ adj short and plump
CUBBYHOLE n small enclosed space or room
CUBE n object with six equal square sides ▷ vb cut into cubes
CUBEB n SE Asian woody climbing plant with brownish berries
CUBEBS > CUBEB
CUBED > CUBE
CUBELIKE adj like a cube
CUBER > CUBE
CUBERS > CUBE
CUBES > CUBE
CUBHOOD n state of being a cub
CUBHOODS > CUBHOOD
CUBIC adj having three dimensions ▷ n cubic equation
CUBICA n fine shalloon-like fabric
CUBICAL adj of or related to volume
CUBICALLY > CUBICAL
CUBICAS > CUBICA
CUBICITY n property of being cubelike
CUBICLE n enclosed part of a large room, screened for privacy
CUBICLES > CUBICLE
CUBICLY > CUBIC
CUBICS > CUBIC
CUBICULA > CUBICULUM
CUBICULUM n underground burial chamber in Imperial Rome, such as those found in the catacombs

CUBIFORM *adj* having the shape of a cube

CUBING > CUBE

CUBISM *n* style of art in which objects are represented by geometrical shapes

CUBISMS > CUBISM

CUBIST > CUBISM

CUBISTIC > CUBISM

CUBISTS > CUBISM

CUBIT *n* old measure of length based on the length of the forearm

CUBITAL *adj* of or relating to the forearm

CUBITI > CUBITUS

CUBITS > CUBIT

CUBITUS *n* elbow

CUBITUSES > CUBITUS

CUBLESS *adj* having no cubs

CUBOID *adj* shaped like a cube ▷ *n* geometric solid whose six faces are rectangles

CUBOIDAL *same as* > CUBOID

CUBOIDS > CUBOID

CUBS > CUB

CUCKING *adj* as in *cucking stool* stool in which suspected witches were tested

CUCKOLD *n* man whose wife has been unfaithful ▷ *vb* be unfaithful to (one's husband)

CUCKOLDED > CUCKOLD

CUCKOLDLY *adj* possessing the qualities of a cuckold

CUCKOLDOM *n* state of being a cuckold

CUCKOLDRY > CUCKOLD

CUCKOLDS > CUCKOLD

CUCKOO *n* migratory bird ▷ *adj* insane or foolish ▷ *interj* imitation or representation of the call of a cuckoo ▷ *vb* repeat over and over

CUCKOOED > CUCKOO

CUCKOOING > CUCKOO

CUCKOOS > CUCKOO

CUCULLATE *adj* shaped like a hood or having a hoodlike part

CUCUMBER *n* long green-skinned fleshy fruit used in salads

CUCUMBERS > CUCUMBER

CUCURBIT *n* type of tropical or subtropical creeping plant

CUCURBITS > CUCURBIT

CUD *n* partially digested food chewed by a ruminant

CUDBEAR *another name for* > ORCHIL

CUDBEARS > CUDBEAR

CUDDEN *n* young coalfish

CUDDENS > CUDDEN

CUDDIE *same as* > CUDDY

CUDDIES > CUDDY

CUDDIN *same as* > CUDDEN

CUDDINS > CUDDIN

CUDDLE *n* hug ▷ *vb* hold close

CUDDLED > CUDDLE

CUDDLER > CUDDLE

CUDDLERS > CUDDLE

CUDDLES > CUDDLE

CUDDLIER > CUDDLE

CUDDLIEST > CUDDLE

CUDDLING > CUDDLE

CUDDLY > CUDDLE

CUDDY *n* small cabin in a boat

CUDGEL *n* short thick stick used as a weapon ▷ *vb* use a cudgel

CUDGELED > CUDGEL

CUDGELER > CUDGEL

CUDGELERS > CUDGEL

CUDGELING > CUDGEL

CUDGELLED > CUDGEL

CUDGELLER > CUDGEL

CUDGELS > CUDGEL

CUDGERIE *n* type of large tropical tree with light-coloured wood

CUDGERIES > CUDGERIE

CUDS > CUD

CUDWEED *n* type of temperate plant

CUDWEEDS > CUDWEED

CUE *n* signal to an actor or musician to begin speaking or playing ▷ *vb* give a cue to

CUED > CUE

CUEING > CUE

CUEINGS > CUEING

CUEIST *n* snooker or billiards player

CUEISTS > CUEIST

CUES > CUE

CUESTA *n* long low ridge with a steep scarp slope and a gentle back slope

CUESTAS > CUESTA

CUFF *n* end of a sleeve ▷ *vb* hit with an open hand

CUFFABLE *n* able to be folded down at the ankle

CUFFED > CUFF

CUFFIN *n* man

CUFFING > CUFF

CUFFINS > CUFFIN

CUFFLE *vb* scuffle

CUFFLED > CUFFLE

CUFFLES > CUFFLE

CUFFLESS *adj* having no cuff(s)

CUFFLING > CUFFLE

CUFFLINK *n* detachable fastener for shirt cuff

CUFFLINKS > CUFFLINK

CUFFO *adv* free of charge

CUFFS > CUFF

CUFFUFFLE *same as* > KERFUFFLE

CUIF *same as* > COOF

CUIFS > CUIF

CUING > CUE

CUIRASS *n* piece of armour, of leather or metal covering the chest and back ▷ *vb* equip with a cuirass

CUIRASSED > CUIRASS

CUIRASSES > CUIRASS

CUISH *same as* > CUISSE

CUISHES > CUISH

CUISINART *n* tradename for a type of food processor

CUISINE *n* style of cooking

CUISINES > CUISINE

CUISINIER *n* cook

CUISSE *n* piece of armour for the thigh

CUISSER *same as* > COOSER

CUISSERS > CUISSER

CUISSES > CUISSE

CUIT *n* ankle

CUITER *vb* pamper

CUITERED > CUITER

CUITERING > CUITER

CUITERS > CUITER

CUITIKIN *n* gaiter

CUITIKINS > CUITIKIN

CUITS > CUIT

CUITTLE *vb* wheedle

CUITTLED > CUITTLE

CUITTLES > CUITTLE

CUITTLING > CUITTLE

CUKE *n* cucumber

CUKES > CUKE

CULCH *n* the basis of an oyster bed

CULCHES > CULCH

CULCHIE *n* rough or unsophisticated country-dweller from outside Dublin ▷ *adj* rough or unsophisticated

CULCHIER > CULCHIE

CULCHIES > CULCHIE

CULCHIEST > CULCHIE

CULET *n* flat face at the bottom of a gem

CULETS > CULET

CULEX *n* type of mosquito

CULEXES > CULEX

CULICES > CULEX

CULICID *n* type of dipterous insect

CULICIDS > CULICID

CULICINE *n* any member of the genus Culex containing mosquitoes

CULICINES > CULICINE

CULINARY *adj* of kitchens or cookery

CULL *vb* choose, gather ▷ *n* culling

CULLAY *n* soapbark tree

CULLAYS > CULLAY

CULLED > CULL

CULLENDER *same as* > COLANDER

CULLER *n* person employed to cull animals

CULLERS > CULLER

CULLET *n* waste glass for melting down to be reused

CULLETS > CULLET

CULLIED > CULLY

CULLIES > CULLY

CULLING > CULL

CULLINGS > CULL

CULLION *n* rascal

CULLIONLY > CULLION

CULLIONS > CULLION

CULLIS *same as* > COULISSE

CULLISES > CULLIS

CULLS > CULL

CULLY *n* pal ▷ *vb* to trick

CULLYING > CULLY

CULLYISM *n* state of being a dupe

CULLYISMS > CULLYISM

CULM *n* coal-mine waste ▷ *vb* form a culm or grass stem

CULMED > CULM

CULMEN *n* summit

CULMINA > CULMEN

CULMINANT *adj* highest or culminating

CULMINATE *vb* reach the highest point or climax

CULMING > CULM

CULMS > CULM

CULOTTE > CULOTTES

CULOTTES *pl n* women's knee-length trousers cut to look like a skirt

CULPA *n* act of neglect

CULPABLE *adj* deserving blame

CULPABLY > CULPABLE

CULPAE > CULPA

CULPATORY *adj* expressing blame

CULPRIT *n* person guilty of an offence or misdeed

CULPRITS > CULPRIT

CULSHIE *n* rough or unsophisticated country-dweller from outside Dublin ▷ *adj* rough or unsophisticated

CULSHIER > CULSHIE

CULSHIES > CULSHIE

CULSHIEST > CULSHIE

CULT *n* specific system of worship ▷ *adj* very popular among a limited group of people

CULTCH *same as* > CULCH

CULTCHES > CULTCH

CULTER *same as* > COULTER

CULTERS > CULTER

CULTI > CULTUS

CULTIC *adj* of or relating to a religious cult

CULTIER > CULTY

CULTIEST > CULTY

CULTIGEN *n* cultivated species of plant that did not come from a wild type

CULTIGENS > CULTIGEN

CULTISH *adj* intended to appeal to a small group of fashionable people

CULTISHLY > CULTISH

CULTISM > CULT

CULTISMS > CULT

CULTIST > CULT

CULTISTS > CULT

CULTIVAR *n* cultivated plant produced from a natural species

CULTIVARS > CULTIVAR

CULTIVATE *vb* prepare (land) to grow crops

CULTLIKE *adj* resembling a cult

CULTRATE *adj* shaped like a knife blade

CULTRATED *same as* > CULTRATE

CULTS > CULT

CULTURAL *adj* of or relating to artistic or social pursuits

CULTURATI *n* people interested in cultural activities

CULTURE *n* ideas, customs, and art of a particular society ▷ *vb* grow (bacteria) for study

CULTURED *adj* showing good taste or manners

CULTURES > CULTURE

CULTURING > CULTURE

CULTURIST > CULTURE

CULTUS another word for > CULT

CULTUSES > CULTUS

CULTY same as > CULTISH

CULVER an archaic or poetic name for > PIGEON

CULVERIN n long-range medium to heavy cannon used during the 15th, 16th, and 17th centuries

CULVERINS > CULVERIN

CULVERS > CULVER

CULVERT n drain under a road or railway ▷ vb direct water through a culvert

CULVERTED > CULVERT

CULVERTS > CULVERT

CUM prep with ▷ n vulgar word for semen ▷ vb ejaculate sperm

CUMACEAN n type of small marine crustacean

CUMACEANS > CUMACEAN

CUMARIC > CUMARIN

CUMARIN same as > COUMARIN

CUMARINS > CUMARIN

CUMARONE variant spelling of > COUMARONE

CUMARONES > CUMARONE

CUMBENT adj lying down

CUMBER vb obstruct or hinder ▷ n hindrance or burden

CUMBERED > CUMBER

CUMBERER > CUMBER

CUMBERERS > CUMBER

CUMBERING > CUMBER

CUMBERS > CUMBER

CUMBIA n Colombian style of music

CUMBIAS > CUMBIA

CUMBRANCE n burden, obstacle, or hindrance

CUMBROUS adj awkward because of size, weight, or height

CUMBUNGI n type of tall Australian marsh plant

CUMBUNGIS > CUMBUNGI

CUMEC n unit of volumetric rate of flow

CUMECS > CUMEC

CUMIN n sweet-smelling seeds of a Mediterranean plant, used in cooking

CUMINS > CUMIN

CUMMED > CUM

CUMMER n gossip

CUMMERS > CUMMER

CUMMIN same as > CUMIN

CUMMING > CUM

CUMMINS > CUMMIN

CUMQUAT same as > KUMQUAT

CUMQUATS > CUMQUAT

CUMS > CUM

CUMSHAW n (used, esp formerly, by beggars in Chinese ports) a present or tip

CUMSHAWS > CUMSHAW

CUMULATE vb accumulate ▷ adj heaped up

CUMULATED > CUMULATE

CUMULATES > CUMULATE

CUMULET n variety of domestic fancy pigeon

CUMULETS > CUMULET

CUMULI > CUMULUS

CUMULOSE adj full of heaps

CUMULOUS adj resembling or consisting of cumulus clouds

CUMULUS n thick white or dark grey cloud

CUMULUSES > CUMULUS

CUNABULA n cradle

CUNCTATOR n person in habit of being late

CUNDIES > CUNDY

CUNDUM n early form of condom

CUNDUMS > CUNDUM

CUNDY n sewer

CUNEAL same as > CUNEIFORM

CUNEATE adj wedge-shaped: cuneate leaves are attached at the narrow end

CUNEATED same as > CUNEATE

CUNEATELY > CUNEATE

CUNEATIC adj cuneiform

CUNEI > CUNEUS

CUNEIFORM adj (written in) an ancient system of writing using wedge-shaped characters ▷ n ancient system of writing using wedge-shaped characters

CUNETTE n small trench dug in the main ditch of a fortification

CUNETTES > CUNETTE

CUNEUS n small wedge-shaped area of the cerebral cortex

CUNIFORM same as > CUNEIFORM

CUNIFORMS > CUNIFORM

CUNIT n one hundred cubic feet

CUNITS > CUNIT

CUNJEVOI n plant of tropical Asia and Australia

CUNJEVOIS > CUNJEVOI

CUNNER n fish of the wrasse family

CUNNERS > CUNNER

CUNNING adj clever at deceiving ▷ n cleverness at deceiving

CUNNINGER > CUNNING

CUNNINGLY > CUNNING

CUNNINGS > CUNNING

CUNT n taboo word for the female genitals

CUNTS > CUNT

CUP n small bowl-shaped drinking container with a handle ▷ vb form (one's hands) into the shape of a cup

CUPBEARER n attendant who fills and serves cups

CUPBOARD n piece of furniture or alcove with a door, for storage ▷ vb store in a cupboard

CUPBOARDS > CUPBOARD

CUPCAKE n small cake baked in a cup-shaped foil or paper case

CUPCAKES > CUPCAKE

CUPEL n refractory pot in which gold or silver is refined ▷ vb refine (gold or silver) by means of cupellation

CUPELED > CUPEL

CUPELER > CUPEL

CUPELERS > CUPEL

CUPELING > CUPEL

CUPELLED > CUPEL

CUPELLER > CUPEL

CUPELLERS > CUPEL

CUPELLING > CUPEL

CUPELS > CUPEL

CUPFERRON n compound used in chemical analysis

CUPFUL n amount a cup will hold

CUPFULS > CUPFUL

CUPGALL n gall found on oakleaves

CUPGALLS > CUPGALL

CUPHEAD n type of bolt or rivet with a cup-shaped head

CUPHEADS > CUPHEAD

CUPHOLDER n device in a car for holding a drinking cup

CUPID n figure representing the Roman god of love

CUPIDITY n greed for money or possessions

CUPIDS > CUPID

CUPLIKE > CUP

CUPMAN n drinking companion

CUPMEN > CUPMAN

CUPOLA n domed roof or ceiling ▷ vb provide with a cupola

CUPOLAED > CUPOLA

CUPOLAING > CUPOLA

CUPOLAR > CUPOLA

CUPOLAS > CUPOLA

CUPOLATED > CUPOLA

CUPPA n cup of tea

CUPPAS > CUPPA

CUPPED > CUP

CUPPER same as > CUPPA

CUPPERS > CUPPER

CUPPIER > CUPPY

CUPPIEST > CUPPY

CUPPING > CUP

CUPPINGS > CUP

CUPPY adj cup-shaped

CUPREOUS adj of copper

CUPRESSUS n type of tree

CUPRIC adj of or containing copper in the divalent state

CUPRITE n red secondary mineral

CUPRITES > CUPRITE

CUPROUS adj of or containing copper in the monovalent state

CUPRUM an obsolete name for > COPPER

CUPRUMS > CUPRUM

CUPS > CUP

CUPSFUL > CUPFUL

CUPULA n dome-shaped structure

CUPULAE > CUPULA

CUPULAR same as > CUPULATE

CUPULATE adj shaped like a small cup

CUPULE n cup-shaped part or structure

CUPULES > CUPULE

CUR n mongrel dog

CURABLE adj capable of being cured

CURABLY > CURABLE

CURACAO n orange-flavoured liqueur

CURACAOS > CURACAO

CURACIES > CURACY

CURACOA same as > CURACAO

CURACOAS > CURACOA

CURACY n work or position of a curate

CURAGH same as > CURRACH

CURAGHS > CURAGH

CURANDERA n female faith healer

CURANDERO n male faith healer

CURARA same as > CURARE

CURARAS > CURARA

CURARE n poisonous resin of a S American tree

CURARES > CURARE

CURARI same as > CURARE

CURARINE n alkaloid extracted from curare, used as a muscle relaxant in surgery

CURARINES > CURARINE

CURARIS > CURARI

CURARISE same as > CURARIZE

CURARISED > CURARISE

CURARISES > CURARISE

CURARIZE vb paralyse or treat with curare

CURARIZED > CURARIZE

CURARIZES > CURARIZE

CURASSOW n gallinaceous ground-nesting bird

CURASSOWS > CURASSOW

CURAT n cuirass

CURATE n clergyman or clergywoman who assists a parish priest ▷ vb be in charge of (an art exhibition or museum)

CURATED > CURATE

CURATES > CURATE

CURATING > CURATE

CURATION n work of a curator

CURATIONS > CURATION

CURATIVE n something able to cure ▷ adj able to cure

CURATIVES > CURATIVE

CURATOR n person in charge of a museum or art gallery

CURATORS > CURATOR

CURATORY > CURATOR

CURATRIX n female curator

CURATS > CURAT

CURB n something that restrains ▷ vb control, restrain

CURBABLE adj capable of being restrained

CURBED > CURB

CURBER > CURB

CURBERS > CURB

CURBING the US spelling of > KERBING

c

CURBINGS > CURBING
CURBLESS adj having no restraint
CURBS > CURB
CURBSIDE n pavement
CURBSIDES > CURBSIDE
CURBSTONE the US spelling of > KERBSTONE
CURCH n woman's plain cap or kerchief
CURCHEF same as > CURCH
CURCHEFS > CURCHEF
CURCHES > CURCH
CURCULIO n type of American weevil
CURCULIOS > CURCULIO
CURCUMA n type of tropical Asian tuberous plant
CURCUMAS > CURCUMA
CURCUMIN n yellow dye derived from turmeric
CURCUMINE same as > CURCUMIN
CURCUMINS > CURCUMIN
CURD n coagulated milk, used to make cheese ▷ vb turn into or become curd
CURDED > CURD
CURDIER > CURD
CURDIEST > CURD
CURDINESS > CURD
CURDING > CURD
CURDLE vb turn into curd, coagulate
CURDLED > CURDLE
CURDLER > CURDLE
CURDLERS > CURDLE
CURDLES > CURDLE
CURDLING > CURDLE
CURDS > CURD
CURDY > CURD
CURE vb get rid of (an illness or problem) ▷ n (treatment causing) curing of an illness or person
CURED > CURE
CURELESS > CURE
CURER > CURE
CURERS > CURE
CURES > CURE
CURET same as > CURETTE
CURETS > CURET
CURETTAGE n process of using a curette
CURETTE n surgical instrument for scraping tissue from body cavities ▷ vb scrape with a curette
CURETTED > CURETTE
CURETTES > CURETTE
CURETTING > CURETTE
CURF n type of limestone
CURFEW n law ordering people to stay inside after a specific time
CURFEWS > CURFEW
CURFS > CURF
CURFUFFLE vb make a kerfuffle
CURIA n papal court and government of the Roman Catholic Church
CURIAE > CURIA
CURIAL > CURIA
CURIALISM n ultramontanism
CURIALIST > CURIALISM

CURIAS > CURIA
CURIE n standard unit of radioactivity
CURIES > CURIE
CURIET n cuirass
CURIETS > CURIET
CURING n act of curing
CURINGS > CURING
CURIO n rare or unusual object valued as a collector's item
CURIOS > CURIO
CURIOSA pl n curiosities
CURIOSITY n eagerness to know or find out
CURIOUS adj eager to learn or know
CURIOUSER > CURIOUS
CURIOUSLY > CURIOUS
CURITE n oxide of uranium and lead
CURITES > CURITE
CURIUM n radioactive element artificially produced from plutonium
CURIUMS > CURIUM
CURL n curved piece of hair ▷ vb make (hair) into curls or (of hair) grow in curls
CURLED > CURL
CURLER n pin or small tube for curling hair
CURLERS > CURLER
CURLEW n long-billed wading bird
CURLEWS > CURLEW
CURLI pl n curled hairlike processes on the surface of the E. coli bacterium
CURLICUE n ornamental curl or twist ▷ vb curl or twist elaborately, as in curlicues
CURLICUED > CURLICUE
CURLICUES > CURLICUE
CURLIER > CURLY
CURLIES pl n as in have by the short and curlies have completely in one's power
CURLIEST > CURLY
CURLILY > CURLY
CURLINESS > CURLY
CURLING n game like bowls, played with heavy stones on ice
CURLINGS > CURLING
CURLPAPER n strip of paper used to roll up and set a section of hair, usually wetted, into a curl
CURLS > CURL
CURLY adj tending to curl
CURLYCUE same as > CURLICUE
CURLYCUES > CURLYCUE
CURN n grain (of corn etc)
CURNEY same as > CURNY
CURNIER > CURNY
CURNIEST > CURNY
CURNS > CURN
CURNY adj granular
CURPEL same as > CRUPPER
CURPELS > CURPEL
CURR vb purr
CURRACH a Scot or Irish name for > CORACLE
CURRACHS > CURRACH

CURRAGH same as > CURRACH
CURRAGHS > CURRAGH
CURRAJONG same as > KURRAJONG
CURRAN n black bun
CURRANS > CURRAN
CURRANT n small dried grape
CURRANTS > CURRANT
CURRANTY > CURRANT
CURRAWONG n Australian songbird
CURRED > CURR
CURREJONG same as > KURRAJONG
CURRENCY n money in use in a particular country
CURRENT adj of the immediate present ▷ n flow of water or air in one direction
CURRENTLY > CURRENT
CURRENTS > CURRENT
CURRICLE n two-wheeled open carriage drawn by two horses side by side
CURRICLES > CURRICLE
CURRICULA n plural form of singular curriculum: course of study in one subject at school or college
CURRIE same as > CURRY
CURRIED > CURRY
CURRIER n person who curries leather
CURRIERS > CURRIER
CURRIERY n trade, work, or place of occupation of a currier
CURRIES > CURRY
CURRIJONG same as > KURRAJONG
CURRING > CURR
CURRISH adj of or like a cur
CURRISHLY > CURRISH
CURRS > CURR
CURRY n Indian dish of meat or vegetables in a hot spicy sauce ▷ vb prepare (food) with curry powder
CURRYCOMB n ridged comb used for grooming horses
CURRYING > CURRY
CURRYINGS > CURRY
CURS > CUR
CURSAL > CURSUS
CURSE vb swear (at) ▷ n swearword
CURSED > CURSE
CURSEDER > CURSED
CURSEDEST > CURSED
CURSEDLY > CURSE
CURSENARY same as > CURSORARY
CURSER > CURSE
CURSERS > CURSE
CURSES > CURSE
CURSI > CURSUS
CURSILLO n short religious retreat
CURSILLOS > CURSILLO
CURSING > CURSE
CURSINGS > CURSE
CURSITOR n clerk in the Court of Chancery
CURSITORS > CURSITOR

CURSITORY > CURSITOR
CURSIVE n handwriting done with joined letters ▷ adj of handwriting or print in which letters are joined in a flowing style
CURSIVELY > CURSIVE
CURSIVES > CURSIVE
CURSOR n movable point of light that shows a specific position on a visual display unit
CURSORARY adj cursory
CURSORES > CURSOR
CURSORIAL adj adapted for running
CURSORILY > CURSORY
CURSORS > CURSOR
CURSORY adj quick and superficial
CURST same as > CURSED
CURSTNESS n peevishness
CURSUS n Neolithic parallel earthworks
CURT adj brief and rather rude
CURTAIL vb cut short
CURTAILED > CURTAIL
CURTAILER > CURTAIL
CURTAILS > CURTAIL
CURTAIN n piece of cloth hung at a window or opening as a screen ▷ vb provide with curtains
CURTAINED > CURTAIN
CURTAINS pl n death or ruin
CURTAL adj cut short ▷ n animal whose tail has been docked
CURTALAX same as > CURTALAXE
CURTALAXE n cutlass
CURTALS > CURTAL
CURTANA n unpointed sword displayed at a coronation as an emblem of mercy
CURTANAS > CURTANA
CURTATE adj shortened
CURTATION > CURTATE
CURTAXE same as > CURTALAXE
CURTAXES > CURTAXE
CURTER > CURT
CURTESIES > CURTESY
CURTEST > CURT
CURTESY n widower's life interest in his wife's estate
CURTILAGE n enclosed area of land adjacent to a dwelling house
CURTLY > CURT
CURTNESS > CURT
CURTSEY same as > CURTSY
CURTSEYED > CURTSEY
CURTSEYS > CURTSEY
CURTSIED > CURTSY
CURTSIES > CURTSY
CURTSY n woman's gesture of respect ▷ vb make a curtsy
CURTSYING > CURTSY
CURULE adj (in ancient Rome) of the highest rank, esp one entitled to use a curule chair
CURVATE adj curved
CURVATED same as > CURVATE

CURVATION > CURVATE
CURVATIVE adj having curved edges
CURVATURE n curved shape
CURVE n continuously bending line with no straight parts ▷ vb form or move in a curve
CURVEBALL n in baseball, a ball pitched in a curving path ▷ vb pitch a curveball
CURVED > CURVE
CURVEDLY > CURVE
CURVES > CURVE
CURVESOME adj curvaceous
CURVET n horse's low leap with all four feet off the ground ▷ vb make such a leap
CURVETED > CURVET
CURVETING > CURVET
CURVETS > CURVET
CURVETTED > CURVET
CURVEY same as **>** CURVY
CURVIER > CURVE
CURVIEST > CURVE
CURVIFORM adj having a curved form
CURVINESS > CURVY
CURVING > CURVE
CURVITAL adj relating to curvature
CURVITIES > CURVITY
CURVITY n curvedness
CURVY adj **>** CURVE
CUSCUS n large Australian nocturnal possum
CUSCUSES > CUSCUS
CUSEC n unit of flow equal to 1 cubic foot per second
CUSECS > CUSEC
CUSH n cushion
CUSHAT n wood pigeon
CUSHATS > CUSHAT
CUSHAW same as **>** CASHAW
CUSHAWS > CUSHAW
CUSHES > CUSH
CUSHIE same as **>** CUSHAT
CUSHIER > CUSHY
CUSHIES > CUSHIE
CUSHIEST > CUSHY
CUSHILY > CUSHY
CUSHINESS > CUSHY
CUSHION n bag filled with soft material, to make a seat more comfortable ▷ vb lessen the effects of
CUSHIONED > CUSHION
CUSHIONET n small cushion
CUSHIONS > CUSHION
CUSHIONY adj like a cushion
CUSHTY interj exclamation of pleasure, agreement, approval, etc
CUSHY adj easy
CUSK n type of food fish of northern coastal waters, with a single long dorsal fin
CUSKS > CUSK
CUSP n pointed end, esp on a tooth
CUSPAL > CUSP
CUSPATE adj having a cusp or cusps
CUSPATED same as **>** CUSPATE
CUSPED same as **>** CUSPATE

CUSPID n tooth having one point
CUSPIDAL same as **>** CUSPIDATE
CUSPIDATE adj having a cusp or cusps
CUSPIDES > CUSPIS
CUSPIDOR another word (esp US) for **>** SPITTOON
CUSPIDORE same as **>** CUSPIDOR
CUSPIDORS > CUSPIDOR
CUSPIDS > CUSPID
CUSPIER > CUSPY
CUSPIEST > CUSPY
CUSPIS n in anatomy, tapering structure
CUSPLIKE adj like a cusp
CUSPS > CUSP
CUSPY adj (of a computer program) well-designed and user-friendly
CUSS n curse, oath ▷ vb swear (at)
CUSSED adj obstinate
CUSSEDLY > CUSSED
CUSSER same as **>** COOSER
CUSSERS > CUSSER
CUSSES > CUSS
CUSSING > CUSS
CUSSO n tree of the rose family
CUSSOS > CUSSO
CUSSWORD n swearword
CUSSWORDS > CUSSWORD
CUSTARD n sweet yellow sauce made from milk and eggs
CUSTARDS > CUSTARD
CUSTARDY adj like custard
CUSTOCK same as **>** CASTOCK
CUSTOCKS > CUSTOCK
CUSTODE n custodian
CUSTODES > CUSTODE
CUSTODIAL > CUSTODY
CUSTODIAN n person in charge of a public building
CUSTODIER n custodian
CUSTODIES > CUSTODY
CUSTODY n protective care
CUSTOM n long-established activity or action ▷ adj made to the specifications of an individual customer
CUSTOMARY adj usual ▷ n statement in writing of customary laws and practices
CUSTOMED adj accustomed
CUSTOMER n person who buys goods or services
CUSTOMERS > CUSTOMER
CUSTOMISE same as **>** CUSTOMIZE
CUSTOMIZE vb make (something) according to a customer's individual requirements
CUSTOMS n duty charged on imports or exports
CUSTOS n superior in the Franciscan religious order
CUSTREL n knave
CUSTRELS > CUSTREL
CUSTUMAL another word for **>** CUSTOMARY

CUSTUMALS > CUSTUMAL
CUSTUMARY n customary
CUSUM n analysis technique used in statistics
CUSUMS > CUSUM
CUT vb open up, penetrate, wound, or divide with a sharp instrument
CUTANEOUS adj of the skin
CUTAWAY adj (of a drawing or model) having part of the outside omitted to reveal the inside ▷ n man's coat cut diagonally from the front waist to the back of the knees
CUTAWAYS > CUTAWAY
CUTBACK n decrease or reduction
CUTBACKS > CUTBACK
CUTBANK n steep banking at a bend in a river
CUTBANKS > CUTBANK
CUTBLOCK n area where logging is permitted
CUTBLOCKS > CUTBLOCK
CUTCH same as **>** CATECHU
CUTCHA adj crude
CUTCHERRY n (formerly, in India) government offices and law courts collectively
CUTCHERY same as **>** CUTCHERRY
CUTCHES > CUTCH
CUTDOWN n decrease
CUTDOWNS > CUTDOWN
CUTE adj appealing or attractive
CUTELY > CUTE
CUTENESS > CUTE
CUTER > CUTE
CUTES > CUTIS
CUTESIE same as **>** CUTESY
CUTESIER > CUTESY
CUTESIEST > CUTESY
CUTEST > CUTE
CUTESY adj affectedly cute or coy
CUTEY same as **>** CUTIE
CUTEYS > CUTEY
CUTGLASS adj (of an accent) upper-class
CUTGRASS n any grass of the genus Leersia
CUTICLE n skin at the base of a fingernail or toenail
CUTICLES > CUTICLE
CUTICULA n cuticle
CUTICULAE > CUTICULA
CUTICULAR > CUTICLE
CUTIE n person regarded as appealing or attractive, esp a girl or woman
CUTIES > CUTIE
CUTIKIN same as **>** CUITIKIN
CUTIKINS > CUTIKIN
CUTIN n waxy waterproof substance
CUTINISE same as **>** CUTINIZE
CUTINISED > CUTINISE
CUTINISES > CUTINISE
CUTINIZE vb become or cause to become covered or impregnated with cutin
CUTINIZED > CUTINIZE

CUTINIZES > CUTINIZE
CUTINS > CUTIN
CUTIS a technical name for the **>** SKIN
CUTISES > CUTIS
CUTLAS same as **>** CUTLASS
CUTLASES > CUTLAS
CUTLASS n curved one-edged sword formerly used by sailors
CUTLASSES > CUTLASS
CUTLER n maker of cutlery
CUTLERIES > CUTLERY
CUTLERS > CUTLER
CUTLERY n knives, forks, and spoons
CUTLET n small piece of meat like a chop
CUTLETS > CUTLET
CUTLETTE n flat croquette of minced meat
CUTLETTES > CUTLETTE
CUTLINE n caption
CUTLINES > CUTLINE
CUTOFF n limit or termination
CUTOFFS > CUTOFF
CUTOUT n something that has been cut out from something else
CUTOUTS > CUTOUT
CUTOVER n transitional period in IT system changeover
CUTOVERS > CUTOVER
CUTPURSE n pickpocket
CUTPURSES > CUTPURSE
CUTS > CUT
CUTSCENE n non-interactive scene in a computer game
CUTSCENES > CUTSCENE
CUTTABLE adj capable of being cut
CUTTAGE n propagation by using parts taken from growing plants
CUTTAGES > CUTTAGE
CUTTER n person or tool that cuts
CUTTERS > CUTTER
CUTTHROAT n person who cuts throats
CUTTIER > CUTTY
CUTTIES > CUTTY
CUTTIEST > CUTTY
CUTTING > CUT
CUTTINGLY > CUT
CUTTINGS > CUT
CUTTLE vb to whisper
CUTTLED > CUTTLE
CUTTLES > CUTTLE
CUTTLING > CUTTLE
CUTTO n large knife
CUTTOE same as **>** CUTTO
CUTTOES > CUTTO
CUTTY adj short or cut short ▷ n something cut short
CUTUP n joker or prankster
CUTUPS > CUTUP
CUTWATER n forward part of the stem of a vessel, which cuts through the water
CUTWATERS > CUTWATER
CUTWORK n type of openwork embroidery
CUTWORKS > CUTWORK

CUTWORM n caterpillar of various types of moth
CUTWORMS > CUTWORM
CUVEE n individual batch or blend of wine
CUVEES > CUVEE
CUVETTE n shallow dish or vessel for holding liquid
CUVETTES > CUVETTE
CUZ n cousin
CUZES > CUZ
CUZZES > CUZ
CUZZIE n close friend or family member
CUZZIES > CUZZIE
CWM same as **>** CIRQUE
CWMS > CWM
CWTCH vb cuddle or be cuddled
CWTCHED > CWTCH
CWTCHES > CWTCH
CWTCHING > CWTCH
CYAN n highly saturated green-blue ▷ adj of this colour
CYANAMID same as **>** CYANAMIDE
CYANAMIDE n white or colourless crystalline soluble weak dibasic acid, which can be hydrolysed to urea
CYANAMIDS > CYANAMID
CYANATE n any salt or ester of cyanic acid
CYANATES > CYANATE
CYANIC adj as in cyanic acid colourless poisonous volatile liquid acid
CYANID same as **>** CYANIDE
CYANIDE n extremely poisonous chemical compound ▷ vb treat with cyanide
CYANIDED > CYANIDE
CYANIDES > CYANIDE
CYANIDING > CYANIDE
CYANIDS > CYANID
CYANIN same as **>** CYANINE
CYANINE n blue dye used in photography
CYANINES > CYANINE
CYANINS > CYANIN
CYANISE vb turn into cyanide
CYANISED > CYANISE
CYANISES > CYANISE
CYANISING > CYANISE
CYANITE a variant spelling of **>** KYANITE
CYANITES > CYANITE
CYANITIC > CYANITE
CYANIZE same as **>** CYANISE
CYANIZED > CYANIZE
CYANIZES > CYANIZE
CYANIZING > CYANIZE
CYANO adj containing cyanogen
CYANOGEN n poisonous colourless flammable gas
CYANOGENS > CYANOGEN
CYANOSE same as **>** CYANOSIS
CYANOSED adj affected by cyanosis
CYANOSES > CYANOSIS

CYANOSIS n blueness of the skin, caused by a deficiency of oxygen in the blood
CYANOTIC > CYANOSIS
CYANOTYPE another name for **>** BLUEPRINT
CYANS > CYAN
CYANURATE n chemical derived from cyanide
CYANURET n cyanide
CYANURETS > CYANURET
CYANURIC adj as in cyanuric acid type of acid
CYATHI > CYATHUS
CYATHIA > CYATHIUM
CYATHIUM n inflorescence of the type found on the poinsettia
CYATHUS n ancient measure of wine
CYBER adj involving computers
CYBERCAFE n café equipped with computer terminals which customers can use to access the internet
CYBERCAST same as **>** WEBCAST
CYBERNATE vb control (a manufacturing process) with a servomechanism or (of a process) to be controlled by a servomechanism
CYBERNAUT n person using internet
CYBERPET n electronic toy that simulates the activities of a pet
CYBERPETS > CYBERPET
CYBERPORN n pornography on the internet
CYBERPUNK n genre of science fiction that features rebellious computer hackers and is set in a dystopian society integrated by computer networks
CYBERSEX n exchanging of sexual messages or information via the internet
CYBERWAR n information warfare
CYBERWARS > CYBERWAR
CYBORG n (in science fiction) a living being enhanced by computer implants
CYBORGS > CYBORG
CYBRARIAN n person in charge of computer archives
CYBRID n cytoplasmic hybrid
CYBRIDS > CYBRID
CYCAD n type of tropical or subtropical plant
CYCADEOID n (now extinct) plant with a woody stem and tough leaves
CYCADS > CYCAD
CYCAS n palm tree of the genus Cycas
CYCASES > CYCAS
CYCASIN n glucoside, toxic to mammals, occurring in cycads
CYCASINS > CYCASIN
CYCLAMATE n salt or ester of cyclamic acid. Certain of

the salts have a very sweet taste and were formerly used as food additives and sugar substitutes
CYCLAMEN n plant with red, pink, or white flowers ▷ adj of a dark reddish-purple colour
CYCLAMENS > CYCLAMEN
CYCLAMIC adj as in cyclamic acid type of acid
CYCLASE n enzyme which acts as a catalyst in the formation of a cyclic compound
CYCLASES > CYCLASE
CYCLE vb ride a bicycle ▷ n bicycle
CYCLECAR n any light car with an engine capacity of 1100cc or less
CYCLECARS > CYCLECAR
CYCLED > CYCLE
CYCLEPATH n special path for bicycles
CYCLER same as **>** CYCLIST
CYCLERIES > CYCLERY
CYCLERS > CYCLER
CYCLERY n business dealing in bicycles and bicycle accessories
CYCLES > CYCLE
CYCLEWAY n path or way designed, and reserved for, cyclists
CYCLEWAYS > CYCLEWAY
CYCLIC adj recurring or revolving in cycles
CYCLICAL n short-term trend, of which reversal is expected ▷ adj cyclic
CYCLICALS > CYCLIC
CYCLICISM > CYCLIC
CYCLICITY > CYCLIC
CYCLICLY > CYCLIC
CYCLIN n type of protein
CYCLING > CYCLE
CYCLINGS > CYCLE
CYCLINS > CYCLIN
CYCLISE same as **>** CYCLIZE
CYCLISED > CYCLISE
CYCLISES > CYCLISE
CYCLISING > CYCLISE
CYCLIST n person who rides a bicycle
CYCLISTS > CYCLIST
CYCLITOL n alicyclic compound
CYCLITOLS > CYCLITOL
CYCLIZE vb be cyclical
CYCLIZED > CYCLIZE
CYCLIZES > CYCLIZE
CYCLIZINE n drug used to relieve the symptoms of motion sickness
CYCLIZING > CYCLIZE
CYCLO n type of rickshaw
CYCLOGIRO n aircraft lifted and propelled by pivoted blades rotating parallel to roughly horizontal transverse axes
CYCLOID adj resembling a circle ▷ n mathematical curve
CYCLOIDAL > CYCLOID
CYCLOIDS > CYCLOID

CYCLOLITH n stone circle
CYCLONAL > CYCLONE
CYCLONE n violent wind moving round a central area
CYCLONES > CYCLONE
CYCLONIC > CYCLONE
CYCLONITE n white crystalline insoluble explosive prepared by the action of nitric acid on hexamethylenetetramine
CYCLOPEAN adj of or relating to the Cyclops
CYCLOPES > CYCLOPS
CYCLOPIAN > CYCLOPS
CYCLOPIC > CYCLOPS
CYCLOPS n type of copepod characterized by having one eye
CYCLORAMA n large picture, such as a battle scene, on the interior wall of a cylindrical room, designed to appear in natural perspective to a spectator in the centre
CYCLOS > CYCLO
CYCLOSES > CYCLOSIS
CYCLOSIS n circulation of cytoplasm or cell organelles, such as food vacuoles in some protozoans
CYCLOTRON n apparatus that accelerates charged particles by means of a strong vertical magnetic field
CYCLUS n cycle
CYCLUSES > CYCLUS
CYDER same as **>** CIDER
CYDERS > CYDER
CYESES > CYESIS
CYESIS the technical name for **>** PREGNANCY
CYGNET n young swan
CYGNETS > CYGNET
CYLICES > CYLIX
CYLIKES > CYLIX
CYLINDER n solid or hollow body with straight sides and circular ends
CYLINDERS > CYLINDER
CYLINDRIC adj shaped like, or characteristic of a cylinder
CYLIX a variant of **>** KYLIX
CYMA n moulding with a double curve, part concave and part convex
CYMAE > CYMA
CYMAGRAPH same as **>** CYMOGRAPH
CYMAR n woman's short fur-trimmed jacket, popular in the 17th and 18th centuries
CYMARS > CYMAR
CYMAS > CYMA
CYMATIA > CYMATIUM
CYMATICS n therapy involving sound waves directed at the body
CYMATIUM n top moulding of a classical cornice or entablature
CYMBAL n percussion instrument
CYMBALEER > CYMBAL
CYMBALER > CYMBAL
CYMBALERS > CYMBAL
CYMBALIST > CYMBAL

CYMBALO another name for > DULCIMER

CYMBALOES > CYMBALO

CYMBALOM same as > CIMBALOM

CYMBALOMS > CYMBALOM

CYMBALOS > CYMBALO

CYMBALS > CYMBAL

CYMBIDIA > CYMBIDIUM

CYMBIDIUM n any orchid of the genus Cymbidium

CYMBIFORM adj shaped like a boat

CYMBLING same as > CYMLING

CYMBLINGS > CYMLING

CYME n type of flower cluster

CYMENE n colourless insoluble liquid

CYMENES > CYMENE

CYMES > CYME

CYMLIN same as > CYMLING

CYMLING n pattypan squash

CYMLINGS > CYMLING

CYMLINS > CYMLIN

CYMOGENE n mixture of volatile flammable hydrocarbons

CYMOGENES > CYMOGENE

CYMOGRAPH n instrument for tracing the outline of an architectural moulding

CYMOID adj resembling a cyme or cyma

CYMOL same as > CYMENE

CYMOLS > CYMOL

CYMOPHANE n yellow or green opalescent variety of chrysoberyl

CYMOSE adj having the characteristics of a cyme

CYMOSELY > CYMOSE

CYMOUS adj relating to a cyme

CYNANCHE n any disease characterized by inflammation and swelling of the throat

CYNANCHES > CYNANCHE

CYNEGETIC adj relating to hunting

CYNIC n person who believes that people always act selfishly ▷ adj of or relating to Sirius, the Dog Star

CYNICAL adj believing that people always act selfishly

CYNICALLY > CYNICAL

CYNICISM n attitude or beliefs of a cynic

CYNICISMS > CYNICISM

CYNICS > CYNIC

CYNODONT n carnivorous mammal-like reptile

CYNODONTS > CYNODONT

CYNOMOLGI n plural form of singular cynomolgus: type of monkey

CYNOSURAL > CYNOSURE

CYNOSURE n centre of attention

CYNOSURES > CYNOSURE

CYPHER same as > CIPHER

CYPHERED > CYPHER

CYPHERING > CYPHER

CYPHERS > CYPHER

CYPRES n legal doctrine

CYPRESES > CYPRES

CYPRESS n evergreen tree with dark green leaves

CYPRESSES > CYPRESS

CYPRIAN n licentious or profligate person

CYPRIANS > CYPRIAN

CYPRID n cypris

CYPRIDES > CYPRIS

CYPRIDS > CYPRID

CYPRINE adj relating to carp ▷ n type of silicate mineral

CYPRINES > CYPRINE

CYPRINID n type of mainly freshwater fish, usu with toothless jaws

CYPRINIDS > CYPRINID

CYPRINOID n type of fish belonging to the suborder which includes cyprinids, electric eels, and loaches

CYPRIS n member of the genus Cypris (small bivalve freshwater crustaceans)

CYPRUS same as > CYPRESS

CYPRUSES > CYPRUS

CYPSELA n dry one-seeded fruit of the daisy and related plants

CYPSELAE > CYPSELA

CYST n (abnormal) sac in the body containing fluid or soft matter

CYSTEIN same as > CYSTEINE

CYSTEINE n sulphur-containing amino acid

CYSTEINES > CYSTEINE

CYSTEINIC > CYSTEINE

CYSTEINS > CYSTEIN

CYSTIC adj of, relating to, or resembling a cyst

CYSTID n cystidean

CYSTIDEAN n any echinoderm of the class Cystoidea, an extinct order of sea lilies

CYSTIDS > CYSTID

CYSTIFORM adj having the form of a cyst

CYSTINE n sulphur-containing amino acid

CYSTINES > CYSTINE

CYSTITIS n inflammation of the bladder

CYSTOCARP n reproductive body in red algae, developed after fertilization and consisting of filaments bearing carpospores

CYSTOCELE n hernia of the urinary bladder

CYSTOID adj resembling a cyst or bladder ▷ n tissue mass that resembles a cyst but lacks an outer membrane

CYSTOIDS > CYSTOID

CYSTOLITH n knoblike deposit of calcium carbonate in the epidermal cells of such plants as the stinging nettle

CYSTOTOMY n surgical incision into the gall bladder or urinary bladder

CYSTS > CYST

CYTASE n cellulose-dissolving enzyme

CYTASES > CYTASE

CYTASTER another word for > ASTER

CYTASTERS > CYTASTER

CYTE n biological cell

CYTES > CYTE

CYTIDINE n nucleoside formed by the condensation of cytosine and ribose

CYTIDINES > CYTIDINE

CYTIDYLIC adj as in cytidylic acid nucleotide that is found in DNA

CYTISI > CYTISUS

CYTISINE n poisonous alkaloid found in laburnum seeds

CYTISINES > CYTISINE

CYTISUS n any plant of the broom genus, Cytisus

CYTODE n mass of protoplasm without a nucleus

CYTODES > CYTODE

CYTOGENY n origin and development of plant cells

CYTOID adj resembling a cell

CYTOKINE n type of protein that carries signals to neighbouring cells

CYTOKINES > CYTOKINE

CYTOKININ n any of a group of plant hormones that promote cell division and retard ageing in plants

CYTOLOGIC > CYTOLOGY

CYTOLOGY n study of plant and animal cells

CYTOLYSES > CYTOLYSIS

CYTOLYSIN n substance that can partially or completely destroy animal cells

CYTOLYSIS n dissolution of cells, esp by the destruction of their membranes

CYTOLYTIC > CYTOLYSIS

CYTOMETER n glass slide used to count and measure blood cells

CYTOMETRY n counting of blood cells using a cytometer

CYTON n main part of a neuron

CYTONS > CYTON

CYTOPATHY n disease of a cell

CYTOPENIA n blood disorder where there is a deficiency in the blood cells

CYTOPLASM n protoplasm of a cell excluding the nucleus

CYTOPLAST n intact cytoplasm of a single cell

CYTOSINE n white crystalline pyrimidine occurring in nucleic acids

CYTOSINES > CYTOSINE

CYTOSOL n solution in a biological cell

CYTOSOLIC > CYTOSOL

CYTOSOLS > CYTOSOL

CYTOSOME n body of a cell excluding its nucleus

CYTOSOMES > CYTOSOME

CYTOTAXES > CYTOTAXIS

CYTOTAXIS n movement of cells due to external stimulation

CYTOTOXIC adj poisonous to living cells: denoting certain drugs used in the treatment of leukaemia and other cancers

CYTOTOXIN n any substance that is poisonous to living cells

CZAPKA n leather and felt peaked military helmet of Polish origin

CZAPKAS > CZAPKA

CZAR same as > TSAR

CZARDAS n Hungarian national dance of alternating slow and fast sections

CZARDASES > CZARDAS

CZARDOM > CZAR

CZARDOMS > CZAR

CZAREVICH n son of a czar

CZAREVNA a variant spelling (esp US) of > TSAREVNA

CZAREVNAS > CZAREVNA

CZARINA variant spelling (esp US) of > TSARINA

CZARINAS > CZARINA

CZARISM a variant spelling (esp US) of > TSARISM

CZARISMS > CZARISM

CZARIST n supporter of the czar

CZARISTS > CZARIST

CZARITSA n Russian empress

CZARITSAS > CZARITSA

CZARITZA same as > CZARINA

CZARITZAS > CZARINA

CZARS > CZAR

Dd

DA n Burmese knife
DAAL n (in Indian cookery) split pulses
DAALS > DAAL
DAB vb pat lightly ▷ n small amount of something soft or moist
DABBA n in Indian cookery, round metal box used to transport hot food
DABBAS > DABBA
DABBED > DAB
DABBER n pad used by printers for applying ink by hand
DABBERS > DABBER
DABBING > DAB
DABBITIES > DABBITY
DABBITY n temporary tattoo
DABBLE vb be involved in something superficially
DABBLED > DABBLE
DABBLER > DABBLE
DABBLERS > DABBLE
DABBLES > DABBLE
DABBLING > DABBLE
DABBLINGS > DABBLE
DABCHICK n type of small grebe
DABCHICKS > DABCHICK
DABS > DAB
DABSTER n incompetent or amateurish worker
DABSTERS > DABSTER
DACE n small European freshwater fish
DACES > DACE
DACHA n country cottage in Russia
DACHAS > DACHA
DACHSHUND n dog with a long body and short legs
DACITE n volcanic rock
DACITES > DACITE
DACK vb remove the trousers from (someone) by force
DACKED > DACK
DACKER vb walk slowly
DACKERED > DACKER
DACKERING > DACKER
DACKERS > DACKER
DACKING > DACK
DACKS > DACK
DACOIT n (in India and Myanmar) a member of a gang of armed robbers
DACOITAGE n robbery by armed gang
DACOITIES > DACOITY
DACOITS > DACOIT

DACOITY n (in India and Myanmar) robbery by an armed gang
DACQUOISE n cake with meringue layers
DACRON n US tradename for a synthetic polyester fibre or fabric
DACRONS > DACRON
DACTYL n metrical foot of three syllables, one long followed by two short
DACTYLAR adj poetry term
DACTYLI > DACTYLUS
DACTYLIC same as **>** DACTYL
DACTYLICS > DACTYLIC
DACTYLIST n poet
DACTYLS > DACTYL
DACTYLUS n tip of a squid's tentacular club
DAD n father ▷ vb act or treat as a father
DADA n nihilistic artistic movement of the early 20th century
DADAH n illegal drugs
DADAHS > DADAH
DADAISM same as **>** DADA
DADAISMS > DADAISM
DADAIST > DADA
DADAISTIC > DADA
DADAISTS > DADA
DADAS > DADA
DADBOD n untoned male physique
DADBODS > DADBOD
DADCHELOR adj as in dadchelor party party held for a prospective father
DADDED > DAD
DADDIES > DADDY
DADDING > DAD
DADDLE vb walk unsteadily
DADDLED > DADDLE
DADDLES > DADDLE
DADDLING > DADDLE
DADDOCK n core of a dead tree
DADDOCKS > DADDOCK
DADDY n father
DADGUM mild form of **>** DAMNED
DADO n lower part of an interior wall decorated differently from the upper part ▷ vb provide with a dado
DADOED > DADO
DADOES > DADO
DADOING > DADO
DADOS > DADO

DADS > DAD
DAE a Scot word for **>** DO
DAEDAL adj skilful or intricate
DAEDALEAN same as **>** DAEDALIAN
DAEDALIAN adj of, relating to, or resembling the work of Daedalus, the Athenian architect and inventor of Greek mythology
DAEDALIC same as **>** DAEDALIAN
DAEING > DAE
DAEMON same as **>** DEMON
DAEMONES > DAEMON
DAEMONIC > DAEMON
DAEMONS > DAEMON
DAES > DAE
DAFF vb frolic
DAFFED > DAFF
DAFFIER > DAFFY
DAFFIES > DAFFY
DAFFIEST > DAFFY
DAFFILY > DAFFY
DAFFINESS > DAFFY
DAFFING > DAFF
DAFFINGS > DAFF
DAFFODIL n yellow trumpet-shaped flower that blooms in spring ▷ adj brilliant yellow
DAFFODILS > DAFFODIL
DAFFS > DAFF
DAFFY adj daft ▷ n daffodil
DAFT adj foolish or crazy
DAFTAR Indian word for **>** OFFICE
DAFTARS > DAFTAR
DAFTER > DAFT
DAFTEST > DAFT
DAFTIE n foolish person
DAFTIES > DAFTIE
DAFTLY > DAFT
DAFTNESS > DAFT
DAG n character ▷ vb cut daglocks from sheep
DAGABA n shrine for Buddhist relics
DAGABAS > DAGABA
DAGGA n cannabis
DAGGAS > DAGGA
DAGGED > DAG
DAGGER n short weapon with pointed blade ▷ vb stab with a dagger
DAGGERED > DAGGER
DAGGERING > DAGGER
DAGGERS > DAGGER
DAGGIER > DAGGY
DAGGIEST > DAGGY
DAGGING > DAG

DAGGINGS > DAG
DAGGLE vb trail through water
DAGGLED > DAGGLE
DAGGLES > DAGGLE
DAGGLING > DAGGLE
DAGGY adj amusing
DAGLOCK n dung-caked lock of wool around the hindquarters of a sheep
DAGLOCKS > DAGLOCK
DAGO n offensive term for a member of a Latin race, esp a Spaniard or Portuguese
DAGOBA n dome-shaped Buddhist shrine
DAGOBAS > DAGOBA
DAGOES > DAGO
DAGOS > DAGO
DAGS > DAG
DAGWOOD n European shrub
DAGWOODS > DAGWOOD
DAH n long sound used in Morse code
DAHABEAH n houseboat used on the Nile
DAHABEAHS > DAHABEAH
DAHABEEAH n Egyptian houseboat
DAHABIAH same as **>** DAHABEAH
DAHABIAHS > DAHABIAH
DAHABIEH n Egyptian houseboat
DAHABIEHS > DAHABIEH
DAHABIYA n Egyptian houseboat
DAHABIYAH n Egyptian houseboat
DAHABIYAS > DAHABIYA
DAHABIYEH n Egyptian houseboat
DAHL same as **>** DHAL
DAHLIA n brightly coloured garden flower
DAHLIAS > DAHLIA
DAHLS > DAHL
DAHOON n evergreen shrub
DAHOONS > DAHOON
DAHS > DAH
DAIDLE vb waddle about
DAIDLED > DAIDLE
DAIDLES > DAIDLE
DAIDLING > DAIDLE
DAIDZEIN n type of protein
DAIDZEINS > DAIDZEIN
DAIKER vb walk slowly
DAIKERED > DAIKER
DAIKERING > DAIKER
DAIKERS > DAIKER
DAIKO n Japanese drum

DAIKON another name for > MOOLI

DAIKONS > DAIKON

DAIKOS > DAIKO

DAILIES > DAILY

DAILINESS > DAILY

DAILY adj occurring every day or every weekday ▷ adv every day ▷ n daily newspaper

DAILYNESS > DAILY

DAIMEN adj occasional

DAIMIO same as > DAIMYO

DAIMIOS > DAIMIO

DAIMOKU n Nichiren Buddhist chant

DAIMOKUS > DAIMOKU

DAIMON same as > DEMON

DAIMONES pl n disembodied souls

DAIMONIC > DAIMON

DAIMONS > DAIMON

DAIMYO n magnate in Japan from the 11th to the 19th century

DAIMYOS > DAIMYO

DAINE vb condescend

DAINED > DAINE

DAINES > DAINE

DAINING > DAINE

DAINT adj dainty ▷ n dainty

DAINTIER > DAINTY

DAINTIES > DAINTY

DAINTIEST > DAINTY

DAINTILY > DAINTY

DAINTS > DAINT

DAINTY adj delicate or elegant ▷ n small cake or sweet

DAIQUIRI n iced drink containing rum, lime juice, and sugar

DAIQUIRIS > DAIQUIRI

DAIRIES > DAIRY

DAIRY n place for the processing or sale of milk and its products ▷ adj of milk or its products

DAIRYING n business of producing, processing, and selling dairy products

DAIRYINGS > DAIRYING

DAIRYMAID n (formerly) woman employed to milk cows

DAIRYMAN n man employed to look after cows

DAIRYMEN > DAIRYMAN

DAIS n raised platform in a hall, used by a speaker

DAISES > DAIS

DAISHIKI n upper garment

DAISHIKIS > DAISHIKI

DAISIED > DAISY

DAISIES > DAISY

DAISY n small wild flower with a yellow centre and white petals

DAISYLIKE adj like a daisy

DAK n system of mail delivery or passenger transport

DAKER vb walk slowly

DAKERED > DAKER

DAKERHEN n European bird

DAKERHENS > DAKERHEN

DAKERING > DAKER

DAKERS > DAKER

DAKOIT same as > DACOIT

DAKOITI same as > DAKOITI

DAKOITIES > DAKOIT

DAKOITIS > DAKOITI

DAKOITS > DAKOIT

DAKOITY n armed robbery

DAKS an informal name for > TROUSERS

DAL same as > DECALITRE

DALAPON n herbicide

DALAPONS > DALAPON

DALASI n standard monetary unit of The Gambia, divided into 100 bututs

DALASIS > DALASI

DALE n (esp in N England) valley

DALED same as > DALETH

DALEDH n letter of Hebrew alphabet

DALEDHS > DALEDH

DALEDS > DALED

DALES > DALE

DALESMAN n person living in a dale, esp in the dales of N England

DALESMEN > DALESMAN

DALETH n fourth letter of the Hebrew alphabet

DALETHS > DALETH

DALGYTE another name for > BILBY

DALGYTES > DALGYTE

DALI n type of tree

DALIS > DALI

DALLE > DALLES

DALLES pl n stretch of a river between high rock walls, with rapids and dangerous currents

DALLIANCE n flirtation

DALLIED > DALLY

DALLIER > DALLY

DALLIERS > DALLY

DALLIES > DALLY

DALLOP n semisolid lump

DALLOPS > DALLOP

DALLY vb waste time

DALLYING > DALLY

DALMAHOY n bushy wig

DALMAHOYS > DALMAHOY

DALMATIAN n breed of dog characterized by its striking spotted markings

DALMATIC n wide-sleeved tunic-like vestment open at the sides, worn by deacons and bishops

DALMATICS > DALMATIC

DALS > DAL

DALT n foster child

DALTON n atomic mass unit

DALTONIAN n colour-blind person

DALTONIC > DALTONISM

DALTONISM n colour blindness, esp the confusion of red and green

DALTONS > DALTON

DALTS > DALT

DAM n barrier built across a river to create a lake ▷ vb build a dam across (a river)

DAMAGE vb harm, spoil ▷ n harm to a person or thing

DAMAGED > DAMAGE

DAMAGER > DAMAGE

DAMAGERS > DAMAGE

DAMAGES pl n money awarded as compensation for injury or loss

DAMAGING > DAMAGE

DAMAN n the Syrian rock hyrax

DAMANS > DAMAN

DAMAR same as > DAMMAR

DAMARS > DAMAR

DAMASCENE vb ornament (metal, esp steel) by etching or by inlaying, usually with gold or silver ▷ n design or article produced by this process ▷ adj of or relating to this process

DAMASK n fabric with a pattern woven into it, used for tablecloths etc ▷ vb ornament (metal) by etching or inlaying, usually with gold or silver

DAMASKED > DAMASK

DAMASKEEN vb decorate metal

DAMASKIN vb decorate metal

DAMASKING > DAMASK

DAMASKINS > DAMASKIN

DAMASKS > DAMASK

DAMASQUIN vb decorate metal

DAMASSIN n patterned damask

DAMASSINS > DAMASSIN

DAMBOARD n draughtboard

DAMBOARDS > DAMBOARD

DAMBROD n draughtboard

DAMBRODS > DAMBROD

DAME n woman

DAMEHOOD n state of being a dame

DAMEHOODS > DAMEHOOD

DAMES > DAME

DAMEWORT n sweet-scented perennial plant with mauve or white flowers

DAMEWORTS > DAMEWORT

DAMFOOL adj foolish ▷ n foolish person

DAMFOOLS > DAMFOOL

DAMIANA n herbal medicine

DAMIANAS > DAMIANA

DAMMAR n any of various resins obtained from SE Asian trees

DAMMARS > DAMMAR

DAMME interj exclamation of surprise

DAMMED > DAM

DAMMER same as > DAMMAR

DAMMERS > DAMMER

DAMMING > DAM

DAMMIT interj exclamation of surprise

DAMN interj exclamation of annoyance ▷ adj extreme(ly) ▷ vb condemn as bad or worthless

DAMNABLE adj annoying

DAMNABLY adv in a detestable manner

DAMNATION interj exclamation of anger ▷ n eternal punishment

DAMNATORY adj threatening or occasioning condemnation

DAMNDEST n utmost

DAMNDESTS > DAMNDEST

DAMNED adj condemned to hell ▷ adv extreme or extremely

DAMNEDER > DAMNED

DAMNEDEST n utmost

DAMNER n person who damns

DAMNERS > DAMNER

DAMNEST same as > DAMNEDEST

DAMNESTS > DAMNEST

DAMNIFIED > DAMNIFY

DAMNIFIES > DAMNIFY

DAMNIFY vb cause loss or damage to (a person)

DAMNING > DAMN

DAMNINGLY > DAMN

DAMNS > DAMN

DAMOISEL same as > DAMSEL

DAMOISELS > DAMOISEL

DAMOSEL same as > DAMSEL

DAMOSELS > DAMOSEL

DAMOZEL n young girl or unmarried woman

DAMOZELS > DAMOZEL

DAMP adj slightly wet ▷ n slight wetness, moisture ▷ vb make damp

DAMPED > DAMP

DAMPEN vb reduce the intensity of

DAMPENED > DAMPEN

DAMPENER > DAMPEN

DAMPENERS > DAMPEN

DAMPENING > DAMPEN

DAMPENS > DAMPEN

DAMPER n movable plate to regulate the draught in a fire

DAMPERS > DAMPER

DAMPEST > DAMP

DAMPIER > DAMPY

DAMPIEST > DAMPY

DAMPING n moistening or wetting

DAMPINGS > DAMPING

DAMPISH > DAMP

DAMPLY > DAMP

DAMPNESS > DAMP

DAMPS > DAMP

DAMPY adj damp

DAMS > DAM

DAMSEL n young woman

DAMSELFLY n type of insect similar to but smaller than a dragonfly

DAMSELS > DAMSEL

DAMSON n small blue-black plumlike fruit

DAMSONS > DAMSON

DAN n in judo, any of the 10 black-belt grades of proficiency

DANAZOL n synthetic male hormone

DANAZOLS > DANAZOL

DANCE vb move the feet and body rhythmically in time to music ▷ n series of steps and movements in time to music

DANCEABLE > DANCE

DANCECORE n type of electronic dance music

DANCED > DANCE
DANCEHALL n style of dance-oriented reggae
DANCELIKE adj like a dance
DANCER > DANCE
DANCERS > DANCE
DANCES > DANCE
DANCETTE another name for > CHEVRON
DANCETTEE adj having a zigzag pattern
DANCETTES > DANCETTE
DANCETTY adj having a zigzag pattern
DANCEWEAR n clothing suitable for dance practice
DANCEY adj of, relating to, or resembling dance music
DANCICAL n type of dance show set to pop music
DANCICALS > DANCICAL
DANCIER > DANCEY
DANCIEST > DANCEY
DANCING > DANCE
DANCINGS > DANCE
DANCY adj (of music) appropriate for dancing
DANDELION n yellow-flowered wild plant
DANDER n stroll ▷ vb stroll
DANDERED > DANDER
DANDERING > DANDER
DANDERS > DANDER
DANDIACAL adj like a dandy
DANDIER > DANDY
DANDIES > DANDY
DANDIEST > DANDY
DANDIFIED > DANDIFY
DANDIFIES > DANDIFY
DANDIFY vb dress like or cause to resemble a dandy
DANDILY > DANDY
DANDIPRAT n small English coin minted in the 16th century
DANDLE vb move (a child) up and down on one's knee
DANDLED > DANDLE
DANDLER > DANDLE
DANDLERS > DANDLE
DANDLES > DANDLE
DANDLING > DANDLE
DANDRIFF same as > DANDRUFF
DANDRIFFS > DANDRIFF
DANDRUFF n loose scales of dry dead skin shed from the scalp
DANDRUFFS > DANDRUFF
DANDRUFFY adj like dandruff
DANDY n man who is overconcerned with the elegance of his appearance ▷ adj very good
DANDYFUNK n ship's biscuit
DANDYISH > DANDY
DANDYISM > DANDY
DANDYISMS > DANDY
DANDYPRAT n English coin
DANEGELD n tax levied in Anglo-Saxon England to provide protection from Viking invaders
DANEGELDS > DANEGELD
DANEGELT same as > DANEGELD

DANEGELTS > DANEGELT
DANELAGH same as > DANELAW
DANELAGIIS > DANELAGH
DANELAW n Danish law in parts of Anglo-Saxon England
DANELAWS > DANELAW
DANEWEED n dwarf elder
DANEWEEDS > DANEWEED
DANEWORT n dwarf elder
DANEWORTS > DANEWORT
DANG vb euphemism for damn, meaning condemn ▷ adj euphemism for damn, meaning extreme(ly)
DANGED > DANG
DANGER n state of being vulnerable to injury, loss, or evil ▷ vb in archaic usage, endanger
DANGERED > DANGER
DANGERING > DANGER
DANGEROUS adj likely or able to cause injury or harm
DANGERS > DANGER
DANGEST > DANG
DANGING > DANG
DANGLE vb hang loosely ▷ n act of dangling or something that dangles
DANGLED > DANGLE
DANGLER > DANGLE
DANGLERS > DANGLE
DANGLES > DANGLE
DANGLIER > DANGLE
DANGLIEST > DANGLE
DANGLING > DANGLE
DANGLINGS > DANGLE
DANGLY > DANGLE
DANGS > DANG
DANIO n type of tropical freshwater fish
DANIOS > DANIO
DANISH n sweet pastry
DANISHES > DANISH
DANK adj unpleasantly damp and chilly ▷ n unpleasant damp and chilliness
DANKER > DANK
DANKEST > DANK
DANKISH > DANK
DANKLY > DANK
DANKNESS > DANK
DANKS > DANK
DANNEBROG n Danish flag
DANNIES > DANNY
DANNY n hand (used esp when addressing children)
DANS > DAN
DANSAK n type of Indian dish
DANSAKS > DANSAK
DANSEUR n male ballet dancer
DANSEURS > DANSEUR
DANSEUSE n female ballet dancer
DANSEUSES > DANSEUSE
DANT vb intimidate
DANTED > DANT
DANTHONIA n type of grass of N temperate regions and S America
DANTING > DANT
DANTON same as > DAUNTON
DANTONED > DANTON
DANTONING > DANTON

DANTONS > DANTON
DANTS > DANT
DAP vb engage in type of fly fishing
DAPHNE n ornamental Eurasian shrub
DAPHNES > DAPHNE
DAPHNIA n type of water flea
DAPHNIAS > DAPHNIA
DAPHNID n water flea
DAPHNIDS > DAPHNID
DAPPED > DAP
DAPPER adj (of a man) neat in appearance ▷ n fisherman or-woman who uses a bobbing bait
DAPPERER > DAPPER
DAPPEREST > DAPPER
DAPPERLY > DAPPER
DAPPERS > DAPPER
DAPPING > DAP
DAPPLE vb mark or become marked with spots or patches of a different colour ▷ n mottled or spotted markings ▷ adj marked with dapples or spots
DAPPLED > DAPPLE
DAPPLES > DAPPLE
DAPPLING > DAPPLE
DAPS > DAP
DAPSONE n antimicrobial drug
DAPSONES > DAPSONE
DAQUIRI n rum cocktail
DAQUIRIS > DAQUIRI
DARAF n unit of elastance equal to a reciprocal farad
DARAFS > DARAF
DARB n something excellent
DARBAR n hall in Sikh temple
DARBARS > DARBAR
DARBIES pl n handcuffs
DARBS > DARB
DARCIES > DARCY
DARCY n unit expressing the permeability coefficient of rock
DARCYS > DARCY
DARE vb be courageous enough to try (to do something) ▷ n challenge to do something risky
DARED > DARE
DAREDEVIL n recklessly bold person ▷ adj recklessly bold or daring
DAREFUL adj daring
DARER > DARE
DARERS > DARE
DARES > DARE
DARESAY vb venture to say
DARG n day's work
DARGA n Muslim shrine
DARGAH n tomb of a Muslim saint
DARGAHS > DARGAH
DARGAS > DARGA
DARGLE n wooded hollow
DARGLES > DARGLE
DARGS > DARG
DARI n variety of sorghum
DARIC n gold coin of ancient Persia
DARICS > DARIC

DARING adj willing to take risks ▷ n courage to do dangerous things
DARINGLY > DARING
DARINGS > DARING
DARIOLE n small cup-shaped mould
DARIOLES > DARIOLE
DARIS > DARI
DARK adj having little or no light ▷ n absence of light ▷ vb in archaic usage, darken
DARKED > DARK
DARKEN vb make or become dark or darker
DARKENED > DARKEN
DARKENER > DARKEN
DARKENERS > DARKEN
DARKENING > DARKEN
DARKENS > DARKEN
DARKER > DARK
DARKEST > DARK
DARKEY same as > DARKY
DARKEYS > DARKEY
DARKFIELD n as in darkfield microscope kind of microscope
DARKIE same as > DARKY
DARKIES > DARKY
DARKING > DARK
DARKISH > DARK
DARKLE vb grow dark
DARKLED > DARKLE
DARKLES > DARKLE
DARKLIER > DARK
DARKLIEST > DARK
DARKLING adj in the dark or night
DARKLINGS adv in darkness
DARKLY > DARK
DARKMANS n slang term for night-time
DARKNESS > DARK
DARKNET n covert communication network on the internet
DARKNETS > DARKNET
DARKROOM n darkened room for processing photographic film
DARKROOMS > DARKROOM
DARKS > DARK
DARKSOME adj dark or darkish
DARKY n offensive word for a Black person
DARLING n much-loved person ▷ adj much-loved
DARLINGLY > DARLING
DARLINGS > DARLING
DARN vb mend (a garment) with a series of interwoven stitches ▷ n patch of darned work
DARNATION mild form of > DAMNATION
DARNDEST n utmost
DARNDESTS > DARNDEST
DARNED adj damned
DARNEDER > DARNED
DARNEDEST a euphemistic word for > DAMNEDEST
DARNEL n weed that grows in grain fields
DARNELS > DARNEL
DARNER > DARN
DARNERS > DARN

DARNEST same as > DARNDEST

DARNESTS > DARNEST

DARNING > DARN

DARNINGS > DARN

DARNS > DARN

DAROGHA n in India, manager

DAROGHAS > DAROGHA

DARRAIGN same as > DERAIGN

DARRAIGNE vb clear from guilt

DARRAIGNS > DARRAIGN

DARRAIN vb clear of guilt

DARRAINE vb clear of guilt

DARRAINED > DARRAINE

DARRAINES > DARRAINE

DARRAINS > DARRAIN

DARRAYN vb clear of guilt

DARRAYNED > DARRAYN

DARRAYNS > DARRAYN

DARRE vb archaic spelling of dare

DARRED > DARRE

DARRES > DARRE

DARRING > DARRE

DARSHAN n Hindu blessing

DARSHANS > DARSHAN

DART n small narrow pointed missile ▷ vb move or direct quickly and suddenly

DARTBOARD n circular board used as the target in the game of darts

DARTED > DART

DARTER n type of aquatic bird

DARTERS > DARTER

DARTING > DART

DARTINGLY > DART

DARTITIS n nervous twitching while playing darts

DARTLE vb move swiftly

DARTLED > DARTLE

DARTLES > DARTLE

DARTLING > DARTLE

DARTRE n skin disease

DARTRES > DARTRE

DARTROUS adj having a skin disease

DARTS n game in which darts are thrown at a dartboard

DARZI n tailor in India

DARZIS > DARZI

DAS > DA

DASH vb move quickly ▷ n sudden quick movement

DASHBOARD n instrument panel in a vehicle

DASHCAM n video camera on a vehicle's dashboard

DASHCAMS > DASHCAM

DASHED > DASH

DASHEEN another name for > TARO

DASHEENS > DASHEEN

DASHEKI n upper garment

DASHEKIS > DASHEKI

DASHER n one of the boards surrounding an ice-hockey rink

DASHERS > DASHER

DASHES > DASH

DASHI n clear stock made from dried fish and kelp

DASHIER > DASHY

DASHIEST > DASHY

DASHIKI n large loose-fitting buttonless upper garment

DASHIKIS > DASHIKI

DASHING adj stylish and attractive

DASHINGLY > DASHING

DASHIS > DASHI

DASHLIGHT n light illuminating the dashboard of an automobile

DASHPOT n device for damping vibrations

DASHPOTS > DASHPOT

DASHY adj showy

DASSIE n type of hoofed rodent-like animal

DASSIES > DASSIE

DASTARD n contemptible sneaking coward

DASTARDLY adj wicked and cowardly

DASTARDS > DASTARD

DASTARDY n cowardice

DASYMETER n device for measuring density of gases

DASYPOD n armadillo

DASYPODS > DASYPOD

DASYURE n small marsupial of Australia, New Guinea, and adjacent islands

DASYURES > DASYURE

DATA n information consisting of observations, measurements, or facts

DATABANK n store of a large amount of information

DATABANKS > DATABANK

DATABASE n store of information in a form that can be easily handled by a computer ▷ vb put data into a database

DATABASED > DATABASE

DATABASES > DATABASE

DATABLE > DATE

DATABUS n computing term

DATABUSES > DATABUS

DATACARD n smart card

DATACARDS > DATACARD

DATACOMMS n computing term

DATAFLOW n as in dataflow architecture means of arranging computer data processing

DATAGLOVE n computing term

DATAGRAM n (in computing) self-contained unit of data transmitted in a packet-switched network

DATAGRAMS > DATAGRAM

DATAL adj slow-witted ▷ n day labour

DATALLER n worker paid by the day

DATALLERS > DATALLER

DATALS > DATAL

DATARIA n Roman Catholic office

DATARIAS > DATARIA

DATARIES > DATARY

DATARY n head of the dataria

DATCHA same as > DACHA

DATCHAS > DATCHA

DATE n specified day of the month ▷ vb mark with the date

DATEABLE > DATE

DATEBOOK n list of forthcoming events

DATEBOOKS > DATEBOOK

DATED adj old-fashioned

DATEDLY > DATED

DATEDNESS > DATED

DATELESS > DATE

DATELINE n information about the place and time an article was written

DATELINED > DATELINE

DATELINES > DATELINE

DATER n person who dates

DATERS > DATER

DATES > DATE

DATING n any of several techniques for establishing the age of objects

DATINGS > DATING

DATIVAL > DATIVE

DATIVE adj denoting a grammatical case ▷ n grammatical case

DATIVELY > DATIVE

DATIVES > DATIVE

DATO n chief of any of certain Muslim tribes in the Philippine Islands

DATOLITE n colourless mineral

DATOLITES > DATOLITE

DATOS > DATO

DATTO n Datsun car

DATTOS > DATTO

DATUM n single piece of information in the form of a fact or statistic

DATUMS > DATUM

DATURA n type of plant

DATURAS > DATURA

DATURIC > DATURA

DATURINE n poisonous alkaloid

DATURINES > DATURINE

DAUB vb smear or spread quickly or clumsily ▷ n crude or badly done painting

DAUBE n braised meat stew

DAUBED > DAUB

DAUBER > DAUB

DAUBERIES > DAUBERY

DAUBERS > DAUB

DAUBERY n act or an instance of daubing

DAUBES > DAUBE

DAUBIER > DAUB

DAUBIEST > DAUB

DAUBING > DAUB

DAUBINGLY > DAUB

DAUBINGS > DAUB

DAUBRIES > DAUBRY

DAUBRY n unskilful painting

DAUBS > DAUB

DAUBY > DAUB

DAUD n lump or chunk of something ▷ vb (in dialect) whack

DAUDED > DAUD

DAUDING > DAUD

DAUDS > DAUD

DAUGHTER n female child ▷ adj denoting a cell, chromosome, etc produced by the division of one of its own kind

DAUGHTERS > DAUGHTER

DAULT n foster child

DAULTS > DAULT

DAUNDER vb stroll

DAUNDERED > DAUNDER

DAUNDERS > DAUNDER

DAUNER vb stroll

DAUNERED > DAUNER

DAUNERING > DAUNER

DAUNERS > DAUNER

DAUNT vb intimidate

DAUNTED > DAUNT

DAUNTER > DAUNT

DAUNTERS > DAUNT

DAUNTING adj intimidating or worrying

DAUNTLESS adj fearless

DAUNTON vb dishearten

DAUNTONED > DAUNTON

DAUNTONS > DAUNTON

DAUNTS > DAUNT

DAUPHIN n (formerly) eldest son of the king of France

DAUPHINE n wife of a dauphin

DAUPHINES > DAUPHINE

DAUPHINS > DAUPHIN

DAUR a Scot word for > DARE

DAURED > DAUR

DAURING > DAUR

DAURS > DAUR

DAUT vb fondle

DAUTED > DAUT

DAUTIE n darling

DAUTIES > DAUTIE

DAUTING > DAUT

DAUTS > DAUT

DAVEN vb pray

DAVENED > DAVEN

DAVENING > DAVEN

DAVENPORT n small writing table with drawers

DAVENS > DAVEN

DAVIDIA n Chinese shrub

DAVIDIAS > DAVIDIA

DAVIES > DAVY

DAVIT n crane, usu one of a pair, at a ship's side, for lowering and hoisting a lifeboat

DAVITS > DAVIT

DAVY n miner's safety lamp

DAW n archaic, dialect, or poetic name for a jackdaw ▷ vb old word for dawn

DAWAH n practice of educating non-Muslims about the message of Islam

DAWAHS > DAWAH

DAWBAKE n foolish or slow-witted person

DAWBAKES > DAWBAKE

DAWBRIES > DAWBRY

DAWBRY n unskilful painting

DAWCOCK n male jackdaw

DAWCOCKS > DAWCOCK

DAWD vb thump

DAWDED > DAWD

DAWDING > DAWD

DAWDLE vb walk slowly, lag behind

d

DAWDLED > DAWDLE
DAWDLER > DAWDLE
DAWDLERS > DAWDLE
DAWDLES > DAWDLE
DAWDLING n act or instance of lagging behind
DAWDLINGS > DAWDLING
DAWDS > DAWD
DAWED > DAW
DAWEN > DAW
DAWING > DAW
DAWISH > DAW
DAWK same as > DAK
DAWKS > DAWK
DAWN n daybreak ▷ vb begin to grow light
DAWNED > DAWN
DAWNER vb stroll
DAWNERED > DAWNER
DAWNERING > DAWNER
DAWNERS > DAWNER
DAWNEY adj (of a person) dull or slow
DAWNING > DAWN
DAWNINGS > DAWN
DAWNLIKE > DAWN
DAWNS > DAWN
DAWS > DAW
DAWSONITE n mineral
DAWT vb fondle
DAWTED > DAWT
DAWTIE n darling
DAWTIES > DAWTIE
DAWTING > DAWT
DAWTS > DAWT
DAY n period of 24 hours
DAYAN n senior rabbi, esp one who sits in a religious court
DAYANIM > DAYAN
DAYANS > DAYAN
DAYBED n narrow bed for day use
DAYBEDS > DAYBED
DAYBOAT n small sailing boat with no sleeping accommodation
DAYBOATS > DAYBOAT
DAYBOOK n book in which transactions are recorded as they occur
DAYBOOKS > DAYBOOK
DAYBOY n boy who attends a boarding school but returns home each evening
DAYBOYS > DAYBOY
DAYBREAK n time in the morning when light first appears
DAYBREAKS > DAYBREAK
DAYCARE n care provided during the working day for people who might be at risk if left on their own
DAYCARES > DAYCARE
DAYCATION n day trip to a place
DAYCENTRE n building used for daycare or other welfare services
DAYCH vb thatch
DAYCHED > DAYCH
DAYCHES > DAYCH
DAYCHING > DAYCH
DAYDREAM n pleasant fantasy indulged in while awake ▷ vb indulge in idle fantasy

DAYDREAMS > DAYDREAM
DAYDREAMT > DAYDREAM
DAYDREAMY adj tending to daydream
DAYFLIES > DAYFLY
DAYFLOWER n type of tropical and subtropical plant with narrow pointed leaves and blue or purplish flowers which wilt quickly
DAYFLY another name for > MAYFLY
DAYGIRL n girl who attends a boarding school but returns home each evening
DAYGIRLS > DAYGIRL
DAYGLO n fluorescent colours
DAYGLOW n fluorescent colours
DAYGLOWS > DAYGLOW
DAYLIGHT n light from the sun
DAYLIGHTS pl n consciousness or wits
DAYLILIES > DAYLILY
DAYLILY n any of various plants having lily-like flowers
DAYLIT > DAYLIGHT
DAYLONG adv lasting the entire day
DAYMARE n bad dream during the day
DAYMARES > DAYMARE
DAYMARK n navigation aid
DAYMARKS > DAYMARK
DAYNT adj dainty ▷ n thing or condition that is extravagant or best
DAYNTS > DAYNT
DAYPACK n small rucksack
DAYPACKS > DAYPACK
DAYROOM n communal living room in a residential institution
DAYROOMS > DAYROOM
DAYS adv during the day, esp regularly
DAYSACK n rucksack
DAYSACKS > DAYSACK
DAYSAIL vb take day trip on a sailing boat or yacht
DAYSAILED > DAYSAIL
DAYSAILER same as > DAYSAILOR
DAYSAILOR n small sailing boat with no sleeping accommodation
DAYSAILS > DAYSAIL
DAYSHELL n thistle
DAYSHELLS > DAYSHELL
DAYSIDE n side of a planet nearest the sun
DAYSIDES > DAYSIDE
DAYSMAN n umpire
DAYSMEN > DAYSMAN
DAYSPRING a poetic word for > DAWN
DAYSTAR a poetic word for > SUN
DAYSTARS > DAYSTAR
DAYTALE n day labour
DAYTALER n worker paid by the day
DAYTALERS > DAYTALER
DAYTALES > DAYTALE
DAYTIME n time from sunrise to sunset

DAYTIMES > DAYTIME
DAYWEAR n clothes for everyday or informal wear
DAYWEARS > DAYWEAR
DAYWORK n daytime work
DAYWORKER > DAYWORK
DAYWORKS > DAYWORK
DAZE vb stun, by a blow or shock ▷ n state of confusion or shock
DAZED > DAZE
DAZEDLY > DAZE
DAZEDNESS > DAZE
DAZER > DAZE
DAZERS > DAZE
DAZES > DAZE
DAZING > DAZE
DAZZLE vb impress greatly ▷ n bright light that dazzles
DAZZLED > DAZZLE
DAZZLER > DAZZLE
DAZZLERS > DAZZLE
DAZZLES > DAZZLE
DAZZLING > DAZZLE
DAZZLINGS > DAZZLING
DE prep of or from
DEACIDIFY vb removal acid from
DEACON n ordained minister ranking immediately below a priest ▷ vb make a deacon of
DEACONED > DEACON
DEACONESS n (in the early church and in some modern Churches) a female member of the laity with duties similar to those of a deacon
DEACONING > DEACON
DEACONRY n office or status of a deacon
DEACONS > DEACON
DEAD adj no longer alive ▷ n period during which coldness or darkness is most intense ▷ adv extremely ▷ vb in archaic usage, die or kill
DEADBEAT n lazy useless person
DEADBEATS > DEADBEAT
DEADBOLT n bolt operated without a spring
DEADBOLTS > DEADBOLT
DEADBOY same as > DEADMAN
DEADBOYS > DEADBOY
DEADED > DEAD
DEADEN vb make less intense
DEADENED > DEADEN
DEADENER > DEADEN
DEADENERS > DEADEN
DEADENING > DEADEN
DEADENS > DEADEN
DEADER > DEAD
DEADERS > DEAD
DEADEST > DEAD
DEADEYE n either of two disclike blocks used to tighten a shroud on a boat
DEADEYES > DEADEYE
DEADFALL n type of trap using a heavy weight to crush prey
DEADFALLS > DEADFALL
DEADHEAD n person who does not pay on a bus, at a game, etc ▷ vb cut off withered flowers from (a plant)

DEADHEADS > DEADHEAD
DEADHOUSE n mortuary
DEADING > DEAD
DEADLIER > DEADLY
DEADLIEST > DEADLY
DEADLIFT vb weightlifting term
DEADLIFTS > DEADLIFT
DEADLIGHT n bull's-eye let into the deck or hull of a vessel to admit light to a cabin
DEADLINE n time limit ▷ vb put a time limit on an action, decision, etc
DEADLINED > DEADLINE
DEADLINES > DEADLINE
DEADLOCK n point in a dispute at which no agreement can be reached ▷ vb bring or come to a deadlock
DEADLOCKS > DEADLOCK
DEADLY adj likely to cause death ▷ adv extremely
DEADMAN n item used in construction
DEADMEN > DEADMAN
DEADNESS > DEAD
DEADPAN adv showing no emotion or expression ▷ adj deliberately emotionless ▷ n deadpan expression or manner
DEADPANS > DEADPAN
DEADS > DEAD
DEADSTOCK n farm equipment
DEADWATER n still water
DEADWOOD n dead trees or branches
DEADWOODS > DEADWOOD
DEAERATE vb remove air from
DEAERATED > DEAERATE
DEAERATES > DEAERATE
DEAERATOR > DEAERATE
DEAF adj unable to hear
DEAFBLIND adj unable to hear or see
DEAFEN vb make deaf, esp temporarily
DEAFENED > DEAFEN
DEAFENING n excessively loud
DEAFENS > DEAFEN
DEAFER > DEAF
DEAFEST > DEAF
DEAFISH > DEAF
DEAFLY > DEAF
DEAFNESS > DEAF
DEAIR vb remove air from
DEAIRED > DEAIR
DEAIRING > DEAIR
DEAIRS > DEAIR
DEAL n agreement or transaction ▷ vb inflict (a blow) on ▷ adj of fir or pine
DEALATE adj (of insects) having lost their wings after mating ▷ n insect that has shed its wings
DEALATED same as > DEALATE
DEALATES > DEALATE
DEALATION > DEALATE
DEALBATE adj bleached

DEALER n person whose business involves buying and selling

DEALERS > DEALER

DEALFISH n long thin fish

DEALIGN vb fall out of agreement with (a political party)

DEALIGNED > DEALIGN

DEALIGNS > DEALIGN

DEALING > DEAL

DEALINGS pl n transactions or business relations

DEALMAKER n person who makes deals

DEALS > DEAL

DEALT > DEAL

DEAMINASE n enzyme that breaks down amino compounds

DEAMINATE vb remove one or more amino groups from (a molecule)

DEAMINISE same as > DEAMINATE

DEAMINIZE same as > DEAMINATE

DEAN n chief administrative official of a college or university faculty ▷ vb punish (a student) by sending them to the dean

DEANED > DEAN

DEANER n shilling

DEANERIES > DEANERY

DEANERS > DEANER

DEANERY n office or residence of a dean

DEANING > DEAN

DEANS > DEAN

DEANSHIP > DEAN

DEANSHIPS > DEAN

DEAR n someone regarded with affection ▷ adj much-loved

DEARE vb harm

DEARED > DEARE

DEARER > DEAR

DEARES > DEARE

DEAREST n term of affection

DEARESTS > DEAREST

DEARIE same as > DEARY

DEARIES > DEARY

DEARING > DEARE

DEARLING n darling

DEARLINGS > DEARLING

DEARLY adv very much

DEARN vb hide

DEARNED > DEARN

DEARNESS > DEAR

DEARNFUL adj secret

DEARNING > DEARN

DEARNLY > DEARN

DEARNS > DEARN

DEARS > DEAR

DEARTH n inadequate amount, scarcity

DEARTHS > DEARTH

DEARY n term of affection: now often sarcastic or facetious

DEASH vb remove ash from

DEASHED > DEASH

DEASHES > DEASH

DEASHING > DEASH

DEASIL adv in the direction of the apparent course of the sun ▷ n motion in this direction

DEASILS > DEASIL

DEASIUL n motion towards the sun

DEASIULS > DEASIUL

DEASOIL n motion towards the sun

DEASOILS > DEASOIL

DEATH n permanent end of life in a person or animal

DEATHBED n bed where a person is about to die or has just died

DEATHBEDS > DEATHBED

DEATHBLOW n thing or event that destroys hope

DEATHCARE adj relating to services helping arrange funerals

DEATHCUP n poisonous fungus

DEATHCUPS > DEATHCUP

DEATHFUL adj murderous

DEATHIER > DEATH

DEATHIEST > DEATH

DEATHLESS adj everlasting, because of fine qualities

DEATHLIER > DEATHLY

DEATHLIKE > DEATH

DEATHLY adv like death ▷ adj resembling death

DEATHS > DEATH

DEATHSMAN n executioner

DEATHSMEN > DEATHSMAN

DEATHTRAP n building, vehicle, etc, that is considered very unsafe

DEATHWARD adv heading towards death

DEATHY > DEATH

DEAVE vb deafen

DEAVED > DEAVE

DEAVES > DEAVE

DEAVING > DEAVE

DEAW n archaic spelling of dew ▷ vb cover with dew

DEAWED > DEAW

DEAWIE > DEAW

DEAWING > DEAW

DEAWS > DEAW

DEAWY > DEAW

DEB n debutante

DEBACLE n disastrous failure

DEBACLES > DEBACLE

DEBAG vb remove the trousers from (someone) by force

DEBAGGED > DEBAG

DEBAGGING > DEBAG

DEBAGS > DEBAG

DEBAR vb prevent, bar

DEBARK vb remove the bark from (a tree)

DEBARKED > DEBARK

DEBARKER > DEBARK

DEBARKERS > DEBARK

DEBARKING > DEBARK

DEBARKS > DEBARK

DEBARMENT > DEBAR

DEBARRASS vb relieve

DEBARRED > DEBAR

DEBARRING > DEBAR

DEBARS > DEBAR

DEBASE vb lower in value, quality, or character

DEBASED > DEBASE

DEBASER > DEBASE

DEBASERS > DEBASE

DEBASES > DEBASE

DEBASING > DEBASE

DEBATABLE adj not absolutely certain

DEBATABLY > DEBATABLE

DEBATE n discussion ▷ vb discuss formally

DEBATED > DEBATE

DEBATEFUL adj quarrelsome

DEBATER > DEBATE

DEBATERS > DEBATE

DEBATES > DEBATE

DEBATING n act of debating

DEBATINGS > DEBATING

DEBAUCH vb make (someone) bad or corrupt ▷ n instance or period of extreme dissipation

DEBAUCHED > DEBAUCH

DEBAUCHEE n man who leads a life of reckless dissipation

DEBAUCHER > DEBAUCH

DEBAUCHES > DEBAUCH

DEBBIER > DEBBY

DEBBIES > DEBBY

DEBBIEST > DEBBY

DEBBY n debutante ▷ adj of, or resembling a debutante

DEBE n tin

DEBEAK vb remove part of the beak of poultry

DEBEAKED > DEBEAK

DEBEAKING > DEBEAK

DEBEAKS > DEBEAK

DEBEARD vb remove beard from mussel

DEBEARDED > DEBEARD

DEBEARDS > DEBEARD

DEBEL vb beat in war

DEBELLED > DEBEL

DEBELLING > DEBEL

DEBELS > DEBEL

DEBENTURE n long-term bond bearing fixed interest, issued by a company or a government agency

DEBES > DEBE

DEBILE adj lacking strength

DEBILITY n weakness, infirmity

DEBIT n sum owing entered on the left side of an account ▷ vb charge (an account) with a debt

DEBITED > DEBIT

DEBITING > DEBIT

DEBITOR n person in debt

DEBITORS > DEBITOR

DEBITS > DEBIT

DEBONAIR adj charming and refined

DEBONAIRE adj suave and refined

DEBONE vb remove bones from

DEBONED > DEBONE

DEBONER > DEBONE

DEBONERS > DEBONE

DEBONES > DEBONE

DEBONING > DEBONE

DEBOSH vb debauch

DEBOSHED > DEBOSH

DEBOSHES > DEBOSH

DEBOSHING > DEBOSH

DEBOSS vb carve a design into

DEBOSSED > DEBOSS

DEBOSSES > DEBOSS

DEBOSSING > DEBOSS

DEBOUCH vb move out from a narrow place to a wider one ▷ n outlet or passage, as for the exit of troops

DEBOUCHE same as > DEBOUCH

DEBOUCHED > DEBOUCH

DEBOUCHES > DEBOUCH

DEBRIDE vb remove dead tissue from

DEBRIDED > DEBRIDE

DEBRIDES > DEBRIDE

DEBRIDING > DEBRIDE

DEBRIEF vb receive a report from (a soldier, diplomat, etc) after an event

DEBRIEFED > DEBRIEF

DEBRIEFER > DEBRIEF

DEBRIEFS > DEBRIEF

DEBRIS n fragments of something destroyed

DEBRUISE vb (in heraldry) overlay or partly cover

DEBRUISED > DEBRUISE

DEBRUISES > DEBRUISE

DEBS > DEB

DEBT n something owed, esp money

DEBTED adj in debt

DEBTEE n person owed a debt

DEBTEES > DEBTEE

DEBTLESS > DEBT

DEBTOR n person who owes money

DEBTORS > DEBTOR

DEBTS > DEBT

DEBUD same as > DISBUD

DEBUDDED > DEBUD

DEBUDDING > DEBUD

DEBUDS > DEBUD

DEBUG vb find and remove defects in (a computer program) ▷ n something that locates and removes defects in a device, system, etc

DEBUGGED > DEBUG

DEBUGGER > DEBUG

DEBUGGERS > DEBUG

DEBUGGING n act of debugging

DEBUGS > DEBUG

DEBUNK vb expose the falseness of

DEBUNKED > DEBUNK

DEBUNKER > DEBUNK

DEBUNKERS > DEBUNK

DEBUNKING > DEBUNK

DEBUNKS > DEBUNK

DEBUR vb remove burs from (a piece of machined metal)

DEBURR vb remove burrs from (a workpiece)

DEBURRED > DEBURR

DEBURRING > DEBURR

DEBURRS > DEBURR

DEBURS > DEBUR

DEBUS vb unload (goods) or (esp of troops) to alight from a motor vehicle

d

DEBUSED > DEBUS

DEBUSES > DEBUS

DEBUSING > DEBUS

DEBUSSED > DEBUS

DEBUSSES > DEBUS

DEBUSSING > DEBUS

DEBUT n first public appearance of a performer ▷ vb make a debut

DEBUTANT n person making a first appearance in a particular capacity

DEBUTANTE n young upper-class woman being formally presented to society

DEBUTANTS > DEBUTANT

DEBUTED > DEBUT

DEBUTING > DEBUT

DEBUTS > DEBUT

DEBYE n unit of electric dipole moment

DEBYES > DEBYE

DECACHORD n instrument with ten strings

DECAD n ten years

DECADAL > DECADE

DECADE n period of ten years

DECADENCE n deterioration in morality or culture

DECADENCY same as > DECADENCE

DECADENT adj characterized by decay or decline, as in being self-indulgent or morally corrupt ▷ n decadent person

DECADENTS > DECADENT

DECADES > DECADE

DECADS > DECAD

DECAF n decaffeinated coffee ▷ adj decaffeinated

DECAFF n decaffeinated coffee

DECAFFS > DECAFF

DECAFS > DECAF

DECAGON n geometric figure with ten faces

DECAGONAL > DECAGON

DECAGONS > DECAGON

DECAGRAM n ten grams

DECAGRAMS > DECAGRAM

DECAHEDRA n plural form of singular decahedron: solid figure with ten plane faces

DECAL vb transfer (a design) by decalcomania

DECALCIFY vb remove calcium or lime from (bones, teeth, etc)

DECALED > DECAL

DECALING > DECAL

DECALITER same as > DECALITRE

DECALITRE n measure of volume equivalent to 10 litres

DECALLED > DECAL

DECALLING > DECAL

DECALOG same as > DECALOGUE

DECALOGS > DECALOG

DECALOGUE n Ten Commandments

DECALS > DECAL

DECAMETER same as > DECAMETRE

DECAMETRE n unit of length equal to ten metres

DECAMP vb depart secretly or suddenly

DECAMPED > DECAMP

DECAMPING > DECAMP

DECAMPS > DECAMP

DECAN n one of three divisions of a sign of the zodiac

DECANAL adj of or relating to a dean or deanery

DECANALLY > DECANAL

DECANE n liquid alkane hydrocarbon

DECANES > DECANE

DECANI adj to be sung by the decanal side of a choir

DECANOIC adj as in decanoic acid white crystalline insoluble carboxylic acid

DECANS > DECAN

DECANT vb pour (a liquid) from one container to another

DECANTATE vb decant

DECANTED > DECANT

DECANTER n stoppered bottle for wine or spirits

DECANTERS > DECANTER

DECANTING > DECANT

DECANTS > DECANT

DECAPOD n creature, such as a crab, with five pairs of walking limbs ▷ adj of, relating to, or belonging to these creatures

DECAPODAL > DECAPOD

DECAPODAN > DECAPOD

DECAPODS > DECAPOD

DECARB vb decoke

DECARBED > DECARB

DECARBING > DECARB

DECARBS > DECARB

DECARE n ten ares or 1000 square metres

DECARES > DECARE

DECASTERE n ten steres

DECASTICH n poem with ten lines

DECASTYLE n portico consisting of ten columns

DECATHLON n athletic contest with ten events

DECAUDATE vb remove the tail from

DECAY vb become weaker or more corrupt ▷ n process of decaying

DECAYABLE > DECAY

DECAYED > DECAY

DECAYER > DECAY

DECAYERS > DECAY

DECAYING > DECAY

DECAYLESS adj immortal

DECAYS > DECAY

DECCIE n decoration

DECCIES > DECCIE

DECEASE n death

DECEASED adj dead ▷ n dead person

DECEASEDS > DECEASED

DECEASES > DECEASE

DECEASING > DECEASE

DECEDENT n deceased person

DECEDENTS > DECEDENT

DECEIT n behaviour intended to deceive

DECEITFUL adj full of deceit

DECEITS > DECEIT

DECEIVE vb mislead by lying

DECEIVED > DECEIVE

DECEIVER > DECEIVE

DECEIVERS > DECEIVE

DECEIVES > DECEIVE

DECEIVING > DECEIVE

DECELERON n type of aileron

DECEMVIR n member of a board of ten magistrates in Ancient Rome

DECEMVIRI > DECEMVIR

DECEMVIRS > DECEMVIR

DECENARY adj of or relating to a tithing

DECENCIES pl n generally accepted standards of good behaviour

DECENCY n conformity to the prevailing standards of what is right

DECENNARY same as > DECENARY

DECENNIA > DECENNIUM

DECENNIAL adj lasting for ten years ▷ n tenth anniversary or its celebration

DECENNIUM a less common word for > DECADE

DECENT adj (of a person) polite and morally acceptable

DECENTER vb put out of centre

DECENTERS > DECENTER

DECENTEST > DECENT

DECENTLY > DECENT

DECENTRE vb put out of centre

DECENTRED > DECENTRE

DECENTRES > DECENTRE

DECEPTION n deceiving

DECEPTIVE adj likely or designed to deceive

DECEPTORY adj deceiving

DECERN vb decree or adjudge

DECERNED > DECERN

DECERNING > DECERN

DECERNS > DECERN

DECERTIFY vb withdraw or remove a certificate or certification from (a person, organization, or country)

DECESSION n departure

DECHEANCE n forfeiting

DECIARE n one tenth of an are or 10 square metres

DECIARES > DECIARE

DECIBEL n unit for measuring the intensity of sound

DECIBELS > DECIBEL

DECIDABLE adj able to be decided

DECIDE vb (cause to) reach a decision

DECIDED adj unmistakable

DECIDEDLY > DECIDED

DECIDER n thing that determines who wins a match or championship

DECIDERS > DECIDER

DECIDES > DECIDE

DECIDING > DECIDE

DECIDUA n membrane lining the uterus of some mammals during pregnancy

DECIDUAE > DECIDUA

DECIDUAL > DECIDUA

DECIDUAS > DECIDUA

DECIDUATE > DECIDUA

DECIDUOUS adj (of a tree) shedding its leaves annually

DECIGRAM n tenth of a gram

DECIGRAMS > DECIGRAM

DECILE n one of nine values of a variable divided into ten equal groups

DECILES > DECILE

DECILITER same as > DECILITRE

DECILITRE n measure of volume equivalent to one tenth of a litre

DECILLION n (in Britain, France, and Germany) the number represented as one followed by 60 zeros (10^{60})

DECIMAL n fraction written in the form of a dot followed by one or more numbers ▷ adj relating to or using powers of ten

DECIMALLY > DECIMAL

DECIMALS > DECIMAL

DECIMATE vb destroy or kill a large proportion of

DECIMATED > DECIMATE

DECIMATES > DECIMATE

DECIMATOR > DECIMATE

DECIME n former French coin

DECIMES > DECIME

DECIMETER same as > DECIMETRE

DECIMETRE n unit of length equal to one tenth of a metre

DECIPHER vb work out the meaning of (something illegible or in code)

DECIPHERS > DECIPHER

DECISION n judgment, conclusion, or resolution

DECISIONS > DECISION

DECISIVE adj having a definite influence

DECISORY adj deciding

DECISTERE n tenth of a stere

DECK n area of a ship that forms a floor ▷ vb dress or decorate

DECKCHAIR n folding wooden and canvas chair designed for use outside

DECKED adj having a wooden deck or platform

DECKEL same as > DECKLE

DECKELS > DECKLE

DECKER > DECK

DECKERS > DECK

DECKHAND n seafarer assigned various duties on the deck of a ship

DECKHANDS > DECKHAND

DECKHOUSE n houselike cabin on the deck of a ship

DECKING n wooden platform in a garden

DECKINGS > DECKING

DECKLE n frame used to contain pulp on the mould in

the making of handmade paper
DECKLED > DECKLE
DECKLES > DECKLE
DECKLESS adj without a deck
DECKO n look ▷ vb have a look
DECKOED > DECKO
DECKOING > DECKO
DECKOS > DECKO
DECKS > DECK
DECLAIM vb speak loudly and dramatically
DECLAIMED > DECLAIM
DECLAIMER > DECLAIM
DECLAIMS > DECLAIM
DECLARANT n person who makes a declaration
DECLARE vb state firmly and forcefully
DECLARED > DECLARE
DECLARER n person who declares
DECLARERS > DECLARER
DECLARES > DECLARE
DECLARING > DECLARE
DECLASS vb lower in social status or position
DECLASSE adj having lost social standing or status
DECLASSED > DECLASS
DECLASSEE adj (of a woman) having lost social standing or status
DECLASSES > DECLASS
DECLAW vb remove claws from
DECLAWED > DECLAW
DECLAWING > DECLAW
DECLAWS > DECLAW
DECLINAL adj bending down ▷ n action of politely refusing or declining
DECLINALS > DECLINAL
DECLINANT adj heraldry term ▷ n person who is diminishing in luck or wealth
DECLINATE adj (esp of plant parts) descending from the horizontal in a curve
DECLINE vb become smaller, weaker, or less important ▷ n gradual weakening or loss
DECLINED > DECLINE
DECLINER > DECLINE
DECLINERS > DECLINE
DECLINES > DECLINE
DECLINING > DECLINE
DECLINIST n person believing something is in decline
DECLIVITY n downward slope
DECLIVOUS adj steep
DECLUTCH vb disengage the clutch of a motor vehicle
DECLUTTER vb simplify or get rid of mess, disorder, complications, etc
DECO adj as in art deco style of art, jewellery, design, etc
DECOCT vb extract the essence from (a substance) by boiling
DECOCTED > DECOCT
DECOCTING > DECOCT

DECOCTION n extraction by boiling
DECOCTIVE > DECOCT
DECOCTS > DECOCT
DECOCTURE n substance obtained by decoction
DECODABLE adj capable of being decoded
DECODE vb convert from code into ordinary language
DECODED > DECODE
DECODER > DECODE
DECODERS > DECODE
DECODES > DECODE
DECODING n act of decoding
DECODINGS > DECODING
DECOHERER n electrical device
DECOKE n decarbonize
DECOKED > DECOKE
DECOKES > DECOKE
DECOKING > DECOKE
DECOLLATE vb separate (continuous stationery, etc) into individual forms
DECOLLETE adj (of a woman's garment) low-cut ▷ n low-cut neckline
DECOLOR vb bleach
DECOLORED > DECOLOR
DECOLORS > DECOLOR
DECOLOUR vb deprive of colour, as by bleaching
DECOLOURS > DECOLOUR
DECOMMIT vb withdraw from a commitment or agreed course of action
DECOMMITS > DECOMMIT
DECOMPLEX adj repeatedly compound
DECOMPOSE vb be broken down through chemical or bacterial action
DECONGEST vb relieve congestion in
DECONTROL vb free of restraints or controls, esp government controls
DECOR n style in which a room or house is decorated
DECORATE vb make more attractive by adding something ornamental
DECORATED > DECORATE
DECORATES > DECORATE
DECORATOR n person whose profession is the painting and wallpapering of buildings
DECOROUS adj polite, calm, and sensible in behaviour
DECORS > DECOR
DECORUM n polite and socially correct behaviour
DECORUMS > DECORUM
DECOS pl n decorations
DECOUPAGE n art or process of decorating a surface with shapes or illustrations cut from paper, card, etc
DECOUPLE vb separate two joined entities or subsystems
DECOUPLED > DECOUPLE
DECOUPLER > DECOUPLE
DECOUPLES > DECOUPLE
DECOY n person or thing used to lure someone into danger ▷ vb lure away by means of a trick

DECOYED > DECOY
DECOYER > DECOY
DECOYERS > DECOY
DECOYING > DECOY
DECOYS > DECOY
DECREASE vb make or become less ▷ n lessening, reduction
DECREASED > DECREASE
DECREASES > DECREASE
DECREE n law made by someone in authority ▷ vb order by decree
DECREED > DECREE
DECREEING > DECREE
DECREER > DECREE
DECREERS > DECREE
DECREES > DECREE
DECREET n final judgment or sentence of a court
DECREETS > DECREET
DECREMENT n act of decreasing
DECREPIT adj weakened or worn out by age or long use
DECRETAL n papal decree ▷ adj of or relating to a decretal or a decree
DECRETALS > DECRETAL
DECRETIST n law student
DECRETIVE adj of a decree
DECRETORY adj of a decree
DECREW vb archaic word for decrease
DECREWED > DECREW
DECREWING > DECREW
DECREWS > DECREW
DECRIAL > DECRY
DECRIALS > DECRY
DECRIED > DECRY
DECRIER > DECRY
DECRIERS > DECRY
DECRIES > DECRY
DECROWN vb depose
DECROWNED > DECROWN
DECROWNS > DECROWN
DECRY vb express disapproval of
DECRYING > DECRY
DECRYPT vb decode (a message)
DECRYPTED > DECRYPT
DECRYPTS > DECRYPT
DECTET n ten musicians
DECTETS > DECTET
DECUBITAL > DECUBITUS
DECUBITI > DECUBITUS
DECUBITUS n posture adopted when lying down
DECUMAN n large wave
DECUMANS > DECUMAN
DECUMBENT adj lying down or lying flat
DECUPLE vb increase by ten times ▷ n amount ten times as large as a given reference ▷ adj increasing tenfold
DECUPLED > DECUPLE
DECUPLES > DECUPLE
DECUPLING > DECUPLE
DECURIA n group of ten
DECURIAS > DECURIA
DECURIES > DECURY
DECURION n local councillor
DECURIONS > DECURION
DECURRENT adj extending down the stem, esp (of a

leaf) having the base of the blade extending down the stem as two wings
DECURSION n state of being decurrent
DECURSIVE adj extending downwards
DECURVE vb curve downwards
DECURVED adj bent or curved downwards
DECURVES > DECURVE
DECURVING > DECURVE
DECURY n (in ancient Rome) a body of ten men
DECUSSATE vb cross or cause to cross in the form of the letter X ▷ adj in the form of the letter X
DEDAL same as > DAEDAL
DEDALIAN adj of Daedalus
DEDANS n open gallery at the server's end of the court
DEDENDA > DEDENDUM
DEDENDUM n radial distance between the pitch circle and root of a gear tooth
DEDENDUMS > DEDENDUM
DEDICANT n person who dedicates
DEDICANTS > DEDICANT
DEDICATE vb commit (oneself or one's time) wholly to a special purpose or cause
DEDICATED adj devoted to a particular purpose or cause
DEDICATEE > DEDICATE
DEDICATES > DEDICATE
DEDICATOR > DEDICATE
DEDIMUS n legal term
DEDIMUSES > DEDIMUS
DEDUCE vb reach (a conclusion) by reasoning from evidence
DEDUCED > DEDUCE
DEDUCES > DEDUCE
DEDUCIBLE > DEDUCE
DEDUCIBLY > DEDUCE
DEDUCING > DEDUCE
DEDUCT vb subtract
DEDUCTED > DEDUCT
DEDUCTING > DEDUCT
DEDUCTION n deducting
DEDUCTIVE adj of or relating to deduction
DEDUCTS > DEDUCT
DEE a Scot word for > DIE
DEED n something that is done ▷ vb convey or transfer (property) by deed ▷ adj Scots form of dead
DEEDED > DEED
DEEDER > DEED
DEEDEST > DEED
DEEDFUL adj full of exploits
DEEDIER > DEEDY
DEEDIEST > DEEDY
DEEDILY > DEEDY
DEEDING > DEED
DEEDLESS adj without exploits
DEEDS > DEED
DEEDY adj hard-working
DEEING > DEE
DEEJAY n disc jockey ▷ vb work or act as a disc jockey
DEEJAYED > DEEJAY

d

d

DEEJAYING n act of deejaying
DEEJAYS > DEEJAY
DEEK interj look at!
DEELY adj as in deely boppers hairband with two bobbing antennae-like attachments
DEEM vb consider, judge
DEEMED > DEEM
DEEMING > DEEM
DEEMS > DEEM
DEEMSTER n title of one of the two justices in the Isle of Man
DEEMSTERS > DEEMSTER
DEEN n din
DEENS > DEEN
DEEP adj extending or situated far down, inwards, backwards, or sideways ▷ n any deep place on land or under water
DEEPEN vb make or become deeper or more intense
DEEPENED > DEEPEN
DEEPENER > DEEPEN
DEEPENERS > DEEPEN
DEEPENING n act of deepening
DEEPENS > DEEPEN
DEEPER > DEEP
DEEPEST > DEEP
DEEPFELT adj sincere
DEEPFROZE vb froze in a freezer
DEEPIE n 3D film
DEEPIES > DEEPIE
DEEPLY > DEEP
DEEPMOST adj deepest
DEEPNESS > DEEP
DEEPS > DEEP
DEEPWATER adj seagoing
DEER n large wild animal, the male of which has antlers
DEERBERRY n huckleberry
DEERE adj serious ▷ n deer
DEERES > DEERE
DEERFLIES > DEERFLY
DEERFLY n insect related to the horsefly
DEERGRASS n type of plant that grows in dense tufts in peat bogs of temperate regions
DEERHORN n horn of a deer
DEERHORNS > DEERHORN
DEERHOUND n very large rough-coated breed of dog of the greyhound type
DEERLET n ruminant mammal
DEERLETS > DEERLET
DEERLIKE adj like a deer
DEERS > DEER
DEERSKIN n hide of a deer
DEERSKINS > DEERSKIN
DEERWEED n forage plant
DEERWEEDS > DEERWEED
DEERYARD n gathering place for deer
DEERYARDS > DEERYARD
DEES > DEE
DEET n insect-repellent
DEETS > DEET
DEEV n mythical monster
DEEVE vb deafen
DEEVED > DEEVE

DEEVES > DEEVE
DEEVING > DEEVE
DEEVS > DEEV
DEEWAN n chief of a village in India
DEEWANS > DEEWAN
DEF adj very good
DEFACE vb deliberately spoil the appearance of
DEFACED > DEFACE
DEFACER > DEFACE
DEFACERS > DEFACE
DEFACES > DEFACE
DEFACING > DEFACE
DEFAECATE same as > DEFECATE
DEFALCATE vb make wrong use of funds entrusted to one
DEFAME vb attack the good reputation of
DEFAMED > DEFAME
DEFAMER > DEFAME
DEFAMERS > DEFAME
DEFAMES > DEFAME
DEFAMING > DEFAME
DEFAMINGS > DEFAME
DEFANG vb remove the fangs of
DEFANGED > DEFANG
DEFANGING > DEFANG
DEFANGS > DEFANG
DEFAST adj defaced
DEFASTE adj defaced
DEFAT vb remove fat from
DEFATS > DEFAT
DEFATTED > DEFAT
DEFATTING > DEFAT
DEFAULT n failure to do something ▷ vb fail to fulfil an obligation
DEFAULTED > DEFAULT
DEFAULTER n person who defaults
DEFAULTS > DEFAULT
DEFEAT vb win a victory over ▷ n defeating
DEFEATED > DEFEAT
DEFEATER > DEFEAT
DEFEATERS > DEFEAT
DEFEATING > DEFEAT
DEFEATISM n ready acceptance or expectation of defeat
DEFEATIST > DEFEATISM
DEFEATS > DEFEAT
DEFEATURE vb deform
DEFECATE vb discharge waste from the body
DEFECATED > DEFECATE
DEFECATES > DEFECATE
DEFECATOR > DEFECATE
DEFECT n imperfection, blemish ▷ vb desert one's cause or country to join the opposing forces
DEFECTED > DEFECT
DEFECTING > DEFECT
DEFECTION n act or an instance of defecting
DEFECTIVE adj imperfect, faulty
DEFECTOR > DEFECT
DEFECTORS > DEFECT
DEFECTS > DEFECT
DEFENCE n resistance against attack ▷ vb provide with defence

DEFENCED > DEFENCE
DEFENCES > DEFENCE
DEFENCING > DEFENCE
DEFEND vb protect from harm or danger
DEFENDANT n person accused of a crime ▷ adj making a defence
DEFENDED > DEFEND
DEFENDER > DEFEND
DEFENDERS > DEFEND
DEFENDING > DEFEND
DEFENDS > DEFEND
DEFENSE same as > DEFENCE
DEFENSED > DEFENSE
DEFENSES > DEFENSE
DEFENSING > DEFENSE
DEFENSIVE adj intended for defence
DEFER vb delay (something) until a future time
DEFERABLE > DEFER
DEFERENCE n polite and respectful behaviour
DEFERENT adj conveying outwards, down, or away ▷ n type of circle in the Ptolemaic system
DEFERENTS > DEFERENT
DEFERMENT n act of deferring or putting off until another time
DEFERRAL same as > DEFERMENT
DEFERRALS > DEFERRAL
DEFERRED adj withheld over a certain period
DEFERRER > DEFER
DEFERRERS > DEFER
DEFERRING > DEFER
DEFERS > DEFER
DEFFER > DEF
DEFFEST > DEF
DEFFLY archaic form of > DEFTLY
DEFFO interj definitely: an expression of agreement or consent
DEFI n challenge
DEFIANCE n open resistance or disobedience
DEFIANCES > DEFIANCE
DEFIANT adj marked by resistance or bold opposition, as to authority
DEFIANTLY > DEFIANT
DEFICIENT adj lacking some essential thing or quality
DEFICIT n amount by which a sum of money is too small
DEFICITS > DEFICIT
DEFIED > DEFY
DEFIER > DEFY
DEFIERS > DEFY
DEFIES > DEFY
DEFILADE n protection provided by obstacles against enemy crossfire from the rear, or observation ▷ vb provide protection for by defilade
DEFILADED > DEFILADE
DEFILADES > DEFILADE

DEFILE vb treat (something sacred or important) without respect ▷ n narrow valley or pass
DEFILED > DEFILE
DEFILER > DEFILE
DEFILERS > DEFILE
DEFILES > DEFILE
DEFILING > DEFILE
DEFINABLE > DEFINE
DEFINABLY > DEFINE
DEFINE vb state precisely the meaning of
DEFINED > DEFINE
DEFINER > DEFINE
DEFINERS > DEFINE
DEFINES > DEFINE
DEFINIENS n word or words used to define or give an account of the meaning of another word, as in a dictionary entry
DEFINING > DEFINE
DEFINITE adj firm, clear, and precise ▷ n something that is firm, clear, and precise
DEFINITES > DEFINITE
DEFIS > DEFI
DEFLATE vb (cause to) collapse through the release of air
DEFLATED > DEFLATE
DEFLATER > DEFLATE
DEFLATERS > DEFLATE
DEFLATES > DEFLATE
DEFLATING > DEFLATE
DEFLATION n reduction in economic activity resulting in lower output and investment
DEFLATOR > DEFLATE
DEFLATORS > DEFLATE
DEFLEA vb remove fleas from
DEFLEAED > DEFLEA
DEFLEAING > DEFLEA
DEFLEAS > DEFLEA
DEFLECT vb (cause to) turn aside from a course
DEFLECTED > DEFLECT
DEFLECTOR > DEFLECT
DEFLECTS > DEFLECT
DEFLEX vb turn downwards
DEFLEXED > DEFLEX
DEFLEXES > DEFLEX
DEFLEXING > DEFLEX
DEFLEXION n deflection
DEFLEXURE n act of deflecting
DEFLORATE vb deflower
DEFLOWER vb deprive (a woman) of her virginity
DEFLOWERS > DEFLOWER
DEFLUENT adj running downwards
DEFLUXION n discharge
DEFO interj (slang) definitely
DEFOAM vb remove foam from
DEFOAMED > DEFOAM
DEFOAMER > DEFOAM
DEFOAMERS > DEFOAM
DEFOAMING > DEFOAM
DEFOAMS > DEFOAM
DEFOCUS vb put out of focus
DEFOCUSED > DEFOCUS
DEFOCUSES > DEFOCUS
DEFOG vb clear of vapour

DEFOGGED > DEFOG
DEFOGGER > DEFOG
DEFOGGERS > DEFOG
DEFOGGING > DEFOG
DEFOGS > DEFOG
DEFOLIANT n chemical sprayed or dusted onto trees to cause their leaves to fall, esp to remove cover from an enemy in warfare
DEFOLIATE vb deprive (a plant) of its leaves ▷ adj (of a plant) having shed its leaves
DEFORCE vb withhold (property, esp land) wrongfully or by force from the rightful owner
DEFORCED > DEFORCE
DEFORCER > DEFORCE
DEFORCERS > DEFORCE
DEFORCES > DEFORCE
DEFORCING > DEFORCE
DEFOREST vb clear of trees
DEFORESTS > DEFOREST
DEFORM vb put out of shape or spoil the appearance of
DEFORMED adj disfigured or misshapen
DEFORMER > DEFORM
DEFORMERS > DEFORM
DEFORMING > DEFORM
DEFORMITY n distortion of a body part
DEFORMS > DEFORM
DEFOUL vb defile
DEFOULED > DEFOUL
DEFOULING > DEFOUL
DEFOULS > DEFOUL
DEFRAG vb defragment
DEFRAGGED > DEFRAG
DEFRAGGER > DEFRAG
DEFRAGS > DEFRAG
DEFRAUD vb cheat out of money, property, etc
DEFRAUDED > DEFRAUD
DEFRAUDER > DEFRAUD
DEFRAUDS > DEFRAUD
DEFRAY vb provide money for (costs or expenses)
DEFRAYAL > DEFRAY
DEFRAYALS > DEFRAY
DEFRAYED > DEFRAY
DEFRAYER > DEFRAY
DEFRAYERS > DEFRAY
DEFRAYING > DEFRAY
DEFRAYS > DEFRAY
DEFREEZE vb defrost
DEFREEZES > DEFREEZE
DEFRIEND vb remove (a person) from the list of one's friends on a social networking website
DEFRIENDS > DEFRIEND
DEFROCK vb deprive (a priest) of priestly status
DEFROCKED > DEFROCK
DEFROCKS > DEFROCK
DEFROST vb make or become free of ice
DEFROSTED > DEFROST
DEFROSTER n device by which the de-icing process of a refrigerator is accelerated, usually by circulating the refrigerant without the expansion process
DEFROSTS > DEFROST

DEFROZE > DEFREEZE
DEFROZEN > DEFREEZE
DEFT adj quick and skilful in movement
DEFTER > DEFT
DEFTEST > DEFT
DEFTLY > DEFT
DEFTNESS > DEFT
DEFUEL vb remove fuel from
DEFUELED > DEFUEL
DEFUELING > DEFUEL
DEFUELLED > DEFUEL
DEFUELS > DEFUEL
DEFUNCT adj no longer existing or operative ▷ n deceased person
DEFUNCTS > DEFUNCT
DEFUND vb stop funds to
DEFUNDED > DEFUND
DEFUNDING > DEFUND
DEFUNDS > DEFUND
DEFUSE vb remove the fuse of (an explosive device)
DEFUSED > DEFUSE
DEFUSER > DEFUSE
DEFUSERS > DEFUSE
DEFUSES > DEFUSE
DEFUSING > DEFUSE
DEFUZE same as > DEFUSE
DEFUZED > DEFUZE
DEFUZES > DEFUZE
DEFUZING > DEFUZE
DEFY vb resist openly and boldly
DEFYING > DEFY
DEG vb water (a plant, etc)
DEGAGE adj unconstrained in manner
DEGAME n tree of South and Central America
DEGAMES > DEGAME
DEGAMI same as > DEGAME
DEGAMIS > DEGAMI
DEGARNISH vb remove ornament from
DEGAS vb remove gas from (a container, vacuum tube, liquid, adsorbent, etc)
DEGASES > DEGAS
DEGASSED > DEGAS
DEGASSER > DEGAS
DEGASSERS > DEGAS
DEGASSES > DEGAS
DEGASSING > DEGAS
DEGAUSS n demagnetize
DEGAUSSED > DEGAUSS
DEGAUSSER > DEGAUSS
DEGAUSSES > DEGAUSS
DEGEARING n process in which a company replaces some or all of its fixed-interest loan stock with ordinary shares
DEGENDER vb remove reference to gender from
DEGENDERS > DEGENDER
DEGERM vb remove germs from
DEGERMED > DEGERM
DEGERMING > DEGERM
DEGERMS > DEGERM
DEGGED > DEG
DEGGING > DEG
DEGLAZE vb dilute meat sediments in (a pan) in order to make a sauce or gravy
DEGLAZED > DEGLAZE

DEGLAZES > DEGLAZE
DEGLAZING > DEGLAZE
DEGOUT n disgust ▷ vb cover (something) with gouts or drops of something
DEGOUTED > DEGOUT
DEGOUTING > DEGOUT
DEGOUTS > DEGOUT
DEGRADE vb reduce to dishonour or disgrace
DEGRADED > DEGRADE
DEGRADER > DEGRADE
DEGRADERS > DEGRADE
DEGRADES > DEGRADE
DEGRADING adj causing humiliation
DEGRAS n emulsion used for dressing hides
DEGREASE vb remove grease from
DEGREASED > DEGREASE
DEGREASER > DEGREASE
DEGREASES > DEGREASE
DEGREE n stage in a scale of relative amount or intensity
DEGREED adj having a degree
DEGREES > DEGREE
DEGS > DEG
DEGU n small S American rodent
DEGUM vb remove gum from
DEGUMMED > DEGUM
DEGUMMING > DEGUM
DEGUMS > DEGUM
DEGUS > DEGU
DEGUST vb taste, esp with care or relish
DEGUSTATE same as > DEGUST
DEGUSTED > DEGUST
DEGUSTING > DEGUST
DEGUSTS > DEGUST
DEHAIR vb remove hair
DEHAIRED > DEHAIR
DEHAIRING > DEHAIR
DEHAIRS > DEHAIR
DEHISCE vb (of the seed capsules of some plants) to burst open spontaneously
DEHISCED > DEHISCE
DEHISCENT adj (of fruits, anthers, etc) opening spontaneously to release seeds or pollen
DEHISCES > DEHISCE
DEHISCING > DEHISCE
DEHORN vb remove or prevent the growth of the horns of (cattle, sheep, or goats)
DEHORNED > DEHORN
DEHORNER > DEHORN
DEHORNERS > DEHORN
DEHORNING > DEHORN
DEHORNS > DEHORN
DEHORS prep apart from
DEHORT vb dissuade
DEHORTED > DEHORT
DEHORTER > DEHORT
DEHORTERS > DEHORT
DEHORTING > DEHORT
DEHORTS > DEHORT
DEHYDRATE vb remove water from (food) to preserve it
DEI > DEUS

DEICE vb free or be freed of ice
DEICED > DEICE
DEICER > DEICE
DEICERS > DEICE
DEICES > DEICE
DEICIDAL > DEICIDE
DEICIDE n act of killing a god
DEICIDES > DEICIDE
DEICING > DEICE
DEICTIC adj proving by direct argument ▷ n term whose reference depends on the context
DEICTICS > DEICTIC
DEID a Scot word for > DEAD
DEIDER > DEID
DEIDEST > DEID
DEIDS > DEID
DEIF a Scot word for > DEAF
DEIFER > DEIF
DEIFEST > DEIF
DEIFIC adj making divine or exalting to the position of a god
DEIFICAL adj divine
DEIFIED > DEIFY
DEIFIER > DEIFY
DEIFIERS > DEIFY
DEIFIES > DEIFY
DEIFORM adj having the form or appearance of a god
DEIFY vb treat or worship as a god
DEIFYING > DEIFY
DEIGN vb agree (to do something), but as if doing someone a favour
DEIGNED > DEIGN
DEIGNING > DEIGN
DEIGNS > DEIGN
DEIL a Scot word for > DEVIL
DEILS > DEIL
DEINDEX vb cause to become no longer index-linked
DEINDEXED > DEINDEX
DEINDEXES > DEINDEX
DEINOSAUR n dinosaur
DEIONISE same as > DEIONIZE
DEIONISED > DEIONISE
DEIONISER > DEIONISE
DEIONISES > DEIONISE
DEIONIZE vb remove ions from (water, etc), esp by ion exchange
DEIONIZED > DEIONIZE
DEIONIZER > DEIONIZE
DEIONIZES > DEIONIZE
DEIPAROUS adj giving birth to a god
DEISEAL n clockwise motion
DEISEALS > DEISEAL
DEISHEAL n clockwise motion
DEISHEALS > DEISHEAL
DEISM n belief in God but not in divine revelation
DEISMS > DEISM
DEIST > DEISM
DEISTIC > DEISM
DEISTICAL > DEISM
DEISTS > DEISM
DEITIES > DEITY

d

DEITY n god or goddess

DEIXES > DEIXIS

DEIXIS n use or reference of a deictic word

DEIXISES > DEIXIS

DEJECT vb have a depressing effect on ▷ adj downcast

DEJECTA pl n waste products excreted from the body

DEJECTED adj unhappy

DEJECTING > DEJECT

DEJECTION n lowness of spirits

DEJECTORY adj causing dejection

DEJECTS > DEJECT

DEJEUNE n lunch

DEJEUNER n lunch

DEJEUNERS > DEJEUNER

DEJEUNES > DEJEUNE

DEKAGRAM n ten grams

DEKAGRAMS > DEKAGRAM

DEKALITER n ten litres

DEKALITRE n ten litres

DEKALOGY n series of ten related works

DEKAMETER n ten meters

DEKAMETRE n ten metres

DEKARE n unit of measurement equal to ten ares

DEKARES > DEKARE

DEKE vb make a deceptive movement ▷ n deceptive movement

DEKED > DEKE

DEKEING > DEKE

DEKES > DEKE

DEKING > DEKE

DEKKO n look ▷ vb have a look

DEKKOED > DEKKO

DEKKOING > DEKKO

DEKKOS > DEKKO

DEL n differential operator

DELAINE n sheer wool or wool and cotton fabric

DELAINES > DELAINE

DELAPSE vb be inherited

DELAPSED > DELAPSE

DELAPSES > DELAPSE

DELAPSING > DELAPSE

DELAPSION n falling down

DELATE vb (formerly) to bring a charge against

DELATED > DELATE

DELATES > DELATE

DELATING > DELATE

DELATION > DELATE

DELATIONS > DELATE

DELATOR > DELATE

DELATORS > DELATE

DELAY vb put off to a later time ▷ n act of delaying

DELAYABLE > DELAY

DELAYED > DELAY

DELAYER > DELAY

DELAYERS > DELAY

DELAYING > DELAY

DELAYS > DELAY

DELE n sign indicating that typeset matter is to be deleted ▷ vb mark (matter to be deleted) with a dele

DELEAD vb remove lead from

DELEADED > DELEAD

DELEADING > DELEAD

DELEADS > DELEAD

DELEAVE vb separate copies

DELEAVED > DELEAVE

DELEAVES > DELEAVE

DELEAVING > DELEAVE

DELEBLE adj able to be deleted

DELECTATE vb delight

DELED > DELE

DELEGABLE > DELEGATE

DELEGACY n elected standing committee at some British universities

DELEGATE n person chosen to represent others, esp at a meeting ▷ vb entrust (duties or powers) to someone

DELEGATED > DELEGATE

DELEGATEE > DELEGATE

DELEGATES > DELEGATE

DELEGATOR > DELEGATE

DELEING > DELE

DELENDA pl n items for deleting

DELES > DELE

DELETABLE > DELETE

DELETE vb remove (something written or printed)

DELETED > DELETE

DELETES > DELETE

DELETING > DELETE

DELETION n act of deleting or fact of being deleted

DELETIONS > DELETION

DELETIVE > DELETE

DELETORY > DELETE

DELF n kind of earthenware

DELFS > DELF

DELFT n tin-glazed earthenware, typically having blue designs on white

DELFTS > DELFT

DELFTWARE same as > DELFT

DELI n delicatessen

DELIBATE vb taste

DELIBATED > DELIBATE

DELIBATES > DELIBATE

DELIBLE adj able to be deleted

DELICACY n being delicate

DELICATE adj fine or subtle in quality or workmanship ▷ n delicacy

DELICATES > DELICATE

DELICE n delicacy

DELICES > DELICE

DELICIOUS adj very appealing to taste or smell

DELICT n wrongful act for which the person injured has the right to a civil remedy

DELICTS > DELICT

DELIGHT n (source of) great pleasure ▷ vb please greatly

DELIGHTED adj greatly pleased ▷ sentence substitute I should be delighted to!

DELIGHTER > DELIGHT

DELIGHTS > DELIGHT

DELIME vb remove lime from

DELIMED > DELIME

DELIMES > DELIME

DELIMING > DELIME

DELIMIT vb mark or lay down the limits of

DELIMITED > DELIMIT

DELIMITER > DELIMIT

DELIMITS > DELIMIT

DELINEATE vb show by drawing

DELINK vb remove or break a link

DELINKED > DELINK

DELINKING > DELINK

DELINKS > DELINK

DELIQUIUM n loss of consciousness

DELIRIA > DELIRIUM

DELIRIANT > DELIRIUM

DELIRIOUS adj suffering from delirium

DELIRIUM n state of excitement and mental confusion, often with hallucinations

DELIRIUMS > DELIRIUM

DELIS > DELI

DELISH adj delicious

DELIST vb remove from a list

DELISTED > DELIST

DELISTING > DELIST

DELISTS > DELIST

DELIVER vb carry (goods etc) to a destination

DELIVERED > DELIVER

DELIVERER > DELIVER

DELIVERLY adv quickly

DELIVERS > DELIVER

DELIVERY n delivering

DELL n small wooded hollow

DELLIER > DELLY

DELLIES > DELLY

DELLIEST > DELLY

DELLS > DELL

DELLY n delicatessen ▷ adj full of dells

DELO an informal word for > DELEGATE

DELOPE vb shoot into the air

DELOPED > DELOPE

DELOPES > DELOPE

DELOPING > DELOPE

DELOS > DELO

DELOUSE vb rid (a person or animal) of lice

DELOUSED > DELOUSE

DELOUSER > DELOUSE

DELOUSERS > DELOUSE

DELOUSES > DELOUSE

DELOUSING > DELOUSE

DELPH n kind of earthenware

DELPHIC adj obscure or ambiguous

DELPHIN n fatty substance from dolphin oil

DELPHINIA n plural form of singular delphinium: garden plant with blue, white or pink flowers

DELPHINS > DELPHIN

DELPHS > DELPH

DELS > DEL

DELT n deltoid muscle

DELTA n fourth letter in the Greek alphabet

DELTAIC > DELTA

DELTAS > DELTA

DELTIC > DELTA

DELTOID n muscle acting to raise the arm ▷ adj shaped like a Greek capital delta

DELTOIDEI n deltoid

DELTOIDS > DELTOID

DELTS > DELT

DELUBRA > DELUBRUM

DELUBRUM n shrine

DELUBRUMS > DELUBRUM

DELUDABLE > DELUDE

DELUDE vb deceive

DELUDED > DELUDE

DELUDER > DELUDE

DELUDERS > DELUDE

DELUDES > DELUDE

DELUDING > DELUDE

DELUGE n great flood ▷ vb flood

DELUGED > DELUGE

DELUGES > DELUGE

DELUGING > DELUGE

DELUNDUNG n spotted mammal

DELUSION n mistaken idea or belief

DELUSIONS > DELUSION

DELUSIVE > DELUSION

DELUSORY > DELUSION

DELUSTER same as > DELUSTRE

DELUSTERS > DELUSTER

DELUSTRE vb remove the lustre from

DELUSTRED > DELUSTRE

DELUSTRES > DELUSTRE

DELUXE adj rich, elegant, superior, or sumptuous

DELVE vb research deeply (for information)

DELVED > DELVE

DELVER > DELVE

DELVERS > DELVE

DELVES > DELVE

DELVING > DELVE

DEMAGOG same as > DEMAGOGUE

DEMAGOGED > DEMAGOG

DEMAGOGIC adj of, characteristic of, relating to, or resembling a demagogue

DEMAGOGS > DEMAGOG

DEMAGOGUE n political agitator who appeals to the prejudice and passions of the mob

DEMAGOGY n demagoguery

DEMAIN n demesne

DEMAINE n demesne

DEMAINES > DEMAINE

DEMAINS > DEMAIN

DEMAN vb reduce the workforce of (a plant, industry, etc)

DEMAND vb request forcefully ▷ n forceful request

DEMANDANT n (formerly) the plaintiff in an action relating to real property

DEMANDED > DEMAND

DEMANDER > DEMAND

DEMANDERS > DEMAND

DEMANDING adj requiring a lot of time or effort

DEMANDS > DEMAND

DEMANNED > DEMAN

DEMANNING > DEMAN

DEMANS > DEMAN

DEMANTOID n bright green variety of andradite garnet

DEMARCATE vb mark, fix, or draw the boundaries, limits, etc, of

DEMARCHE n move, step, or manoeuvre, esp in diplomatic affairs

DEMARCHES > DEMARCHE

DEMARK vb demarcate

DEMARKED > DEMARK

DEMARKET vb discourage consumers from buying

DEMARKETS > DEMARKET

DEMARKING > DEMARK

DEMARKS > DEMARK

DEMAST vb remove the mast from

DEMASTED > DEMAST

DEMASTING > DEMAST

DEMASTS > DEMAST

DEMAYNE n demesne

DEMAYNES > DEMAYNE

DEME n (in preclassical Greece) the territory inhabited by a tribe

DEMEAN vb lower (oneself) in dignity, status, or character

DEMEANE n demesne

DEMEANED > DEMEAN

DEMEANES n demesne

DEMEANING > DEMEAN

DEMEANOR same as > DEMEANOUR

DEMEANORS > DEMEANOR

DEMEANOUR n way a person behaves

DEMEANS > DEMEAN

DEMENT vb deteriorate mentally, esp because of old age

DEMENTATE vb deteriorate mentally

DEMENTED adj mad

DEMENTI n denial

DEMENTIA n state of serious mental deterioration

DEMENTIAL > DEMENTIA

DEMENTIAS > DEMENTIA

DEMENTING > DEMENT

DEMENTIS > DEMENTI

DEMENTS > DEMENT

DEMERARA n brown crystallized cane sugar from the Caribbean and nearby countries

DEMERARAN adj from Demerara

DEMERARAS > DEMERARA

DEMERGE vb separate a company from another

DEMERGED > DEMERGE

DEMERGER n separation of two or more companies which have previously been merged

DEMERGERS > DEMERGER

DEMERGES > DEMERGE

DEMERGING > DEMERGE

DEMERIT n fault, disadvantage ▷ vb deserve

DEMERITED > DEMERIT

DEMERITS > DEMERIT

DEMERSAL adj living or occurring on the bottom of a sea or a lake

DEMERSE vb immerse

DEMERSED > DEMERSE

DEMERSES > DEMERSE

DEMERSING > DEMERSE

DEMERSION > DEMERSE

DEMES > DEME

DEMESNE n land surrounding a house

DEMESNES > DEMESNE

DEMETON n insecticide

DEMETONS > DEMETON

DEMIC adj of population

DEMIES > DEMY

DEMIGOD n being who is part mortal, part god

DEMIGODS > DEMIGOD

DEMIJOHN n large bottle with a short neck, often encased in wicker

DEMIJOHNS > DEMIJOHN

DEMILUNE n outwork in front of a fort, shaped like a crescent moon

DEMILUNES > DEMILUNE

DEMIMONDE n (esp in the 19th century) class of women considered to be outside respectable society because of promiscuity

DEMINER n person who removes mines

DEMINERS > DEMINER

DEMINING n act of removing mines

DEMININGS > DEMINING

DEMIPIQUE n low pique on a saddle

DEMIREP n woman of bad repute, esp a prostitute

DEMIREPS > DEMIREP

DEMISABLE > DEMISE

DEMISE n eventual failure (of something successful) ▷ vb transfer for a limited period

DEMISED > DEMISE

DEMISES > DEMISE

DEMISING > DEMISE

DEMISS adj humble

DEMISSION n relinquishment of or abdication from an office, responsibility, etc

DEMISSIVE adj humble

DEMISSLY > DEMISS

DEMIST vb remove condensation from (a windscreen)

DEMISTED > DEMIST

DEMISTER n device in a motor vehicle to free the windscreen of condensation

DEMISTERS > DEMISTER

DEMISTING n act of removing condensation from (a windscreen)

DEMISTS > DEMIST

DEMIT vb resign (an office, position, etc)

DEMITASSE n small cup used to serve coffee, esp after a meal

DEMITS > DEMIT

DEMITTED > DEMIT

DEMITTING > DEMIT

DEMIURGE n (in the philosophy of Plato) the creator of the universe

DEMIURGES > DEMIURGE

DEMIURGIC > DEMIURGE

DEMIURGUS n demiurge

DEMIVEG n person who eats poultry and fish, but no red meat ▷ adj denoting a person who eats poultry and fish, but no red meat

DEMIVEGES > DEMIVEG

DEMIVOLT n half turn on the hind legs

DEMIVOLTE same as > DEMIVOLT

DEMIVOLTS > DEMIVOLT

DEMIWORLD n demimonde

DEMO n demonstration, organized expression of public opinion ▷ vb demonstrate

DEMOB vb demobilize

DEMOBBED > DEMOB

DEMOBBING > DEMOB

DEMOBS > DEMOB

DEMOCRACY n government by the people or their elected representatives

DEMOCRAT n advocate of democracy

DEMOCRATS > DEMOCRAT

DEMOCRATY n democracy

DEMODE adj out of fashion

DEMODED adj out of fashion

DEMOED > DEMO

DEMOI > DEMOS

DEMOING > DEMO

DEMOLISH vb knock down or destroy (a building)

DEMOLOGY n demography

DEMON n evil spirit

DEMONESS n female demon

DEMONIAC adj appearing to be possessed by a devil ▷ n person possessed by an evil spirit or demon

DEMONIACS > DEMONIAC

DEMONIAN adj of a demon

DEMONIC adj evil

DEMONICAL adj demonic

DEMONISE same as > DEMONIZE

DEMONISED > DEMONISE

DEMONISES > DEMONISE

DEMONISM n study of demons

DEMONISMS > DEMONISM

DEMONIST > DEMONISM

DEMONISTS > DEMONISM

DEMONIZE vb make into a demon

DEMONIZED > DEMONIZE

DEMONIZES > DEMONIZE

DEMONRIES > DEMONRY

DEMONRY > DEMON

DEMONS > DEMON

DEMONYM n name for the inhabitants of a place

DEMONYMS > DEMONYM

DEMOS n people of a nation regarded as a political unit

DEMOSCENE n computer art subculture

DEMOSES > DEMOS

DEMOTE vb reduce in status or rank

DEMOTED > DEMOTE

DEMOTES > DEMOTE

DEMOTIC adj of the common people ▷ n demotic script of ancient Egypt

DEMOTICS > DEMOTIC

DEMOTING > DEMOTE

DEMOTION > DEMOTE

DEMOTIONS > DEMOTE

DEMOTIST > DEMOTIC

DEMOTISTS > DEMOTIC

DEMOUNT vb remove (a motor, gun, etc) from its mounting or setting

DEMOUNTED > DEMOUNT

DEMOUNTS > DEMOUNT

DEMPSTER same as > DEEMSTER

DEMPSTERS > DEMPSTER

DEMPT > DEEM

DEMULCENT adj soothing ▷ n drug or agent that soothes the irritation of inflamed or injured skin surfaces

DEMULSIFY vb undergo or cause to undergo a process in which an emulsion is permanently broken down into its constituents

DEMUR vb raise objections or show reluctance ▷ n act of demurring

DEMURE adj quiet, reserved, and rather shy ▷ vb archaic for look demure ▷ n archaic for demure look

DEMURED > DEMURE

DEMURELY > DEMURE

DEMURER > DEMURE

DEMURES > DEMURE

DEMUREST > DEMURE

DEMURING > DEMURE

DEMURRAGE n delaying of a ship, railway wagon, etc, caused by the charterer's failure to load, unload, etc, before the time of scheduled departure

DEMURRAL n act of demurring

DEMURRALS > DEMURRAL

DEMURRED > DEMUR

DEMURRER n any objection raised

DEMURRERS > DEMURRER

DEMURRING > DEMUR

DEMURS > DEMUR

DEMY n size of printing paper, 17½ by 22½ inches (444.5 × 571.5 mm)

DEMYSHIP n scholarship at Oxford University

DEMYSHIPS > DEMY

DEMYSTIFY vb remove the mystery from

DEMYTHIFY vb remove the mythical characteristics from

DEN n home of a wild animal ▷ vb live in or as if in a den

DENAR n standard monetary unit of Macedonia, divided into 100 deni

DENARI > DENAR

DENARIES > DENARY

DENARII > DENARIUS

DENARIUS n ancient Roman silver coin, often called a penny in translation

DENARS > DENAR

DENARY same as > DENARIUS

DENATURE vb change the nature of

DENATURED > DENATURE

DENATURES > DENATURE

DENAY vb deny

DENAYED > DENAY

DENAYING > DENAY

DENAYS > DENAY

DENAZIFY vb free or declare (people, institutions, etc) freed from Nazi influence or ideology

DENCH adj excellent

DENDRIMER n chemical compound with treelike molecular structure

DENDRITE n threadlike extension of a nerve cell

DENDRITES > DENDRITE

DENDRITIC > DENDRITE

DENDROID adj freely branching ▷ n something that branches freely

DENDROIDS > DENDROID

DENDRON same as > DENDRITE

DENDRONS > DENDRON

DENE n narrow wooded valley

DENERVATE vb deprive (a tissue or organ) of its nerve supply

DENES > DENE

DENET vb remove from the former Net Book Agreement

DENETS > DENET

DENETTED > DENET

DENETTING > DENET

DENGUE n viral disease transmitted by mosquitoes

DENGUES > DENGUE

DENI n monetary unit of Macedonia

DENIABLE adj able to be denied

DENIABLY > DENIABLE

DENIAL n statement that something is not true

DENIALIST n person who refuses to believe an established fact

DENIALS > DENIAL

DENIED > DENY

DENIER n unit of weight used to measure the fineness of nylon or silk

DENIERS > DENIER

DENIES > DENY

DENIGRATE vb criticize unfairly

DENIM n hard-wearing cotton fabric, usu blue

DENIMED adj wearing denim

DENIMS pl n jeans or overalls made of denim

DENIS > DENI

DENITRATE vb undergo or cause to undergo a process in which a compound loses a nitro or nitrate group, nitrogen dioxide, or nitric acid

DENITRIFY vb undergo or cause to undergo loss or removal of nitrogen compounds or nitrogen

DENIZEN n inhabitant ▷ vb make a denizen

DENIZENED > DENIZEN

DENIZENS > DENIZEN

DENNED > DEN

DENNET n carriage for one horse

DENNETS > DENNET

DENNING > DEN

DENOMINAL adj formed from a noun

DENOTABLE > DENOTE

DENOTATE vb denote

DENOTATED > DENOTATE

DENOTATES > DENOTATE

DENOTE vb be a sign of

DENOTED > DENOTE

DENOTES > DENOTE

DENOTING > DENOTE

DENOTIVE > DENOTE

DENOUNCE vb speak vehemently against

DENOUNCED > DENOUNCE

DENOUNCER > DENOUNCE

DENOUNCES > DENOUNCE

DENS > DEN

DENSE adj closely packed

DENSELY > DENSE

DENSENESS > DENSE

DENSER > DENSE

DENSEST > DENSE

DENSIFIED > DENSIFY

DENSIFIER > DENSIFY

DENSIFIES > DENSIFY

DENSIFY vb make or become dense

DENSITIES > DENSITY

DENSITY n degree to which something is filled or occupied

DENT n hollow in the surface of something, made by hitting it ▷ vb make a dent in

DENTAL adj of teeth or dentistry ▷ n dental consonant

DENTALIA > DENTALIUM

DENTALISE same as > DENTALIZE

DENTALITY n use of teeth in pronouncing words

DENTALIUM n type of mollusc

DENTALIZE vb pronounce (a consonant) with the tip of one's tongue against the upper front teeth

DENTALLY > DENTAL

DENTALS > DENTAL

DENTARIA n botanical term

DENTARIAS > DENTARIA

DENTARIES > DENTARY

DENTARY n lower jawbone with teeth

DENTATE adj having teeth or toothlike notches

DENTATED adj having teeth

DENTATELY > DENTATE

DENTATION n state or condition of being dentate

DENTED > DENT

DENTEL n architectural term

DENTELLE n bookbinding term

DENTELLES > DENTELLE

DENTELS > DENTEL

DENTEX n large predatory fish

DENTEXES > DENTEX

DENTICARE n publicly funded dental care

DENTICLE n small tooth or toothlike part, such as any of the placoid scales of sharks

DENTICLES > DENTICLE

DENTIFORM adj shaped like a tooth

DENTIL n architectural ornament

DENTILED > DENTIL

DENTILS > DENTIL

DENTIN same as > DENTINE

DENTINAL > DENTINE

DENTINE n hard dense tissue forming the bulk of a tooth

DENTINES > DENTINE

DENTING > DENT

DENTINS > DENTIN

DENTIST n person qualified to practise dentistry

DENTISTRY n branch of medicine concerned with the teeth and gums

DENTISTS > DENTIST

DENTITION n typical arrangement of teeth in a species

DENTOID adj resembling a tooth

DENTS > DENT

DENTULOUS adj having teeth

DENTURAL > DENTURE

DENTURE n false tooth

DENTURES > DENTURE

DENTURISM n practice of making and fitting dentures

DENTURIST n person who makes dentures

DENUDATE adj denuded ▷ vb denude

DENUDATED > DENUDATE

DENUDATES > DENUDATE

DENUDE vb remove the covering or protection from

DENUDED > DENUDE

DENUDER > DENUDE

DENUDERS > DENUDE

DENUDES > DENUDE

DENUDING > DENUDE

DENY vb declare to be untrue

DENYING > DENY

DENYINGLY > DENY

DEODAND n thing forfeited to charity because it has caused a death

DEODANDS > DEODAND

DEODAR n Himalayan cedar with drooping branches

DEODARA same as > DEODAR

DEODARAS > DEODARA

DEODARS > DEODAR

DEODATE n offering to God

DEODATES > DEODATE

DEODORANT n substance applied to the body to mask the smell of perspiration

DEODORISE same as > DEODORIZE

DEODORIZE vb remove or disguise the smell of

DEONTIC adj of or relating to such ethical concepts as obligation and permissibility

DEONTICS > DEONTIC

DEORBIT vb go out of orbit

DEORBITED > DEORBIT

DEORBITS > DEORBIT

DEOXIDATE vb remove oxygen atoms from

DEOXIDISE same as > DEOXIDIZE

DEOXIDIZE vb remove oxygen atoms from (a compound, molecule, etc)

DEOXY adj having less oxygen than a specified related compound

DEP n small shop where newspapers, sweets, soft drinks, etc are sold

DEPAINT vb depict

DEPAINTED > DEPAINT

DEPAINTS > DEPAINT

DEPANNEUR n (in Quebec) a convenience store

DEPART vb leave

DEPARTED adj dead ▷ n dead person

DEPARTEDS > DEPARTED

DEPARTEE > DEPART

DEPARTEES > DEPART

DEPARTER > DEPART

DEPARTERS > DEPART

DEPARTING > DEPART

DEPARTS > DEPART

DEPARTURE n act of departing

DEPASTURE vb graze or denude by grazing (a pasture, esp a meadow specially grown for the purpose)

DEPECHE n message ▷ vb dispatch; rid oneself of

DEPECHED > DEPECHE

DEPECHES > DEPECHE

DEPECHING > DEPECHE

DEPEINCT vb paint

DEPEINCTS > DEPEINCT

DEPEND vb put trust (in)

DEPENDANT same as > DEPENDENT

DEPENDED > DEPEND

DEPENDENT adj depending on someone or something ▷ n element in a phrase or clause that is not the governor

DEPENDING > DEPEND

DEPENDS > DEPEND

DEPEOPLE vb reduce population

DEPEOPLED > DEPEOPLE

DEPEOPLES > DEPEOPLE

DEPERM vb demagnetize

DEPERMED > DEPERM

DEPERMING > DEPERM

DEPERMS > DEPERM

DEPICT vb produce a picture of

DEPICTED > DEPICT

DEPICTER > DEPICT

DEPICTERS > DEPICT

DEPICTING > DEPICT

DEPICTION > DEPICT

DEPICTIVE > DEPICT

DEPICTOR > DEPICT

DEPICTORS > DEPICT

DEPICTS > DEPICT

DEPICTURE a less common word for > DEPICT

DEPIGMENT vb reduce or remove the normal pigmentation of (the skin)

DEPILATE vb remove the hair from
DEPILATED > DEPILATE
DEPILATES > DEPILATE
DEPILATOR > DEPILATE
DEPLANE vb disembark from an aeroplane
DEPLANED > DEPLANE
DEPLANES > DEPLANE
DEPLANING > DEPLANE
DEPLENISH vb deprive of contents, such as furniture, stock, etc
DEPLETE vb use up
DEPLETED > DEPLETE
DEPLETER > DEPLETE
DEPLETERS > DEPLETE
DEPLETES > DEPLETE
DEPLETING > DEPLETE
DEPLETION > DEPLETE
DEPLETIVE > DEPLETE
DEPLETORY > DEPLETE
DEPLORE vb condemn strongly
DEPLORED > DEPLORE
DEPLORER > DEPLORE
DEPLORERS > DEPLORE
DEPLORES > DEPLORE
DEPLORING > DEPLORE
DEPLOY vb get (troops or resources) ready for immediate action
DEPLOYED > DEPLOY
DEPLOYER > DEPLOY
DEPLOYERS > DEPLOY
DEPLOYING > DEPLOY
DEPLOYS > DEPLOY
DEPLUME vb deprive of feathers
DEPLUMED > DEPLUME
DEPLUMES > DEPLUME
DEPLUMING > DEPLUME
DEPOLISH vb remove the polish from
DEPONE vb declare (something) under oath
DEPONED > DEPONE
DEPONENT n person who makes a statement on oath ▷ adj having a passive form but active meaning
DEPONENTS > DEPONENT
DEPONES > DEPONE
DEPONING > DEPONE
DEPORT vb remove forcibly from a country
DEPORTED > DEPORT
DEPORTEE n person deported or awaiting deportation
DEPORTEES > DEPORTEE
DEPORTER > DEPORT
DEPORTERS > DEPORT
DEPORTING > DEPORT
DEPORTS > DEPORT
DEPOSABLE > DEPOSE
DEPOSAL n deposition; giving of testimony under oath
DEPOSALS > DEPOSAL
DEPOSE vb remove from an office or position of power
DEPOSED > DEPOSE
DEPOSER > DEPOSE
DEPOSERS > DEPOSE
DEPOSES > DEPOSE
DEPOSING > DEPOSE

DEPOSIT vb put down ▷ n sum of money paid into a bank account
DEPOSITED > DEPOSIT
DEPOSITOR n person who places or has money on deposit in a bank or similar organization
DEPOSITS > DEPOSIT
DEPOT n building where goods or vehicles are kept when not in use ▷ adj (of a drug) designed for gradual release
DEPOTS > DEPOT
DEPRAVE vb make morally bad
DEPRAVED adj morally bad
DEPRAVER > DEPRAVE
DEPRAVERS > DEPRAVE
DEPRAVES > DEPRAVE
DEPRAVING > DEPRAVE
DEPRAVITY n moral corruption
DEPRECATE vb express disapproval of
DEPREDATE vb plunder or destroy
DEPREHEND vb apprehend
DEPRENYL n drug combating effects of ageing
DEPRENYLS > DEPRENYL
DEPRESS vb make sad
DEPRESSED adj low in spirits
DEPRESSES > DEPRESS
DEPRESSOR n person or thing that depresses
DEPRIME vb remove the primer from a device
DEPRIMED > DEPRIME
DEPRIMES > DEPRIME
DEPRIMING > DEPRIME
DEPRIVAL > DEPRIVE
DEPRIVALS > DEPRIVE
DEPRIVE vb prevent from (having or enjoying)
DEPRIVED adj lacking adequate living conditions, education, etc
DEPRIVER > DEPRIVE
DEPRIVERS > DEPRIVE
DEPRIVES > DEPRIVE
DEPRIVING > DEPRIVE
DEPROGRAM vb free someone from indoctrination
DEPS > DEP
DEPSIDE n organic chemical compound
DEPSIDES > DEPSIDE
DEPTH n distance downwards, backwards, or inwards
DEPTHLESS adj immeasurably deep
DEPTHS > DEPTH
DEPURANT adj purifying
DEPURANTS > DEPURANT
DEPURATE vb cleanse or purify or to be cleansed or purified
DEPURATED > DEPURATE
DEPURATES > DEPURATE
DEPURATOR > DEPURATE
DEPUTABLE > DEPUTE

DEPUTE vb appoint (someone) to act on one's behalf ▷ n deputy
DEPUTED > DEPUTE
DEPUTES > DEPUTE
DEPUTIES > DEPUTY
DEPUTING > DEPUTE
DEPUTISE same as > DEPUTIZE
DEPUTISED > DEPUTISE
DEPUTISES > DEPUTISE
DEPUTIZE vb act as deputy
DEPUTIZED > DEPUTIZE
DEPUTIZES > DEPUTIZE
DEPUTY n person appointed to act on behalf of another
DEQUEUE vb remove (an item) from a queue of computing tasks
DEQUEUED > DEQUEUE
DEQUEUES > DEQUEUE
DEQUEUING > DEQUEUE
DERACINE adj uprooted from their usual environment ▷ n person who has been uprooted from their usual environment
DERACINES > DERACINE
DERAIGN vb contest (a claim, suit, etc)
DERAIGNED > DERAIGN
DERAIGNS > DERAIGN
DERAIL vb cause (a train) to go off the rails
DERAILED > DERAIL
DERAILER same as > DERAIL
DERAILERS > DERAILER
DERAILING > DERAIL
DERAILS > DERAIL
DERANGE vb disturb the order or arrangement of
DERANGED > DERANGE
DERANGER > DERANGE
DERANGERS > DERANGE
DERANGES > DERANGE
DERANGING > DERANGE
DERAT vb remove rats from
DERATE vb assess the value of some types of property at a lower rate than others for local taxation
DERATED > DERATE
DERATES > DERATE
DERATING > DERATE
DERATINGS > DERATE
DERATION vb end rationing of (food, petrol, etc)
DERATIONS > DERATION
DERATS > DERAT
DERATTED > DERAT
DERATTING > DERAT
DERAY vb go mad
DERAYED > DERAY
DERAYING > DERAY
DERAYS > DERAY
DERBIES > DERBY
DERBY n bowler hat
DERE vb injure
DERECHO n long, fast-moving line of severe storms
DERECHOS > DERECHO
DERED > DERE
DERELICT adj unused and falling into ruins ▷ n social outcast, vagrant

DERELICTS > DERELICT
DEREPRESS vb induce operation of gene
DERES > DERE
DERHAM same as > DIRHAM
DERHAMS > DERHAM
DERIDE vb treat with contempt or ridicule
DERIDED > DERIDE
DERIDER > DERIDE
DERIDERS > DERIDE
DERIDES > DERIDE
DERIDING > DERIDE
DERIG vb remove equipment, eg from stage set
DERIGGED > DERIG
DERIGGING > DERIG
DERIGS > DERIG
DERING > DERE
DERINGER same as > DERRINGER
DERINGERS > DERINGER
DERISIBLE adj subject to or deserving of derision
DERISION n act of deriding
DERISIONS > DERISION
DERISIVE adj mocking, scornful
DERISORY adj too small or inadequate to be considered seriously
DERIVABLE > DERIVE
DERIVABLY > DERIVE
DERIVATE n derivative ▷ vb derive (something)
DERIVATED > DERIVATE
DERIVATES > DERIVATE
DERIVE vb take or develop (from)
DERIVED > DERIVE
DERIVER > DERIVE
DERIVERS > DERIVE
DERIVES > DERIVE
DERIVING > DERIVE
DERM same as > DERMA
DERMA n beef or fowl intestine used as a casing for certain dishes, esp kishke
DERMAL adj of or relating to the skin
DERMAS > DERMA
DERMATIC adj of skin
DERMATOID adj resembling skin
DERMATOME n surgical instrument for cutting thin slices of skin, esp for grafting
DERMESTID n type of beetle whose larva and adult is destructive to many stored organic materials, such as wool and meat
DERMIC > DERMIS
DERMIS another name for > CORIUM
DERMISES > DERMIS
DERMOID adj of or resembling skin ▷ n congenital cystic tumour whose walls are lined with epithelium
DERMOIDS > DERMOID
DERMS > DERM
DERN n concealment ▷ vb keep hidden
DERNED > DERN
DERNFUL adj sorrowful

d

d

DERNIER *adj* last
DERNIES > DERNY
DERNING > DERN
DERNLY *adv* sorrowfully
DERNS > DERN
DERNY *n* bicycle with a small motor
DERNYS > DERNY
DERO *n* tramp or derelict
DEROGATE *vb* detract from ▷ *adj* debased or degraded
DEROGATED > DEROGATE
DEROGATES > DEROGATE
DEROS > DERO
DERRICK *n* simple crane ▷ *vb* raise or lower the jib of (a crane)
DERRICKED > DERRICK
DERRICKS > DERRICK
DERRIERE *n* backside
DERRIERES > DERRIERE
DERRIES > DERRY
DERRINGER *n* small large-bored pistol
DERRIS *n* E Indian woody climbing plant
DERRISES > DERRIS
DERRO *n* vagrant
DERROS > DERRO
DERRY *n* derelict house, esp one used by tramps
DERTH *same as* > DEARTH
DERTHS > DERTH
DERV *n* diesel oil, when used for road transport
DERVISH *n* member of a Muslim religious order noted for a frenzied whirling dance
DERVISHES > DERVISH
DERVS > DERV
DESALT *vb* desalinate
DESALTED > DESALT
DESALTER > DESALT
DESALTERS > DESALT
DESALTING > DESALT
DESALTS > DESALT
DESAND *vb* remove sand from
DESANDED > DESAND
DESANDING > DESAND
DESANDS > DESAND
DESCALE *vb* remove a hard coating from inside (a kettle or pipe)
DESCALED > DESCALE
DESCALER *n* something that removes limescale
DESCALERS > DESCALER
DESCALES > DESCALE
DESCALING > DESCALE
DESCANT *n* tune played or sung above a basic melody ▷ *adj* denoting the highest member in a family of musical instruments ▷ *vb* compose or perform a descant (for a piece of music)
DESCANTED > DESCANT
DESCANTER > DESCANT
DESCANTS > DESCANT
DESCEND *vb* move down (a slope etc)
DESCENDED > DESCEND
DESCENDER > DESCEND
DESCENDS > DESCEND
DESCENT *n* descending
DESCENTS > DESCENT

DESCHOOL *vb* educate by means other than a school
DESCHOOLS > DESCHOOL
DESCRIBE *vb* give an account of (something or someone) in words
DESCRIBED > DESCRIBE
DESCRIBER > DESCRIBE
DESCRIBES > DESCRIBE
DESCRIED > DESCRY
DESCRIER > DESCRY
DESCRIERS > DESCRY
DESCRIES > DESCRY
DESCRIVE *vb* describe
DESCRIVED > DESCRIVE
DESCRIVES > DESCRIVE
DESCRY *vb* catch sight of
DESCRYING > DESCRY
DESECRATE *vb* damage or insult (something sacred)
DESEED *vb* remove the seeds from (eg a fruit)
DESEEDED > DESEED
DESEEDER *n* person who deseeds
DESEEDERS > DESEEDER
DESEEDING > DESEED
DESEEDS > DESEED
DESELECT *vb* refuse to select (an MP) for re-election
DESELECTS > DESELECT
DESERT *n* region with little or no vegetation because of low rainfall ▷ *vb* abandon (a person or place) without intending to return
DESERTED > DESERT
DESERTER > DESERT
DESERTERS > DESERT
DESERTIC *adj* (of soil) developing in hot climates
DESERTIFY *vb* turn into desert
DESERTING > DESERT
DESERTION *n* act of deserting or abandoning or the state of being deserted or abandoned
DESERTS > DESERT
DESERVE *vb* be entitled to or worthy of
DESERVED > DESERVE
DESERVER > DESERVE
DESERVERS > DESERVE
DESERVES > DESERVE
DESERVING *adj* worthy of help, praise, or reward ▷ *n* merit or demerit
DESEX *vb* desexualize
DESEXED > DESEX
DESEXES > DESEX
DESEXING > DESEX
DESHI *same as* > DESI
DESHIS > DESHI
DESI *adj* (in Indian English) indigenous or local ▷ *n* (in Indian English) indigenous or local person
DESICCANT *adj* desiccating or drying ▷ *n* substance, such as calcium oxide, that absorbs water and is used to remove moisture
DESICCATE *vb* remove most of the water from
DESIGN *vb* work out the structure or form of

(something), by making a sketch or plans ▷ *n* preliminary drawing
DESIGNATE *vb* give a name to ▷ *adj* appointed but not yet in office
DESIGNED > DESIGN
DESIGNEE *n* person designated to do something
DESIGNEES > DESIGNEE
DESIGNER *n* person who draws up original sketches or plans from which things are made ▷ *adj* designed by a well-known designer
DESIGNERS > DESIGNER
DESIGNFUL *adj* scheming
DESIGNING *adj* cunning and scheming
DESIGNS > DESIGN
DESILVER *vb* remove silver from
DESILVERS > DESILVER
DESINE *same as* > DESIGN
DESINED > DESINE
DESINENCE *n* ending or termination, esp an inflectional ending of a word
DESINENT > DESINENCE
DESINES > DESINE
DESINING > DESINE
DESIPIENT *adj* foolish
DESIRABLE *adj* worth having ▷ *n* person or thing that is the object of desire
DESIRABLY > DESIRABLE
DESIRE *vb* want very much ▷ *n* wish, longing
DESIRED > DESIRE
DESIRER > DESIRE
DESIRERS > DESIRE
DESIRES > DESIRE
DESIRING > DESIRE
DESIROUS *adj* having a desire for
DESIS > DESI
DESIST *vb* stop (doing something)
DESISTED > DESIST
DESISTING > DESIST
DESISTS > DESIST
DESK *n* piece of furniture with a writing surface and drawers
DESKBOUND *adj* engaged in or involving sedentary work, as at an office desk
DESKFAST *n* breakfast eaten at one's desk at work
DESKFASTS > DESKFAST
DESKILL *vb* mechanize or computerize (a job) thereby reducing the skill required to do it
DESKILLED > DESKILL
DESKILLS > DESKILL
DESKING *n* desks and related furnishings in a given space, eg an office
DESKINGS > DESKING
DESKMAN *n* police officer in charge in police station
DESKMEN > DESKMAN
DESKNOTE *n* small computer
DESKNOTES > DESKNOTE
DESKS > DESK

DESKTOP *adj* (of a computer) small enough to use at a desk ▷ *n* computer small enough to use at a desk
DESKTOPS > DESKTOP
DESMAN *n* either of two molelike amphibious mammals
DESMANS > DESMAN
DESMID *n* type of mainly unicellular freshwater green alga
DESMIDIAN > DESMID
DESMIDS > DESMID
DESMINE *n* type of mineral
DESMINES > DESMINE
DESMODIUM *n* type of plant
DESMOID *adj* resembling a tendon or ligament ▷ *n* very firm tumour of connective tissue
DESMOIDS > DESMOID
DESMOSOME *n* structure in the cell membranes of adjacent cells that binds them together
DESNOOD *vb* remove the snood of a turkey poult to reduce the risk of cannibalism
DESNOODED > DESNOOD
DESNOODS > DESNOOD
DESOEUVRE *adj* with nothing to do
DESOLATE *adj* uninhabited and bleak ▷ *vb* deprive of inhabitants
DESOLATED > DESOLATE
DESOLATER > DESOLATE
DESOLATES > DESOLATE
DESOLATOR > DESOLATE
DESORB *vb* change from an adsorbed state to a gaseous or liquid state
DESORBED > DESORB
DESORBER *n* something that desorbs
DESORBERS > DESORBER
DESORBING > DESORB
DESORBS > DESORB
DESOXY *same as* > DEOXY
DESPAIR *n* total loss of hope ▷ *vb* lose hope
DESPAIRED > DESPAIR
DESPAIRER *n* one who despairs
DESPAIRS > DESPAIR
DESPATCH *same as* > DISPATCH
DESPERADO *n* reckless person ready to commit any violent illegal act
DESPERATE *adj* in despair and reckless
DESPIGHT *obsolete form of* > DESPITE
DESPIGHTS > DESPIGHT
DESPISAL > DESPISE
DESPISALS > DESPISE
DESPISE *vb* regard with contempt
DESPISED > DESPISE
DESPISER > DESPISE
DESPISERS > DESPISE
DESPISES > DESPISE
DESPISING > DESPISE

DESPITE prep in spite of ▷ n contempt ▷ vb show contempt for
DESPITED > DESPITE
DESPITES > DESPITE
DESPITING > DESPITE
DESPOIL vb plunder
DESPOILED > DESPOIL
DESPOILER > DESPOIL
DESPOILS > DESPOIL
DESPOND vb lose heart or hope
DESPONDED > DESPOND
DESPONDS > DESPOND
DESPOT n person in power who acts unfairly or cruelly
DESPOTAT n despot's domain
DESPOTATE same as > DESPOTAT
DESPOTATS > DESPOTAT
DESPOTIC > DESPOT
DESPOTISM n unfair or cruel government or behaviour
DESPOTS > DESPOT
DESPUMATE vb clarify or purify (a liquid) by skimming a scum from its surface
DESSE n desk
DESSERT n sweet course served at the end of a meal
DESSERTS > DESSERT
DESSES > DESSE
DESSYATIN n Russian measure of land
DESTAIN vb remove stain from
DESTAINED > DESTAIN
DESTAINS > DESTAIN
DESTEMPER same as > DISTEMPER
DESTINATE same as > DESTINE
DESTINE vb set apart or appoint
DESTINED adj certain to be or to do something
DESTINES > DESTINE
DESTINIES > DESTINY
DESTINING > DESTINE
DESTINY n future marked out for a person or thing
DESTITUTE adj having no money or possessions
DESTOCK vb reduce the amount of stock
DESTOCKED > DESTOCK
DESTOCKS > DESTOCK
DESTREAM vb take (pupils) out of classes that are organized by ability
DESTREAMS > DESTREAM
DESTRESS vb make or become less stressed
DESTRIER an archaic word for > WARHORSE
DESTRIERS > DESTRIER
DESTROY vb ruin, demolish
DESTROYED > DESTROY
DESTROYER n small heavily armed warship
DESTROYS > DESTROY
DESTRUCT vb destroy intentionally for safety ▷ n act of destructing ▷ adj capable of self-destruction

DESTRUCTO n person who causes havoc or destruction
DESTRUCTS > DESTRUCT
DESUETUDE n condition of not being in use
DESUGAR vb remove sugar from
DESUGARED > DESUGAR
DESUGARS > DESUGAR
DESULFUR same as > DESULPHUR
DESULFURS > DESULFUR
DESULPHUR vb remove sulphur from
DESULTORY adj jumping from one thing to another, disconnected
DESYATIN n Russian unit of area
DESYATINS > DESYATIN
DESYNE same as > DESIGN
DESYNED > DESYNE
DESYNES > DESYNE
DESYNING > DESYNE
DETACH vb disengage and separate
DETACHED adj (of a house) not joined to another house
DETACHER > DETACH
DETACHERS > DETACH
DETACHES > DETACH
DETACHING > DETACH
DETAIL n individual piece of information ▷ vb list fully
DETAILED adj having many details
DETAILER > DETAIL
DETAILERS > DETAIL
DETAILING > DETAIL
DETAILS > DETAIL
DETAIN vb delay (someone)
DETAINED > DETAIN
DETAINEE > DETAIN
DETAINEES > DETAIN
DETAINER n wrongful withholding of the property of another person
DETAINERS > DETAINER
DETAINING > DETAIN
DETAINS > DETAIN
DETANGLE vb remove tangles from (esp hair)
DETANGLED > DETANGLE
DETANGLER n cosmetic product used to detangle hair
DETANGLES > DETANGLE
DETASSEL vb remove top part of corn plant
DETASSELS > DETASSEL
DETECT vb notice
DETECTED > DETECT
DETECTER > DETECT
DETECTERS > DETECT
DETECTING > DETECT
DETECTION n act of noticing, discovering, or sensing something
DETECTIVE n police officer or private agent who investigates crime ▷ adj used in or serving for detection
DETECTOR n instrument used to find something
DETECTORS > DETECTOR
DETECTS > DETECT

DETENT n mechanism to check movement in one direction only
DETENTE n easing of tension between nations
DETENTES > DETENTE
DETENTION n imprisonment
DETENTIST n supporter of detente
DETENTS > DETENT
DETENU n prisoner
DETENUE n female prisoner
DETENUES > DETENUE
DETENUS > DETENU
DETER vb discourage (someone) from doing something by instilling fear or doubt
DETERGE vb wash or wipe away
DETERGED > DETERGE
DETERGENT n chemical substance for washing clothes or dishes ▷ adj having cleansing power
DETERGER n detergent
DETERGERS > DETERGER
DETERGES > DETERGE
DETERGING > DETERGE
DETERMENT > DETER
DETERMINE vb settle (an argument or a question) conclusively
DETERRED > DETER
DETERRENT n something that deters ▷ adj tending to deter
DETERRER > DETER
DETERRERS > DETERRER
DETERRING > DETER
DETERS > DETER
DETERSION n act of cleansing
DETERSIVE same as > DETERGENT
DETEST vb dislike intensely
DETESTED > DETEST
DETESTER > DETEST
DETESTERS > DETEST
DETESTING > DETEST
DETESTS > DETEST
DETHATCH vb remove dead grass from lawn
DETHRONE vb remove from a throne or position of power
DETHRONED > DETHRONE
DETHRONER > DETHRONE
DETHRONES > DETHRONE
DETICK vb remove ticks from
DETICKED > DETICK
DETICKER > DETICK
DETICKERS > DETICK
DETICKING > DETICK
DETICKS > DETICK
DETINUE n action brought by a plaintiff to recover goods wrongfully detained
DETINUES > DETINUE
DETONABLE adj that can be detonated
DETONATE vb explode
DETONATED > DETONATE
DETONATES > DETONATE
DETONATOR n small amount of explosive, or a

device, used to set off an explosion
DETORSION > DETORT
DETORT vb twist or distort
DETORTED > DETORT
DETORTING > DETORT
DETORTION > DETORT
DETORTS > DETORT
DETOUR n route that is not the most direct one ▷ vb deviate or cause to deviate from a direct route or course of action
DETOURED > DETOUR
DETOURING > DETOUR
DETOURS > DETOUR
DETOX n treatment to rid the body of poisonous substances ▷ vb undergo treatment to rid the body of poisonous substances
DETOXED > DETOX
DETOXES > DETOX
DETOXIFY vb remove poison from
DETOXING > DETOX
DETRACT vb make (something) seem less good
DETRACTED > DETRACT
DETRACTOR > DETRACT
DETRACTS > DETRACT
DETRAIN vb leave or cause to leave a railway train, as passengers, etc
DETRAINED > DETRAIN
DETRAINS > DETRAIN
DETRAQUE n insane person
DETRAQUEE n female insane person
DETRAQUES > DETRAQUE
DETRIMENT n disadvantage or damage
DETRITAL > DETRITUS
DETRITION n act of rubbing or wearing away by friction
DETRITUS n loose mass of stones and silt worn away from rocks
DETRUDE vb force down or thrust away or out
DETRUDED > DETRUDE
DETRUDES > DETRUDE
DETRUDING > DETRUDE
DETRUSION > DETRUDE
DETRUSOR n muscle in the wall of the bladder
DETRUSORS > DETRUSOR
DETUNE vb change pitch of (stringed instrument)
DETUNED > DETUNE
DETUNES > DETUNE
DETUNING > DETUNE
DEUCE vb score deuce in tennis ▷ n score of forty all
DEUCED adj damned
DEUCEDLY > DEUCED
DEUCES > DEUCE
DEUCING > DEUCE
DEUDDARN n two-tiered Welsh dresser
DEUDDARNS > DEUDDARN
DEUS n god
DEUTERATE vb treat or combine with deuterium
DEUTERIC adj (of mineral) formed by metasomatic changes

d

d

DEUTERIDE n compound of deuterium with some other element. It is analogous to a hydride

DEUTERIUM n isotope of hydrogen twice as heavy as the normal atom

DEUTERON n nucleus of a deuterium atom, consisting of one proton and one neutron

DEUTERONS > DEUTERON

DEUTON old form of > DEUTERON

DEUTONS > DEUTON

DEUTZIA n shrub with clusters of pink or white flowers

DEUTZIAS > DEUTZIA

DEV same as > DEVA

DEVA n (in Hinduism and Buddhism) divine being or god

DEVALL vb stop

DEVALLED > DEVALL

DEVALLING > DEVALL

DEVALLS > DEVALL

DEVALUATE same as > DEVALUE

DEVALUE vb reduce the exchange value of (a currency)

DEVALUED > DEVALUE

DEVALUES > DEVALUE

DEVALUING > DEVALUE

DEVAS > DEVA

DEVASTATE vb destroy

DEVEIN vb remove vein from

DEVEINED > DEVEIN

DEVEINING > DEVEIN

DEVEINS > DEVEIN

DEVEL same as > DEVVEL

DEVELED > DEVEL

DEVELING > DEVEL

DEVELLED > DEVEL

DEVELLING > DEVEL

DEVELOP vb grow or bring to a later, more elaborate, or more advanced stage

DEVELOPE old form of > DEVELOP

DEVELOPED > DEVELOP

DEVELOPER n person who develops property

DEVELOPES > DEVELOPE

DEVELOPPE n ballet position

DEVELOPS > DEVELOP

DEVELS > DEVEL

DEVERBAL n word deriving from verb

DEVERBALS > DEVERBAL

DEVEST variant spelling of > DIVEST

DEVESTED > DEVEST

DEVESTING > DEVEST

DEVESTS > DEVEST

DEVI n Hindu goddess

DEVIANCE n act or state of being deviant

DEVIANCES > DEVIANCE

DEVIANCY same as > DEVIANCE

DEVIANT adj (person) deviating from what is considered acceptable behaviour ▷ n person whose

behaviour deviates from what is considered to be acceptable

DEVIANTS > DEVIANT

DEVIATE vb differ from others in belief or thought

DEVIATED > DEVIATE

DEVIATES > DEVIATE

DEVIATING > DEVIATE

DEVIATION n act or result of deviating

DEVIATIVE adj tending to deviate

DEVIATOR > DEVIATE

DEVIATORS > DEVIATE

DEVIATORY > DEVIATE

DEVICE n machine or tool used for a specific task

DEVICEFUL adj full of devices

DEVICES > DEVICE

DEVIL n evil spirit ▷ vb prepare (food) with a highly flavoured spiced mixture

DEVILDOM n domain of evil spirits

DEVILDOMS > DEVILDOM

DEVILED > DEVIL

DEVILESS n female devil

DEVILET n young devil

DEVILETS > DEVILET

DEVILFISH n manta fish

DEVILING > DEVIL

DEVILINGS > DEVIL

DEVILISH adj cruel or unpleasant ▷ adv extremely

DEVILISM n doctrine of devil

DEVILISMS > DEVILISM

DEVILKIN n small devil

DEVILKINS > DEVILKIN

DEVILLED > DEVIL

DEVILLING > DEVIL

DEVILMENT n mischievous conduct

DEVILRIES > DEVILRY

DEVILRY n mischievousness

DEVILS > DEVIL

DEVILSHIP n character of devil

DEVILTRY same as > DEVILRY

DEVILWOOD n small US tree

DEVIOUS adj insincere and dishonest

DEVIOUSLY > DEVIOUS

DEVIS > DEVI

DEVISABLE adj (of property, esp realty) capable of being transferred by will

DEVISAL n act of inventing, contriving, or devising

DEVISALS > DEVISAL

DEVISE vb work out (something) in one's mind ▷ n disposition of property by will

DEVISED > DEVISE

DEVISEE n person to whom property, esp realty, is devised by will

DEVISEES > DEVISEE

DEVISER > DEVISE

DEVISERS > DEVISE

DEVISES > DEVISE

DEVISING > DEVISE

DEVISOR n person who devises property, esp realty, by will

DEVISORS > DEVISOR

DEVITRIFY vb change from a vitreous state to a crystalline state

DEVLING n young devil

DEVLINGS > DEVLING

DEVO n short for devolution

DEVOICE vb make (a voiced speech sound) voiceless

DEVOICED > DEVOICE

DEVOICES > DEVOICE

DEVOICING n act of devoicing

DEVOID adj completely lacking (in)

DEVOIR n duty

DEVOIRS > DEVOIR

DEVOLVE vb pass to a successor or substitute

DEVOLVED > DEVOLVE

DEVOLVES > DEVOLVE

DEVOLVING > DEVOLVE

DEVON n bland processed meat in sausage form, eaten cold in slices

DEVONIAN adj denoting the fourth period of the Palaeozoic era

DEVONPORT same as > DAVENPORT

DEVONS > DEVON

DEVORE n velvet fabric with a raised pattern

DEVORES > DEVORE

DEVOS > DEVO

DEVOT n devotee

DEVOTE vb apply or dedicate to a particular purpose

DEVOTED adj showing loyalty or devotion

DEVOTEDLY > DEVOTED

DEVOTEE n person who is very enthusiastic about something

DEVOTEES > DEVOTEE

DEVOTES > DEVOTE

DEVOTING > DEVOTE

DEVOTION n strong affection for or loyalty to someone or something

DEVOTIONS > DEVOTION

DEVOTS > DEVOT

DEVOUR vb eat greedily

DEVOURED > DEVOUR

DEVOURER > DEVOUR

DEVOURERS > DEVOUR

DEVOURING > DEVOUR

DEVOURS > DEVOUR

DEVOUT adj deeply religious

DEVOUTER > DEVOUT

DEVOUTEST > DEVOUT

DEVOUTLY > DEVOUT

DEVS > DEV

DEVVEL vb strike with blow

DEVVELLED > DEVVEL

DEVVELS > DEVVEL

DEW n drops of water that form on the ground at night from vapour in the air ▷ vb moisten with or as with dew

DEWAN n (formerly in India) the chief or finance minister of a state ruled by an Indian prince

DEWANI n post of dewan

DEWANIS > DEWANI

DEWANNIES > DEWANNY

DEWANNY same as > DEWANI

DEWANS > DEWAN

DEWAR n type of vacuum flask

DEWARS > DEWAR

DEWATER vb remove water from

DEWATERED > DEWATER

DEWATERER > DEWATER

DEWATERS > DEWATER

DEWAX vb remove wax from

DEWAXED > DEWAX

DEWAXES > DEWAX

DEWAXING > DEWAX

DEWBERRY n type of bramble with blue-black fruits

DEWCLAW n nonfunctional claw on a dog's leg

DEWCLAWED > DEWCLAW

DEWCLAWS > DEWCLAW

DEWDROP n drop of dew

DEWDROPS > DEWDROP

DEWED > DEW

DEWFALL n formation of dew

DEWFALLS > DEWFALL

DEWFULL obsolete form of > DUE

DEWIER > DEWY

DEWIEST > DEWY

DEWILY > DEWY

DEWINESS > DEWY

DEWING > DEW

DEWITT vb kill, esp hang unlawfully

DEWITTED > DEWITT

DEWITTING > DEWITT

DEWITTS > DEWITT

DEWLAP n loose fold of skin hanging under the throat in dogs, cattle, etc

DEWLAPPED > DEWLAP

DEWLAPS > DEWLAP

DEWLAPT > DEWLAP

DEWLESS > DEW

DEWOOL vb remove wool from

DEWOOLED > DEWOOL

DEWOOLING > DEWOOL

DEWOOLS > DEWOOL

DEWORM vb rid of worms

DEWORMED > DEWORM

DEWORMER > DEWORM

DEWORMERS > DEWORM

DEWORMING > DEWORM

DEWORMS > DEWORM

DEWPOINT n temperature at which water droplets form in the air

DEWPOINTS > DEWPOINT

DEWS > DEW

DEWY adj moist with or as with dew

DEX n dextroamphetamine

DEXES > DEX

DEXIE n pill containing dextroamphetamine

DEXIES > DEXIE

DEXTER adj of or on the right side of a shield, etc, from the bearer's point of view ▷ n small breed of beef cattle

DEXTERITY n skill in using one's hands

DEXTEROUS *adj* possessing or done with dexterity

DEXTERS > DEXTER

DEXTRAL *n* right-handed person

DEXTRALLY > DEXTRAL

DEXTRALS > DEXTRAL

DEXTRAN *n* polysaccharide compound

DEXTRANS > DEXTRAN

DEXTRIN *n* sticky substance obtained from starch

DEXTRINE *same as* > DEXTRIN

DEXTRINES > DEXTRINE

DEXTRINS > DEXTRIN

DEXTRO *adj* dextrorotatory or rotating to the right

DEXTRORSE *adj* (of some climbing plants) growing upwards in a helix from left to right or anticlockwise

DEXTROSE *n* glucose occurring in fruit, honey, and the blood of animals

DEXTROSES > DEXTROSE

DEXTROUS *same as* > DEXTEROUS

DEXY *same as* > DEXIE

DEY *n* title given to commanders or governors of the Janissaries of Algiers

DEYS > DEY

DEZINC *vb* remove zinc from

DEZINCED > DEZINC

DEZINCING > DEZINC

DEZINCKED > DEZINC

DEZINCS > DEZINC

DHABA *n* roadside café in India

DHABAS > DHABA

DHAK *n* tropical Asian tree

DHAKS > DHAK

DHAL *n* curry made from lentils or beans

DHALS > DHAL

DHAMMA *variant of* > DHARMA

DHAMMAS > DHAMMA

DHANSAK *n* any of a variety of Indian dishes

DHANSAKS > DHANSAK

DHARMA *n* moral law or behaviour

DHARMAS > DHARMA

DHARMIC > DHARMA

DHARMSALA *n* Indian hostel

DHARNA *n* (in India) a method of obtaining justice

DHARNAS > DHARNA

DHIKR *n* Sufi religious ceremony

DHIKRS > DHIKR

DHIMMI *n* non-Muslim living in a state governed by sharia law

DHIMMIS > DHIMMI

DHOBI *n* (in India, Malaya, East Africa, etc, esp formerly) a washerman

DHOBIS > DHOBI

DHOL *n* type of Indian drum

DHOLAK *n* type of two-headed drum

DHOLAKS > DHOLAK

DHOLE *n* fierce canine mammal

DHOLES > DHOLE

DHOLL *same as* > DHAL

DHOLLS > DHOLL

DHOLS > DHOL

DHOOLIES > DHOOLY

DHOOLY *same as* > DOOLIE

DHOORA *same as* > DURRA

DHOORAS > DHOORA

DHOOTI *same as* > DHOTI

DHOOTIE *same as* > DHOTI

DHOOTIES > DHOOTIE

DHOOTIS > DHOOTI

DHOTI *n* long loincloth worn by men in India

DHOTIS > DHOTI

DHOURRA *same as* > DURRA

DHOURRAS > DHOURRA

DHOW *n* Arab sailing ship

DHOWS > DHOW

DHURNA *same as* > DHARNA

DHURNAS > DHURNA

DHURRA *same as* > DURRA

DHURRAS > DHURRA

DHURRIE *same as* > DURRIE

DHURRIES > DHURRIE

DHUTI *same as* > DHOTI

DHUTIS > DHUTI

DHYANA *n* type of Hindu meditation

DHYANAS > DHYANA

DI > DEUS

DIABASE *n* altered dolerite

DIABASES > DIABASE

DIABASIC > DIABASE

DIABETES *n* disorder in which an abnormal amount of urine containing an excess of sugar is excreted

DIABETIC *n* person who has diabetes ▷ *adj* of or having diabetes

DIABETICS > DIABETIC

DIABLE *n* type of sauce

DIABLERIE *n* magic or witchcraft connected with devils

DIABLERY *same as* > DIABLERIE

DIABLES > DIABLE

DIABOLIC *adj* of the Devil

DIABOLISE *same as* > DIABOLIZE

DIABOLISM *n* witchcraft, devil worship

DIABOLIST > DIABOLISM

DIABOLIZE *vb* make (someone or something) diabolical

DIABOLO *n* game using a spinning top and a cord fastened to two sticks

DIABOLOGY *n* study of devils

DIABOLOS > DIABOLO

DIACETYL *n* aromatic compound

DIACETYLS > DIACETYL

DIACHRONY *n* change over time

DIACHYLON *n* acid or salt that contains two acidic hydrogen atoms

DIACHYLUM *n* plaster containing glycerin with lead salts

DIACID *n* lead plaster

DIACIDIC *adj* capable of neutralizing two protons with one molecule

DIACIDS > DIACID

DIACODION *n* herbal remedy aiding sleep

DIACODIUM *n* syrup of poppies

DIACONAL *adj* of or associated with a deacon or the diaconate

DIACONATE *n* position or period of office of a deacon

DIACRITIC *n* sign above or below a character to indicate phonetic value or stress

DIACT *same as* > DIACTINE

DIACTINAL *adj* having two pointed ends

DIACTINE *adj* two-rayed ▷ *n* two-rayed sponge spicule

DIACTINES > DIACTINE

DIACTINIC *adj* able to transmit photochemically active radiation

DIACTS > DIACT

DIADEM *n* crown ▷ *vb* adorn or crown with or as with a diadem

DIADEMED > DIADEM

DIADEMING > DIADEM

DIADEMS > DIADEM

DIADOCHI *pl n* six generals who fought for control of the Alexandrian Empire

DIADOCHY *n* replacement of one element in a crystal by another

DIADROM *n* complete course of pendulum

DIADROMS > DIADROM

DIAERESES > DIAERESIS

DIAERESIS *n* mark placed over a vowel to show that it is pronounced separately from the preceding one, for example in *Noël*

DIAERETIC > DIAERESIS

DIAGLYPH *n* figure cut into stone

DIAGLYPHS > DIAGLYPH

DIAGNOSE *vb* determine by diagnosis

DIAGNOSED > DIAGNOSE

DIAGNOSES > DIAGNOSIS

DIAGNOSIS *n* discovery and identification of diseases from the examination of symptoms

DIAGONAL *adj* from corner to corner ▷ *n* diagonal line

DIAGONALS > DIAGONAL

DIAGRAM *n* sketch showing the form or workings of something ▷ *vb* show in or as if in a diagram

DIAGRAMED > DIAGRAM

DIAGRAMS > DIAGRAM

DIAGRAPH *n* device for enlarging or reducing maps, plans, etc

DIAGRAPHS > DIAGRAPH

DIAGRID *n* diagonal structure network

DIAGRIDS > DIAGRID

DIAL *n* face of a clock or watch ▷ *vb* operate the dial or buttons on a telephone in order to contact (a number)

DIALECT *n* form of a language spoken in a particular area

DIALECTAL > DIALECT

DIALECTIC *n* logical debate by question and answer to resolve differences between two views ▷ *adj* of or relating to logical disputation

DIALECTS > DIALECT

DIALED > DIAL

DIALER > DIAL

DIALERS > DIAL

DIALING > DIAL

DIALINGS > DIAL

DIALIST *n* dial-maker

DIALISTS > DIALIST

DIALLAGE *n* green or brownish-black variety of the mineral augite

DIALLAGES > DIALLAGE

DIALLAGIC > DIALLAGE

DIALLED > DIAL

DIALLEL *n* interbreeding among a group of parents ▷ *adj* (of lines) not parallel, meeting, or intersecting

DIALLELS > DIALLEL

DIALLER > DIAL

DIALLERS > DIAL

DIALLING > DIAL

DIALLINGS > DIAL

DIALLIST *same as* > DIALIST

DIALLISTS > DIALLIST

DIALOG *same as* > DIALOGUE

DIALOGED > DIALOG

DIALOGER > DIALOG

DIALOGERS > DIALOG

DIALOGIC > DIALOGUE

DIALOGING > DIALOG

DIALOGISE *same as* > DIALOGIZE

DIALOGISM *n* deduction with one premise and a disjunctive conclusion

DIALOGIST *n* person who writes or takes part in a dialogue

DIALOGITE *n* carbonate mineral

DIALOGIZE *vb* carry on a dialogue

DIALOGS > DIALOG

DIALOGUE *n* conversation between two people, esp in a book, film, or play ▷ *vb* put into the form of a dialogue

DIALOGUED > DIALOGUE

DIALOGUER > DIALOGUE

DIALOGUES > DIALOGUE

DIALS > DIAL

DIALYSATE *n* liquid used in dialysis

DIALYSE *vb* separate by dialysis

DIALYSED > DIALYSE

DIALYSER *n* machine that performs dialysis

DIALYSERS > DIALYSER

DIALYSES > DIALYSIS

DIALYSING > DIALYSE

DIALYSIS *n* filtering of blood through a membrane to remove waste products

d

DIALYTIC > DIALYSIS
DIALYZATE same as
> DIALYSATE
DIALYZE same as
> DIALYSE
DIALYZED > DIALYZE
DIALYZER same as
> DIALYSER
DIALYZERS > DIALYZER
DIALYZES > DIALYZE
DIALYZING > DIALYZE
DIAMAGNET n substance
exhibiting diamagnetism
DIAMANTE adj decorated
with artificial jewels or
sequins ▷ n fabric so covered
DIAMANTES > DIAMANTE
DIAMETER n (length of) a
straight line through the
centre of a circle or sphere
DIAMETERS > DIAMETER
DIAMETRAL same as
> DIAMETRIC
DIAMETRIC adj of a
diameter
DIAMIDE n compound
containing two amido
groups
DIAMIDES > DIAMIDE
DIAMIN same as > DIAMINE
DIAMINE n any chemical
compound containing two
amino groups in its
molecules
DIAMINES > DIAMINE
DIAMINS > DIAMIN
DIAMOND n exceptionally
hard precious stone ▷ adj (of
an anniversary) the sixtieth
▷ vb stud or decorate with
diamonds
DIAMONDED > DIAMOND
DIAMONDS > DIAMOND
DIAMYL adj with two amyl
groups
DIANDRIES > DIANDRY
DIANDROUS adj (of some
flowers or flowering plants)
having two stamens
DIANDRY n practice of
having two husbands
DIANE adj as in steak diane
kind of steak
DIANODAL adj going
through a node
DIANOETIC adj of or
relating to thought, esp to
discursive reasoning rather
than intuition
DIANOIA n perception and
experience regarded as lower
modes of knowledge
DIANOIAS > DIANOIA
DIANTHUS n type of widely
cultivated Eurasian plant
DIAPASE same as
> DIAPASON
DIAPASES > DIAPASE
DIAPASON n either of two
stops found throughout the
range of a pipe organ
DIAPASONS > DIAPASON
DIAPAUSE vb undergo
diapause ▷ n period of
suspended development and
growth
DIAPAUSED > DIAPAUSE
DIAPAUSES > DIAPAUSE

DIAPENTE n (in classical
Greece) the interval of a
perfect fifth
DIAPENTES > DIAPENTE
DIAPER n nappy ▷ vb
decorate with a geometric
pattern
DIAPERED > DIAPER
DIAPERING > DIAPER
DIAPERS > DIAPER
DIAPHONE n set of all
realizations of a given
phoneme in a language
DIAPHONES > DIAPHONE
DIAPHONIC > DIAPHONY
DIAPHONY n style of
two-part polyphonic singing
DIAPHRAGM n muscular
partition that separates the
abdominal cavity and chest
cavity
DIAPHYSES > DIAPHYSIS
DIAPHYSIS n shaft of a
long bone
DIAPIR n type of geologic
formation
DIAPIRIC > DIAPIR
DIAPIRISM > DIAPIR
DIAPIRS > DIAPIR
DIAPSID n reptile with two
holes in rear of skull
DIAPSIDS > DIAPSID
DIAPYESES > DIAPYESIS
DIAPYESIS n discharge of
pus
DIAPYETIC > DIAPYESIS
DIARCH adj (of a vascular
bundle) having two strands
of xylem
DIARCHAL > DIARCHY
DIARCHIC > DIARCHY
DIARCHIES > DIARCHY
DIARCHY n government by
two states, individuals, etc
DIARIAL > DIARY
DIARIAN > DIARY
DIARIES > DIARY
DIARISE same as
> DIARIZE
DIARISED > DIARISE
DIARISES > DIARISE
DIARISING > DIARISE
DIARIST n person who
writes a diary
DIARISTIC > DIARIST
DIARISTS > DIARIST
DIARIZE vb record in diary
DIARIZED > DIARIZE
DIARIZES > DIARIZE
DIARIZING > DIARIZE
DIARRHEA same as
> DIARRHOEA
DIARRHEAL > DIARRHEA
DIARRHEAS > DIARRHEA
DIARRHEIC > DIARRHEA
DIARRHOEA n frequent
discharge of abnormally
liquid faeces
DIARY n (book for) a record
of daily events,
appointments, or
observations
DIASCIA n S African plant,
usu with pink flowers
DIASCIAS > DIASCIA
DIASCOPE n optical
projector used to display
transparencies

DIASCOPES > DIASCOPE
DIASPORA n dispersion or
spreading of a people
DIASPORAS > DIASPORA
DIASPORE n white,
yellowish, or grey mineral
DIASPORES > DIASPORE
DIASPORIC > DIASPORA
DIASTASE n enzyme that
converts starch into sugar
DIASTASES > DIASTASIS
DIASTASIC > DIASTASE
DIASTASIS n separation of
an epiphysis from the long
bone to which it is normally
attached without fracture of
the bone
DIASTATIC > DIASTASIS
DIASTEM same as
> DIASTEMA
DIASTEMA n abnormal
space, fissure, or cleft in a
bodily organ or part
DIASTEMAS > DIASTEMA
DIASTEMS > DIASTEM
DIASTER n stage in cell
division
DIASTERS > DIASTER
DIASTOLE n dilation of the
chambers of the heart
DIASTOLES > DIASTOLE
DIASTOLIC > DIASTOLE
DIASTRAL > DIASTER
DIASTYLE adj having
columns about three
diameters apart ▷ n diastyle
building
DIASTYLES > DIASTYLE
DIATHERMY n local heating
of the body tissues with an
electric current for medical
or surgical purposes
DIATHESES > DIATHESIS
DIATHESIS n hereditary or
acquired susceptibility of the
body to one or more diseases
DIATHETIC > DIATHESIS
DIATOM n microscopic
unicellular alga
DIATOMIC adj containing
two atoms
DIATOMIST n specialist in
diatoms
DIATOMITE n soft very
fine-grained whitish rock
consisting of the siliceous
remains of diatoms
deposited in the ocean or in
ponds or lakes. It is used as
an absorbent, filtering
medium, insulator, filler, etc
DIATOMS > DIATOM
DIATONIC adj of a regular
major or minor scale
DIATREME n volcanic vent
produced by an eruption of gas
DIATREMES > DIATREME
DIATRETA > DIATRETUM
DIATRETUM n Roman glass
bowl
DIATRIBE n bitter critical
attack
DIATRIBES > DIATRIBE
DIATRON n circuit that uses
diodes
DIATRONS > DIATRON
DIATROPIC adj relating to a
type of response in plants to
an external stimulus

DIAXON n bipolar cell
DIAXONS > DIAXON
DIAZEPAM n minor
tranquillizer used to treat
epilepsy
DIAZEPAMS > DIAZEPAM
DIAZEUXES > DIAZEUXIS
DIAZEUXIS n separation of
two tetrachords by interval
of a tone
DIAZIN same as > DIAZINE
DIAZINE n organic
compound
DIAZINES > DIAZINE
DIAZINON n type of
insecticide
DIAZINONS > DIAZINON
DIAZINS > DIAZIN
DIAZO adj relating to a
method for reproducing
documents ▷ n document
produced by this method
DIAZOES > DIAZO
DIAZOLE n type of organic
compound
DIAZOLES > DIAZOLE
DIAZONIUM n type of
chemical group
DIAZOS > DIAZO
DIAZOTISE same as
> DIAZOTIZE
DIAZOTIZE vb cause (an
aryl amine) to react with
nitrous acid to produce a
diazonium salt
DIB vb fish by allowing the
bait to bob and dip on the
surface
DIBASIC adj (of an acid)
containing two acidic
hydrogen atoms
DIBBED > DIB
DIBBER same as > DIBBLE
DIBBERS > DIBBER
DIBBING > DIB
DIBBLE n small gardening
tool ▷ vb make a hole in (the
ground) with a dibble
DIBBLED > DIBBLE
DIBBLER > DIBBLE
DIBBLERS > DIBBLE
DIBBLES > DIBBLE
DIBBLING > DIBBLE
DIBBS n money
DIBBUK variant spelling of
> DYBBUK
DIBBUKIM > DIBBUK
DIBBUKKIM > DIBBUK
DIBBUKS > DIBBUK
DIBROMIDE n chemical
compound that contains
two bromine atoms per
molecule
DIBS > DIB
DIBUTYL adj with two butyl
groups
DICACIOUS adj teasing
DICACITY n playful teasing
DICACODYL n oily slightly
water-soluble poisonous
liquid with garlic-like odour
DICALCIUM n two atoms of
calcium in a compound
DICAMBA n type of
weedkiller
DICAMBAS > DICAMBA
DICAST n juror in ancient
Athens

DICASTERY n congregation

DICASTIC > DICAST

DICASTS > DICAST

DICE n small cube with numbered sides ▷ vb cut (food) into small cubes

DICED > DICE

DICELIKE adj like dice

DICENTRA n Asian or N American ornamental plant

DICENTRAS > DICENTRA

DICENTRIC n abnormal chromosome with two centromeres

DICER > DICE

DICERS > DICE

DICES > DICE

DICEY adj dangerous or risky

DICH interj archaic expression meaning "may it do"

DICHASIA > DICHASIUM

DICHASIAL > DICHASIUM

DICHASIUM n cymose inflorescence in which each branch bearing a flower gives rise to two other flowering branches, as in the stitchwort

DICHOGAMY n maturation of male and female parts of a flower at different times, preventing automatic self-pollination

DICHONDRA n creeping perennial herb

DICHOPTIC adj having the eyes distinctly separate

DICHORD n two-stringed musical instrument

DICHORDS > DICHORD

DICHOTIC adj relating to or involving the stimulation of each ear simultaneously by different sounds

DICHOTOMY n division into two opposed groups or parts

DICHROIC adj having or consisting of only two colours

DICHROISM n property of a uniaxial crystal, such as tourmaline, of showing a perceptible difference in colour when viewed along two different axes in transmitted white light

DICHROITE n grey or violet-blue dichroic material

DICHROMAT n person able to distinguish only two colours

DICHROMIC adj of or involving only two colours

DICHT vb wipe

DICHTED > DICHT

DICHTING > DICHT

DICHTS > DICHT

DICIER > DICEY

DICIEST > DICEY

DICING > DICE

DICINGS > DICE

DICK n fellow ▷ vb vulgar word meaning penetrate with a penis

DICKED > DICK

DICKENS n euphemism for devil

DICKENSES > DICKENS

DICKER vb trade (goods) by bargaining ▷ n petty bargain or barter

DICKERED > DICKER

DICKERER n person who dickers

DICKERERS > DICKERER

DICKERING > DICKER

DICKERS > DICKER

DICKEY same as > DICKY

DICKEYS > DICKEY

DICKHEAD n vulgar word for a stupid or despicable man

DICKHEADS > DICKHEAD

DICKIE same as > DICKY

DICKIER > DICKY

DICKIES > DICKY

DICKIEST > DICKY

DICKING > DICK

DICKINGS > DICKING

DICKS > DICK

DICKTIER > DICKTY

DICKTIEST > DICKTY

DICKTY same as > DICTY

DICKY n false shirt front ▷ adj shaky or weak

DICKYBIRD See > DICKY

DICLINIES > DICLINOUS

DICLINISM > DICLINOUS

DICLINOUS adj (of flowering plants) bearing unisexual flowers

DICLINY > DICLINOUS

DICOT n type of flowering plant

DICOTS > DICOT

DICOTYL n type of flowering plant

DICOTYLS > DICOTYL

DICROTAL same as > DICROTIC

DICROTIC adj having or relating to a double pulse for each heartbeat

DICROTISM > DICROTIC

DICROTOUS same as > DICROTIC

DICT vb dictate

DICTA > DICTUM

DICTATE vb say aloud for someone else to write down ▷ n authoritative command

DICTATED > DICTATE

DICTATES > DICTATE

DICTATING > DICTATE

DICTATION n act of dictating words to be taken down in writing

DICTATOR n ruler who has complete power

DICTATORS > DICTATOR

DICTATORY adj tending to dictate

DICTATRIX > DICTATOR

DICTATURE n dictatorship

DICTED > DICT

DICTIER > DICTY

DICTIEST > DICTY

DICTING > DICT

DICTION n manner of pronouncing words and sounds

DICTIONAL > DICTION

DICTIONS > DICTION

DICTS > DICT

DICTUM n formal statement

DICTUMS > DICTUM

DICTY adj conceited; snobbish

DICTYOGEN n plant with net-veined leaves

DICUMAROL n anticoagulant drug

DICYCLIC adj having the perianth arranged in two whorls

DICYCLIES > DICYCLIC

DICYCLY > DICYCLIC

DID > DO

DIDACT n instructive person

DIDACTIC adj intended to instruct

DIDACTICS n art or science of teaching

DIDACTS > DIDACT

DIDACTYL adj having only two toes on each foot ▷ n animal with only two toes on each foot

DIDACTYLS > DIDACTYL

DIDAKAI same as > DIDICOY

DIDAKAIS > DIDAKAI

DIDAKEI same as > DIDICOY

DIDAKEIS > DIDAKEI

DIDAPPER n small grebe

DIDAPPERS > DIDAPPER

DIDDER vb shake with fear

DIDDERED > DIDDER

DIDDERING > DIDDER

DIDDERS > DIDDER

DIDDICOY same as > DIDICOY

DIDDICOYS > DIDDICOY

DIDDIER > DIDDY

DIDDIES > DIDDY

DIDDIEST > DIDDY

DIDDLE vb swindle

DIDDLED > DIDDLE

DIDDLER > DIDDLE

DIDDLERS > DIDDLE

DIDDLES > DIDDLE

DIDDLEY n worthless amount

DIDDLEYS > DIDDLEY

DIDDLIES > DIDDLY

DIDDLING > DIDDLE

DIDDLY n worthless amount

DIDDUMS interj expression of sympathy, esp to a child

DIDDY n Scots word for a foolish person ▷ adj foolish

DIDELPHIC adj with two genital tubes or ovaries

DIDELPHID n marsupial

DIDICOI same as > DIDICOY

DIDICOIS > DIDICOI

DIDICOY n (in Britain) a person who lives like a Gypsy but is not a true Romany

DIDICOYS > DIDICOY

DIDIE same as > DIDY

DIDIES > DIDY

DIDJERIDU n Australian Aboriginal wind instrument

DIDO n antic

DIDOES > DIDO

DIDOS > DIDO

DIDRACHM n two-drachma piece

DIDRACHMA same as > DIDRACHM

DIDRACHMS > DIDRACHM

DIDST form of the past tense of > DO

DIDY n (US) child's word for nappy

DIDYMIUM n metallic mixture once thought to be an element

DIDYMIUMS > DIDYMIUM

DIDYMO n class of algae

DIDYMOS > DIDYMO

DIDYMOUS adj in pairs or in two parts

DIDYNAMY n (of stamens) being in two unequal pairs

DIE vb cease all biological activity permanently ▷ n shaped block used to cut or form metal

DIEB n N African jackal

DIEBACK n disease of trees and shrubs ▷ vb (of plants) to suffer from dieback

DIEBACKS > DIEBACK

DIEBS > DIEB

DIECIOUS same as > DIOECIOUS

DIED > DIE

DIEDRAL same as > DIHEDRAL

DIEDRALS > DIEDRAL

DIEDRE n large shallow groove or corner in a rock face

DIEDRES > DIEDRE

DIEGESES > DIEGESIS

DIEGESIS n utterance of fact

DIEGETIC adj relating to a factual narrative

DIEHARD n person who resists change

DIEHARDS > DIEHARD

DIEING > DIE

DIEL n 24-hour period ▷ adj of or lasting for any 24-hour period

DIELDRIN n highly toxic insecticide

DIELDRINS > DIELDRIN

DIELS > DIEL

DIELYTRA n genus of herbaceous plants

DIELYTRAS > DIELYTRA

DIEMAKER n one who makes dies

DIEMAKERS > DIEMAKER

DIENE n type of hydrocarbon

DIENES > DIENE

DIEOFF n process of dying in large numbers

DIEOFFS > DIEOFF

DIERESES > DIERESIS

DIERESIS same as > DIAERESIS

DIERETIC > DIERESIS

DIES > DIE

DIESEL vb drive diesel-fuelled vehicle ▷ n diesel engine

DIESELED > DIESEL

DIESELING > DIESEL

DIESELISE same as > DIESELIZE

DIESELIZE vb be equipped with diesel engine

DIESELS > DIESEL

d

DIESES > DIESIS
DIESINKER n person who engraves dies
DIESIS n (in ancient Greek theory) any interval smaller than a whole tone
DIESTER n synthetic lubricant
DIESTERS > DIESTER
DIESTOCK n device holding the dies used to cut an external screw thread
DIESTOCKS > DIESTOCK
DIESTROUS same as > DIOESTRUS
DIESTRUM another word for > DIOESTRUS
DIESTRUMS > DIESTRUM
DIESTRUS same as > DIOESTRUS
DIET n food that a person or animal regularly eats ▷ vb follow a special diet so as to lose weight ▷ adj (of food) suitable for a weight-reduction diet
DIETARIAN n dieter
DIETARIES > DIETARY
DIETARILY > DIETARY
DIETARY adj of or relating to a diet ▷ n regulated diet
DIETED > DIET
DIETER > DIET
DIETERS > DIET
DIETETIC adj prepared for special dietary requirements
DIETETICS n study of diet and nutrition
DIETHER n chemical compound
DIETHERS > DIETHER
DIETHYL adj as in diethyl ether ether
DIETHYLS > DIETHYL
DIETICIAN n person who specializes in dietetics
DIETINE n low-ranking diet
DIETINES > DIETINE
DIETING > DIET
DIETINGS > DIET
DIETIST another word for > DIETITIAN
DIETISTS > DIETIST
DIETITIAN same as > DIETICIAN
DIETS > DIET
DIF same as > DIFF
DIFF n (slang) difference
DIFFER vb be unlike
DIFFERED > DIFFER
DIFFERENT adj unlike
DIFFERING > DIFFER
DIFFERS > DIFFER
DIFFICILE adj difficult
DIFFICULT adj requiring effort or skill to do or understand
DIFFIDENT adj lacking self-confidence
DIFFLUENT adj flowing; not fixed
DIFFORM adj irregular in form
DIFFRACT vb cause to undergo diffraction
DIFFRACTS > DIFFRACT
DIFFS > DIFF

DIFFUSE vb spread over a wide area ▷ adj widely spread
DIFFUSED > DIFFUSE
DIFFUSELY > DIFFUSE
DIFFUSER n person or thing that diffuses
DIFFUSERS > DIFFUSER
DIFFUSES > DIFFUSE
DIFFUSING > DIFFUSE
DIFFUSION n act of diffusing or the fact of being diffused
DIFFUSIVE adj characterized by diffusion
DIFFUSOR same as > DIFFUSER
DIFFUSORS > DIFFUSOR
DIFS > DIF
DIG vb cut into, break up, and turn over or remove (earth), esp with a spade ▷ n digging
DIGAMIES > DIGAMY
DIGAMIST > DIGAMY
DIGAMISTS > DIGAMY
DIGAMMA n letter of the Greek alphabet
DIGAMMAS > DIGAMMA
DIGAMOUS > DIGAMY
DIGAMY n second marriage
DIGASTRIC adj (of certain muscles) having two fleshy portions joined by a tendon ▷ n muscle of the mandible that assists in lowering the lower jaw
DIGENESES > DIGENESIS
DIGENESIS n ability to alternate between means of reproduction
DIGENETIC adj of or relating to digenesis
DIGERATI pl n people who earn large amounts of money through internet-related business
DIGEST vb subject to a process of digestion ▷ n shortened version of a book, report, or article
DIGESTANT same as > DIGESTIVE
DIGESTED > DIGEST
DIGESTER n apparatus or vessel, such as an autoclave, in which digestion is carried out
DIGESTERS > DIGESTER
DIGESTIF n something, esp a drink, taken as an aid to digestion, either before or after a meal
DIGESTIFS > DIGESTIF
DIGESTING > DIGEST
DIGESTION n (body's system for) breaking down food into easily absorbed substances
DIGESTIVE adj relating to digestion
DIGESTOR same as > DIGESTER
DIGESTORS > DIGESTOR
DIGESTS > DIGEST
DIGGABLE adj that can be dug
DIGGED a past tense of > DIG
DIGGER n machine used for digging

DIGGERS > DIGGER
DIGGING > DIG
DIGGINGS pl n material that has been dug out
DIGHT vb adorn or equip, as for battle
DIGHTED > DIGHT
DIGHTING > DIGHT
DIGHTS > DIGHT
DIGICAM n digital camera
DIGICAMS > DIGICAM
DIGIPACK n (esp formerly) type of packaging for a CD or DVD
DIGIPACKS > DIGIPACK
DIGIT n finger or toe
DIGITAL adj displaying information as numbers ▷ n one of the keys on the manuals of an organ or piano, etc
DIGITALIN n poisonous amorphous crystalline mixture of glycosides extracted from digitalis leaves and formerly used in treating heart disease
DIGITALIS n drug made from foxglove leaves, used as a heart stimulant
DIGITALLY > DIGITAL
DIGITALS > DIGITAL
DIGITATE adj (of leaves) having leaflets in the form of a spread hand
DIGITATED same as > DIGITATE
DIGITISE same as > DIGITIZE
DIGITISED > DIGITISE
DIGITISER > DIGITIZE
DIGITISES > DIGITISE
DIGITIZE vb transcribe (data) into a digital form for processing by a computer
DIGITIZED adj recorded or stored in digital form
DIGITIZER > DIGITIZE
DIGITIZES > DIGITIZE
DIGITONIN n type of glycoside
DIGITOXIN same as > DIGOXIN
DIGITRON n type of tube for displaying information
DIGITRONS > DIGITRON
DIGITS > DIGIT
DIGITULE n any small finger-like process
DIGITULES > DIGITULE
DIGLOSSIA n existence in a language of a high, or socially prestigious, and a low, or everyday, form, as German and Swiss German in Switzerland
DIGLOSSIC > DIGLOSSIA
DIGLOT n bilingual book
DIGLOTS > DIGLOT
DIGLOTTIC > DIGLOT
DIGLYPH n ornament in Doric frieze with two grooves
DIGLYPHS > DIGLYPH
DIGNIFIED adj calm, impressive, and worthy of respect
DIGNIFIES > DIGNIFY
DIGNIFY vb add distinction to

DIGNITARY n person of high official position
DIGNITIES > DIGNITY
DIGNITY n serious, calm, and controlled behaviour or manner
DIGONAL adj of or relating to a symmetry operation
DIGOXIN n glycoside extracted from the leaves of the woolly foxglove
DIGOXINS > DIGOXIN
DIGRAPH n two letters used to represent a single sound
DIGRAPHIC > DIGRAPH
DIGRAPHS > DIGRAPH
DIGRESS vb depart from the main subject in speech or writing
DIGRESSED > DIGRESS
DIGRESSER > DIGRESS
DIGRESSES > DIGRESS
DIGS > DIG
DIGYNIAN adj relating to plant class Digynia
DIGYNOUS another word for > DIGYNIAN
DIHEDRA > DIHEDRON
DIHEDRAL adj having or formed by two intersecting planes ▷ n figure formed by two intersecting planes
DIHEDRALS > DIHEDRAL
DIHEDRON n figure formed by two intersecting planes
DIHEDRONS > DIHEDRON
DIHYBRID n offspring of two individuals that differ with respect to two pairs of genes
DIHYBRIDS > DIHYBRID
DIHYDRIC adj (of an alcohol) containing two hydroxyl groups per molecule
DIKA n wild mango
DIKAS > DIKA
DIKAST same as > DICAST
DIKASTS > DIKAST
DIKDIK n small African antelope
DIKDIKS > DIKDIK
DIKE same as > DYKE
DIKED > DIKE
DIKER n builder of dikes
DIKERS > DIKER
DIKES > DIKE
DIKETONE n as in diphenylene diketone compound used in dye manufacture, aka anthraquinone
DIKETONES > DIKETONE
DIKEY adj (of a lesbian) masculine
DIKIER > DIKEY
DIKIEST > DIKEY
DIKING > DIKE
DIKKOP n type of brownish shore bird with a large head and eyes
DIKKOPS > DIKKOP
DIKTAT n dictatorial decree
DIKTATS > DIKTAT
DILATABLE > DILATE
DILATABLY > DILATE
DILATANCY n phenomenon caused by the nature of the

stacking or fitting together of particles or granules in a heterogeneous system, such as the solidification of certain sols under pressure, and the thixotropy of certain gels

DILATANT *adj* tending to dilate ▷ *n* something, such as a catheter, that causes dilation

DILATANTS > DILATANT

DILATATE *same as* > DILATE

DILATATOR *same as* > DILATOR

DILATE *vb* make or become wider or larger

DILATED > DILATE

DILATER *same as* > DILATOR

DILATERS > DILATER

DILATES > DILATE

DILATING > DILATE

DILATION > DILATE

DILATIONS > DILATE

DILATIVE > DILATE

DILATOR *n* something that dilates an object

DILATORS > DILATOR

DILATORY *adj* tending or intended to waste time

DILDO *n* object used as a substitute for an erect penis

DILDOE *same as* > DILDO

DILDOES > DILDOE

DILDOS > DILDO

DILEMMA *n* situation offering a choice between two undesirable alternatives

DILEMMAS > DILEMMA

DILEMMIC > DILEMMA

DILIGENCE *n* steady and careful application

DILIGENT *adj* careful and persevering in carrying out duties

DILL *n* sweet-smelling herb ▷ *vb* flavour with dill

DILLED > DILL

DILLI *n* dilly bag; small bag, esp one made of plaited grass and used for carrying food

DILLIER > DILLY

DILLIES > DILLY

DILLIEST > DILLY

DILLING > DILL

DILLINGS > DILL

DILLIS > DILLI

DILLS > DILL

DILLWEED *n* dill plant or its foliage

DILLWEEDS > DILLWEED

DILLY *adj* foolish ▷ *n* person or thing that is remarkable

DILSCOOP *n* type of shot in cricket in which the ball goes over the wicketkeeper's head

DILSCOOPS > DILSCOOP

DILTIAZEM *n* drug used to treat angina

DILUENT *adj* causing dilution or serving to dilute ▷ *n* substance used for or causing dilution

DILUENTS > DILUENT

DILUTABLE > DILUTE

DILUTE *vb* make (a liquid) less concentrated, esp by adding water ▷ *adj* (of a liquid) thin and watery

DILUTED > DILUTE

DILUTEE > DILUTE

DILUTEES > DILUTE

DILUTER > DILUTE

DILUTERS > DILUTE

DILUTES > DILUTE

DILUTING > DILUTE

DILUTION *n* act of diluting or state of being diluted

DILUTIONS > DILUTION

DILUTIVE *adj* having effect of decreasing earnings per share

DILUTOR *n* thing intended to have a diluting effect

DILUTORS > DILUTOR

DILUVIA > DILUVIUM

DILUVIAL *adj* of a flood, esp the great Flood described in the Old Testament

DILUVIAN *same as* > DILUVIAL

DILUVION *same as* > DILUVIUM

DILUVIONS > DILUVION

DILUVIUM *n* glacial drift

DILUVIUMS > DILUVIUM

DIM *adj* badly lit ▷ *vb* make or become dim

DIMBLE *n* wooded hollow; dingle

DIMBLES > DIMBLE

DIMBO *n* unintelligent person

DIMBOES > DIMBO

DIMBOS > DIMBO

DIME *n* coin of the US and Canada, worth ten cents

DIMENSION *n* measurement of the size of something in a particular direction ▷ *vb* shape or cut to specified dimensions

DIMER *n* type of molecule

DIMERIC *adj* of a dimer

DIMERISE *same as* > DIMERIZE

DIMERISED > DIMERISE

DIMERISES > DIMERISE

DIMERISM > DIMEROUS

DIMERISMS > DIMEROUS

DIMERIZE *vb* react or cause to react to form a dimer

DIMERIZED > DIMERIZE

DIMERIZES > DIMERIZE

DIMEROUS *adj* consisting of or divided into two segments, as the tarsi of some insects

DIMERS > DIMER

DIMES > DIME

DIMETER *n* type of verse

DIMETERS > DIMETER

DIMETHYL *n* ethane

DIMETHYLS > DIMETHYL

DIMETRIC *adj* of, relating to, or shaped like a quadrilateral

DIMIDIATE *adj* divided in halves ▷ *vb* halve (two bearings) so that they can be represented on the same shield

DIMINISH *vb* make or become smaller, fewer, or less

DIMISSORY *adj* granting permission to be ordained

DIMITIES > DIMITY

DIMITY *n* light strong cotton fabric with woven stripes or squares

DIMLY > DIM

DIMMABLE *adj* that can be dimmed

DIMMED > DIM

DIMMER > DIM

DIMMERS > DIM

DIMMEST > DIM

DIMMING *n* as in *global dimming* decrease in the amount of sunlight reaching the earth

DIMMINGS > DIMMING

DIMMISH > DIM

DIMNESS > DIM

DIMNESSES > DIM

DIMORPH *n* either of two forms of a substance that exhibits dimorphism

DIMORPHIC *adj* having two distinct forms

DIMORPHS > DIMORPH

DIMOUT *n* reduction of lighting

DIMOUTS > DIMOUT

DIMP *n* in Northern English dialect, a cigarette butt

DIMPLE *n* small natural dent, esp in the cheeks or chin ▷ *vb* produce dimples by smiling

DIMPLED > DIMPLE

DIMPLES > DIMPLE

DIMPLIER > DIMPLE

DIMPLIEST > DIMPLE

DIMPLING > DIMPLE

DIMPLY > DIMPLE

DIMPS > DIMP

DIMPSIES > DIMPSY

DIMPSY *n* twilight

DIMS > DIM

DIMWIT *n* stupid person

DIMWITS > DIMWIT

DIMWITTED > DIMWIT

DIMYARIAN *adj* with two adductor muscles

DIMYARY *adj* with two adductor muscles

DIN *n* loud unpleasant confused noise ▷ *vb* instil (something) into someone by constant repetition

DINAR *n* monetary unit

DINARCHY *same as* > DIARCHY

DINARS > DINAR

DINDLE *another word for* > DINNLE

DINDLED > DINDLE

DINDLES > DINDLE

DINDLING > DINDLE

DINE *vb* eat dinner

DINED > DINE

DINER *n* person eating a meal

DINERIC *adj* of or concerned with the interface between immiscible liquids

DINERO *n* money

DINEROS > DINERO

DINERS > DINER

DINES > DINE

DINETTE *n* alcove or small area for use as a dining room

DINETTES > DINETTE

DINFUL *adj* noisy

DING *n* small dent in a vehicle ▷ *vb* ring or cause to ring, esp with tedious repetition

DINGBAT *n* any unnamed object

DINGBATS > DINGBAT

DINGDONG *n* sound of a bell or bells ▷ *vb* make such a sound

DINGDONGS > DINGDONG

DINGE *n* dent ▷ *vb* make a dent in (something)

DINGED > DINGE

DINGER *n* (in baseball) home run

DINGERS > DINGER

DINGES *n* jocular word for something whose name is unknown or forgotten

DINGESES > DINGES

DINGEY *same as* > DINGHY

DINGEYS > DINGEY

DINGHIES > DINGHY

DINGHY *n* small boat, powered by sails, oars, or a motor ▷ *vb* ignore or avoid a person or event

DINGIED > DINGY

DINGIER > DINGY

DINGIES > DINGY

DINGIEST > DINGY

DINGILY > DINGY

DINGINESS > DINGY

DINGING > DINGE

DINGLE *n* small wooded hollow or valley

DINGLES > DINGLE

DINGO *n* Australian wild dog ▷ *vb* act in a cowardly manner

DINGOED > DINGO

DINGOES > DINGO

DINGOING > DINGO

DINGOS > DINGO

DINGS > DING

DINGUS *same as* > DINGES

DINGUSES > DINGUS

DINGY *adj* lacking light ▷ *vb* ignore or avoid a person or event

DINGYING > DINGY

DINIC *n* remedy for vertigo

DINICS > DINIC

DINING *n* act of dining

DININGS > DINING

DINITRO *adj* containing two nitro groups

DINK *adj* neat or neatly dressed ▷ *vb* carry (a second person) on a horse, bicycle, etc ▷ *n* ball struck delicately

DINKED > DINK

DINKER > DINK

DINKEST > DINK

DINKEY *n* small locomotive

DINKEYS > DINKEY

DINKIE *n* affluent married childless person ▷ *adj* designed for or appealing to dinkies

d

d

DINKIER > DINKY
DINKIES > DINKIE
DINKIEST > DINKY
DINKING > DINK
DINKLIER > DINKLY
DINKLIEST > DINKLY
DINKLY adj neat
DINKS > DINK
DINKUM n truth or genuineness
DINKUMS > DINKUM
DINKY adj small and neat
DINMONT n neutered sheep
DINMONTS > DINMONT
DINNA vb a Scots word for do not
DINNAE vb (Scots) do not
DINNED > DIN
DINNER vb dine ▷ n main meal of the day
DINNERED > DINNER
DINNERING > DINNER
DINNERS > DINNER
DINNING > DIN
DINNLE vb shake
DINNLED > DINNLE
DINNLES > DINNLE
DINNLING > DINNLE
DINO n dinosaur
DINOCERAS n uintathere, a gigantic fossil ungulate
DINOMANIA n strong interest in dinosaurs
DINOS > DINO
DINOSAUR n type of extinct prehistoric reptile, many of which were of gigantic size
DINOSAURS > DINOSAUR
DINOTHERE n type of extinct elephant-like mammal with tusks curving downwards and backwards
DINS > DIN
DINT variant of > DENT
DINTED > DINT
DINTING > DINT
DINTLESS > DINT
DINTS > DINT
DIOBOL n ancient Greek coin
DIOBOLON same as > DIOBOL
DIOBOLONS > DIOBOLON
DIOBOLS > DIOBOL
DIOCESAN adj of or relating to a diocese ▷ n bishop of a diocese
DIOCESANS > DIOCESAN
DIOCESE n district over which a bishop has control
DIOCESES > DIOCESE
DIODE n semiconductor device
DIODES > DIODE
DIOECIES > DIOECY
DIOECIOUS adj (of plants) having the male and female reproductive organs on separate plants
DIOECISM > DIOECIOUS
DIOECISMS > DIOECIOUS
DIOECY n state of being dioecious
DIOESTRUS n period in mammal's oestral cycle
DIOICOUS same as > DIOECIOUS

DIOL n any of a class of alcohols that have two hydroxyl groups in each molecule
DIOLEFIN n type of polymer
DIOLEFINS > DIOLEFIN
DIOLS > DIOL
DIONYSIAC same as > DIONYSIAN
DIONYSIAN adj relating to the set of creative qualities that encompasses spontaneity and irrationality
DIOPSIDE n colourless or pale-green pyroxene mineral
DIOPSIDES > DIOPSIDE
DIOPSIDIC > DIOPSIDE
DIOPTASE n green glassy mineral
DIOPTASES > DIOPTASE
DIOPTER same as > DIOPTRE
DIOPTERS > DIOPTER
DIOPTRAL > DIOPTRE
DIOPTRATE adj (of compound eye) divided by transverse line
DIOPTRE n unit for measuring the refractive power of a lens
DIOPTRES > DIOPTRE
DIOPTRIC adj of or concerned with dioptrics
DIOPTRICS n branch of geometrical optics concerned with the formation of images by lenses
DIORAMA n miniature three-dimensional scene
DIORAMAS > DIORAMA
DIORAMIC > DIORAMA
DIORISM n definition; clarity
DIORISMS > DIORISM
DIORISTIC > DIORISM
DIORITE n dark coarse-grained igneous plutonic rock
DIORITES > DIORITE
DIORITIC > DIORITE
DIOSGENIN n yam-based substance used in hormone therapy
DIOTA n type of ancient vase
DIOTAS > DIOTA
DIOXAN n colourless insoluble toxic liquid
DIOXANE same as > DIOXAN
DIOXANES > DIOXANE
DIOXANS > DIOXAN
DIOXID same as > DIOXIDE
DIOXIDE n oxide containing two oxygen atoms per molecule
DIOXIDES > DIOXIDE
DIOXIDS > DIOXID
DIOXIN n poisonous chemical by-product of certain weedkillers
DIOXINS > DIOXIN
DIP vb plunge quickly or briefly into a liquid ▷ n dipping
DIPCHICK same as > DABCHICK
DIPCHICKS > DIPCHICK

DIPEPTIDE n compound consisting of two linked amino acids
DIPHASE adj of, having, or concerned with two phases
DIPHASIC same as > DIPHASE
DIPHENYL another name for > BIPHENYL
DIPHENYLS > DIPHENYL
DIPHONE n combination of two speech sounds
DIPHONES > DIPHONE
DIPHTHONG n union of two vowel sounds in a single compound sound
DIPHYSITE n belief in Christ having both divine and human natures
DIPLEGIA n paralysis of corresponding parts on both sides of the body
DIPLEGIAS > DIPLEGIA
DIPLEGIC > DIPLEGIA
DIPLEX adj permitting simultaneous transmission in both directions
DIPLEXER n device that enables the simultaneous transmission of more than one signal
DIPLEXERS > DIPLEXER
DIPLOE n spongy bone separating the two layers of compact bone of the skull
DIPLOES > DIPLOE
DIPLOGEN n heavy hydrogen
DIPLOGENS > DIPLOGEN
DIPLOIC adj relating to diploe
DIPLOID adj denoting a cell or organism with pairs of homologous chromosomes ▷ n diploid cell or organism
DIPLOIDIC > DIPLOID
DIPLOIDS > DIPLOID
DIPLOIDY > DIPLOID
DIPLOMA vb bestow diploma on ▷ n qualification awarded by a college on successful completion of a course
DIPLOMACY n conduct of the relations between nations by peaceful means
DIPLOMAED > DIPLOMA
DIPLOMAS > DIPLOMA
DIPLOMAT n official engaged in diplomacy
DIPLOMATA > DIPLOMA
DIPLOMATE n any person who has been granted a diploma, esp a physician certified as a specialist
DIPLOMATS > DIPLOMAT
DIPLON another name for > DEUTERON
DIPLONEMA a less common name for > DIPLOTENE
DIPLONS > DIPLON
DIPLONT n animal or plant that has the diploid number of chromosomes in its somatic cells
DIPLONTIC > DIPLONT
DIPLONTS > DIPLONT

DIPLOPIA n visual defect in which a single object is seen in duplicate
DIPLOPIAS > DIPLOPIA
DIPLOPIC > DIPLOPIA
DIPLOPOD n type of arthropod such as the millipede
DIPLOPODS > DIPLOPOD
DIPLOSES > DIPLOSIS
DIPLOSIS n doubling of the haploid number of chromosomes
DIPLOTENE n fourth stage of the prophase of meiosis, during which the paired homologous chromosomes separate except at the places where genetic exchange has occurred
DIPLOZOA n type of parasitic worm
DIPLOZOIC adj (of certain animals) bilaterally symmetrical
DIPLOZOON n type of parasitic worm
DIPNET vb fish using fishing net on pole
DIPNETS > DIPNET
DIPNETTED > DIPNET
DIPNOAN n lungfish
DIPNOANS > DIPNOAN
DIPNOOUS adj having lungs and gills
DIPODIC > DIPODY
DIPODIES > DIPODY
DIPODY n metrical unit consisting of two feet
DIPOLAR > DIPOLE
DIPOLE n two equal but opposite electric charges or magnetic poles separated by a small distance
DIPOLES > DIPOLE
DIPPABLE > DIP
DIPPED > DIP
DIPPER n ladle used for dipping
DIPPERFUL n amount held by scoop
DIPPERS > DIPPER
DIPPIER > DIPPY
DIPPIEST > DIPPY
DIPPINESS > DIPPY
DIPPING > DIP
DIPPINGS > DIP
DIPPY adj odd, eccentric, or crazy
DIPROTIC adj having two hydrogen atoms
DIPS > DIP
DIPSADES > DIPSAS
DIPSAS n type of snake
DIPSHIT n vulgar word for a stupid person
DIPSHITS > DIPSHIT
DIPSO n dipsomaniac or alcoholic
DIPSOS > DIPSO
DIPSTICK n notched rod dipped into a container to measure the level of a liquid
DIPSTICKS > DIPSTICK
DIPSWITCH n switch for dipping a vehicle's headlights
DIPT > DIP

DIPTERA n order of insects with two wings

DIPTERAL adj having a double row of columns

DIPTERAN n dipterous insect ▷ adj having two wings or winglike parts

DIPTERANS > DIPTERAN

DIPTERAS > DIPTERA

DIPTERIST n fly expert

DIPTEROI > DIPTEROS

DIPTERON same as > DIPTERAN

DIPTERONS > DIPTERON

DIPTEROS n Greek building with double columns

DIPTEROUS adj having two wings or winglike parts

DIPTYCA same as > DIPTYCH

DIPTYCAS > DIPTYCA

DIPTYCH n painting on two hinged panels

DIPTYCHS > DIPTYCH

DIQUARK n particle in physics

DIQUARKS > DIQUARK

DIQUAT n type of herbicide

DIQUATS > DIQUAT

DIRAM n money unit of Tajikistan

DIRAMS > DIRAM

DIRDAM same as > DIRDUM

DIRDAMS > DIRDAM

DIRDUM n tumult

DIRDUMS > DIRDUM

DIRE adj disastrous, urgent, or terrible

DIRECT adj (of a route) shortest, straight ▷ adv in a direct manner ▷ vb lead and organize

DIRECTED > DIRECT

DIRECTER > DIRECT

DIRECTEST > DIRECT

DIRECTING > DIRECT

DIRECTION n course or line along which a person or thing moves, points, or lies

DIRECTIVE n instruction, order ▷ adj tending to direct

DIRECTLY adv in a direct manner

DIRECTOR n person or thing that directs or controls

DIRECTORS > DIRECTOR

DIRECTORY n book listing names, addresses, and telephone numbers ▷ adj directing

DIRECTRIX n fixed reference line, situated on the convex side of a conic section, that is used when defining or calculating its eccentricity

DIRECTS > DIRECT

DIREFUL same as > DIRE

DIREFULLY > DIREFUL

DIRELY > DIRE

DIREMPT vb separate with force

DIREMPTED > DIREMPT

DIREMPTS > DIREMPT

DIRENESS > DIRE

DIRER > DIRE

DIREST > DIRE

DIRGE n slow sad song of mourning

DIRGEFUL > DIRGE

DIRGELIKE > DIRGE

DIRGES > DIRGE

DIRHAM n standard monetary unit of Morocco

DIRHAMS > DIRHAM

DIRHEM same as > DIRHAM

DIRHEMS > DIRHEM

DIRIGE n dirge

DIRIGENT adj directing

DIRIGES > DIRIGE

DIRIGIBLE adj able to be steered ▷ n airship

DIRIGISM same as > DIRIGISME

DIRIGISME n control by the state of economic and social matters

DIRIGISMS > DIRIGISM

DIRIGISTE > DIRIGISME

DIRIMENT adj (of an impediment to marriage in canon law) totally invalidating

DIRK n dagger, formerly worn by Scottish Highlanders ▷ vb stab with a dirk

DIRKE variant of > DIRK

DIRKED > DIRK

DIRKES > DIRKE

DIRKING > DIRK

DIRKS > DIRK

DIRL vb tingle; vibrate

DIRLED > DIRL

DIRLING > DIRL

DIRLS > DIRL

DIRNDL n full gathered skirt

DIRNDLS > DIRNDL

DIRT vb soil ▷ n unclean substance, filth

DIRTBAG n filthy person

DIRTBAGS > DIRTBAG

DIRTBALL n insulting word for a contemptible person

DIRTBALLS > DIRTBALL

DIRTED > DIRT

DIRTIED > DIRTY

DIRTIER > DIRTY

DIRTIES > DIRTY

DIRTIEST > DIRTY

DIRTILY > DIRTY

DIRTINESS > DIRTY

DIRTING > DIRT

DIRTS > DIRT

DIRTY adj covered or marked with dirt ▷ vb make dirty

DIRTYING > DIRTY

DIS same as > DISS

DISA n type of orchid

DISABLE vb make ineffective, unfit, or incapable

DISABLED adj lacking a physical power, such as the ability to walk

DISABLER > DISABLE

DISABLERS > DISABLE

DISABLES > DISABLE

DISABLING > DISABLE

DISABLISM n discrimination against disabled people

DISABLIST > DISABLISM

DISABUSAL > DISABUSE

DISABUSE vb rid (someone) of a mistaken idea

DISABUSED > DISABUSE

DISABUSES > DISABUSE

DISACCORD n lack of agreement or harmony ▷ vb be out of agreement

DISADORN vb deprive of ornamentation

DISADORNS > DISADORN

DISAFFECT vb cause to lose loyalty or affection

DISAFFIRM vb deny or contradict (a statement)

DISAGREE vb argue or have different opinions

DISAGREED > DISAGREE

DISAGREES > DISAGREE

DISALLIED > DISALLY

DISALLIES > DISALLY

DISALLOW vb reject as untrue or invalid

DISALLOWS > DISALLOW

DISALLY vb separate

DISANCHOR vb raise anchor of

DISANNEX vb disunite

DISANNUL vb cancel

DISANNULS > DISANNUL

DISANOINT vb invalidate anointment of

DISAPPEAR vb cease to be visible

DISAPPLY vb make (law) invalid

DISARM vb deprive of weapons

DISARMED > DISARM

DISARMER > DISARM

DISARMERS > DISARM

DISARMING adj removing hostility or suspicion

DISARMS > DISARM

DISARRAY n confusion and lack of discipline ▷ vb throw into confusion

DISARRAYS > DISARRAY

DISAS > DISA

DISASTER n occurrence that causes great distress or destruction

DISASTERS > DISASTER

DISATTIRE vb remove clothes from

DISATTUNE vb render out of tune

DISAVOUCH archaic form of > DISAVOW

DISAVOW vb deny connection with or responsibility for

DISAVOWAL > DISAVOW

DISAVOWED > DISAVOW

DISAVOWER > DISAVOW

DISAVOWS > DISAVOW

DISBAND vb (cause to) cease to function as a group

DISBANDED > DISBAND

DISBANDS > DISBAND

DISBAR vb deprive (a barrister) of the right to practise

DISBARK same as > DISEMBARK

DISBARKED > DISBARK

DISBARKS > DISBARK

DISBARRED > DISBAR

DISBARS > DISBAR

DISBELIEF n refusal or reluctance to believe

DISBENCH vb remove from bench

DISBODIED adj disembodied

DISBOSOM vb disclose

DISBOSOMS > DISBOSOM

DISBOUND adj unbound

DISBOWEL vb disembowel

DISBOWELS > DISBOWEL

DISBRANCH vb remove or cut a branch or branches from (a tree)

DISBUD vb remove superfluous buds from (a plant, esp a fruit tree)

DISBUDDED > DISBUD

DISBUDS > DISBUD

DISBURDEN vb remove a load from (a person or animal)

DISBURSAL > DISBURSE

DISBURSE vb pay out

DISBURSED > DISBURSE

DISBURSER > DISBURSE

DISBURSES > DISBURSE

DISC n flat circular object ▷ vb work (land) with a disc harrow

DISCAGE vb release from cage

DISCAGED > DISCAGE

DISCAGES > DISCAGE

DISCAGING > DISCAGE

DISCAL adj relating to or resembling a disc

DISCALCED adj barefooted: used to denote friars and nuns who wear sandals

DISCANDIE same as > DISCANDY

DISCANDY vb melt; dissolve

DISCANT same as > DESCANT

DISCANTED > DISCANT

DISCANTER > DISCANT

DISCANTS > DISCANT

DISCARD vb get rid of (something or someone) as useless or undesirable ▷ n person or thing that has been cast aside

DISCARDED > DISCARD

DISCARDER > DISCARD

DISCARDS > DISCARD

DISCASE vb remove case from

DISCASED > DISCASE

DISCASES > DISCASE

DISCASING > DISCASE

DISCED > DISC

DISCEPT vb discuss

DISCEPTED > DISCEPT

DISCEPTS > DISCEPT

DISCERN vb see or be aware of (something) clearly

DISCERNED > DISCERN

DISCERNER > DISCERN

DISCERNS > DISCERN

DISCERP vb divide

DISCERPED > DISCERP

DISCERPS > DISCERP

DISCHARGE vb release, allow to go ▷ n substance that comes out from a place

d

DISCHURCH vb deprive of church membership
DISCI > DISCUS
DISCIDE vb split
DISCIDED > DISCIDE
DISCIDES > DISCIDE
DISCIDING > DISCIDE
DISCIFORM adj disc-shaped
DISCINCT adj loosely dressed, without belt
DISCING > DISC
DISCIPLE vb teach ▷ n follower of the doctrines of a teacher, esp Jesus Christ
DISCIPLED > DISCIPLE
DISCIPLES > DISCIPLE
DISCLAIM vb deny (responsibility for or knowledge of something)
DISCLAIMS > DISCLAIM
DISCLESS adj having no disc
DISCLIKE > DISC
DISCLIMAX n climax community resulting from the activities of human beings or domestic animals in climatic and other conditions that would otherwise support a different type of community
DISCLOSE vb make known
DISCLOSED > DISCLOSE
DISCLOSER > DISCLOSE
DISCLOSES > DISCLOSE
DISCLOST > DISCLOSE
DISCO vb go to a disco ▷ n nightclub where people dance to amplified pop records
DISCOBOLI pl n discus throwers
DISCOED > DISCO
DISCOER > DISCO
DISCOERS > DISCO
DISCOES > DISCO
DISCOID adj like a disc ▷ n disclike object
DISCOIDAL adj like a disc
DISCOIDS > DISCOID
DISCOING > DISCO
DISCOLOGY n study of gramophone records
DISCOLOR same as > DISCOLOUR
DISCOLORS > DISCOLOR
DISCOLOUR vb change in colour, fade
DISCOMFIT vb make uneasy or confused
DISCOMMON vb deprive (land) of the character and status of common, as by enclosure
DISCORD n lack of agreement or harmony between people ▷ vb disagree
DISCORDED > DISCORD
DISCORDS > DISCORD
DISCOS > DISCO
DISCOUNT vb take no account of something ▷ n deduction from the full price of something
DISCOUNTS > DISCOUNT
DISCOURE vb discover
DISCOURED > DISCOURE

DISCOURES > DISCOURE
DISCOURSE n conversation ▷ vb speak or write (about) at length
DISCOVER vb be the first to find or to find out about
DISCOVERS > DISCOVER
DISCOVERT adj (of a woman) not under the protection of a husband
DISCOVERY n discovering
DISCREDIT vb damage the reputation of ▷ n damage to someone's reputation
DISCREET adj careful to avoid embarrassment, esp by keeping confidences secret
DISCRETE adj separate, distinct
DISCRETER > DISCRETE
DISCROWN vb deprive of a crown
DISCROWNS > DISCROWN
DISCS > DISC
DISCUMBER vb disencumber
DISCURE old form of > DISCOVER
DISCURED > DISCURE
DISCURES > DISCURE
DISCURING > DISCURE
DISCURSUS n discursive reasoning
DISCUS n object thrown in sports competitions
DISCUSES > DISCUS
DISCUSS vb consider (something) by talking it over
DISCUSSED > DISCUSS
DISCUSSER > DISCUSS
DISCUSSES > DISCUSS
DISDAIN n feeling of superiority and dislike ▷ vb refuse with disdain
DISDAINED > DISDAIN
DISDAINS > DISDAIN
DISEASE vb make uneasy ▷ n illness, sickness
DISEASED adj having or affected with disease
DISEASES > DISEASE
DISEASING > DISEASE
DISEDGE vb render blunt
DISEDGED > DISEDGE
DISEDGES > DISEDGE
DISEDGING > DISEDGE
DISEMBARK vb get off a ship, aircraft, or bus
DISEMBODY vb free from the body or from physical form
DISEMPLOY vb dismiss from employment
DISENABLE vb cause to become incapable
DISENDOW vb take away an endowment from
DISENDOWS > DISENDOW
DISENGAGE vb release from a connection
DISENROL vb remove from register
DISENROLS > DISENROL
DISENTAIL vb free (an estate) from entail ▷ n act of disentailing

DISENTOMB vb disinter
DISESTEEM vb think little of ▷ n lack of esteem
DISEUR same as > DISEUSE
DISEURS > DISEUR
DISEUSE n (esp formerly) an actress who presents dramatic recitals
DISEUSES > DISEUSE
DISFAME n discredit ▷ vb throw into disrepute or remove fame (from)
DISFAMED > DISFAME
DISFAMES > DISFAME
DISFAMING > DISFAME
DISFAVOR same as > DISFAVOUR
DISFAVORS > DISFAVOR
DISFAVOUR n disapproval or dislike ▷ vb regard or treat with disapproval or dislike
DISFIGURE vb spoil the appearance of
DISFLESH vb reduce flesh of
DISFLUENT adj lacking fluency in speech
DISFOREST same as > DEFOREST
DISFORM vb change form of
DISFORMED > DISFORM
DISFORMS > DISFORM
DISFROCK another word for > UNFROCK
DISFROCKS > DISFROCK
DISGAVEL vb deprive of quality of gavelkind
DISGAVELS > DISGAVEL
DISGEST vb digest
DISGESTED > DISGEST
DISGESTS > DISGEST
DISGODDED adj deprived of religion
DISGORGE vb empty out, discharge
DISGORGED > DISGORGE
DISGORGER n thin notched metal implement for removing hooks from a fish
DISGORGES > DISGORGE
DISGOWN vb remove gown from
DISGOWNED > DISGOWN
DISGOWNS > DISGOWN
DISGRACE n condition of shame, loss of reputation, or dishonour ▷ vb bring shame upon (oneself or others)
DISGRACED > DISGRACE
DISGRACER > DISGRACE
DISGRACES > DISGRACE
DISGRADE vb degrade
DISGRADED > DISGRADE
DISGRADES > DISGRADE
DISGUISE vb change the appearance to conceal the identity ▷ n mask, costume, or manner that disguises
DISGUISED > DISGUISE
DISGUISER > DISGUISE
DISGUISES > DISGUISE
DISGUST n great loathing or distaste ▷ vb sicken, fill with loathing
DISGUSTED > DISGUST
DISGUSTS > DISGUST
DISH n shallow container used for holding or serving food ▷ vb put into a dish

DISHABIT vb dislodge
DISHABITS > DISHABIT
DISHABLE obsolete form of > DISABLE
DISHABLED > DISHABLE
DISHABLES > DISHABLE
DISHALLOW vb make unholy
DISHCLOTH n cloth for washing dishes
DISHCLOUT same as > DISHCLOTH
DISHDASH same as > DISHDASHA
DISHDASHA n long-sleeved collarless white garment worn by some Muslim men
DISHED adj shaped like a dish
DISHELM vb remove helmet from
DISHELMED > DISHELM
DISHELMS > DISHELM
DISHERIT vb disinherit
DISHERITS > DISHERIT
DISHES > DISH
DISHEVEL vb disarrange (the hair or clothes) of (someone)
DISHEVELS > DISHEVEL
DISHFUL n the amount that a dish is able to hold
DISHFULS > DISHFUL
DISHIER > DISHY
DISHIEST > DISHY
DISHING > DISH
DISHINGS > DISH
DISHLIKE > DISH
DISHMOP n mop for cleaning dishes
DISHMOPS > DISHMOP
DISHOARD vb put previously withheld (money) into circulation
DISHOARDS > DISHOARD
DISHOME vb deprive of home
DISHOMED > DISHOME
DISHOMES > DISHOME
DISHOMING > DISHOME
DISHONEST adj not honest or fair
DISHONOR same as > DISHONOUR
DISHONORS > DISHONOR
DISHONOUR vb treat with disrespect ▷ n lack of respect
DISHORN vb remove horns from
DISHORNED > DISHORN
DISHORNS > DISHORN
DISHORSE vb dismount
DISHORSED > DISHORSE
DISHORSES > DISHORSE
DISHOUSE vb deprive of home
DISHOUSED > DISHOUSE
DISHOUSES > DISHOUSE
DISHPAN n large pan for washing dishes, pots, etc
DISHPANS > DISHPAN
DISHRAG n dishcloth
DISHRAGS > DISHRAG
DISHTOWEL n towel for drying dishes and kitchen utensils
DISHUMOUR vb upset; offend

DISHWARE n tableware
DISHWARES > DISHWARE
DISHWATER n water in which dishes and kitchen utensils are or have been washed
DISHY adj good-looking
DISILLUDE vb remove illusions from
DISIMMURE vb release
DISINFECT vb rid of harmful germs, chemically
DISINFEST vb rid of vermin
DISINFORM vb give wrong information
DISINHUME vb dig up
DISINTER vb dig up
DISINTERS > DISINTER
DISINURE vb render unaccustomed
DISINURED > DISINURE
DISINURES > DISINURE
DISINVENT vb undo the invention or existence of
DISINVEST vb remove investment (from)
DISINVITE vb retract invitation to
DISJASKIT adj fatigued
DISJECT vb break apart
DISJECTED > DISJECT
DISJECTS > DISJECT
DISJOIN vb disconnect or become disconnected
DISJOINED > DISJOIN
DISJOINS > DISJOIN
DISJOINT vb take apart or come apart at the joints ▷ adj (of two sets) having no members in common
DISJOINTS > DISJOINT
DISJUNCT adj not united or joined ▷ n one of the propositions or formulas in a disjunction
DISJUNCTS > DISJUNCT
DISJUNE n breakfast ▷ vb breakfast
DISJUNED > DISJUNE
DISJUNES > DISJUNE
DISJUNING > DISJUNE
DISK same as > DISC
DISKED > DISK
DISKER n person who breaks up earth with a type of farm implement
DISKERS > DISKER
DISKETTE n floppy disk
DISKETTES > DISKETTE
DISKING > DISK
DISKLESS > DISK
DISKLIKE > DISK
DISKS > DISK
DISLEAF vb remove leaf or leaves from
DISLEAFED > DISLEAF
DISLEAFS > DISLEAF
DISLEAL archaic form of > DISLOYAL
DISLEAVE variant of > DISLEAF
DISLEAVED > DISLEAVE
DISLEAVES > DISLEAVE
DISLIKE vb consider unpleasant or disagreeable ▷ n feeling of not liking something or someone

DISLIKED > DISLIKE
DISLIKEN vb render dissimilar to
DISLIKENS > DISLIKEN
DISLIKER > DISLIKE
DISLIKERS > DISLIKE
DISLIKES > DISLIKE
DISLIKING > DISLIKE
DISLIMB vb remove limbs from
DISLIMBED > DISLIMB
DISLIMBS > DISLIMB
DISLIMN vb efface
DISLIMNED > DISLIMN
DISLIMNS > DISLIMN
DISLINK vb disunite
DISLINKED > DISLINK
DISLINKS > DISLINK
DISLOAD vb unload
DISLOADED > DISLOAD
DISLOADS > DISLOAD
DISLOCATE vb displace (a bone or joint) from its normal position
DISLODGE vb remove (something) from a previously fixed position
DISLODGED > DISLODGE
DISLODGES > DISLODGE
DISLOIGN vb put at a distance
DISLOIGNS > DISLOIGN
DISLOYAL adj not loyal, deserting one's allegiance
DISLUSTRE vb remove lustre from
DISMAL adj gloomy and depressing
DISMALER > DISMAL
DISMALEST > DISMAL
DISMALITY > DISMAL
DISMALLER > DISMAL
DISMALLY > DISMAL
DISMALS pl n gloomy state of mind
DISMAN vb remove men from
DISMANNED > DISMAN
DISMANS > DISMAN
DISMANTLE vb take apart piece by piece
DISMASK vb remove mask from
DISMASKED > DISMASK
DISMASKS > DISMASK
DISMAST vb break off the mast or masts of (a sailing vessel)
DISMASTED > DISMAST
DISMASTS > DISMAST
DISMAY vb fill with alarm or depression ▷ n alarm mixed with sadness
DISMAYD adj word used by Spenser meaning misshapen
DISMAYED > DISMAY
DISMAYFUL > DISMAY
DISMAYING > DISMAY
DISMAYL vb remove a coat of mail from
DISMAYLED > DISMAYL
DISMAYLS > DISMAYL
DISMAYS > DISMAY
DISME old form of > DIME
DISMEMBER vb remove the limbs of
DISMES > DISME

DISMISS vb remove (an employee) from a job ▷ sentence substitute order to end an activity or give permission to disperse
DISMISSAL n official notice of discharge from employment or service
DISMISSED > DISMISS
DISMISSES > DISMISS
DISMODED adj no longer fashionable
DISMOUNT vb get off a horse or bicycle ▷ n act of dismounting
DISMOUNTS > DISMOUNT
DISNATURE vb cause to be in an unnatural condition
DISNEST vb remove from a nest
DISNESTED > DISNEST
DISNESTS > DISNEST
DISOBEY vb neglect or refuse to obey
DISOBEYED > DISOBEY
DISOBEYER > DISOBEY
DISOBEYS > DISOBEY
DISOBLIGE vb disregard the desires of
DISODIUM n compound containing two sodium atoms
DISOMIC adj having an extra chromosome in the haploid state
DISOMIES > DISOMY
DISOMY > DISOMIC
DISORBED adj thrown out of orbit
DISORDER n state of untidiness and disorganization ▷ vb upset the order of
DISORDERS > DISORDER
DISORIENT vb cause (someone) to lose their bearings
DISOWN vb deny any connection with (someone)
DISOWNED > DISOWN
DISOWNER > DISOWN
DISOWNERS > DISOWN
DISOWNING > DISOWN
DISOWNS > DISOWN
DISPACE vb move or travel about
DISPACED > DISPACE
DISPACES > DISPACE
DISPACING > DISPACE
DISPARAGE vb speak contemptuously of
DISPARATE adj completely different ▷ n unlike things or people
DISPARITY n inequality or difference
DISPARK vb release
DISPARKED > DISPARK
DISPARKS > DISPARK
DISPART vb separate
DISPARTED > DISPART
DISPARTS > DISPART
DISPATCH vb send off to a destination or to perform a task ▷ n official communication or report, sent in haste
DISPATHY obsolete spelling of > DYSPATHY

DISPAUPER vb state that someone is no longer a pauper
DISPEACE n absence of peace
DISPEACES > DISPEACE
DISPEL vb destroy or remove
DISPELLED > DISPEL
DISPELLER > DISPEL
DISPELS > DISPEL
DISPENCE same as > DISPENSE
DISPENCED > DISPENCE
DISPENCES > DISPENCE
DISPEND vb spend
DISPENDED > DISPEND
DISPENDS > DISPEND
DISPENSE vb distribute in portions
DISPENSED > DISPENSE
DISPENSER n device, such as a vending machine, that automatically dispenses a single item or a measured quantity
DISPENSES > DISPENSE
DISPEOPLE vb remove inhabitants from
DISPERSAL n act of dispersing or the condition of being dispersed
DISPERSE vb scatter over a wide area ▷ adj of or consisting of the particles in a colloid or suspension
DISPERSED > DISPERSE
DISPERSER > DISPERSE
DISPERSES > DISPERSE
DISPIRIT vb make downhearted
DISPIRITS > DISPIRIT
DISPLACE vb move from the usual location
DISPLACED > DISPLACE
DISPLACER > DISPLACE
DISPLACES > DISPLACE
DISPLANT vb displace
DISPLANTS > DISPLANT
DISPLAY vb make visible or noticeable ▷ n displaying
DISPLAYED > DISPLAY
DISPLAYER > DISPLAY
DISPLAYS > DISPLAY
DISPLE vb punish
DISPLEASE vb annoy or upset
DISPLED > DISPLE
DISPLES > DISPLE
DISPLING > DISPLE
DISPLODE obsolete word for > EXPLODE
DISPLODED > DISPLODE
DISPLODES > DISPLODE
DISPLUME vb remove feathers from
DISPLUMED > DISPLUME
DISPLUMES > DISPLUME
DISPONDEE n (poetry) double foot of two long syllables
DISPONE vb transfer ownership
DISPONED > DISPONE
DISPONEE vb person whom something is disponed to
DISPONEES > DISPONEE

d

DISPONER > DISPONE
DISPONERS > DISPONE
DISPONES > DISPONE
DISPONGE same as
  > DISPUNGE
DISPONGED > DISPONGE
DISPONGES > DISPONGE
DISPONING > DISPONE
DISPORT vb indulge
  (oneself) in pleasure ▷ n
  amusement
DISPORTED > DISPORT
DISPORTS > DISPORT
DISPOSAL n getting rid of
  something
DISPOSALS > DISPOSAL
DISPOSE vb place in a
  certain order
DISPOSED adj willing or
  eager
DISPOSER > DISPOSE
DISPOSERS > DISPOSE
DISPOSES > DISPOSE
DISPOSING > DISPOSE
DISPOST vb remove from
  post
DISPOSTED > DISPOST
DISPOSTS > DISPOST
DISPOSURE a rare word for
  > DISPOSAL
DISPRAD old form of
  > DISPREAD
DISPRAISE vb express
  disapproval or condemnation
  of ▷ n disapproval, etc,
  expressed
DISPREAD vb spread out
DISPREADS > DISPREAD
DISPRED old spelling of
  > DISPREAD
DISPREDS > DISPRED
DISPRISON vb release from
  captivity
DISPRIZE vb scorn
DISPRIZED > DISPRIZE
DISPRIZES > DISPRIZE
DISPROFIT n loss ▷ vb
  (cause to) fail to profit
DISPROOF n facts that
  disprove something
DISPROOFS > DISPROOF
DISPROOVE vb disapprove
  of
DISPROVAL > DISPROVE
DISPROVE vb show (an
  assertion or claim) to be
  incorrect
DISPROVED > DISPROVE
DISPROVEN > DISPROVE
DISPROVER > DISPROVE
DISPROVES > DISPROVE
DISPUNGE vb expunge
DISPUNGED > DISPUNGE
DISPUNGES > DISPUNGE
DISPURSE another word for
  > DISBURSE
DISPURSED > DISPURSE
DISPURSES > DISPURSE
DISPURVEY vb strip of
  equipment, provisions, etc
DISPUTANT n person who
  argues ▷ adj engaged in
  argument
DISPUTE n disagreement,
  argument ▷ vb argue about
  (something)
DISPUTED > DISPUTE

DISPUTER > DISPUTE
DISPUTERS > DISPUTE
DISPUTES > DISPUTE
DISPUTING > DISPUTE
DISQUIET n feeling of
  anxiety ▷ vb make
  (someone) anxious ▷ adj
  uneasy or anxious
DISQUIETS > DISQUIET
DISRANK vb demote
DISRANKED > DISRANK
DISRANKS > DISRANK
DISRATE vb punish (an
  officer) by lowering in rank
DISRATED > DISRATE
DISRATES > DISRATE
DISRATING > DISRATE
DISREGARD vb give little or
  no attention to ▷ n lack of
  attention or respect
DISRELISH vb have a
  feeling of aversion for ▷ n
  such a feeling
DISREPAIR n condition of
  being worn out or in poor
  working order
DISREPUTE n loss or lack of
  good reputation
DISROBE vb undress
DISROBED > DISROBE
DISROBER > DISROBE
DISROBERS > DISROBE
DISROBES > DISROBE
DISROBING > DISROBE
DISROOT vb uproot
DISROOTED > DISROOT
DISROOTS > DISROOT
DISRUPT vb interrupt the
  progress of
DISRUPTED > DISRUPT
DISRUPTER > DISRUPT
DISRUPTOR > DISRUPT
DISRUPTS > DISRUPT
DISS vb treat (a person) with
  contempt
DISSAVE vb spend savings
DISSAVED > DISSAVE
DISSAVER n person who
  dissaves
DISSAVERS > DISSAVER
DISSAVES > DISSAVE
DISSAVING > DISSAVE
DISSEAT vb unseat
DISSEATED > DISSEAT
DISSEATS > DISSEAT
DISSECT vb cut something
  open to examine it
DISSECTED adj in the form
  of narrow lobes or segments
DISSECTOR > DISSECT
DISSECTS > DISSECT
DISSED > DISS
DISSEISE vb deprive of
  seisin
DISSEISED > DISSEISE
DISSEISEE n person who is
  disseised
DISSEISES > DISSEISE
DISSEISIN n act of
  disseising or state of being
  disseised
DISSEISOR > DISSEISE
DISSEIZE same as
  > DISSEISE
DISSEIZED > DISSEIZE
DISSEIZEE n person who is
  disseized

DISSEIZES > DISSEIZE
DISSEIZIN same as
  > DISSEISIN
DISSEIZOR > DISSEIZE
DISSEMBLE vb conceal
  one's real motives or
  emotions by pretence
DISSEMBLY n dismantling
DISSENSUS n
  disagreement within group
DISSENT vb disagree ▷ n
  disagreement
DISSENTED > DISSENT
DISSENTER > DISSENT
DISSENTS > DISSENT
DISSERT n give or make a
  dissertation; dissertate
DISSERTED > DISSERT
DISSERTS > DISSERT
DISSERVE vb do a disservice
  to
DISSERVED > DISSERVE
DISSERVES > DISSERVE
DISSES > DISS
DISSEVER vb break off or
  become broken off
DISSEVERS > DISSEVER
DISSHIVER vb break in
  pieces
DISSIDENT n person who
  disagrees with and criticizes
  the government ▷ adj
  disagreeing with the
  government
DISSIGHT n eyesore
DISSIGHTS > DISSIGHT
DISSIMILE n comparison
  using contrast
DISSING > DISS
DISSIPATE vb waste or
  squander
DISSOCIAL adj
  incongruous or irreconcilable
DISSOLUTE adj leading an
  immoral life
DISSOLVE vb (cause to)
  become liquid ▷ n scene
  filmed or televised by
  dissolving
DISSOLVED > DISSOLVE
DISSOLVER > DISSOLVE
DISSOLVES > DISSOLVE
DISSONANT adj discordant
DISSUADE vb deter
  (someone) by persuasion
  from doing something
DISSUADED > DISSUADE
DISSUADER > DISSUADE
DISSUADES > DISSUADE
DISSUNDER vb separate
DISTAFF n rod on which
  wool etc is wound for
  spinning
DISTAFFS > DISTAFF
DISTAIN vb stain; tarnish
DISTAINED > DISTAIN
DISTAINS > DISTAIN
DISTAL adj (of a bone, limb,
  etc) situated farthest from
  the point of attachment
DISTALLY > DISTAL
DISTANCE n space between
  two points
DISTANCED > DISTANCE
DISTANCES > DISTANCE
DISTANT adj far apart
DISTANTLY > DISTANT

DISTASTE n dislike, disgust
DISTASTED > DISTASTE
DISTASTES > DISTASTE
DISTAVES > DISTAFF
DISTEMPER n highly
  contagious viral disease of
  dogs ▷ vb paint with
  distemper
DISTEND vb (of part of the
  body) swell
DISTENDED > DISTEND
DISTENDER > DISTEND
DISTENDS > DISTEND
DISTENT adj bloated;
  swollen ▷ n breadth;
  distension
DISTENTS > DISTENT
DISTHENE n bluish-green
  mineral
DISTHENES > DISTHENE
DISTHRONE vb remove from
  throne
DISTICH n unit of two verse
  lines
DISTICHAL > DISTICH
DISTICHS > DISTICH
DISTIL vb subject to or
  obtain by distillation
DISTILL same as > DISTIL
DISTILLED > DISTIL
DISTILLER n person or
  company that makes strong
  alcoholic drink, esp whisky
DISTILLS > DISTILL
DISTILS > DISTIL
DISTINCT adj not the same
DISTINGUE adj
  distinguished or noble
DISTOME n parasitic
  flatworm
DISTOMES > DISTOME
DISTORT vb misrepresent
  (the truth or facts)
DISTORTED > DISTORT
DISTORTER > DISTORT
DISTORTS > DISTORT
DISTRACT vb draw the
  attention of (a person) away
  from something
DISTRACTS > DISTRACT
DISTRAIL n trail made by
  aircraft flying through cloud
DISTRAILS > DISTRAIL
DISTRAIN vb seize
  (personal property) to
  enforce payment of a debt
DISTRAINS > DISTRAIN
DISTRAINT n act or process
  of distraining
DISTRAIT adj absent-
  minded or preoccupied
DISTRAITE feminine form of
  > DISTRAIT
DISTRESS n extreme
  unhappiness ▷ vb upset
  badly
DISTRICT n area of land
  regarded as an
  administrative or
  geographical unit ▷ vb divide
  into districts
DISTRICTS > DISTRICT
DISTRIX n splitting of the
  ends of hairs
DISTRIXES > DISTRIX
DISTRUST vb regard as
  untrustworthy ▷ n feeling of
  suspicion or doubt

DISTRUSTS > DISTRUST
DISTUNE vb cause to be out of tune
DISTUNED > DISTUNE
DISTUNES > DISTUNE
DISTUNING > DISTUNE
DISTURB vb intrude on
DISTURBED adj emotionally upset or maladjusted
DISTURBER > DISTURB
DISTURBS > DISTURB
DISTYLE n temple with two columns
DISTYLES > DISTYLE
DISULFATE n chemical compound containing two sulfate ions
DISULFID same as > DISULFIDE
DISULFIDE n compound of a base with two atoms of sulfur
DISULFIDS > DISULFID
DISUNION > DISUNITE
DISUNIONS > DISUNITE
DISUNITE vb cause disagreement among
DISUNITED > DISUNITE
DISUNITER > DISUNITE
DISUNITES > DISUNITE
DISUNITY n dissension or disagreement
DISUSAGE n disuse
DISUSAGES > DISUSAGE
DISUSE vb stop using ▷ n state of being no longer used
DISUSED adj no longer used
DISUSES > DISUSE
DISUSING > DISUSE
DISVALUE vb belittle
DISVALUED > DISVALUE
DISVALUES > DISVALUE
DISVOUCH vb dissociate oneself from
DISYOKE vb unyoke
DISYOKED > DISYOKE
DISYOKES > DISYOKE
DISYOKING > DISYOKE
DIT vb stop something happening ▷ n short sound used in the spoken representation of telegraphic codes
DITA n tropical shrub
DITAL n key for raising pitch of lute string
DITALS > DITAL
DITAS > DITA
DITCH n narrow channel dug in the earth for drainage or irrigation ▷ vb abandon
DITCHED > DITCH
DITCHER > DITCH
DITCHERS > DITCH
DITCHES > DITCH
DITCHING > DITCH
DITCHLESS > DITCH
DITE vb set down in writing
DITED > DITE
DITES > DITE
DITHECAL adj having two thecae
DITHECOUS another word for > DITHECAL
DITHEISM n belief in two equal gods
DITHEISMS > DITHEISM

DITHEIST > DITHEISM
DITHEISTS > DITHEISM
DITHELETE n one believing that Christ had two wills
DITHELISM n belief that Christ had two wills
DITHER vb be uncertain or indecisive ▷ n state of indecision or agitation
DITHERED > DITHER
DITHERER > DITHER
DITHERERS > DITHER
DITHERIER > DITHER
DITHERING n instance of being uncertain or indecisive
DITHERS > DITHER
DITHERY > DITHER
DITHIOL n chemical compound
DITHIOLS > DITHIOL
DITHIONIC adj as in dithionic acid type of acid
DITHYRAMB n (in ancient Greece) a passionate choral hymn in honour of Dionysus
DITING > DITE
DITOKOUS adj producing two eggs
DITONE n interval of two tones
DITONES > DITONE
DITROCHEE n double metrical foot
DITS > DIT
DITSIER > DITSY
DITSIEST > DITSY
DITSINESS > DITSY
DITSY same as > DITZY
DITT same as > DIT
DITTANDER n type of plant of coastal Europe, N Africa, and SW Asia, with clusters of small white flowers
DITTANIES > DITTANY
DITTANY n aromatic plant
DITTAY n accusation; charge
DITTAYS > DITTAY
DITTED > DIT
DITTIED > DITTY
DITTIES > DITTY
DITTING > DIT
DITTIT > DIT
DITTO n same ▷ adv in the same way ▷ sentence substitute used to avoid repeating or to confirm agreement with an immediately preceding sentence ▷ vb copy
DITTOED > DITTO
DITTOING > DITTO
DITTOLOGY n interpretation in two ways
DITTOS > DITTO
DITTS > DITT
DITTY vb set to music ▷ n short simple poem or song
DITTYING > DITTY
DITZ n silly scatterbrained person
DITZES > DITZ
DITZIER > DITZY
DITZIEST > DITZY
DITZINESS > DITZY
DITZY adj silly and scatterbrained

DIURESES > DIURESIS
DIURESIS n excretion of an unusually large quantity of urine
DIURETIC n drug that increases the flow of urine ▷ adj acting to increase the flow of urine
DIURETICS > DIURETIC
DIURNAL adj happening during the day or daily ▷ n service book containing all the canonical hours except matins
DIURNALLY > DIURNAL
DIURNALS > DIURNAL
DIURON n type of herbicide
DIURONS > DIURON
DIUTURNAL adj long-lasting
DIV n dividend
DIVA n distinguished female singer
DIVAGATE vb digress or wander
DIVAGATED > DIVAGATE
DIVAGATES > DIVAGATE
DIVALENCE > DIVALENT
DIVALENCY > DIVALENT
DIVALENT n element that can unite with two atoms ▷ adj having two valencies or a valency of two
DIVALENTS > DIVALENT
DIVAN n low backless bed
DIVANS > DIVAN
DIVAS > DIVA
DIVE vb plunge headfirst into water ▷ n diving
DIVEBOMB vb bomb while making steep dives
DIVEBOMBS > DIVEBOMB
DIVED > DIVE
DIVELLENT adj separating
DIVER n person who works or explores underwater
DIVERGE vb separate and go in different directions
DIVERGED > DIVERGE
DIVERGENT adj diverging or causing divergence
DIVERGES > DIVERGE
DIVERGING > DIVERGE
DIVERS adj various ▷ determiner various
DIVERSE vb turn away ▷ adj having variety, assorted
DIVERSED > DIVERSE
DIVERSELY > DIVERSE
DIVERSES > DIVERSE
DIVERSIFY vb create different forms of
DIVERSING > DIVERSE
DIVERSION n official detour used by traffic when a main route is closed
DIVERSITY n quality of being different or varied
DIVERSLY > DIVERS
DIVERT vb change the direction of
DIVERTED > DIVERT
DIVERTER > DIVERT
DIVERTERS > DIVERT
DIVERTING > DIVERT
DIVERTIVE > DIVERT
DIVERTS > DIVERT
DIVES > DIVE

DIVEST vb strip (of clothes)
DIVESTED > DIVEST
DIVESTING > DIVEST
DIVESTS > DIVEST
DIVESTURE > DIVEST
DIVI alternative spelling of > DIVVY
DIVIDABLE > DIVIDE
DIVIDANT adj distinct
DIVIDE vb separate into parts ▷ n division, split
DIVIDED adj split
DIVIDEDLY > DIVIDED
DIVIDEND n sum of money representing part of the profit made, paid by a company to its shareholders
DIVIDENDS > DIVIDEND
DIVIDER n screen used to divide a room into separate areas
DIVIDERS pl n compasses with two pointed arms, used for measuring or dividing lines
DIVIDES > DIVIDE
DIVIDING > DIVIDE
DIVIDINGS > DIVIDE
DIVIDIVI n tropical tree
DIVIDIVIS > DIVIDIVI
DIVIDUAL adj divisible
DIVIDUOUS adj divided
DIVIED > DIVI
DIVINABLE > DIVINE
DIVINATOR n diviner
DIVINE adj of God or a god ▷ vb discover (something) by intuition or guessing ▷ n priest who is learned in theology
DIVINED > DIVINE
DIVINELY > DIVINE
DIVINER > DIVINE
DIVINERS > DIVINE
DIVINES > DIVINE
DIVINEST > DIVINE
DIVING > DIVE
DIVINGS > DIVE
DIVINIFY vb give divine status to
DIVINING > DIVINE
DIVINISE same as > DIVINIZE
DIVINISED > DIVINISE
DIVINISES > DIVINISE
DIVINITY n study of religion
DIVINIZE vb make divine
DIVINIZED > DIVINIZE
DIVINIZES > DIVINIZE
DIVIS > DIVI
DIVISIBLE adj capable of being divided
DIVISIBLY > DIVISIBLE
DIVISIM adv separately
DIVISION n dividing, sharing out
DIVISIONS > DIVISION
DIVISIVE adj tending to cause disagreement
DIVISOR n number to be divided into another number
DIVISORS > DIVISOR
DIVNA vb do not
DIVO n male diva
DIVORCE n legal ending of a marriage ▷ vb legally end one's marriage (to)

d

d

DIVORCED > DIVORCE
DIVORCEE n person who is divorced
DIVORCEES > DIVORCEE
DIVORCER > DIVORCE
DIVORCERS > DIVORCE
DIVORCES > DIVORCE
DIVORCING > DIVORCE
DIVORCIVE > DIVORCE
DIVOS > DIVO
DIVOT n small piece of turf
DIVOTS > DIVOT
DIVS > DIV
DIVULGATE vb make publicly known
DIVULGE vb make known, disclose
DIVULGED > DIVULGE
DIVULGER > DIVULGE
DIVULGERS > DIVULGE
DIVULGES > DIVULGE
DIVULGING > DIVULGE
DIVULSE vb tear apart
DIVULSED > DIVULSE
DIVULSES > DIVULSE
DIVULSING > DIVULSE
DIVULSION n tearing or pulling apart
DIVULSIVE > DIVULSION
DIVVIED > DIVVY
DIVVIER > DIVVY
DIVVIES > DIVVY
DIVVIEST > DIVVY
DIVVY vb divide and share ▷ adj dialect word for stupid
DIVVYING > DIVVY
DIVVYING alternative present participle of > DIVVY
DIWAN same as > DEWAN
DIWANS > DIWAN
DIXI interj I have spoken
DIXIE n large metal pot for cooking, brewing tea, etc
DIXIES > DIXIE
DIXIT n statement
DIXITS > DIXIT
DIXY same as > DIXIE
DIYA n small oil lamp, usu made from clay
DIYAS > DIYA
DIZAIN n ten-line poem
DIZAINS > DIZAIN
DIZEN archaic word for ▷ BEDIZEN
DIZENED > DIZEN
DIZENING > DIZEN
DIZENMENT > DIZEN
DIZENS > DIZEN
DIZYGOTIC adj developed from two separately fertilized eggs
DIZYGOUS another word for > DIZYGOTIC
DIZZARD n dunce
DIZZARDS > DIZZARD
DIZZIED > DIZZY
DIZZIER > DIZZY
DIZZIES > DIZZY
DIZZIEST > DIZZY
DIZZILY > DIZZY
DIZZINESS > DIZZY
DIZZY adj having or causing a whirling sensation ▷ vb make dizzy
DIZZYING > DIZZY
DJEBEL a variant spelling of > JEBEL

DJEBELS > DJEBEL
DJELLABAH n kind of loose cloak with a hood, worn by men esp in North Africa and the Middle East
DJELLABAH same as > DJELLABA
DJEMBE n W African drum
DJEMBES > DJEMBE
DJIBBA same as > JUBBAH
DJIBBAH same as > JUBBAH
DJIBBAHS > DJIBBAH
DJIBBAS > DJIBBA
DJIN same as > JINN
DJINN > DJINNI
DJINNI same as > JINNI
DJINNS > DJINNI
DJINNY same as > JINNI
DJINS > DJIN
DO vb perform or complete (a deed or action) ▷ n party, celebration
DOAB n alluvial land between two converging rivers
DOABLE adj capable of being done
DOABS > DOAB
DOAT same as > DOTE
DOATED > DOAT
DOATER > DOAT
DOATERS > DOAT
DOATING > DOAT
DOATINGS > DOAT
DOATS > DOAT
DOB vb as in dob in inform against or report
DOBBED > DOB
DOBBER n informant or traitor
DOBBERS > DOBBER
DOBBIE same as > DOBBY
DOBBIES > DOBBY
DOBBIN n name for a horse
DOBBING > DOB
DOBBINS > DOBBIN
DOBBY n attachment to a loom, used in weaving small figures
DOBCHICK same as > DABCHICK
DOBCHICKS > DOBCHICK
DOBE same as > ADOBE
DOBES > DOBE
DOBHASH n interpreter
DOBHASHES > DOBHASH
DOBIE n cannabis
DOBIES > DOBIE
DOBLA n medieval Spanish gold coin, probably worth 20 maravedis
DOBLAS > DOBLA
DOBLON a variant spelling of > DOUBLOON
DOBLONES > DOBLON
DOBLONS > DOBLON
DOBRA n standard monetary unit of São Tomé e Principe
DOBRAS > DOBRA
DOBRO n type of acoustic guitar
DOBROS > DOBRO
DOBS > DOB
DOBSON n larva of dobsonfly
DOBSONFLY n large North American insect
DOBSONS > DOBSON

DOBY same as > DOBIE
DOC same as > DOCTOR
DOCENT n voluntary worker who acts as a guide
DOCENTS > DOCENT
DOCETIC adj believing that the humanity of Christ was apparent and not real
DOCHMIAC > DOCHMIUS
DOCHMIACS > DOCHMIAC
DOCHMII > DOCHMIUS
DOCHMIUS n five-syllable foot
DOCHT > DOW
DOCIBLE adj easily tamed
DOCILE adj (of a person or animal) easily controlled
DOCILELY > DOCILE
DOCILER > DOCILE
DOCILEST > DOCILE
DOCILITY > DOCILE
DOCIMASY n close examination
DOCK n enclosed area of water where ships are loaded, unloaded, or repaired ▷ vb bring or be brought into dock
DOCKAGE n charge levied upon a vessel for using a dock
DOCKAGES > DOCKAGE
DOCKED > DOCK
DOCKEN n something of no value or importance
DOCKENS > DOCKEN
DOCKER n person employed to load and unload ships
DOCKERS > DOCKER
DOCKET n label on a delivery, stating contents, delivery instructions, etc ▷ vb fix a docket to (a package or other delivery)
DOCKETED > DOCKET
DOCKETING > DOCKET
DOCKETS > DOCKET
DOCKHAND n dock labourer
DOCKHANDS > DOCKHAND
DOCKING > DOCK
DOCKINGS > DOCK
DOCKISE same as > DOCKIZE
DOCKISED > DOCKISE
DOCKISES > DOCKISE
DOCKISING > DOCKISE
DOCKIZE vb convert into docks
DOCKIZED > DOCKIZE
DOCKIZES > DOCKIZE
DOCKIZING > DOCKIZE
DOCKLAND n area around the docks
DOCKLANDS > DOCKLAND
DOCKS > DOCK
DOCKSIDE n area next to dock
DOCKSIDES > DOCKSIDE
DOCKYARD n place where ships are built or repaired
DOCKYARDS > DOCKYARD
DOCO n (slang) documentary
DOCOS > DOCO
DOCQUET same as > DOCKET
DOCQUETED > DOCQUET
DOCQUETS > DOCQUET
DOCS > DOC

DOCTOR n person licensed to practise medicine ▷ vb alter in order to deceive
DOCTORAL > DOCTOR
DOCTORAND n student working towards doctorate
DOCTORATE n highest academic degree in any field of knowledge
DOCTORED > DOCTOR
DOCTORESS n female doctor
DOCTORIAL > DOCTOR
DOCTORING n act of doctoring
DOCTORLY > DOCTOR
DOCTORS > DOCTOR
DOCTRESS same as > DOCTORESS
DOCTRINAL > DOCTRINE
DOCTRINE n body of teachings of a religious, political, or philosophical group
DOCTRINES > DOCTRINE
DOCU n documentary film
DOCUDRAMA n film or television programme based on true events, presented in a dramatized form
DOCUMENT n piece of paper providing an official record of something ▷ vb record or report (something) in detail
DOCUMENTS > DOCUMENT
DOCUS > DOCU
DOCUSOAP n reality television programme in the style of a documentary
DOCUSOAPS > DOCUSOAP
DOD vb clip
DODDARD adj archaic word for missing branches; rotten ▷ n tree missing its top branches through rot
DODDARDS > DODDARD
DODDED > DOD
DODDER vb move unsteadily ▷ n type of rootless parasitic plant
DODDERED > DODDER
DODDERER > DODDER
DODDERERS > DODDER
DODDERIER > DODDER
DODDERING adj shaky, feeble, or infirm, esp from old age
DODDERS > DODDER
DODDERY > DODDER
DODDIER > DODDY
DODDIES > DODDY
DODDIEST > DODDY
DODDING > DOD
DODDIPOLL same as > DODDYPOLL
DODDLE n something easily accomplished
DODDLES > DODDLE
DODDY n bad mood ▷ adj sulky
DODDYPOLL n dunce
DODECAGON n geometric figure with twelve sides
DODGE vb avoid (a blow, being seen, etc) by moving suddenly ▷ n cunning or deceitful trick

DODGEBALL n game in which the players form a circle and try to hit opponents in the circle with a large ball

DODGED > DODGE

DODGEM n bumper car

DODGEMS > DODGEM

DODGER n person who evades a responsibility or duty

DODGERIES > DODGERY

DODGERS > DODGER

DODGERY n deception

DODGES > DODGE

DODGIER > DODGY

DODGIEST > DODGY

DODGINESS > DODGY

DODGING > DODGE

DODGINGS > DODGE

DODGY adj dangerous, risky

DODKIN n coin of little value

DODKINS > DODKIN

DODMAN n snail

DODMANS > DODMAN

DODO n large flightless extinct bird

DODOES > DODO

DODOISM > DODO

DODOISMS > DODO

DODOS > DODO

DODS > DOD

DOE n female deer, hare, or rabbit

DOEK n square of cloth worn on the head by women

DOEKS > DOEK

DOEN > DO

DOER n active or energetic person

DOERS > DOER

DOES > DO

DOESKIN n skin of a deer, lamb, or sheep

DOESKINS > DOESKIN

DOEST > DO

DOETH > DO

DOF informal South African word for > STUPID

DOFF vb take off or lift (one's hat) in polite greeting

DOFFED > DOFF

DOFFER > DOFF

DOFFERS > DOFF

DOFFING > DOFF

DOFFS > DOFF

DOG n domesticated four-legged mammal ▷ vb follow (someone) closely

DOGAN n offensive word for a Catholic

DOGANS > DOGAN

DOGARESSA n wife of doge

DOGATE n office of doge

DOGATES > DOGATE

DOGBANE n N American plant

DOGBANES > DOGBANE

DOGBERRY n any of certain plants that have berry-like fruits

DOGBOLT n bolt on cannon

DOGBOLTS > DOGBOLT

DOGCART n light horse-drawn two-wheeled cart

DOGCARTS > DOGCART

DOGDOM n world of dogs

DOGDOMS > DOGDOM

DOGE n (formerly) chief magistrate of Venice or Genoa

DOGEAR vb fold down the corner of (a page) ▷ n folded-down corner of a page

DOGEARED > DOGEAR

DOGEARING > DOGEAR

DOGEARS > DOGEAR

DOGEATE n office of doge

DOGEATES > DOGEATE

DOGEDOM n domain of doge

DOGEDOMS > DOGEDOM

DOGES > DOGE

DOGESHIP > DOGE

DOGESHIPS > DOGE

DOGEY same as > DOGIE

DOGEYS > DOGEY

DOGFACE n WW2 US soldier

DOGFACES > DOGFACE

DOGFIGHT vb fight in confused way ▷ n close-quarters combat between fighter aircraft

DOGFIGHTS > DOGFIGHT

DOGFISH n small shark

DOGFISHES > DOGFISH

DOGFOOD n food for a dog

DOGFOODS > DOGFOOD

DOGFOUGHT > DOGFIGHT

DOGFOX n male fox

DOGFOXES > DOGFOX

DOGGED adj stubbornly determined

DOGGEDER > DOGGED

DOGGEDEST > DOGGED

DOGGEDLY > DOGGED

DOGGER n Dutch fishing vessel with two masts

DOGGEREL n poorly written poetry, usu comic

DOGGERELS > DOGGEREL

DOGGERIES > DOGGERY

DOGGERMAN n sailor on dogger

DOGGERMEN > DOGGERMAN

DOGGERS > DOGGER

DOGGERY n surly behaviour

DOGGESS n female dog

DOGGESSES > DOGGESS

DOGGIE same as > DOGGY

DOGGIER > DOGGY

DOGGIES > DOGGY

DOGGIEST > DOGGY

DOGGINESS > DOGGY

DOGGING > DOG

DOGGINGS > DOG

DOGGISH adj of or like a dog

DOGGISHLY > DOGGISH

DOGGO adv in hiding and keeping quiet

DOGGONE interj exclamation of annoyance, disappointment, etc ▷ vb damn ▷ adj damnedest

DOGGONED > DOGGONE

DOGGONER > DOGGONE

DOGGONES > DOGGONE

DOGGONEST > DOGGONE

DOGGONING > DOGGONE

DOGGREL same as > DOGGEREL

DOGGRELS > DOGGREL

DOGGY n child's word for a dog ▷ adj of or like a dog

DOGHANGED same as > HANGDOG

DOGHOLE n squalid dwelling place

DOGHOLES > DOGHOLE

DOGHOUSE n kennel

DOGHOUSES > DOGHOUSE

DOGIE n motherless calf

DOGIES > DOGIE

DOGLEG n sharp bend ▷ vb go off at an angle ▷ adj of or with the shape of a dogleg

DOGLEGGED > DOGLEG

DOGLEGS > DOGLEG

DOGLIKE > DOG

DOGMA n doctrine or system of doctrines proclaimed by authority as true

DOGMAN n person who directs a crane whilst riding on an object being lifted by it

DOGMAS > DOGMA

DOGMATA > DOGMA

DOGMATIC adj habitually stating one's opinions forcefully or arrogantly

DOGMATICS n study of religious dogmas and doctrines

DOGMATISE same as > DOGMATIZE

DOGMATISM > DOGMATIZE

DOGMATIST n dogmatic person

DOGMATIZE vb say or state (something) in a dogmatic manner

DOGMATORY > DOGMA

DOGMEN > DOGMAN

DOGNAP vb carry off and hold (a dog), usually for ransom

DOGNAPED > DOGNAP

DOGNAPER > DOGNAP

DOGNAPERS > DOGNAP

DOGNAPING > DOGNAP

DOGNAPPED > DOGNAP

DOGNAPPER > DOGNAP

DOGNAPS > DOGNAP

DOGPILE n pile of bodies formed by people jumping on top of each other

DOGPILES > DOGPILE

DOGREL n doggerel

DOGRELS > DOGREL

DOGROBBER n army cook

DOGS > DOG

DOGSBODY n person who carries out boring tasks for others ▷ vb act as a dogsbody

DOGSHIP n condition of being a dog

DOGSHIPS > DOGSHIP

DOGSHORES n pieces of wood to prop up boat

DOGSHOW n competition in which dogs are judged

DOGSHOWS > DOGSHOW

DOGSKIN n leather from dog's skin

DOGSKINS > DOGSKIN

DOGSLED n sleigh drawn by dogs

DOGSLEDS > DOGSLED

DOGSLEEP n feigned sleep

DOGSLEEPS > DOGSLEEP

DOGSTAIL n type of grass

DOGSTAILS > DOGSTAIL

DOGTAIL same as > DOGSTAIL

DOGTAILS > DOGTAIL

DOGTEETH > DOGTOOTH

DOGTOOTH n medieval carved ornament

DOGTOWN n community of prairie dogs

DOGTOWNS > DOGTOWN

DOGTROT n gently paced trot

DOGTROTS > DOGTROT

DOGVANE n light windvane mounted on the side of a vessel

DOGVANES > DOGVANE

DOGWATCH n either of two watches aboard ship, from four to six pm or from six to eight pm

DOGWOOD n type of tree or shrub

DOGWOODS > DOGWOOD

DOGY same as > DOGIE

DOH n in tonic sol-fa, first degree of any major scale ▷ interj exclamation of annoyance when something goes wrong

DOHS > DOH

DOHYO n sumo wrestling ring

DOHYOS > DOHYO

DOILED same as > DOILT

DOILIED adj having a doily

DOILIES > DOILY

DOILT adj foolish

DOILTER > DOILT

DOILTEST > DOILT

DOILY n decorative lacy paper mat, laid on a plate

DOING > DO

DOINGS pl n deeds or actions

DOIT n former small copper coin of the Netherlands

DOITED adj foolish or childish, as from senility

DOITIT same as > DOITED

DOITKIN same as > DOIT

DOITKINS > DOITKIN

DOITS > DOIT

DOJO n room or hall for the practice of martial arts

DOJOS > DOJO

DOL n unit of pain intensity, as measured by dolorimetry

DOLABRATE adj shaped like a hatchet or axe head

DOLCE n dessert ▷ adv (to be performed) gently and sweetly

DOLCES > DOLCE

DOLCETTO n variety of grape

DOLCETTOS > DOLCETTO

DOLCI > DOLCE

DOLDRUMS pl n depressed state of mind

DOLE n money received from the state while unemployed ▷ vb distribute in small quantities

DOLED > DOLE

DOLEFUL adj dreary, unhappy

DOLEFULLY > DOLEFUL

DOLENT adj sad

d

DOLENTE adv (to be performed) in a sorrowful manner

DOLERITE n dark igneous rock such as augite

DOLERITES > DOLERITE

DOLERITIC > DOLERITE

DOLES > DOLE

DOLESOME same as > DOLEFUL

DOLIA > DOLIUM

DOLICHOS n tropical vine

DOLICHURI n poetic term

DOLINA same as > DOLINE

DOLINAS > DOLINA

DOLINE n depression of the ground surface formed in limestone regions

DOLINES > DOLINE

DOLING > DOLE

DOLIUM n genus of molluscs

DOLL n small model of a human being, used as a toy ▷ vb as in doll up dress up

DOLLAR n standard monetary unit of many countries

DOLLARED adj flagged with a dollar sign

DOLLARISE same as > DOLLARIZE

DOLLARIZE vb replace a country's currency with US dollar

DOLLARS > DOLLAR

DOLLDOM > DOLL

DOLLDOMS > DOLL

DOLLED > DOLL

DOLLHOOD > DOLL

DOLLHOODS > DOLL

DOLLHOUSE n toy house in which dolls and miniature furniture can be put

DOLLIED > DOLLY

DOLLIER n person who operates a dolly

DOLLIERS > DOLLIER

DOLLIES > DOLLY

DOLLINESS > DOLLY

DOLLING > DOLL

DOLLISH > DOLL

DOLLISHLY > DOLL

DOLLOP n lump (of food) ▷ vb serve out (food)

DOLLOPED > DOLLOP

DOLLOPING > DOLLOP

DOLLOPS > DOLLOP

DOLLS > DOLL

DOLLY adj attractive and unintelligent ▷ n wheeled support for a camera ▷ vb wheel a camera on a dolly

DOLLYBIRD n pretty and fashionable young woman

DOLLYING > DOLLY

DOLMA n vine leaf stuffed with a filling of meat and rice

DOLMADES > DOLMA

DOLMAN n long Turkish outer robe

DOLMANS > DOLMAN

DOLMAS > DOLMA

DOLMEN n prehistoric monument

DOLMENIC > DOLMEN

DOLMENS > DOLMEN

DOLOMITE n mineral consisting of calcium magnesium carbonate

DOLOMITES > DOLOMITE

DOLOMITIC > DOLOMITE

DOLOR same as > DOLOUR

DOLORIFIC adj causing pain or sadness

DOLOROSO adv (to be performed) in a sorrowful manner

DOLOROUS adj sad, mournful

DOLORS > DOLOR

DOLOS n knucklebone of a sheep, buck, etc, used esp by diviners

DOLOSSE > DOLOS

DOLOSTONE n rock composed of the mineral dolomite

DOLOUR n grief or sorrow

DOLOURS > DOLOUR

DOLPHIN n sea mammal of the whale family

DOLPHINET n female dolphin

DOLPHINS > DOLPHIN

DOLS > DOL

DOLT n stupid person

DOLTISH > DOLT

DOLTISHLY > DOLT

DOLTS > DOLT

DOM n title given to various monks and to certain of the canons regular

DOMAIN n field of knowledge or activity

DOMAINAL > DOMAIN

DOMAINE n French estate

DOMAINES > DOMAINE

DOMAINS > DOMAIN

DOMAL adj of a house

DOMANIAL > DOMAIN

DOMATIA > DOMATIUM

DOMATIUM n plant cavity inhabited by commensal insects or mites or, occasionally, microorganisms

DOME n rounded roof built on a circular base ▷ vb cover with or as if with a dome

DOMED > DOME

DOMELIKE > DOME

DOMES > DOME

DOMESDAY same as > DOOMSDAY

DOMESDAYS > DOMESDAY

DOMESTIC adj of one's own country or a specific country ▷ n person whose job is to do housework in someone else's house

DOMESTICS > DOMESTIC

DOMETT n wool and cotton cloth

DOMETTS > DOMETT

DOMIC adj dome-shaped

DOMICAL > DOME

DOMICALLY > DOME

DOMICIL same as > DOMICILE

DOMICILE n place where one lives ▷ vb establish or be established in a dwelling place

DOMICILED > DOMICILE

DOMICILES > DOMICILE

DOMICILS > DOMICIL

DOMIER > DOMY

DOMIEST > DOMY

DOMINANCE n control

DOMINANCY > DOMINANCE

DOMINANT adj having authority or influence ▷ n dominant allele or character

DOMINANTS > DOMINANT

DOMINATE vb control or govern

DOMINATED > DOMINATE

DOMINATES > DOMINATE

DOMINATOR > DOMINATE

DOMINE n clergyman or clergywoman

DOMINEE n minister of the Dutch Reformed Church

DOMINEER vb act with arrogance or tyranny

DOMINEERS > DOMINEER

DOMINEES > DOMINEE

DOMINES > DOMINE

DOMING > DOME

DOMINICAL adj of, relating to, or emanating from Jesus Christ as Lord

DOMINICK n breed of chicken

DOMINICKS > DOMINICK

DOMINIE n minister, clergyman or clergywoman: also used as a term of address

DOMINIES > DOMINIE

DOMINION same as > DOMINIUM

DOMINIONS same as > DOMINION

DOMINIQUE n type of chicken

DOMINIUM n ownership or right to possession of property, esp realty

DOMINIUMS > DOMINIUM

DOMINO n small rectangular block marked with dots, used in dominoes

DOMINOES n game in which dominoes with matching halves are laid together

DOMINOS > DOMINO

DOMOIC adj as in domoic acid kind of amino acid

DOMS > DOM

DOMY adj having a dome or domes

DON vb put on (clothing) ▷ n member of the teaching staff at a university or college

DONA n Spanish lady

DONAH n woman

DONAHS > DONAH

DONAIR same as > DONER

DONAIRS > DONAIR

DONARIES > DONARY

DONARY n thing given for holy use

DONAS > DONA

DONATARY n recipient

DONATE vb give, esp to a charity or organization

DONATED > DONATE

DONATES > DONATE

DONATING > DONATE

DONATION n donating

DONATIONS > DONATION

DONATISM n doctrine and beliefs relating to an early Christian sect

DONATISMS > DONATISM

DONATIVE n gift or donation ▷ adj of or like a donation

DONATIVES > DONATIVE

DONATOR > DONATE

DONATORS > DONATE

DONATORY n recipient

DONDER vb beat (someone) up ▷ n wretch

DONDERED > DONDER

DONDERING > DONDER

DONDERS > DONDER

DONE > DO

DONEE n person who receives a gift

DONEES > DONEE

DONEGAL n type of tweed

DONEGALS > DONEGAL

DONENESS n extent to which something is cooked

DONEPEZIL n drug used to treat dementia

DONER n doner kebab, dish of grilled meat served in pitta bread

DONERS > DONER

DONG n deep reverberating sound of a large bell ▷ vb (of a bell) to make a deep reverberating sound

DONGA n steep-sided gully created by soil erosion

DONGAS > DONGA

DONGED > DONG

DONGING > DONG

DONGLE n electronic device

DONGLES > DONGLE

DONGOLA n leather tanned using a particular method

DONGOLAS > DONGOLA

DONGS > DONG

DONING n act of giving blood

DONINGS > DONING

DONJON n heavily fortified central tower of a castle

DONJONS > DONJON

DONKEY n long-eared member of the horse family

DONKEYMAN n person working in a ship's engine room

DONKEYMEN > DONKEYMAN

DONKEYS > DONKEY

DONKO n tearoom or cafeteria in a factory, wharf area, etc

DONKOS > DONKO

DONNA n Italian lady

DONNARD same as > DONNERT

DONNART same as > DONNERT

DONNAS > DONNA

DONNAT n lazy person

DONNATS > DONNAT

DONNE same as > DONNEE

DONNED > DON

DONNEE n subject or theme

DONNEES > DONNEE

DONNERD adj stupid

DONNERED same as > DONNERT

DONNERT adj stunned
DONNES > DONNE
DONNICKER n toilet
DONNIES > DONNY
DONNIKER same as > DONNICKER
DONNIKERS > DONNIKER
DONNING > DON
DONNISH adj serious and academic
DONNISHLY > DONNISH
DONNISM n loftiness
DONNISMS > DONNISM
DONNOT n lazy person
DONNOTS > DONNOT
DONNY same as > DANNY
DONOR n person who gives blood or organs for medical use
DONORS > DONOR
DONORSHIP > DONOR
DONS > DON
DONSHIP n state or condition of being a don
DONSHIPS > DONSHIP
DONSIE adj rather unwell
DONSIER > DONSIE
DONSIEST > DONSIE
DONSY same as > DONSIE
DONUT same as > DOUGHNUT
DONUTS > DONUT
DONUTTED > DONUT
DONUTTING > DONUT
DONZEL n man of high birth
DONZELS > DONZEL
DOO a Scot word for > DOVE
DOOB n type of Indian grass
DOOBIE same as > DOOB
DOOBIES > DOOBIE
DOOBREY n thingumabob
DOOBREYS > DOOBREY
DOOBRIE same as > DOOBREY
DOOBRIES > DOOBRIE
DOOBRY n thing whose name is unknown or forgotten
DOOBS > DOOB
DOOCE vb dismiss (an employee) because of comments they have posted on the internet
DOOCED > DOOCE
DOOCES > DOOCE
DOOCING > DOOCE
DOOCOT n dovecote
DOOCOTS > DOOCOT
DOODAD same as > DOODAH
DOODADS > DOODAD
DOODAH n unnamed thing
DOODAHS > DOODAH
DOODIES > DOODY
DOODLE vb scribble or draw aimlessly ▷ n shape or picture drawn aimlessly
DOODLEBUG n diviner's rod
DOODLED > DOODLE
DOODLER > DOODLE
DOODLERS > DOODLE
DOODLES > DOODLE
DOODLING > DOODLE
DOODOO n excrement
DOODOOS > DOODOO
DOODY same as > DOODOO
DOOFER n thingamajig
DOOFERS > DOOFER

DOOFUS n slow-witted or stupid person
DOOFUSES > DOOFUS
DOOHICKEY another name for > DOODAH
DOOK n wooden plug driven into a wall to hold a nail, screw, etc ▷ vb dip or plunge
DOOKED > DOOK
DOOKET n dovecote
DOOKETS > DOOKET
DOOKING > DOOK
DOOKS > DOOK
DOOL n boundary marker
DOOLALLY adj out of one's mind
DOOLAN n Roman Catholic
DOOLANS > DOOLAN
DOOLE same as > DOOL
DOOLEE same as > DOOLIE
DOOLEES > DOOLEE
DOOLES > DOOLE
DOOLIE n enclosed couch on poles for carrying passengers
DOOLIES > DOOLIE
DOOLS > DOOL
DOOLY same as > DOOLIE
DOOM n death or a terrible fate ▷ vb destine or condemn to death or a terrible fate
DOOMED > DOOM
DOOMFUL > DOOM
DOOMFULLY > DOOM
DOOMIER > DOOMY
DOOMIEST > DOOMY
DOOMILY > DOOMY
DOOMING > DOOM
DOOMS > DOOM
DOOMSAYER n pessimist
DOOMSDAY n day on which the Last Judgment will occur
DOOMSDAYS > DOOMSDAY
DOOMSMAN n pessimist
DOOMSMEN > DOOMSMAN
DOOMSTER n person habitually given to predictions of impending disaster or doom
DOOMSTERS > DOOMSTER
DOOMWATCH n surveillance of the environment to warn of and prevent harm to it from human factors such as pollution or overpopulation
DOOMY adj despondent or pessimistic
DOON same as > DOWN
DOONA n large quilt used as a bed cover
DOONAS > DOONA
DOOR n hinged or sliding panel for closing the entrance to a building, room, etc
DOORBELL n device for visitors to announce presence at a door
DOORBELLS > DOORBELL
DOORCASE same as > DOORFRAME
DOORCASES > DOORCASE
DOORED adj having a door
DOORFRAME n frame that supports a door
DOORJAMB n vertical post forming one side of a door frame

DOORJAMBS > DOORJAMB
DOORKNOB n knob for opening and closing a door
DOORKNOBS > DOORKNOB
DOORKNOCK n fund-raising campaign for charity conducted by seeking donations from door to door
DOORLESS > DOOR
DOORLIKE adj like a door
DOORMAN n man employed to be on duty at the entrance to a large public building
DOORMAT n mat for wiping dirt from shoes before going indoors
DOORMATS > DOORMAT
DOORMEN > DOORMAN
DOORN n thorn
DOORNAIL n as in dead as a doornail dead beyond any doubt
DOORNAILS > DOORNAIL
DOORNBOOM n S African tree with yellow or white flowers
DOORNS > DOORN
DOORPLATE n name-plate on door
DOORPOST same as > DOORJAMB
DOORPOSTS > DOORPOST
DOORS > DOOR
DOORSILL n horizontal member of wood, stone, etc, forming the bottom of a doorframe
DOORSILLS > DOORSILL
DOORSMAN n doorkeeper
DOORSMEN > DOORSMAN
DOORSTEP n step in front of a door
DOORSTEPS > DOORSTEP
DOORSTONE n stone of threshold
DOORSTOP n object which prevents a door from closing or striking a wall
DOORSTOPS > DOORSTOP
DOORWAY n opening into a building or room
DOORWAYS > DOORWAY
DOORWOMAN n female doorman
DOORWOMEN > DOORWOMAN
DOORYARD n yard in front of the front or back door of a house
DOORYARDS > DOORYARD
DOOS > DOO
DOOSES > DOOS
DOOSRA n type of delivery in cricket
DOOSRAS > DOOSRA
DOOWOP n style of singing in harmony
DOOWOPS > DOOWOP
DOOZER same as > DOOZY
DOOZERS > DOOZER
DOOZIE same as > DOOZY
DOOZIES > DOOZIE
DOOZY n something excellent
DOP n small drink ▷ vb fail to reach the required standard in (an examination, course, etc)
DOPA n precursor to dopamine

DOPAMINE n chemical found in the brain that acts as a neurotransmitter
DOPAMINES > DOPAMINE
DOPANT n element or compound used to dope a semiconductor
DOPANTS > DOPANT
DOPAS > DOPA
DOPATTA n headscarf
DOPATTAS > DOPATTA
DOPE n additive used to improve the properties of something ▷ vb apply a dopant ▷ adj excellent
DOPED > DOPE
DOPEHEAD n habitual drug user
DOPEHEADS > DOPEHEAD
DOPER n person who administers dope
DOPERS > DOPER
DOPES > DOPE
DOPESHEET n document giving information on horse races
DOPEST > DOPE
DOPESTER n person who makes predictions, esp in sport or politics
DOPESTERS > DOPESTER
DOPEY adj half-asleep, drowsy
DOPEYNESS > DOPEY
DOPIAZA n Indian meat or fish dish cooked in onion sauce
DOPIAZAS > DOPIAZA
DOPIER > DOPEY
DOPIEST > DOPEY
DOPILY > DOPEY
DOPINESS > DOPEY
DOPING > DOPE
DOPINGS > DOPE
DOPPED > DOP
DOPPER n member of an Afrikaner church which practises a strict Calvinism
DOPPERS > DOPPER
DOPPIE n cartridge case
DOPPIES > DOPPIE
DOPPING > DOP
DOPPINGS > DOP
DOPPIO n double measure, esp of espresso coffee
DOPPIOS > DOPPIO
DOPS > DOP
DOPY same as > DOPEY
DOR n European dung beetle ▷ vb mock
DORAD n South American river fish
DORADO n large marine percoid fish
DORADOS > DORADO
DORADS > DORAD
DORB same as > DORBA
DORBA n stupid, inept, or clumsy person
DORBAS > DORBA
DORBEETLE same as > DOR
DORBS > DORB
DORBUG n type of beetle
DORBUGS > DORBUG
DORE n walleye fish
DOREE n type of fish
DOREES > DOREE

DORES > DORE
DORHAWK n nightjar
DORHAWKS > DORHAWK
DORIC adj rustic
DORIDOID n shell-less mollusc
DORIDOIDS > DORIDOID
DORIES > DORY
DORIS n woman
DORISE same as > DORIZE
DORISED > DORISE
DORISES > DORISE
DORISING > DORISE
DORIZE vb become Doric
DORIZED > DORIZE
DORIZES > DORIZE
DORIZING > DORIZE
DORK n stupid person
DORKIER > DORK
DORKIEST > DORK
DORKINESS > DORK
DORKISH adj stupid or contemptible
DORKS > DORK
DORKY > DORK
DORLACH n quiver of arrows
DORLACHS > DORLACH
DORM same as > DORMITORY
DORMANCY > DORMANT
DORMANT n supporting beam ▷ adj temporarily quiet, inactive, or not being used
DORMANTS > DORMANT
DORMER n window that sticks out from a sloping roof
DORMERED adj having dormer windows
DORMERS > DORMER
DORMICE > DORMOUSE
DORMIE adj (in golf) leading by as many holes as there are left
DORMIENT adj dormant
DORMIN n hormone found in plants
DORMINS > DORMIN
DORMITION n Mary's assumption to heaven
DORMITIVE adj sleep-inducing
DORMITORY n large room, esp at a school, containing several beds ▷ adj (of a town or suburb) having many inhabitants who travel to work in a nearby city
DORMOUSE n small mouselike rodent with a furry tail
DORMS > DORM
DORMY same as > DORMIE
DORNECK same as > DORNICK
DORNECKS > DORNECK
DORNICK n heavy damask cloth
DORNICKS > DORNICK
DORNOCK n type of coarse fabric
DORNOCKS > DORNOCK
DORONICUM n Eurasian and N African plant with yellow daisy-like flowers
DORP n small town
DORPER n breed of sheep
DORPERS > DORPER

DORPS > DORP
DORR same as > DOR
DORRED > DOR
DORRING > DOR
DORRS > DORR
DORS > DOR
DORSA > DORSUM
DORSAD adj towards the back or dorsal aspect
DORSAL adj of or on the back ▷ n dorsal fin
DORSALLY > DORSAL
DORSALS > DORSAL
DORSE n type of small fish
DORSEL another word for > DOSSAL
DORSELS > DORSEL
DORSER n hanging tapestry
DORSERS > DORSER
DORSES > DORSE
DORSIFLEX adj bending towards the back ▷ vb bend towards the back or dorsal
DORSUM n the back
DORT vb sulk
DORTED > DORT
DORTER n dormitory
DORTERS > DORTER
DORTIER > DORTY
DORTIEST > DORTY
DORTINESS > DORTY
DORTING > DORT
DORTOUR same as > DORTER
DORTOURS > DORTOUR
DORTS > DORT
DORTY adj haughty, or sullen
DORY n spiny-finned edible sea fish
DORYMAN n person who fishes from a small boat called a dory
DORYMEN > DORYMAN
DOS > DO
DOSA n Indian pancake made from rice flour
DOSAGE same as > DOSE
DOSAGES > DOSAGE
DOSAI > DOSA
DOSAS > DOSA
DOSE n specific quantity of a medicine taken at one time ▷ vb give a dose to
DOSED > DOSE
DOSEH n former Egyptian religious ceremony
DOSEHS > DOSEH
DOSEMETER same as > DOSIMETER
DOSER > DOSE
DOSERS > DOSE
DOSES > DOSE
DOSH n money
DOSHA n (in Hinduism) any of the three energies believed to be in the body
DOSHAS > DOSHA
DOSHES > DOSH
DOSIMETER n instrument for measuring the dose of X-rays or other radiation absorbed by matter or the intensity of a source of radiation
DOSIMETRY > DOSIMETER
DOSING > DOSE
DOSIOLOGY n study of doses

DOSOLOGY same as > DOSIOLOGY
DOSS vb sleep, esp in a dosshouse ▷ n bed, esp in a dosshouse
DOSSAL n ornamental hanging used in churches
DOSSALS > DOSSAL
DOSSED > DOSS
DOSSEL same as > DOSSAL
DOSSELS > DOSSEL
DOSSER n bag or basket for carrying objects on the back
DOSSERET n stone above column supporting an arch
DOSSERETS > DOSSERET
DOSSERS > DOSSER
DOSSES > DOSS
DOSSHOUSE n cheap lodging house for homeless people
DOSSIER n collection of documents about a subject or person
DOSSIERS > DOSSIER
DOSSIL n lint for dressing wound
DOSSILS > DOSSIL
DOSSING > DOSS
DOST a singular form of the present tense (indicative mood) of > DO
DOT n small round mark ▷ vb mark with a dot
DOTAGE n weakness as a result of old age
DOTAGES > DOTAGE
DOTAL adj of a dowry
DOTANT another word for > DOTARD
DOTANTS > DOTANT
DOTARD n person who is feeble-minded through old age
DOTARDLY adj like a dotard
DOTARDS > DOTARD
DOTATION n act of giving a dowry
DOTATIONS > DOTATION
DOTCOM n company that does most of its business on the internet
DOTCOMMER n person who carries out business on the internet
DOTCOMS > DOTCOM
DOTE vb love to an excessive or foolish degree
DOTED > DOTE
DOTER > DOTE
DOTERS > DOTE
DOTES > DOTE
DOTH a singular form of the present tense of > DO
DOTIER > DOTY
DOTIEST > DOTY
DOTING > DOTE
DOTINGLY > DOTE
DOTINGS > DOTE
DOTISH adj foolish
DOTS > DOT
DOTTED > DOT
DOTTEL same as > DOTTLE
DOTTELS > DOTTEL
DOTTER > DOT
DOTTEREL n rare kind of plover

DOTTERELS > DOTTEREL
DOTTERS > DOT
DOTTIER > DOTTY
DOTTIEST > DOTTY
DOTTILY > DOTTY
DOTTINESS > DOTTY
DOTTING > DOT
DOTTLE n tobacco left in a pipe after smoking ▷ adj relating to dottle
DOTTLED adj foolish
DOTTLER > DOTTLE
DOTTLES > DOTTLE
DOTTLEST > DOTTLE
DOTTREL same as > DOTTEREL
DOTTRELS > DOTTREL
DOTTY adj rather eccentric
DOTY adj (of wood) rotten
DOUANE n customs house
DOUANES > DOUANE
DOUANIER n customs officer
DOUANIERS > DOUANIER
DOUAR same as > DUAR
DOUARS > DOUAR
DOUBLE adj as much again in number, amount, size, etc ▷ adv twice over ▷ n twice the number, amount, size, etc ▷ vb make or become twice as much or as many
DOUBLED > DOUBLE
DOUBLER > DOUBLE
DOUBLERS > DOUBLE
DOUBLES n game between two pairs of players
DOUBLET n man's close-fitting jacket, with or without sleeves
DOUBLETON n original holding of two cards only in a suit
DOUBLETS > DOUBLET
DOUBLING > DOUBLE
DOUBLINGS > DOUBLE
DOUBLOON n former Spanish gold coin
DOUBLOONS > DOUBLOON
DOUBLURE n decorative lining of vellum or leather, etc, on the inside of a book cover
DOUBLURES > DOUBLURE
DOUBLY adv in a greater degree, quantity, or measure
DOUBT n uncertainty about the truth, facts, or existence of something ▷ vb question the truth of
DOUBTABLE > DOUBT
DOUBTABLY > DOUBT
DOUBTED > DOUBT
DOUBTER > DOUBT
DOUBTERS > DOUBT
DOUBTFUL adj unlikely ▷ n person who is undecided or uncertain about an issue
DOUBTFULS > DOUBTFUL
DOUBTING > DOUBT
DOUBTINGS > DOUBT
DOUBTLESS adv probably or certainly ▷ adj certain
DOUBTS > DOUBT
DOUC n Old World monkey
DOUCE adj quiet
DOUCELY > DOUCE
DOUCENESS > DOUCE

DOUCEPERE *same as* > DOUZEPER

DOUCER > DOUCE

DOUCEST > DOUCE

DOUCET *n* former flute-like instrument

DOUCETS > DOUCET

DOUCEUR *n* gratuity, tip, or bribe

DOUCEURS > DOUCEUR

DOUCHE *n* stream of water onto or into the body ▷ *vb* cleanse or treat by means of a douche

DOUCHEBAG *n* despicable person

DOUCHED > DOUCHE

DOUCHES > DOUCHE

DOUCHING *n* act of douching

DOUCHINGS > DOUCHING

DOUCINE *n* type of moulding for cornice

DOUCINES > DOUCINE

DOUCS > DOUC

DOUGH *n* thick mixture used for making bread etc

DOUGHBALL *n* ball of bread used as bait in carp fishing

DOUGHBOY *n* infantryman, esp in World War I

DOUGHBOYS > DOUGHBOY

DOUGHFACE *n* Northern Democrat who sided with the South in the American Civil War

DOUGHIER > DOUGHY

DOUGHIEST > DOUGHY

DOUGHLIKE > DOUGH

DOUGHNUT *n* small cake of sweetened dough fried in deep fat ▷ *vb* surround a speaker to give the impression that Parliament is crowded

DOUGHNUTS > DOUGHNUT

DOUGHS > DOUGH

DOUGHT > DOW

DOUGHTIER > DOUGHTY

DOUGHTILY > DOUGHTY

DOUGHTY *adj* brave and determined

DOUGHY *adj* resembling dough in consistency, colour, etc

DOUK *same as* > DOOK

DOUKED > DOUK

DOUKING > DOUK

DOUKS > DOUK

DOULA *n* woman who supports families during pregnancy and childbirth

DOULAS > DOULA

DOULEIA *same as* > DULIA

DOULEIAS > DOULEIA

DOUM *n* as in *doum palm* variety of palm tree

DOUMA *same as* > DUMA

DOUMAS > DOUMA

DOUMS > DOUM

DOUN *same as* > DOWN

DOUP *n* bottom

DOUPIONI *n* type of fabric

DOUPIONIS > DOUPIONI

DOUPPIONI *n* type of silk yarn

DOUPS > DOUP

DOUR *adj* sullen and unfriendly

DOURA *same as* > DURRA

DOURAH *same as* > DURRA

DOURAHS > DOURAH

DOURAS > DOURA

DOURER > DOUR

DOUREST > DOUR

DOURINE *n* infectious disease of horses

DOURINES > DOURINE

DOURLY > DOUR

DOURNESS > DOUR

DOUSE *vb* drench with water or other liquid ▷ *n* immersion

DOUSED > DOUSE

DOUSER > DOUSE

DOUSERS > DOUSE

DOUSES > DOUSE

DOUSING > DOUSE

DOUT *vb* extinguish

DOUTED > DOUT

DOUTER > DOUT

DOUTERS > DOUT

DOUTING > DOUT

DOUTS > DOUT

DOUX *adj* sweet

DOUZEPER *n* distinguished person

DOUZEPERS > DOUZEPER

DOVE *vb* be semi-conscious ▷ *n* bird with a heavy body, small head, and short legs

DOVECOT *same as* > DOVECOTE

DOVECOTE *n* structure for housing pigeons

DOVECOTES > DOVECOTE

DOVECOTS > DOVECOT

DOVED > DOVE

DOVEISH *adj* dovelike

DOVEISHLY > DOVEISH

DOVEKEY *same as* > DOVEKIE

DOVEKEYS > DOVEKEY

DOVEKIE *n* small short-billed auk

DOVEKIES > DOVEKIE

DOVELET *n* small dove

DOVELETS > DOVELET

DOVELIKE > DOVE

DOVEN *vb* pray

DOVENED > DOVEN

DOVENING > DOVEN

DOVENS > DOVEN

DOVER *vb* doze ▷ *n* doze

DOVERED > DOVER

DOVERING > DOVER

DOVERS > DOVER

DOVES > DOVE

DOVETAIL *n* joint containing wedge-shaped tenons ▷ *vb* fit together neatly

DOVETAILS > DOVETAIL

DOVIE *Scots word for* > STUPID

DOVIER > DOVIE

DOVIEST > DOVIE

DOVING > DOVE

DOVISH > DOVE

DOVISHLY > DOVISH

DOW *vb* archaic word meaning be of worth

DOWABLE *adj* capable of being endowed

DOWAGER *n* widow possessing property or a title obtained from her husband

DOWAGERS > DOWAGER

DOWAR *same as* > DUAR

DOWARS > DOWAR

DOWD *n* woman who wears unfashionable clothes

DOWDIER > DOWDY

DOWDIES > DOWDY

DOWDIEST > DOWDY

DOWDILY > DOWDY

DOWDINESS > DOWDY

DOWDS > DOWD

DOWDY *adj* dull and old-fashioned ▷ *n* dowdy woman

DOWDYISH > DOWDY

DOWDYISM > DOWDY

DOWDYISMS > DOWD

DOWED > DOW

DOWEL *n* wooden or metal peg used as a fastener ▷ *vb* join pieces of wood using dowels

DOWELED > DOWEL

DOWELING *n* joining of two pieces of wood using dowels

DOWELINGS > DOWELING

DOWELLED > DOWEL

DOWELLING *same as* > DOWELING

DOWELS > DOWEL

DOWER *n* life interest in a part of her husband's estate allotted to a widow by law ▷ *vb* endow

DOWERED > DOWER

DOWERIES > DOWERY

DOWERING > DOWER

DOWERLESS > DOWER

DOWERS > DOWER

DOWERY *same as* > DOWRY

DOWF *adj* dull; listless

DOWFNESS > DOWF

DOWIE *adj* dull and dreary

DOWIER > DOWIE

DOWIEST > DOWIE

DOWING > DOW

DOWITCHER *n* type of snipelike shore bird of arctic and subarctic N America

DOWL *n* fluff

DOWLAS *n* coarse fabric

DOWLASES > DOWLAS

DOWLE *same as* > DOWL

DOWLES > DOWLE

DOWLIER > DOWLY

DOWLIEST > DOWLY

DOWLNE *n* obsolete word meaning down (feathers)

DOWLNES > DOWLNE

DOWLNEY > DOWLNE

DOWLS > DOWL

DOWLY *adj* dull

DOWN *adv* indicating movement to or position in a lower place ▷ *adj* depressed, unhappy ▷ *vb* drink quickly ▷ *n* soft fine feathers

DOWNA *obsolete Scots form of* > CANNOT

DOWNBEAT *adj* gloomy ▷ *n* first beat of a bar

DOWNBEATS > DOWNBEAT

DOWNBOUND *adj* travelling south

DOWNBOW *n* (in music) a downward stroke of the bow across the strings

DOWNBOWS > DOWNBOW

DOWNBURST *n* very high-speed downward movement of turbulent air in a limited area for a short time. Near the ground it spreads out from its centre with high horizontal velocities

DOWNCAST *adj* sad, dejected ▷ *n* ventilation shaft

DOWNCASTS > DOWNCAST

DOWNCOME *same as* > DOWNCOMER

DOWNCOMER *n* pipe that connects a cistern to a WC, wash basin, etc

DOWNCOMES > DOWNCOME

DOWNCOURT *adj* in far end a of court

DOWNCRIED > DOWNCRY

DOWNCRIES > DOWNCRY

DOWNCRY *vb* denigrate or disparage

DOWNDRAFT *n* downward air current

DOWNED > DOWN

DOWNER *n* depressing experience

DOWNERS > DOWNER

DOWNFALL *n* sudden loss of success or power

DOWNFALLS > DOWNFALL

DOWNFIELD *adj* at far end of field

DOWNFLOW *n* something that flows down

DOWNFLOWS > DOWNFLOW

DOWNFORCE *n* force produced by air resistance plus gravity that increases the stability of an aircraft or motor vehicle by pressing it downwards

DOWNGRADE *vb* reduce in importance or value

DOWNHAUL *n* line for hauling down a sail or for increasing the tension at its luff

DOWNHAULS > DOWNHAUL

DOWNHILL *adj* going or sloping down ▷ *adv* towards the bottom of a hill ▷ *n* downward slope

DOWNHILLS > DOWNHILL

DOWNHOLE *adj* (in the oil industry) denoting any piece of equipment that is used in the well itself

DOWNIER > DOWNY

DOWNIES > DOWNY

DOWNIEST > DOWNY

DOWNILY *adv* in a manner resembling or indicating a layer of soft fine feathers or hairs

DOWNINESS > DOWNY

DOWNING > DOWN

DOWNLAND *same as* > DOWNS

DOWNLANDS > DOWNLAND

DOWNLESS > DOWN

DOWNLIGHT *n* lamp shining downwards

DOWNLIKE > DOWN

DOWNLINK *n* satellite transmission channel

SECTION 1: Words between 2 and 9 letters in length

d

DOWNLINKS > DOWNLINK

DOWNLOAD vb transfer data from one computer to another ▷ n file transferred in such a way

DOWNLOADS > DOWNLOAD

DOWNLOW n as in on the downlow not widely known

DOWNLOWS > DOWNLOW

DOWNMOST adj lowest

DOWNPIPE n pipe for carrying rainwater from a roof gutter to the ground or to a drain

DOWNPIPES > DOWNPIPE

DOWNPLAY vb play down

DOWNPLAYS > DOWNPLAY

DOWNPOUR n heavy fall of rain

DOWNPOURS > DOWNPOUR

DOWNRANGE adv in the direction of the intended flight path of a rocket or missile

DOWNRATE vb reduce in value or importance

DOWNRATED > DOWNRATE

DOWNRATES > DOWNRATE

DOWNRIGHT adv extreme(ly) ▷ adj absolute

DOWNRIVER adv in direction of current

DOWNRUSH n instance of rushing down

DOWNS pl n low grassy hills, esp in S England

DOWNSCALE vb reduce in scale

DOWNSHIFT vb reduce work hours

DOWNSIDE n disadvantageous aspect of a situation

DOWNSIDES > DOWNSIDE

DOWNSIZE vb reduce the number of people employed by (a company)

DOWNSIZED > DOWNSIZE

DOWNSIZER > DOWNSIZE

DOWNSIZES > DOWNSIZE

DOWNSLIDE n downward trend

DOWNSLOPE adv towards the bottom of a slope ▷ n downward slope

DOWNSPIN n sudden downturn

DOWNSPINS > DOWNSPIN

DOWNSPOUT same as > DOWNPIPE

DOWNSTAGE adj or at the front part of the stage ▷ adv at or towards the front of the stage ▷ n front half of the stage

DOWNSTAIR adj situated on lower floor

DOWNSTATE adj in, or relating to the part of the state away from large cities, esp the southern part ▷ adv towards the southern part of a state ▷ n southern part of a state

DOWNSWEPT adj curved downwards

DOWNSWING n statistical downward trend in business activity, the death rate, etc

DOWNTHROW n state of throwing down or being thrown down

DOWNTICK n small decrease

DOWNTICKS > DOWNTICK

DOWNTIME n time during which a computer or other machine is not working

DOWNTIMES > DOWNTIME

DOWNTOWN n central or lower part of a city, esp the main commercial area ▷ adv towards, to, or into this area ▷ adj of, relating to, or situated in the downtown area

DOWNTOWNS > DOWNTOWN

DOWNTREND n downward trend

DOWNTROD adj downtrodden

DOWNTURN n drop in the success of an economy or a business

DOWNTURNS > DOWNTURN

DOWNVOTE vb publicly disapprove of a social media post

DOWNVOTED > DOWNVOTE

DOWNVOTES > DOWNVOTE

DOWNWARD same as > DOWNWARDS

DOWNWARDS adv from a higher to a lower level, condition, or position

DOWNWARP n wide depression in the earth's surface

DOWNWARPS > DOWNWARP

DOWNWASH n downward deflection of an airflow, esp one caused by an aircraft wing

DOWNWIND adj in the same direction towards which the wind is blowing

DOWNY adj covered with soft fine hair or feathers ▷ n as in the downy bed

DOWNZONE vb reduce density of housing in area

DOWNZONED > DOWNZONE

DOWNZONES > DOWNZONE

DOWP same as > DOUP

DOWPS > DOWP

DOWRIES > DOWRY

DOWRY n property brought by a woman to her husband at marriage

DOWS > DOW

DOWSABEL n sweetheart

DOWSABELS > DOWSABEL

DOWSE same as > DOUSE

DOWSED > DOWSE

DOWSER > DOWSE

DOWSERS > DOWSE

DOWSES > DOWSE

DOWSET same as > DOUCET

DOWSETS > DOWSET

DOWSING n act of dowsing

DOWSINGS > DOWSING

DOWT n cigarette butt

DOWTS > DOWT

DOX vb publish someone's personal information on the internet

DOXAPRAM n drug used to stimulate the respiration

DOXAPRAMS > DOXAPRAM

DOXASTIC adj of or relating to belief ▷ n branch of logic that studies the concept of belief

DOXASTICS > DOXASTIC

DOXED > DOX

DOXES > DOX

DOXIE same as > DOXY

DOXIES > DOXY

DOXING > DOX

DOXOLOGY n short hymn of praise to God

DOXY n opinion or doctrine, esp concerning religious matters

DOY n beloved person: used esp as an endearment

DOYEN n senior member of a group, profession, or society

DOYENNE > DOYEN

DOYENNES > DOYEN

DOYENS > DOYEN

DOYLEY same as > DOILY

DOYLEYS > DOYLEY

DOYLIES > DOYLY

DOYLY same as > DOILY

DOYS > DOY

DOZE vb sleep lightly or briefly ▷ n short sleep

DOZED adj (of timber or rubber) rotten or decayed

DOZEN n set of twelve ▷ vb stun

DOZENED > DOZEN

DOZENING > DOZEN

DOZENS > DOZEN

DOZENTH > DOZEN

DOZENTHS > DOZEN

DOZER > DOZE

DOZERS > DOZE

DOZES > DOZE

DOZIER > DOZY

DOZIEST > DOZY

DOZILY > DOZY

DOZINESS > DOZY

DOZING > DOZE

DOZINGS > DOZE

DOZY adj feeling sleepy

DRAB adj dull and dreary ▷ n light olive-brown colour ▷ vb consort with prostitutes

DRABBED > DRAB

DRABBER n one who frequents prostitutes ▷ adj more drab

DRABBERS > DRABBER

DRABBEST > DRAB

DRABBET n yellowish-brown fabric of coarse linen

DRABBETS > DRABBET

DRABBIER > DRABBY

DRABBIEST > DRABBY

DRABBING > DRAB

DRABBISH adj slightly drab

DRABBLE vb make or become wet or dirty

DRABBLED > DRABBLE

DRABBLER n part fixed to bottom of sail

DRABBLERS > DRABBLER

DRABBLES > DRABBLE

DRABBLING > DRABBLE

DRABBY adj slightly drab

DRABETTE n type of rough linen fabric

DRABETTES > DRABETTE

DRABLER same as > DRABBLER

DRABLERS > DRABLER

DRABLY > DRAB

DRABNESS > DRAB

DRABS > DRAB

DRAC same as > DRACK

DRACAENA n type of tropical plant often cultivated as a house plant for its decorative foliage

DRACAENAS > DRACAENA

DRACENA same as > DRACAENA

DRACENAS > DRACENA

DRACHM same as > DRAM

DRACHMA n former monetary unit of Greece

DRACHMAE > DRACHMA

DRACHMAI > DRACHMA

DRACHMAS > DRACHMA

DRACHMS > DRACHM

DRACK adj (esp of a woman) unattractive

DRACO n as in draco lizard flying lizard

DRACONE n large container towed by a ship

DRACONES > DRACONE

DRACONIAN adj severe, harsh

DRACONIC same as > DRACONIAN

DRACONISM > DRACONIAN

DRACONTIC same as > DRACONIC

DRAD archaic past of > DREAD

DRAFF n residue of husks used as a food for cattle

DRAFFIER > DRAFF

DRAFFIEST > DRAFF

DRAFFISH adj worthless

DRAFFS > DRAFF

DRAFFY > DRAFF

DRAFT same as > DRAUGHT

DRAFTABLE > DRAFT

DRAFTED > DRAFT

DRAFTEE n conscript

DRAFTEES > DRAFTEE

DRAFTER > DRAFT

DRAFTERS > DRAFT

DRAFTIER > DRAFTY

DRAFTIEST > DRAFTY

DRAFTILY > DRAFTY

DRAFTING > DRAFT

DRAFTINGS > DRAFT

DRAFTS > DRAFT

DRAFTSMAN adj person skilled in drawing

DRAFTSMEN > DRAFTSMAN

DRAFTY same as > DRAUGHTY

DRAG vb pull with force, esp along the ground ▷ n person or thing that slows up progress

DRAGEE n sweet made of a nut, fruit, etc, coated with a hard sugar icing

DRAGEES > DRAGEE

DRAGGED > DRAG

DRAGGER > DRAG

DRAGGERS > DRAG

DRAGGIER > DRAGGY

DRAGGIEST > DRAGGY

DRAGGING > DRAG

DRAGGINGS > DRAGGING

DRAGGLE vb make or become wet or dirty by trailing on the ground

DRAGGLED > DRAGGLE

DRAGGLES > DRAGGLE

DRAGGLING > DRAGGLE

DRAGGY adj slow or boring

DRAGHOUND n hound used to follow an artificial trail of scent in a drag hunt

DRAGLINE same as > DRAGROPE

DRAGLINES > DRAGLINE

DRAGNET n net used to scour the bottom of a pond or river

DRAGNETS > DRAGNET

DRAGOMAN n (in some Middle Eastern countries) professional interpreter or guide

DRAGOMANS > DRAGOMAN

DRAGOMEN > DRAGOMAN

DRAGON n mythical fire-breathing monster like a huge lizard

DRAGONESS > DRAGON

DRAGONET n type of small spiny-finned fish with a flat head and a slender brightly coloured body

DRAGONETS > DRAGONET

DRAGONFLY n brightly coloured insect with a long slender body and two pairs of wings

DRAGONISE same as > DRAGONIZE

DRAGONISH > DRAGON

DRAGONISM n vigilance

DRAGONIZE vb turn into dragon

DRAGONNE adj dragonlike

DRAGONS > DRAGON

DRAGOON n heavily armed cavalryman ▷ vb coerce, force

DRAGOONED > DRAGOON

DRAGOONS > DRAGOON

DRAGROPE n rope used to drag military equipment, esp artillery

DRAGROPES > DRAGROPE

DRAGS > DRAG

DRAGSMAN n carriage driver

DRAGSMEN > DRAGSMAN

DRAGSTER n car specially built or modified for drag racing

DRAGSTERS > DRAGSTER

DRAGSTRIP n track for drag racing

DRAGWAY n race course for drag racing

DRAGWAYS > DRAGWAY

DRAIL n weighted hook used in trolling ▷ vb fish with a drail

DRAILED > DRAIL

DRAILING > DRAIL

DRAILS > DRAIL

DRAIN n pipe or channel that carries off water or sewage ▷ vb draw off or remove liquid from

DRAINABLE > DRAIN

DRAINAGE n system of drains

DRAINAGES > DRAINAGE

DRAINED > DRAIN

DRAINER n person or thing that drains

DRAINERS > DRAINER

DRAINING > DRAIN

DRAINPIPE same as > DOWNPIPE

DRAINS > DRAIN

DRAISENE same as > DRAISINE

DRAISENES > DRAISENE

DRAISINE n light rail vehicle

DRAISINES > DRAISINE

DRAKE n male duck

DRAKES > DRAKE

DRAM n small amount of a strong alcoholic drink, esp whisky ▷ vb drink a dram

DRAMA n serious play for theatre, television, or radio

DRAMADIES > DRAMEDY

DRAMADY same as > DRAMEDY

DRAMAS > DRAMA

DRAMATIC adj of or like drama

DRAMATICS n art of acting or producing plays

DRAMATISE same as > DRAMATIZE

DRAMATIST n person who writes plays

DRAMATIZE vb rewrite (a book) in the form of a play

DRAMATURG n literary adviser at a theatre

DRAMEDIES > DRAMEDY

DRAMEDY n television or film drama in which there are important elements of comedy

DRAMMACH n oatmeal mixed with cold water

DRAMMACHS > DRAMMACH

DRAMMED > DRAM

DRAMMING > DRAM

DRAMMOCK same as > DRAMMACH

DRAMMOCKS > DRAMMOCK

DRAMS > DRAM

DRAMSHOP n bar

DRAMSHOPS > DRAMSHOP

DRANGWAY n narrow lane

DRANGWAYS > DRANGWAY

DRANK > DRINK

DRANT vb drone

DRANTED > DRANT

DRANTING > DRANT

DRANTS > DRANT

DRAP a Scot word for > DROP

DRAPABLE > DRAPE

DRAPE vb cover with material, usu in folds ▷ n piece of cloth hung at a window or opening as a screen

DRAPEABLE > DRAPE

DRAPED > DRAPE

DRAPER n person who sells fabrics and sewing materials

DRAPERIED > DRAPERY

DRAPERIES > DRAPERY

DRAPERS > DRAPER

DRAPERY n fabric or clothing arranged and draped

DRAPES pl n material hung at an opening or window to shut out light or to provide privacy

DRAPET n cloth

DRAPETS > DRAPET

DRAPEY adj hanging in loose folds

DRAPIER n draper

DRAPIERS > DRAPIER

DRAPIEST > DRAPEY

DRAPING > DRAPE

DRAPPED > DRAP

DRAPPIE n little drop

DRAPPIES > DRAPPIE

DRAPPING > DRAP

DRAPPY n drop (of liquid)

DRAPS > DRAP

DRASTIC n strong purgative ▷ adj strong and severe

DRASTICS > DRASTIC

DRAT interj exclamation of annoyance ▷ vb curse

DRATCHELL n dialect word meaning a scruffy woman

DRATS > DRAT

DRATTED adj wretched

DRATTING > DRAT

DRAUGHT vb make preliminary plan ▷ n current of cold air, esp in an enclosed space ▷ adj (of an animal) used for pulling heavy loads

DRAUGHTED > DRAUGHT

DRAUGHTER > DRAUGHT

DRAUGHTS n game for two players using a draughtboard and 12 draughtsmen each

DRAUGHTY adj exposed to draughts of air

DRAUNT same as > DRANT

DRAUNTED > DRAUNT

DRAUNTING > DRAUNT

DRAUNTS > DRAUNT

DRAVE archaic past of > DRIVE

DRAW vb sketch (a figure, picture, etc) with a pencil or pen ▷ n attraction

DRAWABLE > DRAW

DRAWBACK n disadvantage ▷ vb move backwards

DRAWBACKS > DRAWBACK

DRAWBAR n strong metal bar on a tractor, locomotive, etc

DRAWBARS > DRAWBAR

DRAWBORE n hole bored through tenon

DRAWBORES > DRAWBORE

DRAWCARD n performer certain to attract a large audience

DRAWCARDS > DRAWCARD

DRAWCORD n cord for drawing tight eg round a hood

DRAWCORDS > DRAWCORD

DRAWDOWN n decrease

DRAWDOWNS > DRAWDOWN

DRAWEE n person or organization on which payment is drawn

DRAWEES > DRAWEE

DRAWER n sliding box-shaped part of a piece of furniture, used for storage

DRAWERFUL n amount contained in drawer

DRAWERS pl n undergarment worn on the lower part of the body

DRAWING > DRAW

DRAWINGS > DRAW

DRAWKNIFE n woodcutting tool with two handles at right angles to the blade, used to shave wood

DRAWL vb speak slowly, with long vowel sounds ▷ n drawling manner of speech

DRAWLED > DRAWL

DRAWLER > DRAWL

DRAWLERS > DRAWL

DRAWLIER > DRAWL

DRAWLIEST > DRAWL

DRAWLING > DRAWL

DRAWLS > DRAWL

DRAWLY > DRAWL

DRAWN > DRAW

DRAWNWORK n type of ornamental needlework

DRAWPLATE n plate used to reduce the diameter of wire by drawing it through conical holes

DRAWS > DRAW

DRAWSHAVE same as > DRAWKNIFE

DRAWTUBE n type of tube used in a telescope

DRAWTUBES > DRAWTUBE

DRAY vb pull using cart ▷ n low cart used for carrying heavy loads

DRAYAGE n act of transporting something a short distance

DRAYAGES > DRAYAGE

DRAYED > DRAY

DRAYHORSE n large powerful horse used for drawing a dray

DRAYING > DRAY

DRAYMAN n driver of a dray

DRAYMEN > DRAYMAN

DRAYS > DRAY

DRAZEL n dirty or immoral woman

DRAZELS > DRAZEL

DREAD vb anticipate with apprehension or fear ▷ n great fear ▷ adj awesome

DREADED > DREAD

DREADER > DREAD

DREADERS > DREAD

DREADEST > DREAD

DREADFUL n cheap, often lurid or sensational book or magazine ▷ adj very disagreeable or shocking

DREADFULS > DREADFUL

DREADING > DREAD

DREADLESS > DREAD

DREADLOCK n Rastafarian hair braid

DREADLY > DREAD

DREADS > DREAD

DREAM n imagined events experienced while asleep ▷ vb see imaginary pictures in the mind while asleep ▷ adj ideal

DREAMBOAT n exceptionally attractive person or thing

DREAMED > DREAM

d

DREAMER n person who dreams habitually
DREAMERS > DREAMER
DREAMERY n dream world
DREAMFUL > DREAM
DREAMHOLE n light-admitting hole in a tower
DREAMIER > DREAMY
DREAMIEST > DREAMY
DREAMILY > DREAMY
DREAMING > DREAM
DREAMINGS > DREAM
DREAMLAND n ideal land existing in dreams or in the imagination
DREAMLESS > DREAM
DREAMLIKE > DREAM
DREAMS > DREAM
DREAMT > DREAM
DREAMTIME n time when the world was new and fresh
DREAMY adj vague or impractical
DREAR same as > DREARY
DREARE obsolete form of > DREAR
DREARER > DREAR
DREARES > DREARE
DREAREST > DREAR
DREARIER > DREARY
DREARIES > DREARY
DREARIEST > DREARY
DREARILY > DREARY
DREARING n sorrow
DREARINGS > DREARING
DREARS > DREAR
DREARY adj dull, boring ▷ n dreary thing or person
DRECK n rubbish
DRECKIER > DRECK
DRECKIEST > DRECK
DRECKISH adj like rubbish
DRECKS > DRECK
DRECKSILL n doorstep
DRECKY > DRECK
DREDGE vb clear or search (a river bed or harbour) by removing silt or mud
DREDGED > DREDGE
DREDGER n machine used to remove mud from a river bed or harbour
DREDGERS > DREDGER
DREDGES > DREDGE
DREDGING > DREDGE
DREDGINGS > DREDGE
DREE vb endure ▷ adj dreary
DREED > DREE
DREEING > DREE
DREER > DREE
DREES > DREE
DREEST > DREE
DREG n small quantity
DREGGIER > DREGGY
DREGGIEST > DREGGY
DREGGISH adj foul
DREGGY adj like or full of dregs
DREGS pl n solid particles that settle at the bottom of some liquids
DREICH adj dreary
DREICHER > DREICH
DREICHEST > DREICH
DREIDEL n spinning top
DREIDELS > DREIDEL

DREIDL same as > DREIDEL
DREIDLS > DREIDL
DREIGH same as > DREICH
DREIGHER > DREIGH
DREIGHEST > DREIGH
DREK same as > DRECK
DREKKIER > DREKKY
DREKKIEST > DREKKY
DREKKY > DREK
DREKS > DREK
DRENCH vb make completely wet ▷ n act or an instance of drenching
DRENCHED > DRENCH
DRENCHER > DRENCH
DRENCHERS > DRENCH
DRENCHES > DRENCH
DRENCHING > DRENCH
DRENT obsolete word for > DRENCHED
DREPANID n type of moth of the superfamily which comprises the hook-tip moths
DREPANIDS > DREPANID
DREPANIUM n type of flower cluster
DRERE obsolete form of > DREAR
DRERES > DRERE
DRERIHEAD n obsolete word for dreary
DRESS n one-piece garment for a woman or girl ▷ vb put clothes on ▷ adj suitable for a formal occasion
DRESSAGE n training of a horse to perform manoeuvres in response to the rider's body signals
DRESSAGES > DRESSAGE
DRESSED > DRESS
DRESSER n piece of furniture with shelves and with cupboards
DRESSERS > DRESSER
DRESSES > DRESS
DRESSIER > DRESSY
DRESSIEST > DRESSY
DRESSILY > DRESSY
DRESSING n sauce for salad
DRESSINGS pl n dressed stonework, mouldings, and carved ornaments used to form quoins, keystones, sills, and similar features
DRESSMADE > DRESSMAKE
DRESSMAKE vb make clothes
DRESSY adj (of clothes) elegant
DREST > DRESS
DREVILL n offensive person
DREVILLS > DREVILL
DREW > DRAW
DREY n squirrel's nest
DREYS > DREY
DRIB vb flow in drops
DRIBBED > DRIB
DRIBBER > DRIB
DRIBBERS > DRIB
DRIBBING > DRIB
DRIBBLE vb (allow to) flow in drops ▷ n small quantity of liquid falling in drops
DRIBBLED > DRIBBLE
DRIBBLER > DRIBBLE

DRIBBLERS > DRIBBLE
DRIBBLES > DRIBBLE
DRIBBLET same as > DRIBLET
DRIBBLETS > DRIBBLET
DRIBBLIER > DRIBBLE
DRIBBLING n act of dribbling
DRIBBLY > DRIBBLE
DRIBLET n small amount
DRIBLETS > DRIBLET
DRIBS > DRIB
DRICE n pellets of frozen carbon dioxide
DRICES > DRICE
DRICKSIE same as > DRUXY
DRICKSIER > DRICKSIE
DRIED > DRY
DRIEGH adj tedious
DRIER > DRY
DRIERS > DRY
DRIES > DRY
DRIEST > DRY
DRIFT vb be carried along by currents of air or water ▷ n something piled up by the wind or current
DRIFTAGE n act of drifting
DRIFTAGES > DRIFTAGE
DRIFTED > DRIFT
DRIFTER n person who moves aimlessly from place to place or job to job
DRIFTERS > DRIFTER
DRIFTIER > DRIFT
DRIFTIEST > DRIFT
DRIFTING n act of drifting
DRIFTINGS > DRIFTING
DRIFTLESS > DRIFT
DRIFTNET n fishing net that drifts with the tide
DRIFTNETS > DRIFTNET
DRIFTPIN same as > DRIFT
DRIFTPINS > DRIFTPIN
DRIFTS > DRIFT
DRIFTWOOD n wood floating on or washed ashore by the sea
DRIFTY > DRIFT
DRILL n tool or machine for boring holes ▷ vb bore a hole in (something) with or as if with a drill
DRILLABLE > DRILL
DRILLED > DRILL
DRILLER > DRILL
DRILLERS > DRILL
DRILLHOLE n hole drilled in the ground, usu for exploratory purposes
DRILLING n type of hard-wearing cloth
DRILLINGS > DRILL
DRILLS > DRILL
DRILLSHIP n floating drilling platform
DRILY adv in a dry manner
DRINK vb swallow (a liquid) ▷ n (portion of) a liquid suitable for drinking
DRINKABLE > DRINK
DRINKABLY > DRINK
DRINKER n person who drinks
DRINKERS > DRINKER
DRINKING > DRINK
DRINKINGS > DRINK

DRINKS > DRINK
DRIP vb (let) fall in drops ▷ n falling of drops of liquid
DRIPLESS > DRIP
DRIPPED > DRIP
DRIPPER > DRIP
DRIPPERS > DRIP
DRIPPIER > DRIPPY
DRIPPIEST > DRIPPY
DRIPPILY > DRIPPY
DRIPPING > DRIP
DRIPPINGS > DRIP
DRIPPY adj mawkish, insipid, or inane
DRIPS > DRIP
DRIPSTONE n form of calcium carbonate existing in stalactites or stalagmites
DRIPT > DRIP
DRISHEEN n pudding made of sheep's intestines filled with meal and sheep's blood
DRISHEENS > DRISHEEN
DRIVABLE > DRIVE
DRIVE vb guide the movement of (a vehicle) ▷ n journey by car, van, etc
DRIVEABLE > DRIVE
DRIVEL n foolish talk ▷ vb speak foolishly
DRIVELED > DRIVEL
DRIVELER > DRIVEL
DRIVELERS > DRIVEL
DRIVELINE n transmission line from engine to wheels of vehicle
DRIVELING > DRIVEL
DRIVELLED > DRIVEL
DRIVELLER > DRIVEL
DRIVELS > DRIVEL
DRIVEN > DRIVE
DRIVER n person who drives a vehicle
DRIVERS > DRIVER
DRIVES > DRIVE
DRIVEWAY n path for vehicles connecting a building to a public road
DRIVEWAYS > DRIVEWAY
DRIVING > DRIVE
DRIVINGLY > DRIVE
DRIVINGS > DRIVE
DRIZZLE n very light rain ▷ vb rain lightly
DRIZZLED > DRIZZLE
DRIZZLES > DRIZZLE
DRIZZLIER > DRIZZLE
DRIZZLING > DRIZZLE
DRIZZLY > DRIZZLE
DROGER n W Indian boat
DROGERS > DROGER
DROGHER same as > DROGER
DROGHERS > DROGHER
DROGUE n any funnel-like device used as a sea anchor
DROGUES > DROGUE
DROGUET n woollen fabric
DROGUETS > DROGUET
DROICH n dwarf
DROICHIER > DROICHY
DROICHS > DROICH
DROICHY adj dwarfish
DROID same as > ANDROID
DROIDS > DROID
DROIL vb carry out boring menial work

DROILED > DROIL
DROILING > DROIL
DROILS > DROIL
DROIT n legal or moral right or claim
DROITS > DROIT
DROKE n small group of trees
DROKES > DROKE
DROLE adj amusing ⊳ n scoundrel
DROLER > DROLE
DROLES > DROLE
DROLEST > DROLE
DROLL vb speak wittily ⊳ adj quaintly amusing
DROLLED > DROLL
DROLLER > DROLL
DROLLERY n humour
DROLLEST > DROLL
DROLLING > DROLL
DROLLINGS > DROLL
DROLLISH adj somewhat droll
DROLLNESS > DROLL
DROLLS > DROLL
DROLLY > DROLL
DROME same as > AERODROME
DROMEDARE obsolete form of > DROMEDARY
DROMEDARY n camel with a single hump
DROMES > DROME
DROMIC adj relating to running track
DROMICAL same as > DROMIC
DROMOI > DROMOS
DROMON same as > DROMOND
DROMOND n sailing vessel of the 12th to 15th centuries
DROMONDS > DROMOND
DROMONS > DROMON
DROMOS n Greek passageway
DRONE n male bee ⊳ vb make a monotonous low dull sound
DRONED > DRONE
DRONER > DRONE
DRONERS > DRONE
DRONES > DRONE
DRONGO n tropical songbird
DRONGOES > DRONGO
DRONGOS > DRONGO
DRONIER > DRONY
DRONIEST > DRONY
DRONING > DRONE
DRONINGLY > DRONE
DRONISH > DRONE
DRONISHLY > DRONE
DRONKLAP n South African word for a drunkard
DRONKLAPS > DRONKLAP
DRONY adj monotonous
DROOB n pathetic person
DROOBS > DROOB
DROOG n ruffian
DROOGISH > DROOG
DROOGS > DROOG
DROOK same as > DROUK
DROOKED > DROOK
DROOKING > DROOK
DROOKINGS > DROOK
DROOKIT same as > DROUKIT
DROOKS > DROOK

DROOL vb show excessive enthusiasm (for)
DROOLED > DROOL
DROOLIER > DROOLY
DROOLIEST > DROOLY
DROOLING > DROOL
DROOLS > DROOL
DROOLY adj tending to drool
DROOME obsolete form of > DRUM
DROOMES > DROOME
DROOP vb hang downwards loosely ⊳ n act or state of drooping
DROOPED > DROOP
DROOPIER > DROOPY
DROOPIEST > DROOPY
DROOPILY > DROOPY
DROOPING > DROOP
DROOPS > DROOP
DROOPY adj hanging or sagging downwards
DROP vb (allow to) fall vertically ⊳ n small quantity of liquid forming a round shape
DROPCLOTH n cloth spread on floor to catch drips while painting
DROPDOWN n menu on a computer screen, beneath a selected item
DROPDOWNS > DROPDOWN
DROPFLIES > DROPFLY
DROPFLY n (angling) artificial fly
DROPFORGE vb forge metal between two dies
DROPHEAD adj as in drophead coupe two-door car with a folding roof and sloping back
DROPHEADS > DROPHEAD
DROPKICK n kick in which a ball is dropped and then kicked
DROPKICKS > DROPKICK
DROPLET n very small drop of liquid
DROPLETS > DROPLET
DROPLIGHT n electric light that may be raised or lowered by means of a pulley or other mechanism
DROPLIKE adj like a drop
DROPLOCK adj as in droplock loan type of bank loan ⊳ n type of bank loan
DROPLOCKS > DROPLOCK
DROPOUT n person who rejects conventional society
DROPOUTS > DROPOUT
DROPPABLE > DROP
DROPPED > DROP
DROPPER n small tube with a rubber part at one end
DROPPERS > DROPPER
DROPPING > DROP
DROPPINGS pl n faeces of certain animals, such as rabbits or birds
DROPPLE n trickle
DROPPLES > DROPPLE
DROPS > DROP
DROPSEED n type of grass
DROPSEEDS > DROPSEED
DROPSHOT n type of tennis shot

DROPSHOTS > DROPSHOT
DROPSICAL > DROPSY
DROPSIED > DROPSY
DROPSIES > DROPSY
DROPSONDE n radiosonde dropped by parachute
DROPSTONE n calcium carbonate in stalactites
DROPSY n illness in which watery fluid collects in the body
DROPT > DROP
DROPTOP n convertible car
DROPTOPS > DROPTOP
DROPWISE adv in form of a drop
DROPWORT n Eurasian plant with cream-coloured flowers, related to the rose
DROPWORTS > DROPWORT
DROSERA n insectivorous plant
DROSERAS > DROSERA
DROSHKIES > DROSHKY
DROSHKY n four-wheeled carriage, formerly used in Russia
DROSKIES > DROSKY
DROSKY same as > DROSHKY
DROSS n scum formed on the surfaces of molten metals
DROSSES > DROSS
DROSSIER > DROSS
DROSSIEST > DROSS
DROSSY > DROSS
DROSTDIES > DROSTDY
DROSTDY n office of landdrost
DROSTDYS > DROSTDY
DROUGHT n prolonged shortage of rainfall
DROUGHTS > DROUGHT
DROUGHTY > DROUGHT
DROUK vb drench
DROUKED > DROUK
DROUKING > DROUK
DROUKINGS > DROUK
DROUKIT adj drenched
DROUKS > DROUK
DROUTH same as > DROUGHT
DROUTHIER > DROUTHY
DROUTHS > DROUTH
DROUTHY adj thirsty or dry
DROVE vb drive livestock ⊳ n moving crowd
DROVED > DROVE
DROVER n person who drives sheep or cattle
DROVERS > DROVER
DROVES > DROVE
DROVING > DROVE
DROVINGS > DROVE
DROW n sea fog
DROWN vb die or kill by immersion in liquid
DROWND dialect form of > DROWN
DROWNDED > DROWND
DROWNDING > DROWND
DROWNDS > DROWND
DROWNED > DROWN
DROWNER > DROWN
DROWNERS > DROWN
DROWNING > DROWN
DROWNINGS > DROWN
DROWNS > DROWN

DROWS > DROW
DROWSE vb be sleepy, dull, or sluggish ⊳ n state of being drowsy
DROWSED > DROWSE
DROWSES > DROWSE
DROWSIER > DROWSY
DROWSIEST > DROWSY
DROWSIHED adj old form of drowsy
DROWSILY > DROWSY
DROWSING > DROWSE
DROWSY adj feeling sleepy
DRUB vb beat as with a stick ⊳ n blow, as from a stick
DRUBBED > DRUB
DRUBBER > DRUB
DRUBBERS > DRUB
DRUBBING > DRUB
DRUBBINGS > DRUB
DRUBS > DRUB
DRUCKEN adj drunken
DRUDGE n person who works hard at uninteresting tasks ⊳ vb work at such tasks
DRUDGED > DRUDGE
DRUDGER > DRUDGE
DRUDGERS > DRUDGE
DRUDGERY n uninteresting work that must be done
DRUDGES > DRUDGE
DRUDGING > DRUDGE
DRUDGISM > DRUDGE
DRUDGISMS > DRUDGE
DRUG n substance used in the treatment or prevention of disease ⊳ vb give a drug to (a person or animal) to cause sleepiness or unconsciousness
DRUGGED > DRUG
DRUGGER n druggist
DRUGGERS > DRUGGER
DRUGGET n coarse fabric used as a protective floor-covering, etc
DRUGGETS > DRUGGET
DRUGGIE n drug addict
DRUGGIER > DRUG
DRUGGIES > DRUGGIE
DRUGGIEST > DRUG
DRUGGING > DRUG
DRUGGIST n pharmacist
DRUGGISTS > DRUGGIST
DRUGGY > DRUG
DRUGLESS adj having no drugs
DRUGLORD n criminal who controls the distribution and sale of large quantities of illegal drugs
DRUGLORDS > DRUGLORD
DRUGMAKER n manufacturer of drugs
DRUGS > DRUG
DRUGSTER n drug addict
DRUGSTERS > DRUGSTER
DRUGSTORE n pharmacy where a wide range of goods are available
DRUID n member of an ancient order of priests in the pre-Christian era
DRUIDESS > DRUID
DRUIDIC > DRUID
DRUIDICAL > DRUID
DRUIDISM > DRUID

d

d

DRUIDISMS > DRUID
DRUIDRIES > DRUID
DRUIDRY > DRUID
DRUIDS > DRUID
DRUM n percussion instrument ▷ vb play (music) on a drum
DRUMBEAT n sound made by beating a drum
DRUMBEATS > DRUMBEAT
DRUMBLE vb be inactive
DRUMBLED > DRUMBLE
DRUMBLES > DRUMBLE
DRUMBLING > DRUMBLE
DRUMFIRE n heavy, rapid, and continuous gunfire, the sound of which resembles rapid drumbeats
DRUMFIRES > DRUMFIRE
DRUMFISH n one of several types of fish that make a drumming sound
DRUMHEAD n part of a drum that is struck
DRUMHEADS > DRUMHEAD
DRUMLIER > DRUMLY
DRUMLIEST > DRUMLY
DRUMLIKE > DRUM
DRUMLIN n streamlined mound of glacial drift
DRUMLINS > DRUMLIN
DRUMLY adj dismal; dreary
DRUMMED > DRUM
DRUMMER n person who plays a drum or drums
DRUMMERS > DRUMMER
DRUMMIES > DRUMMY
DRUMMING n act of drumming
DRUMMINGS > DRUMMING
DRUMMOCK same as > DRAMMOCK
DRUMMOCKS > DRUMMOCK
DRUMMY n (in South Africa) drum majorette
DRUMROLL n continued repeated sound of drum
DRUMROLLS > DRUMROLL
DRUMS > DRUM
DRUMSTICK n stick used for playing a drum
DRUNK adj intoxicated with alcoholic drink ▷ n drunk person
DRUNKARD n person who frequently gets drunk
DRUNKARDS > DRUNKARD
DRUNKEN adj drunk or frequently drunk
DRUNKENLY > DRUNKEN
DRUNKER > DRUNK
DRUNKEST > DRUNK
DRUNKISH adj rather drunk
DRUNKS > DRUNK
DRUPE n fleshy fruit with a stone, such as the peach or cherry
DRUPEL same as > DRUPELET
DRUPELET n small drupe, usually one of a number forming a compound fruit
DRUPELETS > DRUPELET
DRUPELS > DRUPEL
DRUPES > DRUPE
DRUSE n aggregate of small crystals within a cavity

DRUSEN pl n small deposits of material on the retina
DRUSES > DRUSE
DRUSIER > DRUSY
DRUSIEST > DRUSY
DRUSY adj made of tiny crystals
DRUTHER n preference
DRUTHERS n preference
DRUXIER > DRUXY
DRUXIEST > DRUXY
DRUXY adj (of wood) having decayed white spots
DRY adj lacking moisture ▷ vb make or become dry
DRYABLE > DRY
DRYAD n wood nymph
DRYADES > DRYAD
DRYADIC > DRYAD
DRYADS > DRYAD
DRYAS n alpine plant with white flowers
DRYASDUST adj boringly bookish
DRYBEAT vb beat severely
DRYBEATEN > DRYBEAT
DRYBEATS > DRYBEAT
DRYER > DRY
DRYERS > DRY
DRYEST > DRY
DRYING > DRY
DRYINGS > DRY
DRYISH adj fairly dry
DRYLAND n arid area
DRYLANDS > DRYLAND
DRYLOT n livestock enclosure
DRYLOTS > DRYLOT
DRYLY same as > DRILY
DRYMOUTH n condition of insufficient saliva
DRYMOUTHS > DRYMOUTH
DRYNESS > DRY
DRYNESSES > DRY
DRYPOINT n copper engraving technique using a hard steel needle
DRYPOINTS > DRYPOINT
DRYS > DRY
DRYSALTER n dealer in certain chemical products, such as dyestuffs and gums, and in dried, tinned, or salted foods and edible oils
DRYSTONE adj (of a wall) made without mortar
DRYSUIT n waterproof rubber suit for wearing in esp cold water
DRYSUITS > DRYSUIT
DRYWALL n wall built without mortar ▷ vb build a wall without mortar
DRYWALLED > DRYWALL
DRYWALLER n person who builds drystone walls
DRYWALLS > DRYWALL
DRYWELL n type of sewage disposal system
DRYWELLS > DRYWELL
DSO same as > ZHO
DSOBO same as > ZOBO
DSOBOS > DSOBO
DSOMO same as > ZHOMO
DSOMOS > DSOMO
DSOS > DSO
DUAD a rare word for > PAIR

DUADS > DUAD
DUAL adj having two parts, functions, or aspects ▷ n dual number ▷ vb make (a road) into a dual carriageway
DUALIN n explosive substance
DUALINS > DUALIN
DUALISE same as > DUALIZE
DUALISED > DUALISE
DUALISES > DUALISE
DUALISING > DUALISE
DUALISM n state of having two distinct parts
DUALISMS > DUALISM
DUALIST > DUALISM
DUALISTIC > DUALISM
DUALISTS > DUALISM
DUALITIES > DUALITY
DUALITY n state or quality of being two or in two parts
DUALIZE vb cause to have two parts
DUALIZED > DUALIZE
DUALIZES > DUALIZE
DUALIZING > DUALIZE
DUALLED > DUAL
DUALLIE n pickup truck with dual rear tyres
DUALLIES > DUALLIE
DUALLING > DUAL
DUALLY > DUAL
DUALS > DUAL
DUAN n poem
DUANS > DUAN
DUAR n Arab camp
DUARCHIES > DUARCHY
DUARCHY same as > DIARCHY
DUARS > DUAR
DUATHLETE n athlete who competes in duathlons
DUATHLON n athletic contest in which each athlete competes in running and cycling events
DUATHLONS > DUATHLON
DUB vb give (a person or place) a name or nickname ▷ n style of reggae record production
DUBBED > DUB
DUBBER > DUB
DUBBERS > DUB
DUBBIN n thick grease applied to leather to soften and waterproof it ▷ vb apply dubbin to
DUBBINED > DUBBIN
DUBBING > DUB
DUBBINGS > DUB
DUBBINING > DUBBIN
DUBBINS > DUBBIN
DUBBO adj stupid ▷ n stupid person
DUBBOS > DUBBO
DUBIETIES > DUBIETY
DUBIETY n state of being doubtful
DUBIOSITY same as > DUBIETY
DUBIOUS adj feeling or causing doubt
DUBIOUSLY > DUBIOUS
DUBITABLE adj open to doubt

DUBITABLY > DUBITABLE
DUBITANCY > DUBITATE
DUBITATE vb doubt
DUBITATED > DUBITATE
DUBITATES > DUBITATE
DUBNIUM n chemical element
DUBNIUMS > DUBNIUM
DUBONNET n dark purplish-red colour
DUBONNETS > DUBONNET
DUBS > DUB
DUBSTEP n genre of electronic music
DUBSTEPS > DUBSTEP
DUCAL adj of a duke
DUCALLY > DUCAL
DUCAT n former European gold or silver coin
DUCATOON n former silver coin
DUCATOONS > DUCATOON
DUCATS > DUCAT
DUCDAME interj Shakespearean nonsense word
DUCE n leader
DUCES > DUCE
DUCHESS n woman who holds the rank of duke ▷ vb overwhelm with flattering attention
DUCHESSE n type of satin
DUCHESSED > DUCHESS
DUCHESSES > DUCHESS
DUCHIES > DUCHY
DUCHY n territory of a duke or duchess
DUCI > DUCE
DUCK n water bird ▷ vb move (the head or body) quickly downwards
DUCKBILL n duck-billed platypus
DUCKBILLS > DUCKBILL
DUCKBOARD n board or boards laid so as to form a floor or path over wet or muddy ground
DUCKED > DUCK
DUCKER > DUCK
DUCKERS > DUCK
DUCKFOOT adj as in duckfoot quote chevron-shaped quotation mark
DUCKIE same as > DUCKY
DUCKIER > DUCKY
DUCKIES > DUCKY
DUCKIEST > DUCKY
DUCKING > DUCK
DUCKINGS > DUCK
DUCKISH n twilight
DUCKISHES > DUCKISH
DUCKLING n baby duck
DUCKLINGS > DUCKLING
DUCKMOLE another word for > DUCKBILL
DUCKMOLES > DUCKMOLE
DUCKPIN n short bowling pin
DUCKPINS > DUCKPIN
DUCKS > DUCK
DUCKSHOVE vb evade responsibility
DUCKTAIL n Teddy boy's hairstyle
DUCKTAILS > DUCKTAIL
DUCKWALK vb walk in a squatting posture

DUCKWALKS > DUCKWALK
DUCKWEED n type of small stemless aquatic plant
DUCKWEEDS > DUCKWEED
DUCKY n darling or dear ▷ adj delightful
DUCT vb convey via a duct ▷ n tube, pipe, or channel through which liquid or gas is conveyed
DUCTAL > DUCT
DUCTED > DUCT
DUCTILE adj (of a metal) able to be shaped into sheets or wires
DUCTILELY > DUCTILE
DUCTILITY > DUCTILE
DUCTING > DUCT
DUCTINGS > DUCT
DUCTLESS > DUCT
DUCTS > DUCT
DUCTULE n small duct
DUCTULES > DUCTULE
DUCTWORK n system of ducts
DUCTWORKS > DUCTWORK
DUD n ineffectual person or thing ▷ adj bad or useless
DUDDER n door-to-door salesperson ▷ vb tremble or shudder
DUDDERED > DUDDER
DUDDERIES > DUDDERY
DUDDERING > DUDDER
DUDDERS > DUDDER
DUDDERY n place where old clothes are sold
DUDDIE adj ragged ▷ n friend or a chum
DUDDIER > DUDDIE
DUDDIES > DUDDIE
DUDDIEST > DUDDIE
DUDDY same as **>** DUDDIE
DUDE vb dress fashionably ▷ n man
DUDED > DUDE
DUDEEN n clay pipe with a short stem
DUDEENS > DUDEEN
DUDENESS n state of being a dude
DUDES > DUDE
DUDETTE n woman who behaves like a dude
DUDETTES > DUDETTE
DUDGEON n anger or resentment
DUDGEONS > DUDGEON
DUDHEEN n type of pipe
DUDHEENS > DUDHEEN
DUDING > DUDE
DUDISH > DUDE
DUDISHLY > DUDE
DUDISM n being a dude
DUDISMS > DUDISM
DUDS > DUD
DUE vb supply with ▷ adj expected or scheduled to be present or arrive ▷ n something that is owed or required ▷ adv directly or exactly
DUECENTO n thirteenth century (in Italian art)
DUECENTOS > DUECENTO
DUED > DUE
DUEFUL adj proper

DUEL n formal fight with deadly weapons between two people ▷ vb fight in a duel
DUELED > DUEL
DUELER > DUEL
DUELERS > DUELER
DUELING > DUEL
DUELINGS > DUELING
DUELIST > DUEL
DUELISTS > DUELIST
DUELLED > DUEL
DUELLER > DUEL
DUELLERS > DUELLER
DUELLI > DUELLO
DUELLING > DUEL
DUELLINGS > DUELLING
DUELLIST > DUEL
DUELLISTS > DUELLIST
DUELLO n art of duelling
DUELLOS > DUELLO
DUELS > DUEL
DUELSOME adj given to duelling
DUENDE n Spanish goblin
DUENDES > DUENDE
DUENESS > DUE
DUENESSES > DUE
DUENNA n (esp in Spain) elderly woman acting as chaperone to a young woman
DUENNAS > DUENNA
DUES pl n membership fees
DUET n piece of music for two performers ▷ vb perform a duet
DUETED > DUET
DUETING > DUET
DUETS > DUET
DUETT same as **>** DUET
DUETTED > DUET
DUETTI > DUETTO
DUETTING > DUET
DUETTINO n simple duet
DUETTINOS > DUETTINO
DUETTIST > DUET
DUETTISTS > DUET
DUETTO same as **>** DUET
DUETTOS > DUETTO
DUETTS > DUETT
DUFF adj broken or useless ▷ vb change the appearance of or give a false appearance to (old or stolen goods) ▷ n mishit golf shot
DUFFED > DUFF
DUFFEL n heavy woollen cloth with a thick nap
DUFFELS > DUFFEL
DUFFER n dull or incompetent person
DUFFERDOM n condition of being a duffer
DUFFERISM same as **>** DUFFERDOM
DUFFERS > DUFFER
DUFFEST > DUFF
DUFFING > DUFF
DUFFINGS > DUFF
DUFFLE same as **>** DUFFEL
DUFFLES > DUFFLE
DUFFS > DUFF
DUFUS same as **>** DOOFUS
DUFUSES > DUFUS
DUG Scottish word for **>** DOG

DUGITE n medium-sized Australian venomous snake
DUGITES > DUGITE
DUGONG n whalelike mammal of tropical waters
DUGONGS > DUGONG
DUGOUT n (at a sports ground) covered bench where managers and substitutes sit
DUGOUTS > DUGOUT
DUGS > DUG
DUH interj ironic response to a question or statement
DUHKHA same as **>** DUKKHA
DUHKHAS > DUHKHA
DUI > DUO
DUIKER n small African antelope
DUIKERBOK same as **>** DUIKER
DUIKERS > DUIKER
DUING > DUE
DUIT n former Dutch coin
DUITS > DUIT
DUKA n shop
DUKAS > DUKA
DUKE vb fight with fists ▷ n nobleman of the highest rank
DUKED > DUKE
DUKEDOM n title, rank, or position of a duke
DUKEDOMS > DUKEDOM
DUKELING n low-ranking duke
DUKELINGS > DUKELING
DUKERIES > DUKERY
DUKERY n duke's domain
DUKES pl n fists
DUKESHIP > DUKE
DUKESHIPS > DUKE
DUKING > DUKE
DUKKA n mix of ground roast nuts and spices
DUKKAH same as **>** DUKKA
DUKKAHS > DUKKAH
DUKKAS > DUKKA
DUKKHA n Buddhist belief that all things are suffering
DUKKHAS > DUKKHA
DULCAMARA n orange-fruited vine
DULCE n sweet food or drink
DULCES > DULCE
DULCET adj (of a sound) soothing or pleasant ▷ n soft organ stop
DULCETLY > DULCET
DULCETS > DULCET
DULCIAN n precursor to the bassoon
DULCIANA n sweet-toned organ stop, controlling metal pipes of narrow scale
DULCIANAS > DULCIANA
DULCIANS > DULCIAN
DULCIFIED > DULCIFY
DULCIFIES > DULCIFY
DULCIFY vb make pleasant or agreeable
DULCIMER n tuned percussion instrument
DULCIMERS > DULCIMER
DULCIMORE former name for **>** DULCIMER
DULCINEA n man's sweetheart

DULCINEAS > DULCINEA
DULCITE n sweet substance
DULCITES > DULCITE
DULCITOL another word for **>** DULCITE
DULCITOLS > DULCITOL
DULCITUDE n sweetness
DULCOSE another word for **>** DULCITE
DULCOSES > DULCOSE
DULE n suffering; misery
DULES > DULE
DULIA n veneration accorded to saints
DULIAS > DULIA
DULL adj not interesting ▷ vb make or become dull
DULLARD n dull or stupid person
DULLARDS > DULLARD
DULLED > DULL
DULLER > DULL
DULLEST > DULL
DULLIER > DULL
DULLIEST > DULL
DULLING > DULL
DULLISH > DULL
DULLISHLY > DULL
DULLNESS > DULL
DULLS > DULL
DULLY > DULL
DULNESS > DULL
DULNESSES > DULL
DULOCRACY n rule by slaves
DULOSES > DULOSIS
DULOSIS n behaviour where one species of ant forces members of another to work for them
DULOTIC > DULOSIS
DULSE n seaweed with large red edible fronds
DULSES > DULSE
DULY adv in a proper manner
DUM adj steamed
DUMA n elective legislative assembly established by Tsar Nicholas II
DUMAIST n member of duma
DUMAISTS > DUMAIST
DUMAS > DUMA
DUMB vb silence ▷ adj lacking the power to speak
DUMBBELL n short bar with a heavy ball or disc at each end, used for physical exercise
DUMBBELLS > DUMBBELL
DUMBCANE n West Indian aroid plant
DUMBCANES > DUMBCANE
DUMBED > DUMB
DUMBER > DUMB
DUMBEST > DUMB
DUMBFOUND vb strike dumb with astonishment
DUMBHEAD n dunce
DUMBHEADS > DUMBHEAD
DUMBING > DUMB
DUMBLY > DUMB
DUMBNESS > DUMB
DUMBO n slow-witted unintelligent person
DUMBOS > DUMBO
DUMBS > DUMB
DUMBSHIT n vulgar word for a stupid person

d

DUMBSHITS > DUMBSHIT
DUMBSHOW n actions performed without words in a play
DUMBSHOWS > DUMBSHOW
DUMBSIZE vb reduce the number in a workforce to the point it becomes ineffective
DUMBSIZED > DUMBSIZE
DUMBSIZES > DUMBSIZE
DUMDUM n soft-nosed bullet
DUMDUMS > DUMDUM
DUMELA sentence substitute hello
DUMFOUND same as > DUMBFOUND
DUMFOUNDS > DUMFOUND
DUMKA n Slavonic lyrical song
DUMKAS > DUMKA
DUMKY > DUMKA
DUMMERER n archaic word for a person who pretends they cannot speak
DUMMERERS > DUMMERER
DUMMIED > DUMMY
DUMMIER > DUMMY
DUMMIES > DUMMY
DUMMIEST > DUMMY
DUMMINESS > DUMMY
DUMMKOPF n stupid person
DUMMKOPFS > DUMMKOPF
DUMMY n figure representing the human form ▷ adj imitation, substitute ▷ vb prepare an imitation of (a proposed book, page, etc)
DUMMYING > DUMMY
DUMOSE adj bushlike
DUMOSITY > DUMOSE
DUMOUS same as > DUMOSE
DUMP vb drop or let fall in a careless manner ▷ n place where waste materials are left
DUMPBIN n unit in a bookshop displaying a particular publisher's books
DUMPBINS > DUMPBIN
DUMPCART n cart for dumping without handling
DUMPCARTS > DUMPCART
DUMPED > DUMP
DUMPEE n person dumped from a relationship
DUMPEES > DUMPEE
DUMPER > DUMP
DUMPERS > DUMP
DUMPIER > DUMPY
DUMPIES > DUMPY
DUMPIEST > DUMPY
DUMPILY > DUMPY
DUMPINESS > DUMPY
DUMPING > DUMP
DUMPINGS > DUMP
DUMPISH same as > DUMPY
DUMPISHLY > DUMPISH
DUMPLE vb form into dumpling shape
DUMPLED > DUMPLE
DUMPLES > DUMPLE
DUMPLING n small ball of dough cooked and served with stew
DUMPLINGS > DUMPLING
DUMPS pl n state of melancholy or depression
DUMPSITE n location of dump

DUMPSITES > DUMPSITE
DUMPSTER n refuse skip
DUMPSTERS > DUMPSTER
DUMPTRUCK n lorry with a tipping container
DUMPY n dumpy person ▷ adj short and plump
DUN adj brownish-grey ▷ vb demand payment from (a debtor) ▷ n demand for payment
DUNAM n unit of area measurement
DUNAMS > DUNAM
DUNCE n person who is stupid or slow to learn
DUNCEDOM > DUNCE
DUNCEDOMS > DUNCE
DUNCELIKE > DUNCE
DUNCERIES > DUNCERY
DUNCERY n duncelike behaviour
DUNCES > DUNCE
DUNCH vb push against gently
DUNCHED > DUNCH
DUNCHES > DUNCH
DUNCHING > DUNCH
DUNCICAL adj duncelike
DUNCISH adj duncelike
DUNCISHLY > DUNCE
DUNDER n cane juice lees
DUNDERS > DUNDER
DUNE n mound or ridge of drifted sand
DUNELAND n land characterized by dunes
DUNELANDS > DUNELAND
DUNELIKE > DUNE
DUNES > DUNE
DUNG n faeces from animals such as cattle ▷ vb cover (ground) with manure
DUNGAREE n coarse cotton fabric used chiefly for work clothes, etc
DUNGAREED adj wearing dungarees
DUNGAREES > DUNGAREE
DUNGED > DUNG
DUNGEON vb hold captive in dungeon ▷ n underground prison cell
DUNGEONED > DUNGEON
DUNGEONER n jailer
DUNGEONS > DUNGEON
DUNGER n old decrepit car
DUNGERS > DUNGER
DUNGHEAP n pile of dung
DUNGHEAPS > DUNGHEAP
DUNGHILL n heap of dung
DUNGHILLS > DUNGHILL
DUNGIER > DUNG
DUNGIEST > DUNG
DUNGING > DUNG
DUNGMERE n cesspool
DUNGMERES > DUNGMERE
DUNGS > DUNG
DUNGY > DUNG
DUNITE n ultrabasic igneous rock
DUNITES > DUNITE
DUNITIC > DUNITE
DUNK vb dip (a biscuit or bread) in a drink or soup before eating it
DUNKED > DUNK

DUNKER > DUNK
DUNKERS > DUNK
DUNKING n act of dunking
DUNKINGS > DUNKING
DUNKS > DUNK
DUNLIN n small sandpiper
DUNLINS > DUNLIN
DUNNAGE n loose material used for packing cargo
DUNNAGES > DUNNAGE
DUNNAKIN n lavatory
DUNNAKINS > DUNNAKIN
DUNNART n type of insectivorous marsupial
DUNNARTS > DUNNART
DUNNED > DUN
DUNNER > DUN
DUNNESS > DUN
DUNNESSES > DUN
DUNNEST > DUN
DUNNIER > DUNNY
DUNNIES > DUNNY
DUNNIEST > DUNNY
DUNNING > DUN
DUNNINGS > DUNNING
DUNNISH > DUN
DUNNITE n explosive containing ammonium picrate
DUNNITES > DUNNITE
DUNNO vb slang for don't know
DUNNOCK n hedge sparrow
DUNNOCKS > DUNNOCK
DUNNY n in Australia, toilet ▷ adj like or relating to a dunny
DUNS > DUN
DUNSH same as > DUNCH
DUNSHED > DUNSH
DUNSHES > DUNSH
DUNSHING > DUNSH
DUNT n blow ▷ vb strike or hit
DUNTED > DUNT
DUNTING > DUNT
DUNTS > DUNT
DUO same as > DUET
DUOBINARY adj denoting a communications system for coding digital data in which three data bands are used, 0, +1, −1
DUODECIMO n book size resulting from folding a sheet of paper into twelve leaves
DUODENA > DUODENUM
DUODENAL > DUODENUM
DUODENARY adj of or relating to the number 12
DUODENUM n first part of the small intestine, just below the stomach
DUODENUMS > DUODENUM
DUOLOG same as > DUOLOGUE
DUOLOGS > DUOLOG
DUOLOGUE n (in drama) conversation between only two speakers
DUOLOGUES > DUOLOGUE
DUOMI > DUOMO
DUOMO n cathedral in Italy
DUOMOS > DUOMO
DUOPOLIES > DUOPOLY
DUOPOLIST n either of the two suppliers in a duopoly

DUOPOLY n situation when control of a commodity is vested in two producers or suppliers
DUOPSONY n two rival buyers controlling sellers
DUOS > DUO
DUOTONE n process for producing halftone illustrations
DUOTONES > DUOTONE
DUP vb open
DUPABLE > DUPE
DUPATTA n scarf worn in India
DUPATTAS > DUPATTA
DUPE vb deceive or cheat ▷ n person who is easily deceived
DUPED > DUPE
DUPER > DUPE
DUPERIES > DUPERY
DUPERS > DUPE
DUPERY > DUPE
DUPES > DUPE
DUPING n act of duping
DUPINGS > DUPING
DUPION n silk fabric made from the threads of double cocoons
DUPIONS > DUPION
DUPLE adj having two beats in a bar
DUPLET n pair of electrons shared between two atoms in a covalent bond
DUPLETS > DUPLET
DUPLEX vb duplicate ▷ n apartment on two floors ▷ adj having two parts
DUPLEXED > DUPLEX
DUPLEXER n telecommunications system
DUPLEXERS > DUPLEXER
DUPLEXES > DUPLEX
DUPLEXING n act of duplicating
DUPLEXITY > DUPLEX
DUPLICAND n feu duty doubled
DUPLICATE adj copied exactly from an original ▷ n exact copy ▷ vb make an exact copy of
DUPLICITY n deceitful behaviour
DUPLIED > DUPLY
DUPLIES > DUPLY
DUPLY vb give a second reply
DUPLYING > DUPLY
DUPONDII > DUPONDIUS
DUPONDIUS n brass coin of ancient Rome worth half a sesterce
DUPPED > DUP
DUPPIES > DUPPY
DUPPING > DUP
DUPPY n spirit or ghost
DUPS > DUP
DURA same as > DURRA
DURABLE adj long-lasting
DURABLES pl n goods that require infrequent replacement
DURABLY > DURABLE
DURAL n alloy of aluminium and copper
DURALS > DURAL

DURALUMIN n light and strong aluminium alloy containing copper, silicon, magnesium, and manganese

DURAMEN another name for > HEARTWOOD

DURAMENS > DURAMEN

DURANCE n imprisonment

DURANCES > DURANCE

DURANT n tough, leathery cloth

DURANTS > DURANT

DURAS > DURA

DURATION n length of time that something lasts

DURATIONS > DURATION

DURATIVE adj denoting an aspect of verbs that includes the imperfective and the progressive ▷ n durative aspect of a verb

DURATIVES > DURATIVE

DURBAR n (formerly) the court of a native ruler or a governor in India

DURBARS > DURBAR

DURDUM same as > DIRDUM

DURDUMS > DURDUM

DURE vb endure

DURED > DURE

DUREFUL adj lasting

DURES > DURE

DURESS n compulsion by use of force or threats

DURESSE same as > DURESS

DURESSES > DURESS

DURGAH same as > DARGAH

DURGAHS > DURGAH

DURGAN n dwarf

DURGANS > DURGAN

DURGIER > DURGY

DURGIEST > DURGY

DURGY adj dwarflike

DURIAN n SE Asian tree whose very large oval fruits have a hard spiny rind and an evil smell

DURIANS > DURIAN

DURICRUST another name for > CALICHE

DURING prep throughout or within the limit of (a period of time)

DURION same as > DURIAN

DURIONS > DURION

DURMAST n large Eurasian oak tree with lobed leaves

DURMASTS > DURMAST

DURN same as > DARN

DURNDEST same as > DARNEDEST

DURNED > DURN

DURNEDER > DURNED

DURNEDEST > DURN

DURNING > DURN

DURNS > DURN

DURO n silver peso of Spain or Spanish America

DUROC n breed of pig

DUROCS > DUROC

DUROMETER n instrument for measuring hardness

DUROS > DURO

DUROY n coarse woollen fabric

DUROYS > DUROY

DURR same as > DURRA

DURRA n Old World variety of sorghum

DURRAS > DURRA

DURRIE n cotton carpet made in India, often in rectangular pieces fringed at the ends

DURRIES > DURRY

DURRS > DURR

DURRY n cigarette

DURST a past tense of > DARE

DURUKULI n S American monkey

DURUKULIS > DURUKULI

DURUM n variety of wheat

DURUMS > DURUM

DURZI n Indian tailor

DURZIS > DURZI

DUSH vb strike hard

DUSHED > DUSH

DUSHES > DUSH

DUSHING > DUSH

DUSK n time just before nightfall, when it is almost dark ▷ adj shady ▷ vb make or become dark

DUSKED > DUSK

DUSKEN vb grow dark

DUSKENED > DUSKEN

DUSKENING > DUSKEN

DUSKENS > DUSKEN

DUSKER > DUSK

DUSKEST > DUSK

DUSKIER > DUSKY

DUSKIEST > DUSKY

DUSKILY > DUSKY

DUSKINESS > DUSKY

DUSKING > DUSK

DUSKISH > DUSK

DUSKISHLY > DUSK

DUSKLY > DUSK

DUSKNESS > DUSK

DUSKS > DUSK

DUSKY adj dark in colour

DUST n small dry particles of earth, sand, or dirt ▷ vb remove dust from (furniture) by wiping

DUSTBALL n ball of dust

DUSTBALLS > DUSTBALL

DUSTBIN n large container for household rubbish

DUSTBINS > DUSTBIN

DUSTCART n truck for collecting household rubbish

DUSTCARTS > DUSTCART

DUSTCLOTH n cloth used for dusting

DUSTCOAT n light, loose-fitting long coat

DUSTCOATS > DUSTCOAT

DUSTCOVER same as > DUSTSHEET

DUSTED > DUST

DUSTER n cloth used for dusting

DUSTERS > DUSTER

DUSTHEAP n accumulation of refuse

DUSTHEAPS > DUSTHEAP

DUSTIER > DUSTY

DUSTIEST > DUSTY

DUSTILY > DUSTY

DUSTINESS > DUSTY

DUSTING > DUST

DUSTINGS > DUST

DUSTLESS > DUST

DUSTLIKE > DUST

DUSTMAN n man whose job is to collect household rubbish

DUSTMEN > DUSTMAN

DUSTOFF n casualty evacuation helicopter

DUSTOFFS > DUSTOFF

DUSTPAN n short-handled shovel

DUSTPANS > DUSTPAN

DUSTPROOF adj repelling dust

DUSTRAG n cloth for dusting

DUSTRAGS > DUSTRAG

DUSTS > DUST

DUSTSHEET n large cloth cover to protect furniture from dust

DUSTSTORM n storm with whirling column of dust

DUSTUP n quarrel, fight, or argument

DUSTUPS > DUSTUP

DUSTY adj covered with dust

DUTCH n wife

DUTCHES > DUTCH

DUTCHMAN n piece of wood, metal, etc, used to repair or patch faulty workmanship

DUTCHMEN > DUTCHMAN

DUTEOUS adj dutiful or obedient

DUTEOUSLY > DUTEOUS

DUTIABLE adj (of goods) requiring payment of duty

DUTIED adj liable for duty

DUTIES > DUTY

DUTIFUL adj doing what is expected

DUTIFULLY > DUTIFUL

DUTY n work or a task performed as part of one's job

DUUMVIR n one of two coequal magistrates or officers

DUUMVIRAL > DUUMVIR

DUUMVIRI > DUUMVIR

DUUMVIRS > DUUMVIR

DUVET same as > DOONA

DUVETINE same as > DUVETYN

DUVETINES > DUVETINE

DUVETS > DUVET

DUVETYN n soft napped velvety fabric of cotton, silk, wool, or rayon

DUVETYNE same as > DUVETYN

DUVETYNES > DUVETYNE

DUVETYNS > DUVETYN

DUX n (in Scottish and certain other schools) the top pupil in a class or school

DUXELLES n paste of mushrooms and onions

DUXES > DUX

DUYKER same as > DUIKER

DUYKERS > DUYKER

DVANDVA n class of compound words

DVANDVAS > DVANDVA

DVORNIK n Russian doorkeeper

DVORNIKS > DVORNIK

DWAAL n state of absent-mindedness

DWAALS > DWAAL

DWALE n deadly nightshade

DWALES > DWALE

DWALM vb faint

DWALMED > DWALM

DWALMING > DWALM

DWALMS > DWALM

DWAM n stupor or daydream ▷ vb faint or fall ill

DWAMMED > DWAM

DWAMMING > DWAM

DWAMS > DWAM

DWANG n short piece of wood inserted in a timber-framed wall

DWANGS > DWANG

DWARF adj undersized ▷ n person who is smaller than average ▷ vb cause (someone or something) to seem small by being much larger

DWARFED > DWARF

DWARFER > DWARF

DWARFEST > DWARF

DWARFING > DWARF

DWARFISH > DWARF

DWARFISM n condition of being a dwarf

DWARFISMS > DWARFISM

DWARFLIKE > DWARF

DWARFNESS > DWARF

DWARFS > DWARF

DWARVES > DWARF

DWAUM same as > DWAM

DWAUMED > DWAUM

DWAUMING > DWAUM

DWAUMS > DWAUM

DWEEB n stupid or uninteresting person

DWEEBIER > DWEEBY

DWEEBIEST > DWEEBY

DWEEBISH > DWEEBY

DWEEBS > DWEEB

DWEEBY adj like or typical of a dweeb

DWELL vb live, reside ▷ n regular pause in the operation of a machine

DWELLED > DWELL

DWELLER > DWELL

DWELLERS > DWELL

DWELLING > DWELL

DWELLINGS > DWELL

DWELLS > DWELL

DWELT > DWELL

DWILE n floor cloth

DWILES > DWILE

DWINDLE vb grow less in size, strength, or number

DWINDLED > DWINDLE

DWINDLES > DWINDLE

DWINDLING > DWINDLE

DWINE vb languish

DWINED > DWINE

DWINES > DWINE

DWINING > DWINE

DYABLE > DYE

DYAD n operator that is the unspecified product of two vectors

DYADIC adj of or relating to a dyad ▷ n sum of a particular number of dyads

DYADICS > DYADIC

DYADS > DYAD

DYARCHAL > DYARCHY

DYARCHIC > DYARCHY
DYARCHIES > DYARCHY
DYARCHY *same as* > DIARCHY
DYBBUK n (in Jewish folklore) the body of a person possessed by the soul of a dead sinner
DYBBUKIM > DYBBUK
DYBBUKKIM > DYBBUK
DYBBUKS > DYBBUK
DYE n colouring substance ▷ vb colour (hair or fabric) by applying a dye
DYEABLE > DYE
DYED > DYE
DYEING > DYE
DYEINGS > DYE
DYELINE *same as* > DIAZO
DYELINES > DYELINE
DYER > DYE
DYERS > DYE
DYES > DYE
DYESTER n dyer
DYESTERS > DYESTER
DYESTUFF n substance that can be used as a dye or from which a dye can be obtained
DYESTUFFS > DYESTUFF
DYEWEED n plant that produces dye
DYEWEEDS > DYEWEED
DYEWOOD n any wood from which dyes and pigments can be obtained
DYEWOODS > DYEWOOD
DYEWORKS n place where dye is made
DYING > DIE
DYINGLY > DIE
DYINGNESS > DIE
DYINGS > DIE
DYKE n wall built to prevent flooding ▷ vb protect with a dyke
DYKED > DYKE
DYKES > DYKE
DYKEY *same as* > DIKEY
DYKIER > DYKEY
DYKIEST > DYKEY
DYKING > DYKE
DYKON n celebrity admired by lesbians
DYKONS > DYKON
DYNAMETER n instrument for determining the magnifying power of telescopes
DYNAMIC adj full of energy, ambition, and new ideas ▷ n energetic or driving force
DYNAMICAL *same as* > DYNAMIC
DYNAMICS n branch of mechanics concerned with motions of bodies
DYNAMISE *same as* > DYNAMIZE
DYNAMISED > DYNAMISE
DYNAMISES > DYNAMISE

DYNAMISM n great energy and enthusiasm
DYNAMISMS > DYNAMISM
DYNAMIST > DYNAMISM
DYNAMISTS > DYNAMISM
DYNAMITE n explosive made of nitroglycerine ▷ vb blow (something) up with dynamite
DYNAMITED > DYNAMITE
DYNAMITER > DYNAMITE
DYNAMITES > DYNAMITE
DYNAMITIC > DYNAMITE
DYNAMIZE vb cause to be dynamic
DYNAMIZED > DYNAMIZE
DYNAMIZES > DYNAMIZE
DYNAMO n device for converting mechanical energy into electrical energy
DYNAMOS > DYNAMO
DYNAMOTOR n electrical machine having a single magnetic field and two independent armature windings of which one acts as a motor and the other a generator: used to convert direct current from a battery into alternating current
DYNAST n hereditary ruler
DYNASTIC > DYNASTY
DYNASTIES > DYNASTY
DYNASTS > DYNAST
DYNASTY n sequence of hereditary rulers
DYNATRON n as in *dynatron oscillator* type of oscillator
DYNATRONS > DYNATRON
DYNE n cgs unit of force
DYNEIN n class of proteins
DYNEINS > DYNEIN
DYNEL n trade name for synthetic fibre
DYNELS > DYNEL
DYNES > DYNE
DYNODE n electrical component
DYNODES > DYNODE
DYNORPHIN n drug used to treat cocaine addiction
DYSBINDIN n gene associated with schizophrenia
DYSCHROA n discolouration of skin
DYSCHROAS > DYSCHROA
DYSCHROIA *same as* > DYSCHROA
DYSCRASIA n any abnormal physiological condition, esp of the blood
DYSCRASIC > DYSCRASIA
DYSCRATIC > DYSCRASIA
DYSENTERY n infection of the intestine causing severe diarrhoea
DYSFLUENT adj not fluent
DYSGENIC adj referring to the degeneration of a race or strain

DYSGENICS n study of factors capable of reducing the quality of a race or strain, esp the human race
DYSLALIA n defective speech characteristic of those affected by aphasia
DYSLALIAS > DYSLALIA
DYSLECTIC > DYSLEXIA
DYSLEXIA n disorder causing impaired ability to read
DYSLEXIAS > DYSLEXIA
DYSLEXIC > DYSLEXIA
DYSLEXICS > DYSLEXIA
DYSLOGIES > DYSLOGY
DYSLOGY n uncomplimentary remarks
DYSMELIA n condition of missing or stunted limbs
DYSMELIAS > DYSMELIA
DYSMELIC > DYSMELIA
DYSODIL n yellow or green mineral
DYSODILE *same as* > DYSODIL
DYSODILES > DYSODILE
DYSODILS > DYSODIL
DYSODYLE *same as* > DYSODIL
DYSODYLES > DYSODYLE
DYSPATHY n dislike
DYSPEPSIA n indigestion
DYSPEPSY *same as* > DYSPEPSIA
DYSPEPTIC adj relating to or suffering from dyspepsia ▷ n person suffering from dyspepsia
DYSPHAGIA n difficulty in swallowing, caused by obstruction or spasm of the oesophagus
DYSPHAGIC > DYSPHAGIA
DYSPHAGY *same as* > DYSPHAGIA
DYSPHASIA n disorder of language caused by a brain lesion
DYSPHASIC > DYSPHASIA
DYSPHONIA n any impairment in the ability to speak normally, as from spasm or strain of the vocal cords
DYSPHONIC > DYSPHONIA
DYSPHORIA n feeling of being ill at ease
DYSPHORIC > DYSPHORIA
DYSPLASIA n abnormal development of an organ or part of the body, including congenital absence
DYSPNEA *same as* > DYSPNOEA
DYSPNEAL > DYSPNEA
DYSPNEAS > DYSPNEA
DYSPNEIC > DYSPNEA
DYSPNOEA n difficulty in breathing or in catching the breath

DYSPNOEAL > DYSPNOEA
DYSPNOEAS > DYSPNOEA
DYSPNOEIC > DYSPNOEA
DYSPNOIC > DYSPNOEA
DYSPRAXIA n impairment in the control of the motor system
DYSPRAXIC adj suffering from dyspraxia
DYSTAXIA n lack of muscular coordination resulting in shaky limb movements and unsteady gait
DYSTAXIAS > DYSTAXIA
DYSTAXIC adj relating to or affected by dystaxia
DYSTECTIC adj difficult to fuse together
DYSTHESIA n unpleasant skin sensation
DYSTHETIC > DYSTHESIA
DYSTHYMIA n characteristics of the neurotic and introverted, including anxiety, depression, and compulsive behaviour
DYSTHYMIC > DYSTHYMIA
DYSTOCIA n abnormal, slow, or difficult childbirth
DYSTOCIAL > DYSTOCIA
DYSTOCIAS > DYSTOCIA
DYSTONIA n neurological disorder
DYSTONIAS > DYSTONIA
DYSTONIC > DYSTONIA
DYSTOPIA n imaginary place where everything is as bad as it can be
DYSTOPIAN > DYSTOPIA
DYSTOPIAS > DYSTOPIA
DYSTROPHY n any of various bodily disorders, characterized by wasting of tissues
DYSURIA n difficult or painful urination
DYSURIAS > DYSURIA
DYSURIC > DYSURIA
DYSURIES > DYSURY
DYSURY *same as* > DYSURIA
DYTISCID n type of carnivorous aquatic beetle with large flattened back legs used for swimming
DYTISCIDS > DYTISCID
DYVOUR n debtor
DYVOURIES > DYVOURY
DYVOURS > DYVOUR
DYVOURY n bankruptcy
DZEREN n Chinese yellow antelope
DZERENS > DZEREN
DZHO *same as* > ZHO
DZHOS > DZHO
DZIGGETAI *a variant of* > CHIGETAI
DZO *a variant spelling of* ZO
DZOS > DZO

Ee

EA *n* river

EACH *pron* every (one) taken separately ▷ *determiner* every (one) of two or more considered individually ▷ *adv* for, to, or from each one

EACHWHERE *adv* everywhere

EADISH *n* aftermath

EADISHES > EADISH

EAGER *adj* showing or feeling great desire, keen ▷ *n* eagre

EAGERER > EAGER

EAGEREST > EAGER

EAGERLY > EAGER

EAGERNESS > EAGER

EAGERS > EAGER

EAGLE *n* bird of prey ▷ *vb* in golf, score two strokes under par for a hole

EAGLED > EAGLE

EAGLEHAWK *n* large Australian eagle

EAGLES > EAGLE

EAGLET *n* young eagle

EAGLETS > EAGLET

EAGLEWOOD *n* Asian thymelaeaceous tree with fragrant wood that yields a resin used as a perfume

EAGLING > EAGLE

EAGRE *n* tidal bore, esp of the Humber or Severn estuaries

EAGRES > EAGRE

EALDORMAN *n* official of Anglo-Saxon England, appointed by the king, who was responsible for law, order, and justice in his shire and for leading his local fyrd in battle

EALDORMEN > EALDORMAN

EALE *n* beast in Roman legend ▷ *vb* to ail

EALED > EALE

EALES > EALE

EALING > EALE

EAN *vb* give birth

EANED > EAN

EANING > EAN

EANLING *n* newborn lamb

EANLINGS > EANLING

EANS > EAN

EAR *n* organ of hearing, esp the external part of it ▷ *vb* (of cereal plants) to develop such parts

EARACHE *n* pain in the ear

EARACHES > EARACHE

EARBALL *n* device used in acupressure

EARBALLS > EARBALL

EARBASH *vb* talk incessantly

EARBASHED > EARBASH

EARBASHER > EARBASH

EARBASHES > EARBASH

EARBOB *n* earring

EARBOBS > EARBOB

EARBUD *n* small earphone

EARBUDS > EARBUD

EARCON *n* sound representing object or event

EARCONS > EARCON

EARD *vb* bury

EARDED > EARD

EARDING > EARD

EARDROP *n* pendant earring

EARDROPS *pl n* liquid medication for inserting into the external ear

EARDRUM *n* part of the ear which enables one to hear sounds

EARDRUMS > EARDRUM

EARDS > EARD

EARED *adj* having an ear or ears

EARFLAP *n* either of two pieces of fabric or fur attached to a cap

EARFLAPS > EARFLAP

EARFUL *n* scolding or telling-off

EARFULS > EARFUL

EARHOLE *n* the external opening of the ear

EARHOLES > EARHOLE

EARING *n* line fastened to a corner of a sail for reefing

EARINGS > EARING

EARL *n* British nobleman ranking next below a marquess

EARLAP *same as* > EARFLAP

EARLAPS > EARLAP

EARLDOM *n* rank, title, or dignity of an earl or countess

EARLDOMS > EARLDOM

EARLESS > EAR

EARLIER > EARLY

EARLIES > EARLY

EARLIEST > EARLY

EARLIKE > EAR

EARLINESS > EARLY

EARLOBE *n* fleshy lower part of the outer ear

EARLOBES > EARLOBE

EARLOCK *n* curl of hair close to ear

EARLOCKS > EARLOCK

EARLS > EARL

EARLSHIP *n* title or position of earl

EARLSHIPS > EARLSHIP

EARLY *adv* before the expected or usual time ▷ *adj* occurring or arriving before the correct or expected time ▷ *n* something which is early

EARLYWOOD *n* light wood made by tree in spring

EARMARK *vb* set (something) aside for a specific purpose ▷ *n* distinguishing mark

EARMARKED > EARMARK

EARMARKS > EARMARK

EARMUFF *n* item of clothing for keeping the ears warm

EARMUFFS > EARMUFF

EARN *vb* obtain by work or merit

EARNED > EARN

EARNER > EARN

EARNERS > EARN

EARNEST *adj* serious and sincere ▷ *n* part payment given in advance

EARNESTLY > EARNEST

EARNESTS > EARNEST

EARNING > EARN

EARNINGS *pl n* money earned

EARNS > EARN

EARNT > EARN

EARPHONE *n* receiver for a radio etc, held to or put in the ear

EARPHONES > EARPHONE

EARPICK *n* instrument for removing ear wax

EARPICKS > EARPICK

EARPIECE *n* earphone in a telephone receiver

EARPIECES > EARPIECE

EARPLUG *n* piece of soft material placed in the ear to keep out water or noise

EARPLUGS > EARPLUG

EARRING *n* ornament for the lobe of the ear

EARRINGED *adj* wearing earrings

EARRINGS > EARRING

EARS > EAR

EARSHOT *n* hearing range

EARSHOTS > EARSHOT

EARST *adv* first; previously

EARSTONE *n* calcium carbonate crystal in the ear

EARSTONES > EARSTONE

EARTH *n* planet that we live on ▷ *vb* connect (a circuit) to earth

EARTHBORN *adj* of earthly origin

EARTHED > EARTH

EARTHEN *adj* made of baked clay or earth

EARTHFALL *n* landslide

EARTHFAST *adj* method of building

EARTHFLAX *n* type of asbestos

EARTHIER > EARTHY

EARTHIEST > EARTHY

EARTHILY > EARTHY

EARTHING > EARTH

EARTHLIER > EARTHLY

EARTHLIES > EARTHLY

EARTHLIKE > EARTH

EARTHLING *n* (esp in poetry or science fiction) an inhabitant of the earth

EARTHLY *adj* conceivable or possible ▷ *n* chance

EARTHMAN *n* (esp in science fiction) an inhabitant or native of the earth

EARTHMEN > EARTHMAN

EARTHNUT *n* perennial umbelliferous plant of Europe and Asia, with edible dark brown tubers

EARTHNUTS > EARTHNUT

EARTHPEA *n* peanut; groundnut

EARTHPEAS > EARTHPEA

EARTHRISE *n* rising of the earth above the lunar horizon, as seen from a spacecraft emerging from the lunar farside

EARTHS > EARTH

EARTHSET *n* setting of the earth below the lunar horizon

EARTHSETS > EARTHSET

EARTHSTAR *n* type of woodland fungus

EARTHWARD *adv* towards the earth

EARTHWAX *n* ozocerite

EARTHWOLF *n* aardvark

EARTHWORK *n* fortification made of earth

EARTHWORM *n* worm which burrows in the soil

EARTHY *adj* coarse or crude

EARWAX *nontechnical name for* > CERUMEN

EARWAXES > EARWAX

EARWIG *n* small insect with a pincer-like tail ▷ *vb* eavesdrop

EARWIGGED > EARWIG

EARWIGGY *adj* like an earwig

EARWIGS > EARWIG

EARWORM *n* irritatingly catchy tune

e

EARWORMS > EARWORM
EAS > EA
EASE n freedom from difficulty, discomfort, or worry ▷ vb give bodily or mental ease to
EASED > EASE
EASEFUL adj characterized by or bringing ease
EASEFULLY > EASEFUL
EASEL n frame to support an artist's canvas or a blackboard
EASELED adj mounted on easel
EASELESS > EASE
EASELS > EASEL
EASEMENT n right of a landowner to make limited use of a neighbour's land
EASEMENTS > EASEMENT
EASER > EASE
EASERS > EASE
EASES > EASE
EASIED > EASY
EASIER > EASY
EASIES > EASY
EASIEST > EASY
EASILY adv without difficulty
EASINESS n quality or condition of being easy to accomplish, do, obtain, etc
EASING n as in quantitative easing increasing the supply of money to stimulate the economy
EASINGS > EASING
EASLE n hot ash
EASLES > EASLE
EASSEL adv easterly
EASSIL adv easterly
EAST n (direction towards) the part of the horizon where the sun rises ▷ adj in the east ▷ adv in, to, or towards the east ▷ vb move or turn east
EASTABOUT adv in, to, or towards the east
EASTBOUND adj going towards the east
EASTED > EAST
EASTER n most important festival of the Christian Church
EASTERLY adj of or in the east ▷ adv towards the east ▷ n wind from the east
EASTERN adj situated in or towards the east
EASTERNER n person from the east of a country or area
EASTERS > EASTER
EASTING n net distance eastwards made by a vessel moving towards the east
EASTINGS > EASTING
EASTLAND n land in east
EASTLANDS > EASTLAND
EASTLIN adj easterly
EASTLING adj easterly
EASTLINGS adv eastward
EASTLINS adv eastward
EASTMOST adj furthest east
EASTS > EAST
EASTWARD same as > EASTWARDS

EASTWARDS adv towards the east
EASY adj not needing much work or effort ▷ vb stop rowing
EASYGOING adj relaxed in manner
EASYING > EASY
EAT vb take (food) into the mouth and swallow it
EATABLE adj fit or suitable for eating
EATABLES pl n food
EATAGE n grazing rights
EATAGES > EATAGE
EATCHE n adze
EATCHES > EATCHE
EATEN > EAT
EATER > EAT
EATERIE same as > EATERY
EATERIES > EATERY
EATERS > EAT
EATERY n restaurant or eating house
EATH adj easy
EATHE same as > EATH
EATHLY > EATH
EATING > EAT
EATINGS > EAT
EATS > EAT
EAU same as > EA
EAUS > EAU
EAUX > EAU
EAVE vb give cover under the eaves of a building
EAVED adj having eaves
EAVES > EAVE
EAVESDRIP n water dropping from eaves
EAVESDROP vb listen secretly to a private conversation
EAVING > EAVE
EBAUCHE n rough sketch
EBAUCHES > EBAUCHE
EBAYER n any person who uses eBay
EBAYERS > EBAYER
EBAYING n buying or selling using eBay
EBAYINGS > EBAYING
EBB vb (of tide water) flow back ▷ n flowing back of the tide
EBBED > EBB
EBBET n type of newt
EBBETS > EBBET
EBBING > EBB
EBBLESS > EBB
EBBS > EBB
EBENEZER n chapel
EBENEZERS > EBENEZER
EBENISTE n cabinetmaker
EBENISTES > EBENISTE
EBIONISE same as > EBIONIZE
EBIONISED > EBIONISE
EBIONISES > EBIONISE
EBIONISM n doctrine that the poor shall be saved
EBIONISMS > EBIONISM
EBIONITIC > EBIONISM
EBIONIZE vb preach ebionism
EBIONIZED > EBIONIZE
EBIONIZES > EBIONIZE
EBON poetic word for > EBONY

EBONICS n dialect used by African-Americans
EBONIES > EBONY
EBONISE same as > EBONIZE
EBONISED > EBONISE
EBONISES > EBONISE
EBONISING > EBONISE
EBONIST n carver of ebony
EBONISTS > EBONIST
EBONITE another name for > VULCANITE
EBONITES > EBONITE
EBONIZE vb stain or otherwise finish in imitation of ebony
EBONIZED > EBONIZE
EBONIZES > EBONIZE
EBONIZING > EBONIZE
EBONS > EBON
EBONY n hard black wood ▷ adj deep black
EBOOK n book in electronic form
EBOOKS > EBOOK
EBRIATE adj drunk
EBRIATED same as > EBRIATE
EBRIETIES > EBRIETY
EBRIETY n drunkenness
EBRILLADE n jerk on rein, when horse refuses to turn
EBRIOSE adj drunk
EBRIOSITY > EBRIOSE
EBULLIENT adj full of enthusiasm or excitement
EBURNEAN adj made of ivory
EBURNEOUS adj like ivory
ECAD n organism whose form has been affected by its environment
ECADS > ECAD
ECARINATE adj having no carina or keel
ECARTE n card game for two, played with 32 cards and king high
ECARTES > ECARTE
ECAUDATE adj tailless
ECBOLE n digression
ECBOLES > ECBOLE
ECBOLIC adj inducing labour ▷ n drug or agent that induces labour
ECBOLICS > ECBOLIC
ECCE interj behold
ECCENTRIC adj odd or unconventional ▷ n eccentric person
ECCLESIA n (in formal Church usage) a congregation
ECCLESIAE > ECCLESIA
ECCLESIAL adj ecclesiastical
ECCO interj look there
ECCRINE adj of or denoting glands that secrete externally
ECCRISES > ECCRISIS
ECCRISIS n excrement
ECCRITIC n purgative
ECCRITICS > ECCRITIC
ECDEMIC adj not indigenous or endemic
ECDYSES > ECDYSIS
ECDYSIAL > ECDYSIS

ECDYSIAST facetious word for > STRIPPER
ECDYSIS n shedding of the cuticle in arthropods or the outer epidermal layer in reptiles
ECDYSISES > ECDYSIS
ECDYSON same as > ECDYSONE
ECDYSONE n hormone secreted by the prothoracic gland of insects
ECDYSONES > ECDYSONE
ECDYSONS > ECDYSON
ECESIC > ECESIS
ECESIS n establishment of a plant in a new environment
ECESISES > ECESIS
ECH same as > ECHE
ECHAPPE n leap in ballet
ECHAPPES > ECHAPPE
ECHARD n water that is present in the soil but cannot be utilized by plants
ECHARDS > ECHARD
ECHE vb eke out
ECHED > ECHE
ECHELLE n ladder; scale
ECHELLES > ECHELLE
ECHELON n level of power or responsibility ▷ vb assemble in echelon
ECHELONED > ECHELON
ECHELONS > ECHELON
ECHES > ECHE
ECHEVERIA n tropical American plant cultivated for its colourful foliage
ECHIDNA n Australian spiny egg-laying mammal
ECHIDNAE > ECHIDNA
ECHIDNAS > ECHIDNA
ECHIDNINE n snake poison
ECHINACEA n N American plant with purple and black flowers
ECHINATE adj covered with spines, bristles, or bristle-like outgrowths
ECHINATED same as > ECHINATE
ECHING > ECHE
ECHINI > ECHINUS
ECHINOID n type of echinoderm of the class which includes the sea urchins and sand dollars
ECHINOIDS > ECHINOID
ECHINUS n ovolo moulding between the shaft and the abacus of a Doric column
ECHINUSES > ECHINUS
ECHIUM n type of Eurasian and African plant
ECHIUMS > ECHIUM
ECHIURAN n spoonworm
ECHIURANS > ECHIURAN
ECHIUROID n marine worm
ECHO n repetition of sounds by reflection of sound waves off a surface ▷ vb repeat or be repeated as an echo
ECHOED > ECHO
ECHOER > ECHO
ECHOERS > ECHO
ECHOES > ECHO
ECHOEY adj producing echoes

ECHOGRAM n record made by echography

ECHOGRAMS > ECHOGRAM

ECHOGRAPH n device that uses sonic waves to measure the depth of water

ECHOIC adj characteristic of or resembling an echo

ECHOIER > ECHOEY

ECHOIEST > ECHOEY

ECHOING > ECHO

ECHOISE same as > ECHOIZE

ECHOISED > ECHOISE

ECHOISES > ECHOISE

ECHOISING > ECHOISE

ECHOISM n onomatopoeia as a source of word formation

ECHOISMS > ECHOISM

ECHOIST > ECHOISM

ECHOISTS > ECHOISM

ECHOIZE vb repeat like echo

ECHOIZED > ECHOIZE

ECHOIZES > ECHOIZE

ECHOIZING > ECHOIZE

ECHOLALIA n tendency to repeat mechanically words just spoken by another person

ECHOLALIC > ECHOLALIA

ECHOLESS > ECHO

ECHOS > ECHO

ECHOVIRUS n any of a group of viruses that can cause symptoms of mild meningitis, the common cold, or infections of the intestinal and respiratory tracts

ECHT adj real

ECLAIR n finger-shaped pastry filled with cream and covered with chocolate

ECLAIRS > ECLAIR

ECLAMPSIA n serious condition that can develop towards the end of a pregnancy, causing high blood pressure, swelling, and convulsions

ECLAMPSY same as > ECLAMPSIA

ECLAMPTIC > ECLAMPSIA

ECLAT n brilliant success

ECLATS > ECLAT

ECLECTIC adj selecting from various styles, ideas, or sources ▷ n person who takes an eclectic approach

ECLECTICS > ECLECTIC

ECLIPSE n temporary obscuring of one star or planet by another ▷ vb surpass or outclass

ECLIPSED > ECLIPSE

ECLIPSER > ECLIPSE

ECLIPSERS > ECLIPSE

ECLIPSES > ECLIPSIS

ECLIPSING > ECLIPSE

ECLIPSIS same as > ELLIPSIS

ECLIPTIC n apparent path of the sun ▷ adj of or relating to an eclipse

ECLIPTICS > ECLIPTIC

ECLOGITE n rare coarse-grained basic rock

ECLOGITES > ECLOGITE

ECLOGUE n pastoral or idyllic poem, usually in the form of a conversation or soliloquy

ECLOGUES > ECLOGUE

ECLOSE vb emerge

ECLOSED > ECLOSE

ECLOSES > ECLOSE

ECLOSING > ECLOSE

ECLOSION n emergence of an insect larva from the egg or an adult from the pupal case

ECLOSIONS > ECLOSION

ECO n ecology activist

ECOCIDAL > ECOCIDE

ECOCIDE n total destruction of an area of the natural environment

ECOCIDES > ECOCIDE

ECOD same as > EGAD

ECOFREAK n environmentalist

ECOFREAKS > ECOFREAK

ECOGIFT n donation of land for environmental purposes

ECOGIFTS > ECOGIFT

ECOLODGE n eco-friendly tourist accommodation

ECOLODGES > ECOLODGE

ECOLOGIC > ECOLOGY

ECOLOGIES > ECOLOGY

ECOLOGIST > ECOLOGY

ECOLOGY n study of the links between living things and their environment

ECOMAP n diagram showing the links between an individual and their community

ECOMAPS > ECOMAP

ECOMMERCE n business transactions conducted on the internet

ECOMUSEUM n museum exploring the history, culture, and environment of a region

ECONOBOX n fuel efficient utility vehicle

ECONOMIC adj of economics

ECONOMICS n social science concerned with the production and consumption of goods and services

ECONOMIES > ECONOMY

ECONOMISE same as > ECONOMIZE

ECONOMISM n political theory that regards economics as the main factor in society, ignoring or reducing to simplistic economic terms other factors such as culture, nationality, etc

ECONOMIST n specialist in economics

ECONOMIZE vb reduce expense or waste

ECONOMY n system of interrelationship of money, industry, and employment in a country ▷ adj denoting a class of air travel that is cheaper than first-class

ECONUT n derogatory term for a keen environmentalist

ECONUTS > ECONUT

ECOPHOBIA n fear of home

ECORCHE n anatomical figure without the skin

ECORCHES > ECORCHE

ECOREGION n area defined by its environmental conditions, esp climate, landforms, and soil characteristics

ECOS > ECO

ECOSPHERE n planetary ecosystem, consisting of all living organisms and their environment

ECOSSAISE n lively dance in two-four time

ECOSTATE adj with no ribs or nerves

ECOSYSTEM n system involving interactions between a community and its environment

ECOTAGE n sabotage for ecological motives

ECOTAGES > ECOTAGE

ECOTARIAN n person who eats only eco-friendly food

ECOTONAL > ECOTONE

ECOTONE n zone between two major ecological communities

ECOTONES > ECOTONE

ECOTOPIA n ecologically ideal area or society

ECOTOPIAS > ECOTOPIA

ECOTOUR n holiday taking care not to damage environment ▷ vb take an ecotour

ECOTOURED > ECOTOUR

ECOTOURS > ECOTOUR

ECOTOXIC adj harmful to animals, plants or the environment

ECOTYPE n organisms within a species that have adapted to a particular environment

ECOTYPES > ECOTYPE

ECOTYPIC > ECOTYPE

ECOZONE n large area with an ecosystem

ECOZONES > ECOZONE

ECPHRASES > ECPHRASIS

ECPHRASIS same as > EKPHRASIS

ECRASEUR n surgical device consisting of a heavy wire loop

ECRASEURS > ECRASEUR

ECRITOIRE n writing desk with compartments and drawers

ECRU adj pale creamy-brown ▷ n greyish-yellow to a light greyish colour

ECRUS > ECRU

ECSTASES > ECSTASIS

ECSTASIED > ECSTASY

ECSTASIES > ECSTASY

ECSTASIS same as > ECSTASY

ECSTASISE same as > ECSTASIZE

ECSTASIZE vb make or become ecstatic

ECSTASY n state of intense delight

ECSTATIC adj in a trancelike state of great rapture or delight ▷ n person who has periods of intense trancelike joy

ECSTATICS pl n fits of delight or rapture

ECTASES > ECTASIS

ECTASIA n distension or dilation of a duct, vessel, or hollow viscus

ECTASIAS > ECTASIA

ECTASIS same as > ECTASIA

ECTATIC > ECTASIA

ECTHYMA n local inflammation of the skin

ECTHYMAS > ECTHYMA

ECTHYMATA > ECTHYMA

ECTOBLAST same as > EPIBLAST

ECTOCRINE n substance that is released by an organism into the external environment and influences the development, behaviour, etc, of members of the same or different species

ECTODERM n outer germ layer of an animal embryo

ECTODERMS > ECTODERM

ECTOGENE n type of gene

ECTOGENES > ECTOGENE

ECTOGENIC adj capable of developing outside the host

ECTOGENY n (of bacteria, etc) development outside the host

ECTOMERE n any of the blastomeres that later develop into ectoderm

ECTOMERES > ECTOMERE

ECTOMERIC > ECTOMERE

ECTOMORPH n person with a thin body build: said to be correlated with cerebrotonia

ECTOPHYTE n parasitic plant that lives on the surface of its host

ECTOPIA n congenital displacement of an organ or part

ECTOPIAS > ECTOPIA

ECTOPIC > ECTOPIA

ECTOPIES > ECTOPY

ECTOPLASM n substance that supposedly is emitted from the body of a medium during a trance

ECTOPROCT another word for > BRYOZOAN

ECTOPY same as > ECTOPIA

ECTOSARC n ectoplasm of an amoeba or any other protozoan

ECTOSARCS > ECTOSARC

ECTOTHERM n animal whose body temperature is determined by ambient temperature

ECTOZOA > ECTOZOON

ECTOZOAN same as > ECTOZOON

ECTOZOANS > ECTOZOAN

ECTOZOIC > ECTOZOON

ECTOZOON n parasitic organism that lives on the outside of its host

e

ECTROPIC > ECTROPION

ECTROPION n condition in which the eyelid turns over exposing some of the inner lid

ECTROPIUM same as > ECTROPION

ECTYPAL > ECTYPE

ECTYPE n copy as distinguished from a prototype

ECTYPES > ECTYPE

ECU n any of various former French gold or silver coins

ECUELLE n covered soup bowl with handles

ECUELLES > ECUELLE

ECUMENE n inhabited area of the world

ECUMENES > ECUMENE

ECUMENIC adj tending to promote unity among Churches

ECUMENICS > ECUMENIC

ECUMENISM n aim of unity among Christian churches throughout the world

ECUMENIST n believer in ecumenicism

ECURIE n team of motor-racing cars

ECURIES > ECURIE

ECUS > ECU

ECZEMA n skin disease causing intense itching

ECZEMAS > ECZEMA

ED n editor

EDACIOUS adj devoted to eating

EDACITIES > EDACIOUS

EDACITY > EDACIOUS

EDAMAME n immature soybeans boiled in the pod

EDAMAMES > EDAMAME

EDAPHIC adj of or relating to the physical and chemical conditions of the soil

EDDIED > EDDY

EDDIES > EDDY

EDDISH n pasture grass

EDDISHES > EDDISH

EDDO same as > TARO

EDDOES > EDDO

EDDY n circular movement of air, water, etc ▷ vb move with a circular motion

EDDYING > EDDY

EDELWEISS n alpine plant with white flowers

EDEMA same as > OEDEMA

EDEMAS > EDEMA

EDEMATA > EDEMA

EDEMATOSE > EDEMA

EDEMATOUS > EDEMA

EDENIC adj delightful, like the Garden of Eden

EDENTAL adj having few or no teeth

EDENTATE n mammal with few or no teeth, such as an armadillo or a sloth ▷ adj denoting such a mammal

EDENTATES > EDENTATE

EDGE n border or line where something ends or begins ▷ vb provide an edge or border for

EDGEBONE n aitchbone

EDGEBONES > EDGEBONE

EDGED > EDGE

EDGELESS > EDGE

EDGER > EDGE

EDGERS > EDGE

EDGES > EDGE

EDGEWAYS adv with the edge forwards or uppermost

EDGEWISE same as > EDGEWAYS

EDGIER > EDGY

EDGIEST > EDGY

EDGILY > EDGY

EDGINESS > EDGY

EDGING n anything placed along an edge to finish it ▷ adj relating to or used for making an edge

EDGINGS > EDGING

EDGY adj nervous or irritable

EDH n character of the runic alphabet

EDHS > EDH

EDIBILITY > EDIBLE

EDIBLE adj fit to be eaten

EDIBLES pl n articles fit to eat

EDICT n order issued by an authority

EDICTAL > EDICT

EDICTALLY > EDICT

EDICTS > EDICT

EDIFICE n large building

EDIFICES > EDIFICE

EDIFICIAL > EDIFICE

EDIFIED > EDIFY

EDIFIER > EDIFY

EDIFIERS > EDIFY

EDIFIES > EDIFY

EDIFY vb improve morally by instruction

EDIFYING > EDIFY

EDILE variant spelling of > AEDILE

EDILES > EDILE

EDIT vb prepare (a book, film, etc) for publication or broadcast ▷ n act of editing

EDITABLE > EDIT

EDITED > EDIT

EDITING > EDIT

EDITINGS > EDIT

EDITION n number of copies of a new publication printed at one time ▷ vb produce multiple copies of (an original work of art)

EDITIONED > EDITION

EDITIONS > EDITION

EDITOR n person who edits

EDITORIAL n newspaper article stating the opinion of the editor ▷ adj of editing or editors

EDITORS > EDITOR

EDITRESS n female editor

EDITRICES > EDITRIX

EDITRIX n female editor

EDITRIXES > EDITRIX

EDITS > EDIT

EDS > ED

EDUCABLE adj capable of being trained or educated ▷ n person with learning difficulties who is capable of being educated

EDUCABLES > EDUCABLE

EDUCATE vb teach

EDUCATED adj having an education, esp a good one

EDUCATES > EDUCATE

EDUCATING > EDUCATE

EDUCATION n process of acquiring knowledge and understanding

EDUCATIVE adj educating

EDUCATOR n person who educates

EDUCATORS > EDUCATOR

EDUCATORY adj educative or educational

EDUCE vb evolve or develop

EDUCED > EDUCE

EDUCEMENT > EDUCE

EDUCES > EDUCE

EDUCIBLE > EDUCE

EDUCING > EDUCE

EDUCT n substance separated from a mixture without chemical change

EDUCTION n something educed

EDUCTIONS > EDUCTION

EDUCTIVE > EDUCE

EDUCTOR > EDUCE

EDUCTORS > EDUCE

EDUCTS > EDUCT

EE Scots word for > EYE

EECH same as > ECHE

EECHED > EECH

EECHES > EECH

EECHING > EECH

EEEW interj exclamation of disgust

EEJIT Scots and Irish word for > IDIOT

EEJITS > EEJIT

EEK interj indicating shock or fright

EEL n snakelike fish

EELFARE n young eel

EELFARES > EELFARE

EELGRASS n type of submerged marine plant with grasslike leaves

EELIER > EEL

EELIEST > EEL

EELING n practice of catching eels

EELINGS > EELING

EELLIKE adj resembling an eel

EELPOUT n marine eel-like blennioid fish

EELPOUTS > EELPOUT

EELS > EEL

EELWORM n any of various nematode worms

EELWORMS > EELWORM

EELWRACK n grasslike plant growing in seawater

EELWRACKS > EELWRACK

EELY > EEL

EEN > EE

EENSIER > EENSY

EENSIEST > EENSY

EENSY adj very small

EERIE adj uncannily frightening or disturbing

EERIER > EERIE

EERIEST > EERIE

EERILY > EERIE

EERINESS > EERIE

EERY same as > EERIE

EEVEN n evening

EEVENS > EEVEN

EEVN n evening

EEVNING n evening

EEVNINGS > EEVNING

EEVNS > EEVN

EEW interj exclamation of disgust

EF n letter F

EFF vb use bad language

EFFABLE adj capable of being expressed in words

EFFACE vb remove by rubbing

EFFACED > EFFACE

EFFACER > EFFACE

EFFACERS > EFFACE

EFFACES > EFFACE

EFFACING > EFFACE

EFFECT n change or result caused by someone or something ▷ vb cause to happen, accomplish

EFFECTED > EFFECT

EFFECTER > EFFECT

EFFECTERS > EFFECT

EFFECTING > EFFECT

EFFECTIVE adj producing a desired result ▷ n soldier who is equipped and prepared for action

EFFECTOR n nerve ending that terminates in a muscle or gland

EFFECTORS > EFFECTOR

EFFECTS pl n personal belongings

EFFECTUAL adj producing the intended result

EFFED > EFF

EFFEIR vb suit

EFFEIRED > EFFEIR

EFFEIRING > EFFEIR

EFFEIRS > EFFEIR

EFFENDI n (in the Ottoman Empire) a title of respect

EFFENDIS > EFFENDI

EFFERE same as > EFFEIR

EFFERED > EFFERE

EFFERENCE > EFFERENT

EFFERENT adj carrying or conducting outwards ▷ n type of nerve

EFFERENTS > EFFERENT

EFFERES > EFFERE

EFFERING > EFFERE

EFFETE adj powerless, feeble

EFFETELY > EFFETE

EFFICACY n quality of being successful in producing an intended result

EFFICIENT adj functioning effectively with little waste of effort

EFFIERCE vb archaic word meaning make fierce

EFFIERCED > EFFIERCE

EFFIERCES > EFFIERCE

EFFIGIAL > EFFIGY

EFFIGIES > EFFIGY

EFFIGY n image or likeness of a person

EFFING > EFF

EFFINGS > EFF

EFFLUENCE n act or process of flowing out

EFFLUENT *n* liquid discharged as waste ▷ *adj* flowing out or forth

EFFLUENTS > EFFLUENT

EFFLUVIA > EFFLUVIUM

EFFLUVIAL > EFFLUVIUM

EFFLUVIUM *n* unpleasant smell, as of decaying matter or gaseous waste

EFFLUX *same as* **>** EFFLUENCE

EFFLUXES > EFFLUX

EFFLUXION *same as* **>** EFFLUX

EFFORCE *vb* force

EFFORCED > EFFORCE

EFFORCES > EFFORCE

EFFORCING > EFFORCE

EFFORT *n* physical or mental exertion

EFFORTFUL > EFFORT

EFFORTS > EFFORT

EFFRAIDE *archaic form of* **>** AFRAID

EFFRAY *archaic form of* **>** AFFRAY

EFFRAYS > EFFRAY

EFFS > EFF

EFFULGE *vb* radiate

EFFULGED > EFFULGE

EFFULGENT *adj* radiant

EFFULGES > EFFULGE

EFFULGING > EFFULGE

EFFUSE *vb* pour or flow out ▷ *adj* (esp of an inflorescence) spreading out loosely

EFFUSED > EFFUSE

EFFUSES > EFFUSE

EFFUSING > EFFUSE

EFFUSION *n* unrestrained outburst

EFFUSIONS > EFFUSION

EFFUSIVE *adj* openly emotional, demonstrative

EFS > EF

EFT *n* dialect or archaic name for a newt ▷ *adv* again

EFTEST *adj* nearest at hand

EFTS > EFT

EFTSOON > EFTSOONS

EFTSOONS *adv* soon afterwards

EGAD *n* mild oath or expression of surprise

EGADS > EGAD

EGAL *adj* equal

EGALITE *n* equality

EGALITES > EGALITE

EGALITIES > EGALITY

EGALITY *n* equality

EGALLY > EGAL

EGAREMENT *n* confusion

EGENCE *n* need

EGENCES > EGENCE

EGENCIES > EGENCY

EGENCY *same as* **>** EGENCE

EGER *same as* **>** EAGRE

EGERS > EGER

EGEST *vb* excrete (waste material)

EGESTA *pl n* anything egested, as waste material from the body

EGESTED > EGEST

EGESTING > EGEST

EGESTION > EGEST

EGESTIONS > EGEST

EGESTIVE > EGEST

EGESTS > EGEST

EGG *n* object laid by birds and other creatures, containing a developing embryo ▷ *vb* urge or incite, esp to daring or foolish acts

EGGAR *same as* **>** EGGER

EGGARS > EGGAR

EGGBEATER *n* kitchen utensil for beating eggs, whipping cream, etc

EGGCORN *n* misspelling caused by the mishearing of a word

EGGCORNS > EGGCORN

EGGCUP *n* cup for holding a boiled egg

EGGCUPS > EGGCUP

EGGED > EGG

EGGER *n* moth with brown body and wings

EGGERIES > EGGERY

EGGERS > EGGER

EGGERY *n* place where eggs are laid

EGGFRUIT *n* fruit of eggplant

EGGFRUITS > EGGFRUIT

EGGHEAD *n* intellectual person

EGGHEADED > EGGHEAD

EGGHEADS > EGGHEAD

EGGIER > EGGY

EGGIEST > EGGY

EGGING > EGG

EGGLER *n* egg dealer: sometimes itinerant

EGGLERS > EGGLER

EGGLESS > EGG

EGGLIKE *adj* like an egg

EGGMASS *n* intelligentsia

EGGMASSES > EGGMASS

EGGNOG *n* drink made of raw eggs, milk, sugar, spice, and brandy or rum

EGGNOGS > EGGNOG

EGGPLANT *n* dark purple tropical fruit, cooked and eaten as a vegetable

EGGPLANTS > EGGPLANT

EGGS > EGG

EGGSHELL *n* hard covering round the egg of a bird or animal ▷ *adj* (of paint) having a very slight sheen

EGGSHELLS > EGGSHELL

EGGWASH *n* beaten egg for brushing on pastry

EGGWASHES > EGGWASH

EGGWHISK *same as* **>** EGGBEATER

EGGWHISKS > EGGWHISK

EGGY *adj* soaked in or tasting of egg

EGIS *rare spelling of* **>** AEGIS

EGISES > EGIS

EGLANTINE *n* Eurasian rose

EGLATERE *archaic name for* **>** EGLANTINE

EGLATERES > EGLATERE

EGLOMISE *n* gilding

EGLOMISES > EGLOMISE

EGMA *mispronunciation of* **>** ENIGMA

EGMAS > EGMA

EGO *n* conscious mind of an individual

EGOISM *n* excessive concern for one's own interests

EGOISMS > EGOISM

EGOIST *n* person who is preoccupied with their own interests

EGOISTIC > EGOIST

EGOISTS > EGOIST

EGOITIES > EGOITY

EGOITY *n* essence of the ego

EGOLESS *adj* without an ego

EGOMANIA *n* obsessive concern with one's own needs and desires

EGOMANIAC > EGOMANIA

EGOMANIAS > EGOMANIA

EGOS > EGO

EGOSURF *vb* search for one's own name on the internet

EGOSURFED > EGOSURF

EGOSURFS > EGOSURF

EGOTHEISM *n* making god of oneself

EGOTISE *same as* **>** EGOTIZE

EGOTISED > EGOTISE

EGOTISES > EGOTISE

EGOTISING > EGOTISE

EGOTISM *n* concern only for one's own interests and feelings

EGOTISMS > EGOTISM

EGOTIST *n* conceited boastful person

EGOTISTIC > EGOTIST

EGOTISTS > EGOTIST

EGOTIZE *vb* talk or write in self-important way

EGOTIZED > EGOTIZE

EGOTIZES > EGOTIZE

EGOTIZING > EGOTIZE

EGREGIOUS *adj* outstandingly bad

EGRESS *same as* **>** EMERSION

EGRESSED > EGRESS

EGRESSES > EGRESS

EGRESSING > EGRESS

EGRESSION *same as* **>** EGRESS

EGRESSIVE *n* speech sound produced with an exhalation of breath

EGRET *n* lesser white heron

EGRETS > EGRET

EGYPTIAN *n* type of typeface

EGYPTIANS > EGYPTIAN

EH *interj* exclamation of surprise or inquiry ▷ *vb* say 'eh'

EHED > EH

EHING > EH

EHS > EH

EIDE > EIDOS

EIDENT *adj* diligent

EIDER *n* Arctic duck

EIDERDOWN *n* quilt (orig stuffed with eider feathers)

EIDERS > EIDER

EIDETIC *adj* (of images) exceptionally vivid, allowing detailed recall of something ▷ *n* person with eidetic ability

EIDETICS > EIDETIC

EIDOGRAPH *n* device for copying drawings

EIDOLA > EIDOLON

EIDOLIC > EIDOLON

EIDOLON *n* unsubstantial image

EIDOLONS > EIDOLON

EIDOS *n* intellectual character of a culture or a social group

EIGENMODE *n* characteristic vibration pattern

EIGENTONE *n* characteristic acoustic resonance frequency of a system

EIGHT *n* one more than seven

EIGHTBALL *n* black ball in pool

EIGHTEEN *n* eight and ten

EIGHTEENS > EIGHTEEN

EIGHTFOIL *n* eight leaved flower shape in heraldry

EIGHTFOLD *adj* having eight times as many or as much ▷ *adv* by eight times as many or as much

EIGHTFOOT *adj* measuring eight feet

EIGHTH *n* number eight in a series ▷ *adj* coming after the seventh and before the ninth

EIGHTHLY *same as* **>** EIGHTH

EIGHTHS > EIGHTH

EIGHTIES > EIGHTY

EIGHTIETH *n* one of 80 approximately equal parts of something

EIGHTS > EIGHT

EIGHTSMAN *n* member of an eight-man team

EIGHTSMEN > EIGHTSMAN

EIGHTSOME *n* group of eight people

EIGHTVO *another word for* **>** OCTAVO

EIGHTVOS > EIGHTVO

EIGHTY *n* eight times ten

EIGNE *adj* firstborn

EIK *variant form of* **>** EKE

EIKED > EIK

EIKING > EIK

EIKON *variant spelling of* **>** ICON

EIKONES > EIKON

EIKONS > EIKON

EIKS > EIK

EILD *n* old age

EILDING *n* fuel

EILDINGS > EILDING

EILDS > EILD

EINA *interj* exclamation of pain

EINE *pl n* eyes

EINKORN *n* variety of wheat of Greece and SW Asia

EINKORNS > EINKORN

EINSTEIN *n* scientific genius

EINSTEINS > EINSTEIN

EIRACK *n* young hen

EIRACKS > EIRACK

EIRENIC *variant spelling of* **>** IRENIC

EIRENICAL *same as* **>** IRENIC

e

EIRENICON n proposition that attempts to harmonize conflicting viewpoints

EIRENICS n theology concerned with unity among churches

EISEGESES > EISEGESIS

EISEGESIS n interpretation of a text, esp a biblical text, using one's own ideas

EISEL n vinegar

EISELL same as > EISEL

EISELLS > EISELL

EISELS > EISEL

EISH interj South African exclamation

EISWEIN n wine made from grapes frozen on the vine

EISWEINS > EISWEIN

EITHER pron one or the other (of two) ▷ adv likewise ▷ determiner one or the other (of two)

EJACULATE vb utter abruptly

EJECT vb force out, expel

EJECTA pl n matter thrown out by a volcano or during a meteorite impact

EJECTABLE > EJECT

EJECTED > EJECT

EJECTING > EJECT

EJECTION > EJECT

EJECTIONS > EJECT

EJECTIVE adj relating to or causing ejection ▷ n ejective consonant

EJECTIVES > EJECTIVE

EJECTMENT n (formerly) an action brought by a wrongfully dispossessed owner seeking to recover possession of their land

EJECTOR n person or thing that ejects

EJECTORS > EJECTOR

EJECTS > EJECT

EJIDO n communal farmland in Mexico

EJIDOS > EJIDO

EKE vb increase, enlarge, or lengthen

EKED > EKE

EKES > EKE

EKING > EKE

EKISTIC > EKISTICS

EKISTICAL > EKISTICS

EKISTICS n science or study of human settlements

EKKA n type of one-horse carriage

EKKAS > EKKA

EKLOGITE same as > ECLOGITE

EKLOGITES > EKLOGITE

EKPHRASES > EKPHRASIS

EKPHRASIS n description of a visual work of art

EKPWELE n former monetary unit of Equatorial Guinea

EKPWELES > EKPWELE

EKTEXINE n in pollen and spores, the outer of the two layers that make up the exine

EKTEXINES > EKTEXINE

EKUELE same as > EKPWELE

EL n American elevated railway

ELABORATE adj with a lot of fine detail ▷ vb expand upon

ELAEAGNUS n Eurasian ornamental shrub or small tree

ELAEOLITE n nephelite

ELAIN same as > TRIOLEIN

ELAINS > ELAIN

ELAIOSOME n oil-rich body on seeds or fruits that attracts ants, which act as dispersal agents

ELAN n style and vigour

ELANCE vb throw a lance

ELANCED > ELANCE

ELANCES > ELANCE

ELANCING > ELANCE

ELAND n large antelope of southern Africa

ELANDS > ELAND

ELANET n bird of prey

ELANETS > ELANET

ELANS > ELAN

ELAPHINE adj of or like a red deer

ELAPID n mostly tropical type of venomous snake

ELAPIDS > ELAPID

ELAPINE adj of or like an elapid

ELAPSE vb (of time) pass by

ELAPSED > ELAPSE

ELAPSES > ELAPSE

ELAPSING > ELAPSE

ELASTANCE n reciprocal of capacitance

ELASTANE n synthetic fibre that is able to return to its original shape after being stretched

ELASTANES > ELASTANE

ELASTASE n enzyme that digests elastin

ELASTASES > ELASTASE

ELASTIC adj resuming normal shape after distortion ▷ n tape or fabric containing interwoven strands of flexible rubber

ELASTICS > ELASTIC

ELASTIN n fibrous scleroprotein

ELASTINS > ELASTIN

ELASTOMER n any material, such as natural or synthetic rubber, that is able to resume its original shape when a deforming force is removed

ELATE vb fill with high spirits, exhilaration, pride or optimism

ELATED adj extremely happy and excited

ELATEDLY > ELATED

ELATER n elaterid beetle

ELATERID n type of beetle of the family which constitutes the click beetles

ELATERIDS > ELATERID

ELATERIN n white crystalline substance found in elaterium, used as a purgative

ELATERINS > ELATERIN

ELATERITE n dark brown naturally occurring bitumen resembling rubber

ELATERIUM n greenish sediment prepared from the juice of the squirting cucumber, used as a purgative

ELATERS > ELATER

ELATES > ELATE

ELATING > ELATE

ELATION n feeling of great happiness and excitement

ELATIONS > ELATION

ELATIVE adj denoting a grammatical case in Finnish and other languages ▷ n elative case

ELATIVES > ELATIVE

ELBOW n joint between the upper arm and the forearm ▷ vb shove or strike with the elbow

ELBOWED > ELBOW

ELBOWING n act of elbowing

ELBOWINGS > ELBOWING

ELBOWROOM n sufficient scope to move or function

ELBOWS > ELBOW

ELCHEE n ambassador

ELCHEES > ELCHEE

ELCHI same as > ELCHEE

ELCHIS > ELCHI

ELD n old age

ELDER adj older ▷ n older person

ELDERCARE n care of elderly

ELDERLIES > ELDERLY

ELDERLY adj (fairly) old

ELDERS > ELDER

ELDERSHIP > ELDER

ELDEST n oldest child

ELDESTS > ELDEST

ELDIN n fuel

ELDING same as > ELDIN

ELDINGS > ELDING

ELDINS > ELDIN

ELDORADO n place of great riches or fabulous opportunity

ELDORADOS > ELDORADO

ELDRESS n woman elder

ELDRESSES > ELDRESS

ELDRICH same as > ELDRITCH

ELDRITCH adj weird, uncanny

ELDS > ELD

ELECT vb choose by voting ▷ adj appointed but not yet in office

ELECTABLE > ELECT

ELECTED > ELECT

ELECTEE n someone who is elected

ELECTEES > ELECTEE

ELECTING > ELECT

ELECTION n choosing of representatives by voting

ELECTIONS > ELECTION

ELECTIVE adj chosen by election ▷ n optional course or hospital placement undertaken by a medical student

ELECTIVES > ELECTIVE

ELECTOR n someone who has the right to vote in an election

ELECTORAL adj of or relating to elections

ELECTORS > ELECTOR

ELECTRESS n female elector

ELECTRET n permanently polarized dielectric material

ELECTRETS > ELECTRET

ELECTRIC adj produced by, transmitting, or powered by electricity ▷ n electric train, car, etc

ELECTRICS > ELECTRIC

ELECTRIFY vb adapt for operation by electric power

ELECTRISE same as > ELECTRIZE

ELECTRIZE vb electrify

ELECTRO vb (in printing) make a metallic copy of a page

ELECTRODE n conductor through which an electric current enters or leaves a battery, vacuum tube, etc

ELECTROED > ELECTRO

ELECTRON n elementary particle in all atoms that has a negative electrical charge

ELECTRONS > ELECTRON

ELECTROS > ELECTRO

ELECTRUM n alloy of gold (55–88 per cent) and silver used for jewellery and ornaments

ELECTRUMS > ELECTRUM

ELECTS > ELECT

ELECTUARY n paste taken orally, containing a drug mixed with syrup or honey

ELEDOISIN n substance extracted from the salivary glands of a small octopus for medical applications

ELEGANCE n dignified grace in appearance, movement, or behaviour

ELEGANCES > ELEGANCE

ELEGANCY same as > ELEGANCE

ELEGANT adj pleasing or graceful in dress, style, or design

ELEGANTLY > ELEGANT

ELEGIAC adj mournful or plaintive ▷ n elegiac couplet or stanza

ELEGIACAL > ELEGIAC

ELEGIACS > ELEGIAC

ELEGIAST n writer of elegies

ELEGIASTS > ELEGIAST

ELEGIES > ELEGY

ELEGISE same as > ELEGIZE

ELEGISED > ELEGISE

ELEGISES > ELEGISE

ELEGISING > ELEGISE

ELEGIST > ELEGIZE

ELEGISTS > ELEGIZE

ELEGIT n writ delivering debtor's property to plaintiff

ELEGITS > ELEGIT

ELEGIZE vb compose an elegy or elegies (in memory of)

ELEGIZED > ELEGIZE

ELEGIZES > ELEGIZE

ELEGIZING > ELEGIZE

ELEGY n mournful poem, esp a lament for the dead

ELEMENT *n* component part
ELEMENTAL *adj* of primitive natural forces or passions ▷ *n* spirit or force that is said to appear in physical form
ELEMENTS > ELEMENT
ELEMI *n* fragrant resin obtained from various tropical trees
ELEMIS > ELEMI
ELENCH *n* refutation in logic
ELENCHI > ELENCHUS
ELENCHIC > ELENCHUS
ELENCHS > ELENCH
ELENCHTIC *same as* > ELENCTIC
ELENCHUS *n* refutation of an argument by proving the contrary of its conclusion
ELENCTIC *adj* refuting an argument by proving the falsehood of its conclusion
ELEOPTENE *n* liquid part of a volatile oil
ELEPHANT *n* huge four-footed thick-skinned animal with ivory tusks and a long trunk
ELEPHANTS > ELEPHANT
ELEPIDOTE *n* large rhododendron with leathery leaves
ELEUTHERI *pl n* secret society
ELEVATE *vb* raise in rank or status
ELEVATED *adj* higher than normal ▷ *n* railway that runs on an elevated structure
ELEVATEDS > ELEVATED
ELEVATES > ELEVATE
ELEVATING > ELEVATE
ELEVATION *n* raising
ELEVATOR *n* lift for carrying people
ELEVATORS > ELEVATOR
ELEVATORY > ELEVATE
ELEVEN *n* one more than ten
ELEVENS > ELEVEN
ELEVENSES *n* mid-morning snack
ELEVENTH *n* number eleven in a series ▷ *adj* coming after the tenth in numbering or counting order, position, time, etc
ELEVENTHS > ELEVENTH
ELEVON *n* aircraft control surface usually fitted to tailless or delta-wing aircraft
ELEVONS > ELEVON
ELF *n* (in folklore) small mischievous fairy ▷ *vb* entangle (esp hair)
ELFED > ELF
ELFHOOD > ELF
ELFHOODS > ELF
ELFIN *adj* small and delicate ▷ *n* young elf
ELFING > ELF
ELFINS > ELFIN
ELFISH *adj* of, relating to, or like an elf or elves ▷ *n* supposed language of elves
ELFISHES > ELFISH
ELFISHLY > ELFISH
ELFLAND *another name for* > FAIRYLAND

ELFLANDS > ELFLAND
ELFLIKE > ELF
ELFLOCK *n* lock of hair
ELFLOCKS > ELFLOCK
ELFS > ELF
ELHI *adj* informal word for or relating to elementary high school
ELIAD *n* glance
ELIADS > ELIAD
ELICHE *n* pasta in the form of spirals
ELICHES > ELICHE
ELICIT *vb* bring about (a response or reaction)
ELICITED > ELICIT
ELICITING > ELICIT
ELICITOR > ELICIT
ELICITORS > ELICIT
ELICITS > ELICIT
ELIDE *vb* omit (a vowel or syllable) from a spoken word
ELIDED > ELIDE
ELIDES > ELIDE
ELIDIBLE > ELIDE
ELIDING > ELIDE
ELIGIBLE *adj* meeting the requirements or qualifications needed ▷ *n* eligible person or thing
ELIGIBLES > ELIGIBLE
ELIGIBLY > ELIGIBLE
ELIMINANT > ELIMINATE
ELIMINATE *vb* get rid of
ELINT *n* electronic intelligence
ELINTS > ELINT
ELISION *n* omission of a syllable or vowel from a spoken word
ELISIONS > ELISION
ELITE *n* most powerful, rich, or gifted members of a group ▷ *adj* of, relating to, or suitable for an elite
ELITES > ELITE
ELITISM *n* belief that society should be ruled by a small group of superior people
ELITISMS > ELITISM
ELITIST > ELITISM
ELITISTS > ELITISM
ELIXIR *n* legendary liquid
ELIXIRS > ELIXIR
ELK *n* large deer of N Europe and Asia
ELKHORN *n* as in *elkhorn fern* fern with a large leaf like an elk's horn
ELKHOUND *n* powerful breed of dog
ELKHOUNDS > ELKHOUND
ELKS > ELK
ELL *n* obsolete unit of length
ELLAGIC *adj* of an acid derived from gallnuts
ELLIPSE *n* oval shape
ELLIPSES > ELLIPSIS
ELLIPSIS *n* omission of letters or words in a sentence
ELLIPSOID *n* surface whose plane sections are ellipses or circles
ELLIPTIC *adj* relating to or having the shape of an ellipse
ELLOPS *same as* > ELOPS

ELLOPSES > ELLOPS
ELLS > ELL
ELLWAND *n* stick for measuring lengths
ELLWANDS > ELLWAND
ELM *n* tree with serrated leaves
ELMEN *adj* of or relating to elm trees
ELMIER > ELMY
ELMIEST > ELMY
ELMS > ELM
ELMWOOD *n* wood from an elm tree
ELMWOODS > ELMWOOD
ELMY *adj* of or relating to elm trees
ELOCUTE *vb* speak as if practising elocution
ELOCUTED > ELOCUTE
ELOCUTES > ELOCUTE
ELOCUTING > ELOCUTE
ELOCUTION *n* art of speaking clearly in public
ELOCUTORY > ELOCUTION
ELODEA *n* type of American plant
ELODEAS > ELODEA
ELOGE *same as* > EULOGY
ELOGES > ELOGE
ELOGIES > ELOGY
ELOGIST > ELOGY
ELOGISTS > ELOGY
ELOGIUM *same as* > EULOGY
ELOGIUMS > ELOGIUM
ELOGY *same as* > EULOGY
ELOIGN *vb* remove (oneself, one's property, etc) to a distant place
ELOIGNED > ELOIGN
ELOIGNER > ELOIGN
ELOIGNERS > ELOIGN
ELOIGNING > ELOIGN
ELOIGNS > ELOIGN
ELOIN *same as* > ELOIGN
ELOINED > ELOIN
ELOINER > ELOIN
ELOINERS > ELOINER
ELOINING > ELOIN
ELOINMENT > ELOIGN
ELOINS > ELOIN
ELONGATE *vb* make or become longer ▷ *adj* long and narrow
ELONGATED > ELONGATE
ELONGATES > ELONGATE
ELOPE *vb* (of two people) run away secretly to get married
ELOPED > ELOPE
ELOPEMENT > ELOPE
ELOPER > ELOPE **ELOPERS** > ELOPE
ELOPES > ELOPE
ELOPING > ELOPE
ELOPS *n* type of fish
ELOPSES > ELOPS
ELOQUENCE *n* fluent powerful use of language
ELOQUENT *adj* (of speech or writing) fluent and persuasive
ELPEE *n* LP, long-playing record
ELPEES > ELPEE
ELS > EL
ELSE *adv* in addition or more
ELSEWHERE *adv* in or to another place

ELSEWISE *adv* otherwise
ELSHIN *n* cobbler's awl
ELSHINS > ELSHIN
ELSIN *variant of* > ELSHIN
ELSINS > ELSIN
ELT *n* young female pig
ELTCHI *variant of* > ELCHEE
ELTCHIS > ELTCHI
ELTS > ELT
ELUANT *same as* > ELUENT
ELUANTS > ELUANT
ELUATE *n* solution of adsorbed material obtained during the process of elution
ELUATES > ELUATE
ELUCIDATE *vb* make (something difficult) clear
ELUDE *vb* escape from by cleverness or quickness
ELUDED > ELUDE
ELUDER > ELUDE
ELUDERS > ELUDE
ELUDES > ELUDE
ELUDIBLE *adj* able to be eluded
ELUDING > ELUDE
ELUENT *n* solvent used for eluting
ELUENTS > ELUENT
ELUSION > ELUDE
ELUSIONS > ELUDE
ELUSIVE *adj* difficult to catch or remember
ELUSIVELY > ELUSIVE
ELUSORY *adj* avoiding the issue
ELUTE *vb* wash out (a substance) by the action of a solvent
ELUTED > ELUTE
ELUTES > ELUTE
ELUTING > ELUTE
ELUTION > ELUTE
ELUTIONS > ELUTE
ELUTOR > ELUTE
ELUTORS > ELUTE
ELUTRIATE *vb* purify or separate (a substance or mixture) by washing and straining or decanting
ELUVIA > ELUVIUM
ELUVIAL > ELUVIUM
ELUVIATE *vb* remove material suspended in water in a layer of soil by the action of rainfall
ELUVIATED > ELUVIATE
ELUVIATES > ELUVIATE
ELUVIUM *n* mass of sand, silt, etc
ELUVIUMS > ELUVIUM
ELVAN *n* type of rock
ELVANITE *variant of* > ELVAN
ELVANITES > ELVANITE
ELVANS > ELVAN
ELVEN *adj* like an elf
ELVER *n* young eel
ELVERS > ELVER
ELVES > ELF
ELVISH *same as* > ELFISH
ELVISHES > ELVISH
ELVISHLY > ELVISH
ELYSIAN *adj* delightful, blissful
ELYTRA > ELYTRON
ELYTRAL > ELYTRON

ELYTROID > ELYTRON

ELYTRON n either of the horny front wings of beetles and some other insects

ELYTROUS > ELYTRON

ELYTRUM same as > ELYTRON

EM n square of a body of any size of type, used as a unit of measurement

EMACIATE vb become or cause to become abnormally thin

EMACIATED adj abnormally thin

EMACIATES > EMACIATE

EMACS n powerful computer program

EMACSEN > EMACS

EMAIL n electronic mail ▷ vb send a message by electronic mail

EMAILABLE adj capable of being emailed

EMAILED > EMAIL

EMAILER > EMAIL

EMAILERS > EMAILER

EMAILING > EMAIL

EMAILINGS > EMAILING

EMAILS > EMAIL

EMANANT > EMANATE

EMANATE vb issue, proceed from a source

EMANATED > EMANATE

EMANATES > EMANATE

EMANATING > EMANATE

EMANATION n act or instance of emanating

EMANATIST > EMANATE

EMANATIVE > EMANATE

EMANATOR > EMANATE

EMANATORS > EMANATE

EMANATORY > EMANATE

EMBACE variant of > EMBASE

EMBACES > EMBACE

EMBACING > EMBACE

EMBAIL vb enclose in a circle

EMBAILED > EMBAIL

EMBAILING > EMBAIL

EMBAILS > EMBAIL

EMBALE vb bind

EMBALED > EMBALE

EMBALES > EMBALE

EMBALING > EMBALE

EMBALL vb enclose in a circle

EMBALLED > EMBALL

EMBALLING > EMBALL

EMBALLS > EMBALL

EMBALM vb preserve (a corpse) from decay by the use of chemicals etc

EMBALMED > EMBALM

EMBALMER > EMBALM

EMBALMERS > EMBALM

EMBALMING > EMBALM

EMBALMS > EMBALM

EMBANK vb protect, enclose, or confine with an embankment

EMBANKED > EMBANK

EMBANKER > EMBANK

EMBANKERS > EMBANK

EMBANKING > EMBANK

EMBANKS > EMBANK

EMBAR vb close in with bars

EMBARGO n order by a government prohibiting trade with a country ▷ vb put an embargo on

EMBARGOED > EMBARGO

EMBARGOES > EMBARGO

EMBARK vb board a ship or aircraft

EMBARKED > EMBARK

EMBARKING > EMBARK

EMBARKS > EMBARK

EMBARRAS n embarrassment

EMBARRASS vb cause to feel self-conscious or ashamed

EMBARRED > EMBAR

EMBARRING > EMBAR

EMBARS > EMBAR

EMBASE vb degrade or debase

EMBASED > EMBASE

EMBASES > EMBASE

EMBASING > EMBASE

EMBASSADE n embassy

EMBASSAGE n work of an embassy

EMBASSIES > EMBASSY

EMBASSY n offices or official residence of an ambassador

EMBASTE > EMBASE

EMBATHE vb bathe with water

EMBATHED > EMBATHE

EMBATHES > EMBATHE

EMBATHING > EMBATHE

EMBATTLE vb deploy (troops) for battle

EMBATTLED adj having a lot of difficulties

EMBATTLES > EMBATTLE

EMBAY vb form into a bay

EMBAYED > EMBAY

EMBAYING > EMBAY

EMBAYLD archaic past form of > EMBAIL

EMBAYMENT n shape resembling a bay

EMBAYS > EMBAY

EMBED vb fix firmly in something solid ▷ n journalist accompanying an active military unit

EMBEDDED > EMBED

EMBEDDING n practice of assigning or being assigned a journalist to accompany an active military unit

EMBEDMENT > EMBED

EMBEDS > EMBED

EMBELLISH vb decorate

EMBER n glowing piece of wood or coal in a dying fire

EMBERS > EMBER

EMBEZZLE vb steal money that has been entrusted to one

EMBEZZLED > EMBEZZLE

EMBEZZLER > EMBEZZLE

EMBEZZLES > EMBEZZLE

EMBIGGEN vb make bigger

EMBIGGENS > EMBIGGEN

EMBITTER vb make (a person) resentful or bitter

EMBITTERS > EMBITTER

EMBLAZE vb cause to light up

EMBLAZED > EMBLAZE

EMBLAZER > EMBLAZE

EMBLAZERS > EMBLAZE

EMBLAZES > EMBLAZE

EMBLAZING > EMBLAZE

EMBLAZON vb decorate with bright colours

EMBLAZONS > EMBLAZON

EMBLEM n object or design that symbolizes a quality, type, or group ▷ vb represent or signify

EMBLEMA n mosaic decoration

EMBLEMATA > EMBLEMA

EMBLEMED > EMBLEM

EMBLEMING > EMBLEM

EMBLEMISE same as > EMBLEMIZE

EMBLEMIZE vb function as an emblem of

EMBLEMS > EMBLEM

EMBLIC n type of Indian tree

EMBLICS > EMBLIC

EMBLOOM vb adorn with blooms

EMBLOOMED > EMBLOOM

EMBLOOMS > EMBLOOM

EMBLOSSOM vb adorn with blossom

EMBODIED > EMBODY

EMBODIER > EMBODY

EMBODIERS > EMBODY

EMBODIES > EMBODY

EMBODY vb be an example or expression of

EMBODYING > EMBODY

EMBOG vb sink down into a bog

EMBOGGED > EMBOG

EMBOGGING > EMBOG

EMBOGS > EMBOG

EMBOGUE vb go out through a narrow channel or passage

EMBOGUED > EMBOGUE

EMBOGUES > EMBOGUE

EMBOGUING > EMBOGUE

EMBOIL vb enrage or be enraged

EMBOILED > EMBOIL

EMBOILING > EMBOIL

EMBOILS > EMBOIL

EMBOLDEN vb encourage (someone)

EMBOLDENS > EMBOLDEN

EMBOLI > EMBOLUS

EMBOLIC adj of or relating to an embolus or embolism

EMBOLIES > EMBOLY

EMBOLISE same as > EMBOLIZE

EMBOLISED > EMBOLISE

EMBOLISES > EMBOLISE

EMBOLISM n blocking of a blood vessel by a blood clot or air bubble

EMBOLISMS > EMBOLISM

EMBOLIZE vb cause embolism in (a blood vessel)

EMBOLIZED > EMBOLIZE

EMBOLIZES > EMBOLIZE

EMBOLUS n material that blocks a blood vessel

EMBOLUSES > EMBOLUS

EMBOLY n infolding of an outer layer of cells so as to form a pocket in the surface

EMBORDER vb edge or border

EMBORDERS > EMBORDER

EMBOSCATA n sudden attack or raid

EMBOSK vb hide or cover

EMBOSKED > EMBOSK

EMBOSKING > EMBOSK

EMBOSKS > EMBOSK

EMBOSOM vb enclose or envelop, esp protectively

EMBOSOMED > EMBOSOM

EMBOSOMS > EMBOSOM

EMBOSS vb create a decoration that stands out on (a surface)

EMBOSSED adj (of a design or pattern) standing out from a surface

EMBOSSER > EMBOSS

EMBOSSERS > EMBOSS

EMBOSSES > EMBOSS

EMBOSSING n decoration that stands out on (a surface)

EMBOST > EMBOSS

EMBOUND vb surround or encircle

EMBOUNDED > EMBOUND

EMBOUNDS > EMBOUND

EMBOW vb design or create (a structure) in the form of an arch or vault

EMBOWED > EMBOW

EMBOWEL vb bury or embed deeply

EMBOWELED > EMBOWEL

EMBOWELS > EMBOWEL

EMBOWER vb enclose in or as in a bower

EMBOWERED > EMBOWER

EMBOWERS > EMBOWER

EMBOWING > EMBOW

EMBOWMENT > EMBOW

EMBOWS > EMBOW

EMBOX vb put in a box

EMBOXED > EMBOX

EMBOXES > EMBOX

EMBOXING > EMBOX

EMBRACE vb clasp in the arms, hug ▷ n act of embracing

EMBRACED > EMBRACE

EMBRACEOR n person guilty of embracery

EMBRACER > EMBRACE

EMBRACERS > EMBRACE

EMBRACERY n offence of attempting by corrupt means to influence a jury or juror, as by bribery or threats

EMBRACES > EMBRACE

EMBRACING > EMBRACE

EMBRACIVE > EMBRACE

EMBRAID vb braid or interweave

EMBRAIDED > EMBRAID

EMBRAIDS > EMBRAID

EMBRANGLE vb confuse or entangle

EMBRASOR n one who embraces

EMBRASORS > EMBRASOR

EMBRASURE n door or window having splayed sides so that the opening is larger on the inside

EMBRAVE vb adorn or decorate

EMBRAVED > EMBRAVE

EMBRAVES > EMBRAVE

EMBRAVING > EMBRAVE

EMBRAZURE variant of > EMBRASURE

EMBREAD vb braid
EMBREADED > EMBREAD
EMBREADS > EMBREAD
EMBREATHE vb breathe in air
EMBRITTLE vb become brittle
EMBROCATE vb apply a liniment or lotion to (a part of the body)
EMBROGLIO same as **>** IMBROGLIO
EMBROIDER vb decorate with needlework
EMBROIL vb involve (a person) in problems
EMBROILED > EMBROIL
EMBROILER > EMBROIL
EMBROILS > EMBROIL
EMBROWN vb make or become brown
EMBROWNED > EMBROWN
EMBROWNS > EMBROWN
EMBRUE variant spelling of **>** IMBRUE
EMBRUED > EMBRUE
EMBRUES > EMBRUE
EMBRUING > EMBRUE
EMBRUTE variant of **>** IMBRUTE
EMBRUTED > EMBRUTE
EMBRUTES > EMBRUTE
EMBRUTING > EMBRUTE
EMBRYO n unborn creature in the early stages of development
EMBRYOID > EMBRYO
EMBRYOIDS > EMBRYO
EMBRYON variant of **>** EMBRYO
EMBRYONAL same as **>** EMBRYONIC
EMBRYONIC adj at an early stage
EMBRYONS > EMBRYON
EMBRYOS > EMBRYO
EMBRYOTIC variant of **>** EMBRYONIC
EMBUS vb cause (troops) to board a transport vehicle
EMBUSED > EMBUS
EMBUSES > EMBUS
EMBUSIED > EMBUSY
EMBUSIES > EMBUSY
EMBUSING > EMBUS
EMBUSQUE n man who avoids military conscription by obtaining a government job
EMBUSQUES > EMBUSQUE
EMBUSSED > EMBUS
EMBUSSES > EMBUS
EMBUSSING > EMBUS
EMBUSY vb keep occupied
EMBUSYING > EMBUSY
EMCEE n master of ceremonies ▷ vb act as master of ceremonies (for or at)
EMCEED > EMCEE
EMCEEING > EMCEE
EMCEES > EMCEE
EMDASH n long dash in punctuation
EMDASHES > EMDASH
EME n uncle
EMEER variant of **>** EMIR

EMEERATE variant of **>** EMIRATE
EMEERATES > EMEERATE
EMEERS > EMEER
EMEND vb remove errors from
EMENDABLE > EMEND
EMENDALS pl n funds put aside for repairs
EMENDATE vb make corrections
EMENDATED > EMENDATE
EMENDATES > EMENDATE
EMENDATOR n one who emends a text
EMENDED > EMEND
EMENDER > EMEND
EMENDERS > EMEND
EMENDING > EMEND
EMENDS > EMEND
EMERALD n bright green precious stone ▷ adj bright green
EMERALDS > EMERALD
EMERAUDE archaic variant of **>** EMERALD
EMERAUDES > EMERAUDE
EMERG n part of a hospital dealing with emergencies
EMERGE vb come into view
EMERGED > EMERGE
EMERGENCE n act or process of emerging
EMERGENCY n sudden unforeseen occurrence needing immediate action
EMERGENT adj coming into being or notice ▷ n aquatic plant with stem and leaves above the water
EMERGENTS > EMERGENT
EMERGES > EMERGE
EMERGING > EMERGE
EMERGS > EMERG
EMERIED > EMERY
EMERIES > EMERY
EMERITA adj retired, but retaining an honorary title ▷ n woman who is retired, but retains an honorary title
EMERITAE > EMERITA
EMERITAS > EMERITA
EMERITI > EMERITUS
EMERITUS adj retired, but retaining an honorary title ▷ n man who is retired, but retains an honorary title
EMEROD n haemorrhoid
EMERODS > EMEROD
EMEROID variant of **>** EMEROD
EMEROIDS > EMEROID
EMERSE same as **>** EMERSED
EMERSED adj protruding above the surface of the water
EMERSION n act or an instance of emerging
EMERSIONS > EMERSION
EMERY n hard mineral used for smoothing and polishing ▷ vb apply emery to
EMERYING > EMERY
EMES > EME
EMESES > EMESIS
EMESIS technical name for **>** VOMITING
EMESISES > EMESIS

EMETIC n substance that causes vomiting ▷ adj causing vomiting
EMETICAL same as **>** EMETIC
EMETICS > EMETIC
EMETIN same as **>** EMETINE
EMETINE n white bitter poisonous alkaloid
EMETINES > EMETINE
EMETINS > EMETIN
EMEU variant of **>** EMU
EMEUS > EMEU
EMEUTE n uprising or rebellion
EMEUTES > EMEUTE
EMIC adj of or relating to a significant linguistic unit ▷ n emic viewpoint or approach
EMICANT > EMICATE
EMICATE vb twinkle
EMICATED > EMICATE
EMICATES > EMICATE
EMICATING > EMICATE
EMICATION > EMICATE
EMICS > EMIC
EMICTION n passing of urine
EMICTIONS > EMICTION
EMICTORY > EMICTION
EMIGRANT n person who leaves one place or country, esp a native country, to settle in another
EMIGRANTS > EMIGRANT
EMIGRATE vb go and settle in another country
EMIGRATED > EMIGRATE
EMIGRATES > EMIGRATE
EMIGRE n someone who has left his or her native country for political reasons
EMIGREE n female emigre
EMIGREES > EMIGREE
EMIGRES > EMIGRE
EMINENCE n position of superiority or fame
EMINENCES > EMINENCE
EMINENCY same as **>** EMINENCE
EMINENT adj distinguished, well-known
EMINENTLY > EMINENT
EMIR n Muslim ruler
EMIRATE n emir's country
EMIRATES > EMIRATE
EMIRS > EMIR
EMISSARY n agent sent on a mission by a government ▷ adj (of veins) draining blood from sinuses in the dura mater to veins outside the skull
EMISSILE adj able to be emitted
EMISSION n act of giving out heat, light, a smell, etc
EMISSIONS > EMISSION
EMISSIVE > EMISSION
EMIT vb give out
EMITS > EMIT
EMITTANCE > EMIT
EMITTED > EMIT
EMITTER n person or thing that emits
EMITTERS > EMITTER
EMITTING > EMIT

EMLETS pl n as in blood-drop emlets Chilean plant
EMMA n former communications code for the letter A
EMMARBLE vb decorate with marble
EMMARBLED > EMMARBLE
EMMARBLES > EMMARBLE
EMMAS > EMMA
EMMER n variety of wheat
EMMERS > EMMER
EMMESH variant of **>** ENMESH
EMMESHED > EMMESH
EMMESHES > EMMESH
EMMESHING > EMMESH
EMMET n tourist or holiday-maker
EMMETROPE n person whose vision is normal
EMMETS > EMMET
EMMEW vb restrict
EMMEWED > EMMEW
EMMEWING > EMMEW
EMMEWS > EMMEW
EMMOVE vb cause emotion in
EMMOVED > EMMOVE
EMMOVES > EMMOVE
EMMOVING > EMMOVE
EMMY n award for outstanding television performances and productions
EMMYS > EMMY
EMO n type of music
EMOCORE n punk rock with lyrics that deal with emotional subjects
EMOCORES > EMOCORE
EMODIN n type of chemical compound
EMODINS > EMODIN
EMOJI n digital icon used in electronic communication
EMOJIS > EMOJI
EMOLLIATE vb make soft or smooth
EMOLLIENT adj softening, soothing ▷ n substance which softens or soothes the skin
EMOLUMENT n fees or wages from employment
EMONG variant of **>** AMONG
EMONGES variant of **>** AMONG
EMONGEST variant of **>** AMONGST
EMONGST variant of **>** AMONGST
EMOS > EMO
EMOTE vb display exaggerated emotion, as if acting
EMOTED > EMOTE
EMOTER > EMOTE
EMOTERS > EMOTE
EMOTES > EMOTE
EMOTICON n any of several combinations of symbols used in email and texting
EMOTICONS > EMOTICON
EMOTING > EMOTE
EMOTION n strong feeling
EMOTIONAL adj readily affected by or appealing to the emotions
EMOTIONS > EMOTION

EMOTIVE adj tending to arouse emotion
EMOTIVELY > EMOTIVE
EMOTIVISM n theory that moral utterances do not have a truth value but express the feelings of the speaker, so that *murder is wrong* is equivalent to *down with murder*
EMOTIVITY > EMOTIVE
EMOVE vb cause to feel emotion
EMOVED > EMOVE
EMOVES > EMOVE
EMOVING > EMOVE
EMPACKET vb wrap up
EMPACKETS > EMPACKET
EMPAESTIC adj embossed
EMPAIRE variant of > IMPAIR
EMPAIRED > EMPAIRE
EMPAIRES > EMPAIRE
EMPAIRING > EMPAIRE
EMPALE less common spelling of > IMPALE
EMPALED > EMPALE
EMPALER > EMPALE
EMPALERS > EMPALE
EMPALES > EMPALE
EMPALING > EMPALE
EMPANADA n Spanish meat-filled pastry
EMPANADAS > EMPANADA
EMPANEL vb enter on a list (names of persons to be summoned for jury service)
EMPANELED > EMPANEL
EMPANELS > EMPANEL
EMPANOPLY vb put armour on
EMPARE archaic variant of > IMPAIR
EMPARED > EMPARE
EMPARES > EMPARE
EMPARING > EMPARE
EMPARL variant of > IMPARL
EMPARLED > EMPARL
EMPARLING > EMPARL
EMPARLS > EMPARL
EMPART variant of > IMPART
EMPARTED > EMPART
EMPARTING > EMPART
EMPARTS > EMPART
EMPATHIC adj of or relating to empathy
EMPATHIES > EMPATHY
EMPATHISE same as > EMPATHIZE
EMPATHIST > EMPATHY
EMPATHIZE vb sense and understand someone else's feelings as if they were one's own
EMPATHY n ability to understand someone else's feelings
EMPATRON vb treat in the manner of a patron
EMPATRONS > EMPATRON
EMPAYRE archaic variant of > IMPAIR
EMPAYRED > EMPAYRE
EMPAYRES > EMPAYRE
EMPAYRING > EMPAYRE
EMPEACH variant of > IMPEACH

EMPEACHED > EMPEACH
EMPEACHES > EMPEACH
EMPENNAGE n rear part of an aircraft, comprising the fin, rudder, and tailplane
EMPEOPLE vb bring people into
EMPEOPLED > EMPEOPLE
EMPEOPLES > EMPEOPLE
EMPERCE archaic variant of > EMPIERCE
EMPERCED > EMPERCE
EMPERCES > EMPERCE
EMPERCING > EMPERCE
EMPERIES > EMPERY
EMPERISE variant of > EMPERIZE
EMPERISED > EMPERISE
EMPERISES > EMPERISE
EMPERISH vb damage or harm
EMPERIZE vb act like an emperor
EMPERIZED > EMPERIZE
EMPERIZES > EMPERIZE
EMPEROR n ruler of an empire
EMPERORS > EMPEROR
EMPERY n dominion or power
EMPHASES > EMPHASIS
EMPHASIS n special importance or significance
EMPHASISE same as > EMPHASIZE
EMPHASIZE vb give emphasis or prominence to
EMPHATIC adj showing emphasis ▷ n emphatic consonant, as used in Arabic
EMPHATICS > EMPHATIC
EMPHLYSES > EMPHLYSIS
EMPHLYSIS n outbreak of blisters on the body
EMPHYSEMA n condition in which the air sacs of the lungs are grossly enlarged, causing breathlessness
EMPIERCE vb pierce or cut
EMPIERCED > EMPIERCE
EMPIERCES > EMPIERCE
EMPIGHT adj attached or positioned ▷ vb attach or position
EMPIGHTED > EMPIGHT
EMPIGHTS > EMPIGHT
EMPIRE n group of territories under the rule of one state or person
EMPIRES > EMPIRE
EMPIRIC n person who relies on empirical methods
EMPIRICAL adj relying on experiment or experience, not on theory ▷ n posterior probability of an event derived on the basis of its observed frequency in a sample
EMPIRICS > EMPIRIC
EMPLACE vb put in place or position
EMPLACED > EMPLACE
EMPLACES > EMPLACE
EMPLACING > EMPLACE
EMPLANE vb board or put on board an aeroplane

EMPLANED > EMPLANE
EMPLANES > EMPLANE
EMPLANING > EMPLANE
EMPLASTER vb cover with plaster
EMPLASTIC adj sticky
EMPLASTRA n plural of emplastrum, a medicated plaster
EMPLEACH variant of > IMPLEACH
EMPLECTON n type of masonry filled with rubbish
EMPLECTUM variant of > EMPLECTON
EMPLONGE variant of > IMPLUNGE
EMPLONGED > EMPLONGE
EMPLONGES > EMPLONGE
EMPLOY vb engage or make use of the services of (a person) in return for money ▷ n state of being employed
EMPLOYE same as > EMPLOYEE
EMPLOYED > EMPLOY
EMPLOYEE n person who is hired to work for someone in return for payment
EMPLOYEES > EMPLOYEE
EMPLOYER n person or organization that employs someone
EMPLOYERS > EMPLOYER
EMPLOYES > EMPLOYE
EMPLOYING > EMPLOY
EMPLOYS > EMPLOY
EMPLUME vb put a plume on
EMPLUMED > EMPLUME
EMPLUMES > EMPLUME
EMPLUMING > EMPLUME
EMPOISON vb embitter or corrupt
EMPOISONS > EMPOISON
EMPOLDER variant spelling of > IMPOLDER
EMPOLDERS > EMPOLDER
EMPORIA > EMPORIUM
EMPORIUM n large general shop
EMPORIUMS > EMPORIUM
EMPOWER vb enable, authorize
EMPOWERED > EMPOWER
EMPOWERS > EMPOWER
EMPRESS n woman who rules an empire
EMPRESSE adj keen; zealous
EMPRESSES > EMPRESS
EMPRISE n chivalrous or daring enterprise
EMPRISES > EMPRISE
EMPRIZE variant of > EMPRISE
EMPRIZES > EMPRIZE
EMPT vb empty
EMPTED > EMPT
EMPTIABLE > EMPTY
EMPTIED > EMPTY
EMPTIER > EMPTY
EMPTIERS > EMPTY
EMPTIES > EMPTY
EMPTIEST > EMPTY
EMPTILY > EMPTY
EMPTINESS > EMPTY
EMPTING > EMPT
EMPTINGS variant of > EMPTINS

EMPTINS pl n liquid leavening agent made from potatoes
EMPTION n process of buying something
EMPTIONAL > EMPTION
EMPTIONS > EMPTION
EMPTS > EMPT
EMPTY adj containing nothing ▷ vb make or become empty ▷ n empty container, esp a bottle
EMPTYING > EMPTY
EMPTYINGS > EMPTY
EMPTYSES > EMPTYSIS
EMPTYSIS n act of spitting up blood
EMPURPLE vb make or become purple
EMPURPLED > EMPURPLE
EMPURPLES > EMPURPLE
EMPUSA n goblin in Greek mythology
EMPUSAS > EMPUSA
EMPUSE variant of > EMPUSA
EMPUSES > EMPUSE
EMPYEMA n collection of pus in a body cavity
EMPYEMAS > EMPYEMA
EMPYEMATA > EMPYEMA
EMPYEMIC > EMPYEMA
EMPYESES > EMPYESIS
EMPYESIS n pus-filled boil on the skin
EMPYREAL variant of > EMPYREAN
EMPYREAN n heavens or sky ▷ adj of or relating to the sky or the heavens
EMPYREANS > EMPYREAN
EMPYREUMA n smell and taste associated with burning vegetable and animal matter
EMS > EM
EMU n large Australian flightless bird with long legs
EMULATE vb attempt to equal or surpass by imitating
EMULATED > EMULATE
EMULATES > EMULATE
EMULATING > EMULATE
EMULATION n act of emulating or imitating
EMULATIVE > EMULATE
EMULATOR > EMULATE
EMULATORS > EMULATE
EMULE variant of > EMULATE
EMULED > EMULE
EMULES > EMULE
EMULGE vb remove liquid from
EMULGED > EMULGE
EMULGENCE > EMULGE
EMULGENT > EMULGE
EMULGES > EMULGE
EMULGING > EMULGE
EMULING > EMULE
EMULOUS adj desiring or aiming to equal or surpass another
EMULOUSLY > EMULOUS
EMULSIBLE > EMULSIFY
EMULSIFY vb (of two liquids) join together
EMULSIN n enzyme that is found in almonds

EMULSINS > EMULSIN
EMULSION n light-sensitive coating on photographic film ▷ vb paint with emulsion paint
EMULSIONS > EMULSION
EMULSIVE > EMULSION
EMULSOID n sol with a liquid disperse phase
EMULSOIDS > EMULSOID
EMULSOR n device that emulsifies
EMULSORS > EMULSOR
EMUNCTION > EMUNCTORY
EMUNCTORY adj relating to a bodily organ or duct with an excretory function ▷ n excretory organ or duct
EMUNGE vb clean or clear out
EMUNGED > EMUNGE
EMUNGES > EMUNGE
EMUNGING > EMUNGE
EMURE variant of > IMMURE
EMURED > EMURE
EMURES > EMURE
EMURING > EMURE
EMUS > EMU
EMYD n freshwater tortoise or terrapin
EMYDE same as > EMYD
EMYDES > EMYDE
EMYDS > EMYD
EMYS n freshwater tortoise or terrapin
EN n unit of measurement, half the width of an em
ENABLE vb provide (a person) with the means (to do something)
ENABLED > ENABLE
ENABLER > ENABLE
ENABLERS > ENABLE
ENABLES > ENABLE
ENABLING > ENABLE
ENACT vb establish by law
ENACTABLE > ENACT
ENACTED > ENACT
ENACTING > ENACT
ENACTION > ENACT
ENACTIONS > ENACT
ENACTIVE > ENACT
ENACTMENT > ENACT
ENACTOR > ENACT
ENACTORS > ENACT
ENACTORY > ENACT
ENACTS > ENACT
ENACTURE > ENACT
ENACTURES > ENACT
ENALAPRIL n ACE inhibitor used to treat high blood pressure and congestive heart failure
ENALLAGE n act of using one grammatical form in the place of another
ENALLAGES > ENALLAGE
ENAMEL n glasslike coating applied to metal etc to preserve the surface ▷ vb cover with enamel
ENAMELED > ENAMEL
ENAMELER > ENAMEL
ENAMELERS > ENAMEL
ENAMELING > ENAMEL
ENAMELIST > ENAMEL
ENAMELLED > ENAMEL
ENAMELLER > ENAMEL

ENAMELS > ENAMEL
ENAMINE n type of unsaturated compound
ENAMINES > ENAMINE
ENAMOR same as > ENAMOUR
ENAMORADO n beloved one
ENAMORED same as > ENAMOURED
ENAMORING > ENAMOR
ENAMORS > ENAMOR
ENAMOUR vb inspire with love
ENAMOURED adj inspired with love
ENAMOURS > ENAMOUR
ENANTHEMA n ulcer on a mucous membrane
ENARCH variant of > INARCH
ENARCHED > ENARCH
ENARCHES > ENARCH
ENARCHING > ENARCH
ENARGITE n sulphide of copper and arsenic
ENARGITES > ENARGITE
ENARM vb provide with arms
ENARMED > ENARM
ENARMING > ENARM
ENARMS > ENARM
ENATE adj growing out or outwards ▷ n relative on the mother's side
ENATES > ENATE
ENATIC adj related on one's mother's side
ENATION > ENATE
ENATIONS > ENATE
ENAUNTER conj in case that
ENCAENIA n festival of dedication or commemoration
ENCAENIAS > ENCAENIA
ENCAGE vb confine in or as in a cage
ENCAGED > ENCAGE
ENCAGES > ENCAGE
ENCAGING > ENCAGE
ENCALM vb becalm, settle
ENCALMED > ENCALM
ENCALMING > ENCALM
ENCALMS > ENCALM
ENCAMP vb set up in a camp
ENCAMPED > ENCAMP
ENCAMPING > ENCAMP
ENCAMPS > ENCAMP
ENCANTHIS n tumour of the eye
ENCAPSULE vb enclose or be enclosed in or as if in a capsule
ENCARPUS n decoration of fruit or flowers on a frieze
ENCASE vb enclose or cover completely
ENCASED > ENCASE
ENCASES > ENCASE
ENCASH vb exchange (a cheque) for cash
ENCASHED > ENCASH
ENCASHES > ENCASH
ENCASHING > ENCASH
ENCASING > ENCASE
ENCASTRE adj (of a beam) fixed at the ends
ENCAUSTIC adj decorated by any process involving burning in colours, esp by inlaying coloured clays and

baking or by fusing wax colours to the surface ▷ n process of burning in colours
ENCAVE variant of > INCAVE
ENCAVED > ENCAVE
ENCAVES > ENCAVE
ENCAVING > ENCAVE
ENCEINTE n boundary wall enclosing a defended area
ENCEINTES > ENCEINTE
ENCEPHALA n brains
ENCHAFE vb heat up
ENCHAFED > ENCHAFE
ENCHAFES > ENCHAFE
ENCHAFING > ENCHAFE
ENCHAIN vb bind with chains
ENCHAINED > ENCHAIN
ENCHAINS > ENCHAIN
ENCHANT vb delight and fascinate
ENCHANTED > ENCHANT
ENCHANTER > ENCHANT
ENCHANTS > ENCHANT
ENCHARGE vb give into the custody of
ENCHARGED > ENCHARGE
ENCHARGES > ENCHARGE
ENCHARM vb enchant
ENCHARMED > ENCHARM
ENCHARMS > ENCHARM
ENCHASE less common word for > CHASE
ENCHASED > ENCHASE
ENCHASER > ENCHASE
ENCHASERS > ENCHASE
ENCHASES > ENCHASE
ENCHASING > ENCHASE
ENCHEASON n reason
ENCHEER vb cheer up
ENCHEERED > ENCHEER
ENCHEERS > ENCHEER
ENCHILADA n Mexican dish of a tortilla filled with meat, served with chilli sauce
ENCHORIAL adj of or used in a particular country: used esp of the popular (demotic) writing of the ancient Egyptians
ENCHORIC same as > ENCHORIAL
ENCIERRO n Spanish bull run
ENCIERROS > ENCIERRO
ENCINA n type of oak
ENCINAL > ENCINA
ENCINAS > ENCINA
ENCIPHER vb convert (a message, document, etc) from plain text into code or cipher
ENCIPHERS > ENCIPHER
ENCIRCLE vb form a circle around
ENCIRCLED > ENCIRCLE
ENCIRCLES > ENCIRCLE
ENCLASP vb clasp
ENCLASPED > ENCLASP
ENCLASPS > ENCLASP
ENCLAVE n part of a country entirely surrounded by another ▷ vb hold in an enclave
ENCLAVED > ENCLAVE
ENCLAVES > ENCLAVE
ENCLAVING > ENCLAVE

ENCLISES > ENCLISIS
ENCLISIS n state of being enclitic
ENCLITIC adj relating to a monosyllabic word treated as a suffix ▷ n enclitic word or linguistic form
ENCLITICS > ENCLITIC
ENCLOSE vb surround completely
ENCLOSED > ENCLOSE
ENCLOSER > ENCLOSE
ENCLOSERS > ENCLOSE
ENCLOSES > ENCLOSE
ENCLOSING > ENCLOSE
ENCLOSURE n area of land enclosed by a fence, wall, or hedge
ENCLOTHE vb clothe
ENCLOTHED > ENCLOTHE
ENCLOTHES > ENCLOTHE
ENCLOUD vb hide with clouds
ENCLOUDED > ENCLOUD
ENCLOUDS > ENCLOUD
ENCODABLE > ENCODE
ENCODE vb convert (a message) into code
ENCODED > ENCODE
ENCODER > ENCODE
ENCODERS > ENCODE
ENCODES > ENCODE
ENCODING n act of encoding
ENCODINGS > ENCODING
ENCOLOUR vb give a colour to
ENCOLOURS > ENCOLOUR
ENCOLPIA > ENCOLPION
ENCOLPION n religious symbol worn on the breast
ENCOLPIUM variant of > ENCOLPION
ENCOLURE n mane of a horse
ENCOLURES > ENCOLURE
ENCOMIA > ENCOMIUM
ENCOMIAST n person who speaks or writes an encomium
ENCOMION variant of > ENCOMIUM
ENCOMIUM n formal expression of praise
ENCOMIUMS > ENCOMIUM
ENCOMPASS vb surround
ENCORE interj again, once more ▷ n extra performance due to enthusiastic demand ▷ vb demand an extra or repeated performance
ENCORED > ENCORE
ENCORES > ENCORE
ENCORING > ENCORE
ENCOUNTER vb meet unexpectedly ▷ n unexpected meeting
ENCOURAGE vb inspire with confidence
ENCRADLE vb put in a cradle
ENCRADLED > ENCRADLE
ENCRADLES > ENCRADLE
ENCRATIES > ENCRATY
ENCRATY n control of one's desires, actions, etc
ENCREASE variant form of > INCREASE
ENCREASED > ENCREASE

e

e

ENCREASES > ENCREASE
ENCRIMSON vb make crimson
ENCRINAL > ENCRINITE
ENCRINIC > ENCRINITE
ENCRINITE n sedimentary rock formed almost exclusively from the skeletal plates of crinoids
ENCROACH vb intrude gradually on a person's rights or land
ENCRUST vb cover with a layer of something
ENCRUSTED > ENCRUST
ENCRUSTS > ENCRUST
ENCRYPT vb put (a message) into code
ENCRYPTED > ENCRYPT
ENCRYPTS > ENCRYPT
ENCUMBER vb hinder or impede
ENCUMBERS > ENCUMBER
ENCURTAIN vb cover or surround with curtains
ENCYCLIC n letter sent by the Pope to all bishops
ENCYCLICS > ENCYCLIC
ENCYST vb enclose or become enclosed by a cyst, thick membrane, or shell
ENCYSTED > ENCYST
ENCYSTING > ENCYST
ENCYSTS > ENCYST
END n furthest point or part ▷ vb bring or come to a finish
ENDAMAGE vb cause injury to
ENDAMAGED > ENDAMAGE
ENDAMAGES > ENDAMAGE
ENDAMEBA same as > ENDAMOEBA
ENDAMEBAE > ENDAMEBA
ENDAMEBAS > ENDAMEBA
ENDAMEBIC > ENDAMEBA
ENDAMOEBA same as > ENTAMOEBA
ENDANGER vb put in danger
ENDANGERS > ENDANGER
ENDARCH adj having the first-formed xylem internal to that formed later
ENDARCHY n state of being endarch
ENDART variant of > INDART
ENDARTED > ENDART
ENDARTING > ENDART
ENDARTS > ENDART
ENDASH n short dash in punctuation
ENDASHES > ENDASH
ENDBRAIN n part of the brain
ENDBRAINS > ENDBRAIN
ENDCAP n display placed at the end of a shop aisle
ENDCAPS > ENDCAP
ENDEAR vb cause to be liked
ENDEARED > ENDEAR
ENDEARING adj giving rise to love or esteem
ENDEARS > ENDEAR
ENDEAVOR same as > ENDEAVOUR
ENDEAVORS > ENDEAVOR
ENDEAVOUR vb try ▷ n effort

ENDECAGON n figure with eleven sides
ENDED > END
ENDEICTIC > ENDEIXIS
ENDEIXES > ENDEIXIS
ENDEIXIS n sign or mark
ENDEMIAL same as > ENDEMIC
ENDEMIC adj present within a particular area or group of people ▷ n endemic disease or plant
ENDEMICAL adj endemic
ENDEMICS > ENDEMIC
ENDEMISM > ENDEMIC
ENDEMISMS > ENDEMIC
ENDENIZEN vb make a denizen
ENDER > END
ENDERMIC adj (of a medicine) acting by absorption through the skin
ENDERON variant of > ANDIRON
ENDERONS > ENDERON
ENDERS > END
ENDEW variant of > ENDUE
ENDEWED > ENDEW
ENDEWING > ENDEW
ENDEWS > ENDEW
ENDEXINE n inner layer of an exine
ENDEXINES > ENDEXINE
ENDGAME n closing stage of a game of chess
ENDGAMES > ENDGAME
ENDGATE n tailboard of a vehicle
ENDGATES > ENDGATE
ENDING n last part or conclusion of something
ENDINGS > ENDING
ENDIRON variant of > ANDIRON
ENDIRONS > ENDIRON
ENDITE variant of > INDICT
ENDITED > ENDITE
ENDITES > ENDITE
ENDITING > ENDITE
ENDIVE n curly-leaved plant used in salads
ENDIVES > ENDIVE
ENDLANG variant of > ENDLONG
ENDLEAF n endpaper in a book
ENDLEAFS > ENDLEAF
ENDLEAVES > ENDLEAF
ENDLESS adj having no end
ENDLESSLY > ENDLESS
ENDLONG adv lengthways or on end
ENDMOST adj nearest the end
ENDNOTE n note at the end of a section of writing
ENDNOTES > ENDNOTE
ENDOBLAST less common name for > ENDODERM
ENDOCARP n inner layer of a fruit
ENDOCARPS > ENDOCARP
ENDOCAST n cast made of the inside of a cranial cavity to show the size and shape of a brain
ENDOCASTS > ENDOCAST

ENDOCRINE adj relating to the glands which secrete hormones directly into the bloodstream ▷ n endocrine gland
ENDOCYTIC adj involving absorption of cells
ENDODERM n inner germ layer of an animal embryo
ENDODERMS > ENDODERM
ENDODYNE same as > AUTODYNE
ENDOERGIC adj (of a nuclear reaction) occurring with absorption of energy
ENDOGAMIC > ENDOGAMY
ENDOGAMY n marriage within one's own tribe or similar unit
ENDOGEN n plant that increases in size by internal growth
ENDOGENIC adj formed or occurring inside the earth
ENDOGENS > ENDOGEN
ENDOGENY n development by internal growth
ENDOLYMPH n fluid that fills the membranous labyrinth of the internal ear
ENDOMIXES > ENDOMIXIS
ENDOMIXIS n reorganization of certain nuclei with some protozoa
ENDOMORPH n person with a fat and heavy body build: said to be correlated with viscerotonia
ENDOPHAGY n cannibalism within the same group or tribe
ENDOPHYTE n fungus, or occasionally an alga or other organism, that lives within a plant
ENDOPLASM n inner cytoplasm in some cells, esp protozoa, which is more granular and fluid than the outer cytoplasm
ENDOPOD n inner branch of a two-branched crustacean
ENDOPODS > ENDOPOD
ENDOPROCT n small animal living in water
ENDORPHIN n chemical occurring in the brain, which has a similar effect to morphine
ENDORSE vb give approval to
ENDORSED > ENDORSE
ENDORSEE n person in whose favour a negotiable instrument is endorsed
ENDORSEES > ENDORSEE
ENDORSER > ENDORSE
ENDORSERS > ENDORSE
ENDORSES > ENDORSE
ENDORSING > ENDORSE
ENDORSIVE > ENDORSE
ENDORSOR > ENDORSE
ENDORSORS > ENDORSE
ENDOSARC same as > ENDOPLASM
ENDOSARCS > ENDOSARC
ENDOSCOPE n long slender medical instrument used for examining the interior of

hollow organs including the lung, stomach, bladder and bowel
ENDOSCOPY > ENDOSCOPE
ENDOSMOS same as > ENDOSMOSE
ENDOSMOSE n osmosis in which water enters a cell or organism from the surrounding solution
ENDOSOME n sac within a biological cell
ENDOSOMES > ENDOSOME
ENDOSPERM n tissue within the seed of a flowering plant that surrounds and nourishes the developing embryo
ENDOSPORE n small asexual spore produced by some bacteria and algae
ENDOSS vb endorse
ENDOSSED > ENDOSS
ENDOSSES > ENDOSS
ENDOSSING > ENDOSS
ENDOSTEA > ENDOSTEUM
ENDOSTEAL > ENDOSTEUM
ENDOSTEUM n highly vascular membrane lining the marrow cavity of long bones, such as the femur and humerus
ENDOSTYLE n groove or fold in the pharynx of various chordates
ENDOTHERM n animal with warm blood
ENDOTOXIC > ENDOTOXIN
ENDOTOXIN n toxin contained within the protoplasm of an organism, esp a bacterium, and liberated only at death
ENDOW vb provide permanent income for
ENDOWED > ENDOW
ENDOWER > ENDOW
ENDOWERS > ENDOW
ENDOWING > ENDOW
ENDOWMENT n money given to an institution, such as a hospital
ENDOWS > ENDOW
ENDOZOA > ENDOZOON
ENDOZOIC adj (of a plant) living within an animal
ENDOZOON variant of > ENTOZOON
ENDPAPER n either of two leaves pasted to the inside of the cover of a book
ENDPAPERS > ENDPAPER
ENDPLATE n any usually flat platelike structure at the end of something
ENDPLATES > ENDPLATE
ENDPLAY n technique in card games ▷ vb force (an opponent) to make a particular lead near the end of a hand
ENDPLAYED > ENDPLAY
ENDPLAYS > ENDPLAY
ENDPOINT n point at which anything is complete
ENDPOINTS > ENDPOINT
ENDRIN n type of insecticide
ENDRINS > ENDRIN

ENDS > END
ENDSHIP *n* small village
ENDSHIPS > ENDSHIP
ENDUE *vb* invest or provide, as with some quality or trait
ENDUED > ENDUE
ENDUES > ENDUE
ENDUING > ENDUE
ENDUNGEON *vb* put in a dungeon
ENDURABLE > ENDURE
ENDURABLY > ENDURE
ENDURANCE *n* act or power of enduring
ENDURE *vb* bear (hardship) patiently
ENDURED > ENDURE
ENDURER > ENDURE
ENDURERS > ENDURE
ENDURES > ENDURE
ENDURING *adj* long-lasting
ENDURO *n* long-distance race for vehicles
ENDUROS > ENDURO
ENDWAYS *adv* having the end forwards or upwards ▷ *adj* vertical or upright
ENDWISE *same as* **>** ENDWAYS
ENDYSES > ENDYSIS
ENDYSIS *n* formation of new layers of integument after ecdysis
ENDZONE *n* (in American football) area at either end of the playing field
ENDZONES > ENDZONE
ENE *variant of* **>** EVEN
ENEMA *n* medicine that helps to empty the bowels
ENEMAS > ENEMA
ENEMATA > ENEMA
ENEMIES > ENEMY
ENEMY *n* hostile person or nation, opponent ▷ *adj* of or belonging to an enemy
ENERGETIC *adj* having or showing energy and enthusiasm
ENERGIC > ENERGY
ENERGID *n* nucleus and cytoplasm in a syncytium
ENERGIDS > ENERGID
ENERGIES > ENERGY
ENERGISE *same as* **>** ENERGIZE
ENERGISED > ENERGISE
ENERGISER > ENERGISE
ENERGISES > ENERGISE
ENERGIZE *vb* give vigour to
ENERGIZED > ENERGIZE
ENERGIZER > ENERGIZE
ENERGIZES > ENERGIZE
ENERGUMEN *n* person thought to be possessed by an evil spirit
ENERGY *n* capacity for intense activity
ENERVATE *vb* deprive of strength or vitality ▷ *adj* deprived of strength or vitality
ENERVATED > ENERVATE
ENERVATES > ENERVATE
ENERVATOR > ENERVATE
ENERVE *vb* enervate
ENERVED > ENERVE

ENERVES > ENERVE
ENERVING > ENERVE
ENES > ENE
ENEW *vb* force a bird into water
ENEWED > ENEW
ENEWING > ENEW
ENEWS > ENEW
ENFACE *vb* write, print, or stamp (something) on the face of (a document)
ENFACED > ENFACE
ENFACES > ENFACE
ENFACING > ENFACE
ENFANT *n* French child
ENFANTS > ENFANT
ENFEEBLE *vb* weaken
ENFEEBLED > ENFEEBLE
ENFEEBLER > ENFEEBLE
ENFEEBLES > ENFEEBLE
ENFELON *vb* infuriate
ENFELONED > ENFELON
ENFELONS > ENFELON
ENFEOFF *vb* invest (a person) with possession of a freehold estate in land
ENFEOFFED > ENFEOFF
ENFEOFFS > ENFEOFF
ENFESTED *adj* made bitter
ENFETTER *vb* fetter
ENFETTERS > ENFETTER
ENFEVER *vb* make feverish
ENFEVERED > ENFEVER
ENFEVERS > ENFEVER
ENFIERCE *vb* make ferocious
ENFIERCED > ENFIERCE
ENFIERCES > ENFIERCE
ENFILADE *n* burst of gunfire sweeping from end to end along a line of troops ▷ *vb* attack with an enfilade
ENFILADED > ENFILADE
ENFILADES > ENFILADE
ENFILED *adj* passed through
ENFIRE *vb* set alight
ENFIRED > ENFIRE
ENFIRES > ENFIRE
ENFIRING > ENFIRE
ENFIX *variant of* **>** INFIX
ENFIXED > ENFIX
ENFIXES > ENFIX
ENFIXING > ENFIX
ENFLAME *variant of* **>** INFLAME
ENFLAMED > ENFLAME
ENFLAMES > ENFLAME
ENFLAMING > ENFLAME
ENFLESH *vb* make flesh
ENFLESHED > ENFLESH
ENFLESHES > ENFLESH
ENFLOWER *vb* put flowers on
ENFLOWERS > ENFLOWER
ENFOLD *vb* cover by wrapping something around
ENFOLDED > ENFOLD
ENFOLDER > ENFOLD
ENFOLDERS > ENFOLD
ENFOLDING > ENFOLD
ENFOLDS > ENFOLD
ENFORCE *vb* impose obedience (to a law etc)
ENFORCED > ENFORCE
ENFORCER > ENFORCE
ENFORCERS > ENFORCE

ENFORCES > ENFORCE
ENFORCING > ENFORCE
ENFOREST *vb* make into a forest
ENFORESTS > ENFOREST
ENFORM *variant of* **>** INFORM
ENFORMED > ENFORM
ENFORMING > ENFORM
ENFORMS > ENFORM
ENFRAME *vb* put inside a frame
ENFRAMED > ENFRAME
ENFRAMES > ENFRAME
ENFRAMING > ENFRAME
ENFREE *vb* release, make free
ENFREED > ENFREE
ENFREEDOM *variant of* **>** ENFREE
ENFREEING > ENFREE
ENFREES > ENFREE
ENFREEZE *vb* freeze
ENFREEZES > ENFREEZE
ENFROSEN *archaic past participle of* **>** ENFREEZE
ENFROZE > ENFREEZE
ENFROZEN > ENFREEZE
ENG *another name for* **>** AGMA
ENGAGE *vb* take part, participate ▷ *adj* (of an artist) morally or politically committed to some ideology
ENGAGED *adj* pledged to be married
ENGAGEDLY > ENGAGED
ENGAGEE *adj* (of a female artist) morally or politically committed to some ideology
ENGAGER > ENGAGE
ENGAGERS > ENGAGE
ENGAGES > ENGAGE
ENGAGING *adj* charming
ENGAOL *vb* put into gaol
ENGAOLED > ENGAOL
ENGAOLING > ENGAOL
ENGAOLS > ENGAOL
ENGARLAND *vb* cover with garlands
ENGENDER *vb* produce, cause to occur
ENGENDERS > ENGENDER
ENGENDURE > ENGENDER
ENGILD *vb* cover with or as if with gold
ENGILDED > ENGILD
ENGILDING > ENGILD
ENGILDS > ENGILD
ENGILT > ENGILD
ENGINE *n* any machine which converts energy into mechanical work ▷ *vb* put an engine in
ENGINED > ENGINE
ENGINEER *n* person trained in any branch of engineering ▷ *vb* plan in a clever manner
ENGINEERS > ENGINEER
ENGINER > ENGINE
ENGINERS > ENGINE
ENGINERY *n* collection or assembly of engines
ENGINES > ENGINE
ENGINING > ENGINE
ENGINOUS *adj* ingenious or clever
ENGIRD *vb* surround
ENGIRDED > ENGIRD

ENGIRDING > ENGIRD
ENGIRDLE *variant of* **>** ENGIRD
ENGIRDLED > ENGIRDLE
ENGIRDLES > ENGIRDLE
ENGIRDS > ENGIRD
ENGIRT > ENGIRD
ENGLACIAL *adj* embedded in, carried by, or running through a glacier
ENGLISH *vb* put spin on a billiard ball
ENGLISHED > ENGLISH
ENGLISHES > ENGLISH
ENGLOBE *vb* surround as if in a globe
ENGLOBED > ENGLOBE
ENGLOBES > ENGLOBE
ENGLOBING > ENGLOBE
ENGLOOM *vb* make dull or dismal
ENGLOOMED > ENGLOOM
ENGLOOMS > ENGLOOM
ENGLUT *vb* devour ravenously
ENGLUTS > ENGLUT
ENGLUTTED > ENGLUT
ENGOBE *n* liquid put on pottery before glazing
ENGOBES > ENGOBE
ENGORE *vb* pierce or wound
ENGORED > ENGORE
ENGORES > ENGORE
ENGORGE *vb* clog with blood
ENGORGED > ENGORGE
ENGORGES > ENGORGE
ENGORGING > ENGORGE
ENGORING > ENGORE
ENGOULED *adj* (in heraldry) with ends coming from the mouths of animals
ENGOUMENT *n* obsessive liking
ENGRACE *vb* give grace to
ENGRACED > ENGRACE
ENGRACES > ENGRACE
ENGRACING > ENGRACE
ENGRAFF *variant of* **>** ENGRAFT
ENGRAFFED > ENGRAFF
ENGRAFFS > ENGRAFF
ENGRAFT *vb* graft (a shoot, bud, etc) onto a stock
ENGRAFTED > ENGRAFT
ENGRAFTS > ENGRAFT
ENGRAIL *vb* decorate or mark with small carved notches
ENGRAILED > ENGRAIL
ENGRAILS > ENGRAIL
ENGRAIN *variant spelling of* **>** INGRAIN
ENGRAINED > ENGRAIN
ENGRAINER > ENGRAIN
ENGRAINS > ENGRAIN
ENGRAM *n* physical basis of an individual memory in the brain
ENGRAMMA *variant of* **>** ENGRAM
ENGRAMMAS > ENGRAMMA
ENGRAMME *variant of* **>** ENGRAM
ENGRAMMES > ENGRAMME
ENGRAMMIC > ENGRAM
ENGRAMS > ENGRAM
ENGRASP *vb* grasp or seize

ENGRASPED > ENGRASP
ENGRASPS > ENGRASP
ENGRAVE vb carve (a design) onto a hard surface
ENGRAVED > ENGRAVE
ENGRAVEN > ENGRAVE
ENGRAVER > ENGRAVE
ENGRAVERS > ENGRAVE
ENGRAVERY > ENGRAVE
ENGRAVES > ENGRAVE
ENGRAVING n print made from an engraved plate
ENGRENAGE n act of putting into gear
ENGRIEVE vb grieve
ENGRIEVED > ENGRIEVE
ENGRIEVES > ENGRIEVE
ENGROOVE vb put a groove in
ENGROOVED > ENGROOVE
ENGROOVES > ENGROOVE
ENGROSS vb occupy the attention of (a person) completely
ENGROSSED > ENGROSS
ENGROSSER > ENGROSS
ENGROSSES > ENGROSS
ENGS > ENG
ENGUARD vb protect or defend
ENGUARDED > ENGUARD
ENGUARDS > ENGUARD
ENGULF vb cover or surround completely
ENGULFED > ENGULF
ENGULFING > ENGULF
ENGULFS > ENGULF
ENGULPH variant of > ENGULF
ENGULPHED > ENGULPH
ENGULPHS > ENGULPH
ENGYSCOPE n microscope
ENHALO vb surround with or as if with a halo
ENHALOED > ENHALO
ENHALOES > ENHALO
ENHALOING > ENHALO
ENHALOS > ENHALO
ENHANCE vb increase in quality, value, or attractiveness
ENHANCED > ENHANCE
ENHANCER > ENHANCE
ENHANCERS > ENHANCE
ENHANCES > ENHANCE
ENHANCING > ENHANCE
ENHANCIVE > ENHANCE
ENHEARSE variant of > INHEARSE
ENHEARSED > ENHEARSE
ENHEARSES > ENHEARSE
ENHEARTEN vb give heart to, encourage
ENHUNGER vb cause to be hungry
ENHUNGERS > ENHUNGER
ENHYDRITE n type of mineral
ENHYDROS n piece of chalcedony that contains water
ENHYDROUS > ENHYDROS
ENIAC n early type of computer built in the 1940s
ENIACS > ENIAC
ENIGMA n puzzling thing or person
ENIGMAS > ENIGMA

ENIGMATA > ENIGMA
ENIGMATIC > ENIGMA
ENISLE vb put on or make into an island
ENISLED > ENISLE
ENISLES > ENISLE
ENISLING > ENISLE
ENJAMB vb (of a line of verse) run over into the next line
ENJAMBED > ENJAMB
ENJAMBING > ENJAMB
ENJAMBS > ENJAMB
ENJOIN vb order (someone) to do something
ENJOINDER n order
ENJOINED > ENJOIN
ENJOINER > ENJOIN
ENJOINERS > ENJOIN
ENJOINING > ENJOIN
ENJOINS > ENJOIN
ENJOY vb take joy in
ENJOYABLE > ENJOY
ENJOYABLY > ENJOY
ENJOYED > ENJOY
ENJOYER > ENJOY
ENJOYERS > ENJOY
ENJOYING > ENJOY
ENJOYMENT n act or condition of receiving pleasure from something
ENJOYS > ENJOY
ENKERNEL vb put inside a kernel
ENKERNELS > ENKERNEL
ENKINDLE vb set on fire
ENKINDLED > ENKINDLE
ENKINDLER > ENKINDLE
ENKINDLES > ENKINDLE
ENLACE vb bind or encircle with or as with laces
ENLACED > ENLACE
ENLACES > ENLACE
ENLACING > ENLACE
ENLARD vb put lard on
ENLARDED > ENLARD
ENLARDING > ENLARD
ENLARDS > ENLARD
ENLARGE vb make or grow larger
ENLARGED > ENLARGE
ENLARGEN variant of > ENLARGE
ENLARGENS > ENLARGEN
ENLARGER n optical instrument for making enlarged photographs
ENLARGERS > ENLARGER
ENLARGES > ENLARGE
ENLARGING > ENLARGE
ENLEVE adj having been abducted
ENLIGHT vb light up
ENLIGHTED > ENLIGHT
ENLIGHTEN vb give information to
ENLIGHTS > ENLIGHT
ENLINK vb link together
ENLINKED > ENLINK
ENLINKING > ENLINK
ENLINKS > ENLINK
ENLIST vb enter the armed forces
ENLISTED > ENLIST
ENLISTEE > ENLIST
ENLISTEES > ENLIST
ENLISTER > ENLIST

ENLISTERS > ENLIST
ENLISTING > ENLIST
ENLISTS > ENLIST
ENLIT > ENLIGHT
ENLIVEN vb make lively or cheerful
ENLIVENED > ENLIVEN
ENLIVENER > ENLIVEN
ENLIVENS > ENLIVEN
ENLOCK vb lock or secure
ENLOCKED > ENLOCK
ENLOCKING > ENLOCK
ENLOCKS > ENLOCK
ENLUMINE vb illuminate
ENLUMINED > ENLUMINE
ENLUMINES > ENLUMINE
ENMESH vb catch or involve in or as if in a net or snare
ENMESHED > ENMESH
ENMESHES > ENMESH
ENMESHING > ENMESH
ENMEW variant of > EMMEW
ENMEWED > ENMEW
ENMEWING > ENMEW
ENMEWS > ENMEW
ENMITIES > ENMITY
ENMITY n ill will, hatred
ENMOSSED adj having a covering of moss
ENMOVE variant of > EMMOVE
ENMOVED > ENMOVE
ENMOVES > ENMOVE
ENMOVING > ENMOVE
ENNAGE n number of ens in printed matter
ENNAGES > ENNAGE
ENNEAD n group or series of nine
ENNEADIC > ENNEAD
ENNEADS > ENNEAD
ENNEAGON another name for > NONAGON
ENNEAGONS > ENNEAGON
ENNEAGRAM n personality system involving nine distinct but interconnected personality types
ENNOBLE vb make noble, elevate
ENNOBLED > ENNOBLE
ENNOBLER > ENNOBLE
ENNOBLERS > ENNOBLE
ENNOBLES > ENNOBLE
ENNOBLING > ENNOBLE
ENNOG n back alley
ENNOGS > ENNOG
ENNUI n boredom, dissatisfaction ▷ vb bore
ENNUIED > ENNUI
ENNUIS > ENNUI
ENNUYE adj bored
ENNUYED > ENNUI
ENNUYE same as > ENNUYE
ENNUYING > ENNUI
ENODAL adj having no nodes
ENOKI variant of > ENOKITAKE
ENOKIDAKE variant of > ENOKITAKE
ENOKIS > ENOKI
ENOKITAKE n Japanese mushroom
ENOL n type of organic compound
ENOLASE n type of enzyme
ENOLASES > ENOLASE

ENOLIC > ENOL
ENOLOGIES > ENOLOGY
ENOLOGIST n wine expert
ENOLOGY usual US spelling of > OENOLOGY
ENOLS > ENOL
ENOMOTIES > ENOMOTY
ENOMOTY n division of the Spartan army in ancient Greece
ENOPHILE n lover of wine
ENOPHILES > ENOPHILE
ENORM variant of > ENORMOUS
ENORMITY n great wickedness
ENORMOUS adj very big, vast
ENOSES > ENOSIS
ENOSIS n union of Greece and Cyprus
ENOSISES > ENOSIS
ENOUGH adj as much or as many as necessary ▷ n sufficient quantity ▷ adv sufficiently
ENOUGHS > ENOUGH
ENOUNCE vb enunciate
ENOUNCED > ENOUNCE
ENOUNCES > ENOUNCE
ENOUNCING > ENOUNCE
ENOW archaic word for > ENOUGH
ENOWS > ENOW
ENPLANE vb board an aircraft
ENPLANED > ENPLANE
ENPLANES > ENPLANE
ENPLANING > ENPLANE
ENPRINT n standard photographic print
ENPRINTS > ENPRINT
ENQUEUE vb add (an item) to a queue of computing tasks
ENQUEUED > ENQUEUE
ENQUEUES > ENQUEUE
ENQUEUING > ENQUEUE
ENQUIRE same as > INQUIRE
ENQUIRED > ENQUIRE
ENQUIRER > ENQUIRE
ENQUIRERS > ENQUIRE
ENQUIRES > ENQUIRE
ENQUIRIES > ENQUIRE
ENQUIRING > ENQUIRE
ENQUIRY > ENQUIRE
ENRACE vb bring in a race of people
ENRACED > ENRACE
ENRACES > ENRACE
ENRACING > ENRACE
ENRAGE vb make extremely angry
ENRAGED > ENRAGE
ENRAGEDLY > ENRAGE
ENRAGES > ENRAGE
ENRAGING > ENRAGE
ENRANCKLE vb upset, make irate
ENRANGE vb arrange, organize
ENRANGED > ENRANGE
ENRANGES > ENRANGE
ENRANGING > ENRANGE
ENRANK vb put in a row
ENRANKED > ENRANK
ENRANKING > ENRANK
ENRANKS > ENRANK

ENRAPT > ENRAPTURE
ENRAPTURE vb fill with delight
ENRAUNGE archaic variant of > ENRANGE
ENRAUNGED > ENRAUNGE
ENRAUNGES > ENRAUNGE
ENRAVISH vb enchant
ENRHEUM vb pass a cold on to
ENRHEUMED > ENRHEUM
ENRHEUMS > ENRHEUM
ENRICH vb improve in quality
ENRICHED > ENRICH
ENRICHER > ENRICH
ENRICHERS > ENRICH
ENRICHES > ENRICH
ENRICHING > ENRICH
ENRIDGED adj ridged
ENRING vb put a ring round
ENRINGED > ENRING
ENRINGING > ENRING
ENRINGS > ENRING
ENRIVEN adj ripped
ENROBE vb dress in or as if in a robe
ENROBED > ENROBE
ENROBER > ENROBE
ENROBERS > ENROBE
ENROBES > ENROBE
ENROBING > ENROBE
ENROL vb (cause to) become a member
ENROLL same as > ENROL
ENROLLED > ENROLL
ENROLLEE > ENROL
ENROLLEES > ENROL
ENROLLER > ENROL
ENROLLERS > ENROL
ENROLLING > ENROLL
ENROLLS > ENROLL
ENROLMENT n act of enrolling or state of being enrolled
ENROLS > ENROL
ENROOT vb establish (plants) by fixing their roots in the earth
ENROOTED > ENROOT
ENROOTING > ENROOT
ENROOTS > ENROOT
ENROUGH vb roughen
ENROUGHED > ENROUGH
ENROUGHS > ENROUGH
ENROUND vb encircle
ENROUNDED > ENROUND
ENROUNDS > ENROUND
ENS n being or existence in the most general abstract sense
ENSAMPLE n example ▷ vb make an example
ENSAMPLED > ENSAMPLE
ENSAMPLES > ENSAMPLE
ENSATE adj shaped like a sword
ENSCONCE vb settle firmly or comfortably
ENSCONCED > ENSCONCE
ENSCONCES > ENSCONCE
ENSCROLL variant of > INSCROLL
ENSCROLLS > ENSCROLL
ENSEAL vb seal up
ENSEALED > ENSEAL

ENSEALING > ENSEAL
ENSEALS > ENSEAL
ENSEAM vb put a seam on
ENSEAMED > ENSEAM
ENSEAMING > ENSEAM
ENSEAMS > ENSEAM
ENSEAR vb dry
ENSEARED > ENSEAR
ENSEARING > ENSEAR
ENSEARS > ENSEAR
ENSEMBLE n all the parts of something taken together ▷ adv all together or at once ▷ adj (of a film or play) involving several separate but often interrelated story lines
ENSEMBLES > ENSEMBLE
ENSERF vb enslave
ENSERFED > ENSERF
ENSERFING > ENSERF
ENSERFS > ENSERF
ENSEW variant of > ENSUE
ENSEWED > ENSEW
ENSEWING > ENSEW
ENSEWS > ENSEW
ENSHEATH variant of > INSHEATHE
ENSHEATHE variant of > INSHEATHE
ENSHEATHS > ENSHEATH
ENSHELL variant of > INSHELL
ENSHELLED > ENSHELL
ENSHELLS > ENSHELL
ENSHELTER vb shelter
ENSHIELD vb protect
ENSHIELDS > ENSHIELD
ENSHRINE vb cherish or treasure
ENSHRINED > ENSHRINE
ENSHRINEE > ENSHRINE
ENSHRINES > ENSHRINE
ENSHROUD vb cover or hide as with a shroud
ENSHROUDS > ENSHROUD
ENSIFORM adj shaped like a sword blade
ENSIGN n military officer ▷ vb mark with a sign
ENSIGNCY > ENSIGN
ENSIGNED > ENSIGN
ENSIGNING > ENSIGN
ENSIGNS > ENSIGN
ENSILAGE n process of ensiling green fodder ▷ vb make into silage
ENSILAGED > ENSILAGE
ENSILAGES > ENSILAGE
ENSILE vb store and preserve (green fodder) in an enclosed pit or silo
ENSILED > ENSILE
ENSILES > ENSILE
ENSILING > ENSILE
ENSKIED > ENSKY
ENSKIES > ENSKY
ENSKY vb put in the sky
ENSKYED > ENSKY
ENSKYING > ENSKY
ENSLAVE vb make a slave of (someone)
ENSLAVED > ENSLAVE
ENSLAVER > ENSLAVE
ENSLAVERS > ENSLAVE
ENSLAVES > ENSLAVE
ENSLAVING > ENSLAVE

ENSNARE vb catch in or as if in a snare
ENSNARED > ENSNARE
ENSNARER > ENSNARE
ENSNARERS > ENSNARE
ENSNARES > ENSNARE
ENSNARING > ENSNARE
ENSNARL vb become tangled in
ENSNARLED > ENSNARL
ENSNARLS > ENSNARL
ENSORCEL vb enchant
ENSORCELL variant of > ENSORCEL
ENSORCELS > ENSORCEL
ENSOUL vb endow with a soul
ENSOULED > ENSOUL
ENSOULING > ENSOUL
ENSOULS > ENSOUL
ENSPHERE vb enclose in or as if in a sphere
ENSPHERED > ENSPHERE
ENSPHERES > ENSPHERE
ENSTAMP vb imprint with a stamp
ENSTAMPED > ENSTAMP
ENSTAMPS > ENSTAMP
ENSTATITE n grey, green, yellow, or brown pyroxene mineral consisting of magnesium silicate in orthorhombic crystalline form
ENSTEEP vb soak in water
ENSTEEPED > ENSTEEP
ENSTEEPS > ENSTEEP
ENSTYLE vb give a name to
ENSTYLED > ENSTYLE
ENSTYLES > ENSTYLE
ENSTYLING > ENSTYLE
ENSUE vb come next, result
ENSUED > ENSUE
ENSUES > ENSUE
ENSUING adj following subsequently or in order
ENSUITE n bathroom attached to another room
ENSUITES > ENSUITE
ENSURE vb make certain or sure
ENSURED > ENSURE
ENSURER > ENSURE
ENSURERS > ENSURE
ENSURES > ENSURE
ENSURING > ENSURE
ENSWATHE vb bind or wrap
ENSWATHED > ENSWATHE
ENSWATHES > ENSWATHE
ENSWEEP vb sweep across
ENSWEEPS > ENSWEEP
ENSWEPT > ENSWEEP
ENTAIL vb bring about or impose inevitably ▷ n restriction imposed by entailing an estate
ENTAILED > ENTAIL
ENTAILER > ENTAIL
ENTAILERS > ENTAIL
ENTAILING > ENTAIL
ENTAILS > ENTAIL
ENTAME vb make tame
ENTAMEBA same as > ENTAMOEBA
ENTAMEBAE > ENTAMEBA
ENTAMEBAS > ENTAMEBA
ENTAMED > ENTAME

ENTAMES > ENTAME
ENTAMING > ENTAME
ENTAMOEBA n parasitic amoeba that lives in the intestines of humans and causes amoebic dysentery
ENTANGLE vb catch or involve in or as if in a tangle
ENTANGLED > ENTANGLE
ENTANGLER > ENTANGLE
ENTANGLES > ENTANGLE
ENTASES > ENTASIS
ENTASIA same as > ENTASIS
ENTASIAS > ENTASIA
ENTASIS n slightly convex curve given to the shaft of a structure
ENTASTIC adj (of a disease) characterized by spasms
ENTAYLE variant of > ENTAIL
ENTAYLED > ENTAYLE
ENTAYLES > ENTAYLE
ENTAYLING > ENTAYLE
ENTELECHY n (in the philosophy of Aristotle) actuality as opposed to potentiality
ENTELLUS n langur of S Asia
ENTENDER vb make more tender
ENTENDERS > ENTENDER
ENTENTE n friendly understanding between nations
ENTENTES > ENTENTE
ENTER vb come or go in
ENTERA > ENTERON
ENTERABLE > ENTER
ENTERAL same as > ENTERIC
ENTERALLY > ENTERIC
ENTERATE adj with an intestine separate from the outer wall of the body
ENTERED > ENTER
ENTERER > ENTER
ENTERERS > ENTER
ENTERIC adj intestinal ▷ n infectious disease of the intestines
ENTERICS > ENTERIC
ENTERING > ENTER
ENTERINGS > ENTER
ENTERITIS n inflammation of the intestine
ENTERON n alimentary canal
ENTERONS > ENTERON
ENTERS > ENTER
ENTERTAIN vb amuse
ENTERTAKE vb entertain
ENTERTOOK > ENTERTAKE
ENTETE adj obsessed
ENTETEE variant of > ENTETE
ENTHALPY n property of a thermodynamic system
ENTHETIC adj (esp of infectious diseases) introduced into the body from without
ENTHRAL vb hold the attention of
ENTHRALL same as > ENTHRAL
ENTHRALLS > ENTHRALL

e

SECTION 1: Words between 2 and 9 letters in length

e

ENTHRALS > ENTHRAL
ENTHRONE vb place (someone) on a throne
ENTHRONED > ENTHRONE
ENTHRONES > ENTHRONE
ENTHUSE vb (cause to) show enthusiasm
ENTHUSED > ENTHUSE
ENTHUSES > ENTHUSE
ENTHUSING > ENTHUSE
ENTHYMEME n incomplete syllogism, in which one or more premises are unexpressed as their truth is considered to be self-evident
ENTIA > ENS
ENTICE vb attract by exciting hope or desire, tempt
ENTICED > ENTICE
ENTICER > ENTICE
ENTICERS > ENTICE
ENTICES > ENTICE
ENTICING > ENTICE
ENTICINGS > ENTICE
ENTIRE adj including every detail, part, or aspect of something ▷ n state of being entire
ENTIRELY adv without reservation or exception
ENTIRES > ENTIRE
ENTIRETY n state of being entire or whole
ENTITIES > ENTITY
ENTITLE vb give a right to
ENTITLED > ENTITLE
ENTITLES > ENTITLE
ENTITLING > ENTITLE
ENTITY n separate distinct thing
ENTOBLAST less common name for > ENDODERM
ENTODERM same as > ENDODERM
ENTODERMS > ENTODERM
ENTOIL archaic word for > ENSNARE
ENTOILED > ENTOIL
ENTOILING > ENTOIL
ENTOILS > ENTOIL
ENTOMB vb place (a corpse) in a tomb
ENTOMBED > ENTOMB
ENTOMBING > ENTOMB
ENTOMBS > ENTOMB
ENTOMIC adj denoting or relating to insects
ENTOPHYTE variant of > ENDOPHYTE
ENTOPIC adj situated in its normal place or position
ENTOPROCT n type of marine animal
ENTOPTIC adj (of visual sensation) resulting from structures within the eye itself
ENTOPTICS n study of entoptic visions
ENTOTIC adj of or relating to the inner ear
ENTOURAGE n group of people who assist an important person
ENTOZOA > ENTOZOON
ENTOZOAL > ENTOZOON

ENTOZOAN same as > ENTOZOON
ENTOZOANS > ENTOZOAN
ENTOZOIC adj of or relating to an entozoon
ENTOZOON n internal parasite
ENTRAIL vb twist or entangle
ENTRAILED > ENTRAIL
ENTRAILS pl n intestines
ENTRAIN vb board or put aboard a train
ENTRAINED > ENTRAIN
ENTRAINER > ENTRAIN
ENTRAINS > ENTRAIN
ENTRALL variant of > ENTRAILS
ENTRALLES variant of > ENTRAILS
ENTRAMMEL vb hamper or obstruct by entangling
ENTRANCE n way into a place ▷ vb delight ▷ adj necessary in order to enter something
ENTRANCED > ENTRANCE
ENTRANCES > ENTRANCE
ENTRANT n person who enters a university, contest, etc
ENTRANTS > ENTRANT
ENTRAP vb trick into difficulty etc
ENTRAPPED > ENTRAP
ENTRAPPER > ENTRAP
ENTRAPS > ENTRAP
ENTREAT vb ask earnestly
ENTREATED > ENTREAT
ENTREATS > ENTREAT
ENTREATY n earnest request
ENTRECHAT n leap in ballet during which the dancer repeatedly crosses their feet or beats them together
ENTRECOTE n beefsteak cut from between the ribs
ENTREE n dish served before a main course
ENTREES > ENTREE
ENTREMES variant of > ENTREMETS
ENTREMETS n dessert
ENTRENCH vb establish firmly
ENTREPOT n warehouse for commercial goods
ENTREPOTS > ENTREPOT
ENTRESOL another name for > MEZZANINE
ENTRESOLS > ENTRESOL
ENTREZ interj enter
ENTRIES > ENTRY
ENTRISM variant of > ENTRYISM
ENTRISMS > ENTRISM
ENTRIST > ENTRISM
ENTRISTS > ENTRIST
ENTROLD adj word used by Spenser meaning surrounded
ENTROPIC > ENTROPY
ENTROPIES > ENTROPY
ENTROPION n turning inwards of the edge of the eyelid

ENTROPIUM variant of > ENTROPION
ENTROPY n lack of organization
ENTRUST vb put into the care or protection of
ENTRUSTED > ENTRUST
ENTRUSTS > ENTRUST
ENTRY n entrance ▷ adj necessary in order to enter something
ENTRYISM n joining a political party to change its principles
ENTRYISMS > ENTRYISM
ENTRYIST > ENTRYISM
ENTRYISTS > ENTRYISM
ENTRYWAY n entrance passage
ENTRYWAYS > ENTRYWAY
ENTS pl n (college) entertainments
ENTWINE vb twist together or around
ENTWINED > ENTWINE
ENTWINES > ENTWINE
ENTWINING > ENTWINE
ENTWIST vb twist together or around
ENTWISTED > ENTWIST
ENTWISTS > ENTWIST
ENUCLEATE vb remove the nucleus from (a cell) ▷ adj (of cells) deprived of their nuclei
ENUF common intentional literary misspelling of > ENOUGH
ENUMERATE vb name one by one
ENUNCIATE vb pronounce clearly
ENURE variant spelling of > INURE
ENURED > ENURE
ENUREMENT > ENURE
ENURES > ENURE
ENURESES > ENURESIS
ENURESIS n involuntary discharge of urine, esp during sleep
ENURETIC > ENURESIS
ENURETICS > ENURESIS
ENURING > ENURE
ENURN same as > INURN
ENURNED same as > INURNED
ENURNING same as > INURNING
ENURNS same as > INURNS
ENVASSAL vb make a vassal of
ENVASSALS > ENVASSAL
ENVAULT vb enclose in a vault; entomb
ENVAULTED > ENVAULT
ENVAULTS > ENVAULT
ENVEIGLE same as > INVEIGLE
ENVEIGLED > ENVEIGLE
ENVEIGLES > ENVEIGLE
ENVELOP vb wrap up, enclose
ENVELOPE n folded gummed paper cover for a letter
ENVELOPED > ENVELOP
ENVELOPER > ENVELOP

ENVELOPES > ENVELOPE
ENVELOPS > ENVELOP
ENVENOM vb fill or impregnate with venom
ENVENOMED > ENVENOM
ENVENOMS > ENVENOM
ENVERMEIL vb dye vermilion
ENVIABLE adj arousing envy, fortunate
ENVIABLY > ENVIABLE
ENVIED > ENVY
ENVIER > ENVY
ENVIERS > ENVY
ENVIES > ENVY
ENVIOUS adj full of envy
ENVIOUSLY > ENVIOUS
ENVIRO n environmentalist
ENVIRON vb encircle or surround
ENVIRONED > ENVIRON
ENVIRONS pl n surrounding area, esp of a town
ENVIROS > ENVIRO
ENVISAGE vb conceive of as a possibility
ENVISAGED > ENVISAGE
ENVISAGES > ENVISAGE
ENVISION vb conceive of as a possibility, esp in the future
ENVISIONS > ENVISION
ENVOI same as > ENVOY
ENVOIS > ENVOI
ENVOY n messenger
ENVOYS > ENVOY
ENVOYSHIP > ENVOY
ENVY n feeling of discontent aroused by another's good fortune ▷ vb grudge (another's good fortune, success, or qualities)
ENVYING > ENVY
ENVYINGLY > ENVY
ENVYINGS > ENVY
ENWALL vb wall in
ENWALLED > ENWALL
ENWALLING > ENWALL
ENWALLOW vb sink or plunge
ENWALLOWS > ENWALLOW
ENWALLS > ENWALL
ENWHEEL archaic word for > ENCIRCLE
ENWHEELED > ENWHEEL
ENWHEELS > ENWHEEL
ENWIND vb wind or coil around
ENWINDING > ENWIND
ENWINDS > ENWIND
ENWOMB vb enclose in or as if in a womb
ENWOMBED > ENWOMB
ENWOMBING > ENWOMB
ENWOMBS > ENWOMB
ENWOUND > ENWIND
ENWRAP vb wrap or cover up
ENWRAPPED > ENWRAP
ENWRAPS > ENWRAP
ENWRAPT > ENWRAP
ENWREATH vb surround or encircle with or as with a wreath or wreaths
ENWREATHE same as > ENWREATH
ENWREATHS > ENWREATH
ENZIAN n gentian violet
ENZIANS > ENZIAN

ENZONE *vb* enclose in a zone

ENZONED > ENZONE

ENZONES > ENZONE

ENZONING > ENZONE

ENZOOTIC *adj* (of diseases) affecting animals within a limited region ▷ *n* enzootic disease

ENZOOTICS > ENZOOTIC

ENZYM *same as* > ENZYME

ENZYMATIC > ENZYME

ENZYME *n* complex protein that acts as a catalyst

ENZYMES > ENZYME

ENZYMIC > ENZYME

ENZYMS > ENZYM

EOAN *adj* of or relating to the dawn

EOBIONT *n* hypothetical chemical precursor of a living cell

EOBIONTS > EOBIONT

EOCENE *adj* of, denoting, or formed in the second epoch of the Tertiary period

EOHIPPUS *n* extinct dog-sized ancestor of the horse

EOLIAN *adj* of or relating to the wind

EOLIENNE *n* type of fine cloth

EOLIENNES > EOLIENNE

EOLIPILE *variant of* > AEOLIPILE

EOLIPILES > EOLIPILE

EOLITH *n* stone used as a primitive tool in Eolithic times

EOLITHIC > EOLITH

EOLITHS > EOLITH

EOLOPILE *variant of* > AEOLIPILE

EOLOPILES > EOLOPILE

EON *n* two or more eras

EONIAN *adj* of or relating to an eon

EONISM *n* adoption of female dress and behaviour by a male

EONISMS > EONISM

EONS > EON

EORL *n* Anglo-Saxon nobleman

EORLS > EORL

EOSIN *n* red crystalline water-insoluble derivative of fluorescein

EOSINE *same as* > EOSIN

EOSINES > EOSINE

EOSINIC > EOSIN

EOSINS > EOSIN

EOTHEN *adv* from the East

EPACRID *n* type of heath-like plant

EPACRIDS > EPACRID

EPACRIS *n* genus of the epacrids

EPACRISES > EPACRIS

EPACT *n* difference in time between the solar year and the lunar year

EPACTS > EPACT

EPAENETIC *adj* eulogistic

EPAGOGE *n* inductive reasoning

EPAGOGES > EPAGOGE

EPAGOGIC > EPAGOGE

EPANODOS *n* return to main theme after a digression

EPARCH *n* bishop or metropolitan in charge of an eparchy

EPARCHATE *same as* > EPARCHY

EPARCHIAL > EPARCHY

EPARCHIES > EPARCHY

EPARCHS > EPARCH

EPARCHY *n* diocese of the Eastern Christian Church

EPATANT *adj* startling or shocking

EPATER *vb* shock conventional people

EPATERED > EPATER

EPATERING > EPATER

EPATERS > EPATER

EPAULE *n* shoulder of a fortification

EPAULES > EPAULE

EPAULET *same as* > EPAULETTE

EPAULETED *adj* wearing an epaulet

EPAULETS > EPAULET

EPAULETTE *n* shoulder ornament on a uniform

EPAXIAL *adj* above the axis

EPAZOTE *n* type of herb

EPAZOTES > EPAZOTE

EPEDAPHIC *adj* of or relating to atmospheric conditions

EPEE *n* straight-bladed sword used in fencing

EPEEIST *n* one who uses or specializes in using an epee

EPEEISTS > EPEEIST

EPEES > EPEE

EPEIRA *same as* > EPEIRID

EPEIRAS > EPEIRA

EPEIRIC *adj* in, of, or relating to a continent

EPEIRID *n* type of spider

EPEIRIDS > EPEIRID

EPENDYMA *n* membrane lining the ventricles of the brain and the central canal of the spinal cord

EPENDYMAL > EPENDYMA

EPENDYMAS > EPENDYMA

EPEOLATRY *n* worship of words

EPERDU *adj* distracted

EPERDUE *adj* distracted

EPERGNE *n* ornamental centrepiece for a table

EPERGNES > EPERGNE

EPHA *same as* > EPHAH

EPHAH *n* Hebrew unit of dry measure

EPHAHS > EPHAH

EPHAS > EPHA

EPHEBE *n* (in ancient 'Greece) youth about to enter full citizenship

EPHEBES > EPHEBE

EPHEBI > EPHEBE

EPHEBIC > EPHEBE

EPHEBOI > EPHEBOS

EPHEBOS *same as* > EPHEBE

EPHEBUS *same as* > EPHEBE

EPHEDRA *n* gymnosperm shrub

EPHEDRAS > EPHEDRA

EPHEDRIN *same as* > EPHEDRINE

EPHEDRINE *n* alkaloid used for treatment of asthma and hay fever

EPHEDRINS > EPHEDRIN

EPHELIDES > EPHELIS

EPHELIS *n* freckle

EPHEMERA *n* something transitory or short-lived

EPHEMERAE > EPHEMERA

EPHEMERAL *adj* short-lived ▷ *n* short-lived organism, such as the mayfly

EPHEMERAS > EPHEMERA

EPHEMERID *n* mayfly

EPHEMERIS *n* table giving the future positions of a planet, comet, or satellite

EPHEMERON *n* an insect that lives for only one day; anything short-lived

EPHIALTES *n* incubus

EPHOD *n* embroidered vestment worn by priests

EPHODS > EPHOD

EPHOR *n* one of a board of senior magistrates in several ancient Greek states

EPHORAL > EPHOR

EPHORALTY > EPHOR

EPHORATE > EPHOR

EPHORATES > EPHOR

EPHORI > EPHOR

EPHORS > EPHOR

EPIBIOSES > EPIBIOSIS

EPIBIOSIS *n* any relationship between two organisms in which one grows on the other but is not parasitic on it

EPIBIOTIC > EPIBIOSIS

EPIBLAST *n* outermost layer of an embryo, which becomes the ectoderm at gastrulation

EPIBLASTS > EPIBLAST

EPIBLEM *n* outermost cell layer of a root

EPIBLEMS > EPIBLEM

EPIBOLIC > EPIBOLY

EPIBOLIES > EPIBOLY

EPIBOLY *n* process that occurs during gastrulation in vertebrates

EPIC *n* long poem, book, or film about heroic events or actions ▷ *adj* very impressive or ambitious

EPICAL > EPIC

EPICALLY > EPIC

EPICALYX *n* small sepal-like bracts in some flowers

EPICANTHI *n* folds of skin extending vertically over the inner angles of the eyes

EPICARDIA *n* layers of pericardia in direct contact with the heart

EPICARP *n* outermost layer of the pericarp of fruits

EPICARPS > EPICARP

EPICEDE *same as* > EPICEDIUM

EPICEDES > EPICEDE

EPICEDIA > EPICEDIUM

EPICEDIAL > EPICEDIUM

EPICEDIAN > EPICEDIUM

EPICEDIUM *n* funeral ode

EPICENE *adj* having the characteristics of both sexes; hermaphroditic ▷ *n* epicene person or creature

EPICENES > EPICENE

EPICENISM > EPICENE

EPICENTER *same as* > EPICENTRE

EPICENTRA *n* epicentres

EPICENTRE *n* point on the earth's surface immediately above the origin of an earthquake

EPICIER *n* grocer

EPICIERS > EPICIER

EPICISM *n* style or trope characteristic of epics

EPICISMS > EPICISM

EPICIST *n* writer of epics

EPICISTS > EPICIST

EPICLESES > EPICLESIS

EPICLESIS *n* invocation of the Holy Spirit to consecrate the bread and wine of the Eucharist

EPICLIKE *adj* resembling or reminiscent of an epic

EPICORMIC *adj* (of a tree shoot or branch) growing from a dormant bud below the bark

EPICOTYL *n* part of an embryo plant stem above the cotyledons but beneath the terminal bud

EPICOTYLS > EPICOTYL

EPICRANIA *n* tissue covering the cranium

EPICRISES > EPICRISIS

EPICRISIS *n* secondary crisis occurring in the course of a disease

EPICRITIC *adj* (of certain nerve fibres of the skin) serving to perceive and distinguish fine variations of temperature or touch

EPICS > EPIC

EPICURE *n* person who enjoys good food and drink

EPICUREAN *adj* devoted to sensual pleasures, esp food and drink ▷ *n* epicure

EPICURES > EPICURE

EPICURISE *same as* > EPICURIZE

EPICURISM > EPICURE

EPICURIZE *vb* act as an epicure

EPICYCLE *n* (in the Ptolemaic system) a small circle, around which a planet was thought to revolve

EPICYCLES > EPICYCLE

EPICYCLIC > EPICYCLE

EPIDEMIC *n* widespread occurrence of a disease ▷ *adj* (esp of a disease) affecting many people in an area

EPIDEMICS > EPIDEMIC

EPIDERM *same as* > EPIDERMIS

EPIDERMAL > EPIDERMIS

EPIDERMIC > EPIDERMIS

EPIDERMIS *n* outer layer of the skin

e

e

EPIDERMS > EPIDERM
EPIDICTIC adj designed to display something, esp the skill of the speaker in rhetoric
EPIDOSITE n rock formed of quartz and epidote
EPIDOTE n green mineral
EPIDOTES > EPIDOTE
EPIDOTIC > EPIDOTE
EPIDURAL n spinal anaesthetic injected to relieve pain during childbirth ▷ adj on or over the outermost membrane covering the brain and spinal cord
EPIDURALS > EPIDURAL
EPIFAUNA n animals that live on the surface of the seabed
EPIFAUNAE > EPIFAUNA
EPIFAUNAL > EPIFAUNA
EPIFAUNAS > EPIFAUNA
EPIFOCAL adj situated or occurring at an epicentre
EPIGAEAL same as
> EPIGEAL
EPIGAEAN same as
> EPIGEAL
EPIGAEOUS same as
> EPIGEAL
EPIGAMIC adj denoting an animal feature that attracts the opposite sex
EPIGEAL adj of or relating to a form of seed germination
EPIGEAN same as
> EPIGEAL
EPIGEIC same as
> EPIGEAL
EPIGENE adj formed or taking place at or near the surface of the earth
EPIGENIC adj pertaining to the theory of the gradual development of the embryo
EPIGENIST n one who studies or espouses the theory of the gradual development of the embryo
EPIGENOME n group of chemical compounds that modify a genome
EPIGENOUS adj growing on the surface, esp the upper surface, of an organism or part
EPIGEOUS same as
> EPIGEAL
EPIGON same as > EPIGONE
EPIGONE n inferior follower or imitator
EPIGONES > EPIGONE
EPIGONI > EPIGONE
EPIGONIC > EPIGONE
EPIGONISM > EPIGONE
EPIGONOUS > EPIGONE
EPIGONS > EPIGON
EPIGONUS same as
> EPIGONE
EPIGRAM n short witty remark or poem
EPIGRAMS > EPIGRAM
EPIGRAPH n quotation at the start of a book
EPIGRAPHS > EPIGRAPH
EPIGRAPHY n study of ancient inscriptions

EPIGYNIES > EPIGYNOUS
EPIGYNOUS adj (of flowers) having the receptacle enclosing and fused with the gynoecium so that the other floral parts arise above it
EPIGYNY > EPIGYNOUS
EPILATE vb remove hair from
EPILATED > EPILATE
EPILATES > EPILATE
EPILATING > EPILATE
EPILATION > EPILATE
EPILATOR n electrical appliance for plucking unwanted hair
EPILATORS > EPILATOR
EPILEPSY n disorder of the nervous system causing loss of consciousness and sometimes convulsions
EPILEPTIC adj of or having epilepsy ▷ n person who has epilepsy
EPILIMNIA n upper layers of water in lakes
EPILITHIC adj (of plants) growing on the surface of rock
EPILOBIUM n willow-herb
EPILOG same as
> EPILOGUE
EPILOGIC > EPILOGUE
EPILOGISE same as
> EPILOGIZE
EPILOGIST > EPILOGUE
EPILOGIZE vb write or deliver epilogues
EPILOGS > EPILOG
EPILOGUE n short speech or poem at the end of a literary work, esp a play
EPILOGUED adj followed by an epilogue
EPILOGUES > EPILOGUE
EPIMER n isomer
EPIMERASE n enzyme that interconverts epimers
EPIMERE n dorsal part of the mesoderm of a vertebrate embryo
EPIMERES > EPIMERE
EPIMERIC > EPIMERISM
EPIMERISE same as
> EPIMERIZE
EPIMERISM n optical isomerism in which isomers can form about asymmetric atoms within the molecule
EPIMERIZE vb change (a chemical compound) into an epimer
EPIMERS > EPIMER
EPIMYSIA > EPIMYSIUM
EPIMYSIUM n sheath of connective tissue that encloses a skeletal muscle
EPINAOI > EPINAOS
EPINAOS n rear vestibule
EPINASTIC > EPINASTY
EPINASTY n increased growth of the upper surface of a plant part
EPINEURAL adj outside a nerve trunk
EPINEURIA n sheaths of connective tissue around bundles of nerve fibres
EPINICIAN > EPINICION

EPINICION n victory song
EPINIKIAN > EPINICION
EPINIKION same as
> EPINICION
EPINOSIC adj unhealthy
EPIPHANIC > EPIPHANY
EPIPHANY n moment of great or sudden revelation
EPIPHRAGM n disc of calcium phosphate and mucilage secreted by snails over the aperture of their shells before hibernation
EPIPHYSES > EPIPHYSIS
EPIPHYSIS n end of a long bone, initially separated from the shaft (diaphysis) by a section of cartilage that eventually ossifies so that the two portions fuse together
EPIPHYTAL > EPIPHYTE
EPIPHYTE n plant that grows on another plant but is not parasitic on it
EPIPHYTES > EPIPHYTE
EPIPHYTIC > EPIPHYTE
EPIPLOA > EPIPLOON
EPIPLOIC > EPIPLOON
EPIPLOON n greater omentum
EPIPLOONS > EPIPLOON
EPIPOLIC > EPIPOLISM
EPIPOLISM n fluorescence
EPIROGENY n formation and submergence of continents by broad, relatively slow, displacements of the earth's crust
EPIRRHEMA n address in Greek comedy
EPISCIA n creeping plant
EPISCIAS > EPISCIA
EPISCOPAL adj of or governed by bishops
EPISCOPE n optical device that projects an enlarged image
EPISCOPES > EPISCOPE
EPISCOPY n area overseen
EPISEMON n emblem
EPISEMONS > EPISEMON
EPISODAL same as
> EPISODIC
EPISODE n incident in a series of incidents
EPISODES > EPISODE
EPISODIAL same as
> EPISODIC
EPISODIC adj occurring at irregular intervals
EPISOMAL adj of or like an episome
EPISOME n unit of genetic material (DNA) in bacteria that can be replicated
EPISOMES > EPISOME
EPISPERM n protective outer layer of certain seeds
EPISPERMS > EPISPERM
EPISPORE n outer layer of certain spores
EPISPORES > EPISPORE
EPISTASES > EPISTASIS
EPISTASIS n scum on the surface of a liquid, esp on an old specimen of urine
EPISTASY same as
> EPISTASIS

EPISTATIC > EPISTASIS
EPISTAXES > EPISTAXIS
EPISTAXIS technical name for > NOSEBLEED
EPISTEMIC adj of or relating to knowledge or epistemology
EPISTERNA n parts of the sternums of mammals
EPISTLE n letter, esp of an apostle ▷ vb preface
EPISTLED > EPISTLE
EPISTLER n writer of an epistle or epistles
EPISTLERS > EPISTLER
EPISTLES > EPISTLE
EPISTLING > EPISTLE
EPISTOLER same as
> EPISTLER
EPISTOLET n short letter
EPISTOLIC > EPISTLE
EPISTOME n area between the mouth and antennae of crustaceans
EPISTOMES > EPISTOME
EPISTYLE n lowest part of an entablature that bears on the columns
EPISTYLES > EPISTYLE
EPITAPH n commemorative inscription on a tomb ▷ vb compose an epitaph
EPITAPHED > EPITAPH
EPITAPHER > EPITAPH
EPITAPHIC > EPITAPH
EPITAPHS > EPITAPH
EPITASES > EPITASIS
EPITASIS n (in classical drama) part of a play in which the main action develops
EPITAXES > EPITAXIS
EPITAXIAL > EPITAXY
EPITAXIC > EPITAXY
EPITAXIES > EPITAXY
EPITAXIS same as
> EPITAXY
EPITAXY n growth of a thin layer on the surface of a crystal
EPITHECA n outer and older layer of the cell wall of a diatom
EPITHECAE > EPITHECA
EPITHELIA n animal tissues consisting of one or more layers of closely packed cells covering the external and internal surfaces of the body
EPITHEM n external topical application
EPITHEMA > EPITHEM
EPITHEMS > EPITHEM
EPITHESES > EPITHESIS
EPITHESIS n addition of a letter to the end of a word, so that its sense does not change
EPITHET n descriptive word or name ▷ vb name
EPITHETED > EPITHET
EPITHETIC > EPITHET
EPITHETON same as
> EPITHET
EPITHETS > EPITHET
EPITOME n typical example
EPITOMES > EPITOME

EPITOMIC > EPITOME

EPITOMISE same as > EPITOMIZE

EPITOMIST > EPITOMIZE

EPITOMIZE vb be the epitome of

EPITONIC adj undergoing too great a strain

EPITOPE n site on an antigen at which a specific antibody becomes attached

EPITOPES > EPITOPE

EPITRITE n metrical foot with three long syllables and one short one

EPITRITES > EPITRITE

EPIZEUXES > EPIZEUXIS

EPIZEUXIS n deliberate repetition of a word

EPIZOA > EPIZOON

EPIZOAN same as > EPIZOON

EPIZOANS > EPIZOAN

EPIZOIC adj (of an animal or plant) growing or living on the exterior of a living animal

EPIZOISM > EPIZOIC

EPIZOISMS > EPIZOIC

EPIZOITE n organism that lives on an animal but is not parasitic on it

EPIZOITES > EPIZOITE

EPIZOON n animal that lives on the body of another animal

EPIZOOTIC adj (of a disease) suddenly and temporarily affecting a large number of animals over a large area ▷ n epizootic disease

EPIZOOTY n animal disease

EPOCH n period of notable events

EPOCHA same as > EPOCH

EPOCHAL > EPOCH

EPOCHALLY > EPOCH

EPOCHAS > EPOCHA

EPOCHS > EPOCH

EPODE n part of a lyric ode that follows the strophe and the antistrophe

EPODES > EPODE

EPODIC > EPODE

EPONYM n name derived from the name of a real or mythical person

EPONYMIC > EPONYM

EPONYMIES > EPONYMY

EPONYMOUS adj after whom a book, play, etc is named

EPONYMS > EPONYM

EPONYMY n derivation of names of places, etc, from those of persons

EPOPEE n epic poem

EPOPEES > EPOPEE

EPOPOEIA same as > EPOPEE

EPOPOEIAS > EPOPOEIA

EPOPT n one initiated into mysteries

EPOPTS > EPOPT

EPOS n body of poetry in which the tradition of a people is conveyed

EPOSES > EPOS

EPOXIDE n chemical compound

EPOXIDES > EPOXIDE

EPOXIDISE same as > EPOXIDIZE

EPOXIDIZE vb form an epoxide

EPOXIED > EPOXY

EPOXIES > EPOXY

EPOXY adj of or containing a specific type of chemical compound ▷ n epoxy resin ▷ vb glue with epoxy resin

EPOXYED > EPOXY

EPOXYING > EPOXY

EPRIS adj enamoured

EPRISE feminine form of > EPRIS

EPSILON n fifth letter of the Greek alphabet

EPSILONIC adj of or relating to an arbitrary small quantity

EPSILONS > EPSILON

EPSOMITE n sulphate of magnesium

EPSOMITES > EPSOMITE

EPUISE adj exhausted

EPUISEE feminine form of > EPUISE

EPULARY adj of or relating to feasting

EPULATION n feasting

EPULIDES > EPULIS

EPULIS n swelling of the gum

EPULISES > EPULIS

EPULOTIC n scarring

EPULOTICS > EPULOTIC

EPURATE vb purify

EPURATED > EPURATE

EPURATES > EPURATE

EPURATING > EPURATE

EPURATION > EPURATE

EPYLLIA > EPYLLION

EPYLLION n miniature epic

EPYLLIONS > EPYLLION

EQUABLE adj even-tempered

EQUABLY > EQUABLE

EQUAL adj identical in size, quantity, degree, etc ▷ n person or thing equal to another ▷ vb be equal to

EQUALED > EQUAL

EQUALI pl n pieces for a group of instruments of the same kind

EQUALING > EQUAL

EQUALISE same as > EQUALIZE

EQUALISED > EQUALISE

EQUALISER same as > EQUALIZER

EQUALISES > EQUALISE

EQUALITY n state of being equal

EQUALIZE vb make or become equal

EQUALIZED > EQUALIZE

EQUALIZER n person or thing that equalizes, esp a device to counterbalance opposing forces

EQUALIZES > EQUALIZE

EQUALLED > EQUAL

EQUALLING > EQUAL

EQUALLY > EQUAL

EQUALNESS n equality

EQUALS > EQUAL

EQUANT n circle in which a planet was formerly believed to move

EQUANTS > EQUANT

EQUATABLE > EQUATE

EQUATE vb make or regard as equivalent

EQUATED > EQUATE

EQUATES > EQUATE

EQUATING > EQUATE

EQUATION n mathematical statement that two expressions are equal

EQUATIONS > EQUATION

EQUATIVE adj (in grammar) denoting the equivalence or identity of two terms

EQUATOR n imaginary circle round the earth

EQUATORS > EQUATOR

EQUERRIES > EQUERRY

EQUERRY n attendant to a member of a royal family

EQUES n (in ancient Rome) horseman

EQUID n any animal of the horse family

EQUIDS > EQUID

EQUIFINAL adj having the same end or result

EQUIMOLAL adj having an equal number of moles

EQUIMOLAR same as > EQUIMOLAL

EQUINAL same as > EQUINE

EQUINE adj of or like a horse ▷ n any animal of the horse family

EQUINELY > EQUINE

EQUINES > EQUINE

EQUINIA n glanders

EQUINIAS > EQUINIA

EQUINITY n horse-like nature

EQUINOX n time of year when day and night are of equal length

EQUINOXES > EQUINOX

EQUIP vb provide with supplies, components, etc

EQUIPAGE n horse-drawn carriage, esp one elegantly equipped and attended by liveried footmen ▷ vb equip

EQUIPAGED > EQUIPAGE

EQUIPAGES > EQUIPAGE

EQUIPE n (esp in motor racing) team

EQUIPES > EQUIPE

EQUIPMENT n set of tools or devices used for a particular purpose

EQUIPOISE n perfect balance ▷ vb offset or balance in weight or force

EQUIPPED > EQUIP

EQUIPPER > EQUIP

EQUIPPERS > EQUIP

EQUIPPING > EQUIP

EQUIPS > EQUIP

EQUISETA > EQUISETUM

EQUISETIC > EQUISETUM

EQUISETUM n type of plant such as the horsetail

EQUITABLE adj fair and reasonable

EQUITABLY > EQUITABLE

EQUITANT adj having the base folded around the stem

EQUITES pl n cavalry

EQUITIES > EQUITY

EQUITY n fairness

EQUIVALVE adj equipped with identical valves

EQUIVOCAL adj ambiguous

EQUIVOKE same as > EQUIVOQUE

EQUIVOKES > EQUIVOKE

EQUIVOQUE n play on words

ER interj sound made when hesitating in speech

ERA n period of time considered as distinctive

ERADIATE less common word for > RADIATE

ERADIATED > ERADIATE

ERADIATES > ERADIATE

ERADICANT > ERADICATE

ERADICATE vb destroy completely

ERAS > ERA

ERASABLE > ERASE

ERASE vb destroy all traces of

ERASED > ERASE

ERASEMENT > ERASE

ERASER n object for erasing something written

ERASERS > ERASER

ERASES > ERASE

ERASING > ERASE

ERASION n act of erasing

ERASIONS > ERASION

ERASURE n erasing

ERASURES > ERASURE

ERATHEM n stratum of rocks representing a specific geological era

ERATHEMS > ERATHEM

ERBIA n oxide of erbium

ERBIAS > ERBIA

ERBIUM n metallic element of the lanthanide series

ERBIUMS > ERBIUM

ERE prep before ▷ vb plough

ERECT vb build ▷ adj upright

ERECTABLE > ERECT

ERECTED > ERECT

ERECTER same as > ERECTOR

ERECTERS > ERECTER

ERECTILE adj capable of becoming erect

ERECTING > ERECT

ERECTION n act of erecting or the state of being erected

ERECTIONS > ERECTION

ERECTIVE adj tending to erect

ERECTLY > ERECT

ERECTNESS > ERECT

ERECTOR n any muscle that raises a part or makes it erect

ERECTORS > ERECTOR

ERECTS > ERECT

ERED > ERE

ERELONG adv before long

EREMIC adj of or relating to deserts

EREMITAL > EREMITE

EREMITE n Christian hermit

EREMITES > EREMITE

EREMITIC > EREMITE**

e

EREMITISH > EREMITE
EREMITISM > EREMITE
EREMURI > EREMURUS
EREMURUS n type of herb
ERENOW adv long before the present
EREPSIN n mixture of proteolytic enzymes secreted by the small intestine
EREPSINS > EREPSIN
ERES > ERE
ERETHIC > ERETHISM
ERETHISM n abnormally high degree of irritability or sensitivity in any part of the body
ERETHISMS > ERETHISM
ERETHITIC > ERETHISM
EREV n day before
EREVS > EREV
EREWHILE adv short time ago
EREWHILES same as > EREWHILE
ERF n plot of land marked off for building purposes
ERG same as > ERGOMETER
ERGASTIC adj consisting of the non-living by-products of protoplasmic activity
ERGATANER n wingless male ant
ERGATE n worker ant
ERGATES > ERGATE
ERGATIVE adj denoting a verb that takes the same noun as either direct object or subject ▷ n ergative verb
ERGATIVES > ERGATIVE
ERGATOID > ERGATE
ERGATOIDS > ERGATOID
ERGO same as > ERGOMETER
ERGODIC adj of or relating to the probability that any state will recur
ERGOGENIC adj giving energy
ERGOGRAM n tracing produced by an ergograph
ERGOGRAMS > ERGOGRAM
ERGOGRAPH n instrument that measures and records the amount of work a muscle does during contraction, its rate of fatigue, etc
ERGOMANIA n excessive desire to work
ERGOMETER n dynamometer
ERGOMETRY n measurement of work done
ERGON n work
ERGONOMIC adj designed to minimize effort
ERGONS > ERGON
ERGOS > ERGO
ERGOT n fungal disease of cereal
ERGOTIC > ERGOT
ERGOTISE same as > ERGOTIZE
ERGOTISED > ERGOTISE
ERGOTISES > ERGOTISE
ERGOTISM n ergot poisoning
ERGOTISMS > ERGOTISM

ERGOTIZE vb inflict ergotism upon
ERGOTIZED > ERGOTIZE
ERGOTIZES > ERGOTIZE
ERGOTS > ERGOT
ERGS > ERG
ERHU n Chinese two-stringed violin
ERHUS > ERHU
ERIACH same as > ERIC
ERIACHS > ERIACH
ERIC n (in old Irish law) fine paid by a murderer to the family of his or her victim
ERICA n genus of plants including heathers
ERICAS > ERICA
ERICK same as > ERIC
ERICKS > ERICK
ERICOID adj (of leaves) small and tough, resembling those of heather
ERICS > ERIC
ERIGERON n type of plant
ERIGERONS > ERIGERON
ERING > ERE
ERINGO same as > ERYNGO
ERINGOES > ERINGO
ERINGOS > ERINGO
ERINITE n arsenate of copper
ERINITES > ERINITE
ERINUS n type of plant
ERINUSES > ERINUS
ERIOMETER n device for measuring the diameters of minute particles or fibres
ERIONITE n common form of zeolite
ERIONITES > ERIONITE
ERIOPHYID n type of mite
ERISTIC adj of, relating to, or given to controversy or logical disputation ▷ n person who engages in logical disputes
ERISTICAL same as > ERISTIC
ERISTICS > ERISTIC
ERK n aircraftman or naval rating
ERKS > ERK
ERLANG n unit of traffic intensity in a telephone system
ERLANGS > ERLANG
ERLKING n malevolent spirit who carries off children
ERLKINGS > ERLKING
ERM interj expression of hesitation
ERMELIN n ermine
ERMELINS > ERMELIN
ERMINE n stoat in northern regions
ERMINED adj clad in the fur of the ermine
ERMINES > ERMINE
ERN archaic variant of > EARN
ERNE n fish-eating (European) sea eagle
ERNED > ERN
ERNES > ERNE
ERNING > ERN
ERNS > ERN
ERODABLE > ERODE
ERODE vb wear away

ERODED > ERODE
ERODENT > ERODE
ERODENTS > ERODE
ERODES > ERODE
ERODIBLE > ERODE
ERODING > ERODE
ERODIUM n type of geranium
ERODIUMS > ERODIUM
EROGENIC same as > EROGENOUS
EROGENOUS adj sensitive to sexual stimulation
EROS n love
EROSE adj jagged or uneven, as though gnawed or bitten
EROSELY > EROSE
EROSES > EROS
EROSIBLE adj able to be eroded
EROSION n wearing away of rocks or soil
EROSIONAL > EROSION
EROSIONS > EROSION
EROSIVE > EROSION
EROSIVITY > EROSION
EROSTRATE adj without a beak
EROTEMA n rhetorical question
EROTEMAS > EROTEMA
EROTEME same as > EROTEMA
EROTEMES > EROTEME
EROTESES > EROTESIS
EROTESIS same as > EROTEMA
EROTETIC adj pertaining to a rhetorical question
EROTIC adj relating to sexual pleasure or desire ▷ n person who has strong sexual desires
EROTICA n sexual literature or art
EROTICAL adj erotic
EROTICAS > EROTICA
EROTICISE same as > EROTICIZE
EROTICISM n erotic quality or nature
EROTICIST > EROTICISM
EROTICIZE vb regard or present in a sexual way
EROTICS > EROTIC
EROTISE same as > EROTIZE
EROTISED > EROTISE
EROTISES > EROTISE
EROTISING > EROTISE
EROTISM same as > EROTICISM
EROTISMS > EROTISM
EROTIZE vb make erotic
EROTIZED > EROTIZE
EROTIZES > EROTIZE
EROTIZING > EROTIZE
EROTOLOGY n study of erotic stimuli and sexual behaviour
ERR vb make a mistake
ERRABLE adj capable of making a mistake
ERRANCIES > ERRANCY
ERRANCY n state or an instance of erring or a tendency to err
ERRAND n short trip to do something for someone

ERRANDS > ERRAND
ERRANT adj behaving in a manner considered to be unacceptable ▷ n knight-errant
ERRANTLY > ERRANT
ERRANTRY n way of life of a knight errant
ERRANTS > ERRANT
ERRATA > ERRATUM
ERRATAS informal variant of > ERRATA
ERRATIC adj irregular or unpredictable ▷ n rock that has been transported by glacial action
ERRATICAL adj erratic
ERRATICS > ERRATIC
ERRATUM n error in writing or printing
ERRED > ERR
ERRHINE adj causing nasal secretion ▷ n errhine drug or agent
ERRHINES > ERRHINE
ERRING > ERR
ERRINGLY > ERR
ERRINGS > ERRING
ERRONEOUS adj incorrect, mistaken
ERROR n mistake, inaccuracy, or misjudgment
ERRORIST n one who makes errors
ERRORISTS > ERRORIST
ERRORLESS > ERROR
ERRORS > ERROR
ERRS > ERR
ERS same as > ERVIL
ERSATZ adj made in imitation ▷ n ersatz substance or article
ERSATZES > ERSATZ
ERSES > ERS
ERST adv long ago
ERSTWHILE adj former ▷ adv formerly
ERUCIC adj as in erucic acid crystalline fatty acid
ERUCIFORM adj resembling a caterpillar
ERUCT vb belch
ERUCTATE same as > ERUCT
ERUCTATED > ERUCTATE
ERUCTATES > ERUCTATE
ERUCTED > ERUCT
ERUCTING > ERUCT
ERUCTS > ERUCT
ERUDITE adj having great academic knowledge ▷ n erudite person
ERUDITELY > ERUDITE
ERUDITES > ERUDITE
ERUDITION > ERUDITE
ERUGO n verdigris
ERUGOS > ERUGO
ERUMPENT adj bursting out or developing as though bursting through
ERUPT vb eject (steam, water, or volcanic material) violently
ERUPTED > ERUPT
ERUPTIBLE > ERUPT
ERUPTING > ERUPT
ERUPTION > ERUPT
ERUPTIONS > ERUPT

ERUPTIVE adj erupting or tending to erupt ▷ n type of volcanic rock

ERUPTIVES > ERUPTIVE

ERUPTS > ERUPT

ERUV n area within which certain activities forbidden to be done on the Sabbath are permitted

ERUVIM > ERUV

ERUVIN > ERUV

ERUVS > ERUV

ERVALENTA n health food made from lentil and barley flour

ERVEN > ERF

ERVIL n type of vetch

ERVILS > ERVIL

ERYNGIUM n type of temperate and subtropical plant

ERYNGIUMS > ERYNGIUM

ERYNGO n type of plant with toothed or lobed leaves

ERYNGOES > ERYNGO

ERYNGOS > ERYNGO

ERYTHEMA n patchy inflammation of the skin

ERYTHEMAL > ERYTHEMA

ERYTHEMAS > ERYTHEMA

ERYTHEMIC > ERYTHEMA

ERYTHRINA n tropical tree with red flowers

ERYTHRISM n abnormal red coloration, as in plumage or hair

ERYTHRITE n sweet crystalline compound extracted from certain algae and lichens

ERYTHROID adj red or reddish

ERYTHRON n red blood cells and their related tissues

ERYTHRONS > ERYTHRON

ES n letter S

ESCABECHE n (in Mexican cookery) pickled vegetables and peppers, served as a condiment for fish

ESCALADE n assault by the use of ladders, esp on a fortification ▷ vb gain access to (a place) by the use of ladders

ESCALADED > ESCALADE

ESCALADER > ESCALADE

ESCALADES > ESCALADE

ESCALADO n escalade

ESCALATE vb increase in extent or intensity

ESCALATED > ESCALATE

ESCALATES > ESCALATE

ESCALATOR n moving staircase

ESCALIER n staircase

ESCALIERS > ESCALIER

ESCALLOP another word for > SCALLOP

ESCALLOPS > ESCALLOP

ESCALOP another word for > SCALLOP

ESCALOPE n thin slice of meat, esp veal

ESCALOPED > ESCALOP

ESCALOPES > ESCALOPE

ESCALOPS > ESCALOP

ESCAPABLE > ESCAPE

ESCAPADE n mischievous adventure

ESCAPADES > ESCAPADE

ESCAPADO n escaped criminal

ESCAPADOS > ESCAPADO

ESCAPE vb get free (of) ▷ n act of escaping

ESCAPED > ESCAPE

ESCAPEE n person who has escaped

ESCAPEES > ESCAPEE

ESCAPER > ESCAPE

ESCAPERS > ESCAPE

ESCAPES > ESCAPE

ESCAPING > ESCAPE

ESCAPISM n taking refuge in fantasy to avoid unpleasant reality

ESCAPISMS > ESCAPISM

ESCAPIST > ESCAPISM

ESCAPISTS > ESCAPISM

ESCAR same as > ESKER

ESCARGOT n variety of edible snail, usually eaten with a sauce made of melted butter and garlic

ESCARGOTS > ESCARGOT

ESCAROLE n variety of endive with broad leaves, used in salads

ESCAROLES > ESCAROLE

ESCARP n inner side of the ditch separating besiegers and besieged ▷ vb make into a slope

ESCARPED > ESCARP

ESCARPING > ESCARP

ESCARPS > ESCARP

ESCARS > ESCAR

ESCHALOT another name for a > SHALLOT

ESCHALOTS > ESCHALOT

ESCHAR n dry scab or slough

ESCHARS > ESCHAR

ESCHEAT n possessions that become state property in the absence of an heir ▷ vb attain such property

ESCHEATED > ESCHEAT

ESCHEATOR > ESCHEAT

ESCHEATS > ESCHEAT

ESCHEW vb abstain from, avoid

ESCHEWAL > ESCHEW

ESCHEWALS > ESCHEW

ESCHEWED > ESCHEW

ESCHEWER > ESCHEW

ESCHEWERS > ESCHEW

ESCHEWING > ESCHEW

ESCHEWS > ESCHEW

ESCLANDRE n scandal or notoriety

ESCOLAR n slender spiny-finned fish

ESCOLARS > ESCOLAR

ESCOPETTE n carbine

ESCORT n people following another person for protection or as an honour ▷ vb act as an escort to

ESCORTAGE > ESCORT

ESCORTED > ESCORT

ESCORTING > ESCORT

ESCORTS > ESCORT

ESCOT vb maintain

ESCOTED > ESCOT

ESCOTING > ESCOT

ESCOTS > ESCOT

ESCOTTED > ESCOT

ESCOTTING > ESCOT

ESCRIBANO n clerk

ESCRIBE vb make a mathematical drawing

ESCRIBED > ESCRIBE

ESCRIBES > ESCRIBE

ESCRIBING > ESCRIBE

ESCROC n conman

ESCROCS > ESCROC

ESCROL same as > ESCROLL

ESCROLL n scroll

ESCROLLS > ESCROLL

ESCROLS > ESCROL

ESCROW n item delivered to a third party pending fulfilment of a condition ▷ vb place (money, a document, etc) in escrow

ESCROWED > ESCROW

ESCROWING > ESCROW

ESCROWS > ESCROW

ESCUAGE (in medieval Europe) another word for > SCUTAGE

ESCUAGES > ESCUAGE

ESCUDO n former monetary unit of Portugal

ESCUDOS > ESCUDO

ESCULENT adj edible ▷ n any edible substance

ESCULENTS > ESCULENT

ESEMPLASY n unification

ESERINE n crystalline alkaloid

ESERINES > ESERINE

ESES > ES

ESILE n vinegar

ESILES > ESILE

ESKAR same as > ESKER

ESKARS > ESKAR

ESKER n long ridge of gravel, sand, etc

ESKERS > ESKER

ESKIES > ESKY

ESKY n portable insulated container

ESLOIN same as > ELOIGN

ESLOINED > ESLOIN

ESLOINING > ESLOIN

ESLOINS > ESLOIN

ESLOYNE same as > ELOIGN

ESLOYNED > ESLOYNE

ESLOYNES > ESLOYNE

ESLOYNING > ESLOYNE

ESNE n household slave

ESNECIES > ESNECY

ESNECY n inheritance law

ESNES > ESNE

ESOPHAGI > ESOPHAGUS

ESOPHAGUS n part of the alimentary canal between the pharynx and the stomach

ESOTERIC adj understood by only a small number of people with special knowledge

ESOTERICA n (collection of) esoteric things

ESOTERIES > ESOTERIC

ESOTERISM > ESOTERIC

ESOTERY > ESOTERIC

ESOTROPIA n condition in which eye turns inwards

ESOTROPIC > ESOTROPIA

ESPADA n sword

ESPADAS > ESPADA

ESPAGNOLE n tomato and sherry sauce

ESPALIER n shrub or fruit tree trained to grow flat ▷ vb train (a plant) on an espalier

ESPALIERS > ESPALIER

ESPANOL n Spanish person

ESPANOLES > ESPANOL

ESPARTO n grass of S Europe and N Africa

ESPARTOS > ESPARTO

ESPECIAL adj special

ESPERANCE n hope or expectation

ESPIAL n act or fact of being seen or discovered

ESPIALS > ESPIAL

ESPIED > ESPY

ESPIEGLE adj playful

ESPIER > ESPY

ESPIERS > ESPY

ESPIES > ESPY

ESPIONAGE n spying

ESPLANADE n wide open road used as a public promenade

ESPOIR n category of wrestler

ESPOIRS > ESPOIR

ESPOUSAL n adoption or support

ESPOUSALS > ESPOUSAL

ESPOUSE vb adopt or give support to (a cause etc)

ESPOUSED > ESPOUSE

ESPOUSER > ESPOUSE

ESPOUSERS > ESPOUSE

ESPOUSES > ESPOUSE

ESPOUSING > ESPOUSE

ESPRESSO n strong coffee made by forcing steam or boiling water through ground coffee beans

ESPRESSOS > ESPRESSO

ESPRIT n spirit, liveliness, or wit

ESPRITS > ESPRIT

ESPUMOSO n sparkling wine

ESPUMOSOS > ESPUMOSO

ESPY vb catch sight of

ESPYING > ESPY

ESQUIRE n courtesy title placed after a man's name ▷ vb escort

ESQUIRED > ESQUIRE

ESQUIRES > ESQUIRE

ESQUIRESS feminine form of > ESQUIRE

ESQUIRING > ESQUIRE

ESQUISSE n sketch

ESQUISSES > ESQUISSE

ESS n letter S

ESSAY n short literary composition ▷ vb attempt

ESSAYED > ESSAY

ESSAYER > ESSAY

ESSAYERS > ESSAY

ESSAYETTE n short essay

ESSAYING > ESSAY

ESSAYISH > ESSAY

ESSAYIST n person who writes essays

ESSAYISTS > ESSAYIST

ESSAYS > ESSAY

e

ESSE *n* existence
ESSENCE *n* most important feature of a thing which determines its identity
ESSENCES > ESSENCE
ESSENTIAL *adj* vitally important ▷ *n* something fundamental or indispensable
ESSES > ESS
ESSIVE *n* grammatical case
ESSIVES > ESSIVE
ESSOIN *n* excuse ▷ *vb* excuse for not appearing in court
ESSOINED > ESSOIN
ESSOINER > ESSOIN
ESSOINERS > ESSOIN
ESSOINING > ESSOIN
ESSOINS > ESSOIN
ESSONITE *variant spelling of* > HESSONITE
ESSONITES > ESSONITE
ESSOYNE *same as* > ESSOIN
ESSOYNES > ESSOYNE
EST *n* treatment intended to help people towards psychological growth
ESTABLISH *vb* set up on a permanent basis
ESTACADE *n* defensive arrangement of stakes
ESTACADES > ESTACADE
ESTAFETTE *n* mounted courier
ESTAMINET *n* small café, bar, or bistro, esp a shabby one
ESTANCIA *n* (in Spanish America) a large estate or cattle ranch
ESTANCIAS > ESTANCIA
ESTATE *n* landed property ▷ *vb* provide with an estate
ESTATED > ESTATE
ESTATES > ESTATE
ESTATING > ESTATE
ESTEEM *n* high regard ▷ *vb* think highly of
ESTEEMED > ESTEEM
ESTEEMING > ESTEEM
ESTEEMS > ESTEEM
ESTER *n* chemical compound
ESTERASE *n* any of a group of enzymes that hydrolyse esters
ESTERASES > ESTERASE
ESTERIFY *vb* change or cause to change into an ester
ESTERS > ESTER
ESTHESES > ESTHESIS
ESTHESIA *US spelling of* > AESTHESIA
ESTHESIAS > ESTHESIA
ESTHESIS *n* esthesia
ESTHETE *US spelling of* > AESTHETE
ESTHETES > ESTHETE
ESTHETIC > ESTHETE
ESTHETICS > ESTHETE
ESTIMABLE *adj* worthy of respect
ESTIMABLY > ESTIMABLE
ESTIMATE *vb* calculate roughly ▷ *n* approximate calculation

ESTIMATED > ESTIMATE
ESTIMATES > ESTIMATE
ESTIMATOR *n* person or thing that estimates
ESTIVAL *usual US spelling of* > AESTIVAL
ESTIVATE *usual US spelling of* > AESTIVATE
ESTIVATED > ESTIVATE
ESTIVATES > ESTIVATE
ESTIVATOR > ESTIVATE
ESTOC *n* short stabbing sword
ESTOCS > ESTOC
ESTOILE *n* heraldic star with wavy points
ESTOILES > ESTOILE
ESTOP *vb* preclude by estoppel
ESTOPPAGE > ESTOP
ESTOPPED > ESTOP
ESTOPPEL *n* rule precluding a person from denying the truth of a statement of facts
ESTOPPELS > ESTOPPEL
ESTOPPING > ESTOP
ESTOPS > ESTOP
ESTOVER *same as* > ESTOVERS
ESTOVERS *pl n* right allowed by law to tenants of land to cut timber, esp for fuel and repairs
ESTRADE *n* dais or raised platform
ESTRADES > ESTRADE
ESTRADIOL *n* most potent estrogenic hormone secreted by the mammalian ovary
ESTRAGON *another name for* > TARRAGON
ESTRAGONS > ESTRAGON
ESTRAL *US spelling of* > OESTRAL
ESTRANGE *vb* separate and live apart from (one's spouse)
ESTRANGED *adj* no longer living with one's spouse
ESTRANGER > ESTRANGE
ESTRANGES > ESTRANGE
ESTRAPADE *n* attempt by a horse to throw its rider
ESTRAY *n* stray domestic animal of unknown ownership ▷ *vb* stray
ESTRAYED > ESTRAY
ESTRAYING > ESTRAY
ESTRAYS > ESTRAY
ESTREAT *n* true copy of or extract from a court record ▷ *vb* send an extract of the court record
ESTREATED > ESTREAT
ESTREATS > ESTREAT
ESTREPE *vb* lay waste
ESTREPED > ESTREPE
ESTREPES > ESTREPE
ESTREPING > ESTREPE
ESTRICH *n* ostrich
ESTRICHES > ESTRICH
ESTRIDGE *n* ostrich
ESTRIDGES > ESTRIDGE
ESTRILDID *n* weaver finch
ESTRIN *US spelling of* > OESTRIN
ESTRINS > ESTRIN

ESTRIOL *usual US spelling of* > OESTRIOL
ESTRIOLS > ESTRIOL
ESTRO *n* poetic inspiration
ESTROGEN *usual US spelling of* > OESTROGEN
ESTROGENS > ESTROGEN
ESTRONE *usual US spelling of* > OESTRONE
ESTRONES > ESTRONE
ESTROS > ESTRO
ESTROUS > ESTRUS
ESTRUAL > ESTRUS
ESTRUM *usual US spelling of* > OESTRUM
ESTRUMS > ESTRUM
ESTRUS *usual US spelling of* > OESTRUS
ESTRUSES > ESTRUS
ESTS > EST
ESTUARIAL > ESTUARY
ESTUARIAN > ESTUARY
ESTUARIES > ESTUARY
ESTUARINE *adj* formed or deposited in an estuary
ESTUARY *n* mouth of a river
ESURIENCE > ESURIENT
ESURIENCY > ESURIENT
ESURIENT *adj* greedy
ET *dialect past tense of* > EAT
ETA *n* seventh letter in the Greek alphabet
ETACISM *n* pronunciation of eta as a long vowel sound
ETACISMS > ETACISM
ETAERIO *n* aggregate fruit
ETAERIOS > ETAERIO
ETAGE *n* floor in a multi-storey building
ETAGERE *n* stand with open shelves for displaying ornaments, etc
ETAGERES > ETAGERE
ETAGES > ETAGE
ETALAGE *n* display
ETALAGES > ETALAGE
ETALON *n* device used in spectroscopy
ETALONS > ETALON
ETAMIN *same as* > ETAMINE
ETAMINE *n* cotton or worsted fabric of loose weave
ETAMINES > ETAMINE
ETAMINS > ETAMIN
ETAPE *n* public storehouse
ETAPES > ETAPE
ETAS > ETA
ETAT *n* state
ETATISM *same as* > ETATISME
ETATISME *n* authoritarian control by the state
ETATISMES > ETATISME
ETATISMS > ETATISM
ETATIST > ETATISME
ETATISTE > ETATISME
ETATISTES > ETATISME
ETATS > ETAT
ETCETERA *n* number of other items
ETCETERAS *pl n* miscellaneous extra things or people
ETCH *vb* wear away or cut the surface of (metal, glass, etc) with acid

ETCHANT *n* any acid or corrosive used for etching
ETCHANTS > ETCHANT
ETCHED > ETCH
ETCHER > ETCH
ETCHERS > ETCH
ETCHES > ETCH
ETCHING *n* picture printed from an etched metal plate
ETCHINGS > ETCHING
ETEN *n* giant
ETENS > ETEN
ETERNAL *adj* without beginning or end ▷ *n* eternal thing
ETERNALLY > ETERNAL
ETERNALS > ETERNAL
ETERNE *archaic or poetic word for* > ETERNAL
ETERNISE *same as* > ETERNIZE
ETERNISED > ETERNISE
ETERNISES > ETERNISE
ETERNITY *n* infinite time
ETERNIZE *vb* make eternal
ETERNIZED > ETERNIZE
ETERNIZES > ETERNIZE
ETESIAN *adj* (of NW winds) recurring annually in the summer in the E Mediterranean ▷ *n* etesian wind
ETESIANS > ETESIAN
ETH *same as* > EDH
ETHAL *n* cetyl alcohol
ETHALS > ETHAL
ETHANAL *n* colourless volatile pungent liquid
ETHANALS > ETHANAL
ETHANE *n* odourless flammable gas
ETHANES > ETHANE
ETHANOATE *same as* > ACETATE
ETHANOIC *adj* as in ethanoic acid acetic acid
ETHANOL *same as* > ALCOHOL
ETHANOLS > ETHANOL
ETHANOYL *n* type of acyl group or radical
ETHANOYLS > ETHANOYL
ETHE *adj* easy
ETHENE *same as* > ETHYLENE
ETHENES > ETHENE
ETHEPHON *n* synthetic plant-growth regulator
ETHEPHONS > ETHEPHON
ETHER *n* colourless anaesthetic
ETHERCAP *n* spider
ETHERCAPS > ETHERCAP
ETHEREAL *adj* extremely delicate
ETHEREOUS *same as* > ETHEREAL
ETHERIAL *same as* > ETHEREAL
ETHERIC > ETHER
ETHERICAL > ETHER
ETHERIFY *vb* change (a compound, such as an alcohol) into an ether
ETHERION *n* gas formerly believed to exist in air
ETHERIONS > ETHERION

ETHERISE same as > ETHERIZE

ETHERISED > ETHERISE

ETHERISER > ETHERISE

ETHERISES > ETHERISE

ETHERISH > ETHER

ETHERISM n addiction to ether

ETHERISMS > ETHERISM

ETHERIST > ETHERISM

ETHERISTS > ETHERISM

ETHERIZE vb subject (a person) to the anaesthetic influence of ether fumes

ETHERIZED > ETHERIZE

ETHERIZER > ETHERIZE

ETHERIZES > ETHERIZE

ETHERS > ETHER

ETHIC n moral principle

ETHICAL adj of or based on a system of moral beliefs ▷ n drug available only by prescription

ETHICALLY > ETHICAL

ETHICALS > ETHICAL

ETHICIAN > ETHICS

ETHICIANS > ETHICS

ETHICISE same as > ETHICIZE

ETHICISED > ETHICISE

ETHICISES > ETHICISE

ETHICISM > ETHICS

ETHICISMS > ETHICS

ETHICIST > ETHICS

ETHICISTS > ETHICS

ETHICIZE vb make or consider as ethical

ETHICIZED > ETHICIZE

ETHICIZES > ETHICIZE

ETHICS n code of behaviour

ETHINYL same as > ETHYNYL

ETHINYLS > ETHINYL

ETHION n type of pesticide

ETHIONINE n type of amino acid

ETHIONS > ETHION

ETHIOPS n dark-coloured chemical compound

ETHIOPSES > ETHIOPS

ETHMOID adj denoting or relating to a specific bone of the skull ▷ n ethmoid bone

ETHMOIDAL same as > ETHMOID

ETHMOIDS > ETHMOID

ETHNARCH n ruler of a people or province, as in parts of the Roman and Byzantine Empires

ETHNARCHS > ETHNARCH

ETHNARCHY > ETHNARCH

ETHNE > ETHNOS

ETHNIC adj relating to a people or group that shares a culture, religion, or language ▷ n member of an ethnic group, esp a minority group

ETHNICAL same as > ETHNIC

ETHNICISM n paganism

ETHNICITY > ETHNIC

ETHNICS > ETHNIC

ETHNOCIDE n extermination of a race

ETHNOGENY n branch of ethnology that deals with the origin of races or peoples

ETHNOLOGY n study of human races

ETHNONYM n name of ethnic group

ETHNONYMS > ETHNONYM

ETHNOS n ethnic group

ETHNOSES > ETHNOS

ETHOGRAM n description of animal's behaviour

ETHOGRAMS > ETHOGRAM

ETHOLOGIC > ETHOLOGY

ETHOLOGY n study of the behaviour of animals in their normal environment

ETHONONE another name for > KETENE

ETHONONES > ETHONONE

ETHOS n distinctive spirit and attitudes of a people, culture, etc

ETHOSES > ETHOS

ETHOXIDE n any of a class of saltlike compounds

ETHOXIDES > ETHOXIDE

ETHOXIES > ETHOXY

ETHOXY same as > ETHOXYL

ETHOXYL n univalent radical

ETHOXYLS > ETHOXYL

ETHS > ETH

ETHYL adj type of chemical hydrocarbon group

ETHYLATE same as > ETHOXIDE

ETHYLATED > ETHYLATE

ETHYLATES > ETHYLATE

ETHYLENE n poisonous gas used as an anaesthetic and as fuel

ETHYLENES > ETHYLENE

ETHYLENIC > ETHYLENE

ETHYLIC > ETHYL

ETHYLS > ETHYL

ETHYNE another name for > ACETYLENE

ETHYNES > ETHYNE

ETHYNYL n univalent radical

ETHYNYLS > ETHYNYL

ETIC adj relating to linguistic terms analysed without regard to structural function ▷ n etic approach or viewpoint

ETICS > ETIC

ETIOLATE vb become pale and weak

ETIOLATED > ETIOLATE

ETIOLATES > ETIOLATE

ETIOLIN n yellow pigment

ETIOLINS > ETIOLIN

ETIOLOGIC > ETIOLOGY

ETIOLOGY n study of the causes of diseases

ETIQUETTE n conventional code of conduct

ETNA n container used to heat liquids

ETNAS > ETNA

ETOILE n star

ETOILES > ETOILE

ETOUFFEE n spicy Cajun stew

ETOUFFEES > ETOUFFEE

ETOURDI adj foolish

ETOURDIE feminine form of > ETOURDI

ETRANGER n foreigner

ETRANGERE feminine form of > ETRANGER

ETRANGERS > ETRANGER

ETRENNE n New Year's gift

ETRENNES > ETRENNE

ETRIER n short portable ladder or set of webbing loops

ETRIERS > ETRIER

ETTERCAP n spider

ETTERCAPS > ETTERCAP

ETTIN n giant

ETTINS > ETTIN

ETTLE vb intend

ETTLED > ETTLE

ETTLES > ETTLE

ETTLING > ETTLE

ETUDE n short musical composition for a solo instrument

ETUDES > ETUDE

ETUI n small usually ornamented case

ETUIS > ETUI

ETWEE same as > ETUI

ETWEES > ETWEE

ETYMA > ETYMON

ETYMIC > ETYMON

ETYMOLOGY n study of the sources and development of words

ETYMON n earliest form of a word or morpheme from which another is derived

ETYMONS > ETYMON

ETYPIC adj unable to conform to type

ETYPICAL same as > ETYPIC

EUCAIN same as > EUCAINE

EUCAINE n crystalline optically active substance

EUCAINES > EUCAINE

EUCAINS > EUCAIN

EUCALYPT n myrtaceous tree

EUCALYPTI n eucalypts

EUCALYPTS > EUCALYPT

EUCARYON same as > EUKARYOTE

EUCARYONS > EUCARYON

EUCARYOT same as > EUKARYOTE

EUCARYOTE same as > EUKARYOTE

EUCARYOTS > EUCARYOT

EUCHARIS n S American plant cultivated for its large white fragrant flowers

EUCHLORIC > EUCHLORIN

EUCHLORIN n explosive gaseous mixture of chlorine and chlorine dioxide

EUCHOLOGY n prayer formulary

EUCHRE n US and Canadian card game ▷ vb prevent (a player) from making their contracted tricks

EUCHRED > EUCHRE

EUCHRES > EUCHRE

EUCHRING > EUCHRE

EUCLASE n brittle green gem

EUCLASES > EUCLASE

EUCLIDEAN adj of or relating to Euclid (Greek mathematician of Alexandria, 3rd century BC), esp his system of geometry

EUCLIDIAN same as > EUCLIDEAN

EUCRITE n type of stony meteorite

EUCRITES > EUCRITE

EUCRITIC > EUCRITE

EUCRYPHIA n Australian and S American tree or shrub, mostly evergreen, with dark lustrous green leaves and white flowers

EUCYCLIC adj (of plants) having the same number of leaves in each whorl

EUDAEMON same as > EUDEMON

EUDAEMONS > EUDAEMON

EUDAEMONY same as > EUDEMONIA

EUDAIMON same as > EUDEMON

EUDAIMONS > EUDAIMON

EUDEMON n benevolent spirit or demon

EUDEMONIA n happiness, esp (in the philosophy of Aristotle) that resulting from a rational active life

EUDEMONIC > EUDEMONIA

EUDEMONS > EUDEMON

EUDIALYTE n brownish-red mineral

EUGARIE another name for > PIPI

EUGARIES > EUGARIE

EUGE interj well done!

EUGENIA n plant of the clove family

EUGENIAS > EUGENIA

EUGENIC > EUGENICS

EUGENICAL > EUGENICS

EUGENICS n study of methods of improving the human race

EUGENISM > EUGENICS

EUGENISMS > EUGENICS

EUGENIST > EUGENICS

EUGENISTS > EUGENICS

EUGENOL n oily liquid used in perfumery

EUGENOLS > EUGENOL

EUGH archaic form of > YEW

EUGHEN archaic form of > YEW

EUGHS > EUGH

EUGLENA n type of freshwater unicellular organism

EUGLENAS > EUGLENA

EUGLENID same as > EUGLENA

EUGLENIDS > EUGLENID

EUGLENOID > EUGLENA

EUK vb itch

EUKARYON same as > EUKARYOTE

EUKARYONS > EUKARYON

EUKARYOT same as > EUKARYOTE

EUKARYOTE n type of organism whose cells each have a distinct nucleus within which the genetic material is contained

EUKARYOTS > EUKARYOT

EUKED > EUK

EUKING > EUK

EUKS > EUK

e

EULACHAN same as
> EULACHON
EULACHANS > EULACHAN
EULACHON n salmonoid
food fish
EULACHONS > EULACHON
EULOGIA n blessed bread
EULOGIAE > EULOGIA
EULOGIAS > EULOGIA
EULOGIES > EULOGY
EULOGISE same as
> EULOGIZE
EULOGISED > EULOGISE
EULOGISER > EULOGISE
EULOGISES > EULOGISE
EULOGIST > EULOGIZE
EULOGISTS > EULOGIZE
EULOGIUM same as
> EULOGY
EULOGIUMS > EULOGIUM
EULOGIZE vb praise (a
person or thing) highly in
speech or writing
EULOGIZED > EULOGIZE
EULOGIZER > EULOGIZE
EULOGIZES > EULOGIZE
EULOGY n speech or writing
in praise of a person
EUMELANIN n dark melanin
EUMERISM n collection of
similar parts
EUMERISMS > EUMERISM
EUMONG same as > EUMUNG
EUMONGS > EUMONG
EUMUNG n any of various
Australian acacias
EUMUNGS > EUMUNG
EUNUCH n castrated man
EUNUCHISE same as
> EUNUCHIZE
EUNUCHISM > EUNUCH
EUNUCHIZE vb castrate
EUNUCHOID n one suffering
from deficient sexual
development
EUNUCHS > EUNUCH
EUOI n cry of Bacchic
frenzy
EUONYMIN n extract derived
from the bark of the
euonymus
EUONYMINS > EUONYMIN
EUONYMUS n type of
N temperate tree or shrub
EUOUAE n musical term
EUOUAES > EUOUAE
EUPAD n antiseptic powder
EUPADS > EUPAD
EUPATRID n (in ancient
Greece) hereditary noble or
landowner
EUPATRIDS > EUPATRID
EUPEPSIA n good digestion
EUPEPSIAS > EUPEPSIA
EUPEPSIES > EUPEPSY
EUPEPSY same as
> EUPEPSIA
EUPEPTIC > EUPEPSIA
EUPHAUSID n small pelagic
shrimplike crustacean
EUPHEMISE same as
> EUPHEMIZE
EUPHEMISM n inoffensive
word or phrase substituted
for one considered offensive
or upsetting
EUPHEMIST > EUPHEMISM

EUPHEMIZE vb speak in
euphemisms or refer to by
means of a euphemism
EUPHENIC adj of or
pertaining to biological
improvement
EUPHENICS n science of
biological improvement
EUPHOBIA n fear of good
news
EUPHOBIAS > EUPHOBIA
EUPHON n glass harmonica
EUPHONIA same as
> EUPHONY
EUPHONIAS > EUPHONIA
EUPHONIC adj denoting or
relating to euphony
EUPHONIES > EUPHONY
EUPHONISE same as
> EUPHONIZE
EUPHONISM n use of
pleasant-sounding words
EUPHONIUM n brass musical
instrument, tenor tuba
EUPHONIZE vb make
pleasant to hear
EUPHONS > EUPHON
EUPHONY n pleasing sound
EUPHORBIA n type of plant
such as the spurge or
poinsettia
EUPHORIA n sense of
elation
EUPHORIAS > EUPHORIA
EUPHORIC > EUPHORIA
EUPHORIES > EUPHORY
EUPHORY same as
> EUPHORIA
EUPHOTIC adj denoting the
part of a sea or lake with
enough light to enable
photosynthesis
EUPHRASIA n eyebright
EUPHRASY same as
> EYEBRIGHT
EUPHROE n wooden block
through which the lines of a
crowfoot are rove
EUPHROES > EUPHROE
EUPHUISE same as
> EUPHUIZE
EUPHUISED > EUPHUISE
EUPHUISES > EUPHUISE
EUPHUISM n artificial prose
style of the Elizabethan
period
EUPHUISMS > EUPHUISM
EUPHUIST > EUPHUISM
EUPHUISTS > EUPHUISM
EUPHUIZE vb write in
euphuism
EUPHUIZED > EUPHUIZE
EUPHUIZES > EUPHUIZE
EUPLASTIC adj healing
quickly and well
EUPLOID adj having
chromosomes in an exact
multiple of the haploid
number ▷ n euploid cell or
individual
EUPLOIDS > EUPLOID
EUPLOIDY > EUPLOID
EUPNEA same as > EUPNOEA
EUPNEAS > EUPNEA
EUPNEIC > EUPNOEA
EUPNOEA n normal relaxed
breathing
EUPNOEAS > EUPNOEA

EUPNOEIC > EUPNOEA
EUREKA n exclamation of
triumph at finding
something
EUREKAS > EUREKA
EURHYTHMY n rhythmic
movement
EURIPI > EURIPUS
EURIPUS n strait or channel
with a strong current or tide
EURIPUSES > EURIPUS
EURO n unit of the single
currency of the European
Union
EUROBOND n bond issued in
a eurocurrency
EUROBONDS > EUROBOND
EUROCRAT n member, esp a
senior member, of the
administration of the
European Union
EUROCRATS > EUROCRAT
EUROCREEP n gradual
introduction of the euro into
use in Britain
EUROKIES > EUROKY
EUROKOUS > EUROKY
EUROKY n ability of an
organism to live under
different conditions
EUROLAND n area
containing the countries
using the euro
EUROLANDS > EUROLAND
EURONOTE n form of
euro-commercial paper
consisting of short-term
negotiable bearer notes
EURONOTES > EURONOTE
EUROPHILE n person who
admires Europe, Europeans,
or the European Union
EUROPIUM n silvery-white
element of the lanthanide
series
EUROPIUMS > EUROPIUM
EUROPOP n type of pop
music by European artists
EUROPOPS > EUROPOP
EUROS > EURO
EUROZONE n area
containing the countries
using the euro
EUROZONES > EUROZONE
EURYBATH n organism that
can live at different depths
underwater
EURYBATHS > EURYBATH
EURYOKIES > EURYOKY
EURYOKOUS > EURYOKY
EURYOKY same as > EUROKY
EURYTHERM n organism
that can tolerate widely
differing temperatures
EURYTHMIC adj having a
pleasing and harmonious
rhythm, order, or structure
EURYTHMY n dancing style
in which the rhythm of music
is expressed through body
movements
EURYTOPIC adj (of a
species) able to tolerate a
wide range of environments
EUSOCIAL adj using division
of labour
EUSOL n solution of eupad in
water

EUSOLS > EUSOL
EUSTACIES > EUSTATIC
EUSTACY > EUSTATIC
EUSTASIES > EUSTATIC
EUSTASY > EUSTATIC
EUSTATIC adj denoting
worldwide changes in sea
level
EUSTELE n central cylinder
of a seed plant
EUSTELES > EUSTELE
EUSTRESS n type of stress
that is beneficial
EUSTYLE n building with
columns optimally spaced
EUSTYLES > EUSTYLE
EUTAXIA n condition of
being easily melted
EUTAXIAS > EUTAXIA
EUTAXIES > EUTAXY
EUTAXITE n banded
volcanic rock
EUTAXITES > EUTAXITE
EUTAXITIC > EUTAXITE
EUTAXY n good order
EUTECTIC adj having the
lowest freezing point
possible for the mixture ▷ n
eutectic mixture
EUTECTICS > EUTECTIC
EUTECTOID n mixture of
substances similar to a
eutectic, but forming two or
three constituents from a
solid instead of from a melt
▷ adj concerned with or
suitable for eutectoid
mixtures
EUTEXIA same as
> EUTAXIA
EUTEXIAS > EUTEXIA
EUTHANASE same as
> EUTHANIZE
EUTHANASY n the act of
killing someone painlessly
EUTHANAZE same as
> EUTHANIZE
EUTHANISE same as
> EUTHANIZE
EUTHANIZE vb kill
(someone, esp one suffering
from a terminal illness)
painlessly
EUTHENICS n study of the
control of the environment,
esp with a view to improving
the health and living
standards of the human race
EUTHENIST > EUTHENICS
EUTHERIAN n type of
mammal with a placenta,
whose young reach an
advanced state of
development before birth
EUTHYMIA n pleasant state
of mind
EUTHYMIAS > EUTHYMIA
EUTHYROID n condition of
having thyroid glands that
function normally
EUTRAPELY n
conversational skill
EUTROPHIC adj (of lakes
and similar habitats) rich in
organic and mineral
nutrients and supporting an
abundant plant life, which in
the process of decaying

depletes the oxygen supply for animal life

EUTROPHY > EUTROPHIC

EUTROPIC > EUTROPY

EUTROPIES > EUTROPY

EUTROPOUS > EUTROPY

EUTROPY n chemical structure

EUXENITE n rare brownish-black mineral

EUXENITES > EUXENITE

EVACUANT adj serving to promote excretion ▷ n evacuant agent

EVACUANTS > EVACUANT

EVACUATE vb send (someone) away from a place of danger

EVACUATED > EVACUATE

EVACUATES > EVACUATE

EVACUATOR > EVACUATE

EVACUEE n person evacuated from a place of danger

EVACUEES > EVACUEE

EVADABLE > EVADE

EVADE vb get away from or avoid

EVADED > EVADE

EVADER > EVADE

EVADERS > EVADE

EVADES > EVADE

EVADIBLE > EVADE

EVADING > EVADE

EVADINGLY > EVADE

EVAGATION n digression

EVAGINATE vb turn (an organ or part) inside out

EVALUABLE > EVALUATE

EVALUATE vb find or judge the value of

EVALUATED > EVALUATE

EVALUATES > EVALUATE

EVALUATOR > EVALUATE

EVANESCE vb fade gradually from sight

EVANESCED > EVANESCE

EVANESCES > EVANESCE

EVANGEL n gospel of Christianity

EVANGELIC adj of, based upon, or following from the gospels

EVANGELS > EVANGEL

EVANGELY n gospel

EVANISH poetic word for > VANISH

EVANISHED > EVANISH

EVANISHES > EVANISH

EVANITION > EVANISH

EVAPORATE vb change from a liquid or solid to a vapour

EVAPORITE n any sedimentary rock, such as rock salt, gypsum, or anhydrite, formed by evaporation of former seas or salt-water lakes

EVASIBLE > EVASION

EVASION n act of evading something by cunning or illegal means

EVASIONAL > EVASION

EVASIONS > EVASION

EVASIVE adj not straightforward

EVASIVELY > EVASIVE

EVE n evening or day before some special event

EVECTION n irregularity in the moon's motion caused by perturbations of the sun and planets

EVECTIONS > EVECTION

EVEJAR n nightjar

EVEJARS > EVEJAR

EVEN adj flat or smooth ▷ adv equally ▷ vb make even ▷ n eve

EVENED > EVEN

EVENEMENT n event

EVENER > EVEN

EVENERS > EVEN

EVENEST > EVEN

EVENFALL n early evening

EVENFALLS > EVENFALL

EVENING n end of the day or early part of the night ▷ adj of or in the evening

EVENINGS adv in the evening, esp regularly

EVENLY > EVEN

EVENNESS > EVEN

EVENS adv (of a bet) winning the same as the amount staked if successful

EVENSONG n evening prayer

EVENSONGS > EVENSONG

EVENT n anything that takes place ▷ vb take part or ride (a horse) in eventing

EVENTED > EVENT

EVENTER > EVENTING

EVENTERS > EVENTING

EVENTFUL adj full of exciting incidents

EVENTIDE n evening

EVENTIDES > EVENTIDE

EVENTING n riding competitions, usu involving cross-country, jumping, and dressage

EVENTINGS > EVENTING

EVENTIVE adj relating to an event

EVENTLESS > EVENT

EVENTRATE vb open the belly of

EVENTS > EVENT

EVENTUAL adj ultimate

EVENTUATE vb result ultimately (in)

EVER adv at any time

EVERGLADE n large area of submerged marshland

EVERGREEN adj (tree or shrub) having leaves throughout the year ▷ n evergreen tree or shrub

EVERMORE adv for all time to come

EVERNET n hypothetical form of internet

EVERNETS > EVERNET

EVERSIBLE > EVERT

EVERSION > EVERT

EVERSIONS > EVERT

EVERT vb turn (some bodily part) outwards or inside out

EVERTED > EVERT

EVERTING > EVERT

EVERTOR n any muscle that turns a part outwards

EVERTORS > EVERTOR

EVERTS > EVERT

EVERWHERE adv to or in all parts or places

EVERWHICH dialect version of > WHICHEVER

EVERY adj each without exception

EVERYBODY pron every person

EVERYDAY adj usual or ordinary ▷ n ordinary day

EVERYDAYS > EVERYDAY

EVERYMAN n ordinary person; common person

EVERYMEN > EVERYMAN

EVERYONE pron every person

EVERYWAY adv in every way

EVERYWHEN adv to or in all parts or places

EVES > EVE

EVET n eft

EVETS > EVET

EVHOE interj cry of Bacchic frenzy

EVICT vb legally expel (someone) from his or her home

EVICTED > EVICT

EVICTEE > EVICT

EVICTEES > EVICT

EVICTING > EVICT

EVICTION > EVICT

EVICTIONS > EVICT

EVICTOR > EVICT

EVICTORS > EVICT

EVICTS > EVICT

EVIDENCE n ground for belief ▷ vb demonstrate, prove

EVIDENCED > EVIDENCE

EVIDENCES > EVIDENCE

EVIDENT adj easily seen or understood ▷ n item of evidence

EVIDENTLY adv without question

EVIDENTS > EVIDENT

EVIL n wickedness ▷ adj harmful ▷ adv in an evil manner

EVILDOER n wicked person

EVILDOERS > EVILDOER

EVILDOING > EVILDOER

EVILER > EVIL

EVILEST > EVIL

EVILLER > EVIL

EVILLEST > EVIL

EVILLY > EVIL

EVILNESS > EVIL

EVILS > EVIL

EVINCE vb make evident

EVINCED > EVINCE

EVINCES > EVINCE

EVINCIBLE > EVINCE

EVINCIBLY > EVINCE

EVINCING > EVINCE

EVINCIVE > EVINCE

EVIRATE vb deprive of strength or vigour

EVIRATED > EVIRATE

EVIRATES > EVIRATE

EVIRATING > EVIRATE

EVITABLE adj able to be avoided

EVITATE archaic word for > AVOID

EVITATED > EVITATE

EVITATES > EVITATE

EVITATING > EVITATE

EVITATION > EVITATE

EVITE archaic word for > AVOID

EVITED > EVITE

EVITERNAL adj eternal

EVITES > EVITE

EVITING > EVITE

EVO informal word for > EVENING

EVOCABLE > EVOKE

EVOCATE vb evoke

EVOCATED > EVOCATE

EVOCATES > EVOCATE

EVOCATING > EVOCATE

EVOCATION n act of evoking

EVOCATIVE adj tending or serving to evoke

EVOCATOR n person or thing that evokes

EVOCATORS > EVOCATOR

EVOCATORY adj evocative

EVOE interj cry of Bacchic frenzy

EVOHE interj cry of Bacchic frenzy

EVOKE vb call or summon up (a memory, feeling, etc)

EVOKED > EVOKE

EVOKER > EVOKE

EVOKERS > EVOKE

EVOKES > EVOKE

EVOKING > EVOKE

EVOLUE n colonial term for an African educated according to European principles

EVOLUES > EVOLUE

EVOLUTE n geometric curve ▷ adj having the margins rolled outwards ▷ vb evolve

EVOLUTED > EVOLUTE

EVOLUTES > EVOLUTE

EVOLUTING > EVOLUTE

EVOLUTION n gradual change in the characteristics of living things over successive generations, esp to a more complex form

EVOLUTIVE adj relating to, tending to, or promoting evolution

EVOLVABLE > EVOLVE

EVOLVE vb develop gradually

EVOLVED > EVOLVE

EVOLVENT adj evolving ▷ n involute curve

EVOLVENTS > EVOLVENT

EVOLVER > EVOLVE

EVOLVERS > EVOLVE

EVOLVES > EVOLVE

EVOLVING > EVOLVE

EVONYMUS same as > EUONYMUS

EVOS > EVO

EVOVAE n mnemonic used in sacred music

EVOVAES > EVOVAE

EVULGATE vb make public

EVULGATED > EVULGATE

EVULGATES > EVULGATE

EVULSE vb extract by force

EVULSED > EVULSE

EVULSES > EVULSE
EVULSING > EVULSE
EVULSION n act of extracting by force
EVULSIONS > EVULSION
EVZONE n soldier in an elite Greek infantry regiment
EVZONES > EVZONE
EW interj expression of disgust
EWE n female sheep
EWER n large jug with a wide mouth
EWERS > EWER
EWES > EWE
EWEST Scots word for > NEAR
EWFTES Spenserian plural of > EFT
EWGHEN archaic form of > YEW
EWHOW interj expression of pity or regret
EWK vb itch
EWKED > EWK
EWKING > EWK
EWKS > EWK
EWT archaic form of > NEWT
EWTS > EWT
EX prep not including ▷ n former spouse, significant other, etc ▷ vb cross out or delete
EXABYTE n very large unit of computer memory
EXABYTES > EXABYTE
EXACT adj correct and complete in every detail ▷ vb demand (payment or obedience)
EXACTA n horse-racing bet
EXACTABLE > EXACT
EXACTAS > EXACTA
EXACTED > EXACT
EXACTER > EXACT
EXACTERS > EXACT
EXACTEST > EXACT
EXACTING adj making rigorous or excessive demands
EXACTION n act of obtaining or demanding money as a right
EXACTIONS > EXACTION
EXACTLY adv precisely, in every respect ▷ interj just so! precisely!
EXACTMENT n condition of being exact
EXACTNESS > EXACT
EXACTOR > EXACT
EXACTORS > EXACT
EXACTRESS > EXACT
EXACTS > EXACT
EXACUM n type of tropical plant
EXACUMS > EXACUM
EXAHERTZ n very large unit of frequency
EXALT vb praise highly
EXALTED adj high or elevated in rank, position, dignity, etc
EXALTEDLY > EXALTED
EXALTER > EXALT
EXALTERS > EXALT
EXALTING > EXALT
EXALTS > EXALT
EXAM n examination
EXAMEN n examination of conscience

EXAMENS > EXAMEN
EXAMETRE n ten to the power of eighteen metres
EXAMETRES > EXAMETRE
EXAMINANT n examiner
EXAMINATE n examinee
EXAMINE vb look at closely
EXAMINED > EXAMINE
EXAMINEE n person who sits an exam
EXAMINEES > EXAMINEE
EXAMINER > EXAMINE
EXAMINERS > EXAMINE
EXAMINES > EXAMINE
EXAMINING > EXAMINE
EXAMPLAR archaic form of > EXEMPLAR
EXAMPLARS > EXAMPLAR
EXAMPLE n specimen typical of its group
EXAMPLED > EXAMPLE
EXAMPLES > EXAMPLE
EXAMPLING > EXAMPLE
EXAMS > EXAM
EXANIMATE adj lacking life
EXANTHEM same as > EXANTHEMA
EXANTHEMA n skin eruption or rash occurring as a symptom in a disease such as measles or scarlet fever
EXANTHEMS > EXANTHEM
EXAPTED adj biologically adapted
EXAPTIVE adj involving biological adaptation
EXARATE adj (of the pupa of some insects) having legs, wings, antennae, etc, free and movable
EXARATION n writing
EXARCH n head of certain autonomous Orthodox Christian Churches ▷ adj (of a xylem strand) having the first-formed xylem external to that formed later
EXARCHAL > EXARCH
EXARCHATE n office, rank, or jurisdiction of an exarch
EXARCHIES > EXARCHY
EXARCHIST n supporter of an exarch
EXARCHS > EXARCH
EXARCHY same as > EXARCHATE
EXCAMB vb exchange
EXCAMBED > EXCAMB
EXCAMBING > EXCAMB
EXCAMBION n exchange, esp of land
EXCAMBIUM same as > EXCAMBION
EXCAMBS > EXCAMB
EXCARNATE vb remove flesh from
EXCAUDATE adj having no tail or tail-like process
EXCAVATE vb unearth buried objects from (a piece of land) methodically to learn about the past
EXCAVATED > EXCAVATE
EXCAVATES > EXCAVATE
EXCAVATOR n large machine used for digging
EXCEED vb be greater than

EXCEEDED > EXCEED
EXCEEDER > EXCEED
EXCEEDERS > EXCEED
EXCEEDING adj very great
EXCEEDS > EXCEED
EXCEL vb be superior to
EXCELLED > EXCEL
EXCELLENT adj exceptionally good
EXCELLING > EXCEL
EXCELS > EXCEL
EXCELSIOR n excellent: used as a motto and as a trademark for various products, esp in the US for fine wood shavings used for packing breakable objects
EXCENTRIC same as > ECCENTRIC
EXCEPT prep other than, not including ▷ vb leave out; omit; exclude
EXCEPTANT n person taking exception
EXCEPTED > EXCEPT
EXCEPTING prep except
EXCEPTION n excepting
EXCEPTIVE adj relating to or forming an exception
EXCEPTOR > EXCEPT
EXCEPTORS > EXCEPT
EXCEPTS > EXCEPT
EXCERPT n passage taken from a book, speech, etc ▷ vb take a passage from a book, speech, etc
EXCERPTA > EXCERPTUM
EXCERPTED > EXCERPT
EXCERPTER > EXCERPT
EXCERPTOR > EXCERPT
EXCERPTS > EXCERPT
EXCERPTUM n excerpt
EXCESS n state or act of exceeding the permitted limits ▷ vb make (a position) redundant
EXCESSED > EXCESS
EXCESSES > EXCESS
EXCESSING > EXCESS
EXCESSIVE adj exceeding the normal or permitted extents or limits
EXCHANGE vb give or receive (something) in return for something else ▷ n act of exchanging
EXCHANGED > EXCHANGE
EXCHANGER n person or thing that exchanges
EXCHANGES > EXCHANGE
EXCHEAT same as > ESCHEAT
EXCHEATS > EXCHEAT
EXCHEQUER n (in Britain and certain other countries) accounting department of the Treasury, responsible for receiving and issuing funds
EXCIDE vb cut out
EXCIDED > EXCIDE
EXCIDES > EXCIDE
EXCIDING > EXCIDE
EXCIMER n excited dimer which would remain dissociated in the ground state
EXCIMERS > EXCIMER

EXCIPIENT n substance, such as sugar or gum, used to prepare a drug or drugs in a form suitable for administration
EXCIPLE n part of a lichen
EXCIPLES > EXCIPLE
EXCISABLE > EXCISE
EXCISE n tax on goods produced for the home market ▷ vb cut out or away
EXCISED > EXCISE
EXCISEMAN n (formerly) a government agent who collected excise and prevented smuggling
EXCISEMEN > EXCISEMAN
EXCISES > EXCISE
EXCISING > EXCISE
EXCISION > EXCISE
EXCISIONS > EXCISE
EXCITABLE adj easily excited
EXCITABLY > EXCITABLE
EXCITANCY n ability to excite
EXCITANT adj able to excite or stimulate ▷ n something able to excite
EXCITANTS > EXCITANT
EXCITE vb arouse to strong emotion
EXCITED adj emotionally aroused, esp to pleasure or agitation
EXCITEDLY > EXCITED
EXCITER n person or thing that excites
EXCITERS > EXCITER
EXCITES > EXCITE
EXCITING adj causing excitement
EXCITON n excited electron bound to the hole produced by its excitation
EXCITONIC > EXCITON
EXCITONS > EXCITON
EXCITOR n type of nerve
EXCITORS > EXCITOR
EXCLAIM vb speak suddenly, cry out
EXCLAIMED > EXCLAIM
EXCLAIMER > EXCLAIM
EXCLAIMS > EXCLAIM
EXCLAVE n territory owned by a country, but surrounded by another
EXCLAVES > EXCLAVE
EXCLOSURE n area of land, esp in a forest, fenced round to keep out unwanted animals
EXCLUDE vb keep out, leave out
EXCLUDED > EXCLUDE
EXCLUDEE > EXCLUDE
EXCLUDEES > EXCLUDE
EXCLUDER > EXCLUDE
EXCLUDERS > EXCLUDE
EXCLUDES > EXCLUDE
EXCLUDING prep excepting
EXCLUSION n act or an instance of excluding or the state of being excluded
EXCLUSIVE adj excluding everything else ▷ n story reported in only one newspaper

EXCLUSORY > EXCLUDE

EXCORIATE vb censure severely

EXCREMENT n waste matter discharged from the body

EXCRETA n excrement

EXCRETAL > EXCRETA

EXCRETE vb discharge (waste matter) from the body

EXCRETED > EXCRETE

EXCRETER > EXCRETE

EXCRETERS > EXCRETE

EXCRETES > EXCRETE

EXCRETING > EXCRETE

EXCRETION > EXCRETE

EXCRETIVE > EXCRETE

EXCRETORY > EXCRETE

EXCUBANT adj keeping guard

EXCUDIT sentence substitute (named person) made this

EXCULPATE vb free from blame or guilt

EXCURRENT adj having an outward flow, as certain pores in sponges, ducts, etc

EXCURSE vb wander

EXCURSED > EXCURSE

EXCURSES > EXCURSE

EXCURSING > EXCURSE

EXCURSION n short journey, esp for pleasure

EXCURSIVE adj tending to digress

EXCURSUS n incidental digression from the main topic

EXCUSABLE > EXCUSE

EXCUSABLY > EXCUSE

EXCUSAL > EXCUSE

EXCUSALS > EXCUSE

EXCUSE n explanation offered to justify (a fault etc) ▷ vb put forward a reason or justification for (a fault etc)

EXCUSED > EXCUSE

EXCUSER > EXCUSE

EXCUSERS > EXCUSE

EXCUSES > EXCUSE

EXCUSING > EXCUSE

EXCUSIVE adj excusing

EXEAT n leave of absence from school or some other institution

EXEATS > EXEAT

EXEC n executive

EXECRABLE adj of very poor quality

EXECRABLY > EXECRABLE

EXECRATE vb feel and express loathing and hatred of (someone or something)

EXECRATED > EXECRATE

EXECRATES > EXECRATE

EXECRATOR > EXECRATE

EXECS > EXEC

EXECUTANT n performer, esp of musical works

EXECUTARY n person whose job comprises tasks appropriate to a middle-management executive as well as those traditionally carried out by a secretary

EXECUTE vb put (a condemned person) to death

EXECUTED > EXECUTE

EXECUTER > EXECUTE

EXECUTERS > EXECUTE

EXECUTES > EXECUTE

EXECUTING > EXECUTE

EXECUTION n act of executing

EXECUTIVE n person or group in an administrative position ▷ adj having the function of carrying out plans, orders, laws, etc

EXECUTOR n person appointed to perform the instructions of a will

EXECUTORS > EXECUTOR

EXECUTORY adj (of a law, agreement, etc) coming into operation at a future date

EXECUTRIX n female executor

EXECUTRY n condition of being an executor

EXED > EX

EXEDRA n building, room, portico, or apse containing a continuous bench

EXEDRAE > EXEDRA

EXEDRAS > EXEDRA

EXEEM same as **>** EXEME

EXEEMED > EXEEM

EXEEMING > EXEEM

EXEEMS > EXEEM

EXEGESES > EXEGESIS

EXEGESIS n explanation of a text, esp of the Bible

EXEGETE n person who practises exegesis

EXEGETES > EXEGETE

EXEGETIC adj of or relating to exegesis

EXEGETICS n scientific study of exegesis and exegetical methods

EXEGETIST same as **>** EXEGETE

EXEME vb set free

EXEMED > EXEME

EXEMES > EXEME

EXEMING > EXEME

EXEMPLA > EXEMPLUM

EXEMPLAR n person or thing to be copied, model

EXEMPLARS > EXEMPLAR

EXEMPLARY adj being a good example

EXEMPLE same as **>** EXAMPLE

EXEMPLES > EXEMPLE

EXEMPLIFY vb show an example of

EXEMPLUM n anecdote that supports a moral point

EXEMPT adj not subject to an obligation etc ▷ vb release from an obligation etc ▷ n person who is exempt from an obligation, tax, etc

EXEMPTED > EXEMPT

EXEMPTING > EXEMPT

EXEMPTION > EXEMPT

EXEMPTIVE > EXEMPT

EXEMPTS > EXEMPT

EXEQUATUR n official authorization issued by a host country to a consular agent, permitting them to perform their official duties

EXEQUIAL > EXEQUY

EXEQUIES > EXEQUY

EXEQUY n funeral rite

EXERCISE n activity to train the body or mind ▷ vb make use of

EXERCISED > EXERCISE

EXERCISER n device with springs or elasticated cords for muscular exercise

EXERCISES > EXERCISE

EXERCYCLE n exercise bicycle

EXERGIES > EXERGY

EXERGONIC adj (of a biochemical reaction) producing energy and therefore occurring spontaneously

EXERGUAL > EXERGUE

EXERGUE n space on the reverse of a coin or medal

EXERGUES > EXERGUE

EXERGY n maximum amount of useful work obtainable from a system

EXERT vb use (influence, authority, etc) forcefully or effectively

EXERTED > EXERT

EXERTING > EXERT

EXERTION > EXERT

EXERTIONS > EXERT

EXERTIVE > EXERT

EXERTS > EXERT

EXES > EX

EXEUNT vb (they) go out

EXFIL vb exfiltrate

EXFILLED > EXFIL

EXFILLING > EXFIL

EXFILS > EXFIL

EXFOLIANT n cosmetic removing dead skin

EXFOLIATE vb peel in scales or layers

EXHALABLE > EXHALE

EXHALANT adj emitting a vapour or liquid ▷ n organ or vessel that emits a vapour or liquid

EXHALANTS > EXHALANT

EXHALE vb breathe out

EXHALED > EXHALE

EXHALENT same as **>** EXHALANT

EXHALENTS > EXHALENT

EXHALES > EXHALE

EXHALING > EXHALE

EXHAUST vb tire out ▷ n gases ejected from an engine as waste products

EXHAUSTED > EXHAUST

EXHAUSTER > EXHAUST

EXHAUSTS > EXHAUST

EXHEDRA same as **>** EXEDRA

EXHEDRAE > EXHEDRA

EXHIBIT vb display to the public ▷ n object exhibited to the public

EXHIBITED > EXHIBIT

EXHIBITER > EXHIBIT

EXHIBITOR n person or thing that exhibits

EXHIBITS > EXHIBIT

EXHORT vb urge earnestly

EXHORTED > EXHORT

EXHORTER > EXHORT

EXHORTERS > EXHORT

EXHORTING > EXHORT

EXHORTS > EXHORT

EXHUMATE same as **>** EXHUME

EXHUMATED > EXHUMATE

EXHUMATES > EXHUMATE

EXHUME vb dig up (something buried, esp a corpse)

EXHUMED > EXHUME

EXHUMER > EXHUME

EXHUMERS > EXHUME

EXHUMES > EXHUME

EXHUMING > EXHUME

EXIES n hysterics

EXIGEANT adj exacting

EXIGEANTE same as **>** EXIGEANT

EXIGENCE same as **>** EXIGENCY

EXIGENCES > EXIGENCE

EXIGENCY n urgent demand or need

EXIGENT adj urgent ▷ n emergency

EXIGENTLY > EXIGENT

EXIGENTS > EXIGENT

EXIGIBLE adj liable to be exacted or required,

EXIGUITY > EXIGUOUS

EXIGUOUS adj scanty or meagre

EXILABLE > EXILE

EXILE n prolonged, usu enforced, absence from one's country ▷ vb expel from one's country

EXILED > EXILE

EXILEMENT same as **>** EXILE

EXILER > EXILE

EXILERS > EXILE

EXILES > EXILE

EXILIAN > EXILE

EXILIC > EXILE

EXILING > EXILE

EXILITIES > EXILITY

EXILITY n poverty or meagreness

EXIMIOUS adj select and distinguished

EXINE n outermost coat of a pollen grain or a spore

EXINES > EXINE

EXING > EX

EXIST vb have being or reality

EXISTED > EXIST

EXISTENCE n fact or state of being real, live, or actual

EXISTENT adj in existence ▷ n person or a thing that exists

EXISTENTS > EXISTENT

EXISTING > EXIST

EXISTS > EXIST

EXIT n way out ▷ vb go out

EXITANCE n measure of the ability of a surface to emit radiation

EXITANCES > EXITANCE

EXITED > EXIT

EXITING > EXIT

EXITLESS > EXIT

EXITS > EXIT

EXO informal word for **>** EXCELLENT

EXOCARP same as
> EPICARP
EXOCARPS > EXOCARP
EXOCRINE adj relating to a
gland, such as the sweat
gland, that secretes
externally through a duct ▷ n
exocrine gland
EXOCRINES > EXOCRINE
EXOCYCLIC adj (of a cyclic
compound) situated outside
the ring
EXOCYTIC adj outside
biological cell
EXOCYTOSE vb secrete
substance from within cell
EXODE n exodus
EXODERM same as
> ECTODERM
EXODERMAL > EXODERM
EXODERMIS same as
> ECTODERM
EXODERMS > EXODERM
EXODES > EXODE
EXODIC > EXODE
EXODIST > EXODUS
EXODISTS > EXODUS
EXODOI > EXODOS
EXODONTIA n branch of
dental surgery concerned
with the extraction of teeth
EXODOS n processional song
performed at the end of a
play
EXODUS n departure of a
large number of people
EXODUSES > EXODUS
EXOENZYME n extracellular
enzyme
EXOERGIC adj (of a nuclear
reaction) occurring with
evolution of energy
EXOGAMIC > EXOGAMY
EXOGAMIES > EXOGAMY
EXOGAMOUS > EXOGAMY
EXOGAMY n act of marrying a
person from another tribe,
clan, etc
EXOGEN n type of plant
EXOGENIC adj formed or
occurring on the earth's
surface
EXOGENISM > EXOGENOUS
EXOGENOUS adj having an
external origin
EXOGENS > EXOGEN
EXOME n part of the genome
consisting of exons
EXOMES > EXOME
EXOMION same as > EXOMIS
EXOMIONS > EXOMION
EXOMIS n sleeveless jacket
EXOMISES > EXOMIS
EXON n one of the officers
who command the Yeomen
of the Guard
EXONERATE vb free from
blame or a criminal charge
EXONEREE n person who
has been exonerated
EXONEREES > EXONEREE
EXONIC > EXON
EXONS > EXON
EXONUMIA n objects of
interest to numismatists
that are not coins, such as
medals and tokens
EXONUMIST n collector of
medals and tokens

EXONYM n name given to a
place by foreigners
EXONYMS > EXONYM
EXOPHAGY n (among
cannibals) custom of eating
only members of other tribes
EXOPHORIC adj denoting or
relating to a pronoun such as
"I" or "you", the meaning of
which is determined by
reference outside the
discourse rather than by a
preceding or following
expression
EXOPLANET n planet that
orbits a star in a solar system
other than that of Earth
EXOPLASM another name for
> ECTOPLASM
EXOPLASMS > EXOPLASM
EXOPOD same as
> EXOPODITE
EXOPODITE n outer
projection on the hind legs of
some crustaceans
EXOPODS > EXOPOD
EXORABLE adj able to be
persuaded or moved by
pleading
EXORATION n plea
EXORCISE same as
> EXORCIZE
EXORCISED > EXORCISE
EXORCISER > EXORCISE
EXORCISES > EXORCISE
EXORCISM > EXORCIZE
EXORCISMS > EXORCIZE
EXORCIST > EXORCIZE
EXORCISTS > EXORCIZE
EXORCIZE vb expel (evil
spirits) by prayers and
religious rites
EXORCIZED > EXORCIZE
EXORCIZER > EXORCIZE
EXORCIZES > EXORCIZE
EXORDIA > EXORDIUM
EXORDIAL > EXORDIUM
EXORDIUM n introductory
part or beginning, esp of an
oration or discourse
EXORDIUMS > EXORDIUM
EXOSMIC > EXOSMOSIS
EXOSMOSE same as
> EXOSMOSIS
EXOSMOSES > EXOSMOSIS
EXOSMOSIS n osmosis in
which water flows from a cell
or organism into the
surrounding solution
EXOSMOTIC > EXOSMOSIS
EXOSPHERE n outermost
layer of the earth's
atmosphere
EXOSPORAL > EXOSPORE
EXOSPORE n outer layer of
the spores of some algae and
fungi
EXOSPORES > EXOSPORE
EXOSPORIA n exospores
EXOSTOSES > EXOSTOSIS
EXOSTOSIS n abnormal
bony outgrowth from the
surface of a bone
EXOTERIC adj intelligible to
or intended for more than a
select or initiated minority
EXOTIC adj having a strange
allure or beauty ▷ n
non-native plant

EXOTICA pl n (collection of)
exotic objects
EXOTICISE same as
> EXOTICIZE
EXOTICISM > EXOTIC
EXOTICIST > EXOTIC
EXOTICIZE vb regard or
present as exotic
EXOTICS > EXOTIC
EXOTISM n something
exotic
EXOTISMS > EXOTISM
EXOTOXIC > EXOTOXIN
EXOTOXIN n toxin produced
by a microorganism and
secreted into the
surrounding medium
EXOTOXINS > EXOTOXIN
EXOTROPIA n condition in
which eye turns outwards
EXOTROPIC > EXOTROPIA
EXPAND vb make or become
larger
EXPANDED adj (of printer's
type) wider than usual for a
particular height
EXPANDER n device for
exercising and developing
the muscles of the body
EXPANDERS > EXPANDER
EXPANDING > EXPAND
EXPANDOR same as
> EXPANDER
EXPANDORS > EXPANDOR
EXPANDS > EXPAND
EXPANSE n uninterrupted
wide area
EXPANSES > EXPANSE
EXPANSILE adj able to
expand or cause expansion
EXPANSION n act of
expanding
EXPANSIVE adj wide or
extensive
EXPAT n short for expatriate
EXPATIATE vb speak or
write at great length (on)
EXPATS > EXPAT
EXPECT vb regard as
probable
EXPECTANT adj expecting
or hopeful ▷ n person who
expects something
EXPECTED > EXPECT
EXPECTER n person who
expects
EXPECTERS > EXPECTER
EXPECTING adj pregnant
EXPECTS > EXPECT
EXPEDIENT n something
that achieves a particular
purpose ▷ adj suitable to the
circumstances, appropriate
EXPEDITE vb hasten the
progress of ▷ adj unimpeded
or prompt
EXPEDITED > EXPEDITE
EXPEDITER n person who
expedites something, esp a
person employed in an
industry to ensure that work
on each job progresses
efficiently
EXPEDITES > EXPEDITE
EXPEDITOR same as
> EXPEDITER
EXPEL vb drive out with
force

EXPELLANT adj forcing out
or having the capacity to
force out ▷ n medicine used
to expel undesirable
substances or organisms
from the body, esp worms
from the digestive tract
EXPELLED > EXPEL
EXPELLEE > EXPEL
EXPELLEES > EXPEL
EXPELLENT same as
> EXPELLANT
EXPELLER > EXPEL
EXPELLERS pl n residue
remaining after an oilseed
has been crushed to expel
the oil, used for animal
fodder
EXPELLING > EXPEL
EXPELS > EXPEL
EXPEND vb spend, use up
EXPENDED > EXPEND
EXPENDER > EXPEND
EXPENDERS > EXPEND
EXPENDING > EXPEND
EXPENDS > EXPEND
EXPENSE n cost ▷ vb treat
as an expense
EXPENSED > EXPENSE
EXPENSES > EXPENSE
EXPENSING > EXPENSE
EXPENSIVE adj high-priced
EXPERT n person with
extensive skill or knowledge
in a particular field ▷ adj
skilful or knowledgeable ▷ vb
experience
EXPERTED > EXPERT
EXPERTING > EXPERT
EXPERTISE same as
> EXPERTIZE
EXPERTISM > EXPERTIZE
EXPERTIZE vb act as an
expert or give an expert
opinion (on)
EXPERTLY > EXPERT
EXPERTS > EXPERT
EXPIABLE adj capable of
being expiated or atoned for
EXPIATE vb make amends
for
EXPIATED
> EXPIATE **EXPIATES**
> EXPIATE
EXPIATING > EXPIATE
EXPIATION n act, process,
or a means of expiating
EXPIATOR > EXPIATE
EXPIATORS > EXPIATE
EXPIATORY adj capable of
making expiation
EXPIRABLE > EXPIRE
EXPIRANT n one who
expires
EXPIRANTS > EXPIRANT
EXPIRE vb finish or run out
EXPIRED > EXPIRE
EXPIRER > EXPIRE
EXPIRERS > EXPIRE
EXPIRES > EXPIRE
EXPIRIES > EXPIRY
EXPIRING > EXPIRE
EXPIRY n end, esp of a
contract period
EXPISCATE vb find; fish out
EXPLAIN vb make clear and
intelligible

EXPLAINED > EXPLAIN
EXPLAINER > EXPLAIN
EXPLAINS > EXPLAIN
EXPLANT *vb* transfer (living tissue) from its natural site to a new site or to a culture medium ▷ *n* piece of tissue treated in this way
EXPLANTED > EXPLANT
EXPLANTS > EXPLANT
EXPLETIVE *n* swearword ▷ *adj* expressing no particular meaning, esp when filling out a line of verse
EXPLETORY *adj* expletive
EXPLICATE *vb* explain
EXPLICIT *adj* precisely and clearly expressed ▷ *n* word used to indicate the end of a book
EXPLICITS > EXPLICIT
EXPLODE *vb* burst with great violence, blow up
EXPLODED > EXPLODE
EXPLODER > EXPLODE
EXPLODERS > EXPLODE
EXPLODES > EXPLODE
EXPLODING > EXPLODE
EXPLOIT *vb* take advantage of for one's own purposes ▷ *n* notable feat or deed
EXPLOITED > EXPLOIT
EXPLOITER > EXPLOIT
EXPLOITS > EXPLOIT
EXPLORE *vb* investigate
EXPLORED > EXPLORE
EXPLORER > EXPLORE
EXPLORERS > EXPLORE
EXPLORES > EXPLORE
EXPLORING > EXPLORE
EXPLOSION *n* exploding
EXPLOSIVE *adj* tending to explode ▷ *n* substance that causes explosions
EXPO *n* exposition, large public exhibition
EXPONENT *n* person who advocates an idea, cause, etc ▷ *adj* offering a declaration, explanation, or interpretation
EXPONENTS > EXPONENT
EXPONIBLE *adj* able to be explained
EXPORT *n* selling or shipping of goods to a foreign country ▷ *vb* sell or ship (goods) to a foreign country
EXPORTED > EXPORT
EXPORTER > EXPORT
EXPORTERS > EXPORT
EXPORTING > EXPORT
EXPORTS > EXPORT
EXPOS > EXPO
EXPOSABLE > EXPOSE
EXPOSAL > EXPOSE
EXPOSALS > EXPOSE
EXPOSE *vb* uncover or reveal ▷ *n* bringing of a crime, scandal, etc to public notice
EXPOSED *adj* not concealed
EXPOSER > EXPOSE
EXPOSERS > EXPOSE
EXPOSES > EXPOSE
EXPOSING > EXPOSE
EXPOSIT *vb* state

EXPOSITED > EXPOSIT
EXPOSITOR *n* person who expounds
EXPOSITS > EXPOSIT
EXPOSOME *n* collection of environmental factors which can affect a person's health
EXPOSOMES > EXPOSOME
EXPOSTURE *n* exposure
EXPOSURE *n* exposing
EXPOSURES > EXPOSURE
EXPOUND *vb* explain in detail
EXPOUNDED > EXPOUND
EXPOUNDER > EXPOUND
EXPOUNDS > EXPOUND
EXPRESS *vb* put into words ▷ *adj* explicitly stated ▷ *n* fast train or bus stopping at only a few stations ▷ *adv* by express delivery
EXPRESSED > EXPRESS
EXPRESSER > EXPRESS
EXPRESSES > EXPRESS
EXPRESSLY *adv* definitely
EXPRESSO *variant of* > ESPRESSO
EXPRESSOS > EXPRESSO
EXPUGN *vb* storm
EXPUGNED > EXPUGN
EXPUGNING > EXPUGN
EXPUGNS > EXPUGN
EXPULSE *vb* expel
EXPULSED > EXPULSE
EXPULSES > EXPULSE
EXPULSING > EXPULSE
EXPULSION *n* act of expelling or the fact of being expelled
EXPULSIVE *adj* tending or serving to expel
EXPUNCT *vb* expunge
EXPUNCTED > EXPUNCT
EXPUNCTS > EXPUNCT
EXPUNGE *vb* delete, erase, blot out
EXPUNGED > EXPUNGE
EXPUNGER > EXPUNGE
EXPUNGERS > EXPUNGE
EXPUNGES > EXPUNGE
EXPUNGING > EXPUNGE
EXPURGATE *vb* remove objectionable parts from (a book etc)
EXPURGE *vb* purge
EXPURGED > EXPURGE
EXPURGES > EXPURGE
EXPURGING > EXPURGE
EXQUISITE *adj* of extreme beauty or delicacy ▷ *n* dandy
EXSCIND *vb* cut off or out
EXSCINDED > EXSCIND
EXSCINDS > EXSCIND
EXSECANT *n* trigonometric function
EXSECANTS > EXSECANT
EXSECT *vb* cut out
EXSECTED > EXSECT
EXSECTING > EXSECT
EXSECTION > EXSECT
EXSECTS > EXSECT
EXSERT *vb* thrust out ▷ *adj* protruded or stretched out from (something)
EXSERTED > EXSERT
EXSERTILE > EXSERT
EXSERTING > EXSERT
EXSERTION > EXSERT

EXSERTS > EXSERT
EXSICCANT *n* medicine which causes drying or desiccation
EXSICCATE *vb* dry up
EXSTROPHY *n* congenital eversion of a hollow organ, esp the urinary bladder
EXSUCCOUS *adj* without sap or juice
EXTANT *adj* still existing
EXTASIES > EXTASY
EXTASY *same as* > ECSTASY
EXTATIC *same as* > ECSTATIC
EXTEMPORE *adj* without planning or preparation ▷ *adv* without planning or preparation
EXTEND *vb* draw out or be drawn out, stretch
EXTENDANT *adj* (in heraldry) with wings spread
EXTENDED > EXTEND
EXTENDER *n* person or thing that extends
EXTENDERS > EXTENDER
EXTENDING > EXTEND
EXTENDS > EXTEND
EXTENSE *adj* extensive ▷ *n* extension; expanse
EXTENSES > EXTENSE
EXTENSILE *adj* capable of being extended
EXTENSION *n* room or rooms added to an existing building ▷ *adj* denoting something that can be extended or that extends another object
EXTENSITY *n* that part of sensory perception relating to the spatial aspect of objects
EXTENSIVE *adj* having a large extent, widespread
EXTENSOR *n* muscle that extends a part of the body
EXTENSORS > EXTENSOR
EXTENT *n* range over which something extends, area
EXTENTS > EXTENT
EXTENUATE *vb* make (an offence or fault) less blameworthy
EXTERIOR *n* part or surface on the outside ▷ *adj* of, on, or coming from the outside
EXTERIORS > EXTERIOR
EXTERMINE *vb* exterminate
EXTERN *n* person with an official connection to an institution but not residing in it
EXTERNAL *adj* of, situated on, or coming from the outside ▷ *n* external circumstance or aspect, esp one that is superficial or inessential
EXTERNALS > EXTERNAL
EXTERNAT *n* day school
EXTERNATS > EXTERNAT
EXTERNE *same as* > EXTERN
EXTERNES > EXTERNE
EXTERNS > EXTERN
EXTINCT *adj* having died out ▷ *vb* extinguish

EXTINCTED > EXTINCT
EXTINCTS > EXTINCT
EXTINE *same as* > EXINE
EXTINES > EXTINE
EXTIRP *vb* extirpate
EXTIRPATE *vb* destroy utterly
EXTIRPED > EXTIRP
EXTIRPING > EXTIRP
EXTIRPS > EXTIRP
EXTOL *vb* praise highly
EXTOLD *archaic past participle of* > EXTOL
EXTOLL *same as* > EXTOL
EXTOLLED > EXTOLL
EXTOLLER > EXTOL
EXTOLLERS > EXTOL
EXTOLLING > EXTOLL
EXTOLLS > EXTOLL
EXTOLMENT > EXTOL
EXTOLS > EXTOL
EXTORSIVE *adj* intended or tending to extort
EXTORT *vb* get (something) by force or threats
EXTORTED > EXTORT
EXTORTER > EXTORT
EXTORTERS > EXTORT
EXTORTING > EXTORT
EXTORTION *n* act of securing money, favours, etc by intimidation or violence
EXTORTIVE > EXTORT
EXTORTS > EXTORT
EXTRA *adj* more than is usual, expected or needed ▷ *n* additional person or thing ▷ *adv* unusually or exceptionally
EXTRABOLD *n* very bold typeface
EXTRACT *vb* pull out by force ▷ *n* something extracted, such as a passage from a book etc
EXTRACTED > EXTRACT
EXTRACTOR *n* person or thing that extracts
EXTRACTS > EXTRACT
EXTRADITE *vb* send (an accused person) back to his or her own country for trial
EXTRADOS *n* outer curve or surface of an arch or vault
EXTRAIT *n* extract
EXTRAITS > EXTRAIT
EXTRALITY *n* diplomatic immunity
EXTRANET *n* intranet modified to allow outside access
EXTRANETS > EXTRANET
EXTRAPOSE *vb* move (a word or words) to the end of a clause or sentence
EXTRAS > EXTRA
EXTRAUGHT *old past participle of* > EXTRACT
EXTRAVERT *same as* > EXTROVERT
EXTREAT *n* extraction ▷ *vb* extract or eliminate (something)
EXTREATED > EXTREAT
EXTREATS > EXTREAT
EXTREMA > EXTREMUM
EXTREMAL *n* clause in a recursive definition

e

e

EXTREMALS > EXTREMAL
EXTREME *adj* of a high or the highest degree or intensity ▷ *n* either of the two limits of a scale or range
EXTREMELY > EXTREME
EXTREMER > EXTREME
EXTREMES > EXTREME
EXTREMEST > EXTREME
EXTREMISM > EXTREMIST
EXTREMIST *n* person who favours immoderate methods ▷ *adj* holding extreme opinions
EXTREMITY *n* farthest point
EXTREMUM *n* extreme point
EXTREMUMS > EXTREMUM
EXTRICATE *vb* free from complication or difficulty
EXTRINSIC *adj* not contained or included within
EXTROPIAN *n* believer in extropy
EXTROPIES > EXTROPY
EXTROPY *n* supposition that human life will expand throughout the universe via technology
EXTRORSAL *same as* **>** EXTRORSE
EXTRORSE *adj* turned or opening outwards or away from the axis
EXTROVERT *adj* lively and outgoing ▷ *n* extrovert person
EXTRUDE *vb* squeeze or force out
EXTRUDED > EXTRUDE
EXTRUDER > EXTRUDE
EXTRUDERS > EXTRUDE
EXTRUDES > EXTRUDE
EXTRUDING > EXTRUDE
EXTRUSILE *adj* being thrust or forced out
EXTRUSION *n* act or process of extruding
EXTRUSIVE *adj* tending to extrude
EXTRUSORY > EXTRUDE
EXTUBATE *vb* remove tube from hollow organ
EXTUBATED > EXTUBATE
EXTUBATES > EXTUBATE
EXUBERANT *adj* high-spirited
EXUBERATE *vb* be exuberant
EXUDATE *same as* **>** EXUDATION
EXUDATES > EXUDATE
EXUDATION *n* act of exuding or oozing out
EXUDATIVE > EXUDATION
EXUDE *vb* (of a liquid or smell) seep or flow out slowly and steadily
EXUDED > EXUDE
EXUDES > EXUDE
EXUDING > EXUDE
EXUL *vb* exile; banish
EXULLED > EXUL
EXULLING > EXUL

EXULS > EXUL
EXULT *vb* be joyful or jubilant
EXULTANCE > EXULTANT
EXULTANCY > EXULTANT
EXULTANT *adj* elated or jubilant, esp because of triumph or success
EXULTED > EXULT
EXULTING > EXULT
EXULTS > EXULT
EXURB *n* residential area beyond suburbs
EXURBAN > EXURBIA
EXURBIA *n* region outside the suburbs of a city
EXURBIAS > EXURBIA
EXURBS > EXURB
EXUVIA *n* cast-off exoskeleton of animal
EXUVIAE > EXUVIA
EXUVIAL > EXUVIA
EXUVIATE *vb* shed (a skin or similar outer covering)
EXUVIATED > EXUVIATE
EXUVIATES > EXUVIATE
EXUVIUM *n* cast-off exoskeleton of animal
EYALET *n* province of Ottoman Empire
EYALETS > EYALET
EYAS *n* nestling hawk or falcon
EYASES > EYAS
EYASS *same as* **>** EYAS
EYASSES > EYASS
EYE *n* organ of sight ▷ *vb* look at carefully or warily
EYEABLE *adj* pleasant to look at
EYEBALL *n* ball-shaped part of the eye ▷ *vb* eye
EYEBALLED > EYEBALL
EYEBALLS > EYEBALL
EYEBANK *n* place in which corneas are stored
EYEBANKS > EYEBANK
EYEBAR *n* bar with flattened ends with holes for connecting pins
EYEBARS > EYEBAR
EYEBATH *n* small cup for applying medication to the eye
EYEBATHS > EYEBATH
EYEBEAM *n* glance
EYEBEAMS > EYEBEAM
EYEBLACK *another name for* **>** MASCARA
EYEBLACKS > EYEBLACK
EYEBLINK *n* very small amount of time
EYEBLINKS > EYEBLINK
EYEBOLT *n* type of threaded bolt
EYEBOLTS > EYEBOLT
EYEBRIGHT *n* type of plant with small white-and-purple flowers, formerly used to treat eye disorders
EYEBROW *n* line of hair on the bony ridge above the eye ▷ *vb* equip with artificial eyebrows

EYEBROWED > EYEBROW
EYEBROWS > EYEBROW
EYECUP *same as* **>** EYEBATH
EYECUPS > EYECUP
EYED > EYE
EYEDNESS > EYE
EYEDROPS *n* medicine applied to the eyes in drops
EYEFOLD *n* fold of skin above eye
EYEFOLDS > EYEFOLD
EYEFUL *n* view
EYEFULS > EYEFUL
EYEGLASS *n* lens for aiding defective vision
EYEHOLE *n* hole through which something is passed
EYEHOLES > EYEHOLE
EYEHOOK *n* hook attached to a ring at the extremity of a rope or chain
EYEHOOKS > EYEHOOK
EYEING > EYE
EYELASH *n* short hair that grows out from the eyelid
EYELASHES > EYELASH
EYELESS > EYE
EYELET *n* small hole for a lace or cord to be passed through ▷ *vb* supply with an eyelet or eyelets
EYELETED > EYELET
EYELETEER *n* small bodkin or other pointed tool for making eyelet holes
EYELETING > EYELET
EYELETS > EYELET
EYELETTED > EYELET
EYELEVEL *adj* level with a person's eyes
EYELIAD *same as* **>** OEILLADE
EYELIADS > EYELIAD
EYELID *n* fold of skin that covers the eye when it is closed
EYELIDS > EYELID
EYELIFT *n* cosmetic surgery for eyes
EYELIFTS > EYELIFT
EYELIKE > EYE
EYELINE *n* line of sight
EYELINER *n* cosmetic used to outline the eyes
EYELINERS > EYELINER
EYELINES > EYELINE
EYEN *pl n* eyes
EYEOPENER *n* something surprising
EYEPATCH *n* material worn over an injured eye
EYEPIECE *n* lens in a microscope, telescope, etc, into which the person using it looks
EYEPIECES > EYEPIECE
EYEPOINT *n* position of a lens at which the sharpest image is obtained
EYEPOINTS > EYEPOINT
EYEPOPPER *n* something that excites the eye
EYER *n* someone who eyes

EYERS > EYER
EYES > EYE
EYESHADE *n* opaque or tinted translucent visor
EYESHADES > EYESHADE
EYESHADOW *n* coloured cosmetic put around the eyes so as to enhance their colour or shape
EYESHINE *n* reflection of light from animal eye at night
EYESHINES > EYESHINE
EYESHOT *n* range of vision
EYESHOTS > EYESHOT
EYESIGHT *n* ability to see
EYESIGHTS > EYESIGHT
EYESOME *adj* attractive
EYESORE *n* ugly object
EYESORES > EYESORE
EYESPOT *n* small area of pigment
EYESPOTS > EYESPOT
EYESTALK *n* movable stalk bearing a compound eye at its tip
EYESTALKS > EYESTALK
EYESTONE *n* device for removing foreign body from eye
EYESTONES > EYESTONE
EYESTRAIN *n* fatigue or irritation of the eyes, caused by tiredness or a failure to wear glasses
EYETEETH > EYETOOTH
EYETOOTH *n* either of the two canine teeth in the upper jaw
EYEWASH *n* nonsense
EYEWASHES > EYEWASH
EYEWATER *n* lotion for the eyes
EYEWATERS > EYEWATER
EYEWEAR *n* spectacles; glasses
EYEWEARS > EYEWEAR
EYEWINK *n* wink of the eye; instant
EYEWINKS > EYEWINK
EYING > EYE
EYLIAD *same as* **>** OEILLADE
EYLIADS > EYLIAD
EYNE *poetic plural of* **>** EYE
EYOT *n* island
EYOTS > EYOT
EYRA *n* reddish-brown variety of the jaguarondi
EYRAS > EYRA
EYRE *n* obsolete circuit court
EYRES > EYRE
EYRIE *n* nest of an eagle
EYRIES > EYRIE
EYRIR *n* Icelandic monetary unit
EYRY *same as* **>** EYRIE
EZINE *n* magazine available only in electronic form
EZINES > EZINE

Ff

FA same as > FAH
FAA Scot word for > FALL
FAAING > FAA
FAAN > FAA
FAAS > FAA
FAB adj excellent ▷ n fabrication
FABACEOUS adj belonging to the legume family of flowering plants which includes peas and beans
FABBER > FAB
FABBEST > FAB
FABBIER > FABBY
FABBIEST > FABBY
FABBY same as > FAB
FABLE n story with a moral ▷ vb relate or tell (fables)
FABLED adj made famous in legend
FABLER > FABLE
FABLERS > FABLE
FABLES > FABLE
FABLET n large smartphone able to perform many of the functions of a tablet computer
FABLETS > FABLET
FABLIAU n comic usually ribald verse tale
FABLIAUX > FABLIAU
FABLING > FABLE
FABLINGS > FABLE
FABRIC n knitted or woven cloth ▷ vb build
FABRICANT n manufacturer
FABRICATE vb make up (a story or lie)
FABRICKED > FABRIC
FABRICS > FABRIC
FABRIQUE n (in Quebec) group of laypersons who hold church property in trust for the parish
FABRIQUES > FABRIQUE
FABS > FAB
FABULAR adj relating to fables
FABULATE vb make up fables
FABULATED > FABULATE
FABULATES > FABULATE
FABULATOR > FABULATE
FABULISE vb make up fables
FABULISED > FABULISE
FABULISES > FABULISE
FABULISM n literary technique of placing fantastical elements in mundane settings

FABULISMS > FABULISM
FABULIST n person who invents or recounts fables
FABULISTS > FABULIST
FABULIZE vb make up fables
FABULIZED > FABULIZE
FABULIZES > FABULIZE
FABULOUS adj excellent
FABURDEN n early form of counterpoint
FABURDENS > FABURDEN
FACADE n front of a building
FACADES > FACADE
FACE n front of the head ▷ vb look or turn towards
FACEABLE > FACE
FACEBAR n wrestling hold
FACEBARS > FACEBAR
FACEBOOK vb search for (someone) on the Facebook website
FACEBOOKS > FACEBOOK
FACECLOTH n small piece of cloth used to wash the face and hands
FACED > FACE
FACEDOWN vb confront and force (someone or something) to back down
FACEDOWNS > FACEDOWN
FACELESS adj impersonal, anonymous
FACELIFT n cosmetic surgery for the face
FACELIFTS > FACELIFT
FACEMAIL n computer-generated face that delivers messages on screen
FACEMAILS > FACEMAIL
FACEMAN n miner who works at the coalface
FACEMASK n protective mask for the face
FACEMASKS > FACEMASK
FACEMEN > FACEMAN
FACEOFF n when opposing skaters compete for the puck at the start of an ice hockey game
FACEOFFS > FACEOFF
FACEPALM vb bring one's palm to one's face in dismay
FACEPALMS > FACEPALM
FACEPLANT vb fall on one's face
FACEPLATE n perforated circular metal plate that can be attached to the headstock of a lathe in order to hold flat or irregularly shaped workpieces

FACEPRINT n digitally recorded representation of a person's face that can be used for security purposes because it is as individual as a fingerprint
FACER n difficulty or problem
FACERS > FACER
FACES > FACE
FACET n aspect ▷ vb cut facets in (a gemstone)
FACETE adj witty and humorous
FACETED > FACET
FACETELY > FACETE
FACETIAE pl n humorous or witty sayings
FACETIME vb talk with (someone) via the FaceTime application
FACETIMED > FACETIME
FACETIMES > FACETIME
FACETING n act of faceting
FACETINGS > FACETING
FACETIOUS adj funny or trying to be funny, esp at inappropriate times
FACETS > FACET
FACETTED > FACET
FACETTING > FACET
FACEUP adj with the face or surface exposed
FACIA same as > FASCIA
FACIAE > FACIA
FACIAL adj of or relating to the face ▷ n beauty treatment for the face
FACIALIST n beautician who specializes in treatments for the face
FACIALLY > FACIAL
FACIALS > FACIAL
FACIAS > FACIA
FACIEND n multiplicand
FACIENDS > FACIEND
FACIES n general form and appearance
FACILE adj (of a remark, argument, etc) superficial
FACILELY > FACILE
FACILITY n skill
FACING n lining or covering for decoration or reinforcement
FACINGS > FACING
FACONNE adj denoting a fabric with the design woven in ▷ n such a fabric
FACONNES > FACONNE
FACSIMILE n exact copy ▷ vb make an exact copy of
FACT n event or thing known to have happened or existed

FACTA > FACTUM
FACTFUL > FACT
FACTICE n soft rubbery material
FACTICES > FACTICE
FACTICITY n philosophical process
FACTION n (dissenting) minority group within a larger body
FACTIONAL > FACTION
FACTIONS > FACTION
FACTIOUS adj of or producing factions
FACTIS variant of > FACTICE
FACTISES > FACTIS
FACTITIVE adj denoting a verb taking a direct object as well as a noun in apposition, as for example elect in They elected John president, where John is the direct object and president is the complement
FACTIVE adj giving rise to the presupposition that a sentence is true
FACTOID n piece of unreliable information believed to be true
FACTOIDAL > FACTOID
FACTOIDS > FACTOID
FACTOR n element contributing to a result ▷ vb engage in the business of a factor
FACTORAGE n commission payable to a factor
FACTORED > FACTOR
FACTORIAL n product of all the integers from one to a given number ▷ adj of factorials or factors
FACTORIES > FACTORY
FACTORING n business of a factor
FACTORISE same as > FACTORIZE
FACTORIZE vb calculate the factors of (a number)
FACTORS > FACTOR
FACTORY n building where goods are manufactured
FACTOTUM n person employed to do all sorts of work
FACTOTUMS > FACTOTUM
FACTS > FACT
FACTSHEET n printed sheet containing information relating to items covered in a television or radio programme

f

FACTUAL adj concerning facts rather than opinions or theories

FACTUALLY > FACTUAL

FACTUM n something done, deed

FACTUMS > FACTUM

FACTURE n construction

FACTURES > FACTURE

FACULA n any of the bright areas on the sun's surface

FACULAE > FACULA

FACULAR > FACULA

FACULTIES > FACULTY

FACULTY n physical or mental ability

FACUNDITY n eloquence, fluency of speech

FAD n short-lived fashion

FADABLE > FADE

FADAISE n silly remark

FADAISES > FADAISE

FADDIER > FADDY

FADDIEST > FADDY

FADDINESS n excessive fussiness

FADDISH > FAD

FADDISHLY > FAD

FADDISM > FAD

FADDISMS > FAD

FADDIST > FAD

FADDISTS > FAD

FADDLE vb mess around, toy with

FADDLED > FADDLE

FADDLES > FADDLE

FADDLING > FADDLE

FADDY adj unreasonably fussy, particularly about food

FADE vb (cause to) lose brightness, colour, or strength ▷ n act or an instance of fading

FADEAWAY n fading to the point of disappearance

FADEAWAYS > FADEAWAY

FADED > FADE

FADEDLY > FADE

FADEDNESS > FADE

FADEIN n gradual appearance of image on film

FADEINS > FADEIN

FADELESS adj not subject to fading

FADEOUT n gradual disappearance of image on film

FADEOUTS > FADEOUT

FADER > FADE

FADERS > FADE

FADES > FADE

FADEUR n blandness, insipidness

FADEURS > FADEUR

FADGE vb agree ▷ n package of wool in a wool-bale

FADGED > FADGE

FADGES > FADGE

FADGING > FADGE

FADIER > FADY

FADIEST > FADY

FADING n variation in strength of received radio signals

FADINGS > FADING

FADLIKE > FADE

FADO n type of melancholy Portuguese folk song

FADOMETER n instrument used to determine the resistance to fading of a pigment or dye

FADOS > FADO

FADS > FAD

FADY adj faded

FAE Scot word for > FROM

FAECAL adj of, relating to, or consisting of faeces

FAECES pl n waste matter discharged from the body

FAENA n matador's final actions before the kill

FAENAS > FAENA

FAERIE n land of fairies

FAERIES > FAERIE

FAERY same as > FAERIE

FAFF vb dither or fuss

FAFFED > FAFF

FAFFIER > FAFFY

FAFFIEST > FAFFY

FAFFING > FAFF

FAFFS > FAFF

FAFFY adj awkward and time-consuming to do or use

FAG n tiresome work ▷ vb work hard

FAGACEOUS adj relating to a family of trees, including beech, oak, and chestnut, whose fruit is enclosed in a husk

FAGGED > FAG

FAGGERIES > FAGGERY

FAGGERY n offensive term for male homosexuality

FAGGIER > FAG

FAGGIEST > FAG

FAGGING > FAG

FAGGINGS > FAG

FAGGOT n ball of chopped liver, herbs, and bread ▷ vb collect into a bundle or bundles

FAGGOTED > FAGGOT

FAGGOTIER > FAGGOTY

FAGGOTING n decorative needlework done by tying vertical threads together in bundles

FAGGOTRY n offensive term for male homosexuality

FAGGOTS > FAGGOT

FAGGOTY adj like a faggot

FAGGY > FAG

FAGIN n criminal

FAGINS > FAGIN

FAGOT same as > FAGGOT

FAGOTED > FAGOT

FAGOTER > FAGOT

FAGOTERS > FAGOT

FAGOTING same as > FAGGOTING

FAGOTINGS > FAGOTING

FAGOTS > FAGOT

FAGOTTI > FAGOTTO

FAGOTTIST n bassoon player

FAGOTTO n bassoon

FAGOTTOS > FAGOTTO

FAGS > FAG

FAH n (in tonic sol-fa) fourth degree of any major scale

FAHLBAND n thin bed of schistose rock impregnated with metallic sulphides

FAHLBANDS > FAHLBAND

FAHLERZ n copper ore

FAHLERZES > FAHLERZ

FAHLORE n copper ore

FAHLORES > FAHLORE

FAHS > FAH

FAIBLE variant of > FOIBLE

FAIBLES > FAIBLE

FAIENCE n tin-glazed earthenware

FAIENCES > FAIENCE

FAIK vb grasp

FAIKED > FAIK

FAIKES n sandy rock

FAIKING > FAIK

FAIKS > FAIK

FAIL vb be unsuccessful ▷ n instance of not passing an exam or test

FAILED > FAIL

FAILING n weak point ▷ prep in the absence of

FAILINGLY > FAILING

FAILINGS > FAILING

FAILLE n soft light ribbed fabric of silk, rayon, or taffeta

FAILLES > FAILLE

FAILOVER n automatic transfer to a backup computer system in the event of a primary system failure

FAILOVERS > FAILOVER

FAILS > FAIL

FAILURE n act or instance of failing

FAILURES > FAILURE

FAIN adv gladly ▷ adj willing or eager ▷ vb desire

FAINE variant of > FAIN

FAINEANCE > FAINEANT

FAINEANCY > FAINEANT

FAINEANT n lazy person ▷ adj indolent

FAINEANTS > FAINEANT

FAINED > FAIN

FAINER > FAIN

FAINES > FAINE

FAINEST > FAIN

FAINING > FAIN

FAINITES interj cry for truce or respite from the rules of a game

FAINLY > FAIN

FAINNE n badge worn by advocates of the Irish language

FAINNES > FAINNE

FAINNESS > FAIN

FAINS > FAIN

FAINT adj lacking clarity, brightness, or volume ▷ vb lose consciousness temporarily ▷ n temporary loss of consciousness

FAINTED > FAINT

FAINTER > FAINT

FAINTERS > FAINT

FAINTEST > FAINT

FAINTIER > FAINTY

FAINTIEST > FAINTY

FAINTING > FAINT

FAINTINGS > FAINT

FAINTISH > FAINT

FAINTLY > FAINT

FAINTNESS > FAINT

FAINTS > FAINT

FAINTY > FAINT

FAIR adj unbiased and reasonable ▷ adv fairly ▷ n travelling entertainment ▷ vb join together to form a smooth shape

FAIRED > FAIR

FAIRER > FAIR

FAIREST > FAIR

FAIRFACED adj (of brickwork) having a neat smooth unplastered surface

FAIRGOER n person attending fair

FAIRGOERS > FAIRGOER

FAIRIER > FAIRY

FAIRIES > FAIRY

FAIRIEST > FAIRY

FAIRILY > FAIRY

FAIRING n structure fitted round part of a vehicle to reduce drag

FAIRINGS > FAIRING

FAIRISH adj moderately good, well, etc

FAIRISHLY > FAIRISH

FAIRLEAD n block or ring through which a line is rove

FAIRLEADS > FAIRLEAD

FAIRLY adv moderately

FAIRNESS > FAIR

FAIRS > FAIR

FAIRWAY n area between the tee and the green

FAIRWAYS > FAIRWAY

FAIRY n imaginary small creature ▷ adj of or relating to a fairy or fairies

FAIRYDOM > FAIRY

FAIRYDOMS > FAIRY

FAIRYHOOD > FAIRY

FAIRYISM > FAIRY

FAIRYISMS > FAIRY

FAIRYLAND n imaginary place where fairies live

FAIRYLIKE > FAIRY

FAIRYTALE n story about fairies or other mythical or magical beings, esp one of traditional origin told to children

FAITH n strong belief, esp without proof

FAITHCURE n supposed cure or healing through prayer or faith in God

FAITHED adj having faith or a faith

FAITHER Scot word for > FATHER

FAITHERS > FAITHER

FAITHFUL adj loyal

FAITHFULS > FAITHFUL

FAITHING n practising a faith

FAITHINGS > FAITHING

FAITHLESS adj disloyal or dishonest

FAITHS > FAITH

FAITOR n traitor, impostor

FAITORS > FAITOR

FAITOUR n impostor

FAITOURS > FAITOUR

FAIX interj have faith

FAJITA > FAJITAS

FAJITAS pl n Mexican dish

FAKE vb cause something not genuine to appear so by fraud ▷ n person, thing, or act that is not genuine ▷ adj not genuine

FAKED > FAKE

FAKEER same as > FAKIR

FAKEERS > FAKEER

FAKEMENT n something false, counterfeit

FAKEMENTS > FAKEMENT

FAKER > FAKE

FAKERIES > FAKERY

FAKERS > FAKE

FAKERY > FAKE

FAKES > FAKE

FAKEST > FAKE

FAKEY adj (of a skateboarding manoeuvre) travelling backwards ▷ n skateboarding position in which the skateboarder faces backwards

FAKEYS > FAKEY

FAKIE same as > FAKEY

FAKIER > FAKEY

FAKIES > FAKIE

FAKIEST > FAKEY

FAKING > FAKE

FAKIR n Muslim who spurns worldly possessions

FAKIRISM > FAKIR

FAKIRISMS > FAKIR

FAKIRS > FAKIR

FALAFEL n ball or cake made from chickpeas

FALAFELS > FALAFEL

FALAJ n kind of irrigation channel in ancient Oman

FALANGISM > FALANGIST

FALANGIST n member of the Fascist movement founded in Spain in 1933

FALBALA n gathered flounce, frill, or ruffle

FALBALAS > FALBALA

FALCADE n movement of a horse

FALCADES > FALCADE

FALCATE adj shaped like a sickle

FALCATED same as > FALCATE

FALCATION > FALCATE

FALCES > FALX

FALCHION n short and slightly curved medieval sword broader towards the point

FALCHIONS > FALCHION

FALCIFORM same as > FALCATE

FALCON n small bird of prey

FALCONER n person who breeds or trains hawks or who follows the sport of falconry

FALCONERS > FALCONER

FALCONET n type of small falcon

FALCONETS > FALCONET

FALCONINE adj of, relating to, or resembling a falcon

FALCONOID n chemical thought to resist cancer

FALCONRY n art of training falcons

FALCONS > FALCON

FALCULA n sharp curved claw, esp of a bird

FALCULAE > FALCULA

FALCULAS > FALCULA

FALCULATE > FALCULA

FALDAGE n feudal right

FALDAGES > FALDAGE

FALDERAL n showy but worthless trifle ▷ vb sing nonsense words

FALDERALS > FALDERAL

FALDEROL same as > FALDERAL

FALDEROLS > FALDEROL

FALDETTA n Maltese woman's garment with a stiffened hood

FALDETTAS > FALDETTA

FALDSTOOL n backless seat, sometimes capable of being folded, used by bishops and certain other prelates

FALL vb drop through the force of gravity ▷ n falling

FALLACIES > FALLACY

FALLACY n false belief

FALLAL n showy ornament, trinket, or article of dress

FALLALERY > FALLAL

FALLALISH adj foppish

FALLALS > FALLAL

FALLAWAY n friendship that has been withdrawn

FALLAWAYS > FALLAWAY

FALLBACK n something that recedes or retreats

FALLBACKS > FALLBACK

FALLBOARD n cover for piano keyboard

FALLEN > FALL

FALLER n any device that falls or operates machinery by falling

FALLERS > FALLER

FALLFISH n large N American freshwater fish resembling the chub

FALLIBLE adj (of a person) liable to make mistakes

FALLIBLY > FALLIBLE

FALLING > FALL

FALLINGS > FALL

FALLOFF n decline or drop

FALLOFFS > FALLOFF

FALLOUT n radioactive particles spread as a result of a nuclear explosion ▷ vb disagree and quarrel ▷ sentence substitute order to leave a parade or disciplinary formation

FALLOUTS > FALLOUT

FALLOW adj (of land) ploughed but left unseeded to regain fertility ▷ n land treated in this way ▷ vb leave (land) unseeded after ploughing and harrowing it

FALLOWED > FALLOW

FALLOWER > FALLOW

FALLOWEST > FALLOW

FALLOWING > FALLOW

FALLOWS > FALLOW

FALLS > FALL

FALSE adj not true or correct ▷ adv in a false or dishonest manner ▷ vb falsify

FALSED > FALSE

FALSEFACE n mask

FALSEHOOD n quality of being untrue

FALSELY > FALSE

FALSENESS > FALSE

FALSER > FALSE

FALSERS n colloquial term for false teeth

FALSES > FALSE

FALSEST > FALSE

FALSETTO n voice pitched higher than one's natural range

FALSETTOS > FALSETTO

FALSEWORK n framework supporting something under construction

FALSIE n pad used to enlarge breast shape

FALSIES > FALSIE

FALSIFIED > FALSIFY

FALSIFIER > FALSIFY

FALSIFIES > FALSIFY

FALSIFY vb alter fraudulently

FALSING > FALSE

FALSISH > FALSE

FALSISM > FALSE

FALSISMS > FALSE

FALSITIES > FALSITY

FALSITY n state of being false

FALTBOAT n collapsible boat made of waterproof material stretched over a light framework

FALTBOATS > FALTBOAT

FALTER vb be hesitant, weak, or unsure ▷ n uncertainty or hesitancy in speech or action

FALTERED > FALTER

FALTERER > FALTER

FALTERERS > FALTER

FALTERING > FALTER

FALTERS > FALTER

FALX n sickle-shaped anatomical structure

FAME n state of being widely recognized ▷ vb make known or famous

FAMED > FAME

FAMELESS > FAME

FAMES > FAME

FAMILIAL adj of or relating to the family

FAMILIAR adj well-known ▷ n demon supposed to attend a witch

FAMILIARS n attendant demons

FAMILIES > FAMILY

FAMILISM n beliefs of a mystical Christian religious sect

FAMILISMS > FAMILISM

FAMILIST adj relating to familism

FAMILLE n type of Chinese porcelain

FAMILLES > FAMILLE

FAMILY n group of parents and their children ▷ adj suitable for parents and children together

FAMINE n severe shortage of food

FAMINES > FAMINE

FAMING > FAME

FAMISH vb be or make very hungry or weak

FAMISHED adj very hungry

FAMISHES > FAMISH

FAMISHING > FAMISH

FAMOUS adj very well-known ▷ vb make famous

FAMOUSED > FAMOUS

FAMOUSES > FAMOUS

FAMOUSING > FAMOUS

FAMOUSLY adv excellently

FAMULI > FAMULUS

FAMULUS n (formerly) the attendant of a sorcerer or scholar

FAN n object used to create a current of air ▷ vb blow or cool with a fan

FANAL n lighthouse

FANALS > FANAL

FANATIC n person who is excessively enthusiastic about something ▷ adj excessively enthusiastic

FANATICAL adj surpassing what is normal or accepted in enthusiasm for or belief in something

FANATICS > FANATIC

FANBASE n body of admirers

FANBASES > FANBASE

FANBOY n obsessive fan of a subject or hobby

FANBOYS > FANBOY

FANCIABLE adj physically attractive

FANCIED adj imaginary

FANCIER n person interested in plants or animals

FANCIERS > FANCIER

FANCIES > FANCY

FANCIEST > FANCY

FANCIFIED > FANCIFY

FANCIFIES > FANCIFY

FANCIFUL adj not based on fact

FANCIFY vb make more beautiful

FANCILESS > FANCY

FANCILY > FANCY

FANCINESS > FANCY

FANCY adj elaborate, not plain ▷ n sudden irrational liking or desire ▷ vb suppose; imagine

FANCYING > FANCY

FANCYWORK n ornamental needlework

FAND vb try

FANDANGLE n elaborate ornament

FANDANGO n lively Spanish dance

FANDANGOS > FANDANGO

FANDED > FAND

FANDING > FAND

FANDOM n collectively, the fans of a sport, pastime or person

FANDOMS > FANDOM

FANDS > FAND

FANE n temple or shrine

FANEGA n Spanish unit of measurement

f

FANEGADA n Spanish unit of land area

FANEGADAS > FANEGADA

FANEGAS > FANEGA

FANES > FANE

FANFARADE n fanfare

FANFARE n tune played on brass instruments ▷ vb perform a fanfare

FANFARED > FANFARE

FANFARES > FANFARE

FANFARING > FANFARE

FANFARON n braggart

FANFARONA n gold chain

FANFARONS > FANFARON

FANFIC n fiction based on work by other authors

FANFICS > FANFIC

FANFOLD vb fold (paper) like a fan

FANFOLDED > FANFOLD

FANFOLDS > FANFOLD

FANG n snake's tooth which injects poison ▷ vb seize

FANGA same as > FANEGA

FANGAS > FANGA

FANGED > FANG

FANGING > FANG

FANGIRL n enthusiastic female devotee of something

FANGIRLS > FANGIRL

FANGLE vb fashion

FANGLED > FANGLE

FANGLES > FANGLE

FANGLESS > FANG

FANGLIKE > FANG

FANGLING > FANGLE

FANGO n mud from thermal springs in Italy

FANGOS > FANGO

FANGS > FANG

FANION n small flag used by surveyors

FANIONS > FANION

FANJET same as > TURBOFAN

FANJETS > FANJET

FANK n sheep pen ▷ vb put sheep in a pen

FANKED > FANK

FANKING > FANK

FANKLE vb entangle ▷ n tangle

FANKLED > FANKLE

FANKLES > FANKLE

FANKLING > FANKLE

FANKS > FANK

FANLIGHT n semicircular window over a door or window

FANLIGHTS > FANLIGHT

FANLIKE > FAN

FANNED > FAN

FANNEL n ecclesiastical vestment

FANNELL variant of > FANNEL

FANNELLS > FANNELL

FANNELS > FANNEL

FANNER > FAN

FANNERS > FAN

FANNIED > FANNY

FANNIES > FANNY

FANNING > FAN

FANNINGS > FAN

FANNY n vulgar word for the female genitals ▷ vb waste time; misbehave

FANNYING > FANNY

FANO same as > FANON

FANON n collar-shaped vestment

FANONS > FANON

FANOS > FANO

FANS > FAN

FANSITE n website aimed at fans of a celebrity, film, etc

FANSITES > FANSITE

FANSUB n fan-produced subtitling of films

FANSUBS > FANSUB

FANTAD n nervous, agitated state

FANTADS > FANTAD

FANTAIL n small New Zealand bird with a tail like a fan

FANTAILED adj having a tail like a fan

FANTAILS > FANTAIL

FANTASIA n musical composition of an improvised nature

FANTASIAS > FANTASIA

FANTASIE same as > FANTASY

FANTASIED > FANTASY

FANTASIES > FANTASY

FANTASISE same as > FANTASIZE

FANTASIST n person who indulges in fantasies

FANTASIZE vb indulge in daydreams

FANTASM archaic spelling of > PHANTASM

FANTASMAL > FANTASM

FANTASMIC > FANTASM

FANTASMS > FANTASM

FANTASQUE n fantasy

FANTAST n dreamer or visionary

FANTASTIC adj very good ▷ n person who dresses or behaves eccentrically

FANTASTRY n condition of being fantastic

FANTASTS > FANTAST

FANTASY n far-fetched notion ▷ adj of a type of competition ▷ vb fantasize

FANTEEG n nervous, agitated state

FANTEEGS > FANTEEG

FANTIGUE variant of > FANTEEG

FANTIGUES > FANTIGUE

FANTOD n crotchety or faddish behaviour

FANTODS > FANTOD

FANTOM archaic spelling of > PHANTOM

FANTOMS > FANTOM

FANTOOSH adj pretentious

FANUM n temple

FANUMS > FANUM

FANWISE adj like a fan

FANWORT n aquatic plant

FANWORTS > FANWORT

FANZINE n magazine produced by fans

FANZINES > FANZINE

FAP adj drunk

FAQIR same as > FAKIR

FAQIRS > FAQIR

FAQUIR variant of > FAQIR

FAQUIRS > FAQUIR

FAR adv at, to, or from a great distance ▷ adj remote in space or time ▷ vb go far

FARAD n unit of electrical capacitance

FARADAIC same as > FARADIC

FARADAY n quantity of electricity

FARADAYS > FARADAY

FARADIC adj of an intermittent asymmetric alternating current

FARADISE same as > FARADIZE

FARADISED > FARADISE

FARADISER > FARADISE

FARADISES > FARADISE

FARADISM n therapeutic use of faradic currents

FARADISMS > FARADISM

FARADIZE vb treat (an organ or part) with faradic currents

FARADIZED > FARADIZE

FARADIZER > FARADIZE

FARADIZES > FARADIZE

FARADS > FARAD

FARAND adj pleasant or attractive in manner or appearance

FARANDINE n silk and wool cloth

FARANDOLE n lively dance in six-eight or four-four time from Provence

FARANG n Thai for a foreigner

FARANGS > FARANG

FARAWAY adj very distant

FARAWAYS same as > FARAWAY

FARCE n boisterous comedy ▷ vb enliven (a speech, etc) with jokes

FARCED > FARCE

FARCEMEAT same as > FORCEMEAT

FARCER same as > FARCEUR

FARCERS > FARCER

FARCES > FARCE

FARCEUR n writer of or performer in farces

FARCEURS > FARCEUR

FARCEUSE n female farceur

FARCEUSES > FARCEUSE

FARCI adj (of food) stuffed

FARCICAL adj ludicrous

FARCIE same as > FARCI

FARCIED adj afflicted with farcy

FARCIES > FARCY

FARCIFIED > FARCIFY

FARCIFIES > FARCIFY

FARCIFY vb turn into a farce

FARCIN n equine disease

FARCING > FARCE

FARCINGS > FARCE

FARCINS > FARCIN

FARCY n form of glanders, a bacterial disease of horses

FARD n paint for the face, esp white paint ▷ vb paint (the face) with fard

FARDAGE n material laid beneath or between cargo

FARDAGES > FARDAGE

FARDED > FARD

FARDEL n bundle or burden

FARDELS > FARDEL

FARDEN n farthing

FARDENS > FARDEN

FARDING > FARD

FARDINGS > FARD

FARDS > FARD

FARE n charge for a passenger's journey ▷ vb get on (as specified)

FAREBOX n box where money for bus fares is placed

FAREBOXES > FAREBOX

FARED > FARE

FARER > FARE

FARERS > FARE

FARES > FARE

FAREWELL interj goodbye ▷ n act of saying goodbye and leaving ▷ vb say goodbye ▷ adj parting or closing

FAREWELLS > FAREWELL

FARFAL same as > FELAFEL

FARFALLE n pasta in bow shapes

FARFALLES > FARFALLE

FARFALS > FARFAL

FARFEL same as > FELAFEL

FARFELS > FARFEL

FARFET adj far-fetched

FARINA n flour or meal made from any kind of cereal grain

FARINAS > FARINA

FARING > FARE

FARINHA n cassava meal

FARINHAS > FARINHA

FARINOSE adj similar to or yielding farina

FARL n thin cake of oatmeal, often triangular in shape

FARLE same as > FARL

FARLES > FARLE

FARLS > FARL

FARM n area of land for growing crops or rearing livestock ▷ vb cultivate (land)

FARMABLE > FARM

FARMED adj (of fish or game) reared on a farm

FARMER n person who owns or runs a farm

FARMERESS n female farmer

FARMERIES > FARMERY

FARMERS > FARMER

FARMERY n farm buildings

FARMHAND n person who is hired to work on a farm

FARMHANDS > FARMHAND

FARMHOUSE n house attached to a farm

FARMING n business or skill of agriculture

FARMINGS > FARMING

FARMLAND n land that is used for or suitable for farming

FARMLANDS > FARMLAND

FARMOST adj most distant

FARMS > FARM

FARMSTEAD n farm and its buildings

FARMWIFE n woman who works on a farm

FARMWIVES > FARMWIFE

FARMWORK n tasks carried out on a farm

FARMWORKS > FARMWORK

FARMYARD n small area of land enclosed by or around the farm buildings

FARMYARDS > FARMYARD

FARNARKEL vb spend time or act in a careless or inconsequential manner

FARNESOL n type of alcohol

FARNESOLS > FARNESOL

FARNESS > FAR

FARNESSES > FAR

FARO n gambling game

FAROLITO n votive candle

FAROLITOS > FAROLITO

FAROS > FARO

FAROUCHE adj sullen or shy

FARRAGO n jumbled mixture of things

FARRAGOES > FARRAGO

FARRAGOS > FARRAGO

FARRAND variant of > FARAND

FARRANT variant of > FARAND

FARRED > FAR

FARREN n allotted ground

FARRENS > FARREN

FARRIER n person who shoes horses

FARRIERS > FARRIER

FARRIERY n art, work, or establishment of a farrier

FARRING > FAR

FARRO n variety of wheat

FARROS > FARRO

FARROW n litter of piglets ▷ vb (of a sow) give birth ▷ adj (of a cow) not calving in a given year

FARROWED > FARROW

FARROWING n (of a sow) act of giving birth

FARROWS > FARROW

FARRUCA n flamenco dance performed by men

FARRUCAS > FARRUCA

FARS > FAR

FARSE vb insert into

FARSED > FARSE

FARSEEING adj having shrewd judgment

FARSES > FARSE

FARSIDE n part of the Moon facing away from the Earth

FARSIDES > FARSIDE

FARSING > FARSE

FART n emission of gas from the anus ▷ vb emit gas from the anus

FARTED > FART

FARTHEL same as > FARL

FARTHELS > FARTHEL

FARTHER > FAR

FARTHEST > FAR

FARTHING n former British coin equivalent to a quarter of a penny

FARTHINGS > FARTHING

FARTING > FART

FARTLEK n in sport, another name for interval training

FARTLEKS > FARTLEK

FARTS > FART

FAS > FA

FASCES pl n (in ancient Rome) a bundle of rods containing an axe

FASCI > FASCIO

FASCIA n outer surface of a dashboard

FASCIAE > FASCIA

FASCIAL > FASCIA

FASCIAS > FASCIA

FASCIATE adj (of stems and branches) abnormally flattened due to coalescence

FASCIATED same as > FASCIATE

FASCICLE same as > FASCICULE

FASCICLED adj in instalments

FASCICLES > FASCICLE

FASCICULE n one part of a printed work that is published in instalments

FASCICULI > FASCICULE

FASCIITIS n inflammation of the fascia of a muscle

FASCINATE vb attract and interest strongly

FASCINE n bundle of long sticks used in construction

FASCINES > FASCINE

FASCIO n political group

FASCIOLA n band

FASCIOLAS > FASCIOLA

FASCIOLE n band

FASCIOLES > FASCIOLE

FASCIS > FASCI

FASCISM n right-wing totalitarian political system

FASCISMI > FASCISMO

FASCISMO Italian word for > FASCISM

FASCISMS > FASCISM

FASCIST n adherent or practitioner of fascism ▷ adj characteristic of or relating to fascism

FASCISTA Italian word for > FASCIST

FASCISTI > FASCISTA

FASCISTIC > FASCIST

FASCISTS > FASCIST

FASCIITIS same as > FASCIITIS

FASH n worry ▷ vb trouble

FASHED > FASH

FASHERIES > FASHERY

FASHERY n difficulty, trouble

FASHES > FASH

FASHING > FASH

FASHION n style popular at a particular time ▷ vb form or make into a particular shape

FASHIONED > FASHION

FASHIONER > FASHION

FASHIONS > FASHION

FASHIONY adj fashionable, trendy

FASHIOUS adj troublesome

FAST adj (capable of) acting or moving quickly ▷ adv quickly ▷ vb go without food, esp for religious reasons ▷ n period of fasting

FASTBACK n car having a back that forms one continuous slope from roof to rear

FASTBACKS > FASTBACK

FASTBALL n ball pitched at the pitcher's top speed

FASTBALLS > FASTBALL

FASTED > FAST

FASTEN vb make or become firmly fixed or joined

FASTENED > FASTEN

FASTENER > FASTEN

FASTENERS > FASTEN

FASTENING n something that fastens something, such as a clasp or lock

FASTENS > FASTEN

FASTER > FAST

FASTERS > FAST

FASTEST > FAST

FASTI pl n in ancient Rome, business days

FASTIE n deceitful act

FASTIES > FASTIE

FASTIGIUM n highest point

FASTING > FAST

FASTINGS > FAST

FASTISH > FAST

FASTLY > FAST

FASTNESS n fortress, safe place

FASTS > FAST

FASTUOUS adj arrogant

FAT adj having excess flesh on the body ▷ n extra flesh on the body ▷ vb fatten

FATAL adj causing death or ruin

FATALISM n belief that all events are predetermined

FATALISMS > FATALISM

FATALIST > FATALISM

FATALISTS > FATALISM

FATALITY n death caused by an accident or disaster

FATALLY adv resulting in death or disaster

FATALNESS > FATAL

FATBACK n fat from the upper part of a side of pork

FATBACKS > FATBACK

FATBERG n large mass of fat in a sewer

FATBERGS > FATBERG

FATBIRD n nocturnal bird

FATBIRDS > FATBIRD

FATE n power supposed to predetermine events ▷ vb predetermine

FATED adj destined

FATEFUL adj having important, usu disastrous, consequences

FATEFULLY > FATEFUL

FATES > FATE

FATHEAD n stupid person

FATHEADED adj stupid

FATHEADS > FATHEAD

FATHER n male parent ▷ vb be the father of (offspring)

FATHERED > FATHER

FATHERING > FATHER

FATHERLY adj kind or protective, like a father

FATHERS > FATHER

FATHOM n unit of length ▷ vb understand

FATHOMED > FATHOM

FATHOMER > FATHOM

FATHOMERS > FATHOM

FATHOMING > FATHOM

FATHOMS > FATHOM

FATIDIC adj prophetic

FATIDICAL same as > FATIDIC

FATIGABLE > FATIGUE

FATIGATE vb fatigue

FATIGATED > FATIGATE

FATIGATES > FATIGATE

FATIGUE n extreme physical or mental tiredness ▷ vb tire out

FATIGUED > FATIGUE

FATIGUES > FATIGUE

FATIGUING > FATIGUE

FATING > FATE

FATISCENT adj having the appearance of being cracked

FATLESS > FAT

FATLIKE > FAT

FATLING n young farm animal fattened for killing

FATLINGS > FATLING

FATLY > FAT

FATNESS > FAT

FATNESSES > FAT

FATS > FAT

FATSIA n type of shrub

FATSIAS > FATSIA

FATSO n disparaging term for a fat person

FATSOES > FATSO

FATSOS > FATSO

FATSTOCK n livestock fattened and ready for market

FATSTOCKS > FATSTOCK

FATTED > FAT

FATTEN vb (cause to) become fat

FATTENED > FATTEN

FATTENER > FATTEN

FATTENERS > FATTEN

FATTENING > FATTEN

FATTENS > FATTEN

FATTER > FAT

FATTEST > FAT

FATTIER > FATTY

FATTIES > FATTY

FATTIEST > FATTY

FATTILY > FATTY

FATTINESS > FATTY

FATTING > FAT

FATTISH > FAT

FATTISM n discrimination on the basis of weight

FATTISMS > FATTISM

FATTIST > FATTISM

FATTISTS > FATTISM

FATTRELS n ends of ribbon

FATTY adj containing fat ▷ n insulting word for a fat person

FATUITIES > FATUITY

FATUITOUS > FATUITY

FATUITY n foolish thoughtlessness

FATUOUS adj foolish

FATUOUSLY > FATUOUS

FATWA n religious decree issued by a Muslim leader ▷ vb issue a fatwa

f

FATWAED > FATWA
FATWAH same as > FATWA
FATWAHED > FATWAH
FATWAHING > FATWAH
FATWAHS > FATWAH
FATWAING > FATWA
FATWAS > FATWA
FATWOOD n wood used for kindling
FATWOODS > FATWOOD
FAUBOURG n suburb or quarter, esp of a French city
FAUBOURGS > FAUBOURG
FAUCAL adj of or relating to the fauces
FAUCALS > FAUCAL
FAUCES n area of the mouth
FAUCET n tap
FAUCETRY n art or practice of making faucets
FAUCETS > FAUCET
FAUCHION n short sword
FAUCHIONS > FAUCHION
FAUCHON variant of > FAUCHION
FAUCHONS > FAUCHON
FAUCIAL same as > FAUCAL
FAUGH interj exclamation of disgust, scorn, etc
FAULCHION variant of > FAUCHION
FAULD n piece of armour
FAULDS > FAULD
FAULT n responsibility for something wrong ▷ vb criticize or blame
FAULTED > FAULT
FAULTFUL > FAULT
FAULTIER > FAULTY
FAULTIEST > FAULTY
FAULTILY > FAULTY
FAULTING > FAULT
FAULTLESS adj without fault
FAULTLINE n surface of a fault fracture
FAULTS > FAULT
FAULTY adj badly designed or not working properly
FAUN n (in Roman legend) mythological creature
FAUNA n animals of a given place or time
FAUNAE > FAUNA
FAUNAL > FAUNA
FAUNALLY > FAUNA
FAUNAS > FAUNA
FAUNIST > FAUNA
FAUNISTIC > FAUNA
FAUNISTS > FAUNA
FAUNLIKE > FAUN
FAUNS > FAUN
FAUNULA n fauna of a small single environment
FAUNULAE > FAUNULA
FAUNULE same as > FAUNULA
FAUNULES > FAUNULE
FAUR Scot word for > FAR
FAURD adj favoured
FAURER > FAUR
FAUREST > FAUR
FAUSTIAN adj of or relating to Faust, esp reminiscent of his bargain with the devil
FAUT Scot word for > FAULT
FAUTED > FAUT

FAUTEUIL n armchair, the sides of which are not upholstered
FAUTEUILS > FAUTEUIL
FAUTING > FAUT
FAUTOR n patron
FAUTORS > FAUTOR
FAUTS > FAUT
FAUVE adj of the style of the Fauve art movement ▷ n member of the Fauve art movement
FAUVES > FAUVE
FAUVETTE n singing bird, warbler
FAUVETTES > FAUVETTE
FAUVISM > FAUVISM
FAUVISMS > FAUVISM
FAUVIST n artist following the Fauve style of painting
FAUVISTS > FAUVIST
FAUX adj false
FAUXMANCE n fake romance between two celebrities to gain media coverage
FAVA n type of bean
FAVAS > FAVA
FAVE short for > FAVOURITE
FAVEL adj (of a horse) dun-coloured ▷ n fallow-coloured horse
FAVELA n (in Brazil) a shanty or shantytown
FAVELAS > FAVELA
FAVELL variant of > FAVEL
FAVELLA n group of spores
FAVELLAS > FAVELLA
FAVELS > FAVEL
FAVEOLATE adj pitted with cell-like cavities
FAVER > FAVE
FAVES > FAVE
FAVEST > FAVE
FAVICON n icon displayed before a website's URL
FAVICONS > FAVICON
FAVISM n type of anaemia
FAVISMS > FAVISM
FAVONIAN adj of or relating to the west wind
FAVOR same as > FAVOUR
FAVORABLE adj favourable
FAVORABLY adv favourably
FAVORED > FAVOR
FAVORER > FAVOR
FAVORERS > FAVOUR
FAVORING > FAVOR
FAVORITE same as > FAVOURITE
FAVORITES > FAVORITE
FAVORLESS > FAVOR
FAVORS > FAVOR
FAVOSE same as > FAVEOLATE
FAVOUR n approving attitude ▷ vb prefer
FAVOURED > FAVOUR
FAVOURER > FAVOUR
FAVOURERS > FAVOUR
FAVOURING > FAVOUR
FAVOURITE adj most liked ▷ n preferred person or thing
FAVOURS > FAVOUR
FAVOUS adj resembling honeycomb
FAVRILE n type of iridescent glass

FAVRILES > FAVRILE
FAVUS n infectious fungal skin disease
FAVUSES > FAVUS
FAW n gypsy
FAWN n young deer ▷ adj light yellowish-brown ▷ vb seek attention from (someone) by insincere flattery
FAWNED > FAWN
FAWNER > FAWN
FAWNERS > FAWN
FAWNIER > FAWNY
FAWNIEST > FAWNY
FAWNING > FAWN
FAWNINGLY > FAWN
FAWNINGS > FAWN
FAWNLIKE > FAWN
FAWNS > FAWN
FAWNY adj of a fawn colour
FAWS > FAW
FAX n electronic system ▷ vb send (a document) by this system
FAXABLE adj able to be faxed
FAXED > FAX
FAXES > FAX
FAXING > FAX
FAY n fairy or sprite ▷ adj of or resembling a fay ▷ vb fit or be fitted closely or tightly
FAYALITE n rare brown or black mineral
FAYALITES > FAYALITE
FAYED > FAY
FAYENCE variant of > FAIENCE
FAYENCES > FAYENCE
FAYER > FAY
FAYEST > FAY
FAYING > FAY
FAYNE archaic spelling of > FEIGN
FAYNED > FAYNE
FAYNES > FAYNE
FAYNING > FAYNE
FAYRE pseudo-archaic spelling of > FAIR
FAYRES > FAYRE
FAYS > FAY
FAZE vb disconcert or fluster
FAZED adj worried or disconcerted
FAZENDA n large estate or ranch
FAZENDAS > FAZENDA
FAZES > FAZE
FAZING > FAZE
FE n variant of Hebrew letter pe, transliterated as f
FEAGUE vb whip or beat
FEAGUED > FEAGUE
FEAGUES > FEAGUE
FEAGUING > FEAGUE
FEAL vb conceal
FEALED > FEAL
FEALING > FEAL
FEALS > FEAL
FEALTIES > FEALTY
FEALTY n (in feudal society) subordinate's loyalty
FEAR n distress or alarm caused by impending danger or pain ▷ vb be afraid of (something or someone)

FEARE n companion
FEARED > FEAR
FEARER > FEAR
FEARERS > FEAR
FEARES > FEARE
FEARFUL adj feeling fear
FEARFULLY adv in a fearful manner
FEARING > FEAR
FEARLESS > FEAR
FEARS > FEAR
FEARSOME adj terrifying
FEART adj (Scots) afraid
FEASANCE n performance of an act
FEASANCES > FEASANCE
FEASE vb perform an act
FEASED > FEASE
FEASES > FEASE
FEASIBLE adj able to be done, possible
FEASIBLY > FEASIBLE
FEASING > FEASE
FEAST n lavish meal ▷ vb eat a feast
FEASTED > FEAST
FEASTER > FEAST
FEASTERS > FEAST
FEASTFUL adj festive
FEASTING > FEAST
FEASTINGS > FEAST
FEASTLESS > FEAST
FEASTS > FEAST
FEAT n remarkable, skilful, or daring action ▷ adj neat ▷ vb make neat
FEATED > FEAT
FEATEOUS adj neat
FEATER > FEAT
FEATEST > FEAT
FEATHER n one of the barbed shafts forming the plumage of birds ▷ vb fit or cover with feathers
FEATHERED > FEATHER
FEATHERS > FEATHER
FEATHERY > FEATHER
FEATING > FEAT
FEATLIER > FEAT
FEATLIEST > FEAT
FEATLY > FEAT
FEATOUS variant of > FEATEOUS
FEATS > FEAT
FEATUOUS variant of > FEATEOUS
FEATURE n part of the face, such as the eyes ▷ vb have as a feature or be a feature in
FEATURED adj having features as specified
FEATURELY adj handsome
FEATURES > FEATURE
FEATURING > FEATURE
FEAZE same as > FEEZE
FEAZED > FEAZE
FEAZES > FEAZE
FEAZING > FEAZE
FEBLESSE n feebleness
FEBLESSES > FEBLESSE
FEBRICITY n condition of having a fever
FEBRICULA n slight transient fever
FEBRICULE variant of > FEBRICULA

FEBRIFIC *adj* causing or having a fever
FEBRIFUGE *n* any drug or agent for reducing fever ▷ *adj* serving to reduce fever
FEBRILE *adj* very active and nervous
FEBRILITY > FEBRILE
FECAL *same as* > FAECAL
FECES *same as* > FAECES
FECHT *Scot word for* > FIGHT
FECHTER > FECHT
FECHTERS > FECHT
FECHTING > FECHT
FECHTS > FECHT
FECIAL *adj* heraldic
FECIALS > FECIAL
FECIT *vb* (he or she) made it
FECK *vb* euphemism for an expletive
FECKED > FECK
FECKIN *same as* > FECKING
FECKING > FECK
FECKLESS *adj* ineffectual or irresponsible
FECKLY *adv* dialect word meaning mostly
FECKS > FECK
FECULA *n* type of starch
FECULAE > FECULA
FECULAS > FECULA
FECULENCE > FECULENT
FECULENCY > FECULENT
FECULENT *adj* filthy, scummy, muddy, or foul
FECUND *adj* fertile
FECUNDATE *vb* make fruitful
FECUNDITY *n* fertility
FED *n* FBI agent
FEDARIE *n* accomplice
FEDARIES > FEDARIE
FEDAYEE *n* (in Arab states) a commando
FEDAYEEN > FEDAYEE
FEDELINI *n* type of pasta
FEDELINIS > FEDELINI
FEDERACY *n* alliance
FEDERAL *adj* of a system of governance ▷ *n* supporter of federal union or federation
FEDERALLY > FEDERAL
FEDERALS > FEDERAL
FEDERARIE *variant of* > FEDARIE
FEDERARY *variant of* > FEDARIE
FEDERATE *vb* unite in a federation ▷ *adj* federal
FEDERATED > FEDERATE
FEDERATES > FEDERATE
FEDERATOR > FEDERATE
FEDEX *vb* send by FedEx
FEDEXED > FEDEX
FEDEXES > FEDEX
FEDEXING > FEDEX
FEDORA *n* soft hat with a brim
FEDORAS > FEDORA
FEDS > FED
FEE *n* charge paid to be allowed to do something ▷ *vb* pay a fee to
FEEB *n* contemptible person
FEEBLE *adj* lacking physical or mental power ▷ *vb* make feeble

FEEBLED > FEEBLE
FEEBLER > FEEBLE
FEEBLES > FEEBLE
FEEBLEST > FEEBLE
FEEBLING > FEEBLE
FEEBLISH > FEEBLE
FEEBLY > FEEBLE
FEEBS > FEEB
FEED *vb* give food to ▷ *n* act of feeding
FEEDABLE > FEED
FEEDBACK *n* information received in response to something done
FEEDBACKS > FEEDBACK
FEEDBAG *n* any bag in which feed for livestock is sacked
FEEDBAGS > FEEDBAG
FEEDBOX *n* trough, manger
FEEDBOXES > FEEDBOX
FEEDER *n* baby's bib
FEEDERS > FEEDER
FEEDGRAIN *n* cereal grown to feed livestock
FEEDHOLE *n* small hole through which cable etc is inserted
FEEDHOLES > FEEDHOLE
FEEDING > FEED
FEEDINGS > FEED
FEEDLOT *n* area where livestock are fattened rapidly
FEEDLOTS > FEEDLOT
FEEDPIPE *n* pipe through which something is supplied to a machine or system
FEEDPIPES > FEEDPIPE
FEEDS > FEED
FEEDSTOCK *n* main raw material used in the manufacture of a product
FEEDSTUFF *n* any material used as a food, esp for animals
FEEDWATER *n* water, previously purified to prevent scale deposit or corrosion, that is fed to boilers for steam generation
FEEDYARD *n* place where cattle are kept and fed
FEEDYARDS > FEEDYARD
FEEING > FEE
FEEL *vb* have a physical or emotional sensation of ▷ *n* act of feeling
FEELBAD *adj* inducing depression
FEELER *n* organ of touch in some animals
FEELERS > FEELER
FEELESS > FEE
FEELGOOD *adj* causing or characterized by a feeling of self-satisfaction
FEELING > FEEL
FEELINGLY > FEEL
FEELINGS > FEEL
FEELS > FEEL
FEEN *n* in Irish dialect, an informal word for 'man'
FEENS > FEEN
FEER *vb* make a furrow
FEERED > FEER
FEERIE *n* fairyland
FEERIES > FEERIE
FEERIN *n* furrow

FEERING > FEER
FEERINGS > FEER
FEERINS > FEERIN
FEERS > FEER
FEES > FEE
FEESE *vb* perturb
FEESED > FEESE
FEESES > FEESE
FEESING > FEESE
FEET > FOOT
FEETFIRST *adv* with the feet coming first
FEETLESS > FOOT
FEEZE *vb* beat ▷ *n* rush
FEEZED > FEEZE
FEEZES > FEEZE
FEEZING > FEEZE
FEG *same as* > FIG
FEGARIES > FEGARY
FEGARY *variant of* > VAGARY
FEGS > FEG
FEH *same as* > FE
FEHM *n* medieval German court
FEHME > FEHM
FEHMIC > FEHM
FEHS > FEH
FEIGN *vb* pretend
FEIGNED > FEIGN
FEIGNEDLY > FEIGN
FEIGNER > FEIGN
FEIGNERS > FEIGN
FEIGNING > FEIGN
FEIGNINGS > FEIGN
FEIGNS > FEIGN
FEIJOA *n* evergreen myrtaceous shrub of S America
FEIJOADA *n* Brazilian stew of black beans, meat and vegetables
FEIJOADAS > FEIJOADA
FEIJOAS > FEIJOA
FEINT *n* sham attack meant to distract an opponent ▷ *vb* make a feint ▷ *adj* printing term meaning ruled with faint lines
FEINTED > FEINT
FEINTER > FEINT
FEINTEST > FEINT
FEINTING > FEINT
FEINTS *pl n* leavings of the second distillation of Scotch malt whisky
FEIRIE *adj* nimble
FEIRIER > FEIRIE
FEIRIEST > FEIRIE
FEIS *n* Irish music and dance festival
FEISEANNA > FEIS
FEIST *n* small aggressive dog
FEISTIER > FEISTY
FEISTIEST > FEISTY
FEISTILY > FEISTY
FEISTS > FEIST
FEISTY *adj* showing courage or spirit
FELAFEL *same as* > FALAFEL
FELAFELS > FELAFEL
FELCH *vb* taboo word meaning to suck semen from the vagina or anus of (a sexual partner)
FELCHED > FELCH
FELCHES > FELCH

FELCHING > FELCH
FELDGRAU *n* ordinary German soldier (from uniform colour)
FELDGRAUS > FELDGRAU
FELDSCHAR *same as* > FELDSHER
FELDSCHER *same as* > FELDSHER
FELDSHER *n* (in Russia) a medical doctor's assistant
FELDSHERS > FELDSHER
FELDSPAR *n* hard mineral that is the main constituent of igneous rocks
FELDSPARS > FELDSPAR
FELDSPATH *variant of* > FELDSPAR
FELICIA *n* type of African herb
FELICIAS > FELICIA
FELICIFIC *adj* making or tending to make happy
FELICITER *adj* happily, successfully
FELICITY *n* happiness
FELID *n* any animal belonging to the cat family
FELIDS > FELID
FELINE *adj* of cats ▷ *n* member of the cat family
FELINELY > FELINE
FELINES > FELINE
FELINITY > FELINE
FELL *vb* cut or knock down ▷ *adj* cruel or deadly
FELLA *nonstandard variant of* > FELLOW
FELLABLE > FELL
FELLAH *n* peasant in Arab countries
FELLAHEEN > FELLAH
FELLAHIN > FELLAH
FELLAHS > FELLAH
FELLAS > FELLA
FELLATE *vb* perform fellatio on (a person)
FELLATED > FELLATE
FELLATES > FELLATE
FELLATING > FELLATE
FELLATIO *n* sexual activity in which the penis is stimulated by the partner's mouth
FELLATION *same as* > FELLATIO
FELLATIOS > FELLATIO
FELLATOR > FELLATIO
FELLATORS > FELLATIO
FELLATRIX > FELLATIO
FELLED > FELL
FELLER *n* person or thing that fells
FELLERS > FELLER
FELLEST > FELL
FELLFIELD *n* stony tundra area with little vegetation
FELLIES > FELLY
FELLING > FELL
FELLINGS > FELLING
FELLNESS > FELL
FELLOE *n* (segment of) the rim of a wheel
FELLOES > FELLOE
FELLOW *n* man or boy ▷ *adj* in the same group or condition ▷ *vb* join as a companion

f

f

FELLOWED > FELLOW
FELLOWING > FELLOW
FELLOWLY adj friendly, companionable
FELLOWMAN n companion
FELLOWMEN > FELLOWMAN
FELLOWS > FELLOW
FELLS > FELL
FELLY same as > FELLOE
FELON n (formerly) person guilty of a felony ▷ adj evil
FELONIES > FELONY
FELONIOUS adj of, involving, or constituting a felony
FELONOUS adj wicked
FELONRIES > FELONRY
FELONRY n felons collectively
FELONS > FELON
FELONY n serious crime
FELQUISTE n member of paramilitary group seeking independence for Quebec
FELSIC adj relating to igneous rock
FELSITE n any fine-grained igneous rock
FELSITES > FELSITE
FELSITIC > FELSITE
FELSPAR same as > FELDSPAR
FELSPARS > FELSPAR
FELSTONE same as > FELSITE
FELSTONES > FELSTONE
FELT n matted fabric ▷ vb become matted
FELTED > FELT
FELTER vb mat together
FELTERED > FELTER
FELTERING > FELTER
FELTERS > FELTER
FELTIER > FELT
FELTIEST > FELT
FELTING n felted material
FELTINGS > FELTING
FELTLIKE > FELT
FELTS > FELT
FELTY > FELT
FELUCCA n narrow lateen-rigged vessel
FELUCCAS > FELUCCA
FELWORT n type of plant
FELWORTS > FELWORT
FEM n type of igneous rock
FEMAL adj effeminate ▷ n effeminate person
FEMALE adj of the sex which bears offspring ▷ n female person or animal
FEMALES > FEMALE
FEMALITY > FEMALE
FEMALS > FEMAL
FEME n woman or wife
FEMERALL n ventilator or smoke outlet on a roof
FEMERALLS > FEMERALL
FEMERELL n ventilator or smoke outlet in a roof
FEMERELLS > FEMERELL
FEMES > FEME
FEMETARY variant of > FUMITORY
FEMICIDAL > FEMICIDE
FEMICIDE n killing of a woman or girl

FEMICIDES > FEMICIDE
FEMINACY n feminine character
FEMINAL adj feminine, female
FEMINAZI n offensive term for a militant feminist
FEMINAZIS > FEMINAZI
FEMINEITY n quality of being feminine
FEMINIE n women collectively
FEMINIES > FEMINIE
FEMININE adj having qualities traditionally regarded as suitable for, or typical of, women ▷ n short for feminine noun
FEMININES > FEMININE
FEMINISE same as > FEMINIZE
FEMINISED > FEMINISE
FEMINISES > FEMINISE
FEMINISM n advocacy of equal rights for women
FEMINISMS > FEMINISM
FEMINIST n person who advocates equal rights for women ▷ adj of, relating to, or advocating feminism
FEMINISTS > FEMINIST
FEMINITY > FEMINAL
FEMINIZE vb make or become feminine
FEMINIZED > FEMINIZE
FEMINIZES > FEMINIZE
FEMITER variant of > FUMITORY
FEMITERS > FEMITER
FEMME n woman or wife
FEMMES > FEMME
FEMMIER > FEMMY
FEMMIEST > FEMMY
FEMMY adj markedly or exaggeratedly feminine
FEMORA > FEMUR
FEMORAL adj of the thigh
FEMS > FEM
FEMUR n thighbone
FEMURS > FEMUR
FEN n low-lying flat marshy land
FENAGLE variant of > FINAGLE
FENAGLED > FENAGLE
FENAGLES > FENAGLE
FENAGLING > FENAGLE
FENCE n barrier of posts linked by wire or wood ▷ vb enclose with or as if with a fence
FENCED > FENCE
FENCELESS > FENCE
FENCELIKE > FENCE
FENCELINE n continuous extent of fence encompassing a tract of farmland
FENCER n person who fights with a sword
FENCEROW n uncultivated land flanking a fence
FENCEROWS > FENCEROW
FENCERS > FENCER
FENCES > FENCE
FENCEWIRE n wire used in making fences

FENCIBLE n person who undertook military service in defence of their homeland only
FENCIBLES > FENCIBLE
FENCING n sport of fighting with swords
FENCINGS > FENCING
FEND vb give support (to someone, esp oneself) ▷ n shift or effort
FENDED > FEND
FENDER n low metal frame in front of a fireplace
FENDERED adj having a fender
FENDERS > FENDER
FENDIER > FENDY
FENDIEST > FENDY
FENDING > FEND
FENDS > FEND
FENDY adj thrifty
FENESTRA n small opening in or between bones
FENESTRAE > FENESTRA
FENESTRAL > FENESTRA
FENESTRAS > FENESTRA
FENI n Goan alcoholic drink
FENING n small currency unit of Bosnia-Herzegovina
FENINGA > FENING
FENINGS > FENING
FENIS > FENI
FENITAR variant of > FUMITORY
FENITARS > FENITAR
FENKS n whale blubber
FENLAND > FEN
FENLANDS > FEN
FENMAN > FEN
FENMEN > FEN
FENNEC n type of nocturnal desert fox
FENNECS > FENNEC
FENNEL n fragrant plant
FENNELS > FENNEL
FENNIER > FENNY
FENNIES > FENNY
FENNIEST > FENNY
FENNING same as > FENING
FENNISH > FEN
FENNY adj boggy or marshy ▷ n feni
FENS > FEN
FENT n piece of waste fabric
FENTANYL n narcotic drug used in medicine to relieve pain
FENTANYLS > FENTANYL
FENTHION n type of pesticide
FENTHIONS > FENTHION
FENTS > FENT
FENUGREEK n Mediterranean plant grown for its heavily scented seeds
FENURON n type of herbicide
FENURONS > FENURON
FEOD same as > FEUD
FEODAL > FEOD
FEODARIES > FEOD
FEODARY > FEOD
FEODS > FEOD
FEOFF same as > FIEF
FEOFFED > FEOFF
FEOFFEE n (in feudal society) a vassal granted a fief by their lord

FEOFFEES > FEOFFEE
FEOFFER > FEOFF
FEOFFERS > FEOFF
FEOFFING > FEOFF
FEOFFMENT n (in medieval Europe) a lord's act of granting a fief to his man
FEOFFOR > FEOFF
FEOFFORS > FEOFF
FEOFFS > FEOFF
FER same as > FAR
FERACIOUS adj fruitful
FERACITY > FERACIOUS
FERAL adj wild ▷ n person who displays such tendencies and appearance
FERALISED same as > FERALIZED
FERALIZED adj once domesticated, but now wild
FERALS > FERAL
FERBAM n powder used as a fungicide
FERBAMS > FERBAM
FERE n companion ▷ adj fierce
FERER > FERE
FERES > FERE
FEREST > FERE
FERETORY n shrine, usually portable, for a saint's relics
FERIA n weekday on which no feast occurs
FERIAE > FERIA
FERIAL adj of or relating to a feria
FERIAS > FERIA
FERINE same as > FERAL
FERITIES > FERITY
FERITY > FERAL
FERLIE same as > FERLY
FERLIED > FERLY
FERLIER > FERLY
FERLIES > FERLY
FERLIEST > FERLY
FERLY adj wonderful ▷ n wonder ▷ vb wonder
FERLYING > FERLY
FERM variant of > FARM
FERMATA another word for > PAUSE
FERMATAS > FERMATA
FERMATE > FERMATA
FERMENT n any agent that causes fermentation ▷ vb (cause to) undergo fermentation
FERMENTED > FERMENT
FERMENTER > FERMENT
FERMENTOR > FERMENT
FERMENTS > FERMENT
FERMI n unit of length
FERMION n type of particle
FERMIONIC > FERMION
FERMIONS > FERMION
FERMIS > FERMI
FERMIUM n chemical element
FERMIUMS > FERMIUM
FERMS > FERM
FERN n flowerless plant with fine fronds
FERNALLY n seedless plant that is not a true fern
FERNBIRD n small brown and white New Zealand swamp bird with a fernlike tail

FERNBIRDS > FERNBIRD
FERNERIES > FERNERY
FERNERY n place where ferns are grown
FERNIER > FERN
FERNIEST > FERN
FERNING n production of a fern-like pattern
FERNINGS > FERNING
FERNINST same as > FORNENST
FERNLESS > FERN
FERNLIKE > FERN
FERNS > FERN
FERNSHAW n fern thicket
FERNSHAWS > FERNSHAW
FERNTICLE n freckle
FERNY > FERN
FEROCIOUS adj savagely fierce or cruel
FEROCITY > FEROCIOUS
FERRATE n type of salt
FERRATES > FERRATE
FERREL variant of > FERRULE
FERRELED > FERREL
FERRELING > FERREL
FERRELLED > FERREL
FERRELS > FERREL
FERREOUS adj containing or resembling iron
FERRET n tamed polecat ▷ vb hunt with ferrets
FERRETED > FERRET
FERRETER > FERRET
FERRETERS > FERRET
FERRETIER > FERRETY
FERRETING > FERRET
FERRETS > FERRET
FERRETY adj like a ferret
FERRIAGE n transportation by ferry
FERRIAGES > FERRIAGE
FERRIC adj of or containing iron
FERRIED > FERRY
FERRIES > FERRY
FERRITE n type of ceramic compound
FERRITES > FERRITE
FERRITIC > FERRITE
FERRITIN n type of protein
FERRITINS > FERRITIN
FERROCENE n reddish-orange insoluble crystalline compound
FERROGRAM n slide used to illustrate suspended iron particles in the lubricant of a machine
FERROTYPE n photographic print produced directly in a camera by exposing a sheet of iron or tin coated with a sensitized enamel
FERROUS adj of or containing iron in the divalent state
FERRUGO n disease affecting plants
FERRUGOS > FERRUGO
FERRULE n metal cap to strengthen the end of a stick ▷ vb equip (a stick, etc) with a ferrule
FERRULED > FERRULE
FERRULES > FERRULE

FERRULING > FERRULE
FERRUM Latin word for > IRON
FERRUMS > FERRUM
FERRY n boat for transporting people and vehicles ▷ vb carry by ferry
FERRYBOAT same as > FERRY
FERRYING > FERRY
FERRYMAN n someone who provides a ferry service
FERRYMEN > FERRYMAN
FERTIGATE vb fertilize and irrigate at the same time
FERTILE adj capable of producing young, crops, or vegetation
FERTILELY > FERTILE
FERTILER > FERTILE
FERTILEST > FERTILE
FERTILISE same as > FERTILIZE
FERTILITY n ability to produce offspring, esp abundantly
FERTILIZE vb to supply (soil or water) with mineral and organic nutrients to aid the growth of plants
FERULA n large Mediterranean plant
FERULAE > FERULA
FERULAS > FERULA
FERULE same as > FERRULE
FERULED > FERULE
FERULES > FERULE
FERULING > FERULE
FERVENCY another word for > FERVOUR
FERVENT adj intensely passionate and sincere
FERVENTER > FERVENT
FERVENTLY > FERVENT
FERVID same as > FERVENT
FERVIDER > FERVID
FERVIDEST > FERVID
FERVIDITY > FERVID
FERVIDLY > FERVID
FERVOR same as > FERVOUR
FERVOROUS > FERVOUR
FERVORS > FERVOR
FERVOUR n intensity of feeling
FERVOURS > FERVOUR
FES > FE
FESCUE n pasture and lawn grass with stiff narrow leaves
FESCUES > FESCUE
FESS vb confess
FESSE n horizontal band across a shield
FESSED > FESS
FESSES > FESSE
FESSING > FESS
FESSWISE adv in heraldry, with a horizontal band across the shield
FEST n event at which the emphasis is on a particular activity
FESTA n festival
FESTAL adj festive ▷ n festivity
FESTALLY > FESTAL
FESTALS > FESTAL
FESTAS > FESTA

FESTER vb grow worse and increasingly hostile ▷ n small ulcer or sore containing pus
FESTERED > FESTER
FESTERING > FESTER
FESTERS > FESTER
FESTIER > FESTY
FESTIEST > FESTY
FESTILOGY n treatise about church festivals
FESTINATE vb hurry
FESTIVAL n organized series of special events or performances
FESTIVALS > FESTIVAL
FESTIVE adj of or like a celebration
FESTIVELY > FESTIVE
FESTIVITY n happy celebration
FESTIVOUS > FESTIVE
FESTOLOGY variant of > FESTILOGY
FESTOON vb hang decorations in loops ▷ n decorative chain
FESTOONED > FESTOON
FESTOONS > FESTOON
FESTS > FEST
FESTY adj dirty
FET vb fetch
FETA n white salty Greek cheese
FETAL adj of, relating to, or resembling a fetus
FETAS > FETA
FETATION n state of pregnancy
FETATIONS > FETATION
FETCH vb go after and bring back ▷ n ghost or apparition of a living person
FETCHED > FETCH
FETCHER n person or animal that fetches
FETCHERS > FETCHER
FETCHES > FETCH
FETCHING adj attractive
FETE n gala, bazaar, etc, usu held outdoors ▷ vb honour or entertain regally
FETED > FETE
FETERITA n type of sorghum
FETERITAS > FETERITA
FETES > FETE
FETIAL n ancient Roman herald ▷ adj of or relating to the fetiales
FETIALES > FETIAL
FETIALIS n priest in ancient Rome
FETIALS > FETIAL
FETICH same as > FETISH
FETICHE variant of > FETICH
FETICHES > FETICH
FETICHISE variant of > FETICHIZE
FETICHISM same as > FETISHISM
FETICHIST > FETISHISM
FETICHIZE vb be excessively or irrationally devoted to an object, activity, etc
FETICIDAL > FETICIDE

FETICIDE n destruction of a fetus in the uterus
FETICIDES > FETICIDE
FETID adj stinking
FETIDER > FETID
FETIDEST > FETID
FETIDITY > FETID
FETIDLY > FETID
FETIDNESS > FETID
FETING > FETE
FETISH n irrational devotion (to an object, activity, etc)
FETISHES > FETISH
FETISHISE same as > FETISHIZE
FETISHISM n excessive attention or attachment to something
FETISHIST > FETISHISM
FETISHIZE vb be excessively or irrationally devoted to (an object, activity, etc)
FETLOCK n projection behind and above a horse's hoof
FETLOCKED adj having fetlocks
FETLOCKS > FETLOCK
FETOLOGY n branch of medicine concerned with the fetus in the uterus
FETOR n offensive stale or putrid odour
FETORS > FETOR
FETOSCOPE n fibreoptic instrument that can be passed through the abdomen of a pregnant woman to enable examination of the fetus and withdrawal of blood for sampling in prenatal diagnosis
FETOSCOPY > FETOSCOPE
FETS > FET
FETT variant of > FET
FETTA variant of > FETA
FETTAS > FETTA
FETTED > FET
FETTER n chain or shackle for the foot ▷ vb restrict
FETTERED > FETTER
FETTERER > FETTER
FETTERERS > FETTER
FETTERING > FETTER
FETTERS > FETTER
FETTING > FET
FETTLE same as > FETTLING
FETTLED > FETTLE
FETTLER n person employed to maintain railway tracks
FETTLERS > FETTLER
FETTLES > FETTLE
FETTLING n refractory material used to line the hearth of puddling furnaces
FETTLINGS > FETTLING
FETTS > FETT
FETTUCINE n type of pasta in the form of narrow ribbons
FETTUCINI same as > FETTUCINE
FETUS n embryo of a mammal in the later stages of development

f

FETUSES > FETUS
FETWA variant of > FATWA
FETWAS > FETWA
FEU n (in Scotland) type of rent ▷ vb grant land to a person who pays a feu
FEUAR n tenant of a feu
FEUARS > FEUAR
FEUD n long bitter hostility between two people or groups ▷ vb carry on a feud
FEUDAL adj of or like feudalism
FEUDALISE same as > FEUDALIZE
FEUDALISM n medieval system in which people held land from a lord, and in return worked and fought for him
FEUDALIST > FEUDALISM
FEUDALITY n state or quality of being feudal
FEUDALIZE vb make feudal
FEUDALLY > FEUDAL
FEUDARIES > FEUDARY
FEUDARY n holder of land through feudal right
FEUDATORY n person holding a fief ▷ adj relating to or characteristic of the relationship between lord and vassal
FEUDED > FEUD
FEUDING > FEUD
FEUDINGS > FEUD
FEUDIST n person who takes part in a feud or quarrel
FEUDISTS > FEUDIST
FEUDS > FEUD
FEUED > FEU
FEUILLETE n puff pastry
FEUING > FEU
FEUS > FEU
FEUTRE vb place in a resting position
FEUTRED > FEUTRE
FEUTRES > FEUTRE
FEUTRING > FEUTRE
FEVER n (illness causing) high body temperature ▷ vb affect with or as if with fever
FEVERED > FEVER
FEVERFEW n bushy European plant with white flower heads, formerly used medicinally
FEVERFEWS > FEVERFEW
FEVERING > FEVER
FEVERISH adj suffering from fever
FEVERLESS > FEVER
FEVEROUS same as > FEVERISH
FEVERROOT n American wild plant
FEVERS > FEVER
FEVERWEED n plant thought to be medicinal
FEVERWORT n any of several plants considered to have medicinal properties, such as horse gentian and boneset
FEW adj not many ▷ n as in the few small number of people considered as a class
FEWER > FEW
FEWEST > FEW

FEWMET variant of > FUMET
FEWMETS > FEWMET
FEWNESS > FEW
FEWNESSES > FEW
FEWS > FEW
FEWTER variant of > FEUTRE
FEWTERED > FEWTER
FEWTERING > FEUTRE
FEWTERS > FEWTER
FEWTRILS n trifles, trivia
FEY adj whimsically strange ▷ vb clean out
FEYED > FEY
FEYER > FEY
FEYEST > FEY
FEYING > FEY
FEYLY > FEY
FEYNESS > FEY
FEYNESSES > FEY
FEYS > FEY
FEZ n brimless tasselled cap, orig from Turkey
FEZES > FEZ
FEZZED adj wearing a fez
FEZZES > FEZ
FEZZY > FEZ
FIACRE n small four-wheeled horse-drawn carriage
FIACRES > FIACRE
FIANCE n man engaged to be married
FIANCEE n woman who is engaged to be married
FIANCEES > FIANCEE
FIANCES > FIANCE
FIAR n property owner
FIARS n legally fixed price of corn
FIASCHI > FIASCO
FIASCO n ridiculous or humiliating failure
FIASCOES > FIASCO
FIASCOS > FIASCO
FIAT n arbitrary order ▷ vb issue a fiat
FIATED > FIAT
FIATING > FIAT
FIATS > FIAT
FIAUNT n fiat
FIAUNTS > FIAUNT
FIB n trivial lie ▷ vb tell a lie
FIBBED > FIB
FIBBER > FIB
FIBBERIES > FIB
FIBBERS > FIB
FIBBERY > FIB
FIBBING > FIB
FIBER same as > FIBRE
FIBERED > FIBRE
FIBERFILL same as > FIBREFILL
FIBERISE same as > FIBERIZE
FIBERISED > FIBERISE
FIBERISES > FIBERISE
FIBERIZE vb break into fibres
FIBERIZED > FIBERIZE
FIBERIZES > FIBERIZE
FIBERLESS > FIBRE
FIBERLIKE > FIBER
FIBERS > FIBER
FIBRANNE n synthetic fabric
FIBRANNES > FIBRANNE

FIBRATE n drug used to lower fat levels in the body
FIBRATES > FIBRATE
FIBRE n thread that can be spun into yarn
FIBRED > FIBRE
FIBREFILL n synthetic fibre used as a filling for pillows, quilted materials, etc
FIBRELESS > FIBRE
FIBRELIKE adj like a fibre
FIBRES > FIBRE
FIBRIFORM adj having the form of a fibre or fibres
FIBRIL n small fibre
FIBRILAR > FIBRIL
FIBRILLA same as > FIBRIL
FIBRILLAE > FIBRILLA
FIBRILLAR > FIBRIL
FIBRILLIN n kind of protein
FIBRILS > FIBRIL
FIBRIN n white insoluble elastic protein
FIBRINOID > FIBRIN
FIBRINOUS adj of, containing, or resembling fibrin
FIBRINS > FIBRIN
FIBRO n mixture of cement and asbestos fibre
FIBROCYTE n type of fibroblast
FIBROID adj (of structures or tissues) containing or resembling fibres ▷ n benign tumour composed of fibrous connective tissue
FIBROIDS > FIBROID
FIBROIN n tough elastic protein
FIBROINS > FIBROIN
FIBROLINE n type of yarn
FIBROLITE n trademark name for a type of building board containing asbestos and cement
FIBROMA n type of benign tumour
FIBROMAS > FIBROMA
FIBROMATA > FIBROMA
FIBROS > FIBRO
FIBROSE vb become fibrous
FIBROSED > FIBROSE
FIBROSES > FIBROSE
FIBROSING > FIBROSE
FIBROSIS n formation of an abnormal amount of fibrous tissue
FIBROTIC > FIBROSIS
FIBROUS adj consisting of, containing, or resembling fibres
FIBROUSLY > FIBROUS
FIBS > FIB
FIBSTER n fibber
FIBSTERS > FIBSTER
FIBULA n slender outer bone of the lower leg
FIBULAE > FIBULA
FIBULAR > FIBULA
FIBULAS > FIBULA
FICAIN n cysteine proteinase isolated from the latex of figs

FICAINS > FICAIN
FICE n small aggressive dog
FICES > FICE
FICHE n film for storing publications in miniature
FICHES > FICHE
FICHU n woman's shawl or scarf
FICHUS > FICHU
FICIN n enzyme
FICINS > FICIN
FICKLE adj changeable, inconstant ▷ vb puzzle
FICKLED > FICKLE
FICKLER > FICKLE
FICKLES > FICKLE
FICKLEST > FICKLE
FICKLING > FICKLE
FICKLY > FICKLE
FICO n worthless trifle
FICOES > FICO
FICOS > FICO
FICTILE adj moulded or capable of being moulded from clay
FICTION n literary works of the imagination
FICTIONAL > FICTION
FICTIONS > FICTION
FICTIVE adj of, relating to, or able to create fiction
FICTIVELY > FICTIVE
FICTOR n sculptor
FICTORS > FICTOR
FICUS n type of plant
FICUSES > FICUS
FID n spike for separating strands of rope in splicing
FIDDIOUS vb treat someone as Coriolanus, in the eponymous play, dealt with Aufidius
FIDDLE n violin ▷ vb play the violin
FIDDLED > FIDDLE
FIDDLER n person who plays the fiddle
FIDDLERS > FIDDLER
FIDDLES > FIDDLE
FIDDLEY n area of a vessel
FIDDLEYS > FIDDLEY
FIDDLIER > FIDDLY
FIDDLIEST > FIDDLY
FIDDLING adj trivial ▷ n act of fiddling
FIDDLINGS > FIDDLING
FIDDLY adj awkward to do or use
FIDEISM n theological doctrine
FIDEISMS > FIDEISM
FIDEIST > FIDEISM
FIDEISTIC > FIDEISM
FIDEISTS > FIDEISM
FIDELISMO n belief in the principles of Fidel Castro, Cuban Communist statesman
FIDELISTA n advocate of fidelismo
FIDELITY n faithfulness
FIDES n faith or trust
FIDGE obsolete word for > FIDGET
FIDGED > FIDGE
FIDGES > FIDGE

FIDGET *vb* move about restlessly ▷ *n* person who fidgets
FIDGETED > FIDGET
FIDGETER > FIDGET
FIDGETERS > FIDGET
FIDGETIER > FIDGET
FIDGETING > FIDGET
FIDGETS > FIDGET
FIDGETY > FIDGET
FIDGING > FIDGE
FIDIBUS *n* spill for lighting a candle or pipe
FIDIBUSES > FIDIBUS
FIDO *n* generic term for a dog
FIDOS > FIDO
FIDS > FID
FIDUCIAL *adj* used as a standard of reference or measurement
FIDUCIARY *n* person bound to act for someone else's benefit, as a trustee ▷ *adj* of a trust or trustee
FIE *same as* > FEY
FIEF *n* land granted by a lord in return for war service
FIEFDOM *n* (in Feudal Europe) the property owned by a lord
FIEFDOMS > FIEFDOM
FIEFS > FIEF
FIELD *n* piece of land used for pasture or growing crops ▷ *vb* stop, catch, or return (the ball) as a fielder
FIELDBOOT *n* knee-length boot
FIELDED > FIELD
FIELDER *n* (in certain sports) player whose task is to field the ball
FIELDERS > FIELDER
FIELDFARE *n* type of large Old World thrush
FIELDING > FIELD
FIELDINGS > FIELD
FIELDMICE *pl n* nocturnal mice
FIELDS > FIELD
FIELDSMAN *n* fielder
FIELDSMEN > FIELDSMAN
FIELDVOLE *n* small rodent
FIELDWARD *adv* towards a field or fields
FIELDWORK *n* investigation made in the field as opposed to the classroom or the laboratory
FIEND *n* evil spirit
FIENDISH *adj* of or like a fiend
FIENDLIKE > FIEND
FIENDS > FIEND
FIENT *n* fiend
FIENTS > FIENT
FIER *same as* > FERE
FIERCE *adj* wild or aggressive
FIERCELY > FIERCE
FIERCER > FIERCE
FIERCEST > FIERCE
FIERE *same as* > FERE
FIERES > FIERE
FIERIER > FIERY
FIERIEST > FIERY

FIERILY > FIERY
FIERINESS > FIERY
FIERS > FIER
FIERY *adj* consisting of or like fire
FIEST > FIE
FIESTA *n* religious festival, carnival
FIESTAS > FIESTA
FIFE *n* small high-pitched flute ▷ *vb* play (music) on a fife
FIFED > FIFE
FIFER > FIFE
FIFERS > FIFE
FIFES > FIFE
FIFI *n* mountaineering hook
FIFING > FIFE
FIFIS > FIFI
FIFTEEN *n* five and ten
FIFTEENER *n* fifteen-syllable line of poetry
FIFTEENS > FIFTEEN
FIFTEENTH *adj* coming after the fourteenth in order, position, time, etc ▷ *n* one of 15 equal or nearly equal parts of something
FIFTH *n* number five in a series ▷ *adj* of or being number five in a series
FIFTHLY *same as* > FIFTH
FIFTHS > FIFTH
FIFTIES > FIFTY
FIFTIETH *adj* being the number of *fifty* in order ▷ *n* one of 50 equal or parts
FIFTIETHS > FIFTIETH
FIFTY *n* five times ten
FIFTYFOLD *adj* multiplied fifty times
FIFTYISH > FIFTY
FIG *n* soft pear-shaped fruit ▷ *vb* dress (up) or rig (out)
FIGEATER *n* large beetle
FIGEATERS > FIGEATER
FIGGED > FIG
FIGGERIES > FIGGERY
FIGGERY *n* adornment, ornament
FIGGIER > FIGGY
FIGGIEST > FIGGY
FIGGING > FIG
FIGGY *adj* tasting like figs
FIGHT *vb* struggle (against) in battle or physical combat ▷ *n* aggressive conflict between two (groups of) people
FIGHTABLE > FIGHT
FIGHTBACK *n* act or campaign of resistance
FIGHTER *n* boxer
FIGHTERS > FIGHTER
FIGHTING > FIGHT
FIGHTINGS > FIGHT
FIGHTS > FIGHT
FIGJAM *n* very conceited person
FIGJAMS > FIGJAM
FIGLIKE *adj* like a fig
FIGMENT *n* fantastic notion, invention, or fabrication
FIGMENTS > FIGMENT
FIGO *variant of* > FICO
FIGOS > FIGO

FIGS > FIG
FIGTREE *n* tree that produces figs
FIGTREES > FIGTREE
FIGULINE *adj* of or resembling clay ▷ *n* article made of clay
FIGULINES > FIGULINE
FIGURABLE > FIGURE
FIGURAL *adj* composed of or relating to human or animal figures
FIGURALLY > FIGURAL
FIGURANT *n* ballet dancer who does group work but no solo roles
FIGURANTE *n* female figurant
FIGURANTS > FIGURANT
FIGURATE *adj* exhibiting or produced by figuration
FIGURE *n* numerical symbol ▷ *vb* calculate (sums or amounts)
FIGURED *adj* decorated with a design
FIGUREDLY > FIGURED
FIGURER > FIGURE
FIGURERS > FIGURE
FIGURES > FIGURE
FIGURINE *n* statuette
FIGURINES > FIGURINE
FIGURING > FIGURE
FIGURIST *n* user of numbers
FIGURISTS > FIGURIST
FIGWORT *n* N temperate plant
FIGWORTS > FIGWORT
FIKE *vb* fidget
FIKED > FIKE
FIKERIES > FIKERY
FIKERY *n* fuss
FIKES > FIKE
FIKIER > FIKY
FIKIEST > FIKY
FIKING > FIKE
FIKISH *adj* fussy
FIKY *adj* fussy
FIL *same as* > FILS
FILA > FILUM
FILABEG *variant of* > FILIBEG
FILABEGS > FILABEG
FILACEOUS *adj* made of threads
FILACER *n* formerly, English legal officer
FILACERS > FILACER
FILAGGRIN *n* protein found in skin cells
FILAGREE *same as* > FILIGREE
FILAGREED > FILAGREE
FILAGREES > FILAGREE
FILAMENT *n* fine wire in a light bulb that gives out light
FILAMENTS > FILAMENT
FILANDER *n* species of kangaroo
FILANDERS > FILANDER
FILAR *adj* of thread
FILAREE *n* type of storksbill, a weed
FILAREES > FILAREE
FILARIA *n* type of parasitic nematode worm

FILARIAE > FILARIA
FILARIAL > FILARIA
FILARIAN > FILARIA
FILARIID *adj* of or relating to a family of threadlike roundworms
FILARIIDS > FILARIID
FILASSE *n* vegetable fibre such as jute
FILASSES > FILASSE
FILATORY *n* machine for making threads
FILATURE *n* act or process of spinning silk, etc, into threads
FILATURES > FILATURE
FILAZER *variant of* > FILACER
FILAZERS > FILAZER
FILBERD *variant of* > FILBERT
FILBERDS > FILBERD
FILBERT *n* hazelnut
FILBERTS > FILBERT
FILCH *vb* steal (small amounts)
FILCHED > FILCH
FILCHER > FILCH
FILCHERS > FILCH
FILCHES > FILCH
FILCHING > FILCH
FILCHINGS > FILCH
FILE *n* box or folder used to keep documents in order ▷ *vb* place (a document) in a file
FILEABLE > FILE
FILECARD *n* type of brush with sharp steel bristles, used for cleaning the teeth of a file
FILECARDS > FILECARD
FILED > FILE
FILEFISH *n* tropical fish with a narrow body
FILEMOT *n* type of brown colour
FILEMOTS > FILEMOT
FILENAME *n* codified name of a file a computer system
FILENAMES > FILENAME
FILER > FILE
FILERS > FILE
FILES > FILE
FILET *variant of* > FILLET
FILETED > FILET
FILETING > FILET
FILETS > FILET
FILFOT *variant of* > FYLFOT
FILFOTS > FILFOT
FILIAL *adj* of or befitting a son or daughter
FILIALLY > FILIAL
FILIATE *vb* fix judicially the paternity of (a child)
FILIATED > FILIATE
FILIATES > FILIATE
FILIATING > FILIATE
FILIATION *n* line of descent
FILIBEG *n* kilt worn by Scottish Highlanders
FILIBEGS > FILIBEG
FILICIDAL > FILICIDE
FILICIDE *n* act of killing one's own son or daughter
FILICIDES > FILICIDE

f

FILIFORM adj having the form of a thread

FILIGRAIN n filigree

FILIGRANE variant of > FILIGRAIN

FILIGREE n delicate ornamental work of gold or silver wire ▷ adj made of filigree ▷ vb decorate with or as if with filigree

FILIGREED > FILIGREE

FILIGREES > FILIGREE

FILII > FILIUS

FILING > FILE

FILINGS pl n shavings removed by a file

FILIOQUE n theological term found in the Nicene Creed

FILIOQUES > FILIOQUE

FILISTER same as > FILLISTER

FILISTERS > FILISTER

FILIUS n son

FILK n parodic type of folk music with science fiction lyrics

FILKS > FILK

FILL vb make or become full

FILLABLE > FILL

FILLAGREE same as > FILIGREE

FILLE n girl

FILLED > FILL

FILLER n substance that fills a gap or increases bulk

FILLERS > FILLER

FILLES > FILLE

FILLESTER same as > FILLISTER

FILLET n boneless piece of meat or fish ▷ vb remove the bones from

FILLETED > FILLET

FILLETER n person who fillets

FILLETERS > FILLETER

FILLETING > FILLET

FILLETS > FILLET

FILLIBEG same as > FILIBEG

FILLIBEGS > FILLIBEG

FILLIES > FILLY

FILLING n substance that fills a gap or cavity ▷ adj (of food) substantial and satisfying

FILLINGS > FILLING

FILLIP n something that adds stimulation or enjoyment ▷ vb stimulate or excite

FILLIPED > FILLIP

FILLIPEEN n philopoena

FILLIPING > FILLIP

FILLIPS > FILLIP

FILLISTER n adjustable plane for cutting rabbets, grooves, etc

FILLO variant of > FILO

FILLOS > FILLO

FILLS > FILL

FILLY n young female horse

FILM n projected images creating the illusion of movement ▷ vb photograph with a video camera ▷ adj

connected with films or the cinema

FILMABLE > FILM

FILMCARD n cinema loyalty card

FILMCARDS > FILMCARD

FILMDOM n cinema industry

FILMDOMS > FILMDOM

FILMED > FILM

FILMER n film-maker

FILMERS > FILMER

FILMFEST n film festival

FILMFESTS > FILMFEST

FILMGOER n person who goes regularly to the cinema

FILMGOERS > FILMGOER

FILMGOING n activity of going to see films

FILMI adj of or relating to Indian films

FILMIC adj of or suggestive of films or the cinema

FILMIER > FILMY

FILMIEST > FILMY

FILMILY > FILMY

FILMINESS > FILMY

FILMING n act of photographing with a video camera

FILMINGS > FILMING

FILMIS > FILMI

FILMISH > FILM

FILMLAND n cinema industry

FILMLANDS > FILMLAND

FILMLESS > FILM

FILMLIKE > FILM

FILMMAKER n person who makes films

FILMS > FILM

FILMSET vb set (type matter) by filmsetting

FILMSETS > FILMSET

FILMSTRIP n strip of film composed of different images projected separately as slides

FILMY adj very thin, delicate

FILO n type of flaky Greek pastry in very thin sheets

FILOPLUME n any of the hairlike feathers that lack vanes and occur between the contour feathers

FILOPODIA n plural form of singular filopodium: ectoplasmic pseudopodium

FILOS > FILO

FILOSE adj resembling a thread or threadlike process

FILOSELLE n soft silk thread, used esp for embroidery

FILOVIRUS n any member of a family of viruses that includes the agents responsible for Ebola virus disease and Marburg disease

FILS n monetary unit of Bahrain, Iraq, Jordan, and Kuwait

FILTER n device permitting fluid to pass but retaining solids ▷ vb remove impurities from (a substance) with a filter

FILTERED > FILTER

FILTERER > FILTER

FILTERERS > FILTER

FILTERING > FILTER

FILTERS > FILTER

FILTH n disgusting dirt

FILTHIER > FILTHY

FILTHIEST > FILTHY

FILTHILY > FILTHY

FILTHS > FILTH

FILTHY adj characterized by or full of filth ▷ adv extremely

FILTRABLE adj capable of being filtered

FILTRATE n filtered gas or liquid ▷ vb remove impurities with a filter

FILTRATED > FILTRATE

FILTRATES > FILTRATE

FILTRE adj as in cafe filtre a strong black filtered coffee

FILUM n any threadlike structure or part

FIMBLE n male plant of the hemp

FIMBLES > FIMBLE

FIMBRIA n fringe or fringelike margin or border

FIMBRIAE > FIMBRIA

FIMBRIAL > FIMBRIA

FIMBRIATE adj having a fringed margin, as some petals, antennae, etc

FIN n any of the appendages of some aquatic animals ▷ vb provide with fins

FINABLE adj liable to a fine

FINAGLE vb get or achieve by craftiness or trickery

FINAGLED > FINAGLE

FINAGLER > FINAGLE

FINAGLERS > FINAGLE

FINAGLES > FINAGLE

FINAGLING n use of trickery to achieve aims

FINAL adj at the end ▷ n deciding contest

FINALE n concluding part of a performance

FINALES > FINALE

FINALIS n musical finishing note

FINALISE same as > FINALIZE

FINALISED > FINALISE

FINALISER > FINALISE

FINALISES > FINALISE

FINALISM n doctrine that final causes determine the course of all events

FINALISMS > FINALISM

FINALIST n competitor in a final

FINALISTS > FINALIST

FINALITY n condition or quality of being final or settled

FINALIZE vb put into final form

FINALIZED > FINALIZE

FINALIZER > FINALIZE

FINALIZES > FINALIZE

FINALLY adv after a long delay

FINALS pl n deciding part of a competition

FINANCE vb provide or obtain funds for ▷ n system of money, credit, and investment

FINANCED > FINANCE

FINANCES > FINANCE

FINANCIAL adj of or relating to finance, finances, or people who manage money ▷ n financial institution or report

FINANCIER n person involved in large-scale financial business

FINANCING > FINANCE

FINBACK another name for > RORQUAL

FINBACKS > FINBACK

FINCA n Spanish villa

FINCAS > FINCA

FINCH n small songbird with a short strong beak

FINCHED adj with streaks or spots on the back

FINCHES > FINCH

FINCHLIKE adj like a finch

FIND vb discover by chance ▷ n person or thing found, esp when valuable

FINDABLE > FIND

FINDER n small telescope fitted to a larger one

FINDERS > FINDER

FINDING > FIND

FINDINGS > FIND

FINDRAM variant of > FINNAN

FINDRAMS > FINDRAM

FINDS > FIND

FINE adj very good ▷ n payment imposed as a penalty ▷ vb impose a fine on

FINEABLE same as > FINABLE

FINED > FINE

FINEER variant of > VENEER

FINEERED > FINEER

FINEERING > FINEER

FINEERS > FINEER

FINEISH > FINE

FINELESS > FINE

FINELY adv into small pieces

FINENESS n state or quality of being fine

FINER > FINE

FINERIES > FINERY

FINERS > FINE

FINERY n showy clothing

FINES > FINE

FINESPUN adj spun or drawn out to a fine thread

FINESSE n delicate skill ▷ vb bring about with finesse

FINESSED > FINESSE

FINESSER > FINESSE

FINESSERS > FINESSE

FINESSES > FINESSE

FINESSING > FINESSE

FINEST n (in the US) police of a particular city

FINESTS > FINEST

FINFISH n fish with fins, as opposed to shellfish

FINFISHES > FINFISH

FINFOOT n type of aquatic bird

FINFOOTS > FINFOOT

FINGAN variant of > FINJAN

FINGANS > FINGAN

FINGER n one of the four long jointed parts of the

hand ▷ *vb* touch or handle with the fingers

FINGERED *adj* marked or dirtied by handling

FINGERER > FINGER

FINGERERS > FINGER

FINGERING *n* technique of using the fingers in playing a musical instrument

FINGERS > FINGER

FINGERTIP *n* end joint or tip of a finger

FINI *n* end; finish

FINIAL *n* ornament at the apex of a gable or spire

FINIALED *adj* having a finial or finials

FINIALS > FINIAL

FINICAL another word for > FINICKY

FINICALLY > FINICAL

FINICKETY *adj* fussy or tricky

FINICKIER > FINICKY

FINICKIN variant of > FINICKY

FINICKING same as > FINICKY

FINICKY *adj* excessively particular, fussy

FINIKIN variant of > FINICKY

FINIKING variant of > FINICKY

FINING *n* process of removing bubbles from molten glass

FININGS > FINING

FINIS *n* end; finish

FINISES > FINIS

FINISH *vb* bring to an end, stop ▷ *n* end, last part

FINISHED *adj* perfected

FINISHER *n* craftsperson who carries out the final tasks in a manufacturing process

FINISHERS > FINISHER

FINISHES > FINISH

FINISHING *n* act or skill of goal scoring

FINITE *adj* having limits in space, time, or size ▷ *n* verb limited by person, number, tense or mood

FINITELY > FINITE

FINITES > FINITE

FINITISM *n* mathematical philosophy which rejects infinite quantities

FINITISMS > FINITISM

FINITIST *n* one who believes in or advocates finitism

FINITISTS > FINITIST

FINITO *adj* finished

FINITUDE > FINITE

FINITUDES > FINITE

FINJAN *n* small, handleless coffee cup

FINJANS > FINJAN

FINK *n* strikebreaker ▷ *vb* inform (on someone), as to the police

FINKED > FINK

FINKING > FINK

FINKS > FINK

FINLESS > FIN

FINLIKE > FIN

FINLIT *n* understanding of the concepts associated with finance

FINLITS > FINLIT

FINMARK *n* former monetary unit of Finland

FINMARKS > FINMARK

FINNAC variant of > FINNOCK

FINNACK variant of > FINNOCK

FINNACKS > FINNACK

FINNACS > FINNAC

FINNAN *n* smoked haddock

FINNANS > FINNAN

FINNED > FIN

FINNER another name for > RORQUAL

FINNERS > FINNER

FINNESKO *n* reindeer-skin boot

FINNICKY variant of > FINICKY

FINNIER > FINNY

FINNIEST > FINNY

FINNING > FIN

FINNMARK *n* former Finnish monetary unit

FINNMARKS > FINNMARK

FINNOCHIO variant of > FINOCCHIO

FINNOCK *n* young sea trout on its first return to fresh water

FINNOCKS > FINNOCK

FINNSKO variant of > FINNESKO

FINNY *adj* relating to or containing many fishes

FINO *n* very dry sherry

FINOCCHIO *n* variety of fennel with celery-like stalks which are eaten as a vegetable

FINOCHIO same as > FINOCCHIO

FINOCHIOS > FINOCHIO

FINOS > FINO

FINS > FIN

FINSKO variant of > FINNESKO

FINTECH *n* financial services technology

FINTECHS > FINTECH

FIORATURA same as > FIORITURA

FIORD same as > FJORD

FIORDS > FIORD

FIORIN *n* type of temperate perennial grass

FIORINS > FIORIN

FIORITURA *n* embellishment, esp ornamentation added by the performer

FIORITURE > FIORITURA

FIPPENCE *n* fivepence

FIPPENCES > FIPPENCE

FIPPLE *n* wooden plug forming a flue in the end of a pipe

FIPPLES > FIPPLE

FIQH *n* Islamic jurisprudence

FIQHS > FIQH

FIQUE *n* hemp

FIQUES > FIQUE

FIR *n* pyramid-shaped tree

FIRE *n* state of combustion producing heat, flames, and smoke ▷ *vb* operate (a weapon) so that a bullet or missile is released

FIREABLE > FIRE

FIREARM *n* rifle, pistol, or shotgun

FIREARMED *adj* carrying firearm

FIREARMS > FIREARM

FIREBACK *n* ornamental iron slab against the back wall of a hearth

FIREBACKS > FIREBACK

FIREBALL *n* ball of fire at the centre of an explosion

FIREBALLS > FIREBALL

FIREBASE *n* artillery base from which heavy fire is directed at the enemy

FIREBASES > FIREBASE

FIREBIRD *n* any of various songbirds having a bright red plumage, esp the Baltimore oriole

FIREBIRDS > FIREBIRD

FIREBOARD *n* mantelpiece

FIREBOAT *n* motor vessel with fire-fighting apparatus

FIREBOATS > FIREBOAT

FIREBOMB *n* bomb that is designed to cause fires ▷ *vb* detonate such a bomb

FIREBOMBS > FIREBOMB

FIREBOX *n* furnace chamber of a boiler in a steam locomotive

FIREBOXES > FIREBOX

FIREBRAND *n* person who causes unrest

FIREBRAT *n* type of small primitive wingless insect

FIREBRATS > FIREBRAT

FIREBREAK *n* strip of cleared land to stop the advance of a fire

FIREBRICK *n* heat-resistant brick used for lining furnaces, fireplaces, etc

FIREBUG *n* person who deliberately sets fire to property

FIREBUGS > FIREBUG

FIREBUSH *n* as in *Chilean firebush* South American shrub with scarlet flowers

FIRECLAY *n* heat-resistant clay used in the making of firebricks, furnace linings, etc

FIRECLAYS > FIRECLAY

FIRECREST *n* small European warbler with a crown striped with yellow, black, and white

FIRED > FIRE

FIREDAMP *n* explosive gas, composed mainly of methane, formed in mines

FIREDAMPS > FIREDAMP

FIREDOG *n* either of two metal stands supporting logs in a fire

FIREDOGS > FIREDOG

FIREDRAKE *n* fire-breathing dragon

FIREFANG *vb* become overheated through decomposition

FIREFANGS > FIREFANG

FIREFIGHT *n* brief small-scale engagement between opposing military ground forces using short-range light weapons

FIREFLIES > FIREFLY

FIREFLOAT *n* boat used for firefighting

FIREFLOOD *n* method of extracting oil from a well by burning some of the oil to increase the rate of flow

FIREFLY *n* beetle that glows in the dark

FIREGUARD same as > FIREBREAK

FIREHALL *n* US and Canadian word for fire station

FIREHALLS > FIREHALL

FIREHOSE *n* hose used to extinguish fires

FIREHOSES > FIREHOSE

FIREHOUSE *n* fire station

FIRELESS > FIRE

FIRELIGHT *n* light from a fire

FIRELIT *adj* lit by firelight

FIRELOCK *n* obsolete type of gunlock with a priming mechanism ignited by sparks

FIRELOCKS > FIRELOCK

FIREMAN *n* man who puts out fires and rescues people

FIREMANIC > FIREMAN

FIREMARK *n* plaque indicating that a building is insured

FIREMARKS > FIREMARK

FIREMEN > FIREMAN

FIREPAN *n* metal container for a fire in a room

FIREPANS > FIREPAN

FIREPINK *n* wildflower belonging to the pink family

FIREPINKS > FIREPINK

FIREPIT *n* hole dug in the ground for a fire

FIREPITS > FIREPIT

FIREPLACE *n* recess in a room for a fire

FIREPLUG *n* US and New Zealand name for a fire hydrant

FIREPLUGS > FIREPLUG

FIREPOT *n* Chinese fondue-like cooking pot

FIREPOTS > FIREPOT

FIREPOWER *n* amount of fire that may be delivered by a unit or weapon

FIREPROOF *adj* capable of resisting damage by fire ▷ *vb* make resistant to fire

FIRER > FIRE

FIREREEL *n* fire engine

FIREREELS > FIREREEL

FIREROOM *n* stokehold

FIREROOMS > FIREROOM

FIRERS > FIRE

FIRES > FIRE

FIRESCAPE *vb* arrange a garden so that fire cannot spread easily

f

FIRESHIP n vessel set alight and directed among enemy warships

FIRESHIPS > FIRESHIP

FIRESIDE n hearth

FIRESIDES > FIRESIDE

FIRESTONE n sandstone that withstands intense heat, esp one used for lining kilns, furnaces, etc

FIRESTORM n uncontrollable blaze sustained by violent winds that are drawn into the column of rising hot air over the burning area: often the result of heavy bombing

FIRETHORN n type of evergreen spiny shrub of SE Europe and Asia with bright red or orange fruits, cultivated for ornament

FIRETRAP n building that would burn easily or one without fire escapes

FIRETRAPS > FIRETRAP

FIRETRUCK n fire engine

FIREWALL n appliance that prevents unauthorized access to a computer network from the internet ▷ vb protect (a computer system) or block (unwanted access) with a firewall

FIREWALLS > FIREWALL

FIREWATER n any alcoholic spirit

FIREWEED n first vegetation growing in burnt-over areas

FIREWEEDS > FIREWEED

FIREWOMAN n female firefighter

FIREWOMEN > FIREWOMAN

FIREWOOD n wood for burning

FIREWOODS > FIREWOOD

FIREWORK n device ignited to produce colourful sparks and explosions

FIREWORKS pl n show in which fireworks are let off

FIREWORM n cranberry worm

FIREWORMS > FIREWORM

FIRIE n in Australian English, informal word for a firefighter

FIRIES > FIRIE

FIRING n discharge of a firearm

FIRINGS > FIRING

FIRK vb beat

FIRKED > FIRK

FIRKIN n small wooden barrel or similar container

FIRKING > FIRK

FIRKINS > FIRKIN

FIRKS > FIRK

FIRLOT n unit of measurement for grain

FIRLOTS > FIRLOT

FIRM adj not soft or yielding ▷ adv in an unyielding manner ▷ vb make or become firm ▷ n business company

FIRMAMENT n sky or the heavens

FIRMAN n edict of an Oriental sovereign

FIRMANS > FIRMAN

FIRMED > FIRM

FIRMER > FIRM

FIRMERS > FIRM

FIRMEST > FIRM

FIRMING > FIRM

FIRMLESS adj unstable

FIRMLY > FIRM

FIRMNESS > FIRM

FIRMS > FIRM

FIRMWARE n fixed form of software programmed into a read-only memory

FIRMWARES > FIRMWARE

FIRN another name for > NEVE

FIRNS > FIRN

FIRRIER > FIRRY

FIRRIEST > FIRRY

FIRRING n wooden battens used in building construction

FIRRINGS > FIRRING

FIRRY adj of, relating to, or made from fir trees

FIRS > FIR

FIRST adj earliest in time or order ▷ n person or thing coming before all others ▷ adv before anything else

FIRSTBORN adj eldest of the children in a family ▷ n eldest child in a family

FIRSTHAND adj from the original source

FIRSTLING n first, esp the first offspring

FIRSTLY adv coming before other points, questions, etc

FIRSTNESS > FIRST

FIRSTS pl n saleable goods of the highest quality

FIRTH n narrow inlet of the sea, esp in Scotland

FIRTHS > FIRTH

FIRWOOD n wood of the fir tree

FIRWOODS > FIRWOOD

FISC n state or royal treasury

FISCAL adj of government finances, esp taxes ▷ n (in some countries) a public prosecutor

FISCALIST > FISCAL

FISCALLY > FISCAL

FISCALS > FISCAL

FISCS > FISC

FISGIG variant of > FISHGIG

FISGIGS > FISGIG

FISH n cold-blooded vertebrate with gills, that lives in water ▷ vb try to catch fish

FISHABLE > FISH

FISHBALL n fried ball of flaked fish and mashed potato

FISHBALLS > FISHBALL

FISHBOAT n boat used for fishing

FISHBOATS > FISHBOAT

FISHBOLT n bolt used for fastening a fishplate to a rail

FISHBOLTS > FISHBOLT

FISHBONE n bone of a fish

FISHBONES > FISHBONE

FISHBOWL n goldfish bowl

FISHBOWLS > FISHBOWL

FISHCAKE n mixture of flaked fish and mashed potatoes formed into a flat circular shape

FISHCAKES > FISHCAKE

FISHED > FISH

FISHER n fisherman

FISHERIES > FISHERY

FISHERMAN n person who catches fish for a living or for pleasure

FISHERMEN > FISHERMAN

FISHERS > FISHER

FISHERY n area of the sea used for fishing

FISHES > FISH

FISHEYE n type of lens

FISHEYES > FISHEYE

FISHFUL adj teeming with fish

FISHGIG n pole with barbed prongs for impaling fish

FISHGIGS > FISHGIG

FISHHOOK n sharp hook used in angling, esp one with a barb

FISHHOOKS > FISHHOOK

FISHIER > FISHY

FISHIEST > FISHY

FISHIFIED > FISHIFY

FISHIFIES > FISHIFY

FISHIFY vb change into fish

FISHILY > FISHY

FISHINESS > FISHY

FISHING n job or pastime of catching fish

FISHINGS > FISHING

FISHKILL n mass killing of fish by pollution

FISHKILLS > FISHKILL

FISHLESS > FISH

FISHLIKE > FISH

FISHLINE n line used on a fishing-rod

FISHLINES > FISHLINE

FISHMEAL n ground dried fish used as feed for farm animals or as a fertilizer

FISHMEALS > FISHMEAL

FISHNET n open mesh fabric resembling netting

FISHNETS > FISHNET

FISHPLATE n metal plate holding rails together

FISHPOLE n boom arm for a microphone

FISHPOLES > FISHPOLE

FISHPOND > FISH

FISHPONDS > FISH

FISHSKIN n skin of a fish

FISHSKINS > FISHSKIN

FISHTAIL n nozzle placed over a Bunsen burner to produce a fanlike flame ▷ vb slow an aeroplane by swerving the tail

FISHTAILS > FISHTAIL

FISHWAY n fish ladder

FISHWAYS > FISHWAY

FISHWIFE n derogatory term for a coarse scolding woman

FISHWIVES > FISHWIFE

FISHWORM n worm used as fishing bait

FISHWORMS > FISHWORM

FISHY adj of or like fish

FISHYBACK n goods supply chain involving container transfer from lorry to ship

FISK vb frisk

FISKED > FISK

FISKING > FISK

FISKS > FISK

FISNOMIE n physiognomy

FISNOMIES > FISNOMIE

FISSATE > FISSILE

FISSILE adj capable of undergoing nuclear fission

FISSILITY > FISSILE

FISSION n splitting

FISSIONAL > FISSION

FISSIONED adj split or broken into parts

FISSIONS > FISSION

FISSIPED adj having toes separated from one another ▷ n fissiped animal

FISSIPEDE > FISSIPED

FISSIPEDS > FISSIPED

FISSIVE > FISSILE

FISSLE vb rustle

FISSLED > FISSLE

FISSLES > FISSLE

FISSLING > FISSLE

FISSURAL > FISSURE

FISSURE n long narrow cleft or crack ▷ vb crack or split apart

FISSURED > FISSURE

FISSURES > FISSURE

FISSURING > FISSURE

FIST n clenched hand ▷ vb hit with the fist

FISTED > FIST

FISTFIGHT n fight using bare fists

FISTFUL n quantity that can be held in a fist or hand

FISTFULS > FISTFUL

FISTIANA n world of boxing

FISTIANAS > FISTIANA

FISTIC adj of or relating to fisticuffs or boxing

FISTICAL > FISTIC

FISTICUFF n cuff or blow ▷ vb fight or strike with the fists

FISTIER > FIST

FISTIEST > FIST

FISTING n act of fisting

FISTINGS > FISTING

FISTMELE n measurement of the height of the string of a braced bow

FISTMELES > FISTMELE

FISTNOTE n note in printed text preceded by the fist symbol

FISTNOTES > FISTNOTE

FISTS > FIST

FISTULA n long narrow ulcer

FISTULAE > FISTULA

FISTULAR same as > FISTULOUS

FISTULAS > FISTULA

FISTULATE same as > FISTULOUS

FISTULOSE variant of > FISTULOUS

FISTULOUS adj containing, relating to, or resembling a fistula

FISTY > FIST

FIT vb be appropriate or suitable for ▷ adj appropriate ▷ n way in which something fits

FITCH n fur of the polecat or ferret

FITCHE adj pointed

FITCHEE variant of > FITCHE

FITCHES > FITCH

FITCHET same as > FITCH

FITCHETS > FITCHET

FITCHEW archaic name for > POLECAT

FITCHEWS > FITCHEW

FITCHY variant of > FITCHE

FITFUL adj occurring in irregular spells

FITFULLY > FITFUL

FITLIER > FITLY

FITLIEST > FITLY

FITLY adv in a proper manner or place or at a proper time

FITMENT n accessory attached to a machine

FITMENTS > FITMENT

FITNA n state of trouble or chaos

FITNAS > FITNA

FITNESS n state of being fit

FITNESSES > FITNESS

FITS > FIT

FITT n song

FITTABLE > FIT

FITTE variant of > FITT

FITTED > FIT

FITTER > FIT

FITTERS > FIT

FITTES > FITTE

FITTEST > FIT

FITTING > FIT

FITTINGLY > FIT

FITTINGS > FIT

FITTS > FITT

FIVE n one more than four

FIVEFOLD adj having five times as many or as much ▷ adv by five times as many or as much

FIVEPENCE n five-penny coin

FIVEPENNY adj (of a nail) one and three-quarters of an inch in length

FIVEPIN > FIVEPINS

FIVEPINS n bowling game played esp in Canada

FIVER n five-pound note

FIVERS > FIVER

FIVES n ball game resembling squash

FIX vb make or become firm, stable, or secure ▷ n difficult situation

FIXABLE > FIX

FIXATE vb become or cause to become fixed

FIXATED > FIXATE

FIXATES > FIXATE

FIXATIF variant of > FIXATIVE

FIXATIFS > FIXATIF

FIXATING > FIXATE

FIXATION n obsessive interest in something

FIXATIONS > FIXATION

FIXATIVE n liquid used to preserve or hold things in place ▷ adj serving or tending to fix

FIXATIVES > FIXATIVE

FIXATURE n something that holds an object in place

FIXATURES > FIXATURE

FIXED adj attached or placed so as to be immovable

FIXEDLY > FIXED

FIXEDNESS > FIXED

FIXER n solution used to make a photographic image permanent

FIXERS > FIXER

FIXES > FIX

FIXING n means of attaching one thing to another

FIXINGS pl n apparatus or equipment

FIXIT n solution to a complex problem ▷ adj that fixes things

FIXITIES > FIXITY

FIXITS > FIXIT

FIXITY n state of being fixed

FIXIVE > FIX

FIXT adj fixed

FIXTURE n permanently fitted piece of household equipment

FIXTURES > FIXTURE

FIXURE n firmness

FIXURES > FIXURE

FIZ variant of > FIZZ

FIZGIG vb inform on someone to the police

FIZGIGGED > FIZGIG

FIZGIGS > FIZGIG

FIZZ vb make a hissing or bubbling noise ▷ n hissing or bubbling noise

FIZZED > FIZZ

FIZZEN variant of > FOISON

FIZZENS > FIZZEN

FIZZER n anything that fizzes

FIZZERS > FIZZER

FIZZES > FIZZ

FIZZGIG variant of > FISHGIG

FIZZGIGS > FIZZGIG

FIZZIER > FIZZ

FIZZIEST > FIZZ

FIZZILY adv in a fizzy manner

FIZZINESS > FIZZ

FIZZING > FIZZ

FIZZINGS > FIZZ

FIZZLE vb make a weak hissing or bubbling sound ▷ n hissing or bubbling sound

FIZZLED > FIZZLE

FIZZLES > FIZZLE

FIZZLING > FIZZLE

FIZZY > FIZZ

FJELD n high rocky plateau

FJELDS > FJELD

FJORD n long narrow inlet of the sea between cliffs

FJORDIC > FJORD

FJORDS > FJORD

FLAB n unsightly body fat

FLABBIER > FLABBY

FLABBIEST > FLABBY

FLABBILY > FLABBY

FLABBY adj having flabby flesh

FLABELLA > FLABELLUM

FLABELLUM n fan-shaped organ or part, such as the tip of the proboscis of a honeybee

FLABS > FLAB

FLACCID adj soft and limp

FLACCIDER > FLACCID

FLACCIDLY > FLACCID

FLACK vb flutter

FLACKED > FLACK

FLACKER vb flutter like a bird

FLACKERED > FLACKER

FLACKERS > FLACKER

FLACKERY > FLACK

FLACKET n flagon ▷ vb flap or flutter about

FLACKETED > FLACKET

FLACKETS > FLACKET

FLACKING > FLACK

FLACKS > FLACK

FLACON n small stoppered bottle or flask

FLACONS > FLACON

FLAFF vb flap

FLAFFED > FLAFF

FLAFFER vb flutter

FLAFFERED > FLAFFER

FLAFFERS > FLAFFER

FLAFFING > FLAFF

FLAFFS > FLAFF

FLAG n piece of cloth attached to a pole as an emblem or signal ▷ vb mark with a flag or sticker

FLAGELLA > FLAGELLUM

FLAGELLAR > FLAGELLUM

FLAGELLIN n structural protein of bacterial flagella

FLAGELLUM n whiplike outgrowth from a cell that acts as an organ of movement

FLAGEOLET n small instrument like a recorder

FLAGGED > FLAG

FLAGGER > FLAG

FLAGGERS > FLAG

FLAGGIER > FLAGGY

FLAGGIEST > FLAGGY

FLAGGING > FLAG

FLAGGINGS > FLAG

FLAGGY adj drooping

FLAGITATE vb importune

FLAGLESS > FLAG

FLAGMAN n person who has charge of a flag

FLAGMEN > FLAGMAN

FLAGON n wide bottle

FLAGONS > FLAGON

FLAGPOLE n pole for a flag

FLAGPOLES > FLAGPOLE

FLAGRANCE > FLAGRANT

FLAGRANCY > FLAGRANT

FLAGRANT adj openly outrageous

FLAGS > FLAG

FLAGSHIP n admiral's ship

FLAGSHIPS > FLAGSHIP

FLAGSTAFF same as > FLAGPOLE

FLAGSTICK n in golf, pole used to indicate position of hole

FLAGSTONE n flat slab of hard stone for paving

FLAIL vb wave about wildly ▷ n tool formerly used for threshing grain by hand

FLAILED > FLAIL

FLAILING > FLAIL

FLAILS > FLAIL

FLAIR n natural ability

FLAIRS > FLAIR

FLAK n anti-aircraft fire

FLAKE n small thin piece, esp chipped off something ▷ vb peel off in flakes

FLAKED > FLAKE

FLAKER > FLAKE

FLAKERS > FLAKE

FLAKES > FLAKE

FLAKEY same as > FLAKY

FLAKIER > FLAKY

FLAKIES n dandruff

FLAKIEST > FLAKY

FLAKILY > FLAKY

FLAKINESS > FLAKY

FLAKING > FLAKE

FLAKS > FLAK

FLAKY adj like or made of flakes

FLAM n falsehood, deception, or sham ▷ vb cheat or deceive

FLAMBE vb cook or serve (food) in flaming brandy ▷ adj (of food) served in flaming brandy

FLAMBEAU n burning torch, as used in night processions

FLAMBEAUS > FLAMBEAU

FLAMBEAUX > FLAMBEAU

FLAMBEE same as > FLAMBE

FLAMBEED > FLAMBEE

FLAMBEES > FLAMBEE

FLAMBEING > FLAMBE

FLAMBES > FLAMBE

FLAME n luminous burning gas coming from burning material ▷ vb burn brightly

FLAMED > FLAME

FLAMELESS > FLAME

FLAMELET > FLAME

FLAMELETS > FLAME

FLAMELIKE > FLAME

FLAMEN n (in ancient Rome) type of priest

FLAMENCO n rhythmical Spanish dance accompanied by a guitar and vocalist

FLAMENCOS > FLAMENCO

FLAMENS > FLAMEN

FLAMEOUT n failure of an aircraft jet engine in flight due to extinction of the flame ▷ vb (of a jet engine) to fail in flight or to cause (a jet engine) to fail in flight

FLAMEOUTS > FLAMEOUT

FLAMER > FLAME

FLAMERS > FLAME

FLAMES > FLAME

FLAMFEW n fantastic trifle
FLAMFEWS > FLAMFEW
FLAMIER > FLAMY
FLAMIEST > FLAMY
FLAMINES > FLAMEN
FLAMING adj burning with flames ▷ adv extremely
FLAMINGLY > FLAMING
FLAMINGO n large pink wading bird with a long neck and legs
FLAMINGOS > FLAMINGO
FLAMM variant of > FLAM
FLAMMABLE adj easily set on fire
FLAMMED > FLAM
FLAMMING > FLAM
FLAMMS > FLAM
FLAMMULE n small flame
FLAMMULES > FLAMMULE
FLAMS > FLAM
FLAMY > FLAME
FLAN n open sweet or savoury tart
FLANCARD n armour covering a horse's flank
FLANCARDS > FLANCARD
FLANCH variant of > FLAUNCH
FLANCHED > FLANCH
FLANCHES > FLANCH
FLANCHING > FLANCH
FLANE vb walk idly, saunter
FLANED > FLANE
FLANERIE n aimless strolling or lounging
FLANERIES > FLANERIE
FLANES n arrows
FLANEUR n idler or loafer
FLANEURS > FLANEUR
FLANGE n projecting rim or collar ▷ vb attach or provide (a component) with a flange
FLANGED > FLANGE
FLANGER > FLANGE
FLANGERS > FLANGE
FLANGES > FLANGE
FLANGING n act of flanging
FLANGINGS > FLANGING
FLANING > FLANE
FLANK n part of the side between the hips and ribs ▷ vb be at or move along the side of
FLANKED > FLANK
FLANKEN n cut of beef
FLANKENS > FLANKEN
FLANKER n one of a detachment of soldiers guarding the flanks
FLANKERED > FLANKER
FLANKERS > FLANKER
FLANKING > FLANK
FLANKS > FLANK
FLANNEL n small piece of cloth for washing the face ▷ vb talk evasively
FLANNELED > FLANNEL
FLANNELET n cotton imitation of flannel
FLANNELLY adj like flannel
FLANNELS > FLANNEL
FLANNEN adj made of flannel
FLANNENS > FLANNEN
FLANNIE same as > FLANNY
FLANNIES > FLANNIE

FLANNY n shirt made of flannel
FLANS > FLAN
FLAP vb move back and forwards or up and down ▷ n action or sound of flapping
FLAPERON n control flap on aircraft wing
FLAPERONS > FLAPERON
FLAPJACK n chewy biscuit made with oats
FLAPJACKS > FLAPJACK
FLAPLESS > FLAP
FLAPLIKE adj like a flap
FLAPPABLE > FLAP
FLAPPED > FLAP
FLAPPER n (in the 1920s) an unconventional young woman
FLAPPERS > FLAPPER
FLAPPIER > FLAPPY
FLAPPIEST > FLAPPY
FLAPPING > FLAP
FLAPPINGS > FLAP
FLAPPY adj loose
FLAPS > FLAP
FLAPTRACK n component in an aircraft wing
FLARE vb blaze with a sudden unsteady flame ▷ n sudden unsteady flame
FLAREBACK n flame in the breech of a gun when fired
FLARED > FLARE
FLARES pl n trousers with legs that widen below the knee
FLAREUP n outbreak of something
FLAREUPS > FLAREUP
FLARIER > FLARY
FLARIEST > FLARY
FLARING > FLARE
FLARINGLY > FLARE
FLARY adj flare-like
FLASER n type of sedimentary structure in rock
FLASERS > FLASER
FLASH n sudden burst of light or flame ▷ adj vulgarly showy ▷ vb emit or reflect light suddenly or intermittently
FLASHBACK n scene in a book, play, or film, that shows earlier events ▷ vb return in a novel, film, etc, to a past event
FLASHBANG n stun grenade
FLASHBULB n small light bulb that produces a bright flash of light
FLASHCARD n card shown briefly as a memory test
FLASHCUBE n in photography, a cube with a bulb that is attached to a camera
FLASHED > FLASH
FLASHER > FLASH
FLASHERS > FLASHER
FLASHES > FLASH
FLASHEST > FLASH
FLASHGUN n type of electronic flash for a camera
FLASHGUNS > FLASHGUN

FLASHIER > FLASHY
FLASHIEST > FLASHY
FLASHILY > FLASHY
FLASHING n watertight material used to cover joins in a roof
FLASHINGS > FLASHING
FLASHLAMP n electric lamp producing a flash of intense light
FLASHOVER n electric discharge over or around the surface of an insulator
FLASHTUBE n tube used in a flashlamp
FLASHY adj showy in a vulgar way
FLASK n flat bottle
FLASKET n long shallow basket
FLASKETS > FLASKET
FLASKS > FLASK
FLAT adj level and horizontal ▷ adv in or into a flat position ▷ n flat surface ▷ vb live in a flat
FLATBACK n flat-backed ornament, designed for viewing from front
FLATBACKS > FLATBACK
FLATBED n type of printing machine
FLATBEDS > FLATBED
FLATBOAT n flat-bottomed boat for transporting goods on a canal
FLATBOATS > FLATBOAT
FLATBREAD n type of thin unleavened bread
FLATBROD n flatbread made with rye
FLATBRODS > FLATBROD
FLATCAP n Elizabethan man's hat
FLATCAPS > FLATCAP
FLATCAR n flatbed
FLATCARS > FLATCAR
FLATETTE n very small flat
FLATETTES > FLATETTE
FLATFEET > FLATFOOT
FLATFISH n sea fish, such as the sole, which has a flat body
FLATFOOT n flattening of the instep arch
FLATFOOTS > FLATFOOT
FLATFORM n thick, level sole on a shoe
FLATFORMS > FLATFORM
FLATHEAD n common Australian flatfish
FLATHEADS > FLATHEAD
FLATIRON n (formerly) an iron for pressing clothes that was heated by being placed on a stove
FLATIRONS > FLATIRON
FLATLAND n land notable for its levelness
FLATLANDS > FLATLAND
FLATLET n small flat
FLATLETS > FLATLET
FLATLINE vb flat line on medical equipment monitoring one's vital signs
FLATLINED > FLATLINE
FLATLINER > FLATLINE

FLATLINES > FLATLINE
FLATLING adv in a flat or prostrate position ▷ adj with the flat side, as of a sword
FLATLINGS same as > FLATLING
FLATLONG adv prostrate
FLATLY > FLAT
FLATMATE n person with whom one shares a flat
FLATMATES > FLATMATE
FLATNESS > FLAT
FLATPACK n pieces packed into a flat box for home assembly
FLATPACKS > FLATPACK
FLATPICK vb play (a guitar, etc) by plucking individual strings with a plectrum
FLATPICKS > FLATPICK
FLATS > FLAT
FLATSHARE n state of living in a flat where each occupant shares the facilities and expenses ▷ vb live in a flat with other people who are not relatives
FLATSTICK adv with great speed or effort
FLATTED > FLAT
FLATTEN vb make or become flat or flatter
FLATTENED > FLATTEN
FLATTENER > FLATTEN
FLATTENS > FLATTEN
FLATTER vb praise insincerely
FLATTERED > FLATTER
FLATTERER > FLATTER
FLATTERS > FLATTER
FLATTERY n excessive or insincere praise
FLATTEST > FLAT
FLATTIE n flat tyre
FLATTIES > FLATTIE
FLATTING > FLAT
FLATTINGS > FLAT
FLATTISH adj somewhat flat
FLATTOP n informal name for an aircraft carrier
FLATTOPS > FLATTOP
FLATTY n flat shoe
FLATULENT adj suffering from or caused by too much gas in the intestines
FLATUOUS > FLATUS
FLATUS n gas generated in the alimentary canal
FLATUSES > FLATUS
FLATWARE n cutlery
FLATWARES > FLATWARE
FLATWASH n laundry that can be ironed mechanically
FLATWATER n slowly moving water in a river
FLATWAYS adv with the flat or broad side down or in contact with another surface
FLATWISE same as > FLATWAYS
FLATWORK n laundry that can be ironed mechanically
FLATWORKS > FLATWORK
FLATWORM n worm, such as a tapeworm, with a flattened body

FLATWORMS > FLATWORM
FLAUGHT vb flutter
FLAUGHTED > FLAUGHT
FLAUGHTER vb cut peat
FLAUGHTS > FLAUGHT
FLAUNCH n cement or mortar slope to throw off water ▷ vb cause to slope in this manner
FLAUNCHED > FLAUNCH
FLAUNCHES > FLAUNCH
FLAUNE variant of > FLAM
FLAUNES > FLAUNE
FLAUNT vb display (oneself or one's possessions) arrogantly ▷ n act of flaunting
FLAUNTED > FLAUNT
FLAUNTER > FLAUNT
FLAUNTERS > FLAUNT
FLAUNTIER > FLAUNTY
FLAUNTILY > FLAUNTY
FLAUNTING > FLAUNT
FLAUNTS > FLAUNT
FLAUNTY adj characterized by or inclined to ostentatious display
FLAUTA n tortilla rolled around a filling
FLAUTAS > FLAUTA
FLAUTIST n flute player
FLAUTISTS > FLAUTIST
FLAVA n individual style
FLAVANOL n type of flavonoid
FLAVANOLS > FLAVANOL
FLAVANONE n flavone-derived compound
FLAVAS > FLAVA
FLAVIN n heterocyclic ketone
FLAVINE same as > FLAVIN
FLAVINES > FLAVINE
FLAVINS > FLAVIN
FLAVONE n crystalline compound occurring in plants
FLAVONES > FLAVONE
FLAVONOID n any of a group of organic compounds that occur as pigments in fruit and flowers
FLAVONOL n flavonoid said to offer protection against heart disease
FLAVONOLS > FLAVONOL
FLAVOR same as > FLAVOUR
FLAVORED > FLAVOR
FLAVORER > FLAVOR
FLAVORERS > FLAVOR
FLAVORFUL adj flavourful
FLAVORIER > FLAVORY
FLAVORING n flavouring
FLAVORIST n blender of ingredients, to create or enhance flavours
FLAVOROUS adj having flavour
FLAVORS > FLAVOR
FLAVORY adj flavoursome
FLAVOUR n distinctive taste ▷ vb give flavour to
FLAVOURED > FLAVOUR
FLAVOURER > FLAVOUR
FLAVOURS > FLAVOUR
FLAVOURY adj flavoursome

FLAW n imperfection or blemish ▷ vb make or become blemished, defective, or imperfect
FLAWED > FLAW
FLAWIER > FLAW
FLAWIEST > FLAW
FLAWING > FLAW
FLAWLESS > FLAW
FLAWN variant of > FLAM
FLAWNS > FLAWN
FLAWS > FLAW
FLAWY > FLAW
FLAX n plant grown for its stem fibres and seeds
FLAXEN adj (of hair) pale yellow
FLAXES > FLAX
FLAXIER > FLAXY
FLAXIEST > FLAXY
FLAXLIKE adj like flax
FLAXSEED n seed of the flax plant, which yields linseed oil
FLAXSEEDS > FLAXSEED
FLAXY same as > FLAXEN
FLAY same as > FLEY
FLAYED > FLAY
FLAYER > FLAY
FLAYERS > FLAY
FLAYING > FLAY
FLAYS > FLAY
FLAYSOME adj frightening
FLEA n small bloodsucking insect
FLEABAG n dirty or unkempt person, esp a woman
FLEABAGS > FLEABAG
FLEABANE n as in Canadian fleabane small plant thought to ward off fleas
FLEABANES > FLEABANE
FLEABITE n bite of a flea
FLEABITES > FLEABITE
FLEADH n festival of Irish music, dancing, and culture
FLEADHS > FLEADH
FLEAM n lancet used for letting blood
FLEAMS > FLEAM
FLEAPIT n shabby cinema or theatre
FLEAPITS > FLEAPIT
FLEAS > FLEA
FLEASOME adj having fleas
FLEAWORT n type of plant
FLEAWORTS > FLEAWORT
FLECHE n slender spire
FLECHES > FLECHE
FLECHETTE n steel dart or missile dropped from an aircraft, as in World War I
FLECK n small mark, streak, or speck ▷ vb speckle
FLECKED > FLECK
FLECKER same as > FLECK
FLECKERED > FLECKER
FLECKERS > FLECKER
FLECKIER > FLECKY
FLECKIEST > FLECKY
FLECKING > FLECK
FLECKLESS > FLECK
FLECKS > FLECK
FLECKY > FLECK
FLECTION n act of bending or the state of being bent
FLECTIONS > FLECTION

FLED > FLEE
FLEDGE vb feed and care for (a young bird) until it is able to fly
FLEDGED > FLEDGE
FLEDGES > FLEDGE
FLEDGIER > FLEDGY
FLEDGIEST > FLEDGY
FLEDGING > FLEDGE
FLEDGLING n young bird ▷ adj new or inexperienced
FLEDGY adj feathery or feathered
FLEE vb run away (from)
FLEECE n sheep's coat of wool ▷ vb defraud or overcharge
FLEECED > FLEECE
FLEECER > FLEECE
FLEECERS > FLEECE
FLEECES > FLEECE
FLEECH vb flatter
FLEECHED > FLEECH
FLEECHES > FLEECH
FLEECHING > FLEECH
FLEECIE n person who collects fleeces for baling
FLEECIER > FLEECY
FLEECIES > FLEECIE
FLEECIEST > FLEECY
FLEECILY > FLEECY
FLEECING > FLEECE
FLEECY adj made of or like fleece ▷ n person who collects fleeces after shearing and prepares them for baling
FLEEING > FLEE
FLEEK n as in on fleek stylish, on trend
FLEEKS n as in on fleeks stylish, on trend
FLEER vb grin or laugh at ▷ n derisory glance or grin
FLEERED > FLEER
FLEERER > FLEER
FLEERERS > FLEER
FLEERING > FLEER
FLEERINGS > FLEER
FLEERS > FLEER
FLEES > FLEE
FLEET n number of warships organized as a unit ▷ adj swift in movement ▷ vb move rapidly
FLEETED > FLEET
FLEETER n person who sails with a fleet of ships
FLEETERS > FLEETER
FLEETEST > FLEET
FLEETING adj rapid and soon passing
FLEETLY > FLEET
FLEETNESS > FLEET
FLEETS > FLEET
FLEG vb scare
FLEGGED > FLEG
FLEGGING > FLEG
FLEGS > FLEG
FLEHMEN vb (of mammal) grimace
FLEHMENED > FLEHMEN
FLEHMENS > FLEHMEN
FLEISHIG same as > FLEISHIK
FLEISHIK adj containing or derived from meat or meat products

FLEME vb drive out
FLEMED > FLEME
FLEMES > FLEME
FLEMING n inhabitant of Flanders or a Flemish-speaking Belgian
FLEMISH vb stow (a rope) in a Flemish coil
FLEMISHED > FLEMISH
FLEMISHES > FLEMISH
FLEMIT > FLEME
FLENCH same as > FLENSE
FLENCHED > FLENCH
FLENCHER > FLENCH
FLENCHERS > FLENCH
FLENCHES > FLENCH
FLENCHING > FLENCH
FLENSE vb strip (a whale, seal, etc) of (its blubber or skin)
FLENSED > FLENSE
FLENSER > FLENSE
FLENSERS > FLENSE
FLENSES > FLENSE
FLENSING > FLENSE
FLEROVIUM n transuranic element
FLESH n soft part of a human or animal body ▷ vb remove flesh from
FLESHED > FLESH
FLESHER n person or machine that fleshes hides or skins
FLESHERS > FLESHER
FLESHES > FLESH
FLESHHOOD n incarnation
FLESHIER > FLESHY
FLESHIEST > FLESHY
FLESHILY > FLESHY
FLESHING > FLESH
FLESHINGS pl n flesh-coloured tights
FLESHLESS > FLESH
FLESHLIER > FLESHLY
FLESHLING n voluptuary
FLESHLY adj fleshy; fat
FLESHMENT n act of fleshing
FLESHPOT n pot in which meat is cooked
FLESHPOTS pl n places, such as brothels and strip clubs, where sexual desires are catered to
FLESHWORM n flesh-eating worm
FLESHY adj plump
FLETCH same as > FLEDGE
FLETCHED > FLETCH
FLETCHER n person who makes arrows
FLETCHERS > FLETCHER
FLETCHES > FLETCH
FLETCHING > FLETCH
FLETTON n type of brick
FLETTONS > FLETTON
FLEUR n flower emblem used in heraldry
FLEURET same as > FLEURETTE
FLEURETS > FLEURET
FLEURETTE n ornament resembling a flower
FLEURON n decorative piece of pastry
FLEURONS > FLEURON

f

FLEURS > FLEUR
FLEURY same as > FLORY
FLEW > FLY
FLEWED adj having large flews
FLEWS pl n upper lip of a bloodhound or similar dog
FLEX n flexible insulated electric cable ▷ vb bend
FLEXAGON n hexagon made from a single pliable strip of triangles
FLEXAGONS > FLEXAGON
FLEXED > FLEX
FLEXES > FLEX
FLEXI n flexitime
FLEXIBLE adj easily bent
FLEXIBLY > FLEXIBLE
FLEXILE same as > FLEXIBLE
FLEXING > FLEX
FLEXION n act of bending a joint or limb
FLEXIONAL > FLEXION
FLEXIONS > FLEXION
FLEXIS > FLEXI
FLEXITIME n system permitting variation in starting and finishing times of work
FLEXO n flexography
FLEXOR n type of muscle
FLEXORS > FLEXOR
FLEXOS > FLEXO
FLEXTIME same as > FLEXITIME
FLEXTIMER > FLEXTIME
FLEXTIMES > FLEXTIME
FLEXUOSE same as > FLEXUOUS
FLEXUOUS adj full of bends or curves
FLEXURAL > FLEXURE
FLEXURE n act of flexing or the state of being flexed
FLEXURES > FLEXURE
FLEXWING n collapsible fabric wing used in hang gliding
FLEXWINGS > FLEXWING
FLEY vb be afraid or cause to be afraid
FLEYED > FLEY
FLEYING > FLEY
FLEYS > FLEY
FLIBBERT n small piece or bit
FLIBBERTS > FLIBBERT
FLIC n French police officer
FLICHTER vb flutter
FLICHTERS > FLICHTER
FLICK vb touch or move in a quick movement ▷ n tap or quick stroke
FLICKABLE > FLICK
FLICKED > FLICK
FLICKER vb shine unsteadily or intermittently ▷ n unsteady brief light
FLICKERED > FLICKER
FLICKERS > FLICKER
FLICKERY adj flickering
FLICKING > FLICK
FLICKS > FLICK
FLICS > FLIC
FLIED > FLY
FLIER > FLY

FLIERS > FLY
FLIES > FLY
FLIEST > FLY
FLIGHT n journey by air ▷ vb cause (a ball, dart, etc) to float slowly or deceptively towards its target
FLIGHTED > FLIGHT
FLIGHTIER > FLIGHTY
FLIGHTILY > FLIGHTY
FLIGHTING > FLIGHT
FLIGHTS > FLIGHT
FLIGHTY adj frivolous and fickle
FLIM n five-pound note
FLIMFLAM n nonsense ▷ vb deceive
FLIMFLAMS > FLIMFLAM
FLIMP vb steal
FLIMPED > FLIMP
FLIMPING > FLIMP
FLIMPS > FLIMP
FLIMS > FLIM
FLIMSIER > FLIMSY
FLIMSIES > FLIMSY
FLIMSIEST > FLIMSY
FLIMSILY > FLIMSY
FLIMSY adj not strong or substantial ▷ n thin paper used for making carbon copies
FLINCH same as > FLENSE
FLINCHED > FLINCH
FLINCHER > FLINCH
FLINCHERS > FLINCH
FLINCHES > FLINCH
FLINCHING > FLINCH
FLINDER n fragment ▷ vb scamper about flutteringly
FLINDERED > FLINDER
FLINDERS > FLINDER
FLING vb throw, send, or move forcefully or hurriedly ▷ n spell of self-indulgent enjoyment
FLINGER > FLING
FLINGERS > FLING
FLINGING > FLING
FLINGS > FLING
FLINKITE n anhydrous phosphate
FLINKITES > FLINKITE
FLINT n hard grey stone ▷ vb fit or provide with a flint
FLINTED > FLINT
FLINTHEAD n American wading bird
FLINTIER > FLINTY
FLINTIEST > FLINTY
FLINTIFY vb turn to flint
FLINTILY > FLINTY
FLINTING > FLINT
FLINTLIKE > FLINT
FLINTLOCK n obsolete gun in which the powder was lit by a spark from a flint
FLINTS > FLINT
FLINTY adj cruel
FLIP vb throw (something small or light) carelessly ▷ n snap or tap ▷ adj flippant
FLIPBOARD n piece of office equipment consisting of a board to which a flipchart, etc can be attached
FLIPBOOK n book of drawings made to seem animated by flipping pages

FLIPBOOKS > FLIPBOOK
FLIPCHART n pad containing large sheets of paper, mounted on a stand and used to present reports, etc
FLIPFLOP n rubber sandal
FLIPFLOPS > FLIPFLOP
FLIPPANCY > FLIPPANT
FLIPPANT adj treating serious things lightly
FLIPPED > FLIP
FLIPPER n limb of a sea animal adapted for swimming
FLIPPERS > FLIPPER
FLIPPEST > FLIP
FLIPPIER > FLIPPY
FLIPPIEST > FLIPPY
FLIPPING n act or instance of flipping
FLIPPINGS > FLIPPING
FLIPPY adj (of clothes) moving to and fro as the wearer walks
FLIPS > FLIP
FLIPSIDE n reverse or opposite side
FLIPSIDES > FLIPSIDE
FLIR n forward looking infrared radar
FLIRS > FLIR
FLIRT vb behave as if physically attracted to someone ▷ n person who flirts
FLIRTED > FLIRT
FLIRTER > FLIRT
FLIRTERS > FLIRT
FLIRTIER > FLIRT
FLIRTIEST > FLIRT
FLIRTING > FLIRT
FLIRTINGS > FLIRT
FLIRTISH > FLIRT
FLIRTS > FLIRT
FLIRTY > FLIRT
FLISK vb skip
FLISKED > FLISK
FLISKIER > FLISK
FLISKIEST > FLISK
FLISKING > FLISK
FLISKS > FLISK
FLISKY > FLISK
FLIT vb move lightly and rapidly ▷ n act of flitting
FLITCH n side of pork salted and cured ▷ vb cut (a tree trunk) into pieces of timber
FLITCHED > FLITCH
FLITCHES > FLITCH
FLITCHING > FLITCH
FLITE vb scold or rail at ▷ n dispute or scolding
FLITED > FLITE
FLITES > FLITE
FLITING > FLITE
FLITS > FLIT
FLITT adj fleet ▷ vb to flit
FLITTED > FLIT
FLITTER > FLIT
FLITTERED > FLIT
FLITTERN n bark of young oak tree
FLITTERNS > FLITTERN
FLITTERS > FLIT
FLITTING > FLIT
FLITTINGS > FLIT

FLITTS > FLITT
FLIVVER n old, cheap, or battered car
FLIVVERS > FLIVVER
FLIX n fur ▷ vb have fur
FLIXED > FLIX
FLIXES > FLIX
FLIXING > FLIX
FLIXWEED n plant of the mustard family
FLIXWEEDS > FLIXWEED
FLOAT vb rest on the surface of a liquid ▷ n object used to help someone or something float
FLOATABLE > FLOAT
FLOATAGE same as > FLOTAGE
FLOATAGES > FLOATAGE
FLOATANT n substance used in fly-fishing, to help dry flies to float
FLOATANTS > FLOATANT
FLOATBASE n place where seaplanes dock
FLOATCUT adj as in floatcut file file with rows of parallel teeth
FLOATED > FLOAT
FLOATEL same as > FLOTEL
FLOATELS > FLOATEL
FLOATER n person or thing that floats
FLOATERS > FLOATER
FLOATIER > FLOATY
FLOATIEST > FLOATY
FLOATING adj moving about, changing
FLOATINGS > FLOATING
FLOATS pl n footlights
FLOATY adj filmy and light
FLOB vb spit
FLOBBED > FLOB
FLOBBING > FLOB
FLOBS > FLOB
FLOC same as > FLOCK
FLOCCED > FLOC
FLOCCI > FLOCCUS
FLOCCING > FLOC
FLOCCOSE adj consisting of or covered with woolly tufts or hairs
FLOCCULAR > FLOCCUS
FLOCCULE n small aggregate of flocculent material
FLOCCULES > FLOCCULE
FLOCCULI > FLOCCULUS
FLOCCULUS same as > FLOCCULE
FLOCCUS n downy or woolly covering ▷ adj (of a cloud) having the appearance of woolly tufts
FLOCK n number of animals of one kind together ▷ vb gather in a crowd ▷ adj (of wallpaper) with a velvety raised pattern
FLOCKED > FLOCK
FLOCKIER > FLOCK
FLOCKIEST > FLOCK
FLOCKING > FLOCK
FLOCKINGS > FLOCK
FLOCKLESS > FLOCK
FLOCKS > FLOCK
FLOCKY > FLOCK

FLOCS > FLOC
FLOE n sheet of floating ice
FLOES > FLOE
FLOG vb beat with a whip or stick
FLOGGABLE > FLOG
FLOGGED > FLOG
FLOGGER > FLOG
FLOGGERS > FLOG
FLOGGING > FLOG
FLOGGINGS > FLOG
FLOGS > FLOG
FLOKATI n Greek hand-woven shaggy woollen rug
FLOKATIS > FLOKATI
FLONG n material used for making moulds in stereotyping
FLONGS > FLONG
FLOOD n overflow of water onto a normally dry area ▷ vb cover or become covered with water
FLOODABLE > FLOOD
FLOODED > FLOOD
FLOODER > FLOOD
FLOODERS > FLOOD
FLOODGATE n gate used to control the flow of water
FLOODING n submerging of land under water
FLOODINGS > FLOODING
FLOODLESS > FLOOD
FLOODLIT adj illuminated with a floodlight
FLOODMARK n high-water mark
FLOODS > FLOOD
FLOODTIDE n rising tide
FLOODWALL n wall built as a defence against floods
FLOODWAY n conduit for floodwater
FLOODWAYS > FLOODWAY
FLOOEY adj awry
FLOOIE same as > FLOOEY
FLOOR n lower surface of a room ▷ vb knock down
FLOORAGE n area of floor
FLOORAGES > FLOORAGE
FLOORED > FLOOR
FLOORER n coup de grâce
FLOORERS > FLOORER
FLOORHEAD n upper side of a floor timber
FLOORING > FLOOR
FLOORINGS > FLOOR
FLOORLESS > FLOOR
FLOORPAN n bottom part of a motor vehicle's interior
FLOORPANS > FLOORPAN
FLOORS > FLOOR
FLOORSHOW n entertainment on floor of nightclub
FLOOSIE same as > FLOOZY
FLOOSIES > FLOOSIE
FLOOSY variant of > FLOOSIE
FLOOZIE same as > FLOOZY
FLOOZIES > FLOOZY
FLOOZY n derogatory term for a woman considered immodest
FLOP vb bend, fall, or collapse loosely or carelessly ▷ n failure

FLOPHOUSE n cheap lodging house, esp one used by tramps
FLOPOVER n TV visual effect of page being turned
FLOPOVERS > FLOPOVER
FLOPPED > FLOP
FLOPPER > FLOP
FLOPPERS > FLOP
FLOPPIER > FLOPPY
FLOPPIES > FLOPPY
FLOPPIEST > FLOPPY
FLOPPILY > FLOPPY
FLOPPING > FLOP
FLOPPY adj hanging downwards, loose ▷ n floppy disk
FLOPS > FLOP
FLOPTICAL n type of floppy disk
FLOR n type of yeast
FLORA n plants of a given place or time
FLORAE > FLORA
FLORAL adj consisting of or decorated with flowers ▷ n class of perfume
FLORALLY > FLORAL
FLORALS > FLORAL
FLORAS > FLORA
FLOREANT > FLOREAT
FLOREAT vb may (a person, institution, etc) flourish
FLOREATED same as > FLORIATED
FLORENCE n type of fennel
FLORENCES > FLORENCE
FLORET n part of a composite flower head
FLORETS > FLORET
FLORIATED adj having ornamentation based on flowers and leaves
FLORICANE n fruiting stem of plant
FLORID adj with a red or flushed complexion
FLORIDEAN n member of the red seaweed family
FLORIDER > FLORID
FLORIDEST > FLORID
FLORIDITY > FLORID
FLORIDLY > FLORID
FLORIER > FLORY
FLORIEST > FLORY
FLORIFORM adj flower-shaped
FLORIGEN n hypothetical plant hormone
FLORIGENS > FLORIGEN
FLORIN n former British and Australian coin
FLORINS > FLORIN
FLORIST n seller of flowers
FLORISTIC adj of or relating to flowers or a flora
FLORISTRY > FLORIST
FLORISTS > FLORIST
FLORS > FLOR
FLORUIT prep (he or she) flourished in ▷ n such a period in a person's life
FLORUITS > FLORUIT
FLORULA n flora of a small single environment
FLORULAE > FLORULA

FLORULE same as > FLORULA
FLORULES > FLORULE
FLORY adj containing a fleur-de-lys
FLOSCULAR > FLOSCULE
FLOSCULE n floret
FLOSCULES > FLOSCULE
FLOSH n hopper-shaped box
FLOSHES > FLOSH
FLOSS n fine silky fibres ▷ vb clean (between the teeth) with dental floss
FLOSSED > FLOSS
FLOSSER > FLOSS
FLOSSERS > FLOSS
FLOSSES > FLOSS
FLOSSIE variant of > FLOSSY
FLOSSIER > FLOSSY
FLOSSIES > FLOSSY
FLOSSIEST > FLOSSY
FLOSSILY > FLOSSY
FLOSSING > FLOSS
FLOSSINGS > FLOSS
FLOSSY adj consisting of or resembling floss ▷ n floozy
FLOTA n formerly, Spanish commercial fleet
FLOTAGE n act or state of floating
FLOTAGES > FLOTAGE
FLOTANT adj in heraldry, flying in the air
FLOTAS > FLOTA
FLOTATION n launching or financing of a business enterprise
FLOTE n aquatic perennial grass ▷ vb skim (eg milk)
FLOTED > FLOTE
FLOTEL n (in the oil industry) rig or boat used as accommodation
FLOTELS > FLOTEL
FLOTES > FLOTE
FLOTILLA n small fleet or fleet of small ships
FLOTILLAS > FLOTILLA
FLOTING > FLOTE
FLOTSAM n floating wreckage
FLOTSAMS > FLOTSAM
FLOUNCE vb go with emphatic movements ▷ n flouncing movement
FLOUNCED > FLOUNCE
FLOUNCES > FLOUNCE
FLOUNCIER > FLOUNCE
FLOUNCING n material, such as lace or embroidered fabric, used for making flounces
FLOUNCY > FLOUNCE
FLOUNDER vb move with difficulty, as in mud ▷ n edible flatfish
FLOUNDERS > FLOUNDER
FLOUR n powder made by grinding grain, esp wheat ▷ vb sprinkle with flour
FLOURED > FLOUR
FLOURIER > FLOUR
FLOURIEST > FLOUR
FLOURING > FLOUR
FLOURISH vb be active, successful, or widespread ▷ n dramatic waving motion

FLOURISHY adj full of flourishes
FLOURLESS > FLOUR
FLOURS > FLOUR
FLOURY > FLOUR
FLOUSE vb splash
FLOUSED > FLOUSE
FLOUSES > FLOUSE
FLOUSH variant of > FLOUSE
FLOUSHED > FLOUSH
FLOUSHES > FLOUSH
FLOUSHING > FLOUSH
FLOUSING > FLOUSE
FLOUT vb deliberately disobey (a rule, law, etc)
FLOUTED > FLOUT
FLOUTER > FLOUT
FLOUTERS > FLOUT
FLOUTING > FLOUT
FLOUTS > FLOUT
FLOW vb (of liquid) move in a stream ▷ n act, rate, or manner of flowing
FLOWABLE adj capable of flowing
FLOWAGE n act of overflowing or the state of having overflowed
FLOWAGES > FLOWAGE
FLOWCHART n diagrammatic representation of the sequence of operations or equipment in an industrial process, computer program, etc
FLOWED > FLOW
FLOWER n part of a plant that produces seeds ▷ vb produce flowers, bloom
FLOWERAGE n mass of flowers
FLOWERBED n piece of ground for growing flowers
FLOWERED adj decorated with a floral design
FLOWERER n plant that flowers at a specified time or in a specified way
FLOWERERS > FLOWERER
FLOWERET another name for > FLORET
FLOWERETS > FLOWERET
FLOWERFUL adj having plentiful flowers
FLOWERIER > FLOWERY
FLOWERILY > FLOWERY
FLOWERING adj (of certain species of plants) capable of producing conspicuous flowers
FLOWERPOT n pot in which plants are grown
FLOWERS > FLOWER
FLOWERY adj decorated with a floral design
FLOWING > FLOW
FLOWINGLY > FLOW
FLOWMETER n instrument that measures the rate of flow of a liquid or gas within a pipe or tube
FLOWN > FLY
FLOWS > FLOW
FLOWSTONE n type of speleothem
FLOX adj as in flox silk type of silk

FLU n any of various viral infections
FLUATE n fluoride
FLUATES > FLUATE
FLUB vb bungle
FLUBBED > FLUB
FLUBBER > FLUB
FLUBBERS > FLUB
FLUBBING > FLUB
FLUBDUB n bunkum
FLUBDUBS > FLUBDUB
FLUBS > FLUB
FLUCTUANT adj inclined to vary or fluctuate
FLUCTUATE vb change frequently and erratically
FLUE n passage or pipe for smoke or hot air
FLUED adj having a flue
FLUELLEN n type of plant
FLUELLENS > FLUELLEN
FLUELLIN same as > FLUELLEN
FLUELLINS > FLUELLIN
FLUENCE > FLUENCY
FLUENCES > FLUENCY
FLUENCIES > FLUENCY
FLUENCY n quality of being fluent
FLUENT adj able to speak or write with ease ▷ n variable quantity in fluxions
FLUENTLY > FLUENT
FLUENTS > FLUENT
FLUERIC adj of or relating to fluidics
FLUERICS pl n fluidics
FLUES > FLUE
FLUEWORK n collectively, organ stops
FLUEWORKS > FLUEWORK
FLUEY adj involved in, caused by, or like influenza
FLUFF n soft fibres ▷ vb make or become soft and puffy
FLUFFBALL n ball of fluff
FLUFFED > FLUFF
FLUFFER n person employed on a railway to clear the tracks
FLUFFERS > FLUFFER
FLUFFIER > FLUFFY
FLUFFIEST > FLUFFY
FLUFFILY > FLUFFY
FLUFFING > FLUFF
FLUFFS > FLUFF
FLUFFY adj of, resembling, or covered with fluff
FLUGEL n grand piano or harpsichord
FLUGELMAN variant of > FUGLEMAN
FLUGELMEN > FLUGELMAN
FLUGELS > FLUGEL
FLUID n substance able to flow and change its shape ▷ adj able to flow or change shape easily
FLUIDAL > FLUID
FLUIDALLY > FLUID
FLUIDIC > FLUIDICS
FLUIDICS n study and use of the flow of fluids in tubes
FLUIDIFY vb make fluid
FLUIDISE same as > FLUIDIZE

FLUIDISED > FLUIDISE
FLUIDISER > FLUIDISE
FLUIDISES > FLUIDISE
FLUIDITY n state of being fluid
FLUIDIZE vb make fluid
FLUIDIZED > FLUIDIZE
FLUIDIZER > FLUIDIZE
FLUIDIZES > FLUIDIZE
FLUIDLIKE > FLUID
FLUIDLY > FLUID
FLUIDNESS > FLUID
FLUIDRAM n British imperial measure
FLUIDRAMS > FLUIDRAM
FLUIDS > FLUID
FLUIER > FLUEY
FLUIEST > FLUEY
FLUISH > FLU
FLUKE n accidental stroke of luck ▷ vb gain, make, or hit by a fluke
FLUKED > FLUKE
FLUKES > FLUKE
FLUKEY same as > FLUKY
FLUKIER > FLUKY
FLUKIEST > FLUKY
FLUKILY > FLUKY
FLUKINESS > FLUKY
FLUKING > FLUKE
FLUKY adj done or gained by an accident
FLUME n narrow sloping channel for water ▷ vb transport (logs) in a flume
FLUMED > FLUME
FLUMES > FLUME
FLUMING > FLUME
FLUMMERY n silly or trivial talk
FLUMMOX vb puzzle or confuse
FLUMMOXED > FLUMMOX
FLUMMOXES > FLUMMOX
FLUMP vb move or fall heavily
FLUMPED > FLUMP
FLUMPING > FLUMP
FLUMPS > FLUMP
FLUNG > FLING
FLUNK vb fail ▷ n low grade below the pass standard
FLUNKED > FLUNK
FLUNKER > FLUNK
FLUNKERS > FLUNK
FLUNKEY same as > FLUNKY
FLUNKEYS > FLUNKEY
FLUNKIE same as > FLUNKY
FLUNKIES > FLUNKY
FLUNKING > FLUNK
FLUNKS > FLUNK
FLUNKY n servile person
FLUNKYISM > FLUNKY
FLUOR same as > FLUORSPAR
FLUORENE n white insoluble crystalline solid
FLUORENES > FLUORENE
FLUORESCE vb exhibit fluorescence
FLUORIC adj of, concerned with, or produced from fluorine or fluorspar
FLUORID same as > FLUORIDE
FLUORIDE n compound containing fluorine

FLUORIDES > FLUORIDE
FLUORIDS > FLUORID
FLUORIN same as > FLUORINE
FLUORINE n toxic yellow gas: most reactive of all the elements
FLUORINES > FLUORINE
FLUORINS > FLUORIN
FLUORITE same as > FLUORSPAR
FLUORITES > FLUORITE
FLUOROSES > FLUOROSIS
FLUOROSIS n fluoride poisoning, due to ingestion of too much fluoride in drinking water over a long period or to ingestion of pesticides containing fluoride salts. Chronic fluorosis results in mottling of the teeth of children
FLUOROTIC > FLUOROSIS
FLUORS > FLUOR
FLUORSPAR n white or colourless mineral, consisting of calcium fluoride in crystalline form: the chief ore of fluorine
FLURR vb scatter
FLURRED > FLURR
FLURRIED > FLURRY
FLURRIES > FLURRY
FLURRING > FLURR
FLURRS > FLURR
FLURRY n sudden commotion ▷ vb confuse
FLURRYING > FLURRY
FLUS > FLU
FLUSH vb blush or cause to blush ▷ n blush ▷ adj level with the surrounding surface ▷ adv so as to be level
FLUSHABLE > FLUSH
FLUSHED > FLUSH
FLUSHER > FLUSH
FLUSHERS > FLUSH
FLUSHES > FLUSH
FLUSHEST > FLUSH
FLUSHIER > FLUSHY
FLUSHIEST > FLUSHY
FLUSHING n extra feeding given to ewes before mating to increase the lambing percentage
FLUSHINGS > FLUSHING
FLUSHNESS > FLUSH
FLUSHWORK n decorative treatment of the surface of an outside wall with flints split to show their smooth black surface, combined with dressed stone to form patterns such as tracery or initials
FLUSHY adj ruddy
FLUSTER vb make nervous or upset ▷ n nervous or upset state
FLUSTERED > FLUSTER
FLUSTERS > FLUSTER
FLUSTERY adj flustered
FLUSTRATE vb fluster
FLUTE n wind instrument ▷ vb utter in a high-pitched tone
FLUTED adj having decorative grooves

FLUTELIKE > FLUTE
FLUTER n craftsperson who makes flutes or fluting
FLUTERS > FLUTER
FLUTES > FLUTE
FLUTEY adj resembling a flute in sound
FLUTEYER > FLUTEY
FLUTEYEST > FLUTEY
FLUTIER > FLUTEY
FLUTIEST > FLUTEY
FLUTINA n type of accordion
FLUTINAS > FLUTINA
FLUTING n design of decorative grooves
FLUTINGS > FLUTING
FLUTIST same as > FLAUTIST
FLUTISTS > FLUTIST
FLUTTER vb wave rapidly ▷ n flapping movement
FLUTTERED > FLUTTER
FLUTTERER > FLUTTER
FLUTTERS > FLUTTER
FLUTTERY adj flapping rapidly
FLUTY > FLUTE
FLUVIAL adj of rivers
FLUVIATIC > FLUVIAL
FLUX n constant change or instability ▷ vb make or become fluid
FLUXED > FLUX
FLUXES > FLUX
FLUXGATE n type of magnetometer
FLUXGATES > FLUXGATE
FLUXING > FLUX
FLUXION n rate of change of a function
FLUXIONAL > FLUXION
FLUXIONS > FLUXION
FLUXIVE > FLUX
FLUXMETER n any instrument for measuring magnetic flux, usually by measuring the charge that flows through a coil when the flux changes
FLUYT n Dutch sailing ship
FLUYTS > FLUYT
FLY vb move through the air on wings or in an aircraft ▷ n fastening at the front of trousers ▷ adj sharp and cunning
FLYABLE > FLY
FLYAWAY adj (of hair) very fine and soft ▷ n person who is frivolous or flighty
FLYAWAYS > FLYAWAY
FLYBACK n item of electrical equipment
FLYBACKS > FLYBACK
FLYBANE n type of campion
FLYBANES > FLYBANE
FLYBELT n strip of tsetse-infested land
FLYBELTS > FLYBELT
FLYBLEW > FLYBLOW
FLYBLOW vb contaminate ▷ n egg or young larva of a blowfly
FLYBLOWN adj covered with blowfly eggs
FLYBLOWS > FLYBLOW

FLYBOAT *n* any small swift boat
FLYBOATS > FLYBOAT
FLYBOOK *n* small case or wallet for storing artificial flies
FLYBOOKS > FLYBOOK
FLYBOY *n* air force pilot
FLYBOYS > FLYBOY
FLYBRIDGE *n* highest navigational bridge on a ship
FLYBY *n* flight past a particular position or target
FLYBYS > FLYBY
FLYER > FLY
FLYERS > FLY
FLYEST > FLY
FLYFISHER *n* angler who fishes with a fly
FLYHAND *n* device on a printing press
FLYHANDS > FLYHAND
FLYING > FLY
FLYINGS > FLY
FLYLEAF *n* blank leaf at the beginning or end of a book
FLYLEAVES > FLYLEAF
FLYLESS > FLY
FLYLINE *n* type of line used in fly fishing
FLYLINES > FLYLINE
FLYMAKER *n* person who makes fishing flies
FLYMAKERS > FLYMAKER
FLYMAN *n* stagehand
FLYMEN > FLYMAN
FLYOFF *n* all water transferred from the earth to the atmosphere
FLYOFFS > FLYOFF
FLYOVER *n* road passing over another by a bridge
FLYOVERS > FLYOVER
FLYPAPER *n* paper with a sticky poisonous coating, used to kill flies
FLYPAPERS > FLYPAPER
FLYPAST *n* ceremonial flight of aircraft over a given area
FLYPASTS > FLYPAST
FLYPE *vb* fold back
FLYPED > FLYPE
FLYPES > FLYPE
FLYPING > FLYPE
FLYPITCH *n* area for unlicensed stalls at markets
FLYPOSTER *n* person who puts up posters illegally
FLYRODDER *n* angler using artificial fly
FLYSCH *n* type of marine sedimentary facies
FLYSCHES > FLYSCH
FLYSCREEN *n* wire-mesh screen over a window to prevent flies from entering a room
FLYSHEET *n* part of tent
FLYSHEETS > FLYSHEET
FLYSPECK *n* small speck of the excrement of a fly *▷ vb* mark with flyspecks
FLYSPECKS > FLYSPECK
FLYSPRAY *n* insecticide sprayed from an aerosol
FLYSPRAYS > FLYSPRAY

FLYSTRIKE *n* infestation of wounded sheep by blowflies or maggots
FLYTE *same as* > FLITE
FLYTED > FLYTE
FLYTES > FLYTE
FLYTIER *n* person who makes their own fishing flies
FLYTIERS > FLYTIER
FLYTING > FLYTE
FLYTINGS > FLYTE
FLYTRAP *n* any of various insectivorous plants
FLYTRAPS > FLYTRAP
FLYWAY *n* usual route used by birds when migrating
FLYWAYS > FLYWAY
FLYWEIGHT *n* boxer weighing up to 112lb (professional) or 51kg (amateur)
FLYWHEEL *n* heavy wheel regulating the speed of a machine
FLYWHEELS > FLYWHEEL
FOAL *n* young of a horse or related animal *▷ vb* give birth to a foal
FOALED > FOAL
FOALFOOT *n* coltsfoot
FOALFOOTS > FOALFOOT
FOALING *n* act of flanging
FOALINGS > FOALING
FOALS > FOAL
FOAM *n* mass of small bubbles on a liquid *▷ vb* produce foam
FOAMABLE > FOAM
FOAMED > FOAM
FOAMER *n* (possibly obsessive) enthusiast
FOAMERS > FOAMER
FOAMIER > FOAMY
FOAMIEST > FOAMY
FOAMILY > FOAMY
FOAMINESS > FOAMY
FOAMING > FOAM
FOAMINGLY > FOAM
FOAMINGS > FOAM
FOAMLESS > FOAM
FOAMLIKE > FOAM
FOAMS > FOAM
FOAMY *adj* of, resembling, consisting of, or covered with foam
FOB *n* short watch chain *▷ vb* cheat
FOBBED > FOB
FOBBING > FOB
FOBS > FOB
FOCACCIA *n* flat Italian bread made with olive oil and yeast
FOCACCIAS > FOCACCIA
FOCAL *adj* of or at a focus
FOCALISE *same as* > FOCALIZE
FOCALISED > FOCALIZE
FOCALISES > FOCALIZE
FOCALIZE *less common word for* > FOCUS
FOCALIZED > FOCALIZE
FOCALIZES > FOCALIZE
FOCALLY > FOCAL
FOCI > FOCUS
FOCIMETER *n* photographic focusing device

FOCOMETER *n* instrument for measuring the focal length of a lens
FOCUS *n* point at which light or sound waves converge *▷ vb* bring or come into focus
FOCUSABLE > FOCUS
FOCUSED > FOCUS
FOCUSER > FOCUS
FOCUSERS > FOCUS
FOCUSES > FOCUS
FOCUSING > FOCUS
FOCUSINGS > FOCUS
FOCUSLESS > FOCUS
FOCUSSED > FOCUS
FOCUSSES > FOCUS
FOCUSSING > FOCUS
FODDER *n* feed for livestock *▷ vb* supply (livestock) with fodder
FODDERED > FODDER
FODDERER > FODDER
FODDERERS > FODDER
FODDERING > FODDER
FODDERS > FODDER
FODGEL *adj* buxom
FOE *n* enemy, opponent
FOEDARIE *variant of* > FEDARIE
FOEDARIES > FOEDARIE
FOEDERATI *pl n* (in ancient Rome) tribes bound by treaty to support the Roman Empire
FOEFIE *adj* as in *foefie slide* rope along which a person may traverse
FOEHN *same as* > FOHN
FOEHNS > FOEHN
FOEMAN *n* enemy in war
FOEMEN > FOEMAN
FOEN *same as* > FOE
FOES > FOE
FOETAL *same as* > FETAL
FOETATION *same as* > FETATION
FOETICIDE *same as* > FETICIDE
FOETID *same as* > FETID
FOETIDER > FOETID
FOETIDEST > FOETID
FOETIDLY > FOETID
FOETOR *same as* > FETOR
FOETORS > FOETOR
FOETUS *same as* > FETUS
FOETUSES > FOETUS
FOG *n* mass of condensed water vapour in the lower air *▷ vb* cover with steam
FOGASH *n* type of Hungarian pike perch
FOGASHES > FOGASH
FOGBOUND *adj* prevented from operating by fog
FOGBOW *n* faint arc of light sometimes seen in a fog bank
FOGBOWS > FOGBOW
FOGDOG *n* spot sometimes seen in fog near the horizon
FOGDOGS > FOGDOG
FOGEY *n* old-fashioned person
FOGEYDOM > FOGEY
FOGEYDOMS > FOGEY
FOGEYISH > FOGEY
FOGEYISM > FOGEY
FOGEYISMS > FOGEY

FOGEYS > FOGEY
FOGFRUIT *n* wildflower of the verbena family
FOGFRUITS > FOGFRUIT
FOGGAGE *n* grass grown for winter grazing
FOGGAGES > FOGGAGE
FOGGED > FOG
FOGGER *n* device that generates a fog
FOGGERS > FOGGER
FOGGIER > FOG
FOGGIEST > FOG
FOGGILY > FOG
FOGGINESS > FOG
FOGGING *n* act of fogging
FOGGINGS > FOGGING
FOGGY > FOG
FOGHORN *n* large horn sounded to warn ships in fog
FOGHORNS > FOGHORN
FOGIE *variant of* > FOGEY
FOGIES > FOGIE
FOGLE *n* silk handkerchief
FOGLES > FOGLE
FOGLESS > FOG
FOGLIGHT *n* motor-vehicle light used in fog
FOGLIGHTS > FOGLIGHT
FOGMAN *n* person in charge of railway fog-signals
FOGMEN > FOGMAN
FOGOU *n* subterranean building found in Cornwall
FOGOUS > FOGOU
FOGRAM *n* fogey
FOGRAMITE > FOGRAM
FOGRAMITY > FOGRAM
FOGRAMS > FOGRAM
FOGS > FOG
FOGY *same as* > FOGEY
FOGYDOM > FOGY
FOGYDOMS > FOGY
FOGYISH > FOGY
FOGYISM > FOGY
FOGYISMS > FOGY
FOH *interj* expression of disgust
FOHN *n* type of warm dry wind
FOHNS > FOHN
FOIBLE *n* minor weakness or slight peculiarity
FOIBLES > FOIBLE
FOID *n* rock-forming mineral similar to feldspar
FOIDS > FOID
FOIL *vb* ruin (someone's plan) *▷ n* metal in a thin sheet, esp for wrapping food
FOILABLE > FOIL
FOILBORNE *adj* moving by means of hydrofoils
FOILED > FOIL
FOILING > FOIL
FOILINGS > FOIL
FOILIST *n* person who fences with a foil
FOILISTS > FOILIST
FOILS > FOIL
FOILSMAN *n* person who uses or specializes in using a foil
FOILSMEN > FOILSMAN
FOIN *n* thrust or lunge with a weapon *▷ vb* thrust with a weapon

f

f

FOINED > FOIN
FOINING > FOIN
FOININGLY > FOIN
FOINS > FOIN
FOISON n plentiful supply or yield
FOISONS > FOISON
FOIST vb force or impose on
FOISTED > FOIST
FOISTER > FOIST
FOISTERS > FOIST
FOISTING > FOIST
FOISTS > FOIST
FOLACIN n folic acid
FOLACINS > FOLACIN
FOLATE n folic acid
FOLATES > FOLATE
FOLD vb bend so that one part covers another ▷ n folded piece or part
FOLDABLE > FOLD
FOLDAWAY adj (of a bed) able to be folded and put away when not in use
FOLDAWAYS > FOLDAWAY
FOLDBACK n (in multitrack recording) a process for returning a signal to a performer instantly
FOLDBACKS > FOLDBACK
FOLDBOAT another name for > FALTBOAT
FOLDBOATS > FOLDBOAT
FOLDED > FOLD
FOLDER n piece of folded cardboard for holding loose papers
FOLDEROL same as > FALDERAL
FOLDEROLS > FOLDEROL
FOLDERS > FOLDER
FOLDING > FOLD
FOLDINGS > FOLDING
FOLDOUT another name for > GATEFOLD
FOLDOUTS > FOLDOUT
FOLDS > FOLD
FOLDUP n something that folds up
FOLDUPS > FOLDUP
FOLEY n footsteps editor
FOLEYS > FOLEY
FOLIA > FOLIUM
FOLIAGE n leaves
FOLIAGED adj having foliage
FOLIAGES > FOLIAGE
FOLIAR adj of or relating to a leaf or leaves
FOLIATE adj relating to, possessing, or resembling leaves ▷ vb ornament with foliage or with leaf forms such as foils
FOLIATED adj ornamented with or made up of foliage or foils
FOLIATES > FOLIATE
FOLIATING > FOLIATE
FOLIATION n process of producing leaves
FOLIATURE > FOLIATION
FOLIC adj as in folic acid any of a group of vitamins of the B complex
FOLIE n madness
FOLIES > FOLIE

FOLIO n sheet of paper folded in half to make two leaves of a book ▷ adj of or made in the largest book size ▷ vb number the leaves of (a book) consecutively
FOLIOED > FOLIO
FOLIOING > FOLIO
FOLIOLATE adj possessing or relating to leaflets
FOLIOLE n part of a compound leaf
FOLIOLES > FOLIOLE
FOLIOLOSE > FOLIOLE
FOLIOS > FOLIO
FOLIOSE adj (of a tree) leaf-bearing
FOLIOUS adj foliose
FOLIUM n plane geometrical curve
FOLIUMS > FOLIUM
FOLK n people in general ▷ adj traditional to the common people of a country
FOLKIE n devotee of folk music ▷ adj of or relating to folk music
FOLKIER > FOLKIE
FOLKIES > FOLKIE
FOLKIEST > FOLKIE
FOLKINESS n quality of being folky
FOLKISH > FOLK
FOLKLAND n former type of land tenure
FOLKLANDS > FOLKLAND
FOLKLIFE n traditional customs, arts, crafts, and other forms of cultural expression of a people
FOLKLIFES > FOLKLIFE
FOLKLIKE > FOLK
FOLKLIVES > FOLKLIFE
FOLKLORE n traditional beliefs and stories of a people
FOLKLORES > FOLKLORE
FOLKLORIC > FOLKLORE
FOLKMOOT n (in early medieval England) an assembly of the people of a district, town, or shire
FOLKMOOTS > FOLKMOOT
FOLKMOT same as > FOLKMOOT
FOLKMOTE same as > FOLKMOOT
FOLKMOTES > FOLKMOTE
FOLKMOTS > FOLKMOT
FOLKS > FOLK
FOLKSIER > FOLKSY
FOLKSIEST > FOLKSY
FOLKSILY > FOLKSY
FOLKSONG n traditional song
FOLKSONGS > FOLKSONG
FOLKSY adj simple and unpretentious
FOLKTALE n tale or legend from an oral tradition
FOLKTALES > FOLKTALE
FOLKWAY singular form of > FOLKWAYS
FOLKWAYS pl n traditional and customary ways of living
FOLKY same as > FOLKIE
FOLLES > FOLLIS

FOLLICLE n small cavity in the body, esp one from which a hair grows
FOLLICLES > FOLLICLE
FOLLIED > FOLLY
FOLLIES > FOLLY
FOLLIS n Roman coin
FOLLOW vb go or come after
FOLLOWED > FOLLOW
FOLLOWER n disciple or supporter
FOLLOWERS > FOLLOWER
FOLLOWING adj about to be mentioned ▷ n group of supporters ▷ prep as a result of
FOLLOWS > FOLLOW
FOLLOWUP n further action
FOLLOWUPS > FOLLOWUP
FOLLY n foolishness ▷ vb behave foolishly
FOLLYING > FOLLY
FOMENT vb encourage or stir up (trouble)
FOMENTED > FOMENT
FOMENTER > FOMENT
FOMENTERS > FOMENT
FOMENTING > FOMENT
FOMENTS > FOMENT
FOMES n any material that may harbour pathogens
FOMITE same as > FOMES
FOMITES > FOMES
FON vb compel
FOND adj tender, loving ▷ n background of a design, as in lace ▷ vb dote
FONDA n Spanish hotel
FONDANT n (sweet made from) flavoured paste of sugar and water ▷ adj (of a colour) soft
FONDANTS > FONDANT
FONDAS > FONDA
FONDED > FOND
FONDER > FOND
FONDEST > FOND
FONDING > FOND
FONDLE vb caress
FONDLED > FONDLE
FONDLER > FONDLE
FONDLERS > FONDLE
FONDLES > FONDLE
FONDLING > FONDLE
FONDLINGS > FONDLE
FONDLY > FOND
FONDNESS > FOND
FONDS > FOND
FONDU n ballet movement
FONDUE n Swiss dish ▷ vb cook and serve (food) as a fondue
FONDUED > FONDUE
FONDUEING > FONDUE
FONDUES > FONDUE
FONDUING > FONDUE
FONDUS > FONDU
FONE n informal spelling of telephone
FONES > FONE
FONLY adv foolishly
FONNED > FON
FONNING > FON
FONS > FON
FONT n bowl in a church for baptismal water
FONTAL > FONT

FONTANEL n soft membraneous gap in an infant's skull
FONTANELS > FONTANEL
FONTANGE n type of tall headdress
FONTANGES > FONTANGE
FONTICULI pl n fontanelles
FONTINA n mild Italian cheese
FONTINAS > FONTINA
FONTLET > FONT
FONTLETS > FONT
FONTS > FONT
FOO n temporary computer variable or file
FOOBAR same as > FUBAR
FOOD n what one eats; solid nourishment
FOODBANK n charity which distributes food to the needy
FOODBANKS > FOODBANK
FOODBORNE adj (of illness) caused by contaminated food
FOODERIES > FOODERY
FOODERY n restaurant
FOODFUL adj supplying abundant food
FOODIE n gourmet
FOODIES > FOODIE
FOODISM n enthusiasm for and interest in good food
FOODISMS > FOODISM
FOODLAND n land on which food is produced
FOODLANDS > FOODLAND
FOODLESS > FOOD
FOODOIR n book or blog that combines a personal memoir with recipes
FOODOIRS > FOODOIR
FOODS > FOOD
FOODSHED n the area through which food is transported from farm to consumer
FOODSHEDS > FOODSHED
FOODSTUFF n substance used as food
FOODWAYS pl n customs and traditions relating to food and its preparation
FOODY same as > FOODIE
FOOFARAW n vulgar ornamentation
FOOFARAWS > FOOFARAW
FOOL n person lacking sense or judgment ▷ vb deceive (someone)
FOOLED > FOOL
FOOLERIES > FOOLERY
FOOLERY n foolish behaviour
FOOLFISH n orange filefish or winter flounder
FOOLHARDY adj recklessly adventurous
FOOLING > FOOL
FOOLINGS > FOOL
FOOLISH adj unwise, silly, or absurd
FOOLISHER > FOOLISH
FOOLISHLY > FOOLISH
FOOLPROOF adj unable to fail
FOOLS > FOOL

FOOLSCAP n size of paper, 34.3 x 43.2 centimetres

FOOLSCAPS > FOOLSCAP

FOOS > FOO

FOOSBALL n US and Canadian name for table football

FOOSBALLS > FOOSBALL

FOOT n part of the leg below the ankle ▷ vb kick

FOOTAGE n amount of film used

FOOTAGES > FOOTAGE

FOOTBAG n type of sport

FOOTBAGS > FOOTBAG

FOOTBALL n game played by two teams kicking a ball in an attempt to score goals

FOOTBALLS > FOOTBALL

FOOTBAR n any bar used by the foot

FOOTBARS > FOOTBAR

FOOTBATH n vessel for bathing the feet

FOOTBATHS > FOOTBATH

FOOTBED n insole in a boot or shoe

FOOTBEDS > FOOTBED

FOOTBOARD n treadle or foot-operated lever on a machine

FOOTBOY n boy servant

FOOTBOYS > FOOTBOY

FOOTBRAKE n brake operated with the foot

FOOTCLOTH obsolete word for > CAPARISON

FOOTED > FOOT

FOOTER n person who goes on foot ▷ vb potter

FOOTERED > FOOTER

FOOTERING > FOOTER

FOOTERS > FOOTER

FOOTFALL n sound of a footstep

FOOTFALLS > FOOTFALL

FOOTFAULT n fault that occurs when the server fails to keep both feet behind the baseline until he/she has served

FOOTGEAR another name for > FOOTWEAR

FOOTGEARS > FOOTGEAR

FOOTHILL n lower slope of a mountain or a relatively low hill at the foot of a mountain

FOOTHILLS > FOOTHILL

FOOTHOLD n secure position from which progress may be made

FOOTHOLDS > FOOTHOLD

FOOTIE same as > FOOTY

FOOTIER > FOOTY

FOOTIES > FOOTIE

FOOTIEST > FOOTY

FOOTING n basis or foundation

FOOTINGS > FOOTING

FOOTLE vb loiter aimlessly ▷ n foolishness

FOOTLED > FOOTLE

FOOTLER > FOOTLE

FOOTLERS > FOOTLE

FOOTLES > FOOTLE

FOOTLESS > FOOT

FOOTLIGHT n light illuminating the front of a stage

FOOTLIKE > FOOT

FOOTLING adj trivial ▷ n trifle

FOOTLINGS > FOOTLING

FOOTLONG n type of extra-long frankfurter

FOOTLONGS > FOOTLONG

FOOTLOOSE adj free from ties

FOOTMAN n male servant in uniform

FOOTMARK n mark or trace of mud, wetness, etc, left by a person's foot on a surface

FOOTMARKS > FOOTMARK

FOOTMEN > FOOTMAN

FOOTMUFF n muff used to keep the feet warm

FOOTMUFFS > FOOTMUFF

FOOTNOTE n note printed at the foot of a page ▷ vb supply (a page, book, etc) with footnotes

FOOTNOTED > FOOTNOTE

FOOTNOTES > FOOTNOTE

FOOTPACE n normal or walking pace

FOOTPACES > FOOTPACE

FOOTPAD n highwayman, on foot rather than horseback

FOOTPADS > FOOTPAD

FOOTPAGE n errand-boy

FOOTPAGES > FOOTPAGE

FOOTPATH n narrow path for walkers only

FOOTPATHS > FOOTPATH

FOOTPLATE n platform in the cab of a locomotive for the driver

FOOTPOST n post delivered on foot

FOOTPOSTS > FOOTPOST

FOOTPRINT n mark left by a foot

FOOTPUMP n pump operated with the foot

FOOTPUMPS > FOOTPUMP

FOOTRA variant of > FOUTRA

FOOTRACE n race run on foot

FOOTRACES > FOOTRACE

FOOTRAS > FOOTRA

FOOTREST n something that provides a support for the feet, such as a low stool, rail, etc

FOOTRESTS > FOOTREST

FOOTROPE n part of a boltrope to which the foot of a sail is stitched

FOOTROPES > FOOTROPE

FOOTRULE n rigid measure, one foot in length

FOOTRULES > FOOTRULE

FOOTS pl n sediment that accumulates at the bottom of a vessel

FOOTSAL n type of indoor football with five players on each side

FOOTSALS > FOOTSAL

FOOTSIE n flirtation involving the touching together of feet

FOOTSIES > FOOTSIE

FOOTSLOG vb march

FOOTSLOGS > FOOTSLOG

FOOTSORE adj having sore or tired feet, esp from much walking

FOOTSTALK n small supporting stalk in animals and plants

FOOTSTALL n pedestal, plinth, or base of a column, pier, or statue

FOOTSTEP n step in walking

FOOTSTEPS > FOOTSTEP

FOOTSTOCK another name for > TAILSTOCK

FOOTSTONE n memorial stone at the foot of a grave

FOOTSTOOL n low stool used to rest the feet on while sitting

FOOTSY variant of > FOOTSIE

FOOTWALL n rocks on the lower side of an inclined fault plane or mineral vein

FOOTWALLS > FOOTWALL

FOOTWAY n way or path for pedestrians

FOOTWAYS > FOOTWAY

FOOTWEAR n anything worn to cover the feet

FOOTWEARS > FOOTWEAR

FOOTWEARY adj tired from walking

FOOTWELL n part of a car in which the foot pedals are located

FOOTWELLS > FOOTWELL

FOOTWORK n skilful use of the feet, as in sport or dancing

FOOTWORKS > FOOTWORK

FOOTWORN adj footsore

FOOTY n football ▷ adj mean

FOOZLE vb bungle (a shot) ▷ n bungled shot

FOOZLED > FOOZLE

FOOZLER > FOOZLE

FOOZLERS > FOOZLE

FOOZLES > FOOZLE

FOOZLING > FOOZLE

FOOZLINGS > FOOZLE

FOP n man excessively concerned with fashion ▷ vb act like a fop

FOPLING n vain affected dandy

FOPLINGS > FOPLING

FOPPED > FOP

FOPPERIES > FOPPERY

FOPPERY n clothes, affectations, etc, of or befitting a fop

FOPPING > FOP

FOPPISH > FOP

FOPPISHLY > FOP

FOPS > FOP

FOR prep indicating benefit, receipt, timespan, distance, etc

FORA > FORUM

FORAGE vb search about (for) ▷ n food for cattle or horses

FORAGED > FORAGE

FORAGER > FORAGE

FORAGERS > FORAGE

FORAGES > FORAGE

FORAGING > FORAGE

FORAM n marine protozoan

FORAMEN n natural hole

FORAMENS > FORAMEN

FORAMINA > FORAMEN

FORAMINAL > FORAMEN

FORAMS > FORAM

FORANE adj as in vicar forane type of Roman Catholic priest

FORASMUCH conj since

FORAY n brief raid or attack ▷ vb raid or ravage (a town, district, etc)

FORAYED > FORAY

FORAYER > FORAY

FORAYERS > FORAY

FORAYING > FORAY

FORAYS > FORAY

FORB n any herbaceous plant that is not a grass

FORBAD > FORBID

FORBADE > FORBID

FORBARE > FORBEAR

FORBEAR vb cease or refrain (from doing something)

FORBEARER > FORBEAR

FORBEARS > FORBEAR

FORBID vb prohibit, refuse to allow

FORBIDAL > FORBID

FORBIDALS > FORBIDAL

FORBIDDAL n prohibition

FORBIDDEN adj not permitted by order or law

FORBIDDER > FORBID

FORBIDS > FORBID

FORBODE vb obsolete word meaning forbid ▷ n obsolete word meaning forbidding

FORBODED > FORBODE

FORBODES > FORBODE

FORBODING > FORBODE

FORBORE past tense of > FORBEAR

FORBORNE > FORBEAR

FORBS > FORB

FORBY adv besides

FORBYE same as > FORBY

FORCAT n convict or galley slave

FORCATS > FORCAT

FORCE n strength or power ▷ vb compel, make (someone) do something

FORCEABLE > FORCE

FORCEABLY adv in a forcible manner

FORCED adj compulsory

FORCEDLY > FORCED

FORCEFUL adj emphatic and confident

FORCELESS > FORCE

FORCEMEAT n mixture of chopped ingredients used for stuffing

FORCEOUT n play in baseball in which a runner is forced to run to next base and is put out

FORCEOUTS > FORCEOUT

FORCEPS pl n surgical pincers

FORCEPSES > FORCEPS

FORCER > FORCE

FORCERS > FORCE

FORCES > FORCE

FORCIBLE *adj* involving physical force or violence

FORCIBLY > FORCIBLE

FORCING > FORCE

FORCINGLY > FORCE

FORCIPATE > FORCEPS

FORCIPES > FORCEPS

FORD *n* shallow place where a river may be crossed ▷ *vb* cross (a river) at a ford

FORDABLE > FORD

FORDED > FORD

FORDID > FORDO

FORDING > FORD

FORDLESS > FORD

FORDO *vb* destroy

FORDOES > FORDO

FORDOING > FORDO

FORDONE > FORDO

FORDONNE *vb* as in *from fordonne* fordone

FORDS > FORD

FORE *adj* in, at, or towards the front ▷ *n* front part ▷ *interj* golfer's shouted warning

FOREANENT *prep* opposite

FOREARM *n* arm from the wrist to the elbow ▷ *vb* prepare beforehand

FOREARMED > FOREARM

FOREARMS > FOREARM

FOREBAY *n* reservoir or canal

FOREBAYS > FOREBAY

FOREBEAR *n* ancestor

FOREBEARS > FOREBEAR

FOREBITT *n* post at a ship's foremast for securing cables

FOREBITTS > FOREBITT

FOREBODE *vb* warn of or indicate (an event, result, etc) in advance

FOREBODED > FOREBODE

FOREBODER > FOREBODE

FOREBODES > FOREBODE

FOREBODY *n* part of a ship forward of the foremast

FOREBOOM *n* boom of a foremast

FOREBOOMS > FOREBOOM

FOREBRAIN *n* the part of the brain that develops from the anterior portion of the neural tube

FOREBY *variant of* **>** FORBY

FOREBYE *variant of* **>** FORBY

FORECABIN *n* forward cabin on a vessel

FORECADDY *n* caddy who goes ahead of the golfer to point out the ball's location

FORECAR *n* vehicle attached to a motorcycle

FORECARS > FORECAR

FORECAST *vb* predict (weather, events, etc) ▷ *n* prediction

FORECASTS > FORECAST

FORECHECK *vb* in ice-hockey, to try to gain control of the puck while at opponents' end of rink

FORECLOSE *vb* take possession of (property bought with borrowed money which has not been repaid)

FORECLOTH *n* cloth hung over the front of something, especially an altar

FORECOURT *n* courtyard or open space in front of a building

FOREDATE *vb* antedate

FOREDATED > FOREDATE

FOREDATES > FOREDATE

FOREDECK *n* deck between the bridge and the forecastle

FOREDECKS > FOREDECK

FOREDID > FOREDO

FOREDO *same as* **>** FORDO

FOREDOES > FOREDO

FOREDOING > FOREDO

FOREDONE > FOREDO

FOREDOOM *vb* doom or condemn beforehand

FOREDOOMS > FOREDOOM

FOREFACE *n* muzzle of an animal

FOREFACES > FOREFACE

FOREFEEL *vb* have a premonition of

FOREFEELS > FOREFEEL

FOREFEET > FOREFOOT

FOREFELT > FOREFEEL

FOREFEND *same as* **>** FORFEND

FOREFENDS > FOREFEND

FOREFOOT *n* either of the front feet of an animal

FOREFRONT *n* most active or prominent position

FOREGLEAM *n* early or premonitory inkling or indication

FOREGO *same as* **>** FORGO

FOREGOER > FOREGO

FOREGOERS > FOREGO

FOREGOES > FOREGO

FOREGOING *adj* going before, preceding

FOREGONE *adj* gone or completed

FOREGUT *n* anterior part of the digestive tract of vertebrates

FOREGUTS > FOREGUT

FOREHAND *n* stroke played with the palm of the hand facing forward ▷ *adj* (of a stroke) made with the wrist facing the direction of play ▷ *adv* with a forehand stroke ▷ *vb* play (a shot) forehand

FOREHANDS > FOREHAND

FOREHEAD *n* part of the face above the eyebrows

FOREHEADS > FOREHEAD

FOREHENT *vb* seize in advance

FOREHENTS > FOREHENT

FOREHOCK *n* foreleg cut of bacon or pork

FOREHOCKS > FOREHOCK

FOREHOOF *n* front hoof

FOREHOOFS > FOREHOOF

FOREIGN *adj* not of, or in, one's own country

FOREIGNER *n* person from a foreign country

FOREIGNLY > FOREIGN

FOREJUDGE *same as* **>** FORJUDGE

FOREKING *n* previous king

FOREKINGS > FOREKING

FOREKNEW > FOREKNOW

FOREKNOW *vb* know in advance

FOREKNOWN > FOREKNOW

FOREKNOWS > FOREKNOW

FOREL *vb* cover (a book) with parchment

FORELADY *n* forewoman of a jury

FORELAID > FORELAY

FORELAIN > FORELIE

FORELAND *n* headland, cape, or coastal promontory

FORELANDS > FORELAND

FORELAY *archaic word for* **>** AMBUSH

FORELAYS > FORELAY

FORELEG *n* either of the front legs of an animal

FORELEGS > FORELEG

FORELEND *vb* give up

FORELENDS > FORELEND

FORELENT > FORELEND

FORELIE *vb* lie in front of

FORELIES > FORELIE

FORELIFT *vb* lift up in front

FORELIFTS > FORELIFT

FORELIMB *n* front or anterior limb

FORELIMBS > FORELIMB

FORELLED > FOREL

FORELLING > FOREL

FORELOCK *n* lock of hair over the forehead ▷ *vb* secure (a bolt) by means of a forelock

FORELOCKS > FORELOCK

FORELS > FOREL

FORELYING > FORELIE

FOREMAN *n* person in charge of a group of workers

FOREMAST *n* mast nearest the bow of a ship

FOREMASTS > FOREMAST

FOREMEAN *vb* intend in advance

FOREMEANS > FOREMEAN

FOREMEANT > FOREMEAN

FOREMEN > FOREMAN

FOREMILK *n* first milk drawn from a cow's udder prior to milking

FOREMILKS > FOREMILK

FOREMOST *adv* first in time, place, or importance ▷ *adj* first in time, place, or importance

FORENAME *n* first name

FORENAMED *adj* named or mentioned previously

FORENAMES > FORENAME

FORENIGHT *n* evening

FORENOON *n* morning

FORENOONS > FORENOON

FORENSIC *adj* used in or connected with courts of law

FORENSICS *n* art or study of formal debating

FOREPART *n* first or front part in place, order, or time

FOREPARTS > FOREPART

FOREPAST *adj* bygone

FOREPAW *n* either of the front feet of a land mammal

FOREPAWS > FOREPAW

FOREPEAK *n* interior part of a vessel that is furthest forward

FOREPEAKS > FOREPEAK

FOREPLAN *vb* plan in advance

FOREPLANS > FOREPLAN

FOREPLAY *n* sexual stimulation before intercourse

FOREPLAYS > FOREPLAY

FOREPOINT *vb* predetermine or indicate in advance

FORERAN > FORERUN

FORERANK *n* first rank

FORERANKS > FORERANK

FOREREACH *vb* keep moving under momentum without engine or sails

FOREREAD *vb* foretell

FOREREADS > FOREREAD

FORERUN *vb* serve as a herald for

FORERUNS > FORERUN

FORES > FORE

FORESAID *less common word for* **>** AFORESAID

FORESAIL *n* main sail on the foremast of a ship

FORESAILS > FORESAIL

FORESAW > FORESEE

FORESAY *vb* foretell

FORESAYS > FORESAY

FORESEE *vb* see or know beforehand

FORESEEN > FORESEE

FORESEER > FORESEE

FORESEERS > FORESEE

FORESEES > FORESEE

FORESHANK *n* top of the front leg of an animal

FORESHEET *n* sheet of a foresail

FORESHEW *variant of* **>** FORESHOW

FORESHEWN > FORESHEW

FORESHEWS > FORESHEW

FORESHIP *n* fore part of a ship

FORESHIPS > FORESHIP

FORESHOCK *n* relatively small earthquake heralding the arrival of a much larger one. Some large earthquakes are preceded by a series of foreshocks

FORESHORE *n* part of the shore between high- and low-tide marks

FORESHOW *vb* indicate in advance

FORESHOWN > FORESHOW

FORESHOWS > FORESHOW

FORESIDE *n* front or upper side or part

FORESIDES > FORESIDE

FORESIGHT *n* ability to anticipate and provide for future needs

FORESKIN *n* fold of skin covering the tip of the penis

FORESKINS > FORESKIN

FORESKIRT *n* front skirt of a garment (as opposed to the train)

FORESLACK *variant of* **>** FORSLACK

FORESLOW *variant of* > FORSLOW

FORESLOWS > FORESLOW

FORESPAKE > FORESPEAK

FORESPEAK *vb* predict

FORESPEND *variant of* > FORSPEND

FORESPENT > FORESPEND

FORESPOKE > FORESPEAK

FOREST *n* large area with a thick growth of trees ▷ *vb* create a forest (in)

FORESTAGE *n* part of a stage in front of the curtain

FORESTAIR *n* external stair

FORESTAL > FOREST

FORESTALL *vb* prevent or guard against in advance

FORESTAY *n* adjustable stay used on ships

FORESTAYS > FORESTAY

FORESTEAL > FOREST

FORESTED > FOREST

FORESTER *n* person skilled in forestry

FORESTERS > FORESTER

FORESTIAL > FOREST

FORESTINE > FOREST

FORESTING > FOREST

FORESTRY *n* science of planting and caring for trees

FORESTS > FOREST

FORESWEAR *vb* forgo

FORESWORE > FORESWEAR

FORESWORN > FORESWEAR

FORETASTE *n* early limited experience of something to come ▷ *vb* have a foretaste of

FORETEACH *vb* teach beforehand

FORETEETH > FORETOOTH

FORETELL *vb* tell or indicate beforehand

FORETELLS > FORETELL

FORETHINK *vb* have prescience

FORETIME *n* time already gone

FORETIMES > FORETIME

FORETOKEN *n* sign of a future event ▷ *vb* foreshadow

FORETOLD > FORETELL

FORETOOTH *another word for an* > INCISOR

FORETOP *n* platform at the top of the foremast

FORETOPS > FORETOP

FOREVER *adv* without end ▷ *n* very long time

FOREVERS > FOREVER

FOREWARD *n* vanguard ▷ *vb* guard (something) in front

FOREWARDS > FOREWARD

FOREWARN *vb* warn beforehand

FOREWARNS > FOREWARN

FOREWEIGH *vb* assess in advance

FOREWENT *past tense of* > FOREGO

FOREWIND *n* favourable wind

FOREWINDS > FOREWIND

FOREWING *n* either wing of the anterior pair of an insect's two pairs of wings

FOREWINGS > FOREWING

FOREWOMAN *n* woman in charge of a group of workers

FOREWOMEN > FOREWOMAN

FOREWORD *n* introduction to a book

FOREWORDS > FOREWORD

FOREWORN *same as* > FORWORN

FOREX *n* foreign exchange

FOREXES > FOREX

FOREYARD *n* yard for supporting the foresail of a square-rigger

FOREYARDS > FOREYARD

FORFAIR *vb* perish

FORFAIRED > FORFAIR

FORFAIRN *adj* worn out

FORFAIRS > FORFAIR

FORFAITER *n* someone who purchases receivables from exporters

FORFAULT *variant of* > FORFEIT

FORFAULTS > FORFAULT

FORFEIT *n* thing lost or given up as a penalty for a fault or mistake ▷ *vb* lose as a forfeit ▷ *adj* lost as a forfeit

FORFEITED > FORFEIT

FORFEITER > FORFEIT

FORFEITS > FORFEIT

FORFEND *vb* protect or secure

FORFENDED > FORFEND

FORFENDS > FORFEND

FORFEX *n* pair of pincers, esp the paired terminal appendages of an earwig

FORFEXES > FORFEX

FORFICATE *adj* (esp of the tails of certain birds) deeply forked

FORFOCHEN *Scots word for* > EXHAUSTED

FORGAT *past tense of* > FORGET

FORGATHER *vb* gather together

FORGAVE > FORGIVE

FORGE *n* place where metal is worked, smithy ▷ *vb* make a fraudulent imitation of (something)

FORGEABLE > FORGE

FORGED > FORGE

FORGEMAN > FORGE

FORGEMEN > FORGE

FORGER > FORGE

FORGERIES > FORGERY

FORGERS > FORGE

FORGERY *n* illegal copy of something

FORGES > FORGE

FORGET *vb* fail to remember

FORGETFUL *adj* tending to forget

FORGETIVE *adj* imaginative and inventive

FORGETS > FORGET

FORGETTER > FORGET

FORGING *n* process of producing a metal component by hammering

FORGINGS > FORGING

FORGIVE *vb* cease to blame or hold resentment against, pardon

FORGIVEN > FORGIVE

FORGIVER > FORGIVE

FORGIVERS > FORGIVE

FORGIVES > FORGIVE

FORGIVING *adj* willing to forgive

FORGO *vb* do without or give up

FORGOER > FORGO

FORGOERS > FORGO

FORGOES > FORGO

FORGOING > FORGO

FORGONE > FORGO

FORGOT *past tense of* > FORGET

FORGOTTEN *past participle of* > FORGET

FORHAILE *vb* distress

FORHAILED > FORHAILE

FORHAILES > FORHAILE

FORHENT *variant of* > FOREHENT

FORHENTS > FORHENT

FORHOO *vb* forsake

FORHOOED > FORHOO

FORHOOIE *variant of* > FORHOO

FORHOOIED > FORHOOIE

FORHOOIES > FORHOOIE

FORHOOING > FORHOO

FORHOOS > FORHOO

FORHOW *variant of* > FORHOO

FORHOWED > FORHOW

FORHOWING > FORHOW

FORHOWS > FORHOW

FORINSEC *adj* foreign

FORINT *n* standard monetary unit of Hungary

FORINTS > FORINT

FORJASKIT *adj* exhausted

FORJESKIT *variant of* > FORJASKIT

FORJUDGE *vb* deprive of a right by the judgment of a court

FORJUDGED > FORJUDGE

FORJUDGES > FORJUDGE

FORK *n* tool for eating food ▷ *vb* pick up, dig, etc with a fork

FORKBALL *n* method of pitching in baseball

FORKBALLS > FORKBALL

FORKED *adj* having a fork or forklike parts

FORKEDLY > FORKED

FORKER > FORK

FORKERS > FORK

FORKFUL > FORK

FORKFULS > FORK

FORKHEAD *n* forked head of a rod

FORKHEADS > FORKHEAD

FORKIER > FORKY

FORKIEST > FORKY

FORKINESS > FORKY

FORKING > FORK

FORKLESS > FORK

FORKLIFT *n* vehicle for loading goods on wooden pallets

FORKLIFTS > FORKLIFT

FORKLIKE > FORK

FORKS > FORK

FORKSFUL > FORK

FORKTAIL *n* bird belonging to the flycatcher family

FORKTAILS > FORKTAIL

FORKY *adj* forked

FORLANA *n* Venetian dance

FORLANAS > FORLANA

FORLEND *variant of* > FORELEND

FORLENDS > FORLEND

FORLENT > FORLEND

FORLESE *vb* lose, forsake

FORLESES > FORLESE

FORLESING > FORLESE

FORLORE > FORLESE

FORLORN *adj* lonely and unhappy ▷ *n* forsaken person

FORLORNER > FORLORN

FORLORNLY > FORLORN

FORLORNS > FORLORN

FORM *n* shape or appearance ▷ *vb* give a (particular) shape to or take a (particular) shape

FORMABLE > FORM

FORMABLY > FORM

FORMAL *adj* of or characterized by conventions of behaviour ▷ *n* woman's evening gown

FORMALIN *n* solution of formaldehyde in water

FORMALINE *n* forty per cent solution of formaldehyde in water, used as a disinfectant

FORMALINS > FORMALIN

FORMALISE *same as* > FORMALIZE

FORMALISM *n* concern with outward appearances and structure at the expense of content

FORMALIST > FORMALISM

FORMALITY *n* requirement of custom or etiquette

FORMALIZE *vb* make official or formal

FORMALLY > FORMAL

FORMALS > FORMAL

FORMAMIDE *n* amide derived from formic acid

FORMANT *n* any of several frequency ranges

FORMANTS > FORMANT

FORMAT *n* size and shape of a publication ▷ *vb* arrange in a format

FORMATE *n* type of salt or ester of formic acid ▷ *vb* fly aircraft in formation

FORMATED > FORMAT

FORMATES > FORMATE

FORMATING > FORMAT

FORMATION *n* forming

FORMATIVE *adj* of or relating to development ▷ *n* inflectional or derivational affix

FORMATS > FORMAT

FORMATTED > FORMAT

FORMATTER > FORMAT

FORME *n* type matter assembled and ready for printing

FORMED > FORM

FORMEE *n* type of heraldic cross

FORMEES > FORMEE

f

FORMER adj of an earlier time, previous ▷ n person or thing that forms or shapes
FORMERLY adv in the past
FORMERS > FORMER
FORMES > FORME
FORMFUL adj imaginative
FORMIATE variant of > FORMATE
FORMIATES > FORMIATE
FORMIC adj of, relating to, or derived from ants
FORMICA n tradename for any of various laminated plastic sheets
FORMICANT adj low-tension (of pulse)
FORMICARY n ant hill
FORMICAS > FORMICA
FORMICATE vb crawl around like ants
FORMING > FORM
FORMINGS > FORM
FORMLESS adj without a definite shape or form
FORMOL same as > FORMALIN
FORMOLS > FORMOL
FORMS > FORM
FORMULA n written form of a scientific or mathematical rule
FORMULAE > FORMULA
FORMULAIC > FORMULA
FORMULAR adj of or relating to formulas ▷ n model or set form
FORMULARS > FORMULAR
FORMULARY n book of prescribed formulas ▷ adj of, relating to, or of the nature of a formula
FORMULAS > FORMULA
FORMULATE vb plan or describe precisely and clearly
FORMULISE vb express in a formula
FORMULISM n adherence to or belief in formulas
FORMULIST > FORMULISM
FORMULIZE variant of > FORMULISE
FORMWORK n arrangement of wooden boards to shape concrete
FORMWORKS > FORMWORK
FORMYL n the monovalent group CHO-
FORMYLS > FORMYL
FORNENST prep situated against or facing towards
FORNENT variant of > FORNENST
FORNICAL > FORNIX
FORNICATE vb have sexual intercourse without being married ▷ adj arched or hoodlike in form
FORNICES > FORNIX
FORNIX n any archlike structure
FORPET n quarter of a peck (measure)
FORPETS > FORPET
FORPINE vb waste away
FORPINED > FORPINE
FORPINES > FORPINE

FORPINING > FORPINE
FORPIT variant of > FORPET
FORPITS > FORPIT
FORRAD adv forward ▷ n forward
FORRADER > FORRAD
FORRADS > FORRAD
FORRARDER adv further forward
FORRAY archaic variant of > FORAY
FORRAYED > FORRAY
FORRAYING > FORRAY
FORRAYS > FORRAY
FORREN adj foreign
FORRIT adv forward(s)
FORSAID > FORSAY
FORSAKE vb withdraw support or friendship from
FORSAKEN adj completely deserted or helpless
FORSAKER > FORSAKE
FORSAKERS > FORSAKE
FORSAKES > FORSAKE
FORSAKING > FORSAKE
FORSAY vb renounce
FORSAYING > FORSAY
FORSAYS > FORSAY
FORSLACK vb be neglectful
FORSLACKS > FORSLACK
FORSLOE variant of > FORSLOW
FORSLOED > FORSLOE
FORSLOES > FORSLOE
FORSLOW vb hinder
FORSLOWED > FORSLOW
FORSLOWS > FORSLOW
FORSOOK past tense of > FORSAKE
FORSOOTH adv indeed
FORSPEAK vb bewitch
FORSPEAKS > FORSPEAK
FORSPEND vb exhaust
FORSPENDS > FORSPEND
FORSPENT > FORSPEND
FORSPOKE > FORSPEAK
FORSPOKEN > FORSPEAK
FORSWATT adj sweat-covered
FORSWEAR vb renounce or reject
FORSWEARS > FORSWEAR
FORSWINK vb exhaust through toil
FORSWINKS > FORSWINK
FORSWONCK variant of > FORSWUNK
FORSWORE > FORSWEAR
FORSWORN past participle of > FORSWEAR
FORSWUNK adj overworked
FORSYTHIA n shrub with yellow flowers in spring
FORT n fortified building or place ▷ vb fortify
FORTALICE n small fort or outwork of a fortification
FORTE n thing at which a person excels ▷ adv loudly
FORTED > FORT
FORTES > FORTIS
FORTH adv forwards, out, or away ▷ prep out of
FORTHCAME > FORTHCOME
FORTHCOME vb come forth
FORTHINK vb regret

FORTHINKS > FORTHINK
FORTHWITH adv at once
FORTHY adv therefore
FORTIES > FORTY
FORTIETH adj being the number of forty in order ▷ n one of 40 equal parts
FORTIETHS > FORTIETH
FORTIFIED > FORTIFY
FORTIFIER > FORTIFY
FORTIFIES > FORTIFY
FORTIFY vb make (a place) defensible, as by building walls
FORTILAGE n small fort
FORTING > FORT
FORTIS adj (of a consonant) articulated with considerable muscular tension ▷ n type of consonantal pronunciation
FORTITUDE n courage in adversity or pain
FORTLET > FORT
FORTLETS > FORT
FORTNIGHT n two weeks
FORTRESS n large fort or fortified town ▷ vb protect with or as if with a fortress
FORTS > FORT
FORTUITY n chance or accidental occurrence
FORTUNATE adj having good luck
FORTUNE n luck, esp when favourable ▷ vb befall
FORTUNED > FORTUNE
FORTUNES > FORTUNE
FORTUNING > FORTUNE
FORTUNISE same as > FORTUNIZE
FORTUNIZE vb make happy
FORTY n four times ten
FORTYFOLD adj multiplied forty times
FORTYISH > FORTY
FORUM n meeting or medium for open discussion or debate
FORUMS > FORUM
FORWANDER vb wander far
FORWARD same as > FORWARDS
FORWARDED > FORWARD
FORWARDER n person or thing that forwards
FORWARDLY > FORWARD
FORWARDS adv towards or at a place further ahead in space or time
FORWARN archaic word for > FORBID
FORWARNED > FORWARN
FORWARNS > FORWARN
FORWASTE vb lay waste
FORWASTED > FORWASTE
FORWASTES > FORWASTE
FORWEARY vb exhaust
FORWENT past tense of > FORGO
FORWHY adv for what reason
FORWORN adj weary
FORZA n force
FORZANDI > FORZANDO
FORZANDO another word for > SFORZANDO
FORZANDOS > FORZANDO
FORZATI > FORZATO

FORZATO variant of > FORZANDO
FORZATOS > FORZATO
FORZE > FORZA
FOSCARNET n antiviral medication
FOSS same as > FOSSE
FOSSA n anatomical depression, trench, or hollow area
FOSSAE > FOSSA
FOSSAS > FOSSA
FOSSATE adj having cavities or depressions
FOSSE n ditch or moat, esp one dug as a fortification
FOSSED adj having a ditch or moat
FOSSES > FOSSE
FOSSETTE n small depression or fossa, as in a bone
FOSSETTES > FOSSETTE
FOSSICK vb search, esp for gold or precious stones
FOSSICKED > FOSSICK
FOSSICKER > FOSSICK
FOSSICKS > FOSSICK
FOSSIL n hardened remains of an animal or plant preserved in rock ▷ adj of, like, or being a fossil
FOSSILISE same as > FOSSILIZE
FOSSILIZE vb turn into a fossil
FOSSILS > FOSSIL
FOSSOR n grave digger
FOSSORIAL adj (of the forelimbs and skeleton of burrowing animals) adapted for digging
FOSSORS > FOSSOR
FOSSULA n small fossa
FOSSULAE > FOSSULA
FOSSULATE adj hollowed
FOSTER vb promote the growth or development of ▷ adj of or involved in fostering a child
FOSTERAGE n act of caring for or bringing up a foster child
FOSTERED > FOSTER
FOSTERER > FOSTER
FOSTERERS > FOSTER
FOSTERING > FOSTER
FOSTERS > FOSTER
FOSTRESS n female fosterer
FOTHER vb stop a leak in a ship's hull
FOTHERED > FOTHER
FOTHERING > FOTHER
FOTHERS > FOTHER
FOU adj full ▷ n bushel
FOUAT n succulent pink-flowered plant
FOUATS > FOUAT
FOUD n sheriff in Orkney and Shetland
FOUDRIE n foud's district or office
FOUDRIES > FOUDRIE
FOUDS > FOUD
FOUER > FOU
FOUEST > FOU
FOUET n archaic word for a whip

FOUETS > FOUET

FOUETTE n step in ballet

FOUETTES > FOUETTE

FOUGADE n booby-trapped pit or type of mine

FOUGADES > FOUGADE

FOUGASSE n type of bread made with olive oil

FOUGASSES > FOUGASSE

FOUGHT > FIGHT

FOUGHTEN > FIGHT

FOUGHTIER > FOUGHTY

FOUGHTY adj musty

FOUL adj loathsome or offensive ▷ n violation of the rules ▷ vb make dirty or polluted

FOULARD n soft light fabric

FOULARDS > FOULARD

FOULBROOD n disease of honeybees

FOULDER vb flash like lightning

FOULDERED > FOULDER

FOULDERS > FOULDER

FOULE n type of woollen cloth

FOULED > FOUL

FOULER > FOUL

FOULES > FOULE

FOULEST > FOUL

FOULIE n bad mood

FOULIES > FOULIE

FOULING > FOUL

FOULINGS > FOUL

FOULLY > FOUL

FOULMART n polecat

FOULMARTS > FOULMART

FOULNESS n state or quality of being foul

FOULS > FOUL

FOUMART former name for the **>** POLECAT

FOUMARTS > FOUMART

FOUND vb set up or establish (an institution, etc)

FOUNDED > FOUND

FOUNDER vb break down or fail ▷ n person who establishes an institution, etc

FOUNDERED > FOUNDER

FOUNDERS > FOUNDER

FOUNDING > FOUND

FOUNDINGS > FOUND

FOUNDLING n abandoned baby

FOUNDRESS > FOUNDER

FOUNDRIES > FOUNDRY

FOUNDRY n place where metal is melted and cast

FOUNDS > FOUND

FOUNT same as **>** FONT

FOUNTAIN n jet of water

FOUNTAINS > FOUNTAIN

FOUNTFUL adj full of springs

FOUNTS > FOUNT

FOUR n one more than three

FOURBALL n type of golf match for two pairs

FOURBALLS > FOURBALL

FOURCHEE n type of heraldic cross

FOURCHEES > FOURCHEE

FOUREYED adj wearing spectacles

FOURFOLD adj having four times as many or as much ▷ adv by four times as many or as much

FOURGON n long covered wagon

FOURGONS > FOURGON

FOURPENCE n former English silver coin then worth four pennies

FOURPENNY adj blow, esp with the fist

FOURPLAY n supply of television, internet, landline and mobile phone services by one provider

FOURPLAYS > FOURPLAY

FOURPLEX n building that contains four separate dwellings

FOURS > FOUR

FOURSCORE adj eighty

FOURSES n snack eaten at four o'clock

FOURSOME n group of four people

FOURSOMES > FOURSOME

FOURTEEN n four and ten

FOURTEENS > FOURTEEN

FOURTH n number four in a series ▷ adj of or being number four in a series

FOURTHLY > FOURTH

FOURTHS > FOURTH

FOUS > FOU

FOUSSA n Madagascan civet-like animal

FOUSSAS > FOUSSA

FOUSTIER > FOUSTY

FOUSTIEST > FOUSTY

FOUSTY archaic variant of **>** FUSTY

FOUTER same as **>** FOOTER

FOUTERED > FOUTER

FOUTERING > FOUTER

FOUTERS > FOUTER

FOUTH n abundance

FOUTHS > FOUTH

FOUTRA n fig; expression of contempt

FOUTRAS > FOUTRA

FOUTRE vb footer

FOUTRED > FOUTRE

FOUTRES > FOUTRE

FOUTRING > FOUTRE

FOVEA n any small pit in the surface of a bodily organ or part

FOVEAE > FOVEA

FOVEAL > FOVEA

FOVEAS > FOVEA

FOVEATE > FOVEA

FOVEATED > FOVEA

FOVEIFORM adj shaped like small pit

FOVEOLA n small fovea

FOVEOLAE > FOVEOLA

FOVEOLAR > FOVEOLA

FOVEOLAS > FOVEOLA

FOVEOLATE > FOVEOLA

FOVEOLE same as **>** FOVEOLA

FOVEOLES > FOVEOLE

FOVEOLET same as **>** FOVEOLA

FOVEOLETS > FOVEOLET

FOWL n domestic cock or hen ▷ vb hunt or snare wild birds

FOWLED > FOWL

FOWLER > FOWLING

FOWLERS > FOWLING

FOWLING n shooting or trapping of birds for sport or as a livelihood

FOWLINGS > FOWLING

FOWLPOX n viral infection of poultry and other birds

FOWLPOXES > FOWLPOX

FOWLS > FOWL

FOWTH variant of **>** FOUTH

FOWTHS > FOWTH

FOX n reddish-brown bushy-tailed animal of the dog family ▷ vb perplex or deceive

FOXBERRY n lingonberry

FOXED > FOX

FOXES > FOX

FOXFIRE n glow emitted by certain fungi

FOXFIRES > FOXFIRE

FOXFISH n type of shark

FOXFISHES > FOXFISH

FOXGLOVE n tall plant with purple or white flowers

FOXGLOVES > FOXGLOVE

FOXHOLE n small pit dug for protection

FOXHOLES > FOXHOLE

FOXHOUND n dog bred for hunting foxes

FOXHOUNDS > FOXHOUND

FOXHUNT n hunting of foxes with hounds ▷ vb hunt foxes with hounds

FOXHUNTED > FOXHUNT

FOXHUNTER > FOXHUNT

FOXHUNTS > FOXHUNT

FOXIE n fox terrier

FOXIER > FOXY

FOXIES > FOXIE

FOXIEST > FOXY

FOXILY > FOXY

FOXINESS > FOXY

FOXING n piece of leather used on part of the upper of a shoe

FOXINGS > FOXING

FOXLIKE > FOX

FOXSHARK n thresher shark

FOXSHARKS > FOXSHARK

FOXSHIP n cunning

FOXSHIPS > FOXSHIP

FOXSKIN adj made from the skin of a fox ▷ n skin of a fox

FOXSKINS > FOXSKIN

FOXTAIL n type of grass

FOXTAILS > FOXTAIL

FOXTROT n ballroom dance with slow and quick steps ▷ vb perform this dance

FOXTROTS > FOXTROT

FOXY adj of or like a fox, esp in craftiness

FOY n loyalty

FOYBOAT n small rowing boat

FOYBOATS > FOYBOAT

FOYER n entrance hall in a theatre, cinema, or hotel

FOYERS > FOYER

FOYLE variant of **>** FOIL

FOYLED > FOYLE

FOYLES > FOYLE

FOYLING > FOYLE

FOYNE variant of **>** FOIN

FOYNED > FOYNE

FOYNES > FOYNE

FOYNING > FOYNE

FOYS > FOY

FOZIER > FOZY

FOZIEST > FOZY

FOZINESS > FOZY

FOZY adj spongy

FRA n brother: a title given to an Italian monk or friar

FRAB vb nag

FRABBED > FRAB

FRABBING > FRAB

FRABBIT adj peevish

FRABJOUS adj splendid

FRABS > FRAB

FRACAS n noisy quarrel

FRACASES > FRACAS

FRACK adj bold ▷ vb release oil or gas from rock by fracking

FRACKED > FRACK

FRACKER n individual or company which engages in fracking

FRACKERS > FRACKER

FRACKING n method of releasing oil or gas from rock

FRACKINGS > FRACKING

FRACKS > FRACK

FRACT vb break

FRACTAL n mathematically repeating structure ▷ adj of, relating to, or involving such a process

FRACTALS > FRACTAL

FRACTED > FRACT

FRACTI > FRACTUS

FRACTING > FRACT

FRACTION n numerical quantity that is not a whole number ▷ vb divide

FRACTIONS > FRACTION

FRACTIOUS adj easily upset and angered

FRACTS > FRACT

FRACTUR variant of **>** FRAKTUR

FRACTURAL > FRACTURE

FRACTURE n breaking, esp of a bone ▷ vb break

FRACTURED > FRACTURE

FRACTURER > FRACTURE

FRACTURES > FRACTURE

FRACTURS > FRACTUR

FRACTUS n ragged-shaped cloud formation

FRAE Scot word for **>** FROM

FRAENA > FRAENUM

FRAENUM n fold of membrane or skin that supports an organ

FRAENUMS > FRAENUM

FRAG vb kill or wound (a fellow soldier or superior officer) deliberately

FRAGGED > FRAG

FRAGGING > FRAG

FRAGGINGS > FRAG

FRAGILE adj easily broken or damaged

FRAGILELY > FRAGILE

FRAGILER > FRAGILE

FRAGILEST > FRAGILE

FRAGILITY > FRAGILE

f

FRAGMENT *n* piece broken off ▷ *vb* break into pieces
FRAGMENTS > FRAGMENT
FRAGOR *n* sudden sound
FRAGORS > FRAGOR
FRAGRANCE *n* pleasant smell
FRAGRANCY *same as* > FRAGRANCE
FRAGRANT *adj* sweet-smelling
FRAGS > FRAG
FRAICHEUR *n* freshness
FRAIL *adj* physically weak ▷ *n* rush basket for figs or raisins
FRAILER > FRAIL
FRAILEST > FRAIL
FRAILISH > FRAIL
FRAILLY > FRAIL
FRAILNESS > FRAIL
FRAILS > FRAIL
FRAILTEE *variant of* > FRAILTY
FRAILTEES > FRAILTEE
FRAILTIES > FRAILTY
FRAILTY *n* physical or moral weakness
FRAIM *n* stranger
FRAIMS > FRAIM
FRAISE *n* neck ruff worn during the 16th century ▷ *vb* provide a rampart with a palisade
FRAISED > FRAISE
FRAISES > FRAISE
FRAISING > FRAISE
FRAKTUR *n* style of typeface
FRAKTURS > FRAKTUR
FRAMABLE > FRAME
FRAMBESIA *n* infectious disease
FRAMBOISE *n* brandy distilled from raspberries in the Alsace-Lorraine region
FRAME *n* structure giving shape or support ▷ *vb* put together, construct
FRAMEABLE > FRAME
FRAMED > FRAME
FRAMELESS > FRAME
FRAMER > FRAME
FRAMERS > FRAME
FRAMES > FRAME
FRAMEWORK *n* supporting structure
FRAMING *n* frame, framework, or system of frames
FRAMINGS > FRAMING
FRAMPAL *same as* > FRAMPOLD
FRAMPLER *n* quarrelsome person
FRAMPLERS > FRAMPLER
FRAMPOLD *adj* peevish
FRANC *n* monetary unit
FRANCHISE *n* right to vote ▷ *vb* grant (a person, firm, etc) a franchise
FRANCISE *same as* > FRANCIZE
FRANCISED > FRANCISE
FRANCISES > FRANCISE
FRANCIUM *n* radioactive metallic element
FRANCIUMS > FRANCIUM

FRANCIZE *vb* make French
FRANCIZED > FRANCIZE
FRANCIZES > FRANCIZE
FRANCO *adj* post-free
FRANCOLIN *n* African or Asian partridge
FRANCS > FRANC
FRANGER *n* condom
FRANGERS > FRANGER
FRANGIBLE *adj* breakable or fragile
FRANGLAIS *n* informal French containing a high proportion of words of English origin
FRANION *n* lover, paramour
FRANIONS > FRANION
FRANK *adj* honest and straightforward in speech or attitude ▷ *n* official mark on a letter permitting delivery ▷ *vb* put such a mark on (a letter)
FRANKABLE > FRANK
FRANKED > FRANK
FRANKER > FRANK
FRANKERS > FRANK
FRANKEST > FRANK
FRANKFORT *same as* > FRANKFURT
FRANKFURT *n* light brown smoked sausage
FRANKING > FRANK
FRANKLIN *n* (in 14th- and 15th-century England) a landholder of free but not noble birth
FRANKLINS > FRANKLIN
FRANKLY *adv* in truth
FRANKNESS > FRANK
FRANKS > FRANK
FRANKUM *n* spruce resin
FRANKUMS > FRANKUM
FRANSERIA *n* American shrub
FRANTIC *adj* distracted with rage, grief, joy, etc
FRANTICLY > FRANTIC
FRANZIER > FRANZY
FRANZIEST > FRANZY
FRANZY *adj* irritable
FRAP *vb* lash down or together
FRAPE *adj* tightly bound ▷ *vb* alter information on a person's social networking profile
FRAPEAGE *n* act of altering information on a person's social networking profile
FRAPEAGES > FRAPEAGE
FRAPED > FRAPE
FRAPES > FRAPE
FRAPING > FRAPE
FRAPPANT *adj* striking, vivid
FRAPPE *adj* (of drinks) chilled ▷ *n* type of drink
FRAPPED > FRAP
FRAPPEE *same as* > FRAPPE
FRAPPES > FRAPPE
FRAPPING > FRAP
FRAPS > FRAP
FRAS > FRA
FRASCATI *n* dry or semisweet white wine from the Lazio region of Italy
FRASCATIS > FRASCATI

FRASS *n* refuse left by insects and insect larvae
FRASSES > FRASS
FRAT *n* member of a fraternity
FRATCH *n* quarrel
FRATCHES > FRATCH
FRATCHETY *adj* quarrelsome
FRATCHIER > FRATCHY
FRATCHING > FRATCH
FRATCHY *adj* quarrelsome
FRATE *n* friar
FRATER *n* mendicant friar or a lay brother in a monastery or priory
FRATERIES > FRATER
FRATERNAL *adj* of a brother, brotherly
FRATERS > FRATER
FRATERY > FRATER
FRATI > FRATE
FRATRIES > FRATER
FRATRY > FRATER
FRATS > FRAT
FRAU *n* married German woman
FRAUD *n* (criminal) deception, swindle
FRAUDFUL > FRAUD
FRAUDS > FRAUD
FRAUDSMAN *n* practitioner of criminal fraud
FRAUDSMEN > FRAUDSMAN
FRAUDSTER *n* person who commits a fraud
FRAUGHAN *n* small shrub
FRAUGHANS > FRAUGHAN
FRAUGHT *adj* tense or anxious ▷ *vb* archaic word for load ▷ *n* archaic word for freight
FRAUGHTED > FRAUGHT
FRAUGHTER > FRAUGHT
FRAUGHTS > FRAUGHT
FRAULEIN *n* unmarried German woman
FRAULEINS > FRAULEIN
FRAUS > FRAU
FRAUTAGE *n* cargo
FRAUTAGES > FRAUTAGE
FRAWZEY *n* celebration
FRAWZEYS > FRAWZEY
FRAY *n* noisy quarrel or conflict ▷ *vb* make or become ragged at the edge
FRAYED > FRAY
FRAYING > FRAY
FRAYINGS > FRAY
FRAYS > FRAY
FRAZIL *n* small pieces of ice that form in turbulently moving water
FRAZILS > FRAZIL
FRAZZLE *n* exhausted state ▷ *vb* tire out
FRAZZLED > FRAZZLE
FRAZZLES > FRAZZLE
FRAZZLING > FRAZZLE
FREAK *n* abnormal person or thing ▷ *adj* abnormal ▷ *vb* streak with colour
FREAKED > FREAK
FREAKERY *n* as in *control freakery* obsessive need to be in control of events

FREAKFUL *variant of* > FREAKISH
FREAKIER > FREAKY
FREAKIEST > FREAKY
FREAKILY > FREAKY
FREAKING > FREAK
FREAKISH *adj* of, related to, or characteristic of a freak
FREAKOUT *n* heightened emotional state
FREAKOUTS > FREAKOUT
FREAKS > FREAK
FREAKY *adj* weird, peculiar
FRECKLE *n* small brown spot on the skin ▷ *vb* mark or become marked with freckles
FRECKLED > FRECKLE
FRECKLES > FRECKLE
FRECKLIER > FRECKLE
FRECKLING > FRECKLE
FRECKLY > FRECKLE
FREDAINE *n* escapade
FREDAINES > FREDAINE
FREE *adj* able to act at will, not compelled or restrained ▷ *vb* release, liberate
FREEBASE *n* cocaine that has been refined by heating it in ether or some other solvent ▷ *vb* refine (cocaine) in this way
FREEBASED > FREEBASE
FREEBASER > FREEBASE
FREEBASES > FREEBASE
FREEBEE *variant of* > FREEBIE
FREEBEES > FREEBEE
FREEBIE *n* something provided without charge ▷ *adj* without charge
FREEBIES > FREEBIE
FREEBOARD *n* space or distance between the deck of a vessel and the water line
FREEBOOT *vb* act as a freebooter
FREEBOOTS > FREEBOOT
FREEBOOTY > FREEBOOT
FREEBORN *adj* not born in slavery
FREECYCLE *vb* recycle an unwanted item by donating it
FREED > FREE
FREEDIVER *n* person who dives without breathing apparatus
FREEDMAN *n* man freed from slavery
FREEDMEN > FREEDMAN
FREEDOM *n* being free
FREEDOMS > FREEDOM
FREEFALL *adj* as in *freefall parachuting* parachuting in which the jumper manoeuvres in free fall before opening the parachute
FREEFORM *n* irregular flowing shape, often used in industrial or fabric design ▷ *adj* freely flowing, spontaneous
FREEGAN *n* person who avoids buying consumer goods
FREEGANS > FREEGAN

FREEHAND *adj* drawn without guiding instruments
FREEHOLD *n* tenure of land for life without restrictions ▷ *adj* of or held by freehold
FREEHOLDS > FREEHOLD
FREEING > FREE
FREEKEH *n* type of cereal
FREEKEHS > FREEKEH
FREELANCE *n* self-employed person doing specific pieces of work for various employers ▷ *vb* work as a freelance ▷ *adv* of or as a freelance
FREELOAD *vb* act as a freeloader
FREELOADS > FREELOAD
FREELY > FREE
FREEMAN *n* person who has been given the freedom of a city
FREEMASON *n* member of a guild of itinerant skilled stonemasons, who had a system of secret signs and passwords with which they recognized each other
FREEMEN > FREEMAN
FREEMIUM *n* free service with paid additional options
FREEMIUMS > FREEMIUM
FREENESS > FREE
FREEPHONE *n* system of telephone use in which the cost of calls in response to an advertisement is borne by the advertiser
FREEPOST *adj* (of post) able to be posted without charge
FREEPOSTS > FREEPOST
FREER *n* liberator
FREERIDE *n* extreme form of skiing, snowboarding, or mountain biking
FREERIDES > FREERIDE
FREERS > FREER
FREES > FREE
FREESHEET *n* newspaper that is distributed free, paid for by its advertisers
FREESIA *n* plant with fragrant tubular flowers
FREESIAS > FREESIA
FREEST > FREE
FREESTONE *n* any fine-grained stone, esp sandstone or limestone, that can be cut and worked in any direction without breaking
FREESTYLE *n* competition, such as in swimming, in which each participant may use a style of his or her choice ▷ *vb* perform (music, a sport, etc) in a freestyle manner
FREET *n* omen or superstition
FREETIER > FREETY
FREETIEST > FREETY
FREETS > FREET
FREETY *adj* superstitious
FREEWARE *n* computer software that may be distributed and used without payment
FREEWARES > FREEWARE
FREEWAY *n* motorway

FREEWAYS > FREEWAY
FREEWHEEL *vb* travel downhill on a bicycle without pedalling ▷ *n* device in the rear hub of a bicycle wheel that permits it to rotate freely while the pedals are stationary
FREEWILL *n* apparent human ability to make choices that are not externally determined
FREEWOMAN *n* woman who is free or at liberty
FREEWOMEN > FREEWOMAN
FREEWRITE *vb* write freely without stopping or thinking
FREEWROTE > FREEWRITE
FREEZABLE > FREEZE
FREEZE *vb* turn from liquid to solid by the reduction of temperature ▷ *n* period of very cold weather
FREEZER *n* insulated cabinet for cold-storage of perishable foods
FREEZERS > FREEZER
FREEZES > FREEZE
FREEZING > FREEZE
FREEZINGS > FREEZE
FREIGHT *n* commercial transport of goods ▷ *vb* send by freight
FREIGHTED > FREIGHT
FREIGHTER *n* ship or aircraft for transporting goods
FREIGHTS > FREIGHT
FREIT *variant of* > FREET
FREITIER > FREITY
FREITIEST > FREITY
FREITS > FREIT
FREITY *adj* superstitious
FREMD *n* strange person or thing
FREMDS > FREMD
FREMIT *same as* > FREMD
FREMITS > FREMIT
FREMITUS *n* vibration felt by a hand placed on the body
FRENA > FRENUM
FRENCH *vb* cut (food) into thin strips
FRENCHED > FRENCH
FRENCHES > FRENCH
FRENCHIFY *vb* make or become French in appearance, behaviour, etc
FRENCHING > FRENCH
FRENEMIES > FRENEMY
FRENEMY *n* supposed friend who behaves in a treacherous manner
FRENETIC *adj* uncontrolled, excited ▷ *n* madman
FRENETICS > FRENETIC
FRENNE *variant of* > FREMD
FRENNES > FRENNE
FRENULA > FRENULUM
FRENULAR > FRENULUM
FRENULUM *n* group of bristles on the hind wing of some moths
FRENULUMS > FRENULUM
FRENUM *same as* > FRAENUM
FRENUMS > FRENUM
FRENZICAL > FRENZY

FRENZIED *adj* filled with or as if with frenzy
FRENZIES > FRENZY
FRENZILY > FRENZY
FRENZY *n* wild excitement or agitation ▷ *vb* make frantic
FRENZYING > FRENZY
FREON *n* tradename for an aerosol refrigerant
FREONS > FREON
FREQUENCE *same as* > FREQUENCY
FREQUENCY *n* rate of occurrence
FREQUENT *adj* happening often ▷ *vb* visit habitually
FREQUENTS > FREQUENT
FRERE *n* friar
FRERES > FRERE
FRESCADE *n* shady place or cool walk
FRESCADES > FRESCADE
FRESCO *n* watercolour painting done on wet plaster ▷ *vb* paint a fresco
FRESCOED > FRESCO
FRESCOER > FRESCO
FRESCOERS > FRESCO
FRESCOES > FRESCO
FRESCOING > FRESCO
FRESCOIST > FRESCO
FRESCOS > FRESCO
FRESH *adj* newly made, acquired, etc ▷ *adv* recently ▷ *vb* freshen
FRESHED > FRESH
FRESHEN *vb* make or become fresh or fresher
FRESHENED > FRESHEN
FRESHENER > FRESHEN
FRESHENS > FRESHEN
FRESHER *n* first-year student
FRESHERS > FRESHER
FRESHES > FRESH
FRESHEST > FRESH
FRESHET *n* sudden overflowing of a river
FRESHETS > FRESHET
FRESHIE *n* new Indian immigrant to the UK
FRESHIES > FRESHIE
FRESHING > FRESH
FRESHISH > FRESH
FRESHLY > FRESH
FRESHMAN *same as* > FRESHER
FRESHMEN > FRESHMAN
FRESHNESS > FRESH
FRESNEL *n* unit of frequency
FRESNELS > FRESNEL
FRET *vb* be worried ▷ *n* worried state
FRETBOARD *n* fingerboard with frets on a stringed musical instrument
FRETFUL *adj* irritable
FRETFULLY > FRETFUL
FRETLESS > FRET
FRETS > FRET
FRETSAW *n* fine saw with a narrow blade, used for fretwork
FRETSAWS > FRETSAW
FRETSOME *adj* vexing
FRETTED > FRET

FRETTER > FRET
FRETTERS > FRET
FRETTIER > FRETTY
FRETTIEST > FRETTY
FRETTING > FRET
FRETTINGS > FRET
FRETTY *adj* decorated with frets
FRETWORK *n* decorative carving in wood
FRETWORKS > FRETWORK
FRIABLE *adj* easily crumbled
FRIAND *n* small almond cake
FRIANDE *variant of* > FRIAND
FRIANDES > FRIANDE
FRIANDS > FRIAND
FRIAR *n* member of a male Roman Catholic religious order
FRIARBIRD *n* Australian honeyeater with a naked head
FRIARIES > FRIARY
FRIARLY > FRIAR
FRIARS > FRIAR
FRIARY *n* house of friars
FRIB *n* piece of wool removed from a fleece during classing
FRIBBLE *vb* fritter away ▷ *n* wasteful or frivolous person or action ▷ *adj* frivolous
FRIBBLED > FRIBBLE
FRIBBLER > FRIBBLE
FRIBBLERS > FRIBBLE
FRIBBLES > FRIBBLE
FRIBBLING > FRIBBLE
FRIBBLISH *adj* trifling
FRIBS > FRIB
FRICADEL *variant of* > FRIKKADEL
FRICADELS > FRICADEL
FRICANDO *n* larded and braised veal fillet
FRICASSEE *n* stewed meat served in a thick white sauce ▷ *vb* prepare (meat) as a fricassee
FRICATIVE *n* consonant produced by friction of the breath through a partially open mouth, such as (f) or (z) ▷ *adj* relating to or being a fricative
FRICHT *vb* frighten
FRICHTED > FRICHT
FRICHTING > FRICHT
FRICHTS > FRICHT
FRICKING *adj* slang word for absolute
FRICOT *n* Acadian stew of potatoes, meat or fish
FRICOTS > FRICOT
FRICTION *n* resistance met with by a body moving over another
FRICTIONS > FRICTION
FRIDGE *n* apparatus in which food and drinks are kept cool ▷ *vb* archaic word for chafe
FRIDGED > FRIDGE
FRIDGES > FRIDGE
FRIDGING > FRIDGE
FRIED > FRY

f

SECTION 1: Words between 2 and 9 letters in length

f

FRIEDCAKE n type of doughnut

FRIEND n person whom one knows well and likes ▷ vb befriend

FRIENDED > FRIEND

FRIENDING > FRIEND

FRIENDLY adj showing or expressing liking ▷ n match played for its own sake and not as part of a competition

FRIENDS > FRIEND

FRIER same as > FRYER

FRIERS > FRIER

FRIES > FRY

FRIEZE n ornamental band on a wall ▷ vb give a nap to (cloth)

FRIEZED > FRIEZE

FRIEZES > FRIEZE

FRIEZING > FRIEZE

FRIG vb behave foolishly or aimlessly ▷ n fridge

FRIGATE n medium-sized fast warship

FRIGATES > FRIGATE

FRIGATOON n Venetian sailing ship

FRIGES > FRIG

FRIGGED > FRIG

FRIGGER > FRIG

FRIGGERS > FRIG

FRIGGING > FRIG

FRIGGINGS > FRIG

FRIGHT n sudden fear or alarm

FRIGHTED > FRIGHT

FRIGHTEN vb scare or terrify

FRIGHTENS > FRIGHTEN

FRIGHTFUL adj horrifying

FRIGHTING > FRIGHT

FRIGHTS > FRIGHT

FRIGID adj formal or stiff in temperament

FRIGIDER > FRIGID

FRIGIDEST > FRIGID

FRIGIDITY > FRIGID

FRIGIDLY > FRIGID

FRIGOT variant of > FRIGATE

FRIGOTS > FRIGOT

FRIGS > FRIG

FRIJOL n variety of bean

FRIJOLE variant of > FRIJOL

FRIJOLES > FRIJOL

FRIKKADEL n South African meatball

FRILL n gathered strip of fabric attached at one edge ▷ vb adorn or fit with a frill or frills

FRILLED > FRILL

FRILLER > FRILL

FRILLERS > FRILL

FRILLERY n fabric or clothing arranged in frills

FRILLIER > FRILLY

FRILLIES pl n flimsy women's underwear

FRILLIEST > FRILLY

FRILLING > FRILL

FRILLINGS > FRILL

FRILLS > FRILL

FRILLY adj with a frill or frills

FRINGE n hair cut short and hanging over the forehead ▷ vb decorate with a fringe ▷ adj (of theatre) unofficial or unconventional

FRINGED > FRINGE

FRINGES > FRINGE

FRINGIER > FRINGY

FRINGIEST > FRINGY

FRINGING n act of fringing

FRINGINGS > FRINGING

FRINGY adj having a fringe

FRIPON n rogue

FRIPONS > FRIPON

FRIPPER n dealer in old clothes

FRIPPERER same as > FRIPPER

FRIPPERS > FRIPPER

FRIPPERY n useless ornamentation

FRIPPET n frivolous or flamboyant young woman

FRIPPETS > FRIPPET

FRIS same as > FRISKA

FRISBEE n tradename of a light plastic disc for throwing in a game

FRISBEES > FRISBEE

FRISE n fabric with a long normally uncut nap used for upholstery and rugs

FRISEE n endive

FRISEES > FRISEE

FRISES > FRIS

FRISETTE n curly or frizzed fringe, often an artificial hairpiece, worn by women on the forehead

FRISETTES > FRISETTE

FRISEUR n hairdresser

FRISEURS > FRISEUR

FRISK vb move or leap playfully ▷ n playful movement

FRISKA n (in Hungarian music) the fast movement of a piece

FRISKAS > FRISKA

FRISKED > FRISK

FRISKER > FRISK

FRISKERS > FRISK

FRISKET n part of a hand printing press

FRISKETS > FRISKET

FRISKFUL > FRISK

FRISKIER > FRISKY

FRISKIEST > FRISKY

FRISKILY > FRISKY

FRISKING > FRISK

FRISKINGS > FRISK

FRISKS > FRISK

FRISKY adj lively or high-spirited

FRISSON n shiver of fear or excitement

FRISSONS > FRISSON

FRIST archaic word for > POSTPONE

FRISTED > FRIST

FRISTING > FRIST

FRISTS > FRIST

FRISURE n styling the hair into curls

FRISURES > FRISURE

FRIT n basic materials for making glass, glazes for

pottery, etc ▷ vb fuse (materials) in making frit

FRITES pl n chipped potatoes

FRITFLIES > FRITFLY

FRITFLY n type of small black fly

FRITH same as > FIRTH

FRITHBORH n type of pledge

FRITHS > FRITH

FRITS > FRIT

FRITT same as > FRIT

FRITTATA n flat thick Italian omelette

FRITTATAS > FRITTATA

FRITTED > FRIT

FRITTER n piece of food fried in batter ▷ vb waste or squander

FRITTERED > FRITTER

FRITTERER > FRITTER

FRITTERS > FRITTER

FRITTING > FRIT

FRITTS > FRITT

FRITURE archaic word for > FRITTER

FRITURES > FRITURE

FRITZ n as in on the fritz in a state of disrepair ▷ vb (of an appliance, etc) become broken or start malfunctioning

FRITZED > FRITZ

FRITZES > FRITZ

FRITZING > FRITZ

FRIULANO n type of Italian cheese

FRIULANOS > FRIULANO

FRIVOL vb behave frivolously

FRIVOLED > FRIVOL

FRIVOLER > FRIVOL

FRIVOLERS > FRIVOL

FRIVOLING > FRIVOL

FRIVOLITY > FRIVOLOUS

FRIVOLLED > FRIVOL

FRIVOLLER > FRIVOL

FRIVOLOUS adj not serious or sensible

FRIVOLS > FRIVOL

FRIZ variant of > FRIZZ

FRIZADO n fine frieze-like fabric

FRIZADOS > FRIZADO

FRIZE n coarse woollen fabric ▷ vb freeze

FRIZED > FRIZE

FRIZER n person who gives nap to cloth

FRIZERS > FRIZER

FRIZES > FRIZE

FRIZETTE same as > FRISETTE

FRIZETTES > FRIZETTE

FRIZING > FRIZE

FRIZZ vb form (hair) into stiff wiry curls ▷ n hair that has been frizzed

FRIZZANTE adj (of wine) slightly effervescent

FRIZZED > FRIZZ

FRIZZER > FRIZZ

FRIZZERS > FRIZZ

FRIZZES > FRIZZ

FRIZZIER > FRIZZY

FRIZZIES n condition of having frizzy hair

FRIZZIEST > FRIZZY

FRIZZILY > FRIZZY

FRIZZING > FRIZZ

FRIZZLE vb cook or heat until crisp and shrivelled ▷ n tight curl

FRIZZLED > FRIZZLE

FRIZZLER > FRIZZLE

FRIZZLERS > FRIZZLE

FRIZZLES > FRIZZLE

FRIZZLIER > FRIZZLE

FRIZZLING > FRIZZLE

FRIZZLY > FRIZZLE

FRIZZY adj (of the hair) in tight crisp wiry curls

FRO adv away ▷ n afro

FROCK n dress ▷ vb invest (a person) with the office or status of a cleric

FROCKED > FROCK

FROCKING n coarse material suitable for making frocks or work clothes

FROCKINGS > FROCKING

FROCKLESS > FROCK

FROCKS > FROCK

FROE n cutting tool

FROES > FROE

FROG n type of amphibian

FROGBIT n floating aquatic Eurasian plant

FROGBITS > FROGBIT

FROGEYE n plant disease

FROGEYED adj affected by frogeye

FROGEYES > FROGEYE

FROGFISH n type of angler fish

FROGGED adj decorated with frogging

FROGGERY n place where frogs are kept

FROGGIER > FROGGY

FROGGIEST > FROGGY

FROGGING n decorative fastening of looped braid on a coat

FROGGINGS > FROGGING

FROGGY adj like a frog

FROGLET n young frog

FROGLETS > FROGLET

FROGLIKE > FROG

FROGLING n young frog

FROGLINGS > FROGLING

FROGMAN n swimmer with equipment for working under water

FROGMARCH vb force (a resisting person) to move by holding their arms ▷ n method of carrying a resisting person in which each limb is held and the victim is face downwards

FROGMEN > FROGMAN

FROGMOUTH n type of nocturnal insectivorous bird of SE Asia and Australia

FROGS > FROG

FROGSPAWN n jelly-like substance containing frog's eggs

FROIDEUR n coldness

FROIDEURS > FROIDEUR

FROING n as in toing and froing going back and forth

FROINGS > FROING

FROISE n kind of pancake
FROISES > FROISE
FROLIC vb run and play in a lively way ▷ n lively and merry behaviour ▷ adj full of merriment or fun
FROLICKED > FROLIC
FROLICKER > FROLIC
FROLICKY adj frolicsome
FROLICS > FROLIC
FROM prep indicating the point of departure, source, etc
FROMAGE n as in fromage frais low-fat soft cheese
FROMAGES > FROMAGE
FROMENTY same as > FRUMENTY
FROND n long leaf or leaflike part of a fern, palm, or seaweed
FRONDAGE n fronds collectively
FRONDAGES > FRONDAGE
FRONDED adj having fronds
FRONDENT adj leafy
FRONDEUR n 17th-century French rebel
FRONDEURS > FRONDEUR
FRONDLESS > FROND
FRONDOSE adj leafy or like a leaf
FRONDOUS adj leafy or like a leaf
FRONDS > FROND
FRONS n plate on the head of some insects
FRONT n fore part ▷ adj of or at the front ▷ vb face (onto)
FRONTAGE n facade of a building
FRONTAGER n owner of a building or land on the front of a street
FRONTAGES > FRONTAGE
FRONTAL adj of, at, or in the front ▷ n decorative hanging for the front of an altar
FRONTALLY > FRONTAL
FRONTALS > FRONTAL
FRONTED > FRONT
FRONTENIS n racket used in Basque ball game
FRONTER n front side
FRONTERS > FRONTER
FRONTES > FRONS
FRONTEST > FRONT
FRONTIER n area of a country bordering on another
FRONTIERS > FRONTIER
FRONTING > FRONT
FRONTLESS > FRONT
FRONTLET n small decorative loop worn on a woman's forehead
FRONTLETS > FRONTLET
FRONTLINE adj of, relating to, or suitable for the front line of a military formation
FRONTLIST n list of books about to be published
FRONTMAN n nominal leader who lacks real power or authority
FRONTMEN > FRONTMAN

FRONTON n wall against which pelota or jai alai is played
FRONTONS > FRONTON
FRONTOON variant of > FRONTON
FRONTOONS > FRONTOON
FRONTPAGE adj on or suitable for the front page of a newspaper ▷ vb place something on the front page of a newspaper
FRONTS > FRONT
FRONTWARD adv towards the front
FRONTWAYS adv with the front forward
FRONTWISE variant of > FRONTWAYS
FRORE adj very cold or frosty
FROREN variant of > FRORE
FRORN variant of > FRORE
FRORNE variant of > FRORE
FRORY adj frozen
FROS > FRO
FROSH n freshman
FROSHES > FROSH
FROST n white frozen dew or mist ▷ vb become covered with frost
FROSTBIT > FROSTBITE
FROSTBITE n destruction of tissue, esp of the fingers or ears, by cold ▷ vb affect with frostbite
FROSTED adj (of glass) having a rough surface to make it opaque ▷ n type of ice cream dish
FROSTEDS > FROSTED
FROSTFISH n American fish appearing in frosty weather
FROSTIER > FROSTY
FROSTIEST > FROSTY
FROSTILY > FROSTY
FROSTING n sugar icing
FROSTINGS > FROSTING
FROSTLESS > FROST
FROSTLIKE > FROST
FROSTLINE n depth to which ground freezes in winter
FROSTNIP n milder form of frostbite
FROSTNIPS > FROSTNIP
FROSTS > FROST
FROSTWORK n patterns made by frost on glass, metal, etc
FROSTY adj characterized or covered by frost
FROTH n mass of small bubbles ▷ vb foam
FROTHED > FROTH
FROTHER > FROTH
FROTHERS > FROTH
FROTHERY n anything insubstantial, like froth
FROTHIER > FROTH
FROTHIEST > FROTH
FROTHILY > FROTH
FROTHING n act of frothing
FROTHINGS > FROTHING
FROTHLESS > FROTH
FROTHS > FROTH
FROTHY > FROTH

FROTTAGE n act or process of taking a rubbing from a rough surface for a work of art
FROTTAGES > FROTTAGE
FROTTEUR n person who rubs against another person's body for a sexual thrill
FROTTEURS > FROTTEUR
FROUFROU n swishing sound, as made by a long silk dress
FROUFROUS > FROUFROU
FROUGHIER > FROUGHY
FROUGHY adj rancid
FROUNCE vb wrinkle
FROUNCED > FROUNCE
FROUNCES > FROUNCE
FROUNCING > FROUNCE
FROUZIER > FROUZY
FROUZIEST > FROUZY
FROUZILY adv in a frouzy manner
FROUZY same as > FROWZY
FROW same as > FROE
FROWARD adj obstinate
FROWARDLY > FROWARD
FROWARDS same as > FROWARD
FROWIE variant of > FROUGHY
FROWIER > FROWIE
FROWIEST > FROWIE
FROWN vb wrinkle one's brows in worry, anger, or thought ▷ n frowning expression
FROWNED > FROWN
FROWNER > FROWN
FROWNERS > FROWN
FROWNIER > FROWNY
FROWNIEST > FROWNY
FROWNING > FROWN
FROWNS > FROWN
FROWNY adj displaying a frown
FROWS > FROW
FROWSIER > FROWSY
FROWSIEST > FROWSY
FROWSILY adv in a frowsy manner
FROWST n hot and stale atmosphere ▷ vb abandon oneself to such an atmosphere
FROWSTED > FROWST
FROWSTER > FROWST
FROWSTERS > FROWST
FROWSTIER > FROWSTY
FROWSTING > FROWST
FROWSTS > FROWST
FROWSTY adj stale or musty
FROWSY same as > FROWZY
FROWY variant of > FROUGHY
FROWZIER > FROWZY
FROWZIEST > FROWZY
FROWZILY > FROWZY
FROWZY adj dirty or unkempt
FROZE > FREEZE
FROZEN > FREEZE
FROZENLY > FREEZE
FRUCTAN n type of polymer of fructose
FRUCTANS > FRUCTAN
FRUCTED adj fruit-bearing

FRUCTIFY vb (cause to) bear fruit
FRUCTIVE adj fruitful
FRUCTOSE n crystalline sugar occurring in many fruits
FRUCTOSES > FRUCTOSE
FRUCTUARY n archaic word for a person who enjoys the fruits of something
FRUCTUATE vb bear fruit
FRUCTUOUS adj productive or fruitful
FRUG vb perform the frug, a 1960s dance
FRUGAL adj thrifty, sparing
FRUGALIST > FRUGAL
FRUGALITY > FRUGAL
FRUGALLY > FRUGAL
FRUGGED > FRUG
FRUGGING > FRUG
FRUGIVORE adj fruit-eating
FRUGS > FRUG
FRUICT obsolete variant of > FRUIT
FRUICTS > FRUICT
FRUIT n part of a plant containing seeds ▷ vb bear fruit
FRUITAGE n process, state, or season of producing fruit
FRUITAGES > FRUITAGE
FRUITCAKE n cake containing dried fruit
FRUITED > FRUIT
FRUITER n fruit grower
FRUITERER n person who sells fruit
FRUITERS > FRUITER
FRUITERY n fruitage
FRUITFUL adj useful or productive
FRUITIER > FRUITY
FRUITIEST > FRUITY
FRUITILY > FRUITY
FRUITING > FRUIT
FRUITINGS > FRUIT
FRUITION n fulfilment of something worked for or desired
FRUITIONS > FRUITION
FRUITIVE adj enjoying
FRUITLESS adj useless or unproductive
FRUITLET n small fruit
FRUITLETS > FRUITLET
FRUITLIKE > FRUIT
FRUITS > FRUIT
FRUITWOOD n wood of a fruit tree
FRUITWORM n insect larva that feeds on fruit
FRUITY adj of or like fruit
FRUMENTY n kind of porridge made from hulled wheat boiled with milk, sweetened, and spiced
FRUMP n dowdy woman ▷ vb mock or taunt
FRUMPED > FRUMP
FRUMPIER > FRUMPY
FRUMPIEST > FRUMPY
FRUMPILY > FRUMPY
FRUMPING > FRUMP
FRUMPISH same as > FRUMPY

FRUMPLE vb wrinkle or crumple
FRUMPLED > FRUMPLE
FRUMPLES > FRUMPLE
FRUMPLING > FRUMPLE
FRUMPS > FRUMP
FRUMPY adj (of a woman, clothes, etc) dowdy or unattractive
FRUSEMIDE n diuretic used to relieve oedema, for example caused by heart or kidney disease
FRUSH vb break into pieces
FRUSHED > FRUSH
FRUSHES > FRUSH
FRUSHING > FRUSH
FRUST n fragment
FRUSTA > FRUSTUM
FRUSTRATE vb upset or anger ▷ adj frustrated or thwarted
FRUSTS > FRUST
FRUSTULE n hard siliceous cell wall of a diatom
FRUSTULES > FRUSTULE
FRUSTUM n part of a solid
FRUSTUMS > FRUSTUM
FRUTEX n shrub
FRUTICES > FRUTEX
FRUTICOSE adj shrubby
FRUTIFIED > FRUTIFY
FRUTIFIES > FRUTIFY
FRUTIFY vb malapropism for notify
FRY vb cook or be cooked in fat or oil ▷ n dish of fried food
FRYABLE > FRY
FRYBREAD n Native American fried bread
FRYBREADS > FRYBREAD
FRYER n person or thing that fries
FRYERS > FRYER
FRYING > FRY
FRYINGS > FRY
FRYPAN n long-handled shallow pan used for frying
FRYPANS > FRYPAN
FUB vb cheat
FUBAR adj irreparably damaged or bungled
FUBBED > FUB
FUBBERIES > FUBBERY
FUBBERY n cheating
FUBBIER > FUBBY
FUBBIEST > FUBBY
FUBBING > FUB
FUBBY adj chubby
FUBS > FUB
FUBSIER > FUBSY
FUBSIEST > FUBSY
FUBSY adj short and stout
FUCHSIA n ornamental shrub
FUCHSIAS > FUCHSIA
FUCHSIN n greenish crystalline substance
FUCHSINE same as > FUCHSIN
FUCHSINES > FUCHSINE
FUCHSINS > FUCHSIN
FUCHSITE n form of mica
FUCHSITES > FUCHSITE
FUCI > FUCUS
FUCK vb taboo word meaning have sexual intercourse (with) ▷ n act of sexual intercourse
FUCKED > FUCK
FUCKER n taboo word for a despicable or obnoxious person
FUCKERS > FUCKER
FUCKFACE n taboo word for a stupid or contemptible person
FUCKFACES > FUCKFACE
FUCKHEAD n taboo word for a stupid or contemptible person
FUCKHEADS > FUCKHEAD
FUCKING > FUCK
FUCKINGS > FUCK
FUCKOFF n taboo word for an annoying or unpleasant person
FUCKOFFS > FUCKOFF
FUCKS > FUCK
FUCKUP vb taboo word meaning to damage or bungle ▷ n taboo word meaning an act or an instance of bungling
FUCKUPS > FUCKUP
FUCKWIT n taboo word for a fool or idiot
FUCKWITS > FUCKWIT
FUCOID n type of seaweed
FUCOIDAL n type of seaweed
FUCOIDS > FUCOID
FUCOSE n aldose
FUCOSES > FUCOSE
FUCOUS same as > FUCOIDAL
FUCUS n type of seaweed
FUCUSED adj archaic word meaning made up with cosmetics
FUCUSES > FUCUS
FUD n rabbit's tail
FUDDIER > FUDDY
FUDDIES > FUDDY
FUDDIEST > FUDDY
FUDDLE vb cause to be intoxicated or confused ▷ n confused state
FUDDLED > FUDDLE
FUDDLER > FUDDLE
FUDDLERS > FUDDLE
FUDDLES > FUDDLE
FUDDLING > FUDDLE
FUDDLINGS > FUDDLE
FUDDY n old-fashioned person ▷ adj old-fashioned
FUDGE n soft caramel-like sweet ▷ vb make (an issue) less clear deliberately ▷ interj mild exclamation of annoyance
FUDGED > FUDGE
FUDGES > FUDGE
FUDGIER > FUDGY
FUDGIEST > FUDGY
FUDGING > FUDGE
FUDGY adj resembling or containing fudge
FUDS > FUD
FUEHRER n leader: applied esp to Adolf Hitler
FUEHRERS > FUEHRER
FUEL n substance burned or treated to produce heat or power ▷ vb provide with fuel
FUELED > FUEL
FUELER > FUEL
FUELERS > FUEL
FUELING > FUEL
FUELLED > FUEL
FUELLER > FUEL
FUELLERS > FUEL
FUELLING > FUEL
FUELS > FUEL
FUELWOOD n any wood used as a fuel
FUELWOODS > FUELWOOD
FUERO n Spanish code of laws
FUEROS > FUERO
FUFF vb puff
FUFFED > FUFF
FUFFIER > FUFFY
FUFFIEST > FUFFY
FUFFING > FUFF
FUFFS > FUFF
FUFFY adj puffy
FUG n hot stale atmosphere ▷ vb sit in a fug
FUGACIOUS adj passing quickly away
FUGACITY n property of a gas that expresses its tendency to escape or expand
FUGAL adj of, relating to, or in the style of a fugue
FUGALLY > FUGAL
FUGATO adj in the manner or style of a fugue ▷ n movement, section, or piece in this style
FUGATOS > FUGATO
FUGGED > FUG
FUGGIER > FUG
FUGGIEST > FUG
FUGGILY > FUG
FUGGINESS n state or condition of being fuggy
FUGGING > FUG
FUGGY > FUG
FUGHETTA n short fugue
FUGHETTAS > FUGHETTA
FUGIE n runaway
FUGIES > FUGIE
FUGIO n former US copper coin
FUGIOS > FUGIO
FUGITIVE n person who flees, esp from arrest or pursuit ▷ adj fleeing
FUGITIVES > FUGITIVE
FUGLE vb act as a fugleman
FUGLED > FUGLE
FUGLEMAN n (formerly) a soldier used as an example for those learning drill
FUGLEMEN > FUGLEMAN
FUGLES > FUGLE
FUGLIER > FUGLY
FUGLIEST > FUGLY
FUGLING > FUGLE
FUGLY adj offensive word for very ugly
FUGS > FUG
FUGU n puffer fish
FUGUE n type of musical composition ▷ vb be in a dreamlike, altered state of consciousness
FUGUED > FUGUE
FUGUELIKE > FUGUE
FUGUES > FUGUE
FUGUING > FUGUE
FUGUIST n composer of fugues
FUGUISTS > FUGUIST
FUGUS > FUGU
FUHRER same as > FUEHRER
FUHRERS > FUHRER
FUJI n type of African music
FUJIS > FUJI
FULCRA > FULCRUM
FULCRATE > FULCRUM
FULCRUM n pivot about which a lever turns
FULCRUMS > FULCRUM
FULFIL vb achieve (a desire or promise)
FULFILL same as > FULFIL
FULFILLED > FULFILL
FULFILLER > FULFIL
FULFILLS > FULFILL
FULFILS > FULFIL
FULGENCY > FULGENT
FULGENT adj shining brilliantly
FULGENTLY > FULGENT
FULGID same as > FULGENT
FULGOR n brilliance
FULGOROUS > FULGOR
FULGORS > FULGOR
FULGOUR variant of > FULGOR
FULGOURS > FULGOUR
FULGURAL > FULGURATE
FULGURANT > FULGURATE
FULGURATE vb flash like lightning
FULGURITE n tube of glassy mineral matter found in sand and rock, formed by the action of lightning
FULGUROUS adj flashing like or resembling lightning
FULHAM n loaded die
FULHAMS > FULHAM
FULL adj containing as much or as many as possible ▷ adv completely ▷ vb clean, shrink, and press cloth
FULLAGE n price charged for fulling cloth
FULLAGES > FULLAGE
FULLAM variant of > FULHAM
FULLAMS > FULLAM
FULLAN variant of > FULHAM
FULLANS > FULLAN
FULLBACK n defensive player
FULLBACKS > FULLBACK
FULLBLOOD n person of unmixed race
FULLED > FULL
FULLER n person who fulls cloth for a living ▷ vb forge (a groove) or caulk (a riveted joint) with a fuller
FULLERED > FULLER
FULLERENE n any of various carbon molecules with a polyhedral structure similar to that of buckminsterfullerene
FULLERIDE n compound of a fullerene in which atoms are trapped inside the cage of carbon atoms
FULLERIES > FULLERY

FULLERING > FULLER

FULLERITE n crystalline form of a fullerene

FULLERS > FULLER

FULLERY n place where fulling is carried out

FULLEST > FULL

FULLFACE n in printing, a letter that takes up full body size

FULLFACES > FULLFACE

FULLING > FULL

FULLISH > FULL

FULLNESS > FULL

FULLS > FULL

FULLY adv greatest degree or extent

FULMAR n Arctic sea bird

FULMARS > FULMAR

FULMINANT adj sudden and violent

FULMINATE vb criticize or denounce angrily ▷ n any salt or ester of fulminic acid, esp the mercury salt, which is used as a detonator

FULMINE vb fulminate

FULMINED > FULMINE

FULMINES > FULMINE

FULMINIC adj as in fulminic acid, unstable volatile acid

FULMINING > FULMINE

FULMINOUS adj harshly critical

FULNESS > FULL

FULNESSES > FULL

FULSOME adj distastefully excessive or insincere

FULSOMELY > FULSOME

FULSOMER > FULSOME

FULSOMEST > FULSOME

FULVID variant of > FULVOUS

FULVOUS adj of a dull brownish-yellow colour

FUM n phoenix, in Chinese mythology

FUMADO n salted, smoked fish

FUMADOES > FUMADO

FUMADOS > FUMADO

FUMAGE n hearth money

FUMAGES > FUMAGE

FUMARASE n enzyme

FUMARASES > FUMARASE

FUMARATE n salt of fumaric acid

FUMARATES > FUMARATE

FUMARIC adj as in fumaric acid colourless crystalline acid

FUMAROLE n vent in or near a volcano from which hot gases, esp steam, are emitted

FUMAROLES > FUMAROLE

FUMAROLIC > FUMAROLE

FUMATORIA pl n small airtight chambers for fumigating insects or fungi

FUMATORY n chamber where insects and fungi are destroyed by fumigation

FUMBLE vb handle awkwardly ▷ n act of fumbling

FUMBLED > FUMBLE

FUMBLER > FUMBLE

FUMBLERS > FUMBLE

FUMBLES > FUMBLE

FUMBLING > FUMBLE

FUME vb be very angry

FUMED adj (of wood) having been exposed to ammonia fumes

FUMELESS > FUME

FUMELIKE > FUME

FUMER > FUME

FUMEROLE variant of > FUMAROLE

FUMEROLES > FUMEROLE

FUMERS > FUME

FUMES > FUME

FUMET n liquor from cooking fish, meat, or game

FUMETS > FUMET

FUMETTE variant of > FUMET

FUMETTES > FUMETTE

FUMETTI > FUMETTO

FUMETTO n speech balloon in a comic or cartoon

FUMETTOS > FUMETTO

FUMIER > FUME

FUMIEST > FUME

FUMIGANT n substance used for fumigating

FUMIGANTS > FUMIGANT

FUMIGATE vb disinfect with fumes

FUMIGATED > FUMIGATE

FUMIGATES > FUMIGATE

FUMIGATOR > FUMIGATE

FUMING > FUME

FUMINGLY > FUME

FUMITORY n chiefly European plant with spurred flowers, formerly used medicinally

FUMOSITY > FUME

FUMOUS > FUME

FUMS > FUM

FUMULI > FUMULUS

FUMULUS n smokelike cloud

FUMY > FUME

FUN n enjoyment or amusement ▷ vb trick ▷ adj providing amusement or entertainment

FUNBOARD n type of surfboard

FUNBOARDS > FUNBOARD

FUNCKIA n type of plant resembling the lily

FUNCKIAS > FUNCKIA

FUNCTION n purpose something exists for ▷ vb operate or work

FUNCTIONS > FUNCTION

FUNCTOR n performer of a function

FUNCTORS > FUNCTOR

FUND n stock of money for a special purpose ▷ vb provide money to

FUNDABLE > FUND

FUNDAMENT n buttocks

FUNDED > FUND

FUNDER > FUND

FUNDERS > FUND

FUNDI n expert or boffin

FUNDIC > FUNDUS

FUNDIE n fundamentalist Christian

FUNDIES > FUNDIE

FUNDING > FUND

FUNDINGS > FUND

FUNDIS > FUNDI

FUNDLESS > FUND

FUNDRAISE vb raise money for a cause

FUNDS pl n money that is readily available

FUNDUS n base of an organ

FUNDY n fundamentalist

FUNEBRAL variant of > FUNEBRIAL

FUNEBRE adj funereal or mournful

FUNEBRIAL same as > FUNEREAL

FUNERAL n ceremony of burying or cremating a dead person

FUNERALS > FUNERAL

FUNERARY adj of or for a funeral

FUNEREAL adj gloomy or sombre

FUNEST adj lamentable

FUNFAIR n entertainment with machines to ride on and stalls

FUNFAIRS > FUNFAIR

FUNFEST n enjoyable time

FUNFESTS > FUNFEST

FUNG same as > FUNK

FUNGAL adj of, derived from, or caused by a fungus or fungi ▷ n fungus or fungal infection

FUNGALS > FUNGAL

FUNGI > FUNGUS

FUNGIBLE n goods replaceable by similar goods of equal quantity or weight ▷ adj having the quality of fungibles

FUNGIBLES > FUNGIBLE

FUNGIC > FUNGUS

FUNGICIDE n substance that destroys fungi

FUNGIFORM adj shaped like a mushroom or similar fungus

FUNGISTAT n substance that inhibits the growth of fungi

FUNGO n in baseball, act of tossing and hitting the ball ▷ vb toss and hit a ball

FUNGOED > FUNGO

FUNGOES > FUNGO

FUNGOID adj resembling a fungus

FUNGOIDAL > FUNGOID

FUNGOIDS > FUNGOID

FUNGOING > FUNGO

FUNGOS > FUNGO

FUNGOSITY > FUNGOUS

FUNGOUS adj appearing and spreading quickly like a fungus

FUNGS > FUNG

FUNGUS n plant such as a mushroom or mould

FUNGUSES > FUNGUS

FUNHOUSE n amusing place at fairground

FUNHOUSES > FUNHOUSE

FUNICLE n stalk that attaches an ovule to the wall of the ovary

FUNICLES > FUNICLE

FUNICULAR n cable railway on a mountainside or cliff ▷ adj relating to or operated by a rope, cable, etc

FUNICULI > FUNICULUS

FUNICULUS same as > FUNICLE

FUNK n style of dance music with a strong beat ▷ vb avoid (doing something) through fear

FUNKED > FUNK

FUNKER > FUNK

FUNKERS > FUNK

FUNKHOLE n dugout

FUNKHOLES > FUNKHOLE

FUNKIA n hosta

FUNKIAS > FUNKIA

FUNKIER > FUNKY

FUNKIEST > FUNKY

FUNKILY > FUNKY

FUNKINESS > FUNKY

FUNKING > FUNK

FUNKS > FUNK

FUNKSTER n performer or fan of funk music

FUNKSTERS > FUNKSTER

FUNKY adj (of music) having a strong beat

FUNNED > FUN

FUNNEL n cone-shaped tube ▷ vb (cause to) move through or as if through a funnel

FUNNELED > FUNNEL

FUNNELING > FUNNEL

FUNNELLED > FUNNEL

FUNNELS > FUNNEL

FUNNER > FUN

FUNNEST > FUN

FUNNIER > FUNNY

FUNNIES pl n comic strips in a newspaper

FUNNIEST > FUNNY

FUNNILY > FUNNY

FUNNINESS > FUNNY

FUNNING > FUN

FUNNY adj comical, humorous ▷ n joke or witticism

FUNNYMAN n comedian

FUNNYMEN > FUNNYMAN

FUNPLEX n large amusement centre

FUNPLEXES > FUNPLEX

FUNS > FUN

FUNSTER n funnyman or funnywoman

FUNSTERS > FUNSTER

FUR n soft hair of a mammal ▷ vb cover or become covered with fur

FURACIOUS adj thievish

FURACITY > FURACIOUS

FURAL n furfural

FURALS > FURAL

FURAN n colourless flammable toxic liquid heterocyclic compound

FURANE variant of > FURAN

FURANES > FURANE

FURANOSE n simple sugar containing a furan ring

FURANOSES > FURANOSE

FURANS > FURAN

FURBALL n ball of fur regurgitated by an animal

f

f

FURBALLS > FURBALL
FURBEARER n mammal hunted for its pelt or fur
FURBELOW n flounce, ruffle, or other ornamental trim ▷ vb put a furbelow on (a garment)
FURBELOWS > FURBELOW
FURBISH vb smarten up
FURBISHED > FURBISH
FURBISHER > FURBISH
FURBISHES > FURBISH
FURCA n any forklike structure, esp in insects
FURCAE > FURCA
FURCAL > FURCA
FURCATE vb divide into two parts ▷ adj forked, branching
FURCATED > FURCATE
FURCATELY > FURCATE
FURCATES > FURCATE
FURCATING > FURCATE
FURCATION > FURCATE
FURCRAEA n plant belonging to the Agave family
FURCRAEAS > FURCRAEA
FURCULA n any forklike part or organ
FURCULAE > FURCULA
FURCULAR > FURCULA
FURCULUM same as > FURCULA
FURDER same as > FURTHER
FUREUR n rage or anger
FUREURS > FUREUR
FURFAIR variant of > FURFUR
FURFAIRS > FURFAIR
FURFUR n scurf or scaling of the skin
FURFURAL n colourless liquid used as a solvent
FURFURALS > FURFURAL
FURFURAN same as > FURAN
FURFURANS > FURFURAN
FURFURES > FURFUR
FURFUROL variant of > FURFURAL
FURFUROLE variant of > FURFURAL
FURFUROLS > FURFUROL
FURFUROUS > FURFUR
FURFURS > FURFUR
FURIBUND adj furious
FURIES > FURY
FURIOSITY > FURIOUS
FURIOSO adv in a frantically rushing manner ▷ n passage or piece to be performed in this way
FURIOSOS > FURIOSO
FURIOUS adj very angry
FURIOUSLY > FURIOUS
FURKID n companion animal
FURKIDS > FURKID
FURL vb roll up and fasten (a sail, umbrella, or flag) ▷ n act or an instance of furling
FURLABLE > FURL
FURLANA variant of > FORLANA
FURLANAS > FURLANA
FURLED > FURL
FURLER > FURL
FURLERS > FURL

FURLESS > FUR
FURLIKE adj like fur
FURLING > FURL
FURLONG n unit of length
FURLONGS > FURLONG
FURLOUGH n leave of absence ▷ vb grant a furlough to
FURLOUGHS > FURLOUGH
FURLS > FURL
FURMENTY same as > FRUMENTY
FURMETIES > FURMETY
FURMETY same as > FRUMENTY
FURMITIES > FURMITY
FURMITY same as > FRUMENTY
FURNACE n enclosed chamber containing a very hot fire ▷ vb burn in a furnace
FURNACED > FURNACE
FURNACES > FURNACE
FURNACING > FURNACE
FURNIMENT n furniture
FURNISH vb provide with furniture
FURNISHED > FURNISH
FURNISHER > FURNISH
FURNISHES > FURNISH
FURNITURE n large movable articles such as chairs and wardrobes
FUROL variant of > FURFURAL
FUROLE variant of > FURFURAL
FUROLES > FUROLE
FUROLS > FUROL
FUROR same as > FURORE
FURORE n very excited or angry reaction
FURORES > FURORE
FURORS > FUROR
FURPHIES > FURPHY
FURPHY n rumour or fictitious story
FURPIECE n item of clothing made of or decorated with fur
FURPIECES > FURPIECE
FURR vb furrow
FURRED same as > FURRY
FURRIER n dealer in furs
FURRIERS > FURRIER
FURRIERY n occupation of a furrier
FURRIES > FURRY
FURRIEST > FURRY
FURRILY > FURRY
FURRINER n dialect rendering of foreigner
FURRINERS > FURRINER
FURRINESS > FURRY
FURRINGS > FUR
FURRINGS > FUR
FURROW n trench made by a plough ▷ vb make or become wrinkled
FURROWED > FURROW
FURROWER > FURROW
FURROWERS > FURROW
FURROWIER > FURROWY
FURROWING > FURROW
FURROWS > FURROW
FURROWY adj having furrows

FURRS > FURR
FURRY adj like or covered with fur or something furlike ▷ n child's fur-covered toy animal
FURS > FUR
FURTH adv out
FURTHER adv in addition ▷ adj more distant ▷ vb promote
FURTHERED > FURTHER
FURTHERER > FURTHER
FURTHERS > FURTHER
FURTHEST adv to the greatest degree ▷ adj most distant
FURTIVE adj sly and secretive
FURTIVELY > FURTIVE
FURUNCLE technical name for > BOIL
FURUNCLES > FURUNCLE
FURY n wild anger
FURZE n gorse
FURZES > FURZE
FURZIER > FURZE
FURZIEST > FURZE
FURZY > FURZE
FUSAIN n fine charcoal pencil
FUSAINS > FUSAIN
FUSARIA > FUSARIUM
FUSARIUM n type of fungus
FUSARIUMS > FUSARIUM
FUSAROL variant of > FUSAROLE
FUSAROLE n type of architectural moulding
FUSAROLES > FUSAROLE
FUSAROLS > FUSAROL
FUSBALL same as > FOOSBALL
FUSBALLS > FUSBALL
FUSC adj dark or dark-brown
FUSCOUS adj of a brownish-grey colour
FUSE n cord containing an explosive for detonating a bomb ▷ vb (cause to) fail as a result of a blown fuse
FUSED > FUSE
FUSEE n (in early clocks and watches) a spirally grooved spindle
FUSEES > FUSEE
FUSEL n mixture of amyl alcohols, propanol, and butanol
FUSELAGE n body of an aircraft
FUSELAGES > FUSELAGE
FUSELESS > FUSE
FUSELIKE > FUSE
FUSELS > FUSEL
FUSES > FUSE
FUSHION n spirit
FUSHIONS > FUSHION
FUSIBLE adj capable of being melted
FUSIBLY > FUSIBLE
FUSIDIC adj as in fusidic acid kind of acid
FUSIFORM adj elongated and tapering at both ends
FUSIL n light flintlock musket
FUSILE adj easily melted

FUSILEER same as > FUSILIER
FUSILEERS > FUSILEER
FUSILIER n soldier of certain regiments
FUSILIERS > FUSILIER
FUSILLADE n continuous discharge of firearms ▷ vb attack with a fusillade
FUSILLI n spiral-shaped pasta
FUSILLIS > FUSILLI
FUSILS > FUSIL
FUSING > FUSE
FUSION n melting ▷ adj of a style of cooking
FUSIONAL > FUSION
FUSIONISM n favouring of coalitions among political groups
FUSIONIST > FUSIONISM
FUSIONS > FUSION
FUSK vb obtain data from (a website) by using a fusker
FUSKED > FUSK
FUSKER vb obtain data from (a website) by using hacking software
FUSKERED > FUSKER
FUSKERING > FUSKER
FUSKERS > FUSKER
FUSKING > FUSK
FUSKS > FUSK
FUSS n needless activity or worry ▷ vb make a fuss
FUSSBALL same as > FOOSBALL
FUSSBALLS > FUSSBALL
FUSSED > FUSS
FUSSER > FUSS
FUSSERS > FUSS
FUSSES > FUSS
FUSSIER > FUSSY
FUSSIEST > FUSSY
FUSSILY > FUSSY
FUSSINESS > FUSSY
FUSSING > FUSS
FUSSPOT n person who is difficult to please and complains often
FUSSPOTS > FUSSPOT
FUSSY adj inclined to fuss
FUST vb become mouldy
FUSTED > FUST
FUSTET n wood of the Venetian sumach shrub
FUSTETS > FUSTET
FUSTIAN n (formerly) a hard-wearing fabric of cotton mixed with flax or wool ▷ adj cheap
FUSTIANS > FUSTIAN
FUSTIC n large tropical American tree
FUSTICS > FUSTIC
FUSTIER > FUSTY
FUSTIEST > FUSTY
FUSTIGATE vb beat
FUSTILUGS n fat person
FUSTILY > FUSTY
FUSTINESS > FUSTY
FUSTING > FUST
FUSTOC variant of > FUSTIC
FUSTOCS > FUSTOC
FUSTS > FUST
FUSTY adj stale-smelling
FUSULINID n any of various extinct foraminifers

FUSUMA *n* Japanese sliding door
FUSUMAS > FUSUMA
FUTCHEL *n* timber support in a carriage
FUTCHELS > FUTCHEL
FUTHARC *same as* > FUTHARK
FUTHARCS > FUTHARC
FUTHARK *n* phonetic alphabet consisting of runes
FUTHARKS > FUTHARK
FUTHORC *same as* > FUTHARK
FUTHORCS > FUTHORC
FUTHORK *same as* > FUTHARK
FUTHORKS > FUTHORK
FUTILE *adj* unsuccessful or useless
FUTILELY > FUTILE
FUTILER > FUTILE
FUTILEST > FUTILE
FUTILITY *n* lack of effectiveness or success
FUTON *n* Japanese-style bed
FUTONS > FUTON

FUTSAL *n* form of association football
FUTSALS > FUTSAL
FUTTOCK *n* one of the ribs in the frame of a wooden vessel
FUTTOCKS > FUTTOCK
FUTURAL *adj* relating to the future
FUTURE *n* time to come ▷ *adj* yet to come or be
FUTURES *pl n* type of commodity trading
FUTURISM *n* early 20th-century artistic movement
FUTURISMS > FUTURISM
FUTURIST > FUTURISM
FUTURISTS > FUTURISM
FUTURITY *n* future
FUTZ *vb* fritter time away
FUTZED > FUTZ
FUTZES > FUTZ
FUTZING > FUTZ
FUZE *same as* > FUSE
FUZED > FUZE
FUZEE *same as* > FUSEE
FUZEES > FUZEE

FUZELESS *adj* without a fuze
FUZES > FUZE
FUZIL *variant of* > FUSIL
FUZILS > FUZIL
FUZING > FUZE
FUZZ *n* mass of fine or curly hairs or fibres ▷ *vb* make or become fuzzy
FUZZBALL *n* ball of fuzz
FUZZBALLS > FUZZBALL
FUZZBOX *n* device that distorts sound
FUZZBOXES > FUZZBOX
FUZZED > FUZZ
FUZZES > FUZZ
FUZZIER > FUZZY
FUZZIEST > FUZZY
FUZZILY > FUZZY
FUZZINESS > FUZZY
FUZZING > FUZZ
FUZZLE *vb* make drunk
FUZZLED > FUZZLE
FUZZLES > FUZZLE
FUZZLING > FUZZLE
FUZZTONE *n* device distorting electric guitar

sound
FUZZTONES > FUZZTONE
FUZZY *adj* of, like, or covered with fuzz
FY *interj* exclamation of disapproval
FYCE *variant of* > FICE
FYCES > FYCE
FYKE *n* fish trap ▷ *vb* catch fish in this manner
FYKED > FYKE
FYKES > FYKE
FYKING > FYKE
FYLE *variant of* > FILE
FYLES > FYLE
FYLFOT *rare word for* > SWASTIKA
FYLFOTS > FYLFOT
FYNBOS *n* area of low-growing, evergreen vegetation
FYNBOSES > FYNBOS
FYRD *n* militia of an Anglo-Saxon shire
FYRDS > FYRD
FYTTE *n* song
FYTTES > FYTTE

Gg

g

GAB vb talk or chatter ▷ n mechanical device

GABARDINE n strong twill cloth used esp for raincoats

GABBA n type of electronic dance music

GABBARD same as > GABBART

GABBARDS > GABBARD

GABBART n Scottish sailing barge

GABBARTS > GABBART

GABBAS > GABBA

GABBED > GAB

GABBER > GAB

GABBERS > GAB

GABBIER > GABBY

GABBIEST > GABBY

GABBINESS > GABBY

GABBING > GAB

GABBLE vb speak rapidly and indistinctly ▷ n rapid indistinct speech

GABBLED > GABBLE

GABBLER > GABBLE

GABBLERS > GABBLE

GABBLES > GABBLE

GABBLING > GABBLE

GABBLINGS > GABBLE

GABBRO n dark basic plutonic igneous rock

GABBROIC > GABBRO

GABBROID adj gabbro-like

GABBROS > GABBRO

GABBY adj talkative

GABELLE n salt tax levied until 1790

GABELLED > GABELLE

GABELLER n person who collects the gabelle

GABELLERS > GABELLER

GABELLES > GABELLE

GABERDINE same as > GABARDINE

GABFEST n prolonged gossiping or conversation

GABFESTS > GABFEST

GABIES > GABY

GABION n cylindrical metal container filled with stones

GABIONADE n row of gabions submerged in a waterway, stream, river, etc, to control the flow of water

GABIONAGE n structure composed of gabions

GABIONED > GABION

GABIONS > GABION

GABLE n triangular upper part of a wall between sloping roofs

GABLED > GABLE

GABLELIKE > GABLE

GABLES > GABLE

GABLET n small gable

GABLETS > GABLET

GABLING > GABLE

GABNASH n chatter

GABNASHES > GABNASH

GABOON n dark wood

GABOONS > GABOON

GABS > GAB

GABY n simpleton

GACH vb behave boastfully

GACHED > GACH

GACHER n person who gaches

GACHERS > GACHER

GACHES > GACH

GACHING > GACH

GAD vb go about in search of pleasure ▷ n carefree adventure

GADABOUT n pleasure-seeker

GADABOUTS > GADABOUT

GADARENE adj headlong

GADDED > GAD

GADDER > GAD

GADDERS > GAD

GADDI n cushion on an Indian prince's throne

GADDING > GAD

GADDIS > GADDI

GADE same as > GAD

GADES > GADE

GADFLIES > GADFLY

GADFLY n fly that bites cattle

GADGE n man

GADGES > GADGE

GADGET n small mechanical device or appliance

GADGETEER n person who delights in gadgetry

GADGETIER > GADGETY

GADGETRY n gadgets

GADGETS > GADGET

GADGETY adj characterized by gadgets

GADGIE n fellow

GADGIES > GADGIE

GADI n Indian throne

GADID n type of marine fish

GADIDS > GADID

GADIS > GADI

GADJE same as > GADGIE

GADJES > GADJE

GADJO same as > GORGIO

GADJOS > GADJO

GADLING n vagabond

GADLINGS > GADLING

GADMAN n person who drives horses at the plough

GADMEN > GADMAN

GADOID adj of the cod family of marine fishes ▷ n gadoid fish

GADOIDS > GADOID

GADOLINIC adj relating to gadolinium, a silvery white metallic element

GADROON n type of decorative moulding

GADROONED > GADROON

GADROONS > GADROON

GADS > GAD

GADSMAN n person who uses a gad when driving animals

GADSMEN > GADSMAN

GADSO n archaic expression of surprise

GADWALL n type of duck related to the mallard

GADWALLS > GADWALL

GADZOOKS interj mild oath

GAE Scot word for > GO

GAED > GAE

GAEING > GAE

GAELICISE vb adapt to conform to Gaelic spelling and pronunciation

GAELICISM > GAELICISE

GAELICIZE same as > GAELICISE

GAEN > GAE

GAES > GAE

GAFF n stick with an iron hook for landing large fish ▷ vb hook or land (a fish) with a gaff

GAFFE n social blunder

GAFFED > GAFF

GAFFER n foreman or boss

GAFFERS > GAFFER

GAFFES > GAFFE

GAFFING > GAFF

GAFFINGS > GAFF

GAFFS > GAFF

GAFFSAIL n quadrilateral fore-and-aft sail on a sailing vessel

GAFFSAILS > GAFFSAIL

GAG vb choke or retch ▷ n cloth etc put into or tied across the mouth

GAGA adj senile

GAGAKU n type of traditional Japanese music

GAGAKUS > GAGAKU

GAGE vb gauge ▷ n (formerly) an object thrown down as a challenge to fight

GAGEABLE > GAGE

GAGEABLY > GAGE

GAGED > GAGE

GAGER same as > GAUGER

GAGERS > GAGER

GAGES > GAGE

GAGGED > GAG

GAGGER n person or thing that gags

GAGGERIES > GAGGERY

GAGGERS > GAGGER

GAGGERY n practice of telling jokes

GAGGING > GAG

GAGGLE n disorderly crowd ▷ vb (of geese) to cackle

GAGGLED > GAGGLE

GAGGLES > GAGGLE

GAGGLING > GAGGLE

GAGGLINGS > GAGGLE

GAGING > GAGE

GAGMAN n person who writes gags for a comedian

GAGMEN > GAGMAN

GAGS > GAG

GAGSTER n standup comedian

GAGSTERS > GAGSTER

GAHNITE n dark green mineral

GAHNITES > GAHNITE

GAID same as > GAD

GAIDS > GAID

GAIETIES > GAIETY

GAIETY n cheerfulness

GAIJIN n (in Japan) a foreigner

GAILLARD same as > GALLIARD

GAILLARDE same as > GAILLARD

GAILY adv merrily

GAIN vb acquire or obtain ▷ n profit or advantage ▷ adj straight or near

GAINABLE > GAIN

GAINED > GAIN

GAINER n person or thing that gains

GAINERS > GAINER

GAINEST > GAIN

GAINFUL adj useful or profitable

GAINFULLY > GAINFUL

GAINING > GAIN

GAININGS pl n profits or earnings

GAINLESS > GAIN

GAINLIER > GAINLY

GAINLIEST > GAINLY

GAINLY adj graceful or well-formed ▷ adv conveniently or suitably

GAINS pl n profits or winnings

GAINSAID > GAINSAY

GAINSAY *vb* deny or contradict

GAINSAYER > GAINSAY

GAINSAYS > GAINSAY

GAINST *short for* > AGAINST

GAIR *n* strip of green grass on a hillside

GAIRFOWL *same as* > GAREFOWL

GAIRFOWLS > GAIRFOWL

GAIRS > GAIR

GAIT *n* manner of walking ▷ *vb* teach (a horse) a particular gait

GAITA *n* type of bagpipe

GAITAS > GAITA

GAITED > GAIT

GAITER *n* cloth or leather covering for the lower leg

GAITERED *adj* wearing gaiters

GAITERS > GAITER

GAITING > GAIT

GAITS > GAIT

GAITT *Scots word for* > GATE

GAITTS > GAITT

GAJO *same as* > GORGIO

GAJOS > GAJO

GAK *n* cocaine

GAKS > GAK

GAL *n* girl

GALA *n* festival

GALABEA *same as* > DJELLABA

GALABEAH *same as* > DJELLABA

GALABEAHS > GALABEAH

GALABEAS > GALABEA

GALABIA *same as* > DJELLABA

GALABIAH *same as* > DJELLABA

GALABIAHS > GALABIAH

GALABIAS > GALABIA

GALABIEH *same as* > DJELLABA

GALABIEHS > GALABIEH

GALABIYA *same as* > DJELLABA

GALABIYAH *same as* > DJELLABA

GALABIYAS > GALABIYA

GALACTIC *adj* of the Galaxy or other galaxies

GALACTICO *n* famous and highly paid footballer

GALACTOSE *n* white water-soluble monosaccharide found in lactose

GALAGE *same as* > GALOSH

GALAGES > GALAGE

GALAGO *another name for* > BUSHBABY

GALAGOS > GALAGO

GALAH *n* Australian cockatoo

GALAHS > GALAH

GALANGA *same as* > GALINGALE

GALANGAL *same as* > GALINGALE

GALANGALS > GALANGAL

GALANGAS > GALANGA

GALANT *n* 18th-century style of music

GALANTINE *n* cold dish of meat or poultry, which is boned, cooked, stuffed, then pressed into a neat shape and glazed

GALANTS > GALANT

GALANTY *n as in galanty show* pantomime shadow play

GALAPAGO *n* tortoise

GALAPAGOS > GALAPAGO

GALAS > GALA

GALATEA *n* strong twill-weave cotton fabric

GALATEAS > GALATEA

GALAVANT *same as* > GALLIVANT

GALAVANTS > GALAVANT

GALAX *n* coltsfoot

GALAXES > GALAX

GALAXIES > GALAXY

GALAXY *n* system of stars

GALBANUM *n* bitter aromatic gum resin

GALBANUMS > GALBANUM

GALDRAGON *old Scots word for a* > SORCERESS

GALE *n* strong wind ▷ *vb* be very stormy

GALEA *n* part or organ shaped like a helmet

GALEAE > GALEA

GALEAS > GALEA

GALEATE > GALEA

GALEATED > GALEA

GALED > GALE

GALEIFORM > GALEA

GALENA *n* soft bluish-grey mineral

GALENAS > GALENA

GALENGALE *same as* > GALINGALE

GALENIC > GALENA

GALENICAL *n* any drug prepared from plant or animal tissue, esp vegetables, rather than being chemically synthesized ▷ *adj* denoting or belonging to this group of drugs

GALENITE *same as* > GALENA

GALENITES > GALENITE

GALENOID *adj* pertaining to galena

GALERE *n* group of people having a common interest

GALERES > GALERE

GALES > GALE

GALETTE *n* type of savoury pancake

GALETTES > GALETTE

GALILEE *n* type of porch or chapel

GALILEES > GALILEE

GALING > GALE

GALINGALE *n* European plant with rough-edged leaves, reddish spikelets of flowers, and aromatic roots

GALIONGEE *n* sailor

GALIOT *n* small swift galley

GALIOTS > GALIOT

GALIPOT *n* resin obtained from several species of pine

GALIPOTS > GALIPOT

GALIVANT *same as* > GALLIVANT

GALIVANTS > GALIVANT

GALL *n* impudence ▷ *vb* annoy

GALLABEA *same as* > DJELLABA

GALLABEAH *same as* > DJELLABA

GALLABEAS > GALLABEA

GALLABIA *same as* > DJELLABA

GALLABIAH *same as* > DJELLABA

GALLABIAS > GALLABIA

GALLABIEH *same as* > DJELLABA

GALLABIYA *same as* > DJELLABA

GALLAMINE *n* muscle relaxant used in anaesthesia

GALLANT *adj* brave and noble ▷ *n* man who tried to impress with fashionable clothes or daring acts ▷ *vb* court or flirt (with)

GALLANTED > GALLANT

GALLANTER > GALLANT

GALLANTLY > GALLANT

GALLANTRY *n* showy, attentive treatment of women

GALLANTS > GALLANT

GALLATE *n* salt of gallic acid

GALLATES > GALLATE

GALLEASS *n* three-masted lateen-rigged galley

GALLED > GALL

GALLEIN *n* type of dyestuff

GALLEINS > GALLEIN

GALLEON *n* large three-masted sailing ship

GALLEONS > GALLEON

GALLERIA *n* central court through several storeys of a shopping centre

GALLERIAS > GALLERIA

GALLERIED *adj* having a gallery or galleries

GALLERIES > GALLERY

GALLERIST *n* person who owns or runs an art gallery

GALLERY *n* room or building for displaying works of art ▷ *vb* tunnel; form an underground gallery

GALLET *vb* use mixture to support a roof-slate

GALLETA *n* low-growing, coarse grass

GALLETAS > GALLETA

GALLETED > GALLET

GALLETING > GALLET

GALLETS > GALLET

GALLEY *n* kitchen of a ship or aircraft

GALLEYS > GALLEY

GALLFLIES > GALLFLY

GALLFLY *n* any of several small insects

GALLIARD *n* spirited dance in triple time for two persons, popular in the 16th and 17th centuries ▷ *adj* lively

GALLIARDS > GALLIARD

GALLIASS *same as* > GALLEASS

GALLIC *adj* of or containing gallium in the trivalent state

GALLICA *n* variety of rose

GALLICAN *adj* favouring restriction of papal control of the French church

GALLICAS > GALLICA

GALLICISE *same as* > GALLICIZE

GALLICISM *n* word or idiom borrowed from French

GALLICIZE *vb* make or become French in attitude, language, etc

GALLIED > GALLY

GALLIER > GALLY

GALLIES > GALLY

GALLIEST > GALLY

GALLINAZO *n* black vulture

GALLING *adj* annoying or bitterly humiliating

GALLINGLY > GALLING

GALLINULE *n* moorhen

GALLIOT *same as* > GALIOT

GALLIOTS > GALLIOT

GALLIPOT *same as* > GALIPOT

GALLIPOTS > GALLIPOT

GALLISE *vb* use method to increase the quantity of wine produced

GALLISED > GALLISE

GALLISES > GALLISE

GALLISING > GALLISE

GALLISISE *vb* gallise

GALLISIZE *same as* > GALLISE

GALLIUM *n* soft grey metallic element

GALLIUMS > GALLIUM

GALLIVANT *vb* go about in search of pleasure

GALLIVAT *n* Oriental armed vessel

GALLIVATS > GALLIVAT

GALLIWASP *n* type of Central American lizard

GALLIZE *same as* > GALLISE

GALLIZED > GALLIZE

GALLIZES > GALLIZE

GALLIZING > GALLIZE

GALLNUT *n* type of plant gall that resembles a nut

GALLNUTS > GALLNUT

GALLOCK *adj* left-handed

GALLON *n* liquid measure of eight pints, equal to 4.55 litres

GALLONAGE *n* capacity measured in gallons

GALLONS > GALLON

GALLOON *n* narrow band of cord, gold braid, etc

GALLOONED > GALLOON

GALLOONS > GALLOON

GALLOOT *same as* > GALOOT

GALLOOTS > GALLOOT

GALLOP *n* horse's fastest pace ▷ *vb* go or ride at a gallop

GALLOPADE *n* gallop ▷ *vb* perform a gallopade

GALLOPED > GALLOP

GALLOPER > GALLOP

GALLOPERS > GALLOP

g

g

GALLOPING adj progressing at or as if at a gallop

GALLOPS > GALLOP

GALLOUS adj of or containing gallium in the divalent state

GALLOW vb frighten

GALLOWAY n breed of hornless beef cattle

GALLOWAYS > GALLOWAY

GALLOWED > GALLOW

GALLOWING > GALLOW

GALLOWS n wooden structure used for hanging criminals

GALLOWSES > GALLOWS

GALLS > GALL

GALLSTONE n hard mass formed in the gall bladder or its ducts

GALLUMPH same as > GALUMPH

GALLUMPHS > GALLUMPH

GALLUS adj bold ▷ n suspender for trousers

GALLUSED adj held up by galluses

GALLUSES > GALLUS

GALLY vb frighten ▷ adj (of land) damp or barren

GALLYING > GALLY

GALOCHE same as > GALOSH

GALOCHED > GALOCHE

GALOCHES > GALOCHE

GALOCHING > GALOCHE

GALOOT n clumsy or uncouth person

GALOOTS > GALOOT

GALOP n 19th-century dance in quick duple time ▷ vb dance a galop

GALOPADE same as > GALOP

GALOPADES > GALOP

GALOPED > GALOP

GALOPIN n boy who ran errands for a cook

GALOPING > GALOP

GALOPINS > GALOPIN

GALOPPED > GALOP

GALOPPING > GALOP

GALOPS > GALOP

GALORE adv in abundance ▷ adj in abundance ▷ n abundance

GALORES > GALORE

GALOSH n waterproof overshoe ▷ vb cover with galoshes

GALOSHE same as > GALOSH

GALOSHED > GALOSH

GALOSHES > GALOSH

GALOSHING > GALOSH

GALOWSES Shakespearean plural for > GALLOWS

GALRAVAGE same as > GILRAVAGE

GALS > GAL

GALTONIA n type of bulbous plant with waxy white flowers and a fragrant scent

GALTONIAS > GALTONIA

GALUMPH vb leap or move about clumsily

GALUMPHED > GALUMPH

GALUMPHER > GALUMPH

GALUMPHS > GALUMPH

GALUT same as > GALUTH

GALUTH n exile of Jews from Palestine

GALUTHS > GALUTH

GALUTS > GALUT

GALVANIC adj of or producing an electric current generated by chemical means

GALVANISE same as > GALVANIZE

GALVANISM n electricity, esp when produced by chemical means as in a cell or battery

GALVANIST > GALVANISM

GALVANIZE vb stimulate into action ▷ n galvanized iron, usually in the form of corrugated sheets as used in roofing

GALVO n instrument for measuring electric current

GALVOS > GALVO

GALYAC same as > GALYAK

GALYACS > GALYAC

GALYAK n smooth glossy fur

GALYAKS > GALYAK

GAM n school of whales ▷ vb (of whales) form a school

GAMA n tall perennial grass

GAMAHUCHE n vulgar word for cunnilingus or fellatio ▷ vb practise cunnilingus or fellatio on

GAMARUCHE same as > GAMAHUCHE

GAMAS > GAMA

GAMASH n type of gaiter

GAMASHES > GAMASH

GAMAY n red grape variety

GAMAYS > GAMAY

GAMB n in heraldry, the whole foreleg of a beast

GAMBA n second-largest member of the viol family

GAMBADE same as > GAMBADO

GAMBADES > GAMBADE

GAMBADO n leap or gambol; caper ▷ vb perform a gambado

GAMBADOED > GAMBADO

GAMBADOES > GAMBADO

GAMBADOS > GAMBADO

GAMBAS > GAMBA

GAMBE same as > GAMB

GAMBES > GAMBE

GAMBESON n garment worn under mail in the Middle Ages

GAMBESONS > GAMBESON

GAMBET n tattler

GAMBETS > GAMBET

GAMBETTA n redshank

GAMBETTAS > GAMBETTA

GAMBIA same as > GAMBIER

GAMBIAS > GAMBIA

GAMBIER n astringent resinous substance

GAMBIERS > GAMBIER

GAMBIR same as > GAMBIER

GAMBIRS > GAMBIR

GAMBIST n person who plays the (viola da) gamba

GAMBISTS > GAMBIST

GAMBIT n opening move intended to secure an advantage ▷ vb sacrifice a chess piece to gain a better position

GAMBITED > GAMBIT

GAMBITING > GAMBIT

GAMBITS > GAMBIT

GAMBLE vb play games of chance to win money ▷ n risky undertaking

GAMBLED > GAMBLE

GAMBLER > GAMBLE

GAMBLERS > GAMBLE

GAMBLES > GAMBLE

GAMBLING > GAMBLE

GAMBLINGS > GAMBLE

GAMBO n farm cart

GAMBOES > GAMBO

GAMBOGE n gum resin

GAMBOGES > GAMBOGE

GAMBOGIAN > GAMBOGE

GAMBOGIC > GAMBOGE

GAMBOL vb jump about playfully, frolic ▷ n frolic

GAMBOLED > GAMBOL

GAMBOLING > GAMBOL

GAMBOLLED > GAMBOL

GAMBOLS > GAMBOL

GAMBOS > GAMBO

GAMBREL n hock of a horse or similar animal

GAMBRELS > GAMBREL

GAMBROON n type of linen cloth

GAMBROONS > GAMBROON

GAMBS > GAMB

GAMBUSIA n small fish that feeds on mosquito larvae

GAMBUSIAS > GAMBUSIA

GAME n amusement or pastime ▷ vb play games ▷ adj brave

GAMEBAG n bag for carrying hunted game birds

GAMEBAGS > GAMEBAG

GAMEBOOK n book containing a range of possible strategies for a game

GAMEBOOKS > GAMEBOOK

GAMECOCK n cock bred and trained for fighting

GAMECOCKS > GAMECOCK

GAMED > GAME

GAMEFISH n fish caught for sport

GAMEFOWL n cock bred for cockfighting

GAMEFOWLS > GAMEFOWL

GAMELAN n type of percussion orchestra

GAMELANS > GAMELAN

GAMELIKE > GAME

GAMELY adv in a brave or sporting manner

GAMENESS n courage or bravery

GAMEPLAY n plot of a computer or video game or the way that it is played

GAMEPLAYS > GAMEPLAY

GAMER n person who plays computer games

GAMERS > GAMER

GAMES > GAME

GAMESHOW n TV show in which games are played by contestants

GAMESHOWS > GAMESHOW

GAMESIER > GAMESY

GAMESIEST > GAMESY

GAMESMAN n one who practises gamesmanship

GAMESMEN > GAMESMAN

GAMESOME adj full of merriment

GAMEST > GAME

GAMESTER n someone who plays games

GAMESTERS > GAMESTER

GAMESY adj sporty

GAMETAL > GAMETE

GAMETE n reproductive cell

GAMETES > GAMETE

GAMETIC > GAMETE

GAMEY adj having the smell or flavour of game

GAMEYNESS n quality of being gamey

GAMGEE n as in gamgee tissue type of wound-dressing

GAMIC adj (esp of reproduction) requiring the fusion of gametes

GAMIER > GAMEY

GAMIEST > GAMEY

GAMIFIED > GAMIFY

GAMIFIES > GAMIFY

GAMIFY vb add gamelike elements to a task to encourage participation

GAMIFYING > GAMIFY

GAMILY > GAMEY

GAMIN n street urchin

GAMINE n slim boyish young woman

GAMINERIE n impish behaviour

GAMINES > GAMINE

GAMINESS > GAMEY

GAMING n playing games

GAMINGS > GAMING

GAMINS > GAMIN

GAMMA n third letter of the Greek alphabet

GAMMADIA > GAMMADION

GAMMADION n decorative figure composed of a number of Greek capital gammas, esp radiating from a centre, as in a swastika

GAMMAS > GAMMA

GAMMAT n offensive term for a Cape Coloured person

GAMMATIA > GAMMATION

GAMMATION same as > GAMMADION

GAMMATS > GAMMAT

GAMME n musical scale

GAMMED > GAM

GAMMER n dialect word for an old woman

GAMMERS > GAMMER

GAMMES > GAMME

GAMMIER > GAMMY

GAMMIEST > GAMMY

GAMMING > GAM

GAMMOCK vb clown around

GAMMOCKED > GAMMOCK

GAMMOCKS > GAMMOCK

GAMMON n cured or smoked ham ▷ vb score a double victory in backgammon over

GAMMONED > GAMMON

GAMMONER > GAMMON

GAMMONERS > GAMMON
GAMMONING > GAMMON
GAMMONS > GAMMON
GAMMY adj (of the leg) lame
GAMODEME n isolated breeding population
GAMODEMES > GAMODEME
GAMONE n chemical used by gametes
GAMONES > GAMONE
GAMP n umbrella
GAMPISH adj bulging
GAMPS > GAMP
GAMS > GAM
GAMUT n whole range or scale (of music, emotions, etc)
GAMUTS > GAMUT
GAMY same as > GAMEY
GAMYNESS > GAMY
GAN vb go
GANACHE n rich icing or filling
GANACHES > GANACHE
GANCH vb impale
GANCHED > GANCH
GANCHES > GANCH
GANCHING > GANCH
GANDER n male goose ▷ vb look
GANDERED > GANDER
GANDERING > GANDER
GANDERISM > GANDER
GANDERS > GANDER
GANDY adj as in gandy dancer railway track maintenance worker
GANE > GO
GANEF n unscrupulous opportunist
GANEFS > GANEF
GANEV same as > GANEF
GANEVS > GANEV
GANG n (criminal) group ▷ vb become or act as a gang
GANGBANG n sexual intercourse with several men one after the other ▷ vb force to take part in a gangbang
GANGBANGS > GANGBANG
GANGBO n order restricting the activities of a gang member
GANGBOARD n gangway
GANGBOS > GANGBO
GANGED > GANG
GANGER n foreman of a gang of labourers
GANGERS > GANGER
GANGING > GANG
GANGINGS > GANG
GANGLAND n criminal underworld
GANGLANDS > GANGLAND
GANGLE vb move awkwardly
GANGLED > GANGLE
GANGLES > GANGLE
GANGLIA > GANGLION
GANGLIAL > GANGLION
GANGLIAR > GANGLION
GANGLIATE vb form a ganglion
GANGLIER > GANGLY
GANGLIEST > GANGLY
GANGLING adj lanky and awkward

GANGLION n group of nerve cells
GANGLIONS > GANGLION
GANGLY same as > GANGLING
GANGPLANK n portable bridge for boarding or leaving a ship
GANGPLOW n plough designed to produce parallel furrows
GANGPLOWS > GANGPLOW
GANGREL n wandering beggar
GANGRELS > GANGREL
GANGRENE n decay of body tissue as a result of disease or injury ▷ vb become or cause to become affected with gangrene
GANGRENED > GANGRENE
GANGRENES > GANGRENE
GANGS > GANG
GANGSHAG vb participate in group sex with
GANGSHAGS > GANGSHAG
GANGSMAN n foreman
GANGSMEN > GANGSMAN
GANGSTA n member of a street gang
GANGSTAS > GANGSTA
GANGSTER n member of a criminal gang
GANGSTERS > GANGSTER
GANGUE n valueless material in an ore
GANGUES > GANGUE
GANGWAY same as > GANGPLANK
GANGWAYS > GANGWAY
GANISTER n type of sedimentary rock
GANISTERS > GANISTER
GANJA n highly potent form of cannabis
GANJAH same as > GANJA
GANJAHS > GANJAH
GANJAS > GANJA
GANNED > GAN
GANNET n large sea bird
GANNETRY n gannets' breeding-place
GANNETS > GANNET
GANNING > GAN
GANNISTER same as > GANISTER
GANOF same as > GANEF
GANOFS > GANOF
GANOID adj of the scales of certain fishes ▷ n ganoid fish
GANOIDS > GANOID
GANOIN n the outer layer of fish scales
GANOINE same as > GANOIN
GANOINES > GANOINE
GANOINS > GANOIN
GANS > GAN
GANSEY n jersey or pullover
GANSEYS > GANSEY
GANT vb yawn
GANTED > GANT
GANTELOPE same as > GAUNTLET
GANTING > GANT
GANTLET n section of a railway where two tracks overlap ▷ vb make railway tracks form a gantlet

GANTLETED > GANTLET
GANTLETS > GANTLET
GANTLINE n line rove through a sheave for hoisting men or gear
GANTLINES > GANTLINE
GANTLOPE same as > GAUNTLET
GANTLOPES > GANTLOPE
GANTRIES > GANTRY
GANTRY n structure supporting something
GANTS > GANT
GANYMEDE n potboy
GANYMEDES > GANYMEDE
GANZFELD n type of experiment used in parapsychology
GANZFELDS > GANZFELD
GAOL same as > JAIL
GAOLBIRD n person who is or has been confined to gaol, esp repeatedly
GAOLBIRDS > GAOLBIRD
GAOLBREAK less common spelling of > JAILBREAK
GAOLBROKE > GAOLBREAK
GAOLED > GAOL
GAOLER > GAOL
GAOLERESS n female gaoler
GAOLERS > GAOL
GAOLING > GAOL
GAOLLESS adj without a gaol
GAOLS > GAOL
GAP n break or opening
GAPE vb stare in wonder ▷ n act of gaping
GAPED > GAPE
GAPER n person or thing that gapes
GAPERS > GAPER
GAPES n disease of young domestic fowl
GAPESEED n person who stares, mouth agape, at something
GAPESEEDS > GAPESEED
GAPEWORM n type of parasitic worm that lives in the trachea of birds
GAPEWORMS > GAPEWORM
GAPIER > GAPE
GAPIEST > GAPE
GAPING adj wide open ▷ n state of having a gaping mouth
GAPINGLY > GAPING
GAPINGS > GAPING
GAPLESS > GAP
GAPO n forest near a river, flooded in the rainy season
GAPOS > GAPO
GAPOSIS n gap between closed fastenings on a garment
GAPOSISES > GAPOSIS
GAPPED > GAP
GAPPER n person taking a year out of education
GAPPERS > GAPPER
GAPPIER > GAP
GAPPIEST > GAP
GAPPING n the act of taking a gap year
GAPPINGS > GAPPING
GAPPY > GAP

GAPS > GAP
GAPY > GAPE
GAR same as > GARPIKE
GARAGE n building used to house cars ▷ vb put or keep a car in a garage
GARAGED > GARAGE
GARAGEMAN n car mechanic
GARAGEMEN > GARAGEMAN
GARAGES > GARAGE
GARAGEY adj (of music) in a garage style
GARAGIER > GARAGEY
GARAGIEST > GARAGEY
GARAGING n accommodation for housing a motor vehicle
GARAGINGS > GARAGING
GARAGIST n person who runs a garage
GARAGISTE n small-scale wine-maker
GARAGISTS > GARAGIST
GARB n clothes ▷ vb clothe
GARBAGE n rubbish
GARBAGES > GARBAGE
GARBAGEY > GARBAGE
GARBAGIER > GARBAGY
GARBAGY adj like garbage
GARBANZO another name for > CHICKPEA
GARBANZOS > GARBANZO
GARBE n in heraldry, a wheat-sheaf
GARBED > GARB
GARBES > GARB
GARBING > GARB
GARBLE vb jumble (a story, quotation, etc), esp unintentionally ▷ n act of garbling
GARBLED adj (of a story etc) jumbled and confused
GARBLER > GARBLE
GARBLERS > GARBLE
GARBLES > GARBLE
GARBLESS > GARB
GARBLING > GARBLE
GARBLINGS > GARBLE
GARBO n dustman
GARBOARD n bottommost plank of a vessel's hull
GARBOARDS > GARBOARD
GARBOIL n confusion or disturbance
GARBOILS > GARBOIL
GARBOLOGY n study of the contents of domestic dustbins to analyse the consumption patterns of households
GARBOS > GARBO
GARBS > GARB
GARBURE n thick soup from Bearn in France
GARBURES > GARBURE
GARCINIA n tropical tree
GARCINIAS > GARCINIA
GARCON n waiter
GARCONS > GARCON
GARDA n member of the Irish police force
GARDAI > GARDA
GARDANT same as > GUARDANT
GARDANTS > GARDANT

GARDEN n piece of land for growing flowers, fruit, or vegetables ▷ vb cultivate a garden
GARDENED > GARDEN
GARDENER n person who works in or takes care of a garden as an occupation or pastime
GARDENERS > GARDENER
GARDENFUL n quantity that will fill a garden
GARDENIA n large fragrant white waxy flower
GARDENIAS > GARDENIA
GARDENING n planning and cultivation of a garden
GARDENS > GARDEN
GARDEROBE n wardrobe or the contents of a wardrobe
GARDYLOO n act of throwing slops from a window
GARDYLOOS > GARDYLOO
GARE n filth ▷ adj greedy; covetous
GAREFOWL n great auk
GAREFOWLS > GAREFOWL
GARES > GARE
GARFISH same as > GARPIKE
GARFISHES > GARFISH
GARGANEY n small Eurasian duck, closely related to the mallard
GARGANEYS > GARGANEY
GARGANTUA n monster in Japanese film
GARGARISE vb gargle
GARGARISM n gargle
GARGARIZE same as > GARGARISE
GARGET n inflammation of the mammary gland
GARGETS > GARGET
GARGETY > GARGET
GARGLE vb wash the throat ▷ n liquid used for gargling
GARGLED > GARGLE
GARGLER > GARGLE
GARGLERS > GARGLE
GARGLES > GARGLE
GARGLING > GARGLE
GARGOYLE n waterspout carved in the form of a grotesque face, esp on a church ▷ vb provide with gargoyles
GARGOYLED > GARGOYLE
GARGOYLES > GARGOYLE
GARI n thinly sliced pickled ginger
GARIAL same as > GAVIAL
GARIALS > GARIAL
GARIBALDI n woman's loose blouse with long sleeves popular in the 1860s, copied from the red flannel shirt worn by Garibaldi's soldiers
GARIGUE n open shrubby vegetation of dry Mediterranean regions
GARIGUES > GARIGUE
GARIS > GARI
GARISH adj crudely bright or colourful ▷ vb heal
GARISHED > GARISH
GARISHES > GARISH

GARISHING > GARISH
GARISHLY > GARISH
GARJAN same as > GURJUN
GARJANS > GARJAN
GARLAND n wreath of flowers worn or hung as a decoration ▷ vb decorate with garlands
GARLANDED > GARLAND
GARLANDRY n collective term for garlands
GARLANDS > GARLAND
GARLIC n pungent bulb of a plant of the onion family
GARLICKED adj flavoured with garlic
GARLICKY adj containing or resembling the taste or odour of garlic
GARLICS > GARLIC
GARMENT n article of clothing ▷ vb cover or clothe
GARMENTED > GARMENT
GARMENTS > GARMENT
GARMS pl n clothing
GARNER vb collect or store ▷ n place for storage or safekeeping
GARNERED > GARNER
GARNERING > GARNER
GARNERS > GARNER
GARNET n red semiprecious stone
GARNETS > GARNET
GARNI adj garnished
GARNISH vb decorate (food) ▷ n decoration for food
GARNISHED > GARNISH
GARNISHEE n person upon whom a notice of warning has been served ▷ vb attach (a debt or other property) by a notice of warning
GARNISHER > GARNISH
GARNISHES > GARNISH
GARNISHOR n person who or thing that garnishes
GARNISHRY n decoration
GARNITURE n decoration or embellishment
GAROTE same as > GARROTTE
GAROTED > GAROTE
GAROTES > GAROTE
GAROTING > GAROTE
GAROTTE same as > GARROTTE
GAROTTED > GAROTTE
GAROTTER > GAROTTE
GAROTTERS > GAROTTE
GAROTTES > GAROTTE
GAROTTING > GAROTTE
GAROUPA in Chinese and SE Asian cookery, another name for > GROPER
GAROUPAS > GAROUPA
GARPIKE n primitive freshwater bony fish
GARPIKES > GARPIKE
GARRAN same as > GARRON
GARRANS > GARRAN
GARRE vb compel
GARRED > GAR
GARRES > GARRE
GARRET n attic in a house
GARRETED adj living in a garret

GARRETEER n person who lives in a garret
GARRETS > GARRET
GARRIGUE same as > GARIGUE
GARRIGUES > GARRIGUE
GARRING > GAR
GARRISON n troops stationed in a town or fort ▷ vb station troops in
GARRISONS > GARRISON
GARRON n small sturdy pony
GARRONS > GARRON
GARROT n goldeneye duck
GARROTE same as > GARROTTE
GARROTED > GARROTE
GARROTER > GARROTE
GARROTES > GARROTE
GARROTING > GARROTE
GARROTS > GARROT
GARROTTE n Spanish method of execution by strangling ▷ vb kill by this method
GARROTTED > GARROTTE
GARROTTER > GARROTTE
GARROTTES > GARROTTE
GARRULITY > GARRULOUS
GARRULOUS adj talkative
GARRYA n catkin-bearing evergreen shrub
GARRYAS > GARRYA
GARRYOWEN n (in rugby union) high kick forwards followed by a charge to the place where the ball lands
GARS > GAR
GART vb compel
GARTER n band used to hold up a sock or stocking ▷ vb secure with a garter
GARTERED > GARTER
GARTERING > GARTER
GARTERS > GARTER
GARTH n courtyard surrounded by a cloister
GARTHS > GARTH
GARUDA n Hindu god
GARUDAS > GARUDA
GARUM n fermented fish sauce
GARUMS > GARUM
GARVEY n small flat-bottomed yacht
GARVEYS > GARVEY
GARVIE n sprat
GARVIES > GARVIE
GARVOCK n sprat
GARVOCKS > GARVOCK
GAS n airlike substance that is not liquid or solid ▷ vb poison or render unconscious with gas
GASAHOL n mixture of petrol and alcohol used as fuel
GASAHOLS > GASAHOL
GASALIER same as > GASOLIER
GASALIERS > GASALIER
GASBAG n person who talks too much ▷ vb talk in a voluble way
GASBAGGED > GASBAG
GASBAGS > GASBAG
GASCON n boaster

GASCONADE n boastful talk, bragging, or bluster ▷ vb boast, brag, or bluster
GASCONISM > GASCON
GASCONS > GASCON
GASEITIES > GASEITY
GASEITY n state of being gaseous
GASELIER same as > GASOLIER
GASELIERS > GASELIER
GASEOUS adj of or like gas
GASES > GAS
GASFIELD n area in which natural gas is found underground
GASFIELDS > GASFIELD
GASH vb make a long deep cut in ▷ n long deep cut ▷ adj witty
GASHED > GASH
GASHER > GASH
GASHES > GASH
GASHEST > GASH
GASHFUL adj full of gashes
GASHING > GASH
GASHLIER > GASHLY
GASHLIEST > GASHLY
GASHLY adv wittily ▷ adj hideous; ghastly
GASHOLDER n large tank for storing gas
GASHOUSE n gasworks
GASHOUSES > GASHOUSE
GASIFIED > GASIFY
GASIFIER > GASIFY
GASIFIERS > GASIFY
GASIFIES > GASIFY
GASIFORM adj in a gaseous form
GASIFY vb change into a gas
GASIFYING > GASIFY
GASKET n type of seal
GASKETED adj having a gasket
GASKETS > GASKET
GASKIN n lower part of a horse's thigh
GASKING same as > GASKET
GASKINGS > GASKING
GASKINS > GASKIN
GASLESS > GAS
GASLIGHT vb manipulate (a person) by presenting them with lies until they doubt their sanity
GASLIGHTS > GASLIGHT
GASLIT adj lit by gas
GASMAN n man employed by a gas company
GASMEN > GASMAN
GASOGENE n siphon bottle
GASOGENES > GASOGENE
GASOHOL n mixture of petrol and alcohol used as fuel
GASOHOLS > GASOHOL
GASOLENE same as > GASOLINE
GASOLENES > GASOLENE
GASOLIER n branched hanging fitting for gaslights
GASOLIERS > GASOLIER
GASOLINE n petrol
GASOLINES > GASOLINE
GASOLINIC > GASOLINE
GASOMETER same as > GASHOLDER

GASOMETRY n measurement of quantities of gases

GASP vb draw in breath sharply or with difficulty ▷ n convulsive intake of breath

GASPED > GASP

GASPER n person who gasps

GASPEREAU another name for > ALEWIFE

GASPERS > GASPER

GASPIER > GASP

GASPIEST > GASP

GASPINESS > GASP

GASPING > GASP

GASPINGLY > GASP

GASPINGS > GASP

GASPS > GASP

GASPY > GASP

GASSED > GAS

GASSER n drilling or well that yields natural gas

GASSERS > GASSER

GASSES > GAS

GASSIER > GASSY

GASSIEST > GASSY

GASSILY > GASSY

GASSINESS > GASSY

GASSING > GAS

GASSINGS > GAS

GASSY adj filled with gas

GAST vb frighten

GASTED > GAST

GASTER vb frighten

GASTERED > GASTER

GASTERING > GASTER

GASTERS > GASTER

GASTFULL adj dismal

GASTHAUS n guest house

GASTIGHT adj not allowing gas to enter or escape

GASTING > GAST

GASTNESS n dread

GASTNESSE same as > GASTNESS

GASTRAEA n hypothetical primeval form posited by Haeckel

GASTRAEAS > GASTRAEA

GASTRAEUM n underside of the body

GASTRAL adj relating to the stomach

GASTREA same as > GASTRAEA

GASTREAS > GASTREA

GASTRIC adj of the stomach

GASTRIN n polypeptide hormone

GASTRINS > GASTRIN

GASTRITIC > GASTRITIS

GASTRITIS n inflammation of the stomach lining

GASTROPOD n type of mollusc, such as a snail, with a single flattened muscular foot

GASTROPUB n pub specializing in high-quality food

GASTRULA n saclike animal embryo

GASTRULAE > GASTRULA

GASTRULAR > GASTRULA

GASTRULAS > GASTRULA

GASTS > GAST

GASWORKS n plant where coal gas is made

GAT n pistol or revolver

GATCH vb behave boastfully

GATCHED > GATCH

GATCHER n person who gatches

GATCHERS > GATCHER

GATCHES > GATCH

GATCHING > GATCH

GATE n movable barrier, usu hinged, in a wall or fence ▷ vb provide with a gate or gates

GATEAU n rich elaborate cake

GATEAUS > GATEAU

GATEAUX > GATEAU

GATECRASH vb gain entry to (a party, concert, etc) without invitation or payment

GATED > GATE

GATEFOLD n oversize page in a book or magazine that is folded in

GATEFOLDS > GATEFOLD

GATEHOUSE n building at or above a gateway

GATELEG n table having hinged legs that swing out

GATELEGS > GATELEG

GATELESS > GATE

GATELIKE > GATE

GATEMAN n gatekeeper

GATEMEN > GATEMAN

GATEPOST n post on which a gate is hung

GATEPOSTS > GATEPOST

GATER variant of > GATOR

GATERS > GATER

GATES > GATE

GATEWAY n entrance with a gate

GATEWAYS > GATEWAY

GATH n (in Indian music) second section of a raga

GATHER vb assemble ▷ n act of gathering

GATHERED > GATHER

GATHERER > GATHER

GATHERERS > GATHER

GATHERING n assembly

GATHERS > GATHER

GATHS > GATH

GATING > GATE

GATINGS > GATE

GATLING n as in gatling gun kind of machine-gun

GATOR shortened form of > ALLIGATOR

GATORS > GATOR

GATS > GAT

GATVOL adj in South African English, fed up

GAU n district set up by the Nazi Party

GAUCH vb behave boastfully

GAUCHE adj socially awkward ▷ vb make gauche

GAUCHED > GAUCHE

GAUCHELY > GAUCHE

GAUCHER n gauche person

GAUCHERIE n quality of being gauche

GAUCHERS > GAUCHER

GAUCHES > GAUCHE

GAUCHESCO adj relating to the folk traditions of the gauchos

GAUCHEST > GAUCHE

GAUCHING > GAUCHE

GAUCHO n S American cowboy

GAUCHOS > GAUCHO

GAUCIER variant of > GAUCY

GAUCIER > GAUCY

GAUCIEST > GAUCY

GAUCY adj plump or jolly

GAUD n article of cheap finery ▷ vb decorate gaudily

GAUDEAMUS n first word of a traditional graduation song, hence the song itself

GAUDED > GAUD

GAUDERIES > GAUDERY

GAUDERY n cheap finery or display

GAUDGIE same as > GADGIE

GAUDGIES > GAUDGIE

GAUDIER > GAUDY

GAUDIES > GAUDY

GAUDIEST > GAUDY

GAUDILY > GAUDY

GAUDINESS > GAUDY

GAUDING > GAUD

GAUDS > GAUD

GAUDY adj vulgarly bright or colourful ▷ n festival held at some schools and colleges

GAUFER n wafer

GAUFERS > GAUFER

GAUFFER same as > GOFFER

GAUFFERED > GAUFFER

GAUFFERS > GAUFFER

GAUFRE same as > GAUFER

GAUFRES > GAUFRE

GAUGE vb estimate or judge ▷ n measuring instrument ▷ adj of a pressure measurement

GAUGEABLE > GAUGE

GAUGEABLY > GAUGE

GAUGED > GAUGE

GAUGER n person or thing that gauges

GAUGERS > GAUGER

GAUGES > GAUGE

GAUGING > GAUGE

GAUGINGS > GAUGE

GAUJE same as > GADGIE

GAUJES > GAUJE

GAULEITER n person in a position of authority who behaves in an overbearing authoritarian manner

GAULT n stiff compact clay or thick heavy clayey soil

GAULTER n person who digs gault

GAULTERS > GAULTER

GAULTS > GAULT

GAUM vb understand

GAUMED > GAUM

GAUMIER > GAUMY

GAUMIEST > GAUMY

GAUMING > GAUM

GAUMLESS variant spelling of > GORMLESS

GAUMS > GAUM

GAUMY adj clogged

GAUN > GO

GAUNCH same as > GANCH

GAUNCHED > GAUNCH

GAUNCHES > GAUNCH

GAUNCHING > GAUNCH

GAUNT adj lean and haggard ▷ vb yawn

GAUNTED > GAUNT

GAUNTER > GAUNT

GAUNTEST > GAUNT

GAUNTING > GAUNT

GAUNTLET n heavy glove with a long cuff ▷ vb run (or cause to run) the gauntlet

GAUNTLETS > GAUNTLET

GAUNTLY > GAUNT

GAUNTNESS > GAUNT

GAUNTREE same as > GANTRY

GAUNTREES > GAUNTREE

GAUNTRIES > GAUNTRY

GAUNTRY same as > GANTRY

GAUNTS > GAUNT

GAUP same as > GAWP

GAUPED > GAUP

GAUPER > GAUP

GAUPERS > GAUP

GAUPING > GAUP

GAUPS > GAUP

GAUPUS same as > GAWPUS

GAUPUSES > GAUPUS

GAUR n large wild member of the cattle tribe

GAURS > GAUR

GAUS > GAU

GAUSS n cgs unit of magnetic flux density

GAUSSES > GAUSS

GAUSSIAN adj denoting the mathematical principles of K F Gauss

GAUZE n transparent loosely woven fabric

GAUZELIKE > GAUZE

GAUZES > GAUZE

GAUZIER > GAUZY

GAUZIEST > GAUZY

GAUZILY > GAUZY

GAUZINESS > GAUZY

GAUZY adj resembling gauze

GAVAGE n forced feeding by means of a tube

GAVAGES > GAVAGE

GAVE > GIVE

GAVEL n small hammer banged on a table ▷ vb use a gavel to restore order

GAVELED > GAVEL

GAVELING > GAVEL

GAVELKIND n former system of land tenure peculiar to Kent based on the payment of rent to the lord instead of the performance of services by the tenant

GAVELLED > GAVEL

GAVELLING > GAVEL

GAVELMAN n gavelkind tenant

GAVELMEN > GAVELMAN

GAVELOCK n iron crowbar

GAVELOCKS > GAVELOCK

GAVELS > GAVEL

GAVIAL n as in false gavial small crocodile

GAVIALOID adj of or like gavials

GAVIALS > GAVIAL

GAVOT same as > GAVOTTE

GAVOTS > GAVOT**

g

GAVOTTE n old formal dance ▷ vb dance a gavotte
GAVOTTED > GAVOTTE
GAVOTTES > GAVOTTE
GAVOTTING > GAVOTTE
GAW n as in weather gaw partial rainbow
GAWCIER > GAWCY
GAWCIEST > GAWCY
GAWCY same as > GAUCY
GAWD same as > GAUD
GAWDS > GAWD
GAWK vb stare stupidly
GAWKED > GAWK
GAWKER > GAWK
GAWKERS > GAWK
GAWKIER > GAWKY
GAWKIES > GAWKY
GAWKIEST > GAWKY
GAWKIHOOD n state of being gawky
GAWKILY > GAWKY
GAWKINESS > GAWKY
GAWKING > GAWK
GAWKISH same as > GAWKY
GAWKISHLY > GAWKY
GAWKS > GAWK
GAWKY adj clumsy or awkward ▷ n clumsy or awkward person
GAWMOGE n clownish person
GAWMOGES > GAWMOGE
GAWP vb stare stupidly
GAWPED > GAWP
GAWPER > GAWP
GAWPERS > GAWP
GAWPING > GAWP
GAWPS > GAWP
GAWPUS n silly person
GAWPUSES > GAWPUS
GAWS > GAW
GAWSIE same as > GAUCY
GAWSIER > GAWSIE
GAWSIEST > GAWSIE
GAWSY same as > GAUCY
GAY adj carefree and merry ▷ n homosexual person
GAYAL n type of ox
GAYALS > GAYAL
GAYCATION n holiday designed for the gay market
GAYDAR n supposed ability to recognize if another person is homosexual
GAYDARS > GAYDAR
GAYER > GAY
GAYEST > GAY
GAYETIES > GAYETY
GAYETY same as > GAIETY
GAYLY > GAY
GAYNESS > GAY
GAYNESSES > GAY
GAYS > GAY
GAYSOME adj full of merriment
GAYWINGS n flowering wintergreen
GAZABO n fellow or companion
GAZABOES > GAZABO
GAZABOS > GAZABO
GAZAL same as > GHAZAL
GAZALS > GAZAL
GAZANG vb inconvenience a buyer by declining to sell a house just before the purchase is completed

GAZANGED > GAZANG
GAZANGING > GAZANG
GAZANGS > GAZANG
GAZANIA n S African plant
GAZANIAS > GAZANIA
GAZAR n type of silk cloth
GAZARS > GAZAR
GAZE vb look fixedly ▷ n fixed look
GAZEBO n summerhouse with a good view
GAZEBOES > GAZEBO
GAZEBOS > GAZEBO
GAZED > GAZE
GAZEFUL adj gazing
GAZEHOUND n hound such as a greyhound that hunts by sight rather than by scent
GAZELLE n small graceful antelope
GAZELLES > GAZELLE
GAZEMENT n view
GAZEMENTS > GAZEMENT
GAZER > GAZE
GAZERS > GAZE
GAZES > GAZE
GAZETTE n official publication containing announcements ▷ vb announce or report (facts or an event) in a gazette
GAZETTED > GAZETTE
GAZETTEER n (part of) a book that lists and describes places ▷ vb list in a gazetteer
GAZETTES > GAZETTE
GAZETTING > GAZETTE
GAZIER > GAZY
GAZIEST > GAZY
GAZILLION n in informal English, an extremely large but unspecified number, quantity, or amount
GAZING > GAZE
GAZINGS > GAZE
GAZOGENE same as > GASOGENE
GAZOGENES > GAZOGENE
GAZON n sod used to cover a parapet in a fortification
GAZONS > GAZON
GAZOO n kazoo
GAZOOKA same as > GAZOO
GAZOOKAS > GAZOOKA
GAZOON same as > GAZON
GAZOONS > GAZOON
GAZOOS > GAZOO
GAZPACHO n Spanish soup made from tomatoes, peppers, etc, and served cold
GAZPACHOS > GAZPACHO
GAZUMP vb raise the price of a property after verbally agreeing it with (a prospective buyer) ▷ n act or an instance of gazumping
GAZUMPED > GAZUMP
GAZUMPER > GAZUMP
GAZUMPERS > GAZUMP
GAZUMPING n act of gazumping
GAZUMPS > GAZUMP
GAZUNDER vb reduce an offer on a property immediately before purchase ▷ n act or instance of gazundering

GAZUNDERS > GAZUNDER
GAZY adj prone to gazing
GEAL vb congeal
GEALED > GEAL
GEALING > GEAL
GEALOUS Spenserian spelling of > JEALOUS
GEALOUSY Spenserian spelling of > JEALOUSY
GEALS > GEAL
GEAN n white-flowered tree
GEANS > GEAN
GEAR n set of toothed wheels used to change direction or speed ▷ vb prepare or organize for something
GEARBOX n case enclosing a set of gears in a motor vehicle
GEARBOXES > GEARBOX
GEARCASE n protective casing for gears
GEARCASES > GEARCASE
GEARE Spenserian spelling of > JEER
GEARED > GEAR
GEARES > GEARE
GEARHEAD n part in engine gear system
GEARHEADS > GEARHEAD
GEARING n system of gears designed to transmit motion
GEARINGS > GEARING
GEARLESS > GEAR
GEARS > GEAR
GEARSHIFT n lever used to move gearwheels relative to each other, esp in a motor vehicle
GEARSTICK n lever used to move gear wheels in a motor vehicle
GEARWHEEL n one of the toothed wheels in the gears of a motor vehicle
GEASON adj wonderful
GEAT n in casting, the channel which leads to a mould
GEATS > GEAT
GEBUR n tenant farmer
GEBURS > GEBUR
GECK vb beguile
GECKED > GECK
GECKING > GECK
GECKO n small tropical lizard
GECKOES > GECKO
GECKOS > GECKO
GECKS > GECK
GED Scots word for > PIKE
GEDACT n flutelike stopped metal diapason organ pipe
GEDACTS > GEDACT
GEDDIT interj exclamation meaning do you understand it?
GEDECKT same as > GEDACT
GEDECKTS > GEDECKT
GEDS > GED
GEE interj mild exclamation of surprise, admiration, etc ▷ vb move (an animal, esp a horse) ahead
GEEBAG n in Irish slang, a disagreeable woman
GEEBAGS > GEEBAG
GEEBUNG n Australian tree or shrub

GEEBUNGS > GEEBUNG
GEECHEE n offensive name for a Black person from the southern states of the US **GEECHEES** > GEECHEE
GEED > GEE
GEEGAW same as > GEWGAW
GEEGAWS > GEEGAW
GEEING > GEE
GEEK n person skilled in a specific subject
GEEKDOM > GEEK
GEEKDOMS > GEEK
GEEKED adj highly excited
GEEKERIES > GEEKERY
GEEKERY n preoccupation with, or great knowledge about, a specialized subject
GEEKIER > GEEKY
GEEKIEST > GEEKY
GEEKINESS > GEEK
GEEKISH adj of or like a geek
GEEKISM n preoccupation with subjects generally considered unfashionable or boring
GEEKISMS > GEEKISM
GEEKS > GEEK
GEEKSPEAK n slang word for jargon used by geeks, esp computer enthusiasts
GEEKY adj of or like a geek
GEELBEK n edible marine fish
GEELBEKS > GEELBEK
GEEP n cross between a goat and a sheep
GEEPOUND another name for > SLUG
GEEPOUNDS > SLUG
GEEPS > GEEP
GEES > GEE
GEESE > GOOSE
GEEST n area of heathland in N Germany and adjacent areas
GEESTS > GEEST
GEEZ interj expression of surprise
GEEZAH variant spelling of > GEEZER
GEEZAHS > GEEZAH
GEEZER n man
GEEZERS > GEEZER
GEFILTE adj as in gefilte fish dish of fish stuffed with various ingredients
GEFUFFLE same as > KERFUFFLE
GEFUFFLED > GEFUFFLE
GEFUFFLES > GEFUFFLE
GEFULLTE adj as in gefullte fish dish of fish stuffed with various ingredients
GEGGIE Scottish, esp Glaswegian, slang word for the > MOUTH
GEGGIES > GEGGIE
GEHLENITE n green mineral consisting of calcium aluminium silicate in tetragonal crystalline form
GEISHA n (in Japan) professional female companion for men
GEISHAS > GEISHA
GEIST n spirit

GEISTS > GEIST
GEIT n border on clothing ▷ vb put a border on (an article of clothing)
GEITED > GEIT
GEITING > GEIT
GEITS > GEIT
GEL n jelly-like substance ▷ vb form a gel
GELABLE adj capable of forming a gel
GELADA n NE African baboon
GELADAS > GELADA
GELANDE adj as in gelande jump jump made in downhill skiing
GELANT same as > GELLANT
GELANTS > GELANT
GELASTIC adj relating to laughter
GELATE vb form a gel
GELATED > GELATE
GELATES > GELATE
GELATI n layered dessert
GELATIN same as > GELATINE
GELATINE n substance made by boiling animal bones
GELATINES > GELATINE
GELATING > GELATE
GELATINS > GELATIN
GELATION n act or process of freezing a liquid
GELATIONS > GELATION
GELATIS > GELATI
GELATO n Italian frozen dessert, similar to ice cream
GELATOS > GELATO
GELCAP n medicine enclosed in gelatine
GELCAPS > GELCAP
GELCOAT n thin layer of gel or resin applied to the surface
GELCOATS > GELCOAT
GELD vb emasculate; weaken ▷ n tax on land in Anglo-Saxon and Norman England
GELDED > GELD
GELDER > GELD
GELDERS > GELD
GELDING > GELD
GELDINGS > GELD
GELDS > GELD
GELEE n jelly
GELEES > GELEE
GELID adj very cold, icy, or frosty
GELIDER > GELID
GELIDEST > GELID
GELIDITY > GELID
GELIDLY > GELID
GELIDNESS > GELID
GELIGNITE n type of dynamite used for blasting
GELLANT n compound that forms a solid structure
GELLANTS > GELLANT
GELLED > GEL
GELLIES > GELLY
GELLING > GEL
GELLY same as > GELIGNITE
GELOSIES > GELOSY

GELOSY Spenserian spelling of > JEALOUSY
GELS > GEL
GELSEMIA > GELSEMIUM
GELSEMINE n alkaloid obtained from gelsemium
GELSEMIUM n type of climbing shrub of SE Asia and North America, esp the yellow jasmine
GELT n money
GELTS > GELT
GEM n precious stone or jewel ▷ vb set or ornament with gems
GEMATRIA n numerology of the Hebrew language and alphabet
GEMATRIAS > GEMATRIA
GEMCLIP n paperclip
GEMCLIPS > GEMCLIP
GEMEL n in heraldry, parallel bars
GEMELS > GEMEL
GEMFISH n Australian food fish with a delicate flavour
GEMFISHES > GEMFISH
GEMINAL adj occurring in pairs
GEMINALLY > GEMINAL
GEMINATE adj combined in pairs ▷ vb arrange or be arranged in pairs
GEMINATED > GEMINATE
GEMINATES > GEMINATE
GEMINI n expression of surprise
GEMINIES > GEMINY
GEMINOUS adj in pairs
GEMINY n pair
GEMLIKE > GEM
GEMMA n reproductive structure in liverworts, mosses, etc
GEMMAE > GEMMA
GEMMAN dialect form of > GENTLEMAN
GEMMATE adj (of some plants and animals) having gemmae ▷ vb produce or reproduce by gemmae
GEMMATED > GEMMATE
GEMMATES > GEMMATE
GEMMATING > GEMMATE
GEMMATION > GEMMATE
GEMMATIVE adj relating to gemmation
GEMMED > GEM
GEMMEN > GEMMAN
GEMMEOUS adj gem-like
GEMMERIES > GEMMERY
GEMMERY n gems collectively
GEMMIER > GEM
GEMMIEST > GEM
GEMMILY > GEM
GEMMINESS > GEM
GEMMING > GEM
GEMMOLOGY same as > GEMOLOGY
GEMMULE n result of asexual reproduction by sponges
GEMMULES > GEMMULE
GEMMY > GEM
GEMOLOGY n branch of mineralogy that is concerned with gems and gemstones

GEMONY same as > JIMINY
GEMOT n (in Anglo-Saxon England) a legal or administrative assembly
GEMOTE same as > GEMOT
GEMOTES > GEMOTE
GEMOTS > GEMOT
GEMS > GEM
GEMSBOK same as > ORYX
GEMSBOKS > GEMSBOK
GEMSBUCK same as > ORYX
GEMSBUCKS > GEMSBUCK
GEMSHORN n type of medieval flute
GEMSHORNS > GEMSHORN
GEMSTONE n precious or semiprecious stone, esp one which has been cut and polished
GEMSTONES > GEMSTONE
GEMUTLICH adj having a feeling or atmosphere of warmth and friendliness
GEN n information ▷ vb gain information
GENA n cheek
GENAL > GENA
GENAPPE n smooth worsted yarn used for braid, etc
GENAPPES > GENAPPE
GENAS > GENA
GENDARME n member of the French police force
GENDARMES > GENDARME
GENDER n state of being male or female ▷ vb assign a gender to
GENDERED > GENDER
GENDERING > GENDER
GENDERISE same as > GENDERIZE
GENDERIZE vb make distinctions according to gender in or among
GENDERS > GENDER
GENE n part of a cell
GENEALOGY n (study of) the history and descent of a family or families
GENERA > GENUS
GENERABLE adj able to be generated
GENERAL adj common or widespread ▷ n very senior army officer ▷ vb act as a general
GENERALCY n rank of general
GENERALE singular form of > GENERALIA
GENERALIA n generalities
GENERALLY adv usually
GENERALS > GENERAL
GENERANT n something that generates
GENERANTS > GENERANT
GENERATE vb produce or bring into being
GENERATED > GENERATE
GENERATES > GENERATE
GENERATOR n machine for converting mechanical energy into electrical energy
GENERIC adj of a class, group, or genus ▷ n drug, food product, etc that does not have a trademark

GENERICAL same as > GENERIC
GENERICS > GENERIC
GENEROUS adj free in giving
GENES > GENE
GENESES > GENESIS
GENESIS n beginning or origin
GENET n type of agile catlike mammal
GENETIC adj of genes or genetics
GENETICAL same as > GENETIC
GENETICS n study of heredity and variation in organisms
GENETRIX n female progenitor
GENETS > GENET
GENETTE same as > GENET
GENETTES > GENETTE
GENEVA n gin
GENEVAS > GENEVA
GENIAL adj cheerful and friendly
GENIALISE vb make genial
GENIALITY > GENIAL
GENIALIZE same as > GENIALISE
GENIALLY > GENIAL
GENIC adj of or relating to a gene or genes
GENICALLY > GENIC
GENICULAR adj of or relating to the knee
GENIE n (in fairy tales) magical wish-granting servant
GENIES > GENIE
GENII > GENIUS
GENIP same as > GENIPAP
GENIPAP n evergreen Caribbean tree
GENIPAPO n tropical American tree
GENIPAPOS > GENIPAPO
GENIPAPS > GENIPAP
GENIPS > GENIP
GENISTA n any member of the broom family
GENISTAS > GENISTA
GENISTEIN n substance found in plants, thought to fight cancer
GENITAL adj of the reproductive organs
GENITALIA same as > GENITALS
GENITALIC > GENITALIA
GENITALLY > GENITAL
GENITALS pl n external reproductive organs
GENITIVAL > GENITIVE
GENITIVE n grammatical case indicating possession ▷ adj denoting such a grammatical case
GENITIVES > GENITIVE
GENITOR n biological father
GENITORS > GENITOR
GENITRIX same as > GENETRIX
GENITURE n birth
GENITURES > GENITURE
GENIUS n (person with) an exceptional ability

g

g

GENIUSES > GENIUS
GENIZAH n repository for sacred objects which may not be destroyed
GENIZAHS > GENIZAH
GENIZOT > GENIZAH
GENIZOTH > GENIZAH
GENLOCK n generator locking device ▷ vb activate a genlock
GENLOCKED > GENLOCK
GENLOCKS > GENLOCK
GENNAKER n type of sail for boats
GENNAKERS > GENNAKER
GENNED > GEN
GENNEL same as > GINNEL
GENNELS > GENNEL
GENNET n female donkey or ass
GENNETS > GENNET
GENNIES > GENNY
GENNING > GEN
GENNY same as > GENOA
GENOA n large triangular jib sail
GENOAS > GENOA
GENOCIDAL > GENOCIDE
GENOCIDE n murder of a race of people
GENOCIDES > GENOCIDE
GENOGRAM n expanded family tree
GENOGRAMS > GENOGRAM
GENOISE n rich sponge cake
GENOISES > GENOISE
GENOM same as > GENOME
GENOME n all genetic material within an organism
GENOMES > GENOME
GENOMIC > GENOME
GENOMICS n branch of molecular genetics concerned with the study of genomes
GENOMS > GENOM
GENOTOXIC adj harmful to genetic material
GENOTYPE n genetic constitution of an organism ▷ vb determine the genotype of
GENOTYPED > GENOTYPE
GENOTYPES > GENOTYPE
GENOTYPIC > GENOTYPE
GENRE n style of literary, musical, or artistic work
GENRES > GENRE
GENRO n group of Japanese statesmen
GENROS > GENRO
GENS n (in ancient Rome) a group of aristocratic families
GENSENG same as > GINSENG
GENSENGS > GENSENG
GENT n gentleman
GENTEEL adj affectedly proper and polite
GENTEELER > GENTEEL
GENTEELLY > GENTEEL
GENTES > GENS
GENTIAN n mountain plant with deep blue flowers
GENTIANS > GENTIAN
GENTIER > GENTY
GENTIEST > GENTY

GENTIL adj gentle
GENTILE n non-Jewish person ▷ adj used to designate a place or the inhabitants of a place
GENTILES > GENTILE
GENTILIC adj tribal
GENTILISE vb live like a gentile
GENTILISH adj heathenish
GENTILISM n heathenism
GENTILITY n noble birth or ancestry
GENTILIZE same as > GENTILISE
GENTLE adj mild or kindly ▷ vb tame or subdue (a horse) ▷ n maggot, esp when used as bait in fishing
GENTLED > GENTLE
GENTLEMAN n polite well-bred man
GENTLEMEN > GENTLEMAN
GENTLER > GENTLE
GENTLES > GENTLE
GENTLEST > GENTLE
GENTLING > GENTLE
GENTLY > GENTLE
GENTOO n grey-backed penguin
GENTOOS > GENTOO
GENTRICE n high birth
GENTRICES > GENTRICE
GENTRIES > GENTRY
GENTRIFY vb cause a neighbourhood to appeal to the middle classes
GENTRY n term for people just below the nobility in social rank
GENTS n men's public toilet
GENTY adj neat
GENU n any knee-like bend in a structure or part
GENUA > GENU
GENUFLECT vb bend the knee as a sign of reverence or deference
GENUINE adj not fake, authentic
GENUINELY > GENUINE
GENUS n group of animals or plants
GENUSES > GENUS
GEO n (esp in Shetland) a small fjord or gully
GEOBOTANY n study of plants in relation to their geological habitat
GEOCACHE vb search for hidden containers using GPS as a recreational activity
GEOCACHED > GEOCACHE
GEOCACHER n person who participates in geocaching
GEOCACHES > GEOCACHE
GEOCARPIC > GEOCARPY
GEOCARPY n ripening of fruits below ground, as occurs in the peanut
GEOCODE vb assign geographical coordinates to a physical location using a digital code
GEOCODED > GEOCODE
GEOCODES > GEOCODE
GEOCODING > GEOCODE

GEOCORONA n outer layer of earth's atmosphere
GEODATA n information about geographical location held in a digital format
GEODE n cavity within a rock mass or nodule
GEODES > GEODE
GEODESIC adj of the geometry of curved surfaces ▷ n shortest line between two points on a curve
GEODESICS > GEODESIC
GEODESIES > GEODESY
GEODESIST > GEODESY
GEODESY n study of the shape and size of the earth
GEODETIC same as > GEODESIC
GEODETICS same as > GEODETIC
GEODIC > GEODE
GEODUCK n king clam
GEODUCKS > GEODUCK
GEOFACT n rock shaped by natural forces
GEOFACTS > GEOFACT
GEOGENIES > GEOGENY
GEOGENY same as > GEOGONY
GEOGNOSES > GEOGNOSY
GEOGNOSIS same as > GEOGNOSY
GEOGNOST > GEOGNOSY
GEOGNOSTS > GEOGNOSY
GEOGNOSY n early form of geology
GEOGONIC > GEOGONY
GEOGONIES > GEOGONY
GEOGONY n science of the earth's formation
GEOGRAPHY n study of the earth's physical features, climate, population, etc
GEOID n hypothetical surface
GEOIDAL > GEOID
GEOIDS > GEOID
GEOLATRY n worship of the earth
GEOLOGER > GEOLOGY
GEOLOGERS > GEOLOGY
GEOLOGIAN > GEOLOGY
GEOLOGIC > GEOLOGY
GEOLOGIES > GEOLOGY
GEOLOGISE same as > GEOLOGIZE
GEOLOGIST > GEOLOGY
GEOLOGIZE vb study the geological features of (an area)
GEOLOGY n study of the earth
GEOMANCER > GEOMANCY
GEOMANCY n prophecy made from casting down a handful of earth
GEOMANT n geomancer
GEOMANTIC > GEOMANCY
GEOMANTS > GEOMANT
GEOMATICS n branch of science dealing with the collection, storage, and analysis of geographical data
GEOMETER n person who is practised in or who studies geometry

GEOMETERS > GEOMETER
GEOMETRIC adj of geometry
GEOMETRID n type of moth, the larvae of which are called measuring worms, inchworms, or loopers
GEOMETRY n branch of mathematics dealing with points, lines, curves, and surfaces
GEOMYOID adj relating to burrowing rodents of the genus Geomys
GEONOMICS n doctrine holding that those things found in nature belong to no one person but instead belong equally to all
GEOPHAGIA same as > GEOPHAGY
GEOPHAGY n practice of eating earth, clay, chalk, etc, found in some primitive tribes
GEOPHILIC adj soil-loving
GEOPHONE n device for recording seismic movement
GEOPHONES > GEOPHONE
GEOPHYTE n perennial plant that propagates by means of buds below the soil surface
GEOPHYTES > GEOPHYTE
GEOPHYTIC > GEOPHYTE
GEOPONIC adj of or relating to agriculture, esp as a science
GEOPONICS n science of agriculture
GEOPROBE n probing device used for sampling soil
GEOPROBES > GEOPROBE
GEORGETTE n fine silky fabric
GEORGIC adj agricultural ▷ n poem about rural or agricultural life
GEORGICAL same as > GEORGIC
GEORGICS > GEORGIC
GEOS > GEO
GEOSPHERE n the rigid outer layer of the earth
GEOSTATIC adj denoting or relating to the pressure exerted by a mass of rock or a similar substance
GEOTACTIC > GEOTAXIS
GEOTAG n geographical co-ordinates digitally applied to data ▷ vb apply a geotag to data
GEOTAGGED > GEOTAG
GEOTAGS > GEOTAG
GEOTAXES > GEOTAXIS
GEOTAXIS n movement of an organism in response to the stimulus of gravity
GEOTHERM n line or surface within or on the earth connecting points of equal temperature
GEOTHERMS > GEOTHERM
GEOTROPIC adj of geotropism: the response of a plant to the stimulus of gravity

GER n portable Mongolian dwelling

GERAH n ancient Hebrew unit of weight

GERAHS > GERAH

GERANIAL n cis-isomer of citral

GERANIALS > GERANIAL

GERANIOL n type of alcohol with an odour of roses

GERANIOLS > GERANIOL

GERANIUM n cultivated plant with red, pink, or white flowers

GERANIUMS > GERANIUM

GERARDIA n any plant of the genus Gerardia

GERARDIAS > GERARDIA

GERBE same as > GARBE

GERBERA n type of plant

GERBERAS > GERBERA

GERBES > GERBE

GERBIL n burrowing desert rodent of Asia and Africa

GERBILLE same as > GERBIL

GERBILLES > GERBILLE

GERBILS > GERBIL

GERE Spenserian spelling of > GEAR

GERENT n person who rules or manages

GERENTS > GERENT

GERENUK n slender antelope

GERENUKS > GERENUK

GERES > GERE

GERFALCON same as > GYRFALCON

GERIATRIC adj of elderly people

GERLE Spenserian spelling of > GIRL

GERLES > GERLE

GERM n microbe, esp one causing disease ▷ vb sprout

GERMAIN same as > GERMEN

GERMAINE same as > GERMEN

GERMAINES > GERMAINE

GERMAINS > GERMAIN

GERMAN n type of dance ▷ adj having the same parents as oneself

GERMANDER n type of plant

GERMANE adj relevant

GERMANELY > GERMANE

GERMANIC adj of or containing germanium in the tetravalent state

GERMANISE same as > GERMANIZE

GERMANITE n mineral consisting of a complex copper arsenic sulphide containing germanium, gallium, iron, zinc, and lead: an ore of germanium and gallium

GERMANIUM n brittle grey element that is a semiconductor

GERMANIZE vb adopt or cause to adopt German customs, speech, institutions, etc

GERMANOUS adj of or containing germanium in the divalent state

GERMANS > GERMAN

GERMED > GERM

GERMEN n cells that gives rise to the germ cells

GERMENS > GERMEN

GERMFREE > GERM

GERMICIDE n substance that kills germs

GERMIER > GERMY

GERMIEST > GERMY

GERMIN same as > GERMEN

GERMINA > GERMEN

GERMINAL adj of or in the earliest stage of development

GERMINANT adj in the process of germinating

GERMINATE vb (cause to) sprout or begin to grow

GERMINESS > GERMY

GERMING > GERM

GERMINS > GERMIN

GERMLIKE > GERM

GERMPLASM n plant genetic material

GERMPROOF adj protected against the penetration of germs

GERMS > GERM

GERMY adj full of germs

GERNE vb grin

GERNED > GERNE

GERNES > GERNE

GERNING > GERNE

GERONIMO interj shout given by US paratroopers as they jump into battle

GERONTIC adj of or relating to the senescence of an organism

GEROPIGA n grape syrup used to sweeten inferior port wines

GEROPIGAS > GEROPIGA

GERS > GER

GERT adv in dialect, great or very big

GERTCHA interj get out of here!

GERUND n noun formed from a verb

GERUNDIAL > GERUND

GERUNDIVE n (in Latin grammar) an adjective formed from a verb, expressing the desirability of the activity denoted by the verb ▷ adj of or relating to the gerund or gerundive

GERUNDS > GERUND

GESNERIA n S American plant grown for its bright flowers

GESNERIAD > GESNERIA

GESNERIAS > GESNERIA

GESSAMINE another word for > JASMINE

GESSE Spenserian spelling of > GUESS

GESSED > GESSE

GESSES > GESSE

GESSING > GESSE

GESSO n plaster used for painting or in sculpture ▷ vb apply gesso to

GESSOED > GESSO

GESSOES > GESSO

GEST n notable deed or exploit

GESTALT n perceptual pattern or structure

GESTALTEN > GESTALT

GESTALTS > GESTALT

GESTANT adj laden

GESTAPO n any secret state police organization

GESTAPOS > GESTAPO

GESTATE vb carry (young) in the uterus during pregnancy

GESTATED > GESTATE

GESTATES > GESTATE

GESTATING > GESTATE

GESTATION n (period of) carrying of young in the womb between conception and birth

GESTATIVE > GESTATION

GESTATORY > GESTATION

GESTE same as > GEST

GESTES > GESTE

GESTIC adj consisting of gestures

GESTICAL > GESTIC

GESTS > GEST

GESTURAL > GESTURE

GESTURE n movement to convey meaning ▷ vb gesticulate

GESTURED > GESTURE

GESTURER > GESTURE

GESTURERS > GESTURE

GESTURES > GESTURE

GESTURING > GESTURE

GET vb obtain or receive

GETA n type of Japanese wooden sandal

GETABLE > GET

GETAS > GETA

GETATABLE adj accessible

GETAWAY n used in escape

GETAWAYS > GETAWAY

GETOUT n excuse to get out of doing something

GETOUTS > GETOUT

GETS > GET

GETTABLE > GET

GETTER n person or thing that gets ▷ vb remove (a gas) by the action of a getter

GETTERED > GETTER

GETTERING > GETTER

GETTERS > GETTER

GETTING > GET

GETTINGS > GET

GETUP n outfit

GETUPS > GETUP

GEUM n type of herbaceous plant

GEUMS > GEUM

GEWGAW n showy but valueless trinket ▷ adj showy and valueless

GEWGAWED adj decorated gaudily

GEWGAWS > GEWGAW

GEY adv extremely ▷ adj gallant

GEYAN adv somewhat

GEYER > GEY

GEYEST > GEY

GEYSER n spring that discharges steam and hot water ▷ vb erupt like a geyser

GEYSERED > GEYSER

GEYSERING > GEYSER

GEYSERITE n mineral form of hydrated silica resembling opal, deposited from the waters of geysers and hot springs

GEYSERS > GEYSER

GHARIAL same as > GAVIAL

GHARIALS > GHARIAL

GHARRI same as > GHARRY

GHARRIES > GHARRY

GHARRIS > GHARRI

GHARRY n (in India) horse-drawn vehicle

GHAST vb terrify

GHASTED > GHAST

GHASTFUL adj dismal

GHASTING > GHAST

GHASTLIER > GHASTLY

GHASTLY adj unpleasant ▷ adv unhealthily

GHASTNESS n dread

GHASTS > GHAST

GHAT n (in India) steps leading down to a river

GHATS > GHAT

GHAUT n small cleft in a hill

GHAUTS > GHAUT

GHAZAL n Arabic love poem

GHAZALS > GHAZAL

GHAZEL same as > GHAZAL

GHAZELS > GHAZEL

GHAZI n Muslim fighter against infidels

GHAZIES > GHAZI

GHAZIS > GHAZI

GHEE n (in Indian cookery) clarified butter

GHEES > GHEE

GHERAO n form of industrial action in India ▷ vb trap an employer in his or her office, to induce the workforce's discontent

GHERAOED > GHERAO

GHERAOES > GHERAO

GHERAOING > GHERAO

GHERAOS > GHERAO

GHERKIN n small pickled cucumber

GHERKINS > GHERKIN

GHESSE Spenserian spelling of > GUESS

GHESSED > GHESSE

GHESSES > GHESSE

GHESSING > GHESSE

GHEST > GHESSE

GHETTO n slum area inhabited by a deprived minority ▷ vb ghettoize

GHETTOED > GHETTO

GHETTOES > GHETTO

GHETTOING > GHETTO

GHETTOISE same as > GHETTOIZE

GHETTOIZE vb confine (someone or something) to a particular area or category

GHETTOS > GHETTO

GHI same as > GHEE

GHIBLI n fiercely hot wind of North Africa

GHIBLIS > GHIBLI

GHILGAI same as > GILGAI

GHILGAIS > GHILGAI

g

GHILLIE n (in Scotland) attendant for hunting or fishing ▷ vb act as a ghillie

GHILLIED > GHILLIE

GHILLIES > GHILLIE

GHILLYING > GHILLIE

GHIS > GHI

GHOST n disembodied spirit of a dead person ▷ vb ghostwrite

GHOSTED > GHOST

GHOSTIER > GHOSTY

GHOSTIEST > GHOSTY

GHOSTING > GHOST

GHOSTINGS > GHOST

GHOSTLIER > GHOSTLY

GHOSTLIKE > GHOST

GHOSTLY adj frightening in appearance or effect

GHOSTS > GHOST

GHOSTY adj pertaining to ghosts

GHOUL n person with morbid interests

GHOULIE n goblin

GHOULIES > GHOULIE

GHOULISH adj of or relating to ghouls

GHOULS > GHOUL

GHRELIN n hormone that stimulates appetite

GHRELINS > GHRELIN

GHUBAR adj as in ghubar numeral type of numeral

GHYLL same as > GILL

GHYLLS > GHYLL

GI n white suit worn in martial arts

GIAMBEUX n jambeaux; leg armour

GIANT n mythical being of superhuman size ▷ adj huge

GIANTESS same as > GIANT

GIANTHOOD n condition of being a giant

GIANTISM same as > GIGANTISM

GIANTISMS > GIANTISM

GIANTLIER > GIANTLY

GIANTLIKE > GIANT

GIANTLY adj giantlike

GIANTRIES > GIANTRY

GIANTRY n collective term for giants

GIANTS > GIANT

GIANTSHIP n style of address for a giant

GIAOUR n derogatory term for a non-Muslim, esp a Christian, used esp by the Turks

GIAOURS > GIAOUR

GIARDIA n species of parasite

GIARDIAS > GIARDIA

GIB n metal wedge, pad, or thrust bearing ▷ vb fasten or supply with a gib

GIBBED > GIB

GIBBER vb speak or utter rapidly and unintelligibly ▷ n boulder

GIBBERED > GIBBER

GIBBERING n rapid, unintelligible speech

GIBBERISH n rapid unintelligible talk

GIBBERS > GIBBER

GIBBET n gallows for displaying executed criminals ▷ vb put to death by hanging on a gibbet

GIBBETED > GIBBET

GIBBETING > GIBBET

GIBBETS > GIBBET

GIBBETTED > GIBBET

GIBBING > GIB

GIBBON n agile tree-dwelling ape of S Asia

GIBBONS > GIBBON

GIBBOSE same as > GIBBOUS

GIBBOSITY n state of being gibbous

GIBBOUS adj (of the moon) between half and fully illuminated

GIBBOUSLY > GIBBOUS

GIBBSITE n mineral consisting of hydrated aluminium oxide

GIBBSITES > GIBBSITE

GIBE vb make jeering or scoffing remarks (at) ▷ n derisive or provoking remark

GIBED > GIBE

GIBEL n Prussian carp

GIBELS > GIBEL

GIBER > GIBE

GIBERS > GIBE

GIBES > GIBE

GIBING > GIBE

GIBINGLY > GIBE

GIBLET > GIBLETS

GIBLETS pl n gizzard, liver, heart, and neck of a fowl

GIBLI same as > GHIBLI

GIBLIS > GIBLI

GIBS > GIB

GIBSON n martini garnished with onion

GIBSONS > GIBSON

GIBUS n collapsible top hat

GIBUSES > GIBUS

GID n disease of sheep

GIDDAP interj exclamation used to make a horse go faster

GIDDAY interj expression of greeting

GIDDIED > GIDDY

GIDDIER > GIDDY

GIDDIES > GIDDY

GIDDIEST > GIDDY

GIDDILY > GIDDY

GIDDINESS > GIDDY

GIDDUP same as > GIDDYUP

GIDDY adj having or causing a feeling of dizziness ▷ vb make giddy

GIDDYAP same as > GIDDYUP

GIDDYING > GIDDY

GIDDYUP interj exclamation used to make a horse go faster

GIDGEE n small acacia tree

GIDGEES > GIDGEE

GIDJEE same as > GIDGEE

GIDJEES > GIDJEE

GIDS > GID

GIE Scot word for > GIVE

GIED > GIE

GIEING > GIE

GIEN > GIE

GIES > GIE

GIF n file held in GIF format

GIFS > GIF

GIFT n present ▷ vb make a present of

GIFTABLE adj suitable as gift ▷ n something suitable as gift

GIFTABLES > GIFTABLE

GIFTED adj talented

GIFTEDLY > GIFTED

GIFTEE n person given a gift

GIFTEES > GIFTEE

GIFTING n act of gifting

GIFTINGS > GIFTING

GIFTLESS > GIFT

GIFTS > GIFT

GIFTSHOP n shop selling articles suitable for gifts

GIFTSHOPS > GIFTSHOP

GIFTWARE n anything that may be given as a present

GIFTWARES > GIFTWARE

GIFTWRAP vb wrap (a gift) in decorative wrapping paper

GIFTWRAPS > GIFTWRAP

GIG n single performance by pop or jazz musicians ▷ vb play a gig or gigs

GIGA same as > GIGUE

GIGABIT n unit of information in computing

GIGABITS > GIGABIT

GIGABYTE n one thousand and twenty-four megabytes

GIGABYTES > GIGABYTE

GIGACYCLE same as > GIGAHERTZ

GIGAFLOP n measure of computer processing speed

GIGAFLOPS > GIGAFLOP

GIGAHERTZ n unit of frequency equal to 10⁹ hertz

GIGANTEAN adj gigantic

GIGANTIC adj enormous

GIGANTISM n excessive growth of the entire body, caused by overproduction of growth hormone by the pituitary gland during childhood or adolescence

GIGAS > GIGA

GIGATON n unit of explosive force

GIGATONS > GIGATON

GIGAVOLT n billion volts

GIGAVOLTS > GIGAVOLT

GIGAWATT n unit of power equal to 1 billion watts

GIGAWATTS > GIGAWATT

GIGGED > GIG

GIGGING > GIG

GIGGIT vb move quickly

GIGGITED > GIGGIT

GIGGITING > GIGGIT

GIGGITS > GIGGIT

GIGGLE vb laugh nervously or foolishly ▷ n such a laugh

GIGGLED > GIGGLE

GIGGLER > GIGGLE

GIGGLERS > GIGGLE

GIGGLES > GIGGLE

GIGGLIER > GIGGLE

GIGGLIEST > GIGGLE

GIGGLING > GIGGLE

GIGGLINGS > GIGGLE

GIGGLY > GIGGLE

GIGHE > GIGA

GIGLET n flighty girl

GIGLETS > GIGLET

GIGLOT same as > GIGLET

GIGLOTS > GIGLOT

GIGMAN n one who places great importance on respectability

GIGMANITY > GIGMAN

GIGMEN > GIGMAN

GIGOLO n man paid to be an escort

GIGOLOS > GIGOLO

GIGOT n leg of lamb or mutton

GIGOTS > GIGOT

GIGS > GIG

GIGUE n piece of music incorporated into the classical suite

GIGUES > GIGUE

GILA n large venomous brightly coloured lizard

GILAS > GILA

GILBERT n unit of magnetomotive force

GILBERTS > GILBERT

GILCUP same as > GILTCUP

GILCUPS > GILCUP

GILD vb put a thin layer of gold on

GILDED > GILD

GILDEN adj gilded

GILDER > GILD

GILDERS > GILD

GILDHALL same as > GUILDHALL

GILDHALLS > GILDHALL

GILDING > GILD

GILDINGS > GILD

GILDS > GILD

GILDSMAN > GILD

GILDSMEN > GILD

GILET n waist- or hip-length garment

GILETS > GILET

GILGAI n natural water hole

GILGAIS > GILGAI

GILGIE n type of freshwater crayfish

GILGIES > GILGIE

GILL n radiating structure beneath the cap of a mushroom ▷ vb catch (fish) or (of fish) to be caught in a gill net

GILLAROO n type of brown trout

GILLAROOS > GILLAROO

GILLED > GILL

GILLER > GILL

GILLERS > GILL

GILLET n mare

GILLETS > GILLET

GILLFLIRT n flirtatious woman

GILLIE n (in Scotland) attendant for hunting or fishing ▷ vb act as a gillie

GILLIED > GILLIE

GILLIES > GILLY

GILLING > GILL

GILLION n (no longer in technical use) one thousand million

GILLIONS > GILLION

GILLNET n net designed to catch fish by the gills ▷ vb fish using a gillnet

GILLNETS > GILLNET

GILLS pl n breathing organs in fish and other water creatures

GILLY vb act as a gillie

GILLYING > GILLY

GILLYVOR n type of carnation

GILLYVORS > GILLYVOR

GILPEY n mischievous, frolicsome boy or girl

GILPEYS > GILPEY

GILPIES > GILPY

GILPY same as > GILPEY

GILRAVAGE vb make merry, especially to excess

GILSONITE n very pure form of asphalt found in Utah and Colorado

GILT n young sow

GILTCUP n buttercup

GILTCUPS > GILTCUP

GILTHEAD n type of fish

GILTHEADS > GILTHEAD

GILTS > GILT

GILTWOOD adj made of wood and gilded

GIMBAL vb support on gimbals

GIMBALED > GIMBAL

GIMBALING > GIMBAL

GIMBALLED > GIMBAL

GIMBALS pl n set of pivoted rings

GIMCRACK adj showy but cheap ▷ n cheap showy trifle or gadget

GIMCRACKS > GIMCRACK

GIMEL n third letter of the Hebrew alphabet

GIMELS > GIMEL

GIMLET n small tool ▷ adj penetrating or piercing ▷ vb make holes in (wood) using a gimlet

GIMLETED > GIMLET

GIMLETING > GIMLET

GIMLETS > GIMLET

GIMMAL n ring composed of interlocking rings ▷ vb provide with gimmals

GIMMALLED > GIMMAL

GIMMALS > GIMMAL

GIMME interj give me! ▷ n term used in shot putt

GIMMER n year-old ewe

GIMMERS > GIMMER

GIMMES > GIMME

GIMMICK n something designed to attract attention ▷ vb make gimmicky

GIMMICKED > GIMMICK

GIMMICKRY > GIMMICK

GIMMICKS > GIMMICK

GIMMICKY > GIMMICK

GIMMIE n very short putt in golf

GIMMIES > GIMMIE

GIMMOR n mechanical device

GIMMORS > GIMMOR

GIMP n tapelike trimming of silk, wool, or cotton, often stiffened with wire ▷ vb slang term for limp

GIMPED > GIMP

GIMPIER > GIMPY

GIMPIEST > GIMPY

GIMPING > GIMP

GIMPS > GIMP

GIMPY same as > GAMMY

GIN n spirit flavoured with juniper berries ▷ vb free (cotton) of seeds with an engine

GINCH same as > GITCH

GINCHES > GINCH

GING n child's catapult

GINGAL n type of musket mounted on a swivel

GINGALL same as > GINGAL

GINGALLS > GINGALL

GINGALS > GINGAL

GINGE n person with ginger hair

GINGELEY same as > GINGILI

GINGELEYS > GINGELEY

GINGELI same as > GINGILI

GINGELIES > GINGELY

GINGELIS > GINGELI

GINGELLI same as > GINGILI

GINGELLIS > GINGILI

GINGELLY same as > GINGILI

GINGELY same as > GINGILI

GINGER n root of a tropical plant, used as a spice ▷ adj light reddish-brown ▷ vb add the spice ginger to (a dish)

GINGERADE n fizzy drink flavoured with ginger

GINGERED > GINGER

GINGERIER > GINGERY

GINGERING > GINGER

GINGERLY adv cautiously ▷ adj cautious

GINGEROUS adj reddish

GINGERS > GINGER

GINGERY adj like or tasting of ginger

GINGES > GINGE

GINGHAM n cotton cloth, usu checked or striped

GINGHAMS > GINGHAM

GINGILI n oil obtained from sesame seeds

GINGILIS > GINGILI

GINGILLI same as > GINGILI

GINGILLIS > GINGILLI

GINGIVA same as > GUM

GINGIVAE > GINGIVA

GINGIVAL > GINGIVA

GINGKO same as > GINGKO

GINGKOES > GINGKO

GINGKOS > GINGKO

GINGLE same as > JINGLE

GINGLES > GINGLE

GINGLYMI > GINGLYMUS

GINGLYMUS n hinge joint

GINGS > GING

GINHOUSE n building where cotton is ginned

GINHOUSES > GINHOUSE

GINK n man or boy

GINKGO n ornamental Chinese tree

GINKGOES > GINKGO

GINKGOS > GINKGO

GINKS > GINK

GINN same as > JINN

GINNED > GIN

GINNEL n narrow passageway between buildings

GINNELS > GINNEL

GINNER > GIN

GINNERIES > GINHOUSE

GINNERS > GIN

GINNERY another word for > GINHOUSE

GINNIER > GINNY

GINNIEST > GINNY

GINNING > GIN

GINNINGS > GIN

GINNY adj relating to the spirit gin

GINORMOUS adj very large

GINS > GIN

GINSENG n (root of) a plant

GINSENGS > GINSENG

GINSHOP n tavern

GINSHOPS > GINSHOP

GINZO n offensive term for person of Italian descent

GINZOES > GINZO

GINZOS > GINZO

GIO same as > GEO

GIOCOSO adv (of music) to be expressed joyfully or playfully

GIOS > GIO

GIP same as > GYP

GIPON another word for > JUPON

GIPONS > GIPON

GIPPED > GIP

GIPPER > GIP

GIPPERS > GIP

GIPPIES > GIPPY

GIPPING > GIP

GIPPO n gypsy

GIPPOES > GIPPO

GIPPOS > GIPPO

GIPPY n starling

GIPS > GIP

GIPSEN obsolete word for > GYPSY

GIPSENS > GIPSEN

GIPSIED > GIPSY

GIPSIES > GIPSY

GIPSY n member of a nomadic people ▷ vb live like a gypsy

GIPSYDOM > GIPSY

GIPSYDOMS > GIPSY

GIPSYHOOD > GIPSY

GIPSYING > GIPSY

GIPSYISH > GIPSY

GIPSYISM n gipsy custom

GIPSYISMS > GIPSYISM

GIPSYWORT n hairy Eurasian plant with two-lipped white flowers with purple dots on the lower lip

GIRAFFE n African ruminant mammal

GIRAFFES > GIRAFFE

GIRAFFID adj giraffe-like ▷ n member of the Giraffidae family

GIRAFFIDS > GIRAFFID

GIRAFFINE adj relating to a giraffe

GIRAFFISH > GIRAFFE

GIRAFFOID adj giraffe-like

GIRANDOLA same as > GIRANDOLE

GIRANDOLE n ornamental branched wall candleholder, usually incorporating a mirror

GIRASOL n type of opal

GIRASOLE same as > GIRASOL

GIRASOLES > GIRASOLE

GIRASOLS > GIRASOL

GIRD vb put a belt round ▷ n blow or stroke

GIRDED > GIRD

GIRDER n large metal beam

GIRDERS > GIRDER

GIRDING > GIRD

GIRDINGLY > GIRD

GIRDINGS > GIRD

GIRDLE n woman's elastic corset ▷ vb surround or encircle

GIRDLED > GIRDLE

GIRDLER n person or thing that girdles

GIRDLERS > GIRDLER

GIRDLES > GIRDLE

GIRDLING > GIRDLE

GIRDS > GIRD

GIRKIN same as > GHERKIN

GIRKINS > GIRKIN

GIRL n female child

GIRLHOOD n state or time of being a girl

GIRLHOODS > GIRLHOOD

GIRLIE adj suited to young women ▷ n little girl

GIRLIER > GIRLY

GIRLIES > GIRLIE

GIRLIEST > GIRLY

GIRLISH adj of or like a girl in looks, behaviour, innocence, etc

GIRLISHLY > GIRLISH

GIRLOND obsolete word for > GARLAND

GIRLONDS > GIRLOND

GIRLS > GIRL

GIRLY same as > GIRLIE

GIRN vb snarl

GIRNED > GIRN

GIRNEL n large chest for storing meal

GIRNELS > GIRNEL

GIRNER > GIRN

GIRNERS > GIRN

GIRNIE adj peevish

GIRNIER > GIRNIE

GIRNIEST > GIRNIE

GIRNING > GIRN

GIRNS > GIRN

GIRO n system of transferring money

GIROLLE n chanterelle mushroom

GIROLLES > GIROLLE

GIRON n part of a heraldic shield

GIRONIC > GIRON

GIRONNY adj divided into segments from the fesse point

GIRONS > GIRON

GIROS > GIRO

GIROSOL same as > GIRASOL
GIROSOLS > GIROSOL
GIRR same as > GIRD
GIRRS > GIRR
GIRSH n currency unit of Saudi Arabia
GIRSHES > GIRSH
GIRT vb gird; bind
GIRTED > GIRT
GIRTH n measurement round something ▷ vb fasten a girth on (a horse)
GIRTHED > GIRTH
GIRTHING > GIRTH
GIRTHLINE same as > GIRTLINE
GIRTHS > GIRTH
GIRTING > GIRT
GIRTLINE n gantline
GIRTLINES > GIRTLINE
GIRTS > GIRT
GIS > GI
GISARME n long-shafted battle-axe
GISARMES > GISARME
GISM n vulgar word for semen
GISMO same as > GIZMO
GISMOLOGY same as > GIZMOLOGY
GISMOS > GISMO
GISMS > GISM
GIST n substance or main point of a matter
GISTS > GIST
GIT vb dialect version of get
GITANA n female gypsy
GITANAS > GITANA
GITANO n male gypsy
GITANOS > GITANO
GITCH n underwear
GITCHES > GITCH
GITE n self-catering holiday cottage for let in France
GITES > GITE
GITS > GIT
GITTARONE n acoustic bass guitar
GITTED > GIT
GITTERN n obsolete medieval instrument ▷ vb play the gittern
GITTERNED > GITTERN
GITTERNS > GITTERN
GITTIN n Jewish divorce
GITTING > GIT
GIUST same as > JOUST
GIUSTED > GIUST
GIUSTING > GIUST
GIUSTO adv as observed strictly
GIUSTS > GIUST
GIVABLE > GIVE
GIVE vb present (something) to another person ▷ n resilience or elasticity
GIVEABLE > GIVE
GIVEAWAY n something that reveals hidden feelings or intentions ▷ adj very cheap or free
GIVEAWAYS > GIVEAWAY
GIVEBACK n reduction in wages in return for some other benefit, in time of recession

GIVEBACKS > GIVEBACK
GIVED same as > GYVED
GIVEN n assumed fact
GIVENNESS n condition of being given
GIVENS > GIVEN
GIVER > GIVE
GIVERS > GIVE
GIVES > GIVE
GIVING > GIVE
GIVINGS > GIVE
GIZMO n device
GIZMOLOGY n study of gadgets
GIZMOS > GIZMO
GIZZ n wig
GIZZARD n part of a bird's stomach
GIZZARDS > GIZZARD
GIZZEN vb (of wood) to warp
GIZZENED > GIZZEN
GIZZENING > GIZZEN
GIZZENS > GIZZEN
GIZZES > GIZZ
GJETOST n type of Norwegian cheese
GJETOSTS > GJETOST
GJU n type of violin used in Shetland
GJUS > GJU
GLABELLA n elevation of the frontal bone above the nose
GLABELLAE > GLABELLA
GLABELLAR > GLABELLA
GLABRATE same as > GLABROUS
GLABROUS adj without hair or a similar growth
GLACE adj preserved in a thick sugary syrup ▷ vb ice or candy (cakes, fruits, etc)
GLACED > GLACE
GLACEED > GLACE
GLACEING > GLACE
GLACES > GLACE
GLACIAL adj of ice or glaciers ▷ n ice age
GLACIALLY > GLACIAL
GLACIALS > GLACIAL
GLACIATE vb cover or become covered with glaciers or masses of ice
GLACIATED > GLACIATE
GLACIATES > GLACIATE
GLACIER n slow-moving mass of ice
GLACIERED adj having a glacier or glaciers
GLACIERS > GLACIER
GLACIS n slight incline
GLACISES > GLACIS
GLAD adj pleased and happy ▷ vb become glad ▷ n gladiolus
GLADDED > GLAD
GLADDEN vb make glad
GLADDENED > GLADDEN
GLADDENER > GLADDEN
GLADDENS > GLADDEN
GLADDER > GLAD
GLADDEST > GLAD
GLADDIE n gladiolus
GLADDIES > GLADDIE
GLADDING > GLAD
GLADDON n stinking iris

GLADDONS > GLADDON
GLADE n open space in a forest
GLADELIKE > GLADE
GLADES > GLADE
GLADFUL adj full of gladness
GLADIATE adj shaped like a sword
GLADIATOR n (in ancient Rome) man trained to fight in arenas to provide entertainment
GLADIER > GLADE
GLADIEST > GLADE
GLADIOLA same as > GLADIOLUS
GLADIOLAR > GLADIOLUS
GLADIOLAS > GLADIOLA
GLADIOLE same as > GLADIOLUS
GLADIOLES > GLADIOLE
GLADIOLI > GLADIOLUS
GLADIOLUS n garden plant with sword-shaped leaves
GLADIUS n short sword used by Roman legionaries
GLADIUSES > GLADIUS
GLADLIER > GLAD
GLADLIEST > GLAD
GLADLY > GLAD
GLADNESS > GLAD
GLADS > GLAD
GLADSOME adj joyous or cheerful
GLADSOMER > GLADSOME
GLADSTONE n light four-wheeled horse-drawn vehicle
GLADWRAP n in New Zealand English, thin film for wrapping food ▷ vb cover with gladwrap
GLADWRAPS > GLADWRAP
GLADY > GLADE
GLAIK n prank
GLAIKET same as > GLAIKIT
GLAIKIT adj foolish
GLAIKS > GLAIK
GLAIR n white of egg ▷ vb apply glair to (something)
GLAIRE same as > GLAIR
GLAIRED > GLAIR
GLAIREOUS > GLAIR
GLAIRES > GLAIRE
GLAIRIER > GLAIR
GLAIRIEST > GLAIR
GLAIRIN n viscous mineral deposit
GLAIRING > GLAIR
GLAIRINS > GLAIRIN
GLAIRS > GLAIR
GLAIRY > GLAIR
GLAIVE archaic word for > SWORD
GLAIVED adj armed with a sword
GLAIVES > GLAIVE
GLAM n magical illusion ▷ vb make oneself look glamorous ▷ adj glamorous
GLAMMED > GLAM
GLAMMER > GLAM
GLAMMEST > GLAM
GLAMMIER > GLAMMY
GLAMMIEST > GLAMMY
GLAMMING > GLAM

GLAMMY adj glamorous
GLAMOR same as > GLAMOUR
GLAMORED > GLAMOR
GLAMORING > GLAMOR
GLAMORISE same as > GLAMORIZE
GLAMORIZE vb cause to be or seem glamorous
GLAMOROUS adj alluring
GLAMORS > GLAMOR
GLAMOUR n alluring charm or fascination ▷ vb bewitch
GLAMOURED adj bewitched
GLAMOURS > GLAMOUR
GLAMPING n camping with luxurious physical comforts
GLAMPINGS > GLAMPING
GLAMS > GLAM
GLANCE vb look rapidly or briefly ▷ n brief look
GLANCED > GLANCE
GLANCER n log or pole used to protect trees from damage
GLANCERS > GLANCER
GLANCES > GLANCE
GLANCING > GLANCE
GLANCINGS > GLANCE
GLAND n organ that produces and secretes substances
GLANDERED > GLANDERS
GLANDERS n highly infectious bacterial disease of horses, sometimes transmitted to humans
GLANDES > GLANS
GLANDLESS > GLAND
GLANDLIKE > GLAND
GLANDS > GLAND
GLANDULAR adj of or affecting a gland or glands
GLANDULE n small gland
GLANDULES > GLANDULE
GLANS n any small rounded body or glandlike mass
GLARE vb stare angrily ▷ n angry stare ▷ adj smooth and glassy
GLAREAL adj (of a plant) growing in cultivated land
GLARED > GLARE
GLARELESS > GLARE
GLAREOUS adj resembling the white of an egg
GLARES > GLARE
GLARIER > GLARE
GLARIEST > GLARE
GLARINESS > GLARE
GLARING adj conspicuous
GLARINGLY > GLARING
GLARY > GLARE
GLASNOST n policy of openness and accountability, esp, formerly, in the USSR
GLASNOSTS > GLASNOST
GLASS n hard brittle substance ▷ vb cover with, enclose in, or fit with glass
GLASSED > GLASS
GLASSEN adj glassy
GLASSES pl n pair of lenses for correcting faulty vision
GLASSFUL n amount held by a full glass
GLASSFULS > GLASSFUL
GLASSIE same as > GLASSY

GLASSIER > GLASSY

GLASSIES > GLASSY

GLASSIEST > GLASSY

GLASSIFY vb turn into glass

GLASSILY > GLASSY

GLASSINE n glazed translucent paper used for book jackets

GLASSINES > GLASSINE

GLASSING > GLASS

GLASSLESS > GLASS

GLASSLIKE > GLASS

GLASSMAN n man whose work is making or selling glassware

GLASSMEN > GLASSMAN

GLASSWARE n articles made of glass

GLASSWORK n production of glassware

GLASSWORM n larva of gnat

GLASSWORT n type of plant of salt marshes, with fleshy stems and scalelike leaves, formerly used in glass-making

GLASSY adj like glass ▷ n glass marble

GLAUCOMA n eye disease

GLAUCOMAS > GLAUCOMA

GLAUCOUS adj covered with a bluish waxy or powdery bloom

GLAUM vb snatch

GLAUMED > GLAUM

GLAUMING > GLAUM

GLAUMS > GLAUM

GLAUR n mud or mire

GLAURIER > GLAUR

GLAURIEST > GLAUR

GLAURS > GLAUR

GLAURY > GLAUR

GLAZE vb fit or cover with glass ▷ n transparent coating

GLAZED > GLAZE

GLAZEN adj glazed

GLAZER > GLAZE

GLAZERS > GLAZE

GLAZES > GLAZE

GLAZIER n person who fits windows with glass

GLAZIERS > GLAZIER

GLAZIERY > GLAZIER

GLAZIEST > GLAZE

GLAZILY > GLAZE

GLAZINESS > GLAZE

GLAZING n surface of a glazed object

GLAZINGS > GLAZING

GLAZY > GLAZE

GLEAM n small beam or glow of light ▷ vb emit a gleam

GLEAMED > GLEAM

GLEAMER n mirror used to cheat in card games

GLEAMERS > GLEAMER

GLEAMIER > GLEAM

GLEAMIEST > GLEAM

GLEAMING > GLEAM

GLEAMINGS > GLEAM

GLEAMS > GLEAM

GLEAMY > GLEAM

GLEAN vb gather (facts etc) bit by bit

GLEANABLE > GLEAN

GLEANED > GLEAN

GLEANER > GLEAN

GLEANERS > GLEAN

GLEANING > GLEAN

GLEANINGS pl n pieces of information that have been gleaned

GLEANS > GLEAN

GLEAVE same as > SWORD

GLEAVES > GLEAVE

GLEBA n mass of spores

GLEBAE > GLEBA

GLEBE n land granted to a member of the clergy

GLEBELESS > GLEBE

GLEBES > GLEBE

GLEBIER > GLEBY

GLEBIEST > GLEBY

GLEBOUS adj gleby

GLEBY adj relating to a glebe

GLED n kite

GLEDE same as > GLED

GLEDES > GLEDE

GLEDGE vb glance sideways

GLEDGED > GLEDGE

GLEDGES > GLEDGE

GLEDGING > GLEDGE

GLEDS > GLED

GLEE n triumph and delight ▷ vb be full of glee

GLEED n burning ember or hot coal

GLEEDS > GLEED

GLEEFUL adj merry or joyful

GLEEFULLY > GLEEFUL

GLEEING > GLEE

GLEEK vb jeer

GLEEKED > GLEEK

GLEEKING > GLEEK

GLEEKS > GLEEK

GLEEMAN n minstrel

GLEEMEN > GLEEMAN

GLEENIE n guinea fowl

GLEENIES > GLEENIE

GLEES > GLEE

GLEESOME adj full of glee

GLEET n inflammation of the urethra ▷ vb discharge pus

GLEETED > GLEET

GLEETIER > GLEET

GLEETIEST > GLEET

GLEETING > GLEET

GLEETS > GLEET

GLEETY > GLEET

GLEG adj quick

GLEGGER > GLEG

GLEGGEST > GLEG

GLEGLY > GLEG

GLEGNESS > GLEG

GLEI same as > GLEY

GLEIS > GLEI

GLEN n deep narrow valley, esp in Scotland

GLENGARRY n brimless Scottish cap with a crease down the crown

GLENLIKE > GLEN

GLENOID adj resembling or having a shallow cavity ▷ n shallow cavity

GLENOIDAL > GLENOID

GLENOIDS > GLENOID

GLENS > GLEN

GLENT same as > GLINT

GLENTED > GLENT

GLENTING > GLENT

GLENTS > GLENT

GLEY n bluish-grey compact sticky soil ▷ vb squint

GLEYED > GLEY

GLEYING > GLEY

GLEYINGS > GLEY

GLEYS > GLEY

GLIA n web of tissue that supports nerve cells

GLIADIN n protein of cereals with a high proline content

GLIADINE same as > GLIADIN

GLIADINES > GLIADINE

GLIADINS > GLIADIN

GLIAL > GLIA

GLIAS > GLIA

GLIB adj fluent but insincere or superficial ▷ vb render glib, smooth, or slippery

GLIBBED > GLIB

GLIBBER > GLIB

GLIBBERY adj slippery

GLIBBEST > GLIB

GLIBBING > GLIB

GLIBLY > GLIB

GLIBNESS > GLIB

GLIBS > GLIB

GLID adj moving smoothly and easily

GLIDDER > GLID

GLIDDERY adj slippery

GLIDDEST > GLID

GLIDE vb move easily and smoothly ▷ n smooth easy movement

GLIDED > GLIDE

GLIDEPATH n path followed by aircraft coming in to land

GLIDER n flying phalanger

GLIDERS > GLIDER

GLIDES > GLIDE

GLIDING n sport of flying gliders

GLIDINGLY > GLIDE

GLIDINGS > GLIDING

GLIFF n slap

GLIFFING > GLIFF

GLIFFINGS > GLIFF

GLIFFS > GLIFF

GLIFT n moment

GLIFTS > GLIFT

GLIKE same as > GLEEK

GLIKES > GLIKE

GLIM n light or lamp

GLIME vb glance sideways

GLIMED > GLIME

GLIMES > GLIME

GLIMING > GLIME

GLIMMER vb shine faintly, flicker ▷ n faint gleam

GLIMMERED > GLIMMER

GLIMMERS > GLIMMER

GLIMMERY adj glimmering, shimmery

GLIMPSE n brief or incomplete view ▷ vb catch a glimpse of

GLIMPSED > GLIMPSE

GLIMPSER > GLIMPSE

GLIMPSERS > GLIMPSE

GLIMPSES > GLIMPSE

GLIMPSING > GLIMPSE

GLIMS > GLIM

GLINT vb gleam brightly ▷ n bright gleam

GLINTED > GLINT

GLINTIER > GLINT

GLINTIEST > GLINT

GLINTING > GLINT

GLINTS > GLINT

GLINTY > GLINT

GLIOMA n tumour of the brain and spinal cord

GLIOMAS > GLIOMA

GLIOMATA > GLIOMA

GLIOSES > GLIOSIS

GLIOSIS n process leading to scarring in the nervous system

GLISK n glimpse

GLISKS > GLISK

GLISSADE n gliding step in ballet ▷ vb perform a glissade

GLISSADED > GLISSADE

GLISSADER > GLISSADE

GLISSADES > GLISSADE

GLISSANDI > GLISSANDO

GLISSANDO n slide between two notes in which all intermediate notes are played

GLISSE n type of dance step

GLISSES > GLISSE

GLISTEN vb gleam by reflecting light ▷ n gleam or gloss

GLISTENED > GLISTEN

GLISTENS > GLISTEN

GLISTER archaic word for > GLITTER

GLISTERED > GLISTER

GLISTERS > GLISTER

GLIT n slimy matter

GLITCH n small problem that stops something from working

GLITCHES > GLITCH

GLITCHIER > GLITCH

GLITCHY > GLITCH

GLITS > GLIT

GLITTER vb shine with bright flashes ▷ n sparkle or brilliance

GLITTERED > GLITTER

GLITTERS > GLITTER

GLITTERY > GLITTER

GLITZ n ostentatious showiness ▷ vb make something more attractive

GLITZED > GLITZ

GLITZES > GLITZ

GLITZIER > GLITZY

GLITZIEST > GLITZY

GLITZILY > GLITZY

GLITZING > GLITZ

GLITZY adj showily attractive

GLOAM n dusk

GLOAMING n twilight

GLOAMINGS > GLOAMING

GLOAMS > GLOAM

GLOAT vb regard one's own good fortune with pleasure ▷ n act of gloating

GLOATED > GLOAT

GLOATER > GLOAT

GLOATERS > GLOAT

GLOATING n act of gloating

GLOATINGS > GLOATING

GLOATS > GLOAT

g

GLOB n rounded mass of thick fluid
GLOBAL adj worldwide
GLOBALISE same as > GLOBALIZE
GLOBALISM n policy which is worldwide in scope
GLOBALIST > GLOBALISM
GLOBALIZE vb put (something) into effect worldwide
GLOBALLY > GLOBAL
GLOBATE adj shaped like a globe
GLOBATED same as > GLOBATE
GLOBBIER > GLOBBY
GLOBBIEST > GLOBBY
GLOBBY adj thick and lumpy
GLOBE n sphere with a map of the earth on it ▷ vb form or cause to form into a globe
GLOBED > GLOBE
GLOBEFISH another name for > PUFFER
GLOBELIKE > GLOBE
GLOBES > GLOBE
GLOBESITY n informal word for obesity seen as a worldwide social problem
GLOBETROT vb regularly travel internationally
GLOBI > GLOBUS
GLOBIER > GLOBY
GLOBIEST > GLOBY
GLOBIN n protein component
GLOBING > GLOBE
GLOBINS > GLOBIN
GLOBOID adj shaped approximately like a globe ▷ n globoid body
GLOBOIDS > GLOBOID
GLOBOSE adj spherical or approximately spherical ▷ n globose object
GLOBOSELY > GLOBOSE
GLOBOSITY > GLOBOSE
GLOBOUS same as > GLOBOSE
GLOBS > GLOB
GLOBULAR adj shaped like a globe or globule ▷ n globular star cluster
GLOBULARS > GLOBULAR
GLOBULE n small round drop
GLOBULES > GLOBULE
GLOBULET n small globule
GLOBULETS > GLOBULET
GLOBULIN n simple protein found in living tissue
GLOBULINS > GLOBULIN
GLOBULITE n spherical form of crystallite
GLOBULOUS same as > GLOBULAR
GLOBUS n any spherelike structure
GLOBY adj round
GLOCHID n barbed spine on a plant
GLOCHIDIA n plural form of singular glochidium, a barbed hair on some plants
GLOCHIDS > GLOCHID
GLODE > GLIDE

GLOGG n hot alcoholic mixed drink
GLOGGS > GLOGG
GLOIRE n glory
GLOIRES > GLOIRE
GLOM vb attach oneself to or associate oneself with
GLOMERA > GLOMUS
GLOMERATE adj gathered into a compact rounded mass ▷ vb wind into a ball
GLOMERULE n cymose inflorescence in the form of a ball-like cluster of flowers
GLOMERULI n plural of singular glomerulus: a knot of blood vessels in the kidney
GLOMMED > GLOM
GLOMMING > GLOM
GLOMS > GLOM
GLOMUS n small anastomosis in an artery or vein
GLONOIN n nitroglycerin
GLONOINS > GLONOIN
GLOOM n melancholy or depression ▷ vb look sullen or depressed
GLOOMED > GLOOM
GLOOMFUL > GLOOM
GLOOMIER > GLOOMY
GLOOMIEST > GLOOMY
GLOOMILY > GLOOMY
GLOOMING > GLOOM
GLOOMINGS > GLOOM
GLOOMLESS > GLOOM
GLOOMS > GLOOM
GLOOMSTER n person with gloomy outlook
GLOOMY adj despairing or sad
GLOOP vb cover with a viscous substance
GLOOPED > GLOOP
GLOOPIER > GLOOP
GLOOPIEST > GLOOP
GLOOPING > GLOOP
GLOOPS > GLOOP
GLOOPY > GLOOP
GLOP vb cover with a viscous substance
GLOPPED > GLOP
GLOPPIER > GLOP
GLOPPIEST > GLOP
GLOPPING > GLOP
GLOPPY > GLOP
GLOPS > GLOP
GLORIA n silk, wool, cotton, or nylon fabric
GLORIAS > GLORIA
GLORIED > GLORY
GLORIES > GLORY
GLORIFIED > GLORIFY
GLORIFIER > GLORIFY
GLORIFIES > GLORIFY
GLORIFY vb make (something) seem more worthy than it is
GLORIOLE another name for a > HALO
GLORIOLES > GLORIOLE
GLORIOSA n bulbous African tropical plant
GLORIOSAS > GLORIOSA
GLORIOUS adj brilliantly beautiful

GLORY n praise or honour ▷ vb triumph or exalt
GLORYING > GLORY
GLOSS n surface shine or lustre ▷ vb make glossy
GLOSSA n paired tonguelike lobe in the labium of an insect
GLOSSAE > GLOSSA
GLOSSAL > GLOSSA
GLOSSARY n list of special or technical words with definitions
GLOSSAS > GLOSSA
GLOSSATOR n writer of glosses and commentaries, esp (in the Middle Ages) an interpreter of Roman and Canon Law
GLOSSED > GLOSS
GLOSSEME n smallest meaningful unit of a language, such as stress, form, etc
GLOSSEMES > GLOSSEME
GLOSSER > GLOSS
GLOSSERS > GLOSS
GLOSSES > GLOSS
GLOSSIER > GLOSSY
GLOSSIES > GLOSSY
GLOSSIEST > GLOSSY
GLOSSILY > GLOSSY
GLOSSINA n tsetse fly
GLOSSINAS > GLOSSINA
GLOSSING > GLOSS
GLOSSIST same as > GLOSSATOR
GLOSSISTS > GLOSSIST
GLOSSITIC > GLOSSITIS
GLOSSITIS n inflammation of the tongue
GLOSSLESS > GLOSS
GLOSSY adj smooth and shiny ▷ n expensively produced magazine
GLOST n lead glaze used for pottery
GLOSTS > GLOST
GLOTTAL adj of the glottis
GLOTTIC adj of or relating to the tongue or the glottis
GLOTTIDES > GLOTTIS
GLOTTIS n vocal cords and the space between them
GLOTTISES > GLOTTIS
GLOUT vb look sullen
GLOUTED > GLOUT
GLOUTING > GLOUT
GLOUTS > GLOUT
GLOVE n covering for the hand
GLOVEBOX n small compartment in a car for miscellaneous articles
GLOVED > GLOVE
GLOVELESS > GLOVE
GLOVELIKE adj like a glove
GLOVER n person who makes or sells gloves
GLOVERS > GLOVER
GLOVES > GLOVE
GLOVING > GLOVE
GLOVINGS > GLOVE
GLOW vb emit light and heat without flames ▷ n glowing light
GLOWED > GLOW

GLOWER n scowl ▷ vb stare angrily
GLOWERED > GLOWER
GLOWERING > GLOWER
GLOWERS > GLOWER
GLOWFLIES > GLOWFLY
GLOWFLY n firefly
GLOWING adj full of praise
GLOWINGLY > GLOWING
GLOWLAMP n small light consisting of two or more electrodes in an inert gas
GLOWLAMPS > GLOWLAMP
GLOWS > GLOW
GLOWSTICK n plastic tube containing a luminescent material, waved or held aloft esp at gigs, raves, etc
GLOWWORM n European beetle which produces a greenish light
GLOWWORMS > GLOWWORM
GLOXINIA n tropical plant with large bell-shaped flowers
GLOXINIAS > GLOXINIA
GLOZE vb explain away ▷ n flattery or deceit
GLOZED > GLOZE
GLOZES > GLOZE
GLOZING > GLOZE
GLOZINGS > GLOZE
GLUCAGON n hormone that releases glucose into the blood
GLUCAGONS > GLUCAGON
GLUCAN n any polysaccharide consisting of a polymer of glucose
GLUCANS > GLUCAN
GLUCINA n oxide of glucinum
GLUCINAS > GLUCINA
GLUCINIC > GLUCINIUM
GLUCINIUM former name of > BERYLLIUM
GLUCINUM same as > GLUCINIUM
GLUCINUMS > GLUCINUM
GLUCONATE n compound formed when a mineral is bound to gluconic acid
GLUCONIC adj as in gluconic acid acid that occurs naturally in fruit
GLUCOSE n kind of sugar found in fruit
GLUCOSES > GLUCOSE
GLUCOSIC > GLUCOSE
GLUCOSIDE n any of a large group of glycosides that yield glucose on hydrolysis
GLUE n natural or synthetic sticky substance ▷ vb fasten with glue
GLUEBALL n hypothetical composite subatomic particle
GLUEBALLS > GLUEBALL
GLUED > GLUE
GLUEING > GLUE
GLUEISH same as > GLUISH
GLUELIKE > GLUE
GLUEPOT n container for holding glue
GLUEPOTS > GLUEPOT
GLUER > GLUE

GLUERS > GLUE
GLUES > GLUE
GLUEY > GLUE
GLUEYNESS > GLUE
GLUG n word representing a gurgling sound ▷ vb drink noisily, taking big gulps
GLUGGABLE adj (of wine) easy and pleasant to drink
GLUGGED > GLUG
GLUGGING > GLUG
GLUGS > GLUG
GLUHWEIN n mulled wine
GLUHWEINS > GLUHWEIN
GLUIER > GLUE
GLUIEST > GLUE
GLUILY > GLUE
GLUINESS > GLUE
GLUING > GLUE
GLUISH adj having the properties of glue
GLUM adj sullen or gloomy
GLUME n one of a pair of dry membranous bracts in grasses
GLUMELIKE > GLUME
GLUMELLA n palea
GLUMELLAS > GLUMELLA
GLUMES > GLUME
GLUMLY > GLUM
GLUMMER > GLUM
GLUMMEST > GLUM
GLUMNESS > GLUM
GLUMPIER > GLUMPY
GLUMPIEST > GLUMPY
GLUMPILY > GLUMPY
GLUMPISH > GLUMPY
GLUMPS n state of sulking
GLUMPY adj sullen
GLUMS n gloomy feelings
GLUNCH vb look sullen
GLUNCHED > GLUNCH
GLUNCHES > GLUNCH
GLUNCHING > GLUNCH
GLUON n hypothetical particle
GLUONS > GLUON
GLURGE n stories supposed to be true but often fabricated
GLURGES > GLURGE
GLUT n excessive supply ▷ vb oversupply
GLUTAEAL > GLUTAEUS
GLUTAEI > GLUTAEUS
GLUTAEUS same as > GLUTEUS
GLUTAMATE n any salt of glutamic acid, esp its sodium salt
GLUTAMIC adj as in glutamic acid nonessential amino acid that plays a part in nitrogen metabolism
GLUTAMINE n nonessential amino acid occurring in proteins: plays an important role in protein metabolism
GLUTCH vb swallow
GLUTCHED > GLUTCH
GLUTCHES > GLUTCH
GLUTCHING > GLUTCH
GLUTE same as > GLUTEUS
GLUTEAL > GLUTEUS
GLUTEI > GLUTEUS
GLUTELIN n water-insoluble plant protein found in cereals

GLUTELINS > GLUTELIN
GLUTEN n protein found in cereal grain
GLUTENIN n type of protein
GLUTENINS > GLUTENIN
GLUTENOUS > GLUTEN
GLUTENS > GLUTEN
GLUTES > GLUTE
GLUTEUS n any of the three muscles of the buttock
GLUTINOUS adj sticky or gluey
GLUTS > GLUT
GLUTTED > GLUT
GLUTTING > GLUT
GLUTTON n greedy person
GLUTTONS > GLUTTON
GLUTTONY n practice of eating too much
GLYCAEMIA n presence of glucose in blood
GLYCAEMIC > GLYCAEMIA
GLYCAN n polysaccharide
GLYCANS > GLYCAN
GLYCATION n the bonding of a sugar molecule to a protein or lipid
GLYCEMIA US spelling of > GLYCAEMIA
GLYCEMIAS > GLYCEMIA
GLYCEMIC > GLYCEMIA
GLYCERIA n manna grass
GLYCERIAS > GLYCERIA
GLYCERIC adj of, containing, or derived from glycerol
GLYCERIDE n any fatty-acid ester of glycerol
GLYCERIN same as > GLYCEROL
GLYCERINE same as > GLYCEROL
GLYCERINS > GLYCERIN
GLYCEROL n colourless odourless syrupy liquid
GLYCEROLS > GLYCEROL
GLYCERYL n (something) derived from glycerol
GLYCERYLS > GLYCERYL
GLYCIN same as > GLYCINE
GLYCINE n nonessential amino acid
GLYCINES > GLYCINE
GLYCINS > GLYCIN
GLYCOCOLL n glycine
GLYCOGEN n starchlike carbohydrate stored in the liver and muscles of humans and animals
GLYCOGENS > GLYCOGEN
GLYCOL n another name (not in technical usage) for a diol
GLYCOLIC > GLYCOL
GLYCOLLIC > GLYCOL
GLYCOLS > GLYCOL
GLYCONIC n verse consisting of a spondee, choriamb and pyrrhic
GLYCONICS > GLYCONIC
GLYCOSE n any of various monosaccharides
GLYCOSES > GLYCOSE
GLYCOSIDE n any of a group of substances, such as digitoxin, derived from monosaccharides by

replacing the hydroxyl group by another group
GLYCOSYL n glucose-derived radical
GLYCOSYLS > GLYCOSYL
GLYCYL n radical of glycine
GLYCYLS > GLYCYL
GLYPH n carved channel or groove
GLYPHIC > GLYPH
GLYPHS > GLYPH
GLYPTAL n alkyd resin
GLYPTALS > GLYPTAL
GLYPTIC adj of or relating to engraving or carving
GLYPTICS n art of engraving precious stones
GMELINITE n zeolitic mineral
GNAMMA variant of > NAMMA
GNAR same as > GNARL
GNARL n any knotty protuberance or swelling on a tree ▷ vb knot or cause to knot
GNARLED adj rough, twisted, and knobbly
GNARLIER > GNARLY
GNARLIEST > GNARLY
GNARLING > GNARL
GNARLS > GNARL
GNARLY adj good
GNARR same as > GNARL
GNARRED > GNAR
GNARRING > GNAR
GNARRS > GNARR
GNARS > GNAR
GNASH vb grind (the teeth) together ▷ n act of gnashing the teeth
GNASHED > GNASH
GNASHER n tooth
GNASHERS pl n teeth, esp false ones
GNASHES > GNASH
GNASHING > GNASH
GNASHINGS > GNASHING
GNAT n small biting two-winged fly
GNATHAL same as > GNATHIC
GNATHIC adj of or relating to the jaw
GNATHION n lowest point of the midline of the lower jaw: a reference point in craniometry
GNATHIONS > GNATHION
GNATHITE n appendage of an arthropod that is specialized for grasping or chewing
GNATHITES > GNATHITE
GNATHONIC adj deceitfully flattering
GNATLIKE > GNAT
GNATLING n small gnat
GNATLINGS > GNATLING
GNATS > GNAT
GNATTIER > GNATTY
GNATTIEST > GNATTY
GNATTY adj infested with gnats
GNATWREN n small bird of the gnatcatcher family
GNATWRENS > GNATWREN

GNAW vb bite or chew steadily ▷ n act or an instance of gnawing
GNAWABLE > GNAW
GNAWED > GNAW
GNAWER > GNAW
GNAWERS > GNAW
GNAWING > GNAW
GNAWINGLY > GNAW
GNAWINGS > GNAW
GNAWN > GNAW
GNAWS > GNAW
GNEISS n coarse-grained metamorphic rock
GNEISSES > GNEISS
GNEISSIC > GNEISS
GNEISSOID > GNEISS
GNEISSOSE > GNEISS
GNOCCHI n dumplings
GNOMAE > GNOME
GNOME n imaginary creature like a little old man
GNOMELIKE > GNOME
GNOMES > GNOME
GNOMIC adj of pithy sayings
GNOMICAL same as > GNOMIC
GNOMISH > GNOME
GNOMIST n writer of pithy sayings
GNOMISTS > GNOMIST
GNOMON n stationary arm on a sundial
GNOMONIC > GNOMON
GNOMONICS > GNOMON
GNOMONS > GNOMON
GNOSES > GNOSIS
GNOSIS n supposedly revealed knowledge of spiritual truths
GNOSTIC adj of, relating to, or possessing knowledge ▷ n one who knows
GNOSTICAL same as > GNOSTIC
GNOSTICS > GNOSTIC
GNOW n Australian wild bird
GNOWS > GNOW
GNU n ox-like S African antelope
GNUS > GNU
GO vb move to or from a place ▷ n attempt
GOA n Tibetan gazelle
GOAD vb provoke (someone) to take some kind of action, usu in anger ▷ n spur or provocation
GOADED > GOAD
GOADING > GOAD
GOADLIKE > GOAD
GOADS > GOAD
GOADSMAN n person who uses a goad
GOADSMEN > GOADSMAN
GOADSTER n goadsman
GOADSTERS > GOADSTER
GOAF n waste left in old mine workings
GOAFS > GOAF
GOAL n posts through which the ball or puck has to move to score ▷ vb in rugby, to convert a try into a goal
GOALBALL n game played with a ball that emits sound
GOALBALLS > GOALBALL

g

GOALED > GOAL

GOALIE n goalkeeper

GOALIES > GOALIE

GOALING > GOAL

GOALLESS > GOAL

GOALMOUTH n area in front of the goal

GOALPOST n one of the two posts marking the limit of a goal

GOALPOSTS > GOALPOST

GOALS > GOAL

GOALWARD adv towards a goal

GOALWARDS same as > GOALWARD

GOANNA n large Australian lizard

GOANNAS > GOANNA

GOARY variant spelling of > GORY

GOAS > GOA

GOAT n sure-footed ruminant animal with horns

GOATEE n pointed tuft-like beard

GOATEED > GOATEE

GOATEES > GOATEE

GOATFISH n red mullet

GOATHERD n person who looks after a herd of goats

GOATHERDS > GOATHERD

GOATIER > GOATY

GOATIES > GOATY

GOATIEST > GOATY

GOATISH adj of, like, or relating to a goat

GOATISHLY > GOATISH

GOATLIKE > GOAT

GOATLING n young goat

GOATLINGS > GOATLING

GOATS > GOAT

GOATSE n deliberately offensive image placed maliciously into a website

GOATSES > GOATSE

GOATSKIN n leather made from the skin of a goat

GOATSKINS > GOATSKIN

GOATWEED n plant of the genus Capraria

GOATWEEDS > GOATWEED

GOATY n pointed tuft-like beard ⊳ adj resembling a goat

GOB n lump of a soft substance ⊳ vb spit

GOBAN n board on which go is played

GOBANG n Japanese board-game

GOBANGS > GOBANG

GOBANS > GOBAN

GOBAR adj as in gobar numeral kind of numeral

GOBBED > GOB

GOBBELINE same as > GOBLIN

GOBBET n lump, esp of food

GOBBETS > GOBBET

GOBBI > GOBBO

GOBBIER > GOBBY

GOBBIEST > GOBBY

GOBBING > GOB

GOBBLE vb eat hastily and greedily ⊳ n rapid gurgling cry of the male turkey ⊳ interj imitation of this sound

GOBBLED > GOBBLE

GOBBLER n turkey

GOBBLERS > GOBBLER

GOBBLES > GOBBLE

GOBBLING > GOBBLE

GOBBO n hunchback

GOBBY adj loudmouthed and offensive

GOBI n (in Indian cookery) cauliflower

GOBIES > GOBY

GOBIID n member of the genus Gobius

GOBIIDS > GOBIID

GOBIOID n type of spiny-finned fish

GOBIOIDS > GOBIOID

GOBIS > GOBI

GOBLET n drinking cup without handles

GOBLETS > GOBLET

GOBLIN n (in folklore) small malevolent creature

GOBLINS > GOBLIN

GOBO n shield placed around a microphone

GOBOES > GOBO

GOBONEE same as > GOBONY

GOBONY adj in heraldry, composed of a row of small, alternately coloured, squares

GOBOS > GOBO

GOBS > GOB

GOBSHITE n vulgar Irish slang for a stupid person

GOBSHITES > GOBSHITE

GOBURRA n kookaburra

GOBURRAS > GOBURRA

GOBY n small spiny-finned fish

GOCHUJANG n spicy paste used in Korean cuisine

GOD n spirit or being worshipped as having supernatural power ⊳ vb deify

GODAWFUL adj very bad or unpleasant

GODCHILD n child for whom a person stands as godparent

GODDAM vb damn

GODDAMMED > GODDAM

GODDAMMIT interj an oath expressing anger, surprise, irritation, etc

GODDAMN interj oath expressing anger, surprise, etc ⊳ adj extremely ⊳ vb damn

GODDAMNED > GODDAMN

GODDAMNIT interj god damn it

GODDAMNS > GODDAMN

GODDAMS > GODDAM

GODDED > GOD

GODDEN n evening greeting

GODDENS > GODDEN

GODDESS n female divinity

GODDESSES > GODDESS

GODDING > GOD

GODET n triangular piece of material inserted into a garment

GODETIA n plant with showy flowers

GODETIAS > GODETIA

GODETS > GODET

GODFATHER n male godparent ⊳ vb be a godfather to

GODHEAD n essential nature and condition of being a god

GODHEADS > GODHEAD

GODHOOD n state of being divine

GODHOODS > GODHOOD

GODLESS adj wicked or unprincipled

GODLESSLY > GODLESS

GODLIER > GODLY

GODLIEST > GODLY

GODLIKE adj resembling or befitting a god or God

GODLILY > GODLY

GODLINESS > GODLY

GODLING n little god

GODLINGS > GODLING

GODLY adj devout or pious

GODMOTHER n female godparent

GODOWN n (in East Asia and India) warehouse

GODOWNS > GODOWN

GODPARENT n person who promises at a child's baptism to bring the child up as a Christian

GODROON same as > GADROON

GODROONED > GODROON

GODROONS > GODROON

GODS > GOD

GODSEND n something unexpected but welcome

GODSENDS > GODSEND

GODSHIP n divinity

GODSHIPS > GODSHIP

GODSLOT n time in a schedule for religious broadcasts

GODSLOTS > GODSLOT

GODSO same as > GADSO

GODSON n male godchild

GODSONS > GODSON

GODSPEED n expression of one's good wishes for a person's success and safety

GODSPEEDS > GODSPEED

GODSQUAD n evangelical Christians

GODSQUADS > GODSQUAD

GODWARD adv towards God

GODWARDS same as > GODWARD

GODWIT n shore bird with long legs and an upturned bill

GODWITS > GODWIT

GOE same as > GO

GOEL n in Jewish law, blood-avenger

GOELS > GOEL

GOER n person who attends something regularly

GOERS > GOER

GOES > GO

GOEST vb archaic 2nd person sing present of go

GOETH vb archaic 3rd person sing present of go

GOETHITE n black, brown, or yellow mineral

GOETHITES > GOETHITE

GOETIC > GOETY

GOETIES > GOETY

GOETY n witchcraft

GOEY adj go-ahead

GOFER n employee or assistant performing menial tasks

GOFERS > GOFER

GOFF obsolete variant of > GOLF

GOFFED > GOFF

GOFFER vb press pleats into (a frill) ⊳ n ornamental frill made by pressing pleats

GOFFERED > GOFFER

GOFFERING > GOFFER

GOFFERS > GOFFER

GOFFING > GOFF

GOFFS > GOFF

GOGGA n any small insect

GOGGAS > GOGGA

GOGGLE vb (of the eyes) bulge ⊳ n fixed or bulging stare

GOGGLEBOX n television set

GOGGLED > GOGGLE

GOGGLER n big-eyed scad

GOGGLERS > GOGGLER

GOGGLES > GOGGLE

GOGGLIER > GOGGLE

GOGGLIEST > GOGGLE

GOGGLING > GOGGLE

GOGGLINGS > GOGGLE

GOGGLY > GOGGLE

GOGLET n long-necked water-cooling vessel

GOGLETS > GOGLET

GOGO n disco

GOGOS > GOGO

GOHONZON n (in Nichiren Buddhism) paper scroll to which devotional chanting is directed

GOHONZONS > GOHONZON

GOIER > GOEY

GOIEST > GOEY

GOING > GO

GOINGS > GO

GOITER same as > GOITRE

GOITERED > GOITER

GOITERS > GOITER

GOITRE n swelling of the thyroid gland in the neck

GOITRED > GOITRE

GOITRES > GOITRE

GOITROGEN n substance that induces the formation of a goitre

GOITROUS > GOITRE

GOJI same as > WOLFBERRY

GOJIS > GOJI

GOLCONDA n source of wealth or riches, esp a mine

GOLCONDAS > GOLCONDA

GOLD n yellow precious metal ⊳ adj made of gold

GOLDARN euphemistic variant of > GODDAMN

GOLDARNED > GOLDARN

GOLDARNS > GOLDARN

GOLDBRICK vb swindle

GOLDBUG n American beetle with a bright metallic lustre

GOLDBUGS > GOLDBUG

GOLDCREST n small bird with a yellow crown

GOLDEN adj made of gold ⊳ vb gild

GOLDENED > GOLDEN

GOLDENER > GOLDEN

GOLDENEST > GOLDEN

GOLDENEYE *n* type of black-and-white diving duck of northern regions

GOLDENING > GOLDEN

GOLDENLY > GOLDEN

GOLDENROD *n* tall plant with spikes of small yellow flowers

GOLDENS > GOLDEN

GOLDER > GOLD

GOLDEST > GOLD

GOLDEYE *n* N American fish

GOLDEYES > GOLDEYE

GOLDFIELD *n* area in which there are gold deposits

GOLDFINCH *n* kind of finch, the male of which has yellow-and-black wings

GOLDFINNY *same as* > GOLDSINNY

GOLDFISH *n* orange fish kept in ponds or aquariums

GOLDIER > GOLDY

GOLDIES > GOLDY

GOLDIEST > GOLDY

GOLDISH > GOLD

GOLDLESS > GOLD

GOLDMINER *n* miner who works in a gold mine

GOLDS > GOLD

GOLDSINNY *n* small European fish

GOLDSIZE *n* adhesive used to fix gold leaf to a surface

GOLDSIZES > GOLDSIZE

GOLDSMITH *n* dealer in or maker of gold articles

GOLDSPINK *n* goldfinch

GOLDSTICK *n* colonel in the Life Guards who carries out ceremonial duties

GOLDSTONE *n* dark-coloured glass, usually green or brown, spangled with fine particles of gold, copper, or some other metal

GOLDTAIL *n* as in *goldtail moth* European moth with white wings and a soft white furry body with a yellow tail tuft

GOLDTONE *adj* gold-coloured ▷ *n* photographic image printed on a glass-plate with a painted golden backing

GOLDTONES > GOLDTONE

GOLDURN *variant of* > GODDAMN

GOLDURNS > GOLDURN

GOLDWORK *n* gold objects collectively

GOLDWORKS > GOLDWORK

GOLDY *adj* gold-like ▷ *n* goldfinch

GOLE *obsolete spelling of* > GOAL

GOLEM *n* (in Jewish legend) artificially created human

GOLEMS > GOLEM

GOLES > GOLE

GOLF *n* outdoor sport ▷ *vb* play golf

GOLFED > GOLF

GOLFER *n* person who plays golf

GOLFERS > GOLFER

GOLFIANA *n* collection of golfing memorabilia

GOLFIANAS > GOLFIANA

GOLFING > GOLF

GOLFINGS > GOLF

GOLFS > GOLF

GOLGOTHA *n* place of burial

GOLGOTHAS > GOLGOTHA

GOLIARD *n* one of a number of wandering scholars

GOLIARDIC > GOLIARD

GOLIARDS > GOLIARD

GOLIARDY > GOLIARD

GOLIAS *vb* behave outrageously

GOLIASED > GOLIAS

GOLIASES > GOLIAS

GOLIASING > GOLIAS

GOLIATH *n* giant

GOLIATHS > GOLIATH

GOLLAN *n* yellow flower

GOLLAND *same as* > GOLLAN

GOLLANDS > GOLLAND

GOLLANS > GOLLAN

GOLLAR *same as* > GOLLER

GOLLARED > GOLLAR

GOLLARING > GOLLAR

GOLLARS > GOLLAR

GOLLER *vb* roar

GOLLERED > GOLLER

GOLLERING > GOLLER

GOLLERS > GOLLER

GOLLIED > GOLLY

GOLLIES > GOLLY

GOLLIWOG *n* soft black-faced doll

GOLLIWOGG *same as* > GOLLIWOG

GOLLIWOGS > GOLLIWOG

GOLLOP *vb* eat or drink (something) quickly or greedily

GOLLOPED > GOLLOP

GOLLOPER > GOLLOP

GOLLOPERS > GOLLOP

GOLLOPING > GOLLOP

GOLLOPS > GOLLOP

GOLLY *interj* exclamation of mild surprise ▷ *vb* spit

GOLLYING > GOLLY

GOLLYWOG *same as* > GOLLIWOG

GOLLYWOGS > GOLLYWOG

GOLOMYNKA *n* oily fish found only in Lake Baikal

GOLOSH *same as* > GALOSH

GOLOSHE *same as* > GALOSH

GOLOSHED > GOLOSH

GOLOSHES > GOLOSH

GOLOSHING > GOLOSH

GOLOSHOES > GOLOSH

GOLP *same as* > GOLPE

GOLPE *n* in heraldry, a purple circle

GOLPES > GOLPE

GOLPS > GOLP

GOMBEEN *n* usury

GOMBEENS > GOMBEEN

GOMBO *same as* > GUMBO

GOMBOS > GOMBO

GOMBRO *same as* > GUMBO

GOMBROON *n* Persian and Chinese pottery and porcelain wares

GOMBROONS > GOMBROON

GOMBROS > GOMBRO

GOMER *n* unwanted hospital patient

GOMERAL *same as* > GOMERIL

GOMERALS > GOMERAL

GOMEREL *same as* > GOMERIL

GOMERELS > GOMEREL

GOMERIL *n* Scots word for a slow-witted person

GOMERILS > GOMERIL

GOMERS > GOMER

GOMOKU *another word for* > GOBANG

GOMOKUS > GOMOKU

GOMPA *n* Tibetan monastery

GOMPAS > GOMPA

GOMPHOSES > GOMPHOSIS

GOMPHOSIS *n* form of immovable articulation in which a peglike part fits into a cavity, as in the setting of a tooth in its socket

GOMUTI *n* E Indian feather palm

GOMUTIS > GOMUTI

GOMUTO *same as* > GOMUTI

GOMUTOS > GOMUTO

GON *n* geometrical grade

GONAD *n* organ producing reproductive cells

GONADAL > GONAD

GONADIAL > GONAD

GONADIC > GONAD

GONADS > GONAD

GONCH *same as* > GITCH

GONCHES > GONCH

GONDELAY *same as* > GONDOLA

GONDELAYS > GONDELAY

GONDOLA *n* long narrow boat used in Venice

GONDOLAS > GONDOLA

GONDOLIER *n* person who propels a gondola

GONE > GO

GONEF *same as* > GANEF

GONEFS > GONEF

GONENESS *n* faintness from hunger

GONER *n* person or thing beyond help or recovery

GONERS > GONER

GONFALON *n* banner hanging from a crossbar

GONFALONS > GONFALON

GONFANON *same as* > GONFALON

GONFANONS > GONFANON

GONG *n* rimmed metal disc ▷ *vb* sound a gong

GONGED > GONG

GONGING > GONG

GONGLIKE > GONG

GONGS > GONG

GONGSTER *n* person who strikes a gong

GONGSTERS > GONGSTER

GONGYO *n* Buddhist ceremony

GONGYOS > GONGYO

GONIA > GONION

GONIATITE *n* type of extinct cephalopod mollusc similar to an ammonite

GONIDIA > GONIDIUM

GONIDIAL > GONIDIUM

GONIDIC > GONIDIUM

GONIDIUM *n* green algal cell in the thallus of a lichen

GONIF *same as* > GANEF

GONIFF *same as* > GANEF

GONIFFS > GONIFF

GONIFS > GONIF

GONION *n* point or apex of the angle of the lower jaw

GONIUM *n* immature reproductive cell

GONK *n* stuffed toy, often used as a mascot

GONKS > GONK

GONNA *vb* going to

GONOCOCCI *n* plural of singular gonococcus

GONOCYTE *n* any cell which may potentially undergo meiosis

GONOCYTES > GONOCYTE

GONODUCT *n* duct leading from a gonad to the exterior, through which gametes pass

GONODUCTS > GONODUCT

GONOF *same as* > GANEF

GONOFS > GONOF

GONOPH *same as* > GANEF

GONOPHORE *n* polyp in certain coelenterates that bears gonads

GONOPHS > GONOPH

GONOPOD *n* either of the reproductive organs of insects

GONOPODS > GONOPOD

GONOPORE *n* external pore in insects, earthworms, etc, through which the gametes are extruded

GONOPORES > GONOPORE

GONORRHEA *n* infectious venereal disease

GONOSOME *n* individuals, collectively, in a colonial animal that are involved with reproduction

GONOSOMES > GONOSOME

GONS > GON

GONYS *n* lower outline of a bird's bill

GONYSES > GONYS

GONZO *adj* wild or crazy ▷ *n* wild or crazy person

GONZOS > GONZO

GOO *n* sticky substance

GOOBER *another name for* > PEANUT

GOOBERS > GOOBER

GOOBIES > GOOBY

GOOBY *n* spittle

GOOD *adj* giving pleasure ▷ *n* benefit

GOODBY *same as* > GOODBYE

GOODBYE *n* expression used on parting ▷ *interj* expression used on parting ▷ *sentence substitute* farewell

GOODBYES > GOODBYE

GOODBYS > GOODBY

GOODFACED *adj* with a handsome face

GOODFELLA *n* gangster, esp one in the Mafia

GOODIE *same as* > GOODY

GOODIER > GOODY

GOODIES > GOODY

COODTEST > GOODY

GOODINESS > GOODY

GOODISH > GOOD

GOODLIER > GOODLY

GOODLIEST > GOODLY

GOODLY adj considerable

GOODMAN n husband

GOODMEN > GOODMAN

GOODNESS n quality of being good ▷ interj exclamation of surprise

GOODNIGHT n conventional expression of farewell used in the evening or at night

GOODS > GOOD

GOODSIRE n grandfather

GOODSIRES > GOODSIRE

GOODTIME adj wildly seeking pleasure

GOODWIFE n mistress of a household

GOODWILL n kindly feeling

GOODWILLS > GOODWILL

GOODWIVES > GOODWIFE

GOODY n hero in a book or film ▷ interj child's exclamation of pleasure ▷ adj smug and sanctimonious

GOODYEAR n euphemistic term for the Devil

GOODYEARS > GOODYEAR

GOOEY adj sticky and soft

GOOEYNESS > GOOEY

GOOF n mistake ▷ vb make a mistake

GOOFBALL n barbiturate sleeping pill

GOOFBALLS > GOOFBALL

GOOFED > GOOF

GOOFIER > GOOFY

GOOFIEST > GOOFY

GOOFILY > GOOFY

GOOFINESS > GOOFY

GOOFING > GOOF

GOOFS > GOOF

GOOFUS n slow-witted or stupid person

GOOFUSES > GOOFUS

GOOFY adj silly or ridiculous

GOOG n egg

GOOGLE vb search on the internet using a search engine

GOOGLED > GOOGLE

GOOGLES > GOOGLE

GOOGLIES > GOOGLY

GOOGLING > GOOGLE

GOOGLY n ball that spins unexpectedly on the bounce

GOOGOL n number shown as one followed by 100 zeros

GOOGOLS > GOOGOL

GOOGS > GOOG

GOOIER > GOOEY

GOOIEST > GOOEY

GOOILY > GOOEY

GOOINESS n quality of being gooey

GOOK n offensive word for a person from a Far Eastern country

GOOKIER > GOOKY

GOOKIEST > GOOKY

GOOKS > GOOK

GOOKY adj sticky and messy

GOOL n corn marigold

GOOLD Scots word for > GOLD

GOOLDS > GOOLD

GOOLEY same as > GOOLIE

GOOLEYS > GOOLEY

GOOLIE n vulgar word for a testicle

GOOLIES > GOOLIE

GOOLS > GOOL

GOOLY same as > GOOLIE

GOOMBAH n patron or mentor

GOOMBAHS > GOOMBAH

GOOMBAY n Bahamian soft drink

GOOMBAYS > GOOMBAY

GOON n person hired to commit violent acts

GOONDA n (in India) habitual criminal

GOONDAS > GOONDA

GOONERIES > GOONERY

GOONERY n behaviour typical of goons

GOONEY n albatross

GOONEYS > GOONEY

GOONIE Scots word for a > GOWN

GOONIER > GOON

GOONIES > GOONIE

GOONIEST > GOON

GOONS > GOON

GOONY > GOON

GOOP n rude or ill-mannered person

GOOPED adj as in gooped up sticky with goop

GOOPIER > GOOP

GOOPIEST > GOOP

GOOPINESS n quality of being goopy

GOOPS > GOOP

GOOPY > GOOP

GOOR same as > GUR

GOORAL same as > GORAL

GOORALS > GOORAL

GOORIE same as > KURI

GOORIES > GOORIE

GOOROO same as > GURU

GOOROOS > GOOROO

GOORS > GOOR

GOORY same as > KURI

GOOS > GOO

GOOSANDER n type of duck

GOOSE n web-footed bird like a large duck ▷ vb prod (someone) playfully in the bottom

GOOSED > GOOSE

GOOSEFISH another name for > MONKFISH

GOOSEFOOT n type of usu weedy plant with small greenish flowers and leaves shaped like a goose's foot

GOOSEGOB n gooseberry

GOOSEGOBS > GOOSEGOB

GOOSEGOG n gooseberry

GOOSEGOGS > GOOSEGOG

GOOSEHERD n person who herds geese

GOOSELIKE adj like a goose

GOOSENECK n pivot between the forward end of a boom and a mast, to allow the boom to swing freely

GOOSERIES > GOOSERY

GOOSERY n place for keeping geese

GOOSES > GOOSE

GOOSEY same as > GOOSY

GOOSEYS > GOOSEY

GOOSIER > GOOSY

GOOSIES > GOOSY

GOOSIEST > GOOSY

GOOSINESS > GOOSY

GOOSING > GOOSE

GOOSY adj of or like a goose ▷ n goose

GOPAK n Russian peasant dance

GOPAKS > GOPAK

GOPHER n American burrowing rodent ▷ vb burrow

GOPHERED > GOPHER

GOPHERING > GOPHER

GOPHERS > GOPHER

GOPIK n money unit of Azerbaijan

GOPIKS > GOPIK

GOPURA n gateway tower of an Indian temple

GOPURAM same as > GOPURA

GOPURAMS > GOPURAM

GOPURAS > GOPURA

GOR interj God! ▷ n seagull

GORA n (in Indian English) White or fair-skinned male

GORAL n small S Asian goat antelope

GORALS > GORAL

GORAMIES > GORAMY

GORAMY same as > GOURAMI

GORAS > GORA

GORBELLY n large belly

GORBLIMEY interj exclamation of surprise or annoyance ▷ n instance of having uttered this exclamation

GORBLIMY same as > GORBLIMEY

GORCOCK n male of the red grouse

GORCOCKS > GORCOCK

GORCROW n carrion crow

GORCROWS > GORCROW

GORDITA n small thick tortilla

GORDITAS > GORDITA

GORE n blood from a wound ▷ vb pierce with horns

GORED > GORE

GOREFEST n film featuring excessive depictions of bloodshed

GOREFESTS > GOREFEST

GOREHOUND n enthusiast of gory horror films

GORES > GORE

GORGE n deep narrow valley ▷ vb eat greedily

GORGEABLE > GORGE

GORGED > GORGE

GORGEDLY > GORGE

GORGEOUS adj strikingly beautiful or attractive

GORGER > GORGE

GORGERIN another name for > NECKING

GORGERINS > GORGERIN

GORGERS > GORGE

GORGES > GORGE

GORGET n collar-like piece of armour

GORGETED > GORGET

GORGETS > GORGET

GORGIA n improvised sung passage

GORGIAS > GORGIA

GORGING > GORGE

GORGIO n word used by gypsies for a non-gypsy

GORGIOS > GORGIO

GORGON n terrifying or repulsive woman

GORGONEIA n plural of gorgoneion: representation of a Gorgon's head

GORGONIAN n type of coral with a horny or chalky branching skeleton, such as the sea fan and red coral

GORGONISE vb turn to stone

GORGONIZE same as > GORGONISE

GORGONS > GORGON

GORHEN n female red grouse

GORHENS > GORHEN

GORI n (in Indian English) White or fair-skinned female

GORIER > GORY

GORIEST > GORY

GORILLA n largest of the apes, found in Africa

GORILLAS > GORILLA

GORILLIAN > GORILLA

GORILLINE > GORILLA

GORILLOID > GORILLA

GORILY > GORY

GORINESS > GORY

GORING > GORE

GORINGS > GORE

GORIS > GORI

GORM n foolish person ▷ vb understand

GORMAND same as > GOURMAND

GORMANDS > GORMAND

GORMED > GORM

GORMIER > GORMY

GORMIEST > GORMY

GORMING > GORM

GORMLESS adj stupid

GORMS > GORM

GORMY adj gormless

GORP same as > GAWP

GORPED > GORP

GORPING > GORP

GORPS > GORP

GORS > GOR

GORSE n prickly yellow-flowered shrub

GORSEDD n meeting held daily before an eisteddfod

GORSEDDS > GORSEDD

GORSES > GORSE

GORSIER > GORSE

GORSIEST > GORSE

GORSOON n young boy

GORSOONS > GORSOON

GORSY > GORSE

GORY adj horrific or bloodthirsty

GOS > GO

GOSH interj exclamation of mild surprise or wonder

GOSHAWK n large hawk

SECTION 1: Words between 2 and 9 letters in length

GOSHAWKS > GOSHAWK
GOSHT *n* Indian meat dish
GOSHTS > GOSHT
GOSLARITE *n* hydrated zinc sulphate
GOSLET *n* pygmy goose
GOSLETS > GOSLET
GOSLING *n* young goose
GOSLINGS > GOSLING
GOSPEL *n* any of the first four books of the New Testament ▷ *adj* denoting a kind of religious music ▷ *vb* teach the gospel
GOSPELER *same as* > GOSPELLER
GOSPELERS > GOSPELER
GOSPELISE *vb* evangelise
GOSPELIZE *same as* > GOSPELISE
GOSPELLED > GOSPEL
GOSPELLER *n* person who reads or chants the Gospel in a religious service
GOSPELLY *adj* like gospel music
GOSPELS > GOSPEL
GOSPODA > GOSPODIN
GOSPODAR *n* hospodar
GOSPODARS > GOSPODAR
GOSPODIN *n* Russian title of address, often indicating respect
GOSPORT *n* aeroplane communication device
GOSPORTS > GOSPORT
GOSS *vb* spit
GOSSAMER *n* very fine fabric
GOSSAMERS > GOSSAMER
GOSSAMERY *adj* like gossamer
GOSSAN *n* oxidized portion of a mineral vein in rock
GOSSANS > GOSSAN
GOSSE *variant of* > GORSE
GOSSED > GOSS
GOSSES > GOSSE
GOSSIB *n* gossip
GOSSIBS > GOSSIB
GOSSING > GOSS
GOSSIP *n* idle talk, esp about other people ▷ *vb* engage in gossip
GOSSIPED > GOSSIP
GOSSIPER > GOSSIP
GOSSIPERS > GOSSIP
GOSSIPIER > GOSSIPY
GOSSIPING > GOSSIP
GOSSIPPED > GOSSIP
GOSSIPPER > GOSSIP
GOSSIPRY *n* idle talk
GOSSIPS > GOSSIP
GOSSIPY *adj* tending to gossip
GOSSOON *n* boy, esp a servant boy
GOSSOONS > GOSSOON
GOSSYPINE *adj* cottony
GOSSYPOL *n* toxic crystalline pigment that is a constituent of cottonseed oil
GOSSYPOLS > GOSSYPOL
GOSTER *vb* laugh uncontrollably
GOSTERED > GOSTER
GOSTERING > GOSTER
GOSTERS > GOSTER

GOT > GET
GOTCH *same as* > GITCH
GOTCHA *adj* as in *gotcha lizard* Australian name for a crocodile
GOTCHAS > GOTCHA
GOTCHES > GOTCH
GOTCHIES *pl n* underwear
GOTH *n* aficionado of Goth music and fashion
GOTHIC *adj* of or relating to a literary style ▷ *n* family of heavy script typefaces
GOTHICISE *same as* > GOTHICIZE
GOTHICISM > GOTHIC
GOTHICIZE *vb* make gothic in style
GOTHICS > GOTHIC
GOTHIER > GOTHY
GOTHIEST > GOTHY
GOTHITE *same as* > GOETHITE
GOTHITES > GOTHITE
GOTHS > GOTH
GOTHY *adj* characteristic of Gothic clothing or music
GOTTA *vb* got to
GOTTEN *past participle of* > GET
GOUACHE *n* (painting using) watercolours mixed with glue
GOUACHES > GOUACHE
GOUCH *vb* become drowsy or lethargic under the influence of narcotics
GOUCHED > GOUCH
GOUCHES > GOUCH
GOUCHING > GOUCH
GOUGE *vb* scoop or force out ▷ *n* hole or groove
GOUGED > GOUGE
GOUGER *n* person or tool that gouges
GOUGERE *n* choux pastry flavoured with cheese
GOUGERES > GOUGERE
GOUGERS > GOUGER
GOUGES > GOUGE
GOUGING > GOUGE
GOUJEERS *same as* > GOODYEAR
GOUJON *n* small strip of food
GOUJONS > GOUJON
GOUK *same as* > GOWK
GOUKS > GOUK
GOULASH *n* rich stew seasoned with paprika
GOULASHES > GOULASH
GOURA *n* large, crested ground pigeon found in New Guinea
GOURAMI *n* large SE Asian labyrinth fish
GOURAMIES > GOURAMI
GOURAMIS > GOURAMI
GOURAS > GOURA
GOURD *n* fleshy fruit of a climbing plant
GOURDE *n* standard monetary unit of Haiti
GOURDES > GOURDE
GOURDFUL *n* as much as a gourd will hold
GOURDFULS > GOURDFUL
GOURDIER > GOURDY

GOURDIEST > GOURDY
GOURDLIKE > GOURD
GOURDS > GOURD
GOURDY *adj* (of horses) swollen-legged
GOURMAND *n* person who is very keen on food and drink
GOURMANDS > GOURMAND
GOURMET *n* connoisseur of food and drink
GOURMETS > GOURMET
GOUSTIER > GOUSTY
GOUSTIEST > GOUSTY
GOUSTROUS *adj* stormy
GOUSTY *adj* dismal
GOUT *n* drop or splash (of something)
GOUTFLIES > GOUTFLY
GOUTFLY *n* fly whose larvae infect crops
GOUTIER > GOUTY
GOUTIEST > GOUTY
GOUTILY > GOUTY
GOUTINESS > GOUTY
GOUTS > GOUT
GOUTTE *n* heraldic device
GOUTTES > GOUTTE
GOUTWEED *n* Eurasian plant with white flowers and creeping underground stems
GOUTWEEDS > GOUTWEED
GOUTWORT *n* bishop's weed
GOUTWORTS > GOUTWORT
GOUTY *adj* afflicted with the disease gout
GOV *n* boss
GOVERN *vb* rule, direct, or control ▷ *n* ability to be governed
GOVERNALL *n* government
GOVERNED > GOVERN
GOVERNESS *n* woman teacher in a private household ▷ *vb* act as a governess
GOVERNING > GOVERN
GOVERNOR *n* official governing a province or state
GOVERNORS > GOVERNOR
GOVERNS > GOVERN
GOVS > GOV
GOWAN *n* any of various flowers growing in fields
GOWANED > GOWAN
GOWANS > GOWAN
GOWANY > GOWAN
GOWD *Scots word for* > GOLD
GOWDER > GOWD
GOWDEST > GOWD
GOWDS > GOWD
GOWDSPINK *n* goldfinch
GOWF *vb* strike
GOWFED > GOWF
GOWFER > GOWF
GOWFERS > GOWF
GOWFING > GOWF
GOWFS > GOWF
GOWK *n* stupid person
GOWKS > GOWK
GOWL *n* substance in the corner of the eyes after sleep ▷ *vb* howl
GOWLAN *same as* > GOLLAN
GOWLAND *same as* > GOLLAN
GOWLANDS > GOWLAND
GOWLANS > GOWLAN

GOWLED > GOWL
GOWLING > GOWL
GOWLS > GOWL
GOWN *n* woman's long formal dress ▷ *vb* supply with or dress in a gown
GOWNBOY *n* foundationer schoolboy who wears a gown
GOWNBOYS > GOWNBOY
GOWNED > GOWN
GOWNING > GOWN
GOWNMAN *n* professional person who wears a gown
GOWNMEN > GOWNMAN
GOWNS > GOWN
GOWNSMAN *same as* > GOWNMAN
GOWNSMEN > GOWNSMAN
GOWPEN *n* pair of cupped hands
GOWPENFUL *n* amount that can be contained in cupped hands
GOWPENS > GOWPEN
GOX *n* gaseous oxygen
GOXES > GOX
GOY *n* Jewish word for a non-Jew
GOYIM > GOY
GOYISCH > GOY
GOYISH > GOY
GOYISHE *adj* like a goy
GOYLE *n* ravine
GOYLES > GOYLE
GOYS > GOY
GOZZAN *same as* > GOSSAN
GOZZANS > GOZZAN
GRAAL *n* holy grail
GRAALS > GRAAL
GRAB *vb* grasp suddenly, snatch ▷ *n* sudden snatch
GRABBABLE > GRAB
GRABBED > GRAB
GRABBER > GRAB
GRABBERS > GRAB
GRABBIER > GRABBY
GRABBIEST > GRABBY
GRABBING > GRAB
GRABBLE *vb* scratch or feel about with the hands
GRABBLED > GRABBLE
GRABBLER > GRABBLE
GRABBLERS > GRABBLE
GRABBLES > GRABBLE
GRABBLING > GRABBLE
GRABBY *adj* greedy or selfish
GRABEN *n* elongated trough of land
GRABENS > GRABEN
GRABS > GRAB
GRACE *n* beauty and elegance ▷ *vb* honour
GRACED > GRACE
GRACEFUL *adj* having beauty of movement, style, or form
GRACELESS *adj* lacking elegance
GRACES > GRACE
GRACILE *adj* gracefully thin or slender
GRACILES > GRACILIS
GRACILIS *n* thin muscle on the inner thigh
GRACILITY > GRACILE
GRACING > GRACE

g

g

GRACIOSO n clown in Spanish comedy

GRACTOSOS > GRACIOSO

GRACIOUS adj kind and courteous ▷ interj expression of mild surprise or wonder

GRACKLE n American songbird with a dark iridescent plumage

GRACKLES > GRACKLE

GRAD n graduate

GRADABLE adj capable of being graded ▷ n word of this kind

GRADABLES > GRADABLE

GRADATE vb change or cause to change imperceptibly

GRADATED > GRADATE

GRADATES > GRADATE

GRADATIM adv step by step

GRADATING > GRADATE

GRADATION n (stage in) a series of degrees or steps

GRADATORY adj moving step by step ▷ n flight of stairs

GRADDAN vb dress corn

GRADDANED > GRADDAN

GRADDANS > GRADDAN

GRADE n place on a scale of quality, rank, or size ▷ vb arrange in grades

GRADED > GRADE

GRADELESS > GRADE

GRADELIER > GRADELY

GRADELY adj fine

GRADER n person or thing that grades

GRADERS > GRADER

GRADES > GRADE

GRADIENT n (degree of) slope ▷ adj sloping uniformly

GRADIENTS > GRADIENT

GRADIN n ledge above or behind an altar

GRADINE same as > GRADIN

GRADINES > GRADINE

GRADING > GRADE

GRADINGS > GRADING

GRADINI > GRADINO

GRADINO n step above an altar

GRADINS > GRADIN

GRADS > GRAD

GRADUAL adj occurring or moving in small stages ▷ n antiphon or group of several antiphons

GRADUALLY > GRADUAL

GRADUALS > GRADUAL

GRADUAND n person who is about to graduate

GRADUANDS > GRADUAND

GRADUATE vb receive a degree or diploma ▷ n holder of a degree

GRADUATED > GRADUATE

GRADUATES > GRADUATE

GRADUATOR > GRADUATE

GRADUS n book of études or other musical exercises

GRADUSES > GRADUS

GRAECISE same as > GRAECIZE

GRAECISED > GRAECISE

GRAECISES > GRAECISE

GRAECIZE vb make or become like the ancient Greeks

GRAECIZED > GRAECIZE

GRAECIZES > GRAECIZE

GRAFF same as > GRAFT

GRAFFED > GRAFF

GRAFFING > GRAFF

GRAFFITI pl n words or drawings scribbled or sprayed on walls etc

GRAFFITIS > GRAFFITI

GRAFFITO n instance of graffiti

GRAFFS > GRAFF

GRAFT n surgical transplant of skin or tissue ▷ vb transplant (living tissue) surgically

GRAFTAGE n in horticulture, the art of grafting

GRAFTAGES > GRAFTAGE

GRAFTED > GRAFT

GRAFTER > GRAFT

GRAFTERS > GRAFT

GRAFTING > GRAFT

GRAFTINGS > GRAFT

GRAFTS > GRAFT

GRAHAM n cracker made of graham flour

GRAHAMS > GRAHAM

GRAIL n any desired ambition or goal

GRAILE same as > GRAIL

GRAILES > GRAILE

GRAILS > GRAIL

GRAIN n seedlike fruit of a cereal plant ▷ vb paint in imitation of the grain of wood or leather

GRAINAGE n duty paid on grain

GRAINAGES > GRAINAGE

GRAINE n eggs of the silkworm

GRAINED > GRAIN

GRAINER > GRAIN

GRAINERS > GRAIN

GRAINES > GRAINE

GRAINIER > GRAINY

GRAINIEST > GRAINY

GRAINING n pattern or texture of the grain of wood, leather, etc

GRAININGS > GRAINING

GRAINLESS > GRAIN

GRAINS > GRAIN

GRAINY adj resembling, full of, or composed of grain

GRAIP n long-handled gardening fork

GRAIPS > GRAIP

GRAITH vb clothe

GRAITHED > GRAITH

GRAITHING > GRAITH

GRAITHLY > GRAITH

GRAITHS > GRAITH

GRAKLE same as > GRACKLE

GRAKLES > GRAKLE

GRALLOCH n entrails of a deer ▷ vb disembowel (a deer killed in a hunt)

GRALLOCHS > GRALLOCH

GRAM n metric unit of mass

GRAMA n type of grass

GRAMARIES > GRAMARY

GRAMARY same as > GRAMARYE

GRAMARYE n magic, necromancy, or occult learning

GRAMARYES > GRAMARYE

GRAMAS > GRAMA

GRAMASH n type of gaiter

GRAMASHES > GRAMASH

GRAME n sorrow

GRAMERCY interj many thanks

GRAMES > GRAME

GRAMMA n pasture grass of the South American plains

GRAMMAGE n weight of paper expressed as grams per square metre

GRAMMAGES > GRAMMAGE

GRAMMAR n branch of linguistics

GRAMMARS > GRAMMAR

GRAMMAS > GRAMMA

GRAMMATIC adj of or relating to grammar

GRAMME same as > GRAME

GRAMMES > GRAM

GRAMOCHE same as > GRAMASH

GRAMOCHES > GRAMOCHE

GRAMP n grandfather

GRAMPA variant of > GRANDPA

GRAMPAS > GRAMPA

GRAMPIES > GRAMPY

GRAMPS > GRAMP

GRAMPUS n dolphin-like mammal

GRAMPUSES > GRAMPUS

GRAMPY n grandfather

GRAMS > GRAM

GRAN n grandmother

GRANA > GRANUM

GRANARIES > GRANARY

GRANARY n storehouse for grain

GRAND adj large or impressive, imposing ▷ n thousand pounds or dollars

GRANDAD n grandfather

GRANDADDY same as > GRANDAD

GRANDADS > GRANDAD

GRANDAM n archaic word for grandmother

GRANDAME same as > GRANDAM

GRANDAMES > GRANDAME

GRANDAMS > GRANDAM

GRANDAUNT n great-aunt

GRANDBABY n very young grandchild

GRANDDAD same as > GRANDAD

GRANDDADS > GRANDAD

GRANDDAM same as > GRANDAM

GRANDDAMS > GRANDDAM

GRANDE feminine form of > GRAND

GRANDEE n Spanish nobleman of the highest rank

GRANDEES > GRANDEE

GRANDER > GRAND

GRANDEST > GRAND

GRANDEUR n magnificence

GRANDEURS > GRANDEUR

GRANDIOSE adj imposing

GRANDIOSO adv (to be played) in a grand manner

GRANDKID n grandchild

GRANDKIDS > GRANDKID

GRANDLY > GRAND

GRANDMA n grandmother

GRANDMAMA same as > GRANDMA

GRANDMAS > GRANDMA

GRANDNESS > GRAND

GRANDPA n grandfather

GRANDPAPA same as > GRANDPA

GRANDPAS > GRANDPA

GRANDS > GRAND

GRANDSIR same as > GRANDSIRE

GRANDSIRE n grandfather

GRANDSIRS > GRANDSIR

GRANDSON n male grandchild

GRANDSONS > GRANDSON

GRANFER n grandfather

GRANFERS > GRANFER

GRANGE n country house with farm buildings

GRANGER n keeper or member of a grange

GRANGERS > GRANGER

GRANGES > GRANGE

GRANITA n Italian iced drink

GRANITAS > GRANITA

GRANITE n very hard igneous rock

GRANITES > GRANITE

GRANITIC > GRANITE

GRANITISE vb form granite

GRANITITE n any granite with a high content of biotite

GRANITIZE same as > GRANITISE

GRANITOID n rock that contains or resembles granite

GRANIVORE n animal that feeds on seeds and grain

GRANNAM n old woman

GRANNAMS > GRANNAM

GRANNIE same as > GRANNY

GRANNIED > GRANNY

GRANNIES > GRANNY

GRANNOM n type of caddis fly esteemed as a bait by anglers

GRANNOMS > GRANNOM

GRANNY n grandmother ▷ vb defeat without conceding a single point

GRANNYING > GRANNY

GRANNYISH adj typical of or suitable for an elderly woman

GRANOLA n muesli-like breakfast cereal

GRANOLAS > GRANOLA

GRANOLITH n paving material consisting of a mixture of cement and crushed granite or granite chippings

GRANS > GRAN

GRANT vb consent to fulfil (a request) ▷ n money provided by a government for a specific purpose

GRANTABLE > GRANT

GRANTED > GRANT

GRANTEE n person to whom a grant is made

GRANTEES > GRANTEE

GRANTER > GRANT

GRANTERS > GRANT

GRANTING > GRANT

GRANTOR n person who makes a grant

GRANTORS > GRANTOR

GRANTS > GRANT

GRANTSMAN n student who specializes in obtaining grants

GRANTSMEN > GRANTSMAN

GRANULAR adj of or like grains

GRANULARY adj granular

GRANULATE vb make into grains

GRANULE n small grain

GRANULES > GRANULE

GRANULITE n granular foliated metamorphic rock in which the minerals form a mosaic of equal-sized granules

GRANULOMA n tumour composed of granulation tissue produced in response to chronic infection, inflammation, a foreign body, or to unknown causes

GRANULOSE less common word for > GRANULAR

GRANULOUS adj consisting of grains or granules

GRANUM n membrane layer in a chloroplast

GRANUMS > GRANUM

GRAPE n small juicy green or purple berry ▷ vb grope

GRAPED > GRAPE

GRAPELESS > GRAPE

GRAPELICE pl n lice that are destructive to grape plants

GRAPELIKE > GRAPE

GRAPERIES > GRAPERY

GRAPERY n building where grapes are grown

GRAPES n abnormal growth on the fetlock of a horse

GRAPESEED n seed of the grape

GRAPESHOT n bullets which scatter when fired

GRAPETREE n sea grape, a shrubby plant resembling a grapevine

GRAPEVINE n grape-bearing vine

GRAPEY > GRAPE

GRAPH n type of graph ▷ vb draw or represent in a graph

GRAPHED > GRAPH

GRAPHEME n smallest meaningful contrastive unit in a writing system

GRAPHEMES > GRAPHEME

GRAPHEMIC > GRAPHEME

GRAPHENE n layer of graphite one atom thick

GRAPHENES > GRAPHENE

GRAPHIC adj vividly descriptive

GRAPHICAL same as > GRAPHIC

GRAPHICLY > GRAPHIC

GRAPHICS pl n diagrams, graphs, etc, esp as used on a television programme or computer screen

GRAPHING > GRAPH

GRAPHITE n soft black form of carbon, used in pencil leads

GRAPHITES > GRAPHITE

GRAPHITIC > GRAPHITE

GRAPHIUM n stylus (for writing)

GRAPHIUMS > GRAPHIUM

GRAPHS > GRAPH

GRAPIER > GRAPE

GRAPIEST > GRAPE

GRAPINESS > GRAPE

GRAPING > GRAPE

GRAPLE same as > GRAPPLE

GRAPLES > GRAPLE

GRAPLIN same as > GRAPNEL

GRAPLINE same as > GRAPNEL

GRAPLINES > GRAPLINE

GRAPLINS > GRAPLIN

GRAPNEL n device with several hooks

GRAPNELS > GRAPNEL

GRAPPA n type of spirit

GRAPPAS > GRAPPA

GRAPPLE vb try to cope with (something difficult) ▷ n grapnel

GRAPPLED > GRAPPLE

GRAPPLER > GRAPPLE

GRAPPLERS > GRAPPLE

GRAPPLES > GRAPPLE

GRAPPLING n act of gripping or seizing, as in wrestling

GRAPY > GRAPE

GRASP vb grip something firmly ▷ n grip or clasp

GRASPABLE > GRASP

GRASPED > GRASP

GRASPER > GRASP

GRASPERS > GRASP

GRASPING adj greedy or avaricious

GRASPLESS adj relaxed

GRASPS > GRASP

GRASS n common type of plant ▷ vb cover with grass

GRASSBIRD n type of warbler found in long grass and reed beds

GRASSED > GRASS

GRASSER n police informant

GRASSERS > GRASSER

GRASSES > GRASS

GRASSHOOK another name for > SICKLE

GRASSIER > GRASSY

GRASSIEST > GRASSY

GRASSILY > GRASSY

GRASSING > GRASS

GRASSINGS > GRASS

GRASSLAND n land covered with grass

GRASSLESS > GRASS

GRASSLIKE > GRASS

GRASSPLOT n plot of ground overgrown with grass

GRASSQUIT n tropical American finch

GRASSROOT adj relating to the ordinary people, especially as part of the electorate

GRASSUM n in Scots law, sum paid when taking a lease

GRASSUMS > GRASSUM

GRASSY adj covered with, containing, or resembling grass

GRASTE archaic past participle of > GRACE

GRAT > GREET

GRATE vb rub into small bits on a rough surface ▷ n framework of metal bars for holding fuel in a fireplace

GRATED > GRATE

GRATEFUL adj feeling or showing gratitude

GRATELESS > GRATE

GRATER n tool with a sharp surface for grating food

GRATERS > GRATER

GRATES > GRATE

GRATICULE n grid of intersecting lines, esp of latitude and longitude on which a map is drawn

GRATIFIED > GRATIFY

GRATIFIER > GRATIFY

GRATIFIES > GRATIFY

GRATIFY vb satisfy or please ▷ adj giving one satisfaction or pleasure

GRATIN n crust of browned breadcrumbs

GRATINATE vb cook until the juice is absorbed and the surface crisps

GRATINE adj cooked au gratin

GRATINEE vb cook au gratin

GRATINEED > GRATINEE

GRATINEES > GRATINEE

GRATING adj harsh or rasping ▷ n framework of metal bars covering an opening

GRATINGLY > GRATING

GRATINGS > GRATING

GRATINS > GRATIN

GRATIS adj free, for nothing

GRATITUDE n feeling of being thankful for a favour or gift

GRATTOIR n scraper made of flint

GRATTOIRS > GRATTOIR

GRATUITY n money given for services rendered, tip

GRATULANT > GRATULATE

GRATULATE vb greet joyously

GRAUNCH vb crush or destroy

GRAUNCHED > GRAUNCH

GRAUNCHER > GRAUNCH

GRAUNCHES > GRAUNCH

GRAUPEL n soft hail or snow pellets

GRAUPELS > GRAUPEL

GRAV n unit of acceleration

GRAVADLAX same as > GRAVLAX

GRAVAMEN n that part of an accusation weighing most heavily against an accused

GRAVAMENS > GRAVAMEN

GRAVAMINA > GRAVAMEN

GRAVE n hole for burying a corpse ▷ adj causing concern ▷ vb cut, carve, sculpt, or engrave ▷ adv to be performed in a solemn manner

GRAVED > GRAVE

GRAVEL n mixture of small stones and coarse sand ▷ vb cover with gravel

GRAVELED > GRAVEL

GRAVELESS > GRAVE

GRAVELIKE > GRAVE

GRAVELING > GRAVEL

GRAVELISH > GRAVEL

GRAVELLED > GRAVEL

GRAVELLY adj like gravel

GRAVELS > GRAVEL

GRAVELY > GRAVE

GRAVEN > GRAVE

GRAVENESS > GRAVE

GRAVER n any of various tools

GRAVERS > GRAVER

GRAVES > GRAVE

GRAVESIDE n area surrounding a grave

GRAVESITE n site of grave

GRAVEST > GRAVE

GRAVEWARD adj moving towards grave

GRAVEYARD n cemetery

GRAVID adj pregnant

GRAVIDA n pregnant woman

GRAVIDAE > GRAVIDA

GRAVIDAS > GRAVIDA

GRAVIDITY > GRAVID

GRAVIDLY > GRAVID

GRAVIES > GRAVY

GRAVING > GRAVE

GRAVINGS > GRAVE

GRAVIS adj as in myasthenia gravis chronic muscle-weakening disease

GRAVITAS n seriousness or solemnity

GRAVITATE vb be influenced or drawn towards

GRAVITIES > GRAVITY

GRAVITINO n hypothetical subatomic particle

GRAVITON n postulated quantum of gravitational energy

GRAVITONS > GRAVITON

GRAVITY n force of attraction

GRAVLAKS same as > GRAVLAX

GRAVLAX n dry-cured salmon

GRAVLAXES > GRAVLAX

GRAVS > GRAV

GRAVURE n method of intaglio printing

GRAVURES > GRAVURE

GRAVY n juices from meat in cooking

GRAWLIX n sequence of symbols used in text to replace profanity

GRAWLIXES > GRAWLIX

GRAY same as > GREY

GRAYBACK same as > GREYBACK

g

g

GRAYBACKS > GRAYBACK
GRAYBEARD *same as* > GREYBEARD
GRAYED > GRAY
GRAYER > GRAY
GRAYEST > GRAY
GRAYFISH *n* dogfish
GRAYFLIES > GRAYFLY
GRAYFLY *n* trumpet fly
GRAYHEAD *n* one with grey hair
GRAYHEADS > GRAYHEAD
GRAYHEN *n* female of the black grouse
GRAYHENS > GRAYHEN
GRAYHOUND *US spelling of* > GREYHOUND
GRAYING > GRAY
GRAYISH > GRAY
GRAYLAG *same as* > GREYLAG
GRAYLAGS > GRAYLAG
GRAYLE *n* holy grail
GRAYLES > GRAYLE
GRAYLING *n* fish of the salmon family
GRAYLINGS > GRAYLING
GRAYLIST *vb* hold (someone) in suspicion, without actually excluding him or her from a particular activity
GRAYLISTS > GRAYLIST
GRAYLY > GRAY
GRAYMAIL *n* tactic to avoid prosecution in an espionage case
GRAYMAILS > GRAYMAIL
GRAYNESS > GREY
GRAYOUT *n* impairment of vision due to lack of oxygen
GRAYOUTS > GRAYOUT
GRAYS > GRAY
GRAYSCALE *adj* in shades of grey
GRAYSTONE *n* grey igneous rock of volcanic origin
GRAYWACKE *same as* > GREYWACKE
GRAYWATER *n* water that has been used
GRAZABLE > GRAZE
GRAZE *vb* feed on grass ▷ *n* slight scratch or scrape
GRAZEABLE > GRAZE
GRAZED > GRAZE
GRAZER > GRAZE
GRAZERS > GRAZE
GRAZES > GRAZE
GRAZIER *n* person who feeds cattle for market
GRAZIERS > GRAZIER
GRAZING *n* land on which grass for livestock is grown
GRAZINGLY > GRAZE
GRAZINGS > GRAZING
GRAZIOSO *adv* (of music) to be played gracefully
GREASE *n* soft melted animal fat ▷ *vb* apply grease to
GREASED > GREASE
GREASER *n* mechanic, esp of motor vehicles
GREASERS > GREASER
GREASES > GREASE
GREASIER > GREASY

GREASIES > GREASY
GREASIEST > GREASY
GREASILY > GREASY
GREASING > GREASE
GREASY *adj* covered with or containing grease ▷ *n* shearer
GREAT *adj* large in size or number ▷ *n* distinguished person
GREATCOAT *n* heavy overcoat
GREATEN *vb* make or become great
GREATENED > GREATEN
GREATENS > GREATEN
GREATER > GREAT
GREATEST *n* most outstanding individual in a given field
GREATESTS > GREATEST
GREATLY > GREAT
GREATNESS > GREAT
GREATS > GREAT
GREAVE *n* piece of armour for the shin ▷ *vb* grieve
GREAVED > GREAVE
GREAVES *pl n* residue left after the rendering of tallow
GREAVING > GREAVE
GREBE *n* diving water bird
GREBES > GREBE
GREBO *same as* > GREEBO
GREBOES > GREBO
GREBOS > GREBO
GRECE *n* flight of steps
GRECES > GRECE
GRECIAN *same as* > GRECE
GRECIANS > GRECIAN
GRECISE *same as* > GRAECIZE
GRECISED > GRECISE
GRECISES > GRECISE
GRECISING > GRECISE
GRECIZE *same as* > GRAECIZE
GRECIZED > GRECIZE
GRECIZES > GRECIZE
GRECIZING > GRECIZE
GRECQUE *n* ornament of Greek origin
GRECQUES > GRECQUE
GREE *n* superiority or victory ▷ *vb* come or cause to come to agreement or harmony
GREEBO *n* unkempt or dirty-looking rock music fan
GREEBOES > GREEBO
GREEBOS > GREEBO
GREECE *same as* > GRECE
GREECES > GREECE
GREED *n* excessive desire for food, wealth, etc
GREEDHEAD *n* avaricious person
GREEDIER > GREEDY
GREEDIEST > GREEDY
GREEDILY > GREEDY
GREEDLESS > GREED
GREEDS > GREED
GREEDSOME *same as* > GREEDY
GREEDY *adj* having an excessive desire for something
GREEGREE *same as* > GRIGRI

GREEGREES > GREEGREE
GREEING > GREE
GREEK *vb* represent text as grey lines on a computer screen
GREEKED > GREEK
GREEKING > GREEK
GREEKINGS > GREEK
GREEN *adj* of a colour between blue and yellow ▷ *n* colour between blue and yellow ▷ *vb* make or become green
GREENBACK *n* inconvertible legal-tender US currency note originally issued during the Civil War in 1862
GREENBELT *n* zone of farmland, parks, and open country surrounding a town or city
GREENBONE *n* an eel-like food fish
GREENBUG *n* common name for Schizaphis graminum
GREENBUGS > GREENBUG
GREENED > GREEN
GREENER *n* recent immigrant
GREENERS > GREENER
GREENERY *n* vegetation
GREENEST > GREEN
GREENEYE *n* small slender fish with pale green eyes
GREENEYES > GREENEYE
GREENFLY *n* green aphid, a common garden pest
GREENGAGE *n* sweet green plum
GREENHAND *n* greenhorn
GREENHEAD *n* male mallard
GREENHORN *n* novice
GREENIE *n* conservationist
GREENIER > GREEN
GREENIES > GREENIE
GREENIEST > GREEN
GREENING *n* process of making or becoming more aware of environmental considerations
GREENINGS > GREENING
GREENISH > GREEN
GREENLET *n* type of insectivorous songbird
GREENLETS > GREENLET
GREENLING *n* type of food fish of the N Pacific Ocean
GREENLIT *adj* given permission to proceed
GREENLY > GREEN
GREENMAIL *n* practice of a company buying sufficient shares in another company to threaten takeover and making a quick profit as a result of the threatened company buying back its shares at a higher price ▷ *vb* carry out the practice of greenmail
GREENNESS > GREEN
GREENROOM *n* backstage room in a theatre where performers rest or receive visitors
GREENS > GREEN
GREENSAND *n* olive-green sandstone consisting mainly of quartz and glauconite

GREENSICK *adj* suffering from greensickness: same as chlorosis
GREENSOME *n* match for two pairs in which each of the four players tees off and after selecting the better drive the partners of each pair play that ball alternately
GREENTH *n* greenness
GREENTHS > GREENTH
GREENWASH *n* superficial or insincere display of concern for the environment that is shown by an organization ▷ *vb* adopt a 'greenwash' policy
GREENWAY *n* linear open space, with pedestrian and cycle paths
GREENWAYS > GREENWAY
GREENWEED *n* woodwaxen
GREENWING *n* teal
GREENWOOD *n* forest or wood when the leaves are green
GREENY > GREEN
GREES > GREE
GREESE *same as* > GRECE
GREESES > GREESE
GREESING > GREESE
GREESINGS > GREESE
GREET *vb* meet with expressions of welcome ▷ *n* weeping
GREETE *same as* > GREET
GREETED > GREET
GREETER *n* person who greets people
GREETERS > GREETER
GREETES > GREETE
GREETING *n* act or words of welcoming on meeting
GREETINGS > GREETING
GREETS > GREET
GREFFIER *n* registrar
GREFFIERS > GREFFIER
GREGALE *n* northeasterly wind occurring in the Mediterranean
GREGALES > GREGALE
GREGARIAN *adj* gregarious
GREGARINE *n* type of parasitic protozoan typically occurring in other invertebrates
GREGATIM *adv* in flocks or crowds
GREGE *vb* make heavy
GREGED > GREGE
GREGES > GREGE
GREGING > GREGE
GREGO *n* short, thick jacket
GREGOS > GREGO
GREIGE *adj* (of a fabric or material) not yet dyed ▷ *n* unbleached or undyed cloth or yarn
GREIGES > GREIGE
GREIN *vb* desire fervently
GREINED > GREIN
GREINING > GREIN
GREINS > GREIN
GREISEN *n* light-coloured metamorphic rock
GREISENS > GREISEN
GREISLY *same as* > GRISLY

GREMIAL n type of cloth used in Mass

GREMIALS > GREMIAL

GREMLIN n imaginary being

GREMLINS > GREMLIN

GREMMIE n young surfer

GREMMIES > GREMMIE

GREMMY same as > GREMMIE

GREMOLATA n garnish of finely chopped parsley, garlic and lemon

GREN same as > GRIN

GRENACHE n variety of grape

GRENACHES > GRENACHE

GRENADE n small bomb

GRENADES > GRENADE

GRENADIER n soldier of a regiment formerly trained to throw grenades

GRENADINE n syrup made from pomegranates

GRENNED > GREN

GRENNING > GREN

GRENS > GREN

GRESE same as > GRECE

GRESES > GRESE

GRESSING same as > GRECE

GRESSINGS > GRESSING

GREVE same as > GREAVE

GREVES > GREVE

GREVILLEA n any of various Australian evergreen trees and shrubs

GREW vb shudder

GREWED > GREW

GREWHOUND n greyhound

GREWING > GREW

GREWS > GREW

GREWSOME archaic or US spelling of > GRUESOME

GREWSOMER > GREWSOME

GREX n group of plants

GREXES > GREX

GREY adj of a colour between black and white ▷ n grey colour ▷ vb become or make grey

GREYBACK n any of various animals having a grey back, such as the grey whale and the hooded crow

GREYBACKS > GREYBACK

GREYBEARD n old man, esp a sage

GREYED > GREY

GREYER > GREY

GREYEST > GREY

GREYHEAD n one having grey hair

GREYHEADS > GREYHEAD

GREYHEN n female of the black grouse

GREYHENS > GREYHEN

GREYHOUND n swift slender dog used in racing

GREYING > GREY

GREYINGS > GREY

GREYISH > GREY

GREYLAG n large grey goose

GREYLAGS > GREYLAG

GREYLIST vb hold (someone) in suspicion, without actually excluding him or her from a particular activity

GREYLISTS > GREYLIST

GREYLY > GREY

GREYNESS > GREY

GREYS > GREY

GREYSCALE n range of grey shades from white to black

GREYSTONE n type of grey rock

GREYWACKE n any dark sandstone or grit having a matrix of clay minerals

GRIBBLE n type of small marine crustacean

GRIBBLES > GRIBBLE

GRICE vb collect objects concerned with railways ▷ n object collected or place visited by a railway enthusiast

GRICED > GRICE

GRICER > GRICE

GRICERS > GRICE

GRICES > GRICE

GRICING > GRICE

GRICINGS > GRICE

GRID n network of horizontal and vertical lines, bars, etc ▷ vb form a grid pattern

GRIDDED > GRID

GRIDDER n American football player

GRIDDERS > GRIDDER

GRIDDING > GRID

GRIDDLE n flat iron plate for cooking ▷ vb cook (food) on a griddle

GRIDDLED > GRIDDLE

GRIDDLES > GRIDDLE

GRIDDLING > GRIDDLE

GRIDE vb grate or scrape harshly ▷ n harsh or piercing sound

GRIDED > GRIDE

GRIDELIN n greyish violet colour

GRIDELINS > GRIDELIN

GRIDES > GRIDE

GRIDING > GRIDE

GRIDIRON n frame of metal bars for grilling food ▷ vb cover with parallel lines

GRIDIRONS > GRIDIRON

GRIDLOCK n situation where traffic is not moving ▷ vb (of traffic) to obstruct (an area)

GRIDLOCKS > GRIDLOCK

GRIDS > GRID

GRIECE same as > GRECE

GRIECED > GRIECE

GRIECES > GRIECE

GRIEF n deep sadness

GRIEFER n online gamer who spoils the game for others on purpose

GRIEFERS > GRIEFER

GRIEFFUL adj stricken with grief

GRIEFLESS > GRIEF

GRIEFS > GRIEF

GRIESIE same as > GRISY

GRIESLY same as > GRISY

GRIESY same as > GRISY

GRIEVANCE n real or imaginary cause for complaint

GRIEVANT n any person with a grievance

GRIEVANTS > GRIEVANT

GRIEVE vb (cause to) feel grief ▷ n farm manager or overseer

GRIEVED > GRIEVE

GRIEVER > GRIEVE

GRIEVERS > GRIEVE

GRIEVES > GRIEVE

GRIEVING > GRIEVE

GRIEVINGS > GRIEVE

GRIEVOUS adj very severe or painful

GRIFF n information

GRIFFE n carved ornament at the base of a column

GRIFFES > GRIFFE

GRIFFIN n mythical monster

GRIFFINS > GRIFFIN

GRIFFON same as > GRIFFIN

GRIFFONS > GRIFFON

GRIFFS > GRIFF

GRIFT vb swindle

GRIFTED > GRIFT

GRIFTER > GRIFT

GRIFTERS > GRIFT

GRIFTING > GRIFT

GRIFTS > GRIFT

GRIG n lively person ▷ vb fish for grigs

GRIGGED > GRIG

GRIGGING > GRIG

GRIGRI n African talisman, amulet, or charm

GRIGRIS > GRIGRI

GRIGS > GRIG

GRIKE n fissure in rock

GRIKES > GRIKE

GRILL n device on a cooker ▷ vb cook under a grill

GRILLADE n grilled food

GRILLADES > GRILLADE

GRILLAGE n arrangement of beams and crossbeams used as a foundation on soft ground

GRILLAGES > GRILLAGE

GRILLE n grating over an opening

GRILLED adj cooked on a grill or gridiron

GRILLER > GRILL

GRILLERS > GRILL

GRILLERY n place where food is grilled

GRILLES > GRILLE

GRILLING > GRILL

GRILLINGS > GRILL

GRILLION n extremely large but unspecified number, quantity, or amount ▷ determiner amounting to a grillion

GRILLIONS > GRILLION

GRILLROOM n restaurant serving grilled foods

GRILLS > GRILL

GRILLWORK same as > GRILL

GRILSE n salmon on its first return from the sea to fresh water

GRILSES > GRILSE

GRIM adj stern

GRIMACE n ugly or distorted facial expression ▷ vb make a grimace

GRIMACED > GRIMACE

GRIMACER > GRIMACE

GRIMACERS > GRIMACE

GRIMACES > GRIMACE

GRIMACING > GRIMACE

GRIMALKIN n old cat, esp an old female cat

GRIME n ingrained dirt ▷ vb make very dirty

GRIMED > GRIME

GRIMES > GRIME

GRIMIER > GRIME

GRIMIEST > GRIME

GRIMILY > GRIME

GRIMINESS > GRIME

GRIMING > GRIME

GRIMLY > GRIM

GRIMMER > GRIM

GRIMMEST > GRIM

GRIMNESS > GRIM

GRIMOIRE n textbook of sorcery and magic

GRIMOIRES > GRIMOIRE

GRIMY > GRIME

GRIN vb smile broadly, showing the teeth ▷ n broad smile

GRINCH n person whose attitude has a depressing effect

GRINCHES > GRINCH

GRIND vb crush or rub to a powder ▷ n hard work

GRINDED obsolete past participle of > GRIND

GRINDELIA n type of coarse American plant with yellow daisy-like flower heads

GRINDER n device for grinding substances

GRINDERS > GRINDER

GRINDERY n place in which tools and cutlery are sharpened

GRINDING > GRIND

GRINDINGS > GRIND

GRINDS > GRIND

GRINGA n derogatory term (used by Latin Americans) for a woman from an English-speaking country

GRINGAS > GRINGA

GRINGO n derogatory term (used by Latin Americans) for a person from an English-speaking country

GRINGOS > GRINGO

GRINNED > GRIN

GRINNER > GRIN

GRINNERS > GRIN

GRINNING > GRIN

GRINNINGS > GRIN

GRINS > GRIN

GRIOT n (in W Africa) member of a caste recording tribal history

GRIOTS > GRIOT

GRIP n firm hold or grasp ▷ vb grasp or hold tightly

GRIPE vb complain persistently ▷ n complaint

GRIPED > GRIPE

GRIPER > GRIPE

GRIPERS > GRIPE

g

GRIPES > GRIPE
GRIPEY adj causing gripes
GRIPIER > GRIPEY
GRIPIEST > GRIPEY
GRIPING n act of griping
GRIPINGLY > GRIPE
GRIPINGS > GRIPE
GRIPLE same as > GRIPPLE
GRIPMAN n cable-car operator
GRIPMEN > GRIPMAN
GRIPPE former name for > INFLUENZA
GRIPPED > GRIP
GRIPPER > GRIP
GRIPPERS > GRIP
GRIPPES > GRIPPE
GRIPPIER > GRIPPY
GRIPPIEST > GRIPPY
GRIPPING > GRIP
GRIPPLE adj greedy ▷ n hook
GRIPPLES > GRIPPLE
GRIPPY adj having grip
GRIPS > GRIP
GRIPSACK n travel bag
GRIPSACKS > GRIPSACK
GRIPT archaic variant of > GRIPPED
GRIPTAPE n rough tape for sticking to a surface to provide a greater grip
GRIPTAPES > GRIPTAPE
GRIPY same as > GRIPEY
GRIS same as > GRECE
GRISAILLE n technique of monochrome painting in shades of grey, as in an oil painting or a wall decoration, imitating the effect of relief
GRISE vb shudder
GRISED > GRISE
GRISELY same as > GRISLY
GRISEOUS adj streaked or mixed with grey
GRISES > GRISE
GRISETTE n (esp formerly) a French working-class girl, esp a pretty or flirtatious one
GRISETTES > GRISETTE
GRISGRIS same as > GRIGRI
GRISING > GRISE
GRISKIN n lean part of a loin of pork
GRISKINS > GRISKIN
GRISLED another word for > GRIZZLED
GRISLIER > GRISLY
GRISLIES > GRISLY
GRISLIEST > GRISLY
GRISLY adj horrifying or ghastly ▷ n large American bear
GRISON n type of mammal
GRISONS > GRISON
GRISSINI pl n thin crisp breadsticks
GRISSINO n Italian breadstick
GRIST n grain for grinding
GRISTER n device for grinding grain
GRISTERS > GRISTER
GRISTLE n tough stringy animal tissue found in meat

GRISTLES > GRISTLE
GRISTLIER > GRISTLE
GRISTLY > GRISTLE
GRISTMILL n mill, esp one equipped with large grinding stones for grinding grain
GRISTS > GRIST
GRISY adj grim
GRIT n rough particles of sand ▷ vb spread grit on (an icy road etc) ▷ adj great
GRITH n security or peace guaranteed for a period of time
GRITHS > GRITH
GRITLESS > GRIT
GRITS > GRIT
GRITSTONE same as > GRIT
GRITTED > GRIT
GRITTER n vehicle that spreads grit on the roads
GRITTERS > GRITTER
GRITTEST > GRIT
GRITTIER > GRITTY
GRITTIEST > GRITTY
GRITTILY > GRITTY
GRITTING n spreading grit on road surfaces
GRITTINGS > GRITTING
GRITTY adj courageous and tough
GRIVATION n (in navigation) grid variation
GRIVET n E African monkey
GRIVETS > GRIVET
GRIZ n grizzly bear
GRIZE same as > GRECE
GRIZES > GRIZE
GRIZZES > GRIZ
GRIZZLE vb whine or complain ▷ n grey colour
GRIZZLED adj grey-haired
GRIZZLER > GRIZZLE
GRIZZLERS > GRIZZLE
GRIZZLES > GRIZZLE
GRIZZLIER > GRIZZLY
GRIZZLIES > GRIZZLY
GRIZZLING > GRIZZLE
GRIZZLY n large American bear ▷ adj somewhat grey
GROAN n deep sound of grief or pain ▷ vb utter a groan
GROANED > GROAN
GROANER n person or thing that groans
GROANERS > GROANER
GROANFUL adj sad
GROANING > GROAN
GROANINGS > GROAN
GROANS > GROAN
GROAT n fourpenny piece
GROATS pl n hulled and crushed grain of various cereals
GROCER n shopkeeper selling foodstuffs
GROCERIES pl n food and other household supplies
GROCERS > GROCER
GROCERY n business or premises of a grocer
GROCKED same as > GROKKED
GROCKING same as > GROKKING
GROCKLE n tourist in SW England

GROCKLES > GROCKLE
GRODIER > GRODY
GRODIEST > GRODY
GRODY adj unpleasant
GROG n spirit, usu rum, and water ▷ vb drink grog
GROGGED > GROG
GROGGERY n grogshop
GROGGIER > GROGGY
GROGGIEST > GROGGY
GROGGILY > GROGGY
GROGGING > GROG
GROGGY adj faint, shaky, or dizzy
GROGRAM n coarse fabric
GROGRAMS > GROGRAM
GROGS > GROG
GROGSHOP n drinking place, esp one of disreputable character
GROGSHOPS > GROGSHOP
GROIN n place where the legs join the abdomen ▷ vb provide or construct with groins
GROINED > GROIN
GROINING > GROIN
GROININGS > GROIN
GROINS > GROIN
GROK vb understand completely and intuitively
GROKED same as > GROKKED
GROKING same as > GROKKING
GROKKED > GROK
GROKKING > GROK
GROKS > GROK
GROMA n Roman surveying instrument
GROMAS > GROMA
GROMET same as > GROMMET
GROMETS > GROMET
GROMMET n ring or eyelet
GROMMETED adj having grommets
GROMMETS > GROMMET
GROMWELL n hairy flowering plant
GROMWELLS > GROMWELL
GRONE obsolete word for > GROAN
GRONED > GRONE
GRONEFULL same as > GROANFUL
GRONES > GRONE
GRONING > GRONE
GROOF n face, or front of the body
GROOFS > GROOF
GROOLIER > GROOLY
GROOLIEST > GROOLY
GROOLY adj gruesome
GROOM n person who looks after horses ▷ vb make or keep one's clothes and appearance neat and tidy
GROOMED > GROOM
GROOMER > GROOM
GROOMERS > GROOM
GROOMING > GROOM
GROOMINGS > GROOM
GROOMS > GROOM
GROOMSMAN n man who attends the bridegroom at a wedding, usually the best man
GROOMSMEN > GROOMSMAN

GROOVE n long narrow channel in a surface
GROOVED > GROOVE
GROOVER n device that makes grooves
GROOVERS > GROOVER
GROOVES > GROOVE
GROOVIER > GROOVY
GROOVIEST > GROOVY
GROOVILY > GROOVY
GROOVING > GROOVE
GROOVY adj attractive or exciting
GROPE vb feel about or search uncertainly ▷ n instance of groping
GROPED > GROPE
GROPER n type of large fish of warm and tropical seas
GROPERS > GROPER
GROPES > GROPE
GROPING > GROPE
GROPINGLY > GROPE
GROSBEAK n finch with a large powerful bill
GROSBEAKS > GROSBEAK
GROSCHEN n former Austrian monetary unit worth one hundredth of a schilling
GROSCHENS > GROSCHEN
GROSER n gooseberry
GROSERS > GROSER
GROSERT another word for > GROSER
GROSERTS > GROSERT
GROSET another word for > GROSER
GROSETS > GROSET
GROSGRAIN n heavy ribbed silk or rayon fabric
GROSS adj flagrant ▷ n twelve dozen ▷ vb make as total revenue before deductions ▷ interj exclamation indicating disgust
GROSSART another word for > GROSER
GROSSARTS > GROSSART
GROSSED > GROSS
GROSSER > GROSS
GROSSERS > GROSS
GROSSES > GROSS
GROSSEST > GROSS
GROSSING > GROSS
GROSSLY > GROSS
GROSSNESS > GROSS
GROSSULAR n type of garnet
GROSZ n Polish monetary unit
GROSZE > GROSZ
GROSZY > GROSZ
GROT n rubbish
GROTESQUE adj strangely distorted ▷ n grotesque person or thing
GROTS > GROT
GROTTIER > GROTTY
GROTTIEST > GROTTY
GROTTO n small picturesque cave
GROTTOED adj having a grotto
GROTTOES > GROTTO
GROTTOS > GROTTO

GROTTY adj nasty or in bad condition
GROUCH vb grumble or complain ▷ n person who is always complaining
GROUCHED > GROUCH
GROUCHES > GROUCH
GROUCHIER > GROUCHY
GROUCHILY > GROUCHY
GROUCHING > GROUCH
GROUCHY adj bad-tempered
GROUF same as > GROOF
GROUFS > GROUF
GROUGH n natural channel or fissure in a peat moor
GROUGHS > GROUGH
GROUND n surface of the earth ▷ n or of the ground ▷ vb base or establish
GROUNDAGE n fee levied on a vessel entering a port or anchored off a shore
GROUNDED adj sensible and down-to-earth
GROUNDEN obsolete variant of > GROUND
GROUNDER n (in baseball) ball that travels along the ground
GROUNDERS > GROUNDER
GROUNDHOG another name for > WOODCHUCK
GROUNDING n basic knowledge of a subject
GROUNDMAN n groundsman
GROUNDMEN > GROUNDMAN
GROUNDNUT n peanut
GROUNDOUT n (in baseball) being put out after hitting a grounder that is fielded and thrown to first base
GROUNDS > GROUND
GROUNDSEL n yellow-flowered weed
GROUP n number of people or things regarded as a unit ▷ vb place or form into a group
GROUPABLE > GROUP
GROUPAGE n gathering people or objects into a group or groups
GROUPAGES > GROUPAGE
GROUPED > GROUP
GROUPER n large edible sea fish
GROUPERS > GROUPER
GROUPIE n ardent fan of a celebrity or of a sport or activity
GROUPIES > GROUPIE
GROUPING n set of people or organizations who act or work together to achieve a shared aim
GROUPINGS > GROUPING
GROUPIST n follower of a group
GROUPISTS > GROUPIST
GROUPLET n small group
GROUPLETS > GROUPLET
GROUPOID n magma
GROUPOIDS > GROUPOID
GROUPS > GROUP
GROUPWARE n software that enables computers within a group or organization to work together, allowing

users to exchange electronic-mail messages, access shared files and databases, use video conferencing, etc
GROUPWORK n work done by a group acting together
GROUPY same as > GROUPIE
GROUSE n stocky game bird ▷ vb grumble or complain ▷ adj fine or excellent
GROUSED > GROUSE
GROUSER > GROUSE
GROUSERS > GROUSE
GROUSES > GROUSE
GROUSEST > GROUSE
GROUSING > GROUSE
GROUT n thin mortar ▷ vb fill up with grout
GROUTED > GROUT
GROUTER > GROUT
GROUTERS > GROUT
GROUTIER > GROUTY
GROUTIEST > GROUTY
GROUTING > GROUT
GROUTINGS > GROUT
GROUTS pl n sediment or grounds
GROUTY adj sullen or surly
GROVE n small group of trees
GROVED > GROVE
GROVEL vb behave humbly in order to win a superior's favour
GROVELED > GROVEL
GROVELER > GROVEL
GROVELERS > GROVEL
GROVELESS > GROVE
GROVELING > GROVEL
GROVELLED > GROVEL
GROVELLER > GROVEL
GROVELS > GROVEL
GROVES > GROVE
GROVET n wrestling hold
GROVETS > GROVET
GROVIER > GROVY
GROVIEST > GROVY
GROVY adj like a grove
GROW vb develop physically
GROWABLE adj able to be cultivated
GROWER n person who grows plants
GROWERS > GROWER
GROWING > GROW
GROWINGLY > GROW
GROWINGS > GROW
GROWL vb make a low rumbling sound ▷ n growling sound
GROWLED > GROWL
GROWLER n person, animal, or thing that growls
GROWLERS > GROWLER
GROWLERY n place to retreat to, alone, when ill-humoured
GROWLIER > GROWL
GROWLIEST > GROWL
GROWLING > GROWL
GROWLINGS > GROWL
GROWLS > GROWL
GROWLY > GROWL
GROWN > GROW
GROWNUP n adult
GROWNUPS > GROWNUP
GROWS > GROW

GROWTH n growing ▷ adj of or relating to growth
GROWTHIER > GROWTHY
GROWTHIST n advocate of the importance of economic growth
GROWTHS > GROWTH
GROWTHY adj rapid-growing
GROYNE n wall built out from the shore to control erosion
GROYNES > GROYNE
GROZING adj as in grozing iron iron for smoothing joints between lead pipes
GRR interj expressing anger or annoyance
GRRL n as in riot grrl young woman who enjoys feminist punk rock
GRRLS > GRRL
GRRRL n as in riot grrrl young woman who enjoys feminist punk rock
GRRRLS > GRRRL
GRUB n legless insect larva ▷ vb search carefully for something
GRUBBED > GRUB
GRUBBER n person who grubs
GRUBBERS > GRUBBER
GRUBBIER > GRUBBY
GRUBBIEST > GRUBBY
GRUBBILY > GRUBBY
GRUBBING > GRUB
GRUBBLE same as > GRABBLE
GRUBBLED > GRUBBLE
GRUBBLES > GRUBBLE
GRUBBLING > GRUBBLE
GRUBBY adj dirty
GRUBS > GRUB
GRUBSTAKE n supplies provided for a prospector on the condition that the donor has a stake in any finds ▷ vb furnish with such supplies
GRUBWORM another word for > GRUB
GRUBWORMS > GRUBWORM
GRUDGE vb be unwilling to give or allow ▷ n resentment ▷ adj planned or carried out in order to settle a grudge
GRUDGED > GRUDGE
GRUDGEFUL adj envious
GRUDGER > GRUDGE
GRUDGERS > GRUDGE
GRUDGES > GRUDGE
GRUDGING > GRUDGE
GRUDGINGS > GRUDGE
GRUE n shiver or shudder ▷ vb shiver or shudder
GRUED > GRUE
GRUEING > GRUE
GRUEL n thin porridge ▷ vb subject to exhausting experiences
GRUELED > GRUEL
GRUELER > GRUEL
GRUELERS > GRUEL
GRUELING same as > GRUELLING
GRUELINGS > GRUELING
GRUELLED > GRUEL
GRUELLER > GRUEL
GRUELLERS > GRUEL

GRUELLING adj exhausting or severe ▷ n severe experience, esp punishment
GRUELS > GRUEL
GRUES > GRUE
GRUESOME adj causing horror and disgust
GRUESOMER > GRUESOME
GRUFE same as > GROOF
GRUFES > GRUFE
GRUFF adj rough or surly in manner or voice ▷ vb talk gruffly
GRUFFED > GRUFF
GRUFFER > GRUFF
GRUFFEST > GRUFF
GRUFFIER > GRUFFY
GRUFFIEST > GRUFFY
GRUFFILY > GRUFFY
GRUFFING > GRUFF
GRUFFISH > GRUFF
GRUFFLY > GRUFF
GRUFFNESS > GRUFF
GRUFFS > GRUFF
GRUFFY adj gruff
GRUFTED adj dirty
GRUGRU n tropical American palm
GRUGRUS > GRUGRU
GRUIFORM adj relating to an order of birds, including cranes and bustards
GRUING > GRUE
GRUM adj surly
GRUMBLE vb complain ▷ n complaint
GRUMBLED > GRUMBLE
GRUMBLER > GRUMBLE
GRUMBLERS > GRUMBLE
GRUMBLES > GRUMBLE
GRUMBLIER > GRUMBLE
GRUMBLING > GRUMBLE
GRUMBLY > GRUMBLE
GRUME n clot
GRUMES > GRUME
GRUMLY > GRUM
GRUMMER > GRUM
GRUMMEST > GRUM
GRUMMET same as > GROMMET
GRUMMETED adj having grummets
GRUMMETS > GRUMMET
GRUMNESS > GRUM
GRUMOSE same as > GRUMOUS
GRUMOUS adj (esp of plant parts) consisting of granular tissue
GRUMP n surly or bad-tempered person ▷ vb complain or grumble
GRUMPED > GRUMP
GRUMPH vb grunt
GRUMPHED > GRUMPH
GRUMPHIE n pig
GRUMPHIES > GRUMPHIE
GRUMPHING > GRUMPH
GRUMPHS > GRUMPH
GRUMPHY same as > GRUMPHIE
GRUMPIER > GRUMPY
GRUMPIES > GRUMPY
GRUMPIEST > GRUMPY
GRUMPILY > GRUMPY
GRUMPING > GRUMP

g

g

GRUMPISH same as > GRUMPY

GRUMPS > GRUMP

GRUMPY adj bad-tempered ▷ n bad-tempered person

GRUND n as in grund mail payment for right of burial

GRUNDIES pl n men's underpants

GRUNDLE n perineum

GRUNDLES > GRUNDLE

GRUNGE n style of rock music with a fuzzy guitar sound

GRUNGER n fan of grunge music

GRUNGERS > GRUNGER

GRUNGES > GRUNGE

GRUNGEY adj messy or dirty

GRUNGIER > GRUNGY

GRUNGIEST > GRUNGY

GRUNGY adj squalid or seedy

GRUNION n Californian marine fish that spawns on beaches

GRUNIONS > GRUNION

GRUNT vb make a low short gruff sound, like a pig ▷ n pig's sound

GRUNTED > GRUNT

GRUNTER n person or animal that grunts, esp a pig

GRUNTERS > GRUNTER

GRUNTING > GRUNT

GRUNTINGS > GRUNT

GRUNTLE vb grunt or groan

GRUNTLED > GRUNTLE

GRUNTLES > GRUNTLE

GRUNTLING > GRUNTLE

GRUNTS > GRUNT

GRUPPETTI > GRUPPETTO

GRUPPETTO n turn

GRUSHIE adj healthy and strong

GRUTCH vb grudge

GRUTCHED > GRUTCH

GRUTCHES > GRUTCH

GRUTCHING > GRUTCH

GRUTTEN > GREET

GRUYERE n hard flat whole-milk cheese with holes

GRUYERES > GRUYERE

GRYCE same as > GRICE

GRYCES > GRYCE

GRYDE same as > GRIDE

GRYDED > GRYDE

GRYDES > GRYDE

GRYDING > GRYDE

GRYESY adj grey

GRYFON same as > GRIFFIN

GRYFONS > GRYFON

GRYKE same as > GRIKE

GRYKES > GRYKE

GRYPE same as > GRIPE

GRYPES > GRYPE

GRYPHON same as > GRIFFIN

GRYPHONS > GRYPHON

GRYPT archaic form of > GRIPPED

GRYSBOK n small antelope

GRYSBOKS > GRYSBOK

GRYSELY same as > GRISLY

GRYSIE same as > GRISY

GU same as > GJU

GUACAMOLE n spread of mashed avocado, tomato pulp, mayonnaise, and seasoning

GUACHARO another name for > OILBIRD

GUACHAROS > GUACHARO

GUACO n any of several plants used as an antidote to snakebite

GUACOS > GUACO

GUAIAC same as > GUAIACUM

GUAIACOL n yellowish creosote-like liquid

GUAIACOLS > GUAIACOL

GUAIACS > GUAIAC

GUAIACUM n tropical American evergreen tree

GUAIACUMS > GUAIACUM

GUAIOCUM same as > GUAIACUM

GUAIOCUMS > GUAIOCUM

GUAN n type of bird of Central and S America

GUANA another word for > IGUANA

GUANABANA n tropical tree or its fruit

GUANACO n S American animal related to the llama

GUANACOS > GUANACO

GUANAS > GUANA

GUANASE n type of enzyme

GUANASES > GUANASE

GUANAY n type of cormorant

GUANAYS > GUANAY

GUANAZOLO n form of guanine

GUANGO n rain tree

GUANGOS > GUANGO

GUANIDIN same as > GUANIDINE

GUANIDINE n strongly alkaline crystalline substance, soluble in water and found in plant and animal tissues

GUANIDINS > GUANIDIN

GUANIN same as > GUANINE

GUANINE n white almost insoluble compound

GUANINES > GUANINE

GUANINS > GUANIN

GUANO n dried sea-bird manure

GUANOS > GUANO

GUANOSINE n nucleoside consisting of guanine and ribose

GUANS > GUAN

GUANXI n Chinese social concept

GUANXIS > GUANXI

GUANYLIC adj as in guanylic acid nucleotide consisting of guanine, ribose or deoxyribose, and a phosphate group

GUAR n Indian plant

GUARACHA same as > HUARACHE

GUARACHAS > GUARACHA

GUARACHE same as > HUARACHE

GUARACHES > GUARACHE

GUARACHI same as > HUARACHE

GUARACHIS > GUARACHI

GUARANA n type of shrub native to Venezuela

GUARANAS > GUARANA

GUARANI n standard monetary unit of Paraguay

GUARANIES > GUARANI

GUARANIS > GUARANI

GUARANTEE n formal assurance, esp in writing, that a product will meet certain standards ▷ vb give a guarantee

GUARANTOR n person who gives or is bound by a guarantee

GUARANTY n pledge of responsibility for fulfilling another person's obligations in case of default

GUARD vb watch over to protect or to prevent escape ▷ n person or group that guards

GUARDABLE > GUARD

GUARDAGE n state of being in the care of a guardian

GUARDAGES > GUARDAGE

GUARDANT adj (of a beast) shown full face ▷ n guardian

GUARDANTS > GUARDANT

GUARDDOG n dog trained to protect premises

GUARDDOGS > GUARDDOG

GUARDED adj cautious or noncommittal

GUARDEDLY > GUARDED

GUARDEE n guardsman

GUARDEES > GUARDEE

GUARDER > GUARD

GUARDERS > GUARD

GUARDIAN n keeper or protector ▷ adj protecting or safeguarding

GUARDIANS > GUARDIAN

GUARDING > GUARD

GUARDLESS > GUARD

GUARDLIKE > GUARD

GUARDRAIL n railing at the side of a staircase, road, etc, as a safety barrier

GUARDROOM n room used by guards

GUARDS > GUARD

GUARDSHIP n warship responsible for the safety of other ships in its company

GUARDSMAN n member of the Guards

GUARDSMEN > GUARDSMAN

GUARISH vb heal

GUARISHED > GUARISH

GUARISHES > GUARISH

GUARS > GUAR

GUAVA n yellow-skinned tropical American fruit

GUAVAS > GUAVA

GUAYABERA n type of embroidered men's shirt

GUAYULE n bushy shrub of the southwestern US

GUAYULES > GUAYULE

GUB n Scots word for mouth ▷ vb hit or defeat

GUBBAH same as > GUB

GUBBAHS > GUBBAH

GUBBED > GUB

GUBBING > GUB

GUBBINS n object of little or no value

GUBBINSES > GUBBINS

GUBERNIYA n territorial division of imperial Russia

GUBS > GUB

GUCK n slimy matter

GUCKIER > GUCKY

GUCKIEST > GUCKY

GUCKS > GUCK

GUCKY adj slimy and mucky

GUDDLE vb catch (fish) with the hands ▷ n muddle

GUDDLED > GUDDLE

GUDDLES > GUDDLE

GUDDLING > GUDDLE

GUDE Scots word for > GOOD

GUDEMAN n male householder

GUDEMEN > GUDEMAN

GUDES n goods

GUDESIRE n grandfather

GUDESIRES > GUDESIRE

GUDEWIFE n female householder

GUDEWIVES > GUDEWIFE

GUDGEON n small freshwater fish ▷ vb trick or cheat

GUDGEONED > GUDGEON

GUDGEONS > GUDGEON

GUE same as > GJU

GUELDER adj as in guelder rose kind of shrub

GUENON n slender Old World monkey

GUENONS > GUENON

GUERDON n reward or payment ▷ vb give a guerdon to

GUERDONED > GUERDON

GUERDONER > GUERDON

GUERDONS > GUERDON

GUEREZA n handsome colobus monkey

GUEREZAS > GUEREZA

GUERIDON n small ornately carved table

GUERIDONS > GUERIDON

GUERILLA same as > GUERRILLA

GUERILLAS > GUERILLA

GUERITE n turret used by a sentry

GUERITES > GUERITE

GUERNSEY n seaman's knitted woollen sweater

GUERNSEYS > GUERNSEY

GUERRILLA n member of an unofficial armed force fighting regular forces

GUES > GUE

GUESS vb estimate or draw a conclusion without proper knowledge ▷ n estimate or conclusion reached by guessing

GUESSABLE > GUESS

GUESSED > GUESS

GUESSER > GUESS

GUESSERS > GUESS

GUESSES > GUESS

GUESSING > GUESS

GUESSINGS > GUESS

GUESSWORK n process or results of guessing

GUEST n person entertained at another's expense ▷ vb appear as a visiting player or performer

GUESTBOOK n page on a website where users leave comments

GUESTED > GUEST

GUESTEN vb stay as a guest in someone's house

GUESTENED > GUESTEN

GUESTENS > GUESTEN

GUESTING > GUEST

GUESTS > GUEST

GUESTWISE adv as, or in the manner of, a guest

GUFF n nonsense

GUFFAW n crude noisy laugh ▷ vb laugh in this way

GUFFAWED > GUFFAW

GUFFAWING > GUFFAW

GUFFAWS > GUFFAW

GUFFIE Scots word for > PIG

GUFFIES > GUFFIE

GUFFS > GUFF

GUGA n gannet chick

GUGAS > GUGA

GUGGLE vb drink making a gurgling sound

GUGGLED > GUGGLE

GUGGLES > GUGGLE

GUGGLING > GUGGLE

GUGLET same as > GOGLET

GUGLETS > GUGLET

GUICHET n grating, hatch, or small opening in a wall

GUICHETS > GUICHET

GUID Scot word for > GOOD

GUIDABLE > GUIDE

GUIDAGE n guidance

GUIDAGES > GUIDAGE

GUIDANCE n leadership, instruction, or advice

GUIDANCES > GUIDANCE

GUIDE n person who conducts tour expeditions ▷ vb act as a guide for

GUIDEBOOK n handbook with information for visitors to a place

GUIDED > GUIDE

GUIDELESS > GUIDE

GUIDELINE n set principle for doing something

GUIDEPOST n sign on a post by a road indicating directions

GUIDER > GUIDE

GUIDERS > GUIDE

GUIDES > GUIDE

GUIDESHIP n supervision

GUIDEWAY n track controlling the motion of something

GUIDEWAYS > GUIDEWAY

GUIDEWORD n word at top of dictionary page indicating first entry on page

GUIDING > GUIDE

GUIDINGS > GUIDE

GUIDON n small pennant

GUIDONS > GUIDON

GUIDS pl n possessions

GUILD n organization or club

GUILDER n former monetary unit of the Netherlands

GUILDERS > GUILDER

GUILDHALL n hall where members of a guild meet

GUILDRIES > GUILDRY

GUILDRY n in Scotland, corporation of merchants

GUILDS > GUILD

GUILDSHIP n condition of being a member of a guild

GUILDSMAN n man who is a member of a guild

GUILDSMEN > GUILDSMAN

GUILE n cunning or deceit ▷ vb deceive

GUILED > GUILE

GUILEFUL > GUILE

GUILELESS adj free from guile

GUILER n deceiver

GUILERS > GUILER

GUILES > GUILE

GUILING > GUILE

GUILLEMET n (in printing) a duckfoot quote

GUILLEMOT n black-and-white diving sea bird of N hemisphere

GUILLOCHE n ornamental band or border with a repeating pattern of two or more interwoven wavy lines, as in architecture ▷ vb decorate with guilloches

GUILT n fact or state of having done wrong ▷ vb make (a person) feel guilty

GUILTED > GUILT

GUILTIER > GUILTY

GUILTIEST > GUILTY

GUILTILY > GUILTY

GUILTING > GUILT

GUILTLESS adj innocent

GUILTS > GUILT

GUILTY adj responsible for an offence or misdeed

GUIMBARD n Jew's harp

GUIMBARDS > GUIMBARD

GUIMP same as > GUIMPE

GUIMPE n short blouse worn under a pinafore dress ▷ vb make with gimp

GUIMPED > GUIMPE

GUIMPES > GUIMPE

GUIMPING > GUIMPE

GUIMPS > GUIMP

GUINEA n former British monetary unit

GUINEAS > GUINEA

GUINEP n type of tropical American tree

GUINEPS > GUINEP

GUIPURE n heavy lace

GUIPURES > GUIPURE

GUIRO n percussion instrument made from a hollow gourd

GUIROS > GUIRO

GUISARD n guiser

GUISARDS > GUISARD

GUISE n false appearance ▷ vb disguise or be disguised in fancy dress

GUISED > GUISE

GUISER n mummer, esp at Christmas or Halloween revels

GUISERS > GUISER

GUISES > GUISE

GUISING > GUISE

GUISINGS > GUISE

GUITAR n stringed instrument

GUITARIST > GUITAR

GUITARS > GUITAR

GUITGUIT n bird belonging to the family Coerebidae

GUITGUITS > GUITGUIT

GUIZER same as > GUISER

GUIZERS > GUIZER

GUL n design used in oriental carpets

GULA n gluttony

GULAG n forced-labour camp

GULAGS > GULAG

GULAR adj of or situated in the throat or oesophagus ▷ n throat or oesophagus

GULARS > GULAR

GULAS > GULA

GULCH n deep narrow valley ▷ vb swallow fast

GULCHED > GULCH

GULCHES > GULCH

GULCHING > GULCH

GULDEN same as > GUILDER

GULDENS > GULDEN

GULE Scots word for > MARIGOLD

GULES n red in heraldry

GULET n wooden Turkish sailing boat

GULETS > GULET

GULF n large deep bay ▷ vb swallow up

GULFED > GULF

GULFIER > GULF

GULFIEST > GULF

GULFING > GULF

GULFLIKE > GULF

GULFS > GULF

GULFWEED n type of brown seaweed

GULFWEEDS > GULFWEED

GULFY > GULF

GULL n long-winged sea bird ▷ vb cheat or deceive

GULLABLE same as > GULLIBLE

GULLABLY > GULLABLE

GULLED > GULL

GULLER n deceiver

GULLERIES > GULLERY

GULLERS > GULLER

GULLERY n breeding-place for gulls

GULLET n muscular tube from the mouth to the stomach

GULLETS > GULLET

GULLEY same as > GULLY

GULLEYED > GULLEY

GULLEYING > GULLEY

GULLEYS > GULLEY

GULLIBLE adj easily tricked

GULLIBLY > GULLIBLE

GULLIED > GULLY

GULLIES > GULLY

GULLING > GULL

GULLISH adj stupid

GULLS > GULL

GULLWING adj (of vehicle door) opening upwards

GULLY n channel cut by running water ▷ vb make (channels) in (the ground, sand, etc)

GULLYING > GULLY

GULOSITY n greed or gluttony

GULP vb swallow hastily ▷ n gulping

GULPED > GULP

GULPER > GULP

GULPERS > GULP

GULPH archaic word for > GULF

GULPHS > GULPH

GULPIER > GULP

GULPIEST > GULP

GULPING > GULP

GULPINGLY > GULP

GULPS > GULP

GULPY > GULP

GULS > GUL

GULY adj relating to gules

GUM n firm flesh in which the teeth are set ▷ vb stick with gum

GUMBALL n round piece of chewing gum

GUMBALLS > GUMBALL

GUMBO n mucilaginous pods of okra

GUMBOIL n abscess on the gum

GUMBOILS > GUMBOIL

GUMBOOT n rubber boot

GUMBOOTS pl n Wellington boots

GUMBOS > GUMBO

GUMBOTIL n sticky clay formed by the weathering of glacial drift

GUMBOTILS > GUMBOTIL

GUMDROP n hard jelly-like sweet

GUMDROPS > GUMDROP

GUMLANDS pl n infertile land where kauri once grew

GUMLESS > GUM

GUMLIKE > GUM

GUMLINE n line where gums meet teeth

GUMLINES > GUMLINE

GUMMA n rubbery tumour

GUMMAS > GUMMA

GUMMATA > GUMMA

GUMMATOUS > GUMMA

GUMMED > GUM

GUMMER n punch-cutting tool

GUMMERS > GUMMER

GUMMI n gelatin-based flavoured sweet

GUMMIER > GUMMY

GUMMIES > GUMMY

GUMMIEST > GUMMY

GUMMILY > GUMMY

GUMMINESS > GUMMY

GUMMING > GUM

GUMMINGS > GUM

GUMMIS > GUMMI

GUMMITE n orange or yellowish amorphous secondary mineral

GUMMITES > GUMMITE

GUMMOSE same as > GUMMOUS

GUMMOSES > GUMMOSE

g

GUMMOSIS n abnormal production of gum in trees
GUMMOSITY > GUMMOUS
GUMMOUS adj resembling or consisting of gum
GUMMY adj toothless ▷ n type of small crustacean-eating shark
GUMNUT n hardened seed container of the gumtree
GUMNUTS > GUMNUT
GUMP vb guddle
GUMPED > GUMP
GUMPHION n funeral banner
GUMPHIONS > GUMPHION
GUMPING > GUMP
GUMPS > GUMP
GUMPTION n resourcefulness
GUMPTIONS > GUMPTION
GUMPTIOUS > GUMPTION
GUMS > GUM
GUMSHIELD n plate or strip of soft waxy substance used by boxers to protect the teeth and gums
GUMSHOE n waterproof overshoe ▷ vb act stealthily
GUMSHOED > GUMSHOE
GUMSHOES > GUMSHOE
GUMSUCKER n native-born Australian
GUMTREE n any of various trees that yield gum
GUMTREES > GUMTREE
GUMWEED n any of several yellow-flowered plants
GUMWEEDS > GUMWEED
GUMWOOD same as > GUMTREE
GUMWOODS > GUMWOOD
GUN n weapon with a tube from which missiles are fired ▷ vb cause (an engine) to run at high speed
GUNBOAT n small warship
GUNBOATS > GUNBOAT
GUNCOTTON n form of cellulose nitrate used as an explosive
GUNDIES > GUNDY
GUNDOG n dog trained to work with a hunter or gamekeeper
GUNDOGS > GUNDOG
GUNDY n toffee
GUNFIGHT n fight between persons using firearms ▷ vb fight with guns
GUNFIGHTS > GUNFIGHT
GUNFIRE n repeated firing of guns
GUNFIRES > GUNFIRE
GUNFLINT n piece of flint in a flintlock's hammer used to strike the spark that ignites the charge
GUNFLINTS > GUNFLINT
GUNFOUGHT > GUNFIGHT
GUNG adj as in gung ho extremely or excessively enthusiastic about something
GUNGE n sticky unpleasant substance ▷ vb block or encrust with gunge
GUNGED > GUNGE
GUNGES > GUNGE

GUNGIER > GUNGE
GUNGIEST > GUNGE
GUNGING > GUNGE
GUNGY > GUNGE
GUNHOUSE n on a warship, an armoured rotatable enclosure for guns
GUNHOUSES > GUNHOUSE
GUNITE n mortar sprayed in a very dense concrete layer
GUNITES > GUNITE
GUNK n slimy or filthy substance ▷ vb cover with gunk
GUNKED > GUNK
GUNKHOLE vb make a series of short boat excursions
GUNKHOLED > GUNKHOLE
GUNKHOLES > GUNKHOLE
GUNKIER > GUNK
GUNKIEST > GUNK
GUNKING > GUNK
GUNKS > GUNK
GUNKY > GUNK
GUNLAYER n person who aims a ship's gun
GUNLAYERS > GUNLAYER
GUNLESS > GUN
GUNLOCK n mechanism in some firearms
GUNLOCKS > GUNLOCK
GUNMAKER n person who makes guns
GUNMAKERS > GUNMAKER
GUNMAN n armed criminal
GUNMEN > GUNMAN
GUNMETAL n alloy of copper, tin, and zinc ▷ adj dark grey
GUNMETALS > GUNMETAL
GUNNAGE n number of guns carried by a warship
GUNNAGES > GUNNAGE
GUNNED > GUN
GUNNEL same as > GUNWALE
GUNNELS > GUNNEL
GUNNEN > GUN
GUNNER n artillery soldier
GUNNERA n type of herbaceous plant
GUNNERAS > GUNNERA
GUNNERIES > GUNNERY
GUNNERS > GUNNER
GUNNERY n use or science of large guns
GUNNIES > GUNNY
GUNNING > GUN
GUNNINGS > GUN
GUNNY n strong coarse fabric used for sacks
GUNNYBAG same as > GUNNYSACK
GUNNYBAGS > GUNNYBAG
GUNNYSACK n sack made from gunny
GUNPAPER n cellulose nitrate explosive made by treating paper with nitric acid
GUNPAPERS > GUNPAPER
GUNPLAY n use of firearms, as by criminals
GUNPLAYS > GUNPLAY
GUNPOINT n muzzle of a gun
GUNPOINTS > GUNPOINT
GUNPORT n porthole or other opening for a gun

GUNPORTS > GUNPORT
GUNPOWDER n explosive mixture of potassium nitrate, sulphur, and charcoal
GUNROOM n the mess allocated to junior officers
GUNROOMS > GUNROOM
GUNRUNNER n person who smuggles guns and ammunition
GUNS > GUN
GUNSEL n criminal who carries a gun
GUNSELS > GUNSEL
GUNSHIP n ship or helicopter armed with heavy guns
GUNSHIPS > GUNSHIP
GUNSHOT n shot or range of a gun
GUNSHOTS > GUNSHOT
GUNSIGHT n device on a gun which helps the user to aim
GUNSIGHTS > GUNSIGHT
GUNSMITH n person who manufactures or repairs firearms, esp portable guns
GUNSMITHS > GUNSMITH
GUNSTICK n ramrod
GUNSTICKS > GUNSTICK
GUNSTOCK n wooden handle to which the barrel of a rifle is attached
GUNSTOCKS > GUNSTOCK
GUNSTONE n cannonball
GUNSTONES > GUNSTONE
GUNTER n type of gaffing
GUNTERS > GUNTER
GUNWALE n top of a ship's side
GUNWALES > GUNWALE
GUNYAH n hut or shelter in the bush
GUNYAHS > GUNYAH
GUP n gossip
GUPPIES > GUPPY
GUPPY n small colourful aquarium fish
GUPS > GUP
GUQIN n type of Chinese zither
GUQINS > GUQIN
GUR n unrefined cane sugar
GURAMI same as > GOURAMI
GURAMIS > GURAMI
GURDIES > GURDY
GURDWARA n Sikh place of worship
GURDWARAS > GURDWARA
GURDY n winch on a fishing boat
GURGE vb swallow up
GURGED > GURGE
GURGES > GURGE
GURGING > GURGE
GURGLE n bubbling noise ▷ vb (of water) to make low bubbling noises when flowing
GURGLED > GURGLE
GURGLES > GURGLE
GURGLET same as > GOGLET
GURGLETS > GURGLET
GURGLIER > GURGLY
GURGLIEST > GURGLY
GURGLING > GURGLE

GURGLY adj making gurgling sounds
GURGOYLE same as > GARGOYLE
GURGOYLES > GURGOYLE
GURJUN n S or SE Asian tree that yields a resin
GURJUNS > GURJUN
GURL vb snarl
GURLED > GURL
GURLET n type of pickaxe
GURLETS > GURLET
GURLIER > GURLY
GURLIEST > GURLY
GURLING > GURL
GURLS > GURL
GURLY adj stormy
GURN variant spelling of > GIRN
GURNARD n spiny armour-headed sea fish
GURNARDS > GURNARD
GURNED > GURN
GURNET same as > GURNARD
GURNETS > GURNET
GURNEY n wheeled stretcher for transporting hospital patients
GURNEYS > GURNEY
GURNING > GURN
GURNS > GURN
GURRAH n type of coarse muslin
GURRAHS > GURRAH
GURRIER n low-class tough ill-mannered person
GURRIERS > GURRIER
GURRIES > GURRY
GURRY n dog-fight
GURS > GUR
GURSH n unit of currency in Saudi Arabia
GURSHES > GURSH
GURU n Hindu or Sikh religious teacher or leader
GURUDOM n state of being a guru
GURUDOMS > GURUDOM
GURUISM > GURU
GURUISMS > GURU
GURUS > GURU
GURUSHIP > GURU
GURUSHIPS > GURU
GUS > GU
GUSH vb flow out suddenly and profusely ▷ n sudden copious flow
GUSHED > GUSH
GUSHER n spurting oil well
GUSHERS > GUSHER
GUSHES > GUSH
GUSHIER > GUSHY
GUSHIEST > GUSHY
GUSHILY > GUSHY
GUSHINESS > GUSHY
GUSHING > GUSH
GUSHINGLY > GUSH
GUSHY adj displaying excessive sentimentality
GUSLA n Balkan single-stringed musical instrument
GUSLAR n player of the gusla
GUSLARS > GUSLAR
GUSLAS > GUSLA
GUSLE same as > GUSLA
GUSLES > GUSLE

GUSLI *n* Russian harp-like musical instrument

GUSLIS *n* GUSLI

GUSSET *n* piece of material sewn into a garment to strengthen it ▷ *vb* put a gusset in (a garment)

GUSSETED > GUSSET

GUSSETING > GUSSET

GUSSETS > GUSSET

GUSSIE *n* young pig

GUSSIED > GUSSY

GUSSIES > GUSSY

GUSSY *vb* dress elaborately

GUSSYING > GUSSY

GUST *n* sudden blast of wind ▷ *vb* blow in gusts

GUSTABLE *n* anything that can be tasted

GUSTABLES > GUSTABLE

GUSTATION *n* act of tasting or the faculty of taste

GUSTATIVE > GUSTATION

GUSTATORY > GUSTATION

GUSTED > GUST

GUSTFUL *adj* tasty

GUSTIE *adj* tasty

GUSTIER > GUSTY

GUSTIEST > GUSTY

GUSTILY > GUSTY

GUSTINESS > GUSTY

GUSTING > GUST

GUSTLESS *adj* tasteless

GUSTO *n* enjoyment or zest

GUSTOES > GUSTO

GUSTOS > GUSTO

GUSTS > GUST

GUSTY *adj* windy and blustery

GUT *n* intestine ▷ *vb* remove the guts from ▷ *adj* basic or instinctive

GUTBUCKET *n* highly emotional style of jazz playing

GUTCHER *n* grandfather

GUTCHERS > GUTCHER

GUTFUL *n* bellyful

GUTFULS > GUTFUL

GUTLESS *adj* cowardly

GUTLESSLY > GUTLESS

GUTLIKE > GUT

GUTROT *n* upset stomach

GUTROTS > GUTROT

GUTS *vb* devour greedily

GUTSED > GUTS

GUTSER *n* as in *come a gutser* fall heavily to the ground

GUTSERS > GUTSER

GUTSES > GUTS

GUTSFUL *n* bellyful

GUTSFULS > GUTSFUL

GUTSIER > GUTSY

GUTSIEST > GUTSY

GUTSILY > GUTSY

GUTSINESS > GUTSY

GUTSING > GUTS

GUTSY *adj* courageous

GUTTA *n* small drop-like ornament

GUTTAE > GUTTA

GUTTAS > GUTTA

GUTTATE *adj* covered with small drops or drop-like markings ▷ *vb* exude droplets of liquid

GUTTATED *same as* > GUTTATE

GUTTATES > GUTTATE

GUTTATING > GUTTATE

GUTTATION > GUTTATE

GUTTED > GUT

GUTTER *n* shallow channel for carrying away water ▷ *vb* (of a candle) burn unsteadily

GUTTERED > GUTTER

GUTTERIER > GUTTERY

GUTTERING *n* material for gutters

GUTTERS > GUTTER

GUTTERY *adj* vulgar

GUTTIER > GUTTY

GUTTIES > GUTTY

GUTTIEST > GUTTY

GUTTING > GUT

GUTTLE *vb* eat greedily

GUTTLED > GUTTLE

GUTTLER > GUTTLE

GUTTLERS > GUTTLE

GUTTLES > GUTTLE

GUTTLING > GUTTLE

GUTTURAL *adj* (of a sound) produced at the back of the throat ▷ *n* guttural consonant

GUTTURALS > GUTTURAL

GUTTY *n* urchin or delinquent ▷ *adj* courageous

GUTZER *n* bad fall

GUTZERS > GUTZER

GUV *informal name for* > GOVERNOR

GUVS > GUV

GUY *n* man or boy ▷ *vb* make fun of

GUYED > GUY

GUYING > GUY

GUYLE *same as* > GUILE

GUYLED > GUYLE

GUYLER > GUYLE

GUYLERS > GUYLE

GUYLES > GUYLE

GUYLINE *n* guy rope

GUYLINER *n* eyeliner worn by men

GUYLINERS > GUYLINER

GUYLINES > GUYLINE

GUYLING > GUYLE

GUYOT *n* flat-topped submarine mountain

GUYOTS > GUYOT

GUYS > GUY

GUYSE *same as* > GUISE

GUYSES > GUYSE

GUZZLE *vb* eat or drink greedily

GUZZLED > GUZZLE

GUZZLER *n* person or thing that guzzles

GUZZLERS > GUZZLER

GUZZLES > GUZZLE

GUZZLING > GUZZLE

GWEDUC *same as* > GEODUCK

GWEDUCK *same as* > GEODUCK

GWEDUCKS > GWEDUCK

GWEDUCS > GWEDUC

GWINE *dialect form of* > GOING

GWINIAD *n* powan

GWINIADS > GWINIAD

GWYNIAD *n* type of freshwater white fish

GWYNIADS > GWYNIAD

GYAL *same as* > GAYAL

GYALS > GYAL

GYAN *n* (in Indian English) knowledge

GYANS > GYAN

GYRE *vb* (of a sail) swing suddenly from one side to the other ▷ *n* instance of gybing

GYBED > GYBE

GYBES > GYBE

GYBING > GYBE

GYELD *n* guild

GYELDS > GYELD

GYLDEN *adj* golden

GYM *n* gymnasium

GYMBAL *same as* > GIMBAL

GYMBALS > GYMBAL

GYMKHANA *n* horse-riding competition

GYMKHANAS > GYMKHANA

GYMMAL *same as* > GIMMAL

GYMMALS > GYMMAL

GYMNASIA > GYMNASIUM

GYMNASIAL > GYMNASIUM

GYMNASIC > GYMNASIUM

GYMNASIEN > GYMNASIUM

GYMNASIUM *n* large room with equipment for physical training

GYMNAST *n* expert in gymnastics

GYMNASTIC *adj* of, relating to, like, or involving gymnastics

GYMNASTS > GYMNAST

GYMNIC *adj* gymnastic

GYMNOSOPH *n* adherent of gymnosophy: belief that food and clothing are detrimental to purity of thought

GYMP *same as* > GIMP

GYMPED > GYMP

GYMPIE *n* tall tree with stinging hairs on its leaves

GYMPIES > GYMPIE

GYMPING > GYMP

GYMPS > GYMP

GYMS > GYM

GYMSLIP *n* tunic or pinafore formerly worn by schoolgirls

GYMSLIPS > GYMSLIP

GYMSUIT *n* costume worn for gymnastics

GYMSUITS > GYMSUIT

GYNAE *adj* gynaecological ▷ *n* gynaecology

GYNAECEA > GYNAECEUM

GYNAECEUM *same as* > GYNAECIA

GYNAECIA > GYNAECIUM

GYNAECIUM *same as* > GYNOECIUM

GYNAECOID *adj* resembling, relating to, or like a woman

GYNAES > GYNAE

GYNANDRY *n* hermaphroditism

GYNARCHIC > GYNARCHY

GYNARCHY *n* government by women

GYNECIA > GYNECIUM

GYNECIC *adj* relating to the female sex

GYNECIUM *same as* > GYNOECIUM

GYNECOID *same as* > GYNAECOID

GYNIATRY *n* gynaecology: medicine concerned with diseases in women

GYNIE *n* gynaecology

GYNIES > GYNIE

GYNNEY *n* guinea hen

GYNNEYS > GYNNEY

GYNNIES > GYNNY

GYNNY *same as* > GYNNEY

GYNO *n* gynaecologist

GYNOCRACY *n* government by women

GYNOECIA > GYNOECIUM

GYNOECIUM *n* carpels of a flowering plant collectively

GYNOPHOBE *n* person who hates or fears women

GYNOPHORE *n* stalk in some plants that bears the gynoecium above the level of the other flower parts

GYNOS > GYNO

GYNY *n* gynaecology

GYOZA *n* Japanese fried dumpling

GYOZAS > GYOZA

GYP *vb* swindle, cheat, or defraud ▷ *n* act of cheating

GYPLURE *n* synthetic version of a gypsy moth pheromone

GYPLURES > GYPLURE

GYPO *n* small-scale independent logger

GYPOS > GYPO

GYPPED > GYP

GYPPER > GYP

GYPPERS > GYP

GYPPIE *same as* > GIPPY

GYPPIES > GYPPY

GYPPING > GYP

GYPPO *n* offensive term for a gypsy

GYPPOS > GYPPO

GYPPY *same as* > GIPPY

GYPS > GYP

GYPSEIAN *adj* relating to gypsies

GYPSEOUS > GYPSUM

GYPSIED > GYPSY

GYPSIES > GYPSY

GYPSTER *n* swindler

GYPSTERS > GYPSTER

GYPSUM *n* chalklike mineral

GYPSUMS > GYPSUM

GYPSY *n* member of a nomadic people ▷ *vb* live like a gypsy

GYPSYDOM > GYPSY

GYPSYDOMS > GYPSYDOM

GYPSYHOOD > GYPSY

GYPSYING > GYPSY

GYPSYISH > GYPSY

GYPSYISM *n* state of being a gypsy

GYPSYISMS > GYPSYISM

GYPSYWORT *n* type of Eurasian herb with white flowers

GYRAL *adj* having a circular, spiral, or rotating motion

g

GYRALLY > GYRAL

GYRANT *adj* gyrating

GYRASE *n* topoisomerase enzyme

GYRASES > GYRASE

GYRATE *vb* rotate or spiral about a point or axis ▷ *adj* curved or coiled into a circle

GYRATED > GYRATE

GYRATES > GYRATE

GYRATING > GYRATE

GYRATION *n* act or process of gyrating

GYRATIONS > GYRATION

GYRATOR *n* electronic circuit that inverts the impedance

GYRATORS > GYRATOR

GYRATORY > GYRATE

GYRE *n* circular or spiral movement or path ▷ *vb* whirl

GYRED > GYRE

GYRENE *n* nickname for a member of the US Marine Corps

GYRENES > GYRENE

GYRES > GYRE

GYRFALCON *n* very large rare falcon of northern regions

GYRI > GYRUS

GYRING > GYRE

GYRO *n* gyrocompass

GYROCAR *n* two-wheeled car

GYROCARS > GYROCAR

GYRODYNE *n* aircraft with rotor

GYRODYNES > GYRODYNE

GYROIDAL *adj* spiral

GYROLITE *n* silicate

GYROLITES > GYROLITE

GYROMANCY *n* divination by spinning in a circle, then falling on any of various letters that have been written on the ground

GYRON *same as* > GIRON

GYRONIC > GYRON

GYRONNY *same as* > GIRONNY

GYRONS > GYRON

GYROPILOT *n* type of automatic pilot

GYROPLANE *another name for* > AUTOGIRO

GYROS > GYRO

GYROSCOPE *n* disc rotating on an axis that can turn in any direction, so the disc maintains the same position regardless of the movement of the surrounding structure

GYROSE *adj* marked with sinuous lines

GYROSTAT *same as* > GYROSCOPE

GYROSTATS > GYROSTAT

GYROUS *adj* gyrose

GYROVAGUE *n* peripatetic monk

GYRUS *n* convolution

GYRUSES > GYRUS

GYTE *n* spoilt child

GYTES > GYTE

GYTRASH *n* spirit that haunts lonely roads

GYTRASHES > GYTRASH

GYTTJA *n* sediment on lake bottom

GYTTJAS > GYTTJA

GYVE *vb* shackle or fetter ▷ *n* fetters

GYVED > GYVE

GYVES > GYVE

GYVING > GYVE

g

Hh

HA *interj* exclamation of triumph, surprise, or scorn

HAAF *n* fishing ground off the Shetland and Orkney Islands

HAAFS > HAAF

HAANEPOOT *n* variety of grape

HAAR *n* cold sea mist or fog off the North Sea

HAARS > HAAR

HABANERA *n* slow Cuban dance in duple time

HABANERAS > HABANERA

HABANERO *n* variety of chilli pepper

HABANEROS > HABANERO

HABDABS *n* highly nervous state

HABDALAH *n* prayer at end of Jewish sabbath

HABDALAHS > HABDALAH

HABENDUM *n* part of a deed defining the limits of ownership

HABENDUMS > HABENDUM

HABERDINE *n* dried cod

HABERGEON *n* light sleeveless coat of mail worn in the 14th century under the plated hauberk

HABILABLE *adj* able to wear clothes

HABILE *adj* skilful

HABIT *n* established way of behaving ▷ *vb* clothe

HABITABLE *adj* fit to be lived in

HABITABLY > HABITABLE

HABITAN *same as* > HABITANT

HABITANS > HABITAN

HABITANT *n* person who lives in a place

HABITANTS > HABITANT

HABITAT *n* natural home of an animal or plant

HABITATS > HABITAT

HABITED *adj* dressed in a habit

HABITING > HABIT

HABITS > HABIT

HABITUAL *adj* done regularly and repeatedly ▷ *n* person with a habit

HABITUALS > HABITUAL

HABITUATE *vb* accustom

HABITUDE *n* habit or tendency

HABITUDES > HABITUDE

HABITUE *n* frequent visitor to a place

HABITUES > HABITUE

HABITUS *n* general physical state

HABITUSES > HABITUS

HABLE *old form of* > ABLE

HABOOB *n* sandstorm

HABOOBS > HABOOB

HABU *n* large venomous snake

HABUS > HABU

HACEK *n* pronunciation symbol in Slavonic language

HACEKS > HACEK

HACENDADO *n* owner of hacienda

HACHIS *n* hash

HACHURE *n* shading drawn on a map to indicate steepness of a hill ▷ *vb* mark or show by hachures

HACHURED > HACHURE

HACHURES > HACHURE

HACHURING > HACHURE

HACIENDA *n* ranch or large estate in Latin America

HACIENDAS > HACIENDA

HACK *vb* cut or chop violently ▷ *n* (inferior) writer or journalist ▷ *adj* unoriginal or of a low standard

HACKABLE > HACK

HACKAMORE *n* rope or rawhide halter used for unbroken foals

HACKBERRY *n* American tree or shrub with edible cherry-like fruits

HACKBOLT *n* shearwater

HACKBOLTS > HACKBOLT

HACKBUT *another word for* > ARQUEBUS

HACKBUTS > HACKBUT

HACKED > HACK

HACKEE *n* chipmunk

HACKEES > HACKEE

HACKER *n* computer enthusiast

HACKERIES > HACKERY

HACKERS > HACKER

HACKERY *n* journalism

HACKETTE *n* informal, derogatory term for female journalist

HACKETTES > HACKETTE

HACKIE *n* US word meaning cab driver

HACKIES > HACKIE

HACKING > HACK

HACKINGS > HACK

HACKLE *same as* > HECKLE

HACKLED > HACKLE

HACKLER > HACKLE

HACKLERS > HACKLE

HACKLES *pl n* hairs which rise in response to emotion

HACKLET *n* kittiwake

HACKLETS > HACKLET

HACKLIER > HACKLY

HACKLIEST > HACKLY

HACKLING > HACKLE

HACKLY *adj* rough or jagged

HACKMAN *n* taxi driver

HACKMEN > HACKMAN

HACKNEY *n* taxi ▷ *vb* make commonplace and banal by too frequent use

HACKNEYED *adj* (of a word or phrase) unoriginal and overused

HACKNEYS > HACKNEY

HACKS > HACK

HACKSAW *n* small saw for cutting metal ▷ *vb* cut with a hacksaw

HACKSAWED > HACKSAW

HACKSAWN > HACKSAW

HACKSAWS > HACKSAW

HACKWORK *n* dull repetitive work

HACKWORKS > HACKWORK

HACQUETON *n* padded jacket worn under chain mail

HAD *vb* Scots form of hold

HADAL *adj* denoting very deep zones of the oceans

HADARIM > HEDER

HADAWAY *sentence substitute* exclamation urging the hearer to refrain from delay

HADDEN > HAD

HADDEST *same as* > HADST

HADDIE *n* finnan haddock

HADDIES > HADDIE

HADDING > HAD

HADDOCK *n* edible sea fish of N Atlantic

HADDOCKS > HADDOCK

HADE *n* angle made to the vertical by the plane of a fault or vein ▷ *vb* incline from the vertical

HADED > HADE

HADEDAH *n* large grey-green S African ibis

HADEDAHS > HADEDAH

HADES > HADE

HADING > HADE

HADITH *n* body of legend about Mohammed and his followers

HADITHS > HADITH

HADJ *same as* > HAJJ

HADJEE *same as* > HADJI

HADJEES > HADJEE

HADJES > HADJ

HADJI *same as* > HAJJI

HADJIS > HADJI

HADROME *n* part of xylem

HADROMES > HADROME

HADRON *n* type of elementary particle

HADRONIC > HADRON

HADRONS > HADRON

HADROSAUR *n* any one of a large group of duck-billed partly aquatic bipedal dinosaurs

HADS > HAD

HADST *singular form of the past tense (indicative mood) of* > HAVE

HAE *Scot variant of* > HAVE

HAECCEITY *n* property that uniquely identifies an object

HAED > HAE

HAEING > HAE

HAEM *n* red organic pigment containing ferrous iron

HAEMAL *adj* of the blood

HAEMATAL *same as* > HAEMAL

HAEMATEIN *n* dark purple water-insoluble crystalline substance obtained from logwood and used as an indicator and biological stain

HAEMATIC *n* agent that stimulates the production of red blood cells

HAEMATICS > HAEMATIC

HAEMATIN *n* dark bluish or brownish pigment

HAEMATINS > HAEMATIN

HAEMATITE *same as* > HEMATITE

HAEMATOID *adj* resembling blood

HAEMATOMA *n* tumour of clotted or partially clotted blood

HAEMIC *same as* > HAEMATIC

HAEMIN *n* haematin chloride

HAEMINS > HAEMIN

HAEMOCOEL *n* body cavity of many invertebrates, including arthropods and molluscs, developed from part of the blood system

HAEMOCYTE *n* any blood cell, esp a red blood cell

HAEMOID *same as* > HAEMATOID

HAEMOLYSE *same as* > HAEMOLYZE

HAEMOLYZE *vb* break down red blood cells

HAEMONIES > HAEMONY

h

h

HAEMONY n plant mentioned in Milton's poetry

HAEMOSTAT n surgical instrument that stops bleeding by compression of a blood vessel

HAEMS > HAEM

HAEN > HAE

HAEREDES > HAERES

HAEREMAI interj Māori expression of welcome ▷ n act of saying 'haeremai'

HAEREMAIS > HAEREMAI

HAERES same as > HERES

HAES > HAE

HAET n whit

HAETS > HAET

HAFF n lagoon

HAFFET n side of head

HAFFETS > HAFFET

HAFFIT same as > HAFFET

HAFFITS > HAFFIT

HAFFLIN same as > HALFLING

HAFFLINS > HAFFLIN

HAFFS > HAFF

HAFIZ n title for a person who knows the Koran by heart

HAFIZES > HAFIZ

HAFNIUM n metallic element found in zirconium ores

HAFNIUMS > HAFNIUM

HAFT n handle of an axe, knife, or dagger ▷ vb provide with a haft

HAFTARA same as > HAFTARAH

HAFTARAH n short reading from the Prophets

HAFTARAHS > HAFTARAH

HAFTARAS > HAFTARA

HAFTAROS > HAFTARAH

HAFTAROT > HAFTARAH

HAFTAROTH > HAFTARAH

HAFTED > HAFT

HAFTER > HAFT

HAFTERS > HAFT

HAFTING > HAFT

HAFTORAH same as > HAFTARAH

HAFTORAHS > HAFTORAH

HAFTOROS > HAFTORAH

HAFTOROT > HAFTORAH

HAFTOROTH > HAFTORAH

HAFTS > HAFT

HAG n ugly old woman ▷ vb hack

HAGADIC same as > HAGGADIC

HAGADIST same as > HAGGADIST

HAGADISTS > HAGADIST

HAGBERRY same as > HACKBERRY

HAGBOLT same as > HACKBOLT

HAGBOLTS > HAGBOLT

HAGBORN adj born of a witch

HAGBUSH same as > ARQUEBUS

HAGBUSHES > HAGBUSH

HAGBUT same as > ARQUEBUS

HAGBUTEER > HAGBUT

HAGBUTS > HAGBUT

HAGBUTTER > HAGBUT

HAGDEN same as > HACKBOLT

HAGDENS > HAGDEN

HAGDON same as > HACKBOLT

HAGDONS > HAGDON

HAGDOWN same as > HACKBOLT

HAGDOWNS > HAGDOWN

HAGFISH n any of various primitive eel-like vertebrates

HAGFISHES > HAGFISH

HAGG n boggy place

HAGGADA same as > HAGGADAH

HAGGADAH n book containing the order of service of the traditional Jewish Passover meal

HAGGADAHS > HAGGADAH

HAGGADAS > HAGGADA

HAGGADIC > HAGGADAH

HAGGADIST n writer of Aggadoth

HAGGADOT > HAGGADAH

HAGGADOTH > HAGGADAH

HAGGARD adj looking tired and ill ▷ n hawk that has reached maturity before being caught

HAGGARDLY > HAGGARD

HAGGARDS > HAGGARD

HAGGED > HAG

HAGGING > HAG

HAGGIS n Scottish dish

HAGGISES > HAGGIS

HAGGISH > HAG

HAGGISHLY > HAG

HAGGLE vb bargain or wrangle over a price

HAGGLED > HAGGLE

HAGGLER > HAGGLE

HAGGLERS > HAGGLE

HAGGLES > HAGGLE

HAGGLING n act of haggling

HAGGLINGS > HAGGLING

HAGGS > HAGG

HAGIARCHY n government by saints, holy people, or those in holy orders

HAGIOLOGY n literature about the lives and legends of saints

HAGLET same as > HACKLET

HAGLETS > HAGLET

HAGLIKE > HAG

HAGRIDDEN > HAGRIDE

HAGRIDE vb torment or obsess

HAGRIDER > HAGRIDE

HAGRIDERS > HAGRIDE

HAGRIDES > HAGRIDE

HAGRIDING > HAGRIDE

HAGRODE > HAGRIDE

HAGS > HAG

HAH same as > HA

HAHA n wall or other boundary marker that is set in a ditch

HAHAS > HAHA

HAHNIUM n transuranic element

HAHNIUMS > HAHNIUM

HAHS > HAH

HAICK same as > HAIK

HAICKS > HAICK

HAIDUK n rural brigand

HAIDUKS > HAIDUK

HAIK n Arab's outer garment

HAIKA > HAIK

HAIKAI same as > HAIKU

HAIKS > HAIK

HAIKU n Japanese verse form in 17 syllables

HAIKUS > HAIKU

HAIL n (shower of) small pellets of ice ▷ vb fall as or like hail ▷ sentence substitute exclamation of greeting

HAILED > HAIL

HAILER > HAIL

HAILERS > HAIL

HAILIER > HAIL

HAILIEST > HAIL

HAILING > HAIL

HAILS > HAIL

HAILSHOT n small scattering shot

HAILSHOTS > HAILSHOT

HAILSTONE n pellet of hail

HAILSTORM n storm during which hail falls

HAILY > HAIL

HAIMISH same as > HEIMISH

HAIN vb Scots word meaning save

HAINCH Scots form of > HAUNCH

HAINCHED > HAINCH

HAINCHES > HAINCH

HAINCHING > HAINCH

HAINED > HAIN

HAINING > HAIN

HAININGS > HAIN

HAINS > HAIN

HAINT same as > HAUNT

HAINTS > HAINT

HAIQUE same as > HAIK

HAIQUES > HAIQUE

HAIR n threadlike growth on the skin ▷ vb provide with hair

HAIRBALL n mass of hair that forms in the stomach of animals

HAIRBALLS > HAIRBALL

HAIRBAND n band worn around head to control hair

HAIRBANDS > HAIRBAND

HAIRBELL same as > HAREBELL

HAIRBELLS > HAIRBELL

HAIRBRUSH n brush for grooming the hair

HAIRCAP n type of moss

HAIRCAPS > HAIRCAP

HAIRCLOTH n cloth woven from horsehair, used in upholstery

HAIRCUT n act or an instance of cutting the hair

HAIRCUTS > HAIRCUT

HAIRDO n hairstyle

HAIRDOS > HAIRDO

HAIRDRIER same as > HAIRDRYER

HAIRDRYER n hand-held electric device that blows out hot air and is used to dry and, sometimes, assist in styling the hair, as in blow-drying

HAIRED adj with hair

HAIRGRIP n small bent clasp used to fasten the hair

HAIRGRIPS > HAIRGRIP

HAIRIER > HAIRY

HAIRIEST > HAIRY

HAIRIF another name for > CLEAVERS

HAIRIFS > HAIRIF

HAIRILY adv in a hairy manner

HAIRINESS > HAIRY

HAIRING > HAIR

HAIRLESS adj having little or no hair ▷ n as in Mexican hairless small breed of hairless dog

HAIRLIKE > HAIR

HAIRLINE n edge of hair at the top of the forehead ▷ adj very fine or narrow

HAIRLINES > HAIRLINE

HAIRLOCK n lock of hair

HAIRLOCKS > HAIRLOCK

HAIRNET n any of several kinds of light netting worn over the hair

HAIRNETS > HAIRNET

HAIRPIECE n section of false hair added to a person's real hair

HAIRPIN n U-shaped wire used to hold the hair in place

HAIRPINS > HAIRPIN

HAIRS > HAIR

HAIRSPRAY n fixative solution sprayed onto the hair to keep a hairstyle in shape

HAIRST Scots form of > HARVEST

HAIRSTED > HAIRST

HAIRSTING > HAIRST

HAIRSTS > HAIRST

HAIRSTYLE n cut and arrangement of a person's hair

HAIRTAIL n spiny-finned fish

HAIRTAILS > HAIRTAIL

HAIRWING n fishing lure tied with hair

HAIRWINGS > HAIRWING

HAIRWORK n thing made from hair

HAIRWORKS > HAIRWORK

HAIRWORM n any of various hairlike nematode worms

HAIRWORMS > HAIRWORM

HAIRY adj covered with hair

HAIRYBACK n offensive word for an Afrikaner

HAITH interj Scots oath

HAJ same as > HADJ

HAJES > HAJ

HAJI same as > HAJJI

HAJIS > HAJI

HAJJ n pilgrimage a Muslim makes to Mecca

HAJJAH n Muslim woman who has made a pilgrimage to Mecca

HAJJAHS > HAJJAH

HAJJES > HAJJ

HAJJI n Muslim who has made a pilgrimage to Mecca

HAJJIS > HAJJI

HAKA n ceremonial Māori dance with chanting

HAKAM *n* text written by a rabbi
HAKAMS > HAKAM
HAKARI *n* Māori ritual feast
HAKARIS > HAKARI
HAKAS > HAKA
HAKE *n* edible sea fish of N hemisphere
HAKEA *n* Australian tree or shrub with hard woody fruit
HAKEAS > HAKEA
HAKEEM *same as* > HAKIM
HAKEEMS > HAKEEM
HAKES > HAKE
HAKIM *n* Muslim judge, ruler, or administrator
HAKIMS > HAKIM
HAKU *in New Zealand English, same as* > KINGFISH
HAKUS > HAKU
HALACHA *n* Jewish religious law
HALACHAS > HALACHA
HALACHIC > HALACHA
HALACHIST > HALACHA
HALACHOT > HALACHA
HALACHOTH > HALACHA
HALAKAH *same as* > HALACHA
HALAKAHS > HALAKAH
HALAKHA *same as* > HALACHA
HALAKHAH *same as* > HALACHA
HALAKHAHS > HALAKHAH
HALAKHAS > HALAKHA
HALAKHIC > HALAKHAH
HALAKHIST > HALAKHAH
HALAKHOT > HALAKHA
HALAKHOTH > HALAKHAH
HALAKIC > HALAKHA
HALAKIST > HALAKHA
HALAKISTS > HALAKHA
HALAKOTH > HALAKHA
HALAL *n* meat from animals slaughtered according to Muslim law ▷ *adj* of or relating to such meat ▷ *vb* kill (animals) in this way
HALALA *n* money unit in Saudi Arabia
HALALAH *same as* > HALALA
HALALAHS > HALALAH
HALALAS > HALALA
HALALLED > HALAL
HALALLING > HALAL
HALALS > HALAL
HALATION *n* bright ring surrounding a light source
HALATIONS > HALATION
HALAVAH *same as* > HALVAH
HALAVAHS > HALAVAH
HALAZONE *n* type of disinfectant
HALAZONES > HALAZONE
HALBERD *n* spear with an axe blade
HALBERDS > HALBERD
HALBERT *same as* > HALBERD
HALBERTS > HALBERT
HALCYON *adj* peaceful and happy ▷ *n* mythological bird
HALCYONIC *adj* peaceful and happy
HALCYONS > HALCYON

HALE *adj* healthy, robust ▷ *vb* pull or drag
HALED > HALE
HALENESS > HALE
HALER *same as* > HELLER
HALERS > HALER
HALERU > HALER
HALES > HALE
HALEST > HALE
HALF *n* either of two equal parts ▷ *adj* denoting one of two equal parts ▷ *adv* to the extent of half
HALFA *n* African grass
HALFAS > HALFA
HALFBACK *n* player positioned immediately behind the forwards
HALFBACKS > HALFBACK
HALFBEAK *n* type of fish with a short upper jaw and a protruding lower jaw
HALFBEAKS > HALFBEAK
HALFEN *same as* > HALF
HALFLIFE *n* time taken for half of the atoms in a radioactive material to undergo decay
HALFLIN *same as* > HALFLING
HALFLING *n* person only half-grown
HALFLINGS > HALFLING
HALFLINS > HALFLIN
HALFLIVES > HALFLIFE
HALFNESS > HALF
HALFPACE *n* landing on staircase
HALFPACES > HALFPACE
HALFPENCE > HALFPENNY
HALFPENNY *n* former British coin worth half an old penny
HALFPIPE *n* U-shaped object used in skateboarding stunts
HALFPIPES > HALFPIPE
HALFS > HALF
HALFTIME *n* rest period between the two halves of a game
HALFTIMES > HALFTIME
HALFTONE *n* illustration showing lights and shadows by means of very small dots ▷ *adj* relating to, used in, or made by halftone
HALFTONES > HALFTONE
HALFTRACK *n* vehicle with caterpillar tracks and wheels
HALFWAY *adj* at or to half the distance
HALFWIT *n* foolish or stupid person
HALFWITS > HALFWIT
HALIBUT *n* large edible flatfish of N Atlantic
HALIBUTS > HALIBUT
HALICORE *n* dugong
HALICORES > HALICORE
HALID *same as* > HALIDE
HALIDE *n* binary compound
HALIDES > HALIDE
HALIDOM *n* holy place or thing
HALIDOME *same as* > HALIDOM

HALIDOMES > HALIDOME
HALIDOMS > HALIDOM
HALIDS > HALID
HALIER *n* former currency unit of Slovakia
HALIEROV > HALIER
HALIERS > HALIER
HALIEUTIC *adj* of fishing
HALIMOT *n* court held by lord
HALIMOTE *same as* > HALIMOT
HALIMOTES > HALIMOTE
HALIMOTS > HALIMOT
HALING > HALE
HALIOTIS *n* type of shellfish
HALITE *n* colourless or white mineral
HALITES > HALITE
HALITOSES > HALITOSIS
HALITOSIS *n* unpleasant-smelling breath
HALITOTIC > HALITUS
HALITOUS > HALITUS
HALITUS *n* vapour
HALITUSES > HALITUS
HALL *n* entrance passage
HALLAH *variant spelling of* > CHALLAH
HALLAHS > HALLAH
HALLAL *same as* > HALAL
HALLALI *n* bugle call
HALLALIS > HALLALI
HALLALLED > HALLAL
HALLALOO *same as* > HALLOO
HALLALOOS > HALLALOO
HALLALS > HALLAL
HALLAN *n* partition in cottage
HALLANS > HALLAN
HALLEL *n* (in Judaism) section of the liturgy
HALLELS > HALLEL
HALLIAN *same as* > HALLION
HALLIANS > HALLIAN
HALLIARD *same as* > HALYARD
HALLIARDS > HALLIARD
HALLING *n* Norwegian country dance
HALLINGS > HALLING
HALLION *n* lout
HALLIONS > HALLION
HALLMARK *n* typical feature ▷ *vb* stamp with a hallmark
HALLMARKS > HALLMARK
HALLO *same as* > HALLOO
HALLOA *same as* > HALLOO
HALLOAED > HALLOA
HALLOAING > HALLOA
HALLOAS > HALLOA
HALLOED > HALLO
HALLOES > HALLO
HALLOING > HALLO
HALLOO *interj* shout used to call hounds at a hunt ▷ *sentence substitute* shout to attract attention, esp to call hounds at a hunt ▷ *n* shout of "halloo" ▷ *vb* shout (something) to (someone)
HALLOOED > HALLOO
HALLOOING > HALLOO
HALLOOS > HALLOO

HALLOS > HALLO
HALLOT > HALLAH
HALLOTH *same as* > CHALLAH
HALLOUMI *n* salty white sheep's cheese from Greece or Turkey, usually eaten grilled
HALLOUMIS > HALLOUMI
HALLOW *vb* consecrate or set apart as being holy
HALLOWED *adj* regarded as holy
HALLOWER > HALLOW
HALLOWERS > HALLOW
HALLOWING > HALLOW
HALLOWS > HALLOW
HALLS > HALL
HALLSTAND *n* piece of furniture on which are hung coats, hats, etc
HALLUCAL > HALLUX
HALLUCES > HALLUX
HALLUX *n* first digit on the hind foot of an animal
HALLWAY *n* entrance area
HALLWAYS > HALLWAY
HALLYON *same as* > HALLION
HALLYONS > HALLYON
HALM *same as* > HAULM
HALMA *n* board game
HALMAS > HALMA
HALMS > HALM
HALO *n* ring of light round the head of a sacred figure ▷ *vb* surround with a halo
HALOBIONT *n* plant or animal that lives in a salty environment such as the sea
HALOCLINE *n* gradient in salinity of sea
HALOED > HALO
HALOES > HALO
HALOGEN *n* any of a group of nonmetallic elements
HALOGENIC *adj* of or relating to halogens
HALOGENS > HALOGEN
HALOGETON *n* herbaceous plant
HALOID *adj* resembling or derived from a halogen ▷ *n* compound containing halogen atoms in its molecules
HALOIDS > HALOID
HALOING > HALO
HALOLIKE > HALO
HALON *n* any of a class of chemical compounds
HALONS > HALON
HALOPHILE *n* organism that thrives in an extremely salty environment, such as the Dead Sea
HALOPHILY *n* ability to live in salty environment
HALOPHOBE *n* plant unable to live in salty soil
HALOPHYTE *n* plant that grows in very salty soil, as in a salt marsh
HALOS > HALO
HALOSERE *n* plant community that originates and develops in conditions of high salinity

HALOSERES > HALOSERE

HALOTHANE n colourless volatile slightly soluble liquid with an odour resembling that of chloroform

HALOUMI same as > HALLOUMI

HALOUMIS > HALLOUMI

HALSE vb embrace

HALSED > HALSE

HALSER > HALSE

HALSERS > HALSE

HALSES > HALSE

HALSING > HALSE

HALT vb come or bring to a stop ▷ n temporary stop ▷ adj lame

HALTED > HALT

HALTER n strap round a horse's head with a rope to lead it with ▷ vb put a halter on (a horse)

HALTERE n one of a pair of modified hind wings in dipterous insects

HALTERED > HALTER

HALTERES > HALTERE

HALTERING > HALTER

HALTERS > HALTER

HALTING > HALT

HALTINGLY > HALT

HALTINGS > HALT

HALTLESS > HALT

HALTS > HALT

HALUTZ variant spelling of > CHALUTZ

HALUTZIM > HALUTZ

HALVA same as > HALVAH

HALVAH n E Mediterranean, Middle Eastern, or Indian sweetmeat

HALVAHS > HALVAH

HALVAS > HALVA

HALVE vb divide in half

HALVED > HALVE

HALVER > HALVE

HALVERS > HALVE

HALVES > HALVE

HALVING n act of halving

HALVINGS > HALVING

HALWA n type of sweet Indian dish

HALWAS > HALWA

HALYARD n rope for raising a ship's sail or flag

HALYARDS > HALYARD

HAM n smoked or salted meat from a pig's thigh ▷ vb overact

HAMADA n rocky plateau in desert

HAMADAS > HAMADA

HAMADRYAD n one of a class of nymphs, each of which inhabits a tree and dies with it

HAMADRYAS n type of baboon

HAMAL n (in Middle Eastern countries) a porter or servant

HAMALS > HAMAL

HAMAMELIS n any of several trees or shrubs native to E Asia and North America and cultivated as ornamentals

HAMARTIA n flaw in character which leads to the

downfall of the protagonist in a tragedy

HAMARTIAS > HAMARTIA

HAMATE adj hook-shaped ▷ n small bone in the wrist

HAMATES > HAMATE

HAMATSA n Native Canadian dance

HAMATSAS > HAMATSA

HAMAUL same as > HAMAL

HAMAULS > HAMAUL

HAMBA interj usually offensive term for go away

HAMBLE vb mutilate

HAMBLED > HAMBLE

HAMBLES > HAMBLE

HAMBLING > HAMBLE

HAMBONE vb strike body to provide percussion

HAMBONED > HAMBONE

HAMBONES > HAMBONE

HAMBONING > HAMBONE

HAMBURG same as > HAMBURGER

HAMBURGER n minced beef shaped into a flat disc, cooked and usually served in a bread roll

HAMBURGS > HAMBURG

HAME n Scots word for home ▷ vb to home

HAMED > HAME

HAMES > HAME

HAMEWITH adv Scots word meaning homewards

HAMFAT n mediocre performer

HAMFATS > HAMFAT

HAMFATTER n inferior actor or musician

HAMING > HAME

HAMLET n small village

HAMLETS > HAMLET

HAMMADA same as > HAMADA

HAMMADAS > HAMMADA

HAMMAL same as > HAMAL

HAMMALS > HAMMAL

HAMMAM n bathing establishment

HAMMAMS > HAMMAM

HAMMED > HAM

HAMMER n tool ▷ vb hit (as if) with a hammer

HAMMERED > HAMMER

HAMMERER > HAMMER

HAMMERERS > HAMMER

HAMMERING > HAMMER

HAMMERKOP n shark with hammer-shaped head

HAMMERMAN n person working with hammer

HAMMERMEN > HAMMERMAN

HAMMERS > HAMMER

HAMMERTOE n condition in which the toe is permanently bent at the joint

HAMMIER > HAMMY

HAMMIES > HAMMY

HAMMIEST > HAMMY

HAMMILY > HAMMY

HAMMINESS > HAMMY

HAMMING > HAM

HAMMOCK same as > HUMMOCK

HAMMOCKS > HAMMOCK

HAMMY adj (of an actor) overacting or tending to overact ▷ n hamstring

HAMOSE adj shaped like a hook

HAMOUS same as > HAMOSE

HAMPER vb make it difficult for (someone or something) to move or progress ▷ n large basket with a lid

HAMPERED > HAMPER

HAMPERER > HAMPER

HAMPERERS > HAMPER

HAMPERING > HAMPER

HAMPERS > HAMPER

HAMPSTER same as > HAMSTER

HAMPSTERS > HAMPSTER

HAMS > HAM

HAMSTER n small rodent with a short tail and cheek pouches

HAMSTERS > HAMSTER

HAMSTRING n tendon at the back of the knee ▷ vb make it difficult for (someone) to take any action

HAMSTRUNG > HAMSTRING

HAMULAR > HAMULUS

HAMULATE > HAMULUS

HAMULI > HAMULUS

HAMULOSE > HAMULUS

HAMULOUS > HAMULUS

HAMULUS n biological attribute

HAMZA n sign used in Arabic to represent the glottal stop

HAMZAH same as > HAMZA

HAMZAHS > HAMZAH

HAMZAS > HAMZA

HAN archaic inflected form of > HAVE

HANAP n medieval drinking cup

HANAPER n small wickerwork basket

HANAPERS > HANAPER

HANAPS > HANAP

HANCE same as > HAUNCH

HANCES > HANCE

HANCH vb try to bite

HANCHED > HANCH

HANCHES > HANCH

HANCHING > HANCH

HAND n part of the body at the end of the arm ▷ vb pass, give

HANDAX n small axe held in one hand

HANDAXE same as > HANDAX

HANDAXES > HANDAX

HANDBAG n woman's small bag

HANDBAGS pl n incident in which people threaten to fight

HANDBALL n game in which two teams try to throw a ball into their opponent's goal ▷ vb pass (the ball) with a blow of the fist

HANDBALLS > HANDBALL

HANDBELL n bell rung by hand, esp one of a tuned set used in musical performance

HANDBELLS > HANDBELL

HANDBILL n small printed notice

HANDBILLS > HANDBILL

HANDBLOWN adj (of glass) made by hand

HANDBOOK n small reference or instruction book

HANDBOOKS > HANDBOOK

HANDBRAKE n brake in a motor vehicle operated by a hand lever

HANDCAR n small railway vehicle

HANDCARS > HANDCAR

HANDCART n simple cart pushed or pulled by hand, used for transporting goods

HANDCARTS > HANDCART

HANDCLAP n act of clapping hands

HANDCLAPS > HANDCLAP

HANDCLASP another word for > HANDSHAKE

HANDCRAFT n handicraft

HANDCUFF n one of a linked pair of metal rings for locking round wrists ▷ vb put handcuffs on

HANDCUFFS > HANDCUFF

HANDED > HAND

HANDER > HAND

HANDERS > HAND

HANDFAST n agreement, esp of marriage, confirmed by a handshake ▷ vb betroth or marry (two persons or another person) by joining the hands

HANDFASTS > HANDFAST

HANDFED > HANDFEED

HANDFEED vb feed (a person or an animal) by hand

HANDFEEDS > HANDFEED

HANDFUL n amount that can be held in the hand

HANDFULS > HANDFUL

HANDGLASS n hand-held magnifying glass

HANDGRIP n covering on the handle of a racket or club

HANDGRIPS > HANDGRIP

HANDGUN n firearm such as a pistol

HANDGUNS > HANDGUN

HANDHELD adj held in position by the hand ▷ n computer that can be held in the hand

HANDHELDS > HANDHELD

HANDHOLD n object, crevice, etc, that can be used as a grip or support, as in climbing

HANDHOLDS > HANDHOLD

HANDICAP n hindrance or disadvantage ▷ vb make it difficult for (someone) to do something

HANDICAPS > HANDICAP

HANDIER > HANDY

HANDIEST > HANDY

HANDILY adv in a handy way or manner

HANDINESS > HANDY

HANDING > HAND

HANDISM n discrimination against left- or right-handed people

HANDISMS > HANDISM

HANDIWORK n result of someone's work or activity

HANDJAR n Persian dagger

HANDJARS > HANDJAR

HANDJOB n vulgar word for manual stimulation of another person's penis

HANDJOBS > HANDJOB

HANDKNIT n garment knitted by hand

HANDKNITS > HANDKNIT

HANDLE n part of an object that is held so that it can be used ▷ vb hold, feel, or move with the hands

HANDLEBAR adj as in handlebar moustache: bushy extended moustache with curled ends that resembles the handlebars of a bicycle

HANDLED > HANDLE

HANDLER n person who controls an animal

HANDLERS > HANDLER

HANDLES > HANDLE

HANDLESS > HAND

HANDLIKE > HAND

HANDLINE n hand-operated fishing line

HANDLINER n fisherman who fishes with a handline

HANDLINES > HANDLINE

HANDLING n act or an instance of picking up, turning over, or touching something

HANDLINGS > HANDLING

HANDLIST n rough list

HANDLISTS > HANDLIST

HANDLOOM n weaving device operated by hand

HANDLOOMS > HANDLOOM

HANDMADE adj made by hand, not by machine

HANDMAID n person or thing that serves as a useful but subordinate purpose

HANDMAIDS > HANDMAID

HANDOFF n (in rugby) act of warding off an opposing player

HANDOFFS > HANDOFF

HANDOUT n clothing, food, or money given to a needy person

HANDOUTS > HANDOUT

HANDOVER n transfer or surrender

HANDOVERS > HANDOVER

HANDPASS vb pass the ball by striking it with the hand

HANDPHONE n in SE Asian English, mobile phone

HANDPICK vb choose or select with great care, as for a special job or purpose

HANDPICKS > HANDPICK

HANDPLAY n fighting with fists

HANDPLAYS > HANDPLAY

HANDPRESS n printing press operated by hand

HANDPRINT n print of hand

HANDRAIL n rail alongside a stairway, to provide support

HANDRAILS > HANDRAIL

HANDROLL n large dried-seaweed cone filled with cold rice and other ingredients

HANDROLLS > HANDROLL

HANDS > HAND

HANDSAW n any saw for use in one hand only

HANDSAWS > HANDSAW

HANDSEL n gift for good luck ▷ vb give a handsel to (a person)

HANDSELED > HANDSEL

HANDSELS > HANDSEL

HANDSET n telephone mouth- and earpiece in a single unit

HANDSETS > HANDSET

HANDSEWN adj sewn by hand

HANDSFUL > HANDFUL

HANDSHAKE n act of grasping and shaking a person's hand, such as in greeting or when agreeing on a deal

HANDSIER > HANDSY

HANDSIEST > HANDSY

HANDSOME adj (esp of a man) good-looking ▷ n term of endearment for a beloved person

HANDSOMER > HANDSOME

HANDSOMES > HANDSOME

HANDSPIKE n bar or length of pipe used as a lever

HANDSTAFF n staff held in hand

HANDSTAMP vb stamp by hand

HANDSTAND n act of supporting the body on the hands in an upside-down position

HANDSTURN n slightest amount of work

HANDSY adj engaging in unwanted physical contact

HANDTOWEL n towel for drying hands

HANDWHEEL n wheel operated by hand

HANDWORK n work done by hand rather than by machine

HANDWORKS > HANDWORK

HANDWOVEN adj woven by hand

HANDWRIT > HANDWRITE

HANDWRITE vb write by hand

HANDWROTE > HANDWRITE

HANDY adj convenient, useful

HANDYMAN n man who is good at making or repairing things

HANDYMEN > HANDYMAN

HANDYWORK same as > HANDIWORK

HANEPOOT n variety of muscat grape

HANEPOOTS > HANEPOOT

HANG vb attach or be attached at the top with the lower part free

HANGABLE adj suitable for hanging

HANGAR n large shed for storing aircraft ▷ vb put in a hangar

HANGARAGE n combined hangar and garage

HANGARED > HANGAR

HANGARING > HANGAR

HANGARS > HANGAR

HANGBIRD n any bird, esp the Baltimore oriole, that builds a hanging nest

HANGBIRDS > HANGBIRD

HANGDOG adj guilty, ashamed ▷ n furtive or sneaky person

HANGDOGS > HANGDOG

HANGED > HANG

HANGER n curved piece of wood, wire, etc with a hook

HANGERS > HANGER

HANGFIRE n failure to fire

HANGFIRES > HANGFIRE

HANGI n Māori oven

HANGING > HANG

HANGINGS > HANG

HANGIS > HANGI

HANGMAN n man who executes people by hanging

HANGMEN > HANGMAN

HANGNAIL n piece of skin partly torn away from the base or side of a fingernail

HANGNAILS > HANGNAIL

HANGNEST same as > HANGBIRD

HANGNESTS > HANGNEST

HANGOUT n place where one lives or that one frequently visits

HANGOUTS > HANGOUT

HANGOVER n headache and nausea as a result of drinking too much alcohol

HANGOVERS > HANGOVER

HANGRIER > HANGRY

HANGRIEST > HANGRY

HANGRY adj irritable as a result of feeling hungry

HANGS > HANG

HANGTAG n attached label

HANGTAGS > HANGTAG

HANGUL n alphabetic scheme used in Korean

HANGULS > HANGUL

HANGUP n emotional or psychological or problem

HANGUPS > HANGUP

HANIWA n Japanese funeral offering

HANIWAS > HANIWA

HANJAR same as > HANDJAR

HANJARS > HANJAR

HANK n coil, esp of yarn ▷ vb attach (a sail) to a stay by hanks

HANKED > HANK

HANKER vb desire intensely

HANKERED > HANKER

HANKERER > HANKER

HANKERERS > HANKER

HANKERING > HANKER

HANKERS > HANKER

HANKIE same as > HANKY

HANKIES > HANKY

HANKING > HANK

HANKS > HANK

HANKY n handkerchief

HANSA same as > HANSE

HANSAS > HANSA

HANSE n medieval guild of merchants

HANSEATIC > HANSA

HANSEL same as > HANDSEL

HANSELED > HANSEL

HANSELING > HANSEL

HANSELLED > HANSEL

HANSELS > HANSEL

HANSES > HANSE

HANSOM n two-wheeled one-horse carriage

HANSOMS > HANSOM

HANT same as > HAUNT

HANTED > HANT

HANTING > HANT

HANTLE n good deal

HANTLES > HANTLE

HANTS > HANT

HANUKIAH n candelabrum having nine branches that is lit during the festival of Hanukkah

HANUKIAHS > HANUKIAH

HANUMAN n type of monkey

HANUMANS > HANUMAN

HAO n monetary unit of Vietnam

HAOLE n Hawaiian word for White person

HAOLES > HAOLE

HAOMA n type of ritual drink

HAOMAS > HAOMA

HAOS > HAO

HAP n luck ▷ vb cover up

HAPAX n word that appears once in a work of literature

HAPAXES > HAPAX

HAPHAZARD adj not organized or planned ▷ n chance

HAPHTARA same as > HAFTARAH

HAPHTARAH same as > HAFTARAH

HAPHTARAS > HAPHTARA

HAPHTAROT > HAPHTARA

HAPKIDO n Korean martial art

HAPKIDOS > HAPKIDO

HAPLESS adj unlucky

HAPLESSLY > HAPLESS

HAPLITE variant of > APLITE

HAPLITES > HAPLITE

HAPLITIC > HAPLITE

HAPLOID adj denoting a cell or organism with unpaired chromosomes ▷ n haploid cell or organism

HAPLOIDIC adj denoting a cell or organism with unpaired chromosomes

HAPLOIDS > HAPLOID

HAPLOIDY > HAPLOID

HAPLOLOGY n omission of a repeated occurrence of a sound or syllable in fluent speech

HAPLONT n organism with a haploid number of chromosomes

HAPLONTIC > HAPLONT

HAPLONTS > HAPLONT

HAPLOPIA n normal single vision

HAPLOPIAS > HAPLOPIA

HAPLOSES > HAPLOSIS

HAPLOSIS n production of a haploid number of chromosomes during meiosis

HAPLOTYPE n collection of genetic markers usually inherited together

h

HAPLY archaic word for
> PERHAPS
HAPPED > HAP
HAPPEN vb take place,
occur
HAPPENED > HAPPEN
HAPPENING n event,
occurrence ▷ adj fashionable
and up-to-the-minute
HAPPENS > HAPPEN
HAPPI n type of loose
Japanese coat
HAPPIED > HAPPY
HAPPIER > HAPPY
HAPPIES > HAPPY
HAPPIEST > HAPPY
HAPPILY > HAPPY
HAPPINESS > HAPPY
HAPPING > HAP
HAPPIS > HAPPI
HAPPOSHU n beer-like
Japanese drink
HAPPOSHUS > HAPPOSHU
HAPPY adj feeling or causing
joy ▷ vb make happy
HAPPYING > HAPPY
HAPS > HAP
HAPTEN n incomplete
antigen
HAPTENE same as > HAPTEN
HAPTENES > HAPTENE
HAPTENIC > HAPTENE
HAPTENS > HAPTEN
HAPTERON n organ of
attachment in some aquatic
plants
HAPTERONS > HAPTERON
HAPTIC adj relating to or
based on the sense of touch
HAPTICAL same as
> HAPTIC
HAPTICS n science of sense
of touch
HAPU n subtribe
HAPUKA another name for
> GROPER
HAPUKAS > HAPUKA
HAPUKU same as > HAPUKA
HAPUKUS > HAPUKU
HAPUS > HAPU
HAQUETON same as
> HACQUETON
HAQUETONS > HAQUETON
HARAAM same as > HARAM
HARAKEKE in New Zealand
English, another name for
> FLAX
HARAKEKES > HARAKEKE
HARAM n anything that is
forbidden by Islamic law
HARAMBEE n work chant
used on the E African coast
▷ interj cry of harambee
HARAMBEES > HARAMBEE
HARAMDA same as
> HARAMZADA
HARAMDAS > HARAMDA
HARAMDI same as
> HARAMZADI
HARAMDIS > HARAMDI
HARAMS > HARAM
HARAMZADA n in Indian
English, slang word for an
illegitimate male
HARAMZADI n in Indian
English, slang word for an
illegitimate female

HARANGUE vb address
angrily or forcefully ▷ n
angry or forceful speech
HARANGUED > HARANGUE
HARANGUER > HARANGUE
HARANGUES > HARANGUE
HARASS vb annoy or trouble
constantly
HARASSED > HARASS
HARASSER > HARASS
HARASSERS > HARASS
HARASSES > HARASS
HARASSING > HARASS
HARBINGER n someone or
something that announces
the approach of something
▷ vb announce the approach
or arrival of
HARBOR same as > HARBOUR
HARBORAGE n shelter or
refuge, as for a ship
HARBORED > HARBOR
HARBORER > HARBOR
HARBORERS > HARBOR
HARBORFUL n amount a
harbour can hold
HARBORING > HARBOR
HARBOROUS adj hospitable
HARBORS > HARBOR
HARBOUR n sheltered port
▷ vb maintain secretly in the
mind
HARBOURED > HARBOUR
HARBOURER > HARBOUR
HARBOURS > HARBOUR
HARD adj firm, solid, or rigid
▷ adv with great energy or
effort
HARDASS n tough person
HARDASSES > HARDASS
HARDBACK n book with a
stiff cover ▷ adj of or
denoting a hardback
HARDBACKS > HARDBACK
HARDBAG n rigid container
on a motorcycle
HARDBAGS > HARDBAG
HARDBAKE n almond toffee
HARDBAKES > HARDBAKE
HARDBALL n as in play
hardball act in a ruthless or
uncompromising way
HARDBALLS > HARDBALL
HARDBEAM same as
> HORNBEAM
HARDBEAMS > HARDBEAM
HARDBOARD n thin stiff
board made of compressed
sawdust and wood chips
HARDBODY n attractive
person with a muscular
physique
HARDBOOT n type of skiing
boot
HARDBOOTS > HARDBOOT
HARDBOUND same as
> HARDBACK
HARDCASE n tough person
▷ adj relating to a container
that has a rigid structure
HARDCASES > HARDCASE
HARDCORE n style of rock
music with short fast songs
and little melody
HARDCORES > HARDCORE
HARDCOURT adj (of tennis)
played on hard surface

HARDCOVER same as
> HARDBACK
HARDEDGE n style of
painting in which vividly
coloured subjects are clearly
delineated ▷ adj of, relating
to, or denoting this style of
painting
HARDEDGES > HARDEDGE
HARDEN vb make or become
hard ▷ n rough fabric made
from hards
HARDENED adj toughened
by experience
HARDENER n person or thing
that hardens
HARDENERS > HARDENER
HARDENING n act or
process of becoming or
making hard
HARDENS > HARDEN
HARDER > HARD
HARDEST > HARD
HARDFACE n
uncompromising person
HARDFACES > HARDFACE
HARDGOODS same as
> HARDWARE
HARDGRASS n coarse grass
HARDHACK n woody plant
HARDHACKS > HARDHACK
HARDHAT n hat made of a
hard material for protection
▷ adj typical of construction
workers
HARDHATS > HARDHAT
HARDHEAD same as
> HARDHEADS
HARDHEADS n thistle-like
plant
HARDIER > HARDY
HARDIES > HARDY
HARDIEST > HARDY
HARDIHEAD same as
> HARDIHOOD
HARDIHOOD n courage or
daring
HARDILY adv in a hardy
manner
HARDIMENT same as
> HARDIHOOD
HARDINESS n condition or
quality of being hardy,
robust, or bold
HARDISH > HARD
HARDLINE adj
uncompromising
HARDLINER > HARDLINE
HARDLY adv scarcely or not
at all
HARDMAN n tough, ruthless,
or violent man
HARDMEN > HARDMAN
HARDNESS n quality or
condition of being hard
HARDNOSE n tough person
HARDNOSED adj tough,
shrewd, and practical
HARDNOSES > HARDNOSE
HARDOKE n burdock
HARDOKES > HARDOKE
HARDPACK n rigid backpack
HARDPACKS > HARDPACK
HARDPAN n hard impervious
layer of clay below the soil
HARDPANS > HARDPAN
HARDPARTS n skeleton

HARDROCK adj concerned
with extracting minerals
other than coal ▷ n tough
uncompromising man
HARDROCKS > HARDROCK
HARDS pl n coarse fibres and
other refuse from flax and
hemp
HARDSCAPE n man-made
features used in landscape
architecture
HARDSET adj in difficulties
HARDSHELL adj having a
shell or carapace that is
thick, heavy, or hard
HARDSHIP n suffering
HARDSHIPS > HARDSHIP
HARDSTAND n hard surface
on which vehicles may be
parked
HARDTACK n kind of hard
saltless biscuit, formerly
eaten by sailors
HARDTACKS > HARDTACK
HARDTAIL n mountain bike
with no rear suspension
HARDTAILS > HARDTAIL
HARDTOP n car equipped
with a metal or plastic roof
HARDTOPS > HARDTOP
HARDWARE n metal tools or
implements
HARDWARES > HARDWARE
HARDWIRE vb instal
permanently in computer
HARDWIRED adj (of a circuit
or instruction) permanently
wired into a computer,
replacing separate software
HARDWIRES > HARDWIRE
HARDWOOD n wood of a
broad-leaved tree such as
oak or ash
HARDWOODS > HARDWOOD
HARDY adj able to stand
difficult conditions ▷ n any
blacksmith's tool made with
a square shank
HARE n animal like a large
rabbit, with longer ears and
legs ▷ vb run (away) quickly
HAREBELL n blue
bell-shaped flower
HAREBELLS > HAREBELL
HARED > HARE
HAREEM same as > HAREM
HAREEMS > HAREEM
HARELD n long-tailed duck
HARELDS > HARELD
HARELIKE > HARE
HARELIP n slight split in the
upper lip
HARELIPS > HARELIP
HAREM n Muslim man's wives
and concubines
HAREMS > HAREM
HARES > HARE
HARESTAIL n species of
cotton grass
HAREWOOD n sycamore
wood that has been stained
for use in furniture making
HAREWOODS > HAREWOOD
HARIANA n Indian breed of
cattle
HARIANAS > HARIANA
HARICOT n variety of French
bean

HARICOTS > HARICOT
HARIGALDS pl n intestines
HARIGALS same as > HARIGALDS
HARIJAN n member of an Indian caste
HARIJANS > HARIJAN
HARIM same as > HAREM
HARIMS > HARIM
HARING > HARE
HARIOLATE vb practise divination
HARIRA n Moroccan soup
HARIRAS > HARIRA
HARISH adj like hare
HARISSA n hot paste
HARISSAS > HARISSA
HARK vb listen
HARKED > HARK
HARKEN same as > HEARKEN
HARKENED > HARKEN
HARKENER > HARKEN
HARKENERS > HARKEN
HARKENING > HARKEN
HARKENS > HARKEN
HARKING > HARK
HARKS > HARK
HARL same as > HERL
HARLED > HARL
HARLEQUIN n stock comic character with a diamond-patterned costume and mask ⊳ adj in many colours
HARLING > HARL
HARLINGS > HARL
HARLOT n old-fashioned word for a prostitute ⊳ adj of or like a harlot
HARLOTRY > HARLOT
HARLOTS > HARLOT
HARLS > HARL
HARM vb injure physically, mentally, or morally ⊳ n physical, mental, or moral injury
HARMALA n African plant
HARMALAS > HARMALA
HARMALIN n chemical derived from harmala
HARMALINE same as > HARMALIN
HARMALINS > HARMALIN
HARMAN n constable
HARMANS > HARMAN
HARMATTAN n dusty wind from the Sahara blowing towards the W African coast, esp from November to March
HARMDOING n doing of harm
HARMED > HARM
HARMEL same as > HARMALA
HARMELS > HARMEL
HARMER > HARM
HARMERS > HARM
HARMFUL adj causing or tending to cause harm
HARMFULLY > HARMFUL
HARMIN same as > HARMALIN
HARMINE same as > HARMALIN
HARMINES > HARMINE
HARMING > HARM
HARMINS > HARMIN

HARMLESS adj safe to use, touch, or be near
HARMONIC adj of harmony ⊳ n overtone of a musical note produced when that note is played
HARMONICA n small wind instrument played by sucking and blowing
HARMONICS n science of musical sounds
HARMONIES > HARMONY
HARMONISE same as > HARMONIZE
HARMONIST n person skilled in the art and techniques of harmony
HARMONIUM n keyboard instrument like a small organ
HARMONIZE vb sing or play in harmony
HARMONY n peaceful agreement and cooperation
HARMOST n Spartan governor
HARMOSTS > HARMOST
HARMOSTY n office of a harmost
HARMOTOME n mineral of the zeolite group
HARMS > HARM
HARN n coarse linen
HARNESS n arrangement of straps for attaching a horse to a cart or plough ⊳ vb put a harness on
HARNESSED > HARNESS
HARNESSER > HARNESS
HARNESSES > HARNESS
HARNS > HARN
HARO interj cry meaning alas
HAROS > HARO
HAROSET n Jewish dish eaten at Passover
HAROSETH same as > HAROSET
HAROSETHS > HAROSETH
HAROSETS > HAROSET
HARP n large triangular stringed instrument ⊳ vb play the harp
HARPED > HARP
HARPER > HARP
HARPERS > HARP
HARPIES > HARPY
HARPIN n type of protein
HARPING > HARP
HARPINGS pl n wooden members used for strengthening the bow of a vessel
HARPINS same as > HARPINGS
HARPIST > HARP
HARPISTS > HARP
HARPOON n barbed spear attached to a rope for hunting whales ⊳ vb spear with a harpoon
HARPOONED > HARPOON
HARPOONER > HARPOON
HARPOONS > HARPOON
HARPS > HARP
HARPY n nasty or bad-tempered woman
HARPYLIKE > HARPY
HARQUEBUS variant of > ARQUEBUS

HARRIDAN n nagging or vicious woman
HARRIDANS > HARRIDAN
HARRIED > HARRY
HARRIER n cross-country runner
HARRIERS > HARRIER
HARRIES > HARRY
HARROW n implement used to break up lumps of soil ⊳ vb draw a harrow over
HARROWED > HARROW
HARROWER > HARROW
HARROWERS > HARROW
HARROWING > HARROW
HARROWS > HARROW
HARRUMPH vb clear or make the noise of clearing the throat
HARRUMPHS > HARRUMPH
HARRY vb keep asking (someone) to do something
HARRYING > HARRY
HARSH adj severe and difficult to cope with ⊳ vb ruin or end a state of elation
HARSHED > HARSH
HARSHEN vb make harsh
HARSHENED > HARSHEN
HARSHENS > HARSHEN
HARSHER > HARSH
HARSHES > HARSH
HARSHEST > HARSH
HARSHING > HARSH
HARSHLY > HARSH
HARSHNESS > HARSH
HARSLET same as > HASLET
HARSLETS > HARSLET
HART n adult male deer
HARTAL n (in India) closing shops or suspending work
HARTALS > HARTAL
HARTBEES same as > HARTBEEST
HARTBEEST n African antelope
HARTELY archaic spelling of > HEARTILY
HARTEN same as > HEARTEN
HARTENED > HARTEN
HARTENING > HARTEN
HARTENS > HARTEN
HARTLESSE same as > HEARTLESS
HARTS > HART
HARTSHORN n sal volatile
HARUMPH same as > HARRUMPH
HARUMPHED > HARUMPH
HARUMPHS > HARUMPH
HARUSPEX n priest in ancient Rome
HARUSPICY > HARUSPEX
HARVEST n (season for) the gathering of crops ⊳ vb gather (a ripened crop)
HARVESTED > HARVEST
HARVESTER n harvesting machine, esp a combine harvester
HARVESTS > HARVEST
HAS > HAVE
HASBIAN n former lesbian
HASBIANS > HASBIAN
HASH n dish of diced cooked meat and vegetables reheated ⊳ vb chop into small pieces

HASHED > HASH
HASHEESH same as > HASHISH
HASHES > HASH
HASHHEAD n regular marijuana user
HASHHEADS > HASHHEAD
HASHIER > HASH
HASHIEST > HASH
HASHING > HASH
HASHINGS > HASHING
HASHISH n illegal drug made from the cannabis plant
HASHISHES > HASHISH
HASHMARK n character (#)
HASHMARKS > HASHMARK
HASHTAG n word or phrase used to denote the topic of a Twitter post
HASHTAGS > HASHTAG
HASHY > HASH
HASK n archaic name for a basket for transporting fish
HASKS > HASK
HASLET n loaf of cooked minced pig's offal, eaten cold
HASLETS > HASLET
HASP n type of fastening ⊳ vb secure (a door, window, etc) with a hasp
HASPED > HASP
HASPING > HASP
HASPS > HASP
HASS n as in white hass oatmeal pudding made with sheep's gullet
HASSAR n South American catfish
HASSARS > HASSAR
HASSEL variant of > HASSLE
HASSELS > HASSEL
HASSES > HASS
HASSIUM n chemical element
HASSIUMS > HASSIUM
HASSLE n trouble, bother ⊳ vb bother or annoy
HASSLED > HASSLE
HASSLES > HASSLE
HASSLING > HASSLE
HASSOCK n cushion for kneeling on in church
HASSOCKS > HASSOCK
HASSOCKY adj full of hassocks
HAST singular form of the present tense (indicative mood) of > HAVE
HASTA Spanish for > UNTIL
HASTATE adj shaped like a spear
HASTATED same as > HASTATE
HASTATELY > HASTATE
HASTE n (excessive) quickness ⊳ vb hasten
HASTED > HASTE
HASTEFUL > HASTE
HASTEN vb (cause to) hurry
HASTENED > HASTEN
HASTENER > HASTEN
HASTENERS > HASTEN
HASTENING > HASTEN
HASTENS > HASTEN
HASTES > HASTE
HASTIER > HASTY

h

HASTIEST > HASTY
HASTILY > HASTY
HASTINESS > HASTY
HASTING > HASTE
HASTINGS > HASTE
HASTY adj (too) quick
HAT n covering for the head, often with a brim ▷ vb supply (a person) with a hat or put a hat on (someone)
HATABLE > HATE
HATBAND n band or ribbon around a hat
HATBANDS > HATBAND
HATBOX n box or case for a hat or hats
HATBOXES > HATBOX
HATBRUSH n brush for hats
HATCH vb (cause to) emerge from an egg ▷ n hinged door covering an opening in a floor or wall
HATCHABLE > HATCH
HATCHBACK n car with a lifting door at the back
HATCHECK n cloakroom
HATCHECKS > HATCHECK
HATCHED > HATCH
HATCHEL same as > HECKLE
HATCHELED > HATCHEL
HATCHELS > HATCHEL
HATCHER > HATCH
HATCHERS > HATCH
HATCHERY n place where eggs are hatched under artificial conditions
HATCHES > HATCH
HATCHET n small axe
HATCHETS > HATCHET
HATCHETY adj like a hatchet
HATCHING > HATCH
HATCHINGS > HATCH
HATCHLING n young animal that has newly hatched from an egg
HATCHMENT n diamond-shaped tablet displaying the coat of arms of a dead person
HATCHWAY n opening in the deck of a ship
HATCHWAYS > HATCHWAY
HATE vb dislike intensely ▷ n intense dislike
HATEABLE > HATE
HATED > HATE
HATEFUL adj causing or deserving hate
HATEFULLY > HATEFUL
HATELESS > HATE
HATER > HATE
HATERENT same as > HATRED
HATERENTS > HATERENT
HATERS > HATE
HATES > HATE
HATFUL n amount a hat will hold
HATFULS > HATFUL
HATGUARD n string to keep a hat from blowing off
HATGUARDS > HATGUARD
HATH form of the present tense (indicative mood) of > HAVE
HATHA n as in hatha yoga form of yoga
HATINATOR n small fancy hat

HATING > HATE
HATLESS > HAT
HATLIKE > HAT
HATMAKER n maker of hats
HATMAKERS > HATMAKER
HATPEG n peg to hang hat on
HATPEGS > HATPEG
HATPIN n pin used to secure a woman's hat to her hair
HATPINS > HATPIN
HATRACK n rack for hanging hats on
HATRACKS > HATRACK
HATRED n intense dislike
HATREDS > HATRED
HATS > HAT
HATSFUL > HATFUL
HATSTAND n frame or pole equipped with hooks or arms for hanging up hats, coats, etc
HATSTANDS > HATSTAND
HATTED > HAT
HATTER n person who makes and sells hats ▷ vb annoy
HATTERED > HATTER
HATTERIA n species of reptile
HATTERIAS > HATTERIA
HATTERING > HATTER
HATTERS > HATTER
HATTING > HAT
HATTINGS > HAT
HATTOCK n small hat
HATTOCKS > HATTOCK
HAUBERK n long sleeveless coat of mail
HAUBERKS > HAUBERK
HAUBOIS same as > HAUTBOY
HAUD Scot word for > HOLD
HAUDING > HAUD
HAUDS > HAUD
HAUF Scot word for > HALF
HAUFS > HAUF
HAUGH n low-lying often alluvial riverside meadow
HAUGHS > HAUGH
HAUGHT same as > HAUGHTY
HAUGHTIER > HAUGHTY
HAUGHTILY > HAUGHTY
HAUGHTY adj proud, arrogant
HAUL vb pull or drag with effort ▷ n hauling
HAULAGE n (charge for) transporting goods
HAULAGES > HAULAGE
HAULBACK n (in lumbering) line used to bring a cable back
HAULBACKS > HAULBACK
HAULD Scots word for > HOLD
HAULDS > HAULD
HAULED > HAUL
HAULER same as > HAULIER
HAULERS > HAULER
HAULIER n firm or person that transports goods by road
HAULIERS > HAULIER
HAULING n act of hauling
HAULINGS > HAULING
HAULM n stalks of beans, peas, or potatoes collectively

HAULMIER > HAULMY
HAULMIEST > HAULMY
HAULMS > HAULM
HAULMY adj having haulms
HAULOUT n act of hauling a boat out of water
HAULOUTS > HAULOUT
HAULS > HAUL
HAULST same as > HALSE
HAULT same as > HAUGHTY
HAULYARD same as > HALYARD
HAULYARDS > HAULYARD
HAUN n Scot word for hand
HAUNCH n human hip or fleshy hindquarter of an animal ▷ vb cause (an animal) to come down on its haunches
HAUNCHED > HAUNCH
HAUNCHES > HAUNCH
HAUNCHING > HAUNCH
HAUNS > HAUN
HAUNT vb visit in the form of a ghost ▷ n place visited frequently
HAUNTED adj frequented by ghosts
HAUNTER > HAUNT
HAUNTERS > HAUNT
HAUNTING adj memorably beautiful or sad
HAUNTINGS > HAUNT
HAUNTS > HAUNT
HAURIANT adj rising
HAURIENT same as > HAURIANT
HAUSE same as > HALSE
HAUSED > HAUSE
HAUSEN n variety of sturgeon
HAUSENS > HAUSEN
HAUSES > HAUSE
HAUSFRAU n German housewife
HAUSFRAUS > HAUSFRAU
HAUSING > HAUSE
HAUSTELLA n plural of haustellum: tip of the proboscis of an insect
HAUSTORIA n plural of haustorium: organ of a parasitic plant that absorbs food and water from host tissues
HAUT same as > HAUGHTY
HAUTBOIS same as > HAUTBOY
HAUTBOY n type of strawberry
HAUTBOYS > HAUTBOY
HAUTE adj French word meaning high
HAUTER > HAUT
HAUTEST > HAUT
HAUTEUR n haughtiness
HAUTEURS > HAUTEUR
HAUYNE n blue mineral containing calcium
HAUYNES > HAUYNE
HAVARTI n Danish cheese
HAVARTIS > HAVARTI
HAVDALAH n ceremony at the end of the Sabbath
HAVDALAHS > HAVDALAH
HAVDOLOH same as > HAVDALAH

HAVDOLOHS > HAVDOLOH
HAVE vb possess, hold
HAVELOCK n cap flap covering the back of the neck
HAVELOCKS > HAVELOCK
HAVEN n place of safety ▷ vb secure or shelter in or as if in a haven
HAVENED > HAVEN
HAVENING > HAVEN
HAVENLESS > HAVEN
HAVENS > HAVEN
HAVEOUR same as > HAVIOR
HAVEOURS > HAVEOUR
HAVER vb talk nonsense ▷ n nonsense
HAVERED > HAVER
HAVEREL n fool
HAVERELS > HAVEREL
HAVERING > HAVER
HAVERINGS > HAVER
HAVERS > HAVER
HAVERSACK n canvas bag carried on the back or shoulder
HAVERSINE n half the value of the versed sine
HAVES > HAVE
HAVILDAR n noncommissioned officer in the Indian army, equivalent in rank to sergeant
HAVILDARS > HAVILDAR
HAVING > HAVE
HAVINGS > HAVE
HAVIOR same as > HAVIOUR
HAVIORS > HAVIOR
HAVIOUR n possession
HAVIOURS > HAVIOUR
HAVOC n disorder and confusion ▷ vb lay waste
HAVOCKED > HAVOC
HAVOCKER > HAVOC
HAVOCKERS > HAVOC
HAVOCKING > HAVOC
HAVOCS > HAVOC
HAW n hawthorn berry ▷ vb make an inarticulate utterance
HAWALA n Middle Eastern system of money transfer
HAWALAS > HAWALA
HAWBUCK n bumpkin
HAWBUCKS > HAWBUCK
HAWEATER n resident of Manitoulin Island, Ontario
HAWEATERS > HAWEATER
HAWED > HAW
HAWFINCH n European finch with a stout bill and brown plumage with black-and-white wings
HAWING > HAW
HAWK n bird of prey ▷ vb offer (goods) for sale in the street or door-to-door
HAWKBELL n bell fitted to a hawk's leg
HAWKBELLS > HAWKBELL
HAWKBILL same as > HAWKSBILL
HAWKBILLS > HAWKBILL
HAWKBIT n any of three perennial plants
HAWKBITS > HAWKBIT
HAWKED > HAWK
HAWKER n travelling salesperson

HAWKERS > HAWKER
HAWKEY same as **>** HOCKEY
HAWKEYED adj having extremely keen sight
HAWKEYS > HAWKEY
HAWKIE n cow with white stripe on face
HAWKIES > HAWKIE
HAWKING another name for **>** FALCONRY
HAWKINGS > HAWKING
HAWKISH adj favouring the use of force rather than diplomacy
HAWKISHLY > HAWKISH
HAWKIT adj having a white streak
HAWKLIKE > HAWK
HAWKMOTH n narrow-winged moth
HAWKMOTHS > HAWKMOTH
HAWKNOSE n hooked nose
HAWKNOSES > HAWKNOSE
HAWKS > HAWK
HAWKSBILL n type of turtle
HAWKSHAW n private detective
HAWKSHAWS > HAWKSHAW
HAWKWEED n hairy plant with clusters of dandelion-like flowers
HAWKWEEDS > HAWKWEED
HAWM vb be idle and relaxed
HAWMED > HAWM
HAWMING > HAWM
HAWMS > HAWM
HAWS > HAW
HAWSE vb of boats, pitch violently when at anchor
HAWSED > HAWSE
HAWSEHOLE n one of the holes in the upper part of the bows of a vessel through which the anchor ropes pass
HAWSEPIPE n strong metal pipe through which an anchor rope passes
HAWSER n large rope used on a ship
HAWSERS > HAWSER
HAWSES > HAWSE
HAWSING > HAWSE
HAWTHORN n thorny shrub or tree
HAWTHORNS > HAWTHORN
HAWTHORNY adj resembling hawthorns
HAY n grass cut and dried as fodder ▷ vb cut, dry, and store (grass, clover, etc) as fodder
HAYBAND n rope made by twisting hay together
HAYBANDS > HAYBAND
HAYBOX n airtight box used to keep partially cooked food warm
HAYBOXES > HAYBOX
HAYCATION n working holiday at a farm
HAYCOCK n pile of hay left until dry enough to move
HAYCOCKS > HAYCOCK
HAYED > HAY
HAYER n person who makes hay
HAYERS > HAYER

HAYEY > HAY
HAYFIELD n field of hay
HAYFIELDS > HAYFIELD
HAYFORK n long-handled fork
HAYFORKS > HAYFORK
HAYIER > HAYEY
HAYIEST > HAYEY
HAYING > HAY
HAYINGS > HAY
HAYLAGE n type of hay for animal fodder
HAYLAGES > HAYLAGE
HAYLE n welfare
HAYLES > HAYLE
HAYLOFT n loft for storing hay
HAYLOFTS > HAYLOFT
HAYMAKER n person who helps to cut, turn, toss, spread, or carry hay
HAYMAKERS > HAYMAKER
HAYMAKING > HAYMAKER
HAYMOW n part of a barn where hay is stored
HAYMOWS > HAYMOW
HAYRACK n rack for holding hay for feeding to animals
HAYRACKS > HAYRACK
HAYRAKE n large rake used to collect hay
HAYRAKES > HAYRAKE
HAYRICK same as **>** HAYSTACK
HAYRICKS > HAYRICK
HAYRIDE n pleasure trip in hay wagon
HAYRIDES > HAYRIDE
HAYS > HAY
HAYSEED n seeds or fragments of grass or straw
HAYSEEDS > HAYSEED
HAYSEL n season for making hay
HAYSELS > HAYSEL
HAYSTACK n large pile of stored hay
HAYSTACKS > HAYSTACK
HAYWARD n parish officer in charge of enclosures and fences
HAYWARDS > HAYWARD
HAYWIRE adj (of things) not functioning properly ▷ n wire for binding hay
HAYWIRES > HAYWIRE
HAZAN same as **>** CANTOR
HAZANIM > HAZAN
HAZANS > HAZAN
HAZARD n something that could be dangerous ▷ vb put in danger
HAZARDED > HAZARD
HAZARDER > HAZARD
HAZARDERS > HAZARD
HAZARDING > HAZARD
HAZARDIZE same as **>** HAZARD
HAZARDOUS adj involving great risk
HAZARDRY n taking of risks
HAZARDS > HAZARD
HAZE n mist, often caused by heat ▷ vb make or become hazy
HAZED > HAZE

HAZEL n small tree producing edible nuts ▷ adj (of eyes) greenish-brown
HAZELHEN n type of grouse
HAZELHENS > HAZELHEN
HAZELLY > HAZEL
HAZELNUT n nut of a hazel shrub, which has a smooth shiny hard shell
HAZELNUTS > HAZELNUT
HAZELS > HAZEL
HAZELWOOD n the wood of the hazel
HAZER > HAZE
HAZERS > HAZE
HAZES > HAZE
HAZIER > HAZY
HAZIEST > HAZY
HAZILY > HAZY
HAZINESS > HAZY
HAZING > HAZE
HAZINGS > HAZE
HAZMAT n hazardous material
HAZMATS > HAZMAT
HAZY adj not clear, misty
HAZZAN same as **>** CANTOR
HAZZANIM > HAZZAN
HAZZANS > HAZZAN
HE pron male person or animal ▷ n male person or animal ▷ interj expression of amusement or derision
HEAD n upper or front part of the body ▷ adj chief, principal ▷ vb be at the top or front of
HEADACHE n continuous pain in the head
HEADACHES > HEADACHE
HEADACHEY same as **>** HEADACHY
HEADACHY adj suffering from, caused by, or likely to cause a headache
HEADAGE n payment to farmer based on animals owned
HEADAGES > HEADAGE
HEADBAND n ribbon or band worn around the head
HEADBANDS > HEADBAND
HEADBANG vb nod one's head violently to the beat of loud rock music
HEADBANGS > HEADBANG
HEADBOARD n vertical board at the top end of a bed
HEADCASE n insane person
HEADCASES > HEADCASE
HEADCHAIR n chair with support for the head
HEADCLOTH n kerchief worn on the head
HEADCOUNT n count of number of people present
HEADDRESS n decorative head covering
HEADED adj having a head or heads
HEADEND n facility from which cable television is transmitted
HEADENDS > HEADEND
HEADER n striking a ball with the head
HEADERS > HEADER

HEADFAST n mooring rope at the bows of a ship
HEADFASTS > HEADFAST
HEADFIRST adv with the head foremost
HEADFISH same as **>** SUNFISH
HEADFRAME n structure supporting winding machinery at mine
HEADFUCK n taboo slang for experience that is wildly exciting or impressive
HEADFUCKS > HEADFUCK
HEADFUL n amount head will hold
HEADFULS > HEADFUL
HEADGATE n gate used to control the flow of water at the upper end of a lock or conduit
HEADGATES > HEADGATE
HEADGEAR n hats collectively
HEADGEARS > HEADGEAR
HEADGUARD n padded helmet worn to protect the head in contact sports
HEADHUNT vb recruit employee from another company
HEADHUNTS > HEADHUNT
HEADIER > HEADY
HEADIEST > HEADY
HEADILY > HEADY
HEADINESS > HEADY
HEADING same as **>** HEAD
HEADINGS > HEADING
HEADLAMP same as **>** HEADLIGHT
HEADLAMPS > HEADLAMP
HEADLAND n area of land jutting out into the sea
HEADLANDS > HEADLAND
HEADLEASE n main lease often subdivided
HEADLESS adj without a head
HEADLIGHT n powerful light on the front of a vehicle
HEADLIKE > HEAD
HEADLINE n title at the top of a newspaper article, esp on the front page
HEADLINED > HEADLINE
HEADLINER n performer given prominent billing
HEADLINES > HEADLINE
HEADLOCK n wrestling hold
HEADLOCKS > HEADLOCK
HEADLONG adj with the head first ▷ adv with the head foremost
HEADMAN n chief or leader
HEADMARK n characteristic
HEADMARKS > HEADMARK
HEADMEN > HEADMAN
HEADMOST less common word for **>** FOREMOST
HEADNOTE n note at book chapter head
HEADNOTES > HEADNOTE
HEADPEACE archaic form of **>** HEADPIECE
HEADPHONE n small loudspeaker held against the ear

HEADPIECE n decorative band at the top of a page, chapter, etc

HEADPIN another word for > KINGPIN

HEADPINS > HEADPIN

HEADPOND n artificial pond behind a dam

HEADPONDS > HEADPOND

HEADRACE n channel that carries water to a water wheel, turbine, etc

HEADRACES > HEADRACE

HEADRAIL n end of the table from which play is started, nearest the baulkline

HEADRAILS > HEADRAIL

HEADREACH n distance made to windward while tacking ▷ vb gain distance over (another boat) when tacking

HEADREST n support for the head, as on a dentist's chair or car seat

HEADRESTS > HEADREST

HEADRIG n edge of ploughed field

HEADRIGS > HEADRIG

HEADRING n African head decoration

HEADRINGS > HEADRING

HEADROOM n space above person's head in a vehicle

HEADROOMS > HEADROOM

HEADROPE n rope round an animal's head

HEADROPES > HEADROPE

HEADS adv with the side of a coin with a head on it uppermost

HEADSAIL n any sail set forward of the foremast

HEADSAILS > HEADSAIL

HEADSCARF n scarf for the head, often worn tied under the chin

HEADSET n pair of headphones

HEADSETS > HEADSET

HEADSHAKE n gesture of shaking head

HEADSHIP n position or state of being a leader, esp the head teacher of a school

HEADSHIPS > HEADSHIP

HEADSHOT n photo of person's head

HEADSHOTS > HEADSHOT

HEADSMAN n (formerly) an executioner who beheaded condemned persons

HEADSMEN > HEADSMAN

HEADSPACE n space between bolt and cartridge in a rifle

HEADSTALL n part of a bridle that fits round a horse's head

HEADSTAND n act or an instance of balancing on the head, usually with the hands as support

HEADSTAY n rope from mast to bow on ship

HEADSTAYS > HEADSTAY

HEADSTICK n piece of wood formerly used in typesetting

HEADSTOCK n part of a machine that supports and transmits the drive to the chuck

HEADSTONE n memorial stone on a grave

HEADWALL n steep slope at the head of a glacial cirque

HEADWALLS > HEADWALL

HEADWARD same as > HEADWARDS

HEADWARDS adv backwards beyond the original source

HEADWATER n highest part of river

HEADWAY same as > HEADROOM

HEADWAYS > HEADWAY

HEADWIND n wind blowing against the course of an aircraft or ship

HEADWINDS > HEADWIND

HEADWORD n key word placed at the beginning of a line, paragraph, etc, as in a dictionary entry

HEADWORDS > HEADWORD

HEADWORK n intellectual labour

HEADWORKS > HEADWORK

HEADY adj intoxicating or exciting

HEAL vb make or become well

HEALABLE > HEAL

HEALD same as > HEDDLE

HEALDED > HEALD

HEALDING > HEALD

HEALDS > HEALD

HEALED > HEAL

HEALEE n person who is being healed

HEALEES > HEALEE

HEALER > HEAL

HEALERS > HEAL

HEALING > HEAL

HEALINGLY > HEAL

HEALINGS > HEAL

HEALS > HEAL

HEALSOME Scots word for > WHOLESOME

HEALTH n normal (good) condition of someone's body ▷ interj exclamation wishing someone good health as part of a toast

HEALTHFUL same as > HEALTHY

HEALTHIER > HEALTHY

HEALTHILY > HEALTHY

HEALTHISM n lifestyle that prioritizes health and fitness over anything else

HEALTHS > HEALTH

HEALTHY adj having good health

HEAME old form of > HOME

HEAP n pile of things one on top of another ▷ vb gather into a pile

HEAPED > HEAP

HEAPER > HEAP

HEAPERS > HEAP

HEAPIER > HEAPY

HEAPIEST > HEAPY

HEAPING adj (of a spoonful) heaped

HEAPS > HEAP

HEAPSTEAD n buildings at mine

HEAPY adj having many heaps

HEAR vb perceive (a sound) by ear

HEARABLE > HEAR

HEARD same as > HERD

HEARDS > HEARD

HEARE old form of > HAIR

HEARER > HEAR

HEARERS > HEAR

HEARES > HEARE

HEARIE old form of > HAIRY

HEARING > HEAR

HEARINGS > HEAR

HEARKEN vb listen

HEARKENED > HEARKEN

HEARKENER > HEARKEN

HEARKENS > HEARKEN

HEARS > HEAR

HEARSAY n gossip, rumour

HEARSAYS > HEARSAY

HEARSE n funeral car used to carry a coffin ▷ vb put in hearse

HEARSED > HEARSE

HEARSES > HEARSE

HEARSIER > HEARSY

HEARSIEST > HEARSY

HEARSING > HEARSE

HEARSY adj like a hearse

HEART n organ that pumps blood round the body ▷ vb (of vegetables) form a heart

HEARTACHE n intense anguish

HEARTBEAT n one complete pulsation of the heart

HEARTBURN n burning sensation in the chest caused by indigestion

HEARTED > HEART

HEARTEN vb encourage, make cheerful

HEARTENED > HEARTEN

HEARTENER > HEARTEN

HEARTENS > HEARTEN

HEARTFELT adj felt sincerely or strongly

HEARTFREE adj not in love

HEARTH n floor of a fireplace

HEARTHRUG n rug laid before fireplace

HEARTHS > HEARTH

HEARTIER > HEARTY

HEARTIES > HEARTY

HEARTIEST > HEARTY

HEARTIKIN n little heart

HEARTILY adv thoroughly or vigorously

HEARTING > HEART

HEARTLAND n central region of a country or continent

HEARTLESS adj cruel, unkind

HEARTLET n little heart

HEARTLETS > HEART

HEARTLING n little heart

HEARTLY adv vigorously

HEARTPEA same as > HEARTSEED

HEARTPEAS > HEARTPEA

HEARTS n card game

HEARTSEED n type of vine

HEARTSICK adj deeply dejected or despondent

HEARTSINK n patient who visits a doctor with multiple non-specific symptoms that are impossible to treat

HEARTSOME adj cheering or encouraging

HEARTSORE adj greatly distressed ▷ n cause of pain in the heart or the pain itself

HEARTWOOD n central core of dark hard wood in tree trunks

HEARTWORM n parasitic nematode worm that lives in the heart and bloodstream of vertebrates

HEARTY adj substantial, nourishing ▷ n comrade, esp a sailor

HEAST same as > HEST

HEASTE same as > HEST

HEASTES > HEASTE

HEASTS > HEAST

HEAT vb make or become hot ▷ n state of being hot

HEATABLE > HEAT

HEATED adj angry and excited

HEATEDLY > HEATED

HEATER n device for supplying heat

HEATERS > HEATER

HEATH n area of open uncultivated land

HEATHBIRD n black grouse

HEATHCOCK same as > BLACKCOCK

HEATHEN n person who does not believe in an established religion ▷ adj of or relating to heathen peoples

HEATHENRY > HEATHEN

HEATHENS > HEATHEN

HEATHER n low-growing plant ▷ adj of a heather colour

HEATHERED > HEATHER

HEATHERS > HEATHER

HEATHERY > HEATHER

HEATHFOWL Compare > MOORFOWL

HEATHIER > HEATH

HEATHIEST > HEATH

HEATHLAND n area of heath

HEATHLESS > HEATH

HEATHLIKE > HEATH

HEATHS > HEATH

HEATHY > HEATH

HEATING n device or system for supplying heat

HEATINGS > HEATING

HEATLESS > HEAT

HEATPROOF > HEAT

HEATS > HEAT

HEATSPOT n spot on skin produced by heat

HEATSPOTS > HEATSPOT

HEATWAVE n prolonged period of unusually hot weather

HEATWAVES > HEATWAVE

HEAUME n large helmet reaching the shoulders

HEAUMES > HEAUME

HEAVE vb lift with effort ▷ n heaving

HEAVED > HEAVE

HEAVEN *n* place believed to be the home of God

HEAVENLY *adj* of or like heaven

HEAVENS > HEAVEN

HEAVER > HEAVE

HEAVERS > HEAVE

HEAVES > HEAVE

HEAVIER > HEAVY

HEAVIES > HEAVY

HEAVIEST > HEAVY

HEAVILY > HEAVY

HEAVINESS > HEAVY

HEAVING > HEAVE

HEAVINGS > HEAVE

HEAVY *adj* of great weight ▷ *n* person hired to threaten violence

HEAVYISH *n* rather heavy

HEAVYSET *adj* stockily built

HEBDOMAD *n* number seven or a group of seven

HEBDOMADS > HEBDOMAD

HEBE *n* any of various flowering shrubs

HEBEN *old form of >* EBONY

HEBENON *n* source of poison

HEBENONS > HEBENON

HEBENS > HEBEN

HEBES > HEBE

HEBETANT *adj* causing dullness

HEBETATE *adj* (of plant parts) having a blunt or soft point ▷ *vb* make or become blunted

HEBETATED > HEBETATE

HEBETATES > HEBETATE

HEBETIC *adj* of or relating to puberty

HEBETUDE *n* mental dullness or lethargy

HEBETUDES > HEBETUDE

HEBONA *same as >* HEBENON

HEBONAS > HEBONA

HEBRAISE *same as* > HEBRAIZE

HEBRAISED > HEBRAISE

HEBRAISES > HEBRAISE

HEBRAIZE *vb* become or cause to become Hebrew or Hebraic

HEBRAIZED > HEBRAIZE

HEBRAIZES > HEBRAIZE

HECATOMB *n* sacrifice of 100 oxen

HECATOMBS > HECATOMB

HECH *interj* expression of surprise

HECHT *same as >* HIGHT

HECHTING > HECHT

HECHTS > HECHT

HECK *interj* mild exclamation of surprise, irritation, etc ▷ *n* frame for obstructing the passage of fish in a river

HECKLE *vb* interrupt with comments, questions, or taunts ▷ *n* instrument for combing flax or hemp

HECKLED > HECKLE

HECKLER > HECKLE

HECKLERS > HECKLE

HECKLES > HECKLE

HECKLING > HECKLE

HECKLINGS > HECKLE

HECKS > HECK

HECKUVA *adj* heck of a

HECOGENIN *n* plant chemical

HECTARE *n* one hundred ares

HECTARES > HECTARE

HECTIC *adj* rushed or busy ▷ *n* hectic fever or flush

HECTICAL *same as >* HECTIC

HECTICLY > HECTIC

HECTICS > HECTIC

HECTOGRAM *n* one hundred grams. 1 hectogram is equivalent to 3.527 ounces

HECTOR *vb* bully ▷ *n* blustering bully

HECTORED > HECTOR

HECTORER > HECTOR

HECTORERS > HECTOR

HECTORING > HECTOR

HECTORISM > HECTOR

HECTORLY > HECTOR

HECTORS > HECTOR

HEDARIM *same as* > HADARIM

HEDDLE *n* frame on a loom ▷ *vb* pass thread through a heddle

HEDDLED > HEDDLE

HEDDLES > HEDDLE

HEDDLING > HEDDLE

HEDER *variant spelling of* > CHEDER

HEDERA *n* ivy

HEDERAL > HEDERA

HEDERAS > HEDERA

HEDERATED *adj* honoured with crown of ivy

HEDERS > HEDER

HEDGE *n* row of bushes forming a barrier or boundary ▷ *vb* be evasive or noncommittal

HEDGEBILL *n* tool for pruning a hedge

HEDGED > HEDGE

HEDGEHOG *n* small mammal with a protective covering of spines

HEDGEHOGS > HEDGEHOG

HEDGEHOP *vb* (of an aircraft) to fly close to the ground, as in crop spraying

HEDGEHOPS > HEDGEHOP

HEDGEPIG *same as* > HEDGEHOG

HEDGEPIGS > HEDGEPIG

HEDGER > HEDGE

HEDGEROW *n* bushes forming a hedge

HEDGEROWS > HEDGEROW

HEDGERS > HEDGE

HEDGES > HEDGE

HEDGIER > HEDGE

HEDGIEST > HEDGE

HEDGING > HEDGE

HEDGINGLY > HEDGE

HEDGINGS > HEDGE

HEDGY > HEDGE

HEDONIC > HEDONISM

HEDONICS *n* branch of psychology concerned with the study of pleasant and unpleasant sensations

HEDONISM *n* doctrine that pleasure is the most important thing in life

HEDONISMS > HEDONISM

HEDONIST > HEDONISM

HEDONISTS > HEDONISM

HEDYPHANE *n* variety of lead ore

HEDYSARUM *n* leguminous plant of the genus Hedysarum

HEED *n* careful attention ▷ *vb* pay careful attention to

HEEDED > HEED

HEEDER > HEED

HEEDERS > HEED

HEEDFUL > HEED

HEEDFULLY > HEED

HEEDIER > HEEDY

HEEDIEST > HEEDY

HEEDINESS > HEED

HEEDING > HEED

HEEDLESS *adj* taking no notice

HEEDS > HEED

HEEDY *adj* heedful; attentive

HEEHAW *interj* representation of the braying sound of a donkey ▷ *vb* make braying sound

HEEHAWED > HEEHAW

HEEHAWING > HEEHAW

HEEHAWS > HEEHAW

HEEL *n* back part of the foot ▷ *vb* repair the heel of (a shoe)

HEELBALL *n* mixture of beeswax and lampblack used by shoemakers

HEELBALLS > HEELBALL

HEELBAR *n* small shop where shoes are repaired

HEELBARS > HEELBAR

HEELED > HEEL

HEELER *n* dog that herds cattle by biting at their heels

HEELERS > HEELER

HEELING > HEEL

HEELINGS > HEEL

HEELLESS > HEEL

HEELPIECE *n* piece of a shoe, stocking, etc, designed to fit the heel

HEELPLATE *n* reinforcing piece of metal

HEELPOST *n* post for carrying the hinges of a door or gate

HEELPOSTS > HEELPOST

HEELS > HEEL

HEELTAP *n* layer of leather, etc, in the heel of a shoe

HEELTAPS > HEELTAP

HEEZE *Scots word for >* HOIST

HEEZED > HEEZE

HEEZES > HEEZE

HEEZIE *n* act of lifting

HEEZIES > HEEZIE

HEEZING > HEEZE

HEFT *vb* assess the weight of (something) by lifting ▷ *n* weight

HEFTE *same as >* HEAVE

HEFTED > HEFT

HEFTER > HEFT

HEFTERS > HEFT

HEFTIER > HEFTY

HEFTIEST > HEFTY

HEFTILY > HEFTY

HEFTINESS > HEFTY

HEFTING > HEFT

HEFTS > HEFT

HEFTY *adj* large, heavy, or strong

HEGARI *n* African sorghum

HEGARIS > HEGARI

HEGEMON *n* person in authority

HEGEMONIC > HEGEMONY

HEGEMONS > HEGEMON

HEGEMONY *n* political domination

HEGIRA *n* emigration escape or flight

HEGIRAS > HEGIRA

HEGUMEN *n* head of a monastery of the Eastern Church

HEGUMENE *n* head of Greek nunnery

HEGUMENES > HEGUMENE

HEGUMENOI > HEGUMENOS

HEGUMENOS *same as* > HEGUMEN

HEGUMENS > HEGUMEN

HEGUMENY *n* office of hegumen

HEH *interj* exclamation of surprise or inquiry

HEHS > HEH

HEID *Scot word for >* HEAD

HEIDS > HEID

HEIDUC *n* Hungarian guerilla warrior

HEIDUCS > HEIDUC

HEIFER *n* young cow

HEIFERS > HEIFER

HEIGH *same as >* HEY

HEIGHT *n* distance from base to top

HEIGHTEN *vb* make or become higher or more intense

HEIGHTENS > HEIGHTEN

HEIGHTH *obsolete form of* > HEIGHT

HEIGHTHS > HEIGHTH

HEIGHTISM *n* discrimination based on people's heights

HEIGHTS > HEIGHT

HEIL *vb* give a German greeting

HEILED > HEIL

HEILING > HEIL

HEILS > HEIL

HEIMISH *adj* comfortable

HEINIE *n* buttocks

HEINIES > HEINIE

HEINOUS *adj* evil and shocking

HEINOUSLY > HEINOUS

HEIR *n* person entitled to inherit property or rank ▷ *vb* inherit

HEIRDOM *n* succession by right of blood

HEIRDOMS > HEIRDOM

HEIRED > HEIR

HEIRESS *n* woman who inherits or expects to inherit great wealth

HEIRESSES > HEIRESS

HEIRING > HEIR

HEIRLESS > HEIR

HEIRLOOM *n* object that has belonged to a family for generations

SECTION 1: Words between 2 and 9 letters in length

h

HEIRLOOMS > HEIRLOOM

HEIRS > HEIR

HEIRSHIP n state or condition of being an heir

HEIRSHIPS > HEIRSHIP

HEISHI n Native American shell jewellery

HEIST n robbery ▷ vb steal or burgle

HEISTED > HEIST

HEISTER > HEIST

HEISTERS > HEIST

HEISTING > HEIST

HEISTS > HEIST

HEITIKI n Māori neck ornament of greenstone

HEITIKIS > HEITIKI

HEJAB same as > HIJAB

HEJABS > HEJAB

HEJIRA same as > HEGIRA

HEJIRAS > HEJIRA

HEJRA same as > HEGIRA

HEJRAS > HEJRA

HEKETARA n small shrub that has flowers with white petals and yellow centres

HEKETARAS > HEKETARA

HEKTARE same as > HECTARE

HEKTARES > HEKTARE

HEKTOGRAM same as > HECTOGRAM

HELCOID adj having ulcers

HELD > HOLD

HELE vb as in hele in insert (cuttings, etc) into soil

HELED > HELE

HELENIUM n plant with daisy-like yellow or variegated flowers

HELENIUMS > HELENIUM

HELES > HELE

HELIAC same as > HELIACAL

HELIACAL adj as in heliacal rising rising of a celestial object at approximately the same time as the rising of the sun

HELIAST n ancient Greek juror

HELIASTS > HELIAST

HELIBORNE adj carried in helicopter

HELIBUS n helicopter carrying passengers

HELIBUSES > HELIBUS

HELICAL adj spiral

HELICALLY > HELICAL

HELICASE n enzyme vital to all living organisms

HELICASES > HELICASE

HELICES > HELIX

HELICITY n projection of the spin of an elementary particle on the direction of propagation

HELICLINE n spiral-shaped ramp

HELICOID adj shaped like a spiral ▷ n any surface resembling that of a screw thread

HELICOIDS > HELICOID

HELICON n bass tuba

HELICONIA n tropical flowering plant

HELICONS > HELICON

HELICOPT vb transport using a helicopter

HELICOPTS > HELICOPT

HELICTITE n twisted stalactite

HELIDECK n landing deck for helicopters on ships, oil platforms, etc

HELIDECKS > HELIDECK

HELIDROME n small airport for helicopters

HELILIFT vb transport by helicopter

HELILIFTS > HELILIFT

HELIMAN n helicopter pilot

HELIMEN > HELIMAN

HELING > HELE

HELIO n instrument for sending messages in Morse code

HELIODOR n clear yellow form of beryl used as a gemstone

HELIODORS > HELIODOR

HELIOGRAM n message sent by reflecting the sun's rays in a mirror

HELIOLOGY n study of sun

HELIOPSES > HELIOPSIS

HELIOPSIS n type of flowering plant

HELIOS > HELIO

HELIOSES > HELIOSIS

HELIOSIS n bad effect of overexposure to the sun

HELIOSTAT n astronomical instrument used to reflect the light of the sun in a constant direction

HELIOTYPE n printing process in which an impression is taken in ink from a gelatine surface that has been exposed under a negative and prepared for printing

HELIOTYPY same as > HELIOTYPE

HELIOZOAN n type of protozoan, typically having a siliceous shell and stiff radiating cytoplasmic projections

HELIOZOIC > HELIOZOAN

HELIPAD n place for helicopters to land and take off

HELIPADS > HELIPAD

HELIPILOT n helicopter pilot

HELIPORT n airport for helicopters

HELIPORTS > HELIPORT

HELISKI vb ski down a mountain after ascending it by helicopter

HELISKIED > HELISKI

HELISKIS > HELISKI

HELISTOP n landing place for helicopter

HELISTOPS > HELISTOP

HELITACK n use of helicopters to extinguish a forest fire

HELITACKS > HELITACK

HELIUM n very light colourless odourless gas

HELIUMS > HELIUM

HELIX n spiral

HELIXES > HELIX

HELL n believed to be where wicked people go when they die ▷ vb act wildly

HELLBENT adj intent

HELLBOX n (in printing) container for broken type

HELLBOXES > HELLBOX

HELLBROTH n evil concoction

HELLCAT n spiteful fierce-tempered woman

HELLCATS > HELLCAT

HELLDIVER n small greyish-brown North American grebe

HELLEBORE n plant with white flowers that bloom in winter

HELLED > HELL

HELLENISE same as > HELLENIZE

HELLENIZE vb make or become like the ancient Greeks

HELLER n monetary unit of the Czech Republic and Slovakia

HELLERI n Central American fish

HELLERIES > HELLERY

HELLERIS > HELLERI

HELLERS > HELLER

HELLERY n wild or mischievous behaviour

HELLFIRE n torment of hell, imagined as eternal fire

HELLFIRES > HELLFIRE

HELLHOLE n unpleasant or evil place

HELLHOLES > HELLHOLE

HELLHOUND n hound of hell

HELLICAT n evil creature

HELLICATS > HELLICAT

HELLIER n slater

HELLIERS > HELLIER

HELLING > HELL

HELLION n rough or rowdy person, esp a child

HELLIONS > HELLION

HELLISH adj very unpleasant ▷ adv (intensifier) extremely

HELLISHLY > HELLISH

HELLKITE n bird of prey from hell

HELLKITES > HELLKITE

HELLO interj expression of greeting or surprise ▷ n act of saying 'hello' ▷ sentence substitute expression of greeting ▷ vb say hello

HELLOED > HELLO

HELLOES > HELLO

HELLOING > HELLO

HELLOS > HELLO

HELLOVA same as > HELLUVA

HELLS > HELL

HELLSCAPE n harshly unpleasant environment

HELLUVA adj extremely good

HELLWARD adj towards hell

HELLWARDS adv towards hell

HELM n tiller or wheel for steering a ship ▷ vb direct or steer

HELMED > HELM

HELMER n film director

HELMERS > HELMER

HELMET n hard hat worn for protection

HELMETED > HELMET

HELMETING n wearing or provision of a helmet

HELMETS > HELMET

HELMING > HELM

HELMINTH n any parasitic worm, esp a nematode or fluke

HELMINTHS > HELMINTH

HELMLESS > HELM

HELMS > HELM

HELMSMAN n person at the helm who steers the ship

HELMSMEN > HELMSMAN

HELO n helicopter

HELOPHYTE n any perennial marsh plant that bears its overwintering buds in the mud below the surface

HELOS > HELO

HELOT n serf or slave

HELOTAGE same as > HELOTISM

HELOTAGES > HELOTAGE

HELOTISM n condition or quality of being a helot

HELOTISMS > HELOTISM

HELOTRIES > HELOTRY

HELOTRY n serfdom or slavery

HELOTS > HELOT

HELP vb make something easier, better, or quicker for (someone) ▷ n assistance or support

HELPABLE > HELP

HELPDESK n place where advice is given by telephone

HELPDESKS > HELPDESK

HELPED > HELP

HELPER > HELP

HELPERS > HELP

HELPFUL adj giving help

HELPFULLY > HELPFUL

HELPING n single portion of food

HELPINGS > HELPING

HELPLESS adj weak or incapable

HELPLINE n telephone line set aside for callers to contact an organization for help with a problem

HELPLINES > HELPLINE

HELPMATE n companion and helper, esp a spouse

HELPMATES > HELPMATE

HELPMEET less common word for > HELPMATE

HELPMEETS > HELPMEET

HELPS > HELP

HELVE n handle of a hand tool such as an axe or pick ▷ vb fit a helve to (a tool)

HELVED > HELVE

HELVES > HELVE

HELVETIUM same as > ASTATINE

HELVING > HELVE
HEM n bottom edge of a garment ▷ vb provide with a hem
HEMAGOG same as **> HEMAGOGUE**
HEMAGOGS > HEMAGOG
HEMAGOGUE n haemagogue: drug that promotes the flow of blood
HEMAL same as **> HAEMAL**
HEMATAL same as **> HEMAL**
HEMATEIN same as **> HAEMATEIN**
HEMATEINS > HEMATEIN
HEMATIC same as **> HAEMATIC**
HEMATICS > HEMATIC
HEMATIN same as **> HAEMATIN**
HEMATINE n red dye
HEMATINES > HEMATINE
HEMATINIC same as **> HAEMATIC**
HEMATINS > HEMATIN
HEMATITE n red, grey, or black mineral
HEMATITES > HEMATITE
HEMATITIC > HEMATITE
HEMATOID same as **> HAEMATOID**
HEMATOMA same as **> HAEMATOMA**
HEMATOMAS > HEMATOMA
HEMATOSES > HEMATOSIS
HEMATOSIS n haematosis: oxygenation of venous blood in the lungs
HEMATOZOA n plural of hematozoon: protozoan that is parasitic in the blood
HEMATURIA n the presence of blood or red blood cells in the urine
HEMATURIC > HEMATURIA
HEME same as **>** HAEM
HEMELYTRA n plural of hemelytron: forewing of plant bugs
HEMES > HEME
HEMIALGIA n pain limited to one side of the body
HEMIC same as **>** HAEMATIC
HEMICYCLE n semicircular structure, room, arena, wall, etc
HEMIHEDRA n plural of hemihedron, a hemihedral solid
HEMIHEDRY n hemihedral property of crystals
HEMIN same as **>** HAEMIN
HEMINA n old liquid measure
HEMINAS > HEMINA
HEMINS > HEMIN
HEMIOLA n rhythmic device
HEMIOLAS > HEMIOLA
HEMIOLIA same as **> HEMIOLA**
HEMIOLIAS > HEMIOLIA
HEMIOLIC > HEMIOLA
HEMIONE same as **> HEMIONUS**
HEMIONES > HEMIONE
HEMIONUS n Asian wild ass
HEMIOPIA n defective vision seeing only halves of things

HEMIOPIAS > HEMIOPIA
HEMIOPIC > HEMIOPIA
HEMIOPSIA same as **> HEMIOPIA**
HEMIPOD same as **> HEMIPODE**
HEMIPODE n button quail
HEMIPODES > HEMIPODE
HEMIPODS > HEMIPOD
HEMIPTER n insect with beaklike mouthparts
HEMIPTERS > HEMIPTER
HEMISPACE n area in brain
HEMISTICH n half line of verse
HEMITROPE another name for **>** TWIN
HEMITROPY n state of being a twin
HEMLINE n level to which the hem of a skirt hangs
HEMLINES > HEMLINE
HEMLOCK n poisonous plant
HEMLOCKS > HEMLOCK
HEMMED > HEM
HEMMER n attachment on a sewing machine for hemming
HEMMERS > HEMMER
HEMMING > HEM
HEMOCOEL same as **> HAEMOCOEL**
HEMOCOELS > HEMOCOEL
HEMOCONIA n the small particles of matter, thought to be particles of the structure of red blood cells, that are present in blood that is flowing around the body
HEMOCYTE same as **> HAEMOCYTE**
HEMOCYTES > HEMOCYTE
HEMOID same as **> HAEMATOID**
HEMOLYMPH n blood-like fluid in invertebrates
HEMOLYSE vb break down so that haemoglobin is released
HEMOLYSED > HEMOLYSE
HEMOLYSES > HEMOLYSIS
HEMOLYSIN n haemolysin: substance that breaks down red blood cells
HEMOLYSIS n haemolysis: disintegration of red blood cells
HEMOLYTIC adj destroying red blood corpuscles
HEMOLYZE vb undergo or make undergo hemolysis
HEMOLYZED > HEMOLYZE
HEMOLYZES > HEMOLYZE
HEMOPHILE n haemophile: person with haemophilia
HEMOSTAT same as **> HAEMOSTAT**
HEMOSTATS > HEMOSTAT
HEMOTOXIC > HEMOTOXIN
HEMOTOXIN n substance that destroys red blood cells
HEMP n Asian plant with tough fibres
HEMPEN > HEMP
HEMPIE variant of **>** HEMPY
HEMPIER > HEMPY
HEMPIES > HEMPY

HEMPIEST > HEMPY
HEMPLIKE > HEMP
HEMPS > HEMP
HEMPSEED n seed of hemp
HEMPSEEDS > HEMPSEED
HEMPWEED n climbing weed
HEMPWEEDS > HEMPWEED
HEMPY adj of or like hemp ▷ n rogue
HEMS > HEM
HEMSTITCH n decorative edging stitch, usually for a hem, in which the cross threads are stitched in groups ▷ vb decorate (a hem, etc) with hemstitches
HEN n female domestic fowl ▷ vb lose one's courage
HENBANE n poisonous plant with sticky hairy leaves
HENBANES > HENBANE
HENBIT n European plant with small dark red flowers
HENBITS > HENBIT
HENCE adv from this time ▷ interj begone! away!
HENCH adj fit and muscular
HENCHER > HENCH
HENCHEST > HENCH
HENCHMAN n person employed by someone powerful to carry out orders
HENCHMEN > HENCHMAN
HENCOOP n cage for poultry
HENCOOPS > HENCOOP
HEND vb seize
HENDED > HEND
HENDIADYS n rhetorical device by which two nouns joined by a conjunction are used instead of a noun and modifier
HENDING > HEND
HENDS > HEND
HENEQUEN n agave plant native to Yucatán
HENEQUENS > HENEQUEN
HENEQUIN same as **> HENEQUEN**
HENEQUINS > HENEQUIN
HENGE n monument from the Neolithic and Bronze Ages
HENGES > HENGE
HENHOUSE n coop for hens
HENHOUSES > HENHOUSE
HENIQUEN same as **> HENEQUEN**
HENIQUENS > HENIQUEN
HENIQUIN same as **> HENIQUEN**
HENIQUINS > HENIQUIN
HENLEY n type of sweater
HENLEYS > HENLEY
HENLIKE > HEN
HENNA n reddish dye made from a shrub or tree ▷ vb dye (the hair) with henna
HENNAED > HENNA
HENNAING > HENNA
HENNAS > HENNA
HENNED > HEN
HENNER n challenge
HENNERIES > HENNERY
HENNERS > HENNER
HENNERY n place or farm for keeping poultry

HENNIER > HENNY
HENNIES > HENNY
HENNIEST > HENNY
HENNIN n former women's hat
HENNING > HEN
HENNINS > HENNIN
HENNISH > HEN
HENNISHLY ▷ HEN
HENNY adj like a hen ▷ n cock that looks like a hen
HENOTIC adj acting to reconcile
HENPECK vb (of a woman) to harass or torment (a man)
HENPECKED adj (of a man) dominated by his wife
HENPECKS > HENPECK
HENRIES > HENRY
HENRY n unit of electrical inductance
HENRYS > HENRY
HENS > HEN
HENT vb seize ▷ n anything that has been grasped, esp by the mind
HENTED > HENT
HENTING > HENT
HENTS > HENT
HEP same as **>** HIP
HEPAR n compound containing sulphur
HEPARIN n polysaccharide present in most body tissues
HEPARINS > HEPARIN
HEPARS > HEPAR
HEPATIC adj of the liver ▷ n any of various drugs for use in treating diseases of the liver
HEPATICA n woodland plant with white, mauve, or pink flowers
HEPATICAE > HEPATICA
HEPATICAL same as **> HEPATIC**
HEPATICAS > HEPATICA
HEPATICS > HEPATIC
HEPATISE same as **> HEPATIZE**
HEPATISED > HEPATISE
HEPATISES > HEPATISE
HEPATITE n mineral containing sulphur
HEPATITES > HEPATITE
HEPATITIS n inflammation of the liver
HEPATIZE vb turn into liver
HEPATIZED > HEPATIZE
HEPATIZES > HEPATIZE
HEPATOMA n cancer of liver
HEPATOMAS > HEPATOMA
HEPCAT n person who is hep
HEPCATS > HEPCAT
HEPPER > HEP
HEPPEST > HEP
HEPS > HEP
HEPSTER same as **> HIPSTER**
HEPSTERS > HEPSTER
HEPT archaic spelling of **> HEAPED**
HEPTAD n group or series of seven
HEPTADS > HEPTAD
HEPTAGLOT n book written in seven languages

HEPTAGON n geometric figure with seven sides

HEPTAGONS > HEPTAGON

HEPTANE n alkane found in petroleum

HEPTANES > HEPTANE

HEPTAPODY n verse with seven beats in rhythm

HEPTARCH > HEPTARCHY

HEPTARCHS > HEPTARCHY

HEPTARCHY n government by seven rulers

HEPTOSE n any monosaccharide with seven carbon atoms per molecule

HEPTOSES > HEPTOSE

HER pron refers to anything personified as feminine ▷ adj belonging to her ▷ determiner of, belonging to, or associated with her

HERALD n person who announces important news ▷ vb signal the approach of

HERALDED > HERALD

HERALDIC adj of or relating to heraldry

HERALDING > HERALD

HERALDIST > HERALDRY

HERALDRY n study of coats of arms and family trees

HERALDS > HERALD

HERB n plant used for flavouring in cookery, and in medicine

HERBAGE n herbaceous plants collectively

HERBAGED adj with grass growing on it

HERBAGES > HERBAGE

HERBAL adj of or relating to herbs, usually culinary or medicinal herbs ▷ n book describing and listing the properties of plants

HERBALISM n use of herbal medicine

HERBALIST n person who grows or specializes in the use of medicinal herbs

HERBALS > HERBAL

HERBAR same as > HERBARY

HERBARIA > HERBARIUM

HERBARIAL > HERBARIUM

HERBARIAN same as > HERBALIST

HERBARIES > HERBARY

HERBARIUM n collection of dried plants that are mounted and classified systematically

HERBARS > HERBAR

HERBARY n herb garden

HERBED adj flavoured with herbs

HERBELET same as > HERBLET

HERBELETS > HERBELET

HERBICIDE n chemical used to destroy plants, esp weeds

HERBIER > HERBY

HERBIEST > HERBY

HERBIST same as > HERBALIST

HERBISTS > HERBIST

HERBIVORA n animals that eat grass

HERBIVORE n animal that eats only plants

HERBIVORY > HERBIVORE

HERBLESS > HERB

HERBLET n little herb

HERBLETS > HERBLET

HERBLIKE > HERB

HERBOLOGY n use or study of herbal medicine

HERBORISE same as > HERBORIZE

HERBORIST same as > HERBALIST

HERBORIZE vb collect herbs

HERBOSE same as > HERBOUS

HERBOUS adj with abundance of herbs

HERBS > HERB

HERBY adj abounding in herbs

HERCOGAMY n prevention of flower pollination

HERCULEAN adj requiring great strength or effort

HERCULES n as in hercules beetle very large tropical American beetle

HERCYNITE n mineral containing iron

HERD n group of animals feeding and living together ▷ vb collect into a herd

HERDBOY n boy who looks after herd

HERDBOYS > HERDBOY

HERDED > HERD

HERDEN n type of coarse cloth

HERDENS > HERDEN

HERDER same as > HERDSMAN

HERDERS > HERDER

HERDESS n female herder

HERDESSES > HERDESS

HERDIC n small horse-drawn carriage

HERDICS > HERDIC

HERDING n act of herding

HERDINGS > HERDING

HERDLIKE > HERD

HERDMAN same as > HERDSMAN

HERDMEN > HERDMAN

HERDS > HERD

HERDSMAN n man who looks after a herd of animals

HERDSMEN > HERDSMAN

HERDWICK n hardy breed of sheep

HERDWICKS > HERDWICK

HERE adv in, at, or to this place or point ▷ n this place

HEREABOUT adv hereabouts

HEREAFTER adv after this point or time ▷ n life after death

HEREAT adv because of this

HEREAWAY same as > HEREABOUT

HEREAWAYS dialect form of > HERE

HEREBY adv by means of or as a result of this

HEREDES > HERES

HEREDITY n passing on of characteristics from one generation to another

HEREFROM adv from here

HEREIN adv in this place, matter, or document

HEREINTO adv into this place, circumstance, etc

HERENESS n state of being here

HEREOF adv of or concerning this

HEREON archaic word for > HEREUPON

HERES > HERE

HERESIES > HERESY

HERESY n opinion contrary to accepted opinion or belief

HERETIC n person who holds unorthodox opinions

HERETICAL > HERETIC

HERETICS > HERETIC

HERETO adv this place, matter, or document

HERETRIX n in Scots law, female inheritor

HEREUNDER adv (in documents, etc) below this

HEREUNTO archaic word for > HERETO

HEREUPON adv following immediately after this

HEREWITH adv with this

HERIED > HERY

HERIES > HERY

HERIOT n (in medieval England) a death duty paid to the lord

HERIOTS > HERIOT

HERISSE adj with bristles

HERISSON n spiked beam used as fortification

HERISSONS > HERISSON

HERITABLE adj capable of being inherited

HERITABLY > HERITABLE

HERITAGE n something inherited

HERITAGES > HERITAGE

HERITOR n person who inherits

HERITORS > HERITOR

HERITRESS > HERITOR

HERITRIX > HERITOR

HERKOGAMY same as > HERCOGAMY

HERL n barb or barbs of a feather

HERLING n Scots word for a type of fish

HERLINGS > HERLING

HERLS > HERL

HERM n (in ancient Greece) a stone head of Hermes

HERMA same as > HERM

HERMAE > HERMA

HERMAEAN adj type of statue

HERMAI > HERMA

HERMANDAD n organization of middle classes in Spain

HERMETIC adj sealed so as to be airtight

HERMETICS n alchemy

HERMETISM n belief in pagan mystical knowledge

HERMETIST > HERMETISM

HERMIT n person living in solitude, esp for religious reasons

HERMITAGE n home of a hermit

HERMITESS n female hermit

HERMITIC > HERMIT

HERMITISM n act of living as hermit

HERMITRY n life as hermit

HERMITS > HERMIT

HERMS > HERM

HERN archaic or dialect word for > HERON

HERNIA n medical problem

HERNIAE > HERNIA

HERNIAL > HERNIA

HERNIAS > HERNIA

HERNIATE n form hernia

HERNIATED > HERNIA

HERNIATES > HERNIATE

HERNS > HERN

HERNSHAW same as > HERONSHAW

HERNSHAWS > HERNSHAW

HERO n principal character in a film, book, etc

HEROES > HERO

HEROIC adj courageous

HEROICAL same as > HEROIC

HEROICISE same as > HEROICIZE

HEROICIZE same as > HEROIZE

HEROICLY > HERO

HEROICS pl n extravagant behaviour

HEROIN n highly addictive illegal drug derived from morphine

HEROINE n principal female character in a novel, play, etc

HEROINES > HEROINE

HEROINISM n addiction to heroin

HEROINS > HEROIN

HEROISE same as > HEROIZE

HEROISED > HEROISE

HEROISES > HEROISE

HEROISING > HEROISE

HEROISM n great courage and bravery

HEROISMS > HEROISM

HEROIZE vb make into hero

HEROIZED > HEROIZE

HEROIZES > HEROIZE

HEROIZING > HEROIZE

HERON n long-legged wading bird

HERONRIES > HERONRY

HERONRY n colony of breeding herons

HERONS > HERON

HERONSEW same as > HERONSHAW

HERONSEWS > HERONSEW

HERONSHAW n young heron

HEROON n temple or monument dedicated to hero

HEROONS > HEROON

HEROS > HERO

HEROSHIP > HERO

HEROSHIPS > HERO

HERPES n any of several inflammatory skin diseases

HERPESES > HERPES**

HERPETIC *adj* of or relating to herpes ▷ *n* person suffering from herpes

HERPETICS > HERPETIC

HERPETOID *adj* like reptile

HERPTILE *adj* denoting, relating to, or characterizing both reptiles and amphibians

HERRIED > HERRY

HERRIES > HERRY

HERRIMENT *n* act of plundering

HERRING *n* important food fish of northern seas

HERRINGER *n* person or boat catching herring

HERRINGS > HERRING

HERRY *vb* harry

HERRYING > HERRY

HERRYMENT *same as* > HERRIMENT

HERS *pron* something belonging to her

HERSALL *n* rehearsal

HERSALLS > HERSALL

HERSE *n* harrow

HERSED *adj* arranged like a harrow

HERSELF *pron* feminine singular reflexive form

HERSES > HERSE

HERSHIP *n* act of plundering

HERSHIPS > HERSHIP

HERSTORY *n* history from a female point of view or as it relates to women

HERTZ *n* unit of frequency

HERTZES > HERTZ

HERY *vb* praise

HERYE *same as* > HERY

HERYED > HERYE

HERYES > HERYE

HERYING > HERY

HES > HE

HESITANCE > HESITANT

HESITANCY > HESITANT

HESITANT *adj* undecided or wavering

HESITATE *vb* be slow or uncertain in doing something

HESITATED > HESITATE

HESITATER > HESITATE

HESITATES > HESITATE

HESITATOR > HESITATE

HESP *same as* > HASP

HESPED > HESP

HESPERID *n* species of butterfly

HESPERIDS > HESPERID

HESPING > HESP

HESPS > HESP

HESSIAN *n* coarse jute fabric

HESSIANS > HESSIAN

HESSITE *n* black or grey metallic mineral

HESSITES > HESSITE

HESSONITE *n* orange-brown variety of grossularite garnet

HEST *archaic word for* > BEHEST

HESTERNAL *adj* belonging to yesterday

HESTS > HEST

HET *n* short for heterosexual ▷ *adj* Scots word for hot

HETAERA *n* (esp in ancient Greece) a female prostitute

HETAERAE > HETAERA

HETAERAS > HETAERA

HETAERIC > HETAERA

HETAERISM *n* state of being a concubine

HETAERIST > HETAERISM

HETAIRA *same as* > HETAERA

HETAIRAI > HETAIRA

HETAIRAS > HETAIRA

HETAIRIA *n* society

HETAIRIAS > HETAIRIA

HETAIRIC > HETAERA

HETAIRISM *same as* > HETAERISM

HETAIRIST > HETAERISM

HETE *same as* > HIGHT

HETERO *n* short for heterosexual

HETERODOX *adj* differing from accepted doctrines or beliefs

HETERONYM *n* one of two or more words pronounced differently but spelt alike

HETEROPOD *n* marine invertebrate with a foot for swimming

HETEROS > HETERO

HETEROSES > HETEROSIS

HETEROSIS *n* increased size, strength, etc, of a hybrid as compared to either of its parents

HETEROTIC > HETEROSIS

HETES > HETE

HETH *n* eighth letter of the Hebrew alphabet

HETHER *same as* > HITHER

HETHS > HETH

HETING > HETE

HETMAN *another word for* > ATAMAN

HETMANATE > HETMAN

HETMANS > HETMAN

HETMEN > HETMAN

HETS > HET

HETTIE *n* slang term for a heterosexual

HETTIES > HETTIE

HEUCH *Scots word for* > CRAG

HEUCHERA *n* N American plant with heart-shaped leaves and mostly red flowers

HEUCHERAS > HEUCHERA

HEUCHS > HEUCH

HEUGH *same as* > HEUCH

HEUGHS > HEUGH

HEUREKA *same as* > EUREKA

HEUREKAS > HEUREKA

HEURETIC *same as* > HEURISTIC

HEURETICS *n* use of logic

HEURISM *n* use of logic

HEURISMS > HEURISM

HEURISTIC *adj* involving learning by investigation ▷ *n* science of heuristic procedure

HEVEA *n* rubber-producing South American tree

HEVEAS > HEVEA

HEW *vb* cut with an axe

HEWABLE > HEW

HEWED > HEW

HEWER > HEW

HEWERS > HEW

HEWGH *interj* sound made to imitate the flight of an arrow

HEWING > HEW

HEWINGS > HEW

HEWN > HEW

HEWS > HEW

HEX *adj* of or relating to hexadecimal notation ▷ *n* evil spell ▷ *vb* bewitch

HEXACHORD *n* (in medieval musical theory) any of three diatonic scales based upon C, F, and G, each consisting of six notes, from which solmization was developed

HEXACT *n* part of a sponge with six rays

HEXACTS > HEXACT

HEXAD *n* group or series of six

HEXADE *same as* > HEXAD

HEXADECYL *n* univalent radical derived from hexadecane

HEXADES > HEXADE

HEXADIC > HEXAD

HEXADS > HEXAD

HEXAFOIL *n* pattern with six lobes

HEXAFOILS > HEXAFOIL

HEXAGLOT *n* book written in six languages

HEXAGLOTS > HEXAGLOT

HEXAGON *n* geometrical figure with six sides

HEXAGONAL *adj* having six sides and six angles

HEXAGONS > HEXAGON

HEXAGRAM *n* star formed by extending the sides of a regular hexagon to meet at six points

HEXAGRAMS > HEXAGRAM

HEXAHEDRA *n* plural of hexahedron: solid figure with six plane faces

HEXAMERAL *adj* arranged in six groups

HEXAMETER *n* verse line consisting of six metrical feet

HEXAMINE *n* fuel for camping stoves

HEXAMINES > HEXAMINE

HEXANE *n* liquid alkane existing in five isomeric forms

HEXANES > HEXANE

HEXANOIC *adj* as in *hexanoic acid* insoluble oily carboxylic acid found in coconut and palm oils and in milk

HEXAPLA *n* edition of the Old Testament

HEXAPLAR > HEXAPLA

HEXAPLAS > HEXAPLA

HEXAPLOID *adj* with six times the normal number of chromosomes

HEXAPOD *n* six-footed arthropod

HEXAPODAL *adj* relating to the Hexapoda, ie insects

HEXAPODIC > HEXAPODY

HEXAPODS > HEXAPOD

HEXAPODY *n* verse measure consisting of six metrical feet

HEXARCH *adj* (of a plant) with six veins

HEXARCHY *n* alliance of six states

HEXASTICH *n* poem, stanza, or strophe that consists of six lines

HEXASTYLE *n* portico or façade with six columns ▷ *adj* having six columns

HEXATHLON *n* athletic contest comprising six events

HEXED > HEX

HEXENE *same as* > HEXYLENE

HEXENES > HEXENE

HEXER > HEX

HEXEREI *n* witchcraft

HEXEREIS > HEXEREI

HEXERS > HEX **HEXES** > HEX

HEXING > HEX

HEXINGS > HEX

HEXONE *n* colourless insoluble liquid ketone

HEXONES > HEXONE

HEXOSAN *n* form of polysaccharide

HEXOSANS > HEXOSAN

HEXOSE *n* monosaccharide, such as glucose

HEXOSES > HEXOSE

HEXYL *adj* of or consisting of a specific group of atoms

HEXYLENE *n* chemical compound similar to ethylene

HEXYLENES > HEXYLENE

HEXYLIC > HEXYL

HEXYLS > HEXYL

HEY *interj* expression of surprise or for catching attention ▷ *vb* perform a country dance

HEYDAY *n* time of greatest success, prime

HEYDAYS > HEYDAY

HEYDEY *variant of* > HEYDAY

HEYDEYS > HEYDEY

HEYDUCK *same as* > HAIDUK

HEYDUCKS > HEYDUCK

HEYED > HEY

HEYING > HEY

HEYS > HEY

HI *interj* hello

HIANT *adj* gaping

HIATAL > HIATUS

HIATUS *n* pause or interruption in continuity

HIATUSES > HIATUS

HIBACHI *n* portable brazier for heating and cooking food

HIBACHIS > HIBACHI

HIBAKUSHA *n* survivor of either of the atomic-bomb attacks on Hiroshima and Nagasaki in 1945

HIBERNAL *adj* of or occurring in winter

HIBERNATE *vb* (of an animal) pass the winter as if in a deep sleep

HIBERNISE *same as* > HIBERNIZE

h

HIBERNIZE vb make Irish
HIBISCUS n tropical plant with large brightly coloured flowers
HIC interj representation of the sound of a hiccup
HICATEE same as > HICCATEE
HICATEES > HICATEE
HICCATEE n tortoise of West Indies
HICCATEES > HICCATEE
HICCOUGH same as > HICCUP
HICCOUGHS > HICCOUGH
HICCUP n spasm of the breathing organs ▷ vb make a hiccup
HICCUPED > HICCUP
HICCUPIER > HICCUPY
HICCUPING > HICCUP
HICCUPPED > HICCUP
HICCUPS > HICCUP
HICCUPY adj tending to hiccup
HICK n unsophisticated country person ▷ adj unsophisticated
HICKER > HICK
HICKEST > HICK
HICKEY n object or gadget
HICKEYS > HICKEY
HICKIE same as > HICKEY
HICKIES > HICKIE
HICKISH > HICK
HICKORIES > HICKORY
HICKORY n N American nut-bearing tree
HICKS > HICK
HICKWALL n green woodpecker
HICKWALLS > HICKWALL
HICKYMAL n titmouse
HICKYMALS > HICKYMAL
HID > HIDE
HIDABLE > HIDE
HIDAGE n former tax on land
HIDAGES > HIDAGE
HIDALGA n Spanish noblewoman
HIDALGAS > HIDALGA
HIDALGO n member of the lower nobility in Spain
HIDALGOS > HIDALGO
HIDDEN > HIDE
HIDDENITE n green transparent variety of the mineral spodumene, used as a gemstone
HIDDENLY > HIDE
HIDDER n young ram
HIDDERS > HIDDER
HIDE vb put (oneself or an object) somewhere difficult to see or find ▷ n place of concealment, esp for a bird-watcher
HIDEAWAY n private place
HIDEAWAYS > HIDEAWAY
HIDEBOUND adj unwilling to accept new ideas
HIDED > HIDE
HIDELESS > HIDE
HIDEOSITY > HIDEOUS
HIDEOUS adj ugly, revolting
HIDEOUSLY > HIDEOUS
HIDEOUT n hiding place

HIDEOUTS > HIDEOUT
HIDER > HIDE
HIDERS > HIDE
HIDES > HIDE
HIDING > HIDE
HIDINGS > HIDE
HIDLING n hiding place
HIDLINGS adv in secret
HIDLINS same as > HIDLINGS
HIDROSES > HIDROSIS
HIDROSIS n any skin disease affecting the sweat glands
HIDROTIC > HIDROSIS
HIDROTICS > HIDROSIS
HIE vb hurry
HIED > HIE
HIEING > HIE
HIELAMAN n Australian Aboriginal shield
HIELAMANS > HIELAMAN
HIELAND adj characteristic of Highlanders
HIEMAL less common word for > HIBERNAL
HIEMS n winter
HIERACIUM n plant of hawkweed family
HIERARCH n person in a position of high-priestly authority
HIERARCHS > HIERARCH
HIERARCHY n system of people or things arranged in a graded order
HIERATIC adj of or relating to priests ▷ n hieratic script of ancient Egypt
HIERATICA n type of papyrus
HIERATICS > HIERATIC
HIEROCRAT n person who believes in government by religious leaders
HIERODULE n (in ancient Greece) a temple slave
HIEROGRAM n sacred symbol
HIEROLOGY n sacred literature
HIERURGY n performance of religious drama or music
HIES > HIE
HIFALUTIN adj pompous or pretentious
HIGGLE less common word for > HAGGLE
HIGGLED > HIGGLE
HIGGLER > HIGGLE
HIGGLERS > HIGGLE
HIGGLES > HIGGLE
HIGGLING > HIGGLE
HIGGLINGS > HIGGLE
HIGH adj being a relatively great distance from top to bottom; tall ▷ adv at or to a height ▷ n high place or level ▷ vb hie
HIGHBALL n tall drink of whisky with soda water or ginger ale and ice ▷ vb move at great speed
HIGHBALLS > HIGHBALL
HIGHBORN adj of noble or aristocratic birth
HIGHBOY n tall chest of drawers in two sections

HIGHBOYS > HIGHBOY
HIGHBRED adj of noble breeding
HIGHBROW n intellectual and serious person ▷ adj concerned with serious, intellectual subjects
HIGHBROWS > HIGHBROW
HIGHBUSH adj (of bush) growing tall ▷ n tall-growing bush
HIGHCHAIR n long-legged chair with a tray attached, used by a very young child at mealtimes
HIGHED > HIGH
HIGHER n advanced level of the Scottish Certificate of Education ▷ vb raise up
HIGHERED > HIGHER
HIGHERING > HIGHER
HIGHERS > HIGHER
HIGHEST > HIGH
HIGHFLIER same as > HIGHFLYER
HIGHFLYER n person who is extreme in aims, ambition, etc
HIGHING > HIGH
HIGHISH > HIGH
HIGHJACK same as > HIJACK
HIGHJACKS > HIGHJACK
HIGHJINKS n lively enjoyment
HIGHLAND n relatively high ground
HIGHLANDS > HIGHLAND
HIGHLIFE n African music genre
HIGHLIFES > HIGHLIFE
HIGHLIGHT n outstanding part or feature ▷ vb give emphasis to
HIGHLY adv extremely
HIGHMAN n dice weighted to make it fall in particular way
HIGHMEN > HIGHMAN
HIGHMOST adj highest
HIGHNESS n condition of being high or lofty
HIGHRISE n tall building
HIGHRISES > HIGHRISE
HIGHROAD n main road
HIGHROADS > HIGHROAD
HIGHS > HIGH
HIGHSPOT n highlight
HIGHSPOTS > HIGHSPOT
HIGHT vb archaic word for name or call
HIGHTAIL vb go or move in a great hurry
HIGHTAILS > HIGHTAIL
HIGHTED > HIGHT
HIGHTH old form of > HEIGHT
HIGHTHS > HIGHTH
HIGHTING n oath
HIGHTINGS > HIGHTING
HIGHTOP n top of ship's mast
HIGHTOPS > HIGHTOP
HIGHTS > HIGHT
HIGHVELD n high-altitude grassland region of E South Africa
HIGHVELDS > HIGHVELD
HIGHWAY n main road

HIGHWAYS > HIGHWAY
HIJAB n covering for the head and face
HIJABS > HIJAB
HIJACK vb seize control of (an aircraft or other vehicle) while travelling ▷ n instance of hijacking
HIJACKED > HIJACK
HIJACKER > HIJACK
HIJACKERS > HIJACK
HIJACKING > HIJACK
HIJACKS > HIJACK
HIJINKS n lively enjoyment
HIJRA same as > HIJRAH
HIJRAH same as > HEGIRA
HIJRAHS > HIJRAH
HIJRAS > HIJRA
HIKE n long walk in the country, esp for pleasure ▷ vb go for a long walk
HIKED > HIKE
HIKER > HIKE
HIKERS > HIKE
HIKES > HIKE
HIKING n sport of taking long walks in the country
HIKINGS > HIKING
HIKOI n walk or march, esp a Māori protest march ▷ vb take part in such a march
HIKOIED > HIKOI
HIKOIING > HIKOI
HIKOIS > HIKOI
HILA > HILUM
HILAR > HILUS
HILARIOUS adj very funny
HILARITY n mirth and merriment
HILCH vb hobble
HILCHED > HILCH
HILCHES > HILCH
HILCHING > HILCH
HILD same as > HOLD
HILDING n coward
HILDINGS > HILDING
HILI > HILUS
HILL n raised part of the earth's surface ▷ vb form into a hill or mound
HILLBILLY n usually disparaging term for an unsophisticated country person
HILLCREST n crest of hill
HILLED > HILL
HILLER > HILL
HILLERS > HILL
HILLFOLK n people living in the hills
HILLFORT n fortified hilltop
HILLFORTS > HILLFORT
HILLIER > HILL
HILLIEST > HILL
HILLINESS > HILL
HILLING > HILL
HILLINGS > HILLING
HILLMEN same as > HILLFOLK
HILLO same as > HELLO
HILLOA same as > HALLOA
HILLOAED > HILLOA
HILLOAING > HILLOA
HILLOAS > HILLOA
HILLOCK n small hill
HILLOCKED > HILLOCK

HILLOCKS > HILLOCK
HILLOCKY adj having hillocks
HILLOED > HILLO
HILLOES > HILLO
HILLOING > HILLO
HILLOS > HILLO
HILLS > HILL
HILLSIDE n side of a hill
HILLSIDES > HILLSIDE
HILLSLOPE same as > HILLSIDE
HILLTOP n top of hill
HILLTOPS > HILLTOP
HILLY > HILL
HILT n handle of a sword or knife ▷ vb supply with a hilt
HILTED > HILT
HILTING > HILT
HILTLESS > HILT
HILTS > HILT
HILUM n scar on a seed
HILUS rare word for > HILUM
HIM pron refers to a male person or animal ▷ n male person
HIMATIA > HIMATION
HIMATION n (in ancient Greece) a cloak draped around the body
HIMATIONS > HIMATION
HIMBO n derogatory term for an attractive but empty-headed man
HIMBOS > HIMBO
HIMS > HIM
HIMSELF pron masculine singular reflexive form
HIN n Hebrew unit of capacity
HINAHINA same as > MAHOE
HINAHINAS > HINAHINA
HINAU n New Zealand tree
HINAUS > HINAU
HIND adj situated at the back ▷ n female deer
HINDBERRY n raspberry
HINDBRAIN n part of the brain comprising the cerebellum, pons and medulla oblongata
HINDCAST vb test (a mathematical model)
HINDCASTS > HINDCAST
HINDER vb get in the way of ▷ adj situated at the back
HINDERED > HINDER
HINDERER > HINDER
HINDERERS > HINDER
HINDERING > HINDER
HINDERS > HINDER
HINDFEET > HINDFOOT
HINDFOOT n back foot
HINDGUT n part of the vertebrate digestive tract
HINDGUTS > HINDGUT
HINDHEAD n back of head
HINDHEADS > HINDHEAD
HINDLEG n back leg
HINDLEGS > HINDLEG
HINDMILK n breast milk produced after the first part of feeding
HINDMILKS > HINDMILK
HINDMOST > HIND
HINDRANCE n obstruction or snag

HINDS > HIND
HINDSHANK n meat from animal's hind leg
HINDSIGHT n ability to understand, after something has happened, what should have been done
HINDWARD adj at back
HINDWING n back wing
HINDWINGS > HINDWING
HING n asafoetida
HINGE n device for holding two parts so one can swing freely ▷ vb depend (on)
HINGED > HINGE
HINGELESS > HINGE
HINGELIKE > HINGE
HINGER n tool for making hinges
HINGERS > HINGER
HINGES > HINGE
HINGING > HINGE
HINGS > HING
HINKIER > HINKY
HINKIEST > HINKY
HINKY adj strange
HINNIE n sweetheart
HINNIED > HINNY
HINNIES > HINNY
HINNY n offspring of a male horse and a female donkey ▷ vb whinny
HINNYING > HINNY
HINS > HIN
HINT n indirect suggestion ▷ vb suggest indirectly
HINTED > HINT
HINTER > HINT
HINTERS > HINT
HINTING > HINT
HINTINGLY > HINT
HINTINGS > HINT
HINTS > HINT
HIOI n New Zealand plant of the mint family
HIOIS > HIOI
HIP n either side of the body between the pelvis and the thigh ▷ adj aware of or following the latest trends ▷ interj exclamation used to introduce cheers
HIPBONE n either of the bones that form the sides of the pelvis
HIPBONES > HIPBONE
HIPHUGGER adj (of trousers) having a low waist
HIPLESS > HIP
HIPLIKE > HIP
HIPLINE n widest part of a person's hips
HIPLINES > HIPLINE
HIPLY > HIP
HIPNESS > HIP
HIPNESSES > HIP
HIPPARCH n (in ancient Greece) a cavalry commander
HIPPARCHS > HIPPARCH
HIPPED adj having a hip or hips
HIPPEN n baby's nappy
HIPPENS > HIPPEN
HIPPER > HIP
HIPPEST > HIP
HIPPIATRY n treatment of disease in horses

HIPPIC adj of horses
HIPPIE same as > HIPPY
HIPPIEDOM > HIPPIE
HIPPIEISH > HIPPIE
HIPPIER > HIPPY
HIPPIES > HIPPY
HIPPIEST > HIPPY
HIPPIN same as > HIPPEN
HIPPINESS > HIPPY
HIPPING same as > HIPPEN
HIPPINGS > HIPPING
HIPPINS > HIPPIN
HIPPISH adj in low spirits
HIPPO n hippopotamus
HIPPOCRAS n old English drink of wine flavoured with spices
HIPPODAME n sea horse
HIPPOLOGY n study of horses
HIPPOS > HIPPO
HIPPURIC adj as in hippuric acid crystalline solid excreted in the urine of mammals
HIPPURITE n type of fossil
HIPPUS n spasm of eye
HIPPUSES > HIPPUS
HIPPY n person whose behaviour implies a rejection of values ▷ adj having large hips
HIPPYDOM > HIPPY
HIPPYDOMS > HIPPY
HIPPYISH adj pertaining to or like a hippy
HIPS > HIP
HIPSHOT adj having a dislocated hip
HIPSTER n enthusiast of modern jazz
HIPSTERS pl n trousers cut so that the top encircles the hips
HIPT > HIP
HIRABLE > HIRE
HIRAGANA n Japanese system of writing
HIRAGANAS > HIRAGANA
HIRAGE n fee for hiring
HIRAGES > HIRAGE
HIRCINE adj of or like a goat, esp in smell
HIRCOSITY n quality of being like a goat
HIRE vb pay to have temporary use of ▷ n hiring
HIREABLE > HIRE
HIREAGE same as > HIRAGE
HIREAGES > HIREAGE
HIRED > HIRE
HIREE n hired person
HIREES > HIREE
HIRELING n derogatory term for a person who works only for wages
HIRELINGS > HIRELING
HIRER > HIRE
HIRERS > HIRE
HIRES > HIRE
HIRING > HIRE
HIRINGS > HIRE
HIRLING n Scots word for a type of fish
HIRLINGS > HIRLING
HIRPLE vb limp ▷ n limping gait
HIRPLED > HIRPLE

HIRPLES > HIRPLE
HIRPLING > HIRPLE
HIRRIENT n trilled sound
HIRRIENTS > HIRRIENT
HIRSEL vb sort into groups
HIRSELED > HIRSEL
HIRSELING > HIRSEL
HIRSELLED > HIRSEL
HIRSELS > HIRSEL
HIRSLE vb wriggle or fidget
HIRSLED > HIRSLE
HIRSLES > HIRSLE
HIRSLING > HIRSLE
HIRSTIE adj dry
HIRSUTE adj hairy
HIRSUTISM > HIRSUTE
HIRUDIN n anticoagulant
HIRUDINS > HIRUDIN
HIRUNDINE adj of or resembling a swallow
HIS adj belonging to him
HISH same as > HISS
HISHED > HISH
HISHES > HISH
HISHING > HISH
HISN dialect form of > HIS
HISPANISM n Spanish turn of phrase
HISPID adj covered with stiff hairs or bristles
HISPIDITY > HISPID
HISS n sound like that of a long s (as an expression of contempt) ▷ vb utter a hiss ▷ interj exclamation of derision or disapproval
HISSED > HISS
HISSELF dialect form of > HIMSELF
HISSER > HISS
HISSERS > HISS
HISSES > HISS
HISSIER > HISSY
HISSIES > HISSY
HISSIEST > HISSY
HISSING > HISS
HISSINGLY > HISS
HISSINGS > HISS
HISSY n temper tantrum ▷ adj sound similar to a hiss
HIST interj exclamation used to attract attention ▷ vb make hist sound
HISTAMIN variant of > HISTAMINE
HISTAMINE n substance released by the body tissues in allergic reactions
HISTAMINS > HISTAMIN
HISTED > HIST
HISTIDIN variant of > HISTIDINE
HISTIDINE n nonessential amino acid that occurs in most proteins: a precursor of histamine
HISTIDINS > HISTIDIN
HISTIE same as > HIRSTIE
HISTING > HIST
HISTIOID same as > HISTOID
HISTOGEN n obsolete botanical term
HISTOGENS > HISTOGEN
HISTOGENY > HISTOGEN
HISTOGRAM n statistical graph in which the frequency

h

of values is represented by vertical bars of varying heights and widths

HISTOID adj (esp of a tumour)

HISTOLOGY n study of the tissues of an animal or plant

HISTONE n any of a group of proteins present in cell nuclei

HISTONES > HISTONE

HISTORIAN n writer of history

HISTORIC adj famous or significant in history

HISTORIED adj recorded in history

HISTORIES > HISTORY

HISTORIFY vb make part of history

HISTORISM n idea that history influences present

HISTORY n (record or account of) past events

HISTRIO n actor

HISTRION same as > HISTRIO

HISTRIONS > HISTRION

HISTRIOS > HISTRIO

HISTS > HIST

HIT vb strike, touch forcefully ▷ n hitting

HITCH n minor problem ▷ vb obtain (a lift) by hitchhiking

HITCHED > HITCH

HITCHER > HITCH

HITCHERS > HITCH

HITCHES > HITCH

HITCHHIKE vb travel by obtaining free lifts

HITCHIER > HITCH

HITCHIEST > HITCH

HITCHILY > HITCH

HITCHING > HITCH

HITCHY > HITCH

HITHE n small harbour

HITHER adv or towards this place ▷ vb come

HITHERED > HITHER

HITHERING > HITHER

HITHERS > HITHER

HITHERTO adv until this time

HITHES > HITHE

HITLESS > HIT

HITMAKER n successful performer or producer of popular music

HITMAKERS > HITMAKER

HITMAN n professional killer

HITMEN > HITMAN

HITS > HIT

HITTABLE > HIT

HITTER n boxer who has a hard punch rather than skill or finesse

HITTERS > HITTER

HITTING > HIT

HIVE n structure in which social bees live and rear their young ▷ vb cause (bees) to collect or (of bees) to collect inside a hive

HIVED > HIVE

HIVELESS > HIVE

HIVELIKE > HIVE

HIVEMIND n people who share their knowledge with one another, producing

either collective intelligence or conformity

HIVEMINDS > HIVEMIND

HIVER n person who keeps beehives

HIVERS > HIVER

HIVES n allergic reaction

HIVEWARD adj towards hive

HIVEWARDS adv towards hive

HIVING > HIVE

HIYA sentence substitute informal term of greeting

HIZEN n type of Japanese porcelain

HIZENS > HIZEN

HIZZ same as > HISS

HIZZED > HIZZ

HIZZES > HIZZ

HIZZING > HIZZ

HIZZONER n nickname for mayor

HIZZONERS > HIZZONER

HM interj sound made to express hesitation or doubt

HMM same as > HM

HMMM interj expressing thoughtful consideration

HO interj imitation or representation of the sound of a deep laugh ▷ n cry of 'ho' ▷ vb halt

HOA same as > HO

HOACTZIN same as > HOATZIN

HOACTZINS > HOACTZIN

HOAED > HOA

HOAGIE n sandwich made with long bread roll

HOAGIES > HOAGIE

HOAGY same as > HOAGIE

HOAING > HOA

HOAR adj covered with hoarfrost ▷ vb make hoary

HOARD n store hidden away for future use ▷ vb save or store

HOARDED > HOARD

HOARDER > HOARD

HOARDERS > HOARD

HOARDING n large board for displaying advertisements

HOARDINGS > HOARDING

HOARDS > HOARD

HOARED > HOAR

HOARFROST n white ground frost

HOARHEAD n person with white hair

HOARHEADS > HOARHEAD

HOARHOUND same as > HOREHOUND

HOARIER > HOARY

HOARIEST > HOARY

HOARILY > HOARY

HOARINESS > HOARY

HOARING > HOAR

HOARS > HOAR

HOARSE adj (of a voice) rough and unclear

HOARSELY > HOARSE

HOARSEN vb make or become hoarse

HOARSENED > HOARSEN

HOARSENS > HOARSEN

HOARSER > HOARSE

HOARSEST > HOARSE

HOARY adj grey or white(-haired)

HOAS > HOA

HOAST n cough ▷ vb cough

HOASTED > HOAST

HOASTING > HOAST

HOASTMAN n shipper of coal

HOASTMEN > HOASTMAN

HOASTS > HOAST

HOATCHING adj infested

HOATZIN n South American bird

HOATZINES > HOATZIN

HOATZINS > HOATZIN

HOAX n deception or trick ▷ vb deceive or play a trick upon

HOAXED > HOAX

HOAXER > HOAX

HOAXERS > HOAX

HOAXES > HOAX

HOAXING > HOAX

HOB n flat top part of a cooker ▷ vb cut or form with a hob

HOBBED > HOB

HOBBER n machine used in making gears

HOBBERS > HOBBER

HOBBIES > HOBBY

HOBBING > HOB

HOBBISH adj like a clown

HOBBIT n one of an imaginary race of half-size people

HOBBITRY > HOBBIT

HOBBITS > HOBBIT

HOBBLE vb walk lamely ▷ n strap, rope, etc, used to hobble a horse

HOBBLED > HOBBLE

HOBBLER > HOBBLE

HOBBLERS > HOBBLE

HOBBLES > HOBBLE

HOBBLING > HOBBLE

HOBBLINGS > HOBBLE

HOBBY n activity pursued in one's spare time

HOBBYISM > HOBBY

HOBBYISMS > HOBBY

HOBBYIST > HOBBY

HOBBYISTS > HOBBY

HOBBYLESS > HOBBY

HOBDAY vb alleviate a breathing problem in certain horses

HOBDAYED > HOBDAY

HOBDAYING > HOBDAY

HOBDAYS > HOBDAY

HOBGOBLIN n mischievous goblin

HOBJOB vb do odd jobs

HOBJOBBED > HOBJOB

HOBJOBBER > HOBJOB

HOBJOBS > HOBJOB

HOBLIKE > HOB

HOBNAIL n short nail with a large head for protecting soles ▷ vb provide with hobnails

HOBNAILED > HOBNAIL

HOBNAILS > HOBNAIL

HOBNOB vb be on friendly terms (with)

HOBNOBBED > HOBNOB

HOBNOBBER > HOBNOB

HOBNOBBY adj tending to hobnob

HOBNOBS > HOBNOB

HOBO n tramp or vagrant ▷ vb live as hobo

HOBODOM > HOBO

HOBODOMS > HOBO

HOBOED > HOBO

HOBOES > HOBO

HOBOING > HOBO

HOBOISM > HOBO

HOBOISMS > HOBO

HOBOS > HOBO

HOBS > HOB

HOC adj Latin for this

HOCK n joint in the leg of an animal corresponding to a human ankle ▷ vb pawn

HOCKED > HOCK

HOCKER > HOCK

HOCKERS > HOCK

HOCKEY n team sport

HOCKEYS > HOCKEY

HOCKING > HOCK

HOCKLE vb spit

HOCKLED > HOCKLE

HOCKLES > HOCKLE

HOCKLING > HOCKLE

HOCKS > HOCK

HOCKSHOP n pawnshop

HOCKSHOPS > HOCKSHOP

HOCUS vb take in

HOCUSED > HOCUS

HOCUSES > HOCUS

HOCUSING > HOCUS

HOCUSSED > HOCUS

HOCUSSES > HOCUS

HOCUSSING > HOCUS

HOD n open wooden box attached to a pole ▷ vb bob up and down

HODAD n person who pretends to be a surfer

HODADDIES > HODADDY

HODADDY same as > HODAD

HODADS > HODAD

HODDED > HOD

HODDEN n coarse homespun cloth

HODDENS > HODDEN

HODDIN same as > HODDEN

HODDING > HOD

HODDINS > HODDIN

HODDLE vb waddle

HODDLED > HODDLE

HODDLES > HODDLE

HODDLING > HODDLE

HODIERNAL adj of the present day

HODJA n respectful Turkish form of address

HODJAS > HODJA

HODMAN n hod carrier

HODMANDOD n snail

HODMEN > HODMAN

HODOGRAPH n curve of which the radius vector represents the velocity of a moving particle

HODOMETER another name for > ODOMETER

HODOMETRY > HODOMETER

HODOSCOPE n any device for tracing the path of a charged particle, esp a particle found in cosmic rays

HODS > HOD

HOE n long-handled tool used for loosening soil or weeding ▷ vb scrape or weed with a hoe
HOECAKE n maize cake
HOECAKES > HOECAKE
HOED > HOE
HOEDOWN n boisterous square dance
HOEDOWNS > HOEDOWN
HOEING > HOE
HOELIKE > HOE
HOER > HOE
HOERS > HOE
HOES > HOE
HOG n castrated male pig ▷ vb take more than one's share of
HOGAN n wooden dwelling covered with earth
HOGANS > HOGAN
HOGBACK n narrow ridge of steeply inclined rock strata
HOGBACKS > HOGBACK
HOGEN n strong alcoholic drink
HOGENS > HOGEN
HOGFISH n type of fish
HOGFISHES > HOGFISH
HOGG same as > HOG
HOGGED > HOG
HOGGER > HOG
HOGGEREL n year-old sheep
HOGGERELS > HOGGEREL
HOGGERIES > HOGGERY
HOGGERS > HOG
HOGGERY n hogs collectively
HOGGET n young sheep that has yet to be sheared
HOGGETS > HOGGET
HOGGIN n finely sifted gravel
HOGGING same as > HOGGIN
HOGGINGS > HOGGING
HOGGINS > HOGGIN
HOGGISH adj selfish, gluttonous, or dirty
HOGGISHLY > HOGGISH
HOGGS > HOGG
HOGH n ridge of land
HOGHOOD n condition of being hog
HOGHOODS > HOGHOOD
HOGHS > HOGH
HOGLIKE > HOG
HOGMANAY n New Year's Eve
HOGMANAYS > HOGMANAY
HOGMANE n short stiff mane
HOGMANES > HOGMANE
HOGMENAY variant of > HOGMANAY
HOGMENAYS > HOGMENAY
HOGNOSE n as in hognose snake puff adder
HOGNOSED adj as in hognosed skunk any of several American skunks having a broad snoutlike nose
HOGNOSES > HOGNOSE
HOGNUT another name for > PIGNUT
HOGNUTS > HOGNUT
HOGS > HOG
HOGSHEAD n large cask
HOGSHEADS > HOGSHEAD
HOGTIE vb tie together the legs or the arms and legs of
HOGTIED > HOGTIE
HOGTIEING > HOGTIE

HOGTIES > HOGTIE
HOGTYING > HOGTIE
HOGWARD n person looking after hogs
HOGWARDS > HOGWARD
HOGWASH n nonsense
HOGWASHES > HOGWASH
HOGWEED n any of several umbelliferous plants
HOGWEEDS > HOGWEED
HOH same as > HO
HOHA adj bored or annoyed
HOHED > HOH
HOHING > HOH
HOHS > HOH
HOI same as > HOY
HOICK vb raise abruptly and sharply
HOICKED > HOICK
HOICKING > HOICK
HOICKS interj cry used to encourage hounds to hunt ▷ vb shout hoicks
HOICKSED > HOICKS
HOICKSES > HOICKS
HOICKSING > HOICKS
HOIDEN same as > HOYDEN
HOIDENED > HOIDEN
HOIDENING > HOIDEN
HOIDENISH > HOIDEN
HOIDENS > HOIDEN
HOIED > HOI
HOIING > HOI
HOIK same as > HOICK
HOIKED > HOIK
HOIKING > HOIK
HOIKS > HOIK
HOING > HO
HOIS > HOI
HOISE same as > HOIST
HOISED > HOISE
HOISES > HOISE
HOISIN n Chinese sweet spicy sauce
HOISING > HOISE
HOISINS > HOISIN
HOIST vb raise or lift up ▷ n device for lifting things
HOISTED > HOIST
HOISTER > HOIST
HOISTERS > HOIST
HOISTING > HOIST
HOISTINGS > HOIST
HOISTMAN n person operating a hoist
HOISTMEN > HOISTMAN
HOISTS > HOIST
HOISTWAY n shaft for a hoist
HOISTWAYS > HOISTWAY
HOKA n red cod
HOKAS > HOKA
HOKE vb overplay (a part, etc)
HOKED > HOKE
HOKES > HOKE
HOKEY adj corny
HOKEYNESS > HOKEY
HOKI n fish of New Zealand waters
HOKIER > HOKEY
HOKIEST > HOKEY
HOKILY > HOKEY
HOKINESS > HOKEY
HOKING > HOKE
HOKIS > HOKI
HOKKU same as > HAIKU

HOKONUI n illicit whisky
HOKONUIS > HOKONUI
HOKUM n rubbish, nonsense
HOKUMS > HOKUM
HOKYPOKY n trickery
HOLANDRIC adj relating to Y-chromosomal genes
HOLARCHY n system composed of interacting holons
HOLARD n amount of water contained in soil
HOLARDS > HOLARD
HOLD vb keep or support in or with the hands or arms ▷ n act or way of holding
HOLDABLE > HOLD
HOLDALL n large strong travelling bag
HOLDALLS > HOLDALL
HOLDBACK n part of a horse harness
HOLDBACKS > HOLDBACK
HOLDDOWN n control function in a computer
HOLDDOWNS > HOLDDOWN
HOLDEN past participle of > HOLD
HOLDER n person or thing that holds
HOLDERBAT n part of pipe used as fastening
HOLDERS > HOLDER
HOLDFAST n act of gripping strongly
HOLDFASTS > HOLDFAST
HOLDING > HOLD
HOLDINGS > HOLD
HOLDOUT n (in US English) someone or thing that refuses to change
HOLDOUTS > HOLDOUT
HOLDOVER n official who continues in office after his or her term has expired
HOLDOVERS > HOLDOVER
HOLDS > HOLD
HOLDUP n robbery, esp an armed one
HOLDUPS > HOLDUP
HOLE n area hollowed out in a solid ▷ vb make holes in
HOLED > HOLE
HOLELESS > HOLE
HOLES > HOLE
HOLESOM same as > HOLESOME
HOLESOME same as > WHOLESOME
HOLEY adj full of holes
HOLEYER > HOLEY
HOLEYEST > HOLEY
HOLIBUT same as > HALIBUT
HOLIBUTS > HOLIBUT
HOLIDAY n time spent away from home for rest or recreation ▷ vb spend a holiday
HOLIDAYED > HOLIDAY
HOLIDAYER > HOLIDAY
HOLIDAYS > HOLIDAY
HOLIER > HOLY
HOLIES > HOLY
HOLIEST > HOLY
HOLILY adv in a holy, devout, or sacred manner

HOLINESS n state of being holy
HOLING > HOLE
HOLINGS > HOLE
HOLISM n view that a whole is greater than the sum of its parts
HOLISMS > HOLISM
HOLIST > HOLISM
HOLISTIC adj considering the complete person, physically and mentally
HOLISTS > HOLISM
HOLK vb dig
HOLKED > HOLK
HOLKING > HOLK
HOLKS > HOLK
HOLLA same as > HOLLO
HOLLAED > HOLLA
HOLLAING > HOLLA
HOLLAND n coarse linen cloth, used esp for furnishing
HOLLANDS > HOLLAND
HOLLAS > HOLLA
HOLLER vb shout, yell ▷ vb shout or yell
HOLLERED > HOLLER
HOLLERING > HOLLER
HOLLERS > HOLLER
HOLLIDAM same as > HALIDOM
HOLLIDAMS > HOLLIDAM
HOLLIES > HOLLY
HOLLO interj cry for attention, or of encouragement ▷ vb shout
HOLLOA same as > HOLLO
HOLLOAED > HOLLOA
HOLLOAING > HOLLOA
HOLLOAS > HOLLOA
HOLLOED > HOLLO
HOLLOES > HOLLO
HOLLOING > HOLLO
HOLLOO same as > HALLOO
HOLLOOED > HOLLOO
HOLLOOING > HOLLOO
HOLLOOS > HOLLOO
HOLLOS > HOLLO
HOLLOW adj having a hole or space inside ▷ n cavity or space ▷ vb form a hollow in
HOLLOWARE n hollow utensils such as cups
HOLLOWED > HOLLOW
HOLLOWER > HOLLOW
HOLLOWEST > HOLLOW
HOLLOWING > HOLLOW
HOLLOWLY > HOLLOW
HOLLOWS > HOLLOW
HOLLY n evergreen tree with prickly leaves and red berries
HOLLYHOCK n tall garden plant with spikes of colourful flowers
HOLM n island in a river, lake, or estuary
HOLME same as > HOLM
HOLMES > HOLME
HOLMIA n oxide of holmium
HOLMIAS > HOLMIA
HOLMIC adj of or containing holmium
HOLMIUM n silver-white metallic element
HOLMIUMS > HOLMIUM
HOLMS > HOLM
HOLO n short for hologram

HOLOCAINE n type of anaesthetic for the eye
HOLOCAUST n destruction or loss of life on a massive scale
HOLOCENE adj of the most recent epoch of the Quaternary period
HOLOCRINE adj (of the secretion of glands) characterized by disintegration of the entire glandular cell in releasing its product, as in sebaceous glands
HOLOGAMY n condition of having gametes like ordinary cells
HOLOGRAM n three-dimensional photographic image
HOLOGRAMS > HOLOGRAM
HOLOGRAPH n document handwritten by the author
HOLOGYNIC adj passed down through females
HOLOGYNY n inheritance of genetic traits through females only
HOLOHEDRA n geometrical forms with particular symmetry
HOLON n autonomous self-reliant unit, esp in manufacturing
HOLONIC > HOLON
HOLONS > HOLON
HOLOPHOTE n device for directing light from lighthouse
HOLOPHYTE n plant capable of synthesizing food from inorganic molecules
HOLOPTIC adj with eyes meeting at the front
HOLOS > HOLO
HOLOTYPE n original specimen from which a description of a new species is made
HOLOTYPES > HOLOTYPE
HOLOTYPIC > HOLOTYPE
HOLOZOIC adj (of animals) obtaining nourishment by feeding on plants or other animals
HOLP past tense of > HELP
HOLPEN past participle of > HELP
HOLS pl n holidays
HOLSTEIN n breed of cattle
HOLSTEINS > HOLSTEIN
HOLSTER n leather case for a pistol, hung from a belt ▷ vb return (a pistol) to its holster
HOLSTERED > HOLSTER
HOLSTERS > HOLSTER
HOLT n otter's lair
HOLTS > HOLT
HOLUBTSI pl n cabbage rolls
HOLY adj of God or a god ▷ n sacred place
HOLYDAM same as > HALIDOM
HOLYDAME same as > HALIDOM
HOLYDAMES > HOLYDAME
HOLYDAMS > HOLYDAM

HOLYDAY n day on which a religious festival is observed
HOLYDAYS > HOLYDAY
HOLYSTONE n soft sandstone used for scrubbing the decks of a vessel ▷ vb scrub (a vessel's decks) with a holystone
HOLYTIDE n time for special religious observance
HOLYTIDES > HOLYTIDE
HOM n sacred plant of the Parsees and ancient Persians
HOMA same as > HOM
HOMAGE n show of respect or honour towards someone or something ▷ vb render homage to
HOMAGED > HOMAGE
HOMAGER > HOMAGE
HOMAGERS > HOMAGE
HOMAGES > HOMAGE
HOMAGING > HOMAGE
HOMALOID n geometrical plane
HOMALOIDS > HOMALOID
HOMAS > HOMA
HOMBRE slang word for > MAN
HOMBRES > HOMBRE
HOMBURG n man's soft felt hat
HOMBURGS > HOMBURG
HOME n place where one lives ▷ adj of one's home, birthplace, or native country ▷ adv to or at home ▷ vb direct towards (a point or target)
HOMEBIRD n person who is reluctant to leave their home
HOMEBIRDS > HOMEBIRD
HOMEBIRTH n act of giving birth to a child in one's own home
HOMEBODY n person whose life and interests are centred on the home
HOMEBOUND adj heading for home
HOMEBOY n close friend
HOMEBOYS > HOMEBOY
HOMEBRED adj raised or bred at home ▷ n animal bred at home
HOMEBREDS > HOMEBRED
HOMEBREW n home-made beer
HOMEBREWS > HOMEBREW
HOMEBUILT adj built at home
HOMEBUYER n person buying a home
HOMECOMER n person coming home
HOMECRAFT n skills used in the home
HOMED > HOME
HOMEFELT adj felt personally
HOMEGIRL > HOMEBOY
HOMEGIRLS > HOMEBOY
HOMEGROWN adj (esp of fruit and vegetables) produced in one's own country, district, estate, or garden
HOMELAND n country from which a person's ancestors came

HOMELANDS > HOMELAND
HOMELESS adj having nowhere to live ▷ pl n people who have nowhere to live
HOMELIER > HOMELY
HOMELIEST > HOMELY
HOMELIKE > HOME
HOMELILY > HOMELY
HOMELY adj simple, ordinary, and comfortable
HOMELYN n species of ray
HOMELYNS > HOMELYN
HOMEMADE adj made at home
HOMEMAKER n person, esp a housewife, who manages a home
HOMEOBOX adj of genes that regulate cell development
HOMEOMERY n condition of being made up of similar parts
HOMEOPATH n person who treats disease by the use of small amounts of a drug that produces symptoms like those of the disease being treated
HOMEOSES > HOMEOSIS
HOMEOSIS n process of one part coming to resemble another
HOMEOTIC > HOMEOSIS
HOMEOWNER n person who owns the home in which he or she lives
HOMEPAGE n main page of website
HOMEPAGES > HOMEPAGE
HOMEPLACE n person's home
HOMEPORT n port where vessel is registered
HOMEPORTS > HOMEPORT
HOMER n homing pigeon ▷ vb score a home run in baseball
HOMERED > HOMER
HOMERIC adj grand or heroic
HOMERING > HOMER
HOMEROOM n common room at school
HOMEROOMS > HOMEROOM
HOMERS > HOMER
HOMES > HOME
HOMESICK adj sad because missing one's home and family
HOMESITE n site for building house
HOMESITES > HOMESITE
HOMESPUN adj (of philosophies or opinions) plain and unsophisticated ▷ n cloth made at home or made of yarn spun at home
HOMESPUNS > HOMESPUN
HOMESTALL same as > HOMESTEAD
HOMESTAND n series of games played at a team's home ground
HOMESTAY n period spent living as a guest in someone's home
HOMESTAYS > HOMESTAY
HOMESTEAD n farmhouse plus the adjoining land

HOMESTYLE adj (of cooking) simple and unfussy
HOMETOWN n town where one lives or was born
HOMETOWNS > HOMETOWN
HOMEWARD adj going home ▷ adv towards home
HOMEWARDS adv towards home
HOMEWARE n crockery, furniture, and furnishings with which a house, room, etc, is furnished
HOMEWARES > HOMEWARE
HOMEWORK n school work done at home
HOMEWORKS > HOMEWORK
HOMEY same as > HOMY
HOMEYNESS > HOMEY
HOMEYS > HOMEY
HOMICIDAL adj of, involving, or characterized by homicide
HOMICIDE n killing of a human being
HOMICIDES > HOMICIDE
HOMIE short for > HOMEBOY
HOMIER > HOMY
HOMIES > HOMIE
HOMIEST > HOMY
HOMILETIC adj of or relating to a homily or sermon
HOMILIES > HOMILY
HOMILIST > HOMILY
HOMILISTS > HOMILY
HOMILY n speech telling people how they should behave
HOMINES > HOMO
HOMINESS > HOMY
HOMING adj relating to the ability to return home after travelling ▷ n ability to return home after travelling
HOMINGS > HOMING
HOMINIAN same as > HOMINID
HOMINIANS > HOMINIAN
HOMINID n humankind or any extinct forerunner of humankind ▷ adj of or belonging to this family
HOMINIDS > HOMINID
HOMINIES > HOMINY
HOMININ n member of a zoological family
HOMININE adj characteristic of humans
HOMININS > HOMININ
HOMINISE same as > HOMINIZE
HOMINISED > HOMINISE
HOMINISES > HOMINISE
HOMINIZE vb make suitable for humans
HOMINIZED > HOMINIZE
HOMINIZES > HOMINIZE
HOMINOID n humanlike animal ▷ adj of or like a human
HOMINOIDS > HOMINOID
HOMINY n coarsely ground maize
HOMME French word for > MAN
HOMMES > HOMME
HOMMOCK same as > HUMMOCK

HOMMOCKS > HOMMOCK
HOMMOS *same as* > HUMMUS
HOMMOSES > HOMMOS
HOMO *n* homogenized milk
HOMOCERCY *n* condition in fish of having a symmetrical tail
HOMODONT *adj* (of most nonmammalian vertebrates) having teeth that are all of the same type
HOMODYNE *adj* of strengthened radio waves
HOMOEOBOX *same as* > HOMEOBOX
HOMOEOSES > HOMOEOSIS
HOMOEOSIS *n* condition of controlling a system from within
HOMOEOTIC > HOMOEOSIS
HOMOGAMIC > HOMOGAMY
HOMOGAMY *n* simultaneous maturation of all the anthers and stigmas of a flower
HOMOGENY *n* similarity in structure of individuals or parts because of common ancestry
HOMOGONY *n* condition in a plant of having stamens and styles of the same length in all the flowers
HOMOGRAFT *n* tissue graft obtained from an organism of the same species as the recipient
HOMOGRAPH *n* word spelt the same as another, but with a different meaning
HOMOLOG *same as* > HOMOLOGUE
HOMOLOGIC *adj* having a related or similar position, structure, etc
HOMOLOGS > HOMOLOG
HOMOLOGUE *n* homologous part or organ
HOMOLOGY *n* condition of being homologous
HOMOLYSES > HOMOLYSIS
HOMOLYSIS *n* dissociation of a molecule into two neutral fragments
HOMOLYTIC > HOMOLYSIS
HOMOMORPH *n* thing same in form as something else
HOMONYM *n* word that is spelt the same as another
HOMONYMIC > HOMONYM
HOMONYMS > HOMONYM
HOMONYMY *n* the quality of being pronounced or spelt in the same way
HOMOPHILE *n* rare word for homosexual
HOMOPHOBE *n* person who hates homosexuality
HOMOPHONE *n* word pronounced the same as another, but with a different meaning or spelling
HOMOPHONY *n* linguistic phenomenon whereby words of different origins become identical in pronunciation
HOMOPHYLY *n* resemblance due to common ancestry

HOMOPLASY *n* state of being derived from an individual of the same species as the recipient
HOMOPOLAR *adj* of uniform charge
HOMOS > HOMO
HOMOSEX *n* sexual activity between homosexuals
HOMOSEXES > HOMOSEX
HOMOSPORY *n* state of producing spores of one kind only
HOMOSTYLY *n* (in flowers) existence of styles of only one length
HOMOTAXES > HOMOTAXIS
HOMOTAXIC > HOMOTAXIS
HOMOTAXIS *n* similarity of composition and arrangement in rock strata of different ages or in different regions
HOMOTONIC *adj* of same tone
HOMOTONY > HOMOTONIC
HOMOTYPAL *adj* of normal type
HOMOTYPE *n* something with same structure as something else
HOMOTYPES > HOMOTYPE
HOMOTYPIC *same as* > HOMOTYPAL
HOMOTYPY > HOMOTYPE
HOMOUSIAN *adj* believing God the Son and God the Father to be of the same essence
HOMS > HOM
HOMUNCLE *n* homunculus
HOMUNCLES > HOMUNCLE
HOMUNCULE *n* homunculus
HOMUNCULI *n* plural of homunculus: miniature man
HOMY *adj* like a home
HON *short for* > HONEY
HONAN *n* silk fabric of rough weave
HONANS > HONAN
HONCHO *n* person in charge ▷ *vb* supervise or be in charge of
HONCHOED > HONCHO
HONCHOES > HONCHO
HONCHOING > HONCHO
HONCHOS > HONCHO
HOND *old form of* > HAND
HONDA *n* loop used to make a lasso
HONDAS > HONDA
HONDLE *vb* negotiate on price
HONDLED > HONDLE
HONDLES > HONDLE
HONDLING > HONDLE
HONDS > HOND
HONE *vb* sharpen ▷ *n* fine whetstone used for sharpening edged tools and knives
HONED > HONE
HONER > HONE
HONERS > HONE
HONES > HONE
HONEST *adj* truthful and moral

HONESTER > HONEST
HONESTEST > HONEST
HONESTIES > HONESTY
HONESTLY *adv* in an honest manner ▷ *interj* expression of disgust, surprise, etc
HONESTY *n* quality of being honest
HONEWORT *n* European plant that has clusters of small white flowers
HONEWORTS > HONEWORT
HONEY *n* edible substance made by bees; term of endearment ▷ *vb* sweeten with or as if with honey
HONEYBEE *n* bee widely domesticated as a source of honey and beeswax
HONEYBEES > HONEYBEE
HONEYBELL *n* hybrid citrus fruit
HONEYBUN *n* term of endearment
HONEYBUNS > HONEYBUN
HONEYCOMB *n* waxy structure of six-sided cells in which honey is stored by bees in a beehive ▷ *vb* pierce or fill with holes, cavities, etc
HONEYDEW *n* sugary substance produced by aphids and similar insects
HONEYDEWS > HONEYDEW
HONEYED > HONEY
HONEYEDLY > HONEY
HONEYFUL *adj* full of honey
HONEYING > HONEY
HONEYLESS > HONEY
HONEYMOON *n* holiday taken by a newly married couple ▷ *vb* take a honeymoon
HONEYPOT *n* container for honey
HONEYPOTS > HONEYPOT
HONEYS > HONEY
HONEYTRAP *n* scheme in which a victim is lured into a compromising situation by an attractive person
HONG *n* (in China) a factory, warehouse, etc ▷ *vb* archaic form of hang
HONGI *n* Māori greeting in which people touch noses ▷ *vb* touch noses
HONGIED > HONGI
HONGIES > HONGI
HONGIING > HONGI
HONGING > HONG
HONGIS > HONGI
HONGS > HONG
HONIED *same as* > HONEYED
HONIEDLY > HONEY
HONING > HONE
HONK *n* sound made by a car horn ▷ *vb* (cause to) make this sound
HONKED > HONK
HONKER *n* person or thing that honks
HONKERS > HONKER
HONKEY *same as* > HONKY
HONKEYS > HONKEY
HONKIE *same as* > HONKY
HONKIES > HONKY
HONKING > HONK

HONKS > HONK
HONKY *n* derogatory term for a White person or White people collectively
HONOR *same as* > HONOUR
HONORABLE *adj* possessing high principles
HONORABLY *adv* in an honourable way
HONORAND *n* person being honoured
HONORANDS > HONORAND
HONORARIA *n* fee pain for a nominally free service
HONORARY *adj* held or given only as an honour
HONORED > HONOR
HONOREE *same as* > HONORAND
HONOREES > HONOREE
HONORER > HONOUR
HONORERS > HONOUR
HONORIFIC *adj* showing respect
HONORING > HONOR
HONORLESS > HONOUR
HONORS *same as* > HONOURS
HONOUR *n* sense of honesty and fairness ▷ *vb* give praise and attention to
HONOURARY *less common spelling of* > HONORARY
HONOURED > HONOUR
HONOUREE *n* person who is honoured
HONOUREES > HONOUREE
HONOURER > HONOUR
HONOURERS > HONOUR
HONOURING > HONOUR
HONOURS > HONOUR
HONS > HON
HOO *interj* expression of joy, excitement, etc
HOOCH *n* alcoholic drink, esp illicitly distilled spirits
HOOCHES > HOOCH
HOOCHIE *n* immoral woman
HOOCHIES > HOOCHIE
HOOD *n* head covering, often attached to a coat or jacket ▷ *vb* cover with or as if with a hood
HOODED *adj* (of a garment) having a hood
HOODIA *n* any of several southern African succulent plants
HOODIAS > HOODIA
HOODIE *n* hooded sweatshirt
HOODIER > HOOD
HOODIES > HOODIE
HOODIEST > HOOD
HOODING > HOOD
HOODLESS > HOOD
HOODLIKE > HOOD
HOODLUM *n* violent criminal, gangster
HOODLUMS > HOODLUM
HOODMAN *n* blindfolded person in blind man's buff
HOODMEN > HOODMAN
HOODMOLD *n* moulding over door or window
HOODMOLDS > HOODMOLD
HOODOO *n* (cause of) bad luck ▷ *vb* bring bad luck to

h

h

HOODOOED > HOODOO
HOODOOING > HOODOO
HOODOOISM > HOODOO
HOODOOS > HOODOO
HOODS > HOOD
HOODWINK vb trick, deceive
HOODWINKS > HOODWINK
HOODY > HOOD
HOOEY n nonsense ▷ interj nonsense
HOOEYS > HOOEY
HOOF n horny covering of the foot of a horse, deer, etc ▷ vb kick or trample with the hooves
HOOFBEAT n sound made by hoof on the ground
HOOFBEATS > HOOFBEAT
HOOFBOUND adj (of a horse) having dry contracted hooves, with resultant pain and lameness
HOOFED adj having a hoof or hoofs
HOOFER n professional dancer
HOOFERS > HOOFER
HOOFING > HOOF
HOOFLESS > HOOF
HOOFLIKE > HOOF
HOOFPRINT n mark made by hoof on ground
HOOFROT n disease of hoof
HOOFROTS > HOOFROT
HOOFS > HOOF
HOOK n curved object used to hang, hold, or pull something ▷ vb fasten or catch (as if) with a hook
HOOKA same as > HOOKAH
HOOKAH n oriental pipe
HOOKAHS > HOOKAH
HOOKAS > HOOKA
HOOKCHECK n in ice hockey, act of hooking an opposing player
HOOKED adj bent like a hook
HOOKER n person or thing that hooks
HOOKERS > HOOKER
HOOKEY same as > HOOKY
HOOKEYS > HOOKEY
HOOKIER > HOOKY
HOOKIES > HOOKY
HOOKIEST > HOOKY
HOOKING n act of hooking
HOOKINGS > HOOKING
HOOKLESS > HOOK
HOOKLET n little hook
HOOKLETS > HOOKLET
HOOKLIKE > HOOK
HOOKNOSE n nose with a pronounced outward and downward curve
HOOKNOSED > HOOKNOSE
HOOKNOSES > HOOKNOSE
HOOKS > HOOK
HOOKUP n contact of an aircraft with the hose of a tanker aircraft
HOOKUPS > HOOKUP
HOOKWORM n blood-sucking worm with hooked mouthparts
HOOKWORMS > HOOKWORM
HOOKY n truancy, usually from school ▷ adj hooklike

HOOLACHAN n Highland reel
HOOLEY n lively party
HOOLEYS > HOOLEY
HOOLICAN same as > HOOLACHAN
HOOLICANS > HOOLICAN
HOOLIE same as > HOOLEY
HOOLIER > HOOLY
HOOLIES > HOOLIE
HOOLIEST > HOOLY
HOOLIGAN n rowdy young person
HOOLIGANS > HOOLIGAN
HOOLOCK n Indian gibbon
HOOLOCKS > HOOLOCK
HOOLY adj careful or gentle
HOON n loutish youth who drives irresponsibly ▷ vb drive irresponsibly
HOONED > HOON
HOONING > HOON
HOONS > HOON
HOOP n rigid circular band ▷ vb surround with or as if with a hoop
HOOPED > HOOP
HOOPER rare word for > COOPER
HOOPERS > HOOPER
HOOPING > HOOP
HOOPLA n fairground game
HOOPLAS > HOOPLA
HOOPLESS > HOOP
HOOPLIKE > HOOP
HOOPOE n bird with a pinkish-brown plumage
HOOPOES > HOOPOE
HOOPOO same as > HOOPOE
HOOPOOS > HOOPOO
HOOPS > HOOP
HOOPSKIRT n skirt stiffened by hoops
HOOPSTER n basketball player
HOOPSTERS > HOOPSTER
HOOR n unpleasant or difficult thing
HOORAH same as > HURRAH
HOORAHED > HOORAH
HOORAHING > HOORAH
HOORAHS > HOORAH
HOORAY same as > HURRAH
HOORAYED > HOORAY
HOORAYING > HOORAY
HOORAYS > HOORAY
HOORD same as > HOARD
HOORDS > HOORD
HOOROO n cheer of joy or victory ▷ vb shout "hooroo"
HOOROOED > HOOROO
HOOROOING > HOOROO
HOOROOS > HOOROO
HOORS > HOOR
HOOSEGOW slang word for > JAIL
HOOSEGOWS > HOOSEGOW
HOOSGOW same as > JAIL
HOOSGOWS > HOOSGOW
HOOSH vb shoo away
HOOSHED > HOOSH
HOOSHES > HOOSH
HOOSHING > HOOSH
HOOT n sound of a car horn ▷ vb sound (a car horn) ▷ interj exclamation of impatience or dissatisfaction

HOOTCH same as > HOOCH
HOOTCHES > HOOTCH
HOOTED > HOOT
HOOTER n device that hoots
HOOTERS > HOOTER
HOOTIER > HOOT
HOOTIEST > HOOT
HOOTING > HOOT
HOOTNANNY n informal performance by folk singers
HOOTS same as > HOOT
HOOTY > HOOT
HOOVE same as > HEAVE
HOOVED > HOOVE
HOOVEN > HOOVE
HOOVER vb vacuum-clean (a carpet, furniture, etc)
HOOVERED > HOOVER
HOOVERING n act of hoovering
HOOVERS > HOOVER
HOOVES > HOOF
HOOVING > HOOVE
HOP vb jump on one foot ▷ n instance of hopping
HOPAK n type of Ukrainian dance
HOPAKS > HOPAK
HOPBIND n stalk of the hop
HOPBINDS > HOPBIND
HOPBINE same as > HOPBIND
HOPBINES > HOPBINE
HOPDOG n species of caterpillar
HOPDOGS > HOPDOG
HOPE vb want (something) to happen or be true ▷ n expectation of something desired
HOPED > HOPE
HOPEFUL adj having, expressing, or inspiring hope ▷ n person considered to be on the brink of success
HOPEFULLY adv in a hopeful manner
HOPEFULS > HOPEFUL
HOPELESS adj having or offering no hope
HOPER > HOPE
HOPERS > HOPE
HOPES > HOPE
HOPFIELD n field where hops are grown
HOPFIELDS > HOPFIELD
HOPHEAD n heroin or opium addict
HOPHEADS > HOPHEAD
HOPING > HOPE
HOPINGLY > HOPE
HOPLITE n (in ancient Greece) a heavily armed infantryman
HOPLITES > HOPLITE
HOPLITIC > HOPLITE
HOPLOLOGY n study of weapons or armour
HOPPED > HOP
HOPPER n container for storing substances
HOPPERCAR same as > HOPPER
HOPPERS > HOPPER
HOPPIER > HOPPY
HOPPIEST > HOPPY
HOPPINESS n state of tasting or smelling of hops

HOPPING > HOP
HOPPINGS > HOP
HOPPLE same as > HOBBLE
HOPPLED > HOPPLE
HOPPLER > HOPPLE
HOPPLERS > HOPPLE
HOPPLES > HOPPLE
HOPPLING > HOPPLE
HOPPUS adj as in hoppus foot unit of volume for round timber
HOPPY adj tasting of hops
HOPS > HOP
HOPSACK n roughly woven fabric
HOPSACKS > HOPSACK
HOPSCOTCH n children's game of hopping in a pattern drawn on the ground
HOPTOAD n toad
HOPTOADS > HOPTOAD
HORA n traditional Israeli or Romanian circle dance
HORAH same as > HORA
HORAHS > HORAH
HORAL less common word for > HOURLY
HORARY adj relating to the hours
HORAS > HORA
HORDE n large crowd ▷ vb form, move in, or live in a horde
HORDED > HORDE
HORDEIN n simple protein, rich in proline, that occurs in barley
HORDEINS > HORDEIN
HORDEOLA > HORDEOLUM
HORDEOLUM n (in medicine) stye
HORDES > HORDE
HORDING > HORDE
HORDOCK same as > HARDOKE
HORDOCKS > HORDOCK
HORE same as > HOAR
HOREHOUND n plant that produces a bitter juice formerly used as a cough medicine
HORI n offensive term for a Māori
HORIATIKI n traditional Greek salad consisting of tomatoes, cucumber, onion, olives, and feta cheese
HORIS > HORI
HORIZON n apparent line that divides the earth and the sky
HORIZONAL > HORIZON
HORIZONS > HORIZON
HORK vb spit
HORKED > HORK
HORKEY same as > HOCKEY
HORKEYS > HORKEY
HORKING > HORK
HORKS > HORK
HORLICKS n as in make a horlicks make a mistake or a mess
HORME n (in Jungian psychology) fundamental vital energy
HORMES > HORME
HORMESES > HORMES

HORMESIS n beneficial effect of exposure to a very small amount of a toxic substance

HORMETIC adj relating to hormesis

HORMIC > HORME

HORMONAL > HORMONE

HORMONE n substance secreted by certain glands

HORMONES > HORMONE

HORMONIC > HORMONE

HORN n one of a pair of bony growths ▷ vb provide with a horn or horns

HORNBAG n in Australian slang, a promiscuous woman

HORNBAGS > HORNBAG

HORNBEAK n garfish

HORNBEAKS > HORNBEAK

HORNBEAM n tree with smooth grey bark

HORNBEAMS > HORNBEAM

HORNBILL n bird with a bony growth on its large beak

HORNBILLS > HORNBILL

HORNBOOK n page of religious text with flattened cow horn over it

HORNBOOKS > HORNBOOK

HORNBUG n stag beetle

HORNBUGS > HORNBUG

HORNDOG n sexually aggressive man

HORNDOGS > HORNDOG

HORNED adj having a horn, horns, or hornlike parts

HORNER n dealer in horn

HORNERS > HORNER

HORNET n large wasp with a severe sting

HORNETS > HORNET

HORNFELS n hard fine-grained metamorphic rock

HORNFISH n fish of the needlefish family

HORNFUL n amount a horn will hold

HORNFULS > HORNFUL

HORNGELD n feudal rent based on number of cattle

HORNGELDS > HORNGELD

HORNIER > HORNY

HORNIEST > HORNY

HORNILY > HORNY

HORNINESS > HORNY

HORNING > HORN

HORNINGS > HORN

HORNISH adj like horn

HORNIST n horn player

HORNISTS > HORNIST

HORNITO n small vent in volcano

HORNITOS > HORNITO

HORNLESS > HORN

HORNLET n small horn

HORNLETS > HORNLET

HORNLIKE > HORN

HORNPIPE n (music for) a solo dance, traditionally performed by sailors

HORNPIPES > HORNPIPE

HORNPOUT n catfish

HORNPOUTS > HORNPOUT

HORNS > HORN

HORNSTONE same as > HORNFELS

HORNTAIL n wasplike insect

HORNTAILS > HORNTAIL

HORNWORK n bastion in fortifications

HORNWORKS > HORNWORK

HORNWORM n caterpillar of hawk moth

HORNWORMS > HORNWORM

HORNWORT n aquatic plant

HORNWORTS > HORNWORT

HORNWRACK n yellowish bryozoan or sea mat sometimes found on beaches after a storm

HORNY adj of or like horn

HORNYHEAD n species of fish

HORNYWINK n lapwing

HOROEKA n New Zealand tree

HOROEKAS > HOROEKA

HOROKAKA n low-growing New Zealand plant with fleshy leaves and pink or white flowers

HOROKAKAS > HOROKAKA

HOROLOGE rare word for > TIMEPIECE

HOROLOGER n an expert maker of timepieces

HOROLOGES > HOROLOGE

HOROLOGIA n plural of horologium: clocktower

HOROLOGIC > HOROLOGY

HOROLOGY n art of making clocks and watches or of measuring time

HOROMETRY n measurement of time

HOROPITO n New Zealand plant

HOROPITOS > HOROPITO

HOROPTER n locus of points in space that have the same disparity as fixation

HOROPTERS > HOROPTER

HOROSCOPE n prediction of a person's future based on the positions of the planets, sun, and moon at his or her birth

HOROSCOPY n casting and interpretation of horoscopes

HORRENT adj bristling

HORRIBLE adj disagreeable, unpleasant ▷ n horrible thing

HORRIBLES > HORRIBLE

HORRIBLY adv in a horrible manner

HORRID adj disagreeable, unpleasant

HORRIDER > HORRID

HORRIDEST > HORRID

HORRIDLY > HORRID

HORRIFIC adj causing horror

HORRIFIED adj terrified

HORRIFIES > HORRIFY

HORRIFY vb cause to feel horror or shock

HORROR n (thing or person causing) terror or hatred ▷ adj having a frightening subject

HORRORS pl n fit of depression or anxiety ▷ interj expression of dismay, sometimes facetious

HORS adv as in hors d'oeuvre appetizer

HORSE n large animal with hooves, a mane, and a tail ▷ vb provide with a horse

HORSEBACK n horse's back

HORSEBEAN n broad bean

HORSEBOX n trailer used for transporting horses

HORSECAR n streetcar drawn by horses

HORSECARS > HORSECAR

HORSED > HORSE

HORSEFLY n large bloodsucking fly

HORSEHAIR n hair from the tail or mane of a horse

HORSEHEAD n head of a horse

HORSEHIDE n hide of a horse

HORSELESS > HORSE

HORSELIKE > HORSE

HORSEMAN n person skilled in riding

HORSEMEAT n flesh of the horse used as food

HORSEMEN > HORSEMAN

HORSEMINT n European mint plant

HORSEPLAY n rough or rowdy play

HORSEPOND n pond where horses drink

HORSEPOX n viral infection of horses

HORSERACE n race for horses

HORSES > HORSE

HORSESHIT n vulgar word for nonsense, rubbish

HORSESHOD > HORSESHOE

HORSESHOE n protective U-shaped piece of iron nailed to a horse's hoof, regarded as a symbol of good luck ▷ vb fit with a horseshoe

HORSETAIL n plant with small dark toothlike leaves

HORSEWAY n road for horses

HORSEWAYS > HORSEWAY

HORSEWEED n US name for Canadian fleabane

HORSEWHIP n whip with a long thong, used for managing horses ▷ vb beat (a person or animal) with such a whip

HORSEY adj very keen on horses

HORSIE n child's word for a horse

HORSIER > HORSEY

HORSIES > HORSIE

HORSIEST > HORSEY

HORSILY > HORSEY

HORSINESS > HORSEY

HORSING > HORSE

HORSINGS > HORSE

HORSON same as > WHORESON

HORSONS > HORSON

HORST n ridge of land

HORSTE variant of > HORST

HORSTES > HORSTE

HORSTS > HORST

HORSY same as > HORSEY

HORTATION > HORTATORY

HORTATIVE same as > HORTATORY

HORTATORY adj encouraging

HORTENSIA n type of hydrangea

HOS > HO

HOSANNA interj exclamation of praise to God ▷ n act of crying "hosanna" ▷ vb cry hosanna

HOSANNAED > HOSANNA

HOSANNAH same as > HOSANNA

HOSANNAHS > HOSANNAH

HOSANNAS > HOSANNA

HOSE n flexible pipe for conveying liquid ▷ vb water with a hose

HOSED > HOSE

HOSEL n socket in head of golf club

HOSELIKE > HOSE

HOSELS > HOSEL

HOSEMAN n fireman in charge of hose

HOSEMEN > HOSEMAN

HOSEN > HOSE

HOSEPIPE n hose

HOSEPIPES > HOSEPIPE

HOSER n person who swindles or deceives others

HOSERS > HOSER

HOSES > HOSE

HOSEY vb claim possession

HOSEYED > HOSEY

HOSEYING > HOSEY

HOSEYS > HOSEY

HOSIER n person who sells stockings, etc

HOSIERIES > HOSIERY

HOSIERS > HOSIER

HOSIERY n stockings, socks, and tights collectively

HOSING > HOSE

HOSPICE n nursing home for the terminally ill

HOSPICES > HOSPICE

HOSPITAGE n behaviour of guest

HOSPITAL n place where people who are ill are looked after and treated

HOSPITALE n lodging

HOSPITALS > HOSPITAL

HOSPITIA > HOSPITIUM

HOSPITIUM same as > HOSPICE

HOSPODAR n (formerly) the governor or prince of Moldavia or Wallachia under Ottoman rule

HOSPODARS > HOSPODAR

HOSS n horse

HOSSES > HOSS

HOST n person who entertains guests ▷ vb be the host of

HOSTA n ornamental plant

HOSTAGE n person who is illegally held prisoner

HOSTAGES > HOSTAGE

HOSTAS > HOSTA

h

HOSTED > HOST
HOSTEL n building providing accommodation ▷ vb stay in hostels
HOSTELED > HOSTEL
HOSTELER same as > HOSTELLER
HOSTELERS > HOSTELER
HOSTELING n hostelling
HOSTELLED > HOSTEL
HOSTELLER n person who stays at youth hostels
HOSTELRY n inn, pub
HOSTELS > HOSTEL
HOSTESS n woman who receives and entertains guests ▷ vb act as hostess
HOSTESSED > HOSTESS
HOSTESSES > HOSTESS
HOSTIE n informal Australian word for an air hostess
HOSTIES > HOSTIE
HOSTILE adj unfriendly ▷ n hostile person
HOSTILELY > HOSTILE
HOSTILES > HOSTILE
HOSTILITY n unfriendly and aggressive feelings or behaviour
HOSTING > HOST
HOSTINGS > HOST
HOSTLER another name (esp Brit) for > OSTLER
HOSTLERS > HOSTLER
HOSTLESS adj lacking a host
HOSTLESSE adj inhospitable
HOSTLY > HOST
HOSTRIES > HOSTRY
HOSTRY n lodging
HOSTS > HOST
HOT adj having a high temperature ▷ vb make or become hot
HOTBED n any place encouraging a particular activity
HOTBEDS > HOTBED
HOTBLOOD n type of horse
HOTBLOODS > HOTBLOOD
HOTBOX n container maintained at a high temperature to heat its contents ▷ vb smoke marijuana in a closed room
HOTBOXED > HOTBOX
HOTBOXES > HOTBOX
HOTBOXING > HOTBOX
HOTCAKE n pancake
HOTCAKES > HOTCAKE
HOTCH vb jog
HOTCHED > HOTCH
HOTCHES > HOTCH
HOTCHING > HOTCH
HOTCHPOT n collecting of property so that it may be redistributed in equal shares
HOTCHPOTS > HOTCHPOT
HOTDOG vb perform a series of manoeuvres in skiing, etc
HOTDOGGED > HOTDOG
HOTDOGGER > HOTDOG
HOTDOGS > HOTDOG
HOTE > HIGHT
HOTEL n establishment providing lodging and meals

HOTELDOM n hotel business
HOTELDOMS > HOTELDOM
HOTELIER n owner or manager of a hotel
HOTELIERS > HOTELIER
HOTELING n office practice in which desk space is booked in advance by an employee as required
HOTELINGS > HOTELING
HOTELLING same as > HOTELING
HOTELMAN n hotel owner
HOTELMEN > HOTELMAN
HOTELS > HOTEL
HOTEN > HIGHT
HOTFOOT adv quickly and eagerly ▷ vb move quickly
HOTFOOTED > HOTFOOT
HOTFOOTS > HOTFOOT
HOTHEAD n excitable or fiery person
HOTHEADED adj impetuous, rash, or hot-tempered
HOTHEADS > HOTHEAD
HOTHOUSE n greenhouse
HOTHOUSED adj taught intensively
HOTHOUSES > HOTHOUSE
HOTLINE n direct telephone link for emergency use
HOTLINER n person running a phone-in radio programme
HOTLINERS > HOTLINER
HOTLINES > HOTLINE
HOTLINK n area on website connecting to another site
HOTLINKS > HOTLINK
HOTLY > HOT
HOTNESS > HOT
HOTNESSES > HOT
HOTPLATE n heated metal surface on an electric cooker
HOTPLATES > HOTPLATE
HOTPOT n casserole topped with potatoes
HOTPOTS > HOTPOT
HOTPRESS vb subject (paper, cloth, etc) to heat and pressure
HOTROD n car with a modified engine for increased power
HOTRODS > HOTROD
HOTS > HOT
HOTSHOT n important person or expert, esp when showy
HOTSHOTS > HOTSHOT
HOTSPOT n place where wireless broadband is provided
HOTSPOTS > HOTSPOT
HOTSPUR n impetuous or fiery person
HOTSPURS > HOTSPUR
HOTTED > HOT
HOTTENTOT n as in hottentot fig perennial plant with fleshy leaves, showy yellow or purple flowers, and edible fruits
HOTTER vb simmer
HOTTERED > HOTTER
HOTTERING > HOTTER
HOTTERS > HOTTER
HOTTEST > HOT

HOTTIE n attractive person
HOTTIES > HOTTIE
HOTTING n stealing fast cars to put on a show of skilful driving
HOTTINGS > HOTTING
HOTTISH adj fairly hot
HOTTY same as > HOTTIE
HOUDAH same as > HOWDAH
HOUDAHS > HOUDAH
HOUDAN n breed of light domestic fowl
HOUDANS > HOUDAN
HOUF same as > HOWF
HOUFED > HOUF
HOUFF same as > HOWF
HOUFFED > HOUFF
HOUFFING > HOUFF
HOUFFS > HOUFF
HOUFING > HOUF
HOUFS > HOUF
HOUGH n in Scotland, a cut of meat corresponding to shin ▷ vb hamstring (cattle, horses, etc)
HOUGHED > HOUGH
HOUGHING > HOUGH
HOUGHS > HOUGH
HOUHERE n small evergreen New Zealand tree
HOUHERES > HOUHERE
HOUMMOS same as > HUMMUS
HOUMMOSES > HOUMMOS
HOUMOUS same as > HUMMUS
HOUMOUSES > HOUMOUS
HOUMUS same as > HUMMUS
HOUMUSES > HOUMUS
HOUND n hunting dog ▷ vb pursue relentlessly
HOUNDED > HOUND
HOUNDER > HOUND
HOUNDERS > HOUND
HOUNDFISH n name given to various small sharks or dogfish
HOUNDING > HOUND
HOUNDS > HOUND
HOUNGAN n voodoo priest
HOUNGANS > HOUNGAN
HOUR n twenty-fourth part of a day, sixty minutes
HOURGLASS n device with two glass compartments, containing a quantity of sand that takes an hour to trickle from the top section to the bottom one
HOURI n any of the nymphs of paradise
HOURIS > HOURI
HOURLIES > HOURLY
HOURLONG adj lasting an hour
HOURLY adv (happening) every hour ▷ adj of, occurring, or done once every hour ▷ n something that is done by the hour
HOURPLATE n dial of clock
HOURS pl n indefinite time
HOUSE n building used as a home ▷ vb give accommodation to
HOUSEBOAT n stationary boat used as a home
HOUSEBOY n male domestic servant

HOUSEBOYS > HOUSEBOY
HOUSECARL n (in medieval Europe) a household warrior of Danish kings and nobles
HOUSECOAT n woman's long loose coat-shaped garment for wearing at home
HOUSED > HOUSE
HOUSEFLY n common fly often found in houses
HOUSEFUL n full amount or number that can be accommodated in a particular house
HOUSEFULS > HOUSEFUL
HOUSEHOLD n all the people living in a house ▷ adj relating to the running of a household
HOUSEKEEP vb run household
HOUSEKEPT > HOUSEKEEP
HOUSEL vb give the Eucharist to (someone)
HOUSELED > HOUSEL
HOUSELEEK n plant that has a rosette of succulent leaves and pinkish flowers and grows on walls
HOUSELESS > HOUSE
HOUSELIKE adj like a house
HOUSELINE n tarred marline
HOUSELING > HOUSEL
HOUSELLED > HOUSEL
HOUSELS > HOUSEL
HOUSEMAID n female servant employed to do housework
HOUSEMAN n junior hospital doctor
HOUSEMATE n person who is not part of the same family, but with whom one shares a house
HOUSEMEN > HOUSEMAN
HOUSER > HOUSE
HOUSEROOM n room for storage or lodging
HOUSERS > HOUSE
HOUSES > HOUSE
HOUSESAT > HOUSESIT
HOUSESIT vb live in and look after a house during the absence of its owner or owners
HOUSESITS > HOUSESIT
HOUSETOP n rooftop
HOUSETOPS > HOUSETOP
HOUSEWIFE n woman who runs her own household and does not have a job
HOUSEWORK n work of running a home, such as cleaning, cooking, and shopping
HOUSEWRAP n shawl or loose robe worn indoors
HOUSEY adj of or like house music
HOUSIER > HOUSEY
HOUSIEST > HOUSEY
HOUSING n (providing of) houses
HOUSINGS > HOUSING
HOUSLING adj of sacrament ▷ n growing of the climbing

stem of the hop into a dense mass

HOUSLINGS > HOUSLING

HOUSTONIA n small North American plant with blue, white or purple flowers

HOUT same as > HOOT

HOUTED > HOUT

HOUTING n type of fish

HOUTINGS > HOUTING

HOUTS > HOUT

HOVE vb swell

HOVEA n Australian plant with purple flowers

HOVEAS > HOVEA

HOVED > HOVE

HOVEL n small dirty house or hut ▷ vb shelter or be sheltered in a hovel

HOVELED > HOVEL

HOVELING > HOVEL

HOVELLED > HOVEL

HOVELLER n person working on boat

HOVELLERS > HOVELLER

HOVELLING > HOVEL

HOVELS > HOVEL

HOVEN > HEAVE

HOVER vb (of a bird etc) remain suspended in one place in the air ▷ n act of hovering

HOVERED > HOVER

HOVERER > HOVER

HOVERERS > HOVER

HOVERFLY n hovering wasp-like fly

HOVERING > HOVER

HOVERPORT n port for hovercraft

HOVERS > HOVER

HOVES > HOVE

HOVING > HOVE

HOW adv in what way, by what means ▷ n the way a thing is done ▷ sentence substitute supposed Native American greeting

HOWBE same as > HOWBEIT

HOWBEIT adv in archaic usage, however

HOWDAH n canopied seat on an elephant's back

HOWDAHS > HOWDAH

HOWDIE n midwife

HOWDIED > HOWDY

HOWDIES > HOWDY

HOWDY vb greet someone

HOWDYING > HOWDY

HOWE n depression in the earth's surface

HOWES > HOWE

HOWEVER adv nevertheless

HOWF n haunt, esp a public house ▷ vb visit a place frequently

HOWFED > HOWF

HOWFF vb visit a place frequently

HOWFFED > HOWFF

HOWFFING > HOWFF

HOWFFS > HOWFF

HOWFING > HOWF

HOWFS > HOWF

HOWITZER n large gun firing shells at a steep angle

HOWITZERS > HOWITZER

HOWK vb dig (out or up)

HOWKED > HOWK

HOWKER > HOWK

HOWKERS > HOWK

HOWKING > HOWK

HOWKS > HOWK

HOWL n loud wailing cry ▷ vb utter a howl

HOWLBACK same as > HOWLROUND

HOWLBACKS > HOWLBACK

HOWLED > HOWL

HOWLER n stupid mistake

HOWLERS > HOWLER

HOWLET another word for > OWL

HOWLETS > HOWLET

HOWLING adj great ▷ n act of wailing

HOWLINGLY > HOWLING

HOWLINGS > HOWLING

HOWLROUND n condition, resulting in a howling noise, when sound from a loudspeaker is fed back into the microphone of a public-address or recording system

HOWLS > HOWL

HOWRE same as > HOUR

HOWRES > HOWRE

HOWS > HOW

HOWSO same as > HOWSOEVER

HOWSOEVER less common word for > HOWEVER

HOWTOWDIE n Scottish dish of boiled chicken with poached eggs and spinach

HOWZAT interj cry in cricket appealing for dismissal of batsman

HOWZIT informal word for > HELLO

HOX vb hamstring

HOXED > HOX

HOXES > HOX

HOXING > HOX

HOY interj cry used to attract someone's attention ▷ n freight barge ▷ vb drive animal with cry

HOYA n any of various E Asian or Australian plants

HOYAS > HOYA

HOYDEN n wild or boisterous girl ▷ vb behave like a hoyden

HOYDENED > HOYDEN

HOYDENING > HOYDEN

HOYDENISH > HOYDEN

HOYDENISM > HOYDEN

HOYDENS > HOYDEN

HOYED > HOY

HOYING > HOY

HOYLE n archer's mark used as a target

HOYLES > HOYLE

HOYS > HOY

HRYVNA n standard monetary unit of Ukraine

HRYVNAS > HRYVNA

HRYVNIA n money unit of Ukraine

HRYVNIAS > HRYVNIA

HRYVNYA same as > HRYVNA

HRYVNYAS > HRYVNYA

HUANACO same as > GUANACO

HUANACOS > HUANACO

HUAQUERO n Central American tomb robber

HUAQUEROS > HUAQUERO

HUARACHE n Mexican sandal

HUARACHES > HUARACHE

HUARACHO same as > HUARACHE

HUARACHOS > HUARACHO

HUB n centre of a wheel, through which the axle passes

HUBBIES > HUBBY

HUBBLIER > HUBBLY

HUBBLIEST > HUBBLY

HUBBLY adj having an irregular surface

HUBBUB n confused noise of many voices

HUBBUBOO same as > HUBBUB

HUBBUBOOS > HUBBUBOO

HUBBUBS > HUBBUB

HUBBY n husband

HUBCAP n metal disc that protects the hub of a wheel

HUBCAPS > HUBCAP

HUBLESS adj without a hub

HUBRIS n pride, arrogance

HUBRISES > HUBRIS

HUBRISTIC > HUBRIS

HUBS > HUB

HUCK same as > HUCKABACK

HUCKABACK n coarse absorbent linen or cotton fabric used for towels and informal shirts, etc

HUCKED > HUCK

HUCKERY adj ugly

HUCKING > HUCK

HUCKLE n hip or haunch ▷ vb force out or arrest roughly

HUCKLED > HUCKLE

HUCKLES > HUCKLE

HUCKLING > HUCKLE

HUCKS > HUCK

HUCKSTER n person using aggressive methods of selling ▷ vb peddle

HUCKSTERS > HUCKSTER

HUCKSTERY > HUCKSTER

HUDDEN > HAUD

HUDDLE vb hunch (oneself) through cold or fear ▷ n small group

HUDDLED > HUDDLE

HUDDLER > HUDDLE

HUDDLERS > HUDDLE

HUDDLES > HUDDLE

HUDDLING > HUDDLE

HUDDUP interj get up

HUDNA n truce or ceasefire for a fixed duration

HUDNAS > HUDNA

HUDUD n set of laws and punishments in the Koran

HUDUDS > HUDUD

HUE n colour, shade

HUED adj having a hue or colour as specified

HUELESS > HUE

HUER n pilchard fisherman

HUERS > HUER

HUES > HUE

HUFF n passing mood of anger or resentment ▷ vb blow or puff heavily

HUFFED > HUFF

HUFFER > HUFFING

HUFFERS > HUFFING

HUFFIER > HUFF

HUFFIEST > HUFF

HUFFILY > HUFF

HUFFINESS > HUFF

HUFFING n practice of inhaling fumes for intoxicating effects

HUFFINGS > HUFFING

HUFFISH > HUFF

HUFFISHLY > HUFF

HUFFKIN n type of muffin

HUFFKINS > HUFFKIN

HUFFS > HUFF

HUFFY > HUFF

HUG vb clasp tightly in the arms, usu with affection ▷ n tight or fond embrace

HUGE adj very big

HUGELY adv very much

HUGENESS > HUGE

HUGEOUS same as > HUGE

HUGEOUSLY > HUGEOUS

HUGER > HUGE

HUGEST > HUGE

HUGGABLE > HUG

HUGGED > HUG

HUGGER > HUG

HUGGERS > HUG

HUGGIER > HUGGY

HUGGIEST > HUGGY

HUGGING > HUG

HUGGY adj sensitive and caring

HUGS > HUG

HUGY same as > HUGE

HUH interj exclamation of derision or inquiry

HUHU n type of hairy New Zealand beetle

HUHUS > HUHU

HUI n meeting of Māori people

HUIA n extinct bird of New Zealand

HUIAS > HUIA

HUIC interj in hunting, a call to hounds

HUIPIL n Mayan woman's blouse

HUIPILES > HUIPIL

HUIPILS > HUIPIL

HUIS > HUI

HUISACHE n American tree

HUISACHES > HUISACHE

HUISSIER n doorkeeper

HUISSIERS > HUISSIER

HUITAIN n verse of eighteen lines

HUITAINS > HUITAIN

HULA n swaying Hawaiian dance

HULAS > HULA

HULE same as > ULE

HULES > HULE

HULK n body of an abandoned ship ▷ vb move clumsily

HULKED > HULK

HULKIER > HULKY

HULKIEST > HULKY

HULKING adj bulky, unwieldy
HULKS > HULK
HULKY same as > HULKING
HULL n main body of a boat ▷ vb remove the hulls from
HULLED > HULL
HULLER > HULL
HULLERS > HULL
HULLIER > HULLY
HULLIEST > HULLY
HULLING > HULL
HULLO same as > HELLO
HULLOA same as > HALLOA
HULLOAED > HULLOA
HULLOAING > HULLOA
HULLOAS > HULLOA
HULLOED > HULLO
HULLOES > HULLO
HULLOING > HULLO
HULLOO same as > HALLOO
HULLOOED > HULLOO
HULLOOING > HULLOO
HULLOOS > HULLOO
HULLOS > HULLO
HULLS > HULL
HULLY adj having husks
HUM vb make a low continuous vibrating sound ▷ n humming sound
HUMA n mythical bird
HUMAN adj of or typical of people ▷ n human being
HUMANE adj kind or merciful
HUMANELY > HUMANE
HUMANER > HUMANE
HUMANEST > HUMANE
HUMANHOOD n state of being human
HUMANISE same as > HUMANIZE
HUMANISED > HUMANISE
HUMANISER > HUMANISE
HUMANISES > HUMANISE
HUMANISM n belief in human effort rather than religion
HUMANISMS > HUMANISM
HUMANIST > HUMANISM
HUMANISTS > HUMANISM
HUMANITY n human race
HUMANIZE vb make human or humane
HUMANIZED > HUMANIZE
HUMANIZER > HUMANIZE
HUMANIZES > HUMANIZE
HUMANKIND n human race
HUMANLIKE > HUMAN
HUMANLY adv by human powers or means
HUMANNESS > HUMAN
HUMANOID adj resembling a human being in appearance ▷ n (in science fiction) a robot or creature resembling a human being
HUMANOIDS > HUMANOID
HUMANS > HUMAN
HUMAS > HUMA
HUMATE n decomposed plants used as fertilizer
HUMATES > HUMATE
HUMBLE adj conscious of one's failings ▷ vb cause to feel humble, humiliate
HUMBLEBEE another name for the > BUMBLEBEE
HUMBLED > HUMBLE

HUMBLER > HUMBLE
HUMBLERS > HUMBLE
HUMBLES > HUMBLE
HUMBLESSE n quality of being humble
HUMBLEST > HUMBLE
HUMBLING > HUMBLE
HUMBLINGS > HUMBLE
HUMBLY > HUMBLE
HUMBUCKER n twin-coil guitar pick-up
HUMBUG n hard striped peppermint sweet ▷ vb cheat or deceive (someone)
HUMBUGGED > HUMBUG
HUMBUGGER > HUMBUG
HUMBUGS > HUMBUG
HUMBUZZ n type of beetle
HUMBUZZES > HUMBUZZ
HUMDINGER n excellent person or thing
HUMDRUM adj ordinary, dull ▷ n monotonous routine, task, or person
HUMDRUMS > HUMDRUM
HUMECT vb make moist
HUMECTANT adj producing moisture ▷ n substance added to another substance to keep it moist
HUMECTATE vb produce moisture
HUMECTED > HUMECT
HUMECTING > HUMECT
HUMECTIVE > HUMECT
HUMECTS > HUMECT
HUMEFIED > HUMEFY
HUMEFIES > HUMEFY
HUMEFY same as > HUMIFY
HUMEFYING > HUMEFY
HUMERAL adj of or relating to the humerus ▷ n silk shawl worn by a priest at High Mass; humeral veil
HUMERALS > HUMERAL
HUMERI > HUMERUS
HUMERUS n bone from the shoulder to the elbow
HUMF same as > HUMPH
HUMFED > HUMF
HUMFING > HUMF
HUMFS > HUMF
HUMHUM n Indian cotton cloth
HUMHUMS > HUMHUM
HUMIC adj of, derived from, or resembling humus
HUMICOLE n any plant that thrives on humus
HUMICOLES > HUMICOLE
HUMID adj damp and hot
HUMIDER > HUMID
HUMIDEST > HUMID
HUMIDEX n system of measuring discomfort
HUMIDEXES > HUMIDEX
HUMIDICES > HUMIDEX
HUMIDIFY vb make the air in (a room) more humid or damp
HUMIDITY n dampness
HUMIDLY > HUMID
HUMIDNESS > HUMID
HUMIDOR n humid place for storing cigars, tobacco, etc
HUMIDORS > HUMIDOR
HUMIFIED > HUMIFY

HUMIFIES > HUMIFY
HUMIFY vb convert or be converted into humus
HUMIFYING > HUMIFY
HUMILIANT adj humiliating
HUMILIATE vb lower the dignity or hurt the pride of
HUMILITY n quality of being humble
HUMINT n human intelligence
HUMINTS > HUMINT
HUMITE n mineral containing magnesium
HUMITES > HUMITE
HUMITURE n measure of both humidity and temperature
HUMITURES > HUMITURE
HUMLIE n hornless cow
HUMLIES > HUMLIE
HUMMABLE > HUM
HUMMAUM same as > HAMMAM
HUMMAUMS > HUMMAUM
HUMMED > HUM
HUMMEL adj (of cattle) hornless ▷ vb remove horns from
HUMMELLED > HUMMEL
HUMMELLER > HUMMEL
HUMMELS > HUMMEL
HUMMER > HUM
HUMMERS > HUM
HUMMING > HUM
HUMMINGS > HUM
HUMMLE adj as in hummle bonnet type of Scottish cap
HUMMOCK n very small hill ▷ vb form into a hummock or hummocks
HUMMOCKED > HUMMOCK
HUMMOCKS > HUMMOCK
HUMMOCKY adj having hummocks
HUMMUM same as > HAMMAM
HUMMUMS > HUMMUM
HUMMUS n creamy dip
HUMMUSES > HUMMUS
HUMOGEN n type of fertilizer
HUMOGENS > HUMOGEN
HUMONGOUS same as > HUMUNGOUS
HUMOR same as > HUMOUR
HUMORAL adj denoting or relating to a type of immunity
HUMORALLY > HUMORAL
HUMORED > HUMOR
HUMORESK n humorous musical composition
HUMORESKS > HUMORESK
HUMORFUL > HUMOR
HUMORING > HUMOR
HUMORIST n writer or entertainer who uses humour in his or her work
HUMORISTS > HUMORIST
HUMORLESS > HUMOR
HUMOROUS adj amusing, esp in a witty or clever way
HUMORS > HUMOR
HUMORSOME adj capricious
HUMOUR n ability to say or perceive things that are amusing ▷ vb be kind and indulgent to
HUMOURED > HUMOUR

HUMOURFUL > HUMOUR
HUMOURING > HUMOUR
HUMOURS > HUMOUR
HUMOUS same as > HUMUS
HUMOUSES > HUMOUS
HUMP n raised piece of ground ▷ vb carry or heave
HUMPBACK same as > HUNCHBACK
HUMPBACKS > HUMPBACK
HUMPED > HUMP
HUMPEN n old German drinking glass
HUMPENS > HUMPEN
HUMPER > HUMP
HUMPERS > HUMP
HUMPH interj exclamation of annoyance or scepticism ▷ vb exclaim humph
HUMPHED > HUMPH
HUMPHING > HUMPH
HUMPHS > HUMPH
HUMPIER > HUMPY
HUMPIES > HUMPY
HUMPIEST > HUMPY
HUMPINESS > HUMPY
HUMPING > HUMP
HUMPLESS > HUMP
HUMPLIKE > HUMP
HUMPS > HUMP
HUMPTIES > HUMPTY
HUMPTY n low padded seat
HUMPY adj full of humps ▷ n primitive hut
HUMS > HUM
HUMSTRUM n medieval musical instrument
HUMSTRUMS > HUMSTRUM
HUMUNGOUS adj very large
HUMUS n decomposing matter in the soil
HUMUSES > HUMUS
HUMUSIER > HUMUSY
HUMUSIEST > HUMUSY
HUMUSY adj like humus
HUMVEE n military vehicle
HUMVEES > HUMVEE
HUN n member of any of several nomadic peoples
HUNCH n feeling or suspicion not based on facts ▷ vb draw (one's shoulders) up or together
HUNCHBACK n person with an abnormal curvature of the spine
HUNCHED > HUNCH
HUNCHES > HUNCH
HUNCHING > HUNCH
HUNDRED n ten times ten ▷ adj amounting to a hundred
HUNDREDER n inhabitant of a hundred
HUNDREDOR same as > HUNDREDER
HUNDREDS > HUNDRED
HUNDREDTH adj being the ordinal number of 100 in numbering or counting order, position, time, etc ▷ n one of 100 approximately equal parts of something
HUNG > HANG
HUNGAN same as > HOUNGAN
HUNGANS > HUNGAN

HUNGER n discomfort or weakness from lack of food ▷ vb want very much
HUNGERED > HUNGER
HUNGERFUL adj hungry
HUNGERING > HUNGER
HUNGERLY adj hungry
HUNGERS > HUNGER
HUNGOVER adj suffering from hangover
HUNGRIER > HUNGRY
HUNGRIEST > HUNGRY
HUNGRILY > HUNGRY
HUNGRY adj desiring food
HUNH same as > HUH
HUNK n large piece
HUNKER vb squat
HUNKERED > HUNKER
HUNKERING > HUNKER
HUNKERS pl n haunches
HUNKEY n person of Hungarian descent
HUNKEYS > HUNKEY
HUNKIE same as > HUNKEY
HUNKIER > HUNKY
HUNKIES > HUNKIE
HUNKIEST > HUNKY
HUNKS n grumpy old person
HUNKSES > HUNKS
HUNKY adj excellent
HUNNISH > HUN
HUNS > HUN
HUNT vb seek out and kill (wild animals) for food or sport ▷ n hunting
HUNTABLE > HUNT
HUNTAWAY n sheepdog trained to drive sheep by barking
HUNTAWAYS > HUNTAWAY
HUNTED adj harassed and worn
HUNTEDLY > HUNT
HUNTER n person or animal that hunts wild animals
HUNTERS > HUNTER
HUNTING n pursuit and killing or capture of wild animals
HUNTINGS > HUNTING
HUNTRESS same as > HUNTER
HUNTS > HUNT
HUNTSMAN n man who hunts wild animals, esp foxes
HUNTSMEN > HUNTSMAN
HUP vb cry hup to get a horse to move
HUPIRO in New Zealand English, same as > STINKWOOD
HUPIROS > HUPIRO
HUPPAH variant spelling of > CHUPPAH
HUPPAHS > HUPPAH
HUPPED > HUP
HUPPING > HUP
HUPPOT > HUPPAH
HUPPOTH same as > HUPPOT
HUPS > HUP
HURCHEON same as > URCHIN
HURCHEONS > HURCHEON
HURDEN same as > HARDEN
HURDENS > HURDEN
HURDIES pl n buttocks or haunches

HURDLE n light barrier for jumping over in some races ▷ vb jump over (something)
HURDLED > HURDLE
HURDLER > HURDLE
HURDLERS > HURDLE
HURDLES > HURDLE
HURDLING > HURDLE
HURDLINGS > HURDLE
HURDS same as > HARDS
HURL vb throw or utter forcefully ▷ n act or an instance of hurling
HURLBAT same as > WHIRLBAT
HURLBATS > HURLBAT
HURLED > HURL
HURLER > HURL
HURLERS > HURL
HURLEY n another word for the game of hurling
HURLEYS > HURLEY
HURLIES > HURLY
HURLING n Irish game like hockey
HURLINGS > HURLING
HURLS > HURL
HURLY n wheeled barrow
HURRA same as > HURRAH
HURRAED > HURRA
HURRAH interj exclamation of joy or applause ▷ n cheer of joy or victory ▷ vb shout "hurrah"
HURRAHED > HURRAH
HURRAHING > HURRAH
HURRAHS > HURRAH
HURRAING > HURRA
HURRAS > HURRA
HURRAY same as > HURRAH
HURRAYED > HURRAY
HURRAYING > HURRAY
HURRAYS > HURRAY
HURRICANE n very strong, often destructive, wind or storm
HURRICANO same as > HURRICANE
HURRIED adj done quickly or too quickly
HURRIEDLY > HURRIED
HURRIER > HURRY
HURRIERS > HURRY
HURRIES > HURRY
HURRY vb (cause to) move or act very quickly ▷ n doing something or the need to do something quickly
HURRYING > HURRY
HURRYINGS > HURRY
HURST n wood
HURSTS > HURST
HURT vb cause physical or mental pain to ▷ n physical or mental pain ▷ adj injured or pained
HURTER > HURT
HURTERS > HURT
HURTFUL adj unkind
HURTFULLY > HURTFUL
HURTING > HURT
HURTLE vb move quickly or violently
HURTLED > HURTLE
HURTLES > HURTLE
HURTLESS adj uninjured
HURTLING > HURTLE

HURTS > HURT
HUSBAND n man to whom one is married ▷ vb use economically
HUSBANDED > HUSBAND
HUSBANDER > HUSBAND
HUSBANDLY adj of or like a husband
HUSBANDRY n farming
HUSBANDS > HUSBAND
HUSH vb make or be silent ▷ n stillness or silence ▷ interj plea or demand for silence
HUSHABIED > HUSHABY
HUSHABIES > HUSHABY
HUSHABY interj used in quietening a baby or child to sleep ▷ n lullaby ▷ vb quieten to sleep
HUSHABYE same as > HUSHABY
HUSHED > HUSH
HUSHEDLY > HUSH
HUSHER same as > USHER
HUSHERED > HUSHER
HUSHERING > HUSHER
HUSHERS > HUSHER
HUSHES > HUSH
HUSHFUL adj quiet
HUSHIER > HUSHY
HUSHIEST > HUSHY
HUSHING > HUSH
HUSHPUPPY n snack of deep-fried dough
HUSHY adj secret
HUSK n outer covering of certain seeds and fruits ▷ vb remove the husk from
HUSKED > HUSK
HUSKER > HUSK
HUSKERS > HUSK
HUSKIER > HUSKY
HUSKIES > HUSKY
HUSKIEST > HUSKY
HUSKILY > HUSKY
HUSKINESS > HUSKY
HUSKING > HUSK
HUSKINGS > HUSK
HUSKLIKE > HUSK
HUSKS > HUSK
HUSKY adj slightly hoarse ▷ n Arctic sledge dog with thick hair and a curled tail
HUSO n sturgeon
HUSOS > HUSO
HUSS n flesh of the European dogfish
HUSSAR n lightly armed cavalry soldier
HUSSARS > HUSSAR
HUSSES > HUSS
HUSSIES > HUSSY
HUSSIF n sewing kit
HUSSIFS > HUSSIF
HUSSY n derogatory term for a woman considered immodest
HUSTINGS pl n political campaigns and speeches before an election
HUSTLE vb push about, jostle ▷ n lively activity or bustle
HUSTLED > HUSTLE
HUSTLER > HUSTLE
HUSTLERS > HUSTLE
HUSTLES > HUSTLE

HUSTLING > HUSTLE
HUSTLINGS > HUSTLE
HUSWIFE same as > HOUSEWIFE
HUSWIFES > HUSWIFE
HUSWIVES > HUSWIFE
HUT n small house, shelter, or shed ▷ vb equip with huts
HUTCH n cage for pet rabbits etc ▷ vb store or keep in or as if in a hutch
HUTCHED > HUTCH
HUTCHES > HUTCH
HUTCHIE n temporary shelter
HUTCHIES > HUTCHIE
HUTCHING > HUTCH
HUTIA n rodent of West Indies
HUTIAS > HUTIA
HUTLIKE > HUT
HUTMENT n number or group of huts
HUTMENTS > HUTMENT
HUTS > HUT
HUTTED > HUT
HUTTING > HUT
HUTTINGS > HUT
HUTZPA same as > HUTZPAH
HUTZPAH variant spelling of > CHUTZPAH
HUTZPAHS > HUTZPAH
HUTZPAS > HUTZPA
HUZOOR n person of rank in India
HUZOORS > HUZOOR
HUZZA same as > HUZZAH
HUZZAED > HUZZA
HUZZAH archaic word for > HURRAH
HUZZAHED > HUZZAH
HUZZAHING > HUZZAH
HUZZAHS > HUZZAH
HUZZAING > HUZZA
HUZZAS > HUZZA
HUZZIES > HUZZY
HUZZY same as > HUSSY
HWAN another name for > WON
HWYL n emotional fervour, as in the recitation of poetry
HWYLS > HWYL
HYACINE same as > HYACINTH
HYACINES > HYACINE
HYACINTH n sweet-smelling spring flower that grows from a bulb
HYACINTHS > HYACINTH
HYAENA same as > HYENA
HYAENAS > HYAENA
HYAENIC > HYAENA
HYALIN n glassy translucent substance
HYALINE adj clear and translucent, with no fibres or granules ▷ n glassy transparent surface
HYALINES > HYALINE
HYALINISE same as > HYALINIZE
HYALINIZE vb give a glassy consistency to
HYALINS > HYALIN
HYALITE n clear and colourless variety of opal in globular form
HYALITES > HYALITE

HYALOGEN n insoluble substance in body structures

HYALOGENS > HYALOGEN

HYALOID adj clear and transparent ▷ n delicate transparent membrane

HYALOIDS > HYALOID

HYALONEMA n species of sponge

HYBRID n offspring of two plants or animals of different species ▷ adj of mixed origin

HYBRIDISE same as **>** HYBRIDIZE

HYBRIDISM > HYBRID

HYBRIDIST > HYBRID

HYBRIDITY > HYBRID

HYBRIDIZE vb produce or cause (species) to produce hybrids

HYBRIDOMA n hybrid cell formed by the fusion of two different types of cell, esp one capable of producing antibodies, but of limited lifespan, fused with an immortal tumour cell

HYBRIDOUS > HYBRID

HYBRIDS > HYBRID

HYBRIS same as **>** HUBRIS

HYBRISES > HYBRIS

HYBRISTIC > HYBRIS

HYDANTOIN n colourless odourless crystalline compound present in beet molasses and used in the manufacture of pharmaceuticals and synthetic resins

HYDATHODE n pore in plants, esp on the leaves, specialized for discharging water

HYDATID n cyst containing tapeworm larvae

HYDATIDS > HYDATID

HYDATOID adj watery

HYDRA n mythical many-headed water serpent

HYDRACID n acid, such as hydrochloric acid, that does not contain oxygen

HYDRACIDS > HYDRACID

HYDRAE > HYDRA

HYDRAEMIA n wateriness of blood

HYDRAGOG n drug that removes water

HYDRAGOGS > HYDRAGOG

HYDRANGEA n ornamental shrub with clusters of pink, blue, or white flowers

HYDRANT n outlet from a water main with a nozzle for a hose

HYDRANTH n polyp in a colony of hydrozoan coelenterates

HYDRANTHS > HYDRANTH

HYDRANTS > HYDRANT

HYDRAS > HYDRA

HYDRASE n enzyme that removes water

HYDRASES > HYDRASE

HYDRASTIS n any of various Japanese and E North American plants, such as goldenseal, having showy foliage and ornamental red fruits

HYDRATE n chemical compound of water with another substance ▷ vb treat or impregnate with water

HYDRATED adj (of a compound) chemically bonded to water molecules

HYDRATES > HYDRATE

HYDRATING > HYDRATE

HYDRATION > HYDRATE

HYDRATOR > HYDRATE

HYDRATORS > HYDRATE

HYDRAULIC adj operated by pressure forced through a pipe by a liquid such as water or oil

HYDRAZIDE n any of a class of chemical compounds that result when hydrogen in hydrazine or any of its derivatives is replaced by an acid radical

HYDRAZINE n colourless basic liquid made from sodium hypochlorite and ammonia: a strong reducing agent, used chiefly as a rocket fuel

HYDRAZOIC adj as in hydrazoic acid colourless highly explosive liquid

HYDREMIA same as **>** HYDRAEMIA

HYDREMIAS > HYDREMIA

HYDRIA n (in ancient Greece and Rome) a large water jar

HYDRIAE > HYDRIA

HYDRIC adj of or containing hydrogen

HYDRID same as **>** HYDROID

HYDRIDE n compound of hydrogen with another element

HYDRIDES > HYDRIDE

HYDRIDS > HYDRID

HYDRILLA n aquatic plant used as an oxygenator in aquaria and pools

HYDRILLAS > HYDRILLA

HYDRIODIC adj as in hydriodic acid colourless or pale yellow aqueous solution of hydrogen iodide: a strong acid

HYDRO n hotel offering facilities for hydropathy ▷ adj short for hydroelectric

HYDROCAST n gathering of water samples for analysis

HYDROCELE n abnormal collection of fluid in any saclike space

HYDROFOIL n fast light boat with its hull raised out of the water on one or more pairs of fins

HYDROGEL n gel in which the liquid constituent is water

HYDROGELS > HYDROGEL

HYDROGEN n light flammable colourless gas that combines with oxygen to form water

HYDROGENS > HYDROGEN

HYDROID adj of an order of colonial hydrozoan coelenterates ▷ n hydroid colony or individual

HYDROIDS > HYDROID

HYDROLASE n enzyme, such as an esterase, that controls hydrolysis

HYDROLOGY n study of the distribution, conservation, and use of the water of the earth and its atmosphere

HYDROLYSE vb subject to or undergo hydrolysis

HYDROLYTE n substance subjected to hydrolysis

HYDROLYZE same as **>** HYDROLYSE

HYDROMA same as **>** HYGROMA

HYDROMAS > HYDROMA

HYDROMATA > HYDROMA

HYDROMEL n another word for 'mead' (the drink)

HYDROMELS > HYDROMEL

HYDRONAUT n person trained to operate deep submergence vessels

HYDRONIC adj using hot water in heating system

HYDRONIUM n as in hydronium ion positive ion formed by the attachment of a proton to a water molecule

HYDROPATH n exponent of treating disease using large quantities of water

HYDROPIC > HYDROPSY

HYDROPS n anaemia in a fetus

HYDROPSES > HYDROPS

HYDROPSY same as **>** DROPSY

HYDROPTIC > HYDROPSY

HYDROPULT n type of water pump

HYDROS > HYDRO

HYDROSERE n sere that begins in an aquatic environment

HYDROSKI n hydrofoil used on some seaplanes to provide extra lift when taking off

HYDROSKIS > HYDROSKI

HYDROSOL n sol that has water as its liquid phase

HYDROSOLS > HYDROSOL

HYDROSOMA same as **>** HYDROSOME

HYDROSOME n body of a colonial hydrozoan

HYDROSTAT n device that detects the presence of water as a prevention against drying out, overflow, etc, esp one used as a warning in a steam boiler

HYDROUS adj containing water

HYDROVANE n vane on a seaplane conferring stability on water (a sponson) or facilitating take-off (a hydrofoil)

HYDROXIDE n compound containing a hydroxyl group or ion

HYDROXIUM n type of positive ion

HYDROXY adj of a type of chemical compound

HYDROXYL n the monovalent group –OH or the ion OH⁻

HYDROXYLS > HYDROXYL

HYDROZOA > HYDROZOON

HYDROZOAN n type of invertebrate of the class which includes the hydra and Portuguese man-of-war

HYDROZOON same as **>** HYDROZOAN

HYDYNE n type of rocket fuel

HYDYNES > HYDYNE

HYE same as **>** HIE

HYED > HYE

HYEING > HYE

HYEN same as **>** HYENA

HYENA n scavenging doglike mammal of Africa and S Asia

HYENAS > HYENA

HYENIC > HYENA

HYENINE adj of hyenas

HYENOID adj of or like hyenas

HYENS > HYEN

HYES > HYE

HYETAL adj of or relating to rain, rainfall, or rainy regions

HYETOLOGY n study of rainfall

HYGEIST same as **>** HYGIENIST

HYGEISTS > HYGEIST

HYGGE n Danish practice that promotes wellbeing

HYGGES > HYGGE

HYGIEIST same as **>** HYGIENIST

HYGIEISTS > HYGIEIST

HYGIENE n principles of health and cleanliness

HYGIENES > HYGIENE

HYGIENIC adj promoting health or cleanliness

HYGIENICS same as **>** HYGIENE

HYGIENIST n person skilled in the practice of hygiene

HYGRISTOR n electronic component the resistance of which varies with humidity

HYGRODEIK n type of thermometer

HYGROLOGY n study of humidity of air

HYGROMA n swelling soft tissue that occurs over a joint

HYGROMAS > HYGROMA

HYGROMATA > HYGROMA

HYGROPHIL adj moisture-loving

HYGROSTAT n device for maintaining constant humidity

HYING > HIE

HYKE same as **>** HAIK

HYKES > HYKE

HYLA n type of tropical American tree frog

HYLAS > HYLA

HYLDING same as **>** HILDING

HYLDINGS > HYLDING

HYLE n wood

HYLEG n dominant planet when someone is born

HYLEGS > HYLEG

HYLES > HYLE

HYLIC adj solid

HYLICISM n materialism

HYLICISMS > HYLICISM

HYLICIST > HYLICISM

HYLICISTS > HYLICISM

HYLISM same as > HYLICISM

HYLISMS > HYLISM

HYLIST > HYLISM

HYLISTS > HYLISM

HYLOBATE n gibbon

HYLOBATES > HYLOBATE

HYLOIST n materialist

HYLOISTS > HYLOIST

HYLOPHYTE n plant that grows in woods

HYLOZOIC > HYLOZOISM

HYLOZOISM n philosophical doctrine that life is one of the properties of matter

HYLOZOIST > HYLOZOISM

HYMEN n membrane partly covering a girl's vaginal opening

HYMENAEAL same as > HYMENEAL

HYMENAEAN n person who believes there will be no resurrection

HYMENAL > HYMEN

HYMENEAL adj of or relating to marriage ▷ n wedding song or poem

HYMENEALS > HYMENEAL

HYMENEAN n wedding song

HYMENEANS > HYMENEAN

HYMENIA > HYMENIUM

HYMENIAL > HYMENIUM

HYMENIUM n (in some fungi) a layer of cell-producing spores

HYMENIUMS > HYMENIUM

HYMENS > HYMEN

HYMN n Christian song of praise sung to God or a saint ▷ vb express (praises, thanks, etc) by singing hymns

HYMNAL n book of hymns ▷ adj of, relating to, or characteristic of hymns

HYMNALS > HYMNAL

HYMNARIES > HYMNARY

HYMNARY same as > HYMNAL

HYMNBOOK n book containing the words and music of hymns

HYMNBOOKS > HYMNBOOK

HYMNED > HYMN

HYMNIC > HYMN

HYMNING > HYMN

HYMNIST n person who composes hymns

HYMNISTS > HYMNIST

HYMNLESS > HYMN

HYMNLIKE > HYMN

HYMNODIES > HYMNODY

HYMNODIST same as > HYMNIST

HYMNODY n composition or singing of hymns

HYMNOLOGY same as > HYMNODY

HYMNS > HYMN

HYNDE same as > HIND

HYNDES > HYNDE

HYOID adj of or relating to the hyoid bone ▷ n horseshoe-shaped bone

HYOIDAL adj of or relating to the hyoid bone

HYOIDEAN same as > HYOIDAL

HYOIDS > HYOID

HYOSCINE n colourless viscous liquid alkaloid

HYOSCINES > HYOSCINE

HYP n short for hypotenuse ▷ vb offend

HYPALGIA n reduced ability to feel pain

HYPALGIAS > HYPALGIA

HYPALLAGE n figure of speech in which the natural relations of two words in a statement are interchanged, as in *the fire spread the wind*

HYPANTHIA n plural of hypanthium: cup-shaped receptacle of perigynous or epigynous flowers

HYPATE n string of lyre

HYPATES > HYPATE

HYPE n intensive or exaggerated publicity or sales promotion ▷ vb promote (a product) using intensive or exaggerated publicity

HYPED > HYPE

HYPER n excitable person ▷ adj excitable

HYPERACID adj having excess acidity

HYPERARID adj extremely dry

HYPERBOLA n curve produced when a cone is cut by a plane at a steeper angle to its base than its side

HYPERBOLE n deliberate exaggeration for effect

HYPERCUBE n figure in a space of four or more dimensions having all its sides equal and all its angles right angles

HYPEREMIA n excessive blood in an organ or part

HYPEREMIC > HYPEREMIA

HYPERER > HYPER

HYPEREST > HYPER

HYPERFINE adj as in *hyperfine structure* splitting of a spectral line of an atom or molecule into two or more closely spaced components as a result of interaction of the electrons with the magnetic moments of the nuclei

HYPERGAMY n custom that forbids a woman to marry a man of lower social status

HYPERGOL n type of fuel

HYPERGOLS > HYPERGOL

HYPERICIN n antidepressant and antiviral compound

HYPERICUM n herbaceous plant or shrub

HYPERLINK n link from a hypertext file that gives users instant access to related material in another file ▷ vb link (files) in this way

HYPERMART n very large supermarket

HYPERNOVA n exploding star that produces even more energy and light than a supernova

HYPERNYM n superordinate

HYPERNYMS > HYPERNYM

HYPERNYMY > HYPERNYM

HYPERON n any baryon that is not a nucleon

HYPERONS > HYPERON

HYPEROPE n person with hyperopia

HYPEROPES > HYPEROPE

HYPEROPIA n inability to see near objects clearly because the images received by the eye are focused behind the retina

HYPEROPIC > HYPEROPIA

HYPERPNEA n increase in breathing rate

HYPERPURE adj extremely pure

HYPERREAL adj involving or characterized by particularly realistic graphic representation ▷ n that which constitutes hyperreality

HYPERS > HYPE

HYPERTEXT n computer software and hardware that allows users to store and view text and move between related items easily

HYPES > HYPE

HYPESTER n person who gives a product intense publicity

HYPESTERS > HYPESTER

HYPETHRAL adj having no roof

HYPHA n any of the filaments in the mycelium of a fungus

HYPHAE > HYPHA

HYPHAL > HYPHA

HYPHEMIA n bleeding inside eye

HYPHEMIAS > HYPHEMIA

HYPHEN n punctuation mark (-) ▷ vb hyphenate

HYPHENATE vb separate (words) with a hyphen

HYPHENED > HYPHEN

HYPHENIC > HYPHEN

HYPHENING > HYPHEN

HYPHENISE same as > HYPHENIZE

HYPHENISM > HYPHEN

HYPHENIZE same as > HYPHENATE

HYPHENS > HYPHEN

HYPHIES > HYPHY

HYPHY n type of hip-hop music

HYPING > HYPE

HYPINGS > HYPE

HYPINOSES > HYPINOSIS

HYPINOSIS n protein deficiency in blood

HYPNIC n sleeping drug

HYPNICS > HYPNIC

HYPNOGENY n hypnosis

HYPNOID adj of or relating to a state resembling sleep

HYPNOIDAL same as > HYPNOID

HYPNOLOGY n study of sleep and hypnosis

HYPNONE n sleeping drug

HYPNONES > HYPNONE

HYPNOSES > HYPNOSIS

HYPNOSIS n artificially induced state of relaxation

HYPNOTEE n person being hypnotized

HYPNOTEES > HYPNOTEE

HYPNOTIC adj of or (as if) producing hypnosis ▷ n drug that induces sleep

HYPNOTICS > HYPNOTIC

HYPNOTISE same as > HYPNOTIZE

HYPNOTISM n inducing hypnosis in someone

HYPNOTIST n person skilled in the theory and practice of hypnosis

HYPNOTIZE vb induce hypnosis in (a person)

HYPNOTOID adj like hypnosis

HYPNUM n species of moss

HYPNUMS > HYPNUM

HYPO vb inject with a hypodermic syringe

HYPOACID adj abnormally acidic

HYPOBARIC adj below normal pressure

HYPOBLAST n inner layer of an embryo at an early stage of development that becomes the endoderm at gastrulation

HYPOBOLE n act of anticipating objection

HYPOBOLES > HYPOBOLE

HYPOCAUST n ancient Roman heating system in which hot air circulated under the floor and between double walls

HYPOCIST n type of juice

HYPOCISTS > HYPOCIST

HYPOCOTYL n part of an embryo plant between the cotyledons and the radicle

HYPOCRISY n (instance of) pretence of having standards or beliefs that are contrary to one's real character or actual behaviour

HYPOCRITE n person who pretends to be what he or she is not

HYPODERM n layer of thick-walled tissue in some plants

HYPODERMA n layer of skin tissue

HYPODERMS > HYPODERM

HYPOED > HYPO

HYPOGAEA > HYPOGAEUM

HYPOGAEAL > HYPOGAEUM

HYPOGAEAN > HYPOGAEUM

HYPOGAEUM same as > HYPOGEUM

HYPOGEA > HYPOGEUM

HYPOGEAL adj occurring or living below the surface of the ground

HYPOGEAN > HYPOGEUM

HYPOGENE adj formed, taking place, or originating

beneath the surface of the earth

HYPOGENIC > HYPOGENE

HYPOGEOUS *same as* > HYPOGEAL

HYPOGEUM *n* underground vault, esp one used for burials

HYPOGYNY *adj* having the gynoecium above the other floral parts

HYPOID *adj* as in *hypoid gear* type of gear ▷ *n* hypoid gear

HYPOIDS > HYPOID

HYPOING > HYPO

HYPOMANIA *n* abnormal condition of extreme excitement, milder than mania but characterized by great optimism and overactivity and often by reckless spending of money

HYPOMANIC > HYPOMANIA

HYPOMORPH *n* mutant gene

HYPONASTY *n* increased growth of the lower surface of a plant part, resulting in an upward bending of the part

HYPONEA *same as* > HYPOPNEA

HYPONEAS > HYPONEA

HYPONOIA *n* underlying meaning

HYPONOIAS > HYPONOIA

HYPONYM *n* word whose meaning is included as part of another

HYPONYMS > HYPONYM

HYPONYMY > HYPONYM

HYPOPHYGE *another name for* > APOPHYGE

HYPOPLOID *adj* having or designating a chromosome number that is less than a multiple of the haploid number

HYPOPNEA *same as* > HYPOPNOEA

HYPOPNEAS > HYPOPNEA

HYPOPNEIC > HYPOPNEA

HYPOPNOEA *n* abnormally shallow breathing, usually accompanied by a decrease in the breathing rate

HYPOPYON *n* pus in eye

HYPOPYONS > HYPOPYON

HYPOS > HYPO

HYPOSTOME *n* invertebrate body part

HYPOSTYLE *adj* having a roof supported by columns ▷ *n* building constructed in this way

HYPOTAXES > HYPOTAXIS

HYPOTAXIS *n* subordination of one clause to another by a conjunction

HYPOTHEC *n* charge on property in favour of a creditor

HYPOTHECA *n* inner and younger layer of the cell wall of a diatom

HYPOTHECS > HYPOTHEC

HYPOTONIA *n* state of being hypnotized

HYPOTONIC *adj* (of muscles) lacking normal tone or tension

HYPOXEMIA *n* lack of oxygen in blood

HYPOXEMIC > HYPOXEMIA

HYPOXIA *n* deficiency in oxygen delivery

HYPOXIAS > HYPOXIA

HYPOXIC > HYPOXIA

HYPPED > HYP

HYPPING > HYP

HYPS > HYP

HYPURAL *adj* below the tail

HYRACES > HYRAX

HYRACOID *n* hyrax

HYRACOIDS > HYRACOID

HYRAX *n* type of hoofed rodent-like animal of Africa and Asia

HYRAXES > HYRAX

HYSON *n* Chinese green tea

HYSONS > HYSON

HYSSOP *n* sweet-smelling herb used in folk medicine

HYSSOPS > HYSSOP

HYSTERIA *n* state of uncontrolled excitement, anger, or panic

HYSTERIAS > HYSTERIA

HYSTERIC *adj* of or suggesting hysteria

HYSTERICS *pl n* attack of hysteria

HYSTEROID *adj* resembling hysteria

HYTE *adj* insane

HYTHE *same as* > HITHE

HYTHES > HYTHE

Ii

IAMB n metrical foot of two syllables

IAMBI > IAMBUS

IAMBIC adj written in a type of metrical unit ▷ n iambic foot, line, or stanza

IAMBICS > IAMBIC

IAMBIST n one who writes iambs

IAMBISTS > IAMBIST

IAMBS > IAMB

IAMBUS same as > IAMB

IAMBUSES > IAMBUS

IANTHINE adj violet

IATRIC adj relating to medicine or physicians

IATRICAL same as > IATRIC

IATROGENY n disease caused by medical intervention

IBADAH n following of Islamic beliefs and practices

IBADAT > IBADAH

IBERIS n plant with white or purple flowers

IBERISES > IBERIS

IBEX n wild goat

IBEXES > IBEX

IBICES > IBEX

IBIDEM adv in the same place

IBIS n large wading bird with long legs

IBISES > IBIS

IBOGAINE n dopamine blocker

IBOGAINES > IBOGAINE

IBRIK same as > CEZVE

IBRIKS > IBRIK

IBUPROFEN n drug that relieves pain and reduces inflammation

ICE n water in the solid state, formed by freezing liquid water ▷ vb form or cause to form ice

ICEBALL n ball of ice

ICEBALLS > ICEBALL

ICEBERG n large floating mass of ice

ICEBERGS > ICEBERG

ICEBLINK n yellowish-white reflected glare in the sky over an ice field

ICEBLINKS > ICEBLINK

ICEBOAT n boat that breaks up bodies of ice in water ▷ vb pilot an iceboat

ICEBOATED > ICEBOAT

ICEBOATER > ICEBOAT

ICEBOATS > ICEBOAT

ICEBOUND adj covered or made immobile by ice

ICEBOX n refrigerator

ICEBOXES > ICEBOX

ICECAP n mass of ice permanently covering an area

ICECAPPED adj having an icecap

ICECAPS > ICECAP

ICED adj covered with icing

ICEFALL n part of a glacier

ICEFALLS > ICEFALL

ICEFIELD n very large flat expanse of ice floating in the sea; large ice floe

ICEFIELDS > ICEFIELD

ICEFISH vb fish through a hole in the ice on a lake

ICEFISHED > ICEFISH

ICEFISHES > ICEFISH

ICEHOUSE n building for storing ice

ICEHOUSES > ICEHOUSE

ICEKHANA n motor race on a frozen lake

ICEKHANAS > ICEKHANA

ICELESS > ICE

ICELIKE > ICE

ICEMAKER n device for making ice

ICEMAKERS > ICEMAKER

ICEMAN n person who sells or delivers ice

ICEMEN > ICEMAN

ICEPACK n bag or folded cloth containing ice

ICEPACKS > ICEPACK

ICER n person who ices cakes

ICERS > ICER

ICES > ICE

ICESCAPE n landscape covered in ice

ICESCAPES > ICESCAPE

ICESTONE n cryolite

ICESTONES > ICESTONE

ICEWINE n dessert wine made from grapes that have frozen before being harvested

ICEWINES > ICEWINE

ICEWORM n small worm found in glaciers

ICEWORMS > ICEWORM

ICH archaic form of > EKE

ICHABOD interj the glory has departed

ICHED > ICH

ICHES > ICH

ICHING > ICH

ICHNEUMON n greyish-brown mongoose

ICHNITE n trace fossil

ICHNITES > ICHNITE

ICHNOLITE same as > ICHNITE

ICHNOLOGY n study of trace fossils

ICHOR n fluid said to flow in the veins of the gods

ICHOROUS > ICHOR

ICHORS > ICHOR

ICHS > ICH

ICHTHIC same as > ICHTHYIC

ICHTHYIC adj of, relating to, or characteristic of fishes

ICHTHYOID adj resembling a fish ▷ n fishlike vertebrate

ICHTHYS n early Christian emblem

ICHTHYSES > ICHTHYS

ICICLE n tapering spike of ice

ICICLED adj covered with icicles

ICICLES > ICICLE

ICIER > ICY

ICIEST > ICY

ICILY adv in an icy or reserved manner

ICINESS n condition of being icy or very cold

ICINESSES > ICINESS

ICING n mixture used to decorate cakes

ICINGS > ICING

ICK interj expression of disgust

ICKER n ear of corn

ICKERS > ICKER

ICKIER > ICKY

ICKIEST > ICKY

ICKILY > ICKY

ICKINESS > ICKY

ICKLE ironically childish word for > LITTLE

ICKLER > ICKLE

ICKLEST > ICKLE

ICKS > ICK

ICKY adj sticky

ICON n picture of Christ or another religious figure

ICONES > ICON

ICONIC adj relating to the character of an icon

ICONICAL same as > ICONIC

ICONICITY > ICONIC

ICONIFIED > ICONIFY

ICONIFIES > ICONIFY

ICONIFY vb render as an icon

ICONISE same as > ICONIZE

ICONISED > ICONISE

ICONISES > ICONISE

ICONISING > ICONISE

ICONIZE vb render as an icon

ICONIZED > ICONIZE

ICONIZES > ICONIZE

ICONIZING > ICONIZE

ICONOLOGY n study or field of art history concerning icons

ICONOSTAS n screen with doors and icons set in tiers, which separates the from the nave

ICONS > ICON

ICTAL > ICTUS

ICTERIC > ICTERUS

ICTERICAL > ICTERUS

ICTERICS > ICTERUS

ICTERID n bird of the oriole family

ICTERIDS > ICTERID

ICTERINE > ICTERID

ICTERUS n yellowing of plant leaves

ICTERUSES > ICTERUS

ICTIC > ICTUS

ICTUS n metrical or rhythmic stress in verse feet

ICTUSES > ICTUS

ICY adj very cold

ID n mind's instinctive unconscious energies

IDANT n chromosome

IDANTS > IDANT

IDE n silver orfe fish

IDEA n plan or thought formed in the mind

IDEAED > IDEA

IDEAL adj most suitable ▷ n conception of something that is perfect

IDEALESS > IDEA

IDEALISE same as > IDEALIZE

IDEALISED > IDEALISE

IDEALISER > IDEALISE

IDEALISES > IDEALISE

IDEALISM n tendency to seek perfection in everything

IDEALISMS > IDEALISM

IDEALIST > IDEALISM

IDEALISTS > IDEALISM

IDEALITY > IDEAL

IDEALIZE vb regard or portray as perfect or nearly perfect

IDEALIZED > IDEALIZE

IDEALIZER > IDEALIZE

IDEALIZES > IDEALIZE

IDEALLESS > IDEAL

i

IDEALLY > IDEAL
IDEALNESS > IDEAL
IDEALOGUE corruption of > IDEOLOGUE
IDEALOGY corruption of > IDEOLOGY
IDEALS > IDEAL
IDEAS > IDEA
IDEATA > IDEATUM
IDEATE vb form or have an idea of
IDEATED > IDEATE
IDEATES > IDEATE
IDEATING > IDEATE
IDEATION > IDEATE
IDEATIONS > IDEATE
IDEATIVE > IDEATE
IDEATUM n objective reality
IDEE n idea
IDEES > IDEE
IDEM adj same
IDENT n short visual image that works as a logo
IDENTIC adj having the same intention regarding another power
IDENTICAL adj exactly the same
IDENTIFY vb prove or recognize as being a certain person or thing
IDENTIKIT n trademark name for a set of transparencies of various typical facial characteristics that can be superimposed on one another to build up a picture of a person sought by the police
IDENTITY n state of being a specified person or thing
IDENTS > IDENT
IDEOGRAM n symbol that directly represents a concept or thing
IDEOGRAMS > IDEOGRAM
IDEOGRAPH same as > IDEOGRAM
IDEOLOGIC > IDEOLOGY
IDEOLOGUE n ideologist
IDEOLOGY n body of ideas and beliefs of a group, nation, etc
IDEOMOTOR adj designating automatic muscular movements stimulated by ideas
IDEOPHONE n sound that represents a complete idea
IDEOPOLIS n city whose economy mainly consists of intellectual enterprises
IDES n specific date of each month in the Roman calendar
IDIOBLAST n plant cell that differs from those around it in the same tissue
IDIOCIES > IDIOCY
IDIOCY n utter stupidity
IDIOGRAM another name for > KARYOGRAM
IDIOGRAMS > IDIOGRAM
IDIOGRAPH n trademark
IDIOLECT n variety or form of a language used by an individual
IDIOLECTS > IDIOLECT

IDIOM n group of words with special meaning
IDIOMATIC > IDIOM
IDIOMS > IDIOM
IDIOPATHY n any disease of unknown cause
IDIOPHONE n percussion instrument, such as a cymbal or xylophone, made of naturally sonorous material
IDIOPLASM n germ plasm
IDIOT n foolish or stupid person
IDIOTCIES > IDIOTCY
IDIOTCY same as > IDIOCY
IDIOTIC adj of or resembling an idiot
IDIOTICAL same as > IDIOTIC
IDIOTICON n dictionary of dialect
IDIOTISH same as > IDIOTIC
IDIOTISM archaic word for > IDIOCY
IDIOTISMS > IDIOTISM
IDIOTS > IDIOT
IDIOTYPE n unique part of antibody
IDIOTYPES > IDIOTYPE
IDIOTYPIC > IDIOTYPE
IDLE adj not doing anything ▷ vb spend (time) doing very little
IDLED > IDLE
IDLEHOOD > IDLE
IDLEHOODS > IDLE
IDLENESS > IDLE
IDLER n person who idles
IDLERS > IDLER
IDLES > IDLE
IDLESSE > IDLE
IDLESSES > IDLE
IDLEST > IDLE
IDLING > IDLE
IDLY > IDLE
IDOCRASE n green, brown, or yellow mineral
IDOCRASES > IDOCRASE
IDOL n object of excessive devotion
IDOLA > IDOLUM
IDOLATER > IDOLATRY
IDOLATERS > IDOLATRY
IDOLATOR n one who worships idols
IDOLATORS > IDOLATRY
IDOLATRY n worship of idols
IDOLISE same as > IDOLIZE
IDOLISED > IDOLISE
IDOLISER > IDOLISE
IDOLISERS > IDOLISE
IDOLISES > IDOLISE
IDOLISING > IDOLISE
IDOLISM > IDOL
IDOLISMS > IDOL
IDOLIST > IDOLIZE
IDOLISTS > IDOLIZE
IDOLIZE vb love or admire excessively
IDOLIZED > IDOLIZE
IDOLIZER > IDOLIZE
IDOLIZERS > IDOLIZE
IDOLIZES > IDOLIZE
IDOLIZING > IDOLIZE

IDOLON n mental picture
IDOLS > IDOL
IDOLUM n mental picture
IDONEITY > IDONEOUS
IDONEOUS adj appropriate
IDS > ID
IDYL same as > IDYLL
IDYLIST same as > IDYLLIST
IDYLISTS > IDYLIST
IDYLL n scene or time of great peace and happiness
IDYLLIAN same as > IDYLLIC
IDYLLIC adj of or relating to an idyll
IDYLLIST n writer of idylls
IDYLLISTS > IDYLLIST
IDYLLS > IDYLL
IDYLS > IDYL
IF n uncertainty or doubt
IFF conj in logic, a shortened form of if and only if
IFFIER > IFFY
IFFIEST > IFFY
IFFILY adv in an iffy manner
IFFINESS > IFFY
IFFY adj doubtful, uncertain
IFS > IF
IFTAR n meal eaten by Muslims
IFTARS > IFTAR
IGAD same as > EGAD
IGAPO n flooded forest
IGAPOS > IGAPO
IGARAPE n canoe route
IGARAPES > IGARAPE
IGG vb antagonize
IGGED > IGG
IGGING > IGG
IGGS > IGG
IGLOO n Inuit house
IGLOOS > IGLOO
IGLU same as > IGLOO
IGLUS > IGLU
IGNARO n ignoramus
IGNAROES > IGNARO
IGNAROS > IGNARO
IGNATIA n dried seed
IGNATIAS > IGNATIA
IGNEOUS adj (of rock) formed as molten rock cools
IGNESCENT adj giving off sparks when struck, as a flint ▷ n ignescent substance
IGNIFIED > IGNIFY
IGNIFIES > IGNIFY
IGNIFY vb turn into fire
IGNIFYING > IGNIFY
IGNITABLE > IGNITE
IGNITE vb catch fire or set fire to
IGNITED > IGNITE
IGNITER n person or thing that ignites
IGNITERS > IGNITER
IGNITES > IGNITE
IGNITIBLE > IGNITE
IGNITING > IGNITE
IGNITION n system that ignites the fuel-and-air mixture to start an engine
IGNITIONS > IGNITION
IGNITOR same as > IGNITER

IGNITORS > IGNITOR
IGNITRON n mercury-arc rectifier controlled by a subsidiary electrode
IGNITRONS > IGNITRON
IGNOBLE adj dishonourable
IGNOBLER > IGNOBLE
IGNOBLEST > IGNOBLE
IGNOBLY > IGNOBLE
IGNOMIES > IGNOMY
IGNOMINY n humiliating disgrace
IGNOMY Shakespearean variant of > IGNOMINY
IGNORABLE > IGNORE
IGNORAMI > IGNORAMUS
IGNORAMUS n ignorant person
IGNORANCE n lack of knowledge or education
IGNORANT adj lacking knowledge ▷ n ignorant person
IGNORANTS > IGNORANT
IGNORE vb refuse to notice, disregard deliberately ▷ n disregard
IGNORED > IGNORE
IGNORER > IGNORE
IGNORERS > IGNORE
IGNORES > IGNORE
IGNORING > IGNORE
IGUANA n large tropical American lizard
IGUANAS > IGUANA
IGUANIAN > IGUANA
IGUANIANS > IGUANA
IGUANID same as > IGUANA
IGUANIDS > IGUANID
IGUANODON n massive herbivorous long-tailed bipedal dinosaur
IHRAM n white robes worn by Muslim pilgrims to Mecca
IHRAMS > IHRAM
IJTIHAD n effort of deriving a legal ruling from the Koran
IJTIHADS > IJTIHAD
IKAN n (in Malaysia) fish
IKANS > IKAN
IKAT n method of creating patterns in fabric
IKATS > IKAT
IKEBANA n Japanese art of flower arrangement
IKEBANAS > IKEBANA
IKON same as > ICON
IKONS > IKON
ILEA > ILEUM
ILEAC adj of or relating to the ileum
ILEAL same as > ILEAC
ILEITIDES > ILEITIS
ILEITIS n inflammation of the ileum
ILEITISES > ILEITIS
ILEOSTOMY n surgical formation of a permanent opening through the abdominal wall into the ileum
ILEUM n lowest part of the small intestine
ILEUS n obstruction of the intestine
ILEUSES > ILEUS

ILEX n any of a genus of trees or shrubs that includes holly
ILEXES > ILEX
ILIA > ILIUM
ILIAC adj of or relating to the ilium **ILIACI** > ILIACUS
ILIACUS n muscle near the ilium
ILIACUSES > ILIACUS
ILIAD n epic poem
ILIADS > ILIAD
ILIAL > ILIUM
ILICES > ILEX
ILIUM n part of the hipbone
ILK n type ▷ determiner each
ILKA same as > ILK
ILKADAY n every day
ILKADAYS > ILKADAY
ILKS > ILK
ILL adj not in good health ▷ n evil, harm ▷ adv badly
ILLAPSE vb slide in
ILLAPSED > ILLAPSE
ILLAPSES > ILLAPSE
ILLAPSING > ILLAPSE
ILLATION rare word for > INFERENCE
ILLATIONS > ILLATION
ILLATIVE adj of or relating to illation ▷ n illative case
ILLATIVES > ILLATIVE
ILLAWARRA n Australian breed of shorthorn dairy cattle
ILLEGAL adj against the law ▷ n person who entered or attempted to enter a country illegally
ILLEGALLY > ILLEGAL
ILLEGALS > ILLEGAL
ILLEGIBLE adj unable to be read or deciphered
ILLEGIBLY > ILLEGIBLE
ILLER > ILL
ILLEST > ILL
ILLIAD n wink
ILLIADS > ILLIAD
ILLIBERAL adj narrow-minded, intolerant
ILLICIT adj illegal
ILLICITLY > ILLICIT
ILLIMITED adj infinite
ILLINIUM n type of radioactive element
ILLINIUMS > ILLINIUM
ILLIPE n Asian tree
ILLIPES > ILLIPE
ILLIQUID adj (of an asset) not easily convertible into cash
ILLISION n act of striking against
ILLISIONS > ILLISION
ILLITE n clay mineral of the mica group
ILLITES > ILLITE
ILLITIC > ILLITE
ILLNESS n disease or indisposition
ILLNESSES > ILLNESS
ILLOGIC n reasoning characterized by lack of logic
ILLOGICAL adj unreasonable
ILLOGICS > ILLOGIC

ILLS > ILL
ILLTH n condition of poverty or misery
ILLTHS > ILLTH
ILLUDE vb trick or deceive
ILLUDED > ILLUDE
ILLUDES > ILLUDE
ILLUDING > ILLUDE
ILLUME vb illuminate
ILLUMED > ILLUME
ILLUMES > ILLUME
ILLUMINE vb throw light in or into
ILLUMINED > ILLUMINE
ILLUMINER n illuminator
ILLUMINES > ILLUMINE
ILLUMING > ILLUME
ILLUPI same as > ILLIPE
ILLUPIS > ILLUPI
ILLUSION n deceptive appearance or belief
ILLUSIONS > ILLUSION
ILLUSIVE same as > ILLUSORY
ILLUSORY adj seeming to be true, but actually false
ILLUVIA > ILLUVIUM
ILLUVIAL > ILLUVIUM
ILLUVIATE vb deposit illuvium
ILLUVIUM n material washed down from one soil layer to a lower one
ILLUVIUMS > ILLUVIUM
ILLY adv badly
ILMENITE n black mineral found in igneous rocks as layered deposits and in veins
ILMENITES > ILMENITE
IMAGE n mental picture of someone or something ▷ vb picture in the mind
IMAGEABLE > IMAGE
IMAGED > IMAGE
IMAGELESS > IMAGE
IMAGER n device that produces images
IMAGERIES > IMAGERY
IMAGERS > IMAGER
IMAGERY n images collectively, esp in the arts
IMAGES > IMAGE
IMAGINAL adj of, relating to, or resembling an imago
IMAGINARY adj existing only in the imagination
IMAGINE vb form a mental image of ▷ sentence substitute exclamation of surprise
IMAGINED > IMAGINE
IMAGINEER n person skilled in devising or implementing creative ideas ▷ vb devise and implement (a creative idea)
IMAGINER > IMAGINE
IMAGINERS > IMAGINE
IMAGINES > IMAGO
IMAGING > IMAGE
IMAGINGS > IMAGE
IMAGINING > IMAGINE
IMAGINIST n imaginative person
IMAGISM n poetic movement
IMAGISMS > IMAGISM
IMAGIST > IMAGISM

IMAGISTIC > IMAGISM
IMAGISTS > IMAGISM
IMAGO n mature adult insect
IMAGOES > IMAGO
IMAGOS > IMAGO
IMAM n leader of prayers in a mosque
IMAMATE n region or territory governed by an imam
IMAMATES > IMAMATE
IMAMS > IMAM
IMARET n (in Turkey) a hospice for pilgrims or travellers
IMARETS > IMARET
IMARI n Japanese porcelain
IMARIS > IMARI
IMAUM same as > IMAM
IMAUMS > IMAUM
IMBALANCE n lack of balance or proportion
IMBALM same as > EMBALM
IMBALMED > IMBALM
IMBALMER > IMBALM
IMBALMERS > IMBALM
IMBALMING > IMBALM
IMBALMS > IMBALM
IMBAR vb bar in
IMBARK vb cover in bark
IMBARKED > IMBARK
IMBARKING > IMBARK
IMBARKS > IMBARK
IMBARRED > IMBAR
IMBARRING > IMBAR
IMBARS > IMBAR
IMBASE vb degrade
IMBASED > IMBASE
IMBASES > IMBASE
IMBASING > IMBASE
IMBATHE vb bathe
IMBATHED > IMBATHE
IMBATHES > IMBATHE
IMBATHING > IMBATHE
IMBECILE n stupid person ▷ adj stupid or senseless
IMBECILES > IMBECILE
IMBECILIC > IMBECILE
IMBED same as > EMBED
IMBEDDED > IMBED
IMBEDDING > IMBED
IMBEDS > IMBED
IMBIBE vb drink (alcoholic drinks)
IMBIBED > IMBIBE
IMBIBER > IMBIBE
IMBIBERS > IMBIBE
IMBIBES > IMBIBE
IMBIBING > IMBIBE
IMBITTER same as > EMBITTER
IMBITTERS > IMBITTER
IMBIZO n meeting in S Africa
IMBIZOS > IMBIZO
IMBLAZE vb depict heraldically
IMBLAZED > IMBLAZE
IMBLAZES > IMBLAZE
IMBLAZING > IMBLAZE
IMBODIED > IMBODY
IMBODIES > IMBODY
IMBODY same as > EMBODY
IMBODYING > IMBODY
IMBOLDEN same as > EMBOLDEN
IMBOLDENS > IMBOLDEN

IMBORDER vb enclose in a border
IMBORDERS > IMBORDER
IMBOSK vb conceal
IMBOSKED > IMBOSK
IMBOSKING > IMBOSK
IMBOSKS > IMBOSK
IMBOSOM vb hold in one's heart
IMBOSOMED > IMBOSOM
IMBOSOMS > IMBOSOM
IMBOSS same as > EMBOSS
IMBOSSED > IMBOSS
IMBOSSES > IMBOSS
IMBOSSING > IMBOSS
IMBOWER vb enclose in a bower
IMBOWERED > IMBOWER
IMBOWERS > IMBOWER
IMBRANGLE vb entangle
IMBRAST Spenserian past participle of > EMBRACE
IMBREX n curved tile
IMBRICATE adj having tiles or slates that overlap ▷ vb decorate with a repeating pattern resembling scales or overlapping tiles
IMBRICES > IMBREX
IMBROGLIO n confusing and complicated situation
IMBROWN vb make brown
IMBROWNED > IMBROWN
IMBROWNS > IMBROWN
IMBRUE vb stain, esp with blood
IMBRUED > IMBRUE
IMBRUES > IMBRUE
IMBRUING > IMBRUE
IMBRUTE vb reduce to a bestial state
IMBRUTED > IMBRUTE
IMBRUTES > IMBRUTE
IMBRUTING > IMBRUTE
IMBUE vb fill or inspire with (ideals or principles)
IMBUED > IMBUE
IMBUEMENT > IMBUE
IMBUES > IMBUE
IMBUING > IMBUE
IMBURSE vb pay
IMBURSED > IMBURSE
IMBURSES > IMBURSE
IMBURSING > IMBURSE
IMID n immunomodulatory drug
IMIDAZOLE n white crystalline basic heterocyclic compound
IMIDE n any of a class of organic compounds
IMIDES > IMIDE
IMIDIC > IMIDE
IMIDO > IMIDE
IMIDS > IMID
IMINAZOLE same as > IMIDAZOLE
IMINE n any of a class of organic compounds
IMINES > IMINE
IMINO > IMINE
IMINOUREA another name for > GUANIDINE
IMIPENEM n drug used to destroy bacteria
IMIPENEMS > IMIPENEM
IMITABLE > IMITATE

IMITANCY n tendency to imitate

IMITANT same as > IMITATION

IMITANTS > IMITANT

IMITATE vb take as a model

IMITATED > IMITATE

IMITATES > IMITATE

IMITATING > IMITATE

IMITATION n copy of an original ▷ adj made to look like a material of superior quality

IMITATIVE adj imitating or tending to copy

IMITATOR > IMITATE

IMITATORS > IMITATE

IMMANACLE vb fetter

IMMANE adj monstrous

IMMANELY > IMMANE

IMMANENCE > IMMANENT

IMMANENCY > IMMANENT

IMMANENT adj present within and throughout something

IMMANITY > IMMANE

IMMANTLE vb cover with a mantle

IMMANTLED > IMMANTLE

IMMANTLES > IMMANTLE

IMMASK vb disguise

IMMASKED > IMMASK

IMMASKING > IMMASK

IMMASKS > IMMASK

IMMATURE n young animal ▷ adj not fully developed

IMMATURER > IMMATURE

IMMATURES > IMMATURE

IMMEDIACY > IMMEDIATE

IMMEDIATE adj occurring at once

IMMENSE adj extremely large

IMMENSELY > IMMENSE

IMMENSER > IMMENSE

IMMENSEST > IMMENSE

IMMENSITY n state or quality of being immense

IMMERGE archaic word for > IMMERSE

IMMERGED > IMMERGE

IMMERGES > IMMERGE

IMMERGING > IMMERGE

IMMERSE vb involve deeply, engross

IMMERSED adj sunk or submerged

IMMERSER > IMMERSE

IMMERSERS > IMMERSE

IMMERSES > IMMERSE

IMMERSING > IMMERSE

IMMERSION n form of baptism in which part or the whole of a person's body is submerged in the water

IMMERSIVE adj providing information or stimulation for a number of senses, not only sight and sound

IMMESH variant of > ENMESH

IMMESHED > IMMESH

IMMESHES > IMMESH

IMMESHING > IMMESH

IMMEW vb confine

IMMEWED > IMMEW

IMMEWING > IMMEW

IMMEWS > IMMEW

IMMIES > IMMY

IMMIGRANT n person who comes to a foreign country in order to settle there

IMMIGRATE vb come to a place or country of which one is not a native in order to settle there

IMMINENCE > IMMINENT

IMMINENCY > IMMINENT

IMMINENT adj about to happen

IMMINGLE vb blend or mix together

IMMINGLED > IMMINGLE

IMMINGLES > IMMINGLE

IMMINUTE adj reduced

IMMISSION n insertion

IMMIT vb insert

IMMITS > IMMIT

IMMITTED > IMMIT

IMMITTING > IMMIT

IMMIX vb mix in

IMMIXED > IMMIX

IMMIXES > IMMIX

IMMIXING > IMMIX

IMMIXTURE > IMMIX

IMMOBILE adj not moving

IMMODEST adj behaving in an indecent or improper manner

IMMODESTY > IMMODEST

IMMOLATE vb kill as a sacrifice

IMMOLATED > IMMOLATE

IMMOLATES > IMMOLATE

IMMOLATOR > IMMOLATE

IMMOMENT adj of no value

IMMORAL adj morally wrong, corrupt

IMMORALLY > IMMORAL

IMMORTAL adj living forever ▷ n person whose fame will last for all time

IMMORTALS > IMMORTAL

IMMOTILE adj not capable of moving spontaneously and independently

IMMOVABLE adj unable to be moved

IMMOVABLY > IMMOVABLE

IMMUNE adj protected against a specific disease ▷ n immune person or animal

IMMUNER > IMMUNE

IMMUNES > IMMUNE

IMMUNEST > IMMUNE

IMMUNISE same as > IMMUNIZE

IMMUNISED > IMMUNISE

IMMUNISER > IMMUNISE

IMMUNISES > IMMUNISE

IMMUNITY n ability to resist disease

IMMUNIZE vb make immune to a disease

IMMUNIZED > IMMUNIZE

IMMUNIZER > IMMUNIZE

IMMUNIZES > IMMUNIZE

IMMUNOGEN n any substance that evokes an immune response

IMMURE vb imprison

IMMURED > IMMURE

IMMURES > IMMURE

IMMURING > IMMURE

IMMUTABLE adj unchangeable

IMMUTABLY > IMMUTABLE

IMMY n image-orthicon camera

IMP n (in folklore) creature with magical powers ▷ vb method of repairing the wing of a hawk or falcon

IMPACABLE adj incapable of being placated or pacified

IMPACT n strong effect ▷ vb have a strong effect on

IMPACTED > IMPACT

IMPACTER > IMPACT

IMPACTERS > IMPACT

IMPACTFUL > IMPACT

IMPACTING > IMPACT

IMPACTION > IMPACT

IMPACTITE n glassy rock formed in a meteor collision

IMPACTIVE adj of or relating to a physical impact

IMPACTOR > IMPACT

IMPACTORS > IMPACT

IMPACTS > IMPACT

IMPAINT vb paint

IMPAINTED > IMPAINT

IMPAINTS > IMPAINT

IMPAIR vb weaken or damage

IMPAIRED > IMPAIR

IMPAIRER > IMPAIR

IMPAIRERS > IMPAIR

IMPAIRING > IMPAIR

IMPAIRS > IMPAIR

IMPALA n southern African antelope

IMPALAS > IMPALA

IMPALE vb pierce with a sharp object

IMPALED > IMPALE

IMPALER > IMPALE

IMPALERS > IMPALE

IMPALES > IMPALE

IMPALING > IMPALE

IMPANATE adj embodied in bread

IMPANEL variant spelling (esp US) of > EMPANEL

IMPANELED > IMPANEL

IMPANELS > IMPANEL

IMPANNEL same as > IMPANEL

IMPANNELS > IMPANNEL

IMPARITY less common word for > DISPARITY

IMPARK vb make into a park

IMPARKED > IMPARK

IMPARKING > IMPARK

IMPARKS > IMPARK

IMPARL vb parley

IMPARLED > IMPARL

IMPARLING > IMPARL

IMPARLS > IMPARL

IMPART vb communicate (information)

IMPARTED > IMPART

IMPARTER > IMPART

IMPARTERS > IMPART

IMPARTIAL adj not favouring one side or the other

IMPARTING > IMPART

IMPARTS > IMPART

IMPASSE n situation in which progress is impossible

IMPASSES > IMPASSE

IMPASSION vb arouse the passions of

IMPASSIVE adj showing no emotion, calm

IMPASTE vb apply paint thickly to

IMPASTED > IMPASTE

IMPASTES > IMPASTE

IMPASTING > IMPASTE

IMPASTO n technique of applying paint thickly ▷ vb apply impasto

IMPASTOED > IMPASTO

IMPASTOS > IMPASTO

IMPATIENS n plant such as balsam, touch-me-not, busy Lizzie, and policeman's helmet

IMPATIENT adj irritable at any delay or difficulty

IMPAVE vb set in a pavement

IMPAVED > IMPAVE

IMPAVES > IMPAVE

IMPAVID adj fearless

IMPAVIDLY > IMPAVID

IMPAVING > IMPAVE

IMPAWN vb pawn

IMPAWNED > IMPAWN

IMPAWNING > IMPAWN

IMPAWNS > IMPAWN

IMPEACH vb charge with a serious crime against the state

IMPEACHED > IMPEACH

IMPEACHER > IMPEACH

IMPEACHES > IMPEACH

IMPEARL vb adorn with pearls

IMPEARLED > IMPEARL

IMPEARLS > IMPEARL

IMPECCANT adj not sinning

IMPED > IMP

IMPEDANCE n measure of the opposition to the flow of an alternating current

IMPEDE vb hinder in action or progress

IMPEDED > IMPEDE

IMPEDER > IMPEDE

IMPEDERS > IMPEDE

IMPEDES > IMPEDE

IMPEDING > IMPEDE

IMPEDOR n component that offers impedance

IMPEDORS > IMPEDOR

IMPEL vb push or force (someone) to do something

IMPELLED > IMPEL

IMPELLENT > IMPEL

IMPELLER n vaned rotating disc of a centrifugal pump, compressor, etc

IMPELLERS > IMPELLER

IMPELLING > IMPEL

IMPELLOR same as > IMPELLER

IMPELLORS > IMPELLOR

IMPELS > IMPEL

IMPEND vb be about to happen

IMPENDED > IMPEND

IMPENDENT adj impending; threatening

IMPENDING > IMPEND

IMPENDS > IMPEND

IMPENNATE *adj* (of birds) lacking true functional wings or feathers

IMPERATOR *n* (in imperial Rome) a title of the emperor

IMPERFECT *adj* having faults or mistakes ▷ *n* imperfect tense

IMPERIA > IMPERIUM

IMPERIAL *adj* of or like an empire or emperor ▷ *n* wine bottle holding the equivalent of eight normal bottles

IMPERIALS > IMPERIAL

IMPERIL *vb* put in danger

IMPERILED > IMPERIL

IMPERILS > IMPERIL

IMPERIOUS *adj* proud and domineering

IMPERIUM *n* supreme power of Roman consuls and emperors

IMPERIUMS > IMPERIUM

IMPETICOS *vb* put in a pocket

IMPETIGO *n* contagious skin disease

IMPETIGOS > IMPETIGO

IMPETRATE *vb* supplicate or entreat for, esp by prayer

IMPETUOUS *adj* done or acting without thought, rash

IMPETUS *n* incentive, impulse

IMPETUSES > IMPETUS

IMPHEE *n* African sugar cane

IMPHEES > IMPHEE

IMPI *n* group of Zulu warriors

IMPIES > IMPI

IMPIETIES > IMPIETY

IMPIETY *n* lack of respect or religious reverence

IMPING > IMP

IMPINGE *vb* affect or restrict

IMPINGED > IMPINGE

IMPINGENT *adj* striking against or upon

IMPINGER > IMPINGE

IMPINGERS > IMPINGE

IMPINGES > IMPINGE

IMPINGING > IMPINGE

IMPINGS > IMP

IMPIOUS *adj* showing a lack of respect or reverence

IMPIOUSLY > IMPIOUS

IMPIS > IMPI

IMPISH *adj* mischievous

IMPISHLY > IMPISH

IMPLANT *n* something put into someone's body ▷ *vb* put (something) into someone's body

IMPLANTED > IMPLANT

IMPLANTER > IMPLANT

IMPLANTS > IMPLANT

IMPLATE *vb* sheathe

IMPLATED > IMPLATE

IMPLATES > IMPLATE

IMPLATING > IMPLATE

IMPLEACH *vb* intertwine

IMPLEAD *vb* sue or prosecute

IMPLEADED > IMPLEAD

IMPLEADER > IMPLEAD

IMPLEADS > IMPLEAD

IMPLED > IMPLEAD

IMPLEDGE *vb* pledge

IMPLEDGED > IMPLEDGE

IMPLEDGES > IMPLEDGE

IMPLEMENT *vb* carry out (instructions etc) ▷ *n* tool, instrument

IMPLETE *vb* fill

IMPLETED > IMPLETE

IMPLETES > IMPLETE

IMPLETING > IMPLETE

IMPLETION > IMPLETE

IMPLEX *n* part of an arthropod

IMPLEXES > IMPLEX

IMPLEXION *n* complication

IMPLICATE *vb* show to be involved, esp in a crime

IMPLICIT *adj* expressed indirectly

IMPLICITY > IMPLICIT

IMPLIED *adj* hinted at or suggested

IMPLIEDLY > IMPLIED

IMPLIES > IMPLY

IMPLODE *vb* collapse inwards

IMPLODED > IMPLODE

IMPLODENT *n* sound of an implosion

IMPLODES > IMPLODE

IMPLODING > IMPLODE

IMPLORE *vb* beg earnestly

IMPLORED > IMPLORE

IMPLORER > IMPLORE

IMPLORERS > IMPLORE

IMPLORES > IMPLORE

IMPLORING > IMPLORE

IMPLOSION *n* act or process of imploding

IMPLOSIVE *n* consonant pronounced in a particular way

IMPLUNGE *vb* submerge

IMPLUNGED > IMPLUNGE

IMPLUNGES > IMPLUNGE

IMPLUVIA > IMPLUVIUM

IMPLUVIUM *n* rain-filled water tank

IMPLY *vb* indicate by hinting, suggest

IMPLYING > IMPLY

IMPOCKET *vb* put in a pocket

IMPOCKETS > IMPOCKET

IMPOLDER *vb* make into a polder

IMPOLDERS > IMPOLDER

IMPOLICY *n* act or an instance of being injudicious or impolitic

IMPOLITE *adj* showing bad manners

IMPOLITER > IMPOLITE

IMPOLITIC *adj* unwise or inadvisable

IMPONE *vb* impose

IMPONED > IMPONE

IMPONENT *n* person who imposes a duty, etc

IMPONENTS > IMPONENT

IMPONES > IMPONE

IMPONING > IMPONE

IMPOROUS *adj* not porous

IMPORT *vb* bring in (goods) from another country ▷ *n* something imported

IMPORTANT *adj* of great significance or value

IMPORTED > IMPORT

IMPORTER > IMPORT

IMPORTERS > IMPORT

IMPORTING > IMPORT

IMPORTS > IMPORT

IMPORTUNE *vb* harass with persistent requests

IMPOSABLE > IMPOSE

IMPOSE *vb* force the acceptance of

IMPOSED > IMPOSE

IMPOSER > IMPOSE

IMPOSERS > IMPOSE

IMPOSES > IMPOSE

IMPOSEX *n* acquisition by female organisms of male characteristics

IMPOSEXES > IMPOSEX

IMPOSING *adj* grand, impressive

IMPOST *n* tax, esp a customs duty ▷ *vb* classify (imported goods) according to the duty payable on them

IMPOSTED > IMPOST

IMPOSTER > IMPOST

IMPOSTERS > IMPOST

IMPOSTING > IMPOST

IMPOSTOR *n* person who cheats or swindles by pretending to be someone else

IMPOSTORS > IMPOSTOR

IMPOSTS > IMPOST

IMPOSTUME *archaic word for* > ABSCESS

IMPOSTURE *n* deception, esp by pretending to be someone else

IMPOT *n* slang term for the act of imposing

IMPOTENCE > IMPOTENT

IMPOTENCY > IMPOTENT

IMPOTENT *adj* powerless ▷ *n* one who is impotent

IMPOTENTS > IMPOTENT

IMPOTS > IMPOT

IMPOUND *vb* take legal possession of, confiscate

IMPOUNDED > IMPOUND

IMPOUNDER > IMPOUND

IMPOUNDS > IMPOUND

IMPOWER *less common spelling of* > EMPOWER

IMPOWERED > IMPOWER

IMPOWERS > IMPOWER

IMPRECATE *vb* swear, curse, or blaspheme

IMPRECISE *adj* inexact or inaccurate

IMPREGN *vb* impregnate

IMPREGNED > IMPREGN

IMPREGNS > IMPREGN

IMPRESA *n* heraldic device

IMPRESARI *n* impresarios

IMPRESAS > IMPRESA

IMPRESE *same as* > IMPRESA

IMPRESES > IMPRESE

IMPRESS *vb* affect strongly, usu favourably ▷ *n* impressing

IMPRESSE *n* heraldic device

IMPRESSED > IMPRESS

IMPRESSER > IMPRESS

IMPRESSES > IMPRESS

IMPREST *n* fund of cash used to pay incidental expenses

IMPRESTS > IMPREST

IMPRIMIS *adv* in the first place

IMPRINT *n* mark made by printing or stamping ▷ *vb* produce (a mark) by printing or stamping

IMPRINTED > IMPRINT

IMPRINTER > IMPRINT

IMPRINTS > IMPRINT

IMPRISON *vb* put in prison

IMPRISONS > IMPRISON

IMPRO *n* short for improvisation

IMPROBITY *n* dishonesty or wickedness

IMPROMPTU *adj* without planning or preparation ▷ *adv* in a spontaneous or improvised way ▷ *n* short piece of instrumental music resembling improvisation

IMPROPER *adj* indecent

IMPROS > IMPRO

IMPROV *n* improvisational comedy

IMPROVE *vb* make or become better

IMPROVED > IMPROVE

IMPROVER > IMPROVE

IMPROVERS > IMPROVE

IMPROVES > IMPROVE

IMPROVING > IMPROVE

IMPROVISE *vb* make use of whatever materials are available

IMPROVS > IMPROV

IMPRUDENT *adj* not sensible or wise

IMPS > IMP

IMPSONITE *n* asphaltite compound

IMPUDENCE *n* quality of being impudent

IMPUDENCY *same as* > IMPUDENCE

IMPUDENT *adj* cheeky, disrespectful

IMPUGN *vb* challenge the truth or validity of

IMPUGNED > IMPUGN

IMPUGNER > IMPUGN

IMPUGNERS > IMPUGN

IMPUGNING > IMPUGN

IMPUGNS > IMPUGN

IMPULSE *vb* give an impulse to ▷ *n* sudden urge to do something

IMPULSED > IMPULSE

IMPULSES > IMPULSE

IMPULSING > IMPULSE

IMPULSION *n* act of impelling or the state of being impelled

IMPULSIVE *adj* acting or done without careful consideration

IMPUNDULU *n* mythical bird associated with witchcraft, frequently manifested as the secretary bird

IMPUNITY *n* exemption or immunity from punishment or recrimination

IMPURE adj having dirty or unwanted substances mixed in

IMPURELY > IMPURE

IMPURER > IMPURE

IMPUREST > IMPURE

IMPURITY n impure element or thing

IMPURPLE vb colour purple

IMPURPLED > IMPURPLE

IMPURPLES > IMPURPLE

IMPUTABLE adj capable of being imputed

IMPUTABLY > IMPUTABLE

IMPUTE vb attribute responsibility to

IMPUTED > IMPUTE

IMPUTER > IMPUTE

IMPUTERS > IMPUTE

IMPUTES > IMPUTE

IMPUTING > IMPUTE

IMSHI interj go away!

IMSHY same as > IMSHI

IN prep indicating position inside, state or situation, etc ▷ adv indicating position inside, entry into, etc ▷ adj fashionable ▷ n way of approaching or befriending a person ▷ vb take in

INABILITY n lack of means or skill to do something

INACTION n act of doing nothing

INACTIONS > INACTION

INACTIVE adj idle

INAIDABLE adj beyond help

INAMORATA n woman with whom one is in love

INAMORATI > INAMORATO

INAMORATO n man with whom one is in love

INANE adj senseless, silly ▷ n something that is inane

INANELY > INANE

INANENESS > INANE

INANER > INANE

INANES > INANE

INANEST > INANE

INANGA n common type of New Zealand grass tree

INANGAS > INANGA

INANIMATE adj not living

INANITIES > INANITY

INANITION n exhaustion or weakness, as from lack of food

INANITY n lack of intelligence or imagination

INAPT adj not apt or fitting

INAPTER > INAPT

INAPTEST > INAPT

INAPTLY > INAPT

INAPTNESS > INAPT

INARABLE adj not arable

INARCH vb graft (a plant)

INARCHED > INARCH

INARCHES > INARCH

INARCHING > INARCH

INARM vb embrace

INARMED > INARM

INARMING > INARM

INARMS > INARM

INASMUCH conj as in inasmuch as , in view of the fact that

INAUDIBLE adj not loud enough to be heard

INAUDIBLY > INAUDIBLE

INAUGURAL adj of or for an inauguration ▷ n speech made at an inauguration

INAURATE adj gilded ▷ vb cover in gold

INAURATED > INAURATE

INAURATES > INAURATE

INBEING n existence in something else

INBEINGS > INBEING

INBENT adj bent inwards

INBOARD adj (of a boat's engine) inside the hull ▷ adv within the sides of a vessel or aircraft

INBOARDS same as > INBOARD

INBORN adj existing from birth, natural

INBOUND vb pass into the playing area from outside it ▷ adj coming in

INBOUNDED > INBOUND

INBOUNDS > INBOUND

INBOX n folder which stores in-coming email messages

INBOXES > INBOX

INBREAK n breaking in

INBREAKS > INBREAK

INBREATHE vb infuse or imbue

INBRED n inbred person or animal ▷ adj produced as a result of inbreeding

INBREDS > INBRED

INBREED vb breed from closely related individuals

INBREEDER > INBREED

INBREEDS > INBREED

INBRING vb bring in

INBRINGS > INBRING

INBROUGHT > INBRING

INBUILT adj present from the start

INBURNING adj burning within

INBURST n irruption ▷ vb burst in

INBURSTS > INBURST

INBY adv into the house or an inner room ▷ adj located near or nearest to the house

INBYE adv near the house

INCAGE vb confine in or as in a cage

INCAGED > INCAGE

INCAGES > INCAGE

INCAGING > INCAGE

INCANT vb chant (a spell)

INCANTED > INCANT

INCANTING > INCANT

INCANTS > INCANT

INCAPABLE adj unable (to do something)

INCAPABLY > INCAPABLE

INCARNATE adj in human form ▷ vb give a bodily or concrete form to

INCASE variant spelling of > ENCASE

INCASED > INCASE

INCASES > INCASE

INCASING > INCASE

INCAUTION n act of not being cautious

INCAVE vb hide

INCAVED > INCAVE

INCAVES > INCAVE

INCAVI > INCAVO

INCAVING > INCAVE

INCAVO n incised part of a carving

INCEDE vb advance

INCEDED > INCEDE

INCEDES > INCEDE

INCEDING > INCEDE

INCEL n involuntary celibate

INCELS > INCEL

INCENSE vb make very angry ▷ n substance that gives off a perfume when burned

INCENSED > INCENSE

INCENSER n incense burner

INCENSERS > INCENSER

INCENSES > INCENSE

INCENSING > INCENSE

INCENSOR n incense burner

INCENSORS > INCENSOR

INCENSORY less common name for > CENSER

INCENT vb provide incentive

INCENTED > INCENT

INCENTER same as > INCENTRE

INCENTERS > INCENTER

INCENTING > INCENT

INCENTIVE n something that encourages effort or action ▷ adj encouraging greater effort

INCENTRE n centre of an inscribed circle

INCENTRES > INCENTRE

INCENTS > INCENT

INCEPT vb (of organisms) to ingest (food) ▷ n rudimentary organ

INCEPTED > INCEPT

INCEPTING > INCEPT

INCEPTION n beginning

INCEPTIVE adj beginning ▷ n type of verb

INCEPTOR > INCEPT

INCEPTORS > INCEPT

INCEPTS > INCEPT

INCERTAIN archaic form of > UNCERTAIN

INCESSANT adj never stopping

INCEST n sexual intercourse between two closely related people

INCESTS > INCEST

INCH n unit of length ▷ vb move slowly and gradually

INCHASE same as > ENCHASE

INCHASED > INCHASE

INCHASES > INCHASE

INCHASING > INCHASE

INCHED > INCH

INCHER n something measuring given amount of inches

INCHERS > INCHER

INCHES > INCH

INCHING > INCH

INCHMEAL adv gradually

INCHOATE adj just begun and not yet properly developed ▷ vb begin

INCHOATED > INCHOATE

INCHOATES > INCHOATE

INCHPIN n cervine sweetbread

INCHPINS > INCHPIN

INCHTAPE n measuring tape marked out in inches

INCHTAPES > INCHTAPE

INCHWORM n larva of a type of moth

INCHWORMS > INCHWORM

INCIDENCE n extent or frequency of occurrence

INCIDENT n something that happens ▷ adj related (to) or dependent (on)

INCIDENTS > INCIDENT

INCIPIENT adj just starting to appear or happen

INCIPIT n Latin introductory phrase

INCIPITS > INCIPIT

INCISAL adj relating to the cutting edge of incisors and cuspids

INCISE vb cut into with a sharp tool

INCISED > INCISE

INCISES > INCISE

INCISING > INCISE

INCISION n cut, esp one made during a surgical operation

INCISIONS > INCISION

INCISIVE adj direct and forceful

INCISOR n front tooth, used for biting into food

INCISORS > INCISOR

INCISORY > INCISOR

INCISURAL > INCISURE

INCISURE n incision or notch in an organ or part

INCISURES > INCISURE

INCITABLE > INCITE

INCITANT n something that incites

INCITANTS > INCITANT

INCITE vb stir up, provoke

INCITED > INCITE

INCITER > INCITE

INCITERS > INCITE

INCITES > INCITE

INCITING > INCITE

INCIVIL archaic form of > UNCIVIL

INCIVISM n neglect of a citizen's duties

INCIVISMS > INCIVISM

INCLASP vb clasp

INCLASPED > INCLASP

INCLASPS > INCLASP

INCLE same as > INKLE

INCLEMENT adj (of weather) stormy or severe

INCLES > INCLE

INCLINE vb lean, slope ▷ n slope

INCLINED adj having a disposition

INCLINER > INCLINE

INCLINERS > INCLINE

INCLINES > INCLINE

INCLINING > INCLINE

INCLIP vb embrace
INCLIPPED > INCLIP
INCLIPS > INCLIP
INCLOSE less common spelling of > ENCLOSE
INCLOSED > INCLOSE
INCLOSER > INCLOSE
INCLOSERS > INCLOSE
INCLOSES > INCLOSE
INCLOSING > INCLOSE
INCLOSURE > INCLOSE
INCLUDE vb have as part of the whole
INCLUDED adj (of the stamens or pistils of a flower) not protruding beyond the corolla
INCLUDES > INCLUDE
INCLUDING > INCLUDE
INCLUSION n including or being included
INCLUSIVE adj including everything (specified)
INCOG n incognito
INCOGNITA n female who is in disguise or unknown
INCOGNITO adv having adopted a false identity ▷ n false identity ▷ adj under an assumed name or appearance
INCOGS > INCOG
INCOME n amount of money earned
INCOMER n person who comes to a place in which they were not born
INCOMERS > INCOMER
INCOMES > INCOME
INCOMING adj coming in ▷ n act of coming in
INCOMINGS > INCOMING
INCOMMODE vb cause inconvenience to
INCOMPACT adj not compact
INCONDITE adj poorly constructed or composed
INCONIE adj fine or delicate
INCONNU n whitefish of Arctic waters
INCONNUE n unknown woman
INCONNUES > INCONNUE
INCONNUS > INCONNU
INCONY adj fine or delicate
INCORPSE vb incorporate
INCORPSED > INCORPSE
INCORPSES > INCORPSE
INCORRECT adj wrong
INCORRUPT adj free from corruption
INCREASE vb make or become greater in size, number, etc ▷ n rise in number, size, etc
INCREASED > INCREASE
INCREASER > INCREASE
INCREASES > INCREASE
INCREATE adj (esp of gods) never having been created
INCREMATE vb cremate
INCREMENT n increase in money or value, esp a regular salary increase
INCRETION n direct secretion into the

bloodstream, esp of a hormone from an endocrine gland
INCRETORY > INCRETION
INCROSS n variation produced by inbreeding ▷ vb produce by inbreeding
INCROSSED > INCROSS
INCROSSES > INCROSS
INCRUST same as > ENCRUST
INCRUSTED > INCRUST
INCRUSTS > INCRUST
INCUBATE vb (of a bird) hatch (eggs) by sitting on them
INCUBATED > INCUBATE
INCUBATES > INCUBATE
INCUBATOR n heated enclosed apparatus for rearing premature babies
INCUBI > INCUBUS
INCUBOUS adj having overlapping leaves
INCUBUS n (in folklore) type of demon
INCUBUSES > INCUBUS
INCUDAL > INCUS
INCUDATE > INCUS
INCUDES > INCUS
INCULCATE vb fix in someone's mind by constant repetition
INCULPATE vb cause (someone) to be blamed for a crime
INCULT adj (of land) uncultivated
INCUMBENT n person who holds a particular office or position ▷ adj morally binding as a duty
INCUMBER less common spelling of > ENCUMBER
INCUMBERS > INCUMBER
INCUNABLE n early printed book
INCUR vb cause (something unpleasant) to happen
INCURABLE adj not able to be cured ▷ n person with an incurable disease
INCURABLY > INCURABLE
INCURIOUS adj showing no curiosity or interest
INCURRED > INCUR
INCURRENT adj (of anatomical ducts, tubes, channels, etc) having an inward flow
INCURRING > INCUR
INCURS > INCUR
INCURSION n sudden brief invasion
INCURSIVE > INCURSION
INCURVATE vb curve or cause to curve inwards ▷ adj curved inwards
INCURVE vb curve or cause to curve inwards
INCURVED > INCURVE
INCURVES > INCURVE
INCURVING > INCURVE
INCURVITY > INCURVE
INCUS n bone in the ear of mammals
INCUSE n design stamped or hammered onto a coin ▷ vb impress (a design) in a coin

▷ adj stamped or hammered onto a coin
INCUSED > INCUSE
INCUSES > INCUSE
INCUSING > INCUSE
INCUT adj cut or etched in ▷ n indent in rock used as a foothold
INCUTS > INCUT
INDABA n (among South Africans) a meeting to discuss a serious topic
INDABAS > INDABA
INDAGATE vb investigate
INDAGATED > INDAGATE
INDAGATES > INDAGATE
INDAGATOR > INDAGATE
INDAMIN same as > INDAMINE
INDAMINE n organic base used in the production of the dye safranine
INDAMINES > INDAMINE
INDAMINS > INDAMIN
INDART vb dart in
INDARTED > INDART
INDARTING > INDART
INDARTS > INDART
INDEBTED adj owing gratitude for help or favours
INDECENCY n state or quality of being indecent
INDECENT adj morally offensive
INDECORUM n indecorous behaviour or speech
INDEED adv really, certainly ▷ interj expression of indignation or surprise
INDEEDY interj indeed
INDELIBLE adj impossible to erase or remove
INDELIBLY > INDELIBLE
INDEMNIFY vb secure against loss, damage, or liability
INDEMNITY n insurance against loss or damage
INDENE n colourless liquid hydrocarbon
INDENES > INDENE
INDENT vb make a dent in
INDENTED > INDENT
INDENTER > INDENT
INDENTERS > INDENT
INDENTING > INDENT
INDENTION n space between a margin and the start of the line of text
INDENTOR > INDENT
INDENTORS > INDENT
INDENTS > INDENT
INDENTURE n contract, esp one binding an apprentice to his or her employer ▷ vb bind (an apprentice) by indenture
INDEVOUT adj not devout
INDEW same as > INDUE
INDEWED > INDEW
INDEWING > INDEW
INDEWS > INDEW
INDEX n alphabetical list of subjects dealt with in a book ▷ vb provide (a book) with an index
INDEXABLE > INDEX

INDEXAL > INDEX
INDEXED > INDEX
INDEXER > INDEX
INDEXERS > INDEX
INDEXES > INDEX
INDEXICAL adj arranged as or relating to an index or indexes ▷ n term whose reference depends on the context of utterance
INDEXING > INDEX
INDEXINGS > INDEX
INDEXLESS > INDEX
INDIA n code word for the letter I
INDIAS > INDIA
INDICAN n compound secreted in the urine
INDICANS > INDICAN
INDICANT n something that indicates
INDICANTS > INDICANT
INDICATE vb be a sign or symptom of
INDICATED > INDICATE
INDICATES > INDICATE
INDICATOR n something acting as a sign or indication
INDICES plural of > INDEX
INDICIA > INDICIUM
INDICIAL > INDICIUM
INDICIAS > INDICIUM
INDICIUM n notice
INDICIUMS > INDICIUM
INDICT vb formally charge with a crime
INDICTED > INDICT
INDICTEE > INDICT
INDICTEES > INDICT
INDICTER > INDICT
INDICTERS > INDICT
INDICTING > INDICT
INDICTION n recurring fiscal period of 15 years, often used as a unit for dating events
INDICTOR > INDICT
INDICTORS > INDICT
INDICTS > INDICT
INDIE adj (of rock music) released by an independent record label ▷ n independent record company
INDIES > INDIE
INDIGEN same as > INDIGENE
INDIGENCE > INDIGENT
INDIGENCY > INDIGENT
INDIGENE n indigenous person, animal, or thing
INDIGENES > INDIGENE
INDIGENS > INDIGEN
INDIGENT adj extremely poor ▷ n impoverished person
INDIGENTS > INDIGENT
INDIGEST n undigested mass ▷ vb suffer indigestion
INDIGESTS > INDIGEST
INDIGN adj undeserving
INDIGNANT adj feeling or showing indignation
INDIGNIFY vb treat in a humiliating manner
INDIGNITY n embarrassing or humiliating treatment
INDIGNLY > INDIGN**

INDIGO *adj* deep violet-blue ▷ *n* dye of this colour

INDIGOES > INDIGO

INDIGOID *adj* of, concerned with, or resembling indigo or its blue colour ▷ *n* any of a number of synthetic dyes or pigments related in chemical structure to indigo

INDIGOIDS > INDIGOID

INDIGOS > INDIGO

INDIGOTIC > INDIGO

INDIGOTIN *same as* > INDIGO

INDINAVIR *n* drug used to treat AIDS

INDIRECT *adj* done or caused by someone or something else

INDIRUBIN *n* isomer of indigotin

INDISPOSE *vb* make unwilling or opposed

INDITE *vb* write

INDITED > INDITE

INDITER > INDITE

INDITERS > INDITE

INDITES > INDITE

INDITING > INDITE

INDIUM *n* soft silvery-white metallic element

INDIUMS > INDIUM

INDIVIDUA *pl n* indivisible entities

INDOCIBLE *same as* > INDOCILE

INDOCILE *adj* difficult to discipline or instruct

INDOL *same as* > INDOLE

INDOLE *n* crystalline heterocyclic compound

INDOLENCE > INDOLENT

INDOLENCY *n* laziness

INDOLENT *adj* lazy

INDOLES > INDOLE

INDOLS > INDOL

INDOOR *adj* inside a building

INDOORS *adj* inside or into a building

INDORSE *variant spelling of* > ENDORSE

INDORSED > INDORSE

INDORSEE *n* the person to whom a note or bill is indorsed

INDORSEES > INDORSE

INDORSER > INDORSE

INDORSERS > INDORSE

INDORSES > INDORSE

INDORSING > INDORSE

INDORSOR > INDORSE

INDORSORS > INDORSE

INDOW *archaic variant of* > ENDOW

INDOWED > INDOW

INDOWING > INDOW

INDOWS > INDOW

INDOXYL *n* water-soluble crystalline compound

INDOXYLS > INDOXYL

INDRAFT *same as* > INDRAUGHT

INDRAFTS > INDRAFT

INDRAUGHT *n* act of drawing or pulling in

INDRAWN *adj* drawn or pulled in

INDRENCH *vb* submerge

INDRI *same as* > INDRIS

INDRIS *n* large lemuroid primate

INDRISES > INDRIS

INDUBIOUS *adj* certain

INDUCE *vb* persuade or influence

INDUCED > INDUCE

INDUCER > INDUCE

INDUCERS > INDUCE

INDUCES > INDUCE

INDUCIAE *n* time limit for a defendant to appear in court

INDUCIBLE > INDUCE

INDUCING > INDUCE

INDUCT *vb* formally install (someone) in office

INDUCTED > INDUCT

INDUCTEE *n* military conscript

INDUCTEES > INDUCTEE

INDUCTILE *adj* not ductile, pliant, or yielding

INDUCTING > INDUCT

INDUCTION *n* the act of inducing

INDUCTIVE *adj* of or using induction

INDUCTOR *n* device designed to create inductance in an electrical circuit

INDUCTORS > INDUCTOR

INDUCTS > INDUCT

INDUE *variant spelling of* > ENDUE

INDUED > INDUE

INDUES > INDUE

INDUING > INDUE

INDULGE *vb* allow oneself pleasure

INDULGED > INDULGE

INDULGENT *adj* kind or lenient, often to excess

INDULGER > INDULGE

INDULGERS > INDULGE

INDULGES > INDULGE

INDULGING > INDULGE

INDULIN *same as* > INDULINE

INDULINE *n* any of a class of blue dyes obtained from aniline and aminoazobenzene

INDULINES > INDULINE

INDULINS > INDULIN

INDULT *n* type of faculty granted by the Holy See

INDULTS > INDULT

INDUMENTA *pl n* outer coverings of feather, fur, etc

INDUNA *n* (in South Africa) a Black African overseer

INDUNAS > INDUNA

INDURATE *vb* make or become hard or callous ▷ *adj* hardened, callous, or unfeeling

INDURATED > INDURATE

INDURATES > INDURATE

INDUSIA > INDUSIUM

INDUSIAL > INDUSIUM

INDUSIATE *adj* covered in indusia

INDUSIUM *n* outgrowth on the undersurface of fern leaves

INDUSTRY *n* manufacture of goods

INDUVIAE *pl n* withered leaves

INDUVIAL > INDUVIAE

INDUVIATE > INDUVIAE

INDWELL *vb* (of a spirit, principle, etc) to inhabit

INDWELLER > INDWELL

INDWELLS > INDWELL

INDWELT > INDWELL

INDYREF *n* independence referendum

INDYREFS > INDYREF

INEARTH *poetic word for* > BURY

INEARTHED > INEARTH

INEARTHS > INEARTH

INEBRIANT *adj* causing intoxication, esp drunkenness ▷ *n* something that inebriates

INEBRIATE *adj* habitually drunk ▷ *n* person who is habitually drunk ▷ *vb* make drunk

INEBRIETY > INEBRIATE

INEBRIOUS *adj* drunk

INEDIBLE *adj* not fit to be eaten

INEDIBLY > INEDIBLE

INEDITA *pl n* unpublished writings

INEDITED *adj* not edited

INEFFABLE *adj* too great for words

INEFFABLY > INEFFABLE

INELASTIC *adj* not elastic

INELEGANT *adj* lacking elegance or refinement

INEPT *adj* clumsy, lacking skill

INEPTER > INEPT

INEPTEST > INEPT

INEPTLY > INEPT

INEPTNESS > INEPT

INEQUABLE *adj* unfair

INEQUITY *n* injustice or unfairness

INERM *adj* without thorns

INERMOUS *same as* > INERM

INERRABLE *adj* not liable to error ▷ *n* person or thing that is incapable of error

INERRABLY > INERRABLE

INERRANCY > INERRABLE

INERRANT *same as* > INERRABLE

INERT *n* inert thing ▷ *adj* without the power of motion or resistance

INERTER > INERT

INERTEST > INERT

INERTIA *n* feeling of unwillingness to do anything

INERTIAE > INERTIA

INERTIAL > INERTIA

INERTIAS > INERTIA

INERTLY > INERT

INERTNESS > INERT

INERTS > INERT

INERUDITE *adj* not erudite

INESSIVE *n* grammatical case in Finnish

INESSIVES > INESSIVE

INEXACT *adj* not exact or accurate

INEXACTLY > INEXACT

INEXPERT *n* unskilled person ▷ *adj* lacking skill

INEXPERTS > INEXPERT

INFALL *vb* move towards (something) under the influence of gravity

INFALLING > INFALL

INFALLS > INFALL

INFAME *vb* defame

INFAMED > INFAME

INFAMES > INFAME

INFAMIES > INFAMY

INFAMING > INFAME

INFAMISE *same as* > INFAMIZE

INFAMISED > INFAMISE

INFAMISES > INFAMISE

INFAMIZE *vb* make infamous

INFAMIZED > INFAMIZE

INFAMIZES > INFAMIZE

INFAMOUS *adj* well-known for something bad

INFAMY *n* state of being infamous

INFANCIES > INFANCY

INFANCY *n* early childhood

INFANT *n* very young child ▷ *adj* of, relating to, or designed for young children

INFANTA *n* (formerly) daughter of a king of Spain or Portugal

INFANTAS > INFANTA

INFANTE *n* (formerly) any son of a king of Spain or Portugal, except the heir to the throne

INFANTEER *n* solider belonging to the infantry

INFANTES > INFANTE

INFANTILE *adj* childish

INFANTINE *adj* infantile

INFANTRY *n* soldiers who fight on foot

INFANTS > INFANT

INFARCT *n* localized area of dead tissue ▷ *vb* obstruct the blood supply to part of a body

INFARCTED > INFARCT

INFARCTS > INFARCT

INFARE *vb* enter

INFARES > INFARE

INFATUATE *vb* inspire or fill with an intense and unreasoning passion ▷ *n* person who is infatuated

INFAUNA *n* animals that live in ocean and river beds

INFAUNAE > INFAUNA

INFAUNAL > INFAUNA

INFAUNAS > INFAUNA

INFAUST *adj* unlucky

INFECT *vb* affect with a disease ▷ *adj* contaminated or polluted with or as if with a disease

INFECTANT *adj* causing infection ▷ *n* thing that infects or causes infection

INFECTED > INFECT

INFECTER > INFECT

INFECTERS > INFECT

INFECTING > INFECT

INFECTION *n* infectious disease

INFECTIVE adj capable of causing infection

INFECTOR > INFECT

INFECTORS > INFECT

INFECTS > INFECT

INFECUND less common word for > INFERTILE

INFEED n action of supplying a machine with a material

INFEEDS > INFEED

INFEFT vb give possession of heritable property

INFEFTED > INFEFT

INFEFTING > INFEFT

INFEFTS > INFEFT

INFELT adj heartfelt

INFEOFF same as > ENFEOFF

INFEOFFED > INFEOFF

INFEOFFS > INFEOFF

INFER vb work out from evidence

INFERABLE > INFER

INFERABLY > INFER

INFERE adv together

INFERENCE n act or process of reaching a conclusion by reasoning from evidence

INFERIAE pl n offerings made to the spirits of the dead

INFERIBLE > INFER

INFERIOR adj lower in quality, position, or status ▷ n person of lower position or status

INFERIORS > INFERIOR

INFERNAL adj of hell

INFERNO n intense raging fire

INFERNOS > INFERNO

INFERRED > INFER

INFERRER > INFER

INFERRERS > INFER

INFERRING > INFER

INFERS > INFER

INFERTILE adj unable to produce offspring

INFEST vb inhabit or overrun in unpleasantly large numbers

INFESTANT n parasite

INFESTED > INFEST

INFESTER > INFEST

INFESTERS > INFEST

INFESTING > INFEST

INFESTS > INFEST

INFICETE adj not witty

INFIDEL n person with no religion ▷ adj of unbelievers or unbelief

INFIDELIC > INFIDEL

INFIDELS > INFIDEL

INFIELD n area of the field near the pitch

INFIELDER n player positioned in the infield

INFIELDS > INFIELD

INFIGHT vb box at close quarters

INFIGHTER > INFIGHT

INFIGHTS > INFIGHT

INFILL vb fill in ▷ n act of filling or closing gaps in something

INFILLED > INFILL

INFILLING > INFILL

INFILLS > INFILL

INFIMA > INFIMUM

INFIMUM n greatest lower bound

INFIMUMS > INFIMUM

INFINITE adj without any limit or end ▷ n something without any limit or end

INFINITES > INFINITE

INFINITY n endless space, time, or number

INFIRM vb make infirm ▷ adj physically or mentally weak

INFIRMARY n hospital

INFIRMED > INFIRM

INFIRMER > INFIRM

INFIRMEST > INFIRM

INFIRMING > INFIRM

INFIRMITY n state of being infirm

INFIRMLY > INFIRM

INFIRMS > INFIRM

INFIX vb fix firmly in ▷ n affix inserted into the middle of a word

INFIXED > INFIX

INFIXES > INFIX

INFIXING > INFIX

INFIXION > INFIX

INFIXIONS > INFIX

INFLAME vb make angry or excited

INFLAMED > INFLAME

INFLAMER > INFLAME

INFLAMERS > INFLAME

INFLAMES > INFLAME

INFLAMING > INFLAME

INFLATE vb expand by filling with air or gas

INFLATED > INFLATE

INFLATER > INFLATE

INFLATERS > INFLATE

INFLATES > INFLATE

INFLATING > INFLATE

INFLATION n inflating

INFLATIVE adj causing inflation

INFLATOR > INFLATE

INFLATORS > INFLATE

INFLATUS n act of breathing in

INFLECT vb change (the voice) in tone or pitch

INFLECTED > INFLECT

INFLECTOR > INFLECT

INFLECTS > INFLECT

INFLEXED adj curved or bent inwards and downwards towards the axis

INFLEXION n modulation of the voice

INFLEXURE same as > INFLEXION

INFLICT vb impose (something unpleasant) on

INFLICTED > INFLICT

INFLICTER > INFLICT

INFLICTOR > INFLICT

INFLICTS > INFLICT

INFLIGHT adj provided during flight in an aircraft

INFLOW n something, such as liquid or gas, that flows in ▷ vb flow in

INFLOWING same as > INFLOW

INFLOWS > INFLOW

INFLUENCE n effect of one person or thing on another ▷ vb have an effect on

INFLUENT adj flowing in ▷ n something flowing in, esp a tributary

INFLUENTS > INFLUENT

INFLUENZA n contagious viral disease causing headaches, muscle pains, and fever

INFLUX n arrival or entry of many people or things

INFLUXES > INFLUX

INFLUXION same as > INFLUX

INFO n information

INFOBAHN same as > INTERNET

INFOBAHNS > INFOBAHN

INFOLD variant spelling of > ENFOLD

INFOLDED > INFOLD

INFOLDER > INFOLD

INFOLDERS > INFOLD

INFOLDING > INFOLD

INFOLDS > INFOLD

INFOMANIA n obsessive devotion to gathering information

INFORCE same as > ENFORCE

INFORCED > INFORCE

INFORCES > INFORCE

INFORCING > INFORCE

INFORM vb tell ▷ adj without shape

INFORMAL adj relaxed and friendly

INFORMANT n person who gives information

INFORMED > INFORM

INFORMER n person who informs to the police

INFORMERS > INFORMER

INFORMING > INFORM

INFORMS > INFORM

INFORTUNE n misfortune

INFOS > INFO

INFOTECH n information technology

INFOTECHS > INFOTECH

INFOUGHT > INFIGHT

INFRA adv (esp in textual annotation) below

INFRACT vb violate or break (a law, an agreement, etc)

INFRACTED > INFRACT

INFRACTOR > INFRACT

INFRACTS > INFRACT

INFRARED adj of or using rays below the red end of the visible spectrum ▷ n infrared part of the spectrum

INFRAREDS > INFRARED

INFRINGE vb break (a law or agreement)

INFRINGED > INFRINGE

INFRINGER > INFRINGE

INFRINGES > INFRINGE

INFRUGAL adj wasteful

INFULA same as > INFULAE

INFULAE pl n two ribbons hanging from a bishop's mitre

INFURIATE vb make very angry ▷ adj furious

INFUSCATE adj (esp of the wings of an insect) tinged with brown

INFUSE vb fill (with an emotion or quality)

INFUSED > INFUSE

INFUSER n any device used to make an infusion

INFUSERS > INFUSER

INFUSES > INFUSE

INFUSIBLE adj unable to be fused or melted

INFUSING > INFUSE

INFUSION n infusing

INFUSIONS > INFUSION

INFUSIVE > INFUSION

INFUSORIA pl n tiny water-dwelling animals

INFUSORY adj containing infusoria ▷ n infusorian, a tiny water-dwelling mammal

ING n meadow near a river

INGAN Scots word for > ONION

INGANS > INGAN

INGATE n entrance

INGATES > INGATE

INGATHER vb gather together or in (a harvest)

INGATHERS > INGATHER

INGENER Shakespearean form of > ENGINEER

INGENERS > INGENER

INGENIOUS adj showing cleverness and originality

INGENIUM n genius

INGENIUMS > INGENIUM

INGENU n artless or inexperienced boy or young man

INGENUE n inexperienced girl or young woman

INGENUES > INGENUE

INGENUITY n cleverness at inventing things

INGENUOUS adj unsophisticated and trusting

INGENUS > INGENU

INGEST vb take (food or liquid) into the body

INGESTA pl n nourishment taken through the mouth

INGESTED > INGEST

INGESTING > INGEST

INGESTION > INGEST

INGESTIVE > INGEST

INGESTS > INGEST

INGINE n genius

INGINES > INGINE

INGLE n fire in a room or a fireplace

INGLENEUK same as > INGLENOOK

INGLENOOK n corner by a fireplace

INGLES > INGLE

INGLOBE vb shape as a sphere

INGLOBED > INGLOBE

INGLOBES > INGLOBE

INGLOBING > INGLOBE

INGLUVIAL > INGLUVIES

INGLUVIES n bird's craw

INGO n revelation

INGOES > INGO

INGOING same as > INGO

i

INGOINGS > INGOING
INGOT n oblong block of cast metal ▷ vb shape (metal) into ingots
INGOTED > INGOT
INGOTING > INGOT
INGOTS > INGOT
INGRAFT variant spelling of > ENGRAFT
INGRAFTED > INGRAFT
INGRAFTS > INGRAFT
INGRAIN vb impress deeply on the mind or nature ▷ adj (of carpets) made of fibre that is dyed before being spun ▷ n carpet made from ingrained yarn
INGRAINED > INGRAIN
INGRAINER n person who ingrains
INGRAINS > INGRAIN
INGRAM adj ignorant ▷ n ignorant person
INGRAMS > INGRAM
INGRATE n ungrateful person ▷ adj ungrateful
INGRATELY > INGRATE
INGRATES > INGRATE
INGRESS n entrance
INGRESSES > INGRESS
INGROOVE vb cut a groove into
INGROOVED > INGROOVE
INGROOVES > INGROOVE
INGROSS archaic form of > ENGROSS
INGROSSED > INGROSS
INGROSSES > INGROSS
INGROUND adj sunk into ground ▷ vb fix (something) in the ground or in a foundation
INGROUNDS > INGROUND
INGROUP n highly cohesive and relatively closed social group
INGROUPS > INGROUP
INGROWING adj (of a toenail) growing abnormally into the flesh
INGROWN adj grown abnormally into the flesh
INGROWTH n act of growing inwards
INGROWTHS > INGROWTH
INGRUM adj ignorant ▷ n ignorant person
INGRUMS > INGRUM
INGS > ING
INGUINAL adj of or relating to the groin
INGULF variant spelling of > ENGULF
INGULFED > INGULF
INGULFING > INGULF
INGULFS > INGULF
INGULPH archaic form of > ENGULF
INGULPHED > INGULPH
INGULPHS > INGULPH
INHABIT vb live in
INHABITED > INHABIT
INHABITER n inhabitant
INHABITOR n inhabitant
INHABITS > INHABIT
INHALABLE adj that can be inhaled

INHALANT n medical preparation inhaled to help breathing problems ▷ adj inhaled for its soothing or therapeutic effect
INHALANTS > INHALANT
INHALATOR n device for converting drugs into a fine spray for inhaling
INHALE vb breathe in (air, smoke, etc)
INHALED > INHALE
INHALER n container for an inhalant
INHALERS > INHALER
INHALES > INHALE
INHALING > INHALE
INHARMONY n discord
INHAUL n line for hauling in a sail
INHAULER same as > INHAUL
INHAULERS > INHAULER
INHAULS > INHAUL
INHAUST vb drink in
INHAUSTED > INHAUST
INHAUSTS > INHAUST
INHEARSE vb bury
INHEARSED > INHEARSE
INHEARSES > INHEARSE
INHERCE same as > INHEARSE
INHERCED > INHERCE
INHERCES > INHERCE
INHERCING > INHERCE
INHERE vb be an inseparable part (of)
INHERED > INHERE
INHERENCE n state or condition of being inherent
INHERENCY same as > INHERENCE
INHERENT adj existing as an inseparable part
INHERES > INHERE
INHERING > INHERE
INHERIT vb receive (money etc) from someone who has died
INHERITED > INHERIT
INHERITOR > INHERIT
INHERITS > INHERIT
INHESION less common word for > INHERENCE
INHESIONS > INHESION
INHIBIN n peptide hormone
INHIBINS > INHIBIN
INHIBIT vb restrain (an impulse or desire)
INHIBITED > INHIBIT
INHIBITER same as > INHIBITOR
INHIBITOR n person or thing that inhibits
INHIBITS > INHIBIT
INHOLDER n inhabitant
INHOLDERS > INHOLDER
INHOLDING n privately owned land inside a federal reserve
INHOOP vb confine
INHOOPED > INHOOP
INHOOPING > INHOOP
INHOOPS > INHOOP
INHUMAN adj cruel or brutal
INHUMANE adj not humane

INHUMANER > INHUMANE
INHUMANLY > INHUMAN
INHUMATE vb bury
INHUMATED > INHUMATE
INIIUMATES > INHUMATE
INHUME vb inter
INHUMED > INHUME
INHUMER > INHUME
INHUMERS > INHUME
INHUMES > INHUME
INHUMING > INHUME
INIA > INION
INIMICAL adj unfavourable or hostile
INION n most prominent point at the back of the head
INIONS > INION
INIQUITY n injustice or wickedness
INISLE vb put on or make into an island
INISLED > INISLE
INISLES > INISLE
INISLING > INISLE
INITIAL adj first, at the beginning ▷ n first letter, esp of a person's name ▷ vb sign with one's initials
INITIALED > INITIAL
INITIALER > INITIAL
INITIALLY > INITIAL
INITIALS > INITIAL
INITIATE vb begin or set going ▷ n recently initiated person ▷ adj initiated
INITIATED > INITIATE
INITIATES > INITIATE
INITIATOR n person or thing that initiates
INJECT vb put (a fluid) into the body with a syringe
INJECTANT n injected substance
INJECTED > INJECT
INJECTING > INJECT
INJECTION n fluid injected into the body, esp for medicinal purposes
INJECTIVE > INJECTION
INJECTOR > INJECT
INJECTORS > INJECT
INJECTS > INJECT
INJELLIED > INJELLY
INJELLIES > INJELLY
INJELLY vb place in jelly
INJERA n white Ethiopian flatbread, similar to a crepe
INJERAS > INJERA
INJOINT vb join
INJOINTED > INJOINT
INJOINTS > INJOINT
INJUNCT vb issue a legal injunction against (a person)
INJUNCTED > INJUNCT
INJUNCTS > INJUNCT
INJURABLE > INJURE
INJURE vb hurt physically or mentally
INJURED > INJURE
INJURER > INJURE
INJURERS > INJURE
INJURES > INJURE
INJURIES > INJURY
INJURING > INJURE
INJURIOUS adj causing harm
INJURY n physical hurt

INJUSTICE n unfairness
INK n coloured liquid used for writing or printing ▷ vb mark in ink (something already marked in pencil)
INKBERRY n North American holly tree
INKBLOT n abstract patch of ink
INKBLOTS > INKBLOT
INKED > INK
INKER > INK
INKERS > INK
INKHOLDER same as > INKHORN
INKHORN n (formerly) a small portable container for ink
INKHORNS > INKHORN
INKHOSI n Zulu clan chief
INKHOSIS > INKHOSI
INKIER > INKY
INKIEST > INKY
INKINESS > INKY
INKING > INK
INKJET adj of a method of printing ▷ n inkjet printer
INKJETS > INKJET
INKLE n kind of linen tape used for trimmings ▷ vb hint
INKLED > INKLE
INKLES > INKLE
INKLESS > INK
INKLIKE > INK
INKLING n slight idea or suspicion
INKLINGS > INKLING
INKOSI same as > INKHOSI
INKOSIS > INKOSI
INKPAD n pad used for rubber-stamping or fingerprinting
INKPADS > INKPAD
INKPOT n ink-bottle
INKPOTS > INKPOT
INKS > INK
INKSPOT n ink stain
INKSPOTS > INKSPOT
INKSTAIN n stain made by ink
INKSTAINS > INKSTAIN
INKSTAND n stand or tray for holding writing tools and containers for ink
INKSTANDS > INKSTAND
INKSTONE n stone used in making ink
INKSTONES > INKSTONE
INKWELL n small container for ink
INKWELLS > INKWELL
INKWOOD n type of tree
INKWOODS > INKWOOD
INKY adj dark or black
INLACE variant spelling of > ENLACE
INLACED > INLACE
INLACES > INLACE
INLACING > INLACE
INLAID > INLAY
INLAND adv in or towards the interior of a country ▷ adj of or in the interior of a country or region ▷ n interior of a country or region
INLANDER > INLAND
INLANDERS > INLAND

INLANDS > INLAND
INLAY n inlaid substance or pattern ▷ vb decorate by inserting wooden pieces
INLAYER > INLAY
INLAYERS > INLAY
INLAYING > INLAY
INLAYINGS > INLAY
INLAYS > INLAY
INLET n water extending from the sea into the land ▷ vb insert or inlay
INLETS > INLET
INLETTING > INLET
INLIER n outcrop of rocks surrounded by younger rocks
INLIERS > INLIER
INLOCK vb lock up
INLOCKED > INLOCK
INLOCKING > INLOCK
INLOCKS > INLOCK
INLY adv inwardly
INLYING adj situated within or inside
INMATE n person living in an institution such as a prison
INMATES > INMATE
INMESH variant spelling of **>** ENMESH
INMESHED > INMESH
INMESHES > INMESH
INMESHING > INMESH
INMIGRANT adj coming in from another area of the same country ▷ n immigrant person or animal
INMOST adj innermost
INN n pub or small hotel, esp in the country ▷ vb stay at an inn
INNAGE n type of measurement
INNAGES > INNAGE
INNARDS pl n internal organs
INNATE adj being part of someone's nature, inborn
INNATELY > INNATE
INNATIVE adj native
INNED > INN
INNER adj happening or located inside ▷ n red innermost ring on a target
INNERLY > INNER
INNERMOST adj furthest inside
INNERNESS > INNER
INNERS > INNER
INNERSOLE same as **>** INSOLE
INNERVATE vb supply nerves to (a bodily organ or part)
INNERVE vb supply with nervous energy
INNERVED > INNERVE
INNERVES > INNERVE
INNERVING > INNERVE
INNERWEAR n underwear
INNING n division of baseball match
INNINGS > INNING
INNINGSES > INNINGS
INNIT interj isn't it
INNKEEPER n owner or manager of an inn
INNLESS adj without inns

INNOCENCE n quality or state of being innocent
INNOCENCY same as **>** INNOCENCE
INNOCENT adj not guilty of a crime ▷ n innocent person, esp a child
INNOCENTS > INNOCENT
INNOCUITY > INNOCUOUS
INNOCUOUS adj not harmful
INNOVATE vb introduce new ideas or methods
INNOVATED > INNOVATE
INNOVATES > INNOVATE
INNOVATOR > INNOVATE
INNOXIOUS adj not noxious
INNS > INN
INNUENDO n indirect reference to something rude or unpleasant
INNUENDOS > INNUENDO
INNYARD n courtyard of an inn
INNYARDS > INNYARD
INOCULA > INOCULUM
INOCULANT same as **>** INOCULUM
INOCULATE vb protect against disease by injecting with a vaccine
INOCULUM n substance used in giving an inoculation
INOCULUMS > INOCULUM
INODOROUS adj odourless
INOPINATE adj unexpected
INORB vb enclose in or as if in an orb
INORBED > INORB
INORBING > INORB
INORBS > INORB
INORGANIC adj not having the characteristics of living organisms ▷ n material not made from living organisms
INORNATE adj simple
INOSINE n type of molecule making up cell
INOSINES > INOSINE
INOSITE same as **>** INOSITOL
INOSITES > INOSITE
INOSITOL n cyclic alcohol
INOSITOLS > INOSITOL
INOTROPE n drug for controlling muscular contractions
INOTROPES > INOTROPE
INOTROPIC adj affecting or controlling the contraction of muscles, esp those of the heart
INPATIENT n patient who stays in a hospital for treatment
INPAYMENT n money paid into a bank account
INPHASE adj in the same phase
INPOUR vb pour in
INPOURED > INPOUR
INPOURING > INPOUR
INPOURS > INPOUR
INPUT n resources put into a project etc ▷ vb enter (data) in a computer
INPUTS > INPUT
INPUTTED > INPUT

INPUTTER > INPUT
INPUTTERS > INPUT
INPUTTING > INPUT
INQILAB n (in India, Pakistan, etc) revolution
INQILABS > INQILAB
INQUERE Spenserian form of **>** INQUIRE
INQUERED > INQUERE
INQUERES > INQUERE
INQUERING > INQUERE
INQUEST n official inquiry into a sudden death
INQUESTS > INQUEST
INQUIET vb disturb
INQUIETED > INQUIET
INQUIETLY > INQUIET
INQUIETS > INQUIET
INQUILINE n animal that lives in close association with another animal without harming it ▷ adj of or living as an inquiline
INQUINATE vb corrupt
INQUIRE vb seek information or ask (about)
INQUIRED > INQUIRE
INQUIRER > INQUIRE
INQUIRERS > INQUIRE
INQUIRES > INQUIRE
INQUIRIES > INQUIRY
INQUIRING > INQUIRE
INQUIRY n question
INQUORATE adj without enough people present to make a quorum
INRO n Japanese seal-box
INROAD n invasion or hostile attack
INROADS > INROAD
INRUN n slope down which ski jumpers ski
INRUNS > INRUN
INRUSH n sudden and overwhelming inward flow
INRUSHES > INRUSH
INRUSHING same as **>** INRUSH
INS > IN
INSANE adj mentally ill
INSANELY > INSANE
INSANER > INSANE
INSANEST > INSANE
INSANIE n insanity
INSANIES > INSANIE
INSANITY n state of being insane
INSATIATE adj not able to be satisfied
INSATIETY n insatiability
INSCAPE n essential inner nature of a person, etc
INSCAPES > INSCAPE
INSCIENCE n ignorance
INSCIENT adj ignorant
INSCONCE vb fortify
INSCONCED > INSCONCE
INSCONCES > INSCONCE
INSCRIBE vb write or carve words on
INSCRIBED > INSCRIBE
INSCRIBER > INSCRIBE
INSCRIBES > INSCRIBE
INSCROLL vb write on a scroll
INSCROLLS > INSCROLL
INSCULP vb engrave

INSCULPED > INSCULP
INSCULPS > INSCULP
INSCULPT adj engraved
INSEAM vb contain
INSEAMED > INSEAM
INSEAMING > INSEAM
INSEAMS > INSEAM
INSECT n small animal with six legs
INSECTAN > INSECT
INSECTARY n place where insects are kept
INSECTEAN > INSECT
INSECTILE > INSECT
INSECTION n incision
INSECTS > INSECT
INSECURE adj anxious, not confident
INSECURER > INSECURE
INSEEM vb cover with grease
INSEEMED > INSEEM
INSEEMING > INSEEM
INSEEMS > INSEEM
INSELBERG n isolated rocky hill rising abruptly from a flat plain
INSENSATE adj without sensation, unconscious
INSERT vb put inside or include ▷ n something inserted
INSERTED adj (of a muscle) attached to the bone that it moves
INSERTER > INSERT
INSERTERS > INSERT
INSERTING > INSERT
INSERTION n act of inserting
INSERTS > INSERT
INSET n small picture inserted within a larger one ▷ vb place in or within ▷ adj decorated with something inserted
INSETS > INSET
INSETTED > INSET
INSETTER > INSET
INSETTERS > INSET
INSETTING > INSET
INSHALLAH sentence substitute if Allah wills it
INSHEATH vb sheathe
INSHEATHE vb sheathe
INSHEATHS > INSHEATH
INSHELL vb retreat, as into a shell
INSHELLED > INSHELL
INSHELLS > INSHELL
INSHELTER vb put in a shelter
INSHIP vb travel or send by ship
INSHIPPED > INSHIP
INSHIPS > INSHIP
INSHORE adj close to the shore ▷ adv towards the shore
INSHRINE variant spelling of **>** ENSHRINE
INSHRINED > INSHRINE
INSHRINES > INSHRINE
INSIDE prep in or to the interior of ▷ adj on or of the inside ▷ adv on, in, or to the inside, indoors ▷ n inner side, surface, or part

INSIDER n someone who has privileged knowledge

INSIDERS > INSIDER

INSIDES > INSIDE

INSIDIOUS adj subtle or unseen but dangerous

INSIGHT n deep understanding

INSIGHTS > INSIGHT

INSIGNE same as > INSIGNIA

INSIGNIA n badge or emblem of honour or office

INSIGNIAS > INSIGNIA

INSINCERE adj showing false feelings, not genuine

INSINEW vb connect or strengthen, as with sinews

INSINEWED > INSINEW

INSINEWS > INSINEW

INSINUATE vb suggest indirectly

INSIPID adj lacking interest, spirit, or flavour

INSIPIDER > INSIPID

INSIPIDLY > INSIPID

INSIPIENT adj lacking wisdom

INSIST vb demand or state firmly

INSISTED > INSIST

INSISTENT adj making persistent demands

INSISTER > INSIST

INSISTERS > INSIST

INSISTING > INSIST

INSISTS > INSIST

INSNARE less common spelling of > ENSNARE

INSNARED > INSNARE

INSNARER > INSNARE

INSNARERS > INSNARE

INSNARES > INSNARE

INSNARING > INSNARE

INSOFAR adv to the extent

INSOLATE vb expose to sunlight, as for bleaching

INSOLATED > INSOLATE

INSOLATES > INSOLATE

INSOLE n inner sole of a shoe or boot

INSOLENCE > INSOLENT

INSOLENT n insolent person ▷ adj rude and disrespectful

INSOLENTS > INSOLENT

INSOLES > INSOLE

INSOLUBLE adj incapable of being solved

INSOLUBLY > INSOLUBLE

INSOLVENT adj unable to pay one's debts ▷ n person who is insolvent

INSOMNIA n inability to sleep

INSOMNIAC adj exhibiting or causing insomnia ▷ n person experiencing insomnia

INSOMNIAS > INSOMNIA

INSOMUCH adv such an extent

INSOOTH adv indeed

INSOUL variant of > ENSOUL

INSOULED > INSOUL

INSOULING > INSOUL

INSOULS > INSOUL

INSOURCE vb subcontract work to a company under the same general ownership

INSOURCED > INSOURCE

INSOURCES > INSOURCE

INSPAN vb harness (animals) to (a vehicle)

INSPANNED > INSPAN

INSPANS > INSPAN

INSPECT vb check closely or officially

INSPECTED > INSPECT

INSPECTOR n person who inspects

INSPECTS > INSPECT

INSPHERE variant spelling of > ENSPHERE

INSPHERED > INSPHERE

INSPHERES > INSPHERE

INSPIRE vb fill with enthusiasm, stimulate

INSPIRED adj brilliantly creative

INSPIRER > INSPIRE

INSPIRERS > INSPIRE

INSPIRES > INSPIRE

INSPIRING > INSPIRE

INSPIRIT vb fill with vigour

INSPIRITS > INSPIRIT

INSPO n source of inspiration

INSPOS > INSPO

INSTABLE less common word for > UNSTABLE

INSTAGRAM vb share (a photo) using the Instagram app

INSTAL same as > INSTALL

INSTALL vb put in and prepare (equipment) for use

INSTALLED > INSTALL

INSTALLER > INSTALL

INSTALLS > INSTALL

INSTALS > INSTAL

INSTANCE n particular example ▷ vb mention as an example

INSTANCED > INSTANCE

INSTANCES > INSTANCE

INSTANCY n quality of being urgent or imminent

INSTANT n very brief time ▷ adj happening at once

INSTANTER adv without delay

INSTANTLY adv immediately

INSTANTS > INSTANT

INSTAR vb decorate with stars ▷ n stage in the development of an insect

INSTARRED > INSTAR

INSTARS > INSTAR

INSTATE vb place in a position or office

INSTATED > INSTATE

INSTATES > INSTATE

INSTATING > INSTATE

INSTEAD adv as a replacement or substitute

INSTEP n part of the foot

INSTEPS > INSTEP

INSTIGATE vb cause to happen

INSTIL vb introduce (an idea etc) gradually into someone's mind

INSTILL same as > INSTIL

INSTILLED > INSTILL

INSTILLER > INSTILL

INSTILLS > INSTILL

INSTILS > INSTIL

INSTINCT n inborn tendency to behave in a certain way ▷ adj animated or impelled (by)

INSTINCTS > INSTINCT

INSTITUTE n organization set up for a specific purpose, esp research or teaching ▷ vb start or establish

INSTRESS vb create or sustain

INSTROKE n inward stroke

INSTROKES > INSTROKE

INSTRUCT vb order to do something

INSTRUCTS > INSTRUCT

INSUCKEN adj of a sucken

INSULA n pyramid-shaped area of the brain

INSULAE > INSULA

INSULANT n insulation

INSULANTS > INSULANT

INSULAR adj not open to new ideas, narrow-minded ▷ n islander

INSULARLY > INSULAR

INSULARS > INSULAR

INSULATE vb reduce the transfer of electricity, heat, or sound by lining with nonconducting material

INSULATED > INSULATE

INSULATES > INSULATE

INSULATOR n any material or device that insulates

INSULIN n hormone produced in the pancreas

INSULINS > INSULIN

INSULSE adj stupid

INSULSITY n stupidity

INSULT vb behave rudely to, offend ▷ n insulting remark or action

INSULTANT adj insulting

INSULTED > INSULT

INSULTER > INSULT

INSULTERS > INSULT

INSULTING > INSULT

INSULTS > INSULT

INSURABLE > INSURE

INSURANCE n agreement by which one makes regular payments to a company who pay an agreed sum if damage, loss, or death occurs

INSURANT n holder of an insurance policy

INSURANTS > INSURANT

INSURE vb protect by insurance

INSURED adj covered by insurance ▷ n those covered by an insurance policy

INSUREDS > INSURED

INSURER n person or company that sells insurance

INSURERS > INSURER

INSURES > INSURE

INSURGENT adj in revolt against an established authority ▷ n person who takes part in a rebellion

INSURING > INSURE

INSWATHE vb bind or wrap

INSWATHED > INSWATHE

INSWATHES > INSWATHE

INSWEPT adj narrowed towards the front

INSWING n movement of a bowled ball

INSWINGER n ball bowled so as to move from off to leg through the air

INSWINGS > INSWING

INTACT adj not changed or damaged in any way

INTACTLY > INTACT

INTAGLI > INTAGLIO

INTAGLIO n (gem carved with) an engraved design

INTAGLIOS > INTAGLIO

INTAKE n amount or number taken in

INTAKES > INTAKE

INTARSIA n mosaic of inlaid wood

INTARSIAS > INTARSIA

INTEGER n positive or negative whole number or zero

INTEGERS > INTEGER

INTEGRAL adj being an essential part of a whole ▷ n sum of a large number of very small quantities

INTEGRALS > INTEGRAL

INTEGRAND n mathematical function to be integrated

INTEGRANT adj part of a whole ▷ n integrant thing or part

INTEGRATE vb combine into a whole ▷ adj made up of parts

INTEGRIN n protein that acts as a signal receptor between cells

INTEGRINS > INTEGRIN

INTEGRITY n quality of having high moral principles

INTEL n US military intelligence

INTELLECT n power of thinking and reasoning

INTELS > INTEL

INTENABLE adj untenable

INTEND vb propose or plan (to do something)

INTENDANT n provincial or colonial official of France, Spain, or Portugal

INTENDED adj planned or future ▷ n person whom one is to marry

INTENDEDS > INTENDED

INTENDER > INTEND

INTENDERS > INTEND

INTENDING > INTEND

INTENDS > INTEND

INTENIBLE adj incapable of holding

INTENSATE vb intensify

INTENSE adj of great strength or degree

INTENSELY > INTENSE

INTENSER > INTENSE

INTENSEST > INTENSE

INTENSIFY vb make or become more intense

INTENSION n set of characteristics or properties by which the referent or referents of a given word are determined

INTENSITY n state or quality of being intense

INTENSIVE adj using or needing concentrated effort or resources ▷ n intensifier or intensive pronoun or grammatical construction

INTENT n intention ▷ adj paying close attention

INTENTION n something intended

INTENTIVE adj intent

INTENTLY > INTENT

INTENTS > INTENT

INTER vb bury (a dead body)

INTERACT vb act on or in close relation with each other

INTERACTS > INTERACT

INTERAGE adj between different ages

INTERARCH vb have intersecting arches

INTERBANK adj conducted between or involving two or more banks

INTERBED vb lie between strata of different minerals

INTERBEDS > INTERBED

INTERBRED adj having been bred within a single family or strain so as to produce particular characteristics

INTERCEDE vb try to end a dispute between two people or groups

INTERCELL adj occurring between cells

INTERCEPT vb seize or stop in transit ▷ n point at which two figures intersect

INTERCITY adj (in Britain) denoting a fast train or passenger rail service, esp between main towns

INTERCLAN adj occurring between clans

INTERCLUB adj of, relating to, or conducted between two or more clubs

INTERCOM n internal communication system with loudspeakers

INTERCOMS > INTERCOM

INTERCOOL vb cool a car engine by means of an intercooler

INTERCROP n crop grown between the rows of another crop ▷ vb grow (one crop) between the rows of (another)

INTERCUT another word for > CROSSCUT

INTERCUTS > INTERCUT

INTERDASH vb dash between

INTERDEAL vb intrigue or plot

INTERDICT n official prohibition or restraint ▷ vb prohibit or forbid

INTERDINE vb eat together

INTERESS vb interest

INTERESSE vb interest

INTEREST n desire to know or hear more about something ▷ vb arouse the interest of

INTERESTS > INTEREST

INTERFACE n area where two things interact or link ▷ vb connect or be connected with by interface

INTERFERE vb try to influence other people's affairs where one is not involved or wanted

INTERFILE vb place (one or more items) among other items in a file or arrangement

INTERFIRM adj occurring between companies

INTERFLOW vb flow together

INTERFOLD vb fold together

INTERFUSE vb mix or become mixed

INTERGANG adj occurring between gangs

INTERGREW > INTERGROW

INTERGROW vb grow among

INTERIM adj temporary, provisional, or intervening ▷ n intervening time ▷ adv meantime

INTERIMS > INTERIM

INTERIOR n inside ▷ adj inside, inner

INTERIORS > INTERIOR

INTERJECT vb make (a remark) suddenly or as an interruption

INTERJOIN vb join together

INTERKNIT vb knit together

INTERKNOT vb knot together

INTERLACE vb join together as if by weaving

INTERLAID > INTERLAY

INTERLAP less common word for > OVERLAP

INTERLAPS > INTERLAP

INTERLARD vb insert in or occur throughout

INTERLAY vb insert (layers) between ▷ n material, such as paper, placed between a printing plate and its base

INTERLAYS > INTERLAY

INTERLEAF n extra leaf which is inserted

INTERLEND vb lend between libraries

INTERLENT > INTERLEND

INTERLINE vb write or print (matter) between the lines of (a text or book)

INTERLINK vb connect together

INTERLOAN n loan between one library and another

INTERLOCK vb join firmly together ▷ n device used to prevent a mechanism from operating independently or unsafely ▷ adj (of fabric) closely knitted

INTERLOOP vb loop together

INTERLOPE vb intrude

INTERLUDE n short rest or break in an activity or event

INTERMALE adj occurring between males

INTERMAT n patch of seabed devoid of vegetation

INTERMATS > INTERMAT

INTERMENT n burial

INTERMESH vb net together

INTERMIT vb suspend (activity) or (of activity) to be suspended temporarily or at intervals

INTERMITS > INTERMIT

INTERMIX vb mix together

INTERMONT adj located between mountains

INTERMURE vb wall in

INTERN vb imprison, esp during a war ▷ n trainee doctor in a hospital

INTERNAL adj of or on the inside ▷ n medical examination of the inside of the body

INTERNALS > INTERNAL

INTERNE same as > INTERN

INTERNED > INTERN

INTERNEE n person who is interned

INTERNEES > INTERNEE

INTERNES > INTERNE

INTERNET n worldwide computer network

INTERNETS > INTERNET

INTERNING > INTERN

INTERNIST n physician who specializes in internal medicine

INTERNODE n part of a plant stem between two nodes

INTERNS > INTERN

INTERPAGE vb print (matter) on intervening pages

INTERPLAY n action and reaction of two things upon each other

INTERPLED adj having instituted a particular type of proceedings

INTERPONE vb interpose

INTERPOSE vb insert between or among things

INTERPRET vb explain the meaning of

INTERRACE adj between races

INTERRAIL vb travel on an international rail pass

INTERRED > INTER

INTERREX n person who governs during an interregnum

INTERRING > INTER

INTERROW adj occurring between rows

INTERRUPT vb break into (a conversation etc) ▷ n signal to initiate the stopping of the running of one computer program in order to run another

INTERS > INTER

INTERSECT vb (of roads) meet and cross

INTERSERT vb insert between

INTERSEX n condition of having characteristics intermediate between those of a male and a female

INTERTERM adj occurring between terms ▷ n intersession

INTERTEXT adj text seen as modifying another text in literary theory

INTERTIE n short roofing timber

INTERTIES > INTERTIE

INTERTILL vb cultivate between rows of crops

INTERUNIT adj occurring between units

INTERVAL n time between two particular moments or events

INTERVALE dialect form of > INTERVAL

INTERVALS > INTERVAL

INTERVEIN vb intersect

INTERVENE vb involve oneself in a situation, esp to prevent conflict

INTERVIEW n formal discussion, esp between a job-seeker and an employer ▷ vb conduct an interview with

INTERWAR adj of or happening in the period between World War I and World War II

INTERWEB same as > INTERNET

INTERWEBS > INTERWEB

INTERWIND vb wind together

INTERWORD adj between words

INTERWORK vb interweave

INTERWOVE adj having been woven together

INTERZONE n area between two occupied zones

INTESTACY > INTESTATE

INTESTATE adj not having made a will ▷ n person who dies without having made a will

INTESTINE n lower part of the alimentary canal

INTHRAL archaic form of > ENTHRAL

INTHRALL archaic form of > ENTHRAL

INTHRALLS > INTHRALL

INTHRALS > INTHRAL

INTHRONE archaic form of > ENTHRONE

INTHRONED > INTHRONE

INTHRONES > INTHRONE

INTI n former monetary unit of Peru

INTIFADA n Palestinian uprising against Israel in the West Bank and Gaza Strip

INTIFADAH same as > INTIFADA

INTIFADAS > INTIFADA

i

INTIFADEH same as
> INTIFADA
INTIL Scot form of > INTO
INTIMA n innermost layer of an organ or part
INTIMACY n close or warm friendship
INTIMAE > INTIMA
INTIMAL > INTIMA
INTIMAS > INTIMA
INTIMATE adj having a close personal relationship ⊳ n close friend ⊳ vb hint at or suggest
INTIMATED > INTIMATE
INTIMATER > INTIMATE
INTIMATES > INTIMATE
INTIME adj intimate
INTIMISM n school of impressionist painting
INTIMISMS > INTIMISM
INTIMIST > INTIMISM
INTIMISTE > INTIMISM
INTIMISTS > INTIMISM
INTIMITY n intimacy
INTINE n inner wall of a pollen grain or a spore
INTINES > INTINE
INTIRE archaic form of > ENTIRE
INTIS > INTI
INTITLE archaic form of > ENTITLE
INTITLED > INTITLE
INTITLES > INTITLE
INTITLING > INTITLE
INTITULE vb (in Britain) to entitle (an act of parliament)
INTITULED > INTITULE
INTITULES > INTITULE
INTO prep indicating motion towards the centre, result of a change, etc
INTOED adj having inward-turning toes
INTOMB same as > ENTOMB
INTOMBED > INTOMB
INTOMBING > INTOMB
INTOMBS > INTOMB
INTONACO n wet plaster surface on which frescoes are painted
INTONACOS > INTONACO
INTONATE vb pronounce with a rise and fall of the voice
INTONATED > INTONATE
INTONATES > INTONATE
INTONATOR > INTONATE
INTONE vb speak or recite in an unvarying tone of voice
INTONED > INTONE
INTONER > INTONE
INTONERS > INTONE
INTONES > INTONE
INTONING > INTONE
INTONINGS > INTONE
INTORSION n spiral twisting in plant stems or other parts
INTORT vb twist inward
INTORTED > INTORT
INTORTING > INTORT
INTORTION > INTORT
INTORTS > INTORT
INTOWN adj infield
INTRA prep within

INTRACITY same as
> INTERCITY
INTRADA n prelude
INTRADAS > INTRADA
INTRADAY adj occurring within one day
INTRADOS n inner curve or surface of an arch or vault
INTRANET n internal network that makes use of internet technology
INTRANETS > INTRANET
INTRANT n one who enters
INTRANTS > INTRANT
INTREAT archaic spelling of > ENTREAT
INTREATED > INTREAT
INTREATS > INTREAT
INTRENCH less common spelling of > ENTRENCH
INTREPID adj fearless, bold
INTRICACY > INTRICATE
INTRICATE adj involved or complicated
INTRIGANT n person who intrigues
INTRIGUE vb make interested or curious ⊳ n secret plotting
INTRIGUED > INTRIGUE
INTRIGUER > INTRIGUE
INTRIGUES > INTRIGUE
INTRINCE adj intricate
INTRINSIC adj essential to the basic nature of something
INTRO n introduction
INTRODUCE vb present (someone) by name (to another person)
INTROFIED > INTROFY
INTROFIES > INTROFY
INTROFY vb increase the wetting properties
INTROIT n short prayer said or sung
INTROITAL > INTROIT
INTROITS > INTROIT
INTROITUS n entrance to a body cavity
INTROJECT vb (esp of a child) to incorporate ideas of others, or (in fantasy) of objects
INTROLD variant of > ENTROLD
INTROMIT vb enter or insert or allow to enter or be inserted
INTROMITS > INTROMIT
INTRON n stretch of DNA
INTRONIC adj of or like an intron
INTRONS > INTRON
INTRORSE adj turned inwards or towards the axis
INTROS > INTRO
INTROVERT n person concerned more with his or her thoughts and feelings than with the outside world ⊳ adj shy and quiet ⊳ vb turn (a hollow organ or part) inside out
INTRUDE vb come in or join in without being invited
INTRUDED > INTRUDE

INTRUDER n person who enters a place without permission
INTRUDERS > INTRUDER
INTRUDES > INTRUDE
INTRUDING > INTRUDE
INTRUSION n act of intruding
INTRUSIVE adj characterized by intrusion or tending to intrude
INTRUST same as > ENTRUST
INTRUSTED > INTRUST
INTRUSTS > INTRUST
INTUBATE vb insert a tube or cannula into (a hollow organ)
INTUBATED > INTUBATE
INTUBATES > INTUBATE
INTUIT vb know or discover by intuition
INTUITED > INTUIT
INTUITING > INTUIT
INTUITION n instinctive knowledge or insight without conscious reasoning
INTUITIVE adj of, possessing, or resulting from intuition
INTUITS > INTUIT
INTUMESCE vb swell or become swollen
INTURN n inward turn
INTURNED adj turned inward
INTURNS > INTURN
INTUSE n contusion
INTUSES > INTUSE
INTWINE less common spelling of > ENTWINE
INTWINED > INTWINE
INTWINES > INTWINE
INTWINING > INTWINE
INTWIST vb twist together
INTWISTED > INTWIST
INTWISTS > INTWIST
INUKSHUIT > INUKSHUK
INUKSHUK n stone used by Inuit people to mark a location
INUKSHUKS > INUKSHUK
INUKSUIT > INUKSUK
INUKSUK same as > INUKSHUK
INUKSUKS > INUKSUK
INULA n plant of the elecampane genus
INULAS > INULA
INULASE n enzyme
INULASES > INULASE
INULIN n fructose polysaccharide
INULINS > INULIN
INUMBRATE vb shade
INUNCTION n application of an ointment to the skin, esp by rubbing
INUNDANT > INUNDATE
INUNDATE vb flood
INUNDATED > INUNDATE
INUNDATES > INUNDATE
INUNDATOR > INUNDATE
INURBANE adj not urbane
INURE vb cause to accept or become hardened to
INURED > INURE

INUREMENT > INURE
INURES > INURE
INURING > INURE
INURN vb place (esp cremated ashes) in an urn
INURNED > INURN
INURNING > INURN
INURNMENT > INURN
INURNS > INURN
INUSITATE adj out of use
INUST adj burnt in
INUSTION > INUST
INUSTIONS > INUST
INUTILE adj useless
INUTILELY > INUTILE
INUTILITY > INUTILE
INVADABLE > INVADE
INVADE vb enter (a country) by military force
INVADED > INVADE
INVADER > INVADE
INVADERS > INVADE
INVADES > INVADE
INVADING > INVADE
INVALID n disabled or chronically ill person ⊳ vb dismiss from active service because of illness or injury ⊳ adj having no legal force
INVALIDED > INVALID
INVALIDER > INVALID
INVALIDLY > INVALID
INVALIDS > INVALID
INVAR n alloy made from iron and nickel
INVARIANT n entity, quantity, etc, that is unaltered by a particular transformation of coordinates
INVARS > INVAR
INVASION n invading
INVASIONS > INVASION
INVASIVE adj of or relating to an invasion, intrusion, etc
INVEAGLE archaic form of > INVEIGLE
INVEAGLED > INVEAGLE
INVEAGLES > INVEAGLE
INVECKED same as > INVECTED
INVECTED adj bordered with small convex curves
INVECTIVE n abusive speech or writing ⊳ adj characterized by or using abusive language, bitter sarcasm, etc
INVEIGH vb criticize strongly
INVEIGHED > INVEIGH
INVEIGHER > INVEIGH
INVEIGHS > INVEIGH
INVEIGLE vb coax by cunning or trickery
INVEIGLED > INVEIGLE
INVEIGLER > INVEIGLE
INVEIGLES > INVEIGLE
INVENIT sentence substitute (he or she) designed it
INVENT vb think up or create (something new)
INVENTED > INVENT
INVENTER same as > INVENTOR
INVENTERS > INVENTER
INVENTING > INVENT

INVENTION n something invented

INVENTIVE adj creative and resourceful

INVENTOR n person who invents, esp as a profession

INVENTORS > INVENTOR

INVENTORY n detailed list of goods or furnishings ▷ vb make a list of

INVENTS > INVENT

INVERITY n untruth

INVERNESS n type of cape

INVERSE vb make something opposite or contrary in effect ▷ adj reversed in effect, sequence, direction, etc ▷ n exact opposite

INVERSED > INVERSE

INVERSELY > INVERSE

INVERSES > INVERSE

INVERSING > INVERSE

INVERSION n act of inverting or state of being inverted

INVERSIVE > INVERSION

INVERT vb turn upside down or inside out

INVERTASE n enzyme, occurring in the intestinal juice of animals and in yeasts

INVERTED > INVERT

INVERTER n any device for converting a direct current into an alternating current

INVERTERS > INVERTER

INVERTIN same as > INVERTASE

INVERTING > INVERT

INVERTINS > INVERTIN

INVERTOR same as > INVERTER

INVERTORS > INVERTOR

INVERTS > INVERT

INVEST vb spend (money, time, etc) with the expectation of profit

INVESTED > INVEST

INVESTING > INVEST

INVESTOR > INVEST

INVESTORS > INVEST

INVESTS > INVEST

INVEXED adj concave

INVIABLE adj not viable, esp financially

INVIABLY > INVIABLE

INVIDIOUS adj likely to cause resentment

INVIOLACY > INVIOLATE

INVIOLATE adj unharmed, unaffected

INVIOUS adj without paths or roads

INVIRILE adj unmanly

INVISCID adj not viscid

INVISIBLE adj not able to be seen ▷ n invisible item of trade

INVISIBLY > INVISIBLE

INVITAL adj not vital

INVITE vb request the company of ▷ n invitation

INVITED > INVITE

INVITEE n one who is invited

INVITEES > INVITEE

INVITER > INVITE

INVITERS > INVITE

INVITES > INVITE

INVITING adj tempting, attractive ▷ n old word for invitation

INVITINGS > INVITING

INVOCABLE > INVOKE

INVOCATE archaic word for ▸ INVOKE

INVOCATED > INVOCATE

INVOCATES > INVOCATE

INVOCATOR > INVOCATE

INVOICE n bill for goods or services ▷ vb present (a customer) with an invoice

INVOICED > INVOICE

INVOICES > INVOICE

INVOICING n act of presenting an invoice for payment

INVOKE vb put (a law or penalty) into operation

INVOKED > INVOKE

INVOKER > INVOKE

INVOKERS > INVOKE

INVOKES > INVOKE

INVOKING > INVOKE

INVOLUCEL n ring of bracts at the base of the florets of a compound umbel

INVOLUCRA n involucres

INVOLUCRE n ring of bracts at the base of an inflorescence in such plants as the composites

INVOLUTE adj complex, intricate, or involved ▷ n curve described by the free end of a thread as it is wound around another curve ▷ vb become involute

INVOLUTED > INVOLUTE

INVOLUTES > INVOLUTE

INVOLVE vb include as a necessary part

INVOLVED > INVOLVE

INVOLVER > INVOLVE

INVOLVERS > INVOLVE

INVOLVES > INVOLVE

INVOLVING > INVOLVE

INWALL vb surround with a wall

INWALLED > INWALL

INWALLING > INWALL

INWALLS > INWALL

INWARD adj directed towards the middle ▷ adv towards the inside or middle ▷ n inward part

INWARDLY adv within the private thoughts or feelings

INWARDS adv towards the inside or middle of something

INWEAVE vb weave together

INWEAVED > INWEAVE

INWEAVES > INWEAVE

INWEAVING > INWEAVE

INWICK vb perform a type of curling stroke

INWICKED > INWICK

INWICKING > INWICK

INWICKS > INWICK

INWIND vb wind or coil around

INWINDING > INWIND

INWINDS > INWIND

INWIT n conscience

INWITH adv within

INWITS > INWIT

INWORK vb work in

INWORKED > INWORK

INWORKING > INWORK

INWORKS > INWORK

INWORN adj worn in

INWOUND > INWIND

INWOVE > INWEAVE

INWOVEN > INWEAVE

INWRAP less common spelling of > ENWRAP

INWRAPPED > INWRAP

INWRAPS > INWRAP

INWRAPT > INWRAP

INWREATHE same as > ENWREATHE

INWROUGHT adj worked or woven into material, esp decoratively

INYALA n antelope

INYALAS > INYALA

IO interj exclamation of triumph ▷ n cry of 'io'

IODATE same as > IODIZE

IODATED > IODATE

IODATES > IODATE

IODATING > IODATE

IODATION > IODATE

IODATIONS > IODATE

IODIC adj of or containing iodine

IODID same as > IODIDE

IODIDE n chemical compound

IODIDES > IODIDE

IODIDS > IODID

IODIN same as > IODINE

IODINATE vb cause to combine with iodine

IODINATED > IODINATE

IODINATES > IODINATE

IODINE n bluish-black element

IODINES > IODINE

IODINS > IODIN

IODISE same as > IODIZE

IODISED > IODISE

IODISER > IODISE

IODISERS > IODISE

IODISES > IODISE

IODISING > IODISE

IODISM n poisoning caused by iodine or its compounds

IODISMS > IODISM

IODIZE vb treat with iodine

IODIZED > IODIZE

IODIZER > IODIZE

IODIZERS > IODIZE

IODIZES > IODIZE

IODIZING > IODIZE

IODOFORM n yellow crystalline insoluble volatile solid

IODOFORMS > IODOFORM

IODOMETRY n procedure used in volumetric analysis for determining the quantity of substance present that contains iodine

IODOPHILE adj taking an intense iodine stain

IODOPHOR n substance in which iodine is combined with an agent that renders it soluble

IODOPHORS > IODOPHOR

IODOPSIN n violet light-sensitive pigment in the retina

IODOPSINS > IODOPSIN

IODOUS adj of or containing iodine

IODURET n iodide

IODURETS > IODURET

IODYRITE n silver iodide

IODYRITES > IODYRITE

IOLITE n grey or violet-blue dichroic mineral

IOLITES > IOLITE

ION n electrically charged atom

IONIC adj of or in the form of ions

IONICALLY adv in an ionic manner

IONICITY n ionic character

IONICS pl n study of ions

IONISABLE > IONISE

IONISE same as > IONIZE

IONISED > IONISE

IONISER same as > IONIZER

IONISERS > IONISER

IONISES > IONISE

IONISING > IONISE

IONIUM n naturally occurring radioisotope of thorium

IONIUMS > IONIUM

IONIZABLE > IONIZE

IONIZE vb change into ions

IONIZED > IONIZE

IONIZER n person or thing that ionizes

IONIZERS > IONIZER

IONIZES > IONIZE

IONIZING > IONIZE

IONOGEN n compound that exists as ions when dissolved

IONOGENIC adj forming ions

IONOGENS > IONOGEN

IONOMER n type of thermoplastic

IONOMERS > IONOMER

IONONE n yellowish liquid mixture

IONONES > IONONE

IONOPAUSE n transitional zone in the atmosphere between the ionosphere and the exosphere

IONOPHORE n chemical compound capable of forming a complex with an ion and transporting it through a biological membrane

IONOSONDE n instrument measuring ionization

IONOTROPY n reversible interconversion of a pair of organic isomers as a result of the migration of an ionic part of the molecule

IONS > ION

IOPANOIC adj as in iopanoic acid type of acid containing iodine

IOS > IO

IOTA n ninth letter in the Greek alphabet

i

IOTACISM n pronunciation tendency in Modern Greek

IOTACISMS > IOTACISM

IOTAS > IOTA

IPECAC n type of S American shrub

IPECACS > IPECAC

IPOMOEA n convolvulaceous plant

IPOMOEAS > IPOMOEA

IPPON n winning point awarded in a judo or karate competition

IPPONS > IPPON

IPRINDOLE n antidepressant

IRACUND adj easily angered

IRADE n written edict of a Muslim ruler

IRADES > IRADE

IRASCIBLE adj easily angered

IRASCIBLY > IRASCIBLE

IRATE adj very angry

IRATELY > IRATE

IRATENESS > IRATE

IRATER > IRATE

IRATEST > IRATE

IRE vb anger ▷ n anger

IRED > IRE

IREFUL > IRE

IREFULLY > IRE

IRELESS > IRE

IRENIC adj tending to conciliate or promote peace

IRENICAL same as > IRENIC

IRENICISM > IRENICS

IRENICON variant spelling of > EIRENICON

IRENICONS > IRENICON

IRENICS n branch of theology

IRENOLOGY n study of peace

IRES > IRE

IRID n type of iris

IRIDAL > IRID

IRIDEAL > IRID

IRIDES > IRIS

IRIDIAL > IRID

IRIDIAN > IRID

IRIDIC adj of or containing iridium

IRIDISE vb make iridescent

IRIDISED > IRIDISE

IRIDISES > IRIDISE

IRIDISING > IRIDISE

IRIDIUM n very hard corrosion-resistant metal

IRIDIUMS > IRIDIUM

IRIDIZE vb make iridescent

IRIDIZED > IRIDIZE

IRIDIZES > IRIDIZE

IRIDIZING > IRIDIZE

IRIDOCYTE n cell in the skin of fish that gives them iridescence

IRIDOLOGY n technique used in complementary medicine to diagnose illness by studying a patient's eyes

IRIDOTOMY n surgical incision into the iris, esp to create an artificial pupil

IRIDS > IRID

IRING > IRE

IRIS n part of the eye ▷ vb display iridescence

IRISATE vb make iridescent

IRISATED > IRISATE

IRISATES > IRISATE

IRISATING > IRISATE

IRISATION > IRISATE

IRISCOPE n instrument that displays the prismatic colours

IRISCOPES > IRISCOPE

IRISED > IRIS

IRISES > IRIS

IRISING > IRIS

IRITIC > IRITIS

IRITIS n inflammation of the iris of the eye

IRITISES > IRITIS

IRK vb irritate, annoy

IRKED > IRK

IRKING > IRK

IRKS > IRK

IRKSOME adj irritating, annoying

IRKSOMELY > IRKSOME

IROKO n tropical African hardwood tree

IROKOS > IROKO

IRON n strong silvery-white metallic element ▷ adj made of iron ▷ vb smooth (clothes or fabric) with an iron

IRONBARK n Australian eucalyptus with hard rough bark

IRONBARKS > IRONBARK

IRONBOUND adj bound with iron

IRONCLAD adj covered or protected with iron ▷ n large wooden 19th-century warship with armoured plating

IRONCLADS > IRONCLAD

IRONE n fragrant liquid

IRONED > IRON

IRONER > IRON

IRONERS > IRON

IRONES > IRONE

IRONIC adj using irony

IRONICAL same as > IRONIC

IRONIER > IRONY

IRONIES > IRONY

IRONIEST > IRONY

IRONING n clothes to be ironed

IRONINGS > IRONING

IRONISE same as > IRONIZE

IRONISED > IRONISE

IRONISES > IRONISE

IRONISING > IRONISE

IRONIST > IRONIZE

IRONISTS > IRONIZE

IRONIZE vb use or indulge in irony

IRONIZED > IRONIZE

IRONIZES > IRONIZE

IRONIZING > IRONIZE

IRONLESS > IRON

IRONLIKE > IRON

IRONMAN n very strong man

IRONMEN > IRONMAN

IRONNESS > IRON

IRONS > IRON

IRONSIDE n person with great stamina or resistance

IRONSIDES > IRONSIDE

IRONSMITH adj blacksmith

IRONSTONE n rock consisting mainly of iron ore

IRONWARE n domestic articles made of iron

IRONWARES > IRONWARE

IRONWEED n plant with purplish leaves

IRONWEEDS > IRONWEED

IRONWOMAN n very strong woman

IRONWOMEN > IRONWOMAN

IRONWOOD n any of various trees, such as hornbeam, with exceptionally hard wood

IRONWOODS > IRONWOOD

IRONWORK n work done in iron, esp decorative work

IRONWORKS n building in which iron is smelted, cast, or wrought

IRONY n grammatical device ▷ adj of, resembling, or containing iron

IRRADIANT adj radiating light

IRRADIATE vb subject to or treat with radiation

IRREAL adj unreal

IRREALITY n unreality

IRREDENTA same as > IRRIDENTA

IRREGULAR adj not regular or even ▷ n soldier not in a regular army

IRRELATED adj irrelevant

IRRIDENTA n region that is ethnically or historically tied to one country, but which is ruled by another

IRRIGABLE > IRRIGATE

IRRIGABLY > IRRIGATE

IRRIGATE vb supply (land) with water by artificial channels or pipes

IRRIGATED > IRRIGATE

IRRIGATES > IRRIGATE

IRRIGATOR > IRRIGATE

IRRIGUOUS adj well-watered

IRRISION n mockery

IRRISIONS > IRRISION

IRRISORY adj mocking

IRRITABLE adj easily annoyed

IRRITABLY > IRRITABLE

IRRITANCY > IRRITANT

IRRITANT adj causing irritation ▷ n something that annoys or irritates

IRRITANTS > IRRITANT

IRRITATE vb annoy, anger

IRRITATED > IRRITATE

IRRITATES > IRRITATE

IRRITATOR > IRRITATE

IRRUPT vb enter forcibly or suddenly

IRRUPTED > IRRUPT

IRRUPTING > IRRUPT

IRRUPTION > IRRUPT

IRRUPTIVE adj irrupting or tending to irrupt

IRRUPTS > IRRUPT

IRUKANDJI n tiny but highly venomous Australian jellyfish

IS vb form of the present tense of be

ISABEL n brown yellow colour

ISABELLA same as > ISABEL

ISABELLAS > ISABELLA

ISABELS > ISABEL

ISAGOGE n academic introduction

ISAGOGES > ISAGOGE

ISAGOGIC > ISAGOGICS

ISAGOGICS n introductory studies, esp in the history of the Bible

ISALLOBAR n line on a map connecting places with equal pressure changes

ISARITHM n line on a map connecting places with the same population density

ISARITHMS > ISARITHM

ISATIN n yellowish-red crystalline compound

ISATINE same as > ISATIN

ISATINES > ISATINE

ISATINIC > ISATIN

ISATINS > ISATIN

ISBA n log hut

ISBAS > ISBA

ISCHAEMIA n inadequate supply of blood to an organ or part, as from an obstructed blood flow

ISCHAEMIC > ISCHAEMIA

ISCHEMIA same as > ISCHAEMIA

ISCHEMIAS > ISCHEMIA

ISCHEMIC > ISCHAEMIA

ISCHIA > ISCHIUM

ISCHIADIC > ISCHIUM

ISCHIAL > ISCHIUM

ISCHIATIC > ISCHIUM

ISCHIUM n part of the hipbone

ISCHURIA n retention of urine

ISCHURIAS > ISCHURIA

ISEIKONIA n seeing of same image in both eyes

ISEIKONIC > ISEIKONIA

ISENERGIC adj of equal energy

ISH n issue

ISHES > ISH

ISINGLASS n kind of gelatine obtained from some freshwater fish

ISIT sentence substitute expression used in response to a statement

ISLAND n piece of land surrounded by water ▷ vb cause to become an island

ISLANDED > ISLAND

ISLANDER n person who lives on an island

ISLANDERS > ISLANDER

ISLANDING > ISLAND

ISLANDS > ISLAND

ISLE vb make an isle of ▷ n island

ISLED > ISLE

ISLELESS adj without islands

ISLEMAN n islander

ISLEMEN > ISLEMAN

ISLES > ISLE

ISLESMAN same as > ISLEMAN

ISLESMEN > ISLESMAN

ISLET n small island

ISLETED adj having islets

ISLETS > ISLET

ISLING > ISLE

ISLOMANIA n obsessional enthusiasm or partiality for islands

ISM n doctrine, system, or practice

ISMATIC adj following fashionable doctrines

ISMATICAL same as > ISMATIC

ISMS > ISM

ISNA vb is not

ISNAE same as > ISNA

ISO n short segment of film that can be replayed easily

ISOAMYL n as in isoamyl acetate colourless volatile compound

ISOAMYLS > ISOAMYL

ISOBAR n line showing equal pressure

ISOBARE same as > ISOBAR

ISOBARES > ISOBARE

ISOBARIC adj having equal atmospheric pressure

ISOBARISM > ISOBAR

ISOBARS > ISOBAR

ISOBASE n line connecting points of equal land upheaval

ISOBASES > ISOBASE

ISOBATH n line showing equal depth of water

ISOBATHIC > ISOBATH

ISOBATHS > ISOBATH

ISOBRONT n line connecting points of simultaneous storm development

ISOBRONTS > ISOBRONT

ISOBUTANE n form of butane

ISOBUTENE n isomer of butene

ISOBUTYL n as in methyl isobutyl ketone colourless insoluble liquid ketone used as a solvent for organic compounds

ISOBUTYLS > ISOBUTYL

ISOCHASM n line connecting points of equal aurorae frequency

ISOCHASMS > ISOCHASM

ISOCHEIM n line on a map connecting places with the same mean winter temperature

ISOCHEIMS > ISOCHEIM

ISOCHIMAL > ISOCHIME

ISOCHIME same as > ISOCHEIM

ISOCHIMES > ISOCHIME

ISOCHOR n line showing equal pressure and temperature

ISOCHORE same as > ISOCHOR

ISOCHORES > ISOCHORE

ISOCHORIC > ISOCHOR

ISOCHORS > ISOCHOR

ISOCHRON n line on an isotope ratio diagram

ISOCHRONE n line on a map or diagram connecting places from which it takes the same time to travel to a certain point

ISOCHRONS > ISOCHRON

ISOCLINAL adj sloping in the same direction and at the same angle ▷ n imaginary line connecting points on the earth's surface having equal angles of dip

ISOCLINE same as > ISOCLINAL

ISOCLINES > ISOCLINE

ISOCLINIC same as > ISOCLINAL

ISOCRACY n form of government in which all people have equal powers

ISOCRATIC > ISOCRACY

ISOCRYMAL same as > ISOCRYME

ISOCRYME n line connecting points of equal winter temperature

ISOCRYMES > ISOCRYME

ISOCYANIC adj as in isocyanic acid, hypothetical acid known only in the form of its compounds

ISOCYCLIC adj containing a closed ring of atoms of the same kind, esp carbon atoms

ISODICA > ISODICON

ISODICON n short anthem

ISODOMA > ISODOMON

ISODOMON n masonry formed of uniform blocks, with courses are of equal height

ISODOMOUS > ISODOMON

ISODOMUM same as > ISODOMON

ISODONT n animal in which the teeth are of similar size

ISODONTAL same as > ISODONT

ISODONTS > ISODONT

ISODOSE n dose of radiation applied in radiotherapy

ISODOSES > ISODOSE

ISOENZYME same as > ISOZYME

ISOETES n quillwort

ISOFORM n protein similar in function but not form to another

ISOFORMS > ISOFORM

ISOGAMETE n gamete that is similar in size and form to the one with which it unites in fertilization

ISOGAMIC > ISOGAMY

ISOGAMIES > ISOGAMY

ISOGAMOUS > ISOGAMY

ISOGAMY n fusion of similar gametes

ISOGENEIC same as > ISOGENIC

ISOGENIC same as > ISOGENOUS

ISOGENIES > ISOGENOUS

ISOGENOUS adj of similar origin, as parts derived from the same embryonic tissue

ISOGENY > ISOGENOUS

ISOGLOSS n line drawn on a linguistic map

ISOGON n equiangular polygon

ISOGONAL same as > ISOGONIC

ISOGONALS > ISOGONAL

ISOGONE same as > ISOGONIC

ISOGONES > ISOGONE

ISOGONIC adj having, making, or involving equal angles ▷ n imaginary line connecting points on the earth's surface having equal magnetic declination

ISOGONICS > ISOGONIC

ISOGONIES > ISOGONIC

ISOGONS > ISOGON

ISOGONY > ISOGONIC

ISOGRAFT vb grafting tissue from a donor genetically identical to the recipient

ISOGRAFTS > ISOGRAFT

ISOGRAM same as > ISOPLETH

ISOGRAMS > ISOGRAM

ISOGRAPH n line connecting points of the same linguistic usage

ISOGRAPHS > ISOGRAPH

ISOGRIV n line showing equal angular bearing

ISOGRIVS > ISOGRIV

ISOHEL n line showing equal sunshine

ISOHELS > ISOHEL

ISOHYDRIC adj having the same acidity or hydrogen-ion concentration

ISOHYET n line showing equal rainfall

ISOHYETAL same as > ISOHYET

ISOHYETS > ISOHYET

ISOKONT same as > ISOKONTAN

ISOKONTAN n alga whose zoospores have equal cilia

ISOKONTS > ISOKONT

ISOLABLE > ISOLATE

ISOLATE vb place apart or alone ▷ n isolated person or group

ISOLATED > ISOLATE

ISOLATES > ISOLATE

ISOLATING > ISOLATE

ISOLATION > ISOLATE

ISOLATIVE adj concerned with isolation

ISOLATOR > ISOLATE

ISOLATORS > ISOLATE

ISOLEAD n line on a ballistic graph

ISOLEADS > ISOLEAD

ISOLEX n line on map showing where a particular word is used

ISOLEXES > ISOLEX

ISOLINE same as > ISOPLETH

ISOLINES > ISOLINE

ISOLOG > ISOLOGOUS

ISOLOGOUS adj (of two or more organic compounds) having a similar structure

but containing different atoms of the same valency

ISOLOGS > ISOLOGOUS

ISOLOGUE > ISOLOGOUS

ISOLOGUES > ISOLOGOUS

ISOMER n compound that has the same molecular formula as another

ISOMERASE n any enzyme that catalyses the conversion of one isomeric form of a compound to another

ISOMERE same as > ISOMER

ISOMERES > ISOMERE

ISOMERIC > ISOMER

ISOMERISE same as > ISOMERIZE

ISOMERISM n existence of two or more compounds having the same molecular formula but a different arrangement of atoms within the molecule

ISOMERIZE vb change or cause to change from one isomer to another

ISOMEROUS adj having an equal number of parts or markings

ISOMERS > ISOMER

ISOMETRIC adj relating to muscular contraction without shortening of the muscle ▷ n drawing made in this way

ISOMETRY n distance-preserving injective map between metric spaces

ISOMORPH n substance or organism that exhibits isomorphism

ISOMORPHS > ISOMORPH

ISONIAZID n soluble colourless crystalline compound used to treat tuberculosis

ISONOME n line on a map showing equal abundance of a species

ISONOMES > ISONOME

ISONOMIC > ISONOMY

ISONOMIES > ISONOMY

ISONOMOUS > ISONOMY

ISONOMY n equality before the law of the citizens of a state

ISOOCTANE n colourless liquid alkane hydrocarbon produced from petroleum and used in standardizing petrol

ISOPACH n line showing equal thickness

ISOPACHS > ISOPACH

ISOPHONE n isogloss marking off an area in which a particular feature of pronunciation is found

ISOPHONES > ISOPHONE

ISOPHOTAL > ISOPHOTE

ISOPHOTE n line on a diagram of a celestial object joining points of equal brightness

ISOPHOTES > ISOPHOTE

ISOPLETH n line on a map connecting places with the same amount of some geographical phenomenon

ISOPLETHS > ISOPLETH
ISOPOD n type of crustacean ▷ adj of this type of crustacean
ISOPODAN > ISOPOD
ISOPODANS > ISOPOD
ISOPODOUS > ISOPOD
ISOPODS > ISOPOD
ISOPOLITY n equality of political rights
ISOPRENE n colourless volatile liquid with a penetrating odour
ISOPRENES > ISOPRENE
ISOPROPYL n group of atoms
ISOPTERAN n termite
ISOPYCNAL n line on a map connecting points of equal atmospheric density
ISOPYCNIC same as > ISOPYCNAL
ISOS > ISO
ISOSCELES adj (of a triangle) having two sides of equal length
ISOSMOTIC same as > ISOTONIC
ISOSPIN n number used to classify elementary particles
ISOSPINS > ISOSPIN
ISOSPORY n condition of having spores of only one kind
ISOSTACY n state of balance in earth's crust
ISOSTASY same as > ISOSTACY
ISOSTATIC > ISOSTASY
ISOSTERIC adj (of two different molecules) having the same number of atoms and the same number and configuration of valency electrons
ISOTACH n line showing equal wind speed
ISOTACHS > ISOTACH
ISOTACTIC adj (of a stereospecific polymer) having identical steric configurations of the groups on each asymmetric carbon atom on the chain
ISOTHERAL > ISOTHERE
ISOTHERE n line on a map linking places with the same mean summer temperature
ISOTHERES > ISOTHERE
ISOTHERM n line on a map connecting points of equal temperature
ISOTHERMS > ISOTHERM
ISOTONE n atom with same number of neutrons as another
ISOTONES > ISOTONE
ISOTONIC adj (of two or more muscles) having equal tension

ISOTOPE n atom with same atomic number as another
ISOTOPES > ISOTOPE
ISOTOPIC > ISOTOPE
ISOTOPIES > ISOTOPE
ISOTOPY > ISOTOPE
ISOTRON n device for separating small quantities of isotopes
ISOTRONS > ISOTRON
ISOTROPIC adj having uniform physical properties, such as elasticity or conduction in all directions
ISOTROPY > ISOTROPIC
ISOTYPE n pictorial presentation of statistical information
ISOTYPES > ISOTYPE
ISOTYPIC > ISOTYPE
ISOZYME n variant of an enzyme
ISOZYMES > ISOZYME
ISOZYMIC > ISOZYME
ISPAGHULA n dietary fibre derived from seed husks and used as a thickener or stabilizer in the food industry
ISSEI n first-generation Japanese immigrant
ISSEIS > ISSEI
ISSUABLE adj capable of issuing or being issued
ISSUABLY > ISSUABLE
ISSUANCE n act of issuing
ISSUANCES > ISSUANCE
ISSUANT adj emerging or issuing
ISSUE n topic of interest or discussion ▷ vb make (a statement etc) publicly
ISSUED > ISSUE
ISSUELESS > ISSUE
ISSUER > ISSUE
ISSUERS > ISSUE
ISSUES > ISSUE
ISSUING > ISSUE
ISTANA n (in Malaysia) a royal palace
ISTANAS > ISTANA
ISTHMI > ISTHMUS
ISTHMIAN n inhabitant of an isthmus ▷ adj relating to or situated in an isthmus
ISTHMIANS > ISTHMIAN
ISTHMIC > ISTHMUS
ISTHMOID > ISTHMUS
ISTHMUS n narrow strip of land connecting two areas of land
ISTHMUSES > ISTHMUS
ISTLE n fibre obtained from various agave and yucca trees
ISTLES > ISTLE
IT pron refers to a nonhuman, animal, plant, or inanimate object ▷ n player whose turn it is to catch the

others in children's games
ITA n type of palm
ITACISM n pronunciation of the Greek letter eta
ITACISMS > ITACISM
ITACONIC adj as in itaconic acid , white colourless crystalline carboxylic acid
ITALIC adj (of printing type) sloping to the right ▷ n style of printing type
ITALICISE same as > ITALICIZE
ITALICIZE vb put in italics
ITALICS > ITALIC
ITAS > ITA
ITCH n skin irritation causing a desire to scratch ▷ vb have an itch
ITCHED > ITCH
ITCHES > ITCH
ITCHIER > ITCH
ITCHIEST > ITCH
ITCHILY > ITCH
ITCHINESS > ITCH
ITCHING > ITCH
ITCHINGS > ITCH
ITCHWEED n white hellebore
ITCHWEEDS > ITCHWEED
ITCHY > ITCH
ITEM n single thing in a list or collection ▷ adv likewise ▷ vb itemize
ITEMED > ITEM
ITEMING > ITEM
ITEMISE same as > ITEMIZE
ITEMISED > ITEMISE
ITEMISER > ITEMISE
ITEMISERS > ITEMISE
ITEMISES > ITEMISE
ITEMISING > ITEMISE
ITEMIZE vb make a list of
ITEMIZED > ITEMIZE
ITEMIZER > ITEMIZE
ITEMIZERS > ITEMIZER
ITEMIZES > ITEMIZE
ITEMIZING > ITEMIZE
ITEMS > ITEM
ITERANCE > ITERATE
ITERANCES > ITERATE
ITERANT > ITERATE
ITERATE vb repeat
ITERATED > ITERATE
ITERATES > ITERATE
ITERATING > ITERATE
ITERATION > ITERATE
ITERATIVE adj repetitious or frequent
ITERUM adv again
ITHER Scot word for > OTHER
ITINERACY n travelling from place to place
ITINERANT adj travelling from place to place ▷ n itinerant worker or other person

ITINERARY n detailed plan of a journey ▷ adj of or relating to travel or routes of travel
ITINERATE vb travel from place to place
ITS pron belonging to it ▷ adj of or belonging to it
ITSELF pron reflexive form of it
IURE adv by law
IVIED adj covered with ivy
IVIES > IVY
IVORIED > IVORY
IVORIER > IVORY
IVORIES pl n keys of a piano
IVORIEST > IVORY
IVORIST n worker in ivory
IVORISTS > IVORIST
IVORY n bony substance forming the tusks of elephants ▷ adj yellowish-white
IVORYBILL n large American woodpecker
IVORYLIKE > IVORY
IVORYWOOD n yellowish-white wood of an Australian tree, used for engraving, inlaying, and turnery
IVRESSE n drunkenness
IVRESSES > IVRESSE
IVY n evergreen climbing plant
IVYLEAF adj as in ivyleaf geranium type of geranium plant
IVYLIKE > IVY
IWI n Māori tribe
IWIS archaic word for > CERTAINLY
IXIA n southern African plant
IXIAS > IXIA
IXNAY interj nix
IXODIASES > IXODIASIS
IXODIASIS n disease transmitted by ticks
IXODID n hard-bodied tick
IXODIDS > IXODID
IXORA n flowering shrub
IXORAS > IXORA
IXTLE same as > ISTLE
IXTLES > IXTLE
IZAR n long garment worn by Muslim women
IZARD n type of goat-antelope
IZARDS > IZARD
IZARS > IZAR
IZVESTIA n news
IZVESTIAS > IZVESTIA
IZVESTIYA same as > IZVESTIA
IZZARD n letter Z
IZZARDS > IZZARD
IZZAT n honour or prestige
IZZATS > IZZAT

Jj

JA *interj* yes ▷ *sentence substitute* yes

JAAP *n* S African offensive word for a simpleton or country bumpkin

JAAPS > JAAP

JAB *vb* poke sharply ▷ *n* quick punch or poke

JABBED > JAB

JABBER *vb* talk rapidly or incoherently ▷ *n* rapid or incoherent talk

JABBERED > JABBER

JABBERER > JABBER

JABBERERS > JABBER

JABBERING > JABBER

JABBERS > JABBER

JABBING > JAB

JABBINGLY > JAB

JABBLE *vb* ripple

JABBLED > JABBLE

JABBLES > JABBLE

JABBLING > JABBLE

JABERS *interj* Irish exclamation

JABIRU *n* large white-and-black Australian stork

JABIRUS > JABIRU

JABORANDI *n* any of several tropical American rutaceous shrubs

JABOT *n* frill or ruffle on the front of a blouse or shirt

JABOTS > JABOT

JABS > JAB

JACAL *n* Mexican daub hut

JACALES > JACAL

JACALS > JACAL

JACAMAR *n* tropical American bird with an iridescent plumage

JACAMARS > JACAMAR

JACANA *n* long-legged long-toed bird

JACANAS > JACANA

JACARANDA *n* tropical tree with sweet-smelling wood

JACARE *another name for* **>** CAYMAN

JACARES > JACARE

JACCHUS *n* small monkey

JACCHUSES > JACCHUS

JACENT *adj* lying

JACINTH *another name for* **>** HYACINTH

JACINTHE *n* hyacinth

JACINTHES > JACINTHE

JACINTHS > JACINTH

JACK *n* device for raising a motor vehicle or other heavy object ▷ *vb* lift or push (an object) with a jack

JACKAL *n* doglike wild animal of Africa and Asia ▷ *vb* behave like a jackal

JACKALLED > JACKAL

JACKALOPE *n* mythical animal of the western US

JACKALS > JACKAL

JACKAROO *same as* **>** JACKEROO

JACKAROOS > JACKAROO

JACKASS *n* fool

JACKASSES > JACKASS

JACKBOOT *n* high military boot ▷ *vb* oppress

JACKBOOTS > JACKBOOT

JACKDAW *n* Eurasian bird of the crow family

JACKDAWS > JACKDAW

JACKED > JACK

JACKEEN *n* slick self-assertive lower-class Dubliner

JACKEENS > JACKEEN

JACKER *n* labourer

JACKEROO *n* young male management trainee on a sheep or cattle station ▷ *vb* work as a jackeroo

JACKEROOS > JACKEROO

JACKERS > JACKER

JACKET *n* short coat ▷ *vb* put a jacket on (someone or something)

JACKETED > JACKET

JACKETING > JACKET

JACKETS > JACKET

JACKFISH *n* small pike fish

JACKFRUIT *n* tropical Asian tree

JACKIES > JACKY

JACKING > JACK

JACKINGS > JACK

JACKKNIFE *vb* (of an articulated truck) go out of control so that the trailer swings round at a sharp angle to the cab ▷ *n* large clasp knife

JACKLEG *n* unskilled worker

JACKLEGS > JACKLEG

JACKLIGHT *vb* hunt (fish or game) by dazzling them with a light

JACKLING *n* particular way of winning the ball in rugby

JACKLINGS > JACKLING

JACKMAN *n* retainer

JACKMEN > JACKMAN

JACKPLANE *n* large woodworking plane

JACKPOT *n* largest prize that may be won in a game ▷ *vb* accumulate stake money in a prize fund

JACKPOTS > JACKPOT

JACKROLL *vb* gang-rape

JACKROLLS > JACKROLL

JACKS *n* type of game

JACKSCREW *n* lifting device

JACKSHAFT *n* short length of shafting that transmits power from an engine or motor to a machine

JACKSIE *n* buttocks or anus

JACKSIES > JACKSIE

JACKSMELT *n* food fish of the North Pacific

JACKSMITH *n* smith who makes jacks

JACKSNIPE *n* small Eurasian short-billed snipe

JACKSTAFF *n* staff on a ship's bow, for flying the jack

JACKSTAY *n* object to which a sail edge is fastened along a yard

JACKSTAYS > JACKSTAY

JACKSTONE *n* small round pebble

JACKSTRAW *n* straw mannequin

JACKSY *same as* **>** JACKSIE

JACKY *n* offensive word for a native Australian

JACOBIN *n* variety of fancy pigeon

JACOBINS > JACOBIN

JACOBUS *n* English gold coin

JACOBUSES > JACOBUS

JACONET *n* light cotton fabric

JACONETS > JACONET

JACQUARD *n* fabric in which the design is incorporated into the weave

JACQUARDS > JACQUARD

JACQUERIE *n* peasant rising or revolt

JACTATION *n* act of boasting

JACULATE *vb* hurl

JACULATED > JACULATE

JACULATES > JACULATE

JACULATOR > JACULATE

JACUZZI *n* type of bath or pool

JACUZZIS > JACUZZI

JADE *n* semiprecious stone ▷ *adj* bluish-green ▷ *vb* exhaust or make exhausted from work or use

JADED *adj* tired and unenthusiastic

JADEDLY > JADED

JADEDNESS > JADED

JADEITE *n* usually green or white mineral

JADEITES > JADEITE

JADELIKE > JADE

JADERIES > JADERY

JADERY *n* shrewishness

JADES > JADE

JADING > JADE

JADISH > JADE

JADISHLY > JADE

JADITIC > JADE

JAEGER *n* German or Austrian marksman

JAEGERS > JAEGER

JAFA *n* offensive name for a person from Auckland

JAFAS > JAFA

JAFFA *n* (in cricket) well-bowled ball

JAFFAS > JAFFA

JAG *n* period of uncontrolled indulgence in an activity ▷ *vb* cut unevenly

JAGA *n* guard ▷ *vb* guard or watch

JAGAED > JAGA

JAGAING > JAGA

JAGAS > JAGA

JAGDWURST *n* type of cured German sausage

JAGER *same as* **>** JAEGER

JAGERS > JAGER

JAGG *same as* **>** JAG

JAGGARIES > JAGGARY

JAGGARY *same as* **>** JAGGERY

JAGGED > JAG

JAGGEDER > JAGGED

JAGGEDEST > JAG

JAGGEDLY > JAG

JAGGER *n* pedlar

JAGGERIES > JAGGERY

JAGGERS > JAGGER

JAGGERY *n* coarse brown sugar

JAGGHERY *same as* **>** JAGGERY

JAGGIER > JAGGY

JAGGIES > JAGGY

JAGGIEST > JAGGY

JAGGING > JAG

JAGGS > JAGG

JAGGY *adj* prickly ▷ *n* jagged computer image

JAGHIR *n* Indian regional governance

JAGHIRDAR *n* Indian regional governor

JAGHIRE *n* Indian regional governance

JAGHIRES > JAGHIRE

j

JAGHIRS > JAGHIR
JAGIR n Indian regional governance
JAGIRS > JAGIR
JAGLESS > JAG
JAGRA n Hindu festival
JAGRAS > JAGRA
JAGS > JAG
JAGUAR n large S American spotted cat
JAGUARS > JAGUAR
JAI interj victory (to)
JAIL n prison ▷ vb send to prison
JAILABLE > JAIL
JAILBAIT n young women collectively, considered sexually attractive but below the age of consent
JAILBAITS > JAILBAIT
JAILBIRD n person who has often been in prison
JAILBIRDS > JAILBIRD
JAILBREAK n escape from jail ▷ vb adapt an electronic device to use unauthorized software
JAILBROKE > JAILBREAK
JAILED > JAIL
JAILER n person in charge of a jail
JAILERESS > JAILER
JAILERS > JAILER
JAILHOUSE n jail
JAILING > JAIL
JAILLESS > JAIL
JAILOR same as > JAILER
JAILORESS > JAILOR
JAILORS > JAILOR
JAILS > JAIL
JAK same as > JACK
JAKE adj slang word meaning all right
JAKER > JAKE
JAKES n toilet; lavatory
JAKESES > JAKES
JAKEST > JAKE
JAKEY n derogatory Scots word for a homeless alcoholic person
JAKEYS > JAKEY
JAKFRUIT same as > JACKFRUIT
JAKFRUITS > JAKFRUIT
JAKS > JAK
JALABIB > JILBAB
JALAP n Mexican convolvulaceous plant
JALAPENO n very hot type of green chilli pepper, used esp in Mexican cookery
JALAPENOS > JALAPENO
JALAPIC > JALAP
JALAPIN n purgative resin
JALAPINS > JALAPIN
JALAPS > JALAP
JALEBI n type of Asian sweet fried snack
JALEBIS > JALEBI
JALFREZI adj (in Indian cookery) stir-fried with green peppers, onions, and green chillies ▷ n curry made with green peppers, onions, and green chillies
JALFREZIS > JALFREZI
JALLEBI same as > JALEBI

JALLEBIS > JALLEBI
JALOP same as > JALAP
JALOPIES > JALOPY
JALOPPIES > JALOPPY
JALOPPY same as > JALOPY
JALOPS > JALOP
JALOPY n old car
JALOUSE vb suspect
JALOUSED > JALOUSE
JALOUSES > JALOUSE
JALOUSIE n window blind or shutter constructed from angled slats of wood, plastic, etc
JALOUSIED > JALOUSIE
JALOUSIES > JALOUSIE
JALOUSING > JALOUSE
JAM vb pack tightly into a place ▷ n fruit preserve or hold-up of traffic
JAMAAT n Islamic council
JAMAATS > JAMAAT
JAMADAR n Indian army officer
JAMADARS > JAMADAR
JAMB n side post of a door or window frame ▷ vb climb up a crack in rock
JAMBALAYA n Creole dish made of shrimps, ham, rice, onions, etc
JAMBART same as > GREAVE
JAMBARTS > JAMBART
JAMBE same as > JAMB
JAMBEAU another word for > GREAVE
JAMBEAUS > JAMBEAU
JAMBEAUX > JAMBEAU
JAMBED > JAMB
JAMBEE n light cane
JAMBEES > JAMBEE
JAMBER same as > GREAVE
JAMBERS > JAMBER
JAMBES > JAMBE
JAMBEUX > JAMBEAU
JAMBIER n greave
JAMBIERS > JAMBIER
JAMBING > JAMB
JAMBIYA n curved dagger
JAMBIYAH same as > JAMBIYA
JAMBIYAHS > JAMBIYAH
JAMBIYAS > JAMBIYA
JAMBO sentence substitute E African salutation
JAMBOK same as > SJAMBOK
JAMBOKKED > JAMBOK
JAMBOKS > JAMBOK
JAMBOLAN n Asian tree
JAMBOLANA same as > JAMBOLAN
JAMBOLANS > JAMBOLAN
JAMBONE n type of play in the card game euchre
JAMBONES > JAMBONE
JAMBOOL same as > JAMBOLAN
JAMBOOLS > JAMBOOL
JAMBOREE n large gathering or celebration
JAMBOREES > JAMBOREE
JAMBS > JAMB
JAMBU same as > JAMBOLAN
JAMBUL same as > JAMBOLAN
JAMBULS > JAMBUL
JAMBUS > JAMBU

JAMBUSTER n (in Canada) jam-filled doughnut
JAMDANI n patterned muslin
JAMDANIS > JAMDANI
JAMES n jemmy
JAMESES > JAMES
JAMJAR n container for preserves
JAMJARS > JAMJAR
JAMLIKE > JAM
JAMMABLE > JAM
JAMMED > JAM
JAMMER > JAM
JAMMERS > JAM
JAMMIER > JAMMY
JAMMIES informal word for > PYJAMAS
JAMMIEST > JAMMY
JAMMING > JAM
JAMMINGS > JAM
JAMMY adj lucky
JAMON n as in jamon serrano cured ham from Spain
JAMPACKED adj very crowded
JAMPAN n type of sedan chair used in India
JAMPANEE n jampan bearer
JAMPANEES > JAMPANEE
JAMPANI same as > JAMPANEE
JAMPANIS > JAMPANI
JAMPANS > JAMPAN
JAMPOT n container for preserves
JAMPOTS > JAMPOT
JAMS > JAM
JANE n girl or woman
JANES > JANE
JANGLE vb (cause to) make a harsh ringing noise ▷ n harsh ringing noise
JANGLED > JANGLE
JANGLER > JANGLE
JANGLERS > JANGLE
JANGLES > JANGLE
JANGLIER > JANGLY
JANGLIEST > JANGLY
JANGLING > JANGLE
JANGLINGS > JANGLE
JANGLY adj making a jangling sound
JANIFORM adj with two faces
JANISARY same as > JANISSARY
JANISSARY n infantryman in the Turkish army, originally a member of the sovereign's personal guard, from the 14th to the early 19th century
JANITOR n caretaker of a school or other building
JANITORS > JANITOR
JANITRESS > JANITOR
JANITRIX > JANITOR
JANIZAR same as > JANISSARY
JANIZARS > JANIZAR
JANIZARY same as > JANISSARY
JANKER n device for transporting logs
JANKERS > JANKER
JANN n lesser jinn
JANNEY vb act as a disguised reveller at Christmas

JANNEYED > JANNEY
JANNEYING > JANNEY
JANNEYS > JANNEY
JANNIED > JANNY
JANNIES > JANNY
JANNOCK same as > JONNOCK
JANNOCKS > JANNOCK
JANNS > JANN
JANNY n janitor ▷ vb work as a janitor
JANNYING > JANNY
JANNYINGS > JANNYING
JANSKY n unit of flux density
JANSKYS > JANSKY
JANTEE archaic version of > JAUNTY
JANTIER > JANTY
JANTIES > JANTY
JANTIEST > JANTY
JANTY n petty officer ▷ adj (in archaic usage) jaunty
JAP vb splash
JAPAN n very hard varnish, usu black ▷ vb cover with this varnish ▷ adj relating to or varnished with japan
JAPANISE same as > JAPANIZE
JAPANISED > JAPANISE
JAPANISES > JAPANISE
JAPANIZE vb make Japanese
JAPANIZED > JAPANIZE
JAPANIZES > JAPANIZE
JAPANNED > JAPAN
JAPANNER > JAPAN
JAPANNERS > JAPAN
JAPANNING > JAPAN
JAPANS > JAPAN
JAPE n joke or prank ▷ vb joke or jest (about)
JAPED > JAPE
JAPER > JAPE
JAPERIES > JAPE
JAPERS > JAPE
JAPERY > JAPE
JAPES > JAPE
JAPING > JAPE
JAPINGLY > JAPE
JAPINGS > JAPE
JAPONICA n shrub with red flowers
JAPONICAS > JAPONICA
JAPPED > JAP
JAPPING > JAP
JAPS > JAP
JAR n wide-mouthed container ▷ vb have a disturbing or unpleasant effect
JARARACA n South American snake
JARARACAS > JARARACA
JARARAKA same as > JARARACA
JARARAKAS > JARARAKA
JARFUL same as > JAR
JARFULS > JARFUL
JARGON n specialized technical language ▷ vb use or speak in jargon
JARGONED > JARGON
JARGONEER n user of jargon
JARGONEL n pear
JARGONELS > JARGONEL
JARGONIER > JARGONY**

JARGONING > JARGON

JARGONISE *same as* > JARGONIZE

JARGONISH > JARGON

JARGONIST > JARGON

JARGONIZE *vb* render into jargon

JARGONS > JARGON

JARGONY *adj* full of jargon

JARGOON *same as* > JARGON

JARGOONS > JARGON

JARHEAD *n* US Marine

JARHEADS > JARHEAD

JARINA *n* South American palm tree

JARINAS > JARINA

JARK *n* seal or pass

JARKMAN *n* forger of passes or licences

JARKMEN > JARKMAN

JARKS > JARK

JARL *n* Scandinavian chieftain or noble

JARLDOM > JARL

JARLDOMS > JARL

JARLS > JARL

JARLSBERG *n* Norwegian cheese

JAROOL *n* Indian tree

JAROOLS > JAROOL

JAROSITE *n* yellow to brown mineral

JAROSITES > JAROSITE

JAROVISE *same as* > JAROVIZE

JAROVISED > JAROVISE

JAROVISES > JAROVISE

JAROVIZE *vb* vernalize

JAROVIZED > JAROVIZE

JAROVIZES > JAROVIZE

JARP *vb* strike or smash

JARPED > JARP

JARPING > JARP

JARPS > JARP

JARRAH *n* Australian eucalypt yielding valuable timber

JARRAHS > JARRAH

JARRED > JAR

JARRING > JAR

JARRINGLY > JAR

JARRINGS > JAR

JARS > JAR

JARSFUL > JARFUL

JARTA *n* heart

JARTAS > JARTA

JARUL *variant of* > JAROOL

JARULS > JARUL

JARVEY *n* hackney coachman

JARVEYS > JARVEY

JARVIE *same as* > JARVEY

JARVIES > JARVIE

JASEY *n* wig

JASEYS > JASEY

JASIES > JASY

JASMIN *same as* > JASMINE

JASMINE *n* shrub with sweet-smelling yellow or white flowers

JASMINES > JASMINE

JASMINS > JASMIN

JASMONATE *n* plant hormone that regulates growth

JASP *another word for* > JASPER

JASPE *adj* resembling jasper ▷ *n* subtly striped woven fabric

JASPER *n* variety of quartz

JASPERIER > JASPERY

JASPERISE *same as* > JASPERIZE

JASPERIZE *vb* turn into jasper

JASPEROUS > JASPER

JASPERS > JASPER

JASPERY *adj* resembling jasper

JASPES > JASPE

JASPIDEAN > JASPER

JASPILITE *n* rock like jasper

JASPIS *archaic word for* > JASPER

JASPISES > JASPIS

JASPS > JASP

JASS *obsolete variant of* > JAZZ

JASSES > JASS

JASSID *n* leafhopper

JASSIDS > JASSID

JASY *n* wig

JATAKA *n* text describing the birth of Buddha

JATAKAS > JATAKA

JATO *n* jet-assisted takeoff

JATOS > JATO

JATROPHA *n* poisonous shrub of C America used primarily as a biofuel

JATROPHAS > JATROPHA

JAUK *vb* dawdle

JAUKED > JAUK

JAUKING > JAUK

JAUKS > JAUK

JAUNCE *vb* prance

JAUNCED > JAUNCE

JAUNCES > JAUNCE

JAUNCING > JAUNCE

JAUNDICE *n* disease marked by yellowness of the skin ▷ *vb* distort (the judgment, etc) adversely

JAUNDICED > JAUNDICE

JAUNDICES > JAUNDICE

JAUNSE *same as* > JAUNCE

JAUNSED > JAUNSE

JAUNSES > JAUNSE

JAUNSING > JAUNSE

JAUNT *n* short journey for pleasure ▷ *vb* make such a journey

JAUNTED > JAUNT

JAUNTEE *old spelling of* > JAUNTY

JAUNTIE *old spelling of* > JAUNTY

JAUNTIER > JAUNTY

JAUNTIES > JAUNTY

JAUNTIEST > JAUNTY

JAUNTILY > JAUNTY

JAUNTING > JAUNT

JAUNTS > JAUNT

JAUNTY *adj* sprightly and cheerful ▷ *n* master-at-arms on a naval ship

JAUP *same as* > JARP

JAUPED > JAUP

JAUPING > JAUP

JAUPS > JAUP

JAVA *n* coffee or a variety of it

JAVAS > JAVA

JAVEL *adj* as in *javel water* bleach or disinfectant

JAVELIN *n* light spear thrown in sports competitions ▷ *vb* spear with a javelin

JAVELINA *n* collared peccary

JAVELINAS > JAVELINA

JAVELINED > JAVELIN

JAVELINS > JAVELIN

JAVELLE *adj* as in *javelle water*, a bleach and antiseptic

JAVELS > JAVEL

JAW *n* one of the bones in which the teeth are set ▷ *vb* talk lengthily

JAWAN *n* (in India) a soldier

JAWANS > JAWAN

JAWARI *n* variety of sorghum

JAWARIS > JAWARI

JAWBATION *n* scolding

JAWBONE *n* lower jaw of a person or animal ▷ *vb* try to persuade by virtue of one's high office or position

JAWBONED > JAWBONE

JAWBONER > JAWBONE

JAWBONERS > JAWBONE

JAWBONES > JAWBONE

JAWBONING > JAWBONE

JAWBOX *n* metal sink

JAWBOXES > JAWBOX

JAWED > JAW

JAWFALL *n* depression

JAWFALLS > JAWFALL

JAWHOLE *n* cesspit

JAWHOLES > JAWHOLE

JAWING > JAW

JAWINGS > JAW

JAWLESS > JAW

JAWLIKE > JAW

JAWLINE *n* outline of the jaw

JAWLINES > JAWLINE

JAWS > JAW

JAXIE *same as* > JACKSIE

JAXIES > JAXIE

JAXY *same as* > JACKSIE

JAY *n* type of bird

JAYBIRD *n* jay

JAYBIRDS > JAYBIRD

JAYCEE *n* member of a Junior Chamber of Commerce

JAYCEES > JAYCEE

JAYGEE *n* lieutenant junior grade in the US army

JAYGEES > JAYGEE

JAYHAWKER *n* Unionist guerrilla in US Civil War

JAYS > JAY

JAYVEE *n* junior varsity sports team

JAYVEES > JAYVEE

JAYWALK *vb* cross or walk in a street recklessly or illegally

JAYWALKED > JAYWALK

JAYWALKER > JAYWALK

JAYWALKS > JAYWALK

JAZERANT *n* coat of metal plates sewn onto cloth

JAZERANTS > JAZERANT

JAZIES > JAZY

JAZY *n* wig

JAZZ *n* kind of music ▷ *vb* play or dance to jazz music

JAZZBO *n* jazz musician or fan

JAZZBOS > JAZZBO

JAZZED > JAZZ

JAZZER > JAZZ

JAZZERS > JAZZ

JAZZES > JAZZ

JAZZIER > JAZZY

JAZZIEST > JAZZY

JAZZILY > JAZZY

JAZZINESS > JAZZY

JAZZING > JAZZ

JAZZLIKE > JAZZ

JAZZMAN > JAZZ

JAZZMEN > JAZZ

JAZZY *adj* flashy or showy

JEALOUS *adj* fearful of losing (something) to a rival

JEALOUSE *vb* be jealous of

JEALOUSED > JEALOUSE

JEALOUSER > JEALOUSE

JEALOUSES > JEALOUSE

JEALOUSLY > JEALOUS

JEALOUSY *n* state of or an instance of feeling jealous

JEAN *n* tough twill-weave cotton fabric

JEANED *adj* wearing jeans

JEANETTE *n* light jean cloth

JEANETTES > JEANETTE

JEANS *pl n* casual denim trousers

JEANSWEAR *n* clothing made from denim

JEAT *n* jet

JEATS > JEAT

JEBEL *n* hill or mountain in an Arab country

JEBELS > JEBEL

JEDI *n* person claiming to live according to the Jedi philosophy

JEDIS > JEDI

JEE *variant of* > GEE

JEED > JEE

JEEING > JEE

JEEL *vb* make into jelly

JEELED > JEEL

JEELIE *same as* > JEELY

JEELIED > JEELY

JEELIEING > JEELIE

JEELIES > JEELY

JEELING > JEEL

JEELS > JEEL

JEELY *n* jelly ▷ *vb* make into jelly

JEELYING > JEELY

JEEP *n* small military four-wheel drive road vehicle ▷ *vb* travel in a jeep

JEEPED > JEEP

JEEPERS *interj* mild exclamation of surprise

JEEPING > JEEP

JEEPNEY *n* Filipino bus converted from a jeep

JEEPNEYS > JEEPNEY

JEEPS > JEEP

JEER *vb* scoff or deride ▷ *n* cry of derision

JEERED > JEER

JEERER > JEER

JEERERS > JEER

JEERING > JEER

JEERINGLY > JEER
JEERINGS > JEER
JEERS > JEER
JEES > JEE
JEESLY same as **>** JEEZLY
JEEZ interj expression of surprise or irritation
JEEZE same as **>** JEEZ
JEEZELY same as **>** JEEZLY
JEEZLY adj used as an intensifier
JEFE n (in Spanish-speaking countries) a military or political leader
JEFES > JEFE
JEFF vb downsize or close down (an organization)
JEFFED > JEFF
JEFFING > JEFF
JEFFS > JEFF
JEGGINGS pl n women's leggings designed to look like tight denim jeans
JEHAD same as **>** JIHAD
JEHADEEN same as **>** JIHADEEN
JEHADI same as **>** JIHADI
JEHADIS > JEHADI
JEHADISM same as **>** JIHADISM
JEHADISMS > JEHADISM
JEHADIST > JEHADISM
JEHADISTS > JEHADISM
JEHADS > JEHAD
JEHU n fast driver
JEHUS > JEHU
JEJUNA > JEJUNUM
JEJUNAL > JEJUNUM
JEJUNE adj simple or naive
JEJUNELY > JEJUNE
JEJUNITY > JEJUNE
JEJUNUM n part of the small intestine
JEJUNUMS > JEJUNUM
JELAB same as **>** JELLABA
JELABS > JELAB
JELL vb form into a jelly-like substance
JELLABA n loose robe with a hood
JELLABAH same as **>** JELLABA
JELLABAHS > JELLABAH
JELLABAS > JELLABA
JELLED > JELL
JELLIED > JELLY
JELLIES > JELLY
JELLIFIED > JELLIFY
JELLIFIES > JELLIFY
JELLIFY vb make into or become jelly
JELLING > JELL
JELLO n (in US English) type of dessert
JELLOS > JELLO
JELLS > JELL
JELLY n fruit-flavoured clear dessert set with gelatine ▷ vb jellify
JELLYBEAN n bean-shaped sweet with a brightly coloured coating around a gelatinous filling
JELLYFISH n small jelly-like sea animal
JELLYING > JELLY
JELLYLIKE > JELLY

JELLYROLL n type of cake
JELUTONG n Malaysian tree
JELUTONGS > JELUTONG
JEMADAR n native officer serving as a mercenary in India
JEMADARS > JEMADAR
JEMBE n hoe
JEMBES > JEMBE
JEMIDAR same as **>** JEMADAR
JEMIDARS > JEMIDAR
JEMIMA n boot with elastic sides
JEMIMAS > JEMIMA
JEMMIED > JEMMY
JEMMIER > JEMMY
JEMMIES > JEMMY
JEMMIEST > JEMMY
JEMMINESS > JEMMY
JEMMY n short steel crowbar used by burglars ▷ vb prise (something) open with a jemmy ▷ adj neat
JEMMYING > JEMMY
JENNET n female donkey or ass
JENNETING n early-season apple
JENNETS > JENNET
JENNIES > JENNY
JENNY same as **>** JENNET
JEOFAIL n oversight in legal pleading
JEOFAILS > JEOFAIL
JEON n Korean pancake
JEONS > JEON
JEOPARD vb put in jeopardy
JEOPARDED > JEOPARD
JEOPARDER > JEOPARD
JEOPARDS > JEOPARD
JEOPARDY n danger ▷ vb put in jeopardy
JEQUERITY same as **>** JEQUIRITY
JEQUIRITY n seed of the Indian liquorice
JERBIL variant spelling of **>** GERBIL
JERBILS > JERBIL
JERBOA n small mouselike rodent with long hind legs
JERBOAS > JERBOA
JEREED same as **>** JERID
JEREEDS > JEREED
JEREMIAD n long mournful complaint
JEREMIADS > JEREMIAD
JEREPIGO n sweet fortified wine similar to port
JEREPIGOS > JEREPIGO
JERFALCON variant of **>** GYRFALCON
JERID n wooden javelin
JERIDS > JERID
JERK vb move or throw abruptly ▷ n sharp or abruptly stopped movement
JERKED > JERK
JERKER > JERK
JERKERS > JERK
JERKIER > JERKY
JERKIES > JERKY
JERKIEST > JERKY
JERKILY > JERKY
JERKIN n sleeveless jacket
JERKINESS > JERKY

JERKING > JERK
JERKINGLY > JERK
JERKINGS > JERK
JERKINS > JERKIN
JERKS > JERK
JERKWATER adj inferior and insignificant ▷ n railway locomotive
JERKY adj characterized by jerks ▷ n type of cured meat
JEROBOAM n wine bottle holding the equivalent of four normal bottles
JEROBOAMS > JEROBOAM
JERQUE vb search for contraband
JERQUED > JERQUE
JERQUER > JERQUE
JERQUERS > JERQUE
JERQUES > JERQUE
JERQUING > JERQUE
JERQUINGS > JERQUE
JERREED variant spelling of **>** JERID
JERREEDS > JERREED
JERRICAN n five-gallon fuel can
JERRICANS > JERRICAN
JERRID n blunt javelin
JERRIDS > JERRID
JERRIES > JERRY
JERRY short for **>** JEROBOAM
JERRYCAN n flat-sided can used for storing or transporting liquids, esp motor fuel
JERRYCANS > JERRYCAN
JERSEY n knitted jumper
JERSEYED > JERSEY
JERSEYS > JERSEY
JESS n short leather strap used in falconry ▷ vb put jesses on (a hawk or falcon)
JESSAMIES > JESSAMY
JESSAMINE same as **>** JASMINE
JESSAMY n fop
JESSANT adj emerging
JESSE same as **>** JESS
JESSED > JESS
JESSERANT n coat of metal plates sewn onto cloth
JESSES > JESS
JESSIE n derogatory term for a weak or cowardly boy or man
JESSIES > JESSIE
JESSING > JESS
JEST vb joke ▷ n something done or said for amusement
JESTBOOK n book of amusing stories
JESTBOOKS > JESTBOOK
JESTED > JEST
JESTEE n person about whom a joke is made
JESTEES > JESTEE
JESTER n professional clown at court
JESTERS > JESTER
JESTFUL > JEST
JESTING > JEST
JESTINGLY > JEST
JESTINGS > JEST
JESTS > JEST
JESUIT n offensive term for a person given to subtle and equivocating arguments

JESUITIC > JESUIT
JESUITISM > JESUIT
JESUITRY > JESUIT
JESUITS > JESUIT
JESUS n French paper size
JET n aircraft driven by jet propulsion ▷ vb fly by jet aircraft
JETBEAD n ornamental shrub
JETBEADS > JETBEAD
JETE n dance step
JETES > JETE
JETFOIL n type of hydrofoil that is propelled by water jets
JETFOILS > JETFOIL
JETLAG n tiredness caused by crossing timezones in jet flight
JETLAGS > JETLAG
JETLIKE > JET
JETLINER n commercial airliner powered by jet engines
JETLINERS > JETLINER
JETON n gambling chip
JETONS > JETON
JETPACK n wearable harness with jets, used for transport
JETPACKS > JETPACK
JETPORT n airport for jet planes
JETPORTS > JETPORT
JETS > JET
JETSAM n goods thrown overboard to lighten a ship
JETSAMS > JETSAM
JETSOM same as **>** JETSAM
JETSOMS > JETSOM
JETSON archaic form of **>** JETSAM
JETSONS > JETSON
JETSTREAM n narrow belt of high-altitude winds moving east at high speeds)
JETTATURA n evil eye
JETTED > JET
JETTIED > JETTY
JETTIER > JETTY
JETTIES > JETTY
JETTIEST > JETTY
JETTINESS > JETTY
JETTING > JET
JETTISON vb abandon
JETTISONS > JETTISON
JETTON n counter or token
JETTONS > JETTON
JETTY n small pier ▷ adj of or resembling jet, esp in colour or polish ▷ vb equip with a cantilevered floor
JETTYING > JETTY
JETWAY n tradename of device used in airports
JETWAYS > JETWAY
JEU n game
JEUNE adj young
JEUX > JEU
JEW vb obsolete offensive word for haggle ▷ n obsolete offensive word for a haggler
JEWED > JEW
JEWEL n precious or semiprecious stone ▷ vb fit or decorate with a jewel or jewels

JEWELED > JEWEL

JEWELER *same as* > JEWELLER

JEWELERS > JEWELER

JEWELFISH *n* beautifully coloured fish popular in aquaria

JEWELING > JEWEL

JEWELLED > JEWEL

JEWELLER *n* dealer in jewels

JEWELLERS > JEWELLER

JEWELLERY *n* objects decorated with precious stones

JEWELLIKE > JEWEL

JEWELLING > JEWEL

JEWELRIES > JEWELRY

JEWELRY *same as* > JEWELLERY

JEWELS > JEWEL

JEWELWEED *n* small bushy plant

JEWFISH *n* freshwater catfish

JEWFISHES > JEWFISH

JEWIE *n* jewfish

JEWIES > JEWIE

JEWING > JEW

JEWS > JEW

JEZAIL *n* Afghan musket

JEZAILS > JEZAIL

JEZEBEL *n* shameless or scheming woman

JEZEBELS > JEZEBEL

JHALA *n* Indian musical style

JHALAS > JHALA

JHATKA *n* slaughter of animals for food according to Sikh law

JHATKAS > JHATKA

JIAO *n* Chinese currency unit

JIAOS > JIAO

JIB *same as* > JIBE

JIBB *same as* > JIBE

JIBBA *n* long, loose coat worn by Muslim men

JIBBAH *same as* > JUBBAH

JIBBAHS > JIBBAH

JIBBAS > JIBBA

JIBBED > JIBB

JIBBER *variant of* > GIBBER

JIBBERED > JIBBER

JIBBERING > JIBBER

JIBBERS > JIBBER

JIBBING > JIBB

JIBBINGS > JIBB

JIBBONS *pl n* spring onions

JIBBOOM *n* spar forming an extension of the bowsprit

JIBBOOMS > JIBBOOM

JIBBS > JIBB

JIBE *vb* taunt or jeer ▷ *n* insulting or taunting remark

JIBED > JIBE

JIBER > JIBE

JIBERS > JIBE

JIBES > JIBE

JIBING > JIBE

JIBINGLY > JIBE

JIBS > JIB

JICAMA *n* pale brown turnip

JICAMAS > JICAMA

JICKAJOG *vb* engage in sexual intercourse

JICKAJOGS > JICKAJOG

JIFF *same as* > JIFFY

JIFFIES > JIFFY

JIFFS > JIFF

JIFFY *n* very short period of time

JIG *n* type of lively dance ▷ *vb* dance a jig

JIGABOO *n* offensive term for a Black person

JIGABOOS > JIGABOO

JIGAJIG *vb* engage in sexual intercourse

JIGAJIGS > JIGAJIG

JIGAJOG *variant of* > JIGAJIG

JIGAJOGS > JIGAJOG

JIGAMAREE *n* thing

JIGGED > JIG

JIGGER *n* small whisky glass ▷ *vb* interfere or alter

JIGGERED > JIGGER

JIGGERING > JIGGER

JIGGERS > JIGGER

JIGGIER > JIGGY

JIGGIEST > JIGGY

JIGGING > JIG

JIGGINGS > JIG

JIGGISH > JIG

JIGGLE *vb* move up and down with short jerky movements ▷ *n* short jerky motion

JIGGLED > JIGGLE

JIGGLES > JIGGLE

JIGGLIER > JIGGLE

JIGGLIEST > JIGGLE

JIGGLING > JIGGLE

JIGGLY > JIGGLE

JIGGUMBOB *n* thing

JIGGY *adj* resembling a jig

JIGJIG *variant of* > JIGAJIG

JIGJIGS > JIGJIG

JIGLIKE > JIG

JIGOT *same as* > GIGOT

JIGOTS > JIGOT

JIGS > JIG

JIGSAW *n* type of game ▷ *vb* cut with a jigsaw

JIGSAWED > JIGSAW

JIGSAWING > JIGSAW

JIGSAWN > JIGSAW

JIGSAWS > JIGSAW

JIHAD *n* Islamic holy war against unbelievers

JIHADEEN *pl n* jihadists

JIHADI *n* person who takes part in a jihad

JIHADIS > JIHADI

JIHADISM *n* Islamic fundamentalist movement that favours jihads

JIHADISMS > JIHADISM

JIHADIST > JIHADISM

JIHADISTS > JIHADISM

JIHADS > JIHAD

JILBAB *n* long robe worn by Muslim women

JILBABS > JILBAB

JILGIE *n* freshwater crayfish

JILGIES > JILGIE

JILL *variant spelling of* > GILL

JILLAROO *n* female jackeroo

JILLAROOS > JILLAROO

JILLET *n* flighty or capricious woman

JILLETS > JILLET

JILLFLIRT *same as* > JILLET

JILLION *n* extremely large number or amount

JILLIONS > JILLION

JILLIONTH > JILLION

JILLS > JILL

JILT *vb* leave or reject (one's lover) ▷ *n* woman who jilts a lover

JILTED > JILT

JILTER > JILT

JILTERS > JILT

JILTING > JILT

JILTS > JILT

JIMCRACK *same as* > GIMCRACK

JIMCRACKS > JIMCRACK

JIMINY *interj* expression of surprise

JIMJAM > JIMJAMS

JIMJAMS *pl n* state of nervous tension, excitement, or anxiety

JIMMIE *same as* > JIMMY

JIMMIED > JIMMY

JIMMIES > JIMMY

JIMMINY *interj* expression of surprise

JIMMY *same as* > JEMMY

JIMMYING > JIMMY

JIMP *adj* handsome

JIMPER > JIMP

JIMPEST > JIMP

JIMPIER > JIMPY

JIMPIEST > JIMPY

JIMPLY *adv* neatly

JIMPNESS > JIMP

JIMPSON *same as* > JIMSON

JIMPY *adj* neat and tidy

JIMSON *n* as in *jimson weed* type of poisonous plant

JIMSONS > JIMSON

JIN *n* Chinese unit of weight

JINGAL *n* swivel-mounted gun

JINGALL *same as* > JINGAL

JINGALLS > JINGALL

JINGALS > JINGAL

JINGBANG *n* entirety of something

JINGBANGS > JINGBANG

JINGKO *same as* > GINGKO

JINGKOES > JINGKO

JINGLE *n* catchy verse or song used in an advert ▷ *vb* (cause to) make a gentle ringing sound

JINGLED > JINGLE

JINGLER > JINGLE

JINGLERS > JINGLE

JINGLES > JINGLE

JINGLET *n* sleigh-bell clapper

JINGLETS > JINGLET

JINGLIER > JINGLE

JINGLIEST > JINGLE

JINGLING > JINGLE

JINGLY > JINGLE

JINGO *n* loud and bellicose patriot; chauvinism

JINGOES > JINGO

JINGOISH > JINGO

JINGOISM *n* aggressive nationalism

JINGOISMS > JINGOISM

JINGOIST > JINGOISM

JINGOISTS > JINGOISM

JINJILI *n* type of sesame

JINJILIS > JINJILI

JINK *vb* move quickly or jerkily in order to dodge someone ▷ *n* jinking movement

JINKED > JINK

JINKER *n* vehicle for transporting timber ▷ *vb* carry or transport in a jinker

JINKERED > JINKER

JINKERING > JINKER

JINKERS > JINKER

JINKING > JINK

JINKS > JINK

JINN > JINNI

JINNE *interj* South African exclamation

JINNEE *same as* > JINNI

JINNI *n* spirit in Muslim mythology

JINNIS > JINNI

JINNS > JINNI

JINRIKSHA *same as* > RICKSHAW

JINS > JIN

JINX *n* person or thing bringing bad luck ▷ *vb* be or put a jinx on

JINXED > JINX

JINXES > JINX

JINXING > JINX

JIPIJAPA *n* plant whose leaves are used for making panama hats

JIPIJAPAS > JIPIJAPA

JIPYAPA *same as* > JIPIJAPA

JIPYAPAS > JIPYAPA

JIRBLE *vb* pour carelessly

JIRBLED > JIRBLE

JIRBLES > JIRBLE

JIRBLING > JIRBLE

JIRD *n* gerbil

JIRDS > JIRD

JIRGA *n* Afghan council

JIRGAS > JIRGA

JIRKINET *n* bodice

JIRKINETS > JIRKINET

JIRRE *same as* > JINNE

JISM *n* vulgar word for semen

JISMS > JISM

JISSOM *slang word for* > SEMEN

JISSOMS > JISSOM

JITNEY *n* small cheap bus

JITNEYS > JITNEY

JITTER *vb* be anxious or nervous

JITTERBUG *n* fast jerky American dance that was popular in the 1940s ▷ *vb* dance the jitterbug

JITTERED > JITTER

JITTERIER > JITTERY

JITTERING > JITTER

JITTERS > JITTER

JITTERY *adj* nervous

JIUJITSU *variant spelling of* > JUJITSU

JIUJITSUS > JIUJITSU

JIUJUTSU *same as* > JUJITSU

JIUJUTSUS > JIUJUTSU

j

j

JIVE n lively dance of the 1940s and '50s ▷ vb dance the jive ▷ adj pertaining to or indicative of jive

JIVEASS adj misleading or phoney ▷ n person who loves fun and excitement

JIVEASSES > JIVEASS

JIVED > JIVE

JIVER > JIVE

JIVERS > JIVE

JIVES > JIVE

JIVEST > JIVE

JIVEY adj jazzy; lively

JIVIER > JIVEY

JIVIEST > JIVEY

JIVING > JIVE

JIVY same as > JIVEY

JIZ n wig

JIZZ n term for the characteristics that identify a particular species of bird or plant

JIZZES > JIZZ

JNANA n type of yoga

JNANAS > JNANA

JO n Scots word for sweetheart

JOANNA n piano

JOANNAS > JOANNA

JOANNES same as > JOHANNES

JOANNESES > JOANNES

JOB n occupation or paid employment ▷ vb work at casual jobs

JOBATION n scolding

JOBATIONS > JOBATION

JOBBED > JOB

JOBBER n person who jobs

JOBBERIES > JOBBERY

JOBBERS > JOBBER

JOBBERY n practice of making private profit out of a public office

JOBBIE n referring to a thing usually specified in the preceding part of a sentence

JOBBIES > JOBBIE

JOBBING adj doing individual jobs for payment ▷ n act of seeking work

JOBBINGS > JOBBING

JOBCENTRE n office where unemployed people can find out about job vacancies

JOBE vb scold

JOBED > JOBE

JOBERNOWL n stupid person

JOBES > JOBE

JOBHOLDER n person who has a job

JOBING > JOBE

JOBLESS pl n as in the jobless unemployed people ▷ adj unemployed

JOBNAME n title of position

JOBNAMES > JOBNAME

JOBS > JOB

JOBSEEKER n person looking for employment

JOBSHARE n arrangement in which two people divide the duties for one job between them

JOBSHARES > JOBSHARE

JOBSWORTH n person in a position of minor authority who invokes the letter of the law in order to avoid any action requiring initiative, cooperation, etc

JOCK n athlete

JOCKDOM n world of male athletes

JOCKDOMS > JOCKDOM

JOCKETTE n female athlete

JOCKETTES > JOCKETTE

JOCKEY n person who rides horses in races ▷ vb ride (a horse) in a race

JOCKEYED > JOCKEY

JOCKEYING > JOCKEY

JOCKEYISH > JOCKEY

JOCKEYISM n skills and practices of jockeys

JOCKEYS > JOCKEY

JOCKIER > JOCKY

JOCKIEST > JOCKY

JOCKISH adj macho

JOCKNEY n the Scots dialect influenced by cockney speech patterns

JOCKNEYS > JOCKNEY

JOCKO n chimpanzee

JOCKOS > JOCKO

JOCKS > JOCK

JOCKSTRAP n support worn by male athletes

JOCKTELEG n clasp knife

JOCKY adj indicating or appropriate to a male athlete

JOCO adj relaxed ▷ n joke

JOCOS > JOCO

JOCOSE adj playful or humorous

JOCOSELY > JOCOSE

JOCOSER > JOCOSE

JOCOSEST > JOCOSE

JOCOSITY > JOCOSE

JOCULAR adj fond of joking

JOCULARLY > JOCULAR

JOCULATOR n joker

JOCUND adj merry or cheerful

JOCUNDER > JOCUND

JOCUNDEST > JOCUND

JOCUNDITY > JOCUND

JOCUNDLY > JOCUND

JODEL same as > YODEL

JODELLED > JODEL

JODELLING > JODEL

JODELS > JODEL

JODHPUR n as in jodphur boots ankle-length leather riding boots

JODHPURS pl n riding breeches

JOE same as > JO

JOES > JOE

JOEY n young kangaroo

JOEYS > JOEY

JOG vb run at a gentle pace, esp for exercise ▷ n slow run

JOGGED > JOG

JOGGER n person who runs at a jog for exercise

JOGGERS > JOGGER

JOGGING > JOG

JOGGINGS > JOG

JOGGLE vb shake or move jerkily ▷ n act of joggling

JOGGLED > JOGGLE

JOGGLER > JOGGLE

JOGGLERS > JOGGLE

JOGGLES > JOGGLE

JOGGLING > JOGGLE

JOGPANTS pl n trousers worn for jogging

JOGS > JOG

JOGTROT n easy bouncy gait ▷ vb move at a jogtrot

JOGTROTS > JOGTROT

JOHANNES n Portuguese gold coin minted in the early 18th century

JOHN n toilet

JOHNBOAT n small flat-bottomed boat

JOHNBOATS > JOHNBOAT

JOHNNIE same as > JOHNNY

JOHNNIES > JOHNNY

JOHNNY n chap

JOHNS > JOHN

JOHNSON slang word for > PENIS

JOHNSONS > JOHNSON

JOIN vb become a member (of) ▷ n place where two things are joined

JOINABLE > JOIN

JOINDER n act of joining, esp in legal contexts

JOINDERS > JOINDER

JOINED > JOIN

JOINER n maker of finished woodwork

JOINERIES > JOINERY

JOINERS > JOINER

JOINERY n joiner's work

JOINING > JOIN

JOININGS > JOIN

JOINS > JOIN

JOINT adj shared by two or more ▷ n place where bones meet but can move ▷ vb divide meat into joints

JOINTED adj having a joint or joints

JOINTEDLY > JOINTED

JOINTER n tool for pointing mortar joints

JOINTERS > JOINTER

JOINTING > JOINT

JOINTINGS > JOINTING

JOINTLESS > JOINT

JOINTLY > JOINT

JOINTNESS > JOINT

JOINTRESS n woman entitled to a jointure

JOINTS > JOINT

JOINTURE n provision made by a husband for his wife after his death

JOINTURED > JOINTURE

JOINTURES > JOINTURE

JOINTWEED n American wild plant

JOINTWORM n larva of chalcid flies which form galls on the stems of cereal plants

JOIST n horizontal beam ▷ vb construct (a floor, roof, etc) with joists

JOISTED > JOIST

JOISTING > JOIST

JOISTS > JOIST

JOJOBA n shrub of SW North America

JOJOBAS > JOJOBA

JOKE n thing said or done to cause laughter ▷ vb make jokes

JOKED > JOKE

JOKER n person who jokes

JOKERS > JOKER

JOKES > JOKE

JOKESMITH n comedian

JOKESOME > JOKE

JOKESTER n person who makes jokes

JOKESTERS > JOKESTER

JOKEY adj intended as a joke

JOKIER > JOKEY

JOKIEST > JOKEY

JOKILY > JOKE

JOKINESS > JOKE

JOKING n act of joking

JOKINGLY > JOKE

JOKINGS > JOKING

JOKOL Shetland word for > YES

JOKY same as > JOKEY

JOL n party ▷ vb have a good time

JOLE vb knock

JOLED > JOLE

JOLES > JOLE

JOLING > JOLE

JOLIOTIUM n former name proposed for dubnium

JOLL variant of > JOLE

JOLLED > JOL

JOLLER n person who has a good time

JOLLERS > JOLLER

JOLLEY same as > JOLLY

JOLLEYER > JOLLEY

JOLLEYERS > JOLLEY

JOLLEYING > JOLLEY

JOLLEYS > JOLLEY

JOLLIED > JOLLY

JOLLIER n joker

JOLLIERS > JOLLIER

JOLLIES > JOLLY

JOLLIEST > JOLLY

JOLLIFIED > JOLLIFY

JOLLIFIES > JOLLIFY

JOLLIFY vb be or cause to be jolly

JOLLILY > JOLLY

JOLLIMENT > JOLLY

JOLLINESS > JOLLY

JOLLING > JOL

JOLLITIES > JOLLITY

JOLLITY n condition of being jolly

JOLLOF adj as in jollof rice, a W African dish made from rice and meat or fish

JOLLOP n cream or unguent

JOLLOPS > JOLLOP

JOLLS > JOLL

JOLLY adj full of good humour ▷ adv extremely ▷ vb try to make or keep (someone) cheerful ▷ n festivity or celebration

JOLLYBOAT n small boat used as a utility tender for a vessel

JOLLYER > JOLLY

JOLLYERS > JOLLY

JOLLYHEAD same as > JOLLITY

JOLLYING > JOLLY

JOLLYINGS > JOLLY

JOLS > JOL

JOLT n unpleasant surprise or shock ▷ vb surprise or shock

JOLTED > JOLT

JOLTER > JOLT

JOLTERS > JOLT

JOLTHEAD n fool

JOLTHEADS > JOLTHEAD

JOLTIER > JOLT

JOLTIEST > JOLT

JOLTILY > JOLT

JOLTING n act of jolting

JOLTINGLY > JOLT

JOLTINGS > JOLTING

JOLTS > JOLT

JOLTY > JOLT

JOMO same as > ZO

JOMON n particular era in Japanese history

JOMONS > JOMON

JOMOS > JOMON

JONCANOE n Jamaican ceremony

JONCANOES > JONCANOE

JONES vb desire

JONESED > JONES

JONESES > JONES

JONESING > JONES

JONG n friend, often used in direct address

JONGLEUR n (in medieval France) an itinerant minstrel

JONGLEURS > JONGLEUR

JONGS > JONG

JONNOCK adj genuine ▷ adv honestly

JONNYCAKE n type of flat bread

JONQUIL n fragrant narcissus

JONQUILS > JONQUIL

JONTIES > JONTY

JONTY n petty officer

JOOK vb poke or puncture (the skin) ▷ n jab or the resulting wound

JOOKED > JOOK

JOOKERIES > JOOKERY

JOOKERY n mischief

JOOKING > JOOK

JOOKS > JOOK

JOR n movement in Indian music

JORAM same as > JORUM

JORAMS > JORAM

JORDAN n chamber pot

JORDANS > JORDAN

JORDELOO same as > GARDYLOO

JORDELOOS > JORDELOO

JORS > JOR

JORUM n large drinking bowl or vessel or its contents

JORUMS > JORUM

JOSEPH n woman's floor-length riding coat

JOSEPHS > JOSEPH

JOSH vb tease ▷ n teasing or bantering joke

JOSHED > JOSH

JOSHER > JOSH

JOSHERS > JOSH

JOSHES > JOSH

JOSHING n act of joshing

JOSHINGLY > JOSH

JOSHINGS > JOSHING

JOSKIN n bumpkin

JOSKINS > JOSKIN

JOSS n Chinese deity

JOSSER n simpleton

JOSSERS > JOSSER

JOSSES > JOSS

JOSTLE vb knock or push against ▷ n act of jostling

JOSTLED > JOSTLE

JOSTLER > JOSTLE

JOSTLERS > JOSTLE

JOSTLES > JOSTLE

JOSTLING > JOSTLE

JOSTLINGS > JOSTLE

JOT vb write briefly ▷ n very small amount

JOTA n Spanish dance

JOTAS > JOTA

JOTS > JOT

JOTTED > JOT

JOTTER n notebook

JOTTERS > JOTTER

JOTTIER > JOTTY

JOTTIEST > JOTTY

JOTTING > JOT

JOTTINGS > JOT

JOTTY > JOT

JOTUN n giant

JOTUNN same as > JOTUN

JOTUNNS > JOTUNN

JOTUNS > JOTUN

JOUAL n nonstandard variety of Canadian French

JOUALS > JOUAL

JOUGS pl n iron ring for restraining an offender

JOUISANCE n joy

JOUK vb duck or dodge ▷ n sudden evasive movement

JOUKED > JOUK

JOUKERIES > JOUKERY

JOUKERY same as > JOOKERY

JOUKING > JOUK

JOUKS > JOUK

JOULE n unit of work or energy ▷ vb knock

JOULED > JOULE

JOULES > JOULE

JOULING > JOULE

JOUNCE vb shake or jolt or cause to shake or jolt ▷ n jolting movement

JOUNCED > JOUNCE

JOUNCES > JOUNCE

JOUNCIER > JOUNCE

JOUNCIEST > JOUNCE

JOUNCING > JOUNCE

JOUNCY > JOUNCE

JOUR n day

JOURNAL n daily newspaper or magazine ▷ vb record in a journal

JOURNALED > JOURNAL

JOURNALS > JOURNAL

JOURNEY n act of travelling from one place to another ▷ vb travel

JOURNEYED > JOURNEY

JOURNEYER > JOURNEY

JOURNEYS > JOURNEY

JOURNO n journalist

JOURNOS > JOURNO

JOURS > JOUR

JOUST n combat between two knights ▷ vb fight on horseback using lances

JOUSTED > JOUST

JOUSTER > JOUST

JOUSTERS > JOUST

JOUSTING n act of jousting

JOUSTINGS > JOUSTING

JOUSTS > JOUST

JOVIAL adj happy and cheerful

JOVIALITY > JOVIAL

JOVIALLY > JOVIAL

JOVIALTY > JOVIAL

JOW vb ring (a bell)

JOWAR n variety of sorghum

JOWARI same as > JOWAR

JOWARIS > JOWARI

JOWARS > JOWAR

JOWED > JOW

JOWING > JOW

JOWL n lower jaw ▷ vb knock

JOWLED > JOWL

JOWLER n dog with prominent jowls

JOWLERS > JOWLER

JOWLIER > JOWL

JOWLIEST > JOWL

JOWLINESS > JOWL

JOWLING > JOWL

JOWLS > JOWL

JOWLY > JOWL

JOWS > JOW

JOY n feeling of great delight or pleasure ▷ vb feel joy

JOYANCE n joyous feeling or festivity

JOYANCES > JOYANCE

JOYED > JOY

JOYFUL adj feeling or bringing great joy

JOYFULLER > JOYFUL

JOYFULLY > JOYFUL

JOYING > JOY

JOYLESS adj feeling or bringing no joy

JOYLESSLY > JOYLESS

JOYOUS adj extremely happy and enthusiastic

JOYOUSLY > JOYOUS

JOYPAD n computer games console

JOYPADS > JOYPAD

JOYPOP vb take addictive drugs occasionally

JOYPOPPED > JOYPOP

JOYPOPPER > JOYPOP

JOYPOPS > JOYPOP

JOYRIDDEN > JOYRIDE

JOYRIDE n drive in a car one has stolen ▷ vb take such a ride

JOYRIDER > JOYRIDE

JOYRIDERS > JOYRIDE

JOYRIDES > JOYRIDE

JOYRIDING > JOYRIDE

JOYRODE > JOYRIDE

JOYS > JOY

JOYSTICK n control device for an aircraft or computer

JOYSTICKS > JOYSTICK

JUBA n lively African-American dance

JUBAS > JUBA

JUBATE adj possessing a mane

JUBBAH n long loose outer garment with wide sleeves

JUBBAHS > JUBBAH

JUBE n part of a church or cathedral

JUBES > JUBE

JUBHAH same as > JUBBAH

JUBHAHS > JUBHAH

JUBILANCE > JUBILANT

JUBILANCY > JUBILANT

JUBILANT adj feeling or expressing great joy

JUBILATE vb have or express great joy

JUBILATED > JUBILATE

JUBILATES > JUBILATE

JUBILE same as > JUBILEE

JUBILEE n special anniversary, esp 25th or 50th

JUBILEES > JUBILEE

JUBILES > JUBILE

JUCO n junior college in America

JUCOS > JUCO

JUD n large block of coal

JUDAS n peephole

JUDASES > JUDAS

JUDDER vb vibrate violently ▷ n violent vibration

JUDDERED > JUDDER

JUDDERIER > JUDDERY

JUDDERING > JUDDER

JUDDERS > JUDDER

JUDDERY adj shaky

JUDGE n public official ▷ vb act as a judge

JUDGEABLE > JUDGE

JUDGED > JUDGE

JUDGELESS > JUDGE

JUDGELIKE > JUDGE

JUDGEMENT same as > JUDGMENT

JUDGER > JUDGE

JUDGERS > JUDGE

JUDGES > JUDGE

JUDGESHIP n position, office, or function of a judge

JUDGEY adj tending to be judgmental

JUDGIER > JUDGY

JUDGIEST > JUDGY

JUDGING n act of judging

JUDGINGLY > JUDGE

JUDGINGS > JUDGING

JUDGMATIC adj judicious

JUDGMENT n opinion reached after careful thought

JUDGMENTS > JUDGMENT

JUDGY adj tending to be judgmental

JUDICABLE adj capable of being judged, esp in a court of law

JUDICARE n (in Canada) state-paid legal services

JUDICARES > JUDICARE

JUDICATOR n person who acts as a judge

JUDICIAL adj of or by a court or judge

JUDICIARY n system of courts and judges ▷ adj of or relating to courts of law, judgment, or judges

JUDICIOUS adj well-judged and sensible

JUDIES > JUDY

JUDO *n* type of sport

JUDOGI *n* white two-piece cotton costume

JUDOGIS > JUDOGI

JUDOIST > JUDO

JUDOISTS > JUDO

JUDOKA *n* competitor or expert in judo

JUDOKAS > JUDOKA

JUDOS > JUDO

JUDS > JUD

JUDY *n* woman

JUG *n* container for liquids ▷ *vb* stew or boil (meat, esp hare) in an earthenware container

JUGA > JUGUM

JUGAAD *n* (in Indian English) problem-solving

JUGAADS > JUGAAD

JUGAL *adj* of or relating to the zygomatic bone ▷ *n* cheekbone

JUGALS > JUGAL

JUGATE *adj* having parts arranged in pairs

JUGFUL *same as* > JUG

JUGFULS > JUGFUL

JUGGED > JUG

JUGGING > JUG

JUGGINGS > JUG

JUGGINS *n* silly person

JUGGINSES > JUGGINS

JUGGLE *vb* throw and catch (objects) to keep them in the air ▷ *n* act of juggling

JUGGLED > JUGGLE

JUGGLER *n* person who juggles, esp a professional entertainer

JUGGLERS > JUGGLER

JUGGLERY > JUGGLE

JUGGLES > JUGGLE

JUGGLING > JUGGLE

JUGGLINGS > JUGGLE

JUGHEAD *n* clumsy person

JUGHEADS > JUGHEAD

JUGLET *n* small jug

JUGLETS > JUGLET

JUGS > JUG

JUGSFUL > JUGFUL

JUGULA > JUGULUM

JUGULAR *n* one of three large veins of the neck

JUGULARS > JUGULAR

JUGULATE *vb* check (a disease) by extreme measures or remedies

JUGULATED > JUGULATE

JUGULATES > JUGULATE

JUGULUM *n* lower throat

JUGUM *n* part of an insect's forewing

JUGUMS > JUGUM

JUICE *n* liquid part of vegetables, fruit, or meat ▷ *vb* extract juice from fruits and vegetables

JUICED > JUICE

JUICEHEAD *n* alcoholic

JUICELESS > JUICE

JUICER *n* kitchen appliance

JUICERS > JUICER

JUICES > JUICE

JUICIER > JUICY

JUICIEST > JUICY

JUICILY > JUICY

JUICINESS > JUICY

JUICING > JUICE

JUICY *adj* full of juice

JUJITSU *n* Japanese martial art

JUJITSUS > JUJITSU

JUJU *n* W African magic charm or fetish

JUJUBE *n* chewy sweet made of flavoured gelatine

JUJUBES > JUJUBE

JUJUISM > JUJU

JUJUISMS > JUJU

JUJUIST > JUJU

JUJUISTS > JUJU

JUJUS > JUJU

JUJUTSU *same as* > JUJITSU

JUJUTSUS > JUJUTSU

JUKE *vb* dance or play dance music

JUKEBOX *n* coin-operated music box

JUKEBOXES > JUKEBOX

JUKED > JUKE

JUKES > JUKE

JUKING > JUKE

JUKSKEI *n* type of game

JUKSKEIS > JUKSKEI

JUKU *n* Japanese martial art

JUKUS > JUKU

JULEP *n* sweet alcoholic drink

JULEPS > JULEP

JULIENNE *adj* (of vegetables or meat) cut into thin shreds ▷ *n* clear soup containing thinly shredded vegetables ▷ *vb* cut into thin pieces

JULIENNED > JULIENNE

JULIENNES > JULIENNE

JULIET *n* code word for the letter J

JULIETS > JULIET

JUMAR *n* climbing tool ▷ *vb* climb (up a fixed rope) using jumars

JUMARED > JUMAR

JUMARING > JUMAR

JUMARRED > JUMAR

JUMARRING > JUMAR

JUMARS > JUMAR

JUMART *n* mythical offspring of a bull and a mare

JUMARTS > JUMART

JUMBAL *same as* > JUMBLE

JUMBALS > JUMBAL

JUMBIE *n* Caribbean ghost

JUMBIES > JUMBIE

JUMBLE *n* confused heap or state ▷ *vb* mix in a disordered way

JUMBLED > JUMBLE

JUMBLER > JUMBLE

JUMBLERS > JUMBLE

JUMBLES > JUMBLE

JUMBLIER > JUMBLE

JUMBLIEST > JUMBLE

JUMBLING > JUMBLE

JUMBLY > JUMBLE

JUMBO *adj* very large ▷ *n* large jet airliner

JUMBOISE *same as* > JUMBOIZE

JUMBOISED > JUMBOISE

JUMBOISES > JUMBOISE

JUMBOIZE *vb* extend (a ship) by inserting a part between the bow and stern

JUMBOIZED > JUMBOIZE

JUMBOIZES > JUMBOIZE

JUMBOS > JUMBO

JUMBUCK *n* sheep

JUMBUCKS > JUMBUCK

JUMBY *n* Caribbean ghost

JUMELLE *n* paired objects

JUMELLES > JUMELLE

JUMP *vb* leap or spring into the air using the leg muscles ▷ *n* act of jumping

JUMPABLE > JUMP

JUMPED > JUMP

JUMPER *n* sweater or pullover

JUMPERS > JUMPER

JUMPIER > JUMPY

JUMPIEST > JUMPY

JUMPILY > JUMPY

JUMPINESS > JUMPY

JUMPING > JUMP

JUMPINGLY > JUMP

JUMPINGS > JUMP

JUMPOFF *n* round in a showjumping contest

JUMPOFFS > JUMPOFF

JUMPROPE *n* rope held in the hands and jumped over

JUMPROPES > JUMPROPE

JUMPS > JUMP

JUMPSHOT *n* type of shot in basketball in which a player jumps to reach the basket

JUMPSHOTS > JUMPSHOT

JUMPSIES *pl n* game involving jumping over a straight rope

JUMPSUIT *n* one-piece garment of combined trousers and jacket or shirt

JUMPSUITS > JUMPSUIT

JUMPY *adj* nervous

JUN *variant of* > CHON

JUNCATE *same as* > JUNKET

JUNCATES > JUNCATE

JUNCO *n* North American bunting

JUNCOES > JUNCO

JUNCOS > JUNCO

JUNCTION *n* place where routes, railway lines, or roads meet

JUNCTIONS > JUNCTION

JUNCTURAL > JUNCTURE

JUNCTURE *n* point in time, esp a critical one

JUNCTURES > JUNCTURE

JUNCUS *n* type of rush

JUNCUSES > JUNCUS

JUNEATING *n* early-season apple

JUNGLE *n* tropical forest of dense tangled vegetation

JUNGLED *adj* covered with jungle

JUNGLEGYM *n* climbing frame for children

JUNGLES > JUNGLE

JUNGLI *n* uncultured person

JUNGLIER > JUNGLE

JUNGLIEST > JUNGLE

JUNGLIS > JUNGLI

JUNGLIST *n* jungle-music enthusiast

JUNGLISTS > JUNGLIST

JUNGLY > JUNGLE

JUNIOR *adj* of lower standing ▷ *n* junior person ▷ *vb* work as a junior

JUNIORATE *n* preparatory course for candidates for religious orders

JUNIORED > JUNIOR

JUNIORING > JUNIOR

JUNIORITY *n* condition of being junior

JUNIORS > JUNIOR

JUNIPER *n* evergreen shrub with purple berries

JUNIPERS > JUNIPER

JUNK *n* discarded or useless objects ▷ *vb* discard as junk

JUNKANOO *n* Bahamian ceremony

JUNKANOOS > JUNKANOO

JUNKED > JUNK

JUNKER *n* (formerly) young German nobleman

JUNKERDOM *n* condition of being a junker

JUNKERS > JUNKER

JUNKET *n* excursion by public officials ▷ *vb* (of a public official, committee, etc) to go on a junket

JUNKETED > JUNKET

JUNKETEER > JUNKET

JUNKETER > JUNKET

JUNKETERS > JUNKET

JUNKETING > JUNKET

JUNKETS > JUNKET

JUNKETTED > JUNKET

JUNKETTER > JUNKET

JUNKIE *n* slang word for person addicted to something

JUNKIER > JUNKY

JUNKIES > JUNKIE

JUNKIEST > JUNKY

JUNKINESS > JUNKY

JUNKING > JUNK

JUNKMAN *n* man who trades in discarded items

JUNKMEN > JUNKMAN

JUNKS > JUNK

JUNKY *adj* of low quality

JUNKYARD *n* place where junk is stored or collected for sale

JUNKYARDS > JUNKYARD

JUNTA *n* military officers holding power in a country

JUNTAS > JUNTA

JUNTO *same as* > JUNTA

JUNTOS > JUNTO

JUPATI *n* type of palm tree

JUPATIS > JUPATI

JUPE *n* sleeveless jacket

JUPES > JUPE

JUPON *n* short sleeveless padded garment

JUPONS > JUPON

JURA > JUS

JURAL *adj* of or relating to law or to the administration of justice

JURALLY > JURAL

JURANT *n* person taking oath

JURANTS > JURANT

JURASSIC adj of the second period of the Mesozoic era

JURAT n statement at the foot of an affidavit

JURATORY adj of, relating to, or expressed in an oath

JURATS > JURAT

JURE adv by legal right ▷ n legal right

JUREL n edible fish

JURELS > JUREL

JURES > JURE

JURIDIC same as > JURIDICAL

JURIDICAL adj of law or the administration of justice

JURIED > JURY

JURIES > JURY

JURIST n expert in law

JURISTIC adj of or relating to jurists

JURISTS > JURIST

JUROR n member of a jury

JURORS > JUROR

JURY n group of people sworn to deliver a verdict in a court of law ▷ adj makeshift ▷ vb evaluate by jury

JURYING > JURY

JURYLESS > JURY

JURYMAN n member of a jury, esp a man

JURYMAST n replacement mast

JURYMASTS > JURYMAST

JURYMEN > JURYMAN

JURYWOMAN n female member of a jury

JURYWOMEN > JURYWOMAN

JUS n right, power, or authority

JUSSIVE n mood of verbs used for giving orders; imperative

JUSSIVES > JUSSIVE

JUST adv very recently ▷ adj fair or impartial in action or judgment ▷ vb joust

JUSTED > JUST

JUSTER > JUST

JUSTERS > JUST

JUSTEST > JUST **JUSTICE** n quality of being just

JUSTICER n magistrate

JUSTICERS > JUSTICER

JUSTICES > JUSTICE

JUSTICIAR n chief political and legal officer from the time of William I to that of Henry III, who deputized for the king in his absence and presided over the kings' courts

JUSTIFIED > JUSTIFY

JUSTIFIER > JUSTIFY

JUSTIFIES > JUSTIFY

JUSTIFY vb prove right or reasonable

JUSTING > JUST

JUSTLE less common word for > JOSTLE

JUSTLED > JUSTLE

JUSTLES > JUSTLE

JUSTLING > JUSTLE

JUSTLY > JUST

JUSTNESS > JUST

JUSTS same as > JOUST

JUT vb project or stick out ▷ n something that juts out

JUTE n plant fibre, used for rope, canvas, etc

JUTELIKE > JUTE

JUTES > JUTE

JUTS > JUT

JUTTED > JUT

JUTTIED > JUTTY

JUTTIER > JUTTY

JUTTIES > JUTTY

JUTTIEST > JUTTY

JUTTING > JUT

JUTTINGLY > JUT

JUTTY vb project beyond ▷ adj characterized by jutting

JUTTYING > JUTTY

JUVE same as > JUVENILE

JUVENAL variant spelling (esp US) of > JUVENILE

JUVENALS > JUVENAL

JUVENILE adj young ▷ n young person or child

JUVENILES > JUVENILE

JUVENILIA pl n works produced in an author's youth

JUVES > JUVE

JUVIE n juvenile detention centre

JUVIES > JUVIE

JUXTAPOSE vb put side by side

JYMOLD adj having a hinge

JYNX n wryneck

JYNXES > JYNX

Kk

KA *n* (in ancient Egypt) type of spirit ▷ *vb* (in archaic usage) help

KAAL *adj* naked

KAAMA *n* large African antelope with lyre-shaped horns

KAAMAS > KAAMA

KAAS *n* Dutch cabinet or wardrobe

KAB *variant spelling of* > CAB

KABAB *same as* > KEBAB

KABABBED > KABAB

KABABBING > KABAB

KABABS > KABAB

KABADDI *n* type of game

KABADDIS > KABADDI

KABAKA *n* any of the former rulers of the Baganda people

KABAKAS > KABAKA

KABALA *same as* > KABBALAH

KABALAS > KABALA

KABALISM > KABALA

KABALISMS > KABALA

KABALIST > KABALA

KABALISTS > KABALA

KABAR *archaic form of* > CABER

KABARS > KABAR

KABAYA *n* tunic

KABAYAS > KABAYA

KABBALA *same as* > KABBALAH

KABBALAH *n* ancient Jewish mystical tradition

KABBALAHS > KABBALAH

KABBALAS > KABBALA

KABBALISM > KABBALAH

KABBALIST > KABBALAH

KABELE *same as* > KEBELE

KABELES > KABELE

KABELJOU *n* large fish that is an important food fish of South African waters

KABELJOUS > KABELJOU

KABELJOUW *same as* > KABELJOU

KABIKI *n* fruit tree found in India

KABIKIS > KABIKI

KABLOOEY *interj* expressing alarming or surprising abruptness

KABLOOIE *same as* > KABLOOEY

KABLOONA *n* (among Canadian Inuits) person who is not Inuit

KABLOONAS > KABLOONA

KABLOONAT > KABLOONA

KABOB *same as* > KEBAB

KABOBBED > KABOB

KABOBBING > KABOB

KABOBS > KABOB

KABOCHA *n* type of Japanese pumpkin

KABOCHAS > KABOCHA

KABOODLE *same as* > CABOODLE

KABOODLES > KABOODLE

KABOOM *n* loud echoing explosive sound

KABOOMS > KABOOM

KABS > KAB

KABUKI *n* form of Japanese drama

KABUKIS > KABUKI

KACCHA *n* trousers worn traditionally by Sikhs

KACCHAS > KACCHA

KACHA *adj* crude

KACHAHRI *n* Indian courthouse

KACHAHRIS > KACHAHRI

KACHCHA *same as* > KACHA

KACHERI *same as* > KACHAHRI

KACHERIS > KACHERI

KACHINA *n* type of supernatural being

KACHINAS > KACHINA

KACHORI *n* balls of fried dough with various fillings, eaten as a snack

KACHORIS > KACHORI

KACHUMBER *n* salad of onion, tomato, and cucumber

KACK *same as* > CACK

KACKS > KACK

KADAI *same as* > KARAHI

KADAIS > KADAI

KADAITCHA *n* (in certain Central Australian Aboriginal tribes) man with the mission of avenging the death of a tribesman

KADDISH *n* ancient Jewish liturgical prayer

KADDISHES > KADDISH

KADDISHIM > KADDISH

KADE *same as* > KED

KADES > KADE

KADI *variant spelling of* > CADI

KADIS > KADI

KAE *n* dialect word for jackdaw or jay ▷ *vb* (in archaic usage) help

KAED > KAE

KAEING > KAE

KAES > KAE

KAF *n* letter of the Hebrew alphabet

KAFFIR *n* Southern African variety of sorghum

KAFFIRS > KAFFIR

KAFFIYAH *same as* > KAFFIYEH

KAFFIYAHS > KAFFIYAH

KAFFIYEH *same as* > KEFFIYEH

KAFFIYEHS > KAFFIYEH

KAFILA *n* caravan

KAFILAS > KAFILA

KAFIR *same as* > KAFFIR

KAFIRS > KAFIR

KAFS > KAF

KAFTAN *n* long loose Eastern garment

KAFTANS > KAFTAN

KAFUFFLE *n* commotion or disorder

KAFUFFLES > KAFUFFLE

KAGO *n* Japanese sedan chair

KAGOOL *variant spelling of* > CAGOULE

KAGOOLS > KAGOOL

KAGOS > KAGO

KAGOUL *variant spelling of* > CAGOULE

KAGOULE *same as* > KAGOUL

KAGOULES > KAGOULE

KAGOULS > KAGOUL

KAGU *n* crested nocturnal bird

KAGUS > KAGU

KAHAL *n* Jewish community

KAHALS > KAHAL

KAHAWAI *n* food and game fish of New Zealand

KAHAWAIS > KAHAWAI

KAHIKATEA *n* tall New Zealand coniferous tree

KAHIKATOA *n* tall New Zealand coniferous tree

KAHUNA *n* Hawaiian priest, shaman, or expert

KAHUNAS > KAHUNA

KAI *n* food

KAIAK *same as* > KAYAK

KAIAKED > KAIAK

KAIAKING > KAIAK

KAIAKS > KAIAK

KAID *n* North African chieftain or leader

KAIDS > KAID

KAIE *archaic form of* > KEY

KAIES > KAIE

KAIF *same as* > KIF

KAIFS > KAIF

KAIK *same as* > KAINGA

KAIKA *same as* > KAINGA

KAIKAI *n* food

KAIKAIS > KAIKAI

KAIKAS > KAIKA

KAIKAWAKA *n* small pyramid-shaped New Zealand conifer

KAIKOMAKO *n* small New Zealand tree with white flowers and black fruit

KAIKS > KAIK

KAIL *same as* > KALE

KAILS > KAIL

KAILYAIRD *same as* > KALEYARD

KAILYARD *same as* > KALEYARD

KAILYARDS > KAILYARD

KAIM *same as* > KAME

KAIMAKAM *n* Turkish governor

KAIMAKAMS > KAIMAKAM

KAIMS > KAIM

KAIN *variant spelling of* > CAIN

KAING > KA

KAINGA *n* (in New Zealand) a Māori village or small settlement

KAINGAS > KAINGA

KAINIT *same as* > KAINITE

KAINITE *n* white mineral

KAINITES > KAINITE

KAINITS > KAINIT

KAINS > KAIN

KAIROMONE *n* substance secreted by animal

KAIS > KAI

KAISER *n* German or Austro-Hungarian emperor

KAISERDOM > KAISER

KAISERIN *n* empress

KAISERINS > KAISERIN

KAISERISM > KAISER

KAISERS > KAISER

KAIZEN *n* type of philosophy

KAIZENS > KAIZEN

KAJAWAH *n* type of seat or pannier used on a camel

KAJAWAHS > KAJAWAH

KAJEPUT *n* variety of Australian melaleuca

KAJEPUTS > KAJEPUT

KAK *n* South African vulgar slang word for faeces

KAKA *n* parrot of New Zealand

KAKAPO *n* nocturnal New Zealand parrot

KAKAPOS > KAKAPO

KAKARIKI *n* green-feathered New Zealand parrot

KAKARIKIS > KAKARIKI

KAKAS > KAKA

KAKEMONO n Japanese wall hanging

KAKEMONOS > KAKEMONO

KAKI n Asian persimmon tree

KAKIEMON n type of 17th century Japanese porcelain

KAKIEMONS > KAKIEMON

KAKIS > KAKI

KAKIVAK n fish spear used by Inuit people

KAKIVAKS > KAKIVAK

KAKODYL variant spelling of > CACODYL

KAKODYLS > KAKODYL

KAKS > KAK

KAKURO n crossword-style puzzle with numbers

KAKUROS > KAKURO

KALAM n discussion and debate

KALAMANSI n hybrid citrus fruit from the Philippines

KALAMATA n as in kalamata olive aubergine-coloured Greek olive

KALAMATAS > KALAMATA

KALAMDAN n Persian box in which to keep pens

KALAMDANS > KALAMDAN

KALAMKARI n Indian cloth printing and printed Indian cloth

KALAMS > KALAM

KALANCHOE n tropical succulent plant having small brightly coloured flowers and dark shiny leaves

KALE n cabbage with crinkled leaves

KALENDAR variant form of > CALENDAR

KALENDARS > KALENDAR

KALENDS same as > CALENDS

KALES > KALE

KALEWIFE n Scots word for a female vegetable or cabbage seller

KALEWIVES > KALEWIFE

KALEYARD n vegetable garden

KALEYARDS > KALEYARD

KALI another name for > SALTWORT

KALIAN another name for > HOOKAH

KALIANS > KALIAN

KALIF variant spelling of > CALIPH

KALIFATE same as > CALIPHATE

KALIFATES > KALIFATE

KALIFS > KALIF

KALIMBA n musical instrument

KALIMBAS > KALIMBA

KALINITE n alum

KALINITES > KALINITE

KALIPH variant spelling of > CALIPH

KALIPHATE same as > CALIPHATE

KALIPHS > KALIPH

KALIS > KALI

KALIUM n Latin for potassium

KALIUMS > KALIUM

KALLIDIN n type of peptide

KALLIDINS > KALLIDIN

KALLITYPE n old printing process

KALMIA n evergreen ericaceous shrub

KALMIAS > KALMIA

KALONG n fruit bat

KALONGS > KALONG

KALOOKI n card game

KALOOKIE same as > KALOOKI

KALOOKIES > KALOOKIE

KALOOKIS > KALOOKI

KALOTYPE variant spelling of > CALOTYPE

KALOTYPES > KALOTYPE

KALPA n period in Hindu cosmology

KALPAC same as > CALPAC

KALPACS > KALPAC

KALPAK variant spelling of > CALPAC

KALPAKS > KALPAK

KALPAS > KALPA

KALPIS n Greek water jar

KALPISES > KALPIS

KALSOMINE variant of > CALCIMINE

KALUKI same as > KALOOKI

KALUKIS > KALUKI

KALUMPIT n type of Filipino fruit tree or its fruit

KALUMPITS > KALUMPIT

KALYPTRA n Greek veil

KALYPTRAS > KALYPTRA

KAM Shakespearean word for > CROOKED

KAMA n large African antelope with lyre-shaped horns

KAMAAINA n Hawaiian local

KAMAAINAS > KAMAAINA

KAMACITE n alloy of iron and nickel, occurring in meteorites

KAMACITES > KAMACITE

KAMAHI n hardwood tree

KAMAHIS > KAMAHI

KAMALA n East Indian tree

KAMALAS > KAMALA

KAMAS > KAMA

KAME n irregular mound of gravel, sand, etc

KAMEES same as > KAMEEZ

KAMEESES > KAMEES

KAMEEZ n long tunic

KAMEEZES > KAMEEZ

KAMELA same as > KAMALA

KAMELAS > KAMELA

KAMERAD interj shout of surrender ▷ vb surrender

KAMERADED > KAMERAD

KAMERADS > KAMERAD

KAMES > KAME

KAMI n divine being or spiritual force in Shinto

KAMICHI n South American bird

KAMICHIS > KAMICHI

KAMIK n traditional Inuit boot

KAMIKAZE n Japanese pilot who performed a suicide mission ▷ adj undertaken in the knowledge that it will kill the person performing it

KAMIKAZES > KAMIKAZE

KAMIKS > KAMIK

KAMILA same as > KAMALA

KAMILAS > KAMILA

KAMIS same as > KAMEEZ

KAMISES > KAMIS

KAMME same as > KAM

KAMOKAMO n kind of marrow found in New Zealand

KAMOKAMOS > KAMOKAMO

KAMOTIK n type of Inuit sledge

KAMOTIKS > KAMOTIK

KAMOTIQ same as > KAMOTIK

KAMOTIQS > KAMOTIQ

KAMPONG n (in Malaysia) village

KAMPONGS > KAMPONG

KAMSEEN same as > KHAMSIN

KAMSEENS > KAMSEEN

KAMSIN same as > KAMSEEN

KAMSINS > KAMSIN

KANA n Japanese syllabary

KANAE n grey mullet

KANAES > KANAE

KANAKA n Australian word for any native of the South Pacific

KANAKAS > KANAKA

KANAMYCIN n type of antibiotic

KANAS > KANA

KANBAN n just-in-time manufacturing process

KANBANS > KANBAN

KANDIES > KANDY

KANDY same as > CANDIE

KANE n Hawaiian man or boy

KANEH n 6-cubit Hebrew measure

KANEHS > KANEH

KANES > KANE

KANG n Chinese heatable platform

KANGA n piece of gaily decorated thin cotton cloth

KANGAROO n Australian marsupial ▷ vb (of a car) move forward with sudden jerks

KANGAROOS > KANGAROO

KANGAS > KANGA

KANGHA n comb traditionally worn by Sikhs

KANGHAS > KANGHA

KANGS > KANG

KANJI n Japanese writing system

KANJIS > KANJI

KANS n Indian wild sugar cane

KANSES > KANS

KANT archaic spelling of > CANT

KANTAR n unit of weight

KANTARS > KANTAR

KANTED > KANT

KANTELA same as > KANTELE

KANTELAS > KANTELA

KANTELE n Finnish stringed instrument

KANTELES > KANTELE

KANTEN same as > AGAR

KANTENS > KANTEN

KANTHA n Bengali embroidered quilt

KANTHAS > KANTHA

KANTIKOY vb dance ceremonially

KANTIKOYS > KANTIKOY

KANTING > KANT

KANTS > KANT

KANUKA n New Zealand myrtaceous tree

KANUKAS > KANUKA

KANZU n long garment

KANZUS > KANZU

KAOLIANG n any of various E Asian varieties of sorghum

KAOLIANGS > KAOLIANG

KAOLIN n fine white clay

KAOLINE same as > KAOLIN

KAOLINES > KAOLINE

KAOLINIC > KAOLIN

KAOLINISE same as > KAOLINIZE

KAOLINITE n white or grey clay mineral consisting of hydrated aluminium silicate in triclinic crystalline form, the main constituent of kaolin

KAOLINIZE vb change into kaolin

KAOLINS > KAOLIN

KAON n type of meson

KAONIC > KAON

KAONS > KAON

KAPA n Hawaiian cloth made from beaten mulberry bark

KAPAS > KAPA

KAPEEK > KAPEYKA

KAPEYKA n small currency unit of Belarus

KAPH n 11th letter of the Hebrew alphabet

KAPHS > KAPH

KAPOK n fluffy fibre

KAPOKS > KAPOK

KAPOW n sharp explosive sound

KAPOWS > KAPOW

KAPPA n tenth letter in the Greek alphabet

KAPPAS > KAPPA

KAPU n (in Hawaii) system of rules for daily life

KAPUKA same as > BROADLEAF

KAPUKAS > KAPUKA

KAPUS > KAPU

KAPUT adj ruined or broken

KAPUTT same as > KAPUT

KARA n steel bangle traditionally worn by Sikhs

KARABINER n metal clip with a spring for attaching to a piton, belay, etc

KARAHI n type of wok

KARAHIS > KARAHI

KARAISM n beliefs and doctrines of a Jewish sect

KARAISMS > KARAISM

KARAIT same as > KRAIT

KARAITS > KARAIT

KARAKA n New Zealand tree

KARAKAS > KARAKA

KARAKIA n prayer

k

KARAKIAS > KARAKIA
KARAKUL n sheep of central Asia
KARAKULS > KARAKUL
KARAMU n small New Zealand tree
KARAMUS > KARAMU
KARANGA n call or chant of welcome, sung by a female elder ▷ vb perform a karanga
KARANGAED > KARANGA
KARANGAS > KARANGA
KARAOKE n form of entertainment
KARAOKES > KARAOKE
KARAS > KARA
KARAT n measure of the proportion of gold in an alloy
KARATE n Japanese system of unarmed combat
KARATEIST same as > KARATEKA
KARATEKA n competitor or expert in karate
KARATEKAS > KARATEKA
KARATES > KARATE
KARATS > KARAT
KAREAREA n New Zealand falcon
KAREAREAS > KAREAREA
KARENGO n edible type of Pacific seaweed
KARENGOS > KARENGO
KARITE n shea tree
KARITES > KARITE
KARK variant spelling of > CARK
KARKED > KARK
KARKING > KARK
KARKS > KARK
KARMA n person's actions affecting his or her fate in the next reincarnation
KARMAS > KARMA
KARMIC > KARMA
KARN old word for > CAIRN
KARNS > KARN
KARO n small New Zealand tree or shrub
KAROO n high arid plateau
KAROOS > KAROO
KARORO n large seagull
KAROROS > KARORO
KAROS > KARO
KAROSHI n (in Japan) death caused by overwork
KAROSHIS > KAROSHI
KAROSS n type of blanket
KAROSSES > KAROSS
KARRI n Australian eucalypt
KARRIS > KARRI
KARROO same as > KAROO
KARROOS > KARROO
KARSEY variant spelling of > KHAZI
KARSEYS > KARSEY
KARSIES > KARSY
KARST n geological term
KARSTIC > KARST
KARSTIFY vb become karstic
KARSTS > KARST
KARSY variant spelling of > KHAZI
KART n light low-framed vehicle
KARTER > KART

KARTERS > KART
KARTING > KART
KARTINGS > KART
KARTS > KART
KARYOGAMY n fusion of two gametic nuclei during fertilization
KARYOGRAM n diagram or photograph of the chromosomes of a cell, arranged in homologous pairs and in a numbered sequence
KARYOLOGY n study of cell nuclei, esp with reference to the number and shape of the chromosomes
KARYON n nucleus of a cell
KARYONS > KARYON
KARYOSOME n any of the dense aggregates of chromatin in the nucleus of a cell
KARYOTIN less common word for > CHROMATIN
KARYOTINS > KARYOTIN
KARYOTYPE n appearance of the chromosomes in a somatic cell of an individual or species, with reference to their number, size, shape, etc ▷ vb determine the karyotype of (a cell)
KARZIES > KARZY
KARZY variant spelling of > KHAZI
KAS > KA
KASBAH n citadel of any of various North African cities
KASBAHS > KASBAH
KASHA n dish originating in Eastern Europe
KASHAS > KASHA
KASHER vb make fit for use
KASHERED > KASHER
KASHERING > KASHER
KASHERS > KASHER
KASHMIR variant spelling of > CASHMERE
KASHMIRS > KASHMIR
KASHRUS same as > KASHRUTH
KASHRUSES > KASHRUS
KASHRUT same as > KASHRUTH
KASHRUTH n condition of being fit for ritual use in general
KASHRUTHS > KASHRUTH
KASHRUTS > KASHRUT
KASME interj (in Indian English) I swear
KAT same as > KHAT
KATA n form of exercise
KATABASES > KATABASIS
KATABASIS n retreat of the Greek mercenaries of Cyrus the Younger, after his death at Cunaxa, from the Euphrates to the Black Sea in 401–400 BC under the leadership of Xenophon
KATABATIC adj (of winds) blowing downhill through having become denser with cooling, esp at night when heat is lost from the earth's surface

KATABOLIC same as > CATABOLIC
KATAKANA n system of Japanese syllabic writing
KATAKANAS > KATAKANA
KATAL n SI unit of catalytic activity
KATALS > KATAL
KATANA n Japanese samurai sword
KATANAS > KATANA
KATAS > KATA
KATCHINA variant spelling of > KACHINA
KATCHINAS > KATCHINA
KATCINA variant spelling of > KACHINA
KATCINAS > KATCINA
KATHAK n form of dancing
KATHAKALI n form of dance drama of S India using mime and based on Hindu literature
KATHAKS > KATHAK
KATHARSES > KATHARSIS
KATHARSIS variant spelling of > CATHARSIS
KATHODAL > KATHODE
KATHODE variant spelling of > CATHODE
KATHODES > KATHODE
KATHODIC > KATHODE
KATHUMP n sound of a dull heavy blow
KATHUMPS > KATHUMP
KATI variant spelling of > CATTY
KATION variant spelling of > CATION
KATIONS > KATION
KATIPO n small poisonous New Zealand spider
KATIPOS > KATIPO
KATIS > KATI
KATORGA n type of labour camp
KATORGAS > KATORGA
KATS > KAT
KATSINA n (among the Hopi) doll representing spirit messengers
KATSINAM > KATSINA
KATSINAS > KATSINA
KATSURA n Asian tree
KATSURAS > KATSURA
KATTI variant spelling of > CATTY
KATTIS > KATTI
KATYDID n large green grasshopper of N America
KATYDIDS > KATYDID
KAUGH same as > KIAUGH
KAUGHS > KAUGH
KAUMATUA n senior member of a tribe
KAUMATUAS > KAUMATUA
KAUPAPA n strategy, policy, or cause
KAUPAPAS > KAUPAPA
KAURI n large NZ conifer
KAURIES > KAURY
KAURIS > KAURI
KAURU n edible stem of the cabbage tree
KAURUS > KAURU
KAURY variant spelling of > KAURI

KAVA n Polynesian shrub
KAVAKAVA same as > KAVA
KAVAKAVAS > KAVAKAVA
KAVAL n type of flute played in the Balkans
KAVALS > KAVAL
KAVAS > KAVA
KAVASS n armed Turkish constable
KAVASSES > KAVASS
KAW variant spelling of > CAW
KAWA n protocol or etiquette
KAWAII n (in Japan) quality of being lovable or cute
KAWAIIS > KAWAII
KAWAKAWA n aromatic shrub or small tree of New Zealand
KAWAKAWAS > KAWAKAWA
KAWAS > KAWA
KAWAU n New Zealand name for black shag
KAWAUS > KAWAU
KAWED > KAW
KAWING > KAW
KAWS > KAW
KAY n name of the letter K
KAYAK n Inuit canoe ▷ vb travel by kayak
KAYAKED > KAYAK
KAYAKER > KAYAK
KAYAKERS > KAYAK
KAYAKING > KAYAK
KAYAKINGS > KAYAK
KAYAKS > KAYAK
KAYLE n one of a set of ninepins
KAYLES pl n ninepins
KAYLIED adj intoxicated or drunk
KAYO another term for > KNOCKOUT
KAYOED > KAYO
KAYOES > KAYO
KAYOING > KAYO
KAYOINGS > KAYO
KAYOS > KAYO
KAYS > KAY
KAZACHKI same as > KAZACHOK
KAZACHOC n Ukrainian folk dance
KAZACHOCS > KAZACHOC
KAZACHOK n Russian folk dance
KAZACHOKS > KAZACHOK
KAZATSKI same as > KAZACHOK
KAZATSKY same as > KAZACHOK
KAZATZKA same as > KAZACHOK
KAZATZKAS > KAZACHOK
KAZI variant spelling of > KHAZI
KAZILLION same as > GAZILLION
KAZIS > KAZI
KAZOO n musical instrument
KAZOOS > KAZOO
KBAR n kilobar
KBARS > KBAR
KEA n large brownish-green parrot of NZ
KEAS > KEA
KEASAR archaic variant of > KAISER
KEASARS > KEASAR

KEAVIE n archaic or dialect word for a type of crab

KEAVIES > KEAVIE

KEB vb Scots word meaning miscarry or reject a lamb

KEBAB n food grilled on a skewer ▷ vb skewer

KEBABBED > KEBAB

KEBABBING > KEBAB

KEBABS > KEBAB

KEBAR n Scots word for beam or rafter

KEBARS > KEBAR

KEBBED > KEB

KEBBIE n Scots word for shepherd's crook

KEBBIES > KEBBIE

KEBBING > KEB

KEBBOCK n Scots word for a cheese

KEBBOCKS > KEBBOCK

KEBBUCK same as > KEBBOCK

KEBBUCKS > KEBBUCK

KEBELE n Ethiopian local council

KEBELES > KEBELE

KEBLAH same as > KIBLAH

KEBLAHS > KEBLAH

KEBOB same as > KEBAB

KEBOBBED > KEBOB

KEBOBBING > KEBOB

KEBOBS > KEBOB

KEBS > KEB

KECK vb retch or feel nausea

KECKED > KECK

KECKING > KECK

KECKLE Scots variant of > CACKLE

KECKLED > KECKLE

KECKLES > KECKLE

KECKLING > KECKLE

KECKLINGS > KECKLE

KECKS pl n trousers

KECKSES > KECKS

KECKSIES > KECKSY

KECKSY n dialect word meaning hollow plant stalk

KED n as in sheep ked sheep tick

KEDDAH same as > KHEDA

KEDDAHS > KEDDAH

KEDGE vb move (a ship) using cable attached to an anchor ▷ n light anchor used for kedging

KEDGED > KEDGE

KEDGER n small anchor

KEDGEREE n dish of fish with rice and eggs

KEDGEREES > KEDGEREE

KEDGERS > KEDGER

KEDGES > KEDGE

KEDGIER > KEDGY

KEDGIEST > KEDGY

KEDGING > KEDGE

KEDGY adj dialect word for happy or lively

KEDS > KED

KEECH n old word for lump of fat

KEECHES > KEECH

KEEF same as > KIF

KEEFS > KEEF

KEEK Scot word for > PEEP

KEEKED > KEEK

KEEKER > KEEK

KEEKERS > KEEK

KEEKING > KEEK

KEEKS > KEEK

KEEL n part of a ship ▷ vb mark with a stain

KEELAGE n fee charged by certain ports

KEELAGES > KEELAGE

KEELBOAT n river boat with a shallow draught and a keel

KEELBOATS > KEELBOAT

KEELED > KEEL

KEELER n bargeman

KEELERS > KEELER

KEELHALE same as > KEELHAUL

KEELHALED > KEELHALE

KEELHALES > KEELHALE

KEELHAUL vb reprimand (someone) harshly

KEELHAULS > KEELHAUL

KEELIE n kestrel

KEELIES > KEELIE

KEELING > KEEL

KEELINGS > KEEL

KEELIVINE Scots word for > PENCIL

KEELLESS > KEEL

KEELMAN n bargeman

KEELMEN > KEELMAN

KEELS > KEEL

KEELSON n part of a ship

KEELSONS > KEELSON

KEELYVINE same as > KEELIVINE

KEEMA n (in Indian cookery) minced meat

KEEMAS > KEEMA

KEEN adj eager or enthusiastic ▷ vb wail over the dead ▷ n lament for the dead

KEENED > KEEN

KEENER > KEEN

KEENERS > KEEN

KEENEST > KEEN

KEENING > KEEN

KEENINGS > KEEN

KEENLY > KEEN

KEENNESS > KEEN

KEENO same as > KENO

KEENOS > KEENO

KEENS > KEEN

KEEP vb have or retain possession of ▷ n cost of food and everyday expenses

KEEPABLE > KEEP

KEEPER n person who looks after animals in a zoo

KEEPERS > KEEPER

KEEPING > KEEP

KEEPINGS > KEEP

KEEPNET n cylindrical net used to keep fish alive

KEEPNETS > KEEPNET

KEEPS > KEEP

KEEPSAKE n gift treasured for the sake of the giver

KEEPSAKES > KEEPSAKE

KEEPSAKY adj superficially attractive

KEESHOND n breed of dog of the spitz type

KEESHONDS > KEESHOND

KEESTER same as > KEISTER

KEESTERS > KEESTER

KEET short for > PARAKEET

KEETS > KEET

KEEVE n tub or vat

KEEVES > KEEVE

KEF same as > KIF

KEFFEL dialect word for > HORSE

KEFFELS > KEFFEL

KEFFIYAH same as > KAFFIYEH

KEFFIYAHS > KEFFIYAH

KEFFIYEH n cotton headdress worn by Arabs

KEFFIYEHS > KEFFIYEH

KEFIR n effervescent drink

KEFIRS > KEFIR

KEFS > KEF

KEFTEDES n Greek dish of meatballs cooked with herbs and onions

KEFUFFLE same as > KERFUFFLE

KEFUFFLED > KEFUFFLE

KEFUFFLES > KEFUFFLE

KEG n small metal beer barrel ▷ vb put in kegs

KEGELER same as > KEGLER

KEGELERS > KEGELER

KEGGED > KEG

KEGGER > KEG

KEGGERS > KEG

KEGGING > KEG

KEGLER n participant in a game of tenpin bowling

KEGLERS > KEGLER

KEGLING n bowling

KEGLINGS > KEGLING

KEGS > KEG

KEHUA n ghost or spirit

KEHUAS > KEHUA

KEIGHT > KETCH

KEIR same as > KIER

KEIREN n type of track cycling event

KEIRENS > KEIREN

KEIRETSU n group of Japanese businesses

KEIRETSUS > KEIRETSU

KEIRIN n cycling race originating in Japan

KEIRINS > KEIRIN

KEIRS > KEIR

KEISTER n rump

KEISTERS > KEISTER

KEITLOA n type of rhinoceros

KEITLOAS > KEITLOA

KEKENO n New Zealand fur seal

KEKENOS > KEKENO

KEKERENGU n Māori bug

KEKS same as > KECKS

KEKSYE same as > KEX

KEKSYES > KEKSYE

KELEP n large ant found in Central and South America

KELEPS > KELEP

KELIM same as > KILIM

KELIMS > KELIM

KELL dialect word for > HAIRNET

KELLAUT same as > KHILAT

KELLAUTS > KELLAUT

KELLIES > KELLY

KELLS > KELL

KELLY n part of a drill system

KELOID n type of scar tissue

KELOIDAL > KELOID

KELOIDS > KELOID

KELP n large brown seaweed ▷ vb burn seaweed to make a type of ash

KELPED > KELP

KELPER n Falkland Islander

KELPERS > KELPER

KELPFISH n type of fish that lives among kelp

KELPIE n Australian sheepdog

KELPIES > KELPIE

KELPING > KELP

KELPS > KELP

KELPY same as > KELPIE

KELSON same as > KEELSON

KELSONS > KELSON

KELT n salmon that has recently spawned

KELTER same as > KILTER

KELTERS > KELTER

KELTIE variant spelling of > KELTY

KELTIES > KELTY

KELTS > KELT

KELTY n old Scots word for a drink imposed on someone not thought to be drinking enough

KELVIN n SI unit of temperature

KELVINS > KELVIN

KEMB old word for > COMB

KEMBED > KEMB

KEMBING > KEMB

KEMBLA n small change

KEMBLAS > KEMBLA

KEMBO same as > KIMBO

KEMBOED > KEMBO

KEMBOING > KEMBO

KEMBOS > KEMBO

KEMBS > KEMB

KEMP n coarse hair or strand of hair ▷ vb dialect word meaning to compete or try to come first

KEMPED > KEMP

KEMPER > KEMP

KEMPERS > KEMP

KEMPIER > KEMPY

KEMPIEST > KEMPY

KEMPING > KEMP

KEMPINGS > KEMP

KEMPLE n variable Scottish measure for hay or straw

KEMPLES > KEMPLE

KEMPS > KEMP

KEMPT adj (of hair) tidy

KEMPY > KEMP

KEN vb know ▷ n range of knowledge or perception

KENAF another name for > AMBARY

KENAFS > KENAF

KENCH n bin for salting and preserving fish

KENCHES > KENCH

KENDO n Japanese sport of fencing using wooden staves

KENDOIST n person who practises kendo

KENDOISTS > KENDOIST

KENDOS > KENDO

KENNED > KEN

k

KENNEL n hutlike shelter for a dog ▷ vb put or go into a kennel
KENNELED > KENNEL
KENNELING > KENNEL
KENNELLED > KENNEL
KENNELMAN n man who works in a kennels
KENNELMEN > KENNELMAN
KENNELS > KENNEL
KENNER > KEN
KENNERS > KEN
KENNET n old word for a small hunting dog
KENNETS > KENNET
KENNETT vb spoil or destroy ruthlessly
KENNETTED > KENNETT
KENNETTS > KENNETT
KENNING > KEN
KENNINGS > KEN
KENO n game of chance similar to bingo
KENOS > KENO
KENOSES > KENOSIS
KENOSIS n Christ's renunciation of certain divine attributes
KENOSISES > KENOSIS
KENOTIC > KENOSIS
KENOTICS > KENOSIS
KENOTRON n signal-amplifying device
KENOTRONS > KENOTRON
KENS > KEN
KENSPECK adj Scots for easily seen or recognized
KENT dialect word for > PUNT
KENTE n brightly coloured handwoven cloth
KENTED > KENT
KENTES > KENTE
KENTIA n plant name
KENTIAS > KENTIA
KENTING > KENT
KENTLEDGE n scrap metal used as ballast in a vessel
KENTS > KENT
KEP vb catch
KEPHALIC variant spelling of > CEPHALIC
KEPHALICS > KEPHALIC
KEPHALIN same as > CEPHALIN
KEPHALINS > KEPHALIN
KEPHIR same as > KEFIR
KEPHIRS > KEPHIR
KEPI n French military cap with a flat top and a horizontal peak
KEPIS > KEPI
KEPPED > KEP
KEPPEN > KEP
KEPPING > KEP
KEPPIT > KEP
KEPS > KEP
KEPT > KEEP
KERAMIC rare variant of > CERAMIC
KERAMICS rare variant of > CERAMICS
KERATIN n fibrous protein found in the hair and nails
KERATINS > KERATIN
KERATITIS n inflammation of the cornea

KERATOID adj resembling horn
KERATOMA n horny growth on the skin
KERATOMAS > KERATOMA
KERATOSE adj (esp of certain sponges) having a horny skeleton
KERATOSES > KERATOSIS
KERATOSIC > KERATOSE
KERATOSIS n any skin condition marked by a horny growth, such as a wart
KERATOTIC > KERATOSIS
KERB n edging to a footpath ▷ vb provide with or enclose with a kerb
KERBAYA n blouse worn by Malay women
KERBAYAS > KERBAYA
KERBED > KERB
KERBING n material used for a kerb
KERBINGS > KERBING
KERBLOOEY n sound of an explosion
KERBS > KERB
KERBSIDE n edge of a pavement where it drops to the level of the road
KERBSIDES > KERBSIDE
KERBSTONE n one of a series of stones that form a kerb
KERCHIEF n piece of cloth worn over the head or round the neck
KERCHIEFS > KERCHIEF
KERCHOO interj atishoo
KEREL n chap or fellow
KERELS > KEREL
KERERU n New Zealand pigeon
KERERUS > KERERU
KERF n cut made by a saw, an axe, etc ▷ vb cut
KERFED > KERF
KERFING > KERF
KERFLOOEY adv into state of destruction or malfunction
KERFS > KERF
KERFUFFLE n commotion or disorder ▷ vb put into disorder or disarray
KERKIER > KERKY
KERKIEST > KERKY
KERKY adj stupid
KERMA n quantity of radiation
KERMAS > KERMA
KERMES n dried bodies of female scale insects
KERMESES > KERMES
KERMESITE n red antimony
KERMESS same as > KERMIS
KERMESSE same as > KERMIS
KERMESSES > KERMESSE
KERMIS n (formerly) annual country festival or carnival
KERMISES > KERMIS
KERMODE n type of black bear found in Canada
KERMODES > KERMODE
KERN n projection of a printed character ▷ vb

furnish (a typeface) with a kern
KERNE same as > KERN
KERNED > KERNE
KERNEL n seed of a nut, cereal, or fruit stone ▷ vb form kernels
KERNELED > KERNEL
KERNELING > KERNEL
KERNELLED > KERNEL
KERNELLY adj with or like kernels
KERNELS > KERNEL
KERNES > KERNE
KERNING n provision of kerns in printing
KERNINGS > KERNING
KERNISH adj resembling an armed foot soldier or peasant
KERNITE n light soft colourless or white mineral
KERNITES > KERNITE
KERNS > KERN
KERO short for > KEROSENE
KEROGEN n material that produces hydrocarbons when heated
KEROGENS > KEROGEN
KEROS > KERO
KEROSENE n liquid mixture distilled from petroleum and used as a fuel or solvent
KEROSENES > KEROSENE
KEROSINE same as > KEROSENE
KEROSINES > KEROSINE
KERPLUNK vb land noisily
KERPLUNKS > KERPLUNK
KERRIA n type of shrub with yellow flowers
KERRIAS > KERRIA
KERRIES > KERRY
KERRY n breed of dairy cattle
KERSEY n smooth woollen cloth
KERSEYS > KERSEY
KERVE dialect word for > CARVE
KERVED > KERVE
KERVES > KERVE
KERVING > KERVE
KERYGMA n Christian gospel
KERYGMAS > KERYGMA
KERYGMATA > KERYGMA
KESAR old variant of > KAISER
KESARS > KESAR
KESH n beard and uncut hair traditionally worn by Sikhs
KESHES > KESH
KEST old form of > CAST
KESTING > KEST
KESTREL n type of small falcon
KESTRELS > KESTREL
KESTS > KEST
KET n dialect word for carrion
KETA n type of salmon
KETAINE adj in poor taste
KETAMINE n drug used in medicine as an anaesthetic
KETAMINES > KETAMINE
KETAS > KETA
KETCH n two-masted sailing vessel ▷ vb (in archaic usage) catch

KETCHES > KETCH
KETCHING > KETCH
KETCHUP n thick cold sauce, usu made of tomatoes
KETCHUPS > KETCHUP
KETCHUPY adj like ketchup
KETE n basket woven from flax
KETENE n colourless irritating toxic gas
KETENES > KETENE
KETES > KETE
KETMIA n as in bladder ketmia plant with pale yellow flowers
KETMIAS > KETMIA
KETO adj as in keto form form of tautomeric compounds
KETOGENIC adj forming or able to stimulate the production of ketone bodies
KETOL n nitrogenous substance
KETOLS > KETOL
KETONE n type of organic solvent
KETONEMIA n excess of ketone bodies in the blood
KETONES > KETONE
KETONIC > KETONE
KETONURIA n presence of ketone bodies in the urine
KETOSE n any monosaccharide that contains a ketone group
KETOSES > KETOSIS
KETOSIS n high concentration of ketone bodies in the blood
KETOTIC > KETOSIS
KETOXIME n oxime formed by reaction between hydroxylamine and a ketone
KETOXIMES > KETOXIME
KETS > KET
KETTLE n container used for boiling water ▷ vb contain a public protest in an enclosed space
KETTLED > KETTLE
KETTLEFUL > KETTLE
KETTLES > KETTLE
KETTLING > KETTLE
KETUBAH n Jewish marriage contract
KETUBAHS > KETUBAH
KETUBOT > KETUBAH
KETUBOTH > KETUBAH
KEVEL n strong bitt or bollard for securing heavy hawsers
KEVELS > KEVEL
KEVIL old variant of > KEVEL
KEVILS > KEVIL
KEWL nonstandard variant spelling of > COOL
KEWLER > KEWL
KEWLEST > KEWL
KEWPIE n type of brightly coloured doll
KEWPIES > KEWPIE
KEX n any of several hollow-stemmed umbelliferous plants
KEXES > KEX
KEY n device for operating a lock by moving a bolt ▷ adj of

great importance ▷ *vb* enter (text) using a keyboard

KEYBOARD *n* set of keys on a piano, computer, etc ▷ *vb* enter (text) using a keyboard

KEYBOARDS > KEYBOARD

KEYBUGLE *n* bugle with keys

KEYBUGLES > KEYBUGLE

KEYBUTTON *n* on a keyboard, an object which, when pressed, causes the letter, number, or symbol shown on it to be printed in a document

KEYCARD *n* electronic card used as a key

KEYCARDS > KEYCARD

KEYED > KEY

KEYER *n* device that keys signals or information into a device or computing system

KEYERS > KEYER

KEYEST > KEY

KEYFRAME *n* image used to show the start and end of animation sequence

KEYFRAMES > KEYFRAME

KEYHOLE *n* opening for inserting a key into a lock

KEYHOLES > KEYHOLE

KEYING > KEY

KEYINGS > KEY

KEYLESS > KEY

KEYLINE *n* outline image on artwork or plans to show where it is to be placed

KEYLINES > KEYLINE

KEYLOGGER *n* device or software application used for covertly recording and monitoring keystrokes made on a remote computer

KEYNOTE *adj* central or dominating ▷ *n* dominant idea of a speech etc ▷ *vb* deliver a keynote address to (a political convention, etc)

KEYNOTED > KEYNOTE

KEYNOTER *n* person delivering a keynote address

KEYNOTERS > KEYNOTER

KEYNOTES > KEYNOTE

KEYNOTING > KEYNOTE

KEYPAD *n* small panel with a set of buttons

KEYPADS > KEYPAD

KEYPAL *n* person one regularly exchanges emails with for fun

KEYPALS > KEYPAL

KEYPRESS *n* single depression of a keyboard key

KEYPUNCH *n* keyboard device to transfer data onto punched cards ▷ *vb* transfer (data) onto punched cards

KEYRING *n* metal ring for keeping keys together

KEYRINGS > KEYRING

KEYS *interj* children's cry for truce

KEYSET *n* set of computer keys used for a particular purpose

KEYSETS > KEYSET

KEYSTER *same as* > KEISTER

KEYSTERS > KEYSTER

KEYSTONE *n* most important part of a process, organization, etc ▷ *vb* project or provide with a distorted image

KEYSTONED > KEYSTONE

KEYSTONES > KEYSTONE

KEYSTROKE *n* single operation of the mechanism of a typewriter or keyboard-operated typesetting machine by the action of a key ▷ *vb* enter or cause to be recorded by pressing a key

KEYWAY *n* engineering device

KEYWAYS > KEYWAY

KEYWORD *n* word or phrase used to find something on a computer

KEYWORDS > KEYWORD

KEYWORKER *n* public sector worker regarded as providing an essential service

KGOTLA *n* (in South African English) meeting place

KGOTLAS > KGOTLA

KHADDAR *n* cotton cloth

KHADDARS > KHADDAR

KHADI *same as* > KHADDAR

KHADIS > KHADI

KHAF *n* letter of the Hebrew alphabet

KHAFS > KHAF

KHAKI *adj* dull yellowish-brown ▷ *n* fabric of this colour used for military uniforms

KHAKILIKE > KHAKI

KHAKIS > KHAKI

KHALAT *same as* > KHILAT

KHALATS > KHALAT

KHALIF *variant spelling of* > CALIPH

KHALIFA *same as* > CALIPH

KHALIFAH *same as* > CALIPH

KHALIFAHS > KHALIFAH

KHALIFAS > KHALIFA

KHALIFAT *same as* > CALIPHATE

KHALIFATE *same as* > CALIPHATE

KHALIFATS > KHALIFAT

KHALIFS > KHALIF

KHAMSEEN *same as* > KHAMSIN

KHAMSEENS > KHAMSEEN

KHAMSIN *n* hot southerly wind

KHAMSINS > KHAMSIN

KHAN *n* title of respect in Afghanistan and central Asia

KHANATE *n* territory ruled by a khan

KHANATES > KHANATE

KHANDA *n* double-edged sword

KHANDAS > KHANDA

KHANGA *same as* > KANGA

KHANGAS > KHANGA

KHANJAR *n* type of dagger

KHANJARS > KHANJAR

KHANS > KHAN

KHANSAMA *same as* > KHANSAMAH

KHANSAMAH *n* Indian cook or other male servant

KHANSAMAS > KHANSAMA

KHANUM *feminine form of* > KHAN

KHANUMS > KHANUM

KHAPH *n* letter of the Hebrew alphabet

KHAPHS > KHAPH

KHARIF *n* crop harvested at the beginning of winter

KHARIFS > KHARIF

KHAT *n* white-flowered evergreen shrub

KHATS > KHAT

KHAYA *n* type of African tree

KHAYAL *n* kind of Indian classical vocal music

KHAYALS > KHAYAL

KHAYAS > KHAYA

KHAZEN *same as* > CHAZAN

KHAZENIM > KHAZEN

KHAZENS > KHAZEN

KHAZI *n* lavatory

KHAZIS > KHAZI

KHEDA *n* enclosure used to capture wild elephants

KHEDAH *same as* > KHEDA

KHEDAHS > KHEDAH

KHEDAS > KHEDA

KHEDIVA *n* khedive's wife

KHEDIVAL > KHEDIVE

KHEDIVAS > KHEDIVA

KHEDIVATE > KHEDIVE

KHEDIVE *n* viceroy of Egypt under Ottoman suzerainty

KHEDIVES > KHEDIVE

KHEDIVIAL > KHEDIVE

KHET *n* Thai district

KHETH *same as* > HETH

KHETHS > KHETH

KHETS > KHET

KHI *n* letter of the Greek alphabet

KHILAFAT *same as* > CALIPHATE

KHILAFATS > KHILAFAT

KHILAT *n* (in the Middle East) gift given to someone as a mark of honour

KHILATS > KHILAT

KHILIM *same as* > KILIM

KHILIMS > KHILIM

KHIMAR *n* type of headscarf worn by Muslim women

KHIMARS > KHIMAR

KHIRKAH *n* dervish's woollen or cotton outer garment

KHIRKAHS > KHIRKAH

KHIS > KHI

KHODJA *same as* > KHOJA

KHODJAS > KHODJA

KHOJA *n* teacher in a Muslim school

KHOJAS > KHOJA

KHOR *n* watercourse

KHORS > KHOR

KHOTBAH *same as* > KHUTBAH

KHOTBAHS > KHOTBAH

KHOTBEH *same as* > KHUTBAH

KHOTBEHS > KHOTBEH

KHOUM *n* Mauritanian monetary unit

KHOUMS > KHOUM

KHUD *n* Indian ravine

KHUDS > KHUD

KHURTA *same as* > KURTA

KHURTAS > KHURTA

KHUSKHUS *n* aromatic perennial Indian grass whose roots are woven into mats, fans, and baskets

KHUTBAH *n* sermon in a Mosque, especially on a Friday

KHUTBAHS > KHUTBAH

KI *n* vital energy

KIAAT *n* tropical African leguminous tree

KIAATS > KIAAT

KIACK *n* N American fish of the herring family

KIACKS > KIACK

KIANG *n* variety of wild ass

KIANGS > KIANG

KIAUGH *n* (in Scots) anxiety

KIAUGHS > KIAUGH

KIBBE *n* Middle Eastern dish

KIBBEH *same as* > KIBBE

KIBBEHS > KIBBEH

KIBBES > KIBBE

KIBBI *same as* > KIBBE

KIBBIS > KIBBI

KIBBITZ *same as* > KIBITZ

KIBBITZED > KIBBITZ

KIBBITZER > KIBBITZ

KIBBITZES > KIBBITZ

KIBBLE *n* bucket used in wells or in mining for hoisting ▷ *vb* grind into small pieces

KIBBLED > KIBBLE

KIBBLES > KIBBLE

KIBBLING > KIBBLE

KIBBUTZ *n* communal farm or factory in Israel

KIBBUTZIM > KIBBUTZ

KIBE *n* chilblain

KIBEI *n* someone of Japanese ancestry born in the US and educated in Japan

KIBEIS > KIBEI

KIBES > KIBE

KIBIBYTE *n* two to the power of ten bytes

KIBIBYTES > KIBIBYTE

KIBITKA *n* (in Russia) covered sledge or wagon

KIBITKAS > KIBITKA

KIBITZ *vb* interfere or offer unwanted advice

KIBITZED > KIBITZ

KIBITZER > KIBITZ

KIBITZERS > KIBITZ

KIBITZES > KIBITZ

KIBITZING > KIBITZ

KIBLA *same as* > KIBLAH

KIBLAH *n* direction of Mecca

KIBLAHS > KIBLAH

KIBLAS > KIBLA

KIBOSH *vb* put a stop to

KIBOSHED > KIBOSH

KIBOSHES > KIBOSH

KIBOSHING > KIBOSH

KICK *vb* drive, push, or strike with the foot ▷ *n* thrust or blow with the foot

KICKABLE > KICK

k

k

KICKABOUT n informal game of soccer
KICKBACK n money paid illegally for favours done ▷ vb have a strong reaction
KICKBACKS > KICKBACK
KICKBALL n children's ball game or the large ball used in it
KICKBALLS > KICKBALL
KICKBOARD n type of float held on to by a swimmer when practising leg strokes
KICKBOX vb box with hands and feet
KICKBOXED > KICKBOX
KICKBOXER n someone who practises kickboxing, a martial art that resembles boxing but in which kicks are permitted
KICKBOXES > KICKBOX
KICKDOWN n method of changing gear in a car with automatic transmission
KICKDOWNS > KICKDOWN
KICKED > KICK
KICKER n person or thing that kicks
KICKERS > KICKER
KICKFLIP n type of skateboarding manoeuvre ▷ vb perform a kickflip in skateboarding
KICKFLIPS > KICKFLIP
KICKIER > KICKY
KICKIEST > KICKY
KICKING n act of kicking
KICKINGS > KICKING
KICKOFF n kick that starts a game of football
KICKOFFS > KICKOFF
KICKOUT n (in basketball) instance of kicking the ball
KICKOUTS > KICKOUT
KICKPLATE n metal plate at the base of a door
KICKS > KICK
KICKSHAW n valueless trinket
KICKSHAWS same as > KICKSHAW
KICKSTAND n short metal bar on a motorcycle, which when kicked into a vertical position holds the cycle upright when stationary
KICKSTART vb start by kicking pedal
KICKUP n fuss
KICKUPS > KICKUP
KICKY adj excitingly unusual and different
KID n child ▷ vb tease or deceive (someone) ▷ adj younger
KIDDED > KID
KIDDER > KID
KIDDERS > KID
KIDDIE same as > KIDDY
KIDDIED > KIDDY
KIDDIER n old word for a market trader
KIDDIERS > KIDDIER
KIDDIES > KIDDY
KIDDING n act of kidding
KIDDINGLY > KID
KIDDINGS > KIDDING

KIDDISH > KID
KIDDLE n device for catching fish in a river or in the sea
KIDDLES > KIDDLE
KIDDO n very informal term of address for a young person
KIDDOES > KIDDO
KIDDOS > KIDDO
KIDDUSH n (in Judaism) special blessing
KIDDUSHES > KIDDUSH
KIDDY n affectionate word for a child ▷ vb tease or deceive
KIDDYING > KIDDY
KIDDYWINK n humorous word for a child
KIDEL same as > KIDDLE
KIDELS > KIDEL
KIDGE dialect word for > LIVELY
KIDGIE adj dialect word for friendly and welcoming
KIDGIER > KIDGIE
KIDGIEST > KIDGIE
KIDGLOVE adj overdelicate or overrefined
KIDLET n humorous word for small child
KIDLETS > KIDLET
KIDLIKE > KID
KIDLING n young kid
KIDLINGS > KIDLING
KIDLIT n children's literature
KIDLITS > KIDLIT
KIDNAP vb seize and hold (a person) to ransom
KIDNAPED > KIDNAP
KIDNAPEE > KIDNAP
KIDNAPEES > KIDNAP
KIDNAPER > KIDNAP
KIDNAPERS > KIDNAP
KIDNAPING > KIDNAP
KIDNAPPED > KIDNAP
KIDNAPPEE > KIDNAP
KIDNAPPER > KIDNAP
KIDNAPS > KIDNAP
KIDNEY n either of the pair of organs that produce urine
KIDNEYS > KIDNEY
KIDOLOGY n practice of bluffing or deception
KIDS > KID
KIDSKIN n soft smooth leather
KIDSKINS > KIDSKIN
KIDSTAKES pl n pretence
KIDULT n adult interested in entertainments intended for children ▷ adj aimed at or suitable for kidults, or both children and adults
KIDULTS > KIDULT
KIDVID n informal word for children's video or television
KIDVIDS > KIDVID
KIEF same as > KIF
KIEFS > KIEF
KIEKIE n climbing bush plant of New Zealand
KIEKIES > KIEKIE
KIELBASA n Polish sausage
KIELBASAS > KIELBASA
KIELBASI same as > KIELBASA

KIELBASY same as > KIELBASA
KIER n vat in which cloth is bleached
KIERIE n South African cudgel
KIERIES > KIERIE
KIERS > KIER
KIESELGUR n type of mineral
KIESERITE n white mineral consisting of hydrated magnesium sulphate
KIESTER same as > KEISTER
KIESTERS > KIESTER
KIEV n type of chicken dish
KIEVE same as > KEEVE
KIEVES > KIEVE
KIEVS > KIEV
KIF n marijuana
KIFF adj South African slang for excellent
KIFS > KIF
KIGHT n archaic spelling of kite, the bird of prey
KIGHTS > KIGHT
KIKE n offensive word for a Jewish person
KIKES > KIKE
KIKOI n piece of cotton cloth
KIKOIS > KIKOI
KIKUMON n emblem of the imperial family of Japan
KIKUMONS > KIKUMON
KIKUYU n type of grass
KIKUYUS > KIKUYU
KILD old spelling of > KILLED
KILDERKIN n obsolete unit of capacity
KILERG n 1000 ergs
KILERGS > KILERG
KILEY same as > KYLIE
KILEYS > KILEY
KILIKITI n Polynesian version of cricket
KILIKITIS > KILIKITI
KILIM n pileless woven rug
KILIMS > KILIM
KILL vb cause the death of ▷ n act of killing
KILLABLE > KILL
KILLADAR n fort commander or governor
KILLADARS > KILLADAR
KILLAS n Cornish clay slate
KILLASES > KILLAS
KILLCOW n important person
KILLCOWS > KILLCOW
KILLCROP n ever-hungry baby, thought to be a fairy changeling
KILLCROPS > KILLCROP
KILLDEE same as > KILLDEER
KILLDEER n large brown-and-white North American plover with a noisy cry
KILLDEERS > KILLDEER
KILLDEES > KILLDEE
KILLED > KILL
KILLER n person or animal that kills, esp habitually

KILLERS > KILLER
KILLICK n small anchor, esp one made of a heavy stone
KILLICKS > KILLICK
KILLIE same as > KILLIFISH
KILLIES > KILLIE
KILLIFISH n any of various chiefly American minnow-like fishes
KILLING adj very tiring ▷ n sudden financial success
KILLINGLY > KILLING
KILLINGS > KILLING
KILLJOY n person who spoils others' pleasure
KILLJOYS > KILLJOY
KILLOCK same as > KILLICK
KILLOCKS > KILLOCK
KILLOGIE n sheltered place in front of a kiln
KILLOGIES > KILLOGIE
KILLS > KILL
KILLUT same as > KHILAT
KILLUTS > KILLUT
KILN n type of oven ▷ vb fire or process in a kiln
KILNED > KILN
KILNING > KILN
KILNS > KILN
KILO n code word for the letter k
KILOBAR n 1000 bars
KILOBARS > KILOBAR
KILOBASE n unit of measurement for DNA and RNA equal to 1000 base pairs
KILOBASES > KILOBASE
KILOBAUD n 1000 baud
KILOBAUDS > KILOBAUD
KILOBIT n 1024 bits
KILOBITS > KILOBIT
KILOBYTE n 1024 units of information
KILOBYTES > KILOBYTE
KILOCURIE n unit of thousand curies
KILOCYCLE n short for kilocycle per second: a former unit of frequency equal to 1 kilohertz
KILOGAUSS n 1000 gauss
KILOGRAM n one thousand grams
KILOGRAMS > KILOGRAM
KILOGRAY n 1000 gray
KILOGRAYS > KILOGRAY
KILOHERTZ n one thousand hertz
KILOJOULE n 1000 joules
KILOLITER US spelling of > KILOLITRE
KILOLITRE n 1000 litres
KILOMETER same as > KILOMETRE
KILOMETRE n one thousand metres
KILOMOLE n 1000 moles
KILOMOLES > KILOMOLE
KILOPOND n informal unit of gravitational force
KILOPONDS > KILOPOND
KILORAD n 1000 rads
KILORADS > KILORAD
KILOS > KILO

KILOTON *n* one thousand tons

KILOTONNE *same as* > KILOTON

KILOTONS > KILOTON

KILOVOLT *n* one thousand volts

KILOVOLTS > KILOVOLT

KILOWATT *n* one thousand watts

KILOWATTS > KILOWATT

KILP *dialect form of* > KELP

KILPS > KILP

KILT *n* knee-length pleated tartan skirt-like garment ▷ *vb* put pleats in (cloth)

KILTED > KILT

KILTER *n* working order or alignment

KILTERS > KILTER

KILTIE *n* someone wearing a kilt

KILTIES > KILTIE

KILTING > KILT

KILTINGS > KILT

KILTLIKE > KILT

KILTS > KILT

KILTY *same as* > KILTIE

KIMBO *vb* place akimbo

KIMBOED > KIMBO

KIMBOING > KIMBO

KIMBOS > KIMBO

KIMCHEE *same as* > KIMCHI

KIMCHEES > KIMCHEE

KIMCHI *n* Korean dish

KIMCHIS > KIMCHI

KIMMER *same as* > CUMMER

KIMMERS > KIMMER

KIMONO *n* loose wide-sleeved Japanese robe

KIMONOED > KIMONO

KIMONOS > KIMONO

KIN *n* person's relatives collectively ▷ *adj* related by blood

KINA *n* standard monetary unit of Papua New Guinea

KINAKINA *same as* > QUININE

KINAKINAS > KINAKINA

KINARA *n* African candle holder

KINARAS > KINARA

KINAS > KINA

KINASE *n* type of enzyme

KINASES > KINASE

KINCHIN *old slang word for* > CHILD

KINCHINS > KINCHIN

KINCOB *n* fine silk fabric

KINCOBS > KINCOB

KIND *adj* considerate, friendly, and helpful ▷ *n* class or group with common characteristics ▷ *vb* old word for beget or father

KINDA *adv* very informal shortening of kind of

KINDED > KIND

KINDER *adj* more kind ▷ *n* kindergarten or nursery school

KINDERS > KINDER

KINDEST > KIND

KINDIE *same as* > KINDY

KINDIES > KINDY

KINDING > KIND

KINDLE *vb* set (a fire) alight

KINDLED > KINDLE

KINDLER > KINDLE

KINDLERS > KINDLE

KINDLES > KINDLE

KINDLESS *adj* heartless

KINDLIER > KINDLY

KINDLIEST > KINDLY

KINDLILY > KINDLY

KINDLING *n* dry wood or straw for starting fires

KINDLINGS > KINDLING

KINDLY *adj* having a warm-hearted nature ▷ *adv* in a considerate way

KINDNESS *n* quality of being kind

KINDRED *adj* having similar qualities ▷ *n* blood relationship

KINDREDS > KINDRED

KINDS > KIND

KINDY *n* kindergarten

KINE *pl n* cows or cattle ▷ *n* Japanese pestle

KINEMA *same as* > CINEMA

KINEMAS > KINEMA

KINEMATIC *adj* of or relating to the study of the motion of bodies without reference to mass or force

KINES > KINE

KINESCOPE *n* US name for a television tube ▷ *vb* record on film

KINESES > KINESIS

KINESIC *adj* of or relating to kinesics

KINESICS *n* study of the role of body movements in communication

KINESIS *n* movement of an organism

KINESISES > KINESIS

KINETIC *adj* relating to or caused by motion

KINETICAL *same as* > KINETIC

KINETICS *n* branch of mechanics concerned with the study of bodies in motion

KINETIN *n* plant hormone

KINETINS > KINETIN

KINFOLK *another word for* > KINSFOLK

KINFOLKS > KINFOLK

KING *n* male ruler of a monarchy ▷ *vb* make king

KINGBIRD *n* any of several large American flycatchers

KINGBIRDS > KINGBIRD

KINGBOLT *n* pivot bolt that connects the body of a horse-drawn carriage to the front axle

KINGBOLTS > KINGBOLT

KINGCRAFT *n* art of ruling as a king, esp by diplomacy and cunning

KINGCUP *n* yellow-flowered plant

KINGCUPS > KINGCUP

KINGDOM *n* state ruled by a king or queen

KINGDOMED *adj* old word for with a kingdom

KINGDOMS > KINGDOM

KINGED > KING

KINGFISH *n* food and game fish occurring in warm American Atlantic coastal waters

KINGHOOD > KING

KINGHOODS > KING

KINGING > KING

KINGKLIP *n* edible eel-like marine fish of S Africa

KINGKLIPS > KINGKLIP

KINGLE *n* Scots word for a type of hard rock

KINGLES > KINGLE

KINGLESS > KING

KINGLET *n* king of a small or insignificant territory

KINGLETS > KINGLET

KINGLIER > KINGLY

KINGLIEST > KINGLY

KINGLIKE > KING

KINGLING *n* minor king

KINGLINGS > KINGLING

KINGLY *adj* appropriate to a king ▷ *adv* in a manner appropriate to a king

KINGMAKER *n* person who has control over appointments to positions of authority

KINGPIN *n* most important person in an organization

KINGPINS > KINGPIN

KINGPOST *n* vertical post connecting the apex of a triangular roof truss to the tie beam

KINGPOSTS > KINGPOST

KINGS > KING

KINGSHIP *n* position or authority of a king

KINGSHIPS > KINGSHIP

KINGSIDE *n* side of the chessboard on which a particular king is at the start of a game

KINGSIDES > KINGSIDE

KINGSNAKE *n* North American snake

KINGWOOD *n* hard fine-grained violet-tinted wood of a Brazilian leguminous tree

KINGWOODS > KINGWOOD

KININ *n* type of polypeptide

KININS > KININ

KINK *n* twist or bend in rope, wire, hair, etc ▷ *vb* form or cause to form a kink

KINKAJOU *n* arboreal mammal of Central and South America

KINKAJOUS > KINKAJOU

KINKED > KINK

KINKIER > KINKY

KINKIEST > KINKY

KINKILY > KINKY

KINKINESS > KINKY

KINKING > KINK

KINKLE *n* little kink

KINKLES > KINKLE

KINKS > KINK

KINKY *adj* tightly curled or looped

KINLESS *adj* without any relatives

KINO *same as* > KENO

KINONE *n* benzoquinone

KINONES > KINONE

KINOS > KINO

KINRED *old form of* > KINDRED

KINREDS > KINRED

KINS > KIN

KINSFOLK *pl n* one's family or relatives

KINSFOLKS > KINSFOLK

KINSHIP *n* blood relationship

KINSHIPS > KINSHIP

KINSMAN *n* relative

KINSMEN > KINSMAN

KINSWOMAN > KINSMAN

KINSWOMEN > KINSMAN

KINTLEDGE *same as* > KENTLEDGE

KIORE *n* small brown rat native to New Zealand

KIORES > KIORE

KIOSK *n* small booth

KIOSKS > KIOSK

KIP *vb* sleep ▷ *n* sleep or slumber

KIPE *n* dialect word for a basket for catching fish

KIPES > KIPE

KIPP *uncommon variant of* > KIP

KIPPA *n* skullcap worn by male Jews

KIPPAGE *n* Scots word for a state of anger or excitement

KIPPAGES > KIPPAGE

KIPPAH *same as* > KIPPA

KIPPAHS > KIPPAH

KIPPAS > KIPPA

KIPPED > KIP

KIPPEN > KEP

KIPPER *n* cleaned, salted, and smoked herring ▷ *vb* cure (a herring) by salting and smoking it

KIPPERED *adj* (of fish, esp herring) having been cleaned, salted, and smoked

KIPPERER > KIPPER

KIPPERERS > KIPPER

KIPPERING > KIPPER

KIPPERS > KIPPER

KIPPING > KIP

KIPPS > KIPP

KIPS > KIP

KIPSKIN *same as* > KIP

KIPSKINS > KIPSKIN

KIPUNJI *n* Tanzanian species of monkey

KIPUNJIS > KIPUNJI

KIR *n* drink made from dry white wine and cassis

KIRANA *n* small family-owned shop in India

KIRANAS > KIRANA

KIRBEH *n* leather bottle

KIRBEHS > KIRBEH

KIRBIGRIP *n* hairgrip

KIRBY *n* as in *kirby grip* type of hairgrip

KIRIGAMI *n* art, originally Japanese, of folding and cutting paper into decorative shapes

KIRIGAMIS > KIRIGAMI

KIRIMON *n* Japanese imperial crest**

k

k

KIRIMONS > KIRIMON
KIRK Scot word for > CHURCH
KIRKED > KIRK
KIRKING > KIRK
KIRKINGS > KIRK
KIRKMAN n member or strong upholder of the Kirk
KIRKMEN > KIRKMAN
KIRKS > KIRK
KIRKTON n village or town with a parish church
KIRKTONS > KIRKTON
KIRKWARD adv towards the church
KIRKYAIRD same as > KIRKYARD
KIRKYARD n churchyard
KIRKYARDS > KIRKYARD
KIRMESS same as > KERMIS
KIRMESSES > KIRMESS
KIRN dialect word for > CHURN
KIRNED > KIRN
KIRNING > KIRN
KIRNS > KIRN
KIRPAN n short sword traditionally carried by Sikhs
KIRPANS > KIRPAN
KIRRI n Hottentot stick
KIRRIS > KIRRI
KIRS > KIR
KIRSCH n cherry brandy
KIRSCHES > KIRSCH
KIRTAN n devotional singing
KIRTANS > KIRTAN
KIRTLE n woman's skirt or dress ▷ vb dress with a kirtle
KIRTLED > KIRTLE
KIRTLES > KIRTLE
KIS > KI
KISAN n peasant or farmer
KISANS > KISAN
KISH n graphite formed on the surface of molten iron
KISHES > KISH
KISHKA same as > KISHKE
KISHKAS > KISHKA
KISHKE n stuffed beef or fowl intestine, boiled and roasted
KISHKES > KISHKE
KISKADEE n large flycatcher of tropical America
KISKADEES > KISKADEE
KISMAT same as > KISMET
KISMATS > KISMAT
KISMET n fate or destiny
KISMETIC > KISMET
KISMETS > KISMET
KISS vb touch with the lips in affection or greeting ▷ n touch with the lips
KISSABLE > KISS
KISSABLY > KISS
KISSAGRAM n greetings service in which a messenger kisses the person celebrating
KISSED > KISS
KISSEL n Russian dessert
KISSELS > KISSEL
KISSER n mouth or face
KISSERS > KISSER
KISSES > KISS
KISSIER > KISSY
KISSIEST > KISSY
KISSING > KISS
KISSINGS > KISSING

KISSOGRAM same as > KISSAGRAM
KISSY adj showing exaggerated affection
KIST n large wooden chest ▷ vb place in a coffin
KISTED > KIST
KISTFUL > KIST
KISTFULS > KIST
KISTING > KIST
KISTS > KIST
KISTVAEN n stone tomb
KISTVAENS > KISTVAEN
KIT n outfit or equipment for a specific purpose ▷ vb fit or provide
KITBAG n bag for a soldier's or traveller's belongings
KITBAGS > KITBAG
KITCHEN n room used for cooking ▷ vb (in archaic usage) provide with food
KITCHENED > KITCHEN
KITCHENER n someone employed in kitchen work
KITCHENET n small kitchen or part of another room equipped for use as a kitchen
KITCHENS > KITCHEN
KITE n light frame covered with a thin material ▷ vb soar and glide
KITEBOARD n board like a windsurfing board, towed by a large kite
KITED > KITE
KITELIKE > KITE
KITENGE n thick cotton cloth
KITENGES > KITENGE
KITER > KITE
KITERS > KITE
KITES > KITE
KITH n one's friends and acquaintances
KITHARA variant of > CITHARA
KITHARAS > KITHARA
KITHE same as > KYTHE
KITHED > KITHE
KITHES > KITHE
KITHING > KITHE
KITHS > KITH
KITING > KITE
KITINGS > KITE
KITLING dialect word for > KITTEN
KITLINGS > KITLING
KITS > KIT
KITSCH n art or literature with popular sentimental appeal ▷ n object or art that is tawdry, vulgarized, sentimental or pretentious
KITSCHES > KITSCH
KITSCHIER > KITSCH
KITSCHIFY vb make kitsch
KITSCHILY > KITSCH
KITSCHY > KITSCH
KITSET n New Zealand word for furniture supplied in pieces
KITSETS > KITSET
KITTED > KIT
KITTEL n white garment worn for certain Jewish rituals or burial

KITTELS > KITTEL
KITTEN n young cat ▷ vb (of cats) give birth
KITTENED > KITTEN
KITTENIER > KITTENY
KITTENING > KITTEN
KITTENISH adj lively and flirtatious
KITTENS > KITTEN
KITTENY adj like a kitten
KITTIES > KITTY
KITTING > KIT
KITTIWAKE n type of seagull
KITTLE adj capricious and unpredictable ▷ vb be troublesome or puzzling to (someone)
KITTLED > KITTLE
KITTLER > KITTLE
KITTLES > KITTLE
KITTLEST > KITTLE
KITTLIER > KITTLY
KITTLIEST > KITTLY
KITTLING > KITTLE
KITTLY Scots word for > TICKLISH
KITTUL n type of palm from which jaggery sugar comes
KITTULS > KITTUL
KITTY n communal fund
KITUL same as > KITTUL
KITULS > KITUL
KIVA n large room in a Pueblo village
KIVAS > KIVA
KIWI n New Zealand flightless bird with a long beak and no tail
KIWIFRUIT n edible oval fruit of the kiwi plant
KIWIS > KIWI
KLANG n (in music) kind of tone
KLANGS > KLANG
KLAP vb slap or spank
KLAPPED > KLAP
KLAPPING > KLAP
KLAPS > KLAP
KLATCH n gathering, especially over coffee
KLATCHES > KLATCH
KLATSCH same as > KLATCH
KLATSCHES > KLATSCH
KLAVERN n local Ku Klux Klan group
KLAVERNS > KLAVERN
KLAVIER same as > CLAVIER
KLAVIERS > KLAVIER
KLAXON n loud horn used on emergency vehicles ▷ vb hoot with a klaxon
KLAXONED > KLAXON
KLAXONING > KLAXON
KLAXONS > KLAXON
KLEAGLE n person with a particular rank in the Ku Klux Klan
KLEAGLES > KLEAGLE
KLEENEX n tradename for a kind of tissue
KLEENEXES > KLEENEX
KLEFTIKO n type of Greek lamb dish
KLEFTIKOS > KLEFTIKO

KLENDUSIC adj disease-resistant
KLEPHT n group of Greeks
KLEPHTIC > KLEPHT
KLEPHTISM > KLEPHT
KLEPHTS > KLEPHT
KLEPTO n compulsive thief
KLEPTOS > KLEPTO
KLETT n lightweight climbing boot
KLETTS > KLETT
KLEZMER n Jewish folk musician
KLEZMERS > KLEZMER
KLEZMORIM > KLEZMER
KLICK n kilometre
KLICKS > KLICK
KLIEG n as in klieg light intense carbon-arc light
KLIEGS > KLIEG
KLIK US military slang word for > KILOMETRE
KLIKS > KLIK
KLINKER n type of brick used in paving
KLINKERS > KLINKER
KLINOSTAT n rotating and tilting plant holder for studying and experimenting with plant growth
KLIPDAS n rock hyrax
KLIPDASES > KLIPDAS
KLISTER n type of ski dressing for improving grip on snow
KLISTERS > KLISTER
KLONDIKE same as > KLONDYKE
KLONDIKED > KLONDIKE
KLONDIKER same as > KLONDYKER
KLONDIKES > KLONDIKE
KLONDYKE n rich source of something ▷ vb transfer (bulk loads of fish) to factory ships at sea for processing
KLONDYKED > KLONDYKE
KLONDYKER n East European factory ship
KLONDYKES > KLONDYKE
KLONG n type of canal in Thailand
KLONGS > KLONG
KLOOCH same as > KLOOCHMAN
KLOOCHES > KLOOCH
KLOOCHMAN n Native American woman
KLOOCHMEN > KLOOCHMAN
KLOOF n mountain pass or gorge
KLOOFS > KLOOF
KLOOTCH same as > KLOOCHMAN
KLOOTCHES > KLOOTCH
KLUDGE n untidy solution ▷ vb cobble something together
KLUDGED > KLUDGE
KLUDGES > KLUDGE
KLUDGEY > KLUDGE
KLUDGIER > KLUDGE
KLUDGIEST > KLUDGE
KLUDGING > KLUDGE
KLUDGY > KLUDGE
KLUGE same as > KLUDGE
KLUGED > KLUGE

SECTION 1: Words between 2 and 9 letters in length

KLUGES > KLUGE

KLUGING > KLUGE

KLUTZ *n* clumsy or stupid person

KLUTZES > KLUTZ

KLUTZIER > KLUTZ

KLUTZIEST > KLUTZ

KLUTZY > KLUTZ

KLYSTRON *n* electron tube for the amplification of microwaves

KLYSTRONS > KLYSTRON

KNACK *n* skilful way of doing something ⊳ *vb* dialect word for crack or snap

KNACKED *adj* broken or worn out

KNACKER *n* buyer of old horses for killing ⊳ *vb* exhaust

KNACKERED *adj* extremely tired

KNACKERS > KNACKER

KNACKERY *n* slaughterhouse for horses

KNACKIER > KNACKY

KNACKIEST > KNACKY

KNACKING > KNACK

KNACKISH *adj* old word meaning cunning or artful

KNACKS > KNACK

KNACKY *adj* old or dialect word for cunning or artful

KNAG *n* knot in wood

KNAGGIER > KNAGGY

KNAGGIEST > KNAGGY

KNAGGY *adj* knotty

KNAGS > KNAG

KNAIDEL *same as* > KNEIDEL

KNAIDELS > KNAIDEL

KNAIDLACH > KNAIDEL

KNAP *n* crest of a hill ⊳ *vb* hit, hammer, or chip

KNAPPED > KNAP

KNAPPER > KNAP

KNAPPERS > KNAP

KNAPPING > KNAP

KNAPPLE *old word for* > NIBBLE

KNAPPLED > KNAPPLE

KNAPPLES > KNAPPLE

KNAPPLING > KNAPPLE

KNAPS > KNAP

KNAPSACK *n* soldier's or traveller's bag worn strapped on the back

KNAPSACKS > KNAPSACK

KNAPWEED *n* plant with purplish thistle-like flowers

KNAPWEEDS > KNAPWEED

KNAR *old spelling of* > GNAR

KNARL *old spelling of* > GNARL

KNARLIER > KNARLY

KNARLIEST > KNARLY

KNARLS > KNARL

KNARLY *same as* > GNARLY

KNARRED > KNAR

KNARRIER > KNAR

KNARRIEST > KNAR

KNARRING > KNAR

KNARRY > KNAR

KNARS > KNAR

KNAUR *variant form of* > KNUR

KNAURS > KNAUR

KNAVE *n* jack at cards

KNAVERIES > KNAVERY

KNAVERY *n* dishonest behaviour

KNAVES > KNAVE

KNAVESHIP *n* old Scottish legal term for the small proportion of milled grain due to the person doing the milling

KNAVISH > KNAVE

KNAVISHLY > KNAVE

KNAWE *same as* > KNAWEL

KNAWEL *n* type of Old World plant

KNAWELS > KNAWEL

KNAWES > KNAWE

KNEAD *vb* work (dough) into a smooth mixture with the hands

KNEADABLE > KNEAD

KNEADED > KNEAD

KNEADER > KNEAD

KNEADERS > KNEAD

KNEADING > KNEAD

KNEADS > KNEAD

KNEE *n* joint between thigh and lower leg ⊳ *vb* strike or push with the knee

KNEEBOARD *vb* surfboard ridden in kneeling position ⊳ *vb* ride a kneeboard

KNEECAP *nontechnical name for* > PATELLA

KNEECAPS > KNEECAP

KNEED > KNEE

KNEEHOLE *n* space for the knees, esp under a desk

KNEEHOLES > KNEEHOLE

KNEEING > KNEE

KNEEJERK *adj* (of a reply or reaction) automatic and predictable

KNEEL *vb* fall or rest on one's knees ⊳ *n* act or position of kneeling

KNEELED > KNEEL

KNEELER > KNEEL

KNEELERS > KNEEL

KNEELIKE *adj* like a knee

KNEELING > KNEEL

KNEELS > KNEEL

KNEEPAD *n* protective covering for the knee

KNEEPADS > KNEEPAD

KNEEPAN *another word for* > PATELLA

KNEEPANS > KNEEPAN

KNEEPIECE *n* knee-shaped piece of timber in ship

KNEEROOM *n* space to put one's knees

KNEEROOMS > KNEEROOM

KNEES > KNEE

KNEESIES *n* flirtatious touching of knees under table

KNEESOCK *n* type of sock that comes up to the knee

KNEESOCKS > KNEESOCK

KNEIDEL *n* (in Jewish cookery) small dumpling

KNEIDELS > KNEIDEL

KNEIDLACH > KNEIDEL

KNELL *n* sound of a bell, esp at a funeral or death ⊳ *vb* ring a knell

KNELLED > KNELL

KNELLING > KNELL

KNELLS > KNELL

KNELT > KNEEL

KNESSET *n* parliament or assembly

KNESSETS > KNESSET

KNEVELL *vb* old Scots word meaning beat

KNEVELLED > KNEVELL

KNEVELLS > KNEVELL

KNEW > KNOW

KNICKER *n* woman's or girl's undergarment

KNICKERED > KNICKER

KNICKERS *pl n* woman's or girl's undergarment

KNICKS *pl n* knickers

KNIFE *n* sharp-edged blade with a handle ⊳ *vb* cut or stab with a knife

KNIFED > KNIFE

KNIFELESS > KNIFE

KNIFELIKE > KNIFE

KNIFEMAN *n* man who is armed with a knife

KNIFEMEN > KNIFEMAN

KNIFER > KNIFE

KNIFEREST *n* support on which a carving knife or carving fork is placed at the table

KNIFERS > KNIFE

KNIFES > KNIFE

KNIFING > KNIFE

KNIFINGS > KNIFE

KNIGHT *n* man who has been given a knighthood ⊳ *vb* award a knighthood to

KNIGHTAGE *n* group of knights or knights collectively

KNIGHTED > KNIGHT

KNIGHTING > KNIGHT

KNIGHTLY *adj* of, resembling, or appropriate for a knight

KNIGHTS > KNIGHT

KNIPHOFIA *n* any of several perennial southern African flowering plants

KNISH *n* type of dish

KNISHES > KNISH

KNIT *vb* make (a garment) by interlocking a series of loops in wool or other yarn ⊳ *n* fabric made by knitting

KNITBONE *n* comfrey

KNITBONES > KNITBONE

KNITCH *dialect word for* > BUNDLE

KNITCHES > KNITCH

KNITS > KNIT

KNITTABLE > KNIT

KNITTED > KNIT

KNITTER > KNIT

KNITTERS > KNIT

KNITTING > KNIT

KNITTINGS > KNIT

KNITTLE *n* old word for string or cord

KNITTLES > KNITTLE

KNITWEAR *n* knitted clothes, such as sweaters

KNITWEARS > KNITWEAR

KNIVE *rare variant of* > KNIFE

KNIVED > KNIVE

KNIVES > KNIFE

KNIVING > KNIVE

KNOB *n* rounded projection, such as a switch on a radio ⊳ *vb* supply with knobs

KNOBBED > KNOB

KNOBBER *n* two-year-old male deer

KNOBBERS > KNOBBER

KNOBBIER > KNOB

KNOBBIEST > KNOB

KNOBBING > KNOB

KNOBBLE *n* small knob ⊳ *vb* dialect word meaning strike

KNOBBLED *same as* > KNOBBLY

KNOBBLES > KNOBBLE

KNOBBLIER > KNOBBLY

KNOBBLING > KNOBBLE

KNOBBLY *adj* covered with small bumps

KNOBBY > KNOB

KNOBHEAD *n* stupid person

KNOBHEADS > KNOBHEAD

KNOBLIKE > KNOB

KNOBS > KNOB

KNOBSTICK *n* stick with a round knob at the end, used as a club or missile by South African tribespeople

KNOCK *vb* give a blow or push to ⊳ *n* blow or rap

KNOCKBACK *n* rejection, esp of a job application or invitation to go on a date

KNOCKDOWN *adj* (of a price) very low

KNOCKED > KNOCK

KNOCKER *n* metal fitting for knocking on a door

KNOCKERS > KNOCKER

KNOCKING > KNOCK

KNOCKINGS > KNOCK

KNOCKLESS > KNOCK

KNOCKOFF *n* informal word for a cheap, often illegal, copy of something

KNOCKOFFS > KNOCKOFF

KNOCKOUT *n* blow that renders an opponent unconscious ⊳ *vb* render (someone) unconscious

KNOCKOUTS > KNOCKOUT

KNOCKS > KNOCK

KNOLL *n* small rounded hill ⊳ *vb* (in archaic or dialect usage) knell

KNOLLED > KNOLL

KNOLLER > KNOLL

KNOLLERS > KNOLL

KNOLLIER > KNOLL

KNOLLIEST > KNOLL

KNOLLING > KNOLL

KNOLLS > KNOLL

KNOLLY > KNOLL

KNOP *n* knob, esp an ornamental one

KNOPPED > KNOP

KNOPS > KNOP

KNOSP *n* budlike architectural feature

KNOSPS > KNOSP

KNOT *n* type of fastening ⊳ *vb* tie with or into a knot

KNOTGRASS *n* polygonaceous weedy plant whose small green flowers produce numerous seeds

KNOTHEAD *n* stupid person

k

KNOTHEADS > KNOTHEAD
KNOTHOLE n hole in a piece of wood where a knot has been
KNOTHOLES > KNOTHOLE
KNOTLESS > KNOT
KNOTLIKE > KNOT
KNOTS > KNOT
KNOTTED > KNOT
KNOTTER > KNOT
KNOTTERS > KNOT
KNOTTIER > KNOTTY
KNOTTIEST > KNOTTY
KNOTTILY > KNOTTY
KNOTTING > KNOT
KNOTTINGS > KNOT
KNOTTY adj full of knots
KNOTWEED n type of plant with small flowers and jointed stems
KNOTWEEDS > KNOTWEED
KNOTWORK n ornamentation consisting of a mass of intertwined and knotted cords
KNOTWORKS > KNOTWORK
KNOUT n stout whip ▷ vb whip
KNOUTED > KNOUT
KNOUTING > KNOUT
KNOUTS > KNOUT
KNOW vb be or feel certain of the truth of (information etc)
KNOWABLE > KNOW
KNOWE same as > KNOLL
KNOWER > KNOW
KNOWERS > KNOW
KNOWES > KNOWE
KNOWHOW n ingenuity, knack, or skill
KNOWHOWS > KNOWHOW
KNOWING > KNOW
KNOWINGER > KNOW
KNOWINGLY > KNOW
KNOWINGS > KNOW
KNOWLEDGE n facts, feelings or experiences known by a person or group of people ▷ vb (in archaic usage) acknowledge
KNOWN n fact or something that is known
KNOWNS > KNOWN
KNOWS > KNOW
KNUB dialect word for > KNOB
KNUBBIER > KNUBBY
KNUBBIEST > KNUB
KNUBBLE vb dialect word for beat or pound using one's fists
KNUBBLED > KNUBBLE
KNUBBLES > KNUBBLE
KNUBBLIER > KNUBBLY
KNUBBLING > KNUBBLE
KNUBBLY adj having small lumps or protuberances
KNUBBY adj knub
KNUBS > KNUB
KNUCKLE n bone at the finger joint ▷ vb rub with the knuckles
KNUCKLED > KNUCKLE
KNUCKLER n type of pitch in baseball
KNUCKLERS > KNUCKLER
KNUCKLES > KNUCKLE
KNUCKLIER > KNUCKLE

KNUCKLING > KNUCKLE
KNUCKLY > KNUCKLE
KNUR n knot or protuberance in a tree trunk or in wood
KNURL n small ridge, often one of a series ▷ vb impress with a series of fine ridges or serrations
KNURLED > KNURL
KNURLIER > KNURLY
KNURLIEST > KNURLY
KNURLING > KNURL
KNURLINGS > KNURL
KNURLS > KNURL
KNURLY rare word for > GNARLED
KNURR same as > KNUR
KNURRS > KNURR
KNURS > KNUR
KNUT n dandy
KNUTS > KNUT
KO n (in New Zealand) traditional digging tool
KOA n Hawaiian leguminous tree
KOALA n tree-dwelling Australian marsupial with dense grey fur
KOALAS > KOALA
KOAN n (in Zen Buddhism) problem that admits no logical solution
KOANS > KOAN
KOAP n (in Papua New Guinean slang) sexual intercourse
KOAPS > KOAP
KOAS > KOA
KOB n any of several species of antelope
KOBAN n old oval-shaped Japanese gold coin
KOBANG same as > KOBAN
KOBANGS > KOBANG
KOBANS > KOBAN
KOBO n Nigerian monetary unit
KOBOLD n mischievous household sprite
KOBOLDS > KOBOLD
KOBOS > KOBO
KOBS > KOB
KOCHIA n any of several plants whose foliage turns dark red
KOCHIAS > KOCHIA
KOEKOEA n long-tailed cuckoo of New Zealand
KOEKOEAS > KOEKOEA
KOEL n any of several parasitic cuckoos
KOELS > KOEL
KOFF n Dutch masted merchant vessel
KOFFS > KOFF
KOFTA n Indian dish
KOFTAS > KOFTA
KOFTGAR n (in India) person skilled at inlaying steel with gold
KOFTGARI n ornamental Indian metalwork
KOFTGARIS > KOFTGARI
KOFTGARS > KOFTGAR
KOFTWORK same as > KOFTGARI
KOFTWORKS > KOFTWORK

KOGAL n (in Japan) trendy teenage girl
KOGALS > KOGAL
KOHA n gift or donation, esp of cash
KOHANIM > KOHEN
KOHAS > KOHA
KOHEKOHE n New Zealand tree with large glossy leaves and reddish wood
KOHEKOHES > KOHEKOHE
KOHEN n member of the Jewish priestly caste
KOHL n cosmetic powder
KOHLRABI n type of cabbage with an edible stem
KOHLRABIS > KOHLRABI
KOHLS > KOHL
KOI n any of various ornamental forms of the common carp
KOINE n common language among speakers of different languages
KOINES > KOINE
KOIS > KOI
KOJI n Japanese steamed rice
KOJIS > KOJI
KOKA n former type of score in judo
KOKAKO n type of crow
KOKAKOS > KOKAKO
KOKAM same as > KOKUM
KOKAMS > KOKAM
KOKANEE n type of freshwater salmon
KOKANEES > KOKANEE
KOKAS > KOKA
KOKER n Guyanese sluice
KOKERS > KOKER
KOKIRI n type of rough-skinned New Zealand triggerfish
KOKIRIS > KOKIRI
KOKOBEH adj (of certain fruit) having a rough skin
KOKOPU n any of several small freshwater fish of New Zealand
KOKOPUS > KOKOPU
KOKOWAI n type of clay
KOKOWAIS > KOKOWAI
KOKRA n type of wood
KOKRAS > KOKRA
KOKUM n tropical tree
KOKUMS > KOKUM
KOLA n as in kola nut caffeine-containing seed used in medicine and soft drinks
KOLACKIES > KOLACKY
KOLACKY n sweet bun with a fruit, jam, or nut filling
KOLAS > KOLA
KOLBASI same as > KOLBASSI
KOLBASIS > KOLBASI
KOLBASSA same as > KIELBASA
KOLBASSAS > KOLBASSA
KOLBASSI n type of sausage
KOLBASSIS > KOLBASSI
KOLHOZ same as > KOLKHOZ
KOLHOZES > KOLHOZ
KOLHOZY > KOLHOZ

KOLINSKI same as > KOLINSKY
KOLINSKY n Asian mink
KOLKHOS same as > KOLKHOZ
KOLKHOSES > KOLKHOS
KOLKHOSY > KOLKHOS
KOLKHOZ n (formerly) collective farm in the Soviet Union
KOLKHOZES > KOLKHOZ
KOLKHOZY > KOLKHOZ
KOLKOZ same as > KOLKHOZ
KOLKOZES > KOLKOZ
KOLKOZY > KOLKOZ
KOLO n Serbian folk dance
KOLOS > KOLO
KOMATIK n type of sledge
KOMATIKS > KOMATIK
KOMBU n dark brown seaweed
KOMBUS > KOMBU
KOMISSAR same as > COMMISSAR
KOMISSARS > KOMISSAR
KOMITAJI n rebel or revolutionary
KOMITAJIS > KOMITAJI
KOMONDOR n large powerful dog of an ancient Hungarian breed, originally used for sheep herding
KOMONDORS > KOMONDOR
KOMPROMAT n potentially damaging documents, photographs, etc kept for blackmail
KON old word for > KNOW
KONAKI same as > KONEKE
KONAKIS > KONAKI
KONBU same as > KOMBU
KONBUS > KONBU
KOND > KON
KONDO n (in Uganda) thief or armed robber
KONDOS > KONDO
KONEKE n type of farm vehicle
KONEKES > KONEKE
KONFYT n South African fruit preserve
KONFYTS > KONFYT
KONGONI n E African hartbeest
KONIMETER n device for measuring airborne dust concentration in which samples are obtained by sucking the air through a hole and allowing it to pass over a glass plate coated with grease on which the particles collect
KONINI n edible dark purple berry
KONINIS > KONINI
KONIOLOGY n study of atmospheric dust and its effects
KONISCOPE n device for detecting and measuring dust in the air
KONK same as > CONK
KONKED > KONK
KONKING > KONK
KONKS > KONK
KONNING > KON

KONS > KON
KOODOO same as > KUDU
KOODOOS > KOODOO
KOOK n eccentric person ▷ vb dialect word for vanish
KOOKED > KOOK
KOOKIE same as > KOOKY
KOOKIER > KOOKY
KOOKIEST > KOOKY
KOOKILY > KOOKY
KOOKINESS > KOOKY
KOOKING > KOOK
KOOKS > KOOK
KOOKUM same as > KOKUM
KOOKUMS > KOOKUM
KOOKY adj crazy, eccentric, or foolish
KOOLAH old form of > KOALA
KOOLAHS > KOOLAH
KOORI n Australian Aborigine
KOORIES > KOORI
KOORIS > KOORI
KOP n prominent isolated hill or mountain in southern Africa
KOPASETIC same as > COPACETIC
KOPECK n former Russian monetary unit
KOPECKS > KOPECK
KOPEK same as > KOPECK
KOPEKS > KOPEK
KOPH n 19th letter in the Hebrew alphabet
KOPHS > KOPH
KOPIYKA n monetary unit of Ukraine
KOPIYKAS > KOPIYKA
KOPIYKY > KOPIYKA
KOPIYOK > KOPIYKA
KOPJE n small hill
KOPJES > KOPJE
KOPPA n consonantal letter in the Greek alphabet
KOPPAS > KOPPA
KOPPIE same as > KOPJE
KOPPIES > KOPPIE
KOPS > KOP
KOR n ancient Hebrew unit of capacity
KORA n West African instrument
KORAI > KORE
KORARI n native New Zealand flax plant
KORARIS > KORARI
KORAS > KORA
KORAT n as in korat cat rare blue-grey breed of cat
KORATS > KORAT
KORE n ancient Greek statue of a young woman wearing clothes
KORERO n talk or discussion ▷ vb speak or converse
KOREROED > KORERO
KOREROING > KORERO
KOREROS > KORERO
KORES > KORE
KORFBALL n game similar to basketball, in which each team consists of six men and six women
KORFBALLS > KORFBALL
KORIMAKO another name for > BELLBIRD

KORIMAKOS > KORIMAKO
KORKIR n variety of lichen used in dyeing
KORKIRS > KORKIR
KORMA n type of mild Indian dish
KORMAS > KORMA
KORO n elderly Māori man
KOROMIKO n flowering New Zealand shrub
KOROMIKOS > KOROMIKO
KORORA n small New Zealand penguin
KORORAS > KORORA
KOROS > KORO
KOROWAI n decorative woven cloak worn by a Māori chief
KOROWAIS > KOROWAI
KORS > KOR
KORU n stylized curved pattern used esp in carving
KORUN > KORUNA
KORUNA n standard monetary unit of the Czech Republic and Slovakia
KORUNAS > KORUNA
KORUNY > KORUNA
KORUS > KORU
KOS n Indian unit of distance
KOSES > KOS
KOSHER adj conforming to Jewish religious law ▷ n kosher food ▷ vb prepare in accordance with Jewish dietary rules
KOSHERED > KOSHER
KOSHERING > KOSHER
KOSHERS > KOSHER
KOSMOS variant form of > COSMOS
KOSMOSES > KOSMOS
KOSS same as > KOS
KOSSES > KOSS
KOTARE n small greenish-blue kingfisher
KOTARES > KOTARE
KOTCH vb South African slang for vomit
KOTCHED > KOTCH
KOTCHES > KOTCH
KOTCHING > KOTCH
KOTO n Japanese stringed instrument
KOTOS > KOTO
KOTOW same as > KOWTOW
KOTOWED > KOTOW
KOTOWER > KOTOW
KOTOWERS > KOTOW
KOTOWING > KOTOW
KOTOWS > KOTOW
KOTTABOS same as > COTTABUS
KOTUKU n type of white heron
KOTUKUS > KOTUKU
KOTWAL n senior police officer or magistrate in an Indian town
KOTWALS > KOTWAL
KOULAN same as > KULAN
KOULANS > KOULAN
KOUMIS same as > KUMISS
KOUMISES > KOUMIS
KOUMISS same as > KUMISS
KOUMISSES > KOUMISS
KOUMYS same as > KUMISS

KOUMYSES > KOUMYS
KOUMYSS same as > KUMISS
KOUMYSSES > KOUMYSS
KOUPREY n large wild SE Asian ox
KOUPREYS > KOUPREY
KOURA n New Zealand freshwater crayfish
KOURAS > KOURA
KOURBASH same as > KURBASH
KOUROI > KOUROS
KOUROS n ancient Greek statue of a young man
KOUSKOUS same as > COUSCOUS
KOUSSO n Abyssinian tree
KOUSSOS > KOUSSO
KOW old variant of > COW
KOWHAI n New Zealand tree
KOWHAIS > KOWHAI
KOWS > KOW
KOWTOW vb be servile (towards) ▷ n act of kowtowing
KOWTOWED > KOWTOW
KOWTOWER > KOWTOW
KOWTOWERS > KOWTOW
KOWTOWING > KOWTOW
KOWTOWS > KOWTOW
KRAAL n S African village surrounded by a strong fence ▷ adj denoting or relating to the tribal aspects of the Black African way of life ▷ vb enclose (livestock) in a kraal
KRAALED > KRAAL
KRAALING > KRAAL
KRAALS > KRAAL
KRAB same as > KARABINER
KRABS > KRAB
KRAFT n strong wrapping paper
KRAFTS > KRAFT
KRAI n administrative division of Russia
KRAIS > KRAI
KRAIT n brightly coloured venomous snake of S and SE Asia
KRAITS > KRAIT
KRAKEN n legendary sea monster
KRAKENS > KRAKEN
KRAKOWIAK n Polish dance
KRAMERIA another name for > RHATANY
KRAMERIAS > KRAMERIA
KRANG n dead whale from which the blubber has been removed
KRANGS > KRANG
KRANS n sheer rock face
KRANSES > KRANS
KRANTZ same as > KRANS
KRANTZES > KRANTZ
KRANZ same as > KRANS
KRANZES > KRANZ
KRATER same as > CRATER
KRATERS > KRATER
KRAUT n sauerkraut
KRAUTROCK n experimental German rock music
KRAUTS > KRAUT
KRAY same as > KRAI
KRAYS > KRAY

KREASOTE same as > CREOSOTE
KREASOTED > KREASOTE
KREASOTES > KREASOTE
KREATINE same as > CREATINE
KREATINES > KREATINE
KREEP n lunar substance
KREEPS > KREEP
KREESE same as > KRIS
KREESED > KREESE
KREESES > KREESE
KREESING > KREESE
KREMLIN n citadel of any Russian city
KREMLINS > KREMLIN
KRENG same as > KRANG
KRENGS > KRENG
KREOSOTE same as > CREOSOTE
KREOSOTED > KREOSOTE
KREOSOTES > KREOSOTE
KREPLACH pl n small filled dough casings usually served in soup
KREPLECH same as > KREPLACH
KREUTZER n any of various former copper and silver coins of Germany or Austria
KREUTZERS > KREUTZER
KREUZER same as > KREUTZER
KREUZERS > KREUZER
KREWE n club taking part in New Orleans carnival parade
KREWES > KREWE
KRILL n small shrimplike sea creature
KRILLS > KRILL
KRIMMER n tightly curled light grey fur
KRIMMERS > KRIMMER
KRIS n type of Malayan and Indonesian knife ▷ vb stab or slash with a kris
KRISED > KRIS
KRISES > KRIS
KRISING > KRIS
KROMESKY n croquette consisting of a piece of bacon wrapped round minced meat or fish
KRONA n standard monetary unit of Sweden
KRONE n standard monetary unit of Norway and Denmark
KRONEN > KRONE
KRONER > KRONE
KRONOR > KRONA
KRONUR > KRONA
KROON n standard monetary unit of Estonia
KROONI > KROON
KROONS > KROON
KRUBI n aroid plant with an unpleasant smell
KRUBIS > KRUBI
KRUBUT same as > KRUBI
KRUBUTS > KRUBUT
KRULLER variant spelling of > CRULLER
KRULLERS > KRULLER
KRUMHORN variant spelling of > CRUMHORN
KRUMHORNS > KRUMHORN

k

KRUMKAKE n Scandinavian biscuit

KRUMKAKES > KRUMKAKE

KRUMMHOLZ n zone of stunted wind-blown trees growing at high altitudes just above the timberline on tropical mountains

KRUMMHORN variant spelling of > CRUMHORN

KRUMPER > KRUMPING

KRUMPERS > KRUMPER

KRUMPING n type of aggressive dance

KRUMPINGS > KRUMPING

KRUNK n style of hip-hop music

KRUNKED same as > CRUNKED

KRUNKS > KRUNK

KRYOLITE variant spelling of > CRYOLITE

KRYOLITES > KRYOLITE

KRYOLITH same as > CRYOLITE

KRYOLITHS > KRYOLITH

KRYOMETER same as > CRYOMETER

KRYPSES > KRYPSIS

KRYPSIS n idea that Christ made secret use of his divine attributes

KRYPTON n colourless gas

KRYPTONS > KRYPTON

KRYTRON n type of fast electronic gas-discharge switch

KRYTRONS > KRYTRON

KSAR old form of > TSAR

KSARS > KSAR

KUBASA same as > KIELBASA

KUBASAS > KUBASA

KUBIE n Ukrainian roll filled with kielbasa

KUBIES > KUBIE

KUCCHA same as > KACCHA

KUCCHAS > KUCCHA

KUCHCHA same as > KACHA

KUCHEN n breadlike cake

KUCHENS > KUCHEN

KUDLIK n Inuit soapstone seal-oil lamp

KUDLIKS > KUDLIK

KUDO variant of > KUDOS

KUDOS n fame or credit

KUDOSES > KUDOS

KUDU n African antelope with spiral horns

KUDUS > KUDU

KUDZU n hairy leguminous climbing plant

KUDZUS > KUDZU

KUE n name of the letter Q

KUEH n (in Malaysia) any cake of Malay, Chinese, or Indian origin

KUES > KUE

KUFI n cap for Muslim man

KUFIS > KUFI

KUFIYAH same as > KEFFIYEH

KUFIYAHS > KUFIYAH

KUGEL n baked pudding in traditional Jewish cooking

KUGELS > KUGEL

KUIA n Māori female elder or elderly woman

KUIAS > KUIA

KUKRI n heavy, curved knife used by Gurkhas

KUKRIS > KUKRI

KUKU n mussel

KUKUS > KUKU

KULA n ceremonial gift exchange among islanders in the W Pacific

KULAK n (formerly) property-owning Russian peasant

KULAKI > KULAK

KULAKS > KULAK

KULAN n Asiatic wild ass

KULANS > KULAN

KULAS > KULA

KULBASA same as > KIELBASA

KULBASAS > KULBASA

KULFI n Indian dessert

KULFIS > KULFI

KULTUR n German civilization

KULTURS > KULTUR

KUMARA n tropical root vegetable with yellow flesh

KUMARAHOU n New Zealand shrub

KUMARAS > KUMARA

KUMARI n (in Indian English) maiden

KUMARIS > KUMARI

KUMBALOI pl n worry beads

KUMERA same as > KUMARA

KUMERAS > KUMERA

KUMIKUMI same as > KAMOKAMO

KUMIKUMIS > KUMIKUMI

KUMIS same as > KUMISS

KUMISES > KUMIS

KUMISS n drink made from fermented mare's or other milk

KUMISSES > KUMISS

KUMITE n freestyle sparring or fighting

KUMITES > KUMITE

KUMKUM n red pigment used by Hindu women to make a mark on the forehead

KUMKUMS > KUMKUM

KUMMEL n German liqueur

KUMMELS > KUMMEL

KUMQUAT n citrus fruit resembling a tiny orange

KUMQUATS > KUMQUAT

KUMYS same as > KUMISS

KUMYSES > KUMYS

KUNA n standard monetary unit of Croatia

KUNDALINI n (in yoga) life force that resides at the base of the spine

KUNE > KUNA

KUNEKUNE n feral pig

KUNEKUNES > KUNEKUNE

KUNJOOS adj (in Indian English) mean or stingy

KUNKAR n type of limestone

KUNKARS > KUNKAR

KUNKUR same as > KUNKAR

KUNKURS > KUNKUR

KUNZITE n variety of the mineral spodumene

KUNZITES > KUNZITE

KURBASH vb whip with a hide whip

KURBASHED > KURBASH

KURBASHES > KURBASH

KURFUFFLE same as > KERFUFFLE

KURGAN n Russian burial mound

KURGANS > KURGAN

KURI n mongrel dog

KURIS > KURI

KURRAJONG n Australian tree or shrub with tough fibrous bark

KURRE old variant of > CUR

KURRES > KURRE

KURSAAL n public room at a health resort

KURSAALS > KURSAAL

KURTA n long loose garment

KURTAS > KURTA

KURTOSES > KURTOSIS

KURTOSIS n measure of the concentration of a distribution around its mean

KURU n degenerative disease of the nervous system

KURUS > KURU

KURUSH n small currency unit of Turkey

KURUSHES > KURUSH

KURVEY vb (in old South African English) transport goods by ox cart

KURVEYED > KURVEY

KURVEYING > KURVEY

KURVEYOR > KURVEY

KURVEYORS > KURVEY

KURVEYS > KURVEY

KUSSO variant spelling of > KOUSSO

KUSSOS > KUSSO

KUTA n (in Indian English) male dog

KUTAS > KUTA

KUTCH same as > CATECHU

KUTCHA adj makeshift or not solid

KUTCHES > KUTCH

KUTI n (in Indian English) female dog

KUTIS > KUTI

KUTU n body louse

KUTUS > KUTU

KUVASZ n breed of dog from Hungary

KUVASZOK > KUVASZ

KUZU same as > KUDZU

KUZUS > KUZU

KVAS same as > KVASS

KVASES > KVAS

KVASS n alcoholic drink

KVASSES > KVASS

KVELL vb US word meaning be happy

KVELLED > KVELL

KVELLING > KVELL

KVELLS > KVELL

KVETCH vb complain or grumble

KVETCHED > KVETCH

KVETCHER > KVETCH

KVETCHERS > KVETCH

KVETCHES > KVETCH

KVETCHIER > KVETCHY

KVETCHILY > KVETCHY

KVETCHING n act of grumbling or complaining

KVETCHY adj tending to grumble or complain

KWACHA n standard monetary unit of Zambia

KWACHAS > KWACHA

KWAITO n type of South African pop music

KWAITOS > KWAITO

KWANZA n standard monetary unit of Angola

KWANZAS > KWANZA

KWELA n type of pop music

KWELAS > KWELA

KY pl n Scots word for cows

KYACK n type of pannier

KYACKS > KYACK

KYAK same as > KAYAK

KYAKS > KYAK

KYANG same as > KIANG

KYANGS > KYANG

KYANISE same as > KYANIZE

KYANISED > KYANISE

KYANISES > KYANISE

KYANISING > KYANISE

KYANITE n grey, green, or blue mineral

KYANITES > KYANITE

KYANITIC > KYANITE

KYANIZE vb treat (timber) with corrosive sublimate

KYANIZED > KYANIZE

KYANIZES > KYANIZE **KYANIZING > KYANIZE**

KYAR same as > COIR

KYARS > KYAR

KYAT n standard monetary unit of Myanmar

KYATS > KYAT

KYBO n temporary lavatory used when camping

KYBOS > KYBO

KYBOSH same as > KIBOSH

KYBOSHED > KYBOSH

KYBOSHES > KYBOSH

KYBOSHING > KYBOSH

KYDST > KYTHE

KYE n Korean fundraising meeting

KYES > KYE

KYLE n narrow strait or channel

KYLES > KYLE

KYLICES > KYLIX

KYLIE n type of boomerang

KYLIES > KYLIE

KYLIKES > KYLIX

KYLIN n (in Chinese art) mythical animal

KYLINS > KYLIN

KYLIX n drinking vessel used in ancient Greece

KYLIXES > KYLIX

KYLLOSES > KYLLOSIS

KYLLOSIS n club foot

KYLOE n breed of beef cattle

KYLOES > KYLOE

KYMOGRAM n image or other visual record created by a kymograph

KYMOGRAMS > KYMOGRAM

KYMOGRAPH n rotatable drum for holding paper on

which a tracking stylus continuously records variations in blood pressure, respiratory movements, etc

KYND *old variant of >* KIND

KYNDE *old variant of >* KIND

KYNDED > KYND

KYNDES > KYNDE

KYNDING > KYND

KYNDS > KYND

KYNE *pl n* archaic word for cows

KYOGEN *n* type of Japanese drama

KYOGENS > KYOGEN

KYPE *n* hook on the lower jaw of a mature male salmon

KYPES > KYPE

KYPHOSES > KYPHOSIS

KYPHOSIS *n* backward curvature of the thoracic spine

KYPHOTIC > KYPHOSIS

KYRIE *n* type of prayer

KYRIELLE *n* verse form of French origin characterized by repeated lines or words

KYRIELLES > KYRIELLE

KYRIES > KYRIE

KYTE *n* belly

KYTES > KYTE

KYTHE *vb* appear

KYTHED > KYTHE

KYTHES > KYTHE

KYTHING > KYTHE

KYU *n* (in judo) one of the five student grades

KYUS > KYU

L1

LA *n* the sixth note of the musical scale

LAAGER *n* (in Africa) a camp defended by a circular formation of wagons ▷ *vb* form (wagons) into a laager

LAAGERED > LAAGER

LAAGERING > LAAGER

LAAGERS > LAAGER

LAARI *same as* > LARI

LAARIS > LAARI

LAB *n* laboratory

LABARA > LABARUM

LABARUM *n* standard carried in Christian processions

LABARUMS > LABARUM

LABDA *same as* > LAMBDA

LABDACISM *n* excessive use or idiosyncratic pronunciation of (l)

LABDANUM *n* dark resinous juice obtained from various rockroses

LABDANUMS > LABDANUM

LABDAS > LABDA

LABEL *n* piece of card fixed to an object ▷ *vb* give a label to

LABELABLE > LABEL

LABELED > LABEL

LABELER > LABEL

LABELERS > LABEL

LABELING > LABEL

LABELLA > LABELLUM

LABELLATE > LABELLUM

LABELLED > LABEL

LABELLER > LABEL

LABELLERS > LABEL

LABELLING > LABEL

LABELLIST *n* person who wears only clothes with fashionable brand names

LABELLOID > LABELLUM

LABELLUM *n* lip-like part of certain plants

LABELMATE *n* musician or singer who records for the same company as another

LABELS > LABEL

LABIA > LABIUM

LABIAL *adj* of the lips ▷ *n* speech sound that involves the lips

LABIALISE *same as* > LABIALIZE

LABIALISM > LABIALIZE

LABIALITY > LABIAL

LABIALIZE *vb* pronounce with articulation involving rounded lips

LABIALLY > LABIAL

LABIALS > LABIAL

LABIATE *n* plant with square stems, aromatic leaves, and a two-lipped flower ▷ *adj* of this family

LABIATED *adj* having a lip

LABIATES > LABIATE

LABILE *adj* (of a compound) prone to chemical change

LABILITY > LABILE

LABIS *n* cochlear

LABISES > LABIS

LABIUM *n* lip or liplike structure

LABLAB *n* twining leguminous plant

LABLABS > LABLAB

LABNEH *n* Mediterranean soft cheese

LABNEHS > LABNEH

LABOR *same as* > LABOUR

LABORED *same as* > LABOURED

LABOREDLY > LABOURED

LABORER *same as* > LABOURER

LABORERS > LABORER

LABORING > LABOR

LABORIOUS *adj* involving great prolonged effort

LABORISM *same as* > LABOURISM

LABORISMS > LABORISM

LABORIST *same as* > LABOURIST

LABORISTS > LABORIST

LABORITE *n* adherent of the Labour party

LABORITES > LABORITE

LABORS > LABOR

LABORSOME *adj* requiring hard work

LABOUR *n* physical work or exertion ▷ *vb* work hard

LABOURED *adj* uttered or done with difficulty

LABOURER *n* person who labours, esp someone doing manual work for wages

LABOURERS > LABOURER

LABOURING > LABOUR

LABOURISM *n* dominance of the working classes

LABOURIST *n* person who supports workers' rights

LABOURITE *n* person who supports workers' rights

LABOURS > LABOUR

LABRA > LABRUM

LABRADOR *n* large retriever dog with a usu gold or black coat

LABRADORS > LABRADOR

LABRAL *adj* of or like a lip

LABRET *n* piece of bone or shell

LABRETS > LABRET

LABRID *same as* > LABROID

LABRIDS > LABRID

LABROID *n* type of fish ▷ *adj* of or relating to such fish

LABROIDS > LABROID

LABROSE *adj* thick-lipped

LABRUM *n* lip or liplike part

LABRUMS > LABRUM

LABRUSCA *n* grape variety

LABRUSCAS > LABRUSCA

LABRYS *n* type of axe

LABRYSES > LABRYS

LABS > LAB

LABURNUM *n* ornamental tree with yellow hanging flowers

LABURNUMS > LABURNUM

LABYRINTH *n* complicated network of passages

LAC *same as* > LAKH

LACCOLITE *same as* > LACCOLITH

LACCOLITH *n* dome-shaped body of igneous rock between two layers of older sedimentary rock

LACE *n* delicate fabric ▷ *vb* fasten with shoelaces, cords, etc

LACEBARK *n* small evergreen tree

LACEBARKS > LACEBARK

LACED > LACE

LACELESS > LACE

LACELIKE > LACE

LACEMAKER *n* one who makes lace

LACER > LACE

LACERABLE > LACERATE

LACERANT *adj* painfully distressing

LACERATE *vb* tear (flesh) ▷ *adj* having edges that are jagged or torn

LACERATED > LACERATE

LACERATES > LACERATE

LACERS > LACE

LACERTIAN *n* type of reptile

LACERTID *n* type of lizard

LACERTIDS > LACERTID

LACERTINE *adj* relating to lacertids ▷ *n* lacertid lizard

LACES > LACE

LACET *n* braided work in lace

LACETS > LACET

LACEWING *n* any of various neuropterous insects

LACEWINGS > LACEWING

LACEWOOD *n* wood of sycamore tree

LACEWOODS > LACEWOOD

LACEWORK *n* work made from lace

LACEWORKS > LACEWORK

LACEY *same as* > LACY

LACHES *n* unreasonable delay in pursuing a legal remedy

LACHESES > LACHES

LACHRYMAL *same as* > LACRIMAL

LACIER > LACY

LACIEST > LACY

LACILY > LACY

LACINESS > LACY

LACING > LACE

LACINGS > LACE

LACINIA *n* narrow fringe on petal

LACINIAE > LACINIA

LACINIATE *adj* jagged

LACK *n* shortage of something needed ▷ *vb* need

LACKADAY *another word for* > ALAS

LACKED > LACK

LACKER *variant spelling of* > LACQUER

LACKERED > LACKER

LACKERING > LACKER

LACKERS > LACKER

LACKEY *n* servile follower ▷ *vb* act as a lackey (to)

LACKEYED > LACKEY

LACKEYING > LACKEY

LACKEYS > LACKEY

LACKING > LACK

LACKLAND *n* fool

LACKLANDS > LACKLAND

LACKS > LACK

LACMUS *n* old form of litmus

LACMUSES > LACMUS

LACONIC *adj* using only a few words, terse

LACONICAL *same as* > LACONIC

LACONISM *n* economy of expression

LACONISMS > LACONISM

LACQUER *n* hard varnish for wood or metal ▷ *vb* apply lacquer to

LACQUERED > LACQUER

LACQUERER > LACQUER

LACQUERS > LACQUER

LACQUEY *same as* > LACKEY

LACQUEYED > LACQUEY

LACQUEYS > LACQUEY

LACRIMAL *adj* of tears or the glands which produce them ▷ *n* bone near tear gland

LACRIMALS > LACRIMAL

LACRIMARY adj of or relating to tears or to the glands that secrete tears

LACRIMOSO adj tearful

LACROSSE n sport in which teams catch and throw a ball using long sticks with a pouched net

LACROSSES > LACROSSE

LACRYMAL same as > LACRIMAL

LACRYMALS > LACRYMAL

LACS > LAC

LACTAM n any of a group of inner amides

LACTAMS > LACTAM

LACTARIAN n vegetarian who eats dairy products

LACTARY adj relating to milk

LACTASE n any of a group of enzymes that hydrolyse lactose to glucose and galactose

LACTASES > LACTASE

LACTATE vb secrete milk ▷ n ester or salt of lactic acid

LACTATED > LACTATE

LACTATES > LACTATE

LACTATING > LACTATE

LACTATION n secretion of milk by female mammals to feed young

LACTEAL adj of or like milk ▷ n any of the lymphatic vessels that convey chyle from the small intestine to the blood

LACTEALLY > LACTEAL

LACTEALS > LACTEAL

LACTEAN another word for > LACTEOUS

LACTEOUS adj milky

LACTIC adj of or derived from milk

LACTIFIC adj yielding milk

LACTITOL n type of artificial sweetener

LACTITOLS > LACTITOL

LACTIVISM > LACTIVIST

LACTIVIST n person who advocates breast-feeding

LACTONE n any of a class of organic compounds

LACTONES > LACTONE

LACTONIC > LACTONE

LACTOSE n white crystalline sugar found in milk

LACTOSES > LACTOSE

LACTULOSE n synthetic sugar used as a laxative

LACUNA n gap or missing part, esp in a document or series

LACUNAE > LACUNA

LACUNAL > LACUNA

LACUNAR n ceiling, soffit, or vault having coffers ▷ adj having a lacuna

LACUNARIA > LACUNAR

LACUNARS > LACUNAR

LACUNARY > LACUNA

LACUNAS > LACUNA

LACUNATE > LACUNA

LACUNE n hiatus

LACUNES > LACUNE

LACUNOSE > LACUNA

LACY adj fine, like lace

LAD n boy or young man

LADANUM same as > LABDANUM

LADANUMS > LADANUM

LADDER n frame of two poles connected by horizontal steps for climbing ▷ vb cause to have a line of undone stitches

LADDERED > LADDER

LADDERIER > LADDERY

LADDERING > LADDER

LADDERS > LADDER

LADDERY adj (of tights) laddered

LADDIE n familiar term for a male, esp a young man

LADDIER > LADDY

LADDIES > LADDIE

LADDIEST > LADDY

LADDISH adj behaving in a macho or immature manner

LADDISHLY adv in a laddish manner

LADDISM n laddish attitudes and behaviour

LADDISMS > LADDISM

LADDY adj laddish

LADE vb put cargo on board ▷ n watercourse

LADED > LADE

LADEN adj loaded ▷ vb load with cargo

LADENED > LADEN

LADENING > LADEN

LADENS > LADEN

LADER > LADE

LADERS > LADE

LADES > LADE

LADETTE n young woman who behaves like a young man

LADETTES > LADETTE

LADHOOD > LAD

LADHOODS > LAD

LADIES n women's public toilet

LADIFIED > LADIFY

LADIFIES > LADIFY

LADIFY same as > LADYFY

LADIFYING > LADIFY

LADING > LADE

LADINGS > LADE

LADINO n Italian variety of white clover

LADINOS > LADINO

LADLE n long-handled spoon with a large bowl ▷ vb serve out

LADLED > LADLE

LADLEFUL > LADLE

LADLEFULS > LADLE

LADLER n person who serves with a ladle

LADLERS > LADLER

LADLES > LADLE

LADLING > LADLE

LADRON same as > LADRONE

LADRONE n thief

LADRONES > LADRONE

LADRONS > LADRON

LADS > LAD

LADY n woman of good breeding or high rank ▷ adj female

LADYBIRD n small red beetle with black spots

LADYBIRDS > LADYBIRD

LADYBOY n transvestite or transsexual from the Far East

LADYBOYS > LADYBOY

LADYBUG same as > LADYBIRD

LADYBUGS > LADYBUG

LADYCOW another word for > LADYBIRD

LADYCOWS > LADYCOW

LADYFIED > LADYFY

LADYFIES > LADYFY

LADYFISH n type of game fish

LADYFLIES > LADYFLY

LADYFLY another word for > LADYBIRD

LADYFY vb make a lady of (someone)

LADYFYING > LADYFY

LADYHOOD > LADY

LADYHOODS > LADY

LADYISH > LADY

LADYISM > LADY

LADYISMS > LADY

LADYKIN n endearing form of lady

LADYKINS > LADYKIN

LADYLIKE adj polite and dignified

LADYLOVE n beloved woman

LADYLOVES > LADYLOVE

LADYNESS n state of being a lady

LADYPALM n small palm, grown indoors

LADYPALMS > LADYPALM

LADYSHIP n title of a peeress

LADYSHIPS > LADYSHIP

LAER another word for > LAAGER

LAERED > LAER

LAERING > LAER

LAERS > LAER

LAESIE old form of > LAZY

LAETARE n fourth Sunday of Lent

LAETARES > LAETARE

LAETRILE n drug used to treat cancer

LAETRILES > LAETRILE

LAEVIGATE same as > LEVIGATE

LAEVO adj on the left

LAEVULIN n polysaccharide occurring in the tubers of certain helianthus plants

LAEVULINS > LAEVULIN

LAEVULOSE n fructose

LAG vb go too slowly, fall behind ▷ n delay between events

LAGAN n goods or wreckage on the sea bed

LAGANS > LAGAN

LAGENA n bottle with a narrow neck

LAGENAS > LAGENA

LAGEND same as > LAGAN

LAGENDS > LAGEND

LAGER n light-bodied beer ▷ vb ferment into lager

LAGERED > LAGER

LAGERING > LAGER

LAGERS > LAGER

LAGGARD n person who lags behind ▷ adj sluggish, slow

LAGGARDLY adj like a laggard

LAGGARDS > LAGGARD

LAGGED > LAG

LAGGEN n spar of a barrel

LAGGENS > LAGGEN

LAGGER n person who lags pipes

LAGGERS > LAGGER

LAGGIN same as > LAGGEN

LAGGING > LAG

LAGGINGLY > LAG

LAGGINGS > LAG

LAGGINS > LAGGIN

LAGNAPPE same as > LAGNIAPPE

LAGNAPPES > LAGNAPPE

LAGNIAPPE n small gift, esp one given to a customer who makes a purchase

LAGOMORPH n type of placental mammal of the order which includes rabbits and hares

LAGOON n water cut off from the sea by reefs or sand bars

LAGOONAL > LAGOON

LAGOONS > LAGOON

LAGRIMOSO adj mournful

LAGS > LAG

LAGUNA n lagoon

LAGUNAS > LAGUNA

LAGUNE same as > LAGOON

LAGUNES > LAGUNE

LAH n (in tonic sol-fa) sixth degree of any major scale

LAHAL n game played by native peoples of the Pacific Northwest

LAHALS > LAHAL

LAHAR n landslide of volcanic debris and water

LAHARS > LAHAR

LAHS > LAH

LAIC adj laical ▷ n layman

LAICAL adj secular

LAICALLY > LAIC

LAICH n low-lying piece of land

LAICHS > LAICH

LAICISE same as > LAICIZE

LAICISED > LAICISE

LAICISES > LAICISE

LAICISING > LAICISE

LAICISM > LAIC

LAICISMS > LAIC

LAICITIES > LAICITY

LAICITY n state of being laical

LAICIZE vb remove ecclesiastical status from

LAICIZED > LAICIZE

LAICIZES > LAICIZE

LAICIZING > LAICIZE

LAICS > LAIC

LAID Scots form of > LOAD

LAIDED > LAID

LAIDING > LAID

LAIDLIER > LAIDLY

LAIDLIEST > LAIDLY

LAIDLY adj very ugly

LAIDS > LAID

LAIGH adj low-lying ▷ n area of low-lying ground

LAIGHER > LAIGH
LAIGHEST > LAIGH
LAIGHS > LAIGH
LAIK vb play (a game, etc)
LAIKA n type of small dog
LAIKAS > LAIKA
LAIKED > LAIK
LAIKER > LAIK
LAIKERS > LAIK
LAIKING > LAIK
LAIKS > LAIK
LAIN > LIE
LAIPSE vb beat soundly
LAIPSED > LAIPSE
LAIPSES > LAIPSE
LAIPSING > LAIPSE
LAIR n resting place of an animal ▷ vb retreat to or rest in a lair
LAIRAGE n accommodation for farm animals
LAIRAGES > LAIRAGE
LAIRD n Scottish landowner
LAIRDLIER > LAIRDLY
LAIRDLY adj pertaining to laird(s)
LAIRDS > LAIRD
LAIRDSHIP n state of being laird
LAIRED > LAIR
LAIRIER > LAIRY
LAIRIEST > LAIRY
LAIRING > LAIR
LAIRISE same as > LAIRIZE
LAIRISED > LAIRISE
LAIRISES > LAIRISE
LAIRISING > LAIRISE
LAIRIZE vb show off
LAIRIZED > LAIRIZE
LAIRIZES > LAIRIZE
LAIRIZING > LAIRIZE
LAIRS > LAIR
LAIRY adj gaudy or flashy
LAISSE n type of rhyme scheme
LAISSES > LAISSE
LAITANCE n white film forming on drying concrete
LAITANCES > LAITANCE
LAITH Scots form of > LOATH
LAITHLY same as > LAIDLY
LAITIES > LAITY
LAITY n non-clergy
LAKE n expanse of water entirely surrounded by land ▷ vb take time away from work
LAKEBED n bed of lake
LAKEBEDS > LAKEBED
LAKED > LAKE
LAKEFILL n area of land on a filled lake
LAKEFILLS > LAKEFILL
LAKEFRONT n area at edge of lake
LAKEHEAD n shore of a lake farthest from the outlet
LAKEHEADS > LAKEHEAD
LAKELAND n countryside with a lot of lakes
LAKELANDS > LAKELAND
LAKELET n small lake
LAKELETS > LAKELET
LAKELIKE > LAKE
LAKEPORT n port on lake

LAKEPORTS > LAKEPORT
LAKER n lake cargo vessel
LAKERS > LAKER
LAKES > LAKE
LAKESHORE n area at edge of lake
LAKESIDE n area at edge of lake
LAKESIDES > LAKESIDE
LAKEVIEW adj having a view of a lake
LAKEWARD same as > LAKEWARDS
LAKEWARDS adj towards a lake
LAKH n (in India) 100 000, esp referring to this sum of rupees
LAKHS > LAKH
LAKIER > LAKY
LAKIEST > LAKY
LAKIN short form of > LADYKIN
LAKING > LAKE
LAKINGS > LAKE
LAKINS > LAKIN
LAKISH adj similar to poetry of Lake poets
LAKSA n (in Malaysia) Chinese dish of rice noodles in curry or hot soup
LAKSAS > LAKSA
LAKY adj of the reddish colour of the pigment lake
LALANG n coarse weedy Malaysian grass
LALANGS > LALANG
LALDIE n great gusto
LALDIES > LALDIE
LALDY same as > LALDIE
LALIQUE n ornamental glass
LALIQUES > LALIQUE
LALL vb make bad 'l' or 'r' sounds
LALLAN n literary version of the English spoken in Lowland Scotland
LALLAND same as > LALLAN
LALLANDS > LALLAND
LALLANS > LALLAN
LALLATION n defect of speech consisting of the pronunciation of 'r' as 'l'
LALLED > LALL
LALLING > LALL
LALLINGS > LALL
LALLS > LALL
LALLYGAG vb loiter aimlessly
LALLYGAGS > LALLYGAG
LAM vb attack vigorously
LAMA n Buddhist priest in Tibet or Mongolia
LAMAISTIC adj relating to the Mahayana form of Buddhism
LAMANTIN another word for > MANATEE
LAMANTINS > LAMANTIN
LAMAS > LAMA
LAMASERAI same as > LAMASERY
LAMASERY n monastery of lamas
LAMB n young sheep ▷ vb give birth to a lamb or lambs

LAMBADA n type of Brazilian dance
LAMBADAS > LAMBADA
LAMBAST vb beat or thrash
LAMBASTE same as > LAMBAST
LAMBASTED > LAMBAST
LAMBASTES > LAMBASTE
LAMBASTS > LAMBAST
LAMBDA n 11th letter of the Greek alphabet
LAMBDAS > LAMBDA
LAMBDOID adj having the shape of the Greek letter lambda
LAMBED > LAMB
LAMBENCY > LAMBENT
LAMBENT adj (of a flame) flickering softly
LAMBENTLY > LAMBENT
LAMBER n person that attends to lambing ewes
LAMBERS > LAMBER
LAMBERT n cgs unit of illumination, equal to 1 lumen per square centimetre
LAMBERTS > LAMBERT
LAMBIE same as > LAMBKIN
LAMBIER > LAMBY
LAMBIES > LAMBIE
LAMBIEST > LAMBY
LAMBING n birth of lambs at the end of winter
LAMBINGS > LAMBING
LAMBITIVE n medicine taken by licking
LAMBKILL n N American dwarf shrub
LAMBKILLS > LAMBKILL
LAMBKIN n young lamb
LAMBKINS > LAMBKIN
LAMBLIKE > LAMB
LAMBLING n small lamb
LAMBLINGS > LAMBLING
LAMBOYS n skirt-like piece of armour made from metal strips
LAMBRUSCO n Italian sparkling wine
LAMBS > LAMB
LAMBSKIN n skin of a lamb, usually with the wool still on, used to make coats, slippers, etc
LAMBSKINS > LAMBSKIN
LAMBSWOOL n wool from a lamb's first shearing
LAMBY adj lamb-like
LAME adj having an injured or disabled leg or foot ▷ vb make lame ▷ n fabric interwoven with gold or silver threads
LAMEBRAIN n stupid or slow-witted person
LAMED n 12th letter in the Hebrew alphabet
LAMEDH same as > LAMED
LAMEDHS > LAMEDH
LAMEDS > LAMED
LAMELLA n thin layer, plate, etc, like the calcified layers of which bone is formed
LAMELLAE > LAMELLA
LAMELLAR > LAMELLA
LAMELLAS > LAMELLA
LAMELLATE > LAMELLA

LAMELLOID another word for > LAMELLA
LAMELLOSE > LAMELLA
LAMELY > LAME
LAMENESS > LAME
LAMENT vb feel or express sorrow (for) ▷ n passionate expression of grief
LAMENTED adj grieved for
LAMENTER > LAMENT
LAMENTERS > LAMENT
LAMENTING > LAMENT
LAMENTS > LAMENT
LAMER > LAME
LAMES > LAME
LAMEST > LAME
LAMETER Scots form of > LAMIGER
LAMETERS > LAMETER
LAMIA n female monster with a snake's body and a woman's head
LAMIAE > LAMIA
LAMIAS > LAMIA
LAMIGER n disabled person
LAMIGERS > LAMIGER
LAMINA n thin plate, esp of bone or mineral
LAMINABLE > LAMINATE
LAMINAE > LAMINA
LAMINAL n consonant articulated with blade of tongue
LAMINALS > LAMINAL
LAMINAR > LAMINA
LAMINARIA n type of brown seaweed
LAMINARIN n carbohydrate, consisting of repeated glucose units, that is the main storage product of brown algae
LAMINARY > LAMINA
LAMINAS > LAMINA
LAMINATE vb make (a sheet of material) by sticking together thin sheets ▷ n laminated sheet ▷ adj composed of lamina
LAMINATED adj composed of many layers stuck together
LAMINATES > LAMINATE
LAMINATOR > LAMINATE
LAMING > LAME
LAMINGTON n sponge cake coated with a sweet coating
LAMININ n type of protein
LAMININS > LAMININ
LAMINITIS n (in animals with hooves) inflammation of the tissue to which the hoof is attached
LAMINOSE > LAMINA
LAMINOUS > LAMINA
LAMISH adj rather lame
LAMISTER n fugitive
LAMISTERS > LAMISTER
LAMITER same as > LAMETER
LAMITERS > LAMITER
LAMMED > LAM
LAMMER Scots word for > AMBER
LAMMERS > LAMMER
LAMMIE same as > LAMMY
LAMMIES > LAMMY

LAMMIGER *same as* > LAMIGER

LAMMIGERS > LAMIGER

LAMMING > LAM

LAMMINGS > LAM

LAMMY n thick woollen jumper

LAMP n device which produces light from electricity, oil, or gas ▷ vb go quickly with long steps

LAMPAD n candlestick

LAMPADARY n person who lights the lamps in an Orthodox Greek Church

LAMPADIST n prize-winner in a race run by young men with torches

LAMPADS > LAMPAD

LAMPAS n swelling of the mucous membrane of the hard palate of horses

LAMPASES > LAMPAS

LAMPASSE *same as* > LAMPAS

LAMPASSES > LAMPASSE

LAMPBLACK n fine black soot used as a pigment in paint and ink ▷ vb blacken with fine black soot

LAMPBRUSH n as in *lampbrush chromosome* type of chromosome

LAMPED > LAMP

LAMPER n lamprey

LAMPERN n migratory European lamprey

LAMPERNS > LAMPERN

LAMPERS > LAMPER

LAMPERSES > LAMPERS

LAMPHOLE n hole in ground for lowering lamp into sewer

LAMPHOLES > LAMPHOLE

LAMPING > LAMP

LAMPINGS > LAMP

LAMPION n oil-burning lamp

LAMPIONS > LAMPION

LAMPLESS adj without a lamp

LAMPLIGHT n light produced by lamp

LAMPLIT adj lit by lamps

LAMPOON n humorous satire ridiculing someone ▷ vb satirize or ridicule

LAMPOONED > LAMPOON

LAMPOONER > LAMPOON

LAMPOONS > LAMPOON

LAMPPOST n post supporting a lamp in the street

LAMPPOSTS > LAMPPOST

LAMPREY n eel-like fish with a round sucking mouth

LAMPREYS > LAMPREY

LAMPS > LAMP

LAMPSHADE n shade used to reduce light shed by light bulb

LAMPSHELL n brachiopod

LAMPSTAND n stand for a lamp

LAMPUKA *same as* > LAMPUKI

LAMPUKAS > LAMPUKA

LAMPUKI n type of fish

LAMPUKIS > LAMPUKI

LAMPYRID n firefly

LAMPYRIDS > LAMPYRID

LAMS > LAM

LAMSTER n fugitive

LAMSTERS > LAMSTER

LANA n wood from genipap tree

LANAI *Hawaiian word for* > VERANDA

LANAIS > LANAI

LANAS > LANA

LANATE adj having or consisting of a woolly covering of hairs

LANATED *same as* > LANATE

LANCE n long spear used by a mounted soldier ▷ vb pierce (a boil or abscess) with a lancet

LANCED > LANCE

LANCEGAY n kind of ancient spear

LANCEGAYS > LANCEGAY

LANCEJACK n lance corporal

LANCELET n type of marine invertebrate

LANCELETS > LANCELET

LANCELIKE adj like a lance

LANCEOLAR adj narrow and tapering to a point at each end

LANCER n formerly, cavalry soldier armed with a lance

LANCERS n quadrille for eight or sixteen couples

LANCES > LANCE

LANCET n pointed two-edged surgical knife

LANCETED adj having one or more lancet arches or windows

LANCETS > LANCET

LANCEWOOD n New Zealand tree with slender leaves

LANCH *obsolete form of* > LAUNCH

LANCHED > LANCH

LANCHES > LANCH

LANCHING > LANCH

LANCIERS pl n type of dance

LANCIFORM adj in the form of a lance

LANCINATE adj (esp of pain) sharp or cutting

LANCING > LANCE

LAND n solid part of the earth's surface ▷ vb come or bring to earth after a flight, jump, or fall

LANDAMMAN n chairman of the governing council in some Swiss cantons

LANDAU n four-wheeled carriage with two folding hoods

LANDAULET n small landau

LANDAUS > LANDAU

LANDBOARD n narrow board, with wheels larger than those on a skateboard, usually ridden while standing

LANDDAMNE vb Shakespearian word for make (a person's life) unbearable

LANDDROS n sheriff

LANDDROST n South African magistrate

LANDE n type of moorland in SW France

LANDED adj possessing or consisting of lands

LANDER n spacecraft which lands on a planet or other body

LANDERS > LANDER

LANDES > LANDE

LANDFALL n ship's first landing after a voyage

LANDFALLS > LANDFALL

LANDFAST adj (of ice) attached to the shore

LANDFILL n disposing of rubbish by covering it with earth

LANDFILLS > LANDFILL

LANDFORCE n body of people trained for land warfare

LANDFORM n any natural feature of the earth's surface, such as valleys and mountains

LANDFORMS > LANDFORM

LANDGRAB n sudden attempt to establish ownership of something

LANDGRABS > LANDGRAB

LANDGRAVE n (from the 13th century to 1806) a count who ruled over a specified territory

LANDING n floor area at the top of a flight of stairs

LANDINGS > LANDING

LANDLADY n woman who owns and leases property

LANDLER n Austrian country dance

LANDLERS > LANDLER

LANDLESS > LAND

LANDLINE n telecommunications cable laid over land

LANDLINES > LANDLINE

LANDLOPER n vagabond or vagrant

LANDLORD n person who rents out land, houses, etc

LANDLORDS > LANDLORD

LANDMAN n person who lives and works on land

LANDMARK n prominent object in or feature of a landscape

LANDMARKS > LANDMARK

LANDMASS n large continuous area of land

LANDMEN > LANDMAN

LANDMINE n type of bomb laid on or just under the surface of the ground ▷ vb lay (an area) with landmines

LANDMINED > LANDMINE

LANDMINES > LANDMINE

LANDOWNER n person who owns land

LANDRACE n white very long-bodied lop-eared breed of pork pig

LANDRACES > LANDRACE

LANDRAIL n type of bird

LANDRAILS > LANDRAIL

LANDS pl n holdings in land

LANDSCAPE n extensive piece of inland scenery seen from one place ▷ vb improve natural features of (a piece of land) ▷ adj (of a publication or an illustration in a publication) of greater width than height

LANDSHARK n person who makes inordinate profits by buying and selling land

LANDSIDE n part of an airport farthest from the aircraft

LANDSIDES > LANDSIDE

LANDSKIP *another word for* > LANDSCAPE

LANDSKIPS > LANDSKIP

LANDSLEIT > LANDSMAN

LANDSLID > LANDSLIDE

LANDSLIDE vb cause land or rock to fall from hillside

LANDSLIP *same as* > LANDSLIDE

LANDSLIPS > LANDSLIP

LANDSMAN n person who works or lives on land, as distinguished from a seaman

LANDSMEN > LANDSMAN

LANDWARD *same as* > LANDWARDS

LANDWARDS adv towards land

LANDWASH n part of the shore between the high-water mark and the sea

LANDWIND n wind that comes from the land

LANDWINDS > LANDWIND

LANE n narrow road

LANELY *Scots form of* > LONELY

LANES > LANE

LANEWAY n lane

LANEWAYS > LANEWAY

LANG *Scot word for* > LONG

LANGAHA n type of Madagascan snake

LANGAHAS > LANGAHA

LANGAR n dining hall in a gurdwara

LANGARS > LANGAR

LANGER n informal Irish word for penis ▷ adj comparative form of lang

LANGERED adj drunk

LANGERS > LANGER

LANGEST > LANG

LANGLAUF n cross-country skiing

LANGLAUFS > LANGLAUF

LANGLEY n unit of solar radiation

LANGLEYS > LANGLEY

LANGOUSTE n spiny lobster

LANGRAGE n shot consisting of scrap iron packed into a case, formerly used in naval warfare

LANGRAGES > LANGRAGE

LANGREL *same as* > LANGRAGE

LANGRELS > LANGREL

LANGRIDGE *same as* > LANGRAGE

LANGSHAN n breed of chicken

LANGSHANS > LANGSHAN

LANGSPEL *n* type of Scandinavian stringed instrument

LANGSPELS > LANGSPEL

LANGSPIEL *same as* > LANGSPEL

LANGSPIL *n* type of Scandinavian stringed instrument

LANGSPILS > LANGSPIL

LANGSYNE *adv* long ago ▷ *n* times long past, esp those fondly remembered

LANGSYNES > LANGSYNE

LANGUAGE *n* system of sounds, symbols, etc for communicating thought ▷ *vb* express in language

LANGUAGED > LANGUAGE

LANGUAGES > LANGUAGE

LANGUE *n* language considered as an abstract system

LANGUED *adj* having a tongue

LANGUES > LANGUE

LANGUET *n* anything resembling a tongue

LANGUETS > LANGUET

LANGUETTE *same as* > LANGUET

LANGUID *adj* lacking energy

LANGUIDLY > LANGUID

LANGUISH *vb* suffer neglect or hardship

LANGUOR *n* dreamy relaxation

LANGUORS > LANGUOR

LANGUR *n* type of arboreal Old World monkey

LANGURS > LANGUR

LANIARD *same as* > LANYARD

LANIARDS > LANIARD

LANIARIES > LANIARY

LANIARY *adj* adapted for tearing ▷ *n* tooth adapted for tearing

LANITAL *n* fibre used in production of synthetic wool

LANITALS > LANITAL

LANK *adj* straight and limp ▷ *vb* become lank

LANKED > LANK

LANKER > LANK

LANKEST > LANK

LANKIER > LANKY

LANKIEST > LANKY

LANKILY > LANKY

LANKINESS > LANKY

LANKING > LANK

LANKLY > LANK

LANKNESS > LANK

LANKS > LANK

LANKY *adj* tall and thin

LANNER *n* large falcon

LANNERET *n* male or tercel of the lanner falcon

LANNERETS > LANNERET

LANNERS > LANNER

LANOLATED > LANOLIN

LANOLIN *n* grease from sheep's wool used in ointments etc

LANOLINE *same as* > LANOLIN

LANOLINES > LANOLINE

LANOLINS > LANOLIN

LANOSE *same as* > LANATE

LANOSITY > LANOSE

LANT *n* stale urine

LANTANA *n* shrub with orange or yellow flowers

LANTANAS > LANTANA

LANTERLOO *n* old card game

LANTERN *n* light in a transparent protective case ▷ *vb* supply with a lantern

LANTERNED > LANTERN

LANTERNS > LANTERN

LANTHANON *n* one of a group of chemical elements

LANTHANUM *n* silvery-white metallic element

LANTHORN *archaic word for* > LANTERN

LANTHORNS > LANTHORN

LANTS > LANT

LANTSKIP *another word for* > LANDSCAPE

LANTSKIPS > LANTSKIP

LANUGO *n* layer of fine hairs, esp the covering of the human fetus before birth

LANUGOS > LANUGO

LANX *n* dish; plate

LANYARD *n* neck cord to hold a knife or whistle

LANYARDS > LANYARD

LAODICEAN *adj* indifferent, esp in religious matters ▷ *n* person having a lukewarm attitude towards religious matters

LAOGAI *n* forced labour camp in China

LAOGAIS > LAOGAI

LAP *n* part between the waist and knees when sitting ▷ *vb* overtake so as to be one or more circuits ahead

LAPBOARD *n* flat board that can be used on the lap as a makeshift table or desk

LAPBOARDS > LAPBOARD

LAPDOG *n* small pet dog

LAPDOGS > LAPDOG

LAPEL *n* part of the front of a coat or jacket folded back towards the shoulders

LAPELED > LAPEL

LAPELLED > LAPEL

LAPELS > LAPEL

LAPFUL *same as* > LAP

LAPFULS > LAPFUL

LAPHELD *adj* small enough to be used on one's lap

LAPIDARY *adj* of or relating to stones ▷ *n* person who cuts, polishes, sets, or deals in gemstones

LAPIDATE *vb* pelt with stones

LAPIDATED > LAPIDATE

LAPIDATES > LAPIDATE

LAPIDEOUS *adj* having appearance or texture of stone

LAPIDES > LAPIS

LAPIDIFIC *adj* transforming into stone

LAPIDIFY *vb* change into stone

LAPIDIST *n* cutter and engraver of precious stones

LAPIDISTS > LAPIDIST

LAPILLI > LAPILLUS

LAPILLUS *n* small piece of lava thrown from a volcano

LAPIN *n* rabbit fur

LAPINS > LAPIN

LAPIS *n* as in *lapis lazuli* brilliant blue mineral gemstone

LAPISES > LAPIS

LAPJE *same as* > LAPPIE

LAPJES > LAPJE

LAPPED > LAP

LAPPEL *same as* > LAPEL

LAPPELS > LAPPEL

LAPPER *n* one that laps ▷ *vb* curdle

LAPPERED > LAPPER

LAPPERING > LAPPER

LAPPERS > LAPPER

LAPPET *n* small hanging flap

LAPPETED > LAPPET

LAPPETS > LAPPET

LAPPIE *n* rag

LAPPIES > LAPPIE

LAPPING > LAP

LAPPINGS > LAP

LAPS > LAP

LAPSABLE > LAPSE

LAPSANG *n* Chinese tea

LAPSANGS > LAPSANG

LAPSE *n* temporary drop in a standard ▷ *vb* drop in standard

LAPSED > LAPSE

LAPSER > LAPSE

LAPSERS > LAPSE

LAPSES > LAPSE

LAPSIBLE > LAPSE

LAPSING > LAPSE

LAPSTONE *n* device used by a cobbler on which leather is beaten

LAPSTONES > LAPSTONE

LAPSTRAKE *n* clinker-built boat

LAPSTREAK *same as* > LAPSTRAKE

LAPSUS *n* lapse or error

LAPTOP *adj* small enough to fit on a user's lap ▷ *n* small computer

LAPTOPS > LAPTOP

LAPTRAY *n* tray with a cushioned underside

LAPTRAYS > LAPTRAY

LAPWING *n* plover with a tuft of feathers on the head

LAPWINGS > LAPWING

LAPWORK *n* work with lapping edges

LAPWORKS > LAPWORK

LAQUEARIA *n* ceiling made of panels

LAR *n* boy or young man

LARBOARD *n* port (side of a ship)

LARBOARDS > LARBOARD

LARCENER > LARCENY

LARCENIES > LARCENY

LARCENIST > LARCENY

LARCENOUS > LARCENY

LARCENY *n* theft

LARCH *n* deciduous coniferous tree

LARCHEN *adj* of larch

LARCHES > LARCH

LARCHWOOD *n* wood of the larch

LARD *n* soft white pig fat ▷ *vb* insert strips of bacon in before cooking

LARDALITE *n* type of mineral

LARDED > LARD

LARDER *n* storeroom for food

LARDERER *n* person in charge of larder

LARDERERS > LARDERER

LARDERS > LARDER

LARDIER > LARDY

LARDIEST > LARDY

LARDING > LARD

LARDLIKE > LARD

LARDON *n* strip or cube of fat or bacon used in larding meat

LARDONS > LARDON

LARDOON *same as* > LARDON

LARDOONS > LARDOON

LARDS > LARD

LARDY *adj* fat

LARE *another word for* > LORE

LAREE *n* Asian fish-hook

LAREES > LAREE

LARES > LARE

LARGANDO *adv* (music) growing slower and more marked

LARGE *adj* great in size, number ▷ *n* formerly, musical note

LARGELY *adv* principally

LARGEN *another word for* > ENLARGE

LARGENED > LARGEN

LARGENESS > LARGE

LARGENING > LARGEN

LARGENS > LARGEN

LARGER > LARGE

LARGES > LARGE

LARGESS *same as* > LARGESSE

LARGESSE *n* generous giving, esp of money

LARGESSES > LARGESSE

LARGEST > LARGE

LARGHETTO *adv* be performed moderately slowly ▷ *n* piece or passage to be performed in this way

LARGISH *adj* fairly large

LARGITION *n* act of being generous

LARGO *adv* in a slow and dignified manner ▷ *n* performance piece in a slow manner

LARGOS > LARGO

LARI *n* monetary unit of Georgia

LARIAT *n* lasso ▷ *vb* tether with lariat

LARIATED > LARIAT

LARIATING > LARIAT

LARIATS > LARIAT

LARIGAN *n* type of tanned moccasin boot

LARIGANS > LARIGAN

LARINE *adj* of, relating to, or resembling a gull

LARIS > LARI

LARK *n* small brown songbird ▷ *vb* frolic

LARKED > LARK

LARKER > LARK

LARKERS > LARK

LARKIER > LARKY

LARKIEST > LARKY

LARKINESS > LARKY

LARKING > LARK

LARKISH > LARK

LARKS > LARK

LARKSOME *adj* mischievous

LARKSPUR *n* plant with spikes of blue, pink, or white flowers with spurs

LARKSPURS > LARKSPUR

LARKY *adj* frolicsome

LARMIER *n* pouch under lower eyelid of deer

LARMIERS > LARMIER

LARN *vb* learn

LARNAKES > LARNAX

LARNAX *n* terracotta coffin

LARNED > LARN

LARNEY *n* White person ▷ *adj* (of clothes) smart

LARNEYS > LARNEY

LARNIER > LARNEY

LARNIEST > LARNEY

LARNING > LARN

LARNS > LARN

LARNT > LARN

LAROID *adj* relating to Larus genus of gull family

LARRIGAN *n* knee-high oiled leather moccasin boot worn by trappers, etc

LARRIGANS > LARRIGAN

LARRIKIN *n* mischievous or unruly person

LARRIKINS > LARRIKIN

LARRUP *vb* beat or flog

LARRUPED > LARRUP

LARRUPER > LARRUP

LARRUPERS > LARRUP

LARRUPING > LARRUP

LARRUPS > LARRUP

LARS > LAR

LARUM *archaic word for* > ALARM

LARUMS > LARUM

LARVA *n* immature insect

LARVAE > LARVA

LARVAL > LARVA

LARVAS > LARVA

LARVATE *adj* masked; concealed

LARVATED *same as* > LARVATE

LARVICIDE *vb* kill larvae with a chemical

LARVIFORM *adj* in the form of a larva

LARVIKITE *n* type of mineral

LARYNGAL *adj* laryngeal ▷ *n* sound articulated in the larynx

LARYNGALS > LARYNGAL

LARYNGEAL *adj* of or relating to the larynx

LARYNGES > LARYNX

LARYNX *n* part of the throat containing the vocal cords

LARYNXES > LARYNX

LAS > LA

LASAGNA *same as* > LASAGNE

LASAGNAS > LASAGNA

LASAGNE *n* sheet pasta

LASAGNES > LASAGNE

LASCAR *n* East Indian seaman

LASCARS > LASCAR

LASE *vb* to be capable of acting as a laser

LASED > LASE

LASER *n* device producing a very narrow intense beam of light ▷ *vb* use a laser on (something), esp as part of medical treatment

LASERDISC *n* disk similar in size to a long-playing record, on which data is stored in pits in a similar way to data storage on a compact disk

LASERDISK *same as* > LASERDISC

LASERED > LASER

LASERING > LASER

LASERS > LASER

LASERWORT *n* type of plant

LASES > LASE

LASH *n* eyelash ▷ *vb* hit with a whip

LASHED > LASH

LASHER > LASH

LASHERS > LASH

LASHES > LASH

LASHING > LASH

LASHINGLY > LASH

LASHINGS *pl n* great amount of

LASHINS *variant of* > LASHINGS

LASHKAR *n* troop of Indian men with weapons

LASHKARS > LASHKAR

LASHLESS *adj* (of a whip) without a lash

LASING > LASE

LASINGS > LASE

LASKET *n* loop at the foot of a sail onto which an extra sail may be fastened

LASKETS > LASKET

LASQUE *n* flat-cut diamond

LASQUES > LASQUE

LASS *n* girl

LASSES > LASS

LASSI *n* cold drink made of yoghurt or buttermilk, flavoured with sugar, salt, or spice

LASSIE *n* little lass

LASSIES > LASSIE

LASSIS > LASSI

LASSITUDE *n* physical or mental weariness

LASSLORN *adj* abandoned by a young girl

LASSO *n* rope with a noose ▷ *vb* catch with a lasso

LASSOCK *another word for* > LASS

LASSOCKS > LASSOCK

LASSOED > LASSO

LASSOER > LASSO

LASSOERS > LASSO

LASSOES > LASSO

LASSOING *n* act of lassoing

LASSOINGS > LASSOING

LASSOS > LASSO

LASSU *n* slow part of csárdás folk dance

LASSUS > LASSU

LASSY *n* short for molasses

LAST *adv* coming at the end or after all others ▷ *adj* only remaining ▷ *n* last person or thing ▷ *vb* continue

LASTAGE *n* space for storing goods in ship

LASTAGES > LASTAGE

LASTBORN *n* last child to be born

LASTBORNS > LASTBORN

LASTED > LAST

LASTER > LAST

LASTERS > LAST

LASTING *adj* remaining effective for a long time ▷ *n* strong durable fabric used for shoe uppers, etc

LASTINGLY > LASTING

LASTINGS > LASTING

LASTLY *adv* at the end or at the last point

LASTS > LAST

LAT *n* former coin of Latvia

LATAH *n* psychological condition

LATAHS > LATAH

LATAKIA *n* Turkish tobacco

LATAKIAS > LATAKIA

LATCH *n* fastening for a door with a bar and lever ▷ *vb* fasten with a latch

LATCHED > LATCH

LATCHES > LATCH

LATCHET *n* shoe fastening

LATCHETS > LATCHET

LATCHING > LATCH

LATCHKEY *n* key for an outside door or gate, esp one that lifts a latch

LATCHKEYS > LATCHKEY

LATE *adj* after the normal or expected time ▷ *adv* after the normal or expected time

LATECOMER *n* person or thing that comes late

LATED *archaic word for* > BELATED

LATEEN *adj* of a rig with a triangular sail bent to a yard hoisted to the head of a low mast

LATEENER *n* lateen-rigged ship

LATEENERS > LATEEN

LATEENS > LATEEN

LATELY *adv* in recent times

LATEN *vb* become or cause to become late

LATENCE > LATENT

LATENCES > LATENCE

LATENCIES > LATENT

LATENCY > LATENT

LATENED > LATEN

LATENESS > LATE

LATENING > LATEN

LATENS > LATEN

LATENT *adj* hidden and not yet developed ▷ *n* fingerprint that is not visible to the eye

LATENTLY > LATENT

LATENTS > LATENT

LATER *adv* afterwards

LATERAD *adv* towards the side

LATERAL *adj* of or relating to the side or sides ▷ *n* lateral object, part, passage, or movement ▷ *vb* pass laterally

LATERALED > LATERAL

LATERALLY > LATERAL

LATERALS > LATERAL

LATERBORN *adj* born later ▷ *n* one born later

LATERISE *same as* > LATERIZE

LATERISED > LATERISE

LATERISES > LATERISE

LATERITE *n* any of a group of deposits consisting of residual insoluble ferric and aluminium oxides

LATERITES > LATERITE

LATERITIC > LATERITE

LATERIZE *vb* develop into a laterite

LATERIZED > LATERIZE

LATERIZES > LATERIZE

LATESCENT *n* becoming latent

LATEST *n* the most recent news

LATESTS > LATEST

LATEWAKE *n* vigil held over a dead body

LATEWAKES > LATEWAKE

LATEWOOD *n* wood formed later in tree's growing season

LATEWOODS > LATEWOOD

LATEX *n* milky fluid found in some plants

LATEXES > LATEX

LATH *n* thin strip of wood ▷ *vb* attach laths to

LATHE *n* machine for turning wood or metal while it is being shaped ▷ *vb* shape, bore, or cut a screw thread in or on (a workpiece) on a lathe

LATHED > LATHE

LATHEE *same as* > LATHI

LATHEES > LATHEE

LATHEN *adj* covered with laths

LATHER *n* froth of soap and water ▷ *vb* make frothy

LATHERED > LATHER

LATHERER > LATHER

LATHERERS > LATHER

LATHERIER > LATHER

LATHERING > LATHER

LATHERS > LATHER

LATHERY > LATHER

LATHES > LATHE

LATHI *n* long heavy wooden stick used as a weapon in India

LATHIER > LATHY

LATHIEST > LATHY

LATHING > LATHE

LATHINGS > LATHE

LATHIS > LATHI

LATHLIKE > LATH

LATHS > LATH

LATHWORK *n* work made of laths

LATHWORKS > LATHWORK
LATHY adj resembling a lath, esp in being tall and thin
LATHYRISM n neurological disease often resulting in weakness and paralysis of the legs
LATHYRUS n genus of climbing plant
LATI > LAT
LATICES > LATEX
LATICIFER n cell or group of cells in a plant that contains latex
LATICLAVE n broad stripe on Roman senator's tunic
LATIFONDI > LATIFONDO
LATIFONDO n large agricultural estate in ancient Rome
LATIGO n strap on horse's saddle
LATIGOES > LATIGO
LATIGOS > LATIGO
LATILLA n stick making up part of ceiling
LATILLAS > LATILLA
LATIMERIA n type of coelacanth fish
LATINA n US female of Latin American origin
LATINAS > LATINA
LATINISE same as > LATINIZE
LATINISED > LATINISE
LATINISES > LATINISE
LATINITY n facility in the use of Latin
LATINIZE vb translate into Latin
LATINIZED > LATINIZE
LATINIZES > LATINIZE
LATINO n US male of Latin American origin
LATINOS > LATINO
LATISH adv rather late ▷ adj rather late
LATITANCY > LATITANT
LATITANT adj concealed
LATITAT n writ presuming that person accused was hiding
LATITATS > LATITAT
LATITUDE n angular distance measured in degrees N or S of the equator
LATITUDES > LATITUDE
LATKE n crispy Jewish pancake
LATKES > LATKE
LATOSOL n type of deep, well-drained soil
LATOSOLIC > LATOSOL
LATOSOLS > LATOSOL
LATRANT adj barking
LATRATION n instance of barking
LATRIA n adoration that may be offered to God alone
LATRIAS > LATRIA
LATRINE n toilet in a barracks
LATRINES > LATRINE
LATROCINY n banditry
LATRON n bandit
LATRONS > LATRON
LATS > LAT

LATTE n coffee with hot milk
LATTEN n metal or alloy, esp brass, made in thin sheets
LATTENS > LATTEN
LATTER adj second of two ▷ n second of two people or things
LATTERLY adv recently
LATTERS > LATTER
LATTES > LATTE
LATTICE n framework of intersecting strips of wood ▷ vb adorn with a lattice
LATTICED > LATTICE
LATTICES > LATTICE
LATTICING > LATTICE
LATTICINI > LATTICINO
LATTICINO n type of Italian glass
LATTIN n brass alloy beaten into a thin sheet
LATTINS > LATTIN
LATU n type of edible Asian seaweed
LATUS > LATU
LAUAN n type of wood used in furniture-making
LAUANS > LAUAN
LAUCH Scots form of > LAUGH
LAUCHING > LAUCH
LAUCHS > LAUCH
LAUD vb praise or glorify ▷ n praise or glorification
LAUDABLE adj praiseworthy
LAUDABLY > LAUDABLE
LAUDANUM n opium-based sedative
LAUDANUMS > LAUDANUM
LAUDATION formal word for > PRAISE
LAUDATIVE same as > LAUDATORY
LAUDATOR n one who praises highly
LAUDATORS > LAUDATOR
LAUDATORY adj praising or glorifying
LAUDED > LAUD
LAUDER > LAUD
LAUDERS > LAUD
LAUDING > LAUD
LAUDS n traditional morning prayer of the Western Church
LAUF n run in bobsleighing
LAUFS > LAUF
LAUGH vb make sounds with the voice expressing amusement ▷ n act of laughing
LAUGHABLE adj ridiculously inadequate
LAUGHABLY > LAUGHABLE
LAUGHED > LAUGH
LAUGHER > LAUGH
LAUGHERS > LAUGH
LAUGHFUL > LAUGH
LAUGHIER > LAUGHY
LAUGHIEST > LAUGHY
LAUGHING > LAUGH
LAUGHINGS > LAUGH
LAUGHLINE n funny line in dialogue
LAUGHS > LAUGH
LAUGHSOME adj causing laughter
LAUGHTER n sound or action of laughing

LAUGHTERS > LAUGHTER
LAUGHY adj laughing a lot
LAUNCE old form of > LANCE
LAUNCED > LAUNCE
LAUNCES > LAUNCE
LAUNCH vb put into the water for the first time ▷ n launching
LAUNCHED > LAUNCH
LAUNCHER n device for launching projectiles
LAUNCHERS > LAUNCHER
LAUNCHES > LAUNCH
LAUNCHING n act of launching
LAUNCHPAD n platform from which a spacecraft is launched
LAUNCING > LAUNCE
LAUND n open grassy space
LAUNDER vb wash and iron ▷ n water trough
LAUNDERED > LAUNDER
LAUNDERER > LAUNDER
LAUNDERS > LAUNDER
LAUNDRESS n woman who launders clothes, sheets, etc, for a living
LAUNDRIES > LAUNDRY
LAUNDRY n clothes for washing
LAUNDS > LAUND
LAURA n group of monastic cells
LAURAE > LAURA
LAURAS > LAURA
LAUREATE adj crowned with laurel leaves as a sign of honour ▷ n person honoured with an award for art or science ▷ vb crown with laurel
LAUREATED > LAUREATE
LAUREATES > LAUREATE
LAUREL n glossy-leaved shrub, bay tree ▷ vb crown with laurel
LAURELED > LAUREL
LAURELING > LAUREL
LAURELLED > LAUREL
LAURELS > LAUREL
LAURIC adj as in lauric acid dodecanoic acid
LAURYL n as in lauryl alcohol crystalline solid used to make detergents
LAURYLS > LAURYL
LAUWINE n avalanche
LAUWINES > LAUWINE
LAV short for > LAVATORY
LAVA n molten rock thrown out by volcanoes
LAVABO n ritual washing of priest's hands at Mass
LAVABOES > LAVABO
LAVABOS > LAVABO
LAVAFORM n in form of lava
LAVAGE n washing out of a hollow organ
LAVAGES > LAVAGE
LAVAL adj of or relating to lava
LAVALAVA n draped skirtlike garment worn by Polynesians
LAVALAVAS > LAVALAVA

LAVALIER n decorative pendant worn on chain
LAVALIERE same as > LAVALIER
LAVALIERS > LAVALIER
LAVALIKE > LAVA
LAVANDIN n hybrid of two varieties of the lavender plant
LAVANDINS > LAVANDIN
LAVAS > LAVA
LAVASH n Armenian flat bread
LAVASHES > LAVASH
LAVATERA n type of plant closely resembling the mallow
LAVATERAS > LAVATERA
LAVATION n act or process of washing
LAVATIONS > LAVATION
LAVATORY n toilet
LAVE archaic word for > WASH
LAVED > LAVE
LAVEER vb (in sailing) tack
LAVEERED > LAVEER
LAVEERING > LAVEER
LAVEERS > LAVEER
LAVEMENT n washing with injections of water
LAVEMENTS > LAVEMENT
LAVENDER n shrub with fragrant flowers ▷ adj bluish-purple
LAVENDERS > LAVENDER
LAVER n priest's basin for ritual ablutions
LAVEROCK Scot and northern English dialect word for > SKYLARK
LAVEROCKS > LAVEROCK
LAVERS > LAVER
LAVES > LAVE
LAVING > LAVE
LAVISH adj prolific ▷ vb give or spend generously
LAVISHED > LAVISH
LAVISHER > LAVISH
LAVISHERS > LAVISH
LAVISHES > LAVISH
LAVISHEST > LAVISH
LAVISHING > LAVISH
LAVISHLY > LAVISH
LAVOLT same as > LAVOLTA
LAVOLTA n old Italian dance ▷ vb dance the lavolta
LAVOLTAED > LAVOLTA
LAVOLTAS > LAVOLTA
LAVOLTED > LAVOLT
LAVOLTING > LAVOLT
LAVOLTS > LAVOLT
LAVRA same as > LAURA
LAVRAS > LAVRA
LAVROCK same as > LAVEROCK
LAVROCKS > LAVROCK
LAVS > LAV
LAVVIES > LAVVY
LAVVY n lavatory
LAW n rule binding on a community ▷ vb prosecute ▷ adj (in archaic usage) low
LAWBOOK n book on subject of law
LAWBOOKS > LAWBOOK
LAWCOURT n court of law
LAWCOURTS > LAWCOURT

LAWED > LAW
LAWER > LAW
LAWEST > LAW
LAWFARE n use of the law by a country against its enemies
LAWFARES > LAWFARE
LAWFUL adj allowed by law
LAWFULLY > LAWFUL
LAWGIVER n giver of a code of laws
LAWGIVERS > LAWGIVER
LAWGIVING > LAWGIVER
LAWIN n bill or reckoning
LAWINE n avalanche
LAWINES > LAWINE
LAWING same as > LAWIN
LAWINGS > LAWING
LAWINS > LAWIN
LAWK interj used to show surprise
LAWKS same as > LAWK
LAWLAND same as > LOWLAND
LAWLANDS > LAWLAND
LAWLESS adj breaking the law
LAWLESSLY > LAWLESS
LAWLIKE > LAW
LAWMAKER same as > LAWGIVER
LAWMAKERS > LAWMAKER
LAWMAKING n process of legislating
LAWMAN n officer of the law
LAWMEN > LAWMAN
LAWMONGER n inferior lawyer
LAWN n area of tended and mown grass ▷ vb create or make into a lawn
LAWNED adj having a lawn
LAWNIER > LAWN
LAWNIEST > LAWN
LAWNING > LAWN
LAWNMOWER n machine for cutting grass on lawns
LAWNS > LAWN
LAWNY > LAWN
LAWS > LAW
LAWSUIT n court case
LAWSUITS > LAWSUIT
LAWYER n professional legal expert ▷ vb act as lawyer
LAWYERED > LAWYER
LAWYERING > LAWYER
LAWYERLY adj like a lawyer
LAWYERS > LAWYER
LAX adj not strict ▷ vb make lax, loosen
LAXATION n act of making lax or the state of being lax
LAXATIONS > LAXATION
LAXATIVE adj (medicine) inducing the emptying of the bowels ▷ n medicine that induces the emptying of the bowels
LAXATIVES > LAXATIVE
LAXATOR n muscle that loosens body part
LAXATORS > LAXATOR
LAXED > LAX
LAXER > LAX
LAXES > LAX
LAXEST > LAX
LAXING > LAX
LAXISM > LAXIST

LAXISMS > LAXIST
LAXIST n lenient or tolerant person
LAXISTS > LAXIST
LAXITIES > LAX
LAXITY > LAX
LAXLY > LAX
LAXNESS > LAX
LAXNESSES > LAX
LAY vb put in horizontal position
LAYABOUT n lazy person ▷ vb hit out with violent and repeated blows in all directions
LAYABOUTS > LAYABOUT
LAYAWAY n merchandise reserved for future delivery
LAYAWAYS > LAYAWAY
LAYBACK n technique for climbing cracks ▷ vb use layback technique
LAYBACKED > LAYBACK
LAYBACKS > LAYBACK
LAYDEEZ pl n jocular spelling of ladies
LAYED > LAY
LAYER n single thickness of some substance ▷ vb form a layer
LAYERAGE n covering stem or branch with soil to encourage new roots
LAYERAGES > LAYERAGE
LAYERED > LAYER
LAYERING n act of arranging something in layers
LAYERINGS > LAYERING
LAYERS > LAYER
LAYETTE n clothes for a newborn baby
LAYETTES > LAYETTE
LAYIN n basketball score
LAYING > LAY
LAYINGS > LAY
LAYINS > LAYIN
LAYLOCK old form of > LILAC
LAYLOCKS > LAYLOCK
LAYMAN n person who is not a member of the clergy
LAYMANISE same as > LAYMANIZE
LAYMANIZE vb make (information) easier to understand
LAYMEN > LAYMAN
LAYOFF n act of suspending employees
LAYOFFS > LAYOFF
LAYOUT n arrangement, esp of printing matter
LAYOUTS > LAYOUT
LAYOVER n break in a journey
LAYOVERS > LAYOVER
LAYPEOPLE > LAYPERSON
LAYPERSON n person who is not a member of the clergy
LAYS > LAY
LAYSHAFT n auxiliary shaft in a gearbox
LAYSHAFTS > LAYSHAFT
LAYSTALL n place where waste is deposited
LAYSTALLS > LAYSTALL

LAYTIME n time allowed for loading cargo
LAYTIMES > LAYTIME
LAYUP n period of incapacity through illness
LAYUPS > LAYUP
LAYWOMAN n woman who is not a member of the clergy **LAYWOMEN** > LAYWOMAN
LAZAR archaic word for > LEPER
LAZARET same as > LAZARETTO
LAZARETS > LAZARET
LAZARETTE same as > LAZARETTO
LAZARETTO n small locker at the stern of a boat or a storeroom between decks of a ship
LAZARS > LAZAR
LAZE vb be idle or lazy ▷ n time spent lazing
LAZED > LAZE
LAZES > LAZE
LAZIED > LAZY
LAZIER > LAZY
LAZIES > LAZY
LAZIEST > LAZY
LAZILY > LAZY
LAZINESS > LAZY
LAZING > LAZE
LAZO another word for > LASSO
LAZOED > LAZO
LAZOES > LAZO
LAZOING > LAZO
LAZOS > LAZO
LAZULI n lapis lazuli
LAZULIS > LAZULI
LAZULITE n blue mineral
LAZULITES > LAZULITE
LAZURITE n rare blue mineral consisting of a sodium-calcium-aluminium silicate
LAZURITES > LAZURITE
LAZY vb laze ▷ adj not inclined to work or exert oneself
LAZYBONES n lazy person
LAZYING > LAZY
LAZYISH > LAZY
LAZZARONE n Italian street beggar
LAZZARONI > LAZZARONE
LAZZI > LAZZO
LAZZO n comic routine in the commedia dell'arte
LEA n meadow
LEACH vb remove by passing a liquid through ▷ n act or process of leaching
LEACHABLE > LEACH
LEACHATE n water that carries salts dissolved out of materials through which it has percolated
LEACHATES > LEACHATE
LEACHED > LEACH
LEACHER > LEACH
LEACHERS > LEACH
LEACHES > LEACH
LEACHIER > LEACHY
LEACHIEST > LEACHY
LEACHING > LEACH

LEACHINGS > LEACH
LEACHOUR old form of > LECHER
LEACHOURS > LEACHOUR
LEACHY adj porous
LEAD vb guide or conduct ▷ n first or most prominent place ▷ adj acting as a leader or lead
LEADABLE n able to be led
LEADED adj (of windows) made from many small panes of glass held together by lead strips
LEADEN adj heavy or sluggish ▷ vb become or cause to become leaden
LEADENED > LEADEN
LEADENING > LEADEN
LEADENLY > LEADEN
LEADENS > LEADEN
LEADER n person who leads
LEADERENE n strong female leader
LEADERS > LEADER
LEADIER > LEADY
LEADIEST > LEADY
LEADING > LEAD
LEADINGLY > LEAD
LEADINGS > LEAD
LEADLESS adj without lead
LEADMAN n man who leads
LEADMEN > LEADMAN
LEADOFF n initial move
LEADOFFS > LEADOFF
LEADPLANT N American shrub
LEADS > LEAD
LEADSCREW n threaded rod in a lathe
LEADSMAN n sailor who takes soundings with a lead line
LEADSMEN > LEADSMAN
LEADWORK n maintenance work involving lead pipes, etc
LEADWORKS > LEADWORK
LEADWORT n type of tropical or subtropical shrub with red, blue, or white flowers
LEADWORTS > LEADWORT
LEADY adj like lead
LEAF n flat usu green blade attached to the stem of a plant ▷ vb turn (pages) cursorily
LEAFAGE n leaves of plants
LEAFAGES > LEAFAGE
LEAFBUD n bud producing leaves rather than flowers
LEAFBUDS > LEAFBUD
LEAFED > LEAF
LEAFERIES > LEAFERY
LEAFERY n foliage
LEAFIER > LEAFY
LEAFIEST > LEAFY
LEAFINESS > LEAFY
LEAFING > LEAF
LEAFLESS > LEAF
LEAFLET n sheet of printed matter for distribution ▷ vb distribute leaflets (to)
LEAFLETED > LEAFLET
LEAFLETER > LEAFLET
LEAFLETS > LEAFLET
LEAFLIKE > LEAF

LEAFMOLD n fungus on decayed leaves
LEAFMOLDS > LEAFMOLD
LEAFROLL n viral disease of potatoes
LEAFROLLS > LEAFROLL
LEAFS > LEAF
LEAFSTALK n stalk attaching a leaf to a stem or branch
LEAFWORM n cotton plant pest
LEAFWORMS > LEAFWORM
LEAFY adj covered with leaves
LEAGUE n association promoting the interests of its members
LEAGUED > LEAGUE
LEAGUER vb harass; beset ▷ n encampment, esp of besiegers
LEAGUERED > LEAGUER
LEAGUERS > LEAGUER
LEAGUES > LEAGUE
LEAGUING > LEAGUE
LEAK n hole or defect that allows the escape or entrance of liquid, gas, radiation, etc ▷ vb let liquid etc in or out
LEAKAGE n act or instance of leaking
LEAKAGES > LEAKAGE
LEAKED > LEAK
LEAKER > LEAK
LEAKIER > LEAKY
LEAKIEST > LEAKY
LEAKILY > LEAKY
LEAKINESS > LEAKY
LEAKING > LEAK
LEAKLESS > LEAK
LEAKPROOF adj not likely to leak
LEAKS > LEAK
LEAKY adj leaking
LEAL adj loyal
LEALER > LEAL
LEALEST > LEAL
LEALLY > LEAL
LEALTIES > LEAL
LEALTY > LEAL
LEAM vb shine
LEAMED > LEAM
LEAMING > LEAM
LEAMS > LEAM
LEAN vb rest (against) ▷ adj thin but healthy-looking ▷ n lean part of meat
LEANED > LEAN
LEANER > LEAN
LEANERS > LEAN
LEANEST > LEAN
LEANING > LEAN
LEANINGS > LEAN
LEANLY > LEAN
LEANNESS > LEAN
LEANS > LEAN
LEANT > LEAN
LEANY old form of > LEAN
LEAP vb make a sudden powerful jump ▷ n sudden powerful jump
LEAPED > LEAP
LEAPER > LEAP
LEAPEROUS old form of > LEPROUS

LEAPERS > LEAP
LEAPFROG n game in which a player vaults over another bending down ▷ vb play leapfrog
LEAPFROGS > LEAPFROG
LEAPING > LEAP
LEAPOROUS old form of > LEPROUS
LEAPROUS old form of > LEPROUS
LEAPS > LEAP
LEAPT > LEAP
LEAR vb instruct
LEARE same as > LEAR
LEARED > LEAR
LEARES > LEARE
LEARIER > LEARY
LEARIEST > LEARY
LEARINESS > LEARY
LEARING > LEAR
LEARN vb gain skill or knowledge by study, practice, or teaching
LEARNABLE > LEARN
LEARNED > LEARN
LEARNEDLY > LEARN
LEARNER n someone who is learning something
LEARNERS > LEARNER
LEARNING > LEARN
LEARNINGS > LEARN
LEARNS > LEARN
LEARNT > LEARN
LEARS > LEAR
LEARY same as > LEERY
LEAS > LEA
LEASABLE > LEASE
LEASE n contract by which land or property is rented for a stated time ▷ vb let or rent by lease
LEASEBACK n property transaction in which the buyer leases the property to the seller
LEASED > LEASE
LEASEHOLD adj (land or property) held on lease ▷ n land or property held under a lease
LEASER > LEASE
LEASERS > LEASE
LEASES > LEASE
LEASH n lead for a dog ▷ vb control by a leash
LEASHED > LEASH
LEASHES > LEASH
LEASHING > LEASH
LEASING > LEASE
LEASINGS > LEASE
LEASOW vb pasture
LEASOWE same as > LEASOW
LEASOWED > LEASOWE
LEASOWES > LEASOWE
LEASOWING > LEASOW
LEASOWS > LEASOW
LEAST n smallest amount ▷ adj smallest ▷ n smallest one ▷ adv in the smallest degree
LEASTS > LEAST
LEASTWAYS adv at least
LEASTWISE same as > LEASTWAYS
LEASURE old form of > LEISURE

LEASURES > LEASURE
LEAT n trench or ditch that conveys water to a mill wheel
LEATHER n material made from treated animal skins ▷ adj of leather ▷ vb beat or thrash
LEATHERED > LEATHER
LEATHERN adj made of or resembling leather
LEATHERS > LEATHER
LEATHERY adj like leather, tough
LEATS > LEAT
LEAVE vb go away from ▷ n permission to be absent
LEAVED adj with leaves
LEAVEN n substance that causes dough to rise ▷ vb raise with leaven
LEAVENED > LEAVEN
LEAVENER n person or thing that leavens
LEAVENERS > LEAVENER
LEAVENING > LEAVEN
LEAVENOUS adj containing leaven
LEAVENS > LEAVEN
LEAVER > LEAVE
LEAVERS > LEAVE
LEAVES > LEAF
LEAVIER > LEAVY
LEAVIEST > LEAVY
LEAVING > LEAVE
LEAVINGS pl n something remaining, such as refuse
LEAVY same as > LEAFY
LEAZE same as > LEASE
LEAZES > LEAZE
LEBBEK n type of timber tree
LEBBEKS > LEBBEK
LEBEN n semiliquid food made from curdled milk
LEBENS > LEBEN
LEBKUCHEN n biscuit, originating from Germany, usually containing honey, spices, etc
LECANORA n type of lichen
LECANORAS > LECANORA
LECCIES > LECCY
LECCY n electricity
LECH vb behave lecherously ▷ n lecherous act
LECHAIM interj drinking toast ▷ n drink for a toast
LECHAIMS > LECHAIM
LECHAYIM same as > LECHAIM
LECHAYIMS > LECHAYIM
LECHED > LECH
LECHER n man who has or shows excessive sexual desire ▷ vb behave lecherously
LECHERED > LECHER
LECHERIES > LECHERY
LECHERING > LECHER
LECHEROUS adj (of a man) having or showing excessive sexual desire
LECHERS > LECHER
LECHERY n unrestrained and promiscuous sexuality
LECHES > LECH
LECHING > LECH

LECHWE n African antelope
LECHWES > LECHWE
LECITHIN n yellow-brown compound found in plant and animal tissues
LECITHINS > LECITHIN
LECTERN n reading desk
LECTERNS > LECTERN
LECTIN n type of protein
LECTINS > LECTIN
LECTION n variant reading of a passage in a text
LECTIONS > LECTION
LECTOR n university lecturer
LECTORATE > LECTOR
LECTORS > LECTOR
LECTOTYPE n specimen designated by author after the publication of a species name
LECTRESS n female reader
LECTURE n informative talk ▷ vb give a talk
LECTURED > LECTURE
LECTURER n person who lectures, esp in a university or college
LECTURERS > LECTURER
LECTURES > LECTURE
LECTURING > LECTURE
LECTURN old form of > LECTERN
LECTURNS > LECTURN
LECYTHI > LECYTHUS
LECYTHIS n genus of very tall trees
LECYTHUS n (in ancient Greece) a vase with a narrow neck
LED > LEAD
LEDDEN n language; speech
LEDDENS > LEDDEN
LEDE n introductory part of a news story
LEDES > LEDE
LEDGE n narrow shelf
LEDGED > LEDGE
LEDGER n book of debit and credit accounts ▷ vb fish using a wire trace while the bait floats freely and the weight sinks
LEDGERED > LEDGER
LEDGERING > LEDGER
LEDGERS > LEDGER
LEDGES > LEDGE
LEDGIER > LEDGE
LEDGIEST > LEDGE
LEDGY > LEDGE
LEDUM n evergreen shrub
LEDUMS > LEDUM
LEE n sheltered side ▷ vb (Scots) lie
LEEAR Scots form of > LIAR
LEEARS > LEEAR
LEEBOARD n board lowered along the lee side of a vessel to reduce drift
LEEBOARDS > LEEBOARD
LEECH n bloodsucking worm ▷ vb use leeches to suck the blood of
LEECHDOM n remedy
LEECHDOMS > LEECHDOM
LEECHED > LEECH
LEECHEE same as > LITCHI
LEECHEES > LEECHEE

LEECHES > LEECH
LEECHING > LEECH
LEECHLIKE > LEECH
LEED > LEE
LEEING > LEE
LEEK n vegetable with a long bulb and thick stem
LEEKS > LEEK
LEEP vb boil; scald
LEEPED > LEEP
LEEPING > LEEP
LEEPS > LEEP
LEER vb look or grin at in a sneering manner ▷ n sneering look or grin
LEERED > LEER
LEERIER > LEERY
LEERIEST > LEERY
LEERILY > LEERY
LEERINESS > LEERY
LEERING > LEER
LEERINGLY > LEER
LEERINGS > LEER
LEERS > LEER
LEERY adj suspicious or wary (of)
LEES pl n sediment of wine
LEESE old form of > LOOSE
LEESES > LEESE
LEESING > LEESE
LEET n shortlist
LEETLE form of > LITTLE
LEETS > LEET
LEETSPEAK n jargon used by some internet groups
LEEWARD n lee side ▷ adv towards this side ▷ adj towards where the wind blows
LEEWARDLY > LEEWARD
LEEWARDS adv towards the lee side
LEEWAY n room for free movement within limits
LEEWAYS > LEEWAY
LEEZE adj as in leeze me Scots for lief is me, an expression of affection
LEFT adj on the opposite side from right ▷ n left side
LEFTE old past tense of > LIFT
LEFTER > LEFT
LEFTEST > LEFT
LEFTIE same as > LEFTY
LEFTIES > LEFTY
LEFTISH > LEFT
LEFTISM > LEFTIST
LEFTISMS > LEFTIST
LEFTIST adj of the political left ▷ n supporter of the political left
LEFTISTS > LEFTIST
LEFTMOST > LEFT
LEFTMOSTS > LEFT
LEFTOVER n unused portion of food or material ▷ adj left as an unused portion
LEFTOVERS > LEFTOVER
LEFTS > LEFT
LEFTWARD same as > LEFTWARDS
LEFTWARDS adv towards or on the left
LEFTWING adj of or relating to the leftist faction of a party, etc

LEFTY n left-winger
LEG n limb on which a person or animal walks, runs, or stands
LEGACIES > LEGACY
LEGACY n thing left in a will
LEGAL adj established or permitted by law ▷ n legal expert
LEGALESE n conventional language in which legal documents are written
LEGALESES > LEGALESE
LEGALISE same as > LEGALIZE
LEGALISED > LEGALISE
LEGALISER > LEGALISE
LEGALISES > LEGALISE
LEGALISM n strict adherence to the letter of the law
LEGALISMS > LEGALISM
LEGALIST > LEGALISM
LEGALISTS > LEGALISM
LEGALITY n state or quality of being legal or lawful
LEGALIZE vb make legal
LEGALIZED > LEGALIZE
LEGALIZER > LEGALIZE
LEGALIZES > LEGALIZE
LEGALLY > LEGAL
LEGALS > LEGAL
LEGATARY n legatee
LEGATE n messenger or representative, esp from the Pope ▷ vb leave as legacy
LEGATED > LEGATE
LEGATEE n recipient of a legacy
LEGATEES > LEGATEE
LEGATES > LEGATE
LEGATINE > LEGATE
LEGATING > LEGATE
LEGATION n diplomatic minister and his or her staff
LEGATIONS > LEGATION
LEGATO adv smoothly ▷ n playing with no gaps between notes
LEGATOR n person who gives a legacy or makes a bequest
LEGATORS > LEGATOR
LEGATOS > LEGATO
LEGEND n traditional story
LEGENDARY adj famous
LEGENDISE same as > LEGENDIZE
LEGENDIST n writer of legends
LEGENDIZE vb make into legend
LEGENDRY > LEGEND
LEGENDS > LEGEND
LEGER variant of > LEDGER
LEGERING > LEGER
LEGERINGS > LEGER
LEGERITY n agility
LEGERS > LEGER
LEGES > LEX
LEGGE vb lighten or lessen
LEGGED > LEG
LEGGER n person who moves barge through tunnel using legs
LEGGERS > LEGGER
LEGGES > LEGGE

LEGGIE n leg spin bowler
LEGGIER > LEGGY
LEGGIERO adj light; delicate
LEGGIES > LEGGIE
LEGGIEST > LEGGY
LEGGIN same as > LEGGING
LEGGINESS > LEGGY
LEGGING n extra outer covering for the lower leg
LEGGINGED > LEGGING
LEGGINGS > LEGGING
LEGGINS > LEGGIN
LEGGISM n blacklegging
LEGGISMS > LEGGISM
LEGGO sentence substitute let go!
LEGGY adj having long legs
LEGHOLD n type of animal trap that clamps down on the animal's leg
LEGHOLDS > LEGHOLD
LEGHORN n Italian wheat straw woven into hats
LEGHORNS > LEGHORN
LEGIBLE adj easily read
LEGIBLY > LEGIBLE
LEGION n large military force ▷ adj very large or numerous
LEGIONARY adj of or relating to a legion ▷ n soldier belonging to a legion
LEGIONED adj arranged in legions
LEGIONS > LEGION
LEGISLATE vb make laws
LEGIST n legal mind
LEGISTS > LEGIST
LEGIT n legitimate drama ▷ adj legitimate
LEGITIM n inheritance due to children from father
LEGITIMS > LEGITIM
LEGITS > LEGIT
LEGLAN same as > LEGLIN
LEGLANS > LEGLAN
LEGLEN same as > LEGLIN
LEGLENS > LEGLEN
LEGLESS adj without legs
LEGLET n leg jewellery
LEGLETS > LEGLET
LEGLIKE > LEG
LEGLIN n milk-pail
LEGLINS > LEGLIN
LEGMAN n newsman who reports from the scene
LEGMEN > LEGMAN
LEGONG n Indonesian dance
LEGONGS > LEGONG
LEGROOM n space to put one's legs
LEGROOMS > LEGROOM
LEGS > LEG
LEGSIDE n part of a cricket field to the left of a right-handed batsman as they face the bowler
LEGSIDES > LEGSIDE
LEGUAAN n S African lizard
LEGUAANS > LEGUAAN
LEGUAN same as > LEGUAAN
LEGUANS > LEGUAN
LEGUME n pod of a plant of the pea or bean family
LEGUMES > LEGUME
LEGUMIN n protein from leguminous plants

LEGUMINS > LEGUMIN
LEGWARMER n one of a pair of garments resembling stockings without feet
LEGWEAR n clothing for legs
LEGWEARS > LEGWEAR
LEGWORK n work that involves travelling on foot or as if on foot
LEGWORKS > LEGWORK
LEHAIM same as > LECHAIM
LEHAIMS > LEHAIM
LEHAYIM same as > LEHAIM
LEHAYIMS > LEHAYIM
LEHR n long tunnel-shaped oven used for annealing glass
LEHRJAHRE n apprenticeship
LEHRS > LEHR
LEHUA n flower of Hawaii
LEHUAS > LEHUA
LEI n Hawaiian garland
LEIDGER same as > LEDGER
LEIDGERS > LEIDGER
LEIGER same as > LEDGER
LEIGERS > LEIGER
LEIOMYOMA same as > FIBROID
LEIPOA n Australian bird
LEIPOAS > LEIPOA
LEIR same as > LEAR
LEIRED > LEIR
LEIRING > LEIR
LEIRS > LEIR
LEIS > LEI
LEISH adj agile
LEISHER > LEISH
LEISHEST > LEISH
LEISLER n small bat
LEISLERS > LEISLER
LEISTER n pronged fishing spear ▷ vb spear with a leister
LEISTERED > LEISTER
LEISTERS > LEISTER
LEISURE n time for relaxation or hobbies ▷ vb have leisure
LEISURED > LEISURE
LEISURELY adj deliberate, unhurried ▷ adv slowly
LEISURES > LEISURE
LEISURING > LEISURE
LEITMOTIF n recurring theme associated with a person, situation, or thought
LEITMOTIV same as > LEITMOTIF
LEK n bird display area ▷ vb gather at lek
LEKE old form of > LEAK
LEKGOTLA n meeting place for village assemblies, court cases, and meetings of village leaders
LEKGOTLAS > LEKGOTLA
LEKKED > LEK
LEKKER adj attractive or nice
LEKKING > LEK
LEKKINGS > LEK
LEKS > LEK
LEKU > LEK
LEKVAR n prune or apricot pie filling
LEKVARS > LEKVAR
LEKYTHI > LEKYTHOS
LEKYTHOI > LEKYTHOS

LEKYTHOS n Greek flask
LEKYTHUS same as
> LEKYTHOS
LEMAN n beloved
LEMANS > LEMAN
LEME same as > LEAM
LEMED > LEME
LEMEL n metal filings
LEMELS > LEMEL
LEMES > LEME
LEMING > LEME
LEMMA n word in its citation
form
LEMMAS > LEMMA
LEMMATA > LEMMA
LEMMATISE same as
> LEMMATIZE
LEMMATIZE vb group
together the inflected forms
of (a word) for analysis as a
single item
LEMME vb (short for) let me
LEMMING n rodent of Arctic
regions
LEMMINGS > LEMMING
LEMNISCAL adj relating to a
type of closed plane curve
LEMNISCI > LEMNISCUS
LEMNISCUS technical name
for > FILLET
LEMON n yellow oval fruit
▷ adj pale-yellow ▷ vb
flavour with lemon
LEMONADE n lemon-
flavoured soft drink, often
fizzy
LEMONADES > LEMONADE
LEMONED > LEMON
LEMONFISH n type of game
fish
LEMONIER > LEMONY
LEMONIEST > LEMONY
LEMONING > LEMON
LEMONISH > LEMON
LEMONLIKE > LEMON
LEMONS > LEMON
LEMONWOOD n small tree of
New Zealand
LEMONY adj like a lemon
LEMPIRA n monetary unit of
Honduras
LEMPIRAS > LEMPIRA
LEMUR n animal like a small
monkey
LEMURES pl n spirits of the
dead
LEMURIAN same as
> LEMUROID
LEMURIANS > LEMURIAN
LEMURINE same as
> LEMUROID
LEMURINES > LEMURINE
LEMURLIKE > LEMUR
LEMUROID adj relating to
the superfamily which
includes the lemurs ▷ n
animal that resembles or is
closely related to a lemur
LEMUROIDS > LEMUROID
LEMURS > LEMUR
LEND vb give temporary use
of
LENDABLE > LEND
LENDER > LEND
LENDERS > LEND
LENDING > LEND
LENDINGS > LEND

LENDS > LEND
LENES > LENIS
LENG vb linger ▷ adj long
LENGED > LENG
LENGER > LENG
LENGEST > LENG
LENGING > LENG
LENGS > LENG
LENGTH n extent or
measurement from end to
end
LENGTHEN vb make or
become longer
LENGTHENS > LENGTHEN
LENGTHFUL > LENGTH
LENGTHIER > LENGTHY
LENGTHILY > LENGTHY
LENGTHMAN n person
whose job it is to maintain a
particular length of road or
railway line
LENGTHMEN > LENGTHMAN
LENGTHS > LENGTH
LENGTHY adj very long
LENIENCE > LENIENT
LENIENCES > LENIENT
LENIENCY > LENIENT
LENIENT adj tolerant, not
strict or severe ▷ n lenient
person
LENIENTLY > LENIENT
LENIENTS > LENIENT
LENIFIED > LENIFY
LENIFIES > LENIFY
LENIFY vb make lenient
LENIFYING > LENIFY
LENIS adj pronounced with
little muscular tension ▷ n
consonant like this
LENITE vb undergo lenition
LENITED > LENITE
LENITES > LENITE
LENITIES > LENITY
LENITING > LENITE
LENITION n weakening of
consonant sound
LENITIONS > LENITION
LENITIVE adj soothing or
alleviating of pain or distress
▷ n lenitive drug
LENITIVES > LENITIVE
LENITY n mercy or
clemency
LENO n weave in which the
warp yarns are twisted in
pairs between the weft
LENOS > LENO
LENS n piece of glass or
similar material with one or
both sides curved
LENSE same as > LENS
LENSED adj incorporating a
lens
LENSES > LENS
LENSING n materials which
colour and diffuse light
LENSINGS > LENSING
LENSLESS > LENS
LENSLIKE adj like a lens
LENSMAN n camera operator
LENSMEN > LENSMAN
LENT > LEND
LENTANDO adv slowing
down
LENTEN adj of or relating to
Lent
LENTI > LENTO

LENTIC adj of, relating to, or
inhabiting still water
LENTICEL n any of
numerous pores in the stem
of a woody plant
LENTICELS > LENTICEL
LENTICLE n lens-shaped
layer of mineral or rock
embedded in a matrix of
different constitution
LENTICLES > LENTICLE
LENTICULE n small lentil
LENTIFORM adj shaped like
a biconvex lens
LENTIGO technical name for a
> FRECKLE
LENTIL n edible seed
LENTILS > LENTIL
LENTISC same as
> LENTISK
LENTISCS > LENTISC
LENTISK n mastic tree
LENTISKS > LENTISK
LENTO adv slowly ▷ n
movement or passage
performed slowly
LENTOID adj lentiform ▷ n
lentiform object
LENTOIDS > LENTOID
LENTOR n lethargy
LENTORS > LENTOR
LENTOS > LENTO
LENTOUS adj lethargic
LENVOY another word for
> ENVOY
LENVOYS > LENVOY
LEONE n monetary unit of
Sierra Leone
LEONES > LEONE
LEONINE adj like a lion
LEOPARD n large spotted
animal of the cat family
LEOPARDS > LEOPARD
LEOTARD n tight-fitting
garment covering the upper
body
LEOTARDED adj wearing a
leotard
LEOTARDS > LEOTARD
LEP dialect word for > LEAP
LEPER n person with
leprosy
LEPERS > LEPER
LEPID adj amusing
LEPIDOTE adj covered with
scales, scaly leaves, or spots
▷ n lepidote person,
creature, or thing
LEPIDOTES > LEPIDOTE
LEPORID adj of the family of
mammals including rabbits
and hares ▷ n any animal
belonging to this family
LEPORIDAE > LEPORID
LEPORIDS > LEPORID
LEPORINE adj of, relating
to, or resembling a hare
LEPPED > LEP
LEPPING > LEP
LEPRA n leprosy
LEPRAS > LEPRA
LEPROSE adj having or
denoting a whitish scurfy
surface
LEPROSERY n hospital for
leprosy sufferers
LEPROSIES > LEPROSY

LEPROSITY n state of being
leprous
LEPROSY n disease
attacking the nerves and
skin
LEPROTIC adj relating to
leprosy
LEPROUS adj having leprosy
LEPROUSLY > LEPROUS
LEPS > LEP
LEPT > LEAP
LEPTA > LEPTON
LEPTIN n protein that
regulates the amount of fat
in the body
LEPTINS > LEPTIN
LEPTOME n tissue of plant
conducting food
LEPTOMES > LEPTOME
LEPTON n any of a group of
elementary particles with
weak interactions
LEPTONIC > LEPTON
LEPTONS > LEPTON
LEPTOPHOS n type of
pesticide
LEPTOSOME n person with a
small bodily frame and a
slender physique
LEPTOTENE n (in
reproduction) early stage in
cell division
LEQUEAR same as
> LACUNAR
LEQUEARS > LEQUEAR
LERE same as > LEAR
LERED > LERE
LERES > LERE
LERING > LERE
LERNAEAN adj relating to
Lerna, the swamp in which
dwelt the Hydra
LERP n crystallized
honeydew
LERPS > LERP
LES short form of > LESBIAN
LESBIAN n homosexual
woman ▷ adj of homosexual
women
LESBIANS > LESBIAN
LESBIC adj relating to
lesbians
LESBIGAY n characteristic
of or intended for the lesbian,
bisexual, and gay community
LESBIGAYS > LESBIGAY
LESBO n offensive term for a
lesbian
LESBOS > LESBO
LESES > LES
LESION n change in an
organ of the body caused by
injury ▷ vb cause lesions
LESIONED > LESION
LESIONING > LESION
LESIONS > LESION
LESPEDEZA n bush clover
LESS n smaller amount ▷ adj
smaller in extent, degree, or
duration ▷ pron smaller part
or quantity ▷ adv smaller
extent or degree ▷ prep after
deducting, minus
LESSEE n person to whom a
lease is granted
LESSEES > LESSEE
LESSEN vb make or become
smaller or not as much

LESSENED > LESSEN
LESSENING n act of lessening
LESSENS > LESSEN
LESSER adj not as great in quantity, size, or worth
LESSES > LESS
LESSON n class or single period of instruction in a subject ▷ vb censure or punish
LESSONED > LESSON
LESSONING > LESSON
LESSONS > LESSON
LESSOR n person who grants a lease of property
LESSORS > LESSOR
LEST conj so as to prevent any possibility that ▷ vb listen
LESTED > LEST
LESTING > LEST
LESTS > LEST
LESULA n species of monkey inhabiting forests in DR Congo
LESULAS > LESULA
LET n act of letting property ▷ vb obstruct
LETCH same as > LECH
LETCHED > LETCH
LETCHES > LETCH
LETCHING > LETCH
LETCHINGS > LETCH
LETDOWN n disappointment
LETDOWNS > LETDOWN
LETHAL adj deadly ▷ n weapon, etc capable of causing death
LETHALITY > LETHAL
LETHALLY > LETHAL
LETHALS > LETHAL
LETHARGIC > LETHARGY
LETHARGY n sluggishness or dullness
LETHE n forgetfulness
LETHEAN > LETHE
LETHEE n life-blood
LETHEES > LETHEE
LETHES > LETHE
LETHIED adj forgetful
LETOUT n circumstance that serves as an excuse not to do something
LETOUTS > LETOUT
LETROZOLE n drug used to treat breast cancer
LETS > LET
LETTABLE > LET
LETTED > LET
LETTER n written message ▷ vb put letters on
LETTERBOX n slot through which letters are delivered into a building
LETTERED adj learned
LETTERER > LETTER
LETTERERS > LETTER
LETTERING n act, art, or technique of inscribing letters on to something
LETTERMAN n successful college sportsman
LETTERMEN > LETTERMAN
LETTERN another word for > LECTERN
LETTERNS > LETTERN

LETTERS pl n literary knowledge
LETTERSET n method of rotary printing in which ink is transferred from raised surfaces to paper via a rubber-covered cylinder
LETTING > LET
LETTINGS > LET
LETTRE n letter
LETTRES > LETTRE
LETTUCE n plant with large green leaves used in salads
LETTUCES > LETTUCE
LETUP n lessening or abatement
LETUPS > LETUP
LEU n monetary unit of Romania
LEUCAEMIA same as > LEUKAEMIA
LEUCAEMIC > LEUCAEMIA
LEUCEMIA same as > LEUKAEMIA
LEUCEMIAS > LEUCEMIA
LEUCEMIC adj of or like leucemia
LEUCH > LAUCH
LEUCHEN > LAUCH
LEUCIN same as > LEUCINE
LEUCINE n essential amino acid
LEUCINES > LEUCINE
LEUCINS > LEUCIN
LEUCISM n condition causing pale discolouration of hair or skin
LEUCISMS > LEUCISM
LEUCISTIC adj having reduced pigmentation in the skin but normally coloured eyes
LEUCITE n grey or white mineral
LEUCITES > LEUCITE
LEUCITIC > LEUCITE
LEUCO n as in leuco base colourless compound
LEUCOCYTE n white blood cell
LEUCOMA n white opaque scar of the cornea
LEUCOMAS > LEUCOMA
LEUCON n type of sponge
LEUCONS > LEUCON
LEUCOSES > LEUCOSIS
LEUCOSIN n albumin in cereal grains
LEUCOSINS > LEUCOSIN
LEUCOSIS same as > LEUKAEMIA
LEUCOTIC adj of or relating to leucosis
LEUCOTOME n needle used in leucotomy
LEUCOTOMY n surgical operation of cutting some of the nerve fibres in the frontal lobes of the brain
LEUD Scots word for > BREADTH
LEUDES > LEUD
LEUDS > LEUD
LEUGH > LAUCH
LEUGHEN > LAUCH
LEUKAEMIA n disease caused by uncontrolled

overproduction of white blood cells
LEUKAEMIC adj of or relating to leukaemia
LEUKEMIA same as > LEUKAEMIA
LEUKEMIAS > LEUKEMIA
LEUKEMIC > LEUKEMIA
LEUKEMICS > LEUKEMIA
LEUKEMOID adj resembling leukaemia
LEUKOCYTE same as > LEUCOCYTE
LEUKOMA same as > LEUCOMA
LEUKOMAS > LEUKOMA
LEUKON n white blood cell count
LEUKONS > LEUKON
LEUKOSES > LEUKOSIS
LEUKOSIS n abnormal growth of white blood cells
LEUKOTIC > LEUKOSIS
LEUKOTOME same as > LEUCOTOME
LEUKOTOMY n lobotomy
LEV n monetary unit of Bulgaria
LEVA > LEV
LEVANT n leather made from the skins of goats, sheep, or seals ▷ vb bolt or abscond
LEVANTED > LEVANT
LEVANTER n easterly wind in the W Mediterranean area, esp in the late summer
LEVANTERS > LEVANTER
LEVANTINE n cloth of twilled silk
LEVANTING > LEVANT
LEVANTS > LEVANT
LEVAS > LEV
LEVATOR n muscle that raises a part of the body
LEVATORES > LEVATOR
LEVATORS > LEVATOR
LEVE adj darling ▷ adv gladly
LEVEE n natural or artificial river embankment ▷ vb go to the reception of
LEVEED > LEVEE
LEVEEING > LEVEE
LEVEES > LEVEE
LEVEL adj horizontal ▷ vb make even or horizontal ▷ n horizontal line or surface
LEVELED > LEVEL
LEVELER same as > LEVELLER
LEVELERS > LEVELER
LEVELING > LEVEL
LEVELLED > LEVEL
LEVELLER n person or thing that levels
LEVELLERS > LEVELLER
LEVELLEST > LEVEL
LEVELLING > LEVEL
LEVELLY > LEVEL
LEVELNESS > LEVEL
LEVELS > LEVEL
LEVER n handle used to operate machinery ▷ vb prise or move with a lever
LEVERAGE n action or power of a lever ▷ vb borrow capital required
LEVERAGED > LEVERAGE

LEVERAGES > LEVERAGE
LEVERED > LEVER
LEVERET n young hare
LEVERETS > LEVERET
LEVERING > LEVER
LEVERS > LEVER
LEVES > LEVE
LEVIABLE adj (of taxes, tariffs, etc) liable to be levied
LEVIATHAN n sea monster
LEVIED > LEVY
LEVIER > LEVY
LEVIERS > LEVY
LEVIES > LEVY
LEVIGABLE > LEVIGATE
LEVIGATE vb grind into a fine powder or a smooth paste ▷ adj having a smooth polished surface
LEVIGATED > LEVIGATE
LEVIGATES > LEVIGATE
LEVIGATOR > LEVIGATE
LEVIN archaic word for > LIGHTNING
LEVINS > LEVIN
LEVIRATE n practice, required by Old Testament law, of marrying the widow of one's brother
LEVIRATES > LEVIRATE
LEVIRATIC > LEVIRATE
LEVIS n jeans
LEVITATE vb rise or cause to rise into the air
LEVITATED > LEVITATE
LEVITATES > LEVITATE
LEVITATOR > LEVITATE
LEVITE n Christian clergyman or clergywoman
LEVITES > LEVITE
LEVITIC > LEVITE
LEVITICAL > LEVITE
LEVITIES > LEVITY
LEVITY n fickleness
LEVO adj anticlockwise
LEVODOPA n substance occurring naturally in the body and used to treat Parkinson's disease
LEVODOPAS > LEVODOPA
LEVOGYRE n counterclockwise spiral
LEVOGYRES > LEVOGYRE
LEVS > LEV
LEVULIN n substance obtained from certain bulbs
LEVULINS > LEVULIN
LEVULOSE n fructose
LEVULOSES > LEVULOSE
LEVY vb impose and collect (a tax) ▷ n imposition or collection of taxes
LEVYING > LEVY
LEW adj tepid
LEWD adj lustful or indecent
LEWDER > LEWD
LEWDEST > LEWD
LEWDLY > LEWD
LEWDNESS > LEWD
LEWDSBIES > LEWDSBY
LEWDSBY another word for > LEWDSTER
LEWDSTER n lewd person
LEWDSTERS > LEWDSTER
LEWIS n lifting device for heavy stone or concrete blocks

LEWISES > LEWIS
LEWISIA n type of herb
LEWISIAS > LEWISIA
LEWISITE n colourless oily poisonous liquid
LEWISITES > LEWISITE
LEWISSON same as > LEWIS
LEWISSONS > LEWISSON
LEX n system or body of laws
LEXEME n minimal meaningful unit of language
LEXEMES > LEXEME
LEXEMIC > LEXEME
LEXES > LEX
LEXICA > LEXICON
LEXICAL adj relating to the vocabulary of a language
LEXICALLY > LEXICAL
LEXICON n dictionary
LEXICONS > LEXICON
LEXIGRAM n figure or symbol that represents a word
LEXIGRAMS > LEXIGRAM
LEXIS n totality of vocabulary in a language
LEXISES > LEXIS
LEY n land under grass
LEYLANDI same as > LEYLANDII
LEYLANDII n type of fast-growing cypress tree
LEYLANDIS > LEYLANDI
LEYS > LEY
LEZ short form of > LESBIAN
LEZES > LEZ
LEZZ short form of > LESBIAN
LEZZA same as > LEZZIE
LEZZAS > LEZZA
LEZZES > LEZZ
LEZZIE n lesbian
LEZZIES > LEZZIE
LEZZY short form of > LESBIAN
LI n Chinese measurement of distance
LIABILITY n hindrance or disadvantage
LIABLE adj legally obliged or responsible
LIAISE vb establish and maintain communication
LIAISED > LIAISE
LIAISES > LIAISE
LIAISING > LIAISE
LIAISON n communication and contact between groups
LIAISONS > LIAISON
LIANA n climbing plant
LIANAS > LIANA
LIANE same as > LIANA
LIANES > LIANE
LIANG n Chinese unit of weight
LIANGS > LIANG
LIANOID > LIANA
LIAR n person who tells lies
LIARD adj grey ▷ n former small coin
LIARDS > LIARD
LIARS > LIAR
LIART Scots form of > LIARD
LIAS n lowest series of rocks of the Jurassic system
LIASES > LIAS

LIASSIC adj relating to the earliest epoch of the Jurassic period
LIATRIS n North American plant with white flowers
LIATRISES > LIATRIS
LIB n informal word for liberation ▷ vb geld
LIBANT adj touching lightly
LIBATE vb offer as gift to the gods
LIBATED > LIBATE
LIBATES > LIBATE
LIBATING > LIBATE
LIBATION n drink poured as an offering to the gods
LIBATIONS > LIBATION
LIBATORY > LIBATE
LIBBARD another word for > LEOPARD
LIBBARDS > LIBBARD
LIBBED > LIB
LIBBER n liberationist
LIBBERS > LIBBER
LIBBING > LIB
LIBECCHIO same as > LIBECCIO
LIBECCIO n strong westerly or southwesterly wind blowing onto the W coast of Corsica
LIBECCIOS > LIBECCIO
LIBEL n published statement falsely damaging a person's reputation ▷ vb falsely damage the reputation of
LIBELANT same as > LIBELLANT
LIBELANTS > LIBELANT
LIBELED > LIBEL
LIBELEE same as > LIBELLEE
LIBELEES > LIBELEE
LIBELER > LIBEL
LIBELERS > LIBEL
LIBELING > LIBEL
LIBELIST > LIBEL
LIBELISTS > LIBEL
LIBELLANT n party who brings an action in the ecclesiastical courts by presenting a libel
LIBELLED > LIBEL
LIBELLEE n person against whom a libel has been filed in an ecclesiastical court
LIBELLEES > LIBELLEE
LIBELLER > LIBEL
LIBELLERS > LIBEL
LIBELLING > LIBEL
LIBELLOUS > LIBEL
LIBELOUS > LIBEL
LIBELS > LIBEL
LIBER n tome or book
LIBERAL adj having social and political views that favour progress and reform ▷ n person with such views
LIBERALLY > LIBERAL
LIBERALS > LIBERAL
LIBERATE vb set free
LIBERATED adj not bound by traditional social roles
LIBERATES > LIBERATE
LIBERATOR > LIBERATE

LIBERO another name for > SWEEPER
LIBEROS > LIBERO
LIBERS > LIBER
LIBERTIES > LIBERTY
LIBERTINE n immoral person ▷ adj unscrupulous
LIBERTY n freedom
LIBIDINAL > LIBIDO
LIBIDO n psychic energy
LIBIDOS > LIBIDO
LIBKEN n lodging
LIBKENS > LIBKEN
LIBLAB n 19th century British liberal
LIBLABS > LIBLAB
LIBRA n ancient Roman unit of weight
LIBRAE > LIBRA
LIBRAIRE n bookseller
LIBRAIRES > LIBRAIRE
LIBRAIRIE n bookshop
LIBRARIAN n keeper of or worker in a library
LIBRARIES > LIBRARY
LIBRARY n room or building where books are kept
LIBRAS > LIBRA
LIBRATE vb oscillate or waver
LIBRATED > LIBRATE
LIBRATES > LIBRATE
LIBRATING > LIBRATE
LIBRATION n act or an instance of oscillating
LIBRATORY > LIBRATE
LIBRETTI > LIBRETTO
LIBRETTO n words of an opera
LIBRETTOS > LIBRETTO
LIBRI > LIBER
LIBRIFORM adj (of a fibre of woody tissue) elongated and having a pitted thickened cell wall
LIBS > LIB
LICE > LOUSE
LICENCE n document giving official permission ▷ vb (in the US) give permission to
LICENCED > LICENCE
LICENCEE same as > LICENSEE
LICENCEES > LICENCEE
LICENCER > LICENCE
LICENCERS > LICENCE
LICENCES > LICENCE
LICENCING > LICENCE
LICENSE vb grant or give a licence for
LICENSED > LICENSE
LICENSEE n holder of a licence
LICENSEES > LICENSEE
LICENSER > LICENSE
LICENSERS > LICENSE
LICENSES > LICENSE
LICENSING > LICENSE
LICENSOR > LICENSE
LICENSORS > LICENSE
LICENSURE n act of conferring licence
LICENTE adj permitted; allowed
LICH n dead body
LICHANOS n note played using forefinger

LICHEE same as > LITCHI
LICHEES > LICHEE
LICHEN n small flowerless plant forming a crust on rocks, trees, etc ▷ vb cover with lichen
LICHENED > LICHEN
LICHENIN n complex polysaccharide occurring in certain species of moss
LICHENING > LICHEN
LICHENINS > LICHENIN
LICHENISM n an association of fungus and alga as lichen
LICHENIST n person who studies lichens
LICHENOID > LICHEN
LICHENOSE > LICHEN
LICHENOUS > LICHEN
LICHENS > LICHEN
LICHES > LICH
LICHGATE n roofed gate to a churchyard
LICHGATES > LICHGATE
LICHI same as > LITCHI
LICHIS > LICHI
LICHT Scot word for > LIGHT
LICHTED > LICHT
LICHTER > LICHT
LICHTEST > LICHT
LICHTING > LICHT
LICHTLIED > LICHTLY
LICHTLIES > LICHTLY
LICHTLY vb treat discourteously
LICHTS > LICHT
LICHWAKE n night vigil over a dead body
LICHWAKES > LICHWAKE
LICHWAY n path used to carry coffin into church
LICHWAYS > LICHWAY
LICIT adj lawful, permitted
LICITLY > LICIT
LICITNESS > LICIT
LICK vb pass the tongue over ▷ n licking
LICKED > LICK
LICKER > LICK
LICKERISH adj lecherous or lustful
LICKERS > LICK
LICKING n beating
LICKINGS > LICKING
LICKPENNY n something that uses up large amounts of money
LICKS > LICK
LICKSPIT n flattering or servile person
LICKSPITS > LICKSPIT
LICORICE same as > LIQUORICE
LICORICES > LICORICE
LICTOR n one of a group of ancient Roman officials
LICTORIAN > LICTOR
LICTORS > LICTOR
LID n movable cover
LIDAR n radar-type instrument
LIDARS > LIDAR
LIDDED > LID
LIDDING n lids
LIDDINGS > LIDDING

LIDGER variant form of > LEDGER

LIDGERS > LIDGER

LIDLESS adj having no lid or top

LIDO n open-air centre for swimming and water sports

LIDOCAINE n powerful local anaesthetic administered by injection

LIDOS > LIDO

LIDS > LID

LIE vb make a false statement ▷ n falsehood

LIED n setting for solo voice and piano of a poem

LIEDER > LIED

LIEF adv gladly ▷ adj ready ▷ n beloved person

LIEFER > LIEF

LIEFEST > LIEF

LIEFLY > LIEF

LIEFS > LIEF

LIEGE adj bound to give or receive feudal service ▷ n lord

LIEGEDOM > LIEGE

LIEGEDOMS > LIEGE

LIEGELESS > LIEGE

LIEGEMAN n (formerly) the subject of a sovereign or feudal lord

LIEGEMEN > LIEGEMAN

LIEGER same as > LEDGER

LIEGERS > LIEGER

LIEGES > LIEGE

LIEN n right to hold another's property until a debt is paid

LIENABLE adj that can be subject of a lien

LIENAL adj of or relating to the spleen

LIENEE n person against whom a lien has been placed

LIENEES > LIENEE

LIENOR n person who holds a lien

LIENORS > LIENOR

LIENS > LIEN

LIENTERIC > LIENTERY

LIENTERY n passage of undigested food in the faeces

LIER n person who lies down

LIERNE n short secondary rib that connects intersections of the primary ribs

LIERNES > LIERNE

LIERS > LIER

LIES > LIE

LIEU n stead

LIEUS > LIEU

LIEVE same as > LEVE

LIEVER > LIEVE

LIEVES > LIEVE

LIEVEST > LIEVE

LIFE n state of living beings

LIFEBELT n ring filled with air, used to keep a person afloat when in danger of drowning

LIFEBELTS > LIFEBELT

LIFEBLOOD n blood vital to life

LIFEBOAT n boat used for rescuing people at sea

LIFEBOATS > LIFEBOAT

LIFEBUOY n any of various kinds of buoyant device for keeping people afloat

LIFEBUOYS > LIFEBUOY

LIFECARE n care of person's health and welfare

LIFECARES > LIFECARE

LIFEFUL adj full of life

LIFEGUARD n person who saves people from drowning ▷ vb work as lifeguard

LIFEHACK n action that simplifies a task or reduces frustration in everyday life ▷ vb perform a lifehack

LIFEHACKS > LIFEHACK

LIFEHOLD adj (of land) held while one is alive

LIFELESS adj dead

LIFELIKE adj closely resembling or representing life

LIFELINE n means of contact or support

LIFELINES > LIFELINE

LIFELONG adj lasting all of a person's life

LIFER n prisoner sentenced to imprisonment for life

LIFERS > LIFER

LIFES pl n as in still lifes paintings or drawings of inanimate objects

LIFESAVER n saver of a person's life

LIFESOME adj full of life

LIFESPAN n period of time during which a person or animal may be expected to live

LIFESPANS > LIFESPAN

LIFESTYLE n particular attitudes, habits, etc ▷ adj suggestive of a fashionable or desirable lifestyle

LIFETIME n length of time a person is alive

LIFETIMES > LIFETIME

LIFEWAY n way of life

LIFEWAYS > LIFEWAY

LIFEWORK n work to which a person has devoted their life

LIFEWORKS > LIFEWORK

LIFEWORLD n way individual experiences world

LIFT vb move upwards in position, status, volume, etc ▷ n cage raised and lowered in a vertical shaft

LIFTABLE > LIFT

LIFTBACK n hatchback

LIFTBACKS > LIFTBACK

LIFTBOY n person who operates a lift

LIFTBOYS > LIFTBOY

LIFTED > LIFT

LIFTER > LIFT

LIFTERS > LIFT

LIFTGATE n rear opening of hatchback

LIFTGATES > LIFTGATE

LIFTING > LIFT

LIFTMAN same as > LIFTBOY

LIFTMEN > LIFTMAN

LIFTOFF n moment a rocket leaves the ground ▷ vb (of a rocket) to leave its launch pad

LIFTOFFS > LIFTOFF

LIFTS > LIFT

LIFULL obsolete form of > LIFEFUL

LIG n function with free entertainment and refreshments ▷ vb attend such a function

LIGAMENT n band of tissue joining bones

LIGAMENTS > LIGAMENT

LIGAN same as > LAGAN

LIGAND n atom, molecule, radical, or ion forming a complex with a central atom

LIGANDS > LIGAND

LIGANS > LIGAN

LIGASE n any of a class of enzymes

LIGASES > LIGASE

LIGATE vb tie up or constrict (something) with a ligature

LIGATED > LIGATE

LIGATES > LIGATE

LIGATING > LIGATE

LIGATION > LIGATE

LIGATIONS > LIGATE

LIGATIVE > LIGATE

LIGATURE n link, bond, or tie ▷ vb bind with a ligature

LIGATURED > LIGATURE

LIGATURES > LIGATURE

LIGER n hybrid offspring of a female tiger and a male lion

LIGERS > LIGER

LIGGE obsolete form of > LIE

LIGGED > LIG

LIGGER > LIG

LIGGERS > LIG

LIGGES > LIGGE

LIGGING > LIG

LIGGINGS > LIG

LIGHT n electromagnetic radiation by which things are visible ▷ adj bright ▷ vb ignite ▷ adv with little luggage

LIGHTBULB n glass bulb containing gas that emits light when a current is passed through it

LIGHTED > LIGHT

LIGHTEN vb make less dark

LIGHTENED > LIGHTEN

LIGHTENER > LIGHTEN

LIGHTENS > LIGHTEN

LIGHTER n device for lighting cigarettes etc ▷ vb convey in a type of flat-bottomed barge

LIGHTERED > LIGHTER

LIGHTERS > LIGHTER

LIGHTEST > LIGHT

LIGHTFACE n weight of type in printing

LIGHTFAST adj (of a dye) unaffected by light

LIGHTFUL adj full of light

LIGHTING > LIGHT

LIGHTINGS > LIGHT

LIGHTISH > LIGHT

LIGHTLESS > LIGHT

LIGHTLIED > LIGHTLY

LIGHTLIES > LIGHTLY

LIGHTLY adv in a light way ▷ vb belittle

LIGHTNESS n quality of being light

LIGHTNING n visible discharge of electricity in the atmosphere ▷ adj fast and sudden

LIGHTS > LIGHT

LIGHTSHIP n moored ship used as a lighthouse

LIGHTSOME adj lighthearted

LIGHTWAVE adj using light waves

LIGHTWOOD n Australian acacia

LIGNAGE another word for > LINEAGE

LIGNAGES > LIGNAGE

LIGNALOES another name for > EAGLEWOOD

LIGNAN n beneficial substance found in plants

LIGNANS > LIGNAN

LIGNE n unit of measurement

LIGNEOUS adj of or like wood

LIGNES > LIGNE

LIGNICOLE adj growing or living in wood

LIGNIFIED > LIGNIFY

LIGNIFIES > LIGNIFY

LIGNIFORM adj having the appearance of wood

LIGNIFY vb become woody with the deposition of lignin in cell walls

LIGNIN n complex polymer occurring in certain plant cell walls making the plant rigid

LIGNINS > LIGNIN

LIGNITE n woody textured rock used as fuel

LIGNITES > LIGNITE

LIGNITIC > LIGNITE

LIGNOSE n explosive compound

LIGNOSES > LIGNOSE

LIGNUM n wood

LIGNUMS > LIGNUM

LIGROIN n volatile fraction of petroleum

LIGROINE same as > LIGROIN

LIGROINES > LIGROINE

LIGROINS > LIGROIN

LIGS > LIG

LIGULA same as > LIGULE

LIGULAE > LIGULA

LIGULAR > LIGULA

LIGULAS > LIGULA

LIGULATE adj having the shape of a strap

LIGULATED same as > LIGULATE

LIGULE n membranous outgrowth between the leaf blade and sheath

LIGULES > LIGULE

LIGULOID > LIGULA

LIGURE n any of the 12 precious stones used in the breastplates of high priests

LIGURES > LIGURE

LIGUSTRUM n plant of a genus comprising the privets

LIKABLE adj easy to like

LIKABLY > LIKABLE

LIKE adj similar ▷ vb find enjoyable ▷ n favourable feeling, desire, or preference

LIKEABLE same as > LIKABLE

LIKEABLY same as > LIKABLY

LIKED > LIKE

LIKELIER > LIKELY

LIKELIEST > LIKELY

LIKELY adj tending or inclined ▷ adv probably

LIKEN vb compare

LIKENED > LIKEN

LIKENESS n resemblance

LIKENING > LIKEN

LIKENS > LIKEN

LIKER > LIKE

LIKERS > LIKE

LIKES > LIKE

LIKEST > LIKE

LIKEWAKE same as > LYKEWAKE

LIKEWAKES > LIKEWAKE

LIKEWALK same as > LYKEWAKE

LIKEWALKS > LIKEWALK

LIKEWISE adv similarly

LIKIN n historically, Chinese tax

LIKING n fondness

LIKINGS > LIKING

LIKINS > LIKIN

LIKUTA n coin in Zaïre

LILAC n shrub with pale mauve flowers ▷ adj light-purple

LILACS > LILAC

LILANGENI n standard monetary unit of Swaziland, divided into 100 cents

LILIED adj decorated with lilies

LILIES > LILY

LILL obsolete form of > LOLL

LILLED > LILL

LILLING > LILL

LILLIPUT adj tiny ▷ n tiny person or being

LILLIPUTS > LILLIPUT

LILLS > LILL

LILO n inflatable mattress

LILOS > LILO

LILT n musical quality in speech ▷ vb speak with a lilt

LILTED > LILT

LILTING > LILT

LILTINGLY > LILT

LILTS > LILT

LILY n plant which has large, often white, flowers

LILYLIKE adj resembling a lily

LIMA n type of edible bean

LIMACEL n small shell inside some kinds of slug

LIMACELS > LIMACEL

LIMACEOUS adj relating to the slug

LIMACES > LIMAX

LIMACINE adj relating to slugs

LIMACON n heart-shaped curve

LIMACONS > LIMACON

LIMAIL same as > LEMEL

LIMAILS > LIMAIL

LIMAN n lagoon

LIMANS > LIMAN

LIMAS > LIMA

LIMATION n polishing

LIMATIONS > LIMATION

LIMAX n slug

LIMB n arm, leg, or wing ▷ vb dismember

LIMBA n type of African tree

LIMBAS > LIMBA

LIMBATE adj having an edge or border of a different colour from the rest

LIMBEC obsolete form of > ALEMBIC

LIMBECK obsolete form of > ALEMBIC

LIMBECKS > LIMBECK

LIMBECS > LIMBEC

LIMBED > LIMB

LIMBER vb loosen stiff muscles by exercising ▷ adj pliant or supple ▷ n part of a gun carriage

LIMBERED > LIMBER

LIMBERER > LIMBER

LIMBEREST > LIMBER

LIMBERING > LIMBER

LIMBERLY > LIMBER

LIMBERS > LIMBER

LIMBI > LIMBUS

LIMBIC > LIMBUS

LIMBIER > LIMBY

LIMBIEST > LIMBY

LIMBING > LIMB

LIMBLESS > LIMB

LIMBMEAL adv piece by piece

LIMBO n region between Heaven and Hell for the unbaptized ▷ vb perform a Caribbean dance that entails passing under a bar while leaning backwards

LIMBOED > LIMBO

LIMBOES > LIMBO

LIMBOING > LIMBO

LIMBOS > LIMBO

LIMBOUS adj with overlapping edges

LIMBS > LIMB

LIMBUS n border

LIMBUSES > LIMBUS

LIMBY adj with long legs, stem, branches, etc

LIME n calcium compound used as a fertilizer or in making cement ▷ vb spread a calcium compound upon (land) ▷ adj having the flavour of lime fruit

LIMEADE n drink made from sweetened lime juice and plain or carbonated water

LIMEADES > LIMEADE

LIMED > LIME

LIMEKILN n kiln in which calcium carbonate is burned to produce quicklime

LIMEKILNS > LIMEKILN

LIMELESS > LIME

LIMELIGHT n glare of publicity ▷ vb illuminate with limelight

LIMELIT > LIMELIGHT

LIMEN another term for > THRESHOLD

LIMENS > LIMEN

LIMEPIT n pit containing lime in which hides are placed to remove the hair

LIMEPITS > LIMEPIT

LIMERENCE n psychological state resulting from romantic attraction

LIMERICK n humorous verse of five lines

LIMERICKS > LIMERICK

LIMES n fortified boundary of the Roman Empire

LIMESCALE n flaky deposit left in containers such as kettles by the action of heat on water containing calcium salts

LIMESTONE n sedimentary rock used in building

LIMEWASH n mixture of lime and water used to whitewash walls, ceilings, etc

LIMEWATER n clear colourless solution of calcium hydroxide in water

LIMEY n British person ▷ adj British

LIMEYS > LIMEY

LIMIER > LIMY

LIMIEST > LIMY

LIMINA > LIMEN

LIMINAL adj relating to the point beyond which a sensation becomes too faint to be experienced

LIMINESS > LIMY

LIMING > LIME

LIMINGS > LIME

LIMIT n ultimate extent, degree, or amount of something ▷ vb restrict or confine

LIMITABLE > LIMIT

LIMITARY adj of, involving, or serving as a limit

LIMITED adj having a limit ▷ n limited train, bus, etc

LIMITEDLY > LIMITED

LIMITEDS > LIMITED

LIMITER n thing that limits something

LIMITERS > LIMITER

LIMITES > LIMES

LIMITING > LIMIT

LIMITINGS > LIMIT

LIMITLESS > LIMIT

LIMITS > LIMIT

LIMMA n semitone

LIMMAS > LIMMA

LIMMER n scoundrel

LIMMERS > LIMMER

LIMN vb represent in drawing or painting

LIMNAEID n type of snail

LIMNAEIDS > LIMNAEID

LIMNED > LIMN

LIMNER > LIMN

LIMNERS > LIMN

LIMNETIC adj of the open water of lakes down to the depth of light penetration

LIMNIC adj relating to lakes

LIMNING > LIMN

LIMNOLOGY n study of bodies of fresh water with reference to their plant and animal life, physical properties, geographical features, etc

LIMNS > LIMN

LIMO short for > LIMOUSINE

LIMONENE n liquid optically active terpene with a lemon-like odour

LIMONENES > LIMONENE

LIMONITE n common brown, black, or yellow amorphous secondary mineral

LIMONITES > LIMONITE

LIMONITIC > LIMONITE

LIMONIUM n sea plant with funnel-shaped flowers

LIMONIUMS > LIMONIUM

LIMOS > LIMO

LIMOSES > LIMOSIS

LIMOSIS n excessive hunger

LIMOUS adj muddy

LIMOUSINE n large luxurious car

LIMP vb walk with an uneven step ▷ n limping walk ▷ adj without firmness or stiffness

LIMPA n type of rye bread

LIMPAS > LIMPA

LIMPED > LIMP

LIMPER > LIMP

LIMPERS > LIMP

LIMPEST > LIMP

LIMPET n shellfish which sticks to rocks ▷ adj denoting weapons that are magnetically attached to their targets

LIMPETS > LIMPET

LIMPID adj clear or transparent

LIMPIDITY > LIMPID

LIMPIDLY > LIMPID

LIMPING > LIMP

LIMPINGLY > LIMP

LIMPINGS > LIMP

LIMPKIN n rail-like wading bird

LIMPKINS > LIMPKIN

LIMPLY > LIMP

LIMPNESS > LIMP

LIMPS > LIMP

LIMPSEY same as > LIMPSY

LIMPSIER > LIMPSY

LIMPSIEST > LIMPSY

LIMPSY adj limp

LIMULI > LIMULUS

LIMULOID n type of crab

LIMULOIDS > LIMULOID

LIMULUS n horseshoe crab

LIMULUSES > LIMULUS

LIMY adj of, like, or smeared with birdlime

LIN vb cease

LINABLE > LINE

LINAC n linear accelerator

LINACS > LINAC

LINAGE n number of lines in written or printed matter

LINAGES > LINAGE

LINALOL same as > LINALOOL

LINALOLS > LINALOL

LINALOOL n optically active colourless fragrant liquid
LINALOOLS > LINALOOL
LINCH n ledge
LINCHES > LINCH
LINCHET another word for > LINCH
LINCHETS > LINCHET
LINCHPIN n pin to hold a wheel on its axle
LINCHPINS > LINCHPIN
LINCRUSTA n type of wallpaper having a hard embossed surface
LINCTURE n medicine taken by licking
LINCTURES > LINCTURE
LINCTUS n cough medicine
LINCTUSES > LINCTUS
LIND variant of > LINDEN
LINDANE n white poisonous crystalline powder
LINDANES > LINDANE
LINDEN n large tree with heart-shaped leaves and fragrant yellowish flowers
LINDENS > LINDEN
LINDIED > LINDY
LINDIES > LINDY
LINDS > LIND
LINDWORM n wingless serpent-like dragon
LINDWORMS > LINDWORM
LINDY n lively dance ▷ vb perform the lindy
LINDYING > LINDY
LINE n long narrow mark ▷ vb mark with lines
LINEABLE > LINE
LINEAGE n descent from an ancestor
LINEAGES > LINEAGE
LINEAL adj in direct line of descent
LINEALITY > LINEAL
LINEALLY > LINEAL
LINEAMENT n facial feature
LINEAR adj of or in lines
LINEARISE same as > LINEARIZE
LINEARITY > LINEAR
LINEARIZE vb make linear
LINEARLY > LINEAR
LINEATE adj marked with lines
LINEATED same as > LINEATE
LINEATION n act of marking with lines
LINEBRED adj having an ancestor that is common to sire and dam
LINECUT n method of relief printing
LINECUTS > LINECUT
LINED > LINE
LINELESS > LINE
LINELIKE > LINE
LINEMAN same as > LINESMAN
LINEMATE n ice hockey player on the same line as another
LINEMATES > LINEMATE
LINEMEN > LINEMAN
LINEN n cloth or thread made from flax

LINENFOLD n form of decorative wood carving that resembles folded linen
LINENIER > LINENY
LINENIEST > LINENY
LINENS > LINEN
LINENY adj like linen
LINEOLATE adj marked with very fine parallel lines
LINER n large passenger ship
LINERLESS adj having no lining
LINERS > LINER
LINES > LINE
LINESCORE n horizontal chart showing scoring in a game
LINESMAN n (in some sports) an official who helps the referee or umpire
LINESMEN > LINESMAN
LINEUP n row or arrangement of people or things
LINEUPS > LINEUP
LINEY > LINE
LING n slender food fish
LINGA same as > LINGAM
LINGAM n (in Sanskrit) masculine gender
LINGAMS > LINGAM
LINGAS > LINGA
LINGBERRY same as > COWBERRY
LINGCOD n type of food fish
LINGCODS > LINGCOD
LINGEL n shoemaker's thread
LINGELS > LINGEL
LINGER vb delay or prolong departure
LINGERED > LINGER
LINGERER > LINGER
LINGERERS > LINGER
LINGERIE n women's underwear or nightwear
LINGERIES > LINGERIE
LINGERING > LINGER
LINGERS > LINGER
LINGIER > LINGY
LINGIEST > LINGY
LINGLE same as > LINGEL
LINGLES > LINGLE
LINGO n foreign or unfamiliar language or jargon
LINGOES > LINGO
LINGOS > LINGO
LINGOT n ingot
LINGOTS > LINGOT
LINGS > LING
LINGSTER n person able to communicate with aliens
LINGSTERS > LINGSTER
LINGUA n any tongue-like structure
LINGUAE > LINGUA
LINGUAL adj of the tongue ▷ n lingual consonant
LINGUALLY > LINGUAL
LINGUALS > LINGUAL
LINGUAS > LINGUA
LINGUICA n Portuguese sausage
LINGUICAS > LINGUICA
LINGUINE n kind of pasta in the shape of thin flat strands

LINGUINES > LINGUINE
LINGUINI same as > LINGUINE
LINGUINIS > LINGUINI
LINGUISA same as > LINGUICA
LINGUISAS > LINGUISA
LINGUIST n person skilled in foreign languages
LINGUISTS > LINGUIST
LINGULA n small tongue
LINGULAE > LINGULA
LINGULAR > LINGULA
LINGULAS > LINGULA
LINGULATE adj shaped like a tongue
LINGY adj heather-covered
LINHAY n farm building with an open front
LINHAYS > LINHAY
LINIER > LINE
LINIEST > LINE
LINIMENT n medicated liquid rubbed on the skin to relieve pain or stiffness
LINIMENTS > LINIMENT
LININ n network of viscous material in the nucleus of a cell
LINING n layer of cloth attached to the inside of a garment etc
LININGS > LINING
LININS > LININ
LINISH vb polish metal
LINISHED > LINISH
LINISHER > LINISH
LINISHERS > LINISH
LINISHES > LINISH
LINISHING > LINISH
LINK n any of the rings forming a chain ▷ vb connect with or as if with links
LINKABLE > LINK
LINKAGE n act of linking or the state of being linked
LINKAGES > LINKAGE
LINKBOY n (formerly) a boy who carried a torch for pedestrians in dark streets
LINKBOYS > LINKBOY
LINKED > LINK
LINKER n person or thing that links
LINKERS > LINKER
LINKIER > LINKY
LINKIEST > LINKY
LINKING > LINK
LINKMAN same as > LINKBOY
LINKMEN > LINKMAN
LINKROT n state of having expired hyperlinks on a website
LINKROTS > LINKROT
LINKS > LINK
LINKSLAND n land near sea used for golf
LINKSMAN same as > LINKBOY
LINKSMEN > LINKSMAN
LINKSPAN n hinged bridge on a quay, used to move vehicles on or off a vessel
LINKSPANS > LINKSPAN
LINKSTER n interpreter
LINKSTERS > LINKSTER

LINKUP n establishing of a union between objects, groups, organizations, etc
LINKUPS > LINKUP
LINKWORK n something made up of links
LINKWORKS > LINKWORK
LINKY adj (of countryside) consisting of links
LINN n waterfall or a pool at the foot of it
LINNED > LIN
LINNET n songbird of the finch family
LINNETS > LINNET
LINNEY same as > LINHAY
LINNEYS > LINNEY
LINNIES > LINNY
LINNING > LIN
LINNS > LINN
LINNY same as > LINHAY
LINO same as > LINOLEUM
LINOCUT n design cut in relief in lino mounted on a block of wood
LINOCUTS > LINOCUT
LINOLEATE n ester or salt of linoleic acid
LINOLEIC adj as in linoleic acid colourless oily essential fatty acid found in linseed
LINOLENIC adj as in linolenic acid colourless unsaturated essential fatty acid
LINOLEUM n type of floor covering
LINOLEUMS > LINOLEUM
LINOS > LINO
LINOTYPE n line of metal type produced by machine ▷ vb set as line of type
LINOTYPED > LINOTYPE
LINOTYPER > LINOTYPE
LINOTYPES > LINOTYPE
LINS > LIN
LINSANG n any of several forest-dwelling viverrine mammals
LINSANGS > LINSANG
LINSEED n seed of the flax plant
LINSEEDS > LINSEED
LINSEY n type of cloth
LINSEYS > LINSEY
LINSTOCK n long staff holding a lighted match, formerly used to fire a cannon
LINSTOCKS > LINSTOCK
LINT n shreds of fibre, etc ▷ vb shed or remove lint
LINTED adj having lint
LINTEL n horizontal beam at the top of a door or window
LINTELED adj (of a door or window) having a lintel
LINTELLED adj having a lintel
LINTELS > LINTEL
LINTER n machine for stripping the short fibres of ginned cotton seeds
LINTERS > LINTER
LINTIE Scot word for > LINNET

LINTIER > LINT
LINTIES > LINTIE
LINTIEST > LINT
LINTING n process of making lint
LINTINGS > LINTING
LINTLESS > LINT
LINTOL same as > LINTEL
LINTOLS > LINTOL
LINTS > LINT
LINTSEED same as
> LINSEED
LINTSEEDS > LINTSEED
LINTSTOCK same as
> LINSTOCK
LINTWHITE n linnet
LINTY > LINT
LINUM n type of plant of temperate regions
LINUMS > LINUM
LINURON n type of herbicide
LINURONS > LINURON
LINUX n nonproprietary computer operating system
LINUXES > LINUX
LINY > LINE
LION n large animal of the cat family
LIONCEL n (in heraldry) small lion
LIONCELLE same as
> LIONCEL
LIONCELS > LIONCEL
LIONEL same as > LIONCEL
LIONELS > LIONEL
LIONESS n female lion
LIONESSES > LIONESS
LIONET n young lion
LIONETS > LIONET
LIONFISH n any of various scorpion fishes of the Pacific
LIONHEAD n small breed of rabbit with long fur around the face
LIONHEADS > LIONHEAD
LIONISE same as
> LIONIZE
LIONISED > LIONISE
LIONISER > LIONISE
LIONISERS > LIONISE
LIONISES > LIONISE
LIONISING > LIONISE
LIONISM n lion-like appearance of leprosy
LIONISMS > LIONISM
LIONIZE vb treat as a celebrity
LIONIZED > LIONIZE
LIONIZER > LIONIZE
LIONIZERS > LIONIZE
LIONIZES > LIONIZE
LIONIZING > LIONIZE
LIONLIER > LIONLY
LIONLIEST > LIONLY
LIONLIKE > LION
LIONLY adj like a lion
LIONS > LION
LIP n either of the fleshy edges of the mouth ▷ vb touch with the lips
LIPA n monetary unit of Croatia
LIPAEMIA n abnormally large amount of fat in the blood
LIPAEMIAS > LIPAEMIA

LIPARITE n type of igneous rock
LIPARITES > LIPARITE
LIPAS > LIPA
LIPASE n any of a group of enzymes that digest fat
LIPASES > LIPASE
LIPE n lurching or jerking movement
LIPECTOMY n surgical operation to remove fat
LIPEMIA same as
> LIPAEMIA
LIPEMIAS > LIPEMIA
LIPES > LIPE
LIPGLOSS n cosmetic for the lips to give a sheen
LIPID n any of a group of organic compounds including fats, oils, waxes, and sterols
LIPIDE same as > LIPID
LIPIDES > LIPIDE
LIPIDIC > LIPID
LIPIDOSES > LIPIDOSIS
LIPIDOSIS n disorder in lipid metabolism
LIPIDS > LIPID
LIPIN n family of nuclear proteins
LIPINS > LIPIN
LIPLESS > LIP
LIPLIKE > LIP
LIPLINER n cosmetic used to outline the lips
LIPLINERS > LIPLINER
LIPO n liposuction
LIPOCYTE n fat-storing cell
LIPOCYTES > LIPOCYTE
LIPOGRAM n piece of writing in which all words containing a particular letter have been omitted
LIPOGRAMS > LIPOGRAM
LIPOIC adj as in lipoic acid sulphur-containing fatty acid
LIPOID n fatlike substance, such as wax
LIPOIDAL > LIPOID
LIPOIDS > LIPOID
LIPOLITIC same as
> LIPOLYTIC
LIPOLYSES > LIPOLYSIS
LIPOLYSIS n hydrolysis of fats resulting in the production of carboxylic acids and glycerol
LIPOLYTIC adj fat-burning
LIPOMA n benign tumour composed of fatty tissue
LIPOMAS > LIPOMA
LIPOMATA > LIPOMA
LIPOPLAST n small particle in plant cytoplasm, esp that of seeds, in which fat is stored
LIPOS > LIPO
LIPOSOMAL > LIPOSOME
LIPOSOME n particle formed by lipids
LIPOSOMES > LIPOSOME
LIPOSUCK vb subject to liposuction
LIPOSUCKS > LIPOSUCK
LIPOTROPY n breaking down of fat in body
LIPPED > LIP

LIPPEN vb trust
LIPPENED > LIPPEN
LIPPENING > LIPPEN
LIPPENS > LIPPEN
LIPPER Scots word for
> RIPPLE
LIPPERED > LIPPER
LIPPERING > LIPPER
LIPPERS > LIPPER
LIPPIE variant of > LIPPY
LIPPIER > LIPPY
LIPPIES > LIPPY
LIPPIEST > LIPPY
LIPPINESS > LIPPY
LIPPING > LIP
LIPPINGS > LIP
LIPPITUDE n state of having bleary eyes
LIPPY adj insolent or cheeky ▷ n lipstick
LIPREAD vb follow what someone says by watching their lips
LIPREADER > LIPREAD
LIPREADS > LIPREAD
LIPS > LIP
LIPSALVE n substance used to prevent or relieve chapped lips
LIPSALVES > LIPSALVE
LIPSTICK n cosmetic in stick form, for colouring the lips ▷ vb put lipstick on
LIPSTICKS > LIPSTICK
LIPURIA n presence of fat in the urine
LIPURIAS > LIPURIA
LIQUABLE adj that can be melted
LIQUATE vb separate one component of by heating until the more fusible part melts
LIQUATED > LIQUATE
LIQUATES > LIQUATE
LIQUATING > LIQUATE
LIQUATION > LIQUATE
LIQUEFIED > LIQUEFY
LIQUEFIER > LIQUEFY
LIQUEFIES > LIQUEFY
LIQUEFY vb become liquid
LIQUESCE vb become liquid
LIQUESCED > LIQUESCE
LIQUESCES > LIQUESCE
LIQUEUR n flavoured and sweetened alcoholic spirit ▷ vb flavour with liqueur
LIQUEURED > LIQUEUR
LIQUEURS > LIQUEUR
LIQUID n substance in a physical state which can change shape but not size ▷ adj of or being a liquid
LIQUIDATE vb pay (a debt)
LIQUIDIER > LIQUIDY
LIQUIDISE same as
> LIQUIDIZE
LIQUIDITY n state of being able to meet financial obligations
LIQUIDIZE vb make or become liquid
LIQUIDLY > LIQUID
LIQUIDS > LIQUID
LIQUIDUS n line on graph above which a substance is in liquid form

LIQUIDY adj having the nature of liquid
LIQUIFIED > LIQUIFY
LIQUIFIER n something that liquifies
LIQUIFIES > LIQUIFY
LIQUIFY same as
> LIQUEFY
LIQUITAB n soluble plastic capsule containing liquid detergent or medicine
LIQUITABS > LIQUITAB
LIQUOR n alcoholic drink ▷ vb steep in warm water to form wort in brewing
LIQUORED > LIQUOR
LIQUORICE n black substance used in medicine and as a sweet
LIQUORING > LIQUOR
LIQUORISH same as
> LICKERISH
LIQUORS > LIQUOR
LIRA n monetary unit of Turkey, Malta, and formerly of Italy
LIRAS > LIRA
LIRE > LIRA
LIRI > LIRA
LIRIOPE n grasslike plant
LIRIOPES > LIRIOPE
LIRIPIPE n tip of a graduate's hood
LIRIPIPES > LIRIPIPE
LIRIPOOP same as
> LIRIPIPE
LIRIPOOPS > LIRIPOOP
LIRK vb wrinkle
LIRKED > LIRK
LIRKING > LIRK
LIRKS > LIRK
LIROT > LIRA
LIROTH > LIRA
LIS n fleur-de-lis
LISENTE > SENTE
LISK Yorkshire dialect for
> GROIN
LISKS > LISK
LISLE n strong fine cotton thread or fabric
LISLES > LISLE
LISP n speech defect in which s and z are pronounced th ▷ vb speak or utter with a lisp
LISPED > LISP
LISPER > LISP
LISPERS > LISP
LISPING > LISP
LISPINGLY > LISP
LISPINGS > LISP
LISPOUND n unit of weight
LISPOUNDS > LISPOUND
LISPS > LISP
LISPUND same as
> LISPOUND
LISPUNDS > LISPUND
LISSES > LIS
LISSOM adj supple, agile
LISSOME same as > LISSOM
LISSOMELY > LISSOM
LISSOMLY > LISSOM
LIST n item-by-item record of names or things, usu written one below another ▷ vb make a list of
LISTABLE > LIST

LISTBOX n small box on a computer screen, showing a list of options

LISTBOXES > LISTBOX

LISTED > LIST

LISTEE n person on list

LISTEES > LISTEE

LISTEL another name for > FILLET

LISTELS > LISTEL

LISTEN vb concentrate on hearing something

LISTENED > LISTEN

LISTENER > LISTEN

LISTENERS > LISTEN

LISTENING > LISTEN

LISTENS > LISTEN

LISTER n plough with a double mouldboard to throw soil to sides of a central furrow

LISTERIA n type of rodlike Gram-positive bacterium

LISTERIAL > LISTERIA

LISTERIAS > LISTERIA

LISTERS > LISTER

LISTETH > LIST

LISTFUL adj paying attention

LISTICLE n article which consists of a list

LISTICLES > LISTICLE

LISTING n list or an entry in a list

LISTINGS > LISTING

LISTLESS adj lacking interest or energy

LISTS pl n field of combat in a tournament

LISTSERV n email service for those with similar interests

LISTSERVS > LISTSERV

LIT n archaic word for dye or colouring

LITAI > LITAS

LITANIES > LITANY

LITANY n prayer with responses from the congregation

LITAS n monetary unit of Lithuania

LITCHI n Chinese tree with round edible fruits

LITCHIS > LITCHI

LITE same as > LIGHT

LITED > LITE

LITENESS > LITE

LITER same as > LITRE

LITERACY n ability to read and write

LITERAL adj according to the explicit meaning of a word or text ▷ n misspelling in a text

LITERALLY adv in a literal manner

LITERALS > LITERAL

LITERARY adj of or knowledgeable about literature

LITERATE adj able to read and write ▷ n literate person

LITERATES > LITERATE

LITERATI pl n literary people

LITERATIM adv letter for letter

LITERATO > LITERATI

LITERATOR n professional writer

LITERATUS > LITERATI

LITEROSE adj affectedly literary

LITERS > LITER

LITES > LITE

LITEST > LITE

LITH n limb or joint

LITHARGE n lead monoxide

LITHARGES > LITHARGE

LITHATE n salt of uric acid

LITHATES > LITHATE

LITHE adj flexible or supple, pliant ▷ vb listen

LITHED > LITHE

LITHELY > LITHE

LITHEMIA n gout

LITHEMIAS > LITHEMIA

LITHEMIC > LITHEMIA

LITHENESS > LITHE

LITHER > LITHE

LITHERLY adj crafty; cunning

LITHES > LITHE

LITHESOME less common word for > LISSOM

LITHEST > LITHE

LITHIA n lithium present in mineral waters as lithium salts

LITHIAS > LITHIA

LITHIASES > LITHIASIS

LITHIASIS n formation of a calculus

LITHIC adj of stone

LITHIFIED > LITHIFY

LITHIFIES > LITHIFY

LITHIFY vb turn into rock

LITHING > LITHE

LITHISTID n type of sponge

LITHITE n part of cell with sensory element

LITHITES > LITHITE

LITHIUM n chemical element, the lightest known metal

LITHIUMS > LITHIUM

LITHO n lithography ▷ vb print using lithography

LITHOCYST n sac containing otoliths

LITHOED > LITHO

LITHOES > LITHO

LITHOID adj resembling rock

LITHOIDAL same as > LITHOID

LITHOING > LITHO

LITHOLOGY n physical characteristics of a rock

LITHOPONE n white pigment consisting of a mixture of zinc sulphide, zinc oxide, and barium sulphate

LITHOPS n fleshy-leaved plant

LITHOS > LITHO

LITHOSOL n type of azonal soil

LITHOSOLS > LITHOSOL

LITHOTOME n instrument used in lithotomy operation

LITHOTOMY n surgical removal of a calculus, esp one in the urinary bladder

LITHOTYPE n etched surface for printing a design

LITHS > LITH

LITIGABLE adj that may be the subject of litigation

LITIGANT n person involved in a lawsuit ▷ adj engaged in litigation

LITIGANTS > LITIGANT

LITIGATE vb bring or contest a law suit

LITIGATED > LITIGATE

LITIGATES > LITIGATE

LITIGATOR > LITIGATE

LITIGIOUS adj frequently going to law

LITING > LITE

LITMUS n soluble powder obtained from lichens

LITMUSES > LITMUS

LITORAL same as > LITTORAL

LITOTES n ironical understatement used for effect

LITOTIC > LITOTES

LITRE n unit of liquid measure

LITREAGE n volume in litres

LITREAGES > LITREAGE

LITRES > LITRE

LITS > LIT

LITTEN adj lighted

LITTER n untidy rubbish ▷ vb strew with litter

LITTERBAG n bag for putting rubbish in

LITTERBUG n person who tends to drop rubbish in public places

LITTERED > LITTER

LITTERER n one who litters

LITTERERS > LITTERER

LITTERIER > LITTERY

LITTERING > LITTER

LITTERS > LITTER

LITTERY adj covered in litter

LITTLE adj small ▷ adv not a lot ▷ n small amount, extent, or duration

LITTLER > LITTLE

LITTLES > LITTLE

LITTLEST > LITTLE

LITTLIE n young child

LITTLIES > LITTLIE

LITTLIN same as > LITTLING

LITTLING n child

LITTLINGS > LITTLING

LITTLINS > LITTLIN

LITTLISH adj rather small

LITTORAL adj of or by the seashore ▷ n coastal district

LITTORALS > LITTORAL

LITU > LITAS

LITURGIC > LITURGY

LITURGICS n study of liturgies

LITURGIES > LITURGY

LITURGISM > LITURGIST

LITURGIST n student or composer of liturgical forms

LITURGY n prescribed form of public worship

LITUUS n curved trumpet

LITUUSES > LITUUS

LIVABLE adj tolerable or pleasant to live (with)

LIVE vb be alive ▷ adj living, alive ▷ adv in the form of a live performance

LIVEABLE same as > LIVABLE

LIVEBLOG vb blog about (an event) as it happens

LIVEBLOGS > LIVEBLOG

LIVED > LIVE

LIVEDO n reddish discoloured patch on the skin

LIVEDOS > LIVEDO

LIVELIER > LIVELY

LIVELIEST > LIVELY

LIVELILY > LIVELY

LIVELOD n livelihood

LIVELODS > LIVELOD

LIVELONG adj long or seemingly long

LIVELONGS > LIVELONG

LIVELOOD n livelihood

LIVELOODS > LIVELOOD

LIVELY adj full of life or vigour

LIVEN vb make or become lively

LIVENED > LIVEN

LIVENER > LIVEN

LIVENERS > LIVEN

LIVENESS n state of being alive

LIVENING > LIVEN

LIVENS > LIVEN

LIVER n person who lives in a specified way

LIVERED adj having liver

LIVERIED adj wearing livery

LIVERIES > LIVERY

LIVERING n process of liquid becoming lumpy

LIVERINGS > LIVERING

LIVERISH adj having a disorder of the liver

LIVERLEAF n woodland plant

LIVERLESS > LIVER

LIVERS > LIVER

LIVERWORT n plant resembling seaweed or leafy moss

LIVERY n distinctive dress ▷ adj of or resembling liver

LIVERYMAN n member of a livery company

LIVERYMEN > LIVERYMAN

LIVES > LIFE

LIVEST > LIVE

LIVESTOCK n farm animals

LIVETRAP n box constructed to trap an animal without injuring it

LIVETRAPS > LIVETRAP

LIVEWARE n personnel working in a computer system

LIVEWARES > LIVEWARE

LIVEWELL n container of water on a fishing boat used to store live fish

LIVEWELLS > LIVEWELL

LIVEYER n (in Newfoundland) a full-time resident

LIVEYERE same as > LIVEYER

LIVEYERES > LIVEYERE

LIVEYERS > LIVEYER

LIVID adj angry or furious

LIVIDER > LIVID

LIVIDEST > LIVID

LIVIDITY n state of being livid

LIVIDLY > LIVID

LIVIDNESS > LIVID

LIVIER same as > LIVEYER

LIVIERS > LIVIER

LIVING adj possessing life, not dead or inanimate ▷ n condition of being alive

LIVINGLY > LIVING

LIVINGS > LIVING

LIVOR another word for > LIVIDITY

LIVORS > LIVOR

LIVRAISON n one of the numbers of a book published in parts

LIVRE n former French unit of money of account

LIVRES > LIVRE

LIVYER same as > LIVEYER

LIVYERS > LIVYER

LIXIVIA > LIXIVIUM

LIXIVIAL > LIXIVIATE

LIXIVIATE less common word for > LEACH

LIXIVIOUS > LIXIVIUM

LIXIVIUM n alkaline solution obtained by leaching wood ash with water

LIXIVIUMS > LIXIVIUM

LIZARD n four-footed reptile with a long body and tail

LIZARDS > LIZARD

LIZZIE n as in tin lizzie old or decrepit car

LIZZIES > LIZZIE

LLAMA n woolly animal of the camel family

LLAMAS > LLAMA

LLANERO n native of llanos

LLANEROS > LLANERO

LLANO n extensive grassy treeless plain

LLANOS > LLANO

LO interj look!

LOACH n carplike fish

LOACHES > LOACH

LOAD n burden or weight ▷ vb put a load on or into

LOADABLE adj able to be loaded

LOADED adj containing a hidden trap

LOADEN vb load

LOADENED > LOADEN

LOADENING > LOADEN

LOADENS > LOADEN

LOADER n person who loads a gun or other firearm

LOADERS > LOADER

LOADING n load or burden

LOADINGS > LOADING

LOADS pl n lots or a lot

LOADSPACE n area in a motor vehicle where a load can be carried

LOADSTAR same as > LODESTAR

LOADSTARS > LOADSTAR

LOADSTONE same as > LODESTONE

LOAF n shaped mass of baked bread ▷ vb idle, loiter

LOAFED > LOAF

LOAFER n idler

LOAFERISH > LOAFER

LOAFERS > LOAFER

LOAFING > LOAF

LOAFINGS > LOAF

LOAFS > LOAF

LOAM n fertile soil ▷ vb cover, treat, or fill with loam

LOAMED > LOAM

LOAMIER > LOAM

LOAMIEST > LOAM

LOAMINESS > LOAM

LOAMING > LOAM

LOAMLESS > LOAM

LOAMS > LOAM

LOAMY > LOAM

LOAN n money lent at interest ▷ vb lend

LOANABLE > LOAN

LOANBACK n facility by which an individual can borrow from his or her pension fund ▷ vb make use of this facility

LOANBACKS > LOANBACK

LOANED > LOAN

LOANEE n sportsperson who is loaned out

LOANEES > LOANEE

LOANER > LOAN

LOANERS > LOAN

LOANING > LOAN

LOANINGS > LOANING

LOANS > LOAN

LOANSHIFT n adaptation of word from one language by another

LOANWORD n word adopted from one language into another

LOANWORDS > LOANWORD

LOAST > LOSE

LOATH adj unwilling or reluctant (to)

LOATHE vb hate

LOATHED > LOATHE

LOATHER > LOATHE

LOATHERS > LOATHE

LOATHES > LOATHE

LOATHEST > LOATH

LOATHFUL adj causing loathing

LOATHING n strong disgust

LOATHINGS > LOATHING

LOATHLIER > LOATHLY

LOATHLY adj loathsome

LOATHNESS > LOATH

LOATHSOME adj causing loathing

LOATHY obsolete form of > LOATHSOME

LOAVE vb form a loaf

LOAVED > LOAVE

LOAVES > LOAF

LOAVING > LOAVE

LOB n ball struck in a high arc ▷ vb strike in a high arc

LOBAR adj of or affecting a lobe

LOBATE adj with or like lobes

LOBATED same as > LOBATE

LOBATELY > LOBATE

LOBATION n division into lobes

LOBATIONS > LOBATION

LOBBED > LOB

LOBBER n one who lobs

LOBBERS > LOBBER

LOBBIED > LOBBY

LOBBIES > LOBBY

LOBBING > LOB

LOBBY n corridor into which rooms open ▷ vb try to influence (legislators) in the formulation of policy

LOBBYER > LOBBY

LOBBYERS > LOBBY

LOBBYGOW n errand boy

LOBBYGOWS > LOBBYGOW

LOBBYING > LOBBY

LOBBYINGS > LOBBY

LOBBYISM > LOBBYIST

LOBBYISMS > LOBBYIST

LOBBYIST n person who lobbies on behalf of a particular interest

LOBBYISTS > LOBBYIST

LOBE n rounded projection

LOBECTOMY n surgical removal of a lobe from any organ or gland in the body

LOBED > LOBE

LOBEFIN n type of fish

LOBEFINS > LOBEFIN

LOBELESS adj having no lobes

LOBELET n small lobe

LOBELETS > LOBELET

LOBELIA n garden plant

LOBELIAS > LOBELIA

LOBELIKE adj like a lobe

LOBELINE n crystalline alkaloid extracted from the seeds of the Indian tobacco plant

LOBELINES > LOBELINE

LOBES > LOBE

LOBI > LOBUS

LOBING n formation of lobes

LOBINGS > LOBING

LOBIPED adj with lobed toes

LOBLOLLY n southern US pine tree

LOBO n timber wolf

LOBOLA n (in African custom) price paid by a bridegroom's family to his bride's family

LOBOLAS > LOBOLA

LOBOLO same as > LOBOLA

LOBOLOS > LOBOLO

LOBOS > LOBO

LOBOSE another word for > LOBATE

LOBOTOMY n surgical incision into a lobe of the brain to treat certain disorders

LOBS > LOB

LOBSCOUSE n sailor's stew of meat, vegetables, and hardtack

LOBSTER n shellfish ▷ vb fish for lobsters

LOBSTERED > LOBSTER

LOBSTERER n person who catches lobsters

LOBSTERS > LOBSTER

LOBSTICK n tree used as landmark

LOBSTICKS > LOBSTICK

LOBTAIL vb (of a whale) hit a surface of water with the tail

LOBTAILED > LOBTAIL

LOBTAILS > LOBTAIL

LOBULAR > LOBULE

LOBULARLY > LOBULE

LOBULATE > LOBULE

LOBULATED > LOBULE

LOBULE n small lobe or a subdivision of a lobe

LOBULES > LOBULE

LOBULI > LOBULUS

LOBULOSE > LOBULE

LOBULUS n small lobe

LOBUS n lobe

LOBWORM same as > LUGWORM

LOBWORMS > LOBWORM

LOCA > LOCUS

LOCAL adj of a particular place ▷ n person from a particular place

LOCALE n scene of an event

LOCALES > LOCALE

LOCALISE same as > LOCALIZE

LOCALISED > LOCALISE

LOCALISER > LOCALISE

LOCALISES > LOCALISE

LOCALISM n pronunciation, phrase, etc, peculiar to a particular locality

LOCALISMS > LOCALISM

LOCALIST > LOCALISM

LOCALISTS > LOCALISM

LOCALITE n resident of an area

LOCALITES > LOCALITE

LOCALITY n neighbourhood or area

LOCALIZE vb restrict to a particular place

LOCALIZED > LOCALIZE

LOCALIZER > LOCALIZE

LOCALIZES > LOCALIZE

LOCALLY adv within a particular area or place

LOCALNESS > LOCAL

LOCALS > LOCAL

LOCATABLE > LOCATE

LOCATE vb discover the whereabouts of

LOCATED > LOCATE

LOCATER > LOCATE

LOCATERS > LOCATE

LOCATES > LOCATE

LOCATING > LOCATE

LOCATION n site or position

LOCATIONS > LOCATION

LOCATIVE adj (of a word or phrase) indicating place or direction ▷ n locative case

LOCATIVES > LOCATIVE

LOCATOR n part of index that shows where to find information

LOCATORS > LOCATOR

LOCAVORE n person who prefers locally produced food

LOCAVORES > LOCAVORE

LOCELLATE adj split into secondary cells

LOCH n lake

LOCHAN n small inland loch

LOCHANS > LOCHAN

LOCHE n freshwater fish of the cod family

LOCHES > LOCHE

LOCHIA n vaginal discharge following childbirth

LOCHIAL > LOCHIA

LOCHIAS > LOCHIA

LOCHS > LOCH

LOCI > LOCUS

LOCIE n type of logging engine

LOCIES > LOCIE

LOCIS > LOCUS

LOCK n appliance for fastening a door, case, etc ▷ vb fasten or become fastened securely

LOCKABLE > LOCK

LOCKAGE n system of locks in a canal

LOCKAGES > LOCKAGE

LOCKAWAY n investment intended to be held for a relatively long time

LOCKAWAYS > LOCKAWAY

LOCKBOX n system of collecting funds from companies by banks

LOCKBOXES > LOCKBOX

LOCKDOWN n device used to secure equipment, etc

LOCKDOWNS > LOCKDOWN

LOCKED > LOCK

LOCKER n small cupboard with a lock

LOCKERS > LOCKER

LOCKET n small hinged pendant for a portrait etc

LOCKETS > LOCKET

LOCKFAST adj securely fastened with a lock

LOCKFUL n sufficient to fill a canal lock

LOCKFULS > LOCKFUL

LOCKHOUSE n house of lock-keeper

LOCKING > LOCK

LOCKINGS > LOCK

LOCKJAW n tetanus

LOCKJAWS > LOCKJAW

LOCKLESS adj having no lock

LOCKMAKER n maker of locks

LOCKMAN n lock-keeper

LOCKMEN > LOCKMAN

LOCKNUT n nut screwed down on a primary nut to stop it from loosening

LOCKNUTS > LOCKNUT

LOCKOUT n closing of a workplace by an employer to force workers to accept terms

LOCKOUTS > LOCKOUT

LOCKPICK another word for > PICKLOCK

LOCKPICKS > LOCKPICK

LOCKRAM n type of linen cloth

LOCKRAMS > LOCKRAM

LOCKS > LOCK

LOCKSET n hardware used to lock door

LOCKSETS > LOCKSET

LOCKSMAN same as > LOCKMAN

LOCKSMEN > LOCKSMAN

LOCKSMITH n person who makes and mends locks

LOCKSTEP n method of marching in step as closely as possible

LOCKSTEPS > LOCKSTEP

LOCKUP n prison

LOCKUPS > LOCKUP

LOCO n locomotive ▷ adj insane ▷ vb poison with locoweed

LOCOED > LOCO

LOCOES > LOCO

LOCOFOCO n match

LOCOFOCOS > LOCOFOCO

LOCOING > LOCO

LOCOISM n disease of cattle, sheep, and horses caused by eating locoweed

LOCOISMS > LOCOISM

LOCOMAN n railwayman

LOCOMEN > LOCOMAN

LOCOMOTE vb move from one place to another

LOCOMOTED > LOCOMOTE

LOCOMOTES > LOCOMOTE

LOCOMOTOR adj of or relating to locomotion

LOCOPLANT another word for > LOCOWEED

LOCOS > LOCO

LOCOWEED n any of several perennial leguminous plants

LOCOWEEDS > LOCOWEED

LOCULAR adj divided into compartments by septa

LOCULATE same as > LOCULAR

LOCULATED same as > LOCULATE

LOCULE n any of the chambers of an ovary or anther

LOCULED adj having locules

LOCULES > LOCULE

LOCULI > LOCULUS

LOCULUS same as > LOCULE

LOCUM n temporary stand-in for a doctor, or clergyman or clergywoman

LOCUMS > LOCUM

LOCUPLETE adj well-stored

LOCUS n area or place where something happens

LOCUST n destructive insect ▷ vb ravage, as locusts

LOCUSTA n flower cluster unit in grasses

LOCUSTAE > LOCUSTA

LOCUSTAL > LOCUSTA

LOCUSTED > LOCUST

LOCUSTING > LOCUST

LOCUSTS > LOCUST

LOCUTION n manner or style of speech

LOCUTIONS > LOCUTION

LOCUTORY adj room intended for conversation

LOD n type of logarithm

LODE n vein of ore

LODEN n thick waterproof, woollen cloth

LODENS > LODEN

LODES > LODE

LODESMAN n pilot

LODESMEN > LODESMAN

LODESTAR n star used in navigation or astronomy as a point of reference

LODESTARS > LODESTAR

LODESTONE n magnetic iron ore

LODGE n gatekeeper's house ▷ vb live in another's house at a fixed charge

LODGEABLE > LODGE

LODGED > LODGE

LODGEMENT same as > LODGMENT

LODGEPOLE n type of pine tree

LODGER n tenant

LODGERS > LODGER

LODGES > LODGE

LODGING n temporary residence

LODGINGS pl n rented room or rooms in which to live, esp in another person's house

LODGMENT n act of lodging or the state of being lodged

LODGMENTS > LODGMENT

LODICULA n delicate scale in grass

LODICULAE > LODICULA

LODICULE n minute scale at the base of the ovary in grass flowers

LODICULES > LODICULE

LODS > LOD

LOERIE same as > LOURIE

LOERIES > LOERIE

LOESS n fine-grained soil

LOESSAL > LOESS

LOESSES > LOESS

LOESSIAL > LOESS

LOESSIC adj relating to or consisting of loess

LOFT n space between the top storey and roof of a building ▷ vb strike, throw, or kick (a ball) high into the air

LOFTED > LOFT

LOFTER n type of golf club

LOFTERS > LOFTER

LOFTIER > LOFTY

LOFTIEST > LOFTY

LOFTILY > LOFTY

LOFTINESS > LOFTY

LOFTING > LOFT

LOFTLESS > LOFT

LOFTLIKE > LOFT

LOFTS > LOFT

LOFTSMAN n person who reproduces in actual size a draughtsman's design for a ship or an aircraft

LOFTSMEN > LOFTSMAN

LOFTY adj of great height

LOG n portion of a felled tree stripped of branches ▷ vb saw logs from a tree

LOGAN another name for > BOGAN

LOGANIA n type of Australian plant

LOGANIAS > LOGANIA

LOGANS > LOGAN

LOGAOEDIC adj of or relating to verse in which mixed metres are combined within a single line to give the effect of prose ▷ n line or verse of this kind

LOGARITHM n one of a series of arithmetical functions used to make certain calculations easier

LOGBOARD n board used for logging a ship's records

LOGBOARDS > LOGBOARD

LOGBOOK n book recording the details about a car or a ship's journeys

LOGBOOKS > LOGBOOK

LOGE n small enclosure or box in a theatre or opera house

LOGES > LOGE

LOGGAT n small piece of wood

LOGGATS > LOGGAT

LOGGED > LOG

LOGGER n tractor or crane for handling logs

LOGGERS > LOGGER

LOGGETS n old-fashioned game played with sticks

LOGGIA n covered gallery at the side of a building

LOGGIAS > LOGGIA

LOGGIE > LOGGIA

LOGGIER > LOGGY

LOGGIEST > LOGGY

LOGGING > LOG

LOGGINGS > LOG

LOGGISH > LOG

LOGGY adj sluggish

LOGIA > LOGION

LOGIC n philosophy of reasoning

LOGICAL adj of logic

LOGICALLY > LOGICAL

LOGICIAN n person who specializes in or is skilled at logic

LOGICIANS > LOGICIAN

LOGICISE same as > LOGICIZE

LOGICISED > LOGICISE

LOGICISES > LOGICISE

LOGICISM n philosophical theory that all of mathematics can be deduced from logic

LOGICISMS > LOGICISM

LOGICIST > LOGICISM

LOGICISTS > LOGICISM

LOGICIZE vb present reasons for or against

LOGICIZED > LOGICIZE

LOGICIZES > LOGICIZE

LOGICLESS > LOGIC

LOGICS > LOGIC

LOGIE n fire-place of a kiln

LOGIER > LOGY

LOGIES > LOGIE

LOGIEST > LOGY

LOGILY > LOGY

LOGIN n process by which a computer user logs on

LOGINESS > LOGY

LOGINS > LOGY

LOGION n saying of Christ regarded as authentic

LOGIONS > LOGION

LOGISTIC n uninterpreted calculus or system of symbolic logic ▷ adj (of a curve) having a particular form of equation

LOGISTICS n detailed planning and organization of a large, esp military, operation

LOGJAM n blockage of logs in a river ▷ vb cause a logjam

LOGJAMMED > LOGJAM

LOGJAMS > LOGJAM

LOGJUICE n poor quality port wine

LOGJUICES > LOGJUICE

LOGLINE n synopsis of screenplay

LOGLINES > LOGLINE

LOGLOG n logarithm of a logarithm (in equations, etc)

LOGLOGS > LOGLOG

LOGNORMAL adj (maths) having a natural logarithm with normal distribution

LOGO same as > LOGOTYPE

LOGOED adj having a logo

LOGOFF n process by which a computer user logs out

LOGOFFS > LOGOFF

LOGOGRAM n single symbol representing an entire morpheme, word, or phrase

LOGOGRAMS > LOGOGRAM

LOGOGRAPH same as > LOGOGRAM

LOGOGRIPH n word puzzle, esp one based on recombination of the letters of a word

LOGOI > LOGOS

LOGOMACH n one who argues over words

LOGOMACHS > LOGOMACH

LOGOMACHY n argument about words or the meaning of words

LOGON variant of > LOGIN

LOGONS > LOGON

LOGOPEDIC adj of or relating to speech therapy

LOGOPHILE n one who loves words

LOGORRHEA n excessive or uncontrollable talkativeness

LOGOS n reason expressed in words and things, argument, or justification

LOGOTHETE n officer of Byzantine empire

LOGOTYPE n piece of type with several uncombined characters cast on it

LOGOTYPES > LOGOTYPE

LOGOTYPY > LOGOTYPE

LOGOUT variant of > LOGOFF

LOGOUTS > LOGOUT

LOGROLL vb use logrolling in order to procure the passage of (legislation)

LOGROLLED > LOGROLL

LOGROLLER > LOGROLL

LOGROLLS > LOGROLL

LOGS > LOG

LOGWAY another name for > GANGWAY

LOGWAYS > LOGWAY

LOGWOOD n tree of the Caribbean and Central America

LOGWOODS > LOGWOOD

LOGY adj dull or listless

LOHAN another word for > ARHAT

LOHANS > LOHAN

LOIASES > LOIASIS

LOIASIS n disease caused by a tropical eye worm

LOIASISES > LOIASIS

LOID vb open (a lock) using a celluloid strip

LOIDED > LOID

LOIDING > LOID

LOIDS > LOID

LOIN n part of the body between the ribs and the hips

LOINCLOTH n piece of cloth covering the loins only

LOINS pl n hips and the inner surface of the legs

LOIPE n cross-country skiing track

LOIPEN > LOIPE

LOIR n large dormouse

LOIRS > LOIR

LOITER vb stand or wait aimlessly or idly

LOITERED > LOITER

LOITERER > LOITER

LOITERERS > LOITERER

LOITERING > LOITER

LOITERS > LOITER

LOKE n track

LOKES > LOKE

LOKSHEN pl n noodles

LOLIGO n type of squid

LOLIGOS > LOLIGO

LOLIUM n type of grass

LOLIUMS > LOLIUM

LOLL vb lounge lazily ▷ n act or instance of lolling

LOLLED > LOLL

LOLLER > LOLL

LOLLERS > LOLL

LOLLIES > LOLLY

LOLLING > LOLL

LOLLINGLY > LOLL

LOLLIPOP n boiled sweet on a small wooden stick

LOLLIPOPS > LOLLIPOP

LOLLOP vb move clumsily

LOLLOPED > LOLLOP

LOLLOPIER > LOLLOPY

LOLLOPING > LOLLOP

LOLLOPS > LOLLOP

LOLLOPY adj moving with a lollop

LOLLS > LOLL

LOLLY n lollipop or ice lolly

LOLLYGAG same as > LALLYGAG

LOLLYGAGS > LOLLYGAG

LOLLYPOP same as > LOLLIPOP

LOLLYPOPS > LOLLYPOP

LOLOG same as > LOGLOG

LOLOGS > LOLOG

LOLZ same as > LULZ

LOMA n lobe

LOMAS > LOMA

LOMATA > LOMA

LOME n fertile soil ▷ vb cover with lome

LOMED > LOME

LOMEIN n Chinese dish

LOMEINS > LOMEIN

LOMENT n pod of certain leguminous plants

LOMENTA > LOMENTUM

LOMENTS > LOMENT

LOMENTUM same as > LOMENT

LOMENTUMS > LOMENTUM

LOMES > LOME

LOMING > LOME

LOMPISH another word for > LUMPISH

LONE adj solitary

LONELIER > LONELY

LONELIEST > LONELY

LONELILY > LONELY

LONELY adj sad because alone

LONENESS > LONE

LONER n solitary person

LONERS > LONER

LONESOME adj lonely ▷ n own

LONESOMES > LONESOME

LONG adj having length ▷ adv for a certain time ▷ vb have a strong desire (for)

LONGA n long note

LONGAEVAL adj long-lived

LONGAN n sapindaceous tree of tropical and subtropical Asia

LONGANS > LONGAN

LONGAS > LONGA

LONGBOARD n type of surfboard

LONGBOAT n largest boat carried on a ship

LONGBOATS > LONGBOAT

LONGBOW n large powerful bow

LONGBOWS > LONGBOW

LONGCASE n as in longcase clock grandfather clock

LONGCLOTH n fine plain-weave cotton cloth made in long strips

LONGE n rope used in training a horse ▷ vb train using a longe

LONGED > LONG

LONGEING > LONGE

LONGER n line of barrels on a ship

LONGERON n main longitudinal structural member of an aircraft

LONGERONS > LONGERON

LONGERS > LONGER

LONGES > LONGE

LONGEST > LONG

LONGEVAL another word for > LONGAEVAL

LONGEVITY n long life

LONGEVOUS > LONGEVITY

LONGFORM adj (of a text) long in form

LONGHAIR n cat with long hair

LONGHAIRS > LONGHAIR

LONGHAND n ordinary writing, not shorthand or typing

LONGHANDS > LONGHAND

LONGHEAD n person with long head

LONGHEADS > LONGHEAD

LONGHORN n British breed of beef cattle with long curved horns

LONGHORNS > LONGHORN

LONGHOUSE n long communal dwelling of Native American peoples

LONGICORN n type of beetle with long antennae

LONGIES n long johns

LONGING n yearning ▷ adj having or showing desire

LONGINGLY > LONGING

LONGINGS > LONGING

LONGISH adj rather long

LONGITUDE n distance east or west from a standard meridian

LONGJUMP n jumping contest decided by length

LONGJUMPS > LONGJUMP

LONGLEAF n North American pine tree

LONGLINE n (tennis) straight stroke played down court

LONGLINER n person who fishes with a longline

LONGLINES > LONGLINE

LONGLIST n initial list from which a shortlist is selected ▷ vb include (eg a candidate) on a longlist

LONGLISTS > LONGLIST

LONGLY > LONG

LONGNECK n US, Canadian and Australian word for a 330-ml beer bottle with a long narrow neck

LONGNECKS > LONGNECK

LONGNESS > LONG

LONGS pl n full-length trousers

LONGSHIP n narrow open boat with oars and a square sail, used by the Vikings

LONGSHIPS > LONGSHIP

LONGSHORE adj situated on, relating to, or along the shore

LONGSOME adj slow; boring

LONGSPUR n any of various Arctic and North American buntings

LONGSPURS > LONGSPUR

LONGTIME adj of long standing

LONGUEUR n period of boredom or dullness

LONGUEURS > LONGUEUR

LONGWALL n long face in coal mine

LONGWALLS > LONGWALL

LONGWAYS adv lengthways

LONGWISE same as > LONGWAYS

LONGWORM n as in sea longworm kind of marine worm

LONGWORMS > LONGWORM

LONICERA n honeysuckle

LONICERAS > LONICERA

LOO n toilet ▷ vb Scots word meaning love

LOOBIER > LOOBY
LOOBIES > LOOBY
LOOBIEST > LOOBY
LOOBILY > LOOBY
LOOBY adj foolish ▷ n foolish or stupid person
LOOED > LOO
LOOEY n lieutenant
LOOEYS > LOOEY
LOOF n part of ship's side
LOOFA same as > LOOFAH
LOOFAH n sponge made from the dried pod of a gourd
LOOFAHS > LOOFAH
LOOFAS > LOOFA
LOOFFUL n handful
LOOFFULS > LOOFFUL
LOOFS > LOOF
LOOGIE n lump of spit and phlegm
LOOGIES > LOOGIE
LOOIE same as > LOOEY
LOOIES > LOOIE
LOOING > LOO
LOOK vb direct the eyes or attention (towards) ▷ n instance of looking
LOOKALIKE n person who is the double of another
LOOKDOWN n way paper appears when looked at under reflected light
LOOKDOWNS > LOOKDOWN
LOOKED > LOOK
LOOKER n person who looks
LOOKERS > LOOKER
LOOKIE interj look (over here)
LOOKING > LOOK
LOOKISM n discrimination because of appearance
LOOKISMS > LOOKISM
LOOKIST > LOOKISM
LOOKISTS > LOOKISM
LOOKIT interj look at this
LOOKOUT n act of watching for danger or for an opportunity ▷ vb be careful
LOOKOUTS > LOOKOUT
LOOKOVER n inspection, esp a brief one
LOOKOVERS > LOOKOVER
LOOKS > LOOK
LOOKSISM same as > LOOKISM
LOOKSISMS > LOOKSISM
LOOKUP n act of looking up information
LOOKUPS > LOOKUP
LOOKY same as > LOOKIE
LOOM n machine for weaving cloth ▷ vb appear dimly
LOOMED > LOOM
LOOMING > LOOM
LOOMS > LOOM
LOON n diving bird
LOONEY same as > LOONY
LOONEYS > LOONEY
LOONIE n Canadian dollar coin
LOONIER > LOONY
LOONIES > LOONY
LOONIEST > LOONY
LOONILY > LOONY
LOONINESS > LOONY
LOONING n cry of the loon

LOONINGS > LOONING
LOONS > LOON
LOONY adj very foolish ▷ n very foolish person
LOOP n round shape made by a curved line ▷ vb form with a loop
LOOPED > LOOP
LOOPER n person or thing that loops or makes loops
LOOPERS > LOOPER
LOOPHOLE n means of evading a rule without breaking it ▷ vb provide with loopholes
LOOPHOLED > LOOPHOLE
LOOPHOLES > LOOPHOLE
LOOPIER > LOOPY
LOOPIEST > LOOPY
LOOPILY > LOOPY
LOOPINESS > LOOPY
LOOPING > LOOP
LOOPINGS > LOOP
LOOPLIKE adj like a loop
LOOPS > LOOP
LOOPY adj slightly mad or crazy
LOOR > LIEF
LOORD obsolete word for > LOUT
LOORDS > LOORD
LOOS > LOO
LOOSE adj not tight, fastened, fixed, or tense ▷ adv in a loose manner ▷ vb free
LOOSEBOX n enclosed stall with a door in which an animal can be kept
LOOSED > LOOSE
LOOSELY > LOOSE
LOOSEN vb make loose
LOOSENED > LOOSEN
LOOSENER > LOOSEN
LOOSENERS > LOOSEN
LOOSENESS > LOOSE
LOOSENING n act of loosening
LOOSENS > LOOSEN
LOOSER > LOOSE
LOOSES > LOOSE
LOOSEST > LOOSE
LOOSIE n informal word for loose forward
LOOSIES pl n cigarettes sold individually
LOOSING n celebration of one's 21st birthday
LOOSINGS > LOOSING
LOOT vb pillage ▷ n goods stolen during pillaging
LOOTED > LOOT
LOOTEN Scots past form of > LET
LOOTER > LOOT
LOOTERS > LOOT
LOOTING > LOOT
LOOTINGS > LOOT
LOOTS > LOOT
LOOVES > LOOF
LOP vb cut away ▷ n part(s) lopped off
LOPE vb run with long easy strides ▷ n loping stride
LOPED > LOPE
LOPER > LOPE
LOPERS > LOPE

LOPES > LOPE
LOPGRASS n smooth-bladed grass
LOPHODONT adj (of teeth) having elongated ridges
LOPING > LOPE
LOPINGLY adv in a loping manner
LOPOLITH n saucer- or lens-shaped body of intrusive igneous rock
LOPOLITHS > LOPOLITH
LOPPED > LOP
LOPPER n tool for lopping ▷ vb curdle
LOPPERED > LOPPER
LOPPERING > LOPPER
LOPPERS > LOPPER
LOPPET n long-distance cross-country ski race
LOPPETS > LOPPET
LOPPIER > LOPPY
LOPPIES > LOPPY
LOPPIEST > LOPPY
LOPPING > LOP
LOPPINGS > LOP
LOPPY adj floppy ▷ n ranch hand
LOPS > LOP
LOPSIDED adj greater in height, weight, or size on one side
LOPSTICK variant of > LOBSTICK
LOPSTICKS > LOPSTICK
LOQUACITY n tendency to talk a great deal
LOQUAT n ornamental evergreen rosaceous tree
LOQUATS > LOQUAT
LOQUITUR n stage direction meaning he or she speaks
LOR interj exclamation of surprise or dismay
LORAL adj of part of side of bird's head
LORAN n radio navigation system operating over long distances
LORANS > LORAN
LORATE adj like a strap
LORAZEPAM n type of tranquilizer
LORCHA n junk-rigged vessel
LORCHAS > LORCHA
LORD n person with power over others ▷ vb act in a superior way
LORDED > LORD
LORDING n gentleman
LORDINGS > LORDING
LORDKIN n little lord
LORDKINS > LORDKIN
LORDLESS > LORD
LORDLIER > LORDLY
LORDLIEST > LORDLY
LORDLIKE > LORD
LORDLING n young lord
LORDLINGS > LORDLING
LORDLY adj imperious, proud ▷ adv in the manner of a lord
LORDOMA same as > LORDOSIS
LORDOMAS > LORDOMA
LORDOSES > LORDOSIS

LORDOSIS n forward curvature of the lumbar spine
LORDOTIC > LORDOSIS
LORDS > LORD
LORDSHIP n position or authority of a lord
LORDSHIPS > LORDSHIP
LORDY interj exclamation of surprise or dismay
LORE n body of traditions
LOREAL adj concerning or relating to lore
LOREL another word for > LOSEL
LORELS > LOREL
LORES > LORE
LORETTE n concubine
LORETTES > LORETTE
LORGNETTE n pair of spectacles mounted on a long handle
LORGNON n monocle or pair of spectacles
LORGNONS > LORGNON
LORIC same as > LORICA
LORICA n hard outer covering of rotifers, ciliate protozoans, and similar organisms
LORICAE > LORICA
LORICAS > LORICA
LORICATE > LORICA
LORICATED > LORICA
LORICATES > LORICA
LORICS > LORIC
LORIES > LORY
LORIKEET n small brightly coloured Australian parrot
LORIKEETS > LORIKEET
LORIMER n (formerly) a person who made bits and spurs
LORIMERS > LORIMER
LORINER same as > LORIMER
LORINERS > LORINER
LORING n teaching
LORINGS > LORING
LORIOT n golden oriole (bird)
LORIOTS > LORIOT
LORIS n any of several prosimian primates
LORISES > LORIS
LORN adj forsaken or wretched
LORNER > LORN
LORNEST > LORN
LORNNESS > LORN
LORRELL obsolete word for > LOSEL
LORRELLS > LORRELL
LORRIES > LORRY
LORRY n large vehicle for transporting loads by road
LORY n small parrot of Australia and Indonesia
LOS n approval
LOSABLE > LOSE
LOSE vb part with
LOSED > LOSE
LOSEL n worthless person ▷ adj worthless
LOSELS > LOSEL
LOSEN same as > LOSE
LOSER n person or thing that loses

LOSERS > LOSER
LOSES > LOSE
LOSH interj lord
LOSING adj unprofitable; failing
LOSINGEST > LOSING
LOSINGLY > LOSE
LOSINGS pl n losses
LOSLYF n South African slang for a promiscuous female
LOSLYFS > LOSLYF
LOSS n losing
LOSSES > LOSS
LOSSIER > LOSSY
LOSSIEST > LOSSY
LOSSLESS > LOSS
LOSSMAKER n organization, industry, or enterprise that consistently fails to make a profit
LOSSY adj designed to have a high attenuation
LOST adj missing
LOSTNESS > LOST
LOT pron great number ▷ n collection of people or things ▷ vb draw lots for
LOTA n globular water container
LOTAH same as > LOTA
LOTAHS > LOTAH
LOTAS > LOTA
LOTE another word for > LOTUS
LOTES > LOTE
LOTH same as > LOATH
LOTHARIO n rake, libertine, or seducer
LOTHARIOS > LOTHARIO
LOTHEFULL obsolete form of > LOATHFUL
LOTHER > LOTH
LOTHEST > LOTH
LOTHFULL obsolete form of > LOATHFUL
LOTHNESS > LOTH
LOTHSOME same as > LOATHSOME
LOTI n monetary unit of Lesotho
LOTIC adj of communities living in rapidly flowing water
LOTION n medical or cosmetic liquid for use on the skin
LOTIONS > LOTION
LOTO same as > LOTTO
LOTOS same as > LOTUS
LOTOSES > LOTOS
LOTS > LOT
LOTSA determiner lots of
LOTTA n lot of
LOTTE n type of fish
LOTTED > LOT
LOTTER n someone who works an allotment
LOTTERIES > LOTTERY
LOTTERS > LOTTER
LOTTERY n method of raising money by selling tickets that win prizes by chance
LOTTES > LOTTE
LOTTING > LOT
LOTTO n game of chance

LOTTOS > LOTTO
LOTUS n legendary plant whose fruit induces forgetfulness
LOTUSES > LOTUS
LOTUSLAND n idyllic place of contentment
LOU Scot word for > LOVE
LOUCHE adj shifty
LOUCHELY > LOUCHE
LOUCHER > LOUCHE
LOUCHEST > LOUCHE
LOUD adj noisy
LOUDEN vb make louder
LOUDENED > LOUDEN
LOUDENING > LOUDEN
LOUDENS > LOUDEN
LOUDER > LOUD
LOUDEST > LOUD
LOUDISH adj fairly loud
LOUDLIER > LOUD
LOUDLIEST > LOUD
LOUDLY > LOUD
LOUDMOUTH n person who talks too much, esp in a boastful or indiscreet way
LOUDNESS > LOUD
LOUED > LOU
LOUGH n loch
LOUGHS > LOUGH
LOUIE same as > LOOEY
LOUIES > LOUIE
LOUING > LOU
LOUIS n former French gold coin
LOUMA n market in developing countries
LOUMAS > LOUMA
LOUN same as > LOWN
LOUND same as > LOUN
LOUNDED > LOUND
LOUNDER vb beat severely
LOUNDERED > LOUNDER
LOUNDERS > LOUNDER
LOUNDING > LOUND
LOUNDS > LOUND
LOUNED > LOUN
LOUNGE n living room in a private house ▷ vb sit, lie, or stand in a relaxed manner
LOUNGED > LOUNGE
LOUNGER n extending chair
LOUNGERS > LOUNGER
LOUNGES > LOUNGE
LOUNGEY n suggestive of a lounge bar or easy-listening music
LOUNGIER > LOUNGEY
LOUNGIEST > LOUNGEY
LOUNGING > LOUNGE
LOUNGINGS > LOUNGE
LOUNGY adj casual; relaxed
LOUNING > LOUN
LOUNS > LOUN
LOUP Scot word for > LEAP
LOUPE n magnifying glass used by jewellers, horologists, etc
LOUPED > LOUP
LOUPEN > LOUP
LOUPES > LOUPE
LOUPING > LOUP
LOUPIT > LOUP
LOUPS > LOUP
LOUR vb be overcast ▷ n menacing scowl

LOURE n slow, former French dance
LOURED > LOUR
LOURES > LOURE
LOURIE n type of African bird
LOURIER > LOURY
LOURIES > LOURIE
LOURIEST > LOURY
LOURING > LOUR
LOURINGLY > LOUR
LOURINGS > LOUR
LOURS > LOUR
LOURY adj sombre
LOUS > LOU
LOUSE n wingless parasitic insect ▷ vb ruin or spoil
LOUSED > LOUSE
LOUSER n mean nasty person
LOUSERS > LOUSER
LOUSES > LOUSE
LOUSEWORT n any of various N temperate scrophulariaceous plants
LOUSIER > LOUSY
LOUSIEST > LOUSY
LOUSILY > LOUSY
LOUSINESS > LOUSY
LOUSING n act or instance of removing lice
LOUSINGS > LOUSING
LOUSY adj mean or unpleasant
LOUT n crude person ▷ vb bow or stoop
LOUTED > LOUT
LOUTERIES > LOUTERY
LOUTERY n crude or boorish behaviour
LOUTING > LOUT
LOUTISH adj of a lout
LOUTISHLY > LOUTISH
LOUTS > LOUT
LOUVAR n large silvery whalelike scombroid fish
LOUVARS > LOUVAR
LOUVER same as > LOUVRE
LOUVERED same as > LOUVRED
LOUVERS > LOUVER
LOUVRE n one of a set of parallel slats slanted to admit air but not rain
LOUVRED adj having louvres
LOUVRES > LOUVRE
LOVABLE adj attracting or deserving affection
LOVABLY > LOVABLE
LOVAGE n European plant used for flavouring food
LOVAGES > LOVAGE
LOVAT n yellowish-or bluish-green mixture in tweeds
LOVATS > LOVAT
LOVE vb have a great affection for ▷ n great affection
LOVEABLE same as > LOVABLE
LOVEABLY > LOVABLE
LOVEBIRD n small parrot
LOVEBIRDS > LOVEBIRD
LOVEBITE n temporary red mark left on a person's skin by someone biting or sucking it

LOVEBITES > LOVEBITE
LOVEBUG n small US flying insect
LOVEBUGS > LOVEBUG
LOVED > LOVE
LOVEFEST n event when people talk about loving one another
LOVEFESTS > LOVEFEST
LOVELESS adj without love
LOVELIER > LOVELY
LOVELIES > LOVELY
LOVELIEST > LOVELY
LOVELIGHT n brightness of eyes of one in love
LOVELILY > LOVELY
LOVELOCK n long lock of hair worn on the forehead
LOVELOCKS > LOVELOCK
LOVELORN adj miserable because of unhappiness in love
LOVELY adj very attractive ▷ n attractive woman
LOVEMAKER n one involved in lovemaking
LOVER n person who loves something or someone
LOVERED adj having a lover
LOVERLESS > LOVER
LOVERLY adj like a lover
LOVERS > LOVER
LOVES > LOVE
LOVESEAT n armchair for two people
LOVESEATS > LOVESEAT
LOVESICK adj pining or languishing because of love
LOVESOME adj full of love
LOVEVINE n leafless parasitic vine
LOVEVINES > LOVEVINE
LOVEY adj loving; affectionate ▷ n affectionate person
LOVEYS > LOVEY
LOVIE n beloved person
LOVIER > LOVEY
LOVIES > LOVIE
LOVIEST > LOVEY
LOVING adj affectionate, tender ▷ n state of being in love
LOVINGLY > LOVING
LOVINGS > LOVING
LOW adj not high ▷ adv in a low position ▷ n low position ▷ vb moo
LOWAN n type of Australian bird
LOWANS > LOWAN
LOWBALL vb deliberately under-charge
LOWBALLED > LOWBALL
LOWBALLS > LOWBALL
LOWBORN adj of ignoble or common parentage
LOWBOY n table fitted with drawers
LOWBOYS > LOWBOY
LOWBRED same as > LOWBORN
LOWBROW adj with nonintellectual tastes and interests ▷ n person with nonintellectual tastes
LOWBROWED > LOWBROW

LOWBROWS > LOWBROW
LOWBUSH n type of blueberry bush
LOWBUSHES > LOWBUSH
LOWDOWN n inside info
LOWDOWNS > LOWDOWN
LOWE variant of > LOW
LOWED > LOW
LOWER adj below one or more other things ▷ vb cause or allow to move down
LOWERABLE > LOWER
LOWERCASE n small letters ▷ adj non-capitalized
LOWERED > LOWER
LOWERIER > LOWERY
LOWERIEST > LOWERY
LOWERING > LOWER
LOWERINGS > LOWER
LOWERMOST adj lowest
LOWERS > LOWER
LOWERY adj sombre
LOWES > LOWE
LOWEST > LOW
LOWING > LOW
LOWINGS > LOW
LOWISH > LOW
LOWLAND n low-lying country ▷ adj of a lowland or lowlands
LOWLANDER > LOWLAND
LOWLANDS > LOWLAND
LOWLIER > LOWLY
LOWLIEST > LOWLY
LOWLIFE n member or members of the underworld
LOWLIFER > LOWLIFE
LOWLIFERS > LOWLIFE
LOWLIFES > LOWLIFE
LOWLIGHT n unenjoyable or unpleasant part of an event
LOWLIGHTS > LOWLIGHT
LOWLIHEAD n state of being humble
LOWLILY > LOWLY
LOWLINESS > LOWLY
LOWLIVES > LOWLIFE
LOWLY adj modest, humble ▷ adv in a low or lowly manner
LOWN vb calm
LOWND same as > LOWN
LOWNDED > LOWND
LOWNDING > LOWND
LOWNDS > LOWND
LOWNE same as > LOON
LOWNED > LOWN
LOWNES > LOWNE
LOWNESS > LOW
LOWNESSES > LOW
LOWNING > LOWN
LOWNS > LOWN
LOWP same as > LOUP
LOWPASS adj (of a filter) transmitting frequencies below a certain value
LOWPED > LOWP
LOWPING > LOWP
LOWPS > LOWP
LOWRIDER n car with body close to ground
LOWRIDERS > LOWRIDER
LOWRIE another name for > LORY
LOWRIES > LOWRY

LOWRY another name for > LORY
LOWS > LOW
LOWSE vb release or loose ▷ adj loose
LOWSED > LOWSE
LOWSENING same as > LOOSING
LOWSER > LOWSE
LOWSES > LOWSE
LOWSEST > LOWSE
LOWSING > LOWSE
LOWSIT > LOWSE
LOWT same as > LOUT
LOWTED > LOWT
LOWTING > LOWT
LOWTS > LOWT
LOWVELD n low ground in S Africa
LOWVELDS > LOWVELD
LOX vb load fuel tanks of spacecraft with liquid oxygen ▷ n kind of smoked salmon
LOXED > LOX
LOXES > LOX
LOXING > LOX
LOXODROME n line on globe crossing all meridians at same angle
LOXODROMY n technique of navigating using rhumb lines
LOXYGEN n liquid oxygen
LOXYGENS > LOXYGEN
LOY n narrow spade with a single footrest
LOYAL adj faithful
LOYALER > LOYAL
LOYALEST > LOYAL
LOYALISM > LOYALIST
LOYALISMS > LOYALIST
LOYALIST n patriotic supporter of the sovereign or government
LOYALISTS > LOYALIST
LOYALLER > LOYAL
LOYALLEST > LOYAL
LOYALLY > LOYAL
LOYALNESS > LOYAL
LOYALTIES > LOYALTY
LOYALTY n quality of being loyal
LOYS > LOY
LOZELL obsolete form of > LOSEL
LOZELLS > LOZELL
LOZEN n window pane
LOZENGE n medicated tablet
LOZENGED adj decorated with lozenges
LOZENGES > LOZENGE
LOZENGIER > LOZENGY
LOZENGY adj divided by diagonal lines to form a lattice
LOZENS > LOZEN
LUACH n Jewish calendar
LUAU n feast of Hawaiian food
LUAUS > LUAU
LUBBARD same as > LUBBER
LUBBARDS > LUBBARD
LUBBER n big, awkward, or stupid person
LUBBERLY adj big and awkward

LUBBERS > LUBBER
LUBE n lubricating oil ▷ vb lubricate with oil
LUBED > LUBE
LUBES > LUBE
LUBFISH n type of fish
LUBFISHES > LUBFISH
LUBING > LUBE
LUBRA n offensive term for an Aboriginal woman
LUBRAS > LUBRA
LUBRIC adj slippery
LUBRICAL same as > LUBRIC
LUBRICANT n lubricating substance, such as oil ▷ adj serving to lubricate
LUBRICATE vb oil or grease to lessen friction
LUBRICITY n smoothness or slipperiness
LUBRICOUS adj slippery
LUCARNE n type of dormer window
LUCARNES > LUCARNE
LUCE another name for > PIKE
LUCENCE > LUCENT
LUCENCES > LUCENT
LUCENCIES > LUCENT
LUCENCY > LUCENT
LUCENT adj brilliant
LUCENTLY > LUCENT
LUCERN same as > LUCERNE
LUCERNE n alfalfa
LUCERNES > LUCERNE
LUCERNS > LUCERN
LUCES > LUCE
LUCHOT > LUACH
LUCHOTH > LUACH
LUCID adj clear
LUCIDER > LUCID
LUCIDEST > LUCID
LUCIDITY > LUCID
LUCIDLY > LUCID
LUCIDNESS > LUCID
LUCIFER n friction match
LUCIFERIN n substance occurring in bioluminescent organisms, such as glow-worms and fireflies
LUCIFERS > LUCIFER
LUCIGEN n type of lamp
LUCIGENS > LUCIGEN
LUCITE n type of transparent acrylic-based plastic
LUCITES > LUCITE
LUCK n fortune, good or bad ▷ vb have good fortune
LUCKED > LUCK
LUCKEN adj shut
LUCKIE same as > LUCKY
LUCKIER > LUCKY
LUCKIES > LUCKY
LUCKIEST > LUCKY
LUCKILY > LUCKY
LUCKINESS > LUCKY
LUCKING > LUCK
LUCKLESS adj having bad luck
LUCKPENNY n coin kept for luck
LUCKS > LUCK
LUCKY adj having or bringing good luck ▷ n old woman
LUCRATIVE adj very profitable

LUCRE n money or wealth
LUCRES > LUCRE
LUCTATION n effort; struggle
LUCUBRATE vb write or study, esp at night
LUCULENT adj easily understood
LUCUMA n S American tree
LUCUMAS > LUCUMA
LUCUMO n Etruscan king
LUCUMONES > LUCUMO
LUCUMOS > LUCUMO
LUD n lord ▷ interj exclamation of dismay or surprise
LUDE n slang word for drug for relieving anxiety
LUDERICK n Australian fish, usu black or dark brown in colour
LUDERICKS > LUDERICK
LUDES > LUDE
LUDIC adj playful
LUDICALLY > LUDIC
LUDICROUS adj absurd or ridiculous
LUDO n game played with dice and counters on a board
LUDOS > LUDO
LUDS > LUD
LUDSHIP > LUD
LUDSHIPS > LUD
LUES n pestilence
LUETIC > LUES
LUETICS > LUES
LUFF vb sail (a ship) towards the wind ▷ n leading edge of a fore-and-aft sail
LUFFA same as > LOOFAH
LUFFAS > LUFFA
LUFFED > LUFF
LUFFING > LUFF
LUFFS > LUFF
LUG vb carry with great effort ▷ n projection serving as a handle
LUGE n racing toboggan ▷ vb ride on a luge
LUGED > LUGE
LUGEING > LUGE
LUGEINGS > LUGE
LUGER n pistol
LUGERS > LUGER
LUGES > LUGE
LUGGABLE n unwieldy portable computer
LUGGABLES > LUGGABLE
LUGGAGE n suitcases, bags, etc
LUGGAGES > LUGGAGE
LUGGED > LUG
LUGGER n small working boat with an oblong sail
LUGGERS > LUGGER
LUGGIE n wooden bowl
LUGGIES > LUGGIE
LUGGING > LUG
LUGHOLE informal word for > EAR
LUGHOLES > LUGHOLE
LUGING > LUGE
LUGINGS > LUGE
LUGS > LUG
LUGSAIL n four-sided sail
LUGSAILS > LUGSAIL

L

LUGWORM n large worm used as bait

LUGWORMS > LUGWORM

LUIT Scots past form of > LET

LUITEN > LET

LUKE variant of > LUKEWARM

LUKEWARM adj moderately warm, tepid

LULIBUB obsolete form of > LOLLIPOP

LULIBUBS > LULIBUB

LULL vb soothe (someone) by soft sounds or motions ▷ n brief time of quiet in a storm etc

LULLABIED > LULLABY

LULLABIES > LULLABY

LULLABY n quiet song ▷ vb quiet with a lullaby

LULLED > LULL

LULLER > LULL

LULLERS > LULL

LULLING > LULL

LULLINGLY adv in a lulling manner

LULLS > LULL

LULU n person or thing deemed to be outstanding

LULUS > LULU

LULZ pl n laughs at someone else's or one's own expense

LUM n chimney

LUMA n monetary unit of Armenia

LUMAS > LUMA

LUMBAGO n pain in the lower back

LUMBAGOS > LUMBAGO

LUMBANG n type of tree

LUMBANGS > LUMBANG

LUMBAR adj of the part of the body between the lowest ribs and the hipbones ▷ n old-fashioned kind of ship

LUMBARS > LUMBAR

LUMBER n unwanted disused household articles ▷ vb burden with something unpleasant

LUMBERED > LUMBER

LUMBERER > LUMBER

LUMBERERS > LUMBER

LUMBERING n business or trade of cutting, transporting, preparing, or selling timber ▷ adj awkward in movement

LUMBERLY adj heavy; clumsy

LUMBERMAN n person whose work involves felling trees

LUMBERMEN > LUMBERMAN

LUMBERS > LUMBER

LUMBI > LUMBUS

LUMBRICAL adj relating to any of the four wormlike muscles in the hand or foot

LUMBRICI > LUMBRICUS

LUMBRICUS n type of worm

LUMBUS n part of the lower back and sides between the pelvis and the ribs

LUMEN n derived SI unit of luminous flux

LUMENAL > LUMEN

LUMENS > LUMEN

LUMINA > LUMEN

LUMINAIRE n light fixture

LUMINAL > LUMEN

LUMINANCE n state or quality of radiating or reflecting light

LUMINANT n something used to give light

LUMINANTS > LUMINANT

LUMINARIA n type of candle

LUMINARY n famous person ▷ adj of, involving, or characterized by light or enlightenment

LUMINE vb illuminate

LUMINED > LUMINE

LUMINES > LUMINE

LUMINESCE vb exhibit luminescence

LUMINING > LUMINE

LUMINISM n US artistic movement

LUMINISMS > LUMINISM

LUMINIST > LUMINISM

LUMINISTS > LUMINISM

LUMINOUS adj reflecting or giving off light

LUMME interj exclamation of surprise or dismay

LUMMIER > LUMMY

LUMMIEST > LUMMY

LUMMOX n clumsy person

LUMMOXES > LUMMOX

LUMMY interj exclamation of surprise ▷ adj excellent

LUMP n shapeless mass ▷ vb consider as one group

LUMPED > LUMP

LUMPEN adj stupid or unthinking ▷ n member of underclass

LUMPENLY > LUMPEN

LUMPENS > LUMPEN

LUMPER n stevedore

LUMPERS > LUMPER

LUMPFISH n North Atlantic scorpaenoid fish

LUMPIA n type of Indonesian spring roll

LUMPIAS > LUMPIA

LUMPIER > LUMPY

LUMPIEST > LUMPY

LUMPILY > LUMPY

LUMPINESS > LUMPY

LUMPING > LUMP

LUMPINGLY > LUMP

LUMPISH adj stupid or clumsy

LUMPISHLY > LUMPISH

LUMPKIN n lout

LUMPKINS > LUMPKIN

LUMPS > LUMP

LUMPY adj full of lumps

LUMS > LUM

LUN n sheltered spot

LUNA n large American moth

LUNACIES > LUNACY

LUNACY n foolishness

LUNANAUT same as > LUNARNAUT

LUNANAUTS > LUNANAUT

LUNAR adj relating to the moon ▷ n lunar distance

LUNARIAN n inhabitant of the moon

LUNARIANS > LUNARIAN

LUNARIES > LUNARY

LUNARIST n one believing the moon influences weather

LUNARISTS > LUNARIST

LUNARNAUT n astronaut who travels to moon

LUNARS > LUNAR

LUNARY n moonwort herb

LUNAS > LUNA

LUNATE adj shaped like a crescent ▷ n crescent-shaped bone forming part of the wrist

LUNATED variant of > LUNATE

LUNATELY > LUNATE

LUNATES > LUNATE

LUNATIC adj foolish ▷ n foolish person

LUNATICAL variant of > LUNATIC

LUNATICS > LUNATIC

LUNATION See > MONTH

LUNATIONS > LUNATION

LUNCH n meal at midday ▷ vb eat lunch

LUNCHBOX n container for carrying a packed lunch

LUNCHED > LUNCH

LUNCHEON n formal lunch

LUNCHEONS > LUNCHEON

LUNCHER > LUNCH

LUNCHERS > LUNCH

LUNCHES > LUNCH

LUNCHING > LUNCH

LUNCHMEAT n mixture of meat and cereal

LUNCHPAIL n container for carrying a packed lunch

LUNCHROOM n room where lunch is served or people may eat lunches they bring

LUNCHTIME n time at which lunch is usually eaten

LUNE same as > LUNETTE

LUNES > LUNE

LUNET n small moon or satellite

LUNETS > LUNET

LUNETTE n anything that is shaped like a crescent

LUNETTES > LUNETTE

LUNG n organ that allows an animal or bird to breathe air

LUNGAN same as > LONGAN

LUNGANS > LUNGAN

LUNGE n sudden forward motion ▷ vb move with or make a lunge

LUNGED > LUNGE

LUNGEE same as > LUNGI

LUNGEES > LUNGEE

LUNGEING > LUNGE

LUNGER > LUNGE

LUNGERS > LUNGE

LUNGES > LUNGE

LUNGFISH n freshwater bony fish with an air-breathing lung

LUNGFUL > LUNG

LUNGFULS > LUNG

LUNGI n cotton cloth worn as a loincloth, sash, or turban

LUNGIE n guillemot

LUNGIES > LUNGIE

LUNGING > LUNGE

LUNGIS > LUNGI

LUNGLESS adj having no lungs

LUNGLIKE adj like a lung

LUNGS > LUNG

LUNGWORM n type of parasitic worm occurring in the lungs of mammals

LUNGWORMS > LUNGWORM

LUNGWORT n plant with spotted leaves

LUNGWORTS > LUNGWORT

LUNGYI same as > LUNGI

LUNGYIS > LUNGYI

LUNIER > LUNY

LUNIES > LUNY

LUNIEST > LUNY

LUNINESS > LUNY

LUNISOLAR adj resulting from or based on the combined gravitational attraction of the sun and moon

LUNITIDAL adj of or relating to tidal phenomena as produced by the moon

LUNK n awkward person

LUNKER n very large fish

LUNKERS > LUNKER

LUNKHEAD n stupid person

LUNKHEADS > LUNKHEAD

LUNKS > LUNK

LUNS > LUN

LUNT vb produce smoke

LUNTED > LUNT

LUNTING > LUNT

LUNTS > LUNT

LUNULA n white area at base of the fingernail

LUNULAE > LUNULA

LUNULAR same as > LUNULATE

LUNULATE adj having markings shaped like crescents

LUNULATED same as > LUNULATE

LUNULE same as > LUNULA

LUNULES > LUNULE

LUNY same as > LOONY

LUNYIE same as > LUNGIE

LUNYIES > LUNYIE

LUPANAR n brothel

LUPANARS > LUPANAR

LUPIN n garden plant

LUPINE adj like a wolf ▷ n lupin

LUPINES > LUPINE

LUPINS > LUPIN

LUPOID adj suffering from lupus

LUPOUS adj relating to lupus

LUPPEN Scots past form of > LEAP

LUPULIN n resinous powder extracted from the female flowers of the hop plant

LUPULINE adj relating to lupulin

LUPULINIC same as > LUPULINE

LUPULINS > LUPULIN

LUPUS n ulcerous skin disease

LUPUSES > LUPUS

LUR n large bronze musical horn

LURCH *vb* tilt suddenly ▷ *n* lurching movement
LURCHED > LURCH
LURCHER *n* crossbred dog trained to hunt silently
LURCHERS > LURCHER
LURCHES > LURCH
LURCHING > LURCH
LURDAN *n* stupid or dull person ▷ *adj* dull or stupid
LURDANE *same as* > LURDAN
LURDANES > LURDANE
LURDANS > LURDAN
LURDEN *same as* > LURDAN
LURDENS > LURDEN
LURE *vb* tempt by promise of reward ▷ *n* person that lures
LURED > LURE
LURER > LURE
LURERS > LURE
LURES > LURE
LUREX *n* thin glittery thread
LUREXES > LUREX
LURGI *same as* > LURGY
LURGIES > LURGY
LURGIS > LURGI
LURGY *n* any undetermined illness
LURID *adj* sensational
LURIDER > LURID
LURIDEST > LURID
LURIDLY > LURID
LURIDNESS > LURID
LURING > LURE
LURINGLY > LURE
LURINGS > LURING
LURK *vb* lie hidden
LURKED > LURK
LURKER > LURK
LURKERS > LURK
LURKING *adj* lingering
LURKINGLY > LURKING
LURKINGS > LURKING
LURKS > LURK
LURRIES > LURRY
LURRY *n* confused jumble
LURS > LUR
LURVE *n* love
LURVES > LURVE
LUSCIOUS *adj* extremely pleasurable to taste or smell
LUSER *n* humorous term for computer user
LUSERS > LUSER
LUSH *adj* growing thickly ▷ *n* alcoholic ▷ *vb* drink to excess
LUSHED > LUSH
LUSHER *adj* more lush ▷ *n* drunkard
LUSHERS > LUSHER
LUSHES > LUSH
LUSHEST > LUSH
LUSHIER > LUSHY
LUSHIES > LUSHY
LUSHIEST > LUSHY
LUSHING > LUSH
LUSHLY > LUSH
LUSHNESS > LUSH
LUSHY *adj* slightly intoxicated ▷ *n* drunkard
LUSK *vb* lounge around
LUSKED > LUSK
LUSKING > LUSK
LUSKISH *adj* lazy
LUSKS > LUSK

LUST *n* strong desire ▷ *vb* have strong desire (for)
LUSTED > LUST
LUSTER *same as* > LUSTRE
LUSTERED > LUSTER
LUSTERING > LUSTER
LUSTERS > LUSTER
LUSTFUL *adj* driven by strong sexual desire
LUSTFULLY > LUSTFUL
LUSTICK *obsolete word for* > LUSTY
LUSTIER > LUSTY
LUSTIEST > LUSTY
LUSTIHEAD *n* vigour
LUSTIHOOD *n* vigour
LUSTILY > LUSTY
LUSTINESS > LUSTY
LUSTING > LUST
LUSTIQUE *obsolete word for* > LUSTY
LUSTLESS > LUST
LUSTRA > LUSTRUM
LUSTRAL *adj* of or relating to a ceremony of purification
LUSTRATE *vb* purify by means of religious rituals or ceremonies
LUSTRATED > LUSTRATE
LUSTRATES > LUSTRATE
LUSTRE *n* gloss, sheen ▷ *vb* make, be, or become lustrous
LUSTRED > LUSTRE
LUSTRES > LUSTRE
LUSTRINE *same as* > LUSTRING
LUSTRINES > LUSTRINE
LUSTRING *n* glossy silk cloth, formerly used for clothing, upholstery, etc
LUSTRINGS > LUSTRING
LUSTROUS > LUSTRE
LUSTRUM *n* period of five years
LUSTRUMS > LUSTRUM
LUSTS > LUST
LUSTY *adj* vigorous, healthy
LUSUS *n* freak, mutant
LUSUSES > LUSUS
LUTANIST *same as* > LUTENIST
LUTANISTS > LUTANIST
LUTE *n* musical instrument r ▷ *vb* seal with cement and clay
LUTEA *adj* yellow
LUTEAL *adj* relating to the development of the corpus luteum
LUTECIUM *same as* > LUTETIUM
LUTECIUMS > LUTECIUM
LUTED > LUTE
LUTEFISK *n* Scandinavian fish dish
LUTEFISKS > LUTEFISK
LUTEIN *n* xanthophyll pigment
LUTEINISE *same as* > LUTEINIZE
LUTEINIZE *vb* develop into part of corpus luteum
LUTEINS > LUTEIN
LUTELIKE *adj* like a lute
LUTENIST *n* person who plays the lute

LUTENISTS > LUTENIST
LUTEOLIN *n* yellow crystalline compound found in many plants
LUTEOLINS > LUTEOLIN
LUTEOLOUS > LUTEOLIN
LUTEOUS *adj* of a greenish-yellow colour
LUTER *n* lute player
LUTERS > LUTER
LUTES > LUTE
LUTESCENT *adj* yellowish in colour
LUTETIUM *n* silvery-white metallic element
LUTETIUMS > LUTETIUM
LUTEUM *adj* yellow
LUTFISK *same as* > LUTEFISK
LUTFISKS > LUTFISK
LUTHERN *another name for* > DORMER
LUTHERNS > LUTHERN
LUTHIER *n* lute-maker
LUTHIERS > LUTHIER
LUTING *n* cement and clay
LUTINGS > LUTING
LUTIST *same as* > LUTENIST
LUTISTS > LUTIST
LUTITE *another name for* > PELITE
LUTITES > LUTITE
LUTTEN > LOOT
LUTZ *n* skating jump
LUTZES > LUTZ
LUV *n* love ▷ *vb* love
LUVS > LUV
LUVVED > LUV
LUVVIE *n* person who is involved in acting or the theatre
LUVVIEDOM *n* theatrical world
LUVVIES > LUVVIE
LUVVING > LUV
LUVVY *same as* > LUVVIE
LUX *n* unit of illumination ▷ *vb* clean with a vacuum cleaner
LUXATE *vb* put (a shoulder, knee, etc) out of joint
LUXATED > LUXATE
LUXATES > LUXATE
LUXATING > LUXATE
LUXATION > LUXATE
LUXATIONS > LUXATE
LUXE *n* as in *de luxe* luxuriousness ▷ *adj* luxury
LUXED > LUX
LUXER > LUXE
LUXES > LUX
LUXEST > LUXE
LUXING > LUX
LUXMETER *n* device for measuring light
LUXMETERS > LUXMETER
LUXURIANT *adj* rich and abundant
LUXURIATE *vb* take self-indulgent pleasure (in)
LUXURIES > LUXURY
LUXURIOUS *adj* full of luxury, sumptuous
LUXURIST *n* person who loves luxurious things
LUXURISTS > LUXURIST

LUXURY *n* enjoyment of rich, very comfortable living ▷ *adj* of or providing luxury
LUZ *n* supposedly indestructible bone of the human body
LUZERN *n* alfalfa
LUZERNS > LUZERN
LUZZES > LUZ
LWEI *n* Angolan monetary unit
LWEIS > LWEI
LYAM *n* leash
LYAMS > LYAM
LYARD *same as* > LIARD
LYART *same as* > LIARD
LYASE *n* any enzyme that catalyses the separation of two parts of a molecule
LYASES > LYASE
LYCAENID *n* type of butterfly
LYCAENIDS > LYCAENID
LYCEA > LYCEUM
LYCEE *n* secondary school
LYCEES > LYCEE
LYCEUM *n* public building for concerts
LYCEUMS > LYCEUM
LYCH *same as* > LICH
LYCHEE *same as* > LITCHI
LYCHEES > LYCHEE
LYCHES > LYCH
LYCHGATE *same as* > LICHGATE
LYCHGATES > LYCHGATE
LYCHNIS *n* plant with red, pink, or white flowers
LYCHNISES > LYCHNIS
LYCOPENE *n* red pigment
LYCOPENES > LYCOPENE
LYCOPOD *n* type of moss
LYCOPODS > LYCOPOD
LYCOPSID *n* type of club moss
LYCOPSIDS > LYCOPSID
LYCRA *n* type of elastic fabric used for tight-fitting garments
LYCRAS > LYCRA
LYDDITE *n* explosive consisting chiefly of fused picric acid
LYDDITES > LYDDITE
LYE *n* caustic solution
LYES > LYE
LYFULL *obsolete form of* > LIFEFUL
LYING > LIE
LYINGLY > LIE
LYINGS > LIE
LYKEWAKE *n* watch held over a dead person, often with festivities
LYKEWAKES > LYKEWAKE
LYKEWALK *variant of* > LYKEWAKE
LYKEWALKS > LYKEWALK
LYM *obsolete form of* > LYAM
LYME *n* as in *lyme grass* type of perennial dune grass
LYMES > LYME
LYMITER *same as* > LIMITER
LYMITERS > LYMITER
LYMPH *n* colourless bodily fluid

LYMPHAD n ancient rowing boat
LYMPHADS > LYMPHAD
LYMPHATIC adj of, relating to, or containing lymph ▷ n lymphatic vessel
LYMPHOID adj of or resembling lymph, or relating to the lymphatic system
LYMPHOMA n any form of cancer of the lymph nodes
LYMPHOMAS > LYMPHOMA
LYMPHOUS adj resembling lymph
LYMPHS > LYMPH
LYMS > LYM
LYNAGE obsolete form of > LINEAGE
LYNAGES > LYNAGE
LYNCEAN adj of a lynx
LYNCH vb put to death without a trial
LYNCHED > LYNCH
LYNCHER > LYNCH
LYNCHERS > LYNCH
LYNCHES > LYNCH
LYNCHET n ridge formed by ploughing a hillside
LYNCHETS > LYNCHET
LYNCHING > LYNCH
LYNCHINGS > LYNCH
LYNCHPIN same as > LINCHPIN
LYNCHPINS > LYNCHPIN
LYNE n flax
LYNES > LYNE
LYNX n animal of the cat family
LYNXES > LYNX
LYNXLIKE > LYNX
LYOLYSES > LYOLYSIS
LYOLYSIS n formation of

an acid and a base from the interaction of a salt with a solvent
LYOMEROUS adj relating to Lyomeri fish
LYONNAISE adj (of food) cooked or garnished with onions, usually fried
LYOPHIL same as > LYOPHILIC
LYOPHILE same as > LYOPHILIC
LYOPHILED adj lyophilized
LYOPHILIC adj (of a colloid) having a dispersed phase with a high affinity for the continuous phase
LYOPHOBE same as > LYOPHOBIC
LYOPHOBIC adj (of a colloid) having a dispersed phase with little or no affinity for the continuous phase
LYRA n as in lyra viol lutelike musical instrument
LYRATE adj shaped like a lyre
LYRATED same as > LYRATE
LYRATELY > LYRATE
LYRE n ancient musical instrument
LYREBIRD n Australian bird, the male of which spreads its tail into the shape of a lyre
LYREBIRDS > LYREBIRD
LYRES > LYRE
LYRIC adj expressing emotion in songlike style ▷ n short poem in a songlike style
LYRICAL same as > LYRIC
LYRICALLY > LYRIC
LYRICISE same as > LYRICIZE
LYRICISED > LYRICISE

LYRICISES > LYRICISE
LYRICISM n quality or style of lyric poetry
LYRICISMS > LYRICISM
LYRICIST n person who writes the words of songs or musicals
LYRICISTS > LYRICIST
LYRICIZE vb write lyrics
LYRICIZED > LYRICIZE
LYRICIZES > LYRICIZE
LYRICON n wind synthesizer
LYRICONS > LYRICON
LYRICS > LYRIC
LYRIFORM adj lyre-shaped
LYRISM n art or technique of playing the lyre
LYRISMS > LYRISM
LYRIST same as > LYRICIST
LYRISTS > LYRIST
LYSATE n material formed by lysis
LYSATES > LYSATE
LYSE vb undergo lysis
LYSED > LYSE
LYSERGIC adj as in lysergic acid crystalline compound used in medical research
LYSERGIDE n LSD
LYSES > LYSIS
LYSIGENIC adj caused by breaking down of cells
LYSIMETER n instrument for determining solubility, esp the amount of water-soluble matter in soil
LYSIN n antibodies that dissolute cells against which they are directed
LYSINE n essential amino acid that occurs in proteins
LYSINES > LYSINE

LYSING > LYSE
LYSINS > LYSIN
LYSIS n destruction of cells by a lysin
LYSOGEN n lysis-inducing agent
LYSOGENIC > LYSOGEN
LYSOGENS > LYSOGEN
LYSOGENY > LYSOGEN
LYSOL n antiseptic solution
LYSOLS > LYSOL
LYSOSOMAL > LYSOSOME
LYSOSOME n any of numerous small particles that are present in the cytoplasm of most cells
LYSOSOMES > LYSOSOME
LYSOZYME n enzyme occurring in tears, certain body tissues, and egg white
LYSOZYMES > LYSOZYME
LYSSA less common word for > RABIES
LYSSAS > LYSSA
LYTE vb dismount
LYTED > LYTE
LYTES > LYTE
LYTHE n type of fish
LYTHES > LYTHE
LYTHRUM n genus of plants including loosestrife
LYTHRUMS > LYTHRUM
LYTIC adj relating to, causing, or resulting from lysis
LYTICALLY > LYTIC
LYTING > LYTE
LYTTA n mass of cartilage under the tongue in carnivores
LYTTAE > LYTTA
LYTTAS > LYTTA

Mm

MA *n* mother
MAA *vb* (of goats) bleat
MAAED > MAA
MAAING > MAA
MAAR *n* coneless volcanic crater
MAARE > MAAR
MAARS > MAAR
MAAS *n* thick soured milk
MAASES > MAAS
MAATJES *n* pickled herring
MABE *n* type of pearl
MABELA *n* ground sorghum
MABELAS > MABELA
MABES > MABE
MAC *n* macintosh
MACA *n* type of plant
MACABER *same as* > MACABRE
MACABRE *adj* strange and horrible, gruesome
MACABRELY > MACABRE
MACABRER > MACABRE
MACABREST > MACABRE
MACACO *n* type of lemur
MACACOS > MACACO
MACADAM *n* road surface
MACADAMED *adj* (of a road) paved with macadam
MACADAMIA *n* Australian tree with edible nuts
MACADAMS > MACADAM
MACAHUBA *n* South American palm tree
MACAHUBAS > MACAHUBA
MACALLUM *n* ice cream with raspberry sauce
MACALLUMS > MACALLUM
MACAQUE *n* monkey of Asia and Africa
MACAQUES > MACAQUE
MACARISE *vb* congratulate
MACARISED > MACARISE
MACARISES > MACARISE
MACARISM *n* blessing
MACARISMS > MACARISM
MACARIZE *same as* > MACARISE
MACARIZED > MACARIZE
MACARIZES > MACARIZE
MACARON *n* small meringue cake
MACARONI *n* pasta in short tube shapes
MACARONIC *adj* (of verse) characterized by a mixture of vernacular words jumbled together with Latin words or Latinized words or with words from one or more other foreign languages ▷ *n* macaronic verse

MACARONIS > MACARONI
MACARONS > MACARON
MACAROON *n* small biscuit or cake made with ground almonds
MACAROONS > MACAROON
MACAS > MACA
MACASSAR *n* oily preparation formerly put on the hair to make it smooth and shiny
MACASSARS > MACASSAR
MACAW *n* large tropical American parrot
MACAWS > MACAW
MACCABAW *same as* > MACCABOY
MACCABAWS > MACCABAW
MACCABOY *n* dark rose-scented snuff
MACCABOYS > MACCABOY
MACCARONI *same as* > MACARONI
MACCHIA *n* thicket in Italy
MACCHIATO *n* espresso coffee served with a dash of hot or cold milk
MACCHIE > MACCHIA
MACCOBOY *same as* > MACCABOY
MACCOBOYS > MACCOBOY
MACE *n* club ▷ *vb* use a mace
MACED > MACE
MACEDOINE *n* hot or cold mixture of diced vegetables
MACER *n* macebearer, esp (in Scotland) an official who acts as usher in a court of law
MACERAL *n* any of the organic units that constitute coal
MACERALS > MACERAL
MACERATE *vb* soften by soaking
MACERATED > MACERATE
MACERATER > MACERATE
MACERATES > MACERATE
MACERATOR > MACERATE
MACERS > MACER
MACES > MACE
MACH *n* ratio of the speed of a body in a particular medium to the speed of sound in that medium
MACHACA *n* Mexican dish of shredded dried beef
MACHACAS > MACHACA
MACHAIR *n* (in the western Highlands of Scotland) a strip of sandy, grassy land
MACHAIRS > MACHAIR

MACHAN *n* (in India) a raised platform used in tiger hunting
MACHANS > MACHAN
MACHE *n* papier-mâché
MACHER *n* important or influential person
MACHERS > MACHER
MACHES > MACHE
MACHETE *n* broad heavy knife used for cutting or as a weapon
MACHETES > MACHETE
MACHI *n* as in *machi chips* in Indian English, fish and chips
MACHINATE *vb* contrive, plan, or devise (schemes, plots, etc)
MACHINE *n* apparatus designed to perform a task ▷ *vb* make or produce by machine
MACHINED > MACHINE
MACHINERY *n* machines or machine parts collectively
MACHINES > MACHINE
MACHINIMA *n* use of real-time 3-D graphics to generate computer animation
MACHINING > MACHINE
MACHINIST *n* person who operates a machine
MACHISMO *n* exaggerated or strong masculinity
MACHISMOS > MACHISMO
MACHMETER *n* instrument for measuring the Mach number of an aircraft in flight
MACHO *adj* strongly masculine ▷ *n* strong masculinity
MACHOISM > MACHO
MACHOISMS > MACHO
MACHOS > MACHO
MACHREE *n* Irish form of address meaning my dear
MACHREES > MACHREE
MACHS > MACH
MACHZOR *n* Jewish prayer book
MACHZORIM > MACHZOR
MACHZORS > MACHZOR
MACING > MACE
MACINTOSH *n* waterproof raincoat
MACK *same as* > MAC
MACKEREL *n* edible sea fish
MACKERELS > MACKEREL
MACKINAW *n* thick short double-breasted plaid coat
MACKINAWS > MACKINAW

MACKLE *n* blurred impression ▷ *vb* mend hurriedly or in a makeshift way
MACKLED > MACKLE
MACKLES > MACKLE
MACKLING > MACKLE
MACKS > MACK
MACLE *n* crystal consisting of two parts
MACLED > MACLE
MACLES > MACLE
MACON *n* wine from the Mâcon area
MACONS > MACON
MACOYA *n* South American tree
MACOYAS > MACOYA
MACRAME *n* ornamental work of knotted cord
MACRAMES > MACRAME
MACRAMI *same as* > MACRAME
MACRAMIS > MACRAMI
MACRO *n* close-up lens
MACROBIAN *adj* long-lived
MACROCODE *n* computer instruction that triggers many other instructions
MACROCOPY *n* enlargement of printed material for easier reading
MACROCOSM *n* universe
MACROCYST *n* unusually large cyst
MACROCYTE *n* abnormally large red blood cell
MACRODOME *n* dome shape in crystal structure
MACRODONT *adj* having large teeth
MACROGLIA *n* one of the two types of non-nervous tissue (glia) found in the central nervous system: includes astrocytes
MACROLIDE *n* type of antibiotic drug
MACROLOGY *n* verbose but meaningless talk
MACROMERE *n* any of the large yolk-filled cells formed by unequal splitting of a fertilized ovum
MACROMOLE *n* large chemistry mole
MACRON *n* mark placed over a letter to represent a long vowel
MACRONS > MACRON
MACROPOD *n* member of kangaroo family
MACROPODS > MACROPOD

m

MACROPSIA *n* condition of seeing everything in the field of view as larger than it really is, which can occur in diseases of the retina or in some brain disorders
MACROS > MACRO
MACROTOUS *adj* having large ears
MACRURAL *adj* long-tailed
MACRURAN *n* type of decapod crustacean
MACRURANS > MACRURAN
MACRUROID *adj* long-tailed
MACRUROUS *adj* long-tailed
MACS > MAC
MACTATION *n* sacrificial killing
MACULA *n* small spot like a freckle
MACULAE > MACULA
MACULAR > MACULA
MACULAS > MACULA
MACULATE *vb* spot, stain, or pollute ▷ *adj* spotted or polluted
MACULATED > MACULATE
MACULATES > MACULATE
MACULE *same as* > MACKLE
MACULED > MACULE
MACULES > MACULE
MACULING > MACULE
MACULOSE *adj* having spots
MACUMBA *n* religious cult in Brazil
MACUMBAS > MACUMBA
MAD *adj* mentally deranged ▷ *vb* make mad
MADAFU *n* coconut milk
MADAFUS > MADAFU
MADAM *n* polite term of address for a woman ▷ *vb* call someone madam
MADAME *n* French title equivalent to *Mrs*
MADAMED > MADAM
MADAMES > MADAME
MADAMING > MADAM
MADAMS > MADAM
MADAROSES > MADAROSIS
MADAROSIS *n* abnormal loss of eyebrows or eyelashes
MADBRAIN *adj* deranged ▷ *n* rash or deranged person
MADBRAINS > MADBRAIN
MADCAP *adj* foolish or reckless ▷ *n* impulsive or reckless person
MADCAPS > MADCAP
MADDED > MAD
MADDEN *vb* infuriate or irritate
MADDENED > MADDEN
MADDENING *adj* irritating, annoying
MADDENS > MADDEN
MADDER *n* type of rose
MADDERS > MADDER
MADDEST > MAD
MADDING > MAD
MADDINGLY > MAD
MADDISH > MAD
MADDOCK *same as* > MATTOCK
MADDOCKS > MADDOCK
MADE > MAKE
MADEFIED > MADEFY

MADEFIES > MADEFY
MADEFY *vb* make moist
MADEFYING > MADEFY
MADEIRA *n* kind of rich sponge cake
MADEIRAS > MADEIRA
MADELEINE *n* small fancy sponge cake
MADERISE *vb* become reddish
MADERISED > MADERISE
MADERISES > MADERISE
MADERIZE *same as* > MADERISE
MADERIZED > MADERIZE
MADERIZES > MADERIZE
MADEUPPY *adj* artificial or contrived in an obvious way
MADGE *n* type of hammer
MADGES > MADGE
MADHOUSE *n* place filled with uproar or confusion
MADHOUSES > MADHOUSE
MADID *adj* wet
MADISON *n* type of cycle relay race
MADISONS > MADISON
MADLING *n* insane person
MADLINGS > MADLING
MADLY *adv* with great speed and energy
MADMAN *n* person who is insane
MADMEN > MADMAN
MADNESS *n* insanity
MADNESSES > MADNESS
MADONNA *n* picture or statue of the Virgin Mary
MADONNAS > MADONNA
MADOQUA *n* Ethiopian antelope
MADOQUAS > MADOQUA
MADRAS *n* medium-hot curry
MADRASA *same as* > MADRASAH
MADRASAH *n* educational institution, particularly for Islamic religious instruction
MADRASAHS > MADRASAH
MADRASAS > MADRASA
MADRASES > MADRAS
MADRASSA *same as* > MADRASAH
MADRASSAH *same as* > MADRASAH
MADRASSAS > MADRASSA
MADRE *Spanish word for* > MOTHER
MADREPORE *n* type of coral which often occurs in tropical seas and forms large coral reefs
MADRES > MADRE
MADRIGAL *n* 16th–17th-century part song for unaccompanied voices
MADRIGALS > MADRIGAL
MADRILENE *n* cold consommé flavoured with tomato juice
MADRONA *n* N American evergreen tree or shrub
MADRONAS > MADRONA
MADRONE *same as* > MADRONA
MADRONES > MADRONE
MADRONO *same as* > MADRONA

MADRONOS > MADRONO
MADS > MAD
MADTOM *n* species of catfish
MADTOMS > MADTOM
MADURO *adj* (of cigars) dark and strong ▷ *n* cigar of this type
MADUROS > MADURO
MADWOMAN *n* woman who is insane, esp one who behaves violently
MADWOMEN > MADWOMAN
MADWORT *n* low-growing Eurasian plant with small blue flowers
MADWORTS > MADWORT
MADZOON *same as* > MATZOON
MADZOONS > MADZOON
MAE *adj* more
MAELID *n* mythical spirit of apple tree
MAELIDS > MAELID
MAELSTROM *n* great whirlpool
MAENAD *n* female disciple of Dionysus
MAENADES > MAENAD
MAENADIC > MAENAD
MAENADISM > MAENAD
MAENADS > MAENAD
MAERL *n* type of red coralline algae
MAERLS > MAERL
MAES > MAE
MAESTOSO *adv* be performed majestically ▷ *n* piece or passage directed to be played in this way
MAESTOSOS > MAESTOSO
MAESTRI > MAESTRO
MAESTRO *n* outstanding musician or conductor
MAESTROS > MAESTRO
MAFFIA *same as* > MAFIA
MAFFIAS > MAFFIA
MAFFICK *vb* celebrate extravagantly and publicly
MAFFICKED > MAFFICK
MAFFICKER > MAFFICK
MAFFICKS > MAFFICK
MAFFLED *adj* baffled
MAFFLIN *n* half-witted person
MAFFLING *same as* > MAFFLIN
MAFFLINGS > MAFFLING
MAFFLINS > MAFFLIN
MAFIA *n* international secret organization founded in Sicily
MAFIAS > MAFIA
MAFIC *n* minerals present in igneous rock
MAFICS > MAFIC
MAFIOSI > MAFIOSO
MAFIOSO *n* member of the Mafia
MAFIOSOS > MAFIOSO
MAFTED *adj* suffering under oppressive heat
MAFTIR *n* final section of the weekly Torah reading
MAFTIRS > MAFTIR
MAG *vb* talk ▷ *n* talk
MAGAININ *n* substance with antibacterial properties

MAGAININS > MAGAININ
MAGALOG *same as* > MAGALOGUE
MAGALOGS > MAGALOG
MAGALOGUE *n* combination of a magazine and a catalogue
MAGAZINE *n* periodical publication with articles by different writers
MAGAZINES > MAGAZINE
MAGDALEN *n* reformed prostitute
MAGDALENE *same as* > MAGDALEN
MAGDALENS > MAGDALEN
MAGE *archaic word for* > MAGICIAN
MAGENTA *adj* deep purplish-red ▷ *n* deep purplish red
MAGENTAS > MAGENTA
MAGES > MAGE
MAGESHIP > MAGE
MAGESHIPS > MAGE
MAGG *same as* > MAG
MAGGED > MAG
MAGGIE *n* magpie
MAGGIES > MAGGIE
MAGGING > MAG
MAGGOT *n* larva of an insect
MAGGOTIER > MAGGOTY
MAGGOTS > MAGGOT
MAGGOTY *adj* relating to, resembling, or ridden with maggots
MAGGS > MAGG
MAGI > MAGUS
MAGIAN > MAGUS
MAGIANISM > MAGUS
MAGIANS > MAGUS
MAGIC *n* supposed art of invoking supernatural powers to influence events ▷ *vb* transform or produce by or as if by magic ▷ *adj* of, using, or like magic
MAGICAL > MAGIC
MAGICALLY > MAGIC
MAGICIAN *n* conjuror
MAGICIANS > MAGICIAN
MAGICKED > MAGIC
MAGICKING > MAGIC
MAGICS > MAGIC
MAGILP *same as* > MEGILP
MAGILPS > MAGILP
MAGISM > MAGUS
MAGISMS > MAGUS
MAGISTER *n* person entitled to teach in medieval university
MAGISTERS > MAGISTER
MAGISTERY *n* agency or substance, such as the philosopher's stone, believed to transmute other substances
MAGISTRAL *adj* of, relating to, or characteristic of a master ▷ *n* fortification in a determining position
MAGLEV *n* type of high-speed train
MAGLEVS > MAGLEV
MAGMA *n* molten rock inside the earth's crust
MAGMAS > MAGMA

MAGMATA > MAGMA

MAGMATIC > MAGMA

MAGMATISM > MAGMA

MAGNALIUM n alloy of magnesium and aluminium

MAGNATE n influential or wealthy person, esp in industry

MAGNATES > MAGNATE

MAGNES n magnetic iron ore

MAGNESES > MAGNES

MAGNESIA n white tasteless substance used as an antacid and a laxative

MAGNESIAL > MAGNESIA

MAGNESIAN > MAGNESIA

MAGNESIAS > MAGNESIA

MAGNESIC > MAGNESIA

MAGNESITE n white, colourless, or lightly tinted mineral

MAGNESIUM n silvery-white metallic element

MAGNET n piece of iron or steel capable of attracting iron and pointing north when suspended

MAGNETAR n neutron star with intense magnetic field

MAGNETARS > MAGNETAR

MAGNETIC adj having the properties of a magnet

MAGNETICS n branch of physics concerned with magnetism

MAGNETISE same as > MAGNETIZE

MAGNETISM n magnetic property

MAGNETIST > MAGNETISM

MAGNETITE n black magnetizable mineral that is an important source of iron

MAGNETIZE vb make into a magnet

MAGNETO n apparatus for ignition in an internal-combustion engine

MAGNETON n unit of magnetic moment

MAGNETONS > MAGNETON

MAGNETOS > MAGNETO

MAGNETRON n electronic valve used with a magnetic field to generate microwave oscillations, used esp in radar

MAGNETS > MAGNET

MAGNIFIC adj magnificent, grandiose, or pompous

MAGNIFICO n magnate

MAGNIFIED > MAGNIFY

MAGNIFIER > MAGNIFY

MAGNIFIES > MAGNIFY

MAGNIFY vb increase in apparent size, as with a lens

MAGNITUDE n relative importance or size

MAGNOLIA n shrub or tree with showy white or pink flowers

MAGNOLIAS > MAGNOLIA

MAGNON n short for Cro-Magnon

MAGNONS > MAGNON

MAGNOX n alloy used in fuel elements of some nuclear reactors

MAGNOXES > MAGNOX

MAGNUM n large wine bottle holding about 1.5 litres

MAGNUMS > MAGNUM

MAGNUS adj as in magnus hitch knot similar to a clove hitch but having one more turn

MAGOT n Chinese or Japanese figurine in a crouching position, usually grotesque

MAGOTS > MAGOT

MAGPIE n black-and-white bird

MAGPIES > MAGPIE

MAGS > MAG

MAGSMAN n raconteur

MAGSMEN > MAGSMAN

MAGUEY n tropical American agave plant

MAGUEYS > MAGUEY

MAGUS n Zoroastrian priest of the ancient Medes and Persians

MAGYAR adj of or relating to a style of sleeve

MAHA n as in maha yoga form of yoga

MAHANT n chief priest in a Hindu temple

MAHANTS > MAHANT

MAHARAJA same as > MAHARAJAH

MAHARAJAH n former title of some Indian princes

MAHARAJAS > MAHARAJA

MAHARANEE same as > MAHARANI

MAHARANI n wife of a maharaja

MAHARANIS > MAHARANI

MAHARISHI n Hindu religious teacher or mystic

MAHATMA n person revered for holiness and wisdom

MAHATMAS > MAHATMA

MAHEWU n (in South Africa) fermented liquid mealie-meal porridge

MAHEWUS > MAHEWU

MAHIMAHI n Pacific fish

MAHIMAHIS > MAHIMAHI

MAHJONG n game of Chinese origin, using tiles

MAHJONGG same as > MAHJONG

MAHJONGGS > MAHJONGG

MAHJONGS > MAHJONG

MAHLSTICK same as > MAULSTICK

MAHMAL n litter used in Muslim ceremony

MAHMALS > MAHMAL

MAHOE n New Zealand tree

MAHOES > MAHOE

MAHOGANY n hard reddish-brown wood of several tropical trees ▷ adj reddish-brown

MAHONIA n Asian and American evergreen shrub

MAHONIAS > MAHONIA

MAHOUT n (in India and the East Indies) elephant driver or keeper

MAHOUTS > MAHOUT

MAHSEER n large freshwater Indian fish

MAHSEERS > MAHSEER

MAHSIR same as > MAHSEER

MAHSIRS > MAHSIR

MAHUA n Indian tree

MAHUANG n herbal medicine from shrub

MAHUANGS > MAHUANG

MAHUAS > MAHUA

MAHWA same as > MAHUA

MAHWAS > MAHWA

MAHZOR same as > MACHZOR

MAHZORIM > MAHZOR

MAHZORS > MAHZOR

MAIASAUR same as > MAIASAURA

MAIASAURA n species of dinosaur

MAIASAURS > MAIASAUR

MAID n female servant ▷ vb work as maid

MAIDAN n (in Pakistan, India, etc) open area

MAIDANS > MAIDAN

MAIDED > MAID

MAIDEN n young unmarried woman ▷ adj unmarried

MAIDENISH > MAIDEN

MAIDENLY adj modest

MAIDENS > MAIDEN

MAIDHOOD > MAID

MAIDHOODS > MAID

MAIDING > MAID

MAIDISH > MAID

MAIDISM n pellagra

MAIDISMS > MAIDISM

MAIDLESS > MAID

MAIDS > MAID

MAIEUTIC adj of or relating to the Socratic method of eliciting knowledge by a series of questions and answers

MAIEUTICS n Socratic method

MAIGRE adj not containing meat ▷ n species of fish

MAIGRES > MAIGRE

MAIHEM same as > MAYHEM

MAIHEMS > MAIHEM

MAIK n old halfpenny

MAIKO n apprentice geisha

MAIKOS > MAIKO

MAIKS > MAIK

MAIL n letters and packages transported and delivered by the post office ▷ vb send by mail

MAILABLE > MAIL

MAILBAG n large bag for transporting or delivering mail

MAILBAGS > MAILBAG

MAILBOAT n boat that carries mail

MAILBOATS > MAILBOAT

MAILBOX n box into which letters and parcels are delivered

MAILBOXES > MAILBOX

MAILCAR same as > MAILCOACH

MAILCARS > MAILCAR

MAILCOACH n railway coach specially constructed for the transportation of mail

MAILE n halfpenny

MAILED > MAIL

MAILER n person who addresses or mails letters, etc

MAILERS > MAILER

MAILES > MAILE

MAILGRAM n telegram

MAILGRAMS > MAILGRAM

MAILING > MAIL

MAILINGS > MAILING

MAILL n Scots word meaning rent

MAILLESS > MAIL

MAILLOT n tights worn for ballet, gymnastics, etc

MAILLOTS > MAILLOT

MAILLS > MAILL

MAILMAN n postman

MAILMEN > MAILMAN

MAILMERGE n computer program for sending mass mailings

MAILPOUCH same as > MAILBAG

MAILROOM n room where mail to and from building is dealt with

MAILROOMS > MAILROOM

MAILS > MAIL

MAILSACK same as > MAILBAG

MAILSACKS > MAILSACK

MAILSHOT n posting of advertising material to many selected people at once

MAILSHOTS > MAILSHOT

MAILVAN n vehicle used to transport post

MAILVANS > MAILVAN

MAIM vb cripple or mutilate ▷ n injury or defect

MAIMED > MAIM

MAIMER > MAIM

MAIMERS > MAIM

MAIMING > MAIM

MAIMINGS > MAIM

MAIMS > MAIM

MAIN adj chief or principal ▷ n principal pipe or line carrying water, gas, or electricity ▷ vb lower sails

MAINBOOM n spar for mainsail

MAINBOOMS > MAINBOOM

MAINBRACE n brace attached to the mainyard

MAINDOOR n door from street into house

MAINDOORS > MAINDOOR

MAINED > MAIN

MAINER > MAIN

MAINEST > MAIN

MAINFRAME adj denoting a high-speed general-purpose computer ▷ n high-speed general-purpose computer, with a large store capacity

MAINING > MAIN

MAINLAND n stretch of land which forms the main part of a country

MAINLANDS > MAINLAND

MAINLINE n the trunk route between two points ▷ vb inject a drug into a vein ▷ adj having an important position

MAINLINED > MAINLINE

MAINLINER > MAINLINE
MAINLINES > MAINLINE
MAINLY adv for the most part, chiefly
MAINMAST n chief mast of a ship
MAINMASTS > MAINMAST
MAINOR n act of doing something
MAINORS > MAINOR
MAINOUR same as > MAINOR
MAINOURS > MAINOUR
MAINPRISE n former legal surety ▷ vb allow a prisoner to go free based on a guarantee that he or she will appear in court on the designated day
MAINS > MAIN
MAINSAIL n largest sail on a mainmast
MAINSAILS > MAINSAIL
MAINSHEET n line used to control the angle of the mainsail to the wind
MAINSTAGE n largest stage in a theatre complex
MAINSTAY n chief support
MAINSTAYS > MAINSTAY
MAINTAIN vb continue or keep in existence
MAINTAINS > MAINTAIN
MAINTOP n top or platform at the head of the mainmast
MAINTOPS > MAINTOP
MAINYARD n yard for a square mainsail
MAINYARDS > MAINYARD
MAIOLICA same as > MAIOLICA
MAIOLICAS > MAIOLICA
MAIR Scots form of > MORE
MAIRE n New Zealand tree
MAIREHAU n small aromatic shrub of New Zealand
MAIREHAUS > MAIREHAU
MAIRES > MAIRE
MAIRS > MAIR
MAISE n measure of herring
MAISES > MAISE
MAIST Scot word for > MOST
MAISTER Scots word for > MASTER
MAISTERED > MAISTER
MAISTERS > MAISTER
MAISTRIES > MAISTER
MAISTRING > MAISTER
MAISTRY > MAISTER
MAISTS > MAIST
MAIZE n type of corn with spikes of yellow grains
MAIZES > MAIZE
MAJAGUA same as > MAHOE
MAJAGUAS > MAJAGUA
MAJESTIC adj beautiful, dignified, and impressive
MAJESTIES > MAJESTY
MAJESTY n stateliness or grandeur
MAJLIS n (in Arab countries) an assembly
MAJLISES > MAJLIS
MAJOLICA n type of ornamented Italian pottery
MAJOLICAS > MAJOLICA
MAJOR adj greater in number, quality, or extent ▷ n

middle-ranking army officer ▷ vb do one's principal study in (a particular subject)
MAJORAT n estate, the right to which is that of the first born child of a family
MAJORATS > MAJORAT
MAJORDOMO n chief steward or butler of a great household
MAJORED > MAJOR
MAJORETTE n one of a group of girls who practise formation marching and baton twirling
MAJORING > MAJOR
MAJORITY n greater number
MAJORLY adv very
MAJORS > MAJOR
MAJORSHIP > MAJOR
MAJUSCULE n large letter, either capital or uncial, used in printing or writing ▷ adj relating to, printed, or written in such letters
MAK Scot word for > MAKE
MAKABLE > MAKE
MAKAR same as > MAKER
MAKARS > MAKAR
MAKE vb create, construct, or establish ▷ n brand, type, or style
MAKEABLE n rough, unpolished stone
MAKEABLES > MAKEABLE
MAKEBATE n troublemaker
MAKEBATES > MAKEBATE
MAKEFAST n strong support to which a vessel is secured
MAKEFASTS > MAKEFAST
MAKELESS > MAKE
MAKEOVER vb transfer the title of (property, etc) ▷ n alterations to improve a person's appearance
MAKEOVERS > MAKEOVER
MAKER n person or company that makes something
MAKEREADY n process of preparing the forme and the cylinder or platen packing to achieve the correct impression all over the forme
MAKERS > MAKER
MAKES > MAKE
MAKESHIFT adj serving as a temporary substitute ▷ n something serving in this capacity
MAKEUP n cosmetics applied to the face
MAKEUPS > MAKEUP
MAKHANI n Indian dish made with butter or ghee ▷ adj denoting such a dish
MAKHANIS > MAKHANI
MAKI n in Japanese cuisine, rice and other ingredients wrapped in a short seaweed roll
MAKIMONO n Japanese scroll
MAKIMONOS > MAKIMONO
MAKING > MAKE
MAKINGS pl n potentials, qualities, or materials
MAKIS > MAKI

MAKO n powerful shark of the Atlantic and Pacific Oceans
MAKOS > MAKO
MAKS > MAK
MAKUTA plural of > LIKUTA
MAKUTU n Polynesian witchcraft ▷ vb cast a spell on
MAKUTUED > MAKUTU
MAKUTUING > MAKUTU
MAKUTUS > MAKUTU
MAL n illness
MALA n string of beads or knots, used in praying and meditating
MALACCA n stem of the rattan palm
MALACCAS > MALACCA
MALACHITE n green mineral
MALACIA n softening of an organ or tissue
MALACIAS > MALACIA
MALADIES > MALADY
MALADROIT adj clumsy or awkward
MALADY n disease or illness
MALAGUENA n Spanish dance similar to the fandango
MALAISE n something wrong which affects a section of society or area of activity
MALAISES > MALAISE
MALAM same as > MALLAM
MALAMS > MALAM
MALAMUTE n Alaskan sled dog of the spitz type, having a dense usually greyish coat
MALAMUTES > MALAMUTE
MALANDER same as > MALANDERS
MALANDERS pl n disease of horses characterized by an eczematous inflammation behind the knee
MALANGA same as > COCOYAM
MALANGAS > MALANGA
MALAPERT adj saucy or impudent ▷ n saucy or impudent person
MALAPERTS > MALAPERT
MALAPROP n word unintentionally confused with one of similar sound
MALAPROPS > MALAPROP
MALAR n cheekbone ▷ adj of or relating to the cheek or cheekbone
MALARIA n infectious disease caused by mosquito bite
MALARIAL > MALARIA
MALARIAN > MALARIA
MALARIAS > MALARIA
MALARIOUS > MALARIA
MALARKEY n nonsense or rubbish
MALARKEYS > MALARKEY
MALARKIES > MALARKY
MALARKY same as > MALARKEY
MALAROMA n bad smell
MALAROMAS > MALAROMA
MALARS > MALAR

MALAS > MALA
MALATE n any salt or ester of malic acid
MALATES > MALATE
MALATHION n yellow organophosphorus insecticide used as a dust or mist for the control of house flies and garden pests
MALAX vb soften
MALAXAGE > MALAX
MALAXAGES > MALAX
MALAXATE same as > MALAX
MALAXATED > MALAXATE
MALAXATES > MALAXATE
MALAXATOR n machine for kneading or grinding
MALAXED > MALAX
MALAXES > MALAX
MALAXING > MALAX
MALE adj of the sex which can fertilize reproductive cells ▷ n male person or animal
MALEATE n any salt or ester of maleic acid
MALEATES > MALEATE
MALEDICT vb utter a curse against ▷ adj cursed or detestable
MALEDICTS > MALEDICT
MALEFFECT n bad effect
MALEFIC adj causing evil
MALEFICE n wicked deed
MALEFICES > MALEFICE
MALEIC adj as in maleic acid colourless soluble crystalline substance
MALEMIUT same as > MALAMUTE
MALEMIUTS > MALEMIUT
MALEMUTE same as > MALAMUTE
MALEMUTES > MALEMUTE
MALENESS > MALE
MALENGINE n wicked plan
MALES > MALE
MALFED adj having malfunctioned
MALFORMED adj deformed
MALGRADO prep in spite of
MALGRE same as > MAUGRE
MALGRED > MALGRE
MALGRES > MALGRE
MALGRING > MALGRE
MALI n member of an Indian caste
MALIBU n as in malibu board lightweight surfboard
MALIC adj as in malic acid colourless crystalline compound occurring in apples
MALICE n desire to cause harm to others ▷ vb wish harm to
MALICED > MALICE
MALICES > MALICE
MALICHO n mischief
MALICHOS > MALICHO
MALICING > MALICE
MALICIOUS adj characterized by malice
MALIGN vb slander or defame ▷ adj evil in influence or effect
MALIGNANT adj seeking to harm others

MALIGNED > MALIGN

MALIGNER > MALIGN

MALIGNERS > MALIGN

MALIGNING > MALIGN

MALIGNITY n evil disposition

MALIGNLY > MALIGN

MALIGNS > MALIGN

MALIHINI n (in Hawaii) a foreigner or stranger

MALIHINIS > MALIHINI

MALIK n person of authority in India

MALIKS > MALIK

MALINE n stiff net

MALINES > MALINE

MALINGER vb feign illness to avoid work

MALINGERS > MALINGER

MALINGERY > MALINGER

MALIS > MALI

MALISM n belief that evil dominates world

MALISMS > MALISM

MALISON archaic or poetic word for > CURSE

MALISONS > MALISON

MALIST > MALISM

MALKIN archaic or dialect name for a > CAT

MALKINS > MALKIN

MALL n street or shopping area closed to vehicles ▷ vb maul

MALLAM n (in W Africa) expert in the Koran

MALLAMS > MALLAM

MALLANDER same as > MALANDERS

MALLARD n wild duck

MALLARDS > MALLARD

MALLCORE n type of rock music combining heavy metal and hip-hop

MALLCORES > MALLCORE

MALLEABLE adj capable of being hammered or pressed into shape

MALLEABLY > MALLEABLE

MALLEATE vb hammer

MALLEATED > MALLEATE

MALLEATES > MALLEATE

MALLECHO same as > MALICHO

MALLECHOS > MALLECHO

MALLED > MALL

MALLEE n low-growing eucalypt in dry regions

MALLEES > MALLEE

MALLEI > MALLEUS

MALLEMUCK n any of various sea birds, such as the albatross, fulmar, or shearwater

MALLENDER same as > MALANDERS

MALLEOLAR > MALLEOLUS

MALLEOLI > MALLEOLUS

MALLEOLUS n either of two rounded bony projections of the tibia and fibula on the sides of each ankle joint

MALLET n (wooden) hammer

MALLETS > MALLET

MALLEUS n small bone in the middle ear

MALLEUSES > MALLEUS

MALLING > MALL

MALLINGS > MALL

MALLOW n plant with pink or purple flowers

MALLOWS > MALLOW

MALLS > MALL

MALM n soft greyish limestone that crumbles easily

MALMAG n Asian monkey

MALMAGS > MALMAG

MALMIER > MALMY

MALMIEST > MALMY

MALMS > MALM

MALMSEY n sweet Madeira wine

MALMSEYS > MALMSEY

MALMSTONE same as > MALM

MALMY adj looking like malm

MALODOR same as > MALODOUR

MALODORS > MALODOR

MALODOUR n unpleasant smell

MALODOURS > MALODOUR

MALONATE n salt of malonic acid

MALONATES > MALONATE

MALONIC adj as in malonic acid colourless crystalline compound

MALOTI plural of > LOTI

MALPIGHIA n type of tropical shrub

MALPOSED adj in abnormal position

MALS > MAL

MALSTICK same as > MAULSTICK

MALSTICKS > MALSTICK

MALT n grain, such as barley, dried in a kiln ▷ vb make into or make with malt

MALTALENT n evil intention

MALTASE n enzyme that hydrolyses maltose to glucose

MALTASES > MALTASE

MALTED n malted milk drink

MALTEDS > MALT

MALTESE adj as in maltese cross cross-shaped part of a film projector

MALTHA n any of various naturally occurring mixtures of hydrocarbons

MALTHAS > MALTHA

MALTIER > MALTY

MALTIEST > MALTY

MALTINESS > MALTY

MALTING n building in which malt is made or stored

MALTINGS > MALTING

MALTIPOO n cross between a Maltese and a poodle

MALTIPOOS > MALTIPOO

MALTMAN same as > MALTSTER

MALTMEN > MALTMAN

MALTOL n food additive

MALTOLS > MALTOL

MALTOSE n sugar formed by the action of enzymes on starch

MALTOSES > MALTOSE

MALTREAT vb treat badly

MALTREATS > MALTREAT

MALTS > MALT

MALTSTER n person who makes or deals in malt

MALTSTERS > MALTSTER

MALTWORM n heavy drinker

MALTWORMS > MALTWORM

MALTY adj of, like, or containing malt

MALUS n financial penalty incurred by an investor

MALUSES > MALUS

MALVA n mallow plant

MALVAS > MALVA

MALVASIA n type of grape used to make malmsey

MALVASIAN > MALVASIA

MALVASIAS > MALVASIA

MALVESIE same as > MALMSEY

MALVESIES > MALVESIE

MALVOISIE n amber dessert wine made in France, similar to malmsey

MALWA n Ugandan drink brewed from millet

MALWARE n computer program designed to cause damage to a system

MALWARES > MALWARE

MALWAS > MALWA

MAM same as > MOTHER

MAMA n mother

MAMAGUY vb deceive or tease ▷ n deception or flattery

MAMAGUYED > MAMAGUY

MAMAGUYS > MAMAGUY

MAMAKAU same as > MAMAKU

MAMAKAUS > MAMAKAU

MAMAKO same as > MAMAKU

MAMAKOS > MAMAKO

MAMAKU n tall edible New Zealand tree fern

MAMAKUS > MAMAKU

MAMALIGA same as > POLENTA

MAMALIGAS > MAMALIGA

MAMAS > MAMA

MAMASAN n (in Japan) woman in a position of authority

MAMASANS > MAMASAN

MAMATEEK n type of wigwam

MAMATEEKS > MAMATEEK

MAMBA n deadly S African snake

MAMBAS > MAMBA

MAMBO n Latin American dance resembling the rumba ▷ vb perform this dance

MAMBOED > MAMBO

MAMBOES > MAMBO

MAMBOING > MAMBO

MAMBOS > MAMBO

MAMEE same as > MAMEY

MAMEES > MAMEE

MAMELON n small rounded hillock

MAMELONS > MAMELON

MAMELUCO n Brazilian of mixed European and South American descent

MAMELUCOS > MAMELUCO

MAMELUKE n member of a military class once ruling Egypt

MAMELUKES > MAMELUKE

MAMEY n tropical tree

MAMEYES > MAMEY

MAMEYS > MAMEY

MAMIE n tropical tree

MAMIES > MAMIE

MAMILLA n nipple or teat

MAMILLAE > MAMILLA

MAMILLAR adj of the breast

MAMILLARY > MAMILLA

MAMILLATE adj having nipples or nipple-like projections

MAMLUK same as > MAMELUKE

MAMLUKS > MAMLUK

MAMMA n buxom and voluptuous woman

MAMMAE > MAMMA

MAMMAL n animal of the type that suckles its young

MAMMALIAN > MAMMAL

MAMMALITY > MAMMAL

MAMMALOGY n branch of zoology concerned with the study of mammals

MAMMALS > MAMMAL

MAMMARIES > MAMMARY

MAMMARY adj of the breasts or milk-producing glands ▷ n breast

MAMMAS > MAMMA

MAMMATE adj having breasts

MAMMATI > MAMMATUS

MAMMATUS n breast-shaped cloud

MAMMEE same as > MAMEY

MAMMEES > MAMMEE

MAMMER vb hesitate

MAMMERED > MAMMER

MAMMERING > MAMMER

MAMMERS > MAMMER

MAMMET same as > MAUMET

MAMMETRY n worship of idols

MAMMETS > MAMMET

MAMMEY same as > MAMEY

MAMMEYS > MAMMEY

MAMMIE same as > MAMMY

MAMMIES > MAMMY

MAMMIFER same as > MAMMAL

MAMMIFERS > MAMMIFER

MAMMIFORM adj in the form of a breast

MAMMILLA same as > MAMILLA

MAMMILLAE > MAMMILLA

MAMMILLAR same as > MAMILLAR

MAMMITIS same as > MASTITIS

MAMMOCK n fragment ▷ vb tear or shred

MAMMOCKED > MAMMOCK

MAMMOCKS > MAMMOCK

MAMMOGRAM n X-ray of a breast

MAMMON n wealth regarded as a source of evil

MAMMONISH > MAMMON

MAMMONISM > MAMMON

MAMMONIST > MAMMON

MAMMONITE > MAMMON

MAMMONS > MAMMON

MAMMOTH n extinct elephant-like mammal ▷ adj colossal

m

m

MAMMOTHS > MAMMOTH
MAMMY same as **>** MOTHER
MAMPARA n foolish person, idiot
MAMPARAS > MAMPARA
MAMPOER n home-distilled brandy
MAMPOERS > MAMPOER
MAMS > MAM
MAMSELLE n mademoiselle
MAMSELLES > MAMSELLE
MAMZER n child of an incestuous or adulterous union
MAMZERIM > MAMZER
MAMZERS > MAMZER
MAN n adult male ▷ vb supply with sufficient people for operation or defence
MANA n authority, influence
MANACLE vb handcuff or fetter ▷ n metal ring or chain put round the wrists or ankles
MANACLED > MANACLE
MANACLES > MANACLE
MANACLING > MANACLE
MANAGE vb succeed in doing
MANAGED > MANAGE
MANAGER n person in charge of a business, institution, actor, sports team, etc
MANAGERS > MANAGER
MANAGES > MANAGE
MANAGING adj having administrative control or authority
MANAIA n figure in Māori carving
MANAIAS > MANAIA
MANAKIN same as **>** MANIKIN
MANAKINS > MANAKIN
MANANA n tomorrow ▷ adv tomorrow
MANANAS > MANANA
MANAS > MANA
MANAT n standard monetary unit of Azerbaijan
MANATEE n large tropical plant-eating aquatic mammal
MANATEES > MANATEE
MANATI same as **>** MANATEE
MANATIS > MANATI
MANATOID > MANATEE
MANATS > MANAT
MANATU n large flowering deciduous New Zealand tree
MANATUS > MANATU
MANAWA in New Zealand, same as **>** MANGROVE
MANAWAS > MANAWA
MANBAG n small handbag with a shoulder strap, carried by men
MANBAGS > MANBAG
MANBAND n boy band whose members have reached maturity
MANBANDS > MANBÂND
MANCALA n African and Asian board game
MANCALAS > MANCALA
MANCANDO adv musical direction meaning fading away

MANCHE n long sleeve
MANCHEGO n Spanish cheese
MANCHEGOS > MANCHEGO
MANCHES > MANCHE
MANCHET n type of bread
MANCHETS > MANCHET
MANCIPATE vb make legal transfer in ancient Rome
MANCIPLE n steward who buys provisions, esp in a college, Inn of Court, or monastery
MANCIPLES > MANCIPLE
MANCUS n former English coin
MANCUSES > MANCUS
MAND > MAN
MANDALA n circular design symbolizing the universe
MANDALAS > MANDALA
MANDALIC > MANDALA
MANDAMUS n order of a superior court
MANDARIN n high-ranking government official
MANDARINE same as **>** MANDARIN
MANDARINS > MANDARIN
MANDATARY same as **>** MANDATORY
MANDATE n official or authoritative command ▷ vb give authority to
MANDATED > MANDATE
MANDATES > MANDATE
MANDATING > MANDATE
MANDATOR > MANDATE
MANDATORS > MANDATE
MANDATORY adj compulsory ▷ n person or state holding a mandate
MANDI n (in India) a big market
MANDIBLE n lower jawbone or jawlike part
MANDIBLES > MANDIBLE
MANDILION same as **>** MANDYLION
MANDIOC same as **>** MANIOC
MANDIOCA same as **>** MANIOC
MANDIOCAS > MANDIOCA
MANDIOCCA same as **>** MANIOC
MANDIOCS > MANDIOC
MANDIR n Hindu or Jain temple
MANDIRA same as **>** MANDIR
MANDIRAS > MANDIRA
MANDIRS > MANDIR
MANDIS > MANDI
MANDOLA n early type of mandolin
MANDOLAS > MANDOLA
MANDOLIN n musical instrument with four pairs of strings
MANDOLINE same as **>** MANDOLIN
MANDOLINS > MANDOLIN
MANDOM n mankind
MANDOMS > MANDOM
MANDORA n ancestor of mandolin
MANDORAS > MANDORA
MANDORLA n area of light surrounding Christ in a painting

MANDORLAS > MANDORLA
MANDRAKE n plant with a forked root
MANDRAKES > MANDRAKE
MANDREL n shaft on which work is held in a lathe
MANDRELS > MANDREL
MANDRIL same as **>** MANDREL
MANDRILL n large blue-faced baboon
MANDRILLS > MANDRILL
MANDRILS > MANDRIL
MANDUCATE vb eat or chew
MANDYLION n loose garment formerly worn over armour
MANE n long hair on the neck of a horse, lion, etc
MANEB n powdered fungicide
MANEBS > MANEB
MANED > MANE
MANEGE n art of training horses and riders ▷ vb train horse
MANEGED > MANEGE
MANEGES > MANEGE
MANEGING > MANEGE
MANEH same as **>** MINA
MANEHS > MANEH
MANELESS > MANE
MANENT > MANET
MANES pl n spirits of the dead, often revered as minor deities
MANET vb theatre direction, remain on stage
MANEUVER same as **>** MANOEUVRE
MANEUVERS > MANEUVER
MANFUL adj determined and brave
MANFULLER > MANFUL
MANFULLY > MANFUL
MANG vb speak
MANGA n type of Japanese comic book
MANGABEY n large African monkey
MANGABEYS > MANGABEY
MANGABIES > MANGABY
MANGABY same as **>** MANGABEY
MANGAL n Turkish brazier
MANGALS > MANGAL
MANGANATE n salt of manganic acid
MANGANESE n brittle greyish-white metallic element
MANGANIC adj of or containing manganese in the trivalent state
MANGANIN n copper-based alloy
MANGANINS > MANGANIN
MANGANITE n blackish mineral
MANGANOUS adj of or containing manganese in the divalent state
MANGAS > MANGA
MANGE n skin disease of domestic animals
MANGEAO n small New Zealand tree with glossy leaves

MANGEAOS > MANGEAO
MANGED > MANG
MANGEL n Eurasian variety of the beet plant
MANGELS > MANGEL
MANGER n eating trough in a stable or barn
MANGERS > MANGER
MANGES > MANGE
MANGETOUT n variety of pea with an edible pod
MANGEY same as **>** MANGY
MANGIER > MANGY
MANGIEST > MANGY
MANGILY > MANGY
MANGINESS > MANGY
MANGING > MANG
MANGLE vb destroy by crushing and twisting ▷ n machine with rollers for squeezing water from washed clothes
MANGLED > MANGLE
MANGLER > MANGLE
MANGLERS > MANGLE
MANGLES > MANGLE
MANGLING > MANGLE
MANGO n tropical fruit with sweet juicy yellow flesh
MANGOES > MANGO
MANGOLD n type of root vegetable
MANGOLDS > MANGOLD
MANGONEL n war engine for hurling stones
MANGONELS > MANGONEL
MANGOS > MANGO
MANGOSTAN n East Indian tree with thick leathery leaves and edible fruit
MANGOUSTE same as **>** MONGOOSE
MANGROVE n tropical tree with exposed roots, which grows beside water
MANGROVES > MANGROVE
MANGS > MANG
MANGULATE vb bend or twist out of shape
MANGY adj having mange
MANHANDLE vb treat roughly
MANHATTAN n mixed drink consisting of four parts whisky, one part vermouth, and a dash of bitters
MANHOLE n hole with a cover, through which a person can enter a drain or sewer
MANHOLES > MANHOLE
MANHOOD n state or quality of being a man or being manly
MANHOODS > MANHOOD
MANHUNT n organized search, usu by police, for a wanted man
MANHUNTER > MANHUNT
MANHUNTS > MANHUNT
MANI n place to pray
MANIA n extreme enthusiasm
MANIAC n person acting wildly
MANIACAL adj affected with or characteristic of mania

MANIACS > MANIAC

MANIAS > MANIA

MANIC adj extremely excited or energetic ▷ n person with mania

MANICALLY > MANIC

MANICOTTI pl n large tubular noodles, usually stuffed with ricotta cheese and baked in a tomato sauce

MANICS > MANIC

MANICURE n cosmetic care of the fingernails and hands ▷ vb care for (the fingernails and hands) in this way

MANICURED > MANICURE

MANICURES > MANICURE

MANIES > MANY

MANIFEST adj easily noticed, obvious ▷ vb show plainly ▷ n list of cargo or passengers for customs

MANIFESTO n declaration of policy as issued by a political party ▷ vb issued manifesto

MANIFESTS > MANIFEST

MANIFOLD adj numerous and varied ▷ n pipe with several outlets, esp in an internal-combustion engine ▷ vb duplicate (a page, book, etc)

MANIFOLDS > MANIFOLD

MANIFORM adj like hand

MANIHOC variation of > MANIOC

MANIHOCS > MANIHOC

MANIHOT n tropical American plant

MANIHOTS > MANIHOT

MANIKIN n little man or dwarf

MANIKINS > MANIKIN

MANILA n strong brown paper used for envelopes

MANILAS > MANILA

MANILLA n early currency in W Africa in the form of a small bracelet

MANILLAS > MANILLA

MANILLE n (in ombre and quadrille) the second best trump

MANILLES > MANILLE

MANIOC same as > CASSAVA

MANIOCA same as > MANIOC

MANIOCAS > MANIOCA

MANIOCS > MANIOC

MANIPLE n (in ancient Rome) a unit of 120 to 200 foot soldiers

MANIPLES > MANIPLE

MANIPLIES same as > MANYPLIES

MANIPULAR adj of or relating to an ancient Roman maniple

MANIS n pangolin

MANISES > MANIS

MANITO same as > MANITOU

MANITOS > MANITO

MANITOU n Native American deified spirit or force

MANITOUS > MANITOU

MANITU same as > MANITOU

MANITUS > MANITU

MANJACK n single individual

MANJACKS > MANJACK

MANKIER > MANKY

MANKIEST > MANKY

MANKIND n human beings collectively

MANKINDS > MANKIND

MANKINI n revealing man's swimming costume

MANKINIS > MANKINI

MANKY adj worthless, rotten, or in bad taste

MANLESS > MAN

MANLIER > MANLY

MANLIEST > MANLY

MANLIKE adj resembling or befitting a man

MANLIKELY > MANLIKE

MANLILY > MANLY

MANLINESS > MANLY

MANLY adj (possessing qualities) appropriate to a man

MANMADE adj made or produced by human beings

MANNA n miraculous food which sustained the Israelites in the wilderness

MANNAN n drug derived from mannose

MANNANS > MANNAN

MANNAS > MANNA

MANNED > MAN

MANNEQUIN n woman who models clothes at a fashion show

MANNER n way a thing happens or is done

MANNERED adj affected

MANNERISM n person's distinctive habit or trait

MANNERIST > MANNERISM

MANNERLY adj having good manners, polite ▷ adv with good manners

MANNERS pl n person's social conduct

MANNIKIN same as > MANIKIN

MANNIKINS > MANNIKIN

MANNING > MAN

MANNISH adj like a man

MANNISHLY > MANNISH

MANNITE same as > MANNITOL

MANNITES > MANNITE

MANNITIC > MANNITOL

MANNITOL n white crystalline water-soluble sweet-tasting substance

MANNITOLS > MANNITOL

MANNOSE n hexose sugar

MANNOSES > MANNOSE

MANO n stone for grinding grain

MANOAO n New Zealand shrub

MANOAOS > MANOAO

MANOES > MANO

MANOEUVER same as > MANOEUVRE

MANOEUVRE n skilful movement ▷ vb manipulate or contrive skilfully or cunningly

MANOMETER n instrument for comparing pressures

MANOMETRY > MANOMETER

MANOR n large country house and its lands

MANORIAL > MANOR

MANORS > MANOR

MANOS > MANO

MANOSCOPY n measurement of the densities of gases

MANPACK n load carried by one person

MANPACKS > MANPACK

MANPOWER n available number of workers

MANPOWERS > MANPOWER

MANQUE adj would-be ▷ n section on a roulette table

MANQUES > MANQUE

MANRED n homage

MANREDS > MANRED

MANRENT same as > MANRED

MANRENTS > MANRENT

MANRIDER n train carrying miners in coal mine

MANRIDERS > MANRIDER

MANRIDING adj carrying people rather than goods

MANROPE n rope railing

MANROPES > MANROPE

MANS > MAN

MANSARD n type of sloping roof

MANSARDED adj having mansard roof

MANSARDS > MANSARD

MANSCAPE vb groom a man's bodily hair for aesthetics

MANSCAPED > MANSCAPE

MANSCAPES > MANSCAPE

MANSE n house provided for a minister in some religious denominations

MANSES > MANSE

MANSHIFT n work done by one person in one shift

MANSHIFTS > MANSHIFT

MANSION n large house

MANSIONS > MANSION

MANSLAYER n person who kills a man

MANSONRY n mansions collectively

MANSPLAIN vb (of a man) explain something to a woman in a condescending way

MANSPREAD vb (of a man) sit with the legs wide apart, denying others space

MANSUETE adj gentle

MANSWORN adj perjured ▷ n someone who perjures

MANSWORNS > MANSWORN

MANTA n type of large ray with very wide winglike pectoral fins

MANTAS > MANTA

MANTEAU n cloak or mantle

MANTEAUS > MANTEAU

MANTEAUX > MANTEAU

MANTEEL n cloak

MANTEELS > MANTEEL

MANTEL n structure round a fireplace ▷ vb construct a mantel

MANTELET n woman's short mantle, often lace-trimmed, worn in the mid-19th century

MANTELETS > MANTELET

MANTELS > MANTEL

MANTES > MANTIS

MANTIC adj of or relating to divination and prophecy

MANTICORA same as > MANTICORE

MANTICORE n mythical monster with body of lion and human head

MANTID same as > MANTIS

MANTIDS > MANTID

MANTIES > MANTY

MANTILLA n (in Spain) a lace scarf covering a woman's head and shoulders

MANTILLAS > MANTILLA

MANTIS n carnivorous insect like a grasshopper

MANTISES > MANTIS

MANTISSA n part of a common logarithm consisting of the decimal point and the figures following it

MANTISSAS > MANTISSA

MANTLE same as > MANTEL

MANTLED > MANTLE

MANTLES > MANTLE

MANTLET same as > MANTELET

MANTLETS > MANTLET

MANTLING n drapery or scrollwork around a shield

MANTLINGS > MANTLING

MANTO same as > MANTEAU

MANTOES > MANTO

MANTOS > MANTO

MANTRA n any sacred word or syllable used as an object of concentration

MANTRAM same as > MANTRA

MANTRAMS > MANTRAM

MANTRAP n snare for catching people, esp trespassers

MANTRAPS > MANTRAP

MANTRAS > MANTRA

MANTRIC > MANTRA

MANTUA n loose gown of the 17th and 18th centuries

MANTUAS > MANTUA

MANTY Scots variant of > MANTUA

MANTYHOSE n tights that are worn by men

MANUAL adj of or done with the hands ▷ n handbook

MANUALLY > MANUAL

MANUALS > MANUAL

MANUARY same as > MANUAL

MANUBRIA > MANUBRIUM

MANUBRIAL > MANUBRIUM

MANUBRIUM n any handle-shaped part, esp the upper part of the sternum

MANUCODE n bird of Paradise with blue-black plumage

MANUCODES > MANUCODE

MANUHIRI n visitor to a Māori marae

MANUHIRIS > MANUHIRI

MANUKA n New Zealand tree

MANUKAS > MANUKA

MANUL n Asian wildcat

MANULS > MANUL

MANUMATIC adj relating to a type of automatic car transmission

MANUMEA n pigeon of Samoa

MANUMEAS > MANUMEA

MANUMIT vb free from slavery

MANUMITS > MANUMIT

MANURANCE n cultivation of land

MANURE n animal excrement used as a fertilizer ▷ vb fertilize (land) with this

MANURED > MANURE

MANURER > MANURE

MANURERS > MANURE

MANURES > MANURE

MANURIAL > MANURE

MANURING > MANURE

MANURINGS > MANURE

MANUS n wrist and hand

MANWARD adv towards humankind

MANWARDS same as > MANWARD

MANWISE adv in a human way

MANY adj numerous ▷ n large number

MANYATA same as > MANYATTA

MANYATAS > MANYATA

MANYATTA n settlement of Masai people

MANYATTAS > MANYATTA

MANYFOLD adj many in number

MANYPLIES n third component of the stomach of ruminants

MANZANITA n Californian plant

MANZELLO n instrument like saxophone

MANZELLOS > MANZELLO

MAOMAO n fish of New Zealand seas

MAOMAOS > MAOMAO

MAORMOR same as > MORMAOR

MAORMORS > MAORMOR

MAP n representation of the earth's surface or some part of it ▷ vb make a map of

MAPAU n small New Zealand tree

MAPAUS > MAPAU

MAPLE n tree with broad leaves, a variety of which yields sugar

MAPLELIKE > MAPLE

MAPLES > MAPLE

MAPLESS > MAP

MAPLIKE > MAP

MAPMAKER n person who draws maps

MAPMAKERS > MAPMAKER

MAPMAKING > MAPMAKER

MAPPABLE > MAP

MAPPED > MAP

MAPPEMOND n map of world

MAPPER > MAP

MAPPERIES > MAPPERY

MAPPERS > MAP

MAPPERY n making of maps

MAPPING > MAP

MAPPINGS > MAP

MAPPIST > MAP

MAPPISTS > MAP

MAPS > MAP

MAPSTICK same as > MOPSTICK

MAPSTICKS > MAPSTICK

MAPWISE adv like map

MAQUETTE n sculptor's small preliminary model or sketch

MAQUETTES > MAQUETTE

MAQUI n Chilean shrub

MAQUILA n US-owned factory in Mexico

MAQUILAS > MAQUILA

MAQUIS n French underground movement in World War II

MAQUISARD n member of French maquis

MAR vb spoil or impair ▷ n disfiguring mark

MARA n harelike S American rodent

MARABI n kind of music popular in S African townships in the 1930s

MARABIS > MARABI

MARABOU n large black-and-white African stork

MARABOUS > MARABOU

MARABOUT n Muslim holy man or hermit of North Africa

MARABOUTS > MARABOUT

MARABUNTA n any of several social wasps

MARACA n shaken percussion instrument

MARACAS > MARACA

MARAE n enclosed space in front of a Māori meeting house

MARAES > MARAE

MARAGING adj as in maraging steel strong low-carbon steel

MARAGINGS > MARAGING

MARAH n bitterness

MARAHS > MARAH

MARAKA > MARKA

MARANATHA n member of Christian sect

MARANTA n tropical American plant

MARANTAS > MARANTA

MARARI n eel-like blennioid food fish

MARARIS > MARARI

MARAS > MARA

MARASCA n European cherry tree with red acid-tasting fruit

MARASCAS > MARASCA

MARASMIC > MARASMUS

MARASMOID > MARASMUS

MARASMUS n emaciation

MARATHON n long-distance race of 26 miles 385 yards (42.195 kilometres) ▷ adj of or relating to a race on foot of 26 miles 385 yards (42.195 kilometres)

MARATHONS > MARATHON

MARAUD vb wander or raid in search of plunder

MARAUDED > MARAUD

MARAUDER > MARAUD

MARAUDERS > MARAUD

MARAUDING adj wandering or raiding in search of plunder

MARAUDS > MARAUD

MARAVEDI n any of various Spanish coins of copper or gold

MARAVEDIS > MARAVEDI

MARBELISE same as > MARBLEIZE

MARBELIZE same as > MARBLEIZE

MARBLE n kind of limestone with a mottled appearance ▷ vb mottle with variegated streaks in imitation of marble

MARBLED > MARBLE

MARBLEISE same as > MARBLEIZE

MARBLEIZE vb give a marble-like appearance to

MARBLER > MARBLE

MARBLERS > MARBLE

MARBLES n game in which marble balls are rolled at one another

MARBLIER > MARBLE

MARBLIEST > MARBLE

MARBLING n mottled effect or pattern resembling marble

MARBLINGS > MARBLING

MARBLY > MARBLE

MARC n remains of grapes or other fruit that have been pressed for wine-making

MARCASITE n crystals of iron pyrites, used in jewellery

MARCATO adj (of notes) heavily accented ▷ adv with each note heavily accented ▷ n heavily accented note

MARCATOS > MARCATO

MARCEL n hairstyle characterized by repeated regular waves ▷ vb make such waves in (the hair)

MARCELLA n type of fabric

MARCELLAS > MARCELLA

MARCELLED > MARCEL

MARCELLER > MARCEL

MARCELS > MARCEL

MARCH vb walk with a military step ▷ n action of marching

MARCHED > MARCH

MARCHEN n German story

MARCHER n person who marches

MARCHERS > MARCHER

MARCHES > MARCH

MARCHESA n (in Italy) the wife or widow of a marchese

MARCHESAS > MARCHESA

MARCHESE n (in Italy) a nobleman ranking below a prince and above a count

MARCHESI > MARCHESE

MARCHING > MARCH

MARCHLAND n border land

MARCHLIKE adj like march in rhythm

MARCHMAN n person living on border

MARCHMEN > MARCHMAN

MARCHPANE same as > MARZIPAN

MARCONI vb communicate by wireless

MARCONIED > MARCONI

MARCONIS > MARCONI

MARCS > MARC

MARD > MAR

MARDIED > MARDY

MARDIER > MARDY

MARDIES > MARDY

MARDIEST > MARDY

MARDY adj (of a child) spoilt ▷ vb behave in mardy way

MARDYING > MARDY

MARE n female horse or zebra

MAREMMA n marshy unhealthy region near the shore, esp in Italy

MAREMMAS > MAREMMA

MAREMME > MAREMMA

MARENGO adj browned in oil and cooked with tomatoes, mushrooms, garlic, wine, etc

MARERO n member of a C American organized criminal gang

MAREROS > MARERO

MARES > MARE

MARESCHAL same as > MARSHAL

MARG short for > MARGARINE

MARGARIC adj of or resembling pearl

MARGARIN n ester of margaric acid

MARGARINE n butter substitute made from animal or vegetable fats

MARGARINS > MARGARIN

MARGARITA n mixed drink consisting of tequila and lemon juice

MARGARITE n pink pearly micaceous mineral

MARGATE n greyish fish of W Atlantic

MARGATES > MARGATE

MARGAY n feline mammal of Central and S America

MARGAYS > MARGAY

MARGE n margarine

MARGENT same as > MARGIN

MARGENTED > MARGENT

MARGENTS > MARGENT

MARGES > MARGE

MARGIN n edge or border ▷ vb provide with a margin

MARGINAL adj insignificant, unimportant ▷ n marginal constituency

MARGINALS > MARGINAL

MARGINATE vb provide with a margin or margins ▷ adj having a margin of a distinct colour or form

MARGINED > MARGIN

MARGINING > MARGIN

MARGINS > MARGIN

MARGOSA n Indian tree

MARGOSAS > MARGOSA

MARGRAVE n (formerly) a German nobleman ranking above a count

MARGRAVES > MARGRAVE

MARGS > MARG

MARIA > MARE

MARIACHI n small ensemble of street musicians in Mexico

MARIACHIS > MARIACHI

MARIALITE n silicate mineral

MARID n spirit in Muslim mythology

MARIDS > MARID

MARIES > MARY

MARIGOLD n plant with yellow or orange flowers

MARIGOLDS > MARIGOLD

MARIGRAM n graphic record of the tide levels at a particular coastal station

MARIGRAMS > MARIGRAM

MARIGRAPH n gauge for recording the levels of the tides

MARIHUANA same as > MARIJUANA

MARIJUANA n dried flowers and leaves of the cannabis plant

MARIMBA n Latin American percussion instrument

MARIMBAS > MARIMBA

MARIMBIST > MARIMBA

MARINA n harbour for yachts and other pleasure boats

MARINADE n seasoned liquid in which fish or meat is soaked before cooking

MARINADED > MARINADE

MARINADES > MARINADE

MARINARA n Italian pasta sauce

MARINARAS > MARINARA

MARINAS > MARINA

MARINATE vb soak in marinade

MARINATED > MARINATE

MARINATES > MARINATE

MARINE adj of the sea or shipping ▷ n (esp in Britain and the US) soldier trained for land and sea combat

MARINER n sailor

MARINERA n folk dance of Peru

MARINERAS > MARINERA

MARINERS > MARINER

MARINES > MARINE

MARINIERE adj served in white wine and onion sauce

MARIPOSA n plant of southwestern US and Mexico

MARIPOSAS > MARIPOSA

MARISCHAL Scots variant of > MARSHAL

MARISH n marsh

MARISHES > MARISH

MARITAGE n right of a lord to choose the spouses of his wards

MARITAGES > MARITAGE

MARITAL adj relating to marriage

MARITALLY > MARITAL

MARITIME adj relating to shipping

MARJORAM n aromatic herb used for seasoning food and in salads

MARJORAMS > MARJORAM

MARK n line, dot, scar, etc visible on a surface ▷ vb make a mark on

MARKA n unit of currency introduced as an interim currency in Bosnia-Herzegovina

MARKAS > MARKA

MARKDOWN n price reduction ▷ vb reduce in price

MARKDOWNS > MARKDOWN

MARKED adj noticeable

MARKEDLY > MARKED

MARKER n object used to show the position of something

MARKERS > MARKER

MARKET n assembly or place for buying and selling ▷ vb offer or produce for sale

MARKETED > MARKET

MARKETEER n supporter of the European Union and of Britain's membership of it

MARKETER > MARKET

MARKETERS > MARKET

MARKETING n part of a business that controls the way that goods or services are sold

MARKETISE same as > MARKETIZE

MARKETIZE vb convert (a national economy) to a market economy

MARKETS > MARKET

MARKHOOR same as > MARKHOR

MARKHOORS > MARKHOOR

MARKHOR n large wild Himalayan goat

MARKHORS > MARKHOR

MARKING n arrangement of colours on an animal or plant

MARKINGS > MARKING

MARKKA n former standard monetary unit of Finland

MARKKAA > MARKKA

MARKKAS > MARKKA

MARKMAN n person owning land

MARKMEN > MARKMAN

MARKS > MARK

MARKSMAN n person skilled at shooting

MARKSMEN > MARKSMAN

MARKUP n percentage added to the cost of something to give the seller a profit

MARKUPS > MARKUP

MARL n soil formed of clay and lime, used as fertilizer ▷ vb fertilize (land) with marl

MARLE same as > MARVEL

MARLED > MARL

MARLES > MARLE

MARLIER > MARLY

MARLIEST > MARLY

MARLIN same as > MARLINE

MARLINE n light rope, usually tarred, made of two strands laid left-handed

MARLINES > MARLINE

MARLING same as > MARLINE

MARLINGS > MARLING

MARLINS > MARLIN

MARLITE n type of marl that contains clay and calcium carbonate

MARLITES > MARLITE

MARLITIC > MARLITE

MARLS > MARL

MARLSTONE same as > MARLITE

MARLY adj marl-like

MARM same as > MADAM

MARMALADE n jam made from citrus fruits ▷ adj (of cats) streaked orange or yellow and brown

MARMALISE vb beat soundly or defeat utterly

MARMALIZE same as > MARMALISE

MARMARISE same as > MARMARIZE

MARMARIZE vb turn to marble

MARMELISE same as > MARMELIZE

MARMELIZE vb beat soundly

MARMEM n as in marmem alloy type of alloy

MARMITE n large cooking pot

MARMITES > MARMITE

MARMOREAL adj of or like marble

MARMOREAN same as > MARMOREAL

MARMOSE n South American opossum

MARMOSES > MARMOSE

MARMOSET n small bushy-tailed monkey

MARMOSETS > MARMOSET

MARMOT n burrowing rodent

MARMOTS > MARMOT

MARMS > MARM

MAROCAIN n fabric of ribbed crepe

MAROCAINS > MAROCAIN

MARON n freshwater crustacean

MARONS > MARON

MAROON adj reddish-purple ▷ vb abandon ashore, esp on an island ▷ n exploding firework or flare used as a warning signal

MAROONED > MAROON

MAROONER > MAROON

MAROONERS > MAROON

MAROONING > MAROON

MAROONS > MAROON

MAROQUIN n morocco leather

MAROQUINS > MAROQUIN

MAROR n Jewish ceremonial dish of bitter herbs

MARORS > MAROR

MARPLOT n person who spoils a plot

MARPLOTS > MARPLOT

MARQUE n brand of product, esp of a car

MARQUEE n large tent used for a party or exhibition

MARQUEES > MARQUEE

MARQUES > MARQUE

MARQUESS n nobleman of the rank below a duke

MARQUETRY n ornamental inlaid work of wood

MARQUIS n (in some European countries) nobleman of the rank above a count

MARQUISE same as > MARQUEE

MARQUISES > MARQUISE

MARRA n (in N England) friend

MARRAM n as in marram grass any of several grasses that grow on sandy shores

MARRAMS > MARRAM

MARRANO n Spanish or Portuguese Jew of the late Middle Ages who was converted to Christianity

MARRANOS > MARRANO

MARRAS > MARRA

MARRED > MAR

MARRELS same as > MERILS

MARRER > MAR

MARRERS > MAR

MARRI n W Australian eucalyptus

MARRIAGE n state of being married

MARRIAGES > MARRIAGE

MARRIED > MARRY

MARRIEDS pl n married people

MARRIER > MARRY

MARRIERS > MARRY

MARRIES > MARRY

MARRING > MAR

MARRIS > MARRI

MARRON n large edible sweet chestnut

MARRONS > MARRON

MARROW n fatty substance inside bones ▷ vb be mate to

MARROWED > MARROW

MARROWFAT n variety of large pea

MARROWIER > MARROWY

MARROWING > MARROW

MARROWISH > MARROW

MARROWS > MARROW

MARROWSKY n spoonerism

MARROWY adj full of marrow

MARRUM same as > MARRAM

MARRUMS > MARRUM

MARRY vb take as a spouse ▷ interj exclamation of surprise or anger

MARRYING > MARRY

MARRYINGS > MARRY

MARS > MAR

MARSALA n dark sweet dessert wine made in Sicily

MARSALAS > MARSALA

MARSE same as > MASTER

MARSEILLE n strong cotton fabric with a raised pattern, used for bedspreads, etc

MARSES > MARSE

MARSH n low-lying wet land

MARSHAL n officer of the highest rank ▷ vb arrange in order

MARSHALCY > MARSHAL

MARSHALED > MARSHAL

MARSHALER > MARSHAL

MARSHALL n shortened form of Marshall Plan

MARSHALLS > MARSHALL
MARSHALS > MARSHAL
MARSHBUCK n antelope of the central African swamplands, with spreading hoofs adapted to boggy ground
MARSHED adj having a marsh
MARSHES > MARSH
MARSHIER > MARSHY
MARSHIEST > MARSHY
MARSHLAND n land consisting of marshes
MARSHLIKE > MARSH
MARSHWORT n type of creeping aquatic plant with small white flowers
MARSHY adj of, involving, or like a marsh
MARSPORT n spoilsport
MARSPORTS > MARSPORT
MARSQUAKE n Martian equivalent of earthquake
MARSUPIA > MARSUPIUM
MARSUPIAL n animal that carries its young in a pouch, such as a kangaroo ▷ adj of or like a marsupial
MARSUPIAN > MARSUPIAL
MARSUPIUM n external pouch in most female marsupials within which the newly born offspring are suckled and complete their development
MART n market ▷ vb sell or trade
MARTAGON n Eurasian lily plant cultivated for its mottled purplish-red flowers
MARTAGONS > MARTAGON
MARTED > MART
MARTEL n hammer-shaped weapon ▷ vb use such a weapon
MARTELLED > MARTEL
MARTELLO n small circular tower for coastal defence, formerly much used in Europe
MARTELLOS > MARTELLO
MARTELS > MARTEL
MARTEN n weasel-like animal
MARTENS > MARTEN
MARTEXT n preacher who makes many mistakes
MARTEXTS > MARTEXT
MARTIAL adj of war, warlike
MARTIALLY > MARTIAL
MARTIALS pl n as in court martials military courts that try people subject to military law
MARTIAN n inhabitant of Mars
MARTIANS > MARTIAN
MARTIN n bird with a slightly forked tail
MARTINET n person who maintains strict discipline
MARTINETS > MARTINET
MARTING > MART
MARTINGAL n strap of a horse's harness
MARTINI n cocktail of vermouth and gin
MARTINIS > MARTINI

MARTINS > MARTIN
MARTLET n footless bird often found in coats of arms
MARTLETS > MARTLET
MARTS > MART
MARTYR n person who dies or suffers for his or her beliefs ▷ vb make a martyr of
MARTYRDOM n sufferings or death of a martyr
MARTYRED > MARTYR
MARTYRIA > MARTYRIUM
MARTYRIES > MARTYRY
MARTYRING > MARTYR
MARTYRISE > MARTYR
MARTYRISH adj like a martyr
MARTYRIUM same as **> MARTYRY**
MARTYRIZE > MARTYR
MARTYRLY > MARTYR
MARTYRS > MARTYR
MARTYRY n shrine or chapel erected in honour of a martyr
MARVEL vb be filled with wonder ▷ n wonderful thing
MARVELED > MARVEL
MARVELER n (US) person who marvels
MARVELERS > MARVELER
MARVELING > MARVEL
MARVELLED > MARVEL
MARVELLER n person who marvels
MARVELOUS adj causing great wonder
MARVELS > MARVEL
MARVER vb roll molten glass on slab
MARVERED > MARVER
MARVERING > MARVER
MARVERS > MARVER
MARVIER > MARVY
MARVIEST > MARVY
MARVY shortened form of **> MARVELOUS**
MARXISANT adj sympathetic to Marxism
MARY n woman
MARYBUD n bud of marigold
MARYBUDS > MARYBUD
MARYJANE n woman's shoe with strap over the top
MARYJANES > MARYJANE
MARZIPAN n paste of ground almonds, sugar, and egg whites ▷ vb cover with marzipan
MARZIPANS > MARZIPAN
MAS > MA
MASA n Mexican maize dough
MASALA n mixture of spices ground into a paste ▷ adj spicy
MASALAS > MASALA
MASAS > MASA
MASCARA n cosmetic for darkening the eyelashes
MASCARAED adj wearing mascara
MASCARAS > MASCARA
MASCARON n in architecture, a face carved in stone or metal
MASCARONS n grotesque face used as decoration

MASCLE n charge consisting of a lozenge with a lozenge-shaped hole in the middle
MASCLED > MASCLE
MASCLES > MASCLE
MASCON n any of several lunar regions of high gravity
MASCONS > MASCON
MASCOT n person, animal, or thing supposed to bring good luck
MASCOTS > MASCOT
MASCULINE adj relating to males
MASCULIST n advocate of rights of men)
MASCULY > MASCLE
MASE vb function as maser
MASED > MASE
MASER n device for amplifying microwaves
MASERS > MASER
MASES > MASE
MASH n soft pulpy mass ▷ vb crush into a soft mass
MASHALLAH interj what Allah wishes
MASHED > MASH
MASHER > MASH
MASHERS > MASH
MASHES > MASH
MASHGIACH n person who ensures adherence to kosher rules
MASHGIAH same as **> MASHGIACH**
MASHGIHIM > MASHGIACH
MASHIACH n messiah
MASHIACHS > MASHIACH
MASHIE n former golf club, used for approach shots
MASHIER > MASHY
MASHIES > MASHIE
MASHIEST > MASHY
MASHING > MASH
MASHINGS > MASH
MASHLAM same as **> MASLIN**
MASHLAMS > MASHLAM
MASHLIM same as **> MASLIN**
MASHLIMS > MASHLIM
MASHLIN same as **> MASLIN**
MASHLINS > MASHLIN
MASHLOCH same as **> MASLIN**
MASHLOCHS > MASHLOCH
MASHLUM same as **> MASLIN**
MASHLUMS > MASHLUM
MASHMAN n brewery worker
MASHMEN > MASHMAN
MASHUA n South American plant
MASHUAS > MASHUA
MASHUP n piece of music in which a producer or DJ blends together two or more tracks
MASHUPS > MASHUP
MASHY adj like mash
MASING > MASE
MASJID same as **> MOSQUE**
MASJIDS > MASJID
MASK n covering for the face, as a disguise or protection ▷ vb cover with a mask
MASKABLE > MASK
MASKED adj disguised or covered by or as if by a mask

MASKEG n North American bog
MASKEGS > MASKEG
MASKER n person who wears a mask or takes part in a masque
MASKERS > MASKER
MASKING n act or practice of masking
MASKINGS > MASKING
MASKLIKE > MASK
MASKS > MASK
MASLIN n mixture of wheat, rye or other grain
MASLINS > MASLIN
MASOCHISM n gaining of pleasure from feeling pain or humiliation
MASOCHIST > MASOCHISM
MASON n person who works with stone ▷ vb construct or strengthen with masonry
MASONED > MASON
MASONIC adj of, characteristic of, or relating to Freemasons
MASONING > MASON
MASONITE n tradename for a kind of dark brown hardboard used for partitions, lining, etc
MASONITES > MASONITE
MASONRIED adj built of masonry
MASONRIES > MASONRY
MASONRY n stonework
MASONS > MASON
MASOOLAH n Indian boat used in surf
MASOOLAHS > MASOOLAH
MASQUE n 16th–17th-century form of dramatic entertainment
MASQUER same as **> MASKER**
MASQUERS > MASQUER
MASQUES > MASQUE
MASS n coherent body of matter ▷ adj large-scale ▷ vb form into a mass
MASSA old fashioned variant of **> MASTER**
MASSACRE n indiscriminate killing of large numbers of people ▷ vb kill in large numbers
MASSACRED > MASSACRE
MASSACRER > MASSACRE
MASSACRES > MASSACRE
MASSAGE n rubbing and kneading of parts of the body to reduce pain or stiffness ▷ vb give a massage to
MASSAGED > MASSAGE
MASSAGER > MASSAGE
MASSAGERS > MASSAGE
MASSAGES > MASSAGE
MASSAGING > MASSAGE
MASSAGIST > MASSAGE
MASSAS > MASSA
MASSCULT n culture of masses
MASSCULTS > MASSCULT
MASSE n billiard stroke that makes the ball move in a curve around another ball
MASSED > MASS
MASSEDLY > MASS

MASSES pl n body of common people

MASSETER n muscle of the cheek used in moving the jaw, esp in chewing

MASSETERS > MASSETER

MASSEUR n person who gives massages

MASSEURS > MASSEUR

MASSEUSE n woman who gives massages, esp as a profession

MASSEUSES > MASSEUSE

MASSICOT n yellow earthy secondary mineral

MASSICOTS > MASSICOT

MASSIER > MASSY

MASSIEST > MASSY

MASSIF n connected group of mountains

MASSIFS > MASSIF

MASSINESS > MASSY

MASSING > MASS

MASSIVE adj large and heavy ▷ n group of friends or associates

MASSIVELY > MASSIVE

MASSIVES > MASSIVE

MASSLESS > MASS

MASSOOLA same as > MASOOLAH

MASSOOLAS > MASSOOLA

MASSTIGE n impression of exclusivity in mass-produced goods

MASSTIGES > MASSTIGE

MASSY literary word for > MASSIVE

MASSYMORE n underground prison

MAST n tall pole for supporting something, esp a ship's sails ▷ vb equip with a mast

MASTABA n mud-brick superstructure above tombs in ancient Egypt

MASTABAH same as > MASTABA

MASTABAHS > MASTABAH

MASTABAS > MASTABA

MASTED > MAST

MASTER n person in control, such as an employer or an owner of slaves or animals ▷ vb acquire knowledge of or skill in

MASTERATE n status of master

MASTERDOM > MASTER

MASTERED > MASTER

MASTERFUL adj domineering

MASTERIES > MASTERY

MASTERING > MASTER

MASTERLY adj showing great skill

MASTERS > MASTER

MASTERY n expertise

MASTFUL > MAST

MASTHEAD n head of a mast ▷ vb send (a sailor) to the masthead as a punishment

MASTHEADS > MASTHEAD

MASTHOUSE n place for storing masts

MASTIC n gum obtained from certain trees

MASTICATE vb chew

MASTICH same as > MASTIC

MASTICHE same as > MASTIC

MASTICHES > MASTICHE

MASTICHS > MASTICH

MASTICOT same as > MASSICOT

MASTICOTS > MASTICOT

MASTICS > MASTIC

MASTIER > MASTY

MASTIEST > MASTY

MASTIFF n large dog

MASTIFFS > MASTIFF

MASTING > MAST

MASTITIC > MASTITIS

MASTITIS n inflammation of a breast or udder

MASTIX n type of gum

MASTIXES > MASTIX

MASTLESS > MAST

MASTLIKE > MAST

MASTODON n extinct elephant-like mammal

MASTODONS > MASTODON

MASTODONT same as > MASTODON

MASTOID n projection of the bone behind the ear ▷ adj shaped like a nipple or breast

MASTOIDAL > MASTOID

MASTOIDS > MASTOID

MASTOPEXY n cosmetic surgery of breasts

MASTS > MAST

MASTY > MAST

MASU n Japanese salmon

MASULA same as > MASOOLAH

MASULAS > MASULA

MASURIUM n silver-grey metallic element

MASURIUMS > MASURIUM

MASUS > MASU

MAT n piece of fabric used as a floor covering or to protect a surface ▷ vb tangle or become tangled into a dense mass ▷ adj having a dull, lustreless, or roughened surface

MATACHIN n dancer with sword

MATACHINA n female matachin

MATACHINI > MATACHIN

MATACHINS > MATACHIN

MATADOR n bullfighter who kills the bull

MATADORA n female matador

MATADORAS > MATADORA

MATADORE n form of dominoes game

MATADORES > MATADORE

MATADORS > MATADOR

MATAGOURI n thorny bush of New Zealand that forms thickets in open country

MATAI n New Zealand tree, the wood of which is used for timber for building

MATAIS > MATAI

MATAMATA (in Malaysia) a former name for > POLICE

MATAMATAS > MATAMATA

MATAMBALA > TAMBALA

MATATA same as > FERNBIRD

MATATAS > MATATA

MATATU n type of shared taxi used in Kenya

MATATUS > MATATU

MATCH n contest in a game or sport ▷ vb be exactly like, equal to, or in harmony with

MATCHA n Japanese green tea

MATCHABLE > MATCH

MATCHAS > MATCHA

MATCHBOOK n number of cardboard matches attached in folder

MATCHBOX n small box for holding matches

MATCHED > MATCH

MATCHER > MATCH

MATCHERS > MATCH

MATCHES > MATCH

MATCHET same as > MACHETE

MATCHETS > MATCHET

MATCHING > MATCH

MATCHLESS adj unequalled

MATCHLOCK n obsolete type of gunlock igniting the powder by means of a slow match

MATCHMADE > MATCHMAKE

MATCHMAKE vb bring suitable people together for marriage

MATCHMARK n mark made on mating components of an engine, machine, etc, to ensure that the components are assembled in the correct relative positions ▷ vb stamp (an object) with matchmarks

MATCHPLAY adj of a golf scoring system relating to holes won and lost ▷ n (in golf) scoring system in which a point is earned for each hole won

MATCHUP n sports match

MATCHUPS > MATCHUP

MATCHWOOD n small splinters

MATE n friend ▷ vb pair (animals) or (of animals) be paired for reproduction

MATED > MATE

MATELASSE adj (in textiles) having a raised design, as quilting

MATELESS > MATE

MATELOT n sailor

MATELOTE n fish served with a sauce of wine, onions, seasonings, and fish stock

MATELOTES > MATELOTE

MATELOTS > MATELOT

MATELOTTE same as > MATELOTE

MATER n mother: often used facetiously

MATERIAL n substance of which a thing is made ▷ adj of matter or substance

MATERIALS pl n equipment necessary for a particular activity

MATERIEL n materials and equipment of an organization, esp of a military force

MATERIELS > MATERIEL

MATERNAL adj of a mother

MATERNITY n motherhood ▷ adj of or for pregnant women

MATERS > MATER

MATES > MATE

MATESHIP n comradeship of friends, usually male, viewed as an institution

MATESHIPS > MATESHIP

MATEY adj friendly or intimate ▷ n friend or fellow: usually used in direct address

MATEYNESS > MATEY

MATEYS > MATEY

MATFELLON n knapweed

MATFELON n knapweed

MATFELONS > MATFELON

MATGRASS n widespread European grass

MATH same as > MATHS

MATHESES > MATHESIS

MATHESIS n learning or wisdom

MATHS n science concerned with the study of numbers

MATICO n Peruvian shrub

MATICOS > MATICO

MATIER > MATEY

MATIES > MATEY

MATIEST > MATEY

MATILDA n bushman's swag

MATILDAS > MATILDA

MATILY > MATEY

MATIN adj of or relating to matins

MATINAL same as > MATIN

MATINEE n afternoon performance in a theatre or cinema

MATINEES > MATINEE

MATINESS > MATY

MATING > MATE

MATINGS > MATE

MATINS pl n early morning church service

MATIPO n New Zealand shrub

MATIPOS > MATIPO

MATJES same as > MAATJES

MATLESS > MAT

MATLO same as > MATELOT

MATLOS > MATLO

MATLOW same as > MATELOT

MATLOWS > MATLOW

MATOKE n (in Uganda) the flesh of bananas, boiled and mashed as a food

MATOKES > MATOKE

MATOOKE same as > MATOKE

MATOOKES > MATOOKE

MATRASS n long-necked glass flask

MATRASSES > MATRASS

MATRES > MATER

MATRIARCH n female head of a tribe or family

MATRIC n matriculation

MATRICE same as > MATRIX

MATRICES > MATRIX

MATRICIDE n crime of killing one's mother

MATRICS > MATRIC

MATRICULA n register

MATRILINY n attention to descent of kinship through the female line
MATRIMONY n marriage
MATRIX n substance or situation in which something originates, takes form, or is enclosed
MATRIXES > MATRIX
MATRON n staid or dignified married woman
MATRONAGE n state of being a matron
MATRONAL > MATRON
MATRONISE same as > MATRONIZE
MATRONIZE vb make matronly
MATRONLY adj (of a woman) middle-aged and plump
MATRONS > MATRON
MATROSS n gunner's assistant
MATROSSES > MATROSS
MATS > MAT
MATSAH same as > MATZO
MATSAHS > MATSAH
MATSURI n Japanese religious ceremony
MATSURIS > MATSURI
MATSUTAKE n Japanese mushroom
MATT adj dull, not shiny ▷ n dull surface
MATTAMORE n subterranean storehouse or dwelling
MATTE same as > MATT
MATTED > MAT
MATTEDLY > MAT
MATTER n substance of which something is made ▷ vb be of importance
MATTERED > MATTER
MATTERFUL > MATTER
MATTERIER > MATTERY
MATTERING > MATTER
MATTERS > MATTER
MATTERY adj containing pus
MATTES > MATTE
MATTIE n young herring
MATTIES > MATTIE
MATTIFIED > MATTIFY
MATTIFIES > MATTIFY
MATTIFY vb make (the skin of the face) less oily or shiny using cosmetics
MATTIN same as > MATIN
MATTING > MAT
MATTINGS > MAT
MATTINS same as > MATINS
MATTOCK n large pick with one of its blade ends flattened for loosening soil
MATTOCKS > MATTOCK
MATTOID n person displaying eccentric behaviour
MATTOIDS > MATTOID
MATTRASS same as > MATRASS
MATTRESS n large stuffed flat case, often with springs, used on or as a bed
MATTS > MATT
MATURABLE > MATURE
MATURATE vb mature or bring to maturity

MATURATED > MATURATE
MATURATES > MATURATE
MATURE adj fully developed or grown-up ▷ vb make or become mature
MATURED > MATURE
MATURELY > MATURE
MATURER > MATURE
MATURERS > MATURE
MATURES > MATURE
MATUREST > MATURE
MATURING > MATURE
MATURITY n state of being mature
MATUTINAL adj of, occurring in, or during the morning
MATUTINE same as > MATUTINAL
MATWEED n grass found on moors
MATWEEDS > MATWEED
MATY same as > MATEY
MATZA same as > MATZO
MATZAH same as > MATZO
MATZAHS > MATZAH
MATZAS > MATZA
MATZO n large very thin biscuit of unleavened bread
MATZOH same as > MATZO
MATZOHS > MATZOH
MATZOON n fermented milk product similar to yogurt
MATZOONS > MATZOON
MATZOS > MATZO
MATZOT > MATZO
MATZOTH > MATZOH
MAUBIES > MAUBY
MAUBY n Caribbean bittersweet drink
MAUD n shawl or rug of grey wool plaid
MAUDLIN adj foolishly or tearfully sentimental
MAUDLINLY > MAUDLIN
MAUDS > MAUD
MAUGER same as > MAUGRE
MAUGRE prep in spite of ▷ vb behave spitefully towards
MAUGRED > MAUGRE
MAUGRES > MAUGRE
MAUGRING > MAUGRE
MAUL vb handle roughly ▷ n loose scrum
MAULED > MAUL
MAULER > MAUL
MAULERS pl n hands
MAULGRE same as > MAUGRE
MAULGRED > MAULGRE
MAULGRES > MAULGRE
MAULGRING > MAULGRE
MAULING n act of mauling
MAULINGS > MAULING
MAULS > MAUL
MAULSTICK n long stick used by artists to steady the hand holding the brush
MAULVI n expert in Islamic law
MAULVIS > MAULVI
MAUMET n false god
MAUMETRY > MAUMET
MAUMETS > MAUMET
MAUN dialect word for > MUST
MAUND n unit of weight used in Asia ▷ vb beg
MAUNDED > MAUND

MAUNDER vb talk or act aimlessly or idly
MAUNDERED > MAUNDER
MAUNDERER > MAUNDER
MAUNDERS > MAUNDER
MAUNDIES > MAUNDY
MAUNDING > MAUND
MAUNDS > MAUND
MAUNDY n ceremonial washing of the feet of poor people
MAUNGIER > MAUNGY
MAUNGIEST > MAUNGY
MAUNGY adj (esp of a child) sulky, bad-tempered, or peevish
MAUNNA vb Scots term meaning must not
MAURI n soul
MAURIS > MAURI
MAUSIER > MAUSY
MAUSIEST > MAUSY
MAUSOLEA > MAUSOLEUM
MAUSOLEAN > MAUSOLEUM
MAUSOLEUM n stately tomb
MAUSY adj foggy; misty
MAUT same as > MAHOUT
MAUTHER n girl
MAUTHERS > MAUTHER
MAUTS > MAUT
MAUVAIS adj bad
MAUVAISE feminine form of > MAUVAIS
MAUVE adj pale purple ▷ n any of various pale purple colours
MAUVEIN same as > MAUVEINE
MAUVEINE same as > MAUVE
MAUVEINES > MAUVEINE
MAUVEINS > MAUVEIN
MAUVER > MAUVE
MAUVES > MAUVE
MAUVEST > MAUVE
MAUVIN same as > MAUVEINE
MAUVINE same as > MAUVEINE
MAUVINES > MAUVINE
MAUVINS > MAUVIN
MAUZIER > MAUZY
MAUZIEST > MAUZY
MAUZY adj foggy; misty
MAVEN n expert or connoisseur
MAVENS > MAVEN
MAVERICK adj independent and unorthodox (person) ▷ n person of independent or unorthodox views ▷ vb take illegally
MAVERICKS > MAVERICK
MAVIE n type of thrush
MAVIES > MAVIE
MAVIN same as > MAVEN
MAVINS > MAVIN
MAVIS n song thrush
MAVISES > MAVIS
MAVOURNIN n Irish form of address meaning my darling
MAW n animal's mouth, throat, or stomach ▷ vb eat or bite
MAWBOUND adj (of cattle) constipated
MAWED > MAW

MAWGER adj (of persons or animals) thin or lean
MAWING > MAW
MAWK n maggot
MAWKIER > MAWK
MAWKIEST > MAWK
MAWKIN n slovenly woman
MAWKINS > MAWKIN
MAWKISH adj foolishly sentimental
MAWKISHLY > MAWKISH
MAWKS > MAWK
MAWKY > MAWK
MAWMET same as > MAUMET
MAWMETRY > MAWMET
MAWMETS > MAWMET
MAWN n measure of capacity
MAWNS > MAWN
MAWPUS same as > MOPUS
MAWPUSES > MAWPUS
MAWR same as > MAUTHER
MAWRS > MAWR
MAWS > MAW
MAWSEED n poppy seed
MAWSEEDS > MAWSEED
MAWTHER same as > MAUTHER
MAWTHERS > MAWTHER
MAX vb reach the full extent
MAXED > MAX
MAXES > MAX
MAXI adj (of a garment) very long ▷ n type of large racing yacht
MAXIBOAT n large racing yacht
MAXIBOATS > MAXIBOAT
MAXICOAT n long coat
MAXICOATS > MAXICOAT
MAXIDRESS n dress that reaches the ankle
MAXILLA n upper jawbone of a vertebrate
MAXILLAE > MAXILLA
MAXILLAR > MAXILLA
MAXILLARY > MAXILLA
MAXILLAS > MAXILLA
MAXILLULA n jaw in crustacean
MAXIM n general truth or principle
MAXIMA > MAXIMUM
MAXIMAL adj maximum ▷ n maximum
MAXIMALLY > MAXIMAL
MAXIMALS > MAXIMAL
MAXIMAND n something that is to be maximized
MAXIMANDS > MAXIMAND
MAXIMIN n highest of a set of minimum values
MAXIMINS > MAXIMIN
MAXIMISE same as > MAXIMIZE
MAXIMISED > MAXIMISE
MAXIMISER > MAXIMIZE
MAXIMISES > MAXIMISE
MAXIMIST > MAXIM
MAXIMISTS > MAXIM
MAXIMITE n type of explosive
MAXIMITES > MAXIMITE
MAXIMIZE vb increase to a maximum
MAXIMIZED > MAXIMIZE
MAXIMIZER > MAXIMIZE

m

MAXIMIZES > MAXIMIZE
MAXIMS > MAXIM
MAXIMUM n greatest possible (amount or number) ▷ adj of, being, or showing a maximum or maximums
MAXIMUMLY > MAXIMUM
MAXIMUMS > MAXIMUM
MAXIMUS n method rung on twelve bells
MAXIMUSES > MAXIMUS
MAXING > MAX
MAXIS > MAXI
MAXIXE n Brazilian dance in duple time
MAXIXES > MAXIXE
MAXWELL n cgs unit of magnetic flux
MAXWELLS > MAXWELL
MAY vb used as an auxiliary to express possibility, permission, opportunity, etc ▷ vb gather may (hawthorn)
MAYA n illusion, esp the material world of the senses regarded as illusory
MAYAN > MAYA
MAYAPPLE n American plant
MAYAPPLES > MAYAPPLE
MAYAS > MAYA
MAYBE adv perhaps, possibly ▷ sentence substitute possibly ▷ n possibility
MAYBES > MAYBE
MAYBIRD n American songbird
MAYBIRDS > MAYBIRD
MAYBUSH n flowering shrub
MAYBUSHES > MAYBUSH
MAYDAY n international radiotelephone distress signal
MAYDAYS > MAYDAY
MAYED > MAY
MAYEST same as > MAYST
MAYFISH n type of N American fish
MAYFISHES > MAYFISH
MAYFLIES > MAYFLY
MAYFLOWER n any of various plants that bloom in May
MAYFLY n short-lived aquatic insect
MAYHAP archaic word for > PERHAPS
MAYHAPPEN same as > MAYHAP
MAYHEM n violent destruction or confusion
MAYHEMS > MAYHEM
MAYING > MAY
MAYINGS > MAYING
MAYO n mayonnaise
MAYOR n head of a municipality
MAYORAL > MAYOR
MAYORALTY n (term of) office of a mayor
MAYORESS n mayor's wife
MAYORS > MAYOR
MAYORSHIP > MAYOR
MAYOS > MAYO
MAYPOLE n pole set up for dancing round on the first day of May to celebrate spring
MAYPOLES > MAYPOLE

MAYPOP n American wild flower
MAYPOPS > MAYPOP
MAYS > MAY
MAYST singular form of the present tense of > MAY
MAYSTER same as > MASTER
MAYSTERS > MAYSTER
MAYVIN same as > MAVEN
MAYVINS > MAYVIN
MAYWEED n widespread Eurasian weedy plant
MAYWEEDS > MAYWEED
MAZAEDIA > MAZAEDIUM
MAZAEDIUM n part of lichen
MAZARD same as > MAZER
MAZARDS > MAZARD
MAZARINE n blue colour
MAZARINES > MAZARINE
MAZE n complex network of paths or lines
MAZED > MAZE
MAZEDLY adv in a bewildered way
MAZEDNESS n bewilderment
MAZEFUL > MAZE
MAZELIKE > MAZE
MAZELTOV interj congratulations
MAZEMENT > MAZE
MAZEMENTS > MAZE
MAZER n large hardwood drinking bowl
MAZERS > MAZER
MAZES > MAZE
MAZEY adj dizzy
MAZHBI n low-caste Sikh
MAZHBIS > MAZHBI
MAZIER > MAZY
MAZIEST > MAZY
MAZILY > MAZY
MAZINESS > MAZY
MAZING > MAZE
MAZOURKA same as > MAZURKA
MAZOURKAS > MAZOURKA
MAZOUT same as > MAZUT
MAZOUTS > MAZOUT
MAZUMA n money
MAZUMAS > MAZUMA
MAZURKA n lively Polish dance
MAZURKAS > MAZURKA
MAZUT n residue left after distillation of petrol
MAZUTS > MAZUT
MAZY adj of or like a maze
MAZZARD same as > MAZARD
MAZZARDS > MAZZARD
MBAQANGA n style of Black popular music of urban South Africa
MBAQANGAS > MBAQANGA
MBIRA n African musical instrument
MBIRAS > MBIRA
ME n (in tonic sol-fa) third degree of any major scale ▷ pron refers to the speaker or writer
MEACOCK n timid person
MEACOCKS > MEACOCK
MEAD n alcoholic drink made from honey
MEADOW n piece of grassland
MEADOWIER > MEADOWY

MEADOWS > MEADOW
MEADOWY adj consisting of meadows
MEADS > MEAD
MEAGER same as > MEAGRE
MEAGERER > MEAGER
MEAGEREST > MEAGER
MEAGERLY > MEAGRE
MEAGRE adj scanty or insufficient ▷ n Mediterranean fish
MEAGRELY > MEAGRE
MEAGRER > MEAGRE
MEAGRES > MEAGRE
MEAGREST > MEAGRE
MEAL n occasion when food is served and eaten ▷ vb cover with meal
MEALED > MEAL
MEALER n person eating but not lodging at boarding house
MEALERS > MEALER
MEALIE n maize
MEALIER > MEALY
MEALIES > MEALIE
MEALIEST > MEALY
MEALINESS > MEALY
MEALING > MEAL
MEALLESS > MEAL
MEALS > MEAL
MEALTIME n time for meal
MEALTIMES > MEALTIME
MEALWORM n larva of various beetles which feeds on meal, flour, and similar stored foods
MEALWORMS > MEALWORM
MEALY adj resembling meal
MEALYBUG n plant-eating homopterous insect
MEALYBUGS > MEALYBUG
MEAN vb intend to convey or express ▷ adj miserly, ungenerous, or petty ▷ n middle point between two extremes
MEANDER vb follow a winding course ▷ n winding course
MEANDERED > MEANDER
MEANDERER > MEANDER
MEANDERS > MEANDER
MEANDRIAN > MEANDER
MEANDROUS > MEANDER
MEANE vb moan
MEANED > MEANE
MEANER > MEAN
MEANERS > MEAN
MEANES > MEANE
MEANEST > MEAN
MEANIE n unkind or miserly person
MEANIES > MEANIE
MEANING n what something means
MEANINGLY > MEAN
MEANINGS > MEANING
MEANLY > MEAN
MEANNESS > MEAN
MEANS > MEAN
MEANT > MEAN
MEANTIME n intervening period ▷ adv meanwhile
MEANTIMES > MEANTIME
MEANWHILE adv during the intervening period

MEANY same as > MEANIE
MEARE same as > MERE
MEARES > MEARE
MEARING adj forming boundary
MEASE vb assuage
MEASED > MEASE
MEASES > MEASE
MEASLNG > MEASE
MEASLE vb infect with measles
MEASLED adj (of cattle, sheep, or pigs) infested with tapeworm larvae
MEASLES n infectious disease producing red spots
MEASLIER > MEASLY
MEASLIEST > MEASLY
MEASLING > MEASLE
MEASLY adj meagre
MEASURE n size or quantity ▷ vb determine the size or quantity of
MEASURED adj slow and teady
MEASURER > MEASURE
MEASURERS > MEASURE
MEASURES pl n rock strata that contain a particular type of deposit
MEASURING adj used to measure quantities, esp in cooking
MEAT n animal flesh as food
MEATAL > MEATUS
MEATAXE n meat cleaver
MEATAXES > MEATAXE
MEATBALL n minced beef, shaped into a ball before cooking
MEATBALLS > MEATBALL
MEATED adj fattened
MEATH same as > MEAD
MEATHE same as > MEAD
MEATHEAD n stupid person
MEATHEADS > MEATHEAD
MEATHES > MEATHE
MEATHOOK n hook on which to hang meat
MEATHOOKS > MEATHOOK
MEATHS > MEATH
MEATIER > MEATY
MEATIEST > MEATY
MEATILY > MEATY
MEATINESS > MEATY
MEATLESS > MEAT
MEATLOAF n chopped meat served in loaf-shaped mass
MEATMAN n meat seller
MEATMEN > MEATMAN
MEATS > MEAT
MEATSPACE n real physical world, as contrasted with the world of cyberspace
MEATUS n natural opening or channel
MEATUSES > MEATUS
MEATY adj (tasting) of or like meat
MEAWES same as > MEWS
MEAZEL same as > MESEL
MEAZELS > MEAZEL
MEBIBYTE n 2^{20} bytes
MEBIBYTES > MEBIBYTE
MEBOS n South African dish of dried apricots
MEBOSES > MEBOS

m

m

MECCA n place that attracts many visitors

MECCAS > MECCA

MECH n mechanic

MECHANIC n person skilled in repairing or operating machinery

MECHANICS n scientific study of motion and force

MECHANISE same as > MECHANIZE

MECHANISM n way a machine works

MECHANIST same as > MECHANIC

MECHANIZE vb equip with machinery

MECHITZA n screen in synagogue separating men and women

MECHITZAS > MECHITZA

MECHITZOT > MECHITZA

MECHOUI n Canadian dish of meat roasted on a spit

MECHOUIS > MECHOUI

MECHS > MECH

MECK same as > MAIK

MECKS > MECK

MECLIZINE n drug used to treat motion sickness

MECONATE n salt of meconic acid

MECONATES > MECONATE

MECONIC adj derived from poppies

MECONIN n substance found in opium

MECONINS > MECONIN

MECONIUM n dark green mucoid material that forms the first faeces of a newborn infant

MECONIUMS > MECONIUM

MED n doctor

MEDACCA n Japanese freshwater fish

MEDACCAS > MEDACCA

MEDAILLON n small round thin piece of food

MEDAKA same as > MEDACCA

MEDAKAS > MEDAKA

MEDAL n piece of metal with an inscription etc, given as a reward or memento ▷ vb honour with a medal

MEDALED > MEDAL

MEDALET n small medal

MEDALETS > MEDALET

MEDALING > MEDAL

MEDALIST same as > MEDALLIST

MEDALISTS > MEDALIST

MEDALLED > MEDAL

MEDALLIC > MEDAL

MEDALLING > MEDAL

MEDALLION n disc-shaped ornament worn on a chain round the neck

MEDALLIST n winner of a medal

MEDALPLAY n (in golf) scoring system in which the score is based on the total number of strokes taken

MEDALS > MEDAL

MEDCINAL same as > MEDICINAL

MEDDLE vb interfere annoyingly

MEDDLED > MEDDLE

MEDDLER > MEDDLE

MEDDLERS > MEDDLE

MEDDLES > MEDDLE

MEDDLING > MEDDLE

MEDDLINGS > MEDDLE

MEDEVAC n evacuation of casualties ▷ vb transport (a wounded or sick person) to hospital

MEDEVACED > MEDEVAC

MEDEVACS > MEDEVAC

MEDFLIES > MEDFLY

MEDFLY n Mediterranean fruit fly

MEDIA n medium of cultivation, conveyance, or expression

MEDIACIES > MEDIACY

MEDIACY n quality or state of being mediate

MEDIAD adj situated near the median line or plane of an organism

MEDIAE > MEDIA

MEDIAEVAL adj of, relating to, or in the style of the Middle Ages ▷ n person living in medieval times

MEDIAL adj of or in the middle ▷ n speech sound between being fortis and lenis

MEDIALLY > MEDIAL

MEDIALS > MEDIAL

MEDIAN n middle (point or line) ▷ adj of, relating to, situated in, or directed towards the middle

MEDIANLY > MEDIAN

MEDIANS > MEDIAN

MEDIANT n third degree of a major or minor scale

MEDIANTS > MEDIANT

MEDIAS > MEDIA

MEDIATE vb intervene in a dispute to bring about agreement ▷ adj occurring as a result of or dependent upon mediation

MEDIATED > MEDIATE

MEDIATELY > MEDIATE

MEDIATES > MEDIATE

MEDIATING > MEDIATE

MEDIATION n act of mediating

MEDIATISE same as > MEDIATIZE

MEDIATIVE > MEDIATE

MEDIATIZE vb annex (a state) to another state, allowing the former ruler to retain their title and some authority

MEDIATOR > MEDIATE

MEDIATORS > MEDIATE

MEDIATORY > MEDIATE

MEDIATRIX n female mediator

MEDIC n doctor or medical student

MEDICABLE adj potentially able to be treated or cured medically

MEDICABLY > MEDICABLE

MEDICAID n US federal health insurance programme for persons on low income

MEDICAIDS > MEDICAID

MEDICAL adj of the science of medicine ▷ n medical examination

MEDICALLY > MEDICAL

MEDICALS > MEDICAL

MEDICANT n medicinal substance

MEDICANTS > MEDICANT

MEDICARE n US federal health insurance programme for older people

MEDICARES > MEDICARE

MEDICATE vb treat with a medicinal substance

MEDICATED adj (of a patient) having been treated with a medicine or drug

MEDICATES > MEDICATE

MEDICIDE n suicide assisted by doctor

MEDICIDES > MEDICIDE

MEDICINAL adj having therapeutic properties ▷ n medicinal substance

MEDICINE n substance used to treat disease ▷ vb treat with medicine

MEDICINED > MEDICINE

MEDICINER n physician

MEDICINES > MEDICINE

MEDICK n type of small leguminous plant with yellow or purple flowers

MEDICKS > MEDICK

MEDICO n doctor or medical student

MEDICOS > MEDICO

MEDICS > MEDIC

MEDIEVAL adj of the Middle Ages ▷ n person living in medieval times

MEDIEVALS > MEDIEVAL

MEDIGAP n private health insurance

MEDIGAPS > MEDIGAP

MEDII > MEDIUS

MEDINA n ancient quarter of North African city

MEDINAS > MEDINA

MEDIOCRE adj average in quality

MEDITATE vb reflect deeply, esp on spiritual matters

MEDITATED > MEDITATE

MEDITATES > MEDITATE

MEDITATOR > MEDITATE

MEDIUM adj midway between extremes, average ▷ n middle state, degree, or condition

MEDIUMS pl n medium-dated gilt-edged securities

MEDIUS n middle finger

MEDIUSES > MEDIUS

MEDIVAC variant spelling of > MEDEVAC

MEDIVACED > MEDIVAC

MEDIVACS > MEDIVAC

MEDLAR n apple-like fruit of a small tree

MEDLARS > MEDLAR

MEDLE same as > MEDDLE

MEDLED > MEDLE

MEDLES > MEDLE

MEDLEY n miscellaneous mixture ▷ adj of, being, or relating to a mixture or variety

MEDLEYS > MEDLEY

MEDLING > MEDLE

MEDRESA same as > MADRASAH

MEDRESAS > MEDRESA

MEDRESE same as > MADRASAH

MEDRESES > MEDRESE

MEDRESSEH same as > MADRASAH

MEDS > MED

MEDULLA n marrow, pith, or inner tissue

MEDULLAE > MEDULLA

MEDULLAR > MEDULLA

MEDULLARY > MEDULLA

MEDULLAS > MEDULLA

MEDULLATE adj having medulla

MEDUSA n jellyfish

MEDUSAE > MEDUSA

MEDUSAL > MEDUSA

MEDUSAN > MEDUSA

MEDUSANS > MEDUSA

MEDUSAS > MEDUSA

MEDUSOID same as > MEDUSA

MEDUSOIDS > MEDUSOID

MEE n Malaysian noodle dish

MEED n recompense

MEEDS > MEED

MEEK adj submissive or humble

MEEKEN vb make meek

MEEKENED > MEEKEN

MEEKENING > MEEKEN

MEEKENS > MEEKEN

MEEKER > MEEK

MEEKEST > MEEK

MEEKLY > MEEK

MEEKNESS > MEEK

MEEMIE n attack of hysteria

MEEMIES > MEEMIE

MEER same as > MERE

MEERCAT same as > MEERKAT

MEERCATS > MEERCAT

MEERED > MEER

MEERING > MEER

MEERKAT n S African mongoose

MEERKATS > MEERKAT

MEERS > MEER

MEES > MEE

MEET vb come together (with) ▷ n meeting, esp a sports meeting ▷ adj fit or suitable

MEETER > MEET

MEETERS > MEET

MEETEST > MEET

MEETING > MEET

MEETINGS > MEET

MEETLY > MEET

MEETNESS n properness

MEETS > MEET

MEFF dialect word for > TRAMP

MEFFS > MEFF

MEG short for > MEGABYTE

MEGA adj extremely good, great, or successful

MEGABAR n unit of million bars

MEGABARS > MEGABAR

MEGABIT n one million bits

MEGABITS > MEGABIT

MEGABUCK n million dollars

MEGABUCKS > MEGABUCK

MEGABYTE n 2²⁰ or 1 048 576 bytes

MEGABYTES > MEGABYTE

MEGACITY n city with over 10 million inhabitants

MEGACURIE n unit of million curies

MEGACYCLE same as > MEGAHERTZ

MEGADEAL n very good deal

MEGADEALS > MEGADEAL

MEGADEATH n death of a million people, esp in a nuclear war or attack

MEGADOSE n very large dose, as of a medicine, vitamin, etc

MEGADOSES > MEGADOSE

MEGADYNE n unit of million dynes

MEGADYNES > MEGADYNE

MEGAFARAD n unit of million farads

MEGAFAUNA n component of the fauna of a region or period that comprises the larger terrestrial animals

MEGAFLOP n measure of a computer's processing speed

MEGAFLOPS > MEGAFLOP

MEGAFLORA n plants large enough to be seen by naked eye

MEGAFOG n amplified fog signal

MEGAFOGS > MEGAFOG

MEGAGAUSS n unit of million gauss

MEGAHERTZ n one million hertz

MEGAHIT n great success

MEGAHITS > MEGAHIT

MEGAJOULE n unit of million joules

MEGALITH n great stone, esp as part of a prehistoric monument

MEGALITHS > MEGALITH

MEGALITRE n one million litres

MEGALODON n an extinct giant shark of the Cenozoic era

MEGALOPIC adj having large eyes

MEGALOPS n crab in larval stage

MEGAMALL n very large shopping mall

MEGAMALLS > MEGAMALL

MEGAPHONE n cone-shaped instrument used to amplify the voice ▷ vb speak through megaphone

MEGAPHYLL n relatively large type of leaf produced by ferns and seed plants

MEGAPIXEL n one million pixels

MEGAPLEX n large cinema complex

MEGAPOD same as > MEGAPODE

MEGAPODE n bird of Australia, New Guinea, and adjacent islands

MEGAPODES > MEGAPODE

MEGAPODS > MEGAPOD

MEGAQUAKE n very large earthquake

MEGARA > MEGARON

MEGARAD n unit of million rads

MEGARADS > MEGARAD

MEGARON n tripartite rectangular room, found in Bronze Age Greece and Asia Minor

MEGARONS > MEGARON

MEGASCOPE n type of image projector

MEGASPORE n larger of the two types of spore produced by some spore-bearing plants, which develops into the female gametophyte

MEGASS another name for > BAGASSE

MEGASSE same as > MEGASS

MEGASSES > MEGASS

MEGASTAR n very well-known personality in the entertainment business

MEGASTARS > MEGASTAR

MEGASTORE n very large store

MEGASTORM n very large storm

MEGATHERE n type of gigantic extinct American sloth common in late Cenozoic times

MEGATON n explosive power equal to that of one million tons of TNT

MEGATONIC > MEGATON

MEGATONS > MEGATON

MEGAVOLT n one million volts

MEGAVOLTS > MEGAVOLT

MEGAWATT n one million watts

MEGAWATTS > MEGAWATT

MEGILLA same as > MEGILLAH

MEGILLAH n scroll of the Book of Esther, read on the festival of Purim

MEGILLAHS > MEGILLAH

MEGILLAS > MEGILLA

MEGILLOTH > MEGILLAH

MEGILP n oil-painting medium of linseed oil mixed with mastic varnish or turpentine

MEGILPH same as > MEGILP

MEGILPHS > MEGILPH

MEGILPS > MEGILP

MEGOHM n one million ohms

MEGOHMS > MEGOHM

MEGRIM n caprice

MEGRIMS n fit of depression

MEGS > MEG

MEH interj expression of indifference or boredom

MEHNDI n (esp in India) the practice of painting designs on the hands, feet, etc using henna

MEHNDIS > MEHNDI

MEIBOMIAN adj as in meibomian gland any of the small sebaceous glands in the eyelid, beneath the conjunctiva

MEIKLE adj Scots word meaning large

MEIN Scots word for > MOAN

MEINED > MEIN

MEINEY same as > MEINY

MEINEYS > MEINEY

MEINIE same as > MEINY

MEINIES > MEINY

MEINING > MEIN

MEINS > MEIN

MEINT same as > MING

MEINY n retinue or household

MEIOCYTE n cell that divides by meiosis to produce four haploid spores

MEIOCYTES > MEIOCYTE

MEIOFAUNA n component of the fauna of a sea or lake bed comprising small (but not microscopic) animals, such as tiny worms and crustaceans

MEIONITE n mineral containing silica

MEIONITES > MEIONITE

MEIOSES > MEIOSIS

MEIOSIS n type of cell division

MEIOSPORE n haploid spore

MEIOTIC > MEIOSIS

MEISHI n business card in Japan

MEISHIS > MEISHI

MEISTER n person who excels at a particular activity

MEISTERS > MEISTER

MEITH n landmark

MEITHS > MEITH

MEJLIS same as > MAJLIS

MEJLISES > MEJLIS

MEKKA same as > MECCA

MEKKAS > MEKKA

MEKOMETER n device for measuring distance

MEL n pure form of honey

MELA n Asian cultural or religious fair or festival

MELAENA n medical condition

MELAENAS > MELAENA

MELALEUCA n Australian shrub or tree with a white trunk and black branches

MELAMDIM > MELAMED

MELAMED n Hebrew teacher

MELAMINE n colourless crystalline compound used in making synthetic resins

MELAMINES > MELAMINE

MELAMPODE n poisonous plant

MELANGE n mixture

MELANGES > MELANGE

MELANIAN n freshwater mollusc

MELANIANS > MELANIAN

MELANIC adj relating to melanism or melanosis ▷ n darker form of creature

MELANICS > MELANIC

MELANIN n dark pigment found in the hair, skin, and eyes

MELANINS > MELANIN

MELANISE same as > MELANIZE

MELANISED > MELANISE

MELANISES > MELANISE

MELANISM same as > MELANOSIS

MELANISMS > MELANISM

MELANIST > MELANISM

MELANISTS > MELANISM

MELANITE n black variety of andradite garnet

MELANITES > MELANITE

MELANITIC > MELANITE

MELANIZE vb turn into melanin

MELANIZED > MELANIZE

MELANIZES > MELANIZE

MELANO n person with extremely dark skin

MELANOID adj resembling melanin ▷ n dark substance formed in skin

MELANOIDS > MELANOID

MELANOMA n tumour composed of dark-coloured cells, occurring in some skin cancers

MELANOMAS > MELANOMA

MELANOS > MELANO

MELANOSES > MELANOSIS

MELANOSIS n skin condition characterized by excessive deposits of melanin

MELANOTIC > MELANOSIS

MELANOUS adj having a dark complexion and black hair

MELANURIA n presence of melanin in urine

MELANURIC > MELANURIA

MELAPHYRE n type of weathered amygdaloidal basalt or andesite

MELAS > MELA

MELASTOME n tropical flowering plant

MELATONIN n hormone-like secretion of the pineal gland, causing skin colour changes in some animals and thought to be involved in reproductive function

MELBA adj relating to a type of dessert sauce or toast

MELD vb merge or blend ▷ n act of melding

MELDED > MELD

MELDER > MELD

MELDERS > MELD

MELDING > MELD

MELDS > MELD

MELEE n noisy confused fight or crowd

MELEES > MELEE

MELENA n excrement stained by blood

MELENAS > MELENA

MELIC adj (of poetry, esp ancient Greek lyric poems) intended to be sung ▷ n type of grass

MELICK n either of two pale green perennial grasses

MELICKS > MELICK

m

MELICS > MELIC
MELIK same as > MALIK
MELIKS > MELIK
MELILITE n mineral containing calcium
MELILITES > MELILITE
MELILOT n plant with small white or yellow fragrant flowers
MELILOTS > MELILOT
MELINITE n high explosive made from picric acid
MELINITES > MELINITE
MELIORATE vb improve
MELIORISM n notion that the world can be improved by human effort
MELIORIST > MELIORISM
MELIORITY n improved state
MELISMA n expressive vocal phrase or passage consisting of several notes sung to one syllable
MELISMAS > MELISMA
MELISMATA > MELISMA
MELITTIN n main toxic component in bee venom
MELITTINS > MELITTIN
MELL vb mix
MELLAY same as > MELEE
MELLAYS > MELLAY
MELLED > MELL
MELLIFIC adj forming or producing honey
MELLING > MELL
MELLITE n soft yellow mineral
MELLITES > MELLITE
MELLITIC > MELLITE
MELLOTRON n musical synthesizer
MELLOW adj soft, not harsh ▷ vb make or become mellow
MELLOWED > MELLOW
MELLOWER > MELLOW
MELLOWEST > MELLOW
MELLOWIER > MELLOWY
MELLOWING > MELLOW
MELLOWLY > MELLOW
MELLOWS > MELLOW
MELLOWY adj mellow
MELLS > MELL
MELOCOTON n variety of peach
MELODEON n small accordion
MELODEONS > MELODEON
MELODIA same as > MELODICA
MELODIAS > MELODIA
MELODIC adj of melody
MELODICA n type of flute
MELODICAS > MELODICA
MELODICS n study of melody
MELODIES > MELODY
MELODION same as > MELODEON
MELODIONS > MELODION
MELODIOUS adj pleasing to the ear
MELODISE same as > MELODIZE
MELODISED > MELODISE
MELODISER > MELODISE
MELODISES > MELODISE

MELODIST n composer of melodies
MELODISTS > MELODIST
MELODIZE vb provide with a melody
MELODIZED > MELODIZE
MELODIZER > MELODIZE
MELODIZES > MELODIZE
MELODRAMA n play full of extravagant action and emotion
MELODRAME same as > MELODRAMA
MELODY n series of musical notes which make a tune
MELOID n type of long-legged beetle
MELOMANIA n great enthusiasm for music
MELOMANIC > MELOMANIA
MELON n large round juicy fruit with a hard rind
MELONGENE n aubergine
MELONIER > MELONY
MELONIEST > MELONY
MELONS > MELON
MELONY adj like a melon
MELOXICAM n anti-inflammatory drug used to treat osteoarthritis
MELPHALAN n drug used to treat leukaemia
MELS > MEL
MELT vb (cause to) become liquid by heat ▷ n act or process of melting
MELTABLE > MELT
MELTAGE n process or result of melting or the amount melted
MELTAGES > MELTAGE
MELTDOWN n (in a nuclear reactor) melting of the fuel rods, with the possible release of radiation
MELTDOWNS > MELTDOWN
MELTED > MELT
MELTEMI n northerly wind in the northeast Mediterranean
MELTEMIS > MELTEMI
MELTER > MELT
MELTERS > MELT
MELTIER > MELTY
MELTIEST > MELTY
MELTING > MELT
MELTINGLY > MELT
MELTINGS > MELT
MELTITH n meal
MELTITHS > MELTITH
MELTON n heavy smooth woollen fabric with a short nap, used esp for overcoats
MELTONS > MELTON
MELTS > MELT
MELTWATER n melted snow or ice
MELTY adj tending to melt
MELUNGEON n any of a dark-skinned group of people of the Appalachians in E Tennessee, of mixed Indian, White, and Black ancestry
MEM n 13th letter in the Hebrew alphabet, transliterated as m

MEMBER n individual making up a body or society ▷ adj (of a (country or group) belonging to an organization or alliance
MEMBERED adj having members
MEMBERS > MEMBER
MEMBRAL adj of limbs
MEMBRANAL > MEMBRANE
MEMBRANE n thin flexible tissue in a plant or animal body
MEMBRANED adj having membrane
MEMBRANES > MEMBRANE
MEME n idea or element of social behaviour
MEMENTO n thing serving to remind, souvenir
MEMENTOES > MEMENTO
MEMENTOS > MEMENTO
MEMES > MEME
MEMETIC adj of or relating to a meme
MEMETICS n study of genetic transmission of culture
MEMO n memorandum
MEMOIR n biography or historical account based on personal knowledge
MEMOIRISM n writing of memoirs
MEMOIRIST > MEMOIRISM
MEMOIRS pl n collection of reminiscences about a period or series of events
MEMORABLE adj worth remembering, noteworthy
MEMORABLY > MEMORABLE
MEMORANDA n plural of memorandum: written statement of communications
MEMORIAL n something serving to commemorate a person or thing ▷ adj serving as a memorial
MEMORIALS > MEMORIAL
MEMORIES > MEMORY
MEMORISE same as > MEMORIZE
MEMORISED > MEMORISE
MEMORISER > MEMORIZE
MEMORISES > MEMORISE
MEMORITER adv from memory
MEMORIZE vb commit to memory
MEMORIZED > MEMORIZE
MEMORIZER > MEMORIZE
MEMORIZES > MEMORIZE
MEMORY n ability to remember
MEMOS > MEMO
MEMS > MEM
MEMSAHIB n (formerly, in India) term of respect used for a European married woman
MEMSAHIBS > MEMSAHIB
MEN > MAN
MENACE n threat ▷ vb threaten, endanger
MENACED > MENACE
MENACER > MENACE
MENACERS > MENACE

MENACES > MENACE
MENACING > MENACE
MENAD same as > MAENAD
MENADIONE n yellow crystalline compound
MENADS > MENAD
MENAGE old form of > MANAGE
MENAGED > MENAGE
MENAGERIE n collection of wild animals for exhibition
MENAGES > MENAGE
MENAGING > MENAGE
MENARCHE n first occurrence of menstruation
MENARCHES > MENARCHE
MENAZON n type of insecticide
MENAZONS > MENAZON
MEND vb repair or patch ▷ n mended area
MENDABLE > MEND
MENDACITY n (tendency to) untruthfulness
MENDED > MEND
MENDER > MEND
MENDERS > MEND
MENDICANT adj begging ▷ n beggar
MENDICITY > MENDICANT
MENDIGO n Spanish beggar or vagrant
MENDIGOS > MENDIGO
MENDING n something to be mended, esp clothes
MENDINGS > MENDING
MENDS > MEND
MENE Scots form of > MOAN
MENED > MENE
MENEER n S African title of address
MENEERS > MENEER
MENES > MENE
MENFOLK pl n men collectively, esp the men of a particular family
MENFOLKS same as > MENFOLK
MENG vb mix
MENGE same as > MENG
MENGED > MENG
MENGES > MENGE
MENGING > MENG
MENGS > MENG
MENHADEN n marine N American fish, source of fishmeal, fertilizer, and oil
MENHADENS > MENHADEN
MENHIR n single upright prehistoric stone
MENHIRS > MENHIR
MENIAL adj involving boring work of low status ▷ n person with a menial job
MENIALLY > MENIAL
MENIALS > MENIAL
MENILITE n liver opal
MENILITES > MENILITE
MENING > MENE
MENINGEAL > MENINX
MENINGES > MENINX
MENINX n one of three membranes that envelop the brain and spinal cord
MENISCAL > MENISCUS
MENISCATE > MENISCUS
MENISCI > MENISCUS
MENISCOID > MENISCUS

MENISCUS n curved surface of a liquid

MENO adv musical instruction indicating 'less'

MENOLOGY n ecclesiastical calendar of the months

MENOMINEE n whitefish, found in N America and Siberia

MENOMINI same as > MENOMINEE

MENOMINIS > MENOMINI

MENOPAUSE n time when a woman's menstrual cycle ceases

MENOPOLIS n informal word for an area with a high proportion of single men

MENOPOME n American salamander

MENOPOMES > MENOPOME

MENORAH n seven-branched candelabrum used as an emblem of Judaism

MENORAHS > MENORAH

MENORRHEA n normal menstrual flow

MENSA n faint constellation in the S hemisphere

MENSAE n star of the mensa constellation

MENSAL adj monthly

MENSAS > MENSA

MENSCH n decent person

MENSCHEN > MENSCH

MENSCHES > MENSCH

MENSCHIER > MENSCHY

MENSCHY adj decent

MENSE vb grace

MENSED > MENSE

MENSEFUL adj gracious

MENSELESS adj graceless

MENSES n menstruation

MENSH vb mention

MENSHED > MENSH

MENSHEN n Chinese door god

MENSHES > MENSH

MENSHING > MENSH

MENSING > MENSE

MENSTRUA > MENSTRUUM

MENSTRUAL adj of or relating to menstruation

MENSTRUUM n solvent, esp one used in the preparation of a drug

MENSUAL same as > MENSAL

MENSURAL adj of or involving measure

MENSWEAR n clothing for men

MENSWEARS > MENSWEAR

MENT same as > MING

MENTA > MENTUM

MENTAL adj of, in, or done by the mind

MENTALESE n picturing of concepts in mind without words

MENTALISM n doctrine that mind is the fundamental reality and that objects of knowledge exist only as aspects of the subject's consciousness

MENTALIST > MENTALISM

MENTALITY n way of thinking

MENTALLY > MENTAL

MENTATION n process or result of mental activity

MENTEE n person trained by mentor

MENTEES > MENTEE

MENTHENE n liquid obtained from menthol

MENTHENES > MENTHENE

MENTHOL n organic compound found in peppermint

MENTHOLS > MENTHOL

MENTICIDE n destruction of person's mental independence

MENTION vb refer to briefly ▷ n brief reference

MENTIONED > MENTION

MENTIONER > MENTION

MENTIONS > MENTION

MENTO n Jamaican song

MENTOR n adviser or guide ▷ vb act as a mentor to (someone)

MENTORED > MENTOR

MENTORIAL > MENTOR

MENTORING n (in business) the practice of assigning a junior member of staff to the care of a more experienced person who assists them in their career

MENTORS > MENTOR

MENTOS > MENTO

MENTUM n chin

MENU n list of dishes to be served, or from which to order

MENUDO n Mexican soup

MENUDOS > MENUDO

MENUISIER n joiner

MENUS > MENU

MENYIE same as > MEINIE

MENYIES > MENYIE

MEOU same as > MEOW

MEOUED > MEOU

MEOUING > MEOU

MEOUS > MEOU

MEOW vb (of a cat) to make a characteristic crying sound ▷ interj imitation of this sound

MEOWED > MEOW

MEOWING > MEOW

MEOWS > MEOW

MEPACRINE n drug formerly widely used to treat malaria

MEPHITIC adj poisonous

MEPHITIS n foul-smelling discharge

MEPHITISM n poisoning

MERANTI n wood from any of several Malaysian trees

MERANTIS > MERANTI

MERBROMIN n green iridescent crystalline compound

MERC n mercenary

MERCADO n market

MERCADOS > MERCADO

MERCAPTAN another name (not in technical usage) for > THIOL

MERCAPTO adj of a particular chemical group

MERCAT Scots word for > MARKET

MERCATS > MERCAT

MERCENARY adj influenced by greed ▷ n hired soldier

MERCER n dealer in textile fabrics and fine cloth

MERCERIES > MERCER

MERCERISE same as > MERCERIZE

MERCERIZE vb treat (cotton yarn) with an alkali to increase its strength and reception to dye and impart a lustrous silky appearance

MERCERS > MERCER

MERCERY > MERCER

MERCES > MERC

MERCH n merchandise

MERCHANT n person engaged in trade, wholesale trader ▷ adj of ships involved in commercial trade or their crews ▷ vb conduct trade in

MERCHANTS > MERCHANT

MERCHES > MERCH

MERCHET n type of fine paid by feudal tenant to his lord

MERCHETS > MERCHET

MERCHILD n mythical creature with upper body of child and lower body of fish

MERCIABLE adj merciful

MERCIES > MERCY

MERCIFIDE > MERCIFY

MERCIFIED > MERCIFY

MERCIFIES > MERCIFY

MERCIFUL adj compassionate

MERCIFY vb show mercy to

MERCILESS adj without mercy

MERCS > MERC

MERCURATE vb treat or mix with mercury

MERCURIAL adj lively, changeable ▷ n any salt of mercury for use as a medicine

MERCURIC adj of or containing mercury in the divalent state

MERCURIES > MERCURY

MERCURISE same as > MERCURATE

MERCURIZE same as > MERCURISE

MERCUROUS adj of or containing mercury in the monovalent state

MERCURY n silvery liquid metal

MERCY n compassionate treatment

MERDE French word for > EXCREMENT

MERDES > MERDE

MERE adj nothing more than ▷ n lake ▷ vb old form of survey

MERED adj forming a boundary

MEREL same as > MERIL

MERELL same as > MERIL

MERELLS same as > MERILS

MERELS > MEREL

MERELY adv only

MERENGUE n type of lively dance music

MERENGUES > MERENGUE

MEREOLOGY n formal study of the logical properties of the relation of part and whole

MERER > MERE

MERES > MERE

MERESMAN n man who decides on boundaries

MERESMEN > MERESMAN

MEREST > MERE

MERESTONE n stone marking boundary

MERFOLK n mermaids and mermen

MERFOLKS > MERFOLK

MERGANSER n large crested diving duck

MERGE vb combine or blend

MERGED > MERGE

MERGEE n business taken over by merger

MERGEES > MERGEE

MERGENCE > MERGE

MERGENCES > MERGE

MERGER n combination of business firms into one

MERGERS > MERGER

MERGES > MERGE

MERGING > MERGE

MERGINGS > MERGE

MERGUEZ n heavily spiced N African sausage

MERI n Māori war club

MERICARP n part of plant fruit

MERICARPS > MERICARP

MERIDIAN n imaginary circle of the earth passing through both poles ▷ adj along or relating to a meridian

MERIDIANS > MERIDIAN

MERIL n counter used in merils

MERILS n old board game

MERIMAKE n merrymaking

MERIMAKES > MERIMAKE

MERING > MERE

MERINGS > MERING

MERINGUE n baked mixture of egg whites and sugar

MERINGUES > MERINGUE

MERINO n breed of sheep with fine soft wool

MERINOS > MERINO

MERIS > MERI

MERISES > MERISIS

MERISIS n growth by division of cells

MERISM n duplication of biological parts

MERISMS > MERISM

MERISTEM n plant tissue responsible for growth

MERISTEMS > MERISTEM

MERISTIC adj of or relating to the number of organs or parts in an animal or plant body

MERIT n excellence or worth ▷ vb deserve

MERITED > MERIT

MERITING > MERIT

MERITLESS > MERIT

MERITS > MERIT

MERK n old Scots coin

m

MERKIN *n* artificial hairpiece for the pudendum

MERKINS > MERKIN

MERKS > MERK

MERL *same as* > MERLE

MERLE *adj* (of a dog, esp a collie) having a bluish-grey coat with speckles or streaks of black ▷ *n* dog with this coat

MERLES > MERLE

MERLIN *n* small falcon

MERLING *n* whiting

MERLINGS > MERLING

MERLINS > MERLIN

MERLON *n* solid upright section in a crenellated battlement

MERLONS > MERLON

MERLOT *n* type of black grape

MERLOTS > MERLOT

MERLS > MERL

MERMAID *n* imaginary sea creature with the upper part of a woman and the lower part of a fish

MERMAIDEN *same as* > MERMAID

MERMAIDS > MERMAID

MERMAN *n* male counterpart of the mermaid

MERMEN > MERMAN

MEROCRINE *adj* (of the secretion of glands) characterized by formation of the product without undergoing disintegration

MEROGONY *n* development of embryo from part of ovum

MEROISTIC *adj* producing yolk and ova

MEROME *same as* > MEROSOME

MEROMES > MEROME

MERONYM *n* part of something used to refer to the whole

MERONYMS > MERONYM

MERONYMY > MERONYM

MEROPIA *n* partial blindness

MEROPIAS > MEROPIA

MEROPIC > MEROPIA

MEROPIDAN *n* bird of bee-eater family

MEROSOME *n* segment in body of worm

MEROSOMES > MEROSOME

MEROZOITE *n* any of the cells formed by fission of a schizont during the life cycle of sporozoan protozoans, such as the malaria parasite

MERPEOPLE *same as* > MERFOLK

MERRIE *adj* (archaic) merry

MERRIER > MERRY

MERRIES > MERRY

MERRIEST > MERRY

MERRILY > MERRY

MERRIMENT *n* gaiety, fun, or mirth

MERRINESS > MERRY

MERRY *adj* cheerful or jolly ▷ *n* type of cherry

MERRYMAN *n* jester

MERRYMEN > MERRYMAN

MERSALYL *n* salt of sodium

MERSALYLS > MERSALYL

MERSE *n* low level ground by a river or shore

MERSES > MERSE

MERSION *n* dipping in water

MERSIONS > MERSION

MERYCISM *n* rumination

MERYCISMS > MERYCISM

MES > ME

MESA *n* flat-topped hill found in arid regions

MESAIL *n* visor

MESAILS > MESAIL

MESAL *same as* > MESIAL

MESALLY > MESAL

MESARAIC *adj* of mesentery

MESARCH *adj* having the first-formed xylem surrounded by that formed later

MESAS > MESA

MESCAL *n* spineless globe-shaped cactus

MESCALIN *same as* > MESCALINE

MESCALINE *n* hallucinogenic drug obtained from the tops of mescals

MESCALINS > MESCALIN

MESCALISM *n* addiction to mescal

MESCALS > MESCAL

MESCLUM *same as* > MESCLUN

MESCLUMS > MESCLUM

MESCLUN *n* type of green salad

MESCLUNS > MESCLUN

MESDAMES > MADAM

MESE *n* middle string on lyre

MESEEMED > MESEEMS

MESEEMETH *same as* > MESEEMS

MESEEMS *vb* it seems to me

MESEL *n* person with leprosy

MESELED *adj* afflicted by leprosy

MESELS > MESEL

MESENTERA *n* plural of mesenteron, the midgut

MESENTERY *n* double layer of peritoneum that is attached to the back wall of the abdominal cavity and supports most of the small intestine

MESES > MESE

MESETA *n* plateau in Spain

MESETAS > MESETA

MESH *n* network or net ▷ *vb* (of gear teeth) engage ▷ *adj* made from mesh

MESHED > MESH

MESHES > MESH

MESHIER > MESH

MESHIEST > MESH

MESHING > MESH

MESHINGS > MESH

MESHUGA *n* crazy person

MESHUGAAS *n* madness

MESHUGAH *same as* > MESHUGA

MESHUGAS *adj* crazy

MESHUGGA *same as* > MESHUGA

MESHUGGAH *same as* > MESHUGA

MESHUGGE *same as* > MESHUGA

MESHWORK *n* network

MESHWORKS > MESHWORK

MESHY > MESH

MESIAD *adj* relating to or situated at the middle or centre

MESIAL *another word for* > MEDIAL

MESIALLY > MESIAL

MESIAN *same as* > MESIAL

MESIC > MESON

MESICALLY > MESON

MESMERIC *adj* holding (someone) as if spellbound

MESMERISE *same as* > MESMERIZE

MESMERISM *n* hypnotic state induced by the operator's imposition of their will on that of the patient

MESMERIST > MESMERISM

MESMERIZE *vb* hold spellbound

MESNALTY *n* lands of a mesne lord

MESNE *adj* (in law) intermediate or intervening

MESNES > MESNE

MESOBLAST *another name for* > MESODERM

MESOCARP *n* middle layer of the pericarp of a fruit, such as the flesh of a peach

MESOCARPS > MESOCARP

MESOCRANY *n* medium skull breadth

MESODERM *n* middle germ layer of an animal embryo

MESODERMS > MESODERM

MESOGLEA *n* gelatinous material found in jellyfish

MESOGLEAL > MESOGLEA

MESOGLEAS > MESOGLEA

MESOGLOEA *same as* > MESOGLEA

MESOLITE *n* type of mineral

MESOLITES > MESOLITE

MESOMERE *n* cell in fertilized ovum

MESOMERES > MESOMERE

MESOMORPH *n* person with a muscular body build: said to be correlated with somatotonia

MESON *n* elementary atomic particle

MESONIC > MESON

MESONS > MESON

MESOPAUSE *n* zone of minimum temperature between the mesosphere and the thermosphere

MESOPHILE *n* ideal growth temperature of 20-45 degrees

MESOPHYL *same as* > MESOPHYLL

MESOPHYLL *n* soft chlorophyll-containing tissue of a leaf between the upper and lower layers of epidermis: involved in photosynthesis

MESOPHYLS > MESOPHYL

MESOPHYTE *n* any plant that grows in surroundings receiving an average supply of water

MESOSAUR *n* extinct aquatic reptile

MESOSAURS > MESOSAUR

MESOSCALE *adj* of weather phenomena of medium duration

MESOSOME *n* part of bacterial cell

MESOSOMES > MESOSOME

MESOTRON *same as* > MESON

MESOTRONS > MESOTRON

MESOZOAN *n* type of parasite

MESOZOANS > MESOZOAN

MESOZOIC *adj* of, denoting, or relating to an era of geological time

MESPIL *n* type of N American tree

MESPILS > MESPIL

MESPRISE *same as* > MISPRISE

MESPRISES > MESPRISE

MESPRIZE *same as* > MISPRISE

MESPRIZES > MESPRIZE

MESQUIN *adj* mean

MESQUINE *same as* > MESQUIN

MESQUIT *same as* > MESQUITE

MESQUITE *n* small tree whose sugary pods are used as animal fodder

MESQUITES > MESQUITE

MESQUITS > MESQUIT

MESS *n* untidy or dirty confusion ▷ *vb* muddle or dirty

MESSAGE *n* communication sent ▷ *vb* send as a message

MESSAGED > MESSAGE

MESSAGES > MESSAGE

MESSAGING *n* sending and receiving of messages

MESSALINE *n* light lustrous twilled-silk fabric

MESSAN *Scots word for* > DOG

MESSANS > MESSAN

MESSED > MESS

MESSENGER *n* bearer of a message ▷ *vb* send by messenger

MESSES > MESS

MESSIAH *n* exceptional or hoped for liberator

MESSIAHS > MESSIAH

MESSIANIC *adj* of or relating to the Messiah, his awaited deliverance of the Jews, or the new age of peace expected to follow this

MESSIAS *same as* > MESSIAH

MESSIASES > MESSIAS

MESSIER > MESSY

MESSIEST > MESSY

MESSIEURS > MONSIEUR

MESSILY > MESSY

MESSINESS > MESSY

MESSING > MESS

MESSMAN *n* sailor working in ship's mess**

MESSMATE n person with whom one shares meals in a mess, esp in the army
MESSMATES > MESSMATE
MESSMEN > MESSMAN
MESSUAGE n house together with outbuildings and adjacent land
MESSUAGES > MESSUAGE
MESSY adj dirty, confused, or untidy
MESTEE same as > MUSTEE
MESTEES > MESTEE
MESTER n master: used as a term of address for a man who is the head of a house
MESTERS > MESTER
MESTESO n Spanish music genre
MESTESOES > MESTESO
MESTESOS > MESTESO
MESTINO n person of mixed race
MESTINOES > MESTINO
MESTINOS > MESTINO
MESTIZA > MESTIZO
MESTIZAS > MESTIZO
MESTIZO n person of mixed parentage
MESTIZOES > MESTIZO
MESTIZOS > MESTIZO
MESTO adj sad
MESTOM same as > MESTOME
MESTOME n conducting tissue associated with parenchyma
MESTOMES > MESTOME
MESTOMS > MESTOM
MESTRANOL n synthetic oestrogen
MET n meteorology
META adj in a self-parodying style
METABASES > METABASIS
METABASIS n change
METABATIC > METABASIS
METABOLIC adj of or related to the sum total of the chemical processes that occurs in living organisms, resulting in growth, production of energy, elimination of waste material, etc
METABOLY n ability of some cells, esp protozoans, to alter their shape
METACARPI n skeleton of the hand between the wrist and the fingers
METADATA n data which accompanies digital data
METADATAS > METADATA
METAFILE n (in computing) file format that can hold other types of file
METAFILES > METAFILE
METAGE n official measuring of weight or contents
METAGENIC adj of or relating to metagenesis
METAGES > METAGE
METAIRIE n area of land on which farmer pays rent in kind
METAIRIES > METAIRIE
METAL n malleable element able to conduct heat and

electricity ▷ adj made of metal ▷ vb fit or cover with metal
METALED > METAL
METALHEAD n fan of heavy metal music
METALING > METAL
METALISE same as > METALLIZE
METALISED > METALISE
METALISES > METALISE
METALIST same as > METALLIST
METALISTS > METALIST
METALIZE same as > METALLIZE
METALIZED > METALIZE
METALIZES > METALIZE
METALLED > METAL
METALLIC adj of or consisting of metal ▷ n something metallic
METALLICS > METALLIC
METALLIKE > METAL
METALLINE adj of, resembling, or relating to metals
METALLING > METAL
METALLISE same as > METALLIZE
METALLIST n person who works with metals
METALLIZE vb make metallic or to coat or treat with metal
METALLOID n nonmetallic element, such as arsenic or silicon, that has some of the properties of a metal ▷ adj of or being a metalloid
METALLY adj like metal
METALMARK n variety of butterfly
METALS > METAL
METALWARE n items made of metal
METALWORK n craft of making objects from metal
METAMALE n sterile male organism
METAMALES > METAMALE
METAMER n any of two or more isomeric compounds exhibiting metamerism
METAMERAL > METAMERE
METAMERE n body segment of invertebrates
METAMERES > METAMERE
METAMERIC adj divided into or consisting of metameres
METAMERS > METAMER
METAMICT adj of the amorphous state of a substance that has lost its crystalline structure
METANOIA n repentance
METANOIAS > METANOIA
METAPELET n foster mother
METAPHASE n second stage of mitosis during which the condensed chromosomes attach to the centre of the spindle
METAPHOR n type of figure of speech
METAPHORS > METAPHOR
METAPLASM n nonliving constituents, such as starch

and pigment granules, of the cytoplasm of a cell
METAPLOT > METAPELET
METARCHON n nontoxic substance, such as a chemical to mask pheromones, that reduces the persistence of a pest
METASOMA n posterior part of an arachnid's abdomen (opisthosoma) that never carries appendages
METASOMAS > METASOMA
METATAG n element of HTML code used by search engines to index pages
METATAGS > METATAG
METATARSI pl n skeleton of human foot between toes and tarsus
METATE n stone for grinding grain on
METATES > METATE
METAVERSE n virtual universe, eg one of a computer or role-playing game
METAXYLEM n xylem tissue that consists of rigid thick-walled cells and occurs in parts of the plant that have finished growing
METAYAGE n farming in which rent is paid in kind
METAYAGES > METAYAGE
METAYER n farmer who pays rent in kind
METAYERS > METAYER
METAZOA > METAZOAN
METAZOAL > METAZOAN
METAZOAN n animal having a body composed of many cells ▷ adj of the metazoans
METAZOANS > METAZOAN
METAZOIC adj relating to the group of multicellular animals that includes all animals except sponges
METAZOON same as > METAZOAN
METCAST n weather forecast
METCASTS > METCAST
METE vb deal out as punishment ▷ n measure
METED > METE
METEOR n small fast-moving heavenly body
METEORIC adj of a meteor
METEORISM n distension of the abdomen
METEORIST n person who studies meteors
METEORITE n meteor that has fallen to earth
METEOROID n any of the small celestial bodies that are thought to orbit the sun. When they enter the earth's atmosphere, they become visible as meteors
METEOROUS > METEOR
METEORS > METEOR
METEPA n type of pesticide
METEPAS > METEPA
METER same as > METRE
METERAGE n act of measuring
METERAGES > METERAGE

METERED > METER
METERING > METER
METERS > METER
METES > METE
METESTICK n measuring rod
METESTRUS n period following oestrus
METEWAND same as > METESTICK
METEWANDS > METEWAND
METEYARD same as > METESTICK
METEYARDS > METEYARD
METFORMIN n drug used to treat diabetes
METH n methylated spirits
METHADON same as > METHADONE
METHADONE n drug similar to morphine
METHADONS > METHADON
METHANAL n colourless poisonous irritating gas
METHANALS > METHANAL
METHANE n colourless inflammable gas
METHANES > METHANE
METHANOIC adj as in methanoic acid systematic name for formic acid
METHANOL n colourless poisonous liquid used as a solvent and fuel
METHANOLS > METHANOL
METHANOYL n organic chemical compound
METHEGLIN n (esp formerly) spiced or medicated mead
METHINK same as > METHINKS
METHINKS vb it seems to me
METHO n methylated spirits
METHOD n way or manner
METHODIC same as > METHOD
METHODISE same as > METHODIZE
METHODISM n system and practices of the Methodist Church, developed by the English preacher John Wesley (1703–91) and his followers
METHODIST > METHODISM
METHODIZE vb organize according to a method
METHODS > METHOD
METHOS > METHO
METHOUGHT > METHINKS
METHOXIDE n saltlike compound in which the hydrogen atom in the hydroxyl group of methanol has been replaced by a metal atom
METHOXIES > METHOXY
METHOXY n steroid drug
METHOXYL n chemical compound of methyl and hydroxyl
METHOXYLS > METHOXYL
METHS n methylated spirits
METHYL n compound containing a saturated hydrocarbon group of atoms
METHYLAL n colourless volatile flammable liquid

m

m

METHYLALS > METHYLAL
METHYLASE n enzyme
METHYLATE vb mix with methanol
METHYLENE n divalent hydrocarbon group
METHYLIC > METHYL
METHYLS > METHYL
METHYSES > METHYSIS
METHYSIS n drunkenness
METHYSTIC adj intoxicating
METIC n (in ancient Greece) alien having some rights of citizenship
METICA n monetary unit of Mozambique
METICAIS > METICAL
METICAL n money unit in Mozambique
METICALS > METICAL
METICAS > METICA
METICS > METIC
METIER n profession or trade
METIERS > METIER
METIF n person of mixed race
METIFS > METIF
METING > METE
METIS n person of mixed parentage
METISSE > METIS
METISSES > METIS
METOL n organic substance used as a photographic developer
METOLS > METOL
METONYM n word used in a metonymy
METONYMIC > METONYMY
METONYMS > METONYM
METONYMY n figure of speech in which one thing is replaced by another associated with it
METOPAE > METOPE
METOPE n square space between two triglyphs in a Doric frieze
METOPES > METOPE
METOPIC adj of or relating to the forehead
METOPISM n congenital disfigurement of forehead
METOPISMS > METOPISM
METOPON n painkilling drug
METOPONS > METOPON
METOPRYL n type of anaesthetic
METOPRYLS > METOPRYL
METRALGIA n pain in the uterus
METRAZOL n drug used to improve blood circulation
METRAZOLS > METRAZOL
METRE n unit of length ▷ vb express in poetry
METRED > METRE
METRES > METRE
METRIC adj of the decimal system of weights and measures based on the metre
METRICAL adj of measurement
METRICATE vb convert a measuring system or instrument to metric units

METRICIAN n writer of metrical verse
METRICISE vb study metre of poetry
METRICISM > METRICTSE
METRICIST same as > METRICIAN
METRICIZE same as > METRICISE
METRICS n art of using poetic metre
METRIFIED > METRIFY
METRIFIER > METRIFY
METRIFIES > METRIFY
METRIFY vb render into poetic metre
METRING > METRE
METRIST n person skilled in the use of poetic metre
METRISTS > METRIST
METRITIS n inflammation of the uterus
METRO n underground railway system, esp in Paris
METROLOGY n science of weights and measures
METRONOME n instrument which marks musical time by means of a ticking pendulum
METROPLEX n large urban area
METROS > METRO
METS > MET
METTLE n courage or spirit
METTLED adj spirited, courageous, or valiant
METTLES > METTLE
METUMP n band for carrying a load or burden
METUMPS > METUMP
MEU another name for > SPIGNEL
MEUNIERE adj cooked in ~ butter with lemon juice and parsley
MEUS > MEU
MEUSE n gap through which an animal passed ▷ vb go through this gap
MEUSED > MEUSE
MEUSES > MEUSE
MEUSING > MEUSE
MEVE same as > MOVE
MEVED > MEVE
MEVES > MEVE
MEVING > MEVE
MEVROU n S African title of address
MEVROUS > MEVROU
MEW n cry of a cat ▷ vb utter this cry
MEWED > MEW
MEWING > MEW
MEWL vb (esp of a baby) to cry weakly ▷ n weak or whimpering cry
MEWLED > MEWL
MEWLER > MEWL
MEWLERS > MEWL
MEWLING > MEWL
MEWLS > MEWL
MEWS same as > MEUSE
MEWSED > MEWS
MEWSES > MEWS
MEWSING > MEWS
MEYNT > MING
MEZAIL same as > MESAIL

MEZAILS > MEZAIL
MEZCAL variant spelling of > MESCAL
MEZCALINE variant spelling of > MESCALINE
MEZCALS > MEZCAL
MEZE n type of hors d'oeuvre
MEZEREON same as > MEZEREUM
MEZEREONS > MEZEREON
MEZEREUM n dried bark of certain shrubs, formerly used to treat arthritis
MEZEREUMS > MEZEREUM
MEZES > MEZE
MEZQUIT same as > MESQUITE
MEZQUITE same as > MESQUITE
MEZQUITES > MEZQUITE
MEZQUITS > MEZQUIT
MEZUZA same as > MEZUZAH
MEZUZAH n piece of parchment inscribed with biblical passages
MEZUZAHS > MEZUZAH
MEZUZAS > MEZUZA
MEZUZOT > MEZUZAH
MEZUZOTH > MEZUZAH
MEZZ same as > MEZZANINE
MEZZALUNA n half-moon shaped kitchen chopper
MEZZANINE n intermediate storey, esp between the ground and first floor ▷ adj of or relating to an intermediate stage in a financial process
MEZZE same as > MEZE
MEZZES > MEZZE
MEZZO adv moderately ▷ n singer with voice between soprano and contralto
MEZZOS > MEZZO
MEZZOTINT n method of engraving by scraping the roughened surface of a metal plate ▷ vb engrave (a copper plate) in this fashion
MGANGA n witch doctor
MGANGAS > MGANGA
MHO former name for > SIEMENS
MHORR n African gazelle
MHORRS > MHORR
MHOS > MHO
MI n (in tonic sol-fa) the third degree of any major scale
MIAOU same as > MEOW
MIAOUED > MIAOU
MIAOUING > MIAOU
MIAOUS > MIAOU
MIAOW same as > MEOW
MIAOWED > MIAOW
MIAOWING > MIAOW
MIAOWS > MIAOW
MIASM same as > MIASMA
MIASMA n unwholesome or foreboding atmosphere
MIASMAL > MIASMA
MIASMAS > MIASMA
MIASMATA > MIASMA
MIASMATIC > MIASMA
MIASMIC > MIASMA
MIASMOUS > MIASMA
MIASMS > MIASM
MIAUL same as > MEOW

MIAULED > MIAUL
MIAULING > MIAUL
MIAULS > MIAUL
MIB n marble used in games
MIBS > MIB
MIBUNA n type of Japanese leafy vegetable
MIBUNAS > MIBUNA
MIC n microphone
MICA n glasslike mineral used as an electrical insulator
MICACEOUS > MICA
MICAS > MICA
MICATE vb add mica to
MICATED > MICATE
MICATES > MICATE
MICATING > MICATE
MICAWBER n person who idles and trusts to fortune
MICAWBERS > MICAWBER
MICE > MOUSE
MICELL same as > MICELLE
MICELLA same as > MICELLE
MICELLAE > MICELLA
MICELLAR > MICELLE
MICELLAS > MICELLA
MICELLE n charged aggregate of molecules of colloidal size in a solution
MICELLES > MICELLE
MICELLS > MICELL
MICH same as > MITCH
MICHAEL n as in take the michael teasing
MICHAELS > MICHAEL
MICHE same as > MICH
MICHED > MICH
MICHER > MICH
MICHERS > MICH
MICHES > MICH
MICHIGAN US name for > NEWMARKET
MICHIGANS > MICHIGAN
MICHING > MICH
MICHINGS > MICH
MICHT n Scots word for might
MICHTS > MICHT
MICK n derogatory term for an Irish person
MICKERIES > MICKERY
MICKERY n waterhole, esp in a dry riverbed
MICKEY n young bull ▷ vb drug a person's drink
MICKEYED > MICKEY
MICKEYING > MICKEY
MICKEYS > MICKEY
MICKIES > MICKY
MICKLE adj large or abundant ▷ adv much ▷ n great amount
MICKLER > MICKLE
MICKLES > MICKLE
MICKLEST > MICKLE
MICKS > MICK
MICKY same as > MICKEY
MICO n marmoset
MICOS > MICO
MICRA > MICRON
MICRIFIED > MICRIFY
MICRIFIES > MICRIFY
MICRIFY vb make very small
MICRO n small computer

MICROBAR n millionth of bar of pressure

MICROBARS > MICROBAR

MICROBE n minute organism, esp one causing disease

MICROBEAD n very small plastic particle

MICROBEAM n X-ray machine with narrow focussed beam

MICROBES > MICROBE

MICROBIAL > MICROBE

MICROBIAN > MICROBE

MICROBIC > MICROBE

MICROBLOG vb contribute to a blog which limits the length of individual postings

MICROBREW n beer made in small brewery

MICROBUS n small bus

MICROCAP adj (of investments) involving very small amounts of capital

MICROCAR n small car

MICROCARD n card containing microprint

MICROCARS > MICROCAR

MICROCHIP n small wafer of silicon containing electronic circuits ▷ vb implant (an animal) with a microchip tag for purposes of identification

MICROCODE n set of computer instructions

MICROCOPY n greatly reduced photographic copy of a printed page, drawing, etc, on microfilm or microfiche

MICROCOSM n miniature representation of something

MICROCYTE n unusually small red blood cell

MICRODONT adj having unusually small teeth

MICRODOT n photographic copy of a document reduced to pinhead size

MICRODOTS > MICRODOT

MICROFILM n miniaturized recording of books or documents on a roll of film ▷ vb photograph a page or document on microfilm

MICROFINE adj composed of tiny particles

MICROFORM n method of storing symbolic information by using photographic reduction techniques, such as microfilm, microfiche, etc

MICROGLIA n one of the two types of non-nervous tissue (glia) found in the central nervous system, having macrophage activity

MICROGRAM n photograph or drawing of an object as viewed through a microscope

MICROHM n millionth of ohm

MICROHMS > MICROHM

MICROINCH n millionth of inch

MICROJET n light jet-propelled aircraft

MICROJETS > MICROJET

MICROLITE n small private aircraft carrying no more than two people, with an empty weight of not more than 150 kg and a wing area not less than 10 square metres: used in pleasure flying and racing

MICROLITH n small Mesolithic flint tool which was made from a blade and formed part of hafted tools

MICROLOAN n very small loan

MICROLOGY n study of microscopic things

MICROLUX n millionth of a lux

MICROMERE n any of the small cells formed by unequal splitting of a fertilized ovum

MICROMESH n very fine mesh

MICROMHO n millionth of mho

MICROMHOS > MICROMHO

MICROMINI n very short skirt

MICROMOLE n millionth of mole

MICROMORT n unit of risk

MICRON n unit of length equal to one millionth of a metre

MICRONISE same as > MICRONIZE

MICRONIZE vb break down to very small particles

MICRONS > MICRON

MICROPORE n very small pore

MICROPSIA n defect of vision in which objects appear to be smaller than they appear to a person with normal vision

MICROPUMP n small pump inserted in skin to automatically deliver medicine

MICROPYLE n small opening in the integuments of a plant ovule through which the male gametes pass

MICROS > MICRO

MICROSITE n website that is intended for a specific limited purpose and is often temporary

MICROSOME n any of the small particles consisting of ribosomes and fragments of attached endoplasmic reticulum that can be isolated from cells by centrifugal action

MICROTOME n instrument used for cutting thin sections, esp of biological material, for microscopical examination

MICROTOMY n cutting of sections with a microtome

MICROTONE n any musical interval smaller than a semitone

MICROTUBE n tiny tube

MICROVOLT n millionth of volt

MICROWATT n millionth of watt

MICROWAVE n electromagnetic wave with a wavelength of a few centimetres, used in radar and cooking ▷ vb cook in a microwave oven

MICROWIRE n very fine wire

MICRURGY n manipulation and examination of single cells under a microscope

MICS > MIC

MICTION n urination

MICTIONS > MICTION

MICTURATE vb urinate

MID adj intermediate, middle ▷ n middle ▷ prep amid

MIDAIR n some point above ground level, in the air

MIDAIRS > MIDAIR

MIDBAND adj using a range of frequencies between narrowband and broadband

MIDBRAIN n part of the brain that develops from the middle portion of the embryonic neural tube

MIDBRAINS > MIDBRAIN

MIDCALF n garment reaching to middle of the calf

MIDCALVES > MIDCALF

MIDCAP adj (of investments) involving medium-sized amounts of capital

MIDCOURSE adj in middle of course

MIDCULT n middlebrow culture

MIDCULTS > MIDCULT

MIDDAY n noon

MIDDAYS > MIDDAY

MIDDEN n rubbish heap

MIDDENS > MIDDEN

MIDDEST adj in middle

MIDDIE same as > MIDDY

MIDDIES > MIDDY

MIDDLE adj equidistant from two extremes ▷ n middle point or part ▷ vb place in the middle

MIDDLED > MIDDLE

MIDDLEMAN n trader who buys from the producer and sells to the consumer

MIDDLEMEN > MIDDLEMAN

MIDDLER n pupil in middle years at school

MIDDLERS > MIDDLER

MIDDLES > MIDDLE

MIDDLING adj mediocre ▷ adv moderately

MIDDLINGS pl n poorer or coarser part of flour or other products

MIDDORSAL adj in middle or back

MIDDY n middle-sized glass of beer

MIDFIELD n area between the two opposing defences

MIDFIELDS > MIDFIELD

MIDGE n small mosquito-like insect

MIDGES > MIDGE

MIDGET n very small person or thing ▷ adj much smaller than normal

MIDGETS > MIDGET

MIDGIE n informal word for a midge

MIDGIER > MIDGY

MIDGIES > MIDGIE

MIDGIEST > MIDGY

MIDGUT n middle part of the digestive tract

MIDGUTS > MIDGUT

MIDGY adj characterized by midges

MIDI adj (of a skirt, coat, etc) reaching to below the knee or midcalf ▷ n skirt, coat, etc reaching to below the knee or midcalf

MIDIBUS n medium-sized bus

MIDIBUSES > MIDIBUS

MIDINETTE n Parisian seamstress or salesgirl in a clothes shop

MIDIRON n golf club used for medium-length approach shots

MIDIRONS > MIDIRON

MIDIS > MIDI

MIDISKIRT n skirt of medium length

MIDLAND n middle part of a country

MIDLANDER n person living in the midlands

MIDLANDS > MIDLAND

MIDLEG n middle of leg

MIDLEGS > MIDLEG

MIDLIFE n middle age

MIDLIFER n middle-aged person

MIDLIFERS > MIDLIFER

MIDLINE n line at middle of something

MIDLINES > MIDLINE

MIDLIST n books in publisher's range that sell reasonably well

MIDLISTS > MIDLIST

MIDLIVES > MIDLIFE

MIDMONTH n middle of month

MIDMONTHS > MIDMONTH

MIDMOST adv in the middle or midst ▷ n the middle or midst

MIDMOSTS > MIDMOST

MIDNIGHT n twelve o'clock at night

MIDNIGHTS > MIDNIGHT

MIDNOON n noon

MIDNOONS > MIDNOON

MIDPAY adj paying more than an unskilled job but less than a high-income one

MIDPOINT n point on a line equally distant from either end

MIDPOINTS > MIDPOINT

MIDRANGE n part of loudspeaker

MIDRANGES > MIDRANGE

MIDRASH n homily on a Jewish scriptural passage

MIDRASHIC > MIDRASH

MIDRASHIM > MIDRASH

m

m

MIDRASHOT > MIDRASH
MIDRIB n main vein of a leaf
MIDRIBS > MIDRIB
MIDRIFF n middle part of the body
MIDRIFFS > MIDRIFF
MIDS > MID
MIDSEASON adj taking place in the middle of the season
MIDSHIP adj in, of, or relating to the middle of a vessel ▷ n middle of a vessel
MIDSHIPS See > AMIDSHIPS
MIDSHORE adj between the inshore and the offshore
MIDSIZE adj medium-sized
MIDSIZED same as > MIDSIZE
MIDSOLE n layer between the inner and the outer sole of a shoe
MIDSOLES > MIDSOLE
MIDSPACE n area in middle of space
MIDSPACES > MIDSPACE
MIDST See > AMID
MIDSTORY n level of forest trees between smallest and tallest
MIDSTREAM n middle of a stream or river ▷ adj in or towards the middle of a stream or river
MIDSTS > MIDST
MIDSUMMER n middle of summer
MIDTERM n middle of a term in a school, university, etc
MIDTERMS > MIDTERM
MIDTHIGH n garment reaching to the middle of the thigh
MIDTHIGHS > MIDTHIGH
MIDTOWN n centre of a town
MIDTOWNS > MIDTOWN
MIDWATCH n naval watch period beginning at midnight
MIDWATER n middle part of a body of water
MIDWATERS > MIDWATER
MIDWAY adv halfway ▷ adj in or at the middle of the distance ▷ n place in a fair, carnival, etc, where sideshows are located
MIDWAYS > MIDWAY
MIDWEEK n middle of the week
MIDWEEKLY > MIDWEEK
MIDWEEKS > MIDWEEK
MIDWIFE n trained person who assists at childbirth ▷ vb act as midwife
MIDWIFED > MIDWIFE
MIDWIFERY n art or practice of a midwife
MIDWIFES > MIDWIFE
MIDWIFING > MIDWIFE
MIDWINTER n middle or depth of winter
MIDWIVE vb act as midwife
MIDWIVED > MIDWIVE
MIDWIVES > MIDWIVE
MIDWIVING > MIDWIVE
MIDYEAR n middle of the year

MIDYEARS > MIDYEAR
MIELIE same as > MEALIE
MIELIES > MIELIE
MIEN n person's bearing, demeanour, or appearance
MIENS > MIEN
MIEVE same as > MOVE
MIEVED > MIEVE
MIEVES > MIEVE
MIEVING > MIEVE
MIFF vb take offence or offend ▷ n petulant mood
MIFFED > MIFF
MIFFIER > MIFFY
MIFFIEST > MIFFY
MIFFILY > MIFFY
MIFFINESS > MIFFY
MIFFING > MIFF
MIFFS > MIFF
MIFFY adj easily upset
MIFTY same as > MIFFY
MIG n marble used in games
MIGAWD interj interjection used to express surprise
MIGG same as > MIG
MIGGLE n US word for playing marble
MIGGLES > MIGGLE
MIGGS > MIGG
MIGHT n physical strength
MIGHTEST > MAY
MIGHTFUL same as > MIGHTY
MIGHTIER > MIGHTY
MIGHTIEST > MIGHTY
MIGHTILY adv great extent, amount, or degree
MIGHTS > MIGHT
MIGHTST > MAY
MIGHTY adj powerful ▷ adv very
MIGMATITE n composite rock body containing two types of rock (esp igneous and metamorphic rock) that have interacted with each other but are nevertheless still distinguishable
MIGNON adj small and pretty ▷ n tender boneless cut of meat
MIGNONNE > MIGNON
MIGNONNES > MIGNON
MIGNONS > MIGNON
MIGRAINE n severe headache, often with nausea and visual disturbances
MIGRAINES > MIGRAINE
MIGRANT n person or animal that moves from one place to another ▷ adj moving from one place to another
MIGRANTS > MIGRANT
MIGRATE vb move from one place to settle in another
MIGRATED > MIGRATE
MIGRATES > MIGRATE
MIGRATING > MIGRATE
MIGRATION n act or an instance of migrating
MIGRATOR > MIGRATE
MIGRATORS > MIGRATE
MIGRATORY adj (of an animal) migrating every year
MIGS > MIG
MIHA n young fern frond which has not yet opened

MIHAS > MIHA
MIHI n Māori ceremonial greeting ▷ vb greet
MIHIED > MIHI
MIHIING > MIHI
MIHIS > MIHI
MIHRAB n niche in a mosque showing the direction of Mecca
MIHRABS > MIHRAB
MIJNHEER same as > MYNHEER
MIJNHEERS > MIJNHEER
MIKADO n Japanese emperor
MIKADOS > MIKADO
MIKE n microphone ▷ vb supply with a microphone
MIKED > MIKE
MIKES > MIKE
MIKING > MIKE
MIKRA > MIKRON
MIKRON same as > MICRON
MIKRONS > MIKRON
MIKVA n place for ritual bathing by Orthodox Jews
MIKVAH n pool used for ritual purification
MIKVAHS > MIKVAH
MIKVAS > MIKVA
MIKVEH same as > MIKVAH
MIKVEHS > MIKVEH
MIKVOS > MIKVEH
MIKVOT > MIKVEH
MIKVOTH > MIKVAH
MIL n unit of length equal to one thousandth of an inch
MILADI same as > MILADY
MILADIES > MILADY
MILADIS > MILADI
MILADY n (formerly) a continental title for an English gentlewoman
MILAGE same as > MILEAGE
MILAGES > MILAGE
MILCH adj (of a cow) giving milk
MILCHIG same as > MILCHIK
MILCHIK adj containing or used in the preparation of milk products
MILD adj not strongly flavoured ▷ n dark beer flavoured with fewer hops than bitter ▷ vb become gentle
MILDED > MILD
MILDEN vb make or become mild or milder
MILDENED > MILDEN
MILDENING > MILDEN
MILDENS > MILDEN
MILDER > MILD
MILDEST > MILD
MILDEW same as > MOULD
MILDEWED > MILDEW
MILDEWIER > MILDEWY
MILDEWING > MILDEW
MILDEWS > MILDEW
MILDEWY adj covered with mildew
MILDING > MILD
MILDISH adj rather mild
MILDLY > MILD
MILDNESS > MILD
MILDS > MILD

MILE n unit of length equal to 1760 yards or 1.609 kilometres
MILEAGE n distance travelled in miles
MILEAGES > MILEAGE
MILEPOST n signpost that shows the distance in miles to or from a place
MILEPOSTS > MILEPOST
MILER n athlete, horse, etc, that specializes in races of one mile
MILERS > MILER
MILES > MILE
MILESIAN adj Irish
MILESIMO n Spanish word meaning thousandth
MILESIMOS > MILESIMO
MILESTONE same as > MILEPOST
MILF n sexually attractive older woman
MILFOIL same as > YARROW
MILFOILS > MILFOIL
MILFS > MILF
MILIA > MILIUM
MILIARIA n acute itching eruption of the skin, caused by blockage of the sweat glands
MILIARIAL > MILIARIA
MILIARIAS > MILIARIA
MILIARY adj resembling or relating to millet seeds
MILIEU n environment or surroundings
MILIEUS > MILIEU
MILIEUX > MILIEU
MILING n activity of running one mile
MILINGS > MILING
MILITANCE n the condition or fact of being militant, esp in pursuing a political or social end
MILITANCY > MILITANT
MILITANT adj aggressive or vigorous in support of a cause ▷ n militant person
MILITANTS > MILITANT
MILITAR same as > MILITARY
MILITARIA pl n items of military interest, such as weapons, uniforms, medals, etc, esp from the past
MILITARY adj of or for soldiers, armies, or war ▷ n armed services
MILITATE vb have a strong influence or effect
MILITATED > MILITATE
MILITATES > MILITATE
MILITIA n military force of trained citizens
MILITIAS > MILITIA
MILIUM n pimple
MILK n white fluid produced by female mammals to feed their young ▷ vb draw milk from
MILKED > MILK
MILKEN adj of or like milk
MILKER n cow, goat, etc, that yields milk
MILKERS > MILKER

MILKFISH n type of large silvery tropical food and game fish

MILKIER > MILKY

MILKIEST > MILKY

MILKILY > MILKY

MILKINESS > MILKY

MILKING > MILK

MILKINGS > MILKING

MILKLESS > MILK

MILKLIKE > MILK

MILKMAID n (esp in former times) woman who milks cows

MILKMAIDS > MILKMAID

MILKMAN n man who delivers milk to people's houses

MILKMEN > MILKMAN

MILKO informal name for > MILKMAN

MILKOS > MILKO

MILKS > MILK

MILKSHAKE n drink of flavoured milk

MILKSHED n area where milk is produced

MILKSHEDS > MILKSHED

MILKSOP n feeble man

MILKSOPPY adj like a milksop

MILKSOPS > MILKSOP

MILKTOAST n meek, submissive, or timid person

MILKWEED n monarch butterfly

MILKWEEDS > MILKWEED

MILKWOOD n tree producing latex

MILKWOODS > MILKWOOD

MILKWORT n plant with small flowers

MILKWORTS > MILKWORT

MILKY adj of or like milk

MILL n factory ▷ vb grind, press, or process in or as if in a mill

MILLABLE > MILL

MILLAGE adj American tax rate calculated in thousandths per dollar

MILLAGES > MILLAGE

MILLBOARD n strong pasteboard, used esp in book covers

MILLCAKE n food for livestock

MILLCAKES > MILLCAKE

MILLDAM n dam built to raise the water level to turn a millwheel

MILLDAMS > MILLDAM

MILLE French word for > THOUSAND

MILLED adj crushed or ground in a mill

MILLENARY adj of or relating to a thousand or to a thousand years ▷ n adherent of millenarianism

MILLENNIA n plural of millennium: period or cycle of one thousand years

MILLEPED same as > MILLEPEDE

MILLEPEDE same as > MILLIPEDE

MILLEPEDS > MILLEPED

MILLEPORE n type of tropical colonial coral-like hydrozoan

MILLER n person who works in a mill

MILLERITE n yellow mineral consisting of nickel sulphide

MILLERS > MILLER

MILLES > MILLE

MILLET n type of cereal grass

MILLETS > MILLET

MILLHAND n person who works in a mill

MILLHANDS > MILLHAND

MILLHOUSE n house attached to mill

MILLIAMP n one thousandth of an ampere

MILLIAMPS > MILLIAMP

MILLIARD n one thousand millions

MILLIARDS > MILLIARD

MILLIARE n ancient Roman unit of distance

MILLIARES > MILLIARE

MILLIARY adj relating to or marking a distance equal to an ancient Roman mile of a thousand paces

MILLIBAR n unit of atmospheric pressure

MILLIBARS > MILLIBAR

MILLIE n insulting name for a young working-class woman

MILLIEME n Tunisian monetary unit worth one thousandth of a dinar

MILLIEMES > MILLIEME

MILLIER n metric weight of million grams

MILLIERS > MILLIER

MILLIES > MILLIE

MILLIGAL n unit of gravity

MILLIGALS > MILLIGAL

MILLIGRAM n thousandth part of a gram

MILLILUX n thousandth of lux

MILLIME same as > MILLIEME

MILLIMES > MILLIME

MILLIMHO n thousandth of mho

MILLIMHOS > MILLIMHO

MILLIMOLE n thousandth of mole

MILLINE n measurement of advertising space

MILLINER n maker or seller of women's hats

MILLINERS > MILLINER

MILLINERY n hats, trimmings, etc, sold by a milliner

MILLINES > MILLINE

MILLING n act or process of grinding, cutting, pressing, or crushing in a mill

MILLINGS > MILLING

MILLIOHM n thousandth of ohm

MILLIOHMS > MILLIOHM

MILLION n one thousand thousands

MILLIONS > MILLION

MILLIONTH n one of 1 000 000 approximately equal parts of something ▷ adj being the ordinal number of 1 000 000 in numbering or counting order, etc

MILLIPED same as > MILLIPEDE

MILLIPEDE n small animal with a jointed body and many pairs of legs

MILLIPEDS > MILLIPED

MILLIREM n unit of radiation

MILLIREMS > MILLIREM

MILLIVOLT n thousandth of volt

MILLIWATT n thousandth of watt

MILLOCRAT n member of a government of mill owners

MILLPOND n pool which provides water to turn a millwheel

MILLPONDS > MILLPOND

MILLRACE n current of water that turns a millwheel

MILLRACES > MILLRACE

MILLRIND n iron support fitted across an upper millstone

MILLRINDS > MILLRIND

MILLRUN same as > MILLRACE

MILLRUNS > MILLRUN

MILLS > MILL

MILLSCALE n scale on metal being heated

MILLSTONE n flat circular stone for grinding corn

MILLTAIL n channel carrying water away from mill

MILLTAILS > MILLTAIL

MILLWHEEL n waterwheel that drives a mill

MILLWORK n work done in a mill

MILLWORKS > MILLWORK

MILNEB n type of pesticide

MILNEBS > MILNEB

MILO n variety of sorghum with heads of yellow or pinkish seeds

MILOMETER n device that records the number of miles that a bicycle or motor vehicle has travelled

MILOR same as > MILORD

MILORD n (formerly) a continental title used for an English gentleman

MILORDS > MILORD

MILORS > MILOR

MILOS > MILO

MILPA n form of subsistence agriculture in Mexico

MILPAS > MILPA

MILREIS n former monetary unit of Portugal and Brazil

MILS > MIL

MILSEY n milk strainer

MILSEYS > MILSEY

MILT n reproductive fluid of male fish ▷ vb fertilize (the roe of a female fish) with milt

MILTED > MILT

MILTER n male fish that is mature and ready to breed

MILTERS > MILTER

MILTIER > MILTY

MILTIEST > MILTY

MILTING > MILT

MILTONIA n tropical American orchid

MILTONIAS > MILTONIA

MILTS > MILT

MILTY adj full of milt

MILTZ same as > MILT

MILTZES > MILTZ

MILVINE adj of kites and related birds

MIM adj prim, modest, or demure

MIMBAR n pulpit in mosque

MIMBARS > MIMBAR

MIME n acting without the use of words ▷ vb act in mime

MIMED > MIME

MIMEO vb mimeograph

MIMEOED > MIMEO

MIMEOING > MIMEO

MIMEOS > MIMEO

MIMER > MIME

MIMERS > MIME

MIMES > MIME

MIMESES > MIMESIS

MIMESIS n imitative representation of nature or human behaviour

MIMESISES > MIMESIS

MIMESTER > MIME

MIMESTERS > MIME

MIMETIC adj imitating or representing something

MIMETICAL > MIMETIC

MIMETITE n rare secondary mineral

MIMETITES > MIMETITE

MIMIC vb imitate (a person or manner), esp for satirical effect ▷ n person or animal that is good at mimicking ▷ adj of, relating to, or using mimicry

MIMICAL > MIMIC

MIMICKED > MIMIC

MIMICKER > MIMIC

MIMICKERS > MIMIC

MIMICKING > MIMIC

MIMICRIES > MIMICRY

MIMICRY n act or art of copying or imitating closely

MIMICS > MIMIC

MIMING > MIME

MIMIVIRUS n type of large virus

MIMMER > MIM

MIMMEST > MIM

MIMMICK same as > MINNICK

MIMMICKED > MIMMICK

MIMMICKS > MIMMICK

MIMOSA n shrub with fluffy yellow flowers and sensitive leaves

MIMOSAE > MIMOSA

MIMOSAS > MIMOSA

MIMSEY same as > MIMSY

MIMSIER > MIMSY

MIMSIEST > MIMSY

MIMSY adj prim, underwhelming, and ineffectual

MIMULUS n plants cultivated for their yellow or red flowers

MIMULUSES > MIMULUS

MINA n ancient unit of weight and money, used in Asia Minor

MINABLE > MINE

MINACIOUS adj threatening

MINACITY > MINACIOUS

MINAE > MINA

MINAR n tower

MINARET n tall slender tower of a mosque

MINARETED > MINARET

MINARETS > MINARET

MINARS > MINAR

MINAS > MINA

MINATORY adj threatening or menacing

MINBAR same as **>** MIMBAR

MINBARS > MINBAR

MINCE vb cut or grind into very small pieces ▷ n minced meat

MINCED > MINCE

MINCEMEAT n sweet mixture of dried fruit and spices

MINCER n machine for mincing meat

MINCERS > MINCER

MINCES > MINCE

MINCEUR adj (of food) low-fat

MINCIER > MINCY

MINCIEST > MINCY

MINCING adj affectedly elegant in manner

MINCINGLY > MINCING

MINCY adj excessively particular or fussy

MIND n thinking faculties ▷ vb take offence at

MINDED adj having an inclination as specified

MINDEDLY adv in the manner of a person with the kind of mind specified

MINDER n aide or bodyguard

MINDERS > MINDER

MINDFUCK n taboo term for deliberate infliction of psychological damage

MINDFUCKS > MINDFUCK

MINDFUL adj heedful

MINDFULLY > MINDFUL

MINDING > MIND

MINDINGS > MIND

MINDLESS adj stupid

MINDS > MIND

MINDSCAPE n extent of the imagination

MINDSET n ideas and attitudes with which a person approaches a situation

MINDSETS > MINDSET

MINDSHARE n level of awareness in the minds of consumers that a particular product commands

MINE pron belonging to me ▷ n deep hole for digging out coal, ores, etc ▷ vb dig for minerals

MINEABLE > MINE

MINED > MINE

MINEFIELD n area of land or water containing mines

MINELAYER n warship or aircraft for carrying and laying mines

MINEOLA same as **>** MINNEOLA

MINEOLAS > MINEOLA

MINER n person who works in a mine

MINERAL n naturally occurring inorganic substance, such as metal ▷ adj of, containing, or like minerals

MINERALS > MINERAL

MINERS > MINER

MINES > MINE

MINESHAFT n vertical entrance into mine

MINESTONE n ore

MINETTE n type of rock

MINETTES > MINETTE

MINEVER same as **>** MINIVER

MINEVERS > MINEVER

MING vb mix

MINGE n vulgar word for female genitals

MINGED > MING

MINGER n insulting word for an unattractive person

MINGERS > MINGER

MINGES > MINGE

MINGIER > MINGY

MINGIEST > MINGY

MINGILY adv in a miserly manner

MINGINESS > MINGY

MINGING adj unattractive or unpleasant

MINGLE vb mix or blend

MINGLED > MINGLE

MINGLER > MINGLE

MINGLERS > MINGLE

MINGLES > MINGLE

MINGLING > MINGLE

MINGLINGS > MINGLE

MINGS > MING

MINGY adj miserly

MINI same as **>** MINIDRESS

MINIATE vb paint with minium

MINIATED > MINIATE

MINIATES > MINIATE

MINIATING > MINIATE

MINIATION > MINIATE

MINIATURE n small portrait, model, or copy ▷ adj small-scale ▷ vb reproduce in miniature

MINIBAR n selection of drinks and confectionery provided in a hotel room

MINIBARS > MINIBAR

MINIBIKE n light motorcycle

MINIBIKER > MINIBIKE

MINIBIKES > MINIBIKE

MINIBREAK n short holiday

MINIBUS n small bus

MINIBUSES > MINIBUS

MINICAB n ordinary car used as a taxi

MINICABS > MINICAB

MINICAM n portable television camera

MINICAMP n period spent together in isolation by sports team

MINICAMPS > MINICAMP

MINICAMS > MINICAM

MINICAR n small car

MINICARS > MINICAR

MINICOM n device allowing typed telephone messages to be sent and received

MINICOMS > MINICOM

MINIDISC n (esp formerly) small recordable compact disc

MINIDISCS > MINIDISC

MINIDISH n small parabolic aerial for reception or transmission to a communications satellite

MINIDISK same as **>** MINIDISC

MINIDISKS > MINIDISK

MINIDRESS n very short dress, at least four inches above the knee

MINIER > MINY

MINIEST > MINY

MINIFIED > MINIFY

MINIFIES > MINIFY

MINIFY vb minimize or lessen the size or importance of (something)

MINIFYING > MINIFY

MINIGOLF n putting game played via various obstacles

MINIGOLFS > MINIGOLF

MINIKIN n small, dainty, or affected person or thing ▷ adj dainty, prim, or affected

MINIKINS > MINIKIN

MINILAB n equipment for processing photographic film

MINILABS > MINILAB

MINIM n note half the length of a semibreve ▷ adj very small

MINIMA > MINIMUM

MINIMAL adj minimum ▷ n small surfboard

MINIMALLY > MINIMAL

MINIMALS > MINIMAL

MINIMART n convenience store

MINIMARTS > MINIMART

MINIMAX n lowest of a set of maximum values ▷ vb make maximum as low as possible

MINIMAXED > MINIMAX

MINIMAXES > MINIMAX

MINIMENT same as **>** MUNIMENT

MINIMENTS > MINIMENT

MINIMILL n small mill

MINIMILLS > MINIMILL

MINIMISE same as **>** MINIMIZE

MINIMISED > MINIMISE

MINIMISER > MINIMIZE

MINIMISES > MINIMISE

MINIMISM n desire to reduce to minimum

MINIMISMS > MINIMISM

MINIMIST > MINIMISM

MINIMISTS > MINIMISM

MINIMIZE vb reduce to a minimum

MINIMIZED > MINIMIZE

MINIMIZER > MINIMIZE

MINIMIZES > MINIMIZE

MINIMOTO n reduced-size replica motorcycle used for racing

MINIMOTOS > MINIMOTO

MINIMS > MINIM

MINIMUM n least possible (amount or number) ▷ adj of, being, or showing a minimum or minimums

MINIMUMS > MINIMUM

MINIMUS adj youngest: used after the surname of a schoolboy with elder brothers at the same school

MINIMUSES > MINIMUS

MINING n act, process, or industry of extracting coal or ores from the earth

MININGS > MINING

MINION n servile assistant ▷ adj dainty, pretty, or elegant

MINIONS > MINION

MINIPARK n small park

MINIPARKS > MINIPARK

MINIPILL n low-dose oral contraceptive containing a progestogen only

MINIPILLS > MINIPILL

MINIRUGBY n version of rugby with fewer players

MINIS > MINI

MINISCULE same as **>** MINUSCULE

MINISH vb diminish

MINISHED > MINISH

MINISHES > MINISH

MINISHING > MINISH

MINISKI n short ski

MINISKIRT n very short skirt

MINISKIS > MINISKI

MINISODE n episode of a television series shortened for broadcast on the internet

MINISODES > MINISODE

MINISTATE n small independent state

MINISTER n head of a government department ▷ vb attend to the needs of

MINISTERS > MINISTER

MINISTRY n profession or duties of a member of the clergy

MINITOWER n computer in small vertical cabinet

MINITRACK n satellite tracking system

MINIUM n bright red poisonous insoluble oxide of lead

MINIUMS > MINIUM

MINIVAN n small van, esp one with seats in the back for carrying passengers

MINIVANS > MINIVAN

MINIVER n white fur, used in ceremonial costumes

MINIVERS > MINIVER

MINIVET n brightly coloured tropical Asian cuckoo shrike

MINIVETS > MINIVET
MINK n stoat-like animal
MINKE n as in minke whale type of small whalebone whale or rorqual
MINKES > MINKE
MINKS > MINK
MINNEOLA n juicy citrus fruit that is a cross between a tangerine and a grapefruit
MINNEOLAS > MINNEOLA
MINNICK vb behave in fussy way
MINNICKED > MINNICK
MINNICKS > MINNICK
MINNIE n mother
MINNIES > MINNIE
MINNOCK same as > MINNICK
MINNOCKED > MINNOCK
MINNOCKS > MINNOCK
MINNOW n small freshwater fish
MINNOWS > MINNOW
MINNY same as > MINNIE
MINO same as > MYNAH
MINOR adj lesser ⊳ n person regarded legally as a child ⊳ vb take a minor
MINORCA n breed of light domestic fowl
MINORCAS > MINORCA
MINORED > MINOR
MINORING > MINOR
MINORITY n lesser number
MINORS > MINOR
MINORSHIP > MINOR
MINOS > MINO
MINOTAUR n as in minotaur beetle kind of dung-beetle
MINOXIDIL n drug used to counter baldness
MINSHUKU n guesthouse in Japan
MINSHUKUS > MINSHUKU
MINSTER n cathedral or large church
MINSTERS > MINSTER
MINSTREL n medieval singer or musician
MINSTRELS > MINSTREL
MINT n plant with aromatic leaves ⊳ vb make (coins)
MINTAGE n process of minting
MINTAGES > MINTAGE
MINTED > MINT
MINTER > MINT
MINTERS > MINT
MINTIER > MINT
MINTIEST > MINT
MINTING > MINT
MINTLIKE adj like mint
MINTS > MINT
MINTY > MINT
MINUEND n number from which another number is to be subtracted
MINUENDS > MINUEND
MINUET n stately dance ⊳ vb dance the minuet
MINUETED > MINUET
MINUETING > MINUET
MINUETS > MINUET
MINUS adj indicating subtraction ⊳ n sign (-) denoting subtraction or a

number less than zero ⊳ prep reduced by the subtraction of
MINUSCULE adj very small ⊳ n lower-case letter
MINUSES > MINUS
MINUTE n 60th part of an hour or degree ⊳ vb record in the minutes ⊳ adj very small
MINUTED > MINUTE
MINUTELY adv in great detail ⊳ adj occurring every minute
MINUTEMAN n (in the War of American Independence) colonial militiaman who promised to be ready to fight at one minute's notice
MINUTEMEN > MINUTEMAN
MINUTER > MINUTE
MINUTES pl n official record of the proceedings of a meeting or conference
MINUTEST > MINUTE
MINUTIA singular noun of > MINUTIAE
MINUTIAE pl n trifling or precise details
MINUTIAL > MINUTIAE
MINUTING > MINUTE
MINUTIOSE > MINUTIAE
MINX n bold girl
MINXES > MINX
MINXISH > MINX
MINY adj of or like mines
MINYAN n number of persons required by Jewish law to be present for a religious service
MINYANIM > MINYAN
MINYANS > MINYAN
MIOCENE adj of, denoting, or formed in the fourth epoch of the Tertiary period
MIOMBO n (in E Africa) a dry wooded area with sparse deciduous growth
MIOMBOS > MIOMBO
MIOSES > MIOSIS
MIOSIS n excessive contraction of the pupil of the eye
MIOSISES > MIOSIS
MIOTIC > MIOSIS
MIOTICS > MIOSIS
MIPS n unit used to express the speed of a computer's central processing unit
MIQUELET n type of lock on old firearm
MIQUELETS > MIQUELET
MIR n peasant commune in prerevolutionary Russia
MIRABELLE n small sweet yellow-orange fruit that is a variety of greengage
MIRABILIA n wonders
MIRABILIS n tropical American plant
MIRABLE adj wonderful
MIRACIDIA n plural form of singular miracidium: flat ciliated larva of flukes that hatches from the egg and gives rise asexually to other larval forms
MIRACLE n wonderful supernatural event
MIRACLES > MIRACLE

MIRADOR n window, balcony, or turret
MIRADORS > MIRADOR
MIRAGE n optical illusion, esp one caused by hot air
MIRAGES > MIRAGE
MIRANDISE same as > MIRANDIZE
MIRANDIZE vb (in USA) inform arrested person of rights
MIRBANE n substance used in perfumes
MIRBANES > MIRBANE
MIRCHI Indian English word for > HOT
MIRE n swampy ground ⊳ vb sink or be stuck in a mire
MIRED > MIRE
MIREPOIX n mixture of sautéed root vegetables
MIRES > MIRE
MIREX n type of insecticide
MIREXES > MIREX
MIRI > MIR
MIRID n variety of leaf bug
MIRIDS > MIRID
MIRIER > MIRE
MIRIEST > MIRE
MIRIFIC adj achieving wonderful things
MIRIFICAL same as > MIRIFIC
MIRIN n Japanese rice wine
MIRINESS > MIRE
MIRING > MIRE
MIRINS > MIRIN
MIRITI n South American palm
MIRITIS > MIRITI
MIRK same as > MURK
MIRKER > MIRK
MIRKEST > MIRK
MIRKIER > MIRK
MIRKIEST > MIRKY
MIRKILY > MIRK
MIRKINESS > MIRK
MIRKS > MIRK
MIRKY > MIRK
MIRLIER > MIRLY
MIRLIEST > MIRLY
MIRLIGOES n dizzy feeling
MIRLITON another name (chiefly US) for > CHAYOTE
MIRLITONS > MIRLITON
MIRLY same as > MARLY
MIRO n tall New Zealand tree
MIROMIRO n small New Zealand bird
MIROMIROS > MIROMIRO
MIROS > MIRO
MIRROR n coated glass surface for reflecting images ⊳ vb reflect in or as if in a mirror
MIRRORED > MIRROR
MIRRORING n act of mirroring
MIRRORS > MIRROR
MIRS > MIR
MIRTH n laughter, merriment, or gaiety
MIRTHFUL > MIRTH
MIRTHLESS > MIRTH
MIRTHS > MIRTH
MIRV n missile that has several warheads, each one

being directed to different enemy targets ⊳ vb arm with mirvs
MIRVED > MIRV
MIRVING > MIRV
MIRVS > MIRV
MIRY > MIRE
MIRZA n title of respect placed before the surname of a distinguished man
MIRZAS > MIRZA
MIS > MI
MISACT vb act wrongly
MISACTED > MISACT
MISACTING > MISACT
MISACTS > MISACT
MISADAPT vb adapt badly
MISADAPTS > MISADAPT
MISADD vb add badly
MISADDED > MISADD
MISADDING > MISADD
MISADDS > MISADD
MISADJUST vb adjust wrongly
MISADVICE n bad advice
MISADVISE vb give bad advice to
MISAGENT n bad agent
MISAGENTS > MISAGENT
MISAIM vb aim badly
MISAIMED > MISAIM
MISAIMING > MISAIM
MISAIMS > MISAIM
MISALIGN vb align badly
MISALIGNS > MISALIGN
MISALLEGE vb allege wrongly
MISALLIED > MISALLY
MISALLIES > MISALLY
MISALLOT vb allot wrongly
MISALLOTS > MISALLOT
MISALLY vb form unsuitable alliance
MISALTER vb alter wrongly
MISALTERS > MISALTER
MISANDRY n hatred of men
MISAPPLY vb use something for a purpose for which it is not intended or is not suited
MISARRAY n disarray
MISARRAYS > MISARRAY
MISASSAY vb assay wrongly
MISASSAYS > MISASSAY
MISASSIGN vb assign wrongly
MISASSUME vb assume wrongly
MISATE > MISEAT
MISATONE vb atone wrongly
MISATONED > MISATONE
MISATONES > MISATONE
MISAUNTER n misadventure
MISAVER vb claim wrongly
MISAVERS > MISAVER
MISAVISED adj badly advised
MISAWARD vb award wrongly
MISAWARDS > MISAWARD
MISBECAME > MISBECOME
MISBECOME vb be unbecoming to or unsuitable for
MISBEGAN > MISBEGIN

m

MISBEGIN vb begin badly
MISBEGINS >MISBEGIN
MISBEGOT adj illegitimate
MISBEGUN >MISBEGIN
MISBEHAVE vb behave badly
MISBELIEF n false or unorthodox belief
MISBESEEM vb be unsuitable for
MISBESTOW vb bestow wrongly
MISBIAS vb prejudice wrongly
MISBIASED >MISBIAS
MISBIASES >MISBIAS
MISBILL vb present inaccurate bill
MISBILLED >MISBILL
MISBILLS >MISBILL
MISBIND vb bind wrongly
MISBINDS >MISBIND
MISBIRTH n abortion
MISBIRTHS >MISBIRTH
MISBORN adj born prematurely
MISBOUND >MISBIND
MISBRAND vb put misleading label on
MISBRANDS >MISBRAND
MISBUILD vb build badly
MISBUILDS >MISBUILD
MISBUILT >MISBUILD
MISBUTTON vb button wrongly
MISCALL vb call by the wrong name
MISCALLED >MISCALL
MISCALLER >MISCALL
MISCALLS >MISCALL
MISCARRY vb have a miscarriage
MISCAST vb cast (a role or actor) inappropriately
MISCASTS >MISCAST
MISCEGEN n person of mixed race
MISCEGENE same as >MISCEGEN
MISCEGENS >MISCEGEN
MISCEGINE same as >MISCEGEN
MISCH adj as in misch metal alloy of cerium and other rare earth metals
MISCHANCE n unlucky event
MISCHANCY adj unlucky
MISCHARGE vb charge wrongly
MISCHIEF n annoying but not malicious behaviour
MISCHIEFS >MISCHIEF
MISCHOICE n bad choice
MISCHOOSE vb make bad choice
MISCHOSE >MISCHOOSE
MISCHOSEN >MISCHOOSE
MISCIBLE adj able to be mixed
MISCITE vb cite wrongly
MISCITED >MISCITE
MISCITES >MISCITE
MISCITING >MISCITE
MISCLAIM vb claim wrongly
MISCLAIMS >MISCLAIM
MISCLASS adj class badly

MISCODE vb code wrongly
MISCODED >MISCODE
MISCODES >MISCODE
MISCODING >MISCODE
MISCOIN vb coin wrongly
MISCOINED >MISCOIN
MISCOINS >MISCOIN
MISCOLOR same as >MISCOLOUR
MISCOLORS >MISCOLOR
MISCOLOUR vb give wrong colour to
MISCOOK vb cook badly
MISCOOKED >MISCOOK
MISCOOKS >MISCOOK
MISCOPIED >MISCOPY
MISCOPIES >MISCOPY
MISCOPY vb copy badly
MISCOUNT vb count or calculate incorrectly ▷ n false count or calculation
MISCOUNTS >MISCOUNT
MISCREANT n wrongdoer ▷ adj evil or villainous
MISCREATE vb create (something) badly or incorrectly ▷ adj badly or unnaturally formed or made
MISCREDIT vb disbelieve
MISCREED n false creed
MISCREEDS >MISCREED
MISCUE n faulty stroke in snooker, etc ▷ vb make a miscue
MISCUED >MISCUE
MISCUEING >MISCUE
MISCUES >MISCUE
MISCUING >MISCUE
MISCUT n cut wrongly
MISCUTS >MISCUT
MISDATE vb date (a letter, event, etc) wrongly
MISDATED >MISDATE
MISDATES >MISDATE
MISDATING >MISDATE
MISDEAL vb deal out cards incorrectly ▷ n faulty deal
MISDEALER >MISDEAL
MISDEALS >MISDEAL
MISDEALT >MISDEAL
MISDEED n wrongful act
MISDEEDS >MISDEED
MISDEEM vb form bad opinion of
MISDEEMED >MISDEEM
MISDEEMS >MISDEEM
MISDEFINE vb define badly
MISDEMEAN rare word for >MISBEHAVE
MISDEMPT >MISDEEM
MISDESERT n quality of being undeserving
MISDIAL vb dial telephone number incorrectly
MISDIALED >MISDIAL
MISDIALS >MISDIAL
MISDID >MISDO
MISDIET n wrong diet ▷ vb diet or eat improperly
MISDIETED >MISDIET
MISDIETS >MISDIET
MISDIGHT adj done badly ▷ vb mismanage or treat badly
MISDIGHTS >MISDIGHT
MISDIRECT vb give (someone) wrong directions or instructions

MISDIVIDE vb divide wrongly
MISDO vb do badly or wrongly
MISDOER >MISDO
MISDOERS >MISDO
MISDOES >MISDO
MISDOING >MISDO
MISDOINGS >MISDO
MISDONE adj done badly
MISDONNE same as >MISDONE
MISDOUBT archaic word for >DOUBT
MISDOUBTS >MISDOUBT
MISDRAW vb draw poorly
MISDRAWN >MISDRAW
MISDRAWS >MISDRAW
MISDREAD n fear of approaching evil ▷ vb fear or dread
MISDREADS >MISDREAD
MISDREW >MISDRAW
MISDRIVE vb drive badly
MISDRIVEN >MISDRIVE
MISDRIVES >MISDRIVE
MISDROVE >MISDRIVE
MISE n issue in the obsolete writ of right
MISEASE n unease
MISEASES >MISEASE
MISEAT vb eat unhealthy food
MISEATEN >MISEAT
MISEATING >MISEAT
MISEATS >MISEAT
MISEDIT vb edit badly
MISEDITED >MISEDIT
MISEDITS >MISEDIT
MISEMPLOY vb employ badly
MISENROL vb enrol wrongly
MISENROLL same as >MISENROL
MISENROLS >MISENROL
MISENTER vb enter wrongly
MISENTERS >MISENTER
MISENTRY n wrong or mistaken entry
MISER n person who hoards money and hates spending it
MISERABLE adj very unhappy, wretched ▷ n wretched person
MISERABLY >MISERABLE
MISERE n call in solo whist and other card games declaring a hand that will win no tricks
MISERERE n type of psalm
MISERERES >MISERERE
MISERES >MISERE
MISERIES >MISERY
MISERLIER >MISERLY
MISERLY adj of or resembling a miser
MISERS >MISER
MISERY n great unhappiness
MISES >MISE
MISESTEEM n lack of respect
MISEVENT n mishap
MISEVENTS >MISEVENT
MISFAITH n distrust
MISFAITHS >MISFAITH
MISFALL vb happen as piece of bad luck

MISFALLEN >MISFALL
MISFALLS >MISFALL
MISFALNE >MISFALL
MISFARE vb get on badly
MISFARED >MISFARE
MISFARES >MISFARE
MISFARING >MISFARE
MISFEASOR n someone who carries out the improper performance of an act that is lawful in itself
MISFED >MISFEED
MISFEED vb feed wrongly
MISFEEDS >MISFEED
MISFEIGN vb feign with evil motive
MISFEIGNS >MISFEIGN
MISFELL >MISFALL
MISFIELD vb fail to field properly
MISFIELDS >MISFIELD
MISFILE vb file (papers, records, etc) wrongly
MISFILED >MISFILE
MISFILES >MISFILE
MISFILING >MISFILE
MISFIRE vb (of a firearm or engine) fail to fire correctly ▷ n act or an instance of misfiring
MISFIRED >MISFIRE
MISFIRES >MISFIRE
MISFIRING >MISFIRE
MISFIT n person not suited to his or her social environment ▷ vb fail to fit or be fitted
MISFITS >MISFIT
MISFITTED >MISFIT
MISFOCUS n wrong or poor focus
MISFOLD vb fold wrongly
MISFOLDED >MISFOLD
MISFOLDS >MISFOLD
MISFORM vb form badly
MISFORMED >MISFORM
MISFORMS >MISFORM
MISFRAME vb frame wrongly
MISFRAMED >MISFRAME
MISFRAMES >MISFRAME
MISGAGE vb gage wrongly
MISGAGED >MISGAGE
MISGAGES >MISGAGE
MISGAGING >MISGAGE
MISGAUGE vb gauge badly
MISGAUGED >MISGAUGE
MISGAUGES >MISGAUGE
MISGAVE >MISGIVE
MISGENDER vb refer to a person as the wrong gender
MISGIVE vb make or be apprehensive or suspicious
MISGIVEN >MISGIVE
MISGIVES >MISGIVE
MISGIVING n feeling of fear or doubt
MISGO vb go wrong way
MISGOES >MISGO
MISGOING >MISGO
MISGONE >MISGO
MISGOTTEN adj obtained dishonestly
MISGOVERN vb govern badly
MISGRADE vb grade wrongly
MISGRADED >MISGRADE
MISGRADES >MISGRADE

MISGRAFF *adj* badly done
MISGRAFT *vb* graft wrongly
MISGRAFTS > MISGRAFT
MISGREW > MISGROW
MISGROW *vb* grow in unsuitable way
MISGROWN > MISGROW
MISGROWS > MISGROW
MISGROWTH > MISGROW
MISGUESS *vb* guess wrongly
MISGUGGLE *vb* handle incompetently
MISGUIDE *vb* guide or direct wrongly or badly
MISGUIDED *adj* mistaken or unwise
MISGUIDER > MISGUIDE
MISGUIDES > MISGUIDE
MISHANDLE *vb* handle badly or inefficiently
MISHANTER *n* misfortune
MISHAP *n* minor accident ▷ *vb* happen as bad luck
MISHAPPED > MISHAP
MISHAPPEN *vb* happen as bad luck
MISHAPS > MISHAP
MISHAPT *same as* > MISSHAPEN
MISHEAR *vb* hear (what someone says) wrongly
MISHEARD > MISHEAR
MISHEARS > MISHEAR
MISHEGAAS *same as* > MESHUGAAS
MISHEGOSS *same as* > MESHUGAAS
MISHIT *n* faulty shot, kick, or stroke ▷ *vb* hit or kick a ball with a faulty stroke
MISHITS > MISHIT
MISHMASH *n* confused collection or mixture
MISHMEE *n* root of Asian plant
MISHMEES > MISHMEE
MISHMI *n* evergreen perennial plant
MISHMIS > MISHMI
MISHMOSH *same as* > MISHMASH
MISHUGAS *same as* > MESHUGAAS
MISINFER *vb* infer wrongly
MISINFERS > MISINFER
MISINFORM *vb* give incorrect information to
MISINTEND *vb* intend to harm
MISINTER *vb* bury wrongly
MISINTERS > MISINTER
MISJOIN *vb* join badly
MISJOINED > MISJOIN
MISJOINS > MISJOIN
MISJUDGE *vb* judge wrongly or unfairly
MISJUDGED > MISJUDGE
MISJUDGER > MISJUDGE
MISJUDGES > MISJUDGE
MISKAL *n* unit of weight in Iran
MISKALS > MISKAL
MISKEEP *vb* keep wrongly
MISKEEPS > MISKEEP
MISKEN *vb* be unaware of
MISKENNED > MISKEN
MISKENS > MISKEN

MISKENT > MISKEN
MISKEPT > MISKEEP
MISKEY *vb* key wrongly
MISKEYED > MISKEY
MISKEYING > MISKEY
MISKEYS > MISKEY
MISKICK *vb* fail to kick properly
MISKICKED > MISKICK
MISKICKS > MISKICK
MISKNEW > MISKNOW
MISKNOW *vb* have wrong idea about
MISKNOWN > MISKNOW
MISKNOWS > MISKNOW
MISLABEL *vb* label badly
MISLABELS > MISLABEL
MISLABOR *vb* labour wrongly
MISLABORS > MISLABOR
MISLABOUR *vb* labour wrongly
MISLAID > MISLAY
MISLAIN > MISLAY
MISLAY *vb* lose (something) temporarily
MISLAYER > MISLAY
MISLAYERS > MISLAY
MISLAYING > MISLAY
MISLAYS > MISLAY
MISLEAD *vb* give false or confusing information to
MISLEADER > MISLEAD
MISLEADS > MISLEAD
MISLEARED *adj* badly brought up
MISLEARN *vb* learn wrongly
MISLEARNS > MISLEARN
MISLEARNT > MISLEARN
MISLED > MISLEAD
MISLEEKE *same as* > MISLIKE
MISLEEKED > MISLEEKE
MISLEEKES > MISLEEKE
MISLETOE *same as* > MISTLETOE
MISLETOES > MISLETOE
MISLIE *vb* lie wrongly
MISLIES > MISLIE
MISLIGHT *vb* use light to lead astray
MISLIGHTS > MISLIGHT
MISLIKE *vb* dislike ▷ *n* dislike or aversion
MISLIKED > MISLIKE
MISLIKER > MISLIKE
MISLIKERS > MISLIKE
MISLIKES > MISLIKE
MISLIKING > MISLIKE
MISLIPPEN *vb* distrust
MISLIT > MISLIGHT
MISLIVE *vb* live wickedly
MISLIVED > MISLIVE
MISLIVES > MISLIVE
MISLIVING > MISLIVE
MISLOCATE *vb* put in wrong place
MISLODGE *vb* lodge wrongly
MISLODGED > MISLODGE
MISLODGES > MISLODGE
MISLUCK *vb* have bad luck
MISLUCKED > MISLUCK
MISLUCKS > MISLUCK
MISLYING > MISLIE
MISMADE > MISMAKE
MISMAKE *vb* make badly

MISMAKES > MISMAKE
MISMAKING > MISMAKE
MISMANAGE *vb* organize or run (something) badly
MISMARK *vb* mark wrongly
MISMARKED > MISMARK
MISMARKS > MISMARK
MISMARRY *vb* make unsuitable marriage
MISMATCH *vb* form an unsuitable partner, opponent, or set ▷ *n* unsuitable match
MISMATE *vb* mate wrongly
MISMATED > MISMATE
MISMATES > MISMATE
MISMATING *n* unintended breeding of domesticated animals
MISMEET *vb* fail to meet
MISMEETS > MISMEET
MISMET > MISMEET
MISMETRE *vb* fail to follow the metre of a poem
MISMETRED > MISMETRE
MISMETRES > MISMETRE
MISMOVE *vb* move badly
MISMOVED > MISMOVE
MISMOVES > MISMOVE
MISMOVING > MISMOVE
MISNAME *vb* name badly
MISNAMED > MISNAME
MISNAMES > MISNAME
MISNAMING > MISNAME
MISNOMER *n* incorrect or unsuitable name ▷ *vb* apply a misnomer to
MISNOMERS > MISNOMER
MISNUMBER *vb* number wrongly
MISO *n* thick brown salty paste made from soya beans
MISOCLERE *adj* hostile to clergy
MISOGAMIC > MISOGAMY
MISOGAMY *n* hatred of marriage
MISOGYNIC *adj* hating women
MISOGYNY *n* hatred of women
MISOLOGY *n* hatred of reasoning or reasoned argument
MISONEISM *n* hatred of anything new
MISONEIST > MISONEISM
MISORDER *vb* order badly
MISORDERS > MISORDER
MISORIENT *vb* orient incorrectly
MISOS > MISO
MISPAGE *vb* page wrongly
MISPAGED > MISPAGE
MISPAGES > MISPAGE
MISPAGING > MISPAGE
MISPAINT *vb* paint badly or wrongly
MISPAINTS > MISPAINT
MISPARSE *vb* parse wrongly
MISPARSED > MISPARSE
MISPARSES > MISPARSE
MISPART *vb* part wrongly
MISPARTED > MISPART
MISPARTS > MISPART
MISPATCH *vb* patch wrongly
MISPEN *vb* write wrongly

MISPENNED > MISPEN
MISPENS > MISPEN
MISPHRASE *vb* phrase badly
MISPICKEL *n* white or grey metallic mineral consisting of a sulphide of iron and arsenic that forms monoclinic crystals with an orthorhombic shape. an ore of arsenic
MISPLACE *vb* mislay
MISPLACED *adj* (of an emotion or action) directed towards a person or thing that does not deserve it
MISPLACES > MISPLACE
MISPLAN *vb* plan badly or wrongly
MISPLANS > MISPLAN
MISPLANT *vb* plant badly or wrongly
MISPLANTS > MISPLANT
MISPLAY *vb* play badly or wrongly in games or sports ▷ *n* wrong or unskilful play
MISPLAYED > MISPLAY
MISPLAYS > MISPLAY
MISPLEAD *vb* plead incorrectly
MISPLEADS > MISPLEAD
MISPLEASE *vb* displease
MISPLED > MISPLEAD
MISPOINT *vb* punctuate badly
MISPOINTS > MISPOINT
MISPOISE *n* lack of poise ▷ *vb* lack poise
MISPOISED > MISPOISE
MISPOISES > MISPOISE
MISPRAISE *vb* fail to praise properly
MISPRICE *vb* give the wrong price to
MISPRICED > MISPRICE
MISPRICES > MISPRICE
MISPRINT *n* printing error ▷ *vb* print a letter incorrectly
MISPRINTS > MISPRINT
MISPRISE *same as* > MISPRIZE
MISPRISED > MISPRISE
MISPRISES > MISPRISE
MISPRIZE *vb* fail to appreciate the value of
MISPRIZED > MISPRIZE
MISPRIZER > MISPRIZE
MISPRIZES > MISPRIZE
MISPROUD *adj* undeservedly proud
MISQUOTE *vb* quote inaccurately
MISQUOTED > MISQUOTE
MISQUOTER > MISQUOTE
MISQUOTES > MISQUOTE
MISRAISE *vb* raise wrongly or excessively
MISRAISED > MISRAISE
MISRAISES > MISRAISE
MISRATE *vb* rate wrongly
MISRATED > MISRATE
MISRATES > MISRATE
MISRATING > MISRATE
MISREAD *vb* misinterpret (a situation etc)
MISREADS > MISREAD
MISRECKON *vb* reckon wrongly

MISRECORD *vb* record wrongly

MISREFER *vb* refer wrongly

MISREFERS > MISREFER

MISREGARD *n* lack of attention ▷ *vb* have no regard for; disregard

MISRELATE *vb* relate badly

MISRELIED > MISRELY

MISRELIES > MISRELY

MISRELY *vb* rely wrongly

MISRENDER *vb* render wrongly

MISREPORT *vb* report falsely or inaccurately ▷ *n* inaccurate or false report

MISRHYMED *adj* badly rhymed

MISROUTE *vb* send wrong way

MISROUTED > MISROUTE

MISROUTES > MISROUTE

MISRULE *vb* govern inefficiently or unjustly ▷ *n* inefficient or unjust government

MISRULED > MISRULE

MISRULES > MISRULE

MISRULING > MISRULE

MISS *vb* fail to notice, hear, hit, reach, find, or catch ▷ *n* fact or instance of missing

MISSA *n* Roman Catholic mass

MISSABLE > MISS

MISSAE > MISSA

MISSAID > MISSAY

MISSAL *n* book containing the prayers and rites of the Mass

MISSALS > MISSAL

MISSAW > MISSEE

MISSAY *vb* say wrongly

MISSAYING > MISSAY

MISSAYS > MISSAY

MISSEAT *vb* seat wrongly

MISSEATED > MISSEAT

MISSEATS > MISSEAT

MISSED > MISS

MISSEE *vb* see wrongly

MISSEEING > MISSEE

MISSEEM *vb* be unsuitable for

MISSEEMED > MISSEEM

MISSEEMS > MISSEEM

MISSEEN > MISSEE

MISSEES > MISSEE

MISSEL *adj* as in *missel thrush* large European thrush

MISSELL *vb* sell (a product, esp a financial one) misleadingly

MISSELLS > MISSELL

MISSELS > MISSEL

MISSEND *vb* send wrongly

MISSENDS > MISSEND

MISSENSE *n* type of genetic mutation ▷ *vb* give a wrong sense or meaning

MISSENSED > MISSENSE

MISSENSES > MISSENSE

MISSENT > MISSEND

MISSES > MISS

MISSET *vb* set wrongly

MISSETS > MISSET

MISSHAPE *vb* shape badly ▷ *n* something that is badly shaped

MISSHAPED > MISSHAPE

MISSHAPEN *adj* badly shaped, deformed

MTSSHAPER > MISSHAPE

MISSHAPES > MISSHAPE

MISSHOD *adj* badly shod

MISSHOOD *n* state of being an unmarried woman

MISSHOODS > MISSHOOD

MISSIER > MISSY

MISSIES > MISSY

MISSIEST > MISSY

MISSILE *n* rocket with an exploding warhead

MISSILEER *n* serviceman or servicewoman who is responsible for firing missiles

MISSILERY *n* missiles collectively

MISSILES > MISSILE

MISSILRY *same as* > MISSILERY

MISSING *adj* lost or absent

MISSINGLY > MISSING

MISSION *n* specific task or duty ▷ *vb* direct a mission to or establish a mission in

MISSIONAL *adj* emphasizing preaching of gospel

MISSIONED > MISSION

MISSIONER *n* person heading a parochial mission in a Christian country

MISSIONS > MISSION

MISSIS *same as* > MISSUS

MISSISES > MISSIS

MISSISH *adj* like a schoolgirl

MISSIVE *n* letter ▷ *adj* sent or intended to be sent

MISSIVES > MISSIVE

MISSOLD > MISSELL

MISSORT *vb* sort wrongly

MISSORTED > MISSORT

MISSORTS > MISSORT

MISSOUND *vb* sound wrongly

MISSOUNDS > MISSOUND

MISSOUT *n* someone who has been overlooked

MISSOUTS > MISSOUT

MISSPACE *vb* space out wrongly

MISSPACED > MISSPACE

MISSPACES > MISSPACE

MISSPEAK *vb* speak wrongly

MISSPEAKS > MISSPEAK

MISSPELL *vb* spell (a word) wrongly

MISSPELLS > MISSPELL

MISSPELT > MISSPELL

MISSPEND *vb* waste or spend unwisely

MISSPENDS > MISSPEND

MISSPENT > MISSPEND

MISSPOKE > MISSPEAK

MISSPOKEN > MISSPEAK

MISSTAMP *vb* stamp badly

MISSTAMPS > MISSTAMP

MISSTART *vb* start wrongly

MISSTARTS > MISSTART

MISSTATE *vb* state incorrectly

MISSTATED > MISSTATE

MISSTATES > MISSTATE

MISSTEER *vb* steer badly

MISSTEERS > MISSTEER

MISSTEP *n* false step ▷ *vb* take a false step

MISSTEPS > MISSTEP

MISSTOP *vb* stop wrongly

MISSTOPS > MISSTOP

MISSTRIKE *vb* fail to strike properly

MISSTRUCK > MISSTRIKE

MISSTYLE *vb* call by the wrong name

MISSTYLED > MISSTYLE

MISSTYLES > MISSTYLE

MISSUIT *vb* be unsuitable for

MISSUITED > MISSUIT

MISSUITS > MISSUIT

MISSUS *n* one's wife or the wife of the person addressed or referred to

MISSUSES > MISSUS

MISSY *n* affectionate or disparaging form of address to a girl ▷ *adj* missish

MIST *n* thin fog ▷ *vb* cover or be covered with mist

MISTAKE *n* error or blunder ▷ *vb* misunderstand

MISTAKEN *adj* wrong in judgment or opinion

MISTAKER > MISTAKE

MISTAKERS > MISTAKE

MISTAKES > MISTAKE

MISTAKING > MISTAKE

MISTAL *n* cow shed

MISTALS > MISTAL

MISTAUGHT > MISTEACH

MISTBOW *same as* > FOGBOW

MISTBOWS > MISTBOW

MISTEACH *vb* teach badly

MISTED > MIST

MISTELL *vb* tell wrongly

MISTELLS > MISTELL

MISTEMPER *vb* make disordered

MISTEND *vb* tend wrongly

MISTENDED > MISTEND

MISTENDS > MISTEND

MISTER *n* informal form of address for a man ▷ *vb* call (someone) mister

MISTERED > MISTER

MISTERIES > MISTERY

MISTERING > MISTER

MISTERM *vb* term badly

MISTERMED > MISTERM

MISTERMS > MISTERM

MISTERS > MISTER

MISTERY *same as* > MYSTERY

MISTEUK *Scots variant of* > MISTOOK

MISTFUL > MIST

MISTHINK *vb* have poor opinion of

MISTHINKS > MISTHINK

MISTHREW > MISTHROW

MISTHROW *vb* fail to throw properly

MISTHROWN > MISTHROW

MISTHROWS > MISTHROW

MISTICO *n* small Mediterranean sailing ship

MISTICOS > MISTICO

MISTIER > MISTY

MISTIEST > MISTY

MISTIGRIS *n* joker or a blank card used as a wild card in a variety of draw poker

MISTILY > MISTY

MISTIME *vb* do (something) at the wrong time

MISTIMED > MISTIME

MISTIMES > MISTIME

MISTIMING *n* act of mistiming

MISTINESS > MISTY

MISTING *n* application of a fake suntan by spray

MISTINGS > MISTING

MISTITLE *vb* name badly

MISTITLED > MISTITLE

MISTITLES > MISTITLE

MISTLE *same as* > MIZZLE

MISTLED > MISTLE

MISTLES > MISTLE

MISTLETOE *n* evergreen plant with white berries growing as a parasite on trees

MISTLING > MISTLE

MISTOLD > MISTELL

MISTOOK *past tense of* > MISTAKE

MISTOUCH *vb* fail to touch properly

MISTRACE *vb* trace wrongly

MISTRACED > MISTRACE

MISTRACES > MISTRACE

MISTRAIN *vb* train wrongly

MISTRAINS > MISTRAIN

MISTRAL *n* strong dry northerly wind of S France

MISTRALS > MISTRAL

MISTREAT *vb* treat (a person or animal) badly

MISTREATS > MISTREAT

MISTRESS *n* woman in a position of authority, ownership, or control ▷ *vb* become a mistress

MISTRIAL *n* trial made void because of some error

MISTRIALS > MISTRIAL

MISTRUST *vb* have doubts or suspicions about ▷ *n* lack of trust

MISTRUSTS > MISTRUST

MISTRUTH *n* something untrue

MISTRUTHS > MISTRUTH

MISTRYST *vb* fail to keep an appointment with

MISTRYSTS > MISTRYST

MISTS > MIST

MISTUNE *vb* fail to tune properly

MISTUNED > MISTUNE

MISTUNES > MISTUNE

MISTUNING > MISTUNE

MISTUTOR *vb* instruct badly

MISTUTORS > MISTUTOR

MISTY *adj* full of mist

MISTYPE *vb* type badly

MISTYPED > MISTYPE

MISTYPES > MISTYPE

MISTYPING > MISTYPE

MISUNION *n* wrong or bad union

MISUNIONS > MISUNION

MISUSAGE > MISUSE

MISUSAGES > MISUSE

MISUSE n incorrect, improper, or careless use ▷ vb use wrongly

MISUSED > MISUSE

MISUSER n abuse of some right, privilege, office, etc

MISUSERS > MISUSER

MISUSES > MISUSE

MISUSING > MISUSE

MISUST > MISUSE

MISVALUE vb value badly

MISVALUED > MISVALUE

MISVALUES > MISVALUE

MISWEEN vb assess wrongly

MISWEENED > MISWEEN

MISWEENS > MISWEEN

MISWEND vb become lost

MISWENDS > MISWEND

MISWENT > MISWEND

MISWORD vb word badly

MISWORDED > MISWORD

MISWORDS > MISWORD

MISWRIT > MISWRITE

MISWRITE vb write badly

MISWRITES > MISWRITE

MISWROTE > MISWRITE

MISYOKE vb join wrongly

MISYOKED > MISYOKE

MISYOKES > MISYOKE

MISYOKING > MISYOKE

MITCH vb play truant from school

MITCHED > MITCH

MITCHES > MITCH

MITCHING > MITCH

MITE n very small spider-like animal

MITER same as > MITRE

MITERED > MITER

MITERER > MITER

MITERERS > MITER

MITERING > MITER

MITERS > MITER

MITERWORT same as > MITREWORT

MITES > MITE

MITHER vb fuss over or moan about something

MITHERED > MITHER

MITHERING > MITHER

MITHERS > MITHER

MITICIDAL > MITICIDE

MITICIDE n any drug or agent that destroys mites

MITICIDES > MITICIDE

MITIER > MITY

MITIEST > MITY

MITIGABLE > MITIGATE

MITIGANT adj acting to mitigate ▷ n means of easing, lessening, or assuaging

MITIGANTS > MITIGANT

MITIGATE vb make less severe

MITIGATED > MITIGATE

MITIGATES > MITIGATE

MITIGATOR > MITIGATE

MITIS n malleable iron

MITISES > MITIS

MITOGEN n any agent that induces mitosis

MITOGENIC > MITOGEN

MITOGENS > MITOGEN

MITOMYCIN n kind of antibiotic

MITOSES > MITOSIS

MITOSIS n type of cell division

MITOTIC > MITOSIS

MITRAILLE n hail of bullets

MITRAL adj of or like a mitre

MITRE n bishop's pointed headdress ▷ vb join with a mitre joint

MITRED > MITRE

MITRES > MITRE

MITREWORT n Asian and N American plant with clusters of small white flowers and capsules resembling a bishop's mitre

MITRIFORM adj shaped like a mitre

MITRING > MITRE

MITSVAH same as > MITZVAH

MITSVAHS > MITSVAH

MITSVOTH > MITSVAH

MITT same as > MITTEN

MITTEN n glove with one section for the thumb and one for the four fingers together

MITTENED adj wearing mittens

MITTENS > MITTEN

MITTIMUS n warrant of commitment to prison

MITTS > MITT

MITUMBA n used clothes imported for sale in African countries

MITUMBAS > MITUMBA

MITY adj having mites

MITZVAH n commandment or precept, esp one found in the Bible

MITZVAHS > MITZVAH

MITZVOTH > MITZVAH

MIURUS n type of rhythm in poetry

MIURUSES > MIURUS

MIX vb combine or blend into one mass ▷ n mixture

MIXABLE > MIX

MIXDOWN n (in sound recording) the transfer of a multitrack master mix to two-track stereo tape

MIXDOWNS > MIXDOWN

MIXED adj formed or blended together by mixing

MIXEDLY > MIXED

MIXEDNESS > MIXED

MIXEN n dunghill

MIXENS > MIXEN

MIXER n kitchen appliance used for mixing foods

MIXERS > MIXER

MIXES > MIX

MIXIBLE > MIX

MIXIER > MIXY

MIXIEST > MIXY

MIXING n act of mixing

MIXINGS > MIXING

MIXMASTER n disc jockey

MIXOLOGY n art of mixing cocktails

MIXT > MIX

MIXTAPE n compilation of songs from various sources

MIXTAPES > MIXTAPE

MIXTE adj of a type of bicycle frame

MIXTION n amber-based mixture used in making gold leaf

MIXTIONS > MIXTION

MIXTURE n something mixed

MIXTURES > MIXTURE

MIXUP n something that is mixed up

MIXUPS > MIXUP

MIXY adj mixed

MIZ shortened form of > MISERY

MIZEN same as > MIZZEN

MIZENMAST n (on a yawl, ketch, or dandy) the after mast

MIZENS > MIZEN

MIZMAZE n maze

MIZMAZES > MIZMAZE

MIZUNA n Japanese variety of lettuce

MIZUNAS > MIZUNA

MIZZ same as > MIZ

MIZZEN n sail set on a mizzenmast ▷ adj of or relating to any kind of gear used with a mizzenmast

MIZZENS > MIZZEN

MIZZES > MIZ

MIZZLE vb decamp

MIZZLED > MIZZLE

MIZZLES > MIZZLE

MIZZLIER > MIZZLE

MIZZLIEST > MIZZLE

MIZZLING > MIZZLE

MIZZLINGS > MIZZLE

MIZZLY > MIZZLE

MIZZONITE n mineral containing sodium

MIZZY adj as in mizzy maze dialect expression meaning state of confusion

MM interj expression of enjoyment of taste or smell

MMM interj interjection expressing agreement or enjoyment

MNA same as > MINA

MNAS > MNA

MNEME n ability to retain memory

MNEMES > MNEME

MNEMIC > MNEME

MNEMON n unit of memory

MNEMONIC adj intended to help the memory ▷ n something, for instance a verse, intended to help the memory

MNEMONICS n art or practice of improving or of aiding the memory

MNEMONIST > MNEMONICS

MNEMONS > MNEMON

MO n moment

MOA n large extinct flightless New Zealand bird

MOAI n any of the gigantic carved stone figures found on Easter Island (Rapa Nui)

MOAN n low cry of pain ▷ vb make or utter with a moan

MOANED > MOAN

MOANER > MOAN

MOANERS > MOAN

MOANFUL > MOAN

MOANFULLY > MOAN

MOANING > MOAN

MOANINGLY > MOAN

MOANINGS > MOAN

MOANS > MOAN

MOAS > MOA

MOAT n deep wide ditch, esp round a castle ▷ vb surround with or as if with a moat

MOATED > MOAT

MOATING > MOAT

MOATLIKE > MOAT

MOATS > MOAT

MOB n disorderly crowd ▷ vb surround in a mob

MOBBED > MOB

MOBBER > MOB

MOBBERS > MOB

MOBBIE same as > MOBBY

MOBBIES > MOBBY

MOBBING > MOB

MOBBINGS > MOB

MOBBISH > MOB

MOBBISHLY > MOB

MOBBISM n behaviour as mob

MOBBISMS > MOBBISM

MOBBLE same as > MOBLE

MOBBLED > MOBBLE

MOBBLES > MOBBLE

MOBBLING > MOBBLE

MOBBY n West Indian drink

MOBCAP n woman's 18th-century cotton cap

MOBCAPS > MOBCAP

MOBCAST vb create and upload a podcast directly from a mobile phone

MOBCASTED > MOBCAST

MOBCASTS > MOBCAST

MOBE n mobile phone

MOBES > MOBE

MOBEY same as > MOBY

MOBEYS > MOBEY

MOBIE same as > MOBY

MOBIES > MOBY

MOBILE adj able to move ▷ n hanging structure designed to move in air currents

MOBILES > MOBILE

MOBILISE same as > MOBILIZE

MOBILISED > MOBILISE

MOBILISER > MOBILISE

MOBILISES > MOBILISE

MOBILITY n ability to move physically

MOBILIZE vb (of the armed services) prepare for active service

MOBILIZED > MOBILIZE

MOBILIZER > MOBILIZE

MOBILIZES > MOBILIZE

MOBISODE n episode of a TV show made for viewing on a mobile phone

MOBISODES > MOBISODE

MOBLE vb muffle

MOBLED > MOBLE

MOBLES > MOBLE

MOBLING > MOBLE

MOBLOG n blog recorded in the form of mobile phone calls, text messages, and photographs

m

MOBLOGGER > MOBLOG
MOBLOGS > MOBLOG
MOBOCRACY n rule or domination by a mob
MOBOCRAT > MOBOCRACY
MOBOCRATS > MOBOCRACY
MOBS > MOB
MOBSMAN n person in mob
MOBSMEN > MOBSMAN
MOBSTER n member of a criminal organization
MOBSTERS > MOBSTER
MOBY n mobile phone
MOC shortening of
  > MOCCASIN
MOCASSIN same as
  > MOCCASIN
MOCASSINS > MOCASSIN
MOCCASIN n soft leather shoe
MOCCASINS > MOCCASIN
MOCCIES pl n informal Australian word for moccasins
MOCH n spell of humid weather ⊳ vb (of foods) become musty or spoiled
MOCHA n kind of strong dark coffee
MOCHAS > MOCHA
MOCHED > MOCH
MOCHELL same as > MUCH
MOCHELLS > MOCHELL
MOCHI n confection made with rice flour and sweetened bean paste
MOCHIE adj damp or humid
MOCHIER > MOCHIE
MOCHIEST > MOCHIE
MOCHILA n South American shoulder bag
MOCHILAS > MOCHILA
MOCHINESS > MOCHIE
MOCHING > MOCH
MOCHIS > MOCHI
MOCHS > MOCH
MOCHY same as > MOCHIE
MOCK vb make fun of ⊳ adj sham or imitation ⊳ n act of mocking
MOCKABLE > MOCK
MOCKADO n imitation velvet
MOCKADOES > MOCKADO
MOCKAGE same as
  > MOCKERY
MOCKAGES > MOCKAGE
MOCKED > MOCK
MOCKER vb dress up
MOCKERED > MOCKER
MOCKERIES > MOCKERY
MOCKERING > MOCKER
MOCKERNUT n type of smooth-barked hickory with fragrant foliage that turns bright yellow in autumn
MOCKERS > MOCKER
MOCKERY n derision
MOCKING > MOCK
MOCKINGLY > MOCK
MOCKINGS > MOCK
MOCKNEY n person who affects a cockney accent ⊳ adj denoting an affected cockney accent or a person who has one
MOCKNEYS > MOCKNEY
MOCKS > MOCK

MOCKTAIL n cocktail without alcohol
MOCKTAILS > MOCKTAIL
MOCKUP n working full-scale model of a machine, apparatus, etc, for testing, research, etc
MOCKUPS > MOCKUP
MOCOCK n Native American birchbark container
MOCOCKS > MOCOCK
MOCS > MOC
MOCUCK same as > MOCOCK
MOCUCKS > MOCUCK
MOCUDDUM same as
  > MUQADDAM
MOCUDDUMS > MOCUDDUM
MOD n member of a group of fashionable young people, orig in the 1960s ⊳ vb modify (a piece of software or hardware)
MODAFINIL n type of drug used as a stimulant
MODAL adj of or relating to mode or manner ⊳ n modal word
MODALISM n type of Christian doctrine
MODALISMS > MODALISM
MODALIST > MODALISM
MODALISTS > MODALISM
MODALITY n condition of being modal
MODALLY > MODAL
MODALS > MODAL
MODDED > MOD
MODDER n person who modifies a piece of hardware or software
MODDERS > MODDER
MODDING n practice of modifying a car to alter its appearance or performance
MODDINGS > MODDING
MODE n method or manner
MODEL n (miniature) representation ⊳ adj excellent or perfect ⊳ vb make a model of
MODELED > MODEL
MODELER > MODEL
MODELERS > MODEL
MODELING same as
  > MODELLING
MODELINGS > MODELING
MODELIST same as
  > MODELLIST
MODELISTS > MODELIST
MODELLED > MODEL
MODELLER > MODEL
MODELLERS > MODEL
MODELLI > MODELLO
MODELLING n act or an instance of making a model
MODELLIST n person who makes models
MODELLO n artist's preliminary sketch or model
MODELLOS > MODELLO
MODELS > MODEL
MODEM n device for connecting two computers by a telephone line ⊳ vb send or receive by modem
MODEMED > MODEM
MODEMING > MODEM

MODEMS > MODEM
MODENA n popular variety of domestic fancy pigeon
MODENAS > MODENA
MODER n intermediate layer in humus
MODERATE adj not extreme ⊳ n person of moderate views ⊳ vb make or become less violent or extreme
MODERATED > MODERATE
MODERATES > MODERATE
MODERATO adv at a moderate speed ⊳ n moderato piece
MODERATOR n (Presbyterian Church) minister appointed to preside over a Church court, general assembly, etc
MODERATOS > MODERATO
MODERN adj of present or recent times ⊳ n contemporary person
MODERNE n style of architecture and design of the late 1920s and 1930s ⊳ adj of or relating to this style of architecture and design
MODERNER > MODERN
MODERNES > MODERNE
MODERNEST > MODERN
MODERNISE same as
  > MODERNIZE
MODERNISM n (support of) modern tendencies, thoughts, or styles
MODERNIST > MODERNISM
MODERNITY n quality or state of being modern
MODERNIZE vb bring up to date
MODERNLY > MODERN
MODERNS > MODERN
MODERS > MODER
MODES > MODE
MODEST adj not vain or boastful
MODESTER > MODEST
MODESTEST > MODEST
MODESTIES > MODESTY
MODESTLY > MODEST
MODESTY n quality or condition of being modest
MODGE vb do shoddily
MODGED > MODGE
MODGES > MODGE
MODGING > MODGE
MODI > MODUS
MODICA > MODICUM
MODICUM n small quantity
MODICUMS > MODICUM
MODIFIED > MODIFY
MODIFIER n word that qualifies the sense of another
MODIFIERS > MODIFIER
MODIFIES > MODIFY
MODIFY vb change slightly
MODIFYING > MODIFY
MODII > MODIUS
MODILLION n one of a set of ornamental brackets under a cornice, esp as used in the Corinthian order
MODIOLAR > MODIOLUS
MODIOLI > MODIOLUS
MODIOLUS n central bony pillar of the cochlea

MODISH adj in fashion
MODISHLY > MODISH
MODIST n follower of fashion
MODISTE n fashionable dressmaker or milliner
MODISTES > MODISTE
MODISTS > MODIST
MODIUS n ancient Roman quantity measure
MODIWORT Scots variant of
  > MOULDWARP
MODIWORTS > MODIWORT
MODS > MOD
MODULAR adj of, consisting of, or resembling a module or modulus ⊳ n thing comprised of modules
MODULARLY > MODULAR
MODULARS > MODULAR
MODULATE vb vary in tone
MODULATED > MODULATE
MODULATES > MODULATE
MODULATOR > MODULATE
MODULE n self-contained unit, section, or component with a specific function
MODULES > MODULE
MODULI > MODULUS
MODULO adv with reference to modulus
MODULUS n coefficient expressing a specified property
MODUS n way of doing something
MOE adv more ⊳ n wry face
MOELLON n rubble
MOELLONS > MOELLON
MOER n in South Africa, vulgar word for the womb ⊳ vb in South Africa, attack (someone or something) violently
MOERED > MOER
MOERING > MOER
MOERS > MOER
MOES > MOE
MOFETTE n opening in a region of nearly extinct volcanic activity, through which gases pass
MOFETTES > MOFETTE
MOFFETTE same as
  > MOFETTE
MOFFETTES > MOFFETTE
MOFFIE n offensive word for a homosexual man
MOFFIES > MOFFIE
MOFO n taboo term, a shortened form of motherfucker
MOFOS > MOFO
MOFUSSIL n provincial area in India
MOFUSSILS > MOFUSSIL
MOG vb go away
MOGGAN n stocking without foot
MOGGANS > MOGGAN
MOGGED > MOG
MOGGIE same as > MOGGY
MOGGIES > MOGGY
MOGGING > MOG
MOGGY n cat
MOGHUL same as > MOGUL
MOGHULS > MOGHUL
MOGS > MOG

MOGUL n important or powerful person
MOGULED adj having moguls
MOGULS > MOGUL
MOHAIR n fine hair of the Angora goat
MOHAIRS > MOHAIR
MOHALIM same as > MOHELIM
MOHAWK n half turn from either edge of either skate to the corresponding edge of the other skate
MOHAWKS > MOHAWK
MOHEL n man qualified to conduct circumcisions
MOHELIM > MOHEL
MOHELS > MOHEL
MOHICAN n punk hairstyle
MOHICANS > MOHICAN
MOHO n boundary between the earth's crust and mantle
MOHOS > MOHO
MOHR same as > MHORR
MOHRS > MOHR
MOHUA n small New Zealand bird
MOHUAS > MOHUA
MOHUR n former Indian gold coin worth 15 rupees
MOHURS > MOHUR
MOI pron (used facetiously) me
MOIDER same as > MOITHER
MOIDERED > MOIDER
MOIDERING > MOIDER
MOIDERS > MOIDER
MOIDORE n former Portuguese gold coin
MOIDORES > MOIDORE
MOIETIES > MOIETY
MOIETY n half
MOIL vb moisten or soil or become moist, soiled, etc ▷ n toil
MOILE n type of rice pudding made with almond milk
MOILED > MOIL
MOILER > MOIL
MOILERS > MOIL
MOILES > MOILE
MOILING > MOIL
MOILINGLY > MOIL
MOILS > MOIL
MOINEAU n small fortification
MOINEAUS > MOINEAU
MOIRA n fate
MOIRAI > MOIRA
MOIRE adj having a watered or wavelike pattern ▷ n any fabric that has such a pattern
MOIRES > MOIRE
MOISER n informer
MOISERS > MOISER
MOIST adj slightly wet ▷ vb moisten
MOISTED > MOIST
MOISTEN vb make or become moist
MOISTENED > MOISTEN
MOISTENER > MOISTEN
MOISTENS > MOISTEN
MOISTER > MOIST
MOISTEST > MOIST
MOISTFUL adj full of moisture

MOISTIFY vb moisten
MOISTING > MOIST
MOISTLY > MOIST
MOISTNESS > MOIST
MOISTS > MOIST
MOISTURE n liquid diffused as vapour or condensed in drops
MOISTURES > MOISTURE
MOIT same as > MOTE
MOITHER vb bother or bewilder
MOITHERED > MOITHER
MOITHERS > MOITHER
MOITS > MOIT
MOJAHEDIN pl n fundamentalist Muslim guerrillas
MOJARRA n tropical American sea fish
MOJARRAS > MOJARRA
MOJITO n rum-based cocktail
MOJITOS > MOJITO
MOJO n charm or magic spell
MOJOES > MOJO
MOJOS > MOJO
MOKADDAM same as > MUQADDAM
MOKADDAMS > MOKADDAM
MOKE n donkey
MOKES > MOKE
MOKI n edible sea fish of New Zealand
MOKIHI n Māori raft
MOKIHIS > MOKIHI
MOKIS > MOKI
MOKO n Māori tattoo or tattoo pattern
MOKOMOKO n type of skink found in New Zealand
MOKOMOKOS > MOKOMOKO
MOKOPUNA n grandchild or young person
MOKOPUNAS > MOKOPUNA
MOKORO n (in Botswana) the traditional dugout canoe of the people of the Okavango Delta
MOKOROS > MOKORO
MOKOS > MOKO
MOKSHA n freedom from the endless cycle of transmigration into a state of bliss
MOKSHAS > MOKSHA
MOL n the SI unit mole
MOLA another name for > SUNFISH
MOLAL adj of a solution containing one mole of solute per thousand grams of solvent
MOLALITY n measure of solvent concentration
MOLAR n large back tooth used for grinding ▷ adj of any of these teeth
MOLARITY n concentration
MOLARS > MOLAR
MOLAS > MOLA
MOLASSE n sediment from the erosion of mountain ranges
MOLASSES n dark syrup, a by-product of sugar refining
MOLD same as > MOULD

MOLDABLE > MOLD
MOLDAVITE n green tektite found in the Czech Republic, thought to be the product of an ancient meteorite impact in Germany
MOLDBOARD n curved blade of a plough
MOLDED > MOLD
MOLDER same as > MOULDER
MOLDERED > MOLDER
MOLDERING > MOLDER
MOLDERS > MOLDER
MOLDIER > MOLDY
MOLDIEST > MOLDY
MOLDINESS > MOLDY
MOLDING same as > MOULDING
MOLDINGS > MOLDING
MOLDS > MOLD
MOLDWARP same as > MOULDWARP
MOLDWARPS > MOLDWARP
MOLDY same as > MOULDY
MOLE n small dark raised spot on the skin ▷ vb as in mole out seek as if by burrowing
MOLECAST n molehill
MOLECASTS > MOLECAST
MOLECULAR adj of or relating to molecules
MOLECULE n simplest freely existing chemical unit, composed of two or more atoms
MOLECULES > MOLECULE
MOLED > MOLE
MOLEHILL n small mound of earth thrown up by a burrowing mole
MOLEHILLS > MOLEHILL
MOLEHUNT n hunt for a mole
MOLEHUNTS > MOLEHUNT
MOLELIKE adj like a mole
MOLES > MOLE
MOLESKIN n dark grey dense velvety pelt of a mole, used as a fur
MOLESKINS pl n clothing of moleskin
MOLEST vb disturb or annoy
MOLESTED > MOLEST
MOLESTER > MOLEST
MOLESTERS > MOLEST
MOLESTFUL adj molesting
MOLESTING > MOLEST
MOLESTS > MOLEST
MOLIES > MOLY
MOLIMEN n effort needed to perform bodily function
MOLIMENS > MOLIMEN
MOLINE adj (of a cross) having arms of equal length, forked and curved back at the ends ▷ n moline cross
MOLINES > MOLINE
MOLINET n stick for whipping chocolate
MOLINETS > MOLINET
MOLING > MOLE
MOLL n gangster's female accomplice
MOLLA same as > MOLLAH
MOLLAH same as > MULLAH
MOLLAHS > MOLLAH
MOLLAS > MOLLA
MOLLIE same as > MOLLY

MOLLIES > MOLLY
MOLLIFIED > MOLLIFY
MOLLIFIER > MOLLIFY
MOLLIFIES > MOLLIFY
MOLLIFY vb pacify or soothe
MOLLITIES n softness
MOLLS > MOLL
MOLLUSC n soft-bodied, usu hard-shelled, animal
MOLLUSCA n molluscs collectively
MOLLUSCAN > MOLLUSC
MOLLUSCS > MOLLUSC
MOLLUSCUM n viral skin infection
MOLLUSK same as > MOLLUSC
MOLLUSKAN > MOLLUSK
MOLLUSKS > MOLLUSK
MOLLY n American freshwater fish
MOLLYHAWK n juvenile of the southern black-backed gull
MOLLYMAWK informal name for > MALLEMUCK
MOLOCH n spiny Australian desert-living lizard
MOLOCHISE vb sacrifice to deity
MOLOCHIZE same as > MOLOCHISE
MOLOCHS > MOLOCH
MOLOSSI > MOLOSSUS
MOLOSSUS n division of metre in poetry
MOLS > MOL
MOLT same as > MOULT
MOLTED > MOLT
MOLTEN > MELT
MOLTENLY > MELT
MOLTER > MOLT
MOLTERS > MOLT
MOLTING > MOLT
MOLTO adv very
MOLTS > MOLT
MOLY n mythical magic herb
MOLYBDATE n salt or ester of a molybdic acid
MOLYBDIC adj of or containing molybdenum in the trivalent or hexavalent state
MOLYBDOUS adj of or containing molybdenum, esp in a low valence state
MOLYS > MOLY
MOM same as > MOTHER
MOME n fool
MOMENT n short space of time
MOMENTA > MOMENTUM
MOMENTANY same as > MOMENTARY
MOMENTARY adj lasting only a moment
MOMENTLY same as > MOMENT
MOMENTO same as > MEMENTO
MOMENTOES > MOMENTO
MOMENTOS > MOMENTO
MOMENTOUS adj of great significance
MOMENTS > MOMENT
MOMENTUM n impetus to go forward, develop, or get stronger

m

MOMENTUMS > MOMENTUM
MOMES > MOME
MOMI same as > MOM
MOMISM n excessive domination of a child by his or her mother
MOMISMS > MOMISM
MOMMA same as > MAMMA
MOMMAS > MOMMA
MOMMET same as > MAMMET
MOMMETS > MOMMET
MOMMIES > MOMMY
MOMMY same as > MOM
MOMOIR n memoir written by a woman about motherhood
MOMOIRS > MOMOIR
MOMS > MOM
MOMSER same as > MOMZER
MOMSERS > MOMSER
MOMUS n person who ridicules
MOMUSES > MOMUS
MOMZER same as > MAMZER
MOMZERIM > MOMZER
MOMZERS > MOMZER
MON dialect variant of > MAN
MONA n W African guenon monkey
MONACHAL less common word for > MONASTIC
MONACHISM > MONACHAL
MONACHIST > MONACHAL
MONACID same as > MONOACID
MONACIDIC same as > MONACID
MONACIDS > MONACID
MONACT adj (of sponge) with single-spiked structures in skeleton
MONACTINE n monactinal sponge spicule
MONACTS > MONACT
MONAD n any fundamental singular metaphysical entity
MONADAL > MONAD
MONADES > MONAS
MONADIC adj being or relating to a monad
MONADICAL > MONAD
MONADISM n doctrine that monads are the ultimate units of reality
MONADISMS > MONADISM
MONADNOCK n residual hill that consists of hard rock in an otherwise eroded area
MONADS > MONAD
MONAL n S Asian pheasant
MONALS > MONAL
MONAMINE n type of amine
MONAMINES > MONAMINE
MONANDRY n custom of having only one male partner over a period of time
MONARCH n sovereign ruler of a state
MONARCHAL > MONARCH
MONARCHIC > MONARCH
MONARCHS > MONARCH
MONARCHY n government by or a state ruled by a sovereign
MONARDA n mintlike N American plant
MONARDAS > MONARDA

MONAS same as > MONAD
MONASES > MONAS
MONASTERY n residence of a community of monks
MONASTIC adj of monks, nuns, or monasteries ▷ n person who is committed to this way of life, esp a monk
MONASTICS > MONASTIC
MONATOMIC adj consisting of single atoms
MONAUL same as > MONAL
MONAULS > MONAUL
MONAURAL adj relating to, having, or hearing with only one ear
MONAXIAL another word for > UNIAXIAL
MONAXON n type of sponge
MONAXONIC > MONAXON
MONAXONS > MONAXON
MONAZITE n yellow to reddish-brown mineral
MONAZITES > MONAZITE
MONDAIN n man who moves in fashionable society ▷ adj characteristic of fashionable society
MONDAINE n woman who moves in fashionable society ▷ adj characteristic of fashionable society
MONDAINES > MONDAINE
MONDAINS > MONDAIN
MONDE n French word meaning world or society
MONDES > MONDE
MONDIAL adj of or involving the whole world
MONDO n Buddhist questioning technique
MONDOS > MONDO
MONECIAN same as > MONECIOUS
MONECIOUS adj (of some flowering plants) having the male and female reproductive organs in separate flowers on the same plant
MONELLIN n sweet protein
MONELLINS > MONELLIN
MONEME less common word for > MORPHEME
MONEMES > MONEME
MONER n hypothetical simple organism
MONERA > MONER
MONERAN n type of bacterium
MONERANS > MONERAN
MONERGISM n Christian doctrine on spiritual regeneration
MONERON same as > MONER
MONETARY adj of money or currency
MONETH same as > MONTH
MONETHS > MONETH
MONETISE same as > MONETIZE
MONETISED > MONETISE
MONETISES > MONETISE
MONETIZE vb establish as the legal tender of a country
MONETIZED > MONETIZE
MONETIZES > MONETIZE

MONEY n medium of exchange, coins or banknotes
MONEYBAG n bag for money
MONEYBAGS n very rich person
MONEYBELT n belt with compartments for money
MONEYBOX n box for keeping money in
MONEYED adj rich
MONEYER n person who coins money
MONEYERS > MONEYER
MONEYLESS > MONEY
MONEYMAN n person supplying money
MONEYMEN > MONEY
MONEYS > MONEY
MONEYWORT n European and N American creeping plant with round leaves and yellow flowers
MONG n offensive word meaning a foolish person
MONGCORN same as > MASLIN
MONGCORNS > MONGCORN
MONGED adj offensive term meaning under the influence of drugs
MONGEESE > MONGOOSE
MONGER n trader or dealer ▷ vb deal in
MONGERED > MONGER
MONGERIES > MONGER
MONGERING > MONGER
MONGERS > MONGER
MONGERY > MONGER
MONGO same as > MUNGO
MONGOE same as > MONGO
MONGOES > MONGOE
MONGOL adj offensive word for a person affected by Down's syndrome
MONGOLIAN adj offensive term meaning affected by Down's syndrome
MONGOLISM > MONGOL
MONGOLOID n offensive word for a person affected by Down's syndrome
MONGOLS > MONGOL
MONGOOSE n stoat-like mammal of Asia and Africa that kills snakes
MONGOOSES > MONGOOSE
MONGOS > MONGO
MONGREL n animal, esp a dog, of mixed breed ▷ adj of mixed breed or origin
MONGRELLY adj like a mongrel
MONGRELS > MONGREL
MONGS > MONG
MONGST short for > AMONGST
MONIAL n mullion
MONIALS > MONIAL
MONIC adj denoting a type of polynomial
MONICKER same as > MONIKER
MONICKERS > MONICKER
MONIE Scots word for > MANY
MONIED same as > MONEYED
MONIES > MONEY

MONIKER n person's name or nickname
MONIKERED adj having a moniker
MONIKERS > MONIKER
MONILIA n type of fungus
MONILIAE > MONILIA
MONILIAL adj denoting a thrush infection caused by a fungus
MONILIAS > MONILIA
MONIMENT same as > MONUMENT
MONIMENTS > MONIMENT
MONIPLIES same as > MANYPLIES
MONISH same as > ADMONISH
MONISHED > MONISH
MONISHES > MONISH
MONISHING > MONISH
MONISM n doctrine that reality consists of only one basic substance or element
MONISMS > MONISM
MONIST > MONISM
MONISTIC > MONISM
MONISTS > MONISM
MONITION n warning or caution
MONITIONS > MONITION
MONITIVE adj reproving
MONITOR n person or device that checks, controls, warns, or keeps a record of something ▷ vb watch and check on
MONITORED > MONITOR
MONITORS > MONITOR
MONITORY adj acting as or giving a warning ▷ n letter containing a monition
MONITRESS > MONITOR
MONK n member of an all-male religious community
MONKERIES > MONKERY
MONKERY n derogatory word for monastic life or practices
MONKEY n long-tailed primate ▷ vb meddle or fool
MONKEYED > MONKEY
MONKEYING > MONKEY
MONKEYISH > MONKEY
MONKEYISM n practice of behaving like monkey
MONKEYPOD n Central American tree
MONKEYPOT n type of tropical tree
MONKEYPOX n rare viral disease found in Africa
MONKEYS > MONKEY
MONKFISH n type of fish
MONKHOOD n condition of being a monk
MONKHOODS > MONKHOOD
MONKISH adj of, relating to, or resembling a monk or monks
MONKISHLY > MONKISH
MONKS > MONK
MONKSHOOD n poisonous plant with hooded flowers
MONO n monophonic sound
MONOACID adj base which is capable of reacting with only

one molecule of a monobasic acid

MONOACIDS > MONOACID

MONOAMINE *n* substance, such as adrenaline, noradrenaline, or serotonin, that contains a single amine group

MONOAO *n* New Zealand plant with rigid leaves

MONOAOS > MONOAO

MONOBASIC *adj* (of an acid, such as hydrogen chloride) having only one replaceable hydrogen atom per molecule

MONOBLOC *adj* made from a single piece of something

MONOBROW *n* appearance of a single eyebrow as a result of the eyebrows joining above a person's nose

MONOBROWS > MONOBROW

MONOCARPIC *n* plant that is monocarpic

MONOCARPS > MONOCARP

MONOCEROS *n* faint constellation on the celestial equator crossed by the Milky Way and lying close to Orion and Canis Major

MONOCHORD *n* instrument employed in acoustic analysis or investigation, consisting usually of one string stretched over a resonator of wood

MONOCLE *n* eyeglass for one eye only

MONOCLED > MONOCLE

MONOCLES > MONOCLE

MONOCLINE *n* fold in stratified rocks in which the strata are inclined in the same direction from the horizontal

MONOCOQUE *n* vehicle body moulded from a single piece of material with no separate load-bearing parts ▷ *adj* of or relating to the design characteristic of a monocoque

MONOCOT *n* type of flowering plant with a single embryonic seed leaf

MONOCOTS > MONOCOT

MONOCOTYL *same as* > MONOCOT

MONOCRACY *n* government by one person

MONOCRAT > MONOCRACY

MONOCRATS > MONOCRACY

MONOCROP *vb* plant the same crop in a field every year

MONOCROPS > MONOCROP

MONOCULAR *adj* having or for one eye only ▷ *n* device for use with one eye, such as a field glass

MONOCYCLE *another name for* > UNICYCLE

MONOCYTE *n* large phagocytic leucocyte with a spherical nucleus and clear cytoplasm

MONOCYTES > MONOCYTE

MONOCYTIC > MONOCYTE

MONODIC > MONODY

MONODICAL > MONODY

MONODIES > MONODY

MONODIST > MONODY

MONODISTS > MONODY

MONODONT *adj* (of certain animals, esp the male narwhal) having a single tooth throughout life

MONODRAMA *n* play or other dramatic piece for a single performer

MONODY *n* (in Greek tragedy) an ode sung by a single actor

MONOECIES > MONOECY

MONOECISM *n* being both male and female

MONOECY *same as* > MONOECISM

MONOESTER *n* type of ester

MONOFIL *n* synthetic thread or yarn composed of a single strand rather than a twisted fibres

MONOFILS > MONOFIL

MONOFUEL *n* single type of fuel

MONOFUELS > MONOFUEL

MONOGAMIC > MONOGAMY

MONOGAMY *n* custom of being married to one person at a time

MONOGENIC *adj* of or relating to an inherited character difference that is controlled by a single gene

MONOGENY *n* the hypothetical descent of all organisms from a single cell or organism

MONOGERM *adj* containing single seed

MONOGLOT *n* person speaking only one language

MONOGLOTS > MONOGLOT

MONOGONY *n* asexual reproduction

MONOGRAM *n* design of combined letters, esp a person's initials ▷ *vb* decorate (clothing, stationery, etc) with a monogram

MONOGRAMS > MONOGRAM

MONOGRAPH *n* book or paper on a single subject ▷ *vb* write a monograph on

MONOGYNY *n* custom of having only one female partner over a period of time

MONOHULL *n* sailing vessel with a single hull

MONOHULLS > MONOHULL

MONOICOUS *adj* (of some flowering plants) having the male and female reproductive organs in separate flowers on the same plant

MONOKINE *n* type of protein

MONOKINES > MONOKINE

MONOKINI *n* bottom half of a bikini

MONOKINIS > MONOKINI

MONOLATER > MONOLATRY

MONOLATRY *n* exclusive worship of one god without excluding the existence of others

MONOLAYER *n* single layer of atoms or molecules adsorbed on a surface

MONOLINE *adj* as in *monoline insurer* insurer who pays the principal and interest on a bond in the event of a default

MONOLITH *n* large upright block of stone

MONOLITHS > MONOLITH

MONOLOG *same as* > MONOLOGUE

MONOLOGIC > MONOLOGUE

MONOLOGS > MONOLOG

MONOLOGUE *n* long speech by one person

MONOLOGY > MONOLOGUE

MONOMACHY *n* combat between two individuals

MONOMANIA *n* obsession with one thing

MONOMARK *n* series of letters or figures to identify goods, personal articles, etc

MONOMARKS > MONOMARK

MONOMER *n* compound whose molecules can join together to form a polymer

MONOMERIC > MONOMER

MONOMERS > MONOMER

MONOMETER *n* line of verse consisting of one metrical foot

MONOMIAL *n* expression consisting of a single term, such as *5ax* ▷ *adj* consisting of a single algebraic term

MONOMIALS > MONOMIAL

MONOMODE *adj* denoting a type of optical fibre

MONONYM *n* person who is famous enough to be known only by one name

MONONYMS > MONONYM

MONOPHAGY *n* feeding on only one type of food

MONOPHASE *adj* having single alternating electric current ▷ *n* type of matter that contains only one phase or a clear-cut and unattached type of matter

MONOPHONY > MONO

MONOPHYLY *n* group of ancestor and all descendants

MONOPITCH *adj* (of a roof) having only one slope ▷ *n* a monotone

MONOPLANE *n* aeroplane with one pair of wings

MONOPLOID *less common word for* > HAPLOID

MONOPOD *same as* > MONOPODE

MONOPODE *n* member of a legendary one-legged race of Africa

MONOPODES > MONOPODE

MONOPODIA *pl n* main axes of growth in the pine tree and similar plants

MONOPODS > MONOPOD

MONOPODY *n* single-foot measure in poetry

MONOPOLE *n* magnetic pole considered in isolation

MONOPOLES > MONOPOLE

MONOPOLY *n* exclusive possession of or right to do something

MONOPRINT *n* single impression created from a design

MONOPSONY *n* situation in which the entire market demand for a product or service consists of only one buyer

MONOPTERA *n* plural of monopteron: circular classical building, esp a temple, that has a single ring of columns surrounding it

MONOPTOTE *n* word with only one form

MONOPULSE *n* radar transmitting single pulse only

MONORAIL *n* single-rail railway

MONORAILS > MONORAIL

MONORCHID *adj* having one testicle ▷ *n* animal or person with one testicle

MONORHINE *adj* having single nostril ▷ *n* animal that has one nasal orifice

MONORHYME *n* poem in which all lines rhyme

MONOS > MONO

MONOSEMIC *adj* having only a single meaning

MONOSEMY *n* fact of having only a single meaning

MONOSES > MONOSIS

MONOSIES > MONOSY

MONOSIS *n* abnormal separation

MONOSKI *n* wide ski on which the skier stands with both feet ▷ *vb* ski on a monoski

MONOSKIED > MONOSKI

MONOSKIER > MONOSKI

MONOSKIS > MONOSKI

MONOSOME *n* unpaired chromosome, esp an X-chromosome in an otherwise diploid cell

MONOSOMES > MONOSOME

MONOSOMIC > MONOSOME

MONOSOMY *n* condition with a missing pair of chromosomes

MONOSTELE *n* type of plant tissue

MONOSTELY > MONOSTELE

MONOSTICH *n* poem of a single line

MONOSTOME *adj* having only one mouth, pore, or similar opening

MONOSTYLE *adj* having single shaft

MONOSY *same as* > MONOSIS

MONOTASK *vb* perform only one task at a time

MONOTASKS > MONOTASK

MONOTINT *n* black-and-white photograph or transparency

MONOTINTS > MONOTINT

MONOTONE *n* unvaried pitch in speech or sound ▷ *adj* unvarying ▷ *vb* speak in monotone

m

MONOTONED > MONOTONE

MONOTONES > MONOTONE

MONOTONIC same as > MONOTONE

MONOTONY n wearisome routine, dullness

MONOTREME n type of primitive egg-laying toothless mammal of Australia and New Guinea

MONOTROCH n wheelbarrow

MONOTYPE n single print made from a metal or glass plate on which a picture has been painted

MONOTYPES > MONOTYPE

MONOTYPIC adj (of a genus or species) consisting of only one type of animal or plant

MONOVULAR adj of a single ovum

MONOXIDE n oxide that contains one oxygen atom per molecule

MONOXIDES > MONOXIDE

MONOXYLON n canoe made from one log

MONS > MON

MONSIEUR n French title of address equivalent to sir or Mr

MONSIGNOR n ecclesiastical title attached to certain offices or distinctions usually bestowed by the Pope

MONSOON n seasonal wind of SE Asia

MONSOONAL > MONSOON

MONSOONS > MONSOON

MONSTER n imaginary, usu frightening, beast ▷ adj huge ▷ vb criticize (a person or group) severely

MONSTERA n type of tropical climbing plant

MONSTERAS > MONSTERA

MONSTERED > MONSTER

MONSTERS > MONSTER

MONSTROUS adj unnatural or ugly

MONTADALE n breed of sheep

MONTAGE n (making of) a picture composed from pieces of others ▷ vb make as a montage

MONTAGED > MONTAGE

MONTAGES > MONTAGE

MONTAGING > MONTAGE

MONTAN adj as in montan wax hard wax obtained from lignite and peat

MONTANE n area of mountain dominated by vegetation ▷ adj of or inhabiting mountainous regions

MONTANES > MONTANE

MONTANT n vertical part in woodwork

MONTANTO n rising blow

MONTANTOS > MONTANTO

MONTANTS > MONTANT

MONTARIA n Brazilian canoe

MONTARIAS > MONTARIA

MONTE n gambling card game of Spanish origin

MONTEITH n large ornamental bowl

MONTEITHS > MONTEITH

MONTEM n former money-raising practice at Eton school

MONTEMS > MONTEM

MONTERO n round cap with a flap at the back worn by hunters

MONTEROS > MONTERO

MONTES > MONTE

MONTH n one of the twelve divisions of the calendar year

MONTHLIES > MONTHLY

MONTHLING n month-old child

MONTHLONG adj lasting all month

MONTHLY adj happening or payable once a month ▷ adv once a month ▷ n monthly magazine

MONTHS > MONTH

MONTICLE same as > MONTICULE

MONTICLES > MONTICLE

MONTICULE n small hill or mound, such as a secondary volcanic cone

MONTIES > MONTY

MONTRE n pipes of organ

MONTRES > MONTRE

MONTURE n mount or frame

MONTURES > MONTURE

MONTY n complete form of something

MONUMENT n something, esp a building or statue, that commemorates something

MONUMENTS > MONUMENT

MONURON n type of weedkiller

MONURONS > MONURON

MONY Scot word for > MANY

MONYPLIES same as > MANYPLIES

MONZONITE n coarse-grained plutonic igneous rock consisting of equal amounts of plagioclase and orthoclase feldspar, with ferromagnesian minerals

MOO n long deep cry of a cow ▷ vb make this noise ▷ interj instance or imitation of this sound

MOOBIES same as > MOOBS

MOOBS pl n overdeveloped breasts on a man

MOOCH vb loiter about aimlessly

MOOCHED > MOOCH

MOOCHER > MOOCH

MOOCHERS > MOOCH

MOOCHES > MOOCH

MOOCHING > MOOCH

MOOD n temporary (gloomy) state of mind

MOODIED > MOODY

MOODIER > MOODY

MOODIES > MOODY

MOODIEST > MOODY

MOODILY > MOODY

MOODINESS > MOODY

MOODS > MOOD

MOODY adj sullen or gloomy ▷ vb flatter

MOODYING > MOODY

MOOED > MOO

MOOI adj pleasing or nice

MOOING > MOO

MOOK n person regarded with contempt, esp a stupid person

MOOKS > MOOK

MOOKTAR same as > MUKHTAR

MOOKTARS > MOOKTAR

MOOL same as > MOULD

MOOLA same as > MOOLAH

MOOLAH slang word for > MONEY

MOOLAHS > MOOLAH

MOOLAS > MOOLA

MOOLED > MOOL

MOOLEY same as > MOOLY

MOOLEYS > MOOLEY

MOOLI n type of large white radish

MOOLIES > MOOLY

MOOLING > MOOL

MOOLIS > MOOLI

MOOLOO n person from the Waikato

MOOLOOS > MOOLOO

MOOLS > MOOL

MOOLVI same as > MOOLVIE

MOOLVIE n (esp in India) Muslim learned man

MOOLVIES > MOOLVIE

MOOLVIS > MOOLVI

MOOLY same as > MULEY

MOON n natural satellite of the earth ▷ vb be idle in a listless or dreamy way

MOONBEAM n ray of moonlight

MOONBEAMS > MOONBEAM

MOONBLIND adj (of horses) having a disorder which causes inflammation of the eyes and sometimes blindness

MOONBOOTS pl n thickly padded boots

MOONBOW n rainbow made by moonlight

MOONBOWS > MOONBOW

MOONCAKE n type of round Chinese cake

MOONCAKES > MOONCAKE

MOONCALF n person who idles time away

MOONCHILD n someone who is born under the Cancer star sign

MOONCRAFT n lunar module

MOONDOG n bright spot in the sky caused by moonlight

MOONDOGS > MOONDOG

MOONDUST n dust on surface of moon

MOONDUSTS > MOONDUST

MOONED adj decorated with a moon

MOONER > MOON

MOONERS > MOON

MOONEYE n N American large-eyed freshwater fish

MOONEYES > MOONEYE

MOONFACE n big round face ▷ vb have a moon face

MOONFACED > MOONFACE

MOONFACES > MOONFACE

MOONFISH n type of tropical fish

MOONG n as in moong bean kind of bean

MOONGATE n circular gateway in a wall

MOONGATES > MOONGATE

MOONIER > MOONY

MOONIES > MOONY

MOONIEST > MOONY

MOONILY > MOONY

MOONINESS > MOONY

MOONING > MOON

MOONISH > MOON

MOONISHLY > MOON

MOONLESS > MOON

MOONLET n small moon

MOONLETS > MOONLET

MOONLIGHT n light from the moon ▷ adj illuminated by the moon ▷ vb work at a secondary job, esp illegally

MOONLIKE > MOON

MOONLIT adj illuminated by the moon

MOONPHASE n phase of moon

MOONPORT n place from which flights leave for moon

MOONPORTS > MOONPORT

MOONQUAKE n light tremor of the moon, detected on the moon's surface

MOONRAKER n small square sail set above a skysail

MOONRISE n moment when the moon appears above the horizon

MOONRISES > MOONRISE

MOONROCK n rock from moon

MOONROCKS > MOONROCK

MOONROOF same as > SUNROOF

MOONROOFS > MOONROOF

MOONS > MOON

MOONSAIL n small sail high on a mast

MOONSAILS > MOONSAIL

MOONSCAPE n surface of the moon or a picture or model of it

MOONSEED n type of climbing plant with red or black fruits

MOONSEEDS > MOONSEED

MOONSET n moment when the moon disappears below the horizon

MOONSETS > MOONSET

MOONSHEE same as > MUNSHI

MOONSHEES > MOONSHEE

MOONSHINE same as > MOONLIGHT

MOONSHINY adj lacking substance

MOONSHIP n lunar module

MOONSHIPS > MOONSHIP

MOONSHOT n launching of a spacecraft to the moon

MOONSHOTS > MOONSHOT

MOONSTONE n translucent semiprecious stone

MOONWALK *n* instance of walking on the moon
MOONWALKS > MOONWALK
MOONWARD *adj* towards moon
MOONWARDS *adv* towards the moon
MOONWORT *n* type of fern with crescent-shaped leaflets
MOONWORTS > MOONWORT
MOONY *adj* dreamy or listless ▷ *n* crazy or foolish person
MOOP *same as* > MOUP
MOOPED > MOOP
MOOPING > MOOP
MOOPS > MOOP
MOOR *n* tract of open uncultivated ground covered with grass and heather ▷ *vb* secure (a ship) with ropes etc
MOORAGE *n* place for mooring a vessel
MOORAGES > MOORAGE
MOORBURN *n* practice of burning off old growth on a heather moor
MOORBURNS > MOORBURN
MOORCOCK *n* male of the red grouse
MOORCOCKS > MOORCOCK
MOORED > MOOR
MOORFOWL *n* red grouse
MOORFOWLS > MOORFOWL
MOORHEN *n* small black water bird
MOORHENS > MOORHEN
MOORIER > MOOR
MOORIEST > MOOR
MOORILL *n* disease of cattle on moors
MOORILLS > MOORILL
MOORING *n* place for mooring a ship
MOORINGS *pl n* ropes and anchors used in mooring a vessel
MOORISH *adj* of or relating to the Moor people of North Africa
MOORLAND *n* area of moor
MOORLANDS > MOORLAND
MOORLOG *n* rotted wood below the surface of a moor
MOORLOGS > MOORLOG
MOORMAN *n* person living on a moor
MOORMEN > MOORMAN
MOORS > MOOR
MOORVA *same as* > MURVA
MOORVAS > MOORVA
MOORWORT *n* low-growing pink-flowered shrub that grows in peaty bogs
MOORWORTS > MOORWORT
MOORY > MOOR
MOOS > MOO
MOOSE *n* large N American deer
MOOSEBIRD *n* North American jay
MOOSEHAIR *n* hair of a moose
MOOSEHIDE *n* hide of a moose
MOOSEWOOD *n* North American tree

MOOSEYARD *n* place where moose spend winter
MOOT *adj* debatable ▷ *vb* bring up for discussion ▷ *n* (in Anglo-Saxon England) a local administrative assembly
MOOTABLE > MOOT
MOOTED > MOOT
MOOTER > MOOT
MOOTERS > MOOT
MOOTEST > MOOT
MOOTING > MOOT
MOOTINGS > MOOT
MOOTMAN *n* person taking part in a moot
MOOTMEN > MOOTMAN
MOOTNESS > MOOT
MOOTS > MOOT
MOOVE *same as* > MOVE
MOOVED > MOOVE
MOOVES > MOOVE
MOOVING > MOOVE
MOP *n* long stick with twists of cotton or a sponge on the end, used for cleaning ▷ *vb* clean or soak up with or as if with a mop
MOPANE *same as* > MOPANI
MOPANES > MOPANE
MOPANI *n* S African tree that is highly resistant to drought
MOPANIS > MOPANI
MOPBOARD *n* wooden border fixed round the base of an interior wall
MOPBOARDS > MOPBOARD
MOPE *vb* be gloomy and apathetic ▷ *n* gloomy person
MOPED *n* light motorized cycle
MOPEDS > MOPED
MOPEHAWK *same as* > MOPOKE
MOPEHAWKS > MOPEHAWK
MOPER > MOPE
MOPERIES > MOPERY
MOPERS > MOPE
MOPERY *n* gloominess
MOPES > MOPE
MOPEY *same as* > MOPY
MOPHEAD *n* person with shaggy hair
MOPHEADS > MOPHEAD
MOPIER > MOPE
MOPIEST > MOPE
MOPILY > MOPY
MOPINESS > MOPY
MOPING > MOPE
MOPINGLY > MOPE
MOPISH > MOPE
MOPISHLY > MOPE
MOPOKE *n* species of owl
MOPOKES > MOPOKE
MOPPED > MOP
MOPPER > MOP
MOPPERS > MOP
MOPPET *same as* > POPPET
MOPPETS > MOPPET
MOPPIER > MOPPY
MOPPIEST > MOPPY
MOPPING > MOP
MOPPY *adj* (of hair) thick, dishevelled
MOPS > MOP
MOPSIES > MOPSY
MOPSTICK *n* mop handle

MOPSTICKS > MOPSTICK
MOPSY *n* untidy or dowdy person
MOPUS *n* person who mopes
MOPUSES > MOPUS
MOPY > MOPE
MOQUETTE *n* thick velvety fabric used for carpets and upholstery
MOQUETTES > MOQUETTE
MOR *n* layer of acidic humus formed in cool moist areas
MORA *n* quantity of a short syllable in verse
MORACEOUS *adj* relating to a mostly tropical and subtropical family of trees and shrubs which includes the mulberry, fig, and breadfruit
MORAE > MORA
MORAINAL > MORAINE
MORAINE *n* accumulated mass of debris deposited by a glacier
MORAINES > MORAINE
MORAINIC > MORAINE
MORAL *adj* concerned with right and wrong conduct ▷ *n* lesson to be obtained from a story or event ▷ *vb* moralize
MORALE *n* degree of confidence or hope of a person or group
MORALES > MORALE
MORALISE *same as* > MORALIZE
MORALISED > MORALISE
MORALISER > MORALIZE
MORALISES > MORALISE
MORALISM *n* habit or practice of moralizing
MORALISMS > MORALISM
MORALIST *n* person with a strong sense of right and wrong
MORALISTS > MORALIST
MORALITY *n* good moral conduct
MORALIZE *vb* make moral pronouncements
MORALIZED > MORALIZE
MORALIZER > MORALIZE
MORALIZES > MORALIZE
MORALL *same as* > MURAL
MORALLED > MORALL
MORALLER > MORAL
MORALLERS > MORAL
MORALLING > MORALL
MORALLS > MORALL
MORALLY > MORAL
MORALS > MORAL
MORAS > MORA
MORASS *n* marsh
MORASSES > MORASS
MORASSIER > MORASSY
MORASSY *adj* swampy
MORAT *n* drink containing mulberry juice
MORATORIA *pl n* legally authorized postponements of the fulfilment of an obligation
MORATORY > MORATORIA
MORATS > MORAT
MORAY *n* large voracious eel
MORAYS > MORAY

MORBID *adj* unduly interested in death or unpleasant events
MORBIDER > MORBID
MORBIDEST > MORBID
MORBIDITY *n* state of being morbid
MORBIDLY > MORBID
MORBIFIC *adj* causing disease
MORBILLI *same as* > MEASLES
MORBUS *n* disease
MORBUSES > MORBUS
MORCEAU *n* fragment or morsel
MORCEAUX > MORCEAU
MORCHA *n* (in India) hostile demonstration
MORCHAS > MORCHA
MORDACITY *n* quality of sarcasm
MORDANCY > MORDANT
MORDANT *adj* sarcastic or scathing ▷ *n* substance used to fix dyes ▷ *vb* treat (a fabric, yarn, etc) with a mordant
MORDANTED > MORDANT
MORDANTLY > MORDANT
MORDANTS > MORDANT
MORDENT *n* melodic ornament in music
MORDENTS > MORDENT
MORE *adj* greater in amount or degree ▷ *adv* greater extent ▷ *pron* greater or additional amount or number
MOREEN *n* heavy, usually watered, fabric of wool or wool and cotton
MOREENS > MOREEN
MOREISH *adj* (of food) causing a desire for more
MOREL *n* edible mushroom with a pitted cap
MORELLE *n* nightshade
MORELLES > MORELLE
MORELLO *n* variety of small very dark sour cherry
MORELLOS > MORELLO
MORELS > MOREL
MORENDO *adv* (in music) dying away ▷ *n* gentle decrescendo at the end of a musical strain
MORENDOS > MORENDO
MORENESS > MORE
MOREOVER *adv* in addition to what has already been said
MOREPORK *same as* > MOPOKE
MOREPORKS > MOREPORK
MORES *pl n* customs and conventions embodying the fundamental values of a community
MORESQUE *adj* (esp of decoration and architecture) of Moorish style ▷ *n* Moorish design or decoration
MORESQUES > MORESQUE
MORGAN *n* American breed of small compact saddle horse
MORGANITE *n* pink variety of beryl, used as a gemstone
MORGANS > MORGAN

m

SECTION 1: Words between 2 and 9 letters in length

MORGAY n small dogfish

MORGAYS > MORGAY

MORGEN n South African unit of area

MORGENS > MORGEN

MORGUE same as > MORTUARY

MORGUES > MORGUE

MORIA n folly

MORIAS > MORIA

MORIBUND adj without force or vitality

MORICHE same as > MIRITI

MORICHES > MORICHE

MORION n 16th-century helmet with a brim and wide comb

MORIONS > MORION

MORISCO n morris dance

MORISCOES > MORISCO

MORISCOS > MORISCO

MORISH same as > MOREISH

MORKIN n animal dying in accident

MORKINS > MORKIN

MORLING n sheep killed by disease

MORLINGS > MORLING

MORMAOR n former high-ranking Scottish nobleman

MORMAORS > MORMAOR

MORN n morning

MORNAY adj served with a cheese sauce

MORNAYS > MORNAY

MORNE same as > MOURN

MORNED > MORNE

MORNES > MORNE

MORNING n part of the day before noon

MORNINGS > MORNING

MORNS > MORN

MOROCCO n goatskin leather

MOROCCOS > MOROCCO

MORON n insulting term for a foolish or stupid person

MORONIC > MORON

MORONISM > MORON

MORONISMS > MORON

MORONITY > MORON

MORONS > MORON

MOROSE adj sullen or moody

MOROSELY > MOROSE

MOROSER > MOROSE

MOROSEST > MOROSE

MOROSITY > MOROSE

MORPH n phonological representation of a morpheme ▷ vb undergo or cause to undergo morphing

MORPHEAN adj of or relating to Morpheus, the god of sleep and dreams

MORPHED > MORPH

MORPHEME n speech element that cannot be subdivided

MORPHEMES > MORPHEME

MORPHEMIC > MORPHEME

MORPHETIC same as > MORPHEAN

MORPHEW n blemish on skin

MORPHEWS > MORPHEW

MORPHIA same as > MORPHINE

MORPHIAS > MORPHIA

MORPHIC adj as in morphic resonance idea that an event can lead to similar events in the future through a telepathic effect

MORPHIN variant form of > MORPHINE

MORPHINE n drug extracted from opium, used as an anaesthetic and sedative

MORPHINES > MORPHINE

MORPHING n one image changing to another by small gradual steps using computer animation

MORPHINGS > MORPHING

MORPHINIC > MORPHINE

MORPHINS > MORPHIN

MORPHO n type of butterfly

MORPHOGEN n chemical in body that influences growth

MORPHOS > MORPHO

MORPHOSES > MORPHOSIS

MORPHOSIS n development in an organism or its parts characterized by structural change

MORPHOTIC > MORPHOSIS

MORPHS > MORPH

MORRA same as > MORA

MORRAS > MORRA

MORRELL n tall SW Australian eucalyptus with pointed buds

MORRELLS > MORRELL

MORRHUA n cod

MORRHUAS > MORRHUA

MORRICE same as > MORRIS

MORRICES > MORRICE

MORRION same as > MORION

MORRIONS > MORRION

MORRIS vb perform morris dance

MORRISED > MORRIS

MORRISES > MORRIS

MORRISING > MORRIS

MORRO n rounded hill or promontory

MORROS > MORRO

MORROW n next day

MORROWS > MORROW

MORS > MOR

MORSAL same as > MORSEL

MORSALS > MORSAL

MORSE n clasp or fastening on a cope

MORSEL n small piece, esp of food ▷ vb divide into morsels

MORSELED > MORSEL

MORSELING > MORSEL

MORSELLED > MORSEL

MORSELS > MORSEL

MORSES > MORSE

MORSURE n bite

MORSURES > MORSURE

MORT n call blown on a hunting horn to signify the death of the animal hunted

MORTAL adj subject to death ▷ n human being

MORTALISE same as > MORTALIZE

MORTALITY n state of being mortal

MORTALIZE vb make mortal

MORTALLY > MORTAL

MORTALS > MORTAL

MORTAR n small cannon with a short range ▷ vb fire on with mortars

MORTARED > MORTAR

MORTARIER > MORTARY

MORTARING > MORTAR

MORTARMAN n person firing mortar

MORTARMEN > MORTAR

MORTARS > MORTAR

MORTARY adj of or like mortar

MORTBELL n bell rung for funeral

MORTBELLS > MORTBELL

MORTCLOTH n cloth spread over coffin

MORTGAGE n conditional pledging of property as security for the repayment of a loan ▷ vb pledge (property) as security thus ▷ adj of or relating to a mortgage

MORTGAGED > MORTGAGE

MORTGAGEE n creditor in a mortgage

MORTGAGER same as > MORTGAGOR

MORTGAGES > MORTGAGE

MORTGAGOR n debtor in a mortgage

MORTICE same as > MORTISE

MORTICED > MORTICE

MORTICER > MORTICE

MORTICERS > MORTICE

MORTICES > MORTICE

MORTICIAN n undertaker

MORTICING > MORTICE

MORTIFIC adj causing death

MORTIFIED > MORTIFY

MORTIFIER > MORTIFY

MORTIFIES > MORTIFY

MORTIFY vb humiliate

MORTISE n slot cut into a piece of wood, stone, etc ▷ vb cut a slot in (a piece of wood, stone, etc)

MORTISED > MORTISE

MORTISER > MORTISE

MORTISERS > MORTISE

MORTISES > MORTISE

MORTISING > MORTISE

MORTLING n dead body

MORTLINGS > MORTLING

MORTMAIN n status of lands held inalienably by a church

MORTMAINS > MORTMAIN

MORTS > MORT

MORTSAFE n cage placed over a grave to deter body snatchers

MORTSAFES > MORTSAFE

MORTUARY n building where corpses are kept before burial or cremation ▷ adj of or relating to death or burial

MORULA n solid ball of cells resulting from the splitting of a fertilized ovum

MORULAE > MORULA

MORULAR > MORULA

MORULAS > MORULA

MORWONG n food fish of Australasian coastal waters

MORWONGS > MORWONG

MORYAH interj exclamation of annoyance, disbelief, etc

MOS > MO

MOSAIC n design or decoration using small pieces of coloured stone or glass

MOSAICISM n occurrence of different types of tissue side by side

MOSAICIST > MOSAIC

MOSAICKED adj arranged in mosaic form

MOSAICS > MOSAIC

MOSASAUR n type of extinct Cretaceous giant marine lizard, typically with paddle-like limbs

MOSASAURI > MOSASAUR

MOSASAURS > MOSASAUR

MOSCATO n type of sweet dessert wine

MOSCATOS > MOSCATO

MOSCHATE n odour like musk

MOSCHATEL n small N temperate plant with greenish-white musk-scented flowers

MOSCOVIUM n highly radioactive element

MOSE vb have glanders

MOSED > MOSE

MOSELLE n German white wine from the Moselle valley

MOSELLES > MOSELLE

MOSES > MOSE

MOSEY vb walk in a leisurely manner

MOSEYED > MOSEY

MOSEYING > MOSEY

MOSEYS > MOSEY

MOSH n dance performed to loud rock music ▷ vb dance in this manner

MOSHAV n cooperative settlement in Israel

MOSHAVIM > MOSHAV

MOSHED > MOSH

MOSHER > MOSH

MOSHERS > MOSH

MOSHES > MOSH

MOSHING > MOSH

MOSHINGS > MOSH

MOSING > MOSE

MOSK same as > MOSQUE

MOSKONFYT n South African grape syrup

MOSKS > MOSK

MOSLINGS n shavings from animal skin being prepared

MOSQUE n Muslim temple

MOSQUES > MOSQUE

MOSQUITO n blood-sucking flying insect

MOSQUITOS > MOSQUITO

MOSS n small flowerless plant growing in masses on moist surfaces ▷ vb gather moss

MOSSBACK n old turtle, shellfish, etc, that has a growth of algae on its back

MOSSBACKS > MOSSBACK

MOSSED > MOSS

MOSSER > MOSS

MOSSERS > MOSS

MOSSES > MOSS

MOSSGROWN adj covered in moss

MOSSIE n common sparrow

MOSSIER > MOSS

MOSSIES > MOSSIE

MOSSIEST > MOSS

MOSSINESS > MOSS

MOSSING > MOSS

MOSSLAND n land covered in peat

MOSSLANDS > MOSSLAND

MOSSLIKE > MOSS

MOSSO adv to be performed with rapidity

MOSSPLANT n individual plant in moss

MOSSY > MOSS

MOST n greatest number or degree ▷ adj greatest in number or degree ▷ adv in the greatest degree

MOSTE > MOTE

MOSTEST > MOST

MOSTESTS > MOST

MOSTLY adv for the most part, generally

MOSTS > MOST

MOSTWHAT adv mostly

MOT n girl or young woman, esp one's girlfriend

MOTE n tiny speck ▷ vb may or might

MOTED adj containing motes

MOTEL n roadside hotel for motorists

MOTELIER n person running motel

MOTELIERS > MOTELIER

MOTELS > MOTEL

MOTEN > MOTE

MOTES > MOTE

MOTET n short sacred choral song

MOTETS > MOTET

MOTETT same as > MOTET

MOTETTIST > MOTET

MOTETTS > MOTETT

MOTEY adj containing motes ▷ n pigment made from earth

MOTEYS > MOTEY

MOTH n nocturnal insect like a butterfly

MOTHBALL n small ball of camphor or naphthalene used to repel moths from stored clothes ▷ vb store (something operational) for future use

MOTHBALLS > MOTHBALL

MOTHED adj damaged by moths

MOTHER n female parent ▷ adj native or inborn ▷ vb look after as a mother

MOTHERED > MOTHER

MOTHERESE n simplified and repetitive type of speech, with exaggerated intonation and rhythm, often used by adults when speaking to babies

MOTHERIER > MOTHERY

MOTHERING > MOTHER

MOTHERLY adj of or resembling a mother, esp in warmth, or protectiveness

MOTHERS > MOTHER

MOTHERY adj like mother of vinegar

MOTHIER > MOTHY

MOTHIEST > MOTHY

MOTHLIKE > MOTH

MOTHPROOF adj (esp of clothes) chemically treated so as to repel clothes moths ▷ vb make mothproof

MOTHS > MOTH

MOTHY adj ragged

MOTI n derogatory Indian English word for a fat woman or girl

MOTIER > MOTEY

MOTIEST > MOTEY

MOTIF n (recurring) theme or design

MOTIFIC adj causing motion

MOTIFS > MOTIF

MOTILE adj capable of independent movement ▷ n person whose mental imagery strongly reflects movement

MOTILES > MOTILE

MOTILITY > MOTILE

MOTION n process, action, or way of moving ▷ vb direct (someone) by gesture

MOTIONAL > MOTION

MOTIONED > MOTION

MOTIONER > MOTION

MOTIONERS > MOTION

MOTIONING > MOTION

MOTIONIST n person proposing many motions

MOTIONS > MOTION

MOTIS > MOTI

MOTIVATE vb give incentive to

MOTIVATED > MOTIVATE

MOTIVATES > MOTIVATE

MOTIVATOR > MOTIVATE

MOTIVE n reason for a course of action ▷ adj causing motion ▷ vb motivate

MOTIVED > MOTIVE

MOTIVES > MOTIVE

MOTIVIC adj of musical motif

MOTIVING > MOTIVE

MOTIVITY n power of moving or of initiating motion

MOTLEY adj miscellaneous ▷ n costume of a jester

MOTLEYER > MOTLEY

MOTLEYEST > MOTLEY

MOTLEYS > MOTLEY

MOTLIER > MOTLEY

MOTLIEST > MOTLEY

MOTMOT n tropical American bird with a long tail and blue and brownish-green plumage

MOTMOTS > MOTMOT

MOTOCROSS n motorcycle race over a rough course

MOTOR n engine, esp of a vehicle ▷ vb travel by car ▷ adj of or relating to cars and other vehicles powered by engines

MOTORABLE adj (of a road) suitable for use by motor vehicles

MOTORAIL n transport of cars by train

MOTORAILS > MOTORAIL

MOTORBIKE n motorcycle

MOTORBOAT n any boat powered by a motor

MOTORBUS n bus driven by an internal-combustion engine

MOTORCADE n procession of cars carrying important people

MOTORCAR n self-propelled electric railway car

MOTORCARS > MOTORCAR

MOTORDOM n world of motor cars

MOTORDOMS > MOTORDOM

MOTORED > MOTOR

MOTORHOME n large motor vehicle with living quarters behind the driver's compartment

MOTORIAL > MOTOR

MOTORIC n person trained in the muscular causes of vocal changes ▷ adj pertaining to motion

MOTORICS > MOTORIC

MOTORING > MOTOR

MOTORINGS > MOTOR

MOTORISE same as > MOTORIZE

MOTORISED > MOTORISE

MOTORISES > MOTORISE

MOTORIST n driver of a car

MOTORISTS > MOTORIST

MOTORIUM n area of nervous system involved in movement

MOTORIUMS > MOTORIUM

MOTORIZE vb equip with a motor

MOTORIZED > MOTORIZE

MOTORIZES > MOTORIZE

MOTORLESS > MOTOR

MOTORMAN n driver of an electric train

MOTORMEN > MOTORMAN

MOTORS > MOTOR

MOTORSHIP n ship with motor

MOTORWAY n main road for fast-moving traffic

MOTORWAYS > MOTORWAY

MOTORY > MOTOR

MOTOSCAFI > MOTOSCAFO

MOTOSCAFO n motorboat

MOTS > MOT

MOTSER n large sum of money, esp a gambling win

MOTSERS > MOTSER

MOTT n clump of trees

MOTTE n mound on which a castle was built

MOTTES > MOTTE

MOTTIER > MOTTY

MOTTIES > MOTTY

MOTTIEST > MOTTY

MOTTLE vb colour with streaks or blotches of different shades ▷ n mottled appearance, as of the surface of marble

MOTTLED > MOTTLE

MOTTLER n paintbrush for mottled effects

MOTTLERS > MOTTLER

MOTTLES > MOTTLE

MOTTLING > MOTTLE

MOTTLINGS > MOTTLE

MOTTO n saying expressing an ideal or rule of conduct

MOTTOED adj having motto

MOTTOES > MOTTO

MOTTOS > MOTTO

MOTTS > MOTT

MOTTY n target at which coins are aimed in pitch-and-toss ▷ adj containing motes

MOTU n derogatory Indian English word for a fat man or boy

MOTUCA n Brazilian fly

MOTUCAS > MOTUCA

MOTUS > MOTU

MOTZA same as > MOTSER

MOTZAS > MOTZA

MOU Scots word for > MOUTH

MOUCH same as > MOOCH

MOUCHARD n police informer

MOUCHARDS > MOUCHARD

MOUCHED > MOUCH

MOUCHER > MOUCH

MOUCHERS > MOUCH

MOUCHES > MOUCH

MOUCHING > MOUCH

MOUCHOIR n handkerchief

MOUCHOIRS > MOUCHOIR

MOUDIWART same as > MOULDWARP

MOUDIWORT same as > MOULDWARP

MOUE n disdainful or pouting look

MOUES > MOUE

MOUFFLON same as > MOUFLON

MOUFFLONS > MOUFFLON

MOUFLON n wild mountain sheep of Corsica and Sardinia

MOUFLONS > MOUFLON

MOUGHT > MAY

MOUILLE adj palatalized, as in the sounds represented by Spanish ll or ñ

MOUJIK same as > MUZHIK

MOUJIKS > MOUJIK

MOULAGE n mould making

MOULAGES > MOULAGE

MOULD n hollow container in which metal etc is cast ▷ vb shape

MOULDABLE > MOULD

MOULDED > MOULD

MOULDER vb decay into dust ▷ n person who moulds or makes moulds

MOULDERED > MOULDER

MOULDERS > MOULDER

MOULDIER > MOULDY

MOULDIEST > MOULDY

MOULDING n moulded ornamental edging

MOULDINGS > MOULDING

MOULDS > MOULD

MOULDWARP archaic or dialect name for a > MOLE

MOULDY adj stale or musty

MOULIN n vertical shaft in a glacier

m

MOULINET n device for bending crossbow
MOULINETS > MOULINET
MOULINS > MOULIN
MOULS Scots word for > MOULD
MOULT vb shed feathers, hair, or skin to make way for new growth ▷ n process of moulting
MOULTED > MOULT
MOULTEN adj having moulted
MOULTER > MOULT
MOULTERS > MOULT
MOULTING > MOULT
MOULTINGS > MOULT
MOULTS > MOULT
MOUND n heap, esp of earth or stones ▷ vb gather into a mound
MOUNDBIRD n Australian bird laying eggs in mounds
MOUNDED > MOUND
MOUNDING > MOUND
MOUNDS > MOUND
MOUNSEER same as > MONSIEUR
MOUNSEERS > MOUNSEER
MOUNT vb climb or ascend ▷ n backing or support on which something is fixed
MOUNTABLE > MOUNT
MOUNTAIN n hill of great size ▷ adj of, found on, or for use on a mountain or mountains
MOUNTAINS > MOUNTAIN
MOUNTAINY adj mountainous
MOUNTANT n adhesive for mounting pictures
MOUNTANTS > MOUNTANT
MOUNTED adj riding horses
MOUNTER > MOUNT
MOUNTERS > MOUNT
MOUNTING same as > MOUNT
MOUNTINGS > MOUNTING
MOUNTS > MOUNT
MOUP n nibble
MOUPED > MOUP
MOUPING > MOUP
MOUPS > MOUP
MOURN vb feel or express sorrow for (a dead person or lost thing)
MOURNED > MOURN
MOURNER n person attending a funeral
MOURNERS > MOURNER
MOURNFUL adj sad or dismal
MOURNING n grieving ▷ adj of or relating to mourning
MOURNINGS > MOURNING
MOURNIVAL n card game
MOURNS > MOURN
MOURVEDRE n type of red wine grape
MOUS > MOU
MOUSAKA same as > MOUSSAKA
MOUSAKAS > MOUSAKA
MOUSE n small long-tailed rodent ▷ vb stalk and catch mice
MOUSEBIRD another name for > COLY
MOUSED > MOUSE
MOUSEKIN n little mouse

MOUSEKINS > MOUSEKIN
MOUSELIKE > MOUSE
MOUSEMAT n piece of material on which a computer mouse is moved
MOUSEMATS > MOUSEMAT
MOUSEOVER n on a web page, any item that changes or pops up when the pointer of a mouse moves over it
MOUSEPAD n pad for computer mouse
MOUSEPADS > MOUSEPAD
MOUSER n cat used to catch mice
MOUSERIES > MOUSERY
MOUSERS > MOUSER
MOUSERY n place infested with mice
MOUSES > MOUSE
MOUSETAIL n N temperate plant with tail-like flower spikes
MOUSETRAP n spring-loaded trap for killing mice
MOUSEY same as > MOUSY
MOUSIE n little mouse
MOUSIER > MOUSY
MOUSIES > MOUSIE
MOUSIEST > MOUSY
MOUSILY > MOUSY
MOUSINESS > MOUSY
MOUSING n device for closing off a hook
MOUSINGS > MOUSING
MOUSLE vb handle roughly
MOUSLED > MOUSLE
MOUSLES > MOUSLE
MOUSLING > MOUSLE
MOUSME n Japanese girl
MOUSMEE same as > MOUSME
MOUSMEES > MOUSMEE
MOUSMES > MOUSME
MOUSSAKA n dish made with meat, aubergines, and tomatoes, topped with cheese sauce
MOUSSAKAS > MOUSSAKA
MOUSSE n dish of flavoured cream whipped and set ▷ vb apply mousse to
MOUSSED > MOUSSE
MOUSSES > MOUSSE
MOUSSEUX n type of sparkling wine
MOUSSING > MOUSSE
MOUST same as > MUST
MOUSTACHE n hair on the upper lip
MOUSTED > MOUST
MOUSTING > MOUST
MOUSTS > MOUST
MOUSY adj like a mouse, esp in hair colour
MOUTAN n variety of peony
MOUTANS > MOUTAN
MOUTER same as > MULTURE
MOUTERED > MOUTER
MOUTERER > MOUTER
MOUTERERS > MOUTER
MOUTERING > MOUTER
MOUTERS > MOUTER
MOUTH n opening in the head for eating and issuing sounds ▷ vb form (words) with the lips without speaking

MOUTHABLE adj able to be recited
MOUTHED > MOUTH
MOUTHER > MOUTH
MOUTHERS > MOUTH
MOUTHFEEL n texture of a substance as it is perceived in the mouth
MOUTHFUL n amount of food or drink put into the mouth at any one time when eating or drinking
MOUTHFULS > MOUTHFUL
MOUTHIER > MOUTHY
MOUTHIEST > MOUTHY
MOUTHILY > MOUTHY
MOUTHING > MOUTH
MOUTHLESS > MOUTH
MOUTHLIKE > MOUTH
MOUTHPART n any of the paired appendages in arthropods that surround the mouth and are specialized for feeding
MOUTHS > MOUTH
MOUTHWASH n medicated liquid for gargling and cleansing the mouth
MOUTHY adj bombastic
MOUTON n sheepskin processed to resemble the fur of another animal
MOUTONNEE adj rounded by action of glacier
MOUTONS > MOUTON
MOVABLE adj able to be moved or rearranged ▷ n movable article, esp a piece of furniture
MOVABLES > MOVABLE
MOVABLY > MOVABLE
MOVANT n person who applies to a court of law
MOVANTS > MOVANT
MOVE vb change in place or position ▷ n moving
MOVEABLE same as > MOVABLE
MOVEABLES > MOVEABLE
MOVEABLY > MOVEABLE
MOVED > MOVE
MOVELESS adj immobile
MOVEMENT n action or process of moving
MOVEMENTS > MOVEMENT
MOVER n person or animal that moves in a particular way
MOVERS > MOVER
MOVES > MOVE
MOVIE n cinema film
MOVIEDOM n world of cinema
MOVIEDOMS > MOVIEDOM
MOVIEGOER n person who goes to cinema
MOVIELAND same as > MOVIEDOM
MOVIEOKE n entertainment in which people act out scenes from movies
MOVIEOKES > MOVIEOKE
MOVIEOLA same as > MOVIOLA
MOVIEOLAS > MOVIEOLA
MOVIES > MOVIE
MOVING adj arousing or touching the emotions

MOVINGLY > MOVING
MOVIOLA n viewing machine used in cutting and editing film
MOVIOLAS > MOVIOLA
MOW vb cut (grass or crops) ▷ n part of a barn where hay, straw, etc, is stored
MOWA same as > MAHUA
MOWAS > MOWA
MOWBURN vb heat up in mow
MOWBURNED > MOWBURN
MOWBURNS > MOWBURN
MOWBURNT adj (of hay, straw, etc) damaged by overheating in a mow
MOWDIE Scot words for > MOLE
MOWDIES > MOWDIE
MOWED > MOW
MOWER > MOW
MOWERS > MOW
MOWING > MOW
MOWINGS > MOW
MOWN > MOW
MOWRA same as > MAHUA
MOWRAS > MOWRA
MOWS > MOW
MOXA n downy material obtained from various plants
MOXAS > MOXA
MOXIE n courage, nerve, or vigour
MOXIES > MOXIE
MOY n coin
MOYA n mud emitted from a volcano
MOYAS > MOYA
MOYGASHEL n type of Irish linen
MOYITIES > MOYITY
MOYITY same as > MOIETY
MOYL same as > MOYLE
MOYLE vb toil
MOYLED > MOYLE
MOYLES > MOYLE
MOYLING > MOYLE
MOYLS > MOYL
MOYS > MOY
MOZ n hex
MOZE vb give nap to
MOZED > MOZE
MOZES > MOZE
MOZETTA same as > MOZZETTA
MOZETTAS > MOZETTA
MOZETTE > MOZETTA
MOZING > MOZE
MOZO n porter in southwest USA
MOZOS > MOZO
MOZZ same as > MOZ
MOZZES > MOZZ
MOZZETTA n short hooded cape worn by the pope, cardinals, etc
MOZZETTAS > MOZZETTA
MOZZETTE > MOZZETTA
MOZZIE same as > MOSSIE
MOZZIES > MOZZIE
MOZZLE n luck ▷ vb hamper or impede (someone)
MOZZLED > MOZZLE
MOZZLES > MOZZLE
MOZZLING > MOZZLE
MPRET n former Albanian ruler

MPRETS > MPRET
MRIDAMGAM same as **>** MRIDANG
MRIDANG n drum used in Indian music
MRIDANGA same as **>** MRIDANG
MRIDANGAM same as **>** MRIDANG
MRIDANGAS > MRIDANGA
MRIDANGS > MRIDANG
MU n twelfth letter in the Greek alphabet
MUCATE n salt of mucic acid
MUCATES > MUCATE
MUCH adj large amount or degree of **>** n large amount or degree **>** adv great degree
MUCHACHA n (in Spain etc) young woman or female servant
MUCHACHAS > MUCHACHA
MUCHACHO n young man
MUCHACHOS > MUCHACHO
MUCHEL same as **>** MUCH
MUCHELL same as **>** MUCH
MUCHELLS > MUCHELL
MUCHELS > MUCHEL
MUCHES > MUCH
MUCHLY > MUCH
MUCHNESS n magnitude
MUCHO adv Spanish for very
MUCIC adj as in mucic acid colourless crystalline solid carboxylic acid
MUCID adj mouldy, musty, or slimy
MUCIDITY > MUCID
MUCIDNESS > MUCID
MUCIGEN n substance present in mucous cells that is converted into mucin
MUCIGENS > MUCIGEN
MUCILAGE n gum or glue
MUCILAGES > MUCILAGE
MUCIN n any of a group of nitrogenous mucoproteins occurring in saliva, skin, tendon, etc
MUCINOGEN n substance forming mucin
MUCINOID adj of or like mucin
MUCINOUS > MUCIN
MUCINS > MUCIN
MUCK n dirt, filth
MUCKAMUCK n food **>** vb consume food
MUCKED > MUCK
MUCKENDER n handkerchief
MUCKER n person who shifts broken rock or waste **>** vb hoard
MUCKERED > MUCKER
MUCKERING > MUCKER
MUCKERISH > MUCKER
MUCKERS > MUCKER
MUCKHEAP n dunghill
MUCKHEAPS > MUCKHEAP
MUCKIER > MUCKY
MUCKIEST > MUCKY
MUCKILY > MUCKY
MUCKINESS > MUCKY
MUCKING > MUCK
MUCKLE adj large
MUCKLER > MUCKLE
MUCKLES > MUCKLE

MUCKLEST > MUCKLE
MUCKLUCK same as **>** MUKLUK
MUCKLUCKS > MUCKLUCK
MUCKRAKE n agricultural rake for spreading manure **>** vb seek out and expose scandal, esp concerning public figures
MUCKRAKED > MUCKRAKE
MUCKRAKER > MUCKRAKE
MUCKRAKES > MUCKRAKE
MUCKS > MUCK
MUCKSWEAT n profuse sweat
MUCKWORM n any larva or worm that lives in mud
MUCKWORMS > MUCKWORM
MUCKY adj dirty or muddy
MUCKYMUCK n person who is or appears to be very important
MUCLUC same as **>** MUKLUK
MUCLUCS > MUCLUC
MUCOID adj of the nature of or resembling mucin **>** n substance like mucin
MUCOIDAL same as **>** MUCOID
MUCOIDS > MUCOID
MUCOLYTIC adj breaking down mucus **>** n agent that is able to break down mucus
MUCOR n type of fungus
MUCORS > MUCOR
MUCOSA n mucus-secreting membrane that lines body cavities
MUCOSAE > MUCOSA
MUCOSAL > MUCOSA
MUCOSAS > MUCOSA
MUCOSE same as **>** MUCOUS
MUCOSITY > MUCOUS
MUCOUS adj of, resembling, or secreting mucus
MUCRO n short pointed projection from certain parts or organs
MUCRONATE adj terminating in a sharp point
MUCRONES > MUCRO
MUCROS > MUCRO
MUCULENT adj like mucus
MUCUS n slimy secretion of the mucous membranes
MUCUSES > MUCUS
MUD n wet soft earth **>** vb cover in mud
MUDBANK n sloping area of mud beside a body of water
MUDBANKS > MUDBANK
MUDBATH n medicinal bath in heated mud
MUDBATHS > MUDBATH
MUDBUG n crayfish
MUDBUGS > MUDBUG
MUDCAP vb use explosive charge in blasting
MUDCAPPED > MUDCAP
MUDCAPS > MUDCAP
MUDCAT n any of several large North American catfish
MUDCATS > MUDCAT
MUDDED > MUD
MUDDER n horse that runs well in mud
MUDDERS > MUDDER

MUDDIED > MUDDY
MUDDIER > MUDDY
MUDDIES > MUDDY
MUDDIEST > MUDDY
MUDDILY > MUDDY
MUDDINESS > MUDDY
MUDDING > MUD
MUDDLE vb confuse **>** n state of confusion
MUDDLED > MUDDLE
MUDDLER n person who muddles or muddles through
MUDDLERS > MUDDLER
MUDDLES > MUDDLE
MUDDLIER > MUDDLE
MUDDLIEST > MUDDLE
MUDDLING > MUDDLE
MUDDLINGS > MUDDLE
MUDDLY > MUDDLE
MUDDY adj covered or filled with mud **>** vb make muddy
MUDDYING > MUDDY
MUDEJAR n Spanish Moor **>** adj of or relating to a style of architecture
MUDEJARES > MUDEJAR
MUDEYE n larva of the dragonfly
MUDEYES > MUDEYE
MUDFISH n fish that lives in the muddy bottoms of rivers, lakes, etc
MUDFISHES > MUDFISH
MUDFLAP n flap above wheel to deflect mud
MUDFLAPS > MUDFLAP
MUDFLAT n tract of low muddy land
MUDFLATS > MUDFLAT
MUDFLOW n flow of soil mixed with water down a steep unstable slope
MUDFLOWS > MUDFLOW
MUDGE vb speak vaguely
MUDGED > MUDGE
MUDGER > MUDGE
MUDGERS > MUDGE
MUDGES > MUDGE
MUDGING > MUDGE
MUDGUARD n cover over a wheel to prevent mud or water being thrown up by it
MUDGUARDS > MUDGUARD
MUDHEN n water bird living in muddy place
MUDHENS > MUDHEN
MUDHOLE n hole with mud at bottom
MUDHOLES > MUDHOLE
MUDHOOK n anchor
MUDHOOKS > MUDHOOK
MUDHOPPER n type of amphibious fish found on mud flats and in mangrove swamps
MUDIR n local governor
MUDIRIA n province of mudir
MUDIRIAS > MUDIRIA
MUDIRIEH same as **>** MUDIRIA
MUDIRIEHS > MUDIRIEH
MUDIRS > MUDIR
MUDLARK n street urchin **>** vb play in mud
MUDLARKED > MUDLARK
MUDLARKS > MUDLARK

MUDLOGGER n person checking mud for traces of oil
MUDPACK n cosmetic paste applied to the face
MUDPACKS > MUDPACK
MUDPIE n small mass of mud moulded into a pie shape
MUDPIES > MUDPIE
MUDPUPPY n type of salamander
MUDRA n hand movement in Hindu religious dancing
MUDRAS > MUDRA
MUDROCK n type of sedimentary rock
MUDROCKS > MUDROCK
MUDROOM n room where muddy shoes may be left
MUDROOMS > MUDROOM
MUDS > MUD
MUDSCOW n boat for travelling over mudflats
MUDSCOWS > MUDSCOW
MUDSILL n support for building at or below ground
MUDSILLS > MUDSILL
MUDSLIDE n landslide of mud
MUDSLIDES > MUDSLIDE
MUDSLING vb make accusations against a rival candidate
MUDSLINGS > MUDSLING
MUDSLUNG > MUDSLING
MUDSTONE n dark grey clay rock similar to shale but with the lamination less well developed
MUDSTONES > MUDSTONE
MUDWORT n plant growing in mud
MUDWORTS > MUDWORT
MUEDDIN same as **>** MUEZZIN
MUEDDINS > MUEDDIN
MUENSTER n whitish-yellow semihard whole milk cheese, often flavoured with caraway or aniseed
MUENSTERS > MUENSTER
MUESLI n mixture of grain, nuts, and dried fruit
MUESLIS > MUESLI
MUEZZIN n official who summons Muslims to prayer
MUEZZINS > MUEZZIN
MUFF n tube-shaped covering to keep the hands warm **>** vb bungle (an action)
MUFFED > MUFF
MUFFETTEE n small muff worn over the wrist
MUFFIN n light round flat yeast cake
MUFFINEER n muffin dish
MUFFING > MUFF
MUFFINS > MUFFIN
MUFFISH > MUFF
MUFFLE vb wrap up for warmth or to deaden sound **>** n something that muffles
MUFFLED > MUFFLE
MUFFLER n scarf
MUFFLERED adj with muffler
MUFFLERS > MUFFLER

m

MUFFLES > MUFFLE
MUFFLING > MUFFLE
MUFFS > MUFF
MUFLON same as
> MOUFFLON
MUFLONS > MUFLON
MUFTI n civilian clothes worn by a person who usually wears a uniform
MUFTIS > MUFTI
MUG n large drinking cup ▷ vb attack in order to rob
MUGEARITE n crystalline rock
MUGFUL same as **>** MUG
MUGFULS > MUGFUL
MUGG same as **>** MUG
MUGGA n Australian eucalyptus tree
MUGGAR same as **>** MUGGER
MUGGARS > MUGGAR
MUGGAS > MUGGA
MUGGED > MUG
MUGGEE n mugged person
MUGGEES > MUGGEE
MUGGER n person who commits robbery with violence
MUGGERS > MUGGER
MUGGIER > MUGGY
MUGGIEST > MUGGY
MUGGILY > MUGGY
MUGGINESS > MUGGY
MUGGING > MUG
MUGGINGS > MUG
MUGGINS n stupid or gullible person
MUGGINSES > MUGGINS
MUGGISH same as **>** MUGGY
MUGGLE n person who does not possess supernatural powers
MUGGLES > MUGGLE
MUGGS > MUG
MUGGUR same as **>** MUGGER
MUGGURS > MUGGUR
MUGGY adj (of weather) damp and stifling
MUGHAL same as **>** MOGUL
MUGHALS > MUGHAL
MUGS > MUG
MUGSHOT n police photograph of person's face
MUGSHOTS > MUGSHOT
MUGWORT n N temperate herbaceous plant with aromatic leaves
MUGWORTS > MUGWORT
MUGWUMP n neutral or independent person
MUGWUMPS > MUGWUMP
MUHLIES > MUHLY
MUHLY n American grass
MUID n former French measure of capacity
MUIDS > MUID
MUIL same as **>** MULE
MUILS > MUIL
MUIR same as **>** MOOR
MUIRBURN same as
> MOORBURN
MUIRBURNS > MUIRBURN
MUIRS > MUIR
MUIST same as **>** MUST
MUISTED > MUIST
MUISTING > MUIST
MUISTS > MUIST

MUJAHEDIN same as
> MUJAHEDDIN
MUJAHIDIN same as
> MUJAHEDDIN
MUJIK same as **>** MUZHIK
MUJIKS > MUJIK
MUKHTAR n lawyer in India
MUKHTARS > MUKHTAR
MUKLUK n soft boot, usually of sealskin
MUKLUKS > MUKLUK
MUKTUK n thin outer skin of the beluga, used as food
MUKTUKS > MUKTUK
MULATRESS n offensive term for a woman with one Black and one White parent
MULATTA n offensive term for a woman with mixed racial ancestry
MULATTAS > MULATTA
MULATTO n offensive term for a child with mixed racial ancestry ▷ adj of a light brown colour
MULATTOES > MULATTO
MULATTOS > MULATTO
MULBERRY n tree whose leaves are used to feed silkworms ▷ adj dark purple
MULCH n mixture of wet straw, leaves, etc ▷ vb cover (land) with mulch
MULCHED > MULCH
MULCHES > MULCH
MULCHING > MULCH
MULCT vb cheat or defraud ▷ n fine or penalty
MULCTED > MULCT
MULCTING > MULCT
MULCTS > MULCT
MULE n offspring of a horse and a donkey ▷ vb strike coin with different die on each side
MULED > MULE
MULES vb surgically remove folds of skin from a sheep
MULESED > MULES
MULESES > MULES
MULESING > MULES
MULESINGS > MULESING
MULETA n small cape attached to a stick used by a matador
MULETAS > MULETA
MULETEER n mule driver
MULETEERS > MULETEER
MULEY adj (of cattle) having no horns ▷ n any hornless cow
MULEYS > MULEY
MULGA n Australian acacia shrub growing in desert regions
MULGAS > MULGA
MULIE n type of N American deer
MULIES > MULIE
MULING > MULE
MULISH adj obstinate
MULISHLY > MULISH
MULL vb think (over) or ponder ▷ n promontory or headland
MULLA same as **>** MULLAH
MULLAH n Muslim scholar, teacher, or religious leader

MULLAHED same as
> MULLERED
MULLAHING same as
> MULLERING
MULLAHISM n rule by mullahs
MULLAHS > MULLAH
MULLARKY same as
> MALARKEY
MULLAS > MULLA
MULLED > MULL
MULLEIN n type of European plant
MULLEINS > MULLEIN
MULLEN same as **>** MULLEIN
MULLENS > MULLEN
MULLER n flat heavy implement used to grind material ▷ vb beat up or defeat thoroughly
MULLERED adj drunk
MULLERIAN adj relating to animal mimicry in which two or more harmful species resemble each other
MULLERING > MULLER
MULLERS > MULLER
MULLET n edible sea fish
MULLETS > MULLET
MULLEY same as **>** MULEY
MULLEYS > MULLEY
MULLIGAN n stew made from odds and ends of food
MULLIGANS > MULLIGAN
MULLING > MULL
MULLION n vertical dividing bar in a window ▷ vb furnish with mullions
MULLIONED > MULLION
MULLIONS > MULLION
MULLITE n colourless mineral
MULLITES > MULLITE
MULLOCK n waste material from a mine
MULLOCKS > MULLOCK
MULLOCKY adj like mullock
MULLOWAY n large Australian sea fish, valued for sport and food
MULLOWAYS > MULLOWAY
MULLS > MULL
MULMUL n muslin
MULMULL same as **>** MULMUL
MULMULLS > MULMULL
MULMULS > MULMUL
MULSE n drink containing honey
MULSES > MULSE
MULSH same as **>** MULCH
MULSHED > MULSH
MULSHES > MULSH
MULSHING > MULSH
MULTEITY n manifoldness
MULTIAGE adj involving different age groups
MULTIATOM adj involving many atoms
MULTIBAND adj involving more than one waveband
MULTIBANK adj involving more than one bank
MULTICAR adj involving several cars
MULTICAST n broadcast from one source

simultaneously to several receivers on a network
MULTICELL adj involving many cells
MULTICIDE n mass murder
MULTICITY adj involving more than one city
MULTICOPY adj involving many copies ▷ n any of several or many copies (of a book, document, record, etc)
MULTICORE adj having multiple cores
MULTICULT adj multicultural
MULTIDAY adj involving more than one day
MULTIDISC adj involving more than one disc
MULTIDISK adj involving more than one disk
MULTIDRUG adj involving more than one drug
MULTIFID adj having or divided into many lobes or similar segments
MULTIFIL n fibre made up of many filaments
MULTIFILS > MULTIFIL
MULTIFOIL n ornamental design having a large number of foils
MULTIFOLD adj many times doubled
MULTIFORM adj having many shapes or forms
MULTIGENE n one of a group of closely related genes
MULTIGERM adj (of plants) having the ability to multiply germinate
MULTIGRID adj involving several grids
MULTIGYM n exercise apparatus incorporating a variety of weights, used for toning the muscles
MULTIGYMS > MULTIGYM
MULTIHUED adj having many colours
MULTIHULL n sailing vessel with two or more hulls
MULTIJET adj involving more than one jet
MULTILANE adj having several lanes
MULTILINE adj involving several lines ▷ n variety of crop with several lines, each having different genes to improve disease resistance
MULTILOBE adj having more than one lobe
MULTIMODE n device with several modes
MULTIPACK n form of packaging of foodstuffs, etc, that contains several units and is offered at a price below that of the equivalent number of units
MULTIPAGE adj involving many pages
MULTIPARA n woman who has given birth to more than one viable fetus or living child
MULTIPART adj involving many parts

MULTIPATH adj relating to television or radio signals that travel by more than one route from a transmitter and arrive at slightly different times, causing ghost images or audio distortion

MULTIPED adj having many feet ▷ n insect or animal having many feet

MULTIPEDE same as > MULTIPED

MULTIPEDS > MULTIPED

MULTIPION adj involving many pions

MULTIPLE adj having many parts ▷ n quantity which contains another an exact number of times

MULTIPLES > MULTIPLE

MULTIPLET n set of closely spaced lines in a spectrum, resulting from small differences between the energy levels of atoms or molecules

MULTIPLEX n purpose-built complex containing several cinemas and usu restaurants and bars ▷ adj having many elements, complex ▷ vb send (messages or signals) or (of messages or signals) be sent by multiplex

MULTIPLY vb increase in number or degree

MULTIPOLE adj involving more than one pole

MULTIPORT adj involving more than one port

MULTIRISK adj (of insurance) covering several risks

MULTIROLE adj having a number of roles, functions, etc

MULTIROOM adj having many rooms

MULTISITE adj involving more than one site

MULTISIZE adj involving more than size

MULTISTEP adj involving several steps

MULTITASK vb work at several different tasks simultaneously

MULTITIER adj having many tiers

MULTITON adj weighing several tons

MULTITONE adj involving more than one tone

MULTITOOL n device containing various tools attached to one handle

MULTITUDE n great number

MULTIUNIT adj involving more than one unit

MULTIUSE adj suitable for more than one use

MULTIUSER > MULTIUSE

MULTIWALL adj involving several layers

MULTIWAY adj having several paths or routes

MULTIYEAR adj involving more than one year

MULTUM n substance used in brewing

MULTUMS > MULTUM

MULTURE n fee formerly paid to a miller for grinding grain ▷ vb take multure

MULTURED > MULTURE

MULTURER > MULTURE

MULTURERS > MULTURE

MULTURES > MULTURE

MULTURING > MULTURE

MUM n mother ▷ vb act in a mummer's play

MUMBLE vb speak indistinctly, mutter ▷ n indistinct utterance

MUMBLED > MUMBLE

MUMBLER > MUMBLE

MUMBLERS > MUMBLE

MUMBLES > MUMBLE

MUMBLIER > MUMBLY

MUMBLIEST > MUMBLY

MUMBLING > MUMBLE

MUMBLINGS > MUMBLE

MUMBLY > MUMBLE

MUMCHANCE adj silent

MUMM same as > MUM

MUMMED > MUM

MUMMER n actor in a traditional English folk play ▷ vb perform as a mummer

MUMMERED > MUMMER

MUMMERIES > MUMMERY

MUMMERING n Christmas tradition of house-visiting in parts of Canada

MUMMERS > MUMMER

MUMMERY n performance by mummers

MUMMIA n mummified flesh used as medicine

MUMMIAS > MUMMIA

MUMMICHOG n small American fish

MUMMIED > MUMMY

MUMMIES > MUMMY

MUMMIFIED > MUMMIFY

MUMMIFIES > MUMMIFY

MUMMIFORM adj like a mummy ▷ n sarcophagus

MUMMIFY vb preserve a body as a mummy

MUMMING > MUM

MUMMINGS > MUM

MUMMOCK same as > MAMMOCK

MUMMOCKS > MUMMOCK

MUMMS > MUMM

MUMMY n body embalmed and wrapped for burial in ancient Egypt ▷ vb mummify

MUMMYING > MUMMY

MUMP vb be silent

MUMPED > MUMP

MUMPER > MUMP

MUMPERS > MUMP

MUMPING > MUMP

MUMPISH > MUMPS

MUMPISHLY > MUMPS

MUMPS n infectious disease with swelling in the glands of the neck

MUMPSIMUS n opinion held obstinately

MUMS > MUM

MUMSIER > MUMSY

MUMSIES > MUMSY

MUMSIEST > MUMSY

MUMSINESS n the state of being mumsy

MUMSY adj (of a woman) wearing clothes that are old-fashioned and unflattering ▷ n mother

MUMU n oven in Papua New Guinea

MUMUS > MUMU

MUN same as > MAUN

MUNCH vb chew noisily and steadily

MUNCHABLE > MUNCH

MUNCHED > MUNCH

MUNCHER > MUNCH

MUNCHERS > MUNCH

MUNCHES > MUNCH

MUNCHIE n small amount of food eaten between meals

MUNCHIER > MUNCHY

MUNCHIES pl n craving for food

MUNCHIEST > MUNCHY

MUNCHING > MUNCH

MUNCHKIN n undersized person or a child, esp an appealing one

MUNCHKINS > MUNCHKIN

MUNCHY adj suitable for snacking

MUNDANE adj everyday

MUNDANELY > MUNDANE

MUNDANER > MUNDANE

MUNDANEST > MUNDANE

MUNDANITY > MUNDANE

MUNDIC n iron pyrites

MUNDICS > MUNDIC

MUNDIFIED > MUNDIFY

MUNDIFIES > MUNDIFY

MUNDIFY vb cleanse

MUNDUNGO n tripe in Spain

MUNDUNGOS > MUNDUNGO

MUNDUNGUS n smelly tobacco

MUNG vb process (computer data)

MUNGA n army canteen

MUNGAS > MUNGA

MUNGCORN n maslin

MUNGCORNS > MUNGCORN

MUNGE vb modify a password into an unguessable state

MUNGED > MUNG

MUNGES > MUNGE

MUNGING > MUNG

MUNGO n cheap felted fabric made from waste wool

MUNGOES > MUNGO

MUNGOOSE same as > MONGOOSE

MUNGOOSES > MUNGOOSE

MUNGOS > MUNGO

MUNGS > MUNG

MUNI n municipal radio broadcast

MUNICIPAL adj relating to a city or town

MUNIFIED > MUNIFY

MUNIFIES > MUNIFY

MUNIFY vb fortify

MUNIFYING > MUNIFY

MUNIMENT n means of defence

MUNIMENTS pl n title deeds or similar documents

MUNIS > MUNI

MUNITE vb strengthen

MUNITED > MUNITE

MUNITES > MUNITE

MUNITING > MUNITE

MUNITION vb supply with munitions

MUNITIONS pl n military stores

MUNNION archaic word for > MULLION

MUNNIONS > MUNNION

MUNS > MUN

MUNSHI n secretary in India

MUNSHIS > MUNSHI

MUNSTER variant of > MUENSTER

MUNSTERS > MUNSTER

MUNT n offensive word for a Black African

MUNTED adj destroyed or ruined

MUNTER n insulting word for an unattractive person

MUNTERS > MUNTER

MUNTIN n supporting or strengthening bar

MUNTINED adj having a muntin

MUNTING same as > MUNTIN

MUNTINGS > MUNTING

MUNTINS > MUNTIN

MUNTJAC n small Asian deer

MUNTJACS > MUNTJAC

MUNTJAK same as > MUNTJAC

MUNTJAKS > MUNTJAK

MUNTRIE n Australian shrub with green-red edible berries

MUNTRIES > MUNTRIE

MUNTS > MUNT

MUNTU same as > MUNT

MUNTUS > MUNTU

MUON n elementary particle with a mass 207 times that of an electron

MUONIC > MUON

MUONIUM n form of hydrogen

MUONIUMS > MUONIUM

MUONS > MUON

MUPPET n stupid person

MUPPETS > MUPPET

MUQADDAM n person of authority in India

MUQADDAMS > MUQADDAM

MURA n group of people living together in Japanese countryside

MURAENA n moray eel

MURAENAS > MURAENA

MURAENID n eel of moray family

MURAENIDS > MURAENID

MURAGE n tax levied for the construction or maintenance of town walls

MURAGES > MURAGE

MURAL n painting on a wall ▷ adj of or relating to a wall

MURALED same as > MURALLED

MURALIST > MURAL

MURALISTS > MURAL

MURALLED adj decorated with mural

MURALS > MURAL

MURAS > MURA

MURDABAD interj down with

m

MURDER n unlawful intentional killing of a human being ▷ vb kill in this way
MURDERED > MURDER
MURDEREE n murder victim
MURDEREES > MURDEREE
MURDERER > MURDER
MURDERERS > MURDER
MURDERESS > MURDER
MURDERING > MURDER
MURDEROUS adj intending, capable of, or guilty of murder
MURDERS > MURDER
MURE archaic or literary word for > IMMURE
MURED > MURE
MUREIN n polymer found in cells
MUREINS > MUREIN
MURENA same as > MURAENA
MURENAS > MURENA
MURES > MURE
MUREX n marine gastropod formerly used as a source of purple dye
MUREXES > MUREX
MURGEON vb grimace at
MURGEONED > MURGEON
MURGEONS > MURGEON
MURIATE obsolete name for a > CHLORIDE
MURIATED > MURIATE
MURIATES > MURIATE
MURIATIC adj as in muriatic acid former name for a strong acid used in many industrial processes
MURICATE adj having a surface roughened by numerous short points
MURICATED same as > MURICATE
MURICES > MUREX
MURID n animal of mouse family
MURIDS > MURID
MURIFORM adj like mouse
MURINE n animal belonging to the family that includes rats and mice
MURINES > MURINE
MURING > MURE
MURK n thick darkness ▷ adj dark or gloomy ▷ vb murder (a person)
MURKED > MURK
MURKER > MURK
MURKEST > MURK
MURKIER > MURKY
MURKIEST > MURKY
MURKILY > MURKY
MURKINESS > MURKY
MURKING > MURK
MURKISH > MURK
MURKLY > MURK
MURKS > MURK
MURKSOME > MURK
MURKY adj dark or gloomy
MURL vb crumble
MURLAIN n type of basket
MURLAINS > MURLAIN
MURLAN same as > MURLAIN
MURLANS > MURLAN
MURLED > MURL
MURLIER > MURL

MURLIEST > MURL
MURLIN same as > MURLAIN
MURLING > MURL
MURLINS > MURLIN
MURLS > MURL
MURLY > MURL
MURMUR vb speak or say in a quiet indistinct way ▷ n continuous low indistinct sound
MURMURED > MURMUR
MURMURER > MURMUR
MURMURERS > MURMUR
MURMURING > MURMUR
MURMUROUS > MURMUR
MURMURS > MURMUR
MURPHIES > MURPHY
MURPHY dialect or informal word for > POTATO
MURR n former name for a cold
MURRA same as > MURRHINE
MURRAGH n type of large caddis fly
MURRAGHS > MURRAGH
MURRAIN n cattle plague
MURRAINED > MURRAIN
MURRAINS > MURRAIN
MURRAM n type of gravel
MURRAMS > MURRAM
MURRAS > MURRA
MURRAY n large Australian freshwater fish
MURRAYS > MURRAY
MURRE n type of guillemot
MURREE n native Australian
MURREES > MURREE
MURRELET n type of small diving bird related to the auks
MURRELETS > MURRELET
MURREN same as > MURRAIN
MURRENS > MURREN
MURRES > MURRE
MURREY adj mulberry colour
MURREYS > MURREY
MURRHA same as > MURRA
MURRHAS > MURRHA
MURRHINE adj of or relating to an unknown substance used in ancient Rome to make vases, cups, etc ▷ n substance so used
MURRHINES > MURRHINE
MURRI same as > MURREE
MURRIES > MURRY
MURRIN same as > MURRAIN
MURRINE same as > MURRHINE
MURRINES > MURRINE
MURRINS > MURRIN
MURRION same as > MURRAIN
MURRIONS > MURRION
MURRIS > MURRI
MURRS > MURR
MURRY same as > MORAY
MURSHID n Sufi master or guide
MURSHIDS > MURSHID
MURTHER same as > MURDER
MURTHERED > MURTHER
MURTHERER > MURTHER
MURTHERS > MURTHER
MURTI n image of a deity, which itself is considered divine

MURTIS > MURTI
MURVA n type of hemp
MURVAS > MURVA
MUS > MU
MUSACEOUS adj of, relating to, a family of tropical flowering plants with large leaves and clusters of elongated berry fruits: includes the banana, edible plantain, and Manila hemp
MUSANG n catlike animal of Malaysia
MUSANGS > MUSANG
MUSAR n rabbinic literature concerned with ethics
MUSARS > MUSAR
MUSCA n small constellation in the S hemisphere
MUSCADEL same as > MUSCATEL
MUSCADELS > MUSCADEL
MUSCADET n white grape, used for making wine
MUSCADETS > MUSCADET
MUSCADIN n Parisian dandy
MUSCADINE n woody climbing plant of the southeastern US
MUSCADINS > MUSCADIN
MUSCAE > MUSCA
MUSCARINE n poisonous alkaloid occurring in certain mushrooms
MUSCAT same as > MUSCATEL
MUSCATEL n rich sweet wine made from muscat grapes
MUSCATELS > MUSCATEL
MUSCATS > MUSCAT
MUSCAVADO same as > MUSCOVADO
MUSCID n type of fly
MUSCIDS > MUSCID
MUSCLE n tissue in the body which produces movement ▷ vb force one's way (in)
MUSCLED > MUSCLE
MUSCLEMAN n man with highly developed muscles
MUSCLEMEN > MUSCLEMAN
MUSCLES > MUSCLE
MUSCLEY adj of a muscular build
MUSCLIER > MUSCLEY
MUSCLIEST > MUSCLEY
MUSCLING > MUSCLE
MUSCLINGS > MUSCLE
MUSCLY same as > MUSCLEY
MUSCOID adj moss-like ▷ n moss-like plant
MUSCOIDS > MUSCOID
MUSCOLOGY n branch of botany
MUSCONE same as > MUSKONE
MUSCONES > MUSCONE
MUSCOSE adj like moss
MUSCOVADO n raw sugar obtained from the juice of sugar cane by evaporating the molasses
MUSCOVITE n pale brown, or green, or colourless mineral of the mica group
MUSCOVY adj as in muscovy duck a kind of duck

MUSCULAR adj with well-developed muscles
MUSCULOUS adj muscular
MUSE vb ponder quietly ▷ n state of abstraction
MUSED > MUSE
MUSEFUL > MUSE
MUSEFULLY > MUSE
MUSEOLOGY n science of museum organization
MUSER > MUSE
MUSERS > MUSE
MUSES > MUSE
MUSET same as > MUSIT
MUSETS > MUSET
MUSETTE n type of bagpipe formerly popular in France
MUSETTES > MUSETTE
MUSEUM n building where objects are exhibited and preserved
MUSEUMS > MUSEUM
MUSH n soft pulpy mass ▷ interj order to dogs in a sled team to start up or go faster ▷ vb travel by or drive a dogsled
MUSHA interj Irish exclamation of surprise
MUSHED > MUSH
MUSHER > MUSH
MUSHERS > MUSH
MUSHES > MUSH
MUSHIE n mushroom
MUSHIER > MUSHY
MUSHIES > MUSHIE
MUSHIEST > MUSHY
MUSHILY > MUSHY
MUSHINESS > MUSHY
MUSHING n act of mushing
MUSHINGS > MUSHING
MUSHMOUTH n person speaking indistinctly
MUSHRAT same as > MUSKRAT
MUSHRATS same as > MUSHRAT
MUSHROOM n edible fungus with a stem and cap ▷ vb grow rapidly
MUSHROOMS > MUSHROOM
MUSHROOMY adj like a mushroom
MUSHY adj soft and pulpy
MUSIC n art form using a melodious and harmonious combination of notes ▷ vb play music
MUSICAL adj of or like music ▷ n play or film with songs and dancing
MUSICALE n party or social evening with a musical programme
MUSICALES > MUSICALE
MUSICALLY > MUSICAL
MUSICALS > MUSICAL
MUSICIAN n person who plays or composes music, esp as a profession
MUSICIANS > MUSICIAN
MUSICK same as > MUSIC
MUSICKED > MUSIC
MUSICKER > MUSIC
MUSICKERS > MUSIC
MUSICKING > MUSIC
MUSICKS > MUSICK

MUSICLESS > MUSIC

MUSICS > MUSIC

MUSIMON same as > MOUFFLON

MUSIMONS > MUSIMON

MUSING > MUSE

MUSINGLY > MUSE

MUSINGS > MUSE

MUSIT n gap in fence

MUSITS > MUSIT

MUSIVE adj mosaic

MUSJID same as > MASJID

MUSJIDS > MUSJID

MUSK n scent obtained from a gland of the musk deer or produced synthetically ▷ vb perfume with musk

MUSKED > MUSK

MUSKEG n area of undrained boggy land

MUSKEGS > MUSKEG

MUSKET n long-barrelled gun

MUSKETEER n (formerly) a soldier armed with a musket

MUSKETOON n small musket

MUSKETRY n (use of) muskets

MUSKETS > MUSKET

MUSKIE n large North American freshwater game fish

MUSKIER > MUSKY

MUSKIES > MUSKIE

MUSKIEST > MUSKY

MUSKILY > MUSKY

MUSKINESS > MUSKY

MUSKING > MUSK

MUSKIT same as > MESQUITE

MUSKITS > MUSKIT

MUSKLE same as > MUSSEL

MUSKLES > MUSKLE

MUSKMELON n any of several varieties of melon, such as the cantaloupe and honeydew

MUSKONE n substance in musk

MUSKONES > MUSKONE

MUSKOX n large Canadian mammal

MUSKOXEN > MUSKOX

MUSKRAT n N American beaver-like rodent

MUSKRATS > MUSKRAT

MUSKROOT same as > MOSCHATEL

MUSKROOTS > MUSKROOT

MUSKS > MUSK

MUSKY adj smelling of musk

MUSLIN n fine cotton fabric

MUSLINED adj wearing muslin

MUSLINET n coarse muslin

MUSLINETS > MUSLINET

MUSLINS > MUSLIN

MUSMON same as > MUSIMON

MUSMONS > MUSMON

MUSO n musician who is concerned with technique rather than content or expression

MUSOS > MUSO

MUSPIKE n Canadian freshwater fish

MUSPIKES > MUSPIKE

MUSQUASH same as > MUSKRAT

MUSROL n part of bridle

MUSROLS > MUSROL

MUSS vb make untidy ▷ n state of disorder

MUSSE same as > MUSS

MUSSED > MUSS

MUSSEL n edible shellfish with a dark hinged shell

MUSSELLED adj poisoned through eating bad mussels

MUSSELS > MUSSEL

MUSSES > MUSS

MUSSIER > MUSSY

MUSSIEST > MUSSY

MUSSILY > MUSSY

MUSSINESS > MUSSY

MUSSING > MUSS

MUSSITATE vb mutter

MUSSY adj untidy or disordered

MUST vb used as an auxiliary to express obligation, certainty, or resolution ▷ n essential or necessary thing

MUSTACHE same as > MOUSTACHE

MUSTACHED > MUSTACHE

MUSTACHES > MUSTACHE

MUSTACHIO n moustache, esp a bushy or elaborate one

MUSTANG n wild horse of SW USA

MUSTANGS > MUSTANG

MUSTARD n paste made from the powdered seeds of a plant ▷ adj brownish-yellow

MUSTARDS > MUSTARD

MUSTARDY adj like mustard

MUSTED > MUST

MUSTEE n person of mixed racial ancestry

MUSTEES > MUSTEE

MUSTELID n member of weasel family

MUSTELIDS > MUSTELID

MUSTELINE n type of predatory mammal of the family which includes weasels, ferrets, polecats, badgers, and otters

MUSTER vb summon up ▷ n assembly of military personnel

MUSTERED > MUSTER

MUSTERER > MUSTER

MUSTERERS > MUSTER

MUSTERING > MUSTER

MUSTERS > MUSTER

MUSTH n state of frenzied excitement in the males of certain large mammals

MUSTHS > MUSTH

MUSTIER > MUSTY

MUSTIEST > MUSTY

MUSTILY > MUSTY

MUSTINESS > MUSTY

MUSTING > MUST

MUSTS > MUST

MUSTY adj smelling mouldy and stale

MUT another word for > EM

MUTABLE adj liable to change

MUTABLY > MUTABLE

MUTAGEN n any substance that can induce genetic mutation

MUTAGENIC > MUTAGEN

MUTAGENS > MUTAGEN

MUTANDA > MUTANDUM

MUTANDUM n something to be changed

MUTANT n mutated animal, plant, etc ▷ adj of or resulting from mutation

MUTANTS > MUTANT

MUTASE n type of enzyme

MUTASES > MUTASE

MUTATE vb (cause to) undergo mutation

MUTATED > MUTATE

MUTATES > MUTATE

MUTATING > MUTATE

MUTATION same as > MUTANT

MUTATIONS > MUTATION

MUTATIVE > MUTATE

MUTATOR n something that causes a mutation

MUTATORS > MUTATOR

MUTATORY adj subject to change

MUTCH n close-fitting linen cap ▷ vb cadge

MUTCHED > MUTCH

MUTCHES > MUTCH

MUTCHING > MUTCH

MUTCHKIN n Scottish unit of liquid measure equal to slightly less than one pint

MUTCHKINS > MUTCHKIN

MUTE adj silent ▷ vb reduce the volume or soften the tone of a musical instrument

MUTED adj (of sound or colour) softened

MUTEDLY > MUTED

MUTELY > MUTE

MUTENESS > MUTE

MUTER > MUTE

MUTES > MUTE

MUTEST > MUTE

MUTHA n taboo slang word derived from motherfucker

MUTHAS > MUTHA

MUTI n medicine, esp herbal medicine

MUTICATE same as > MUTICOUS

MUTICOUS adj lacking an awn, spine, or point

MUTILATE vb deprive of a limb or other part

MUTILATED > MUTILATE

MUTILATES > MUTILATE

MUTILATOR > MUTILATE

MUTINE vb mutiny

MUTINED > MUTINE

MUTINEER n person who mutinies

MUTINEERS > MUTINEER

MUTINES > MUTINE

MUTING > MUTE

MUTINIED > MUTINY

MUTINIES > MUTINY

MUTINING > MUTINE

MUTINOUS adj openly rebellious

MUTINY n rebellion against authority, esp by soldiers or sailors ▷ vb commit mutiny

MUTINYING > MUTINY

MUTIS > MUTI

MUTISM n state of being mute

MUTISMS > MUTISM

MUTON n part of gene

MUTONS > MUTON

MUTOSCOPE n early form of cine camera

MUTS > MUT

MUTT n mongrel dog

MUTTER vb utter or speak indistinctly ▷ n muttered sound or grumble

MUTTERED > MUTTER

MUTTERER > MUTTER

MUTTERERS > MUTTER

MUTTERING > MUTTER

MUTTERS > MUTTER

MUTTON n flesh of sheep, used as food

MUTTONIER > MUTTONY

MUTTONS > MUTTON

MUTTONY adj like mutton

MUTTS > MUTT

MUTUAL adj felt or expressed by each of two people about the other ▷ n mutual company

MUTUALISE same as > MUTUALIZE

MUTUALISM another name for > SYMBIOSIS

MUTUALIST > MUTUALISM

MUTUALITY > MUTUAL

MUTUALIZE vb make or become mutual

MUTUALLY > MUTUAL

MUTUALS > MUTUAL

MUTUCA same as > MOTUCA

MUTUCAS > MUTUCA

MUTUEL n system of betting

MUTUELS > MUTUEL

MUTULAR > MUTULE

MUTULE n flat block in a Doric cornice

MUTULES > MUTULE

MUTUUM n contract for loan of goods

MUTUUMS > MUTUUM

MUUMUU n loose brightly coloured dress worn by women in Hawaii

MUUMUUS > MUUMUU

MUX vb spoil

MUXED > MUX

MUXES > MUX

MUXING > MUX

MUZAK n piped background music

MUZAKIER > MUZAKY

MUZAKIEST > MUZAKY

MUZAKS > MUZAK

MUZAKY adj having a bland sound

MUZHIK n Russian peasant, esp under the tsars

MUZHIKS > MUZHIK

MUZJIK same as > MUZHIK

MUZJIKS > MUZJIK

MUZZ vb make (something) muzzy

MUZZED > MUZZ

MUZZES > MUZZ

MUZZIER > MUZZY

MUZZIEST > MUZZY

m

MUZZILY > MUZZY
MUZZINESS > MUZZY
MUZZING > MUZZ
MUZZLE n animal's mouth and nose ▷ vb prevent from being heard or noticed
MUZZLED > MUZZLE
MUZZLER > MUZZLE
MUZZLERS > MUZZLE
MUZZLES > MUZZLE
MUZZLING > MUZZLE
MUZZY adj confused or muddled
MVULE n tropical African tree
MVULES > MVULE
MWAH interj representation of the sound of a kiss
MWALIMU n teacher
MWALIMUS > MWALIMU
MY adj belonging to me ▷ interj exclamation of surprise or awe
MYAL > MYALISM
MYALGIA n pain in a muscle or a group of muscles
MYALGIAS > MYALGIA
MYALGIC > MYALGIA
MYALISM n kind of witchcraft
MYALISMS > MYALISM
MYALIST > MYALISM
MYALISTS > MYALISM
MYALL n Australian acacia with hard scented wood
MYALLS > MYALL
MYASES > MYASIS
MYASIS same as > MYIASIS
MYC n oncogene that aids the growth of tumorous cells
MYCELE n microscopic spike-like structure in mucus
MYCELES > MYCELE
MYCELIA > MYCELIUM
MYCELIAL > MYCELIUM
MYCELIAN > MYCELIUM
MYCELIUM n mass forming the body of a fungus
MYCELLA n blue-veined Danish cream cheese
MYCELLAS > MYCELLA
MYCELOID > MYCELIUM
MYCETES n fungus
MYCETOMA n chronic fungal infection
MYCETOMAS > MYCETOMA
MYCOBIONT n fungal constituent of a lichen
MYCOFLORA n all fungus growing in particular place
MYCOLOGIC > MYCOLOGY
MYCOLOGY n study of fungi
MYCOPHAGY n eating of mushrooms
MYCOPHILE n person who likes eating mushrooms
MYCORHIZA n association of a fungus and a plant in which the fungus lives within or on the outside of the plant's roots forming a symbiotic or parasitic relationship
MYCOSES > MYCOSIS
MYCOSIS n any infection or disease caused by fungus
MYCOTIC > MYCOSIS

MYCOTOXIN n any of various toxic substances produced by fungi some of which may affect food and others of which are alleged to have been used in warfare
MYCOVIRUS n virus attacking fungi
MYCS > MYC
MYDRIASES > MYDRIASIS
MYDRIASIS n abnormal dilation of the pupil of the eye
MYDRIATIC adj relating to or causing mydriasis ▷ n mydriatic drug
MYELIN n white tissue forming an insulating sheath around certain nerve fibres
MYELINE same as > MYELIN
MYELINES > MYELINE
MYELINIC > MYELIN
MYELINS > MYELIN
MYELITES > MYELITIS
MYELITIS n inflammation of the spinal cord or of the bone marrow
MYELOCYTE n immature granulocyte, normally occurring in the bone marrow but detected in the blood in certain diseases
MYELOGRAM n X-ray of the spinal cord, after injection with a radio-opaque medium
MYELOID adj of or relating to the spinal cord or the bone marrow
MYELOMA n tumour of the bone marrow
MYELOMAS > MYELOMA
MYELOMATA > MYELOMA
MYELON n spinal cord
MYELONS > MYELON
MYGALE n large American spider
MYGALES > MYGALE
MYIASES > MYIASIS
MYIASIS n infestation of the body by the larvae of flies
MYIOPHILY same as > MYOPHILY
MYLAR n tradename for a kind of strong polyester film
MYLARS > MYLAR
MYLODON n prehistoric giant sloth
MYLODONS > MYLODON
MYLODONT same as > MYLODON
MYLODONTS > MYLODONT
MYLOHYOID n muscle in neck
MYLONITE n fine-grained metamorphic rock
MYLONITES > MYLONITE
MYLONITIC > MYLONITE
MYNA same as > MYNAH
MYNAH n tropical Asian starling which can mimic human speech
MYNAHS > MYNAH
MYNAS > MYNA
MYNHEER n Dutch title of address
MYNHEERS > MYNHEER
MYOBLAST n cell from which muscle develops

MYOBLASTS > MYOBLAST
MYOCARDIA pl n muscular tissues of the heart
MYOCLONIC > MYOCLONUS
MYOCLONUS n sudden involuntary muscle contraction
MYOFIBRIL n type of cell in muscle
MYOGEN n albumin found in muscle
MYOGENIC adj originating in or forming muscle tissue
MYOGENS > MYOGEN
MYOGLOBIN n protein that is the main oxygen-carrier of muscle
MYOGRAM n tracings of muscular contractions
MYOGRAMS > MYOGRAM
MYOGRAPH n instrument for recording tracings of muscular contractions
MYOGRAPHS > MYOGRAPH
MYOGRAPHY > MYOGRAPH
MYOID adj like muscle ▷ n section of a retinal cone or rod which is sensitive to changes in light intensity
MYOIDS > MYOID
MYOLOGIC > MYOLOGY
MYOLOGIES > MYOLOGY
MYOLOGIST > MYOLOGY
MYOLOGY n study of the structure and diseases of muscles
MYOMA n benign tumour composed of muscle tissue
MYOMANCY n divination through observing mice
MYOMANTIC > MYOMANCY
MYOMAS > MYOMA
MYOMATA > MYOMA
MYOMATOUS > MYOMA
MYOMERE n part of a vertebrate embryo
MYOMERES > MYOMERE
MYONEURAL adj involving muscle and nerve
MYOPATHIC > MYOPATHY
MYOPATHY n any disease affecting muscles or muscle tissue
MYOPE n any person afflicted with myopia
MYOPES > MYOPE
MYOPHILY n pollination of plants by flies
MYOPIA n short-sightedness
MYOPIAS > MYOPIA
MYOPIC n shortsighted person
MYOPICS > MYOPIC
MYOPIES > MYOPY
MYOPS same as > MYOPE
MYOPSES > MYOPS
MYOPY same as > MYOPIA
MYOSCOPE n electrical instrument for stimulating muscles
MYOSCOPES > MYOSCOPE
MYOSES > MYOSIS
MYOSIN n protein found in muscle
MYOSINS > MYOSIN
MYOSIS same as > MIOSIS
MYOSISES > MYOSIS

MYOSITIS n inflammation of muscle
MYOSOTE same as > MYOSOTIS
MYOSOTES > MYOSOTE
MYOSOTIS n type of hairy-leaved flowering plant, such as the forget-me-not
MYOSTATIN n protein that inhibits muscle tissue growth
MYOTIC > MIOSIS
MYOTICS > MIOSIS
MYOTOME n any segment of embryonic mesoderm that develops into skeletal muscle
MYOTOMES > MYOTOME
MYOTONIA n lack of muscle tone, frequently including muscle spasm or rigidity
MYOTONIAS > MYOTONIA
MYOTONIC > MYOTONIA
MYOTUBE n cylindrical cell in muscle
MYOTUBES > MYOTUBE
MYRBANE same as > MIRBANE
MYRBANES > MYRBANE
MYRIAD adj innumerable ▷ n large indefinite number
MYRIADS > MYRIAD
MYRIADTH > MYRIAD
MYRIADTHS > MYRIAD
MYRIAPOD n type of invertebrate with a long segmented body and many legs, such as a centipede
MYRIAPODS > MYRIAPOD
MYRICA n dried root bark of the wax myrtle
MYRICAS > MYRICA
MYRINGA n eardrum
MYRINGAS > MYRINGA
MYRIOPOD same as > MYRIAPOD
MYRIOPODS > MYRIOPOD
MYRIORAMA n picture made up of different parts
MYRISTIC adj of nutmeg plant family
MYRMECOID adj ant-like
MYRMIDON n follower or henchperson
MYRMIDONS > MYRMIDON
MYROBALAN n dried plumlike fruit of various tropical trees, used in dyeing, tanning, ink, and medicine
MYRRH n aromatic gum used in perfume, incense, and medicine
MYRRHIC > MYRRH
MYRRHIER > MYRRHY
MYRRHIEST > MYRRHY
MYRRHINE > MURRA
MYRRHOL n oil of myrrh
MYRRHOLS > MYRRHOL
MYRRHS > MYRRH
MYRRHY adj of or like myrrh
MYRTLE n flowering evergreen shrub
MYRTLES > MYRTLE
MYSELF pron reflexive form of I or me
MYSID n small shrimplike crustacean
MYSIDS > MYSID

MYSOST *n* Norwegian cheese
MYSOSTS > MYSOST
MYSPACE *vb* search for (someone) on the MySpace website
MYSPACED > MYSPACE
MYSPACES > MYSPACE
MYSPACING > MYSPACE
MYSTAGOG *n* person instructing others in religious mysteries
MYSTAGOGS > MYSTAGOG
MYSTAGOGY *n* instruction of those who are preparing for initiation into the mysteries
MYSTERIES > MYSTERY
MYSTERY *n* strange or inexplicable thing
MYSTIC *n* person who seeks spiritual knowledge ▷ *adj* mystical
MYSTICAL *adj* having a spiritual or religious significance beyond human understanding
MYSTICETE *n* species of whale
MYSTICISM *n* belief in or experience of a reality beyond normal human understanding or experience
MYSTICLY > MYSTIC

MYSTICS > MYSTIC
MYSTIFIED > MYSTIFY
MYSTIFIER > MYSTIFY
MYSTIFIES > MYSTIFY
MYSTIFY *vb* bewilder or puzzle
MYSTIQUE *n* aura of mystery or power
MYSTIQUES > MYSTIQUE
MYTH *n* tale with supernatural characters
MYTHI > MYTHOS
MYTHIC *same as* **>** MYTHICAL
MYTHICAL *adj* of or relating to myth
MYTHICISE *same as* **>** MYTHICIZE
MYTHICISM *n* theory that explains miracles as myths
MYTHICIST > MYTHICIZE
MYTHICIZE *vb* make into or treat as a myth
MYTHIER > MYTHY
MYTHIEST > MYTHY
MYTHISE *same as* **>** MYTHIZE
MYTHISED > MYTHISE
MYTHISES > MYTHISE
MYTHISING > MYTHISE
MYTHISM *same as* **>** MYTHICISM

MYTHISMS > MYTHISM
MYTHIST > MYTHISM
MYTHISTS > MYTHISM
MYTHIZE *same as* **>** MYTHICIZE
MYTHIZED > MYTHIZE
MYTHIZES > MYTHIZE
MYTHIZING > MYTHIZE
MYTHMAKER *n* person who creates myth
MYTHOI > MYTHOS
MYTHOLOGY *n* myths collectively
MYTHOMANE *n* obsession with lying, exaggerating, or relating incredible imaginary adventures as if they had really happened
MYTHOPEIC *adj* of myths
MYTHOPOET *n* poet writing on mythical theme
MYTHOS *n* beliefs of a specific group or society
MYTHS > MYTH
MYTHUS *same as* **>** MYTHOS
MYTHY *adj* of or like myth
MYTILOID *adj* like mussel
MYXAMEBA *same as* **>** MYXAMOEBA
MYXAMEBAE > MYXAMEBA
MYXAMEBAS > MYXAMEBA

MYXAMOEBA *n* cell produced by spore
MYXEDEMA *same as* **>** MYXOEDEMA
MYXEDEMAS > MYXEDEMA
MYXEDEMIC > MYXOEDEMA
MYXO *n* viral disease of rabbits
MYXOCYTE *n* cell in mucous tissue
MYXOCYTES > MYXOCYTE
MYXOEDEMA *n* disease caused by an underactive thyroid gland
MYXOID *adj* containing mucus
MYXOMA *n* tumour composed of mucous connective tissue
MYXOMAS > MYXOMA
MYXOMATA > MYXOMA
MYXOS > MYXO
MYXOVIRAL > MYXOVIRUS
MYXOVIRUS *n* any of a group of viruses that cause influenza, mumps, and certain other diseases
MZEE *n* old person ▷ *adj* advanced in years
MZEES > MZEE
MZUNGU *n* (in E Africa) White person
MZUNGUS > MZUNGU

Nn

NA *same as* > NAE
NAAM *same as* > NAM
NAAMS > NAAM
NAAN *n* slightly leavened flat Indian bread
NAANS > NAAN
NAARTJE *same as* > NAARTJIE
NAARTJES > NAARTJE
NAARTJIE *n* tangerine
NAARTJIES > NAARTJIE
NAB *vb* arrest (someone)
NABBED > NAB
NABBER *n* thief
NABBERS > NABBER
NABBING > NAB
NABE *n* Japanese hotpot
NABES > NABE
NABIS *n* Parisian art movement
NABK *n* edible berry
NABKS > NABK
NABLA *another name for* > DEL
NABLAS > NABLA
NABOB *n* rich, powerful, or important man
NABOBERY > NABOB
NABOBESS > NABOB
NABOBISH > NABOB
NABOBISM > NABOB
NABOBISMS > NABOB
NABOBS > NABOB
NABS > NAB
NACARAT *n* red-orange colour
NACARATS > NACARAT
NACELLE *n* streamlined enclosure on an aircraft
NACELLES > NACELLE
NACH *n* Indian dance
NACHAS *n* pleasure
NACHE *n* rump
NACHES > NACHE
NACHO *n* snack of a piece of tortilla with a topping
NACHOS > NACHO
NACHTMAAL *same as* > NAGMAAL
NACKET *n* light lunch, snack
NACKETS > NACKET
NACRE *n* mother of pearl
NACRED > NACRE
NACREOUS > NACRE
NACRES > NACRE
NACRITE *n* mineral
NACRITES > NACRITE
NACROUS > NACRE
NADA *n* nothing
NADAS > NADA
NADIR *n* point in the sky opposite the zenith

NADIRAL > NADIR
NADIRS > NADIR
NADORS *n* thirst brought on by excess of alcohol
NADS *pl n* vulgar word for testicles
NAE *Scot word for* > NO
NAEBODIES > NAEBODY
NAEBODY *Scots variant of* > NOBODY
NAES > NAE
NAETHING *Scots variant of* > NOTHING
NAETHINGS > NAETHING
NAEVE *n* birthmark
NAEVES > NAEVE
NAEVI > NAEVUS
NAEVOID > NAEVUS
NAEVUS *n* birthmark or mole
NAFF *adj* lacking quality or taste ▷ *vb* go away
NAFFED > NAFF
NAFFER > NAFF
NAFFEST > NAFF
NAFFING > NAFF
NAFFLY > NAFF
NAFFNESS > NAFF
NAFFS > NAFF
NAG *vb* scold or find fault constantly ▷ *n* person who nags
NAGA *n* cobra
NAGANA *n* disease of all domesticated animals of central and southern Africa
NAGANAS > NAGANA
NAGAPIE *n* bushbaby
NAGAPIES > NAGAPIE
NAGARI *n* scripts for writing several languages of India
NAGARIS > NAGARI
NAGAS > NAGA
NAGGED > NAG
NAGGER > NAG
NAGGERS > NAG
NAGGIER > NAG
NAGGIEST > NAG
NAGGING > NAG
NAGGINGLY > NAG
NAGGINGS > NAGGING
NAGGY > NAG
NAGMAAL *n* Communion
NAGMAALS > NAGMAAL
NAGOR *another name for* > REEDBUCK
NAGORS > NAGOR
NAGS > NAG
NAGWARE *n* software that is initially free and then requires payment
NAGWARES > NAGWARE
NAH *same as* > NO

NAHAL *n* agricultural settlement run by an Israeli military youth organization
NAHALS > NAHAL
NAIAD *n* nymph living in a lake or river
NAIADES > NAIAD
NAIADS > NAIAD
NAIANT *adj* swimming
NAIF *less common word for* > NAIVE
NAIFER > NAIF
NAIFEST > NAIF
NAIFLY > NAIF
NAIFNESS > NAIF
NAIFS > NAIF
NAIK *n* chief
NAIKS > NAIK
NAIL *n* pointed piece of metal used to join two objects together ▷ *vb* attach (something) with nails
NAILBITER *n* person who bites his or her nails
NAILBRUSH *n* small stiff-bristled brush for cleaning the fingernails
NAILED > NAIL
NAILER > NAIL
NAILERIES > NAILERY
NAILERS > NAIL
NAILERY *n* nail factory
NAILFILE *n* small metal file used to shape and smooth the nails
NAILFILES > NAILFILE
NAILFOLD *n* skin at base of fingernail
NAILFOLDS > NAILFOLD
NAILHEAD *n* decorative device, as on tooled leather, resembling the round head of a nail
NAILHEADS > NAILHEAD
NAILING > NAIL
NAILINGS > NAIL
NAILLESS > NAIL
NAILS > NAIL
NAILSET *n* punch for driving down the head of a nail
NAILSETS > NAILSET
NAIN *adj* own
NAINSELL *n* own self
NAINSELLS > NAINSELL
NAINSOOK *n* light soft plain-weave cotton fabric, used esp for babies' wear
NAINSOOKS > NAINSOOK
NAIRA *n* standard monetary unit of Nigeria, divided into 100 kobo
NAIRAS > NAIRA

NAIRU *n* Non-Accelerating Inflation Rate of Unemployment
NAIRUS > NAIRU
NAISSANCE *French for* > BIRTH
NAISSANT *adj* (of a beast) having only the forepart shown above a horizontal division of a shield
NAIVE *adj* innocent and gullible ▷ *n* person who is naive, esp in artistic style
NAIVELY > NAIVE
NAIVENESS > NAIVE
NAIVER > NAIVE
NAIVES > NAIVE
NAIVEST > NAIVE
NAIVETE *variant of* > NAIVETY
NAIVETES > NAIVETE
NAIVETIES > NAIVETY
NAIVETY *n* state or quality of being naive
NAIVIST > NAIVE
NAKED *adj* without clothes
NAKEDER > NAKED
NAKEDEST > NAKED
NAKEDLY > NAKED
NAKEDNESS > NAKED
NAKER *n* small kettledrum used in medieval music
NAKERS > NAKER
NAKFA *n* standard currency unit of Eritrea
NAKFAS > NAKFA
NALA *n* ravine
NALAS > NALA
NALED *n* type of insecticide
NALEDS > NALED
NALIDIXIC *adj* as in *nalidixic acid* type of acid
NALLA *n* ravine
NALLAH *same as* > NALLA
NALLAHS > NALLAH
NALLAS > NALLA
NALOXONE *n* substance that counteracts opiates
NALOXONES > NALOXONE
NAM *n* distraint
NAMABLE > NAME
NAMASKAR *n* salutation used in India
NAMASKARS > NAMASKAR
NAMASTE *n* Indian greeting
NAMASTES > NAMASTE
NAMAYCUSH *n* North American freshwater fish
NAME *n* word by which a person or thing is known ▷ *vb* give a name to
NAMEABLE > NAME

n

NAMECHECK vb mention (someone) by name ▷ n mention of someone's name, for example on a radio programme
NAMED > NAME
NAMELESS adj without a name
NAMELY adv that is to say
NAMEPLATE n small sign on or by a door giving the occupant's name and, sometimes, profession
NAMER > NAME
NAMERS > NAME
NAMES > NAME
NAMESAKE n person with the same name as another
NAMESAKES > NAMESAKE
NAMETAG n identification badge
NAMETAGS > NAMETAG
NAMETAPE n narrow cloth tape bearing the owner's name and attached to an article
NAMETAPES > NAMETAPE
NAMING > NAME
NAMINGS > NAME
NAMMA adj as in namma hole Australian word for a natural well in rock
NAMS > NAM
NAMU n black New Zealand sandfly
NAMUS > NAMU
NAN n grandmother
NANA same as > NAN
NANAS > NANA
NANCE n offensive word for a homosexual man
NANCES > NANCE
NANCIER > NANCY
NANCIES > NANCY
NANCIEST > NANCY
NANCIFIED adj offensive word meaning effeminate
NANCY n offensive word for a homosexual man ▷ adj effeminate or homosexual
NANDIN same as > NANDINA
NANDINA n type of shrub
NANDINAS > NANDINA
NANDINE n African palm civet
NANDINES > NANDINE
NANDINS > NANDIN
NANDOO same as > NANDU
NANDOOS > NANDOO
NANDU n type of ostrich
NANDUS > NANDU
NANE Scot word for > NONE
NANG adj excellent; cool
NANISM n dwarfism
NANISMS > NANISM
NANITE n microscopically small machine or robot
NANITES > NANITE
NANKEEN n hard-wearing buff-coloured cotton fabric
NANKEENS > NANKEEN
NANKIN same as > NANKEEN
NANKINS > NANKIN
NANNA same as > NAN
NANNAS > NANNA
NANNIE same as > NANNY
NANNIED > NANNY

NANNIES > NANNY
NANNY n woman whose job is looking after young children ▷ vb be too protective towards
NANNYGAI n edible sea fish of Australia which is red in colour and has large prominent eyes
NANNYGAIS > NANNYGAI
NANNYING n act of nannying
NANNYINGS > NANNYING
NANNYISH > NANNY
NANO n science concerned with materials on a molecular scale
NANOBE n microbe that is smaller than the smallest known bacterium
NANOBEE n artificial nanoparticle
NANOBEES > NANOBEE
NANOBES > NANOBE
NANOBOT n microscopically small robot
NANOBOTS > NANOBOT
NANODOT n microscopic cluster of atoms used to store data in a computer chip
NANODOTS > NANODOT
NANOGRAM n unit of measurement
NANOGRAMS > NANOGRAM
NANOGRASS n type of synthetic surface
NANOMETER same as > NANOMETRE
NANOMETRE n one thousand-millionth of a metre
NANOOK n polar bear
NANOOKS > NANOOK
NANOPORE n microscopically small pore in an electrically insulating membrane
NANOPORES > NANOPORE
NANOS > NANO
NANOSCALE adj on very small scale
NANOTECH n technology of very small objects
NANOTECHS > NANOTECH
NANOTESLA n unit of measurement
NANOTUBE n cylindrical molecule of carbon
NANOTUBES > NANOTUBE
NANOWATT n unit of measurement
NANOWATTS > NANOWATT
NANOWIRE n microscopically thin wire
NANOWIRES > NANOWIRE
NANOWORLD n world at a microscopic level, as dealt with by nanotechnology
NANS > NAN
NANUA same as > MOKI
NANUAS > NANUA
NAOI > NAOS
NAOS n ancient classical temple
NAOSES > NAOS
NAP n short sleep ▷ vb have a short sleep
NAPA n type of leather

NAPALM n highly inflammable jellied petrol, used in bombs ▷ vb attack (people or places) with napalm
NAPALMED > NAPALM
NAPALMING > NAPALM
NAPALMS > NAPALM
NAPAS > NAPA
NAPE n back of the neck ▷ vb attack with napalm
NAPED > NAPE
NAPERIES > NAPERY
NAPERY n household linen, esp table linen
NAPES > NAPE
NAPHTHA n liquid mixture used as a solvent and in petrol
NAPHTHAS > NAPHTHA
NAPHTHENE n any of a class of cycloalkanes found in petroleum
NAPHTHOL n white crystalline solid used in dyes
NAPHTHOLS > NAPHTHOL
NAPHTHOUS > NAPHTHA
NAPHTHYL n type of monovalent radical
NAPHTHYLS > NAPHTHYL
NAPHTOL same as > NAPHTHOL
NAPHTOLS > NAPHTOL
NAPIFORM adj shaped like a turnip
NAPING > NAPE
NAPKIN same as > NAPPY
NAPKINS > NAPKIN
NAPLESS adj threadbare
NAPOLEON n former French gold coin worth 20 francs
NAPOLEONS > NAPOLEON
NAPOO vb military slang meaning kill
NAPOOED > NAPOO
NAPOOING > NAPOO
NAPOOS > NAPOO
NAPPA n soft leather
NAPPAS > NAPPA
NAPPE n mass of rock that has been thrust from its original position by earth movements
NAPPED > NAP
NAPPER n person or thing that raises the nap on cloth
NAPPERS > NAPPER
NAPPES > NAPPE
NAPPIE same as > NAPPY
NAPPIER > NAPPY
NAPPIES > NAPPY
NAPPIEST > NAPPY
NAPPINESS > NAPPY
NAPPING > NAP
NAPPY n piece of absorbent material fastened round a baby's lower torso ▷ adj having a nap
NAPRON same as > APRON
NAPRONS > NAPRON
NAPROXEN n pain-killing drug
NAPROXENS > NAPROXEN
NAPS > NAP
NARAS same as > NARRAS
NARASES > NARAS
NARC n narcotics agent

NARCEEN same as > NARCEINE
NARCEENS > NARCEEN
NARCEIN same as > NARCEINE
NARCEINE n narcotic alkaloid that occurs in opium
NARCEINES > NARCEINE
NARCEINS > NARCEIN
NARCISM n exceptional admiration for oneself
NARCISMS > NARCISM
NARCISSI > NARCISSUS
NARCISSUS n yellow, orange, or white flower related to the daffodil
NARCIST n narcissist
NARCISTIC adj excessively admiring of oneself
NARCISTS > NARCIST
NARCO same as > NARC
NARCOMA n coma caused by intake of narcotic drugs
NARCOMAS > NARCOMA
NARCOMATA > NARCOMA
NARCOS > NARCO
NARCOSE same as > NARCOSIS
NARCOSES > NARCOSIS
NARCOSIS n effect of a narcotic
NARCOTIC adj of a drug which produces numbness and drowsiness ▷ n such a drug
NARCOTICS > NARCOTIC
NARCOTINE n type of drug
NARCOTISE same as > NARCOTIZE
NARCOTISM n addiction to narcotic drugs
NARCOTIST n person affected by narcotics
NARCOTIZE vb place under the influence of a narcotic drug
NARCS > NARC
NARD n any of several plants with aromatic roots ▷ vb anoint with nard oil
NARDED > NARD
NARDINE > NARD
NARDING > NARD
NARDOO n cloverlike fern which grows in swampy areas
NARDOOS > NARDOO
NARDS > NARD
NARE n nostril
NARES pl n nostrils
NARGHILE another name for > HOOKAH
NARGHILES > NARGHILE
NARGHILLY same as > NARGHILE
NARGHILY same as > NARGHILE
NARGILE same as > NARGHILE
NARGILEH same as > NARGHILE
NARGILEHS > NARGILEH
NARGILES > NARGILE
NARGILIES > NARGILE
NARGILY same as > NARGHILE
NARGUILEH n hookah

n

NARIAL adj of or relating to the nares
NARIC > NARES
NARICORN n bird's nostril
NARICORNS > NARICORN
NARINE same as > NARIAL
NARIS > NARES
NARK vb annoy ⊳ n informer or spy
NARKED > NARK
NARKIER > NARKY
NARKIEST > NARKY
NARKING > NARK
NARKS > NARK
NARKY adj irritable or complaining
NARQUOIS adj malicious
NARRAS n type of shrub
NARRASES > NARRAS
NARRATE vb tell (a story)
NARRATED > NARRATE
NARRATER same as > NARRATOR
NARRATERS > NARRATER
NARRATES > NARRATE
NARRATING > NARRATE
NARRATION n narrating
NARRATIVE n account, story ⊳ adj telling a story
NARRATOR n person who tells a story or gives an account of something
NARRATORS > NARRATOR
NARRATORY > NARRATIVE
NARRE adj nearer
NARROW adj small in breadth in comparison to length ⊳ vb make or become narrow
NARROWED > NARROW
NARROWER > NARROW
NARROWEST > NARROW
NARROWING > NARROW
NARROWISH > NARROW
NARROWLY > NARROW
NARROWS pl n narrow part of a strait, river, or current
NARTHEX n portico at the west end of a basilica or church
NARTHEXES > NARTHEX
NARTJIE same as > NAARTJIE
NARTJIES > NARTJIE
NARWAL same as > NARWHAL
NARWALS > NARWAL
NARWHAL n Arctic whale with a long spiral tusk
NARWHALE same as > NARWHAL
NARWHALES > NARWHALE
NARWHALS > NARWHAL
NARY adv not
NAS vb has not
NASAL adj of the nose ⊳ n nasal speech sound, such as English m, n, or ng
NASALISE same as > NASALIZE
NASALISED > NASALISE
NASALISES > NASALISE
NASALISM n nasal pronunciation
NASALISMS > NASALISM
NASALITY > NASAL
NASALIZE vb pronounce nasally
NASALIZED > NASALIZE

NASALIZES > NASALIZE
NASALLY > NASAL
NASALS > NASAL
NASARD n organ stop
NASARDS > NASARD
NASCENCE > NASCENT
NASCENCES > NASCENT
NASCENCY > NASCENT
NASCENT adj starting to grow or develop
NASEBERRY another name for > SAPODILLA
NASHGAB n chatter
NASHGABS > NASHGAB
NASHI n fruit of the Japanese pear
NASHIS > NASHI
NASIAL > NASION
NASION n craniometric point where the top of the nose meets the ridge of the forehead
NASIONS > NASION
NASSELLA n as in nassella tussock type of tussock grass
NASTALIK n type of script
NASTALIKS > NASTALIK
NASTIC adj (of movement of plants) independent of the direction of the external stimulus
NASTIER > NASTY
NASTIES > NASTY
NASTIEST > NASTY
NASTILY > NASTY
NASTINESS > NASTY
NASTY adj unpleasant ⊳ n something unpleasant
NASUTE n type of termite
NASUTES > NASUTE
NAT n supporter of nationalism
NATAL adj of or relating to birth
NATALITY n birth rate in a given place
NATANT adj (of aquatic plants) floating on the water
NATANTLY adv in a floating manner
NATATION n swimming
NATATIONS > NATATION
NATATORIA pl n indoor swimming pools
NATATORY adj of or relating to swimming
NATCH sentence substitute naturally ⊳ n notch
NATCHES > NATCH
NATES pl n buttocks
NATHELESS prep notwithstanding
NATHEMO same as > NATHEMORE
NATHEMORE adv nevermore
NATHLESS same as > NATHELESS
NATIFORM adj resembling buttocks
NATION n people of one or more cultures or races organized as a single state
NATIONAL adj of or serving a nation as a whole ⊳ n citizen of a nation
NATIONALS > NATIONAL
NATIONS > NATION

NATIS > NATES
NATIVE adj relating to a place where a person was born ⊳ n person born in a place
NATIVELY > NATIVE
NATIVES > NATIVE
NATIVISM n policy of favouring the natives of a country over the immigrants
NATIVISMS > NATIVISM
NATIVIST > NATIVISM
NATIVISTS > NATIVISM
NATIVITY n birth or origin
NATRIUM obsolete name for > SODIUM
NATRIUMS > NATRIUM
NATROLITE n colourless, white, or yellow zeolite mineral
NATRON n whitish or yellow mineral
NATRONS > NATRON
NATS > NAT
NATTER vb talk idly or chatter ⊳ n long idle chat
NATTERED > NATTER
NATTERER > NATTER
NATTERERS > NATTER
NATTERIER > NATTERY
NATTERING > NATTER
NATTERS > NATTER
NATTERY adj irritable
NATTIER > NATTY
NATTIEST > NATTY
NATTILY > NATTY
NATTINESS > NATTY
NATTY adj smart and spruce
NATURA n nature
NATURAE > NATURA
NATURAL adj normal or to be expected ⊳ n person with an inborn talent or skill
NATURALLY > NATURAL
NATURALS > NATURAL
NATURE n whole system of the physical world not controlled by human beings
NATURED adj having a certain disposition
NATURES > NATURE
NATURING adj creative
NATURISM n nudism
NATURISMS > NATURISM
NATURIST > NATURISM
NATURISTS > NATURISM
NAUCH same as > NAUTCH
NAUCHES > NAUCH
NAUGAHYDE n type of vinyl-coated fabric
NAUGHT n nothing ⊳ adv not at all
NAUGHTIER > NAUGHTY
NAUGHTIES > NAUGHTY
NAUGHTILY > NAUGHTY
NAUGHTS > NAUGHT
NAUGHTY adj disobedient or mischievous ⊳ n act of sexual intercourse
NAUMACHIA n mock sea fight performed as an entertainment
NAUMACHY same as > NAUMACHIA
NAUNT n aunt
NAUNTS > NAUNT

NAUPLIAL adj of or like a nauplius, the larval form of certain crustaceans
NAUPLII > NAUPLIUS
NAUPLIOID > NAUPLIUS
NAUPLIUS n larva of many crustaceans
NAUSEA n feeling of being about to vomit
NAUSEANT n substance inducing nausea
NAUSEANTS > NAUSEANT
NAUSEAS > NAUSEA
NAUSEATE vb make (someone) feel sick
NAUSEATED > NAUSEATE
NAUSEATES > NAUSEATE
NAUSEOUS adj as if about to vomit
NAUTCH n intricate traditional Indian dance
NAUTCHES > NAUTCH
NAUTIC same as > NAUTICAL
NAUTICAL adj of the sea or ships
NAUTICS n science of navigation
NAUTILI > NAUTILUS
NAUTILOID n type of mollusc ⊳ adj of this type of mollusc
NAUTILUS n shellfish with many tentacles
NAV n (short for) navigation
NAVAID n navigational aid
NAVAIDS > NAVAID
NAVAL adj of or relating to a navy or ships
NAVALISM n domination of naval interests
NAVALISMS > NAVALISM
NAVALLY > NAVAL
NAVAR n system of air navigation
NAVARCH n admiral
NAVARCHS > NAVARCH
NAVARCHY n navarch's term of office
NAVARHO n aircraft navigation system
NAVARHOS > NAVARHO
NAVARIN n stew of mutton or lamb with root vegetables
NAVARINS > NAVARIN
NAVARS > NAVAR
NAVE n long central part of a church
NAVEL n hollow in the middle of the abdomen
NAVELS > NAVEL
NAVELWORT another name for > PENNYWORT
NAVES > NAVE
NAVETTE n gem cut
NAVETTES > NAVETTE
NAVEW another name for > TURNIP
NAVEWS > NAVEW
NAVICERT n certificate specifying the contents of a neutral ship's cargo
NAVICERTS > NAVICERT
NAVICULA n incense holder
NAVICULAR adj shaped like a boat ⊳ n small boat-shaped bone of the wrist or foot

NAVICULAS > NAVICULA
NAVIES > NAVY
NAVIGABLE adj wide, deep, or safe enough to be sailed through
NAVIGABLY > NAVIGABLE
NAVIGATE vb direct or plot the path or position of a ship, aircraft, or car
NAVIGATED > NAVIGATE
NAVIGATES > NAVIGATE
NAVIGATOR n person who is skilled in or performs navigation, esp on a ship or aircraft
NAVS > NAV
NAVVIED > NAVVY
NAVVIES > NAVVY
NAVVY n labourer employed on a road or a building site ▷ vb work as a navvy
NAVVYING > NAVVY
NAVY n warships with their crews and organization ▷ adj navy-blue
NAW same as > NO
NAWAB n (formerly) a Muslim ruler or landowner in India
NAWABS > NAWAB
NAY interj no ▷ n person who votes against a motion ▷ adv used for emphasis ▷ sentence substitute no
NAYS > NAY
NAYSAID > NAYSAY
NAYSAY vb say no
NAYSAYER > NAYSAY
NAYSAYERS > NAYSAYER
NAYSAYING > NAYSAY
NAYSAYS > NAYSAY
NAYTHLES same as > NATHELESS
NAYWARD n towards denial
NAYWARDS same as > NAYWARD
NAYWORD n proverb
NAYWORDS > NAYWORD
NAZE n flat marshy headland
NAZES > NAZE
NAZI n person who thinks or acts in a brutal or dictatorial way
NAZIFIED > NAZIFY
NAZIFIES > NAZIFY
NAZIFY vb make nazi in character
NAZIFYING > NAZIFY
NAZIR n Muslim official
NAZIRS > NAZIR
NAZIS > NAZI
NDUJA n spicy pork paste
NDUJAS > NDUJA
NE conj nor
NEAFE same as > NIEVE
NEAFES > NEAFE
NEAFFE same as > NIEVE
NEAFFES > NEAFFE
NEAL same as > ANNEAL
NEALED > NEAL
NEALING > NEAL
NEALS > NEAL
NEANIC adj of or relating to the early stages in a life cycle
NEAP adj of, relating to, or constituting a neap tide ▷ vb be grounded by a neap tide
NEAPED > NEAP

NEAPING > NEAP
NEAPS > NEAP
NEAR adj indicating a place or time not far away ▷ vb draw close (to) ▷ prep at or to a place or time not far away from ▷ adv at or to a place or time not far away ▷ n left side of a horse or vehicle
NEARBY adj not far away ▷ adv close at hand
NEARED > NEAR
NEARER > NEAR
NEAREST > NEAR
NEARING > NEAR
NEARISH adj quite near
NEARLIER > NEARLY
NEARLIEST > NEARLY
NEARLY adv almost
NEARNESS > NEAR
NEARS > NEAR
NEARSHORE n area of coastline water ▷ adj situated close to a shore ▷ vb get business services carried out in a neighbouring country
NEARSIDE n side of a vehicle that is nearer the kerb
NEARSIDES > NEARSIDE
NEAT adj tidy and clean ▷ n domestic bovine animal
NEATEN vb make neat
NEATENED > NEATEN
NEATENING > NEATEN
NEATENS > NEATEN
NEATER > NEAT
NEATEST > NEAT
NEATH short for > BENEATH
NEATHERD n cowherd
NEATHERDS > NEATHERD
NEATLY > NEAT
NEATNESS > NEAT
NEATNIK n very neat and tidy person
NEATNIKS > NEATNIK
NEATS > NEAT
NEB n beak of a bird or the nose of an animal ▷ vb look around nosily
NEBBED > NEB
NEBBICH same as > NEBBISH
NEBBICHS > NEBBICH
NEBBING > NEB
NEBBISH n timid man
NEBBISHE same as > NEBBISH
NEBBISHER same as > NEBBISH
NEBBISHES > NEBBISH
NEBBISHY adj timid
NEBBUK n type of shrub
NEBBUKS > NEBBUK
NEBECK same as > NEBBUK
NEBECKS > NEBECK
NEBEK same as > NEBBUK
NEBEKS > NEBEK
NEBEL n Hebrew musical instrument
NEBELS > NEBEL
NEBENKERN n component of insect sperm
NEBISH same as > NEBBISH
NEBISHES > NEBISH
NEBRIS n fawn-skin
NEBRISES > NEBRIS

NEBS > NEB
NEBULA n hazy cloud of particles and gases
NEBULAE > NEBULA
NEBULAR > NEBULA
NEBULAS > NEBULA
NEBULE n cloud
NEBULES > NEBULE
NEBULISE same as > NEBULIZE
NEBULISED > NEBULISE
NEBULISER same as > NEBULIZER
NEBULISES > NEBULISE
NEBULIUM n element
NEBULIUMS > NEBULIUM
NEBULIZE vb turn (a liquid) into a fine spray
NEBULIZED > NEBULIZE
NEBULIZER n device which turns a drug from a liquid into a fine spray which can be inhaled
NEBULIZES > NEBULIZE
NEBULOSE same as > NEBULOUS
NEBULOUS adj vague and unclear
NEBULY adj wavy
NECESSARY adj needed to obtain the desired result
NECESSITY n circumstances that inevitably require a certain result
NECK n part of the body joining the head to the shoulders ▷ vb kiss and cuddle
NECKATEE n piece of ornamental cloth worn around the neck
NECKATEES > NECKATEE
NECKBAND n band around the neck of a garment
NECKBANDS > NECKBAND
NECKBEEF n cheap cattle flesh
NECKBEEFS > NECKBEEF
NECKCLOTH n large ornamental usually white cravat worn formerly by men
NECKED > NECK
NECKER > NECK
NECKERS > NECK
NECKGEAR n any neck covering
NECKGEARS > NECKGEAR
NECKING n activity of kissing and embracing passionately
NECKINGS > NECKING
NECKLACE n decorative piece of jewellery worn around the neck ▷ vb kill (someone) by placing a burning tyre round his or her neck
NECKLACED > NECKLACE
NECKLACES > NECKLACE
NECKLESS > NECK
NECKLET n ornament worn round the neck
NECKLETS > NECKLET
NECKLIKE > NECK
NECKLINE n shape or position of the upper edge of a dress or top

NECKLINES > NECKLINE
NECKPIECE n piece of fur, cloth, etc, worn around the neck or neckline
NECKS > NECK
NECKSHOT n shot in the neck of an animal
NECKSHOTS > NECKSHOT
NECKTIE same as > TIE
NECKTIES > NECKTIE
NECKVERSE n verse read to prove clergy membership
NECKWEAR n articles of clothing, such as ties, scarves, etc, worn around the neck
NECKWEARS > NECKWEAR
NECKWEED n type of plant
NECKWEEDS > NECKWEED
NECROLOGY n list of people recently dead
NECROPHIL n person who is sexually attracted to dead bodies
NECROPOLI pl n burial sites or cemeteries
NECROPSY n postmortem examination ▷ vb carry out a necropsy
NECROSE vb cause or undergo necrosis
NECROSED > NECROSE
NECROSES > NECROSE
NECROSING > NECROSE
NECROSIS n death of cells in the body
NECROTIC > NECROSIS
NECROTISE same as > NECROTIZE
NECROTIZE vb undergo necrosis
NECROTOMY n dissection of a dead body
NECTAR n sweet liquid collected from flowers by bees
NECTAREAL adj of or like nectar
NECTAREAN adj of or like nectar
NECTARED adj filled with nectar
NECTARIAL > NECTARY
NECTARIED adj having nectaries
NECTARIES > NECTARY
NECTARINE n smooth-skinned peach
NECTAROUS > NECTAR
NECTARS > NECTAR
NECTARY n structure secreting nectar in a plant
NED n derogatory name for an adolescent hooligan
NEDDIER > NEDDY
NEDDIES > NEDDY
NEDDIEST > NEDDY
NEDDISH > NED
NEDDY n donkey ▷ adj of or relating to neds
NEDETTE n derogatory name for a female adolescent hooligan
NEDETTES > NEDETTE
NEDS > NED
NEE prep indicating the maiden name of a married woman ▷ adj indicating the

n

maiden name of a married woman

NEED vb require or be in want of ▷ n condition of lacking something

NEEDED > NEED

NEEDER > NEED

NEEDERS > NEED

NEEDFIRE n beacon

NEEDFIRES > NEEDFIRE

NEEDFUL adj necessary or required

NEEDFULLY > NEEDFUL

NEEDFULS n must-haves

NEEDIER > NEEDY

NEEDIEST > NEEDY

NEEDILY > NEEDY

NEEDINESS n state of being needy

NEEDING > NEED

NEEDLE n thin pointed piece of metal with an eye through which thread is passed for sewing ▷ vb goad or provoke

NEEDLED > NEEDLE

NEEDLEFUL n length of thread cut for use in a needle

NEEDLER n needle maker

NEEDLERS > NEEDLER

NEEDLES > NEEDLE

NEEDLESS adj unnecessary

NEEDLIER > NEEDLY

NEEDLIEST > NEEDLE

NEEDLING > NEEDLE

NEEDLINGS > NEEDLE

NEEDLY adj like or full of needles

NEEDMENT n a necessity

NEEDMENTS > NEED

NEEDS adv necessarily ▷ pl n what is required

NEEDY adj poor, in need of financial support

NEELD same as > NEEDLE

NEELDS > NEELD

NEELE same as > NEEDLE

NEELES > NEELE

NEEM n type of large Indian tree

NEEMB same as > NEEM

NEEMBS > NEEMB

NEEMS > NEEM

NEEP dialect name for > TURNIP

NEEPS > NEEP

NEESBERRY same as > NASEBERRY

NEESE same as > NEEZE

NEESED > NEESE

NEESES > NEESE

NEESING > NEESE

NEEZE vb sneeze

NEEZED > NEEZE

NEEZES > NEEZE

NEEZING > NEEZE

NEF n church nave

NEFANDOUS adj unmentionable

NEFARIOUS adj wicked

NEFAST adj wicked

NEFS > NEF

NEG n photographic negative

NEGATE vb invalidate

NEGATED > NEGATE

NEGATER > NEGATE

NEGATERS > NEGATE

NEGATES > NEGATE

NEGATING > NEGATE

NEGATION n opposite or absence of something

NEGATIONS > NEGATION

NEGATIVE adj expressing a denial or refusal ▷ n negative word or statement

NEGATIVED > NEGATIVE

NEGATIVES > NEGATIVE

NEGATON same as > NEGATRON

NEGATONS > NEGATON

NEGATOR > NEGATE

NEGATORS > NEGATE

NEGATORY adj relating to the act of negation

NEGATRON obsolete word for > ELECTRON

NEGATRONS > NEGATRON

NEGLECT vb take no care of ▷ n neglecting or being neglected

NEGLECTED > NEGLECT

NEGLECTER > NEGLECT

NEGLECTOR > NEGLECT

NEGLECTS > NEGLECT

NEGLIGE variant of > NEGLIGEE

NEGLIGEE n woman's lightweight usu lace-trimmed dressing gown

NEGLIGEES > NEGLIGEE

NEGLIGENT adj habitually neglecting duties, responsibilities, etc

NEGLIGES > NEGLIGE

NEGOCIANT n wine merchant

NEGOTIANT n person, nation, organization, etc, involved in a negotiation

NEGOTIATE vb discuss in order to reach (an agreement)

NEGRESS n old-fashioned offensive word for a Black woman

NEGRESSES > NEGRESS

NEGRITUDE n old-fashioned offensive word for the fact of being a Black person

NEGRO n old-fashioned offensive word for a Black man

NEGROES > NEGRO

NEGROHEAD n old-fashioned offensive word for a type of rubber

NEGROID n member of one of the major racial groups

NEGROIDAL same as > NEGROID

NEGROIDS > NEGROID

NEGROISM > NEGRO

NEGROISMS > NEGRO

NEGRONI n type of cocktail

NEGRONIS > NEGRONI

NEGROPHIL n old-fashioned offensive word for a person who admires Black people and their culture

NEGS > NEG

NEGUS n hot drink of port and lemon juice

NEGUSES > NEGUS

NEIF same as > NIEVE

NEIFS > NEIF

NEIGH n loud high-pitched sound made by a horse ▷ vb make this sound

NEIGHBOR same as > NEIGHBOUR

NEIGHBORS > NEIGHBOR

NEIGHBOUR n person who lives or is situated near another ▷ vb be or live close (to a person or thing)

NEIGHED > NEIGH

NEIGHING n act of neighing

NEIGHINGS > NEIGHING

NEIGHS > NEIGH

NEINEI n type of plant

NEINEIS > NEINEI

NEIST Scots variant of > NEXT

NEITHER pron not one nor the other ▷ adj not one nor the other (of two)

NEIVE same as > NIEVE

NEIVES > NEIVE

NEK n mountain pass

NEKS > NEK

NEKTON n free-swimming animals in the middle depths of a sea or lake

NEKTONIC > NEKTON

NEKTONS > NEKTON

NELIES same as > NELIS

NELIS n type of pear

NELLIE n type of albatross

NELLIES > NELLIE

NELLY n as in not on your nelly not under any circumstances

NELSON n type of wrestling hold

NELSONS > NELSON

NELUMBIUM same as > NELUMBO

NELUMBO n type of aquatic plant

NELUMBOS > NELUMBO

NEMA n filament

NEMAS > NEMA

NEMATIC n substance having a mesomorphic state

NEMATICS > NEMATIC

NEMATODE n slender cylindrical unsegmented worm

NEMATODES > NEMATODE

NEMATOID > NEMATODE

NEMERTEAN n type of ribbon-like marine worm ▷ adj of this worm

NEMERTIAN same as > NEMERTEAN

NEMERTINE same as > NEMERTEAN

NEMESES > NEMESIS

NEMESIA n type of southern African plant

NEMESIAS > NEMESIA

NEMESIS n retribution or vengeance

NEMN vb name

NEMNED > NEMN

NEMNING > NEMN

NEMNS > NEMN

NEMOPHILA n any of a genus of low-growing hairy annual plants

NEMORAL adj of a wood

NEMOROUS adj woody

NEMPT adj named

NENE n rare black-and-grey short-winged Hawaiian goose

NENES > NENE

NENNIGAI same as > NANNYGAI

NENNIGAIS > NENNIGAI

NENUPHAR n type of water lily

NENUPHARS > NENUPHAR

NEOBLAST n worm cell

NEOBLASTS > NEOBLAST

NEOCON n supporter of conservative politics

NEOCONS > NEOCON

NEOCORTEX n part of the brain

NEODYMIUM n silvery-white metallic element of lanthanide series

NEOGENE adj of, denoting, or formed during the Miocene and Pliocene epochs

NEOGOTHIC n style of architecture popular in Britain in the 18th and 19th centuries

NEOLITH n Neolithic stone implement

NEOLITHIC n historical period characterized by polished stone tools and weapons ▷ adj relating to this period

NEOLITHS > NEOLITH

NEOLOGIAN > NEOLOGY

NEOLOGIC > NEOLOGISM

NEOLOGIES > NEOLOGY

NEOLOGISE same as > NEOLOGIZE

NEOLOGISM n newly coined word or an established word used in a new sense

NEOLOGIST > NEOLOGISM

NEOLOGIZE vb invent or use neologisms

NEOLOGY same as > NEOLOGISM

NEOMORPH n genetic component

NEOMORPHS > NEOMORPH

NEOMYCIN n type of antibiotic obtained from a bacterium

NEOMYCINS > NEOMYCIN

NEON n element used in illuminated signs and lights ▷ adj of or illuminated by neon

NEONATAL adj relating to the first few weeks of a baby's life

NEONATE n newborn child

NEONATES > NEONATE

NEONED adj lit with neon

NEONOMIAN n Christian religious belief

NEONS > NEON

NEOPAGAN n advocate of the revival of paganism

NEOPAGANS > NEOPAGAN

NEOPHILE n person who welcomes new things

NEOPHILES > NEOPHILE

NEOPHILIA n tendency to like anything new

NEOPHOBE > NEOPHOBIA

NEOPHOBES > NEOPHOBIA

NEOPHOBIA *n* tendency to dislike anything new
NEOPHOBIC > NEOPHOBIA
NEOPHYTE *n* beginner or novice
NEOPHYTES > NEOPHYTE
NEOPHYTIC > NEOPHYTE
NEOPILINA *n* type of mollusc
NEOPLASIA *n* abnormal growth of tissue
NEOPLASM *n* any abnormal new growth of tissue
NEOPLASMS > NEOPLASM
NEOPLASTY *n* surgical formation of new tissue structures or repair of damaged structures
NEOPRENE *n* synthetic rubber used in waterproof products
NEOPRENES > NEOPRENE
NEOSOUL *n* soul music combined with other genres
NEOSOULS > NEOSOUL
NEOTEINIA *n* state of prolonged immaturity
NEOTENIC > NEOTENY
NEOTENIES > NEOTENY
NEOTENOUS > NEOTENY
NEOTENY *n* persistence of larval or fetal features in the adult form of an animal
NEOTERIC *adj* belonging to a new fashion or trend ▷ *n* new writer or philosopher
NEOTERICS > NEOTERIC
NEOTERISE *same as* > NEOTERIZE
NEOTERISM *n* the introduction of new things, especially words
NEOTERIST *n* one who introduces new words or phrases
NEOTERIZE *vb* introduce new things
NEOTOXIN *n* harmful agent
NEOTOXINS > NEOTOXIN
NEOTROPIC *adj* of tropical America
NEOTYPE *n* specimen selected to replace a type specimen that has been lost or destroyed
NEOTYPES > NEOTYPE
NEP *n* catmint
NEPENTHE *n* drug that ancient writers referred to as a means of forgetting grief or trouble
NEPENTHES > NEPENTHE
NEPER *n* unit expressing the ratio of two quantities
NEPERS > NEPER
NEPETA *same as* > CATMINT
NEPETAS > NEPETA
NEPHALISM *n* teetotalism
NEPHALIST *n* one who advocates or practices nephalism
NEPHELINE *n* whitish mineral
NEPHELITE *same as* > NEPHELINE
NEPHEW *n* son of one's sister or brother
NEPHEWS > NEPHEW

NEPHOGRAM *n* photograph of a cloud
NEPHOLOGY *n* study of clouds
NEPHRALGY *n* pain in a kidney
NEPHRIC *adj* renal
NEPHRIDIA *pl n* simple excretory organs of many invertebrates
NEPHRISM *n* chronic kidney disease
NEPHRISMS > NEPHRISM
NEPHRITE *n* tough fibrous amphibole mineral
NEPHRITES > NEPHRITE
NEPHRITIC *adj* of or relating to the kidneys
NEPHRITIS *n* inflammation of a kidney
NEPHROID *adj* kidney-shaped
NEPHRON *n* urine-secreting tubule in the kidney
NEPHRONS > NEPHRON
NEPHROSES > NEPHROSIS
NEPHROSIS *n* any noninflammatory degenerative kidney disease
NEPHROTIC > NEPHROSIS
NEPIONIC *adj* of or relating to the juvenile period in the life cycle of an organism
NEPIT *n* unit of information equal to 1.44 bits
NEPITS > NEPIT
NEPOTIC > NEPOTISM
NEPOTISM *n* favouritism in business shown to relatives and friends
NEPOTISMS > NEPOTISM
NEPOTIST > NEPOTISM
NEPOTISTS > NEPOTISM
NEPS > NEP
NEPTUNIUM *n* synthetic radioactive metallic element
NERAL *n* isomer of citral
NERALS > NERAL
NERD *n* boring person obsessed with a particular subject
NERDIC *same as* > GEEKSPEAK
NERDICS > NERDIC
NERDIER > NERDY
NERDIEST > NERDY
NERDINESS > NERD
NERDISH > NERD
NERDS > NERD
NERDY *adj* clumsy, socially inept
NEREID *n* sea nymph in Greek mythology
NEREIDES > NEREID
NEREIDS > NEREID
NEREIS *n* type of marine worm
NERINE *n* type of S African plant related to the amaryllis
NERINES > NERINE
NERITE *n* type of sea snail
NERITES > NERITE
NERITIC *adj* of or formed in shallow seas near a coastline
NERK *n* fool
NERKA *n* type of salmon
NERKAS > NERKA

NERKS > NERK
NEROL *n* scented liquid
NEROLI *n* brown oil used in perfumery
NEROLIS > NEROLI
NEROLS > NEROL
NERTS *interj* nuts
NERTZ *same as* > NERTS
NERVAL > NERVE
NERVATE *adj* (of leaves) with veins
NERVATION *less common word for* > VENATION
NERVATURE *same as* > NERVATION
NERVE *n* bundle of fibres that conducts impulses between the brain and body ▷ *vb* give courage to oneself
NERVED > NERVE
NERVELESS *adj* numb, without feeling
NERVELET *n* small nerve
NERVELETS > NERVELET
NERVER *n* someone or something which nerves
NERVERS > NERVER
NERVES > NERVE
NERVIER > NERVY
NERVIEST > NERVY
NERVILY > NERVY
NERVINE *adj* having a soothing effect upon the nerves ▷ *n* nervine drug or agent
NERVINES > NERVINE
NERVINESS > NERVY
NERVING > NERVE
NERVINGS > NERVE
NERVOSITY *n* nervousness
NERVOUS *adj* apprehensive or worried
NERVOUSLY > NERVOUS
NERVULAR *adj* relating to a nervule
NERVULE *n* small vein
NERVULES > NERVULE
NERVURE *n* stiff rod in an insect's wing
NERVURES > NERVURE
NERVY *adj* excitable or nervous
NESCIENCE *formal or literary word for* > IGNORANCE
NESCIENT > NESCIENCE
NESCIENTS > NESCIENCE
NESH *adj* sensitive to the cold
NESHER > NESH
NESHEST > NESH
NESHNESS > NESH
NESS *n* headland, cape
NESSES > NESS
NEST *n* place or structure in which birds or certain animals lay eggs or give birth to young ▷ *vb* make or inhabit a nest
NESTABLE > NEST
NESTED > NEST
NESTER > NEST
NESTERS > NEST
NESTFUL *n* the contents of a nest
NESTFULS > NESTFUL
NESTING > NEST
NESTINGS > NEST
NESTLE *vb* snuggle

NESTLED > NESTLE
NESTLER > NESTLE
NESTLERS > NESTLE
NESTLES > NESTLE
NESTLIKE > NEST
NESTLING *n* bird too young to leave the nest
NESTLINGS > NESTLING
NESTMATE *n* bird that shares a nest with another bird
NESTMATES > NESTMATE
NESTOR *n* wise old man
NESTORS > NESTOR
NESTS > NEST
NET *n* fabric of meshes of string, thread, or wire with many openings ▷ *vb* catch (a fish or animal) in a net ▷ *adj* left after all deductions
NETBALL *n* team game in which a ball has to be thrown through a high net
NETBALLER > NETBALL
NETBALLS > NETBALL
NETBOOK *n* type of small laptop computer
NETBOOKS > NETBOOK
NETE *n* lyre string
NETES > NETE
NETFUL *n* the contents of a net
NETFULS > NETFUL
NETHEAD *n* expert on the internet
NETHEADS > NETHEAD
NETHELESS *same as* > NATHELESS
NETHER *adj* lower
NETIZEN *n* person who regularly uses the internet
NETIZENS > NETIZEN
NETLESS *adj* without a net
NETLIKE *adj* resembling a net
NETMINDER *n* goalkeeper
NETOP *n* friend
NETOPS > NETOP
NETROOT *n* activist who promotes a cause via the internet
NETROOTS > NETROOT
NETS > NET
NETSPEAK *n* jargon, abbreviations, and emoticons typically used by frequent internet users
NETSPEAKS > NETSPEAK
NETSUKE *n* (in Japan) a carved ornamental toggle
NETSUKES > NETSUKE
NETSURF *vb* browse the internet for information
NETSURFED > NETSURF
NETSURFER *n* person who surfs the internet
NETSURFS > NETSURF
NETT *same as* > NET
NETTABLE *adj* that can be netted
NETTED > NET
NETTER *n* person that makes nets
NETTERS > NETTER
NETTIE *n* enthusiastic user of the internet
NETTIER > NETTY

n

NETTIES > NETTY
NETTIEST > NETTY
NETTING > NET
NETTINGS > NET
NETTLE n plant with stinging hairs on the leaves ▷ vb bother or irritate
NETTLED > NETTLE
NETTLER n one that nettles
NETTLERS > NETTLER
NETTLES > NETTLE
NETTLIER > NETTLY
NETTLIEST > NETTLE
NETTLING > NETTLE
NETTLY adj like a nettle
NETTS > NETT
NETTY n lavatory ▷ adj resembling a net
NETWORK n system of intersecting lines, roads, etc ▷ vb broadcast (a programme) over a network
NETWORKED > NETWORK
NETWORKER n person who forms business contacts through informal social meetings
NETWORKS > NETWORK
NEUK Scot word for > NOOK
NEUKS > NEUK
NEUM same as > NEUME
NEUMATIC adj relating to a neume
NEUME n notational symbol
NEUMES > NEUME
NEUMIC > NEUME
NEUMS > NEUM
NEURAL adj of a nerve or the nervous system
NEURALGIA n severe pain along a nerve
NEURALGIC > NEURALGIA
NEURALLY > NEURAL
NEURATION n arrangement of veins
NEURAXON n biological cell component
NEURAXONS > NEURAXON
NEURILITY n properties of the nerves
NEURINE n poisonous alkaloid
NEURINES > NEURINE
NEURISM n nerve force
NEURISMS > NEURISM
NEURITE n biological cell component
NEURITES > NEURITE
NEURITIC > NEURITIS
NEURITICS > NEURITIS
NEURITIS n inflammation of a nerve or nerves
NEUROCHIP n neutrino semiconductor chip designed for use in an electronic neural network
NEUROCOEL n cavity in brain
NEUROGLIA another name for > GLIA
NEUROGRAM same as > ENGRAM
NEUROID adj resembling a nerve ▷ n either of the halves of a neural arch
NEUROIDS > NEUROID
NEUROLOGY n scientific study of the nervous system

NEUROMA n any tumour composed of nerve tissue
NEUROMAS > NEUROMA
NEUROMAST n sensory cell in fish
NEUROMATA > NEUROMA
NEURON same as > NEURONE
NEURONAL > NEURONE
NEURONE n cell specialized to conduct nerve impulses
NEURONES > NEURONE
NEURONIC > NEURONE
NEURONS > NEURON
NEUROPATH n person suffering from or predisposed to a disorder of the nervous system
NEUROPIL n dense network of neurons and glia in the central nervous system
NEUROPILS > NEUROPIL
NEUROSAL adj relating to neurosis
NEUROSES > NEUROSIS
NEUROSIS n disorder producing anxiety or obsessive behaviour
NEUROTIC adj emotionally unstable ▷ n neurotic person
NEUROTICS > NEUROTIC
NEUROTOMY n surgical cutting of a nerve, esp to relieve intractable pain
NEURULA n stage of embryonic development
NEURULAE > NEURULA
NEURULAR > NEURULA
NEURULAS > NEURULA
NEUSTIC n part of a sentence that differs with mood
NEUSTICS > NEUSTIC
NEUSTON n organisms that float on the surface of open water
NEUSTONIC > NEUSTON
NEUSTONS > NEUSTON
NEUTER adj belonging to a particular class of grammatical inflections in some languages ▷ vb castrate (an animal) ▷ n neuter gender
NEUTERED > NEUTER
NEUTERING n act of castrating or spaying an animal
NEUTERS > NEUTER
NEUTRAL adj taking neither side in a war or dispute ▷ n neutral person or nation
NEUTRALLY > NEUTRAL
NEUTRALS > NEUTRAL
NEUTRETTO n neutrino associated with the muon
NEUTRINO n elementary particle with no mass or electrical charge
NEUTRINOS > NEUTRINO
NEUTRON n electrically neutral elementary particle
NEUTRONIC > NEUTRON
NEUTRONS > NEUTRON
NEVE n mass of porous ice, formed from snow
NEVEL vb beat with the fists
NEVELLED > NEVEL
NEVELLING > NEVEL

NEVELS > NEVEL
NEVER adv at no time ▷ sentence substitute at no time ▷ interj surely not!
NEVERMIND n difference
NEVERMORE adv never again
NEVES > NEVE
NEVI > NEVUS
NEVOID > NAEVUS
NEVUS same as > NAEVUS
NEW adj not existing before ▷ adv recently ▷ vb make new
NEWB n newbie
NEWBIE n person new to a job, club, etc
NEWBIES > NEWBIE
NEWBORN adj recently or just born ▷ n newborn baby
NEWBORNS > NEWBORN
NEWBS > NEWB
NEWCOME adj recently arrived
NEWCOMER n recent arrival or participant
NEWCOMERS > NEWCOMER
NEWED > NEW
NEWEL n post at the top or bottom of a flight of stairs
NEWELL n new thing
NEWELLED > NEWEL
NEWELLS > NEWELL
NEWELS > NEWEL
NEWER > NEW
NEWEST > NEW
NEWFANGLE adj newly come into existence or fashion ▷ n newfangled thing
NEWFOUND adj newly or recently discovered
NEWIE n fresh idea or thing
NEWIES > NEWIE
NEWING > NEW
NEWISH adj fairly new
NEWISHLY > NEWISH
NEWLY adv recently
NEWLYWED n recently married person
NEWLYWEDS > NEWLYWED
NEWMARKET n double-breasted waisted coat with a full skirt
NEWMOWN adj freshly cut
NEWNESS > NEW
NEWNESSES > NEW
NEWS n important or interesting new happenings ▷ vb report
NEWSAGENT n shopkeeper who sells newspapers and magazines
NEWSBEAT n particular area of news reporting
NEWSBEATS > NEWSBEAT
NEWSBOY n boy who sells or delivers newspapers
NEWSBOYS > NEWSBOY
NEWSBREAK n newsflash
NEWSCAST n radio or television broadcast of the news
NEWSCASTS > NEWSCAST
NEWSCLIP n brief extract from news broadcast
NEWSCLIPS > NEWSCLIP
NEWSDESK n news gathering and reporting department

NEWSDESKS > NEWSDESK
NEWSED > NEWS
NEWSES > NEWS
NEWSFEED n service that provides news articles for distribution
NEWSFEEDS > NEWSFEED
NEWSFLASH n brief important news item, which interrupts a radio or television programme
NEWSGIRL n female newsreader or reporter
NEWSGIRLS > NEWSGIRL
NEWSGROUP n forum where subscribers exchange information about a specific subject by e-mail
NEWSHAWK n newspaper reporter
NEWSHAWKS > NEWSHAWK
NEWSHOUND same as > NEWSHAWK
NEWSIE same as > NEWSY
NEWSIER > NEWSY
NEWSIES > NEWSY
NEWSIEST > NEWSY
NEWSINESS > NEWSY
NEWSING > NEWS
NEWSLESS > NEWS
NEWSMAKER n person whose activities are reported in news
NEWSMAN n male newsreader or reporter
NEWSMEN > NEWSMAN
NEWSPAPER n weekly or daily publication containing news ▷ vb do newspaper related work
NEWSPEAK n deliberately ambiguous and misleading language of politicians and officials
NEWSPEAKS > NEWSPEAK
NEWSPRINT n inexpensive paper used for newspapers
NEWSREEL n short film giving news
NEWSREELS > NEWSREEL
NEWSROOM n room where news is received and prepared for publication or broadcasting
NEWSROOMS > NEWSROOM
NEWSSHEET n sheet giving news and information
NEWSSTAND n portable stand from which newspapers are sold
NEWSTRADE n newspaper retail
NEWSWIRE n electronic means of delivering up-to-the-minute news
NEWSWIRES > NEWSWIRE
NEWSWOMAN n female newsreader or reporter
NEWSWOMEN > NEWSWOMAN
NEWSY adj full of news ▷ n newsagent
NEWT n small amphibious creature
NEWTON n unit of force
NEWTONS > NEWTON
NEWTS > NEWT
NEWWAVER n member of new wave

NEWWAVERS > NEWWAVER
NEXT adv immediately following ▷ n next person or thing
NEXTDOOR adj in or at the adjacent house or building
NEXTLY > NEXT
NEXTNESS > NEXT
NEXTS > NEXT
NEXUS n connection or link
NEXUSES > NEXUS
NGAI n clan or tribe
NGAIO n small New Zealand tree
NGAIOS > NGAIO
NGANA same as > NAGANA
NGANAS > NGANA
NGARARA n lizard found in New Zealand
NGARARAS > NGARARA
NGATI n (occurring as part of the tribe name) a tribe or clan
NGATIS > NGATI
NGOMA n type of drum
NGOMAS > NGOMA
NGULTRUM n standard monetary unit of Bhutan, divided into 100 chetrum
NGULTRUMS > NGULTRUM
NGWEE n Zambian monetary unit
NGWEES > NGWEE
NHANDU n type of spider
NHANDUS > NHANDU
NIACIN n vitamin of the B complex
NIACINS > NIACIN
NIAGARA n deluge or outpouring
NIAGARAS > NIAGARA
NIAISERIE n simplicity
NIALAMIDE n type of drug
NIB n writing point of a pen ▷ vb provide with a nib
NIBBED > NIB
NIBBING > NIB
NIBBLE vb take little bites (of) ▷ n little bite
NIBBLED > NIBBLE
NIBBLER n person, animal, or thing that nibbles
NIBBLERS > NIBBLER
NIBBLES > NIBBLE
NIBBLIES > NIBBLY
NIBBLING > NIBBLE
NIBBLINGS > NIBBLE
NIBBLY n small item of food
NIBLET n very small piece of food
NIBLETS > NIBLET
NIBLICK n former golf club giving a great deal of lift
NIBLICKS > NIBLICK
NIBLIKE > NIB
NIBS > NIB
NICAD n rechargeable dry-cell battery
NICADS > NICAD
NICCOLITE n copper-coloured mineral
NICE adj pleasant
NICEISH > NICE
NICELY > NICE
NICENESS > NICE
NICER > NICE

NICEST > NICE
NICETIES > NICETY
NICETY n subtle point
NICHE n hollow area in a wall ▷ adj of or aimed at a specialist group or market ▷ vb place (a statue) in a niche
NICHED > NICHE
NICHER vb snigger
NICHERED > NICHER
NICHERING > NICHER
NICHERS > NICHER
NICHES > NICHE
NICHING > NICHE
NICHROME n (tradename) alloy of nickel and chrome
NICHROMES > NICHROME
NICHT Scot word for > NIGHT
NICHTS > NICHT
NICISH > NICE
NICK vb make a small cut in ▷ n small cut
NICKAR n hard seed
NICKARS > NICKAR
NICKED > NICK
NICKEL n silvery-white metal often used in alloys ▷ vb plate with nickel
NICKELED > NICKEL
NICKELIC adj of or containing metallic nickel
NICKELINE another name for > NICCOLITE
NICKELING > NICKEL
NICKELISE same as > NICKELIZE
NICKELIZE vb treat with nickel
NICKELLED > NICKEL
NICKELOUS adj of or containing nickel, esp in the divalent state
NICKELS > NICKEL
NICKER n pound sterling ▷ vb (of a horse) to neigh softly
NICKERED > NICKER
NICKERING > NICKER
NICKERNUT n nut of the bonduc tree
NICKERS > NICKER
NICKING > NICK
NICKLE same as > NICKEL
NICKLED > NICKLE
NICKLES > NICKLE
NICKLING > NICKLE
NICKNACK n cheap ornament or trinket
NICKNACKS > NICKNACK
NICKNAME n familiar name given to a person or place ▷ vb call by a nickname
NICKNAMED > NICKNAME
NICKNAMER > NICKNAME
NICKNAMES > NICKNAME
NICKPOINT n break in the slope of a river caused by renewed erosion
NICKS > NICK
NICKSTICK n tally
NICKUM n mischievous person
NICKUMS > NICKUM
NICOISE adj prepared with tomatoes, black olives, garlic and anchovies

NICOL n device for producing plane-polarized light
NICOLS > NICOL
NICOMPOOP n stupid person
NICOTIAN n tobacco user
NICOTIANA n American and Australian plant such as tobacco, with white, yellow, or purple fragrant flowers
NICOTIANS > NICOTIAN
NICOTIN same as > NICOTINE
NICOTINE n poisonous substance found in tobacco
NICOTINED > NICOTINE
NICOTINES > NICOTINE
NICOTINIC > NICOTINE
NICOTINS same as > NICOTIN
NICTATE same as > NICTITATE
NICTATED > NICTATE
NICTATES > NICTATE
NICTATING > NICTATE
NICTATION n act of blinking
NICTITANT adj blinking
NICTITATE vb blink
NID same as > NIDE
NIDAL > NIDUS
NIDAMENTA pl n egg capsules
NIDATE vb undergo nidation
NIDATED > NIDATE
NIDATES > NIDATE
NIDATING > NIDATE
NIDATION n implantation
NIDATIONS > NIDATION
NIDDERING n coward ▷ adj cowardly
NIDDICK n nape of the neck
NIDDICKS > NIDDICK
NIDE vb nest
NIDED > NIDE
NIDERING same as > NIDDERING
NIDERINGS > NIDERING
NIDERLING same as > NIDDERING
NIDES > NIDE
NIDGET n type of hoe ▷ vb assist a woman in labour
NIDGETED > NIDGET
NIDGETING > NIDGET
NIDGETS > NIDGET
NIDI > NIDUS
NIDIFIED > NIDIFY
NIDIFIES > NIDIFY
NIDIFY vb (of a bird) to make or build a nest
NIDIFYING > NIDIFY
NIDING n coward
NIDINGS > NIDING
NIDOR n cooking smell
NIDOROUS > NIDOR
NIDORS > NIDOR
NIDS > NID
NIDUS n nest in which insects or spiders deposit their eggs
NIDUSES > NIDUS
NIE archaic spelling of > NIGH
NIECE n daughter of one's sister or brother
NIECES > NIECE
NIED > NIE

NIEF same as > NIEVE
NIEFS > NIEF
NIELLATED > NIELLO
NIELLI > NIELLO
NIELLIST > NIELLO
NIELLISTS > NIELLO
NIELLO n black compound of sulphur and silver, lead, or copper ▷ vb decorate or treat with niello
NIELLOED > NIELLO
NIELLOING > NIELLO
NIELLOS > NIELLO
NIENTE adv softly fading away
NIES > NIE
NIEVE n closed hand
NIEVEFUL n closed handful
NIEVEFULS > NIEVE
NIEVES > NIEVE
NIFE n earth's core
NIFES > NIFE
NIFF n stink ▷ vb stink
NIFFED > NIFF
NIFFER vb barter
NIFFERED > NIFFER
NIFFERING > NIFFER
NIFFERS > NIFFER
NIFFIER > NIFF
NIFFIEST > NIFF
NIFFING > NIFF
NIFFNAFF vb trifle
NIFFNAFFS > NIFFNAFF
NIFFS > NIFF
NIFFY > NIFF
NIFTIER > NIFTY
NIFTIES > NIFTY
NIFTIEST > NIFTY
NIFTILY > NIFTY
NIFTINESS > NIFTY
NIFTY adj neat or smart ▷ n nifty thing
NIGELLA n type of Mediterranean plant
NIGELLAS > NIGELLA
NIGER n obsolete offensive term for a Black person
NIGERS > NIGER
NIGGARD n stingy person ▷ adj miserly ▷ vb act in a niggardly way
NIGGARDED > NIGGARD
NIGGARDLY adj stingy ▷ adv stingily
NIGGARDS > NIGGARD
NIGGER n offensive name for a Black person ▷ vb burn
NIGGERDOM > NIGGER
NIGGERED > NIGGER
NIGGERIER > NIGGERY
NIGGERING > NIGGER
NIGGERISH > NIGGER
NIGGERISM n offensive term for an idiom supposedly characteristic of Black people
NIGGERS > NIGGER
NIGGERY adj offensive term meaning suggestive of Black people
NIGGLE vb worry slightly ▷ n small worry or doubt
NIGGLED > NIGGLE
NIGGLER > NIGGLE
NIGGLERS > NIGGLE
NIGGLES > NIGGLE

n

NIGGLIER > NIGGLE
NIGGLIEST > NIGGLE
NIGGLING adj petty ▷ n act or instance of niggling
NIGGLINGS > NIGGLING
NIGGLY > NIGGLE
NIGH prep near ▷ adv nearly ▷ adj near ▷ vb approach
NIGHED > NIGH
NIGHER > NIGH
NIGHEST > NIGH
NIGHING > NIGH
NIGHLY > NIGH
NIGHNESS > NIGH
NIGHS > NIGH
NIGHT n time of darkness between sunset and sunrise ▷ adj of, occurring, or working at night
NIGHTBIRD same as **>** NIGHTHAWK
NIGHTCAP n drink taken just before bedtime
NIGHTCAPS > NIGHTCAP
NIGHTCLUB n establishment for dancing, music, etc, open late at night ▷ vb go to nightclubs
NIGHTED adj darkened
NIGHTFALL n approach of darkness
NIGHTFIRE n fire burned at night
NIGHTGEAR n nightclothes
NIGHTGLOW n faint light from the upper atmosphere in the night sky, esp in low latitudes
NIGHTGOWN n loose dress worn in bed by women
NIGHTHAWK n type of American nightjar
NIGHTIE n nightgown
NIGHTIES > NIGHTIE
NIGHTJAR n nocturnal bird with a harsh cry
NIGHTJARS > NIGHTJAR
NIGHTLESS > NIGHT
NIGHTLIFE n entertainment and social activities available at night in a town or city
NIGHTLIKE > NIGHT
NIGHTLONG adv throughout the night
NIGHTLY adv (happening) each night ▷ adj happening each night
NIGHTMARE n very bad dream
NIGHTMARY adj characterized by nightmares
NIGHTS adv at night or on most nights
NIGHTSIDE n dark side
NIGHTSPOT n nightclub
NIGHTTIDE same as **>** NIGHTTIME
NIGHTTIME n time from sunset to sunrise
NIGHTWARD > NIGHT
NIGHTWEAR n apparel worn in bed or before retiring to bed
NIGHTY same as **>** NIGHTIE
NIGIRI n small oval block of cold rice, wasabi and fish
NIGIRIS > NIGIRI

NIGRICANT adj black
NIGRIFIED > NIGRIFY
NIGRIFIES > NIGRIFY
NIGRIFY vb blacken
NIGRITUDE n blackness
NIGROSIN same as **>** NIGROSINE
NIGROSINE n type of black pigment and dye used in inks and shoe polishes
NIGROSINS > NIGROSIN
NIHIL n nil
NIHILISM n rejection of all established authority and institutions
NIHILISMS > NIHILISM
NIHILIST > NIHILISM
NIHILISTS > NIHILISM
NIHILITY n state or condition of being nothing
NIHILS > NIHIL
NIHONGA n Japanese form of painting
NIHONGAS > NIHONGA
NIHONIUM n highly radioactive element
NIHONIUMS > NIHONIUM
NIKAB same as **>** NIQAB
NIKABS > NIKAB
NIKAH n Islamic marriage contract
NIKAHS > NIKAH
NIKAU n palm tree native to New Zealand
NIKAUS > NIKAU
NIL n nothing, zero
NILGAI n large Indian antelope
NILGAIS > NILGAI
NILGAU same as **>** NILGHAU
NILGAUS > NILGAU
NILGHAI same as **>** NILGAI
NILGHAIS > NILGHAI
NILGHAU same as **>** NILGAI
NILGHAUS > NILGHAU
NILL vb be unwilling
NILLED > NILL
NILLING > NILL
NILLS > NILL
NILPOTENT n mathematical term
NILS > NIL
NIM n game involving removing one or more small items from several rows or piles ▷ vb steal
NIMB n halo
NIMBED > NIMB
NIMBI > NIMBUS
NIMBLE adj agile and quick
NIMBLER > NIMBLE
NIMBLESSE > NIMBLE
NIMBLEST > NIMBLE
NIMBLEWIT n alert, bright, and clever person
NIMBLY > NIMBLE
NIMBS > NIMB
NIMBUS n dark grey rain cloud
NIMBUSED > NIMBUS
NIMBUSES > NIMBUS
NIMBYISM n practice of objecting to something that will affect one or take place in one's locality
NIMBYISMS > NIMBYISM

NIMBYNESS same as **>** NIMBYISM
NIMIETIES > NIMIETY
NIMIETY rare word for **>** EXCESS
NIMIOUS > NIMTETY
NIMMED > NIM
NIMMER > NIM
NIMMERS > NIM
NIMMING > NIM
NIMONIC adj as in nimonic alloy type of nickel-based alloy
NIMPS adj easy
NIMROD n hunter
NIMRODS > NIMROD
NIMS > NIM
NINCOM same as **>** NICOMPOOP
NINCOMS > NINCOM
NINCUM same as **>** NICOMPOOP
NINCUMS > NINCUM
NINE n one more than eight
NINEBARK n North American shrub
NINEBARKS > NINEBARK
NINEFOLD adj having nine times as many or as much ▷ adv by nine times as much or as many
NINEHOLES n type of game
NINEPENCE n coin worth nine pennies
NINEPENNY same as **>** NINEPENCE
NINEPIN n skittle used in ninepins
NINEPINS n game of skittles
NINER n (US) student in the ninth grade
NINERS > NINER
NINES > NINE
NINESCORE n product of nine times twenty
NINETEEN n ten and nine
NINETEENS > NINETEEN
NINETIES > NINETY
NINETIETH adj being the ordinal number of ninety in numbering order ▷ n one of 90 approximately equal parts of something
NINETY n ten times nine
NINHYDRIN n chemical reagent used for the detection and analysis of primary amines
NINJA n person skilled in ninjutsu
NINJAS > NINJA
NINJITSU same as **>** NINJUTSU
NINJITSUS > NINJITSU
NINJUTSU n Japanese martial art
NINJUTSUS > NINJUTSU
NINNIES > NINNY
NINNY n stupid person
NINNYISH > NINNY
NINON n fine strong silky fabric
NINONS > NINON
NINTH n number nine in a series ▷ adj coming after the eighth

NINTHLY same as **>** NINTH
NINTHS > NINTH
NIOBATE n type of salt crystal
NIOBATES > NIOBATE
NIOBIC adj of or containing niobium in the pentavalent state
NIOBITE another name for **>** COLUMBITE
NIOBITES > NIOBITE
NIOBIUM n white metallic element
NIOBIUMS > NIOBIUM
NIOBOUS adj of or containing niobium in the trivalent state
NIP vb hurry ▷ n pinch or light bite
NIPA n palm tree of S and SE Asia
NIPAS > NIPA
NIPCHEESE n ship's purser
NIPPED > NIP
NIPPER n small child ▷ vb secure with rope
NIPPERED > NIPPER
NIPPERING > NIPPER
NIPPERKIN n small quantity of alcohol
NIPPERS pl n instrument or tool for pinching or squeezing
NIPPIER > NIPPY
NIPPIEST > NIPPY
NIPPILY > NIPPY
NIPPINESS > NIPPY
NIPPING > NIP
NIPPINGLY > NIP
NIPPLE n projection in the centre of a breast ▷ vb provide with a nipple
NIPPLED > NIPPLE
NIPPLES > NIPPLE
NIPPLING > NIPPLE
NIPPY adj frosty or chilly
NIPS > NIP
NIPTER n type of religious ceremony
NIPTERS > NIPTER
NIQAAB same as **>** NIQAB
NIQAABS > NIQAAB
NIQAB n type of veil worn by some Muslim women
NIQABS > NIQAB
NIRAMIAI n sumo wrestling procedure
NIRAMIAIS > NIRAMIAI
NIRL vb shrivel
NIRLED > NIRL
NIRLIE variant of **>** NIRLY
NIRLIER > NIRLY
NIRLIEST > NIRLY
NIRLING > NIRL
NIRLIT > NIRL
NIRLS > NIRL
NIRLY adj shrivelled
NIRVANA n absolute spiritual enlightenment and bliss
NIRVANAS > NIRVANA
NIRVANIC > NIRVANA
NIS n friendly goblin
NISBERRY same as **>** NASEBERRY
NISEI n native-born citizen of the US or Canada whose parents were Japanese

NISEIS > NISEI
NISGUL n smallest and weakest bird in a brood of chickens
NISGULS > NISGUL
NISH n nothing
NISHES > NISH
NISI adj (of a court order) coming into effect on a specified date
NISSE same as > NIS
NISSES > NISSE
NISUS n impulse towards or striving after a goal
NIT n egg or larva of a louse
NITCHIE n offensive term for a Native American person
NITCHIES > NITCHIE
NITE variant of > NIGHT
NITER same as > NITRE
NITERIE n nightclub
NITERIES > NITERIE
NITERS > NITER
NITERY > NITER
NITES > NITE
NITHER vb shiver
NITHERED > NITHER
NITHERING > NITHER
NITHERS > NITHER
NITHING n coward
NITHINGS > NITHING
NITID adj bright
NITINOL n metal alloy
NITINOLS > NITINOL
NITON less common name for > RADON
NITONS > NITON
NITPICK vb criticize unnecessarily
NITPICKED > NITPICK
NITPICKER > NITPICK
NITPICKS > NITPICK
NITPICKY > NITPICK
NITRAMINE another name for > TETRYL
NITRATE n compound of nitric acid, used as a fertilizer ▷ vb treat with nitric acid or a nitrate
NITRATED > NITRATE
NITRATES > NITRATE
NITRATINE n type of mineral
NITRATING > NITRATE
NITRATION > NITRATE
NITRATOR > NITRATE
NITRATORS > NITRATE
NITRE n potassium nitrate
NITREOUS adj as in nitreous silica another name for quartz glass
NITRES > NITRE
NITRIC adj of or containing nitrogen
NITRID same as > NITRIDE
NITRIDE n compound of nitrogen ▷ vb make into a nitride
NITRIDED > NITRIDE
NITRIDES > NITRIDE
NITRIDING > NITRIDE
NITRIDS > NITRID
NITRIFIED > NITRIFY
NITRIFIER > NITRIFY
NITRIFIES > NITRIFY
NITRIFY vb treat or cause to react with nitrogen

NITRIL same as > NITRILE
NITRILE n any one of a particular class of organic compounds
NITRILES > NITRILE
NITRILS > NITRIL
NITRITE n salt or ester of nitrous acid
NITRITES > NITRITE
NITRO n nitroglycerine
NITROGEN n colourless odourless gas that forms four fifths of the air
NITROGENS > NITROGEN
NITROLIC adj pertaining to a group of acids
NITROS > NITRO
NITROSO adj of a particular monovalent group
NITROSYL another word for > NITROSO
NITROSYLS > NITROSYL
NITROUS adj derived from or containing nitrogen in a low valency state
NITROX n mixture of nitrogen and oxygen used in diving
NITROXES > NITROX
NITROXYL n type of chemical
NITROXYLS > NITROXYL
NITRY adj nitrous
NITRYL n chemical compound
NITRYLS > NITRYL
NITS > NIT
NITTIER > NITTY
NITTIEST > NITTY
NITTY adj infested with nits
NITWIT n stupid person
NITWITS > NITWIT
NITWITTED > NITWIT
NIVAL adj of or growing in or under snow
NIVATION n weathering of rock around a patch of snow by alternate freezing and thawing
NIVATIONS > NIVATION
NIVEOUS adj resembling snow, esp in colour
NIX sentence substitute be careful! watch out! ▷ n rejection or refusal ▷ vb veto, deny, reject, or forbid (plans, suggestions, etc)
NIXE n water sprite
NIXED > NIX
NIXER n spare-time job
NIXERS > NIXER
NIXES > NIX
NIXIE n female water sprite, usually unfriendly to humans
NIXIES > NIXIE
NIXING > NIX
NIXY same as > NIXIE
NIZAM n (formerly) a Turkish regular soldier
NIZAMATE n territory of the nizam
NIZAMATES > NIZAMATE
NIZAMS > NIZAM
NKOSI n term of address to a superior
NKOSIS > NKOSI

NO interj expresses denial, disagreement, or refusal ▷ adj not any, not a ▷ adv not at all ▷ n answer or vote of 'no'
NOAH n shark
NOAHS > NOAH
NOB n person of wealth or social distinction
NOBBIER > NOB
NOBBIEST > NOB
NOBBILY > NOB
NOBBINESS > NOB
NOBBLE vb attract the attention of
NOBBLED > NOBBLE
NOBBLER > NOBBLE
NOBBLERS > NOBBLE
NOBBLES > NOBBLE
NOBBLING > NOBBLE
NOBBUT adv nothing but
NOBBY > NOB
NOBELIUM n artificially produced radioactive element
NOBELIUMS > NOBELIUM
NOBILESSE same as > NOBLESSE
NOBILIARY adj of or relating to the nobility
NOBILITY n quality of being noble
NOBLE adj showing or having high moral qualities ▷ n member of the nobility
NOBLEMAN n person of noble rank
NOBLEMEN > NOBLEMAN
NOBLENESS > NOBLE
NOBLER > NOBLE
NOBLES > NOBLE
NOBLESSE n noble birth or condition
NOBLESSES > NOBLESSE
NOBLEST > NOBLE
NOBLY > NOBLE
NOBODIES > NOBODY
NOBODY pron no person ▷ n person of no importance
NOBS > NOB
NOCAKE n Indian meal made from dried corn
NOCAKES > NOCAKE
NOCEBO n harmless substance that causes harmful effects in patients who expect it to be harmful
NOCEBOS > NOCEBO
NOCENT n guilty person
NOCENTLY > NOCENT
NOCENTS > NOCENT
NOCHEL same as > NOTCHEL
NOCHELED same as > NOTCHELED
NOCHELING n refusal to pay another person's debts
NOCHELLED > NOCHEL
NOCHELS > NOCHEL
NOCK n notch on an arrow or a bow for the bowstring ▷ vb fit (an arrow) on a bowstring
NOCKED > NOCK
NOCKET same as > NACKET
NOCKETS > NOCKET
NOCKING > NOCK
NOCKS > NOCK
NOCTILIO n type of bat

NOCTILIOS > NOCTILIO
NOCTILUCA n type of bioluminescent unicellular marine organism
NOCTUA n type of moth
NOCTUARY n nightly journal
NOCTUAS > NOCTUA
NOCTUID n type of nocturnal moth ▷ adj of or relating to this type of moth
NOCTUIDS > NOCTUID
NOCTULE n any of several large Old World insectivorous bats
NOCTULES > NOCTULE
NOCTUOID adj of or like a noctuid ▷ n member of the family of moths Noctuidae
NOCTUOIDS > NOCTUOID
NOCTURIA n excessive urination during the night
NOCTURIAS > NOCTURIA
NOCTURN n any of the main sections of the office of matins
NOCTURNAL adj of the night ▷ n something active at night
NOCTURNE n short dreamy piece of music
NOCTURNES > NOCTURNE
NOCTURNS > NOCTURN
NOCUOUS adj harmful
NOCUOUSLY > NOCUOUS
NOD vb lower and raise (one's head) briefly in agreement or greeting ▷ n act of nodding
NODAL adj of or like a node
NODALISE same as > NODALIZE
NODALISED same as > NODALISE
NODALISES same as > NODALISE
NODALITY > NODAL
NODALIZE vb make something nodal
NODALIZED > NODALIZE
NODALIZES > NODALIZE
NODALLY > NODAL
NODATED adj knotted
NODATION n knottiness
NODATIONS > NODATION
NODDED > NOD
NODDER > NOD
NODDERS > NOD
NODDIER > NODDY
NODDIES > NODDY
NODDIEST > NODDY
NODDING > NOD
NODDINGLY > NOD
NODDINGS > NOD
NODDLE n head ▷ vb nod (the head), as through drowsiness
NODDLED > NODDLE
NODDLES > NODDLE
NODDLING > NODDLE
NODDY n tropical tern with a dark plumage ▷ adj very easy to use or understand
NODE n point on a plant stem from which leaves grow
NODES > NODE
NODI > NODUS
NODICAL adj of or relating to the nodes of a celestial body

n

NODOSE adj having nodes or knotlike swellings

NODOSITY > NODOSE

NODOUS same as > NODOSE

NODS > NOD

NODULAR > NODULE

NODULATED > NODULE

NODULE n small knot or lump

NODULED > NODULE

NODULES > NODULE

NODULOSE > NODULE

NODULOUS > NODULE

NODUS n problematic idea, situation, etc

NOEL n Christmas

NOELS > NOEL

NOES > NO

NOESES > NOESIS

NOESIS n exercise of reason

NOESISES > NOESIS

NOETIC adj of or relating to the mind

NOG same as > NOGGING

NOGAKU n Japanese style of drama

NOGG same as > NOG

NOGGED adj built with timber and brick

NOGGIN n head

NOGGING n short horizontal timber member

NOGGINGS > NOGGING

NOGGINS > NOGGIN

NOGGS > NOGG

NOGOODNIK n worthless person

NOGS > NOG

NOH n stylized classic drama of Japan

NOHOW adv under any conditions

NOHOWISH > NOHOW

NOIL n short or knotted fibres that are separated from the long fibres by combing

NOILIER > NOILY

NOILIES > NOILY

NOILIEST > NOILY

NOILS > NOIL

NOILY n dry white vermouth drink from France ▷ adj resembling a noil

NOINT vb anoint

NOINTED > NOINT

NOINTER n mischievous child

NOINTERS > NOINTER

NOINTING > NOINT

NOINTS > NOINT

NOIR adj (of a film) showing characteristics of a film noir, in plot or style ▷ n film noir

NOIRISH > NOIR

NOIRS > NOIR

NOISE n sound, usu a loud or disturbing one ▷ vb spread (news or gossip)

NOISED > NOISE

NOISEFUL > NOISE

NOISELESS adj making little or no sound

NOISENIK n rock musician who performs loud harsh music

NOISENIKS > NOISENIK

NOISES > NOISE

NOISETTE n hazelnut chocolate ▷ adj flavoured or made with hazelnuts

NOISETTES > NOISETTE

NOISIER > NOISY

NOISIEST > NOISY

NOISILY > NOISY

NOISINESS > NOISY

NOISING > NOISE

NOISOME adj (of smells) offensive

NOISOMELY > NOISOME

NOISY adj making a lot of noise

NOLE same as > NOLL

NOLES > NOLE

NOLITION n unwillingness

NOLITIONS > NOLITION

NOLL n head

NOLLS > NOLL

NOLO n as in nolo contendere plea indicating that the defendant does not wish to contest the case

NOLOS > NOLO

NOM n name

NOMA n gangrenous inflammation of the mouth

NOMAD n member of a tribe with no fixed dwelling place

NOMADE same as > NOMAD

NOMADES > NOMADE

NOMADIC adj relating to or characteristic of nomads

NOMADIES > NOMADY

NOMADISE same as > NOMADIZE

NOMADISED > NOMADISE

NOMADISES > NOMADISE

NOMADISM > NOMAD

NOMADISMS > NOMAD

NOMADIZE vb live as nomads

NOMADIZED > NOMADIZE

NOMADIZES > NOMADIZE

NOMADS > NOMAD

NOMADY n practice of living like nomads

NOMARCH n head of an ancient Egyptian nome

NOMARCHS > NOMARCH

NOMARCHY n any of the provinces of modern Greece

NOMAS > NOMA

NOMBLES variant spelling of > NUMBLES

NOMBRIL n point on a shield

NOMBRILS > NOMBRIL

NOME n any of the former provinces of modern Greece

NOMEN n ancient Roman's second name

NOMENS > NOMEN

NOMES > NOME

NOMIC adj normal or habitual

NOMINA > NOMEN

NOMINABLE adj that can be nominated

NOMINAL adj in name only ▷ n nominal element

NOMINALLY > NOMINAL

NOMINALS > NOMINAL

NOMINATE vb suggest as a candidate ▷ adj having a particular name

NOMINATED > NOMINATE

NOMINATES > NOMINATE

NOMINATOR > NOMINATE

NOMINEE n candidate

NOMINEES > NOMINEE

NOMISM n adherence to laws as a primary exercise of religion

NOMISMS > NOMISM

NOMISTIC > NOMISM

NOMOCRACY n government based on the rule of law rather than arbitrary will, terror, etc

NOMOGENY n law of life originating as a natural process

NOMOGRAM n arrangement of two linear or logarithmic scales

NOMOGRAMS > NOMOGRAM

NOMOGRAPH same as > NOMOGRAM

NOMOI > NOMOS

NOMOLOGIC > NOMOLOGY

NOMOLOGY n science of law and law-making

NOMOS n convention

NOMOTHETE n legislator

NOMS > NOM

NON adv not

NONA n sleeping sickness

NONACID adj not acid ▷ n nonacid substance

NONACIDIC adj not acidic

NONACIDS > NONACID

NONACTING adj not acting ▷ n acting of poor quality

NONACTION n not action

NONACTIVE adj not active

NONACTOR n person who is not an actor

NONACTORS > NONACTOR

NONADDICT n person who is not an addict

NONADULT n person who is not an adult

NONADULTS > NONADULT

NONAGE n state of being under full legal age

NONAGED > NONAGE

NONAGES > NONAGE

NONAGON n geometric figure with nine sides

NONAGONAL > NONAGON

NONAGONS > NONAGON

NONANE n type of chemical compound

NONANES > NONANE

NONANIMAL adj not animal

NONANOIC adj as in nonanoic acid colourless oily fatty acid with a rancid odour

NONANSWER n unsatisfactory reply ▷ vb decline to answer

NONARABLE adj not arable

NONARIES > NONARY

NONART n something that does not constitute art

NONARTIST n person who is not an artist

NONARTS > NONART

NONARY n set or group of nine

NONAS same as > NONES

NONATOMIC adj not atomic

NONAUTHOR n person who is not the author

NONAVIAN adj not relating to birds

NONBANK n business or institution that is not a bank but provides similar services

NONBANKS > NONBANK

NONBASIC adj not basic

NONBEING n philosophical problem relating to the question of existence

NONBEINGS > NONBEING

NONBELIEF n state of not believing

NONBINARY adj not binary

NONBITING adj not biting

NONBLACK n person who is not Black

NONBLACKS > NONBLACK

NONBODIES > NONBODY

NONBODY n nonphysical nature of a person

NONBONDED adj not bonded

NONBOOK n book with little substance

NONBOOKS > NONBOOK

NONBRAND adj not produced by a well-known company

NONBUYING adj not buying

NONCAKING adj not liable to cake

NONCAMPUS adj not on campus

NONCAREER adj not career-related

NONCASH adj other than cash

NONCASUAL adj not casual

NONCAUSAL adj not causal

NONCE n present time or occasion

NONCEREAL adj not cereal

NONCES > NONCE

NONCHURCH adj not related to the church ▷ vb take away the status of a church

NONCLASS n lack of class

NONCLING adj not liable to stick

NONCODING adj (of DNA) not containing instructions for making protein

NONCOITAL adj not involving sexual intercourse

NONCOKING adj not liable to coke

NONCOLA n soft drink other than cola

NONCOLAS > NONCOLA

NONCOLOR same as > NONCOLOUR

NONCOLORS > NONCOLOR

NONCOLOUR n colour such as black or white

NONCOM n person not involved in combat

NONCOMBAT adj not involved in combat

NONCOMS > NONCOM

NONCONCUR vb disagree

NONCORE adj not central or essential

NONCOUNT adj not capable of being counted

NONCOUNTY adj not controlled or run by a county

NONCREDIT adj relating to an educational course not providing a credit towards a degree

NONCRIME n incident that is not a crime

NONCRIMES > NONCRIME

NONCRISES > NONCRISIS

NONCRISIS n situation that is not a crisis

NONCYCLIC adj not cyclic

NONDAIRY adj not containing dairy products

NONDANCE n series of movements that do not constitute a dance

NONDANCER n person who is not a dancer

NONDANCES > NONDANCE

NONDEALER adj person who is not a dealer

NONDEGREE adj not leading to a degree

NONDEMAND adj not involving demand

NONDESERT adj not belonging to the desert

NONDOCTOR n person who is not a doctor

NONDOLLAR adj not involving the dollar

NONDRIP adj (of paint) specially formulated to minimize dripping during application

NONDRIVER n person who does not drive

NONDRUG adj not involving the use of drugs

NONDRYING adj not drying

NONE pron not any

NONEDIBLE n not edible

NONEGO n everything that is outside one's conscious self

NONEGOS > NONEGO

NONELECT n person not chosen

NONELECTS > NONELECT

NONELITE adj not elite

NONEMPTY adj mathematical term

NONENDING adj not ending

NONENERGY adj without energy

NONENTITY n insignificant person or thing

NONENTRY n failure to enter

NONEQUAL adj not equal ▷ n person who is not the equal of another person

NONEQUALS > NONEQUAL

NONEROTIC adj not erotic

NONES n (in the Roman calendar) the ninth day before the ides of each month

NONESUCH n matchless person or thing

NONET n piece of music composed for a group of nine instruments

NONETHNIC n not ethnic

NONETS > NONET

NONETTE same as > NONET

NONETTES > NONETTE

NONETTI > NONETTO

NONETTO same as > NONET

NONETTOS > NONETTO

NONEVENT n disappointing or insignificant occurrence

NONEVENTS > NONEVENT

NONEXEMPT adj not exempt

NONEXOTIC adj not exotic

NONEXPERT n person who is not an expert

NONEXTANT adj no longer in existence

NONFACT n event or thing not provable

NONFACTOR n something that is not a factor

NONFACTS > NONFACT

NONFADING adj colourfast

NONFAMILY n household that does not consist of a family

NONFAN n person who is not a fan

NONFANS > NONFAN

NONFARM adj not connected with a farm

NONFARMER n person who is not a farmer

NONFAT adj fat free

NONFATAL adj not resulting in or capable of causing death

NONFATTY adj not fatty

NONFEUDAL adj not feudal

NONFILIAL adj not involving parent-child relationship

NONFINAL adj not final

NONFINITE adj not finite

NONFISCAL adj not involving government funds

NONFLUID adj not fluid ▷ n something that is not a fluid

NONFLUIDS > NONFLUID

NONFLYING adj not capable of flying

NONFOCAL adj not focal

NONFOOD n item that is not food ▷ adj relating to items other than food

NONFOODS > NONFOOD

NONFORMAL adj not formal

NONFOSSIL adj not consisting of fossils

NONFROZEN adj not frozen

NONFUEL adj not relating to fuel ▷ n energy not used for generating heat, power, or electricity

NONFUELS > NONFUEL

NONFUNDED adj not receiving funding

NONG n stupid or incompetent person

NONGAME adj not pursued for competitive sport purposes

NONGAY n person who is not gay

NONGAYS > NONGAY

NONGHETTO adj not belonging to the ghetto

NONGLARE adj not causing glare ▷ n any of various nonglare materials

NONGLARES > NONGLARE

NONGLAZED adj not glazed

NONGLOSSY adj not glossy

NONGOLFER n person who is not a golfer

NONGRADED adj not graded

NONGREASY adj not greasy

NONGREEN adj not green

NONGROWTH n failure to grow ▷ adj characterized by a lack of growth

NONGS > NONG

NONGUEST n person who is not a guest

NONGUESTS > NONGUEST

NONGUILT n state of being innocent

NONGUILTS > NONGUILT

NONHARDY adj fragile

NONHEME adj of dietary iron, obtained from vegetable foods

NONHERO n person who is not a hero

NONHEROES > NONHERO

NONHEROIC adj not heroic

NONHOME adj not of the home

NONHUMAN n something not human

NONHUMANS > NONHUMAN

NONHUNTER n person or thing that does not hunt

NONI n tree of SE Asia and the Pacific islands

NONIDEAL adj not ideal

NONILLION n (in Britain, France, and Germany) the number represented as one followed by 54 zeros

NONIMAGE n person who is not a celebrity

NONIMAGES > NONIMAGE

NONIMMUNE adj not immune

NONIMPACT adj not involving impact ▷ n lack of impact

NONINERT adj not inert

NONINJURY adj not involving injury

NONINSECT n animal that is not an insect

NONIONIC adj not ionic

NONIRON adj not requiring ironing

NONIS > NONI

NONISSUE n matter of little importance

NONISSUES > NONISSUE

NONJOINER n person who does not join (an organisation, etc)

NONJURIES > NONJURY

NONJURING adj refusing the oath of allegiance

NONJUROR n person who refuses to take an oath, as of allegiance

NONJURORS > NONJUROR

NONJURY n trial without a jury

NONKIN n those who are not related to a person

NONKINS > NONKIN

NONKOSHER adj not kosher

NONLABOR same as > NONLABOUR

NONLABOUR adj not concerned with labour

NONLAWYER n person who is not a lawyer

NONLEADED adj not leaded

NONLEAFY adj not leafy

NONLEAGUE adj not belonging to a league

NONLEGAL adj not legal

NONLEGUME n not a pod of the pea or bean family

NONLETHAL adj not resulting in or capable of causing death

NONLEVEL adj not level

NONLIABLE adj not liable

NONLIFE n matter which is not living

NONLINEAL same as > NONLINEAR

NONLINEAR adj not of, in, along, or relating to a line

NONLIQUID n substance which is not liquid

NONLIVES > NONLIFE

NONLIVING adj not living

NONLOCAL adj not of, affecting, or confined to a limited area or part ▷ n person who is not local to an area

NONLOCALS > NONLOCAL

NONLOVING adj not loving

NONLOYAL adj not loyal

NONLYRIC adj without lyrics

NONMAJOR n student who is not majoring in a specified subject

NONMAJORS > NONMAJOR

NONMAN n being that is not a man

NONMANUAL adj not manual

NONMARKET adj not relating to markets

NONMATURE adj not mature

NONMEAT n substance that does not contain meat ▷ adj not containing meat

NONMEATS > NONMEAT

NONMEMBER n person who is not a member of a particular club or organization

NONMEN > NONMAN

NONMENTAL adj not mental

NONMETAL n chemical element that forms acidic oxides and is a poor conductor of heat and electricity

NONMETALS > NONMETAL

NONMETRIC adj not metric

NONMETRO adj not metropolitan

NONMOBILE adj not mobile

NONMODAL adj not modal

NONMODERN adj not modern

NONMONEY adj not involving money

NONMORAL adj not involving morality

NONMORTAL adj not fatal

NONMOTILE adj not capable of movement

NONMOVING adj not moving

NONMUSIC n (unpleasant) noise

NONMUSICS > NONMUSIC

NONMUTANT n person or thing that is not mutated

NONMUTUAL adj not mutual

NONNASAL adj not nasal

NONNATIVE adj not native ▷ n person who is not native to a place

n

NONNAVAL adj not belonging to the navy

NONNEURAL adj not neural

NONNEWS adj not concerned with news

NONNIES > NONNY

NONNOBLE adj not noble

NONNORMAL adj not normal

NONNOVEL n literary work that is not a novel

NONNOVELS > NONNOVEL

NONNY n meaningless word

NONOBESE adj not obese

NONOHMIC adj not having electrical resistance

NONOILY adj not oily

NONORAL adj not oral

NONORALLY > NONORAL

NONOWNER n person who is not an owner

NONOWNERS > NONOWNER

NONPAGAN n person who is not a pagan

NONPAGANS > NONPAGAN

NONPAID adj without payment

NONPAPAL adj not of the pope

NONPAPIST adj not papist

NONPAR adj nonparticipating

NONPAREIL n person or thing that is unsurpassed ▷ adj having no match or equal

NONPARENT n person who is not a parent

NONPARITY n state of not being equal

NONPAROUS adj never having given birth

NONPARTY adj not connected with a political party

NONPAST n grammatical term

NONPASTS > NONPAST

NONPAYING adj (of guests, customers, etc) not expected or requested to pay

NONPEAK n period of low demand

NONPEAKS > NONPEAK

NONPERSON n person regarded as nonexistent or unimportant

NONPLANAR adj not planar

NONPLAY n social behaviour that is not classed as play

NONPLAYER n person not playing

NONPLAYS > NONPLAY

NONPLIANT adj not pliant

NONPLUS vb put at a loss ▷ n state of utter perplexity prohibiting action or speech

NONPLUSED > NONPLUS

NONPLUSES > NONPLUS

NONPOETIC adj not poetic

NONPOINT adj without a specific site

NONPOLAR adj not polar

NONPOLICE adj not related to the police

NONPOOR adj not poor ▷ n person who is not poor

NONPOORS > NONPOOR

NONPOROUS adj not permeable to water, air, or other fluids

NONPOSTAL adj not postal

NONPRINT adj published in a format other than print on paper

NONPROFIT n organization that is not intended to make a profit

NONPROS vb enter a judgment of non prosequitur

NONPROVEN adj not tried and tested

NONPUBLIC adj not public

NONQUOTA adj not included in a quota

NONRACIAL adj not related to racial factors or discrimination

NONRACISM n absence of racism

NONRANDOM adj not random

NONRATED adj not rated

NONREADER n person who does not or cannot read

NONRETURN adj denoting a mechanism that permits flow in a pipe in one direction only

NONRHOTIC adj denoting or speaking a dialect of English in which preconsonantal r s are not pronounced

NONRIGID adj not rigid

NONRIOTER n person who does not participate in a riot

NONRIVAL n person or thing not competing for success

NONRIVALS > NONRIVAL

NONROYAL adj not royal ▷ n person who is not a member of a royal family

NONROYALS > NONROYAL

NONRUBBER adj not containing rubber

NONRULING adj not ruling

NONRUN adj (of tights) not laddering

NONRUNNER n person who is not a runner

NONRURAL adj not rural

NONSACRED adj not sacred

NONSALINE adj not containing salt

NONSCHOOL adj not relating to school

NONSECRET adj not sacred

NONSECURE adj not secure

NONSELF n foreign molecule in the body

NONSELVES > NONSELF

NONSENSE n something that has or makes no sense ▷ interj exclamation of disagreement

NONSENSES > NONSENSE

NONSERIAL adj not serial

NONSEXIST adj not discriminating on the basis of gender, esp not against women

NONSEXUAL adj not sexual

NONSHRINK adj not likely to shrink

NONSIGNER n person who cannot use sign language

NONSKATER n person who does not skate

NONSKED n non-scheduled aeroplane

NONSKEDS > NONSKED

NONSKID adj designed to reduce skidding

NONSKIER n person who does not ski

NONSKIERS > NONSKIER

NONSLIP adj designed to prevent slipping

NONSMOKER n person who does not smoke

NONSOCIAL adj not social

NONSOLAR adj not related to the sun

NONSOLID n substance that is not a solid

NONSOLIDS > NONSOLID

NONSPEECH adj not involving speech ▷ n absence of speech

NONSTAPLE adj not staple

NONSTATE adj not relating to the state

NONSTATIC adj not static

NONSTEADY adj not steady

NONSTICK adj coated with a substance that food will not stick to when cooked

NONSTICKY adj not sticky

NONSTOP adv without a stop ▷ adj without a stop ▷ n nonstop flight

NONSTOPS > NONSTOP

NONSTORY n story of little substance or importance

NONSTYLE n style that cannot be identified

NONSTYLES > NONSTYLE

NONSUCH same as > NONESUCH

NONSUCHES > NONSUCH

NONSUGAR n substance that is not a sugar

NONSUGARS > NONSUGAR

NONSUIT n order of a judge dismissing a suit ▷ vb order the dismissal of the suit of (a person)

NONSUITED > NONSUIT

NONSUITS > NONSUIT

NONSYSTEM adj having no system

NONTALKER n person who does not talk

NONTARGET adj not being a target

NONTARIFF adj without tariff

NONTAX n tax that has little real effect

NONTAXES > NONTAX

NONTHEISM n belief there is no God

NONTHEIST n person who believes the existence or non-existence of God is irrelevant

NONTIDAL adj not having a tide

NONTITLE adj without title

NONTONAL adj not written in a key

NONTONIC adj not tonic

NONTOXIC n substance which is not poisonous ▷ adj not poisonous

NONTOXICS > NONTOXIC

NONTRAGIC adj not tragic

NONTRIBAL adj not tribal

NONTRUMP adj not of the trump suit

NONTRUTH same as > UNTRUTH

NONTRUTHS > NONTRUTH

NONUNION adj (of a company) not employing trade union members ▷ n failure of broken bones or bone fragments to heal

NONUNIONS > NONUNION

NONUNIQUE adj not unique

NONUPLE adj ninefold ▷ n ninefold number

NONUPLES > NONUPLE

NONUPLET n child born in a multiple birth of nine siblings

NONUPLETS > NONUPLET

NONURBAN adj not rural

NONURGENT adj not urgent

NONUSABLE adj not usable

NONUSE n failure to use

NONUSER > NONUSE

NONUSERS > NONUSE

NONUSES > NONUSE

NONUSING > NONUSE

NONVACANT adj not vacant

NONVALID adj not valid

NONVECTOR n quantity without size and direction

NONVENOUS adj not venous

NONVERBAL adj not involving the use of language

NONVESTED adj not vested

NONVIABLE adj not viable

NONVIEWER n person who does not watch (television)

NONVIRAL adj not caused by a virus

NONVIRGIN n person who is not a virgin

NONVIRILE adj not virile

NONVISUAL adj not visual

NONVITAL adj not vital

NONVOCAL n music track without singing

NONVOCALS > NONVOCAL

NONVOTER n person who does not vote

NONVOTERS > NONVOTER

NONVOTING adj (of shares in a company) not entitling the owner to vote at company meetings

NONWAGE adj not part of wages

NONWAR n state of nonviolence

NONWARS > NONWAR

NONWHITE n person who is not White

NONWHITES > NONWHITE

NONWINGED adj without wings

NONWOODY adj not woody

NONWOOL adj not wool

NONWORD n series of letters not recognised as a word

NONWORDS > NONWORD

NONWORK adj not involving work ▷ n part of life which does not involve work

NONWORKER n person who does not work

SECTION 1: Words between 2 and 9 letters in length

NONWORKS > NONWORK

NONWOVEN n material made by a method other than weaving

NONWOVENS > NONWOVEN

NONWRITER n person who is not a writer

NONYL n type of chemical

NONYLS > NONYL

NONZERO adj not equal to zero

NOO n type of Japanese musical drama

NOOB same as > NEWBIE

NOOBS > NOOB

NOODGE vb annoy persistently

NOODGED > NOODGE

NOODGES > NOODGE

NOODGING > NOODGE

NOODLE n ribbon-like strip of pasta ▷ vb improvise aimlessly on a musical instrument

NOODLED > NOODLE

NOODLEDOM n state of being a simpleton

NOODLES > NOODLE

NOODLING n aimless musical improvisation

NOODLINGS > NOODLING

NOOGIE n act of inflicting pain by rubbing head hard

NOOGIES > NOOGIE

NOOIT interj South African exclamation of surprise

NOOK n corner or recess

NOOKIE same as > NOOKY

NOOKIER > NOOKY

NOOKIES > NOOKIE

NOOKIEST > NOOKY

NOOKLIKE > NOOK

NOOKS > NOOK

NOOKY n sexual intercourse ▷ adj resembling a nook

NOOLOGIES > NOOLOGY

NOOLOGY n study of intuition

NOOMETRY n mind measurement

NOON n twelve o'clock midday ▷ vb take a rest at noon

NOONDAY adj happening at noon ▷ n middle of the day

NOONDAYS > NOONDAY

NOONED > NOON

NOONER n event taking place in the middle of the day

NOONERS > NOONER

NOONING n midday break for rest or food

NOONINGS > NOONING

NOONS > NOON

NOONTIDE same as > NOONTIME

NOONTIDES > NOONTIDE

NOONTIME n middle of the day

NOONTIMES > NOONTIME

NOOP n point of the elbow

NOOPS > NOOP

NOOSE n loop in the end of a rope, tied with a slipknot ▷ vb catch in a noose

NOOSED > NOOSE

NOOSELIKE adj like a noose

NOOSER n person who uses a noose

NOOSERS > NOOSER

NOOSES > NOOSE

NOOSING > NOOSE

NOOSPHERE n sphere of human thought

NOOTROPIC adj acting on mind

NOPAL n type of cactus

NOPALES > NOPAL

NOPALITO n small cactus

NOPALITOS > NOPALITO

NOPALS > NOPAL

NOPE interj no

NOPLACE same as > NOWHERE

NOR prep and not

NORDIC adj of competitions in cross-country racing and ski-jumping

NORDICITY n quality of being Nordic

NORI n edible seaweed

NORIA n water wheel with buckets attached to its rim

NORIAS > NORIA

NORIMON n Japanese passenger vehicle

NORIMONS > NORIMON

NORIS > NORI

NORITE n variety of gabbro

NORITES > NORITE

NORITIC > NORITE

NORK n vulgar word for a female breast

NORKS > NORK

NORLAND n north part of a country or the earth

NORLANDS > NORLAND

NORM n standard that is regarded as normal

NORMA n norm or standard

NORMAL adj usual, regular, or typical ▷ n usual or regular state, degree or form

NORMALCY > NORMAL

NORMALISE same as > NORMALIZE

NORMALITY > NORMAL

NORMALIZE vb make or become normal

NORMALLY adv as a rule

NORMALS > NORMAL

NORMAN n post used for winding on a ship

NORMANDE n type of cattle

NORMANDES > NORMANDE

NORMANS > NORMAN

NORMAS > NORMA

NORMATIVE adj of or setting a norm or standard

NORMCORE n deliberately normal style of dress

NORMCORES > NORMCORE

NORMED n mathematical term

NORMLESS adj without a norm

NORMS > NORM

NOROVIRUS n virus that causes gastroenteritis

NORSEL vb fit with short lines for fastening hooks

NORSELLED > NORSEL

NORSELLER > NORSEL

NORSELS > NORSEL

NORTENA same as > NORTENO

NORTENAS > NORTENA

NORTENO n type of Mexican music

NORTENOS > NORTENO

NORTH n direction towards the North Pole, opposite south ▷ adj in the north ▷ adv in, to, or towards the north ▷ vb move north

NORTHEAST adv (in or to) direction between north and east ▷ n point of the compass or direction midway between north and east ▷ adj of or denoting the northeastern part of a specified country, area, etc

NORTHED > NORTH

NORTHER n wind or storm from the north ▷ vb move north

NORTHERED > NORTHER

NORTHERLY adj of or in the north ▷ adv towards the north ▷ n wind from the north

NORTHERN adj situated in or towards the north ▷ n person from the north

NORTHERNS > NORTHERN

NORTHERS > NORTHER

NORTHING n movement or distance covered in a northerly direction

NORTHINGS > NORTHING

NORTHLAND n lands that are far to the north

NORTHMOST adj situated furthest north

NORTHS > NORTH

NORTHWARD adv towards the north

NORTHWEST adv (in or to) direction between north and west ▷ n point of the compass or direction midway between north and west ▷ adj of or denoting the northwestern part of a specified country, area, etc

NORWARD same as > NORTHWARD

NORWARDS same as > NORWARD

NOS > NO

NOSE n organ of smell, used also in breathing ▷ vb move forward slowly and carefully

NOSEAN n type of mineral

NOSEANS > NOSEAN

NOSEBAG n bag containing feed fastened round a horse's head

NOSEBAGS > NOSEBAG

NOSEBAND n part of a horse's bridle that goes around the nose

NOSEBANDS > NOSEBAND

NOSEBLEED n bleeding from the nose

NOSED > NOSE

NOSEDIVE vb (of an aircraft) plunge suddenly with the nose pointing downwards

NOSEDIVED > NOSEDIVE

NOSEDIVES > NOSEDIVE

NOSEDOVE > NOSEDIVE

NOSEGAY n small bunch of flowers

NOSEGAYS > NOSEGAY

NOSEGUARD n position in American football

NOSELESS > NOSE

NOSELIKE > NOSE

NOSELITE same as > NOSEAN

NOSELITES > NOSELITE

NOSEPIECE same as > NOSEBAND

NOSER n strong headwind

NOSERS > NOSER

NOSES > NOSE

NOSEWHEEL n wheel fitted under the nose of an aircraft

NOSEY adj prying or inquisitive ▷ n nosey person

NOSEYS > NOSEY

NOSH n food ▷ vb eat

NOSHED > NOSH

NOSHER > NOSH

NOSHERIE same as > NOSHERY

NOSHERIES > NOSHERIE

NOSHERS > NOSH

NOSHERY n restaurant or other place where food is served

NOSHES > NOSH

NOSHING > NOSH

NOSIER > NOSY

NOSIES > NOSY

NOSIEST > NOSY

NOSILY > NOSY

NOSINESS > NOSY

NOSING n edge of a step or stair tread

NOSINGS > NOSING

NOSODE n homeopathic remedy

NOSODES > NOSODE

NOSOLOGIC > NOSOLOGY

NOSOLOGY n branch of medicine concerned with the classification of diseases

NOSTALGIA n sentimental longing for the past

NOSTALGIC adj of or characterized by nostalgia ▷ n person who indulges in nostalgia

NOSTOC n type of bacterium occurring in moist places

NOSTOCS > NOSTOC

NOSTOI > NOSTOS

NOSTOLOGY n scientific study of ageing

NOSTOS n story of a return home

NOSTRIL n one of the two openings at the end of the nose

NOSTRILS > NOSTRIL

NOSTRO adj as in nostro account bank account conducted by a British bank with a foreign bank

NOSTRUM n quack medicine

NOSTRUMS > NOSTRUM

NOSY adj prying or inquisitive ▷ n inquisitive person

NOT adv expressing negation, refusal, or denial

NOTA > NOTUM

NOTABILIA n things worthy of notice

NOTABLE adj worthy of being noted, remarkable ▷ n person of distinction

NOTABLES > NOTABLE

NOTABLY adv particularly or especially

NOTAEUM n back of a bird's body

NOTAEUMS > NOTAEUM

NOTAIRE n (in France) notary

NOTAIRES > NOTAIRE

NOTAL > NOTUM

NOTANDA > NOTANDUM

NOTANDUM n notable fact

NOTAPHILY n study of paper money

NOTARIAL > NOTARY

NOTARIES > NOTARY

NOTARISE same as > NOTARIZE

NOTARISED > NOTARISE

NOTARISES > NOTARISE

NOTARIZE vb attest to or authenticate (a document, contract, etc), as a notary

NOTARIZED > NOTARIZE

NOTARIZES > NOTARIZE

NOTARY n person authorized to witness legal documents

NOTATE vb write (esp music) in notation

NOTATED > NOTATE

NOTATES > NOTATE

NOTATING > NOTATE

NOTATION n representation of numbers or quantities in a system by a series of symbols

NOTATIONS > NOTATION

NOTATOR n person who notates

NOTATORS > NOTATOR

NOTCH n V-shaped cut ▷ vb make a notch in

NOTCHBACK n type of car

NOTCHED > NOTCH

NOTCHEL vb refuse to pay another person's debts

NOTCHELED > NOTCHEL

NOTCHELS > NOTCHEL

NOTCHER n person who cuts notches

NOTCHERS > NOTCHER

NOTCHES > NOTCH

NOTCHIER > NOTCHY

NOTCHIEST > NOTCHY

NOTCHING > NOTCH

NOTCHINGS > NOTCH

NOTCHY adj (of a motor vehicle gear mechanism) requiring careful gear-changing

NOTE n short letter ▷ vb notice, pay attention to

NOTEBANDI n (in India) demonetization

NOTEBOOK n book for writing in

NOTEBOOKS > NOTEBOOK

NOTECARD n greetings card with space to write note

NOTECARDS > NOTECARD

NOTECASE same as > WALLET

NOTECASES > NOTECASE

NOTED adj well-known

NOTEDLY > NOTED

NOTEDNESS > NOTED

NOTELESS > NOTE

NOTELET n small folded card with a design on the front

NOTELETS > NOTELET

NOTEPAD n number of sheets of paper fastened together

NOTEPADS > NOTEPAD

NOTEPAPER n paper used for writing letters

NOTER n person who takes notes

NOTERS > NOTER

NOTES > NOTE

NOTHER same as > OTHER

NOTHING pron not anything ▷ adv not at all ▷ n person or thing of no importance

NOTHINGS > NOTHING

NOTICE n observation or attention ▷ vb observe, become aware of

NOTICED > NOTICE

NOTICER n person who takes notice

NOTICERS > NOTICER

NOTICES > NOTICE

NOTICING > NOTICE

NOTIFIED > NOTIFY

NOTIFIER > NOTIFY

NOTIFIERS > NOTIFY

NOTIFIES > NOTIFY

NOTIFY vb inform

NOTIFYING > NOTIFY

NOTING > NOTE

NOTION n idea or opinion

NOTIONAL adj speculative, imaginary, or unreal

NOTIONIST n person whose opinions are merely notions

NOTIONS > NOTION

NOTITIA n register or list, esp of ecclesiastical districts

NOTITIAE > NOTITIA

NOTITIAS > NOTITIA

NOTOCHORD n fibrous longitudinal rod in all embryo and some adult chordate animals

NOTORIETY > NOTORIOUS

NOTORIOUS adj well known for something bad

NOTORNIS n rare flightless rail of New Zealand

NOTOUR adj notorious

NOTT same as > NOT

NOTTURNI > NOTTURNO

NOTTURNO n piece of music

NOTUM n cuticular plate on an insect

NOUGAT n chewy sweet containing nuts and fruit

NOUGATINE n type of brown nougat with a firm texture

NOUGATS > NOUGAT

NOUGHT n figure o

NOUGHTIES pl n decade from 2000 to 2009

NOUGHTS > NOUGHT

NOUL same as > NOLL

NOULD vb would not

NOULDE same as > NOULD

NOULE same as > NOLL

NOULES > NOULE

NOULS > NOUL

NOUMENA > NOUMENON

NOUMENAL > NOUMENON

NOUMENON n thing as it is in itself

NOUN n word that refers to a person, place, or thing

NOUNAL > NOUN

NOUNALLY > NOUN

NOUNIER > NOUNY

NOUNIEST > NOUNY

NOUNLESS > NOUN

NOUNS > NOUN

NOUNY adj like a noun

NOUP n steep headland

NOUPS > NOUP

NOURICE n nurse

NOURICES > NOURICE

NOURISH vb feed

NOURISHED > NOURISH

NOURISHER > NOURISH

NOURISHES > NOURISH

NOURITURE n nourishment

NOURSLE vb nurse

NOURSLED > NOURSLE

NOURSLES > NOURSLE

NOURSLING > NOURSLE

NOUS n common sense

NOUSELL vb foster

NOUSELLED > NOUSELL

NOUSELLS > NOUSELL

NOUSES > NOUS

NOUSLE vb nuzzle

NOUSLED > NOUSLE

NOUSLES > NOUSLE

NOUSLING > NOUSLE

NOUT same as > NOUGHT

NOUVEAU adj having recently become the thing specified

NOUVEAUX same as > NOUVEAU

NOUVELLE n long short story

NOUVELLES > NOUVELLE

NOVA n type of star

NOVAE > NOVA

NOVALIA n newly reclaimed land

NOVALIKE adj resembling a nova

NOVAS > NOVA

NOVATE vb substitute one thing in place of another

NOVATED adj as in novated lease Australian system of employer-aided car purchase

NOVATES > NOVATE

NOVATING > NOVATE

NOVATION n substitution of a new obligation for an old one by mutual agreement

NOVATIONS > NOVATION

NOVEL n long fictitious story in book form ▷ adj fresh, new, or original

NOVELDOM n realm of fiction

NOVELDOMS > NOVELDOM

NOVELESE n style of writing characteristic of poor novels

NOVELESES > NOVELESE

NOVELETTE n short novel, esp one regarded as trivial or sentimental

NOVELISE same as > NOVELIZE

NOVELISED > NOVELISE

NOVELISER n person who novelizes

NOVELISES > NOVELISE

NOVELISH adj resembling a novel

NOVELISM n innovation

NOVELISMS > NOVELISM

NOVELIST n writer of novels

NOVELISTS > NOVELIST

NOVELIZE vb convert (a true story, film, etc) into a novel

NOVELIZED > NOVELIZE

NOVELIZER n person who novelizes

NOVELIZES > NOVELIZE

NOVELLA n short novel

NOVELLAE > NOVELLA

NOVELLAS > NOVELLA

NOVELLE > NOVELLA

NOVELLY > NOVEL

NOVELS > NOVEL

NOVELTIES > NOVELTY

NOVELTY n newness

NOVEMBER n code word for the letter N

NOVEMBERS > NOVEMBER

NOVENA n set of prayers or services on nine consecutive days

NOVENAE > NOVENA

NOVENARY n set of nine

NOVENAS > NOVENA

NOVENNIAL adj recurring every ninth year

NOVERCAL adj stepmotherly

NOVERINT n writ

NOVERINTS > NOVERINT

NOVICE n beginner

NOVICES > NOVICE

NOVICHOK n powerful nerve agent developed in the former USSR

NOVICHOKS > NOVICHOK

NOVICIATE same as > NOVITIATE

NOVITIATE n period of being a novice

NOVITIES > NOVITY

NOVITY n novelty

NOVOCAINE n tradename of a painkilling substance used as a local anaesthetic

NOVODAMUS n type of charter

NOVUM n game played with dice

NOVUMS > NOVUM

NOW adv at or for the present time ▷ n the present time

NOWADAYS adv in these times

NOWAY adv in no manner

NOWAYS same as > NOWAY

NOWCAST n report on current weather conditions

NOWCASTS > NOWCAST

NOWED adj knotted

NOWHENCE adv from no place

NOWHERE adv not anywhere ▷ n nonexistent or insignificant place

NOWHERES > NOWHERE

NOWHITHER adv no place

NOWISE another word for > NOWAY

NOWL *n* crown of the head
NOWLS > NOWL
NOWN *same as* > OWN
NOWNESS > NOWN
NOWNESSES > NOWN
NOWS > NOW
NOWT *n* nothing
NOWTIER > NOWTY
NOWTIEST > NOWTY
NOWTS > NOWT
NOWTY *adj* bad-tempered
NOWY *adj* having a small projection at the centre (of a cross)
NOX *n* nitrogen oxide
NOXAL *adj* relating to damage done by something belonging to another
NOXES > NOX
NOXIOUS *adj* poisonous or harmful
NOXIOUSLY > NOXIOUS
NOY *vb* harass
NOYADE *n* execution by drowning
NOYADES > NOYADE
NOYANCE *n* nuisance
NOYANCES > NOYANCE
NOYAU *n* brandy-based liqueur
NOYAUS > NOYAU
NOYAUX > NOYAU
NOYED > NOY
NOYES *archaic form of* > NOISE
NOYESES > NOYES
NOYING > NOY
NOYOUS > NOY
NOYS > NOY
NOYSOME > NOY
NOZZER *n* new recruit (in the Navy)
NOZZERS > NOZZER
NOZZLE *n* projecting spout through which fluid is discharged
NOZZLES > NOZZLE
NTH *adj* of an unspecified number
NU *n* 13th letter in the Greek alphabet
NUANCE *n* subtle difference in colour, meaning, or tone ▷ *vb* give subtle differences to
NUANCED > NUANCE
NUANCES > NUANCE
NUANCING > NUANCE
NUB *n* point or gist (of a story etc) ▷ *vb* hang from the gallows
NUBBED > NUB
NUBBER *n* weakly hit ball in baseball
NUBBERS > NUBBER
NUBBIER > NUBBY
NUBBIEST > NUBBY
NUBBIN *n* something small or undeveloped, esp a fruit or ear of corn
NUBBINESS > NUBBY
NUBBING *n* act of hanging (a criminal)
NUBBINGS > NUBBING
NUBBINS > NUBBIN
NUBBLE *n* small lump ▷ *vb* dialect word for beat or pound using one's fists

NUBBLED > NUBBLE
NUBBLES > NUBBLE
NUBBLIER > NUBBLY
NUBBLIEST > NUBBLY
NUBBLING > NUBBLE
NUBBLY > NUBBLE
NUBBY *adj* having small lumps or protuberances
NUBECULA *n* small irregular galaxy near the S celestial pole
NUBECULAE > NUBECULA
NUBIA *n* fleecy scarf for the head, worn by women
NUBIAS > NUBIA
NUBIFORM *adj* cloudlike
NUBILE *adj* (of a girl or woman) mature enough for marriage
NUBILITY > NUBILE
NUBILOSE *same as* > NUBILOUS
NUBILOUS *adj* cloudy
NUBS > NUB
NUBUCK *n* type of leather with a velvety finish
NUBUCKS > NUBUCK
NUCELLAR > NUCELLUS
NUCELLI > NUCELLUS
NUCELLUS *n* central part of a plant ovule containing the embryo sac
NUCHA *n* back or nape of the neck
NUCHAE > NUCHA
NUCHAL *n* scale on a reptile's neck
NUCHALS > NUCHAL
NUCLEAL > NUCLEUS
NUCLEAR *adj* of nuclear weapons or energy
NUCLEASE *n* any of a group of enzymes that hydrolyse nucleic acids to simple nucleotides
NUCLEASES > NUCLEASE
NUCLEATE *adj* having a nucleus ▷ *vb* form a nucleus
NUCLEATED > NUCLEATE
NUCLEATES > NUCLEATE
NUCLEATOR > NUCLEATE
NUCLEI > NUCLEUS
NUCLEIC *adj* as in *nucleic acid* type of complex compound that is a vital constituent of living cells
NUCLEIDE *same as* > NUCLIDE
NUCLEIDES > NUCLEIDE
NUCLEIN *n* protein that occurs in the nuclei of living cells
NUCLEINIC > NUCLEIN
NUCLEINS > NUCLEIN
NUCLEOID *n* component of a bacterium
NUCLEOIDS > NUCLEOID
NUCLEOLAR > NUCLEOLUS
NUCLEOLE *variant of* > NUCLEOLUS
NUCLEOLES > NUCLEOLE
NUCLEOLI > NUCLEOLUS
NUCLEOLUS *n* small rounded body within a resting nucleus that contains RNA and proteins

NUCLEON *n* proton or neutron
NUCLEONIC *adj* relating to the branch of physics concerned with the applications of nuclear energy
NUCLEONS > NUCLEON
NUCLEUS *n* centre, esp of an atom or cell
NUCLEUSES > NUCLEUS
NUCLIDE *n* species of atom characterized by its atomic number and its mass number
NUCLIDES > NUCLIDE
NUCLIDIC > NUCLIDE
NUCULE *n* small seed
NUCULES > NUCULE
NUDATION *n* act of removing a covering
NUDATIONS > NUDATION
NUDDIES > NUDDY
NUDDY *n* as in *in the nuddy* in the nude
NUDE *adj* naked ▷ *n* naked figure in painting, sculpture, or photography
NUDELY > NUDE
NUDENESS > NUDE
NUDER > NUDE
NUDES > NUDE
NUDEST > NUDE
NUDGE *vb* push gently, esp with the elbow ▷ *n* gentle push or touch
NUDGED > NUDGE
NUDGER > NUDGE
NUDGERS > NUDGE
NUDGES > NUDGE
NUDGING > NUDGE
NUDICAUL *adj* (of plants) having stems without leaves
NUDIE *n* film, show, or magazine depicting nudity
NUDIES > NUDIE
NUDISM *n* practice of not wearing clothes
NUDISMS > NUDISM
NUDIST > NUDISM
NUDISTS > NUDISM
NUDITIES > NUDITY
NUDITY *n* state or fact of being nude
NUDNICK *same as* > NUDNIK
NUDNICKS > NUDNICK
NUDNIK *n* boring person
NUDNIKS > NUDNIK
NUDZH *same as* > NUDGE
NUDZHED > NUDZH
NUDZHES > NUDZH
NUDZHING > NUDZH
NUFF *slang form of* > ENOUGH
NUFFIN *slang form of* > NOTHING
NUFFINS > NUFFIN
NUFFS > NUFF
NUG *n* lump of wood sawn from a log
NUGAE *n* jests
NUGATORY *adj* of little value
NUGGAR *n* sailing boat used to carry cargo on the Nile
NUGGARS > NUGGAR
NUGGET *n* small lump of gold in its natural state ▷ *vb* polish footwear
NUGGETED > NUGGET

NUGGETIER > NUGGETY
NUGGETING > NUGGET
NUGGETS > NUGGET
NUGGETTED > NUGGET
NUGGETY *adj* of or resembling a nugget
NUGS > NUG
NUISANCE *n* something or someone that causes annoyance or bother
NUISANCER *n* person or thing causing a nuisance
NUISANCES > NUISANCE
NUKE *vb* attack with nuclear weapons ▷ *n* nuclear weapon
NUKED > NUKE
NUKES > NUKE
NUKING > NUKE
NULL *adj* without legal force ▷ *vb* make negative
NULLA *same as* > NULLAH
NULLAH *n* stream or drain
NULLAHS > NULLAH
NULLAS > NULLA
NULLED > NULL
NULLIFIED > NULLIFY
NULLIFIER > NULLIFY
NULLIFIES > NULLIFY
NULLIFY *vb* make ineffective
NULLING *n* knurling
NULLINGS > NULLING
NULLIPARA *n* woman who has never borne a child
NULLIPORE *n* any of several red seaweeds
NULLITIES > NULLITY
NULLITY *n* state of being null
NULLNESS > NULL
NULLS > NULL
NUMB *adj* without feeling, as through cold, shock, or fear ▷ *vb* make numb
NUMBAT *n* small Australian marsupial
NUMBATS > NUMBAT
NUMBED > NUMB
NUMBER *n* sum or quantity ▷ *vb* count
NUMBERED > NUMBER
NUMBERER *n* person who numbers
NUMBERERS > NUMBERER
NUMBERING > NUMBER
NUMBERS > NUMBER
NUMBEST > NUMB
NUMBFISH *n* any of several electric ray fish
NUMBHEAD *n* insulting word for a stupid person
NUMBHEADS > NUMBHEAD
NUMBING > NUMB
NUMBINGLY > NUMB
NUMBLES *pl n* animal organs, cooked for food
NUMBLY > NUMB
NUMBNESS > NUMB
NUMBNUT *n* insulting word for a stupid person
NUMBNUTS *n* insulting word for a stupid person
NUMBS > NUMB
NUMBSKULL *n* stupid person
NUMCHUCK *same as* > NUNCHAKU

n

NUMCHUCKS > NUMCHUCK
NUMDAH n coarse felt made esp in India
NUMDAHS > NUMDAH
NUMEN n deity or spirit presiding over a thing or place
NUMERABLE adj able to be numbered or counted
NUMERABLY > NUMERABLE
NUMERACY n ability to use numbers, esp in arithmetical operations
NUMERAIRE n unit in which prices are measured
NUMERAL n word or symbol used to express a sum or quantity ▷ adj of, consisting of, or denoting a number
NUMERALLY > NUMERAL
NUMERALS > NUMERAL
NUMERARY adj of or relating to numbers
NUMERATE adj able to do basic arithmetic ▷ vb read (a numerical expression)
NUMERATED > NUMERATE
NUMERATES > NUMERATE
NUMERATOR n number above the line in a fraction
NUMERIC n number or numeral
NUMERICAL adj measured or expressed in numbers
NUMERICS > NUMERIC
NUMEROUS adj existing or happening in large numbers
NUMINA plural of > NUMEN
NUMINOUS adj arousing religious or spiritual emotions ▷ n something that arouses religious or spiritual emotions
NUMMARY adj of or relating to coins
NUMMIER > NUMMY
NUMMIEST > NUMMY
NUMMULAR adj shaped like a coin
NUMMULARY > NUMMULAR
NUMMULINE n coin-shaped fossil
NUMMULITE n type of large fossil protozoan
NUMMY adj delicious
NUMNAH same as > NUMDAH
NUMNAHS > NUMNAH
NUMPKIN n stupid person
NUMPKINS > NUMPKIN
NUMPTIES > NUMPTY
NUMPTY n stupid person
NUMSKULL same as > NUMBSKULL
NUMSKULLS > NUMSKULL
NUN n female member of a religious order
NUNATAK n isolated mountain peak projecting through glacial ice
NUNATAKER > NUNATAK
NUNATAKS > NUNATAK
NUNCHAKU n throwing weapon used in martial arts
NUNCHAKUS > NUNCHAKU
NUNCHEON n light snack
NUNCHEONS > NUNCHEON

NUNCHUCK same as > NUNCHUK
NUNCHUCKS > NUNCHUCK
NUNCHUK n throwing weapon used in martial arts
NUNCHUKS > NUNCHUK
NUNCIO n pope's ambassador
NUNCIOS > NUNCIO
NUNCLE archaic or dialect word for > UNCLE
NUNCLES > NUNCLE
NUNCUPATE vb declare publicly
NUNDINAL n any of seven Roman letters indicating the days of the week
NUNDINALS > NUNDINAL
NUNDINE n market day
NUNDINES > NUNDINE
NUNHOOD n condition, practice, or character of a nun
NUNHOODS > NUNHOOD
NUNLIKE > NUN
NUNNATION n pronunciation of n at the end of words
NUNNERIES > NUNNERY
NUNNERY n convent
NUNNISH > NUN
NUNNY n as in nunny bag small sealskin haversack used in Canada
NUNS > NUN
NUNSHIP > NUN
NUNSHIPS > NUN
NUPTIAL adj relating to marriage
NUPTIALLY > NUPTIAL
NUPTIALS pl n wedding
NUR n wooden ball
NURAGHE n Sardinian round tower
NURAGHI > NURAGHE
NURAGHIC > NURAGHE
NURD same as > NERD
NURDIER > NURD
NURDIEST > NURD
NURDISH > NERD
NURDLE vb score runs in cricket by soft deflections
NURDLED > NURDLE
NURDLES > NURDLE
NURDLING > NURDLE
NURDS > NURD
NURDY > NURD
NURHAG n Sardinian round tower
NURHAGS > NURHAG
NURL variant of > KNURL
NURLED > NURL
NURLING > NURL
NURLS > NURL
NURR n wooden ball
NURRS > NURR
NURS > NUR
NURSE n person employed to look after sick people ▷ vb look after (a sick person)
NURSED > NURSE
NURSELIKE > NURSE
NURSELING same as > NURSLING
NURSEMAID n woman employed to look after children

NURSER n person who treats something carefully
NURSERIES > NURSERY
NURSERS > NURSER
NURSERY n room where children sleep or play
NURSES > NURSE
NURSING n practice or profession of caring for the sick and injured
NURSINGS > NURSING
NURSLE vb nuzzle
NURSLED > NURSLE
NURSLES > NURSLE
NURSLING n child or young animal that is being suckled, nursed, or fostered
NURSLINGS > NURSLING
NURTURAL > NURTURE
NURTURANT > NURTURE
NURTURE n act or process of promoting development ▷ vb promote or encourage development
NURTURED > NURTURE
NURTURER > NURTURE
NURTURERS > NURTURE
NURTURES > NURTURE
NURTURING > NURTURE
NUS > NU
NUT n fruit consisting of a hard shell and a kernel ▷ vb gather nuts
NUTANT adj having the apex hanging down
NUTARIAN n person whose diet is based around nuts
NUTARIANS > NUTARIAN
NUTATE vb nod
NUTATED > NUTATE
NUTATES > NUTATE
NUTATING > NUTATE
NUTATION n periodic variation in the precession of the earth's axis
NUTATIONS > NUTATION
NUTBAR n bar made from chopped nuts
NUTBARS > NUTBAR
NUTBROWN adj of a brownish colour, esp a reddish-brown
NUTBUTTER n ground nuts blended with butter
NUTCASE n slang word for a foolish or crazy person
NUTCASES > NUTCASE
NUTGALL n nut-shaped gall caused by gall wasps on the oak and other trees
NUTGALLS > NUTGALL
NUTGRASS n type of plant
NUTHATCH n small songbird
NUTHIN n nothing
NUTHOUSE n offensive name for a psychiatric hospital
NUTHOUSES > NUTHOUSE
NUTJOB n slang word for a foolish or crazy person
NUTJOBBER n nuthatch
NUTJOBS > NUTJOB
NUTLET n portion of a fruit that fragments when mature
NUTLETS > NUTLET
NUTLIKE > NUT
NUTLOAF n savoury loaf made from nuts

NUTLOAVES > NUTLOAF
NUTMEAL n type of grain
NUTMEALS > NUTMEAL
NUTMEAT n kernel of a nut
NUTMEATS > NUTMEAT
NUTMEG n spice made from the seed of a tropical tree ▷ vb kick or hit the ball between the legs of (an opposing player)
NUTMEGGED > NUTMEG
NUTMEGGY adj of or similar to nutmeg
NUTMEGS > NUTMEG
NUTPECKER n nuthatch
NUTPICK n tool used to dig the meat from nuts
NUTPICKS > NUTPICK
NUTRIA n fur of the coypu
NUTRIAS > NUTRIA
NUTRIENT n substance that provides nourishment ▷ adj providing nourishment
NUTRIENTS > NUTRIENT
NUTRIMENT n food or nourishment required by all living things to grow and stay healthy
NUTRITION n process of taking in and absorbing nutrients
NUTRITIVE adj of nutrition ▷ n nutritious food
NUTS > NUT
NUTSEDGE same as > NUTGRASS
NUTSEDGES > NUTSEDGE
NUTSHELL n shell around the kernel of a nut
NUTSHELLS > NUTSHELL
NUTSIER > NUTSY
NUTSIEST > NUTSY
NUTSO n slang word for a foolish or crazy person
NUTSOS > NUTSO
NUTSY adj slang word for foolish or crazy
NUTTED > NUT
NUTTER n slang word for a foolish or crazy person
NUTTERIES > NUTTERY
NUTTERS > NUTTER
NUTTERY n place where nut trees grow
NUTTIER > NUTTY
NUTTIEST > NUTTY
NUTTILY > NUTTY
NUTTINESS > NUTTY
NUTTING n act of gathering nuts
NUTTINGS > NUTTING
NUTTY adj containing or resembling nuts
NUTWOOD n any of various nut-bearing trees, such as walnut
NUTWOODS > NUTWOOD
NUZZER n present given to a superior in India
NUZZERS > NUZZER
NUZZLE vb push or rub gently with the nose or snout
NUZZLED > NUZZLE
NUZZLER n person or thing that nuzzles
NUZZLERS > NUZZLER
NUZZLES > NUZZLE

n

NUZZLING > NUZZLE

NY *same as* > NIGH

NYAFF *n* small or contemptible person ▷ *vb* yelp like a small dog

NYAFFED > NYAFF

NYAFFING > NYAFF

NYAFFS > NYAFF

NYAH *interj* interjection used to express contempt

NYALA *n* spiral-horned southern African antelope

NYALAS > NYALA

NYANZA *n* (in E Africa) a lake

NYANZAS > NYANZA

NYAOPE *n* narcotic substance

NYAOPES > NYAOPE

NYAS *n* young hawk

NYASES > NYAS

NYBBLE *n* small byte

NYBBLES > NYBBLE

NYCTALOPE *n* person affected by nyctalopia

NYCTALOPS *n* person or thing with night-vision

NYE *n* flock of pheasants ▷ *vb* near

NYED > NYE

NYES > NYE

NYING > NYE

NYLGHAI *same as* > NILGAI

NYLGHAIS > NYLGHAI

NYLGHAU *same as* > NILGAI

NYLGHAUS > NYLGHAU

NYLON *n* synthetic material used for clothing etc

NYLONED *adj* wearing nylons

NYLONS *pl n* stockings made of nylon

NYM *adj* as in *nym war* dispute about publishing material online under a pseudonym

NYMPH *n* mythical spirit of nature, represented as a beautiful young woman ▷ *vb*

fish with a particular type of fly on the hook

NYMPHA *n* either one of the labia minora

NYMPHAE > NYMPHA

NYMPHAEA *n* water lily

NYMPHAEAS > NYMPHAEA

NYMPHAEUM *n* shrine of the nymphs

NYMPHAL > NYMPH

NYMPHALID *n* butterfly of the family that includes the fritillaries and red admirals ▷ *adj* of this family of butterflies

NYMPHEAN > NYMPH

NYMPHED > NYMPH

NYMPHET *n* sexually precocious young girl

NYMPHETIC > NYMPHET

NYMPHETS > NYMPHET

NYMPHETTE *same as* > NYMPHET

NYMPHIC > NYMPH

NYMPHICAL > NYMPH

NYMPHING > NYMPH

NYMPHISH > NYMPH

NYMPHLIER > NYMPHLY

NYMPHLIKE > NYMPH

NYMPHLY *adj* resembling a nymph

NYMPHO *n* nymphomaniac

NYMPHOS > NYMPHO

NYMPHS > NYMPH

NYS > NY

NYSSA *n* type of tree

NYSSAS > NYSSA

NYSTAGMIC > NYSTAGMUS

NYSTAGMUS *n* involuntary movement of the eye comprising a smooth drift followed by a flick back

NYSTATIN *n* type of antibiotic obtained from a bacterium

NYSTATINS > NYSTATIN

n

Oo

OAF n stupid or clumsy person

OAFISH > OAF

OAFISHLY > OAF

OAFS > OAF

OAK n deciduous forest tree

OAKED adj relating to wine that is stored for a time in oak barrels prior to bottling

OAKEN adj made of the wood of the oak

OAKENSHAW n small forest of oaks

OAKER same as > OCHRE

OAKERS > OAKER

OAKIER > OAKY

OAKIES > OAKY

OAKIEST > OAKY

OAKINESS n quality of being oaky

OAKLEAF n the leaf of the oak

OAKLEAVES > OAKLEAF

OAKLIKE > OAK

OAKLING n young oak

OAKLINGS > OAKLING

OAKMOSS n type of lichen

OAKMOSSES > OAKMOSS

OAKS > OAK

OAKUM n fibre obtained by unravelling old rope

OAKUMS > OAKUM

OAKWOOD n the wood of the oak

OAKWOODS > OAKWOOD

OAKY adj hard like the wood of an oak ▷ n ice cream

OANSHAGH n foolish girl or woman

OANSHAGHS > OANSHAGH

OAR n pole with a broad blade, used for rowing a boat ▷ vb propel with oars

OARAGE n use or number of oars

OARAGES > OARAGE

OARED adj equipped with oars

OARFISH n very long ribbonfish with long slender ventral fins

OARFISHES > OARFISH

OARIER > OARY

OARIEST > OARY

OARING > OAR

OARLESS > OAR

OARLIKE > OAR

OARLOCK n swivelling device that holds an oar in place

OARLOCKS > OARLOCK

OARS > OAR

OARSMAN n person who rows

OARSMEN > OARSMAN

OARSWOMAN n female oarsman

OARSWOMEN > OARSWOMAN

OARWEED n type of brown seaweed

OARWEEDS > OARWEED

OARY adj of or like an oar

OASES > OASIS

OASIS n fertile area in a desert

OAST n oven for drying hops

OASTHOUSE n building with kilns for drying hops

OASTS > OAST

OAT n hard cereal grown as food

OATCAKE n thin flat biscuit of oatmeal

OATCAKES > OATCAKE

OATEN adj made of oats or oat straw

OATER n film about the American Wild West

OATERS > OATER

OATH n solemn promise, esp to be truthful in court

OATHABLE adj able to take an oath

OATHS > OATH

OATIER > OATY

OATIEST > OATY

OATLIKE > OAT

OATMEAL n coarse flour made from oats ▷ adj pale brownish-cream

OATMEALS > OATMEAL

OATS > OAT

OATY adj of, like, or containing oats

OAVES > OAF

OB n expression of opposition

OBA n (in W Africa) a Yoruba chief or ruler

OBANG n former Japanese coin

OBANGS > OBANG

OBAS > OBA

OBBLIGATI > OBBLIGATO

OBBLIGATO n essential part or accompaniment ▷ adj not to be omitted in performance

OBCONIC adj shaped like a cone and attached at the pointed end

OBCONICAL same as > OBCONIC

OBCORDATE adj heart-shaped and attached at the pointed end

OBDURACY > OBDURATE

OBDURATE adj hardhearted or stubborn ▷ vb make obdurate

OBDURATED > OBDURATE

OBDURATES > OBDURATE

OBDURE vb make obdurate

OBDURED > OBDURE

OBDURES > OBDURE

OBDURING > OBDURE

OBE n ancient Laconian village

OBEAH vb cast spell on

OBEAHED > OBEAH

OBEAHING > OBEAH

OBEAHISM > OBEAH

OBEAHISMS > OBEAH

OBEAHS > OBEAH

OBECHE n African tree

OBECHES > OBECHE

OBEDIENCE n condition or quality of being obedient

OBEDIENT adj obeying or willing to obey

OBEISANCE n attitude of respect

OBEISANT > OBEISANCE

OBEISM n belief in obeah

OBEISMS > OBEISM

OBELI > OBELUS

OBELIA n type of jellyfish

OBELIAS > OBELIA

OBELION n area of skull

OBELISCAL > OBELISK

OBELISE same as > OBELIZE

OBELISED > OBELISE

OBELISES > OBELISE

OBELISING > OBELISE

OBELISK n stone column tapering to a pyramid at the top

OBELISKS > OBELISK

OBELISM n practice of marking passages in text

OBELISMS > OBELISM

OBELIZE vb mark (a word or passage) with an obelus

OBELIZED > OBELIZE

OBELIZES > OBELIZE

OBELIZING > OBELIZE

OBELUS n mark used to indicate spurious words or passages

OBENTO n Japanese lunch box

OBENTOS > OBENTO

OBES > OBE

OBESE adj very fat

OBESELY > OBESE

OBESENESS > OBESE

OBESER > OBESE

OBESEST > OBESE

OBESITIES > OBESE

OBESITY > OBESE

OBESOGEN n agent causing obesity

OBESOGENS > OBESOGEN

OBEY vb carry out instructions or orders

OBEYABLE > OBEY

OBEYED > OBEY

OBEYER > OBEY

OBEYERS > OBEY

OBEYING > OBEY

OBEYS > OBEY

OBFUSCATE vb make (something) confusing

OBI n broad sash tied in a large flat bow at the back ▷ vb bewitch

OBIA same as > OBEAH

OBIAS > OBIA

OBIED > OBI

OBIING > OBI

OBIISM > OBI

OBIISMS > OBI

OBIIT vb died

OBIS > OBI

OBIT n memorial service

OBITAL adj of obits

OBITER adv by the way

OBITS > OBIT

OBITUAL adj of obits

OBITUARY n announcement of someone's death, esp in a newspaper

OBJECT n physical thing ▷ vb express disapproval

OBJECTED > OBJECT

OBJECTIFY vb represent concretely

OBJECTING > OBJECT

OBJECTION n expression or feeling of opposition or disapproval

OBJECTIVE n aim or purpose ▷ adj not biased

OBJECTOR > OBJECT

OBJECTORS > OBJECT

OBJECTS > OBJECT

OBJET n object

OBJETS > OBJET

OBJURE vb put on oath

OBJURED > OBJURE

OBJURES > OBJURE

OBJURGATE vb scold or reprimand

OBJURING > OBJURE

OBLAST n administrative division of the constituent republics of Russia

OBLASTI > OBLAST

OBLASTS > OBLAST

o

OBLATE adj (of a sphere) flattened at the poles ▷ n person dedicated to a monastic or religious life
OBLATELY > OBLATE
OBLATES > OBLATE
OBLATION n religious offering
OBLATIONS > OBLATION
OBLATORY > OBLATION
OBLIGABLE > OBLIGATE
OBLIGANT n person promising to pay a sum
OBLIGANTS > OBLIGANT
OBLIGATE vb compel, constrain, or oblige morally or legally ▷ adj compelled, bound, or restricted
OBLIGATED > OBLIGATE
OBLIGATES > OBLIGATE
OBLIGATI > OBLIGATO
OBLIGATO same as > OBBLIGATO
OBLIGATOR > OBLIGATE
OBLIGATOS > OBLIGATO
OBLIGE vb compel (someone) morally or by law
OBLIGED > OBLIGE
OBLIGEE n person in whose favour an obligation, contract, or bond is created
OBLIGEES > OBLIGEE
OBLIGER > OBLIGE
OBLIGERS > OBLIGE
OBLIGES > OBLIGE
OBLIGING adj ready to help other people
OBLIGOR n person who binds themself by contract
OBLIGORS > OBLIGOR
OBLIQUE adj slanting ▷ n symbol (/) ▷ vb take or have an oblique direction
OBLIQUED > OBLIQUE
OBLIQUELY > OBLIQUE
OBLIQUER > OBLIQUE
OBLIQUES > OBLIQUE
OBLIQUEST > OBLIQUE
OBLIQUID adj oblique
OBLIQUING > OBLIQUE
OBLIQUITY n state or condition of being oblique
OBLIVION n state of being forgotten
OBLIVIONS > OBLIVION
OBLIVIOUS adj unaware
OBLONG adj having two long sides, two short sides, and four right angles ▷ n oblong figure
OBLONGLY > OBLONG
OBLONGS > OBLONG
OBLOQUIAL > OBLOQUY
OBLOQUIES > OBLOQUY
OBLOQUY n verbal abuse
OBNOXIOUS adj offensive
OBO n ship carrying oil and ore
OBOE n double-reeded woodwind instrument
OBOES > OBOE
OBOIST > OBOE
OBOISTS > OBOE
OBOL same as > OBOLUS
OBOLARY adj very poor
OBOLE n former weight unit in pharmacy

OBOLES > OBOLE
OBOLI > OBOLUS
OBOLS > OBOL
OBOLUS n Greek unit of weight
OBOS > OBO
OBOVATE adj shaped like the longitudinal section of an egg
OBOVATELY > OBOVATE
OBOVOID adj (of a fruit) egg-shaped with the narrower end at the base
OBREPTION n obtaining of something by giving false information
OBS > OB
OBSCENE adj indecent
OBSCENELY > OBSCENE
OBSCENER > OBSCENE
OBSCENEST > OBSCENE
OBSCENITY n state or quality of being obscene
OBSCURANT n opposer of reform and enlightenment ▷ adj of or relating to an obscurant
OBSCURE adj not well known ▷ vb make (something) obscure
OBSCURED > OBSCURE
OBSCURELY > OBSCURE
OBSCURER > OBSCURE
OBSCURERS > OBSCURE
OBSCURES > OBSCURE
OBSCUREST > OBSCURE
OBSCURING > OBSCURE
OBSCURITY n state or quality of being obscure
OBSECRATE rare word for > BESEECH
OBSEQUENT adj (of a river) flowing into a subsequent stream in the opposite direction to the original slope of the land
OBSEQUIAL > OBSEQUIES
OBSEQUIE same as > OBSEQUY
OBSEQUIES pl n funeral rites
OBSEQUY singular of > OBSEQUIES
OBSERVANT adj quick to notice things
OBSERVE vb see or notice
OBSERVED > OBSERVE
OBSERVER n person who observes, esp one who watches someone or something carefully
OBSERVERS > OBSERVER
OBSERVES > OBSERVE
OBSERVING > OBSERVE
OBSESS vb preoccupy (someone) compulsively
OBSESSED > OBSESS
OBSESSES > OBSESS
OBSESSING > OBSESS
OBSESSION n something that preoccupies a person to the exclusion of other things
OBSESSIVE adj motivated by a persistent overriding idea or impulse ▷ n person subject to obsession
OBSESSOR > OBSESS
OBSESSORS > OBSESS

OBSIDIAN n dark glassy volcanic rock
OBSIDIANS > OBSIDIAN
OBSIGN vb confirm
OBSIGNATE same as > OBSIGN
OBSIGNED > OBSIGN
OBSIGNING > OBSIGN
OBSIGNS > OBSIGN
OBSOLESCE vb become obsolete
OBSOLETE adj no longer in use ▷ vb make obsolete
OBSOLETED > OBSOLETE
OBSOLETES > OBSOLETE
OBSTACLE n something that makes progress difficult
OBSTACLES > OBSTACLE
OBSTETRIC adj of or relating to childbirth
OBSTINACY n state or quality of being obstinate
OBSTINATE adj stubborn
OBSTRUCT vb block with an obstacle
OBSTRUCTS > OBSTRUCT
OBSTRUENT adj causing obstruction, esp of the intestinal tract ▷ n anything that causes obstruction
OBTAIN vb acquire intentionally
OBTAINED > OBTAIN
OBTAINER > OBTAIN
OBTAINERS > OBTAIN
OBTAINING > OBTAIN
OBTAINS > OBTAIN
OBTECT adj (of a pupa) encased in a hardened secretion
OBTECTED same as > OBTECT
OBTEMPER vb comply (with)
OBTEMPERS > OBTEMPER
OBTEND vb put forward
OBTENDED > OBTEND
OBTENDING > OBTEND
OBTENDS > OBTEND
OBTENTION n act of obtaining
OBTEST vb beg (someone) earnestly
OBTESTED > OBTEST
OBTESTING > OBTEST
OBTESTS > OBTEST
OBTRUDE vb push oneself or one's ideas on others
OBTRUDED > OBTRUDE
OBTRUDER > OBTRUDE
OBTRUDERS > OBTRUDE
OBTRUDES > OBTRUDE
OBTRUDING > OBTRUDE
OBTRUSION > OBTRUDE
OBTRUSIVE adj unpleasantly noticeable
OBTUND vb deaden or dull
OBTUNDED > OBTUND
OBTUNDENT > OBTUND
OBTUNDING > OBTUND
OBTUNDITY n semi-conscious state
OBTUNDS > OBTUND
OBTURATE vb stop up (an opening, esp the breech of a gun)
OBTURATED > OBTURATE
OBTURATES > OBTURATE

OBTURATOR > OBTURATE
OBTUSE adj not sharp or pointed
OBTUSELY > OBTUSE
OBTUSER > OBTUSE
OBTUSEST > OBTUSE
OBTUSITY > OBTUSE
OBUMBRATE vb overshadow
OBVENTION n incidental expense
OBVERSE n opposite way of looking at an idea ▷ adj facing or turned towards the observer
OBVERSELY > OBVERSE
OBVERSES > OBVERSE
OBVERSION > OBVERT
OBVERT vb deduce the obverse of (a proposition)
OBVERTED > OBVERT
OBVERTING > OBVERT
OBVERTS > OBVERT
OBVIABLE > OBVIATE
OBVIATE vb make unnecessary
OBVIATED > OBVIATE
OBVIATES > OBVIATE
OBVIATING > OBVIATE
OBVIATION > OBVIATE
OBVIATOR > OBVIATE
OBVIATORS > OBVIATE
OBVIOUS adj easy to see or understand, evident
OBVIOUSLY adv in a way that is easy to see or understand
OBVOLUTE adj (of leaves or petals in the bud) folded so that the margins overlap each other
OBVOLUTED same as > OBVOLUTE
OBVOLVENT adj curving around something
OBVS adv obviously
OCA n any of various South American herbaceous plants
OCARINA n small oval wind instrument
OCARINAS > OCARINA
OCAS > OCA
OCCAM n computer programming language
OCCAMIES > OCCAMY
OCCAMS > OCCAM
OCCAMY n type of alloy
OCCASION n time at which a particular thing happens ▷ vb cause
OCCASIONS pl n needs
OCCIDENT literary or formal word for > WEST
OCCIDENTS > OCCIDENT
OCCIES > OCCY
OCCIPITA > OCCIPUT
OCCIPITAL adj of or relating to the back of the head or skull
OCCIPUT n back of the head
OCCIPUTS > OCCIPUT
OCCLUDE vb obstruct
OCCLUDED > OCCLUDE
OCCLUDENT > OCCLUDE
OCCLUDER > OCCLUDE
OCCLUDERS > OCCLUDE
OCCLUDES > OCCLUDE
OCCLUDING > OCCLUDE

o

OCCLUSAL > OCCLUSION

OCCLUSION n act or process of occluding or the state of being occluded

OCCLUSIVE adj of or relating to the act of occlusion ▷ n occlusive speech sound

OCCLUSOR n muscle for closing opening

OCCLUSORS > OCCLUSOR

OCCULT adj relating to the supernatural ▷ vb (of a celestial body) to hide (another celestial body) from view

OCCULTED > OCCULT

OCCULTER n something that obscures

OCCULTERS > OCCULTER

OCCULTING > OCCULT

OCCULTISM n belief in and the study and practice of magic, astrology, etc

OCCULTIST > OCCULTISM

OCCULTLY > OCCULT

OCCULTS > OCCULT

OCCUPANCE same as > OCCUPANCY

OCCUPANCY n (length of) a person's stay in a specified place

OCCUPANT n person occupying a specified place

OCCUPANTS > OCCUPANT

OCCUPATE same as > OCCUPY

OCCUPATED > OCCUPATE

OCCUPATES > OCCUPATE

OCCUPIED > OCCUPY

OCCUPIER n person who lives in a particular house, whether as owner or tenant

OCCUPIERS > OCCUPIER

OCCUPIES > OCCUPY

OCCUPY vb live or work in (a building)

OCCUPYING > OCCUPY

OCCUR vb happen

OCCURRED > OCCUR

OCCURRENT adj (of a property) relating to some observable feature of its bearer

OCCURRING > OCCUR

OCCURS > OCCUR

OCCY n as in all over the occy dialect expression meaning in every direction

OCEAN n vast area of sea between continents

OCEANARIA pl n large saltwater aquaria for marine life

OCEANAUT n undersea explorer

OCEANAUTS > OCEANAUT

OCEANIC adj of or relating to the ocean

OCEANID n ocean nymph in Greek mythology

OCEANIDES > OCEANID

OCEANIDS > OCEANID

OCEANS > OCEAN

OCEANSIDE adj beside the ocean

OCEANVIEW adj with a view of the ocean

OCEANWARD adv towards the ocean

OCELLAR > OCELLUS

OCELLATE > OCELLUS

OCELLATED > OCELLUS

OCELLI > OCELLUS

OCELLUS n simple eye of insects and some other invertebrates

OCELOID adj of or like an ocelot

OCELOT n American wild cat with a spotted coat

OCELOTS > OCELOT

OCH interj expression of surprise, annoyance, or disagreement

OCHE n (in darts) mark behind which a player must stand

OCHER same as > OCHRE

OCHERED > OCHER

OCHERIER > OCHERY

OCHERIEST > OCHERY

OCHERING > OCHER

OCHERISH adj (US) resembling ochre

OCHEROID adj (US) of or like ochre

OCHEROUS > OCHER

OCHERS > OCHER

OCHERY same as > OCHRY

OCHES > OCHE

OCHIDORE n type of crab

OCHIDORES > OCHIDORE

OCHLOCRAT n supporter of rule by the mob

OCHONE interj expression of sorrow or regret

OCHRE n brownish-yellow earth ▷ adj moderate yellow-orange to orange ▷ vb colour with ochre

OCHREA n cup-shaped structure that sheathes the stems of certain plants

OCHREAE > OCHREA

OCHREAS > OCHREA

OCHREATE same as > OCREATE

OCHRED > OCHRE

OCHREOUS > OCHRE

OCHRES > OCHRE

OCHREY > OCHRE

OCHRIER > OCHRY

OCHRIEST > OCHRY

OCHRING > OCHRE

OCHROID > OCHRE

OCHROUS > OCHRE

OCHRY adj containing or resembling ochre

OCICAT n breed of cat with a spotted coat

OCICATS > OCICAT

OCKER n uncultivated or boorish Australian

OCKERISM n Australian boorishness

OCKERISMS > OCKERISM

OCKERS > OCKER

OCKODOLS pl n one's feet when wearing boots

OCOTILLO n cactus-like tree

OCOTILLOS > OCOTILLO

OCREA same as > OCHREA

OCREAE > OCREA

OCREAS > OCREA

OCREATE adj possessing an ocrea

OCTA same as > OKTA

OCTACHORD n eight-stringed musical instrument

OCTAD n group or series of eight

OCTADIC > OCTAD

OCTADS > OCTAD

OCTAGON n geometric figure with eight sides

OCTAGONAL adj having eight sides and eight angles

OCTAGONS > OCTAGON

OCTAHEDRA pl n solid eight-sided figures; octahedrons

OCTAL n number system with a base 8

OCTALS > OCTAL

OCTAMETER n verse line consisting of eight metrical feet

OCTAN n illness that occurs weekly

OCTANE n hydrocarbon found in petrol

OCTANES > OCTANE

OCTANGLE same as > OCTAGON

OCTANGLES > OCTANGLE

OCTANOL n alcohol containing eight carbon atoms

OCTANOLS > OCTANOL

OCTANS > OCTAN

OCTANT n any of the eight parts into which the three planes containing the Cartesian coordinate axes divide space

OCTANTAL > OCTANT

OCTANTS > OCTANT

OCTAPLA n book with eight texts

OCTAPLAS > OCTAPLA

OCTAPLOID adj having eight parts

OCTAPODIC > OCTAPODY

OCTAPODY n line of verse with eight metrical feet

OCTARCHY n government by eight rulers

OCTAROON same as > OCTOROON

OCTAROONS > OCTAROON

OCTAS > OCTA

OCTASTICH n verse of eight lines

OCTASTYLE adj (of building) having eight columns

OCTAVAL > OCTAVE

OCTAVE n (interval between the first and) eighth note of a scale ▷ adj consisting of eight parts

OCTAVES > OCTAVE

OCTAVO n book size in which the sheets are folded into eight leaves

OCTAVOS > OCTAVO

OCTENNIAL adj occurring every eight years

OCTET n group of eight performers

OCTETS > OCTET

OCTETT same as > OCTET

OCTETTE same as > OCTET

OCTETTES > OCTETTE

OCTETTS > OCTETT

OCTILLION n (in Britain and Germany) the number represented as one followed by 48 zeros

OCTOFID adj divided into eight

OCTOHEDRA same as > OCTAHEDRA

OCTONARII pl n lines with eight feet

OCTONARY adj relating to or based on the number eight ▷ n stanza of eight lines

OCTOPI > OCTOPUS

OCTOPLOID same as > OCTAPLOID

OCTOPOD n type of mollusc ▷ adj of these molluscs

OCTOPODAN > OCTOPOD

OCTOPODES > OCTOPOD

OCTOPODS > OCTOPOD

OCTOPOID adj of or like an octopus

OCTOPUS n sea creature with a soft body and eight tentacles

OCTOPUSES > OCTOPUS

OCTOPUSH n hockey-like game played underwater

OCTOROON n offensive term for person of mixed racial ancestry

OCTOROONS > OCTOROON

OCTOSTYLE same as > OCTASTYLE

OCTOTHORP n type of symbol in printing

OCTROI n duty on various goods brought into certain European towns

OCTROIS > OCTROI

OCTUOR n octet

OCTUORS > OCTUOR

OCTUPLE n quantity or number eight times as great as another ▷ adj eight times as much or as many ▷ vb multiply by eight

OCTUPLED > OCTUPLE

OCTUPLES > OCTUPLE

OCTUPLET n one of eight offspring from one birth

OCTUPLETS > OCTUPLET

OCTUPLEX n something made up of eight parts

OCTUPLING > OCTUPLE

OCTUPLY adv by eight times

OCTYL n group of atoms

OCTYLS > OCTYL

OCULAR adj relating to the eyes or sight ▷ n lens in an optical instrument

OCULARIST n person who makes artificial eyes

OCULARLY > OCULAR

OCULARS > OCULAR

OCULATE adj possessing eyes

OCULATED same as > OCULATE

OCULI > OCULUS

OCULIST n ophthalmologist

OCULISTS > OCULIST

OCULUS n round window

OD n hypothetical force

ODA *n* room or chamber
ODAH *same as* > ODA
ODAHS > ODAH
ODAL *same as* > UDAL
ODALIQUE *same as*
 > ODALISQUE
ODALIQUES > ODALIQUE
ODALISK *same as*
 > ODALISQUE
ODALISKS > ODALISK
ODALISQUE *n* female slave
 in a harem
ODALLER > ODAL
ODALLERS > ODAL
ODALS > ODAL
ODAS > ODA
ODD *adj* unusual
ODDBALL *n* eccentric person
 ▷ *adj* strange or peculiar
ODDBALLS > ODDBALL
ODDER > ODD
ODDEST > ODD
ODDISH > ODD
ODDITIES > ODDITY
ODDITY *n* odd person or
 thing
ODDLY > ODD
ODDMENT *n* odd piece or
 thing
ODDMENTS > ODDMENT
ODDNESS > ODD
ODDNESSES > ODD
ODDS *pl n* probability of
 something happening
ODDSMAKER *n* person
 setting odds in betting
ODDSMAN *n* umpire
ODDSMEN > ODDSMAN
ODE *n* lyric poem, usu
 addressed to a particular
 subject
ODEA > ODEUM
ODEON *same as* > ODEUM
ODEONS > ODEON
ODES > ODE
ODEUM *n* ancient building for
 musical performances
ODEUMS > ODEUM
ODIC > OD
ODIFEROUS *adj* having
 odour
ODIOUS *adj* offensive
ODIOUSLY > ODIOUS
ODISM > OD
ODISMS > OD
ODIST > OD
ODISTS > OD
ODIUM *n* widespread dislike
ODIUMS > ODIUM
ODOGRAPH *same as*
 > ODOMETER
ODOGRAPHS > ODOGRAPH
ODOMETER *n* device that
 records the number of miles
 that a bicycle or motor
 vehicle has travelled
ODOMETERS > ODOMETER
ODOMETRY > ODOMETER
ODONATA *pl n* insects of an
 order that includes
 dragonflies
ODONATE *n* dragonfly or
 related insect
ODONATES > ODONATE
ODONATIST *n* dragonfly
 expert
ODONTALGY *n* toothache

ODONTIC *adj* of teeth
ODONTIST *n* dentist
ODONTISTS > ODONTIST
ODONTOID *adj* toothlike ▷ *n*
 bone in the spine
ODONTOIDS > ODONTOID
ODONTOMA *n* tumour near
 teeth
ODONTOMAS > ODONTOMA
ODOR *same as* > ODOUR
ODORANT *n* something with
 a strong smell
ODORANTS > ODORANT
ODORATE *adj* having a
 strong smell
ODORED *same as* > ODOURED
ODORFUL *same as*
 > ODOURFUL
ODORISE *same as*
 > ODORIZE
ODORISED > ODORISE
ODORISER *same as*
 > ODORIZER
ODORISERS > ODORISER
ODORISES > ODORISE
ODORISING > ODORISE
ODORIZE *vb* give an odour to
ODORIZED > ODORIZE
ODORIZER *n* something
 that odorizes
ODORIZERS > ODORIZER
ODORIZES > ODORIZE
ODORIZING > ODORIZE
ODORLESS > ODOR
ODOROUS *adj* having or
 emitting a characteristic
 smell
ODOROUSLY > ODOROUS
ODORS > ODOR
ODOUR *n* particular smell
ODOURED *adj* having an
 odour
ODOURFUL *adj* full of odour
ODOURLESS > ODOUR
ODOURS > ODOUR
ODS > OD
ODSO *n* cry of surprise
ODYL *same as* > OD
ODYLE *same as* > OD
ODYLES > ODYLE
ODYLISM > ODYL
ODYLISMS > ODYL
ODYLS > ODYL
ODYSSEAN *adj* of or like an
 odyssey
ODYSSEY *n* long eventful
 journey
ODYSSEYS > ODYSSEY
ODZOOKS *interj* cry of
 surprise
OE *n* grandchild
OECIST *n* colony founder
OECISTS > OECIST
OECOLOGIC *same as*
 > ECOLOGIC
OECOLOGY *less common*
 spelling of > ECOLOGY
OECUMENIC *variant of*
 > ECUMENIC
OEDEMA *n* abnormal swelling
OEDEMAS > OEDEMA
OEDEMATA > OEDEMA
OEDIPAL *adj* relating to a
 complex whereby a male
 child wants to replace his
 father
OEDIPALLY > OEDIPAL

OEDIPEAN *same as*
 > OEDIPAL
OEDOMETER *n* instrument
 for measuring the
 consolidation of a soil
 specimen under pressure
OEILLADE *n* suggestive
 glance
OEILLADES > OEILLADE
OENANTHIC *adj* smelling of
 or like wine
OENOLOGY *n* study of wine
OENOMANCY *n* divination by
 studying the colour of wine
OENOMANIA *n* craving for
 wine
OENOMEL *n* drink made of
 wine and honey
OENOMELS > OENOMEL
OENOMETER *n* device for
 measuring the strength of
 wine
OENOPHIL *same as*
 > OENOPHILE
OENOPHILE *n* lover or
 connoisseur of wines
OENOPHILS > OENOPHIL
OENOPHILY *n* love of wine
OENOTHERA *n* type of
 American plant with yellow
 flowers that open in the
 evening
OERLIKON *n* type of cannon
OERLIKONS > OERLIKON
OERSTED *n* cgs unit of
 magnetic field strength
OERSTEDS > OERSTED
OES > OE
OESOPHAGI *pl n* gullets
OESTRAL > OESTRUS
OESTRIN *obsolete term for*
 > OESTROGEN
OESTRINS > OESTRIN
OESTRIOL *n* weak
 oestrogenic hormone
 secreted by the mammalian
 ovary
OESTRIOLS > OESTRIOL
OESTROGEN *n* female
 hormone
OESTRONE *n* weak
 oestrogenic hormone
 secreted by the mammalian
 ovary
OESTRONES > OESTRONE
OESTROUS > OESTRUS
OESTRUAL *adj* relating to
 oestrus
OESTRUM *same as*
 > OESTRUS
OESTRUMS > OESTRUM
OESTRUS *n* regularly
 occurring period of fertility in
 female mammals
OESTRUSES > OESTRUS
OEUVRE *n* work of art,
 literature, music, etc
OEUVRES > OEUVRE
OF *prep* belonging to
OFAY *n* derogatory term for a
 White person
OFAYS > OFAY
OFF *prep* away from ▷ *adv*
 away ▷ *adj* not operating ▷ *n*
 side of the field to which the
 batsman's feet point ▷ *vb*
 take off
OFFA *prep* off

OFFAL *n* edible organs of an
 animal, such as liver or
 kidneys
OFFALS > OFFAL
OFFBEAT *adj* unusual or
 eccentric ▷ *n* any of the
 normally unaccented beats
 in a bar
OFFBEATS > OFFBEAT
OFFCAST *n* cast-off
OFFCASTS > OFFCAST
OFFCUT *n* piece remaining
 after the required parts have
 been cut out
OFFCUTS > OFFCUT
OFFED > OFF
OFFENCE *n* (cause of) hurt
 feelings or annoyance
OFFENCES > OFFENCE
OFFEND *vb* hurt the feelings
 of, insult
OFFENDED > OFFEND
OFFENDER > OFFEND
OFFENDERS > OFFEND
OFFENDING > OFFEND
OFFENDS > OFFEND
OFFENSE *same as*
 > OFFENCE
OFFENSES > OFFENSE
OFFENSIVE *adj*
 disagreeable ▷ *n* position or
 action of attack
OFFER *vb* present
 (something) for acceptance
 or rejection ▷ *n* something
 offered
OFFERABLE > OFFER
OFFERED > OFFER
OFFEREE *n* person to whom
 an offer is made
OFFEREES > OFFEREE
OFFERER > OFFER
OFFERERS > OFFER
OFFERING *n* thing offered
OFFERINGS > OFFERING
OFFEROR > OFFER
OFFERORS > OFFER
OFFERS > OFFER
OFFERTORY *n* offering of
 the bread and wine for
 Communion
OFFHAND *adj* casual, curt
 ▷ *adv* without preparation
OFFHANDED *adj* without
 care or consideration
OFFICE *n* room or building
 where people work at desks
OFFICER *n* person in
 authority in the armed
 services ▷ *vb* furnish with
 officers
OFFICERED > OFFICER
OFFICERS > OFFICER
OFFICES > OFFICE
OFFICIAL *adj* of a position
 of authority ▷ *n* person who
 holds a position of authority
OFFICIALS > OFFICIAL
OFFICIANT *n* person who
 presides and officiates at a
 religious ceremony
OFFICIARY *n* body of
 officials ▷ *adj* of, relating to,
 or derived from office
OFFICIATE *vb* act in an
 official role
OFFICINAL *adj* (of
 pharmaceutical products)

O

available without prescription ▷ n officinal preparation or plant

OFFICIOUS adj interfering unnecessarily

OFFIE n off-licence

OFFIES > OFFIE

OFFING n area of the sea visible from the shore

OFFINGS > OFFING

OFFISH adj aloof or distant in manner

OFFISHLY > OFFISH

OFFKEY adj out of tune

OFFLINE adj disconnected from a computer or the internet

OFFLOAD vb pass responsibility to someone else

OFFLOADED > OFFLOAD

OFFLOADS > OFFLOAD

OFFPEAK adj relating to times outside periods of intensive use

OFFPRINT n separate reprint of an article that originally appeared in a larger publication ▷ vb reprint (an article taken from a larger publication) separately

OFFPRINTS > OFFPRINT

OFFPUT n act of putting off

OFFPUTS > OFFPUT

OFFRAMP n road allowing traffic to leave a motorway

OFFRAMPS > OFFRAMP

OFFS > OFF

OFFSADDLE vb unsaddle

OFFSCREEN adj unseen by film viewers

OFFSCUM n scum

OFFSCUMS > OFFSCUM

OFFSEASON n period of little trade in a business

OFFSET vb cancel out ▷ n printing method

OFFSETS > OFFSET

OFFSHOOT n something developed from something else

OFFSHOOTS > OFFSHOOT

OFFSHORE adv away from or at some distance from the shore ▷ adj sited or conducted at sea ▷ n company operating abroad where the tax system is more advantageous than at home ▷ vb transfer (work) to another country where wages are lower

OFFSHORED > OFFSHORE

OFFSHORES > OFFSHORE

OFFSIDE adv (positioned) illegally ahead of the ball ▷ n side of a vehicle nearest the centre of the road

OFFSIDER n partner or assistant

OFFSIDERS > OFFSIDER

OFFSIDES > OFFSIDE

OFFSPRING n child

OFFSTAGE adv out of the view of the audience ▷ n something that happens offstage

OFFSTAGES > OFFSTAGE

OFFTAKE n act of taking off

OFFTAKES > OFFTAKE

OFFTRACK adj not at a racetrack

OFFY same as > OFFIE

OFLAG n prisoner-of-war camp for officers in World War II

OFLAGS > OFLAG

OFT adv often

OFTEN adv frequently, much of the time

OFTENER > OFTEN

OFTENEST > OFTEN

OFTENNESS > OFTEN

OFTER > OFT

OFTEST > OFT

OFTTIMES same as > OFTEN

OGAM same as > OGHAM

OGAMIC > OGAM

OGAMS > OGAM

OGANESSON n highly radioactive element

OGDOAD n group of eight

OGDOADS > OGDOAD

OGEE n moulding having a cross section in the form of a letter S

OGEED adj (of an arch or moulding) having an ogee

OGEES > OGEE

OGGIN n sea

OGGINS > OGGIN

OGHAM n ancient writing system used by the Celts

OGHAMIC > OGHAM

OGHAMIST > OGHAM

OGHAMISTS > OGHAM

OGHAMS > OGHAM

OGIVAL > OGIVE

OGIVE n diagonal rib or groin of a Gothic vault

OGIVES > OGIVE

OGLE vb stare or gape at ▷ n flirtatious look

OGLED > OGLE

OGLER > OGLE

OGLERS > OGLE

OGLES > OGLE

OGLING > OGLE

OGLINGS > OGLE

OGMIC > OGAM

OGRE n giant that eats human flesh

OGREISH > OGRE

OGREISHLY > OGRE

OGREISM > OGRE

OGREISMS > OGRE

OGRES > OGRE

OGRESS > OGRE

OGRESSES > OGRE

OGRISH > OGRE

OGRISHLY > OGRE

OGRISM > OGRE

OGRISMS > OGRE

OH interj exclamation of surprise, pain, etc ▷ vb say 'oh'

OHED > OH

OHIA n Hawaiian plant

OHIAS > OHIA

OHING > OH

OHM n unit of electrical resistance

OHMAGE n electrical resistance in ohms

OHMAGES > OHMAGE

OHMIC adj of or relating to a circuit element

OHMICALLY > OHMIC

OHMMETER n instrument for measuring electrical resistance

OHMMETERS > OHMMETER

OHMS > OHM

OHO n exclamation expressing surprise, exultation, or derision

OHS > OH

OI interj shout to attract attention ▷ n grey-faced petrel

OIDIA > OIDIUM

OIDIOID > OIDIUM

OIDIUM n type of fungal spore

OIK n insulting word for person regarded as inferior because ignorant or lower-class

OIKIST same as > OECIST

OIKISTS > OIKIST

OIKS > OIK

OIL n viscous liquid, insoluble in water and usu flammable ▷ vb lubricate (a machine) with oil

OILBIRD n type of nocturnal gregarious cave-dwelling bird

OILBIRDS > OILBIRD

OILCAMP n camp for oil workers

OILCAMPS > OILCAMP

OILCAN n container with a long nozzle for applying oil to machinery

OILCANS > OILCAN

OILCLOTH n waterproof material

OILCLOTHS > OILCLOTH

OILCUP n cup-shaped oil reservoir in a machine providing continuous lubrication for a bearing

OILCUPS > OILCUP

OILED > OIL

OILER n person, device, etc, that lubricates or supplies oil

OILERIES > OILERY

OILERS > OILER

OILERY n oil business

OILFIELD n area containing oil reserves

OILFIELDS > OILFIELD

OILFIRED adj using oil as fuel

OILGAS n gaseous mixture of hydrocarbons used as a fuel

OILGASES > OILGAS

OILHOLE n hole for oil

OILHOLES > OILHOLE

OILIER > OILY

OILIEST > OILY

OILILY > OILY

OILINESS > OILY

OILING > OIL

OILLET same as > EYELET

OILLETS > OILLET

OILMAN n person who owns or operates oil wells

OILMEN > OILMAN

OILNUT n nut from which oil is extracted

OILNUTS > OILNUT

OILPAN n sump

OILPANS > OILPAN

OILPAPER n oiled paper

OILPAPERS > OILPAPER

OILPROOF adj resistant to oil

OILS > OIL

OILSEED n seed from which oil is extracted

OILSEEDS > OILSEED

OILSKIN n (garment made from) waterproof material

OILSKINS > OILSKIN

OILSTONE n stone with a fine grain lubricated with oil and used for sharpening cutting tools

OILSTONES > OILSTONE

OILTIGHT adj not allowing oil through

OILWAY n channel for oil

OILWAYS > OILWAY

OILY adj soaked or covered with oil

OINK n grunt of a pig or an imitation of this ▷ interj imitation or representation of the grunt of a pig ▷ vb make noise of pig

OINKED > OINK

OINKING > OINK

OINKS > OINK

OINOLOGY same as > OENOLOGY

OINOMEL same as > OENOMEL

OINOMELS > OINOMEL

OINT vb anoint

OINTED > OINT

OINTING > OINT

OINTMENT n greasy substance used for healing skin or as a cosmetic

OINTMENTS > OINTMENT

OINTS > OINT

OIS > OI

OITICICA n South American tree

OITICICAS > OITICICA

OJIME n Japanese bead used to secure cords

OJIMES > OJIME

OK interj expression of approval

OKA n unit of weight used in Turkey

OKAPI n African animal related to the giraffe but with a shorter neck

OKAPIS > OKAPI

OKAS > OKA

OKAY adj satisfactory ▷ vb approve or endorse ▷ n approval or agreement ▷ interj expression of approval

OKAYED > OKAY

OKAYING > OKAY

OKAYS > OKAY

OKE same as > OKA

OKEH variant of > OKAY

OKEHS > OKEH

OKES > OKE

OKEYDOKE *variant of* **>** OKAY

OKEYDOKEY *variant of*
> OKAY

OKIMONO *n* Japanese
ornamental item

OKIMONOS > OKIMONO

OKRA *n* tropical plant with
edible green pods

OKRAS > OKRA

OKTA *n* unit used in
meteorology to measure
cloud cover

OKTAS > OKTA

OLD *adj* having lived or
existed for a long time ▷ *n*
earlier or past time

OLDE *adj* old-world or quaint,
used facetiously

OLDEN *adj* old ▷ *vb* grow old

OLDENED > OLDEN

OLDENING > OLDEN

OLDENS > OLDEN

OLDER > OLD

OLDEST > OLD

OLDIE *n* old but popular
song or film

OLDIES > OLDIE

OLDISH > OLD

OLDNESS > OLD

OLDNESSES > OLD

OLDS > OLD

OLDSQUAW *n* type of
long-tailed sea duck

OLDSQUAWS > OLDSQUAW

OLDSTER *n* older person

OLDSTERS > OLDSTER

OLDSTYLE *n* printing type
style

OLDSTYLES > OLDSTYLE

OLDWIFE *n* any of various
fishes, esp the menhaden or
the alewife

OLDWIVES > OLDWIFE

OLDY *same as* **>** OLDIE

OLE *interj* exclamation of
approval or encouragement
customary at bullfights ▷ *n*
cry of olé

OLEA > OLEUM

OLEACEOUS *adj* relating to a
family of trees and shrubs,
including the ash, jasmine,
and olive

OLEANDER *n* Mediterranean
flowering evergreen shrub

OLEANDERS > OLEANDER

OLEARIA *n* daisy bush

OLEARIAS > OLEARIA

OLEASTER *n* type of shrub
with silver-white twigs and
yellow flowers

OLEASTERS > OLEASTER

OLEATE *n* any salt or ester of
oleic acid

OLEATES > OLEATE

OLECRANAL > OLECRANON

OLECRANON *n* bony
projection of the ulna behind
the elbow joint

OLEFIANT *adj* forming oil

OLEFIN *same as* **>** OLEFINE

OLEFINE *another name for*
> ALKENE

OLEFINES > OLEFINE

OLEFINIC > OLEFINE

OLEFINS > OLEFIN

OLEIC *adj* as in *oleic acid*
colourless oily liquid used in
making soap

OLEIN *another name for*
> TRIOLEIN

OLEINE *same as* **>** OLEIN

OLEINES > OLEINE

OLEINS > OLEIN

OLENT *adj* having smell

OLEO *n* as in *oleo oil* oil
extracted from beef fat

OLEOGRAPH *n*
chromolithograph printed in
oil colours to imitate the
appearance of an oil painting

OLEORESIN *n* semisolid
mixture of a resin and
essential oil

OLEOS > OLEO

OLES > OLE

OLESTRA *n* trademark term
for an artificial fat

OLESTRAS > OLESTRA

OLEUM *n* type of sulphuric
acid

OLEUMS > OLEUM

OLFACT *vb* smell something

OLFACTED > OLFACT

OLFACTING > OLFACT

OLFACTION *n* sense of smell

OLFACTIVE *adj* of sense of
smell

OLFACTORY *adj* relating to
the sense of smell ▷ *n* organ
or nerve concerned with the
sense of smell

OLFACTS > OLFACT

OLIBANUM *n* frankincense

OLIBANUMS > OLIBANUM

OLICOOK *n* doughnut

OLICOOKS > OLICOOK

OLID *adj* foul-smelling

OLIGAEMIA *n* reduction in
the volume of the blood, as
occurs after haemorrhage

OLIGAEMIC > OLIGAEMIA

OLIGARCH *n* member of an
oligarchy

OLIGARCHS > OLIGARCH

OLIGARCHY *n* government
by a small group of people

OLIGEMIA *same as*
> OLIGAEMIA

OLIGEMIAS > OLIGEMIA

OLIGEMIC > OLIGAEMIA

OLIGIST *n* type of iron ore

OLIGISTS > OLIGIST

OLIGOCENE *adj* belonging
to geological time period

OLIGOGENE *n* type of gene

OLIGOMER *n* compound of
relatively low molecular
weight containing up to five
monomer units

OLIGOMERS > OLIGOMER

OLIGOPOLY *n* market
situation in which control
over the supply of a
commodity is held by a small
number of producers

OLIGURIA *n* excretion of an
abnormally small volume of
urine

OLIGURIAS > OLIGURIA

OLIGURIC *adj* relating to
oliguria

OLINGO *n* South American
mammal

OLINGOS > OLINGO

OLINGUITO *n* type of small
S American mammal

OLIO *n* dish of many different
ingredients

OLIOS > OLIO

OLIPHANT *archaic variant of*
> ELEPHANT

OLIPHANTS > OLIPHANT

OLITORIES > OLITORY

OLITORY *n* kitchen garden

OLIVARY *adj* shaped like an
olive

OLIVE *n* small green or black
fruit used as food or pressed
for its oil ▷ *adj* greyish-green

OLIVENITE *n* green to
black rare secondary mineral

OLIVER *n* as in *Bath oliver*
type of unsweetened biscuit

OLIVERS > OLIVER

OLIVES > OLIVE

OLIVET *n* button shaped like
olive

OLIVETS > OLIVET

OLIVEWOOD *n* the wood of
the olive tree

OLIVINE *n* olive-green
mineral of the olivine group

OLIVINES > OLIVINE

OLIVINIC *adj* containing
olivine

OLLA *n* cooking pot

OLLAMH *n* old Irish term for a
wise man

OLLAMHS > OLLAMH

OLLAS > OLLA

OLLAV *same as* **>** OLLAMH

OLLAVS > OLLAV

OLLER *n* waste ground

OLLERS > OLLER

OLLIE *n* type of
skateboarding jump ▷ *vb*
perform an ollie

OLLIED > OLLIE

OLLIEING > OLLIE

OLLIES > OLLIE

OLM *n* pale blind eel-like
salamander

OLMS > OLM

OLOGIES > OLOGY

OLOGIST *n* scientist

OLOGISTS > OLOGIST

OLOGOAN *vb* complain loudly
without reason

OLOGOANED > OLOGOAN

OLOGOANS > OLOGOAN

OLOGY *n* science or other
branch of knowledge

OLOLIUQUI *n* medicinal
plant used by the Aztecs

OLOROSO *n* golden-coloured
sweet sherry

OLOROSOS > OLOROSO

OLPAE > OLPE

OLPE *n* ancient Greek jug

OLPES > OLPE

OLYCOOK *same as*
> OLYKOEK

OLYCOOKS > OLYCOOK

OLYKOEK *n* American type of
doughnut

OLYKOEKS > OLYKOEK

OLYMPIAD *n* staging of the
modern Olympic Games

OLYMPIADS > OLYMPIAD

OLYMPICS *pl n* modern
revival of the ancient Greek
games, featuring sporting
contests

OM *n* sacred syllable in
Hinduism

OMA *n* grandmother

OMADHAUN *n* foolish man or
boy

OMADHAUNS > OMADHAUN

OMAS > OMA

OMASA > OMASUM

OMASAL > OMASUM

OMASUM *n* compartment in
the stomach of a ruminant
animal

OMBER *same as* **>** OMBRE

OMBERS > OMBER

OMBRE *n* 18th-century card
game

OMBRELLA *old form of*
> UMBRELLA

OMBRELLAS > OMBRELLA

OMBRES > OMBRE

OMBROPHIL *n* plant
flourishing in rainy
conditions

OMBU *n* South American tree

OMBUDSMAN *n* official who
investigates complaints
against government
organizations

OMBUDSMEN > OMBUDSMAN

OMBUS > OMBU

OMEGA *n* last letter in the
Greek alphabet

OMEGAS > OMEGA

OMELET *same as*
> OMELETTE

OMELETS > OMELET

OMELETTE *n* dish of eggs
beaten and fried

OMELETTES > OMELETTE

OMEN *n* happening or object
thought to foretell success or
misfortune ▷ *vb* portend

OMENED > OMEN

OMENING > OMEN

OMENS > OMEN

OMENTA > OMENTUM

OMENTAL > OMENTUM

OMENTUM *n* double fold of
the peritoneum

OMENTUMS > OMENTUM

OMER *n* ancient Hebrew unit
of dry measure

OMERS > OMER

OMERTA *n* conspiracy of
silence

OMERTAS > OMERTA

OMICRON *n* 15th letter in the
Greek alphabet

OMICRONS > OMICRON

OMIGOD *interj* exclamation
of surprise, pleasure, dismay,
etc

OMIKRON *same as*
> OMICRON

OMIKRONS > OMIKRON

OMINOUS *adj* worrying,
seeming to foretell
misfortune

OMINOUSLY > OMINOUS

OMISSIBLE > OMIT

OMISSION *n* something
that has been left out or
passed over

O

O

OMISSIONS > OMISSION
OMISSIVE > OMISSION
OMIT *vb* leave out
OMITS > OMIT
OMITTANCE *n* omission
OMITTED > OMIT
OMITTER > OMIT
OMITTERS > OMIT
OMITTING > OMIT
OMLAH *n* staff team in India
OMLAHS > OMLAH
OMMATEA > OMMATEUM
OMMATEUM *n* insect eye
OMMATIDIA *pl n*
cone-shaped parts of the
eyes of some arthropods
OMNEITIES > OMNEITY
OMNEITY *n* state of being all
OMNIANA *n* miscellaneous
collection
OMNIANAS > OMNIANA
OMNIARCH *n* ruler of
everything
OMNIARCHS > OMNIARCH
OMNIBUS *n* several books or
TV or radio programmes
made into one ▷ *adj*
consisting of or dealing with
several different things at
once
OMNIBUSES > OMNIBUS
OMNIETIES > OMNIETY
OMNIETY *same as*
> OMNEITY
OMNIFIC *adj* creating all
things
OMNIFIED > OMNIFY
OMNIFIES > OMNIFY
OMNIFORM *adj* of all forms
OMNIFY *vb* make something
universal
OMNIFYING > OMNIFY
OMNIMODE *adj* of all
functions
OMNIRANGE *n* very-high-
frequency ground radio
navigational system
OMNIUM *n* total value
OMNIUMS > OMNIUM
OMNIVORA *n* group of
omnivorous mammals
OMNIVORE *n* omnivorous
animal
OMNIVORES > OMNIVORE
OMNIVORY *n* state of being
omnivorous
OMOHYOID *n* muscle in
shoulder
OMOHYOIDS > OMOHYOID
OMOPHAGIA *n* eating of raw
food, esp meat
OMOPHAGIC > OMOPHAGIA
OMOPHAGY *same as*
> OMOPHAGIA
OMOPHORIA *pl n* stole-like
bands worn by some bishops
OMOPLATE *n* shoulder blade
OMOPLATES > OMOPLATE
OMOV *n* voting system in
which each voter has one
vote to cast
OMOVS > OMOV
OMPHACITE *n* type of
mineral
OMPHALI > OMPHALOS
OMPHALIC > OMPHALOS
OMPHALOI > OMPHALOS

OMPHALOID *adj* like navel
OMPHALOS *n* (in the ancient
world) a sacred conical
object, esp a stone
OMRAH *n* Muslim noble
OMRAHS > OMRAH
OMS > OM
ON *prep* indicating position
above, attachment,
closeness, etc ▷ *adv* in
operation ▷ *adj* operating
▷ *n* side of the field on which
the batsman stands ▷ *vb* go
on
ONAGER *n* wild ass of Persia
ONAGERS > ONAGER
ONAGRI > ONAGER
ONANISM *n* withdrawal in
sexual intercourse before
ejaculation
ONANISMS > ONANISM
ONANIST > ONANISM
ONANISTIC > ONANISM
ONANISTS > ONANISM
ONBEAT *n* first and third
beats in a bar of four-four
time
ONBEATS > ONBEAT
ONBOARD *vb* incorporate (a
person) into a group
ONBOARDED > ONBOARD
ONBOARDS > ONBOARD
ONCE *adv* on one occasion
▷ *n* one occasion
ONCER *n* (formerly) a
one-pound note
ONCERS > ONCER
ONCES > ONCE
ONCET *dialect form of* > ONCE
ONCIDIUM *n* American
orchid
ONCIDIUMS > ONCIDIUM
ONCOGEN *n* substance
causing tumours to form
ONCOGENE *n* gene that can
cause cancer when
abnormally activated
ONCOGENES > ONCOGENE
ONCOGENIC *adj* causing the
formation of a tumour
ONCOGENS > ONCOGEN
ONCOLOGIC > ONCOLOGY
ONCOLOGY *n* branch of
medicine concerned with the
study, classification, and
treatment of tumours
ONCOLYSES > ONCOLYSIS
ONCOLYSIS *n* destruction
of tumours
ONCOLYTIC *adj* destroying
tumours
ONCOME *n* act of coming on
ONCOMES > ONCOME
ONCOMETER *n* instrument
for measuring body organs
ONCOMICE > ONCOMOUSE
ONCOMING *adj* approaching
from the front ▷ *n* approach
or onset
ONCOMINGS > ONCOMING
ONCOMOUSE *n* mouse bred
for cancer treatment
research
ONCOST *same as*
> OVERHEADS
ONCOSTMAN *n* miner paid
daily
ONCOSTMEN > ONCOSTMAN

ONCOSTS > ONCOST
ONCOTOMY *n* surgical
cutting of a tumour
ONCOVIRUS *n* virus causing
cancer
ONCUS *same as* > ONKUS
ONDATRA *same as*
> MUSQUASH
ONDATRAS > ONDATRA
ONDINE *same as* > UNDINE
ONDINES > ONDINE
ONDING *Scots word for*
> ONSET
ONDINGS > ONDING
ONDOGRAM *n* record made by
ondograph
ONDOGRAMS > ONDOGRAM
ONDOGRAPH *n* instrument
for producing a graphical
recording of an alternating
current
ONE *adj* single, lone ▷ *n*
number or figure 1 ▷ *pron* any
person
ONEFOLD *adj* simple
ONEIRIC *adj* of or relating to
dreams
ONELY *same as* > ONLY
ONENESS *n* unity
ONENESSES > ONENESS
ONER *n* single continuous
action
ONERIER > ONERY
ONERIEST > ONERY
ONEROUS *adj* (of a task)
difficult to carry out
ONEROUSLY > ONEROUS
ONERS > ONER
ONERY *same as* > ORNERY
ONES > ONE
ONESELF *pron* reflexive form
of *one*
ONESIE *n* one-piece
garment combining a top
with trousers
ONESIES > ONESIE
ONETIME *adj* at some time in
the past
ONEYER *old form of* > ONE
ONEYERS > ONEYER
ONEYRE *same as* > ONEYER
ONEYRES > ONEYRE
ONFALL *n* attack or onset
ONFALLS > ONFALL
ONFLOW *n* flowing on
ONFLOWS > ONFLOW
ONGAONGA *n* New Zealand
nettle with a severe or fatal
sting
ONGAONGAS > ONGAONGA
ONGOING *adj* in progress,
continuing
ONGOINGS *pl n* things that
are happening
ONIE *variant spelling of* > ONY
ONION *n* strongly flavoured
edible bulb ▷ *vb* add onion to
ONIONED > ONION
ONIONIER > ONION
ONIONIEST > ONION
ONIONING > ONION
ONIONS > ONION
ONIONSKIN *n* glazed
translucent paper
ONIONY > ONION
ONIRIC *same as* > ONEIRIC
ONISCOID *adj* of or like
woodlice

ONIUM *n* as in *onium
compound* type of chemical
salt
ONIUMS > ONIUM
ONKUS *adj* bad
ONLAY *n* artificial veneer for
a tooth
ONLAYS > ONLAY
ONLIEST *same as* > ONLY
ONLINE *adj* connected to a
computer or the internet
ONLINER *n* person who uses
the internet regularly
ONLINERS > ONLINER
ONLOAD *vb* load files on to a
computer
ONLOADED > ONLOAD
ONLOADING > ONLOAD
ONLOADS > ONLOAD
ONLOOKER *n* person who
watches without taking part
ONLOOKERS > ONLOOKER
ONLOOKING > ONLOOKER
ONLY *adj* alone of its kind
▷ *adv* exclusively
ONNED > ON
ONNING > ON
ONO *n* Hawaiian fish
ONOMAST *n* person who
studies proper names
ONOMASTIC *adj* of or
relating to proper names
ONOMASTS > ONOMAST
ONOS > ONO
ONRUSH *n* forceful forward
rush or flow
ONRUSHES > ONRUSH
ONRUSHING *adj*
approaching quickly
ONS > ON
ONSCREEN *adj* appearing on
screen
ONSET *n* beginning
ONSETS > ONSET
ONSETTER *n* attacker
ONSETTERS > ONSET
ONSETTING *n* attack
ONSHORE *adv* towards the
land
ONSHORING *n* practice of
employing white-collar
workers from abroad
ONSIDE *adv* (of a player in
various sports) in a legal
position ▷ *adj* taking one's
part or side ▷ *n* part of
cricket field where a
batsman stands
ONSIDES > ONSIDE
ONSLAUGHT *n* violent attack
ONST *same as* > ONCE
ONSTAGE *adj* visible by
audience
ONSTEAD *Scots word for*
> FARMSTEAD
ONSTEADS > ONSTEAD
ONSTREAM *adj* in operation
ONTIC *adj* having real
existence
ONTICALLY > ONTIC
ONTO *prep* a position on
ONTOGENIC > ONTOGENY
ONTOGENY *n* entire
sequence of events involved
in the development of an
individual organism
ONTOLOGIC > ONTOLOGY

ONTOLOGY n branch of philosophy concerned with existence

ONUS n responsibility or burden

ONUSES > ONUS

ONWARD same as > ONWARDS

ONWARDLY > ONWARD

ONWARDS adv at or towards a point or position ahead

ONY Scots word for > ANY

ONYCHA n part of mollusc

ONYCHAS > ONYCHA

ONYCHIA n inflammation of the nails or claws of animals

ONYCHIAS > ONYCHIA

ONYCHITE n type of stone

ONYCHITES > ONYCHITE

ONYCHITIS n inflammation of nails

ONYCHIUM n part of insect foot

ONYCHIUMS > ONYCHIUM

ONYMOUS adj (of a book) bearing its author's name

ONYX n type of quartz with coloured layers

ONYXES > ONYX

OO Scots word for > WOOL

OOBIT n hairy caterpillar

OOBITS > OOBIT

OOCYST n type of zygote

OOCYSTS > OOCYST

OOCYTE n immature female germ cell that gives rise to an ovum

OOCYTES > OOCYTE

OODLES pl n great quantities

OODLINS same as > OODLES

OOF n money

OOFIER > OOF

OOFIEST > OOF

OOFS > OOF

OOFTISH n money

OOFTISHES > OOFTISH

OOFY > OOF

OOGAMETE n female gamete

OOGAMETES > OOGAMETE

OOGAMIES > OOGAMY

OOGAMOUS > OOGAMY

OOGAMY n type of reproduction

OOGENESES > OOGENESIS

OOGENESIS n formation and maturation of ova from undifferentiated cells in the ovary

OOGENETIC > OOGENESIS

OOGENIES > OOGENY

OOGENY same as > OOGENESIS

OOGONIA > OOGONIUM

OOGONIAL > OOGONIUM

OOGONIUM n immature female germ cell forming oocytes by repeated divisions

OOGONIUMS > OOGONIUM

OOH interj exclamation of surprise, pleasure, pain, etc ▷ vb say ooh

OOHED > OOH

OOHING n act of exclaiming 'ooh'

OOHINGS > OOHING

OOHS > OOH

OOIDAL adj shaped like egg

OOLACHAN same as > EULACHON

OOLACHANS > OOLACHAN

OOLAKAN same as > EULACHON

OOLAKANS > OOLAKAN

OOLICHAN n north Pacific candlefish

OOLICHANS > OOLICHAN

OOLITE n limestone made up of tiny grains of calcium carbonate

OOLITES > OOLITE

OOLITH n tiny spherical grain of sedimentary rock

OOLITHS > OOLITH

OOLITIC > OOLITE

OOLOGIC > OOLOGY

OOLOGICAL > OOLOGY

OOLOGIES > OOLOGY

OOLOGIST > OOLOGY

OOLOGISTS > OOLOGY

OOLOGY n study of birds' eggs

OOLONG n kind of dark tea

OOLONGS > OOLONG

OOM n title of respect used to refer to an elderly man

OOMIAC same as > UMIAK

OOMIACK same as > UMIAK

OOMIACKS > OOMIACK

OOMIACS > OOMIAC

OOMIAK same as > UMIAK

OOMIAKS > OOMIAK

OOMPAH n representation of the sound made by a deep brass instrument ▷ vb make the noise of a brass instrument

OOMPAHED > OOMPAH

OOMPAHING > OOMPAH

OOMPAHPAH n representation of the sound made by a deep brass instrument

OOMPAHS > OOMPAH

OOMPH n enthusiasm, vigour, or energy

OOMPHS > OOMPH

OOMS > OOM

OOMYCETE n organism formerly classified as fungi

OOMYCETES > OOMYCETE

OON Scots word for > OVEN

OONS > OON

OONT n camel

OONTS > OONT

OOP vb Scots word meaning to bind

OOPED > OOP

OOPHORON n ovary

OOPHORONS > OOPHORON

OOPHYTE n gametophyte in mosses, liverworts, and ferns

OOPHYTES > OOPHYTE

OOPHYTIC > OOPHYTE

OOPING > OOP

OOPS interj exclamation of surprise or apology

OOR Scots form of > OUR

OORALI n member of Indian people

OORALIS > OORALI

OORIAL n Himalayan sheep

OORIALS > OORIAL

OORIE adj Scots word meaning shabby

OORIER > OORIE

OORIEST > OORIE

OOS > OO

OOSE n dust

OOSES > OOSE

OOSIER > OOSE

OOSIEST > OOSE

OOSPERM n fertilized ovum

OOSPERMS > OOSPERM

OOSPHERE n large female gamete produced in the oogonia of algae and fungi

OOSPHERES > OOSPHERE

OOSPORE n thick-walled spore developed from a fertilized oosphere

OOSPORES > OOSPORE

OOSPORIC > OOSPORE

OOSPOROUS > OOSPORE

OOSY > OOSE

OOT Scots word for > OUT

OOTHECA n capsule containing eggs

OOTHECAE > OOTHECA

OOTHECAL > OOTHECA

OOTID n immature female gamete that develops into an ovum

OOTIDS > OOTID

OOTS > OOT

OOZE vb flow slowly ▷ n sluggish flow

OOZED > OOZE

OOZES > OOZE

OOZIER > OOZY

OOZIEST > OOZY

OOZILY > OOZY

OOZINESS > OOZY

OOZING > OOZE

OOZY adj moist or dripping

OP n operation

OPA n grandfather

OPACIFIED > OPACIFY

OPACIFIER > OPACIFY

OPACIFIES > OPACIFY

OPACIFY vb become or make opaque

OPACITIES > OPACITY

OPACITY n state or quality of being opaque

OPACOUS same as > OPAQUE

OPAH n large soft-finned deep-sea fish

OPAHS > OPAH

OPAL n iridescent precious stone

OPALED adj made like opal

OPALESCE vb exhibit a milky iridescence

OPALESCED > OPALESCE

OPALESCES > OPALESCE

OPALINE adj opalescent ▷ n opaque or semiopaque whitish glass

OPALINES > OPALINE

OPALISED same as > OPALIZED

OPALIZED adj made into opal

OPALS > OPAL

OPAQUE adj not able to be seen through, not transparent ▷ n opaque pigment used to block out particular areas on a negative ▷ vb make opaque

OPAQUED > OPAQUE

OPAQUELY > OPAQUE

OPAQUER > OPAQUE

OPAQUES > OPAQUE

OPAQUEST > OPAQUE

OPAQUING > OPAQUE

OPAS > OPA

OPCODE n computer code containing operating instructions

OPCODES > OPCODE

OPE archaic or poetic word for > OPEN

OPED > OPE

OPEN adj not closed ▷ vb (cause to) become open ▷ n competition which all may enter

OPENABLE > OPEN

OPENCAST n as in opencast mining mining by excavating from the surface

OPENED > OPEN

OPENER n tool for opening cans and bottles

OPENERS > OPENER

OPENEST > OPEN

OPENING n beginning ▷ adj first

OPENINGS > OPENING

OPENLY > OPEN

OPENNESS > OPEN

OPENS > OPEN

OPENSIDE n in rugby, flanker who plays on the open side of the scrum

OPENSIDES > OPENSIDE

OPENWORK n ornamental work, as of metal or embroidery, having a pattern of openings or holes

OPENWORKS > OPENWORK

OPEPE n African tree

OPEPES > OPEPE

OPERA n drama in which the text is sung to an orchestral accompaniment

OPERABLE adj capable of being treated by a surgical operation

OPERABLY > OPERABLE

OPERAGOER n person who goes to operas

OPERAND n quantity, variable, or function upon which an operation is performed

OPERANDS > OPERAND

OPERANT adj producing effects ▷ n person or thing that operates

OPERANTLY > OPERANT

OPERANTS > OPERANT

OPERAS > OPERA

OPERATE vb (cause to) work

OPERATED > OPERATE

OPERATES > OPERATE

OPERATIC adj of or relating to opera

OPERATICS n performance of operas

OPERATING > OPERATE

OPERATION n method or procedure of working

OPERATISE same as > OPERATIZE

OPERATIVE adj working ▷ n worker with a special skill

OPERATIZE vb turn (a play, novel, etc) into an opera

OPERATOR n person who operates a machine or instrument

OPERATORS > OPERATOR

OPERCELE same as > OPERCULE

OPERCELES > OPERCELE

OPERCULA > OPERCULUM

OPERCULAR > OPERCULUM

OPERCULE n gill cover

OPERCULES > OPERCULE

OPERCULUM n covering flap or structure in animals or plants

OPERETTA n light-hearted comic opera

OPERETTAS > OPERETTA

OPERON n group of adjacent genes in bacteria

OPERONS > OPERON

OPEROSE adj laborious

OPEROSELY > OPEROSE

OPEROSITY > OPEROSE

OPES > OPE

OPGEFOK adj South African taboo slang for damaged or bungled

OPHIDIAN n reptile of the suborder which comprises the snakes

OPHIDIANS > OPHIDIAN

OPHIOLITE n type of mineral

OPHIOLOGY n branch of zoology that is concerned with the study of snakes

OPHITE n any of several greenish mottled rocks

OPHITES > OPHITE

OPHITIC adj having small elongated feldspar crystals enclosed

OPHIURA n sea creature like a starfish

OPHIURAN same as > OPHIURA

OPHIURANS > OPHIURAN

OPHIURAS > OPHIURA

OPHIURID same as > OPHIURA

OPHIURIDS > OPHIURID

OPHIUROID adj of or like ophiura

OPIATE n narcotic drug containing opium ▷ adj containing or consisting of opium ▷ vb treat with an opiate

OPIATED > OPIATE

OPIATES > OPIATE

OPIATING > OPIATE

OPIFICER n craftsperson

OPIFICERS > OPIFICER

OPINABLE adj thinkable

OPINE vb express an opinion

OPINED > OPINE

OPINES > OPINE

OPING > OPE

OPINICUS n mythical monster

OPINING > OPINE

OPINION n personal belief or judgment

OPINIONED adj having strong opinions

OPINIONS > OPINION

OPIOID n substance that resembles morphine

OPIOIDS > OPIOID

OPIUM n addictive narcotic drug made from poppy seeds

OPIUMISM n addiction to opium

OPIUMISMS > OPIUMISM

OPIUMS > OPIUM

OPOBALSAM n soothing ointment

OPODELDOC n medical ointment

OPOPANAX n medical resin from plant

OPORICE n former medicine made from fruit

OPORICES > OPORICE

OPOSSUM n small marsupial of America or Australasia

OPOSSUMS > OPOSSUM

OPPIDAN adj of a town ▷ n person living in a town

OPPIDANS > OPPIDAN

OPPILANT > OPPILATE

OPPILATE vb block (the pores, bowels, etc)

OPPILATED > OPPILATE

OPPILATES > OPPILATE

OPPO n counterpart in another organization

OPPONENCY > OPPONENT

OPPONENS n muscle of the thumb

OPPONENT n person one is working against in a contest, battle, or argument ▷ adj opposite, as in position

OPPONENTS > OPPONENT

OPPORTUNE adj happening at a suitable time

OPPOS > OPPO

OPPOSABLE adj (of the thumb) capable of touching the tip of all the other fingers

OPPOSABLY > OPPOSABLE

OPPOSE vb work against

OPPOSED > OPPOSE

OPPOSER > OPPOSE

OPPOSERS > OPPOSE

OPPOSES > OPPOSE

OPPOSING > OPPOSE

OPPOSITE adj situated on the other side ▷ n person or thing that is opposite ▷ prep facing ▷ adv on the other side

OPPOSITES > OPPOSITE

OPPRESS vb control by cruelty or force

OPPRESSED > OPPRESS

OPPRESSES > OPPRESS

OPPRESSOR > OPPRESS

OPPUGN vb call into question

OPPUGNANT adj combative, antagonistic, or contrary

OPPUGNED > OPPUGN

OPPUGNER > OPPUGN

OPPUGNERS > OPPUGN

OPPUGNING > OPPUGN

OPPUGNS > OPPUGN

OPS > OP

OPSIMATH n person who learns late in life

OPSIMATHS > OPSIMATH

OPSIMATHY > OPSIMATH

OPSIN n type of protein

OPSINS > OPSIN

OPSOMANIA n extreme enthusiasm for a particular food

OPSONIC > OPSONIN

OPSONIFY same as > OPSONIZE

OPSONIN n constituent of blood serum

OPSONINS > OPSONIN

OPSONISE same as > OPSONIZE

OPSONISED > OPSONISE

OPSONISES > OPSONISE

OPSONIUM n relish eaten with bread

OPSONIUMS > OPSONIUM

OPSONIZE vb subject (bacteria) to the action of opsonins

OPSONIZED > OPSONIZE

OPSONIZES > OPSONIZE

OPT vb show a preference, choose

OPTANT n person who opts

OPTANTS > OPTANT

OPTATIVE adj indicating or expressing choice, preference, or wish ▷ n optative mood

OPTATIVES > OPTATIVE

OPTED > OPT

OPTER > OPT

OPTERS > OPT

OPTIC adj relating to the eyes or sight

OPTICAL adj of or involving light or optics

OPTICALLY > OPTICAL

OPTICIAN n person qualified to prescribe glasses

OPTICIANS > OPTICIAN

OPTICIST n optics expert

OPTICISTS > OPTICIST

OPTICS n science of sight and light

OPTIMA > OPTIMUM

OPTIMAL adj best or most favourable

OPTIMALLY > OPTIMAL

OPTIMATE n Roman aristocrat

OPTIMATES > OPTIMATE

OPTIME n mathematics student at Cambridge University

OPTIMES > OPTIME

OPTIMISE same as > OPTIMIZE

OPTIMISED > OPTIMISE

OPTIMISER > OPTIMISE

OPTIMISES > OPTIMISE

OPTIMISM n tendency to take the most hopeful view

OPTIMISMS > OPTIMISM

OPTIMIST > OPTIMISM

OPTIMISTS > OPTIMISM

OPTIMIZE vb make the most of

OPTIMIZED > OPTIMIZE

OPTIMIZER > OPTIMIZE

OPTIMIZES > OPTIMIZE

OPTIMUM n best possible conditions ▷ adj most favourable

OPTIMUMS > OPTIMUM

OPTING > OPT

OPTION n choice ▷ vb obtain an option on

OPTIONAL adj possible but not compulsory ▷ n optional thing

OPTIONALS > OPTIONAL

OPTIONED > OPTION

OPTIONEE n holder of a financial option

OPTIONEES > OPTIONEE

OPTIONING > OPTION

OPTIONS > OPTION

OPTOLOGY n science of sight

OPTOMETER n any of various instruments for measuring the refractive power of the eye

OPTOMETRY n science or practice of testing visual acuity and prescribing corrective lenses

OPTOPHONE n device for blind people that converts printed words into sounds

OPTRONIC adj relating to optronics

OPTRONICS n science of electronic and light signals

OPTS > OPT

OPULENCE > OPULENT

OPULENCES > OPULENT

OPULENCY > OPULENT

OPULENT adj having or indicating wealth

OPULENTLY > OPULENT

OPULUS n flowering shrub

OPULUSES > OPULUS

OPUNTIA n type of cactus

OPUNTIAS > OPUNTIA

OPUS n artistic creation, esp a musical work

OPUSCLE same as > OPUSCULE

OPUSCLES > OPUSCLE

OPUSCULA > OPUSCULUM

OPUSCULAR > OPUSCULE

OPUSCULE n small or insignificant artistic work

OPUSCULES > OPUSCULE

OPUSCULUM same as > OPUSCULE

OPUSES > OPUS

OQUASSA n American trout

OQUASSAS > OQUASSA

OR prep before ▷ adj of the metal gold ▷ n gold

ORA > OS

ORACH same as > ORACHE

ORACHE n type of plant

ORACHES > ORACHE

ORACIES > ORACY

ORACLE n shrine of an ancient god ▷ vb utter as an oracle

ORACLED > ORACLE

ORACLES > ORACLE

ORACLING > ORACLE

ORACULAR adj of or like an oracle

ORACULOUS adj of an oracle

ORACY n capacity to use speech

ORAD adv towards the mouth

ORAGIOUS adj stormy

ORAL adj spoken ▷ n spoken examination

ORALISM n oral method of communicating with deaf people

ORALISMS > ORALISM

ORALIST > ORALISM

ORALISTS > ORALISM

ORALITIES > ORALITY

ORALITY n state of being oral

ORALLY > ORAL

ORALS > ORAL

ORANG n orangutan

ORANGE n reddish-yellow citrus fruit ▷ adj reddish-yellow

ORANGEADE n orange-flavoured, usu fizzy drink

ORANGER > ORANGE

ORANGERIE archaic variant of > ORANGERY

ORANGERY n greenhouse for growing orange trees

ORANGES > ORANGE

ORANGEST > ORANGE

ORANGEY > ORANGE

ORANGIER > ORANGE

ORANGIEST > ORANGE

ORANGISH > ORANGE

ORANGS > ORANG

ORANGUTAN n large ape with shaggy reddish-brown hair

ORANGY > ORANGE

ORANT n artistic representation of worshipper

ORANTS > ORANT

ORARIA > ORARIUM

ORARIAN n person who lives on the coast

ORARIANS > ORARIAN

ORARION n garment worn by Greek clergyman

ORARIONS > ORARION

ORARIUM n handkerchief

ORATE vb make or give an oration

ORATED > ORATE

ORATES > ORATE

ORATING > ORATE

ORATION n formal speech

ORATIONS > ORATION

ORATOR n skilful public speaker

ORATORIAL adj of oratory

ORATORIAN n clergyman of a particular type of church

ORATORIES > ORATORY

ORATORIO n musical composition for choir and orchestra

ORATORIOS > ORATORIO

ORATORS > ORATOR

ORATORY n art of making speeches

ORATRESS n female orator

ORATRICES > ORATRIX

ORATRIX n female orator

ORATRIXES > ORATRIX

ORATURE n oral forms of literature

ORATURES > ORATURE

ORB n ceremonial decorated sphere ▷ vb make or become circular or spherical

ORBED > ORB

ORBICULAR adj circular or spherical

ORBIER > ORBY

ORBIEST > ORBY

ORBING > ORB

ORBIT n curved path ▷ vb move in an orbit around

ORBITA same as > ORBIT

ORBITAL adj of or denoting an orbit ▷ n region surrounding an atomic nucleus

ORBITALLY > ORBITAL

ORBITALS > ORBITAL

ORBITAS > ORBITA

ORBITED > ORBIT

ORBITER n spacecraft or satellite designed to orbit a planet without landing on it

ORBITERS > ORBITER

ORBITIES > ORBITY

ORBITING > ORBIT

ORBITS > ORBIT

ORBITY n bereavement

ORBLESS > ORB

ORBLIKE adj like an orb

ORBS > ORB

ORBY adj orb-shaped

ORC n any of various whales, such as the killer and grampus

ORCA n killer whale

ORCAS > ORCA

ORCEIN n brown crystalline material

ORCEINS > ORCEIN

ORCHARD n area where fruit trees are grown

ORCHARDS > ORCHARD

ORCHAT same as > ORCHARD

ORCHATS > ORCHAT

ORCHEL same as > ORCHIL

ORCHELLA same as > ORCHIL

ORCHELLAS > ORCHELLA

ORCHELS > ORCHEL

ORCHESES > ORCHESIS

ORCHESIS n art of dance

ORCHESTIC adj of dance

ORCHESTRA n large group of musicians, esp playing a variety of instruments

ORCHID n plant with flowers that have unusual lip-shaped petals

ORCHIDIST n orchid grower

ORCHIDS > ORCHID

ORCHIL n any of various lichens

ORCHILLA same as > ORCHIL

ORCHILLAS > ORCHILLA

ORCHILS > ORCHIL

ORCHIS n type of orchid

ORCHISES > ORCHIS

ORCHITIC > ORCHITIS

ORCHITIS n inflammation of one or both testicles

ORCIN same as > ORCINOL

ORCINE same as > ORCINOL

ORCINES > ORCINE

ORCINOL n colourless crystalline water-soluble solid

ORCINOLS > ORCINOL

ORCINS > ORCIN

ORCS > ORC

ORD n pointed weapon

ORDAIN vb make (someone) a member of the clergy

ORDAINED > ORDAIN

ORDAINER > ORDAIN

ORDAINERS > ORDAIN

ORDAINING > ORDAIN

ORDAINS > ORDAIN

ORDALIAN adj of an ordeal

ORDALIUM same as > ORDEAL

ORDALIUMS > ORDALIUM

ORDEAL n painful or difficult experience

ORDEALS > ORDEAL

ORDER n instruction to be carried out ▷ vb give an instruction to

ORDERABLE > ORDER

ORDERED > ORDER

ORDERER > ORDER

ORDERERS > ORDER

ORDERING > ORDER

ORDERINGS > ORDER

ORDERLESS > ORDER

ORDERLIES > ORDERLY

ORDERLY adj well-organized ▷ n hospital attendant ▷ adv according to custom or rule

ORDERS > ORDER

ORDINAIRE adj ordinary

ORDINAL adj denoting a certain position in a sequence of numbers ▷ n book containing the forms of services for the ordination of ministers

ORDINALLY > ORDINAL

ORDINALS > ORDINAL

ORDINANCE n official rule or order

ORDINAND n candidate for ordination

ORDINANDS > ORDINAND

ORDINANT n person who ordains

ORDINANTS > ORDINANT

ORDINAR Scots word for > ORDINARY

ORDINARS > ORDINAR

ORDINARY adj usual or normal

ORDINATE n vertical coordinate of a point in a two-dimensional system of coordinates ▷ vb ordain

ORDINATED > ORDINATE

ORDINATES > ORDINATE

ORDINEE n person being ordained

ORDINEES > ORDINEE

ORDINES > ORDO

ORDNANCE n weapons and military supplies

ORDNANCES > ORDNANCE

ORDO n religious order

ORDOS > ORDO

ORDS > ORD

ORDURE n excrement

ORDURES > ORDURE

ORDUROUS > ORDURE

ORE n (rock containing) a mineral which yields metal

OREAD n mountain nymph

OREADES > OREAD

OREADS > OREAD

OREBODIES > OREBODY

OREBODY n mass of ore in a mine

ORECTIC adj of or relating to the desires

ORECTIVE > OREXIS

OREGANO n sweet-smelling herb used in cooking

OREGANOS > OREGANO

OREIDE same as > OROIDE

OREIDES > OREIDE

OREODONT n extinct prehistoric mammal

OREODONTS > OREODONT

OREOLOGY same as > OROLOGY

OREPEARCH same as > OVERPERCH

ORES > ORE

ORESTUNCK > OVERSTINK

OREWEED n seaweed

OREWEEDS > OREWEED

OREXIN n hormone that promotes wakefulness and stimulates the appetite

OREXINS > OREXIN

OREXIS n appetite

OREXISES > OREXIS

ORF n infectious disease of sheep

ORFE n small slender European fish

ORFES > ORFE

ORFRAY same as > ORPHREY

ORFRAYS > ORFRAY

ORFS > ORF

ORG n organization

ORGAN n part of an animal or plant that has a particular function

ORGANA > ORGANON

ORGANDIE n fine cotton fabric

ORGANDIES > ORGANDY

ORGANDY same as > ORGANDIE

ORGANELLE n structural and functional unit in a cell

ORGANIC adj of or produced from animals or plants ▷ n substance that is derived from animal or vegetable matter

ORGANICAL same as > ORGANIC

ORGANICS > ORGANIC

ORGANISE same as > ORGANIZE

ORGANISED same as > ORGANIZED

ORGANISER same as > ORGANIZER

ORGANISES > ORGANISE

ORGANISM n any living animal or plant

ORGANISMS > ORGANISM

ORGANIST n organ player

ORGANISTS > ORGANIST

ORGANITY same as > ORGANISM

ORGANIZE vb make arrangements for

ORGANIZED > ORGANIZE

ORGANIZER n person who organizes or is capable of organizing

ORGANIZES > ORGANIZE

O

ORGANON n system of logical or scientific rules

ORGANONS > ORGANON

ORGANOSOL n resin-based coating

ORGANOTIN adj of an organic compound used as a pesticide

ORGANS > ORGAN

ORGANUM same as > ORGANON

ORGANUMS > ORGANUM

ORGANZA n thin stiff fabric of silk, cotton, or synthetic fibre

ORGANZAS > ORGANZA

ORGANZINE n strong thread made of twisted strands of raw silk

ORGASM n most intense point of sexual pleasure ▷ vb experience orgasm

ORGASMED > ORGASM

ORGASMIC > ORGASM

ORGASMING > ORGASM

ORGASMS > ORGASM

ORGASTIC > ORGASM

ORGEAT n drink made with orange flower water

ORGEATS > ORGEAT

ORGIA same as > ORGY

ORGIAC > ORGY

ORGIAS > ORGIA

ORGIAST n person who indulges immoderately in an activity

ORGIASTIC > ORGY

ORGIASTS > ORGIAST

ORGIC > ORGY

ORGIES > ORGY

ORGILLOUS same as > ORGULOUS

ORGONE n substance claimed to be needed for mental health

ORGONES > ORGONE

ORGS > ORG

ORGUE n number of stakes lashed together

ORGUES > ORGUE

ORGULOUS adj proud

ORGY n act of immoderate indulgence

ORIBATID n type of mite

ORIBATIDS > ORIBATID

ORIBI n small African antelope

ORIBIS > ORIBI

ORICALCHE same as > ORICHALC

ORICHALC n type of alloy

ORICHALCS > ORICHALC

ORIEL n type of bay window

ORIELLED adj having an oriel

ORIELS > ORIEL

ORIENCIES > ORIENCY

ORIENCY n state of being iridescent

ORIENT vb position (oneself) according to one's surroundings ▷ n eastern sky or the dawn ▷ adj eastern

ORIENTAL adj eastern ▷ n native of the orient

ORIENTALS > ORIENTAL

ORIENTATE vb position (oneself) according to one's surroundings

ORIENTED > ORIENT

ORIENTEER vb take part in orienteering ▷ n person who takes part in orienteering

ORIENTER > ORIENT

ORIENTERS > ORIENT

ORIENTING > ORIENT

ORIENTS > ORIENT

ORIFEX same as > ORIFICE

ORIFEXES > ORIFEX

ORIFICE n opening or hole

ORIFICES > ORIFICE

ORIFICIAL > ORIFICE

ORIFLAMME n scarlet flag adopted as the national banner of France in the Middle Ages

ORIGAMI n Japanese decorative art of paper folding

ORIGAMIS > ORIGAMI

ORIGAN another name for > MARJORAM

ORIGANE same as > ORIGAN

ORIGANES > ORIGANE

ORIGANS > ORIGAN

ORIGANUM n type of aromatic plant

ORIGANUMS > ORIGANUM

ORIGIN n point from which something develops

ORIGINAL adj first or earliest ▷ n first version, from which others are copied

ORIGINALS > ORIGINAL

ORIGINARY adj native, indigenous

ORIGINATE vb come or bring into existence

ORIGINS > ORIGIN

ORIHOU n small New Zealand tree

ORIHOUS > ORIHOU

ORILLION n part of bastion

ORILLIONS > ORILLION

ORINASAL adj pronounced with simultaneous oral and nasal articulation ▷ n orinasal speech sound

ORINASALS > ORINASAL

ORIOLE n tropical or American songbird

ORIOLES > ORIOLE

ORISHA n any of the minor gods or spirits of traditional Yoruba religion

ORISHAS > ORISHA

ORISON another word for > PRAYER

ORISONS > ORISON

ORIXA same as > ORISHA

ORIXAS > ORIXA

ORLE n border around a shield

ORLEANS n type of fabric

ORLEANSES > ORLEANS

ORLES > ORLE

ORLISTAT n drug used for slimming

ORLISTATS > ORLISTAT

ORLON n crease-resistant acrylic fibre or fabric

ORLONS > ORLON

ORLOP n (in a vessel with four or more decks) the lowest deck

ORLOPS > ORLOP

ORMER n edible marine mollusc

ORMERS > ORMER

ORMOLU n gold-coloured alloy used for decoration

ORMOLUS > ORMOLU

ORNAMENT n decorative object ▷ vb decorate

ORNAMENTS > ORNAMENT

ORNATE adj highly decorated, elaborate

ORNATELY > ORNATE

ORNATER > ORNATE

ORNATEST > ORNATE

ORNERIER > ORNERY

ORNERIEST > ORNERY

ORNERY adj stubborn or vile-tempered

ORNIS less common word for > AVIFAUNA

ORNISES > ORNIS

ORNITHES n birds in Greek myth

ORNITHIC adj of or relating to birds or a bird fauna

ORNITHINE n type of amino acid

ORNITHOID adj like bird

OROGEN n part of earth subject to orogeny

OROGENIC > OROGENY

OROGENIES > OROGENY

OROGENS > OROGEN

OROGENY n formation of mountain ranges

OROGRAPHY n study or mapping of relief, esp of mountains

OROIDE n alloy containing copper, tin, and other metals

OROIDES > OROIDE

OROLOGIES > OROLOGY

OROLOGIST > OROGRAPHY

OROLOGY same as > OROGRAPHY

OROMETER n aneroid barometer with an altitude scale

OROMETERS > OROMETER

ORONASAL adj of or relating to the mouth and nose

OROPESA n float used in minesweeping

OROPESAS > OROPESA

OROTUND adj (of the voice) resonant and booming

OROTUNDLY adv in an orotund manner

ORPHAN n child whose parents are dead ▷ vb deprive of parents

ORPHANAGE n children's home for orphans

ORPHANED > ORPHAN

ORPHANING > ORPHAN

ORPHANISM n state of being an orphan

ORPHANS > ORPHAN

ORPHARION n large lute in use during the 16th and 17th centuries

ORPHIC adj mystical or occult

ORPHICAL same as > ORPHIC

ORPHISM n style of abstract art

ORPHISMS > ORPHISM

ORPHREY n richly embroidered band or border

ORPHREYED adj embroidered with gold

ORPHREYS > ORPHREY

ORPIMENT n yellow mineral

ORPIMENTS > ORPIMENT

ORPIN same as > ORPINE

ORPINE n type of plant

ORPINES > ORPINE

ORPINS > ORPIN

ORRA adj odd or unmatched

ORRAMAN n man who does odd jobs

ORRAMEN > ORRAMAN

ORRERIES > ORRERY

ORRERY n mechanical model of the solar system

ORRICE same as > ORRIS

ORRICES > ORRICE

ORRIS n kind of iris

ORRISES > ORRIS

ORRISROOT n rhizome of a type of iris, used as perfume

ORS > OR

ORSEILLE same as > ORCHIL

ORSEILLES > ORSEILLE

ORSELLIC > ORSEILLE

ORT n fragment

ORTANIQUE n hybrid between an orange and a tangerine

ORTHIAN adj having high pitch

ORTHICON n type of television camera tube

ORTHICONS > ORTHICON

ORTHO n type of photographic plate

ORTHOAXES > ORTHOAXIS

ORTHOAXIS n axis in a crystal

ORTHODOX adj conforming to established views

ORTHODOXY n orthodox belief or practice

ORTHOEPIC > ORTHOEPY

ORTHOEPY n study of correct or standard pronunciation

ORTHOPEDY n treatment of deformity

ORTHOPOD n surgeon

ORTHOPODS > ORTHOPOD

ORTHOPTER n type of aircraft propelled by flapping wings

ORTHOPTIC adj relating to normal binocular vision

ORTHOS > ORTHO

ORTHOSES > ORTHOSIS

ORTHOSIS n artificial or mechanical aid to support a weak part of the body

ORTHOTIC > ORTHOTICS

ORTHOTICS n use of artificial or mechanical aids to assist movement of weak joints or muscles

ORTHOTIST n person who is qualified to practise orthotics

ORTHOTONE adj (of a word) having an independent accent ▷ n independently accented word

ORTHROS n canonical hour in the Greek Church

ORTHROSES > ORTHROS

ORTOLAN n small European songbird eaten as a delicacy

ORTOLANS > ORTOLAN

ORTS pl n scraps or leavings

ORVAL n plant of sage family

ORVALS > ORVAL

ORYX n large African antelope

ORYXES > ORYX

ORZO n pasta in small grain shapes

ORZOS > ORZO

OS n mouth or mouthlike part or opening

OSAR > OS

OSCAR n cash

OSCARS > OSCAR

OSCHEAL adj of the scrotum

OSCILLATE vb swing back and forth

OSCINE n songbird ▷ adj of songbirds

OSCINES > OSCINE

OSCININE > OSCINE

OSCITANCE same as > OSCITANCY

OSCITANCY n state of being drowsy, lazy, or inattentive

OSCITANT > OSCITANCY

OSCITATE vb yawn

OSCITATED > OSCITATE

OSCITATES > OSCITATE

OSCULA > OSCULUM

OSCULANT adj possessing some of the characteristics of two different taxonomic groups

OSCULAR adj of or relating to an osculum

OSCULATE vb kiss

OSCULATED > OSCULATE

OSCULATES > OSCULATE

OSCULE n small mouth or opening

OSCULES > OSCULE

OSCULUM n mouthlike aperture

OSE same as > ESKER

OSES > OSE

OSETRA n type of caviar

OSETRAS > OSETRA

OSHAC n plant smelling of ammonia

OSHACS > OSHAC

OSIER n willow tree

OSIERED adj covered with osiers

OSIERIES > OSIERY

OSIERS > OSIER

OSIERY n work done with osiers

OSMATE n salt of osmic acid

OSMATES > OSMATE

OSMATIC adj relying on sense of smell

OSMETERIA pl n glands in some caterpillars that secrete foul-smelling substances to deter predators

OSMIATE same as > OSMATE

OSMIATES > OSMIATE

OSMIC adj of or containing osmium in a high valence state

OSMICALLY > OSMIC

OSMICS n science of smell

OSMIOUS same as > OSMOUS

OSMIUM n heaviest known metallic element

OSMIUMS > OSMIUM

OSMOL same as > OSMOLE

OSMOLAL > OSMOLE

OSMOLAR adj containing one osmole per litre

OSMOLE n unit of osmotic pressure

OSMOLES > OSMOLE

OSMOLS > OSMOL

OSMOMETER n instrument for measuring osmotic pressure

OSMOMETRY > OSMOMETER

OSMOSE vb undergo or cause to undergo osmosis

OSMOSED > OSMOSE

OSMOSES > OSMOSE

OSMOSING > OSMOSE

OSMOSIS n movement of a liquid through a membrane

OSMOTIC > OSMOSIS

OSMOUS adj of or containing osmium in a low valence state

OSMUND same as > OSMUNDA

OSMUNDA n type of fern

OSMUNDAS > OSMUNDA

OSMUNDINE n type of compost

OSMUNDS > OSMUND

OSNABURG n coarse plain-woven cotton used for sacks, furnishings, etc

OSNABURGS > OSNABURG

OSPREY n large fish-eating bird of prey

OSPREYS > OSPREY

OSSA > OS

OSSARIUM same as > OSSUARY

OSSARIUMS > OSSARIUM

OSSATURE n skeleton

OSSATURES > OSSATURE

OSSEIN n protein that forms the organic matrix of bone

OSSEINS > OSSEIN

OSSELET n growth on knee of horse

OSSELETS > OSSELET

OSSEOUS adj consisting of or like bone

OSSEOUSLY > OSSEOUS

OSSETER n sturgeon

OSSETERS > OSSETER

OSSETRA same as > OSETRA

OSSETRAS > OSSETRA

OSSIA n alternate version or passage ▷ conj or

OSSIAS > OSSIA

OSSICLE n small bone, esp one of those in the middle ear

OSSICLES > OSSICLE

OSSICULAR > OSSICLE

OSSIFIC adj making something turn to bone

OSSIFIED adj converted into bone

OSSIFIER > OSSIFY

OSSIFIERS > OSSIFY

OSSIFIES > OSSIFY

OSSIFRAGA n large sea bird

OSSIFRAGE n osprey

OSSIFY vb (cause to) become bone, harden

OSSIFYING > OSSIFY

OSSOBUCO n Italian dish of veal shank and vegetables stewed in wine

OSSOBUCOS > OSSOBUCO

OSSUARIES > OSSUARY

OSSUARY n any container for the burial of human bones, such as an urn or vault

OSTEAL adj of or relating to bone or to the skeleton

OSTEITIC > OSTEITIS

OSTEITIS n inflammation of a bone

OSTENSIVE adj directly showing or pointing out

OSTENSORY n (in the RC Church) receptacle for displaying the consecrated Host

OSTENT n appearance ▷ vb display boastfully

OSTENTED > OSTENT

OSTENTING > OSTENT

OSTENTS > OSTENT

OSTEOCYTE n bone cell

OSTEODERM n bony area in skin

OSTEOGEN n material from which bone forms

OSTEOGENS > OSTEOGEN

OSTEOGENY n forming of bone

OSTEOID adj of or resembling bone ▷ n bony deposit

OSTEOIDS > OSTEOID

OSTEOLOGY n study of the structure and function of bones

OSTEOMA n tumour composed of bone or bonelike tissue

OSTEOMAS > OSTEOMA

OSTEOMATA > OSTEOMA

OSTEOPATH n person who practises osteopathy

OSTEOSES > OSTEOSIS

OSTEOSIS n forming of bony tissue

OSTEOTOME n surgical instrument for cutting bone, usually a special chisel

OSTEOTOMY n surgical cutting or dividing of bone

OSTIA > OSTIUM

OSTIAL > OSTIUM

OSTIARIES > OSTIARY

OSTIARY another word for > PORTER

OSTIATE adj having ostium

OSTINATI > OSTINATO

OSTINATO n persistently repeated phrase or rhythm

OSTINATOS > OSTINATO

OSTIOLAR > OSTIOLE

OSTIOLATE > OSTIOLE

OSTIOLE n pore in the reproductive bodies of certain algae and fungi

OSTIOLES > OSTIOLE

OSTIUM n pore through which water enters the body

OSTLER n stableman at an inn

OSTLERESS n female ostler

OSTLERS > OSTLER

OSTMARK n currency of the former East Germany

OSTMARKS > OSTMARK

OSTOMATE n person with an ostomy

OSTOMATES > OSTOMATE

OSTOMIES > OSTOMY

OSTOMY n surgically made opening

OSTOSES > OSTOSIS

OSTOSIS n formation of bone

OSTOSISES > OSTOSIS

OSTRACA > OSTRACON

OSTRACEAN adj of oysters ▷ n type of bivalve

OSTRACISE same as > OSTRACIZE

OSTRACISM > OSTRACIZE

OSTRACIZE vb exclude (a person) from a group

OSTRACOD n type of minute crustacean

OSTRACODE adj of ostracods

OSTRACODS > OSTRACOD

OSTRACON n (in ancient Greece) a potsherd used for ostracizing

OSTRAKA > OSTRAKON

OSTRAKON same as > OSTRACON

OSTREGER n keeper of hawks

OSTREGERS > OSTREGER

OSTRICH n large African bird that runs fast but cannot fly

OSTRICHES > OSTRICH

OTAKU n Japanese computer geek

OTAKUS > OTAKU

OTALGIA technical name for > EARACHE

OTALGIAS > OTALGIA

OTALGIC > OTALGIA

OTALGIES > OTALGY

OTALGY same as > OTALGIA

OTARID adj of or like an otary, an eared seal

OTARIES > OTARY

OTARINE > OTARY

OTARY n seal with ears

OTHER vb regard (a person or people) as different from oneself or one's group

OTHERED > OTHER

OTHERING > OTHER

OTHERNESS n quality of being different or distinct in appearance, character, etc

OTHERS > OTHER

OTHERWISE adv differently, in another way ▷ adj of an unexpected nature ▷ pron something different in outcome

OTIC adj of or relating to the ear

OTIOSE adj not useful

OTIOSELY > OTIOSE

OTIOSITY > OTIOSE

OTITIC > OTITIS

OTITIDES > OTITIS

OTITIS *n* inflammation of the ear

OTITISES > OTITIS

OTOCYST *n* embryonic structure in vertebrates that develops into the inner ear

OTOCYSTIC > OTOCYST

OTOCYSTS > OTOCYST

OTOLITH *n* granule of calcium carbonate in the inner ear of vertebrates

OTOLITHIC > OTOLITH

OTOLITHS > OTOLITH

OTOLOGIC *adj* relating to otology

OTOLOGIES > OTOLOGY

OTOLOGIST > OTOLOGY

OTOLOGY *n* branch of medicine concerned with the ear

OTOPLASTY *n* cosmetic surgery on ears

OTORRHOEA *n* discharge from the ears

OTOSCOPE *another name for* **>** AURISCOPE

OTOSCOPES > OTOSCOPE

OTOSCOPIC > OTOSCOPY

OTOSCOPY *n* examination of ear using otoscope

OTOTOXIC *adj* toxic to the ear

OTTAR *variant of* **>** ATTAR

OTTARS > OTTAR

OTTAVA *n* interval of an octave

OTTAVAS > OTTAVA

OTTAVINO *n* piccolo

OTTAVINOS > OTTAVINO

OTTER *n* small brown freshwater mammal that eats fish ▷ *vb* fish using an otter board

OTTERED > OTTER

OTTERING > OTTER

OTTERS > OTTER

OTTO *another name for* **>** ATTAR

OTTOMAN *n* storage chest with a padded lid for use as a seat

OTTOMANS > OTTOMAN

OTTOS > OTTO

OTTRELITE *n* type of mineral

OU *interj* expressing concession ▷ *n* man, bloke, or chap

OUABAIN *n* poisonous white crystalline glycoside

OUABAINS > OUABAIN

OUAKARI *n* South American monkey

OUAKARIS > OUAKARI

OUBAAS *n* man in authority

OUBAASES > OUBAAS

OUBIT *n* hairy caterpillar

OUBITS > OUBIT

OUBLIETTE *n* dungeon entered only by a trapdoor

OUCH *interj* exclamation of sudden pain ▷ *n* brooch or clasp set with gems ▷ *vb* say ouch

OUCHED > OUCH

OUCHES > OUCH

OUCHING > OUCH

OUCHT *Scots word for* **>** ANYTHING

OUCHTS > OUCHT

OUD *n* Arabic stringed musical instrument

OUDS > OUD

OUENS > OU

OUGHLIED > OUGHLY

OUGHLIES > OUGHLY

OUGHLY *variant of* **>** UGLY

OUGHLYING > OUGHLY

OUGHT *vb* have an obligation ▷ *n* zero

OUGHTED > OUGHT

OUGHTING > OUGHT

OUGHTNESS *n* state of being right

OUGHTS > OUGHT

OUGIYA *n* monetary unit of Mauretania

OUGIYAS > OUGIYA

OUGLIE *variant of* **>** UGLY

OUGLIED > OUGLIE

OUGLIEING > OUGLIE

OUGLIES > OUGLIE

OUGUIYA *n* standard monetary unit of Mauritania

OUGUIYAS > OUGUIYA

OUIJA *n* tradename for a board through which spirits supposedly answer questions

OUIJAS > OUIJA

OUISTITI *n* marmoset

OUISTITIS > OUISTITI

OUK *Scots word for* **>** WEEK

OUKS > OUK

OULACHON *same as* **>** EULACHON

OULACHONS > OULACHON

OULAKAN *same as* **>** EULACHON

OULAKANS > OULAKAN

OULD *Scots or Irish form of* **>** OLD

OULDER > OULD

OULDEST > OULD

OULK *Scots form of* **>** WEEK

OULKS > OULK

OULONG *same as* **>** OOLONG

OULONGS > OULONG

OUMA *n* grandmother, often as a title with a surname

OUMAS > OUMA

OUNCE *n* unit of weight equal to one sixteenth of a pound

OUNCES > OUNCE

OUNDIER > OUNDY

OUNDIEST > OUNDY

OUNDY *adj* wavy

OUP *same as* **>** OOP

OUPA *n* grandfather, often as a title with a surname

OUPAS > OUPA

OUPED > OUP

OUPH *same as* **>** OAF

OUPHE *same as* **>** OAF

OUPHES > OUPHE

OUPHS > OUPH

OUPING > OUP

OUPS > OUP

OUR *adj* belonging to us ▷ *determiner* of, belonging to, or associated in some way with us

OURALI *n* plant from which curare comes

OURALIS > OURALI

OURANG *same as* **>** ORANG

OURANGS > OURANG

OURARI *same as* **>** OURALI

OURARIS > OURARI

OUREBI *same as* **>** ORIBI

OUREBIS > OUREBI

OURIE *same as* **>** OORIE

OURIER > OURIE

OURIEST > OURIE

OURN *dialect form of* **>** OUR

OUROBOROS *n* mythical serpent

OUROLOGY *same as* **>** UROLOGY

OUROSCOPY *same as* **>** UROSCOPY

OURS *pron* thing(s) belonging to us

OURSELF *pron* formal word for *myself* used by monarchs

OURSELVES *pron* reflexive form of *we* or *us*

OUS > OU

OUSEL *same as* **>** OUZEL

OUSELS > OUSEL

OUST *vb* force (someone) out, expel

OUSTED > OUST

OUSTER *n* act of forcing someone out of a position

OUSTERS > OUSTER

OUSTING > OUST

OUSTITI *n* device for opening locked door

OUSTITIS > OUSTITI

OUSTS > OUST

OUT *adj* denoting movement or distance away from ▷ *vb* put or throw out

OUTA *prep* informal contraction of out of

OUTACT *vb* surpass in acting

OUTACTED > OUTACT

OUTACTING > OUTACT

OUTACTS > OUTACT

OUTADD *vb* beat or surpass at adding

OUTADDED > OUTADD

OUTADDING > OUTADD

OUTADDS > OUTADD

OUTAGE *n* period of power failure

OUTAGES > OUTAGE

OUTARGUE *vb* defeat in argument

OUTARGUED > OUTARGUE

OUTARGUES > OUTARGUE

OUTASIGHT *adj* excellent or wonderful

OUTASITE *adj* amazing, excellent

OUTASK *vb* declare wedding banns

OUTASKED > OUTASK

OUTASKING > OUTASK

OUTASKS > OUTASK

OUTATE > OUTEAT

OUTBACK *n* remote bush country of Australia

OUTBACKER > OUTBACK

OUTBACKS > OUTBACK

OUTBAKE *vb* bake more or better than

OUTBAKED > OUTBAKE

OUTBAKES > OUTBAKE

OUTBAKING > OUTBAKE

OUTBAR *vb* keep out

OUTBARK *vb* bark more or louder than

OUTBARKED > OUTBARK

OUTBARKS > OUTBARK

OUTBARRED > OUTBAR

OUTBARS > OUTBAR

OUTBAWL *vb* bawl more or louder than

OUTBAWLED > OUTBAWL

OUTBAWLS > OUTBAWL

OUTBEAM *vb* beam more or brighter than

OUTBEAMED > OUTBEAM

OUTBEAMS > OUTBEAM

OUTBEG *vb* beg more or better than

OUTBEGGED > OUTBEG

OUTBEGS > OUTBEG

OUTBID *vb* offer a higher price than

OUTBIDDEN > OUTBID

OUTBIDDER > OUTBID

OUTBIDS > OUTBID

OUTBITCH *vb* bitch more or better than

OUTBLAZE *vb* blaze more or hotter than

OUTBLAZED > OUTBLAZE

OUTBLAZES > OUTBLAZE

OUTBLEAT *vb* bleat more or louder than

OUTBLEATS > OUTBLEAT

OUTBLESS *vb* bless more than

OUTBLOOM *vb* bloom more or better than

OUTBLOOMS > OUTBLOOM

OUTBLUFF *vb* surpass in bluffing

OUTBLUFFS > OUTBLUFF

OUTBLUSH *vb* blush more than

OUTBOARD *adj* (of a boat's engine) portable, with its own propeller ▷ *adv* away from the centre line of a vessel or aircraft ▷ *n* outboard motor

OUTBOARDS > OUTBOARD

OUTBOAST *vb* surpass in boasting

OUTBOASTS > OUTBOAST

OUTBOUGHT > OUTBUY

OUTBOUND *adj* going out

OUTBOUNDS *n* boundaries

OUTBOX *vb* surpass in boxing

OUTBOXED > OUTBOX

OUTBOXES > OUTBOX

OUTBOXING > OUTBOX

OUTBRAG *vb* brag more or better than

OUTBRAGS > OUTBRAG

OUTBRAVE *vb* surpass in bravery

OUTBRAVED > OUTBRAVE

OUTBRAVES > OUTBRAVE

OUTBRAWL *vb* defeat in a brawl

OUTBRAWLS > OUTBRAWL

OUTBRAZEN *vb* be more brazen than

OUTBREAK *n* sudden occurrence (of something unpleasant) ▷ *vb* break out

OUTBREAKS > OUTBREAK

OUTBRED > OUTBREED**

OUTBREED *vb* produce offspring outside a particular family or tribe
OUTBREEDS > OUTBREED
OUTBRIBE *vb* bribe more than
OUTBRIBED > OUTBRIBE
OUTBRIBES > OUTBRIBE
OUTBROKE > OUTBREAK
OUTBROKEN > OUTBREAK
OUTBUILD *vb* exceed in building
OUTBUILDS > OUTBUILD
OUTBUILT > OUTBUILD
OUTBULGE *vb* bulge outwards
OUTBULGED > OUTBULGE
OUTBULGES > OUTBULGE
OUTBULK *vb* exceed in bulk
OUTBULKED > OUTBULK
OUTBULKS > OUTBULK
OUTBULLY *vb* exceed in bullying
OUTBURN *vb* burn longer or brighter than
OUTBURNED > OUTBURN
OUTBURNS > OUTBURN
OUTBURNT > OUTBURN
OUTBURST *n* sudden expression of emotion ▷ *vb* burst out
OUTBURSTS > OUTBURST
OUTBUY *vb* buy more than
OUTBUYING > OUTBUY
OUTBUYS > OUTBUY
OUTBY *adv* outside
OUTBYE *same as* > OUTBY
OUTCALL *n* visit to customer's home by professional ▷ *vb* bid higher than another player in a card game
OUTCALLED > OUTCALL
OUTCALLS > OUTCALL
OUTCAPER *vb* exceed in capering
OUTCAPERS > OUTCAPER
OUTCAST *n* person rejected by a particular group ▷ *adj* rejected, abandoned, or discarded
OUTCASTE *n* person who has been expelled from a caste ▷ *vb* cause (someone) to lose his or her caste
OUTCASTED > OUTCASTE
OUTCASTES > OUTCASTE
OUTCASTS > OUTCAST
OUTCATCH *vb* catch more than
OUTCAUGHT > OUTCATCH
OUTCAVIL *vb* exceed in cavilling
OUTCAVILS > OUTCAVIL
OUTCHARGE *vb* charge more than
OUTCHARM *vb* exceed in charming
OUTCHARMS > OUTCHARM
OUTCHEAT *vb* exceed in cheating
OUTCHEATS > OUTCHEAT
OUTCHID > OUTCHIDE
OUTCHIDE *vb* exceed in chiding
OUTCHIDED > OUTCHIDE
OUTCHIDES > OUTCHIDE

OUTCITIES > OUTCITY
OUTCITY *n* anywhere outside a city's confines
OUTCLASS *vb* surpass in quality
OUTCLIMB *vb* exceed in climbing
OUTCLIMBS > OUTCLIMB
OUTCLOMB > OUTCLIMB
OUTCOACH *vb* exceed in coaching
OUTCOME *n* result
OUTCOMES > OUTCOME
OUTCOOK *vb* cook more or better than
OUTCOOKED > OUTCOOK
OUTCOOKS > OUTCOOK
OUTCOUNT *vb* exceed in counting
OUTCOUNTS > OUTCOUNT
OUTCRAFTY *vb* be craftier than
OUTCRAWL *vb* crawl further or faster than
OUTCRAWLS > OUTCRAWL
OUTCRIED > OUTCRY
OUTCRIES > OUTCRY
OUTCROP *n* part of a rock formation that sticks out of the earth ▷ *vb* (of rock strata) to protrude through the surface of the earth
OUTCROPS > OUTCROP
OUTCROSS *vb* breed (animals or plants of the same breed but different strains) ▷ *n* animal or plant produced as a result of outcrossing
OUTCROW *vb* exceed in crowing
OUTCROWD *vb* have more crowd than
OUTCROWDS > OUTCROWD
OUTCROWED > OUTCROW
OUTCROWS > OUTCROW
OUTCRY *n* vehement or widespread protest ▷ *vb* cry louder or make more noise than (someone or something)
OUTCRYING > OUTCRY
OUTCURSE *vb* exceed in cursing
OUTCURSED > OUTCURSE
OUTCURSES > OUTCURSE
OUTCURVE *n* baseball thrown to curve away from batter
OUTCURVES > OUTCURVE
OUTDANCE *vb* surpass in dancing
OUTDANCED > OUTDANCE
OUTDANCES > OUTDANCE
OUTDARE *vb* be more brave than
OUTDARED > OUTDARE
OUTDARES > OUTDARE
OUTDARING > OUTDARE
OUTDATE *vb* make or become old-fashioned or obsolete
OUTDATED *adj* old-fashioned
OUTDATES > OUTDATE
OUTDATING > OUTDATE
OUTDAZZLE *vb* exceed in dazzling

OUTDEBATE *vb* exceed in debate
OUTDESIGN *vb* exceed in designing
OUTDID > OUTDO
OUTDO *vb* surpass in performance
OUTDODGE *vb* surpass in dodging
OUTDODGED > OUTDODGE
OUTDODGES > OUTDODGE
OUTDOER > OUTDO
OUTDOERS > OUTDO
OUTDOES > OUTDO
OUTDOING > OUTDO
OUTDONE > OUTDO
OUTDOOR *adj* taking place in the open air
OUTDOORS *adv* in(to) the open air ▷ *n* open air
OUTDOORSY *adj* taking part in activities relating to the outdoors
OUTDRAG *vb* beat in drag race
OUTDRAGS > OUTDRAG
OUTDRANK > OUTDRINK
OUTDRAW *vb* draw (a gun) faster than
OUTDRAWN > OUTDRAW
OUTDRAWS > OUTDRAW
OUTDREAM *vb* exceed in dreaming
OUTDREAMS > OUTDREAM
OUTDREAMT > OUTDREAM
OUTDRESS *vb* dress better than
OUTDREW > OUTDRAW
OUTDRINK *vb* drink more alcohol than
OUTDRINKS > OUTDRINK
OUTDRIVE *vb* exceed in driving
OUTDRIVEN > OUTDRIVE
OUTDRIVES > OUTDRIVE
OUTDROP *same as* > OUTCROP
OUTDROPS > OUTDROP
OUTDROVE > OUTDRIVE
OUTDRUNK > OUTDRINK
OUTDUEL *vb* defeat in duel
OUTDUELED > OUTDUEL
OUTDUELS > OUTDUEL
OUTDURE *vb* last longer than
OUTDURED > OUTDURE
OUTDURES > OUTDURE
OUTDURING > OUTDURE
OUTDWELL *vb* live outside something
OUTDWELLS > OUTDWELL
OUTDWELT > OUTDWELL
OUTEARN *vb* earn more than
OUTEARNED > OUTEARN
OUTEARNS > OUTEARN
OUTEAT *vb* eat more than
OUTEATEN > OUTEAT
OUTEATING > OUTEAT
OUTEATS > OUTEAT
OUTECHO *vb* echo more than
OUTECHOED > OUTECHO
OUTECHOES > OUTECHO
OUTED > OUT
OUTEDGE *n* furthest limit
OUTEDGES > OUTEDGE
OUTER *adj* on the outside ▷ *n* white outermost ring on a target

OUTERCOAT *same as* > OVERCOAT
OUTERMOST *adj* furthest out
OUTERS > OUTER
OUTERWEAR *n* clothes worn on top of other clothes
OUTFABLE *vb* exceed in creating fables
OUTFABLED > OUTFABLE
OUTFABLES > OUTFABLE
OUTFACE *vb* subdue or disconcert by staring
OUTFACED > OUTFACE
OUTFACES > OUTFACE
OUTFACING > OUTFACE
OUTFALL *n* mouth of a river or drain
OUTFALLS > OUTFALL
OUTFAST *vb* fast longer than
OUTFASTED > OUTFAST
OUTFASTS > OUTFAST
OUTFAWN *vb* exceed in fawning
OUTFAWNED > OUTFAWN
OUTFAWNS > OUTFAWN
OUTFEAST *vb* exceed in feasting
OUTFEASTS > OUTFEAST
OUTFEEL *vb* exceed in feeling
OUTFEELS > OUTFEEL
OUTFELT > OUTFEEL
OUTFENCE *vb* surpass at fencing
OUTFENCED > OUTFENCE
OUTFENCES > OUTFENCE
OUTFIELD *n* area far from the pitch
OUTFIELDS > OUTFIELD
OUTFIGHT *vb* surpass in fighting
OUTFIGHTS > OUTFIGHT
OUTFIGURE *same as* > OUTTHINK
OUTFIND *vb* exceed in finding
OUTFINDS > OUTFIND
OUTFIRE *vb* exceed in firing
OUTFIRED > OUTFIRE
OUTFIRES > OUTFIRE
OUTFIRING > OUTFIRE
OUTFISH *vb* catch more fish than
OUTFISHED > OUTFISH
OUTFISHES > OUTFISH
OUTFIT *n* matching set of clothes ▷ *vb* furnish or be furnished with an outfit
OUTFITS > OUTFIT
OUTFITTED > OUTFIT
OUTFITTER *n* supplier of clothes
OUTFLANK *vb* get round the side of (an enemy army)
OUTFLANKS > OUTFLANK
OUTFLASH *vb* be flashier than
OUTFLEW > OUTFLY
OUTFLIES > OUTFLY
OUTFLING *n* cutting remark ▷ *vb* whip out
OUTFLINGS > OUTFLING
OUTFLOAT *vb* surpass at floating
OUTFLOATS > OUTFLOAT
OUTFLOW *n* anything that flows out, such as liquid or money ▷ *vb* flow faster than

OUTFLOWED > OUTFLOW
OUTFLOWN > OUTFLY
OUTFLOWS > OUTFLOW
OUTFLUNG > OUTFLING
OUTFLUSH n burst of light
OUTFLY vb fly better or faster than
OUTFLYING > OUTFLY
OUTFOOL vb be more foolish than
OUTFOOLED > OUTFOOL
OUTFOOLS > OUTFOOL
OUTFOOT vb (of a boat) to go faster than (another boat)
OUTFOOTED > OUTFOOT
OUTFOOTS > OUTFOOT
OUTFOUGHT > OUTFIGHT
OUTFOUND > OUTFIND
OUTFOX vb defeat or foil by being more cunning
OUTFOXED > OUTFOX
OUTFOXES > OUTFOX
OUTFOXING > OUTFOX
OUTFROWN vb dominate by frowning more than
OUTFROWNS > OUTFROWN
OUTFUMBLE vb exceed in fumbling
OUTGAIN vb gain more than
OUTGAINED > OUTGAIN
OUTGAINS > OUTGAIN
OUTGALLOP vb gallop faster than
OUTGAMBLE vb defeat at gambling
OUTGAS vb undergo the removal of adsorbed or absorbed gas from solids
OUTGASES > OUTGAS
OUTGASSED > OUTGAS
OUTGASSES > OUTGAS
OUTGATE n way out
OUTGATES > OUTGATE
OUTGAVE > OUTGIVE
OUTGAZE vb gaze beyond
OUTGAZED > OUTGAZE
OUTGAZES > OUTGAZE
OUTGAZING > OUTGAZE
OUTGIVE vb exceed in giving
OUTGIVEN > OUTGIVE
OUTGIVES > OUTGIVE
OUTGIVING > OUTGIVE
OUTGLARE vb exceed in glaring
OUTGLARED > OUTGLARE
OUTGLARES > OUTGLARE
OUTGLEAM vb gleam more than
OUTGLEAMS > OUTGLEAM
OUTGLOW vb glow more than
OUTGLOWED > OUTGLOW
OUTGLOWS > OUTGLOW
OUTGNAW vb exceed in gnawing
OUTGNAWED > OUTGNAW
OUTGNAWN > OUTGNAW
OUTGNAWS > OUTGNAW
OUTGO vb exceed or outstrip ▷ n cost
OUTGOER > OUTGO
OUTGOERS > OUTGO
OUTGOES > OUTGO
OUTGOING adj leaving ▷ n act of going out
OUTGOINGS pl n expenses
OUTGONE > OUTGO

OUTGREW > OUTGROW
OUTGRIN vb exceed in grinning
OUTGRTNS > OUTGRIN
OUTGROSS vb earn more than
OUTGROUP n group of people outside one's own group of people
OUTGROUPS > OUTGROUP
OUTGROW vb become too large or too old for
OUTGROWN > OUTGROW
OUTGROWS > OUTGROW
OUTGROWTH n natural development
OUTGUARD n guard furthest away from main party
OUTGUARDS > OUTGUARD
OUTGUESS vb surpass in guessing
OUTGUIDE n folder in filing system ▷ vb beat or surpass at guiding
OUTGUIDED > OUTGUIDE
OUTGUIDES > OUTGUIDE
OUTGUN vb surpass in fire power
OUTGUNNED > OUTGUN
OUTGUNS > OUTGUN
OUTGUSH vb gush out
OUTGUSHED > OUTGUSH
OUTGUSHES > OUTGUSH
OUTHANDLE vb handle better than
OUTHARBOR n city or town in Newfoundland having a harbor
OUTHAUL n line or cable for tightening the foot of a sail
OUTHAULER same as > OUTHAUL
OUTHAULS > OUTHAUL
OUTHEAR vb exceed in hearing
OUTHEARD > OUTHEAR
OUTHEARS > OUTHEAR
OUTHER same as > OTHER
OUTHIRE vb hire out
OUTHIRED > OUTHIRE
OUTHIRES > OUTHIRE
OUTHIRING > OUTHIRE
OUTHIT vb hit something further than (someone else)
OUTHITS > OUTHIT
OUTHOMER vb score more home runs than
OUTHOMERS > OUTHOMER
OUTHOUSE n building near a main building
OUTHOUSES > OUTHOUSE
OUTHOWL vb exceed in howling
OUTHOWLED > OUTHOWL
OUTHOWLS > OUTHOWL
OUTHUMOR same as > OUTHUMOUR
OUTHUMORS > OUTHUMOR
OUTHUMOUR vb exceed in humouring
OUTHUNT vb exceed in hunting
OUTHUNTED > OUTHUNT
OUTHUNTS > OUTHUNT
OUTHUSTLE vb be more competitive than
OUTHYRE same as > OUTHIRE

OUTHYRED > OUTHYRE
OUTHYRES > OUTHYRE
OUTHYRING > OUTHYRE
OUTING n leisure trip
OUTINGS > OUTING
OUTJEST vb exceed in jesting
OUTJESTED > OUTJEST
OUTJESTS > OUTJEST
OUTJET n projecting part
OUTJETS > OUTJET
OUTJINX vb exceed in jinxing
OUTJINXED > OUTJINX
OUTJINXES > OUTJINX
OUTJOCKEY vb outwit by deception
OUTJUGGLE vb surpass at juggling
OUTJUMP vb jump higher or farther than
OUTJUMPED > OUTJUMP
OUTJUMPS > OUTJUMP
OUTJUT vb jut out ▷ n projecting part
OUTJUTS > OUTJUT
OUTJUTTED > OUTJUT
OUTKEEP vb beat or surpass at keeping
OUTKEEPS > OUTKEEP
OUTKEPT > OUTKEEP
OUTKICK vb exceed in kicking
OUTKICKED > OUTKICK
OUTKICKS > OUTKICK
OUTKILL vb exceed in killing
OUTKILLED > OUTKILL
OUTKILLS > OUTKILL
OUTKISS vb exceed in kissing
OUTKISSED > OUTKISS
OUTKISSES > OUTKISS
OUTLAID > OUTLAY
OUTLAIN > OUTLAY
OUTLAND adj outlying or distant ▷ n outlying areas of a country or region
OUTLANDER n foreigner or stranger
OUTLANDS > OUTLAND
OUTLASH n sudden attack ▷ vb shed tears
OUTLASHED > OUTLASH
OUTLASHES > OUTLASH
OUTLAST vb last longer than
OUTLASTED > OUTLAST
OUTLASTS > OUTLAST
OUTLAUGH vb laugh longer or louder than
OUTLAUGHS > OUTLAUGH
OUTLAUNCE same as > OUTLAUNCH
OUTLAUNCH vb send out
OUTLAW n criminal deprived of legal protection, bandit ▷ vb make illegal
OUTLAWED > OUTLAW
OUTLAWING > OUTLAW
OUTLAWRY n act of outlawing or the state of being outlawed
OUTLAWS > OUTLAW
OUTLAY n expenditure ▷ vb spend (money)
OUTLAYING > OUTLAY
OUTLAYS > OUTLAY

OUTLEAD vb be better leader than
OUTLEADS > OUTLEAD
OUTLEAP vb leap higher or farther than
OUTLEAPED > OUTLEAP
OUTLEAPS > OUTLEAP
OUTLEAPT > OUTLEAP
OUTLEARN vb exceed in learning
OUTLEARNS > OUTLEARN
OUTLEARNT > OUTLEARN
OUTLED > OUTLEAD
OUTLER n farm animal kept out of doors
OUTLERS > OUTLER
OUTLET n means of expressing emotion
OUTLETS > OUTLET
OUTLIE vb lie outside a particular place
OUTLIED > OUTLIE
OUTLIER n outcrop of rocks that is entirely surrounded by older rocks
OUTLIERS > OUTLIER
OUTLIES > OUTLIE
OUTLINE n short general explanation ▷ vb summarize
OUTLINEAR > OUTLINE
OUTLINED > OUTLINE
OUTLINER > OUTLINE
OUTLINERS > OUTLINE
OUTLINES > OUTLINE
OUTLINING > OUTLINE
OUTLIVE vb live longer than
OUTLIVED > OUTLIVE
OUTLIVER > OUTLIVE
OUTLIVERS > OUTLIVE
OUTLIVES > OUTLIVE
OUTLIVING > OUTLIVE
OUTLOOK n attitude ▷ vb look out
OUTLOOKED > OUTLOOK
OUTLOOKS > OUTLOOK
OUTLOVE vb exceed in loving
OUTLOVED > OUTLOVE
OUTLOVES > OUTLOVE
OUTLOVING > OUTLOVE
OUTLUSTER same as > OUTLUSTRE
OUTLUSTRE vb outshine
OUTLYING adj distant from the main area
OUTMAN vb surpass in manpower
OUTMANNED > OUTMAN
OUTMANS > OUTMAN
OUTMANTLE vb be better dressed than
OUTMARCH vb exceed in marching
OUTMASTER vb surpass
OUTMATCH vb surpass or outdo (someone)
OUTMODE vb make unfashionable
OUTMODED adj no longer fashionable or accepted
OUTMODES > OUTMODE
OUTMODING > OUTMODE
OUTMOST another word for > OUTERMOST
OUTMOVE vb move faster or better than
OUTMOVED > OUTMOVE
OUTMOVES > OUTMOVE**

OUTMOVING > OUTMOVE
OUTMUSCLE *vb* dominate by physical strength
OUTNAME *vb* be more notorious than
OUTNAMED > OUTNAME
OUTNAMES > OUTNAME
OUTNAMING > OUTNAME
OUTNESS *n* state or quality of being external
OUTNESSES > OUTNESS
OUTNIGHT *vb* refer to night more often than
OUTNIGHTS > OUTNIGHT
OUTNUMBER *vb* exceed in number
OUTOFFICE *n* outbuilding
OUTPACE *vb* go faster than (someone)
OUTPACED > OUTPACE
OUTPACES > OUTPACE
OUTPACING > OUTPACE
OUTPAINT *vb* exceed in painting
OUTPAINTS > OUTPAINT
OUTPART *n* remote region
OUTPARTS > OUTPART
OUTPASS *vb* exceed in passing
OUTPASSED > OUTPASS
OUTPASSES > OUTPASS
OUTPEEP *vb* peep out
OUTPEEPED > OUTPEEP
OUTPEEPS > OUTPEEP
OUTPEER *vb* surpass
OUTPEERED > OUTPEER
OUTPEERS > OUTPEER
OUTPEOPLE *vb* rid a country of its people
OUTPITCH *vb* exceed in pitching
OUTPITIED > OUTPITY
OUTPITIES > OUTPITY
OUTPITY *vb* exceed in pitying
OUTPLACE *vb* find job for ex-employee
OUTPLACED > OUTPLACE
OUTPLACER > OUTPLACE
OUTPLACES > OUTPLACE
OUTPLAN *vb* exceed in planning
OUTPLANS > OUTPLAN
OUTPLAY *vb* perform better than one's opponent
OUTPLAYED > OUTPLAY
OUTPLAYS > OUTPLAY
OUTPLOD *vb* exceed in plodding
OUTPLODS > OUTPLOD
OUTPLOT *vb* exceed in plotting
OUTPLOTS > OUTPLOT
OUTPOINT *vb* score more points than
OUTPOINTS > OUTPOINT
OUTPOLL *vb* win more votes than
OUTPOLLED > OUTPOLL
OUTPOLLS > OUTPOLL
OUTPORT *n* isolated fishing village, esp in Newfoundland
OUTPORTER *n* inhabitant or native of a Newfoundland outport
OUTPORTS > OUTPORT
OUTPOST *n* outlying settlement

OUTPOSTS > OUTPOST
OUTPOUR *n* act of flowing or pouring out ▷ *vb* pour or cause to pour out freely or rapidly
OUTPOURED > OUTPOUR
OUTPOURER > OUTPOUR
OUTPOURS > OUTPOUR
OUTPOWER *vb* have more power than
OUTPOWERS > OUTPOWER
OUTPRAY *vb* exceed in praying
OUTPRAYED > OUTPRAY
OUTPRAYS > OUTPRAY
OUTPREACH *vb* outdo in preaching
OUTPREEN *vb* exceed in preening
OUTPREENS > OUTPREEN
OUTPRESS *vb* exceed in pressing
OUTPRICE *vb* sell at better price than
OUTPRICED > OUTPRICE
OUTPRICES > OUTPRICE
OUTPRIZE *vb* prize more highly than
OUTPRIZED > OUTPRIZE
OUTPRIZES > OUTPRIZE
OUTPSYCH *vb* defeat by psychological means
OUTPSYCHS > OUTPSYCH
OUTPULL *vb* exceed in pulling
OUTPULLED > OUTPULL
OUTPULLS > OUTPULL
OUTPUNCH *vb* punch better than
OUTPUPIL *n* student sent to a different school to the one he or she would normally attend
OUTPUPILS > OUTPUPIL
OUTPURSUE *vb* pursue farther than
OUTPUSH *vb* exceed in pushing
OUTPUSHED > OUTPUSH
OUTPUSHES > OUTPUSH
OUTPUT *n* amount produced ▷ *vb* produce (data) at the end of a process
OUTPUTS > OUTPUT
OUTPUTTED > OUTPUT
OUTQUOTE *vb* exceed in quoting
OUTQUOTED > OUTQUOTE
OUTQUOTES > OUTQUOTE
OUTRACE *vb* surpass in racing
OUTRACED > OUTRACE
OUTRACES > OUTRACE
OUTRACING > OUTRACE
OUTRAGE *n* great moral indignation ▷ *vb* offend morally
OUTRAGED > OUTRAGE
OUTRAGES > OUTRAGE
OUTRAGING > OUTRAGE
OUTRAISE *vb* raise more money than
OUTRAISED > OUTRAISE
OUTRAISES > OUTRAISE
OUTRAN > OUTRUN
OUTRANCE *n* furthest extreme

OUTRANCES > OUTRANCE
OUTRANG > OUTRING
OUTRANGE *vb* have a greater range than
OUTRANGED > OUTRANGE
OUTRANGES > OUTRANGE
OUTRANK *vb* be of higher rank than (someone)
OUTRANKED > OUTRANK
OUTRANKS > OUTRANK
OUTRATE *vb* offer better rate than
OUTRATED > OUTRATE
OUTRATES > OUTRATE
OUTRATING > OUTRATE
OUTRAVE *vb* outdo in raving
OUTRAVED > OUTRAVE
OUTRAVES > OUTRAVE
OUTRAVING > OUTRAVE
OUTRE *adj* shockingly eccentric
OUTREACH *vb* surpass in reach ▷ *n* act or process of reaching out
OUTREAD *vb* outdo in reading
OUTREADS > OUTREAD
OUTREASON *vb* surpass in reasoning
OUTRECKON *vb* surpass in reckoning
OUTRED *vb* be redder than
OUTREDDED > OUTRED
OUTREDDEN *same as* **>** OUTRED
OUTREDS > OUTRED
OUTREIGN *vb* reign for longer than
OUTREIGNS > OUTREIGN
OUTRELIEF *n* aid given outdoors
OUTREMER *n* land overseas
OUTREMERS > OUTREMER
OUTRIDDEN > OUTRIDE
OUTRIDE *vb* outdo by riding faster, farther, or better than ▷ *n* extra unstressed syllable within a metrical foot
OUTRIDER *n* motorcyclist acting as an escort
OUTRIDERS > OUTRIDER
OUTRIDES > OUTRIDE
OUTRIDING *n* act or instance of riding faster, farther, or better than
OUTRIG *vb* supply with outfit
OUTRIGGED > OUTRIG
OUTRIGGER *n* stabilizing frame projecting from a boat
OUTRIGHT *adv* absolute(ly) ▷ *adj* complete
OUTRIGS > OUTRIG
OUTRING *vb* exceed in ringing
OUTRINGS > OUTRING
OUTRIVAL *vb* surpass
OUTRIVALS > OUTRIVAL
OUTRO *n* instrumental passage that concludes a piece of music
OUTROAR *vb* roar louder than
OUTROARED > OUTROAR
OUTROARS > OUTROAR
OUTROCK *vb* outdo in rocking

OUTROCKED > OUTROCK
OUTROCKS > OUTROCK
OUTRODE > OUTRIDE
OUTROLL *vb* exceed in rolling
OUTROLLED > OUTROLL
OUTROLLS > OUTROLL
OUTROOP *n* auction
OUTROOPER > OUTROOP
OUTROOPS > OUTROOP
OUTROOT *vb* root out
OUTROOTED > OUTROOT
OUTROOTS > OUTROOT
OUTROPE *same as* **>** OUTROOP
OUTROPER > OUTROPE
OUTROPERS > OUTROPE
OUTROPES > OUTROPE
OUTROS > OUTRO
OUTROW *vb* outdo in rowing
OUTROWED > OUTROW
OUTROWING > OUTROW
OUTROWS > OUTROW
OUTRUN *vb* run faster than
OUTRUNG > OUTRING
OUTRUNNER *n* attendant who runs in front of a carriage, etc
OUTRUNS > OUTRUN
OUTRUSH *n* flowing or rushing out ▷ *vb* rush out
OUTRUSHED > OUTRUSH
OUTRUSHES > OUTRUSH
OUTS > OUT
OUTSAID > OUTSAY
OUTSAIL *vb* sail better than
OUTSAILED > OUTSAIL
OUTSAILS > OUTSAIL
OUTSANG > OUTSING
OUTSAT > OUTSIT
OUTSAVOR *same as* **>** OUTSAVOUR
OUTSAVORS > OUTSAVOR
OUTSAVOUR *vb* exceed in savouring
OUTSAW > OUTSEE
OUTSAY *vb* say something out loud
OUTSAYING > OUTSAY
OUTSAYS > OUTSAY
OUTSCHEME *vb* outdo in scheming
OUTSCOLD *vb* outdo in scolding
OUTSCOLDS > OUTSCOLD
OUTSCOOP *vb* outdo in achieving scoops
OUTSCOOPS > OUTSCOOP
OUTSCORE *vb* score more than
OUTSCORED > OUTSCORE
OUTSCORES > OUTSCORE
OUTSCORN *vb* defy with scorn
OUTSCORNS > OUTSCORN
OUTSCREAM *vb* scream louder than
OUTSEE *vb* exceed in seeing
OUTSEEING > OUTSEE
OUTSEEN > OUTSEE
OUTSEES > OUTSEE
OUTSELL *vb* be sold in greater quantities than
OUTSELLS > OUTSELL
OUTSERT *another word for* **>** WRAPROUND
OUTSERTS > OUTSERT

OUTSERVE vb serve better at tennis than

OUTSERVED > OUTSERVE

OUTSERVES > OUTSERVE

OUTSET n beginning

OUTSETS > OUTSET

OUTSHAME vb greatly shame

OUTSHAMED > OUTSHAME

OUTSHAMES > OUTSHAME

OUTSHINE vb surpass (someone) in excellence

OUTSHINED > OUTSHINE

OUTSHINES > OUTSHINE

OUTSHONE > OUTSHINE

OUTSHOOT vb surpass or excel in shooting ▷ n thing that projects or shoots out

OUTSHOOTS > OUTSHOOT

OUTSHOT n projecting part

OUTSHOTS > OUTSHOT

OUTSHOUT vb shout louder than

OUTSHOUTS > OUTSHOUT

OUTSIDE adv indicating movement to or position on the exterior ▷ adj unlikely ▷ n external area or surface

OUTSIDER n person outside a specific group

OUTSIDERS > OUTSIDER

OUTSIDES > OUTSIDE

OUTSIGHT n power of seeing

OUTSIGHTS > OUTSIGHT

OUTSIN vb sin more than

OUTSING vb sing better or louder than

OUTSINGS > OUTSING

OUTSINNED > OUTSIN

OUTSINS > OUTSIN

OUTSIT vb sit longer than

OUTSITS > OUTSIT

OUTSIZE adj larger than normal ▷ n outsize garment

OUTSIZED same as > OUTSIZE

OUTSIZES > OUTSIZE

OUTSKATE vb skate better than

OUTSKATED > OUTSKATE

OUTSKATES > OUTSKATE

OUTSKIRT singular of > OUTSKIRTS

OUTSKIRTS pl n outer areas, esp of a town

OUTSLEEP vb sleep longer than

OUTSLEEPS > OUTSLEEP

OUTSLEPT > OUTSLEEP

OUTSLICK vb outsmart

OUTSLICKS > OUTSLICK

OUTSMART vb outwit

OUTSMARTS > OUTSMART

OUTSMELL vb surpass in smelling

OUTSMELLS > OUTSMELL

OUTSMELT > OUTSMELL

OUTSMILE vb outdo in smiling

OUTSMILED > OUTSMILE

OUTSMILES > OUTSMILE

OUTSMOKE vb smoke more than

OUTSMOKED > OUTSMOKE

OUTSMOKES > OUTSMOKE

OUTSNORE vb outdo in snoring

OUTSNORED > OUTSNORE

OUTSNORES > OUTSNORE

OUTSOAR vb fly higher than

OUTSOARED > OUTSOAR

OUTSOARS > OUTSOAR

OUTSOLD > OUTSELL

OUTSOLE n outermost sole of a shoe

OUTSOLES > OUTSOLE

OUTSOURCE vb subcontract (work) to another company

OUTSPAN vb relax

OUTSPANS > OUTSPAN

OUTSPEAK vb speak better or louder than

OUTSPEAKS > OUTSPEAK

OUTSPED > OUTSPEED

OUTSPEED vb go faster than

OUTSPEEDS > OUTSPEED

OUTSPELL vb exceed at spelling

OUTSPELLS > OUTSPELL

OUTSPELT > OUTSPELL

OUTSPEND vb spend more than

OUTSPENDS > OUTSPEND

OUTSPENT > OUTSPEND

OUTSPOKE > OUTSPEAK

OUTSPOKEN adj tending to say what one thinks

OUTSPORT vb sport in excess of

OUTSPORTS > OUTSPORT

OUTSPRANG > OUTSPRING

OUTSPREAD adj spread or stretched out as far as possible ▷ vb spread out or cause to spread out ▷ n spreading out

OUTSPRING vb spring out

OUTSPRINT vb run faster than (someone)

OUTSPRUNG > OUTSPRING

OUTSTAND vb be outstanding or excel

OUTSTANDS > OUTSTAND

OUTSTARE vb stare longer than

OUTSTARED > OUTSTARE

OUTSTARES > OUTSTARE

OUTSTART vb jump out ▷ n outset

OUTSTARTS > OUTSTART

OUTSTATE vb surpass in stating

OUTSTATED > OUTSTATE

OUTSTATES > OUTSTATE

OUTSTAY vb overstay

OUTSTAYED > OUTSTAY

OUTSTAYS > OUTSTAY

OUTSTEER vb steer better than

OUTSTEERS > OUTSTEER

OUTSTEP vb step farther than

OUTSTEPS > OUTSTEP

OUTSTOOD > OUTSTAND

OUTSTRAIN vb strain too much

OUTSTRIDE vb surpass in striding

OUTSTRIKE vb exceed in striking

OUTSTRIP vb surpass

OUTSTRIPS > OUTSTRIP

OUTSTRIVE vb strive harder than

OUTSTRODE > OUTSTRIDE

OUTSTROKE n outward stroke

OUTSTROVE > OUTSTRIVE

OUTSTRUCK > OUTSTRIKE

OUTSTUDY vb outdo in studying

OUTSTUNT vb outdo in performing stunts

OUTSTUNTS > OUTSTUNT

OUTSULK vb outdo in sulking

OUTSULKED > OUTSULK

OUTSULKS > OUTSULK

OUTSUM vb add up to more than

OUTSUMMED > OUTSUM

OUTSUMS > OUTSUM

OUTSUNG > OUTSING

OUTSWAM > OUTSWIM

OUTSWARE > OUTSWEAR

OUTSWEAR vb swear more than

OUTSWEARS > OUTSWEAR

OUTSWEEP n outward movement of arms in swimming breaststroke

OUTSWEEPS > OUTSWEEP

OUTSWELL vb exceed in swelling

OUTSWELLS > OUTSWELL

OUTSWEPT adj curving outwards

OUTSWIM vb outdo in swimming

OUTSWIMS > OUTSWIM

OUTSWING n (in cricket) movement of a ball from leg to off through the air

OUTSWINGS > OUTSWING

OUTSWORE > OUTSWEAR

OUTSWORN > OUTSWEAR

OUTSWUM > OUTSWIM

OUTSWUNG adj made to curve outwards

OUTTA prep informal contraction of out of

OUTTAKE n unreleased take from a recording session, film, or TV programme ▷ vb take out

OUTTAKEN > OUTTAKE

OUTTAKES > OUTTAKE

OUTTAKING > OUTTAKE

OUTTALK vb talk more, longer, or louder than (someone)

OUTTALKED > OUTTALK

OUTTALKS > OUTTALK

OUTTASK vb assign task to staff outside organization

OUTTASKED > OUTTASK

OUTTASKS > OUTTASK

OUTTELL vb make known

OUTTELLS > OUTTELL

OUTTHANK vb outdo in thanking

OUTTHANKS > OUTTHANK

OUTTHIEVE vb surpass in stealing

OUTTHINK vb outdo in thinking

OUTTHINKS > OUTTHINK

OUTTHREW > OUTTHROW

OUTTHROB vb outdo in throbbing

OUTTHROBS > OUTTHROB

OUTTHROW vb throw better than

OUTTHROWN > OUTTHROW

OUTTHROWS > OUTTHROW

OUTTHRUST vb extend outwards

OUTTOLD > OUTTELL

OUTTONGUE vb speak louder than

OUTTOOK > OUTTAKE

OUTTOP vb rise higher than

OUTTOPPED > OUTTOP

OUTTOPS > OUTTOP

OUTTOWER vb tower over

OUTTOWERS > OUTTOWER

OUTTRADE vb surpass in trading

OUTTRADED > OUTTRADE

OUTTRADES > OUTTRADE

OUTTRAVEL vb outdo in travelling

OUTTRICK vb outdo in trickery

OUTTRICKS > OUTTRICK

OUTTROT vb exceed at trotting

OUTTROTS > OUTTROT

OUTTRUMP vb count for more than

OUTTRUMPS > OUTTRUMP

OUTTURN same as > OUTPUT

OUTTURNS > OUTTURN

OUTVALUE vb surpass in value

OUTVALUED > OUTVALUE

OUTVALUES > OUTVALUE

OUTVAUNT vb outdo in boasting

OUTVAUNTS > OUTVAUNT

OUTVENOM vb surpass in venomousness

OUTVENOMS > OUTVENOM

OUTVIE vb outdo in competition

OUTVIED > OUTVIE

OUTVIES > OUTVIE

OUTVOICE vb surpass in noise

OUTVOICED > OUTVOICE

OUTVOICES > OUTVOICE

OUTVOTE vb defeat by getting more votes than

OUTVOTED > OUTVOTE

OUTVOTER > OUTVOTE

OUTVOTERS > OUTVOTE

OUTVOTES > OUTVOTE

OUTVOTING > OUTVOTE

OUTVYING > OUTVIE

OUTWAIT vb wait longer than

OUTWAITED > OUTWAIT

OUTWAITS > OUTWAIT

OUTWALK vb walk farther or longer than

OUTWALKED > OUTWALK

OUTWALKS > OUTWALK

OUTWAR vb surpass or exceed in warfare

OUTWARD same as > OUTWARDS

OUTWARDLY adv in outward appearance

OUTWARDS adv towards the outside

OUTWARRED > OUTWAR

OUTWARS > OUTWAR

OUTWASH n gravel carried and deposited by water from melting glaciers

OUTWASHES > OUTWASH

OUTWASTE vb outdo in wasting

OUTWASTED > OUTWASTE

OUTWASTES > OUTWASTE

OUTWATCH vb surpass in watching

OUTWEAR vb use up or destroy by wearing

OUTWEARS > OUTWEAR

OUTWEARY vb exhaust

OUTWEED vb root out

OUTWEEDED > OUTWEED

OUTWEEDS > OUTWEED

OUTWEEP vb outdo in weeping

OUTWEEPS > OUTWEEP

OUTWEIGH vb be more important, significant, or influential than

OUTWEIGHS > OUTWEIGH

OUTWELL vb pour out

OUTWELLED > OUTWELL

OUTWELLS > OUTWELL

OUTWENT > OUTGO

OUTWEPT > OUTWEEP

OUTWHIRL vb surpass at whirling

OUTWHIRLS > OUTWHIRL

OUTWICK vb move one curling stone by striking with another

OUTWICKED > OUTWICK

OUTWICKS > OUTWICK

OUTWILE vb surpass in cunning

OUTWILED > OUTWILE

OUTWILES > OUTWILE

OUTWILING > OUTWILE

OUTWILL vb demonstrate stronger will than

OUTWILLED > OUTWILL

OUTWILLS > OUTWILL

OUTWIN vb get out of

OUTWIND vb unwind

OUTWINDED > OUTWIND

OUTWINDS > OUTWIND

OUTWING vb surpass in flying

OUTWINGED > OUTWING

OUTWINGS > OUTWING

OUTWINS > OUTWIN

OUTWISH vb surpass in wishing

OUTWISHED > OUTWISH

OUTWISHES > OUTWISH

OUTWIT vb get the better of (someone) by cunning

OUTWITH prep outside

OUTWITS > OUTWIT

OUTWITTED > OUTWIT

OUTWON > OUTWIN

OUTWORE > OUTWEAR

OUTWORK n defences which lie outside main defensive works ▷ vb work better, harder, etc, than

OUTWORKED > OUTWORK

OUTWORKER > OUTWORK

OUTWORKS > OUTWORK

OUTWORN adj no longer in use

OUTWORTH vb be more valuable than

OUTWORTHS > OUTWORTH

OUTWOUND > OUTWIND

OUTWREST vb extort

OUTWRESTS > OUTWREST

OUTWRIT > OUTWRITE

OUTWRITE vb outdo in writing

OUTWRITES > OUTWRITE

OUTWROTE > OUTWRITE

OUTYELL vb outdo in yelling

OUTYELLED > OUTYELL

OUTYELLS > OUTYELL

OUTYELP vb outdo in yelping

OUTYELPED > OUTYELP

OUTYELPS > OUTYELP

OUTYIELD vb yield more than

OUTYIELDS > OUTYIELD

OUVERT adj open

OUVERTE feminine form of > OUVERT

OUVRAGE n work

OUVRAGES > OUVRAGE

OUVRIER n worker

OUVRIERE feminine form of > OUVRIER

OUVRIERES > OUVRIERE

OUVRIERS > OUVRIER

OUZEL n type of bird

OUZELS > OUZEL

OUZO n strong aniseed-flavoured spirit from Greece

OUZOS > OUZO

OVA > OVUM

OVAL adj egg-shaped ▷ n anything that is oval in shape

OVALBUMIN n albumin in egg whites

OVALITIES > OVAL

OVALITY > OVAL

OVALLY > OVAL

OVALNESS > OVAL

OVALS > OVAL

OVARIAL > OVARY

OVARIAN > OVARY

OVARIES > OVARY

OVARIOLE n tube in insect ovary

OVARIOLES > OVARIOLE

OVARIOUS adj of eggs

OVARITIS n inflammation of an ovary

OVARY n female egg-producing organ

OVATE adj shaped like an egg ▷ vb give ovation

OVATED > OVATE

OVATELY > OVATE

OVATES > OVATE

OVATING > OVATE

OVATION n enthusiastic round of applause

OVATIONAL > OVATION

OVATIONS > OVATION

OVATOR > OVATE

OVATORS > OVATE

OVEL n mourner, esp during the first seven days after a death

OVELS > OVEL

OVEN n heated compartment or container for cooking ▷ vb cook in an oven

OVENABLE adj (of food) suitable for cooking in an oven

OVENBIRD n type of small brownish South American bird

OVENBIRDS > OVENBIRD

OVENED > OVEN

OVENING > OVEN

OVENLIKE > OVEN

OVENPROOF adj able to be used in an oven

OVENS > OVEN

OVENWARE n heat-resistant dishes in which food can be both cooked and served

OVENWARES > OVENWARE

OVENWOOD n pieces of wood for burning in an oven

OVENWOODS > OVENWOOD

OVER adv indicating position on the top of, amount greater than, etc ▷ adj finished ▷ n (in cricket) series of six balls bowled from one end ▷ vb jump over

OVERABLE adj too able

OVERACT vb act in an exaggerated way

OVERACTED > OVERACT

OVERACTS > OVERACT

OVERACUTE adj too acute

OVERAGE adj beyond a specified age ▷ n amount beyond given limit

OVERAGED adj very old

OVERAGES > OVERAGE

OVERALERT adj abnormally alert

OVERALL adv in total ▷ n coat-shaped protective garment ▷ adj from one end to the other

OVERALLED adj wearing overalls

OVERALLS > OVERALL

OVERAPT adj tending excessively

OVERARCH vb form an arch over

OVERARM adv with the arm above the shoulder ▷ adj bowled, thrown, or performed with the arm raised above the shoulder ▷ vb throw (a ball) overarm

OVERARMED > OVERARM

OVERARMS > OVERARM

OVERATE > OVEREAT

OVERAWE vb affect (someone) with an overpowering sense of awe

OVERAWED > OVERAWE

OVERAWES > OVERAWE

OVERAWING > OVERAWE

OVERBAKE vb bake too long

OVERBAKED > OVERBAKE

OVERBAKES > OVERBAKE

OVERBANK n sediment deposited on the flood plain of a river

OVERBANKS > OVERBANK

OVERBEAR vb dominate or overcome

OVERBEARS > OVERBEAR

OVERBEAT vb beat too much

OVERBEATS > OVERBEAT

OVERBED adj fitting over bed

OVERBET vb bet too much

OVERBETS > OVERBET

OVERBID vb bid for more tricks than one can expect to win ▷ n bid higher than someone else's bid

OVERBIDS > OVERBID

OVERBIG adj too big

OVERBILL vb charge too much money

OVERBILLS > OVERBILL

OVERBITE n extension of the upper front teeth over the lower front teeth when the mouth is closed

OVERBITES > OVERBITE

OVERBLEW > OVERBLOW

OVERBLOW vb blow into (a wind instrument) with greater force than normal

OVERBLOWN adj excessive

OVERBLOWS > OVERBLOW

OVERBOARD adv from a boat into the water

OVERBOIL vb boil too much

OVERBOILS > OVERBOIL

OVERBOLD adj too bold

OVERBOOK vb accept too many bookings

OVERBOOKS > OVERBOOK

OVERBOOT n protective boot worn over an ordinary boot or shoe

OVERBOOTS > OVERBOOT

OVERBORE > OVERBEAR

OVERBORN > OVERBEAR

OVERBORNE > OVERBEAR

OVERBOUND vb jump over

OVERBRAKE vb brake too much

OVERBRED adj produced by too much selective breeding

OVERBREED vb produce by too much selective breeding

OVERBRIEF adj too brief

OVERBRIM vb overflow

OVERBRIMS > OVERBRIM

OVERBROAD adj not specific enough

OVERBROW vb hang over

OVERBROWS > OVERBROW

OVERBUILD vb build over or on top of

OVERBUILT > OVERBUILD

OVERBULK vb loom large over

OVERBULKS > OVERBULK

OVERBURN vb (formerly) copy information onto CD

OVERBURNS > OVERBURN

OVERBURNT > OVERBURN

OVERBUSY adj too busy ▷ vb make too busy

OVERBUY vb buy too much or too many

OVERBUYS > OVERBUY

OVERBY adv Scots expression meaning over the road or across the way

OVERCALL n bid higher than the preceding one ▷ vb bid higher than (an opponent)

OVERCALLS > OVERCALL

OVERCAME > OVERCOME

OVERCARRY vb carry too far or too many

OVERCAST adj (of the sky) covered by clouds ▷ vb make or become overclouded or gloomy ▷ n covering, as of clouds or mist

OVERCASTS > OVERCAST

OVERCATCH vb overtake

OVERCHEAP adj too cheap

OVERCHECK n thin leather strap attached to a horse's bit to keep its head up

OVERCHILL vb make too cold

OVERCIVIL adj too civil

OVERCLAD adj wearing too many clothes

OVERCLAIM vb claim too much

OVERCLASS n dominant group in society

OVERCLEAN adj too clean

OVERCLEAR adj too clear

OVERCLOCK vb modify a computer to run at greater speeds than originally intended

OVERCLOSE adj too close

OVERCLOUD vb make or become covered with clouds

OVERCLOY vb weary with excess

OVERCLOYS > OVERCLOY

OVERCLUB vb (in golf) use a club which causes the shot to go too far

OVERCLUBS > OVERCLUB

OVERCOACH vb coach too much

OVERCOAT n heavy coat

OVERCOATS > OVERCOAT

OVERCOLD adj too cold

OVERCOLOR vb colour too highly

OVERCOME vb gain control over after an effort

OVERCOMER > OVERCOME

OVERCOMES > OVERCOME

OVERCOOK vb spoil food by cooking it for too long

OVERCOOKS > OVERCOOK

OVERCOOL vb cool too much

OVERCOOLS > OVERCOOL

OVERCOUNT vb outnumber

OVERCOVER vb cover up

OVERCOY adj too modest

OVERCRAM vb fill too full

OVERCRAMS > OVERCRAM

OVERCRAW same as > OVERCROW

OVERCRAWS > OVERCRAW

OVERCROP vb exhaust (land) by excessive cultivation

OVERCROPS > OVERCROP

OVERCROW vb crow over

OVERCROWD vb fill with more people or things than is desirable

OVERCROWS > OVERCROW

OVERCURE vb take curing process too far

OVERCURED > OVERCURE

OVERCURES > OVERCURE

OVERCUT vb cut too much

OVERCUTS > OVERCUT

OVERDARE vb dare too much

OVERDARED > OVERDARE

OVERDARES > OVERDARE

OVERDATED adj outdated

OVERDEAR adj too dear

OVERDECK n upper deck

OVERDECKS > OVERDECK

OVERDID > OVERDO

OVERDIGHT adj covered up

OVERDO vb do to excess

OVERDOER > OVERDO

OVERDOERS > OVERDO

OVERDOES > OVERDO

OVERDOG n person or side in an advantageous position

OVERDOGS > OVERDOG

OVERDOING > OVERDO

OVERDONE > OVERDO

OVERDOSE n excessive dose of a drug ▷ vb take an overdose

OVERDOSED > OVERDOSE

OVERDOSES > OVERDOSE

OVERDRAFT n overdrawing

OVERDRANK > OVERDRINK

OVERDRAW vb withdraw more money than is in (one's bank account)

OVERDRAWN > OVERDRAW

OVERDRAWS > OVERDRAW

OVERDRESS vb dress (oneself or another) too elaborately or finely ▷ n dress that may be worn over a jumper, blouse, etc

OVERDREW > OVERDRAW

OVERDRIED > OVERDRY

OVERDRIES > OVERDRY

OVERDRINK vb drink too much alcohol

OVERDRIVE n very high gear in a motor vehicle

OVERDROVE > OVERDRIVE

OVERDRUNK > OVERDRINK

OVERDRY vb dry too much

OVERDUB vb add (new sounds) to an audio recording so that the old and the new sounds can be heard ▷ n sound or series of sounds added by this method

OVERDUBS > OVERDUB

OVERDUE adj still due after the time allowed

OVERDUST vb dust too much

OVERDUSTS > OVERDUST

OVERDYE vb dye (a fabric, yarn, etc) excessively

OVERDYED > OVERDYE

OVERDYER > OVERDYE

OVERDYERS > OVERDYE

OVERDYES > OVERDYE

OVEREAGER adj excessively eager or keen

OVEREASY adj too easy

OVEREAT vb eat more than is necessary or healthy

OVEREATEN > OVEREAT

OVEREATER > OVEREAT

OVEREATS > OVEREAT

OVERED > OVER

OVEREDIT vb edit too much

OVEREDITS > OVEREDIT

OVEREGG vb exaggerate absurdly

OVEREGGED > OVEREGG

OVEREGGS > OVEREGG

OVEREMOTE vb emote too much

OVEREQUIP vb equip, furnish with, or supply excessively

OVEREXERT vb exhaust or injure (oneself) by doing too much

OVEREYE vb survey

OVEREYED > OVEREYE

OVEREYES > OVEREYE

OVEREYING > OVEREYE

OVERFALL n turbulent stretch of water caused by marine currents over an underwater ridge ▷ vb fall over

OVERFALLS > OVERFALL

OVERFAR adv too far

OVERFAST adj too fast

OVERFAT adj too fat

OVERFAVOR vb favour too much

OVERFEAR vb fear too much

OVERFEARS > OVERFEAR

OVERFED > OVERFEED

OVERFEED vb give (a person, plant, or animal) more food than is necessary or healthy

OVERFEEDS > OVERFEED

OVERFELL > OVERFALL

OVERFILL vb put more into (something) than there is room for

OVERFILLS > OVERFILL

OVERFINE adj too fine

OVERFISH vb fish too much

OVERFIT adj too fit

OVERFLEW > OVERFLY

OVERFLIES > OVERFLY

OVERFLOOD vb flood excessively

OVERFLOW vb flow over ▷ n something that overflows

OVERFLOWN > OVERFLY

OVERFLOWS > OVERFLOW

OVERFLUSH adj too flush

OVERFLY vb fly over (a territory) or past (a point)

OVERFOCUS vb focus too much

OVERFOLD n fold in which one or both limbs have been inclined more than 90°

OVERFOLDS > OVERFOLD

OVERFOND adj excessively keen (on)

OVERFOUL adj too foul

OVERFRANK adj too frank

OVERFREE adj too forward

OVERFULL adj excessively full

OVERFUND vb supply with too much money

OVERFUNDS > OVERFUND

OVERFUSSY adj too fussy

OVERGALL vb make sore all over

OVERGALLS > OVERGALL

OVERGANG vb dominate

OVERGANGS > OVERGANG

OVERGAVE > OVERGIVE

OVERGEAR vb cause (a company) to have too high a proportion of loan stock

OVERGEARS > OVERGEAR

OVERGET vb overtake

OVERGETS > OVERGET

OVERGILD vb gild too much

OVERGILDS > OVERGILD

OVERGILT > OVERGILD

OVERGIRD vb gird too tightly

OVERGIRDS > OVERGIRD

OVERGIRT > OVERGIRD

OVERGIVE vb give up

OVERGIVEN > OVERGIVE

OVERGIVES > OVERGIVE

OVERGLAD adj too glad

OVERGLAZE adj (of decoration or colours) applied to porcelain above the glaze

OVERGLOOM vb make gloomy

OVERGO vb go beyond

OVERGOAD vb goad too much

OVERGOADS > OVERGOAD

OVERGOES > OVERGO

OVERGOING > OVERGO

OVERGONE > OVERGO

OVERGORGE vb overeat

OVERGOT > OVERGET

OVERGRADE vb grade too highly

OVERGRAIN vb apply grainy texture to

OVERGRASS vb grow grass on top of

OVERGRAZE vb graze (land) too intensively

OVERGREAT adj too great

OVERGREEN vb cover with vegetation

OVERGREW > OVERGROW

OVERGROW vb grow over or across (an area, path, lawn, etc)

OVERGROWN > OVERGROW

OVERGROWS > OVERGROW

OVERHAILE vb pull over

OVERHAIR n outer coat of animal

OVERHAIRS > OVERHAIR

OVERHALE same as > OVERHAILE

OVERHALED > OVERHALE

OVERHALES > OVERHALE

OVERHAND adj thrown or performed with the hand raised above the shoulder ▷ adv with the hand above the shoulder ▷ vb sew with the thread passing over two edges in one direction

OVERHANDS > OVERHAND

OVERHANG vb project beyond something ▷ n overhanging part

OVERHANGS > OVERHANG

OVERHAPPY adj too happy

OVERHARD adj too hard

OVERHASTE n excessive haste

OVERHASTY > OVERHASTE

OVERHATE vb hate too much

OVERHATED > OVERHATE

OVERHATES > OVERHATE

OVERHAUL vb examine and repair ▷ n examination and repair

OVERHAULS > OVERHAUL

OVERHEAD adj above one's head ▷ adv over or above head height ▷ n stroke in racket games played from above head height

OVERHEADS pl n general cost of maintaining a business

OVERHEAP vb supply too much

OVERHEAPS > OVERHEAP
OVERHEAR vb hear (a speaker or remark) unintentionally
OVERHEARD > OVERHEAR
OVERHEARS > OVERHEAR
OVERHEAT vb make or become excessively hot ▷ n condition of being overheated
OVERHEATS > OVERHEAT
OVERHELD > OVERHOLD
OVERHENT vb overtake
OVERHENTS > OVERHENT
OVERHIGH adj too high
OVERHIT vb hit too strongly
OVERHITS > OVERHIT
OVERHOLD vb value too highly
OVERHOLDS > OVERHOLD
OVERHOLY adj too holy
OVERHONOR vb honour too highly
OVERHOPE vb hope too much
OVERHOPED > OVERHOPE
OVERHOPES > OVERHOPE
OVERHOT adj too hot
OVERHUNG > OVERHANG
OVERHUNT vb hunt too much
OVERHUNTS > OVERHUNT
OVERHYPE vb hype too much
OVERHYPED > OVERHYPE
OVERHYPES > OVERHYPE
OVERIDLE adj too idle
OVERING > OVER
OVERINKED adj printed using too much ink
OVERISSUE vb issue (shares, banknotes, etc) in excess of demand or ability to pay ▷ n shares, banknotes, etc, thus issued
OVERJOY vb give great delight to
OVERJOYED adj extremely pleased
OVERJOYS > OVERJOY
OVERJUMP vb jump too far
OVERJUMPS > OVERJUMP
OVERJUST adj too just
OVERKEEN adj too keen
OVERKEEP vb keep too long
OVERKEEPS > OVERKEEP
OVERKEPT > OVERKEEP
OVERKEST same as
 > OVERCAST
OVERKILL n treatment that is greater than required
OVERKILLS > OVERKILL
OVERKIND adj too kind
OVERKING n supreme king
OVERKINGS > OVERKING
OVERKNEE adj reaching to above knee
OVERLABOR vb spend too much work on
OVERLADE vb overburden
OVERLADED > OVERLADE
OVERLADEN > OVERLADE
OVERLADES > OVERLADE
OVERLAID > OVERLAY
OVERLAIN > OVERLIE
OVERLAND adv by land ▷ vb drive (cattle or sheep) overland

OVERLANDS > OVERLAND
OVERLAP vb share part of the same space or period of time (as) ▷ n area overlapping
OVERLAPS > OVERLAP
OVERLARD vb cover with lard
OVERLARDS > OVERLARD
OVERLARGE adj excessively large
OVERLATE adj too late
OVERLAX adj too lax
OVERLAY vb cover with a thin layer ▷ n something that is laid over something else
OVERLAYS > OVERLAY
OVERLEAF adv on the back of the current page
OVERLEAP vb leap too far
OVERLEAPS > OVERLEAP
OVERLEAPT > OVERLEAP
OVERLEARN vb study too intensely
OVERLEND vb lend too much
OVERLENDS > OVERLEND
OVERLENT > OVERLEND
OVERLET vb let to too many
OVERLETS > OVERLET
OVERLEWD adj too lewd
OVERLIE vb lie on or cover (something or someone)
OVERLIER > OVERLIE
OVERLIERS > OVERLIE
OVERLIES > OVERLIE
OVERLIGHT vb illuminate too brightly
OVERLIT > OVERLIGHT
OVERLIVE vb live longer than (another person)
OVERLIVED > OVERLIVE
OVERLIVES > OVERLIVE
OVERLOAD vb put too large a load on or in ▷ n excessive load
OVERLOADS > OVERLOAD
OVERLOCK vb sew fabric with interlocking stitch
OVERLOCKS > OVERLOCK
OVERLONG adj too or excessively long
OVERLOOK vb fail to notice ▷ n high place affording a view
OVERLOOKS > OVERLOOK
OVERLORD n supreme lord or master
OVERLORDS > OVERLORD
OVERLOUD adj too loud
OVERLOVE vb love too much
OVERLOVED > OVERLOVE
OVERLOVES > OVERLOVE
OVERLUSH adj too lush
OVERLUSTY adj too lusty
OVERLY adv excessively
OVERLYING > OVERLIE
OVERMAN vb provide with too many staff ▷ n man who oversees others
OVERMANS > OVERMAN
OVERMANY adj too many ▷ n excess of people
OVERMAST vb provide mast that is too big
OVERMASTS > OVERMAST
OVERMATCH vb be more

than a match for ▷ n person superior in ability
OVERMEEK adj too meek
OVERMELT vb melt too much
OVERMELTS > OVERMELT
OVERMEN > OVERMAN
OVERMERRY adj very merry
OVERMILD adj too mild
OVERMILK vb milk too much
OVERMILKS > OVERMILK
OVERMINE vb mine too much
OVERMINED > OVERMINE
OVERMINES > OVERMINE
OVERMIX vb mix too much
OVERMIXED > OVERMIX
OVERMIXES > OVERMIX
OVERMOUNT vb surmount
OVERMUCH adj too much ▷ n excessive amount
OVERNAME vb repeat (someone's) name
OVERNAMED > OVERNAME
OVERNAMES > OVERNAME
OVERNEAR adj too near
OVERNEAT adj too neat
OVERNET vb cover with net
OVERNETS > OVERNET
OVERNEW adj too new
OVERNICE adj too fastidious, precise, etc
OVERNIGHT adv (taking place) during one night ▷ adj done in, occurring in, or lasting the night ▷ vb stay the night
OVERPACK vb pack too much
OVERPACKS > OVERPACK
OVERPAGE same as
 > OVERLEAF
OVERPAID > OVERPAY
OVERPAINT vb apply too much paint
OVERPART vb give an actor too difficult a role
OVERPARTS > OVERPART
OVERPASS vb pass over, through, or across
OVERPAST > OVERPASS
OVERPAY vb pay (someone) at too high a rate
OVERPAYS > OVERPAY
OVERPEDAL vb use piano pedal too much
OVERPEER vb look down over
OVERPEERS > OVERPEER
OVERPERCH vb fly up to perch on
OVERPERT adj too insolent
OVERPITCH vb bowl (a cricket ball) so that it pitches too close to the stumps
OVERPLAID n plaid in double layer
OVERPLAN vb plan excessively
OVERPLANS > OVERPLAN
OVERPLANT vb plant more than is necessary
OVERPLAST adj put above
OVERPLAY same as
 > OVERACT
OVERPLAYS > OVERPLAY
OVERPLIED > OVERPLY

OVERPLIES > OVERPLY
OVERPLOT vb plot onto existing graph or map
OVERPLOTS > OVERPLOT
OVERPLUS n surplus or excess quantity
OVERPLY vb ply too much
OVERPOISE vb weigh more than
OVERPOST vb hurry over
OVERPOSTS > OVERPOST
OVERPOWER vb subdue or overcome (someone)
OVERPRESS vb oppress
OVERPRICE vb put too high a price on
OVERPRINT vb print (additional matter) onto (something already printed) ▷ n additional matter printed onto something already printed
OVERPRIZE vb prize too highly
OVERPROOF adj containing more alcohol than standard spirit ▷ n spirit with a higher content of alcohol than standard spirit
OVERPROUD adj too proud
OVERPUMP vb pump too much
OVERPUMPS > OVERPUMP
OVERQUICK adj too quick
OVERRACK vb strain too much
OVERRACKS > OVERRACK
OVERRAKE vb rake over
OVERRAKED > OVERRAKE
OVERRAKES > OVERRAKE
OVERRAN > OVERRUN
OVERRANK adj too rank ▷ vb assign an unnecessarily high rank to
OVERRANKS > OVERRANK
OVERRASH adj too rash
OVERRATE vb have too high an opinion of
OVERRATED > OVERRATE
OVERRATES > OVERRATE
OVERREACH vb defeat or thwart (oneself) by attempting to do or gain too much
OVERREACT vb react more strongly than is necessary
OVERREAD vb read over
OVERREADS > OVERREAD
OVERRED vb paint over in red
OVERREDS > OVERRED
OVERREN same as
 > OVERRUN
OVERRENS > OVERREN
OVERRICH adj (of food) excessively flavoursome or fatty
OVERRIDE vb overrule ▷ n device or system that can override an automatic control
OVERRIDER > OVERRIDE
OVERRIDES > OVERRIDE
OVERRIFE adj too rife
OVERRIGID adj too rigid
OVERRIPE adj (of a fruit or vegetable) so ripe that it has started to decay
OVERRIPEN vb become overripe

OVERROAST *vb* roast too long

OVERRODE > OVERRIDE

OVERRUDE *adj* very rude

OVERRUFF *vb* defeat trump card by playing higher trump

OVERRUFFS > OVERRUFF

OVERRULE *vb* reverse the decision of (a person with less power)

OVERRULED > OVERRULE

OVERRULER > OVERRULE

OVERRULES > OVERRULE

OVERRUN *vb* conquer rapidly ▷ *n* act or an instance of overrunning

OVERRUNS > OVERRUN

OVERS > OVER

OVERSAD *adj* too sad

OVERSAIL *vb* project beyond

OVERSAILS > OVERSAIL

OVERSALE *n* selling of more than is available

OVERSALES > OVERSALE

OVERSALT *vb* put too much salt in

OVERSALTS > OVERSALT

OVERSAUCE *vb* put too much sauce on

OVERSAVE *vb* put too much money in savings

OVERSAVED > OVERSAVE

OVERSAVES > OVERSAVE

OVERSAW > OVERSEE

OVERSCALE *adj* at higher scale than standard

OVERSCORE *vb* cancel by drawing a line or lines over or through

OVERSEA *same as* > OVERSEAS

OVERSEAS *adj* to, of, or from a distant country ▷ *adv* across the sea ▷ *n* foreign country or foreign countries collectively

OVERSEE *vb* watch over from a position of authority

OVERSEED *vb* plant too much seed in

OVERSEEDS > OVERSEED

OVERSEEN > OVERSEE

OVERSEER *n* person who oversees others, esp workmen

OVERSEERS > OVERSEER

OVERSEES > OVERSEE

OVERSELL *vb* exaggerate the merits or abilities of

OVERSELLS > OVERSELL

OVERSET *vb* disturb or upset

OVERSETS > OVERSET

OVERSEW *vb* sew (two edges) with stitches that pass over them both

OVERSEWED > OVERSEW

OVERSEWN > OVERSEW

OVERSEWS > OVERSEW

OVERSEXED *adj* more interested in sex than is thought decent

OVERSHADE *vb* appear more important than

OVERSHARE *vb* share too much about oneself

OVERSHARP *adj* too sharp

OVERSHINE *vb* shine down on

OVERSHIRT *n* shirt worn over lighter clothes

OVERSHOE *n* protective shoe worn over an ordinary shoe

OVERSHOES > OVERSHOE

OVERSHONE > OVERSHINE

OVERSHOOT *vb* go beyond (a mark or target) ▷ *n* act or instance of overshooting

OVERSHOT *adj* (of a water wheel) driven by a flow of water that passes over the wheel ▷ *n* type of fishing rod

OVERSHOTS > OVERSHOT

OVERSICK *adj* too sick

OVERSIDE *adv* over the side (of a ship) ▷ *n* top side

OVERSIDES > OVERSIDE

OVERSIGHT *n* mistake caused by not noticing something

OVERSIZE *adj* larger than the usual size ▷ *n* size larger than the usual or proper size

OVERSIZED *same as* > OVERSIZE

OVERSIZES > OVERSIZE

OVERSKATE *vb* (in ice hockey) skate beyond the puck

OVERSKIP *vb* skip over

OVERSKIPS > OVERSKIP

OVERSKIRT *n* outer skirt, esp one that reveals a decorative underskirt

OVERSLEEP *vb* sleep beyond the intended time

OVERSLEPT > OVERSLEEP

OVERSLIP *vb* slip past

OVERSLIPS > OVERSLIP

OVERSLIPT > OVERSLIP

OVERSLOW *adj* too slow

OVERSMAN *n* overseer

OVERSMEN > OVERSMAN

OVERSMOKE *vb* smoke something too much

OVERSOAK *vb* soak too much

OVERSOAKS > OVERSOAK

OVERSOFT *adj* too soft

OVERSOLD > OVERSELL

OVERSOON *adv* too soon

OVERSOUL *n* universal divine essence

OVERSOULS > OVERSOUL

OVERSOW *vb* sow again after first sowing

OVERSOWED > OVERSOW

OVERSOWN > OVERSOW

OVERSOWS > OVERSOW

OVERSPEND *vb* spend more than one can afford ▷ *n* amount by which someone or something is overspent

OVERSPENT > OVERSPEND

OVERSPICE *vb* add too much spice to

OVERSPILL *n* rehousing of people from crowded cities in smaller towns ▷ *vb* overflow

OVERSPILT > OVERSPILL

OVERSPIN *n* forward spinning motion

OVERSPINS > OVERSPIN

OVERSTAFF *vb* provide an excessive number of staff for (a factory, hotel, etc)

OVERSTAIN *vb* stain too much

OVERSTAND *vb* remain longer than

OVERSTANK > OVERSTINK

OVERSTARE *vb* outstare

OVERSTATE *vb* state too strongly

OVERSTAY *vb* stay beyond the limit or duration of

OVERSTAYS > OVERSTAY

OVERSTEER *vb* (of a vehicle) to turn more sharply than is desirable or anticipated

OVERSTEP *vb* go beyond (a certain limit)

OVERSTEPS > OVERSTEP

OVERSTINK *vb* exceed in stinking

OVERSTIR *vb* stir too much

OVERSTIRS > OVERSTIR

OVERSTOCK *vb* hold or supply (a commodity) in excess of requirements

OVERSTOOD > OVERSTAND

OVERSTORY *n* highest level of trees in a rainforest

OVERSTREW *vb* scatter over

OVERSTUDY *vb* study too much

OVERSTUFF *vb* force too much into

OVERSTUNK > OVERSTINK

OVERSUDS *vb* produce too much lather

OVERSUP *vb* sup too much

OVERSUPS > OVERSUP

OVERSURE *adj* too sure

OVERSWAM > OVERSWIM

OVERSWAY *vb* overrule

OVERSWAYS > OVERSWAY

OVERSWEAR *vb* swear again

OVERSWEET *adj* too sweet

OVERSWELL *vb* overflow

OVERSWIM *vb* swim across

OVERSWIMS > OVERSWIM

OVERSWING *vb* swing too much or too far

OVERSWORE > OVERSWEAR

OVERSWORN > OVERSWEAR

OVERSWUM > OVERSWIM

OVERSWUNG > OVERSWING

OVERT *adj* open, not hidden

OVERTAKE *vb* move past (a vehicle or person) travelling in the same direction

OVERTAKEN > OVERTAKE

OVERTAKES > OVERTAKE

OVERTALK *vb* talk over

OVERTALKS > OVERTALK

OVERTAME *adj* too tame

OVERTART *adj* too bitter

OVERTASK *vb* impose too heavy a task upon

OVERTASKS > OVERTASK

OVERTAX *vb* put too great a strain on

OVERTAXED > OVERTAX

OVERTAXES > OVERTAX

OVERTEACH *vb* teach too much

OVERTEEM *vb* be too full of something

OVERTEEMS > OVERTEEM

OVERTHICK *adj* too thick

OVERTHIN *vb* make too thin

OVERTHINK *vb* give too much thought to

OVERTHINS > OVERTHIN

OVERTHREW > OVERTHROW

OVERTHROW *vb* defeat and replace ▷ *n* downfall, destruction

OVERTIGHT *adj* too tight

OVERTIME *adv* in addition to one's normal working hours ▷ *n* work at a regular job done in addition to regular working hours ▷ *vb* exceed the required time for (a photographic exposure)

OVERTIMED > OVERTIME

OVERTIMER > OVERTIME

OVERTIMES > OVERTIME

OVERTIMID *adj* too timid

OVERTIP *vb* give too much money as a tip

OVERTIPS > OVERTIP

OVERTIRE *vb* make too tired

OVERTIRED > OVERTIRE

OVERTIRES > OVERTIRE

OVERTLY > OVERT

OVERTNESS > OVERT

OVERTOIL *vb* work too hard

OVERTOILS > OVERTOIL

OVERTONE *n* additional meaning

OVERTONES > OVERTONE

OVERTOOK > OVERTAKE

OVERTOP *vb* exceed in height

OVERTOPS > OVERTOP

OVERTOWER *vb* tower above

OVERTRADE *vb* (of an enterprise) to trade in excess of working capital

OVERTRAIN *vb* train too much

OVERTREAT *vb* give too much medical treatment to

OVERTRICK *n* trick by which a player exceeds their contract

OVERTRIM *vb* trim too much

OVERTRIMS > OVERTRIM

OVERTRIP *vb* tread lightly over

OVERTRIPS > OVERTRIP

OVERTRUMP *vb* (in cards) play a trump higher than (one previously played to the trick)

OVERTRUST *vb* trust too much

OVERTURE *n* orchestral introduction ▷ *vb* make or present an overture to

OVERTURED > OVERTURE

OVERTURES > OVERTURE

OVERTURN *vb* turn upside down ▷ *n* act of overturning or the state of being overturned

OVERTURNS > OVERTURN

OVERTYPE *vb* type over existing text

OVERTYPED > OVERTYPE

OVERTYPES > OVERTYPE

OVERURGE *vb* urge too strongly

OVERURGED > OVERURGE

OVERURGES > OVERURGE

OVERUSE vb use excessively ▷ n excessive use

OVERUSED > OVERUSE

OVERUSES > OVERUSE

OVERUSING > OVERUSE

OVERVALUE vb regard (someone or something) as much more important than is the case

OVERVEIL vb cover over

OVERVEILS > OVERVEIL

OVERVIEW n general survey

OVERVIEWS > OVERVIEW

OVERVIVID adj too vivid

OVERVOTE vb vote more times than is allowed

OVERVOTED > OVERVOTE

OVERVOTES > OVERVOTE

OVERWARM vb make too warm

OVERWARMS > OVERWARM

OVERWARY adj excessively wary

OVERWASH n act of washing over something

OVERWATCH vb watch over

OVERWATER vb give too much water to

OVERWEAK adj too weak

OVERWEAR vb wear out

OVERWEARS > OVERWEAR

OVERWEARY vb make too tired

OVERWEEN vb think too highly of

OVERWEENS > OVERWEEN

OVERWEIGH vb exceed in weight

OVERWENT > OVERGO

OVERWET vb make too wet

OVERWETS > OVERWET

OVERWHELM vb overpower, esp emotionally

OVERWIDE adj too wide

OVERWILY adj too crafty

OVERWIND vb wind (a watch) beyond the proper limit

OVERWINDS > OVERWIND

OVERWING vb fly above

OVERWINGS > OVERWING

OVERWISE adj too wise

OVERWORD n repeated word or phrase

OVERWORDS > OVERWORD

OVERWORE > OVERWEAR

OVERWORK vb work too much ▷ n excessive work

OVERWORKS > OVERWORK

OVERWORN > OVERWEAR

OVERWOUND > OVERWIND

OVERWRAP vb cover with a wrapping

OVERWRAPS > OVERWRAP

OVERWRAPT > OVERWRAP

OVERWREST vb strain too much

OVERWRITE vb write (something) in an excessively ornate or prolix style

OVERWROTE > OVERWRITE

OVERYEAR vb keep for later year

OVERYEARS > OVERYEAR

OVERZEAL n excess of zeal

OVERZEALS > OVERZEAL

OVIBOS n type of ox

OVIBOSES > OVIBOS

OVIBOVINE > OVIBOS

OVICIDAL > OVICIDE

OVICIDE n killing of sheep

OVICIDES > OVICIDE

OVIDUCAL > OVIDUCT

OVIDUCT n tube through which eggs are conveyed

OVIDUCTAL > OVIDUCT

OVIDUCTS > OVIDUCT

OVIFEROUS adj carrying or producing eggs or ova

OVIFORM adj shaped like an egg

OVIGEROUS same as > OVIFEROUS

OVINE adj of or like a sheep ▷ n member of sheep family

OVINES > OVINE

OVIPARA n all oviparous animals

OVIPARITY > OVIPAROUS

OVIPAROUS adj producing eggs that hatch outside the body of the mother

OVIPOSIT vb (of insects and fishes) to deposit eggs through an ovipositor

OVIPOSITS > OVIPOSIT

OVIRAPTOR n egg-eating dinosaur

OVISAC n capsule or sac in which egg cells are produced

OVISACS > OVISAC

OVIST n person believing ovum contains all subsequent generations

OVISTS > OVIST

OVOID adj egg-shaped ▷ n something that is ovoid

OVOIDAL adj ovoid ▷ n something that is ovoid

OVOIDALS > OVOIDAL

OVOIDS > OVOID

OVOLI > OVOLO

OVOLO n type of convex moulding

OVOLOS > OVOLO

OVONIC adj using particular electronic storage batteries

OVONICS n science of ovonic equipment

OVOTESTES > OVOTESTIS

OVOTESTIS n reproductive organ of snails

OVULAR > OVULE

OVULARY > OVULE

OVULATE vb produce or release an egg cell from an ovary

OVULATED > OVULATE

OVULATES > OVULATE

OVULATING > OVULATE

OVULATION > OVULATE

OVULATORY > OVULATE

OVULE n plant part that contains the egg cell

OVULES > OVULE

OVUM n unfertilized egg cell

OW interj exclamation of pain

OWCHE same as > OUCH

OWCHES > OWCHE

OWE vb be obliged to pay (a sum of money) to (a person)

OWED > OWE

OWELTIES > OWELTY

OWELTY n equality, esp in financial transactions

OWER Scots word for > OVER

OWERBY adv over there

OWERLOUP n Scots word meaning encroachment

OWERLOUPS > OWERLOUP

OWES > OWE

OWIE n minor injury

OWIES > OWIE

OWING > OWE

OWL n night bird of prey ▷ vb act like an owl

OWLED > OWL

OWLER n smuggler

OWLERIES > OWLERY

OWLERS > OWLER

OWLERY n place where owls live

OWLET n young or nestling owl

OWLETS > OWLET

OWLIER > OWLY

OWLIEST > OWLY

OWLING > OWL

OWLISH adj like an owl

OWLISHLY > OWLISH

OWLLIKE > OWL

OWLS > OWL

OWLY same as > OWLISH

OWN adj used to emphasize possession ▷ pron thing(s) belonging to a particular person ▷ vb possess

OWNABLE adj able to be owned

OWNED > OWN

OWNER n person who owns

OWNERLESS > OWNER

OWNERS > OWNER

OWNERSHIP n state or fact of being an owner

OWNING > OWN

OWNS > OWN

OWNSOME n solitary state

OWNSOMES > OWNSOME

OWRE same as > OWER

OWRECAME > OWRECOME

OWRECOME n chorus of song ▷ vb overcome

OWRECOMES > OWRECOME

OWRELAY Scots form of > OVERLAY

OWRELAYS > OWRELAY

OWRES > OWRE

OWREWORD variant of > OVERWORD

OWREWORDS > OWREWORD

OWRIE same as > OORIE

OWRIER > OWRIE

OWRIEST > OWRIE

OWSE Scots form of > OX

OWSEN Scots word for > OXEN

OWT dialect word for > ANYTHING

OWTS > OWT

OX n castrated bull

OXACILLIN n antibiotic drug

OXALATE n salt or ester of oxalic acid ▷ vb treat with oxalate

OXALATED > OXALATE

OXALATES > OXALATE

OXALATING > OXALATE

OXALIC adj as in oxalic acid poisonous acid found in many plants

OXALIS n type of plant

OXALISES > OXALIS

OXAZEPAM n drug used to relieve anxiety

OXAZEPAMS > OXAZEPAM

OXAZINE n type of chemical compound

OXAZINES > OXAZINE

OXAZOLE n type of liquid chemical compound

OXAZOLES > OXAZOLE

OXBLOOD n dark reddish-brown colour ▷ adj of this colour

OXBLOODS > OXBLOOD

OXBOW n piece of wood fitted around the neck of a harnessed ox

OXBOWS > OXBOW

OXCART n cart pulled by ox

OXCARTS > OXCART

OXEN > OX

OXER n high fence

OXERS > OXER

OXES > OX

OXEYE n daisy-like flower

OXEYES > OXEYE

OXFORD n type of stout laced shoe with a low heel

OXFORDS > OXFORD

OXGANG n old measure of farmland

OXGANGS > OXGANG

OXGATE same as > OXGANG

OXGATES > OXGATE

OXHEAD n head of an ox

OXHEADS > OXHEAD

OXHEART n heart-shaped cherry

OXHEARTS > OXHEART

OXHERD n person who tends oxen

OXHERDS > OXHERD

OXHIDE n leather made from the hide of an ox

OXHIDES > OXHIDE

OXIC adj involving oxygen

OXID same as > OXIDE

OXIDABLE adj able to undergo oxidation

OXIDANT n substance that acts or is used as an oxidizing agent

OXIDANTS > OXIDANT

OXIDASE n enzyme that brings about oxidation

OXIDASES > OXIDASE

OXIDASIC > OXIDASE

OXIDATE another word for > OXIDIZE

OXIDATED > OXIDATE

OXIDATES > OXIDATE

OXIDATING > OXIDATE

OXIDATION n oxidizing

OXIDATIVE > OXIDATION

OXIDE n compound of oxygen and one other element

OXIDES > OXIDE

OXIDIC > OXIDE

OXIDISE same as > OXIDIZE

OXIDISED > OXIDISE

OXIDISER same as > OXIDIZER

OXIDISERS > OXIDISER
OXIDISES > OXIDISE
OXIDISING > OXIDISE
OXIDIZE vb combine chemically with oxygen
OXIDIZED > OXIDIZE
OXIDIZER same as > OXIDANT
OXIDIZERS > OXIDIZER
OXIDIZES > OXIDIZE
OXIDIZING > OXIDIZE
OXIDS > OXID
OXIES > OXY
OXIM same as > OXIME
OXIME n type of chemical compound
OXIMES > OXIME
OXIMETER n instrument for measuring oxygen in blood
OXIMETERS > OXIMETER
OXIMETRY > OXIMETER
OXIMS > OXIM
OXLAND same as > OXGANG
OXLANDS > OXLAND
OXLIKE > OX
OXLIP n type of woodland plant
OXLIPS > OXLIP
OXO n as in oxo acid acid that contains oxygen
OXONIUM n as in oxonium compound type of salt derived from an organic ether
OXONIUMS > OXONIUM
OXPECKER n type of African starling
OXPECKERS > OXPECKER
OXSLIP same as > OXLIP
OXSLIPS > OXSLIP
OXTAIL n tail of an ox, used in soups and stews
OXTAILS > OXTAIL
OXTER n armpit ▷ vb grip under arm
OXTERED > OXTER
OXTERING > OXTER
OXTERS > OXTER

OXTONGUE n type of plant
OXTONGUES > OXTONGUE
OXY > OX
OXYACID n any acid that contains oxygen
OXYACIDS > OXYACID
OXYANION n anion containing oxygen atoms
OXYANIONS > OXYANION
OXYCODONE n as in oxycodone hydrochloride opiate drug used as a painkiller
OXYGEN n gaseous element essential to life and combustion
OXYGENASE n enzyme
OXYGENATE vb add oxygen to
OXYGENIC > OXYGEN
OXYGENISE variant of > OXYGENIZE
OXYGENIZE vb add oxygen to
OXYGENOUS > OXYGEN
OXYGENS > OXYGEN
OXYMEL n mixture of vinegar and honey
OXYMELS > OXYMEL
OXYMORA > OXYMORON
OXYMORON n figure of speech that combines two apparently contradictory ideas
OXYMORONS > OXYMORON
OXYNTIC adj of or denoting stomach cells that secrete acid
OXYPHIL n type of cell found in glands
OXYPHILE same as > OXYPHIL
OXYPHILES > OXYPHILE
OXYPHILIC > OXYPHIL
OXYPHILS > OXYPHIL
OXYSALT n any salt of an oxyacid
OXYSALTS > OXYSALT

OXYSOME n group of molecules
OXYSOMES > OXYSOME
OXYTOCIC adj accelerating childbirth by stimulating uterine contractions ▷ n oxytocic drug or agent
OXYTOCICS > OXYTOCIC
OXYTOCIN n hormone that stimulates the ejection of milk in mammals
OXYTOCINS > OXYTOCIN
OXYTONE adj having an accent on the final syllable ▷ n oxytone word
OXYTONES > OXYTONE
OXYTONIC adj (of a word) having the stress or acute accent on the last syllable
OXYTROPE n type of flowering plant
OXYTROPES > OXYTROPE
OY n grandchild
OYE same as > OY
OYER n (in the 13th century) an assize
OYERS > OYER
OYES same as > OYEZ
OYESES > OYES
OYESSES > OYES
OYEZ interj shouted three times by a public crier calling for attention ▷ n such a cry
OYEZES > OYEZ
OYS > OY
OYSTER n edible shellfish ▷ vb dredge for, gather, or raise oysters
OYSTERED > OYSTER
OYSTERER n person fishing for oysters
OYSTERERS > OYSTERER
OYSTERING > OYSTER
OYSTERMAN n person who gathers, cultivates, or sells oysters
OYSTERMEN > OYSTERMAN
OYSTERS > OYSTER

OYSTRIGE archaic variant of > OSTRICH
OYSTRIGES > OYSTRIGE
OZAENA n inflammation of nasal mucous membrane
OZAENAS > OZAENA
OZALID n method of duplicating writing or illustrations
OZALIDS > OZALID
OZEKI n sumo wrestling champion
OZEKIS > OZEKI
OZOCERITE n brown or greyish wax
OZOKERITE same as > OZOCERITE
OZONATE vb add ozone to
OZONATED > OZONATE
OZONATES > OZONATE
OZONATING > OZONATE
OZONATION > OZONATE
OZONE n strong-smelling form of oxygen
OZONES > OZONE
OZONIC > OZONE
OZONIDE n type of unstable explosive compound
OZONIDES > OZONIDE
OZONISE same as > OZONIZE
OZONISED > OZONISE
OZONISER > OZONISE
OZONISERS > OZONISE
OZONISES > OZONISE
OZONISING > OZONISE
OZONIZE vb convert (oxygen) into ozone
OZONIZED > OZONIZE
OZONIZER > OZONIZE
OZONIZERS > OZONIZE
OZONIZES > OZONIZE
OZONIZING > OZONIZE
OZONOUS > OZONE
OZZIE n hospital
OZZIES > OZZIE

Pp

PA n (formerly) fortified Māori settlement

PAAL n stake driven into the ground

PAALS > PAAL

PAAN n leaf of the betel tree

PAANS > PAAN

PABLUM same as > PABULUM

PABLUMS > PABLUM

PABOUCHE n soft shoe

PABOUCHES > PABOUCHE

PABULAR > PABULUM

PABULOUS > PABULUM

PABULUM n food

PABULUMS > PABULUM

PAC n soft shoe

PACA n large burrowing rodent

PACABLE adj easily appeased

PACAS > PACA

PACATION n act of making peace

PACATIONS > PACATION

PACE n single step in walking ▷ vb walk up and down, esp in anxiety ▷ prep with due respect to: used to express polite disagreement

PACED > PACE

PACEMAKER n electronic device surgically implanted in a person with heart disease to regulate the heartbeat

PACEMAN n (in cricket) fast bowler

PACEMEN > PACEMAN

PACER n horse trained to move at a special gait, esp for racing

PACERS > PACER

PACES > PACE

PACEWAY n racecourse for trotting and pacing

PACEWAYS > PACEWAY

PACEY adj fast-moving, quick, lively

PACHA same as > PASHA

PACHADOM n rank of pacha

PACHADOMS > PACHADOM

PACHAK n fragrant roots of Asian plant

PACHAKS > PACHAK

PACHALIC n jurisdiction of pasha

PACHALICS > PACHALIC

PACHAS > PACHA

PACHINKO n Japanese game similar to pinball

PACHINKOS > PACHINKO

PACHISI n Indian game resembling backgammon

PACHISIS > PACHISI

PACHOULI same as > PATCHOULI

PACHOULIS > PACHOULI

PACHUCO n young Mexican living in the US

PACHUCOS > PACHUCO

PACHYDERM n thick-skinned animal such as an elephant

PACHYTENE n third stage of the prophase of meiosis during which the chromosomes become shorter and thicker and divide into chromatids

PACIER > PACY

PACIEST > PACY

PACIFIC adj tending to bring peace

PACIFICAE pl n medieval letters of introduction from the Church

PACIFICAL > PACIFIC

PACIFIED > PACIFY

PACIFIER n baby's dummy

PACIFIERS > PACIFIER

PACIFIES > PACIFY

PACIFISM n belief that violence is unjustifiable

PACIFISMS > PACIFISM

PACIFIST n person who refuses on principle to take part in war ▷ adj advocating, relating to, or characterized by pacifism

PACIFISTS > PACIPIST

PACIFY vb soothe, calm

PACIFYING > PACIFY

PACING n act of pacing

PACINGS > PACING

PACK vb put (clothes etc) together in a suitcase or bag ▷ n bag carried on a person's or animal's back

PACKABLE > PACK

PACKAGE same as > PACKET

PACKAGED > PACKAGE

PACKAGER n independent firm specializing in design and production

PACKAGERS > PACKAGER

PACKAGES > PACKAGE

PACKAGING n box or wrapping in which a product is offered for sale

PACKBOARD n frame for carrying goods

PACKCLOTH n cloth used for packing

PACKED adj completely filled

PACKER n person or company who packs goods

PACKERS > PACKER

PACKET n small container (and contents) ▷ vb wrap up in a packet or as a packet

PACKETED > PACKET

PACKETING > PACKET

PACKETISE same as > PACKETIZE

PACKETIZE vb form data into packets

PACKETS > PACKET

PACKFONG n Chinese alloy

PACKFONGS > PACKFONG

PACKFRAME n light metal frame with shoulder straps, used for carrying heavy or awkward loads

PACKHORSE n horse used for carrying goods

PACKING n material, such as paper or plastic, used to protect packed goods

PACKINGS > PACKING

PACKLY > PACK

PACKMAN n man carrying a pack

PACKMEN > PACKMAN

PACKMULE n mule used to carry burdens

PACKMULES > PACKMULE

PACKNESS > PACK

PACKS > PACK

PACKSACK n bag carried strapped on the back or shoulder

PACKSACKS > PACKSACK

PACKSHEET n cover for pack

PACKSTAFF n staff for supporting pack

PACKWAX n neck ligament

PACKWAXES > PACKWAX

PACKWAY n path for pack animals

PACKWAYS > PACKWAY

PACO n S American mammal

PACOS > PACO

PACS > PAC

PACT n formal agreement

PACTA > PACTUM

PACTION vb concur with

PACTIONAL > PACTION

PACTIONED > PACTION

PACTIONS > PACTION

PACTS > PACT

PACTUM n pact

PACY same as > PACEY

PACZKI n round filled doughnut

PACZKIS > PACZKI

PAD n piece of soft material used for protection, support, absorption of liquid, etc ▷ vb protect or fill with soft material

PADANG n (in Malaysia) playing field

PADANGS > PADANG

PADAUK n tropical African or Asian tree

PADAUKS > PADAUK

PADDED > PAD

PADDER n highwayman who robs on foot

PADDERS > PADDER

PADDIES > PADDY

PADDING > PAD

PADDINGS > PAD

PADDLE n short oar with a broad blade at one or each end ▷ vb move (a canoe etc) with a paddle

PADDLED > PADDLE

PADDLER > PADDLE

PADDLERS > PADDLE

PADDLES > PADDLE

PADDLING > PADDLE

PADDLINGS > PADDLE

PADDOCK n small field or enclosure for horses ▷ vb place (a horse) in a paddock

PADDOCKED > PADDOCK

PADDOCKS > PADDOCK

PADDY n fit of temper

PADDYWACK vb spank or smack

PADELLA n type of candle

PADELLAS > PADELLA

PADEMELON n small Australian wallaby

PADERERO same as > PATERERO

PADEREROS > PADERERO

PADI same as > PADDY

PADIS > PADI

PADISHAH n Iranian ruler

PADISHAHS > PADISHAH

PADKOS n snacks and provisions for a journey

PADLE another name for > LUMPFISH

PADLES > PADLE

PADLOCK n detachable lock with a hinged hoop ▷ vb fasten (something) with a padlock

PADLOCKED > PADLOCK

PADLOCKS > PADLOCK

PADMA n type of lotus

PADMAS > PADMA

PADNAG n ambling horse

PADNAGS > PADNAG

PADOUK same as > PADAUK

PADOUKS > PADOUK

PADRE n chaplain to the armed forces

PADRES > PADRE
PADRI > PADRE
PADRONA n female boss or employer
PADRONAS > PADRONA
PADRONE n owner or proprietor of an inn, esp in Italy
PADRONES > PADRONE
PADRONI > PADRONE
PADRONISM n system of work controlled by a padrone
PADS > PAD
PADSAW n small narrow saw used for cutting curves
PADSAWS > PADSAW
PADSHAH same as > PADISHAH
PADSHAHS > PADSHAH
PADUASOY n rich strong silk fabric used for hangings, vestments, etc
PADUASOYS > PADUASOY
PADYMELON same as > PADEMELON
PAEAN n song of triumph or thanksgiving
PAEANISM > PAEAN
PAEANISMS > PAEAN
PAEANS > PAEAN
PAEDERAST same as > PEDERAST
PAEDEUTIC adj of or relating to the study of teaching
PAEDIATRY n branch of medical science concerned with children and their diseases
PAEDO n paedophile
PAEDOLOGY n study of the character, growth, and development of children
PAEDOS > PAEDO
PAELLA n Spanish dish of rice, chicken, shellfish, and vegetables
PAELLAS > PAELLA
PAENULA n ancient Roman cloak
PAENULAE > PAENULA
PAENULAS > PAENULA
PAEON n metrical foot of four syllables
PAEONIC > PAEON
PAEONICS > PAEON
PAEONIES > PAEONY
PAEONS > PAEON
PAEONY same as > PEONY
PAESAN n fellow countryman
PAESANI > PAESANO
PAESANO n Italian-American man
PAESANOS > PAESANO
PAESANS > PAESAN
PAGAN adj not belonging to one of the world's main religions ▷ n pagan person
PAGANDOM > PAGAN
PAGANDOMS > PAGAN
PAGANISE same as > PAGANIZE
PAGANISED > PAGANISE
PAGANISER > PAGANISE
PAGANISES > PAGANISE
PAGANISH > PAGAN

PAGANISM > PAGAN
PAGANISMS > PAGAN
PAGANIST > PAGAN
PAGANISTS > PAGAN
PAGANIZE vb become pagan, render pagan, or convert to paganism
PAGANIZED > PAGANIZE
PAGANIZER > PAGANIZE
PAGANIZES > PAGANIZE
PAGANS > PAGAN
PAGE n (one side of) sheet of paper forming a book etc ▷ vb summon (someone) by bleeper or loudspeaker
PAGEANT n parade or display of people in costume
PAGEANTRY n spectacular display or ceremony
PAGEANTS > PAGEANT
PAGEBOY n type of hairstyle
PAGEBOYS > PAGEBOY
PAGED > PAGE
PAGEFUL n amount (of text, etc) that a page will hold
PAGEFULS > PAGEFUL
PAGEHOOD n state of being a page
PAGEHOODS > PAGEHOOD
PAGER n small electronic device, capable of receiving short messages
PAGERS > PAGER
PAGES > PAGE
PAGEVIEW n electronic page of information displayed at the request of a user
PAGEVIEWS > PAGEVIEW
PAGINAL adj page-for-page
PAGINATE vb number the pages of (a book, manuscript, etc) in sequence
PAGINATED > PAGINATE
PAGINATES > PAGINATE
PAGING > PAGE
PAGINGS > PAGE
PAGLE same as > PAIGLE
PAGLES > PAGLE
PAGOD n oriental idol
PAGODA n pyramid-shaped Asian temple or tower
PAGODAS > PAGODA
PAGODITE n type of soft mineral used for carving
PAGODITES > PAGODITE
PAGODS > PAGOD
PAGRI n type of turban
PAGRIS > PAGRI
PAGURIAN n type of decapod crustacean of the family which includes the hermit crabs
PAGURIANS > PAGURIAN
PAGURID same as > PAGURIAN
PAGURIDS > PAGURID
PAH same as > PA
PAHAUTEA same as > KAIKAWAKA
PAHAUTEAS > PAHAUTEA
PAHLAVI n Iranian coin
PAHLAVIS > PAHLAVI
PAHOEHOE n hardened lava
PAHOEHOES > PAHOEHOE
PAHS > PAH
PAID > PAY
PAIDEUTIC same as > PAEDEUTIC

PAIDLE Scots variant of > PADDLE
PAIDLES > PAIDLE
PAIGLE n cowslip
PAIGLES > PAIGLE
PAIK vb thump or whack
PAIKED > PAIK
PAIKING > PAIK
PAIKS > PAIK
PAIL n bucket
PAILFUL same as > PAIL
PAILFULS > PAILFUL
PAILLARD n thin slice of meat
PAILLARDS > PAILLARD
PAILLASSE same as > PALLIASSE
PAILLETTE n sequin or spangle sewn onto a costume
PAILLON n thin leaf of metal
PAILLONS > PAILLON
PAILS > PAIL
PAILSFUL > PAILFUL
PAIN n physical or mental suffering ▷ vb cause (someone) mental or physical suffering
PAINCH Scots variant of > PAUNCH
PAINCHES > PAINCH
PAINED adj having or suggesting pain or distress
PAINFUL adj causing pain or distress
PAINFULLY > PAINFUL
PAINIM n heathen or pagan
PAINIMS > PAINIM
PAINING > PAIN
PAINLESS adj not causing pain or distress
PAINS pl n care or trouble
PAINT n coloured substance, spread on a surface with a brush or roller ▷ vb colour or coat with paint
PAINTABLE > PAINT
PAINTBALL n game in which teams of players simulate a military skirmish, shooting each other with paint pellets
PAINTBOX n box containing a tray of dry watercolour paints
PAINTED > PAINT
PAINTER n rope at the front of a boat, for tying it up
PAINTERLY adj having qualities peculiar to painting, esp the depiction of shapes by means of solid masses of colour, rather than by lines
PAINTERS > PAINTER
PAINTIER > PAINT
PAINTIEST > PAINT
PAINTING n picture produced by using paint
PAINTINGS > PAINTING
PAINTPOT n pot for holding paint
PAINTPOTS > PAINTPOT
PAINTRESS n female painter
PAINTS > PAINT
PAINTURE n art of painting

PAINTURES > PAINTURE
PAINTWORK n covering of paint on parts of a vehicle; building, etc
PAINTY > PAINT
PAIOCK obsolete word for > PEACOCK
PAIOCKE obsolete word for > PEACOCK
PAIOCKES > PAIOCKE
PAIOCKS > PAIOCK
PAIR n set of two things matched for use together ▷ vb group or be grouped in twos
PAIRE obsolete spelling of > PAIR
PAIRED > PAIR
PAIRER > PAIR
PAIRES > PAIRE
PAIREST > PAIR
PAIRIAL variant of > PRIAL
PAIRIALS > PAIRIAL
PAIRING > PAIR
PAIRINGS > PAIR
PAIRS > PAIR
PAIRWISE adv in pairs
PAIS n country
PAISA n monetary unit of Bangladesh, Bhutan, India, Nepal, and Pakistan
PAISAN n fellow countryman
PAISANA n female peasant
PAISANAS > PAISANA
PAISANO n friend
PAISANOS > PAISANO
PAISANS > PAISAN
PAISAS > PAISA
PAISE > PAISA
PAISLEY n pattern of small curving shapes with intricate detailing
PAISLEYS > PAISLEY
PAITRICK Scots word for > PARTRIDGE
PAITRICKS > PAITRICK
PAJAMA same as > PYJAMA
PAJAMAED adj wearing pajamas
PAJAMAS > PAJAMA
PAJOCK obsolete word for > PEACOCK
PAJOCKE obsolete word for > PEACOCK
PAJOCKES > PAJOCKE
PAJOCKS > PAJOCK
PAK n pack
PAKAHI n acid land that is unsuitable for cultivation
PAKAHIS > PAKAHI
PAKAPOO n Chinese lottery
PAKAPOOS > PAKAPOO
PAKEHA n person of European descent, as distinct from a Māori
PAKEHAS > PAKEHA
PAKFONG same as > PACKFONG
PAKFONGS > PAKFONG
PAKIHI n area of swampy infertile land
PAKIHIS > PAKIHI
PAKKA variant of > PUKKA
PAKOKO n small freshwater fish
PAKOKOS > PAKOKO

PAKORA n fried battered pieces of vegetable, chicken, etc
PAKORAS > PAKORA
PAKS > PAK
PAKTHONG n white alloy containing copper, zinc, and nickel
PAKTHONGS > PAKTHONG
PAKTONG same as > PAKTHONG
PAKTONGS > PAKTONG
PAL n friend ▷ vb associate as friends
PALABRA n word
PALABRAS > PALABRA
PALACE n residence of a king, bishop, etc
PALACED adj having palaces
PALACES > PALACE
PALACINKE n thin pancake of Central and Eastern Europe
PALADIN n knight who did battle for a monarch
PALADINS > PALADIN
PALAEOSOL n an ancient soil horizon
PALAESTRA n (in ancient Greece or Rome) public place devoted to the training of athletes
PALAFITTE n prehistoric dwelling
PALAGI n (in Samoa) European
PALAGIS > PALAGI
PALAIS n dance hall
PALAMA n webbing on bird's feet
PALAMAE > PALAMA
PALAMATE > PALAMA
PALAMINO same as > PALOMINO
PALAMINOS > PALAMINO
PALAMPORE same as > PALEMPORE
PALANKEEN same as > PALANQUIN
PALANQUIN n (formerly, in the Orient) covered bed in which someone could be carried on the shoulders of four men
PALAPA n open-sided tropical building
PALAPAS > PALAPA
PALAS n East Indian tree
PALASES > PALAS
PALATABLE adj pleasant to taste
PALATABLY > PALATABLE
PALATAL adj of or relating to the palate ▷ n bony plate that forms the palate
PALATALLY > PALATAL
PALATALS > PALATAL
PALATE n roof of the mouth ▷ vb perceive by taste
PALATED > PALATE
PALATES > PALATE
PALATIAL adj like a palace, magnificent
PALATINE same as > PALATAL
PALATINES > PALATINE
PALATING > PALATE

PALAVER n time-wasting fuss ▷ vb (often used humorously) have a conference
PALAVERED > PALAVER
PALAVERER > PALAVER
PALAVERS > PALAVER
PALAY n type of rubber
PALAYS > PALAY
PALAZZI > PALAZZO
PALAZZO n Italian palace
PALAZZOS > PALAZZO
PALE adj light, whitish ▷ vb become pale ▷ n wooden or metal post used in fences
PALEA n bract in a grass spikelet
PALEAE > PALEA
PALEAL > PALEA
PALEATE adj having scales
PALEBUCK n small African antelope
PALEBUCKS > PALEBUCK
PALED > PALE
PALEFACE n White person, said to have been used by Native Americans
PALEFACES > PALEFACE
PALELY > PALE
PALEMPORE n bed covering
PALENESS > PALE
PALEOCENE adj belonging to geological time period
PALEOCON n extremely right-wing conservative
PALEOCONS > PALEOCON
PALEOGENE adj of early geological time period
PALEOLITH n Stone Age artefact
PALEOLOGY n study of prehistory
PALEOSOL n ancient soil horizon
PALEOSOLS > PALEOSOL
PALEOZOIC adj belonging to geological time period
PALER > PALE
PALES > PALE
PALEST > PALE
PALESTRA same as > PALAESTRA
PALESTRAE > PALESTRA
PALESTRAL > PALESTRA
PALESTRAS > PALESTRA
PALET n perpendicular band on escutcheon
PALETOT n loose outer garment
PALETOTS > PALETOT
PALETS > PALET
PALETTE n artist's flat board for mixing colours on
PALETTES > PALETTE
PALEWAYS same as > PALEWISE
PALEWISE adv by perpendicular lines
PALFREY n light saddle horse, esp ridden by women
PALFREYED > PALFREY
PALFREYS > PALFREY
PALI n cliff in Hawaii
PALIER > PALY
PALIEST > PALY
PALIFORM adj resembling coral

PALIKAR n Greek soldier
PALIKARS > PALIKAR
PALILALIA n speech disorder in which a word or phrase is rapidly repeated
PALILLOGY n repetition of word or phrase
PALIMONY n alimony awarded to a nonmarried partner after the break-up of a long-term relationship
PALING n wooden or metal post used in fences
PALINGS > PALING
PALINKA n type of apricot brandy
PALINKAS > PALINKA
PALINODE n poem in which the poet recants something he or she has said in a former poem
PALINODES > PALINODE
PALINODY > PALINODE
PALINOPIA n visual disorder in which the patient perceives a prolonged afterimage
PALIS > PALI
PALISADE n fence made of wooden posts driven into the ground ▷ vb enclose with a palisade
PALISADED > PALISADE
PALISADES > PALISADE
PALISADO same as > PALISADE
PALISH adj rather pale
PALKEE n covered Oriental litter
PALKEES > PALKEE
PALKI same as > PALKEE
PALKIS > PALKI
PALL n cloth spread over a coffin ▷ vb become boring
PALLA n ancient Roman cloak
PALLADIA > PALLADIUM
PALLADIC adj of or containing palladium in the trivalent or tetravalent state
PALLADIUM n silvery-white element of the platinum metal group
PALLADOUS adj of or containing palladium in the divalent state
PALLAE > PALLA
PALLAH n S African antelope
PALLAHS > PALLAH
PALLASITE n meteorite composed of iron and olivine
PALLED > PALL
PALLET same as > PALETTE
PALLETED > PALLET
PALLETING > PALLET
PALLETISE same as > PALLETIZE
PALLETIZE vb stack or transport on a pallet or pallets
PALLETS > PALLET
PALLETTE n armpit plate of a suit of armour
PALLETTES > PALLETTE
PALLIA > PALLIUM
PALLIAL adj relating to cerebral cortex

PALLIARD n person who begs
PALLIARDS > PALLIARD
PALLIASSE n straw-filled mattress
PALLIATE vb lessen the severity of (something) without curing it
PALLIATED > PALLIATE
PALLIATES > PALLIATE
PALLIATOR > PALLIATE
PALLID adj pale, esp because ill or weak
PALLIDER > PALLID
PALLIDEST > PALLID
PALLIDITY > PALLID
PALLIDLY > PALLID
PALLIED > PALLY
PALLIER > PALLY
PALLIES > PALLY
PALLIEST > PALLY
PALLING > PALL
PALLIUM n garment worn by men in ancient Greece or Rome
PALLIUMS > PALLIUM
PALLONE n Italian ball game
PALLONES > PALLONE
PALLOR n paleness of complexion
PALLORS > PALLOR
PALLS > PALL
PALLY adj on friendly terms ▷ vb as in pally up become friends with
PALLYING > PALLY
PALM n inner surface of the hand ▷ vb conceal in or about the hand, as in sleight-of-hand tricks
PALMAR adj of or relating to the palm of the hand
PALMARIAN adj pre-eminent
PALMARY adj worthy of praise
PALMATE adj shaped like an open hand
PALMATED same as > PALMATE
PALMATELY > PALMATE
PALMATION n state of being palmate
PALMBALL n baseball pitched from the palm and thumb
PALMBALLS > PALMBALL
PALMED > PALM
PALMER n medieval pilgrim
PALMERS > PALMER
PALMETTE n ornament or design resembling the palm leaf
PALMETTES > PALMETTE
PALMETTO n small palm tree with fan-shaped leaves
PALMETTOS > PALMETTO
PALMFUL n amount that can be held in the palm of a hand
PALMFULS > PALMFUL
PALMHOUSE n greenhouse for palms, etc
PALMIE n palmtop computer
PALMIER n type of French pastry
PALMIERS > PALMIER

PALMIES > PALMIE
PALMIEST > PALMY
PALMIET n South African rush
PALMIETS > PALMIET
PALMING > PALM
PALMIPED n web-footed bird
PALMIPEDE same as > PALMIPED
PALMIPEDS > PALMIPED
PALMIST > PALMISTRY
PALMISTER n person telling fortunes by reading palms
PALMISTRY n fortune-telling from lines on the palm of the hand
PALMISTS > PALMISTRY
PALMITATE n any salt or ester of palmitic acid
PALMITIC adj as in palmitic acid white crystalline solid that is a saturated fatty acid
PALMITIN n colourless glyceride of palmitic acid
PALMITINS > PALMITIN
PALMLIKE > PALM
PALMPRINT n print of a palm
PALMS > PALM
PALMTOP adj small enough to be held in the hand ▷ n computer small enough to be held in the hand
PALMTOPS > PALMTOP
PALMY adj successful, prosperous and happy
PALMYRA n tall tropical Asian palm
PALMYRAS > PALMYRA
PALOLO n polychaete worm of the S Pacific Ocean
PALOLOS > PALOLO
PALOMINO n gold-coloured horse with a white mane and tail
PALOMINOS > PALOMINO
PALOOKA n stupid or clumsy boxer or other person
PALOOKAS > PALOOKA
PALOVERDE n thorny American shrub
PALP n sensory appendage in crustaceans and insects ▷ vb feel
PALPABLE adj obvious
PALPABLY > PALPABLE
PALPAL > PALP
PALPATE vb examine (an area of the body) by touching ▷ adj of, relating to, or possessing a palp or palps
PALPATED > PALPATE
PALPATES > PALPATE
PALPATING > PALPATE
PALPATION > PALPATE
PALPATOR n type of beetle
PALPATORS > PALPATOR
PALPATORY > PALPATE
PALPEBRA n eyelid
PALPEBRAE > PALPEBRA
PALPEBRAL adj of or relating to the eyelid
PALPEBRAS > PALPEBRA
PALPED > PALP
PALPI > PALPUS
PALPING > PALP

PALPITANT > PALPITATE
PALPITATE vb (of the heart) beat rapidly
PALPS > PALP
PALPUS same as > PALP
PALPUSES > PALPUS
PALS > PAL
PALSA n landform of subarctic regions
PALSAS > PALSA
PALSGRAVE n German count palatine
PALSHIP n state of being pals
PALSHIPS > PALSHIP
PALSIED > PALSY
PALSIER > PALSY
PALSIES > PALSY
PALSIEST > PALSY
PALSTAFF variant of > PALSTAVE
PALSTAFFS > PALSTAFF
PALSTAVE n chisel made to fit into a split wooden handle
PALSTAVES > PALSTAVE
PALSY n paralysis ▷ vb paralyse ▷ adj friendly
PALSYING > PALSY
PALSYLIKE > PALSY
PALTER vb act or talk insincerely
PALTERED > PALTER
PALTERER > PALTER
PALTERERS > PALTER
PALTERING > PALTER
PALTERS > PALTER
PALTRIER > PALTRY
PALTRIEST > PALTRY
PALTRILY > PALTRY
PALTRY adj insignificant
PALUDAL adj of, relating to, or produced by marshes
PALUDIC adj of malaria
PALUDINAL adj inhabiting swamps
PALUDINE adj relating to marsh
PALUDISM rare word for > MALARIA
PALUDISMS > PALUDISM
PALUDOSE adj growing or living in marshes
PALUDOUS adj marshy
PALUSTRAL adj marshy
PALY adj vertically striped
PAM n knave of clubs
PAMPA n grassland area
PAMPAS pl n vast grassy plains in S America
PAMPASES > PAMPAS
PAMPEAN > PAMPAS
PAMPEANS > PAMPAS
PAMPER vb treat (someone) with great indulgence, spoil
PAMPERED > PAMPER
PAMPERER > PAMPER
PAMPERERS > PAMPER
PAMPERING n act of treating (someone) with great indulgence
PAMPERO n dry cold wind in South America
PAMPEROS > PAMPERO
PAMPERS > PAMPER
PAMPHLET n thin paper-covered booklet ▷ vb produce pamphlets

PAMPHLETS > PAMPHLET
PAMPHREY n cabbage
PAMPHREYS > PAMPHREY
PAMPOEN n pumpkin
PAMPOENS > PAMPOEN
PAMPOOTIE n rawhide slipper worn by men in the Aran Islands
PAMS > PAM
PAN n wide long-handled metal container used in cooking ▷ vb sift gravel from (a river) in a pan to search for gold
PANACEA n remedy for all diseases or problems
PANACEAN > PANACEA
PANACEAS > PANACEA
PANACHAEA variant of > PANACEA
PANACHE n confident elegant style
PANACHES > PANACHE
PANADA n mixture used as a thickening in cookery
PANADAS > PANADA
PANAMA n hat made of plaited leaves
PANAMAS > PANAMA
PANARIES > PANARY
PANARY n storehouse for bread
PANATELA same as > PANATELLA
PANATELAS > PANATELA
PANATELLA n long slender cigar
PANAX n genus of perennial herbs
PANAXES > PANAX
PANBROIL vb broil in a pan
PANBROILS > PANBROIL
PANCAKE n thin flat circle of fried batter ▷ vb cause (an aircraft) to make a pancake landing
PANCAKED > PANCAKE
PANCAKES > PANCAKE
PANCAKING > PANCAKE
PANCE n pansy
PANCES > PANCE
PANCETTA n lightly spiced cured bacon from Italy
PANCETTAS > PANCETTA
PANCHAX n brightly coloured tropical Asian cyprinodont fish
PANCHAXES > PANCHAX
PANCHAYAT n village council in India
PANCHEON n shallow bowl
PANCHEONS > PANCHEON
PANCHION same as > PANCHEON
PANCHIONS > PANCHION
PANCOSMIC adj of every cosmos
PANCRATIA n wrestling and boxing contests
PANCRATIC > PANCRATIA
PANCREAS n large gland behind the stomach that produces insulin and helps digestion
PAND n valance
PANDA n large black-and-white bearlike mammal from China

PANDAN n type of palm of S E Asia
PANDANI n tropical tree
PANDANIS > PANDANI
PANDANS > PANDAN
PANDANUS n Old World tropical palmlike plant
PANDAR rare variant of > PANDER
PANDARED > PANDAR
PANDARING > PANDAR
PANDARS > PANDAR
PANDAS > PANDA
PANDATION n warping
PANDECT n treatise covering all aspects of a particular subject
PANDECTS > PANDECT
PANDEMIA n epidemic affecting everyone
PANDEMIAN adj sensual
PANDEMIAS > PANDEMIA
PANDEMIC adj (of a disease) occurring over a wide area ▷ n pandemic disease
PANDEMICS > PANDEMIC
PANDER vb indulge (a person his or her desires) ▷ n someone who indulges a person in his or her desires
PANDERED > PANDER
PANDERER n someone who indulges a person in his or her desires
PANDERERS > PANDERER
PANDERESS n female panderer
PANDERING n act or instance of gratifying someone's weaknesses or desires
PANDERISM > PANDER
PANDERLY > PANDER
PANDEROUS > PANDER
PANDERS > PANDER
PANDIED > PANDY
PANDIES > PANDY
PANDIT same as > PUNDIT
PANDITS > PANDIT
PANDOOR same as > PANDOUR
PANDOORS > PANDOOR
PANDORA n handsome red sea bream
PANDORAS > PANDORA
PANDORE another word for > BANDORE
PANDORES > PANDORE
PANDOUR n one of an 18th-century force of Croatian soldiers
PANDOURS > PANDOUR
PANDOWDY n deep-dish pie made from fruit, esp apples, with a cake topping
PANDROP n hard mint-flavoured sweet
PANDROPS > PANDROP
PANDS > PAND
PANDURA n ancient stringed instrument
PANDURAS > PANDURA
PANDURATE adj (of plant leaves) shaped like the body of a fiddle
PANDY n (in schools) stroke on the hand with a strap as a

punishment ▷ *vb* punish with such strokes

PANDYING > PANDY

PANE *n* sheet of glass in a window or door ▷ *adj* (of fish, meat, etc) dipped or rolled in breadcrumbs before cooking

PANED > PANE

PANEER *n* soft white cheese, used in Indian cookery

PANEERS > PANEER

PANEGOISM *n* form of scepticism

PANEGYRIC *n* formal public commendation

PANEGYRY *n* formal public commendation; panegyric

PANEITIES > PANEITY

PANEITY *n* state of being bread

PANEL *n* flat distinct section of a larger surface, for example in a door ▷ *vb* cover or decorate with panels ▷ *adj* of a group acting as a panel

PANELED > PANEL

PANELESS > PANE

PANELING *same as* **> PANELLING**

PANELINGS > PANELING

PANELISED *same as* **> PANELIZED**

PANELIST *same as* **> PANELLIST**

PANELISTS > PANELIST

PANELIZED *adj* made in sections for quick assembly

PANELLED > PANEL

PANELLING *n* panels collectively, esp on a wall

PANELLIST *n* member of a panel

PANELS > PANEL

PANES > PANE

PANETELA *same as* **> PANATELA**

PANETELAS > PANETELA

PANETELLA *n* long thin cigar

PANETTONE *n* kind of Italian spiced brioche containing sultanas

PANETTONI > PANETTONE

PANFISH *n* small food fish ▷ *vb* fish for panfish

PANFISHED > PANFISH

PANFISHES > PANFISH

PANFORTE *n* hard spicy cake

PANFORTES > PANFORTE

PANFRIED > PANFRY

PANFRIES > PANFRY

PANFRY *vb* fry in a pan

PANFRYING > PANFRY

PANFUL *n* the contents of a pan

PANFULS > PANFUL

PANG *n* sudden sharp feeling of pain or sadness ▷ *vb* cause pain

PANGA *n* broad heavy knife of E Africa, used as a tool or weapon

PANGAMIC *adj* relating to pangamy

PANGAMIES > PANGAMY

PANGAMY *n* unrestricted mating

PANGAS > PANGA

PANGED > PANG

PANGEN *same as* **> PANGENE**

PANGENE *n* hypothetical particle of protoplasm

PANGENES > PANGENE

PANGENS > PANGEN

PANGING > PANG

PANGLESS *adj* without pangs

PANGOLIN *n* mammal with very long snout

PANGOLINS > PANGOLIN

PANGRAM *n* sentence incorporating all the letters of the alphabet

PANGRAMS > PANGRAM

PANGS > PANG

PANHANDLE *n* (in the US) narrow strip of land that projects from one state into another ▷ *vb* accost and beg from (passers-by), esp in the street

PANHUMAN *adj* relating to all humanity

PANIC *n* sudden overwhelming fear ▷ *vb* feel or cause to feel panic ▷ *adj* of or resulting from such terror

PANICALLY > PANIC

PANICK *old word for* **> PANIC**

PANICKED > PANIC

PANICKIER > PANIC

PANICKING > PANIC

PANICKS > PANICK

PANICKY > PANIC

PANICLE *n* loose, irregularly branched cluster of flowers

PANICLED > PANICLE

PANICLES > PANICLE

PANICS > PANIC

PANICUM *n* type of grass

PANICUMS > PANICUM

PANIER *same as* **> PANNIER**

PANIERS > PANIER

PANIM *n* heathen or pagan

PANIMS > PANIM

PANING > PANE

PANINI > PANINO

PANINIS > PANINI

PANINO *n* Italian sandwich

PANISC *n* faun; attendant of Pan

PANISCS > PANISC

PANISK *same as* **> PANISC**

PANISKS > PANISK

PANISLAM *n* all of Islam or the Muslim world

PANISLAMS > PANISLAM

PANJANDRA *n* pompous self-important officials of people of rank

PANKO *n* flaky breadcrumbs used in Japanese cookery

PANKOS > PANKO

PANLIKE *adj* resembling a pan

PANLOGISM *n* metaphysics of Leibniz

PANMICTIC > PANMIXIA

PANMIXES > PANMIXIS

PANMIXIA *n* (in population genetics) random mating within an interbreeding population

PANMIXIAS > PANMIXIA

PANMIXIS *same as* **> PANMIXIA**

PANNAGE *n* pasturage for pigs, esp in a forest

PANNAGES > PANNAGE

PANNE *n* lightweight velvet fabric

PANNED > PAN

PANNELLED *adj* divided into panels

PANNER > PAN

PANNERS > PAN

PANNES > PANNE

PANNI > PANNUS

PANNICK *old spelling of the noun* **> PANIC**

PANNICKS > PANNICK

PANNICLE *n* thin layer of body tissue

PANNICLES > PANNICLE

PANNIER *n* bag fixed on the back of a cycle

PANNIERED > PANNIER

PANNIERS > PANNIER

PANNIKEL *n* skull

PANNIKELL *same as* **> PANNIKEL**

PANNIKELS > PANNIKEL

PANNIKIN *n* small metal cup or pan

PANNIKINS > PANNIKIN

PANNING > PAN

PANNINGS > PAN

PANNIST *n* person who plays a steel drum

PANNISTS > PANNIST

PANNOSE *adj* like felt

PANNUS *n* inflammatory fleshy lesion on the surface of the eye

PANNUSES > PANNUS

PANOCHA *n* coarse grade of sugar made in Mexico

PANOCHAS > PANOCHA

PANOCHE *n* type of dark sugar

PANOCHES > PANOCHE

PANOISTIC *adj* producing ova

PANOPLIED > PANOPLY

PANOPLIES > PANOPLY

PANOPLY *n* magnificent array

PANOPTIC *adj* taking in all parts, aspects, etc, in a single view

PANORAMA *n* wide unbroken view of a scene

PANORAMAS > PANORAMA

PANORAMIC > PANORAMA

PANPIPE *n* wind instrument

PANPIPES > PANPIPE

PANS > PAN

PANSEXUAL *n* person open to any sexual activity

PANSIED *adj* covered with pansies

PANSIES > PANSY

PANSOPHIC > PANSOPHY

PANSOPHY *n* universal knowledge

PANSPERMY *n* 19th-century evolutionary theory

PANSTICK *n* type of cosmetic in stick form

PANSTICKS > PANSTICK

PANSY *n* small garden flower

PANT *vb* breathe quickly and noisily during or after exertion ▷ *n* act of panting

PANTABLE *n* soft shoe

PANTABLES > PANTABLE

PANTAGAMY *n* marriage to everyone

PANTALEON *n* percussion instrument

PANTALET *same as* **> PANTALETS**

PANTALETS *pl n* long drawers, usually trimmed with ruffles, extending below the skirts

PANTALON *n* keyboard instrument

PANTALONE *n* Italian comic character

PANTALONS > PANTALON

PANTALOON *n* (in pantomime) absurd old man, the butt of the clown's tricks

PANTDRESS *n* dress with divided skirt

PANTED > PANT

PANTER *n* person who pants

PANTERS > PANTER

PANTHEISM *n* belief that God is present in everything

PANTHEIST > PANTHEISM

PANTHENOL *n* pantothenyl alcohol

PANTHEON *n* (in ancient Greece and Rome) temple built to honour all the gods

PANTHEONS > PANTHEON

PANTHER *n* leopard, esp a black one

PANTHERS > PANTHER

PANTIE *same as* **> PANTY**

PANTIES *pl n* women's underpants

PANTIHOSE *same as* **> PANTYHOSE**

PANTILE *n* roofing tile with an S-shaped cross section ▷ *vb* tile roof with pantiles

PANTILED > PANTILE

PANTILES > PANTILE

PANTILING > PANTILE

PANTINE *n* pasteboard puppet

PANTINES > PANTINE

PANTING > PANT

PANTINGLY > PANT

PANTINGS > PANT

PANTLEG *n* leg part of a pair of trousers

PANTLEGS > PANTLEG

PANTLER *n* pantry servant

PANTLERS > PANTLER

PANTO *same as* **> PANTOMIME**

PANTOFFLE *same as* **> PANTOFLE**

PANTOFLE *n* kind of slipper

PANTOFLES > PANTOFLE

PANTOMIME *n* play based on a fairy tale, performed at Christmas time

PANTON *n* type of horseshoe

PANTONS > PANTON

PANTOS > PANTO

PANTOUFLE *same as* **> PANTOFLE**

PANTOUM *n* verse form

P

PANTOUMS > PANTOUM
PANTRIES > PANTRY
PANTROPIC adj found throughout tropics
PANTRY n small room or cupboard for storing food
PANTRYMAN n pantry servant
PANTRYMEN > PANTRYMAN
PANTS pl n undergarment for the lower part of the body
PANTSUIT n woman's suit of a jacket or top and trousers
PANTSUITS > PANTSUIT
PANTUN n Malayan poetry
PANTUNS > PANTUN
PANTY n woman's undergarment
PANTYHOSE pl n women's tights
PANZER n German tank
PANZERS > PANZER
PANZOOTIC n disease that affects all the animals in a geographical area
PAOLI > PAOLO
PAOLO n Italian silver coin
PAP n soft food for babies or invalids ▷ vb (of the paparazzi) to follow and photograph (a famous person)
PAPA n father
PAPABLE adj suitable for papacy
PAPACIES > PAPACY
PAPACY n position or term of office of a pope
PAPADAM variant of > POPPODAM
PAPADAMS > PAPADAM
PAPADOM variant of > POPPODAM
PAPADOMS > PAPADOM
PAPADUM variant of > POPPODAM
PAPADUMS > PAPADUM
PAPAIN n enzyme in the unripe fruit of the papaya
PAPAINS > PAPAIN
PAPAL adj of the pope
PAPALISE same as . > PAPALIZE
PAPALISED > PAPALISE
PAPALISES > PAPALISE
PAPALISM n papal system
PAPALISMS > PAPALISM
PAPALIST n supporter of a pope
PAPALISTS > PAPALIST
PAPALIZE vb make papal
PAPALIZED > PAPALIZE
PAPALIZES > PAPALIZE
PAPALLY > PAPAL
PAPARAZZI > PAPARAZZO
PAPARAZZO n photographer specializing in candid photographs of famous people
PAPAS > PAPA
PAPASAN n bowl-shaped chair
PAPASANS > PAPASAN
PAPAUMA n New Zealand word for broadleaf
PAPAUMAS > PAPAUMA

PAPAVER n genus of poppies
PAPAVERS > PAPAVER
PAPAW same as > PAPAYA
PAPAWS > PAPAW
PAPAYA n large sweet West Indian fruit
PAPAYAN > PAPAYA
PAPAYAS > PAPAYA
PAPE n spiritual father
PAPER n material made in sheets from wood pulp or other fibres ▷ vb cover (walls) with wallpaper
PAPERBACK n book with covers made of flexible card ▷ adj of a paperback or publication of paperbacks ▷ vb publish in paperback
PAPERBARK n Australian tree of swampy regions, with spear-shaped leaves and papery bark
PAPERBOY n boy employed to deliver newspapers to people's homes
PAPERBOYS > PAPERBOY
PAPERCLIP n bent wire clip for holding sheets of paper together
PAPERED > PAPER
PAPERER > PAPER
PAPERERS > PAPER
PAPERGIRL n girl employed to deliver newspapers to people's homes
PAPERIER > PAPERY
PAPERIEST > PAPERY
PAPERING > PAPER
PAPERINGS > PAPER
PAPERLESS adj of, relating to, or denoting a means of communication, record keeping, etc, esp electronic, that does not use paper
PAPERS > PAPER
PAPERWARE n printed matter
PAPERWORK n clerical work, such as writing reports and letters
PAPERY adj like paper, esp in thinness, flimsiness, or dryness
PAPES > PAPE
PAPETERIE n box or case for papers and other writing materials
PAPHIAN n prostitute .
PAPHIANS > PAPHIAN
PAPILIO n butterfly
PAPILIOS > PAPILIO
PAPILLA n small projection of tissue
PAPILLAE > PAPILLA
PAPILLAR > PAPILLA
PAPILLARY > PAPILLA
PAPILLATE > PAPILLA
PAPILLOMA n benign tumour derived from epithelial tissue and forming a rounded or lobulated mass
PAPILLON n breed of toy spaniel with large ears
PAPILLONS > PAPILLON
PAPILLOSE > PAPILLA
PAPILLOTE n paper frill around cutlets, etc
PAPILLOUS > PAPILLA

PAPILLULE n tubercle
PAPISH n derogatory term for a Roman Catholic
PAPISHER n derogatory term for a Roman Catholic
PAPISHERS > PAPISHER
PAPISHES > PAPISH
PAPISM n derogatory term for Roman Catholicism
PAPISMS > PAPISM
PAPIST n derogatory term for a Roman Catholic
PAPISTIC > PAPIST
PAPISTRY > PAPIST
PAPISTS > PAPIST
PAPOOSE n Native American child
PAPOOSES > PAPOOSE
PAPPADAM same as > POPPODAM
PAPPADAMS > PAPPADAM
PAPPADOM same as > POPPODAM
PAPPADOMS > PAPPADOM
PAPPADUM n thin circle of dough fried in oil until crisp
PAPPADUMS > PAPPADUM
PAPPED > PAP
PAPPI > PAPPUS
PAPPIER > PAPPY
PAPPIES > PAPPY
PAPPIEST > PAPPY
PAPPING > PAP
PAPPOOSE same as > PAPOOSE
PAPPOOSES > PAPPOOSE
PAPPOSE > PAPPUS
PAPPOUS > PAPPUS
PAPPUS n ring of hairs surrounding the fruit in composite plants
PAPPUSES > PAPPUS
PAPPY adj resembling pap
PAPRICA same as > PAPRIKA
PAPRICAS > PAPRICA
PAPRIKA n mild powdered seasoning
PAPRIKAS same as > PAPRIKASH
PAPRIKASH n chicken dish from Hungary
PAPS > PAP
PAPULA same as > PAPULE
PAPULAE > PAPULA
PAPULAR > PAPULE
PAPULAS > PAPULA
PAPULE n small solid usually round elevation of the skin
PAPULES > PAPULE
PAPULOSE > PAPULE
PAPULOUS > PAPULE
PAPYRAL > PAPYRUS
PAPYRI > PAPYRUS
PAPYRIAN > PAPYRUS
PAPYRINE > PAPYRUS
PAPYRUS n tall water plant
PAPYRUSES > PAPYRUS
PAR n usual or average condition ▷ vb play (a golf hole) in par
PARA n paratrooper
PARABASES > PARABASIS
PARABASIS n (in classical Greek comedy) address from the chorus to the audience
PARABEMA n architectural feature

PARABEN n carcinogenic ester
PARABENS > PARABEN
PARABLAST n yolk of an egg, such as a hen's egg, that undergoes meroblastic splitting
PARABLE n story that illustrates a religious teaching ▷ vb write a parable
PARABLED > PARABLE
PARABLES > PARABLE
PARABLING > PARABLE
PARABOLA n regular curve resembling the course of an object thrown forward and up
PARABOLAE > PARABOLA
PARABOLAS > PARABOLA
PARABOLE n similitude
PARABOLES > PARABOLE
PARABOLIC adj of, relating to, or shaped like a parabola
PARABRAKE n parachute attached to the rear of a vehicle and opened to assist braking
PARACHOR n quantity constant over range of temperatures
PARACHORS > PARACHOR
PARACHUTE n large fabric canopy that slows the descent of a person or object from an aircraft ▷ vb land or drop by parachute
PARACLETE n mediator or advocate
PARACME n phase where fever lessens
PARACMES > PARACME
PARACRINE adj of signalling between biological cells
PARACUSES > PARACUSIS
PARACUSIS n hearing disorder
PARADE n procession or march ▷ vb display or flaunt
PARADED > PARADE
PARADER > PARADE
PARADERS > PARADE
PARADES > PARADE
PARADIGM n example or model
PARADIGMS > PARADIGM
PARADING > PARADE
PARADISAL adj of, relating to, or resembling paradise
PARADISE n heaven
PARADISES > PARADISE
PARADISIC > PARADISE
PARADOR n state-run hotel in Spain
PARADORES > PARADOR
PARADORS > PARADOR
PARADOS n bank behind a trench or other fortification
PARADOSES > PARADOS
PARADOX n person or thing made up of contradictory elements
PARADOXAL adj paradoxical
PARADOXER n proposer of paradox
PARADOXES > PARADOX
PARADOXY n state of being paradoxical

PARADROP n delivery of personnel or equipment from an aircraft by parachute

PARADROPS > PARADROP

PARAE n type of fish

PARAFFIN n liquid mixture distilled from petroleum and used as a fuel or solvent ▷ vb treat with paraffin or paraffin wax

PARAFFINE same as > PARAFFIN

PARAFFINS > PARAFFIN

PARAFFINY adj like paraffin

PARAFFLE n extravagant display

PARAFFLES > PARAFFLE

PARAFLE same as > PARAFFLE

PARAFLES > PARAFLE

PARAFOIL n airfoil used on a paraglider

PARAFOILS > PARAFOIL

PARAFORM n paraformaldehyde

PARAFORMS > PARAFORM

PARAGE n type of feudal land tenure

PARAGES > PARAGE

PARAGLIDE vb glide through the air on a special parachute

PARAGOGE n addition of a sound or a syllable to the end of a word

PARAGOGES > PARAGOGE

PARAGOGIC > PARAGOGE

PARAGOGUE same as > PARAGOGE

PARAGON n model of perfection ▷ vb equal or surpass

PARAGONED > PARAGON

PARAGONS > PARAGON

PARAGRAM n pun

PARAGRAMS > PARAGRAM

PARAGRAPH n section of a piece of writing starting on a new line ▷ vb put (a piece of writing) into paragraphs

PARAKEET n small long-tailed parrot

PARAKEETS > PARAKEET

PARAKELIA n succulent herb with purple flowers that thrives in inland Australia

PARAKITE n series of linked kites

PARAKITES > PARAKITE

PARALALIA n any of various speech disorders, esp the production of a sound different from that intended

PARALEGAL n person trained to assist lawyers but not qualified to practise law ▷ adj of or designating such a person

PARALEXIA n disorder of the ability to read in which words and syllables are meaninglessly transposed

PARALEXIC > PARALEXIA

PARALLAX n apparent change in an object's position due to a change in the observer's position

PARALLEL adj separated by an equal distance at every point ▷ n line separated from another by an equal distance at every point ▷ vb correspond to

PARALLELS > PARALLEL

PARALOGIA n self-deception

PARALOGUE n either of a pair of genes derived from the same ancestral gene

PARALOGY n anatomical similarity

PARALYSE vb affect with paralysis

PARALYSED > PARALYSE

PARALYSER > PARALYSE

PARALYSES > PARALYSIS

PARALYSIS n inability to move or feel, because of damage to the nervous system

PARALYTIC adj affected with paralysis ▷ n person who is paralysed

PARALYZE same as > PARALYSE

PARALYZED > PARALYZE

PARALYZER > PARALYZE

PARALYZES > PARALYZE

PARAMATTA n lightweight twill-weave fabric of wool with silk or cotton

PARAMECIA n freshwater protozoans

PARAMEDIC n person working in support of the medical profession ▷ adj of or designating such a person

PARAMENT n ecclesiastical vestment or decorative hanging

PARAMENTA > PARAMENT

PARAMENTS > PARAMENT

PARAMESE n note in ancient Greek music

PARAMESES > PARAMESE

PARAMETER n limiting factor, boundary

PARAMO n high plateau in the Andes

PARAMORPH n mineral that has undergone paramorphism

PARAMOS > PARAMO

PARAMOUNT adj of the greatest importance ▷ n supreme ruler

PARAMOUR n lover

PARAMOURS > PARAMOUR

PARAMYLUM n starch-like substance

PARANETE n note in ancient Greek music

PARANETES > PARANETE

PARANG n knife used by the Dyaks of Borneo

PARANGS > PARANG

PARANOEA same as > PARANOIA

PARANOEAS > PARANOEA

PARANOEIC same as > PARANOIAC

PARANOIA n disorder causing delusions of grandeur or persecution

PARANOIAC > PARANOIA

PARANOIAS > PARANOIA

PARANOIC > PARANOIA

PARANOICS > PARANOIA

PARANOID adj of, characterized by, or resembling paranoia ▷ n person who shows the behaviour patterns associated with paranoia

PARANOIDS > PARANOID

PARANYM n euphemism

PARANYMPH n bridesmaid or best man

PARANYMS > PARANYM

PARAPARA n small carnivorous New Zealand tree

PARAPARAS > PARAPARA

PARAPENTE n sport of jumping off high mountains wearing skis and a light parachute

PARAPET n low wall or railing along the edge of a balcony or roof ▷ vb provide with a parapet

PARAPETED > PARAPET

PARAPETS > PARAPET

PARAPH n flourish after a signature ▷ vb embellish signature

PARAPHED > PARAPH

PARAPHING > PARAPH

PARAPHS > PARAPH

PARAPODIA n paired unjointed lateral appendages of polychaete worms

PARAQUAT n yellow extremely poisonous soluble solid used in solution as a weedkiller

PARAQUATS > PARAQUAT

PARAQUET n long-tailed parrot

PARAQUETS > PARAQUET

PARAQUITO n parakeet

PARARHYME n type of rhyme

PARAS > PARA

PARASAIL vb glide through air on parachute towed by boat

PARASAILS > PARASAIL

PARASANG n Persian unit of distance equal to about 5.5 km or 3.4 miles

PARASANGS > PARASANG

PARASCEVE n preparation

PARASHAH n section of the Torah read in the synagogue

PARASHAHS > PARASHAH

PARASHOT > PARASHAH

PARASHOTH > PARASHAH

PARASITE n animal or plant living in or on another

PARASITES > PARASITE

PARASITIC > PARASITE

PARASOL n umbrella-like sunshade

PARASOLED adj having a parasol

PARASOLS > PARASOL

PARATAXES > PARATAXIS

PARATAXIS n juxtaposition of clauses in a sentence without the use of a conjunction

PARATHA n (in Indian cookery) flat unleavened bread

PARATHAS > PARATHA

PARATHION n slightly water-soluble toxic oil, odourless and colourless when pure, used as an insecticide

PARATONIC adj (of a plant movement) occurring in response to an external stimulus

PARATROOP n paratrooper

PARAVAIL adj lowest

PARAVANE n device that cuts the anchors of moored mines

PARAVANES > PARAVANE

PARAVANT adv pre-eminently ▷ n pre-eminent person or thing

PARAVANTS > PARAVANT

PARAVAUNT same as > PARAVANT

PARAWING n paraglider

PARAWINGS > PARAWING

PARAXIAL adj (of a light ray) parallel to the axis of an optical system

PARAZOA > PARAZOAN

PARAZOAN n sea sponge

PARAZOANS > PARAZOAN

PARAZOON n parasitic animal

PARBAKE vb partially bake

PARBAKED > PARBAKE

PARBAKES > PARBAKE

PARBAKING > PARBAKE

PARBOIL vb boil until partly cooked

PARBOILED > PARBOIL

PARBOILS > PARBOIL

PARBREAK vb vomit

PARBREAKS > PARBREAK

PARBUCKLE n rope sling for lifting or lowering a heavy cylindrical object, such as a cask or tree trunk ▷ vb raise or lower (an object) with such a sling

PARCEL n something wrapped up, package ▷ vb wrap up

PARCELED > PARCEL

PARCELING > PARCEL

PARCELLED > PARCEL

PARCELS > PARCEL

PARCENARY n joint heirship

PARCENER n person who takes an equal share with another or others

PARCENERS > PARCENER

PARCH vb make very hot and dry

PARCHED > PARCH

PARCHEDLY > PARCH

PARCHEESI n modern board game derived from the ancient game of pachisi

PARCHES > PARCH

PARCHESI same as > PARCHEESI

PARCHESIS > PARCHESI

PARCHING > PARCH

PARCHISI same as > PARCHEESI

PARCHISIS > PARCHISI

P

p

PARCHMENT n thick smooth writing material made from animal skin

PARCIMONY obsolete variant of > PARSIMONY

PARCLOSE n screen or railing in a church separating off an altar, chapel, etc

PARCLOSES > PARCLOSE

PARD n leopard or panther

PARDAH same as > PURDAH

PARDAHS > PARDAH

PARDAL variant spelling of > PARDALE

PARDALE n leopard

PARDALES > PARDALE

PARDALIS n leopard

PARDALOTE n small Australian songbird

PARDALS > PARDAL

PARDED adj having spots

PARDEE adv certainly

PARDI same as > PARDEE

PARDIE same as > PARDEE

PARDINE adj spotted

PARDNER n friend or partner: used as a term of address

PARDNERS > PARDNER

PARDON vb forgive, excuse ▷ n forgiveness ▷ interj sorry ▷ sentence substitute sorry

PARDONED > PARDON

PARDONER n (before the Reformation) person licensed to sell ecclesiastical indulgences

PARDONERS > PARDONER

PARDONING > PARDON

PARDONS > PARDON

PARDS > PARD

PARDY same as > PARDEE

PARE vb cut off the skin or top layer of

PARECIOUS adj having the male and female reproductive organs at different levels on the same stem

PARECISM n state of having male and female organs close together

PARECISMS > PARECISM

PARED > PARE

PAREGORIC n medicine containing opium, benzoic acid, camphor or ammonia, and anise oil

PAREIRA n root of a South American climbing plant

PAREIRAS > PAREIRA

PARELLA n type of lichen

PARELLAS > PARELLA

PARELLE same as > PARELLA

PARELLES > PARELLE

PAREN n parenthesis

PARENESES > PARENESIS

PARENESIS n exhortation

PARENS > PAREN

PARENT n father or mother ▷ vb raise offspring

PARENTAGE n ancestry or family

PARENTAL adj of or relating to a parent or parenthood

PARENTED > PARENT

PARENTING n activity of bringing up children

PARENTS > PARENT

PAREO same as > PAREU

PAREOS > PAREO

PARER > PARE

PARERA n New Zealand duck

PARERAS > PARERA

PARERGA > PARERGON

PARERGON n work that is not one's main employment

PARERS > PARE

PARES > PARE

PARESES > PARESIS

PARESIS n incomplete or slight paralysis of motor functions

PARETIC > PARESIS

PARETICS > PARESIS

PAREU n Polynesian skirt or loincloth

PAREUS > PAREU

PAREV adj containing neither meat nor milk products

PAREVE same as > PAREV

PARFAIT n dessert consisting of layers of ice cream, fruit, and sauce

PARFAITS > PARFAIT

PARFLECHE n sheet of rawhide that has been dried after soaking in lye and water to remove the hair

PARFLESH same as > PARFLECHE

PARFOCAL adj with focal points in the same plane

PARGANA n Indian sub-district

PARGANAS > PARGANA

PARGASITE n dark green mineral

PARGE vb coat with plaster

PARGED > PARGE

PARGES > PARGE

PARGET n plaster, mortar, etc, used to line chimney flues or cover walls ▷ vb cover or decorate with parget

PARGETED > PARGET

PARGETER n one who pargets

PARGETERS > PARGET

PARGETING same as > PARGET

PARGETS > PARGET

PARGETTED > PARGET

PARGETTER n plasterer

PARGING > PARGE

PARGINGS > PARGE

PARGO n sea bream

PARGOES > PARGO

PARGOS > PARGO

PARGYLINE n monoamine oxidase inhibitor

PARHELIA > PARHELION

PARHELIC > PARHELION

PARHELION n one of several bright spots on the parhelic circle or solar halo

PARHYPATE n note in ancient Greek music

PARIAH n social outcast

PARIAHS > PARIAH

PARIAL n pair royal of playing cards

PARIALS > PARIAL

PARIAN n type of marble or porcelain

PARIANS > PARIAN

PARIES n wall of an organ or bodily cavity

PARIETAL adj of the walls of a body cavity such as the skull ▷ n parietal bone

PARIETALS > PARIETAL

PARIETES > PARIES

PARING n piece pared off

PARINGS > PARING

PARIS n type of herb

PARISCHAN variant of > PAROCHIN

PARISES > PARIS

PARISH n area that has its own church and a priest or pastor

PARISHAD n Indian assembly

PARISHADS > PARISHAD

PARISHEN n member of parish

PARISHENS > PARISHEN

PARISHES > PARISH

PARISON n unshaped mass of glass

PARISONS > PARISON

PARITIES > PARITY

PARITOR n official who summons witnesses

PARITORS > PARITOR

PARITY n equality or equivalence

PARK n area of open land for recreational use by the public ▷ vb stop and leave (a vehicle) temporarily

PARKA n large waterproof jacket with a hood

PARKADE n building used as a car park

PARKADES > PARKADE

PARKAS > PARKA

PARKED > PARK

PARKEE n Inuit outer garment

PARKEES > PARKEE

PARKER > PARK

PARKERS > PARK

PARKETTE n small public car park

PARKETTES > PARKETTE

PARKI variant of > PARKA

PARKIE n park keeper

PARKIER > PARKY

PARKIES > PARKIE

PARKIEST > PARKY

PARKIN n moist spicy ginger cake

PARKING > PARK

PARKINGS > PARK

PARKINS > PARKIN

PARKIS > PARKI

PARKISH adj like a park

PARKLAND n grassland with scattered trees

PARKLANDS > PARKLAND

PARKLIKE > PARK

PARKLY adj having many parks or resembling a park

PARKOUR n sport of running in urban areas over obstacles

PARKOURS > PARKOUR

PARKS > PARK

PARKWARD adv towards a park

PARKWARDS adv towards a park

PARKWAY n wide road planted with trees, turf, etc

PARKWAYS > PARKWAY

PARKY adj (of the weather) chilly

PARLANCE n particular way of speaking, idiom

PARLANCES > PARLANCE

PARLANDO adv to be performed as though speaking

PARLANTE same as > PARLANDO

PARLAY vb stake (winnings from one bet) on a subsequent wager ▷ n bet in which winnings are parlayed

PARLAYED > PARLAY

PARLAYING > PARLAY

PARLAYS > PARLAY

PARLE vb speak

PARLED > PARLE

PARLEMENT n parliament

PARLES > PARLE

PARLEY n meeting between opponents to discuss terms ▷ vb have a parley

PARLEYED > PARLEY

PARLEYER > PARLEY

PARLEYERS > PARLEY

PARLEYING > PARLEY

PARLEYS > PARLEY

PARLEYVOO vb speak French ▷ n French language

PARLIES pl n small Scottish biscuits

PARLING > PARLE

PARLOR same as > PARLOUR

PARLORS > PARLOR

PARLOUR n living room for receiving visitors

PARLOURS > PARLOUR

PARLOUS adj dire ▷ adv extremely

PARLOUSLY > PARLOUS

PARLY n short form of parliament

PARMA n breaded chicken dish

PARMAS > PARMA

PARMESAN n Italian hard cheese

PARMESANS > PARMESAN

PAROCHIAL adj narrow in outlook

PAROCHIN n old Scottish parish

PAROCHINE same as > PAROCHIN

PAROCHINS > PAROCHIN

PARODIC > PARODY

PARODICAL > PARODY

PARODIED > PARODY

PARODIES > PARODY

PARODIST > PARODY

PARODISTS > PARODY

PARODOI n path leading to Greek theatre

PARODOS n ode sung by Greek chorus

PARODY n exaggerated and amusing imitation of someone else's style ▷ vb make a parody of

PARODYING > PARODY

PAROECISM n state of being paroecious

PAROEMIA n proverb

PAROEMIAC adj of proverbs

PAROEMIAL adj of proverbs

PAROEMIAS > PAROEMIA

PAROICOUS same as > PARECIOUS

PAROL n (formerly) pleadings in an action when presented by word of mouth ▷ adj (of a contract, lease, etc) not made under seal

PAROLABLE > PAROLE

PAROLE n early freeing of a prisoner on condition that he or she behaves well ▷ vb put on parole

PAROLED > PAROLE

PAROLEE > PAROLE

PAROLEES > PAROLE

PAROLES > PAROLE

PAROLING > PAROLE

PAROLS > PAROL

PARONYM n cognate word

PARONYMIC > PARONYM

PARONYMS > PARONYM

PARONYMY > PARONYM

PAROQUET n small long-tailed parrot

PAROQUETS > PAROQUET

PARORE n type of fish found around Australia and New Zealand

PARORES > PARORE

PAROSMIA n any disorder of the sense of smell

PAROSMIAS > PAROSMIA

PAROTIC adj situated near the ear

PAROTID adj relating to or situated near the parotid gland ▷ n parotid gland

PAROTIDES > PAROTID

PAROTIDS > PAROTID

PAROTIS n parotid gland

PAROTISES > PAROTIS

PAROTITIC > PAROTITIS

PAROTITIS n inflammation of the parotid gland

PAROTOID n poison gland on certain toads and salamanders ▷ adj resembling a parotid gland

PAROTOIDS > PAROTOID

PAROUS adj having given birth

PAROUSIA n Second Coming

PAROUSIAS > PAROUSIA

PAROXYSM n uncontrollable outburst of rage, delight, etc

PAROXYSMS > PAROXYSM

PARP vb make a honking sound

PARPANE n parapet on bridge

PARPANES > PARPANE

PARPED > PARP

PARPEN same as > PARPEND

PARPEND same as > PERPEND

PARPENDS > PARPEND

PARPENS > PARPEN

PARPENT n parapet on bridge

PARPENTS > PARPENT

PARPING > PARP

PARPOINT n parapet on bridge

PARPOINTS > PARPOINT

PARPS > PARP

PARQUET n floor covering made of wooden blocks ▷ vb cover with parquet

PARQUETED > PARQUET

PARQUETRY n pieces of wood arranged in a geometric pattern, used to cover floors

PARQUETS > PARQUET

PARR n salmon up to two years of age

PARRA n tourist or non-resident on a beach

PARRAKEET same as > PARAKEET

PARRAL same as > PARREL

PARRALS > PARRAL

PARRAS > PARRA

PARRED > PAR

PARREL n ring that holds the jaws of a boom to the mast

PARRELS > PARREL

PARRHESIA n boldness of speech

PARRICIDE n crime of killing either of one's parents

PARRIDGE Scottish variant of > PORRIDGE

PARRIDGES > PARRIDGE

PARRIED > PARRY

PARRIER > PARRY

PARRIERS > PARRY

PARRIES > PARRY

PARRING > PAR

PARRITCH Scottish variant of > PORRIDGE

PARROCK vb put (an animal) in a small field

PARROCKED > PARROCK

PARROCKS > PARROCK

PARROKET n small long-tailed parrot

PARROKETS > PARROKET

PARROQUET n small long-tailed parrot

PARROT n tropical bird with a short hooked beak ▷ vb repeat (someone else's words) without thinking

PARROTED > PARROT

PARROTER n person who repeats what is said

PARROTERS > PARROTER

PARROTIER > PARROTY

PARROTING > PARROT

PARROTRY > PARROT

PARROTS > PARROT

PARROTY adj like a parrot; chattering

PARRS > PARR

PARRY vb ward off (an attack) ▷ n parrying

PARRYING > PARRY

PARS > PAR

PARSABLE > PARSE

PARSE vb analyse (a sentence) in terms of grammar

PARSEC n unit of astronomical distance

PARSECS > PARSEC

PARSED > PARSE

PARSER n program that interprets input to a computer

PARSERS > PARSER

PARSES > PARSE

PARSIMONY n extreme caution in spending money

PARSING > PARSE

PARSINGS > PARSE

PARSLEY n herb used for seasoning and decorating food ▷ vb garnish with parsley

PARSLEYED > PARSLEY

PARSLEYS > PARSLEY

PARSLIED > PARSLEY

PARSNEP same as > PARSNIP

PARSNEPS > PARSNEP

PARSNIP n long tapering cream-coloured root vegetable

PARSNIPS > PARSNIP

PARSON n Anglican parish priest

PARSONAGE n parson's house

PARSONIC > PARSON

PARSONISH adj like a parson

PARSONS > PARSON

PART n one of the pieces that make up a whole ▷ vb divide or separate

PARTAKE vb take (food or drink)

PARTAKEN > PARTAKE

PARTAKER > PARTAKE

PARTAKERS > PARTAKE

PARTAKES > PARTAKE

PARTAKING > PARTAKE

PARTAN Scottish word for > CRAB

PARTANS > PARTAN

PARTED adj divided almost to the base

PARTER n thing that parts

PARTERRE n formally patterned flower garden

PARTERRES > PARTERRE

PARTERS > PARTER

PARTI n concept of architectural design

PARTIAL adj not complete ▷ n any of the component tones of a single musical sound ▷ vb remove (a factor) from a set of statistics

PARTIALLY > PARTIAL

PARTIALS > PARTIAL

PARTIBLE adj (esp of property or an inheritance) divisible

PARTICLE n extremely small piece or amount

PARTICLES > PARTICLE

PARTIED > PARTY

PARTIER n person who parties

PARTIERS > PARTIER

PARTIES > PARTY

PARTIEST > PARTY

PARTIM adv in part

PARTING same as > PART

PARTINGS > PARTING

PARTIS > PARTI

PARTISAN n strong supporter of a party or group ▷ adj prejudiced or one-sided

PARTISANS > PARTISAN

PARTITA n type of suite

PARTITAS > PARTITA

PARTITE adj composed of or divided into a specified number of parts

PARTITION n screen or thin wall that divides a room ▷ vb divide with a partition

PARTITIVE adj (of a noun) referring to part of something ▷ n partitive word

PARTITURA n music score for several parts

PARTIZAN same as > PARTISAN

PARTIZANS > PARTIZAN

PARTLET n woman's garment

PARTLETS > PARTLET

PARTLY adv not completely

PARTNER n either member of a couple in a relationship or activity ▷ vb be the partner of

PARTNERED > PARTNER

PARTNERS > PARTNER

PARTON n hypothetical elementary particle

PARTONS > PARTON

PARTOOK > PARTAKE

PARTRIDGE n game bird of the grouse family

PARTS pl n abilities or talents

PARTURE n departure

PARTURES > PARTURE

PARTWAY adv some of the way

PARTWORK n series of magazines issued at regular intervals

PARTWORKS > PARTWORK

PARTY n social gathering for pleasure ▷ vb celebrate, have fun ▷ adj divided into different colours

PARTYER n person who parties

PARTYERS > PARTYER

PARTYGOER n person who goes to party

PARTYING n act of partying

PARTYINGS > PARTYING

PARTYISM n devotion to political party

PARTYISMS > PARTYISM

PARULIDES > PARULIS

PARULIS another name for > GUMBOIL

PARULISES > PARULIS

PARURA same as > PARURE

PARURAS > PARURA

PARURE n set of jewels or other ornaments

PARURES > PARURE

PARURESES > PARURES

PARURESIS n inability urinate in the presence of others

PARURETIC n person unable to urinate in the presence of others

PARVE same as > PAREV

PARVENU n person newly risen to a position of power or wealth ▷ adj of or characteristic of a parvenu

PARVENUE n woman newly risen to a position of power or wealth ▷ adj of a parvenue

PARVENUES > PARVENUE

PARVENUS > PARVENU

PARVIS n court or portico in front of a building, esp a church

PARVISE same as > PARVIS

PARVISES > PARVISE

PARVO n disease of cattle and dogs

PARVOLIN n substance resulting from the putrefaction of flesh

PARVOLINE n liquid derived from coal tar

PARVOLINS > PARVOLIN

PARVOS > PARVO

PAS n dance step or movement, esp in ballet

PASCALS > PASCAL

PASCHAL adj of the Passover or Easter ▷ n Passover or Easter

PASCHALS > PASCHAL

PASCUAL adj relating to pasture ▷ n plant that grows in pasture

PASCUALS > PASCUAL

PASE n movement of the cape or muleta by a matador

PASEAR vb go for a rambling walk

PASEARED > PASEAR

PASEARING > PASEAR

PASEARS > PASEAR

PASELA same as > BONSELA

PASELAS > PASELA

PASEO n bullfighters' procession

PASEOS > PASEO

PASES > PASE

PASH n infatuation ▷ vb throw or be thrown and break or be broken to bits

PASHA n high official of the Ottoman Empire

PASHADOM n territory of a pasha

PASHADOMS > PASHADOM

PASHALIC same as > PASHALIK

PASHALICS > PASHALIC

PASHALIK n province or jurisdiction of a pasha

PASHALIKS > PASHALIK

PASHAS > PASHA

PASHED > PASH

PASHES > PASH

PASHIM same as > PASHM

PASHIMS > PASHIM

PASHING > PASH

PASHKA n rich Russian dessert

PASHKAS > PASHKA

PASHM n underfur of various Tibetan animals, esp goats, used for cashmere shawls

PASHMINA n type of cashmere scarf or shawl made from the underfur of Tibetan goats

PASIMINAS > PASHMINA

PASHMS > PASHM

PASKA same as > PASKHA

PASKAS > PASKA

PASKHA n Russian dessert eaten at Easter

PASKHAS > PASKHA

PASODOBLE n fast modern ballroom dance

PASPALUM n type of grass with wide leaves

PASPALUMS > PASPALUM

PASPIES > PASPY

PASPY n piece of music in triple time

PASQUIL n abusive lampoon or satire ▷ vb ridicule with pasquil

PASQUILER n person who lampoons

PASQUILS > PASQUIL

PASS vb go by, past, or through ▷ n successful result in a test or examination

PASSABLE adj (just) acceptable

PASSABLY adv fairly

PASSADE n act of moving back and forth in the same place

PASSADES > PASSADE

PASSADO n forward thrust with sword

PASSADOES > PASSADO

PASSADOS > PASSADO

PASSAGE n channel or opening providing a way through ▷ vb move or cause to move at a passage

PASSAGED > PASSAGE

PASSAGER n as in passager hawk young hawk or falcon caught while on migration

PASSAGES > PASSAGE

PASSAGING > PASSAGE

PASSALONG adj (of plants) easily propagated and given to others

PASSAMENT vb sew border on garment

PASSANT adj (of a heraldic beast) walking

PASSATA n sauce made from sieved tomatoes

PASSATAS > PASSATA

PASSBAND n frequency band within which signals are transmitted by a filter

PASSBANDS > PASSBAND

PASSBOOK n record of a person's bank transactions

PASSBOOKS > PASSBOOK

PASSCODE n password composed of digits

PASSCODES > PASSCODE

PASSE adj out-of-date

PASSED > PASS

PASSEE adj out-of-date

PASSEL n group or quantity of no fixed number

PASSELS > PASSEL

PASSEMENT vb sew border on garment

PASSENGER n person travelling in a vehicle driven by someone else

PASSEPIED n lively minuet of Breton origin

PASSER n person or thing that passes

PASSERBY n person that is passing or going by, esp on foot

PASSERINE adj belonging to the order of perching birds ▷ n any bird of this order

PASSERS > PASSER

PASSERSBY > PASSERBY

PASSES > PASS

PASSIBLE adj susceptible to emotion or suffering

PASSIBLY > PASSIBLE

PASSIM adv everywhere, throughout

PASSING adj brief or transitory ▷ n death

PASSINGLY > PASSING

PASSINGS > PASSING

PASSION n intense love ▷ vb give passionate character to

PASSIONAL adj of, relating to, or due to passion or the passions ▷ n book recounting the sufferings of Christian martyrs or saints

PASSIONED > PASSION

PASSIONS > PASSION

PASSIVATE vb render (a metal) less susceptible to corrosion by coating the surface with a substance, such as an oxide

PASSIVE adj not playing an active part ▷ n passive form of a verb

PASSIVELY > PASSIVE

PASSIVES > PASSIVE

PASSIVISM n theory, belief, or practice of passive resistance

PASSIVIST > PASSIVISM

PASSIVITY > PASSIVE

PASSKEY n private key

PASSKEYS > PASSKEY

PASSLESS adj having no pass

PASSMAN n student who passes without honours

PASSMEN > PASSMAN

PASSMENT same as > PASSEMENT

PASSMENTS > PASSMENT

PASSOUT n (in ice hockey) pass by an attacking player from behind the opposition goal line

PASSOUTS > PASSOUT

PASSOVER n lamb eaten during Passover

PASSOVERS > PASSOVER

PASSPORT n official document of nationality granting permission to travel abroad ▷ vb (in the European Economic Area) award a firm the right to do business in every member state

PASSPORTS > PASSPORT

PASSUS n division or section of a poem, story, etc

PASSUSES > PASSUS

PASSWORD n secret word or phrase that ensures admission

PASSWORDS > PASSWORD

PAST adj of the time before the present ▷ n period of time before the present ▷ adv ago ▷ prep beyond

PASTA n type of food that is made from flour and water

PASTALIKE > PASTA

PASTANCE n activity that passes time

PASTANCES > PASTANCE

PASTAS > PASTA

PASTE n moist soft mixture, such as toothpaste ▷ vb fasten with paste

PASTED > PASTE

PASTEDOWN n portion of endpaper pasted to cover of book

PASTEL n coloured chalk crayon for drawing ▷ adj pale and delicate in colour

PASTELIKE adj like paste

PASTELIST > PASTEL

PASTELS > PASTEL

PASTER n person or thing that pastes

PASTERN n part of a horse's foot

PASTERNS > PASTERN

PASTERS > PASTER

PASTES > PASTE

PASTEUP n material pasted on a sheet of paper or board

PASTEUPS > PASTEUP

PASTICCI > PASTICCIO

PASTICCIO n art work borrowing various styles

PASTICHE n work of art that mixes styles or copies the style of another artist

PASTICHES > PASTICHE

PASTIE n decorative cover for nipple

PASTIER > PASTY

PASTIES > PASTY

PASTIEST > PASTY

PASTIL same as > PASTILLE

PASTILLE n small fruit-flavoured and sometimes medicated sweet

PASTILLES > PASTILLE

PASTILS > PASTIL

PASTILY > PASTY

PASTIME n activity that makes time pass pleasantly

PASTIMES > PASTIME

PASTINA n small pieces of pasta

PASTINAS > PASTINA

PASTINESS > PASTY

PASTING n heavy defeat

PASTINGS > PASTING

PASTIS n anise-flavoured alcoholic drink

PASTISES > PASTIS

PASTITSIO n Greek dish consisting of minced meat and macaroni topped with bechamel sauce

PASTITSO n Greek dish of baked pasta

PASTITSOS > PASTITSO

p

PASTLESS adj having no past

PASTNESS n quality of being past

PASTOR n member of the clergy in charge of a congregation ⊳ vb act as a pastor

PASTORAL adj of or depicting country life ⊳ n poem or picture portraying country life

PASTORALE n musical composition that suggests country life

PASTORALI > PASTORALE

PASTORALS > PASTORAL

PASTORATE n office or term of office of a pastor

PASTORED > PASTOR

PASTORING > PASTOR

PASTORIUM n residence of pastor

PASTORLY adj like a pastor

PASTORS > PASTOR

PASTRAMI n highly seasoned smoked beef

PASTRAMIS > PASTRAMI

PASTRIES > PASTRY

PASTROMI same as > PASTRAMI

PASTROMIS > PASTROMI

PASTRY n baking dough made of flour, fat, and water

PASTS > PAST

PASTURAGE n business of grazing cattle

PASTURAL adj of pasture

PASTURE n grassy land for farm animals to graze on ⊳ vb cause (livestock) to graze

PASTURED > PASTURE

PASTURER n person who tends cattle

PASTURERS > PASTURER

PASTURES > PASTURE

PASTURING > PASTURE

PASTY adj (of a complexion) pale and unhealthy ⊳ n round of pastry folded over a savoury filling

PAT vb tap lightly ⊳ n gentle tap or stroke ⊳ adj quick, ready, or glib

PATACA n monetary unit of Macao

PATACAS > PATACA

PATAGIA > PATAGIUM

PATAGIAL > PATAGIUM

PATAGIUM n web of skin acting as wings in bats

PATAKA n building on stilts, used for storing provisions

PATAKAS > PATAKA

PATAMAR n type of boat

PATAMARS > PATAMAR

PATBALL n game like squash but using hands

PATBALLS > PATBALL

PATCH n piece of material sewn on a garment ⊳ vb mend with a patch

PATCHABLE > PATCH

PATCHED > PATCH

PATCHER > PATCH

PATCHERS > PATCH

PATCHERY n bungling work

PATCHES > PATCH

PATCHIER > PATCHY

PATCHIEST > PATCHY

PATCHILY > PATCHY

PATCHING > PATCH

PATCHINGS > PATCH

PATCHOCKE Spenserian word for > CLOWN

PATCHOULI n Asiatic tree, the leaves of which yield a heavy fragrant oil

PATCHOULY same as > PATCHOULI

PATCHWORK n needlework made of pieces of different materials sewn together

PATCHY adj of uneven quality or intensity

PATE n head

PATED > PATE

PATELLA n kneecap

PATELLAE > PATELLA

PATELLAR > PATELLA

PATELLAS > PATELLA

PATELLATE adj having the shape of a patella

PATEN n plate used for the bread at Communion

PATENCIES > PATENCY

PATENCY n condition of being obvious

PATENS > PATEN

PATENT n document giving the exclusive right to make or sell an invention ⊳ adj open to public inspection ⊳ vb obtain a patent for

PATENTED > PATENT

PATENTEE n person, group, company, etc, that has been granted a patent

PATENTEES > PATENTEE

PATENTING > PATENT

PATENTLY adv obviously

PATENTOR n person who or official body that grants a patent or patents

PATENTORS > PATENTOR

PATENTS > PATENT

PATER n father

PATERA n shallow ancient Roman bowl

PATERAE > PATERA

PATERCOVE n fraudulent priest

PATERERO n type of cannon

PATEREROS > PATERERO

PATERNAL adj fatherly

PATERNITY n fact or state of being a father

PATERS > PATER

PATES > PATE

PATH n surfaced walk or track ⊳ vb make a path

PATHED > PATH

PATHETIC adj causing feelings of pity or sadness ⊳ pl n pathetic sentiments ⊳ n pathetic person

PATHETICS > PATHETIC

PATHIC n person who suffers ⊳ adj of or relating to suffering

PATHICS > PATHIC

PATHING > PATH

PATHLESS > PATH

PATHNAME n description of where a file is found in a hierarchy of directories

PATHNAMES > PATHNAME

PATHOGEN n thing that causes disease

PATHOGENE same as > PATHOGEN

PATHOGENS > PATHOGEN

PATHOGENY n origin, development, and resultant effects of a disease

PATHOLOGY n scientific study of diseases

PATHOS n power of arousing pity or sadness

PATHOSES > PATHOS

PATHS > PATH

PATHWAY n path

PATHWAYS > PATHWAY

PATIBLE adj endurable

PATIENCE n quality of being patient

PATIENCES > PATIENCE

PATIENT adj enduring difficulties or delays calmly ⊳ n person receiving medical treatment ⊳ vb make calm

PATIENTED > PATIENT

PATIENTER > PATIENT

PATIENTLY > PATIENT

PATIENTS > PATIENT

PATIKI n New Zealand sand flounder or dab

PATIKIS > PATIKI

PATIN same as > PATEN

PATINA n fine layer on a surface

PATINAE > PATINA

PATINAED adj having a patina

PATINAS > PATINA

PATINATE vb coat with patina

PATINATED > PATINATE

PATINATES > PATINATE

PATINE vb cover with patina

PATINED > PATINE

PATINES > PATINE

PATINING > PATINE

PATINISE same as > PATINIZE

PATINISED > PATINISE

PATINISES > PATINISE

PATINIZE vb coat with patina

PATINIZED > PATINIZE

PATINIZES > PATINIZE

PATINS > PATIN

PATIO n paved area adjoining a house

PATIOS > PATIO

PATISSIER n pastry chef

PATKA n head covering worn by Sikh men

PATKAS > PATKA

PATLY adv fitly

PATNESS n appropriateness

PATNESSES > PATNESS

PATOIS n regional dialect, esp of French

PATONCE adj (of cross) with limbs which broaden from centre

PATOOT same as > PATOOTIE

PATOOTIE n person's bottom

PATOOTIES > PATOOTIE

PATOOTS > PATOOT

PATRIAL n (in Britain, formerly) person with a right to live in the United Kingdom

PATRIALS > PATRIAL

PATRIARCH n male head of a family or tribe

PATRIATE vb bring under the authority of an autonomous country

PATRIATED > PATRIATE

PATRIATES > PATRIATE

PATRICIAN n member of the nobility ⊳ adj of noble birth

PATRICIDE n crime of killing one's father

PATRICK n former Irish coin

PATRICKS > PATRICK

PATRICO n fraudulent priest

PATRICOES > PATRICO

PATRICOS > PATRICO

PATRILINY n tracing of family descent through males

PATRIMONY n property inherited from ancestors

PATRIOT n person who loves his or her country

PATRIOTIC > PATRIOT

PATRIOTS > PATRIOT

PATRISTIC adj of or relating to the Fathers of the Church, their writings, or the study of these

PATROL n regular circuit by a guard ⊳ vb go round on guard, or reconnoitring

PATROLLED > PATROL

PATROLLER > PATROL

PATROLMAN n man, esp a policeman, who patrols a certain area

PATROLMEN > PATROLMAN

PATROLOGY n study of the writings of the Fathers of the Church

PATROLS > PATROL

PATRON n person who gives financial support

PATRONAGE n support given by a patron

PATRONAL > PATRONESS

PATRONESS n woman who sponsors or aids artists, charities, etc

PATRONISE same as > PATRONIZE

PATRONIZE vb treat in a condescending way

PATRONLY adj like a patron

PATRONNE n woman who owns or manages a hotel, restaurant, or bar

PATRONNES > PATRONNE

PATRONS > PATRON

PATROON n Dutch land-holder in New Netherland and New York

PATROONS > PATROON

PATS > PAT

PATSIES > PATSY

PATSY n person who is easily cheated, victimized, etc

PATTAMAR n Indian courier

PATTAMARS > PATTAMAR

PATTE n band keeping belt in place

P

PATTED > PAT
PATTEE *adj* (of a cross) having triangular arms widening outwards
PATTEN *n* wooden clog or sandal ▷ *vb* wear pattens
PATTENED > PATTEN
PATTENING > PATTEN
PATTENS > PATTEN
PATTER *vb* make repeated soft tapping sounds ▷ *n* quick succession of taps
PATTERED > PATTER
PATTERER > PATTER
PATTERERS > PATTER
PATTERING > PATTER
PATTERN *n* arrangement of repeated parts or decorative designs ▷ *vb* model
PATTERNED > PATTERN
PATTERNS > PATTERN
PATTERS > PATTER
PATTES > PATTE
PATTEST > PAT
PATTIE *same as* > PATTY
PATTIES > PATTY
PATTING > PAT
PATTLE *dialect for* > PADDLE
PATTLES > PATTLE
PATTRESS *n* box for the space behind electrical sockets and switches
PATTY *n* small flattened cake of minced food
PATTYPAN *n* small round flattish squash
PATTYPANS > PATTYPAN
PATU *n* short Māori club, now used ceremonially
PATULENT *adj* spreading widely
PATULIN *n* toxic antibiotic
PATULINS > PATULIN
PATULOUS *adj* spreading widely or expanded
PATUS > PATU
PATUTUKI *n* blue cod
PATUTUKIS > PATUTUKI
PATY *adj* (of cross) having arms of equal length
PATZER *n* novice chess player
PATZERS > PATZER
PAUA *n* edible shellfish of New Zealand
PAUAS > PAUA
PAUCAL *n* grammatical number for words in contexts where a few of their referents are described ▷ *adj* relating to or inflected for this number
PAUCALS > PAUCAL
PAUCITIES > PAUCITY
PAUCITY *n* scarcity
PAUGHTIER > PAUGHTY
PAUGHTY *Scots word for* > HAUGHTY
PAUL *same as* > PAWL
PAULDRON *n* either of two metal plates worn with armour to protect the shoulders
PAULDRONS > PAULDRON
PAULIN *n* tarpaulin
PAULINS > PAULIN

PAULOWNIA *n* Japanese tree with large heart-shaped leaves and clusters of purplish or white flowers
PAULS > PAUL
PAUNCE *n* pansy
PAUNCES > PAUNCE
PAUNCH *n* protruding belly ▷ *vb* stab in the stomach
PAUNCHED > PAUNCH
PAUNCHES > PAUNCH
PAUNCHIER > PAUNCHY
PAUNCHING > PAUNCH
PAUNCHY *adj* having a protruding belly or abdomen
PAUPER *n* very poor person ▷ *vb* reduce to beggary
PAUPERDOM *n* state of being a pauper
PAUPERED > PAUPER
PAUPERESS *n* female pauper
PAUPERING > PAUPER
PAUPERISE *same as* > PAUPERIZE
PAUPERISM > PAUPER
PAUPERIZE *vb* make a pauper of
PAUPERS > PAUPER
PAUPIETTE *n* rolled stuffed fish or meat
PAURAQUE *n* type of long-tailed nocturnal bird
PAURAQUES > PAURAQUE
PAUROPOD *n* minute myriapod
PAUROPODS > PAUROPOD
PAUSAL > PAUSE
PAUSE *vb* stop for a time ▷ *n* stop or rest in speech or action
PAUSED > PAUSE
PAUSEFUL *adj* taking pauses
PAUSELESS *adj* without pauses
PAUSER > PAUSE
PAUSERS > PAUSE
PAUSES > PAUSE
PAUSING > PAUSE
PAUSINGLY *adv* with pauses
PAUSINGS > PAUSE
PAV *short for* > PAVLOVA
PAVAGE *n* tax towards paving streets
PAVAGES > PAVAGE
PAVAN *same as* > PAVANE
PAVANE *n* slow and stately dance
PAVANES > PAVANE
PAVANS > PAVAN
PAVE *vb* form (a surface) with stone or brick ▷ *n* paved surface, esp an uneven one
PAVED > PAVE
PAVEED *adj* (of jewels) set close together
PAVEMENT *n* paved path for pedestrians ▷ *vb* provide with pavement
PAVEMENTS > PAVEMENT
PAVEN *same as* > PAVANE
PAVENS > PAVEN
PAVER > PAVE
PAVERS > PAVE
PAVES > PAVE

PAVID *adj* fearful
PAVILION *n* building on a playing field etc ▷ *vb* place or set in or as if in a pavilion
PAVILIONS > PAVILION
PAVILLON *n* bell of wind instrument
PAVILLONS > PAVILLON
PAVIN *same as* > PAVANE
PAVING *n* paved surface ▷ *adj* of or for a paved surface or pavement
PAVINGS > PAVING
PAVINS > PAVIN
PAVIOR *same as* > PAVIOUR
PAVIORS > PAVIOR
PAVIOUR *n* person who lays paving
PAVIOURS > PAVIOUR
PAVIS *n* large square shield
PAVISE *same as* > PAVIS
PAVISER *n* soldier holding a pavis
PAVISERS > PAVISER
PAVISES > PAVISE
PAVISSE *same as* > PAVIS
PAVISSES > PAVISSE
PAVLOVA *n* meringue cake topped with whipped cream and fruit
PAVLOVAS > PAVLOVA
PAVONAZZO *n* white Italian marble
PAVONE *n* peacock
PAVONES > PAVONE
PAVONIAN *same as* > PAVONINE
PAVONINE *adj* of or resembling a peacock or the colours, design, or iridescence of a peacock's tail
PAVS > PAV
PAW *n* animal's foot with claws and pads ▷ *vb* scrape with the paw or hoof
PAWA *old word for* > PEACOCK
PAWAS > PAWA
PAWAW *vb* recite N American incantation
PAWAWED > PAWAW
PAWAWING > PAWAW
PAWAWS > PAWAW
PAWED > PAW
PAWER *n* person or animal that paws
PAWERS > PAWER
PAWING > PAW
PAWK *Scots word for* > TRICK
PAWKIER > PAWKY
PAWKIEST > PAWKY
PAWKILY > PAWKY
PAWKINESS > PAWKY
PAWKS > PAWK
PAWKY *adj* having or characterized by a dry wit
PAWL *n* pivoted lever shaped to engage with a ratchet
PAWLS > PAWL
PAWN *vb* deposit (an article) as security for money borrowed ▷ *n* chessman of the lowest value
PAWNABLE > PAWN
PAWNAGE > PAWN
PAWNAGES > PAWN
PAWNCE *old word for* > PANSY
PAWNCES > PAWNCE

PAWNED > PAWN
PAWNEE *n* one who accepts goods in pawn
PAWNEES > PAWNEE
PAWNER *n* one who pawns his or her possessions
PAWNERS > PAWNER
PAWNING > PAWN
PAWNOR *same as* > PAWNER
PAWNORS > PAWNOR
PAWNS > PAWN
PAWNSHOP *n* premises of a pawnbroker
PAWNSHOPS > PAWNSHOP
PAWPAW *same as* > PAPAW
PAWPAWS > PAWPAW
PAWS > PAW
PAX *n* peace ▷ *interj* call signalling a desire to end hostilities
PAXES > PAX
PAXIUBA *n* tropical tree
PAXIUBAS > PAXIUBA
PAXWAX *n* strong ligament in the neck of many mammals
PAXWAXES > PAXWAX
PAY *vb* give money etc in return for goods or services ▷ *n* wages or salary
PAYABLE *adj* due to be paid ▷ *n* debt to be paid
PAYABLES > PAYABLE
PAYABLY > PAYABLE
PAYBACK *n* return on an investment
PAYBACKS > PAYBACK
PAYCHECK *n* payment for work done
PAYCHECKS > PAYCHECK
PAYCHEQUE *n* payment for work done
PAYDAY *n* day on which wages or salaries are paid
PAYDAYS > PAYDAY
PAYDOWN *n* reduction of debt through repayment
PAYDOWNS > PAYDOWN
PAYED > PAY
PAYEE *n* person to whom money is paid or due
PAYEES > PAYEE
PAYER *n* person who pays
PAYERS > PAYER
PAYESS *pl n* uncut sideburns worn by some Jewish men
PAYFONE *US spelling of* > PAYPHONE
PAYFONES > PAYFONE
PAYGRADE *n* military rank
PAYGRADES > PAYGRADE
PAYING > PAY
PAYINGS > PAY
PAYLIST *n* list of people to be paid
PAYLISTS > PAYLIST
PAYLOAD *n* passengers or cargo of an aircraft
PAYLOADS > PAYLOAD
PAYMASTER *n* official responsible for the payment of wages and salaries
PAYMENT *n* act of paying
PAYMENTS > PAYMENT
PAYNIM *n* heathen or pagan
PAYNIMRY *n* state of being heathen
PAYNIMS > PAYNIM

PAYOFF n final settlement, esp in retribution

PAYOFFS > PAYOFF

PAYOLA n bribe to promote a commercial product

PAYOLAS > PAYOLA

PAYOR same as > PAYER

PAYORS > PAYOR

PAYOUT n sum of money paid out

PAYOUTS > PAYOUT

PAYPHONE n coin-operated telephone

PAYPHONES > PAYPHONE

PAYROLL n list of employees who receive regular pay

PAYROLLS > PAYROLL

PAYS > PAY

PAYSAGE n landscape

PAYSAGES > PAYSAGE

PAYSAGIST n painter of landscapes

PAYSD Spenserian form of > POISED

PAYSLIP n note of payment given to employee

PAYSLIPS > PAYSLIP

PAYWALL n system that denies access to a website unless a payment is made

PAYWALLS > PAYWALL

PAZAZZ same as > PIZZAZZ

PAZAZZES > PAZAZZ

PAZZAZZ same as > PIZZAZZ

PAZZAZZES > PAZZAZZ

PE n 17th letter of the Hebrew alphabet, transliterated as p

PEA n climbing plant with seeds growing in pods

PEABERRY n coffee berry containing one seed

PEABRAIN n stupid person

PEABRAINS > PEABRAIN

PEACE n calm, quietness

PEACEABLE adj inclined towards peace

PEACEABLY > PEACEABLE

PEACED > PEACE

PEACEFUL adj not in a state of war or disagreement

PEACELESS adj without peace

PEACENIK n activist who opposes war

PEACENIKS > PEACENIK

PEACES > PEACE

PEACETIME n period without war

PEACH n soft juicy fruit ▷ adj pinkish-orange ▷ vb inform against an accomplice

PEACHBLOW n type of glaze on porcelain

PEACHED > PEACH

PEACHER > PEACH

PEACHERS > PEACH

PEACHES > PEACH

PEACHICK n young peafowl

PEACHICKS > PEACHICK

PEACHIER > PEACHY

PEACHIEST > PEACHY

PEACHILY > PEACHY

PEACHING > PEACH

PEACHY adj of or like a peach, esp in colour or texture

PEACING > PEACE

PEACOAT n woollen jacket

PEACOATS > PEACOAT

PEACOCK n large male bird with a brilliantly coloured fanlike tail ▷ vb display (oneself) proudly

PEACOCKED > PEACOCK

PEACOCKS > PEACOCK

PEACOCKY > PEACOCK

PEACOD same as > PEACOD

PEACODS > PEACOD

PEAFOWL n peacock or peahen

PEAFOWLS > PEAFOWL

PEAG n (formerly) money used by Native Americans

PEAGE same as > PEAG

PEAGES > PEAGE

PEAGS > PEAG

PEAHEN > PEACOCK

PEAHENS > PEACOCK

PEAK n pointed top, esp of a mountain ▷ vb form or reach a peak ▷ adj of or at the point of greatest demand

PEAKED adj having a peak

PEAKIER > PEAK

PEAKIEST > PEAK

PEAKINESS n state of being peaky

PEAKING n act of peaking

PEAKINGS > PEAKING

PEAKISH adj sickly

PEAKLESS adj without a peak

PEAKLIKE > PEAK

PEAKS > PEAK

PEAKY > PEAK

PEAL n long loud echoing sound, esp of bells or thunder ▷ vb sound with a peal or peals

PEALED > PEAL

PEALIKE > PEA

PEALING > PEAL

PEALS > PEAL

PEAN same as > PEEN

PEANED > PEAN

PEANING > PEAN

PEANS > PEAN

PEANUT n pea-shaped nut that ripens underground

PEANUTS > PEANUT

PEANUTTY adj having the taste of peanuts

PEAPOD n pod of the pea plant

PEAPODS > PEAPOD

PEAR n sweet juicy fruit with a narrow top and rounded base

PEARCE old spelling of > PIERCE

PEARCED > PEARCE

PEARCES > PEARCE

PEARCING > PEARCE

PEARE obsolete spelling of > PEAR

PEARES > PEARE

PEARL same as > PURL

PEARLASH n granular crystalline form of potassium carbonate

PEARLED > PEARL

PEARLER n person who dives for or trades in pearls ▷ adj excellent

PEARLERS > PEARLER

PEARLIER > PEARLY

PEARLIES > PEARLY

PEARLIEST > PEARLY

PEARLIN n type of lace used to trim clothes

PEARLING > PEARL

PEARLINGS > PEARL

PEARLINS n type of lace

PEARLISED same as > PEARLIZED

PEARLITE same as > PERLITE

PEARLITES > PEARLITE

PEARLITIC > PEARLITE

PEARLIZED adj having or given a pearly lustre

PEARLS > PEARL

PEARLWARE n goods made from pearl

PEARLWORT n plant with small white flowers that are spherical in bud

PEARLY adj resembling a pearl, esp in lustre ▷ n London costermonger who wears pearl buttons

PEARMAIN n any of several varieties of apple having a red skin

PEARMAINS > PEARMAIN

PEARS > PEAR

PEARST archaic variant of > PIERCED

PEART adj lively

PEARTER > PEART

PEARTEST > PEART

PEARTLY > PEART

PEARTNESS > PEART

PEARWOOD n wood from pear tree

PEARWOODS > PEARWOOD

PEAS > PEA

PEASANT n person working on the land

PEASANTRY n peasants collectively

PEASANTS > PEASANT

PEASANTY adj having qualities ascribed to traditional country life or people

PEASCOD same as > COD

PEASCODS > PEASCOD

PEASE n archaic or dialect word for pea ▷ vb appease

PEASECOD n pod of a pea plant

PEASECODS > PEASECOD

PEASED > PEASE

PEASEN obsolete plural of > PEASE

PEASES > PEASE

PEASING > PEASE

PEASON obsolete plural of > PEASE

PEASOUPER n thick fog

PEAT n decayed vegetable material found in bogs

PEATARIES > PEATARY

PEATARY n area covered with peat

PEATERIES > PEATERY

PEATERY same as > PEATARY

PEATIER > PEAT

PEATIEST > PEAT

PEATLAND n area of land consisting of peat bogs

PEATLANDS > PEATLAND

PEATMAN n person who collects peat

PEATMEN > PEATMAN

PEATS > PEAT

PEATSHIP n ship carrying peat

PEATSHIPS > PEATSHIP

PEATY > PEAT

PEAVEY n wooden lever used for handling logs

PEAVEYS > PEAVEY

PEAVIES > PEAVY

PEAVY same as > PEAVEY

PEAZE same as > PEASE

PEAZED > PEAZE

PEAZES > PEAZE

PEAZING > PEAZE

PEBA n type of armadillo

PEBAS > PEBA

PEBBLE n small roundish stone ▷ vb cover with pebbles

PEBBLED > PEBBLE

PEBBLES > PEBBLE

PEBBLIER > PEBBLE

PEBBLIEST > PEBBLE

PEBBLING n (in curling) act of spraying the rink with drops of hot water to slow down the stone

PEBBLINGS > PEBBLING

PEBBLY > PEBBLE

PEBIBYTE n two to the power of fifty bytes

PEBIBYTES > PEBIBYTE

PEBRINE n disease of silkworms

PEBRINES > PEBRINE

PEC n pectoral muscle

PECAN n edible nut of a N American tree

PECANS > PECAN

PECCABLE adj liable to sin

PECCANCY > PECCANT

PECCANT adj guilty of an offence

PECCANTLY > PECCANT

PECCARIES > PECCARY

PECCARY n piglike animal of American forests

PECCAVI n confession of guilt

PECCAVIS > PECCAVI

PECH Scottish word for > PANT

PECHAN Scots word for > STOMACH

PECHANS > PECHAN

PECHED > PECH

PECHING > PECH

PECHS > PECH

PECK vb strike or pick up with the beak ▷ n pecking movement

PECKE n quarter of bushel

PECKED > PECK

PECKER n short for woodpecker

PECKERS > PECKER

PECKES > PECKE

PECKIER > PECKY

PECKIEST > PECKY

PECKING > PECK

PECKINGS > PECK

P

PECKISH adj slightly hungry
PECKISHLY > PECKISH
PECKS > PECK
PECKY adj discoloured
PECORINI > PECORINO
PECORINO n Italian cheese made from ewes' milk
PECORINOS > PECORINO
PECS pl n pectoral muscles
PECTASE n enzyme occurring in certain ripening fruits
PECTASES > PECTASE
PECTATE n salt or ester of pectic acid
PECTATES > PECTATE
PECTEN n comblike structure in the eye of birds and reptiles
PECTENS > PECTEN
PECTIC > PECTIN
PECTIN n substance in fruit that makes jam set
PECTINAL adj resembling a comb ▷ n fish with bones or a spine resembling a comb
PECTINALS > PECTINAL
PECTINATE adj shaped like a comb
PECTINEAL adj relating to pubic bone
PECTINEI > PECTINEUS
PECTINES > PECTEN
PECTINEUS n muscle in the thigh
PECTINOUS > PECTIN
PECTINS > PECTIN
PECTISE same as > PECTIZE
PECTISED > PECTISE
PECTISES > PECTISE
PECTISING > PECTISE
PECTIZE vb change into a jelly
PECTIZED > PECTIZE
PECTIZES > PECTIZE
PECTIZING > PECTIZE
PECTOLITE n silicate of lime and soda
PECTORAL adj of the chest or thorax ▷ n pectoral muscle or fin
PECTORALS > PECTORAL
PECTOSE n insoluble carbohydrate found in unripe fruit
PECTOSES > PECTOSE
PECULATE vb embezzle (public money)
PECULATED > PECULATE
PECULATES > PECULATE
PECULATOR > PECULATE
PECULIA > PECULIUM
PECULIAR adj strange ▷ n special sort, esp an accented letter
PECULIARS > PECULIAR
PECULIUM n property that a father or master allowed his child or slave to hold as his own
PECUNIARY adj relating to, or consisting of, money
PECUNIOUS adj having lots of money
PED n pannier
PEDAGOG same as > PEDAGOGUE

PEDAGOGIC > PEDAGOGUE
PEDAGOGS > PEDAGOG
PEDAGOGUE n schoolteacher, esp a pedantic one
PEDAGOGY n principles, practice, or profession of teaching
PEDAL n foot-operated lever ▷ vb propel (a bicycle) by using its pedals ▷ adj of or relating to the foot or the feet
PEDALBOAT n boat that is propelled by operating the pedals
PEDALCAR n child's vehicle that is operated by pedals
PEDALCARS > PEDALCAR
PEDALED > PEDAL
PEDALER > PEDAL
PEDALERS > PEDAL
PEDALFER n type of zonal soil deficient in lime but containing deposits of aluminium and iron
PEDALFERS > PEDALFER
PEDALIER n pedal piano
PEDALIERS > PEDALIER
PEDALING > PEDAL
PEDALLED > PEDAL
PEDALLER n person who pedals
PEDALLERS > PEDALLER
PEDALLING > PEDAL
PEDALO n pedal-operated pleasure craft
PEDALOES > PEDALO
PEDALOS > PEDALO
PEDALS > PEDAL
PEDANT n person who is excessively concerned with details and rules
PEDANTIC adj of, relating to, or characterized by pedantry
PEDANTISE same as > PEDANTIZE
PEDANTISM > PEDANT
PEDANTIZE vb make pedantic comments
PEDANTRY n practice of being a pedant, esp in the minute observance of petty rules or details
PEDANTS > PEDANT
PEDATE adj (of a plant leaf) divided into several lobes arising at a common point
PEDATELY > PEDATE
PEDATIFID adj (of a plant leaf) pedately divided, with the divisions less deep than in a pedate leaf
PEDDER old form of > PEDLAR
PEDDERS > PEDDER
PEDDLE vb sell (goods) from door to door
PEDDLED > PEDDLE
PEDDLER same as > PEDLAR
PEDDLERS > PEDDLER
PEDDLERY n business of peddler
PEDDLES > PEDDLE
PEDDLING > PEDDLE
PEDDLINGS > PEDDLE
PEDERAST n man who has sexual relations with boys

PEDERASTS > PEDERAST
PEDERASTY n homosexual relations between men and boys
PEDERERO n type of cannon
PEDEREROS > PEDERERO
PEDES > PES
PEDESES > PEDESIS
PEDESIS n random motion of small particles
PEDESTAL n base supporting a column, statue, etc
PEDESTALS > PEDESTAL
PEDETIC adj of feet
PEDI n pedicure
PEDIATRIC adj of or relating to the medical science of children and their diseases
PEDICAB n pedal-operated tricycle, available for hire
PEDICABS > PEDICAB
PEDICEL n stalk bearing a single flower of an inflorescence
PEDICELS > PEDICEL
PEDICLE n any small stalk
PEDICLED > PEDICLE
PEDICLES > PEDICLE
PEDICULAR adj relating to, infested with, or caused by lice
PEDICULI > PEDICULUS
PEDICULUS n wingless parasite
PEDICURE n medical or cosmetic treatment of the feet ▷ vb give a pedicure
PEDICURED > PEDICURE
PEDICURES > PEDICURE
PEDIFORM adj shaped like a foot
PEDIGREE n register of ancestors, esp of a purebred animal
PEDIGREED > PEDIGREE
PEDIGREES > PEDIGREE
PEDIMENT n triangular part over a door etc
PEDIMENTS > PEDIMENT
PEDIPALP n either member of the second pair of head appendages of arachnids
PEDIPALPI > PEDIPALP
PEDIPALPS > PEDIPALP
PEDIS > PEDI
PEDLAR n person who sells goods from door to door
PEDLARIES > PEDLARY
PEDLARS > PEDLAR
PEDLARY same as > PEDLERY
PEDLER same as > PEDLAR
PEDLERIES > PEDLERY
PEDLERS > PEDLER
PEDLERY n business of pedler
PEDOCAL n type of soil that is rich in lime
PEDOCALIC > PEDOCAL
PEDOCALS > PEDOCAL
PEDOGENIC adj relating to soil
PEDOLOGIC > PEDOLOGY
PEDOLOGY same as > PAEDOLOGY

PEDOMETER n instrument which measures the distance walked
PEDOPHILE n person who is sexually attracted to children
PEDORTHIC adj (of footwear) designed to alleviate foot problems
PEDRAIL n device replacing wheel on rough surfaces
PEDRAILS > PEDRAIL
PEDRERO n type of cannon
PEDREROES > PEDRERO
PEDREROS > PEDRERO
PEDRO n card game
PEDROS > PEDRO
PEDS > PED
PEDUNCLE same as > PEDICEL
PEDUNCLED > PEDUNCLE
PEDUNCLES > PEDUNCLE
PEDWAY n walkway for pedestrians only
PEDWAYS > PEDWAY
PEE vb urinate ▷ n urine
PEEBEEN n type of large evergreen
PEEBEENS > PEEBEEN
PEECE obsolete variant of > PIECE
PEECES > PEECE
PEED > PEE
PEEING > PEE
PEEK n peep or glance ▷ vb glance quickly or secretly
PEEKABO same as > PEEKABOO
PEEKABOO n game in which one person hides his or her face and suddenly reveals it ▷ adj made of fabric that is almost transparent
PEEKABOOS > PEEKABOO
PEEKABOS > PEEKABO
PEEKAPOO n dog which is cross between Pekingese and poodle
PEEKAPOOS > PEEKAPOO
PEEKED > PEEK
PEEKING > PEEK
PEEKS > PEEK
PEEL vb remove the skin or rind of (a vegetable or fruit) ▷ n rind or skin
PEELABLE > PEEL
PEELED > PEEL
PEELER n device for peeling vegetables, fruit, etc
PEELERS > PEELER
PEELING n strip that has been peeled off
PEELINGS > PEELING
PEELS > PEEL
PEEN n end of a hammer head opposite the striking face ▷ vb strike with the peen of a hammer
PEENED > PEEN
PEENGE vb complain
PEENGED > PEENGE
PEENGEING > PEENGE
PEENGES > PEENGE
PEENING > PEENGE
PEENING n act of peening
PEENINGS > PEENING
PEENS > PEEN
PEEOY n homemade firework

PEEOYS > PEEOY

PEEP *vb* look slyly or quickly ▷ *n* peeping look

PEEPBO *n* game of peekaboo

PEEPBOS > PEEPBO

PEEPE *old spelling of >* PIP

PEEPED > PEEP

PEEPER *n* person who peeps

PEEPERS > PEEPER

PEEPES *archaic spelling of > PEEPS*

PEEPHOLE *n* small aperture for observation

PEEPHOLES > PEEPHOLE

PEEPING > PEEP

PEEPS > PEEP

PEEPSHOW *n* box containing a series of pictures that can be seen through a small hole

PEEPSHOWS > PEEPSHOW

PEEPTOE *adj* of a shoe in which the toe is not covered

PEEPUL *n* Indian moraceous tree

PEEPULS > PEEPUL

PEER *n* (in Britain) member of the nobility ▷ *vb* look closely and intently

PEERAGE *n* whole body of peers

PEERAGES > PEERAGE

PEERED > PEER

PEERESS *n* (in Britain) woman holding the rank of a peer

PEERESSES > PEERESS

PEERIE *n* spinning top ▷ *adj* small

PEERIER > PEERIE

PEERIES > PEERIE

PEERIEST > PEERIE

PEERING > PEER

PEERLESS *adj* unequalled, unsurpassed

PEERS > PEER

PEERY *n* child's spinning top

PEES > PEE

PEESWEEP *n* early spring storm

PEESWEEPS > PEESWEEP

PEETWEET *n* spotted sandpiper

PEETWEETS > PEETWEET

PEEVE *vb* irritate or annoy ▷ *n* something that irritates

PEEVED > PEEVE

PEEVER *n* hopscotch

PEEVERS > PEEVER

PEEVES > PEEVE

PEEVING > PEEVE

PEEVISH *adj* fretful or irritable

PEEVISHLY > PEEVISH

PEEWEE *same as >* PEWEE

PEEWEES > PEEWEE

PEEWIT *same as >* LAPWING

PEEWITS > PEEWIT

PEG *n* pin or clip for joining, fastening, marking, etc ▷ *vb* fasten with pegs

PEGASUS *n* winged horse

PEGASUSES > PEGASUS

PEGBOARD *n* board with holes into which pegs can be fitted

PEGBOARDS > PEGBOARD

PEGBOX *n* part of stringed instrument that holds tuning pegs

PEGBOXES > PEGBOX

PEGGED > PEG

PEGGIER > PEGGY

PEGGIES > PEGGY

PEGGIEST > PEGGY

PEGGING > PEG

PEGGINGS > PEG

PEGGY *n* type of small warbler ▷ *adj* resembling a peg

PEGH *variant of >* PECH

PEGHED > PEGH

PEGHING > PEGH

PEGHS > PEGH

PEGLEGGED *adj* having wooden leg

PEGLESS > PEG

PEGLIKE > PEG

PEGMATITE *n* exceptionally coarse-grained intrusive igneous rock

PEGS > PEG

PEGTOP *n* type of spinning top

PEGTOPS > PEGTOP

PEH *same as >* PE

PEHS > PEH

PEIGNOIR *n* woman's light dressing gown

PEIGNOIRS > PEIGNOIR

PEIN *same as >* PEEN

PEINCT *vb* paint

PEINCTED > PEINCT

PEINCTING > PEINCT

PEINCTS > PEINCT

PEINED > PEIN

PEINING > PEIN

PEINS > PEIN

PEIRASTIC *adj* experimental

PEISE *same as >* PEIZE

PEISED > PEISE

PEISES > PEISE

PEISHWA *n* Indian leader

PEISHWAH *same as > PEISHWA*

PEISHWAHS > PEISHWAH

PEISHWAS > PEISHWA

PEISING > PEISE

PEIZE *vb* weight or poise

PEIZED > PEIZE

PEIZES > PEIZE

PEIZING > PEIZE

PEJORATE *vb* change for the worse

PEJORATED > PEJORATE

PEJORATES > PEJORATE

PEKAN *n* large North American marten

PEKANS > PEKAN

PEKE *n* Pekingese dog

PEKEPOO *same as > PEEKAPOO*

PEKEPOOS > PEKEPOO

PEKES > PEKE

PEKIN *n* silk fabric

PEKINS > PEKIN

PEKOE *n* high-quality tea

PEKOES > PEKOE

PEL *n* pixel

PELA *n* insect living on wax

PELAGE *n* coat of a mammal, consisting of hair, wool, fur, etc

PELAGES > PELAGE

PELAGIAL *adj* of the open sea ▷ *n* open body of water such as a lake or the sea

PELAGIALS > PELAGIAL

PELAGIAN *adj* of or inhabiting the open sea ▷ *n* pelagic creature

PELAGIANS > PELAGIAN

PELAGIC *adj* of or relating to the open sea ▷ *n* any pelagic creature

PELAGICS > PELAGIC

PELAS > PELA

PELAU *n* dish made with meat, rice, and pigeon peas

PELAUS > PELAU

PELE *Spenserian variant of > PEAL*

PELECYPOD *another word for > BIVALVE*

PELERINE *n* woman's narrow cape with long pointed ends in front

PELERINES > PELERINE

PELES > PELE

PELF *n* money or wealth

PELFS > PELF

PELHAM *n* horse's bit for a double bridle

PELHAMS > PELHAM

PELICAN *n* large water bird with a pouch beneath its bill

PELICANS > PELICAN

PELISSE *n* cloak or loose coat which is usually fur-trimmed

PELISSES > PELISSE

PELITE *n* any argillaceous rock such as shale

PELITES > PELITE

PELITIC > PELITE

PELL *n* hide of an animal ▷ *vb* hit violently

PELLACH *same as > PELLACK*

PELLACHS > PELLACH

PELLACK *n* porpoise

PELLACKS > PELLACK

PELLAGRA *n* disease caused by lack of vitamin B

PELLAGRAS > PELLAGRA

PELLAGRIN *n* person who suffers from pellagra

PELLED > PELL

PELLET *n* small ball of something ▷ *vb* strike with pellets

PELLETAL > PELLET

PELLETED > PELLET

PELLETIFY *vb* shape into pellets

PELLETING > PELLET

PELLETISE *vb* shape into pellets

PELLETIZE *vb* shape into pellets

PELLETS > PELLET

PELLICLE *n* thin skin or film

PELLICLES > PELLICLE

PELLING > PELL

PELLITORY *n* urticaceous plant

PELLMELL *n* disorder

PELLMELLS > PELLMELL

PELLOCK *n* porpoise

PELLOCKS > PELLOCK

PELLS > PELL

PELLUCID *adj* very clear

PELLUM *n* dust

PELLUMS > PELLUM

PELMA *n* sole of the foot

PELMANISM *n* memory card game

PELMAS > PELMA

PELMATIC > PELMA

PELMET *n* ornamental drapery or board, concealing a curtain rail

PELMETS > PELMET

PELOID *n* mud used therapeutically

PELOIDS > PELOID

PELOLOGY *n* study of therapeutic uses of mud

PELON *adj* hairless ▷ *n* hairless person or animal

PELONS > PELON

PELORIA *n* abnormal production of flowers in a plant

PELORIAN > PELORIA

PELORIAS > PELORIA

PELORIC > PELORIA

PELORIES > PELORY

PELORISED *adj* affected by peloria

PELORISM *n* floral mutation

PELORISMS > PELORISM

PELORIZED *same as > PELORISED*

PELORUS *n* sighting device

PELORUSES > PELORUS

PELORY *n* floral mutation

PELOTA *n* game where players propel a ball against a wall

PELOTAS > PELOTA

PELOTON *n* main field of riders in a bicycle road race

PELOTONS > PELOTON

PELS > PEL

PELT *vb* throw missiles at ▷ *n* skin of a fur-bearing animal

PELTA *n* small ancient shield

PELTAE > PELTA

PELTAS > PELTA

PELTAST *n* (in ancient Greece) lightly armed foot soldier

PELTASTS > PELTAST

PELTATE *adj* (of leaves) having the stalk attached to the centre of the lower surface

PELTATELY > PELTATE

PELTATION > PELTATE

PELTED > PELT

PELTER *vb* rain heavily

PELTERED > PELTER

PELTERING > PELT

PELTERS > PELTER

PELTING > PELT

PELTINGLY > PELT

PELTINGS > PELT

PELTLESS > PELT

PELTRIES > PELTRY

PELTRY *n* pelts of animals collectively

PELTS > PELT

PELVES > PELVIS

PELVIC *adj* of, near, or relating to the pelvis ▷ *n* pelvic bone

P

PELVICS > PELVIC
PELVIFORM adj shaped like pelvis
PELVIS n framework of bones at the base of the spine
PELVISES > PELVIS
PEMBINA n type of cranberry
PEMBINAS > PEMBINA
PEMBROKE n small table
PEMBROKES > PEMBROKE
PEMICAN same as > PEMMICAN
PEMICANS > PEMICAN
PEMMICAN n pressed cake of meat with fat and berries or dried fruits
PEMMICANS > PEMMICAN
PEMOLINE n mild stimulant
PEMOLINES > PEMOLINE
PEMPHIGI > PEMPHIGUS
PEMPHIGUS n any of a group of blistering skin diseases
PEMPHIX n type of crustacean
PEMPHIXES > PEMPHIX
PEN n instrument for writing in ink ▷ vb write or compose
PENAL adj of or used in punishment
PENALISE same as > PENALIZE
PENALISED > PENALISE
PENALISES > PENALISE
PENALITY > PENAL
PENALIZE vb impose a penalty on
PENALIZED > PENALIZE
PENALIZES > PENALIZE
PENALLY > PENAL
PENALTIES > PENALTY
PENALTY n punishment for a crime or offence
PENANCE n voluntary self-punishment ▷ vb impose a penance upon (a sinner)
PENANCED > PENANCE
PENANCES > PENANCE
PENANCING > PENANCE
PENANG variant of > PINANG
PENANGS > PENANG
PENATES pl n household gods
PENCE > PENNY
PENCEL n small pennon
PENCELS > PENCEL
PENCES > PENNY
PENCHANT n inclination or liking
PENCHANTS > PENCHANT
PENCIL n thin cylindrical instrument for writing or drawing ▷ vb draw, write, or mark with a pencil
PENCILED > PENCIL
PENCILER > PENCIL
PENCILERS > PENCIL
PENCILING > PENCIL
PENCILLED > PENCIL
PENCILLER > PENCIL
PENCILS > PENCIL
PENCRAFT n skill in writing
PENCRAFTS > PENCRAFT
PEND vb await judgment or settlement ▷ n archway or vaulted passage

PENDANT n ornament worn on a chain round the neck
PENDANTLY > PENDANT
PENDANTS > PENDANT
PENDED > PEND
PENDENCY > PENDENT
PENDENT adj hanging ▷ n pendant
PENDENTLY > PENDENT
PENDENTS > PENDENT
PENDICLE n something dependent on another
PENDICLER n person who rents a croft
PENDICLES > PENDICLE
PENDING prep while waiting for ▷ adj not yet decided or settled
PENDRAGON n supreme war chief or leader of the ancient Britons
PENDS > PEND
PENDU adj in informal Indian English, culturally backward
PENDULAR adj pendulous
PENDULATE vb swing as pendulum
PENDULE n type of climbing manoeuvre
PENDULES > PENDULE
PENDULINE adj building nests that hang down
PENDULOUS adj hanging, swinging
PENDULUM same as > PENDULE
PENDULUMS > PENDULUM
PENE variant of > PEEN
PENED > PENE
PENEPLAIN n relatively flat land surface produced by a long period of erosion
PENEPLANE same as > PENEPLAIN
PENES > PENIS
PENETRANT adj sharp ▷ n substance that lowers the surface tension of a liquid and thus causes it to penetrate or be absorbed more easily
PENETRATE vb find or force a way into or through
PENFOLD same as > PINFOLD
PENFOLDS > PENFOLD
PENFRIEND n person with whom one regularly exchanges letters
PENFUL n contents of pen
PENFULS > PENFUL
PENGO n former monetary unit of Hungary
PENGOS > PENGO
PENGUIN n flightless black-and-white sea bird
PENGUINRY n breeding place of penguins
PENGUINS > PENGUIN
PENHOLDER n container for pens
PENI old spelling of > PENNY
PENIAL > PENIS
PENICIL n small pad for wounds
PENICILLI n plural of penicillus, small pad for wounds

PENICILS > PENICIL
PENIE old spelling of > PENNY
PENIES > PENIE
PENILE adj of or relating to the penis
PENILL > PENILLION
PENILLION pl n Welsh art or practice of singing poetry in counterpoint to a traditional melody played on the harp
PENING > PENE
PENINSULA n strip of land nearly surrounded by water
PENIS n organ of copulation and urination in male mammals
PENISES > PENIS
PENISTONE n coarse woollen cloth
PENITENCE > PENITENT
PENITENCY > PENITENT
PENITENT adj feeling sorry for having done wrong ▷ n someone who is penitent
PENITENTS > PENITENT
PENK n small fish
PENKNIFE n small knife with blade(s) that fold into the handle
PENKNIVES > PENKNIFE
PENKS > PENK
PENLIGHT n small thin flashlight
PENLIGHTS > PENLIGHT
PENLIKE adj like a pen
PENLITE same as > PENLIGHT
PENLITES > PENLITE
PENMAN n person skilled in handwriting
PENMEN > PENMAN
PENNA n large feather
PENNAE > PENNA
PENNAL n first-year student of Protestant university
PENNALISM n menial choring at college
PENNALS > PENNAL
PENNAME n author's pseudonym
PENNAMES > PENNAME
PENNANT same as > PENDANT
PENNANTS > PENNANT
PENNATE adj having feathers, wings, or winglike structures
PENNATED same as > PENNATE
PENNATULA n sea pen
PENNE n pasta in the form of short tubes
PENNED > PEN
PENNEECH n card game
PENNEECHS > PENNEECH
PENNEECK same as > PENNEECH
PENNEECKS > PENNEECK
PENNER n person who writes
PENNERS > PENNER
PENNES > PENNE
PENNI n former Finnish monetary unit
PENNIA > PENNI
PENNIED adj having money
PENNIES > PENNY

PENNIFORM adj shaped like a feather
PENNILESS adj very poor
PENNILL n stanza in a Welsh poem
PENNINE n mineral found in the Pennine Alps
PENNINES > PENNINE
PENNING > PEN
PENNINITE n bluish-green variety of chlorite occurring in the form of thick crystals
PENNIS > PENNI
PENNON n triangular or tapering flag
PENNONCEL n small narrow flag
PENNONED adj equipped with a pennon
PENNONS > PENNON
PENNY n coin worth one hundredth of a pound
PENNYBOY n employee whose duties include menial tasks, such as running errands
PENNYBOYS > PENNYBOY
PENNYFEE n small payment
PENNYFEES > PENNYFEE
PENNYLAND n old Scottish division of land
PENNYWISE adj careful with small amounts of money
PENNYWORT n Eurasian rock plant with whitish-green tubular flowers and rounded leaves
PENOCHE n type of fudge
PENOCHES > PENOCHE
PENOLOGY n study of punishment and prison management
PENONCEL n small narrow flag
PENONCELS > PENONCEL
PENPOINT n tip of pen
PENPOINTS > PENPOINT
PENPUSHER n person whose work involves a lot of boring paperwork
PENS > PEN
PENSEE n thought put down on paper
PENSEES > PENSEE
PENSEL same as > PENCEL
PENSELS > PENSEL
PENSEROSO n pensive person
PENSIL same as > PENCEL
PENSILE adj designating or building a hanging nest
PENSILITY > PENSILE
PENSILS > PENSIL
PENSION n regular payment to people above a certain age, etc ▷ vb grant a pension to
PENSIONE n Italian boarding house
PENSIONED > PENSION
PENSIONER n person receiving a pension
PENSIONES > PENSIONE
PENSIONI > PENSIONE
PENSIONS > PENSION
PENSIVE adj deeply thoughtful, often with a tinge of sadness

PENSIVELY > PENSIVE
PENSTEMON n North American flowering plant with five stamens
PENSTER n writer
PENSTERS > PENSTER
PENSTOCK n conduit that supplies water to a hydroelectric power plant
PENSTOCKS > PENSTOCK
PENSUM n school exercise
PENSUMS > PENSUM
PENT n penthouse
PENTACLE same as > PENTAGRAM
PENTACLES > PENTACLE
PENTACT n sponge spicule with five rays
PENTACTS > PENTACT
PENTAD n group or series of five
PENTADIC > PENTAD
PENTADS > PENTAD
PENTAGON n geometric figure with five sides
PENTAGONS > PENTAGON
PENTAGRAM n five-pointed star
PENTALOGY n combination of five closely related symptoms
PENTALPHA n five-pointed star
PENTAMERY n state of consisting of five parts
PENTANE n alkane hydrocarbon with three isomers
PENTANES > PENTANE
PENTANGLE same as > PENTAGRAM
PENTANOIC adj as in pentanoic acid colourless liquid carboxylic acid
PENTANOL n colourless oily liquid
PENTANOLS > PENTANOL
PENTAPODY n series or measure of five feet
PENTARCH n member of pentarchy
PENTARCHS > PENTARCH
PENTARCHY n government by five rulers
PENTATHLA n pentathlons
PENTEL n type of pen
PENTELS > PENTEL
PENTENE n colourless flammable liquid alkene
PENTENES > PENTENE
PENTHIA n child born fifth
PENTHIAS > PENTHIA
PENTHOUSE n flat built on the roof or top floor of a building
PENTICE vb accommodate in a penthouse
PENTICED > PENTICE
PENTICES > PENTICE
PENTICING > PENTICE
PENTISE same as > PENTICE
PENTISED > PENTISE
PENTISES > PENTISE
PENTISING > PENTISE
PENTITI > PENTITO

PENTITO n criminal who offers information to the police
PENTODE n electronic valve having five electrodes
PENTODES > PENTODE
PENTOMIC adj denoting the subdivision of an army division into five battle groups
PENTOSAN n polysaccharide occurring in plants, humus, etc
PENTOSANE same as > PENTOSAN
PENTOSANS > PENTOSAN
PENTOSE n monosaccharide containing five atoms of carbon per molecule
PENTOSES > PENTOSE
PENTOSIDE n compound containing sugar
PENTOXIDE n oxide of an element with five atoms of oxygen per molecule
PENTROOF n lean-to
PENTROOFS > PENTROOF
PENTS > PENT
PENTYL n one of a particular chemical group
PENTYLENE n type of chemical
PENTYLS > PENTYL
PENUCHE same as > PANOCHA
PENUCHES > PENUCHE
PENUCHI same as > PANOCHA
PENUCHIS > PENUCHI
PENUCHLE same as > PINOCHLE
PENUCHLES > PENUCHLE
PENUCKLE same as > PENUCHLE
PENUCKLES > PENUCKLE
PENULT n last syllable but one in a word
PENULTIMA same as > PENULT
PENULTS > PENULT
PENUMBRA n (in an eclipse) partially shadowed region which surrounds the full shadow
PENUMBRAE > PENUMBRA
PENUMBRAL > PENUMBRA
PENUMBRAS > PENUMBRA
PENURIES > PENURY
PENURIOUS adj niggardly with money
PENURY n extreme poverty
PENWIPER n something for cleaning the ink from a pen
PENWIPERS > PENWIPER
PENWOMAN n female writer
PENWOMEN > PENWOMAN
PEON n Spanish-American farm labourer or unskilled worker
PEONAGE n state of being a peon
PEONAGES > PEONAGE
PEONES > PEON
PEONIES > PEONY
PEONISM same as > PEONAGE
PEONISMS > PEONISM

PEONS > PEON
PEONY n garden plant
PEOPLE pl n persons generally ▷ vb provide with inhabitants
PEOPLED > PEOPLE
PEOPLER n settler
PEOPLERS > PEOPLER
PEOPLES > PEOPLE
PEOPLING > PEOPLE
PEP n high spirits, energy, or enthusiasm ▷ vb liven by imbuing with new vigour
PEPERINO n type of volcanic rock
PEPERINOS > PEPERINO
PEPEROMIA n plant from tropical and subtropical America with slightly fleshy ornamental leaves
PEPERONI same as > PEPPERONI
PEPERONIS > PEPPERONI
PEPFUL adj full of vitality
PEPINO n purple-striped yellow fruit
PEPINOS > PEPINO
PEPITA n edible dried seed of a squash
PEPITAS > PEPITA
PEPLA > PEPLUM
PEPLOS n part of a woman's attire in ancient Greece
PEPLOSES > PEPLOS
PEPLUM same as > PEPLOS
PEPLUMED > PEPLUM
PEPLUMS > PEPLUM
PEPLUS same as > PEPLOS
PEPLUSES > PEPLUS
PEPO n fruit such as the melon, squash, cucumber, or pumpkin
PEPONIDA variant of > PEPO
PEPONIDAS > PEPO
PEPONIUM variant of > PEPO
PEPONIUMS > PEPONIUM
PEPOS > PEPO
PEPPED > PEP
PEPPER n sharp hot condiment ▷ vb season with pepper
PEPPERBOX n container for pepper
PEPPERED > PEPPER
PEPPERER > PEPPER
PEPPERERS > PEPPER
PEPPERIER > PEPPERY
PEPPERING > PEPPER
PEPPERONI n dry sausage of pork and beef spiced with pepper
PEPPERS > PEPPER
PEPPERY adj tasting of pepper
PEPPIER > PEPPY
PEPPIEST > PEPPY
PEPPILY > PEPPY
PEPPINESS > PEPPY
PEPPING > PEP
PEPPY adj full of vitality
PEPS > PEP
PEPSI n (tradename) brand of soft drink
PEPSIN n enzyme produced in the stomach
PEPSINATE vb treat (a patient) with pepsin

PEPSINE same as > PEPSIN
PEPSINES > PEPSINE
PEPSINS > PEPSIN
PEPSIS > PEPSI
PEPTALK n talk meant to inspire ▷ vb give a peptalk to
PEPTALKED > PEPTALK
PEPTALKS > PEPTALK
PEPTIC adj relating to digestion or the digestive juices ▷ n substance that aids digestion
PEPTICITY > PEPTIC
PEPTICS > PEPTIC
PEPTID variant of > PEPTIDE
PEPTIDASE n any of a group of proteolytic enzymes that hydrolyse peptides to amino acids
PEPTIDE n organic chemical compound
PEPTIDES > PEPTIDE
PEPTIDIC adj of peptides
PEPTIDS > PEPTID
PEPTISE same as > PEPTIZE
PEPTISED > PEPTISE
PEPTISER > PEPTISE
PEPTISERS > PEPTISE
PEPTISES > PEPTISE
PEPTISING > PEPTISE
PEPTIZE vb disperse into a colloidal state
PEPTIZED > PEPTIZE
PEPTIZER > PEPTIZE
PEPTIZERS > PEPTIZE
PEPTIZES > PEPTIZE
PEPTIZING > PEPTIZE
PEPTONE n any of a group of organic compounds
PEPTONES > PEPTONE
PEPTONIC > PEPTONE
PEPTONISE same as > PEPTONIZE
PEPTONIZE vb hydrolyse (a protein) to peptones by enzymic action, esp by pepsin or pancreatic extract
PEQUISTE n in Canada, member or supporter of the Parti Québécois
PEQUISTES > PEQUISTE
PER prep for each
PERACID n acid in which the element forming the acid radical exhibits its highest valency
PERACIDS > PERACID
PERACUTE adj very acute
PERAEA > PERAEON
PERAEON same as > PEREION
PERAEONS > PERAEON
PERAEOPOD same as > PEREIOPOD
PERAI another name for > PIRANHA
PERAIS > PERAI
PERBORATE n salt derived, or apparently derived, from perboric acid
PERBORIC adj as in perboric acid
PERC n perchloride
PERCALE n close-textured woven cotton fabric

PERCALES > PERCALE
PERCALINE *n* fine light cotton fabric, used esp for linings
PERCASE *adv* perchance
PERCE *obsolete word for* > PIERCE
PERCEABLE *adj* pierceable
PERCEANT *adj* piercing
PERCED > PERCE
PERCEIVE *vb* become aware of (something) through the senses
PERCEIVED > PERCEIVE
PERCEIVER > PERCEIVE
PERCEIVES > PERCEIVE
PERCEN > PERCE
PERCENT *n* percentage or proportion
PERCENTAL > PERCENT
PERCENTS > PERCENT
PERCEPT *n* concept that depends on recognition of some external object or phenomenon
PERCEPTS > PERCEPT
PERCES > PERCE
PERCH *n* resting place for a bird ▷ *vb* alight, rest, or place on or as if on a perch
PERCHANCE *adv* perhaps
PERCHED > PERCH
PERCHER > PERCH
PERCHERON *n* compact heavy breed of carthorse
PERCHERS > PERCH
PERCHERY *n* barn in which hens are allowed to move without restriction
PERCHES > PERCH
PERCHING > PERCH
PERCHINGS > PERCH
PERCID *n* type of freshwater fish
PERCIDS > PERCID
PERCIFORM *n* perch-like fish ▷ *adj* of perch-like fish
PERCINE *adj* of perches ▷ *n* type of perch-like fish
PERCINES > PERCINE
PERCING > PERCE
PERCOCT *adj* well-cooked ▷ *vb* cook thoroughly
PERCOCTED > PERCOCT
PERCOCTS > PERCOCT
PERCOID *n* type of spiny-finned teleost fish
PERCOIDS > PERCOID
PERCOLATE *vb* pass or filter through small holes ▷ *n* product of percolation
PERCOLIN *n* pain-relieving drug
PERCOLINS > PERCOLIN
PERCS > PERC
PERCUSS *vb* strike sharply, rapidly, or suddenly
PERCUSSED > PERCUSS
PERCUSSES > PERCUSS
PERCUSSOR > PERCUSS
PERDENDO *adj* (of music) getting gradually quieter and slower
PERDIE *adv* certainly
PERDITION *n* spiritual ruin
PERDU *adj* (of a soldier) placed on hazardous sentry

duty ▷ *n* soldier placed on hazardous sentry duty
PERDUE *same as* > PERDU
PERDUES > PERDUE
PERDURE *vb* last for long time
PERDURED > PERDURE
PERDURES > PERDURE
PERDURING > PERDURE
PERDUS > PERDU
PERDY *adv* certainly
PERE *n* addition to a French surname to specify the father
PEREA > PEREON
PEREGAL *adj* equal ▷ *n* equal
PEREGALS > PEREGAL
PEREGRIN *variant spelling of* > PEREGRINE
PEREGRINE *adj* coming from abroad
PEREGRINS > PEREGRIN
PEREIA > PEREION
PEREION *n* thorax of some crustaceans
PEREIONS > PEREION
PEREIOPOD *n* appendage of the pereion
PEREIRA *n* bark of a South American apocynaceous tree
PEREIRAS > PEREIRA
PERENNATE *vb* (of plants) live from one growing season to another
PERENNIAL *adj* lasting through many years ▷ *n* plant lasting more than two years
PERENNITY *n* state of being perennial
PERENTIE *n* large dark-coloured Australian monitor lizard
PERENTIES > PERENTY
PERENTY *same as* > PERENTIE
PEREON *same as* > PEREION
PEREONS > PEREON
PEREOPOD *same as* > PEREIOPOD
PEREOPODS > PEREOPOD
PERES > PERE
PERFAY *interj* by my faith
PERFECT *adj* having all the essential elements ▷ *n* perfect tense ▷ *vb* improve
PERFECTA *n* bet on the order of the first and second in a race
PERFECTAS > PERFECTA
PERFECTED > PERFECT
PERFECTER *same as* > PERFECTOR
PERFECTI *n* ascetic group of elite Cathars
PERFECTLY *adv* completely, utterly, or absolutely
PERFECTO *n* large cigar that is tapered from both ends
PERFECTOR *n* person who completes or makes something perfect
PERFECTOS > PERFECTO
PERFECTS > PERFECT
PERFERVID *adj* extremely ardent, enthusiastic, or zealous

PERFERVOR *n* zealous person
PERFET *obsolete variant of* > PERFECT
PERFIDIES > PERFIDY
PERFIDY *n* perfidious act
PERFIN *former name for* > SPIF
PERFING *n* practice of taking early retirement from the police force
PERFINGS > PERFING
PERFINS > PERFIN
PERFORANS *adj* perforating or penetrating
PERFORANT *adj* perforating
PERFORATE *vb* make holes in ▷ *adj* pierced by small holes
PERFORCE *adv* of necessity
PERFORM *vb* carry out (an action)
PERFORMED > PERFORM
PERFORMER > PERFORM
PERFORMS > PERFORM
PERFUME *n* liquid cosmetic worn for its pleasant smell ▷ *vb* give a pleasant smell to
PERFUMED > PERFUME
PERFUMER *n* person who makes or sells perfume
PERFUMERS > PERFUMER
PERFUMERY *n* perfumes in general
PERFUMES > PERFUME
PERFUMIER *same as* > PERFUMER
PERFUMING > PERFUME
PERFUMY *adj* like perfume
PERFUSATE *n* fluid flowing through tissue or organ
PERFUSE *vb* permeate through or over
PERFUSED > PERFUSE
PERFUSES > PERFUSE
PERFUSING > PERFUSE
PERFUSION > PERFUSE
PERFUSIVE > PERFUSE
PERGOLA *n* framework of trellis supporting climbing plants
PERGOLAS > PERGOLA
PERGUNNAH *same as* > PARGANA
PERHAPS *adv* possibly, maybe ▷ *sentence substitute* it may happen, be so, etc ▷ *n* something that might have happened
PERHAPSES > PERHAPS
PERI *n* (in Persian folklore) one of a race of beautiful supernatural beings
PERIAGUA *n* dugout canoe
PERIAGUAS > PERIAGUA
PERIAKTOI > PERIAKTOS
PERIAKTOS *n* ancient device for changing theatre scenery
PERIANTH *n* outer part of a flower
PERIANTHS > PERIANTH
PERIAPSES > PERIAPSIS
PERIAPSIS *n* closest point to a central body reached by a body in orbit
PERIAPT *n* charm or amulet

PERIAPTS > PERIAPT
PERIBLAST *n* tissue surrounding blastoderm in meroblastic eggs
PERIBLEM *n* layer of meristematic tissue in stems and roots that gives rise to the cortex
PERIBLEMS > PERIBLEM
PERIBOLI > PERIBOLOS
PERIBOLOI > PERIBOLOS
PERIBOLOS *n* enclosed court surrounding ancient temple
PERIBOLUS *same as* > PERIBOLOS
PERICARP *n* part of a fruit enclosing the seed that develops from the wall of the ovary
PERICARPS > PERICARP
PERICLASE *n* mineral consisting of magnesium oxide in the form of isometric crystals or grains
PERICLINE *n* white translucent variety of albite in the form of elongated crystals
PERICON *n* Argentinian dance
PERICONES > PERICON
PERICOPAE > PERICOPE
PERICOPAL > PERICOPE
PERICOPE *n* selection from a book, esp a passage from the Bible read at religious services
PERICOPES > PERICOPE
PERICOPIC > PERICOPE
PERICYCLE *n* layer of plant tissue beneath the endodermis
PERIDERM *n* outer corky protective layer of woody stems and roots
PERIDERMS > PERIDERM
PERIDIA > PERIDIUM
PERIDIAL > PERIDIUM
PERIDINIA *n* genus of flagellate organisms
PERIDIUM *n* distinct outer layer of the spore-bearing organ in many fungi
PERIDIUMS > PERIDIUM
PERIDOT *n* pale green transparent gemstone
PERIDOTE *same as* > PERIDOT
PERIDOTES > PERIDOTE
PERIDOTIC > PERIDOT
PERIDOTS > PERIDOT
PERIDROME *n* space between the columns and inner room of a classical temple
PERIGEAL > PERIGEE
PERIGEAN > PERIGEE
PERIGEE *n* point in the orbit of the moon or a satellite that is nearest the earth
PERIGEES > PERIGEE
PERIGON *n* angle of 360°
PERIGONE *n* part enclosing the essential organs of a flower
PERIGONES > PERIGONE
PERIGONIA *n* perigones

PERIGONS > PERIGON

PERIGYNY n condition of having the stamens and other floral parts at the same level as the carpels

PERIHELIA n points in the orbits of planets at which they are nearest the sun

PERIKARYA n parts of nerve cells that contain the nuclei

PERIL n great danger ▷ vb expose to danger

PERILED > PERIL

PERILING > PERIL

PERILLA n type of mint

PERILLAS > PERILLA

PERILLED > PERIL

PERILLING > PERIL

PERILOUS adj very hazardous or dangerous

PERILS > PERIL

PERILUNE n point in a lunar orbit when a spacecraft launched from the moon is nearest the moon

PERILUNES > PERILUNE

PERILYMPH n fluid filling the space between the membranous and bony labyrinths of the internal ear

PERIMETER n outer edge of an area

PERIMETRY > PERIMETER

PERIMORPH n mineral that encloses another mineral of a different type

PERIMYSIA n sheaths of fibrous connective tissue surrounding the primary bundles of muscle fibres

PERINAEUM same as > PERINEUM

PERINATAL adj of or in the weeks shortly before or after birth

PERINEA > PERINEUM

PERINEAL > PERINEUM

PERINEUM n region of the body between the anus and the genitals

PERINEUMS > PERINEUM

PERIOD n particular portion of time ▷ adj (of furniture, dress, a play, etc) dating from or in the style of an earlier time ▷ vb divide into periods

PERIODATE n any salt or ester of a periodic acid

PERIODED > PERIOD

PERIODIC adj recurring at intervals

PERIODID n kind of iodide

PERIODIDE variant of > PERIODID

PERIODIDS > PERIODID

PERIODING > PERIOD

PERIODISE same as > PERIODIZE

PERIODIZE vb divide (a portion of time) into periods

PERIODS > PERIOD

PERIOST n thick fibrous two-layered membrane covering the surface of bones

PERIOSTEA > PERIOSTS

PERIOSTS > PERIOST

PERIOTIC adj of or relating to the structures situated around the internal ear ▷ n periotic bone

PERIOTICS > PERIOTIC

PERIPATUS n wormlike arthropod with a segmented body and short unjointed limbs

PERIPETIA n abrupt turn of events or reversal of circumstances

PERIPETY n abrupt turn of events or reversal of circumstances

PERIPHERY n boundary or edge

PERIPLASM n region inside wall of biological cell

PERIPLAST n nutritive and supporting tissue in animal organ

PERIPLUS n circumnavigation

PERIPROCT n tough membrane surrounding anus in echinoderms

PERIPTER n type of ancient temple

PERIPTERS > PERIPTER

PERIPTERY n region surrounding moving body

PERIQUE n strong highly flavoured tobacco

PERIQUES > PERIQUE

PERIS > PERI

PERISARC n outer chitinous layer secreted by colonial hydrozoan coelenterates

PERISARCS > PERISARC

PERISCIAN adj person whose shadow moves round every point of compass during day

PERISCOPE n instrument used, esp in submarines, to give a view of objects on a different level

PERISH vb be destroyed or die

PERISHED adj (of a person, part of the body, etc) extremely cold

PERISHER n mischievous person

PERISHERS > PERISHER

PERISHES > PERISH

PERISHING adj very cold

PERISPERM n nutritive tissue surrounding the embryo in certain seeds, and developing from the nucellus of the ovule

PERISTOME n fringe of pointed teeth surrounding the opening of a moss capsule

PERISTYLE n colonnade that surrounds a court or building

PERITI > PERITUS

PERITONEA n thin translucent serous sacs that line the walls of abdominal cavities and cover the viscera

PERITRACK another name for > TAXIWAY

PERITRICH n ciliate protozoan in which the cilia are restricted to a spiral around the mouth

PERITUS n Catholic theology consultant

PERIWIG same as > PERUKE

PERIWIGS > PERIWIG

PERJINK adj prim or finicky

PERJURE vb render (oneself) guilty of perjury

PERJURED adj having sworn falsely

PERJURER > PERJURE

PERJURERS > PERJURE

PERJURES > PERJURE

PERJURIES > PERJURY

PERJURING > PERJURE

PERJUROUS > PERJURY

PERJURY n act or crime of lying while under oath in a court

PERK n incidental benefit gained from a job, such as a company car ▷ adj pert ▷ vb (of coffee) percolate

PERKED > PERK

PERKIER > PERKY

PERKIEST > PERKY

PERKILY > PERKY

PERKIN same as > PARKIN

PERKINESS > PERKY

PERKING > PERK

PERKINS > PERKIN

PERKISH adj perky

PERKS > PERK

PERKY adj lively or cheerful

PERLEMOEN n edible sea creature with a shell lined with mother of pearl

PERLITE n variety of obsidian

PERLITES > PERLITE

PERLITIC > PERLITE

PERLOUS same as > PERILOUS

PERM n long-lasting curly hairstyle ▷ vb give (hair) a perm

PERMABEAR n an investor who consistently acts in the expectation that the value of stocks and shares will fall

PERMABULL n an investor who consistently acts in the expectation that the value of stocks and shares will rise

PERMALINK n permanent internet hyperlink

PERMALLOY n any of various alloys containing iron and nickel

PERMANENT adj lasting forever

PERMATAN n permanent tan, esp artificial

PERMATANS > PERMATAN

PERMEABLE adj able to be permeated, esp by liquid

PERMEABLY > PERMEABLE

PERMEANCE n act of permeating

PERMEANT > PERMEANCE

PERMEANTS > PERMEANCE

PERMEASE n carrier protein

PERMEASES > PERMEASE

PERMEATE vb pervade or pass through the whole of (something)

PERMEATED > PERMEATE

PERMEATES > PERMEATE

PERMEATOR > PERMEATE

PERMED > PERM

PERMIAN adj of, denoting, or formed in the last period of the Palaeozoic era

PERMIE n person, esp an office worker, employed by a firm on a permanent basis

PERMIES > PERMIE

PERMING > PERM

PERMIT vb give permission, allow ▷ n document giving permission to do something

PERMITS > PERMIT

PERMITTED > PERMIT

PERMITTEE n person given a permit

PERMITTER > PERMIT

PERMS > PERM

PERMUTATE vb alter the sequence or arrangement (of)

PERMUTE vb change the sequence of

PERMUTED > PERMUTE

PERMUTES > PERMUTE

PERMUTING > PERMUTE

PERN n type of buzzard ▷ vb spin

PERNANCY n receiving of rents

PERNED > PERN

PERNING > PERN

PERNIO n chilblain

PERNIONES > PERNIO

PERNOD n aniseed-flavoured aperitif from France

PERNODS > PERNOD

PERNS > PERN

PEROG same as > PIROG

PEROGEN > PEROG

PEROGI n type of Polish dumpling

PEROGIE same as > PEROGI

PEROGIES > PEROGI

PEROGIS > PEROGI

PEROGS > PEROG

PEROGY same as > PEROGI

PERONE n fibula

PERONEAL adj of or relating to the fibula or the outer side of the leg

PERONEI > PERONEUS

PERONES > PERONE

PERONEUS n lateral muscle of the leg

PERORAL adj administered through mouth

PERORALLY > PERORAL

PERORATE vb speak at length, esp in a formal manner

PERORATED > PERORATE

PERORATES > PERORATE

PERORATOR > PERORATE

PEROVSKIA n Russian sage

PEROXID variant of > PEROXIDE

PEROXIDE n hydrogen peroxide used as a hair bleach ▷ adj bleached with or resembling peroxide ▷ vb bleach (the hair) with peroxide

PEROXIDED > PEROXIDE

PEROXIDES > PEROXIDE

PEROXIDIC > PEROXIDE

PEROXIDS > PEROXID
PEROXO n type of acid
PEROXY adj containing the peroxide group
PERP n someone who has committed a crime
PERPEND n large stone that passes through a wall from one side to the other ▷ vb ponder
PERPENDED > PERPEND
PERPENDS > PERPEND
PERPENT same as > PERPEND
PERPENTS > PERPENT
PERPETUAL adj lasting forever ▷ n (of a crop plant) continually producing edible parts
PERPLEX vb puzzle, bewilder
PERPLEXED > PERPLEX
PERPLEXER > PERPLEX
PERPLEXES > PERPLEX
PERPS > PERP
PERRADIAL adj situated around radii of radiate
PERRADII > PERRADIUS
PERRADIUS n primary tentacle of a polyp
PERRIER n short mortar
PERRIERS > PERRIER
PERRIES > PERRY
PERRON n external flight of steps
PERRONS > PERRON
PERRUQUE old spelling of > PERUKE
PERRUQUES > PERRUQUE
PERRY n alcoholic drink made from fermented pears
PERSALT n any salt of a peracid
PERSALTS > PERSALT
PERSANT adj piercing
PERSAUNT adj piercing
PERSE old variant of > PIERCE
PERSECUTE vb treat cruelly because of race, religion, etc
PERSEITY n quality of having substance independently of real objects
PERSELINE same as > PURSLANE
PERSES > PERSE
PERSEVERE vb keep making an effort despite difficulties
PERSICO same as > PERSICOT
PERSICOS > PERSICO
PERSICOT n cordial made from apricots
PERSICOTS > PERSICOT
PERSIENNE n printed calico
PERSIMMON n sweet red tropical fruit
PERSING > PERSE
PERSIST vb continue to be or happen, last
PERSISTED > PERSIST
PERSISTER > PERSIST
PERSISTS > PERSIST
PERSON n human being
PERSONA n someone's personality as presented to others
PERSONAE > PERSONA

PERSONAGE n important person
PERSONAL adj individual or private ▷ n item of movable property
PERSONALS > PERSONAL
PERSONAS > PERSONA
PERSONATE vb assume the identity of (another person) with intent to deceive ▷ adj (of the corollas of certain flowers) having two lips in the form of a face
PERSONIFY vb give human characteristics to
PERSONISE same as > PERSONIZE
PERSONIZE vb personify
PERSONNED adj manned
PERSONNEL n people employed in an organization
PERSONS > PERSON
PERSPEX n any of various clear acrylic resins
PERSPEXES > PERSPEX
PERSPIRE vb sweat
PERSPIRED > PERSPIRE
PERSPIRES > PERSPIRE
PERSPIRY adj perspiring
PERST adj perished
PERSUADE vb make (someone) do something by argument, charm, etc
PERSUADED > PERSUADE
PERSUADER > PERSUADE
PERSUADES > PERSUADE
PERSUE obsolete form of > PURSUE
PERSUED > PERSUE
PERSUES > PERSUE
PERSUING > PERSUE
PERSWADE obsolete form of > PERSUADE
PERSWADED > PERSWADE
PERSWADES > PERSWADE
PERT adj saucy and cheeky ▷ n pert person
PERTAIN vb belong or be relevant (to)
PERTAINED > PERTAIN
PERTAINS > PERTAIN
PERTAKE obsolete form of > PARTAKE
PERTAKEN > PERTAKE
PERTAKES > PERTAKE
PERTAKING > PERTAKE
PERTER > PERT
PERTEST > PERT
PERTHITE n type of feldspar
PERTHITES > PERTHITE
PERTHITIC > PERTHITE
PERTINENT adj relevant
PERTLY > PERT
PERTNESS > PERT
PERTOOK > PERTAKE
PERTS > PERT
PERTURB vb disturb greatly
PERTURBED > PERTURB
PERTURBER > PERTURB
PERTURBS > PERTURB
PERTUSATE adj pierced at apex
PERTUSE adj having holes
PERTUSED adj having holes
PERTUSION n punched hole
PERTUSSAL > PERTUSSIS
PERTUSSES > PERTUSSIS

PERTUSSIS n whooping cough
PERUKE n wig for men worn in the 17th and 18th centuries
PERUKED adj wearing wig
PERUKES > PERUKE
PERUSABLE > PERUSE
PERUSAL > PERUSE
PERUSALS > PERUSE
PERUSE vb read in a careful or leisurely manner
PERUSED > PERUSE
PERUSER > PERUSE
PERUSERS > PERUSE
PERUSES > PERUSE
PERUSING > PERUSE
PERV n pervert ▷ vb give a person an erotic look
PERVADE vb spread right through (something)
PERVADED > PERVADE
PERVADER > PERVADE
PERVADERS > PERVADE
PERVADES > PERVADE
PERVADING > PERVADE
PERVASION > PERVADE
PERVASIVE adj pervading or tending to pervade
PERVE same as > PERV
PERVED > PERV
PERVERSE adj deliberately doing something different from what is thought normal or proper
PERVERSER > PERVERSE
PERVERT vb use or alter for a wrong purpose ▷ n person who practises sexual perversion
PERVERTED adj deviating greatly from what is regarded as normal or right
PERVERTER > PERVERT
PERVERTS > PERVERT
PERVES > PERV
PERVIATE vb perforate or burrow
PERVIATED > PERVIATE
PERVIATES > PERVIATE
PERVICACY n obstinacy
PERVIER > PERVY
PERVIEST > PERVY
PERVING > PERV
PERVIOUS adj able to be penetrated, permeable
PERVO n pervert
PERVOS > PERVO
PERVS > PERV
PERVY adj perverted
PES n animal part corresponding to the foot
PESADE n position in which the horse stands on the hind legs with the forelegs in the air
PESADES > PESADE
PESANT obsolete spelling of > PEASANT
PESANTE adv to be performed clumsily
PESANTS > PESANT
PESAUNT obsolete spelling of > PEASANT
PESAUNTS > PESAUNT
PESETA n former monetary unit of Spain
PESETAS > PESETA

PESEWA n Ghanaian monetary unit
PESEWAS > PESEWA
PESHMERGA n armed forces of Kurdish region of Iraq
PESHWA same as > PEISHWA
PESHWAS > PESHWA
PESKIER > PESKY
PESKIEST > PESKY
PESKILY > PESKY
PESKINESS > PESKY
PESKY adj troublesome
PESO n monetary unit of Argentina, Mexico, etc
PESOS > PESO
PESSARIES > PESSARY
PESSARY n appliance worn in the vagina
PESSIMA n lowest point
PESSIMAL adj (of animal's environment) least favourable for survival
PESSIMISM n tendency to expect the worst in all things
PESSIMIST > PESSIMISM
PESSIMUM same as > PESSIMAL
PEST n annoying person
PESTER vb annoy or nag continually
PESTERED > PESTER
PESTERER > PESTER
PESTERERS > PESTER
PESTERING > PESTER
PESTEROUS adj inclined to annoy
PESTERS > PESTER
PESTFUL adj causing annoyance
PESTHOLE n breeding ground for disease
PESTHOLES > PESTHOLE
PESTHOUSE n hospital for treating persons with infectious diseases
PESTICIDE n chemical for killing insect pests
PESTIER > PESTY
PESTIEST > PESTY
PESTILENT adj annoying, troublesome
PESTLE n club-shaped implement for grinding ▷ vb pound with or as if with a pestle
PESTLED > PESTLE
PESTLES > PESTLE
PESTLING > PESTLE
PESTO n sauce for pasta
PESTOLOGY n study of pests
PESTOS > PESTO
PESTS > PEST
PESTY adj persistently annoying
PET n animal kept for pleasure and companionship ▷ adj kept as a pet ▷ vb treat as a pet
PETABYTE n in computing, 10^{15} or 2^{50} bytes
PETABYTES > PETABYTE
PETAFLOP n (in computing) unit of processing speed
PETAFLOPS > PETAFLOP
PETAHERTZ n very large unit of electrical frequency**

PETAL *n* one of the brightly coloured outer parts of a flower

PETALED > PETAL

PETALINE > PETAL

PETALISM *n* ostracism in ancient Syracuse

PETALISMS > PETALISM

PETALLED > PETAL

PETALLIKE *adj* like a petal

PETALODIC > PETALODY

PETALODY *n* condition in which stamens or other flower parts assume the form and function of petals

PETALOID *adj* resembling a petal, esp in shape

PETALOUS *adj* bearing or having petals

PETALS > PETAL

PETAMETER *same as* > PETAMETRE

PETAMETRE *n* ten to the power of fifteen metres

PETANQUE *n* French game similar to bowls

PETANQUES > PETANQUE

PETAR *obsolete variant of* > PETARD

PETARA *n* clothes basket

PETARAS > PETARA

PETARD *n* device containing explosives

PETARDS > PETARD

PETARIES > PETARY

PETARS > PETAR

PETARY *n* weapon for hurling stones

PETASOS *same as* > PETASUS

PETASOSES > PETASOS

PETASUS *n* broad-brimmed hat worn by the ancient Greeks

PETASUSES > PETASUS

PETAURINE *adj* similar to a flying phalanger ▷ *n* a flying phalanger

PETAURIST *n* flying phalanger

PETCHARY *n* type of kingbird

PETCOCK *n* small valve

PETCOCKS > PETCOCK

PETECHIA *n* small discoloured spot on the skin

PETECHIAE > PETECHIA

PETECHIAL > PETECHIA

PETER *vb* fall (off) in volume, intensity, etc, and finally cease ▷ *n* act of petering

PETERED > PETER

PETERING > PETER

PETERMAN *n* burglar skilled in safe-breaking

PETERMEN > PETERMAN

PETERS > PETER

PETERSHAM *n* thick corded ribbon used to stiffen belts, button bands, etc

PETHER *old variant of* > PEDLAR

PETHERS > PETHER

PETHIDINE *n* white crystalline water-soluble drug used to relieve pain

PETILLANT *adj* (of wine) slightly effervescent

PETIOLAR > PETIOLE

PETIOLATE *adj* (of a plant or leaf) having a leafstalk

PETIOLE *n* stalk which attaches a leaf to a plant

PETIOLED > PETIOLE

PETIOLES > PETIOLE

PETIOLULE *n* stalk of any of the leaflets making up a compound leaf

PETIT *adj* of little or lesser importance

PETITE *adj* (of a woman) small and dainty ▷ *n* clothing size for small women

PETITES > PETITE

PETITIO *n* as in petitio principii, a form of fallacious reasoning

PETITION *n* formal request, esp one signed by many people and presented to parliament ▷ *vb* present a petition to

PETITIONS > PETITION

PETITIOS > PETITIO

PETITORY *adj* soliciting

PETNAP *vb* steal pet

PETNAPER > PETNAP

PETNAPERS > PETNAP

PETNAPING > PETNAP

PETNAPPED > PETNAP

PETNAPPER > PETNAP

PETNAPS > PETNAP

PETRALE *n* type of sole

PETRALES > PETRALE

PETRARIES > PETRARY

PETRARY *n* weapon for hurling stones

PETRE *same as* > SALTPETRE

PETREL *n* sea bird with a hooked bill and tubular nostrils

PETRELS > PETREL

PETRES > PETRE

PETRI *n* as in petri dish shallow glass dish used for cultures of bacteria

PETRICHOR *n* sweet smell caused by rain falling on parched earth

PETRIFIC *adj* petrifying

PETRIFIED > PETRIFY

PETRIFIER > PETRIFY

PETRIFIES > PETRIFY

PETRIFY *vb* frighten severely

PETROGENY *n* origin of rocks

PETROGRAM *n* prehistoric rock painting

PETROL *n* flammable liquid obtained from petroleum ▷ *vb* supply with petrol

PETROLAGE *n* addition of petrol (to a body of water) to get rid of mosquitoes

PETROLEUM *n* thick dark oil found underground

PETROLEUR *n* person using petrol to cause explosions

PETROLIC *adj* of, relating to, containing, or obtained from petroleum

PETROLLED > PETROL

PETROLOGY *n* study of the composition, origin, structure, and formation of rocks

PETROLS > PETROL

PETRONEL *n* obsolete cavalry firearm

PETRONELS > PETRONEL

PETROSAL *adj* of the dense part of the temporal bone that surrounds the inner ear ▷ *n* petrosal bone

PETROSALS > PETROSAL

PETROUS *adj* denoting the dense part of the temporal bone around the inner ear

PETS > PET

PETSAI *n* Chinese cabbage

PETSAIS > PETSAI

PETTABLE > PET

PETTED > PET

PETTEDLY > PET

PETTER > PET

PETTERS > PET

PETTI *n* petticoat

PETTICOAT *n* woman's skirt-shaped undergarment

PETTIER > PETTY

PETTIES > PETTI

PETTIEST > PETTY

PETTIFOG *vb* quibble or fuss over details

PETTIFOGS > PETTIFOG

PETTILY > PETTY

PETTINESS > PETTY

PETTING > PET

PETTINGS > PET

PETTIS > PETTI

PETTISH *adj* peevish or fretful

PETTISHLY > PETTISH

PETTITOES *pl n* pig's trotters, esp when used as food

PETTLE *vb* pat animal

PETTLED > PETTLE

PETTLES > PETTLE

PETTLING > PETTLE

PETTO *n* breast of an animal

PETTY *adj* unimportant, trivial

PETULANCE > PETULANT

PETULANCY > PETULANT

PETULANT *adj* childishly irritable or peevish

PETUNIA *n* garden plant with funnel-shaped flowers

PETUNIAS > PETUNIA

PETUNTSE *n* fusible feldspathic mineral used in hard-paste porcelain

PETUNTSES > PETUNTSE

PETUNTZE *same as* > PETUNTSE

PETUNTZES > PETUNTZE

PEW *n* fixed benchlike seat in a church

PEWEE *n* small N American flycatcher

PEWEES > PEWEE

PEWHOLDER *n* renter of pew

PEWIT *another name for* > LAPWING

PEWITS > PEWIT

PEWS > PEW

PEWTER *n* greyish metal made of tin and lead

PEWTERER > PEWTER

PEWTERERS > PEWTER

PEWTERIER > PEWTERY

PEWTERS > PEWTER

PEWTERY *adj* of or like pewter

PEYOTE *another name for* > MESCAL

PEYOTES > PEYOTE

PEYOTISM *n* ritual use of peyote

PEYOTISMS > PEYOTISM

PEYOTIST *n* person who uses peyote

PEYOTISTS > PEYOTIST

PEYOTL *same as* > PEYOTE

PEYOTLS > PEYOTL

PEYSE *vb* weight or poise

PEYSED > PEYSE

PEYSES > PEYSE

PEYSING > PEYSE

PEYTRAL *same as* > PEYTREL

PEYTRALS > PEYTRAL

PEYTREL *n* breastplate of horse's armour

PEYTRELS > PEYTREL

PEZANT *obsolete spelling of* > PEASANT

PEZANTS > PEZANT

PEZIZOID *adj* having cup-like form

PFENNIG *n* former German monetary unit

PFENNIGE > PFENNIG

PFENNIGS > PFENNIG

PFENNING *old variant of* > PFENNIG

PFENNINGS > PFENNING

PFFT *interj* sound indicating sudden disappearance of something

PFUI *interj* phooey

PHABLET *n* type of handheld personal computer

PHABLETS > PHABLET

PHACELIA *n* plant grown for its large, deep blue bell flowers

PHACELIAS > PHACELIA

PHACOID *adj* lentil- or lens-shaped

PHACOIDAL *same as* > PHACOID

PHACOLITE *n* colourless variety of chabazite

PHACOLITH *n* lens-shaped igneous rock structure

PHAEIC *adj* (of animals) having dusky coloration

PHAEISM > PHAEIC

PHAEISMS > PHAEIC

PHAENOGAM *n* seed-bearing plant

PHAETON *n* light four-wheeled horse-drawn carriage

PHAETONS > PHAETON

PHAGE *n* parasitic virus that destroys its host

PHAGEDENA *n* rapidly spreading ulcer that destroys tissues as it increases in size

PHAGES > PHAGE

PHAGOCYTE *n* cell or protozoan that engulfs particles, such as microorganisms

PHAGOSOME *n* part of biological cell
PHALANGAL > PHALANGE
PHALANGE *another name for* > PHALANX
PHALANGER *same as* > POSSUM
PHALANGES > PHALANX
PHALANGID *n* type of arachnid
PHALANX *n* closely grouped mass of people
PHALANXES > PHALANX
PHALAROPE *n* aquatic shore bird of northern oceans and lakes
PHALLI > PHALLUS
PHALLIC *adj* of or resembling a penis
PHALLIN *n* poisonous substance from mushroom
PHALLINS > PHALLIN
PHALLISM *n* worship or veneration of the phallus
PHALLISMS > PHALLISM
PHALLIST *n* worshipper or venerator of the phallus
PHALLISTS > PHALLIST
PHALLOID *adj* resembling a penis
PHALLUS *n* penis
PHALLUSES > PHALLUS
PHANG *old variant spelling of* > FANG
PHANGED > PHANG
PHANGING > PHANG
PHANGS > PHANG
PHANSIGAR *n* Indian assassin
PHANTASIM *same as* > PHANTASM
PHANTASM *n* unreal vision, illusion
PHANTASMA *same as* > PHANTASM
PHANTASMS > PHANTASM
PHANTAST *same as* > FANTAST
PHANTASTS > PHANTAST
PHANTASY *same as* > FANTASY
PHANTOM *n* ghost ▷ *adj* deceptive or unreal
PHANTOMS > PHANTOM
PHANTOMY *adj* of phantoms
PHANTOSME *old spelling of* > PHANTASM
PHARAOH *n* ancient Egyptian king
PHARAOHS > PHARAOH
PHARAONIC *adj* of or relating to the Pharaohs
PHARE *n* beacon tower
PHARES > PHARE
PHARISAIC *n* righteously hypocritical
PHARISEE *n* self-righteous or hypocritical person
PHARISEES > PHARISEE
PHARM *vb* redirect (a website user) to another, bogus website
PHARMA *n* pharmaceutical companies considered together as an industry
PHARMACY *n* preparation and dispensing of drugs and medicines

PHARMAS > PHARMA
PHARMED > PHARM
PHARMER *n* person who pharms
PHARMERS > PHARMER
PHARMING *n* rearing or growing genetically modified animals or plants in order to develop pharmaceuticals
PHARMINGS > PHARMING
PHARMS > PHARM
PHAROS *n* lighthouse
PHAROSES > PHAROS
PHARYNGAL *adj* of, relating to, or situated in or near the pharynx
PHARYNGES > PHARYNX
PHARYNX *n* cavity forming the back part of the mouth
PHARYNXES > PHARYNX
PHASE *n* distinct or characteristic stage in a development or chain of events ▷ *vb* arrange or carry out in stages
PHASEAL > PHASE
PHASED > PHASE
PHASEDOWN *n* gradual reduction
PHASELESS > PHASE
PHASEOLIN *n* anti-fungal substance from kidney bean
PHASEOUT *n* gradual reduction
PHASEOUTS > PHASEOUT
PHASER *n* type of science-fiction weapon
PHASERS > PHASER
PHASES > PHASE
PHASIC > PHASE
PHASING *n* effect achieved by varying the phase relationship of two similar audio signals
PHASINGS > PHASING
PHASIS *another word for* > PHASE
PHASMID *n* stick insect or leaf insect
PHASMIDS > PHASMID
PHASOR *n* rotating vector representing a quantity that varies sinusoidally
PHASORS > PHASOR
PHAT *adj* terrific
PHATIC *adj* (of speech) used to express sociability rather than specific meaning
PHATTER > PHAT
PHATTEST > PHAT
PHEASANT *n* game bird with bright plumage
PHEASANTS > PHEASANT
PHEAZAR *old variant of* > VIZIER
PHEAZARS > PHEAZAR
PHEER *same as* > FERE
PHEERE *same as* > FERE
PHEERES > PHEERE
PHEERS > PHEER
PHEESE *vb* worry
PHEESED > PHEESE
PHEESES > PHEESE
PHEESING > PHEESE
PHEEZE *same as* > PHEESE
PHEEZED > PHEEZE

PHEEZES > PHEEZE
PHEEZING > PHEEZE
PHELLEM *technical name for* > CORK
PHELLEMS > PHELLEM
PHELLOGEN *n* cork cambium
PHELLOID *adj* like cork
PHELONIA > PHELONION
PHELONION *n* vestment for an Orthodox priest
PHENACITE *n* colourless or white glassy mineral
PHENAKISM *n* deception
PHENAKITE *same as* > PHENACITE
PHENATE *n* ester or salt of phenol
PHENATES > PHENATE
PHENAZIN *same as* > PHENAZINE
PHENAZINE *n* yellow crystalline tricyclic compound
PHENAZINS > PHENAZIN
PHENE *n* genetically determined characteristic of organism
PHENES > PHENE
PHENETIC > PHENETICS
PHENETICS *n* system of classification based on similarities between organisms without regard to their evolutionary relationships
PHENETOL *same as* > PHENETOLE
PHENETOLE *n* colourless oily compound
PHENETOLS > PHENETOL
PHENGITE *n* type of alabaster
PHENGITES > PHENGITE
PHENIC *adj* of phenol
PHENIX *same as* > PHOENIX
PHENIXES > PHENIX
PHENOBARB *n* phenobarbital
PHENOCOPY *n* noninheritable change in an organism that is caused by environmental influence during development but resembles the effects of a genetic mutation
PHENOGAM *same as* > PHAENOGAM
PHENOGAMS > PHENOGAM
PHENOL *n* chemical used in disinfectants and antiseptics
PHENOLATE *vb* treat or disinfect with phenol
PHENOLIC *adj* of, containing, or derived from phenol ▷ *n* derivative of phenol
PHENOLICS > PHENOLIC
PHENOLOGY *n* study of recurring phenomena, such as animal migration, esp as influenced by climatic conditions
PHENOLS > PHENOL
PHENOM *n* person or thing of outstanding abilities
PHENOME *n* full complement of phenotypical traits of an organism, species, etc

PHENOMENA *n* phenomenons
PHENOMES > PHENOME
PHENOMS > PHENOM
PHENOTYPE *n* physical form of an organism as determined by the interaction of its genetic make-up and its environment
PHENOXIDE *n* any of a class of salts of phenol
PHENOXY *modifier* as in *phenoxy resin* any of a class of resins derived from polyhydroxy ethers
PHENYL *n* chemical substance
PHENYLENE *n* compound derived from benzene
PHENYLIC > PHENYL
PHENYLS > PHENYL
PHENYTOIN *n* anticonvulsant drug
PHEON *n* barbed iron head of dart
PHEONS > PHEON
PHERESES > PHERESIS
PHERESIS *n* specialized form of blood donation
PHEROMONE *n* chemical substance, secreted externally by certain animals, such as insects, affecting the behaviour or physiology of other animals of the same species
PHESE *same as* > PHEESE
PHESED > PHESE
PHESES > PHESE
PHESING > PHESE
PHEW *interj* exclamation of relief, surprise, etc
PHI *n* 21st letter in the Greek alphabet
PHIAL *n* small bottle for medicine etc ▷ *vb* put in phial
PHIALLED > PHIAL
PHIALLING > PHIAL
PHIALS > PHIAL
PHILABEG *same as* > FILIBEG
PHILABEGS > PHILABEG
PHILAMOT *variant of* > FILEMOT
PHILAMOTS > PHILAMOT
PHILANDER *vb* (of a man) flirt or have many casual love affairs with women
PHILATELY *n* stamp collecting
PHILAVERY *n* collection of rare and obscure words
PHILHORSE *n* last horse in a team
PHILIBEG *variant spelling of* > FILIBEG
PHILIBEGS > PHILIBEG
PHILIPPIC *n* bitter or impassioned speech of denunciation, invective
PHILISTIA *n* domain of cultural philistine
PHILLABEG *same as* > FILIBEG
PHILLIBEG *same as* > FILIBEG

PHILOGYNY n fondness for women

PHILOLOGY n science of the structure and development of languages

PHILOMATH n lover of learning

PHILOMEL n nightingale

PHILOMELA same as > PHILOMEL

PHILOMELS > PHILOMEL

PHILOMOT n colour of dead leaf

PHILOMOTS > PHILOMOT

PHILOPENA n gift made as forfeit in game

PHILTER same as > PHILTRE

PHILTERED > PHILTER

PHILTERS > PHILTER

PHILTRA > PHILTRUM

PHILTRE n magic drink supposed to arouse love in the person who drinks it ▷ vb mix with love potion

PHILTRED > PHILTRE

PHILTRES > PHILTRE

PHILTRING > PHILTRE

PHILTRUM n indentation above the upper lip

PHIMOSES > PHIMOSIS

PHIMOSIS n abnormal tightness of the foreskin

PHIMOTIC > PHIMOSIS

PHINNOCK variant spelling of > FINNOCK

PHINNOCKS > PHINNOCK

PHIS > PHI

PHISH vb engage in phishing

PHISHED > PHISH

PHISHER n person who phishes

PHISHERS > PHISHER

PHISHES > PHISH

PHISHING n internet fraud to extract personal and financial details

PHISHINGS > PHISHING

PHISNOMY n physiognomy

PHIZ n face or a facial expression

PHIZES > PHIZ

PHIZOG same as > PHIZ

PHIZOGS > PHIZOG

PHIZZ n face

PHIZZES > PHIZ

PHLEBITIC > PHLEBITIS

PHLEBITIS n inflammation of a vein

PHLEGM n thick yellowish substance formed in the nose and throat during a cold

PHLEGMIER > PHLEGM

PHLEGMON n inflammatory mass that may progress to abscess

PHLEGMONS > PHLEGMON

PHLEGMS > PHLEGM

PHLEGMY > PHLEGM

PHLOEM n plant tissue that acts as a path for the distribution of food

PHLOEMS > PHLOEM

PHLOMIS n plant of Phlomis genus

PHLOMISES > PHLOMIS

PHLORIZIN n chemical found in root bark of fruit trees

PHLOX n flowering garden plant

PHLOXES > PHLOX

PHLYCTENA n small blister, vesicle, or pustule

PHO n Vietnamese noodle soup

PHOBIA n intense and unreasoning fear or dislike

PHOBIAS > PHOBIA

PHOBIC adj of, relating to, or arising from a phobia ▷ n person suffering from a phobia

PHOBICS > PHOBIC

PHOBISM n phobia

PHOBISMS > PHOBISM

PHOBIST > PHOBISM

PHOBISTS > PHOBISM

PHOCA n genus of seals

PHOCAE > PHOCA

PHOCAS > PHOCA

PHOCINE adj of, relating to, or resembling a seal

PHOCOMELY n congenital deformity resulting from prenatal interference with the development of the fetal limbs, characterized esp by short stubby hands or feet attached close to the body

PHOEBE n greyish-brown North American flycatcher

PHOEBES > PHOEBE

PHOEBUS n sun

PHOEBUSES > PHOEBUS

PHOENIX n legendary bird said to set fire to itself and rise anew from its ashes

PHOENIXES > PHOENIX

PHOH variant of > FOH

PHOLADES > PHOLAS

PHOLAS n type of bivalve mollusc

PHON n unit of loudness

PHONAL adj relating to voice

PHONATE vb articulate speech sounds

PHONATED > PHONATE

PHONATES > PHONATE

PHONATHON n telephone-based fund-raising campaign

PHONATING > PHONATE

PHONATION > PHONATE

PHONATORY > PHONATE

PHONE vb telephone ▷ n single uncomplicated speech sound

PHONECAM n digital camera incorporated in a mobile phone

PHONECAMS > PHONECAM

PHONECARD n card used to operate certain public telephones

PHONED > PHONE

PHONEME n one of the set of speech sounds in a language

PHONEMES > PHONEME

PHONEMIC adj of or relating to the phoneme

PHONEMICS n classification and analysis of the phonemes of a language

PHONER n person making a telephone call

PHONERS > PHONER

PHONES > PHONE

PHONETIC adj of speech sounds

PHONETICS n science of speech sounds

PHONETISE same as > PHONETIZE

PHONETISM n phonetic writing

PHONETIST n person who advocates or uses a system of phonetic spelling

PHONETIZE vb represent by phonetic signs

PHONEY adj not genuine ▷ n phoney person or thing ▷ vb fake

PHONEYED > PHONEY

PHONEYING > PHONEY

PHONEYS > PHONEY

PHONIC > PHONICS

PHONICS n method of teaching people to read

PHONIED > PHONY

PHONIER > PHONY

PHONIES > PHONY

PHONIEST > PHONY

PHONILY > PHONY

PHONINESS > PHONY

PHONING > PHONE

PHONMETER n instrument measuring sound levels

PHONO n phonograph

PHONOGRAM n any written symbol standing for a sound, syllable, morpheme, or word

PHONOLITE n fine-grained volcanic igneous rock consisting of alkaline feldspars and nepheline

PHONOLOGY n study of the speech sounds in a language

PHONON n quantum of vibrational energy

PHONONS > PHONON

PHONOPORE n device for conveying sound

PHONOS > PHONO

PHONOTYPE n letter or symbol representing a sound

PHONOTYPY n transcription of speech into phonetic symbols

PHONS > PHON

PHONY vb fake

PHONYING > PHONY

PHOOEY interj exclamation of scorn or contempt

PHORATE n type of insecticide

PHORATES > PHORATE

PHORESIES > PHORESY

PHORESY n association in which one animal clings to another to ensure movement from place to place

PHORETIC adj relating to phoresy

PHORMINX n ancient Greek stringed instrument

PHORMIUM n New Zealand plant

PHORMIUMS > PHORMIUM

PHORONID n small wormlike marine animal

PHORONIDS > PHORONID

PHOS > PHO

PHOSGENE n poisonous gas used in warfare

PHOSGENES > PHOSGENE

PHOSPHATE n compound of phosphorus

PHOSPHENE n sensation of light caused by pressure on the eyelid of a closed eye or by other mechanical or electrical interference with the visual system

PHOSPHID same as > PHOSPHIDE

PHOSPHIDE n any compound of phosphorus with another element, esp a more electropositive element

PHOSPHIDS > PHOSPHID

PHOSPHIN same as > PHOSPHINE

PHOSPHINE n colourless flammable gas that is slightly soluble in water and has a strong fishy odour

PHOSPHINS > PHOSPHIN

PHOSPHITE n any salt or ester of phosphorous acid

PHOSPHOR n synthetic fluorescent or phosphorescent substance

PHOSPHORE same as > PHOSPHOR

PHOSPHORI n plural of phosphorus

PHOSPHORS > PHOSPHOR

PHOSSY adj as in phossy jaw gangrenous condition of the lower jawbone

PHOT n unit of illumination

PHOTIC adj of or concerned with light

PHOTICS n science of light

PHOTINIA n genus of garden plants

PHOTINIAS > PHOTINIA

PHOTINO n hypothetical elementary particle

PHOTINOS > PHOTINO

PHOTISM n sensation of light or colour caused by stimulus of another sense

PHOTISMS > PHOTISM

PHOTO n photograph ▷ vb take a photograph of

PHOTOBLOG n blog in which the main content consists of photographs ▷ vb keep a photoblog

PHOTOBOMB vb intrude into the background of a photograph without the subject's knowledge

PHOTOCALL n occasion when people have their photograph taken together

PHOTOCARD n identity card containing a photograph of the bearer

PHOTOCELL n cell which produces a current or voltage when exposed to light or other electromagnetic radiation

P

PHOTOCOPY n photographic reproduction ▷ vb make a photocopy of

PHOTODISK n computer disk that contains photographs

PHOTOED > PHOTO

PHOTOFIT n combining of photographs of facial features into a composite picture of a face

PHOTOFITS > PHOTOFIT

PHOTOG n photograph

PHOTOGEN same as > PHOTOGENE

PHOTOGENE n afterimage

PHOTOGENS > PHOTOGEN

PHOTOGENY n photography

PHOTOGRAM n picture, usually abstract, produced on a photographic material without the use of a camera, as by placing an object on the material and exposing to light

PHOTOGS > PHOTOG

PHOTOING > PHOTO

PHOTOLYSE vb cause to undergo photolysis

PHOTOLYZE same as > PHOTOLYSE

PHOTOMAP n map constructed by adding grid lines, place names, etc, to aerial photographs ▷ vb map (an area) using aerial photography

PHOTOMAPS > PHOTOMAP

PHOTOMASK n material on which etching pattern for integrated circuit is drawn

PHOTON n quantum of electromagnetic radiation energy

PHOTONIC > PHOTON

PHOTONICS n study and design of devices and systems, such as optical fibres, that depend on the transmission, modulation, or amplification of streams of photons

PHOTONS > PHOTON

PHOTOPHIL n light-seeking organism

PHOTOPIA n normal adaptation of the eye to light

PHOTOPIAS > PHOTOPIA

PHOTOPIC > PHOTOPIA

PHOTOPLAY n play filmed as movie

PHOTOPSIA n appearance of flashes due to retinal irritation

PHOTOPSY same as > PHOTOPSIA

PHOTOS > PHOTO

PHOTOSCAN n photographic scan

PHOTOSET vb set (type matter) by photosetting

PHOTOSETS > PHOTOSET

PHOTOSHOP vb edit or alter a picture digitally, usu with Adobe Photoshop

PHOTOSTAT n copy made by photocopying machine ▷ vb make a photostat copy (of)

PHOTOTAXY n movement of an entire organism in response to light

PHOTOTUBE n type of photocell in which radiation falling on a photocathode causes electrons to flow to an anode and thus produce an electric current

PHOTOTYPE n printing plate produced by photography ▷ vb reproduce (an illustration) using a phototype

PHOTOTYPY n process of producing phototypes

PHOTS > PHOT

PHPHT interj expressing irritation or reluctance

PHRASAL adj of, relating to, or composed of phrases

PHRASALLY > PHRASAL

PHRASE n group of words forming a unit of meaning, esp within a sentence ▷ vb express in words

PHRASED > PHRASE

PHRASEMAN n coiner of phrases

PHRASEMEN > PHRASEMAN

PHRASER > PHRASE

PHRASERS > PHRASE

PHRASES > PHRASE

PHRASIER > PHRASY

PHRASIEST > PHRASY

PHRASING n exact words used to say or write something

PHRASINGS > PHRASING

PHRASY adj containing phrases

PHRATRAL > PHRATRY

PHRATRIC > PHRATRY

PHRATRIES > PHRATRY

PHRATRY n group of people within a tribe who have a common ancestor

PHREAK vb hack into a telecommunications system

PHREAKED > PHREAK

PHREAKER > PHREAK

PHREAKERS > PHREAK

PHREAKING > PHREAK

PHREAKS > PHREAK

PHREATIC adj of or relating to ground water occurring below the water table

PHRENESES > PHRENESIS

PHRENESIS n mental confusion

PHRENETIC obsolete spelling of > FRENETIC

PHRENIC adj of or relating to the diaphragm ▷ n (a nerve, blood vessel, etc) located in the diaphragm

PHRENICS > PHRENIC

PHRENISM n belief in non-physical life force

PHRENISMS > PHRENISM

PHRENITIC > PHRENITIS

PHRENITIS n state of frenzy

PHRENSIED > PHRENSY

PHRENSIES > PHRENSY

PHRENSY obsolete spelling of > FRENZY

PHRENTICK obsolete spelling of > PHRENETIC

PHRYGANA another name for > GARIGUE

PHRYGANAS > PHRYGANA

PHT same as > PHPHT

PHTHALATE n salt or ester of phthalic acid

PHTHALEIN n any of a class of organic compounds obtained by the reaction of phthalic anhydride with a phenol and used in dyes

PHTHALIC adj as in phthalic anhydride white crystalline substance used mainly in producing dyestuffs

PHTHALIN n colourless compound formed by reduction of phthalein

PHTHALINS > PHTHALIN

PHTHISES > PHTHISIS

PHTHISIC adj relating to or affected with phthisis ▷ n person suffering from phthisis

PHTHISICS > PHTHISIC

PHTHISIS n any disease that causes wasting of the body, esp pulmonary tuberculosis

PHUT vb make muffled explosive sound

PHUTS > PHUT

PHUTTED > PHUT

PHUTTING > PHUT

PHWOAH same as > PHWOAR

PHWOAR interj expression of attraction

PHYCOCYAN n type of protein found in some algae

PHYCOLOGY n study of algae

PHYLA > PHYLUM

PHYLACTIC adj defending or protecting against disease

PHYLAE > PHYLE

PHYLAR > PHYLUM

PHYLARCH n chief of tribe

PHYLARCHS > PHYLARCH

PHYLARCHY > PHYLARCH

PHYLAXIS n protection against infection

PHYLE n tribe or clan of an ancient Greek people

PHYLESES > PHYLESIS

PHYLESIS n evolutionary events that modify taxon without causing speciation

PHYLETIC adj of or relating to the evolution of a species or group of organisms

PHYLETICS n study of the evolution of species

PHYLIC > PHYLE

PHYLLARY n bract subtending flower head of composite plant

PHYLLID n leaf of a liverwort or moss

PHYLLIDS > PHYLLID

PHYLLITE n compact lustrous metamorphic rock

PHYLLITES > PHYLLITE

PHYLLITIC > PHYLLITE

PHYLLO variant of > FILO

PHYLLODE n flattened leafstalk that resembles and functions as a leaf

PHYLLODES > PHYLLODE

PHYLLODIA > PHYLLODE

PHYLLODY n abnormal development of leaves from parts of flower

PHYLLOID adj resembling a leaf ▷ n leaf-like organ

PHYLLOIDS > PHYLLOID

PHYLLOME n leaf or a leaflike organ

PHYLLOMES > PHYLLOME

PHYLLOMIC > PHYLLOME

PHYLLOPOD n crustacean with leaf-like appendages

PHYLLOS > PHYLLO

PHYLOGENY n sequence of events involved in the evolution of a species, genus, etc

PHYLON n tribe

PHYLUM n major taxonomic division of animals and plants

PHYSALIA n Portuguese man-of-war

PHYSALIAS > PHYSALIA

PHYSALIS n strawberry tomato

PHYSED n physical education

PHYSEDS > PHYSED

PHYSES > PHYSIS

PHYSETER n machine for filtering

PHYSETERS > PHYSETER

PHYSIATRY n treatment of injury by physical means

PHYSIC n medicine or drug, esp a cathartic or purge ▷ vb treat (a patient) with medicine

PHYSICAL adj of the body, as contrasted with the mind or spirit

PHYSICALS pl n commodities that can be purchased and used, as opposed to those bought and sold in a futures market

PHYSICIAN n doctor of medicine

PHYSICISM n belief in the physical as opposed to the spiritual

PHYSICIST n person skilled in or studying physics

PHYSICKED > PHYSIC

PHYSICKY > PHYSIC

PHYSICS n science of the properties of matter and energy

PHYSIO n physiotherapist

PHYSIOS > PHYSIO

PHYSIQUE n person's bodily build and muscular development

PHYSIQUED adj having particular physique

PHYSIQUES > PHYSIQUE

PHYSIS n part of bone responsible for lengthening

PHYTANE n hydrocarbon found in fossilised plant remains

PHYTANES > PHYTANE

PHYTIN n substance from plants used as an energy supplement

PHYTINS > PHYTIN

PHYTOGENY n branch of botany that is concerned with the detailed description of plants

PHYTOID adj resembling plant

PHYTOL n alcohol used to synthesize some vitamins

PHYTOLITH n microscopic particle in plants

PHYTOLOGY rare name for > BOTANY

PHYTOLS > PHYTOL

PHYTON n unit of plant structure

PHYTONIC > PHYTON

PHYTONS > PHYTON

PHYTOSES > PHYTOSIS

PHYTOSIS n disease caused by vegetable parasite

PHYTOTOMY n dissection of plants

PHYTOTRON n building in which plants can be grown on a large scale, under controlled conditions

PI n sixteenth letter in the Greek alphabet ▷ vb spill and mix (set type) indiscriminately

PIA n innermost of the three membranes that cover the brain and the spinal cord

PIACEVOLE adv to be performed in playful manner

PIACULAR adj making expiation for a sacrilege

PIAFFE n passage done on the spot ▷ vb strut on the spot

PIAFFED > PIAFFE

PIAFFER > PIAFFE

PIAFFERS > PIAFFE

PIAFFES > PIAFFE

PIAFFING > PIAFFE

PIAL adj relating to pia mater

PIAN n contagious tropical skin disease

PIANETTE n small piano

PIANETTES > PIANETTE

PIANI > PIANO

PIANIC adj of piano

PIANINO n small upright piano

PIANINOS > PIANINO

PIANISM n technique, skill, or artistry in playing the piano

PIANISMS > PIANISM

PIANIST n person who plays the piano

PIANISTE variant of > PIANIST

PIANISTES > PIANISTE

PIANISTIC > PIANISM

PIANISTS > PIANIST

PIANO n musical instrument with strings which are struck by hammers worked by a keyboard ▷ adv quietly

PIANOLA n type of player piano

PIANOLAS > PIANOLA

PIANOLESS adj without a piano

PIANOLIST n person who plays the Pianola

PIANOS > PIANO

PIANS > PIAN

PIARIST n member of a Roman religious order

PIARISTS > PIARIST

PIAS > PIA

PIASABA same as > PIASSAVA

PIASABAS > PIASABA

PIASAVA same as > PIASSAVA

PIASAVAS > PIASAVA

PIASSABA same as > PIASSAVA

PIASSABAS > PIASSABA

PIASSAVA n South American palm tree

PIASSAVAS > PIASSAVA

PIASTER same as > PIASTRE

PIASTERS > PIASTER

PIASTRE n fractional monetary unit of Egypt, Lebanon, Sudan, South Sudan, and Syria

PIASTRES > PIASTRE

PIAZZA n square or marketplace, esp in Italy

PIAZZAS > PIAZZA

PIAZZE > PIAZZA

PIAZZIAN > PIAZZA

PIBAL n method of measuring wind

PIBALS > PIBAL

PIBROCH n form of bagpipe music

PIBROCHS > PIBROCH

PIC n photograph or illustration

PICA n abnormal craving to ingest substances

PICACHO n pointed solitary mountain

PICACHOS > PICACHO

PICADILLO n Mexican dish

PICADOR n mounted bullfighter with a lance

PICADORES > PICADOR

PICADORS > PICADOR

PICAL adj relating to pica

PICAMAR n hydrocarbon extract of beechwood tar

PICAMARS > PICAMAR

PICANINNY n offensive word for a Black child

PICANTE adj spicy

PICARA n female adventurer

PICARAS > PICARA

PICARIAN n tree-haunting bird

PICARIANS > PICARIAN

PICARO n roguish adventurer

PICAROON n adventurer or rogue

PICAROONS > PICAROON

PICAROS > PICARO

PICAS > PICA

PICAYUNE adj of small value or importance ▷ n any coin of little value, such as a five-cent piece

PICAYUNES > PICAYUNE

PICCADILL n high stiff collar

PICCANIN n offensive word for a Black child

PICCANINS > PICCANIN

PICCATA adj sautéed and served in a lemon sauce ▷ n dish of food sautéed and served in a lemon sauce

PICCATAS > PICCATA

PICCIES > PICCY

PICCOLO n small flute

PICCOLOS > PICCOLO

PICCY n picture or photograph

PICE n former Indian coin worth one sixty-fourth of a rupee

PICENE n type of hydrocarbon

PICENES > PICENE

PICEOUS adj of, relating to, or resembling pitch

PICHOLINE n variety of olive

PICHURIM n S American laurel tree

PICHURIMS > PICHURIM

PICIFORM adj relating to certain tree-haunting birds

PICINE adj relating to woodpeckers

PICK vb choose ▷ n choice

PICKABACK same as > PIGGYBACK

PICKABLE > PICK

PICKADIL same as > PICCADILL

PICKADILL same as > PICCADILL

PICKADILS > PICKADIL

PICKAPACK same as > PICKABACK

PICKAROON same as > PICAROON

PICKAX same as > PICKAXE

PICKAXE n large pick ▷ vb use a pickaxe on (earth, rocks, etc)

PICKAXED > PICKAXE

PICKAXES > PICKAXE

PICKAXING > PICKAXE

PICKBACK vb carry by piggyback

PICKBACKS > PICKBACK

PICKED > PICK

PICKEER vb make raid for booty

PICKEERED > PICKEER

PICKEERER > PICKEER

PICKEERS > PICKEER

PICKER n person or thing that picks

PICKEREL n North American freshwater game fish

PICKERELS > PICKEREL

PICKERIES > PICKERY

PICKERS > PICKER

PICKERY n petty theft

PICKET n person or group standing outside a workplace during a strike ▷ vb form a picket outside (a workplace)

PICKETED > PICKET

PICKETER > PICKET

PICKETERS > PICKET

PICKETING > PICKET

PICKETS > PICKET

PICKIER > PICKY

PICKIEST > PICKY

PICKILY > PICKY

PICKIN n small child

PICKINESS > PICKY

PICKING > PICK

PICKINGS pl n money easily acquired

PICKINS > PICKIN

PICKLE n food preserved in vinegar or salt water ▷ vb preserve in vinegar or salt water

PICKLED adj (of food) preserved

PICKLER > PICKLE

PICKLERS > PICKLE

PICKLES > PICKLE

PICKLING > PICKLE

PICKLOCK n person who picks locks, esp one who gains unlawful access to premises by this means

PICKLOCKS > PICKLOCK

PICKMAW n type of gull

PICKMAWS > PICKMAW

PICKNEY n (in Jamaica) child

PICKNEYS > PICKNEY

PICKOFF n baseball play

PICKOFFS > PICKOFF

PICKPROOF adj (of a lock) unable to be picked

PICKS > PICK

PICKTHANK n flatterer

PICKUP n small truck with an open body and low sides

PICKUPS > PICKUP

PICKWICK n tool for raising the short wick of an oil lamp

PICKWICKS > PICKWICK

PICKY adj fussy

PICLORAM n type of herbicide

PICLORAMS > PICLORAM

PICNIC n informal meal out of doors ▷ vb have a picnic

PICNICKED > PICNIC

PICNICKER > PICNIC

PICNICKY adj like a picnic

PICNICS > PICNIC

PICOCURIE n unit of radioactivity

PICOFARAD n unit of capacitance

PICOGRAM n trillionth of gram

PICOGRAMS > PICOGRAM

PICOLIN variant of > PICOLINE

PICOLINE n liquid derivative of pyridine found in bone oil and coal tar

PICOLINES > PICOLINE

PICOLINIC > PICOLINE

PICOLINS > PICOLIN

PICOMETER same as > PICOMETRE

PICOMETRE n trillionth fraction of metre

PICOMOLE n trillionth of a mole

PICOMOLES > PICOMOLE

PICONG n any teasing or satirical banter

PICONGS > PICONG

PICOT n any of pattern of small loops, as on lace ▷ vb decorate material with small loops

PICOTE adj (of material) picoted

PICOTED > PICOT

PICOTEE n type of carnation

PICOTEES > PICOTEE

PICOTING > PICOT

PICOTITE n dark-brown mineral

PICOTITES > PICOTITE

PICOTS > PICOT

PICOWAVE vb treat food with gamma waves

PICOWAVED > PICOWAVE

PICOWAVES > PICOWAVE

PICQUET vb provide early warning of attack

PICQUETED > PICQUET

PICQUETS > PICQUET

PICRA n powder of aloes and canella

PICRAS > PICRA

PICRATE n any salt or ester of picric acid

PICRATED adj containing picrate

PICRATES > PICRATE

PICRIC adj as in picric acid toxic sparingly soluble crystalline yellow acid

PICRITE n coarse-grained ultrabasic igneous rock

PICRITES > PICRITE

PICRITIC > PICRITE

PICS > PIC

PICTARNIE Scots word for > TERN

PICTOGRAM n picture or symbol standing for a word or group of words, as in written Chinese

PICTORIAL adj of or in painting or pictures ▷ n newspaper etc with many pictures

PICTURAL n picture

PICTURALS > PICTURAL

PICTURE n drawing or painting ▷ vb visualize, imagine

PICTURED > PICTURE

PICTURES > PICTURE

PICTURING > PICTURE

PICTURISE same as > PICTURIZE

PICTURIZE vb adorn with pictures

PICUL n unit of weight, used in China, Japan, and SE Asia

PICULET n small tropical woodpecker with a short tail

PICULETS > PICULET

PICULS > PICUL

PIDDLE vb urinate

PIDDLED > PIDDLE

PIDDLER > PIDDLE

PIDDLERS > PIDDLE

PIDDLES > PIDDLE

PIDDLIER > PIDDLY

PIDDLIEST > PIDDLY

PIDDLING adj small or unimportant

PIDDLY adj trivial

PIDDOCK n marine bivalve that bores into rock, clay, or wood

PIDDOCKS > PIDDOCK

PIDGEON variant of > PIDGIN

PIDGEONS > PIDGEON

PIDGIN n language made up of elements of other languages

PIDGINISE same as > PIDGINIZE

PIDGINIZE vb create pidgin language

PIDGINS > PIDGIN

PIE n dish of meat, fruit, etc baked in pastry

PIEBALD adj (horse) with irregular black-and-white markings ▷ n black-and-white horse

PIEBALDS > PIEBALD

PIECE n separate bit or part

PIECED > PIECE

PIECELESS > PIECE

PIECEMEAL adv bit by bit ▷ adj fragmentary or unsystematic

PIECEN vb join broken threads

PIECENED > PIECEN

PIECENER > PIECEN

PIECENERS > PIECEN

PIECENING > PIECEN

PIECENS > PIECEN

PIECER n person who mends, repairs, or joins something

PIECERS > PIECER

PIECES > PIECE

PIECEWISE adv with respect to number of discrete pieces

PIECEWORK n work paid for according to the quantity produced

PIECING > PIECE

PIECINGS > PIECE

PIECRUST n pastry used for making pies

PIECRUSTS > PIECRUST

PIED > PI

PIEDFORT n coin thicker than normal

PIEDFORTS > PIEDFORT

PIEDISH n container for baking pies

PIEDISHES > PIEDISH

PIEDMONT adj (of glaciers, plains, etc) formed or situated at the foot of a mountain or mountain range ▷ n gentle slope leading from mountains to flat land

PIEDMONTS > PIEDMONT

PIEDNESS n state of being pied

PIEFORT same as > PIEDFORT

PIEFORTS > PIEFORT

PIEHOLE n person's mouth

PIEHOLES > PIEHOLE

PIEING n act of pushing a pie into a person's face

PIEINGS > PIEING

PIEMAN n seller of pies

PIEMEN > PIEMAN

PIEND n salient angle

PIENDS > PIEND

PIEPLANT n rhubarb

PIEPLANTS > PIEPLANT

PIEPOWDER n former court for dealing with certain disputes

PIER n platform on stilts sticking out into the sea

PIERAGE n accommodation for ships at piers

PIERAGES > PIERAGE

PIERCE vb make a hole in or through with a sharp instrument

PIERCED > PIERCE

PIERCER > PIERCE

PIERCERS > PIERCE

PIERCES > PIERCE

PIERCING adj (of a sound) shrill and high-pitched ▷ n art or practice of piercing body parts for the insertion of jewellery

PIERCINGS > PIERCING

PIERHEAD n end of a pier farthest from the shore

PIERHEADS > PIERHEAD

PIERID n type of butterfly

PIERIDINE adj relating to the family Pieridae of butterflies, that includes the whites, brimstones, and sulphurs

PIERIDS > PIERID

PIERIS n American or Asiatic shrub

PIERISES > PIERIS

PIEROG same as > PIROG

PIEROGEN > PIEROG

PIEROGI n Polish dumpling

PIEROGIES > PIEROGI

PIEROGS > PIEROG

PIERRETTE n female pierrot

PIERROT n clown or masquerader with a whitened face

PIERROTS > PIERROT

PIERS > PIER

PIERST archaic spelling of > PIERCED

PIERT n small plant with small greenish flowers

PIERTS > PIERT

PIES > PIE

PIET n magpie

PIETA n sculpture, painting, or drawing of the dead Christ, supported by the Virgin Mary

PIETAS > PIETA

PIETIES > PIETY

PIETISM n exaggerated piety

PIETISMS > PIETISM

PIETIST > PIETISM

PIETISTIC > PIETISM

PIETISTS > PIETISM

PIETS > PIET

PIETY n deep devotion to God and religion

PIEZO adj piezoelectric

PIFFERARI > PIFFERARO

PIFFERARO n player of piffero

PIFFERO n small rustic flute

PIFFEROS > PIFFERO

PIFFLE n nonsense ▷ vb talk or behave feebly

PIFFLED > PIFFLE

PIFFLER n talker of nonsense

PIFFLERS > PIFFLER

PIFFLES > PIFFLE

PIFFLING adj worthless

PIG n animal kept and killed for pork, ham, and bacon ▷ vb eat greedily

PIGBOAT n submarine

PIGBOATS > PIGBOAT

PIGEON n bird with a heavy body and short legs ▷ vb pigeonhole

PIGEONED > PIGEON

PIGEONING > PIGEON

PIGEONITE n brownish mineral

PIGEONRY n loft for keeping pigeons

PIGEONS > PIGEON

PIGFACE n creeping succulent plant

PIGFACES > PIGFACE

PIGFEED n food for pigs

PIGFEEDS > PIGFEED

PIGFISH n grunting fish of the North American Atlantic coast

PIGFISHES > PIGFISH

PIGGED > PIG

PIGGERIES > PIGGERY

PIGGERY n place for keeping and breeding pigs

PIGGIE same as > PIGGY

PIGGIER > PIGGY

PIGGIES > PIGGY

PIGGIEST > PIGGY

PIGGIN n small wooden bucket or tub

PIGGINESS > PIGGY

PIGGING > PIG

PIGGINGS > PIG

PIGGINS > PIGGIN

PIGGISH adj like a pig, esp in appetite or manners

PIGGISHLY > PIGGISH

PIGGY n child's word for a pig ▷ adj like a pig

PIGGYBACK n ride on someone's shoulders ▷ adv carried on someone's shoulders ▷ adj on the back and shoulders of another person ▷ vb give (a person) a piggyback on one's back and shoulders

PIGHEADED adj stupidly stubborn

PIGHT vb pierce

PIGHTED > PIGHT

PIGHTING > PIGHT

PIGHTLE n small enclosure

PIGHTLES > PIGHTLE

PIGHTS > PIGHT

PIGLET n young pig

PIGLETS > PIGLET

PIGLIKE > PIG

PIGLING n young pig

PIGLINGS > PIGLING

PIGMAEAN same as > PYGMAEAN

PIGMAN n male pig farmer

PIGMEAN same as > PYGMAEAN

PIGMEAT *less common name for* > PORK

PIGMEATS > PIGMEAT

PIGMEN > PIGMAN

PIGMENT *n* colouring matter, paint or dye ▷ *vb* colour with pigment

PIGMENTAL > PIGMENT

PIGMENTED > PIGMENT

PIGMENTS > PIGMENT

PIGMIES > PIGMY

PIGMOID *adj* of pygmies ▷ *n* pygmy

PIGMOIDS > PIGMOID

PIGMY *same as* > PYGMY

PIGNERATE *vb* pledge or pawn

PIGNOLI *same as* > PIGNOLIA

PIGNOLIA *n* edible seed of nut pine

PIGNOLIAS > PIGNOLIA

PIGNOLIS > PIGNOLI

PIGNORA > PIGNUS

PIGNORATE *same as* > PIGNERATE

PIGNUS *n* pawn or pledge

PIGNUT *n* bitter nut of hickory trees

PIGNUTS > PIGNUT

PIGOUT *n* binge

PIGOUTS > PIGOUT

PIGPEN *same as* > PIGSTY

PIGPENS > PIGPEN

PIGS > PIG

PIGSCONCE *n* foolish person

PIGSKIN *n* skin of the domestic pig ▷ *adj* made of pigskin

PIGSKINS > PIGSKIN

PIGSNEY *same as* > PIGSNY

PIGSNEYS > PIGSNEY

PIGSNIE *same as* > PIGSNY

PIGSNIES > PIGSNIE

PIGSNY *n* former pet name for girl

PIGSTICK *vb* (esp in India) hunt and spear wild boar, esp from horseback

PIGSTICKS > PIGSTICK

PIGSTIES > PIGSTY

PIGSTUCK > PIGSTICK

PIGSTY *same as* > PIGPEN

PIGSWILL *n* waste food or other edible matter fed to pigs

PIGSWILLS > PIGSWILL

PIGTAIL *n* plait of hair hanging from the back or either side of the head

PIGTAILED > PIGTAIL

PIGTAILS > PIGTAIL

PIGWASH *n* wet feed for pigs

PIGWASHES > PIGWASH

PIGWEED *n* coarse North American weed

PIGWEEDS > PIGWEED

PIHOIHOI *n* variety of New Zealand pipit

PIHOIHOIS > PIHOIHOI

PIING > PI

PIKA *n* burrowing mammal

PIKAKE *n* type of Asian vine

PIKAKES > PIKAKE

PIKAS > PIKA

PIKAU *n* pack, knapsack, or rucksack

PIKAUS > PIKAU

PIKE *n* large predatory freshwater fish ▷ *vb* stab or pierce using a pike ▷ *adj* (of the body position of a diver) bent at the hips but with the legs straight

PIKED > PIKE

PIKELET *n* small thick pancake

PIKELETS > PIKELET

PIKELIKE *adj* like a pike

PIKEMAN *n* (formerly) soldier armed with a pike

PIKEMEN > PIKEMAN

PIKEPERCH *n* pikelike freshwater teleost fish

PIKER *n* shirker

PIKERS > PIKER

PIKES > PIKE

PIKESTAFF *n* wooden handle of a pike

PIKEY *n* in British English, derogatory word for gypsy or vagrant

PIKEYS > PIKEY

PIKI *n* bread made from blue cornmeal

PIKING > PIKE

PIKINGS > PIKE

PIKIS > PIKI

PIKUL *same as* > PICUL

PIKULS > PIKUL

PILA *n* pillar-like anatomical structure

PILAE > PILA

PILAF *same as* > PILAU

PILAFF *same as* > PILAU

PILAFFS > PILAFF

PILAFS > PILAF

PILAO *same as* > PILAU

PILAOS > PILAO

PILAR *adj* relating to hair

PILASTER *n* square column, usu set in a wall

PILASTERS > PILASTER

PILAU *n* Middle Eastern dish

PILAUS > PILAU

PILAW *same as* > PILAU

PILAWS > PILAW

PILCH *n* outer garment, originally one made of skin

PILCHARD *n* small edible sea fish of the herring family

PILCHARDS > PILCHARD

PILCHER *n* scabbard for sword

PILCHERS > PILCHER

PILCHES > PILCH

PILCORN *n* type of oat

PILCORNS > PILCORN

PILCROW *n* paragraph mark

PILCROWS > PILCROW

PILE *n* number of things lying on top of each other ▷ *vb* collect into a pile

PILEA *n* plant which releases a cloud of pollen when shaken

PILEAS > PILEA

PILEATE *adj* (of birds) having a crest

PILEATED *same as* > PILEATE

PILED > PILE

PILEI > PILEUS

PILELESS > PILE

PILEOUS *adj* hairy

PILER *n* placer of things on pile

PILERS > PILER

PILES *pl n* swollen veins in the rectum, haemorrhoids

PILEUM *n* top of a bird's head

PILEUP *n* multiple collision of vehicles

PILEUPS > PILEUP

PILEUS *n* upper cap-shaped part of a mushroom

PILEWORK *n* construction built from heavy stakes or cylinders

PILEWORKS > PILEWORK

PILEWORT *n* plant used to treat piles

PILEWORTS > PILEWORT

PILFER *vb* steal in small quantities

PILFERAGE *n* act or practice of stealing small quantities or articles

PILFERED > PILFER

PILFERER > PILFER

PILFERERS > PILFER

PILFERIES > PILFERY

PILFERING > PILFER

PILFERS > PILFER

PILFERY *n* theft

PILGARLIC *n* bald head or a man with a bald head

PILGRIM *n* person who journeys to a holy place ▷ *vb* travel as a pilgrim

PILGRIMED > PILGRIM

PILGRIMER *n* one who undertakes a pilgrimage

PILGRIMS > PILGRIM

PILI *n* Philippine tree with edible seeds resembling almonds

PILIER > PILY

PILIEST > PILY

PILIFORM *adj* resembling a long hair

PILING *n* act of driving piles

PILINGS > PILING

PILINUT *n* type of nut found in the Philippines

PILINUTS > PILINUT

PILIS > PILI

PILL *n* small ball of medicine swallowed whole ▷ *vb* peel or skin (something)

PILLAGE *vb* steal property by violence in war ▷ *n* violent seizure of goods, esp in war

PILLAGED > PILLAGE

PILLAGER > PILLAGE

PILLAGERS > PILLAGE

PILLAGES > PILLAGE

PILLAGING *n* act of pillaging

PILLAR *n* upright post, usu supporting a roof ▷ *vb* provide or support with pillars

PILLARED > PILLAR

PILLARING > PILLAR

PILLARIST *n* recluse who sat on high pillar

PILLARS > PILLAR

PILLAU *same as* > PILAU

PILLAUS > PILLAU

PILLBOX *n* small box for pills

PILLBOXES > PILLBOX

PILLBUG *n* type of woodlouse

PILLBUGS > PILLBUG

PILLED > PILL

PILLHEAD *n* person addicted to pills

PILLHEADS > PILLHEAD

PILLICOCK *n* penis

PILLIE *n* pilchard

PILLIES > PILLIE

PILLING > PILL

PILLINGS > PILL

PILLION *n* seat for a passenger behind the rider of a motorcycle ▷ *adv* on a pillion ▷ *vb* ride pillion

PILLIONED > PILLION

PILLIONS > PILLION

PILLOCK *n* stupid or annoying person

PILLOCKS > PILLOCK

PILLORIED > PILLORY

PILLORIES > PILLORY

PILLORISE *same as* > PILLORIZE

PILLORIZE *vb* put in pillory

PILLORY *n* frame in which an offender was locked and exposed to public abuse ▷ *vb* ridicule publicly

PILLOW *n* stuffed cloth bag for supporting the head in bed ▷ *vb* rest as if on a pillow

PILLOWED > PILLOW

PILLOWIER > PILLOWY

PILLOWING > PILLOW

PILLOWS > PILLOW

PILLOWY *adj* like a pillow

PILLS > PILL

PILLWORM *n* worm that rolls up spirally

PILLWORMS > PILLWORM

PILLWORT *n* small Eurasian water fern

PILLWORTS > PILLWORT

PILOMOTOR *adj* causing movement of hairs

PILONIDAL *adj* of the crease above the buttocks

PILOSE *adj* covered with fine soft hairs

PILOSITY > PILOSE

PILOT *n* person qualified to fly an aircraft or spacecraft ▷ *adj* experimental and preliminary ▷ *vb* act as the pilot of

PILOTAGE *n* act of piloting an aircraft or ship

PILOTAGES > PILOTAGE

PILOTED > PILOT

PILOTFISH *n* fish that accompanies sharks

PILOTING *n* navigational handling of a ship near land

PILOTINGS > PILOTING

PILOTIS *pl n* posts raising a building up from the ground

PILOTLESS > PILOT

PILOTMAN *n* railway worker who directs trains through hazardous stretches of track

PILOTMEN > PILOTMAN

PILOTS > PILOT

PILOUS *same as* > PILOSE

PILOW *same as* > PILAU

PILOWS > PILOW
PILSENER same as > PILSNER
PILSENERS > PILSENER
PILSNER n type of pale beer with a strong flavour of hops
PILSNERS > PILSNER
PILULA n pill
PILULAE > PILULA
PILULAR > PILULE
PILULAS > PILULA
PILULE n small pill
PILULES > PILULE
PILUM n ancient Roman javelin
PILUS > PILI
PILY adj like wool or pile
PIMA n type of cotton
PIMAS > PIMA
PIMENT n wine flavoured with spices
PIMENTO same as > PIMIENTO
PIMENTON n smoked chilli powder
PIMENTONS > PIMENTON
PIMENTOS > PIMENTO
PIMENTS > PIMENT
PIMIENTO n Spanish pepper with a red fruit used as a vegetable
PIMIENTOS > PIMIENTO
PIMP n person who gets customers for a prostitute ▷ vb embellish
PIMPED > PIMP
PIMPERNEL n wild plant with small star-shaped flowers
PIMPING > PIMP
PIMPINGS > PIMPING
PIMPLE n small pus-filled spot on the skin
PIMPLED > PIMPLE
PIMPLES > PIMPLE
PIMPLIER > PIMPLE
PIMPLIEST > PIMPLE
PIMPLY > PIMPLE
PIMPS > PIMP
PIN n short thin piece of stiff wire with a point and head, for fastening things ▷ vb fasten with a pin
PINA n cone of silver amalgam
PINACEOUS adj relating to a family of conifers with needle-like leaves which includes the pine, spruce, fir, larch, and cedar
PINACOID n pair of opposite parallel faces of crystal
PINACOIDS > PINACOID
PINAFORE n apron
PINAFORED > PINAFORE
PINAFORES > PINAFORE
PINAKOID same as > PINACOID
PINAKOIDS > PINAKOID
PINANG n areca tree
PINANGS > PINANG
PINAS > PINA
PINASTER n Mediterranean pine tree
PINASTERS > PINASTER

PINATA n papier-mâché party decoration filled with sweets
PINATAS > PINATA
PINBALL vb ricochet
PINBALLED > PINBALL
PINBALLS > PINBALL
PINBOARD n cork board for pinning notices, messages etc on
PINBOARDS > PINBOARD
PINBONE n part of sirloin
PINBONES > PINBONE
PINCASE n case for holding pins
PINCASES > PINCASE
PINCER vb grip with pincers
PINCERED > PINCER
PINCERING > PINCER
PINCERS pl n tool consisting of two hinged arms, for gripping
PINCH vb squeeze between finger and thumb ▷ n act of pinching
PINCHBECK n alloy of zinc and copper, used as imitation gold ▷ adj sham or cheap
PINCHBUG n type of crab
PINCHBUGS > PINCHBUG
PINCHCOCK n clamp used to compress a flexible tube to control the flow of fluid through it
PINCHECK n small check woven into fabric
PINCHECKS > PINCHECK
PINCHED > PINCH
PINCHER > PINCH
PINCHERS > PINCH
PINCHES > PINCH
PINCHFIST n mean person
PINCHGUT n miserly person
PINCHGUTS > PINCHGUT
PINCHING > PINCH
PINCHINGS > PINCH
PINCURL n curl secured by a hairpin
PINCURLS > PINCURL
PINDAN n desert region of Western Australia
PINDANS > PINDAN
PINDAREE same as > PINDARI
PINDAREES > PINDAREE
PINDARI n former irregular Indian horseman
PINDARIS > PINDARI
PINDER n person who impounds
PINDERS > PINDER
PINDLING adj peevish or fractious
PINDOWN n wrestling manoeuvre
PINDOWNS > PINDOWN
PINE n evergreen coniferous tree ▷ vb feel great longing (for)
PINEAL adj resembling a pine cone ▷ n pineal gland
PINEALS > PINEAL
PINEAPPLE n large tropical fruit with juicy yellow flesh and a hard skin
PINECONE n seed-producing structure of a pine tree

PINECONES > PINECONE
PINED > PINE
PINEDROPS n parasitic herb of pine trees
PINELAND n area covered with pine forest
PINELANDS > PINELAND
PINELIKE > PINE
PINENE n isomeric terpene found in many essential oils
PINENES > PINENE
PINERIES > PINERY
PINERY n place, esp a hothouse, where pineapples are grown
PINES > PINE
PINESAP n red herb of N America
PINESAPS > PINESAP
PINETA > PINETUM
PINETUM n area of land where pine trees are grown
PINEWOOD n wood of pine trees
PINEWOODS > PINEWOOD
PINEY > PINE
PINFALL another name for > FALL
PINFALLS > PINFALL
PINFISH n small porgy of the Atlantic
PINFISHES > PINFISH
PINFOLD n pound for stray cattle ▷ vb gather or confine in or as if in a pinfold
PINFOLDED > PINFOLD
PINFOLDS > PINFOLD
PING n short high-pitched sound ▷ vb make such a noise
PINGED > PING
PINGER n device, esp a timer, that makes a pinging sound
PINGERS > PINGER
PINGING > PING
PINGLE vb enclose small area of ground
PINGLED > PINGLE
PINGLER > PINGLE
PINGLERS > PINGLE
PINGLES > PINGLE
PINGLING > PINGLE
PINGO n mound of earth or gravel formed in Arctic regions
PINGOES > PINGO
PINGOS > PINGO
PINGPONG n Australian football
PINGPONGS > PINGPONG
PINGRASS n weed with fernlike leaves
PINGS > PING
PINGUEFY vb become greasy or fat
PINGUID adj fatty, oily, or greasy
PINGUIN same as > PENGUIN
PINGUINS > PINGUIN
PINHEAD n head of a pin
PINHEADED adj stupid or silly
PINHEADS > PINHEAD
PINHOLE n small hole made with or as if with a pin

PINHOLES > PINHOLE
PINHOOKER n trader of young thoroughbred horses
PINIER > PINY
PINIES > PINY
PINIEST > PINY
PINING > PINE
PINION n bird's wing ▷ vb immobilize (someone) by tying or holding his or her arms
PINIONED > PINION
PINIONING > PINION
PINIONS > PINION
PINITE n greyish-green or brown mineral
PINITES > PINITE
PINITOL n compound found in pinewood
PINITOLS > PINITOL
PINK n pale reddish colour ▷ adj of the colour pink ▷ vb (of an engine) make a metallic noise because not working properly
PINKED > PINK
PINKEN vb turn pink
PINKENED > PINKEN
PINKENING > PINKEN
PINKENS > PINKEN
PINKER n something that pinks
PINKERS > PINKER
PINKERTON n private detective
PINKEST > PINK
PINKEY n type of ship
PINKEYE n acute inflammation of the conjunctiva of the eye
PINKEYES > PINKEYE
PINKEYS > PINKEY
PINKIE n little finger
PINKIER > PINKY
PINKIES > PINKIE
PINKIEST > PINKY
PINKINESS n quality of being pink
PINKING > PINK
PINKINGS > PINK
PINKISH > PINK
PINKLY > PINK
PINKNESS > PINK
PINKO n person regarded as mildly left-wing
PINKOES > PINKO
PINKOS > PINKO
PINKROOT n plant with red-and-yellow flowers and pink roots
PINKROOTS > PINKROOT
PINKS > PINK
PINKY adj of a pink colour
PINLESS adj without a pin
PINNA n external part of the ear
PINNACE n ship's boat
PINNACES > PINNACE
PINNACLE n highest point of fame or success ▷ vb set on or as if on a pinnacle
PINNACLED > PINNACLE
PINNACLES > PINNACLE
PINNAE > PINNA
PINNAL > PINNA
PINNAS > PINNA

PINNATE adj (of compound leaves) having leaflets growing opposite each other in pairs

PINNATED same as > PINNATE

PINNATELY > PINNATE

PINNATION > PINNATE

PINNED > PIN

PINNER n person or thing that pins

PINNERS > PINNER

PINNET n pinnacle

PINNETS > PINNET

PINNIE same as > PINNY

PINNIES > PINNIE

PINNING > PIN

PINNINGS > PIN

PINNIPED n aquatic placental mammal such as the seal, sea lion, walrus, etc

PINNIPEDE same as > PINNIPED

PINNIPEDS > PINNIPED

PINNOCK n small bird

PINNOCKS > PINNOCK

PINNOED adj held or bound by the arms

PINNULA same as > PINNULE

PINNULAE > PINNULA

PINNULAR > PINNULE

PINNULAS > PINNULA

PINNULATE > PINNULE

PINNULE n lobe of a leaflet of a pinnate compound leaf

PINNULES > PINNULE

PINNY informal or child's name for > PINAFORE

PINOCHLE n card game for two to four players similar to bezique

PINOCHLES > PINOCHLE

PINOCLE same as > PINOCHLE

PINOCLES > PINOCLE

PINOCYTIC adj of process of pinocytosis

PINOLE n flour made in the southwestern United States

PINOLES > PINOLE

PINON n low-growing pine

PINONES > PINON

PINONS > PINON

PINOT n any of several grape varieties

PINOTAGE n variety of red grape

PINOTAGES > PINOTAGE

PINOTS > PINOT

PINPOINT vb locate or identify exactly ▷ adj exact ▷ n insignificant or trifling thing

PINPOINTS > PINPOINT

PINPRICK n small irritation or annoyance ▷ vb puncture with or as if with a pin

PINPRICKS > PINPRICK

PINS > PIN

PINSCHER n breed of dog

PINSCHERS > PINSCHER

PINSETTER n device that sets pins in bowling alley

PINSPOT vb illuminate with a small spotlight

PINSPOTS > PINSPOT

PINSTRIPE n very narrow stripe in fabric

PINSWELL n small boil

PINSWELLS > PINSWELL

PINT n liquid measure, 1/8 gallon (.568 litre)

PINTA n pint of milk

PINTABLE n pinball machine

PINTABLES > PINTABLE

PINTADA same as > PINTADO

PINTADAS > PINTADA

PINTADERA n decorative stamp, usually made of clay, found in the Neolithic of the E Mediterranean and in many American cultures

PINTADO n species of seagoing petrel

PINTADOES > PINTADO

PINTADOS > PINTADO

PINTAIL n greyish-brown duck with a pointed tail

PINTAILED adj having tapered tail

PINTAILS > PINTAIL

PINTANO n tropical reef fish

PINTANOS > PINTANO

PINTAS > PINTA

PINTLE n pin or bolt forming the pivot of a hinge

PINTLES > PINTLE

PINTO adj marked with patches of white ▷ n pinto horse

PINTOES > PINTO

PINTOS > PINTO

PINTS > PINT

PINTSIZE same as > PINTSIZED

PINTSIZED adj very small

PINTUCK vb tuck with a narrow fold of fabric

PINTUCKED > PINTUCK

PINTUCKS > PINTUCK

PINUP n picture of a physically attractive person

PINUPS > PINUP

PINWALE n fabric with narrow ridges

PINWALES > PINWALE

PINWEED n herb with tiny flowers

PINWEEDS > PINWEED

PINWHEEL n cogwheel whose teeth are formed by small pins

PINWHEELS > PINWHEEL

PINWORK n (in needlepoint lace) fine raised stitches

PINWORKS > PINWORK

PINWORM n parasitic nematode worm

PINWORMS > PINWORM

PINWRENCH n wrench with a projection to fit a hole

PINXIT vb (he or she) painted (it)

PINY variant of > PEONY

PINYIN n system of romanized spelling for the Chinese language

PINYINS > PINYIN

PINYON n low-growing pine

PINYONS > PINYON

PIOLET n type of ice axe

PIOLETS > PIOLET

PION n type of subatomic particle

PIONED adj abounding in marsh marigolds

PIONEER n explorer or early settler of a new country ▷ vb be the pioneer or leader of

PIONEERED > PIONEER

PIONEERS > PIONEER

PIONER obsolete spelling of > PIONEER

PIONERS > PIONER

PIONEY same as > PEONY

PIONEYS > PIONEY

PIONIC > PION

PIONIES > PIONY

PIONING n work of pioneers

PIONINGS > PIONING

PIONS > PION

PIONY same as > PEONY

PIOPIO n New Zealand thrush, thought to be extinct

PIOPIOS > PIOPIO

PIOSITIES > PIOSITY

PIOSITY n grandiose display of piety

PIOTED adj pied

PIOUS adj deeply religious, devout

PIOUSLY > PIOUS

PIOUSNESS > PIOUS

PIOY variant of > PEEOY

PIOYE variant of > PEEOY

PIOYES > PIOYE

PIOYS > PIOY

PIP n small seed in a fruit ▷ vb chirp

PIPA n tongueless S American toad

PIPAGE n pipes collectively

PIPAGES > PIPAGE

PIPAL same as > PEEPUL

PIPALS > PIPAL

PIPAS > PIPA

PIPE n tube for conveying liquid or gas ▷ vb play on a pipe

PIPEAGE same as > PIPAGE

PIPEAGES > PIPEAGE

PIPECLAY n fine white clay used in tobacco pipes ▷ vb whiten with pipeclay

PIPECLAYS > PIPECLAY

PIPED > PIPE

PIPEFISH n fish with a long tubelike snout and an elongated body

PIPEFUL n as much tobacco, etc as will fill a pipe

PIPEFULS > PIPEFUL

PIPELESS > PIPE

PIPELIKE > PIPE

PIPELINE n long pipe for transporting oil, water, etc

PIPELINED > PIPELINE

PIPELINES > PIPELINE

PIPER n player on a pipe or bagpipes

PIPERIC > PIPERINE

PIPERINE n crystalline insoluble alkaloid that is the active ingredient of pepper

PIPERINES > PIPERINE

PIPERONAL n white fragrant aldehyde used in flavourings, perfumery, and suntan lotions

PIPERS > PIPER

PIPES > PIPE

PIPESTEM n hollow stem of pipe

PIPESTEMS > PIPESTEM

PIPESTONE n variety of consolidated red clay used by Native Americans to make tobacco pipes

PIPET same as > PIPETTE

PIPETS > PIPET

PIPETTE n slender glass tube used to transfer or measure fluids ▷ vb transfer or measure out (a liquid) using a pipette

PIPETTED > PIPETTE

PIPETTES > PIPETTE

PIPETTING > PIPETTE

PIPEWORK n stops and flues on pipe organ

PIPEWORKS > PIPEWORK

PIPEWORT n perennial plant with a twisted flower stalk and a greenish-grey scaly flower head

PIPEWORTS > PIPEWORT

PIPI n edible mollusc often used as bait

PIPIER > PIPE

PIPIEST > PIPE

PIPINESS n material's suitability for use as pipe

PIPING n system of pipes

PIPINGLY > PIPING

PIPINGS > PIPING

PIPIS > PIPI

PIPISTREL n species of bat

PIPIT n small brownish songbird

PIPITS > PIPIT

PIPKIN same as > PIGGIN

PIPKINS > PIPKIN

PIPLESS > PIP

PIPPED > PIP

PIPPIER > PIPPY

PIPPIEST > PIPPY

PIPPIN n type of eating apple

PIPPING > PIP

PIPPINS > PIPPIN

PIPPY adj containing many pips

PIPS > PIP

PIPSQUEAK n insignificant or contemptible person

PIPUL n Indian fig tree

PIPULS > PIPUL

PIPY > PIPE

PIQUANCE same as > PIQUANT

PIQUANCES > PIQUANT

PIQUANCY > PIQUANT

PIQUANT adj having a pleasant spicy taste

PIQUANTLY > PIQUANT

PIQUE n feeling of hurt pride, baffled curiosity, or resentment ▷ vb hurt the pride of

PIQUED > PIQUE

PIQUES > PIQUE

PIQUET n card game for two ▷ vb play game of piquet

PIQUETED > PIQUET

PIQUETING > PIQUET

PIQUETS > PIQUET

P

PIQUILLO n variety of sweet red pepper
PIQUILLOS > PIQUILLO
PIQUING > PIQUE
PIR n Sufi master
PIRACETAM n drug used to treat muscle spasm
PIRACIES > PIRACY
PIRACY n robbery on the seas
PIRAGUA same as > PIROGUE
PIRAGUAS > PIRAGUA
PIRAI n large S American fish
PIRAIS > PIRAI
PIRANA same as > PIRANHA
PIRANAS > PIRANA
PIRANHA n fierce fish of tropical America
PIRANHAS > PIRANHA
PIRARUCU n large S American food fish
PIRARUCUS > PIRARUCU
PIRATE n sea robber ⊳ vb sell or reproduce (artistic work etc) illegally
PIRATED > PIRATE
PIRATES > PIRATE
PIRATIC > PIRATE
PIRATICAL > PIRATE
PIRATING n act of pirating
PIRATINGS > PIRATING
PIRAYA same as > PIRAI
PIRAYAS > PIRAYA
PIRIFORM adj shaped like pear
PIRL n ripple in water
PIRLICUE same as > PURLICUE
PIRLICUED > PIRLICUE
PIRLICUES > PIRLICUE
PIRLS > PIRL
PIRN n reel or bobbin
PIRNIE n stripy nightcap
PIRNIES > PIRNIE
PIRNIT adj striped
PIRNS > PIRN
PIROG n type of large Russian pie
PIROGEN n turnovers made from kneaded dough
PIROGHI > PIROG
PIROGI > PIROG
PIROGIES > PIROG
PIROGUE n any of various kinds of dugout canoes
PIROGUES > PIROGUE
PIROJKI same as > PIROSHKI
PIROPLASM n parasite of red blood cells
PIROQUE same as > PIROGUE
PIROQUES > PIROQUE
PIROSHKI same as > PIROZHKI
PIROUETTE n spinning turn balanced on the toes of one foot ⊳ vb perform a pirouette
PIROZHKI > PIROZHOK
PIROZHOK n small triangular pastry filled with meat, vegetables, etc
PIRS > PIR
PIS > PI
PISCARIES > PISCARY

PISCARY n place where fishing takes place
PISCATOR n fisherman
PISCATORS > PISCATOR
PISCATORY adj of or relating to fish, fishing, or fishermen
PISCATRIX n female angler
PISCIFORM adj having form of fish
PISCINA n stone basin where water used at Mass is poured away
PISCINAE > PISCINA
PISCINAL > PISCINA
PISCINAS > PISCINA
PISCINE n pond or pool
PISCINES > PISCINE
PISCIVORE n eater of fish
PISCO n S American brandy
PISCOS > PISCO
PISE n rammed earth or clay used to make floors or walls
PISES > PISE
PISH interj exclamation of impatience or contempt ⊳ vb make this exclamation at (someone or something)
PISHED > PISH
PISHEOG same as > PISHOGUE
PISHEOGS > PISHEOG
PISHER n Yiddish term for small boy
PISHERS > PISHER
PISHES > PISH
PISHING > PISH
PISHOGE same as > PISHOGUE
PISHOGES > PISHOGE
PISHOGUE n sorcery
PISHOGUES > PISHOGUE
PISIFORM adj resembling a pea ⊳ n small pealike bone on the ulnar side of the carpus
PISIFORMS > PISIFORM
PISKIES > PISKY
PISKY n Cornish fairy
PISMIRE archaic or dialect word for > ANT
PISMIRES > PISMIRE
PISO n peso of the Philippines
PISOLITE n sedimentary rock
PISOLITES > PISOLITE
PISOLITH same as > PISOLITE
PISOLITHS > PISOLITH
PISOLITIC > PISOLITE
PISOS > PISO
PISS vb vulgar slang word for urinate ⊳ n act of urinating
PISSANT n vulgar slang for an insignificant person
PISSANTS > PISSANT
PISSED adj slang word for drunk
PISSER n vulgar word meaning someone or something that pisses
PISSERS > PISSER
PISSES > PISS
PISSHEAD n vulgar slang for a drunkard

PISSHEADS > PISSHEAD
PISSHOLE n vulgar word for a hole made in soluble matter by urinating
PISSHOLES > PISSHOLE
PISSIER > PISSY
PISSIEST > PISSY
PISSING > PISS
PISSOIR n public urinal, usu enclosed by a wall or screen
PISSOIRS > PISSOIR
PISSY adj vulgar word meaning soiled with urine
PISTACHE n tree yielding pistachio nut
PISTACHES > PISTACHE
PISTACHIO n edible nut of a Mediterranean tree ⊳ adj of a yellowish-green colour
PISTAREEN n Spanish coin, used in the US and the West Indies until the 18th century
PISTE n ski slope
PISTED adj marked off into pistes
PISTES > PISTE
PISTIL n seed-bearing part of a flower
PISTILLAR adj relating to a pistil
PISTILS > PISTIL
PISTOL n short-barrelled handgun ⊳ vb shoot with a pistol
PISTOLE n gold coin formerly used in Europe
PISTOLED > PISTOL
PISTOLEER n person, esp a soldier, who is armed with or fires a pistol
PISTOLERO n shooter of pistols
PISTOLES > PISTOLE
PISTOLET n small pistol
PISTOLETS > PISTOLET
PISTOLIER n shooter of pistols
PISTOLING > PISTOL
PISTOLLED > PISTOL
PISTOLS > PISTOL
PISTON n cylindrical part in an engine that slides to and fro in a cylinder
PISTONS > PISTON
PISTOU n French sauce
PISTOUS > PISTOU
PIT n deep hole in the ground ⊳ vb mark with small dents or scars
PITA n any of several agave plants yielding a strong fibre
PITAHAYA n any giant cactus of Central America and the SW United States
PITAHAYAS > PITAHAYA
PITAPAT adv with quick light taps ⊳ n such taps ⊳ vb make quick light taps or beats
PITAPATS > PITAPAT
PITARA variant of > PETARA
PITARAH variant of > PETARA
PITARAHS > PITARAH
PITARAS > PITARA
PITAS > PITA

PITAYA same as > PITAHAYA
PITAYAS > PITAYA
PITCH vb throw, hurl ⊳ n area marked out for playing sport
PITCHBEND n electronic device that enables a player to bend the pitch of a note being sounded on a synthesizer, usually with a pitch wheel, strip, or lever
PITCHED > PITCH
PITCHER n large jug with a narrow neck
PITCHERS > PITCHER
PITCHES > PITCH
PITCHFORK n large long-handled fork for lifting hay ⊳ vb thrust abruptly or violently
PITCHIER > PITCHY
PITCHIEST > PITCHY
PITCHILY > PITCHY
PITCHING > PITCH
PITCHINGS > PITCH
PITCHMAN n itinerant pedlar of small merchandise who operates from a stand at a fair, etc
PITCHMEN > PITCHMAN
PITCHOUT n type of baseball pitch
PITCHOUTS > PITCHOUT
PITCHPINE n large N American pine tree
PITCHPIPE n small one-note pipe used for tuning instruments
PITCHPOLE vb turn end over end
PITCHY adj full of or covered with pitch
PITEOUS adj arousing pity
PITEOUSLY > PITEOUS
PITFALL n hidden difficulty or danger
PITFALLS > PITFALL
PITH n soft white lining of the rind of oranges etc ⊳ vb destroy the brain and spinal cord of a laboratory animal
PITHBALL n type of conductor
PITHBALLS > PITHBALL
PITHEAD n top of a mine shaft and the buildings and hoisting gear around it
PITHEADS > PITHEAD
PITHECOID adj relating to apes ⊳ n ape, esp an anthropoid ape
PITHED > PITH
PITHFUL > PITH
PITHIER > PITHY
PITHIEST > PITHY
PITHILY > PITHY
PITHINESS > PITHY
PITHING > PITH
PITHLESS > PITH
PITHLIKE > PITH
PITHOI > PITHOS
PITHOS n large ceramic container for oil or grain
PITHS > PITH
PITHY adj short and full of meaning

PITIABLE *adj* arousing or deserving pity or contempt
PITIABLY > PITIABLE
PITIED > PITY
PITIER > PITY
PITIERS > PITY
PITIES > PITY
PITIETH *vb* as in *it pitieth me* archaic inflection of 'pity'
PITIFUL *adj* arousing pity
PITIFULLY > PITIFUL
PITIKINS *n* as in *ods pitikins* mild oath
PITILESS *adj* feeling no pity or mercy
PITLIKE *adj* like a pit
PITMAN *n* coal miner ▷ *n* connecting rod (in a machine)
PITMANS > PITMAN
PITMEN > PITMAN
PITON *n* metal spike used in climbing to secure a rope
PITONS > PITON
PITOT *n* tube used to measure the pressure of a liquid stream
PITOTS > PITOT
PITPROP *n* support beam in mine shaft
PITPROPS > PITPROP
PITS > PIT
PITSAW *n* large saw formerly used for cutting logs into planks
PITSAWS > PITSAW
PITTA *n* small brightly coloured ground-dwelling tropical bird
PITTANCE *n* very small amount of money
PITTANCES > PITTANCE
PITTAS > PITTA
PITTED > PIT
PITTEN *adj* having been put
PITTER *vb* make pattering sound
PITTERED > PITTER
PITTERING > PITTER
PITTERS > PITTER
PITTING > PIT
PITTINGS > PIT
PITTITE *n* occupant of a theatre pit
PITTITES > PITTITE
PITUITA *n* thick nasal secretion
PITUITARY *n* gland at the base of the brain, that helps to control growth ▷ *adj* of or relating to the pituitary gland
PITUITAS > PITUITA
PITUITE *n* mucus
PITUITES > PITUITE
PITUITRIN *n* extract from pituitary gland
PITURI *n* Australian solanaceous shrub
PITURIS > PITURI
PITY *n* sympathy or sorrow for others' suffering ▷ *vb* feel pity for
PITYING > PITY
PITYINGLY > PITY
PITYROID *adj* resembling bran

PIU *adv* more (quickly, softly, etc)
PIUM *n* stinging insect
PIUMS > PIUM
PIUPIU *n* skirt worn by Māoris on ceremonial occasions
PIUPIUS > PIUPIU
PIVOT *n* central shaft on which something turns ▷ *vb* provide with or turn on a pivot
PIVOTABLE > PIVOT
PIVOTAL *adj* of crucial importance
PIVOTALLY > PIVOTAL
PIVOTED > PIVOT
PIVOTER > PIVOT
PIVOTERS > PIVOT
PIVOTING > PIVOT
PIVOTINGS > PIVOT
PIVOTMAN *n* person in rank around whom others wheel
PIVOTMEN > PIVOTMAN
PIVOTS > PIVOT
PIX *less common spelling of* > PYX
PIXEL *n* any of a number of very small picture elements
PIXELATE *vb* divide an image into pixels
PIXELATED > PIXELATE
PIXELATES > PIXELATE
PIXELLATE *same as* > PIXELATE
PIXELS > PIXEL
PIXES > PIX
PIXIE *n* (in folklore) fairy
PIXIEISH > PIXIE
PIXIES > PIXY
PIXILATE *same as* > PIXELATE
PIXILATED *adj* eccentric or whimsical
PIXILATES > PIXILATE
PIXILLATE *same as* > PIXELATE
PIXINESS > PIXIE
PIXY *same as* > PIXIE
PIXYISH > PIXY
PIZAZZ *same as* > PIZZAZZ
PIZAZZES > PIZAZZ
PIZAZZIER > PIZAZZY
PIZAZZY *adj* exciting and lively
PIZE *vb* strike (someone a blow)
PIZED > PIZE
PIZES > PIZE
PIZING > PIZE
PIZZA *n* flat disc of dough covered with a wide variety of savoury toppings and baked
PIZZAIOLA *adj* having a type of tomato sauce
PIZZALIKE > PIZZA
PIZZAS > PIZZA
PIZZAZ *same as* > PZAZZ
PIZZAZES > PIZZAZ
PIZZAZZ *n* attractive combination of energy and style
PIZZAZZES > PIZZAZZ
PIZZAZZY *same as* > PIZZAZZY

PIZZELLE *n* Italian sweet wafer
PIZZELLES > PIZZELLE
PIZZERIA *n* place where pizzas are made, sold, or eaten
PIZZERIAS > PIZZERIA
PIZZICATI > PIZZICATO
PIZZICATO *adj* played by plucking the string of a violin etc with the finger ▷ *adv* (in music for the violin family) to be plucked with the finger ▷ *n* style or technique of playing a normally bowed stringed instrument in this manner
PIZZLE *n* penis of an animal, esp a bull
PIZZLES > PIZZLE
PLAAS *n* farm
PLAASES > PLAAS
PLACABLE *adj* easily placated or appeased
PLACABLY > PLACABLE
PLACARD *n* notice that is carried or displayed in public ▷ *vb* attach placards to
PLACARDED > PLACARD
PLACARDS > PLACARD
PLACATE *vb* make (someone) stop feeling angry or upset
PLACATED > PLACATE
PLACATER > PLACATE
PLACATERS > PLACATE
PLACATES > PLACATE
PLACATING > PLACATE
PLACATION > PLACATE
PLACATIVE *same as* > PLACATORY
PLACATORY *adj* placating or intended to placate
PLACCAT *variant of* > PLACKET
PLACCATE *variant of* > PLACKET
PLACCATES > PLACCATE
PLACCATS > PLACCAT
PLACE *n* particular part of an area or space ▷ *vb* put in a particular place
PLACEABLE > PLACE
PLACEBO *n* pill given to a patient instead of an active drug
PLACEBOES > PLACEBO
PLACEBOS > PLACEBO
PLACED > PLACE
PLACEKICK *n* (in football) kick in which the ball is placed in position before it is kicked ▷ *vb* take a placekick
PLACELESS *adj* not rooted in a specific place or community
PLACEMAN *n* person who holds a public office as a reward for political support
PLACEMAT *n* table mat for a person to put their plate on
PLACEMATS > PLACEMAT
PLACEMEN > PLACEMAN
PLACEMENT *n* arrangement
PLACENTA *n* organ formed in the womb during pregnancy, providing nutrients for the fetus

PLACENTAE > PLACENTA
PLACENTAL *adj* (esp of animals) having a placenta
PLACENTAS > PLACENTA
PLACER *n* surface sediment containing particles of gold or some other valuable mineral
PLACERS > PLACER
PLACES > PLACE
PLACET *n* vote or expression of assent
PLACETS > PLACET
PLACID *adj* not easily excited or upset, calm
PLACIDER > PLACID
PLACIDEST > PLACID
PLACIDITY > PLACID
PLACIDLY > PLACID
PLACING *n* method of issuing securities to the public using an intermediary
PLACINGS > PLACING
PLACIT *n* decree or dictum
PLACITA > PLACITUM
PLACITORY > PLACIT
PLACITS > PLACIT
PLACITUM *n* court or assembly in Middle Ages
PLACK *n* small former Scottish coin
PLACKET *n* opening at the waist of a dress or skirt
PLACKETS > PLACKET
PLACKLESS *adj* lacking money
PLACKS > PLACK
PLACODERM *n* extinct bony-plated fishlike vertebrate
PLACOID *adj* platelike or flattened ▷ *n* fish with placoid scales
PLACOIDS > PLACOID
PLAFOND *n* ceiling, esp one having ornamentation
PLAFONDS > PLAFOND
PLAGAL *adj* (of a cadence) progressing from the subdominant to the tonic chord
PLAGE *n* bright patch in the sun's chromosphere
PLAGES > PLAGE
PLAGIARY *n* person who plagiarizes or a piece of plagiarism
PLAGIUM *n* crime of kidnapping
PLAGIUMS > PLAGIUM
PLAGUE *n* fast-spreading fatal disease ▷ *vb* trouble or annoy continually
PLAGUED > PLAGUE
PLAGUER > PLAGUE
PLAGUERS > PLAGUE
PLAGUES > PLAGUE
PLAGUEY *same as* > PLAGUY
PLAGUIER > PLAGUEY
PLAGUIEST > PLAGUEY
PLAGUILY > PLAGUY
PLAGUING > PLAGUE
PLAGUY *adj* disagreeable or vexing ▷ *adv* disagreeably or annoyingly
PLAICE *n* edible European flatfish

PLAICES > PLAICE
PLAID n long piece of tartan cloth worn as part of Highland dress ▷ vb weave cloth into plaid
PLAIDED > PLAID
PLAIDING > PLAID
PLAIDINGS > PLAID
PLAIDMAN n wearer of plaid
PLAIDMEN > PLAIDMAN
PLAIDS > PLAID
PLAIN adj easy to see or understand ▷ n large stretch of level country ▷ adv clearly or simply ▷ vb complain
PLAINANT n plaintiff
PLAINANTS > PLAINANT
PLAINED > PLAIN
PLAINER > PLAIN
PLAINEST > PLAIN
PLAINFUL adj apt to complain
PLAINING > PLAIN
PLAININGS > PLAIN
PLAINISH > PLAIN
PLAINLY > PLAIN
PLAINNESS > PLAIN
PLAINS pl n extensive tracts of flat treeless countryside
PLAINSMAN n person who lives in a plains region, esp in the Great Plains of North America
PLAINSMEN > PLAINSMAN
PLAINSONG n unaccompanied singing, esp in a medieval church
PLAINT n complaint or lamentation
PLAINTEXT n (in telecommunications) message set in a directly readable form rather than in coded groups
PLAINTFUL adj complaining
PLAINTIFF n person who sues in a court of law
PLAINTIVE adj sad, mournful
PLAINTS > PLAINT
PLAINWORK n weaving
PLAISTER n plaster
PLAISTERS > PLAISTER
PLAIT n intertwined length of hair ▷ vb intertwine separate strands in a pattern
PLAITED > PLAIT
PLAITER > PLAIT
PLAITERS > PLAIT
PLAITING > PLAIT
PLAITINGS > PLAIT
PLAITS > PLAIT
PLAN n way thought out to do or achieve something ▷ vb arrange beforehand
PLANAR adj of or relating to a plane
PLANARIA n type of flatworm
PLANARIAN n type of flatworm
PLANARIAS > PLANARIA
PLANARITY > PLANAR
PLANATE adj having been flattened

PLANATION n erosion of a land surface until it is basically flat
PLANCH vb cover with planks
PLANCHE same as > PLANCH
PLANCHED > PLANCH
PLANCHES > PLANCH
PLANCHET n piece of metal ready to be stamped as a coin, medal, etc
PLANCHETS > PLANCHET
PLANCHING > PLANCH
PLANE n aeroplane ▷ adj perfectly flat or level ▷ vb glide or skim
PLANED > PLANE
PLANELOAD n amount or number carried by plane
PLANENESS > PLANE
PLANER n machine with a cutting tool that makes repeated horizontal strokes
PLANERS > PLANER
PLANES > PLANE
PLANESIDE n area next to aeroplane
PLANET n large body in space that revolves round the sun or another star
PLANETARY adj of or relating to a planet ▷ n train of planetary gears
PLANETIC > PLANET
PLANETOID See > ASTEROID
PLANETS > PLANET
PLANFORM n outline or silhouette of an object, esp an aircraft, as seen from above
PLANFORMS > PLANFORM
PLANGENCY > PLANGENT
PLANGENT adj (of sounds) mournful and resounding
PLANIGRAM n X-ray photograph of a plane section of something
PLANING > PLANE
PLANISH vb give a smooth surface to (a metal)
PLANISHED > PLANISH
PLANISHER > PLANISH
PLANISHES > PLANISH
PLANK n long flat piece of sawn timber ▷ vb cover or provide (an area) with planks
PLANKED > PLANK
PLANKING n number of planks
PLANKINGS > PLANKING
PLANKLIKE adj like a plank
PLANKS > PLANK
PLANKTER n organism in plankton
PLANKTERS > PLANKTER
PLANKTIC adj relating to plankton
PLANKTON n minute animals and plants floating in the surface water of a sea or lake
PLANKTONS > PLANKTON
PLANLESS adj having no plan
PLANNED > PLAN
PLANNER n person who makes plans
PLANNERS > PLANNER

PLANNING > PLAN
PLANNINGS > PLAN
PLANOGRAM n type of schematic plan for displaying merchandise in a shop
PLANOSOL n soil of humid or subhumid uplands
PLANOSOLS > PLANOSOL
PLANS > PLAN
PLANT n living organism that grows in the ground and has no power to move ▷ vb put in the ground to grow
PLANTA n sole of foot
PLANTABLE > PLANT
PLANTAE > PLANTA
PLANTAGE n plants
PLANTAGES > PLANTAGE
PLANTAIN n low-growing wild plant with broad leaves
PLANTAINS > PLANTAIN
PLANTAR adj of, relating to, or occurring on the sole of the foot
PLANTAS > PLANTA
PLANTED > PLANT
PLANTER n owner of a plantation
PLANTERS > PLANTER
PLANTING > PLANT
PLANTINGS > PLANT
PLANTLESS > PLANT
PLANTLET n small plant
PLANTLETS > PLANTLET
PLANTLIKE > PLANT
PLANTLING n young plant
PLANTS > PLANT
PLANTSMAN n experienced gardener who specializes in collecting rare or interesting plants
PLANTSMEN > PLANTSMAN
PLANTULE n embryo in act of germination
PLANTULES > PLANTULE
PLANULA n free-swimming larva of hydrozoan coelenterates
PLANULAE > PLANULA
PLANULAR > PLANULA
PLANULATE adj flat
PLANULOID adj of planula
PLANURIA n expulsion of urine from abnormal opening
PLANURIAS > PLANURIA
PLANURIES > PLANURY
PLANURY another name for > PLANURIA
PLANXTIES > PLANXTY
PLANXTY n Celtic melody for harp
PLAP same as > PLOP
PLAPPED > PLAP
PLAPPING > PLAP
PLAPS > PLAP
PLAQUE n inscribed commemorative stone or metal plate
PLAQUES > PLAQUE
PLAQUETTE n small plaque
PLASH same as > PLEACH
PLASHED > PLASH
PLASHER n type of farm tool
PLASHERS > PLASHER
PLASHES > PLASH
PLASHET n small pond

PLASHETS > PLASHET
PLASHIER > PLASHY
PLASHIEST > PLASHY
PLASHING > PLASH
PLASHINGS > PLASH
PLASHY adj wet or marshy
PLASM same as > PLASMA
PLASMA n clear liquid part of blood
PLASMAGEL another name for > ECTOPLASM
PLASMAS > PLASMA
PLASMASOL another name for > ENDOPLASM
PLASMATIC > PLASMA
PLASMIC > PLASMA
PLASMID n small circle of bacterial DNA
PLASMIDS > PLASMID
PLASMIN n proteolytic enzyme that causes fibrinolysis in blood clots
PLASMINS > PLASMIN
PLASMODIA n amoeboid masses of protoplasm, each containing many nuclei
PLASMOID n section of a plasma having a characteristic shape
PLASMOIDS > PLASMOID
PLASMON n sum total of plasmagenes in a cell
PLASMONS > PLASMON
PLASMS > PLASM
PLAST archaic past participle of > PLACE
PLASTE archaic past participle of > PLACE
PLASTER n mixture of lime, sand, etc for coating walls ▷ vb cover with plaster
PLASTERED adj drunk
PLASTERER > PLASTER
PLASTERS > PLASTER
PLASTERY adj like plaster
PLASTIC n synthetic material that can be moulded when soft but sets in a hard long-lasting shape ▷ adj made of plastic
PLASTICKY adj made of or resembling plastic
PLASTICLY > PLASTIC
PLASTICS > PLASTIC
PLASTID n small particle in the cells of plants and some animals
PLASTIDS > PLASTID
PLASTIQUE n easily moulded plastic explosive
PLASTISOL n suspension of resin particles convertible into solid plastic
PLASTRAL > PLASTRON
PLASTRON n bony plate forming the ventral part of the shell of a tortoise or turtle
PLASTRONS > PLASTRON
PLASTRUM variant of > PLASTRON
PLASTRUMS > PLASTRUM
PLAT n small area of ground
PLATAN n plane tree
PLATANE same as > PLATAN
PLATANES > PLATANE
PLATANNA n S African frog

SECTION 1: Words between 2 and 9 letters in length

PLATANNAS > PLATANNA

PLATANS > PLATAN

PLATBAND n border of flowers in garden

PLATBANDS > PLATBAND

PLATE n shallow dish for holding food ▷ vb cover with a thin coating of gold, silver, or other metal

PLATEASM n talking with mouth open too wide

PLATEASMS > PLATEASM

PLATEAU n area of level high land ▷ vb remain stable for a long period

PLATEAUED > PLATEAU

PLATEAUS > PLATEAU

PLATEAUX > PLATEAU

PLATED adj coated with a layer of metal

PLATEFUL same as > PLATE

PLATEFULS > PLATEFUL

PLATELESS adj having no plate

PLATELET n minute particle occurring in blood of vertebrates and involved in clotting of blood

PLATELETS > PLATELET

PLATELIKE > PLATE

PLATEMAN n one of crew of steam train

PLATEMARK another name for > HALLMARK

PLATEMEN > PLATEMAN

PLATEN n roller of a typewriter, against which the paper is held

PLATENS > PLATEN

PLATER n person or thing that plates

PLATERS > PLATER

PLATES > PLATE

PLATESFUL > PLATEFUL

PLATFORM n raised floor

PLATFORMS > PLATFORM

PLATIER > PLATY

PLATIES > PLATY

PLATIEST > PLATY

PLATINA n alloy of platinum and several other metals

PLATINAS > PLATINA

PLATING n coating of metal

PLATINGS > PLATING

PLATINIC adj of or containing platinum, esp in the tetravalent state

PLATINISE same as > PLATINIZE

PLATINIZE vb coat with platinum

PLATINOID adj containing or resembling platinum

PLATINOUS adj of or containing platinum, esp in the divalent state

PLATINUM n valuable silvery-white metal

PLATINUMS > PLATINUM

PLATITUDE n remark that is true but not interesting or original

PLATONIC adj (of a relationship) friendly or affectionate but not romantic ▷ n platonic friend

PLATONICS > PLATONIC

PLATONISM n philosophy of Plato

PLATOON n smaller unit within a company of soldiers ▷ vb organise into platoons

PLATOONED > PLATOON

PLATOONS > PLATOON

PLATS > PLAT

PLATT adj as in scale and platt denoting a modern straight staircase with landings as opposed to a spiral staircase

PLATTED > PLAT

PLATTER n large dish

PLATTERS > PLATTER

PLATTING > PLAT

PLATTINGS > PLAT

PLATY adj of, relating to, or designating rocks the constituents of which occur in flaky layers ▷ n brightly coloured freshwater fish

PLATYFISH same as > PLATY

PLATYPI > PLATYPUS

PLATYPUS n Australian egg-laying amphibious mammal

PLATYS > PLATY

PLATYSMA n muscle located on side of neck

PLATYSMAS > PLATYSMA

PLAUDIT n expression of enthusiastic approval

PLAUDITE interj give a round of applause!

PLAUDITS > PLAUDIT

PLAUSIBLE adj apparently true or reasonable

PLAUSIBLY > PLAUSIBLE

PLAUSIVE adj expressing praise or approval

PLAUSTRAL adj relating to wagons

PLAY vb occupy oneself in (a game or recreation) ▷ n story performed on stage or broadcast

PLAYA n (in the US) temporary lake in a desert basin

PLAYABLE > PLAY

PLAYACT vb pretend or make believe

PLAYACTED > PLAYACT

PLAYACTOR > PLAYACT

PLAYACTS > PLAYACT

PLAYAS > PLAYA

PLAYBACK n reproducing of a recording, esp formerly on magnetic tape ▷ vb listen to or watch (something recorded)

PLAYBACKS > PLAYBACK

PLAYBILL n poster or bill advertising a play

PLAYBILLS > PLAYBILL

PLAYBOOK n book containing a range of possible set plays

PLAYBOOKS > PLAYBOOK

PLAYBOY n rich man who lives only for pleasure

PLAYBOYS > PLAYBOY

PLAYBUS n mobile playground in a bus

PLAYBUSES > PLAYBUS

PLAYDATE n gathering of children at house for play

PLAYDATES > PLAYDATE

PLAYDAY n day given to play

PLAYDAYS > PLAYDAY

PLAYDOUGH n soft modelling material used by children

PLAYDOWN same as > PLAYOFF

PLAYDOWNS > PLAYDOWN

PLAYED > PLAY

PLAYER n person who plays a game or sport

PLAYERS > PLAYER

PLAYFIELD n field for sports

PLAYFUL adj lively

PLAYFULLY > PLAYFUL

PLAYGIRL n rich woman devoted to pleasure

PLAYGIRLS > PLAYGIRL

PLAYGOER n person who goes often to the theatre

PLAYGOERS > PLAYGOER

PLAYGOING > PLAYGOER

PLAYGROUP n playschool

PLAYHOUSE n theatre

PLAYING n act of playing

PLAYINGS > PLAYING

PLAYLAND n playground

PLAYLANDS > PLAYLAND

PLAYLESS > PLAY

PLAYLET n short play

PLAYLETS > PLAYLET

PLAYLIKE > PLAY

PLAYLIST n list of songs chosen for playing, such as on a radio station ▷ vb put (a song) on a playlist

PLAYLISTS > PLAYLIST

PLAYMAKER n player who creates scoring opportunities for his or her team-mates

PLAYMATE n companion in play

PLAYMATES > PLAYMATE

PLAYOFF n extra contest to decide the winner when two or more competitors are tied

PLAYOFFS > PLAYOFF

PLAYPEN n small portable enclosure in which a young child can safely be left to play

PLAYPENS > PLAYPEN

PLAYROOM n recreation room, esp for children

PLAYROOMS > PLAYROOM

PLAYS > PLAY

PLAYSET n outdoor equipment for children to play on

PLAYSETS > PLAYSET

PLAYSLIP n form used to select numbers in a lottery draw

PLAYSLIPS > PLAYSLIP

PLAYSOME adj playful

PLAYSUIT n woman's or child's outfit, usually comprising shorts and a top

PLAYSUITS > PLAYSUIT

PLAYTHING n toy

PLAYTIME n time for play or recreation, such as a school break

PLAYTIMES > PLAYTIME

PLAYWEAR n clothes suitable for playing in

PLAYWEARS > PLAYWEAR

PLAZA n open space or square

PLAZAS > PLAZA

PLEA n serious or urgent request, entreaty ▷ vb entreat

PLEACH vb interlace the stems or boughs of (a tree or hedge)

PLEACHED > PLEACH

PLEACHES > PLEACH

PLEACHING > PLEACH

PLEAD vb ask urgently or with deep feeling

PLEADABLE > PLEAD

PLEADED > PLEAD

PLEADER > PLEAD

PLEADERS > PLEAD

PLEADING > PLEAD

PLEADINGS > PLEAD

PLEADS > PLEAD

PLEAED > PLEA

PLEAING > PLEA

PLEAS > PLEA

PLEASABLE > PLEASE

PLEASANCE n secluded part of a garden laid out with trees, walks, etc

PLEASANT adj pleasing, enjoyable

PLEASE vb give pleasure or satisfaction to ▷ adv polite word of request

PLEASED > PLEASE

PLEASEDLY > PLEASE

PLEASEMAN n person who courts favour

PLEASEMEN > PLEASEMAN

PLEASER > PLEASE

PLEASERS > PLEASE

PLEASES > PLEASE

PLEASETH obsolete inflection of > PLEASE

PLEASING adj giving pleasure or satisfaction ▷ n act of giving pleasure

PLEASINGS > PLEASING

PLEASURE n feeling of happiness and satisfaction ▷ vb give pleasure to or take pleasure (in)

PLEASURED > PLEASURE

PLEASURER > PLEASURE

PLEASURES > PLEASURE

PLEAT n fold made by doubling material back on itself ▷ vb arrange (material) in pleats

PLEATED > PLEAT

PLEATER n attachment on a sewing machine that makes pleats

PLEATERS > PLEATER

PLEATHER n synthetic leather

PLEATHERS > PLEATHER

PLEATING n act of pleating

PLEATINGS > PLEATING

PLEATLESS > PLEAT

PLEATS > PLEAT

PLEB n common vulgar person

PLEBBIER > PLEBBY

PLEBBIEST > PLEBBY
PLEBBY adj common or vulgar
PLEBE n member of the lowest class at the US Naval Academy or Military Academy
PLEBEAN old variant of > PLEBEIAN
PLEBEIAN adj of the lower social classes ▷ n member of the lower social classes
PLEBEIANS > PLEBEIAN
PLEBES > PLEBE
PLEBIFIED > PLEBIFY
PLEBIFIES > PLEBIFY
PLEBIFY vb make plebeian
PLEBS n common people
PLECTRA > PLECTRUM
PLECTRE variant of > PLECTRUM
PLECTRES > PLECTRE
PLECTRON same as > PLECTRUM
PLECTRONS > PLECTRON
PLECTRUM n small implement for plucking the strings of a guitar etc
PLECTRUMS > PLECTRUM
PLED > PLEAD
PLEDGABLE > PLEDGE
PLEDGE n solemn promise ▷ vb promise solemnly
PLEDGED > PLEDGE
PLEDGEE n person to whom a pledge is given
PLEDGEES > PLEDGEE
PLEDGEOR same as > PLEDGOR
PLEDGEORS > PLEDGEOR
PLEDGER same as > PLEDGOR
PLEDGERS > PLEDGER
PLEDGES > PLEDGE
PLEDGET n small flattened pad of wool, cotton, etc
PLEDGETS > PLEDGET
PLEDGING > PLEDGE
PLEDGOR n person who gives or makes a pledge
PLEDGORS > PLEDGOR
PLEIAD n brilliant or talented group, esp one with seven members
PLEIADES > PLEIAD
PLEIADS > PLEIAD
PLEIOCENE variant spelling of > PLIOCENE
PLEIOMERY n state of having more than normal number
PLEIOTAXY n increase in whorls in flower
PLENA > PLENUM
PLENARIES > PLENARY
PLENARILY > PLENARY
PLENARTY n state of endowed church office when occupied
PLENARY adj (of a meeting) attended by all members ▷ n book read at the Eucharist
PLENCH n tool combining wrench and pliers
PLENCHES > PLENCH
PLENILUNE n full moon
PLENIPO n plenipotentiary diplomat

PLENIPOES > PLENIPO
PLENIPOS > PLENIPO
PLENISH vb fill, stock, or resupply
PLENISHED > PLENISH
PLENISHER > PLENISH
PLENISHES > PLENISH
PLENISM n philosophical theory
PLENISMS > PLENISM
PLENIST > PLENISM
PLENISTS > PLENISM
PLENITUDE n completeness, abundance
PLENTEOUS adj plentiful
PLENTIES > PLENTY
PLENTIFUL adj existing in large amounts or numbers
PLENTY n large amount or number ▷ adj very many ▷ adv more than adequately
PLENUM n enclosure containing gas at a high pressure
PLENUMS > PLENUM
PLEON n abdomen of crustacean
PLEONAL adj of the abdomen of a crustacean
PLEONASM n use of more words than necessary
PLEONASMS > PLEONASM
PLEONAST n person using more words than necessary
PLEONASTE n type of black mineral
PLEONASTS > PLEONAST
PLEONEXIA n greed
PLEONIC > PLEON
PLEONS > PLEON
PLEOPOD another name for > SWIMMERET
PLEOPODS > PLEOPOD
PLERION n filled-centre supernova remnant
PLERIONS > PLERION
PLEROMA n abundance
PLEROMAS > PLEROMA
PLEROME n central column in growing stem or root
PLEROMES > PLEROME
PLESH n small pool
PLESHES > PLESH
PLESSOR same as > PLEXOR
PLESSORS > PLESSOR
PLETHORA n excess
PLETHORAS > PLETHORA
PLETHORIC > PLETHORA
PLEUCH same as > PLEUGH
PLEUCHED > PLEUCH
PLEUCHING > PLEUCH
PLEUCHS > PLEUCH
PLEUGH Scottish word for > PLOUGH
PLEUGHED > PLEUGH
PLEUGHING > PLEUGH
PLEUGHS > PLEUGH
PLEURA n membrane covering the lungs
PLEURAE > PLEURA
PLEURAL > PLEURA
PLEURAS > PLEURA
PLEURISY n inflammation of the membrane covering the lungs
PLEURITIC > PLEURISY
PLEURITIS n pleurisy

PLEURON n part of the cuticle of arthropods
PLEURONIA n combined disorder of pleurisy and pneumonia
PLEUSTON n mass of small organisms, esp algae, floating at the surface of shallow pools
PLEUSTONS > PLEUSTON
PLEW n (formerly in Canada) beaver skin used as a standard unit of value in the fur trade
PLEWS > PLEW
PLEX n shortening of multiplex ▷ vb make a plexus
PLEXAL > PLEXUS
PLEXED > PLEX
PLEXES > PLEX
PLEXIFORM adj like or having the form of a network or plexus
PLEXING > PLEX
PLEXOR n small hammer with a rubber head
PLEXORS > PLEXOR
PLEXURE n act of weaving together
PLEXURES > PLEXURE
PLEXUS n complex network of nerves or blood vessels
PLEXUSES > PLEXUS
PLIABLE adj easily bent
PLIABLY > PLIABLE
PLIANCIES > PLIANT
PLIANCY > PLIANT
PLIANT adj pliable
PLIANTLY > PLIANT
PLICA n folding over of parts, such as a fold of skin, muscle, peritoneum, etc
PLICAE > PLICA
PLICAL > PLICA
PLICAS > PLICA
PLICATE adj having or arranged in parallel folds or ridges ▷ vb arrange into parallel folds
PLICATED > PLICATE
PLICATELY > PLICATE
PLICATES > PLICATE
PLICATING > PLICATE
PLICATION n act of folding or the condition of being folded or plicate
PLICATURE same as > PLICATION
PLIE n classic ballet practice posture with back erect and knees bent
PLIED > PLY
PLIER n person who plies a trade
PLIERS pl n tool with hinged arms and jaws for gripping
PLIES > PLY
PLIGHT n difficult or dangerous situation
PLIGHTED > PLIGHT
PLIGHTER > PLIGHT
PLIGHTERS > PLIGHT
PLIGHTFUL > PLIGHT
PLIGHTING > PLIGHT
PLIGHTS > PLIGHT
PLIM vb swell with water
PLIMMED > PLIM

PLIMMING > PLIM
PLIMS > PLIM
PLIMSOL same as > PLIMSOLE
PLIMSOLE same as > PLIMSOLL
PLIMSOLES > PLIMSOLE
PLIMSOLL n light rubber-soled canvas shoe worn for various sports
PLIMSOLLS > PLIMSOLL
PLIMSOLS > PLIMSOL
PLING n (in computer jargon) an exclamation mark ▷ vb beg from
PLINGED > PLING
PLINGING > PLING
PLINGS > PLING
PLINK n short sharp often metallic sound ▷ vb make such a noise
PLINKED > PLINK
PLINKER > PLINK
PLINKERS > PLINK
PLINKIER > PLINKY
PLINKIEST > PLINKY
PLINKING > PLINK
PLINKINGS > PLINK
PLINKS > PLINK
PLINKY adj (of a sound) short, sharp, and often metallic
PLINTH n slab forming the base of a statue, column, etc
PLINTHS > PLINTH
PLIOCENE adj of the Pliocene geological time period
PLIOFILM n transparent plastic material
PLIOFILMS > PLIOFILM
PLIOSAUR n type of dinosaur
PLIOSAURS > PLIOSAUR
PLIOTRON n type of vacuum tube
PLIOTRONS > PLIOTRON
PLISKIE n practical joke ▷ adj tricky or mischievous
PLISKIER > PLISKIE
PLISKIES > PLISKIE
PLISKIEST > PLISKIE
PLISKY same as > PLISKIE
PLISSE n fabric with a wrinkled finish, achieved by treatment involving caustic soda
PLISSES > PLISSE
PLOAT vb thrash
PLOATED > PLOAT
PLOATING > PLOAT
PLOATS > PLOAT
PLOD vb walk with slow heavy steps ▷ n act of plodding
PLODDED > PLOD
PLODDER n person who plods
PLODDERS > PLODDER
PLODDING > PLOD
PLODDINGS > PLOD
PLODGE vb wade in water, esp the sea ▷ n act of wading
PLODGED > PLODGE
PLODGES > PLODGE
PLODGING > PLODGE
PLODS > PLOD

p

PLOGGING n picking up litter while jogging

PLOGGINGS > PLOGGING

PLOIDIES > PLOIDY

PLOIDY n number of copies of set of chromosomes in cell

PLONG obsolete variant of > PLUNGE

PLONGD > PLONG

PLONGE same as > PLUNGE

PLONGED > PLONGE

PLONGES > PLONGE

PLONGING > PLONGE

PLONGS > PLONG

PLONK vb put (something) down heavily and carelessly ▷ n act of plonking ▷ interj exclamation imitative of this sound

PLONKED > PLONK

PLONKER n stupid person

PLONKERS > PLONKER

PLONKIER > PLONK

PLONKIEST > PLONK

PLONKING > PLONK

PLONKINGS > PLONK

PLONKO n alcoholic, esp one who drinks wine

PLONKOS > PLONKO

PLONKS > PLONK

PLONKY > PLONK

PLOOK same as > PLOUK

PLOOKIE same as > PLOUKY

PLOOKIER > PLOOK

PLOOKIEST > PLOOK

PLOOKS > PLOOK

PLOOKY > PLOOK

PLOP n sound of an object falling into water without a splash ▷ vb make this sound ▷ interj exclamation imitative of this sound

PLOPPED > PLOP

PLOPPING > PLOP

PLOPS > PLOP

PLOSION n sound of an abrupt break or closure, esp the audible release of a stop

PLOSIONS > PLOSION

PLOSIVE adj pronounced with a sudden release of breath ▷ n plosive consonant

PLOSIVES > PLOSIVE

PLOT n secret plan to do something illegal or wrong ▷ vb plan secretly, conspire

PLOTFUL > PLOT

PLOTLESS > PLOT

PLOTLINE n literary or dramatic plot

PLOTLINES > PLOTLINE

PLOTS > PLOT

PLOTTAGE n land that makes up plot

PLOTTAGES > PLOTTAGE

PLOTTED > PLOT

PLOTTER same as > PLOUTER

PLOTTERED > PLOTTER

PLOTTERS > PLOTTER

PLOTTIE n hot spiced drink

PLOTTIER > PLOTTY

PLOTTIES > PLOTTIE

PLOTTIEST > PLOTTY

PLOTTING > PLOT

PLOTTINGS > PLOT

PLOTTY adj intricately plotted

PLOTZ vb faint or collapse

PLOTZED > PLOTZ

PLOTZES > PLOTZ

PLOTZING > PLOTZ

PLOUGH n agricultural tool for turning over soil ▷ vb turn over (earth) with a plough

PLOUGHBOY n boy who guides the animals drawing a plough

PLOUGHED > PLOUGH

PLOUGHER > PLOUGH

PLOUGHERS > PLOUGH

PLOUGHING n act of ploughing

PLOUGHMAN n man who ploughs

PLOUGHMEN > PLOUGHMAN

PLOUGHS > PLOUGH

PLOUK n pimple

PLOUKIE > PLOUK

PLOUKIER > PLOUK

PLOUKIEST > PLOUK

PLOUKS > PLOUK

PLOUKY > PLOUK

PLOUTER same as > PLOWTER

PLOUTERED > PLOUTER

PLOUTERS > PLOUTER

PLOVER n shore bird with a straight bill and long pointed wings

PLOVERIER > PLOVERY

PLOVERS > PLOVER

PLOVERY adj characterized by plovers

PLOW same as > PLOUGH

PLOWABLE > PLOW

PLOWBACK n reinvestment of profits

PLOWBACKS > PLOWBACK

PLOWBOY same as > PLOUGHBOY

PLOWBOYS > PLOWBOY

PLOWED > PLOW

PLOWER > PLOW

PLOWERS > PLOW

PLOWHEAD n draught iron of plow

PLOWHEADS > PLOWHEAD

PLOWING > PLOUGHING

PLOWINGS > PLOWING

PLOWLAND n land plowed

PLOWLANDS > PLOWLAND

PLOWMAN same as > PLOUGHMAN

PLOWMEN > PLOWMAN

PLOWS > PLOW

PLOWSHARE n horizontal pointed cutting blade of a mouldboard plow

PLOWSTAFF n one of the handles of a plow

PLOWTAIL n the end of a plough where the handles are

PLOWTAILS > PLOWTAIL

PLOWTER vb work or play in water or mud ▷ n act of plowtering

PLOWTERED > PLOWTER

PLOWTERS > PLOWTER

PLOWWISE adv as in ploughing

PLOY n manoeuvre designed to gain an advantage ▷ vb form a column from a line of troops

PLOYE n buckwheat pancake

PLOYED > PLOY

PLOYES > PLOYE

PLOYING > PLOY

PLOYS > PLOY

PLU same as > PLEW

PLUCK vb pull or pick off ▷ n courage

PLUCKED > PLUCK

PLUCKER > PLUCK

PLUCKERS > PLUCK

PLUCKIER > PLUCKY

PLUCKIEST > PLUCKY

PLUCKILY > PLUCKY

PLUCKING > PLUCK

PLUCKS > PLUCK

PLUCKY adj brave

PLUE same as > PLEW

PLUES > PLUE

PLUFF vb expel in puffs

PLUFFED > PLUFF

PLUFFIER > PLUFF

PLUFFIEST > PLUFF

PLUFFING > PLUFF

PLUFFS > PLUFF

PLUFFY > PLUFF

PLUG n thing fitting into and filling a hole ▷ vb block or seal (a hole or gap) with a plug

PLUGBOARD n device with a large number of sockets in which electrical plugs can be inserted to form many different temporary circuits

PLUGGED > PLUG

PLUGGER > PLUG

PLUGGERS > PLUG

PLUGGING > PLUG

PLUGGINGS > PLUG

PLUGHOLE n hole at the bottom of a bath or sink which can be closed with a plug

PLUGHOLES > PLUGHOLE

PLUGLESS > PLUG

PLUGOLA n plugging of products on television

PLUGOLAS > PLUGOLA

PLUGS > PLUG

PLUGUGLY n city tough; ruffian

PLUM n oval usu dark red fruit with a stone in the middle ▷ adj dark purplish-red

PLUMAGE n bird's feathers

PLUMAGED > PLUMAGE

PLUMAGES > PLUMAGE

PLUMATE adj of, relating to, or possessing one or more feathers or plumes

PLUMB vb understand (something obscure) ▷ adv exactly ▷ n weight suspended at the end of a line

PLUMBABLE > PLUMB

PLUMBAGO n plant of warm regions with clusters of blue, white, or red flowers

PLUMBAGOS > PLUMBAGO

PLUMBATE n compound formed from lead oxide

PLUMBATES > PLUMBATE

PLUMBED > PLUMB

PLUMBEOUS adj made of or relating to lead or resembling lead in colour

PLUMBER n person who fits and repairs pipes and fixtures for water and drainage systems

PLUMBERS > PLUMBER

PLUMBERY same as > PLUMBING

PLUMBIC adj of or containing lead in the tetravalent state

PLUMBING n pipes and fixtures used in water and drainage systems

PLUMBINGS > PLUMBING

PLUMBISM n chronic lead poisoning

PLUMBISMS > PLUMBISM

PLUMBITE n substance containing lead oxide

PLUMBITES > PLUMBITE

PLUMBLESS adj incapable of being sounded

PLUMBNESS > PLUMB

PLUMBOUS adj of or containing lead in the divalent state

PLUMBS > PLUMB

PLUMBUM n obsolete name for lead (the metal)

PLUMBUMS > PLUMBUM

PLUMCAKE n cake with raisins in it

PLUMCAKES > PLUMCAKE

PLUMCOT n hybrid of apricot and plum

PLUMCOTS > PLUMCOT

PLUMDAMAS n prune

PLUME n feather, esp one worn as an ornament ▷ vb adorn or decorate with feathers or plumes

PLUMED > PLUME

PLUMELESS > PLUME

PLUMELET n small plume

PLUMELETS > PLUMELET

PLUMELIKE > PLUME

PLUMERIA n tropical tree with candelabra-like branches

PLUMERIAS > PLUMERIA

PLUMERIES > PLUMERY

PLUMERY n plumes collectively

PLUMES > PLUME

PLUMIER > PLUMY

PLUMIEST > PLUMY

PLUMING > PLUME

PLUMIPED n bird with feathered feet

PLUMIPEDS > PLUMIPED

PLUMIST n person who makes plumes

PLUMISTS > PLUMIST

PLUMLIKE > PLUM

PLUMMER > PLUM

PLUMMEST > PLUM

PLUMMET vb plunge downward ▷ n weight on a plumb line or fishing line

PLUMMETED > PLUMMET

P

PLUMMETS > PLUMMET
PLUMMIER > PLUMMY
PLUMMIEST > PLUMMY
PLUMMY adj of, full of, or like plums
PLUMOSE same as > PLUMATE
PLUMOSELY > PLUMOSE
PLUMOSITY > PLUMOSE
PLUMOUS adj having plumes or feathers
PLUMP adj moderately or attractively fat ▷ vb sit or fall heavily and suddenly ▷ n heavy abrupt fall or the sound of this ▷ adv suddenly or heavily
PLUMPED > PLUMP
PLUMPEN vb make or become plump
PLUMPENED > PLUMPEN
PLUMPENS > PLUMPEN
PLUMPER n pad carried in the mouth by actors to round out the cheeks
PLUMPERS > PLUMPER
PLUMPEST > PLUMP
PLUMPIE same as > PLUMPY
PLUMPIER > PLUMPY
PLUMPIEST > PLUMPY
PLUMPING > PLUMP
PLUMPISH adj on the plump side
PLUMPLY > PLUMP
PLUMPNESS > PLUMP
PLUMPS > PLUMP
PLUMPY adj plump
PLUMS > PLUM
PLUMULA n down feather
PLUMULAE > PLUMULA
PLUMULAR > PLUMULE
PLUMULATE adj covered with soft fine feathers
PLUMULE n embryonic shoot of seed-bearing plants
PLUMULES > PLUMULE
PLUMULOSE adj having hairs branching out like feathers
PLUMY adj like a feather
PLUNDER vb take by force, esp in time of war ▷ n things plundered, spoils
PLUNDERED > PLUNDER
PLUNDERER > PLUNDER
PLUNDERS > PLUNDER
PLUNGE vb put or throw forcibly or suddenly (into) ▷ n plunging dive
PLUNGED > PLUNGE
PLUNGER n rubber suction cup used to clear blocked pipes
PLUNGERS > PLUNGER
PLUNGES > PLUNGE
PLUNGING > PLUNGE
PLUNGINGS > PLUNGE
PLUNK vb pluck the strings of (a banjo etc) to produce a twanging sound ▷ n act or sound of plunking ▷ interj exclamation imitative of the sound of something plunking ▷ adv exactly
PLUNKED > PLUNK
PLUNKER > PLUNK
PLUNKERS > PLUNK
PLUNKIER > PLUNKY

PLUNKIEST > PLUNKY
PLUNKING > PLUNK
PLUNKS > PLUNK
PLUNKY adj sounding like plucked banjo string
PLUOT n hybrid fruit of the plum and apricot
PLUOTS > PLUOT
PLURAL adj of or consisting of more than one ▷ n word indicating more than one
PLURALISE same as > PLURALIZE
PLURALISM n existence and toleration of a variety of peoples, opinions, etc in a society
PLURALIST > PLURALISM
PLURALITY n state of being plural
PLURALIZE vb make or become plural
PLURALLY > PLURAL
PLURALS > PLURAL
PLURIPARA n woman who has borne more than one child
PLURISIE same as > PLEURISY
PLURISIES > PLURISIE
PLURRY euphemism for > BLOODY
PLUS vb make or become greater in value
PLUSAGE same as > PLUSSAGE
PLUSAGES > PLUSAGE
PLUSED > PLUS
PLUSES > PLUS
PLUSH n fabric with long velvety pile ▷ adj luxurious
PLUSHED adj showily luxurious
PLUSHER > PLUSH
PLUSHES > PLUSH
PLUSHEST > PLUSH
PLUSHIER > PLUSHY
PLUSHIEST > PLUSHY
PLUSHILY > PLUSHY
PLUSHLY > PLUSH
PLUSHNESS > PLUSH
PLUSHY same as > PLUSH
PLUSING > PLUS
PLUSSAGE n amount over and above another amount
PLUSSAGES > PLUSSAGE
PLUSSED > PLUS
PLUSSES > PLUS
PLUSSING > PLUS
PLUTEAL > PLUTEUS
PLUTEI > PLUTEUS
PLUTEUS n larva of sea urchin
PLUTEUSES > PLUTEUS
PLUTO vb reduce in importance
PLUTOCRAT n person who is powerful because of being very rich
PLUTOED > PLUTO
PLUTOES > PLUTO
PLUTOID n dwarf planet whose orbit is beyond Neptune's
PLUTOIDS > PLUTOID
PLUTOING > PLUTO

PLUTOLOGY n study of wealth
PLUTON n any mass of igneous rock that has solidified below the surface of the earth
PLUTONIAN adj of or relating to the underworld
PLUTONIC adj formed from molten rock that has solidified below the earth's surface
PLUTONISM n theory that the earth's crust was formed by volcanoes
PLUTONIUM n radioactive metallic element used esp in nuclear reactors and weapons
PLUTONOMY n economics
PLUTONS > PLUTON
PLUTOS > PLUTO
PLUVIAL n period of high rainfall
PLUVIALS > PLUVIAL
PLUVIAN n crocodile bird
PLUVIANS > PLUVIAN
PLUVIOSE same as > PLUVIOUS
PLUVIOUS adj of or relating to rain
PLUVIUS adj as in pluvius insurance insurance against rain
PLY vb work at (a job or trade) ▷ n thickness of wool, fabric, etc
PLYER n person who plies trade
PLYERS > PLYER
PLYING > PLY
PLYINGLY > PLY
PLYWOOD n board made of thin layers of wood glued together
PLYWOODS > PLYWOOD
PNEUMA n person's vital spirit, soul, or creative energy
PNEUMAS > PNEUMA
PNEUMATIC adj worked by or inflated with wind or air
PNEUMONIA n inflammation of the lungs
PNEUMONIC adj of, relating to, or affecting the lungs
PO n chamberpot
POA n type of grass
POACEOUS adj relating to the plant family which comprises grasses
POACH vb catch (animals) illegally on someone else's land
POACHABLE > POACH
POACHED > POACH
POACHER n person who catches animals illegally on someone else's land
POACHERS > POACHER
POACHES > POACH
POACHIER > POACHY
POACHIEST > POACHY
POACHING > POACH
POACHINGS > POACH
POACHY adj (of land) wet and soft

POAKA n type of stilt (bird) native to New Zealand
POAKAS > POAKA
POAKE n waste matter from tanning of hides
POAKES > POAKE
POAS > POA
POBLANO n variety of chilli pepper
POBLANOS > POBLANO
POBOY n New Orleans sandwich
POBOYS > POBOY
POCHARD n European diving duck
POCHARDS > POCHARD
POCHAY n closed horse-drawn four-wheeled coach ▷ vb transport by pochay
POCHAYED > POCHAY
POCHAYING > POCHAY
POCHAYS > POCHAY
POCHETTE n envelope-shaped handbag used by women and men
POCHETTES > POCHETTE
POCHOIR n print made from stencils
POCHOIRS > POCHOIR
POCK n pus-filled blister resulting from smallpox ▷ vb mark with scars
POCKARD variant of > POCHARD
POCKARDS > POCKARD
POCKED > POCK
POCKET n small bag sewn into clothing for carrying things ▷ vb put into one's pocket ▷ adj small
POCKETED > POCKET
POCKETER > POCKET
POCKETERS > POCKET
POCKETFUL n as much as a pocket will hold
POCKETING > POCKET
POCKETS > POCKET
POCKIER > POCK
POCKIES pl n woollen mittens
POCKIEST > POCK
POCKILY > POCK
POCKING > POCK
POCKMANKY n portmanteau
POCKMARK n pitted scar left on the skin after the healing of a smallpox or similar pustule ▷ vb scar or pit (a surface) with pockmarks
POCKMARKS > POCKMARK
POCKPIT n mark left on skin after a pock has gone
POCKPITS > POCKPIT
POCKS > POCK
POCKY > POCK
POCO adv little
POCOSEN same as > POCOSIN
POCOSENS > POCOSEN
POCOSIN n swamp in US upland coastal region
POCOSINS > POCOSIN
POCOSON same as > POCOSIN
POCOSONS > POCOSON

POD n long narrow seed case of peas, beans, etc ⊳ vb remove the pod from

PODAGRA n gout of the foot or big toe

PODAGRAL > PODAGRA

PODAGRAS > PODAGRA

PODAGRIC > PODAGRA

PODAGROUS > PODAGRA

PODAL adj relating to feet

PODALIC adj relating to feet

PODARGUS n bird of SE Asia and Australia

PODCAST n audio file able to be downloaded and listened to on a computer or MP3 player ⊳ vb make available in this format

PODCASTED > PODCAST

PODCASTER > PODCAST

PODCASTS > PODCAST

PODDED > POD

PODDIE n user of or enthusiast for the iPod, a portable digital music player

PODDIER > PODDY

PODDIES > PODDY

PODDIEST > PODDY

PODDING > POD

PODDLE vb move or travel in a leisurely manner

PODDLED > PODDLE

PODDLES > PODDLE

PODDLING > PODDLE

PODDY n handfed calf or lamb ⊳ adj fat

PODESTA n (in modern Italy) subordinate magistrate in some towns

PODESTAS > PODESTA

PODEX n posterior

PODEXES > PODEX

PODGE n short chubby person

PODGES > PODGE

PODGIER > PODGY

PODGIEST > PODGY

PODGILY > PODGY

PODGINESS > PODGY

PODGY adj short and fat

PODIA > PODIUM

PODIAL > PODIUM

PODIATRIC > PODIATRY

PODIATRY another word for > CHIROPODY

PODITE n crustacean leg

PODITES > PODITE

PODITIC adj similar to the limb segment of an arthropod

PODIUM n small raised platform for a conductor or speaker ⊳ vb finish in the top three places in a sporting competition

PODIUMED > PODIUM

PODIUMING > PODIUM

PODIUMS > PODIUM

PODLEY n young coalfish

PODLEYS > PODLEY

PODLIKE > POD

PODOCARP n stem supporting fruit

PODOCARPS > PODOCARP

PODOLOGY n study of feet

PODOMERE n segment of limb of arthropod

PODOMERES > PODOMERE

PODS > POD

PODSOL same as > PODZOL

PODSOLIC > PODZOL

PODSOLISE same as > PODZOLIZE

PODSOLISE same as > PODZOLIZE

PODSOLS > PODSOL

PODUNK adj small or unimportant ⊳ n small or unimportant thing

PODUNKS > PODUNK

PODZOL n type of soil characteristic of coniferous forest regions

PODZOLIC > PODZOL

PODZOLISE same as > PODZOLIZE

PODZOLIZE vb make into or form a podzol

PODZOLS > PODZOL

POECHORE n dry region

POECHORES > POECHORE

POEM n imaginative piece of writing in rhythmic lines

POEMATIC adj of poetry

POEMS > POEM

POENOLOGY same as > PENOLOGY

POEP n emission of gas from the anus ⊳ vb break wind

POEPED > POEP

POEPING > POEP

POEPOL n South African slang for anus

POEPOLS > POEPOL

POEPS > POEP

POESIED > POESY

POESIES > POESY

POESY n poetry ⊳ vb write poems

POESYING > POESY

POET n writer of poems

POETASTER n writer of inferior verse

POETASTRY > POETASTER

POETESS n female poet

POETESSES > POETESS

POETIC adj of or like poetry

POETICAL n poet

POETICALS > POETICAL

POETICISE same as > POETICIZE

POETICISM > POETICISE

POETICIZE vb put into poetry or make poetic

POETICS n principles and forms of poetry or the study of these

POETICULE n inferior poet

POETISE same as > POETICIZE

POETISED > POETISE

POETISER > POETISE

POETISERS > POETISE

POETISES > POETISE

POETISING > POETISE

POETIZE same as > POETICIZE

POETIZED > POETIZE

POETIZER > POETIZE

POETIZERS > POETIZE

POETIZES > POETIZE

POETIZING > POETIZE

POETLESS > POET

POETLIKE > POET

POETRESSE old variant of > POETESS

POETRIES > POETRY

POETRY n poems

POETS > POET

POETSHIP n state of being poet

POETSHIPS > POETSHIP

POFFLE n small piece of land

POFFLES > POFFLE

POGEY n financial or other relief given to the unemployed by the government

POGEYS > POGEY

POGGE n European marine scorpaenoid fish

POGGES > POGGE

POGIES > POGY

POGO vb jump up and down on one spot

POGOED > POGO

POGOER > POGO

POGOERS > POGO

POGOES > POGO

POGOING > POGO

POGONIA n orchid with pink or white fragrant flowers

POGONIAS > POGONIA

POGONIP n icy winter fog

POGONIPS > POGONIP

POGOS > POGO

POGROM n organized persecution and massacre ⊳ vb carry out a pogrom

POGROMED > POGROM

POGROMING > POGROM

POGROMIST > POGROM

POGROMS > POGROM

POGY same as > POGEY

POH interj exclamation expressing contempt or disgust ⊳ vb reject contemptuously

POHED > POH

POHING > POH

POHIRI variant spelling of > POWHIRI

POHIRIS > POHIRI

POHS > POH

POI n ball of woven flax swung rhythmically by Māori women during poi dances

POIGNADO old variant of > PONIARD

POIGNANCE > POIGNANT

POIGNANCY > POIGNANT

POIGNANT adj sharply painful to the feelings

POILU n infantryman in the French Army

POILUS > POILU

POINADO old variant of > PONIARD

POINADOES > POINADO

POINCIANA n tropical leguminous tree with large orange or red flowers

POIND vb take (property of a debtor) in execution or by way of distress

POINDED > POIND

POINDER > POIND

POINDERS > POIND

POINDING > POIND

POINDINGS > POIND

POINDS > POIND

POINT n main idea in a discussion ⊳ vb show the position of something by extending a finger towards it

POINTABLE > POINT

POINTE n tip of the toe

POINTED adj having a sharp end

POINTEDLY > POINTED

POINTEL n engraver's tool

POINTELLE n fabric design in form of chevrons

POINTELS > POINTEL

POINTER n helpful hint

POINTERS > POINTER

POINTES > POINTE

POINTIER > POINTY

POINTIEST > POINTY

POINTILLE n dotted lines and curves impressed on cover of book

POINTING n insertion of mortar between the joints in brickwork

POINTINGS > POINTING

POINTLESS adj meaningless, irrelevant

POINTLIKE adj like a point

POINTMAN n soldier who walks at the front of an infantry patrol in combat

POINTMEN > POINTMAN

POINTS > POINT

POINTSMAN n person who operates railway points

POINTSMEN > POINTSMAN

POINTY adj having a sharp point or points

POIS > POI

POISE n calm dignified manner ⊳ vb be balanced or suspended

POISED adj absolutely ready

POISER n balancing organ of some insects

POISERS > POISER

POISES > POISE

POISHA n monetary unit of Bangladesh

POISHAS > POISHA

POISING > POISE

POISON n substance that kills or injures when swallowed or absorbed ⊳ vb give poison to

POISONED > POISON

POISONER > POISON

POISONERS > POISON

POISONING n the act of giving poison to someone

POISONOUS adj of or like a poison

POISONS > POISON

POISSON n fish

POISSONS > POISSON

POITIN variant spelling of > POTEEN

POITINS > POITIN

POITREL n breastplate of horse's armour

POITRELS > POITREL

POITRINE n woman's bosom

POITRINES > POITRINE

POKABLE > POKE

POKAL n tall drinking cup

POKALS > POKAL**

p

POKE *vb* jab or prod with one's finger, a stick, etc ▷ *n* poking

POKEBERRY *same as* > POKEWEED

POKED > POKE

POKEFUL *n* contents of small bag

POKEFULS > POKEFUL

POKELOGAN *another name for* > BOGAN

POKER *n* metal rod for stirring a fire

POKERISH *adj* stiff like poker

POKEROOT *same as* > POKEWEED

POKEROOTS > POKEROOT

POKERS > POKER

POKERWORK *n* art of producing pictures or designs on wood by burning it with a heated metal point

POKES > POKE

POKEWEED *n* plant with a poisonous root used medicinally

POKEWEEDS > POKEWEED

POKEY *same as* > POKIE

POKEYS > POKEY

POKIE *n* poker machine

POKIER > POKY

POKIES > POKY

POKIEST > POKY

POKILY > POKY

POKINESS > POKY

POKING > POKE

POKY *adj* small and cramped

POL *n* political campaigner

POLACCA *same as* > POLACRE

POLACCAS > POLACCA

POLACK *n* derogatory name for a person of Polish birth or descent

POLACKS > POLACK

POLACRE *n* three-masted sailing vessel

POLACRES > POLACRE

POLAR *adj* of or near either of the earth's poles ▷ *n* type of line in geometry

POLARISE *same as* > POLARIZE

POLARISED > POLARISE

POLARISER *same as* > POLARIZER

POLARISES > POLARISE

POLARITY *n* state of having two directly opposite tendencies or opinions

POLARIZE *vb* form or cause to form into groups with directly opposite views

POLARIZED > POLARIZE

POLARIZER *n* person or a device that causes polarization

POLARIZES > POLARIZE

POLARON *n* kind of electron

POLARONS > POLARON

POLARS > POLAR

POLDER *n* land reclaimed from the sea, esp in the Netherlands ▷ *vb* reclaim land from the sea

POLDERED > POLDER

POLDERING > POLDER

POLDERS > POLDER

POLE *n* long rounded piece of wood etc ▷ *vb* strike or push with a pole

POLEAX *same as* > POLEAXE

POLEAXE *vb* hit or stun with a heavy blow ▷ *n* axe formerly used in battle or used by a butcher

POLEAXED > POLEAXE

POLEAXES > POLEAXE

POLEAXING > POLEAXE

POLECAT *n* small animal of the weasel family

POLECATS > POLECAT

POLED > POLE

POLEIS > POLIS

POLELESS > POLE

POLEMARCH *n* (in ancient Greece) civilian official, originally a supreme general

POLEMIC *n* fierce attack on or defence of a particular opinion, belief, etc ▷ *adj* of or involving dispute or controversy

POLEMICAL *adj* related to polemics, debate

POLEMICS *n* art of dispute

POLEMISE *same as* > POLEMIZE

POLEMISED > POLEMISE

POLEMISES > POLEMISE

POLEMIST > POLEMIC

POLEMISTS > POLEMIC

POLEMIZE *vb* engage in controversy

POLEMIZED > POLEMIZE

POLEMIZES > POLEMIZE

POLENTA *n* thick porridge made in Italy, usually from maize

POLENTAS > POLENTA

POLER *n* person or thing that poles, esp a punter

POLERS > POLER

POLES > POLE

POLESTAR *n* guiding principle, rule, standard, etc

POLESTARS > POLESTAR

POLEWARD *adv* towards a pole

POLEY *adj* (of cattle) hornless or polled ▷ *n* animal with horns removed

POLEYN *n* piece of armour for protecting the knee

POLEYNS > POLEYN

POLEYS > POLEY

POLIANITE *n* manganese dioxide occurring as hard crystals

POLICE *n* organized force in a state which keeps law and order ▷ *vb* control or watch over with police or a similar body

POLICED > POLICE

POLICEMAN *n* member of a police force

POLICEMEN > POLICEMAN

POLICER *n* computer device controlling use

POLICERS > POLICER

POLICES > POLICE

POLICIER *n* film featuring police investigating crimes

POLICIERS > POLICIER

POLICIES > POLICY

POLICING > POLICE

POLICINGS > POLICE

POLICY *n* plan of action adopted by a person, group, or state

POLIES > POLY

POLING > POLE

POLINGS > POLE

POLIO *n* acute viral disease

POLIOS > POLIO

POLIS *n* ancient Greek city-state

POLISES > POLIS

POLISH *vb* make smooth and shiny by rubbing ▷ *n* substance used for polishing

POLISHED *adj* accomplished

POLISHER > POLISH

POLISHERS > POLISH

POLISHES > POLISH

POLISHING > POLISH

POLITBURO *n* supreme policy-making authority in most communist countries

POLITE *adj* showing consideration for others in one's manners, speech, etc

POLITELY > POLITE

POLITER > POLITE

POLITESSE *n* formal or genteel politeness

POLITEST > POLITE

POLITIC *adj* wise and likely to prove advantageous

POLITICAL *adj* of the state, government, or public administration

POLITICK *vb* engage in politics

POLITICKS > POLITICK

POLITICLY > POLITIC

POLITICO *n* politician

POLITICOS > POLITICO

POLITICS *n* winning and using of power to govern society

POLITIES > POLITY

POLITIQUE *n* 16th-century French moderate

POLITY *n* politically organized state, church, or society

POLJE *n* large elliptical depression in karst regions

POLJES > POLJE

POLK *vb* dance a polka

POLKA *n* lively 19th-century dance ▷ *vb* dance a polka

POLKAED > POLKA

POLKAING > POLKA

POLKAS > POLKA

POLKED > POLK

POLKING > POLK

POLKS > POLK

POLL *n* questioning of a random sample of people to find out general opinion ▷ *vb* receive (votes)

POLLACKS > POLLACK

POLLAN *n* whitefish that occurs in lakes in Northern Ireland

POLLANS > POLLAN

POLLARD *n* animal that has shed its horns or has had them removed ▷ *vb* cut off the top of (a tree) to make it grow bushy

POLLARDED > POLLARD

POLLARDS > POLLARD

POLLAXE *same as* > POLEAXE

POLLAXED > POLLAXE

POLLAXES > POLLAXE

POLLAXING > POLLAXE

POLLED *adj* (of animals, esp cattle) having the horns cut off or being naturally hornless

POLLEE > POLL

POLLEES > POLL

POLLEN *n* fine dust produced by flowers to fertilize other flowers ▷ *vb* collect pollen

POLLENATE *same as* > POLLINATE

POLLENED > POLLEN

POLLENING > POLLEN

POLLENS > POLLEN

POLLENT *adj* strong

POLLER > POLL

POLLERS > POLL

POLLEX *n* first digit of the forelimb of amphibians, reptiles, birds, and mammals

POLLICAL > POLLEX

POLLICES > POLLEX

POLLICIE *obsolete spelling of* > POLICY

POLLICIES > POLLICIE

POLLICY *obsolete spelling of* > POLICY

POLLIES > POLLY

POLLINATE *vb* fertilize with pollen

POLLING *n* casting or registering of votes at an election

POLLINGS > POLLING

POLLINIA > POLLINIUM

POLLINIC > POLLEN

POLLINISE *same as* > POLLINIZE

POLLINIUM *n* mass of cohering pollen grains, produced by plants such as orchids and transported as a whole during pollination

POLLINIZE *same as* > POLLINATE

POLLIST *n* one advocating the use of polls

POLLISTS > POLLIST

POLLIWIG *same as* > POLLIWOG

POLLIWIGS > POLLIWOG

POLLIWOG *n* sailor who has not crossed the equator

POLLIWOGS > POLLIWOG

POLLMAN *n* one passing a degree without honours

POLLMEN > POLLMAN

POLLOCK *same as* > POLLACK

POLLOCKS > POLLOCK

POLLS > POLL

POLLSTER *n* person who conducts opinion polls

POLLSTERS > POLLSTER

POLLACK *n* food fish related to the cod, found in northern seas

POLLTAKER n person conducting poll

POLLUCITE n colourless rare mineral consisting of a hydrated caesium aluminium silicate

POLLUSION n comic Shakespearian character's version of "allusion"

POLLUTANT n something that pollutes

POLLUTE vb contaminate with something poisonous or harmful

POLLUTED adj made unclean or impure

POLLUTER > POLLUTE

POLLUTERS > POLLUTE

POLLUTES > POLLUTE

POLLUTING > POLLUTE

POLLUTION n act of polluting or the state of being polluted

POLLUTIVE adj causing pollution

POLLY n politician

POLLYANNA n person who is constantly or excessively optimistic

POLLYWIG same as > POLLIWOG

POLLYWIGS > POLLYWIG

POLLYWOG same as > POLLIWOG

POLLYWOGS > POLLYWOG

POLO n game like hockey played by teams of players on horseback

POLOIDAL adj relating to a type of magnetic field

POLOIST n devotee of polo

POLOISTS > POLOIST

POLONAISE n old stately dance

POLONIE same as > POLONY

POLONIES > POLONY

POLONISE same as > POLONIZE

POLONISED > POLONISE

POLONISES > POLONISE

POLONISM > POLONISE

POLONISMS > POLONISE

POLONIUM n radioactive element that occurs in trace amounts in uranium ores

POLONIUMS > POLONIUM

POLONIZE vb make Polish

POLONIZED > POLONIZE

POLONIZES > POLONIZE

POLONY n bologna sausage

POLOS > POLO

POLS > POL

POLT n thump or blow ▷ vb strike

POLTED > POLT

POLTFEET > POLTFOOT

POLTFOOT adj having a club foot ▷ n club foot

POLTING > POLT

POLTROON n utter coward

POLTROONS > POLTROON

POLTS > POLT

POLVERINE n glassmakers' potash

POLY n polytechnic

POLYACID adj having two or more hydroxyl groups ▷ n compound made up of two or more hydroxyl groups

POLYACIDS > POLYACID

POLYACT adj (of a sea creature) having many tentacles or limb-like protrusions

POLYADIC adj (of a relation, operation, etc) having several argument places

POLYAMIDE n synthetic polymeric material

POLYAMINE n compound containing two or more amine groups

POLYAMORY n practice of openly having more than one romantic relationship at a time

POLYANDRY n practice of having more than one husband at the same time

POLYANTHA n type of flower

POLYANTHI n hybrid garden primroses

POLYARCH n member of polyarchy

POLYARCHY n political system in which power is dispersed

POLYAXIAL n joint in which movement occurs in more than one axis

POLYAXON n nerve cell with multiple branches

POLYAXONS > POLYAXON

POLYBAG vb put into a polythene bag

POLYBAGS > POLYBAG

POLYBASIC adj (of an acid) having two or more replaceable hydrogen atoms per molecule

POLYBRID n hybrid plant with more than two parental groups

POLYBRIDS > POLYBRID

POLYCARPY n condition of being able to produce flowers and fruit several times in successive years or seasons

POLYCHETE n variety of worm

POLYCONIC adj as in polyconic projection type of projection used in making maps of large areas

POLYCOT n plant that has or appears to have more than two cotyledons

POLYCOTS > POLYCOT

POLYDEMIC adj growing in or inhabiting more than two regions

POLYDRUG adj relating to using several drugs together

POLYENE n organic chemical compound

POLYENES > POLYENE

POLYENIC > POLYENE

POLYESTER n synthetic material used to make plastics and textile fibres

POLYGALA n herbaceous plant or small shrub

POLYGALAS > POLYGALA

POLYGAM n plant of the Polygamia class

POLYGAMIC > POLYGAMY

POLYGAMS > POLYGAM

POLYGAMY n practice of having more than one husband or wife at the same time

POLYGENE n any of a group of genes that each produce a small effect on a particular characteristic of the phenotype

POLYGENES > POLYGENE

POLYGENIC adj of, relating to, or controlled by polygenes

POLYGENY > POLYGENIC

POLYGLOT adj (person) able to speak or write several languages ▷ n person who can speak many languages

POLYGLOTS > POLYGLOT

POLYGLOTT variant of > POLYGLOT

POLYGON n geometrical figure with three or more angles and sides

POLYGONAL > POLYGON

POLYGONS > POLYGON

POLYGONUM n plant with stems with knotlike joints and spikes of small white, green, or pink flowers

POLYGONY > POLYGON

POLYGRAPH n instrument for recording pulse rate and perspiration, used esp as a lie detector

POLYGYNE adj (of a colony of insects) having more than one egg-laying queen

POLYGYNY n practice of having more than one female partner at the same time

POLYHEDRA n solid figures, each consisting of four or more plane faces

POLYIMIDE n type of polymer

POLYLEMMA n debate forcing choice between contradictory positions

POLYMASTY n the presence of more than two breasts

POLYMATH n person of great and varied learning

POLYMATHS > POLYMATH

POLYMATHY > POLYMATH

POLYMER n chemical compound with large molecules made of simple molecules of the same kind

POLYMERIC adj of or being a polymer

POLYMERS > POLYMER

POLYMERY > POLYMER

POLYMORPH n species of animal or plant that exhibits polymorphism

POLYMYXIN n polypeptide antibiotic

POLYNIA same as > POLYNYA

POLYNIAS > POLYNIA

POLYNYA n stretch of open water surrounded by ice

POLYNYAS > POLYNYA

POLYNYI > POLYNYA

POLYOL n type of alcohol

POLYOLS > POLYOL

POLYOMA n type of tumour caused by virus

POLYOMAS > POLYOMA

POLYOMINO n polygon made from joining identical squares at their edges

POLYONYM n object with many names

POLYONYMS > POLYONYM

POLYONYMY > POLYONYM

POLYP n small simple sea creature with a hollow cylindrical body

POLYPARIA n polyparies

POLYPARY n common base and connecting tissue of a colony of coelenterate polyps, esp coral

POLYPE variant of > POLYP

POLYPED same as > POLYPED

POLYPEDS > POLYPED

POLYPES > POLYPE

POLYPHAGY n insatiable appetite

POLYPHASE adj (of an electrical system, circuit, or device) having, generating, or using two or more alternating voltages of the same frequency, the phases of which are cyclically displaced by fractions of a period

POLYPHON n musical instrument resembling a lute

POLYPHONE n letter or character with more than one phonetic value

POLYPHONS > POLYPHON

POLYPHONY n polyphonic style of composition or a piece of music using it

POLYPI > POLYPUS

POLYPIDE n polyp forming part of a colonial animal

POLYPIDES > POLYPIDE

POLYPIDOM same as > POLYPARY

POLYPILL n pill containing a number of medicines that all treat the same condition

POLYPILLS > POLYPILL

POLYPINE adj of or relating to polyps

POLYPITE same as > POLYPIDE

POLYPITES > POLYPITE

POLYPLOID adj (of cells, organisms, etc) having more than twice the basic (haploid) number of chromosomes ▷ n individual or cell of this type

POLYPNEA n rapid breathing

POLYPNEAS > POLYPNEA

POLYPNEIC > POLYPNEA

POLYPOD adj (esp of insect larvae) having many legs or similar appendages ▷ n animal of this type

POLYPODS > POLYPOD

POLYPODY n fern with deeply divided leaves and round naked sori

P

POLYPOID > POLYP

POLYPORE n type of fungi

POLYPORES > POLYPORE

POLYPOSES > POLYPOSIS

POLYPOSIS n formation of many polyps

POLYPOUS > POLYP

POLYPS > POLYP

POLYPTYCH n altarpiece consisting of more than three panels, set with paintings or carvings, and usually hinged for folding

POLYPUS same as > POLYP

POLYPUSES > POLYPUS

POLYS > POLY

POLYSEME n word with many meanings

POLYSEMES > POLYSEME

POLYSEMIC > POLYSEME

POLYSEMY n existence of several meanings in a single word

POLYSOME n assemblage of ribosomes associated with a messenger RNA molecule

POLYSOMES > POLYSOME

POLYSOMIC adj of, relating to, or designating a basically diploid chromosome complement, in which some but not all the chromosomes are represented more than twice

POLYSOMY > POLYSOME

POLYSTYLE adj with many columns ▷ n building with many columns

POLYTENE adj denoting a type of giant-size chromosome

POLYTENY > POLYTENE

POLYTHENE n light plastic used for bags etc

POLYTONAL adj using more than two different tones or keys simultaneously

POLYTYPE n crystal occurring in more than one form ▷ vb produce by use of a polytype

POLYTYPED > POLYTYPE

POLYTYPES > POLYTYPE

POLYTYPIC adj existing in, consisting of, or incorporating several types or forms

POLYURIA n state of discharging abnormally large quantities of urine

POLYURIAS > POLYURIA

POLYURIC > POLYURIA

POLYVINYL n designating a plastic or resin formed by polymerization of a vinyl derivative

POLYWATER n liquid formerly supposed to be polymeric form of water

POLYZOA n small mosslike aquatic creatures

POLYZOAN another word for > BRYOZOAN

POLYZOANS > POLYZOAN

POLYZOARY n colony of bryozoan animals

POLYZOIC adj (of certain colonial animals) having

many zooids or similar polyps

POLYZONAL adj having many zones

POLYZOOID adj resembling a polyzoon

POLYZOON n individual zooid within polyzoan

POM same as > POMMY

POMACE n apple pulp left after pressing for juice

POMACEOUS adj of, relating to, or bearing pomes, such as the apple, pear, and quince trees

POMACES > POMACE

POMADE n perfumed oil put on the hair to make it smooth and shiny ▷ vb put pomade on

POMADED > POMADE

POMADES > POMADE

POMADING > POMADE

POMANDER n mixture of sweet-smelling petals, herbs, etc

POMANDERS > POMANDER

POMATO n hybrid of tomato and potato

POMATOES > POMATO

POMATUM n pomade ▷ vb put pomatum on

POMATUMED > POMATUM

POMATUMS > POMATUM

POMBE n any alcoholic drink

POMBES > POMBE

POME n fleshy fruit of the apple and related plants

POMELIKE adj like a pome

POMELO n edible yellow fruit, like a grapefruit

POMELOS > POMELO

POMEROY n bullet used to down airships

POMEROYS > POMEROY

POMES > POME

POMFRET n small black rounded liquorice sweet

POMFRETS > POMFRET

POMMEE adj (of cross) having end of each arm ending in disk

POMMEL same as > PUMMEL

POMMELE adj having a pommel

POMMELED > POMMEL

POMMELING > POMMEL

POMMELLED > POMMEL

POMMELS > POMMEL

POMMETTY adj having a pommel

POMMIE same as > POMMY

POMMIES > POMMY

POMMY n word used by Australians and New Zealanders for a British person

POMO n postmodernist

POMOERIUM n space around town within city walls

POMOLOGY n branch of horticulture that is concerned with the study and cultivation of fruit

POMOS > POMO

POMP n stately display or ceremony

POMPADOUR n early 18th-century hairstyle for women, having the front hair arranged over a pad to give it greater height and bulk

POMPANO n deep-bodied carangid food fish

POMPANOS > POMPANO

POMPELO n large Asian citrus fruit

POMPELOS > POMPELO

POMPEY vb mollycoddle

POMPEYED > POMPEY

POMPEYING > POMPEY

POMPEYS > POMPEY

POMPHOLYX n type of eczema

POMPIER adj slavishly conventional ▷ n conventional or imitative artist

POMPIERS > POMPIER

POMPILID n spider-hunting wasp

POMPILIDS > POMPILID

POMPION n pumpkin

POMPIONS > POMPION

POMPOM n decorative ball of tufted wool, silk, etc

POMPOMS > POMPOM

POMPON same as > POMPOM

POMPONS > POMPON

POMPOON variant of > POMPOM

POMPOONS > POMPOON

POMPOSITY n vain or ostentatious display of dignity or importance

POMPOSO adj (of music) to be played in a ceremonial manner

POMPOUS adj foolishly serious and grand, self-important

POMPOUSLY > POMPOUS

POMPS > POMP

POMROY variant of > POMEROY

POMROYS > POMROY

POMS > POM

POMWATER n kind of apple

POMWATERS > POMWATER

PONCE vb act stupidly or waste time

PONCEAU n scarlet red

PONCEAUS > PONCEAU

PONCEAUX > PONCEAU

PONCED > PONCE

PONCES > PONCE

PONCEY adj ostentatious or pretentious

PONCHO n loose circular cloak with a hole for the head

PONCHOED adj wearing poncho

PONCHOS > PONCHO

PONCIER > PONCEY

PONCIEST > PONCEY

PONCING > PONCE

PONCY same as > PONCEY

POND n small area of still water ▷ vb hold back (flowing water)

PONDAGE n water held in reservoir

PONDAGES > PONDAGE

PONDED > POND

PONDER vb think thoroughly or deeply (about)

PONDERAL adj relating to weight

PONDERATE vb consider

PONDERED > PONDER

PONDERER > PONDER

PONDERERS > PONDER

PONDERING > PONDER

PONDEROSA n N American pine tree

PONDEROUS adj serious and dull

PONDERS > PONDER

PONDING > POND

PONDOK n (in southern Africa) crudely made house or shack

PONDOKKIE same as > PONDOK

PONDOKS > PONDOK

PONDS > POND

PONDWEED n plant that grows in ponds

PONDWEEDS > PONDWEED

PONE n bread made of maize

PONENT adj westerly ▷ n the west

PONENTS > PONENT

PONES > PONE

PONEY same as > PONY

PONEYS > PONEY

PONG n strong unpleasant smell ▷ vb give off a strong unpleasant smell

PONGA n tall New Zealand tree fern

PONGAL n Indian dish of cooked rice

PONGALS > PONGAL

PONGAS > PONGA

PONGED > PONG

PONGEE n thin plain-weave silk fabric

PONGEES > PONGEE

PONGID n primate of the family which includes the gibbons and the great apes

PONGIDS > PONGID

PONGIER > PONG

PONGIEST > PONG

PONGING > PONG

PONGO n anthropoid ape, esp an orang-utan or (formerly) a gorilla

PONGOES > PONGO

PONGOS > PONGO

PONGS > PONG

PONGY > PONG

PONIARD n small slender dagger ▷ vb stab with a poniard

PONIARDED > PONIARD

PONIARDS > PONIARD

PONIED > PONY

PONIES > PONY

PONK n evil spirit ▷ vb stink

PONKED > PONK

PONKING > PONK

PONKS > PONK

PONS n bridge of connecting tissue

PONT n (in South Africa) river ferry

PONTAGE n tax paid for repairing bridge

PONTAGES > PONTAGE

PONTAL adj of or relating to the pons

PONTES > PONS

PONTIANAC same as > PONTIANAK

PONTIANAK n (in Malay folklore) female vampire

PONTIC adj of or relating to the pons

PONTIE same as > PONTY

PONTIES > PONTY

PONTIFEX n (in ancient Rome) any of the senior members of the Pontifical College

PONTIFF n Pope

PONTIFFS > PONTIFF

PONTIFIC > PONTIFF

PONTIFICE n structure of bridge

PONTIFIED > PONTIFY

PONTIFIES > PONTIFY

PONTIFY vb speak or behave in a pompous or dogmatic manner

PONTIL same as > PUNTY

PONTILE adj relating to pons ▷ n metal bar used in glass-making

PONTILES > PONTILE

PONTILS > PONTIL

PONTINE adj of or relating to bridges

PONTLEVIS n horse rearing repeatedly

PONTON variant of > PONTOON

PONTONEER same as > PONTONIER

PONTONIER n person in charge of or involved in building a pontoon bridge

PONTONS > PONTON

PONTOON n floating platform supporting a temporary bridge ▷ vb cross a river using pontoons

PONTOONED > PONTOON

PONTOONER > PONTOON

PONTOONS > PONTOON

PONTS > PONT

PONTY n rod used for shaping molten glass

PONY n small horse ▷ vb settle bill or debt

PONYING > PONY

PONYSKIN n leather from pony hide

PONYSKINS > PONYSKIN

PONYTAIL n long hair tied in one bunch at the back of the head

PONYTAILS > PONYTAIL

PONZU n type of Japanese dipping sauce

PONZUS > PONZU

POO vb defecate

POOBAH n influential person

POOBAHS > POOBAH

POOCH n slang word for dog ▷ vb bulge or protrude

POOCHED > POOCH

POOCHES > POOCH

POOCHING > POOCH

POOD n unit of weight, used in Russia

POODLE n dog with curly hair often clipped fancifully

POODLES > POODLE

POODS > POOD

POOED > POO

POOF n offensive word for a homosexual man

POOFIER > POOF

POOFIEST > POOF

POOFS > POOF

POOFTAH same as > POOFTER

POOFTAHS > POOFTAH

POOFTER n offensive word for a homosexual man

POOFTERS > POOFTER

POOFY > POOF

POOGYE n Hindu nose-flute

POOGYES > POOGYE

POOH interj exclamation of disdain, contempt, or disgust ▷ vb make such an exclamation

POOHED > POOH

POOHING > POOH

POOHS > POOH

POOING > POO

POOJA variant of > PUJA

POOJAH variant of > PUJA

POOJAHS > POOJAH

POOJAS > POOJA

POOK vb pluck

POOKA n malevolent Irish spirit

POOKAS > POOKA

POOKING > POOK

POOKIT > POOK

POOKS > POOK

POOL n small body of still water ▷ vb put in a common fund

POOLED > POOL

POOLER n person taking part in pool

POOLERS > POOLER

POOLHALL n room containing pool tables

POOLHALLS > POOLHALL

POOLING > POOL

POOLROOM n hall or establishment where pool, billiards, etc, are played

POOLROOMS > POOLROOM

POOLS pl n organized nationwide gambling pool

POOLSIDE n area surrounding swimming pool

POOLSIDES > POOLSIDE

POON n SE Asian tree

POONAC n coconut residue

POONACS > POONAC

POONCE n offensive word for a homosexual man ▷ vb behave effeminately

POONCED > POONCE

POONCES > POONCE

POONCING > POONCE

POONS > POON

POONTANG n vulgar word for the female pudenda

POONTANGS > POONTANG

POOP n raised part at the back of a sailing ship ▷ vb (of a wave or sea) break over the stern of (a vessel)

POOPED > POOP

POOPER n as in party pooper person who spoils other people's enjoyment

POOPERS > POOPER

POOPIER > POOPY

POOPIEST > POOPY

POOPING > POOP

POOPS > POOP

POOPY adj stupid or ineffectual

POOR adj having little money and few possessions

POORBOX n box used for the collection of money for the poor

POORBOXES > POORBOX

POORER > POOR

POOREST > POOR

POORHOUSE n (formerly) publicly maintained institution offering accommodation to the poor

POORI n unleavened Indian bread

POORIS > POORI

POORISH > POOR

POORLIER > POORLY

POORLIEST > POORLY

POORLY adv in a poor manner ▷ adj not in good health

POORMOUTH vb complain about being poor

POORNESS > POOR

POORT n (in South Africa) steep narrow mountain pass

POORTITH same as > PUIRTITH

POORTITHS > POORTITH

POORTS > POORT

POORWILL n bird of N America

POORWILLS > POORWILL

POOS > POO

POOT vb break wind

POOTED > POOT

POOTER vb hurry away

POOTERED > POOTER

POOTERING > POOTER

POOTERS > POOT

POOTING > POOT

POOTLE vb travel or go in a relaxed or leisurely manner

POOTLED > POOTLE

POOTLES > POOTLE

POOTLING > POOTLE

POOTS > POOT

POOVE same as > POOF

POOVERIES > POOVERY

POOVERY n offensive word for male homosexuality

POOVES > POOVE

POOVIER > POOVE

POOVIEST > POOVE

POOVY > POOVE

POP vb make or cause to make a small explosive sound ▷ n small explosive sound ▷ adj popular

POPADUM same as > POPPADOM

POPADUMS > POPADUM

POPCORN n grains of maize heated until they puff up and burst

POPCORNS > POPCORN

POPE n bishop of Rome as head of the Roman Catholic Church

POPEDOM n office or dignity of a pope

POPEDOMS > POPEDOM

POPEHOOD > POPE

POPEHOODS > POPE

POPELESS > POPE

POPELIKE > POPE

POPELING n deputy or supporter of pope

POPELINGS > POPELING

POPERA n music drawing on opera or classical music and aiming for popular appeal

POPERAS > POPERA

POPERIES > POPERY

POPERIN n kind of pear

POPERINS > POPERIN

POPERY n derogatory word for Roman Catholicism

POPES > POPE

POPESEYE adj denoting a cut of steak

POPESHIP > POPE

POPESHIPS > POPE

POPETTE n young female fan or performer of pop music

POPETTES > POPETTE

POPEYED adj staring in astonishment

POPGUN n toy gun that fires a pellet or cork by means of compressed air

POPGUNS > POPGUN

POPINAC n type of thorny shrub

POPINACK same as > POPINAC

POPINACKS > POPINACK

POPINACS > POPINAC

POPINJAY n conceited, foppish, or overly talkative person

POPINJAYS > POPINJAY

POPISH adj derogatory word for Roman Catholic

POPISHLY > POPISH

POPJOY vb amuse oneself

POPJOYED > POPJOY

POPJOYING > POPJOY

POPJOYS > POPJOY

POPLAR n tall slender tree

POPLARS > POPLAR

POPLIN n ribbed cotton material

POPLINS > POPLIN

POPLITEAL adj of, relating to, or near the part of the leg behind the knee

POPLITEI > POPLITEUS

POPLITEUS n muscle in leg

POPLITIC same as > POPLITEAL

POPOUT n type of out in baseball

POPOUTS > POPOUT

POPOVER n individual Yorkshire pudding, often served with roast beef

POPOVERS > POPOVER

POPPA same as > PAPA

POPPADOM n thin round crisp Indian bread

POPPADOMS > POPPADOM

P

POPPADUM same as > POPPADUM

POPPADUMS > POPPADUM

POPPAS > POPPA

POPPED > POP

POPPER n press stud

POPPERING n method of fishing

POPPERS > POPPER

POPPET n term of affection for a small child or sweetheart

POPPETS > POPPET

POPPIED adj covered with poppies

POPPIER > POPPY

POPPIES > POPPY

POPPIEST > POPPY

POPPING > POP

POPPISH adj like pop music

POPPIT n bead used to form necklace

POPPITS > POPPIT

POPPLE vb (of boiling water or a choppy sea) to heave or toss

POPPLED > POPPLE

POPPLES > POPPLE

POPPLIER > POPPLY

POPPLIEST > POPPLY

POPPLING > POPPLE

POPPLY adj covered in small bumps

POPPY n plant with a large red flower ▷ adj reddish-orange

POPPYCOCK n nonsense

POPPYHEAD n hard dry seed-containing capsule of a poppy

POPPYSEED adj made with the seed of the poppy

POPRIN same as > POPERIN

POPS > POP

POPSICLE n tradename for a kind of ice lolly

POPSICLES > POPSICLE

POPSIE same as > POPSY

POPSIES > POPSY

POPSOCK n women's knee-length nylon stocking

POPSOCKS > POPSOCK

POPSTER n pop star

POPSTERS > POPSTER

POPSTREL n young, attractive female pop star

POPSTRELS > POPSTREL

POPSY n attractive young woman

POPTASTIC adj (of pop music) very good

POPULACE n ordinary people

POPULACES > POPULACE

POPULAR adj widely liked and admired ▷ n cheap newspapers with mass circulation

POPULARLY adv by the public as a whole

POPULARS > POPULAR

POPULATE vb live in, inhabit

POPULATED > POPULATE

POPULATES > POPULATE

POPULISM n political strategy based on an appeal to the prejudices of ordinary people

POPULISMS > POPULISM

POPULIST adj appealing to the interests or prejudices of ordinary people ▷ n person who appeals to the interests or prejudices of ordinary people

POPULISTS > POPULIST

POPULOUS adj densely populated

PORAE n large edible sea fish of New Zealand waters

PORAES > PORAE

PORAL adj relating to pores

PORANGI adj crazy

PORBEAGLE n kind of shark

PORCELAIN n fine china

PORCH n covered approach to the entrance of a building

PORCHED adj having a porch

PORCHES > PORCH

PORCHETTA n Italian boneless stuffed pork cut from a whole roast pig

PORCHLESS adj without a porch

PORCINE adj of or like a pig

PORCINI > PORCINO

PORCINIS > PORCINO

PORCINO n edible woodland fungus

PORCUPINE n animal covered with long pointed quills

PORCUPINY adj like a porcupine

PORE n tiny opening in the skin or in the surface of a plant ▷ vb make a close intent examination or study

PORED > PORE

PORER n person who pores

PORERS > PORER

PORES > PORE

PORGE vb cleanse (slaughtered animal) ceremonially

PORGED > PORGE

PORGES > PORGE

PORGIE same as > PORGY

PORGIES > PORGY

PORGING > PORGE

PORGY n any of various sparid fishes

PORIER > PORY

PORIEST > PORY

PORIFER n type of invertebrate

PORIFERAL > PORIFERAN

PORIFERAN n invertebrate of the phylum which comprises the sponges

PORIFERS > PORIFER

PORIN n protein through which molecules can pass

PORINA n moth the larva of which causes damage to grassland

PORINAS > PORINA

PORINESS > PORY

PORING > PORE

PORINS > PORIN

PORISM n type of mathematical proposition

PORISMS > PORISM

PORISTIC > PORISM

PORK vb eat ravenously ▷ n the flesh of pigs used as food

PORKED > PORK

PORKER n pig raised for food

PORKERS > PORKER

PORKIER > PORKY

PORKIES > PORKY

PORKIEST > PORKY

PORKINESS > PORKY

PORKING > PORK

PORKLING n pig

PORKLINGS > PORKLING

PORKPIE n hat with a round flat crown and a brim that can be turned up or down

PORKPIES > PORKPIE

PORKS > PORK

PORKWOOD n wood of small American tree

PORKWOODS > PORKWOOD

PORKY adj of or like pork ▷ n lie

PORLOCK vb interrupt or intrude at an awkward moment

PORLOCKED > PORLOCK

PORLOCKS > PORLOCK

PORN n pornography

PORNIER > PORNY

PORNIEST > PORNY

PORNO same as > PORN

PORNOMAG n pornographic magazine

PORNOMAGS > PORNOMAG

PORNOS > PORNO

PORNS > PORN

PORNY adj pornographic

POROGAMIC > POROGAMY

POROGAMY n fertilization of seed plants

POROMERIC adj (of a plastic) permeable to water vapour ▷ n substance having this characteristic, esp one based on polyurethane and used in place of leather in making shoe uppers

POROSCOPE n instrument for assessing porosity

POROSCOPY > POROSCOPE

POROSE adj pierced with small pores

POROSES > POROSIS

POROSIS n porous condition of bones

POROSITY n state or condition of being porous

POROUS adj allowing liquid to pass through gradually

POROUSLY > POROUS

PORPESS n type of fish

PORPESSE same as > PORPOISE

PORPESSES > PORPESS

PORPHYRIA n hereditary disease of body metabolism, producing abdominal pain, mental confusion, etc

PORPHYRIC > PORPHYRIA

PORPHYRIN n any of a group of pigments occurring widely in animal and plant tissues and having a heterocyclic structure formed from four pyrrole rings linked by four methylene groups

PORPHYRIO n aquatic bird

PORPHYRY n reddish rock with large crystals in it

PORPOISE n fishlike sea mammal ▷ vb (of an aeroplane) nose-dive during landing

PORPOISED > PORPOISE

PORPOISES > PORPOISE

PORPORATE adj wearing purple

PORRECT adj extended forwards ▷ vb stretch forward

PORRECTED > PORRECT

PORRECTS > PORRECT

PORRENGER same as > PORRINGER

PORRIDGE n breakfast food made of oatmeal cooked in water or milk

PORRIDGES > PORRIDGE

PORRIDGY adj having the consistency of porridge

PORRIGO n disease of the scalp

PORRIGOS > PORRIGO

PORRINGER n small dish, often with a handle, used esp formerly for soup or porridge

PORT same as > PORTHOLE

PORTA n aperture in an organ

PORTABLE adj easily carried ▷ n article designed to be easily carried, such as a television or typewriter

PORTABLES > PORTABLE

PORTABLY > PORTABLE

PORTAGE n (route for) transporting boats overland ▷ vb transport (boats) in this way

PORTAGED > PORTAGE

PORTAGES > PORTAGE

PORTAGING > PORTAGE

PORTAGUE n former Portuguese gold coin

PORTAGUES > PORTAGUE

PORTAL n large imposing doorway or gate

PORTALED > PORTAL

PORTALS > PORTAL

PORTANCE n person's bearing

PORTANCES > PORTANCE

PORTAPACK n the first combined videotape recorder and camera

PORTAPAK same as > PORTAPACK

PORTAPAKS > PORTAPAK

PORTAS > PORTA

PORTASES variant of > PORTESSE

PORTATE adj diagonally athwart escutcheon

PORTATILE adj portable

PORTATIVE adj concerned with the act of carrying

PORTED > PORT

PORTEND vb be a sign of

PORTENDED > PORTEND

PORTENDS > PORTEND

PORTENT n sign of a future event

PORTENTS > PORTENT

PORTEOUS variant of > PORTESSE

PORTER n person who carries luggage ▷ vb carry luggage

PORTERAGE n work of carrying supplies, goods, etc, done by porters

PORTERED > PORTER

PORTERESS n female porter

PORTERING > PORTER

PORTERLY adj like a porter

PORTERS > PORTER

PORTESS variant of > PORTESSE

PORTESSE n prayer book

PORTESSES > PORTESSE

PORTFIRE n slow-burning fuse formerly used in fireworks

PORTFIRES > PORTFIRE

PORTFOLIO n (flat case for carrying) examples of an artist's work

PORTHOLE n small round window in a ship or aircraft

PORTHOLES > PORTHOLE

PORTHORS same as > PORTESSE

PORTHOS same as > PORTESSE

PORTHOSES > PORTHOS

PORTHOUSE n company producing port

PORTICO n porch or covered walkway with columns supporting the roof

PORTICOED > PORTICO

PORTICOES > PORTICO

PORTICOS > PORTICO

PORTIER > PORT

PORTIERE n curtain hung in a doorway

PORTIERED adj having a portiere, a curtain hanging across a doorway

PORTIERES > PORTIERE

PORTIEST > PORTY

PORTIGUE same as > PORTAGUE

PORTIGUES > PORTIGUE

PORTING > PORT

PORTION n part or share ▷ vb divide (something) into shares

PORTIONED > PORTION

PORTIONER > PORTION

PORTIONS > PORTION

PORTLAND n type of rose

PORTLANDS > PORTLAND

PORTLAST n gunwale of ship

PORTLASTS > PORTLAST

PORTLESS > PORT

PORTLIER > PORTLY

PORTLIEST > PORTLY

PORTLY adj rather fat

PORTMAN n inhabitant of port

PORTMEN > PORTMAN

PORTOISE same as > PORTLAST

PORTOISES > PORTOISE

PORTOLAN n book of sailing charts

PORTOLANI > PORTOLANO

PORTOLANO variant of > PORTOLAN

PORTOLANS > PORTOLAN

PORTOUS variant of > PORTESSE

PORTOUSES > PORTOUS

PORTRAIT n picture of a person ▷ adj (of a publication or an illustration in a publication) of greater height than width

PORTRAITS > PORTRAIT

PORTRAY vb describe or represent by artistic means, as in writing or film

PORTRAYAL > PORTRAY

PORTRAYED > PORTRAY

PORTRAYER > PORTRAY

PORTRAYS > PORTRAY

PORTREEVE n Saxon magistrate

PORTRESS n female porter, esp a doorkeeper

PORTS > PORT

PORTSIDE adj beside port

PORTULACA n tropical American plant with yellow, pink, or purple showy flowers

PORTULAN same as > PORTOLAN

PORTULANS > PORTULAN

PORTY adj like port

PORWIGGLE n tadpole

PORY adj containing pores

POS > PO

POSABLE > POSE

POSADA n inn in a Spanish-speaking country

POSADAS > POSADA

POSAUNE n organ chorus reed

POSAUNES > POSAUNE

POSE vb place in or take up a particular position to be photographed or drawn ▷ n position while posing

POSEABLE adj able to be manipulated into poses

POSED > POSE

POSER n puzzling question

POSERISH same as > POSEY

POSERS > POSER

POSES > POSE

POSEUR n person who behaves in an affected way to impress others

POSEURS > POSEUR

POSEUSE n female poseur

POSEUSES > POSEUSE

POSEY adj (of a place) for, characteristic of, or full of posers

POSH adj smart, luxurious ▷ adv in a manner associated with the upper class ▷ vb make posh

POSHED > POSH

POSHER > POSH

POSHES > POSH

POSHEST > POSH

POSHING > POSH

POSHLY > POSH

POSHNESS > POSH

POSHO n corn meal

POSHOS > POSHO

POSHTEEN same as > POSTEEN

POSHTEENS > POSHTEEN

POSIDRIVE adj having a patent screwhead that allows greater torque

POSIER > POSY

POSIES > POSY

POSIEST > POSY

POSIGRADE adj producing positive thrust

POSING > POSE

POSINGLY > POSE

POSINGS > POSE

POSIT vb lay down as a basis for argument ▷ n fact, idea, etc, that is posited

POSITED > POSIT

POSITIF n (on older organs) manual controlling soft stops

POSITIFS > POSITIF

POSITING > POSIT

POSITION n place ▷ vb place

POSITIONS > POSITION

POSITIVE same as > PLUS

POSITIVER > POSITIVE

POSITIVES > POSITIVE

POSITON n part of chromosome

POSITONS > POSITON

POSITRON n particle with same mass as electron but positive charge

POSITRONS > POSITRON

POSITS > POSIT

POSNET n small basin or dish

POSNETS > POSNET

POSOLE n Central American stew

POSOLES > POSOLE

POSOLOGIC > POSOLOGY

POSOLOGY n branch of medicine concerned with appropriate doses of drugs

POSS vb wash (clothes) by agitating them with a long rod, pole, etc

POSSE n group of people organized to maintain law and order

POSSED > POSS

POSSER n short stick used for stirring clothes in a washtub

POSSERS > POSSER

POSSES > POSSE

POSSESS vb have as one's property

POSSESSED adj owning or having

POSSESSES > POSSESS

POSSESSOR > POSSESS

POSSET n drink of hot milk curdled with ale, beer, etc, flavoured with spices ▷ vb treat with a posset

POSSETED > POSSET

POSSETING > POSSET

POSSETS > POSSET

POSSIBLE adj able to exist, happen, or be done ▷ n person or thing that might be suitable or chosen

POSSIBLER > POSSIBLE

POSSIBLES > POSSIBLE

POSSIBLY adv perhaps, not necessarily

POSSIE n place

POSSIES > POSSIE

POSSING > POSS

POSSUM vb pretend to be dead, asleep, ignorant, etc

POSSUMED > POSSUM

POSSUMING > POSSUM

POSSUMS > POSSUM

POST n official system of delivering letters and parcels ▷ vb send by post

POSTAGE n charge for sending a letter or parcel by post

POSTAGES > POSTAGE

POSTAL adj of a Post Office or the mail-delivery service ▷ n postcard

POSTALLY > POSTAL

POSTALS > POSTAL

POSTANAL adj behind the anus

POSTAXIAL adj situated or occurring behind the axis of the body

POSTBAG n postperson's bag

POSTBAGS > POSTBAG

POSTBASE n morpheme used as a suffix on a root word

POSTBASES > POSTBASE

POSTBOX n box into which mail is put for collection by the postal service

POSTBOXES > POSTBOX

POSTBOY n man or boy who brings the post round to offices

POSTBOYS > POSTBOY

POSTBURN adj after injury from burns

POSTBUS n vehicle carrying the mail that also carries passengers

POSTBUSES > POSTBUS

POSTCARD n card for sending a message by post without an envelope

POSTCARDS > POSTCARD

POSTCAVA n inferior vena cava

POSTCAVAE > POSTCAVA

POSTCAVAL > POSTCAVA

POSTCAVAS > POSTCAVA

POSTCODE n system of letters and numbers used to aid the sorting of mail ▷ vb put a postcode on a letter

POSTCODED > POSTCODE

POSTCODES > POSTCODE

POSTCOUP adj after a coup

POSTCRASH adj after a crash

POSTDATE vb write a date on (a cheque) that is later than the actual date

POSTDATED > POSTDATE

POSTDATES > POSTDATE

POSTDIVE adj following a dive

POSTDOC n postdoctoral degree

POSTDOCS > POSTDOC

POSTDRUG adj of time after drug has been taken

POSTED > POST

POSTEEN n Afghan leather jacket

p

POSTEENS > POSTEEN

POSTER n large picture or notice stuck on a wall ▷ vb cover with posters

POSTERED > POSTER

POSTERING > POSTER

POSTERIOR n buttocks ▷ adj behind, at the back of

POSTERISE same as > POSTERIZE

POSTERITY n future generations, descendants

POSTERIZE vb humiliate (a sporting opponent) by performing a dramatic feat against them

POSTERN n small back door or gate ▷ adj situated at the rear or the side

POSTERNS > POSTERN

POSTERS > POSTER

POSTFACE n note added to the end of a text

POSTFACES > POSTFACE

POSTFACT n relating to a culture in which appeals to the emotions prevail over facts

POSTFAULT adj after a fault

POSTFIRE adj of the period after a fire

POSTFIX vb add or append at the end of something

POSTFIXAL > POSTFIX

POSTFIXED > POSTFIX

POSTFIXES > POSTFIX

POSTFORM vb mould or shape (plastic) while it hot from reheating

POSTFORMS > POSTFORM

POSTGAME adj of period after sports match

POSTGRAD n graduate taking further degree

POSTGRADS > POSTGRAD

POSTHASTE adv with great speed ▷ n great haste

POSTHEAT n industrial heating process ▷ vb heat a material after welding to relieve stresses

POSTHEATS > POSTHEAT

POSTHOLE n hole dug in ground to hold fence post

POSTHOLES > POSTHOLE

POSTHORSE n horse kept at an inn or posthouse for use by postriders or for hire to travellers

POSTHOUSE n house or inn where horses were kept for postriders or for hire to travellers

POSTICAL adj (of the position of plant parts) behind another part

POSTICHE adj (of architectural ornament) inappropriately applied ▷ n imitation, counterfeit, or substitute

POSTICHES > POSTICHE

POSTICOUS same as > POSTICAL

POSTIE n postman or postwoman

POSTIES > POSTIE

POSTIL n commentary or marginal note, as in a Bible ▷ vb annotate (a biblical passage)

POSTILED > POSTIL

POSTILING > POSTIL

POSTILION n person riding one of a pair of horses drawing a carriage

POSTILLED > POSTIL

POSTILLER > POSTIL

POSTILS > POSTIL

POSTIN variant of > POSTEEN

POSTING n job to which someone is assigned

POSTINGS > POSTING

POSTINS > POSTIN

POSTIQUE variant of > POSTICHE

POSTIQUES > POSTIQUE

POSTLIKE adj like a post

POSTLUDE n final or concluding piece or movement

POSTLUDES > POSTLUDE

POSTMAN n person who collects and delivers post

POSTMARK n official mark stamped on letters showing place and date of posting ▷ vb put such a mark on (mail)

POSTMARKS > POSTMARK

POSTMEN > POSTMAN

POSTNASAL adj situated at the back of the nose

POSTNATAL adj occurring after childbirth

POSTNATI pl n those born in Scotland after its union with England

POSTOP n person recovering from surgery

POSTOPS > POSTOP

POSTORAL adj situated at the back of the mouth

POSTPAID adj with the postage prepaid

POSTPONE vb put off to a later time

POSTPONED > POSTPONE

POSTPONER > POSTPONE

POSTPONES > POSTPONE

POSTPOSE vb place (word or phrase) after other constituents in sentence

POSTPOSED > POSTPOSE

POSTPOSES > POSTPOSE

POSTPUNK adj (of pop music) belonging to a style that followed punk rock ▷ n musician of the musical trend after punk

POSTPUNKS > POSTPUNK

POSTRACE adj of the period after a race

POSTRIDER n (formerly) person who delivered post on horseback

POSTRIOT adj of the period after a riot

POSTS > POST

POSTSHOW adj of the period after a show

POSTSYNC vb add a sound recording to (and synchronize with) an existing video or film recording

POSTSYNCS > POSTSYNC

POSTTAX adj of the period after tax is paid

POSTTEEN n young adult

POSTTEENS > POSTTEEN

POSTTEST n test taken after a lesson

POSTTESTS > POSTTEST

POSTTRIAL adj of the period after a trial

POSTTRUTH adj relating to a culture in which appeals to the emotions prevail over facts

POSTULANT n candidate for admission to a religious order

POSTULATA pl n things postulated

POSTULATE vb assume to be true as the basis of an argument or theory ▷ n something postulated

POSTURAL > POSTURE

POSTURE n position or way in which someone stands, walks, etc ▷ vb behave in an exaggerated way to get attention

POSTURED > POSTURE

POSTURER > POSTURE

POSTURERS > POSTURE

POSTURES > POSTURE

POSTURING n act of posturing

POSTURISE same as > POSTURIZE

POSTURIST > POSTURE

POSTURIZE less common word for > POSTURE

POSTVIRAL adj as in postviral syndrome debilitating condition occurring as a sequel to viral illness

POSTWAR adj occurring or existing after a war

POSTWOMAN n woman who carries and delivers mail as a profession

POSTWOMEN > POSTWOMAN

POSY n small bunch of flowers

POT n round deep container ▷ vb plant in a pot

POTABLE adj drinkable ▷ n something fit to drink

POTABLES > POTABLE

POTAE n hat

POTAES > POTAE

POTAGE n thick soup

POTAGER n small kitchen garden

POTAGERS > POTAGER

POTAGES > POTAGE

POTALE n residue from a grain distillery, used as animal feed

POTALES > POTALE

POTAMIC adj of or relating to rivers

POTASH n white powdery substance obtained from ashes and used as fertilizer ▷ vb treat with potash

POTASHED > POTASH

POTASHES > POTASH

POTASHING > POTASH

POTASS abbreviated form of > POTASSIUM

POTASSA n potassium oxide

POTASSAS > POTASSA

POTASSES > POTASS

POTASSIC > POTASSIUM

POTASSIUM n silvery metallic element

POTATION n act of drinking

POTATIONS > POTATION

POTATO n roundish starchy vegetable that grows underground

POTATOBUG n Colorado beetle

POTATOES > POTATO

POTATORY adj of, relating to, or given to drinking

POTBELLY n bulging belly

POTBOIL vb boil in a pot

POTBOILED > POTBOIL

POTBOILER n inferior work of art produced quickly to make money

POTBOILS > POTBOIL

POTBOUND adj (of plant) unable to grow because pot is too small

POTBOY n (esp formerly) youth or man employed at a public house to serve beer, etc

POTBOYS > POTBOY

POTCH n inferior quality opal used in jewellery for mounting precious opals

POTCHE vb stab

POTCHED > POTCHE

POTCHER > POTCHE

POTCHERS > POTCHE

POTCHES > POTCH

POTCHING > POTCHE

POTE vb push

POTED > POTE

POTEEN n (in Ireland) illegally made alcoholic drink

POTEENS > POTEEN

POTENCE same as > POTENCY

POTENCES > POTENCE

POTENCIES > POTENCY

POTENCY n state or quality of being potent

POTENT adj having great power or influence ▷ n potentate or ruler

POTENTATE n ruler or monarch

POTENTIAL adj possible but not yet actual ▷ n ability or talent not yet fully used

POTENTISE same as > POTENTIZE

POTENTIZE vb make more potent

POTENTLY > POTENT

POTENTS > POTENT

POTES > POTE

POTFUL n amount held by a pot

POTFULS > POTFUL

POTGUN n pot-shaped mortar

POTGUNS > POTGUN

POTHEAD n habitual user of cannabis

POTHEADS > POTHEAD

POTHECARY n pharmacist
POTHEEN rare variant of
> POTEEN
POTHEENS > POTHEEN
POTHER n fuss or
commotion ▷ vb make or be
troubled or upset
POTHERB n plant whose
leaves, flowers, or stems are
used in cooking
POTHERBS > POTHERB
POTHERED > POTHER
POTHERIER > POTHERY
POTHERING > POTHER
POTHERS > POTHER
POTHERY adj stuffy
POTHOLDER n piece of
material used to protect
hands while lifting pot from
oven
POTHOLE n hole in the
surface of a road
POTHOLED > POTHOLE
POTHOLER > POTHOLING
POTHOLERS > POTHOLING
POTHOLES > POTHOLE
POTHOLING n sport of
exploring underground caves
POTHOOK n S-shaped hook
for suspending a pot over a
fire
POTHOOKS > POTHOOK
POTHOS n climbing plant
POTHOSES > POTHOS
POTHOUSE n (formerly)
small tavern or pub
POTHOUSES > POTHOUSE
POTHUNTER n person who
hunts for food or for profit
without regard to the rules of
sport
POTICARY obsolete spelling of
> POTHECARY
POTICHE n tall vase or jar
that narrows towards the
neck
POTICHES > POTICHE
POTIN n bronze alloy with
high tin content
POTING > POTE
POTINS > POTIN
POTION n dose of medicine
or poison
POTIONS > POTION
POTJIE n three-legged iron
pot used for cooking
POTJIES > POTJIE
POTLACH same as
> POTLATCH
POTLACHE same as
> POTLATCH
POTLACHES > POTLACHE
POTLATCH n competitive
ceremonial activity among
certain Native American
tribes
POTLIKE > POT
POTLINE n row of
electrolytic cells for reducing
metals
POTLINES > POTLINE
POTLUCK n whatever food
happens to be available
without special preparation
POTLUCKS > POTLUCK
POTMAN same as > POTBOY
POTMEN > POTMAN

POTOMETER n apparatus
that measures the rate of
water uptake by a plant or
plant part
POTOO n nocturnal tropical
bird
POTOOS > POTOO
POTOROO n Australian
leaping rodent
POTOROOS > POTOROO
POTPIE n meat and
vegetable stew with a pie
crust on top
POTPIES > POTPIE
POTPOURRI n fragrant
mixture of dried flower
petals
POTS > POT
POTSHARD same as
> POTSHERD
POTSHARDS > POTSHARD
POTSHARE same as
> POTSHERD
POTSHARES > POTSHARE
POTSHERD n broken
fragment of pottery
POTSHERDS > POTSHERD
POTSHOP n public house
POTSHOPS > POTSHOP
POTSHOT n shot taken
without careful aim
POTSHOTS > POTSHOT
POTSIE same as > POTSY
POTSIES > POTSY
POTSTONE n impure
massive variety of
soapstone, formerly used for
making cooking vessels
POTSTONES > POTSTONE
POTSY n hopscotch
POTT old variant of > POT
POTTABLE adj (esp of a
snooker ball) easily potted
POTTAGE n thick soup or
stew
POTTAGES > POTTAGE
POTTED > POT
POTTEEN same as
> POTEEN
POTTEENS > POTTEEN
POTTER same as > PUTTER
POTTERED > POTTER
POTTERER > POTTER
POTTERERS > POTTER
POTTERIES > POTTERY
POTTERING > POTTER
POTTERS > POTTER
POTTERY n articles made
from baked clay
POTTIER > POTTY
POTTIES > POTTY
POTTIEST > POTTY
POTTINESS > POTTY
POTTING > POT
POTTINGAR same as
> POTTINGER
POTTINGER n apothecary
POTTLE n liquid measure
equal to half a gallon
POTTLES > POTTLE
POTTO n short-tailed
prosimian primate
POTTOS > POTTO
POTTS > POTT
POTTY adj silly or eccentric
▷ n bowl used by a small
child as a toilet

POTWALLER n man entitled
to the franchise before 1832
by virtue of possession of his
own fireplace
POTZER same as > PATZER
POTZERS > POTZER
POUCH n small bag ▷ vb
place in or as if in a pouch
POUCHED > POUCH
POUCHES > POUCH
POUCHFUL n amount a
pouch will hold
POUCHFULS > POUCHFUL
POUCHIER > POUCH
POUCHIEST > POUCH
POUCHING > POUCH
POUCHLIKE adj like a
pouch
POUCHY > POUCH
POUDER obsolete spelling of
> POWDER
POUDERS > POUDER
POUDRE old spelling of
> POWDER
POUDRES > POUDRE
POUF n large solid cushion
used as a seat ▷ vb pile up
hair into rolled puffs
POUFED > POUF
POUFF same as > POUF
POUFFE same as > POUF
POUFFED > POUFFE
POUFFES > POUFFE
POUFFIER > POUFFY
POUFFIEST > POUFFY
POUFFING > POUFFE
POUFFS > POUFF
POUFFY same as > POOFY
POUFING > POUF
POUFS > POUF
POUFTAH same as
> POOFTER
POUFTAHS > POUFTAH
POUFTER same as
> POOFTER
POUFTERS > POUFTER
POUK Scots variant of > POKE
POUKE n mischievous spirit
POUKES > POUKE
POUKING > POUK
POUKIT > POUK
POUKS > POUK
POULAINE n tapering toe of
shoe
POULAINES > POULAINE
POULARD n hen that has
been spayed for fattening
POULARDE same as
> POULARD
POULARDES > POULARDE
POULARDS > POULARD
POULDER obsolete spelling of
> POWDER
POULDERS > POULDER
POULDRE archaic spelling of
> POWDER
POULDRES > POULDRE
POULDRON same as
> PAULDRON
POULDRONS > POULDRON
POULE n fowl suitable for
slow stewing
POULES > POULE
POULP n octopus
POULPE variant of > POULP
POULPES > POULPE
POULPS > POULP

POULT n young of a
gallinaceous bird
POULTER n poultry dealer
POULTERER same as
> POULTER
POULTERS > POULTER
POULTICE n moist dressing,
often heated, applied to
inflamed skin ▷ vb apply
poultice to
POULTICED > POULTICE
POULTICES > POULTICE
POULTRIES > POULTRY
POULTRY n domestic fowls
POULTS > POULT
POUNCE vb spring upon
suddenly to attack or
capture ▷ n pouncing
POUNCED > POUNCE
POUNCER > POUNCE
POUNCERS > POUNCE
POUNCES > POUNCE
POUNCET n box with a
perforated top used for
perfume
POUNCETS > POUNCET
POUNCING old variant of
> PUNCHING
POUNCING > POUNCE
POUND n monetary unit of
Britain and some other
countries ▷ vb hit heavily
and repeatedly
POUNDAGE n charge of so
much per pound of weight or
sterling
POUNDAGES > POUNDAGE
POUNDAL n fps unit of force
POUNDALS > POUNDAL
POUNDCAKE n cake
containing a pound of each
ingredient
POUNDED > POUND
POUNDER > POUND
POUNDERS > POUND
POUNDING > POUND
POUNDINGS > POUNDING
POUNDS > POUND
POUPE vb make sudden
blowing sound
POUPED > POUPE
POUPES > POUPE
POUPING > POUPE
POUPT > POUPE
POUR vb flow or cause to flow
out in a stream
POURABLE > POUR
POURBOIRE n tip or gratuity
POURED > POUR
POURER > POUR
POURERS > POUR
POURIE n jug
POURIES > POURIE
POURING > POUR
POURINGLY > POUR
POURINGS > POUR
POURPOINT n man's stuffed
quilted doublet of a kind
worn between the Middle
Ages and the 17th century
POURS > POUR
POURSEW obsolete spelling of
> PURSUE
POURSEWED > POURSEW
POURSEWS > POURSEW
POURSUE obsolete spelling of
> PURSUE

P

POURSUED > POURSUE
POURSUES > POURSUE
POURSUING > POURSUE
POURSUIT same as
> PURSUIT
POURSUITS > POURSUIT
POURTRAY obsolete spelling of
> PORTRAY
POURTRAYD > POURTRAY
POURTRAYS > POURTRAY
POUSADA n traditional
Portuguese hotel
POUSADAS > POUSADA
POUSOWDIE n Scottish stew
made from sheep's head
POUSSE same as > PEASE
POUSSES > POUSSE
POUSSETTE n figure in
country dancing in which
couples hold hands and
move up or down the set to
change positions ▷ vb
perform such a figure
POUSSIE old variant of
> PUSSY
POUSSIES > POUSSIE
POUSSIN n young chicken
reared for eating
POUSSINS > POUSSIN
POUT vb thrust out one's lips,
look sulky ▷ n pouting look
POUTASSOU n another
name for the blue whiting
POUTED > POUT
POUTER n pigeon that can
puff out its crop
POUTERS > POUTER
POUTFUL adj tending to
pout
POUTHER Scots variant of
> POWDER
POUTHERED > POUTHER
POUTHERS > POUTHER
POUTIER > POUT
POUTIEST > POUT
POUTINE n dish of chipped
potatoes topped with cheese
and sauce
POUTINES > POUTINE
POUTING > POUT
POUTINGLY > POUT
POUTINGS > POUT
POUTS > POUT
POUTY > POUT
POVERTIES > POVERTY
POVERTY n state of being
without enough food or
money
POW interj exclamation to
indicate that a collision or
explosion has taken place ▷ n
head or a head of hair
POWAN n type of freshwater
whitefish occurring in some
Scottish lakes
POWANS > POWAN
POWDER n substance in the
form of tiny loose particles
▷ vb apply powder to
POWDERED > POWDER
POWDERER > POWDER
POWDERERS > POWDER
POWDERIER > POWDER
POWDERING n sprinkling of
something on a surface
POWDERMAN n person who
handles explosives in a
demolition team

POWDERMEN > POWDERMAN
POWDERS > POWDER
POWDERY > POWDER
POWELLISE same as
> POWELLIZE
POWELLITE n type of
mineral
POWELLIZE vb treat wood
with a sugar solution
POWER n ability to do or act
▷ vb give or provide power to
POWERBAND n range of
speeds allowing efficient
operation of an engine
POWERBOAT n fast powerful
motorboat
POWERED > POWER
POWERFUL adj having great
power or influence ▷ adv
extremely
POWERING > POWER
POWERLESS adj without
power or authority
POWERPLAY n behaviour
intended to maximise
person's power
POWERS > POWER
POWFAGGED adj exhausted
POWHIRI n Māori ceremony
of welcome, esp to a marae
POWHIRIS > POWHIRI
POWIN n peacock
POWINS > POWIN
POWN variant of > POWIN
POWND obsolete spelling of
> POUND
POWNDED > POWND
POWNDING > POWND
POWNDS > POWND
POWNEY old Scots spelling of
> PONY
POWNEYS > POWNEY
POWNIE old Scots spelling of
> PONY
POWNIES > POWNIE
POWNS > POWN
POWNY old Scots spelling of
> PONY
POWRE obsolete spelling of
> POWER
POWRED > POWRE
POWRES > POWRE
POWRING > POWRE
POWS > POW
POWSOWDY same as
> POUSOWDIE
POWTER vb scrabble about
POWTERED > POWTER
POWTERING > POWTER
POWTERS > POWTER
POWWAW interj expression of
disbelief or contempt
POWWOW n talk or conference
▷ vb hold a powwow
POWWOWED > POWWOW
POWWOWING > POWWOW
POWWOWS > POWWOW
POX n disease in which skin
pustules form ▷ vb infect
with pox
POXED > POX
POXES > POX
POXIER > POXY
POXIEST > POXY
POXING > POX
POXVIRUS n virus such as
smallpox

POXY adj of poor quality;
rotten
POYNANT old variant of
> POIGNANT
POYNT obsolete spelling of
> POINT
POYNTED > POYNT
POYNTING > POYNT
POYNTS > POYNT
POYOU n type of armadillo
POYOUS > POYOU
POYSE obsolete variant of
> POISE
POYSED > POYSE
POYSES > POYSE
POYSING > POYSE
POYSON obsolete spelling of
> POISON
POYSONED > POYSON
POYSONING > POYSON
POYSONS > POYSON
POZ adj positive
POZIDRIVE same as
> POSIDRIVE
POZOLE same as > POSOLE
POZOLES > POZOLE
POZZ adj positive
POZZIES > POZZY
POZZOLAN same as
> POZZOLANA
POZZOLANA n type of
porous volcanic ash
POZZOLANS > POZZOLAN
POZZY same as > POSSIE
PRAAM same as > PRAM
PRAAMS > PRAAM
PRABBLE variant of
> BRABBLE
PRABBLES > PRABBLE
PRACHARAK n (in India)
person appointed to
propagate a cause through
personal contact, meetings,
public lectures, etc
PRACTIC adj practical ▷ n
practice ▷ vb put (a theory)
into practice
PRACTICAL adj involving
experience or actual use
rather than theory ▷ n
examination in which
something has to be done
or made
PRACTICE same as
> PRACTISE
PRACTICED > PRACTICE
PRACTICER > PRACTICE
PRACTICES > PRACTICE
PRACTICK obsolete word for
> PRACTICE
PRACTICKS > PRACTICK
PRACTICS > PRACTIC
PRACTICUM n course in
which theory is put into
practice
PRACTIQUE variant of
> PRACTIC
PRACTISE vb do repeatedly
so as to gain skill
PRACTISED > PRACTISE
PRACTISER > PRACTISE
PRACTISES > PRACTISE
PRACTIVE obsolete word for
> ACTIVE
PRACTOLOL n type of drug
PRAD n horse
PRADHAN n (in India) chief or
leader

PRADHANS > PRADHAN
PRADS > PRAD
PRAEAMBLE same as
> PREAMBLE
PRAECIPE n written
request addressed to court
PRAECIPES > PRAECIPE
PRAECOCES n division of
birds whose young are able
to run when first hatched
PRAEDIAL adj of or relating
to land, farming, etc ▷ n
slave attached to a farm
PRAEDIALS > PRAEDIAL
PRAEFECT same as
> PREFECT
PRAEFECTS > PRAEFECT
PRAELECT same as
> PRELECT
PRAELECTS > PRAELECT
PRAELUDIA n musical
preludes
PRAENOMEN n ancient
Roman's first or given name
PRAESES n Roman governor
PRAESIDIA n presidiums
PRAETOR n (in ancient
Rome) senior magistrate
ranking just below the
consuls
PRAETORS > PRAETOR
PRAGMATIC adj concerned
with practical consequences
rather than theory
PRAHU same as > PROA
PRAHUS > PRAHU
PRAIRIE n large treeless
area of grassland
PRAIRIED > PRAIRIE
PRAIRIES > PRAIRIE
PRAISE vb express approval
of (someone or something)
▷ n something said or
written to show approval
PRAISEACH n type of
porridge
PRAISED > PRAISE
PRAISEFUL > PRAISE
PRAISER > PRAISE
PRAISERS > PRAISE
PRAISES > PRAISE
PRAISING > PRAISE
PRAISINGS > PRAISE
PRAJNA n wisdom or
understanding
PRAJNAS > PRAJNA
PRALINE n sweet made of
nuts and caramelized sugar
PRALINES > PRALINE
PRAM n four-wheeled
carriage for a baby, pushed
by hand
PRAMS > PRAM
PRANA n cosmic energy
believed to come from the
sun
PRANAS > PRANA
PRANAYAMA n breath
control in yoga
PRANCE vb walk with
exaggerated bouncing steps
▷ n act of prancing
PRANCED > PRANCE
PRANCER > PRANCE
PRANCERS > PRANCE
PRANCES > PRANCE
PRANCING > PRANCE

PRANCINGS > PRANCE
PRANCK obsolete variant of
> PRANK
PRANCKE obsolete variant of
> PRANK
PRANCKED > PRANK
PRANCKES > PRANCKE
PRANCKING > PRANCK
PRANCKS > PRANCK
PRANDIAL adj of or relating
to a meal
PRANG n crash in a car or
aircraft ▷ vb crash or
damage (an aircraft or car)
PRANGED > PRANG
PRANGING > PRANG
PRANGS > PRANG
PRANK n mischievous trick
▷ vb dress or decorate
showily or gaudily
PRANKED > PRANK
PRANKFUL > PRANK
PRANKIER > PRANK
PRANKIEST > PRANK
PRANKING > PRANK
PRANKINGS > PRANK
PRANKISH > PRANK
PRANKLE obsolete variant of
> PRANCE
PRANKLED > PRANKLE
PRANKLES > PRANKLE
PRANKLING > PRANKLE
PRANKS > PRANK
PRANKSOME > PRANK
PRANKSTER n practical
joker
PRANKY > PRANK
PRAO same as > PROA
PRAOS > PRAO
PRASE n light green
translucent variety of
chalcedony
PRASES > PRASE
PRAT n stupid person
PRATE vb talk idly and at
length ▷ n chatter
PRATED > PRATE
PRATER > PRATE
PRATERS > PRATE
PRATES > PRATE
PRATFALL vb fall upon one's
buttocks
PRATFALLS > PRATFALL
PRATFELL > PRATFALL
PRATIE n potato
PRATIES > PRATIE
PRATING > PRATE
PRATINGLY > PRATE
PRATINGS > PRATE
PRATIQUE n formal
permission given to a vessel
to use a foreign port
PRATIQUES > PRATIQUE
PRATS > PRAT
PRATT n buttocks ▷ vb hit on
the buttocks
PRATTED > PRATT
PRATTING > PRATT
PRATTLE vb chatter in a
childish or foolish way ▷ n
childish or foolish talk
PRATTLED > PRATTLE
PRATTLER > PRATTLE
PRATTLERS > PRATTLE
PRATTLES > PRATTLE
PRATTLING > PRATTLE
PRATTS > PRATT

PRATY obsolete variant of
> PRETTY
PRAU same as > PROA
PRAUNCE obsolete variant of
> PRANCE
PRAUNCED > PRAUNCE
PRAUNCES > PRAUNCE
PRAUNCING > PRAUNCE
PRAUS > PRAU
PRAVITIES > PRAVITY
PRAVITY n moral
degeneracy
PRAWLE n Shakespearian
spelling of "brawl"
PRAWLES > PRAWLE
PRAWLIN variant of
> PRALINE
PRAWLINS > PRAWLIN
PRAWN n edible shellfish like
a large shrimp ▷ vb catch
prawns
PRAWNED > PRAWN
PRAWNER > PRAWN
PRAWNERS > PRAWN
PRAWNING > PRAWN
PRAWNS > PRAWN
PRAXES > PRAXIS
PRAXIS n practice as
opposed to theory
PRAXISES > PRAXIS
PRAY vb say prayers ▷ adv I
beg you ▷ interj I beg you
PRAYED > PRAY
PRAYER n thanks or appeal
addressed to one's God
PRAYERFUL adj inclined to
or characterized by prayer
PRAYERS > PRAYER
PRAYING > PRAY
PRAYINGLY > PRAY
PRAYINGS > PRAY
PRAYS > PRAY
PRE prep before
PREABSORB vb absorb
beforehand
PREACCUSE vb accuse
beforehand
PREACE obsolete variant of
> PRESS
PREACED > PREACE
PREACES > PREACE
PREACH vb give a talk on a
religious theme as part of a
church service
PREACHED > PREACH
PREACHER n person who
preaches, esp in church
PREACHERS > PREACHER
PREACHES > PREACH
PREACHIER > PREACHY
PREACHIFY vb preach or
moralize in a tedious manner
PREACHILY > PREACHY
PREACHING > PREACH
PREACHY adj inclined to or
marked by preaching
PREACING > PREACE
PREACT vb act beforehand
PREACTED > PREACT
PREACTING > PREACT
PREACTS > PREACT
PREADAMIC adj of or
relating to the belief that
there were people on earth
before Adam
PREADAPT vb adapt
beforehand

PREADAPTS > PREADAPT
PREADJUST vb adjust
beforehand
PREADMIT vb prepare
patient prior to treatment
PREADMITS > PREADMIT
PREADOPT vb adopt in
advance
PREADOPTS > PREADOPT
PREADULT n animal or
person who has not reached
adulthood
PREADULTS > PREADULT
PREAGED adj treated to
appear older
PREALLOT vb allot
beforehand
PREALLOTS > PREALLOT
PREALTER vb alter
beforehand
PREALTERS > PREALTER
PREAMBLE n introductory
part to something said or
written ▷ vb write a
preamble
PREAMBLED > PREAMBLE
PREAMBLES > PREAMBLE
PREAMP n electronic
amplifier
PREAMPS > PREAMP
PREANAL adj situated in
front of anus
PREAPPLY vb apply
beforehand
PREARM vb arm beforehand
PREARMED > PREARM
PREARMING > PREARM
PREARMS > PREARM
PREASE vb crowd or press
PREASED > PREASE
PREASES > PREASE
PREASING > PREASE
PREASSE obsolete spelling of
> PRESS
PREASSED > PREASSE
PREASSES > PREASSE
PREASSIGN vb assign
beforehand
PREASSING > PREASSE
PREASSURE vb assure
beforehand
PREATOMIC adj before the
atomic age
PREATTUNE vb attune
beforehand
PREAUDIT n examination of
contracts before a
transaction
PREAUDITS > PREAUDIT
PREAVER vb aver in advance
PREAVERS > PREAVER
PREAXIAL adj situated or
occurring in front of the axis
of the body
PREBADE > PREBID
PREBAKE vb bake before
further cooking
PREBAKED > PREBAKE
PREBAKES > PREBAKE
PREBAKING > PREBAKE
PREBASAL adj in front of a
base
PREBATTLE adj of the
period before a battle
PREBEND n allowance paid
to a canon or member of the
cathedral chapter

PREBENDAL > PREBEND
PREBENDS > PREBEND
PREBID vb bid beforehand
PREBIDDEN > PREBID
PREBIDS > PREBID
PREBILL vb issue an invoice
before the service has been
provided
PREBILLED > PREBILL
PREBILLS > PREBILL
PREBIND vb bind a book in a
hard-wearing binding
PREBINDS > PREBIND
PREBIOTIC adj of the
period before the existence
of life on earth
PREBIRTH n period of life
before birth
PREBIRTHS > PREBIRTH
PREBLESS vb bless a couple
before they marry
PREBOARD vb board an
aircraft before other
passengers
PREBOARDS > PREBOARD
PREBOIL vb boil beforehand
PREBOILED > PREBOIL
PREBOILS > PREBOIL
PREBOOK vb book well in
advance
PREBOOKED > PREBOOK
PREBOOKS > PREBOOK
PREBOOM adj of the period
before an economic boom
PREBORN adj unborn
PREBOUGHT > PREBUY
PREBOUND > PREBIND
PREBUDGET adj before
budget
PREBUILD vb build
beforehand
PREBUILDS > PREBUILD
PREBUILT > PREBUILD
PREBUTTAL n prepared
response to an anticipated
criticism
PREBUY vb buy in advance
PREBUYING > PREBUY
PREBUYS > PREBUY
PRECANCEL vb cancel
(postage stamps) before
placing them on mail ▷ n
precancelled stamp
PRECANCER n condition
that may develop into cancer
PRECARIAT n people
without a long-term source
of income
PRECAST adj cast in a
particular form before being
used ▷ vb cast (concrete) in a
particular form before use
PRECASTS > PRECAST
PRECATIVE same as
> PRECATORY
PRECATORY adj of,
involving, or expressing
entreaty
PRECAUDAL adj in front of
the caudal fin
PRECAVA n superior vena
cava
PRECAVAE > PRECAVA
PRECAVAL n type of vein
PRECAVALS > PRECAVAL
PRECEDE vb go or be before
PRECEDED > PRECEDE

PRECEDENT n previous case or occurrence regarded as an example to be followed ▷ adj preceding

PRECEDES > PRECEDE

PRECEDING adj going or coming before

PRECEESE Scots variant of > PRECISE

PRECENSOR vb censor (a film, play, book, etc) before its publication

PRECENT vb issue a command or law

PRECENTED > PRECENT

PRECENTOR n person who leads the singing in a church

PRECENTS > PRECENT

PRECEPIT old word for > PRECIPICE

PRECEPITS > PRECEPIT

PRECEPT n rule of behaviour

PRECEPTOR n instructor

PRECEPTS > PRECEPT

PRECES pl n prayers

PRECESS vb undergo or cause to undergo precession

PRECESSED > PRECESS

PRECESSES > PRECESS

PRECHARGE vb charge beforehand

PRECHECK vb check beforehand

PRECHECKS > PRECHECK

PRECHILL vb chill beforehand

PRECHILLS > PRECHILL

PRECHOOSE vb choose in advance

PRECHOSE > PRECHOOSE

PRECHOSEN > PRECHOOSE

PRECIEUSE n pretentious female

PRECIEUX n pretentious male

PRECINCT n area in a town closed to traffic

PRECINCTS pl n surrounding region

PRECIOUS adj of great value and importance ▷ adv very

PRECIP n precipitation

PRECIPE n type of legal document

PRECIPES > PRECIPE

PRECIPICE n very steep face of a cliff

PRECIPS > PRECIP

PRECIS n short written summary of a longer piece ▷ vb make a precis of

PRECISE adj exact, accurate in every detail

PRECISED > PRECIS

PRECISELY adv in a precise manner

PRECISER > PRECISE

PRECISES > PRECIS

PRECISEST > PRECISE

PRECISIAN n punctilious observer of rules or forms, esp in the field of religion

PRECISING > PRECIS

PRECISION n quality of being precise ▷ adj accurate

PRECISIVE adj limiting by cutting off all that is unnecessary

PRECITED adj cited previously

PRECLEAN vb clean beforehand

PRECLEANS > PRECLEAN

PRECLEAR vb approve in advance

PRECLEARS > PRECLEAR

PRECLUDE vb make impossible to happen

PRECLUDED > PRECLUDE

PRECLUDES > PRECLUDE

PRECOCIAL adj (of the young of some species of birds after hatching) covered with down, having open eyes, and capable of leaving the nest within a few days of hatching ▷ n precocial bird

PRECOCITY n early maturing or development

PRECODE vb code beforehand

PRECODED > PRECODE

PRECODES > PRECODE

PRECODING > PRECODE

PRECOITAL adj before sex

PRECONISE same as > PRECONIZE

PRECONIZE vb announce or commend publicly

PRECOOK vb cook (food) beforehand

PRECOOKED > PRECOOK

PRECOOKER n device for preparing food before cooking

PRECOOKS > PRECOOK

PRECOOL vb cool in advance

PRECOOLED > PRECOOL

PRECOOLS > PRECOOL

PRECOUP adj of the period before a coup

PRECRASH adj of the period before a crash

PRECREASE vb provide with a crease in advance

PRECRISIS adj occurring before a crisis

PRECURE vb cure in advance

PRECURED > PRECURE

PRECURES > PRECURE

PRECURING > PRECURE

PRECURRER > PRECURE

PRECURSE n forerunning ▷ vb be a precursor of

PRECURSED > PRECURSE

PRECURSES > PRECURSE

PRECURSOR n something that precedes and is a signal of something else, forerunner

PRECUT vb cut in advance

PRECUTS > PRECUT

PRECYCLE vb preemptive approach to waste reduction involving minimal use of packaging

PRECYCLED > PRECYCLE

PRECYCLES > PRECYCLE

PREDACITY n predatory nature

PREDATE vb occur at an earlier date than

PREDATED > PREDATE

PREDATES > PREDATE

PREDATING > PREDATE

PREDATION n relationship between two species of animal in a community, in which one (the predator) hunts, kills, and eats the other (the prey)

PREDATISM n state of preying on other animals

PREDATIVE > PREDATE

PREDATOR n predatory animal

PREDATORS > PREDATOR

PREDATORY adj habitually hunting and killing other animals for food

PREDAWN n period before dawn

PREDAWNS > PREDAWN

PREDEATH n period immediately before death

PREDEATHS > PREDEATH

PREDEBATE adj before a debate

PREDEDUCT vb deduct beforehand

PREDEFINE vb define in advance

PREDELLA n series of small paintings or sculptures in a long narrow strip on an altarpiece

PREDELLAS > PREDELLA

PREDELLE > PREDELLA

PREDESIGN vb design beforehand

PREDEVOTE adj preordained ▷ vb devote or dedicate beforehand

PREDIAL same as > PRAEDIAL

PREDIALS > PREDIAL

PREDICANT same as > PREDIKANT

PREDICATE n part of a sentence in which something is said about the subject ▷ vb declare or assert ▷ adj of or relating to something that has been predicated

PREDICT vb tell about in advance, prophesy

PREDICTED > PREDICT

PREDICTER > PREDICT

PREDICTOR n person or thing that predicts

PREDICTS > PREDICT

PREDIED > PREDY

PREDIES > PREDY

PREDIGEST vb treat (food) artificially to aid subsequent digestion in the body

PREDIKANT n minister in the Dutch Reformed Church in South Africa

PREDILECT adj chosen or preferred

PREDINNER adj of the period before dinner

PREDIVE adj happening before a dive

PREDOOM vb pronounce (someone or something's) doom beforehand

PREDOOMED > PREDOOM

PREDOOMS > PREDOOM

PREDRAFT adj before a draft ▷ n preliminary draft prior to an official draft

PREDRAFTS > PREDRAFT

PREDRIED > PREDRY

PREDRIES > PREDRY

PREDRILL vb drill in advance

PREDRILLS > PREDRILL

PREDRY vb dry beforehand

PREDRYING > PREDRY

PREDUSK n period before dusk

PREDUSKS > PREDUSK

PREDY vb prepare for action

PREDYING > PREDY

PREE vb try or taste

PREED > PREE

PREEDIT vb edit beforehand

PREEDITED > PREEDIT

PREEDITS > PREEDIT

PREEING > PREE

PREELECT vb elect beforehand

PREELECTS > PREELECT

PREEMIE n premature infant

PREEMIES > PREEMIE

PREEMPT vb acquire in advance of or to the exclusion of others

PREEMPTED > PREEMPT

PREEMPTOR n one who preempts

PREEMPTS > PREEMPT

PREEN vb (of a bird) clean or trim (feathers) with the beak ▷ n pin, esp a decorative one

PREENACT vb enact beforehand

PREENACTS > PREENACT

PREENED > PREEN

PREENER > PREEN

PREENERS > PREEN

PREENING > PREEN

PREENS > PREEN

PREERECT vb erect beforehand

PREERECTS > PREERECT

PREES > PREE

PREEVE old form of > PROVE

PREEVED > PREEVE

PREEVES > PREEVE

PREEVING > PREEVE

PREEXCITE vb stimulate in preparation

PREEXEMPT vb exempt beforehand

PREEXILIC adj prior to the Babylonian exile of the Jews

PREEXIST vb exist beforehand

PREEXISTS > PREEXIST

PREEXPOSE vb expose beforehand

PREFAB n prefabricated house ▷ vb manufacture sections of (building) in factory

PREFABBED > PREFAB

PREFABS > PREFAB

PREFACE n introduction to a book ▷ vb serve as an introduction to (a book, speech, etc)

PREFACED > PREFACE

PREFACER > PREFACE

PREFACERS > PREFACE

PREFACES > PREFACE

PREFACIAL adj anterior to face

PREFACING > PREFACE

PREFADE vb fade beforehand

PREFADED > PREFADE

PREFADES > PREFADE

PREFADING > PREFADE

PREFARD vb old form of preferred **PREFATORY** adj concerning a preface

PREFECT n senior pupil in a school, with limited power over others

PREFECTS > PREFECT

PREFER vb like better

PREFERRED > PREFER

PREFERRER > PREFER

PREFERS > PREFER

PREFEUDAL adj of the period before the feudal era

PREFIGHT adj of the period before a boxing match

PREFIGURE vb represent or suggest in advance

PREFILE vb file beforehand

PREFILED > PREFILE

PREFILES > PREFILE

PREFILING > PREFILE

PREFILLED adj having been filled beforehand

PREFIRE vb fire beforehand

PREFIRED > PREFIRE

PREFIRES > PREFIRE

PREFIRING > PREFIRE

PREFIX n letters put at the beginning of a word to make a new word ▷ vb put as an introduction or prefix (to)

PREFIXAL > PREFIX

PREFIXED > PREFIX

PREFIXES > PREFIX

PREFIXING > PREFIX

PREFIXION > PREFIX

PREFLAME adj of the period before combustion

PREFLIGHT adj of or relating to the period just prior to a plane taking off

PREFOCUS vb focus in advance

PREFORM vb form beforehand

PREFORMAT vb format in advance

PREFORMED > PREFORM

PREFORMS > PREFORM

PREFRANK vb frank in advance

PREFRANKS > PREFRANK

PREFREEZE vb freeze beforehand

PREFROZE > PREFREEZE

PREFROZEN > PREFREEZE

PREFUND vb pay for in advance

PREFUNDED > PREFUND

PREFUNDS > PREFUND

PREGAME vb consume alcoholic drinks before going to a social gathering

PREGAMED > PREGAME

PREGAMES > PREGAME

PREGAMING > PREGAME

PREGGERS informal word for > PREGNANT

PREGGIER > PREGGY

PREGGIEST > PREGGY

PREGGO adj slang word for pregnant

PREGGY informal word for > PREGNANT

PREGNABLE adj capable of being assailed or captured

PREGNANCE obsolete word for > PREGNANCY

PREGNANCY n state or condition of being pregnant

PREGNANT adj carrying a fetus in the womb

PREGROWTH n period before something begins to grow

PREGUIDE vb give guidance in advance

PREGUIDED > PREGUIDE

PREGUIDES > PREGUIDE

PREHAB n any programme of training designed to prevent sports injury

PREHABS > PREHAB

PREHALLUX n extra first toe

PREHANDLE vb handle beforehand

PREHARDEN vb harden beforehand

PREHEAT vb heat (an oven, grill, pan, etc) beforehand

PREHEATED > PREHEAT

PREHEATER > PREHEAT

PREHEATS > PREHEAT

PREHEND vb take hold of

PREHENDED > PREHEND

PREHENDS > PREHEND

PREHENSOR n part that grasps

PREHIRING adj relating to early hiring

PREHNITE n green mineral

PREHNITES > PREHNITE

PREHUMAN n hominid that predates human beings

PREHUMANS > PREHUMAN

PREIF old form of > PROOF

PREIFE old form of > PROOF

PREIFES > PREIFE

PREIFS > PREIF

PREIMPOSE vb impose beforehand

PREINFORM vb inform beforehand

PREINSERT vb insert beforehand

PREINVITE vb invite before others

PREJINK variant of > PERJINK

PREJUDGE vb judge beforehand without sufficient evidence

PREJUDGED > PREJUDGE

PREJUDGER > PREJUDGE

PREJUDGES > PREJUDGE

PREJUDICE n unreasonable or unfair dislike or preference ▷ vb cause (someone) to have a prejudice

PREJUDIZE old form of > PREJUDICE

PRELACIES > PRELACY

PRELACY n office or status of a prelate

PRELATE n bishop or other churchman of high rank

PRELATES > PRELATE

PRELATESS n female prelate

PRELATIAL > PRELATE

PRELATIC > PRELATE

PRELATIES > PRELATY

PRELATION n setting of one above another

PRELATISE same as > PRELATIZE

PRELATISH adj like a prelate

PRELATISM same as > PRELACY

PRELATIST > PRELATISM

PRELATIZE vb exercise prelatical power

PRELATURE same as > PRELACY

PRELATY n prelacy

PRELAUNCH adj of the period before a launch

PRELAW adj before taking up study of law

PRELECT vb lecture or discourse in public

PRELECTED > PRELECT

PRELECTOR > PRELECT

PRELECTS > PRELECT

PRELEGAL adj of the period before the start of a law course

PRELIFE n life lived before one's life on earth

PRELIM n event which precedes another

PRELIMIT vb limit beforehand

PRELIMITS > PRELIMIT

PRELIMS pl n pages of a book which come before the main text

PRELIVES > PRELIFE

PRELOAD vb load beforehand

PRELOADED > PRELOAD

PRELOADS > PRELOAD

PRELOCATE vb locate beforehand

PRELOVED adj previously owned or used

PRELUDE n introductory movement in music ▷ vb act as a prelude to (something)

PRELUDED > PRELUDE

PRELUDER > PRELUDE

PRELUDERS > PRELUDE

PRELUDES > PRELUDE

PRELUDI > PRELUDIO

PRELUDIAL > PRELUDE

PRELUDING > PRELUDE

PRELUDIO n musical prelude

PRELUDIOS > PRELUDIO

PRELUNCH adj of the period before lunch

PRELUSION > PRELUDE

PRELUSIVE > PRELUDE

PRELUSORY > PRELUDE

PREM n informal word for a premature infant

PREMADE adj made in advance

PREMAKE vb make beforehand

PREMAKES > PREMAKE

PREMAKING > PREMAKE

PREMAN n hominid

PREMARKET adj of the period before a product is available

PREMATURE adj happening or done before the normal or expected time

PREMEAL adj of the period before a meal

PREMED n premedical student

PREMEDIC same as > PREMED

PREMEDICS > PREMEDIC

PREMEDS > PREMED

PREMEET adj happening before a meet

PREMEN > PREMAN

PREMERGER adj of the period prior to a merger

PREMIA > PREMIUM

PREMIE same as > PREEMIE

PREMIER n prime minister ▷ adj chief, leading

PREMIERE n first performance of a play, film, etc ▷ vb give, or (of a film, play, or opera) be, a premiere

PREMIERED > PREMIERE

PREMIERES > PREMIERE

PREMIERS > PREMIER

PREMIES > PREMIE

PREMISE n statement used as the basis of reasoning ▷ vb state or assume (a proposition) as a premise

PREMISED > PREMISE

PREMISES > PREMISE

PREMISING > PREMISE

PREMISS same as > PREMISE

PREMISSED > PREMISS

PREMISSES > PREMISS

PREMIUM n additional sum of money, as on a wage or charge

PREMIUMS > PREMIUM

PREMIX vb mix beforehand

PREMIXED > PREMIX

PREMIXES > PREMIX

PREMIXING > PREMIX

PREMIXT > PREMIX

PREMODERN adj of the period before a modern era

PREMODIFY vb modify in advance

PREMOLAR n tooth between the canine and first molar in adult humans ▷ adj situated before a molar tooth

PREMOLARS > PREMOLAR

PREMOLD same as > PREMOULD

PREMOLDED > PREMOLD

PREMOLDS > PREMOLD

PREMOLT same as > PREMOULT

PREMONISH vb admonish beforehand

PREMORAL adj not governed by sense of right and wrong

PREMORSE adj appearing as though the end had been bitten off

PREMOSAIC adj of the period before Moses

PREMOTION n previous motion

PREMOTOR adj relating to a part of the frontal lobe of the brain
PREMOULD vb mould in advance
PREMOULDS > PREMOULD
PREMOULT adj happening in the period before an animal moults
PREMOVE vb prompt to action
PREMOVED > PREMOVE
PREMOVES > PREMOVE
PREMOVING > PREMOVE
PREMS > PREM
PREMUNE adj having immunity to a disease as a result of latent infection
PREMY variant of > PREEMIE
PRENAME n forename
PRENAMES > PRENAME
PRENASAL n bone in the front of the nose
PRENASALS > PRENASAL
PRENATAL adj before birth, during pregnancy ▷ n prenatal examination
PRENATALS > PRENATAL
PRENEED adj arranged in advance of eventual requirements
PRENOMEN less common spelling of > PRAENOMEN
PRENOMENS > PRENOMEN
PRENOMINA > PRENOMEN
PRENOON adj of the period before noon
PRENOTIFY vb notify in advance
PRENOTION n preconception
PRENT Scots variant of > PRINT
PRENTED > PRENT
PRENTICE vb bind as an apprentice
PRENTICED > PRENTICE
PRENTICES > PRENTICE
PRENTING > PRENT
PRENTS > PRENT
PRENUBILE adj of the period from birth to puberty
PRENUMBER vb number in advance
PRENUP n prenuptial agreement
PRENUPS > PRENUP
PRENZIE adj Shakespearian word supposed by some to mean "princely"
PREOBTAIN vb obtain in advance
PREOCCUPY vb fill the thoughts or attention of (someone) to the exclusion of other things
PREOCULAR adj relating to the scale in front of the eye of a reptile or fish ▷ n scale in front of the eye of a reptile or fish
PREON n (in particle physics) hypothetical subcomponent of a quark
PREONS > PREON
PREOP n patient being prepared for surgery
PREOPS > PREOP

PREOPTION n right of first choice
PREORAL adj situated in front of mouth
PREORDAIN vb ordain, decree, or appoint beforehand
PREORDER vb order in advance
PREORDERS > PREORDER
PREOWNED adj second-hand
PREP vb prepare
PREPACK vb pack in advance of sale
PREPACKED adj sold already wrapped
PREPACKS > PREPACK
PREPAID > PREPAY
PREPARE vb make or get ready
PREPARED > PREPARE
PREPARER > PREPARE
PREPARERS > PREPARE
PREPARES > PREPARE
PREPARING > PREPARE
PREPASTE vb paste in advance
PREPASTED > PREPASTE
PREPASTES > PREPASTE
PREPAVE vb pave beforehand
PREPAVED > PREPAVE
PREPAVES > PREPAVE
PREPAVING > PREPAVE
PREPAY vb pay for in advance
PREPAYING > PREPAY
PREPAYS > PREPAY
PREPENSE adj (usually in legal contexts) arranged in advance ▷ vb consider beforehand
PREPENSED > PREPENSE
PREPENSES > PREPENSE
PREPILL adj of the period before the contraceptive pill became available
PREPLACE vb place in advance
PREPLACED > PREPLACE
PREPLACES > PREPLACE
PREPLAN vb plan beforehand
PREPLANS > PREPLAN
PREPLANT adj planted in advance
PREPOLLEX n additional digit on thumb of some animals
PREPONE vb bring forward to an earlier time
PREPONED > PREPONE
PREPONES > PREPONE
PREPONING > PREPONE
PREPOSE vb place before
PREPOSED > PREPOSE
PREPOSES > PREPOSE
PREPOSING > PREPOSE
PREPOSTOR n prefect in certain public schools
PREPOTENT adj greater in power, force, or influence
PREPPED > PREP
PREPPIE same as > PREPPY
PREPPIER > PREPPY
PREPPIES > PREPPY
PREPPIEST > PREPPY

PREPPILY > PREPPY
PREPPING > PREP
PREPPY adj denoting a fashion style of neat, understated clothes ▷ n person exhibiting such style
PREPREG n material already impregnated with synthetic resin
PREPREGS > PREPREG
PREPRESS adj before printing
PREPRICE vb price in advance
PREPRICED > PREPRICE
PREPRICES > PREPRICE
PREPRINT vb print in advance
PREPRINTS > PREPRINT
PREPS > PREP
PREPUBES > PREPUBIS
PREPUBIS n animal hip bone
PREPUCE n foreskin
PREPUCES > PREPUCE
PREPUEBLO adj belonging to the period before the Pueblo Indians
PREPUNCH vb pierce with holes in advance
PREPUPA n insect in stage of life before pupa
PREPUPAE > PREPUPA
PREPUPAL adj of the period between the larval and pupal stages
PREPUPAS > PREPUPA
PREPUTIAL > PREPUCE
PREQUEL n film or book about an earlier stage of a story
PREQUELS > PREQUEL
PRERACE adj of the period before a race
PRERADIO adj before the invention of radio
PRERECORD vb record (music or a programme) in advance so that it can be played or broadcast later
PRERECTAL adj in front of the rectum
PREREFORM adj before reform
PRERENAL adj anterior to kidney
PRERETURN adj of the period before return
PREREVIEW vb make a preliminary review
PRERINSE vb treat before rinsing
PRERINSED > PRERINSE
PRERINSES > PRERINSE
PRERIOT adj of the period before a riot
PREROCK adj of the era before rock music
PRERUPT adj abrupt
PRESA n musical sign or symbol to indicate the entry of a part
PRESAGE vb be a sign or warning of ▷ n omen
PRESAGED > PRESAGE
PRESAGER > PRESAGE
PRESAGERS > PRESAGE
PRESAGES > PRESAGE

PRESAGING > PRESAGE
PRESALE n practice of arranging the sale of a product before it is available
PRESALES > PRESALE
PRESBYOPE n person with presbyopy
PRESBYOPY n diminishing ability of the eye to focus
PRESBYTE n person with presbyopy
PRESBYTER n (in some episcopal Churches) official with administrative and priestly duties
PRESBYTES > PRESBYTE
PRESBYTIC > PRESBYTE
PRESCHOOL adj of or for children below the age of five
PRESCIENT adj having knowledge of events before they take place
PRESCIND vb withdraw attention (from something)
PRESCINDS > PRESCIND
PRESCIOUS adj prescient
PRESCORE vb record (the score of a film) before shooting
PRESCORED > PRESCORE
PRESCORES > PRESCORE
PRESCREEN vb screen in advance
PRESCRIBE vb recommend the use of (a medicine)
PRESCRIPT n something laid down or prescribed ▷ adj prescribed as a rule
PRESCUTA > PRESCUTUM
PRESCUTUM n part of an insect's thorax
PRESE > PRESA
PRESEASON n period before the start of a sport season
PRESELECT vb select beforehand
PRESELL vb promote in advance of appearance
PRESELLS > PRESELL
PRESENCE n fact of being in a specified place
PRESENCES > PRESENCE
PRESENILE adj occurring before the onset of old age
PRESENT adj being in a specified place ▷ n present time or tense ▷ vb introduce formally or publicly
PRESENTED > PRESENT
PRESENTEE n person who is presented, as at court
PRESENTER n person introducing a TV or radio show
PRESENTLY adv soon
PRESENTS pl n used in a deed or document to refer to itself
PRESERVE vb keep from being damaged, changed, or ended ▷ n area of interest restricted to a particular person or group
PRESERVED > PRESERVE
PRESERVER > PRESERVE
PRESERVES > PRESERVE
PRESES variant of > PRAESES

PRESET *vb* set a timer so that equipment starts to work at a specific time ▷ *adj* (of equipment) with the controls set in advance ▷ *n* control that is used to set initial conditions

PRESETS > PRESET

PRESETTLE *vb* settle beforehand

PRESHAPE *vb* shape beforehand

PRESHAPED > PRESHAPE

PRESHAPES > PRESHAPE

PRESHIP *vb* ship in advance

PRESHIPS > PRESHIP

PRESHOW *vb* show in advance

PRESHOWED > PRESHOW

PRESHOWN > PRESHOW

PRESHOWS > PRESHOW

PRESHRANK > PRESHRINK

PRESHRINK *vb* subject to a shrinking process so that further shrinkage will not occur

PRESHRUNK > PRESHRINK

PRESIDE *vb* be in charge, esp of a meeting

PRESIDED > PRESIDE

PRESIDENT *n* head of state in many countries

PRESIDER > PRESIDE

PRESIDERS > PRESIDE

PRESIDES > PRESIDE

PRESIDIA > PRESIDIUM

PRESIDIAL *adj* presidential

PRESIDING > PRESIDE

PRESIDIO *n* military post or establishment, esp in countries formerly under Spanish control

PRESIDIOS > PRESIDIO

PRESIDIUM *n* (in Communist countries) permanent administrative committee

PRESIFT *vb* sift beforehand

PRESIFTED > PRESIFT

PRESIFTS > PRESIFT

PRESIGNAL *vb* signal in advance

PRESLEEP *adj* of the period before sleep

PRESLICE *vb* slice in advance

PRESLICED > PRESLICE

PRESLICES > PRESLICE

PRESOAK *vb* soak beforehand

PRESOAKED > PRESOAK

PRESOAKS > PRESOAK

PRESOLD > PRESELL

PRESOLVE *vb* solve beforehand

PRESOLVED > PRESOLVE

PRESOLVES > PRESOLVE

PRESONG *adj* of the period before a song is sung

PRESORT *vb* sort in advance

PRESORTED > PRESORT

PRESORTS > PRESORT

PRESPLIT *adj* of the period prior to a split

PRESS *vb* apply force or weight to ▷ *n* printing machine

PRESSBACK *adj* (of an antique chair) with a pattern pressed into the back rail

PRESSED > PRESS

PRESSER > PRESS

PRESSERS > PRESS

PRESSES > PRESS

PRESSFAT *n* wine vat

PRESSFATS > PRESSFAT

PRESSFUL > PRESS

PRESSFULS > PRESS

PRESSIE *informal word for* > PRESENT

PRESSIES > PRESSIE

PRESSING *adj* urgent ▷ *n* large number of gramophone records produced at one time

PRESSINGS > PRESSING

PRESSION *n* act of pressing

PRESSIONS > PRESSION

PRESSMAN *n* person who works for the press

PRESSMARK *n* location mark on a book indicating a specific bookcase

PRESSMEN > PRESSMAN

PRESSOR *n* something that produces an increase in blood pressure

PRESSORS > PRESSOR

PRESSROOM *n* room in a printing establishment that houses the printing presses

PRESSRUN *n* number of books printed at one time

PRESSRUNS > PRESSRUN

PRESSURE *n* force produced by pressing ▷ *vb* persuade forcefully

PRESSURED > PRESSURE

PRESSURES > PRESSURE

PRESSWORK *n* operation of a printing press

PRESSY *same as* > PRESSIE

PREST *adj* prepared for action or use ▷ *n* loan of money ▷ *vb* give as a loan

PRESTAMP *vb* stamp in advance

PRESTAMPS > PRESTAMP

PRESTED > PREST

PRESTER > PREST

PRESTERNA *adj* anterior to sternum

PRESTERS > PREST

PRESTIGE *n* high status or respect resulting from success or achievements

PRESTIGES > PRESTIGE

PRESTING > PREST

PRESTO *adv* very quickly ▷ *n* passage to be played very quickly

PRESTORE *vb* store in advance

PRESTORED > PRESTORE

PRESTORES > PRESTORE

PRESTOS > PRESTO

PRESTRESS *vb* apply tensile stress to (the steel cables, wires, etc, of a precast concrete part) before the load is applied

PRESTRIKE *adj* of the period before a strike

PRESTS > PREST

PRESUME *vb* suppose to be the case

PRESUMED > PRESUME

PRESUMER > PRESUME

PRESUMERS > PRESUME

PRESUMES > PRESUME

PRESUMING > PRESUME

PRESUMMIT *n* meeting held prior to a summit

PRESURVEY *vb* survey in advance

PRETAPE *vb* (formerly) tape in advance

PRETAPED > PRETAPE

PRETAPES > PRETAPE

PRETAPING > PRETAPE

PRETASTE *vb* taste in advance

PRETASTED > PRETASTE

PRETASTES > PRETASTE

PRETAX *adj* before tax

PRETEEN *n* boy or girl approaching his or her teens

PRETEENS > PRETEEN

PRETELL *vb* predict

PRETELLS > PRETELL

PRETENCE *n* behaviour intended to deceive, pretending

PRETENCES > PRETENCE

PRETEND *vb* claim (something untrue) ▷ *adj* fanciful

PRETENDED > PRETEND

PRETENDER *n* person who makes a false or disputed claim to a position of power

PRETENDS > PRETEND

PRETENSE *same as* > PRETENCE

PRETENSES > PRETENSE

PRETERIST *n* person interested in past

PRETERIT *same as* > PRETERITE

PRETERITE *n* past tense of verbs, such as *jumped, swam* ▷ *adj* expressing such a past tense

PRETERITS > PRETERIT

PRETERM *n* premature baby

PRETERMIT *vb* overlook intentionally

PRETERMS > PRETERM

PRETEST *vb* test (something) before presenting it to its intended public or client ▷ *n* act or instance of pretesting

PRETESTED > PRETEST

PRETESTS > PRETEST

PRETEXT *n* false reason given to hide the real one ▷ *vb* get personal information under false pretences

PRETEXTED > PRETEXT

PRETEXTS > PRETEXT

PRETOLD > PRETELL

PRETONIC *adj* relating to the syllable before the one bearing the primary stress in a word

PRETOR *same as* > PRAETOR

PRETORIAL > PRETOR

PRETORIAN *n* person with the rank of praetor

PRETORS > PRETOR

PRETRAIN *vb* train in advance

PRETRAINS > PRETRAIN

PRETRAVEL *adj* of the period before travel

PRETREAT *vb* treat in advance

PRETREATS > PRETREAT

PRETRIAL *n* hearing prior to a trial

PRETRIALS > PRETRIAL

PRETRIM *vb* trim in advance

PRETRIMS > PRETRIM

PRETTIED > PRETTY

PRETTIER > PRETTY

PRETTIES > PRETTY

PRETTIEST > PRETTY

PRETTIFY *vb* make pretty

PRETTILY > PRETTY

PRETTY *adj* pleasing to look at ▷ *adv* fairly, moderately ▷ *vb* pretty

PRETTYING > PRETTY

PRETTYISH *adj* quite pretty

PRETTYISM *n* affectedly pretty style

PRETYPE *vb* type in advance

PRETYPED > PRETYPE

PRETYPES > PRETYPE

PRETYPING > PRETYPE

PRETZEL *n* brittle salted biscuit ▷ *vb* bend or twist

PRETZELS > PRETZEL

PREUNION *n* early form of trade union

PREUNIONS > PREUNION

PREUNITE *vb* unite in advance

PREUNITED > PREUNITE

PREUNITES > PREUNITE

PREVAIL *vb* gain mastery

PREVAILED > PREVAIL

PREVAILER > PREVAIL

PREVAILS > PREVAIL

PREVALENT *adj* widespread, common

PREVALUE *vb* value beforehand

PREVALUED > PREVALUE

PREVALUES > PREVALUE

PREVE *vb* prove

PREVED > PREVE

PREVENE *vb* come before

PREVENED > PREVENE

PREVENES > PREVENE

PREVENING > PREVENE

PREVENT *vb* keep from happening or doing

PREVENTED > PREVENT

PREVENTER *n* person or thing that prevents

PREVENTS > PREVENT

PREVERB *n* particle preceding root of verb

PREVERBAL > PREVERB

PREVERBS > PREVERB

PREVES > PREVE

PREVIABLE *adj* not yet viable

PREVIEW *n* advance showing of a film or exhibition before it is shown to the public ▷ *vb* view in advance

PREVIEWED > PREVIEW
PREVIEWER > PREVIEW
PREVIEWS > PREVIEW
PREVING > PREVE
PREVIOUS adj coming or happening before
PREVISE vb predict or foresee
PREVISED > PREVISE
PREVISES > PREVISE
PREVISING > PREVISE
PREVISION n act or power of foreseeing
PREVISIT vb visit beforehand
PREVISITS > PREVISIT
PREVISOR > PREVISE
PREVISORS > PREVISE
PREVUE same as > PREVIEW
PREVUED > PREVUE
PREVUES > PREVUE
PREVUING > PREVUE
PREWAR adj relating to the period before a war, esp before World War I or II
PREWARM vb warm beforehand
PREWARMED > PREWARM
PREWARMS > PREWARM
PREWARN vb warn in advance
PREWARNED > PREWARN
PREWARNS > PREWARN
PREWASH vb give a preliminary wash to (clothes) ▷ n preliminary wash
PREWASHED > PREWASH
PREWASHES > PREWASH
PREWEANED adj not yet weaned
PREWEIGH vb weigh beforehand
PREWEIGHS > PREWEIGH
PREWIRE vb wire beforehand
PREWIRED > PREWIRE
PREWIRES > PREWIRE
PREWIRING > PREWIRE
PREWORK vb work in advance
PREWORKED > PREWORK
PREWORKS > PREWORK
PREWORN adj (of clothes) second-hand
PREWRAP vb wrap in advance
PREWRAPS > PREWRAP
PREWRITE vb write beforehand
PREWRITES > PREWRITE
PREWROTE > PREWRITE
PREWYN obsolete spelling of > PRUNE
PREWYNS > PREWYN
PREX same as > PREXY
PREXES > PREX
PREXIE same as > PREXY
PREXIES > PREXY
PREXY n US college president
PREY n animal hunted and killed for food by another animal ▷ vb hunt or seize food by killing other animals
PREYED > PREY
PREYER > PREY
PREYERS > PREY

PREYFUL adj rich in prey
PREYING > PREY
PREYS > PREY
PREZ n president
PREZES > PREZ
PREZZIE same as > PRESSIE
PREZZIES > PREZZIE
PRIAL n pair royal of cards
PRIALS > PRIAL
PRIAPEAN same as > PRIAPIC
PRIAPI > PRIAPUS
PRIAPIC adj phallic
PRIAPISM n prolonged painful erection of the penis
PRIAPISMS > PRIAPISM
PRIAPUS n representation of the penis
PRIAPUSES > PRIAPUS
PRIBBLE variant of > PRABBLE
PRIBBLES > PRIBBLE
PRICE n amount of money for which a thing is bought or sold ▷ vb fix or ask the price of
PRICEABLE > PRICE
PRICED > PRICE
PRICELESS adj very valuable
PRICER > PRICE
PRICERS > PRICE
PRICES > PRICE
PRICEY adj expensive
PRICIER > PRICY
PRICIEST > PRICY
PRICILY > PRICEY
PRICINESS > PRICEY
PRICING > PRICE
PRICINGS > PRICE
PRICK vb pierce lightly with a sharp point ▷ n sudden sharp pain caused by pricking
PRICKED > PRICK
PRICKER n person or thing that pricks
PRICKERS > PRICKER
PRICKET n male deer in the second year of life
PRICKETS > PRICKET
PRICKIER > PRICKY
PRICKIEST > PRICKY
PRICKING > PRICK
PRICKINGS > PRICK
PRICKLE n thorn or spike on a plant ▷ vb have a tingling or pricking sensation
PRICKLED > PRICKLE
PRICKLES > PRICKLE
PRICKLIER > PRICKLY
PRICKLING > PRICKLE
PRICKLY adj having prickles
PRICKS > PRICK
PRICKWOOD n shrub with wood used for skewers
PRICKY adj covered with pricks
PRICY same as > PRICEY
PRIDE n feeling of pleasure and satisfaction when one has done well
PRIDED > PRIDE
PRIDEFUL > PRIDE
PRIDELESS > PRIDE
PRIDES > PRIDE

PRIDIAN adj relating to yesterday
PRIDING > PRIDE
PRIED > PRY
PRIEDIEU n piece of furniture for use when kneeling to pray
PRIEDIEUS > PRIEDIEU
PRIEDIEUX > PRIEDIEU
PRIEF obsolete variant of > PROOF
PRIEFE obsolete variant of > PROOF
PRIEFES > PRIEFE
PRIEFS > PRIEF
PRIER n person who pries
PRIERS > PRIER
PRIES > PRY
PRIEST n (in the Christian church) person who can administer the sacraments and preach ▷ vb make a priest
PRIESTED > PRIEST
PRIESTESS n female official who offers sacrifice on behalf of the people and performs various other religious ceremonies
PRIESTING > PRIEST
PRIESTLY adj of, relating to, characteristic of, or befitting a priest
PRIESTS > PRIEST
PRIEVE obsolete variant of > PROOF
PRIEVED > PRIEVE
PRIEVES > PRIEVE
PRIEVING > PRIEVE
PRIG n self-righteous person who acts as if superior to others
PRIGGED > PRIG
PRIGGER n thief
PRIGGERS > PRIGGER
PRIGGERY > PRIG
PRIGGING > PRIG
PRIGGINGS > PRIG
PRIGGISH > PRIG
PRIGGISM > PRIG
PRIGGISMS > PRIG
PRIGS > PRIG
PRILL vb convert (a material) into a granular free-flowing form ▷ n prilled material
PRILLED > PRILL
PRILLING > PRILL
PRILLS > PRILL
PRIM adj formal, proper, and rather prudish ▷ vb make prim
PRIMA same as > PRIMO
PRIMACIES > PRIMACY
PRIMACY n state of being first in rank, grade, etc
PRIMAEVAL same as > PRIMEVAL
PRIMAGE n tax added to customs duty
PRIMAGES > PRIMAGE
PRIMAL adj of basic causes or origins
PRIMALITY n state of being prime
PRIMALLY > PRIMAL
PRIMARIES > PRIMARY

PRIMARILY adv chiefly or mainly
PRIMARY adj chief, most important ▷ n person or thing that is first in position, time, or importance
PRIMAS > PRIMA
PRIMATAL n primate
PRIMATALS > PRIMATAL
PRIMATE n member of an order of mammals including monkeys and humans
PRIMATES > PRIMATE
PRIMATIAL > PRIMATE
PRIMATIC > PRIMATE
PRIMAVERA n springtime
PRIME adj main, most important ▷ n time when someone is most vigorous ▷ vb give (someone) information in advance
PRIMED > PRIME
PRIMELY > PRIME
PRIMENESS > PRIME
PRIMER n special paint applied to bare wood etc before the main paint
PRIMERO n 16th- and 17th-century card game
PRIMEROS > PRIMERO
PRIMERS > PRIMER
PRIMES > PRIME
PRIMETIME adj occurring during or designed for prime time
PRIMEUR n anything (esp fruit) produced early
PRIMEURS > PRIMEUR
PRIMEVAL adj of the earliest age of the world
PRIMI > PRIMO
PRIMINE n integument surrounding an ovule or the outer of two such integuments
PRIMINES > PRIMINE
PRIMING same as > PRIMER
PRIMINGS > PRIMING
PRIMIPARA n woman who has borne only one child
PRIMITIAE pl n first fruits of the season
PRIMITIAL > PRIMITIAE
PRIMITIAS > PRIMITIAE
PRIMITIVE adj of an early simple stage of development ▷ n primitive person or thing
PRIMLY > PRIM
PRIMMED > PRIM
PRIMMER n elementary textbook
PRIMMERS > PRIMMER
PRIMMEST > PRIM
PRIMMING > PRIM
PRIMNESS > PRIM
PRIMO n upper or right-hand part in a piano duet
PRIMORDIA pl n organs or parts in the earliest stage of development
PRIMOS > PRIMO
PRIMP vb tidy (one's hair or clothes) fussily
PRIMPED > PRIMP
PRIMPING > PRIMP
PRIMPS > PRIMP

PRIMROSE n pale yellow spring flower ▷ adj pale yellow

PRIMROSED > PRIMROSE

PRIMROSES > PRIMROSE

PRIMROSY adj abounding in primroses

PRIMS > PRIM

PRIMSIE Scots variant of > PRIM

PRIMSIER > PRIMSIE

PRIMSIEST > PRIMSIE

PRIMULA n type of primrose with brightly coloured flowers

PRIMULAS > PRIMULA

PRIMULINE n type of dye

PRIMUS n presiding bishop in the Synod

PRIMUSES > PRIMUS

PRIMY adj prime

PRINCE n son of a king or queen ▷ vb act like a prince

PRINCED > PRINCE

PRINCEDOM n dignity, rank, or position of a prince

PRINCEKIN n young prince

PRINCELET n petty or minor prince

PRINCELY adj of or like a prince ▷ adv in a princely manner

PRINCES > PRINCE

PRINCESS n female member of a royal family, esp the daughter of the king or queen

PRINCESSE same as > PRINCESS

PRINCING > PRINCE

PRINCIPAL adj main, most important ▷ n head of a school or college

PRINCIPE n prince

PRINCIPI > PRINCIPE

PRINCIPIA n principles

PRINCIPLE n moral rule guiding behaviour

PRINCOCK same as > PRINCOX

PRINCOCKS > PRINCOCK

PRINCOX n pert youth

PRINCOXES > PRINCOX

PRINK vb dress (oneself) finely

PRINKED > PRINK

PRINKER > PRINK

PRINKERS > PRINK

PRINKING > PRINK

PRINKS > PRINK

PRINT vb reproduce (a newspaper, book, etc) in large quantities by mechanical or electronic means ▷ n printed words etc

PRINTABLE adj capable of being printed or of producing a print

PRINTED > PRINT

PRINTER n person or company engaged in printing

PRINTERS > PRINTER

PRINTERY n establishment in which printing is carried out

PRINTHEAD n component in a printer that forms a printed character

PRINTING n process of producing printed matter

PRINTINGS > PRINTING

PRINTLESS > PRINT

PRINTOUT n printed information produced by a computer output device

PRINTOUTS > PRINTOUT

PRINTS > PRINT

PRION n dovelike petrel with a serrated bill

PRIONS > PRION

PRIOR adj earlier ▷ n head monk in a priory

PRIORATE n office, status, or term of office of a prior

PRIORATES > PRIORATE

PRIORESS n deputy head nun in a convent

PRIORIES > PRIORY

PRIORITY n most important thing that must be dealt with first

PRIORLY > PRIOR

PRIORS > PRIOR

PRIORSHIP n office of prior

PRIORY n place where certain orders of monks or nuns live

PRISAGE n customs duty levied until 1809 upon wine imported into England

PRISAGES > PRISAGE

PRISE same as > PRY

PRISED > PRISE

PRISER > PRISE

PRISERE n primary sere or succession from bare ground to the community climax

PRISERES > PRISERE

PRISERS > PRISE

PRISES > PRISE

PRISING > PRISE

PRISM n transparent block used to disperse light into a spectrum

PRISMATIC adj of or shaped like a prism

PRISMOID n prism-like geometrical shape

PRISMOIDS > PRISMOID

PRISMS > PRISM

PRISMY > PRISM

PRISON n building where criminals and accused people are held ▷ vb imprison

PRISONED > PRISON

PRISONER n person held captive

PRISONERS > PRISONER

PRISONING > PRISON

PRISONOUS > PRISON

PRISONS > PRISON

PRISS n prissy person ▷ vb act prissily

PRISSED > PRISS

PRISSES > PRISS

PRISSIER > PRISSY

PRISSIES > PRISSY

PRISSIEST > PRISSY

PRISSILY > PRISSY

PRISSING > PRISS

PRISSY adj prim, correct, and easily shocked ▷ n prissy person

PRISTANE n colourless combustible liquid

PRISTANES > PRISTANE

PRISTINE adj clean, new, and unused

PRITHEE interj pray thee

PRIVACIES > PRIVACY

PRIVACY n condition of being private

PRIVADO n close friend

PRIVADOES > PRIVADO

PRIVADOS > PRIVADO

PRIVATE adj for the use of one person or group only ▷ n soldier of the lowest rank

PRIVATEER n privately owned armed vessel authorized by the government to take part in a war ▷ vb competitor, esp in motor racing, who is privately financed rather than sponsored by a manufacturer

PRIVATELY > PRIVATE

PRIVATER > PRIVATE

PRIVATES > PRIVATE

PRIVATEST > PRIVATE

PRIVATION n loss or lack of the necessities of life

PRIVATISE same as > PRIVATIZE

PRIVATISM n lack of concern for public life

PRIVATIST > PRIVATISM

PRIVATIVE adj causing privation

PRIVATIZE vb sell (a publicly owned company) to individuals or a private company

PRIVET n bushy evergreen shrub used for hedges

PRIVETS > PRIVET

PRIVIER > PRIVY

PRIVIES > PRIVY

PRIVIEST > PRIVY

PRIVILEGE n advantage or favour that only some people have ▷ vb bestow a privilege or privileges upon

PRIVILY adv in a secret way

PRIVITIES > PRIVITY

PRIVITY n legally recognized relationship between two parties

PRIVY adj sharing knowledge of something secret ▷ n toilet, esp an outside one

PRIZABLE adj of worth

PRIZE n reward given for success in a competition etc ▷ adj winning or likely to win a prize ▷ vb value highly

PRIZED > PRIZE

PRIZEMAN n winner of prize

PRIZEMEN > PRIZEMAN

PRIZER n contender for prize

PRIZERS > PRIZER

PRIZES > PRIZE

PRIZING > PRIZE

PRO prep in favour of ▷ n professional ▷ adv in favour of a motion etc

PROA n canoe-like boat used in the South Pacific

PROACTION n action that initiates change as opposed to reaction to events

PROACTIVE adj tending to initiate change rather than reacting to events

PROAS > PROA

PROB n problem

PROBABLE adj likely to happen or be true ▷ n person who is likely to be chosen for a team, event, etc

PROBABLES > PROBABLE

PROBABLY adv in all likelihood ▷ sentence substitute I believe such a thing or situation may be the case

PROBALL adj believable

PROBAND n first patient to be investigated in a family study

PROBANDS > PROBAND

PROBANG n long flexible rod used to apply medication

PROBANGS > PROBANG

PROBATE n process of proving the validity of a will ▷ vb establish officially the authenticity and validity of (a will)

PROBATED > PROBATE

PROBATES > PROBATE

PROBATING > PROBATE

PROBATION n system of dealing with law-breakers, esp juvenile ones, by placing them under supervision

PROBATIVE adj serving to test or designed for testing

PROBATORY same as > PROBATIVE

PROBE vb search into or examine closely ▷ n surgical instrument used to examine a wound, cavity, etc

PROBEABLE > PROBE

PROBED > PROBE

PROBER > PROBE

PROBERS > PROBE

PROBES > PROBE

PROBING n act of making a thorough enquiry

PROBINGLY > PROBE

PROBINGS > PROBING

PROBIOTIC n bacterium that protects the body from harmful bacteria

PROBIT n statistical measurement

PROBITIES > PROBITY

PROBITS > PROBIT

PROBITY n honesty, integrity

PROBLEM n something difficult to deal with or solve ▷ adj of a literary work that deals with difficult moral questions

PROBLEMS > PROBLEM

PROBOSCIS n long trunk or snout

PROBS > PROB

PROCACITY n insolence

PROCAINE n colourless or white crystalline water-soluble substance

PROCAINES > PROCAINE

PROCAMBIA n plant part in stem and root

PROCARP n female reproductive organ in red algae
PROCARPS > PROCARP
PROCARYON same as > PROKARYON
PROCEDURE n way of doing something, esp the correct or usual one
PROCEED vb start or continue doing
PROCEEDED > PROCEED
PROCEEDER > PROCEED
PROCEEDS pl n money obtained from an event or activity
PROCERITY n tallness
PROCESS n series of actions or changes ▷ vb handle or prepare by a special method of manufacture
PROCESSED > PROCESS
PROCESSER same as > PROCESSOR
PROCESSES > PROCESS
PROCESSOR n person or thing that carries out a process
PROCHAIN variant of > PROCHEIN
PROCHEIN adj next or nearest
PROCHOICE adj in favour of women's right to abortion
PROCHURCH adj favourable to church
PROCIDENT adj relating to prolapsus
PROCINCT n state of preparedness
PROCINCTS > PROCINCT
PROCLAIM vb declare publicly
PROCLAIMS > PROCLAIM
PROCLISES > PROCLITIC
PROCLISIS > PROCLITIC
PROCLITIC adj relating to or denoting a monosyllabic word or form having no stress or accent and pronounced as a prefix of the following word, as in English 't for it in 'twas ▷ n proclitic word or form
PROCLIVE adj prone
PROCONSUL n administrator or governor of a colony, occupied territory, or other dependency
PROCREANT > PROCREATE
PROCREATE vb produce offspring
PROCTAL adj relating to the rectum
PROCTITIS n inflammation of the rectum
PROCTODEA pl n parts of the anus
PROCTOR n university worker who enforces discipline ▷ vb invigilate (an examination)
PROCTORED > PROCTOR
PROCTORS > PROCTOR
PROCURACY n office of a procurator
PROCURAL > PROCURE
PROCURALS > PROCURE

PROCURE vb get, provide
PROCURED > PROCURE
PROCURER n person who provides something
PROCURERS > PROCURER
PROCURES > PROCURE
PROCURESS same as > PROCURER
PROCUREUR n law officer in Guernsey
PROCURING > PROCURE
PROCYONID n animal of the raccoon family
PROD vb poke with something pointed ▷ n prodding
PRODDED > PROD
PRODDER > PROD
PRODDERS > PROD
PRODDING n act of prodding
PRODDINGS > PRODDING
PRODIGAL adj recklessly extravagant, wasteful ▷ n person who spends lavishly or squanders money
PRODIGALS > PRODIGAL
PRODIGIES > PRODIGY
PRODIGY n person with some marvellous talent
PRODITOR n traitor
PRODITORS > PRODITOR
PRODITORY > PRODITOR
PRODNOSE vb make uninvited inquiries (about someone else's business, for example)
PRODNOSED > PRODNOSE
PRODNOSES > PRODNOSE
PRODROMA n symptom that signals the onset of a disease
PRODROMAL > PRODROME
PRODROME n any symptom that signals the impending onset of a disease
PRODROMES > PRODROME
PRODROMI > PRODROME
PRODROMIC > PRODROME
PRODROMUS same as > PRODROME
PRODRUG n compound that is metabolized in the body to produce an active drug
PRODRUGS > PRODRUG
PRODS > PROD
PRODUCE vb bring into existence ▷ n food grown for sale
PRODUCED > PRODUCE
PRODUCER n person with control over the making of a film, record, etc
PRODUCERS > PRODUCER
PRODUCES > PRODUCE
PRODUCING > PRODUCE
PRODUCT n something produced
PRODUCTS > PRODUCT
PROEM n introduction or preface
PROEMBRYO n stage prior to embryo in plants
PROEMIAL > PROEM
PROEMS > PROEM
PROENZYME n inactive form of an enzyme
PROESTRUS n period in the estrous cycle that immediately precedes estrus

PROETTE n female golfing professional
PROETTES > PROETTE
PROF short for > PROFESSOR
PROFACE interj much good may it do you
PROFAMILY adj in favour of family
PROFANE adj showing disrespect for religion or holy things ▷ vb treat (something sacred) irreverently, desecrate
PROFANED > PROFANE
PROFANELY > PROFANE
PROFANER > PROFANE
PROFANERS > PROFANE
PROFANES > PROFANE
PROFANING > PROFANE
PROFANITY n profane talk or behaviour, blasphemy
PROFESS vb state or claim (something as true), sometimes falsely
PROFESSED adj supposed
PROFESSES > PROFESS
PROFESSOR n teacher of the highest rank in a university
PROFFER vb offer ▷ n act of proffering
PROFFERED > PROFFER
PROFFERER > PROFFER
PROFFERS > PROFFER
PROFILE n outline, esp of the face, as seen from the side ▷ vb draw, write, or make a profile of
PROFILED > PROFILE
PROFILER n device that creates a profile
PROFILERS > PROFILER
PROFILES > PROFILE
PROFILING > PROFILE
PROFILIST > PROFILE
PROFIT n money gained ▷ vb gain or benefit
PROFITED > PROFIT
PROFITEER n person who makes excessive profits at the expense of the public ▷ vb make excessive profits
PROFITER > PROFIT
PROFITERS > PROFIT
PROFITING > PROFIT
PROFITS > PROFIT
PROFLUENT adj flowing smoothly or abundantly
PROFORMA n invoice issued before an order is placed
PROFORMAS > PROFORMA
PROFOUND adj showing or needing great knowledge ▷ n great depth
PROFOUNDS > PROFOUND
PROFS > PROF
PROFUSE adj plentiful
PROFUSELY > PROFUSE
PROFUSER > PROFUSE
PROFUSERS > PROFUSE
PROFUSION > PROFUSE
PROFUSIVE same as > PROFUSE
PROG vb prowl about for or as if for food or plunder ▷ n food obtained by begging
PROGENIES > PROGENY

PROGENY n children
PROGERIA n premature old age in children
PROGERIAS > PROGERIA
PROGESTIN n type of steroid hormone
PROGGED > PROG
PROGGER n fan of progressive rock
PROGGERS > PROGGER
PROGGING > PROG
PROGGINS n proctor
PROGNOSE vb predict course of disease
PROGNOSED > PROGNOSE
PROGNOSES > PROGNOSIS
PROGNOSIS n doctor's forecast about the progress of an illness
PROGRADE vb (of beach) advance towards sea
PROGRADED > PROGRADE
PROGRADES > PROGRADE
PROGRAM same as > PROGRAMME
PROGRAMED > PROGRAM
PROGRAMER n US spelling of programmer
PROGRAMME same as > PROGRAM
PROGRAMS > PROGRAM
PROGRESS n improvement, development ▷ vb become more advanced or skilful
PROGS > PROG
PROGUN adj in favour of public owning firearms
PROHIBIT vb forbid or prevent from happening
PROHIBITS > PROHIBIT
PROIGN same as > PROIN
PROIGNED > PROIGN
PROIGNING > PROIGN
PROIGNS > PROIGN
PROIN vb trim or prune
PROINE same as > PROIN
PROINED > PROIN
PROINES > PROINE
PROINING > PROIN
PROINS > PROIN
PROJECT n planned scheme to do or examine something over a period ▷ vb make a forecast based on known data
PROJECTED > PROJECT
PROJECTOR n apparatus for projecting photographic images, films, or slides on a screen
PROJECTS > PROJECT
PROJET n draft of a proposed treaty
PROJETS > PROJET
PROKARYON n nucleus of a prokaryote
PROKARYOT n any organism having cells in each of which the genetic material is in a single DNA chain, not enclosed in a nucleus
PROKE vb thrust or poke
PROKED > PROKE
PROKER > PROKE
PROKERS > PROKE
PROKES > PROKE
PROKING > PROKE

PROLABOR adj favouring the Labor party

PROLABOUR adj favouring an organized labour movement

PROLACTIN n gonadotrophic hormone secreted by the anterior lobe of the pituitary gland

PROLAMIN same as > PROLAMINE

PROLAMINE n any of a group of simple plant proteins, including gliadin, hordein, and zein

PROLAMINS > PROLAMIN

PROLAN n constituent of human pregnancy urine

PROLANS > PROLAN

PROLAPSE n slipping down of an internal organ of the body from its normal position ▷ vb (of an internal organ) slip from its normal position

PROLAPSED > PROLAPSE

PROLAPSES > PROLAPSE

PROLAPSUS same as > PROLAPSE

PROLATE adj having a polar diameter which is longer than the equatorial diameter ▷ vb pronounce or utter

PROLATED > PROLATE

PROLATELY > PROLATE

PROLATES > PROLATE

PROLATING > PROLATE

PROLATION > PROLATE

PROLATIVE > PROLATE

PROLE old form of > PROWL

PROLED > PROLE

PROLEG n appendage on abdominal segment of a caterpillar

PROLEGS > PROLEG

PROLEPSES > PROLEPSIS

PROLEPSIS n rhetorical device by which objections are anticipated and answered in advance

PROLEPTIC > PROLEPSIS

PROLER n prowler

PROLERS > PROLER

PROLES > PROLE

PROLETARY n member of the proletariat

PROLICIDE n killing of one's child

PROLIFIC adj very productive

PROLINE n nonessential amino acid that occurs in protein

PROLINES > PROLINE

PROLING > PROLE

PROLIX adj (of speech or a piece of writing) overlong and boring

PROLIXITY > PROLIX

PROLIXLY > PROLIX

PROLL vb prowl or search

PROLLED > PROLL

PROLLER > PROLL

PROLLERS > PROLL

PROLLING > PROLL

PROLLS > PROLL

PROLLY adv probably

PROLOG same as > PROLOGUE

PROLOGED > PROLOG

PROLOGING > PROLOG

PROLOGISE same as > PROLOGIZE

PROLOGIST n prologue writer

PROLOGIZE vb write a prologue

PROLOGS > PROLOG

PROLOGUE n introduction to a play or book ▷ vb introduce or preface with or as if with a prologue

PROLOGUED > PROLOGUE

PROLOGUES > PROLOGUE

PROLONG vb make (something) last longer

PROLONGE n (formerly) rope used as part of the towing equipment of a gun carriage

PROLONGED > PROLONG

PROLONGER > PROLONG

PROLONGES > PROLONGE

PROLONGS > PROLONG

PROLUSION n preliminary written exercise

PROLUSORY > PROLUSION

PROM n formal dance held at a high school or college

PROMACHOS n defender or champion

PROMENADE n paved walkway along the seafront at a holiday resort ▷ vb take a leisurely walk

PROMETAL n type of cast iron

PROMETALS > PROMETAL

PROMETRIC adj in favour of the metric system

PROMINE n substance promoting cell growth

PROMINENT n feature that projects outwards ▷ adj very noticeable

PROMINES > PROMINE

PROMISE vb say that one will definitely do or not do something ▷ n undertaking to do or not to do something

PROMISED > PROMISE

PROMISEE n person to whom a promise is made

PROMISEES > PROMISEE

PROMISER > PROMISE

PROMISERS > PROMISE

PROMISES > PROMISE

PROMISING adj likely to succeed or turn out well

PROMISOR n person who makes a promise

PROMISORS > PROMISOR

PROMISSOR n (in law) person who makes a promise

PROMMER n spectator at promenade concert

PROMMERS > PROMMER

PROMO vb promote (something)

PROMODERN adj in favour of the modern

PROMOED > PROMO

PROMOING > PROMO

PROMOS > PROMO

PROMOTE vb help to make (something) happen or increase

PROMOTED > PROMOTE

PROMOTER n person who organizes or finances an event etc

PROMOTERS > PROMOTER

PROMOTES > PROMOTE

PROMOTING > PROMOTE

PROMOTION > PROMOTE

PROMOTIVE adj tending to promote

PROMOTOR variant of > PROMOTER

PROMOTORS > PROMOTOR

PROMPT vb cause (an action) ▷ adj done without delay ▷ adv exactly ▷ n anything that serves to remind

PROMPTED > PROMPT

PROMPTER n person offstage who prompts actors

PROMPTERS > PROMPTER

PROMPTEST > PROMPT

PROMPTING > PROMPT

PROMPTLY > PROMPT

PROMPTS > PROMPT

PROMPTURE n prompting

PROMS > PROM

PROMULGE vb bring to public knowledge

PROMULGED > PROMULGE

PROMULGES > PROMULGE

PROMUSCES > PROMUSCIS

PROMUSCIS n proboscis of certain insects

PRONAOI > PRONAOS

PRONAOS n inner area of the portico of a classical temple

PRONATE vb turn (a limb, hand, or foot) so that the palm or sole is directed downwards

PRONATED > PRONATE

PRONATES > PRONATE

PRONATING > PRONATE

PRONATION > PRONATE

PRONATOR n any muscle whose contractions produce or affect pronation

PRONATORS > PRONATOR

PRONE n sermon ▷ adj sloping downwards

PRONELY > PRONE

PRONENESS > PRONE

PRONEPHRA n parts of the kidneys of lower vertebrates

PRONER > PRONE

PRONES > PRONE

PRONEST > PRONE

PRONEUR n flatterer

PRONEURS > PRONEUR

PRONG n one spike of a fork or similar instrument ▷ vb prick or spear with or as if with a prong

PRONGBUCK n horned N American ruminant

PRONGED > PRONG

PRONGHORN n ruminant mammal inhabiting rocky deserts of North America and having small branched horns

PRONGING > PRONG

PRONGS > PRONG

PRONK vb jump straight up

PRONKED > PRONK

PRONKING > PRONK

PRONKINGS > PRONKING

PRONKS > PRONK

PRONOTA > PRONOTUM

PRONOTAL > PRONOTUM

PRONOTUM n notum of the prothorax of an insect

PRONOUN n word, such as she or it, used to replace a noun

PRONOUNCE vb form the sounds of (words or letters), esp clearly or in a particular way

PRONOUNS > PRONOUN

PRONTO adv at once

PRONUCLEI n plural of pronucleus, nucleus of a germ cell after meiosis

PRONUNCIO n papal ambassador

PROO interj (to a horse) stop!

PROOEMION n preface

PROOEMIUM n preface

PROOF n evidence that shows that something is true or has happened ▷ adj able to withstand ▷ vb take a proof from (type matter)

PROOFED > PROOF

PROOFER n reader of proofs

PROOFERS > PROOFER

PROOFING > PROOF

PROOFINGS > PROOF

PROOFLESS > PROOF

PROOFREAD vb read and correct (printer's proofs)

PROOFROOM n room for proofreading

PROOFS > PROOF

PROOTIC n bone in front of ear

PROOTICS > PROOTIC

PROP vb support (something) so that it stays upright or in place ▷ n pole, beam, etc used as a support

PROPAGATE vb spread (information and ideas)

PROPAGE vb propagate

PROPAGED > PROPAGE

PROPAGES > PROPAGE

PROPAGING > PROPAGE

PROPAGULA > PROPAGULE

PROPAGULE n plant part, such as a bud, that becomes detached from the rest of the plant and grows into a new plant

PROPALE vb publish (something)

PROPALED > PROPALE

PROPALES > PROPALE

PROPALING > PROPALE

PROPANE n flammable gas found in petroleum and used as a fuel

PROPANES > PROPANE

PROPANOIC adj as in propanoic acid colourless liquid carboxylic acid

PROPANOL n colourless alcohol

PROPANOLS > PROPANOL

PROPANONE n systematic name of acetone

PROPEL vb cause to move forward

PROPELLED > PROPEL

PROPELLER n revolving shaft with blades for driving a ship or aircraft

PROPELLOR same as > PROPELLER

PROPELS > PROPEL

PROPENAL n type of aldehyde used as a herbicide and tear gas

PROPENALS > PROPENAL

PROPEND vb be inclined or disposed

PROPENDED > PROPEND

PROPENDS > PROPEND

PROPENE n colourless gaseous alkene obtained by cracking petroleum

PROPENES > PROPENE

PROPENOIC adj as in propenoic acid systematic name of acrylic acid

PROPENOL n liquid used to make allylic alcohol

PROPENOLS > PROPENOL

PROPENSE adj inclining forward

PROPENYL n three-carbon radical

PROPENYLS > PROPENYL

PROPER adj real or genuine ▷ n service or psalm regarded as appropriate to a specific day, season, etc

PROPERDIN n protein present in blood serum that, acting with complement, is involved in the destruction of alien cells, such as bacteria

PROPERER > PROPER

PROPEREST > PROPER

PROPERLY > PROPER

PROPERS > PROPER

PROPERTY same as > PROPRIUM

PROPHAGE n type of virus in a bacterial cell

PROPHAGES > PROPHAGE

PROPHASE n first stage of mitosis

PROPHASES > PROPHASE

PROPHASIC > PROPHASE

PROPHECY n prediction

PROPHESY vb foretell

PROPHET n person chosen by God to spread His word

PROPHETIC adj foretelling what will happen

PROPHETS > PROPHET

PROPHYLL n leaf-shaped plant structure

PROPHYLLS > PROPHYLL

PROPINE vb drink a toast to

PROPINED > PROPINE

PROPINES > PROPINE

PROPINING > PROPINE

PROPIONIC adj as in propionic acid former name for propanoic acid

PROPJET another name for > TURBOPROP

PROPJETS > PROPJET

PROPMAN n member of the stage crew in charge of the stage props

PROPMEN > PROPMAN

PROPODEON n part of an insect's thorax

PROPODEUM variant of > PROPODEON

PROPOLIS n resinous aromatic substance collected by bees from trees

PROPONE vb propose or put forward, esp before a court

PROPONED > PROPONE

PROPONENT n person who argues in favour of something

PROPONES > PROPONE

PROPONING > PROPONE

PROPOSAL n act of proposing

PROPOSALS > PROPOSAL

PROPOSE vb put forward for consideration

PROPOSED > PROPOSE

PROPOSER > PROPOSE

PROPOSERS > PROPOSE

PROPOSES > PROPOSE

PROPOSING > PROPOSE

PROPOSITA n woman from whom a line of descent is traced

PROPOSITI n people from whom lines of descent are traced

PROPOUND vb put forward for consideration

PROPOUNDS > PROPOUND

PROPPANT n material used in the oil extraction process

PROPPANTS > PROPPANT

PROPPED > PROP

PROPPING > PROP

PROPRETOR n (in ancient Rome) citizen, esp an ex-praetor, granted a praetor's imperium, to be exercised outside Rome

PROPRIA > PROPRIUM

PROPRIETY n quality of being appropriate or fitting

PROPRIUM n attribute that is not essential to a species but is common and peculiar to it

PROPS > PROP

PROPTOSES > PROPTOSIS

PROPTOSIS n forward displacement of an organ or part, such as the eyeball

PROPULSOR n propeller

PROPYL n type of monovalent radical

PROPYLA > PROPYLON

PROPYLAEA n porticos, esp those that form the entrances to temples

PROPYLENE n gas found in petroleum and used to produce many organic compounds

PROPYLIC > PROPYL

PROPYLITE n altered andesite or similar rock containing calcite, chlorite, etc, produced by the action of hot water

PROPYLON n portico, esp one that forms the entrance to a temple

PROPYLONS > PROPYLON

PROPYLS > PROPYL

PROPYNE n type of gaseous methyl acetylene

PROPYNES > PROPYNE

PRORATE vb divide, assess, or distribute (something) proportionately

PRORATED > PRORATE

PRORATES > PRORATE

PRORATING > PRORATE

PRORATION > PRORATE

PRORE n forward part of ship

PRORECTOR n official in German academia

PROREFORM adj in favour of or supporting reform, esp within politics

PRORES > PRORE

PROROGATE vb discontinue legislative meetings

PROROGUE vb suspend (parliament) without dissolving it

PROROGUED > PROROGUE

PROROGUES > PROROGUE

PROS > PRO

PROSAIC adj lacking imagination, dull

PROSAICAL same as > PROSAIC

PROSAISM n prosaic quality or style

PROSAISMS > PROSAISM

PROSAIST > PROSAISM

PROSAISTS > PROSAISM

PROSATEUR n writer of prose

PROSCENIA pl n arches or openings separating stages from auditoria together with the areas immediately in front of the arches

PROSCRIBE vb prohibit, outlaw

PROSCRIPT n proscription or prohibition

PROSE n ordinary speech or writing in contrast to poetry ▷ vb speak or write in a tedious style

PROSECCO n Italian sparkling white wine

PROSECCOS > PROSECCO

PROSECT vb dissect a cadaver for a public demonstration

PROSECTED > PROSECT

PROSECTOR n person who prepares or dissects anatomical subjects for demonstration

PROSECTS > PROSECT

PROSECUTE vb bring a criminal charge against

PROSED > PROSE

PROSELIKE > PROSE

PROSELYTE n recent convert

PROSEMAN n writer of prose

PROSEMEN > PROSEMAN

PROSER n writer of prose

PROSERS > PROSER

PROSES > PROSE

PROSEUCHA n place of prayer

PROSEUCHE n prayer

PROSIER > PROSY

PROSIEST > PROSY

PROSIFIED > PROSIFY

PROSIFIES > PROSIFY

PROSIFY vb write prose

PROSILY > PROSY

PROSIMIAN n primate of the primitive suborder which includes lemurs, lorises, and tarsiers

PROSINESS > PROSY

PROSING > PROSE

PROSINGS > PROSE

PROSIT interj good health! cheers!

PROSO n millet

PROSOCIAL adj acting to the benefit of society

PROSODIAL adj of prosody

PROSODIAN n writer of prose

PROSODIC > PROSODY

PROSODIES > PROSODY

PROSODIST > PROSODY

PROSODY n study of poetic metre and techniques

PROSOMA n head and thorax of an arachnid

PROSOMAL > PROSOMA

PROSOMAS > PROSOMA

PROSOMATA > PROSOMA

PROSOPON n (in Christianity) manifestation of any of the persons of the Trinity

PROSOPONS > PROSOPON

PROSOS > PROSO

PROSPECT n something anticipated ▷ vb explore, esp for gold

PROSPECTS > PROSPECT

PROSPER vb be successful

PROSPERED > PROSPER

PROSPERS > PROSPER

PROSS n prostitute

PROSSES > PROSS

PROSSIE n prostitute

PROSSIES > PROSSIE

PROST same as > PROSIT

PROSTATE n gland in male mammals that surrounds the neck of the bladder ▷ adj of or relating to the prostate gland

PROSTATES > PROSTATE

PROSTATIC same as > PROSTATE

PROSTERNA n sternums or thoraces of insects

PROSTIE n prostitute

PROSTIES > PROSTIE

PROSTOMIA pl n lobes at the head ends of earthworms and other annelids

PROSTRATE adj lying face downwards ▷ vb lie face downwards

PROSTYLE adj (of a building) having a row of columns in front ▷ n prostyle building, portico, etc

PROSTYLES > PROSTYLE

PROSUMER n amateur user of electronic equipment suitable for professionals

PROSUMERS > PROSUMER

PROSY adj dull and long-winded

PROTAMIN same as > PROTAMINE

PROTAMINE n any of a group of basic simple proteins that occur in the sperm of some fish

P

PROTAMINS > PROTAMIN

PROTANDRY n condition (in hermaphrodite plants) of maturing the anthers before the stigma

PROTANOPE n person with type of colour blindness

PROTASES > PROTASIS

PROTASIS n antecedent of a conditional statement

PROTATIC > PROTASIS

PROTEA n African shrub with showy flowers

PROTEAN adj constantly changing ▷ n creature that can change shape

PROTEANS > PROTEAN

PROTEAS > PROTEA

PROTEASE n any enzyme involved in proteolysis

PROTEASES > PROTEASE

PROTECT vb defend from trouble, harm, or loss

PROTECTED > PROTECT

PROTECTER same as > PROTECTOR

PROTECTOR n person or thing that protects

PROTECTS > PROTECT

PROTEGE n person who is protected and helped by another

PROTEGEE n woman or girl who is protected and helped by another

PROTEGEES > PROTEGEE

PROTEGES > PROTEGE

PROTEI > PROTEUS

PROTEID n protein

PROTEIDE variant of > PROTEID

PROTEIDES > PROTEIDE

PROTEIDS > PROTEID

PROTEIN n any of a group of complex organic compounds that are essential for life

PROTEINIC > PROTEIN

PROTEINS > PROTEIN

PROTEND vb hold out or stretch

PROTENDED > PROTEND

PROTENDS > PROTEND

PROTENSE n extension

PROTENSES > PROTENSE

PROTEOME n full complement of proteins that occur within a cell, tissue, or organism

PROTEOMES > PROTEOME

PROTEOMIC > PROTEOME

PROTEOSE n compound formed during proteolysis

PROTEOSES > PROTEOSE

PROTEST n declaration or demonstration of objection ▷ vb object, disagree

PROTESTED > PROTEST

PROTESTER > PROTEST

PROTESTOR > PROTEST

PROTESTS > PROTEST

PROTEUS n aerobic bacterium

PROTEUSES > PROTEUS

PROTHALLI n small flat free-living gametophytes in ferns, club mosses etc

PROTHESES > PROTHESIS

PROTHESIS n process in the development of a language by which a phoneme or syllable is prefixed to a word to facilitate pronunciation

PROTHETIC > PROTHESIS

PROTHORAX n first segment of the thorax of an insect, which bears the first pair of walking legs

PROTHYL variant of > PROTYLE

PROTHYLS > PROTHYL

PROTIST n organism belonging to the protozoans, unicellular algae, and simple fungi

PROTISTAN > PROTIST

PROTISTIC > PROTIST

PROTISTS > PROTIST

PROTIUM n most common isotope of hydrogen

PROTIUMS > PROTIUM

PROTO adj as in proto team team of people trained to deal with underground rescues, etc

PROTOAVIS n bird-like fossil

PROTOCOL n rules of behaviour for formal occasions

PROTOCOLS > PROTOCOL

PROTODERM n outer primary meristem of a plant

PROTOGINE n type of granite

PROTOGYNY n (in hermaphrodite plants and animals) condition of producing female gametes before male ones

PROTON n positively charged particle in the nucleus of an atom

PROTONATE vb provide atom with proton

PROTONEMA n branched threadlike structure that grows from a moss spore and eventually develops into the moss plant

PROTONIC adj (of a solvent, such as water) able to donate hydrogen ions to solute molecules

PROTONS > PROTON

PROTOPOD n part of crustacean's leg

PROTOPODS > PROTOPOD

PROTORE n primary mineral deposit

PROTORES > PROTORE

PROTOSTAR n cloud of interstellar gas and dust that gradually collapses, forming a hot dense core, and evolves into a star once nuclear fusion can occur in the core

PROTOTYPE n original or model to be copied or developed

PROTOXID variant of > PROTOXIDE

PROTOXIDE n oxide of an element that contains the smallest amount of oxygen of any of its oxides

PROTOXIDS > PROTOXID

PROTOZOA > PROTOZOAN

PROTOZOAL > PROTOZOAN

PROTOZOAN n microscopic one-celled creature ▷ adj of or relating to protozoans

PROTOZOIC adj of or pertaining to the protozoa

PROTOZOON same as > PROTOZOAN

PROTRACT vb lengthen or extend (a situation etc)

PROTRACTS > PROTRACT

PROTRADE adj in favour of trade

PROTRUDE vb stick out, project

PROTRUDED > PROTRUDE

PROTRUDES > PROTRUDE

PROTURAN n any of an order of white wingless insects

PROTURANS > PROTURAN

PROTYL same as > PROTYLE

PROTYLE n hypothetical primitive substance

PROTYLES > PROTYLE

PROTYLS > PROTYL

PROUD adj feeling pleasure and satisfaction

PROUDER > PROUD

PROUDEST > PROUD

PROUDFUL adj full of pride

PROUDISH adj rather proud

PROUDLY > PROUD

PROUDNESS > PROUD

PROUL variant of > PROWL

PROULED > PROUL

PROULER Scots variant of > PROWLER

PROULERS > PROULER

PROULING > PROUL

PROULS > PROUL

PROUNION adj in favour of or supporting the constitutional union between two or more countries

PROUSTITE n red mineral consisting of silver arsenic sulphide in hexagonal crystalline form

PROVABLE > PROVE

PROVABLY > PROVE

PROVAND n food

PROVANDS > PROVAND

PROVANT adj supplied with provisions ▷ vb supply with provisions

PROVANTED > PROVANT

PROVANTS > PROVANT

PROVE vb establish the validity of

PROVEABLE adj able to be proved

PROVEABLY > PROVEABLE

PROVED > PROVE

PROVEDOR variant of > PROVEDORE

PROVEDORE n purveyor

PROVEDORS > PROVEDOR

PROVEN > PROVE

PROVEND same as > PROVAND

PROVENDER n fodder

PROVENDS > PROVEND

PROVENLY > PROVE

PROVER > PROVE

PROVERB n short saying that expresses a truth or gives a warning ▷ vb utter or describe (something) in the form of a proverb

PROVERBED > PROVERB

PROVERBS > PROVERB

PROVERS > PROVE

PROVES > PROVE

PROVIANT variant of > PROVAND

PROVIANTS > PROVIANT

PROVIDE vb make available

PROVIDED > PROVIDE

PROVIDENT adj thrifty

PROVIDER > PROVIDE

PROVIDERS > PROVIDE

PROVIDES > PROVIDE

PROVIDING > PROVIDE

PROVIDOR variant of > PROVEDORE

PROVIDORS > PROVIDOR

PROVINCE n area governed as a unit of a country or empire

PROVINCES > PROVINCE

PROVINE vb plant branch of vine in ground for propagation

PROVINED > PROVINE

PROVINES > PROVINE

PROVING > PROVE

PROVINGS > PROVE

PROVINING > PROVINE

PROVIRAL > PROVIRUS

PROVIRUS n inactive form of a virus in a host cell

PROVISION n act of supplying something ▷ vb supply with food

PROVISO n condition, stipulation

PROVISOES > PROVISO

PROVISOR n person who receives provision

PROVISORS > PROVISOR

PROVISORY adj containing a proviso

PROVISOS > PROVISO

PROVOCANT n provocateur; one who deliberately behaves controversially to provoke argument or other strong reactions

PROVOKE vb deliberately anger

PROVOKED > PROVOKE

PROVOKER > PROVOKE

PROVOKERS > PROVOKE

PROVOKES > PROVOKE

PROVOKING > PROVOKE

PROVOLONE n mellow, pale yellow, soft, and sometimes smoked cheese, made of cow's milk: usually moulded in the shape of a pear

PROVOST n head of certain university colleges in Britain

PROVOSTRY n office of provost

PROVOSTS > PROVOST

PROW n bow of a vessel ▷ adj gallant

PROWAR adj in favour of or supporting war

PROWER > PROW

PROWESS n superior skill or ability

PROWESSED adj brave or skilful

P

PROWESSES > PROWESS
PROWEST > PROW
PROWL *vb* move stealthily around a place as if in search of prey or plunder ▷ *n* prowling
PROWLED > PROWL
PROWLER > PROWL
PROWLERS > PROWL
PROWLING > PROWL
PROWLINGS > PROWL
PROWLS > PROWL
PROWS > PROW
PROXEMIC > PROXEMICS
PROXEMICS *n* study of spatial interrelationships in humans or in populations of animals of the same species
PROXIES > PROXY
PROXIMAL *same as* **>** PROXIMATE
PROXIMATE *adj* next or nearest in space or time
PROXIMITY *n* nearness in space or time
PROXIMO *adv* in or during the next or coming month
PROXY *n* person authorized to act on behalf of someone else
PROYN *obsolete spelling of* **>** PROYNE
PROYNE *obsolete spelling of* **>** PRUNE
PROYNED > PROYN
PROYNES > PROYNE
PROYNING > PROYN
PROYNS > PROYN
PROZYMITE *n* Christian using leavened bread for the Eucharist
PROZZIE *n* slang word for a prostitute
PROZZIES > PROZZIE
PRUDE *n* person who is excessively modest, prim, or proper
PRUDENCE *n* caution in practical affairs
PRUDENCES > PRUDENCE
PRUDENT *adj* cautious, discreet, and sensible
PRUDENTLY > PRUDENT
PRUDERIES > PRUDE
PRUDERY > PRUDE
PRUDES > PRUDE
PRUDISH > PRUDE
PRUDISHLY > PRUDE
PRUH *variant of* **>** PROO
PRUINA *n* woolly white covering on some lichens
PRUINAS > PRUINA
PRUINE *obsolete spelling of* **>** PRUNE
PRUINES > PRUINE
PRUINOSE *adj* coated with a powdery or waxy bloom
PRUNABLE > PRUNE
PRUNE *n* dried plum ▷ *vb* cut off dead parts or excessive branches from (a tree or plant)
PRUNED > PRUNE
PRUNELLA *n* strong fabric, esp a twill-weave worsted, used for gowns and the uppers of some shoes

PRUNELLAS > PRUNELLA
PRUNELLE *same as* **>** PRUNELLA
PRUNELLES > PRUNELLE
PRUNELLO *same as* **>** PRUNELLA
PRUNELLOS > PRUNELLO
PRUNER > PRUNE
PRUNERS > PRUNE
PRUNES > PRUNE
PRUNEY *adj* resembling a prune
PRUNIER > PRUNEY
PRUNIEST > PRUNEY
PRUNING > PRUNE
PRUNINGS > PRUNE
PRUNT *n* glass ornamentation
PRUNTED > PRUNT
PRUNTS > PRUNT
PRUNUS *n* type of ornamental tree or shrub
PRUNUSES > PRUNUS
PRURIENCE > PRURIENT
PRURIENCY *n* sexual desire
PRURIENT *adj* excessively interested in sexual matters
PRURIGO *n* chronic inflammatory disease of the skin
PRURIGOS > PRURIGO
PRURITIC > PRURITUS
PRURITUS *n* any intense sensation of itching
PRUSIK *n* sliding knot used in climbing ▷ *vb* climb (up a rope) using prusiks
PRUSIKED > PRUSIK
PRUSIKING > PRUSIK
PRUSIKS > PRUSIK
PRUSSIAN *adj* as in *prussian blue* colour pigment, discovered in Berlin
PRUSSIATE *n* any cyanide, ferrocyanide, or ferricyanide
PRUSSIC *adj* as in *prussic acid* weakly acidic extremely poisonous aqueous solution of hydrogen cyanide
PRUTA *same as* **>** PRUTAH
PRUTAH *n* former Israeli coin
PRUTOT > PRUTAH
PRUTOTH > PRUTAH
PRY *vb* make an impertinent or uninvited inquiry into a private matter ▷ *n* act of prying
PRYER *same as* **>** PRIER
PRYERS > PRYER
PRYING > PRY
PRYINGLY > PRY
PRYINGS > PRY
PRYS *old variant of* **>** PRICE
PRYSE *old variant of* **>** PRICE
PRYSED > PRYSE
PRYSES > PRYSE
PRYSING > PRYSE
PRYTANEA > PRYTANEUM
PRYTANEUM *n* public hall of a city in ancient Greece
PRYTHEE *same as* **>** PRITHEE
PSALM *n* sacred song ▷ *vb* sing a psalm
PSALMBOOK *n* book of psalms
PSALMED > PSALM

PSALMIC > PSALM
PSALMING > PSALM
PSALMIST *n* writer of psalms
PSALMISTS > PSALMIST
PSALMODIC > PSALMODY
PSALMODY *n* singing of sacred music
PSALMS > PSALM
PSALTER *n* book containing a version of Psalms
PSALTERIA *n* omasa
PSALTERS > PSALTER
PSALTERY *n* ancient instrument played by plucking strings
PSALTRESS *n* woman who sings psalms
PSALTRIES > PSALTRY
PSALTRY *same as* **>** PSALTERY
PSAMMITE *rare name for* **>** SANDSTONE
PSAMMITES > PSAMMITE
PSAMMITIC > PSAMMITE
PSAMMON *n* microscopic life forms living between grains of sand
PSAMMONS > PSAMMON
PSCHENT *n* ancient Egyptian crown
PSCHENTS > PSCHENT
PSELLISM *n* stammering
PSELLISMS > PSELLISM
PSEPHISM *n* proposition adopted by a majority vote
PSEPHISMS > PSEPHISM
PSEPHITE *n* any rock that consists of large fragments embedded in a finer matrix
PSEPHITES > PSEPHITE
PSEPHITIC > PSEPHITE
PSEUD *n* pretentious person
PSEUDAXES > PSEUDAXIS
PSEUDAXIS *another name for* **>** SYMPODIUM
PSEUDERY *n* pretentious talk
PSEUDISH > PSEUD
PSEUDO *n* pretentious person
PSEUDONYM *n* fictitious name adopted esp by an author
PSEUDOPOD *n* temporary projection from the body of a single-celled animal
PSEUDOS > PSEUDO
PSEUDS > PSEUD
PSHAW *n* exclamation of disgust, impatience, disbelief, etc ▷ *vb* make this exclamation
PSHAWED > PSHAW
PSHAWING > PSHAW
PSHAWS > PSHAW
PSI *n* 23rd letter of the Greek alphabet
PSILOCIN *n* hallucinogenic substance
PSILOCINS > PSILOCIN
PSILOSES > PSILOSIS
PSILOSIS *n* disease of the small intestine
PSILOTIC > PSILOSIS
PSION *n* type of elementary particle

PSIONIC > PSIONICS
PSIONICS *n* study of the practical use of psychic powers
PSIONS > PSION
PSIS > PSI
PSOAE > PSOAS
PSOAI > PSOAS
PSOAS *n* either of two muscles of the loins that aid in flexing and rotating the thigh
PSOASES > PSOAS
PSOATIC > PSOAS
PSOCID *n* tiny wingless insect
PSOCIDS > PSOCID
PSORA *n* itching skin complaint
PSORALEA *n* type of tropical and subtropical plant with curly leaves and white or purple flowers
PSORALEAS > PSORALEA
PSORALEN *n* treatment for some skin diseases
PSORALENS > PSORALEN
PSORAS > PSORA
PSORIASES > PSORIASIS
PSORIASIS *n* skin disease with reddish spots and patches covered with silvery scales
PSORIATIC > PSORIASIS
PSORIC > PSORA
PSST *interj* sound made to attract someone's attention
PST *interj* sound made to attract someone's attention
PSYCH *vb* psychoanalyse
PSYCHE *same as* **>** PSYCH
PSYCHED > PSYCH
PSYCHES > PSYCH
PSYCHIC *adj* having mental powers which cannot be explained by natural laws ▷ *n* person with psychic powers
PSYCHICAL > PSYCHIC
PSYCHICS > PSYCHIC
PSYCHING > PSYCH
PSYCHISM *n* belief in a universal soul
PSYCHISMS > PSYCHISM
PSYCHIST > PSYCHISM
PSYCHISTS > PSYCHISM
PSYCHO *n* slang word for a psychopath
PSYCHOGAS *n* gas with a mind-altering effect
PSYCHOID *n* name for an animal's innate impetus to perform actions
PSYCHOIDS > PSYCHOID
PSYCHOS > PSYCHO
PSYCHOSES > PSYCHOSIS
PSYCHOSIS *n* severe mental disorder in which the sufferer's contact with reality becomes distorted
PSYCHOTIC *adj* of, relating to, or characterized by psychosis ▷ *n* person suffering from psychosis
PSYCHS > PSYCH
PSYLLA *same as* **>** PSYLLID
PSYLLAS > PSYLLA

PSYLLID n type of insect of the family which comprises the jumping plant lice

PSYLLIDS > PSYLLID

PSYLLIUM n grain, the husks of which are used as a laxative

PSYLLIUMS > PSYLLIUM

PSYOP n psychological operation

PSYOPS > PSYOP

PSYWAR n psychological warfare

PSYWARS > PSYWAR

PTARMIC n material that causes sneezing

PTARMICS > PTARMIC

PTARMIGAN n bird of the grouse family which turns white in winter

PTERIA > PTERION

PTERIDINE n yellow crystalline base

PTERIN n compound such as folic acid

PTERINS > PTERIN

PTERION n point on the side of the skull where a number of bones meet

PTEROIC adj as in pteroic acid a kind of acid found in spinach

PTEROPOD n small marine gastropod mollusc

PTEROPODS > PTEROPOD

PTEROSAUR n extinct flying reptile

PTERYGIA > PTERYGIUM

PTERYGIAL adj of or relating to a fin or wing

PTERYGIUM n abnormal tissue over corner of eye

PTERYGOID n either of two long bony plates extending downwards from each side of the sphenoid bone within the skull

PTERYLA n any of the tracts of skin that bear contour feathers

PTERYLAE > PTERYLA

PTILOSES > PTILOSIS

PTILOSIS n falling out of eye lashes

PTISAN n grape juice drained off without pressure

PTISANS > PTISAN

PTOMAIN same as **>** PTOMAINE

PTOMAINE n any of a group of poisonous alkaloids found in decaying matter

PTOMAINES > PTOMAINE

PTOMAINIC > PTOMAINE

PTOMAINS > PTOMAIN

PTOOEY interj imitation of the sound of spitting

PTOSES > PTOSIS

PTOSIS n prolapse or drooping of a part, esp the eyelid

PTOTIC > PTOSIS

PTUI same as **>** PTOOEY

PTYALIN n amylase secreted in the saliva of human beings and other animals

PTYALINS > PTYALIN

PTYALISE same as **>** PTYALIZE

PTYALISED > PTYALISE

PTYALISES > PTYALISE

PTYALISM n excessive secretion of saliva

PTYALISMS > PTYALISM

PTYALIZE vb expel saliva from the mouth

PTYALIZED > PTYALIZE

PTYALIZES > PTYALIZE

PTYXES > PTYXIS

PTYXIS n folding of a leaf in a bud

PTYXISES > PTYXIS

PUB n building with a bar licensed to sell alcoholic drinks ▷ vb visit a pub or pubs

PUBBED > PUB

PUBBING > PUB

PUBBINGS > PUBBING

PUBCO n company operating a chain of pubs

PUBCOS > PUBCO

PUBE n vulgar word for a pubic hair

PUBERAL adj relating to puberty

PUBERTAL > PUBERTY

PUBERTIES > PUBERTY

PUBERTY n period at the beginning of adolescence

PUBES > PUBE

PUBESCENT adj reaching or having reached puberty

PUBIC adj of the lower abdomen

PUBIS n one of the three sections of the hipbone that forms part of the pelvis

PUBISES > PUBIS

PUBLIC adj of or concerning the people as a whole ▷ n community, people in general

PUBLICAN n person who owns or runs a pub

PUBLICANS > PUBLICAN

PUBLICISE same as **>** PUBLICIZE

PUBLICIST n person, esp a press agent or journalist, who publicizes something

PUBLICITY n process or information used to arouse public attention

PUBLICIZE vb bring to public attention

PUBLICLY adv in a public manner

PUBLICS > PUBLIC

PUBLISH vb produce and issue (printed matter) for sale

PUBLISHED > PUBLISH

PUBLISHER n company or person that publishes books, periodicals, music, etc

PUBLISHES > PUBLISH

PUBS > PUB

PUCAN n traditional Connemara open sailing boat

PUCANS > PUCAN

PUCCOON n N American plant that yields a red dye

PUCCOONS > PUCCOON

PUCE adj purplish-brown ▷ n colour varying from deep red to dark purplish-brown

PUCELAGE n state of being a maid or girl

PUCELAGES > PUCELAGE

PUCELLE n maid or girl

PUCELLES > PUCELLE

PUCER > PUCE

PUCES > PUCE

PUCELOT > PUCE

PUCK n mischievous or evil spirit ▷ vb strike (the ball) in hurling

PUCKA same as **>** PUKKA

PUCKED > PUCK

PUCKER vb gather into wrinkles ▷ n wrinkle or crease

PUCKERED > PUCKER

PUCKERER > PUCKER

PUCKERERS > PUCKER

PUCKERIER > PUCKERY

PUCKERIES > PUCKERY

PUCKERING > PUCKER

PUCKEROOD adj (NZ informal) ruined; exhausted

PUCKERS > PUCKER

PUCKERY adj tending to pucker ▷ n puckishness

PUCKFIST n puffball

PUCKFISTS > PUCKFIST

PUCKING > PUCK

PUCKISH > PUCK

PUCKISHLY > PUCK

PUCKLE n early type of machine gun

PUCKLES > PUCKLE

PUCKOUT n (in hurling) free hit made by the goalkeeper

PUCKOUTS > PUCKOUT

PUCKS > PUCK

PUCKSTER n hockey player

PUCKSTERS > PUCKSTER

PUD short for **>** PUDDING

PUDDEN dialect spelling of **>** PUDDING

PUDDENING n rope fender on boat

PUDDENS > PUDDEN

PUDDER vb make bother or fuss

PUDDERED > PUDDER

PUDDERING > PUDDER

PUDDERS > PUDDER

PUDDIER > PUDDY

PUDDIES > PUDDY

PUDDIEST > PUDDY

PUDDING n dessert, esp a cooked one served hot

PUDDINGS > PUDDING

PUDDINGY adj having the consistency of a pudding

PUDDLE n small pool of water, esp of rain ▷ vb make (clay etc) into puddle

PUDDLED > PUDDLE

PUDDLER > PUDDLE

PUDDLERS > PUDDLE

PUDDLES > PUDDLE

PUDDLIER > PUDDLE

PUDDLIEST > PUDDLE

PUDDLING n process for converting pig iron into wrought iron

PUDDLINGS > PUDDLING

PUDDLY > PUDDLE

PUDDOCK same as **>** PADDOCK

PUDDOCKS > PUDDOCK

PUDDY n paw ▷ adj short and podgy

PUDENCIES > PUDENCY

PUDENCY n modesty, shame, or prudishness

PUDENDA > PUDENDUM

PUDENDAL > PUDENDUM

PUDENDOUS adj shameful

PUDENDUM n human external genital organs collectively, esp of a female

PUDENT adj lacking in ostentation; humble

PUDEUR n sense of shame or embarrassment

PUDEURS > PUDEUR

PUDGE same as **>** PODGE

PUDGES > PUDGE

PUDGIER > PUDGY

PUDGIEST > PUDGY

PUDGILY > PUDGY

PUDGINESS > PUDGY

PUDGY adj podgy

PUDIBUND adj prudish

PUDIC > PUDENDUM

PUDICITY n modesty

PUDOR n sense of shame

PUDORS > PUDOR

PUDS > PUD

PUDSEY variant of **>** PUDSY

PUDSIER > PUDSY

PUDSIES > PUDSY

PUDSIEST > PUDSY

PUDSY adj plump ▷ n plump person

PUDU n diminutive Andean antelope

PUDUS > PUDU

PUEBLO n communal village of flat-roofed houses

PUEBLOS > PUEBLO

PUER vb steep hides in an alkaline substance from the dung of dogs

PUERED > PUER

PUERILE adj silly and childish

PUERILELY > PUERILE

PUERILISM n immature or childish behaviour by an adult

PUERILITY > PUERILE

PUERING > PUER

PUERPERA n woman who has recently given birth

PUERPERAE > PUERPERA

PUERPERAL adj concerning the period following childbirth

PUERPERIA n periods of around six weeks following childbirths when uteruses return to their normal size and shape

PUERS > PUER

PUFF n (sound of) short blast of breath, wind, etc ▷ vb blow or breathe in short quick draughts

PUFFA adj type of quilted and padded jacket

PUFFBACK n type of small African bird

PUFFBACKS > PUFFBACK

PUFFBALL n ball-shaped fungus
PUFFBALLS > PUFFBALL
PUFFBIRD n brownish tropical American bird with a large head
PUFFBIRDS > PUFFBIRD
PUFFED > PUFF
PUFFER n person or thing that puffs
PUFFERIES > PUFFERY
PUFFERS > PUFFER
PUFFERY n exaggerated praise, esp in publicity or advertising
PUFFIER > PUFFY
PUFFIEST > PUFFY
PUFFILY > PUFFY
PUFFIN n sea bird with a brightly coloured beak
PUFFINESS > PUFFY
PUFFING > PUFF
PUFFINGLY > PUFF
PUFFINGS > PUFF
PUFFINS > PUFFIN
PUFFS > PUFF
PUFFY adj short of breath
PUFTALOON n Australian fried scone
PUG n small snub-nosed dog ▷ vb mix or knead (clay) with water to form a malleable mass or paste
PUGAREE same as > PUGGREE
PUGAREES > PUGAREE
PUGGAREE same as > PUGGREE
PUGGAREES > PUGGAREE
PUGGED > PUG
PUGGERIES > PUGGERY
PUGGERY same as > PUGGREE
PUGGIE n Scottish word for fruit machine
PUGGIER > PUGGY
PUGGIES > PUGGIE
PUGGIEST > PUGGY
PUGGINESS > PUGGY
PUGGING > PUG
PUGGINGS > PUG
PUGGISH > PUG
PUGGLE vb stir up by poking
PUGGLED > PUGGLE
PUGGLES > PUGGLE
PUGGLING > PUGGLE
PUGGREE n scarf, usually pleated, around the crown of some hats, esp sun helmets
PUGGREES > PUGGREE
PUGGRIES > PUGGRY
PUGGRY same as > PUGGREE
PUGGY adj sticky, claylike ▷ n term of endearment
PUGH interj exclamation of disgust
PUGIL n pinch or small handful
PUGILISM n art, practice, or profession of fighting with the fists
PUGILISMS > PUGILISM
PUGILIST > PUGILISM
PUGILISTS > PUGILISM
PUGILS > PUGIL
PUGMARK n trail of an animal
PUGMARKS > PUGMARK

PUGNACITY n readiness to fight
PUGREE same as > PUGGREE
PUGREES > PUGREE
PUGS > PUG
PUH interj exclamation expressing contempt or disgust
PUHA n sow thistle
PUHAS > PUHA
PUIR Scottish word for > POOR
PUIRER > PUIR
PUIREST > PUIR
PUIRTITH n poverty
PUIRTITHS > PUIRTITH
PUISNE adj (esp of a subordinate judge) of lower rank ▷ n judge of lower rank
PUISNES > PUISNE
PUISNY adj younger or inferior
PUISSANCE n showjumping competition that tests a horse's ability to jump large obstacles
PUISSANT adj powerful
PUISSAUNT same as > PUISSANT
PUJA n ritual in honour of the gods, performed either at home or in the mandir (temple)
PUJAH same as > PUJA
PUJAHS > PUJAH
PUJARI n Hindu priest
PUJARIS > PUJARI
PUJAS > PUJA
PUKA in New Zealand English, same as > BROADLEAF
PUKAS > PUKA
PUKATEA n aromatic New Zealand tree
PUKATEAS > PUKATEA
PUKE vb vomit ▷ n act of vomiting
PUKED > PUKE
PUKEKO n brightly coloured New Zealand wading bird
PUKEKOS > PUKEKO
PUKER n person who vomits
PUKERS > PUKER
PUKES > PUKE
PUKEY adj of or like vomit
PUKIER > PUKEY
PUKIEST > PUKEY
PUKING > PUKE
PUKKA adj properly done, constructed, etc
PUKKAH adj genuine
PUKU n belly or stomach
PUKUS > PUKU
PUKY same as > PUKEY
PUL n Afghan monetary unit
PULA n standard monetary unit of Botswana
PULAO same as > PILAU
PULAOS > PULAO
PULAS > PULA
PULDRON same as > PAULDRON
PULDRONS > PULDRON
PULE vb whine or whimper
PULED > PULE
PULER > PULE
PULERS > PULE
PULES > PULE
PULI n Hungarian sheepdog

PULICENE adj flea-ridden
PULICIDE n flea-killing substance
PULICIDES > PULICIDE
PULIER > PULY
PULIEST > PULY
PULIK > PUL
PULING > PULE
PULINGLY > PULE
PULINGS > PULE
PULIS > PULI
PULK same as > PULKA
PULKA n reindeer-drawn sleigh
PULKAS > PULKA
PULKHA same as > PULKA
PULKHAS > PULKHA
PULKS > PULK
PULL vb exert force on (an object) to move it towards the source of the force ▷ n act of pulling
PULLBACK n act of pulling back
PULLBACKS > PULLBACK
PULLED > PULL
PULLER > PULL
PULLERS > PULL
PULLET n young hen
PULLETS > PULLET
PULLEY n device for lifting weights by a downward pull ▷ vb lift with a pulley
PULLEYED > PULLEY
PULLEYING > PULLEY
PULLEYS > PULLEY
PULLI > PULLUS
PULLIES > PULLY
PULLING > PULL
PULLMAN n luxurious railway coach, esp a sleeping car
PULLMANS > PULLMAN
PULLORUM n as in pullorum disease acute serious bacterial disease of very young birds
PULLOUT n removable section of a magazine, etc
PULLOUTS > PULLOUT
PULLOVER n sweater that is pulled on over the head
PULLOVERS > PULLOVER
PULLS > PULL
PULLULATE vb (of animals, etc) breed rapidly or abundantly
PULLUP n exercise in which the body is raised by the arms pulling on a horizontal bar
PULLUPS > PULLUP
PULLUS n technical term for a chick or young bird
PULLY n pullover
PULMO n lung
PULMONARY adj of the lungs
PULMONATE adj having lungs or lung-like organs ▷ n any pulmonate mollusc
PULMONES > PULMO
PULMONIC adj of or relating to the lungs ▷ n person with lung disease
PULMONICS > PULMONIC
PULMOTOR n apparatus for pumping oxygen into the lungs during artificial respiration

PULMOTORS > PULMOTOR
PULP n soft wet substance made from crushed or beaten matter ▷ vb reduce to pulp
PULPAL > PULP
PULPALLY > PULP
PULPBOARD n board made from wood pulp
PULPED > PULP
PULPER > PULP
PULPERS > PULP
PULPIER > PULPY
PULPIEST > PULPY
PULPIFIED > PULPIFY
PULPIFIES > PULPIFY
PULPIFY vb reduce to pulp
PULPILY > PULPY
PULPINESS > PULPY
PULPING n act of pulping
PULPINGS > PULPING
PULPIT n raised platform for a preacher
PULPITAL > PULPIT
PULPITED > PULPIT
PULPITEER n deliverer of sermon ▷ vb preach from a pulpit
PULPITER n preacher
PULPITERS > PULPITER
PULPITRY n art of delivering sermons
PULPITS > PULPIT
PULPITUM n stone screen dividing nave and choir
PULPITUMS > PULPITUM
PULPLESS > PULP
PULPMILL n mill making raw material for paper
PULPMILLS > PULPMILL
PULPOUS n soft and yielding
PULPS > PULP
PULPSTONE n calcified mass in a tooth cavity
PULPWOOD n pine, spruce, or any other soft wood used to make paper
PULPWOODS > PULPWOOD
PULPY adj having a soft or soggy consistency
PULQUE n light alcoholic drink from Mexico
PULQUES > PULQUE
PULS > PUL
PULSANT adj vibrant
PULSAR n small dense star which emits regular bursts of radio waves
PULSARS > PULSAR
PULSATE vb throb, quiver
PULSATED > PULSATE
PULSATES > PULSATE
PULSATILE adj beating rhythmically
PULSATING > PULSATE
PULSATION n act of pulsating
PULSATIVE > PULSATE
PULSATOR n device that stimulates rhythmic motion of a body
PULSATORS > PULSATOR
PULSATORY adj of or relating to pulsation
PULSE n regular beating of blood through the arteries at each heartbeat ▷ vb beat, throb, or vibrate

PULSEBEAT n the pulse
PULSED > PULSE
PULSEJET n type of ramjet engine
PULSEJETS > PULSEJET
PULSELESS > PULSE
PULSER n thing that pulses
PULSERS > PULSER
PULSES > PULSE
PULSIDGE archaic word for > PULSE
PULSIDGES > PULSIDGE
PULSIFIC adj causing the pulse to increase
PULSING > PULSE
PULSION n act of driving forward
PULSIONS > PULSION
PULSOJET same as > PULSEJET
PULSOJETS > PULSOJET
PULTAN n native Indian regiment
PULTANS > PULTAN
PULTON same as > PULTAN
PULTONS > PULTON
PULTOON same as > PULTAN
PULTOONS > PULTOON
PULTRUDE vb produce reinforced plastic process by pultrusion
PULTRUDED > PULTRUDE
PULTRUDES > PULTRUDE
PULTUN same as > PULTAN
PULTUNS > PULTUN
PULTURE n food and drink claimed by foresters
PULTURES > PULTURE
PULU n substance used for stuffing cushions
PULUS > PULU
PULVER vb make into powder
PULVERED > PULVER
PULVERINE n ashes of the barilla plant
PULVERING > PULVER
PULVERISE same as > PULVERIZE
PULVERIZE vb reduce to fine pieces
PULVEROUS adj consisting of tiny particles
PULVERS > PULVER
PULVIL vb apply perfumed powder
PULVILIO n perfumed powder
PULVILIOS > PULVILIO
PULVILLAR adj like cushion
PULVILLE same as > PULVIL
PULVILLED > PULVIL
PULVILLES > PULVILLE
PULVILLI > PULVILLUS
PULVILLIO same as > PULVILIO
PULVILLUS n small pad between the claws at the end of an insect's leg
PULVILS > PULVIL
PULVINAR n part of the thalamus
PULVINARS > PULVINAR
PULVINATE adj (of a frieze) curved convexly
PULVINI > PULVINUS

PULVINULE n part of a leaf
PULVINUS n swelling at the base of a leafstalk
PULWAR n light Indian river boat
PULWARS > PULWAR
PULY adj whiny
PUMA n large American wild cat with a greyish-brown coat
PUMAS > PUMA
PUMELO same as > POMELO
PUMELOS > PUMELO
PUMICATE vb pound fruit with pumice to make juice
PUMICATED > PUMICATE
PUMICATES > PUMICATE
PUMICE n light porous stone used for scouring ▷ vb rub or polish with pumice
PUMICED > PUMICE
PUMICEOUS > PUMICE
PUMICER > PUMICE
PUMICERS > PUMICE
PUMICES > PUMICE
PUMICING > PUMICE
PUMICITE n fine-grained variety of pumice
PUMICITES > PUMICITE
PUMIE n small stone
PUMIES > PUMIE
PUMMEL vb strike repeatedly with or as if with the fists
PUMMELED > PUMMEL
PUMMELING > PUMMEL
PUMMELLED > PUMMEL
PUMMELO same as > POMELO
PUMMELOS > PUMMELO
PUMMELS > PUMMEL
PUMP n machine used to force a liquid or gas to move in a particular direction ▷ vb raise or drive with a pump
PUMPABLE adj capable of being pumped
PUMPED > PUMP
PUMPER > PUMP
PUMPERS > PUMP
PUMPHOOD n cover for the upper wheel of a chain pump
PUMPHOODS > PUMPHOOD
PUMPHOUSE n building where pumping equipment has been installed
PUMPING > PUMP
PUMPINGS > PUMPING
PUMPION archaic word for > PUMPKIN
PUMPIONS > PUMPION
PUMPJACK n pumping apparatus at an oil well
PUMPJACKS > PUMPJACK
PUMPKIN n large round fruit with an orange rind
PUMPKING n programmer with authority to change the master source code
PUMPKINGS > PUMPKING
PUMPKINS > PUMPKIN
PUMPLESS > PUMP
PUMPLIKE > PUMP
PUMPS > PUMP
PUMY adj large and round
PUN n use of words to exploit double meanings for humorous effect ▷ vb make puns

PUNA n high cold dry plateau, esp in the Andes
PUNAANI same as > PUNANI
PUNAANY same as > PUNANI
PUNALUA n marriage between the sisters of one family to the brothers of another
PUNALUAN > PUNALUA
PUNALUAS > PUNALUA
PUNANI n vulgar word for vagina
PUNANY same as > PUNANI
PUNAS > PUNA
PUNCE n kick ▷ vb kick
PUNCED > PUNCE
PUNCES > PUNCE
PUNCH vb strike at with a clenched fist ▷ n blow with a clenched fist
PUNCHBAG n stuffed bag punched for boxing training
PUNCHBAGS > PUNCHBAG
PUNCHBALL n stuffed or inflated ball supported by a flexible rod, that is punched for exercise, esp boxing training
PUNCHBOWL n large bowl for serving punch
PUNCHED > PUNCH
PUNCHEON n large cask of variable capacity, usually between 70 and 120 gallons
PUNCHEONS > PUNCHEON
PUNCHER > PUNCH
PUNCHERS > PUNCH
PUNCHES > PUNCH
PUNCHIER > PUNCHY
PUNCHIEST > PUNCHY
PUNCHILY > PUNCHY
PUNCHING > PUNCH
PUNCHLESS > PUNCH
PUNCHLINE n funny ending of a joke
PUNCHOUT n fist fight
PUNCHOUTS > PUNCHOUT
PUNCHY adj forceful
PUNCING > PUNCE
PUNCTA > PUNCTUM
PUNCTATE adj having or marked with minute spots, holes, or depressions
PUNCTATED same as > PUNCTATE
PUNCTATOR n marker of points
PUNCTILIO n strict attention to minute points of etiquette
PUNCTO n tip of a fencing sword
PUNCTOS > PUNCTO
PUNCTUAL adj arriving or taking place at the correct time
PUNCTUATE vb put punctuation marks in
PUNCTULE n very small opening
PUNCTULES > PUNCTULE
PUNCTUM n tip or small point
PUNCTUMS > PUNCTUM
PUNCTURE n small hole made by a sharp object, esp in a tyre ▷ vb pierce a hole in
PUNCTURED > PUNCTURE

PUNCTURER > PUNCTURE
PUNCTURES > PUNCTURE
PUNDIT n expert who speaks publicly on a subject
PUNDITIC adj of or relating to pundits
PUNDITRY n expressing of expert opinions
PUNDITS > PUNDIT
PUNDONOR n point of honour
PUNG n horse-drawn sleigh with a boxlike body on runners
PUNGA variant spelling of > PONGA
PUNGAS > PUNGA
PUNGENCE n pungency
PUNGENCES > PUNGENCE
PUNGENCY > PUNGENT
PUNGENT adj having a strong sharp bitter flavour
PUNGENTLY > PUNGENT
PUNGLE vb make payment
PUNGLED > PUNGLE
PUNGLES > PUNGLE
PUNGLING > PUNGLE
PUNGS > PUNG
PUNIER > PUNY
PUNIEST > PUNY
PUNILY > PUNY
PUNINESS > PUNY
PUNISH vb cause (someone) to suffer or undergo a penalty for some wrongdoing
PUNISHED > PUNISH
PUNISHER > PUNISH
PUNISHERS > PUNISH
PUNISHES > PUNISH
PUNISHING > PUNISH
PUNITION n punishment
PUNITIONS > PUNITION
PUNITIVE adj relating to punishment
PUNITORY same as > PUNITIVE
PUNJI n sharpened bamboo stick ▷ vb fortify with punjis
PUNJIED > PUNJI
PUNJIES > PUNJI
PUNJIING > PUNJI
PUNJIS > PUNJI
PUNK n style of rock music of the late 1970s ▷ adj relating to the punk movement
PUNKA n fan made of a palm leaf or leaves
PUNKAH same as > PUNKA
PUNKAHS > PUNKAH
PUNKAS > PUNKA
PUNKER > PUNK
PUNKERS > PUNK
PUNKEST > PUNK
PUNKETTE n female follower of punk music
PUNKETTES > PUNKETTE
PUNKEY n small winged insect
PUNKEYS > PUNKEY
PUNKIE same as > PUNKEY
PUNKIER > PUNKY
PUNKIES > PUNKIE
PUNKIEST > PUNKY
PUNKIN same as > PUMPKIN
PUNKINESS > PUNKY
PUNKINS > PUNKIN

PUNKISH > PUNK
PUNKS > PUNK
PUNKY adj of punk music
PUNNED > PUN
PUNNER > PUN
PUNNERS > PUN
PUNNET n small basket for fruit
PUNNETS > PUNNET
PUNNIER > PUNNY
PUNNIEST > PUNNY
PUNNING > PUN
PUNNINGLY > PUN
PUNNINGS > PUN
PUNNY adj of puns
PUNS > PUN
PUNSTER n person who is fond of making puns
PUNSTERS > PUNSTER
PUNT n open flat-bottomed boat propelled by a pole ▷ vb travel in a punt
PUNTED > PUNT
PUNTEE same as > PUNTY
PUNTEES > PUNTEE
PUNTER n informal word for a member of the public
PUNTERS > PUNTER
PUNTIES > PUNTY
PUNTING > PUNT
PUNTO n hit in fencing
PUNTOS > PUNTO
PUNTS > PUNT
PUNTSMAN n man in charge of a river punt
PUNTSMEN > PUNTSMAN
PUNTY n long iron rod used in the finishing process of glass-blowing
PUNY adj small and feeble
PUP n young of certain animals, such as dogs and seals ▷ vb (of dogs, seals, etc) to give birth to pups
PUPA n insect at the stage of development between a larva and an adult
PUPAE > PUPA
PUPAL > PUPA
PUPARIA > PUPARIUM
PUPARIAL > PUPARIUM
PUPARIUM n case enclosing the pupae of certain insects
PUPAS > PUPA
PUPATE vb (of an insect larva) to develop into a pupa
PUPATED > PUPATE
PUPATES > PUPATE
PUPATING > PUPATE
PUPATION > PUPATE
PUPATIONS > PUPATE
PUPFISH n type of small fish
PUPFISHES > PUPFISH
PUPIL n person who is taught by a teacher
PUPILAGE same as > PUPILLAGE
PUPILAGES > PUPILAGE
PUPILAR > PUPIL
PUPILARY same as > PUPILLARY
PUPILLAGE n condition of being a pupil or duration for which one is a pupil
PUPILLAR > PUPIL
PUPILLARY adj of or relating to a pupil or a legal ward

PUPILLATE adj with a spot of a different colour in the middle ▷ vb cry in the manner of a peacock
PUPILS > PUPIL
PUPILSHIP n state of being a pupil
PUPPED > PUP
PUPPET n small doll or figure moved by strings or by the operator's hand
PUPPETEER n person who operates puppets
PUPPETRY n art of making and manipulating puppets and presenting puppet shows
PUPPETS > PUPPET
PUPPIED > PUPPY
PUPPIES > PUPPY
PUPPING > PUP
PUPPODUM same as > POPPADOM
PUPPODUMS > PUPPODUM
PUPPY n young dog ▷ vb have puppies
PUPPYDOM n state of being a puppy
PUPPYDOMS > PUPPYDOM
PUPPYHOOD > PUPPY
PUPPYING > PUPPY
PUPPYISH > PUPPY
PUPPYISM n impudence
PUPPYISMS > PUPPYISM
PUPPYLIKE > PUPPY
PUPS > PUP
PUPU n Hawaiian dish
PUPUNHA n fruit of a type of palm tree
PUPUNHAS > PUPUNHA
PUPUS > PUPU
PUR same as > PURR
PURANA n type of Sanskrit sacred writing
PURANAS > PURANA
PURANIC > PURANA
PURBLIND adj partly or nearly blind
PURCHASE vb obtain by payment ▷ n thing that is bought
PURCHASED > PURCHASE
PURCHASER > PURCHASE
PURCHASES > PURCHASE
PURDA same as > PURDAH
PURDAH n Muslim and Hindu custom of keeping women in seclusion
PURDAHED > PURDAH
PURDAHS > PURDAH
PURDAS > PURDA
PURDONIUM n type of coal scuttle having a slanted cover that is raised to open it, and an inner removable metal container for the coal
PURE adj unmixed, untainted ▷ vb make pure
PUREBLOOD n purebred animal
PUREBRED adj denoting a pure strain obtained through many generations of controlled breeding ▷ n purebred animal
PUREBREDS > PUREBRED
PURED > PURE

PUREE n smooth thick pulp of cooked and sieved fruit, vegetables, meat, or fish ▷ vb make (cooked foods) into a puree
PUREED > PUREE
PUREEING > PUREE
PUREES > PUREE
PURELY adv in a pure manner
PURENESS > PURE
PURER > PURE
PURES > PURE
PUREST > PURE
PURFLE n ruffled or curved ornamental band ▷ vb decorate with such a band or bands
PURFLED > PURFLE
PURFLER > PURFLE
PURFLERS > PURFLE
PURFLES > PURFLE
PURFLING same as > PURFLE
PURFLINGS > PURFLING
PURFLY > PURFLE
PURGATION n act of purging or state of being purged
PURGATIVE adj (medicine) designed to cause defecation ▷ n medicine for emptying the bowels
PURGATORY n place or state of temporary suffering
PURGE vb rid (a thing or place) of (unwanted things or people) ▷ n purging
PURGEABLE > PURGE
PURGED > PURGE
PURGER > PURGE
PURGERS > PURGE
PURGES > PURGE
PURGING > PURGE
PURGINGS > PURGE
PURI n unleavened flaky Indian bread, that is deep-fried in ghee and served hot
PURIFIED > PURIFY
PURIFIER n device or substance that frees something of extraneous, contaminating, or debasing matter
PURIFIERS > PURIFIER
PURIFIES > PURIFY
PURIFY vb make or become pure
PURIFYING > PURIFY
PURIN same as > PURINE
PURINE n colourless crystalline solid that can be prepared from uric acid
PURINES > PURINE
PURING > PURE
PURINS > PURIN
PURIRI n forest tree of New Zealand
PURIRIS > PURIRI
PURIS > PURI
PURISM n strict insistence on the correct usage or style
PURISMS > PURISM
PURIST > PURISM
PURISTIC > PURISM
PURISTS > PURISM

PURITAN n person who follows strict moral or religious principles ▷ adj of or like a puritan
PURITANIC adj of or like a puritan
PURITANS > PURITAN
PURITIES > PURITY
PURITY n state or quality of being pure
PURL n stitch made by knitting a plain stitch backwards ▷ vb knit in purl
PURLED > PURL
PURLER n headlong or spectacular fall
PURLERS > PURLER
PURLICUE vb finish a pen stroke with a flourish
PURLICUED > PURLICUE
PURLICUES > PURLICUE
PURLIEU n land on the edge of a royal forest
PURLIEUS > PURLIEU
PURLIEUX > PURLIEU
PURLIN n horizontal beam that supports the rafters of a roof
PURLINE same as > PURLIN
PURLINES > PURLINE
PURLING > PURL
PURLINGS > PURL
PURLINS > PURLIN
PURLOIN vb steal
PURLOINED > PURLOIN
PURLOINER > PURLOIN
PURLOINS > PURLOIN
PURLS > PURL
PUROMYCIN n type of antibiotic
PURPIE old Scots word for > PURSLANE
PURPIES > PURPIE
PURPLE n colour between red and blue ▷ adj of a colour between red and blue ▷ vb make purple
PURPLED > PURPLE
PURPLER > PURPLE
PURPLES > PURPLE
PURPLEST > PURPLE
PURPLIER > PURPLE
PURPLIEST > PURPLE
PURPLING > PURPLE
PURPLISH > PURPLE
PURPLY > PURPLE
PURPORT vb claim (to be or do something) ▷ n apparent meaning, significance
PURPORTED adj alleged
PURPORTS > PURPORT
PURPOSE n reason for which something is done or exists
PURPOSED > PURPOSE
PURPOSELY adv intentionally
PURPOSES > PURPOSE
PURPOSING > PURPOSE
PURPOSIVE adj having or showing a definite intention
PURPURA n blood disease causing purplish spots
PURPURAS > PURPURA
PURPURE n purple
PURPUREAL adj having a purple colour
PURPURES > PURPURE

PURPURIC > PURPURA

PURPURIN n red crystalline compound used as a stain for biological specimens

PURPURINS > PURPURIN

PURPY variant of > PURPIE

PURR vb (of cats) make low vibrant sound, usu when pleased ▷ n this sound

PURRED > PURR

PURRING > PURR

PURRINGLY > PURR

PURRINGS > PURR

PURRS > PURR

PURS > PUR

PURSE n small bag for money ▷ vb draw (one's lips) together into a small round shape

PURSED > PURSE

PURSEFUL n that which can be contained in purse

PURSEFULS > PURSEFUL

PURSELIKE > PURSE

PURSER n ship's officer who keeps the accounts

PURSERS > PURSER

PURSES > PURSE

PURSEW archaic spelling of > PURSUE

PURSEWED > PURSEW

PURSEWING > PURSEW

PURSEWS > PURSEW

PURSIER > PURSY

PURSIEST > PURSY

PURSILY > PURSY

PURSINESS > PURSY

PURSING > PURSE

PURSLAIN same as > PURSLANE

PURSLAINS > PURSLAIN

PURSLANE n weedy plant used in salads

PURSLANES > PURSLANE

PURSUABLE > PURSUE

PURSUAL n act of pursuit

PURSUALS > PURSUAL

PURSUANCE n carrying out of an action or plan

PURSUANT adj in agreement or conformity

PURSUE vb chase

PURSUED > PURSUE

PURSUER > PURSUE

PURSUERS > PURSUE

PURSUES > PURSUE

PURSUING > PURSUE

PURSUINGS > PURSUE

PURSUIT n pursuing

PURSUITS > PURSUIT

PURSY adj short-winded

PURTIER > PURTY

PURTIEST > PURTY

PURTRAID variant of > PURTRAYD

PURTRAYD adj archaic spelling of portrayed

PURTY adj pretty

PURULENCE > PURULENT

PURULENCY > PURULENT

PURULENT adj of or containing pus

PURVEY vb supply (provisions) ▷ n food and drink laid on at a wedding reception, etc

PURVEYED > PURVEY

PURVEYING > PURVEY

PURVEYOR n person, organization, etc, that supplies food and provisions

PURVEYORS > PURVEYOR

PURVEYS > PURVEY

PURVIEW n scope or range of activity or outlook

PURVIEWS > PURVIEW

PUS n yellowish matter produced by infected tissue

PUSES > PUS

PUSH vb move or try to move by steady force ▷ n act of pushing

PUSHBACK n negative or unfavourable response

PUSHBACKS > PUSHBACK

PUSHBALL n game in which two teams try to push a heavy ball towards opposite goals

PUSHBALLS > PUSHBALL

PUSHBIKE n pedal-driven bicycle

PUSHBIKES > PUSHBIKE

PUSHCART n handcart, typically having two wheels and a canvas roof, used esp by street vendors

PUSHCARTS > PUSHCART

PUSHCHAIR n folding chair on wheels for a baby

PUSHDOWN n list in which the last item added is at the top

PUSHDOWNS > PUSHDOWN

PUSHED adj short of

PUSHER n person who or thing that pushes

PUSHERS > PUSHER

PUSHES > PUSH

PUSHFUL > PUSH

PUSHFULLY > PUSH

PUSHIER > PUSHY

PUSHIEST > PUSHY

PUSHILY > PUSHY

PUSHINESS > PUSHY

PUSHING prep almost or nearly (a certain age, speed, etc) ▷ adj aggressively ambitious ▷ adv almost or nearly (a certain age, speed, etc)

PUSHINGLY > PUSHING

PUSHOVER n something easily achieved

PUSHOVERS > PUSHOVER

PUSHPIN n pin with a small ball-shaped head

PUSHPINS > PUSHPIN

PUSHPIT n safety rail at the stern of a boat

PUSHPITS > PUSHPIT

PUSHROD n metal rod transmitting motion in an engine

PUSHRODS > PUSHROD

PUSHUP n exercise in which the body is raised and lowered to the floor by the arms

PUSHUPS > PUSHUP

PUSHY adj too assertive or ambitious

PUSLE old spelling of > PUZZLE

PUSLED > PUSLE

PUSLES > PUSLE

PUSLEY same as > PURSLANE

PUSLEYS > PUSLEY

PUSLIKE > PUS

PUSLING > PUSLE

PUSS same as > PUSSY

PUSSEL n girl

PUSSELS > PUSSEL

PUSSER n naval purser

PUSSERS > PUSSER

PUSSES > PUSS

PUSSIER > PUSSY

PUSSIES > PUSSY

PUSSIEST > PUSSY

PUSSLEY n weedy trailing herb

PUSSLEYS > PUSSLEY

PUSSLIES > PUSSLY

PUSSLIKE > PUSS

PUSSLY variant of > PUSSLEY

PUSSY n cat ▷ adj containing or full of pus

PUSSYCAT same as > PUSSY

PUSSYCATS > PUSSYCAT

PUSSYFOOT vb behave too cautiously ▷ n person who pussyfoots

PUSSYTOES n type of low-growing plant

PUSTULANT adj causing the formation of pustules ▷ n agent causing such formation

PUSTULAR > PUSTULE

PUSTULATE vb form into pustules ▷ adj covered with pustules

PUSTULE n pimple containing pus

PUSTULED > PUSTULE

PUSTULES > PUSTULE

PUSTULOUS > PUSTULE

PUT vb cause to be (in a position, state, or place) ▷ n throw in putting the shot

PUTAMEN n hard endocarp or stone of fruit

PUTAMENS > PUTAMEN

PUTAMINA > PUTAMEN

PUTATIVE adj reputed, supposed

PUTCHEON n trap for catching salmon

PUTCHEONS > PUTCHEON

PUTCHER n trap for catching salmon

PUTCHERS > PUTCHER

PUTCHOCK same as > PACHAK

PUTCHOCKS > PUTCHOCK

PUTCHUK same as > PACHAK

PUTCHUKS > PUTCHUK

PUTDOWN n snub or insult

PUTDOWNS > PUTDOWN

PUTEAL n enclosure around a well

PUTEALS > PUTEAL

PUTELI n (in India) type of boat

PUTELIS > PUTELI

PUTID adj having an unpleasant odour

PUTLOCK same as > PUTLOG

PUTLOCKS > PUTLOCK

PUTLOG n short horizontal beam that with others supports the floor planks of a scaffold

PUTLOGS > PUTLOG

PUTOFF n pretext or delay

PUTOFFS > PUTOFF

PUTOIS n brush to paint pottery

PUTON n hoax or piece of mockery

PUTONGHUA n Chinese language

PUTONS > PUTON

PUTOUT n baseball play in which the batter or runner is put out

PUTOUTS > PUTOUT

PUTREFIED > PUTREFY

PUTREFIER > PUTREFY

PUTREFIES > PUTREFY

PUTREFY vb rot and produce an offensive smell

PUTRID adj rotten and foul-smelling

PUTRIDER > PUTRID

PUTRIDEST > PUTRID

PUTRIDITY > PUTRID

PUTRIDLY > PUTRID

PUTS > PUT

PUTSCH n sudden violent attempt to remove a government from power

PUTSCHES > PUTSCH

PUTSCHIST n person taking part in putsch

PUTT n stroke on the putting green to roll the ball into or near the hole ▷ vb strike (the ball) in this way

PUTTED > PUTT

PUTTEE n strip of cloth worn wound around the leg

PUTTEES > PUTTEE

PUTTEN old Scots past participle of > PUT

PUTTER n golf club for putting ▷ vb busy oneself in a desultory though agreeable manner

PUTTERED > PUTTER

PUTTERER > PUTTER

PUTTERERS > PUTTER

PUTTERING > PUTTER

PUTTERS > PUTTER

PUTTI > PUTTO

PUTTIE same as > PUTTEE

PUTTIED > PUTTY

PUTTIER n glazier

PUTTIERS > PUTTIER

PUTTIES > PUTTY

PUTTING > PUT

PUTTINGS > PUT

PUTTO n representation of a small boy

PUTTOCK n type of bird of prey

PUTTOCKS > PUTTOCK

PUTTS > PUTT

PUTTY n stiff paste of whiting and linseed oil ▷ vb fill, fix, or coat with putty

PUTTYING > PUTTY

PUTTYLESS > PUTTY

PUTTYLIKE > PUTTY

PUTTYROOT n North American orchid

p

PUTURE n claim of foresters for food

PUTURES > PUTURE

PUTZ n despicable or stupid person ▷ vb waste time

PUTZED > PUTZ

PUTZES > PUTZ

PUTZING > PUTZ

PUY n small volcanic cone

PUYS > PUY

PUZEL same as > PUCELLE

PUZELS > PUZEL

PUZZEL same as > PUCELLE

PUZZELS > PUZZEL

PUZZLE vb perplex and confuse or be perplexed or confused ▷ n problem that cannot be easily solved

PUZZLED > PUZZLE

PUZZLEDLY > PUZZLE

PUZZLEDOM > PUZZLE

PUZZLER n person or thing that puzzles

PUZZLERS > PUZZLER

PUZZLES > PUZZLE

PUZZLING > PUZZLE

PUZZOLANA same as > POZZOLANA

PWN vb defeat (an opponent) in conclusive and humiliating fashion

PWNED > PWN

PWNING > PWN

PWNS > PWN

PYA n monetary unit of Myanmar worth one hundredth of a kyat

PYAEMIA n blood poisoning with pus-forming microorganisms in the blood

PYAEMIAS > PYAEMIA

PYAEMIC > PYAEMIA

PYAS > PYA

PYAT n magpie ▷ adj pied

PYATS > PYAT

PYCNIC same as > PYKNIC

PYCNIDIA > PYCNIDIUM

PYCNIDIAL > PYCNIDIUM

PYCNIDIUM n small flask-shaped structure containing spores that occurs in ascomycetes and certain other fungi

PYCNITE n variety of topaz

PYCNITES > PYCNITE

PYCNON old word for > SEMITONE

PYCNONS > PYCNON

PYCNOSES > PYCNOSIS

PYCNOSIS n process of shrinking in a cell nucleus

PYCNOSOME n stocky body type

PYCNOTIC > PYCNOSIS

PYE same as > PIE

PYEBALD same as > PIEBALD

PYEBALDS > PYEBALD

PYEING > PYE

PYELITIC > PYELITIS

PYELITIS n inflammation of the pelvis of the kidney

PYELOGRAM n film produced by pyelography

PYEMIA same as > PYAEMIA

PYEMIAS > PYEMIA

PYEMIC > PYAEMIA

PYENGADU variant of > PYINKADO

PYENGADUS > PYENGADU

PYES > PYE

PYET same as > PYAT

PYETS > PYET

PYGAL n rear part

PYGALS > PYGAL

PYGARG n type of horned mammal

PYGARGS > PYGARG

PYGARGUS n white-tailed bird of prey

PYGIDIA > PYGIDIUM

PYGIDIAL > PYGIDIUM

PYGIDIUM n terminal division in certain invertebrates

PYGMAEAN > PYGMY

PYGMEAN > PYGMY

PYGMIES > PYGMY

PYGMOID adj of or like pygmies ▷ n pygmy

PYGMOIDS > PYGMOID

PYGMY n something that is a very small example of its type ▷ adj very small

PYGMYISH > PYGMY

PYGMYISM > PYGMY

PYGMYISMS > PYGMY

PYGOSTYLE n vertebral bone in birds

PYIC adj relating to pus

PYIN n constituent of pus

PYINKADO n leguminous tree native to India and Myanmar

PYINKADOS > PYINKADO

PYINS > PYIN

PYJAMA same as > PYJAMAS

PYJAMAED > PYJAMAS

PYJAMAS pl n loose-fitting trousers and top worn in bed

PYKNIC adj characterized by a broad squat fleshy physique ▷ n person with this physical type

PYKNICS > PYKNIC

PYKNOSES > PYKNOSIS

PYKNOSIS n thickening of a cell

PYKNOSOME n stocky body type

PYKNOTIC > PYKNOSIS

PYLON n steel tower-like structure supporting electrical cables

PYLONS > PYLON

PYLORI > PYLORUS

PYLORIC > PYLORUS

PYLORUS n small circular opening at the base of the stomach

PYLORUSES > PYLORUS

PYNE archaic variant of > PINE

PYNED > PYNE

PYNES > PYNE

PYNING > PYNE

PYODERMA n any skin eruption characterized by pustules or the formation of pus

PYODERMAS > PYODERMA

PYODERMIC > PYODERMA

PYOGENIC adj of or relating to the formation of pus

PYOID adj resembling pus

PYONER old variant of > PIONEER

PYONERS > PYONER

PYONINGS n old term for the work of pioneers

PYORRHEA same as > PYORRHOEA

PYORRHEAL > PYORRHOEA

PYORRHEAS > PYORRHEA

PYORRHEIC > PYORRHOEA

PYORRHOEA n a disease of the gums and tooth sockets which causes bleeding of the gums and the formation of pus

PYOSES > PYOSIS

PYOSIS n formation of pus

PYOT same as > PYAT

PYOTS > PYOT

PYRACANTH n type of thorny shrub

PYRAL > PYRE

PYRALID n tropical moth

PYRALIDID same as > PYRALID

PYRALIDS > PYRALID

PYRALIS same as > PYRALID

PYRALISES > PYRALIS

PYRAMID n solid figure with a flat base and triangular sides sloping upwards to a point ▷ vb build up or be arranged in the form of a pyramid

PYRAMIDAL > PYRAMID

PYRAMIDED > PYRAMID

PYRAMIDES > PYRAMIS

PYRAMIDIA n plural of pyramidion, small pyramid on top of obelisk

PYRAMIDIC > PYRAMID

PYRAMIDON n type of pipe for an organ

PYRAMIDS > PYRAMID

PYRAMIS n pyramid-shaped structure

PYRAMISES > PYRAMIS

PYRAN n unsaturated heterocyclic organic compound

PYRANOID > PYRAN

PYRANOSE n structure in many sugars

PYRANOSES > PYRANOSE

PYRANS > PYRAN

PYRAZOLE n crystalline soluble basic heterocyclic compound

PYRAZOLES > PYRAZOLE

PYRE n pile of wood for burning a corpse on

PYRENE n solid polynuclear aromatic hydrocarbon extracted from coal tar

PYRENEITE n dark mineral found in the Pyrenees

PYRENES > PYRENE

PYRENOID n any of various small protein granules that occur in certain algae

PYRENOIDS > PYRENOID

PYRES > PYRE

PYRETHRIN n oily water-insoluble compound used as an insecticide

PYRETHRUM n Eurasian chrysanthemum with white, pink, red, or purple flowers

PYRETIC adj of, relating to, or characterized by fever

PYREX n tradename for glass used in cookery and chemical apparatus

PYREXES > PYREX

PYREXIA technical name for > FEVER

PYREXIAL > PYREXIA

PYREXIAS > PYREXIA

PYREXIC > PYREXIA

PYRIC adj of or relating to burning

PYRIDIC > PYRIDINE

PYRIDINE n colourless hygroscopic liquid with a characteristic odour

PYRIDINES > PYRIDINE

PYRIDOXAL n naturally occurring derivative of pyridoxine that is a precursor of a coenzyme involved in several enzymic reactions

PYRIDOXIN n derivative of pyridine

PYRIFORM adj (esp of organs of the body) pear-shaped

PYRITE n yellow mineral consisting of iron sulphide in cubic crystalline form

PYRITES same as > PYRITE

PYRITIC > PYRITE

PYRITICAL > PYRITE

PYRITISE same as > PYRITIZE

PYRITISED > PYRITISE

PYRITISES > PYRITISE

PYRITIZE vb convert into pyrites

PYRITIZED > PYRITIZE

PYRITIZES > PYRITIZE

PYRITOUS > PYRITE

PYRO n pyromaniac

PYROBORIC adj as in pyroboric acid

PYROCERAM n transparent ceramic material

PYROCLAST n piece of lava ejected from a volcano

PYROGEN n any of a group of substances that cause a rise in temperature in an animal body

PYROGENIC adj produced by or producing heat

PYROGENS > PYROGEN

PYROGIES > PYROGY

PYROGY same as > PIEROGI

PYROHIES > PYROHY

PYROHY same as > PEROGI

PYROLA n evergreen perennial

PYROLAS > PYROLA

PYROLATER n worshipper of fire

PYROLATRY > PYROLATER

PYROLISE same as > PYROLIZE

PYROLISED > PYROLISE

PYROLISES > PYROLISE

PYROLIZE vb subject to pyrolysis

PYROLIZED > PYROLIZE

PYROLIZES > PYROLIZE

PYROLOGY n study of heat

PYROLYSE vb subject to pyrolysis

PYROLYSED > PYROLYSE

PYROLYSER > PYROLYSE

PYROLYSES > PYROLYSE

PYROLYSIS *n* application of heat to chemical compounds in order to cause decomposition

PYROLYTIC > PYROLYSIS

PYROLYZE *same as* > PYROLYSE

PYROLYZED > PYROLYZE

PYROLYZER > PYROLYSE

PYROLYZES > PYROLYZE

PYROMANCY *n* divination by fire or flames

PYROMANIA *n* uncontrollable urge to set things on fire

PYROMETER *n* instrument for measuring high temperatures

PYROMETRY > PYROMETER

PYRONE *n* type of heterocyclic compound

PYRONES > PYRONE

PYRONIN *n* red dye used as a biological stain

PYRONINE *same as* > PYRONIN

PYRONINES > PYRONINE

PYRONINS > PYRONIN

PYROPE *n* deep yellowish-red garnet used as a gemstone

PYROPES > PYROPE

PYROPHONE *n* musical instrument using hydrogen flames

PYROPUS *variant of* > PYROPE

PYROPUSES > PYROPUS

PYROS > PYRO

PYROSCOPE *n* instrument for measuring intensity of heat

PYROSES > PYROSIS

PYROSIS *technical name for* > HEARTBURN

PYROSISES > PYROSIS

PYROSOME *n* tube-shaped glowing marine creature

PYROSOMES > PYROSOME

PYROSTAT *n* device that activates an alarm or extinguisher in the event of a fire

PYROSTATS > PYROSTAT

PYROXENE *n* silicate mineral

PYROXENES > PYROXENE

PYROXENIC > PYROXENE

PYROXYLE *same as* > PYROXYLIN

PYROXYLES > PYROXYLE

PYROXYLIC > PYROXYLIN

PYROXYLIN *n* yellow substance obtained by nitrating cellulose with a mixture of nitric and sulphuric acids

PYRRHIC *n* metrical foot of two short or unstressed syllables ▷ *adj* of or relating to such a metrical foot

PYRRHICS > PYRRHIC

PYRRHOUS *adj* ruddy or reddish

PYRROL *same as* > PYRROLE

PYRROLE *n* colourless insoluble toxic liquid

PYRROLES > PYRROLE

PYRROLIC > PYRROLE

PYRROLS > PYRROL

PYRUVATE *n* ester or salt of pyruvic acid

PYRUVATES > PYRUVATE

PYRUVIC *adj* as in *pyruvic acid* colourless pleasant-smelling liquid

PYSANKA *n* hand-painted Ukrainian Easter egg

PYSANKY > PYSANKA

PYTHIUM *n* type of fungi

PYTHIUMS > PYTHIUM

PYTHON *n* large nonpoisonous snake that crushes its prey

PYTHONESS *n* woman, such as Apollo's priestess at Delphi, believed to be possessed by an oracular spirit

PYTHONIC > PYTHON

PYTHONE > PYTHON

PYURIA *n* any condition characterized by the presence of pus in the urine

PYURIAS > PYURIA

PYX *n* any receptacle for the Eucharistic Host ▷ *vb* put (something) in a pyx

PYXED > PYX

PYXES > PYX

PYXIDES > PYXIS

PYXIDIA > PYXIDIUM

PYXIDIUM *n* dry fruit of such plants as the plantain

PYXIE *n* creeping evergreen shrub of the eastern US

PYXIES > PYXIE

PYXING > PYX

PYXIS *same as* > PYXIDIUM

PZAZZ *same as* > PIZZAZZ

PZAZZES > PZAZZ

Qq

QABALA same as > KABBALAH
QABALAH same as > KABBALAH
QABALAHS > QABALAH
QABALAS > QABALA
QABALISM > QABALAH
QABALISMS > QABALAH
QABALIST > QABALAH
QABALISTS > QABALAH
QADI variant spelling of > CADI
QADIS > QADI
QAID n chief
QAIDS > QAID
QAIMAQAM n Turkish officer or official
QAIMAQAMS > QAIMAQAM
QAJAQ n kayak
QAJAQS > QAJAQ
QALAMDAN n writing case
QALAMDANS > QALAMDAN
QAMUTIK n sledge with wooden runners
QAMUTIKS > QAMUTIK
QANAT n underground irrigation channel
QANATS > QANAT
QAPIK n monetary unit of Azerbaijan
QAPIKS > QAPIK
QASIDA n Arabic verse form
QASIDAS > QASIDA
QAT variant spelling of > KHAT
QATS > QAT
QAWWAL n qawwali singer
QAWWALI n Islamic religious song, esp in Asia
QAWWALIS > QAWWALI
QAWWALS > QAWWAL
QI n vital energy
QIBLA variant of > KIBLAH
QIBLAS > QIBLA
QIGONG n system of breathing and exercise
QIGONGS > QIGONG
QIN n Chinese stringed instrument related to the zither
QINDAR n Albanian monetary unit
QINDARKA > QINDAR
QINDARS > QINDAR
QINGHAOSU n Chinese herb
QINS > QIN
QINTAR same as > QINDAR
QINTARKA > QINTAR
QINTARS > QINTAR
QIS > QI
QIVIUT n soft muskox wool
QIVIUTS > QIVIUT

QOPH variant of > KOPH
QOPHS > QOPH
QORMA variant spelling of > KORMA
QORMAS > QORMA
QUA prep in the capacity of
QUAALUDE n methaqualone
QUAALUDES > QUAALUDE
QUACK vb (of a duck) utter a harsh guttural sound ▷ n unqualified person who claims medical knowledge
QUACKED > QUACK
QUACKER > QUACK
QUACKERS > QUACK
QUACKERY n activities or methods of a quack
QUACKIER > QUACK
QUACKIEST > QUACK
QUACKING > QUACK
QUACKISH > QUACK
QUACKISM same as > QUACKERY
QUACKISMS > QUACKISM
QUACKLE same as > QUACK
QUACKLED > QUACKLE
QUACKLES > QUACKLE
QUACKLING > QUACKLE
QUACKS > QUACK
QUACKY > QUACK
QUAD n quadrangle
QUADDED adj formed of multiple quads
QUADDING n birdwatching in a specified area
QUADDINGS > QUADDING
QUADPLAY same as > FOURPLAY
QUADPLAYS > QUADPLAY
QUADPLEX n apartment on four floors
QUADRANS n Roman coin
QUADRANT n quarter of a circle
QUADRANTS > QUADRANT
QUADRAT n area marked out for study of the plants in the surrounding area
QUADRATE n cube or square, or a square or cubelike object ▷ vb make square or rectangular ▷ adj square or rectangular
QUADRATED > QUADRATE
QUADRATES > QUADRATE
QUADRATI > QUADRATUS
QUADRATIC n equation in which the variable is raised to the power of two, but nowhere raised to a higher power ▷ adj of the second power

QUADRATS > QUADRAT
QUADRATUS n type of muscle
QUADRELLA n four nominated horseraces in which the punter bets on selecting the four winners
QUADRIC adj having or characterized by an equation of the second degree ▷ n quadric curve, surface, or function
QUADRICEP n muscle in thigh
QUADRICS > QUADRIC
QUADRIFID adj divided into four lobes or other parts
QUADRIGA n (in the classical world) a two-wheeled chariot drawn by four horses abreast
QUADRIGAE > QUADRIGA
QUADRIGAS > QUADRIGA
QUADRILLE n square dance for four couples
QUADRIVIA n higher divisions of the seven liberal arts
QUADROON n offensive term for person of mixed racial ancestry
QUADROONS > QUADROON
QUADRUMAN n nonhuman primate
QUADRUPED n any animal with four legs ▷ adj having four feet
QUADRUPLE vb multiply by four ▷ adj four times as much or as many ▷ n quantity or number four times as great as another
QUADRUPLY n reply to a triply
QUADS > QUAD
QUAERE n query or question ▷ interj ask or inquire ▷ vb ask
QUAERED > QUAERE
QUAEREING > QUAERE
QUAERES > QUAERE
QUAERITUR sentence substitute question is asked
QUAESITUM n object sought
QUAESTOR n any of several magistrates of ancient Rome, usually a financial administrator
QUAESTORS > QUAESTOR
QUAFF vb drink heartily or in one draught
QUAFFABLE > QUAFF
QUAFFED > QUAFF

QUAFFER > QUAFF
QUAFFERS > QUAFF
QUAFFING > QUAFF
QUAFFS > QUAFF
QUAG another word for > QUAGMIRE
QUAGGA n recently extinct zebra
QUAGGAS > QUAGGA
QUAGGIER > QUAGGY
QUAGGIEST > QUAGGY
QUAGGY adj resembling a marsh or quagmire
QUAGMIRE n soft wet area of land ▷ vb bog down
QUAGMIRED > QUAGMIRE
QUAGMIRES > QUAGMIRE
QUAGMIRY > QUAGMIRE
QUAGS > QUAG
QUAHAUG same as > QUAHOG
QUAHAUGS > QUAHAUG
QUAHOG n edible clam
QUAHOGS > QUAHOG
QUAI same as > QUAY
QUAICH n small shallow drinking cup
QUAICHES > QUAICH
QUAICHS > QUAICH
QUAIGH same as > QUAICH
QUAIGHS > QUAIGH
QUAIL n small game bird of the partridge family ▷ vb shrink back with fear
QUAILED > QUAIL
QUAILING > QUAIL
QUAILINGS > QUAIL
QUAILS > QUAIL
QUAINT adj attractively unusual, esp in an old-fashioned style
QUAINTER > QUAINT
QUAINTEST > QUAINT
QUAINTLY > QUAINT
QUAIR n book
QUAIRS > QUAIR
QUAIS > QUAI
QUAKE vb shake or tremble with or as if with fear ▷ n earthquake
QUAKED > QUAKE
QUAKER > QUAKE
QUAKERS > QUAKE
QUAKES > QUAKE
QUAKIER > QUAKY
QUAKIEST > QUAKY
QUAKILY > QUAKY
QUAKINESS > QUAKY
QUAKING > QUAKE
QUAKINGLY > QUAKE
QUAKINGS > QUAKE
QUAKY adj inclined to quake

q

QUALE n essential property or quality

QUALIA > QUALE

QUALIFIED > QUALIFY

QUALIFIER n person or thing that qualifies, esp a contestant in a competition who wins a preliminary heat or contest and so earns the right to take part in the next round

QUALIFIES > QUALIFY

QUALIFY vb provide or be provided with the abilities necessary

QUALITIED adj possessing qualities

QUALITIES > QUALITY

QUALITY n degree or standard of excellence ▷ adj excellent or superior

QUALM n pang of conscience

QUALMIER > QUALM

QUALMIEST > QUALM

QUALMING adj having a qualm ▷ n state of having a qualm

QUALMINGS > QUALMING

QUALMISH > QUALM

QUALMLESS > QUALM

QUALMS > QUALM

QUALMY > QUALM

QUAMASH another name for > CAMASS

QUAMASHES > QUAMASH

QUANDANG same as > QUANDONG

QUANDANGS > QUANDANG

QUANDARY n difficult situation or dilemma

QUANDONG n small Australian tree with edible fruit and nuts used in preserves

QUANDONGS > QUANDONG

QUANGO n partly independent official body set up by a government

QUANGOS > QUANGO

QUANNET n flat file with handle at one end

QUANNETS > QUANNET

QUANT n long pole for propelling a boat ▷ vb propel (a boat) with a quant

QUANTA > QUANTUM

QUANTAL adj of or relating to a quantum or an entity that is quantized

QUANTALLY > QUANTAL

QUANTED > QUANT

QUANTIC n mathematical function

QUANTICAL > QUANTIC

QUANTICS > QUANTIC

QUANTIFY vb discover or express the quantity of

QUANTILE n element of a division

QUANTILES > QUANTILE

QUANTING > QUANT

QUANTISE same as > QUANTIZE

QUANTISED > QUANTISE

QUANTISER > QUANTISE

QUANTISES > QUANTISE

QUANTITY n specified or definite amount or number

QUANTIZE vb restrict (a physical quantity) to one of a set of values characterized by quantum numbers

QUANTIZED > QUANTIZE

QUANTIZER > QUANTIZE

QUANTIZES > QUANTIZE

QUANTONG same as > QUANDONG

QUANTONGS > QUANTONG

QUANTS > QUANT

QUANTUM n desired or required amount ▷ adj of or designating a major breakthrough

QUANTUMS > QUANTUM

QUARE adj remarkable or strange

QUARENDEN n dark-red apple

QUARENDER same as > QUARENDEN

QUARER > QUARE

QUAREST > QUARE

QUARK n subatomic particle thought to be the fundamental unit of matter

QUARKS > QUARK

QUARREL n angry disagreement ▷ vb have a disagreement or dispute

QUARRELED > QUARREL

QUARRELER > QUARREL

QUARRELS > QUARREL

QUARRIAN n cockatiel of scrub and woodland regions of inland Australia

QUARRIANS > QUARRIAN

QUARRIED > QUARRY

QUARRIER another word for > QUARRYMAN

QUARRIERS > QUARRIER

QUARRIES > QUARRY

QUARRION same as > QUARRIAN

QUARRIONS > QUARRION

QUARRY n place where stone is dug from the surface of the earth ▷ vb extract (stone) from a quarry

QUARRYING > QUARRY

QUARRYMAN n man who works in or manages a quarry

QUARRYMEN > QUARRYMAN

QUART n unit of liquid measure equal to two pints (1.136 litres)

QUARTAN adj (esp of a malarial fever) occurring every third day ▷ n quartan malaria

QUARTANS > QUARTAN

QUARTE n fourth of eight basic positions from which a parry or attack can be made in fencing

QUARTER n one of four equal parts of something ▷ vb divide into four equal parts ▷ adj being or consisting of one of four equal parts

QUARTERED adj (of a shield) divided into four sections, each having contrasting arms or having two sets of arms, each repeated in diagonally opposite corners

QUARTERER > QUARTER

QUARTERLY adj occurring, due, or issued at intervals of three months ▷ n magazine issued every three months ▷ adv once every three months

QUARTERN n fourth part of certain weights or measures, such as a peck or a pound

QUARTERNS > QUARTERN

QUARTERS pl n accommodation, esp as provided for military personnel

QUARTES > QUARTE

QUARTET n group of four performers

QUARTETS > QUARTET

QUARTETT same as > QUARTET

QUARTETTE same as > QUARTET

QUARTETTI > QUARTETTO

QUARTETTO same as > QUARTET

QUARTETTS > QUARTETT

QUARTIC n biquadratic equation

QUARTICS > QUARTIC

QUARTIER n city district

QUARTIERS > QUARTIER

QUARTILE n one of three values of a variable dividing its distribution into four groups with equal frequencies ▷ adj of a quartile

QUARTILES > QUARTILE

QUARTO n book size in which the sheets are folded into four leaves

QUARTOS > QUARTO

QUARTS > QUART

QUARTZ n hard glossy mineral

QUARTZES > QUARTZ

QUARTZIER > QUARTZ

QUARTZITE n very hard metamorphic rock consisting of a mosaic of intergrown quartz crystals

QUARTZOSE > QUARTZ

QUARTZOUS > QUARTZ

QUARTZY > QUARTZ

QUASAR n extremely distant starlike object that emits powerful radio waves

QUASARS > QUASAR

QUASH vb annul or make void

QUASHED > QUASH

QUASHEE same as > QUASHIE

QUASHEES > QUASHEE

QUASHER > QUASH

QUASHERS > QUASH

QUASHES > QUASH

QUASHIE n in the Carribbean, derogatory term for an unsophisticated or gullible peasant

QUASHIES > QUASHIE

QUASHING > QUASH

QUASI adv as if

QUASS variant of > KVASS

QUASSES > QUASS

QUASSIA n tropical American tree

QUASSIAS > QUASSIA

QUASSIN n bitter crystalline substance

QUASSINS > QUASSIN

QUAT n spot ▷ vb beat down or squash

QUATCH vb move

QUATCHED > QUATCH

QUATCHES > QUATCH

QUATCHING > QUATCH

QUATE n fortune

QUATES > QUATE

QUATORZE n cards worth 14 points in piquet

QUATORZES > QUATORZE

QUATRAIN n stanza or poem of four lines

QUATRAINS > QUATRAIN

QUATRE n playing card with four pips

QUATRES > QUATRE

QUATS > QUAT

QUATTED > QUAT

QUATTING > QUAT

QUAVER vb (of a voice) quiver or tremble ▷ n note half the length of a crotchet

QUAVERED > QUAVER

QUAVERER > QUAVER

QUAVERERS > QUAVER

QUAVERIER > QUAVER

QUAVERING > QUAVER

QUAVERS > QUAVER

QUAVERY > QUAVER

QUAY n wharf built parallel to the shore

QUAYAGE n system of quays

QUAYAGES > QUAYAGE

QUAYD archaic past participle of > QUAIL

QUAYLIKE > QUAY

QUAYS > QUAY

QUAYSIDE n edge of a quay along the water

QUAYSIDES > QUAYSIDE

QUAZZIER > QUAZZY

QUAZZIEST > QUAZZY

QUAZZY adj unwell

QUBIT n quantum bit

QUBITS > QUBIT

QUBYTE n unit of eight qubits

QUBYTES > QUBYTE

QUEACH n thicket

QUEACHES > QUEACH

QUEACHIER > QUEACHY

QUEACHY adj unwell

QUEAN n Scots word for a young unmarried woman

QUEANS > QUEAN

QUEASIER > QUEASY

QUEASIEST > QUEASY

QUEASILY > QUEASY

QUEASY adj having the feeling that one is about to vomit

QUEAZIER > QUEAZY

QUEAZIEST > QUEAZY

QUEAZY same as > QUEASY

QUEBEC n code word for the letter Q

QUEBECS > QUEBEC

QUEBRACHO n anacardiaceous South American tree

QUEECHIER > QUEECHY

QUEECHY *same as* > QUEACHY

QUEEN *n* female sovereign who is the official ruler or head of state ▷ *vb* crown as queen

QUEENCAKE *n* small light cake containing currants

QUEENCUP *n* type of flowering plant

QUEENCUPS > QUEENCUP

QUEENDOM *n* territory, state, people, or community ruled over by a queen

QUEENDOMS > QUEENDOM

QUEENED > QUEEN

QUEENFISH *n* type of Californian marine fish

QUEENHOOD > QUEEN

QUEENIE *n* scallop

QUEENIER > QUEENY

QUEENIES > QUEENIE

QUEENIEST > QUEENY

QUEENING > QUEEN

QUEENINGS > QUEEN

QUEENITE *n* supporter of a queen

QUEENITES > QUEENITE

QUEENLESS > QUEEN

QUEENLET *n* queen of a small realm

QUEENLETS > QUEENLET

QUEENLIER > QUEENLY

QUEENLIKE *adj* like a queen

QUEENLY *adj* resembling or appropriate to a queen ▷ *adv* in a manner appropriate to a queen

QUEENS > QUEEN

QUEENSHIP > QUEEN

QUEENSIDE *n* half of a chessboard in which the queen starts

QUEENY *adj* resembling a queen

QUEER *adj* not normal or usual ▷ *vb* spoil or thwart

QUEERCORE *n* type of gay-oriented punk music

QUEERDOM *n* offensive word for gay culture

QUEERDOMS > QUEERDOM

QUEERED > QUEER

QUEERER > QUEER

QUEEREST > QUEER

QUEERING > QUEER

QUEERISH > QUEER

QUEERITY > QUEER

QUEERLY > QUEER

QUEERNESS > QUEER

QUEERS > QUEER

QUEEST *n* wood pigeon

QUEESTS > QUEEST

QUEINT *same as* > QUAINT

QUELCH *same as* > SQUELCH

QUELCHED > QUELCH

QUELCHES > QUELCH

QUELCHING > QUELCH

QUELEA *n* East African weaver bird

QUELEAS > QUELEA

QUELL *vb* suppress

QUELLABLE > QUELL

QUELLED > QUELL

QUELLER > QUELL

QUELLERS > QUELL

QUELLING > QUELL

QUELLS > QUELL

QUEME *vb* please

QUEMED > QUEME

QUEMES > QUEME

QUEMING > QUEME

QUENA *n* Andean flute

QUENAS > QUENA

QUENCH *vb* satisfy (one's thirst)

QUENCHED > QUENCH

QUENCHER > QUENCH

QUENCHERS > QUENCH

QUENCHES > QUENCH

QUENCHING > QUENCH

QUENELLE *n* finely sieved mixture of cooked meat or fish shaped into various forms

QUENELLES > QUENELLE

QUEP *interj* expression of derision

QUERCETIC > QUERCETIN

QUERCETIN *n* yellow crystalline pigment found naturally in the rind and bark of many plants

QUERCETUM *n* group of oak trees

QUERCINE *adj* of or relating to oak trees

QUERCITIN *same as* > QUERCETIN

QUERIDA *n* sweetheart

QUERIDAS > QUERIDA

QUERIED > QUERY

QUERIER > QUERY

QUERIERS > QUERY

QUERIES > QUERY

QUERIMONY *n* complaint

QUERIST *n* person who makes inquiries or queries

QUERISTS > QUERIST

QUERN *n* stone hand mill for grinding corn

QUERNS > QUERN

QUERULOUS *adj* complaining or whining

QUERY *n* question, esp one raising doubt ▷ *vb* express uncertainty, doubt, or an objection

QUERYING > QUERY

QUERYINGS > QUERY

QUEST *n* long and difficult search ▷ *vb* go in search of

QUESTANT *n* one who quests

QUESTANTS > QUEST

QUESTED > QUEST

QUESTER > QUEST

QUESTERS > QUEST

QUESTING > QUEST

QUESTINGS > QUEST

QUESTION *n* form of words addressed to a person in order to obtain an answer ▷ *vb* put a question or questions to (a person)

QUESTIONS > QUESTION

QUESTOR *same as* > QUAESTOR

QUESTORS > QUESTOR

QUESTRIST *n* one who quests

QUESTS > QUEST

QUETCH *vb* move

QUETCHED > QUETCH

QUETCHES > QUETCH

QUETCHING > QUETCH

QUETHE *vb* say

QUETHES > QUETHE

QUETHING > QUETHE

QUETSCH *n* plum brandy

QUETSCHES > QUETSCH

QUETZAL *n* crested bird of Central and N South America

QUETZALES > QUETZAL

QUETZALS > QUETZAL

QUEUE *n* line of people or vehicles waiting for something ▷ *vb* form or remain in a line while waiting

QUEUED > QUEUE

QUEUEING > QUEUE

QUEUEINGS > QUEUE

QUEUER > QUEUE

QUEUERS > QUEUE

QUEUES > QUEUE

QUEUING > QUEUE

QUEUINGS > QUEUE

QUEY *n* young cow

QUEYN *n* girl

QUEYNIE *same as* > QUEYN

QUEYNIES > QUEYNIE

QUEYNS > QUEYN

QUEYS > QUEY

QUEZAL *same as* > QUETZAL

QUEZALES > QUEZAL

QUEZALS > QUEZAL

QUIBBLE *vb* make trivial objections ▷ *n* trivial objection

QUIBBLED > QUIBBLE

QUIBBLER > QUIBBLE

QUIBBLERS > QUIBBLE

QUIBBLES > QUIBBLE

QUIBBLING > QUIBBLE

QUIBLIN *same as* > QUIBBLE

QUIBLINS > QUIBLIN

QUICH *vb* move

QUICHE *n* savoury flan with an egg custard filling

QUICHED > QUICH

QUICHES > QUICHE

QUICHING > QUICH

QUICK *adj* speedy, fast ▷ *n* area of sensitive flesh under a nail ▷ *adv* in a rapid manner

QUICKBEAM *n* rowan tree

QUICKEN *vb* make or become faster ▷ *n* rowan tree

QUICKENED > QUICKEN

QUICKENER > QUICKEN

QUICKENS > QUICKEN

QUICKER > QUICK

QUICKEST > QUICK

QUICKFIRE *adj* designed for rapid continuous gunfire

QUICKIE *n* anything done or made hurriedly ▷ *adj* made or done rapidly

QUICKIES > QUICKIE

QUICKLIME *n* white solid used in the manufacture of glass and steel

QUICKLY > QUICK

QUICKNESS > QUICK

QUICKS > QUICK

QUICKSAND *n* deep mass of loose wet sand that sucks anything on top of it into it

QUICKSET *adj* (of plants or cuttings) planted so as to form a hedge ▷ *n* hedge composed of such plants

QUICKSETS > QUICKSET

QUICKSTEP *n* fast modern ballroom dance ▷ *vb* perform this dance

QUICKY *same as* > QUICKIE

QUID *n* pound (sterling)

QUIDAM *n* specified person

QUIDAMS > QUIDAM

QUIDDANY *n* quince jelly ▷ *vb* make into quince jelly

QUIDDIT *same as* > QUIDDITY

QUIDDITCH *n* imaginary game in which players fly on broomsticks

QUIDDITS > QUIDDIT

QUIDDITY *n* essential nature of something

QUIDDLE *vb* waste time

QUIDDLED > QUIDDLE

QUIDDLER > QUIDDLE

QUIDDLERS > QUIDDLE

QUIDDLES > QUIDDLE

QUIDDLING > QUIDDLE

QUIDNUNC *n* person eager to learn news and scandal

QUIDNUNCS > QUIDNUNC

QUIDS > QUID

QUIESCE *vb* quieten

QUIESCED > QUIESCE

QUIESCENT *adj* quiet, inactive, or dormant

QUIESCES > QUIESCE

QUIESCING > QUIESCE

QUIET *adj* with little noise ▷ *n* quietness ▷ *vb* make or become quiet

QUIETED > QUIET

QUIETEN *vb* make or become quiet

QUIETENED > QUIETEN

QUIETENER > QUIETEN

QUIETENS > QUIETEN

QUIETER > QUIET

QUIETERS > QUIET

QUIETEST > QUIET

QUIETING > QUIET

QUIETINGS > QUIET

QUIETISM *n* passivity and calmness of mind towards external events

QUIETISMS > QUIETISM

QUIETIST > QUIETISM

QUIETISTS > QUIETISM

QUIETIVE *n* sedative drug

QUIETIVES > QUIETIVE

QUIETLY > QUIET

QUIETNESS > QUIET

QUIETS > QUIET

QUIETSOME > QUIET

QUIETUDE *n* quietness, peace, or tranquillity

QUIETUDES > QUIETUDE

QUIETUS *n* release from life

QUIETUSES > QUIETUS

QUIFF *n* tuft of hair brushed up above the forehead

QUIFFED *adj* having a quiff

QUIFFS > QUIFF

QUIGHT *vb* quit

QUIGHTED > QUIGHT

QUIGHTING > QUIGHT

QUIGHTS > QUIGHT

SECTION 1: Words between 2 and 9 letters in length

QUILL *n* pen made from the feather of a bird's wing or tail ▷ *vb* wind (thread, yarn, etc) onto a spool or bobbin
QUILLAI *another name for* > SOAPBARK
QUILLAIA *same as* > QUILLAI
QUILLAIAS > QUILLAIA
QUILLAIS > QUILLAI
QUILLAJA *same as* > QUILLAT
QUILLAJAS > QUILLAJA
QUILLBACK *n* freshwater fish
QUILLED > QUILL
QUILLET *n* quibble or subtlety
QUILLETS > QUILLET
QUILLING *n* craftwork in which material is formed into small bands that form the basis of a design
QUILLINGS > QUILLING
QUILLMAN *n* clerk
QUILLMEN > QUILLMAN
QUILLON *n* either half of the extended crosspiece of a sword or dagger
QUILLONS > QUILLON
QUILLOW *n* quilt folded to make a pillow
QUILLOWS > QUILLOW
QUILLS > QUILL
QUILLWORK *n* embroidery using porcupine quills
QUILLWORT *n* aquatic tracheophyte plant with quill-like leaves
QUILT *n* padded covering for a bed ▷ *vb* stitch together two layers of (fabric) with padding between them
QUILTED > QUILT
QUILTER > QUILT
QUILTERS > QUILT
QUILTING *n* material used for making a quilt
QUILTINGS > QUILTING
QUILTS > QUILT
QUIM *n* vulgar word for the female genitals
QUIMS > QUIM
QUIN *n* short for quintuplet
QUINA *n* quinine
QUINARIES > QUINARY
QUINARY *adj* consisting of fives or by fives ▷ *n* set of five
QUINAS > QUINA
QUINATE *adj* arranged in or composed of five parts
QUINCE *n* acid-tasting pear-shaped fruit
QUINCES > QUINCE
QUINCHE *vb* move
QUINCHED > QUINCHE
QUINCHES > QUINCHE
QUINCHING > QUINCHE
QUINCUNX *n* five objects arranged in the shape of a rectangle with the fifth in the centre
QUINE *variant of* > QUEAN
QUINELA *same as* > QUINELLA
QUINELAS > QUINELA

QUINELLA *n* form of betting in which the punter bets on selecting the first and second place-winners in any order
QUINELLAS > QUINELLA
QUINES > QUINE
QUINIC *adj* as in *quinic acid* white crystalline soluble optically active carboxylic acid
QUINIDINE *n* crystalline alkaloid drug
QUINIE *n* girl
QUINIELA *same as* > QUINELLA
QUINIELAS > QUINIELA
QUINIES > QUINIE
QUININ *same as* > QUININE
QUININA *same as* > QUININE
QUININAS > QUININA
QUININE *n* bitter drug used as a tonic and formerly to treat malaria
QUININES > QUININE
QUININS > QUININ
QUINNAT *n* Pacific salmon
QUINNATS > QUINNAT
QUINO *same as* > KENO
QUINOA *n* type of grain high in nutrients
QUINOAS > QUINOA
QUINOID *same as* > QUINONOID
QUINOIDAL > QUINOID
QUINOIDS > QUINOID
QUINOL *n* white crystalline soluble phenol used as a photographic developer
QUINOLIN *same as* > QUINOLINE
QUINOLINE *n* oily colourless insoluble basic heterocyclic compound
QUINOLINS > QUINOLIN
QUINOLONE *n* any of a group of synthetic antibiotics
QUINOLS > QUINOL
QUINONE *n* yellow crystalline water-soluble unsaturated ketone
QUINONES > QUINONE
QUINONOID *adj* of, resembling, or derived from quinone
QUINOS > QUINO
QUINQUINA *same as* > QUININE
QUINS > QUIN
QUINSIED > QUINSY
QUINSIES > QUINSY
QUINSY *n* inflammation of the throat or tonsils
QUINT *same as* > QUIN
QUINTA *n* Portuguese vineyard where grapes for wine or port are grown
QUINTAIN *n* post or target set up for tilting exercises for mounted knights or foot soldiers
QUINTAINS > QUINTAIN
QUINTAL *n* unit of weight
QUINTALS > QUINTAL
QUINTAN *adj* (of a fever) occurring every fourth day ▷ *n* quintan fever

QUINTANS > QUINTAN
QUINTAR *n* Albanian unit of currency
QUINTARS > QUINTAR
QUINTAS > QUINTA
QUINTE *n* fifth of eight basic positions from which a parry or attack can be made in fencing
QUINTES > QUINTE
QUINTET *n* group of five performers
QUINTETS > QUINTET
QUINTETT *same as* > QUINTET
QUINTETTE *same as* > QUINTET
QUINTETTI > QUINTETTO
QUINTETTO *same as* > QUINTET
QUINTETTS > QUINTETT
QUINTIC *adj* of or relating to the fifth degree ▷ *n* mathematical function
QUINTICS > QUINTIC
QUINTILE *n* aspect of 72° between two heavenly bodies
QUINTILES > QUINTILE
QUINTIN *same as* > QUINTAIN
QUINTINS > QUINTIN
QUINTROON *n* offensive term for person of mixed racial ancestry
QUINTS > QUINT
QUINTUPLE *vb* multiply by five ▷ *adj* five times as much or as many ▷ *n* quantity or number five times as great as another
QUINTUPLY *n* reply to a quadruply
QUINZE *n* card game where players aim to score 15
QUINZES > QUINZE
QUINZHEE *n* shelter made from hollowed-out snow
QUINZHEES > QUINZHEE
QUINZIE *same as* > QUINZHEE
QUINZIES > QUINZIE
QUIP *n* witty saying ▷ *vb* make a quip
QUIPO *same as* > QUIPU
QUIPOS > QUIPO
QUIPPED > QUIP
QUIPPER > QUIP
QUIPPERS > QUIP
QUIPPIER > QUIP
QUIPPIEST > QUIP
QUIPPING > QUIP
QUIPPISH > QUIP
QUIPPU *same as* > QUIPU
QUIPPUS > QUIPPU
QUIPPY > QUIP
QUIPS > QUIP
QUIPSTER *n* person inclined to make sarcastic or witty remarks
QUIPSTERS > QUIPSTER
QUIPU *n* device of the Incas used to record information using knotted cords
QUIPUS > QUIPU
QUIRE *n* set of 24 or 25 sheets of paper ▷ *vb* arrange in quires

QUIRED > QUIRE
QUIRES > QUIRE
QUIRING > QUIRE
QUIRISTER *same as* > CHORISTER
QUIRK *n* peculiarity of character ▷ *vb* quip
QUIRKED > QUIRK
QUIRKIER > QUIRK
QUIRKIEST > QUIRK
QUIRKILY > QUIRK
QUIRKING > QUIRK
QUIRKISH > QUIRK
QUIRKS > QUIRK
QUIRKY > QUIRK
QUIRT *n* whip with a leather thong at one end ▷ *vb* strike with a quirt
QUIRTED > QUIRT
QUIRTING > QUIRT
QUIRTS > QUIRT
QUISLING *n* traitor who aids an occupying enemy force
QUISLINGS > QUISLING
QUIST *n* wood pigeon
QUISTS > QUIST
QUIT *vb* stop (doing something) ▷ *adj* free (from)
QUITCH *vb* move
QUITCHED > QUITCH
QUITCHES > QUITCH
QUITCHING > QUITCH
QUITCLAIM *n* formal renunciation of any claim against a person or of a right to land ▷ *vb* renounce (a claim) formally
QUITE *archaic form of* > QUIT
QUITED > QUITE
QUITES > QUITE
QUITING > QUITE
QUITRENT *n* former rent payable by a freeholder to their lord that released them from performing services
QUITRENTS > QUITRENT
QUITS > QUIT
QUITTAL *n* repayment of an action with a similar action
QUITTALS > QUITTAL
QUITTANCE *n* release from debt or other obligation
QUITTED > QUIT
QUITTER *n* person who lacks perseverance
QUITTERS > QUITTER
QUITTING > QUIT
QUITTOR *n* infection of the cartilages on the side of a horse's foot
QUITTORS > QUITTOR
QUIVER *vb* shake with a tremulous movement ▷ *n* shaking or trembling
QUIVERED > QUIVER
QUIVERER > QUIVER
QUIVERERS > QUIVER
QUIVERFUL *n* amount that a quiver can hold
QUIVERIER > QUIVER
QUIVERING > QUIVER
QUIVERISH > QUIVER
QUIVERS > QUIVER
QUIVERY > QUIVER
QUIXOTE *n* impractical idealist**

9

QUIXOTES > QUIXOTE

QUIXOTIC *adj* romantic and unrealistic

QUIXOTISM > QUIXOTIC

QUIXOTRY > QUIXOTE

QUIZ *n* entertainment in which the knowledge of the players is tested by a series of questions ▷ *vb* investigate by close questioning

QUIZZED > QUIZ

QUIZZER > QUIZ

QUIZZERS > QUIZ

QUIZZERY > QUIZ

QUIZZES > QUIZ

QUIZZICAL *adj* questioning and mocking

QUIZZIFY > QUIZ

QUIZZING > QUIZ

QUIZZINGS > QUIZ

QULLIQ *n* type of oil lamp used by Inuit people

QULLIQS > QULLIQ

QUOAD *adv* as far as

QUOD *n* jail ▷ *vb* say

QUODDED > QUOD

QUODDING > QUOD

QUODLIBET *n* light piece of music based on two or more popular tunes

QUODLIN *n* cooking apple

QUODLINS > QUODLIN

QUODS > QUOD

QUOHOG *n* edible clam

QUOHOGS > QUOHOG

QUOIF *vb* arrange (the hair)

QUOIFED > QUOIF

QUOIFING > QUOIF

QUOIFS > QUOIF

QUOIN *n* external corner of a building ▷ *vb* wedge

QUOINED > QUOIN

QUOINING > QUOIN

QUOININGS > QUOINING

QUOINS > QUOIN

QUOIST *n* wood pigeon

QUOISTS > QUOIST

QUOIT *n* large ring used in the game of quoits ▷ *vb* throw as a quoit

QUOITED > QUOIT

QUOITER > QUOIT

QUOITERS > QUOIT

QUOITING > QUOIT

QUOITS *n* game in which quoits are tossed at a stake in the ground

QUOKKA *n* small Australian wallaby

QUOKKAS > QUOKKA

QUOLL *n* Australian catlike carnivorous marsupial

QUOLLS > QUOLL

QUOMODO *n* manner

QUOMODOS > QUOMODO

QUONDAM *adj* of an earlier time

QUONK *vb* make an accidental noise while broadcasting

QUONKED > QUONK

QUONKING > QUONK

QUONKS > QUONK

QUOOKE *archaic past participle of* **>** QUAKE

QUOP *vb* pulsate or throb

QUOPPED > QUOP

QUOPPING > QUOP

QUOPS > QUOP

QUORATE *adj* having or being a quorum

QUORUM *n* minimum number of people required to be present at a meeting

QUORUMS > QUORUM

QUOTA *n* share that is due from, due to, or allocated to a group or person

QUOTABLE *adj* apt or suitable for quotation

QUOTABLY > QUOTABLE

QUOTAS > QUOTA

QUOTATION *n* written or spoken passage repeated exactly in a later work, speech, or conversation

QUOTATIVE *n* word indicating quotation ▷ *adj* introducing quoted words

QUOTE *vb* repeat (words) exactly ▷ *n* quotation ▷ *interj* expression used to indicate that the words that follow form a quotation

QUOTED > QUOTE

QUOTER > QUOTE

QUOTERS > QUOTE

QUOTES > QUOTE

QUOTH *vb* said

QUOTHA *interj* expression of mild sarcasm, used in picking up a word or phrase used by someone else

QUOTIDIAN *adj* daily ▷ *n* malarial fever characterized by attacks that recur daily

QUOTIENT *n* result of the division of one number or quantity by another

QUOTIENTS > QUOTIENT

QUOTING > QUOTE

QUOTITION *n* division by repeated subtraction

QUOTUM *same as* **>** QUOTA

QUOTUMS > QUOTUM

QURSH *same as* **>** QURUSH

QURSHES > QURSH

QURUSH *n* former Saudi Arabian currency unit

QURUSHES > QURUSH

QUYTE *same as* **>** QUIT

QUYTED > QUYTE

QUYTES > QUYTE

QUYTING > QUYTE

QWERTIES > QWERTY

QWERTY *n* standard English-language typewriter or computer keyboard

QWERTYS > QWERTY

Rr

RABANNA n Madagascan woven raffia

RABANNAS > RABANNA

RABASKA n large canoe

RABASKAS > RABASKA

RABAT vb rotate so that the plane rotated coincides with another

RABATINE n type of collar

RABATINES > RABATINE

RABATMENT > RABAT

RABATO n wired or starched collar

RABATOES > RABATO

RABATOS > RABATO

RABATS > RABAT

RABATTE same as > RABAT

RABATTED > RABATTE

RABATTES > RABATTE

RABATTING > RABAT

RABBET n recess cut into a surface ▷ vb cut or form a rabbet in (timber)

RABBETED > RABBET

RABBETING > RABBET

RABBETS > RABBET

RABBI n Jewish spiritual leader

RABBIES > RABBI

RABBIN same as > RABBI

RABBINATE n position, function, or tenure of office of a rabbi

RABBINIC adj of or relating to rabbis

RABBINICS n study of rabbinic literature of the post-Talmudic period

RABBINISM n teachings and traditions of the rabbis of the Talmudic period

RABBINIST > RABBINISM

RABBINITE > RABBINISM

RABBINS > RABBIN

RABBIS > RABBI

RABBIT n small burrowing mammal with long ears ▷ vb talk too much

RABBITED > RABBIT

RABBITER n person who traps and sells rabbits

RABBITERS > RABBITER

RABBITIER > RABBITY

RABBITING n activity of hunting rabbits

RABBITO same as > RABBITOH

RABBITOH n (formerly) an itinerant seller of rabbits for eating

RABBITOHS > RABBITOH

RABBITOS > RABBITO

RABBITRY n place where tame rabbits are kept and bred

RABBITS > RABBIT

RABBITY adj like a rabbit

RABBLE n disorderly crowd of noisy people ▷ vb stir, mix, or skim (the molten charge) in a roasting furnace

RABBLED > RABBLE

RABBLER n device for stirring, mixing, or skimming a molten charge in a furnace

RABBLERS > RABBLER

RABBLES > RABBLE

RABBLING > RABBLE

RABBLINGS > RABBLE

RABBONI n very respectful Jewish title or form of address

RABBONIS > RABBONI

RABI n (in Pakistan, India, etc) a crop that is harvested at the end of winter

RABIC > RABIES

RABID adj fanatical

RABIDER > RABID

RABIDEST > RABID

RABIDITY > RABID

RABIDLY > RABID

RABIDNESS > RABID

RABIES n usu fatal viral disease transmitted by dogs and certain other animals

RABIETIC > RABIES

RABIS > RABI

RABONA n method of kicking a football

RABONAS > RABONA

RACA adj biblical word meaning worthless or empty-headed

RACAHOUT n acorn flour or drink made from it

RACAHOUTS > RACAHOUT

RACCAHOUT same as > RACAHOUT

RACCOON n small N American mammal with a long striped tail

RACCOONS > RACCOON

RACE n contest of speed ▷ vb compete with in a race

RACEABLE adj fit for racing

RACECARD n card providing information about a race meeting

RACECARDS > RACECARD

RACED > RACE

RACEGOER n one who attends a race meeting, esp a habitual frequenter of race meetings

RACEGOERS > RACEGOER

RACEGOING > RACEGOER

RACEHORSE n horse specially bred for racing

RACEMATE n racemic compound

RACEMATES > RACEMATE

RACEME n cluster of flowers along a central stem, as in the foxglove

RACEMED adj with or in racemes

RACEMES > RACEME

RACEMIC adj being a mixture of equal amounts of enantiomers

RACEMISE same as > RACEMIZE

RACEMISED > RACEMISE

RACEMISES > RACEMISE

RACEMISM > RACEMIC

RACEMISMS > RACEMIC

RACEMIZE vb change or cause to change into a racemic mixture

RACEMIZED > RACEMIZE

RACEMIZES > RACEMIZE

RACEMOID adj resembling a raceme

RACEMOSE adj being or resembling a raceme

RACEMOUS same as > RACEMOSE

RACEPATH same as > RACETRACK

RACEPATHS > RACEPATH

RACER n person, animal, or machine that races

RACERS > RACER

RACES > RACE

RACETRACK n track for racing

RACEWALK vb race by walking fast rather than running

RACEWALKS > RACEWALK

RACEWAY n racetrack, esp one for banger racing

RACEWAYS > RACEWAY

RACH n scent hound

RACHE same as > RACH

RACHES > RACH

RACHET same as > RATCHET

RACHETED > RACHET

RACHETING > RACHET

RACHETS > RACHET

RACHIAL > RACHIS

RACHIDES > RACHIS

RACHIDIAL > RACHIS

RACHIDIAN > RACHIS

RACHILLA n (in grasses) the short stem of a spikelet that bears the florets

RACHILLAE > RACHILLA

RACHILLAS > RACHILLA

RACHIS n main axis or stem of an inflorescence or compound leaf

RACHISES > RACHIS

RACHITIC > RACHITIS

RACHITIS another name for > RICKETS

RACIAL adj relating to the division of the human species into races

RACIALISE same as > RACIALIZE

RACIALISM same as > RACISM

RACIALIST > RACIALISM

RACIALIZE vb render racial in tone or content

RACIALLY > RACIAL

RACIATION n evolutionary development of races

RACIER > RACY

RACIEST > RACY

RACILY > RACY

RACINESS > RACY

RACING adj denoting or associated with horse races ▷ n practice of engaging in contests of speed

RACINGS > RACING

RACINO n combined racetrack and casino

RACINOS > RACINO

RACISM n hostile attitude or behaviour to members of other races

RACISMS > RACISM

RACIST > RACISM

RACISTS > RACISM

RACK n framework for holding particular articles, such as coats or luggage ▷ vb cause great suffering to

RACKED > RACK

RACKER > RACK

RACKERS > RACK

RACKET n bat with strings stretched in an oval frame, used in tennis etc ▷ vb strike with a racket

RACKETED > RACKET

RACKETEER n person making illegal profits ▷ vb operate a racket

RACKETER n someone making a racket

RACKETERS > RACKETER

RACKETIER > RACKETY

RACKETING > RACKET

RACKETRY n noise and commotion

RACKETS n ball game played in a paved walled court

RACKETT n early double-reeded wind instrument

RACKETTS > RACKETT

RACKETY adj involving noise, commotion and excitement

RACKFUL > RACK

RACKFULS > RACK

RACKING > RACK

RACKINGLY > RACK

RACKINGS > RACK

RACKLE n (Scot) chain

RACKLES > RACKLE

RACKS > RACK

RACKWORK n mechanism with a rack and pinion

RACKWORKS > RACKWORK

RACLETTE n Swiss dish of melted cheese served on boiled potatoes

RACLETTES > RACLETTE

RACLOIR n scraper

RACLOIRS > RACLOIR

RACON n radar beacon

RACONS > RACON

RACONTEUR n skilled storyteller

RACOON same as **>** RACCOON

RACOONS > RACOON

RACQUET same as **>** RACKET

RACQUETED > RACQUET

RACQUETS > RACQUET

RACY adj slightly shocking

RAD n former unit of absorbed ionizing radiation dose ▷ vb fear ▷ adj slang term for great

RADAR n device for tracking distant objects

RADARS > RADAR

RADDED > RAD

RADDER > RAD

RADDEST > RAD

RADDING > RAD

RADDLE same as **>** RUDDLE

RADDLED adj (of a person) unkempt or run-down in appearance

RADDLEMAN same as **>** RUDDLEMAN

RADDLEMEN > RADDLEMAN

RADDLES > RADDLE

RADDLING > RADDLE

RADDOCKE same as **>** RUDDOCK

RADDOCKES > RADDOCKE

RADE (in Scots dialect) past tense of **>** RIDE

RADGE adj angry or uncontrollable ▷ n person acting in such a way

RADGER > RADGE

RADGES > RADGE

RADGEST > RADGE

RADIABLE adj able to be X-rayed

RADIAL adj spreading out from a common central point ▷ n radial-ply tyre

RADIALE n bone in the wrist

RADIALIA > RADIALE

RADIALISE same as **>** RADIALIZE

RADIALITY > RADIAL

RADIALIZE vb arrange in a pattern of radii

RADIALLY > RADIAL

RADIALS > RADIAL

RADIAN n unit for measuring angles, equal to 57.296°

RADIANCE n quality or state of being radiant

RADIANCES > RADIANCE

RADIANCY same as **>** RADIANCE

RADIANS > RADIAN

RADIANT adj looking happy ▷ n point or object that emits radiation

RADIANTLY > RADIANT

RADIANTS > RADIANT

RADIATA n type of pine tree

RADIATAS > RADIATA

RADIATE vb spread out from a centre ▷ adj having rays or a radial structure

RADIATED > RADIATE

RADIATELY > RADIATE

RADIATES > RADIATE

RADIATING > RADIATE

RADIATION n transmission of energy from one body to another

RADIATIVE adj emitting or causing the emission of radiation

RADIATOR n arrangement of pipes containing hot water or steam to heat a room

RADIATORS > RADIATOR

RADIATORY same as **>** RADIATIVE

RADICAL adj fundamental ▷ n person advocating fundamental (political) change

RADICALLY adv thoroughly

RADICALS > RADICAL

RADICAND n number from which a root is to be extracted

RADICANDS > RADICAND

RADICANT adj forming roots from the stem

RADICATE vb root or cause to take root

RADICATED > RADICATE

RADICATES > RADICATE

RADICCHIO n Italian variety of chicory, with purple leaves streaked with white that are eaten raw in salads

RADICEL n very small root

RADICELS > RADICEL

RADICES > RADIX

RADICLE n small or developing root

RADICLES > RADICLE

RADICULAR adj root-related

RADICULE same as **>** RADICLE

RADICULES > RADICULE

RADII > RADIUS

RADIO n use of electromagnetic waves for broadcasting, communication, etc ▷ vb transmit (a message) by radio ▷ adj of, relating to, or using radio

RADIOED > RADIO

RADIOES less common spelling of **>** RADIOS

RADIOGOLD n radioactive isotope of gold

RADIOGRAM n image produced on a specially sensitized photographic film or plate by radiation, usually by X-rays or gamma rays

RADIOING > RADIO

RADIOLOGY n science of using X-rays in medicine

RADIOMAN n radio operator

RADIOMEN > RADIOMAN

RADIONICS n dowsing technique using a pendulum to detect the energy fields that are emitted by all forms of matter

RADIOS > RADIO

RADIOTHON n lengthy radio programme to raise charity funds, etc

RADISH n small hot-flavoured root vegetable eaten raw in salads

RADISHES > RADISH

RADIUM n radioactive metallic element

RADIUMS > RADIUM

RADIUS n (length of) a straight line from the centre to the circumference of a circle ▷ vb give a round shape

RADIUSED > RADIUS

RADIUSES > RADIUS

RADIUSING > RADIUS

RADIX n any number that is the base of a number system or of a system of logarithms

RADIXES > RADIX

RADOME n protective housing for a radar antenna

RADOMES > RADOME

RADON n radioactive gaseous element

RADONS > RADON

RADS > RAD

RADULA n horny tooth-bearing strip on the tongue of molluscs

RADULAE > RADULA

RADULAR > RADULA

RADULAS > RADULA

RADULATE > RADULA

RADWASTE n radioactive waste

RADWASTES > RADWASTE

RAFALE n burst of artillery fire

RAFALES > RAFALE

RAFF n rubbish

RAFFIA n prepared palm fibre for weaving mats etc

RAFFIAS > RAFFIA

RAFFINATE n liquid left after a solute has been extracted by solvent extraction

RAFFINOSE n trisaccharide of fructose, glucose, and galactose that occurs in sugar beet, cotton seed, certain cereals, etc

RAFFISH adj slightly disreputable

RAFFISHLY > RAFFISH

RAFFLE n lottery with goods as prizes ▷ vb offer as a prize in a raffle

RAFFLED > RAFFLE

RAFFLER > RAFFLE

RAFFLERS > RAFFLE

RAFFLES > RAFFLE

RAFFLESIA n any of various tropical Asian parasitic leafless plants whose flowers smell of putrid meat and are pollinated by carrion flies

RAFFLING > RAFFLE

RAFFS > RAFF

RAFT n floating platform of logs, planks, etc ▷ vb convey on or travel by raft, or make a raft from

RAFTED > RAFT

RAFTER n one of the main beams of a roof ▷ vb fit with rafters

RAFTERED > RAFTER

RAFTERING > RAFTER

RAFTERS > RAFTER

RAFTING > RAFT

RAFTINGS > RAFT

RAFTMAN same as **>** RAFTSMAN

RAFTMEN > RAFTMAN

RAFTS > RAFT

RAFTSMAN n someone who does rafting

RAFTSMEN > RAFTSMAN

RAG n fragment of cloth ▷ vb tease ▷ adj of various charitable events at a British university

RAGA n pattern of melody and rhythm in Indian music

RAGAS > RAGA

RAGBAG n confused assortment, jumble

RAGBAGS > RAGBAG

RAGBOLT n bolt that has angled projections on it

RAGBOLTS > RAGBOLT

RAGDE archaic past form of **>** RAGE

RAGDOLL n breed of cat

RAGDOLLS > RAGDOLL

RAGE n violent anger or passion ▷ vb speak or act with fury

RAGED > RAGE

RAGEE same as **>** RAGI

RAGEES > RAGEE

RAGEFUL > RAGE

RAGER > RAGE

RAGERS > RAGE

RAGES > RAGE

RAGG same as **>** RAGSTONE

RAGGA n dance-oriented style of reggae

RAGGAS > RAGGA

RAGGED > RAG

RAGGEDER > RAG

RAGGEDEST > RAG

RAGGEDIER > RAGGEDY

RAGGEDLY > RAG

RAGGEDY adj somewhat ragged

RAGGEE same as **>** RAGI

RAGGEES > RAGGEE

RAGGERIES > RAGGERY

RAGGERY n rags

RAGGIER > RAGGY

RAGGIES > RAGGY
RAGGIEST > RAGGY
RAGGING > RAG
RAGGINGS > RAG
RAGGLE n thin groove cut in stone or brickwork ▷ vb cut a raggle in
RAGGLED > RAGGLE
RAGGLES > RAGGLE
RAGGLING > RAGGLE
RAGGS > RAGG
RAGGY adj ragged ▷ n cereal grass cultivated in Africa and Asia for its edible grain
RAGHEAD n offensive term for an Arab person
RAGHEADS > RAGHEAD
RAGI n cereal grass cultivated in Africa and Asia for its edible grain
RAGING > RAGE
RAGINGLY > RAGE
RAGINGS > RAGE
RAGINI n Indian musical form related to a raga
RAGINIS > RAGINI
RAGIS > RAGI
RAGLAN adj (of a sleeve) joined to a garment from the neck to the underarm ▷ n coat with sleeves that continue to the collar
RAGLANS > RAGLAN
RAGMAN n rag-and-bone man
RAGMANS > RAGMAN
RAGMEN > RAGMAN
RAGMENT n statute, roll, or list
RAGMENTS > RAGMENT
RAGOUT n richly seasoned stew of meat and vegetables ▷ vb make into a ragout
RAGOUTED > RAGOUT
RAGOUTING > RAGOUT
RAGOUTS > RAGOUT
RAGPICKER n rag-and-bone man
RAGS > RAG
RAGSTONE n hard sandstone or limestone, esp when used for building
RAGSTONES > RAGSTONE
RAGTAG n disparaging term for common people
RAGTAGS > RAGTAG
RAGTAIL adj ragged; shabby
RAGTIME n style of jazz piano music
RAGTIMER > RAGTIME
RAGTIMERS > RAGTIME
RAGTIMES > RAGTIME
RAGTOP n informal word for a car with a folding or removable roof
RAGTOPS > RAGTOP
RAGU n Italian meat and tomato sauce
RAGULED same as > RAGULY
RAGULY adj (in heraldry) having toothlike projections
RAGUS > RAGU
RAGWEED n any of several plants
RAGWEEDS > RAGWEED
RAGWHEEL n toothed wheel
RAGWHEELS > RAGWHEEL

RAGWORK n weaving or needlework using rags
RAGWORKS > RAGWORK
RAGWORM n type of worm that lives chiefly in burrows in sand or mud
RAGWORMS > RAGWORM
RAGWORT n plant with ragged leaves and yellow flowers
RAGWORTS > RAGWORT
RAH informal US word for > CHEER
RAHED > RAH
RAHING > RAH
RAHS > RAH
RAHUI n Māori prohibition
RAHUIS > RAHUI
RAI n type of Algerian popular music ·
RAIA same as > RAYAH
RAIAS > RAIA
RAID n sudden surprise attack or search ▷ vb make a raid on
RAIDED > RAID
RAIDER > RAID
RAIDERS > RAID
RAIDING > RAID
RAIDINGS > RAID
RAIDS > RAID
RAIK n wander ▷ vb wander
RAIKED > RAIK
RAIKING > RAIK
RAIKS > RAIK
RAIL n horizontal bar, esp as part of a fence or track ▷ vb complain bitterly or loudly
RAILAGE n cost of transporting goods by rail
RAILAGES > RAILAGE
RAILBED n ballast layer supporting the sleepers of a railway track
RAILBEDS > RAILBED
RAILBIRD n racing aficionado
RAILBIRDS > RAILBIRD
RAILBUS n bus-like vehicle for use on railway lines
RAILBUSES > RAILBUS
RAILCAR n passenger-carrying railway vehicle consisting of a single coach
RAILCARD n card entitling the holder to cheaper rail travel
RAILCARDS > RAILCARD
RAILCARS > RAILCAR
RAILE archaic spelling of > RAIL
RAILED > RAIL
RAILER > RAIL
RAILERS > RAIL
RAILES > RAILE
RAILHEAD n terminal of a railway
RAILHEADS > RAILHEAD
RAILING n fence made of rails supported by posts
RAILINGLY > RAIL
RAILINGS > RAILING
RAILLERY n teasing or joking
RAILLESS > RAIL
RAILLIES > RAILLY
RAILLY old word for > MOCK

RAILMAN n railway employee
RAILMEN > RAILMAN
RAILROAD same as > RAILWAY
RAILROADS > RAILROAD
RAILS > RAIL
RAILWAY n track of iron rails on which trains run
RAILWAYS > RAILWAY
RAILWOMAN n female railway employee
RAILWOMEN > RAILWOMAN
RAIMENT n clothing
RAIMENTS > RAIMENT
RAIN n water falling in drops from the clouds ▷ vb fall or pour down as rain
RAINBAND n dark band in the solar spectrum caused by water in the atmosphere
RAINBANDS > RAINBAND
RAINBIRD n bird whose call is believed to be a sign of impending rain
RAINBIRDS > RAINBIRD
RAINBOW n arch of colours in the sky
RAINBOWED adj resembling or involving a rainbow
RAINBOWS > RAINBOW
RAINBOWY adj resembling a rainbow
RAINCHECK n ticket stub allowing readmission to a game on a later date should bad weather prevent play
RAINCOAT n water-resistant overcoat
RAINCOATS > RAINCOAT
RAINDATE n US term for an alternative date in case of rain
RAINDATES > RAINDATE
RAINDROP n water droplet that falls from the sky when it is raining
RAINDROPS > RAINDROP
RAINE archaic spelling of > REIGN
RAINED > RAIN
RAINES > RAINE
RAINFALL n amount of rain
RAINFALLS > RAINFALL
RAINIER > RAINY
RAINIEST > RAINY
RAINILY > RAINY
RAININESS > RAINY
RAINING > RAIN
RAINLESS > RAIN
RAINMAKER n (among Native Americans) a professional practitioner of ritual incantations or other actions intended to cause rain to fall
RAINOUT n radioactive fallout or atmospheric pollution carried to the earth by rain
RAINOUTS > RAINOUT
RAINPROOF adj (of garments, materials, buildings, etc) impermeable to rainwater ▷ vb make rainproof
RAINS > RAIN
RAINSPOUT n waterspout

RAINSTICK n musical instrument consisting of a tube filled with sand or pebbles
RAINSTORM n storm with heavy rain
RAINSUIT n waterproof jacket and trousers
RAINSUITS > RAINSUIT
RAINSWEPT adj (of a place) characterized by frequent heavy rain
RAINTIGHT same as > RAINPROOF
RAINWASH n action of rain ▷ vb erode or wet as a result of rain
RAINWATER n water from rain
RAINWEAR n protective garments intended for use in wet weather
RAINWEARS > RAINWEAR
RAINY adj characterized by a large rainfall
RAIRD same as > REIRD
RAIRDS > RAIRD
RAIS > RAI
RAISABLE > RAISE
RAISE vb lift up ▷ n increase in pay
RAISEABLE > RAISE
RAISED > RAISE
RAISER > RAISE
RAISERS > RAISE
RAISES > RAISE
RAISIN n dried grape
RAISING n rule that moves a constituent from an embedded clause into the main clause
RAISINGS > RAISING
RAISINIER > RAISINY
RAISINS > RAISIN
RAISINY adj tasting of raisins
RAISONNE adj carefully thought out
RAIT same as > RET
RAITA n Indian dish of chopped cucumber, mint, etc, in yogurt
RAITAS > RAITA
RAITED > RAIT
RAITING > RAIT
RAITS > RAIT
RAIYAT same as > RYOT
RAIYATS > RAIYAT
RAJ n (in India) government
RAJA same as > RAJAH
RAJAH n Indian ruler
RAJAHS > RAJAH
RAJAHSHIP > RAJAH
RAJAS > RAJA
RAJASHIP > RAJA
RAJASHIPS > RAJA
RAJES > RAJ
RAKE n tool used for smoothing earth or gathering leaves, hay, etc ▷ vb gather or smooth with a rake
RAKED > RAKE
RAKEE same as > RAKI
RAKEES > RAKEE
RAKEHELL n dissolute man ▷ adj profligate

RAKEHELLS > RAKEHELL
RAKEHELLY adj profligate
RAKELIKE adj like a rake
RAKEOFF n share of profits, esp one that is illegal or given as a bribe
RAKEOFFS > RAKEOFF
RAKER n person who rakes
RAKERIES > RAKERY
RAKERS > RAKER
RAKERY n rakish behaviour
RAKES > RAKE
RAKESHAME n old word for someone shamefully dissolute
RAKI n strong spirit distilled from grain
RAKIA n strong fruit-based alcoholic drink popular in the Balkans
RAKIAS > RAKIA
RAKIJA same as > RAKIA
RAKIJAS > RAKIJA
RAKING n (in rugby) offence of scraping an opponent with the studs
RAKINGS > RAKING
RAKIS > RAKI
RAKISH adj dashing or jaunty
RAKISHLY > RAKISH
RAKSHAS same as > RAKSHASA
RAKSHASA n Hindu demon
RAKSHASAS > RAKSHASA
RAKSHASES > RAKSHAS
RAKU n type of Japanese pottery
RAKUS > RAKU
RALE n abnormal coarse crackling sound heard on auscultation of the chest
RALES > RALE
RALLIED > RALLY
RALLIER > RALLY
RALLIERS > RALLY
RALLIES > RALLY
RALLIFORM adj of rail family of birds
RALLINE adj relating to a family of birds that includes the rails, crakes, and coots
RALLY n large gathering of people for a meeting ▷ vb bring or come together after dispersal or for a common cause
RALLYE US variant of > RALLY
RALLYES > RALLYE
RALLYING > RALLY
RALLYINGS > RALLY
RALLYIST > RALLY
RALLYISTS > RALLY
RALPH vb slang word meaning vomit
RALPHED > RALPH
RALPHING > RALPH
RALPHS > RALPH
RAM n male sheep ▷ vb strike against with force
RAMADA n outdoor eating area with roof but open sides
RAMADAS > RAMADA
RAMAKIN same as > RAMEKIN
RAMAKINS > RAMAKIN

RAMAL adj relating to a branch or branches
RAMATE adj with branches
RAMBLA n dried-up riverbed
RAMBLAS > RAMBLA
RAMBLE vb walk without a definite route ▷ n walk, esp in the country
RAMBLED > RAMBLE
RAMBLER n person who rambles
RAMBLERS > RAMBLER
RAMBLES > RAMBLE
RAMBLING adj large and irregularly shaped ▷ n activity of going for long walks in the country
RAMBLINGS > RAMBLING
RAMBUTAN n SE Asian tree that has bright red edible fruit
RAMBUTANS > RAMBUTAN
RAMCAT n dialect word for a male cat
RAMCATS > RAMCAT
RAMEAL same as > RAMAL
RAMEE same as > RAMIE
RAMEES > RAMEE
RAMEKIN n small ovenproof dish for a single serving of food
RAMEKINS > RAMEKIN
RAMEN n Japanese dish consisting of a clear broth containing thin white noodles
RAMENS > RAMEN
RAMENTA > RAMENTUM
RAMENTUM n any of the thin brown scales that cover the stems and leaves of young ferns
RAMEOUS same as > RAMAL
RAMEQUIN same as > RAMEKIN
RAMEQUINS > RAMEQUIN
RAMET n any of the individuals in a group of clones
RAMETS > RAMET
RAMI same as > RAMIE
RAMIE n woody Asian shrub with broad leaves
RAMIES > RAMIE
RAMIFIED > RAMIFY
RAMIFIES > RAMIFY
RAMIFORM adj having a branchlike shape
RAMIFY vb become complex
RAMIFYING > RAMIFY
RAMILIE same as > RAMILLIE
RAMILIES > RAMILIE
RAMILLIE n wig with a plait at the back fashionable in the 18th century
RAMILLIES > RAMILLIE
RAMIN n swamp-growing tree found in Malaysia and Indonesia
RAMINS > RAMIN
RAMIS > RAMI
RAMJET n type of jet engine
RAMJETS > RAMJET
RAMMED > RAM
RAMMEL n discarded or waste matter

RAMMELS > RAMMEL
RAMMER > RAM
RAMMERS > RAM
RAMMIER > RAMMY
RAMMIES > RAMMY
RAMMIEST > RAMMY
RAMMING > RAM
RAMMISH adj like a ram, esp in being foul-smelling
RAMMISHLY > RAMMISH
RAMMLE n collection of items saved in case they become useful
RAMMLES > RAMMLE
RAMMY n noisy disturbance or free-for-all ▷ vb make a rammy ▷ adj like a ram
RAMONA same as > SAGEBRUSH
RAMONAS > RAMONA
RAMOSE adj having branches
RAMOSELY > RAMOSE
RAMOSITY > RAMOSE
RAMOUS same as > RAMOSE
RAMOUSLY > RAMOSE
RAMP n slope joining two level surfaces ▷ vb (esp of animals) to rush around in a wild excited manner
RAMPAGE vb dash about violently
RAMPAGED > RAMPAGE
RAMPAGER > RAMPAGE
RAMPAGERS > RAMPAGE
RAMPAGES > RAMPAGE
RAMPAGING > RAMPAGE
RAMPANCY > RAMPANT
RAMPANT adj growing or spreading uncontrollably
RAMPANTLY > RAMPANT
RAMPART n mound or wall for defence ▷ vb provide with a rampart
RAMPARTED > RAMPART
RAMPARTS > RAMPART
RAMPAUGE Scots variant of > RAMPAGE
RAMPAUGED > RAMPAUGE
RAMPAUGES > RAMPAUGE
RAMPED > RAMP
RAMPER > RAMP
RAMPERS > RAMP
RAMPICK same as > RAMPIKE
RAMPICKED > RAMPICK
RAMPICKS > RAMPICK
RAMPIKE n US or dialect word for a dead tree
RAMPIKES > RAMPIKE
RAMPING > RAMP
RAMPINGS > RAMP
RAMPION n European and Asian plant
RAMPIONS > RAMPION
RAMPIRE archaic variant of > RAMPART
RAMPIRED > RAMPIRE
RAMPIRES > RAMPIRE
RAMPOLE same as > RAMPIKE
RAMPOLES > RAMPOLE
RAMPS > RAMP
RAMPSMAN n mugger
RAMPSMEN > RAMPSMAN
RAMROD n long thin rod used for cleaning the barrel of a gun ▷ adj (of someone's

posture) very straight and upright ▷ vb drive
RAMRODDED > RAMROD
RAMRODS > RAMROD
RAMS > RAM
RAMSHORN n any of various freshwater snails
RAMSHORNS > RAMSHORN
RAMSON n type of garlic
RAMSONS > RAMSON
RAMSTAM adv headlong ▷ adj headlong
RAMTIL n African plant grown in India esp for its oil
RAMTILLA same as > RAMTIL
RAMTILLAS > RAMTILLA
RAMTILS > RAMTIL
RAMULAR adj relating to a branch or branches
RAMULI > RAMULUS
RAMULOSE adj (of the parts or organs of animals and plants) having many small branches
RAMULOUS same as > RAMULOSE
RAMULUS n small branch
RAMUS n barb of a bird's feather
RAN > RUN
RANA n genus of frogs
RANARIAN adj of or relating to frogs
RANARIUM n place for keeping frogs
RANARIUMS > RANARIUM
RANAS > RANA
RANCE Scots word for > PROP
RANCED > RANCE
RANCEL vb (in Shetland and Orkney) carry out a search
RANCELLED > RANCEL
RANCELS > RANCEL
RANCES > RANCE
RANCH n large cattle farm in the American West ▷ vb run a ranch
RANCHED > RANCH
RANCHER n person who owns, manages, or works on a ranch
RANCHERA n type of Mexican country music
RANCHERAS > RANCHERA
RANCHERIA n Native American settlement or home of a rancher
RANCHERIE n (in British Columbia, Canada) a settlement of Native Americans, esp on a reserve
RANCHERO another word for > RANCHER
RANCHEROS > RANCHERO
RANCHERS > RANCHER
RANCHES > RANCH
RANCHETTE n small ranch
RANCHING > RANCH
RANCHINGS > RANCH
RANCHLAND n land occupied by a ranch
RANCHLESS > RANCH
RANCHLIKE > RANCH
RANCHMAN n man who owns, manages, or works on a ranch

RANCHMEN > RANCHMAN

RANCHO n hut or group of huts for housing ranch workers

RANCHOS > RANCHO

RANCID adj (of butter, bacon, etc) stale and having an offensive smell

RANCIDER > RANCID

RANCIDEST > RANCID

RANCIDITY > RANCID

RANCIDLY > RANCID

RANCING > RANCE

RANCOR same as > RANCOUR

RANCORED > RANCOR

RANCOROUS > RANCOUR

RANCORS > RANCOR

RANCOUR n deep bitter hate

RANCOURED > RANCOUR

RANCOURS > RANCOUR

RAND n leather strip on the heel of a shoe ▷ vb cut into rands

RANDAN n boat rowed by three people

RANDANS > RANDAN

RANDED > RAND

RANDEM adv with three horses harnessed together as a team ▷ n carriage or team of horses so driven

RANDEMS > RANDEM

RANDIE same as > RANDY

RANDIER > RANDY

RANDIES > RANDY

RANDIEST > RANDY

RANDILY > RANDY

RANDINESS > RANDY

RANDING > RAND

RANDLORD n mining magnate during the 19th-century gold boom in Johannesburg

RANDLORDS > RANDLORD

RANDOM adj made or done by chance or without plan ▷ n (in mining) the course of a vein of ore

RANDOMISE same as > RANDOMIZE

RANDOMIZE vb set up (a selection process, sample, etc) in a deliberately random way in order to enhance the statistical validity of any results obtained

RANDOMLY > RANDOM

RANDOMS > RANDOM

RANDON old variant of > RANDOM

RANDONS > RANDON

RANDS > RAND

RANDY adj rude or reckless ▷ n rude or reckless person

RANEE same as > RANI

RANEES > RANEE

RANG n (Scot) rank

RANGA n derogatory term for a person with red hair

RANGAS > RANGA

RANGATIRA n Māori chief of either gender

RANGE n limits of effectiveness or variation ▷ vb vary between one point and another

RANGED > RANGE

RANGELAND n land that naturally produces forage plants suitable for grazing but where rainfall is too low or erratic for growing crops

RANGER n official in charge of a nature reserve etc

RANGERS > RANGER

RANGES > RANGE

RANGI n sky

RANGIER > RANGY

RANGIEST > RANGY

RANGILY > RANGY

RANGINESS > RANGY

RANGING > RANGE

RANGINGS > RANGE

RANGIORA n evergreen New Zealand shrub or small tree

RANGIORAS > RANGIORA

RANGIS > RANGI

RANGOLI n traditional Indian ground decoration

RANGOLIS > RANGOLI

RANGS > RANG

RANGY adj having long slender limbs

RANI n wife or widow of a rajah

RANID n frog

RANIDS > RANID

RANIFORM n froglike

RANINE adj relating to frogs

RANIS > RANI

RANK n relative place or position ▷ vb have a specific rank or position ▷ adj complete or absolute

RANKE archaic variant of > RANK

RANKED > RANK

RANKER n soldier in the ranks

RANKERS > RANKER

RANKES > RANKE

RANKEST > RANK

RANKING adj prominent ▷ n position on a scale

RANKINGS > RANKING

RANKISH adj old word meaning rather rank

RANKISM n discrimination against people on the grounds of rank

RANKISMS > RANKISM

RANKIST n person who discriminates on the grounds of rank

RANKISTS > RANKIST

RANKLE vb continue to cause resentment or bitterness

RANKLED > RANKLE

RANKLES > RANKLE

RANKLESS > RANK

RANKLING > RANKLE

RANKLY > RANK

RANKNESS > RANK

RANKS > RANK

RANKSHIFT n phenomenon in which a unit at one rank in the grammar has the function of a unit at a lower rank, as for example in the phrase the house on the corner, where the words on the corner shift down from the rank of group to the rank of word

▷ vb shift or be shifted from (one linguistic rank to another)

RANPIKE same as > RAMPIKE

RANPIKES > RANPIKE

RANSACK vb search thoroughly

RANSACKED > RANSACK

RANSACKER > RANSACK

RANSACKS > RANSACK

RANSEL same as > RANCEL

RANSELS > RANSEL

RANSHAKLE Scots word for > RANSACK

RANSOM n money demanded for the release of a kidnapped person ▷ vb pay money to obtain the release of a captive

RANSOMED > RANSOM

RANSOMER > RANSOM

RANSOMERS > RANSOM

RANSOMING > RANSOM

RANSOMS > RANSOM

RANT vb talk in a loud and excited way ▷ n loud excited speech

RANTED > RANT

RANTER > RANT

RANTERISM > RANT

RANTERS > RANT

RANTING > RANT

RANTINGLY > RANT

RANTINGS > RANT

RANTIPOLE n reckless person ▷ vb behave like a rantipole

RANTS > RANT

RANULA n saliva-filled cyst that develops under the tongue

RANULAR adj of a cyst under the tongue

RANULAS > RANULA

RANUNCULI pl n plants of the genus that includes the buttercup, crowfoot, spearwort, and lesser celandine

RANZEL same as > RANCEL

RANZELMAN n (in Shetland and Orkney) type of constable

RANZELMEN > RANZELMAN

RANZELS > RANZEL

RAOULIA n flowering plant of New Zealand

RAOULIAS > RAOULIA

RAP vb hit with a sharp quick blow ▷ n quick sharp blow

RAPACIOUS adj greedy or grasping

RAPACITY > RAPACIOUS

RAPE n violent sexual crime ▷ vb commit rape

RAPED > RAPE

RAPER > RAPE

RAPERS > RAPE

RAPES > RAPE

RAPESEED n seed of the oilseed rape plant

RAPESEEDS > RAPESEED

RAPHAE > RAPHE

RAPHANIA n type of ergotism possibly resulting from consumption of radish seeds

RAPHANIAS > RAPHANIA

RAPHE n elongated ridge of conducting tissue along the side of certain seeds

RAPHES > RAPHE

RAPHIA same as > RAFFIA

RAPHIAS > RAPHIA

RAPHIDE n needle-shaped crystal that occurs in many plant cells

RAPHIDES > RAPHIDE

RAPHIS same as > RAPHIDE

RAPID adj quick, swift

RAPIDER > RAPID

RAPIDEST > RAPID

RAPIDITY > RAPID

RAPIDLY > RAPID

RAPIDNESS > RAPID

RAPIDS pl n part of a river with a fast, turbulent current

RAPIER n fine-bladed sword

RAPIERED adj carrying a rapier

RAPIERS > RAPIER

RAPINE n pillage or plundering

RAPINES > RAPINE

RAPING > RAPE

RAPINI n type of leafy vegetable

RAPINIS > RAPINI

RAPIST n person who commits rape

RAPISTS > RAPIST

RAPLOCH n Scots word for homespun woollen material ▷ adj Scots word meaning coarse or homemade

RAPLOCHS > RAPLOCH

RAPPAREE n Irish irregular soldier of the late 17th century

RAPPAREES > RAPPAREE

RAPPE n Arcadian dish of grated potatoes and pork or chicken

RAPPED > RAP

RAPPEE n moist English snuff of the 18th and 19th centuries

RAPPEES > RAPPEE

RAPPEL n (formerly) a drumbeat to call soldiers to arms ▷ vb abseil

RAPPELED > RAPPEL

RAPPELING > RAPPEL

RAPPELLED > RAPPEL

RAPPELS > RAPPEL

RAPPEN n Swiss coin equal to one hundredth of a franc

RAPPER n something used for rapping, such as a knocker on a door

RAPPERS > RAPPER

RAPPES > RAPPE

RAPPING > RAP

RAPPINGS > RAP

RAPPINI same as > RAPINI

RAPPORT n harmony or agreement

RAPPORTS > RAPPORT

RAPS > RAP

RAPT adj engrossed or spellbound

RAPTLY > RAPT

RAPTNESS > RAPT

RAPTOR n any bird of prey

r

RAPTORIAL adj (of the feet of birds) adapted for seizing prey

RAPTORS > RAPTOR

RAPTURE n ecstasy ▷ vb entrance

RAPTURED > RAPTURE

RAPTURES > RAPTURE

RAPTURING > RAPTURE

RAPTURISE same as > RAPTURIZE

RAPTURIST > RAPTURE

RAPTURIZE vb go into ecstasies

RAPTUROUS adj experiencing or manifesting ecstatic joy or delight

RARE adj uncommon ▷ vb rear

RAREBIT n as in Welsh rarebit dish made from melted cheese served on toast

RAREBITS > RAREBIT

RARED > RARE

RAREE n as in raree show street show or carnival

RAREFIED adj highly specialized, exalted

RAREFIER > RAREFY

RAREFIERS > RAREFY

RAREFIES > RAREFY

RAREFY vb make or become rarer or less dense

RAREFYING > RAREFY

RARELY adv seldom

RARENESS > RARE

RARER > RARE

RARERIPE adj ripening early ▷ n fruit or vegetable that ripens early

RARERIPES > RARERIPE

RARES > RARE

RAREST > RARE

RARIFIED same as > RAREFIED

RARIFIES > RARIFY

RARIFY same as > RAREFY

RARIFYING > RARIFY

RARING adj ready

RARITIES > RARITY

RARITY n something that is valuable because it is unusual

RARK vb as in rark up informal New Zealand expression meaning reprimand severely

RARKED > RARK

RARKING > RARK

RARKS > RARK

RAS n headland

RASBORA n often brightly coloured tropical fish

RASBORAS > RASBORA

RASCAILLE n rabble

RASCAL n rogue ▷ adj belonging to the mob or rabble

RASCALDOM > RASCAL

RASCALISM > RASCAL

RASCALITY n mischievous, disreputable, or dishonest character, behaviour, or action

RASCALLY adj dishonest or mean ▷ adv in a dishonest or mean fashion

RASCALS > RASCAL

RASCASSE n any of various fishes with venomous spines on the fins

RASCASSES > RASCASSE

RASCHEL n type of loosely knitted fabric

RASCHELS > RASCHEL

RASE same as > RAZE

RASED > RASE

RASER > RASE

RASERS > RASE

RASES > RASE

RASH adj hasty, reckless, or incautious ▷ n eruption of spots or patches on the skin ▷ vb (in old usage) cut

RASHED > RASH

RASHER n thin slice of bacon

RASHERS > RASHER

RASHES > RASH

RASHEST > RASH

RASHIE n protective shirt worn by surfers

RASHIES > RASHIE

RASHING > RASH

RASHLIKE > RASH

RASHLY > RASH

RASHNESS > RASH

RASING > RASE

RASMALAI n Indian dessert made from cheese, milk, and almonds

RASMALAIS > RASMALAI

RASORIAL adj (of birds such as domestic poultry) adapted for scratching the ground for food

RASP n harsh grating noise ▷ vb speak in a grating voice

RASPATORY n surgical instrument for abrading

RASPBERRY n red juicy edible berry

RASPED > RASP

RASPER > RASP

RASPERS > RASP

RASPIER > RASPY

RASPIEST > RASPY

RASPINESS > RASPY

RASPING adj (esp of a noise) harsh or grating

RASPINGLY > RASPING

RASPINGS pl n browned breadcrumbs for coating fish and other foods before frying, baking, etc

RASPISH > RASP

RASPS > RASP

RASPY same as > RASPING

RASSE n small S Asian civet

RASSES > RASSE

RASSLE dialect variant of > WRESTLE

RASSLED > RASSLE

RASSLER n wrestler

RASSLERS > RASSLER

RASSLES > RASSLE

RASSLING > RASSLE

RAST archaic past form of > RACE

RASTA adj rastafarian

RASTAFARI n Jamaican religious movement ▷ adj of or relating to the rastafari movement

RASTER n image consisting of rows of pixel information

▷ vb turn a digital image into a large picture

RASTERED > RASTER

RASTERING > RASTER

RASTERISE same as > RASTERIZE

RASTERIZE vb (in computing) convert into pixels for screen output

RASTERS > RASTER

RASTRUM n pen for drawing the five lines of a musical stave simultaneously

RASTRUMS > RASTRUM

RASURE n scraping

RASURES > RASURE

RAT n small rodent ▷ vb inform (on)

RATA n New Zealand hardwood forest tree

RATABLE adj able to be rated or evaluated ▷ n something that can be rated or evaluated

RATABLES pl n property that is liable to rates

RATABLY > RATABLE

RATAFEE same as > RATAFIA

RATAFEES > RATAFEE

RATAFIA n liqueur made from fruit

RATAFIAS > RATAFIA

RATAL n amount on which rates are assessed ▷ adj of or relating to rates (local taxation)

RATALS > RATAL

RATAN same as > RATTAN

RATANIES > RATANY

RATANS > RATAN

RATANY n flowering desert shrub

RATAPLAN n drumming sound ▷ vb drum

RATAPLANS > RATAPLAN

RATAS > RATA

RATATAT n sound of knocking on a door

RATATATS > RATATAT

RATBAG n insulting term for an eccentric or unreliable person

RATBAGS > RATBAG

RATBITE n as in ratbite fever acute infectious disease that can be caught from rats

RATCH same as > RATCHET

RATCHED > RATCH

RATCHES > RATCH

RATCHET n set of teeth on a bar or wheel allowing motion in one direction only ▷ vb move using or as if using a ratchet system

RATCHETED > RATCHET

RATCHETS > RATCHET

RATCHING > RATCH

RATE n degree of speed or progress ▷ vb consider or value

RATEABLE same as > RATABLE

RATEABLES > RATEABLE

RATEABLY > RATEABLE

RATED > RATE

RATEEN same as > RATINE

RATEENS > RATEEN

RATEL n large African and S Asian musteline mammal

RATELS > RATEL

RATEMETER n device for counting and averaging the number of events in a given time

RATEPAYER n person who pays local rates on a building

RATER > RATE

RATERS > RATE

RATES pl n (in some countries) a tax on property levied by a local authority

RATFINK n contemptible or undesirable person

RATFINKS > RATFINK

RATFISH n deep-sea fish with a whiplike tail

RATFISHES > RATFISH

RATH same as > RATHE

RATHA n (in India) a four-wheeled carriage drawn by horses or bullocks

RATHAS > RATHA

RATHE adj blossoming or ripening early in the season

RATHER adv to some extent ▷ interj expression of strong affirmation, often in answer to a question

RATHEREST adv archaic word equivalent to soonest

RATHERIPE same as > RATHRIPE

RATHERISH adv (in informal English) quite or fairly

RATHEST adv dialect or archaic word meaning soonest

RATHOLE n rat's hiding place or burrow

RATHOLES > RATHOLE

RATHOUSE n offensive term for a psychiatric hospital

RATHOUSES > RATHOUSE

RATHRIPE adj dialect word meaning mature or ripe ahead of time ▷ n variety of apple or other fruit that is quick to ripen

RATHRIPES > RATHRIPE

RATHS > RATH

RATICIDE n rat poison

RATICIDES > RATICIDE

RATIFIED > RATIFY

RATIFIER > RATIFY

RATIFIERS > RATIFY

RATIFIES > RATIFY

RATIFY vb give formal approval to

RATIFYING > RATIFY

RATINE n coarse loosely woven cloth

RATINES > RATINE

RATING n valuation or assessment

RATINGS > RATING

RATIO n relationship between two numbers or amounts expressed as a proportion

RATION n fixed allowance of food etc ▷ vb limit to a certain amount per person

RATIONAL adj reasonable, sensible ▷ n rational number

RATIONALE n reason for an action or decision

RATIONALS > RATIONAL

RATIONED > RATION

RATIONING n act of restricting the use or consumption of certain things

RATIONS pl n fixed daily allowance of food

RATIOS > RATIO

RATITE adj (of flightless birds) having a breastbone that lacks a keel ⊳ n bird that belongs to this group

RATITES > RATITE

RATLIKE > RAT

RATLIN same as > RATLINE

RATLINE n light line tied across the shrouds of a sailing vessel

RATLINES > RATLINE

RATLING n young rat

RATLINGS > RATLING

RATLINS > RATLIN

RATO n rocket-assisted take-off

RATOO same as > RATU

RATOON n new shoot that grows from near the root or crown of crop plants ⊳ vb propagate by such a growth

RATOONED > RATOON

RATOONER n plant that spreads by ratooning

RATOONERS > RATOONER

RATOONING > RATOON

RATOONS > RATOON

RATOOS > RATOO

RATOS > RATO

RATPACK n members of the press who pursue celebrities

RATPACKS > RATPACK

RATPROOF adj impenetrable by rats

RATS > RAT

RATSBANE n rat poison, esp arsenic oxide

RATSBANES > RATSBANE

RATTAIL n type of fish

RATTAILED adj having a tail like a rat

RATTAILS > RATTAIL

RATTAN n climbing palm with jointed stems used for canes

RATTANS > RATTAN

RATTED > RAT

RATTEEN same as > RATINE

RATTEENS > RATTEEN

RATTEN vb sabotage or steal tools in order to disrupt the work of

RATTENED > RATTEN

RATTENER > RATTEN

RATTENERS > RATTEN

RATTENING > RATTEN

RATTENS > RATTEN

RATTER n dog or cat that catches and kills rats

RATTERIES > RATTERY

RATTERS > RATTER

RATTERY n rats' dwelling area

RATTIER > RATTY

RATTIEST > RATTY

RATTILY > RATTY

RATTINESS > RATTY

RATTING > RAT

RATTINGS > RAT

RATTISH adj of, resembling, or infested with rats

RATTLE vb give out a succession of short sharp sounds ⊳ n short sharp sound

RATTLEBAG n rattle made out of a bag containing a variety of different things

RATTLEBOX n any of various tropical and subtropical leguminous plants that have inflated pods within which the seeds rattle

RATTLED > RATTLE

RATTLER n something that rattles

RATTLERS > RATTLER

RATTLES > RATTLE

RATTLIER > RATTLY

RATTLIEST > RATTLY

RATTLIN same as > RATLINE

RATTLINE same as > RATLINE

RATTLINES > RATTLINE

RATTLING adv exceptionally, very ⊳ n succession of short sharp sounds

RATTLINGS > RATTLING

RATTLINS > RATTLIN

RATTLY adj having a rattle

RATTON n dialect word for a little rat

RATTONS > RATTON

RATTOON same as > RATOON

RATTOONED > RATTOON

RATTOONS > RATTOON

RATTRAP n device for catching rats

RATTRAPS > RATTRAP

RATTY adj bad-tempered, irritable

RATU n title used by Fijian chiefs or nobles

RATUS > RATU

RAUCID adj raucous

RAUCITIES > RAUCOUS

RAUCITY > RAUCOUS

RAUCLE adj Scots word for rough or tough

RAUCLER > RAUCLE

RAUCLEST > RAUCLE

RAUCOUS adj hoarse or harsh

RAUCOUSLY > RAUCOUS

RAUGHT archaic past form of > REACH

RAUN n fish roe or spawn

RAUNCH n lack of polish or refinement ⊳ vb behave in a raunchy manner

RAUNCHED > RAUNCH

RAUNCHES > RAUNCH

RAUNCHIER > RAUNCHY

RAUNCHILY > RAUNCHY

RAUNCHING > RAUNCHY

RAUNCHY adj earthy, sexy

RAUNGE archaic word for > RANGE

RAUNGED > RAUNGE

RAUNGES > RAUNGE

RAUNGING > RAUNGE

RAUNS > RAUN

RAUPATU n confiscation or seizure of land

RAUPATUS > RAUPATU

RAUPO n New Zealand bulrush

RAUPOS > RAUPO

RAURIKI n any of various plants with prickly leaves

RAURIKIS > RAURIKI

RAUWOLFIA n tropical tree or shrub

RAV n Hebrew word for rabbi

RAVAGE vb cause extensive damage to ⊳ n destructive action

RAVAGED > RAVAGE

RAVAGER > RAVAGE

RAVAGERS > RAVAGE

RAVAGES > RAVAGE

RAVAGING > RAVAGE

RAVE vb talk wildly or with enthusiasm ⊳ n enthusiastically good review

RAVED > RAVE

RAVEL vb tangle or become entangled ⊳ n tangle or complication

RAVELED > RAVEL

RAVELER > RAVEL

RAVELERS > RAVEL

RAVELIN n outwork having two embankments at a salient angle

RAVELING > RAVEL

RAVELINGS > RAVEL

RAVELINS > RAVELIN

RAVELLED > RAVEL

RAVELLER > RAVEL

RAVELLERS > RAVEL

RAVELLIER > RAVELLY

RAVELLING > RAVEL

RAVELLY adj tangled

RAVELMENT n ravel or tangle

RAVELS > RAVEL

RAVEN n black bird like a large crow ⊳ adj (of hair) shiny black ⊳ vb seize or seek (plunder, prey, etc)

RAVENED > RAVEN

RAVENER > RAVEN

RAVENERS > RAVEN

RAVENEST > RAVEN

RAVENING adj (of animals) hungrily searching for prey

RAVENINGS pl n rapacious behaviour and activities

RAVENLIKE > RAVEN

RAVENOUS adj very hungry

RAVENS > RAVEN

RAVER n person who leads a wild or uninhibited social life

RAVERS > RAVER

RAVES > RAVE

RAVEY adj characteristic of a rave

RAVIER > RAVEY

RAVIEST > RAVEY

RAVIGOTE n rich white sauce with herbs and shallots

RAVIGOTES > RAVIGOTE

RAVIGOTTE n French salad sauce

RAVIN archaic spelling of > RAVEN

RAVINE n narrow steep-sided valley worn by a stream

RAVINED > RAVIN

RAVINES > RAVINE

RAVING adj delirious ⊳ n frenzied, irrational, or wildly extravagant talk or utterances

RAVINGLY > RAVING

RAVINGS > RAVING

RAVINING > RAVIN

RAVINS > RAVIN

RAVIOLI n small squares of pasta with a savoury filling

RAVIOLIS > RAVIOLI

RAVISH vb enrapture

RAVISHED > RAVISH

RAVISHER > RAVISH

RAVISHERS > RAVISH

RAVISHES > RAVISH

RAVISHING adj lovely or entrancing

RAVS > RAV

RAW n as in in the raw without clothes ⊳ adj uncooked

RAWARU n New Zealand name for blue cod

RAWARUS > RAWARU

RAWBONE archaic variant of > RAWBONED

RAWBONED adj having a lean bony physique

RAWER > RAW

RAWEST > RAW

RAWHEAD n bogeyman

RAWHEADS > RAWHEAD

RAWHIDE n untanned hide ⊳ vb whip

RAWHIDED > RAWHIDE

RAWHIDES > RAWHIDE

RAWHIDING > RAWHIDE

RAWIN n monitoring of winds in the upper atmosphere using radar and a balloon

RAWING (in dialect) same as > ROWEN

RAWINGS > RAWING

RAWINS > RAWIN

RAWISH > RAW

RAWLY > RAW

RAWMAISH n Irish word for foolish or exaggerated talk

RAWN (in dialect) same as > ROWEN

RAWNESS > RAW

RAWNESSES > RAW

RAWNS > RAWN

RAWS > RAW

RAX vb stretch or extend ⊳ n act of stretching or straining

RAXED > RAX

RAXES > RAX

RAXING > RAX

RAY n single line or narrow beam of light ⊳ vb (of an object) to emit (light) in rays or (of light) to issue in the form of rays

RAYA same as > RAYAH

RAYAH n (formerly) a non-Muslim subject of the Ottoman Empire

RAYAHS > RAYAH

RAYAS > RAYA

RAYED > RAY

RAYGRASS *same as*
> RYEGRASS
RAYING > RAY
RAYLE *archaic spelling of*
> RAIL
RAYLED > RAYLE
RAYLES > RAYLE
RAYLESS *adj* dark
RAYLESSLY > RAYLESS
RAYLET *n* small ray
RAYLETS > RAYLET
RAYLIKE *adj* resembling a
ray
RAYLING > RAYLE
RAYNE *archaic spelling of*
> REIGN
RAYNES > RAYNE
RAYON *n* (fabric made of) a
synthetic fibre
RAYONS > RAYON
RAYS > RAY
RAZE *vb* destroy (buildings or
a town) completely
RAZED > RAZE
RAZEE *n* sailing ship that has
had its upper deck or decks
removed ▷ *vb* remove the
upper deck or decks of (a
sailing ship)
RAZEED > RAZEE
RAZEEING > RAZEE
RAZEES > RAZEE
RAZER > RAZE
RAZERS > RAZE
RAZES > RAZE
RAZING > RAZE
RAZMATAZ *n* noisy or showy
fuss or activity
RAZOO *n* imaginary coin
RAZOOS > RAZOO
RAZOR *n* sharp instrument
for shaving ▷ *vb* cut or shave
with a razor
RAZORABLE *adj* able to be
shaved
RAZORBACK *n* another
name for the common
rorqual
RAZORBILL *n* sea bird of the
North Atlantic with a stout
sideways flattened bill
RAZORCLAM *n* type of
mollusc with a long, narrow
shell
RAZORED > RAZOR
RAZORFISH *n* type of
mollusc with a long, narrow
shell
RAZORING > RAZOR
RAZORS > RAZOR
RAZURE *same as* > RASURE
RAZURES > RAZURE
RAZZ *vb* make fun of
RAZZBERRY *US variant of*
> RASPBERRY
RAZZED > RAZZ
RAZZES > RAZZ
RAZZIA *n* raid for plunder or
slaves
RAZZIAS > RAZZIA
RAZZING *n* act of making
fun of someone
RAZZINGS > RAZZING
RAZZLE *n* as in *on the razzle*
out enjoying oneself or
celebrating
RAZZLES > RAZZLE

RE *prep* concerning ▷ *n* the
second note of the musical
scale
REABSORB *vb* absorb again
REABSORBS > REABSORB
REACCEDE *vb* accede again
REACCEDED > REACCEDE
REACCEDES > REACCEDE
REACCENT *vb* accent again
REACCENTS > REACCENT
REACCEPT *vb* accept again
REACCEPTS > REACCEPT
REACCLAIM *vb* acclaim
again
REACCUSE *vb* accuse again
REACCUSED > REACCUSE
REACCUSES > REACCUSE
REACH *vb* arrive at ▷ *n*
distance that one can reach
REACHABLE > REACH
REACHED > REACH
REACHER > REACH
REACHERS > REACH
REACHES > REACH
REACHING > REACH
REACHLESS *adj*
unreachable or unattainable
REACQUIRE *vb* get or gain
(something) again which
one has owned
REACT *vb* act in response (to)
REACTANCE *n* resistance to
the flow of an alternating
current caused by the
inductance or capacitance of
the circuit
REACTANT *n* substance that
participates in a chemical
reaction
REACTANTS > REACTANT
REACTED > REACT
REACTING > REACT
REACTION *n* physical or
emotional response to a
stimulus
REACTIONS > REACTION
REACTIVE *adj* chemically
active
REACTOR *n* apparatus in
which a nuclear reaction is
controlled to produce energy
REACTORS > REACTOR
REACTS > REACT
REACTUATE *vb* activate
again
READ *vb* look at and
understand or take in
(written or printed matter)
▷ *n* matter suitable for
reading
READABLE *adj* enjoyable to
read
READABLY > READABLE
READAPT *vb* adapt again
READAPTED > READAPT
READAPTS > READAPT
READD *vb* add again
READDED > READD
READDICT *vb* cause to
become addicted again
READDICTS > READDICT
READDING > READD
READDRESS *vb* look at or
discuss (an issue, situation,
etc) from a new or different
point of view
READDS > READD

READER *n* person who reads
READERLY *adj* pertaining to
or suitable for a reader
READERS > READER
READIED > READY
READIER > READY
READIES *pl n* ready money
READIEST > READY
READILY *adv* promptly
READINESS *n* state of being
ready or prepared
READING > READ
READINGS > READ
READJUST *vb* adapt to a
new situation
READJUSTS > READJUST
README *n* document which
accompanies computer files
or software
READMES > README
READMIT *vb* let (a person,
country, etc) back in to a
place or organization
READMITS > READMIT
READOPT *vb* adopt again
READOPTED > READOPT
READOPTS > READOPT
READORN *vb* adorn again
READORNED > READORN
READORNS > READORN
READOUT *n* act of retrieving
information from a
computer memory or
storage device
READOUTS > READOUT
READS > READ
READVANCE *vb* advance
again
READVISE *vb* advise again
READVISED > READVISE
READVISES > READVISE
READY *adj* prepared for use
or action ▷ *vb* prepare
READYING > READY
READYMADE *adj* made for
purchase and immediate use
by any customer
REAEDIFY *vb* rebuild
REAEDIFYE *same as*
> REAEDIFY
REAFFIRM *vb* state again,
confirm
REAFFIRMS > REAFFIRM
REAFFIX *vb* affix again
REAFFIXED > REAFFIX
REAFFIXES > REAFFIX
REAGENCY > REAGENT
REAGENT *n* chemical
substance that reacts with
another
REAGENTS > REAGENT
REAGIN *n* type of antibody
that is formed against an
allergen
REAGINIC > REAGIN
REAGINS > REAGIN
REAIS > REAL
REAK *same as* > RECK
REAKED > REAK
REAKING > REAK
REAKS > REAK
REAL *adj* existing in fact ▷ *n*
standard monetary unit of
Brazil
REALER > REAL
REALES > REAL
REALEST > REAL

REALGAR *n* rare orange-red
soft mineral
REALGARS > REALGAR
REALIA *pl n* real-life facts
and material used in
teaching
REALIGN *vb* change or put
back to a new or former place
or position
REALIGNED > REALIGN
REALIGNS > REALIGN
REALISE *same as*
> REALIZE
REALISED > REALISE
REALISER > REALISE
REALISERS > REALISE
REALISES > REALISE
REALISING > REALISE
REALISM *n* awareness or
acceptance of things as they
are
REALISMS > REALISM
REALIST *n* person who
accepts events, etc, as they
are
REALISTIC *adj* seeing and
accepting things as they
really are, practical
REALISTS > REALIST
REALITIES > REALITY
REALITY *n* state of things as
they are
REALIZE *vb* become aware
or grasp the significance of
REALIZED > REALIZE
REALIZER > REALIZE
REALIZERS > REALIZE
REALIZES > REALIZE
REALIZING > REALIZE
REALLIE *old or dialect variant
of* > REALLY
REALLIED > REALLY
REALLIES > REALLY
REALLOT *vb* allot again
REALLOTS > REALLOT
REALLY *adv* very ▷ *interj*
exclamation of dismay,
doubt, or surprise ▷ *vb* (in
archaic usage) rally
REALLYING > REALLY
REALM *n* kingdom
REALMLESS > REALM
REALMS > REALM
REALNESS > REAL
REALO *n* member of the
German Green party with
moderate views
REALOS > REALO
REALS > REAL
REALTER *vb* alter again
REALTERED > REALTER
REALTERS > REALTER
REALTIE *n* archaic word
meaning sincerity
REALTIES > REALTY
REALTIME *adj* (of a
data-processing system)
constantly updating to
reflect the latest changes in
data
REALTONE *n* audio clip of an
original recording, used as a
mobile phone ringtone
REALTONES > REALTONE
REALTOR *n* estate agent
REALTORS > REALTOR
REALTY *n* immovable
property

REAM *n* twenty quires of paper, generally 500 sheets ▷ *vb* enlarge (a hole) by use of a reamer

REAME *archaic variant of* > REALM

REAMED > REAM

REAMEND *vb* amend again

REAMENDED > REAMEND

REAMENDS > REAMEND

REAMER *n* tool used for smoothing the bores of holes accurately to size

REAMERS > REAMER

REAMES > REAME

REAMIER > REAMY

REAMIEST > REAMY

REAMING > REAM

REAMS > REAM

REAMY *Scots for* > CREAMY

REAN *same as* > REEN

REANALYSE *vb* analyse again

REANALYZE *US spelling of* > REANALYSE

REANIMATE *vb* refresh or enliven (something) again

REANNEX *vb* annex again

REANNEXED > REANNEX

REANNEXES > REANNEX

REANOINT *vb* anoint again

REANOINTS > REANOINT

REANS > REAN

REANSWER *vb* answer again

REANSWERS > REANSWER

REAP *vb* cut and gather (a harvest)

REAPABLE > REAP

REAPED > REAP

REAPER *n* person who reaps or machine for reaping

REAPERS > REAPER

REAPHOOK *n* sickle

REAPHOOKS > REAPHOOK

REAPING *n* act of reaping

REAPINGS > REAPING

REAPPAREL *vb* clothe again

REAPPEAR *vb* appear again

REAPPEARS > REAPPEAR

REAPPLIED > REAPPLY

REAPPLIES > REAPPLY

REAPPLY *vb* put or spread (something) on again

REAPPOINT *vb* assign (a person, committee, etc) to a post or role again

REAPPROVE *vb* approve again

REAPS > REAP

REAR *n* back part ▷ *vb* care for and educate (children)

REARED > REAR

REARER > REAR

REARERS > REAR

REARGUARD *n* troops protecting the rear of an army

REARGUE *vb* argue again

REARGUED > REARGUE

REARGUES > REARGUE

REARGUING > REARGUE

REARHORSE *n* mantis

REARING *n* act of rearing

REARINGS > REARING

REARISE *vb* arise again

REARISEN > REARISE

REARISES > REARISE

REARISING > REARISE

REARLY *old word for* > EARLY

REARM *vb* arm again

REARMED > REARM

REARMICE > REARMOUSE

REARMING > REARM

REARMOST *adj* nearest the back

REARMOUSE *same as* > REREMOUSE

REARMS > REARM

REAROSE > REARISE

REAROUSAL > REAROUSE

REAROUSE *vb* arouse again

REAROUSED > REAROUSE

REAROUSES > REAROUSE

REARRANGE *vb* organize differently, alter

REARREST *vb* arrest again

REARRESTS > REARREST

REARS > REAR

REARWARD *adj* in the rear ▷ *adv* towards the rear ▷ *n* position in the rear, esp the rear division of a military formation

REARWARDS *same as* > REARWARD

REASCEND *vb* ascend again

REASCENDS > REASCEND

REASCENT *n* new ascent

REASCENTS > REASCENT

REASON *n* cause or motive ▷ *vb* think logically in forming conclusions

REASONED *adj* well thought out or well presented

REASONER > REASON

REASONERS > REASON

REASONING *n* process of drawing conclusions from facts or evidence

REASONS > REASON

REASSAIL *vb* assail again

REASSAILS > REASSAIL

REASSERT *vb* assert (rights, claims, etc) again

REASSERTS > REASSERT

REASSESS *vb* reconsider the value or importance of

REASSIGN *vb* move (personnel, resources, etc) to a new post, department, location, etc

REASSIGNS > REASSIGN

REASSORT *vb* assort again

REASSORTS > REASSORT

REASSUME *vb* assume again

REASSUMED > REASSUME

REASSUMES > REASSUME

REASSURE *vb* restore confidence to

REASSURED > REASSURE

REASSURER > REASSURE

REASSURES > REASSURE

REAST *same as* > REEST

REASTED > REAST

REASTIER > REASTY

REASTIEST > REASTY

REASTING > REAST

REASTS > REAST

REASTY *adj* (in dialect) rancid

REATA *n* lasso

REATAS > REATA

REATE *n* type of crowfoot

REATES > REATE

REATTACH *vb* attach again

REATTACK *vb* attack again

REATTACKS > REATTACK

REATTAIN *vb* attain again

REATTAINS > REATTAIN

REATTEMPT *vb* attempt again

REAVAIL *vb* avail again

REAVAILED > REAVAIL

REAVAILS > REAVAIL

REAVE *vb* carry off (property, prisoners, etc) by force

REAVED > REAVE

REAVER > REAVE

REAVERS > REAVE

REAVES > REAVE

REAVING > REAVE

REAVOW *vb* avow again

REAVOWED > REAVOW

REAVOWING > REAVOW

REAVOWS > REAVOW

REAWAKE *vb* awake again

REAWAKED > REAWAKE

REAWAKEN *vb* emerge or rouse from sleep

REAWAKENS > REAWAKEN

REAWAKES > REAWAKE

REAWAKING > REAWAKE

REAWOKE > REAWAKE

REAWOKEN > REAWAKE

REB *n* Confederate soldier in the American Civil War

REBACK *vb* provide with a new back, backing, or lining

REBACKED > REBACK

REBACKING > REBACK

REBACKS > REBACK

REBADGE *vb* relaunch (a product) under a new name, brand, or logo

REBADGED > REBADGE

REBADGES > REBADGE

REBADGING > REBADGE

REBAIT *vb* bait again

REBAITED > REBAIT

REBAITING > REBAIT

REBAITS > REBAIT

REBALANCE *vb* balance again

REBAPTISE *same as* > REBAPTIZE

REBAPTISM *n* new baptism

REBAPTIZE *vb* baptize again

REBAR *n* rod providing reinforcement in concrete structures

REBARS > REBAR

REBASE *vb* set on a new foundation

REBASED > REBASE

REBASES > REBASE

REBASING > REBASE

REBATABLE > REBATE

REBATE *n* discount or refund ▷ *vb* cut a rabbet in

REBATED > REBATE

REBATER > REBATE

REBATERS > REBATE

REBATES > REBATE

REBATING > REBATE

REBATO *same as* > RABATO

REBATOES > REBATO

REBATOS > REBATO

REBBE *n* individual's chosen spiritual mentor

REBBES > REBBE

REBBETZIN *n* wife of a rabbi

REBEC *n* medieval stringed instrument resembling the violin

REBECK *same as* > REBEC

REBECKS > REBECK

REBECS > REBEC

REBEGAN > REBEGIN

REBEGIN *vb* begin again

REBEGINS > REBEGIN

REBEGUN > REBEGIN

REBEL *vb* revolt against the ruling power ▷ *n* person who rebels ▷ *adj* rebelling

REBELDOM > REBEL

REBELDOMS > REBEL

REBELLED > REBEL

REBELLER > REBEL

REBELLERS > REBEL

REBELLING > REBEL

REBELLION *n* organized open resistance to authority

REBELLOW *vb* reecho loudly

REBELLOWS > REBELLOW

REBELS > REBEL

REBID *vb* bid again

REBIDDEN > REBID

REBIDDING > REBID

REBIDS > REBID

REBILL *vb* bill again

REBILLED > REBILL

REBILLING > REBILL

REBILLS > REBILL

REBIND *vb* bind again

REBINDING > REBIND

REBINDS > REBIND

REBIRTH *n* revival or renaissance

REBIRTHER *n* person who has undergone rebirthing therapy

REBIRTHS > REBIRTH

REBIT > REBITE

REBITE *vb* (in printing) to give another application of acid

REBITES > REBITE

REBITING > REBITE

REBITTEN > REBITE

REBLEND *vb* blend again

REBLENDED > REBLEND

REBLENDS > REBLEND

REBLENT *same as* > REBLEND

REBLOCHON *n* type of soft French cheese

REBLOOM *vb* bloom again

REBLOOMED > REBLOOM

REBLOOMER *n* flower that blooms more than once

REBLOOMS > REBLOOM

REBLOSSOM *vb* blossom again

REBOANT *adj* resounding or reverberating

REBOARD *vb* board again

REBOARDED > REBOARD

REBOARDS > REBOARD

REBOATION *n* repeated bellow

REBODIED > REBODY

REBODIES > REBODY

REBODY *vb* give a new body to

REBODYING > REBODY

REBOIL vb boil again
REBOILED > REBOIL
REBOILING > REBOIL
REBOILS > REBOIL
REBOOK vb book again
REBOOKED > REBOOK
REBOOKING > REBOOK
REBOOKS > REBOOK
REBOOT vb shut down and then restart (a computer system)
REBOOTED > REBOOT
REBOOTING > REBOOT
REBOOTS > REBOOT
REBOP same as > BEBOP
REBOPS > REBOP
REBORE n boring of a cylinder to restore its true shape ▷ vb carry out this process
REBORED > REBORE
REBORES > REBORE
REBORING > REBORE
REBORN adj active again after a period of inactivity
REBORROW vb borrow again
REBORROWS > REBORROW
REBOTTLE vb bottle again
REBOTTLED > REBOTTLE
REBOTTLES > REBOTTLE
REBOUGHT > REBUY
REBOUND vb spring back ▷ n act of rebounding
REBOUNDED > REBOUND
REBOUNDER > REBOUND
REBOUNDS > REBOUND
REBOZO n long scarf covering the shoulders and head
REBOZOS > REBOZO
REBRACE vb brace again
REBRACED > REBRACE
REBRACES > REBRACE
REBRACING > REBRACE
REBRANCH vb branch again
REBRAND vb change or update the image of (an organization or product)
REBRANDED > REBRAND
REBRANDS > REBRAND
REBRED > REBREED
REBREED vb breed again
REBREEDS > REBREED
REBS > REB
REBUFF vb reject or snub ▷ n blunt refusal, snub
REBUFFED > REBUFF
REBUFFING > REBUFF
REBUFFS > REBUFF
REBUILD vb build (a building or town) again, after severe damage
REBUILDED archaic past form of > REBUILD
REBUILDS > REBUILD
REBUILT > REBUILD
REBUKABLE > REBUKE
REBUKE vb scold sternly ▷ n stern scolding
REBUKED > REBUKE
REBUKEFUL > REBUKE
REBUKER > REBUKE
REBUKERS > REBUKE
REBUKES > REBUKE
REBUKING > REBUKE
REBURIAL > REBURY

REBURIALS > REBURY
REBURIED > REBURY
REBURIES > REBURY
REBURY vb bury again
REBURYING > REBURY
REBUS n puzzle consisting of pictures and symbols representing words or syllables
REBUSES > REBUS
REBUT vb prove that (a claim) is untrue
REBUTMENT > REBUT
REBUTS > REBUT
REBUTTAL > REBUT
REBUTTALS > REBUT
REBUTTED > REBUT
REBUTTER n defendant's pleading in reply to a claimant's surrejoinder
REBUTTERS > REBUTTER
REBUTTING > REBUT
REBUTTON vb button again
REBUTTONS > REBUTTON
REBUY vb buy again
REBUYING > REBUY
REBUYS > REBUY
REC n short for recreation
RECAL same as > RECALL
RECALESCE vb glow again
RECALL vb recollect or remember ▷ n ability to remember
RECALLED > RECALL
RECALLER > RECALL
RECALLERS > RECALL
RECALLING > RECALL
RECALLS > RECALL
RECALMENT > RECAL
RECALS > RECAL
RECAMIER n shade of pink
RECAMIERS > RECAMIER
RECANE vb cane again
RECANED > RECANE
RECANES > RECANE
RECANING > RECANE
RECANT vb withdraw (a statement or belief) publicly
RECANTED > RECANT
RECANTER > RECANT
RECANTERS > RECANT
RECANTING > RECANT
RECANTS > RECANT
RECAP vb recapitulate ▷ n recapitulation
RECAPPED > RECAP
RECAPPING > RECAP
RECAPS > RECAP
RECAPTION n process of taking back one's property or persons under one's protection without causing a breach of the peace
RECAPTOR > RECAPTURE
RECAPTORS > RECAPTURE
RECAPTURE vb experience again ▷ n act of recapturing
RECARPET vb replace one carpet with another
RECARPETS > RECARPET
RECARRIED > RECARRY
RECARRIES > RECARRY
RECARRY vb carry again
RECAST vb organize or set out in a different way
RECASTING > RECAST

RECASTS > RECAST
RECATALOG vb catalogue again
RECATCH vb catch again
RECATCHES > RECATCH
RECAUGHT > RECATCH
RECAUTION vb caution again
RECCE vb reconnoitre ▷ n reconnaissance
RECCED > RECCE
RECCEED > RECCE
RECCEING > RECCE
RECCES > RECCE
RECCIED > RECCY
RECCIES > RECCY
RECCO same as > RECCE
RECCOS > RECCO
RECCY same as > RECCE
RECCYING > RECCY
RECEDE vb move to a more distant place
RECEDED > RECEDE
RECEDES > RECEDE
RECEDING > RECEDE
RECEIPT n written acknowledgment of money or goods received ▷ vb acknowledge payment of (a bill), as by marking it
RECEIPTED > RECEIPT
RECEIPTOR n person who receipts
RECEIPTS > RECEIPT
RECEIVAL n act of receiving or state of being received
RECEIVALS > RECEIVAL
RECEIVE vb take, accept, or get
RECEIVED adj generally accepted
RECEIVER n part of telephone that is held to the ear
RECEIVERS > RECEIVER
RECEIVES > RECEIVE
RECEIVING > RECEIVE
RECEMENT vb cement again
RECEMENTS > RECEMENT
RECENCIES > RECENT
RECENCY > RECENT
RECENSE vb revise
RECENSED > RECENSE
RECENSES > RECENSE
RECENSING > RECENSE
RECENSION n critical revision of a literary work
RECENSOR vb censor again
RECENSORS > RECENSOR
RECENT adj having happened lately
RECENTER > RECENT
RECENTEST > RECENT
RECENTLY > RECENT
RECENTRE vb centre again
RECENTRED > RECENTRE
RECENTRES > RECENTRE
RECEPT n idea or image formed in the mind by repeated experience
RECEPTION n area for receiving guests, clients, etc
RECEPTIVE adj willing to accept new ideas, suggestions, etc
RECEPTOR n sensory nerve ending that changes specific stimuli into nerve impulses

RECEPTORS > RECEPTOR
RECEPTS > RECEPT
RECERTIFY vb certify again
RECESS n niche or alcove ▷ vb place or set (something) in a recess
RECESSED > RECESS
RECESSES > RECESS
RECESSING > RECESS
RECESSION n period of economic difficulty when little is being bought or sold
RECESSIVE adj receding ▷ n recessive gene or character
RECHANGE vb change again
RECHANGED > RECHANGE
RECHANGES > RECHANGE
RECHANNEL vb channel again
RECHARGE vb cause (a battery etc) to take in and store electricity again
RECHARGED > RECHARGE
RECHARGER > RECHARGE
RECHARGES > RECHARGE
RECHART vb chart again
RECHARTED > RECHART
RECHARTER vb charter again
RECHARTS > RECHART
RECHATE same as > RECHEAT
RECHATES > RECHATE
RECHAUFFE n warmed-up leftover food
RECHEAT n (in a hunt) sounding of the horn to call back the hounds ▷ vb sound the horn to call back the hounds
RECHEATED > RECHEAT
RECHEATS > RECHEAT
RECHECK vb check again
RECHECKED > RECHECK
RECHECKS > RECHECK
RECHERCHE adj refined or elegant
RECHEW vb chew again
RECHEWED > RECHEW
RECHEWING > RECHEW
RECHEWS > RECHEW
RECHIE adj smoky
RECHIP vb put a new chip into (a stolen mobile phone) so it can be reused
RECHIPPED > RECHIP
RECHIPS > RECHIP
RECHLESSE archaic form of > RECKLESS
RECHOOSE vb choose again
RECHOOSES > RECHOOSE
RECHOSE > RECHOOSE
RECHOSEN > RECHOOSE
RECIPE n directions for cooking a dish
RECIPES > RECIPE
RECIPIENT n person who receives something
RECIRCLE vb circle again
RECIRCLED > RECIRCLE
RECIRCLES > RECIRCLE
RECISION n act of cancelling or rescinding
RECISIONS > RECISION
RECIT n narrative
RECITABLE > RECITE

RECITAL n musical performance by a soloist or soloists

RECITALS > RECITAL

RECITE vb repeat (a poem, story, etc) aloud to an audience

RECITED > RECITE

RECITER > RECITE

RECITERS > RECITE

RECITES > RECITE

RECITING > RECITE

RECITS > RECIT

RECK vb mind or care about (something)

RECKAN adj strained, tormented, or twisted ▷ n chain or hook for hanging a pot over a fire

RECKANS > RECKAN

RECKED > RECK

RECKING > RECK

RECKLESS adj heedless of danger

RECKLING dialect word for > RUNT

RECKLINGS > RECKLING

RECKON vb consider or think

RECKONED > RECKON

RECKONER n any of various devices or tables used to facilitate reckoning, esp a ready reckoner

RECKONERS > RECKONER

RECKONING n counting or calculating

RECKONS > RECKON

RECKS > RECK

RECLAD vb cover in a different substance

RECLADDED > RECLAD

RECLADS > RECLAD

RECLAIM vb regain possession of ▷ n act of reclaiming or state of being reclaimed

RECLAIMED > RECLAIM

RECLAIMER > RECLAIM

RECLAIMS > RECLAIM

RECLAME n public acclaim or attention

RECLAMES > RECLAME

RECLASP vb clasp again

RECLASPED > RECLASP

RECLASPS > RECLASP

RECLEAN vb clean again

RECLEANED > RECLEAN

RECLEANS > RECLEAN

RECLIMB vb climb again

RECLIMBED > RECLIMB

RECLIMBS > RECLIMB

RECLINATE adj (esp of a leaf or stem) naturally curved or bent backwards so that the upper part rests on the ground

RECLINE vb rest in a leaning position

RECLINED > RECLINE

RECLINER n armchair with adjustable back

RECLINERS > RECLINER

RECLINES > RECLINE

RECLINING > RECLINE

RECLOSE vb close again

RECLOSED > RECLOSE

RECLOSES > RECLOSE

RECLOSING > RECLOSE

RECLOTHE vb clothe again

RECLOTHED > RECLOTHE

RECLOTHES > RECLOTHE

RECLUSE n person who avoids other people ▷ adj solitary

RECLUSELY > RECLUSE

RECLUSES > RECLUSE

RECLUSION > RECLUSE

RECLUSIVE > RECLUSE

RECLUSORY n recluse's dwelling or cell

RECOAL vb supply or be supplied with fresh coal

RECOALED > RECOAL

RECOALING > RECOAL

RECOALS > RECOAL

RECOAT vb coat again

RECOATED > RECOAT

RECOATING > RECOAT

RECOATS > RECOAT

RECOCK vb cock again

RECOCKED > RECOCK

RECOCKING > RECOCK

RECOCKS > RECOCK

RECODE vb put into a new code

RECODED > RECODE

RECODES > RECODE

RECODIFY vb codify again

RECODING > RECODE

RECOGNISE same as > RECOGNIZE

RECOGNIZE vb identify as (a person or thing) already known

RECOIL vb jerk or spring back ▷ n backward jerk

RECOILED > RECOIL

RECOILER > RECOIL

RECOILERS > RECOIL

RECOILING > RECOIL

RECOILS > RECOIL

RECOIN vb coin again

RECOINAGE n new coinage

RECOINED > RECOIN

RECOINING > RECOIN

RECOINS > RECOIN

RECOLLECT vb call back to mind, remember

RECOLLET n member of a particular Franciscan order

RECOLLETS > RECOLLET

RECOLOR same as > RECOLOUR

RECOLORED > RECOLOR

RECOLORS > RECOLOR

RECOLOUR vb give a new colour to

RECOLOURS > RECOLOUR

RECOMB vb comb again

RECOMBED > RECOMB

RECOMBINE vb join together again

RECOMBING > RECOMB

RECOMBS > RECOMB

RECOMFORT archaic word for > COMFORT

RECOMMEND vb advise or counsel

RECOMMIT vb send (a bill) back to a committee for further consideration

RECOMMITS > RECOMMIT

RECOMPACT vb compact again

RECOMPILE vb compile again

RECOMPOSE vb restore to composure or calmness

RECOMPUTE vb compute again

RECON vb make a preliminary survey

RECONCILE vb harmonize (conflicting beliefs etc)

RECONDITE adj difficult to understand

RECONDUCT vb conduct again

RECONFER vb confer again

RECONFERS > RECONFER

RECONFINE vb confine again

RECONFIRM vb confirm (an arrangement, agreement, etc) again

RECONNECT vb link or be linked together again

RECONNED > RECON

RECONNING > RECON

RECONQUER vb conquer again

RECONS > RECON

RECONSIGN vb consign again

RECONSOLE vb console again

RECONSULT vb consult again

RECONTACT vb contact again

RECONTOUR vb contour again

RECONVENE vb gather together again after an interval

RECONVERT vb change (something) back to a previous state or form

RECONVEY vb convey again

RECONVEYS > RECONVEY

RECONVICT vb convict again

RECOOK vb cook again

RECOOKED > RECOOK

RECOOKING > RECOOK

RECOOKS > RECOOK

RECOPIED > RECOPY

RECOPIES > RECOPY

RECOPY vb copy again

RECOPYING > RECOPY

RECORD n document or other thing that preserves information ▷ vb put in writing

RECORDED > RECORD

RECORDER n person or machine that records, esp audio or video material

RECORDERS > RECORDER

RECORDING n something, esp music, that has been recorded

RECORDIST n person that records

RECORDS > RECORD

RECORK vb cork again

RECORKED > RECORK

RECORKING > RECORK

RECORKS > RECORK

RECOUNT vb tell in detail

RECOUNTAL > RECOUNT

RECOUNTED > RECOUNT

RECOUNTER n narrator of a story

RECOUNTS > RECOUNT

RECOUP vb regain or make good (a loss)

RECOUPE vb (in law) keep back or withhold

RECOUPED > RECOUP

RECOUPES > RECOUPE

RECOUPING > RECOUP

RECOUPLE vb couple again

RECOUPLED > RECOUPLE

RECOUPLES > RECOUPLE

RECOUPS > RECOUP

RECOURE archaic variant of > RECOVER

RECOURED > RECOURE

RECOURES > RECOURE

RECOURING > RECOURE

RECOURSE archaic word for > RETURN

RECOURSED > RECOURSE

RECOURSES > RECOURSE

RECOVER vb become healthy again

RECOVERED > RECOVER

RECOVEREE n (in law) person found against in a recovery case

RECOVERER > RECOVER

RECOVEROR n (in law) person successfully demanding a right in a recovery case

RECOVERS > RECOVER

RECOVERY n act of recovering from sickness, a shock, or a setback

RECOWER archaic variant of > RECOVER

RECOWERED > RECOWER

RECOWERS > RECOWER

RECOYLE archaic spelling of > RECOIL

RECOYLED > RECOYLE

RECOYLES > RECOYLE

RECOYLING > RECOYLE

RECRATE vb crate again

RECRATED > RECRATE

RECRATES > RECRATE

RECRATING > RECRATE

RECREANCE > RECREANT

RECREANCY > RECREANT

RECREANT n disloyal or cowardly person ▷ adj cowardly

RECREANTS > RECREANT

RECREATE vb amuse (oneself or someone else)

RECREATED > RECREATE

RECREATES > RECREATE

RECREATOR > RECREATE

RECREMENT n any substance, such as bile, that is secreted from a part of the body and later reabsorbed

RECROSS vb move or go across (something) again

RECROSSED > RECROSS

RECROSSES > RECROSS

RECROWN vb crown again

RECROWNED > RECROWN

RECROWNS > RECROWN

RECRUIT vb enlist (new soldiers, members, etc) ▷ n newly enlisted soldier

r

RECRUITAL n act of recruiting

RECRUITED > RECRUIT

RECRUITER > RECRUIT

RECRUITS > RECRUIT

RECS > REC

RECTA > RECTUM

RECTAL adj of the rectum

RECTALLY > RECTAL

RECTANGLE n oblong four-sided figure with four right angles

RECTI > RECTUS

RECTIFIED > RECTIFY

RECTIFIER n electronic device, such as a semiconductor diode or valve, that converts an alternating current to a direct current by suppression or inversion of alternate half cycles

RECTIFIES > RECTIFY

RECTIFY vb put right, correct

RECTION n (in grammar) the determination of the form of one word by another word

RECTIONS > RECTION

RECTITIC > RECTITIS

RECTITIS n inflammation of the rectum

RECTITUDE n moral correctness

RECTO n right-hand page of a book

RECTOCELE n protrusion or herniation of the rectum into the vagina

RECTOR n member of the clergy in charge of a parish

RECTORAL adj of or relating to God's rule or to a rector

RECTORATE > RECTOR

RECTORESS n female rector or the wife or widow of a rector

RECTORIAL adj of or relating to a rector ▷ n election of a rector

RECTORIES > RECTORY

RECTORS > RECTOR

RECTORY n rector's house

RECTOS > RECTO

RECTRESS same as > RECTORESS

RECTRICES > RECTRIX

RECTRIX n any of the large stiff feathers of a bird's tail

RECTUM n final section of the large intestine

RECTUMS > RECTUM

RECTUS n straight muscle

RECUILE archaic variant of > RECOIL

RECUILED > RECUILE

RECUILES > RECUILE

RECUILING > RECUILE

RECULE archaic variant of > RECOIL

RECULED > RECULE

RECULES > RECULE

RECULING > RECULE

RECUMBENT adj lying down

RECUR vb happen again

RECURE vb archaic word for cure or recover

RECURED > RECURE

RECURES > RECURE

RECURING > RECURE

RECURRED > RECUR

RECURRENT adj happening or tending to happen again or repeatedly

RECURRING > RECUR

RECURS > RECUR

RECURSION n act or process of returning or running back

RECURSIVE > RECURSION

RECURVATE adj bent back

RECURVE vb curve or bend (something) back or down

RECURVED > RECURVE

RECURVES > RECURVE

RECURVING > RECURVE

RECUSAL n withdrawal of a judge from a case

RECUSALS > RECUSAL

RECUSANCE > RECUSANT

RECUSANCY > RECUSANT

RECUSANT n Roman Catholic who did not attend the services of the Church of England ▷ adj (formerly, of Catholics) refusing to attend services of the Church of England

RECUSANTS > RECUSANT

RECUSE vb (in law) object to or withdraw (a judge)

RECUSED > RECUSE

RECUSES > RECUSE

RECUSING > RECUSE

RECUT vb cut again

RECUTS > RECUT

RECUTTING > RECUT

RECYCLATE n recyclable material

RECYCLE vb reprocess (used materials) for further use ▷ n repetition of a fixed sequence of events

RECYCLED > RECYCLE

RECYCLER > RECYCLE

RECYCLERS > RECYCLE

RECYCLES > RECYCLE

RECYCLING n act of recycling

RECYCLIST > RECYCLE

RED adj of a colour varying from crimson to orange and seen in blood, fire, etc ▷ n red colour

REDACT vb compose or draft (an edict, proclamation, etc)

REDACTED > REDACT

REDACTING > REDACT

REDACTION > REDACT

REDACTOR > REDACT

REDACTORS > REDACT

REDACTS > REDACT

REDAMAGE vb damage again

REDAMAGED > REDAMAGE

REDAMAGES > REDAMAGE

REDAN n fortification of two parapets at a salient angle

REDANS > REDAN

REDARGUE vb archaic word for disprove or refute

REDARGUED > REDARGUE

REDARGUES > REDARGUE

REDATE vb change date of

REDATED > REDATE

REDATES > REDATE

REDATING > REDATE

REDBACK n small venomous Australian spider

REDBACKS > REDBACK

REDBAIT vb harass those with leftwing leanings

REDBAITED > REDBAIT

REDBAITER n person who harasses those with leftwing leanings

REDBAITS > REDBAIT

REDBAY n type of tree

REDBAYS > REDBAY

REDBELLY n any of various animals having red underparts

REDBIRD n type of bird, the male of which has bright red plumage

REDBIRDS > REDBIRD

REDBONE n type of American dog

REDBONES > REDBONE

REDBREAST n robin

REDBRICK n provincial British university of relatively recent foundation

REDBRICKS > REDBRICK

REDBUD n American tree with heart-shaped leaves

REDBUDS > REDBUD

REDBUG another name for > CHIGGER

REDBUGS > REDBUG

REDCAP n member of the military police

REDCAPS > REDCAP

REDCOAT n British soldier

REDCOATS > REDCOAT

REDD vb bring order to ▷ n act or an instance of redding

REDDED > REDD

REDDEN vb make or become red

REDDENDA > REDDENDUM

REDDENDO n Scottish legal clause specifying what duties are required in exchange for something

REDDENDOS > REDDENDO

REDDENDUM n legal clause specifying what shall be given in return for the granting of a lease

REDDENED > REDDEN

REDDENING > REDDEN

REDDENS > REDDEN

REDDER > REDD

REDDERS > REDD

REDDEST > RED

REDDIER > REDDY

REDDIEST > REDDY

REDDING > REDD

REDDINGS > REDD

REDDISH adj somewhat red

REDDISHLY > REDDISH

REDDLE same as > RUDDLE

REDDLED > REDDLE

REDDLEMAN same as > RUDDLEMAN

REDDLEMEN > REDDLEMAN

REDDLES > REDDLE

REDDLING > REDDLE

REDDS > REDD

REDDY adj reddish

REDE n advice or counsel ▷ vb advise

REDEAL vb deal again

REDEALING > REDEAL

REDEALS > REDEAL

REDEALT > REDEAL

REDEAR n variety of sunfish with a red flash above the gills

REDEARS > REDEAR

REDECIDE vb decide again

REDECIDED > REDECIDE

REDECIDES > REDECIDE

REDECRAFT n logic

REDED > REDE

REDEEM vb make up for

REDEEMED > REDEEM

REDEEMER > REDEEM

REDEEMERS > REDEEM

REDEEMING adj making up for faults or deficiencies

REDEEMS > REDEEM

REDEFEAT vb defeat again

REDEFEATS > REDEFEAT

REDEFECT vb defect back or again

REDEFECTS > REDEFECT

REDEFIED > REDEFY

REDEFIES > REDEFY

REDEFINE vb define (something) again or differently

REDEFINED > REDEFINE

REDEFINES > REDEFINE

REDEFY vb defy again

REDEFYING > REDEFY

REDELESS > REDE

REDELIVER vb deliver again

REDEMAND vb demand again

REDEMANDS > REDEMAND

REDENIED > REDENY

REDENIES > REDENY

REDENY vb deny again

REDENYING > REDENY

REDEPLOY vb assign to a new position or task

REDEPLOYS > REDEPLOY

REDEPOSIT vb deposit again

REDES > REDE

REDESCEND vb descend again

REDESIGN vb change the design of (something) ▷ n something that has been redesigned

REDESIGNS > REDESIGN

REDEVELOP vb rebuild or renovate (an area or building)

REDEYE n inferior whiskey

REDEYES > REDEYE

REDFIN n any of various small fishes with reddish fins that are popular aquarium fishes

REDFINS > REDFIN

REDFISH n male salmon that has recently spawned

REDFISHES > REDFISH

REDFOOT n fatal disease of newborn lambs

REDFOOTS > REDFOOT

REDHANDED adj in the act of doing something criminal, wrong, or shameful

REDHEAD n person with reddish hair

REDHEADED > REDHEAD

REDHEADS > REDHEAD

REDHORSE *n* type of fish

REDHORSES > REDHORSE

REDIA *n* parasitic larva of flukes

REDIAE > REDIA

REDIAL *vb* dial (a telephone number) again

REDIALED > REDIAL

REDIALING > REDIAL

REDIALLED > REDIAL

REDIALS > REDIAL

REDIAS > REDIA

REDICTATE *vb* dictate again

REDID > REDO

REDIGEST *vb* digest again

REDIGESTS > REDIGEST

REDIGRESS *vb* digress again

REDING > REDE

REDINGOTE *n* woman's coat with a close-fitting top and a full skirt

REDIP *vb* dip again

REDIPPED > REDIP

REDIPPING > REDIP

REDIPS > REDIP

REDIPT *archaic past form of* **>** REDIP

REDIRECT *vb* send in a new direction or course

REDIRECTS > REDIRECT

REDISCUSS *vb* discuss again

REDISPLAY *vb* display again

REDISPOSE *vb* dispose again

REDISTIL *vb* distil again

REDISTILL *US spelling of* **>** REDISTIL

REDISTILS > REDISTIL

REDIVIDE *vb* divide again

REDIVIDED > REDIVIDE

REDIVIDES > REDIVIDE

REDIVIVUS *adj* returned to life

REDIVORCE *vb* divorce again

REDLEG *n* derogatory term for a poor White person

REDLEGS > REDLEG

REDLINE *vb* refuse a loan to (a person or country) because of the presumed risks involved

REDLINED > REDLINE

REDLINER > REDLINE

REDLINERS > REDLINE

REDLINES > REDLINE

REDLINING > REDLINE

REDLY > RED

REDNECK *n* poor uneducated White farm worker ⊳ *adj* reactionary and bigoted

REDNECKED *adj* with a red neck

REDNECKS > REDNECK

REDNESS > RED

REDNESSES > RED

REDO *vb* do over again in order to improve ⊳ *n* instance of redoing something

REDOCK *vb* dock again

REDOCKED > REDOCK

REDOCKING > REDOCK

REDOCKS > REDOCK

REDOES > REDO

REDOING > REDO

REDOLENCE > REDOLENT

REDOLENCY > REDOLENT

REDOLENT *adj* reminiscent (of)

REDON *vb* don again

REDONE > REDO

REDONNED > REDON

REDONNING > REDON

REDONS > REDON

REDOS > REDO

REDOUBLE *vb* increase, multiply, or intensify ⊳ *n* act of redoubling

REDOUBLED > REDOUBLE

REDOUBLER > REDOUBLE

REDOUBLES > REDOUBLE

REDOUBT *n* small fort defending a hilltop or pass ⊳ *vb* fear

REDOUBTED > REDOUBT

REDOUBTS > REDOUBT

REDOUND *vb* cause advantage or disadvantage (to)

REDOUNDED > REDOUND

REDOUNDS > REDOUND

REDOUT *n* reddened vision caused by a rush of blood to the head

REDOUTS > REDOUT

REDOWA *n* Bohemian folk dance similar to the waltz

REDOWAS > REDOWA

REDOX *n* chemical reaction in which one substance is reduced and the other is oxidized

REDOXES > REDOX

REDPOLL *n* mostly grey-brown finch with a red crown and pink breast

REDPOLLS > REDPOLL

REDRAFT *vb* write a second copy of (a letter, proposal, essay, etc) ⊳ *n* second draft

REDRAFTED > REDRAFT

REDRAFTS > REDRAFT

REDRAW *vb* draw or draw up (something) again or differently

REDRAWER > REDRAW

REDRAWERS > REDRAW

REDRAWING > REDRAW

REDRAWN > REDRAW

REDRAWS > REDRAW

REDREAM *vb* dream again

REDREAMED > REDREAM

REDREAMS > REDREAM

REDREAMT > REDREAM

REDRESS *vb* make amends for ⊳ *n* compensation or amends

REDRESSAL *n* act of redressing

REDRESSED > REDRESS

REDRESSER > REDRESS

REDRESSES > REDRESS

REDRESSOR > REDRESS

REDREW > REDRAW

REDRIED > REDRY

REDRIES > REDRY

REDRILL *vb* drill again

REDRILLED > REDRILL

REDRILLS > REDRILL

REDRIVE *vb* drive again

REDRIVEN > REDRIVE

REDRIVES > REDRIVE

REDRIVING > REDRIVE

REDROOT *n* yellow-flowered bog plant whose roots yield a red dye

REDROOTS > REDROOT

REDROVE > REDRIVE

REDRY *vb* dry again

REDRYING > REDRY

REDS > RED

REDSEAR *same as* **>** REDSHORT

REDSHANK *n* large Eurasian sandpiper with red legs

REDSHANKS > REDSHANK

REDSHARE *n* red algae

REDSHIFT *n* shift in the lines of the spectrum of an astronomical object

REDSHIFTS > REDSHIFT

REDSHIRE *same as* **>** REDSHARE

REDSHIRT *vb* take a year out of a sports team

REDSHIRTS > REDSHIRT

REDSHORT *vb* become brittle at red-hot temperatures

REDSKIN *n* offensive term for a Native American

REDSKINS > REDSKIN

REDSTART *n* European bird of the thrush family

REDSTARTS > REDSTART

REDSTREAK *n* variety of apple

REDTAIL *n* variety of bird with red colouring on its tail

REDTAILS > REDTAIL

REDTOP *n* sensationalist tabloid newspaper

REDTOPS > REDTOP

REDUB *vb* fix or repair

REDUBBED > REDUB

REDUBBING > REDUB

REDUBS > REDUB

REDUCE *vb* bring down, lower

REDUCED > REDUCE

REDUCER *n* chemical solution used to lessen the density of a negative or print

REDUCERS > REDUCER

REDUCES > REDUCE

REDUCIBLE > REDUCE

REDUCIBLY > REDUCE

REDUCING > REDUCE

REDUCTANT *n* reducing agent

REDUCTASE *n* any enzyme that catalyses a biochemical reduction reaction

REDUCTION *n* act of reducing

REDUCTIVE *n* relating to chemical reduction

REDUCTOR *n* apparatus in which substances can be reduced

REDUCTORS > REDUCTOR

REDUIT *n* fortified part from which a garrison may fight on once an enemy has taken outworks

REDUITS > REDUIT

REDUNDANT *adj* (of a worker) no longer needed

REDUVIID *n* type of insect

REDUVIIDS > REDUVIID

REDUX *adj* brought back or returned

REDWARE *another name for* **>** KELP

REDWARES > REDWARE

REDWATER *n* tick-borne disease of cattle

REDWATERS > REDWATER

REDWING *n* small European thrush

REDWINGS > REDWING

REDWOOD *n* giant Californian conifer with reddish bark

REDWOODS > REDWOOD

REDYE *vb* dye again

REDYED > REDYE

REDYEING > REDYE

REDYES > REDYE

REE *n* Scots word for walled enclosure

REEARN *vb* earn again

REEARNED > REEARN

REEARNING > REEARN

REEARNS > REEARN

REEBOK *same as* **>** RHEBOK

REEBOKS > REEBOK

REECH *vb* (in dialect) smoke

REECHED > REECH

REECHES > REECH

REECHIE *same as* **>** REECHY

REECHIER > REECHY

REECHIEST > REECHY

REECHING > REECH

REECHO *vb* echo again

REECHOED > REECHO

REECHOES > REECHO

REECHOING > REECHO

REECHY *adj* (in dialect) smoky

REED *n* tall grass that grows in swamps and shallow water

REEDBED *n* area of wetland with reeds growing in it

REEDBEDS > REEDBED

REEDBIRD *n* any of several birds that frequent reed beds, esp (in the US and Canada) the bobolink

REEDBIRDS > REEDBIRD

REEDBUCK *n* buff-coloured African antelope with inward-curving horns

REEDBUCKS > REEDBUCK

REEDE *obsolete variant of* **>** RED

REEDED > REED

REEDEN *adj* of or consisting of reeds

REEDER *n* thatcher

REEDERS > REEDER

REEDES > REEDE

REEDIER > REEDY

REEDIEST > REEDY

REEDIFIED > REEDIFY

REEDIFIES > REEDIFY

REEDIFY *vb* edify again or rebuild

REEDILY > REEDY

REEDINESS > REEDY

REEDING *n* set of small semicircular architectural mouldings

r

READINGS > READING
REEDIT vb edit again
REEDITED > REEDIT
REEDITING > REEDIT
REEDITION n new edition
REEDITS > REEDIT
REEDLIKE adj resembling a reed
REEDLING n tawny titlike Eurasian songbird common in reed beds
REEDLINGS > REEDLING
REEDMAN n musician who plays a wind instrument that has a reed
REEDMEN > REEDMAN
REEDS > REED
REEDSTOP n organ stop that controls a rank of reed pipes
REEDSTOPS > REEDSTOP
REEDUCATE vb educate again
REEDY adj harsh and thin in tone
REEF n ridge of rock or coral near the surface of the sea ▷ vb roll up part of a sail
REEFABLE > REEF
REEFED > REEF
REEFER n short thick jacket worn esp by sailors
REEFERS > REEFER
REEFIER > REEFY
REEFIEST > REEFY
REEFING > REEF
REEFINGS > REEF
REEFPOINT n short piece of rope for securing a sail
REEFS > REEF
REEFY adj with reefs
REEJECT vb eject again
REEJECTED > REEJECT
REEJECTS > REEJECT
REEK vb smell strongly ▷ n strong unpleasant smell
REEKED > REEK
REEKER > REEK
REEKERS > REEK
REEKIE same as **>** REEKY
REEKIER > REEKY
REEKIEST > REEKY
REEKING > REEK
REEKINGLY > REEK
REEKS > REEK
REEKY adj steamy or smoky
REEL n cylindrical object on which film, tape, thread, or wire is wound ▷ vb stagger, sway, or whirl
REELABLE > REEL
REELECT vb elect again
REELECTED > REELECT
REELECTS > REELECT
REELED > REEL
REELER > REEL
REELERS > REEL
REELEVATE vb elevate again
REELING > REEL
REELINGLY > REEL
REELINGS > REEL
REELMAN n (formerly) member of a beach life-saving team operating a winch
REELMEN > REELMAN

REELS > REEL
REEMBARK vb embark again
REEMBARKS > REEMBARK
REEMBODY vb embody again
REEMBRACE vb embrace again
REEMERGE vb emerge again
REEMERGED > REEMERGE
REEMERGES > REEMERGE
REEMIT vb emit again
REEMITS > REEMIT
REEMITTED > REEMIT
REEMPLOY vb employ again
REEMPLOYS > REEMPLOY
REEN n ditch, esp a drainage channel
REENACT vb enact again
REENACTED > REENACT
REENACTOR > REENACT
REENACTS > REENACT
REENDOW vb endow again
REENDOWED > REENDOW
REENDOWS > REENDOW
REENFORCE vb enforce again
REENGAGE vb engage again
REENGAGED > REENGAGE
REENGAGES > REENGAGE
REENGRAVE vb engrave again
REENJOY vb enjoy again
REENJOYED > REENJOY
REENJOYS > REENJOY
REENLARGE vb enlarge again
REENLIST vb enlist again
REENLISTS > REENLIST
REENROLL vb enrol again
REENROLLS > REENROLL
REENS > REEN
REENSLAVE vb enslave again
REENTER vb enter again
REENTERED > REENTER
REENTERS > REENTER
REENTRANT n reentering angle ▷ adj (of an angle) pointing inwards
REENTRIES > REENTRY
REENTRY n return of a spacecraft into the earth's atmosphere
REEQUIP vb equip again
REEQUIPS > REEQUIP
REERECT vb erect again
REERECTED > REERECT
REERECTS > REERECT
REES > REE
REEST vb (esp of horses) to be noisily uncooperative
REESTED > REEST
REESTIER > REESTY
REESTIEST > REESTY
REESTING > REEST
REESTS > REEST
REESTY same as **>** REASTY
REEVE n local representative of the king in a shire until the early 11th century ▷ vb pass (a rope or cable) through an eye or other narrow opening
REEVED > REEVE
REEVES > REEVE
REEVESHIP n office of a reeve
REEVING > REEVE

REEVOKE vb evoke again
REEVOKED > REEVOKE
REEVOKES > REEVOKE
REEVOKING > REEVOKE
REEXAMINE vb examine again
REEXECUTE vb execute again
REEXHIBIT vb exhibit again
REEXPEL vb expel again
REEXPELS > REEXPEL
REEXPLAIN vb explain again
REEXPLORE vb explore again
REEXPORT vb export again
REEXPORTS > REEXPORT
REEXPOSE vb expose again
REEXPOSED > REEXPOSE
REEXPOSES > REEXPOSE
REEXPRESS vb express again
REF n referee in sport ▷ vb referee
REFACE vb repair or renew the facing of (a wall)
REFACED > REFACE
REFACES > REFACE
REFACING > REFACE
REFALL vb fall again
REFALLEN > REFALL
REFALLING > REFALL
REFALLS > REFALL
REFASHION vb give a new form to (something)
REFASTEN vb fasten again
REFASTENS > REFASTEN
REFECT vb archaic word for restore or refresh with food and drink
REFECTED > REFECT
REFECTING > REFECT
REFECTION n refreshment with food and drink
REFECTIVE > REFECT
REFECTORY n room for meals in a college etc
REFECTS > REFECT
REFED > REFEED
REFEED vb feed again
REFEEDING n act or instance of feeding again
REFEEDS > REFEED
REFEEL vb feel again
REFEELING > REFEEL
REFEELS > REFEEL
REFEL vb refute
REFELL > REFALL
REFELLED > REFEL
REFELLING > REFEL
REFELS > REFEL
REFELT > REFEEL
REFENCE vb fence again
REFENCED > REFENCE
REFENCES > REFENCE
REFENCING > REFENCE
REFER vb allude (to)
REFERABLE > REFER
REFEREE n umpire in sports, esp soccer or boxing ▷ vb act as referee of
REFEREED > REFEREE
REFEREES > REFEREE
REFERENCE n act of referring

REFERENDA pl n polls to determine the view of the electorate on something; referendums
REFERENT n object or idea to which a word or phrase refers
REFERENTS > REFERENT
REFERRAL > REFER
REFERRALS > REFER
REFERRED > REFER
REFERRER > REFER
REFERRERS > REFER
REFERRING > REFER
REFERS > REFER
REFFED > REF
REFFING n act or instance of refereeing a sports match
REFFINGS > REFFING
REFFO n offensive name for a European refugee after World War II
REFFOS > REFFO
REFI n refinancing of a debt
REFIGHT vb fight again ▷ n second or new fight
REFIGHTS > REFIGHT
REFIGURE vb figure again
REFIGURED > REFIGURE
REFIGURES > REFIGURE
REFILE vb file again
REFILED > REFILE
REFILES > REFILE
REFILING > REFILE
REFILL vb fill again ▷ n second or subsequent filling
REFILLED > REFILL
REFILLING > REFILL
REFILLS > REFILL
REFILM vb film again
REFILMED > REFILM
REFILMING > REFILM
REFILMS > REFILM
REFILTER vb filter again
REFILTERS > REFILTER
REFINABLE > REFINE
REFINANCE vb finance again
REFIND vb find again
REFINDING > REFIND
REFINDS > REFIND
REFINE vb purify
REFINED adj cultured or polite
REFINEDLY > REFINED
REFINER n person, device, or substance that removes impurities, etc
REFINERS > REFINER
REFINERY n place where sugar, oil, etc is refined
REFINES > REFINE
REFINING > REFINE
REFININGS > REFINE
REFINISH vb finish again
REFIRE vb fire again
REFIRED > REFIRE
REFIRES > REFIRE
REFIRING > REFIRE
REFIS > REFI
REFIT vb make ready for use again by repairing or reequipping ▷ n repair or reequipping for further use
REFITMENT > REFIT
REFITS > REFIT
REFITTED > REFIT

REFITTING > REFIT

REFIX vb fix again

REFIXED > REFIX

REFIXES > REFIX

REFIXING > REFIX

REFLAG vb flag again

REFLAGGED > REFLAG

REFLAGS > REFLAG

REFLATE vb inflate or be inflated again

REFLATED > REFLATE

REFLATES > REFLATE

REFLATING > REFLATE

REFLATION n increase in the supply of money and credit designed to encourage economic activity

REFLECT vb throw back, esp rays of light, heat, etc

REFLECTED > REFLECT

REFLECTER n archaic word for a critic

REFLECTOR n polished surface for reflecting light etc

REFLECTS > REFLECT

REFLET n iridescent glow or lustre, as on ceramic ware

REFLETS > REFLET

REFLEW > REFLY

REFLEX n involuntary response to a stimulus or situation ▷ adj (of a muscular action) involuntary ▷ vb bend, turn, or reflect backwards

REFLEXED > REFLEX

REFLEXES > REFLEX

REFLEXING > REFLEX

REFLEXION n act of reflecting or the state of being reflected

REFLEXIVE adj denoting a pronoun that refers back to the subject of a sentence or clause ▷ n reflexive pronoun or verb

REFLEXLY > REFLEX

REFLIES > REFLY

REFLOAT vb float again

REFLOATED > REFLOAT

REFLOATS > REFLOAT

REFLOOD vb flood again

REFLOODED > REFLOOD

REFLOODS > REFLOOD

REFLOW vb flow again

REFLOWED > REFLOW

REFLOWER vb flower again

REFLOWERS > REFLOWER

REFLOWING > REFLOW

REFLOWN > REFLY

REFLOWS > REFLOW

REFLUENCE > REFLUENT

REFLUENT adj flowing back

REFLUX vb boil in a vessel attached to a condenser, so that the vapour condenses and flows back in ▷ n act of refluxing

REFLUXED > REFLUX

REFLUXES > REFLUX

REFLUXING > REFLUX

REFLY vb fly again

REFLYING > REFLY

REFOCUS vb focus again or anew

REFOCUSED > REFOCUS

REFOCUSES > REFOCUS

REFOLD vb fold again

REFOLDED > REFOLD

REFOLDING > REFOLD

REFOLDS > REFOLD

REFOOT vb foot again

REFOOTED > REFOOT

REFOOTING > REFOOT

REFOOTS > REFOOT

REFOREST vb replant (an area that was formerly forested) with trees

REFORESTS > REFOREST

REFORGE vb forge again

REFORGED > REFORGE

REFORGES > REFORGE

REFORGING > REFORGE

REFORM n improvement ▷ vb improve

REFORMADE archaic variant of > REFORMADO

REFORMADO n formerly, an officer whose troops have been disbanded

REFORMAT vb format again

REFORMATE n gas formed in certain processes

REFORMATS > REFORMAT

REFORMED > REFORM

REFORMER n > REFORM

REFORMERS > REFORM

REFORMING > REFORM

REFORMISM n doctrine or movement advocating reform, esp political or religious reform, rather than abolition

REFORMIST > REFORMISM

REFORMS > REFORM

REFORTIFY vb fortify again or further

REFOUGHT > REFIGHT

REFOUND vb found again

REFOUNDED > REFOUND

REFOUNDER > REFOUND

REFOUNDS > REFOUND

REFRACT vb change the course of (light etc) passing from one medium to another

REFRACTED > REFRACT

REFRACTOR n object or material that refracts

REFRACTS > REFRACT

REFRAIN n frequently repeated part of a song ▷ vb abstain (from action)

REFRAINED > REFRAIN

REFRAINER > REFRAIN

REFRAINS > REFRAIN

REFRAME vb support or enclose (a picture, photograph, etc) in a new or different frame

REFRAMED > REFRAME

REFRAMES > REFRAME

REFRAMING > REFRAME

REFREEZE vb freeze or be frozen again after having defrosted

REFREEZES > REFREEZE

REFRESH vb revive or reinvigorate, as through food, drink, or rest

REFRESHED > REFRESH

REFRESHEN vb freshen again

REFRESHER n something that refreshes, such as a cold drink

REFRESHES > REFRESH

REFRIED > REFRY

REFRIES > REFRY

REFRINGE formerly used to mean > REFRACT

REFRINGED > REFRINGE

REFRINGES > REFRINGE

REFRONT vb put a new front on

REFRONTED > REFRONT

REFRONTS > REFRONT

REFROZE > REFREEZE

REFROZEN > REFREEZE

REFRY vb fry again

REFRYING > REFRY

REFS > REF

REFT > REAVE

REFUEL vb supply or be supplied with fresh fuel

REFUELED > REFUEL

REFUELING n act of refueling

REFUELLED > REFUEL

REFUELS > REFUEL

REFUGE n (source of) shelter or protection ▷ vb take refuge or give refuge to

REFUGED > REFUGE

REFUGEE n person who seeks refuge, esp in a foreign country

REFUGEES > REFUGEE

REFUGES > REFUGE

REFUGIA > REFUGIUM

REFUGING > REFUGE

REFUGIUM n region that has remained unaltered by a climatic change affecting surrounding regions

REFULGENT adj shining, radiant

REFUND vb pay back ▷ n return of money

REFUNDED > REFUND

REFUNDER > REFUND

REFUNDERS > REFUND

REFUNDING n act or instance of returning money spent

REFUNDS > REFUND

REFURB vb refurbish ▷ n (act or instance of) refurbishment

REFURBED > REFURB

REFURBING > REFURB

REFURBISH vb renovate and brighten up

REFURBS > REFURB

REFURNISH vb furnish again

REFUSABLE > REFUSE

REFUSAL n denial of anything demanded or offered

REFUSALS > REFUSAL

REFUSE vb decline, deny, or reject ▷ n rubbish or useless matter

REFUSED > REFUSE

REFUSENIK n person who refuses to obey a law or cooperate with the government because of strong beliefs

REFUSER > REFUSE

REFUSERS > REFUSE

REFUSES > REFUSE

REFUSING > REFUSE

REFUSION n new or further fusion

REFUSIONS > REFUSION

REFUSNIK same as > REFUSENIK

REFUSNIKS > REFUSNIK

REFUTABLE > REFUTE

REFUTABLY > REFUTE

REFUTAL n act or process of refuting

REFUTALS > REFUTAL

REFUTE vb disprove

REFUTED > REFUTE

REFUTER > REFUTE

REFUTERS > REFUTE

REFUTES > REFUTE

REFUTING > REFUTE

REG n large expanse of stony desert terrain

REGAIN vb get back or recover ▷ n process of getting something back, esp lost weight

REGAINED > REGAIN

REGAINER > REGAIN

REGAINERS > REGAIN

REGAINING > REGAIN

REGAINS > REGAIN

REGAL adj of or like a king or queen ▷ n portable organ equipped only with small reed pipes

REGALE vb entertain (someone) with stories etc ▷ n feast

REGALED > REGALE

REGALER > REGALE

REGALERS > REGALE

REGALES > REGALE

REGALIA pl n ceremonial emblems of royalty or high office

REGALIAN adj royal

REGALIAS > REGALIA

REGALING > REGALE

REGALISM n principle that the sovereign has supremacy in church affairs

REGALISMS > REGALISM

REGALIST > REGALISM

REGALISTS > REGALISM

REGALITY n state or condition of being royal

REGALLY > REGAL

REGALNESS > REGAL

REGALS > REGAL

REGAR same as > REGUR

REGARD vb consider ▷ n respect or esteem

REGARDANT adj (of a beast) shown looking backwards over its shoulder

REGARDED > REGARD

REGARDER > REGARD

REGARDERS > REGARD

REGARDFUL adj showing regard (for)

REGARDING prep on the subject of

REGARDS > REGARD

REGARS > REGAR

REGATHER vb gather again

REGATHERS > REGATHER

REGATTA n meeting for yacht or boat races
REGATTAS > REGATTA
REGAUGE vb gauge again
REGAUGED > REGAUGE
REGAUGES > REGAUGE
REGAUGING > REGAUGE
REGAVE > REGIVE
REGEAR vb readjust
REGEARED > REGEAR
REGEARING > REGEAR
REGEARS > REGEAR
REGELATE vb undergo or cause to undergo regelation, a type of refreezing
REGELATED > REGELATE
REGELATES > REGELATE
REGENCE old variant of > REGENCY
REGENCES > REGENCE
REGENCIES > REGENCY
REGENCY n status or period of office of a regent
REGENT n ruler of a kingdom during the absence, childhood, or illness of its monarch ▷ adj ruling as a regent
REGENTAL > REGENT
REGENTS > REGENT
REGES > REX
REGEST n archaic word for register ▷ vb register
REGESTED > REGEST
REGESTING > REGEST
REGESTS > REGEST
REGGAE n style of Jamaican popular music with a strong beat
REGGAES > REGGAE
REGGAETON n popular music genre from Puerto Rico
REGGO same as > REGO
REGGOS > REGGO
REGICIDAL > REGICIDE
REGICIDE n killing of a king
REGICIDES > REGICIDE
REGIE n government-directed management or government monopoly
REGIES > REGIE
REGIFT vb give (a previously received gift) to someone else
REGIFTED > REGIFT
REGIFTER n person who regifts something
REGIFTERS > REGIFTER
REGIFTING > REGIFT
REGIFTS > REGIFT
REGILD vb gild again
REGILDED > REGILD
REGILDING > REGILD
REGILDS > REGILD
REGILT archaic past form of > REGILD
REGIME n system of government
REGIMEN n prescribed system of diet etc
REGIMENS > REGIMEN
REGIMENT n organized body of troops as a unit of the army ▷ vb force discipline or order on, esp in a domineering manner

REGIMENTS > REGIMENT
REGIMES > REGIME
REGIMINAL adj regimen-related
REGINA n queen
REGINAE > REGINA
REGINAL adj queenly
REGINAS > REGINA
REGION n administrative division of a country
REGIONAL adj of, characteristic of, or limited to a region ▷ n regional heat of a competition
REGIONALS > REGIONAL
REGIONARY same as > REGIONAL
REGIONS > REGION
REGISSEUR n official in a dance company with varying duties, usually including directing productions
REGISTER n (book containing) an official list or record of things ▷ vb enter in a register or set down in writing
REGISTERS > REGISTER
REGISTRAR n keeper of official records
REGISTRY n place where official records are kept
REGIUS adj as in regius professor Crown-appointed holder of a university chair
REGIVE vb give again or back
REGIVEN > REGIVE
REGIVES > REGIVE
REGIVING > REGIVE
REGLAZE vb glaze again
REGLAZED > REGLAZE
REGLAZES > REGLAZE
REGLAZING > REGLAZE
REGLET n flat narrow architectural moulding
REGLETS > REGLET
REGLORIFY vb glorify again
REGLOSS vb gloss again or give a new gloss to
REGLOSSED > REGLOSS
REGLOSSES > REGLOSS
REGLOW vb glow again
REGLOWED > REGLOW
REGLOWING > REGLOW
REGLOWS > REGLOW
REGLUE vb glue again
REGLUED > REGLUE
REGLUES > REGLUE
REGLUING > REGLUE
REGMA n type of fruit with cells that break open and break away when ripe
REGMAKER n drink taken to relieve the symptoms of a hangover
REGMAKERS > REGMAKER
REGMATA > REGMA
REGNA > REGNUM
REGNAL adj of a sovereign, reign, or kingdom
REGNANCY > REGNANT
REGNANT adj reigning
REGNUM n reign or rule
REGO n registration of a motor vehicle

REGOLITH n layer of loose material covering the bedrock of the earth and moon
REGOLITHS > REGOLITH
REGORGE vb vomit up
REGORGED > REGORGE
REGORGES > REGORGE
REGORGING > REGORGE
REGOS > REGO
REGOSOL n type of azonal soil
REGOSOLS > REGOSOL
REGRADE vb grade again
REGRADED > REGRADE
REGRADES > REGRADE
REGRADING > REGRADE
REGRAFT vb graft again
REGRAFTED > REGRAFT
REGRAFTS > REGRAFT
REGRANT vb grant again
REGRANTED > REGRANT
REGRANTS > REGRANT
REGRATE vb buy up (commodities) in advance so as to raise their price for resale
REGRATED > REGRATE
REGRATER > REGRATE
REGRATERS > REGRATE
REGRATES > REGRATE
REGRATING > REGRATE
REGRATOR > REGRATE
REGRATORS > REGRATE
REGREDE vb go back
REGREDED > REGREDE
REGREDES > REGREDE
REGREDING > REGREDE
REGREEN vb green again
REGREENED > REGREEN
REGREENS > REGREEN
REGREET vb greet again or return greetings of
REGREETED > REGREET
REGREETS > REGREET
REGRESS vb revert to a former worse condition ▷ n return to a former and worse condition
REGRESSED > REGRESS
REGRESSES > REGRESS
REGRESSOR > REGRESS
REGRET vb feel sorry about ▷ n feeling of repentance, guilt, or sorrow
REGRETFUL > REGRET
REGRETS > REGRET
REGRETTED > REGRET
REGRETTER > REGRET
REGREW > REGROW
REGRIND vb grind again
REGRINDS > REGRIND
REGROOM vb groom again
REGROOMED > REGROOM
REGROOMS > REGROOM
REGROOVE vb groove again
REGROOVED > REGROOVE
REGROOVES > REGROOVE
REGROUND > REGRIND
REGROUP vb reorganize (military forces) after an attack or a defeat
REGROUPED > REGROUP
REGROUPS > REGROUP
REGROW vb grow or be grown again after having been cut or having died or withered

REGROWING > REGROW
REGROWN > REGROW
REGROWS > REGROW
REGROWTH n growing back of hair, plants, etc
REGROWTHS > REGROWTH
REGS > REG
REGUERDON vb reward
REGULA n rule
REGULABLE adj able to be regulated
REGULAE > REGULA
REGULAR adj normal, customary, or usual ▷ n regular soldier
REGULARLY > REGULAR
REGULARS > REGULAR
REGULATE vb control, esp by rules
REGULATED > REGULATE
REGULATES > REGULATE
REGULATOR n device that automatically controls pressure, temperature, etc
REGULI > REGULUS
REGULINE > REGULUS
REGULISE variant spelling of > REGULIZE
REGULISED > REGULISE
REGULISES > REGULISE
REGULIZE vb turn into regulus
REGULIZED > REGULIZE
REGULIZES > REGULIZE
REGULO n any of a number of temperatures to which a gas oven may be set
REGULOS > REGULO
REGULUS n impure metal forming beneath the slag during the smelting of ores
REGULUSES > REGULUS
REGUR n black loamy Indian soil
REGURS > REGUR
REH n (in India) salty surface crust on the soil
REHAB vb help (a person) to readapt to society or a new job ▷ n treatment or help given to an addict, etc
REHABBED > REHAB
REHABBER > REHAB
REHABBERS > REHAB
REHABBING > REHAB
REHABS > REHAB
REHAMMER vb hammer again
REHAMMERS > REHAMMER
REHANDLE vb handle again
REHANDLED > REHANDLE
REHANDLES > REHANDLE
REHANG vb hang again
REHANGED > REHANG
REHANGING > REHANG
REHANGS > REHANG
REHARDEN vb harden again
REHARDENS > REHARDEN
REHASH vb rework or reuse ▷ n old ideas presented in a new form
REHASHED > REHASH
REHASHES > REHASH
REHASHING > REHASH
REHEAR vb hear again
REHEARD > REHEAR
REHEARING > REHEAR

REHEARS > REHEAR

REHEARSAL *n* preparatory practice session

REHEARSE *vb* practise (a play, concert, etc)

REHEARSED > REHEARSE

REHEARSER > REHEARSE

REHEARSES > REHEARSE

REHEAT *vb* heat or be heated again

REHEATED > REHEAT

REHEATER > REHEAT

REHEATERS > REHEAT

REHEATING > REHEAT

REHEATS > REHEAT

REHEEL *vb* put a new heel or new heels on

REHEELED > REHEEL

REHEELING > REHEEL

REHEELS > REHEEL

REHEM *vb* hem again

REHEMMED > REHEM

REHEMMING > REHEM

REHEMS > REHEM

REHINGE *vb* put a new hinge or new hinges on

REHINGED > REHINGE

REHINGES > REHINGE

REHINGING > REHINGE

REHIRE *vb* hire again

REHIRED > REHIRE

REHIRES > REHIRE

REHIRING > REHIRE

REHOBOAM *n* wine bottle holding the equivalent of six normal bottles (approximately 156 ounces)

REHOBOAMS > REHOBOAM

REHOME *vb* find a new home for (esp a pet)

REHOMED > REHOME

REHOMES > REHOME

REHOMING *n* act of rehoming

REHOMINGS > REHOMING

REHOUSE *vb* provide with a new (and better) home

REHOUSED > REHOUSE

REHOUSES > REHOUSE

REHOUSING > REHOUSE

REHS > REH

REHUNG > REHANG

REHYDRATE *vb* hydrate again

REI *n* name for a former Portuguese coin

REIF *n* Scots word meaning robbery or plunder

REIFIED > REIFY

REIFIER > REIFY

REIFIERS > REIFY

REIFIES > REIFY

REIFS > REIF

REIFY *vb* consider or make (an abstract idea or concept) real or concrete

REIFYING > REIFY

REIGN *n* period of a sovereign's rule ▷ *vb* rule (a country)

REIGNED > REIGN

REIGNING > REIGN

REIGNITE *vb* catch fire or cause to catch fire again

REIGNITED > REIGNITE

REIGNITES > REIGNITE

REIGNS > REIGN

REIK *Scots word for* > SMOKE

REIKI *n* form of therapy to encourage healing or restore wellbeing

REIKIS > REIKI

REIKS > REIK

REILLUME *vb* relight

REILLUMED > REILLUME

REILLUMES > REILLUME

REIMAGE *vb* image again

REIMAGED > REIMAGE

REIMAGES > REIMAGE

REIMAGINE *vb* imagine again

REIMAGING > REIMAGE

REIMBURSE *vb* refund, pay back

REIMMERSE *vb* immerse again

REIMPLANT *vb* implant again

REIMPORT *vb* import (goods manufactured from exported raw materials) ▷ *n* act of reimporting

REIMPORTS > REIMPORT

REIMPOSE *vb* establish previously imposed laws, controls, etc again

REIMPOSED > REIMPOSE

REIMPOSES > REIMPOSE

REIN *vb* check or manage with reins

REINCITE *vb* incite again

REINCITED > REINCITE

REINCITES > REINCITE

REINCUR *vb* incur again

REINCURS > REINCUR

REINDEER *n* deer of Arctic regions with large branched antlers

REINDEERS > REINDEER

REINDEX *vb* index again

REINDEXED > REINDEX

REINDEXES > REINDEX

REINDICT *vb* indict again

REINDICTS > REINDICT

REINDUCE *vb* induce again

REINDUCED > REINDUCE

REINDUCES > REINDUCE

REINDUCT *vb* induct again

REINDUCTS > REINDUCT

REINED > REIN

REINETTE *n* variety of apple

REINETTES > REINETTE

REINFECT *vb* infect or contaminate again

REINFECTS > REINFECT

REINFLAME *vb* inflame again

REINFLATE *vb* inflate again

REINFORCE *vb* give added emphasis to

REINFORM *vb* inform again

REINFORMS > REINFORM

REINFUND *vb* archaic word for pour in again

REINFUNDS > REINFUND

REINFUSE *vb* infuse again

REINFUSED > REINFUSE

REINFUSES > REINFUSE

REINHABIT *vb* inhabit again

REINING > REIN

REINJECT *vb* inject again

REINJECTS > REINJECT

REINJURE *vb* injure again

REINJURED > REINJURE

REINJURES > REINJURE

REINJURY *n* further injury

REINK *vb* ink again

REINKED > REINK

REINKING > REINK

REINKS > REINK

REINLESS > REIN

REINS *pl n* narrow straps attached to a bit to guide a horse

REINSERT *vb* insert again

REINSERTS > REINSERT

REINSMAN *n* driver in a trotting race

REINSMEN > REINSMAN

REINSPECT *vb* inspect again

REINSPIRE *vb* inspire again

REINSTAL *same as* > REINSTALL

REINSTALL *vb* put in place and connect (machinery, equipment, etc) again

REINSTALS > REINSTAL

REINSTATE *vb* restore to a former position

REINSURE *vb* insure again

REINSURED > REINSURE

REINSURER > REINSURE

REINSURES > REINSURE

REINTER *vb* inter again

REINTERS > REINTER

REINVADE *vb* invade again

REINVADED > REINVADE

REINVADES > REINVADE

REINVENT *vb* replace (a product, etc) with an entirely new version

REINVENTS > REINVENT

REINVEST *vb* put back profits from a previous investment into the same enterprise

REINVESTS > REINVEST

REINVITE *vb* invite again

REINVITED > REINVITE

REINVITES > REINVITE

REINVOKE *vb* invoke again

REINVOKED > REINVOKE

REINVOKES > REINVOKE

REINVOLVE *vb* involve again

REIRD *Scots word for* > DIN

REIRDS > REIRD

REIS *n* small branch

REISES > REIS

REISHI *n* type of mushroom with a shiny cap

REISHIS > REISHI

REISSUE *n* book, record, etc, that is released again after being unavailable ▷ *vb* release (a book, record, etc) again after a period of unavailability

REISSUED > REISSUE

REISSUER > REISSUE

REISSUERS > REISSUE

REISSUES > REISSUE

REISSUING > REISSUE

REIST *same as* > REEST

REISTAFEL *same as* > RIJSTAFEL

REISTED > REIST

REISTING > REIST

REISTS > REIST

REITBOK *same as* > REEDBUCK

REITBOKS > REITBOK

REITER *n* soldier in the German cavalry ▷ *vb* repeat something

REITERANT > REITERATE

REITERATE *vb* repeat again and again

REITERED > REITER

REITERING > REITER

REITERS > REITER

REIVE *vb* go on a plundering raid

REIVED > REIVE

REIVER > REIVE

REIVERS > REIVE

REIVES > REIVE

REIVING *n* act of going on a plundering raid

REIVINGS > REIVING

REJACKET *n* put a new jacket on

REJACKETS > REJACKET

REJECT *vb* refuse to accept or believe ▷ *n* person or thing rejected as not up to standard

REJECTED > REJECT

REJECTEE *n* someone who has been rejected

REJECTEES > REJECTEE

REJECTER > REJECT

REJECTERS > REJECT

REJECTING > REJECT

REJECTION > REJECT

REJECTIVE > REJECT

REJECTOR > REJECT

REJECTORS > REJECT

REJECTS > REJECT

REJIG *vb* reequip (a factory or plant) ▷ *n* act or process of rejigging

REJIGGED > REJIG

REJIGGER > REJIG

REJIGGERS > REJIG

REJIGGING > REJIG

REJIGS > REJIG

REJOICE *vb* feel or express great happiness

REJOICED > REJOICE

REJOICER > REJOICE

REJOICERS > REJOICE

REJOICES > REJOICE

REJOICING > REJOICE

REJOIN *vb* join again

REJOINDER *n* answer, retort

REJOINED > REJOIN

REJOINING > REJOIN

REJOINS > REJOIN

REJON *n* bullfighting lance

REJONEO *n* bullfighting activity in which a mounted bullfighter spears the bull with lances

REJONEOS > REJONEO

REJONES > REJON

REJOURN *vb* archaic word meaning postpone or adjourn

REJOURNED > REJOURN

REJOURNS > REJOURN

REJUDGE *vb* judge again

REJUDGED > REJUDGE

REJUDGES > REJUDGE

REJUDGING > REJUDGE

r

REJUGGLE vb juggle again
REJUGGLED > REJUGGLE
REJUGGLES > REJUGGLE
REJUSTIFY vb justify again
REKE same as > RECK
REKED > REKE
REKES > REKE
REKEY vb key again
REKEYED > REKEY
REKEYING > REKEY
REKEYS > REKEY
REKINDLE vb arouse former emotions or interests
REKINDLED > REKINDLE
REKINDLES > REKINDLE
REKING > REKE
REKNIT vb knit again
REKNITS > REKNIT
REKNITTED > REKNIT
REKNOT vb knot again
REKNOTS > REKNOT
REKNOTTED > REKNOT
RELABEL vb label again
RELABELED > RELABEL
RELABELS > RELABEL
RELACE vb lace again
RELACED > RELACE
RELACES > RELACE
RELACHE n break
RELACHES > RELACHE
RELACING > RELACE
RELACQUER vb apply a new coat of lacquer to
RELAID > RELAY
RELAND vb land again
RELANDED > RELAND
RELANDING > RELAND
RELANDS > RELAND
RELAPSE vb fall back into bad habits, illness, etc ▷ n return of bad habits, illness, etc
RELAPSED > RELAPSE
RELAPSER > RELAPSE
RELAPSERS > RELAPSE
RELAPSES > RELAPSE
RELAPSING > RELAPSE
RELATA > RELATUM
RELATABLE > RELATE
RELATE vb establish a relation between
RELATED adj linked by kinship or marriage
RELATEDLY > RELATED
RELATER > RELATE
RELATERS > RELATE
RELATES > RELATE
RELATING > RELATE
RELATION n connection between things
RELATIONS pl n social or political dealings between individuals or groups
RELATIVAL adj of or relating to a relative
RELATIVE adj true to a certain degree or extent ▷ n person connected by blood or marriage
RELATIVES > RELATIVE
RELATOR n person who relates a story
RELATORS > RELATOR
RELATUM n one of the objects between which a relation is said to hold

RELAUNCH vb launch again ▷ n another launching, or something that is relaunched
RELAUNDER vb launder again
RELAX vb make or become looser, less tense, or less rigid
RELAXABLE > RELAX
RELAXANT n drug or agent that relaxes, esp one that relaxes tense muscles ▷ adj of, relating to, or tending to produce relaxation
RELAXANTS > RELAXANT
RELAXED > RELAX
RELAXEDLY > RELAX
RELAXER n person or thing that relaxes
RELAXERS > RELAXER
RELAXES > RELAX
RELAXIN n hormone secreted during pregnancy
RELAXING > RELAX
RELAXINS > RELAXIN
RELAY n fresh set of people or animals relieving others ▷ vb pass on (a message)
RELAYED > RELAY
RELAYING > RELAY
RELAYS > RELAY
RELEARN vb learn (something previously known) again
RELEARNED > RELEARN
RELEARNS > RELEARN
RELEARNT > RELEARN
RELEASE vb set free ▷ n setting free
RELEASED > RELEASE
RELEASEE n someone to whom an estate is released or someone released from captivity
RELEASEES > RELEASEE
RELEASER > RELEASE
RELEASERS > RELEASE
RELEASES > RELEASE
RELEASING > RELEASE
RELEASOR n someone releasing an estate to someone else
RELEASORS > RELEASOR
RELEGABLE adj able to be relegated
RELEGATE vb put in a less important position
RELEGATED > RELEGATE
RELEGATES > RELEGATE
RELEND vb lend again
RELENDING > RELEND
RELENDS > RELEND
RELENT vb give up a harsh intention, become less severe
RELENTED > RELENT
RELENTING > RELENT
RELENTS > RELENT
RELET vb let again
RELETS > RELET
RELETTER vb redo lettering of
RELETTERS > RELETTER
RELETTING > RELET
RELEVANCE > RELEVANT
RELEVANCY > RELEVANT

RELEVANT adj connected with the matter in hand
RELEVE n dance move in which heels are off the ground
RELEVES > RELEVE
RELIABLE adj able to be trusted, dependable ▷ n something or someone believed to be reliable
RELIABLES > RELIABLE
RELIABLY > RELIABLE
RELIANCE n dependence, confidence, or trust
RELIANCES > RELIANCE
RELIANT > RELIANCE
RELIANTLY > RELIANCE
RELIC n something that has survived from the past
RELICENSE vb license again
RELICS > RELIC
RELICT n relic
RELICTION n process by which sea water or fresh water recedes over time, changing the waterline and leaving land exposed
RELICTS > RELICT
RELIDE archaic past form of > RELY
RELIE archaic spelling of > RELY
RELIED > RELY
RELIEF n gladness at the end or removal of pain, distress, etc
RELIEFS > RELIEF
RELIER > RELY
RELIERS > RELY
RELIES > RELY
RELIEVE vb bring relief to
RELIEVED adj experiencing relief, esp from worry or anxiety
RELIEVER n person or thing that relieves
RELIEVERS > RELIEVER
RELIEVES > RELIEVE
RELIEVING > RELIEVE
RELIEVO same as > RELIEF
RELIEVOS > RELIEVO
RELIGHT vb ignite or cause to ignite again
RELIGHTED > RELIGHT
RELIGHTS > RELIGHT
RELIGIEUX n member of a monastic order or clerical body
RELIGION n system of belief in and worship of a supernatural power or god
RELIGIONS > RELIGION
RELIGIOSE adj affectedly or extremely pious
RELIGIOSO adj religious ▷ adv in a religious manner ▷ n musical piece meant to be played devotionally
RELIGIOUS adj of religion ▷ n monk or nun
RELINE vb line again or anew
RELINED > RELINE
RELINES > RELINE
RELINING > RELINE
RELINK vb link again

RELINKED > RELINK
RELINKING > RELINK
RELINKS > RELINK
RELIQUARY n case or shrine for holy relics
RELIQUE archaic spelling of > RELIC
RELIQUEFY vb liquefy again
RELIQUES > RELIQUE
RELIQUIAE pl n fossil remains of animals or plants
RELIQUIFY same as > RELIQUEFY
RELISH vb enjoy, like very much ▷ n liking or enjoyment
RELISHED > RELISH
RELISHES > RELISH
RELISHING > RELISH
RELIST vb list again
RELISTED > RELIST
RELISTEN vb listen again
RELISTENS > RELISTEN
RELISTING > RELIST
RELISTS > RELIST
RELIT > RELIGHT
RELIVABLE > RELIVE
RELIVE vb experience (a sensation etc) again, esp in the imagination
RELIVED > RELIVE
RELIVER vb deliver up again
RELIVERED > RELIVER
RELIVERS > RELIVER
RELIVES > RELIVE
RELIVING > RELIVE
RELLENO n Mexican dish of stuffed vegetable
RELLENOS > RELLENO
RELLIE n relative
RELLIES pl n relatives or relations
RELLISH (in music) variant of > RELISH
RELLISHED > RELLISH
RELLISHES > RELLISH
RELLO n relative
RELLOS > RELLO
RELOAD vb put fresh ammunition into (a firearm)
RELOADED > RELOAD
RELOADER > RELOAD
RELOADERS > RELOAD
RELOADING > RELOAD
RELOADS > RELOAD
RELOAN vb loan again
RELOANED > RELOAN
RELOANING > RELOAN
RELOANS > RELOAN
RELOCATE vb move to a new place to live or work
RELOCATED > RELOCATE
RELOCATEE n someone who is relocated
RELOCATES > RELOCATE
RELOCATOR n program designed to transfer files from one computer to another
RELOCK vb lock again
RELOCKED > RELOCK
RELOCKING > RELOCK
RELOCKS > RELOCK
RELOOK vb look again
RELOOKED > RELOOK
RELOOKING > RELOOK

RELOOKS > RELOOK
RELUCENT adj bright
RELUCT vb struggle or rebel
RELUCTANT adj unwilling or disinclined
RELUCTATE vb be or appear reluctant
RELUCTED > RELUCT
RELUCTING > RELUCT
RELUCTS > RELUCT
RELUME vb light or brighten again
RELUMED > RELUME
RELUMES > RELUME
RELUMINE same as > RELUME
RELUMINED > RELUMINE
RELUMINES > RELUMINE
RELUMING > RELUME
RELY vb depend (on)
RELYING > RELY
REM n dose of ionizing radiation
REMADE n object that has been reconstructed from original materials
REMADES > REMADE
REMAIL vb mail again
REMAILED > REMAIL
REMAILER n internet service that forwards emails anonymously
REMAILERS > REMAILER
REMAILING n act or instance of sending (an email) again
REMAILS > REMAIL
REMAIN vb continue
REMAINDER n part which is left ▷ vb offer (copies of a poorly selling book) at reduced prices
REMAINED > REMAIN
REMAINER n person who remains
REMAINERS > REMAINER
REMAINING > REMAIN
REMAINS pl n relics, esp of ancient buildings
REMAKE vb make again in a different way ▷ n new version of an old film
REMAKER > REMAKE
REMAKERS > REMAKE
REMAKES > REMAKE
REMAKING > REMAKE
REMAN vb man again or afresh
REMAND vb send back into custody or put on bail before trial
REMANDED > REMAND
REMANDING > REMAND
REMANDS > REMAND
REMANENCE n ability of a material to retain magnetization, equal to the magnetic flux density of the material after the removal of the magnetizing field
REMANENCY archaic variant of > REMANENCE
REMANENT adj remaining or left over ▷ n archaic word meaning remainder
REMANENTS > REMANENT
REMANET n something left over

REMANETS > REMANET
REMANIE n fragments and fossils of older origin found in a more recent deposit
REMANIES > REMANIE
REMANNED > REMAN
REMANNING > REMAN
REMANS > REMAN
REMAP vb map again
REMAPPED > REMAP
REMAPPING > REMAP
REMAPS > REMAP
REMARK vb make a casual comment (on) ▷ n observation or comment
REMARKED > REMARK
REMARKER > REMARK
REMARKERS > REMARK
REMARKET vb market again
REMARKETS > REMARKET
REMARKING > REMARK
REMARKS > REMARK
REMARQUE n printing mark in the margin of a plate
REMARQUED adj having had a remarque put on
REMARQUES > REMARQUE
REMARRIED > REMARRY
REMARRIES > REMARRY
REMARRY vb marry again
REMASTER vb make a new master audio recording from an earlier recording
REMASTERS > REMASTER
REMATCH n second or return game or contest between two players ▷ vb match (two contestants) again
REMATCHED > REMATCH
REMATCHES > REMATCH
REMATE vb mate (animals) again ▷ n finishing pass in bullfighting
REMATED > REMATE
REMATES > REMATE
REMATING > REMATE
REMBLAI n earth used for an embankment or rampart
REMBLAIS > REMBLAI
REMBLE dialect word for > REMOVE
REMBLED > REMBLE
REMBLES > REMBLE
REMBLING > REMBLE
REMEAD archaic or dialect word for > REMEDY
REMEADED > REMEAD
REMEADING > REMEAD
REMEADS > REMEAD
REMEASURE vb measure again
REMEDE archaic or dialect word for > REMEDY
REMEDED > REMEDE
REMEDES > REMEDE
REMEDIAL adj intended to correct a specific disability, etc
REMEDIAT archaic word for > REMEDIAL
REMEDIATE archaic word for > REMEDIAL
REMEDIED > REMEDY
REMEDIES > REMEDY
REMEDING > REMEDE
REMEDY n means of curing pain or disease ▷ vb put right

REMEDYING > REMEDY
REMEET vb meet again
REMEETING > REMEET
REMEETS > REMEET
REMEID archaic or dialect word for > REMEDY
REMEIDED > REMEID
REMEIDING > REMEID
REMEIDS > REMEID
REMELT vb melt again
REMELTED > REMELT
REMELTING > REMELT
REMELTS > REMELT
REMEMBER vb retain in or recall to one's memory
REMEMBERS > REMEMBER
REMEN n ancient Egyptian measurement unit
REMEND vb mend again
REMENDED > REMEND
REMENDING > REMEND
REMENDS > REMEND
REMENS > REMEN
REMERCIED > REMERCY
REMERCIES > REMERCY
REMERCY vb archaic word for thank
REMERGE vb merge again
REMERGED > REMERGE
REMERGES > REMERGE
REMERGING > REMERGE
REMET > REMEET
REMEX n any of the large flight feathers of a bird's wing
REMIGATE vb row
REMIGATED > REMIGATE
REMIGATES > REMIGATE
REMIGES > REMEX
REMIGIAL > REMEX
REMIGRATE vb migrate again
REMIND vb cause to remember
REMINDED > REMIND
REMINDER n something that recalls the past
REMINDERS > REMINDER
REMINDFUL adj serving to remind
REMINDING > REMIND
REMINDS > REMIND
REMINISCE vb talk or write of past times, experiences, etc
REMINT vb mint again
REMINTED > REMINT
REMINTING > REMINT
REMINTS > REMINT
REMISE vb give up or relinquish (a right, claim, etc) ▷ n second thrust made on the same lunge after the first has missed
REMISED > REMISE
REMISES > REMISE
REMISING > REMISE
REMISS adj negligent or careless
REMISSION n reduction in the length of a prison term
REMISSIVE > REMISSION
REMISSLY > REMISS
REMISSORY adj liable to or intended to gain remission
REMIT vb send (money) for goods, services, etc, esp by post ▷ n area of competence or authority

REMITMENT n archaic word for remittance or remission
REMITS > REMIT
REMITTAL > REMIT
REMITTALS > REMIT
REMITTED > REMIT
REMITTEE n recipient of a remittance
REMITTEES > REMITTEE
REMITTENT adj (of a disease) periodically less severe
REMITTER n person who remits
REMITTERS > REMITTER
REMITTING > REMIT
REMITTOR same as > REMITTER
REMITTORS > REMITTOR
REMIX vb change the relative prominence of each performer's part of (a recording) ▷ n remixed version of a recording
REMIXED > REMIX
REMIXER n person who remixes a recording
REMIXERS > REMIXER
REMIXES > REMIX
REMIXING > REMIX
REMIXT informal past form of > REMIX
REMIXTURE > REMIX
REMNANT n small piece, esp of fabric, left over ▷ adj remaining
REMNANTAL adj existing as remnant
REMNANTS > REMNANT
REMODEL vb give a different shape or form to ▷ n something that has been remodelled
REMODELED > REMODEL
REMODELER n person who remodels
REMODELS > REMODEL
REMODIFY vb modify again
REMOISTEN vb moisten again
REMOLADE same as > REMOULADE
REMOLADES > REMOLADE
REMOLD US spelling of > REMOULD
REMOLDED > REMOLD
REMOLDING > REMOLD
REMOLDS > REMOLD
REMONTANT adj (esp of cultivated roses) flowering more than once in a single season ▷ n rose having such a growth
REMONTOIR n any of various devices used in watches, clocks, etc, to compensate for errors arising from the changes in the force driving the escapement
REMORA n spiny-finned fish
REMORAS > REMORA
REMORID > REMORA
REMORSE n feeling of sorrow and regret for something one did
REMORSES > REMORSE
REMOTE adj far away, distant ▷ n (in informal usage) remote control

REMOTELY > REMOTE
REMOTER > REMOTE
REMOTES > REMOTE
REMOTEST > REMOTE
REMOTION n removal
REMOTIONS > REMOTION
REMOUD Spenserian variant of > REMOVED
REMOULADE n mayonnaise sauce flavoured with herbs, mustard, and capers, served with salads, cold meat, etc
REMOULD vb change completely ▷ n renovated tyre
REMOULDED > REMOULD
REMOULDS > REMOULD
REMOUNT vb get on (a horse, bicycle, etc) again ▷ n fresh horse
REMOUNTED > REMOUNT
REMOUNTS > REMOUNT
REMOVABLE > REMOVE
REMOVABLY > REMOVE
REMOVAL n act of removing, esp changing residence
REMOVALS > REMOVAL
REMOVE vb take away or off ▷ n degree of difference
REMOVED adj very different or distant
REMOVEDLY adv at a distance
REMOVER > REMOVE
REMOVERS > REMOVE
REMOVES > REMOVE
REMOVING > REMOVE
REMS > REM
REMUAGE n process of turning wine bottles to let the sediment out
REMUAGES > REMUAGE
REMUDA n stock of horses enabling riders to change mounts
REMUDAS > REMUDA
REMUEUR n person carrying out remuage
REMUEURS > REMUEUR
REMURMUR vb murmur again or murmur in reply
REMURMURS > REMURMUR
REN archaic variant of > RUN
RENAGUE same as > RENEGE
RENAGUED > RENAGUE
RENAGUES > RENAGUE
RENAGUING > RENAGUE
RENAIL vb nail again
RENAILED > RENAIL
RENAILING > RENAIL
RENAILS > RENAIL
RENAL adj of the kidneys
RENAME vb change the name of (someone or something)
RENAMED > RENAME
RENAMES > RENAME
RENAMING > RENAME
RENASCENT adj becoming active or vigorous again
RENATURE vb return to natural state
RENATURED > RENATURE
RENATURES > RENATURE
RENAY vb archaic word meaning renounce
RENAYED > RENAY
RENAYING > RENAY

RENAYS > RENAY
RENCONTRE n unexpected meeting ▷ vb meet, esp under negative circumstances
REND vb tear or wrench apart
RENDANG n spicy Indonesian meat dish
RENDANGS > RENDANG
RENDED > REND
RENDER vb cause to become ▷ n first thin coat of plaster applied to a surface
RENDERED > RENDER
RENDERER > RENDER
RENDERERS > RENDER
RENDERING n act or instance of performing a play, piece of music, etc
RENDERS > RENDER
RENDIBLE > REND
RENDING > REND
RENDITION n performance ▷ vb subject someone to an extra-judiciary trial
RENDS > REND
RENDZINA n dark soil found in grassy or formerly grassy areas of moderate rainfall
RENDZINAS > RENDZINA
RENEAGUE same as > RENEGE
RENEAGUED > RENEAGUE
RENEAGUES > RENEAGUE
RENEGADE n person who deserts a cause ▷ vb become a renegade
RENEGADED > RENEGADE
RENEGADES > RENEGADE
RENEGADO archaic word for > RENEGADE
RENEGADOS > RENEGADO
RENEGATE old variant of > RENEGADE
RENEGATES > RENEGATE
RENEGE vb go back (on a promise etc)
RENEGED > RENEGE
RENEGER > RENEGE
RENEGERS > RENEGE
RENEGES > RENEGE
RENEGING > RENEGE
RENEGUE same as > RENEGE
RENEGUED > RENEGUE
RENEGUER > RENEGUE
RENEGUERS > RENEGUE
RENEGUES > RENEGUE
RENEGUING > RENEGUE
RENEST vb nest again or form a new nest
RENESTED > RENEST
RENESTING > RENEST
RENESTS > RENEST
RENEW vb begin again
RENEWABLE > RENEW
RENEWABLY > RENEW
RENEWAL n act of renewing or state of being renewed
RENEWALS > RENEWAL
RENEWED > RENEW
RENEWEDLY > RENEW
RENEWER > RENEW
RENEWERS > RENEW
RENEWING > RENEW
RENEWINGS > RENEW
RENEWS > RENEW
RENEY same as > RENAY

RENEYED > RENEY
RENEYING > RENEY
RENEYS > RENEY
RENFIERST adj archaic word for turned fierce
RENFORCE vb archaic word for reinforce
RENFORCED > RENFORCE
RENFORCES > RENFORCE
RENFORST > RENFORCE
RENGA n type of collaborative poetry found in Japan
RENGAS > RENGA
RENIED > RENY
RENIES > RENY
RENIFORM adj having the shape or profile of a kidney
RENIG same as > RENEGE
RENIGGED > RENIG
RENIGGING > RENIG
RENIGS > RENIG
RENIN n enzyme secreted by the kidneys
RENINS > RENIN
RENITENCE > RENITENT
RENITENCY > RENITENT
RENITENT adj reluctant
RENK adj unpleasant
RENKER > RENK
RENKEST > RENK
RENMINBI same as > YUAN
RENMINBIS > RENMINBI
RENNASE same as > RENNIN
RENNASES > RENNASE
RENNE archaic variant of > RUN
RENNED > REN
RENNES > RENNE
RENNET n substance for curdling milk to make cheese
RENNETS > RENNET
RENNIN n enzyme that occurs in gastric juice
RENNING > REN
RENNINGS > REN
RENNINS > RENNIN
RENO n renovated house
RENOGRAM n X-ray kidney image
RENOGRAMS > RENOGRAM
RENOS > RENO
RENOTIFY vb notify again
RENOUNCE vb give up (a belief, habit, etc) voluntarily ▷ n failure to follow suit in a card game
RENOUNCED > RENOUNCE
RENOUNCER > RENOUNCE
RENOUNCES > RENOUNCE
RENOVATE vb restore to good condition
RENOVATED > RENOVATE
RENOVATES > RENOVATE
RENOVATOR > RENOVATE
RENOWN n widespread good reputation ▷ vb make famous
RENOWNED adj famous
RENOWNER n renown giver
RENOWNERS > RENOWNER
RENOWNING > RENOWN
RENOWNS > RENOWN
RENS > REN
RENT n payment made by a tenant to a landlord or owner of a property ▷ vb grant the

right to use one's property for payment
RENTABLE > REND
RENTAL n sum payable as rent ▷ adj of or relating to rent
RENTALLER n (in Scots law) tenant with very favourable terms
RENTALS > RENTAL
RENTE n annual income from capital investment
RENTED > RENT
RENTER n person who lets his or her property in return for rent
RENTERS > RENTER
RENTES > RENTE
RENTIER n person who lives off unearned income such as rents or interest
RENTIERS > RENTIER
RENTING > RENT
RENTINGS > RENT
RENTS > RENT
RENUMBER vb number again or afresh
RENUMBERS > RENUMBER
RENVERSE vb archaic word meaning overturn
RENVERSED > RENVERSE
RENVERSES > RENVERSE
RENVERST > RENVERSE
RENVOI n referring of a dispute to a jurisdiction other than that in which it arose
RENVOIS > RENVOI
RENVOY old variant of > RENVOI
RENVOYS > RENVOY
RENY same as > RENAY
RENYING > RENY
REO n New Zealand language
REOBJECT vb object again
REOBJECTS > REOBJECT
REOBSERVE vb observe again
REOBTAIN vb obtain again
REOBTAINS > REOBTAIN
REOCCUPY vb occupy (a building, area, etc) again
REOCCUR vb happen, take place, or come about again
REOCCURS > REOCCUR
REOFFEND vb commit another offence
REOFFENDS > REOFFEND
REOFFER vb offer again
REOFFERED > REOFFER
REOFFERS > REOFFER
REOIL vb oil again
REOILED > REOIL
REOILING > REOIL
REOILS > REOIL
REOPEN vb open again after a period of being closed or suspended
REOPENED > REOPEN
REOPENER n clause in a legal document allowing for an issue to be revisited at a subsequent date
REOPENERS > REOPENER
REOPENING n act of reopening
REOPENS > REOPEN

REOPERATE *vb* operate again

REOPPOSE *vb* oppose again

REOPPOSED > REOPPOSE

REOPPOSES > REOPPOSE

REORDAIN *vb* ordain again

REORDAINS > REORDAIN

REORDER *vb* change the order of

REORDERED > REORDER

REORDERS > REORDER

REORG *vb* reorganize

REORGED > REORG

REORGING > REORG

REORGS > REORG

REORIENT *vb* adjust or align (something) in a new or different way

REORIENTS > REORIENT

REOS > REO

REOUTFIT *vb* outfit again

REOUTFITS > REOUTFIT

REOVIRUS *n* type of virus

REOXIDISE *same as* **>** REOXIDIZE

REOXIDIZE *vb* oxidize again

REP *n* sales representative ▷ *vb* work as a representative

REPACIFY *vb* pacify again

REPACK *vb* place or arrange (articles) in (a container) again or in a different way

REPACKAGE *vb* wrap or put (something) in a package again

REPACKED > REPACK

REPACKING > REPACK

REPACKS > REPACK

REPAID > REPAY

REPAINT *vb* apply a new or fresh coat of paint

REPAINTED > REPAINT

REPAINTS > REPAINT

REPAIR *vb* restore to good condition, mend ▷ *n* act of repairing

REPAIRED > REPAIR

REPAIRER > REPAIR

REPAIRERS > REPAIR

REPAIRING > REPAIR

REPAIRMAN *n* man whose job it is to repair machines, appliances, etc

REPAIRMEN > REPAIRMAN

REPAIRS > REPAIR

REPAND *adj* having a wavy margin

REPANDLY > REPAND

REPANEL *vb* panel again or anew

REPANELED > REPANEL

REPANELS > REPANEL

REPAPER *vb* paper again or afresh

REPAPERED > REPAPER

REPAPERS > REPAPER

REPARABLE *adj* able to be repaired or remedied

REPARABLY > REPARABLE

REPARK *vb* park again

REPARKED > REPARK

REPARKING > REPARK

REPARKS > REPARK

REPARTEE *n* interchange of witty retorts ▷ *vb* retort

REPARTEED > REPARTEE

REPARTEES > REPARTEE

REPASS *vb* pass again

REPASSAGE *n* passage back or return

REPASSED > REPASS

REPASSES > REPASS

REPASSING > REPASS

REPAST *n* meal ▷ *vb* feed (on)

REPASTED > REPAST

REPASTING > REPAST

REPASTS > REPAST

REPASTURE *old word for* **>** FOOD

REPATCH *vb* patch again

REPATCHED > REPATCH

REPATCHES > REPATCH

REPATTERN *vb* pattern again

REPAVE *vb* pave again

REPAVED > REPAVE

REPAVES > REPAVE

REPAVING > REPAVE

REPAY *vb* pay back, refund

REPAYABLE > REPAY

REPAYING > REPAY

REPAYMENT > REPAY

REPAYS > REPAY

REPEAL *vb* cancel (a law) officially ▷ *n* act of repealing

REPEALED > REPEAL

REPEALER > REPEAL

REPEALERS > REPEAL

REPEALING > REPEAL

REPEALS > REPEAL

REPEAT *vb* say or do again ▷ *n* act or instance of repeating

REPEATED *adj* done, made, or said again and again

REPEATER *n* firearm that may be discharged many times without reloading

REPEATERS > REPEATER

REPEATING > REPEAT

REPEATS > REPEAT

REPECHAGE *n* extra heat or test providing second chance to previous losers or failing candidates

REPEG *vb* peg again

REPEGGED > REPEG

REPEGGING > REPEG

REPEGS > REPEG

REPEL *vb* be disgusting to

REPELLANT *same as* **>** REPELLENT

REPELLED > REPEL

REPELLENT *adj* distasteful ▷ *n* something that repels, esp a chemical to repel insects

REPELLER > REPEL

REPELLERS > REPEL

REPELLING > REPEL

REPELS > REPEL

REPENT *vb* feel regret for (a deed or omission) ▷ *adj* lying or creeping along the ground

REPENTANT *adj* reproaching oneself for one's past actions or sins

REPENTED > REPENT

REPENTER > REPENT

REPENTERS > REPENT

REPENTING > REPENT

REPENTS > REPENT

REPEOPLE *vb* people again

REPEOPLED > REPEOPLE

REPEOPLES > REPEOPLE

REPERCUSS *vb* have repercussions

REPEREPE *n* New Zealand word for the elephant fish

REPEREPES > REPEREPE

REPERK *vb* perk again

REPERKED > REPERK

REPERKING > REPERK

REPERKS > REPERK

REPERTORY *n* repertoire

REPERUSAL *n* fresh perusal

REPERUSE *vb* peruse again

REPERUSED > REPERUSE

REPERUSES > REPERUSE

REPETEND *n* digit or series of digits in a recurring decimal that repeats itself

REPETENDS > REPETEND

REPHRASE *vb* express in different words

REPHRASED > REPHRASE

REPHRASES > REPHRASE

REPIGMENT *vb* pigment again

REPIN *vb* pin again

REPINE *vb* fret or complain

REPINED > REPINE

REPINER > REPINE

REPINERS > REPINE

REPINES > REPINE

REPINING > REPINE

REPININGS > REPINE

REPINNED > REPIN

REPINNING > REPIN

REPINS > REPIN

REPIQUE *n* score of 30 in the card-game piquet ▷ *vb* score a repique against (someone)

REPIQUED > REPIQUE

REPIQUES > REPIQUE

REPIQUING > REPIQUE

REPLA > REPLUM

REPLACE *vb* substitute for

REPLACED > REPLACE

REPLACER > REPLACE

REPLACERS > REPLACE

REPLACES > REPLACE

REPLACING > REPLACE

REPLAN *vb* plan again

REPLANNED > REPLAN

REPLANS > REPLAN

REPLANT *vb* plant again

REPLANTED > REPLANT

REPLANTS > REPLANT

REPLASTER *vb* plaster again

REPLATE *vb* plate again

REPLATED > REPLATE

REPLATES > REPLATE

REPLATING > REPLATE

REPLAY *n* immediate reshowing on TV of an incident in sport ▷ *vb* play (a match, recording, etc) again

REPLAYED > REPLAY

REPLAYING > REPLAY

REPLAYS > REPLAY

REPLEAD *vb* plead again

REPLEADED > REPLEAD

REPLEADER *n* right to plead again

REPLEADS > REPLEAD

REPLED > REPLEAD

REPLEDGE *vb* pledge again

REPLEDGED > REPLEDGE

REPLEDGES > REPLEDGE

REPLENISH *vb* fill up again, resupply

REPLETE *adj* filled or gorged ▷ *vb* fill again

REPLETED > REPLETE

REPLETELY > REPLETE

REPLETES > REPLETE

REPLETING > REPLETE

REPLETION *n* state or condition of being replete

REPLEVIED > REPLEVY

REPLEVIES > REPLEVY

REPLEVIN *n* recovery of goods unlawfully taken

REPLEVINS > REPLEVIN

REPLEVY *vb* recover possession of (goods) by replevin

REPLICA *n* exact copy

REPLICANT *n* (in science fiction) android indistinguishable from a human being

REPLICAS > REPLICA

REPLICASE *n* type of enzyme

REPLICATE *vb* make or be a copy of ▷ *adj* folded back on itself

REPLICON *n* region of a DNA molecule that is replicated from a single origin

REPLICONS > REPLICON

REPLIED > REPLY

REPLIER > REPLY

REPLIERS > REPLY

REPLIES > REPLY

REPLOT *vb* plot again

REPLOTS > REPLOT

REPLOTTED > REPLOT

REPLOUGH *vb* plough again

REPLOUGHS > REPLOUGH

REPLOW *vb* plow again

REPLOWED > REPLOW

REPLOWING > REPLOW

REPLOWS > REPLOW

REPLUM *n* internal separating wall in some fruits

REPLUMB *vb* plumb again

REPLUMBED > REPLUMB

REPLUMBS > REPLUMB

REPLUNGE *vb* plunge again

REPLUNGED > REPLUNGE

REPLUNGES > REPLUNGE

REPLY *vb* answer or respond ▷ *n* answer or response

REPLYING > REPLY

REPO *n* act of repossessing

REPOINT *vb* repair the joints of (brickwork, masonry, etc) with mortar or cement

REPOINTED > REPOINT

REPOINTS > REPOINT

REPOLISH *vb* polish again

REPOLL *vb* poll again

REPOLLED > REPOLL

REPOLLING > REPOLL

REPOLLS > REPOLL

REPOMAN *n* man employed to repossess goods in cases of non-payment

REPOMEN > REPOMAN

REPONE vb restore (someone) to his or her former status, office, etc

REPONED > REPONE

REPONES > REPONE

REPONING > REPONE

REPORT vb give an account of ⊳ n account or statement

REPORTAGE n act or process of reporting news or other events of general interest

REPORTED > REPORT

REPORTER n person who gathers news for a newspaper, TV, etc

REPORTERS > REPORTER

REPORTING > REPORT

REPORTS > REPORT

REPOS > REPO

REPOSAL n repose

REPOSALL archaic spelling of > REPOSAL

REPOSALLS > REPOSALL

REPOSALS > REPOSAL

REPOSE n peace ⊳ vb lie or lay at rest

REPOSED > REPOSE

REPOSEDLY > REPOSE

REPOSEFUL > REPOSE

REPOSER > REPOSE

REPOSERS > REPOSE

REPOSES > REPOSE

REPOSING > REPOSE

REPOSIT vb put away, deposit, or store up

REPOSITED > REPOSIT

REPOSITOR n any instrument used for correcting the position of displaced organs or bones

REPOSITS > REPOSIT

REPOSSESS vb (of a lender) take back property from a customer who is behind with payments

REPOST vb post again

REPOSTED > REPOST

REPOSTING > REPOST

REPOSTS > REPOST

REPOSURE old word for > REPOSE

REPOSURES > REPOSURE

REPOT vb put (a house plant) into a new usually larger pot

REPOTS > REPOT

REPOTTED > REPOT

REPOTTING > REPOT

REPOUR vb pour back or again

REPOURED > REPOUR

REPOURING > REPOUR

REPOURS > REPOUR

REPOUSSE adj raised in relief ⊳ n design or surface made in this way

REPOUSSES > REPOUSSE

REPOWER vb put new engine in

REPOWERED > REPOWER

REPOWERS > REPOWER

REPP same as > REP

REPPED > REP

REPPING > REP

REPPINGS > REP

REPPS > REPP

REPREEVE archaic spelling of > REPRIEVE

REPREEVED > REPREEVE

REPREEVES > REPREEVE

REPREHEND vb find fault with

REPRESENT vb act as a delegate or substitute for

REPRESS vb keep (feelings) in check

REPRESSED adj (of a person) repressing feelings, instincts, desires, etc

REPRESSER > REPRESS

REPRESSES > REPRESS

REPRESSOR n protein synthesized under the control of a repressor gene, which has the capacity to bind to the operator gene and thereby shut off the expression of the structural genes of an operon

REPRICE vb price again

REPRICED > REPRICE

REPRICES > REPRICE

REPRICING > REPRICE

REPRIEFE n (in archaic usage) reproof

REPRIEFES > REPRIEFE

REPRIEVAL old word for > REPRIEVE

REPRIEVE vb postpone the execution of (a condemned person) ⊳ n (document granting) postponement or cancellation of a punishment

REPRIEVED > REPRIEVE

REPRIEVER > REPRIEVE

REPRIEVES > REPRIEVE

REPRIMAND vb blame (someone) officially for a fault ⊳ n official blame

REPRIME vb prime again

REPRIMED > REPRIME

REPRIMES > REPRIME

REPRIMING > REPRIME

REPRINT vb print further copies of (a book) ⊳ n reprinted copy

REPRINTED > REPRINT

REPRINTER > REPRINT

REPRINTS > REPRINT

REPRISAL n retaliation

REPRISALS > REPRISAL

REPRISE n repeating of an earlier theme ⊳ vb repeat an earlier theme

REPRISED > REPRISE

REPRISES > REPRISE

REPRISING > REPRISE

REPRIVE archaic spelling of > REPRIEVE

REPRIVED > REPRIVE

REPRIVES > REPRIVE

REPRIVING > REPRIVE

REPRIZE archaic spelling of > REPRISE

REPRIZED > REPRIZE

REPRIZES > REPRIZE

REPRIZING > REPRIZE

REPRO n imitation or facsimile of a work of art; reproduction

REPROACH vb blame, rebuke

REPROBACY > REPROBATE

REPROBATE n depraved or disreputable (person) ⊳ adj morally unprincipled ⊳ vb disapprove of

REPROBE vb probe again

REPROBED > REPROBE

REPROBES > REPROBE

REPROBING > REPROBE

REPROCESS vb treat or prepare (something) by a special method again

REPRODUCE vb produce a copy of

REPROGRAM vb program again

REPROOF n severe blaming of someone for a fault ⊳ vb treat (a coat, jacket, etc) so as to renew its texture, etc

REPROOFED > REPROOF

REPROOFS > REPROOF

REPROS > REPRO

REPROVAL same as > REPROOF

REPROVALS > REPROVAL

REPROVE vb speak severely to (someone) about a fault

REPROVED > REPROVE

REPROVER > REPROVE

REPROVERS > REPROVE

REPROVES > REPROVE

REPROVING > REPROVE

REPRYVE archaic spelling of > REPRIEVE

REPRYVED > REPRYVE

REPRYVES > REPRYVE

REPRYVING > REPRYVE

REPS > REP

REPTANT adj creeping, crawling, or lying along the ground

REPTATION n creeping action

REPTILE n cold-blooded egg-laying vertebrate with horny scales or plates ⊳ adj creeping, crawling, or squirming

REPTILES > REPTILE

REPTILIA > REPTILIUM

REPTILIAN adj of, relating to, resembling, or characteristic of reptiles

REPTILIUM n place where live reptiles are kept for show

REPTILOID n reptile or organism resembling a reptile

REPUBLIC n government in which the people possess the supreme power

REPUBLICS > REPUBLIC

REPUBLISH vb publish again

REPUDIATE vb reject the authority or validity of

REPUGN vb oppose or conflict (with)

REPUGNANT adj offensive or distasteful

REPUGNED > REPUGN

REPUGNING > REPUGN

REPUGNS > REPUGN

REPULP vb pulp again

REPULPED > REPULP

REPULPING > REPULP

REPULPS > REPULP

REPULSE vb be disgusting to ⊳ n act of driving back

REPULSED > REPULSE

REPULSER > REPULSE

REPULSERS > REPULSE

REPULSES > REPULSE

REPULSING > REPULSE

REPULSION n distaste or aversion

REPULSIVE adj loathsome, disgusting

REPUMP vb pump again

REPUMPED > REPUMP

REPUMPING > REPUMP

REPUMPS > REPUMP

REPUNIT n any number that consists entirely of the same repeated digits

REPUNITS > REPUNIT

REPURE vb archaic word meaning make pure again

REPURED > REPURE

REPURES > REPURE

REPURIFY vb purify again

REPURING > REPURE

REPURPOSE vb find new purpose for

REPURSUE vb pursue again

REPURSUED > REPURSUE

REPURSUES > REPURSUE

REPUTABLE adj of good reputation, respectable

REPUTABLY > REPUTABLE

REPUTE n reputation ⊳ vb consider (a person or thing) to be as specified

REPUTED adj supposed

REPUTEDLY adv according to general belief or supposition

REPUTES > REPUTE

REPUTING > REPUTE

REPUTINGS > REPUTE

REQUALIFY vb qualify again

REQUERE archaic variant of > REQUIRE

REQUERED > REQUERE

REQUERES > REQUERE

REQUERING > REQUERE

REQUEST vb ask ⊳ n asking

REQUESTED > REQUEST

REQUESTER > REQUEST

REQUESTOR > REQUEST

REQUESTS > REQUEST

REQUICKEN vb quicken again

REQUIEM n Mass celebrated for the dead

REQUIEMS > REQUIEM

REQUIGHT archaic spelling of > REQUITE

REQUIGHTS > REQUIGHT

REQUIN vb type of shark

REQUINS > REQUIN

REQUINTO n type of small guitar

REQUINTOS > REQUINTO

REQUIRE vb want or need

REQUIRED > REQUIRE

REQUIRER > REQUIRE

REQUIRERS > REQUIRE

REQUIRES > REQUIRE

REQUIRING > REQUIRE

REQUISITE adj necessary, essential ⊳ n essential thing

REQUIT vb quit again

REQUITAL n act or an instance of requiting

REQUITALS > REQUITAL

REQUITE vb return to someone (the same

treatment or feeling as received)
REQUITED > REQUITE
REQUITER > REQUITE
REQUITERS > REQUITE
REQUITES > REQUITE
REQUITING > REQUITE
REQUITS > REQUIT
REQUITTED > REQUIT
REQUOTE vb quote again
REQUOTED > REQUOTE
REQUOTES > REQUOTE
REQUOTING > REQUOTE
REQUOYLE archaic spelling of > RECOIL
REQUOYLED > REQUOYLE
REQUOYLES > REQUOYLE
RERACK vb rack again
RERACKED > RERACK
RERACKING > RERACK
RERACKS > RERACK
RERADIATE vb radiate again
RERAIL vb put back on a railway line
RERAILED > RERAIL
RERAILING n replacement of existing rails on a railway line
RERAILS > RERAIL
RERAISE vb raise again
RERAISED > RERAISE
RERAISES > RERAISE
RERAISING > RERAISE
RERAN > RERUN
REREAD vb read (something) again
REREADING > REREAD
REREADS > REREAD
REREBRACE n armour worn on the upper arm
RERECORD vb record again
RERECORDS > RERECORD
REREDOS n ornamental screen behind an altar
REREDOSES > REREDOS
REREDOSSE same as > REREDOS
RERELEASE vb release again
REREMAI n New Zealand word for the basking shark
REREMAIS > REREMAI
REREMICE > REREMOUSE
REREMIND vb remind again
REREMINDS > REREMIND
REREMOUSE n archaic or dialect word for 'bat' (the animal)
RERENT vb rent again
RERENTED > RERENT
RERENTING > RERENT
RERENTS > RERENT
REREPEAT vb repeat again
REREPEATS > REREPEAT
REREVIEW vb review again
REREVIEWS > REREVIEW
REREVISE vb revise again
REREVISED > REREVISE
REREVISES > REREVISE
REREWARD archaic spelling of > REARWARD
REREWARDS archaic spelling of > REARWARDS
RERIG vb rig again
RERIGGED > RERIG

RERIGGING > RERIG
RERIGS > RERIG
RERISE vb rise again
RERISEN > RERISE
RERISES > RERISE
RERISING > RERISE
REROLL vb roll again
REROLLED > REROLL
REROLLER > REROLL
REROLLERS > REROLL
REROLLING > REROLL
REROLLS > REROLL
REROOF vb put a new roof or roofs on
REROOFED > REROOF
REROOFING > REROOF
REROOFS > REROOF
REROSE > RERISE
REROUTE vb send or direct by a different route
REROUTED > REROUTE
REROUTES > REROUTE
REROUTING > REROUTE
RERUN n film or programme that is broadcast again, repeat ▷ vb put on (a film or programme) again
RERUNNING > RERUN
RERUNS > RERUN
RES informal word for > RESIDENCE
RESADDLE vb saddle again
RESADDLED > RESADDLE
RESADDLES > RESADDLE
RESAID > RESAY
RESAIL vb sail again
RESAILED > RESAIL
RESAILING > RESAIL
RESAILS > RESAIL
RESALABLE > RESALE
RESALE n selling of something purchased earlier
RESALES > RESALE
RESALGAR archaic variant of > REALGAR
RESALGARS > RESALGAR
RESALUTE vb salute back or again
RESALUTED > RESALUTE
RESALUTES > RESALUTE
RESAMPLE vb (in graphics or digital photography) change the size or resolution of
RESAMPLED > RESAMPLE
RESAMPLES > RESAMPLE
RESAT > RESIT
RESAW vb saw again
RESAWED > RESAW
RESAWING > RESAW
RESAWN > RESAW
RESAWS > RESAW
RESAY vb say again or in response
RESAYING > RESAY
RESAYS > RESAY
RESCALE vb resize
RESCALED > RESCALE
RESCALES > RESCALE
RESCALING > RESCALE
RESCHOOL vb retrain
RESCHOOLS > RESCHOOL
RESCIND vb annul or repeal
RESCINDED > RESCIND
RESCINDER > RESCIND
RESCINDS > RESCIND
RESCORE vb score afresh

RESCORED > RESCORE
RESCORES > RESCORE
RESCORING > RESCORE
RESCREEN vb screen again
RESCREENS > RESCREEN
RESCRIPT n ordinance taking the form of a reply by the Roman emperor to a point of law
RESCRIPTS > RESCRIPT
RESCUABLE > RESCUE
RESCUE vb deliver from danger or trouble, save ▷ n act of rescuing
RESCUED > RESCUE
RESCUEE n person who is rescued
RESCUEES > RESCUEE
RESCUER > RESCUE
RESCUERS > RESCUE
RESCUES > RESCUE
RESCUING > RESCUE
RESCULPT vb sculpt again
RESCULPTS > RESCULPT
RESEAL vb close or secure tightly again
RESEALED > RESEAL
RESEALING > RESEAL
RESEALS > RESEAL
RESEARCH n systematic investigation to discover facts or collect information ▷ vb carry out investigations
RESEASON vb season again
RESEASONS > RESEASON
RESEAT vb show (a person) to a new seat
RESEATED > RESEAT
RESEATING > RESEAT
RESEATS > RESEAT
RESEAU n mesh background to a lace or other pattern
RESEAUS > RESEAU
RESEAUX > RESEAU
RESECT vb cut out part of (a bone, an organ, or other structure or part)
RESECTED > RESECT
RESECTING > RESECT
RESECTION n excision of part of a bone, organ, or other part
RESECTS > RESECT
RESECURE vb secure again
RESECURED > RESECURE
RESECURES > RESECURE
RESEDA n plant that has small spikes of grey-green flowers ▷ adj of a greyish-green colour
RESEDAS > RESEDA
RESEE vb see again
RESEED vb form seed and reproduce naturally, forming a constant plant population
RESEEDED > RESEED
RESEEDING > RESEED
RESEEDS > RESEED
RESEEING > RESEE
RESEEK vb seek again
RESEEKING > RESEEK
RESEEKS > RESEEK
RESEEN > RESEE
RESEES > RESEE
RESEIZE vb seize again
RESEIZED > RESEIZE
RESEIZES > RESEIZE

RESEIZING > RESEIZE
RESEIZURE > RESEIZE
RESELECT vb choose (someone or something) again
RESELECTS > RESELECT
RESELL vb sell (something) one has previously bought
RESELLER > RESELL
RESELLERS > RESELL
RESELLING > RESELL
RESELLS > RESELL
RESEMBLE vb be or look like
RESEMBLED > RESEMBLE
RESEMBLER > RESEMBLE
RESEMBLES > RESEMBLE
RESEND vb send again
RESENDING > RESEND
RESENDS > RESEND
RESENT vb feel bitter about
RESENTED > RESENT
RESENTER > RESENT
RESENTERS > RESENT
RESENTFUL adj feeling or characterized by resentment
RESENTING > RESENT
RESENTIVE archaic word for > RESENTFUL
RESENTS > RESENT
RESERPINE n insoluble alkaloid used medicinally to lower blood pressure and as a sedative
RESERVE vb set aside, keep for future use ▷ n something, esp money or troops, kept for emergencies
RESERVED adj not showing one's feelings, lacking friendliness
RESERVER > RESERVE
RESERVERS > RESERVE
RESERVICE vb service again
RESERVING > RESERVE
RESERVIST n member of a military reserve
RESERVOIR n natural or artificial lake storing water for community supplies
RESES > RES
RESET vb set again (a broken bone, matter in type, a gemstone, etc) ▷ n act or an instance of setting again
RESETS > RESET
RESETTED same as > RESET
RESETTER > RESET
RESETTERS > RESET
RESETTING > RESET
RESETTLE vb settle to live in a different place
RESETTLED > RESETTLE
RESETTLES > RESETTLE
RESEW vb sew again
RESEWED > RESEW
RESEWING > RESEW
RESEWN > RESEW
RESEWS > RESEW
RESH n 20th letter of the Hebrew alphabet
RESHAPE vb shape (something) again or differently
RESHAPED > RESHAPE
RESHAPER > RESHAPE

r

RESHAPERS > RESHAPE
RESHAPES > RESHAPE
RESHAPING n act of reshaping
RESHARPEN vb sharpen again
RESHAVE vb shave again
RESHAVED > RESHAVE
RESHAVEN > RESHAVE
RESHAVES > RESHAVE
RESHAVING > RESHAVE
RESHES > RESH
RESHINE vb shine again
RESHINED > RESHINE
RESHINES > RESHINE
RESHINGLE vb put new shingles on
RESHINING > RESHINE
RESHIP vb ship again
RESHIPPED > RESHIP
RESHIPPER > RESHIP
RESHIPS > RESHIP
RESHOD > RESHOE
RESHOE vb put a new shoe or shoes on
RESHOED > RESHOE
RESHOEING > RESHOE
RESHOES > RESHOE
RESHONE > RESHINE
RESHOOT vb shoot again
RESHOOTS > RESHOOT
RESHOT > RESHOOT
RESHOW vb show again
RESHOWED > RESHOW
RESHOWER vb have another shower
RESHOWERS > RESHOWER
RESHOWING n act or instance of showing (a film, etc) again
RESHOWN > RESHOW
RESHOWS > RESHOW
RESHUFFLE n reorganization ▷ vb reorganize
RESIANCE archaic word for > RESIDENCE
RESIANCES > RESIANCE
RESIANT archaic word for > RESIDENT
RESIANTS > RESIANT
RESID n residual oil left over from the petroleum distillation process
RESIDE vb dwell permanently
RESIDED > RESIDE
RESIDENCE n home or house
RESIDENCY n regular series of concerts by a band or singer at one venue
RESIDENT n person who lives in a place ▷ adj living in a place
RESIDENTS > RESIDENT
RESIDER > RESIDE
RESIDERS > RESIDE
RESIDES > RESIDE
RESIDING > RESIDE
RESIDS > RESID
RESIDUA > RESIDUUM
RESIDUAL adj of or being a remainder ▷ n something left over as a residue
RESIDUALS > RESIDUAL
RESIDUARY adj of, relating to, or constituting a residue

RESIDUE n what is left, remainder
RESIDUES > RESIDUE
RESIDUOUS adj residual
RESIDUUM n residue
RESIDUUMS > RESIDUUM
RESIFT vb sift again
RESIFTED > RESIFT
RESIFTING > RESIFT
RESIFTS > RESIFT
RESIGHT vb sight again
RESIGHTED > RESIGHT
RESIGHTS > RESIGHT
RESIGN vb give up office, a job, etc
RESIGNED adj content to endure
RESIGNER > RESIGN
RESIGNERS > RESIGN
RESIGNING > RESIGN
RESIGNS > RESIGN
RESILE vb spring or shrink back
RESILED > RESILE
RESILES > RESILE
RESILIENT adj (of a person) recovering quickly from a shock etc
RESILIN n substance found in insect bodies
RESILING > RESILE
RESILINS > RESILIN
RESILVER vb silver again
RESILVERS > RESILVER
RESIN n sticky substance from plants, esp pines ▷ vb treat or coat with resin
RESINATA n type of wine
RESINATAS > RESINATA
RESINATE vb impregnate with resin
RESINATED > RESINATE
RESINATES > RESINATE
RESINED > RESIN
RESINER n applier or collector of resin
RESINERS > RESINER
RESINIER > RESINY
RESINIEST > RESINY
RESINIFY vb become or cause to be resinous
RESINING > RESIN
RESINISE variant spelling of > RESINIZE
RESINISED > RESINISE
RESINISES > RESINISE
RESINIZE vb apply resin to
RESINIZED > RESINIZE
RESINIZES > RESINIZE
RESINLIKE > RESIN
RESINOID adj resembling, characteristic of, or containing resin ▷ n any resinoid substance, esp a synthetic compound
RESINOIDS > RESINOID
RESINOSES > RESINOSIS
RESINOSIS n excessive resin loss in diseased or damaged conifers
RESINOUS > RESIN
RESINS > RESIN
RESINY adj resembling, containing or covered with resin
RESIST vb withstand or oppose ▷ n substance used to protect something

RESISTANT adj characterized by or showing resistance ▷ n person or thing that resists
RESISTED > RESIST
RESISTENT same as > RESISTANT
RESISTER > RESIST
RESISTERS > RESIST
RESISTING > RESIST
RESISTIVE adj exhibiting electrical resistance
RESISTOR n component of an electrical circuit producing resistance
RESISTORS > RESISTOR
RESISTS > RESIST
RESIT vb take (an exam) again ▷ n exam that has to be taken again
RESITE vb move to a different site
RESITED > RESITE
RESITES > RESITE
RESITING > RESITE
RESITS > RESIT
RESITTING > RESIT
RESITUATE vb situate elsewhere
RESIZABLE adj capable of being resized
RESIZE vb change size of
RESIZED > RESIZE
RESIZES > RESIZE
RESIZING > RESIZE
RESKETCH vb sketch again
RESKEW archaic spelling of > RESCUE
RESKEWED > RESKEW
RESKEWING > RESKEW
RESKEWS > RESKEW
RESKILL vb train (workers) to acquire new skills
RESKILLED > RESKILL
RESKILLS > RESKILL
RESKIN vb replace the outermost layer of an aircraft
RESKINNED > RESKIN
RESKINS > RESKIN
RESKUE archaic spelling of > RESCUE
RESKUED > RESKUE
RESKUES > RESKUE
RESKUING > RESKUE
RESLATE vb slate again
RESLATED > RESLATE
RESLATES > RESLATE
RESLATING > RESLATE
RESMELT vb smelt again
RESMELTED > RESMELT
RESMELTS > RESMELT
RESMOOTH vb smooth again
RESMOOTHS > RESMOOTH
RESNATRON n tetrode used to generate high power at high frequencies
RESOAK vb soak again
RESOAKED > RESOAK
RESOAKING > RESOAK
RESOAKS > RESOAK
RESOD vb returf
RESODDED > RESOD
RESODDING > RESOD
RESODS > RESOD
RESOFTEN vb soften again
RESOFTENS > RESOFTEN

RESOJET n type of jet engine
RESOJETS > RESOJET
RESOLD > RESELL
RESOLDER vb solder again
RESOLDERS > RESOLDER
RESOLE vb put a new sole or new soles on
RESOLED > RESOLE
RESOLES > RESOLE
RESOLING > RESOLE
RESOLUBLE adj able to be resolved
RESOLUTE adj firm in purpose ▷ n someone resolute
RESOLUTER > RESOLUTE
RESOLUTES > RESOLUTE
RESOLVE vb decide with an effort of will ▷ n absolute determination
RESOLVED adj determined
RESOLVENT adj serving to dissolve or separate something into its elements ▷ n something that resolves
RESOLVER > RESOLVE
RESOLVERS > RESOLVE
RESOLVES > RESOLVE
RESOLVING > RESOLVE
RESONANCE n echoing, esp with a deep sound
RESONANT adj resounding or reechoing ▷ n type of unobstructed speech sound
RESONANTS > RESONANT
RESONATE vb resound or cause to resound
RESONATED > RESONATE
RESONATES > RESONATE
RESONATOR n any body or system that displays resonance, esp a tuned electrical circuit or a conducting cavity in which microwaves are generated by a resonant current
RESORB vb absorb again
RESORBED > RESORB
RESORBENT > RESORB
RESORBING > RESORB
RESORBS > RESORB
RESORCIN n substance used principally in dyeing
RESORCINS > RESORCIN
RESORT vb have recourse (to) for help etc ▷ n place for holidays
RESORTED > RESORT
RESORTER > RESORT
RESORTERS > RESORT
RESORTING > RESORT
RESORTS > RESORT
RESOUGHT > RESEEK
RESOUND vb echo or ring with sound
RESOUNDED > RESOUND
RESOUNDS > RESOUND
RESOURCE n thing resorted to for support ▷ vb provide funding or other resources for
RESOURCED > RESOURCE
RESOURCES > RESOURCE
RESOW vb sow again
RESOWED > RESOW
RESOWING > RESOW

RESOWN > RESOW
RESOWS > RESOW
RESPACE vb change the spacing of
RESPACED > RESPACE
RESPACES > RESPACE
RESPACING > RESPACE
RESPADE vb dig over
RESPADED > RESPADE
RESPADES > RESPADE
RESPADING > RESPADE
RESPEAK vb speak further
RESPEAKS > RESPEAK
RESPECIFY vb specify again
RESPECT n consideration ▷ vb treat with esteem
RESPECTED > RESPECT
RESPECTER n person who respects someone or something
RESPECTS > RESPECT
RESPELL vb spell again
RESPELLED > RESPELL
RESPELLS > RESPELL
RESPELT > RESPELL
RESPIRE vb breathe
RESPIRED > RESPIRE
RESPIRES > RESPIRE
RESPIRING > RESPIRE
RESPITE n pause, interval of rest ▷ vb grant a respite to
RESPITED > RESPITE
RESPITES > RESPITE
RESPITING > RESPITE
RESPLEND vb be resplendent
RESPLENDS > RESPLEND
RESPLICE vb splice again
RESPLICED > RESPLICE
RESPLICES > RESPLICE
RESPLIT vb split again
RESPLITS > RESPLIT
RESPOKE > RESPEAK
RESPOKEN > RESPEAK
RESPOND vb answer ▷ n pilaster or an engaged column that supports an arch or a lintel
RESPONDED > RESPOND
RESPONDER > RESPOND
RESPONDS > RESPOND
RESPONSA n that part of rabbinic literature concerned with written rulings in answer to questions
RESPONSE n answer
RESPONSER n radio or radar receiver used in conjunction with an interrogator to receive and display signals from a transponder
RESPONSES > RESPONSE
RESPONSOR same as > RESPONSER
RESPONSUM n written answer from a rabbinic authority to a question submitted
RESPOOL vb rewind onto spool
RESPOOLED > RESPOOL
RESPOOLS > RESPOOL
RESPOT vb (in billiards) replace on one of the spots
RESPOTS > RESPOT
RESPOTTED > RESPOT

RESPRANG > RESPRING
RESPRAY n new coat of paint applied to a car, van, etc ▷ vb spray (a car, wheels, etc) with a new coat of paint
RESPRAYED > RESPRAY
RESPRAYS > RESPRAY
RESPREAD vb spread again
RESPREADS > RESPREAD
RESPRING vb put new springs in
RESPRINGS > RESPRING
RESPROUT vb sprout again
RESPROUTS > RESPROUT
RESPRUNG > RESPRING
RESSALDAR n Indian cavalry commander in mixed Anglo-Indian army
REST n freedom from exertion etc ▷ vb take a rest
RESTABLE vb put in stable again or elsewhere
RESTABLED > RESTABLE
RESTABLES > RESTABLE
RESTACK vb stack again
RESTACKED > RESTACK
RESTACKS > RESTACK
RESTAFF vb staff again
RESTAFFED > RESTAFF
RESTAFFS > RESTAFF
RESTAGE vb produce or perform a new production of (a play)
RESTAGED > RESTAGE
RESTAGES > RESTAGE
RESTAGING > RESTAGE
RESTAMP vb stamp again
RESTAMPED > RESTAMP
RESTAMPS > RESTAMP
RESTART vb commence (something) or set (something) in motion again ▷ n act or an instance of starting again
RESTARTED > RESTART
RESTARTER > RESTART
RESTARTS > RESTART
RESTATE vb state or affirm (something) again or in a different way
RESTATED > RESTATE
RESTATES > RESTATE
RESTATING > RESTATE
RESTATION vb station elsewhere
RESTED > REST
RESTEM vb stem again
RESTEMMED > RESTEM
RESTEMS > RESTEM
RESTER > REST
RESTERS > REST
RESTFUL adj relaxing or soothing
RESTFULLY > RESTFUL
RESTIER > RESTY
RESTIEST > RESTY
RESTIFF same as > RESTIVE
RESTIFORM adj (esp of bundles of nerve fibres) shaped like a cord or rope
RESTING > REST
RESTINGS > REST
RESTITCH vb stitch again
RESTITUTE vb restore
RESTIVE adj restless or impatient

RESTIVELY > RESTIVE
RESTLESS adj bored or dissatisfied
RESTO n restored antique, vintage car, etc
RESTOCK vb replenish stores or supplies
RESTOCKED > RESTOCK
RESTOCKS > RESTOCK
RESTOKE vb stoke again
RESTOKED > RESTOKE
RESTOKES > RESTOKE
RESTOKING > RESTOKE
RESTORAL n restoration
RESTORALS > RESTORAL
RESTORE vb return (a building, painting, etc) to its original condition
RESTORED > RESTORE
RESTORER > RESTORE
RESTORERS > RESTORE
RESTORES > RESTORE
RESTORING > RESTORE
RESTOS > RESTO
RESTRAIN vb hold (someone) back from action
RESTRAINS > RESTRAIN
RESTRAINT n something that restrains
RESTRESS vb stress again or differently
RESTRETCH vb stretch again
RESTRICT vb confine to certain limits
RESTRICTS > RESTRICT
RESTRIKE vb strike again
RESTRIKES > RESTRIKE
RESTRING vb string again or anew
RESTRINGE vb restrict
RESTRINGS > RESTRING
RESTRIVE vb strive again
RESTRIVEN > RESTRIVE
RESTRIVES > RESTRIVE
RESTROOM n room in a public building having lavatories and washing facilities
RESTROOMS > RESTROOM
RESTROVE > RESTRIVE
RESTRUCK > RESTRIKE
RESTRUNG > RESTRING
RESTS > REST
RESTUDIED > RESTUDY
RESTUDIES > RESTUDY
RESTUDY vb study again
RESTUFF vb put new stuffing in
RESTUFFED > RESTUFF
RESTUFFS > RESTUFF
RESTUMP vb provide with new stumps
RESTUMPED > RESTUMP
RESTUMPS > RESTUMP
RESTY adj restive
RESTYLE vb style again
RESTYLED > RESTYLE
RESTYLES > RESTYLE
RESTYLING > RESTYLE
RESUBJECT vb subject again
RESUBMIT vb submit again
RESUBMITS > RESUBMIT
RESULT n outcome or consequence ▷ vb be the outcome or consequence (of)

RESULTANT adj arising as a result ▷ n sum of two or more vectors, such as the force resulting from two or more forces acting on a single point
RESULTED > RESULT
RESULTFUL > RESULT
RESULTING > RESULT
RESULTS > RESULT
RESUMABLE > RESUME
RESUME vb begin again ▷ n summary
RESUMED > RESUME
RESUMER > RESUME
RESUMERS > RESUME
RESUMES > RESUME
RESUMING > RESUME
RESUMMON vb summon again
RESUMMONS > RESUMMON
RESUPINE adj lying on the back
RESUPPLY vb provide (with something) again
RESURFACE vb arise or occur again
RESURGE vb rise again from or as if from the dead
RESURGED > RESURGE
RESURGENT adj rising again, as to new life, vigour, etc
RESURGES > RESURGE
RESURGING > RESURGE
RESURRECT vb restore to life
RESURVEY vb survey again
RESURVEYS > RESURVEY
RESUS n (short for) resuscitation room
RESUSES > RESUS
RESUSPEND vb put back into suspension
RESUSSES > RESUS
RESWALLOW vb swallow again
RET vb moisten or soak (flax, hemp, jute, etc) to facilitate separation of fibres
RETABLE n ornamental screenlike structure above and behind an altar
RETABLES > RETABLE
RETABLO n shelf for panels behind an altar
RETABLOS > RETABLO
RETACK vb tack again
RETACKED > RETACK
RETACKING > RETACK
RETACKLE vb tackle again
RETACKLED > RETACKLE
RETACKLES > RETACKLE
RETACKS > RETACK
RETAG vb tag again
RETAGGED > RETAG
RETAGGING > RETAG
RETAGS > RETAG
RETAIL n selling of goods individually or in small amounts to the public ▷ adj of or engaged in such selling ▷ adv by retail ▷ vb sell or be sold retail
RETAILED > RETAIL
RETAILER > RETAIL
RETAILERS > RETAIL

RETAILING > RETAIL
RETAILOR vb tailor afresh
RETAILORS > RETAILOR
RETAILS > RETAIL
RETAIN vb keep in one's possession
RETAINED > RETAIN
RETAINER n fee to retain someone's services
RETAINERS > RETAINER
RETAINING > RETAIN
RETAINS > RETAIN
RETAKE vb recapture ▷ n act of rephotographing a scene
RETAKEN > RETAKE
RETAKER > RETAKE
RETAKERS > RETAKE
RETAKES > RETAKE
RETAKING > RETAKE
RETAKINGS > RETAKE
RETALIATE vb repay an injury or wrong in kind
RETALLIED > RETALLY
RETALLIES > RETALLY
RETALLY vb count up again
RETAMA n type of shrub
RETAMAS > RETAMA
RETAPE vb tape again
RETAPED > RETAPE
RETAPES > RETAPE
RETAPING > RETAPE
RETARD vb delay or slow (progress or development)
RETARDANT n substance that reduces the rate of a chemical reaction ▷ adj having a slowing effect
RETARDATE n offensive word for a person with learning difficulties
RETARDED > RETARD
RETARDER n substance that slows down chemical change
RETARDERS > RETARDER
RETARDING > RETARD
RETARDS > RETARD
RETARGET vb target afresh or differently
RETARGETS > RETARGET
RETASTE vb taste again
RETASTED > RETASTE
RETASTES > RETASTE
RETASTING > RETASTE
RETAUGHT > RETEACH
RETAX vb tax again
RETAXED > RETAX
RETAXES > RETAX
RETAXING > RETAX
RETCH vb try to vomit ▷ n involuntary spasm of the stomach
RETCHED > RETCH
RETCHES > RETCH
RETCHING n act of retching
RETCHINGS > RETCHING
RETCHLESS archaic variant of > RECKLESS
RETE n any network of nerves or blood vessels
RETEACH vb teach again
RETEACHES > RETEACH
RETEAM vb team up again
RETEAMED > RETEAM
RETEAMING > RETEAM
RETEAMS > RETEAM

RETEAR vb tear again
RETEARING > RETEAR
RETEARS > RETEAR
RETELL vb relate (a story, etc) again or differently
RETELLER > RETELL
RETELLERS > RETELL
RETELLING > RETELL
RETELLS > RETELL
RETEM n type of shrub
RETEMPER vb temper again
RETEMPERS > RETEMPER
RETEMS > RETEM
RETENE n yellow crystalline hydrocarbon found in tar oils
RETENES > RETENE
RETENTION n retaining
RETENTIVE adj capable of retaining or remembering
RETEST vb test (something) again or differently
RETESTED > RETEST
RETESTIFY vb testify again
RETESTING > RETEST
RETESTS > RETEST
RETEXTURE vb restore natural texture to
RETHINK vb consider again, esp with a view to changing one's tactics ▷ n act or an instance of thinking again
RETHINKER > RETHINK
RETHINKS > RETHINK
RETHOUGHT > RETHINK
RETHREAD vb thread again
RETHREADS > RETHREAD
RETIA > RETE
RETIAL > RETE
RETIARII > RETIARIUS
RETIARIUS n (in ancient Rome) a gladiator armed with a net and trident
RETIARY adj of, relating to, or resembling a net or web
RETICELLA n form of lace
RETICENCE > RETICENT
RETICENCY > RETICENT
RETICENT adj uncommunicative, reserved
RETICLE n network of fine lines, wires, etc, used in optical instruments
RETICLES > RETICLE
RETICULA > RETICULUM
RETICULAR adj in the form of a network or having a network of parts
RETICULE same as > RETICLE
RETICULES > RETICULE
RETICULUM n any fine network, esp one in the body composed of cells, fibres, etc
RETIE vb tie again
RETIED > RETIE
RETIEING > RETIE
RETIES > RETIE
RETIFORM adj netlike
RETIGHTEN vb tighten again
RETILE vb put new tiles in or on
RETILED > RETILE
RETILES > RETILE
RETILING > RETILE
RETIME vb time again or alter time of

RETIMED > RETIME
RETIMES > RETIME
RETIMING > RETIME
RETINA n light-sensitive membrane at the back of the eye
RETINAE > RETINA
RETINAL adj of or relating to the retina ▷ n aldehyde form of the polyene retinol
RETINALS > RETINAL
RETINAS > RETINA
RETINE n chemical found in body cells that slows cell growth and division
RETINENE n aldehyde form of the polyene retinol
RETINENES > RETINENE
RETINES > RETINE
RETINITE n any of various resins of fossil origin, esp one derived from lignite
RETINITES > RETINITE
RETINITIS n inflammation of the retina
RETINOIC adj containing or derived from retinoid
RETINOID adj resinlike ▷ n derivative of vitamin A
RETINOIDS > RETINOID
RETINOL n another name for vitamin A and rosin oil
RETINOLS > RETINOL
RETINT vb tint again or change tint of
RETINTED > RETINT
RETINTING > RETINT
RETINTS > RETINT
RETINUE n band of attendants
RETINUED > RETINUE
RETINUES > RETINUE
RETINULA n part of the compound eye in certain arthropods
RETINULAE > RETINULA
RETINULAR > RETINULA
RETINULAS > RETINULA
RETIRACY n (in US English) retirement
RETIRAL n act of retiring from office, one's work, etc
RETIRALS > RETIRAL
RETIRANT n (in US English) retired person
RETIRANTS > RETIRANT
RETIRE vb (cause to) give up office or work, esp through age
RETIRED adj having retired from work etc
RETIREDLY > RETIRED
RETIREE n person who has retired from work
RETIREES > RETIREE
RETIRER > RETIRE
RETIRERS > RETIRE
RETIRES > RETIRE
RETIRING adj shy
RETITLE vb give a new title to
RETITLED > RETITLE
RETITLES > RETITLE
RETITLING > RETITLE
RETOLD > RETELL
RETOOK > RETAKE

RETOOL vb replace, reequip, or rearrange the tools in (a factory, etc)
RETOOLED > RETOOL
RETOOLING > RETOOL
RETOOLS > RETOOL
RETORE > RETEAR
RETORN > RETEAR
RETORSION n retaliatory action taken by a state whose citizens have been mistreated by a foreign power by treating the subjects of that power similarly
RETORT vb reply quickly, wittily, or angrily ▷ n quick, witty, or angry reply
RETORTED > RETORT
RETORTER > RETORT
RETORTERS > RETORT
RETORTING > RETORT
RETORTION n act of retorting
RETORTIVE > RETORT
RETORTS > RETORT
RETOTAL vb add up again
RETOTALED > RETOTAL
RETOTALS > RETOTAL
RETOUCH vb restore or improve by new touches, esp of paint ▷ n art or practice of retouching
RETOUCHED > RETOUCH
RETOUCHER > RETOUCH
RETOUCHES > RETOUCH
RETOUR vb (in Scottish law) to return as heir
RETOURED > RETOUR
RETOURING > RETOUR
RETOURS > RETOUR
RETOX vb embark on a binge of something unhealthy after a period of abstinence
RETOXED > RETOX
RETOXES > RETOX
RETOXING > RETOX
RETRACE vb go back over (a route etc) again
RETRACED > RETRACE
RETRACER > RETRACE
RETRACERS > RETRACE
RETRACES > RETRACE
RETRACING > RETRACE
RETRACK vb track again
RETRACKED > RETRACK
RETRACKS > RETRACK
RETRACT vb withdraw (a statement etc)
RETRACTED > RETRACT
RETRACTOR n any of various muscles that retract an organ or part
RETRACTS > RETRACT
RETRAICT archaic form of > RETREAT
RETRAICTS > RETRAICT
RETRAIN vb train to do a new or different job
RETRAINED > RETRAIN
RETRAINEE > RETRAIN
RETRAINS > RETRAIN
RETRAIT archaic form of > RETREAT
RETRAITE archaic form of > RETREAT
RETRAITES > RETRAITE

r

RETRAITS > RETRAIT

RETRAITT n archaic word meaning portrait

RETRAITTS > RETRAITT

RETRAL adj at, near, or towards the back

RETRALLY > RETRAL

RETRATE archaic form of > RETREAT

RETRATED > RETRATE

RETRATES > RETRATE

RETRATING > RETRATE

RETREAD n remould ▷ vb remould

RETREADED > RETREAD

RETREADS > RETREAD

RETREAT vb move back from a position, withdraw ▷ n act of or military signal for retiring or withdrawal

RETREATED > RETREAT

RETREATER > RETREAT

RETREATS > RETREAT

RETREE n imperfectly made paper

RETREES > RETREE

RETRENCH vb reduce expenditure, cut back

RETRIAL n second trial of a case or defendant in a court of law

RETRIALS > RETRIAL

RETRIBUTE vb give back

RETRIED > RETRY

RETRIES > RETRY

RETRIEVAL n act or process of retrieving

RETRIEVE vb fetch back again ▷ n chance of being retrieved

RETRIEVED > RETRIEVE

RETRIEVER n dog trained to retrieve shot game

RETRIEVES > RETRIEVE

RETRIM vb trim again

RETRIMMED > RETRIM

RETRIMS > RETRIM

RETRO adj associated with or revived from the past ▷ n a retro style of art

RETROACT vb act in opposition

RETROACTS > RETROACT

RETROCEDE vb give back

RETROD > RETREAD

RETRODDEN > RETREAD

RETRODICT vb make surmises about the past using information from the present

RETROFIRE n act of firing a retrorocket

RETROFIT vb equip (a piece of equipment) with new parts after manufacture

RETROFITS > RETROFIT

RETROFLEX adj bent or curved backwards ▷ vb bend or turn backwards

RETROJECT vb throw backwards

RETRONYM n word coined for existing thing to distinguish it from new thing

RETRONYMS > RETRONYM

RETROPACK n system of retrorockets on a spacecraft

RETRORSE adj (esp of plant parts) pointing backwards or in a direction opposite to normal

RETROS > RETRO

RETROUSSE adj (of a nose) turned upwards

RETROVERT vb turn back

RETRY vb try again (a case already determined)

RETRYING > RETRY

RETS > RET

RETSINA n Greek wine flavoured with resin

RETSINAS > RETSINA

RETTED > RET

RETTERIES > RETTERY

RETTERY n flax-retting place

RETTING > RET

RETUND vb weaken or blunt

RETUNDED > RETUND

RETUNDING > RETUND

RETUNDS > RETUND

RETUNE vb tune (a musical instrument) differently or again

RETUNED > RETUNE

RETUNES > RETUNE

RETUNING > RETUNE

RETURF vb turf again

RETURFED > RETURF

RETURFING > RETURF

RETURFS > RETURF

RETURN vb go or come back ▷ n returning ▷ adj of or being a return

RETURNED > RETURN

RETURNEE n person who returns to his or her native country, esp after war service

RETURNEES > RETURNEE

RETURNER n person or thing that returns

RETURNERS > RETURNER

RETURNIK n someone returning to the former Soviet Union

RETURNIKS > RETURNIK

RETURNING > RETURN

RETURNS > RETURN

RETUSE adj having a rounded apex and a central depression

RETWEET vb post (another user's post) on the Twitter website for one's own followers

RETWEETED > RETWEET

RETWEETS > RETWEET

RETWIST vb twist again

RETWISTED > RETWIST

RETWISTS > RETWIST

RETYING > RETIE

RETYPE vb type again

RETYPED > RETYPE

RETYPES > RETYPE

RETYPING > RETYPE

REUNIFIED > REUNIFY

REUNIFIES > REUNIFY

REUNIFY vb bring together again something previously divided

REUNION n meeting of people who have been apart

REUNIONS > REUNION

REUNITE vb bring or come together again after a separation

REUNITED > REUNITE

REUNITER > REUNITE

REUNITERS > REUNITE

REUNITES > REUNITE

REUNITING > REUNITE

REUPTAKE vb absorb again ▷ n act of reabsorbing

REUPTAKEN > REUPTAKE

REUPTAKES > REUPTAKE

REUPTOOK > REUPTAKE

REURGE vb urge again

REURGED > REURGE

REURGES > REURGE

REURGING > REURGE

REUSABLE adj able to be used more than once

REUSABLES pl n products which can be used more than once

REUSE vb use again ▷ n act of using something again

REUSED > REUSE

REUSES > REUSE

REUSING > REUSE

REUTILISE same as > REUTILIZE

REUTILIZE vb utilize again

REUTTER vb utter again

REUTTERED > REUTTER

REUTTERS > REUTTER

REV n revolution (of an engine) ▷ vb increase the speed of revolution of (an engine)

REVALENTA n lentil flour

REVALUATE same as > REVALUE

REVALUE vb adjust the exchange value of (a currency) upwards

REVALUED > REVALUE

REVALUES > REVALUE

REVALUING > REVALUE

REVAMP vb renovate or restore ▷ n something that has been renovated or revamped

REVAMPED > REVAMP

REVAMPER > REVAMP

REVAMPERS > REVAMP

REVAMPING > REVAMP

REVAMPS > REVAMP

REVANCHE n revenge

REVANCHES > REVANCHE

REVARNISH vb varnish again

REVEAL vb make known ▷ n vertical side of an opening in a wall

REVEALED > REVEAL

REVEALER > REVEAL

REVEALERS > REVEAL

REVEALING adj disclosing information that one did not know

REVEALS > REVEAL

REVEHENT adj (in anatomy) carrying back

REVEILLE n morning bugle call to waken soldiers

REVEILLES > REVEILLE

REVEL vb take pleasure (in) ▷ n occasion of noisy merrymaking

REVELATOR n revealer

REVELED > REVEL

REVELER > REVEL

REVELERS > REVEL

REVELING > REVEL

REVELLED > REVEL

REVELLER > REVEL

REVELLERS > REVEL

REVELLING > REVEL

REVELMENT > REVEL

REVELRIES > REVELRY

REVELROUS > REVELRY

REVELRY n festivity

REVELS > REVEL

REVENANT n something, esp a ghost, that returns

REVENANTS > REVENANT

REVENGE n retaliation for wrong done ▷ vb make retaliation for

REVENGED > REVENGE

REVENGER > REVENGE

REVENGERS > REVENGE

REVENGES > REVENGE

REVENGING > REVENGE

REVENGIVE > REVENGE

REVENUAL > REVENUE

REVENUE n income, esp of a state

REVENUED > REVENUE

REVENUER n revenue officer or cutter

REVENUERS > REVENUER

REVENUES > REVENUE

REVERABLE > REVERE

REVERB n electronic device that creates artificial acoustics ▷ vb reverberate

REVERBED > REVERB

REVERBING > REVERB

REVERBS > REVERB

REVERE vb be in awe of and respect greatly

REVERED > REVERE

REVERENCE n awe mingled with respect and esteem

REVEREND adj worthy of reverence ▷ n clergyman

REVERENDS > REVEREND

REVERENT adj showing reverence

REVERER > REVERE

REVERERS > REVERE

REVERES > REVERE

REVERIE n absent-minded daydream

REVERIES > REVERIE

REVERIFY vb verify again

REVERING > REVERE

REVERIST n someone given to reveries

REVERISTS > REVERIST

REVERS n turned back part of a garment, such as the lapel

REVERSAL n act or an instance of reversing

REVERSALS > REVERSAL

REVERSE vb turn upside down or the other way round ▷ n opposite ▷ adj opposite or contrary

REVERSED > REVERSE

REVERSELY > REVERSE

REVERSER > REVERSE

REVERSERS > REVERSE

REVERSES > REVERSE

REVERSI n game played on a draughtsboard

REVERSING > REVERSE

r

REVERSION *n* return to a former state, practice, or belief

REVERSIS *n* type of card game

REVERSO *another name for* > VERSO

REVERSOS > REVERSO

REVERT *vb* return to a former state

REVERTANT *n* mutant that has reverted to an earlier form ▷ *adj* having mutated to an earlier form

REVERTED > REVERT

REVERTER > REVERT

REVERTERS > REVERT

REVERTING > REVERT

REVERTIVE > REVERT

REVERTS > REVERT

REVERY *same as* > REVERIE

REVEST *vb* restore (former power, authority, status, etc, to a person)

REVESTED > REVEST

REVESTING > REVEST

REVESTRY *same as* > VESTRY

REVESTS > REVEST

REVET *vb* face (a wall or embankment) with stones

REVETMENT *n* facing of stones, sandbags, etc, to protect a wall, embankment, or earthworks

REVETS > REVET

REVETTED > REVET

REVETTING > REVET

REVEUR *n* daydreamer

REVEURS > REVEUR

REVEUSE *n* female daydreamer

REVEUSES > REVEUSE

REVIBRATE *vb* vibrate again

REVICTUAL *vb* victual again

REVIE *vb* archaic cards term meaning challenge by placing a larger stake

REVIED > REVIE

REVIES > REVIE

REVIEW *n* critical assessment of a book, concert, etc ▷ *vb* hold or write a review of

REVIEWAL *same as* > REVIEW

REVIEWALS > REVIEWAL

REVIEWED > REVIEW

REVIEWER > REVIEW

REVIEWERS > REVIEW

REVIEWING > REVIEW

REVIEWS > REVIEW

REVILE *vb* be abusively scornful of

REVILED > REVILE

REVILER > REVILE

REVILERS > REVILE

REVILES > REVILE

REVILING > REVILE

REVILINGS > REVILE

REVIOLATE *vb* violate again

REVISABLE > REVISE

REVISAL > REVISE

REVISALS > REVISE

REVISE *vb* change or alter ▷ *n* act, process, or result of revising

REVISED > REVISE

REVISER > REVISE

REVISERS > REVISE

REVISES > REVISE

REVISING > REVISE

REVISION *n* act of revising

REVISIONS > REVISION

REVISIT *vb* visit again

REVISITED > REVISIT

REVISITS > REVISIT

REVISOR > REVISE

REVISORS > REVISE

REVISORY *adj* of or having the power of revision

REVIVABLE > REVIVE

REVIVABLY > REVIVE

REVIVAL *n* reviving or renewal

REVIVALS > REVIVAL

REVIVE *vb* bring or come back to life, vigour, use, etc

REVIVED > REVIVE

REVIVER > REVIVE

REVIVERS > REVIVE

REVIVES > REVIVE

REVIVIFY *vb* give new life to

REVIVING > REVIVE

REVIVINGS > REVIVE

REVIVOR *n* means of reviving a lawsuit that has been suspended

REVIVORS > REVIVOR

REVOCABLE *adj* capable of being revoked

REVOCABLY > REVOCABLE

REVOICE *vb* utter again

REVOICED > REVOICE

REVOICES > REVOICE

REVOICING > REVOICE

REVOKABLE *same as* > REVOCABLE

REVOKABLY > REVOCABLE

REVOKE *vb* cancel (a will, agreement, etc) ▷ *n* act of revoking

REVOKED > REVOKE

REVOKER > REVOKE

REVOKERS > REVOKE

REVOKES > REVOKE

REVOKING > REVOKE

REVOLT *n* uprising against authority ▷ *vb* rise in rebellion

REVOLTED > REVOLT

REVOLTER > REVOLT

REVOLTERS > REVOLT

REVOLTING *adj* disgusting, horrible

REVOLTS > REVOLT

REVOLUTE *adj* (esp of the margins of a leaf) rolled backwards and downwards

REVOLVE *vb* turn round, rotate ▷ *n* circular section of a stage that can be rotated

REVOLVED > REVOLVE

REVOLVER *n* repeating pistol

REVOLVERS > REVOLVER

REVOLVES > REVOLVE

REVOLVING *adj* denoting or relating to an engine, such as a radial aero engine, in which

the cylinders revolve about a fixed shaft

REVOTE *vb* decide or grant again by a new vote

REVOTED > REVOTE

REVOTES > REVOTE

REVOTING > REVOTE

REVS > REV

REVUE *n* theatrical entertainment with topical sketches and songs

REVUES > REVUE

REVUIST > REVUE

REVUISTS > REVUE

REVULSED *adj* filled with disgust

REVULSION *n* strong disgust

REVULSIVE *adj* of or causing revulsion ▷ *n* counterirritant

REVVED > REV

REVVING > REV

REVYING > REVIE

REW *archaic spelling of* > RUE

REWAKE *vb* awaken again

REWAKED > REWAKE

REWAKEN *vb* awaken again

REWAKENED > REWAKEN

REWAKENS > REWAKEN

REWAKES > REWAKE

REWAKING > REWAKE

REWAN *archaic past form of* > REWIN

REWARD *n* something given in return for a service ▷ *vb* pay or give something to (someone) for a service, information, etc

REWARDED > REWARD

REWARDER > REWARD

REWARDERS > REWARD

REWARDFUL > REWARD

REWARDING *adj* giving personal satisfaction, worthwhile

REWARDS > REWARD

REWAREWA *n* New Zealand tree

REWAREWAS > REWAREWA

REWARM *vb* warm again

REWARMED > REWARM

REWARMING > REWARM

REWARMS > REWARM

REWASH *vb* wash again

REWASHED > REWASH

REWASHES > REWASH

REWASHING > REWASH

REWATER *vb* water again

REWATERED > REWATER

REWATERS > REWATER

REWAX *vb* wax again

REWAXED > REWAX

REWAXES > REWAX

REWAXING > REWAX

REWEAR *vb* wear again

REWEARING > REWEAR

REWEARS > REWEAR

REWEAVE *vb* weave again

REWEAVED > REWEAVE

REWEAVES > REWEAVE

REWEAVING > REWEAVE

REWED *vb* wed again

REWEDDED > REWED

REWEDDING > REWED

REWEDS > REWED

REWEIGH *vb* weigh again

REWEIGHED > REWEIGH

REWEIGHS > REWEIGH

REWELD *vb* weld again

REWELDED > REWELD

REWELDING > REWELD

REWELDS > REWELD

REWET *vb* wet again

REWETS > REWET

REWETTED > REWET

REWETTING > REWET

REWIDEN *vb* widen again

REWIDENED > REWIDEN

REWIDENS > REWIDEN

REWILD *vb* return areas of land to a wild state

REWILDED > REWILD

REWILDING *n* process of returning land areas to a wild state

REWILDS > REWILD

REWIN *vb* win again

REWIND *vb* wind again

REWINDED > REWIND

REWINDER > REWIND

REWINDERS > REWIND

REWINDING *n* act of rewinding

REWINDS > REWIND

REWINNING > REWIN

REWINS > REWIN

REWIRABLE > REWIRE

REWIRE *vb* provide (a house, engine, etc) with new wiring

REWIRED > REWIRE

REWIRES > REWIRE

REWIRING *n* act of rewiring

REWIRINGS > REWIRING

REWOKE > REWAKE

REWOKEN > REWAKE

REWON > REWIN

REWORD *vb* alter the wording of

REWORDED > REWORD

REWORDING > REWORD

REWORDS > REWORD

REWORE > REWEAR

REWORK *vb* improve or bring up to date

REWORKED > REWORK

REWORKING > REWORK

REWORKS > REWORK

REWORN > REWEAR

REWOUND > REWIND

REWOVE > REWEAVE

REWOVEN > REWEAVE

REWRAP *vb* wrap again

REWRAPPED > REWRAP

REWRAPS > REWRAP

REWRAPT > REWRAP

REWRITE *vb* write again in a different way ▷ *n* something rewritten

REWRITER > REWRITE

REWRITERS > REWRITE

REWRITES > REWRITE

REWRITING > REWRITE

REWRITTEN > REWRITE

REWROTE > REWRITE

REWROUGHT > REWORK

REWS > REW

REWTH *archaic variant of* > RUTH

REWTHS > REWTH

REX *n* king

REXES > REX

REXINE n tradename for a form of artificial leather
REXINES > REXINE
REYNARD n fox
REYNARDS > REYNARD
REZ n informal word for an instance of reserving; reservation
REZERO vb reset to zero
REZEROED > REZERO
REZEROES > REZERO
REZEROING > REZERO
REZEROS > REZERO
REZES > REZ
REZONE vb zone again
REZONED > REZONE
REZONES > REZONE
REZONING n act of changing the land use classification of an area
REZONINGS > REZONING
REZZES > REZ
RHABDOID adj rod-shaped ▷ n rod-shaped structure found in cells of some plants and animals
RHABDOIDS > RHABDOID
RHABDOM n rodlike structures found in the eye of insects
RHABDOMAL > RHABDOM
RHABDOME same as > RHABDOM
RHABDOMES > RHABDOME
RHABDOMS > RHABDOM
RHABDUS n sponge spicule
RHABDUSES > RHABDUS
RHACHIAL > RACHIS
RHACHIDES > RHACHIS
RHACHILLA same as > RACHILLA
RHACHIS same as > RACHIS
RHACHISES > RHACHIS
RHACHITIS same as > RACHITIS
RHAGADES pl n cracks found in the skin
RHAMNOSE n type of plant sugar
RHAMNOSES > RHAMNOSE
RHAMNUS n buckthorn
RHAMNUSES > RHAMNUS
RHAMPHOID adj beaklike
RHANJA n Indian English word for a male lover
RHANJAS > RHANJA
RHAPHAE > RHAPHE
RHAPHE same as > RAPHE
RHAPHES > RHAPHE
RHAPHIDE same as > RAPHIDE
RHAPHIDES > RHAPHIDE
RHAPHIS same as > RAPHIDE
RHAPONTIC n rhubarb
RHAPSODE n (in ancient Greece) professional reciter of poetry
RHAPSODES > RHAPSODE
RHAPSODIC adj of or like a rhapsody
RHAPSODY n freely structured emotional piece of music
RHATANIES > RHATANY
RHATANY n South American leguminous shrub

RHEA n S American three-toed ostrich
RHEAS > RHEA
RHEBOK n woolly brownish-grey southern African antelope
RHEBOKS > RHEBOK
RHEMATIC adj of or relating to word formation
RHEME n constituent of a sentence that adds most new information
RHEMES > RHEME
RHENIUM n silvery-white metallic element with a high melting point
RHENIUMS > RHENIUM
RHEOBASE n minimum nerve impulse required to elicit a response from a tissue
RHEOBASES > RHEOBASE
RHEOBASIC > RHEOBASE
RHEOCHORD n wire inserted into an electrical circuit to vary or regulate the current
RHEOCORDS > RHEOCORD
RHEOLOGIC > RHEOLOGY
RHEOLOGY n branch of physics concerned with the flow and change of shape of matter
RHEOMETER n instrument for measuring the velocity of the blood flow
RHEOMETRY > RHEOMETER
RHEOPHIL adj liking flowing water
RHEOPHILE n something that likes flowing water
RHEOSCOPE n device that detects an electric current
RHEOSTAT n instrument for varying the resistance of an electrical circuit
RHEOSTATS > RHEOSTAT
RHEOTAXES > RHEOTAXIS
RHEOTAXIS n movement of an organism towards or away from a current of water
RHEOTOME n interrupter
RHEOTOMES > RHEOTOME
RHEOTROPE n electric-current-reversing device
RHESUS n macaque monkey
RHESUSES > RHESUS
RHETOR n teacher of rhetoric
RHETORIC n art of effective speaking or writing
RHETORICS > RHETORIC
RHETORISE same as > RHETORIZE
RHETORIZE vb make use of rhetoric
RHETORS > RHETOR
RHEUM n watery discharge from the eyes or nose
RHEUMATIC adj (person) affected by rheumatism ▷ n person suffering from rheumatism
RHEUMATIZ n dialect word meaning rheumatism, any painful disorder of joints, muscles, or connective tissue
RHEUMED adj rheumy

RHEUMIC adj of or relating to rheum
RHEUMIER > RHEUMY
RHEUMIEST > RHEUMY
RHEUMS > RHEUM
RHEUMY adj of the nature of rheum
RHEXES > RHEXIS
RHEXIS n rupture
RHEXISES > RHEXIS
RHIES > RHY
RHIGOLENE n volatile liquid obtained from petroleum and used as a local anaesthetic
RHIME old spelling of > RHYME
RHIMES > RHIME
RHINAL adj of or relating to the nose
RHINE n dialect word for a ditch
RHINES > RHINE
RHINITIC > RHINITIS
RHINITIS n inflammation of the mucous membrane that lines the nose
RHINO n rhinoceros
RHINOCERI n rhinoceroses
RHINOLITH n calculus formed in the nose
RHINOLOGY n branch of medical science concerned with the nose and its diseases
RHINOS > RHINO
RHIPIDATE adj shaped like a fan
RHIPIDION n fan found in Greek Orthodox churches
RHIPIDIUM n on a plant, a fan-shaped arrangement of flowers
RHIZIC adj of or relating to the root of an equation
RHIZINE same as > RHIZOID
RHIZINES > RHIZINE
RHIZOBIA > RHIZOBIUM
RHIZOBIAL > RHIZOBIUM
RHIZOBIUM n type of rod-shaped bacterium typically occurring in the root nodules of leguminous plants
RHIZOCARP n plant that fruits underground or whose root remains intact while the leaves die off annually
RHIZOCAUL n rootlike stem
RHIZOID n hairlike structure in mosses, ferns, and related plants
RHIZOIDAL > RHIZOID
RHIZOIDS > RHIZOID
RHIZOMA same as > RHIZOME
RHIZOMATA > RHIZOMA
RHIZOME n thick underground stem producing new plants
RHIZOMES > RHIZOME
RHIZOMIC > RHIZOME
RHIZOPI > RHIZOPUS
RHIZOPOD n type of protozoan of the phylum which includes the amoebas
RHIZOPODS > RHIZOPOD
RHIZOPUS n type of fungus

RHIZOTOMY n surgical incision into the roots of spinal nerves, esp for the relief of pain
RHO n 17th letter in the Greek alphabet
RHODAMIN same as > RHODAMINE
RHODAMINE n any one of a group of synthetic red or pink basic dyestuffs used for wool and silk. They are made from phthalic anhydride and aminophenols
RHODAMINS > RHODAMIN
RHODANATE n a salt of thiocyanic acid
RHODANIC adj of or relating to thiocyanic acid
RHODANISE same as > RHODANIZE
RHODANIZE vb plate with rhodium
RHODIC adj of or containing rhodium, esp in the tetravalent state
RHODIE same as > RHODY
RHODIES > RHODY
RHODINAL n substance with a lemon-like smell found esp in citronella and certain eucalyptus oils
RHODINALS > RHODINAL
RHODIUM n hard metallic element
RHODIUMS > RHODIUM
RHODOLITE n pale violet or red variety of garnet, used as a gemstone
RHODONITE n brownish translucent mineral
RHODOPSIN n red pigment in the rods of the retina in vertebrates
RHODORA n type of shrub
RHODORAS > RHODORA
RHODOUS adj of or containing rhodium (but proportionally more than a rhodic compound)
RHODY n rhododendron
RHOEADINE n alkaloid found in the poppy
RHOMB same as > RHOMBUS
RHOMBI > RHOMBUS
RHOMBIC adj relating to or having the shape of a rhombus
RHOMBICAL same as > RHOMBIC
RHOMBOI > RHOMBOS
RHOMBOID n parallelogram with adjacent sides of unequal length ▷ adj having such a shape
RHOMBOIDS > RHOMBOID
RHOMBOS n wooden slat attached to a thong that makes a roaring sound when the thong is whirled
RHOMBS > RHOMB
RHOMBUS n diamond-shaped figure
RHOMBUSES > RHOMBUS
RHONCHAL > RHONCHUS
RHONCHI > RHONCHUS
RHONCHIAL > RHONCHUS
RHONCHUS n respiratory sound resembling snoring

RHONCUS n rattling or whistling respiratory sound resembling snoring
RHONCUSES > RHONCUS
RHONE same as **>** RONE
RHONES > RHONE
RHOPALIC adj (of verse) with each word having one more syllable than the word before
RHOPALISM > RHOPALIC
RHOS > RHO
RHOTACISE same as **>** RHOTACIZE
RHOTACISM n excessive use or idiosyncratic pronunciation of r
RHOTACIST > RHOTACISM
RHOTACIZE vb pronounce r excessively or idiosyncratically
RHOTIC adj denoting or speaking a dialect of English in which postvocalic rs are pronounced
RHOTICITY > RHOTIC
RHUBARB n garden plant with fleshy stalks ▷ interj noise made by actors to simulate conversation ▷ vb simulate conversation in this way
RHUBARBED > RHUBARB
RHUBARBS > RHUBARB
RHUBARBY adj tasting of rhubarb
RHUMB n imaginary line on the surface of a sphere that intersects all meridians at the same angle
RHUMBA same as **>** RUMBA
RHUMBAED > RHUMBA
RHUMBAING > RHUMBA
RHUMBAS > RHUMBA
RHUMBS > RHUMB
RHUS n genus of shrubs and small trees
RHUSES > RHUS
RHY archaic spelling of **>** RYE
RHYME n sameness of the final sounds at the ends of lines of verse, or in words ▷ vb make a rhyme
RHYMED > RHYME
RHYMELESS > RHYME
RHYMER same as **>** RHYMESTER
RHYMERS > RHYMER
RHYMES > RHYME
RHYMESTER n mediocre poet
RHYMING > RHYME
RHYMIST > RHYME
RHYMISTS > RHYME
RHYNE same as **>** RHINE
RHYNES > RHYNE
RHYOLITE n fine-grained igneous rock
RHYOLITES > RHYOLITE
RHYOLITIC > RHYOLITE
RHYTA > RHYTON
RHYTHM n any regular movement or beat
RHYTHMAL adj rhythmic
RHYTHMED > RHYTHM
RHYTHMI > RHYTHMUS

RHYTHMIC adj of, relating to, or characterized by rhythm, as in movement or sound
RHYTHMICS n study of rhythmic movement
RHYTHMISE same as **>** RHYTHMIZE
RHYTHMIST n person who has a good sense of rhythm
RHYTHMIZE vb make rhythmic
RHYTHMS > RHYTHM
RHYTHMUS n rhythm
RHYTIDOME n bark
RHYTINA n type of sea cow
RHYTINAS > RHYTINA
RHYTON n (in ancient Greece) horn-shaped drinking vessel
RHYTONS > RHYTON
RIA n long narrow inlet of the seacoast
RIAD n traditional Moroccan house with an interior garden
RIADS > RIAD
RIAL n standard monetary unit of Iran
RIALS > RIAL
RIALTO n market or exchange
RIALTOS > RIALTO
RIANCIES > RIANT
RIANCY > RIANT
RIANT adj laughing
RIANTLY > RIANT
RIAS > RIA
RIATA same as **>** REATA
RIATAS > RIATA
RIB n one of the curved bones forming the framework of the upper part of the body ▷ vb provide or mark with ribs
RIBA n (in Islam) interest or usury
RIBALD adj humorously or mockingly rude ▷ n ribald person
RIBALDER > RIBALD
RIBALDEST > RIBALD
RIBALDLY > RIBALD
RIBALDRY n ribald language or behaviour
RIBALDS > RIBALD
RIBAND n ribbon awarded for some achievement
RIBANDS > RIBAND
RIBAS > RIBA
RIBATTUTA n (in music) type of trill
RIBAUD archaic variant of **>** RIBALD
RIBAUDRED archaic variant of **>** RIBALD
RIBAUDRY archaic variant of **>** RIBALDRY
RIBAUDS > RIBAUD
RIBAVIRIN n type of antiviral drug
RIBBAND same as **>** RIBAND
RIBBANDS > RIBBAND
RIBBED > RIB
RIBBER n someone who ribs
RIBBERS > RIBBER

RIBBIE n baseball run batted in
RIBBIER > RIBBY
RIBBIES > RIBBIE
RIBBIEST > RIBBY
RIBBING > RIB
RIBBINGS > RIB
RIBBIT n sound a frog makes
RIBBITS > RIBBIT
RIBBON n narrow band of fabric used for trimming, tying, etc ▷ vb adorn with a ribbon or ribbons
RIBBONED > RIBBON
RIBBONIER > RIBBONY
RIBBONING > RIBBON
RIBBONRY n ribbons or ribbon work
RIBBONS > RIBBON
RIBBONY adj resembling ribbons
RIBBY adj with noticeable ribs
RIBCAGE n bony structure of ribs enclosing the lungs
RIBCAGES > RIBCAGE
RIBES n genus of shrubs that includes currants
RIBEYE n beefsteak cut from the outer side of the rib section
RIBEYES > RIBEYE
RIBGRASS same as **>** RIBWORT
RIBIBE n rebeck
RIBIBES > RIBIBE
RIBIBLE same as **>** RIBIBE
RIBIBLES > RIBIBLE
RIBIER n variety of grape
RIBIERS > RIBIER
RIBLESS > RIB
RIBLET n small rib
RIBLETS > RIBLET
RIBLIKE > RIB
RIBOSE n pentose sugar that occurs in RNA and riboflavin
RIBOSES > RIBOSE
RIBOSOMAL > RIBOSOME
RIBOSOME n any of numerous minute particles in the cytoplasm of cells
RIBOSOMES > RIBOSOME
RIBOZYMAL > RIBOZYME
RIBOZYME n RNA molecule capable of catalysing a chemical reaction
RIBOZYMES > RIBOZYME
RIBS > RIB
RIBSTON n variety of apple
RIBSTONE same as **>** RIBSTON
RIBSTONES > RIBSTONE
RIBSTONS > RIBSTON
RIBULOSE n type of sugar
RIBULOSES > RIBULOSE
RIBWORK n work or structure involving ribs
RIBWORKS > RIBWORK
RIBWORT n Eurasian plant with lancelike ribbed leaves
RIBWORTS > RIBWORT
RICE n cereal plant grown on wet ground in warm countries ▷ vb sieve (vegetables) to a coarse mashed consistency

RICEBIRD n any of various birds frequenting rice fields, esp the Java sparrow
RICEBIRDS > RICEBIRD
RICED > RICE
RICEFIELD n field used for growing rice
RICEGRASS n type of grass
RICER n kitchen utensil through which soft foods are pressed to form a coarse mash
RICERCAR same as **>** RICERCARE
RICERCARE n elaborate polyphonic composition making extensive use of contrapuntal imitation and usually very slow in tempo
RICERCARI > RICERCARE
RICERCARS > RICERCAR
RICERCATA same as **>** RICERCARE
RICERS > RICER
RICES > RICE
RICEY adj resembling or containing rice
RICH adj owning a lot of money or property, wealthy ▷ vb (in archaic usage) enrich
RICHED > RICH
RICHEN vb enrich
RICHENED > RICHEN
RICHENING > RICHEN
RICHENS > RICHEN
RICHER > RICH
RICHES pl n wealth
RICHESSE n wealth or richness
RICHESSES > RICHESSE
RICHEST > RICH
RICHING > RICH
RICHLY adv elaborately
RICHNESS n state or quality of being rich
RICHT adj right ▷ adv right ▷ n right ▷ vb right
RICHTED > RICHT
RICHTER > RICHT
RICHTEST > RICHT
RICHTING > RICHT
RICHTS > RICHT
RICHWEED n type of plant
RICHWEEDS > RICHWEED
RICIER > RICY
RICIEST > RICY
RICIN n highly toxic protein, a lectin, derived from castor-oil seeds
RICING > RICE
RICINS > RICIN
RICINUS n genus of plants
RICINUSES > RICINUS
RICK n stack of hay etc ▷ vb wrench or sprain (a joint)
RICKED > RICK
RICKER n young kauri tree of New Zealand
RICKERS > RICKER
RICKET n mistake
RICKETIER > RICKETY
RICKETILY > RICKETY
RICKETS n disease of children marked by softening of the bones, bow legs, etc
RICKETTY same as **>** RICKETY

RICKETY adj shaky or unstable

RICKEY n cocktail consisting of gin or vodka, lime juice, and soda water, served iced

RICKEYS > RICKEY

RICKING > RICK

RICKLE n unsteady or shaky structure

RICKLES > RICKLE

RICKLIER > RICKLY

RICKLIEST > RICKLY

RICKLY adj archaic word for run-down or rickety

RICKRACK n zigzag braid used for trimming

RICKRACKS > RICKRACK

RICKS > RICK

RICKSHA same as > RICKSHAW

RICKSHAS > RICKSHA

RICKSHAW n light two-wheeled vehicle pulled by one or two people

RICKSHAWS > RICKSHAW

RICKSTAND n platform on which to put a rick

RICKSTICK n tool used when making hayricks

RICKYARD n place where hayricks are put

RICKYARDS > RICKYARD

RICOCHET vb (of a bullet) rebound from a solid surface ▷ n such a rebound

RICOCHETS > RICOCHET

RICOTTA n soft white unsalted Italian cheese made from sheep's milk

RICOTTAS > RICOTTA

RICRAC same as > RICKRACK

RICRACS > RICRAC

RICTAL > RICTUS

RICTUS n gape or cleft of an open mouth or beak

RICTUSES > RICTUS

RICY same as > RICEY

RID vb clear or relieve (of)

RIDABLE > RIDE

RIDDANCE n act of getting rid of something undesirable or unpleasant

RIDDANCES > RIDDANCE

RIDDED > RID

RIDDEN > RIDE

RIDDER > RID

RIDDERS > RID

RIDDING > RID

RIDDLE n question made puzzling to test one's ingenuity ▷ vb speak in riddles

RIDDLED > RIDDLE

RIDDLER > RIDDLE

RIDDLERS > RIDDLE

RIDDLES > RIDDLE

RIDDLING > RIDDLE

RIDDLINGS > RIDDLE

RIDE vb sit on and control or propel (a horse, bicycle, etc) ▷ n journey on a horse etc

RIDEABLE > RIDE

RIDENT adj laughing, smiling, or happy

RIDER n person who rides

RIDERED > RIDER

RIDERLESS > RIDER

RIDERS > RIDER

RIDERSHIP > RIDER

RIDES > RIDE

RIDGE n long narrow hill ▷ vb form into a ridge or ridges

RIDGEBACK n as in Rhodesian ridgeback breed of dog characterized by a ridge of hair growing along the back in the opposite direction to the rest of the coat

RIDGED > RIDGE

RIDGEL same as > RIDGELING

RIDGELIKE > RIDGE

RIDGELINE n ridge

RIDGELING n domestic male animal with one testicle

RIDGELS > RIDGEL

RIDGEPOLE n timber along the ridge of a roof, to which the rafters are attached

RIDGER n plough used to form furrows and ridges

RIDGERS > RIDGER

RIDGES > RIDGE

RIDGETOP n summit of ridge

RIDGETOPS > RIDGETOP

RIDGETREE another name for > RIDGEPOLE

RIDGEWAY n road or track along a ridge, esp one of great antiquity

RIDGEWAYS > RIDGEWAY

RIDGIER > RIDGE

RIDGIEST > RIDGE

RIDGIL same as > RIDGELING

RIDGILS > RIDGIL

RIDGING > RIDGE

RIDGINGS > RIDGE

RIDGLING same as > RIDGELING

RIDGLINGS > RIDGLING

RIDGY > RIDGE

RIDIC adj ridiculous

RIDICULE n treatment of a person or thing as ridiculous ▷ vb laugh at, make fun of

RIDICULED > RIDICULE

RIDICULER > RIDICULE

RIDICULES > RIDICULE

RIDING > RIDE

RIDINGS > RIDE

RIDLEY n marine turtle

RIDLEYS > RIDLEY

RIDOTTO n entertainment with music and dancing, often in masquerade

RIDOTTOS > RIDOTTO

RIDS > RID

RIEL n standard monetary unit of Cambodia

RIELS > RIEL

RIEM n strip of hide

RIEMPIE n leather thong or lace used mainly to make chair seats

RIEMPIES > RIEMPIE

RIEMS > RIEM

RIESLING n type of white wine

RIESLINGS > RIESLING

RIEVE vb archaic word for rob or plunder

RIEVED > RIEVE

RIEVER n archaic word for robber or plunderer

RIEVERS > RIEVER

RIEVES > RIEVE

RIEVING > RIEVE

RIF vb lay off

RIFAMPIN n drug used in the treatment of tuberculosis, meningitis, and leprosy

RIFAMPINS > RIFAMPIN

RIFAMYCIN n antibiotic

RIFE adj widespread or common

RIFELY > RIFE

RIFENESS > RIFE

RIFER > RIFE

RIFEST > RIFE

RIFF n short repeated melodic figure ▷ vb play or perform riffs in jazz or rock music

RIFFAGE n (in jazz or rock music) act or an instance of playing a short series of chords

RIFFAGES > RIFFAGE

RIFFED > RIFF

RIFFING > RIFF

RIFFLE vb flick through (pages etc) quickly ▷ n rapid in a stream

RIFFLED > RIFFLE

RIFFLER n file with a curved face for filing concave surfaces

RIFFLERS > RIFFLER

RIFFLES > RIFFLE

RIFFLING > RIFFLE

RIFFOLA n use of an abundance of dominant riffs

RIFFOLAS > RIFFOLA

RIFFRAFF n rabble, disreputable people

RIFFRAFFS > RIFFRAFF

RIFFS > RIFF

RIFLE n firearm with a long barrel ▷ vb cut spiral grooves inside the barrel of a gun

RIFLEBIRD n any of various birds of paradise

RIFLED > RIFLE

RIFLEMAN n person skilled in the use of a rifle, esp a soldier

RIFLEMEN > RIFLEMAN

RIFLER > RIFLE

RIFLERIES > RIFLERY

RIFLERS > RIFLE

RIFLERY n rifle shots

RIFLES > RIFLE

RIFLING n cutting of spiral grooves on the inside of a firearm's barrel

RIFLINGS > RIFLING

RIFLIP n genetic difference between two individuals

RIFLIPS > RIFLIP

RIFS > RIF

RIFT n break in friendly relations ▷ vb burst or cause to burst open

RIFTE archaic word for > RIFT

RIFTED > RIFT

RIFTIER > RIFT

RIFTIEST > RIFT

RIFTING > RIFT

RIFTLESS > RIFT

RIFTS > RIFT

RIFTY > RIFT

RIG vb arrange in a dishonest way ▷ n apparatus for drilling for oil and gas

RIGADOON n old Provençal dance in lively duple time

RIGADOONS > RIGADOON

RIGATONI n macaroni in the form of short ridged often slightly curved pieces

RIGATONIS > RIGATONI

RIGAUDON same as > RIGADOON

RIGAUDONS > RIGAUDON

RIGG n type of fish

RIGGALD same as > RIDGELING

RIGGALDS > RIGGALD

RIGGED > RIG

RIGGER n workman who rigs vessels, etc

RIGGERS > RIGGER

RIGGING > RIG

RIGGINGS > RIG

RIGGISH adj dialect word meaning wanton

RIGGS > RIGG

RIGHT adj just ▷ adv correctly ▷ n claim, title, etc allowed or due ▷ vb bring or come back to a normal or correct state

RIGHTABLE adj capable of being righted

RIGHTABLY > RIGHTABLE

RIGHTED > RIGHT

RIGHTEN vb set right

RIGHTENED > RIGHTEN

RIGHTENS > RIGHTEN

RIGHTEOUS adj upright, godly, or virtuous

RIGHTER > RIGHT

RIGHTERS > RIGHT

RIGHTEST > RIGHT

RIGHTFUL adj in accordance with what is right

RIGHTIER > RIGHTY

RIGHTIES > RIGHTY

RIGHTIEST > RIGHTY

RIGHTING > RIGHT

RIGHTINGS > RIGHT

RIGHTISH adj somewhat right, esp politically

RIGHTISM > RIGHTIST

RIGHTISMS > RIGHTIST

RIGHTIST adj on the political right ▷ n supporter of the political right

RIGHTISTS > RIGHTIST

RIGHTLESS > RIGHT

RIGHTLY adv in accordance with the true facts or justice

RIGHTMOST > RIGHT

RIGHTNESS n state or quality of being right

RIGHTO interj expression of agreement or compliance

RIGHTS > RIGHT

RIGHTSIZE vb restructure (an organization) to cut costs and improve effectiveness without ruthlessly downsizing

RIGHTWARD adj situated on or directed towards the right ▷ adv towards or on the right

RIGHTY n right-handed person ▷ adj right-handed

RIGID adj inflexible or strict ▷ adv completely or excessively ▷ n strict and unbending person

RIGIDER > RIGID

RIGIDEST > RIGID

RIGIDIFY vb make or become rigid

RIGIDISE same as > RIGIDIZE

RIGIDISED > RIGIDISE

RIGIDISES > RIGIDISE

RIGIDITY > RIGID

RIGIDIZE vb make or become rigid

RIGIDIZED > RIGIDIZE

RIGIDIZES > RIGIDIZE

RIGIDLY > RIGID

RIGIDNESS > RIGID

RIGIDS > RIGID

RIGLIN same as > RIDGELING

RIGLING same as > RIDGELING

RIGLINGS > RIGLING

RIGLINS > RIGLIN

RIGMAROLE n long complicated procedure

RIGOL n (in dialect) ditch or gutter

RIGOLL same as > RIGOL

RIGOLLS > RIGOLL

RIGOLS > RIGOL

RIGOR same as > RIGOUR

RIGORISM n strictness in judgment or conduct

RIGORISMS > RIGORISM

RIGORIST > RIGORISM

RIGORISTS > RIGORISM

RIGOROUS adj harsh, severe, or stern

RIGORS > RIGOR

RIGOUR n harshness, severity, or strictness

RIGOURS > RIGOUR

RIGOUT n person's clothing

RIGOUTS > RIGOUT

RIGS > RIG

RIGSDALER n any of various former Scandinavian or Dutch small silver coins

RIGWIDDIE n part of the carthorse's harness to which the shafts of the cart attach

RIGWOODIE same as > RIGWIDDIE

RIJSTAFEL n assortment of Indonesian rice dishes

RIKISHA same as > RICKSHAW

RIKISHAS > RIKISHA

RIKISHI n sumo wrestler

RIKSHAW same as > RICKSHAW

RIKSHAWS > RIKSHAW

RILE vb anger or annoy

RILED > RILE

RILES > RILE

RILEY adj cross or irritable

RILIER > RILEY

RILIEST > RILEY

RILIEVI > RILIEVO

RILIEVO same as > RELIEF

RILING > RILE

RILL n small stream ▷ vb trickle

RILLE same as > RILL

RILLED > RILL

RILLES > RILLE

RILLET n little rill

RILLETS > RILLET

RILLETTES pl n potted meat

RILLING > RILL

RILLMARK n mark left by the trickle of a rill

RILLMARKS > RILLMARK

RILLS > RILL

RIM n edge or border ▷ vb put a rim on (a pot, cup, wheel, etc)

RIMA n long narrow opening

RIMAE > RIMA

RIMAYE n crevasse at the head of a glacier

RIMAYES > RIMAYE

RIME same as > RHYME

RIMED > RIME

RIMELESS > RHYME

RIMER same as > RHYMESTER

RIMERS > RIMER

RIMES > RIME

RIMESTER same as > RHYMESTER

RIMESTERS > RIMESTER

RIMFIRE adj (of a cartridge) having the primer in the rim of the base ▷ n cartridge of this type

RIMFIRES > RIMFIRE

RIMIER > RIMY

RIMIEST > RIMY

RIMINESS > RIMY

RIMING > RIME

RIMLAND n area situated on the outer edges of a region

RIMLANDS > RIMLAND

RIMLESS > RIM

RIMMED > RIM

RIMMER n tool for shaping the edge of something

RIMMERS > RIMMER

RIMMING > RIM

RIMMINGS > RIM

RIMOSE adj (esp of plant parts) having the surface marked by a network of intersecting cracks

RIMOSELY > RIMOSE

RIMOSITY > RIMOSE

RIMOUS same as > RIMOSE

RIMPLE vb crease or wrinkle

RIMPLED > RIMPLE

RIMPLES > RIMPLE

RIMPLING > RIMPLE

RIMROCK n rock forming the boundaries of a sandy or gravelly alluvial deposit

RIMROCKS > RIMROCK

RIMS > RIM

RIMSHOT n deliberate simultaneous striking of skin and rim of drum

RIMSHOTS > RIMSHOT

RIMU n New Zealand tree

RIMUS > RIMU

RIMY adj coated with rime

RIN Scots variant of > RUN

RIND n tough outer coating of fruits, cheese, or bacon ▷ vb take the bark off

RINDED > RIND

RINDIER > RINDY

RINDIEST > RINDY

RINDING > RIND

RINDLESS > RIND

RINDS > RIND

RINDY adj with a rind or rindlike skin

RINE archaic variant of > RIND

RINES > RINE

RING vb give out a clear resonant sound, as a bell ▷ n instance of ringing

RINGBARK same as > RING

RINGBARKS > RINGBARK

RINGBIT n type of bit worn by a horse

RINGBITS > RINGBIT

RINGBOLT n bolt with a ring fitted through an eye attached to the bolt head

RINGBOLTS > RINGBOLT

RINGBONE n abnormal bony growth affecting the pastern of a horse, often causing lameness

RINGBONES > RINGBONE

RINGDOVE n large Eurasian pigeon with white patches on the wings and neck

RINGDOVES > RINGDOVE

RINGED > RING

RINGENT adj (of the corolla of plants) consisting of two gaping lips

RINGER n person or thing apparently identical to another

RINGERS > RINGER

RINGETTE n team sport played on ice, using straight sticks to control a rubber ring

RINGETTES > RINGETTE

RINGGIT n standard monetary unit of Malaysia

RINGGITS > RINGGIT

RINGHALS n variety of cobra

RINGING > RING

RINGINGLY > RING

RINGINGS > RING

RINGLESS > RING

RINGLET n curly lock of hair

RINGLETED > RINGLET

RINGLETS > RINGLET

RINGLETY adj resembling a ringlet

RINGLIKE > RING

RINGMAN n (in dialect) ring finger

RINGMEN > RINGMAN

RINGNECK n any bird that has ringlike markings round its neck

RINGNECKS > RINGNECK

RINGS > RING

RINGSIDE n row of seats nearest a boxing or circus ring ▷ adj providing a close uninterrupted view

RINGSIDER n someone with a ringside seat or position

RINGSIDES > RINGSIDE

RINGSTAND n stand for laboratory equipment

RINGSTER n member of a ring controlling a market in antiques, art treasures, etc

RINGSTERS > RINGSTER

RINGTAIL n possum with a curling tail used to grip branches while climbing

RINGTAILS > RINGTAIL

RINGTAW n game in which the aim is to knock marbles out of a ring

RINGTAWS > RINGTAW

RINGTONE n musical tune played by a mobile phone when a call is received

RINGTONES > RINGTONE

RINGTOSS n game in which participants try to throw hoops onto an upright stick

RINGWAY n bypass

RINGWAYS > RINGWAY

RINGWISE adj used to being in the ring and able to respond appropriately

RINGWOMB n complication at lambing resulting from failure of the cervix to open

RINGWOMBS > RINGWOMB

RINGWORK n circular earthwork

RINGWORKS > RINGWORK

RINGWORM n fungal skin disease in circular patches

RINGWORMS > RINGWORM

RINK n sheet of ice for skating or curling ▷ vb skate on a rink

RINKED > RINK

RINKHALS n S African cobra that can spit venom

RINKING > RINK

RINKS > RINK

RINKSIDE n area at the side of a rink

RINKSIDES > RINKSIDE

RINNING > RIN

RINS > RIN

RINSABLE > RINSE

RINSE vb remove soap from (washed clothes, hair, etc) by applying clean water ▷ n act of rinsing

RINSEABLE > RINSE

RINSED > RINSE

RINSER > RINSE

RINSERS > RINSE

RINSES > RINSE

RINSIBLE > RINSE

RINSING > RINSE

RINSINGS > RINSE

RIOJA n red or white Spanish wine with a vanilla bouquet and flavour

RIOJAS > RIOJA

RIOT n disorderly unruly disturbance ▷ vb take part in a riot

RIOTED > RIOT

RIOTER > RIOT

RIOTERS > RIOT

RIOTING > RIOT

RIOTINGS > RIOT
RIOTISE n archaic word for riotous behaviour and excess
RIOTISES > RIOTISE
RIOTIZE same as **>** RIOTISE
RIOTIZES > RIOTIZE
RIOTOUS adj unrestrained
RIOTOUSLY > RIOTOUS
RIOTRIES > RIOTRY
RIOTRY n riotous behaviour
RIOTS > RIOT
RIP vb tear violently **▷** n split or tear
RIPARIAL > RIPARIAN
RIPARIALS > RIPARIAL
RIPARIAN adj of or on the banks of a river **▷** n person who owns land on a riverbank
RIPARIANS > RIPARIAN
RIPCORD n cord pulled to open a parachute
RIPCORDS > RIPCORD
RIPE adj ready to be reaped, eaten, etc **▷** vb ripen
RIPECK same as **>** RYEPECK
RIPECKS > RIPECK
RIPED > RIPE
RIPELY > RIPE
RIPEN vb grow ripe
RIPENED > RIPEN
RIPENER > RIPEN
RIPENERS > RIPEN
RIPENESS > RIPE
RIPENING > RIPEN
RIPENS > RIPEN
RIPER adj more ripe **▷** n old Scots word meaning plunderer
RIPERS > RIPER
RIPES > RIPE
RIPEST > RIPE
RIPIENI > RIPIENO
RIPIENIST n orchestral member who is there to swell the sound rather than play solo
RIPIENO n (in baroque concertos and concerti grossi) the full orchestra
RIPIENOS > RIPIENO
RIPING > RIPE
RIPOFF n grossly overpriced article
RIPOFFS > RIPOFF
RIPOST same as **>** RIPOSTE
RIPOSTE n verbal retort **▷** vb make a riposte
RIPOSTED > RIPOSTE
RIPOSTES > RIPOSTE
RIPOSTING > RIPOSTE
RIPOSTS > RIPOST
RIPP n old Scots word for a handful of grain
RIPPABLE > RIP
RIPPED > RIP
RIPPER n person who rips
RIPPERS > RIPPER
RIPPIER n archaic word for fish seller
RIPPIERS > RIPPIER
RIPPING > RIP
RIPPINGLY > RIP
RIPPINGS > RIPPING
RIPPLE n slight wave or ruffling of a surface **▷** vb flow or form into little waves (on)

RIPPLED > RIPPLE
RIPPLER > RIPPLE
RIPPLERS > RIPPLE
RIPPLES > RIPPLE
RIPPLET n tiny ripple
RIPPLETS > RIPPLET
RIPPLIER > RIPPLE
RIPPLIEST > RIPPLE
RIPPLING > RIPPLE
RIPPLINGS > RIPPLE
RIPPLY > RIPPLE
RIPPS > RIPP
RIPRAP vb deposit broken stones in or on
RIPRAPPED > RIPRAP
RIPRAPS > RIPRAP
RIPS > RIP
RIPSAW n handsaw for cutting along the grain of timber **▷** vb saw with a ripsaw
RIPSAWED > RIPSAW
RIPSAWING > RIPSAW
RIPSAWN > RIPSAW
RIPSAWS > RIPSAW
RIPSTOP n tear-resistant cloth
RIPSTOPS > RIPSTOP
RIPT archaic past form of **>** RIP
RIPTIDE n stretch of turbulent water in the sea
RIPTIDES > RIPTIDE
RIRORIRO n small NZ bush bird that hatches the eggs of the shining cuckoo
RIRORIROS > RIRORIRO
RISALDAR n Indian cavalry officer
RISALDARS > RISALDAR
RISE vb get up from a lying, sitting, or kneeling position **▷** n act of rising
RISEN > RISE
RISER n person who rises, esp from bed
RISERS > RISER
RISES > RISE
RISHI n Indian seer or sage
RISHIS > RISHI
RISIBLE adj causing laughter, ridiculous
RISIBLES pl n sense of humour
RISIBLY > RISIBLE
RISING > RISE
RISINGS > RISE
RISK n chance of disaster or loss **▷** vb act in spite of the possibility of (injury or loss)
RISKED > RISK
RISKER > RISK
RISKERS > RISK
RISKFUL > RISK
RISKIER > RISKY
RISKIEST > RISKY
RISKILY > RISKY
RISKINESS > RISKY
RISKING > RISK
RISKLESS > RISK
RISKS > RISK
RISKY adj full of risk, dangerous
RISOLUTO adj musical term meaning firm and decisive **▷** adv firmly and decisively
RISORII > RISORIUS

RISORIUS n facial muscle responsible for smiling
RISOTTO n dish of rice cooked in stock with vegetables, meat, etc
RISOTTOS > RISOTTO
RISP vb Scots word meaning rasp
RISPED > RISP
RISPETTI > RISPETTO
RISPETTO n kind of folk song
RISPING > RISP
RISPINGS > RISP
RISPS > RISP
RISQUE same as **>** RISK
RISQUES > RISQUE
RISSOLE n cake of minced meat, coated with breadcrumbs and fried
RISSOLES > RISSOLE
RISTRA n string of dried chilli peppers
RISTRAS > RISTRA
RISTRETTO n strong espresso coffee
RISUS n involuntary grinning expression
RISUSES > RISUS
RIT vb Scots word for cut or slit
RITARD n (in music) a slowing down
RITARDS > RITARD
RITE n formal practice or custom, esp religious
RITELESS > RITE
RITENUTO adv held back momentarily **▷** n (in music) a slowing down
RITENUTOS > RITENUTO
RITES > RITE
RITONAVIR n drug used to treat HIV
RITORNEL n (in music) orchestral passage
RITORNELL same as **>** RITORNEL
RITORNELS > RITORNEL
RITS > RIT
RITT same as **>** RIT
RITTED > RIT
RITTER n knight or horseman/horsewoman
RITTERS > RITTER
RITTING > RIT
RITTS > RITT
RITUAL n prescribed order of rites **▷** adj concerning rites
RITUALISE same as **>** RITUALIZE
RITUALISM n exaggerated emphasis on the importance of rites and ceremonies
RITUALIST > RITUALISM
RITUALIZE vb engage in ritualism or devise rituals
RITUALLY > RITUAL
RITUALS > RITUAL
RITUXIMAB n drug used to treat non-Hodgkin's lymphoma
RITZ modifier as in put on the ritz assume a superior air or make an ostentatious display
RITZES > RITZ

RITZIER > RITZY
RITZIEST > RITZY
RITZILY > RITZY
RITZINESS > RITZY
RITZY adj luxurious or elegant
RIVA n rock cleft
RIVAGE n bank, shore, or coast
RIVAGES > RIVAGE
RIVAL n person or thing that competes with another **▷** adj in the position of a rival **▷** vb (try to) equal
RIVALED > RIVAL
RIVALESS n female rival
RIVALING > RIVAL
RIVALISE same as **>** RIVALIZE
RIVALISED > RIVALISE
RIVALISES > RIVALISE
RIVALITY > RIVAL
RIVALIZE vb become a rival
RIVALIZED > RIVALIZE
RIVALIZES > RIVALIZE
RIVALLED > RIVAL
RIVALLESS > RIVAL
RIVALLING > RIVAL
RIVALRIES > RIVALRY
RIVALROUS > RIVALRY
RIVALRY n keen competition
RIVALS > RIVAL
RIVALSHIP > RIVAL
RIVAS > RIVA
RIVE vb split asunder
RIVED > RIVE
RIVEL vb archaic word meaning wrinkle
RIVELLED > RIVEL
RIVELLING > RIVEL
RIVELS > RIVEL
RIVEN > RIVE
RIVER n large natural stream of water
RIVERAIN same as **>** RIPARIAN
RIVERAINS > RIVERAIN
RIVERBANK n bank of a river
RIVERBED n bed of a river
RIVERBEDS > RIVERBOAT
RIVERBOAT n boat, especially a barge, designed for use on rivers
RIVERED adj with a river or rivers
RIVERET n archaic word for rivulet or stream
RIVERETS > RIVERET
RIVERHEAD n source of river
RIVERIER > RIVERY
RIVERIEST > RIVERY
RIVERINE same as **>** RIPARIAN
RIVERLESS > RIVER
RIVERLIKE adj resembling a river
RIVERMAN n boatman or man earning his living working on a river
RIVERMEN > RIVERMAN
RIVERS > RIVER
RIVERSIDE n area beside a river

r

RIVERWALK n paved walkway along the side of a river

RIVERWARD adj towards the river ▷ adv towards the river

RIVERWAY n river serving as a waterway

RIVERWAYS > RIVERWAY

RIVERWEED n type of plant found growing near rivers

RIVERY adj riverlike

RIVES > RIVE

RIVET n bolt for fastening metal plates ▷ vb fasten with rivets

RIVETED > RIVET

RIVETER > RIVET

RIVETERS > RIVET

RIVETING > RIVET

RIVETINGS > RIVET

RIVETS > RIVET

RIVETTED > RIVET

RIVETTING > RIVET

RIVIERA n coastline resembling the Mediterranean Riviera

RIVIERAS > RIVIERA

RIVIERE n necklace of diamonds which gradually increase in size

RIVIERES > RIVIERE

RIVING > RIVE

RIVLIN n Scots word for rawhide shoe

RIVLINS > RIVLIN

RIVO interj (in the past) an informal toast

RIVULET n small stream

RIVULETS > RIVULET

RIVULOSE adj having meandering lines

RIVULUS n type of small tropical American fish

RIVULUSES > RIVULUS

RIYAL n standard monetary unit of Qatar, divided into 100 dirhams

RIYALS > RIYAL

RIZ (in some dialects) past form of > RISE

RIZA n partial icon cover made from precious metal

RIZARD n redcurrant

RIZARDS > RIZARD

RIZAS > RIZA

RIZZAR n Scots word for redcurrant ▷ vb Scots word for sun-dry

RIZZARED > RIZZAR

RIZZARING > RIZZAR

RIZZARS > RIZZAR

RIZZART n Scots word for redcurrant

RIZZARTS > RIZZART

RIZZER same as > RIZZAR

RIZZERED > RIZZER

RIZZERING > RIZZER

RIZZERS > RIZZER

RIZZOR vb dry

RIZZORED > RIZZOR

RIZZORING > RIZZOR

RIZZORS > RIZZOR

ROACH n Eurasian freshwater fish ▷ vb clip (mane) short so that it stands upright

ROACHED adj arched convexly, as the back of certain breeds of dog, such as the whippet

ROACHES > ROACH

ROACHING > ROACH

ROAD n way prepared for passengers, vehicles, etc

ROADBED n material used to make a road

ROADBEDS > ROADBED

ROADBLOCK n barricade across a road to stop traffic for inspection etc

ROADCRAFT n skills and knowledge of a road user

ROADEO n competition testing driving skills

ROADEOS > ROADEO

ROADHOG n selfish or aggressive driver

ROADHOGS > ROADHOG

ROADHOUSE n pub or restaurant on a country road

ROADIE n person who transports and sets up equipment for a band

ROADIES > ROADIE

ROADING n road building

ROADINGS > ROADING

ROADKILL n remains of an animal or animals killed on the road by motor vehicles

ROADKILLS > ROADKILL

ROADLESS > ROAD

ROADMAN n someone involved in road repair or construction

ROADMEN > ROADMAN

ROADS > ROAD

ROADSHOW n radio show broadcast live from a place being visited by a touring disc jockey

ROADSHOWS > ROADSHOW

ROADSIDE n side of a road ▷ adj situated beside a road

ROADSIDES > ROADSIDE

ROADSMAN same as > ROADMAN

ROADSMEN > ROADSMAN

ROADSTEAD same as > ROAD

ROADSTER n open car with only two seats

ROADSTERS > ROADSTER

ROADWAY n part of a road used by vehicles

ROADWAYS > ROADWAY

ROADWORK n sports training by running along roads

ROADWORKS pl n repairs to a road, esp blocking part of the road

ROAM vb wander about ▷ n act of roaming

ROAMED > ROAM

ROAMER > ROAM

ROAMERS > ROAM

ROAMING > ROAM

ROAMINGS > ROAM

ROAMS > ROAM

ROAN adj (of a horse) having a brown or black coat sprinkled with white hairs ▷ n roan horse

ROANPIPE n drainpipe leading down from a gutter

ROANPIPES > ROANPIPE

ROANS > ROAN

ROAR vb make or utter a loud deep hoarse sound like that of a lion ▷ n such a sound

ROARED > ROAR

ROARER > ROAR

ROARERS > ROAR

ROARIE Scots word for > NOISY

ROARIER > ROARY

ROARIEST > ROARY

ROARING > ROAR

ROARINGLY > ROARING

ROARINGS > ROAR

ROARMING adj severe

ROARS > ROAR

ROARY adj sounding like a roar or tending to roar

ROAST vb cook by dry heat, as in an oven ▷ n roasted joint of meat ▷ adj roasted

ROASTED > ROAST

ROASTER n person or thing that roasts

ROASTERS > ROASTER

ROASTIE n roast potato

ROASTIES > ROASTIE

ROASTING adj extremely hot ▷ n severe criticism or scolding

ROASTINGS > ROASTING

ROASTS > ROAST

ROATE archaic form of > ROTE

ROATED > ROATE

ROATES > ROATE

ROATING > ROATE

ROB vb steal from

ROBALO n tropical fish

ROBALOS > ROBALO

ROBAND n piece of marline used for fastening a sail to a spar

ROBANDS > ROBAND

ROBATA n grill used for Japanese cooking

ROBATAS > ROBATA

ROBBED > ROB

ROBBER > ROB

ROBBERIES > ROBBERY

ROBBERS > ROB

ROBBERY n stealing of property from a person by using or threatening to use force

ROBBIN same as > ROBAND

ROBBING > ROB

ROBBINS > ROBBIN

ROBE n long loose outer garment ▷ vb put a robe on

ROBED > ROBE

ROBELIKE adj like a robe

ROBES > ROBE

ROBIN n small brown bird with a red breast

ROBING > ROBE

ROBINGS > ROBE

ROBINIA n type of leguminous tree

ROBINIAS > ROBINIA

ROBINS > ROBIN

ROBLE n oak tree

ROBLES > ROBLE

ROBOCALL n automated telephone call that delivers a message to a large number of people

ROBOCALLS > ROBOCALL

ROBORANT adj tending to fortify or increase strength ▷ n drug or agent that increases strength

ROBORANTS > ROBORANT

ROBOT n automated machine, esp one performing functions in a human manner

ROBOTIC > ROBOT

ROBOTICS n science of designing and using robots

ROBOTISE same as > ROBOTIZE

ROBOTISED > ROBOTISE

ROBOTISES > ROBOTISE

ROBOTISM > ROBOT

ROBOTISMS > ROBOT

ROBOTIZE vb automate

ROBOTIZED > ROBOTIZE

ROBOTIZES > ROBOTIZE

ROBOTRIES > ROBOT

ROBOTRY > ROBOT

ROBOTS > ROBOT

ROBS > ROB

ROBURITE n flameless explosive

ROBURITES > ROBURITE

ROBUST adj very strong and healthy

ROBUSTA n species of coffee tree

ROBUSTAS > ROBUSTA

ROBUSTER > ROBUST

ROBUSTEST > ROBUST

ROBUSTLY > ROBUST

ROC n monstrous bird of Arabian mythology

ROCAILLE n decorative rock or shell work

ROCAILLES > ROCAILLE

ROCAMBOLE n variety of sand leek whose garlic-like bulb is used for seasoning

ROCH same as > ROTCH

ROCHES > ROCH

ROCHET n white surplice with tight sleeves, worn by Church dignitaries

ROCHETS > ROCHET

ROCK n hard mineral substance that makes up part of the earth's crust, stone ▷ vb (cause to) sway to and fro ▷ adj of or relating to rock music

ROCKABIES > ROCKABY

ROCKABLE > ROCK

ROCKABY same as > ROCKABYE

ROCKABYE n lullaby or rocking motion used with a baby during lullabies

ROCKABYES > ROCKABYE

ROCKAWAY n four-wheeled horse-drawn carriage, usually with two seats and a hard top

ROCKAWAYS > ROCKAWAY

ROCKBOUND adj hemmed in or encircled by rocks .

ROCKBURST n sudden rupture of rock in a mine

ROCKCRESS n any plant of the annual or perennial genus Arabis

ROCKED > ROCK

ROCKER n rocking chair

ROCKERIES > ROCKERY

ROCKERS > ROCKER

ROCKERY n mound of stones in a garden for rock plants

ROCKET n self-propelling device powered by the burning of explosive contents ▷ vb move fast, esp upwards

ROCKETED > ROCKET

ROCKETEER n engineer or scientist concerned with the design, operation, or launching of rockets

ROCKETER n bird that launches itself into the air like a rocket when flushed

ROCKETERS > ROCKETER

ROCKETING > ROCKET

ROCKETRY n science and technology of the design and operation of rockets

ROCKETS > ROCKET

ROCKFALL n instance of rocks breaking away and falling from an outcrop

ROCKFALLS > ROCKFALL

ROCKFISH n any of various fishes that live among rocks

ROCKHOUND n person interested in rocks and minerals

ROCKIER n archaic or dialect word for rock pigeon

ROCKIERS > ROCKIER

ROCKIEST > ROCKY

ROCKILY > ROCKY

ROCKINESS > ROCKY

ROCKING > ROCK

ROCKINGLY > ROCKING

ROCKINGS > ROCK

ROCKLAY same as > ROKELAY

ROCKLAYS > ROCKLAY

ROCKLESS > ROCK

ROCKLIKE > ROCK

ROCKLING n any of various small sea fishes having an elongated body and barbels around the mouth

ROCKLINGS > ROCKLING

ROCKOON n rocket fired from a balloon at high altitude

ROCKOONS > ROCKOON

ROCKROSE n any of various shrubs or herbaceous plants cultivated for their roselike flowers

ROCKROSES > ROCKROSE

ROCKS > ROCK

ROCKSHAFT n shaft that rotates backwards and forwards rather than continuously, esp one used in the valve gear of a steam engine

ROCKSLIDE n fall of rocks down hillside

ROCKWATER n water that comes out of rock

ROCKWEED n any of various seaweeds that grow on rocks exposed at low tide

ROCKWEEDS > ROCKWEED

ROCKWOOL n mineral wool used for insulation

ROCKWOOLS > ROCKWOOL

ROCKWORK n structure made of rock

ROCKWORKS > ROCKWORK

ROCKY adj having many rocks

ROCOCO adj (of furniture, architecture, etc) having much elaborate decoration ▷ n style of architecture and decoration characterized by elaborate ornamentation

ROCOCOS > ROCOCO

ROCQUET n another name for the salad plant rocket

ROCQUETS > ROCQUET

ROCS > ROC

ROD n slender straight bar, stick ▷ vb clear with a rod

RODDED > ROD

RODDING > ROD

RODDINGS > ROD

RODE vb (of the male woodcock) to perform a display flight

RODED > RODE

RODENT n animal with teeth specialized for gnawing

RODENTIAL adj relating to rodents

RODENTS > RODENT

RODEO n display of skill by cowboys, such as bareback riding ▷ vb take part in a rodeo

RODEOED > RODEO

RODEOING > RODEO

RODEOS > RODEO

RODES > RODE

RODEWAY archaic spelling of > ROADWAY

RODEWAYS > RODEWAY

RODFISHER n angler

RODGERSIA n flowering plant

RODING > RODE

RODINGS > RODE

RODLESS > ROD

RODLIKE > ROD

RODMAN n someone who uses or fishes with a rod

RODMEN > RODMAN

RODNEY n type of small fishing boat used in Canada

RODNEYS > RODNEY

RODS > ROD

RODSMAN same as > RODMAN

RODSMEN > RODSMAN

RODSTER n angler

RODSTERS > RODSTER

ROE n mass of eggs in a fish, sometimes eaten as food

ROEBUCK n male of the roe deer

ROEBUCKS > ROEBUCK

ROED adj with roe inside

ROEMER n drinking glass, typically having an ovoid bowl on a short stem

ROEMERS > ROEMER

ROENTGEN n unit measuring a radiation dose

ROENTGENS > ROENTGEN

ROES > ROE

ROESTI same as > ROSTI

ROESTIS > ROESTI

ROESTONE same as > OOLITE

ROESTONES > ROESTONE

ROGALLO n flexible fabric delta wing

ROGALLOS > ROGALLO

ROGATION n solemn supplication, esp in a form of ceremony prescribed by the Church

ROGATIONS > ROGATION

ROGATORY adj (esp in legal contexts) seeking or authorized to seek information

ROGER interj (used in signalling) message received ▷ vb acknowledge a received message

ROGERED > ROGER

ROGERING > ROGER

ROGERINGS > ROGER

ROGERS > ROGER

ROGNON n isolated rock outcrop on a glacier

ROGNONS > ROGNON

ROGUE n dishonest or unprincipled person ▷ adj (of a wild beast) living apart from the herd ▷ vb rid (a field or crop) of inferior or unwanted plants

ROGUED > ROGUE

ROGUEING > ROGUE

ROGUER n rogue

ROGUERIES > ROGUERY

ROGUERS > ROGUER

ROGUERY n dishonest or immoral behaviour

ROGUES > ROGUE

ROGUESHIP n condition of being a rogue

ROGUIER > ROGUY

ROGUIEST > ROGUY

ROGUING > ROGUE

ROGUISH adj dishonest or unprincipled

ROGUISHLY > ROGUISH

ROGUY adj roguish

ROHE n territory of a Māori tribal group

ROHES > ROHE

ROID adj short form of steroid

ROIDS > ROID

ROIL vb make (a liquid) cloudy or turbid by stirring up dregs or sediment

ROILED > ROIL

ROILIER > ROILY

ROILIEST > ROILY

ROILING > ROIL

ROILS > ROIL

ROILY adj cloudy or muddy

ROIN same as > ROYNE

ROINED > ROIN

ROINING > ROIN

ROINISH same as > ROYNISH

ROINS > ROIN

ROIST archaic variant of > ROISTER

ROISTED > ROIST

ROISTER vb make merry noisily or boisterously

ROISTERED > ROISTER

ROISTERER > ROISTER

ROISTERS > ROISTER

ROISTING > ROIST

ROISTS > ROIST

ROJAK n (in Malaysia) a salad dish served in chilli sauce

ROJAKS > ROJAK

ROJI n Japanese tea garden or its path of stones

ROJIS > ROJI

ROK same as > ROC

ROKE vb (in dialect) steam or smoke

ROKED > ROKE

ROKELAY n type of cloak

ROKELAYS > ROKELAY

ROKER n variety of ray

ROKERS > ROKER

ROKES > ROKE

ROKIER > ROKY

ROKIEST > ROKY

ROKING > ROKE

ROKKAKU n hexagonal Japanese kite

ROKS > ROK

ROKY adj (in dialect) steamy or smoky

ROLAG n roll of carded wool ready for spinning

ROLAGS > ROLAG

ROLAMITE n type of bearing using two rollers and a moving flexible band

ROLAMITES > ROLAMITE

ROLE n task or function

ROLES > ROLE

ROLF vb massage following a particular technique

ROLFED > ROLF

ROLFER > ROLF

ROLFERS > ROLF

ROLFING > ROLF

ROLFINGS > ROLF

ROLFS > ROLF

ROLL vb move by turning over and over ▷ n act of rolling over or from side to side

ROLLABLE > ROLL

ROLLAWAY n mounted on rollers so as to be easily moved, esp to be stored away after use

ROLLAWAYS > ROLLAWAY

ROLLBACK n reduction to a previous price

ROLLBACKS > ROLLBACK

ROLLBAR n bar that reinforces the frame of a car

ROLLBARS > ROLLBAR

ROLLED > ROLL

ROLLER n rotating cylinder

ROLLERS > ROLLER

ROLLICK vb behave in a boisterous manner ▷ n boisterous or carefree escapade

ROLLICKED > ROLLICK

ROLLICKS > ROLLICK

ROLLICKY adj rollicking

ROLLIE n hand-rolled cigarette

ROLLIES > ROLLIE

ROLLING > ROLL

ROLLINGS > ROLL

ROLLMOP n herring fillet rolled round onion slices and pickled

ROLLMOPS > ROLLMOP

ROLLNECK adj (of a garment) having a high neck that is worn rolled over ▷ n rollneck sweater or other garment

ROLLNECKS > ROLLNECK

ROLLOCK same as > ROWLOCK

ROLLOCKS > ROLLOCK

ROLLOUT n presentation to the public of a new aircraft, product, etc; launch

ROLLOUTS > ROLLOUT

ROLLOVER n instance of a prize continuing in force for an additional period

ROLLOVERS > ROLLOVER

ROLLS > ROLL

ROLLTOP n as in rolltop desk desk having a slatted wooden panel that can be pulled down over the writing surface

ROLLUP n something rolled into a tube shape

ROLLUPS > ROLLUP

ROLLWAY n incline down which logs are rolled

ROLLWAYS > ROLLWAY

ROM n male gypsy

ROMA n gypsy

ROMAGE archaic variant of > RUMMAGE

ROMAGES > ROMAGE

ROMAIKA n Greek dance

ROMAIKAS > ROMAIKA

ROMAINE n usual US and Canadian name for 'cos' (lettuce)

ROMAINES > ROMAINE

ROMAJI n Roman alphabet as used to write Japanese

ROMAJIS > ROMAJI

ROMAL same as > RUMAL

ROMALS > ROMAL

ROMAN adj in or relating to the vertical style of printing type used for most printed matter ▷ n roman type

ROMANCE n love affair ▷ vb exaggerate or fantasize

ROMANCED > ROMANCE

ROMANCER > ROMANCE

ROMANCERS > ROMANCE

ROMANCES > ROMANCE

ROMANCING > ROMANCE

ROMANESCO n type of green cauliflower

ROMANISE same as > ROMANIZE

ROMANISED > ROMANISE

ROMANISES > ROMANISE

ROMANIZE vb impart a Roman Catholic character to (a ceremony, practice, etc)

ROMANIZED > ROMANIZE

ROMANIZES > ROMANIZE

ROMANO n hard light-coloured sharp-tasting cheese

ROMANOS > ROMANO

ROMANS > ROMAN

ROMANTIC adj of or dealing with love ▷ n romantic person or artist

ROMANTICS > ROMANTIC

ROMANZA n short instrumental piece of song-like character

ROMANZAS > ROMANZA

ROMAUNT n verse romance

ROMAUNTS > ROMAUNT

ROMCOM n comedy based around the romantic relationships of the characters

ROMCOMS > ROMCOM

ROMELDALE n type of sheep

ROMEO n male sweetheart

ROMEOS > ROMEO

ROMNEYA n bushy type of poppy

ROMNEYAS > ROMNEYA

ROMP vb play wildly and joyfully ▷ n boisterous activity

ROMPED > ROMP

ROMPER n playful or boisterous child

ROMPERS pl n child's overalls

ROMPING > ROMP

ROMPINGLY > ROMP

ROMPISH adj inclined to romp

ROMPISHLY > ROMP

ROMPS > ROMP

ROMS > ROM

RONCADOR n any of several types of fish

RONCADORS > RONCADOR

RONDACHE n round shield

RONDACHES > RONDACHE

RONDAVEL n circular building, often thatched

RONDAVELS > RONDAVEL

RONDE n round dance

RONDEAU n poem with the opening words of the first line used as a refrain

RONDEAUX > RONDEAU

RONDEL n rondeau with a two-line refrain appearing twice or three times

RONDELET n brief rondeau, having five or seven lines and a refrain taken from the first line

RONDELETS > RONDELET

RONDELLE n type of bead

RONDELLES > RONDELLE

RONDELS > RONDEL

RONDES > RONDE

RONDINO n short rondo

RONDINOS > RONDINO

RONDO n piece of music with a leading theme continually returned to

RONDOS > RONDO

RONDURE n circle or curve

RONDURES > RONDURE

RONE n drainpipe or gutter for carrying rainwater from a roof

RONEO vb duplicate (a document) from a stencil ▷ n document reproduced by this process

RONEOED > RONEO

RONEOING > RONEO

RONEOS > RONEO

RONEPIPE same as > RONE

RONEPIPES > RONEPIPE

RONES > RONE

RONG archaic past participle of > RING

RONGGENG n Malay traditional dance

RONGGENGS > RONGGENG

RONIN n lordless samurai, esp one whose feudal lord had been deprived of his territory

RONINS > RONIN

RONION same as > RUNNION

RONIONS > RONION

RONNE archaic form of > RUN

RONNEL n type of pesticide

RONNELS > RONNEL

RONNIE n Dublin slang word for moustache

RONNIES > RONNIE

RONNING > RONNE

RONT archaic variant of > RUNT

RONTE archaic variant of > RUNT

RONTES > RONTE

RONTGEN variant spelling of > ROENTGEN

RONTGENS > RONTGEN

RONTS > RONT

RONYON same as > RUNNION

RONYONS > RONYON

RONZ n rest of New Zealand (in relation to Auckland)

RONZER n New Zealand word for a New Zealander not from Auckland

RONZERS > RONZER

ROO n kangaroo

ROOD n Cross

ROODS > ROOD

ROOF n outside upper covering of a building, car, etc ▷ vb put a roof on

ROOFED > ROOF

ROOFER > ROOF

ROOFERS > ROOF

ROOFIE n tablet of sedative drug

ROOFIER > ROOFY

ROOFIES > ROOFIE

ROOFIEST > ROOFY

ROOFING n material used to build a roof

ROOFINGS > ROOFING

ROOFLESS > ROOF

ROOFLIKE > ROOF

ROOFLINE n uppermost edge of a roof

ROOFLINES > ROOFLINE

ROOFS > ROOF

ROOFSCAPE n view of the rooftops of a town, city, etc

ROOFTOP n outside part of the roof of a building

ROOFTOPS > ROOFTOP

ROOFTREE same as > RIDGEPOLE

ROOFTREES > ROOFTREE

ROOFY adj with roofs

ROOIBOS n tea prepared from the dried leaves of an African plant

ROOIBOSES > ROOIBOS

ROOIKAT n South African lynx

ROOIKATS > ROOIKAT

ROOINEK n contemptuous name for an Englishman

ROOINEKS > ROOINEK

ROOK n Eurasian bird of the crow family ▷ vb swindle

ROOKED > ROOK

ROOKERIES > ROOKERY

ROOKERY n colony of rooks, penguins, or seals

ROOKIE n new recruit

ROOKIER > ROOKY

ROOKIES > ROOKIE

ROOKIEST > ROOKY

ROOKING > ROOK

ROOKISH > ROOK

ROOKS > ROOK

ROOKY adj abounding in rooks

ROOM n enclosed area in a building ▷ vb occupy or share a room

ROOMED > ROOM

ROOMER > ROOM

ROOMERS > ROOM

ROOMETTE n self-contained compartment in a railway sleeping carriage

ROOMETTES > ROOMETTE

ROOMFUL n number or quantity sufficient to fill a room

ROOMFULS > ROOMFUL

ROOMIE n roommate

ROOMIER > ROOMY

ROOMIES > ROOMIE

ROOMIEST > ROOMY

ROOMILY > ROOMY

ROOMINESS > ROOMY

ROOMING > ROOM

ROOMMATE n person with whom one shares a room or apartment

ROOMMATES > ROOMMATE

ROOMS > ROOM

ROOMSFUL > ROOMFUL

ROOMSOME adj archaic word meaning roomy

ROOMY adj spacious

ROON n Scots word for shred or strip

ROONS > ROON

ROOP same as > ROUP

ROOPED > ROOP

ROOPIER > ROOPY

ROOPIEST > ROOPY

ROOPING > ROOP

ROOPIT same as > ROOPY

ROOPS > ROOP

ROOPY adj (in dialect) hoarse

ROORBACH same as > ROORBACK

ROORBACHS > ROORBACH

ROORBACK n false or distorted report or account, used to obtain political advantage

ROORBACKS > ROORBACK

ROOS > ROO

ROOSA n type of grass

ROOSAS > ROOSA

ROOSE vb flatter

ROOSED > ROOSE

ROOSER > ROOSE

ROOSERS > ROOSE

ROOSES > ROOSE

ROOSING > ROOSE

ROOST n perch for fowls ▷ vb perch

ROOSTED > ROOST

ROOSTER n domestic cock

ROOSTERS > ROOSTER

ROOSTING > ROOST
ROOSTS > ROOST
ROOT n part of a plant that grows down into the earth obtaining nourishment ▷ vb establish a root and start to grow
ROOTAGE n root system
ROOTAGES > ROOTAGE
ROOTBALL n mass of the roots of a plant
ROOTBALLS > ROOTBALL
ROOTBOUND adj (of a pot plant) having outgrown its pot, so that the roots are cramped and tangled
ROOTCAP n layer of cells at root tip
ROOTCAPS > ROOTCAP
ROOTED > ROOT
ROOTEDLY > ROOT
ROOTER > ROOT
ROOTERS > ROOT
ROOTHOLD > ROOT
ROOTHOLDS > ROOT
ROOTIER > ROOTY
ROOTIES > ROOTY
ROOTIEST > ROOTY
ROOTINESS > ROOT
ROOTING > ROOT
ROOTINGS > ROOT
ROOTKIT n set of programs used to gain unauthorized access to a computer system
ROOTKITS > ROOTKIT
ROOTLE vb search unsystematically
ROOTLED > ROOTLE
ROOTLES > ROOTLE
ROOTLESS adj having no sense of belonging
ROOTLET n small root or branch of a root
ROOTLETS > ROOTLET
ROOTLIKE > ROOT
ROOTLING > ROOTLE
ROOTS adj (of popular music) going back to the origins of a style
ROOTSIER > ROOTS
ROOTSIEST > ROOTS
ROOTSTALK same as **>** RHIZOME
ROOTSTOCK same as **>** RHIZOME
ROOTSY > ROOTS
ROOTWORM n beetle larva feeding on roots
ROOTWORMS > ROOTWORM
ROOTY adj rootlike ▷ n (in military slang) bread
ROPABLE adj capable of being roped
ROPE n thick cord ▷ vb bind or fasten with rope
ROPEABLE same as **>** ROPABLE
ROPED > ROPE
ROPELIKE > ROPE
ROPER n someone who makes ropes
ROPERIES > ROPERY
ROPERS > ROPER
ROPERY n place where ropes are made
ROPES > ROPE

ROPEWALK n long narrow usually covered path or shed where ropes are made
ROPEWALKS > ROPEWALK
ROPEWAY n type of aerial lift
ROPEWAYS > ROPEWAY
ROPEWORK n making, mending, or tying ropes
ROPEWORKS > ROPEWORK
ROPEY adj inferior or inadequate
ROPIER > ROPY
ROPIEST > ROPY
ROPILY > ROPEY
ROPINESS > ROPEY
ROPING > ROPE
ROPINGS > ROPE
ROPY same as **>** ROPEY
ROQUE n game developed from croquet
ROQUEFORT n type of French blue cheese
ROQUES > ROQUE
ROQUET vb drive one's ball against (another person's ball) in croquet ▷ n act of roqueting
ROQUETED > ROQUET
ROQUETING > ROQUET
ROQUETS > ROQUET
ROQUETTE n another name for the salad plant rocket
ROQUETTES > ROQUETTE
RORAL archaic word for **>** DEWY
RORE archaic spelling of **>** ROAR
RORES > RORE
RORIC same as **>** RORAL
RORID same as **>** RORAL
RORIE same as **>** ROARY
RORIER > RORY
RORIEST > RORY
RORQUAL n toothless whale with a dorsal fin
RORQUALS > RORQUAL
RORT n dishonest scheme ▷ vb take unfair advantage of something
RORTED > RORT
RORTER n small-scale confidence trickster
RORTERS > RORTER
RORTIER > RORT
RORTIEST > RORT
RORTING > RORT
RORTINGS > RORTING
RORTS > RORT
RORTY > RORT
RORY adj dewy
ROSACE another name for **>** ROSETTE
ROSACEA n chronic inflammatory disease affecting the skin of the face
ROSACEAS > ROSACEA
ROSACEOUS adj of or belonging to a family of plants typically having five-petalled flowers, which includes the rose, strawberry, and many fruit trees
ROSACES > ROSACE
ROSAKER archaic word for **>** REALGAR
ROSAKERS > ROSAKER

ROSALIA n melody which is repeated but at a higher pitch each time
ROSALIAS > ROSALIA
ROSANILIN n reddish-brown crystalline insoluble derivative of aniline used as a red dye
ROSARIA > ROSARIUM
ROSARIAN n person who cultivates roses, esp professionally
ROSARIANS > ROSARIAN
ROSARIES > ROSARY
ROSARIUM n rose garden
ROSARIUMS > ROSARIUM
ROSARY n series of prayers
ROSBIF n term used in France for an English person
ROSBIFS > ROSBIF
ROSCID adj dewy
ROSCOE slang word for **>** GUN
ROSCOES > ROSCOE
ROSE n flowering plant ▷ vb cause to redden
ROSEAL adj rosy or roselike
ROSEATE adj rose-coloured
ROSEATELY > ROSEATE
ROSEBAY n perennial plant with spikes of deep pink flowers
ROSEBAYS > ROSEBAY
ROSEBED n part of a garden where roses grow
ROSEBEDS > ROSEBED
ROSEBOWL n bowl for displaying roses or other flowers
ROSEBOWLS > ROSEBOWL
ROSEBUD n rose which has not yet fully opened
ROSEBUDS > ROSEBUD
ROSEBUSH n flowering shrub
ROSED > ROSE
ROSEFINCH n any of various finches with pink patches
ROSEFISH n red food fish of North Atlantic coastal waters
ROSEHIP n berry-like fruit of a rose plant
ROSEHIPS > ROSEHIP
ROSELESS > RISE
ROSELIKE > RISE
ROSELLA n type of Australian parrot
ROSELLAS > ROSELLA
ROSELLE n Indian flowering plant
ROSELLES > ROSELLE
ROSEMARY n fragrant flowering shrub
ROSEOLA n feverish condition of young children caused by a virus
ROSEOLAR > ROSEOLA
ROSEOLAS > ROSEOLA
ROSERIES > ROSERY
ROSEROOT n Eurasian mountain plant
ROSEROOTS > ROSEROOT
ROSERY n bed or garden of roses
ROSES > ROSE
ROSESLUG n one of various types of pest that feed on roses

ROSESLUGS > ROSESLUG
ROSET n Scots word meaning rosin ▷ vb rub rosin on
ROSETED > ROSET
ROSETING > ROSET
ROSETS > ROSET
ROSETTE n rose-shaped ornament
ROSETTED > ROSET
ROSETTES > ROSETTE
ROSETTING n abnormal leaf formation in a plant due to disease
ROSETTY > ROSET
ROSETY > ROSET
ROSEWATER n scented water used as a perfume and in cooking, made by the distillation of rose petals or by impregnation with oil of roses
ROSEWOOD n fragrant wood used to make furniture
ROSEWOODS > ROSEWOOD
ROSHAMBO n the game of rock-paper-scissors
ROSHAMBOS > ROSHAMBO
ROSHI n teacher of Zen Buddhism
ROSHIS > ROSHI
ROSIED > ROSY
ROSIER archaic word for **>** ROSEBUSH
ROSIERE archaic word for **>** ROSEBUSH
ROSIERES > ROSIERE
ROSIERS > ROSIER
ROSIES > ROSY
ROSIEST > ROSY
ROSILY > ROSY
ROSIN n resin used for treating the bows of violins etc ▷ vb apply rosin to
ROSINATE n chemical compound
ROSINATES > ROSINATE
ROSINED > ROSIN
ROSINER n strong alcoholic drink
ROSINERS > ROSINER
ROSINESS > ROSY
ROSING > ROSE
ROSINIER > ROSINY
ROSINIEST > ROSINY
ROSINING > ROSIN
ROSINOL n yellowish fluorescent oily liquid obtained from certain resins
ROSINOLS > ROSINOL
ROSINOUS adj rosiny
ROSINS > ROSIN
ROSINWEED n N American plant with resinous juice, sticky foliage, and a strong smell
ROSINY adj resembling rosin
ROSIT same as **>** ROSET
ROSITED > ROSIT
ROSITING > ROSIT
ROSITS > ROSIT
ROSMARINE archaic form of **>** ROSEMARY
ROSOGLIO same as **>** ROSOLIO
ROSOGLIOS > ROSOGLIO
ROSOLIO n type of cordial

r

r

ROSOLIOS > ROSOLIO
ROSSER n bark-removing machine
ROSSERS > ROSSER
ROST archaic spelling of **>** ROAST
ROSTED > ROST
ROSTELLA > ROSTELLUM
ROSTELLAR > ROSTELLUM
ROSTELLUM n small beaklike process, such as the hooked projection from the top of the head in tapeworms or the outgrowth from the stigma of an orchid
ROSTER n list of people and their turns of duty ▷ vb place on a roster
ROSTERED > ROSTER
ROSTERING > ROSTER
ROSTERS > ROSTER
ROSTI n cheese-topped fried Swiss dish of grated potato
ROSTING > ROST
ROSTIS > ROSTI
ROSTRA > ROSTRUM
ROSTRAL adj of or like a beak or snout
ROSTRALLY > ROSTRAL
ROSTRATE adj having a beak or beaklike process
ROSTRATED same as **>** ROSTRATE
ROSTRUM n platform or stage
ROSTRUMS > ROSTRUM
ROSTS > ROST
ROSULA n rosette
ROSULAS > ROSULA
ROSULATE adj in the form of a rose
ROSY adj pink-coloured ▷ vb redden or make pink
ROSYING > ROSY
ROT vb decompose or decay ▷ n decay
ROTA n list of people who take it in turn to do a particular task
ROTACHUTE n device like a parachute, with rotor blades instead of a canopy
ROTAL adj of or relating to wheels or rotation
ROTAMETER n device for measuring the flow of a liquid
ROTAN another name for **>** RATTAN
ROTANS > ROTAN
ROTAPLANE n aircraft that derives its lift from freely revolving rotor blades
ROTARIES > ROTARY
ROTARY adj revolving ▷ n traffic roundabout
ROTAS > ROTA
ROTATABLE > ROTATE
ROTATE vb (cause to) move round a centre or on a pivot
ROTATED > ROTATE
ROTATES > ROTATE
ROTATING adj revolving around a central axis, line, or point
ROTATION n act of rotating
ROTATIONS > ROTATION

ROTATIVE same as **>** ROTATORY
ROTATOR n person, device, part, or muscle that rotates or causes rotation
ROTATORES > ROTATOR
ROTATORS > ROTATOR
ROTATORY adj of, relating to, possessing, or causing rotation
ROTAVATE same as **>** ROTOVATE
ROTAVATED > ROTAVATE
ROTAVATES > ROTAVATE
ROTAVATOR n type of machine with rotating blades that will break up soil
ROTAVIRAL adj of or caused by a rotavirus
ROTAVIRUS n any member of a genus of viruses that cause worldwide endemic infections
ROTCH n little auk
ROTCHE same as **>** ROTCH
ROTCHES > ROTCH
ROTCHIE same as **>** ROTCH
ROTCHIES > ROTCHIE
ROTE n mechanical repetition ▷ vb learn by rote
ROTED > ROTE
ROTELY adv by rote
ROTENONE n white odourless crystalline substance
ROTENONES > ROTENONE
ROTES > ROTE
ROTGRASS n type of grass blamed for sheeprot
ROTGUT n alcoholic drink of inferior quality
ROTGUTS > ROTGUT
ROTHER dialect word for **>** OX
ROTHERS > ROTHER
ROTI n (in India and the Caribbean) a type of unleavened bread
ROTIFER n minute aquatic multicellular invertebrate
ROTIFERAL > ROTIFER
ROTIFERAN > ROTIFER
ROTIFERS > ROTIFER
ROTIFORM adj in the shape of a wheel
ROTING > ROTE
ROTINI n type of small spiral-shaped pasta
ROTINIS > ROTINI
ROTIS > ROTI
ROTL n unit of weight used in Muslim countries
ROTLS > ROTL
ROTO n printing process using a cylinder etched with many small recesses in a rotary press
ROTOGRAPH n photograph which is printed white on black ▷ vb create such a photograph
ROTOLI > ROTOLO
ROTOLO n (in Italian cuisine) a roll
ROTOLOS > ROTOLO
ROTON n quantum of vortex motion
ROTONS > ROTON

ROTOR n revolving portion of a dynamo, motor, or turbine
ROTORS > ROTOR
ROTOS > ROTO
ROTOSCOPE n projection device used for creating animated images out of live-action ones ▷ vb create animated images using a rotoscope
ROTOTILL vb break up the soil using a rototiller
ROTOTILLS > ROTOTILL
ROTOVATE vb break up (the surface of the earth, or an area of ground) using a rotavator
ROTOVATED > ROTOVATE
ROTOVATES > ROTOVATE
ROTOVATOR same as **>** ROTAVATOR
ROTPROOF adj proof against rot
ROTS > ROT
ROTTAN n (in dialect) a rat
ROTTANS > ROTTAN
ROTTE n ancient stringed instrument
ROTTED > ROT
ROTTEN adj decaying ▷ adv extremely ▷ n (in dialect) a rat
ROTTENER > ROTTEN
ROTTENEST > ROTTEN
ROTTENLY > ROTTEN
ROTTENS > ROTTEN
ROTTER n despicable person
ROTTERS > ROTTER
ROTTES > ROTTE
ROTTING > ROT
ROTULA n kneecap
ROTULAE > ROTULA
ROTULAS > ROTULA
ROTUND adj round and plump ▷ vb make round
ROTUNDA n circular building or room, esp with a dome
ROTUNDAS > ROTUNDA
ROTUNDATE adj rounded
ROTUNDED > ROTUND
ROTUNDER > ROTUND
ROTUNDEST > ROTUND
ROTUNDING > ROTUND
ROTUNDITY > ROTUND
ROTUNDLY > ROTUND
ROTUNDS > ROTUND
ROTURIER n freeholder or ordinary person
ROTURIERS > ROTURIER
ROUBLE n monetary unit of Russia, Belarus, and Tajikistan
ROUBLES > ROUBLE
ROUCHE same as **>** RUCHE
ROUCHED adj trimmed with a rouche
ROUCHES > ROUCHE
ROUCHING n lace trimming
ROUCHINGS > ROUCHING
ROUCOU another name for **>** ANNATTO
ROUCOUS > ROUCOU
ROUE n man given to immoral living
ROUEN n breed of duck
ROUENS > ROUEN
ROUES > ROUE

ROUGE n red cosmetic used to colour the cheeks ▷ vb apply rouge to
ROUGED > ROUGE
ROUGES > ROUGE
ROUGH adj uneven or irregular ▷ vb make rough ▷ n rough state or area
ROUGHAGE n indigestible constituents of food which aid digestion
ROUGHAGES > ROUGHAGE
ROUGHBACK n rough-skinned flatfish
ROUGHCAST n mixture of plaster and small stones for outside walls ▷ vb coat with this ▷ adj covered with or denoting roughcast
ROUGHDRY vb dry (clothes or linen) without smoothing
ROUGHED > ROUGH
ROUGHEN vb make or become rough
ROUGHENED > ROUGHEN
ROUGHENS > ROUGHEN
ROUGHER n person that does the rough preparatory work on something ▷ adj more rough
ROUGHERS > ROUGHER
ROUGHEST > ROUGH
ROUGHHEW vb cut or hew (timber, stone, etc) roughly without finishing the surface
ROUGHHEWN > ROUGHHEW
ROUGHHEWS > ROUGHHEW
ROUGHIE n small food fish found in Australian waters
ROUGHIES > ROUGHIE
ROUGHING n (in ice hockey) excessive use of force
ROUGHINGS > ROUGHING
ROUGHISH adj somewhat rough
ROUGHLEG n any of several kinds of large hawk with feathered legs
ROUGHLEGS > ROUGHLEG
ROUGHLY adv without being exact or fully authenticated
ROUGHNECK n violent person
ROUGHNESS > ROUGH
ROUGHOUT n unfinished roughly shaped artefact
ROUGHOUTS > ROUGHOUT
ROUGHS > ROUGH
ROUGHSHOD adj (of a horse) shod with rough-bottomed shoes to prevent sliding
ROUGHT archaic past form of **>** REACH
ROUGHY spelling variant of **>** ROUGHIE
ROUGING > ROUGE
ROUILLE n kind of sauce
ROUILLES > ROUILLE
ROUL archaic form of **>** ROLL
ROULADE n slice of meat rolled and cooked
ROULADES > ROULADE
ROULE archaic form of **>** ROLL
ROULEAU n roll of paper containing coins
ROULEAUS > ROULEAU
ROULEAUX > ROULEAU
ROULES > ROULE

ROULETTE n gambling game played with a revolving wheel and a ball ▷ vb use a toothed wheel on (something), as in engraving, making stationery, etc

ROULETTED > ROULETTE

ROULETTES > ROULETTE

ROULS > ROUL

ROUM archaic spelling of > ROOM

ROUMING n pasture given for an animal

ROUMINGS > ROUMING

ROUMS > ROUM

ROUNCE n handle that is turned to move paper and plates on a printing press

ROUNCES > ROUNCE

ROUNCEVAL n giant or monster

ROUNCIES > ROUNCY

ROUNCY archaic word for > HORSE

ROUND adj spherical, cylindrical, circular, or curved ▷ prep indicating an encircling movement, presence on all sides, etc ▷ vb move round ▷ n round shape

ROUNDARCH adj with rounded arches

ROUNDBALL n form of basketball

ROUNDED adj round or curved

ROUNDEDLY > ROUNDED

ROUNDEL same as > ROUNDELAY

ROUNDELAY n simple song with a refrain

ROUNDELS > ROUNDEL

ROUNDER n run round all four bases after one hit in rounders

ROUNDERS n bat-and-ball team game

ROUNDEST > ROUND

ROUNDHAND n style of handwriting with large rounded curves

ROUNDHEEL n derogatory term for a woman considered immodest

ROUNDING n process in which a number within a fraction is approximated as the closest number up or down

ROUNDINGS > ROUNDING

ROUNDISH adj somewhat round

ROUNDLE same as > ROUNDEL

ROUNDLES > ROUNDLE

ROUNDLET n small circle

ROUNDLETS > ROUNDLET

ROUNDLY adv thoroughly

ROUNDNESS > ROUND

ROUNDS > ROUND

ROUNDSMAN n person who makes rounds, as for inspection or to deliver goods

ROUNDSMEN > ROUNDSMAN

ROUNDTRIP n US term for return trip

ROUNDUP n act of gathering together

ROUNDUPS > ROUNDUP

ROUNDURE n archaic word meaning roundness

ROUNDURES > ROUNDURE

ROUNDWOOD n small pieces of timber (about 5–15 cm, or 2–6 in.) in diameter

ROUNDWORM n worm that is a common intestinal parasite of human beings

ROUP n any of various chronic respiratory diseases of birds, esp poultry ▷ vb sell by auction

ROUPED > ROUP

ROUPET adj Scots word meaning hoarse or croaky

ROUPIER > ROUP

ROUPIEST > ROUP

ROUPILY > ROUP

ROUPING > ROUP

ROUPIT same as > ROUPET

ROUPS > ROUP

ROUPY > ROUP

ROUSABLE adj capable of being roused

ROUSANT adj (in heraldry) rising

ROUSE same as > REVEILLE

ROUSED > ROUSE

ROUSEMENT n stirring up

ROUSER n person or thing that rouses people

ROUSERS > ROUSER

ROUSES > ROUSE

ROUSING adj lively, vigorous

ROUSINGLY > ROUSING

ROUSSEAU n pemmican fried in its own fat

ROUSSEAUS > ROUSSEAU

ROUSSETTE n dogfish

ROUST vb rout or stir, as out of bed

ROUSTED > ROUST

ROUSTER n unskilled labourer on an oil rig

ROUSTERS > ROUSTER

ROUSTING > ROUST

ROUSTS > ROUST

ROUT n overwhelming defeat ▷ vb defeat and put to flight

ROUTE n roads taken to reach a destination ▷ vb send by a particular route

ROUTED > ROUTE

ROUTEING > ROUTE

ROUTEMAN n (in US English) delivery man or salesman doing a particular round

ROUTEMEN > ROUTEMAN

ROUTER n device that allows data to be moved between points on a network

ROUTERS > ROUTER

ROUTES > ROUTE

ROUTEWAY n track, road, or waterway, etc, used as a route to somewhere

ROUTEWAYS > ROUTEWAY

ROUTH n abundance ▷ adj abundant

ROUTHIE adj abundant, plentiful, or well filled

ROUTHIER > ROUTHIE

ROUTHIEST > ROUTHIE

ROUTHS > ROUTH

ROUTINE n usual or regular method of procedure ▷ adj ordinary or regular

ROUTINEER n someone who believes in routine

ROUTINELY > ROUTINE

ROUTINES > ROUTINE

ROUTING > ROUT

ROUTINGS > ROUT

ROUTINISE same as > ROUTINIZE

ROUTINISM > ROUTINE

ROUTINIST > ROUTINE

ROUTINIZE vb make routine

ROUTOUS > ROUT

ROUTOUSLY > ROUT

ROUTS > ROUT

ROUX n fat and flour cooked together as a basis for sauces

ROVE vb wander about

ROVED > ROVE

ROVEN > ROVE

ROVER n wanderer, traveller

ROVERS > ROVER

ROVES > ROVE

ROVING > ROVE

ROVINGLY > ROVE

ROVINGS > ROVE

ROW n straight line of people or things ▷ vb propel (a boat) by oars

ROWABLE > ROW

ROWAN n tree producing bright red berries; mountain ash

ROWANS > ROWAN

ROWBOAT n small boat propelled by one or more pairs of oars

ROWBOATS > ROWBOAT

ROWDEDOW same as > ROWDYDOW

ROWDEDOWS > ROWDEDOW

ROWDIER > ROWDY

ROWDIES > ROWDY

ROWDIEST > ROWDY

ROWDILY > ROWDY

ROWDINESS > ROWDY

ROWDY adj disorderly, noisy, and rough ▷ n person like this

ROWDYDOW n hullabaloo ▷ vb make noise

ROWDYDOWS > ROWDYDOW

ROWDYISH > ROWDY

ROWDYISM n rowdy behaviour or tendencies or a habitual pattern of rowdy behaviour

ROWDYISMS > ROWDYISM

ROWED > ROW

ROWEL n small spiked wheel on a spur ▷ vb goad (a horse) using a rowel

ROWELED > ROWEL

ROWELING > ROWEL

ROWELLED > ROWEL

ROWELLING > ROWEL

ROWELS > ROWEL

ROWEN another word for > AFTERMATH

ROWENS > ROWEN

ROWER > ROW

ROWERS > ROW

ROWIE n Scottish bread roll made with butter and fat

ROWIES > ROWIE

ROWING > ROW

ROWINGS > ROW

ROWLOCK n device on a boat that holds an oar in place

ROWLOCKS > ROWLOCK

ROWME archaic variant of ▶ ROOM

ROWMES > ROWME

ROWND archaic variant of > ROUND

ROWNDED > ROWND

ROWNDELL archaic variant of > ROUNDEL

ROWNDELLS > ROWNDELL

ROWNDING > ROWND

ROWNDS > ROWND

ROWOVER n act of winning a rowing race unopposed

ROWOVERS > ROWOVER

ROWS > ROW

ROWT archaic variant of > ROUT

ROWTED > ROWT

ROWTH same as > ROUTH

ROWTHS > ROWTH

ROWTING > ROWT

ROWTS > ROWT

ROYAL adj of, befitting, or supported by a king or queen ▷ n member of a royal family

ROYALET n minor king

ROYALETS > ROYALET

ROYALISE same as > ROYALIZE

ROYALISED > ROYALISE

ROYALISES > ROYALISE

ROYALISM > ROYALIST

ROYALISMS > ROYALIST

ROYALIST n supporter of monarchy ▷ adj of or relating to royalists

ROYALISTS > ROYALIST

ROYALIZE vb make royal

ROYALIZED > ROYALIZE

ROYALIZES > ROYALIZE

ROYALLER > ROYAL

ROYALLEST > ROYAL

ROYALLY > ROYAL

ROYALMAST n highest part of mast

ROYALS > ROYAL

ROYALTIES > ROYALTY

ROYALTY n royal people

ROYNE archaic word for > GNAW

ROYNED > ROYNE

ROYNES > ROYNE

ROYNING > ROYNE

ROYNISH archaic word for > MANGY

ROYST same as > ROIST

ROYSTED > ROYST

ROYSTER same as > ROISTER

ROYSTERED > ROYSTER

ROYSTERER > ROYSTER

ROYSTERS > ROYSTER

ROYSTING > ROYST

ROYSTS > ROYST

ROZELLE same as > ROSELLE

ROZELLES > ROZELLE

ROZET same as > ROSET

ROZETED > ROZET

r

ROZETING > ROZET

ROZETS > ROZET

ROZIT *same as* **>** ROSET

ROZITED > ROZIT

ROZITING > ROZIT

ROZITS > ROZIT

ROZZER *n* policeman or policewoman

ROZZERS > ROZZER

RUANA *n* woollen wrap resembling a poncho

RUANAS > RUANA

RUB *vb* apply pressure with a circular or backwards-and-forwards movement ▷ *n* act of rubbing

RUBABOO *n* soup or stew made by boiling pemmican with, if available, flour and vegetables

RUBABOOS > RUBABOO

RUBACE *same as* **>** RUBASSE

RUBACES > RUBACE

RUBAI *n* verse form of Persian origin consisting of four-line stanzas

RUBAIS > RUBAI

RUBAIYAT *n* (in Persian poetry) a verse form consisting of four-line stanzas

RUBASSE *n* type of quartz containing red haematite

RUBASSES > RUBASSE

RUBATI > RUBATO

RUBATO *n* expressive flexibility of tempo ▷ *adv* with a flexible tempo

RUBATOS > RUBATO

RUBBABOO *same as* **>** RUBABOO

RUBBABOOS > RUBABOO

RUBBED > RUB

RUBBER *n* strong waterproof elastic material ▷ *adj* made of or producing rubber ▷ *vb* provide with rubber coating

RUBBERED > RUBBER

RUBBERIER > RUBBERY

RUBBERING > RUBBER

RUBBERISE *same as* **>** RUBBERIZE

RUBBERIZE *vb* coat or treat with rubber

RUBBERS > RUBBER

RUBBERY *adj* having the texture of or resembling rubber, esp in flexibility or toughness

RUBBET *old Scots past form of* **>** ROB

RUBBIDIES > RUBBIDY

RUBBIDY *same as* **>** RUBBITY

RUBBIES > RUBBY

RUBBING > RUB

RUBBINGS > RUB

RUBBISH *n* waste matter ▷ *vb* criticize

RUBBISHED > RUBBISH

RUBBISHES > RUBBISH

RUBBISHLY *adj* like rubbish

RUBBISHY *adj* worthless, of poor quality, or useless

RUBBIT *old Scots past form of* **>** ROB

RUBBITIES > RUBBITY

RUBBITY *n* pub

RUBBLE *n* fragments of broken stone, brick, etc ▷ *vb* turn into rubble

RUBBLED > RUBBLE

RUBBLES > RUBBLE

RUBBLIER > RUBBLE

RUBBLIEST > RUBBLE

RUBBLING > RUBBLE

RUBBLY > RUBBLE

RUBBOARD *n* board for scrubbing clothes on

RUBBOARDS > RUBBOARD

RUBBY *n* slang word for rubbing alcohol

RUBBYDUB *n* person who drinks cheap alcohol mixtures

RUBBYDUBS > RUBBYDUB

RUBDOWN *n* act of drying or cleaning vigorously

RUBDOWNS > RUBDOWN

RUBE *n* unsophisticated countryman

RUBEFIED > RUBEFY

RUBEFIES > RUBEFY

RUBEFY *vb* make red

RUBEFYING > RUBEFY

RUBEL *n* currency unit of Belarus

RUBELLA *n* mild contagious viral disease

RUBELLAN *n* red-coloured mineral

RUBELLANS > RUBELLAN

RUBELLAS > RUBELLA

RUBELLITE *n* red transparent variety of tourmaline, used as a gemstone

RUBELS > RUBEL

RUBEOLA *technical name for* **>** MEASLES

RUBEOLAR > RUBEOLA

RUBEOLAS > RUBEOLA

RUBES > RUBE

RUBESCENT *adj* reddening

RUBICELLE *n* variety of spinel that is orange or yellow in colour

RUBICON *n* point of no return ▷ *vb* (in bezique) to beat before the loser has managed to gain as many as 1000 points

RUBICONED > RUBICON

RUBICONS > RUBICON

RUBICUND *adj* ruddy

RUBIDIC > RUBIDIUM

RUBIDIUM *n* soft highly reactive radioactive element

RUBIDIUMS > RUBIDIUM

RUBIED > RUBY

RUBIER > RUBY

RUBIES > RUBY

RUBIEST > RUBY

RUBIFIED > RUBIFY

RUBIFIES > RUBIFY

RUBIFY *same as* **>** RUBEFY

RUBIFYING > RUBIFY

RUBIGO *old Scots word for* **>** PENIS

RUBIGOS > RUBIGO

RUBIN *archaic word for* **>** RUBY

RUBINE *archaic word for* **>** RUBY

RUBINEOUS *same as* **>** RUBIOUS

RUBINES > RUBINE

RUBINS > RUBIN

RUBIOUS *adj* of the colour ruby

RUBLE *same as* **>** ROUBLE

RUBLES > RUBLE

RUBLI > RUBLE

RUBOFF *n* resulting effect on something else; consequences

RUBOFFS > RUBOFF

RUBOUT *n* killing or elimination

RUBOUTS > RUBOUT

RUBRIC *n* set of rules for behaviour ▷ *adj* written, printed, or marked in red

RUBRICAL > RUBRIC

RUBRICATE *vb* print (a book or manuscript) with red titles, headings, etc

RUBRICIAN *n* authority on liturgical rubrics

RUBRICS > RUBRIC

RUBS > RUB

RUBSTONE *n* stone used for sharpening or smoothing, esp a whetstone

RUBSTONES > RUBSTONE

RUBUS *n* fruit-bearing genus of shrubs

RUBUSES > RUBUS

RUBY *n* red precious gemstone ▷ *adj* deep red ▷ *vb* redden

RUBYING > RUBY

RUBYLIKE > RUBY

RUC *same as* **>** ROC

RUCHE *n* pleat or frill of lace etc as a decoration ▷ *vb* put a ruche on

RUCHED > RUCHE

RUCHES > RUCHE

RUCHING *n* material used for a ruche

RUCHINGS > RUCHING

RUCK *n* rough crowd of common people ▷ *vb* wrinkle or crease

RUCKED > RUCK

RUCKING > RUCK

RUCKLE *another word for* **>** RUCK

RUCKLED > RUCKLE

RUCKLES > RUCKLE

RUCKLING > RUCKLE

RUCKMAN *n* person who plays in the ruck

RUCKMEN > RUCKMAN

RUCKS > RUCK

RUCKSACK *n* large pack carried on the back

RUCKSACKS > RUCKSACK

RUCKSEAT *n* seat fixed to or forming part of a rucksack

RUCKSEATS > RUCKSEAT

RUCKUS *n* uproar

RUCKUSES > RUCKUS

RUCOLA *n* another name for the salad plant rocket

RUCOLAS > RUCOLA

RUCS > RUC

RUCTATION *n* archaic word meaning eructation or belch

RUCTION *n* uproar

RUCTIONS > RUCTION

RUCTIOUS *adj* tending or likely to cause ructions

RUD *n* red or redness ▷ *vb* redden

RUDACEOUS *adj* (of conglomerate, breccia, and similar rocks) composed of coarse-grained material

RUDAS *n* Scots word for a coarse, rude old woman

RUDASES > RUDAS

RUDBECKIA *n* N American plant cultivated for its showy flowers

RUDD *n* European freshwater fish

RUDDED > RUD

RUDDER *n* device for steering a boat or aircraft

RUDDERS > RUDDER

RUDDIED > RUDDY

RUDDIER > RUDDY

RUDDIES > RUDDY

RUDDIEST > RUDDY

RUDDILY > RUDDY

RUDDINESS > RUDDY

RUDDING > RUD

RUDDLE *n* red ochre, used esp to mark sheep ▷ *vb* mark (sheep) with ruddle

RUDDLED > RUDDLE

RUDDLEMAN *n* ruddle dealer

RUDDLEMEN > RUDDLEMAN

RUDDLES > RUDDLE

RUDDLING > RUDDLE

RUDDOCK *dialect name for the* **>** ROBIN

RUDDOCKS > RUDDOCK

RUDDS > RUDD

RUDDY *adj* of a fresh healthy red colour ▷ *adv* bloody ▷ *vb* redden

RUDDYING > RUDDY

RUDE *archaic spelling of* **>** ROOD

RUDELY > RUDE

RUDENESS > RUDE

RUDER > RUDE

RUDERAL *n* plant that grows on waste ground ▷ *adj* growing in waste places

RUDERALS > RUDERAL

RUDERIES > RUDE

RUDERY > RUDE

RUDES > RUDE

RUDESBIES > RUDESBY

RUDESBY *n* archaic word for rude person

RUDEST > RUDE

RUDI *same as* **>** RUDIE

RUDIE *n* member of a youth movement originating in the 1960s

RUDIES > RUDIE

RUDIMENT *n* first principles or elementary stages of a subject

RUDIMENTS > RUDIMENT

RUDIS > RUDI

RUDISH *adj* somewhat rude

RUDIST *n* cone-shaped extinct mollusc

RUDISTID *same as* **>** RUDIST

RUDISTIDS > RUDISTID

RUDISTS > RUDIST

RUDS > RUD
RUDY same as > RUDIE
RUE vb feel regret for ▷ n plant with evergreen bitter leaves
RUED > RUE
RUEDA n type of Cuban round dance
RUEDAS > RUEDA
RUEFUL adj regretful or sorry
RUEFULLY > RUEFUL
RUEING > RUE
RUEINGS > RUE
RUELLE n area between bed and wall
RUELLES > RUELLE
RUELLIA n genus of plants
RUELLIAS > RUELLIA
RUER > RUE
RUERS > RUE
RUES > RUE
RUFESCENT adj tinged with red or becoming red
RUFF n circular pleated, gathered, or fluted collar ▷ vb trump
RUFFE n European freshwater fish
RUFFED > RUFF
RUFFES > RUFFE
RUFFIAN n violent lawless person ▷ vb act like a ruffian
RUFFIANED > RUFFIAN
RUFFIANLY > RUFFIAN
RUFFIANS > RUFFIAN
RUFFIN archaic name for > RUFFE
RUFFING > RUFF
RUFFINS > RUFFIN
RUFFLE vb disturb the calm of ▷ n frill or pleat
RUFFLED > RUFFLE
RUFFLER n person or thing that ruffles
RUFFLERS > RUFFLER
RUFFLES > RUFFLE
RUFFLIER > RUFFLY
RUFFLIEST > RUFFLY
RUFFLIKE > RUFF
RUFFLING > RUFFLE
RUFFLINGS > RUFFLE
RUFFLY adj ruffled
RUFFS > RUFF
RUFIYAA n standard monetary unit of the Maldives
RUFIYAAS > RUFIYAA
RUFOUS n reddish-brown colour
RUFOUSES > RUFOUS
RUG n small carpet ▷ vb (in dialect) tug
RUGA n fold, wrinkle, or crease
RUGAE > RUGA
RUGAL adj (in anatomy) with ridges or folds
RUGALACH same as > RUGELACH
RUGATE same as > RUGOSE
RUGBIES > RUGBY
RUGBY n form of football played with an oval ball which may be handled by the players
RUGELACH n fruit and nut pastry shaped like a croissant

RUGELACHS > RUGELACH
RUGGED adj rocky or steep
RUGGEDER > RUGGED
RUGGEDEST > RUGGED
RUGGEDISE same as > RUGGEDIZE
RUGGEDIZE vb make durable, as for military use
RUGGEDLY > RUGGED
RUGGELACH same as > RUGELACH
RUGGER same as > RUGBY
RUGGERS > RUGGER
RUGGIER > RUGGY
RUGGIEST > RUGGY
RUGGING > RUG
RUGGINGS > RUG
RUGGY adj (in dialect) rough or rugged
RUGLIKE > RUG
RUGOLA n another name for the salad plant rocket
RUGOLAS > RUGOLA
RUGOSA n any of various shrubs descended from a particular type of wild rose
RUGOSAS > RUGOSA
RUGOSE adj wrinkled
RUGOSELY > RUGOSE
RUGOSITY > RUGOSE
RUGOUS same as > RUGOSE
RUGRAT n young child
RUGRATS > RUGRAT
RUGS > RUG
RUGULOSE adj with little wrinkles
RUIN vb destroy or spoil completely ▷ n destruction or decay
RUINABLE > RUIN
RUINATE vb archaic word for bring or come to ruin
RUINATED > RUINATE
RUINATES > RUINATE
RUINATING > RUINATE
RUINATION n act of ruining
RUINED > RUIN
RUINER > RUIN
RUINERS > RUIN
RUING > RUE
RUINGS > RUE
RUINING > RUIN
RUININGS > RUIN
RUINOUS adj causing ruin
RUINOUSLY > RUINOUS
RUINS > RUIN
RUKH same as > ROC
RUKHS > RUKH
RULABLE > RULE
RULE n statement of what is allowed, for example in a game or procedure ▷ vb govern
RULED > RULE
RULELESS > RULE
RULER n person who governs ▷ vb punish by hitting with a ruler
RULERED > RULER
RULERING > RULER
RULERS > RULER
RULERSHIP > RULER
RULES > RULE
RULESSE adj archaic word meaning ruleless or without rules
RULIER > RULY

RULIEST > RULY
RULING n formal decision ▷ adj controlling or exercising authority
RULINGS > RULING
RULLION n Scots word for rawhide shoe
RULLIONS > RULLION
RULLOCK same as > ROWLOCK
RULLOCKS > RULLOCK
RULY adj orderly
RUM n alcoholic drink distilled from sugar cane ▷ adj odd, strange
RUMAKI n savoury of chicken liver and sliced water chestnut wrapped in bacon
RUMAKIS > RUMAKI
RUMAL n handkerchief or type of cloth
RUMALS > RUMAL
RUMBA n lively ballroom dance of Cuban origin ▷ vb dance the rumba
RUMBAED > RUMBA
RUMBAING > RUMBA
RUMBAS > RUMBA
RUMBELOW n nonsense word used in the refrain of certain sea shanties
RUMBELOWS > RUMBELOW
RUMBLE vb make a low continuous noise ▷ n deep resonant sound
RUMBLED > RUMBLE
RUMBLER > RUMBLE
RUMBLERS > RUMBLE
RUMBLES > RUMBLE
RUMBLIER > RUMBLY
RUMBLIEST > RUMBLY
RUMBLING > RUMBLE
RUMBLINGS > RUMBLE
RUMBLY adj rumbling or liable to rumble
RUMBO n rum-based cocktail
RUMBOS > RUMBO
RUMDUM n alcoholic
RUMDUMS > RUMDUM
RUME archaic form of > RHEUM
RUMEN n first compartment of the stomach of ruminants
RUMENS > RUMEN
RUMES > RUME
RUMINA > RUMEN
RUMINAL > RUMEN
RUMINANT n cud-chewing (animal, such as a cow, sheep, or deer) ▷ adj of ruminants
RUMINANTS > RUMINANT
RUMINATE vb chew the cud
RUMINATED > RUMINATE
RUMINATES > RUMINATE
RUMINATOR > RUMINATE
RUMKIN n archaic term for a drinking vessel
RUMKINS > RUMKIN
RUMLY > RUM
RUMMAGE vb search untidily and at length ▷ n untidy search through a collection of things
RUMMAGED > RUMMAGE
RUMMAGER > RUMMAGE
RUMMAGERS > RUMMAGE
RUMMAGES > RUMMAGE

RUMMAGING > RUMMAGE
RUMMER n drinking glass
RUMMERS > RUMMER
RUMMEST > RUM
RUMMIER > RUMMY
RUMMIES > RUMMY
RUMMIEST > RUMMY
RUMMILY > RUMMY
RUMMINESS > RUMMY
RUMMISH adj rather strange, peculiar, or odd ▷ vb roar or protest
RUMMISHED > RUMMISH
RUMMISHES > RUMMISH
RUMMY n card game in which players try to collect sets or sequences ▷ adj of or like rum in taste or smell
RUMNESS > RUM
RUMNESSES > RUM
RUMOR same as > RUMOUR
RUMORED > RUMOR
RUMORER n person given to spreading rumours
RUMORERS > RUMORER
RUMORING > RUMOR
RUMOROUS adj involving or containing rumours
RUMORS > RUMOR
RUMOUR n unproved statement ▷ vb pass around or circulate in the form of a rumour
RUMOURED > RUMOUR
RUMOURER n someone given to spreading rumours
RUMOURERS > RUMOURER
RUMOURING > RUMOUR
RUMOURS > RUMOUR
RUMP n buttocks ▷ vb turn back on
RUMPED > RUMP
RUMPIER > RUMPY
RUMPIES > RUMPY
RUMPIEST > RUMPY
RUMPING > RUMP
RUMPLE vb make untidy, crumpled, or dishevelled ▷ n wrinkle, fold, or crease
RUMPLED > RUMPLE
RUMPLES > RUMPLE
RUMPLESS > RUMP
RUMPLIER > RUMPLE
RUMPLIEST > RUMPLE
RUMPLING > RUMPLE
RUMPLY > RUMPLE
RUMPO n slang word for sexual intercourse
RUMPOS > RUMPO
RUMPOT n alcoholic
RUMPOTS > RUMPOT
RUMPS > RUMP
RUMPUS n noisy commotion
RUMPUSES > RUMPUS
RUMPY n tailless Manx cat ▷ adj with a large or noticeable rump
RUMRUNNER n alcohol smuggler
RUMS > RUM
RUN vb move with a more rapid gait than walking ▷ n act or spell of running
RUNABOUT n small car used for short journeys ▷ vb move busily from place to place
RUNABOUTS > RUNABOUT

r

RUNAGATE n vagabond, fugitive, or renegade

RUNAGATES > RUNAGATE

RUNANGA n Māori assembly or council

RUNANGAS > RUNANGA

RUNAROUND n deceitful or evasive treatment of a person

RUNAWAY n person or animal that runs away

RUNAWAYS > RUNAWAY

RUNBACK n (in tennis) the areas behind the baselines of the court

RUNBACKS > RUNBACK

RUNCH n another name for white charlock

RUNCHES > RUNCH

RUNCIBLE adj as in runcible spoon forklike utensil with two prongs and one sharp curved prong

RUNCINATE adj (of a leaf) having a saw-toothed margin with the teeth or lobes pointing backwards

RUND same as > ROON

RUNDALE n system of land tenure in Ireland

RUNDALES > RUNDALE

RUNDLE n rung of a ladder

RUNDLED adj rounded

RUNDLES > RUNDLE

RUNDLET n liquid measure, generally about 15 gallons

RUNDLETS > RUNDLET

RUNDOWN adj tired; exhausted ▷ n brief review, résumé, or summary

RUNDOWNS > RUNDOWN

RUNDS > RUND

RUNE n any character of the earliest Germanic alphabet

RUNECRAFT n understanding of and skill working with runes

RUNED n with runes on

RUNELIKE adj resembling a rune or runes

RUNES > RUNE

RUNFLAT adj having a safety feature that prevents tyres becoming dangerous when flat

RUNFLATS > RUNFLAT

RUNG n crosspiece on ladder

RUNGED adj having rungs

RUNGLESS > RUNG

RUNGS > RUNG

RUNIC > RUNE

RUNKLE vb (in dialect) crease or wrinkle

RUNKLED > RUNKLE

RUNKLES > RUNKLE

RUNKLING > RUNKLE

RUNLESS > RUN

RUNLET n cask for wine, beer, etc

RUNLETS > RUNLET

RUNNABLE > RUN

RUNNEL n small brook

RUNNELS > RUNNEL

RUNNER n competitor in a race

RUNNERS > RUNNER

RUNNET dialect word for > RENNET

RUNNETS > RUNNET

RUNNIER > RUNNY

RUNNIEST > RUNNY

RUNNINESS > RUNNY

RUNNING > RUN

RUNNINGLY > RUN

RUNNINGS > RUN

RUNNION n archaic pejorative term for a woman

RUNNIONS > RUNNION

RUNNY adj tending to flow

RUNOFF n extra race to decide the winner after a tie

RUNOFFS > RUNOFF

RUNOUT n dismissal of a batsman by running them out

RUNOUTS > RUNOUT

RUNOVER n incident in which someone is run over by a vehicle

RUNOVERS > RUNOVER

RUNPROOF adj (of stockings or tights) designed to be especially resistant to being ripped

RUNRIG same as > RUNDALE

RUNRIGS > RUNRIG

RUNROUND same as > RUNAROUND

RUNROUNDS > RUNROUND

RUNS > RUN

RUNT n smallest animal in a litter

RUNTED adj stunted

RUNTIER > RUNT

RUNTIEST > RUNT

RUNTINESS > RUNT

RUNTISH > RUNT

RUNTISHLY > RUNT

RUNTS > RUNT

RUNTY > RUNT

RUNWAY n hard level roadway where aircraft take off and land

RUNWAYS > RUNWAY

RUPEE n monetary unit of India and Pakistan

RUPEES > RUPEE

RUPIA n type of skin eruption

RUPIAH n standard monetary unit of Indonesia

RUPIAHS > RUPIAH

RUPIAS > RUPIA

RUPTURE n breaking, breach ▷ vb break, burst, or sever

RUPTURED > RUPTURE

RUPTURES > RUPTURE

RUPTURING > RUPTURE

RURAL adj in or of the countryside ▷ n country dweller

RURALISE same as > RURALIZE

RURALISED > RURALISE

RURALISES > RURALISE

RURALISM > RURAL

RURALISMS > RURAL

RURALIST > RURAL

RURALISTS > RURAL

RURALITE > RURAL

RURALITES > RURAL

RURALITY > RURAL

RURALIZE vb make rural in character, appearance, etc

RURALIZED > RURALIZE

RURALIZES > RURALIZE

RURALLY > RURAL

RURALNESS > RURAL

RURALS > RURAL

RURBAN adj part country, part urban

RURP n very small piton

RURPS > RURP

RURU another name for > MOPOKE

RURUS > RURU

RUSA n type of deer with a mane

RUSALKA n water nymph or spirit

RUSALKAS > RUSALKA

RUSAS > RUSA

RUSCUS n type of shrub

RUSCUSES > RUSCUS

RUSE n stratagem or trick

RUSES > RUSE

RUSH vb move or do very quickly ▷ n sudden quick or violent movement ▷ adj done with speed, hasty

RUSHED > RUSH

RUSHEE n someone interested in gaining fraternity or sorority membership

RUSHEES > RUSHEE

RUSHEN adj made of rushes

RUSHER > RUSH

RUSHERS > RUSH

RUSHES pl n (in film-making) the initial prints of a scene or scenes before editing

RUSHIER > RUSHY

RUSHIEST > RUSHY

RUSHINESS > RUSHY

RUSHING > RUSH

RUSHINGS > RUSH

RUSHLIGHT n narrow candle, formerly in use, made of the pith of various types of rush dipped in tallow

RUSHLIKE > RUSH

RUSHY adj full of rushes

RUSINE adj of or relating to rusa deer

RUSK n hard brown crisp biscuit, used esp for feeding babies

RUSKS > RUSK

RUSMA n Turkish depilatory

RUSMAS > RUSMA

RUSSE adj as in charlotte russe cold dessert made from cream, etc, surrounded by sponge fingers

RUSSEL n type of woollen fabric

RUSSELS > RUSSEL

RUSSET adj reddish-brown ▷ n apple with rough reddish-brown skin ▷ vb become russet-coloured

RUSSETED > RUSSET

RUSSETIER > RUSSETY

RUSSETING > RUSSET

RUSSETS > RUSSET

RUSSETY adj of a russet colour

RUSSIA n Russia leather

RUSSIAS > RUSSIA

RUSSIFIED > RUSSIFY

RUSSIFIES > RUSSIFY

RUSSIFY vb cause to become Russian in character

RUSSULA n type of fungus, typically of toadstool shape

RUSSULAE > RUSSULA

RUSSULAS > RUSSULA

RUST n reddish-brown coating formed on iron etc that has been exposed to moisture ▷ adj reddish-brown ▷ vb become coated with rust

RUSTABLE adj liable to rust

RUSTED > RUST

RUSTIC adj of or resembling country people ▷ n person from the country

RUSTICAL n rustic

RUSTICALS > RUSTICAL

RUSTICANA pl n objects, such as agricultural implements, garden furniture, etc, relating to the countryside or made in imitation of rustic styles

RUSTICATE vb banish temporarily from university as a punishment

RUSTICIAL made-up variant of > RUSTIC

RUSTICISE same as > RUSTICIZE

RUSTICISM > RUSTIC

RUSTICITY > RUSTIC

RUSTICIZE vb make rustic

RUSTICLY > RUSTIC

RUSTICS > RUSTIC

RUSTIER > RUSTY

RUSTIEST > RUSTY

RUSTILY > RUSTY

RUSTINESS > RUSTY

RUSTING > RUST

RUSTINGS > RUST

RUSTLE n low whispering sound ▷ vb steal (cattle)

RUSTLED > RUSTLE

RUSTLER n cattle thief

RUSTLERS > RUSTLER

RUSTLES > RUSTLE

RUSTLESS > RUST

RUSTLING > RUSTLE

RUSTLINGS > RUSTLE

RUSTPROOF adj treated against rusting

RUSTRE n (in heraldry) lozenge with a round hole in the middle showing the background colour

RUSTRED > RUSTRE

RUSTRES > RUSTRE

RUSTS > RUST

RUSTY adj coated with rust

RUT n furrow made by wheels ▷ vb make ruts in

RUTABAGA n plant with a bulbous edible root

RUTABAGAS > RUTABAGA

RUTACEOUS adj relating to a family of tropical and temperate flowering plants which includes rue and citrus trees

RUTH n pity

RUTHENIC *adj* of or containing ruthenium, esp in a high valency state

RUTHENIUM *n* rare hard brittle white element

RUTHER *adv* rather

RUTHFUL *adj* full of or causing sorrow or pity

RUTHFULLY > RUTHFUL

RUTHLESS *adj* pitiless, merciless

RUTHS > RUTH

RUTILANT *adj* of a reddish colour or glow

RUTILATED *adj* (of minerals, esp quartz) containing needles of rutile

RUTILE *n* black, yellowish, or reddish-brown mineral

RUTILES > RUTILE

RUTIN *n* bioflavonoid found in various plants including rue

RUTINS > RUTIN

RUTS > RUT

RUTTED > RUT

RUTTER *n* (in history) type of cavalry soldier

RUTTERS > RUTTER

RUTTIER > RUTTY

RUTTIEST > RUTTY

RUTTILY > RUTTY

RUTTINESS > RUTTY

RUTTING > RUT

RUTTINGS > RUT

RUTTISH *adj* (of an animal) in a condition of rut

RUTTISHLY > RUTTISH

RUTTY *adj* full of ruts or holes

RYA *n* type of rug originating in Scandinavia

RYAL *n* one of several old coins

RYALS > RYAL

RYAS > RYA

RYBAT *n* polished stone piece forming the side of a window or door

RYBATS > RYBAT

RYBAUDRYE *archaic variant of* > RIBALDRY

RYE *n* kind of grain used for fodder and bread

RYEBREAD *n* bread made from rye flour

RYEBREADS > RYEBREAD

RYEFLOUR *n* flour made from rye

RYEFLOURS > RYEFLOUR

RYEGRASS *n* type of grass, widely cultivated as a forage crop

RYEPECK *n* punt-mooring pole

RYEPECKS > RYEPECK

RYES > RYE

RYFE *archaic variant of* > RIFE

RYKE *Scots variant of* > REACH

RYKED > RYKE

RYKES > RYKE

RYKING > RYKE

RYMME *same as* > RIM

RYMMED > RYMME

RYMMES > RYMME

RYMMING > RYMME

RYND *n* (in milling) crossbar piece forming part of the support structure of the upper millstone

RYNDS > RYND

RYOKAN *n* traditional Japanese inn

RYOKANS > RYOKAN

RYOT *n* (in India) a peasant or tenant farmer

RYOTS > RYOT

RYOTWARI *n* (in India) system of land tenure in which land taxes are paid to the state

RYOTWARIS > RYOTWARI

RYPE *n* ptarmigan

RYPECK *same as* > RYEPECK

RYPECKS > RYPECK

RYPER > RYPE

RYU *n* school of Japanese martial arts

RYUS > RYU

Ss

SAAG n (in Indian cookery) spinach

SAAGS > SAAG

SAB n person engaged in direct action to prevent a targeted activity taking place ▷ vb take part in such action

SABADILLA n tropical American liliaceous plant

SABAL n variety of palm tree

SABALS > SABAL

SABATON n foot covering in suit of armour

SABATONS > SABATON

SABAYON n dessert or sweet sauce made with egg yolks, sugar, and wine

SABAYONS > SABAYON

SABBAT n midnight meeting of witches

SABBATH n period of rest

SABBATHS > SABBATH

SABBATIC n period of leave granted to university staff

SABBATICS > SABBATIC

SABBATINE adj of Saturday

SABBATISE same as
> SABBATIZE

SABBATISM n sabbath observance

SABBATIZE vb observe as sabbath

SABBATS > SABBAT

SABBED > SAB

SABBING > SAB

SABBINGS > SABBING

SABE n very informal word meaning sense or savvy ▷ vb very informal word meaning know or savvy

SABED > SABE

SABEING > SABE

SABELLA n marine worm

SABELLAS > SABELLA

SABER same as > SABRE

SABERED > SABER

SABERING > SABER

SABERLIKE > SABER

SABERS > SABER

SABES > SABE

SABHA n set of Muslim prayer beads

SABHAS > SABHA

SABICU n type of Caribbean tree

SABICUS > SABICU

SABIN n unit of acoustic absorption

SABINE variant of > SAVIN

SABINES > SABINE

SABINS > SABIN

SABIR n member of ancient Turkic people

SABIRS > SABIR

SABKHA n flat coastal plain with a salt crust, common in Arabia

SABKHAH n sabkha

SABKHAHS > SABKHAH

SABKHAS > SABKHA

SABKHAT n sabkha

SABKHATS > SABKHAT

SABLE n dark fur from a small weasel-like Arctic animal ▷ adj black

SABLED > SABLE

SABLEFISH n North American fish

SABLER > SABLE

SABLES > SABLE

SABLEST > SABLE

SABLING > SABLE

SABOT n wooden shoe traditionally worn by peasants in France

SABOTAGE n intentional damage done to machinery, systems, etc ▷ vb damage intentionally

SABOTAGED > SABOTAGE

SABOTAGES > SABOTAGE

SABOTED adj wearing sabots

SABOTEUR n person who commits sabotage

SABOTEURS > SABOTEUR

SABOTIER n wearer of wooden clogs

SABOTIERS > SABOTIER

SABOTS > SABOT

SABRA n native-born Israeli Jew

SABRAS > SABRA

SABRE n curved cavalry sword ▷ vb injure or kill with a sabre

SABRED > SABRE

SABRELIKE > SABERLIKE

SABRES > SABRE

SABREUR n person wielding sabre

SABREURS > SABREUR

SABREWING n large type of hummingbird with long curved wings

SABRING > SABRE

SABS > SAB

SABULINE same as
> SABULOUS

SABULOSE same as
> SABULOUS

SABULOUS adj like sand in texture

SABURRA n granular deposit

SABURRAL > SABURRA

SABURRAS > SABURRA

SAC n pouchlike structure in an animal or plant

SACATON n coarse grass of the southwestern US and Mexico

SACATONS > SACATON

SACBUT n medieval trombone

SACBUTS > SACBUT

SACCADE n movement of the eye when it makes a sudden change of fixation, as in reading

SACCADES > SACCADE

SACCADIC > SACCADE

SACCATE adj in the form of a sac

SACCHARIC adj as in saccharic acid white soluble solid acid

SACCHARIN n artificial sweetener

SACCHARUM n cane sugar

SACCIFORM adj like a sac

SACCOI > SACCOS

SACCOS n bishop's garment in the Orthodox Church

SACCOSES > SACCOS

SACCULAR adj of or resembling a sac

SACCULATE adj of, relating to, or possessing a saccule, saccules, or a sacculus

SACCULE n small sac

SACCULES > SACCULE

SACCULI > SACCULUS

SACCULUS same as
> SACCULE

SACELLA > SACELLUM

SACELLUM n tomb within a church

SACHEM same as
> SAGAMORE

SACHEMDOM > SACHEM

SACHEMIC > SACHEM

SACHEMS > SACHEM

SACHET n small envelope or bag containing a single portion

SACHETED adj contained in a sachet

SACHETS > SACHET

SACK n large bag made of coarse material ▷ vb dismiss

SACKABLE adj of an offence that is sufficiently serious to warrant dismissal from a job

SACKAGE n act of sacking a place ▷ vb sack or plunder

SACKAGED > SACKAGE

SACKAGES > SACKAGE

SACKAGING > SACKAGE

SACKBUT n medieval form of trombone

SACKBUTS > SACKBUT

SACKCLOTH n coarse fabric used for sacks, formerly worn as a penance

SACKED > SACK

SACKER > SACK

SACKERS > SACK

SACKFUL > SACK

SACKFULS > SACKFUL

SACKING n rough woven material used for sacks

SACKINGS > SACKING

SACKLESS adj old word meaning innocent

SACKLIKE > SACK

SACKLOAD n amount of something that a sack contains

SACKLOADS > SACKLOAD

SACKS > SACK

SACKSFUL > SACKFUL

SACLESS adj old word meaning unchallengeable

SACLIKE > SAC

SACQUE same as > SACK

SACQUES > SACQUE

SACRA > SACRUM

SACRAL adj of or associated with sacred rites ▷ n sacral vertebra

SACRALGIA n pain in sacrum

SACRALISE same as
> SACRALIZE

SACRALITY n sacredness

SACRALIZE vb make sacred

SACRALS > SACRAL

SACRAMENT n ceremony of the Christian Church, esp Communion

SACRARIA > SACRARIUM

SACRARIAL > SACRARIUM

SACRARIUM n sanctuary of a church

SACRED adj holy

SACREDER > SACRED

SACREDEST > SACRED

SACREDLY > SACRED

SACRIFICE n giving something up ▷ vb offer as a sacrifice

SACRIFIDE vb old form of sacrifice

SACRIFIED > SACRIFY

SACRIFIES > SACRIFY

SACRIFY vb old form of sacrifice

SACRILEGE *n* misuse or desecration of something sacred

SACRING *n* act or ritual of consecration

SACRINGS > SACRING

SACRIST *same as* **>** SACRISTAN

SACRISTAN *n* person in charge of the contents of a church

SACRISTS > SACRIST

SACRISTY *n* room in a church where sacred objects are kept

SACRUM *n* wedge-shaped bone at the base of the spine

SACRUMS > SACRUM

SACS > SAC

SAD *adj* sorrowful, unhappy **>** *vb* New Zealand word meaning express sadness or displeasure strongly

SADDED > SAD

SADDEN *vb* make (someone) sad

SADDENED > SADDEN

SADDENING > SADDEN

SADDENS > SADDEN

SADDER > SAD

SADDEST > SAD

SADDHU *same as* **>** SADHU

SADDHUS > SADDHU

SADDIE *same as* **>** SADDO

SADDIES > SADDIE

SADDING > SAD

SADDISH > SAD

SADDLE *n* rider's seat on a horse or bicycle **>** *vb* put a saddle on (a horse)

SADDLEBAG *n* pouch or small bag attached to the saddle of a horse, bicycle, or motorcycle

SADDLEBOW *n* pommel of a saddle

SADDLED > SADDLE

SADDLER *n* maker or seller of saddles

SADDLERS > SADDLER

SADDLERY *n* saddles and harness for horses collectively

SADDLES > SADDLE

SADDLING > SADDLE

SADDO *vb* make sad **>** *n* socially inadequate or pathetic person

SADDOES > SADDO

SADDOS > SADDO

SADE *same as* **>** SADHE

SADES > SADE

SADHANA *n* one of a number of spiritual practices which lead to perfection

SADHANAS > SADHANA

SADHE *n* 18th letter in the Hebrew alphabet

SADHES > SADHE

SADHU *n* Hindu wandering holy man

SADHUS > SADHU

SADI *variant of* **>** SADHE

SADIRON *n* heavy iron pointed at both ends, for pressing clothes

SADIRONS > SADIRON

SADIS > SADI

SADISM *n* gaining of pleasure from inflicting suffering

SADISMS > SADISM

SADIST > SADISM

SADISTIC > SADISM

SADISTS > SADISM

SADLY > SAD

SADNESS > SAD

SADNESSES > SAD

SADO *variant of* **>** CHADO

SADOS > SADO

SADS > SAD

SADZA *n* southern African porridge

SADZAS > SADZA

SAE *Scot word for* **>** SO

SAECULA > SAECULUM

SAECULUM *n* age in astronomy

SAECULUMS > SAECULUM

SAETER *n* upland pasture in Norway

SAETERS > SAETER

SAFARI *n* expedition to hunt or observe wild animals, esp in Africa **>** *vb* go on safari

SAFARIED > SAFARI

SAFARIING > SAFARI

SAFARIS > SAFARI

SAFARIST *n* person on safari

SAFARISTS > SAFARIST

SAFE *adj* secure, protected **>** *n* strong lockable container **>** *vb* make safe

SAFED > SAFE

SAFEGUARD *vb* protect **>** *n* protection

SAFELIGHT *n* light that can be used in a room in which photographic material is handled, transmitting only those colours to which a particular type of film, plate, or paper is relatively insensitive

SAFELY > SAFE

SAFENESS > SAFE

SAFER > SAFE

SAFES > SAFE

SAFEST > SAFE

SAFETIED > SAFETY

SAFETIES > SAFETY

SAFETY *n* state of being safe **>** *vb* make safe

SAFETYING > SAFETY

SAFETYMAN *n* defensive player in American football

SAFETYMEN > SAFETYMAN

SAFFIAN *n* leather tanned with sumach and usually dyed a bright colour

SAFFIANS > SAFFIAN

SAFFLOWER *n* thistle-like plant with flowers used for dye and oil

SAFFRON *n* orange-coloured flavouring obtained from a crocus **>** *adj* orange

SAFFRONED *adj* containing saffron

SAFFRONS > SAFFRON

SAFFRONY *adj* like saffron

SAFING > SAFE

SAFRANIN *same as* **>** SAFRANINE

SAFRANINE *n* any of a class of azine dyes, used for textiles and biological stains

SAFRANINS > SAFRANIN

SAFROL *n* oily liquid obtained from sassafras

SAFROLE *n* colourless or yellowish oily water-insoluble liquid

SAFROLES > SAFROLE

SAFROLS > SAFROL

SAFRONAL *n* oily liquid derived from saffron

SAFRONALS > SAFRONAL

SAFT *Scot word for* **>** SOFT

SAFTER > SAFT

SAFTEST > SAFT

SAG *vb* sink in the middle **>** *n* droop

SAGA *n* legend of Norse heroes

SAGACIOUS *adj* wise

SAGACITY *n* foresight, discernment, or keen perception

SAGAMAN *n* person reciting Norse sagas

SAGAMEN > SAGAMAN

SAGAMORE *n* (among some Native Americans) a chief or eminent man

SAGAMORES > SAGAMORE

SAGANASH *n* Algonquian term for an Englishman

SAGAPENUM *n* resin formerly used as drug

SAGAS > SAGA

SAGATHIES > SAGATHY

SAGATHY *n* type of light fabric

SAGBUT *n* medieval trombone

SAGBUTS > SAGBUT

SAGE *n* very wise man **>** *adj* wise

SAGEBRUSH *n* aromatic plant of West N America

SAGEHOOD *n* state of being wise

SAGEHOODS > SAGEHOOD

SAGELY > SAGE

SAGENE *n* fishing net

SAGENES > SAGENE

SAGENESS > SAGE

SAGENITE *n* mineral found in crystal form

SAGENITES > SAGENITE

SAGENITIC > SAGENITE

SAGER > SAGE

SAGES > SAGE

SAGEST > SAGE

SAGGAR *n* box in which fragile ceramic wares are placed for protection **>** *vb* put in a saggar

SAGGARD *n* saggar

SAGGARDS > SAGGARD

SAGGARED > SAGGAR

SAGGARING > SAGGAR

SAGGARS > SAGGAR

SAGGED > SAG

SAGGER *same as* **>** SAGGAR

SAGGERED > SAGGER

SAGGERING > SAGGER

SAGGERS > SAGGER

SAGGIER > SAGGY

SAGGIEST > SAGGY

SAGGING > SAG

SAGGINGS > SAG

SAGGY *adj* tending to sag

SAGIER > SAGY

SAGIEST > SAGY

SAGINATE *vb* fatten livestock

SAGINATED > SAGINATE

SAGINATES > SAGINATE

SAGITTA *n* sine of an arc

SAGITTAL *adj* resembling an arrow

SAGITTARY *n* centaur

SAGITTAS > SAGITTA

SAGITTATE *adj* (esp of leaves) shaped like the head of an arrow

SAGO *n* starchy cereal from the powdered pith of the sago palm tree

SAGOIN *n* South American monkey

SAGOINS > SAGOIN

SAGOS > SAGO

SAGOUIN *n* South American monkey

SAGOUINS > SAGOUIN

SAGRADA *adj* as in *cascara sagrada* dried bark of the cascara buckthorn

SAGS > SAG

SAGUARO *n* giant cactus of desert regions

SAGUAROS > SAGUARO

SAGUIN *n* South American monkey

SAGUINS > SAGUIN

SAGUM *n* Roman soldier's cloak

SAGY *adj* like or containing sage

SAHEB *same as* **>** SAHIB

SAHEBS > SAHEB

SAHIB *n* Indian term of address placed after a man's name as a mark of respect

SAHIBA *n* respectful Indian term of address for woman

SAHIBAH *n* sahiba

SAHIBAHS > SAHIBAH

SAHIBAS > SAHIBA

SAHIBS > SAHIB

SAHIWAL *n* breed of cattle in India

SAHIWALS > SAHIWAL

SAHUARO *same as* **>** SAGUARO

SAHUAROS > SAHUARO

SAI *n* South American monkey

SAIBLING *n* freshwater fish

SAIBLINGS > SAIBLING

SAIC *n* boat of eastern Mediterranean

SAICE *same as* **>** SYCE

SAICES > SAICE

SAICK *n* boat of eastern Mediterranean

SAICKS > SAICK

SAICS > SAIC

SAID *same as* **>** SAYYID

SAIDEST > SAY

SAIDS > SAID

SAIDST > SAY

SAIGA *n* either of two antelopes of the plains of central Asia

SAIGAS > SAIGA

SAIKEI n Japanese ornamental miniature landscape

SAIKEIS > SAIKEI

SAIKLESS old Scots word for > INNOCENT

SAIL n sheet of fabric stretched to catch the wind for propelling a sailing boat ▷ vb travel by water

SAILABLE > SAIL

SAILBOARD n board with a mast and single sail, used for windsurfing

SAILBOAT n boat propelled chiefly by sail

SAILBOATS > SAILBOAT

SAILCLOTH n fabric for making sails

SAILED > SAIL

SAILER n vessel, esp one equipped with sails, with specified sailing characteristics

SAILERS > SAILER

SAILFISH n large tropical game fish, with a long sail-like fin on its back

SAILING n practice, art, or technique of sailing a vessel

SAILINGS > SAILING

SAILLESS > SAIL

SAILMAKER n person who makes sails

SAILOR n member of a ship's crew

SAILORING n activity of working as sailor

SAILORLY adj like a sailor

SAILORS > SAILOR

SAILPAST n sailing of ships past a particular place

SAILPASTS > SAILPAST

SAILPLANE n high-performance glider

SAILROOM n space on ship for storing sails

SAILROOMS > SAILROOM

SAILS > SAIL

SAIM Scots word for > LARD

SAIMIN n Hawaiian dish of noodles

SAIMINS > SAIMIN

SAIMIRI n South American monkey

SAIMIRIS > SAIMIRI

SAIMS > SAIM

SAIN vb make the sign of the cross over so as to bless or protect from evil or sin

SAINE vb old form of say

SAINED > SAIN

SAINFOIN n Eurasian plant with pink flowers, widely grown as feed for grazing farm animals

SAINFOINS > SAINFOIN

SAINING > SAIN

SAINS > SAIN

SAINT n person venerated after death as specially holy ▷ vb canonize

SAINTDOM > SAINT

SAINTDOMS > SAINT

SAINTED adj formally recognized by a Christian Church as a saint

SAINTESS n female saint

SAINTFOIN n sainfoin

SAINTHOOD n state or character of being a saint

SAINTING > SATNT

SAINTISH > SAINT

SAINTISM n quality of being saint

SAINTISMS > SAINTISM

SAINTLESS > SAINT

SAINTLIER > SAINTLY

SAINTLIKE > SAINT

SAINTLILY > SAINTLY

SAINTLING n little saint

SAINTLY adj behaving in a very good, patient, or holy way

SAINTS > SAINT

SAINTSHIP > SAINT

SAIQUE n boat in eastern Mediterranean

SAIQUES > SAIQUE

SAIR Scot word for > SORE

SAIRED > SAIR

SAIRER > SAIR

SAIREST > SAIR

SAIRING > SAIR

SAIRS > SAIR

SAIS > SAI

SAIST > SAY

SAITH form of the present tense (indicative mood) of > SAY

SAITHE n dark-coloured food fish found in northern seas

SAITHES > SAITHE

SAITHS > SAITH

SAIYID n Muslim descended from Mohammed's grandson

SAIYIDS > SAIYID

SAJOU n South American monkey

SAJOUS > SAJOU

SAKAI n Malaysian aborigine

SAKAIS > SAKAI

SAKE n benefit

SAKER n large falcon of E Europe and central Asia

SAKERET n male saker

SAKERETS > SAKERET

SAKERS > SAKER

SAKES > SAKE

SAKI n small arboreal monkey

SAKIA n water wheel in Middle East

SAKIAS > SAKIA

SAKIEH same as > SAKIA

SAKIEHS > SAKIEH

SAKIS > SAKI

SAKIYEH same as > SAKIA

SAKIYEHS > SAKIYEH

SAKKOI > SAKKOS

SAKKOS n bishop's garment in Orthodox Church

SAKKOSES > SAKKOS

SAKSAUL n Asian tree

SAKSAULS > SAKSAUL

SAKTI n wife of a Hindu god

SAKTIS > SAKTI

SAL pharmacological term for > SALT

SALAAM n low bow of greeting among Muslims ▷ vb make a salaam

SALAAMED > SALAAM

SALAAMING > SALAAM

SALAAMS > SALAAM

SALABLE same as > SALEABLE

SALABLY > SALEABLY

SALACIOUS adj excessively concerned with sexual matters

SALACITY n excessive interest in sexual matters

SALAD n dish of raw vegetables, eaten as a meal or part of a meal

SALADANG n variety of ox

SALADANGS > SALADANG

SALADE same as > SALLET

SALADES > SALADE

SALADING n ingredients for salad

SALADINGS > SALADING

SALADS > SALAD

SALAL n North American shrub

SALALS > SALAL

SALAMI n highly spiced sausage

SALAMIS > SALAMI

SALAMON n word used in old oaths

SALAMONS > SALAMON

SALANGANE n Asian swift

SALARIAT n salary-earning class

SALARIATS > SALARIAT

SALARIED adj earning or providing a salary

SALARIES > SALARY

SALARY n fixed regular payment, usu monthly, to an employee ▷ vb pay a salary to

SALARYING > SALARY

SALARYMAN n (in Japan) an office worker

SALARYMEN > SALARYMAN

SALAT n obligatory series of Islamic prayers facing towards Mecca

SALATS > SALAT

SALBAND n coating of mineral

SALBANDS > SALBAND

SALCHOW n type of figure-skating jump

SALCHOWS > SALCHOW

SALE n exchange of goods for money

SALEABLE adj fit or likely to be sold

SALEABLY > SALEABLE

SALEP n dried ground starchy tubers of various orchids

SALEPS > SALEP

SALERATUS n sodium bicarbonate when used in baking powder

SALERING n enclosed area for livestock at market

SALERINGS > SALERING

SALEROOM n place where goods are sold by auction

SALEROOMS > SALEROOM

SALES > SALE

SALESGIRL n person who sells goods

SALESLADY n person who sells goods

SALESMAN n person who sells goods

SALESMEN > SALESMAN

SALESROOM n room in which merchandise on sale is displayed

SALET same as > SALLET

SALETS > SALET

SALEWD > SALUE

SALEYARD n area with pens for holding animals before auction

SALEYARDS > SALEYARD

SALFERN n plant of borage family

SALFERNS > SALFERN

SALIAUNCE n old word meaning onslaught

SALIC adj (of rocks and minerals) having a high content of silica and alumina

SALICES > SALIX

SALICET n soft-toned organ stop

SALICETA > SALICETUM

SALICETS > SALICET

SALICETUM n plantation of willows

SALICIN n colourless or white crystalline water-soluble glucoside

SALICINE same as > SALICIN

SALICINES > SALICINE

SALICINS > SALICIN

SALICYLIC adj as in salicylic acid white crystalline substance with a sweet taste and a bitter aftertaste

SALIENCE > SALIENT

SALIENCES > SALIENT

SALIENCY n quality of being prominent

SALIENT adj prominent, noticeable ▷ n projecting part of a front line

SALIENTLY > SALIENT

SALIENTS > SALIENT

SALIFIED > SALIFY

SALIFIES > SALIFY

SALIFY vb treat, mix with, or cause to combine with a salt

SALIFYING > SALIFY

SALIGOT n water chestnut

SALIGOTS > SALIGOT

SALIMETER n hydrometer for measuring salt in a solution

SALIMETRY > SALIMETER

SALINA n salt marsh, lake, or spring

SALINAS > SALINA

SALINE adj containing salt ▷ n solution of sodium chloride and water

SALINES > SALINE

SALINISE same as > SALINIZE

SALINISED > SALINISE

SALINISES > SALINISE

SALINITY > SALINE

SALINIZE vb treat with salt

SALINIZED > SALINIZE

SALINIZES > SALINIZE

SALIVA *n* liquid that forms in the mouth, spittle
SALIVAL > SALIVA
SALIVARY > SALIVA
SALIVAS > SALIVA
SALIVATE *vb* produce saliva
SALIVATED > SALIVATE
SALIVATES > SALIVATE
SALIVATOR > SALIVATE
SALIX *n* plant or tree of willow family
SALL *archaic form of* > SHALL
SALLAD *old spelling of* > SALAD
SALLADS > SALLAD
SALLAL *n* North American shrub
SALLALS > SALLAL
SALLE *n* hall
SALLEE *n* SE Australian eucalyptus
SALLEES > SALLEE
SALLES > SALLE
SALLET *n* light round helmet
SALLETS > SALLET
SALLIED > SALLY
SALLIER > SALLY
SALLIERS > SALLY
SALLIES > SALLY
SALLOW *adj* of an unhealthy pale or yellowish colour ▷ *vb* make sallow ▷ *n* any of several small willow trees
SALLOWED > SALLOW
SALLOWER > SALLOW
SALLOWEST > SALLOW
SALLOWIER > SALLOWY
SALLOWING > SALLOW
SALLOWISH > SALLOW
SALLOWLY > SALLOW
SALLOWS > SALLOW
SALLOWY *adj* full of sallows
SALLY *n* violent excursion ▷ *vb* set or rush out
SALLYING > SALLY
SALLYPORT *n* opening in a fortified place from which troops may make a sally
SALMI *n* ragout of game stewed in a rich brown sauce
SALMIS *same as* > SALMI
SALMON *n* large fish with orange-pink flesh valued as food ▷ *adj* orange-pink
SALMONET *n* young salmon
SALMONETS > SALMONET
SALMONID *n* type of soft-finned fish of the family which includes the salmon
SALMONIDS > SALMONID
SALMONIER > SALMONY
SALMONOID *adj* belonging to the order of soft-finned teleost fishes that includes the salmon, whitefish, grayling, and char ▷ *n* any of these fish
SALMONS > SALMON
SALMONY *adj* of or like a salmon
SALOL *n* white sparingly soluble crystalline compound
SALOLS > SALOL
SALOMETER *n* instrument for measuring salt in solution

SALON *n* commercial premises of a hairdresser, beautician, etc
SALONS > SALON
SALOON *n* closed car with four or more seats
SALOONS > SALOON
SALOOP *n* infusion of aromatic herbs or other plant parts formerly used as a tonic or cure
SALOOPS > SALOOP
SALOP *variant of* > SALOOP
SALOPIAN > SALOOP
SALOPS > SALOP
SALP *n* minute animal floating in sea
SALPA *n* any of various minute floating animals of warm oceans
SALPAE > SALPA
SALPAS > SALPA
SALPIAN *n* minute animal floating in sea
SALPIANS > SALPIAN
SALPICON *n* mixture of chopped fish, meat, or vegetables in a sauce
SALPICONS > SALPICON
SALPID *n* minute animal floating in sea
SALPIDS > SALPID
SALPIFORM > SALPA
SALPINGES > SALPINX
SALPINX *n* Fallopian tube or Eustachian tube
SALPINXES > SALPINX
SALPS > SALP
SALS > SAL
SALSA *n* lively Puerto Rican dance ▷ *vb* dance the salsa
SALSAED > SALSA
SALSAING > SALSA
SALSAS > SALSA
SALSE *n* volcano expelling mud
SALSES > SALSE
SALSIFIES > SALSIFY
SALSIFY *n* Mediterranean plant with a long white edible root
SALSILLA *n* tropical American vine
SALSILLAS > SALSILLA
SALT *n* white crystalline substance used to season food ▷ *vb* season or preserve with salt
SALTANDO *n* staccato piece of violin playing
SALTANDOS > SALTANDO
SALTANT *adj* (of an organism) differing from others of its species because of a saltation ▷ *n* saltant organism
SALTANTS > SALTANT
SALTATE *vb* go through saltation
SALTATED > SALTATE
SALTATES > SALTATE
SALTATING > SALTATE
SALTATION *n* abrupt variation in the appearance of an organism, usu caused by genetic mutation
SALTATO *n* saltando

SALTATORY *adj* specialized for jumping
SALTATOS > SALTATO
SALTBOX *n* box for salt with a sloping lid
SALTBOXES > SALTBOX
SALTBUSH *n* shrub that grows in alkaline desert regions
SALTCAT *n* salty medicine for pigeons
SALTCATS > SALTCAT
SALTCHUCK *n* any body of salt water
SALTED *adj* seasoned, preserved, or treated with salt
SALTER *n* person who deals in or manufactures salt
SALTERIES > SALTERY
SALTERN *n* place where salt is obtained from pools of evaporated sea water
SALTERNS > SALTERN
SALTERS > SALTER
SALTERY *n* factory where fish is salted for storage
SALTEST > SALT
SALTFISH *n* salted cod
SALTIE *n* saltwater crocodile
SALTIER *same as* > SALTIRE
SALTIERS > SALTIER
SALTIES > SALTIE
SALTIEST > SALTY
SALTILY > SALTY
SALTINE *n* salty biscuit
SALTINES > SALTINE
SALTINESS > SALTY
SALTING *n* area of low ground regularly inundated with salt water
SALTINGS > SALTING
SALTIRE *n* diagonal cross on a shield
SALTIRES > SALTIRE
SALTISH > SALT
SALTISHLY > SALT
SALTLESS > SALT
SALTLIKE > SALT
SALTLY > SALT
SALTNESS > SALT
SALTO *n* daring jump ▷ *vb* perform a daring jump
SALTOED > SALTO
SALTOING > SALTO
SALTOS > SALTO
SALTPAN *n* shallow basin containing salt from an evaporated salt lake
SALTPANS > SALTPAN
SALTPETER *same as* > SALTPETRE
SALTPETRE *n* compound used in gunpowder and as a preservative
SALTS > SALT
SALTUS *n* break in the continuity of a sequence
SALTUSES > SALTUS
SALTWATER *n* sea water ▷ *adj* living in the sea
SALTWORK *n* place where salt is refined
SALTWORKS *n* place, building, or factory where salt is produced

SALTWORT *n* any of several chenopodiaceous plants
SALTWORTS > SALTWORT
SALTY *adj* of, tasting of, or containing salt
SALUBRITY *n* quality of being favourable to health or wholesome
SALUE *vb* old word meaning salute
SALUED > SALUE
SALUES > SALUE
SALUING > SALUE
SALUKI *n* type of tall hound with a smooth coat
SALUKIS > SALUKI
SALURETIC *n* drug that increases secretion of salt in urine
SALUT *interj* cheers!
SALUTARY *adj* producing a beneficial result
SALUTE *n* motion of the arm as a formal military sign of respect ▷ *vb* greet with a salute
SALUTED > SALUTE
SALUTER > SALUTE
SALUTERS > SALUTE
SALUTES > SALUTE
SALUTING > SALUTE
SALVABLE *adj* capable of or suitable for being saved or salvaged
SALVABLY > SALVABLE
SALVAGE *n* saving of a ship or other property from destruction ▷ *vb* save from destruction or waste
SALVAGED > SALVAGE
SALVAGEE *n* rope on sailing ship
SALVAGEES > SALVAGEE
SALVAGER > SALVAGE
SALVAGERS > SALVAGE
SALVAGES > SALVAGE
SALVAGING > SALVAGE
SALVARSAN *n* old medicine containing arsenic
SALVATION *n* fact or state of being saved from harm or the consequences of sin
SALVATORY *n* place for storing something safely
SALVE *n* healing or soothing ointment ▷ *vb* soothe or appease
SALVED > SALVE
SALVER *same as* > SALVOR
SALVERS > SALVER
SALVES > SALVE
SALVETE *n* Latin greeting
SALVETES > SALVETE
SALVIA *n* plant with blue or red flowers
SALVIAS > SALVIA
SALVIFIC *adj* acting to salve
SALVING > SALVE
SALVINGS > SALVE
SALVO *n* simultaneous discharge of guns etc ▷ *vb* attack with a salvo
SALVOED > SALVO
SALVOES > SALVO
SALVOING > SALVO

S

SECTION 1: Words between 2 and 9 letters in length

SALVOR n person instrumental in salvaging a vessel or its cargo

SALVORS > SALVOR

SALVOS > SALVO

SALWAR n pair of loose-fitting trousers narrowing around the ankles

SALWARS > SALWAR

SAM vb collect

SAMA n Japanese title of respect

SAMAAN n South American tree

SAMAANS > SAMAAN

SAMADHI n state of deep meditative contemplation

SAMADHIS > SAMADHI

SAMAN n South American tree

SAMANS > SAMAN

SAMARA n dry indehiscent one-seeded fruit

SAMARAS > SAMARA

SAMARITAN n kindly person who helps another in distress

SAMARIUM n silvery metallic element

SAMARIUMS > SAMARIUM

SAMAS > SAMA

SAMBA n lively Brazilian dance ▷ vb perform such a dance

SAMBAED > SAMBA

SAMBAING > SAMBA

SAMBAL n Malaysian dish

SAMBALS > SAMBAL

SAMBAR n S Asian deer with three-tined antlers

SAMBARS > SAMBAR

SAMBAS > SAMBA

SAMBHAR n Indian dish

SAMBHARS > SAMBHAR

SAMBHUR n Asian deer

SAMBHURS > SAMBHUR

SAMBO n offensive word for a Black person

SAMBOES > SAMBO

SAMBOS > SAMBO

SAMBUCA n Italian liqueur

SAMBUCAS > SAMBUCA

SAMBUKE n ancient Greek stringed instrument

SAMBUKES > SAMBUKE

SAMBUR same as > SAMBAR

SAMBURS > SAMBUR

SAME adj identical, not different, unchanged ▷ n something identical

SAMECH n letter in Hebrew alphabet

SAMECHS > SAMECH

SAMEK variant of > SAMEKH

SAMEKH n 15th letter in the Hebrew alphabet

SAMEKHS > SAMEKH

SAMEKS > SAMEK

SAMEL adj of brick, not sufficiently fired

SAMELY adj the same

SAMEN old Scots form of > SAME

SAMENESS n state or quality of being the same

SAMES > SAME

SAMEY adj monotonous

SAMEYNESS n quality of being samey

SAMFOO n style of casual dress worn by Chinese women

SAMFOOS > SAMFOO

SAMFU n Chinese female outfit

SAMFUS > SAMFU

SAMIEL same as > SIMOOM

SAMIELS > SAMIEL

SAMIER > SAMEY

SAMIEST > SAMEY

SAMISEN n Japanese plucked stringed instrument with a long neck

SAMISENS > SAMISEN

SAMITE n heavy fabric of silk used in the Middle Ages

SAMITES > SAMITE

SAMITHI same as > SAMITI

SAMITHIS > SAMITHI

SAMITI n (in India) an association, esp one formed to organize political activity

SAMITIS > SAMITI

SAMIZDAT n system of secret printing and distribution of banned literature in the former USSR

SAMIZDATS > SAMIZDAT

SAMLET n young salmon

SAMLETS > SAMLET

SAMLOR n motor vehicle in Thailand

SAMLORS > SAMLOR

SAMMED > SAM

SAMMIE n sandwich

SAMMIES > SAMMY

SAMMING > SAM

SAMMY n (in South Africa) an Indian fruit and vegetable vendor

SAMNITES n poisonous plant mentioned by Spenser

SAMOSA n (in Indian cookery) a small fried triangular spiced meat or vegetable pasty

SAMOSAS > SAMOSA

SAMOVAR n Russian tea urn

SAMOVARS > SAMOVAR

SAMOYED n Siberian breed of dog with a tightly curled tail

SAMOYEDS > SAMOYED

SAMP n crushed maize used for porridge

SAMPAN n small boat with oars used in China

SAMPANS > SAMPAN

SAMPHIRE n plant found on rocks by the seashore

SAMPHIRES > SAMPHIRE

SAMPI n old Greek number character

SAMPIRE n samphire

SAMPIRES > SAMPIRE

SAMPIS > SAMPI

SAMPLE n part taken as representative of a whole ▷ vb take and test a sample of

SAMPLED > SAMPLE

SAMPLER n piece of embroidery showing the embroiderer's skill

SAMPLERS > SAMPLER

SAMPLERY n making of samplers

SAMPLES > SAMPLE

SAMPLING n process of selecting a random sample

SAMPLINGS > SAMPLING

SAMPS > SAMP

SAMS > SAM

SAMSARA n endless cycle of birth, death, and rebirth

SAMSARAS > SAMSARA

SAMSARIC adj relating to the eternal cycle of birth, suffering, death and rebirth in Indian religions

SAMSHOO same as > SAMSHU

SAMSHOOS > SAMSHOO

SAMSHU n alcoholic drink made from fermented rice

SAMSHUS > SAMSHU

SAMSKARA n Hindu purification ceremony

SAMSKARAS > SAMSKARA

SAMURAI n member of an ancient Japanese warrior caste

SAMURAIS > SAMURAI

SAN n sanatorium

SANATIVE less common word for > CURATIVE

SANATORIA pl n institutions for the care of chronically ill people

SANATORY adj healing

SANBENITO n yellow garment bearing a red cross, worn by penitent heretics in the Inquisition

SANCAI n glaze in Chinese pottery

SANCAIS > SANCAI

SANCHO n African stringed instrument

SANCHOS > SANCHO

SANCTA > SANCTUM

SANCTIFY vb make holy

SANCTION n permission, authorization ▷ vb allow, authorize

SANCTIONS > SANCTION

SANCTITY n sacredness, inviolability

SANCTUARY n holy place

SANCTUM n sacred place

SANCTUMS > SANCTUM

SAND n substance consisting of small grains of rock, esp on a beach or in a desert ▷ vb smooth with sandpaper

SANDABLE > SAND

SANDAL n light shoe consisting of a sole attached by straps ▷ vb put sandals on

SANDALED > SANDAL

SANDALING > SANDAL

SANDALLED > SANDAL

SANDALS > SANDAL

SANDARAC n either of two coniferous trees having hard fragrant dark wood

SANDARACH same as > SANDARAC

SANDARACS > SANDARAC

SANDBAG n bag filled with sand, used as protection against flood water ▷ vb protect with sandbags

SANDBAGS > SANDBAG

SANDBANK n bank of sand below the surface of a river or sea

SANDBANKS > SANDBANK

SANDBAR n ridge of sand in a river or sea, often exposed at low tide

SANDBARS > SANDBAR

SANDBLAST n jet of sand blown from a nozzle under pressure ▷ vb clean or decorate (a surface) with a sandblast

SANDBOX n container on a locomotive from which sand is released onto the rails

SANDBOXES > SANDBOX

SANDBOY n as in happy as a sandboy very happy or high-spirited

SANDBOYS > SANDBOY

SANDBUR n variety of wild grass

SANDBURR n variety of wild grass

SANDBURRS > SANDBURR

SANDBURS > SANDBUR

SANDCRACK n crack in horse's hoof

SANDDAB n type of small Pacific flatfish

SANDDABS > SANDDAB

SANDED > SAND

SANDEK n man who holds a baby being circumcised

SANDEKS > SANDEK

SANDER n power tool for smoothing surfaces

SANDERS > SANDER

SANDERSES > SANDER

SANDFISH n burrowing Pacific fish

SANDFLIES > SANDFLY

SANDFLY n any of various small mothlike flies

SANDGLASS less common word for > HOURGLASS

SANDHEAP n heap of sand

SANDHEAPS > SANDHEAP

SANDHI n modification of a word under the influence of an adjacent word

SANDHILL n hill of sand

SANDHILLS > SANDHILL

SANDHIS > SANDHI

SANDHOG n person who works in underground or underwater construction projects

SANDHOGS > SANDHOG

SANDIER > SANDY

SANDIEST > SANDY

SANDINESS > SANDY

SANDING > SAND

SANDINGS > SAND

SANDIVER n scum forming on molten glass

SANDIVERS > SANDIVER

SANDLESS > SAND

SANDLIKE > SAND

SANDLING n sand eel

SANDLINGS > SANDLING

SANDLOT n area of vacant ground used for children's games

SANDLOTS > SANDLOT

SANDMAN n (in folklore) a magical person supposed to put children to sleep

SANDMEN > SANDMAN

S

SANDPAPER n paper coated with sand for smoothing a surface ▷ vb smooth with sandpaper

SANDPEEP n small sandpiper

SANDPEEPS > SANDPEEP

SANDPILE n pile of sand

SANDPILES > SANDPILE

SANDPIPER n shore bird with a long bill and slender legs

SANDPIT n shallow pit or container holding sand for children to play in

SANDPITS > SANDPIT

SANDPUMP n pump for wet sand

SANDPUMPS > SANDPUMP

SANDS > SAND

SANDSHOE n light canvas shoe with a rubber sole

SANDSHOES > SANDSHOE

SANDSOAP n gritty general-purpose soap

SANDSOAPS > SANDSOAP

SANDSPIT n small point of land created by sand dunes

SANDSPITS > SANDSPIT

SANDSPOUT n sand sucked into air by whirlwind

SANDSPUR n American wild grass

SANDSPURS > SANDSPUR

SANDSTONE n rock composed of sand

SANDSTORM n desert wind that whips up clouds of sand

SANDWICH n two slices of bread with a layer of food between ▷ vb insert between two other things

SANDWORM n any of various polychaete worms that live in burrows on sandy shores, esp the lugworm

SANDWORMS > SANDWORM

SANDWORT n any of numerous caryophyllaceous plants

SANDWORTS > SANDWORT

SANDY adj covered with sand

SANDYISH adj somewhat sandy or covered with sand

SANE adj of sound mind ▷ vb heal

SANED > SANE

SANELY > SANE

SANENESS > SANE

SANER > SANE

SANES > SANE

SANEST > SANE

SANG Scots word for > SONG

SANGA n Ethiopian ox

SANGAR n breastwork of stone or sods

SANGAREE n spiced drink similar to sangria

SANGAREES > SANGAREE

SANGARS > SANGAR

SANGAS > SANGA

SANGEET n Indian pre-wedding celebration

SANGEETS > SANGEET

SANGER n sandwich

SANGERS > SANGER

SANGFROID n composure or self-possession

SANGH n Indian union or association

SANGHA n Buddhist monastic order or community

SANGHAS > SANGHA

SANGHAT n local Sikh community or congregation

SANGHATS > SANGHAT

SANGHS > SANGH

SANGLIER n wild boar

SANGLIERS > SANGLIER

SANGO same as > SANGER

SANGOMA n witch doctor or herbalist

SANGOMAS > SANGOMA

SANGOS > SANGO

SANGRAIL n legendary cup used by Christ at the Last Supper

SANGRAILS > SANGRAIL

SANGREAL same as > SANGRAIL

SANGREALS > SANGREAL

SANGRIA n Spanish drink of red wine and fruit

SANGRIAS > SANGRIA

SANGS > SANG

SANGUIFY vb turn into blood

SANGUINE adj cheerful, optimistic ▷ n red pencil containing ferric oxide, used in drawing

SANGUINED > SANGUINE

SANGUINES > SANGUINE

SANICLE n type of plant with clusters of small white flowers

SANICLES > SANICLE

SANIDINE n alkali feldspar that is found in lavas

SANIDINES > SANIDINE

SANIES n thin greenish foul-smelling discharge from a wound, etc

SANIFIED > SANIFY

SANIFIES > SANIFY

SANIFY vb make healthy

SANIFYING > SANIFY

SANING > SANE

SANIOUS > SANIES

SANITARIA variant of > SANATORIA

SANITARY adj promoting health by getting rid of dirt and germs

SANITATE vb make sanitary

SANITATED > SANITATE

SANITATES > SANITATE

SANITIES > SANITY

SANITISE same as > SANITIZE

SANITISED > SANITISE

SANITISER > SANITISE

SANITISES > SANITISE

SANITIZE vb omit unpleasant details to make (news) more acceptable

SANITIZED > SANITIZE

SANITIZER > SANITIZE

SANITIZES > SANITIZE

SANITORIA variant of > SANATORIA

SANITY n state of having a normal healthy mind

SANJAK n (in the Turkish Empire) a subdivision of a vilayet

SANJAKS > SANJAK

SANK > SINK

SANKO n African stringed instrument

SANKOS > SANKO

SANNIE Scots word for > SANDSHOE

SANNIES > SANNIE

SANNOP n Native American married man

SANNOPS > SANNOP

SANNUP n Native American married man

SANNUPS > SANNUP

SANNYASI n Brahman who having attained the last stage of life as a beggar will not be reborn

SANNYASIN same as > SANNYASI

SANNYASIS > SANNYASI

SANPAN n sampan

SANPANS > SANPAN

SANPRO n sanitary-protection products collectively

SANPROS > SANPRO

SANS archaic word for > WITHOUT

SANSA n African musical instrument

SANSAR n name of a wind that blows in Iran

SANSARS > SANSAR

SANSAS > SANSA

SANSEI n American whose parents were Japanese immigrants

SANSEIS > SANSEI

SANSERIF n style of printer's typeface

SANSERIFS > SANSERIF

SANT n devout person in India

SANTAL n sandalwood

SANTALIC adj of sandalwood

SANTALIN n substance giving sandalwood its colour

SANTALINS > SANTALIN

SANTALOL n liquid from sandalwood used in perfume

SANTALOLS > SANTALOL

SANTALS > SANTAL

SANTERA n priestess of santeria

SANTERAS > SANTERA

SANTERIA n Caribbean religious cult

SANTERIAS > SANTERIA

SANTERO n priest of santeria

SANTEROS > SANTERO

SANTIM n coin formerly used in Latvia

SANTIMI > SANTIMS

SANTIMS n former money unit in Latvia

SANTIMU same as > SANTIMS

SANTIR n Middle Eastern stringed instrument

SANTIRS > SANTIR

SANTO n saint or representation of one

SANTOKU n type of Japanese knife

SANTOKUS > SANTOKU

SANTOL n fruit from Southeast Asia

SANTOLINA n any plant of an evergreen Mediterranean genus grown for its silvery-grey felted foliage

SANTOLS > SANTOL

SANTON n French figurine

SANTONICA n oriental wormwood plant

SANTONIN n soluble substance extracted from santonica

SANTONINS > SANTONIN

SANTONS > SANTON

SANTOOR same as > SANTIR

SANTOORS > SANTOOR

SANTOS > SANTO

SANTOUR n Middle Eastern stringed instrument

SANTOURS > SANTOUR

SANTS > SANT

SANTUR n Middle Eastern stringed instrument

SANTURS > SANTUR

SANYASI same as > SANNYASI

SANYASIS > SANYASI

SAOLA n small, very rare bovine mammal of Vietnam and Laos

SAOLAS > SAOLA

SAOUARI n tropical American tree

SAOUARIS > SAOUARI

SAP n moisture that circulates in plants ▷ vb undermine

SAPAJOU n capuchin monkey

SAPAJOUS > SAPAJOU

SAPAN n tropical tree

SAPANS > SAPAN

SAPANWOOD n small S Asian tree

SAPEGO n skin disease

SAPEGOES > SAPEGO

SAPELE n type of W African tree

SAPELES > SAPELE

SAPFUL adj full of sap

SAPHEAD n simpleton, idiot, or fool

SAPHEADED > SAPHEAD

SAPHEADS > SAPHEAD

SAPHENA n either of two large superficial veins of the legs

SAPHENAE > SAPHENA

SAPHENAS > SAPHENA

SAPHENOUS > SAPHENA

SAPID adj having a pleasant taste

SAPIDER > SAPID

SAPIDEST > SAPID

SAPIDITY > SAPID

SAPIDLESS adj lacking flavour

SAPIDNESS > SAPID

SAPIENCE > SAPIENT

SAPIENCES > SAPIENT

SAPIENCY > SAPIENT

SAPIENS adj relating to or like modern human beings

S

SAPIENT adj wise, shrewd ▷ n wise person
SAPIENTLY > SAPIENT
SAPIENTS > SAPIENT
SAPLESS > SAP
SAPLING n young tree
SAPLINGS > SAPLING
SAPODILLA n large tropical American evergreen tree
SAPOGENIN n substance derived from saponin
SAPONARIA See > SOAPWORT
SAPONATED adj treated or combined with soap
SAPONIFY vb convert (a fat) into a soap by treatment with alkali
SAPONIN n any of a group of plant glycosides
SAPONINE n saponin
SAPONINES > SAPONINE
SAPONINS > SAPONIN
SAPONITE n type of clay mineral
SAPONITES > SAPONITE
SAPOR n quality in a substance that is perceived by the sense of taste
SAPORIFIC > SAPOR
SAPOROUS > SAPOR
SAPORS > SAPOR
SAPOTA same as > SAPODILLA
SAPOTAS > SAPOTA
SAPOTE n Central American tree
SAPOTES > SAPOTE
SAPOUR variant of > SAPOUR
SAPOURS > SAPOUR
SAPPAN n tropical tree
SAPPANS > SAPPAN
SAPPED > SAP
SAPPER n soldier in an engineering unit
SAPPERS > SAPPER
SAPPHIC adj lesbian ▷ n verse written in a particular form
SAPPHICS > SAPPHIC
SAPPHIRE n blue precious stone ▷ adj deep blue
SAPPHIRED adj blue-coloured
SAPPHIRES > SAPPHIRE
SAPPHISM n lesbianism
SAPPHISMS > SAPPHISM
SAPPHIST n lesbian
SAPPHISTS > SAPPHIST
SAPPIER > SAPPY
SAPPIEST > SAPPY
SAPPILY > SAPPY
SAPPINESS > SAPPY
SAPPING n act of sapping
SAPPINGS > SAPPING
SAPPLE vb Scots word meaning wash in water
SAPPLED > SAPPLE
SAPPLES > SAPPLE
SAPPLING > SAPPLE
SAPPY adj (of plants) full of sap
SAPRAEMIA n blood poisoning caused by toxins of putrefactive bacteria
SAPRAEMIC > SAPRAEMIA
SAPREMIA American spelling of > SAPRAEMIA

SAPREMIAS > SAPREMIA
SAPREMIC > SAPREMIA
SAPROBE n organism that lives on decaying organisms
SAPROBES > SAPROBE
SAPROBIAL > SAPROBE
SAPROBIC > SAPROBE
SAPROBITY n state of being a saprobe
SAPROLITE n deposit of earth, etc, formed by decomposition of rocks that has remained in its original site
SAPROPEL n decomposed remains of aquatic organisms at the bottoms of lakes and oceans
SAPROPELS > SAPROPEL
SAPROZOIC adj (of animals or plants) feeding on dead organic matter
SAPS > SAP
SAPSAGO n hard greenish Swiss cheese
SAPSAGOS > SAPSAGO
SAPSUCKER n either of two North American woodpeckers
SAPUCAIA n Brazilian tree
SAPUCAIAS > SAPUCAIA
SAPWOOD n soft wood, just beneath the bark in tree trunks, that consists of living tissue
SAPWOODS > SAPWOOD
SAR n marine fish ▷ vb Scots word meaning savour
SARABAND same as > SARABANDE
SARABANDE n slow stately Spanish dance
SARABANDS > SARABAND
SARAFAN n Russian woman's cloak
SARAFANS > SARAFAN
SARAN n any one of a class of thermoplastic resins
SARANGI n stringed instrument of India played with a bow
SARANGIS > SARANGI
SARANS > SARAN
SARAPE n serape
SARAPES > SARAPE
SARBACANE n type of blowpipe
SARCASM n (use of) bitter or wounding ironic language
SARCASMS > SARCASM
SARCASTIC adj full of or showing sarcasm
SARCENET n fine soft silk fabric formerly from Italy and used for clothing, ribbons, etc
SARCENETS > SARCENET
SARCINA n type of bacterium
SARCINAE > SARCINA
SARCINAS > SARCINA
SARCOCARP n fleshy mesocarp of such fruits as the peach or plum
SARCODE n material making up living cell
SARCODES > SARCODE
SARCODIC > SARCODE

SARCOID adj of, relating to, or resembling flesh ▷ n tumour resembling a sarcoma
SARCOIDS > SARCOID
SARCOLOGY n study of flesh
SARCOMA n malignant tumour beginning in connective tissue
SARCOMAS > SARCOMA
SARCOMATA > SARCOMA
SARCOMERE n any of the units that together comprise skeletal muscle
SARCONET n type of silk
SARCONETS > SARCONET
SARCOPTIC adj relating to mange
SARCOSOME n energy-producing tissue in muscle
SARCOUS adj (of tissue) muscular or fleshy
SARD n orange, red, or brown variety of chalcedony
SARDANA n Catalan dance
SARDANAS > SARDANA
SARDAR n title used before the name of Sikh men
SARDARS > SARDAR
SARDEL n small fish
SARDELLE n small fish
SARDELLES > SARDELLE
SARDELS > SARDEL
SARDINE n small fish of the herring family ▷ vb cram together
SARDINED > SARDINE
SARDINES > SARDINE
SARDINING > SARDINE
SARDIUS same as > SARD
SARDIUSES > SARDIUS
SARDONIAN adj sardonic ▷ n person who flatters with harmful intent
SARDONIC adj mocking or scornful
SARDONYX n brown-and-white gemstone
SARDS > SARD
SARED > SAR
SAREE same as > SARI
SAREES > SAREE
SARGASSA > SARGASSUM
SARGASSO same as > SARGASSUM
SARGASSOS > SARGASSO
SARGASSUM n type of floating seaweed
SARGE n sergeant
SARGES > SARGE
SARGO same as > SARGUS
SARGOS variant of > SARGUS
SARGOSES > SARGOS
SARGUS n species of sea fish
SARGUSES > SARGUS
SARI n long piece of cloth draped around the body and over one shoulder
SARIN n chemical used in warfare as a lethal nerve gas producing asphyxia
SARING > SAR
SARINS > SARIN
SARIS > SARI
SARK n shirt or (formerly) chemise
SARKIER > SARKY

SARKIEST > SARKY
SARKILY > SARKY
SARKINESS n quality of being sarcastic
SARKING n flat planking supporting the roof cladding of a building
SARKINGS > SARKING
SARKS > SARK
SARKY adj sarcastic
SARMENT n thin twig
SARMENTA > SARMENTUM
SARMENTS > SARMENT
SARMENTUM n runner on plant
SARMIE n sandwich
SARMIES > SARMIE
SARNEY n sandwich
SARNEYS > SARNEY
SARNIE n sandwich
SARNIES > SARNIE
SAROD n Indian stringed musical instrument
SARODE n Indian stringed instrument
SARODES > SARODE
SARODIST n sarod player
SARODISTS > SARODIST
SARODS > SAROD
SARONG n long piece of cloth tucked around the waist or under the armpits
SARONGS > SARONG
SARONIC > SAROS
SAROS n cycle in which eclipses of the sun and moon occur in the same sequence
SAROSES > SAROS
SARPANCH n head of a panchayat
SARRASIN n buckwheat
SARRASINS > SARRASIN
SARRAZIN same as > SARRASIN
SARRAZINS > SARRAZIN
SARS > SAR
SARSAR same as > SANSAR
SARSARS > SARSAR
SARSDEN n sarsen
SARSDENS > SARSDEN
SARSEN n boulder of silicified sandstone
SARSENET same as > SARCENET
SARSENETS > SARSENET
SARSENS > SARSEN
SARSNET n type of silk
SARSNETS > SARSNET
SARTOR humorous or literary word for > TAILOR
SARTORIAL adj of clothes or tailoring
SARTORIAN adj of tailoring
SARTORII > SARTORIUS
SARTORIUS n long ribbon-shaped muscle that aids in flexing the knee
SARTORS > SARTOR
SARUS n Indian bird of crane family
SARUSES > SARUS
SASANQUA n type of camellia
SASANQUAS > SASANQUA
SASARARA n scolding
SASARARAS > SASARARA
SASER n device for amplifying ultrasound

SASERS > SASER
SASH n decorative strip of cloth worn round the waist or over one shoulder ▷ vb furnish with a sash, sashes, or sash windows
SASHAY vb move or walk in a casual or a showy manner
SASHAYED > SASHAY
SASHAYING > SASHAY
SASHAYS > SASHAY
SASHED > SASH
SASHES > SASH
SASHIMI n Japanese dish of thin fillets of raw fish
SASHIMIS > SASHIMI
SASHING > SASH
SASHLESS > SASH
SASIN another name for **>** BLACKBUCK
SASINE n granting of legal possession of feudal property
SASINES > SASINE
SASINS > SASIN
SASKATOON n species of serviceberry of W Canada
SASQUATCH n (in Canadian folklore) hairy beast or manlike monster said to leave huge footprints
SASS n insolent or impudent talk or behaviour ▷ vb talk or answer back in such a way
SASSABIES > SASSABY
SASSABY n African antelope of grasslands and semideserts
SASSAFRAS n American tree with aromatic bark used medicinally
SASSARARA n scolding
SASSE n old word meaning canal lock
SASSED > SASS
SASSES > SASS
SASSIER > SASSY
SASSIES > SASSY
SASSIEST > SASSY
SASSILY > SASSY
SASSINESS > SASSY
SASSING > SASS
SASSOLIN n boric acid
SASSOLINS > SASSOLIN
SASSOLITE n boric acid
SASSWOOD same as **>** SASSY
SASSWOODS > SASSWOOD
SASSY adj insolent, impertinent ▷ n W African leguminous tree with poisonous bark
SASSYWOOD n trial by ordeal in Liberia
SASTRA same as **>** SHASTRA
SASTRAS > SASTRA
SASTRUGA n ridge on a snow-covered plain
SASTRUGI > SASTRUGA
SAT > SIT
SATAI same as **>** SATAY
SATAIS > SATAI
SATANG n monetary unit of Thailand worth one hundredth of a baht
SATANGS > SATANG
SATANIC adj of Satan
SATANICAL same as **>** SATANIC

SATANISM n worship of the devil
SATANISMS > SATANISM
SATANIST > SATANISM
SATANISTS > SATANISM
SATANITY n quality of being satanic
SATARA n type of cloth
SATARAS > SATARA
SATAY n Indonesian and Malaysian dish
SATAYS > SATAY
SATCHEL n bag, usu with a shoulder strap, for carrying books
SATCHELED adj carrying a satchel
SATCHELS > SATCHEL
SATCOM n satellite communications
SATCOMS > SATCOM
SATE vb satisfy (a desire or appetite) fully
SATED > SATE
SATEDNESS > SATE
SATEEN n glossy linen or cotton fabric, woven in such a way that it resembles satin
SATEENS > SATEEN
SATELESS adj old word meaning insatiable
SATELLES n species of bacteria
SATELLITE n man-made device orbiting in space ▷ adj of or used in the transmission of television signals from a satellite to the home ▷ vb transmit by communications satellite
SATEM adj denoting or belonging to a particular group of Indo-European languages
SATES > SATE
SATI n Indian widow suicide
SATIABLE adj capable of being satiated
SATIABLY > SATIABLE
SATIATE vb provide with more than enough, so as to disgust
SATIATED > SATIATE
SATIATES > SATIATE
SATIATING > SATIATE
SATIATION > SATIATE
SATIETIES > SATIETY
SATIETY n feeling of having had too much
SATIN n silky fabric with a glossy surface on one side ▷ adj like satin in texture ▷ vb cover with satin
SATINED > SATIN
SATINET n thin or imitation satin
SATINETS > SATINET
SATINETTA n thin satin
SATINETTE same as **>** SATINET
SATING > SATE
SATINIER > SATINY
SATINIEST > SATINY
SATINING > SATIN
SATINPOD n honesty (the plant)
SATINPODS > SATINPOD

SATINS > SATIN
SATINWOOD n tropical tree yielding hard wood
SATINY adj like satin
SATIRE n use of ridicule to expose vice or folly
SATIRES > SATIRE
SATIRIC same as **>** SATIRICAL
SATIRICAL adj of, relating to, or containing satire
SATIRISE same as **>** SATIRIZE
SATIRISED > SATIRISE
SATIRISER > SATIRIZE
SATIRISES > SATIRISE
SATIRIST n writer of satire
SATIRISTS > SATIRIST
SATIRIZE vb ridicule by means of satire
SATIRIZED > SATIRIZE
SATIRIZER > SATIRIZE
SATIRIZES > SATIRIZE
SATIS > SATI
SATISFICE vb act in such a way as to satisfy the minimum requirements for achieving a particular result
SATISFIED > SATISFY
SATISFIER > SATISFY
SATISFIES > SATISFY
SATISFY vb please, content
SATIVE adj old word meaning cultivated
SATNAV n satellite navigation system
SATNAVS > SATNAV
SATORI n state of sudden indescribable intuitive enlightenment
SATORIS > SATORI
SATRAP n (in ancient Persia) a provincial governor or subordinate ruler
SATRAPAL > SATRAP
SATRAPIES > SATRAPY
SATRAPS > SATRAP
SATRAPY n province, office, or period of rule of a satrap
SATSANG n sacred gathering in Hinduism
SATSANGS > SATSANG
SATSUMA n kind of small orange
SATSUMAS > SATSUMA
SATURABLE adj capable of being saturated
SATURANT n substance that causes a solution, etc, to be saturated ▷ adj (of a substance) causing saturation
SATURANTS > SATURANT
SATURATE vb soak thoroughly
SATURATED adj (of a solution or solvent) containing the maximum amount of solute that can normally be dissolved at a given temperature and pressure
SATURATER > SATURATE
SATURATES > SATURATE
SATURATOR > SATURATE
SATURNIC adj poisoned by lead

SATURNIID n type of mainly tropical moth, usu with large brightly coloured wings
SATURNINE adj gloomy in temperament or appearance
SATURNISM n lead poisoning
SATURNIST n old word meaning glum person
SATYR n woodland god, part man, part goat
SATYRA n female satyr
SATYRAL n mythical beast in heraldry
SATYRALS > SATYRAL
SATYRAS > SATYRA
SATYRE n as in sea satyre sea creature mentioned in Spenser's poetry
SATYRES > SATYRE
SATYRESS n female satyr
SATYRIC > SATYR
SATYRICAL > SATYR
SATYRID n butterfly with typically brown or dark wings with paler markings
SATYRIDS > SATYRID
SATYRISK n small satyr
SATYRISKS > SATYRISK
SATYRLIKE > SATYR
SATYRS > SATYR
SAU archaic past tense of **>** SEE
SAUBA n South American ant
SAUBAS > SAUBA
SAUCE n liquid added to food to enhance flavour ▷ vb prepare (food) with sauce
SAUCEBOAT n gravy boat
SAUCEBOX n saucy person
SAUCED > SAUCE
SAUCELESS > SAUCE
SAUCEPAN n cooking pot with a long handle
SAUCEPANS > SAUCEPAN
SAUCEPOT n cooking pot with lid
SAUCEPOTS > SAUCEPOT
SAUCER n small round dish put under a cup
SAUCERFUL > SAUCER
SAUCERS > SAUCER
SAUCES > SAUCE
SAUCH n sallow or willow
SAUCHS > SAUCH
SAUCIER n chef who makes sauces
SAUCIERS > SAUCIER
SAUCIEST > SAUCY
SAUCILY > SAUCY
SAUCINESS > SAUCY
SAUCING > SAUCE
SAUCISSE n type of explosive fuse
SAUCISSES > SAUCISSE
SAUCISSON n type of explosive fuse
SAUCY adj impudent
SAUFGARD old form of **>** SAFEGUARD
SAUFGARDS > SAUFGARD
SAUGER n small North American pikeperch
SAUGERS > SAUGER
SAUGH same as **>** SAUCH
SAUGHS > SAUGH
SAUGHY adj Scots word meaning made of willow

SAUL Scots word for > SOUL
SAULGE n old word for sage plant
SAULGES > SAULGE
SAULIE n Scots word meaning professional mourner
SAULIES > SAULIE
SAULS > SAUL
SAULT n waterfall in Canada
SAULTS > SAULT
SAUNA n Finnish-style steam bath ▷ vb have a sauna
SAUNAED > SAUNA
SAUNAING > SAUNA
SAUNAS > SAUNA
SAUNT Scots form of > SAINT
SAUNTED > SAUNT
SAUNTER vb walk in a leisurely manner, stroll ▷ n leisurely walk
SAUNTERED > SAUNTER
SAUNTERER > SAUNTER
SAUNTERS > SAUNTER
SAUNTING > SAUNT
SAUNTS > SAUNT
SAUREL n type of mackerel
SAURELS > SAUREL
SAURIAN n lizard
SAURIANS > SAURIAN
SAURIES > SAURY
SAUROID adj like a lizard ▷ n type of fish
SAUROIDS > SAUROID
SAUROPOD n type of herbivorous dinosaur including the brontosaurus and the diplodocus
SAUROPODS > SAUROPOD
SAURY n type of fish of tropical and temperate seas
SAUSAGE n minced meat in an edible tube-shaped skin
SAUSAGES > SAUSAGE
SAUT Scot word for > SALT
SAUTE vb fry quickly in a little fat ▷ n dish of sautéed food ▷ adj sautéed until lightly brown
SAUTED > SAUT
SAUTEED > SAUTE
SAUTEEING > SAUTE
SAUTEING > SAUTE
SAUTERNE n sauternes
SAUTERNES n sweet white French wine
SAUTES > SAUTE
SAUTING > SAUT
SAUTOIR n long necklace or pendant
SAUTOIRE variant of > SAUTOIR
SAUTOIRES > SAUTOIRE
SAUTOIRS > SAUTOIR
SAUTS > SAUT
SAV short for > SAVELOY
SAVABLE > SAVE
SAVAGE adj wild, untamed ▷ n uncivilized person ▷ vb attack ferociously
SAVAGED > SAVAGE
SAVAGEDOM > SAVAGE
SAVAGELY > SAVAGE
SAVAGER > SAVAGE
SAVAGERY n viciousness and cruelty
SAVAGES > SAVAGE

SAVAGEST > SAVAGE
SAVAGING > SAVAGE
SAVAGISM > SAVAGE
SAVAGISMS > SAVAGE
SAVANNA n open grasslands of tropical Africa
SAVANNAH same as > SAVANNA
SAVANNAHS > SAVANNAH
SAVANNAS > SAVANNA
SAVANT n learned person
SAVANTE > SAVANT
SAVANTES > SAVANT
SAVANTS > SAVANT
SAVARIN n type of cake
SAVARINS > SAVARIN
SAVASANA n type of pose in yoga
SAVASANAS > SAVASANA
SAVATE n form of boxing in which blows may be delivered with the feet
SAVATES > SAVATE
SAVE vb rescue or preserve from harm, protect ▷ n act of preventing a goal ▷ prep except
SAVEABLE > SAVE
SAVED > SAVE
SAVEGARD vb old word meaning protect
SAVEGARDS > SAVEGARD
SAVELOY n spicy smoked sausage
SAVELOYS > SAVELOY
SAVER > SAVE
SAVERS > SAVE
SAVES > SAVE
SAVEY vb understand
SAVEYED > SAVEY
SAVEYING > SAVEY
SAVEYS > SAVEY
SAVIN n small spreading juniper bush of Europe, N Asia, and North America
SAVINE same as > SAVIN
SAVINES > SAVINE
SAVING n economy ▷ prep except ▷ adj tending to save or preserve
SAVINGLY > SAVING
SAVINGS > SAVING
SAVINS > SAVIN
SAVIOR same as > SAVIOUR
SAVIORS > SAVIOR
SAVIOUR n person who rescues another
SAVIOURS > SAVIOUR
SAVOR same as > SAVOUR
SAVORED > SAVOR
SAVORER > SAVOR
SAVORERS > SAVOR
SAVORIER > SAVORY
SAVORIES > SAVORY
SAVORIEST > SAVORY
SAVORILY > SAVOUR
SAVORING > SAVOR
SAVORLESS > SAVOUR
SAVOROUS > SAVOUR
SAVORS > SAVOR
SAVORY same as > SAVOURY
SAVOUR vb enjoy, relish ▷ n characteristic taste or odour
SAVOURED > SAVOUR
SAVOURER > SAVOUR
SAVOURERS > SAVOUR

SAVOURIER > SAVOURY
SAVOURIES > SAVOURY
SAVOURILY > SAVOURY
SAVOURING > SAVOUR
SAVOURLY adv old word meaning refreshingly
SAVOURS > SAVOUR
SAVOURY adj salty or spicy ▷ n savoury dish served before or after a meal
SAVOY n variety of cabbage
SAVOYARD n person keenly interested in the operettas of Gilbert and Sullivan
SAVOYARDS > SAVOYARD
SAVOYS > SAVOY
SAVS > SAV
SAVVEY vb understand
SAVVEYED > SAVVEY
SAVVEYING > SAVVEY
SAVVEYS > SAVVEY
SAVVIED > SAVVY
SAVVIER > SAVVY
SAVVIES > SAVVY
SAVVIEST > SAVVY
SAVVILY > SAVVY
SAVVINESS > SAVVY
SAVVY vb understand ▷ n understanding, intelligence ▷ adj shrewd
SAVVYING > SAVVY
SAW n hand tool for cutting wood and metal ▷ vb cut with a saw
SAWAH n paddy field
SAWAHS > SAWAH
SAWBILL n type of hummingbird
SAWBILLS > SAWBILL
SAWBLADE n blade of a saw
SAWBLADES > SAWBLADE
SAWBONES n surgeon or doctor
SAWBUCK n sawhorse, esp one having an X-shaped supporting structure
SAWBUCKS > SAWBUCK
SAWDER n flattery ▷ vb flatter
SAWDERED > SAWDER
SAWDERING > SAWDER
SAWDERS > SAWDER
SAWDUST n fine wood fragments made in sawing ▷ vb cover with sawdust
SAWDUSTED > SAWDUST
SAWDUSTS > SAWDUST
SAWDUSTY adj covered in sawdust
SAWED > SAW
SAWER > SAW
SAWERS > SAW
SAWFISH n fish with a long toothed snout
SAWFISHES > SAWFISH
SAWFLIES > SAWFLY
SAWFLY n any of various hymenopterous insects
SAWGRASS n type of sedge with serrated leaves
SAWHORSE n structure for supporting wood that is being sawn
SAWHORSES > SAWHORSE
SAWING > SAW
SAWINGS > SAW
SAWLIKE > SAW

SAWLOG n log suitable for sawing
SAWLOGS > SAWLOG
SAWMILL n mill where timber is sawn into planks
SAWMILLER n person who operates a sawmill
SAWMILLS > SAWMILL
SAWN past participle of > SAW
SAWNEY n derogatory word for a fool
SAWNEYS > SAWNEY
SAWPIT n pit above which a log is sawn into planks
SAWPITS > SAWPIT
SAWS > SAW
SAWSHARK n shark with long sawlike snout
SAWSHARKS > SAWSHARK
SAWTEETH > SAWTOOTH
SAWTIMBER n wood for sawing
SAWTOOTH adj (of a waveform) having an amplitude that varies linearly with time between two values
SAWYER n person who saws timber for a living
SAWYERS > SAWYER
SAX same as > SAXOPHONE
SAXATILE adj living among rocks
SAXAUL n Asian tree
SAXAULS > SAXAUL
SAXE adj as in saxe blue light greyish-blue colour
SAXES > SAX
SAXHORN n valved brass instrument used chiefly in brass and military bands
SAXHORNS > SAXHORN
SAXICOLE variant of > SAXATILE
SAXIFRAGE n alpine rock plant with small flowers
SAXIST n saxophone player
SAXISTS > SAXIST
SAXITOXIN n poison extracted from mollusc
SAXMAN n saxophone player
SAXMEN > SAXMAN
SAXONIES > SAXONY
SAXONITE n igneous rock
SAXONITES > SAXONITE
SAXONY n fine three-ply yarn
SAXOPHONE n brass wind instrument with keys and a curved body
SAXTUBA n bass saxhorn
SAXTUBAS > SAXTUBA
SAY vb speak or utter ▷ n right or chance to speak
SAYABLE n anything that can be said
SAYABLES > SAYABLE
SAYED same as > SAYYID
SAYEDS > SAYED
SAYER > SAY
SAYERS > SAY
SAYEST > SAY
SAYID same as > SAYYID
SAYIDS > SAYID
SAYING > SAY
SAYINGS > SAY
SAYNE > SAY
SAYON n type of tunic

SAYONARA n Japanese farewell
SAYONARAS > SAYONARA
SAYONS > SAYON
SAYS > SAY
SAYST > SAY
SAYYID n Muslim claiming descent from Mohammed's grandson Husain
SAYYIDS > SAYYID
SAZ n Middle Eastern stringed instrument
SAZERAC n mixed drink of whisky, Pernod, syrup, bitters, and lemon
SAZERACS > SAZERAC
SAZES > SAZ
SAZHEN n Russian measure of length
SAZHENS > SAZHEN
SAZZES > SAZ
SBIRRI > SBIRRO
SBIRRO n Italian police officer
SCAB n crust formed over a wound ▷ vb become covered with a scab
SCABBARD n sheath for a sword or dagger
SCABBARDS > SCABBARD
SCABBED > SCAB
SCABBIER > SCABBY
SCABBIEST > SCABBY
SCABBILY > SCABBY
SCABBING > SCAB
SCABBLE vb shape (stone) roughly
SCABBLED > SCABBLE
SCABBLES > SCABBLE
SCABBLING > SCABBLE
SCABBY adj covered with scabs
SCABIES n itchy skin disease
SCABIETIC > SCABIES
SCABIOSA n flowering plant
SCABIOSAS > SCABIOSA
SCABIOUS n plant with showy blue, red, or whitish dome-shaped flower heads ▷ adj having or covered with scabs
SCABLAND n barren rocky land
SCABLANDS pl n type of terrain consisting of bare rock surfaces, with little or no soil cover and scanty vegetation
SCABLIKE > SCAB
SCABRID adj having a rough or scaly surface
SCABROUS adj rough and scaly
SCABS > SCAB
SCAD n any of various carangid fishes
SCADS pl n large amount or number
SCAFF n Scots word meaning food ▷ vb ask for (food) in a mean or rude manner
SCAFFED > SCAFF
SCAFFIE n Scots word meaning street cleaner
SCAFFIER > SCAFFY

SCAFFIES > SCAFFIE
SCAFFIEST > SCAFFY
SCAFFING > SCAFF
SCAFFOLD n temporary platform for builders or other tradespeople ▷ vb provide with a scaffold
SCAFFOLDS > SCAFFOLD
SCAFFS > SCAFF
SCAFFY adj having little value, cheap
SCAG n tear in a garment or piece of cloth ▷ vb make a tear in (cloth)
SCAGGED > SCAG
SCAGGING > SCAG
SCAGLIA n type of limestone
SCAGLIAS > SCAGLIA
SCAGLIOLA n type of imitation marble made of glued gypsum
SCAGS > SCAG
SCAIL vb Scots word meaning disperse
SCAILED > SCAIL
SCAILING > SCAIL
SCAILS > SCAIL
SCAITH vb old word meaning injure
SCAITHED > SCAITH
SCAITHING > SCAITH
SCAITHS > SCAITH
SCALA n passage inside the cochlea
SCALABLE adj capable of being scaled or climbed
SCALABLY > SCALABLE
SCALADE short for > ESCALADE
SCALADES > SCALADE
SCALADO same as > SCALADE
SCALADOS > SCALADO
SCALAE > SCALA
SCALAGE n percentage deducted from the price of goods liable to shrink or leak
SCALAGES > SCALAGE
SCALAR adj having magnitude but no direction ▷ n quantity that has magnitude but not direction
SCALARE another name for > ANGELFISH
SCALARES > SCALARE
SCALARS > SCALAR
SCALATION n way scales are arranged
SCALAWAG same as > SCALLYWAG
SCALAWAGS > SCALAWAG
SCALD vb burn with hot liquid ▷ n (in ancient Scandinavia) a bard or minstrel
SCALDED > SCALD
SCALDER > SCALD
SCALDERS > SCALDER
SCALDFISH n small European flatfish
SCALDHEAD n diseased scalp
SCALDIC > SCALD
SCALDING n instance of burning with hot liquid
SCALDINGS > SCALDING

SCALDINI > SCALDINO
SCALDINO n Italian brazier
SCALDS > SCALD
SCALDSHIP n (in ancient Scandinavia) position of bard
SCALE n one of the thin overlapping plates covering fishes and reptiles ▷ vb remove scales from
SCALEABLE same as > SCALABLE
SCALEABLY same as > SCALABLY
SCALED > SCALE
SCALELESS > SCALE
SCALELIKE > SCALE
SCALENE n triangle with three unequal sides
SCALENES > SCALENE
SCALENI > SCALENUS
SCALENUS n any one of the three muscles situated on each side of the neck
SCALEPAN n part of scales holding weighed object
SCALEPANS > SCALEPAN
SCALER n person or thing that scales
SCALERS > SCALER
SCALES > SCALE
SCALETAIL n type of squirrel
SCALEUP n increase
SCALEUPS > SCALEUP
SCALEWORK n artistic representation of scales
SCALIER > SCALY
SCALIEST > SCALY
SCALINESS > SCALY
SCALING > SCALE
SCALINGS > SCALE
SCALL n disease of the scalp characterized by itching and scab formation
SCALLAWAG same as > SCALLYWAG
SCALLED > SCALL
SCALLIES > SCALLY
SCALLION same as > SHALLOT
SCALLIONS > SCALLION
SCALLOP n edible shellfish with two fan-shaped shells ▷ vb decorate (an edge) with scallops
SCALLOPED > SCALLOP
SCALLOPER > SCALLOP
SCALLOPS > SCALLOP
SCALLS > SCALL
SCALLY n rascal
SCALLYWAG n scamp, rascal
SCALOGRAM n scale for measuring opinion
SCALP n skin and hair on top of the head ▷ vb cut off the scalp of
SCALPED > SCALP
SCALPEL n small surgical knife
SCALPELS > SCALPEL
SCALPER > SCALP
SCALPERS > SCALP
SCALPING n process in which the top portion of a metal ingot is machined away before use
SCALPINGS > SCALPING

SCALPINS n small stones
SCALPLESS > SCALP
SCALPRUM n large scalpel
SCALPRUMS > SCALPRUM
SCALPS > SCALP
SCALY adj resembling or covered in scales
SCAM n dishonest scheme ▷ vb swindle (someone) by means of a trick
SCAMBLE vb scramble
SCAMBLED > SCAMBLE
SCAMBLER > SCAMBLE
SCAMBLERS > SCAMBLE
SCAMBLES > SCAMBLE
SCAMBLING > SCAMBLE
SCAMEL n Shakespearian word of uncertain meaning
SCAMELS > SCAMEL
SCAMMED > SCAM
SCAMMER n person who perpetrates a scam
SCAMMERS > SCAMMER
SCAMMING > SCAM
SCAMMONY n twining Asian convolvulus plant
SCAMP n mischievous child ▷ vb perform without care
SCAMPED > SCAMP
SCAMPER vb run about hurriedly or in play ▷ n scampering
SCAMPERED > SCAMP
SCAMPERER > SCAMPER
SCAMPERS > SCAMPER
SCAMPI pl n large prawns
SCAMPIES > SCAMPI
SCAMPING > SCAMP
SCAMPINGS > SCAMP
SCAMPIS > SCAMPI
SCAMPISH > SCAMP
SCAMPS > SCAMP
SCAMS > SCAM
SCAMSTER same as > SCAMMER
SCAMSTERS > SCAMSTER
SCAMTO n argot of urban Black people in South Africa
SCAMTOS > SCAMTO
SCAN vb scrutinize carefully ▷ n scanning
SCAND > SCAN
SCANDAL n disgraceful action or event ▷ vb disgrace
SCANDALED > SCANDAL
SCANDALS > SCANDAL
SCANDENT adj (of plants) having a climbing habit
SCANDIA n scandium oxide
SCANDIAS > SCANDIA
SCANDIC adj of or containing scandium
SCANDIUM n rare silvery-white metallic element
SCANDIUMS > SCANDIUM
SCANNABLE > SCAN
SCANNED > SCAN
SCANNER n electronic device used for scanning
SCANNERS > SCANNER
SCANNING > SCAN
SCANNINGS > SCAN
SCANS > SCAN
SCANSION n metrical scanning of verse
SCANSIONS > SCANSION

SCANT *adj* barely sufficient, meagre ▷ *vb* limit in size or quantity ▷ *adv* scarcely
SCANTED > SCANT
SCANTER > SCANT
SCANTEST > SCANT
SCANTIER > SCANTY
SCANTIES *n* women's underwear
SCANTIEST > SCANTY
SCANTILY > SCANTY
SCANTING > SCANT
SCANTITY *n* quality of being scant
SCANTLE *vb* stint
SCANTLED > SCANTLE
SCANTLES > SCANTLE
SCANTLING *n* piece of sawn timber, such as a rafter, that has a small cross section
SCANTLY > SCANT
SCANTNESS > SCANT
SCANTS > SCANT
SCANTY *adj* barely sufficient or not sufficient
SCAPA *variant of* > SCARPER
SCAPAED > SCAPA
SCAPAING > SCAPA
SCAPAS > SCAPA
SCAPE *n* leafless stalk in plants ▷ *vb* archaic word for escape
SCAPED > SCAPE
SCAPEGOAT *n* person made to bear the blame for others ▷ *vb* make a scapegoat of
SCAPELESS *adj* allowing no escape
SCAPEMENT *n* escapement
SCAPES > SCAPE
SCAPHOID *obsolete word for* > NAVICULAR
SCAPHOIDS > SCAPHOID
SCAPHOPOD *n* type of marine mollusc of the class which includes tusk (or tooth) shells
SCAPI > SCAPUS
SCAPING > SCAPE
SCAPOLITE *n* any of a group of colourless, white, grey, or violet fluorescent minerals
SCAPOSE > SCAPE
SCAPPLE *vb* shape roughly
SCAPPLED > SCAPPLE
SCAPPLES > SCAPPLE
SCAPPLING > SCAPPLE
SCAPULA *n* shoulder blade
SCAPULAE > SCAPULA
SCAPULAR *adj* of the scapula ▷ *n* loose sleeveless garment worn by monks over their habits
SCAPULARS > SCAPULAR
SCAPULARY *same as* > SCAPULAR
SCAPULAS > SCAPULA
SCAPUS *n* flower stalk
SCAR *n* mark left by a healed wound ▷ *vb* mark or become marked with a scar
SCARAB *n* sacred beetle of ancient Egypt
SCARABAEI *pl n* scarabs
SCARABEE *n* old word for scarab beetle

SCARABEES > SCARABEE
SCARABOID *adj* resembling a scarab beetle ▷ *n* beetle that resembles a scarab
SCARABS > SCARAB
SCARCE *adj* insufficient to meet demand
SCARCELY *adv* hardly at all
SCARCER > SCARCE
SCARCEST > SCARCE
SCARCITY *n* inadequate supply
SCARE *vb* frighten or be frightened ▷ *n* fright, sudden panic ▷ *adj* causing (needless) fear or alarm
SCARECROW *n* figure dressed in old clothes, set up to scare birds away from crops
SCARED > SCARE
SCAREDER > SCARE
SCAREDEST > SCARE
SCAREDIES > SCAREDY
SCAREDY *n* someone who is easily frightened
SCAREHEAD *n* newspaper headline intended to shock
SCARER > SCARE
SCARERS > SCARE
SCARES > SCARE
SCAREWARE *n* type of malware which tricks the user into downloading it
SCAREY *adj* frightening
SCARF *n* piece of material worn round the neck, head, or shoulders ▷ *vb* join
SCARFED > SCARF
SCARFER > SCARF
SCARFERS > SCARF
SCARFING > SCARF
SCARFINGS > SCARF
SCARFISH *n* type of fish
SCARFPIN *n* decorative pin securing a scarf
SCARFPINS > SCARFPIN
SCARFS > SCARF
SCARFSKIN *n* outermost layer of the skin
SCARFWISE *adv* like a scarf
SCARIER > SCARY
SCARIEST > SCARY
SCARIFIED > SCARIFY
SCARIFIER > SCARIFY
SCARIFIES > SCARIFY
SCARIFY *vb* scratch or cut slightly all over
SCARILY > SCARY
SCARINESS > SCARY
SCARING > SCARE
SCARIOSE *same as* > SCARIOUS
SCARIOUS *adj* (of plant parts) membranous, dry, and brownish in colour
SCARLESS > SCAR
SCARLET *n* brilliant red ▷ *adj* bright red ▷ *vb* make scarlet
SCARLETED > SCARLET
SCARLETS > SCARLET
SCARMOGE *n* old form of skirmish
SCARMOGES > SCARMOGE
SCARP *n* steep slope ▷ *vb* wear or cut so as to form a steep slope

SCARPA *vb* run away
SCARPAED > SCARPA
SCARPAING > SCARPA
SCARPAS > SCARPA
SCARPED > SCARP
SCARPER *vb* run away ▷ *n* hasty departure
SCARPERED > SCARPER
SCARPERS > SCARPER
SCARPETTI > SCARPETTO
SCARPETTO *n* type of shoe
SCARPH *vb* join with scarf joint
SCARPHED > SCARPH
SCARPHING > SCARPH
SCARPHS > SCARPH
SCARPINES *n* device for torturing feet
SCARPING > SCARP
SCARPINGS > SCARP
SCARPS > SCARP
SCARRE *n* Shakespearian word of unknown meaning
SCARRED > SCAR
SCARRES > SCARRE
SCARRIER > SCAR
SCARRIEST > SCAR
SCARRING > SCAR
SCARRINGS > SCAR
SCARRY > SCAR
SCARS > SCAR
SCART *vb* scratch or scrape ▷ *n* scratch or scrape
SCARTED > SCART
SCARTH *Scots word for* > CORMORANT
SCARTHS > SCARTH
SCARTING > SCART
SCARTS > SCART
SCARVED *adj* wearing a scarf
SCARVES > SCARF
SCARY *adj* frightening
SCAT *vb* go away ▷ *n* jazz singing using improvised vocal sounds instead of words
SCATBACK *n* American football player
SCATBACKS > SCATBACK
SCATCH *same as* > STILT
SCATCHES > SCATCH
SCATH *vb* old word meaning injure
SCATHE *vb* attack with severe criticism ▷ *n* harm
SCATHED > SCATHE
SCATHEFUL *adj* old word meaning harmful
SCATHES > SCATHE
SCATHING *adj* harshly critical
SCATHS > SCATH
SCATOLE *n* substance found in coal
SCATOLES > SCATOLE
SCATOLOGY *n* scientific study of excrement
SCATS > SCAT
SCATT *n* old word meaning tax ▷ *vb* tax
SCATTED > SCATT
SCATTER *vb* throw about in various directions ▷ *n* scattering
SCATTERED > SCATTER
SCATTERER > SCATTER
SCATTERS > SCATTER

SCATTERY *adj* dispersed
SCATTIER > SCATTY
SCATTIEST > SCATTY
SCATTILY > SCATTY
SCATTING > SCAT
SCATTINGS > SCAT
SCATTS > SCATT
SCATTY *adj* empty-headed
SCAUD *Scot word for* > SCALD
SCAUDED > SCAUD
SCAUDING > SCAUD
SCAUDS > SCAUD
SCAUP *variant of* > SCALP
SCAUPED > SCAUP
SCAUPER *same as* > SCORPER
SCAUPERS > SCAUPER
SCAUPING > SCAUP
SCAUPS > SCAUP
SCAUR *same as* > SCAR
SCAURED > SCAUR
SCAURIES > SCAURY
SCAURING > SCAUR
SCAURS > SCAUR
SCAURY *n* young seagull
SCAVAGE *n* old word meaning toll ▷ *vb* scavenge
SCAVAGED > SCAVAGE
SCAVAGER > SCAVAGE
SCAVAGERS > SCAVAGE
SCAVAGES > SCAVAGE
SCAVAGING > SCAVAGE
SCAVENGE *vb* search for (anything usable) among discarded material
SCAVENGED > SCAVENGE
SCAVENGER *n* person who scavenges
SCAVENGES > SCAVENGE
SCAW *n* headland
SCAWS > SCAW
SCAWTITE *n* mineral containing calcium
SCAWTITES > SCAWTITE
SCAZON *n* metre in poetry
SCAZONS > SCAZON
SCAZONTES > SCAZON
SCAZONTIC > SCAZON
SCEAT *n* Anglo-Saxon coin
SCEATS > SCEAT
SCEATT *same as* > SCEAT
SCEATTAS > SCEAT
SCEATTS > SCEAT
SCEDULE *old spelling of* > SCHEDULE
SCEDULED > SCEDULE
SCEDULES > SCEDULE
SCEDULING > SCEDULE
SCELERAT *n* villain
SCELERATE *n* villain
SCELERATS > SCELERAT
SCENA *n* scene in an opera, usually longer than a single aria
SCENARIES > SCENARY
SCENARIO *n* summary of the plot of a play or film
SCENARIOS > SCENARIO
SCENARISE *same as* > SCENARIZE
SCENARIST > SCENARIO
SCENARIZE *vb* create scenario
SCENARY *n* scenery
SCENAS > SCENA

SCEND vb (of a vessel) to surge upwards in a heavy sea ▷ n upward heaving of a vessel pitching

SCENDED > SCEND

SCENDING > SCEND

SCENDS > SCEND

SCENE n place of action of a real or imaginary event ▷ vb set in a scene

SCENED > SCENE

SCENEMAN n person shifting stage scenery

SCENEMEN > SCENEMAN

SCENERIES > SCENERY

SCENERY n natural features of a landscape

SCENES > SCENE

SCENESTER n person who tries to fit into a particular cultural scene

SCENIC adj picturesque ▷ n something scenic

SCENICAL > SCENE

SCENICS > SCENIC

SCENING > SCENE

SCENT n pleasant smell ▷ vb detect by smell

SCENTED > SCENT

SCENTFUL adj old word meaning having scent

SCENTING > SCENT

SCENTINGS > SCENT

SCENTLESS > SCENT

SCENTS > SCENT

SCEPSIS n doubt

SCEPSISES > SCEPSIS

SCEPTER same as > SCEPTRE

SCEPTERED > SCEPTER

SCEPTERS > SCEPTER

SCEPTIC n person who habitually doubts generally accepted beliefs ▷ adj of or relating to sceptics

SCEPTICAL adj not convinced that something is true

SCEPTICS > SCEPTIC

SCEPTRAL adj royal

SCEPTRE n ornamental rod symbolizing royal power ▷ vb invest with authority

SCEPTRED > SCEPTRE

SCEPTRES > SCEPTRE

SCEPTRING > SCEPTRE

SCEPTRY adj having sceptre

SCERNE vb old word meaning discern

SCERNED > SCERNE

SCERNES > SCERNE

SCERNING > SCERNE

SCHANSE > SCHANTZE

SCHANSES > SCHANSE

SCHANTZE n stones heaped to shelter soldier in battle

SCHANTZES > SCHANTZE

SCHANZE same as > SCHANTZE

SCHANZES > SCHANZE

SCHAPPE n yarn or fabric made from waste silk

SCHAPPED > SCHAPPE

SCHAPPES > SCHAPPE

SCHAPSKA n cap worn by lancer

SCHAPSKAS > SCHAPSKA

SCHATCHEN same as > SHADCHAN

SCHAV n Polish soup

SCHAVS > SCHAV

SCHECHITA n slaughter of animals according to Jewish law

SCHEDULAR > SCHEDULE

SCHEDULE n plan of procedure for a project ▷ vb plan to occur at a certain time

SCHEDULED adj arranged or planned according to a programme, timetable, etc

SCHEDULER > SCHEDULE

SCHEDULES > SCHEDULE

SCHEELITE n white, brownish, or greenish mineral

SCHELLIES > SCHELLY

SCHELLUM n Scots word meaning rascal

SCHELLUMS > SCHELLUM

SCHELLY n freshwater whitefish of the English Lake District

SCHELM n South African word meaning rascal

SCHELMS > SCHELM

SCHEMA n overall plan or diagram

SCHEMAS > SCHEMA

SCHEMATA > SCHEMA

SCHEMATIC adj presented as a plan or diagram ▷ n schematic diagram, esp of an electrical circuit

SCHEME n systematic plan ▷ vb plan in an underhand manner

SCHEMED > SCHEME

SCHEMER > SCHEME

SCHEMERS > SCHEME

SCHEMES > SCHEME

SCHEMIE n insulting Scots word for a resident of a housing scheme

SCHEMIES > SCHEMIE

SCHEMING adj given to making plots ▷ n intrigues

SCHEMINGS > SCHEMING

SCHERZI > SCHERZO

SCHERZO n brisk lively piece of music

SCHERZOS > SCHERZO

SCHIAVONE n type of sword

SCHIEDAM n type of gin produced in the Netherlands

SCHIEDAMS > SCHIEDAM

SCHILLER n unusual iridescent or metallic lustre in some minerals

SCHILLERS > SCHILLER

SCHILLING n former monetary unit of Austria

SCHIMMEL n roan horse

SCHIMMELS > SCHIMMEL

SCHISM n (group resulting from) division in an organization

SCHISMA n musical term

SCHISMAS > SCHISMA

SCHISMS > SCHISM

SCHIST n crystalline rock which splits into layers

SCHISTOSE > SCHIST

SCHISTOUS > SCHIST

SCHISTS > SCHIST

SCHIZIER > SCHIZY

SCHIZIEST > SCHIZY

SCHIZO n offensive term for a schizophrenic person

SCHIZOID adj abnormally introverted ▷ n person with a schizoid personality

SCHIZOIDS > SCHIZOID

SCHIZONT n cell formed from a trophozoite during the asexual stage of the life cycle of sporozoan protozoans

SCHIZONTS > SCHIZONT

SCHIZOPOD n any of various shrimplike crustaceans

SCHIZOS > SCHIZO

SCHIZY adj offensive term meaning schizophrenic

SCHIZZIER > SCHIZZY

SCHIZZY adj offensive term meaning schizophrenic

SCHLAGER n German duelling sword

SCHLAGERS > SCHLAGER

SCHLEMIEL n awkward or unlucky person whose endeavours usually fail

SCHLEMIHL same as > SCHLEMIEL

SCHLEP vb drag or lug (oneself or an object) with difficulty ▷ n arduous journey or procedure

SCHLEPP vb schlep

SCHLEPPED > SCHLEP

SCHLEPPER n incompetent person

SCHLEPPS > SCHLEPP

SCHLEPPY same as > SHLEPPY

SCHLEPS > SCHLEP

SCHLICH n finely crushed ore

SCHLICHS > SCHLICH

SCHLIERE n (in physics or geology) streak of different density or composition from surroundings

SCHLIEREN > SCHLIERE

SCHLIERIC > SCHLIERE

SCHLOCK n goods or produce of cheap or inferior quality ▷ adj cheap, inferior, or trashy

SCHLOCKER n thing of poor quality

SCHLOCKEY adj of inferior quality ▷ n something of inferior quality

SCHLOCKS > SCHLOCK

SCHLOCKY adj of poor quality

SCHLONG vulgar slang word for > PENIS

SCHLONGS > SCHLONG

SCHLOSS n German castle

SCHLOSSES > SCHLOSS

SCHLUB n coarse or contemptible person

SCHLUBS > SCHLUB

SCHLUMP vb move in lazy way

SCHLUMPED > SCHLUMP

SCHLUMPS > SCHLUMP

SCHLUMPY > SCHLUMP

SCHMALTZ n excessive sentimentality

SCHMALTZY adj excessively sentimental

SCHMALZ same as > SCHMALTZ

SCHMALZES > SCHMALZ

SCHMALZY adj schmaltzy

SCHMATTE same as > SCHMUTTER

SCHMATTES > SCHMATTE

SCHMEAR n situation, matter, or affair ▷ vb spread or smear

SCHMEARED > SCHMEAR

SCHMEARS > SCHMEAR

SCHMECK n taste ▷ vb taste good

SCHMECKED > SCHMECK

SCHMECKER n heroin user

SCHMECKS > SCHMECK

SCHMEER same as > SCHMEAR

SCHMEERED > SCHMEER

SCHMEÊRS > SCHMEER

SCHMELZ n ornamental glass

SCHMELZE variant of > SCHMELZ

SCHMELZES > SCHMELZ

SCHMICK adj (in Australia) excellent, elegant, or stylish

SCHMICKER > SCHMICK

SCHMO n dull, stupid, or boring person

SCHMOCK n stupid person

SCHMOCKS > SCHMOCK

SCHMOE n stupid person

SCHMOES > SCHMO

SCHMOOS variant of > SCHMOOSE

SCHMOOSE vb chat

SCHMOOSED > SCHMOOSE

SCHMOOSES > SCHMOOSE

SCHMOOZ n chat

SCHMOOZE vb chat or gossip ▷ n trivial conversation

SCHMOOZED > SCHMOOZE

SCHMOOZER > SCHMOOZE

SCHMOOZES > SCHMOOZE

SCHMOOZY > SCHMOOZE

SCHMOS > SCHMO

SCHMUCK n stupid or contemptible person ▷ vb act as a schmuck

SCHMUCKED > SCHMUCK

SCHMUCKS > SCHMUCK

SCHMUCKY adj foolish

SCHMUTTER n cloth or clothing

SCHMUTZ n dirt; grime

SCHMUTZES > SCHMUTZ

SCHNAPPER same as > SNAPPER

SCHNAPPS n strong alcoholic spirit

SCHNAPS same as > SCHNAPPS

SCHNAPSES > SCHNAPS

SCHNAUZER n wire-haired breed of dog of the terrier type, originally from Germany

SCHNECKE > SCHNECKEN

SCHNECKEN pl n sweet spiral-shaped bread roll flavoured with cinnamon and nuts

S

SCHNEID n succession of losses

SCHNEIDS > SCHNEID

SCHNELL adj German word meaning quick

SCHNITZEL n thin slice of meat, esp veal

SCHNOODLE n cross between a schnauzer and a poodle

SCHNOOK n stupid or gullible person

SCHNOOKS > SCHNOOK

SCHNORKEL less common variant of > SNORKEL

SCHNORR vb beg

SCHNORRED > SCHNORR

SCHNORRER n person who lives off the charity of others

SCHNORRS > SCHNORR

SCHNOZ n nose

SCHNOZES > SCHNOZ

SCHNOZZ n nose

SCHNOZZES > SCHNOZZ

SCHNOZZLE slang word for > NOSE

SCHOLAR n learned person

SCHOLARCH n head of school

SCHOLARLY > SCHOLAR

SCHOLARS > SCHOLAR

SCHOLIA > SCHOLIUM

SCHOLIAST n medieval annotator, esp of classical texts

SCHOLION n scholarly annotation

SCHOLIUM n commentary or annotation, esp on a classical text

SCHOLIUMS > SCHOLIUM

SCHOOL n place where children are taught or instruction is given in a subject ▷ vb educate or train

SCHOOLBAG n school pupil's bag

SCHOOLBOY n child attending school

SCHOOLDAY n day for going to school

SCHOOLE n old form of shoal

SCHOOLED > SCHOOL

SCHOOLER n pupil at a school of a specified kind

SCHOOLERS > SCHOOLER

SCHOOLERY n old word meaning something taught

SCHOOLES > SCHOOLE

SCHOOLIE n schoolteacher or a high-school student

SCHOOLIES > SCHOOLIE

SCHOOLING n education

SCHOOLKID n child who goes to school

SCHOOLMAN n scholar versed in the learning of the Schoolmen

SCHOOLMEN > SCHOOLMAN

SCHOOLS > SCHOOL

SCHOONER n sailing ship rigged fore-and-aft

SCHOONERS > SCHOONER

SCHORL n type of black tourmaline

SCHORLS > SCHORL

SCHOUT n council officer in Netherlands

SCHOUTS > SCHOUT

SCHRIK variant of > SKRIK

SCHRIKS > SCHRIK

SCHROD n young cod

SCHRODS > SCHROD

SCHTICK same as > SHTICK

SCHTICKS > SCHTICK

SCHTIK n schtick

SCHTIKS > SCHTIK

SCHTOOK n trouble

SCHTOOKS > SCHTOOK

SCHTOOM adj silent

SCHTUCK n trouble

SCHTUCKS > SCHTUCK

SCHTUM adj silent or dumb

SCHTUP same as > SHTUP

SCHTUPPED > SCHTUP

SCHTUPS > SCHTUP

SCHUIT n Dutch boat with flat bottom

SCHUITS > SCHUIT

SCHUL same as > SHUL

SCHULN > SCHUL

SCHULS > SCHUL

SCHUSS n straight high-speed downhill run ▷ vb perform a schuss

SCHUSSED > SCHUSS

SCHUSSER > SCHUSS

SCHUSSERS > SCHUSS

SCHUSSES > SCHUSS

SCHUSSING > SCHUSS

SCHUYT n Dutch boat with flat bottom

SCHUYTS > SCHUYT

SCHVARTZE n offensive Yiddish word for Black person

SCHVITZ same as > SHVITZ

SCHVITZED > SCHVITZ

SCHVITZES > SCHVITZ

SCHWA n vowel representing the sound in unstressed syllables

SCHWAG n promotional material given away for free

SCHWAGS > SCHWAG

SCHWARTZE same as > SCHVARTZE

SCHWAS > SCHWA

SCIAENID adj of or relating to a family of mainly tropical and subtropical marine percoid fishes ▷ n any of these fish

SCIAENIDS > SCIAENID

SCIAENOID same as > SCIAENID

SCIAMACHY n fight with an imaginary enemy

SCIARID n small fly

SCIARIDS > SCIARID

SCIATIC adj of the hip ▷ n sciatic part of the body

SCIATICA n severe pain in the large nerve in the back of the leg

SCIATICAL > SCIATICA

SCIATICAS > SCIATICA

SCIATICS > SCIATIC

SCIENCE n systematic study and knowledge of natural or physical phenomena

SCIENCED adj old word meaning learned

SCIENCES > SCIENCE

SCIENT adj old word meaning scientific

SCIENTER adv knowingly

SCIENTIAL adj of or relating to science

SCIENTISE same as > SCIENTIZE

SCIENTISM n application of, or belief in, the scientific method

SCIENTIST n person who studies or practises a science

SCIENTIZE vb treat scientifically

SCILICET adv namely

SCILLA n plant with small bell-shaped flowers

SCILLAS > SCILLA

SCIMETAR n scimitar

SCIMETARS > SCIMETAR

SCIMITAR n curved oriental sword

SCIMITARS > SCIMITAR

SCIMITER n scimitar

SCIMITERS > SCIMITER

SCINCOID adj of, relating to, or resembling a skink ▷ n any animal, esp a lizard, resembling a skink

SCINCOIDS > SCINCOID

SCINTILLA n very small amount

SCIOLISM n practice of opinionating on subjects of which one has only superficial knowledge

SCIOLISMS > SCIOLISM

SCIOLIST > SCIOLISM

SCIOLISTS > SCIOLISM

SCIOLOUS > SCIOLISM

SCIOLTO adv musical direction meaning freely

SCIOMACHY same as > SCIAMACHY

SCIOMANCY n divination with the help of ghosts

SCION n descendant or heir

SCIONS > SCION

SCIOPHYTE n any plant that grows best in the shade

SCIOSOPHY n unscientific system of knowledge

SCIROC > SCIROCCO

SCIROCCO n hot Mediterranean wind

SCIROCCOS > SCIROCCO

SCIROCS > SCIROC

SCIRRHI > SCIRRHUS

SCIRRHOID > SCIRRHUS

SCIRRHOUS adj of or resembling a scirrhus

SCIRRHUS n hard cancerous growth composed of fibrous tissues

SCISSEL n waste metal left over from sheet metal after discs have been punched out of it

SCISSELS > SCISSEL

SCISSIL n scissel

SCISSILE adj capable of being cut or divided

SCISSILS > SCISSIL

SCISSION n act or an instance of cutting, splitting, or dividing

SCISSIONS > SCISSION

SCISSOR vb cut (an object) with scissors

SCISSORED > SCISSOR

SCISSORER > SCISSOR

SCISSORS pl n cutting instrument with two crossed pivoted blades

SCISSURE n longitudinal cleft

SCISSURES > SCISSURE

SCIURID n squirrel or related rodent

SCIURIDS > SCIURID

SCIURINE adj relating to a family of rodents that includes squirrels, marmots, and chipmunks ▷ n any sciurine animal

SCIURINES > SCIURINE

SCIUROID adj (of an animal) resembling a squirrel

SCLAFF vb cause (the club) to hit (the ground behind the ball) when making a stroke ▷ n sclaffing stroke or shot

SCLAFFED > SCLAFF

SCLAFFER > SCLAFF

SCLAFFERS > SCLAFF

SCLAFFING > SCLAFF

SCLAFFS > SCLAFF

SCLATE vb (Scots) slate ▷ n (Scots) slate

SCLATED > SCLATE

SCLATES > SCLATE

SCLATING > SCLATE

SCLAUNDER n old form of slander

SCLAVE n old form of slave

SCLAVES > SCLAVE

SCLERA n tough white substance that forms the outer covering of the eyeball

SCLERAE > SCLERA

SCLERAL > SCLERA

SCLERAS > SCLERA

SCLERE n supporting anatomical structure

SCLEREID n type of biological cell

SCLEREIDE n type of biological cell

SCLEREIDS > SCLEREID

SCLEREMA n condition in which body tissues harden

SCLEREMAS > SCLEREMA

SCLERES > SCLERE

SCLERITE n any of the hard chitinous plates that make up the exoskeleton of an arthropod

SCLERITES > SCLERITE

SCLERITIC > SCLERITE

SCLERITIS n inflammation of the sclera

SCLEROID adj (of organisms and their parts) hard or hardened

SCLEROMA n any small area of abnormally hard tissue, esp in a mucous membrane

SCLEROMAS > SCLEROMA

SCLEROSAL > SCLEROSIS

SCLEROSE vb affect with sclerosis

SCLEROSED adj hardened

SCLEROSES > SCLEROSIS

SCLEROSIS n abnormal hardening of body tissues

SCLEROTAL n bony area in sclerotic

SCLEROTIA pl n masses of hyphae formed in certain fungi

SCLEROTIC same as > SCLERA

SCLEROTIN n protein in the cuticle of insects that becomes hard and dark

SCLEROUS adj hard

SCLIFF n Scots word for small piece

SCLIFFS > SCLIFF

SCLIM vb Scots word meaning climb

SCLIMMED > SCLIM

SCLIMMING > SCLIM

SCLIMS > SCLIM

SCODIER > SCODY

SCODIEST > SCODY

SCODY adj unkempt

SCOFF vb express derision ▷ n mocking expression

SCOFFED > SCOFF

SCOFFER > SCOFF

SCOFFERS > SCOFF

SCOFFING > SCOFF

SCOFFINGS > SCOFF

SCOFFLAW n person who habitually flouts or violates the law

SCOFFLAWS > SCOFFLAW

SCOFFS > SCOFF

SCOG vb shelter

SCOGGED > SCOG

SCOGGING > SCOG

SCOGS > SCOG

SCOINSON n part of door or window frame

SCOINSONS > SCOINSON

SCOLD vb find fault with, reprimand ▷ n person who scolds

SCOLDABLE > SCOLD

SCOLDED > SCOLD

SCOLDER > SCOLD

SCOLDERS > SCOLD

SCOLDING > SCOLD

SCOLDINGS > SCOLD

SCOLDS > SCOLD

SCOLECES > SCOLEX

SCOLECID n variety of worm

SCOLECIDS > SCOLECID

SCOLECITE n white zeolite mineral

SCOLECOID adj like scolex

SCOLEX n headlike part of a tapeworm

SCOLIA > SCOLION

SCOLICES > SCOLEX

SCOLIOMA n condition with abnormal curvature of spine

SCOLIOMAS > SCOLIOMA

SCOLION n ancient Greek drinking song

SCOLIOSES > SCOLIOSIS

SCOLIOSIS n abnormal lateral curvature of the spine

SCOLIOTIC > SCOLIOSIS

SCOLLOP variant of > SCALLOP

SCOLLOPED > SCOLLOP

SCOLLOPS > SCOLLOP

SCOLYTID n type of beetle

SCOLYTIDS > SCOLYTID

SCOLYTOID n type of beetle

SCOMBRID n fish of mackerel family

SCOMBRIDS > SCOMBRID

SCOMBROID adj relating to a suborder of marine spiny-finned fishes ▷ n any fish belonging to this suborder

SCOMFISH vb Scots word meaning stifle

SCONCE n bracket on a wall for holding candles or lights ▷ vb challenge (a fellow student) to drink a large quantity of beer

SCONCED > SCONCE

SCONCES > SCONCE

SCONCHEON n part of door or window frame

SCONCING > SCONCE

SCONE n small plain cake baked in an oven or on a griddle

SCONES > SCONE

SCONTION n part of door or window frame

SCONTIONS > SCONTION

SCOOBIES > SCOOBY

SCOOBY n slang for a clue, notion

SCOOCH vb compress one's body into smaller space

SCOOCHED > SCOOCH

SCOOCHES > SCOOCH

SCOOCHING > SCOOCH

SCOOG vb shelter

SCOOGED > SCOOG

SCOOGING > SCOOG

SCOOGS > SCOOG

SCOOP n shovel-like tool for ladling or hollowing out ▷ vb take up or hollow out with or as if with a scoop

SCOOPABLE > SCOOP

SCOOPED > SCOOP

SCOOPER > SCOOP

SCOOPERS > SCOOP

SCOOPFUL > SCOOP

SCOOPFULS > SCOOP

SCOOPING > SCOOP

SCOOPINGS > SCOOP

SCOOPS > SCOOP

SCOOPSFUL > SCOOP

SCOOSH vb squirt ▷ n squirt or rush of liquid

SCOOSHED > SCOOSH

SCOOSHES > SCOOSH

SCOOSHING > SCOOSH

SCOOT vb leave or move quickly ▷ n act of scooting

SCOOTCH same as > SCOOCH

SCOOTCHED > SCOOTCH

SCOOTCHES > SCOOTCH

SCOOTED > SCOOT

SCOOTER n child's vehicle propelled by pushing on the ground with one foot ▷ vb go on a scooter

SCOOTERED > SCOOTER

SCOOTERS > SCOOTER

SCOOTING > SCOOT

SCOOTS > SCOOT

SCOP n (in Anglo-Saxon England) a bard or minstrel

SCOPA n tuft of hairs on the abdomen or hind legs of bees

SCOPAE > SCOPA

SCOPAS > SCOPA

SCOPATE adj having tuft-type hairs

SCOPE n opportunity for using abilities ▷ vb look at or examine carefully

SCOPED > SCOPE

SCOPELID n deep-sea fish

SCOPELIDS > SCOPELID

SCOPELOID n deep-sea fish

SCOPES > SCOPE

SCOPING > SCOPE

SCOPOLINE n soluble crystalline alkaloid

SCOPS > SCOP

SCOPULA n small tuft of dense hairs on the legs and chelicerae of some spiders

SCOPULAE > SCOPULA

SCOPULAS > SCOPULA

SCOPULATE > SCOPULA

SCORBUTIC adj of or having scurvy

SCORCH vb burn on the surface ▷ n slight burn

SCORCHED > SCORCH

SCORCHER n very hot day

SCORCHERS > SCORCHER

SCORCHES > SCORCH

SCORCHING > SCORCH

SCORDATO adj musical term meaning out of tune

SCORE n points gained in a game or competition ▷ vb gain (points) in a game

SCORECARD n card on which scores are recorded in games such as golf

SCORED > SCORE

SCORELESS adj without anyone scoring

SCORELINE n final score in game

SCOREPAD n pad for recording score in game

SCOREPADS > SCOREPAD

SCORER > SCORE

SCORERS > SCORE

SCORES > SCORE

SCORIA n mass of solidified lava containing many cavities

SCORIAC > SCORIA

SCORIAE > SCORIA

SCORIFIED > SCORIFY

SCORIFIER > SCORIFY

SCORIFIES > SCORIFY

SCORIFY vb remove (impurities) from metals by forming scoria

SCORING n act or practice of scoring

SCORINGS > SCORING

SCORIOUS > SCORIA

SCORN n open contempt ▷ vb despise

SCORNED > SCORN

SCORNER > SCORN

SCORNERS > SCORN

SCORNFUL > SCORN

SCORNING > SCORN

SCORNINGS > SCORN

SCORNS > SCORN

SCORODITE n mineral containing iron and aluminium

SCORPER n kind of fine chisel with a square or curved tip

SCORPERS > SCORPER

SCORPIOID adj of, relating to, or resembling scorpions

SCORPION n small lobster-shaped animal with a sting at the end of a jointed tail

SCORPIONS > SCORPION

SCORRENDO adj musical term meaning gliding

SCORSE vb exchange

SCORSED > SCORSE

SCORSER > SCORSE

SCORSERS > SCORSE

SCORSES > SCORSE

SCORSING > SCORSE

SCOT n payment or tax

SCOTCH vb put an end to ▷ n gash

SCOTCHED > SCOTCH

SCOTCHES > SCOTCH

SCOTCHING > SCOTCH

SCOTER n type of sea duck

SCOTERS > SCOTER

SCOTIA n deep concave moulding

SCOTIAS > SCOTIA

SCOTOMA n blind spot

SCOTOMAS > SCOTOMA

SCOTOMATA > SCOTOMA

SCOTOMIA n dizziness

SCOTOMIAS > SCOTOMIA

SCOTOMIES > SCOTOMY

SCOTOMY n dizziness

SCOTOPHIL adj liking darkness

SCOTOPIA n ability of the eye to adjust for night vision

SCOTOPIAS > SCOTOPIA

SCOTOPIC > SCOTOPIA

SCOTS > SCOT

SCOTTIE n type of small sturdy terrier

SCOTTIES > SCOTTIE

SCOUG vb shelter

SCOUGED > SCOUG

SCOUGING > SCOUG

SCOUGS > SCOUG

SCOUNDREL n cheat or deceiver

SCOUP vb Scots word meaning jump

SCOUPED > SCOUP

SCOUPING > SCOUP

SCOUPS > SCOUP

SCOUR vb clean or polish by rubbing with something rough ▷ n scouring

SCOURED > SCOUR

SCOURER > SCOUR

SCOURERS > SCOUR

SCOURGE n person or thing causing severe suffering ▷ vb cause severe suffering to

SCOURGED > SCOURGE

SCOURGER > SCOURGE

SCOURGERS > SCOURGE

SCOURGES > SCOURGE

SCOURGING n act of scourging

SCOURIE n young seagull

SCOURIES > SCOURIE

SCOURING > SCOUR

SCOURINGS pl n residue left after cleaning grain

SCOURS > SCOUR

SCOURSE vb exchange

SCOURSED > SCOURSE
SCOURSES > SCOURSE
SCOURSING > SCOURSE
SCOUSE n stew made from left-over meat
SCOUSER n inhabitant of Liverpool
SCOUSERS > SCOUSER
SCOUSES > SCOUSE
SCOUT n person sent out to reconnoitre ▷ vb act as a scout
SCOUTED > SCOUT
SCOUTER > SCOUT
SCOUTERS > SCOUT
SCOUTH n Scots word meaning plenty of scope
SCOUTHER n Scots word meaning scorch
SCOUTHERS > SCOUTHER
SCOUTHERY > SCOUTHER
SCOUTHS > SCOUTH
SCOUTING > SCOUT
SCOUTINGS > SCOUT
SCOUTS > SCOUT
SCOW n unpowered barge used for carrying freight ▷ vb transport by scow
SCOWDER vb Scots word meaning scorch
SCOWDERED > SCOWDER
SCOWDERS > SCOWDER
SCOWED > SCOW
SCOWING > SCOW
SCOWL vb have an angry or sullen expression
SCOWLED > SCOWL
SCOWLER n person who scowls
SCOWLERS > SCOWLER
SCOWLING > SCOWL
SCOWLS > SCOWL
SCOWP vb Scots word meaning jump
SCOWPED > SCOWP
SCOWPING > SCOWP
SCOWPS > SCOWP
SCOWRER n old word meaning hooligan
SCOWRERS > SCOWRER
SCOWRIE n young seagull
SCOWRIES > SCOWRIE
SCOWS > SCOW
SCOWTH n Scots word meaning plenty of scope
SCOWTHER vb Scots word meaning scorch
SCOWTHERS > SCOWTHER
SCOWTHS > SCOWTH
SCOZZA n rowdy person, esp one who drinks a lot of alcohol
SCOZZAS > SCOZZA
SCRAB vb scratch
SCRABBED > SCRAB
SCRABBING > SCRAB
SCRABBLE vb scrape at with the hands, feet, or claws ▷ n board game in which words are formed by letter tiles
SCRABBLED > SCRABBLE
SCRABBLER > SCRABBLE
SCRABBLES > SCRABBLE
SCRABBLY adj covered with stunted trees
SCRABS > SCRAB
SCRAE Scots word for > SCREE

SCRAES > SCRAE
SCRAG n thin end of a neck of mutton ▷ vb wring the neck of
SCRAGGED > SCRAG
SCRAGGIER > SCRAGGY
SCRAGGILY > SCRAGGY
SCRAGGING > SCRAG
SCRAGGLY adj untidy or irregular
SCRAGGY adj thin, bony
SCRAGS > SCRAG
SCRAICH vb Scots word meaning scream
SCRAICHED > SCRAICH
SCRAICHS > SCRAICH
SCRAIGH same as > SCRAICH
SCRAIGHED > SCRAIGH
SCRAIGHS > SCRAIGH
SCRAM vb go away quickly ▷ n emergency shutdown of a nuclear reactor
SCRAMB vb scratch with nails or claws
SCRAMBED > SCRAMB
SCRAMBING > SCRAMB
SCRAMBLE vb climb or crawl hastily or awkwardly ▷ n scrambling
SCRAMBLED > SCRAMBLE
SCRAMBLER n electronic device that makes transmitted speech unintelligible
SCRAMBLES > SCRAMBLE
SCRAMBS > SCRAMB
SCRAMJET n type of jet engine
SCRAMJETS > SCRAMJET
SCRAMMED > SCRAM
SCRAMMING > SCRAM
SCRAMS > SCRAM
SCRAN n food
SCRANCH vb crunch
SCRANCHED > SCRANCH
SCRANCHES > SCRANCH
SCRANNEL adj thin ▷ n thin person or thing
SCRANNELS > SCRANNEL
SCRANNIER > SCRANNY
SCRANNY adj scrawny
SCRANS > SCRAN
SCRAP n small piece ▷ vb discard as useless
SCRAPABLE > SCRAPE
SCRAPBOOK n book with blank pages in which newspaper cuttings or pictures are stuck ▷ vb keep (cuttings etc) in a scrapbook
SCRAPE vb rub with something rough or sharp ▷ n act or sound of scraping
SCRAPED > SCRAPE
SCRAPEGUT n old word for fiddle player
SCRAPER > SCRAPE
SCRAPERS > SCRAPE
SCRAPES > SCRAPE
SCRAPHEAP n pile of discarded material
SCRAPIE n disease of sheep and goats
SCRAPIES > SCRAPIE
SCRAPING n act of scraping
SCRAPINGS > SCRAPING

SCRAPPAGE n act of scrapping
SCRAPPED > SCRAP
SCRAPPER n person who scraps
SCRAPPERS > SCRAPPER
SCRAPPIER > SCRAPPY
SCRAPPILY > SCRAPPY
SCRAPPING n act of scrapping
SCRAPPLE n scraps of pork cooked with cornmeal and formed into a loaf
SCRAPPLES > SCRAPPLE
SCRAPPY adj fragmentary, disjointed
SCRAPS > SCRAP
SCRAPYARD n place for scrap metal
SCRAT vb scratch
SCRATCH vb mark or cut with anything rough or sharp ▷ n wound, mark, or sound made by scratching ▷ adj put together at short notice
SCRATCHED > SCRATCH
SCRATCHER n person, animal, or thing that scratches
SCRATCHES n disease of horses characterized by dermatitis in the region of the fetlock
SCRATCHIE n scratchcard
SCRATCHY > SCRATCH
SCRATS > SCRAT
SCRATTED > SCRAT
SCRATTING > SCRAT
SCRATTLE vb dialect word meaning scratch
SCRATTLED > SCRATTLE
SCRATTLES > SCRATTLE
SCRAUCH vb squawk
SCRAUCHED > SCRAUCH
SCRAUCHS > SCRAUCH
SCRAUGH vb squawk
SCRAUGHED > SCRAUGH
SCRAUGHS > SCRAUGH
SCRAVEL vb move quickly
SCRAVELED > SCRAVEL
SCRAVELS > SCRAVEL
SCRAW n sod from the surface of a peat bog or from a field
SCRAWB same as > SCROB
SCRAWBED > SCRAWB
SCRAWBING > SCRAWB
SCRAWBS > SCRAWB
SCRAWL vb write carelessly or hastily ▷ n scribbled writing
SCRAWLED > SCRAWL
SCRAWLER > SCRAWL
SCRAWLERS > SCRAWL
SCRAWLIER > SCRAWL
SCRAWLING > SCRAWL
SCRAWLS > SCRAWL
SCRAWLY > SCRAWL
SCRAWM vb dialect word meaning scratch
SCRAWMED > SCRAWM
SCRAWMING > SCRAWM
SCRAWMS > SCRAWM
SCRAWNIER > SCRAWNY
SCRAWNILY > SCRAWNY
SCRAWNY adj thin and bony
SCRAWP vb scratch (the skin) to relieve itching

SCRAWPED > SCRAWP
SCRAWPING > SCRAWP
SCRAWPS > SCRAWP
SCRAWS > SCRAW
SCRAY n tern
SCRAYE n tern
SCRAYES > SCRAYE
SCRAYS > SCRAY
SCREAK vb screech or creak ▷ n screech or creak
SCREAKED > SCREAK
SCREAKIER > SCREAK
SCREAKING n screeching or creaking
SCREAKS > SCREAK
SCREAKY > SCREAK
SCREAM vb utter a piercing cry, esp of fear or pain ▷ n shrill piercing cry
SCREAMED > SCREAM
SCREAMER n person or thing that screams
SCREAMERS > SCREAMER
SCREAMING n act or instance of screaming
SCREAMO n type of emo music featuring screaming vocals
SCREAMOS > SCREAMO
SCREAMS > SCREAM
SCREE n slope of loose shifting stones
SCREECH n shrill cry ▷ vb utter a shrill cry
SCREECHED > SCREECH
SCREECHER > SCREECH
SCREECHES > SCREECH
SCREECHY adj loud and shrill
SCREED n long tedious piece of writing ▷ vb rip
SCREEDED > SCREED
SCREEDER > SCREED
SCREEDERS > SCREED
SCREEDING > SCREED
SCREEDS > SCREED
SCREEN n surface of a television set, VDU, etc ▷ vb shelter or conceal with or as if with a screen
SCREENED > SCREEN
SCREENER > SCREEN
SCREENERS > SCREEN
SCREENFUL > SCREEN
SCREENIE n informal Australian word for screensaver
SCREENIES > SCREENIE
SCREENING > SCREEN
SCREENS > SCREEN
SCREES > SCREE
SCREET vb shed tears ▷ n act or sound of crying
SCREETED > SCREET
SCREETING > SCREET
SCREETS > SCREET
SCREEVE vb write
SCREEVED > SCREEVE
SCREEVER > SCREEVE
SCREEVERS > SCREEVE
SCREEVES > SCREEVE
SCREEVING > SCREEVE
SCREICH same as > SCREIGH
SCREICHED > SCREICH
SCREICHS > SCREICH
SCREIGH Scot word for > SCREECH

SCREIGHED > SCREIGH
SCREIGHS > SCREIGH
SCREW n metal pin with a spiral ridge along its length ▷ vb turn (a screw)
SCREWABLE > SCREW
SCREWBALL n odd or eccentric person ▷ adj crazy or eccentric
SCREWBEAN n variety of mesquite
SCREWED adj fastened by a screw or screws
SCREWER > SCREW
SCREWERS > SCREW
SCREWHEAD n head of a screw
SCREWIER > SCREWY
SCREWIEST > SCREWY
SCREWING > SCREW
SCREWINGS > SCREW
SCREWLIKE > SCREW
SCREWS > SCREW
SCREWTOP n lid with a threaded rim that is turned to close it securely
SCREWTOPS > SCREWTOP
SCREWUP n something done badly
SCREWUPS > SCREWUP
SCREWWORM n larva of a fly that develops beneath the skin of living mammals often causing illness or death
SCREWY adj crazy or eccentric
SCRIBABLE > SCRIBE
SCRIBAL > SCRIBE
SCRIBBLE vb write hastily or illegibly ▷ n something scribbled
SCRIBBLED > SCRIBBLE
SCRIBBLER n often derogatory term for a writer of poetry, novels, journalism, etc
SCRIBBLES > SCRIBBLE
SCRIBBLY > SCRIBBLE
SCRIBE n person who copies documents ▷ vb score a line with a pointed instrument
SCRIBED > SCRIBE
SCRIBER n pointed steel tool used to score materials as a guide to cutting, etc
SCRIBERS > SCRIBER
SCRIBES > SCRIBE
SCRIBING > SCRIBE
SCRIBINGS > SCRIBE
SCRIBISM > SCRIBE
SCRIBISMS > SCRIBE
SCRIECH vb Scots word meaning screech
SCRIECHED > SCRIECH
SCRIECHS > SCRIECH
SCRIED > SCRY
SCRIENE n old form of screen
SCRIENES > SCRIENE
SCRIES > SCRY
SCRIEVE vb Scots word meaning write
SCRIEVED > SCRIEVE
SCRIEVES > SCRIEVE
SCRIEVING > SCRIEVE
SCRIGGLE vb wriggle
SCRIGGLED > SCRIGGLE

SCRIGGLES > SCRIGGLE
SCRIGGLY > SCRIGGLE
SCRIKE vb old word meaning shriek
SCRIKED > SCRIKE
SCRIKES > SCRIKE
SCRIKING > SCRIKE
SCRIM n open-weave muslin or hessian fabric
SCRIMMAGE n rough or disorderly struggle ▷ vb engage in a scrimmage
SCRIMP vb be very economical
SCRIMPED > SCRIMP
SCRIMPER > SCRIMP
SCRIMPERS > SCRIMP
SCRIMPIER > SCRIMP
SCRIMPILY > SCRIMP
SCRIMPING n act of scrimping
SCRIMPIT adj Scots word meaning ungenerous
SCRIMPLY adv sparingly
SCRIMPS > SCRIMP
SCRIMPY > SCRIMP
SCRIMS > SCRIM
SCRIMSHAW n art of decorating or carving shells, etc, done by sailors as a leisure activity ▷ vb produce scrimshaw (from)
SCRIMURE old word for > FENCER
SCRIMURES > SCRIMURE
SCRINE n old form of shrine
SCRINES > SCRINE
SCRIP n certificate representing a claim to stocks or shares
SCRIPPAGE n contents of scrip
SCRIPS > SCRIP
SCRIPT n text of a film, play, or TV programme ▷ vb write a script for
SCRIPTED > SCRIPT
SCRIPTER n person who writes scripts for films, play, or television dramas
SCRIPTERS > SCRIPTER
SCRIPTING > SCRIPT
SCRIPTORY adj of writing
SCRIPTS > SCRIPT
SCRIPTURE n sacred writings of a religion
SCRITCH vb screech
SCRITCHED > SCRITCH
SCRITCHES > SCRITCH
SCRIVE Scots word for > WRITE
SCRIVED > SCRIVE
SCRIVENER n person who writes out deeds, letters, etc
SCRIVES > SCRIVE
SCRIVING > SCRIVE
SCROB vb scrape with claws
SCROBBED > SCROB
SCROBBING > SCROB
SCROBBLE vb record a person's music preferences in order to recommend similar music
SCROBBLED > SCROBBLE
SCROBBLES > SCROBBLE
SCROBE n groove
SCROBES > SCROBE

SCROBS > SCROB
SCROD n young cod or haddock
SCRODDLED adj made of scraps of pottery
SCRODS > SCROD
SCROFULA n tuberculosis of the lymphatic glands
SCROFULAS > SCROFULA
SCROG n Scots word meaning small tree
SCROGGIE adj having scrogs upon it
SCROGGIER > SCROGGIE
SCROGGIN n mixture of nuts and dried fruits
SCROGGINS > SCROGGIN
SCROGGY variant of > SCROGGIE
SCROGS > SCROG
SCROLL n roll of parchment or paper ▷ vb move (text) up or down on a VDU screen
SCROLLED > SCROLL
SCROLLER n person or thing that scrolls
SCROLLERS > SCROLLER
SCROLLING > SCROLL
SCROLLS > SCROLL
SCROME vb crawl or climb
SCROMED > SCROME
SCROMES > SCROME
SCROMING > SCROME
SCROOCH vb scratch (the skin) to relieve itching
SCROOCHED > SCROOCH
SCROOCHES > SCROOCH
SCROOGE variant of > SCROUGE
SCROOGED > SCROOGE
SCROOGES > SCROOGE
SCROOGING > SCROOGE
SCROOP vb emit a grating or creaking sound ▷ n such a sound
SCROOPED > SCROOP
SCROOPING > SCROOP
SCROOPS > SCROOP
SCROOTCH vb hunch up
SCRORP n deep scratch or weal
SCRORPS > SCRORP
SCROTA > SCROTUM
SCROTAL > SCROTUM
SCROTE n slang derogatory word meaning a worthless fellow
SCROTES > SCROTE
SCROTUM n pouch of skin containing the testicles
SCROTUMS > SCROTUM
SCROUGE vb crowd or press
SCROUGED > SCROUGE
SCROUGER n American word meaning whopper
SCROUGERS > SCROUGER
SCROUGES > SCROUGE
SCROUGING > SCROUGE
SCROUNGE vb get by cadging or begging
SCROUNGED > SCROUNGE
SCROUNGER > SCROUNGE
SCROUNGES > SCROUNGE
SCROUNGY adj shabby
SCROW n scroll
SCROWDGE vb squeeze
SCROWDGED > SCROWDGE

SCROWDGES > SCROWDGE
SCROWL vb old form of scroll
SCROWLE vb old form of scroll
SCROWLED > SCROWL
SCROWLES > SCROWLE
SCROWLING > SCROWL
SCROWLS > SCROWL
SCROWS > SCROW
SCROYLE n old word meaning wretch
SCROYLES > SCROYLE
SCRUB vb clean by rubbing, often with a hard brush and water ▷ n instance of scrubbing ▷ adj stunted or inferior
SCRUBBED > SCRUB
SCRUBBER n person or thing that scrubs
SCRUBBERS > SCRUBBER
SCRUBBIER > SCRUBBY
SCRUBBILY > SCRUBBY
SCRUBBING > SCRUB
SCRUBBY adj covered with scrub
SCRUBLAND n area of scrub vegetation
SCRUBS > SCRUB
SCRUFF same as > SCUM
SCRUFFED > SCRUFF
SCRUFFIER > SCRUFFY
SCRUFFILY > SCRUFFY
SCRUFFING > SCRUFF
SCRUFFS > SCRUFF
SCRUFFY adj unkempt or shabby
SCRUM n restarting of play in rugby ▷ vb form a scrum
SCRUMDOWN n forming of scrum in rugby
SCRUMMAGE same as > SCRUM
SCRUMMED > SCRUM
SCRUMMIE n informal word for a scrum half
SCRUMMIER > SCRUMMY
SCRUMMIES > SCRUMMIE
SCRUMMING > SCRUM
SCRUMMY adj delicious
SCRUMP vb steal (apples) from an orchard or garden
SCRUMPED > SCRUMP
SCRUMPIES > SCRUMPY
SCRUMPING > SCRUMP
SCRUMPLE vb crumple or crush
SCRUMPLED > SCRUMPLE
SCRUMPLES > SCRUMPLE
SCRUMPOX n skin infection spread among players in scrum
SCRUMPS > SCRUMP
SCRUMPY n rough dry cider
SCRUMS > SCRUM
SCRUNCH vb crumple or crunch or be crumpled or crunched ▷ n act or sound of scrunching
SCRUNCHED > SCRUNCH
SCRUNCHES > SCRUNCH
SCRUNCHIE n loop of elastic covered loosely with fabric, used to hold the hair in a ponytail
SCRUNCHIN n piece of deep-fried pork fat

SCRUNCHY adj crunchy

SCRUNT n Scots word meaning stunted thing

SCRUNTIER > SCRUNT

SCRUNTS > SCRUNT

SCRUNTY > SCRUNT

SCRUPLE n doubt produced by one's conscience or morals ▷ vb have doubts on moral grounds

SCRUPLED > SCRUPLE

SCRUPLER > SCRUPLE

SCRUPLERS > SCRUPLE

SCRUPLES > SCRUPLE

SCRUPLING > SCRUPLE

SCRUTABLE adj open to or able to be understood by scrutiny

SCRUTATOR n person who examines or scrutinizes

SCRUTINY n close examination

SCRUTO n trapdoor on stage

SCRUTOIRE n writing desk

SCRUTOS > SCRUTO

SCRUZE vb old word meaning squeeze

SCRUZED > SCRUZE

SCRUZES > SCRUZE

SCRUZING > SCRUZE

SCRY vb divine, esp by crystal gazing

SCRYDE > SCRY

SCRYER > SCRY

SCRYERS > SCRY

SCRYING > SCRY

SCRYINGS > SCRY

SCRYNE n old form of shrine

SCRYNES > SCRYNE

SCUBA n apparatus used in diving ▷ vb dive using scuba equipment

SCUBAED > SCUBA

SCUBAING > SCUBA

SCUBAS > SCUBA

SCUCHIN n old form of scutcheon

SCUCHINS > SCUCHIN

SCUD vb move along swiftly ▷ n act of scudding

SCUDDALER n Scots word meaning leader of festivities

SCUDDED > SCUD

SCUDDER > SCUD

SCUDDERS > SCUD

SCUDDING > SCUD

SCUDDLE vb scuttle

SCUDDLED > SCUDDLE

SCUDDLES > SCUDDLE

SCUDDLING > SCUDDLE

SCUDI > SCUDO

SCUDLER n Scots word meaning leader of festivities

SCUDLERS > SCUDLER

SCUDO n any of several former Italian coins

SCUDS > SCUD

SCUFF vb drag (the feet) while walking ▷ n mark caused by scuffing

SCUFFED > SCUFF

SCUFFER n type of sandal

SCUFFERS > SCUFFER

SCUFFING > SCUFF

SCUFFLE vb fight in a disorderly manner ▷ n disorderly struggle

SCUFFLED > SCUFFLE

SCUFFLER > SCUFFLE

SCUFFLERS > SCUFFLE

SCUFFLES > SCUFFLE

SCUFFLING n act of scuffling

SCUFFS > SCUFF

SCUFT n dialect word meaning nape of neck

SCUFTS > SCUFT

SCUG vb shelter

SCUGGED > SCUG

SCUGGING > SCUG

SCUGS > SCUG

SCUL n old form of school

SCULCH n rubbish

SCULCHES > SCULCH

SCULK vb old form of skulk

SCULKED > SCULK

SCULKER > SCULK

SCULKERS > SCULK

SCULKING > SCULK

SCULKS > SCULK

SCULL n small oar ▷ vb row (a boat) using sculls

SCULLE n old form of school

SCULLED > SCULL

SCULLER > SCULL

SCULLERS > SCULL

SCULLERY n small room where washing-up and other kitchen work is done

SCULLES > SCULLE

SCULLING > SCULL

SCULLINGS > SCULL

SCULLION n servant employed to do the hard work in a kitchen

SCULLIONS > SCULLION

SCULLS > SCULL

SCULP variant of > SCULPTURE

SCULPED > SCULP

SCULPIN n type of fish of the family which includes bullheads and sea scorpions

SCULPING > SCULP

SCULPINS > SCULPIN

SCULPS > SCULP

SCULPSIT vb (he or she) sculptured it: used formerly on sculptures next to a sculptor's name

SCULPT same as > SCULPTURE

SCULPTED > SCULPT

SCULPTING n act or practice of sculpting

SCULPTOR n person who makes sculptures

SCULPTORS > SCULPTOR

SCULPTS > SCULPT

SCULPTURE n art of making figures or designs in wood, stone, etc ▷ vb represent in sculpture

SCULS > SCUL

SCULTCH same as > SCULCH

SCULTCHES > SCULTCH

SCUM n impure or waste matter on the surface of a liquid ▷ vb remove scum from

SCUMBAG n offensive or despicable person

SCUMBAGS > SCUMBAG

SCUMBALL n contemptible person

SCUMBALLS > SCUMBALL

SCUMBER vb old word meaning defecate

SCUMBERED > SCUMBER

SCUMBERS > SCUMBER

SCUMBLE vb soften or blend (an outline or colour) with a thin upper coat of opaque colour ▷ n upper layer of colour applied in this way

SCUMBLED > SCUMBLE

SCUMBLES > SCUMBLE

SCUMBLING > SCUMBLE

SCUMFISH vb Scots word meaning disgust

SCUMLESS > SCUM

SCUMLIKE > SCUM

SCUMMED > SCUM

SCUMMER > SCUM

SCUMMERS > SCUM

SCUMMIER > SCUMMY

SCUMMIEST > SCUMMY

SCUMMILY > SCUMMY

SCUMMING > SCUM

SCUMMINGS > SCUM

SCUMMY adj of, resembling, consisting of, or covered with scum

SCUMS > SCUM

SCUNCHEON n inner part of a door jamb or window frame

SCUNDERED adj Irish dialect word for embarrassed

SCUNGE vb borrow ▷ n dirty or worthless person

SCUNGED > SCUNGE

SCUNGES > SCUNGE

SCUNGIER > SCUNGY

SCUNGIEST > SCUNGY

SCUNGILE same as > SCUNGILLE

SCUNGILI same as > SCUNGILLI

SCUNGILLE n meat of a conch, eaten as a delicacy

SCUNGILLI n seafood dish of conch

SCUNGING > SCUNGE

SCUNGY adj sordid or dirty

SCUNNER vb feel aversion ▷ n strong aversion

SCUNNERED adj annoyed, discontented, or bored

SCUNNERS > SCUNNER

SCUP n common sparid fish of American coastal regions of the Atlantic

SCUPPAUG n sea fish

SCUPPAUGS > SCUPPAUG

SCUPPER vb defeat or ruin ▷ n drain in the side of a ship

SCUPPERED > SCUPPER

SCUPPERS > SCUPPER

SCUPS > SCUP

SCUR n small unattached growth of horn at the site of a normal horn in cattle

SCURF n flaky skin on the scalp

SCURFIER > SCURF

SCURFIEST > SCURF

SCURFS > SCURF

SCURFY > SCURF

SCURRED > SCUR

SCURRIED > SCURRY

SCURRIER n old word meaning scout

SCURRIERS > SCURRIER

SCURRIES > SCURRY

SCURRIL adj old word meaning vulgar

SCURRILE adj old word meaning vulgar

SCURRING > SCUR

SCURRIOUR n old word meaning scout

SCURRY vb move hastily ▷ n act or sound of scurrying

SCURRYING > SCURRY

SCURS > SCUR

SCURVIER > SCURVY

SCURVIES > SCURVY

SCURVIEST > SCURVY

SCURVILY > SCURVY

SCURVY n disease caused by lack of vitamin C ▷ adj mean and despicable

SCUSE shortened form of > EXCUSE

SCUSED > SCUSE

SCUSES > SCUSE

SCUSING > SCUSE

SCUT n short tail of the hare, rabbit, or deer

SCUTA > SCUTUM

SCUTAGE n payment to a lord from his vassal in lieu of military service

SCUTAGES > SCUTAGE

SCUTAL > SCUTE

SCUTATE adj (of animals) having or covered with large bony or horny plates

SCUTATION > SCUTATE

SCUTCH vb separate the fibres from the woody part of (flax) by pounding ▷ n tool used for this

SCUTCHED > SCUTCH

SCUTCHEON same as > SHIELD

SCUTCHER same as > SCUTCH

SCUTCHERS > SCUTCHER

SCUTCHES > SCUTCH

SCUTCHING > SCUTCH

SCUTE n horny or chitinous plate that makes up part of the exoskeleton in armadillos, etc

SCUTELLA > SCUTELLUM

SCUTELLAR > SCUTELLUM

SCUTELLUM n last of three plates into which the notum of an insect's thorax is divided

SCUTES > SCUTE

SCUTIFORM adj (esp of plant parts) shaped like a shield

SCUTIGER n species of centipede

SCUTIGERS > SCUTIGER

SCUTS > SCUT

SCUTTER informal word for > SCURRY

SCUTTERED > SCUTTER

SCUTTERS > SCUTTER

SCUTTLE n fireside container for coal ▷ vb run with short quick steps

SCUTTLED > SCUTTLE

SCUTTLER > SCUTTLE
SCUTTLERS > SCUTTLE
SCUTTLES > SCUTTLE
SCUTTLING n act of scuttling
SCUTUM n middle of three plates into which the notum of an insect's thorax is divided
SCUTWORK n menial or dull work
SCUTWORKS > SCUTWORK
SCUZZ n dirt
SCUZZBAG n disagreeable or disgusting person
SCUZZBAGS > SCUZZBAG
SCUZZBALL n despicable person
SCUZZES > SCUZZ
SCUZZIER > SCUZZY
SCUZZIEST > SCUZZY
SCUZZY adj unkempt, dirty, or squalid
SCYBALA > SCYBALUM
SCYBALOUS > SCYBALUM
SCYBALUM n hard faeces in stomach
SCYE n Scots word meaning sleeve-hole
SCYES > SCYE
SCYPHATE adj shaped like cup
SCYPHI > SCYPHUS
SCYPHUS n ancient Greek two-handled drinking cup
SCYTALE n coded message in ancient Sparta
SCYTALES > SCYTALE
SCYTHE n long-handled tool with a curved blade for cutting grass ▷ vb cut with a scythe
SCYTHED > SCYTHE
SCYTHEMAN n scythe user
SCYTHEMEN > SCYTHEMAN
SCYTHER > SCYTHE
SCYTHERS > SCYTHE
SCYTHES > SCYTHE
SCYTHING > SCYTHE
SDAINE vb old form of disdain
SDAINED > SDAINE
SDAINES > SDAINE
SDAINING > SDAINE
SDAYN vb old form of disdain
SDAYNED > SDAYN
SDAYNING > SDAYN
SDAYNS > SDAYN
SDEIGN vb old form of disdain
SDEIGNE vb old form of disdain
SDEIGNED > SDEIGN
SDEIGNES > SDEIGNE
SDEIGNING > SDEIGN
SDEIGNS > SDEIGN
SDEIN vb old form of disdain
SDEINED > SDEIN
SDEINING > SDEIN
SDEINS > SDEIN
SEA n mass of salt water covering three quarters of the earth's surface
SEABAG n canvas bag for holding a sailor's belongings
SEABAGS > SEABAG
SEABANK n sea shore

SEABANKS > SEABANK
SEABEACH n beach at seaside
SEABED n bottom of sea
SEABEDS > SEABED
SEABIRD n bird that lives on the sea
SEABIRDS > SEABIRD
SEABLITE n prostrate annual plant of the goosefoot family
SEABLITES > SEABLITE
SEABOARD n coast
SEABOARDS > SEABOARD
SEABOOT n sailor's waterproof boot
SEABOOTS > SEABOOT
SEABORNE adj carried on or by the sea
SEABOTTLE n type of seaweed
SEABREAM n type of food fish of European seas
SEABREAMS > SEABREAM
SEACOAST n land bordering on the sea
SEACOASTS > SEACOAST
SEACOCK n valve in the hull of a vessel below the water line
SEACOCKS > SEACOCK
SEACRAFT n skill of a sailor
SEACRAFTS > SEACRAFT
SEACUNNY n steersman on an Indian ship
SEADOG another word for > FOGBOW
SEADOGS > SEADOG
SEADROME n aerodrome floating on sea
SEADROMES > SEADROME
SEAFARER n traveller who goes by sea
SEAFARERS > SEAFARER
SEAFARING adj working or travelling by sea ▷ n act of travelling by sea
SEAFLOOR n bottom of the sea
SEAFLOORS > SEAFLOOR
SEAFOAM n foam formed on the sea
SEAFOAMS > SEAFOAM
SEAFOLK n people who sail the sea
SEAFOLKS > SEAFOLK
SEAFOOD n edible saltwater fish or shellfish
SEAFOODS > SEAFOOD
SEAFOWL n seabird
SEAFOWLS > SEAFOWL
SEAFRONT n built-up area facing the sea
SEAFRONTS > SEAFRONT
SEAGIRT adj surrounded by the sea
SEAGOING adj built for travelling on the sea
SEAGRASS n grass which grows by or in the sea
SEAGULL n gull
SEAGULLS > SEAGULL
SEAHAWK n skua
SEAHAWKS > SEAHAWK
SEAHOG n porpoise
SEAHOGS > SEAHOG

SEAHORSE n marine fish with a horselike head that swims upright
SEAHORSES > SEAHORSE
SEAHOUND n dogfish
SEAHOUNDS > SEAHOUND
SEAKALE n European coastal plant
SEAKALES > SEAKALE
SEAKINDLY adj (of a ship) easy to sail
SEAL n piece of wax, etc attached to a document as a mark of authentication ▷ vb close with or as if with a seal
SEALABLE > SEAL
SEALANT n any substance used for sealing
SEALANTS > SEALANT
SEALCH Scots word for > SEAL
SEALCHS > SEALCH
SEALED adj (of a road) having a hard surface
SEALER n person or thing that seals
SEALERIES > SEALERY
SEALERS > SEALER
SEALERY n occupation of hunting seals
SEALGH Scots word for > SEAL
SEALGHS > SEALGH
SEALIFT vb transport by ship
SEALIFTED > SEALIFT
SEALIFTS > SEALIFT
SEALINE n company running regular sailings
SEALINES > SEALINE
SEALING > SEAL
SEALINGS > SEAL
SEALLIKE adj resembling a seal
SEALPOINT n popular variety of Siamese cat
SEALS > SEAL
SEALSKIN n skin or prepared fur of a seal, used to make coats
SEALSKINS > SEALSKIN
SEALWAX n sealing wax
SEALWAXES > SEALWAX
SEALYHAM n type of short-legged terrier
SEALYHAMS > SEALYHAM
SEAM n line where two edges are joined, as by stitching ▷ vb mark with furrows or wrinkles
SEAMAID n mermaid
SEAMAIDS > SEAMAID
SEAMAN n sailor
SEAMANLY adj like or appropriate to a seaman
SEAMARK n conspicuous object on a shore used as a guide
SEAMARKS > SEAMARK
SEAME n old word meaning grease
SEAMED > SEAM
SEAMEN > SEAMAN
SEAMER n bowler who makes the ball bounce on its seam
SEAMERS > SEAMER

SEAMES > SEAME
SEAMFREE adj having no seam
SEAMIER > SEAMY
SEAMIEST > SEAMY
SEAMINESS > SEAMY
SEAMING > SEAM
SEAMINGS > SEAMING
SEAMLESS adj (of a garment) without seams
SEAMLIKE > SEAM
SEAMOUNT n submarine mountain rising more than 1000 metres above the surrounding ocean floor
SEAMOUNTS > SEAMOUNT
SEAMS > SEAM
SEAMSET n tool for flattening seams in metal
SEAMSETS > SEAMSET
SEAMSTER n person who sews
SEAMSTERS > SEAMSTER
SEAMY adj sordid
SEAN vb fish with seine net
SEANCE n meeting at which spiritualists attempt to communicate with the dead
SEANCES > SEANCE
SEANED > SEAN
SEANING > SEAN
SEANNACHY n Highland genealogist, chronicler, or bard
SEANS > SEAN
SEAPIECE n artwork depicting sea
SEAPIECES > SEAPIECE
SEAPLANE n aircraft designed to take off from and land on water
SEAPLANES > SEAPLANE
SEAPORT n town or city with a harbour for boats and ships
SEAPORTS > SEAPORT
SEAQUAKE n agitation and disturbance of the sea caused by an earthquake at the sea bed
SEAQUAKES > SEAQUAKE
SEAQUARIA pl n areas of salt water where sea animals are kept
SEAR vb scorch, burn the surface of ▷ n mark caused by searing ▷ adj dried up
SEARAT n pirate
SEARATS > SEARAT
SEARCE vb sift
SEARCED > SEARCE
SEARCES > SEARCE
SEARCH vb examine closely in order to find something ▷ n instance of searching
SEARCHED > SEARCH
SEARCHER > SEARCH
SEARCHERS > SEARCH
SEARCHES > SEARCH
SEARCHING n act of searching
SEARCING > SEARCE
SEARE adj old word meaning dry and withered
SEARED > SEAR
SEARER > SEAR
SEAREST > SEAR
SEARING > SEAR

SEARINGLY > SEAR

SEARINGS > SEAR

SEARNESS > SEAR

SEAROBTN n type of American gurnard

SEAROBINS > SEAROBIN

SEARS > SEAR

SEAS > SEA

SEASCAPE n picture of a scene at sea

SEASCAPES > SEASCAPE

SEASCOUT n member of seagoing scouts

SEASCOUTS > SEASCOUT

SEASE vb old form of seize

SEASED > SEASE

SEASES > SEASE

SEASHELL n empty shell of a mollusc

SEASHELLS > SEASHELL

SEASHORE n land bordering on the sea

SEASHORES > SEASHORE

SEASICK adj suffering from nausea caused by the motion of a ship

SEASICKER > SEASICK

SEASIDE n area, esp a holiday resort, on the coast

SEASIDES > SEASIDE

SEASING > SEASE

SEASON n one of four divisions of the year ▷ vb flavour with salt, herbs, etc

SEASONAL adj depending on or varying with the seasons ▷ n seasonal thing

SEASONALS > SEASONAL

SEASONED > SEASON

SEASONER > SEASON

SEASONERS > SEASON

SEASONING n salt, herbs, etc added to food to enhance flavour

SEASONS > SEASON

SEASPEAK n language used by sailors

SEASPEAKS > SEASPEAK

SEASTRAND n seashore

SEASURE n old form of seizure

SEASURES > SEASURE

SEAT n thing designed or used for sitting on ▷ vb cause to sit

SEATBACK n back of seat

SEATBACKS > SEATBACK

SEATBELT n safety belt in vehicle

SEATBELTS > SEATBELT

SEATED > SEAT

SEATER n person or thing that seats

SEATERS > SEATER

SEATING n supply or arrangement of seats ▷ adj of or relating to the provision of places to sit

SEATINGS > SEATING

SEATLESS > SEAT

SEATMATE n person sitting in next seat

SEATMATES > SEATMATE

SEATRAIN n ship that can carry a train

SEATRAINS > SEATRAIN

SEATROUT n trout living in the sea

SEATROUTS > SEATROUT

SEATS > SEAT

SEATWORK n school work done at pupils' desks

SEATWORKS > SEATWORK

SEAWALL n wall built to prevent encroachment or erosion by the sea

SEAWALLED adj having a seawall

SEAWALLS > SEAWALL

SEAWAN n shell beads used by certain Native Americans as money

SEAWANS > SEAWAN

SEAWANT n Native American name for silver coins

SEAWANTS > SEAWANT

SEAWARD same as > SEAWARDS

SEAWARDLY > SEAWARD

SEAWARDS adv towards the sea

SEAWARE n any of numerous large coarse seaweeds

SEAWARES > SEAWARE

SEAWATER n water from sea

SEAWATERS > SEAWATER

SEAWAY n waterway giving access to an inland port

SEAWAYS > SEAWAY

SEAWEED n plant growing in the sea

SEAWEEDS > SEAWEED

SEAWEEDY adj full of seaweed

SEAWIFE n variety of sea fish

SEAWIVES > SEAWIFE

SEAWOMAN n mermaid

SEAWOMEN > SEAWOMAN

SEAWORM n marine worm

SEAWORMS > SEAWORM

SEAWORTHY adj (of a ship) in fit condition for a sea voyage

SEAZE vb old form of seize

SEAZED > SEAZE

SEAZES > SEAZE

SEAZING > SEAZE

SEBACEOUS adj of, like, or secreting fat or oil

SEBACIC adj derived from sebacic acid, a white crystalline acid

SEBASIC same as > SEBACIC

SEBATE n salt of sebacic acid

SEBATES > SEBATE

SEBESTEN n Asian tree

SEBESTENS > SEBESTEN

SEBIFIC adj producing fat

SEBORRHEA n skin disease in which excessive oil is secreted

SEBUM n oily substance secreted by the sebaceous glands

SEBUMS > SEBUM

SEBUNDIES > SEBUNDY

SEBUNDY n irregular soldier in India

SEC same as > SECANT

SECALOSE n type of sugar

SECALOSES > SECALOSE

SECANT n the ratio of the length of the hypotenuse to the length of the adjacent side

SECANTLY > SECANT

SECANTS > SECANT

SECATEUR n secateurs

SECATEURS pl n small pruning shears

SECCO n wall painting done on dried plaster with tempera

SECCOS > SECCO

SECEDE vb withdraw formally from a political alliance or federation

SECEDED > SECEDE

SECEDER > SECEDE

SECEDERS > SECEDE

SECEDES > SECEDE

SECEDING > SECEDE

SECERN vb (of a gland or follicle) to secrete

SECERNED > SECERN

SECERNENT > SECERN

SECERNING > SECERN

SECERNS > SECERN

SECESH n secessionist in US Civil War

SECESHER n secessionist in US Civil War

SECESHERS > SECESHER

SECESHES > SECESH

SECESSION n act of seceding

SECH n hyperbolic secant

SECHS > SECH

SECKEL variant of > SECKLE

SECKELS > SECKEL

SECKLE n type of pear

SECKLES > SECKLE

SECLUDE vb keep (a person) from contact with others

SECLUDED adj private, sheltered

SECLUDES > SECLUDE

SECLUDING > SECLUDE

SECLUSION n state of being secluded

SECLUSIVE adj tending to seclude

SECO adj (of wine) dry

SECODONT n animal with cutting back teeth

SECODONTS > SECODONT

SECONAL n tradename for secobarbital

SECONALS > SECONAL

SECOND adj coming directly after the first ▷ n person or thing coming second ▷ vb express formal support for (a motion proposed in a meeting)

SECONDARY adj of less importance ▷ n person or thing that is secondary

SECONDE n second of eight positions from which a parry or attack can be made in fencing

SECONDED > SECOND

SECONDEE n person who is seconded

SECONDEES > SECONDEE

SECONDER > SECOND

SECONDERS > SECOND

SECONDES > SECONDE

SECONDI > SECONDO

SECONDING n act of seconding

SECONDLY same as > SECOND

SECONDO n left-hand part in a piano duet

SECONDS > SECOND

SECPAR n distance unit in astronomy

SECPARS > SECPAR

SECRECIES > SECRECY

SECRECY n state of being secret

SECRET adj kept from the knowledge of others ▷ n something kept secret

SECRETA n secretions

SECRETAGE n use of mercury in treating furs

SECRETARY n person who deals with correspondence and general clerical work

SECRETE vb (of an organ, gland, etc) produce and release (a substance)

SECRETED > SECRETE

SECRETER > SECRET

SECRETES > SECRETE

SECRETEST > SECRET

SECRETIN n peptic hormone secreted by the mucosae of the duodenum and jejunum

SECRETING > SECRETE

SECRETINS > SECRETIN

SECRETION n substance that is released from a cell, organ, or gland

SECRETIVE adj inclined to keep things secret

SECRETLY > SECRET

SECRETOR > SECRETE

SECRETORS > SECRETE

SECRETORY adj of, relating to, or producing a secretion

SECRETS > SECRET

SECS > SEC

SECT n subdivision of a religious or political group

SECTARIAL > SECT

SECTARIAN adj of a sect ▷ n member of a sect

SECTARIES > SECTARY

SECTARY n member of a sect

SECTATOR n member of sect

SECTATORS > SECTATOR

SECTILE adj able to be cut smoothly

SECTILITY > SECTILE

SECTION n part cut off ▷ vb cut or divide into sections

SECTIONAL adj concerned with a particular area or group within a country or community

SECTIONED > SECTION

SECTIONS > SECTION

SECTOR n part or subdivision ▷ vb divide into sectors

SECTORAL > SECTOR

SECTORED > SECTOR

SECTORIAL adj of or relating to a sector

SECTORING > SECTOR

SECTORISE same as > SECTORIZE

SECTORIZE vb split into sectors

SECTORS > SECTOR

SECTS > SECT

SECULA > SECULUM

SECULAR adj worldly, as opposed to sacred ▷ n member of the secular clergy

SECULARLY > SECULAR

SECULARS > SECULAR

SECULUM n age in astronomy

SECULUMS > SECULUM

SECUND adj having or designating parts arranged on or turned to one side of the axis

SECUNDINE n one of the two integuments surrounding the ovule of a plant

SECUNDLY > SECUND

SECUNDUM adj according to

SECURABLE > SECURE

SECURANCE > SECURE

SECURE adj free from danger ▷ vb obtain

SECURED > SECURE

SECURELY > SECURE

SECURER > SECURE

SECURERS > SECURE

SECURES > SECURE

SECUREST > SECURE

SECURING > SECURE

SECURITAN n person believing they are secure

SECURITY n precautions against theft, espionage, or other danger

SED old spelling of > SAID

SEDAN same as > SALOON

SEDANS > SEDAN

SEDARIM > SEDER

SEDATE adj calm and dignified ▷ vb give a sedative drug to

SEDATED > SEDATE

SEDATELY > SEDATE

SEDATER > SEDATE

SEDATES > SEDATE

SEDATEST > SEDATE

SEDATING > SEDATE

SEDATION n state of calm, esp when brought about by sedatives

SEDATIONS > SEDATION

SEDATIVE adj having a soothing or calming effect ▷ n sedative drug

SEDATIVES > SEDATIVE

SEDENT adj seated

SEDENTARY adj done sitting down, involving little exercise

SEDER n Jewish ceremonial meal held on the first night or first two nights of Passover

SEDERS > SEDER

SEDERUNT n sitting of an ecclesiastical assembly, court, etc

SEDERUNTS > SEDERUNT

SEDES Latin word for > SEAT

SEDGE n coarse grasslike plant growing on wet ground

SEDGED adj having sedge

SEDGELAND n land covered with sedge

SEDGES > SEDGE

SEDGIER > SEDGE

SEDGIEST > SEDGE

SEDGY > SEDGE

SEDILE n seat for clergy in church

SEDILIA n group of three seats where the celebrant and ministers sit during High Mass

SEDILIUM n seat for clergy in church

SEDIMENT n matter which settles to the bottom of a liquid

SEDIMENTS > SEDIMENT

SEDITION n speech or action encouraging rebellion against the government

SEDITIONS > SEDITION

SEDITIOUS adj of, like, or causing sedition

SEDUCE vb win over or attract

SEDUCED > SEDUCE

SEDUCER n person who entices, allures, or seduces

SEDUCERS > SEDUCER

SEDUCES > SEDUCE

SEDUCIBLE > SEDUCE

SEDUCING > SEDUCE

SEDUCINGS > SEDUCE

SEDUCIVE adj seductive

SEDUCTION n act of seducing or the state of being seduced

SEDUCTIVE adj attractive, enticing

SEDUCTOR n person who seduces

SEDUCTORS > SEDUCTOR

SEDULITY > SEDULOUS

SEDULOUS adj diligent or persevering

SEDUM n rock plant

SEDUMS > SEDUM

SEE vb perceive with the eyes or mind ▷ n diocese of a bishop

SEEABLE > SEE

SEECATCH n male seal in Aleutians

SEED n mature fertilized grain of a plant ▷ vb sow with seed

SEEDBED n area of soil prepared for the growing of seedlings before they are transplanted

SEEDBEDS > SEEDBED

SEEDBOX n part of plant that contains seeds

SEEDBOXES > SEEDBED

SEEDCAKE n sweet cake flavoured with caraway seeds and lemon rind or essence

SEEDCAKES > SEEDCAKE

SEEDCASE n part of a fruit enclosing the seeds

SEEDCASES > SEEDCASE

SEEDEATER n bird feeding on seeds

SEEDED > SEED

SEEDER n person or thing that seeds

SEEDERS > SEEDER

SEEDHEAD n seed-containing part of a plant

SEEDHEADS > SEEDHEAD

SEEDIER > SEEDY

SEEDIEST > SEEDY

SEEDILY > SEEDY

SEEDINESS > SEEDY

SEEDING > SEED

SEEDINGS > SEED

SEEDLESS > SEED

SEEDLIKE > SEED

SEEDLING n young plant raised from a seed

SEEDLINGS > SEEDLING

SEEDLIP n basket holding seeds to be sown

SEEDLIPS > SEEDLIP

SEEDMAN n seller of seeds

SEEDMEN > SEEDMAN

SEEDNESS n old word meaning sowing of seeds

SEEDPOD n carpel enclosing the seeds of a flowering plant

SEEDPODS > SEEDPOD

SEEDS > SEED

SEEDSMAN n seller of seeds

SEEDSMEN > SEEDSMAN

SEEDSTOCK n livestock used for breeding

SEEDTIME n season when seeds are sown

SEEDTIMES > SEEDTIME

SEEDY adj shabby

SEEING > SEE

SEEINGS > SEE

SEEK vb try to find or obtain

SEEKER > SEEK

SEEKERS > SEEK

SEEKING > SEEK

SEEKS > SEEK

SEEL vb sew up the eyelids of (a hawk or falcon) so as to render it quiet and tame

SEELD adj old word meaning rare

SEELED > SEEL

SEELIE pl n good benevolent fairies

SEELIER > SEELY

SEELIEST > SEELY

SEELING > SEEL

SEELINGS > SEEL

SEELS > SEEL

SEELY adj old word meaning happy

SEEM vb appear to be

SEEMED > SEEM

SEEMER > SEEM

SEEMERS > SEEM

SEEMING adj apparent but not real ▷ n outward or false appearance

SEEMINGLY adv in appearance but not necessarily in actuality

SEEMINGS > SEEMING

SEEMLESS adj old word meaning unseemly

SEEMLIER > SEEMLY

SEEMLIEST > SEEMLY

SEEMLIHED n old word meaning seemliness

SEEMLY adj proper or fitting ▷ adv properly or decorously

SEEMLYHED n old word meaning seemliness

SEEMS > SEEM

SEEN > SEE

SEEP vb trickle through slowly, ooze ▷ n small spring or place where water, oil, etc has oozed through the ground

SEEPAGE n act or process of seeping

SEEPAGES > SEEPAGE

SEEPED > SEEP

SEEPIER > SEEPY

SEEPIEST > SEEPY

SEEPING > SEEP

SEEPS > SEEP

SEEPY adj tending to seep

SEER n person who sees

SEERESS > SEER

SEERESSES > SEER

SEERS > SEER

SEES > SEE

SEESAW n plank balanced in the middle so that two people seated on either end ride up and down alternately ▷ vb move up and down

SEESAWED > SEESAW

SEESAWING > SEESAW

SEESAWS > SEESAW

SEETHE vb be very agitated ▷ n act or state of seething

SEETHED > SEETHE

SEETHER > SEETHE

SEETHERS > SEETHE

SEETHES > SEETHE

SEETHING adj boiling or foaming as if boiling

SEETHINGS > SEETHING

SEEWING n suing

SEEWINGS > SEEWING

SEFER n scrolls of the Law

SEG n metal stud on shoe sole

SEGAR n cigar

SEGARS > SEGAR

SEGETAL adj (of weeds) growing amongst crops

SEGGAR n box in which pottery is baked

SEGGARS > SEGGAR

SEGHOL n pronunciation mark in Hebrew

SEGHOLATE n vowel sound in Hebrew

SEGHOLS > SEGHOL

SEGMENT n one of several sections into which something may be divided ▷ vb divide into segments

SEGMENTAL adj of, like, or having the form of a segment

SEGMENTED > SEGMENT

SEGMENTS > SEGMENT

SEGNI > SEGNO

SEGNO n sign at the beginning or end of a section directed to be repeated

SEGNOS > SEGNO

SEGO n American variety of lily

SEGOL variant of > SEGHOL

SEGOLATE variant of > SEGHOLATE

SEGOLATES > SEGOLATE

SEGOLS > SEGOL
SEGOS > SEGO
SEGREANT *adj* having raised wings in heraldry
SEGREGANT *n* organism different because of segregation
SEGREGATE *vb* set apart
SEGS > SEG
SEGUE *vb* proceed from one section or piece of music to another without a break ▷ *n* practice or an instance of playing music in this way
SEGUED > SEGUE
SEGUEING > SEGUE
SEGUES > SEGUE
SEGUGIO *n* Italian breed of dog
SEGUGIOS > SEGUGIO
SEHRI *n* meal eaten before sunrise by Muslims fasting during Ramadan
SEHRIS > SEHRI
SEI *n* type of rorqual
SEICENTO *n* 17th century with reference to Italian art and literature
SEICENTOS > SEICENTO
SEICHE *n* periodic oscillation of the surface of an enclosed or partially enclosed body of water
SEICHES > SEICHE
SEIDEL *n* vessel for drinking beer
SEIDELS > SEIDEL
SEIF *n* long ridge of blown sand in a desert
SEIFS > SEIF
SEIGNEUR *n* feudal lord
SEIGNEURS > SEIGNEUR
SEIGNEURY *n* estate of a seigneur
SEIGNIOR *n* (in England) the lord of a seigniory
SEIGNIORS > SEIGNIOR
SEIGNIORY *n* (in England) the fee or manor of a seignior
SEIGNORAL *adj* relating to the quality of being a lord
SEIGNORY *n* lordship
SEIK *Scot word for* **>** SICK
SEIKER > SEIK
SEIKEST > SEIK
SEIL *vb* dialect word meaning strain
SEILED > SEIL
SEILING > SEIL
SEILS > SEIL
SEINE *n* large fishing net that hangs vertically from floats ▷ *vb* catch (fish) using this net
SEINED > SEINE
SEINER > SEINE
SEINERS > SEINE
SEINES > SEINE
SEINING > SEINE
SEININGS > SEINE
SEIR *n* fish of Indian seas
SEIRS > SEIR
SEIS > SEI
SEISABLE > SEISE
SEISE *vb* put into legal possession of (property, etc)
SEISED > SEISE

SEISER > SEISE
SEISERS > SEISE
SEISES > SEISE
SEISIN *n* feudal possession of an estate in land
SEISING > SEISE
SEISINGS > SEISE
SEISINS > SEISIN
SEISM *n* earthquake
SEISMAL *adj* of earthquakes
SEISMIC *adj* relating to earthquakes
SEISMICAL *same as* **>** SEISMIC
SEISMISM *n* occurrence of earthquakes
SEISMISMS > SEISMISM
SEISMS > SEISM
SEISOR *n* person who takes seisin
SEISORS > SEISOR
SEISURE *n* act of seisin
SEISURES > SEISURE
SEITAN *same as* **>** SEITEN
SEITANS > SEITAN
SEITEN *n* gluten from wheat
SEITENS > SEITEN
SEITIES > SEITY
SEITY *n* selfhood
SEIZA *n* traditional Japanese kneeling position
SEIZABLE > SEIZE
SEIZAS > SEIZA
SEIZE *vb* take hold of forcibly or quickly
SEIZED > SEIZE
SEIZER > SEIZE
SEIZERS > SEIZE
SEIZES > SEIZE
SEIZIN *same as* **>** SEISIN
SEIZING *n* binding used for holding together two ropes, two spars, etc
SEIZINGS > SEIZING
SEIZINS > SEIZIN
SEIZOR *n* person who takes seisin
SEIZORS > SEIZOR
SEIZURE *n* sudden violent attack of an illness
SEIZURES > SEIZURE
SEJANT *adj* (of a beast) shown seated
SEJEANT *same as* **>** SEJANT
SEKOS *n* holy place
SEKOSES > SEKOS
SEKT *n* German sparkling wine
SEKTS > SEKT
SEL *Scot word for* **>** SELF
SELACHIAN *adj* relating to a large subclass of cartilaginous fishes including the sharks, rays, dogfish, and skates ▷ *n* any fish belonging to this subclass
SELADANG *n* Malaysian tapir
SELADANGS > SELADANG
SELAH *n* Hebrew word of unknown meaning occurring in the Old Testament psalms
SELAHS > SELAH
SELAMLIK *n* men's quarters in Turkish house

SELAMLIKS > SELAMLIK
SELCOUTH *adj* old word meaning strange
SELD *adj* old word meaning rare
SELDOM *adv* not often, rarely
SELDOMLY > SELDOM
SELDSEEN *adj* old word meaning seldom seen
SELDSHOWN *adj* old word meaning seldom shown
SELE *n* old word meaning happiness
SELECT *vb* pick out or choose ▷ *adj* chosen in preference to others
SELECTA *n* disc jockey
SELECTAS > SELECTA
SELECTED > SELECT
SELECTEE *n* person who is selected, esp for military service
SELECTEES > SELECTEE
SELECTING > SELECT
SELECTION *n* selecting
SELECTIVE *adj* chosen or choosing carefully
SELECTLY > SELECT
SELECTMAN *n* any of the members of the local boards of most New England towns
SELECTMEN > SELECTMAN
SELECTOR *n* person or thing that selects
SELECTORS > SELECTOR
SELECTS > SELECT
SELENATE *n* any salt or ester formed by replacing one or both of the hydrogens of selenic acid with metal ions or organic groups
SELENATES > SELENATE
SELENIAN *adj* of the moon
SELENIC *adj* of or containing selenium, esp in the hexavalent state
SELENIDE *n* compound containing selenium
SELENIDES > SELENIDE
SELENIOUS *adj* of or containing selenium in the divalent or tetravalent state
SELENITE *n* colourless glassy variety of gypsum
SELENITES > SELENITE
SELENITIC > SELENITE
SELENIUM *n* nonmetallic element with photoelectric properties
SELENIUMS > SELENIUM
SELENOSES > SELENOSIS
SELENOSIS *n* poisoned condition caused by selenium
SELENOUS *same as* **>** SELENIOUS
SELES > SELE
SELF *n* distinct individuality or identity of a person or thing ▷ *pron* myself, yourself, himself, or herself ▷ *vb* reproduce by oneself
SELFDOM *n* selfhood
SELFDOMS > SELFDOM
SELFED > SELF
SELFHEAL *n* low-growing European herbaceous plant
SELFHEALS > SELFHEAL

SELFHOOD *n* state of having a distinct identity
SELFHOODS > SELFHOOD
SELFIE *n* photograph taken by pointing a camera at oneself
SELFIES > SELFIE
SELFING > SELF
SELFINGS > SELF
SELFISH *adj* caring too much about oneself and not enough about others
SELFISHLY > SELFISH
SELFISM *n* emphasis on self
SELFISMS > SELFISM
SELFIST > SELFISM
SELFISTS > SELFISM
SELFLESS *adj* unselfish
SELFNESS *n* egotism
SELFS > SELF
SELFSAME *adj* very same
SELFWARD *adj* toward self
SELFWARDS *adv* towards self
SELICTAR *n* Turkish sword-bearer
SELICTARS > SELICTAR
SELKIE *same as* **>** SILKIE
SELKIES > SELKIE
SELL *vb* exchange (something) for money ▷ *n* manner of selling
SELLABLE > SELL
SELLAE > SELLA
SELLAS > SELLA
SELLE *n* old word meaning seat
SELLER *n* person who sells
SELLERS > SELLER
SELLES > SELLE
SELLING *n* providing goods or services to customers in exchange for money
SELLINGS > SELLING
SELLOFF *n* act of selling cheaply
SELLOFFS > SELLOFF
SELLOTAPE *n* tradename for a type of transparent adhesive tape
SELLOUT *n* performance of a show etc for which all the tickets are sold
SELLOUTS > SELLOUT
SELLS > SELL
SELS > SEL
SELSYN *same as* **>** SYNCHRO
SELSYNS > SELSYN
SELTZER *n* natural effervescent water containing minerals
SELTZERS > SELTZER
SELVA *n* dense equatorial forest
SELVAGE *n* edge of cloth, woven so as to prevent unravelling ▷ *vb* edge or border
SELVAGED > SELVAGE
SELVAGEE *n* rope used as strap
SELVAGEES > SELVAGEE
SELVAGES > SELVAGE
SELVAGING > SELVAGE
SELVAS > SELVA
SELVEDGE *same as* **>** SELVAGE

SELLA *n* area of bone in body

SEIGUGIO (entry) — *Italian breed of dog*

SELVEDGED > SELVEDGE

SELVEDGES > SELVEDGE

SELVES > SELF

SEMAINIER n chest of drawers

SEMANTEME same as > SEMEME

SEMANTIC adj relating to the meaning of words

SEMANTICS n study of linguistic meaning

SEMANTIDE n type of molecule

SEMANTRA > SEMANTRON

SEMANTRON n bar struck instead of bell in Orthodox church

SEMAPHORE n system of signalling by holding two flags in different positions to represent letters of the alphabet ▷ vb signal (information) by semaphore

SEMATIC adj acting as a warning, esp to potential predators

SEMBLABLE adj resembling or similar ▷ n something that resembles another thing

SEMBLABLY > SEMBLABLE

SEMBLANCE n outward or superficial appearance

SEMBLANT n semblance

SEMBLANTS > SEMBLANT

SEMBLE vb seem

SEMBLED > SEMBLE

SEMBLES > SEMBLE

SEMBLING > SEMBLE

SEME adj dotted (with)

SEMEE variant of > SEME

SEMEED adj seme

SEMEIA > SEMEION

SEMEION n unit of metre in ancient poetry

SEMEIOTIC same as > SEMIOTIC

SEMEME n meaning of a morpheme

SEMEMES > SEMEME

SEMEMIC > SEMEME

SEMEN n sperm-carrying fluid produced by male animals

SEMENS > SEMEN

SEMES > SEME

SEMESTER vb organize the academic year into two divisions

SEMESTERS > SEMESTER

SEMESTRAL > SEMESTER

SEMI n semidetached house

SEMIANGLE n half angle

SEMIARID adj denoting land that lies on the edges of a desert but has a slightly higher rainfall

SEMIBALD adj partly bald

SEMIBOLD adj denoting a weight of typeface between medium and bold face ▷ n semibold type

SEMIBOLDS > SEMIBOLD

SEMIBREVE n musical note four beats long

SEMIBULL n papal bull issued before coronation

SEMIBULLS > SEMIBULL

SEMICOLON n punctuation mark (;)

SEMICOMA n condition similar to a coma

SEMICOMAS > SEMICOMA

SEMICURED adj partly cured

SEMIDEAF adj partly deaf

SEMIDEIFY vb treat almost as a god

SEMIDOME n half-dome, esp one used to cover a semicircular apse

SEMIDOMED adj having semidome

SEMIDOMES > SEMIDOME

SEMIDRIER > SEMIDRY

SEMIDRY adj partly dry

SEMIDWARF adj smaller than standard variety

SEMIE n historical name for a student in second year at a Scottish university

SEMIERECT adj partly erect

SEMIES > SEMIE

SEMIFINAL n match or round before the final

SEMIFIT adj not fully fit

SEMIFLUID adj having properties between those of a liquid and those of a solid ▷ n substance that has such properties because of high viscosity

SEMIGALA adj characterized by quite a lot of celebration and fun ▷ n occasion that is festive but not to the degree of a gala

SEMIGALAS > SEMIGALA

SEMIGLOBE n half globe

SEMIGLOSS adj (of paint) giving finish between matt and gloss

SEMIGROUP n type of set in mathematics

SEMIHARD adj partly hard

SEMIHIGH adj moderately high

SEMIHOBO n person looking almost like hobo

SEMIHOBOS > SEMIHOBO

SEMILLON n grape used to make wine

SEMILLONS > SEMILLON

SEMILOG adj semilogarithmic

SEMILUNAR adj shaped like a crescent or half-moon

SEMILUNE n half-moon shape

SEMILUNES > SEMILUNE

SEMIMAT adj semimatt

SEMIMATT adj with surface midway between matt and gloss

SEMIMATTE adj semimatt

SEMIMETAL n metal not fully malleable

SEMIMICRO adj using microwaves

SEMIMILD adj somewhat mild

SEMIMOIST adj slightly wet

SEMIMUTE adj old-fashioned word meaning having a speech impairment ▷ n old-fashioned word for a person who has a speech impairment

SEMIMUTES > SEMIMUTE

SEMINA > SEMEN

SEMINAL adj original and influential

SEMINALLY > SEMINAL

SEMINAR n meeting of a group of students for discussion

SEMINARS > SEMINAR

SEMINARY n college for priests

SEMINATE vb sow

SEMINATED > SEMINATE

SEMINATES > SEMINATE

SEMINOMA n malignant tumour of the testicle

SEMINOMAD n person living partly nomadic life

SEMINOMAS > SEMINOMA

SEMINUDE adj partly nude

SEMIOLOGY same as > SEMIOTICS

SEMIOPEN adj half-open

SEMIOSES > SEMIOSIS

SEMIOSIS n action involving establishing a relationship between signs

SEMIOTIC adj relating to signs and symbols, esp spoken or written signs

SEMIOTICS n study of human communications, esp signs and symbols

SEMIOVAL adj shaped like half of an oval

SEMIPED n measure in poetic metre

SEMIPEDS > SEMIPED

SEMIPIOUS adj quite pious

SEMIPLUME n type of bird feather

SEMIPOLAR adj as in semipolar bond type of chemical bond

SEMIPRO n semiprofessional

SEMIPROS > SEMIPRO

SEMIRAW adj not fully cooked or processed

SEMIRIGID adj (of an airship) maintaining shape by means of a main supporting keel and internal gas pressure

SEMIROUND adj with one flat side and one round side ▷ n something semiround

SEMIRURAL adj partly rural

SEMIS n ancient Roman coin

SEMISES > SEMIS

SEMISOFT adj partly soft

SEMISOLID adj having a viscosity and rigidity intermediate between that of a solid and a liquid ▷ n substance in this state

SEMISOLUS n advertisement that appears on the same page as another advertisement but not adjacent to it

SEMISTIFF adj partly stiff

SEMISWEET adj partly sweet

SEMITAR old spelling of > SCIMITAR

SEMITARS > SEMITAR

SEMITAUR old spelling of > SCIMITAR

SEMITAURS > SEMITAR

SEMITIST n student of Semitic languages and culture

SEMITISTS > SEMITIST

SEMITONAL > SEMITONE

SEMITONE n smallest interval between two notes in Western music

SEMITONES > SEMITONE

SEMITONIC > SEMITONE

SEMITRUCK n articulated lorry

SEMIURBAN adj suburban

SEMIVOCAL adj of or relating to a semivowel

SEMIVOWEL n vowel-like sound that acts like a consonant, such as the sound w in well

SEMIWATER adj as in semiwater gas a mixed gas of steam and air

SEMIWILD adj not fully domesticated

SEMIWORKS adj equipped to manufacture but not in great numbers

SEMMIT n Scots word meaning a vest

SEMMITS > SEMMIT

SEMOLINA n hard grains of wheat left after the milling of flour, used to make puddings and pasta

SEMOLINAS > SEMOLINA

SEMPER adv Latin word meaning always

SEMPLE adj Scots word meaning simple

SEMPLER > SEMPLE

SEMPLEST > SEMPLE

SEMPLICE adv performed in a simple manner

SEMPRE adv (preceding a tempo or dynamic marking) always

SEMPSTER n person who sews

SEMPSTERS > SEMPSTER

SEMSEM n sesame

SEMSEMS > SEMSEM

SEMUNCIA n ancient Roman coin

SEMUNCIAE > SEMUNCIA

SEMUNCIAL > SEMUNCIA

SEMUNCIAS > SEMUNCIA

SEN n monetary unit of Brunei, Cambodia, Indonesia, Malaysia, and formerly of Japan

SENA n (in India) the army

SENARIES > SENARY

SENARII > SENARIUS

SENARIUS n type of poem

SENARY adj of or relating to the number six

SENAS > SENA

SENATE n main governing body at some universities

SENATES > SENATE

SENATOR n member of a senate

SENATORS > SENATOR

SEND vb cause (a person or thing) to go to or be taken or transmitted to a place

SENDABLE > SEND

SENDAL n fine silk fabric used for ceremonial clothing, etc

SENDALS > SENDAL

SENDED vb old word meaning sent

SENDER > SEND

SENDERS > SEND

SENDING > SEND

SENDINGS > SEND

SENDOFF n demonstration of good wishes at a person's departure ▷ vb dispatch (something, such as a letter)

SENDOFFS > SENDOFF

SENDS > SEND

SENDUP n parody or imitation

SENDUPS > SENDUP

SENE n money unit in Samoa

SENECA variant of > SENEGA

SENECAS > SENECA

SENECIO n type of plant of the genus which includes groundsels and ragworts

SENECIOS > SENECIO

SENEGA n milkwort plant of the eastern US

SENEGAS > SENEGA

SENES > SENE

SENESCE vb grow old

SENESCED > SENESCE

SENESCENT adj growing old

SENESCES > SENESCE

SENESCHAL n steward of the household of a medieval prince or nobleman

SENESCING > SENESCE

SENGI n African shrew

SENGIS > SENGI

SENGREEN n house leek

SENGREENS > SENGREEN

SENHOR n Portuguese term of address for man

SENHORA n Portuguese term of address for woman

SENHORAS > SENHORA

SENHORES > SENHOR

SENHORITA n Portuguese term of address for girl

SENHORS > SENHOR

SENILE adj mentally or physically weak because of old age ▷ n senile person

SENILELY > SENILE

SENILES > SENILE

SENILITY > SENILE

SENIOR adj superior in rank or standing ▷ n senior person

SENIORITY n state of being senior

SENIORS > SENIOR

SENITI n money unit in Tonga

SENITIS > SENITI

SENNA n tropical plant

SENNACHIE n Gaelic storyteller

SENNAS > SENNA

SENNET n fanfare: used as a stage direction in Elizabethan drama

SENNETS > SENNET

SENNIGHT archaic word for > WEEK

SENNIGHTS > SENNIGHT

SENNIT n flat braided cordage used on ships

SENNITS > SENNIT

SENOPIA n short-sightedness in old age

SENOPIAS > SENOPIA

SENOR n Spanish term of address equivalent to sir or Mr

SENORA n Spanish term of address equivalent to madam or Mrs

SENORAS > SENORA

SENORES > SENOR

SENORITA n Spanish term of address equivalent to madam or Miss

SENORITAS > SENORITA

SENORS > SENOR

SENRYU n Japanese short poem

SENS > SEN

SENSA > SENSUM

SENSATE adj perceived by the senses ▷ vb make sensate

SENSATED > SENSATE

SENSATELY > SENSATE

SENSATES > SENSATE

SENSATING > SENSATE

SENSATION n ability to feel things physically

SENSE n any of the faculties of perception or feeling ▷ vb perceive

SENSED > SENSE

SENSEFUL adj full of sense

SENSEI n martial arts teacher

SENSEIS > SENSEI

SENSELESS adj foolish

SENSES > SENSE

SENSI same as > SENSEI

SENSIBLE adj having or showing good sense ▷ n sensible thing or person

SENSIBLER > SENSIBLE

SENSIBLES > SENSIBLE

SENSIBLY > SENSIBLE

SENSILE adj capable of feeling

SENSILLA > SENSILLUM

SENSILLAE > SENSILLUM

SENSILLUM n sense organ in insects

SENSING > SENSE

SENSINGS > SENSE

SENSIS > SENSI

SENSISM n theory that ideas spring from senses

SENSISMS > SENSISM

SENSIST > SENSISM

SENSISTS > SENSISM

SENSITISE same as > SENSITIZE

SENSITIVE adj easily hurt or offended

SENSITIZE vb make sensitive

SENSOR n device that detects or measures the presence of something, such as radiation

SENSORIA > SENSORIUM

SENSORIAL same as > SENSORY

SENSORILY > SENSORY

SENSORIUM n area of the brain considered responsible for receiving and integrating sensations from the outside world

SENSORS > SENSOR

SENSORY adj of the senses or sensation

SENSUAL adj giving pleasure to the body and senses rather than the mind

SENSUALLY > SENSUAL

SENSUM n sensation detached from the information it conveys

SENSUOUS adj pleasing to the senses

SENT n former monetary unit of Estonia ▷ vb old spelling of scent

SENTE n money unit in Lesotho

SENTED > SENT

SENTENCE n sequence of words capable of standing alone as a statement, question, or command ▷ vb pass sentence on (a convicted person)

SENTENCED > SENTENCE

SENTENCER > SENTENCE

SENTENCES > SENTENCE

SENTENTIA n opinion

SENTI > SENT

SENTIENCE n state or quality of being sentient

SENTIENCY same as > SENTIENCE

SENTIENT adj capable of feeling ▷ n sentient person or thing

SENTIENTS > SENTIENT

SENTIMENT n thought, opinion, or attitude

SENTIMO n money unit in Philippines

SENTIMOS > SENTIMO

SENTINEL n sentry ▷ vb guard as a sentinel

SENTINELS > SENTINEL

SENTING > SENT

SENTRIES > SENTRY

SENTRY n soldier on watch

SENTS > SENT

SENVIES > SENVY

SENVY n mustard

SENZA prep without

SEPAD vb suppose

SEPADDED > SEPAD

SEPADDING > SEPAD

SEPADS > SEPAD

SEPAL n leaflike division of the calyx of a flower

SEPALED > SEPAL

SEPALINE same as > SEPALOID

SEPALLED > SEPAL

SEPALODY n changing of a flower part into a sepal

SEPALOID adj (esp of petals) resembling a sepal in structure and function

SEPALOUS adj with sepals

SEPALS > SEPAL

SEPARABLE adj able to be separated

SEPARABLY > SEPARABLE

SEPARATA > SEPARATUM

SEPARATE vb act as a barrier between ▷ adj not the same, different ▷ n item of clothing that only covers half the body

SEPARATED > SEPARATE

SEPARATES > SEPARATE

SEPARATOR n person or thing that separates

SEPARATUM n separate printing of article from magazine

SEPHEN n stingray

SEPHENS > SEPHEN

SEPIA n reddish-brown pigment ▷ adj dark reddish-brown

SEPIAS > SEPIA

SEPIC adj of sepia

SEPIMENT n hedge

SEPIMENTS > SEPIMENT

SEPIOLITE n meerschaum

SEPIOST n cuttlefish bone

SEPIOSTS > SEPIOST

SEPIUM n cuttlefish bone

SEPIUMS > SEPIUM

SEPMAG adj designating a film, etc for which the sound is recorded on separate magnetic material

SEPOY n (formerly) Indian soldier in the service of the British

SEPOYS > SEPOY

SEPPUKU n Japanese ritual suicide

SEPPUKUS > SEPPUKU

SEPS n species of lizard

SEPSES > SEPSIS

SEPSIS n poisoning caused by pus-forming bacteria

SEPT n clan, esp in Ireland or Scotland

SEPTA > SEPTUM

SEPTAGE n waste removed from septic tank

SEPTAGES > SEPTAGE

SEPTAL adj of or relating to a septum

SEPTARIA > SEPTARIUM

SEPTARIAN > SEPTARIUM

SEPTARIUM n mass of mineral substance having cracks filled with another mineral

SEPTATE adj divided by septa

SEPTATION n division by partitions

SEPTEMFID adj divided into seven

SEPTEMVIR n member of government of seven people

SEPTENARY adj of or relating to the number seven ▷ n number seven

SEPTENNIA pl n cycles of seven years

SEPTET n group of seven performers

SEPTETS > SEPTET

SEPTETTE same as > SEPTET

SEPTETTES > SEPTETTE

SEPTIC adj (of a wound) infected ▷ n infected wound

SEPTICAL > SEPTIC

SEPTICITY > SEPTIC
SEPTICS > SEPTIC
SEPTIFORM adj acting as partition
SEPTIMAL adj of number seven
SEPTIME n seventh of eight basic positions from which a parry can be made in fencing
SEPTIMES > SEPTIME
SEPTIMOLE n group of seven musical notes
SEPTLEVA n gambling term from old card game
SEPTLEVAS > SEPTLEVA
SEPTORIA n any of various parasitic fungi
SEPTORIAS > SEPTORIA
SEPTS > SEPT
SEPTUM n dividing partition between two cavities in the body
SEPTUMS > SEPTUM
SEPTUOR n group of seven musicians
SEPTUORS > SEPTUOR
SEPTUPLE vb multiply by seven ▷ adj seven times as much or as many ▷ n quantity or number seven times as great as another
SEPTUPLED > SEPTUPLE
SEPTUPLES > SEPTUPLE
SEPTUPLET n group of seven notes played in a time value of six, eight, etc
SEPULCHER same as > SEPULCHRE
SEPULCHRE n tomb or burial vault ▷ vb bury in a sepulchre
SEPULTURE n act of placing in a sepulchre
SEQUACITY n quality of being pliant or controllable
SEQUEL n novel, play, or film that continues the story of an earlier one.
SEQUELA n disease related to or arising from a pre-existing disease
SEQUELAE > SEQUELA
SEQUELISE same as > SEQUELIZE
SEQUELIZE vb create sequel to
SEQUELS > SEQUEL
SEQUENCE n arrangement of two or more things in successive order ▷ vb arrange in a sequence
SEQUENCED > SEQUENCE
SEQUENCER n electronic device that determines the order in which a number of operations occur
SEQUENCES > SEQUENCE
SEQUENCY n number of changes in a mathematical list
SEQUENT adj following in order or succession ▷ n something that follows
SEQUENTLY > SEQUENT
SEQUENTS > SEQUENT
SEQUESTER vb seclude
SEQUESTRA pl n detached pieces of necrotic bone that often migrate to wounds

SEQUIN n small ornamental metal disc on a garment ▷ vb apply sequins
SEQUINED > SEQUIN
SEQUINING > SEQUIN
SEQUINNED > SEQUIN
SEQUINS > SEQUIN
SEQUITUR n conclusion that follows from the premises
SEQUITURS > SEQUITUR
SEQUOIA n giant Californian coniferous tree
SEQUOIAS > SEQUOIA
SER n unit of weight used in India
SERA > SERUM
SERAC n pinnacle of ice among crevasses on a glacier, usually on a steep slope
SERACS > SERAC
SERAFILE n line of soldiers
SERAFILES > SERAFILE
SERAFIN n old silver coin of Goa
SERAFINS > SERAFIN
SERAGLIO n sultan's palace
SERAGLIOS > SERAGLIO
SERAI n caravanserai or inn
SERAIL same as > SERAGLIO
SERAILS > SERAIL
SERAIS > SERAI
SERAL > SERE
SERANG n native captain of a crew of sailors in the East Indies
SERANGS > SERANG
SERAPE n blanket-like shawl often of brightly-coloured wool
SERAPES > SERAPE
SERAPH n member of the highest order of angels
SERAPHIC adj of or resembling a seraph
SERAPHIM > SERAPH
SERAPHIMS > SERAPH
SERAPHIN n angel
SERAPHINE n old keyboard instrument
SERAPHINS > SERAPHIN
SERAPHS > SERAPH
SERASKIER n Turkish military leader
SERDAB n secret chamber in an ancient Egyptian tomb
SERDABS > SERDAB
SERE adj dried up or withered ▷ n series of changes occurring in the ecological succession of a particular community ▷ vb sear
SERED > SERE
SEREIN n fine rain falling from a clear sky after sunset
SEREINS > SEREIN
SERENADE n music played or sung to a person by an admirer ▷ vb sing or play a serenade to (someone)
SERENADED > SERENADE
SERENADER > SERENADE
SERENADES > SERENADE
SERENATA n 18th-century cantata, often dramatic in form

SERENATAS > SERENATA
SERENATE n old form of serenade ▷ vb make serene
SERENATED > SERENATE
SERENATES > SERENATE
SERENE adj calm, peaceful ▷ vb make serene
SERENED > SERENE
SERENELY > SERENE
SERENER > SERENE
SERENES > SERENE
SERENEST > SERENE
SERENING > SERENE
SERENITY n state or quality of being serene
SERER > SERE
SERES > SERE
SEREST > SERE
SERF n medieval farm labourer who could not leave the land they worked on
SERFAGE > SERF
SERFAGES > SERF
SERFDOM > SERF
SERFDOMS > SERF
SERFHOOD > SERF
SERFHOODS > SERF
SERFISH > SERF
SERFLIKE > SERF
SERFS > SERF
SERFSHIP > SERF
SERFSHIPS > SERF
SERGE n strong woollen fabric
SERGEANCY > SERGEANT
SERGEANT n noncommissioned officer in the army
SERGEANTS > SERGEANT
SERGEANTY n form of feudal tenure
SERGED adj with sewn seam
SERGER n sewing machine attachment for finishing seams
SERGERS > SERGER
SERGES > SERGE
SERGING n type of sewing
SERGINGS > SERGING
SERIAL n story or play produced in successive instalments ▷ adj of or forming a series
SERIALISE same as > SERIALIZE
SERIALISM n musical technique using a sequence of notes in a definite order
SERIALIST n writer of serials
SERIALITY > SERIAL
SERIALIZE vb publish or present as a serial
SERIALLY > SERIAL
SERIALS > SERIAL
SERIATE adj forming a series ▷ vb form into a series
SERIATED > SERIATE
SERIATELY > SERIATE
SERIATES > SERIATE
SERIATIM adv in a series
SERIATING > SERIATE
SERIATION > SERIATE
SERIC adj of silk
SERICEOUS adj covered with a layer of small silky hairs

SERICIN n gelatinous protein found on the fibres of raw silk
SERICINS > SERICIN
SERICITE n type of mica
SERICITES > SERICITE
SERICITIC > SERICITE
SERICON n solution used in alchemy
SERICONS > SERICON
SERIEMA n either of two cranelike South American birds
SERIEMAS > SERIEMA
SERIES n group or succession of related things, usu arranged in order
SERIF n small line at the extremities of a main stroke in a type character
SERIFED adj having serifs
SERIFFED adj having serifs
SERIFS > SERIF
SERIGRAPH n colour print made by an adaptation of the silk-screen process
SERIN n any of various small yellow-and-brown finches
SERINE n sweet-tasting amino acid
SERINES > SERINE
SERINETTE n barrel organ
SERING > SERE
SERINGA n any of several trees that yield rubber
SERINGAS > SERINGA
SERINS > SERIN
SERIOUS adj giving cause for concern
SERIOUSLY adv in a serious manner or to a serious degree
SERIPH same as > SERIF
SERIPHS > SERIPH
SERJEANCY n rank of sergeant
SERJEANT same as > SERGEANT
SERJEANTS > SERJEANT
SERJEANTY n type of feudal tenure
SERK Scots word for > SHIRT
SERKALI n government in Africa
SERKALIS > SERKALI
SERKS > SERK
SERMON n speech on a religious or moral subject ▷ vb deliver a sermon
SERMONED > SERMON
SERMONEER n preacher
SERMONER variant of > SERMONEER
SERMONERS > SERMONER
SERMONET n short sermon
SERMONETS > SERMONET
SERMONIC > SERMON
SERMONING n preaching a sermon
SERMONISE same as > SERMONIZE
SERMONIZE vb make a long moralizing speech
SERMONS > SERMON
SEROGROUP n group of bacteria with a common antigen

S

SEROLOGIC > SEROLOGY
SEROLOGY *n* science concerned with serums
SEROMA *n* abnormal pocket of clear fluid in the body
SEROMAS > SEROMA
SERON *n* crate
SERONS > SERON
SEROON *n* crate
SEROONS > SEROON
SEROPUS *n* liquid consisting of serum and pus
SEROPUSES > SEROPUS
SEROSA *n* one of the thin membranes surrounding the embryo in an insect's egg
SEROSAE > SEROSA
SEROSAL > SEROSA
SEROSAS > SEROSA
SEROSITY > SEROUS
SEROTINAL *same as* > SEROTINE
SEROTINE *adj* produced, flowering, or developing late in the season ▷ *n* either of two insectivorous bats
SEROTINES > SEROTINE
SEROTINY *n* state of being serotinous
SEROTONIN *n* compound that occurs in the brain, intestines, and blood platelets and acts as a neurotransmitter
SEROTYPE *n* category into which material is placed based on its serological activity ▷ *vb* class according to serotype
SEROTYPED > SEROTYPE
SEROTYPES > SEROTYPE
SEROTYPIC *adj* relating to a serotype
SEROUS *adj* of, containing, or like serum
SEROVAR *n* subdivision of species
SEROVARS > SEROVAR
SEROW *n* either of two antelopes of mountainous regions of S and SE Asia
SEROWS > SEROW
SERPENT *n* snake
SERPENTRY *n* serpents
SERPENTS > SERPENT
SERPIGO *n* any progressive skin eruption
SERPIGOES > SERPIGO
SERPIGOS > SERPIGO
SERPULA *n* type of marine mollusc
SERPULAE > SERPULA
SERPULAS > SERPULA
SERPULID *n* marine polychaete worm
SERPULIDS > SERPULID
SERPULITE *n* variety of fossil
SERR *vb* press close together
SERRA *n* sawlike part or organ
SERRAE > SERRA
SERRAN *n* species of fish
SERRANID *n* type of marine fish of the family which includes the sea bass and sea perch

SERRANIDS > SERRANID
SERRANO *n* type of Spanish ham
SERRANOID *same as* > SERRANID
SERRANOS > SERRANO
SERRANS > SERRAN
SERRAS > SERRA
SERRATE *adj* (of leaves) having a margin of forward pointing teeth ▷ *vb* make serrate
SERRATED *adj* having a notched or sawlike edge
SERRATES > SERRATE
SERRATI > SERRATUS
SERRATING > SERRATE
SERRATION *n* state or condition of being serrated
SERRATURE *same as* > SERRATION
SERRATUS *n* muscle in thorax
SERRE *vb* press close together
SERRED > SERRE
SERREFILE *n* file of soldiers
SERRES > SERRE
SERRICORN *n* beetle with serrate antennae ▷ *adj* (of a beetle) with serrate antennae
SERRIED *adj* in close formation
SERRIEDLY > SERRIED
SERRIES > SERRY
SERRIFORM *adj* resembling a notched or sawlike edge
SERRING > SERRE
SERRS > SERR
SERRULATE *adj* (esp of leaves) minutely serrate
SERRY *vb* close together
SERRYING > SERRY
SERS > SER
SERUEWE *vb* old word meaning survey
SERUEWED > SERUEWE
SERUEWES > SERUEWE
SERUEWING > SERUEWE
SERUM *n* watery fluid left after blood has clotted
SERUMAL > SERUM
SERUMS > SERUM
SERVABLE > SERVE
SERVAL *n* feline African mammal
SERVALS > SERVAL
SERVANT *n* person employed to do household work for another ▷ *vb* work as a servant
SERVANTED > SERVANT
SERVANTRY *n* servants
SERVANTS > SERVANT
SERVE *vb* work for (a person, community, or cause) ▷ *n* act of serving the ball
SERVEABLE > SERVE
SERVED > SERVE
SERVER *n* player who serves in racket games
SERVERIES > SERVERY
SERVERS > SERVER
SERVERY *n* room from which food is served
SERVES > SERVE

SERVEWARE *n* articles by or on which food is served
SERVEWE *vb* old word meaning survey
SERVEWED > SERVEWE
SERVEWES > SERVEWE
SERVEWING > SERVEWE
SERVICE *n* serving ▷ *adj* serving the public rather than producing goods ▷ *vb* provide a service or services to
SERVICED > SERVICE
SERVICER > SERVICE
SERVICERS > SERVICE
SERVICES > SERVICE
SERVICING *n* act of servicing
SERVIENT *adj* subordinate
SERVIETTE *n* table napkin
SERVILE *adj* too eager to obey people, fawning ▷ *n* servile person
SERVILELY > SERVILE
SERVILES > SERVILE
SERVILISM *n* condition of being servile
SERVILITY > SERVILE
SERVING *n* portion of food
SERVINGS > SERVING
SERVITOR *n* servant or attendant
SERVITORS > SERVITOR
SERVITUDE *n* bondage or slavery
SERVLET *n* small program that runs on a web server
SERVLETS > SERVLET
SERVO *n* servomechanism ▷ *adj* of a servomechanism
SERVOS > SERVO
SERVQUAL *n* provision of high-quality products backed by a high level of customer service
SERVQUALS > SERVQUAL
SESAME *n* plant cultivated for its seeds and oil
SESAMES > SESAME
SESAMOID *adj* of or relating to various small bones formed in tendons ▷ *n* sesamoid bone
SESAMOIDS > SESAMOID
SESE *interj* exclamation found in Shakespeare
SESELI *n* garden plant
SESELIS > SESELI
SESEY *interj* exclamation found in Shakespeare
SESH *short for* > SESSION
SESHES > SESH
SESS *n* old word meaning tax ▷ *vb* assess or impose (a tax)
SESSA *interj* exclamation found in Shakespeare
SESSED > SESS
SESSES > SESS
SESSILE *adj* (of flowers or leaves) having no stalk
SESSILITY > SESSILE
SESSING > SESS
SESSION *n* period spent in an activity
SESSIONAL > SESSION
SESSIONS > SESSION
SESSPOOL *n* cesspool

SESSPOOLS > SESSPOOL
SESTERCE *n* silver or, later, bronze coin of ancient Rome worth a quarter of a denarius
SESTERCES > SESTERCE
SESTERTIA *pl n* ancient Roman money accounts
SESTERTII *pl n* sesterces
SESTET *n* last six lines of a sonnet
SESTETS > SESTET
SESTETT *n* group of six
SESTETTE *n* group of six
SESTETTES > SESTETTE
SESTETTO *n* composition for six musicians
SESTETTOS > SESTETTO
SESTETTS > SESTETT
SESTINA *n* elaborate verse form of Italian origin
SESTINAS > SESTINA
SESTINE *n* poem of six lines
SESTINES > SESTINE
SESTON *n* type of plankton
SESTONS > SESTON
SET *vb* put in a specified position or state ▷ *n* setting or being set ▷ *adj* fixed or established beforehand
SETA *n* bristle or bristle-like appendage
SETACEOUS > SETA
SETAE > SETA
SETAL > SETA
SETBACK *n* anything that delays progress
SETBACKS > SETBACK
SETENANT *n* pair of postage stamps of different values joined together
SETENANTS > SETENANT
SETIFORM *adj* shaped like a seta
SETLINE *n* any of various types of fishing line
SETLINES > SETLINE
SETNESS > SET
SETNESSES > SET
SETOFF *n* counterbalance
SETOFFS > SETOFF
SETON *n* surgical thread inserted below the skin
SETONS > SETON
SETOSE *adj* covered with setae
SETOUS > SETA
SETOUT *n* beginning or outset
SETOUTS > SETOUT
SETS > SET
SETSCREW *n* screw that fits into the boss or hub of a wheel
SETSCREWS > SETSCREW
SETT *n* badger's burrow
SETTEE *n* couch
SETTEES > SETTEE
SETTER *n* long-haired gun dog ▷ *vb* treat with a piece of setterwort
SETTERED > SETTER
SETTERING > SETTER
SETTERS > SETTER
SETTING > SET
SETTINGS > SET
SETTLE *vb* arrange or put in order ▷ *n* long wooden

bench with high back and arms

SETTLED > SETTLE

SETTLER n colonist

SETTLERS > SETTLER

SETTLES > SETTLE

SETTLING > SETTLE

SETTLINGS pl n any matter or substance that has settled at the bottom of a liquid

SETTLOR n person who settles property on someone

SETTLORS > SETTLOR

SETTS > SETT

SETUALE n valerian

SETUALES > SETUALE

SETULE n small bristle

SETULES > SETULE

SETULOSE > SETULE

SETULOUS > SETULE

SETUP n way in which anything is organized or arranged

SETUPS > SETUP

SETWALL n valerian

SETWALLS > SETWALL

SEV n Indian snack of deep-fried noodles

SEVEN n one more than six

SEVENFOLD adj having seven times as many or as much ▷ adv by seven times as many or as much

SEVENISH adj about seven

SEVENS n Rugby Union match or series of matches played with seven players on each side

SEVENTEEN n ten and seven

SEVENTH n number seven in a series ▷ adj coming after the sixth and before the eighth

SEVENTHLY same as > SEVENTH

SEVENTHS > SEVENTH

SEVENTIES > SEVENTY

SEVENTY n ten times seven

SEVER vb cut through or off

SEVERABLE adj able to be severed

SEVERAL adj some, a few ▷ n individual person

SEVERALLY adv separately

SEVERALS > SEVERAL

SEVERALTY n state of being several or separate

SEVERANCE n act of severing or state of being severed

SEVERE adj strict or harsh

SEVERED > SEVER

SEVERELY > SEVERE

SEVERER > SEVERE

SEVEREST > SEVERE

SEVERIES > SEVERY

SEVERING > SEVER

SEVERITY > SEVERE

SEVERS > SEVER

SEVERY n part of vaulted ceiling

SEVICHE n Mexican fish dish

SEVICHES > SEVICHE

SEVRUGA n species of sturgeon

SEVRUGAS > SEVRUGA

SEVS > SEV

SEW vb join with thread repeatedly passed through with a needle

SEWABLE > SEW

SEWAGE n waste matter carried away in sewers

SEWAGES > SEWAGE

SEWAN same as > SEAWAN

SEWANS > SEWAN

SEWAR n Asian dagger

SEWARS > SEWAR

SEWED > SEW

SEWEL n scarecrow

SEWELLEL n mountain beaver

SEWELLELS > SEWELLEL

SEWELS > SEWEL

SEWEN same as > SEWIN

SEWENS > SEWEN

SEWER n drain to remove waste water and sewage ▷ vb provide with sewers

SEWERAGE n system of sewers

SEWERAGES > SEWERAGE

SEWERED > SEWER

SEWERING > SEWER

SEWERINGS > SEWER

SEWERLESS > SEWER

SEWERLIKE > SEWER

SEWERS > SEWER

SEWIN n sea trout

SEWING > SEW

SEWINGS > SEW

SEWINS > SEWIN

SEWN > SEW

SEWS > SEW

SEX n state of being male or female ▷ vb find out the sex of

SEXAHOLIC n person who is addicted to sex

SEXCAPADE n sexual escapade

SEXED > SEX

SEXENNIAL adj occurring once every six years or over a period of six years ▷ n sixth anniversary

SEXER n person checking the gender of chickens

SEXERCISE n sexual activity, regarded as a way of keeping fit

SEXERS > SEXER

SEXES > SEX

SEXFID adj split into six

SEXFOIL n flower with six petals or leaves

SEXFOILS > SEXFOIL

SEXIER > SEXY

SEXIEST > SEXY

SEXILY > SEXY

SEXINESS > SEXY

SEXING > SEX

SEXINGS > SEXING

SEXISM n discrimination on the basis of a person's gender

SEXISMS > SEXISM

SEXIST > SEXISM

SEXISTS > SEXISM

SEXLESS adj neither male nor female

SEXLESSLY > SEXLESS

SEXLINKED adj (of a gene) found on a sex chromosome

SEXOLOGIC > SEXOLOGY

SEXOLOGY n study of sexual behaviour in human beings

SEXPERT n person who professes a knowledge of sexual matters

SEXPERTS > SEXPERT

SEXPOT n person considered as sexually very attractive

SEXPOTS > SEXPOT

SEXT n sexually explicit text message ▷ vb send a sexually explicit text message

SEXTAIN same as > SESTINA

SEXTAINS > SEXTAIN

SEXTAN adj (of a fever) marked by paroxysms that recur after an interval of five days

SEXTANS n ancient Roman coin

SEXTANSES > SEXTANS

SEXTANT n navigator's instrument for measuring angles

SEXTANTAL > SEXTANT

SEXTANTS > SEXTANT

SEXTARII > SEXTARIUS

SEXTARIUS n ancient Roman quantity measure

SEXTED > SEXT

SEXTET n group of six performers

SEXTETS > SEXTET

SEXTETT n sextet

SEXTETTE same as > SEXTET

SEXTETTES > SEXTETTE

SEXTETTS > SEXTETT

SEXTILE n value of a variable dividing its distribution into six groups with equal frequencies

SEXTILES > SEXTILE

SEXTING n practice of sending sexually explicit text messages

SEXTINGS > SEXTING

SEXTO same as > SIXMO

SEXTOLET n group of six musical notes

SEXTOLETS > SEXTOLET

SEXTON n official in charge of a church and churchyard

SEXTONESS n female sexton

SEXTONS > SEXTON

SEXTOS > SEXTO

SEXTS > SEXT

SEXTUOR n sextet

SEXTUORS > SEXTUOR

SEXTUPLE vb multiply by six ▷ adj six times as much or as many ▷ n quantity or number six times as great as another

SEXTUPLED > SEXTUPLE

SEXTUPLES > SEXTUPLE

SEXTUPLET n one of six children born at one birth

SEXTUPLY > SEXTUPLE

SEXUAL adj of or characterized by sex

SEXUALISE same as > SEXUALIZE

SEXUALISM n emphasizing of sexuality

SEXUALIST > SEXUALISM

SEXUALITY n state of being sexual

SEXUALIZE vb make or become sexual

SEXUALLY > SEXUAL

SEXVALENT adj with valency of six

SEXY adj exciting or attractive

SEY n Scots word meaning part of a cow carcase

SEYEN n old form of scion

SEYENS > SEYEN

SEYS > SEY

SEYSURE n old form of seizure

SEYSURES > SEYSURE

SEZ vb informal spelling of 'says'

SFERICS same as > SPHERICS

SFORZANDI > SFORZANDO

SFORZANDO adv to be played with strong initial attack ▷ n symbol written above a note, indicating this

SFORZATI > SFORZATO

SFORZATO same as > SFORZANDO

SFORZATOS > SFORZATO

SFUMATO n gradual transition between areas of different colour in painting

SFUMATOS > SFUMATO

SGRAFFITI > SGRAFFITO

SGRAFFITO n technique in mural or ceramic decoration in which the top layer of glaze is incised with a design to reveal parts of the ground

SH interj hush

SHA interj be quiet

SHABASH interj (in Indian English) bravo or well done

SHABBATOT pl n Jewish sabbaths

SHABBIER > SHABBY

SHABBIEST > SHABBY

SHABBILY > SHABBY

SHABBLE n Scots word meaning old sword

SHABBLES > SHABBLE

SHABBY adj worn or dilapidated in appearance

SHABRACK n cavalryman's saddle cloth

SHABRACKS > SHABRACK

SHACK n rough hut ▷ vb evade (work or responsibility)

SHACKED > SHACK

SHACKIER > SHACKY

SHACKIEST > SHACKY

SHACKING > SHACK

SHACKLE n metal ring for securing a person's wrists or ankles ▷ vb fasten with shackles

SHACKLED > SHACKLE

SHACKLER > SHACKLE

SHACKLERS > SHACKLE

SHACKLES > SHACKLE

SHACKLING > SHACKLE

SHACKO same as > SHAKO

SHACKOES > SHACKO

SHACKOS > SHACKO

SHACKS > SHACK
SHACKTOWN n collection of huts or other temporary housing
SHACKY adj resembling a shack; dilapidated
SHAD n herring-like fish
SHADBERRY n edible purplish berry of the shadbush
SHADBLOW n type of shrub
SHADBLOWS > SHADBLOW
SHADBUSH n type of N American tree or shrub
SHADCHAN n Jewish marriage broker
SHADCHANS > SHADCHAN
SHADDOCK another name for > POMELO
SHADDOCKS > SHADDOCK
SHADDUP interj shut up
SHADE n relative darkness ▷ vb screen from light
SHADED > SHADE
SHADELESS > SHADE
SHADER > SHADE
SHADERS > SHADE
SHADES pl n gathering darkness at nightfall
SHADFLIES > SHADFLY
SHADFLY American name for > MAYFLY
SHADIER > SHADY
SHADIEST > SHADY
SHADILY > SHADY
SHADINESS > SHADY
SHADING n graded areas of tone indicating light and dark in a painting or drawing
SHADINGS > SHADING
SHADKHAN same as > SHADCHAN
SHADKHANS > SHADKHAN
SHADOOF n mechanism for raising water
SHADOOFS > SHADOOF
SHADOW n dark shape cast on a surface when something stands between a light and the surface ▷ vb cast a shadow over
SHADOWBOX vb practise boxing against an imaginary opponent
SHADOWED > SHADOW
SHADOWER > SHADOW
SHADOWERS > SHADOW
SHADOWIER > SHADOWY
SHADOWILY > SHADOWY
SHADOWING > SHADOW
SHADOWS > SHADOW
SHADOWY adj (of a place) full of shadows
SHADRACH n lump of iron that has not been melted in the furnace
SHADRACHS > SHADRACH
SHADS > SHAD
SHADUF same as > SHADOOF
SHADUFS > SHADUF
SHADY adj situated in or giving shade
SHAFT n long narrow straight handle of a tool or weapon ▷ vb treat badly
SHAFTED > SHAFT
SHAFTER > SHAFT

SHAFTERS > SHAFT
SHAFTING n assembly of rotating shafts for transmitting power
SHAFTINGS > SHAFTING
SHAFTLESS > SHAFT
SHAFTS > SHAFT
SHAG n cormorant ▷ adj (of a carpet) having a long pile ▷ vb make shaggy
SHAGBARK n North American hickory tree
SHAGBARKS > SHAGBARK
SHAGGABLE adj vulgar word meaning sexually attractive
SHAGGED n shaggy
SHAGGER n vulgar word for a person who has sexual intercourse
SHAGGERS > SHAGGER
SHAGGIER > SHAGGY
SHAGGIEST > SHAGGY
SHAGGILY > SHAGGY
SHAGGING > SHAG
SHAGGY adj covered with rough hair or wool
SHAGPILE adj (of carpet) having long fibres
SHAGREEN n sharkskin
SHAGREENS > SHAGREEN
SHAGROON n nineteenth-century Australian settler in Canterbury
SHAGROONS > SHAGROON
SHAGS > SHAG
SHAH n formerly, ruler of Iran
SHAHADA n Islamic declaration of faith
SHAHADAH same as > SHAHADA
SHAHADAHS > SHAHADAH
SHAHADAS > SHAHADA
SHAHDOM > SHAH
SHAHDOMS > SHAH
SHAHEED same as > SHAHID
SHAHEEDS > SHAHEED
SHAHID n Muslim martyr
SHAHIDS > SHAHID
SHAHS > SHAH
SHAHTOOSH n soft wool that comes from the protected Tibetan antelope
SHAIKH n sheikh
SHAIKHS > SHAIKH
SHAIRD n Scots word meaning shred
SHAIRDS > SHAIRD
SHAIRN Scots word for > DUNG
SHAIRNS > SHAIRN
SHAITAN n (in Muslim countries) an evil spirit
SHAITANS > SHAITAN
SHAKABLE > SHAKE
SHAKE vb move quickly up and down or back and forth ▷ n act of shaking
SHAKEABLE > SHAKE
SHAKED vb old form of shook
SHAKEDOWN n act of extortion
SHAKEN > SHAKE
SHAKEOUT n process of reducing the number of people in a workforce
SHAKEOUTS > SHAKEOUT

SHAKER n container in which drinks are mixed or from which powder is shaken
SHAKERS > SHAKER
SHAKES > SHAKE
SHAKEUP n radical reorganization
SHAKEUPS > SHAKEUP
SHAKIER > SHAKY
SHAKIEST > SHAKY
SHAKILY > SHAKY
SHAKINESS > SHAKY
SHAKING > SHAKE
SHAKINGS > SHAKE
SHAKO n tall cylindrical peaked military hat with a plume
SHAKOES > SHAKO
SHAKOS > SHAKO
SHAKT vb old form of shook
SHAKUDO n Japanese alloy of copper and gold
SHAKUDOS > SHAKUDO
SHAKY adj unsteady
SHALE n flaky sedimentary rock
SHALED > SHALE
SHALELIKE > SHALE
SHALES > SHALE
SHALEY > SHALE
SHALIER > SHALE
SHALIEST > SHALE
SHALING > SHALE
SHALL vb used as an auxiliary to make the future tense
SHALLI n type of fabric
SHALLIS > SHALLI
SHALLON n American shrub
SHALLONS > SHALLON
SHALLOON n light twill-weave woollen fabric used chiefly for coat linings, etc
SHALLOONS > SHALLOON
SHALLOP n light boat used for rowing in shallow water
SHALLOPS > SHALLOP
SHALLOT n kind of small onion
SHALLOTS > SHALLOT
SHALLOW adj not deep ▷ n shallow place in a body of water ▷ vb make or become shallow
SHALLOWED > SHALLOW
SHALLOWER > SHALLOW
SHALLOWLY > SHALLOW
SHALLOWS > SHALLOW
SHALM n old woodwind instrument
SHALMS > SHALM
SHALOM n Jewish greeting meaning 'peace be with you'
SHALOMS > SHALOM
SHALOT n shallot
SHALOTS > SHALOT
SHALT singular form of the present tense (indicative mood) of > SHALL
SHALWAR n pair of loose-fitting trousers narrowing around the ankles
SHALWARS > SHALWAR
SHALY > SHALE
SHAM n thing or person that is not genuine ▷ adj not genuine ▷ vb fake, feign

SHAMA n Indian songbird
SHAMABLE > SHAME
SHAMABLY > SHAME
SHAMAL n hot northwesterly wind
SHAMALS > SHAMAL
SHAMAN n priest of shamanism
SHAMANIC > SHAMAN
SHAMANISM n religion of northern Asia, based on a belief in good and evil spirits
SHAMANIST > SHAMANISM
SHAMANS > SHAMAN
SHAMAS > SHAMA
SHAMATEUR n sportsperson who is officially an amateur but accepts payment
SHAMBA n (in E Africa) any field used for growing crops
SHAMBAS > SHAMBA
SHAMBLE vb walk in a shuffling awkward way ▷ n awkward or shuffling walk
SHAMBLED > SHAMBLE
SHAMBLES n disorderly event or place
SHAMBLIER > SHAMBLE
SHAMBLING > SHAMBLE
SHAMBLY > SHAMBLE
SHAMBOLIC adj completely disorganized
SHAME n painful emotion caused by awareness of having done something foolish ▷ vb cause to feel shame
SHAMEABLE > SHAME
SHAMEABLY > SHAME
SHAMED > SHAME
SHAMEFAST adj old form of shamefaced
SHAMEFUL adj causing or deserving shame
SHAMELESS adj with no sense of shame
SHAMER n cause of shame
SHAMERS > SHAMER
SHAMES > SHAME
SHAMIANA n tent in India
SHAMIANAH n tent in India
SHAMIANAS > SHAMIANA
SHAMINA n wool blend of pashm and shahtoosh
SHAMINAS > SHAMINA
SHAMING n act or attempt to embarrass someone
SHAMINGS > SHAMING
SHAMISEN n Japanese stringed instrument
SHAMISENS > SHAMISEN
SHAMMAS same as > SHAMMES
SHAMMASH same as > SHAMMES
SHAMMASIM > SHAMMES
SHAMMED > SHAM
SHAMMER > SHAM
SHAMMERS > SHAM
SHAMMES n official acting as the beadle, sexton, and caretaker of a synagogue
SHAMMIED > SHAMMY
SHAMMIES > SHAMMY
SHAMMING > SHAM
SHAMMOS same as > SHAMMES

SHAMMOSIM > SHAMMES
SHAMMY n piece of chamois leather ▷ vb rub with a shammy
SHAMMYING > SHAMMY
SHAMOIS n chamois ▷ vb clean with shamois
SHAMOISED > SHAMOIS
SHAMOISES > SHAMOIS
SHAMOS same as **>** SHAMMES
SHAMOSIM > SHAMMES
SHAMOY n chamois ▷ vb rub with a shamoy
SHAMOYED > SHAMOY
SHAMOYING > SHAMOY
SHAMOYS > SHAMOY
SHAMPOO n liquid soap for washing hair, carpets, or upholstery ▷ vb wash with shampoo
SHAMPOOED > SHAMPOO
SHAMPOOER > SHAMPOO
SHAMPOOS > SHAMPOO
SHAMROCK n clover leaf, esp as the Irish emblem
SHAMROCKS > SHAMROCK
SHAMS > SHAM
SHAMUS n police or private detective
SHAMUSES > SHAMUS
SHAN variant of **>** SHAND
SHANACHIE n Gaelic storyteller
SHAND n old word meaning fake coin
SHANDIES > SHANDY
SHANDRIES > SHANDRY
SHANDRY n light horse-drawn cart
SHANDS > SHAND
SHANDY n drink made of beer and lemonade
SHANGHAI vb force or trick (someone) into doing something ▷ n catapult
SHANGHAIS > SHANGHAI
SHANK n lower leg ▷ vb (of fruits, roots, etc) to show disease symptoms
SHANKBONE n bone in lower leg
SHANKED > SHANK
SHANKING > SHANK
SHANKS > SHANK
SHANNIES > SHANNY
SHANNY n European blenny of rocky coastal waters
SHANS > SHAN
SHANTEY same as **>** SHANTY
SHANTEYS > SHANTEY
SHANTI n peace
SHANTIES > SHANTY
SHANTIH same as **>** SHANTI
SHANTIHS > SHANTIH
SHANTIS > SHANTI
SHANTUNG n soft Chinese silk with a knobbly surface
SHANTUNGS > SHANTUNG
SHANTY n shack or crude dwelling
SHANTYMAN n man living in shanty
SHANTYMEN > SHANTYMAN
SHAPABLE > SHAPE
SHAPE n outward form of an object ▷ vb form or mould
SHAPEABLE > SHAPE

SHAPED > SHAPE
SHAPELESS adj (of a person or object) lacking a pleasing shape
SHAPELIER > SHAPELY
SHAPELY adj having an attractive shape
SHAPEN vb shape
SHAPENED > SHAPEN
SHAPENING > SHAPEN
SHAPENS > SHAPEN
SHAPER > SHAPE
SHAPERS > SHAPE
SHAPES > SHAPE
SHAPEUP n system of hiring dockers for a day's work
SHAPEUPS > SHAPEUP
SHAPEWEAR n underwear that shapes body
SHAPING > SHAPE
SHAPINGS > SHAPE
SHAPS n leather over-trousers worn by cowboys
SHARABLE > SHARE
SHARD n broken piece of pottery or glass
SHARDED adj old word meaning hidden under dung
SHARDS > SHARD
SHARE n part of something that belongs to or is contributed by a person ▷ vb give or take a share of (something)
SHAREABLE adj that can be shared
SHARECROP vb cultivate (farmland) as a sharecropper
SHARED > SHARE
SHAREMAN n member of fishing-boat crew who shares profits
SHAREMEN > SHAREMAN
SHARER > SHARE
SHARERS > SHARE
SHARES > SHARE
SHARESMAN n member of fishing-boat crew who shares profits
SHARESMEN > SHARESMAN
SHAREWARE n software available to all users without the need for a licence
SHARIA n body of doctrines that regulate the lives of Muslims
SHARIAH same as **>** SHARIA
SHARIAHS > SHARIAH
SHARIAS > SHARIA
SHARIAT n Islamic religious law
SHARIATS > SHARIAT
SHARIF same as **>** SHERIF
SHARIFIAN > SHARIF
SHARIFS > SHARIF
SHARING > SHARE
SHARINGS > SHARE
SHARK n large usu predatory sea fish ▷ vb obtain (something) by cheating or deception
SHARKED > SHARK
SHARKER n shark hunter
SHARKERS > SHARKER
SHARKING > SHARK
SHARKINGS > SHARK

SHARKISH adj resembling or behaving like a shark
SHARKLIKE > SHARK
SHARKS > SHARK
SHARKSKIN n stiff glossy fabric
SHARN Scots word for **>** DUNG
SHARNIER > SHARNY
SHARNIES > SHARNY
SHARNIEST > SHARN
SHARNS > SHARN
SHARNY n (Scot) person who cleans a cow-house ▷ adj (Scot) covered in dung
SHARON n as in sharon fruit persimmon
SHARP adj having a keen cutting edge or fine point ▷ adv promptly ▷ n symbol raising a note one semitone above natural pitch ▷ vb make sharp
SHARPED > SHARP
SHARPEN vb make or become sharp or sharper
SHARPENED > SHARPEN
SHARPENER > SHARPEN
SHARPENS > SHARPEN
SHARPER n person who cheats
SHARPERS > SHARPER
SHARPEST > SHARP
SHARPIE n member of a teenage group having short hair and distinctive clothes
SHARPIES > SHARPIE
SHARPING > SHARP
SHARPINGS > SHARP
SHARPISH adj fairly sharp ▷ adv promptly
SHARPLY > SHARP
SHARPNESS > SHARP
SHARPS > SHARP
SHARPTAIL n type of grouse
SHARPY n swindler
SHASH vb old form of sash
SHASHED > SHASH
SHASHES > SHASH
SHASHING > SHASH
SHASHLICK same as **>** SHASHLIK
SHASHLIK n type of kebab
SHASHLIKS > SHASHLIK
SHASLIK n type of kebab
SHASLIKS > SHASLIK
SHASTA n plant of the daisy family
SHASTAS > SHASTA
SHASTER same as **>** SHASTRA
SHASTERS > SHASTER
SHASTRA n any of the sacred writings of Hinduism
SHASTRAS > SHASTRA
SHAT past tense and past participle of **>** SHIT
SHATOOSH same as **>** SHAHTOOSH
SHATTER vb break into pieces ▷ n fragment
SHATTERED adj completely exhausted
SHATTERER > SHATTER
SHATTERS > SHATTER
SHATTERY adj liable to shatter

SHAUCHLE vb Scots word meaning shuffle
SHAUCHLED > SHAUCHLE
SHAUCHLES > SHAUCHLE
SHAUCHLY > SHAUCHLE
SHAUGH n old word meaning small wood
SHAUGHS > SHAUGH
SHAUL vb old form of shawl
SHAULED > SHAUL
SHAULING > SHAUL
SHAULS > SHAUL
SHAVABLE > SHAVE
SHAVASANA n type of yoga posture
SHAVE vb remove (hair) from (the face, head, or body) with a razor or shaver ▷ n act of shaving
SHAVEABLE > SHAVE
SHAVED > SHAVE
SHAVELING n derogatory term for a priest or clergyman with a shaven head
SHAVEN adj closely shaved or tonsured
SHAVER n electric razor
SHAVERS > SHAVER
SHAVES > SHAVE
SHAVETAIL n American slang for second lieutenant
SHAVIE n Scots word meaning trick
SHAVIES > SHAVIE
SHAVING > SHAVE
SHAVINGS > SHAVE
SHAW n small wood ▷ vb show
SHAWARMA n strips of lamb, usu served in a pitta
SHAWARMAS > SHAWARMA
SHAWED > SHAW
SHAWING > SHAW
SHAWL n piece of cloth worn over a woman's shoulders or wrapped around a baby ▷ vb cover with a shawl
SHAWLED > SHAWL
SHAWLEY same as **>** SHAWLIE
SHAWLEYS > SHAWLEY
SHAWLIE n insulting term for a working-class woman who wears a shawl
SHAWLIES > SHAWLIE
SHAWLING > SHAWL
SHAWLINGS > SHAWL
SHAWLLESS > SHAWL
SHAWLS > SHAWL
SHAWM n medieval form of the oboe with a conical bore and flaring bell
SHAWMS > SHAWM
SHAWN variant of **>** SHAWM
SHAWS > SHAW
SHAY dialect word for **>** CHAISE
SHAYA n Indian plant
SHAYAS > SHAYA
SHAYKH same as **>** SHEIKH
SHAYKHS > SHAYKH
SHAYS > SHAY
SHAZAM interj magic slogan
SHCHI n Russian cabbage soup
SHCHIS > SHCHI

SHE pron female person or animal previously mentioned ▷ n female person or animal
SHEA n tropical African tree
SHEADING n any of the six subdivisions of the Isle of Man
SHEADINGS > SHEADING
SHEAF n bundle of papers ▷ vb tie into a sheaf
SHEAFED > SHEAF
SHEAFIER > SHEAF
SHEAFIEST > SHEAF
SHEAFING > SHEAF
SHEAFLIKE > SHEAF
SHEAFS > SHEAF
SHEAFY > SHEAF
SHEAL vb old word meaning shell
SHEALED > SHEAL
SHEALING > SHEAL
SHEALINGS > SHEAL
SHEALS > SHEAL
SHEAR vb clip hair or wool from ▷ n breakage caused through strain or twisting
SHEARED > SHEAR
SHEARER > SHEAR
SHEARERS > SHEAR
SHEARING > SHEAR
SHEARINGS > SHEAR
SHEARLEG n one spar of shearlegs
SHEARLEGS same as > SHEERLEGS
SHEARLING n young sheep after its first shearing
SHEARMAN n person who trims cloth
SHEARMEN > SHEARMAN
SHEARS > SHEAR
SHEAS > SHEA
SHEATFISH n European catfish
SHEATH n close-fitting cover, esp for a knife or sword
SHEATHE vb put into a sheath
SHEATHED > SHEATHE
SHEATHER > SHEATHE
SHEATHERS > SHEATHE
SHEATHES > SHEATHE
SHEATHIER > SHEATHE
SHEATHING n any material used as an outer layer
SHEATHS > SHEATH
SHEATHY > SHEATHE
SHEAVE vb gather or bind into sheaves ▷ n wheel with a grooved rim
SHEAVED > SHEAVE
SHEAVES > SHEAF
SHEAVING > SHEAVE
SHEBANG n situation, matter, or affair
SHEBANGS > SHEBANG
SHEBEAN same as > SHEBEEN
SHEBEANS > SHEBEAN
SHEBEEN n place where alcohol is sold illegally ▷ vb run a shebeen
SHEBEENED > SHEBEEN
SHEBEENER > SHEBEEN
SHEBEENS > SHEBEEN
SHECHITA n Jewish method of killing animals for food

SHECHITAH same as > SHECHITA
SHECHITAS > SHECHITA
SHED n building used for storage or shelter or as a workshop ▷ vb get rid of
SHEDABLE > SHED
SHEDDABLE > SHED
SHEDDED > SHED
SHEDDER n person or thing that sheds
SHEDDERS > SHEDDER
SHEDDING > SHED
SHEDDINGS > SHED
SHEDFUL n quantity or amount contained in a shed
SHEDFULS > SHEDFUL
SHEDHAND n labourer working in a shearing shed
SHEDHANDS > SHEDHAND
SHEDLIKE > SHED
SHEDLOAD n very large amount or number
SHEDLOADS > SHEDLOAD
SHEDS > SHED
SHEEL vb old word meaning shell
SHEELED > SHEEL
SHEELING > SHEEL
SHEELS > SHEEL
SHEEN n glistening brightness on the surface of something ▷ adj shining and beautiful ▷ vb give a sheen to
SHEENED > SHEEN
SHEENEY n offensive word for a Jew
SHEENEYS > SHEENEY
SHEENFUL > SHEEN
SHEENIE n offensive word for a Jew
SHEENIER > SHEEN
SHEENIES > SHEENIE
SHEENIEST > SHEEN
SHEENING > SHEEN
SHEENS > SHEEN
SHEENY > SHEEN
SHEEP n ruminant animal bred for wool and meat
SHEEPCOT n sheepcote
SHEEPCOTE another word for > SHEEPFOLD
SHEEPCOTS > SHEEPCOT
SHEEPDOG n dog used for herding sheep
SHEEPDOGS > SHEEPDOG
SHEEPFOLD n pen or enclosure for sheep
SHEEPHEAD n species of fish
SHEEPIER > SHEEP
SHEEPIEST > SHEEP
SHEEPISH adj embarrassed because of feeling foolish
SHEEPLE n people who follow the majority in matters of opinion, taste, etc, collectively
SHEEPLES > SHEEPLE
SHEEPLIKE > SHEEP
SHEEPMAN n person who keeps sheep
SHEEPMEN > SHEEPMAN
SHEEPO n person employed to bring sheep to the catching pen in a shearing shed
SHEEPOS > SHEEPO

SHEEPSKIN n skin of a sheep with the fleece still on, used for clothing or rugs
SHEEPWALK n tract of land for grazing sheep
SHEEPY > SHEEP
SHEER adj absolute, complete ▷ adv steeply ▷ vb change course suddenly ▷ n any transparent fabric used for making garments
SHEERED > SHEER
SHEERER > SHEER
SHEEREST > SHEER
SHEERING > SHEER
SHEERLEG n one spar of sheerlegs
SHEERLEGS n device for lifting heavy weights
SHEERLY > SHEER
SHEERNESS > SHEER
SHEERS > SHEER
SHEESH interj exclamation of surprise or annoyance
SHEESHA n Oriental water-pipe for smoking tobacco
SHEESHAS > SHEESHA
SHEET n large piece of cloth used as an inner bed cover ▷ vb provide with, cover, or wrap in a sheet
SHEETED > SHEET
SHEETER > SHEET
SHEETERS > SHEET
SHEETFED adj printing on separate sheets of paper
SHEETIER > SHEET
SHEETIEST > SHEET
SHEETING n material from which sheets are made
SHEETINGS > SHEETING
SHEETLESS > SHEET
SHEETLIKE > SHEET
SHEETROCK n brand name for plasterboard
SHEETS > SHEET
SHEETY > SHEET
SHEEVE n part of mine winding gear
SHEEVES > SHEEVE
SHEGETZ n offensive word for a non-Jew
SHEHITA n slaughter of animals according to Jewish religious law
SHEHITAH same as > SHEHITA
SHEHITAHS > SHEHITAH
SHEHITAS > SHEHITA
SHEHNAI n Indian wind instrument
SHEHNAIS > SHEHNAI
SHEIK same as > SHEIKH
SHEIKDOM same as > SHEIKHDOM
SHEIKDOMS > SHEIKDOM
SHEIKH n Arab chief
SHEIKHA n chief wife of a sheikh
SHEIKHAS > SHEIKHA
SHEIKHDOM n territory ruled by a sheikh
SHEIKHS > SHEIKH
SHEIKS > SHEIK
SHEILA n girl or woman
SHEILAS > SHEILA

SHEILING n hut used by shepherds
SHEILINGS > SHEILING
SHEITAN n Muslim demon
SHEITANS > SHEITAN
SHEITEL n traditional wig worn by Orthodox Jewish women
SHEITELS > SHEITEL
SHEKALIM > SHEKEL
SHEKEL n monetary unit of Israel
SHEKELIM > SHEKEL
SHEKELS > SHEKEL
SHELDDUCK n species of large duck
SHELDRAKE same as > SHELDUCK
SHELDUCK n large brightly coloured wild duck of Europe and Asia
SHELDUCKS > SHELDUCK
SHELF n board fixed horizontally for holding things ▷ vb put on a shelf
SHELFED > SHELF
SHELFFUL > SHELF
SHELFFULS > SHELF
SHELFIER > SHELF
SHELFIEST > SHELF
SHELFING > SHELF
SHELFLIKE > SHELF
SHELFROOM n space on shelf
SHELFS > SHELF
SHELFY > SHELF
SHELL n hard outer covering of an egg, nut, or certain animals ▷ vb take the shell from
SHELLAC n resin used in varnishes ▷ vb coat with shellac
SHELLACK vb shellac
SHELLACKS > SHELLAC
SHELLACS > SHELLAC
SHELLBACK n sailor who has crossed the equator
SHELLBARK same as > SHAGBARK
SHELLDUCK n shelduck
SHELLED > SHELL
SHELLER > SHELL
SHELLERS > SHELL
SHELLFIRE n firing of artillery shells
SHELLFISH n sea-living animal, esp one that can be eaten, with a shell
SHELLFUL > SHELL
SHELLFULS > SHELL
SHELLIER > SHELL
SHELLIEST > SHELL
SHELLING > SHELL
SHELLINGS > SHELL
SHELLS > SHELL
SHELLWORK n decoration with shells
SHELLY > SHELL
SHELTA n secret language used by some travelling people in Britain and Ireland
SHELTAS > SHELTA
SHELTER n structure providing protection from danger or the weather ▷ vb give shelter to

SHELTERED adj protected from wind and rain
SHELTERER > SHELTER
SHELTERS > SHELTER
SHELTERY adj giving shelter
SHELTIE n small dog similar to a collie
SHELTIES > SHELTY
SHELTY same as > SHELTIE
SHELVE vb put aside or postpone
SHELVED > SHELVE
SHELVER > SHELVE
SHELVERS > SHELVE
SHELVES > SHELF
SHELVIER > SHELVY
SHELVIEST > SHELVY
SHELVING n (material for) shelves
SHELVINGS > SHELVING
SHELVY adj having shelves
SHEMALE n male who has acquired female physical characteristics through surgery
SHEMALES > SHEMALE
SHEMOZZLE n noisy confusion or dispute
SHEN n (in Chinese thought) spiritual element of the psyche
SHENAI same as > SHEHNAI
SHENAIS > SHENAI
SHEND vb put to shame
SHENDING > SHEND
SHENDS > SHEND
SHENT > SHEND
SHEOL n hell
SHEOLS > SHEOL
SHEPHERD n person who tends sheep ▷ vb guide or watch over (people)
SHEPHERDS > SHEPHERD
SHEQALIM n plural of sheqel
SHEQEL same as > SHEKEL
SHEQELS > SHEQEL
SHERANG n person in charge
SHERANGS > SHERANG
SHERBERT same as > SHERBET
SHERBERTS > SHERBERT
SHERBET n fruit-flavoured fizzy powder
SHERBETS > SHERBET
SHERD same as > SHARD
SHERDS > SHERD
SHERE old spelling of > SHEER
SHEREEF same as > SHERIF
SHEREEFS > SHEREEF
SHERIA same as > SHARIA
SHERIAS > SHERIA
SHERIAT n Muslim religious law
SHERIATS > SHERIAT
SHERIF n descendant of Mohammed through his daughter Fatima
SHERIFF n (in the US) chief law enforcement officer of a county
SHERIFFS > SHERIFF
SHERIFIAN > SHERIF
SHERIFS > SHERIF
SHERLOCK n detective ▷ vb investigate (something)
SHERLOCKS > SHERLOCK
SHERO n woman considered a hero

SHEROES > SHERO
SHEROOT n cheroot
SHEROOTS > SHEROOT
SHERPA n official who assists at a summit meeting
SHERPAS > SHERPA
SHERRIED adj flavoured with sherry
SHERRIES > SHERRY
SHERRIS n old form of sherry
SHERRISES > SHERRIS
SHERRY n pale or dark brown fortified wine
SHERWANI n long coat closed up to the neck, worn by men in India
SHERWANIS > SHERWANI
SHES > SHE
SHET vb old form of shut
SHETLAND n type of wool spun in the Shetland islands
SHETLANDS > SHETLAND
SHETS > SHET
SHETTING > SHET
SHEUCH n ditch or trough ▷ vb dig
SHEUCHED > SHEUCH
SHEUCHING > SHEUCH
SHEUCHS > SHEUCH
SHEUGH same as > SHEUCH
SHEUGHED > SHEUGH
SHEUGHING > SHEUGH
SHEUGHS > SHEUGH
SHEVA n mark in Hebrew writing
SHEVAS > SHEVA
SHEW archaic spelling of > SHOW
SHEWBREAD n loaves of bread placed every Sabbath on the table beside the altar of incense in the tabernacle of ancient Israel
SHEWED > SHEW
SHEWEL n old word meaning scarecrow
SHEWELS > SHEWEL
SHEWER > SHEW
SHEWERS > SHEW
SHEWING > SHEW
SHEWN > SHEW
SHEWS > SHEW
SHH interj sound made to ask for silence
SHHH interj interjection requesting quietness
SHIAI n judo contest
SHIAIS > SHIAI
SHIATSU n type of massage
SHIATSUS > SHIATSU
SHIATZU n shiatzu
SHIATZUS > SHIATZU
SHIBAH n Jewish period of mourning
SHIBAHS > SHIBAH
SHIBUICHI n Japanese alloy of copper and silver
SHICKER n alcoholic drink
SHICKERED adj drunk
SHICKERS > SHICKER
SHICKSA n non-Jewish girl
SHICKSAS > SHICKSA
SHIDDER n old word meaning a female animal
SHIDDERS > SHIDDER

SHIDDUCH n arranged marriage
SHIED > SHY
SHIEL vb sheal
SHIELD n piece of armour carried on the arm to protect the body from blows or missiles ▷ vb protect
SHIELDED > SHIELD
SHIELDER > SHIELD
SHIELDERS > SHIELD
SHIELDING > SHIELD
SHIELDS > SHIELD
SHIELED > SHIEL
SHIELING n rough hut or shelter used by people tending cattle on high or remote ground
SHIELINGS > SHIELING
SHIELS > SHIEL
SHIER n horse that shies habitually
SHIERS > SHIER
SHIES > SHY
SHIEST > SHY
SHIFT vb move ▷ n shifting
SHIFTABLE > SHIFT
SHIFTED > SHIFT
SHIFTER > SHIFT
SHIFTERS > SHIFT
SHIFTIER > SHIFTY
SHIFTIEST > SHIFTY
SHIFTILY > SHIFTY
SHIFTING > SHIFT
SHIFTINGS > SHIFT
SHIFTLESS adj lacking in ambition or initiative
SHIFTS > SHIFT
SHIFTWORK n system of employment where an individual's normal hours of work are outside the period of normal day working
SHIFTY adj evasive or untrustworthy
SHIGELLA n type of rod-shaped Gram-negative bacterium
SHIGELLAE > SHIGELLA
SHIGELLAS > SHIGELLA
SHIITAKE n kind of mushroom widely used in Oriental cookery
SHIITAKES > SHIITAKE
SHIKAR n hunting, esp big-game hunting ▷ vb hunt (game, esp big game)
SHIKARA n (in Kashmir) light, flat-bottomed boat
SHIKARAS > SHIKARA
SHIKAREE same as > SHIKARI
SHIKAREES > SHIKAREE
SHIKARI n (in India) a hunter
SHIKARIS > SHIKARI
SHIKARRED > SHIKAR
SHIKARS > SHIKAR
SHIKKER n Yiddish term for drunk person
SHIKKERED same as > SHICKERED
SHIKKERS > SHIKKER
SHIKRA n small Asian sparrowhawk
SHIKRAS > SHIKRA

SHIKSA n often derogatory term for a non-Jewish girl
SHIKSAS > SHIKSA
SHIKSE n non-Jewish girl
SHIKSEH same as > SHIKSE
SHIKSEHS > SHIKSEH
SHIKSES > SHIKSE
SHILINGI n money unit in Tanzania
SHILINGIS > SHILINGI
SHILL n confidence trickster's assistant ▷ vb act as a shill
SHILLABER n keen customer
SHILLALA n short Irish club or cudgel
SHILLALAH same as > SHILLALA
SHILLALAS > SHILLALA
SHILLED > SHILL
SHILLELAH same as > SHILLALA
SHILLING n former British coin
SHILLINGS > SHILLING
SHILLS > SHILL
SHILPIT adj puny
SHILY > SHY
SHIM n thin strip of material placed between two close surfaces to fill a gap ▷ vb fit or fill up with a shim
SHIMAAL n hot Middle Eastern wind
SHIMAALS > SHIMAAL
SHIMMED > SHIM
SHIMMER n faint unsteady light ▷ vb shine with a faint unsteady light
SHIMMERED > SHIMMER
SHIMMERS > SHIMMER
SHIMMERY adj shining with a glistening or tremulous light
SHIMMEY n chemise
SHIMMEYS > SHIMMEY
SHIMMIED > SHIMMY
SHIMMIES > SHIMMY
SHIMMING > SHIM
SHIMMY n American ragtime dance ▷ vb dance the shimmy
SHIMMYING > SHIMMY
SHIMOZZLE n predicament
SHIMS > SHIM
SHIN n front of the lower leg ▷ vb climb by using the hands or arms and legs
SHINBONE n tibia
SHINBONES > SHINBONE
SHINDIES > SHINDY
SHINDIG n noisy party
SHINDIGS > SHINDIG
SHINDY n quarrel or commotion
SHINDYS > SHINDY
SHINE vb give out or reflect light; cause to gleam ▷ n brightness or lustre
SHINED > SHINE
SHINELESS > SHINE
SHINER n black eye
SHINERS > SHINER
SHINES > SHINE
SHINESS > SHY
SHINESSES > SHY

SHINGLE n wooden roof tile ▷ vb cover (a roof) with shingles
SHINGLED > SHINGLE
SHINGLER > SHINGLE
SHINGLERS > SHINGLE
SHINGLES n disease causing a rash of small blisters along a nerve
SHINGLIER > SHINGLE
SHINGLING > SHINGLE
SHINGLY > SHINGLE
SHINGUARD n rigid piece of plastic to protect footballer's shin
SHINIER > SHINY
SHINIES > SHINY
SHINIEST > SHINY
SHINILY > SHINY
SHININESS > SHINY
SHINING > SHINE
SHININGLY > SHINE
SHINJU n (formerly, in Japan) a ritual double suicide of lovers
SHINJUS > SHINJU
SHINKIN n worthless person
SHINKINS > SHINKIN
SHINLEAF n wintergreen
SHINLEAFS > SHINLEAF
SHINNE n old form of chin
SHINNED > SHIN
SHINNERY n American oak tree
SHINNES > SHINNE
SHINNEY vb climb with hands and legs
SHINNEYED > SHINNEY
SHINNEYS > SHINNEY
SHINNIED > SHINNY
SHINNIES > SHINNY
SHINNING > SHIN
SHINNY same as > SHINTY
SHINNYING > SHINNY
SHINOLA n tradename of a kind of boot polish
SHINOLAS > SHINOLA
SHINS > SHIN
SHINTIED > SHINTY
SHINTIES > SHINTY
SHINTY n game like hockey ▷ vb play shinty
SHINTYING > SHINTY
SHINY adj bright and polished
SHIP n large seagoing vessel ▷ vb send or transport by carrier, esp a ship
SHIPBOARD adj taking place or used aboard a ship
SHIPBORNE adj carried on ship
SHIPFUL n amount carried by ship
SHIPFULS > SHIPFUL
SHIPLAP n method of constructing ship hull
SHIPLAPS > SHIPLAP
SHIPLESS > SHIP
SHIPLOAD n quantity carried by a ship
SHIPLOADS > SHIPLOAD
SHIPMAN n master or captain of a ship
SHIPMATE n sailor serving on the same ship as another

SHIPMATES > SHIPMATE
SHIPMEN > SHIPMAN
SHIPMENT n act of shipping cargo
SHIPMENTS > SHIPMENT
SHIPOWNER n person who owns or has shares in a ship or ships
SHIPPABLE > SHIP
SHIPPED > SHIP
SHIPPEN n dialect word for cattle shed
SHIPPENS > SHIPPEN
SHIPPER n person or company that ships
SHIPPERS > SHIPPER
SHIPPIE n prostitute who solicits at a port
SHIPPIES > SHIPPIE
SHIPPING > SHIP
SHIPPINGS > SHIP
SHIPPO n Japanese enamel work
SHIPPON n dialect word for cattle shed
SHIPPONS > SHIPPON
SHIPPOS > SHIPPO
SHIPPOUND n Baltic weight measure
SHIPS > SHIP
SHIPSHAPE adj orderly or neat ▷ adv in a neat and orderly manner
SHIPSIDE n part of wharf next to ship
SHIPSIDES > SHIPSIDE
SHIPTIME n arrival time of a supply ship
SHIPTIMES > SHIPTIME
SHIPWAY n structure on which a vessel is built, then launched
SHIPWAYS > SHIPWAY
SHIPWORM n type of wormlike marine bivalve mollusc
SHIPWORMS > SHIPWORM
SHIPWRECK n destruction of a ship through storm or collision ▷ vb cause to undergo shipwreck
SHIPYARD n place where ships are built
SHIPYARDS > SHIPYARD
SHIR n gathering in material
SHIRALEE n swag
SHIRALEES > SHIRALEE
SHIRAZ n variety of black grape used for wine
SHIRAZES > SHIRAZ
SHIRE n county ▷ vb refresh or rest
SHIRED > SHIRE
SHIREMAN n sheriff
SHIREMEN > SHIREMAN
SHIRES > SHIRE
SHIRETOWN n chief town of a shire
SHIRING > SHIRE
SHIRK vb avoid (duty or work) ▷ n person who shirks
SHIRKED > SHIRK
SHIRKER > SHIRK
SHIRKERS > SHIRK
SHIRKING > SHIRK
SHIRKS > SHIRK

SHIRR vb gather (fabric) into parallel rows to decorate a dress, etc ▷ n series of gathered rows decorating a dress, etc
SHIRRA old Scots word for > SHERIFF
SHIRRALEE n swagman's bundle of possessions
SHIRRAS > SHIRRA
SHIRRED > SHIRR
SHIRRING > SHIRR
SHIRRINGS > SHIRR
SHIRRS > SHIRR
SHIRS > SHIR
SHIRT n garment for the upper part of the body ▷ vb put a shirt on
SHIRTBAND n neckband on shirt
SHIRTED > SHIRT
SHIRTIER > SHIRTY
SHIRTIEST > SHIRTY
SHIRTILY > SHIRTY
SHIRTING n fabric used in making men's shirts
SHIRTINGS > SHIRTING
SHIRTLESS > SHIRT
SHIRTLIKE adj like a shirt
SHIRTS > SHIRT
SHIRTTAIL n part of a shirt that extends below the waist
SHIRTY adj bad-tempered or annoyed
SHISH adj as in shish kebab dish of meat and vegetables grilled on skewers
SHISHA same as > HOOKAH
SHISHAS > SHISHA
SHISO n Asian plant with aromatic leaves
SHISOS > SHISO
SHIST n schist
SHISTS > SHIST
SHIT vb vulgar word for defecate ▷ n excrement
SHITAKE same as > SHIITAKE
SHITAKES > SHITAKE
SHITBAG n vulgar word for a contemptible person
SHITBAGS > SHITBAG
SHITCAN vb vulgar word meaning discard
SHITCANS > SHITCAN
SHITE same as > SHIT
SHITED > SHITE
SHITES > SHITE
SHITFACE n vulgar word for a despicable person
SHITFACED adj vulgar word for drunk
SHITFACES > SHITFACE
SHITHEAD n vulgar word for a fool
SHITHEADS > SHITHEAD
SHITHEEL n vulgar word for a contemptible person
SHITHEELS > SHITHEEL
SHITHOLE n vulgar word for a dirty place
SHITHOLES > SHITHOLE
SHITHOUSE n vulgar word for a lavatory
SHITING > SHITE
SHITLESS adj vulgar word for very frightened

SHITLIST n vulgar word for a list of hated things
SHITLISTS > SHITLIST
SHITLOAD n vulgar word for a lot
SHITLOADS > SHITLOAD
SHITS > SHIT
SHITSTORM n vulgar word for a very difficult situation
SHITTAH n tree mentioned in the Old Testament
SHITTAHS > SHITTAH
SHITTED > SHIT
SHITTER n vulgar word for a toilet
SHITTERS > SHITTER
SHITTIER > SHIT
SHITTIEST > SHIT
SHITTILY > SHIT
SHITTIM > SHITTAH
SHITTIMS > SHITTAH
SHITTING > SHIT
SHITTY > SHIT
SHITWORK n vulgar word for work considered to be menial
SHITWORKS > SHITWORK
SHITZU n breed of small dog with long, silky fur
SHITZUS > SHITZU
SHIUR n lesson in which a passage of the Talmud is studied
SHIURIM > SHIUR
SHIV variant spelling of > CHIV
SHIVA variant of > SHIVAH
SHIVAH n Jewish period of formal mourning
SHIVAHS > SHIVAH
SHIVAREE n discordant mock serenade to newlyweds, made with pans, kettles, etc
SHIVAREED > SHIVAREE
SHIVAREES > SHIVAREE
SHIVAS > SHIVA
SHIVE n flat cork or bung for wide-mouthed bottles
SHIVER vb tremble, as from cold or fear ▷ n shivering
SHIVERED > SHIVER
SHIVERER > SHIVER
SHIVERERS > SHIVER
SHIVERIER > SHIVERY
SHIVERING > SHIVER
SHIVERS > SHIVER
SHIVERY adj inclined to shiver or tremble
SHIVES > SHIVE
SHIVITI n Jewish decorative plaque with religious message
SHIVITIS > SHIVITI
SHIVOO n Australian word meaning rowdy party
SHIVOOS > SHIVOO
SHIVS > SHIV
SHIVVED > SHIV
SHIVVING > SHIV
SHIZZLE n form of US rap slang
SHIZZLES > SHIZZLE
SHKOTZIM n plural of shegetz
SHLEMIEHL Yiddish word for > FOOL

SHLEMIEL *same as* > SCHLEMIEL
SHLEMIELS > SHLEMIEL
SHLEP *vb* schlep
SHLEPP *vb* schlep
SHLEPPED > SHLEP
SHLEPPER > SHLEP
SHLEPPERS > SHLEP
SHLEPPIER > SHLEPPY
SHLEPPING > SHLEP
SHLEPPS > SHLEPP
SHLEPPY *adj* dingy, shabby, or rundown
SHLEPS > SHLEP
SHLIMAZEL *n* unlucky person
SHLOCK *n* something of poor quality
SHLOCKIER > SHLOCK
SHLOCKS > SHLOCK
SHLOCKY > SHLOCK
SHLONG *same as* > SCHLONG
SHLONGS > SHLONG
SHLOSHIM *n* period of thirty days' deep mourning following a death
SHLOSHIMS > SHLOSHIM
SHLUB *same as* > SCHLUB
SHLUBS > SHLUB
SHLUMP *vb* move in lazy way
SHLUMPED > SHLUMP
SHLUMPIER > SHLUMPY
SHLUMPING > SHLUMP
SHLUMPS > SHLUMP
SHLUMPY > SHLUMP
SHMALTZ *n* schmaltz
SHMALTZES > SHMALTZ
SHMALTZY > SHMALTZ
SHMATTE *n* rag
SHMATTES > SHMATTE
SHMEAR *same as* > SCHMEAR
SHMEARED > SHMEAR
SHMEARING > SHMEAR
SHMEARS > SHMEAR
SHMEER *same as* > SCHMEAR
SHMEERED > SHMEER
SHMEERING > SHMEER
SHMEERS > SHMEER
SHMEK *n* smell
SHMEKS > SHMEK
SHMO *same as* > SCHMO
SHMOCK *n* despicable person
SHMOCKS > SHMOCK
SHMOE *same as* > SCHMOE
SHMOES > SHMO
SHMOOSE *variant of* > SCHMOOZE
SHMOOSED > SHMOOSE
SHMOOSES > SHMOOSE
SHMOOSING > SHMOOSE
SHMOOZE *variant of* > SCHMOOZE
SHMOOZED > SHMOOZE
SHMOOZER *same as* > SCHMOOZER
SHMOOZERS > SHMOOZER
SHMOOZES > SHMOOZE
SHMOOZIER > SHMOOZY
SHMOOZING > SHMOOZE
SHMOOZY *adj* talking casually, gossipy
SHMUCK *n* despicable person
SHMUCKIER > SHMUCKY
SHMUCKS > SHMUCK
SHMUCKY *same as* > SCHMUCKY

SHNAPPS *same as* > SCHNAPPS
SHNAPS *n* schnaps
SHNOOK *n* stupid person
SHNOOKS > SHNOOK
SHNORRER *same as* > SCHNORRER
SHNORRERS > SHNORRER
SHO *adj* sure, as pronounced in southern US
SHOAL *n* large number of fish swimming together ▷ *vb* make or become shallow ▷ *adj* (of the draught of a vessel) drawing little water
SHOALED > SHOAL
SHOALER > SHOAL
SHOALEST > SHOAL
SHOALIER > SHOALY
SHOALIEST > SHOALY
SHOALING > SHOAL
SHOALINGS > SHOAL
SHOALNESS > SHOAL
SHOALS > SHOAL
SHOALWISE *adv* in a large group or in large groups
SHOALY *adj* shallow
SHOAT *n* piglet that has recently been weaned
SHOATS > SHOAT
SHOCHET *n* (in Judaism) a person licensed to slaughter animals and birds
SHOCHETIM > SHOCHET
SHOCHETS > SHOCHET
SHOCHU *n* type of Japanese alcoholic spirit
SHOCHUS > SHOCHU
SHOCK *vb* horrify, disgust, or astonish ▷ *n* sudden violent emotional disturbance ▷ *adj* bushy
SHOCKABLE > SHOCK
SHOCKED > SHOCK
SHOCKER *n* person or thing that shocks or horrifies
SHOCKERS > SHOCKER
SHOCKING *adj* causing horror, disgust, or astonishment
SHOCKS > SHOCK
SHOD > SHOE
SHODDEN *vb* old form of shod
SHODDIER > SHODDY
SHODDIES > SHODDY
SHODDIEST > SHODDY
SHODDILY > SHODDY
SHODDY *adj* made or done badly ▷ *n* yarn or fabric made from wool waste or clippings
SHODER *n* skins used in making gold leaf
SHODERS > SHODER
SHOE *n* outer covering for the foot, ending below the ankle ▷ *vb* fit with a shoe or shoes
SHOEBILL *n* large wading bird of tropical E African swamps
SHOEBILLS > SHOEBILL
SHOEBLACK *n* (esp formerly) a person who shines boots and shoes
SHOEBOX *n* cardboard box for shoes
SHOEBOXES > SHOEBOX

SHOEBRUSH *n* brush for cleaning shoes
SHOED > SHOE
SHOEHORN *n* smooth curved implement inserted at the heel of a shoe to ease the foot into it ▷ *vb* cram (people or things) into a very small space
SHOEHORNS > SHOEHORN
SHOEING > SHOE
SHOEINGS > SHOE
SHOELACE *n* cord for fastening shoes
SHOELACES > SHOELACE
SHOELESS > SHOE
SHOEMAKER *n* person who makes or repairs shoes or boots
SHOEPAC *n* waterproof boot
SHOEPACK *n* waterproof boot
SHOEPACKS > SHOEPACK
SHOEPACS > SHOEPAC
SHOER *n* person who shoes horses
SHOERS > SHOER
SHOES > SHOE
SHOESHINE *n* act or an instance of polishing a pair of shoes
SHOETREE *n* piece of metal, wood, or plastic inserted in a shoe to keep its shape
SHOETREES > SHOETREE
SHOFAR *n* ram's horn sounded in Jewish synagogue
SHOFARS > SHOFAR
SHOFROTH > SHOFAR
SHOG *vb* shake
SHOGGED > SHOG
SHOGGING > SHOG
SHOGGLE *vb* shake
SHOGGLED > SHOGGLE
SHOGGLES > SHOGGLE
SHOGGLIER > SHOGGLE
SHOGGLING > SHOGGLE
SHOGGLY > SHOGGLE
SHOGI *n* Japanese chess
SHOGIS > SHOGI
SHOGS > SHOG
SHOGUN *n* Japanese chief military commander
SHOGUNAL > SHOGUN
SHOGUNATE *n* office or rule of a shogun
SHOGUNS > SHOGUN
SHOJI *n* Japanese rice-paper screen in a sliding wooden frame
SHOJIS > SHOJI
SHOJO *n* genre of Japanese comics intended for girls
SHOLA *n* Indian plant
SHOLAS > SHOLA
SHOLOM *n* Hebrew greeting
SHOLOMS > SHOLOM
SHONE > SHINE
SHONEEN *n* Irishman who imitates English ways
SHONEENS > SHONEEN
SHONKIER > SHONKY
SHONKIEST > SHONKY
SHONKY *adj* unreliable or unsound
SHOO *interj* go away! ▷ *vb* drive away as by saying 'shoo'

SHOOED > SHOO
SHOOFLIES > SHOOFLY
SHOOFLY *n* as in *shoofly pie* US dessert similar to treacle tart
SHOOGIE *vb* Scots word meaning swing
SHOOGIED > SHOOGIE
SHOOGIES > SHOOGIE
SHOOGLE *vb* shake, sway, or rock back and forth ▷ *n* rocking motion
SHOOGLED > SHOOGLE
SHOOGLES > SHOOGLE
SHOOGLIER > SHOOGLE
SHOOGLING > SHOOGLE
SHOOGLY > SHOOGLE
SHOOING > SHOO
SHOOK *n* set of parts ready for assembly
SHOOKS > SHOOK
SHOOL *dialect word for* > SHOVEL
SHOOLE *dialect word for* > SHOVEL
SHOOLED > SHOOL
SHOOLES > SHOOLE
SHOOLING > SHOOL
SHOOLS > SHOOL
SHOON *plural of* > SHOE
SHOORA *same as* > SHURA
SHOORAS > SHOORA
SHOOS > SHOO
SHOOSH *vb* make a rushing sound when moving
SHOOSHED > SHOOSH
SHOOSHES > SHOOSH
SHOOSHING > SHOOSH
SHOOT *vb* hit, wound, or kill with a missile fired from a weapon ▷ *n* new branch or sprout of a plant
SHOOTABLE > SHOOT
SHOOTDOWN *n* act of shooting down aircraft
SHOOTER *n* person or thing that shoots
SHOOTERS > SHOOTER
SHOOTIE *n* type of shoe that covers the ankle
SHOOTIES > SHOOTIE
SHOOTING > SHOOT
SHOOTINGS > SHOOT
SHOOTIST *n* person who shoots
SHOOTISTS > SHOOTIST
SHOOTOUT *n* conclusive gunfight
SHOOTOUTS > SHOOTOUT
SHOOTS > SHOOT
SHOP *n* place for sale of goods and services ▷ *vb* visit a shop or shops to buy goods
SHOPBOARD *n* shop counter
SHOPBOT *n* price-comparison website
SHOPBOTS > SHOPBOT
SHOPBOY *n* boy working in shop
SHOPBOYS > SHOPBOY
SHOPE *n* old form of shape
SHOPFRONT *n* area of shop facing street
SHOPFUL *n* amount stored in shop
SHOPFULS > SHOPFUL
SHOPGIRL *n* girl working in shop

S

SHOPGIRLS > SHOPGIRL
SHOPHAR same as > SHOFAR
SHOPHARS > SHOPHAR
SHOPHOUSE n (in SE Asia) shop that is also the owner's residence
SHOPHROTH > SHOPHAR
SHOPLESS adj (of an area) having no shops
SHOPLIFT vb steal from shop
SHOPLIFTS > SHOPLIFT
SHOPMAN n man working in shop
SHOPMEN > SHOPMAN
SHOPPE old-fashioned spelling of > SHOP
SHOPPED > SHOP
SHOPPER n person who buys goods in a shop
SHOPPERS > SHOPPER
SHOPPES > SHOPPE
SHOPPIER > SHOPPY
SHOPPIES > SHOPPY
SHOPPIEST > SHOPPY
SHOPPING > SHOP
SHOPPINGS > SHOP
SHOPPY adj of a shop ▷ n shop assistant
SHOPS > SHOP
SHOPTALK n conversation about one's work, carried on outside working hours
SHOPTALKS > SHOPTALK
SHOPWOMAN n woman working in a shop
SHOPWOMEN > SHOPWOMAN
SHOPWORN adj worn or faded from being displayed in a shop
SHORAN n short-range radar system
SHORANS > SHORAN
SHORE n edge of a sea or lake ▷ vb prop or support
SHOREBIRD n bird that lives close to the water
SHORED > SHORE
SHOREFAST adj (of ice) attached to the shore
SHORELESS adj without a shore suitable for landing
SHORELINE n edge of a sea, lake, or wide river
SHOREMAN n person who lives on the shore
SHOREMEN > SHOREMAN
SHORER > SHORE
SHORERS > SHORE
SHORES > SHORE
SHORESIDE n area at the shore
SHORESMAN n fishing industry worker on the shore
SHORESMEN > SHORESMAN
SHOREWARD adj near or facing the shore ▷ adv towards the shore
SHOREWEED n tufty aquatic perennial plant
SHORING > SHORE
SHORINGS > SHORE
SHORL n black mineral
SHORLS > SHORL
SHORN past participle of > SHEAR

SHORT adj not long ▷ adv abruptly ▷ n drink of spirits ▷ vb short-circuit
SHORTAGE n deficiency
SHORTAGES > SHORTAGE
SHORTARM adj (of a punch) with the arm bent
SHORTARSE n short person
SHORTCAKE n shortbread
SHORTCUT n route that is shorter than the usual one
SHORTCUTS > SHORTCUT
SHORTED > SHORT
SHORTEN vb make or become shorter
SHORTENED > SHORTEN
SHORTENER > SHORTEN
SHORTENS > SHORTEN
SHORTER > SHORT
SHORTEST > SHORT
SHORTFALL n deficit
SHORTGOWN n old Scots word meaning woman's jacket
SHORTHAIR n cat with short fur
SHORTHAND n system of rapid writing using symbols to represent words
SHORTHEAD n species of fish
SHORTHOLD n as in shorthold tenancy letting of a dwelling for between one and five years at a fair rent
SHORTHORN n member of a breed of cattle with short horns
SHORTIA n American flowering plant
SHORTIAS > SHORTIA
SHORTIE n person or thing that is extremely short
SHORTIES > SHORTIE
SHORTING > SHORT
SHORTISH > SHORT
SHORTLIST n list of suitable applicants for a job, etc
SHORTLY adv soon
SHORTNESS > SHORT
SHORTS pl n trousers reaching the top of the thigh or partway to the knee
SHORTSTOP n fielding position to the left of second base viewed from home plate
SHORTWAVE n radio wave with a wavelength in the range 10–100 metres
SHORTY same as > SHORTIE
SHOT vb load with shot
SHOTCRETE n type of concrete sprayed from a hose
SHOTE same as > SHOAT
SHOTES > SHOTE
SHOTFIRER n person detonating a blasting charge
SHOTGUN n gun for firing a charge of shot at short range ▷ adj involving coercion or duress ▷ vb shoot or threaten with or as if with a shotgun
SHOTGUNS > SHOTGUN
SHOTHOLE n drilled hole into which explosive is put for blasting
SHOTHOLES > SHOTHOLE

SHOTMAKER n sport player making good shots
SHOTPROOF adj able to withstand shot
SHOTS > SHOT
SHOTT n shallow temporary salt lake or marsh in the North African desert
SHOTTE n old form of shoat
SHOTTED > SHOT
SHOTTEN adj (of fish, esp herring) having recently spawned
SHOTTES > SHOTTE
SHOTTING > SHOT
SHOTTLE n small drawer
SHOTTLES > SHOTTLE
SHOTTS > SHOTT
SHOUGH n old word meaning lapdog
SHOUGHS > SHOUGH
SHOULD > SHALL
SHOULDER n part of the body to which an arm, foreleg, or wing is attached ▷ vb bear (a burden or responsibility)
SHOULDERS > SHOULDER
SHOULDEST same as > SHOULDST
SHOULDST form of the past tense of > SHALL
SHOUSE n toilet ▷ adj unwell or in poor spirits
SHOUSES > SHOUSE
SHOUT n loud cry ▷ vb cry out loudly
SHOUTED > SHOUT
SHOUTER > SHOUT
SHOUTERS > SHOUT
SHOUTHER Scots form of > SHOULDER
SHOUTHERS > SHOUTHER
SHOUTIER > SHOUTY
SHOUTIEST > SHOUTY
SHOUTING > SHOUT
SHOUTINGS > SHOUT
SHOUTLINE n line in advertisement made prominent to catch attention
SHOUTOUT n public greeting, esp one broadcast via television or radio
SHOUTOUTS > SHOUTOUT
SHOUTS > SHOUT
SHOUTY adj characterized by or involving shouting
SHOVE vb push roughly ▷ n rough push
SHOVED > SHOVE
SHOVEL n tool for lifting or moving loose material ▷ vb lift or move as with a shovel
SHOVELED > SHOVEL
SHOVELER n type of duck
SHOVELERS > SHOVELER
SHOVELFUL > SHOVEL
SHOVELING > SHOVEL
SHOVELLED > SHOVEL
SHOVELLER > SHOVEL
SHOVELS > SHOVEL
SHOVER > SHOVE
SHOVERS > SHOVE
SHOVES > SHOVE
SHOVING n act of pushing hard

SHOVINGS > SHOVING
SHOW vb make, be, or become noticeable or visible ▷ n public exhibition
SHOWABLE > SHOW
SHOWBIZ n entertainment industry including theatre, films, and TV
SHOWBIZZY adj characteristic of showbiz
SHOWBOAT n paddle-wheel river steamer with a theatre and a repertory company ▷ vb perform or behave in a showy and flamboyant way
SHOWBOATS > SHOWBOAT
SHOWBOX n box containing showman's material
SHOWBOXES > SHOWBOX
SHOWBREAD same as > SHEWBREAD
SHOWCASE n situation in which something is displayed to best advantage ▷ vb exhibit or display ▷ adj displayed or meriting display as in a showcase
SHOWCASED > SHOWCASE
SHOWCASES > SHOWCASE
SHOWD vb rock or sway to and fro ▷ n rocking motion
SHOWDED > SHOWD
SHOWDING > SHOWD
SHOWDOWN n confrontation that settles a dispute
SHOWDOWNS > SHOWDOWN
SHOWDS > SHOWD
SHOWED > SHOW
SHOWER n kind of bath in which a person stands while being sprayed with water ▷ vb wash in a shower
SHOWERED > SHOWER
SHOWERER > SHOWER
SHOWERERS > SHOWER
SHOWERFUL > SHOWER
SHOWERIER > SHOWER
SHOWERING > SHOWER
SHOWERS > SHOWER
SHOWERY > SHOWER
SHOWGHE n old word meaning lapdog
SHOWGHES > SHOWGHE
SHOWGIRL n girl who appears in shows, etc, esp as a singer or dancer
SHOWGIRLS > SHOWGIRL
SHOWGOER n member of the audience of a play, film, or show
SHOWGOERS > SHOWGOER
SHOWIER > SHOWY
SHOWIEST > SHOWY
SHOWILY > SHOWY
SHOWINESS > SHOWY
SHOWING > SHOW
SHOWINGS > SHOW
SHOWJUMP vb take part in a showjumping competition
SHOWJUMPS > SHOWJUMP
SHOWMAN n man skilled at presenting anything spectacularly
SHOWMANCE n romance between two stars that lasts only for the run of the show they are in

SHOWMANLY *adj* like a showman

SHOWMEN > SHOWMAN

SHOWN > SHOW

SHOWOFF *n* person who makes a vain display of himself or herself

SHOWOFFS > SHOWOFF

SHOWPIECE *n* excellent specimen shown for display or as an example

SHOWPLACE *n* place visited for its beauty or interest

SHOWRING *n* area where animals are displayed for sale or competition

SHOWRINGS > SHOWRING

SHOWROOM *n* room in which goods for sale are on display

SHOWROOMS > SHOWROOM

SHOWS > SHOW

SHOWTIME *n* time when show begins

SHOWTIMES > SHOWTIME

SHOWY *adj* gaudy

SHOWYARD *n* yard where cattle are displayed

SHOWYARDS > SHOWYARD

SHOYU *n* Japanese variety of soy sauce

SHOYUS > SHOYU

SHRADDHA *n* Hindu offering to an ancestor

SHRADDHAS > SHRADDHA

SHRANK > SHRINK

SHRAPNEL *n* artillery shell filled with pellets which scatter on explosion

SHRAPNELS > SHRAPNEL

SHRED *n* long narrow strip torn from something ▷ *vb* tear to shreds

SHREDDED > SHRED

SHREDDER > SHRED

SHREDDERS > SHRED

SHREDDIER > SHRED

SHREDDING > SHRED

SHREDDY > SHRED

SHREDLESS > SHRED

SHREDS > SHRED

SHREEK *old spelling of* > SHRIEK

SHREEKED > SHREEK

SHREEKING > SHREEK

SHREEKS > SHREEK

SHREIK *old spelling of* > SHRIEK

SHREIKED > SHREIK

SHREIKING > SHREIK

SHREIKS > SHREIK

SHREW *n* small mouselike animal ▷ *vb* curse or damn

SHREWD *adj* clever and perceptive

SHREWDER > SHREWD

SHREWDEST > SHREWD

SHREWDIE *n* shrewd person

SHREWDIES > SHREWDIE

SHREWDLY > SHREWD

SHREWED > SHREW

SHREWING > SHREW

SHREWISH *adj* bad-tempered and nagging

SHREWLIKE > SHREW

SHREWMICE *pl n* shrews

SHREWS > SHREW

SHRI *n* Indian title of respect

SHRIECH *old spelling of* > SHRIEK

SHRIECHED > SHRIECH

SHRIECHES > SHRIECH

SHRIEK *n* shrill cry ▷ *vb* utter (with) a shriek

SHRIEKED > SHRIEK

SHRIEKER > SHRIEK

SHRIEKERS > SHRIEK

SHRIEKIER > SHRIEK

SHRIEKING > SHRIEK

SHRIEKS > SHRIEK

SHRIEKY > SHRIEK

SHRIEVAL *adj* of or relating to a sheriff

SHRIEVE *archaic word for* > SHERIFF

SHRIEVED > SHRIEVE

SHRIEVES > SHRIEVE

SHRIEVING > SHRIEVE

SHRIFT *n* act or an instance of shriving or being shriven

SHRIFTS > SHRIFT

SHRIGHT *n* old word meaning shriek

SHRIGHTS > SHRIGHT

SHRIKE *n* songbird with a heavy hooked bill ▷ *vb* archaic word for shriek

SHRIKED > SHRIKE

SHRIKES > SHRIKE

SHRIKING > SHRIKE

SHRILL *adj* (of a sound) sharp and high-pitched ▷ *vb* utter shrilly

SHRILLED > SHRILL

SHRILLER > SHRILL

SHRILLEST > SHRILL

SHRILLIER > SHRILL

SHRILLING > SHRILL

SHRILLS > SHRILL

SHRILLY > SHRILL

SHRIMP *n* small edible shellfish ▷ *vb* fish for shrimps

SHRIMPED > SHRIMP

SHRIMPER > SHRIMP

SHRIMPERS > SHRIMP

SHRIMPIER > SHRIMP

SHRIMPING > SHRIMP

SHRIMPS > SHRIMP

SHRIMPY > SHRIMP

SHRINAL > SHRINE

SHRINE *n* place of worship associated with a sacred person or object ▷ *vb* enshrine

SHRINED > SHRINE

SHRINES > SHRINE

SHRINING > SHRINE

SHRINK *vb* become or make smaller ▷ *n* psychiatrist

SHRINKAGE *n* decrease in size, value, or weight

SHRINKER > SHRINK

SHRINKERS > SHRINK

SHRINKING > SHRINK

SHRINKS > SHRINK

SHRIS > SHRI

SHRITCH *vb* old word meaning shriek

SHRITCHED > SHRITCH

SHRITCHES > SHRITCH

SHRIVE *vb* hear the confession of (a penitent)

SHRIVED > SHRIVE

SHRIVEL *vb* shrink and wither

SHRIVELED > SHRIVEL

SHRIVELS > SHRIVEL

SHRIVEN > SHRIVE

SHRIVER > SHRIVE

SHRIVERS > SHRIVE

SHRIVES > SHRIVE

SHRIVING > SHRIVE

SHRIVINGS > SHRIVE

SHROFF *n* (in China and Japan) expert employed to identify counterfeit money ▷ *vb* test (money) and separate out the counterfeit and base

SHROFFAGE > SHROFF

SHROFFED > SHROFF

SHROFFING > SHROFF

SHROFFS > SHROFF

SHROOM *n* slang for magic mushroom ▷ *vb* take magic mushrooms

SHROOMED > SHROOM

SHROOMER > SHROOM

SHROOMERS > SHROOM

SHROOMING > SHROOM

SHROOMS > SHROOM

SHROUD *n* piece of cloth used to wrap a dead body ▷ *vb* conceal

SHROUDED > SHROUD

SHROUDIER > SHROUD

SHROUDING > SHROUD

SHROUDS > SHROUD

SHROUDY > SHROUD

SHROVE *vb* dialect word meaning to observe Shrove-tide

SHROVED > SHROVE

SHROVES > SHROVE

SHROVING > SHROVE

SHROW *vb* old form of shrew

SHROWD *adj* old form of shrewd

SHROWED > SHROW

SHROWING > SHROW

SHROWS > SHROW

SHRUB *n* woody plant smaller than a tree ▷ *vb* plant shrubs

SHRUBBED > SHRUB

SHRUBBERY *n* area planted with shrubs

SHRUBBIER > SHRUBBY

SHRUBBING > SHRUB

SHRUBBY *adj* consisting of, planted with, or abounding in shrubs

SHRUBLAND *n* land covered by shrubs

SHRUBLESS > SHRUB

SHRUBLIKE > SHRUB

SHRUBS > SHRUB

SHRUG *vb* raise and then drop (the shoulders) as a sign of indifference or doubt ▷ *n* shrugging

SHRUGGED > SHRUG

SHRUGGING > SHRUG

SHRUGS > SHRUG

SHRUNK > SHRINK

SHRUNKEN *adj* reduced in size

SHTCHI *n* Russian cabbage soup

SHTCHIS > SHTCHI

SHTETEL *same as* > SHTETL

SHTETELS > SHTETEL

SHTETL *n* Jewish community in Eastern Europe

SHTETLACH > SHTETL

SHTETLS > SHTETL

SHTICK *n* comedian's routine

SHTICKIER > SHTICK

SHTICKS > SHTICK

SHTICKY > SHTICK

SHTIK *n* shtick

SHTIKS > SHTIK

SHTOOK *n* trouble

SHTOOKS > SHTOOK

SHTOOM *adj* silent

SHTOOMER > SHTOOM

SHTOOMEST > SHTOOM

SHTREIMEL *n* broad-brimmed hat worn by some Hasidic Jews

SHTUCK *n* trouble

SHTUCKS > SHTUCK

SHTUM *adj* silent

SHTUMM *adj* silent

SHTUMMER > SHTUMM

SHTUMMEST > SHTUMM

SHTUP *vb* vulgar slang word meaning to have sex (with)

SHTUPPED > SHTUP

SHTUPPING > SHTUP

SHTUPS > SHTUP

SHUBUNKIN *n* type of goldfish

SHUCK *n* outer covering of something ▷ *vb* remove the shucks from

SHUCKED > SHUCK

SHUCKER > SHUCK

SHUCKERS > SHUCK

SHUCKING > SHUCK

SHUCKINGS > SHUCK

SHUCKS *pl n* something of little value ▷ *interj* exclamation of disappointment, annoyance, etc

SHUDDER *vb* shake or tremble violently, esp with horror ▷ *n* instance of shaking or trembling

SHUDDERED > SHUDDER

SHUDDERS > SHUDDER

SHUDDERY *adj* shuddering

SHUFFLE *vb* walk without lifting the feet ▷ *n* act of shuffling

SHUFFLED > SHUFFLE

SHUFFLER > SHUFFLE

SHUFFLERS > SHUFFLE

SHUFFLES > SHUFFLE

SHUFFLING > SHUFFLE

SHUFTI *same as* > SHUFTY

SHUFTIES > SHUFTY

SHUFTIS > SHUFTY

SHUFTY *n* look

SHUGGIES > SHUGGY

SHUGGY *n* swing, as at a fairground

SHUL *Yiddish word for* > SYNAGOGUE

SHULE *vb* saunter

SHULED > SHULE

SHULES > SHULE

SHULING > SHULE

SHULN > SHUL

SHULS > SHUL

SHUMAI *pl n* (in Japan) small stuffed dumplings

SHUN vb avoid
SHUNLESS adj old word meaning not to be shunned
SHUNNABLE > SHUN
SHUNNED > SHUN
SHUNNER > SHUN
SHUNNERS > SHUN
SHUNNING > SHUN
SHUNPIKE vb take side road to avoid toll at turnpike
SHUNPIKED > SHUNPIKE
SHUNPIKER > SHUNPIKE
SHUNPIKES > SHUNPIKE
SHUNS > SHUN
SHUNT vb move (objects or people) to a different position ▷ n shunting
SHUNTED > SHUNT
SHUNTER n small railway locomotive used for manoeuvring coaches
SHUNTERS > SHUNTER
SHUNTING > SHUNT
SHUNTINGS > SHUNT
SHUNTS > SHUNT
SHURA n consultative council or assembly
SHURAS > SHURA
SHURIKEN n Japanese weapon with blades or points, thrown by hand
SHURIKENS > SHURIKEN
SHUSH interj be quiet! ▷ vb quiet by saying 'shush'
SHUSHED > SHUSH
SHUSHER > SHUSH
SHUSHERS > SHUSH
SHUSHES > SHUSH
SHUSHING > SHUSH
SHUT vb bring together or fold, close
SHUTDOWN n closing of a factory, shop, or other business ▷ vb discontinue operations permanently
SHUTDOWNS > SHUTDOWN
SHUTE variant of > CHUTE
SHUTED > SHUTE
SHUTES > SHUTE
SHUTEYE n sleep
SHUTEYES > SHUTEYE
SHUTING > SHUTE
SHUTOFF n device that shuts something off
SHUTOFFS > SHUTOFF
SHUTOUT n game in which the opposing team does not score
SHUTOUTS > SHUTOUT
SHUTS > SHUT
SHUTTER n hinged doorlike cover for closing off a window ▷ vb close or equip with a shutter
SHUTTERED > SHUTTER
SHUTTERS > SHUTTER
SHUTTING > SHUT
SHUTTLE n bobbin-like device used in weaving ▷ vb move by or as if by a shuttle
SHUTTLED > SHUTTLE
SHUTTLER > SHUTTLE
SHUTTLERS > SHUTTLE
SHUTTLES > SHUTTLE
SHUTTLING > SHUTTLE
SHVARTZE same as > SCHVARTZE

SHVARTZES > SHVARTZE
SHVITZ vb sweat
SHVITZED > SHVITZ
SHVTTZES > SHVITZ
SHVITZING > SHVITZ
SHWA same as > SCHWA
SHWANPAN same as > SWANPAN
SHWANPANS > SHWANPAN
SHWAS > SHWA
SHWESHWE n African cotton print fabric
SHWESHWES > SHWESHWE
SHY adj not at ease in company ▷ vb start back in fear ▷ n throw
SHYER > SHY
SHYERS > SHY
SHYEST > SHY
SHYING > SHY
SHYISH > SHY
SHYLOCK vb lend money at an exorbitant rate of interest
SHYLOCKED > SHYLOCK
SHYLOCKS > SHYLOCK
SHYLY > SHY
SHYNESS > SHY
SHYNESSES > SHY
SHYPOO n liquor of poor quality
SHYPOOS > SHYPOO
SHYSTER n person who uses discreditable or unethical methods
SHYSTERS > SHYSTER
SI same as > TE
SIAL n silicon-rich and aluminium-rich rocks of the earth's continental upper crust
SIALIC > SIAL
SIALID n species of fly
SIALIDAN > SIALID
SIALIDANS > SIALID
SIALIDS > SIALID
SIALOGRAM n X-ray of salivary gland
SIALOID adj resembling saliva
SIALOLITH n hard deposit formed in salivary gland
SIALON n type of ceramic
SIALONS > SIALON
SIALS > SIAL
SIAMANG n large black gibbon
SIAMANGS > SIAMANG
SIAMESE variant of > SIAMEZE
SIAMESED > SIAMESE
SIAMESES > SIAMESE
SIAMESING > SIAMESE
SIAMEZE vb join together
SIAMEZED > SIAMEZE
SIAMEZES > SIAMEZE
SIAMEZING > SIAMEZE
SIB n blood relative
SIBB n sib
SIBBS > SIBB
SIBILANCE > SIBILANT
SIBILANCY > SIBILANT
SIBILANT adj hissing ▷ n consonant pronounced with a hissing sound
SIBILANTS > SIBILANT
SIBILATE vb pronounce or utter (words or speech) with a hissing sound

SIBILATED > SIBILATE
SIBILATES > SIBILATE
SIBILATOR > SIBILATE
SIBILOUS > SIBILANT
SIBLING n brother or sister
SIBLINGS > SIBLING
SIBS > SIB
SIBSHIP n group of children of the same parents
SIBSHIPS > SIBSHIP
SIBYL n (in ancient Greece and Rome) prophetess
SIBYLIC > SIBYL
SIBYLLIC > SIBYL
SIBYLLINE > SIBYL
SIBYLS > SIBYL
SIC adv thus ▷ vb attack
SICARIO n hired gunman, esp in Latin America
SICARIOS > SICARIO
SICCAN adj Scots word meaning such
SICCAR adj sure
SICCATIVE n substance added to a liquid to promote drying
SICCED > SIC
SICCING > SIC
SICCTTIES > SICCITY
SICCITY n dryness
SICE same as > SYCE
SICES > SICE
SICH adj old form of such
SICHT Scot word for > SIGHT
SICHTED > SICHT
SICHTING > SICHT
SICHTS > SICHT
SICILIANA n Sicilian dance
SICILIANE > SICILIANA
SICILIANO n old dance in six-beat or twelve-beat time
SICK adj vomiting or likely to vomit ▷ n vomit ▷ vb vomit
SICKBAY n room for the treatment of sick people
SICKBAYS > SICKBAY
SICKBED n bed where sick person lies
SICKBEDS > SICKBED
SICKED > SICK
SICKEE n person off work through illness
SICKEES > SICKEE
SICKEN vb make nauseated or disgusted
SICKENED > SICKEN
SICKENER n something that induces sickness or nausea
SICKENERS > SICKENER
SICKENING adj causing horror or disgust
SICKENS > SICKEN
SICKER > SICK
SICKERLY adv Scots word meaning surely
SICKEST > SICK
SICKIE n day of sick leave from work
SICKIES > SICKIE
SICKING > SICK
SICKISH > SICK
SICKISHLY > SICK
SICKLE n tool with a curved blade for cutting grass or grain ▷ vb cut with a sickle
SICKLED > SICKLE

SICKLEMAN n person reaping with sickle
SICKLEMEN > SICKLEMAN
SICKLEMIA n form of anaemia
SICKLEMIC > SICKLEMIA
SICKLES > SICKLE
SICKLIED > SICKLY
SICKLIER > SICKLY
SICKLIES > SICKLY
SICKLIEST > SICKLY
SICKLILY > SICKLY
SICKLING > SICKLE
SICKLY adj unhealthy, weak ▷ adv suggesting sickness ▷ vb make sickly
SICKLYING > SICKLY
SICKNESS n particular illness or disease
SICKNURSE n person nursing sick person ▷ vb act as a sicknurse
SICKO n person who is mentally disturbed or perverted ▷ adj perverted or in bad taste
SICKOS > SICKO
SICKOUT n industrial action in which all workers report sick simultaneously
SICKOUTS > SICKOUT
SICKROOM n room to which a person who is ill is confined
SICKROOMS > SICKROOM
SICKS > SICK
SICKY n day off work due to illness
SICLIKE adj Scots word meaning suchlike
SICS > SIC
SIDA n Australian hemp plant
SIDALCEA n type of perennial N American plant
SIDALCEAS > SIDALCEA
SIDAS > SIDA
SIDDHA n (in Hinduism) person who has achieved perfection
SIDDHAS > SIDDHA
SIDDHI n (in Hinduism) power attained with perfection
SIDDHIS > SIDDHI
SIDDHUISM n (in Indian English) any contrived metaphor or simile
SIDDUR n Jewish prayer book
SIDDURIM > SIDDUR
SIDDURS > SIDDUR
SIDE n line or surface that borders anything ▷ adj at or on the side
SIDEARM n weapon worn on belt ▷ vb provide with a sidearm
SIDEARMED > SIDEARM
SIDEARMER n person who pitches a ball with the arm parallel to the ground
SIDEARMS > SIDEARM
SIDEBAND n frequency band either above or below the carrier frequency
SIDEBANDS > SIDEBAND
SIDEBAR n small newspaper article beside larger one

SIDEBARS > SIDEBAR
SIDEBOARD n piece of furniture for holding plates, cutlery, etc in a dining room
SIDEBONE n damage to the cartilage in a horse's hoof
SIDEBONES n part of horse's hoof
SIDEBURN n strip of whiskers down one side of a man's face
SIDEBURNS > SIDEBURN
SIDECAR n small passenger car on the side of a motorcycle
SIDECARS > SIDECAR
SIDECHAIR n chair without arms
SIDECHECK n part of horse's harness
SIDED > SIDE
SIDEDLY adv pertaining to given number of sides
SIDEDNESS > SIDE
SIDEDRESS vb place fertilizer in the soil near the roots of a plant
SIDEHILL n side of hill
SIDEHILLS > SIDEHILL
SIDEKICK n close friend or associate
SIDEKICKS > SIDEKICK
SIDELESS adj without sides
SIDELIGHT n either of two small lights on the front of a vehicle
SIDELINE n subsidiary interest or source of income ▷ vb prevent (a player) from taking part in a game
SIDELINED > SIDELINE
SIDELINER > SIDELINE
SIDELINES pl n area immediately outside the playing area, where substitute players sit
SIDELING adj to one side ▷ adv sideways ▷ n slope, esp on the side of a road
SIDELINGS > SIDELING
SIDELOCK n long lock of hair on side of head
SIDELOCKS > SIDELOCK
SIDELONG adj sideways ▷ adv obliquely
SIDEMAN n member of a dance band or a jazz group other than the leader
SIDEMEAT n meat from the side of a pig
SIDEMEATS > SIDEMEAT
SIDEMEN > SIDEMAN
SIDENOTE n note written in margin
SIDENOTES > SIDENOTE
SIDEPATH n minor path
SIDEPATHS > SIDEPATH
SIDEPIECE n part forming side of something
SIDER n one who sides with another
SIDERAL adj from the stars
SIDERATE vb strike violently
SIDERATED > SIDERATE
SIDERATES > SIDERATE
SIDEREAL adj of or determined with reference to the stars

SIDERITE n pale yellow to brownish-black mineral
SIDERITES > SIDERITE
SIDERITIC > SIDERITE
SIDEROAD n (esp in Ontario) a road going at right angles to concession roads
SIDEROADS > SIDEROAD
SIDEROSES > SIDEROSIS
SIDEROSIS n lung disease caused by breathing in fine particles of iron or other metallic dust
SIDEROTIC > SIDEROSIS
SIDERS > SIDER
SIDES > SIDE
SIDESHOOT n minor shoot growing on plant
SIDESHOW n entertainment offered along with the main show
SIDESHOWS > SIDESHOW
SIDESLIP same as > SLIP
SIDESLIPS > SIDESLIP
SIDESMAN n man elected to help the parish church warden
SIDESMEN > SIDESMAN
SIDESPIN n horizontal spin put on ball
SIDESPINS > SIDESPIN
SIDESPLIT n house with a higher storey at the side
SIDESTEP vb dodge (an issue) ▷ n movement to one side, such as in dancing or boxing
SIDESTEPS > SIDESTEP
SIDESWIPE n unexpected criticism of someone or something while discussing another subject ▷ vb make a sideswipe
SIDETABLE n small table at the side of a room
SIDETRACK vb divert from the main topic ▷ n railway siding
SIDEWALK n paved path for pedestrians, at the side of a road
SIDEWALKS > SIDEWALK
SIDEWALL n either of the sides of a pneumatic tyre between the tread and the rim
SIDEWALLS > SIDEWALL
SIDEWARD adj directed or moving towards one side ▷ adv towards one side
SIDEWARDS adv towards one side
SIDEWAY variant of > SIDEWAYS
SIDEWAYS adv or from the side ▷ adj moving or directed to or from one side
SIDEWHEEL n one of the paddle wheels of a sidewheeler
SIDEWISE adv sideways
SIDH pl n fairy people
SIDHA n (in Hinduism) person who has achieved perfection
SIDHAS > SIDHA
SIDHE pl n inhabitants of fairyland

SIDHUISM n contrived metaphor or simile
SIDHUISMS > SIDHUISM
SIDING n short stretch of railway track on which trains are shunted from the main line
SIDINGS > SIDING
SIDLE vb walk in a furtive manner ▷ n sideways movement
SIDLED > SIDLE
SIDLER > SIDLE
SIDLERS > SIDLE
SIDLES > SIDLE
SIDLING > SIDLE
SIDLINGLY > SIDLE
SIECLE n century, period, or era
SIECLES > SIECLE
SIEGE n surrounding and blockading of a place ▷ vb lay siege to
SIEGED > SIEGE
SIEGER n person who besieges
SIEGERS > SIEGER
SIEGES > SIEGE
SIEGING > SIEGE
SIELD adj (archaic) provided with a ceiling
SIEMENS n SI unit of electrical conductance
SIEMENSES > SIEMENS
SIEN n old word meaning scion
SIENITE n type of igneous rock
SIENITES > SIENITE
SIENNA n reddish- or yellowish-brown pigment made from natural earth
SIENNAS > SIENNA
SIENS > SIEN
SIENT n old word meaning scion
SIENTS > SIENT
SIEROZEM n type of soil
SIEROZEMS > SIEROZEM
SIERRA n range of mountains in Spain or America with jagged peaks
SIERRAN > SIERRA
SIERRAS > SIERRA
SIES interj in South Africa, an exclamation of disgust
SIESTA n afternoon nap, taken in hot countries
SIESTAS > SIESTA
SIETH n old form of scythe
SIETHS > SIETH
SIEUR n French word meaning lord
SIEURS > SIEUR
SIEVE n utensil with mesh through which a substance is sifted or strained ▷ vb sift or strain through a sieve
SIEVED > SIEVE
SIEVELIKE > SIEVE
SIEVERT n derived SI unit of dose equivalent, equal to 1 joule per kilogram
SIEVERTS > SIEVERT
SIEVES > SIEVE
SIEVING > SIEVE
SIF adj South African slang for disgusting

SIFAKA n either of two large rare arboreal lemuroid primates
SIFAKAS > SIFAKA
SIFFLE vb whistle
SIFFLED > SIFFLE
SIFFLES > SIFFLE
SIFFLEUR n male professional whistler
SIFFLEURS > SIFFLEUR
SIFFLEUSE n female professional whistler
SIFFLING > SIFFLE
SIFREI > SEFER
SIFT vb remove the coarser particles from a substance with a sieve
SIFTED > SIFT
SIFTER > SIFT
SIFTERS > SIFT
SIFTING > SIFT
SIFTINGLY > SIFT
SIFTINGS pl n material or particles separated out by or as if by a sieve
SIFTS > SIFT
SIG n short for signature
SIGANID n tropical fish
SIGANIDS > SIGANID
SIGH n long audible breath expressing sadness, tiredness, relief, or longing ▷ vb utter a sigh
SIGHED > SIGH
SIGHER > SIGH
SIGHERS > SIGH
SIGHFUL > SIGH
SIGHING n act of sighing
SIGHINGLY > SIGH
SIGHINGS > SIGHING
SIGHLESS > SIGH
SIGHLIKE > SIGH
SIGHS > SIGH
SIGHT n ability to see ▷ vb catch sight of
SIGHTABLE > SIGHT
SIGHTED adj not blind
SIGHTER n any of six practice shots allowed to each competitor in a tournament
SIGHTERS > SIGHTER
SIGHTING > SIGHT
SIGHTINGS > SIGHT
SIGHTLESS adj blind
SIGHTLIER > SIGHTLY
SIGHTLINE n uninterrupted line of vision
SIGHTLY adj pleasing or attractive to see
SIGHTS > SIGHT
SIGHTSAW > SIGHTSEE
SIGHTSEE vb visit the famous or interesting sights of (a place)
SIGHTSEEN > SIGHTSEE
SIGHTSEER > SIGHTSEE
SIGHTSEES > SIGHTSEE
SIGHTSMAN n tourist guide
SIGHTSMEN > SIGHTSMAN
SIGIL n seal or signet
SIGILLARY > SIGIL
SIGILLATE adj closed with seal
SIGILS > SIGIL
SIGISBEI > SIGISBEO
SIGISBEO n male escort for a married woman

S

S

SIGLA *n* list of symbols used in a book
SIGLAS > SIGLA
SIGLOI > SIGLOS
SIGLOS *n* silver coin of ancient Persia
SIGLUM *n* symbol used in book
SIGMA *n* 18th letter in the Greek alphabet
SIGMAS > SIGMA
SIGMATE *adj* shaped like the Greek letter sigma or the Roman S ▷ *n* sigmate thing ▷ *vb* add a sigma
SIGMATED > SIGMATE
SIGMATES > SIGMATE
SIGMATIC > SIGMATE
SIGMATING > SIGMATE
SIGMATION > SIGMATE
SIGMATISM *n* repetition of letter s
SIGMATRON *n* machine for generating X-rays
SIGMOID *adj* shaped like the letter S ▷ *n* S-shaped bend in the final portion of the large intestine
SIGMOIDAL *variant of* > SIGMOID
SIGMOIDS > SIGMOID
SIGN *n* indication of something not immediately or outwardly observable ▷ *vb* write (one's name) on (a document or letter) to show its authenticity
SIGNA *pl n* symbols
SIGNABLE > SIGN
SIGNAGE *n* signs collectively
SIGNAGES > SIGNAGE
SIGNAL *n* sign or gesture to convey information ▷ *adj* very important ▷ *vb* convey (information) by signal
SIGNALED > SIGNAL
SIGNALER > SIGNAL
SIGNALERS > SIGNAL
SIGNALING > SIGNAL
SIGNALISE *same as* > SIGNALIZE
SIGNALIZE *vb* make noteworthy or conspicuous
SIGNALLED > SIGNAL
SIGNALLER > SIGNAL
SIGNALLY *adv* conspicuously or especially
SIGNALMAN *n* railwayman in charge of signals and points
SIGNALMEN > SIGNALMAN
SIGNALS > SIGNAL
SIGNARIES > SIGNARY
SIGNARY *n* set of symbols
SIGNATORY *n* one of the parties who sign a document ▷ *adj* having signed a document or treaty
SIGNATURE *n* person's name written by himself or herself in signing something
SIGNBOARD *n* board carrying a sign or notice, often to advertise a business or product
SIGNED > SIGN
SIGNEE *n* person signing document

SIGNEES > SIGNEE
SIGNER *n* person who signs something
SIGNERS > STGNER
SIGNET *n* small seal used to authenticate documents ▷ *vb* stamp or authenticate with a signet
SIGNETED > SIGNET
SIGNETING > SIGNET
SIGNETS > SIGNET
SIGNEUR *old spelling of* > SENIOR
SIGNEURIE *n* old word meaning seniority
SIGNIEUR *n* old word meaning lord
SIGNIEURS > SIGNIEUR
SIGNIFICS *n* study of meaning
SIGNIFIED > SIGNIFY
SIGNIFIER > SIGNIFY
SIGNIFIES > SIGNIFY
SIGNIFY *vb* indicate or suggest
SIGNING *n* system of communication using hand and arm movements
SIGNINGS > SIGNING
SIGNIOR *same as* > SIGNOR
SIGNIORI > SIGNIOR
SIGNIORS > SIGNIOR
SIGNIORY *n* old word meaning lordship
SIGNLESS > SIGN
SIGNOR *n* Italian term of address equivalent to sir or Mr
SIGNORA *n* Italian term of address equivalent to madam or Mrs
SIGNORAS > SIGNORA
SIGNORE *n* Italian man: a title of respect equivalent to sir
SIGNORES > SIGNORE
SIGNORI > SIGNORE
SIGNORIA *n* government of Italian city
SIGNORIAL > SIGNORIA
SIGNORIAS > SIGNORIA
SIGNORIES > SIGNORY
SIGNORINA *n* Italian term of address equivalent to madam or Miss
SIGNORINE > SIGNORINA
SIGNORINI > SIGNORINO
SIGNORINO *n* young gentleman
SIGNORS > SIGNOR
SIGNORY *same as* > SEIGNIORY
SIGNPOST *n* post bearing a sign that shows the way ▷ *vb* mark with signposts
SIGNPOSTS > SIGNPOST
SIGNS > SIGN
SIGS > SIG
SIJO *n* Korean poem
SIJOS > SIJO
SIK *adj* excellent
SIKA *n* Japanese forest-dwelling deer
SIKAS > SIKA
SIKE *n* small stream
SIKER *adj* old spelling of sicker

SIKES > SIKE
SIKORSKY *n* type of helicopter
SIKSIK *n* Arctic ground squirrel
SIKSIKS > SIKSIK
SILAGE *n* fodder crop harvested while green and partially fermented in a silo ▷ *vb* make silage
SILAGED > SILAGE
SILAGEING > SILAGE
SILAGES > SILAGE
SILAGING > SILAGE
SILANE *n* gas containing silicon
SILANES > SILANE
SILASTIC *n* tradename for a type of flexible silicone rubber
SILASTICS > SILASTIC
SILD *n* any of various small young herrings
SILDS > SILD
SILE *vb* pour with rain
SILED > SILE
SILEN *n* god of woodland
SILENCE *n* absence of noise or speech ▷ *vb* make silent
SILENCED *adj* (of a member of the clergy) forbidden to preach or perform clerical functions
SILENCER *n* device to reduce the noise of an engine exhaust or gun
SILENCERS > SILENCER
SILENCES > SILENCE
SILENCING > SILENCE
SILENE *n* type of plant with mostly red or pink flowers, often grown as a garden plant
SILENES > SILENE
SILENI > SILENUS
SILENS > SILEN
SILENT *adj* tending to speak very little ▷ *n* silent film
SILENTER > SILENT
SILENTEST > SILENT
SILENTLY > SILENT
SILENTS > SILENT
SILENUS *n* woodland deity
SILER *n* strainer
SILERS > SILER
SILES > SILE
SILESIA *n* twill-weave fabric of cotton or other fibre
SILESIAS > SILESIA
SILEX *n* type of heat-resistant glass made from fused quartz
SILEXES > SILEX
SILICA *n* hard glossy mineral found as quartz and in sandstone
SILICAS > SILICA
SILICATE *n* compound of silicon, oxygen, and a metal
SILICATED > SILICATE
SILICATES > SILICATE
SILICEOUS *adj* of, relating to, or containing abundant silica
SILICIC *adj* of, concerned with, or containing silicon or an acid obtained from silicon

SILICIDE *n* any one of a class of binary compounds formed between silicon and certain metals
SILICIDES > SILICIDE
SILICIFY *vb* convert or be converted into silica
SILICIOUS *same as* > SILICEOUS
SILICIUM *rare name for* > SILICON
SILICIUMS > SILICIUM
SILICLE *same as* > SILICULA
SILICLES > SILICLE
SILICON *n* brittle nonmetallic element ▷ *adj* denoting an area that contains much high-technology industry
SILICONE *n* tough synthetic substance made from silicon and used in lubricants
SILICONES > SILICONE
SILICONS > SILICON
SILICOSES > SILICOSIS
SILICOSIS *n* lung disease caused by inhaling silica dust
SILICOTIC *n* person suffering from silicosis
SILICULA *n* short broad siliqua occurring in cruciferous plants
SILICULAE > SILICULA
SILICULAS > SILICULA
SILICULE *same as* > SILICULA
SILICULES > SILICULE
SILING > SILE
SILIQUA *n* long dry dehiscent fruit of cruciferous plants such as the wallflower
SILIQUAE > SILIQUA
SILIQUAS > SILIQUA
SILIQUE *same as* > SILIQUA
SILIQUES > SILIQUE
SILIQUOSE > SILIQUA
SILIQUOUS > SILIQUA
SILK *n* fibre made by the larva of a certain moth ▷ *vb* (of maize) develop long hairlike styles
SILKALENE *same as* > SILKALINE
SILKALINE *n* fine smooth cotton fabric used for linings, etc
SILKED > SILK
SILKEN *adj* made of silk ▷ *vb* make like silk
SILKENED > SILKEN
SILKENING > SILKEN
SILKENS > SILKEN
SILKIE *n* Scots word for a seal
SILKIER > SILKY
SILKIES > SILKIE
SILKIEST > SILKY
SILKILY > SILKY
SILKINESS > SILKY
SILKING > SILK
SILKLIKE > SILK
SILKOLINE *n* material like silk
SILKS > SILK

SILKTAIL n waxwing
SILKTAILS > SILKTAIL
SILKWEED another name for > MILKWEED
SILKWEEDS > SILKWEED
SILKWORM n caterpillar that spins a cocoon of silk
SILKWORMS > SILKWORM
SILKY adj of or like silk
SILL n ledge at the bottom of a window or door
SILLABUB same as > SYLLABUB
SILLABUBS > SILLABUB
SILLADAR n Indian irregular cavalryman
SILLADARS > SILLADAR
SILLER n silver ▷ adj silver
SILLERS > SILLER
SILLIBUB n syllabub
SILLIBUBS > SILLIBUB
SILLIER > SILLY
SILLIES > SILLY
SILLIEST > SILLY
SILLILY > SILLY
SILLINESS > SILLY
SILLOCK n young coalfish
SILLOCKS > SILLOCK
SILLS > SILL
SILLY adj foolish ▷ n foolish person
SILO n pit or airtight tower for storing silage or grains ▷ vb put in a silo
SILOED > SILO
SILOING > SILO
SILOS > SILO
SILOXANE n any of a class of compounds containing alternate silicon and oxygen atoms
SILOXANES > SILOXANE
SILPHIA > SILPHIUM
SILPHIUM n American flowering wild plant
SILPHIUMS > SILPHIUM
SILT n mud deposited by moving water ▷ vb fill or be choked with silt
SILTATION > SILT
SILTED > SILT
SILTIER > SILT
SILTIEST > SILT
SILTING > SILT
SILTS > SILT
SILTSTONE n variety of fine sandstone formed from consolidated silt
SILTY > SILT
SILURIAN adj formed in the third period of the Palaeozoic
SILURID n type of freshwater fish of the family which includes catfish
SILURIDS > SILURID
SILURIST n member of ancient Silurian tribe
SILURISTS > SILURIST
SILUROID n freshwater fish
SILUROIDS > SILUROID
SILVA same as > SYLVA
SILVAE > SILVA
SILVAN same as > SYLVAN
SILVANS > SILVAN
SILVAS > SILVA
SILVATIC adj wild, not domestic

SILVER n white precious metal ▷ adj made of or of the colour of silver ▷ vb coat with silver
SILVERED > SILVER
SILVERER > SILVER
SILVERERS > SILVER
SILVEREYE n greenish-coloured songbird of Africa, Australia, New Zealand, and Asia
SILVERIER > SILVERY
SILVERING > SILVER
SILVERISE same as > SILVERIZE
SILVERIZE vb coat with silver
SILVERLY adv like silver
SILVERN adj silver
SILVERS > SILVER
SILVERTIP n mature grizzly bear
SILVERY adj like silver
SILVEX n type of weedkiller
SILVEXES > SILVEX
SILVICAL adj of trees
SILVICS n study of trees
SILYMARIN n antioxidant found in milk thistle
SIM n computer game that simulates an activity
SIMA n silicon-rich and magnesium-rich rocks of the earth's oceanic crust
SIMAR variant spelling of > CYMAR
SIMAROUBA n tropical American tree with divided leaves and fleshy fruits
SIMARRE n woman's loose gown
SIMARRES > SIMARRE
SIMARS > SIMAR
SIMARUBA same as > SIMAROUBA
SIMARUBAS > SIMARUBA
SIMAS > SIMA
SIMATIC > SIMA
SIMAZINE n organic weedkiller
SIMAZINES > SIMAZINE
SIMBA E African word for > LION
SIMBAS > SIMBA
SIMCHA n Jewish celebration or festival
SIMCHAS > SIMCHA
SIMI n East African sword
SIMIAL adj of apes
SIMIAN n monkey or ape ▷ adj of or resembling a monkey or ape
SIMIANS > SIMIAN
SIMILAR adj alike but not identical
SIMILARLY > SIMILAR
SIMILE n figure of speech comparing one thing to another, using 'as' or 'like'
SIMILES > SIMILE
SIMILISE same as > SIMILIZE
SIMILISED > SIMILISE
SIMILISES > SIMILISE
SIMILIZE vb use similes
SIMILIZED > SIMILIZE
SIMILIZES > SIMILIZE

SIMILOR n alloy used in cheap jewellery
SIMILORS > SIMILOR
SIMIOID adj of apes
SIMIOUS adj of apes
SIMIS > SIMI
SIMITAR same as > SCIMITAR
SIMITARS > SIMITAR
SIMKIN word used in India for > CHAMPAGNE
SIMKINS > SIMKIN
SIMLIN n American variety of squash plant
SIMLINS > SIMLIN
SIMMER vb cook gently at just below boiling point ▷ n state of simmering
SIMMERED > SIMMER
SIMMERING > SIMMER
SIMMERS > SIMMER
SIMNEL n fruit cake with marzipan eaten at Easter
SIMNELS > SIMNEL
SIMOLEON n American slang for dollar
SIMOLEONS > SIMOLEON
SIMONIAC n person who is guilty of practising simony
SIMONIACS > SIMONIAC
SIMONIES > SIMONY
SIMONIOUS > SIMONY
SIMONISE same as > SIMONIZE
SIMONISED > SIMONISE
SIMONISES > SIMONISE
SIMONIST > SIMONY
SIMONISTS > SIMONY
SIMONIZE vb polish with wax
SIMONIZED > SIMONIZE
SIMONIZES > SIMONIZE
SIMONY n practice of buying or selling Church benefits
SIMOOM n hot suffocating sand-laden desert wind
SIMOOMS > SIMOOM
SIMOON same as > SIMOOM
SIMOONS > SIMOON
SIMORG n bird in Persian myth
SIMORGS > SIMORG
SIMP short for > SIMPLETON
SIMPAI n Indonesian monkey
SIMPAIS > SIMPAI
SIMPATICO adj pleasant or congenial
SIMPER vb smile in a silly or affected way ▷ n simpering smile
SIMPERED > SIMPER
SIMPERER > SIMPER
SIMPERERS > SIMPER
SIMPERING > SIMPER
SIMPERS > SIMPER
SIMPKIN word used in India for > CHAMPAGNE
SIMPKINS > SIMPKIN
SIMPLE adj easy to understand or do ▷ n simpleton ▷ vb archaic word meaning to look for medicinal herbs
SIMPLED > SIMPLE
SIMPLER > SIMPLE
SIMPLERS > SIMPLE

SIMPLES > SIMPLE
SIMPLESSE n old word meaning simplicity
SIMPLEST > SIMPLE
SIMPLETON n foolish or half-witted person
SIMPLEX adj permitting the transmission of signals in only one direction in a radio circuit ▷ n simple not a compound word
SIMPLEXES > SIMPLEX
SIMPLICES > SIMPLEX
SIMPLICIA n species of moth
SIMPLIFY vb make less complicated
SIMPLING > SIMPLE
SIMPLINGS > SIMPLE
SIMPLISM n quality of being extremely naive
SIMPLISMS > SIMPLISM
SIMPLIST n old word meaning expert in herbal medicine
SIMPLISTE adj simplistic ▷ n person who tends to oversimplify
SIMPLISTS > SIMPLIST
SIMPLY adv in a simple manner
SIMPS > SIMP
SIMS > SIM
SIMUL adj simultaneous ▷ n simultaneous broadcast
SIMULACRA pl n representations of things
SIMULACRE n resemblance
SIMULANT adj simulating ▷ n simulant thing
SIMULANTS > SIMULANT
SIMULAR n person or thing that simulates or imitates ▷ adj fake
SIMULARS > SIMULAR
SIMULATE vb make a pretence of ▷ adj assumed or simulated
SIMULATED adj being an imitation of the genuine article, usually made from cheaper material
SIMULATES > SIMULATE
SIMULATOR n device that simulates specific conditions for the purposes of research or training
SIMULCAST vb broadcast (a programme) simultaneously on radio and television ▷ n programme broadcast in this way
SIMULIUM n tropical fly
SIMULIUMS > SIMULIUM
SIMULS > SIMUL
SIMURG same as > SIMURGH
SIMURGH n bird in Persian myth
SIMURGHS > SIMURGH
SIMURGS > SIMURG
SIN n offence or transgression ▷ vb commit a sin
SINAPISM n mixture of black mustard seeds and an adhesive, applied to the skin
SINAPISMS > SINAPISM

S

SINCE prep during the period of time after ▷ adv from that time

SINCERE adj without pretence or deceit

SINCERELY > SINCERE

SINCERER > SINCERE

SINCEREST > SINCERE

SINCERITY > SINCERE

SINCIPITA > SINCIPUT

SINCIPUT n forward upper part of the skull

SINCIPUTS > SINCIPUT

SIND variant of > SYNE

SINDED > SIND

SINDING > SIND

SINDINGS > SIND

SINDON n type of cloth

SINDONS > SINDON

SINDS > SIND

SINE same as > SYNE

SINECURE n paid job with minimal duties

SINECURES > SINECURE

SINED > SINE

SINES > SINE

SINEW n tough fibrous tissue joining muscle to bone ▷ vb make strong

SINEWED adj having sinews

SINEWIER > SINEWY

SINEWIEST > SINEWY

SINEWING > SINEW

SINEWLESS > SINEW

SINEWS > SINEW

SINEWY adj lean and muscular

SINFONIA n symphony orchestra

SINFONIAS > SINFONIA

SINFONIE > SINFONIA

SINFUL adj guilty of sin

SINFULLY > SINFUL

SING vb make musical sounds with the voice ▷ n act or performance of singing

SINGABLE > SING

SINGALONG n act of singing along with a performer

SINGE vb burn the surface of ▷ n superficial burn

SINGED > SINGE

SINGEING > SINGE

SINGER n person who sings, esp professionally

SINGERS > SINGER

SINGES > SINGE

SINGING > SING

SINGINGLY > SING

SINGINGS > SING

SINGLE adj one only ▷ n single thing ▷ vb pick out from others

SINGLED > SINGLE

SINGLEDOM n state of being unmarried or not involved in a long-term relationship

SINGLES pl n match played with one person on each side

SINGLET n sleeveless vest

SINGLETON n only card of a particular suit held by a player

SINGLETS > SINGLET

SINGLING > SINGLE

SINGLINGS > SINGLE

SINGLY adv one at a time

SINGS > SING

SINGSONG n informal singing session ▷ adj (of the voice) repeatedly rising and falling in pitch

SINGSONGS > SINGSONG

SINGSONGY adj having a singsong rhythm

SINGSPIEL n type of German comic opera with spoken dialogue

SINGULAR adj (of a word or form) denoting one person or thing ▷ n singular form of a word

SINGULARS > SINGULAR

SINGULARY adj (of an operator) monadic

SINGULT n old word meaning sob

SINGULTS > SINGULT

SINGULTUS technical name for > HICCUP

SINH n hyperbolic sine

SINHS > SINH

SINICAL > SINE

SINICISE same as > SINICIZE

SINICISED > SINICISE

SINICISES > SINICISE

SINICIZE vb make Chinese

SINICIZED > SINICIZE

SINICIZES > SINICIZE

SINING > SINE

SINISTER adj threatening or suggesting evil or harm

SINISTRAL adj of, relating to, or located on the left side, esp the left side of the body

SINK vb submerge (in liquid) ▷ n fixed basin with a water supply and drainage pipe

SINKABLE > SINK

SINKAGE n act of sinking or degree to which something sinks or has sunk

SINKAGES > SINKAGE

SINKER n weight for a fishing line

SINKERS > SINKER

SINKFUL n amount that can be held in a sink

SINKFULS > SINKFUL

SINKHOLE n depression in the ground surface where a stream disappears underground

SINKHOLES > SINKHOLE

SINKIER > SINKY

SINKIEST > SINKY

SINKING > SINK

SINKINGS > SINK

SINKS > SINK

SINKY adj giving underfoot

SINLESS adj free from sin or guilt

SINLESSLY > SINLESS

SINNED > SIN

SINNER n person that sins ▷ vb behave like a sinner

SINNERED > SINNER

SINNERING > SINNER

SINNERS > SINNER

SINNET n braided rope

SINNETS > SINNET

SINNING > SIN

SINNINGIA n tropical flowering plant

SINOLOGUE n person who studies Chinese culture, etc

SINOLOGY n study of Chinese culture, etc

SINOPIA n pigment made from iron ore

SINOPIAS > SINOPIA

SINOPIE > SINOPIA

SINOPIS n pigment made from iron ore

SINOPISES > SINOPIS

SINOPITE n iron ore

SINOPITES > SINOPITE

SINS > SIN

SINSYNE adv Scots word meaning since

SINTER n whitish porous incrustation deposited from hot springs ▷ vb form large particles from (powders) by heating or pressure

SINTERED > SINTER

SINTERIER > SINTERY

SINTERING > SINTER

SINTERS > SINTER

SINTERY adj consisting of sinter

SINUATE vb wind

SINUATED same as > SINUATE

SINUATELY > SINUATE

SINUATES > SINUATE

SINUATING > SINUATE

SINUATION same as > SINUOSITY

SINUITIS variant of > SINUSITIS

SINUOSE adj sinuous

SINUOSITY n quality of being sinuous

SINUOUS adj full of turns or curves

SINUOUSLY > SINUOUS

SINUS n hollow space in a bone, esp an air passage opening into the nose

SINUSES > SINUS

SINUSITIS n inflammation of a sinus membrane

SINUSLIKE > SINUS

SINUSOID n blood vessel in certain organs ▷ adj resembling a sinus

SINUSOIDS > SINUSOID

SIP vb drink in small mouthfuls ▷ n amount sipped

SIPE vb soak

SIPED > SIPE

SIPES > SIPE

SIPHON n bent tube which uses air pressure to draw liquid from a container ▷ vb draw off thus

SIPHONAGE > SIPHON

SIPHONAL adj like a siphon

SIPHONATE adj having a syphon

SIPHONED > SIPHON

SIPHONET n sucking tube on an aphid

SIPHONETS > SIPHONET

SIPHONIC same as > SIPHONAL

SIPHONING > SIPHON

SIPHONS > SIPHON

SIPHUNCLE n tube inside shellfish

SIPING > SIPE

SIPPABLE adj able to be sipped

SIPPED > SIP

SIPPER > SIP

SIPPERS > SIP

SIPPET n small piece of toast eaten with soup or gravy

SIPPETS > SIPPET

SIPPING > SIP

SIPPLE vb sip

SIPPLED > SIPPLE

SIPPLES > SIPPLE

SIPPLING > SIPPLE

SIPPY adj as in sippy cup infant's drinking cup with a tight-fitting lid and perforated spout

SIPS > SIP

SIR n polite term of address for a man ▷ vb call someone 'sir'

SIRCAR n government in India

SIRCARS > SIRCAR

SIRDAR same as > SARDAR

SIRDARS > SIRDAR

SIRE n male parent of a horse or other domestic animal ▷ vb father

SIRED > SIRE

SIREE emphasized form of > SIR

SIREES > SIREE

SIREN n device making a loud wailing noise as a warning

SIRENIAN n animal such as the dugong and manatee

SIRENIANS > SIRENIAN

SIRENIC > SIREN

SIRENISE variant of > SIRENIZE

SIRENISED > SIRENISE

SIRENISES > SIRENISE

SIRENIZE vb bewitch

SIRENIZED > SIRENIZE

SIRENIZES > SIRENIZE

SIRENS > SIREN

SIRES > SIRE

SIRGANG n Asian bird

SIRGANGS > SIRGANG

SIRI n betel

SIRIASES > SIRIASIS

SIRIASIS n sunstroke

SIRIH n betel

SIRIHS > SIRIH

SIRING > SIRE

SIRINGS > SIRING

SIRIS > SIRI

SIRKAR n government in India

SIRKARS > SIRKAR

SIRLOIN n prime cut of loin of beef

SIRLOINS > SIRLOIN

SIRNAME vb old form of surname

SIRNAMED > SIRNAME

SIRNAMES > SIRNAME

SIRNAMING > SIRNAME

SIROC n sirocco

SIROCCO *n* hot wind blowing from N Africa into S Europe

SIROCCOS > SIROCCO

SIROCS > SIROC

SIRONISE *same as* > SIRONIZE

SIRONISED > SIRONISE

SIRONISES > SIRONISE

SIRONIZE *vb* treat (a woollen fabric) chemically to prevent it wrinkling after being washed

SIRONIZED > SIRONIZE

SIRONIZES > SIRONIZE

SIROSET *adj* of the chemical treatment of woollen fabrics to give a permanent-press effect

SIRRA *disrespectful form of* > SIR

SIRRAH *n* contemptuous term used in addressing a man or boy

SIRRAHS > SIRRAH

SIRRAS > SIRRA

SIRRED > SIR

SIRREE *n* form of 'sir' used for emphasis

SIRREES > SIRREE

SIRRING > SIR

SIRS > SIR

SIRTUIN *n* protein that regulates cell metabolism and ageing

SIRTUINS > SIRTUIN

SIRUP *same as* > SYRUP

SIRUPED > SIRUP

SIRUPIER > SIRUP

SIRUPIEST > SIRUP

SIRUPING > SIRUP

SIRUPS > SIRUP

SIRUPY > SIRUP

SIRVENTE *n* verse form employed by the troubadours of Provence to satirize political themes

SIRVENTES > SIRVENTE

SIS *n* sister

SISAL *n* (fibre of) plant used in making ropes

SISALS > SISAL

SISERARY *n* scolding

SISES > SIS

SISKIN *n* yellow-and-black finch

SISKINS > SISKIN

SISS *shortening of* > SISTER

SISSES > SISS

SISSIER > SISSY

SISSIES > SISSY

SISSIEST > SISSY

SISSIFIED > SISSY

SISSINESS > SISSY

SISSOO *n* Indian tree

SISSOOS > SISSOO

SISSY *n* derogatory word for a weak or cowardly (person) ▷ *adj* weak or cowardly

SISSYISH > SISSY

SISSYNESS > SISSY

SIST *vb* Scottish law term meaning stop

SISTA *n* informal term for an African-American woman

SISTAS > SISTA

SISTED > SIST

SISTER *n* girl or woman with the same parents as another person ▷ *adj* closely related, similar ▷ *vb* be or be like a sister

SISTERED > SISTER

SISTERING > SISTER

SISTERLY *adj* of or like a sister

SISTERS > SISTER

SISTING > SIST

SISTRA > SISTRUM

SISTROID *adj* contained between the convex sides of two intersecting curves

SISTRUM *n* musical instrument of ancient Egypt consisting of a metal rattle

SISTRUMS > SISTRUM

SISTS > SIST

SIT *vb* rest one's body upright on the buttocks

SITAR *n* Indian stringed musical instrument

SITARIST > SITAR

SITARISTS > SITAR

SITARS > SITAR

SITATUNGA *another name for* > MARSHBUCK

SITCOM *n* situation comedy

SITCOMS > SITCOM

SITE *n* place where something is, was, or is intended to be located ▷ *vb* provide with a site

SITED > SITE

SITELLA *n* type of small generally black-and-white bird

SITELLAS > SITELLA

SITES > SITE

SITFAST *n* sore on a horse's back caused by rubbing of the saddle

SITFASTS > SITFAST

SITH *archaic word for* > SINCE

SITHE *vb* old form of scythe

SITHED > SITHE

SITHEE *interj* look here! listen!

SITHEN *adv* old word meaning since

SITHENCE *adv* old word meaning since

SITHENS *adv* old word meaning since

SITHES > SITHE

SITHING > SITHE

SITING *n* act of siting

SITINGS > SITING

SITIOLOGY *n* study of diet and nutrition

SITKA *modifier* as in *sitka spruce* tall North American spruce tree

SITKAMER *n* sitting room

SITKAMERS > SITKAMER

SITOLOGY *n* scientific study of food, diet, and nutrition

SITREP *n* military situation report

SITREPS > SITREP

SITS > SIT

SITTAR *n* sitar

SITTARS > SITTAR

SITTELLA *variant spelling of* > SITELLA

SITTELLAS > SITTELLA

SITTEN *adj* dialect word for in the saddle

SITTER *n* baby-sitter

SITTERS > SITTER

SITTINE *adj* of nuthatch bird family ▷ *n* type of nuthatch

SITTINES > SITTINE

SITTING > SIT

SITTINGS > SIT

SITUATE *vb* place ▷ *adj* (now used esp in legal contexts) situated

SITUATED > SITUATE

SITUATES > SITUATE

SITUATING > SITUATE

SITUATION *n* state of affairs

SITULA *n* bucket-shaped container

SITULAE > SITULA

SITUP *n* exercise in which the body is brought into a sitting position

SITUPS > SITUP

SITUS *n* position or location

SITUSES > SITUS

SITUTUNGA *n* African antelope

SITZ *n* as in *sitz bath* bath in which the buttocks and hips are immersed in hot water

SITZKRIEG *n* period during a war in which both sides change positions very slowly or not at all

SITZMARK *n* depression in the snow where a skier has fallen

SITZMARKS > SITZMARK

SIVER *same as* > SYVER

SIVERS > SIVER

SIWASH *vb* (in the Pacific Northwest) to camp out with only natural shelter

SIWASHED > SIWASH

SIWASHES > SIWASH

SIWASHING > SIWASH

SIX *n* one more than five

SIXAIN *n* stanza or poem of six lines

SIXAINE *n* six-line stanza of poetry

SIXAINES > SIXAINE

SIXAINS > SIXAIN

SIXER *same as* > SIX

SIXERS > SIXER

SIXES > SIX

SIXFOLD *adj* having six times as many or as much ▷ *adv* by six times as many or as much

SIXISH *adj* around six years of age

SIXMO *n* book size resulting from folding a sheet of paper into six leaves

SIXMOS > SIXMO

SIXPENCE *n* former British and Australian coin worth six pennies

SIXPENCES > SIXPENCE

SIXPENNY *adj* (of a nail) two inches in length

SIXSCORE *n* hundred and twenty

SIXSCORES > SIXSCORE

SIXTE *n* sixth of eight basic positions from which a parry or attack can be made in fencing

SIXTEEN *n* six and ten

SIXTEENER *n* poem verse with sixteen syllables

SIXTEENMO *n* book size resulting from folding a sheet of paper into 16 leaves or 32 pages

SIXTEENS > SIXTEEN

SIXTEENTH *adj* coming after the fifteenth in numbering order ▷ *n* one of 16 equal or nearly equal parts of something

SIXTES > SIXTE

SIXTH *n* number six in a series ▷ *adj* coming after the fifth and before the seventh in numbering order

SIXTHLY *same as* > SIXTH

SIXTHS > SIXTH

SIXTIES > SIXTY

SIXTIETH *adj* being the ordinal number of *sixty* in numbering order ▷ *n* one of 60 approximately equal parts of something

SIXTIETHS > SIXTIETH

SIXTY *n* six times ten

SIXTYFOLD *adj* multiplied sixty times

SIXTYISH > SIXTY

SIZABLE *adj* quite large

SIZABLY > SIZABLE

SIZAR *n* undergraduate receiving a maintenance grant from the college

SIZARS > SIZAR

SIZARSHIP > SIZAR

SIZE *n* dimensions, bigness ▷ *vb* arrange according to size

SIZEABLE *same as* > SIZABLE

SIZEABLY > SIZEABLE

SIZED *adj* of a specified size

SIZEISM *n* discrimination on the basis of a person's size

SIZEISMS > SIZEISM

SIZEIST > SIZEISM

SIZEISTS > SIZEISM

SIZEL *n* scrap metal clippings

SIZELS > SIZEL

SIZER > SIZE

SIZERS > SIZE

SIZES > SIZE

SIZIER > SIZE

SIZIEST > SIZE

SIZINESS > SIZE

SIZING > SIZE

SIZINGS > SIZE

SIZISM *n* discrimination against people because of weight

SIZISMS > SIZISM

SIZIST > SIZISM

SIZISTS > SIZISM

SIZY > SIZE

SIZZLE *vb* make a hissing sound like frying fat ▷ *n* hissing sound

S

SIZZLED > SIZZLE
SIZZLER n something that sizzles
SIZZLERS > SIZZLER
SIZZLES > SIZZLE
SIZZLING adj extremely hot
SIZZLINGS > SIZZLING
SJAMBOK n whip or riding crop made of hide ▷ vb beat with a sjambok
SJAMBOKED > SJAMBOK
SJAMBOKS > SJAMBOK
SJOE interj South African exclamation of surprise, admiration, exhaustion, etc
SKA n type of West Indian pop music of the 1960s
SKAG same as > SCAG
SKAGS > SKAG
SKAIL vb Scots word meaning disperse
SKAILED > SKAIL
SKAILING > SKAIL
SKAILS > SKAIL
SKAITH vb Scots word meaning injure
SKAITHED > SKAITH
SKAITHING > SKAITH
SKAITHS > SKAITH
SKALD n (in ancient Scandinavia) a bard or minstrel
SKALDIC > SKALD
SKALDS > SKALD
SKALDSHIP n (in ancient Scandinavia) position of bard
SKANGER n insulting Irish word for a young working-class person who wears casual sports clothes
SKANGERS > SKANGER
SKANK n fast dance to reggae music ▷ vb perform this dance
SKANKED > SKANK
SKANKER > SKANK
SKANKERS > SKANK
SKANKIER > SKANKY
SKANKIEST > SKANKY
SKANKING > SKANK
SKANKINGS > SKANK
SKANKS > SKANK
SKANKY adj dirty or unattractive
SKART Scots word for > CORMORANT
SKARTH Scots word for > CORMORANT
SKARTHS > SKARTH
SKARTS > SKART
SKAS > SKA
SKAT n three-handed card game using 32 cards
SKATE n boot with a steel blade or sets of wheels attached to the sole ▷ vb glide on or as if on skates
SKATED > SKATE
SKATEPARK n place for skateboarding
SKATEPUNK n member of a skateboarding subculture
SKATER n person who skates
SKATERS > SKATER
SKATES > SKATE

SKATING > SKATE
SKATINGS > SKATE
SKATOL n skatole
SKATOLE n white or brownish crystalline solid
SKATOLES > SKATOLE
SKATOLS > SKATOL
SKATS > SKAT
SKATT n dialect word meaning throw
SKATTS > SKATT
SKAW variant of > SCAW
SKAWS > SKAW
SKEAN n kind of double-edged dagger
SKEANE same as > SKEIN
SKEANES > SKEANE
SKEANS > SKEAN
SKEAR dialect form of > SCARE
SKEARED > SKEAR
SKEARIER > SKEARY
SKEARIEST > SKEARY
SKEARING > SKEAR
SKEARS > SKEAR
SKEARY dialect form of > SCARY
SKED vb short for schedule
SKEDADDLE vb run off ▷ n hasty retreat
SKEDDED > SKED
SKEDDING > SKED
SKEDS > SKED
SKEE variant spelling of > SKI
SKEECHAN n old Scots type of beer
SKEECHANS > SKEECHAN
SKEED > SKEE
SKEEF adj South African slang for at an oblique angle
SKEEING > SKEE
SKEELIER > SKEELY
SKEELIEST > SKEELY
SKEELY adj Scots word meaning skilful
SKEEN n type of ibex
SKEENS > SKEEN
SKEER dialect form of > SCARE
SKEERED > SKEER
SKEERIER > SKEERY
SKEERIEST > SKEERY
SKEERING > SKEER
SKEERS > SKEER
SKEERY dialect form of > SCARY
SKEES > SKEE
SKEESICKS American word meaning > ROGUE
SKEET n form of clay-pigeon shooting
SKEETER informal word for > MOSQUITO
SKEETERS > SKEETER
SKEETS > SKEET
SKEEVIER > SKEEVY
SKEEVIEST > SKEEVY
SKEEVY adj repulsive
SKEG n reinforcing brace between the after end of a keel and the rudderpost
SKEGG n skeg
SKEGGER n young salmon
SKEGGERS > SKEGGER
SKEGGS > SKEGG
SKEGS > SKEG

SKEIGH adj Scots word meaning shy
SKEIGHER > SKEIGH
SKEIGHEST > SKEIGH
SKEIN n yarn wound in a loose coil ▷ vb wind into a skein
SKEINED > SKEIN
SKEINING > SKEIN
SKEINS > SKEIN
SKELDER vb beg
SKELDERED > SKELDER
SKELDERS > SKELDER
SKELETAL > SKELETON
SKELETON n framework of bones inside a person's or animal's body ▷ adj reduced to a minimum
SKELETONS > SKELETON
SKELF n splinter of wood, esp when embedded accidentally in the skin
SKELFS > SKELF
SKELL n homeless person
SKELLIE adj skelly
SKELLIED > SKELLY
SKELLIER > SKELLY
SKELLIES > SKELLY
SKELLIEST > SKELLY
SKELLOCH n Scots word meaning scream
SKELLOCHS > SKELLOCH
SKELLS > SKELL
SKELLUM n rogue
SKELLUMS > SKELLUM
SKELLY n whitefish of certain lakes in the Lake District ▷ vb look sideways or squint ▷ adj cross-eyed
SKELLYING > SKELLY
SKELM n villain or crook
SKELMS > SKELM
SKELP vb slap ▷ n slap
SKELPED > SKELP
SKELPING > SKELP
SKELPINGS > SKELP
SKELPIT vb Scots word meaning skelped
SKELPS > SKELP
SKELTER vb scurry
SKELTERED > SKELTER
SKELTERS > SKELTER
SKELUM n Scots word meaning rascal
SKELUMS > SKELUM
SKEN vb squint or stare
SKENE n Scots word meaning dagger
SKENES > SKENE
SKENNED > SKEN
SKENNING > SKEN
SKENS > SKEN
SKEO n Scots dialect word meaning hut
SKEOES > SKEO
SKEOS > SKEO
SKEP n beehive, esp one constructed of straw ▷ vb gather into a hive
SKEPFUL n amount skep will hold
SKEPFULS > SKEPFUL
SKEPPED > SKEP
SKEPPING > SKEP
SKEPS > SKEP
SKEPSIS n doubt
SKEPSISES > SKEPSIS

SKEPTIC same as > SCEPTIC
SKEPTICAL > SKEPTIC
SKEPTICS > SKEPTIC
SKER vb scour
SKERRED > SKER
SKERRICK n small fragment or amount
SKERRICKS > SKERRICK
SKERRIES > SKERRY
SKERRING > SKER
SKERRY n rocky island or reef
SKERS > SKER
SKET vb splash (water)
SKETCH n rough drawing ▷ vb make a sketch (of)
SKETCHED > SKETCH
SKETCHER > SKETCH
SKETCHERS > SKETCH
SKETCHES > SKETCH
SKETCHIER > SKETCHY
SKETCHILY > SKETCHY
SKETCHING > SKETCH
SKETCHPAD n pad of paper for sketching
SKETCHY adj incomplete or inadequate
SKETS > SKET
SKETTED > SKET
SKETTING > SKET
SKEW vb make slanting or crooked ▷ adj slanting or crooked ▷ n slanting position
SKEWBACK n sloping surface on both sides of a segmental arch that takes the thrust
SKEWBACKS > SKEWBACK
SKEWBALD adj (horse) marked with patches of white and another colour ▷ n horse with this marking
SKEWBALDS > SKEWBALD
SKEWED > SKEW
SKEWER n pin to hold meat together during cooking ▷ vb fasten with a skewer
SKEWERED > SKEWER
SKEWERING > SKEWER
SKEWERS > SKEWER
SKEWEST > SKEW
SKEWING > SKEW
SKEWNESS n quality or condition of being skew
SKEWS > SKEW
SKEWWHIFF adj crooked or slanting
SKI n one of a pair of long runners fastened to boots for gliding over snow or water ▷ vb travel on skis
SKIABLE > SKI
SKIAGRAM n picture made from shadows
SKIAGRAMS > SKIAGRAM
SKIAGRAPH n skiagram
SKIAMACHY same as > SCIAMACHY
SKIASCOPE n medical instrument for examining the eye to detect errors of refraction
SKIASCOPY n retinoscopy
SKIATRON n type of cathode ray tube
SKIATRONS > SKIATRON

SKIBOB n vehicle made of two short skis for gliding down snow slopes

SKIBOBBED > SKIBOB

SKIBOBBER > SKIBOB

SKIBOBS > SKIBOB

SKID vb (of a moving vehicle) slide sideways uncontrollably ▷ n skidding

SKIDDED > SKID

SKIDDER > SKID

SKIDDERS > SKID

SKIDDIER > SKID

SKIDDIEST > SKID

SKIDDING n act of skidding

SKIDDINGS > SKIDDING

SKIDDOO vb go away quickly

SKIDDOOED > SKIDDOO

SKIDDOOS > SKIDDOO

SKIDDY > SKID

SKIDLID n crash helmet

SKIDLIDS > SKIDLID

SKIDMARK n mark left by a skid

SKIDMARKS > SKIDMARK

SKIDOO n snowmobile ▷ vb travel on a skidoo

SKIDOOED > SKIDOO

SKIDOOER n person who rides a skidoo

SKIDOOERS > SKIDOOER

SKIDOOING n act or instance of riding a snowmobile

SKIDOOS > SKIDOO

SKIDPAD n area of road used to test skidding

SKIDPADS > SKIDPAD

SKIDPAN n area made slippery so that vehicle drivers can practise controlling skids

SKIDPANS > SKIDPAN

SKIDPROOF adj (of a road surface, tyre, etc) preventing or resistant to skidding

SKIDS > SKID

SKIDWAY n platform on which logs ready for sawing are piled

SKIDWAYS > SKIDWAY

SKIED > SKY

SKIER > SKI

SKIERS > SKI

SKIES > SKY

SKIEY adj of the sky

SKIEYER > SKIEY

SKIEYEST > SKIEY

SKIFF n small boat ▷ vb travel in a skiff

SKIFFED > SKIFF

SKIFFING > SKIFF

SKIFFLE n style of popular music of the 1950s ▷ vb play this style of music

SKIFFLED > SKIFFLE

SKIFFLES > SKIFFLE

SKIFFLESS > SKIFF

SKIFFLING > SKIFFLE

SKIFFS > SKIFF

SKIING > SKI

SKIINGS > SKI

SKIJORER > SKIJORING

SKIJORERS > SKIJORING

SKIJORING n sport in which a skier is pulled over snow or ice, usually by a horse

SKIJUMPER n one who engages in the sport of skijumping

SKIJORER n one who engages in the sport of skijoring

SKILFUL adj having or showing skill

SKILFULL less common spelling of > SKILFUL

SKILFULLY > SKILFUL

SKILL n special ability or expertise

SKILLED adj possessing or demonstrating skill, or special training

SKILLESS > SKILL

SKILLET n small frying pan or shallow cooking pot

SKILLETS > SKILLET

SKILLFUL same as > SKILFUL

SKILLIER > SKILLY

SKILLIES > SKILLY

SKILLIEST > SKILLY

SKILLING n former Scandinavian coin of low denomination

SKILLINGS > SKILLING

SKILLION n part of a building having a lower, esp sloping, roof

SKILLIONS > SKILLION

SKILLS > SKILL

SKILLY n thin soup or gruel ▷ adj skilled

SKIM vb remove floating matter from the surface of (a liquid) ▷ n act or process of skimming

SKIMBOARD n type of surfboard, shorter than standard and rounded at both ends ▷ vb surf on a skimboard

SKIMMED > SKIM

SKIMMER n person or thing that skims

SKIMMERS > SKIMMER

SKIMMIA n shrub of S and SE Asia

SKIMMIAS > SKIMMIA

SKIMMING > SKIM

SKIMMINGS pl n material that is skimmed off a liquid

SKIMO n informal and offensive word for an Inuit

SKIMOBILE n motor vehicle with skis for travelling on snow

SKIMOS > SKIMO

SKIMP vb not invest enough time, money, material, etc

SKIMPED > SKIMP

SKIMPIER > SKIMPY

SKIMPIEST > SKIMPY

SKIMPILY > SKIMPY

SKIMPING > SKIMP

SKIMPS > SKIMP

SKIMPY adj scanty or insufficient

SKIMS > SKIM

SKIN n outer covering of the body ▷ vb remove the skin of

SKINCARE n use of cosmetics in taking care of skin

SKINCARES > SKINCARE

SKINFLICK n film containing much nudity and sex

SKINFLINT n miser

SKINFOOD n cosmetic cream for the skin

SKINFOODS > SKINFOOD

SKINFUL n sufficient alcoholic drink to make one drunk

SKINFULS > SKINFUL

SKINHEAD n youth with very short hair

SKINHEADS > SKINHEAD

SKINK n type of lizard with reduced limbs and smooth scales ▷ vb serve a drink

SKINKED > SKINK

SKINKER > SKINK

SKINKERS > SKINK

SKINKING > SKINK

SKINKS > SKINK

SKINLESS > SKIN

SKINLIKE > SKIN

SKINNED > SKIN

SKINNER n person who prepares or deals in animal skins

SKINNERS > SKINNER

SKINNIER > SKINNY

SKINNIES > SKINNY

SKINNIEST > SKINNY

SKINNING > SKIN

SKINNY adj thin ▷ n information

SKINS > SKIN

SKINSUIT n skintight one-piece garment worn by cyclists to reduce friction

SKINSUITS > SKINSUIT

SKINT adj having no money

SKINTER > SKINT

SKINTEST > SKINT

SKINTIGHT adj fitting tightly over the body ▷ n tight-fitting garment

SKIO n Scots dialect word meaning hut

SKIOES > SKIO

SKIORER n one who engages in the sport of skioring

SKIORERS > SKIORER

SKIORING n sport of being towed on skis by horse

SKIORINGS > SKIORING

SKIOS > SKIO

SKIP vb leap lightly from one foot to the other ▷ n skipping

SKIPJACK n important food fish of tropical seas

SKIPJACKS > SKIPJACK

SKIPLANE n aircraft fitted with skis to enable it to land on and take off from snow

SKIPLANES > SKIPLANE

SKIPPABLE > SKIP

SKIPPED > SKIP

SKIPPER vb captain ▷ n captain of a ship or aircraft

SKIPPERED > SKIPPER

SKIPPERS > SKIPPER

SKIPPET n small round box for preserving a document or seal

SKIPPETS > SKIPPET

SKIPPIER > SKIPPY

SKIPPIEST > SKIPPY

SKIPPING > SKIP

SKIPPINGS > SKIP

SKIPPY adj in high spirits

SKIPS > SKIP

SKIRL n sound of bagpipes ▷ vb (of bagpipes) to give out a shrill sound

SKIRLED > SKIRL

SKIRLING > SKIRL

SKIRLINGS > SKIRL

SKIRLS > SKIRL

SKIRMISH n brief or minor fight or argument ▷ vb take part in a skirmish

SKIRR vb move, run, or fly rapidly ▷ n whirring or grating sound, as of the wings of birds in flight

SKIRRED > SKIRR

SKIRRET n umbelliferous Old World plant

SKIRRETS > SKIRRET

SKIRRING > SKIRR

SKIRRS > SKIRR

SKIRT n woman's garment hanging from the waist ▷ vb border

SKIRTED > SKIRT

SKIRTER n person who skirts fleeces

SKIRTERS > SKIRTER

SKIRTING n border fixed round the base of an interior wall to protect it from kicks, dirt, etc

SKIRTINGS pl n ragged edges trimmed from the fleece of a sheep

SKIRTLESS > SKIRT

SKIRTLIKE > SKIRT

SKIRTS > SKIRT

SKIS > SKI

SKIT n brief satirical sketch

SKITCH vb (of a dog) to attack

SKITCHED > SKITCH

SKITCHES > SKITCH

SKITCHING > SKITCH

SKITE n boast ▷ vb boast

SKITED > SKITE

SKITES > SKITE

SKITING > SKITE

SKITS > SKIT

SKITTER vb move or run rapidly or lightly

SKITTERED > SKITTER

SKITTERS > SKITTER

SKITTERY adj moving lightly and rapidly

SKITTISH adj playful or lively

SKITTLE n bottle-shaped object used as a target in some games ▷ vb play skittles

SKITTLED > SKITTLE

SKITTLES > SKITTLE

SKITTLING > SKITTLE

SKIVE vb evade work or responsibility

SKIVED > SKIVE

SKIVER n tanned outer layer split from a skin ▷ vb cut leather

SKIVERED > SKIVER

SKIVERING > SKIVER

SKIVERS > SKIVER

SKIVES > SKIVE

SKIVIE *adj* old Scots word meaning disarranged

SKIVIER > SKIVIE

SKIVIEST > SKIVIE

SKIVING > SKIVE

SKIVINGS > SKIVE

SKIVVIED > SKIVVY

SKIVVIES > SKIVVY

SKIVVY *n* female servant who does menial work ▷ *vb* work as a skivvy

SKIVVYING > SKIVVY

SKIVY > SKIVE

SKIWEAR *n* clothes for skiing in

SKIWEARS > SKIWEAR

SKLATE Scots word for > SLATE

SKLATED > SKLATE

SKLATES > SKLATE

SKLATING > SKLATE

SKLENT Scots word for > SLANT

SKLENTED > SKLENT

SKLENTING > SKLENT

SKLENTS > SKLENT

SKLIFF *n* Scots word meaning little piece ▷ *vb* shuffle (the feet)

SKLIFFED > SKLIFF

SKLIFFING > SKLIFF

SKLIFFS > SKLIFF

SKLIM *vb* Scots word meaning climb

SKLIMMED > SKLIM

SKLIMMING > SKLIM

SKLIMS > SKLIM

SKOAL same as > SKOL

SKOALED > SKOAL

SKOALING > SKOAL

SKOALS > SKOAL

SKODIER > SKODY

SKODIEST > SKODY

SKODY *adj* dirty, unkempt

SKOFF *vb* eat greedily

SKOFFED > SKOFF

SKOFFING > SKOFF

SKOFFS > SKOFF

SKOG same as > SCOG

SKOGGED > SKOG

SKOGGING > SKOG

SKOGS > SKOG

SKOKIAAN *n* (in South Africa) a potent alcoholic beverage

SKOKIAANS > SKOKIAAN

SKOL sentence substitute good health! (a drinking toast) ▷ *vb* down (an alcoholic drink) in one go

SKOLED > SKOL

SKOLIA > SKOLION

SKOLING > SKOL

SKOLION *n* ancient Greek drinking song

SKOLLED > SKOL

SKOLLIE same as > SKOLLY

SKOLLIES > SKOLLY

SKOLLING > SKOL

SKOLLY *n* hooligan, usually one of a gang

SKOLS > SKOL

SKOOKUM *adj* strong or brave ▷ *n* strong or brave person

SKOOKUMS > SKOOKUM

SKOOL ironically illiterate or childish spelling of > SCHOOL

SKOOLS > SKOOL

SKOOSH *vb* Scots word meaning squirt

SKOOSHED > SKOOSH

SKOOSHES > SKOOSH

SKOOSHING > SKOOSH

SKORDALIA *n* Greek potato and garlic dip

SKORT *n* pair of shorts with a front panel which gives the appearance of a skirt

SKORTS > SKORT

SKOSH *n* little bit

SKOSHES > SKOSH

SKRAN *n* food

SKRANS > SKRAN

SKREEGH same as > SKREIGH

SKREEGHED > SKREEGH

SKREEGHS > SKREEGH

SKREEN *n* screen

SKREENS > SKREEN

SKREIGH *vb* Scots word meaning screech

SKREIGHED > SKREIGH

SKREIGHS > SKREIGH

SKRIECH same as > SKREIGH

SKRIECHED > SKRIECH

SKRIECHS > SKRIECH

SKRIED > SKRY

SKRIEGH same as > SKREIGH

SKRIEGHED > SKRIEGH

SKRIEGHS > SKRIEGH

SKRIES > SKRY

SKRIK *n* South African word meaning fright

SKRIKE *vb* cry

SKRIKED > SKRIKE

SKRIKES > SKRIKE

SKRIKING > SKRIKE

SKRIKS > SKRIK

SKRIMMAGE *vb* scrimmage

SKRIMP *vb* steal apples

SKRIMPED > SKRIMP

SKRIMPING > SKRIMP

SKRIMPS > SKRIMP

SKRONK *n* type of dissonant, grating popular music

SKRONKS > SKRONK

SKRUMP *vb* steal apples

SKRUMPED > SKRUMP

SKRUMPING > SKRUMP

SKRUMPS > SKRUMP

SKRY *vb* try to tell future

SKRYER > SKRY

SKRYERS > SKRY

SKRYING > SKRY

SKUA *n* large predatory gull

SKUAS > SKUA

SKUDLER *n* Scots word meaning leader of festivities

SKUDLERS > SKUDLER

SKUG *vb* shelter

SKUGGED > SKUG

SKUGGING > SKUG

SKUGS > SKUG

SKULK *vb* move stealthily ▷ *n* person who skulks

SKULKED > SKULK

SKULKER > SKULK

SKULKERS > SKULK

SKULKING > SKULK

SKULKINGS > SKULK

SKULKS > SKULK

SKULL *n* bony framework of the head ▷ *vb* strike on the head

SKULLCAP *n* close-fitting brimless cap

SKULLCAPS > SKULLCAP

SKULLED > SKULL

SKULLING > SKULL

SKULLS > SKULL

SKULPIN *n* North American fish

SKULPINS > SKULPIN

SKUMMER same as > SCUMBER

SKUMMERED > SKUMMER

SKUMMERS > SKUMMER

SKUNK *n* small mammal which emits a foul-smelling fluid when attacked ▷ *vb* defeat overwhelmingly in a game

SKUNKBIRD *n* North American songbird

SKUNKED > SKUNK

SKUNKIER > SKUNK

SKUNKIEST > SKUNK

SKUNKING > SKUNK

SKUNKS > SKUNK

SKUNKWEED *n* low-growing fetid swamp plant of N America

SKUNKY > SKUNK

SKURRIED > SKURRY

SKURRIES > SKURRY

SKURRY *vb* scurry

SKURRYING > SKURRY

SKUTTLE *vb* scuttle

SKUTTLED > SKUTTLE

SKUTTLES > SKUTTLE

SKUTTLING > SKUTTLE

SKY *n* upper atmosphere as seen from the earth ▷ *vb* hit high in the air

SKYBOARD *n* small board used for skysurfing

SKYBOARDS > SKYBOARD

SKYBORN *adj* born in heaven

SKYBORNE *adj* flying through sky

SKYBOX *n* luxurious suite high up in the stand of a sports stadium

SKYBOXES > SKYBOX

SKYBRIDGE *n* covered, elevated bridge connecting two buildings

SKYCAP *n* luggage porter at American airport

SKYCAPS > SKYCAP

SKYCLAD *adj* naked

SKYDIVE *vb* take part in skydiving

SKYDIVED > SKYDIVE

SKYDIVER > SKYDIVE

SKYDIVERS > SKYDIVE

SKYDIVES > SKYDIVE

SKYDIVING *n* sport of jumping from an aircraft and performing manoeuvres before opening one's parachute

SKYDOVE > SKYDIVE

SKYED > SKY

SKYER *n* cricket ball hit up into air

SKYERS > SKYER

SKYEY *adj* of the sky

SKYEYER > SKYEY

SKYEYEST > SKYEY

SKYF *n* South African slang for a cigarette or substance for smoking ▷ *vb* smoke a cigarette

SKYFED > SKYF

SKYFING > SKYF

SKYFS > SKYF

SKYGLOW *n* glow in the night sky caused by urban lights

SKYGLOWS > SKYGLOW

SKYHOME *n* Australian slang for a sub-penthouse flat in a tall building

SKYHOMES > SKYHOME

SKYHOOK *n* hook hung from a helicopter

SKYHOOKS > SKYHOOK

SKYIER > SKYEY

SKYIEST > SKYEY

SKYING > SKY

SKYISH > SKY

SKYJACK *vb* hijack (an aircraft)

SKYJACKED > SKYJACK

SKYJACKER > SKYJACK

SKYJACKS > SKYJACK

SKYLAB *n* orbiting space station

SKYLABS > SKYLAB

SKYLARK *n* lark that sings while soaring at a great height ▷ *vb* play or frolic

SKYLARKED > SKYLARK

SKYLARKER > SKYLARK

SKYLARKS > SKYLARK

SKYLESS *adj* having no sky

SKYLIGHT *n* window in a roof or ceiling

SKYLIGHTS > SKYLIGHT

SKYLIKE > SKY

SKYLINE *n* outline of buildings, trees, etc against the sky

SKYLINES > SKYLINE

SKYLIT *adj* having skylight

SKYMAN *n* paratrooper

SKYMEN > SKYMAN

SKYPHOI > SKYPHOS

SKYPHOS *n* ancient Greek drinking cup

SKYR *n* Scandinavian cheese

SKYRE *vb* Scots word meaning shine

SKYRED > SKYRE

SKYRES > SKYRE

SKYRING > SKYRE

SKYRMION *n* (in theoretical physics) mathematical model used to model baryons

SKYRMIONS > SKYRMION

SKYROCKET *vb* rise very quickly

SKYRS > SKYR

SKYSAIL *n* square sail set above the royal on a square-rigger

SKYSAILS > SKYSAIL

SKYSCAPE *n* painting, drawing, photograph, etc, representing or depicting the sky

S

SKYSCAPES > SKYSCAPE
SKYSURF vb perform freefall aerobatics
SKYSURFED > SKYSURF
SKYSURFER n someone who performs stunts with a small board attached to his or her feet while in free fall
SKYSURFS > SKYSURF
SKYTE vb Scots word meaning slide
SKYTED > SKYTE
SKYTES > SKYTE
SKYTING > SKYTE
SKYWALK n tightrope walk at great height
SKYWALKS > SKYWALK
SKYWARD adj towards the sky ▷ adv towards the sky
SKYWARDS same as **>** SKYWARD
SKYWATCH vb watch the sky in search of celestial bodies or aircraft
SKYWAY n air route
SKYWAYS > SKYWAY
SKYWRITE vb write message in sky with smoke from aircraft
SKYWRITER > SKYWRITE
SKYWRITES > SKYWRITE
SKYWROTE > SKYWRITE
SLAB n broad flat piece ▷ vb cut or make into a slab or slabs
SLABBED > SLAB
SLABBER vb dribble from the mouth
SLABBERED > SLABBER
SLABBERER > SLABBER
SLABBERS > SLABBER
SLABBERY > SLABBER
SLABBIER > SLAB
SLABBIES > SLABBY
SLABBIEST > SLAB
SLABBING n act of slabbing
SLABBINGS > SLABBING
SLABBY n person who works with slabs of timber
SLABLIKE > SLAB
SLABS > SLAB
SLABSTONE n flagstone
SLACK same as **>** SLAKE
SLACKED > SLACK
SLACKEN vb make or become slack
SLACKENED > SLACKEN
SLACKENER > SLACKEN
SLACKENS > SLACKEN
SLACKER n person who evades work or duty
SLACKERS > SLACKER
SLACKEST > SLACK
SLACKING > SLACK
SLACKLY > SLACK
SLACKNESS > SLACK
SLACKS pl n casual trousers
SLADANG n Malayan tapir
SLADANGS > SLADANG
SLADE n little valley
SLADES > SLADE
SLAE Scots word for **>** SLOE
SLAES > SLAE
SLAG n waste left after metal is smelted ▷ vb criticize
SLAGGED > SLAG
SLAGGIER > SLAG

SLAGGIEST > SLAG
SLAGGING > SLAG
SLAGGINGS > SLAG
SLAGGY > SLAG
SLAGHEAP n heap of slag waste
SLAGHEAPS > SLAGHEAP
SLAGS > SLAG
SLAHAL same as **>** LAHAL
SLAHALS > SLAHAL
SLAID vb (Scot) sledge
SLAIDS > SLAID
SLAIN > SLAY
SLAINTE interj cheers!
SLAIRG Scots word for **>** SPREAD
SLAIRGED > SLAIRG
SLAIRGING > SLAIRG
SLAIRGS > SLAIRG
SLAISTER vb cover with a sloppy mess ▷ n sloppy mess
SLAISTERS > SLAISTER
SLAISTERY > SLAISTER
SLAKABLE > SLAKE
SLAKE vb satisfy (thirst or desire)
SLAKEABLE > SLAKE
SLAKED > SLAKE
SLAKELESS adj impossible to slake
SLAKER > SLAKE
SLAKERS > SLAKE
SLAKES > SLAKE
SLAKING > SLAKE
SLALOM n skiing or canoeing race over a winding course ▷ vb take part in a slalom
SLALOMED > SLALOM
SLALOMER > SLALOM
SLALOMERS > SLALOM
SLALOMING > SLALOM
SLALOMIST > SLALOM
SLALOMS > SLALOM
SLAM vb shut, put down, or hit violently and noisily ▷ n act or sound of slamming
SLAMDANCE vb dance aggressively, bumping into others
SLAMMAKIN n woman's loose dress
SLAMMED > SLAM
SLAMMER n prison
SLAMMERS > SLAMMER
SLAMMING > SLAM
SLAMMINGS > SLAM
SLAMS > SLAM
SLANDER n false and malicious statement about a person ▷ vb utter slander about
SLANDERED > SLANDER
SLANDERER > SLANDER
SLANDERS > SLANDER
SLANE n spade for cutting turf
SLANES > SLANE
SLANG n very informal language ▷ vb use insulting language to (someone)
SLANGED > SLANG
SLANGER n street vendor
SLANGERS > SLANGER
SLANGIER > SLANG
SLANGIEST > SLANG
SLANGILY > SLANG
SLANGING > SLANG

SLANGINGS > SLANG
SLANGISH > SLANG
SLANGS > SLANG
SLANGUAGE n language using slang
SLANGULAR adj of or using slang
SLANGY > SLANG
SLANK dialect word for **>** LANK
SLANT vb lean at an angle ▷ n slope
SLANTED > SLANT
SLANTER same as **>** SLINTER
SLANTERS > SLANTER
SLANTIER > SLANTY
SLANTIEST > SLANTY
SLANTING > SLANT
SLANTLY > SLANT
SLANTS > SLANT
SLANTWAYS same as **>** SLANTWISE
SLANTWISE adj in a slanting or oblique direction
SLANTY adj slanting
SLAP n blow with the open hand or a flat object ▷ vb strike with the open hand or a flat object
SLAPDASH adj careless and hasty ▷ adv carelessly or hastily ▷ n slapdash activity or work ▷ vb do in a hurried and careless manner
SLAPHAPPY adj cheerfully irresponsible or careless
SLAPHEAD n derogatory term for a bald person
SLAPHEADS > SLAPHEAD
SLAPJACK n simple card game
SLAPJACKS > SLAPJACK
SLAPPED > SLAP
SLAPPER > SLAP
SLAPPERS > SLAP
SLAPPING > SLAP
SLAPPINGS > SLAPPING
SLAPS > SLAP
SLAPSHOT n hard, fast, often wild, shot executed with a powerful downward swing
SLAPSHOTS > SLAPSHOT
SLAPSTICK n boisterous knockabout comedy
SLART vb spill (something)
SLARTED > SLART
SLARTING > SLART
SLARTS > SLART
SLASH vb cut with a sweeping stroke ▷ n sweeping stroke
SLASHED > SLASH
SLASHER n machine used for cutting scrub or undergrowth in the bush
SLASHERS > SLASHER
SLASHES > SLASH
SLASHFEST n film or computer game that features bloody killings involving blades
SLASHING adj aggressively critical ▷ n act of slashing
SLASHINGS > SLASHING
SLAT n narrow strip of wood or metal ▷ vb provide with slats

SLATCH n slack part of rope
SLATCHES > SLATCH
SLATE n rock which splits easily into thin layers ▷ vb cover with slates ▷ adj dark grey
SLATED > SLATE
SLATELIKE > SLATE
SLATER n person trained in laying roof slates
SLATERS > SLATER
SLATES > SLATE
SLATEY adj slightly mad
SLATHER vb spread quickly or lavishly
SLATHERED > SLATHER
SLATHERS > SLATHER
SLATIER > SLATY
SLATIEST > SLATY
SLATINESS > SLATY
SLATING n act or process of laying slates
SLATINGS > SLATING
SLATS > SLAT
SLATTED > SLAT
SLATTER vb be slovenly
SLATTERED > SLATTER
SLATTERN n derogatory term for a slovenly woman
SLATTERNS > SLATTERN
SLATTERS > SLATTER
SLATTERY adj slovenly
SLATTING > SLAT
SLATTINGS > SLAT
SLATY adj consisting of or resembling slate
SLAUGHTER vb kill (animals) for food ▷ n slaughtering
SLAVE n person owned by another for whom he or she has to work ▷ vb work like a slave
SLAVED > SLAVE
SLAVER n person or ship engaged in the slave trade ▷ vb dribble saliva from the mouth
SLAVERED > SLAVER
SLAVERER > SLAVER
SLAVERERS > SLAVER
SLAVERIES > SLAVERY
SLAVERING > SLAVER
SLAVERS > SLAVER
SLAVERY n state or condition of being a slave
SLAVES > SLAVE
SLAVEY n female general servant
SLAVEYS > SLAVEY
SLAVING > SLAVE
SLAVISH adj of or like a slave
SLAVISHLY > SLAVISH
SLAVOCRAT n US slaveholder before the Civil War
SLAVOPHIL n person who admires the Slavs or their cultures
SLAW short for **>** COLESLAW
SLAWS > SLAW
SLAY vb kill
SLAYABLE > SLAY
SLAYED > SLAY
SLAYER > SLAY
SLAYERS > SLAY
SLAYING n act of slaying
SLAYINGS > SLAYING

SLAYS > SLAY
SLEAVE n tangled thread ▷ vb disentangle (twisted thread, etc)
SLEAVED > SLEAVE
SLEAVES > SLEAVE
SLEAVING > SLEAVE
SLEAZE n behaviour considered dishonest or disreputable ▷ vb behave in a sleazy manner
SLEAZEBAG n disgusting person
SLEAZED > SLEAZE
SLEAZES > SLEAZE
SLEAZIER > SLEAZY
SLEAZIEST > SLEAZY
SLEAZILY > SLEAZY
SLEAZING > SLEAZE
SLEAZO n sleazy person
SLEAZOID n sleazy person
SLEAZOIDS > SLEAZOID
SLEAZOS > SLEAZO
SLEAZY adj run-down or sordid
SLEB n celebrity
SLEBS > SLEB
SLED same as > SLEDGE
SLEDDED > SLED
SLEDDER > SLED
SLEDDERS > SLED
SLEDDING > SLED
SLEDDINGS > SLED
SLEDED > SLED
SLEDGE n carriage on runners for sliding on snow ▷ vb travel by sledge
SLEDGED > SLEDGE
SLEDGER > SLEDGE
SLEDGERS > SLEDGE
SLEDGES > SLEDGE
SLEDGING > SLEDGE
SLEDGINGS > SLEDGE
SLEDS > SLED
SLEE Scots word for > SLY
SLEECH n slippery mud
SLEECHES > SLEECH
SLEECHIER > SLEECH
SLEECHY > SLEECH
SLEEK adj glossy, smooth, and shiny ▷ vb make smooth and glossy, as by grooming, etc
SLEEKED > SLEEK
SLEEKEN vb make sleek
SLEEKENED > SLEEKEN
SLEEKENS > SLEEKEN
SLEEKER > SLEEK
SLEEKERS > SLEEK
SLEEKEST > SLEEK
SLEEKIER > SLEEK
SLEEKIEST > SLEEK
SLEEKING > SLEEK
SLEEKINGS > SLEEK
SLEEKIT adj smooth
SLEEKLY > SLEEK
SLEEKNESS > SLEEK
SLEEKS > SLEEK
SLEEKY > SLEEK
SLEEP n state of rest characterized by unconsciousness ▷ vb be in or as if in a state of sleep
SLEEPAWAY adj describing a type of camp for teenagers
SLEEPER n railway car fitted for sleeping in

SLEEPERS > SLEEPER
SLEEPERY Scots word for > SLEEPY
SLEEPIER > SLEEPY
SLEEPIEST > SLEEPY
SLEEPILY > SLEEPY
SLEEPING > SLEEP
SLEEPINGS > SLEEP
SLEEPLESS adj (of a night) one during which one does not sleep
SLEEPLIKE > SLEEP
SLEEPOUT n small building for sleeping in
SLEEPOUTS > SLEEPOUT
SLEEPOVER n occasion when a person stays overnight at a friend's house
SLEEPRY Scots word for > SLEEPY
SLEEPS > SLEEP
SLEEPSUIT n baby's sleeping garment
SLEEPWALK vb walk while asleep
SLEEPWEAR n clothes for sleeping in
SLEEPY adj needing sleep
SLEER > SLEE
SLEEST > SLEE
SLEET n rain and snow or hail falling together ▷ vb fall as sleet
SLEETED > SLEET
SLEETIER > SLEET
SLEETIEST > SLEET
SLEETING > SLEET
SLEETS > SLEET
SLEETY > SLEET
SLEEVE n part of a garment which covers the arm
SLEEVED > SLEEVE
SLEEVEEN n sly obsequious smooth-tongued person
SLEEVEENS > SLEEVEEN
SLEEVELET n protective covering for forearm
SLEEVER n old beer measure
SLEEVERS > SLEEVER
SLEEVES > SLEEVE
SLEEVING n tubular flexible insulation into which bare wire can be inserted
SLEEVINGS > SLEEVING
SLEEZIER > SLEEZY
SLEEZIEST > SLEEZY
SLEEZY adj sleazy
SLEIDED adj old word meaning separated
SLEIGH same as > SLEDGE
SLEIGHED > SLEIGH
SLEIGHER > SLEIGH
SLEIGHERS > SLEIGH
SLEIGHING > SLEIGH
SLEIGHS > SLEIGH
SLEIGHT n skill or cunning
SLEIGHTS > SLEIGHT
SLENDER adj slim
SLENDERER > SLENDER
SLENDERLY > SLENDER
SLENTER same as > SLINTER
SLENTERS > SLENTER
SLEPT > SLEEP
SLEUTH n detective ▷ vb track or follow

SLEUTHED > SLEUTH
SLEUTHING > SLEUTH
SLEUTHS > SLEUTH
SLEW vb twist sideways, esp awkwardly
SLEWED > SLEW
SLEWING > SLEW
SLEWS > SLEW
SLEY n weaver's tool for separating threads
SLEYS > SLEY
SLICE n thin flat piece cut from something ▷ vb cut into slices
SLICEABLE > SLICE
SLICED > SLICE
SLICER > SLICE
SLICERS > SLICE
SLICES > SLICE
SLICING > SLICE
SLICINGS > SLICE
SLICK adj persuasive and glib ▷ n patch of oil on water ▷ vb make smooth or sleek
SLICKED > SLICK
SLICKEN vb make smooth
SLICKENED > SLICKEN
SLICKENER > SLICKEN
SLICKENS > SLICKEN
SLICKER n sly or untrustworthy person
SLICKERED adj wearing a waterproof jacket
SLICKERS > SLICKER
SLICKEST > SLICK
SLICKING > SLICK
SLICKINGS > SLICK
SLICKLY > SLICK
SLICKNESS > SLICK
SLICKROCK n weathered and smooth sandstone or other rock
SLICKS > SLICK
SLICKSTER n dishonest person
SLID > SLIDE
SLIDABLE > SLIDE
SLIDDEN > SLIDE
SLIDDER vb slip
SLIDDERED > SLIDDER
SLIDDERS > SLIDDER
SLIDDERY adj slippery
SLIDE vb slip smoothly along (a surface) ▷ n act of sliding
SLIDED > SLIDE
SLIDER > SLIDE
SLIDERS > SLIDE
SLIDES > SLIDE
SLIDESHOW n display in the form of a series of images
SLIDEWAY n sloping channel down which things are slid
SLIDEWAYS > SLIDEWAY
SLIDING > SLIDE
SLIDINGLY > SLIDE
SLIDINGS > SLIDE
SLIER > SLY
SLIEST > SLY
SLIEVE n Irish mountain
SLIEVES > SLIEVE
SLIGHT adj small in quantity or extent ▷ n snub ▷ vb insult (someone) by behaving rudely
SLIGHTED > SLIGHT

SLIGHTER > SLIGHT
SLIGHTERS > SLIGHT
SLIGHTEST > SLIGHT
SLIGHTING adj characteristic of a slight
SLIGHTISH > SLIGHT
SLIGHTLY adv in small measure or degree
SLIGHTS > SLIGHT
SLILY > SLY
SLIM adj not heavy or stout, thin ▷ vb make or become slim by diet and exercise
SLIMDOWN n instance of an organization cutting staff
SLIMDOWNS > SLIMDOWN
SLIME n unpleasant thick slippery substance ▷ vb cover with slime
SLIMEBAG n odious and contemptible person
SLIMEBAGS > SLIMEBAG
SLIMEBALL n odious and contemptible person
SLIMED > SLIME
SLIMES > SLIME
SLIMIER > SLIMY
SLIMIEST > SLIMY
SLIMILY > SLIMY
SLIMINESS > SLIMY
SLIMING > SLIME
SLIMLINE adj slim
SLIMLY > SLIM
SLIMMED > SLIM
SLIMMER > SLIM
SLIMMERS > SLIM
SLIMMEST > SLIM
SLIMMING > SLIM
SLIMMINGS > SLIM
SLIMMISH > SLIM
SLIMNESS > SLIM
SLIMPSIER > SLIMPSY
SLIMPSY adj thin and flimsy
SLIMS > SLIM
SLIMSIER > SLIMSY
SLIMSIEST > SLIMSY
SLIMSY adj frail
SLIMY adj of, like, or covered with slime
SLING n bandage hung from the neck to support an injured hand or arm ▷ vb throw
SLINGBACK n shoe with a strap that goes around the back of the heel
SLINGER > SLING
SLINGERS > SLING
SLINGIER > SLINGY
SLINGIEST > SLINGY
SLINGING > SLING
SLINGS > SLING
SLINGSHOT n Y-shaped implement with a loop of elastic fastened to the ends of the two prongs, used for shooting small stones, etc
SLINGY adj resembling the act of using a sling
SLINK vb move furtively or guiltily ▷ n animal, esp a calf, born prematurely
SLINKED > SLINK
SLINKER > SLINK
SLINKERS > SLINK
SLINKIER > SLINKY
SLINKIEST > SLINKY

SLINKILY > SLINKY
SLINKING > SLINK
SLINKS > SLINK
SLINKSKIN n skin of premature calf
SLINKWEED n plant believed to make cow give birth prematurely
SLINKY adj (of clothes) figure-hugging
SLINTER n dodge, trick, or stratagem
SLINTERS > SLINTER
SLIOTAR n ball used in hurling
SLIOTARS > SLIOTAR
SLIP vb lose balance by sliding ▷ n slipping
SLIPCASE n protective case for a book
SLIPCASED adj having a slipcase
SLIPCASES > SLIPCASE
SLIPCOVER n fitted but easily removable cloth cover for a chair, sofa, etc
SLIPDRESS n silky sleeveless dress
SLIPE n wool removed from the pelt of a slaughtered sheep ▷ vb remove skin
SLIPED > SLIPE
SLIPES > SLIPE
SLIPFORM n mould used in building
SLIPFORMS > SLIPFORM
SLIPING > SLIPE
SLIPKNOT n knot tied so that it will slip along the rope round which it is made
SLIPKNOTS > SLIPKNOT
SLIPLESS > SLIP
SLIPNOOSE n noose made with a slipknot, so that it tightens when pulled
SLIPOUT n instance of slipping out
SLIPOUTS > SLIPOUT
SLIPOVER adj of or denoting a garment that can be put on easily over the head ▷ n such a garment, esp a sleeveless pullover
SLIPOVERS > SLIPOVER
SLIPPAGE n act or an instance of slipping
SLIPPAGES > SLIPPAGE
SLIPPED > SLIP
SLIPPER n light shoe for indoor wear ▷ vb hit or beat with a slipper
SLIPPERED > SLIPPER
SLIPPERS > SLIPPER
SLIPPERY adj so smooth or wet as to cause slipping or be difficult to hold
SLIPPIER > SLIPPY
SLIPPIEST > SLIPPY
SLIPPILY > SLIPPY
SLIPPING > SLIP
SLIPPY adj slippery
SLIPRAIL n rail in a fence that can be slipped out of place to make an opening
SLIPRAILS > SLIPRAIL
SLIPS > SLIP
SLIPSHEET n sheet of paper that is interleaved

between freshly printed sheets
SLIPSHOD adj (of an action) careless
SLIPSLOP n weak or unappetizing food or drink
SLIPSLOPS > SLIPSLOP
SLIPSOLE n separate sole on shoe
SLIPSOLES > SLIPSOLE
SLIPT vb old form of slipped
SLIPUP n mistake or mishap
SLIPUPS > SLIPUP
SLIPWARE n pottery that has been decorated with clay
SLIPWARES > SLIPWARE
SLIPWAY n launching slope on which ships are built or repaired
SLIPWAYS > SLIPWAY
SLISH n old word meaning cut
SLISHES > SLISH
SLIT n long narrow cut or opening ▷ vb make a long straight cut in
SLITHER vb slide unsteadily ▷ n slithering movement
SLITHERED > SLITHER
SLITHERS > SLITHER
SLITHERY adj moving with a slithering motion
SLITLESS > SLIT
SLITLIKE > SLIT
SLITS > SLIT
SLITTED > SLIT
SLITTER > SLIT
SLITTERS > SLIT
SLITTIER > SLIT
SLITTIEST > SLIT
SLITTING > SLIT
SLITTY > SLIT
SLIVE vb slip
SLIVED > SLIVE
SLIVEN > SLIVE
SLIVER n small thin piece ▷ vb cut into slivers
SLIVERED > SLIVER
SLIVERER > SLIVER
SLIVERERS > SLIVER
SLIVERING > SLIVER
SLIVERS > SLIVER
SLIVES > SLIVE
SLIVING > SLIVE
SLIVOVIC n plum brandy
SLIVOVICA n plum brandy
SLIVOVITZ n plum brandy from E Europe
SLIVOWITZ n plum brandy
SLOAN n severe telling-off
SLOANS > SLOAN
SLOB n lazy and untidy person ▷ vb behave like a slob
SLOBBED > SLOB
SLOBBER vb dribble or drool ▷ n liquid or saliva spilt from the mouth
SLOBBERED > SLOBBER
SLOBBERER > SLOBBER
SLOBBERS > SLOBBER
SLOBBERY > SLOBBER
SLOBBIER > SLOB
SLOBBIEST > SLOB
SLOBBING > SLOB
SLOBBISH > SLOB
SLOBBY > SLOB

SLOBLAND n muddy ground
SLOBLANDS > SLOBLAND
SLOBS > SLOB
SLOCKEN vb Scots word meaning slake
SLOCKENED > SLOCKEN
SLOCKENS > SLOCKEN
SLOE n sour blue-black fruit
SLOEBUSH n bush on which sloes grow
SLOES > SLOE
SLOETHORN n sloe plant
SLOETREE n sloe plant
SLOETREES > SLOETREE
SLOG vb work hard and steadily ▷ n long and exhausting work or walk
SLOGAN n catchword or phrase used in politics or advertising
SLOGANED adj having a slogan
SLOGANEER n person who coins or employs slogans frequently ▷ vb coin or employ slogans so as to sway opinion
SLOGANISE same as > SLOGANIZE
SLOGANIZE vb use slogans
SLOGANS > SLOGAN
SLOGGED > SLOG
SLOGGER > SLOG
SLOGGERS > SLOG
SLOGGING > SLOG
SLOGS > SLOG
SLOID n Swedish woodwork
SLOIDS > SLOID
SLOJD same as > SLOID
SLOJDS > SLOJD
SLOKEN vb Scots word meaning slake
SLOKENED > SLOKEN
SLOKENING > SLOKEN
SLOKENS > SLOKEN
SLOMMOCK vb walk assertively with a hip-rolling gait
SLOMMOCKS > SLOMMOCK
SLOMO n slow-motion sequence in a film
SLOMOS > SLOMO
SLOOM vb slumber
SLOOMED > SLOOM
SLOOMIER > SLOOM
SLOOMIEST > SLOOM
SLOOMING > SLOOM
SLOOMS > SLOOM
SLOOMY > SLOOM
SLOOP n small single-masted ship
SLOOPS > SLOOP
SLOOSH vb wash with water
SLOOSHED > SLOOSH
SLOOSHES > SLOOSH
SLOOSHING > SLOOSH
SLOOT n ditch for irrigation or drainage
SLOOTS > SLOOT
SLOP vb splash or spill ▷ n spilt liquid
SLOPE vb slant ▷ n sloping surface
SLOPED > SLOPE
SLOPER > SLOPE
SLOPERS > SLOPE
SLOPES > SLOPE

SLOPESIDE n side of a slope
SLOPEWISE > SLOPE
SLOPIER > SLOPE
SLOPIEST > SLOPE
SLOPING > SLOPE
SLOPINGLY > SLOPE
SLOPPED > SLOP
SLOPPIER > SLOPPY
SLOPPIEST > SLOPPY
SLOPPILY > SLOPPY
SLOPPING > SLOP
SLOPPY adj careless or untidy
SLOPS > SLOP
SLOPWORK n manufacture of cheap shoddy clothing or the clothes so produced
SLOPWORKS > SLOPWORK
SLOPY > SLOPE
SLORM vb wipe carelessly
SLORMED > SLORM
SLORMING > SLORM
SLORMS > SLORM
SLOSH vb pour carelessly ▷ n splashing sound
SLOSHED > SLOSH
SLOSHES > SLOSH
SLOSHIER > SLOSH
SLOSHIEST > SLOSH
SLOSHING > SLOSH
SLOSHINGS > SLOSH
SLOSHY > SLOSH
SLOT n narrow opening for inserting something ▷ vb make a slot or slots in
SLOTBACK n American football player
SLOTBACKS > SLOTBACK
SLOTH n slow-moving animal of tropical America ▷ vb be lazy
SLOTHED > SLOTH
SLOTHFUL adj lazy or idle
SLOTHING > SLOTH
SLOTHS > SLOTH
SLOTS > SLOT
SLOTTED > SLOT
SLOTTER > SLOT
SLOTTERS > SLOT
SLOTTING > SLOT
SLOUCH vb sit, stand, or move with a drooping posture ▷ n drooping posture
SLOUCHED > SLOUCH
SLOUCHER > SLOUCH
SLOUCHERS > SLOUCH
SLOUCHES > SLOUCH
SLOUCHIER > SLOUCHY
SLOUCHILY > SLOUCHY
SLOUCHING > SLOUCH
SLOUCHY adj slouching
SLOUGH n bog ▷ vb (of a snake) shed (its skin)
SLOUGHED > SLOUGH
SLOUGHI n N African breed of dog resembling a greyhound
SLOUGHIER > SLOUGHY
SLOUGHING > SLOUGH
SLOUGHIS > SLOUGHI
SLOUGHS > SLOUGH
SLOUGHY > SLOUGH
SLOVE > SLIVE
SLOVEN n habitually dirty or untidy person

SLOVENLY adj dirty or untidy ▷ adv in a slovenly manner

SLOVENRY n quality of being slovenly

SLOVENS > SLOVEN

SLOW adj taking a longer time than is usual or expected ▷ adv slowly ▷ vb reduce the speed (of)

SLOWBACK n lazy person

SLOWBACKS > SLOWBACK

SLOWCOACH n person who moves or works slowly

SLOWDOWN n any slackening of pace

SLOWDOWNS > SLOWDOWN

SLOWED > SLOW

SLOWER > SLOW

SLOWEST > SLOW

SLOWING > SLOW

SLOWINGS > SLOW

SLOWISH > SLOW

SLOWLY > SLOW

SLOWNESS > SLOW

SLOWPOKE same as > SLOWCOACH

SLOWPOKES > SLOWPOKE

SLOWS > SLOW

SLOWWORM n small legless lizard

SLOWWORMS > SLOWWORM

SLOYD n Swedish woodwork

SLOYDS > SLOYD

SLUB n lump in yarn or fabric ▷ vb draw out and twist (a sliver of fibre) before spinning ▷ adj (of material) having an irregular appearance

SLUBB same as > SLUB

SLUBBED > SLUB

SLUBBER vb smear

SLUBBERED > SLUBBER

SLUBBERS > SLUBBER

SLUBBEST > SLUB

SLUBBIER > SLUB

SLUBBIEST > SLUB

SLUBBING > SLUB

SLUBBINGS > SLUB

SLUBBS > SLUBB

SLUBBY > SLUB

SLUBS > SLUB

SLUDGE n thick mud ▷ vb convert into sludge

SLUDGED > SLUDGE

SLUDGES > SLUDGE

SLUDGIER > SLUDGY

SLUDGIEST > SLUDGY

SLUDGING > SLUDGE

SLUDGY adj consisting of, containing, or like sludge

SLUE same as > SLEW

SLUED > SLUE

SLUEING > SLUE

SLUES > SLUE

SLUFF same as > SLOUGH

SLUFFED > SLUFF

SLUFFING > SLUFF

SLUFFS > SLUFF

SLUG n land snail with no shell ▷ vb hit hard

SLUGABED n person who remains in bed through laziness

SLUGABEDS > SLUGABED

SLUGFEST n fist fight

SLUGFESTS > SLUGFEST

SLUGGABED same as > SLUGABED

SLUGGARD n lazy person ▷ adj lazy **SLUGGARDS** > SLUGGARD

SLUGGED > SLUG

SLUGGER n (esp in boxing, baseball, etc) a person who strikes hard

SLUGGERS > SLUGGER

SLUGGING > SLUG

SLUGGISH adj slow-moving, lacking energy

SLUGHORN same as > SLOGAN

SLUGHORNE same as > SLOGAN

SLUGHORNS > SLUGHORN

SLUGLIKE adj like a slug

SLUGS > SLUG

SLUICE n channel that carries a rapid current of water ▷ vb drain water by means of a sluice

SLUICED > SLUICE

SLUICES > SLUICE

SLUICEWAY same as > SLUICE

SLUICIER > SLUICE

SLUICIEST > SLUICE

SLUICING > SLUICE

SLUICY > SLUICE

SLUING > SLUE

SLUIT n water channel in South Africa

SLUITS > SLUIT

SLUM n squalid overcrowded house or area ▷ vb experience poorer places or conditions than usual

SLUMBER n sleep ▷ vb sleep

SLUMBERED > SLUMBER

SLUMBERER > SLUMBER

SLUMBERS > SLUMBER

SLUMBERY adj sleepy

SLUMBROUS adj sleepy

SLUMBRY same as > SLUMBERY

SLUMGUM n material left after wax is extracted from honeycomb

SLUMGUMS > SLUMGUM

SLUMISM n existence of slums

SLUMISMS > SLUMISM

SLUMLORD n absentee landlord of slum property, esp one who profiteers

SLUMLORDS > SLUMLORD

SLUMMED > SLUM

SLUMMER > SLUM

SLUMMERS > SLUM

SLUMMIER > SLUM

SLUMMIEST > SLUM

SLUMMING > SLUM

SLUMMINGS > SLUM

SLUMMOCK vb move slowly and heavily

SLUMMOCKS > SLUMMOCK

SLUMMY > SLUM

SLUMP vb (of prices or demand) decline suddenly ▷ n sudden decline in prices or demand

SLUMPED > SLUMP

SLUMPIER > SLUMPY

SLUMPIEST > SLUMPY

SLUMPING > SLUMP

SLUMPS > SLUMP

SLUMPY adj boggy

SLUMS > SLUM

SLUNG > SLING

SLUNGSHOT n weight attached to the end of a cord and used as a weapon

SLUNK > SLINK

SLUR vb pronounce or utter (words) indistinctly ▷ n slurring of words

SLURB n suburban slum

SLURBAN > SLURB

SLURBS > SLURB

SLURP vb eat or drink noisily ▷ n slurping sound

SLURPED > SLURP

SLURPER > SLURP

SLURPERS > SLURP

SLURPIER > SLURPY

SLURPIEST > SLURPY

SLURPING > SLURP

SLURPS > SLURP

SLURPY adj making a slurping noise

SLURRED > SLUR

SLURRIED > SLURRY

SLURRIES > SLURRY

SLURRING > SLUR

SLURRY n muddy liquid mixture ▷ vb spread slurry

SLURRYING > SLURRY

SLURS > SLUR

SLURVE n pitch in baseball combining elements of the slider and the curveball

SLURVES > SLURVE

SLUSE same as > SLUICE

SLUSES > SLUSE

SLUSH n watery muddy substance ▷ vb make one's way through or as if through slush

SLUSHED > SLUSH

SLUSHES > SLUSH

SLUSHIER > SLUSHY

SLUSHIES > SLUSHY

SLUSHIEST > SLUSHY

SLUSHILY > SLUSHY

SLUSHING > SLUSH

SLUSHY adj of, resembling, or consisting of slush ▷ n unskilled kitchen assistant

SLUT n derogatory term for a woman considered immoral

SLUTCH n mud

SLUTCHES > SLUTCH

SLUTCHIER > SLUTCH

SLUTCHY > SLUTCH

SLUTS > SLUT

SLUTTERY n state of being a slut

SLUTTIER > SLUT

SLUTTIEST > SLUT

SLUTTILY > SLUTTY

SLUTTISH > SLUT

SLUTTY > SLUT

SLY adj crafty

SLYBOOTS pl n person who is sly

SLYER > SLY

SLYEST > SLY

SLYISH > SLY

SLYLY > SLY

SLYNESS > SLY

SLYNESSES > SLY

SLYPE n covered passageway in a church

SLYPES > SLYPE

SMA Scots word for > SMALL

SMAAK vb South African slang for like or love

SMAAKED > SMAAK

SMAAKING > SMAAK

SMAAKS > SMAAK

SMACK vb slap sharply ▷ n sharp slap ▷ adv squarely or directly

SMACKDOWN n severe beating or defeat

SMACKED > SMACK

SMACKER n loud kiss

SMACKEROO n loud kiss

SMACKERS > SMACKER

SMACKHEAD n person who is addicted to heroin

SMACKING adj brisk

SMACKINGS > SMACKING

SMACKS > SMACK

SMAIK n Scots word meaning rascal

SMAIKS > SMAIK

SMALL adj not large in size, number, or amount ▷ n narrow part of the lower back ▷ adv into small pieces ▷ vb make small

SMALLAGE n wild celery

SMALLAGES > SMALLAGE

SMALLBOY n steward's assistant or deputy steward in European households in W Africa

SMALLBOYS > SMALLBOY

SMALLED > SMALL

SMALLER > SMALL

SMALLEST > SMALL

SMALLING > SMALL

SMALLISH > SMALL

SMALLNESS > SMALL

SMALLPOX n contagious disease with blisters that leave scars

SMALLS > SMALL

SMALLSAT n small communications satellite

SMALLSATS > SMALLSAT

SMALLTIME adj unimportant

SMALM same as > SMARM

SMALMED > SMALM

SMALMIER > SMALMY

SMALMIEST > SMALMY

SMALMILY > SMALMY

SMALMING > SMALM

SMALMS > SMALM

SMALMY same as > SMARMY

SMALT n type of silica glass coloured deep blue with cobalt oxide

SMALTI > SMALTO

SMALTINE n mineral containing cobalt

SMALTINES > SMALTINE

SMALTITE n silver-white to greyish mineral

SMALTITES > SMALTITE

SMALTO n coloured glass, etc, used in mosaics

SMALTOS > SMALTO

SMALTS > SMALT

SMARAGD *n* any green gemstone, such as the emerald

SMARAGDE *same as* > SMARAGD

SMARAGDES > SMARAGDE

SMARAGDS > SMARAGD

SMARM *vb* bring (oneself) into favour (with) ▷ *n* obsequious flattery

SMARMED ▷ SMARM

SMARMIER > SMARMY

SMARMIEST > SMARMY

SMARMILY > SMARMY

SMARMING > SMARM

SMARMS > SMARM

SMARMY *adj* unpleasantly suave or flattering

SMART *adj* well-kept and neat ▷ *vb* feel or cause stinging pain ▷ *n* stinging pain ▷ *adv* in a smart manner

SMARTARSE *n* derogatory term for a clever person, esp one who parades their knowledge offensively

SMARTASS *same as* > SMARTARSE

SMARTED > SMART

SMARTEN *vb* make or become smart

SMARTENED > SMARTEN

SMARTENS > SMARTEN

SMARTER > SMART

SMARTEST > SMART

SMARTIE *same as* > SMARTY

SMARTIES > SMARTY

SMARTING > SMART

SMARTISH > SMART

SMARTLY > SMART

SMARTNESS > SMART

SMARTS *pl n* know-how, intelligence, or wits

SMARTWEED *n* grass with acrid smell

SMARTY *n* would-be clever person

SMASH *vb* break violently and noisily ▷ *n* act or sound of smashing ▷ *adv* with a smash

SMASHABLE > SMASH

SMASHED > SMASH

SMASHER *n* attractive person or thing

SMASHEROO *n* excellent person or thing

SMASHERS > SMASHER

SMASHES > SMASH

SMASHING *adj* excellent

SMASHINGS > SMASHING

SMASHUP *n* bad collision of cars

SMASHUPS > SMASHUP

SMATCH *less common word for* > SMACK

SMATCHED > SMATCH

SMATCHES > SMATCH

SMATCHING > SMATCH

SMATTER *n* smattering ▷ *vb* prattle

SMATTERED > SMATTER

SMATTERER > SMATTER

SMATTERS > SMATTER

SMAZE *n* smoky haze, less damp than fog

SMAZES > SMAZE

SMEAR *vb* spread with a greasy or sticky substance ▷ *n* dirty mark or smudge

SMEARCASE *n* American type of cottage cheese

SMEARED > SMEAR

SMEARER > SMEAR

SMEARERS > SMEAR

SMEARIER > SMEARY

SMEARIEST > SMEARY

SMEARILY > SMEARY

SMEARING > SMEAR

SMEARS > SMEAR

SMEARY *adj* smeared, dirty

SMEATH *n* duck

SMEATHS > SMEATH

SMECTIC *adj* (of a substance) existing in state in which the molecules are oriented in layers

SMECTITE *n* type of clay mineral

SMECTITES > SMECTITE

SMECTITIC > SMECTITE

SMEDDUM *n* any fine powder

SMEDDUMS > SMEDDUM

SMEE *n* duck

SMEECH *Southwest English dialect form of* > SMOKE

SMEECHED > SMEECH

SMEECHES > SMEECH

SMEECHING > SMEECH

SMEEK *vb* smoke

SMEEKED > SMEEK

SMEEKING > SMEEK

SMEEKS > SMEEK

SMEES > SMEE

SMEETH *n* duck ▷ *vb* make smooth

SMEETHED > SMEETH

SMEETHING > SMEETH

SMEETHS > SMEETH

SMEGMA *n* whitish sebaceous secretion that accumulates beneath the prepuce

SMEGMAS > SMEGMA

SMEIK *same as* > SMEKE

SMEIKED > SMEIK

SMEIKING *same as* > SMEKING

SMEIKS > SMEIK

SMEKE *n* smoke ▷ *vb* smoke

SMEKED > SMEKE

SMEKES > SMEKE

SMEKING > SMEKE

SMELL *vb* perceive (a scent or odour) by means of the nose ▷ *n* ability to perceive odours by the nose

SMELLABLE *adj* capable of being smelled

SMELLED > SMELL

SMELLER > SMELL

SMELLERS > SMELL

SMELLIER > SMELLY

SMELLIES *pl n* pleasant-smelling products such as perfumes, body lotions, bath salts, etc

SMELLIEST > SMELLY

SMELLING > SMELL

SMELLINGS > SMELL

SMELLS > SMELL

SMELLY *adj* having a nasty smell

SMELT *vb* extract metal from an ore

SMELTED > SMELT

SMELTER *n* industrial plant where smelting is carried out

SMELTERS > SMELTER

SMELTERY *variant of* > SMELTER

SMELTING > SMELT

SMELTINGS > SMELL

SMELTS > SMELT

SMERK *same as* > SMIRK

SMERKED > SMERK

SMERKING > SMERK

SMERKS > SMERK

SMEUSE *n* way through hedge

SMEUSES > SMEUSE

SMEW *n* duck of N Europe and Asia

SMEWS > SMEW

SMICKER *vb* smirk

SMICKERED > SMICKER

SMICKERS > SMICKER

SMICKET *n* smock

SMICKETS > SMICKET

SMICKLY *adv* amorously

SMIDDIED > SMIDDY

SMIDDIES > SMIDDY

SMIDDY *Scots word for* > SMITHY

SMIDDYING > SMIDDY

SMIDGE *n* very small amount or part

SMIDGEN *n* very small amount or part

SMIDGENS > SMIDGEN

SMIDGEON *same as* > SMIDGEN

SMIDGEONS > SMIDGEON

SMIDGES > SMIDGE

SMIDGIN *same as* > SMIDGEN

SMIDGINS > SMIDGIN

SMIERCASE *same as* > SMEARCASE

SMIGHT *same as* > SMITE

SMIGHTING > SMIGHT

SMIGHTS > SMIGHT

SMILAX *n* type of climbing shrub

SMILAXES > SMILAX

SMILE *n* turning up of the corners of the mouth to show pleasure or friendliness ▷ *vb* give a smile

SMILED > SMILE

SMILEFUL *adj* full of smiles

SMILELESS > SMILE

SMILER > SMILE

SMILERS > SMILE

SMILES > SMILE

SMILET *n* little smile

SMILETS > SMILET

SMILEY *n* symbol depicting a smile or other facial expression, used in e-mail ▷ *adj* cheerful

SMILEYS > SMILEY

SMILIER > SMILEY

SMILIES > SMILEY

SMILIEST > SMILEY

SMILING > SMILE

SMILINGLY > SMILE

SMILINGS > SMILE

SMILODON *n* extinct sabre-toothed tiger

SMILODONS > SMILODON

SMIR *n* drizzly rain ▷ *vb* drizzle lightly

SMIRCH *n* stain ▷ *vb* disgrace

SMIRCHED > SMIRCH

SMIRCHER > SMIRCH

SMIRCHERS > SMIRCH

SMIRCHES > SMIRCH

SMIRCHING > SMIRCH

SMIRK *n* smug smile ▷ *vb* give a smirk

SMIRKED > SMIRK

SMIRKER > SMIRK

SMIRKERS > SMIRK

SMIRKIER > SMIRK

SMIRKIEST > SMIRK

SMIRKILY > SMIRK

SMIRKING > SMIRK

SMIRKS > SMIRK

SMIRKY > SMIRK

SMIRR *same as* > SMIR

SMIRRED > SMIRR

SMIRRIER > SMIRR

SMIRRIEST > SMIRR

SMIRRING > SMIRR

SMIRRS > SMIRR

SMIRRY > SMIRR

SMIRS > SMIR

SMIRTING *n* flirting amongst those smoking outside a non-smoking office, pub, etc

SMIRTINGS > SMIRTING

SMISHING *n* phishing via text messages

SMISHINGS > SMISHING

SMIT > SMITE

SMITE *vb* strike hard

SMITER > SMITE

SMITERS > SMITE

SMITES > SMITE

SMITH *n* worker in metal ▷ *vb* work in metal

SMITHED > SMITH

SMITHERS *pl n* little shattered pieces

SMITHERY *n* trade or craft of a blacksmith

SMITHIED > SMITHY

SMITHIES > SMITHY

SMITHING *n* act of working as a smith

SMITHINGS > SMITHING

SMITHS > SMITH

SMITHY *n* blacksmith's workshop ▷ *vb* work as a smith

SMITHYING > SMITHY

SMITING > SMITE

SMITS > SMIT

SMITTED > SMIT

SMITTEN > SMITE

SMITTING > SMIT

SMITTLE *adj* infectious

SMOCK *n* loose overall ▷ *vb* gather (material) by sewing in a honeycomb pattern

SMOCKED > SMOCK

SMOCKING *n* ornamental needlework used to gather material

SMOCKINGS > SMOCKING

SMOCKLIKE > SMOCK

SMOCKS > SMOCK

SMOG *n* mixture of smoke and fog

SMOGGIER > SMOG

SMOGGIEST > SMOG
SMOGGY > SMOG
SMOGLESS > SMOG
SMOGS > SMOG
SMOILE *same as* > SMILE
SMOILED > SMOILE
SMOILES > SMOILE
SMOILING > SMOILE
SMOKABLE > SMOKE
SMOKE *n* cloudy mass that rises from something burning ▷ *vb* give off smoke or treat with smoke
SMOKEABLE > SMOKE
SMOKEBOX *n* part of a steam engine or boiler
SMOKEBUSH *n* plant with purple leaves and small flowers that turn grey-white
SMOKED > SMOKE
SMOKEHO *same as* > SMOKO
SMOKEHOOD *n* hood worn to keep out smoke
SMOKEHOS > SMOKEHO
SMOKEJACK *n* device formerly used for turning a roasting spit, operated by the movement of ascending gases in a chimney
SMOKELESS *adj* having or producing little or no smoke
SMOKELIKE > SMOKE
SMOKEPOT *n* device for producing smoke
SMOKEPOTS > SMOKEPOT
SMOKER *n* person who habitually smokes tobacco
SMOKERS > SMOKER
SMOKES > SMOKE
SMOKEY > SMOKY
SMOKEYS > SMOKEY
SMOKIE *n* smoked haddock
SMOKIER > SMOKY
SMOKIES > SMOKY
SMOKIEST > SMOKY
SMOKILY > SMOKY
SMOKINESS > SMOKY
SMOKING > SMOKE
SMOKINGS > SMOKING
SMOKO *n* short break from work for tea or a cigarette
SMOKOS > SMOKO
SMOKY *adj* filled with or giving off smoke, sometimes excessively ▷ *n* haddock that has been smoked
SMOLDER *same as* > SMOULDER
SMOLDERED > SMOLDER
SMOLDERS > SMOLDER
SMOLT *n* young salmon at the stage when it migrates to the sea
SMOLTS > SMOLT
SMOOCH *vb* kiss and cuddle ▷ *n* smooching
SMOOCHED > SMOOCH
SMOOCHER > SMOOCH
SMOOCHERS > SMOOCH
SMOOCHES > SMOOCH
SMOOCHIER > SMOOCHY
SMOOCHING > SMOOCH
SMOOCHY *adj* romantic
SMOODGE *same as* > SMOOCH
SMOODGED > SMOODGE
SMOODGES > SMOODGE
SMOODGING > SMOODGE

SMOOGE *same as* > SMOOCH
SMOOGED > SMOOGE
SMOOGES > SMOOGE
SMOOGING > SMOOGE
SMOOR *vb* Scots word meaning put out fire
SMOORED > SMOOR
SMOORING > SMOOR
SMOORS > SMOOR
SMOOSH *vb* paint to give softened look
SMOOSHED > SMOOSH
SMOOSHES > SMOOSH
SMOOSHING > SMOOSH
SMOOT *vb* work as printer
SMOOTED > SMOOT
SMOOTH *adj* even in surface, texture, or consistency ▷ *vb* make smooth ▷ *adv* in a smooth manner ▷ *n* smooth part of something
SMOOTHE *same as* > SMOOTH
SMOOTHED > SMOOTH
SMOOTHEN *vb* make or become smooth
SMOOTHENS > SMOOTHEN
SMOOTHER > SMOOTH
SMOOTHERS > SMOOTH
SMOOTHES > SMOOTH
SMOOTHEST > SMOOTH
SMOOTHIE *n* smooth thick drink made with fruit and milk and sometimes ice cream
SMOOTHIES > SMOOTHY
SMOOTHING > SMOOTH
SMOOTHISH > SMOOTH
SMOOTHLY > SMOOTH
SMOOTHS > SMOOTH
SMOOTHY *same as* > SMOOTHIE
SMOOTING > SMOOT
SMOOTS > SMOOT
SMORBROD *n* Danish hors d'oeuvre
SMORBRODS > SMORBROD
SMORE *same as* > SMOOR
SMORED > SMORE
SMORES > SMORE
SMORG *n* short for smorgasbord
SMORGS > SMORG
SMORING > SMORE
SMORZANDO *adv* musical instruction meaning fading away gradually
SMORZATO *same as* > SMORZANDO
SMOTE > SMITE
SMOTHER *vb* suffocate or stifle ▷ *n* anything, such as a cloud of smoke, that stifles
SMOTHERED > SMOTHER
SMOTHERER > SMOTHER
SMOTHERS > SMOTHER
SMOTHERY *adj* tending to smother
SMOUCH *vb* kiss
SMOUCHED > SMOUCH
SMOUCHES > SMOUCH
SMOUCHING > SMOUCH
SMOULDER *vb* burn slowly with smoke but no flame ▷ *n* dense smoke, as from a smouldering fire
SMOULDERS > SMOULDER
SMOULDRY *adj* smouldering

SMOUSE *vb* South African word meaning peddle
SMOUSED > SMOUSE
SMOUSER > SMOUSE
SMOUSERS > SMOUSE
SMOUSES > SMOUSE
SMOUSING > SMOUSE
SMOUT *n* child or undersized person ▷ *vb* creep or sneak
SMOUTED > SMOUT
SMOUTING > SMOUT
SMOUTS > SMOUT
SMOWT *same as* > SMOUT
SMOWTS > SMOWT
SMOYLE *same as* > SMILE
SMOYLED > SMOYLE
SMOYLES > SMOYLE
SMOYLING > SMOYLE
SMRITI *n* class of Hindu sacred literature
SMRITIS > SMRITI
SMUDGE *vb* make or become smeared or soiled ▷ *n* dirty mark
SMUDGED > SMUDGE
SMUDGEDLY > SMUDGE
SMUDGER > SMUDGE
SMUDGERS > SMUDGE
SMUDGES > SMUDGE
SMUDGIER > SMUDGY
SMUDGIEST > SMUDGY
SMUDGILY > SMUDGE
SMUDGING > SMUDGE
SMUDGINGS > SMUDGE
SMUDGY *adj* smeared, blurred, or soiled, or likely to become so
SMUG *adj* self-satisfied ▷ *vb* make neat
SMUGGED > SMUG
SMUGGER > SMUG
SMUGGERY *n* condition or an instance of being smug
SMUGGEST > SMUG
SMUGGING > SMUG
SMUGGLE *vb* import or export (goods) secretly and illegally
SMUGGLED > SMUGGLE
SMUGGLER > SMUGGLE
SMUGGLERS > SMUGGLE
SMUGGLES > SMUGGLE
SMUGGLING > SMUGGLE
SMUGLY > SMUG
SMUGNESS > SMUG
SMUGS > SMUG
SMUR *same as* > SMIR
SMURFING *n* intentionally overwhelming a computer network with messages
SMURFINGS > SMURFING
SMURRED > SMUR
SMURRIER > SMUR
SMURRIEST > SMUR
SMURRING > SMUR
SMURRY > SMUR
SMURS > SMUR
SMUSH *vb* crush
SMUSHED > SMUSH
SMUSHES > SMUSH
SMUSHING > SMUSH
SMUT *n* small dark smudge or stain ▷ *vb* mark or become marked or smudged
SMUTCH *vb* smudge ▷ *n* mark

SMUTCHED > SMUTCH
SMUTCHES > SMUTCH
SMUTCHIER > SMUTCH
SMUTCHING > SMUTCH
SMUTCHY > SMUTCH
SMUTS > SMUT
SMUTTED > SMUT
SMUTTIER > SMUT
SMUTTIEST > SMUT
SMUTTILY > SMUT
SMUTTING > SMUT
SMUTTY > SMUT
SMYTRIE *n* Scots word meaning collection
SMYTRIES > SMYTRIE
SNAB *same as* > SNOB
SNABBLE *same as* > SNAFFLE
SNABBLED > SNABBLE
SNABBLES > SNABBLE
SNABBLING > SNABBLE
SNABS > SNAB
SNACK *n* light quick meal ▷ *vb* eat a snack
SNACKED > SNACK
SNACKER > SNACK
SNACKERS > SNACK
SNACKETTE *n* snack bar
SNACKIER > SNACKY
SNACKIEST > SNACKY
SNACKING > SNACK
SNACKS > SNACK
SNACKY *adj* of the nature of a snack
SNAFFLE *n* jointed bit for a horse ▷ *vb* steal
SNAFFLED > SNAFFLE
SNAFFLES > SNAFFLE
SNAFFLING > SNAFFLE
SNAFU *n* confusion or chaos regarded as the normal state ▷ *adj* confused or muddled up, as usual ▷ *vb* throw into chaos
SNAFUED > SNAFU
SNAFUING > SNAFU
SNAFUS > SNAFU
SNAG *n* difficulty or disadvantage ▷ *vb* catch or tear on a point
SNAGGED > SNAG
SNAGGER *n* type of fishing hook
SNAGGERS > SNAGGER
SNAGGIER > SNAGGY
SNAGGIEST > SNAGGY
SNAGGING > SNAG
SNAGGLE *n* tangled mass
SNAGGLES > SNAGGLE
SNAGGY *adj* having sharp protuberances
SNAGLIKE > SNAG
SNAGS > SNAG
SNAIL *n* slow-moving mollusc with a spiral shell ▷ *vb* move slowly
SNAILED > SNAIL
SNAILERY *n* place where snails are bred
SNAILFISH *n* sea snail
SNAILIER > SNAIL
SNAILIEST > SNAIL
SNAILING > SNAIL
SNAILLIKE *adj* resembling a snail
SNAILS > SNAIL

SNAILY > SNAIL
SNAKE n long thin scaly limbless reptile ▷ vb move in a winding course like a snake
SNAKEBIRD n darter bird
SNAKEBIT adj bitten by snake
SNAKEBITE n bite of a snake
SNAKED > SNAKE
SNAKEFISH n fish resembling snake
SNAKEHEAD n Chinese criminal involved in the illegal transport of Chinese citizens to other parts of the world
SNAKELIKE > SNAKE
SNAKEPIT n pit filled with snakes
SNAKEPITS > SNAKEPIT
SNAKEROOT n any of various North American plants
SNAKES > SNAKE
SNAKESKIN n skin of a snake, esp when made into a leather valued for handbags, shoes, etc
SNAKEWEED same as > SNAKEROOT
SNAKEWISE adv in snakelike way
SNAKEWOOD n South American tree
SNAKEY same as > SNAKY
SNAKIER > SNAKY
SNAKIEST > SNAKY
SNAKILY > SNAKY
SNAKINESS > SNAKY
SNAKING > SNAKE
SNAKISH > SNAKE
SNAKY adj twisted or winding
SNAP vb break suddenly ▷ n act or sound of snapping ▷ adj made on the spur of the moment ▷ adv with a snap
SNAPBACK n sudden rebound or change in direction
SNAPBACKS > SNAPBACK
SNAPHANCE n flintlock gun
SNAPLESS > SNAP
SNAPLINK n metal link used in mountaineering
SNAPLINKS > SNAPLINK
SNAPPABLE > SNAP
SNAPPED > SNAP
SNAPPER n food fish of Australia and New Zealand ▷ vb stumble
SNAPPERED > SNAPPER
SNAPPERS > SNAPPER
SNAPPIER > SNAPPY
SNAPPIEST > SNAPPY
SNAPPILY > SNAPPY
SNAPPING > SNAP
SNAPPINGS > SNAP
SNAPPISH same as > SNAPPY
SNAPPY adj irritable
SNAPS > SNAP
SNAPSHOT n informal photograph
SNAPSHOTS > SNAPSHOT
SNAPTIN n container for food

SNAPTINS > SNAPTIN
SNAPWEED n impatiens
SNAPWEEDS > SNAPWEED
SNAR same as > SNARL
SNARE n trap with a noose ▷ vb catch in or as if in a snare
SNARED > SNARE
SNARELESS > SNARE
SNARER > SNARE
SNARERS > SNARE
SNARES > SNARE
SNARF vb eat or drink greedily
SNARFED > SNARF
SNARFING > SNARF
SNARFLE vb (of an animal) grunt and snort while rooting for food
SNARFLED > SNARFLE
SNARFLES > SNARFLE
SNARFLING > SNARFLE
SNARFS > SNARF
SNARIER > SNARE
SNARIEST > SNARE
SNARING > SNARE
SNARINGS > SNARE
SNARK n imaginary creature in Lewis Carroll's poetry
SNARKIER > SNARKY
SNARKIEST > SNARKY
SNARKILY > SNARKY
SNARKS > SNARK
SNARKY adj unpleasant and scornful
SNARL vb (of an animal) growl with bared teeth ▷ n act or sound of snarling
SNARLED > SNARL
SNARLER > SNARL
SNARLERS > SNARL
SNARLIER > SNARL
SNARLIEST > SNARL
SNARLING > SNARL
SNARLINGS > SNARL
SNARLS > SNARL
SNARLY > SNARL
SNARRED > SNAR
SNARRING > SNAR
SNARS > SNAR
SNARY > SNAR
SNASH vb Scots word meaning speak cheekily
SNASHED > SNASH
SNASHES > SNASH
SNASHING > SNASH
SNASTE n candle wick
SNASTES > SNASTE
SNATCH vb seize or try to seize suddenly ▷ n snatching
SNATCHED > SNATCH
SNATCHER > SNATCH
SNATCHERS > SNATCH
SNATCHES > SNATCH
SNATCHIER > SNATCHY
SNATCHILY > SNATCHY
SNATCHING > SNATCH
SNATCHY adj disconnected or spasmodic
SNATH n handle of a scythe
SNATHE same as > SNATH
SNATHES > SNATHE
SNATHS > SNATH
SNAW Scots variant of > SNOW
SNAWED > SNAW
SNAWING > SNAW
SNAWS > SNAW

SNAZZIER > SNAZZY
SNAZZIEST > SNAZZY
SNAZZILY > SNAZZY
SNAZZY adj stylish and flashy
SNEAD n scythe handle
SNEADS > SNEAD
SNEAK vb move furtively ▷ n cowardly or underhand person ▷ adj without warning
SNEAKBOX n small camouflaged boat, used for wildfowl hunting
SNEAKED > SNEAK
SNEAKER n canvas shoe with rubber sole
SNEAKERED adj wearing sneakers
SNEAKERS > SNEAKER
SNEAKEUP n sneaky person
SNEAKEUPS > SNEAKEUP
SNEAKIER > SNEAK
SNEAKIEST > SNEAK
SNEAKILY > SNEAK
SNEAKING adj slight but persistent
SNEAKISH adj typical of a sneak
SNEAKS > SNEAK
SNEAKSBY n sneak
SNEAKY > SNEAK
SNEAP vb nip
SNEAPED > SNEAP
SNEAPING > SNEAP
SNEAPS > SNEAP
SNEATH same as > SNATH
SNEATHS > SNEATH
SNEB same as > SNIB
SNEBBE same as > SNUB
SNEBBED > SNEB
SNEBBES > SNEBBE
SNEBBING > SNEB
SNEBS > SNEB
SNECK n small squared stone used in a rubble wall to fill spaces between stones ▷ vb fasten (a latch)
SNECKED > SNECK
SNECKING > SNECK
SNECKS > SNECK
SNED vb prune or trim
SNEDDED > SNED
SNEDDING > SNED
SNEDS > SNED
SNEE vb cut
SNEED > SNEE
SNEEING > SNEE
SNEER n contemptuous expression or remark ▷ vb show contempt by a sneer
SNEERED > SNEER
SNEERER > SNEER
SNEERERS > SNEER
SNEERFUL > SNEER
SNEERIER > SNEERY
SNEERIEST > SNEERY
SNEERING > SNEER
SNEERINGS > SNEER
SNEERS > SNEER
SNEERY adj contemptuous or scornful
SNEES > SNEE
SNEESH n Scots word meaning pinch of snuff ▷ vb take snuff

SNEESHAN n Scots word meaning pinch of snuff
SNEESHANS > SNEESHAN
SNEESHED > SNEESH
SNEESHES > SNEESH
SNEESHIN same as > SNEESHAN
SNEESHING same as > SNEESHAN
SNEESHINS > SNEESHIN
SNEEZE vb expel air from the nose suddenly, involuntarily, and noisily ▷ n act or sound of sneezing
SNEEZED > SNEEZE
SNEEZER > SNEEZE
SNEEZERS > SNEEZE
SNEEZES > SNEEZE
SNEEZIER > SNEEZE
SNEEZIEST > SNEEZE
SNEEZING > SNEEZE
SNEEZINGS > SNEEZE
SNEEZY > SNEEZE
SNELL adj biting ▷ vb attach hook to fishing line
SNELLED > SNELL
SNELLER > SNELL
SNELLEST > SNELL
SNELLING > SNELL
SNELLS > SNELL
SNELLY > SNELL
SNIB n catch of a door or window ▷ vb bolt or fasten (a door)
SNIBBED > SNIB
SNIBBING > SNIB
SNIBS > SNIB
SNICK n small cut or notch ▷ vb make a small cut or notch in (something)
SNICKED > SNICK
SNICKER same as > SNIGGER
SNICKERED > SNICKER
SNICKERER > SNICKER
SNICKERS > SNICKER
SNICKERY adj tending to snicker
SNICKET n passageway between walls or fences
SNICKETS > SNICKET
SNICKING > SNICK
SNICKS > SNICK
SNIDE adj critical in an unfair and nasty way ▷ n sham jewellery ▷ vb fill or load
SNIDED > SNIDE
SNIDELY > SNIDE
SNIDENESS > SNIDE
SNIDER > SNIDE
SNIDES > SNIDE
SNIDEST > SNIDE
SNIDEY same as > SNIDE
SNIDIER > SNIDEY
SNIDIEST > SNIDEY
SNIDING > SNIDE
SNIES > SNY
SNIFF vb inhale through the nose in short audible breaths ▷ n act or sound of sniffing
SNIFFABLE > SNIFF
SNIFFED > SNIFF
SNIFFER n device for detecting hidden substances such as drugs
SNIFFERS > SNIFFER
SNIFFIER > SNIFFY

SNIFFIEST > SNIFFY
SNIFFILY > SNIFFY
SNIFFING > SNIFF
SNIFFINGS > SNIFF
SNIFFISH *adj* disdainful
SNIFFLE *vb* sniff repeatedly, as when suffering from a cold ▷ *n* slight cold
SNIFFLED > SNIFFLE
SNIFFLER > SNIFFLE
SNIFFLERS > SNIFFLE
SNIFFLES > SNIFFLE
SNIFFLIER > SNIFFLE
SNIFFLING > SNIFFLE
SNIFFLY > SNIFFLE
SNIFFS > SNIFF
SNIFFY *adj* contemptuous or scornful
SNIFT *same as* **>** SNIFF
SNIFTED > SNIFT
SNIFTER *n* small quantity of alcoholic drink ▷ *vb* sniff
SNIFTERED > SNIFTER
SNIFTERS > SNIFTER
SNIFTIER > SNIFTY
SNIFTIEST > SNIFTY
SNIFTING > SNIFT
SNIFTS > SNIFT
SNIFTY *adj* slang word meaning excellent
SNIG *vb* drag (a felled log) by a chain or cable
SNIGGED > SNIG
SNIGGER *n* sly laugh ▷ *vb* laugh slyly
SNIGGERED > SNIGGER
SNIGGERER > SNIGGER
SNIGGERS > SNIGGER
SNIGGING > SNIG
SNIGGLE *vb* fish for eels by dangling or thrusting a baited hook into cavities ▷ *n* baited hook used for sniggling eels
SNIGGLED > SNIGGLE
SNIGGLER > SNIGGLE
SNIGGLERS > SNIGGLE
SNIGGLES > SNIGGLE
SNIGGLING > SNIGGLE
SNIGLET *n* invented word
SNIGLETS > SNIGLET
SNIGS > SNIG
SNIP *vb* cut in small quick strokes with scissors or shears ▷ *n* bargain ▷ *interj* representation of the sound of scissors or shears closing
SNIPE *n* wading bird with a long straight bill ▷ *vb* shoot at (a person) from cover
SNIPED > SNIPE
SNIPEFISH *n* type of fish of tropical and temperate seas, with a long snout and a single dorsal fin
SNIPELIKE > SNIPE
SNIPER *n* person who shoots at someone from cover
SNIPERS > SNIPER
SNIPES > SNIPE
SNIPIER > SNIPY
SNIPIEST > SNIPY
SNIPING > SNIPE
SNIPINGS > SNIPE
SNIPPED > SNIP
SNIPPER > SNIP

SNIPPERS > SNIP
SNIPPET *n* small piece
SNIPPETS > SNIPPET
SNIPPETY > SNIPPET
SNIPPIER > SNIPPY
SNIPPIEST > SNIPPY
SNIPPILY > SNIPPY
SNIPPING > SNIP
SNIPPINGS > SNIP
SNIPPY *adj* scrappy
SNIPS > SNIP
SNIPY *adj* like a snipe
SNIRT *n* Scots word meaning suppressed laugh ▷ *vb* to snigger
SNIRTED > SNIRT
SNIRTING > SNIRT
SNIRTLE *vb* Scots word meaning snicker
SNIRTLED > SNIRTLE
SNIRTLES > SNIRTLE
SNIRTLING > SNIRTLE
SNIRTS > SNIRT
SNIT *n* fit of temper
SNITCH *vb* act as an informer ▷ *n* informer
SNITCHED > SNITCH
SNITCHER > SNITCH
SNITCHERS > SNITCH
SNITCHES > SNITCH
SNITCHIER > SNITCHY
SNITCHING > SNITCH
SNITCHY *adj* bad-tempered or irritable
SNITS > SNIT
SNITTIER > SNITTY
SNITTIEST > SNITTY
SNITTY *adj* cross or irritable
SNIVEL *vb* cry in a whining way ▷ *n* act of snivelling
SNIVELED > SNIVEL
SNIVELER > SNIVEL
SNIVELERS > SNIVEL
SNIVELIER > SNIVELY
SNIVELING *n* act or instance of crying in a whining way
SNIVELLED > SNIVEL
SNIVELLER > SNIVEL
SNIVELLY *adj* tending to snivel
SNIVELS > SNIVEL
SNIVELY *adj* tending to snivel
SNOB *n* person who judges others by social rank
SNOBBERY > SNOB
SNOBBIER > SNOB
SNOBBIEST > SNOB
SNOBBILY > SNOB
SNOBBISH > SNOB
SNOBBISM > SNOB
SNOBBISMS > SNOB
SNOBBY > SNOB
SNOBLING *n* little snob
SNOBLINGS > SNOBLING
SNOBS > SNOB
SNOCOACH *n* bus-like vehicle for travelling on snow
SNOD *adj* Scots word meaning tidy ▷ *vb* make tidy
SNODDED > SNOD
SNODDER > SNOD
SNODDEST > SNOD
SNODDING > SNOD
SNODDIT > SNOD

SNODS > SNOD
SNOEK *n* edible marine fish
SNOEKS > SNOEK
SNOEP *adj* mean or tight-fisted
SNOG *vb* kiss and cuddle ▷ *n* act of kissing and cuddling
SNOGGED > SNOG
SNOGGER *n* person who snogs
SNOGGERS > SNOGGER
SNOGGING > SNOG
SNOGS > SNOG
SNOKE *same as* **>** SNOOK
SNOKED > SNOKE
SNOKES > SNOKE
SNOKING > SNOKE
SNOOD *n* pouch loosely holding a woman's hair at the back ▷ *vb* hold (the hair) in a snood
SNOODED > SNOOD
SNOODING > SNOOD
SNOODS > SNOOD
SNOOK *n* any of several large game fishes ▷ *vb* lurk
SNOOKED > SNOOK
SNOOKER *n* game played on a billiard table ▷ *vb* leave (a snooker opponent) unable to hit the target ball
SNOOKERED > SNOOKER
SNOOKERS > SNOOKER
SNOOKING > SNOOK
SNOOKS > SNOOK
SNOOL *vb* Scots word meaning dominate
SNOOLED > SNOOL
SNOOLING > SNOOL
SNOOLS > SNOOL
SNOOP *vb* pry ▷ *n* snooping
SNOOPED > SNOOP
SNOOPER *n* person who snoops
SNOOPERS > SNOOPER
SNOOPIER > SNOOP
SNOOPIEST > SNOOP
SNOOPILY > SNOOP
SNOOPING > SNOOP
SNOOPS > SNOOP
SNOOPY > SNOOP
SNOOSE *n* snuff
SNOOSES > SNOOSE
SNOOT *n* nose ▷ *vb* look contemptuously at
SNOOTED > SNOOT
SNOOTFUL *n* enough alcohol to make someone drunk
SNOOTFULS > SNOOTFUL
SNOOTIER > SNOOTY
SNOOTIEST > SNOOTY
SNOOTILY > SNOOTY
SNOOTING > SNOOT
SNOOTS > SNOOT
SNOOTY *adj* haughty
SNOOZE *vb* take a brief light sleep ▷ *n* brief light sleep
SNOOZED > SNOOZE
SNOOZER > SNOOZE
SNOOZERS > SNOOZE
SNOOZES > SNOOZE
SNOOZIER > SNOOZE
SNOOZIEST > SNOOZE
SNOOZING > SNOOZE

SNOOZLE *vb* cuddle and sleep
SNOOZLED > SNOOZLE
SNOOZLES > SNOOZLE
SNOOZLING > SNOOZLE
SNOOZY > SNOOZE
SNORE *vb* make snoring sounds while sleeping ▷ *n* sound of snoring
SNORED > SNORE
SNORER > SNORE
SNORERS > SNORE
SNORES > SNORE
SNORING > SNORE
SNORINGS > SNORE
SNORKEL *n* tube allowing a swimmer to breathe ▷ *vb* swim using a snorkel
SNORKELED > SNORKEL
SNORKELER > SNORKEL
SNORKELS > SNORKEL
SNORT *vb* exhale noisily through the nostrils ▷ *n* act or sound of snorting
SNORTED > SNORT
SNORTER *n* person or animal that snorts
SNORTERS > SNORTER
SNORTIER > SNORT
SNORTIEST > SNORT
SNORTING > SNORT
SNORTINGS > SNORT
SNORTS > SNORT
SNORTY > SNORT
SNOT *n* mucus from the nose ▷ *vb* blow one's nose
SNOTRAG *n* handkerchief
SNOTRAGS > SNOTRAG
SNOTS > SNOT
SNOTTED > SNOT
SNOTTER *vb* breathe through obstructed nostrils
SNOTTERED > SNOTTER
SNOTTERS > SNOTTER
SNOTTERY *n* snot
SNOTTIE *n* midshipman
SNOTTIER > SNOTTY
SNOTTIES > SNOTTY
SNOTTIEST > SNOTTY
SNOTTILY > SNOTTY
SNOTTING > SNOT
SNOTTY *adj* covered with mucus from the nose
SNOUT *n* animal's projecting nose and jaws ▷ *vb* have or give a snout
SNOUTED > SNOUT
SNOUTIER > SNOUT
SNOUTIEST > SNOUT
SNOUTING > SNOUT
SNOUTISH > SNOUT
SNOUTLESS > SNOUT
SNOUTLIKE > SNOUT
SNOUTS > SNOUT
SNOUTY > SNOUT
SNOW *n* frozen vapour falling from the sky in flakes ▷ *vb* fall as or like snow
SNOWBALL *n* snow pressed into a ball for throwing ▷ *vb* increase rapidly
SNOWBALLS > SNOWBALL
SNOWBANK *n* bank of snow
SNOWBANKS > SNOWBANK
SNOWBELL *n* Asian shrub
SNOWBELLS > SNOWBELL

SNOWBELT n northern states of USA
SNOWBELTS > SNOWBELT
SNOWBERRY n shrub grown for its white berries
SNOWBIRD n bird of Arctic regions
SNOWBIRDS > SNOWBIRD
SNOWBLINK n whitish glare in the sky reflected from snow
SNOWBOARD n board on which a person stands to slide across the snow
SNOWBOOT n boot for walking in snow
SNOWBOOTS > SNOWBOOT
SNOWBOUND adj shut in by snow
SNOWBRUSH n brush for clearing snow
SNOWBUSH n North American plant
SNOWCAP n cap of snow on top of a mountain
SNOWCAPS > SNOWCAP
SNOWCAT n tracked vehicle for travelling over snow
SNOWCATS > SNOWCAT
SNOWCLONE n reusable verbal formula
SNOWCOACH n bus equipped to travel on snow
SNOWDOME n leisure centre with facilities for skiing, skating, etc
SNOWDOMES > SNOWDOME
SNOWDRIFT n bank of deep snow
SNOWDROP n small white bell-shaped spring flower
SNOWDROPS > SNOWDROP
SNOWED > SNOW
SNOWFALL n fall of snow
SNOWFALLS > SNOWFALL
SNOWFIELD n large area of permanent snow
SNOWFLAKE n single crystal of snow
SNOWFLEA n wingless insect that lives on or in snow
SNOWFLEAS > SNOWFLEA
SNOWFLECK n snow bunting
SNOWFLICK same as > SNOWFLECK
SNOWGLOBE n transparent sphere filled with water and white particles which resemble snow falling when shaken
SNOWIER > SNOWY
SNOWIEST > SNOWY
SNOWILY > SNOWY
SNOWINESS > SNOWY
SNOWING > SNOW
SNOWISH adj like snow
SNOWK same as > SNOOK
SNOWKED > SNOWK
SNOWKING > SNOWK
SNOWKS > SNOWK
SNOWLAND n area where snow lies
SNOWLANDS > SNOWLAND
SNOWLESS > SNOW
SNOWLIKE > SNOW
SNOWLINE n limit of permanent snow

SNOWLINES > SNOWLINE
SNOWMAKER n machine making artificial snow
SNOWMAN n figure shaped out of snow
SNOWMELT n melting of snow in spring
SNOWMELTS > SNOWMELT
SNOWMEN > SNOWMAN
SNOWMOLD same as > SNOWMOULD
SNOWMOLDS > SNOWMOLD
SNOWMOULD n fungus growing on grass under snow
SNOWPACK n body of hard-packed snow
SNOWPACKS > SNOWPACK
SNOWPLOW n implement or vehicle for clearing snow away
SNOWPLOWS > SNOWPLOW
SNOWS > SNOW
SNOWSCAPE n snow-covered landscape
SNOWSHED n shelter built over an exposed section of railway track
SNOWSHEDS > SNOWSHED
SNOWSHOE n racket-shaped frame with a network of thongs stretched across it for walking on snow ▷ vb walk using snowshoes
SNOWSHOED > SNOWSHOE
SNOWSHOER > SNOWSHOE
SNOWSHOES > SNOWSHOE
SNOWSLIDE n snow avalanche
SNOWSLIP n small snow avalanche
SNOWSLIPS > SNOWSLIP
SNOWSNAKE n Native American game in which a wooden rod is slid over snow
SNOWSTORM n storm with heavy snow
SNOWSUIT n one-piece winter outer garment for child
SNOWSUITS > SNOWSUIT
SNOWY adj covered with or abounding in snow
SNUB vb insult deliberately ▷ n deliberate insult ▷ adj (of a nose) short and blunt
SNUBBE n stub
SNUBBED > SNUB
SNUBBER > SNUB
SNUBBERS > SNUB
SNUBBES > SNUBBE
SNUBBEST > SNUB
SNUBBIER > SNUB
SNUBBIEST > SNUB
SNUBBING > SNUB
SNUBBINGS > SNUB
SNUBBISH > SNUB
SNUBBY > SNUB
SNUBFIN adj as in snubfin dolphin Australian dolphin with a small dorsal fin
SNUBNESS > SNUB
SNUBS > SNUB
SNUCK past tense and past participle of > SNEAK
SNUDGE vb be miserly
SNUDGED > SNUDGE

SNUDGES > SNUDGE
SNUDGING > SNUDGE
SNUFF n powdered tobacco for sniffing up the nostrils ▷ vb extinguish (a candle)
SNUFFBOX n small container for holding snuff
SNUFFED > SNUFF
SNUFFER > SNUFF
SNUFFERS > SNUFF
SNUFFIER > SNUFFY
SNUFFIEST > SNUFFY
SNUFFILY > SNUFFY
SNUFFING > SNUFF
SNUFFINGS > SNUFF
SNUFFLE vb breathe noisily or with difficulty ▷ n act or the sound of snuffling
SNUFFLED > SNUFFLE
SNUFFLER > SNUFFLE
SNUFFLERS > SNUFFLE
SNUFFLES same as > SNIFFLES
SNUFFLIER > SNUFFLE
SNUFFLING > SNUFFLE
SNUFFLY > SNUFFLE
SNUFFS > SNUFF
SNUFFY adj of, relating to, or resembling snuff
SNUG adj warm and comfortable ▷ n small peg that stops a bolt from turning ▷ vb make or become comfortable and warm
SNUGGED > SNUG
SNUGGER > SNUG
SNUGGERIE n small bar in pub
SNUGGERY n cosy and comfortable place or room
SNUGGEST > SNUG
SNUGGIES pl n specially warm underwear
SNUGGING > SNUG
SNUGGLE vb nestle into a person or thing for warmth or from affection ▷ n act of snuggling
SNUGGLED > SNUGGLE
SNUGGLES > SNUGGLE
SNUGGLIER > SNUGGLY
SNUGGLING > SNUGGLE
SNUGGLY adj comfortably warm and suitable for snuggling
SNUGLY > SNUG
SNUGNESS > SNUG
SNUGS > SNUG
SNUSH vb take snuff
SNUSHED > SNUSH
SNUSHES > SNUSH
SNUSHING > SNUSH
SNUZZLE vb root in ground
SNUZZLED > SNUZZLE
SNUZZLES > SNUZZLE
SNUZZLING > SNUZZLE
SNY same as > SNYE
SNYE n side channel of a river
SNYES > SNYE
SO adv such an extent ▷ interj exclamation of surprise, triumph, or realization ▷ n the fifth note of the musical scale
SOAK vb make wet ▷ n soaking

SOAKAGE n process or a period in which a permeable substance is soaked in a liquid
SOAKAGES > SOAKAGE
SOAKAWAY n pit filled with rubble, etc, into which rain or waste water drains
SOAKAWAYS > SOAKAWAY
SOAKED > SOAK
SOAKEN > SOAK
SOAKER > SOAK
SOAKERS > SOAK
SOAKING > SOAK
SOAKINGLY > SOAK
SOAKINGS > SOAK
SOAKS > SOAK
SOAP n compound of alkali and fat, used with water as a cleaning agent ▷ vb apply soap to
SOAPBARK n W South American rosaceous tree
SOAPBARKS > SOAPBARK
SOAPBERRY n any of various chiefly tropical American sapindaceous trees
SOAPBOX n crate used as a platform for speech-making ▷ vb deliver a speech from a soapbox
SOAPBOXED > SOAPBOX
SOAPBOXES > SOAPBOX
SOAPDISH n dish for holding soap
SOAPED > SOAP
SOAPER n soap opera
SOAPERS > SOAPER
SOAPFISH n tropical fish with toxic mucus
SOAPIE n soap opera
SOAPIER > SOAPY
SOAPIES > SOAPIE
SOAPIEST > SOAPY
SOAPILY > SOAPY
SOAPINESS > SOAPY
SOAPING > SOAP
SOAPLAND n Japanese massage parlour and brothel
SOAPLANDS > SOAPLAND
SOAPLESS > SOAP
SOAPLIKE > SOAP
SOAPROOT n plant with roots used as soap substitute
SOAPROOTS > SOAPROOT
SOAPS > SOAP
SOAPSTONE n soft mineral used for making table tops and ornaments
SOAPSUDS pl n foam or lather produced when soap is mixed with water
SOAPSUDSY adj like soapsuds
SOAPWORT n Eurasian plant with clusters of fragrant pink or white flowers
SOAPWORTS > SOAPWORT
SOAPY adj covered with soap
SOAR vb rise or fly upwards ▷ n act of soaring
SOARAWAY adj exceedingly successful
SOARE n young hawk
SOARED > SOAR
SOARER > SOAR
SOARERS > SOAR

SOARES > SOARE

SOARING > SOAR

SOARINGLY > SOAR

SOARINGS > SOAR

SOARS > SOAR

SOAVE n dry white Italian wine

SOAVES > SOAVE

SOB vb weep with convulsive gasps ▷ n act or sound of sobbing

SOBA n (in Japanese cookery) noodles made from buckwheat flour

SOBAS > SOBA

SOBBED > SOB

SOBBER > SOB

SOBBERS > SOB

SOBBING > SOB

SOBBINGLY > SOB

SOBBINGS > SOB

SOBEIT conj provided that

SOBER adj not drunk ▷ vb make or become sober

SOBERED > SOBER

SOBERER > SOBER

SOBEREST > SOBER

SOBERING > SOBER

SOBERISE same as > SOBERIZE

SOBERISED > SOBERISE

SOBERISES > SOBERISE

SOBERIZE vb make sober

SOBERIZED > SOBERIZE

SOBERIZES > SOBERIZE

SOBERLY > SOBER

SOBERNESS > SOBER

SOBERS > SOBER

SOBFUL adj tearful

SOBOLE n creeping underground stem that produces roots and buds

SOBOLES > SOBOLE

SOBRIETY n state of being sober

SOBRIQUET n nickname

SOBS > SOB

SOC n feudal right to hold court

SOCA n mixture of soul and calypso music

SOCAGE n tenure of land by certain services

SOCAGER > SOCAGE

SOCAGERS > SOCAGE

SOCAGES > SOCAGE

SOCAS > SOCA

SOCCAGE same as > SOCAGE

SOCCAGES > SOCCAGE

SOCCER n football played by two teams of eleven kicking a spherical ball

SOCCERS > SOCCER

SOCES > SOC

SOCIABLE adj friendly or companionable ▷ n type of open carriage with two seats facing each other

SOCIABLES > SOCIABLE

SOCIABLY > SOCIABLE

SOCIAL adj living in a community ▷ n informal gathering

SOCIALISE same as > SOCIALIZE

SOCIALISM n political system which advocates

public ownership of industries, resources, and transport

SOCIALIST n supporter or advocate of socialism ▷ adj of or relating to socialism

SOCIALITE n member of fashionable society

SOCIALITY n tendency of groups and persons to develop social links and live in communities

SOCIALIZE vb meet others socially

SOCIALLY > SOCIAL

SOCIALS > SOCIAL

SOCIATE n associate

SOCIATES > SOCIATE

SOCIATION n plant community

SOCIATIVE adj of association

SOCIETAL adj of or relating to society, esp human society or social relations

SOCIETIES > SOCIETY

SOCIETY n human beings considered as a group

SOCIOGRAM n chart showing social relationships

SOCIOLECT n language spoken by particular social class

SOCIOLOGY n study of human societies

SOCIOPATH n person with a personality disorder characterized by a tendency to commit antisocial acts without any feelings of guilt

SOCK n knitted covering for the foot ▷ vb hit hard

SOCKED > SOCK

SOCKET n hole or recess into which something fits ▷ vb furnish with or place into a socket

SOCKETED > SOCKET

SOCKETING > SOCKET

SOCKETS > SOCKET

SOCKETTE n sock not covering ankle

SOCKETTES > SOCKETTE

SOCKEYE n Pacific salmon with red flesh

SOCKEYES > SOCKEYE

SOCKING > SOCK

SOCKLESS > SOCK

SOCKMAN same as > SOCMAN

SOCKMEN > SOCKMAN

SOCKO adj excellent

SOCKS > SOCK

SOCLE another name for > PLINTH

SOCLES > SOCLE

SOCMAN n tenant holding land by socage

SOCMEN > SOCMAN

SOCS > SOC

SOD n (piece of) turf ▷ vb cover with sods

SODA n compound of sodium

SODAIC adj containing soda

SODAIN same as > SUDDEN

SODAINE same as > SUDDEN

SODALESS > SODA

SODALIST n member of sodality

SODALISTS > SODALIST

SODALITE n blue, grey, yellow, or colourless mineral

SODALITES > SODALITE

SODALITY n religious or charitable society

SODAMIDE n white crystalline compound used as a dehydrating agent

SODAMIDES > SODAMIDE

SODAS > SODA

SODBUSTER n farmer who grows crops

SODDED > SOD

SODDEN adj soaked ▷ vb make or become sodden

SODDENED > SODDEN

SODDENING > SODDEN

SODDENLY > SODDEN

SODDENS > SODDEN

SODDIE n house made of sod

SODDIER > SODDY

SODDIES > SODDIE

SODDIEST > SODDY

SODDING > SOD

SODDY adj covered with turf

SODGER dialect variant of > SOLDIER

SODGERED > SODGER

SODGERING > SODGER

SODGERS > SODGER

SODIC adj containing sodium

SODICITY > SODIC

SODIUM n silvery-white metallic element

SODIUMS > SODIUM

SODOM n person who performs sodomy

SODOMIES > SODOMY

SODOMISE same as > SODOMIZE

SODOMISED > SODOMISE

SODOMISES > SODOMISE

SODOMIST > SODOMY

SODOMISTS > SODOMY

SODOMITE n person who practises sodomy

SODOMITES > SODOMITE

SODOMITIC > SODOMY

SODOMIZE vb be the active partner in anal intercourse

SODOMIZED > SODOMIZE

SODOMIZES > SODOMIZE

SODOMS > SODOM

SODOMY n anal intercourse

SODS > SOD

SOEVER adv in any way at all

SOFA n couch

SOFABED n sofa that converts into a bed

SOFABEDS > SOFABED

SOFAR n system for determining a position at sea

SOFARS > SOFAR

SOFAS > SOFA

SOFFIONI n holes in volcano that emit steam

SOFFIT n underside of a part of a building or a structural component

SOFFITS > SOFFIT

SOFT adj easy to shape or cut ▷ adv softly ▷ vb soften

SOFTA n Muslim student of divinity and jurisprudence

SOFTAS > SOFTA

SOFTBACK n paperback

SOFTBACKS > SOFTBACK

SOFTBALL n game similar to baseball, played using a larger softer ball

SOFTBALLS > SOFTBALL

SOFTBOUND adj having paperback binding

SOFTCORE adj describing pornography that is not explicit

SOFTCOVER n book with paper covers

SOFTED > SOFT

SOFTEN vb make or become soft or softer

SOFTENED > SOFTEN

SOFTENER n substance added to another substance to increase its softness

SOFTENERS > SOFTENER

SOFTENING > SOFTEN

SOFTENS > SOFTEN

SOFTER > SOFT

SOFTEST > SOFT

SOFTGOODS n clothing and soft furniture

SOFTHEAD n insulting word for a stupid person

SOFTHEADS > SOFTHEAD

SOFTIE n person who is easily upset

SOFTIES > SOFTY

SOFTING > SOFT

SOFTISH > SOFT

SOFTLING n weakling

SOFTLINGS > SOFTLING

SOFTLY > SOFT

SOFTNESS n quality or an instance of being soft

SOFTPASTE adj as in softpaste porcelain a type of porcelain

SOFTS > SOFT

SOFTSCAPE n vegetation featuring in a landscape

SOFTSHELL n crab or turtle with a soft shell

SOFTWARE n computer programs

SOFTWARES > SOFTWARE

SOFTWOOD n wood of a coniferous tree

SOFTWOODS > SOFTWOOD

SOFTY same as > SOFTIE

SOG vb soak

SOGER same as > SODGER

SOGERS > SOGER

SOGGED > SOG

SOGGIER > SOGGY

SOGGIEST > SOGGY

SOGGILY > SOGGY

SOGGINESS > SOGGY

SOGGING > SOG

SOGGINGS > SOG

SOGGY adj soaked

SOGS > SOG

SOH n (in tonic sol-fa) fifth degree of any major scale

SOHO interj exclamation announcing the sighting of a hare

SOHS > SOH

SOHUR same as > SUHUR

SOHURS > SOHUR

SOIGNE adj well-groomed, elegant

SOIGNEE variant of > SOIGNE

SOIL n top layer of earth ▷ vb make or become dirty

SOILAGE n green fodder

SOILAGES > SOILAGE

SOILBORNE adj carried in soil

SOILED > SOIL

SOILIER > SOIL

SOILIEST > SOIL

SOILINESS > SOIL

SOILING > SOIL

SOILINGS > SOIL

SOILLESS > SOIL

SOILS > SOIL

SOILURE n act of soiling or the state of being soiled

SOILURES > SOILURE

SOILY > SOIL

SOIREE n evening party or gathering

SOIREES > SOIREE

SOJA same as > SOYA

SOJAS > SOJA

SOJOURN n temporary stay ▷ vb stay temporarily

SOJOURNED > SOJOURN

SOJOURNER > SOJOURN

SOJOURNS > SOJOURN

SOJU n type of Korean vodka

SOJUS > SOJU

SOKAH same as > SOCA

SOKAHS > SOKAH

SOKAIYA n Japanese extortionist

SOKE n right to hold a local court

SOKEMAN same as > SOCMAN

SOKEMANRY n feudal tenure by socage

SOKEMEN > SOKEMAN

SOKEN n feudal district

SOKENS > SOKEN

SOKES > SOKE

SOKOL n Czech gymnastic association

SOKOLS > SOKOL

SOL n liquid colloidal solution

SOLA n Indian plant

SOLACE vb comfort in distress ▷ n comfort in misery or disappointment

SOLACED > SOLACE

SOLACER > SOLACE

SOLACERS > SOLACE

SOLACES > SOLACE

SOLACING > SOLACE

SOLACIOUS adj providing solace

SOLAH n Indian plant

SOLAHS > SOLAH

SOLAN archaic name for > GANNET

SOLAND n solan goose

SOLANDER n box for specimens, maps, etc, in the form of a book with a lid

SOLANDERS > SOLANDER

SOLANDS > SOLAND

SOLANIN same as > SOLANINE

SOLANINE n poisonous alkaloid found in various solanaceous plants

SOLANINES > SOLANINE

SOLANINS > SOLANIN

SOLANO n hot wind in Spain

SOLANOS > SOLANO

SOLANS > SOLAN

SOLANUM n any plant of the genus that includes the potato

SOLANUMS > SOLANUM

SOLAR adj of the sun ▷ n upper room

SOLARIA > SOLARIUM

SOLARISE same as > SOLARIZE

SOLARISED > SOLARISE

SOLARISES > SOLARISE

SOLARISM n explanation of myths in terms of the movements and influence of the sun

SOLARISMS > SOLARISM

SOLARIST > SOLARISM

SOLARISTS > SOLARISM

SOLARIUM n place with beds and ultraviolet lights used for acquiring an artificial suntan

SOLARIUMS > SOLARIUM

SOLARIZE vb treat by exposure to the sun's rays

SOLARIZED > SOLARIZE

SOLARIZES > SOLARIZE

SOLARS > SOLAR

SOLAS > SOLA

SOLATE vb change from gel to liquid

SOLATED > SOLATE

SOLATES > SOLATE

SOLATIA > SOLATIUM

SOLATING > SOLATE

SOLATION n liquefaction of a gel

SOLATIONS > SOLATION

SOLATIUM n compensation awarded for injury to the feelings

SOLD n obsolete word for salary

SOLDADO n soldier

SOLDADOES > SOLDADO

SOLDADOS > SOLDADO

SOLDAN archaic word for > SULTAN

SOLDANS > SOLDAN

SOLDE n wages

SOLDER n soft alloy used to join two metal surfaces ▷ vb join with solder

SOLDERED > SOLDER

SOLDERER > SOLDER

SOLDERERS > SOLDER

SOLDERING > SOLDER

SOLDERS > SOLDER

SOLDES > SOLDE

SOLDI > SOLDO

SOLDIER n member of an army ▷ vb serve in an army

SOLDIERED > SOLDIER

SOLDIERLY adj of or befitting a good soldier

SOLDIERS > SOLDIER

SOLDIERY n soldiers collectively

SOLDO n former Italian copper coin

SOLDS > SOLD

SOLE adj one and only ▷ n underside of the foot ▷ vb provide (a shoe) with a sole

SOLECISE variant of > SOLECIZE

SOLECISED > SOLECISE

SOLECISES > SOLECISE

SOLECISM n minor grammatical mistake

SOLECISMS > SOLECISM

SOLECIST > SOLECISM

SOLECISTS > SOLECISM

SOLECIZE vb commit a solecism

SOLECIZED > SOLECIZE

SOLECIZES > SOLECIZE

SOLED > SOLE

SOLEI > SOLEUS

SOLEIN same as > SULLEN

SOLELESS > SOLE

SOLELY adv only, completely

SOLEMN adj serious, deeply sincere

SOLEMNER > SOLEMN

SOLEMNESS > SOLEMN

SOLEMNEST > SOLEMN

SOLEMNIFY vb make serious or grave

SOLEMNISE same as > SOLEMNIZE

SOLEMNITY n state or quality of being solemn

SOLEMNIZE vb celebrate or perform (a ceremony)

SOLEMNLY > SOLEMN

SOLENESS > SOLE

SOLENETTE n small European sole

SOLENODON n either of two rare shrewlike nocturnal mammals of the Caribbean

SOLENOID n coil of wire magnetized by passing a current through it

SOLENOIDS > SOLENOID

SOLEPLATE n joist forming the lowest member of a timber frame

SOLEPRINT n print of sole of foot

SOLER same as > SOLE

SOLERA n system for aging sherry and other fortified wines

SOLERAS > SOLERA

SOLERET n armour for foot

SOLERETS > SOLERET

SOLERS > SOLER

SOLES > SOLE

SOLEUS n muscle in calf of leg

SOLEUSES > SOLEUS

SOLFATARA n volcanic vent emitting only sulphurous gases and water vapour or sometimes hot mud

SOLFEGE variant of > SOLFEGGIO

SOLFEGES > SOLFEGE

SOLFEGGI > SOLFEGGIO

SOLFEGGIO n voice exercise in which runs, scales, etc, are sung to the same syllable or syllables

SOLFERINO n moderate purplish-red colour

SOLGEL adj changing between sol and gel

SOLI adv to be performed by or with soloists

SOLICIT vb request

SOLICITED > SOLICIT

SOLICITOR n lawyer who advises clients and prepares documents and cases

SOLICITS > SOLICIT

SOLICITY n act of making a request

SOLID adj (of a substance) keeping its shape ▷ n three-dimensional shape

SOLIDAGO n chiefly American plant of the genus which includes the goldenrods

SOLIDAGOS > SOLIDAGO

SOLIDARE n old coin

SOLIDARES > SOLIDARE

SOLIDARY adj marked by unity of interests, responsibilities, etc

SOLIDATE vb consolidate

SOLIDATED > SOLIDATE

SOLIDATES > SOLIDATE

SOLIDER > SOLID

SOLIDEST > SOLID

SOLIDI > SOLIDUS

SOLIDIFY vb make or become solid or firm

SOLIDISH > SOLID

SOLIDISM n belief that diseases spring from damage to solid parts of body

SOLIDISMS > SOLIDISM

SOLIDIST > SOLIDISM

SOLIDISTS > SOLIDISM

SOLIDITY > SOLID

SOLIDLY > SOLID

SOLIDNESS > SOLID

SOLIDS > SOLID

SOLIDUM n part of pedestal

SOLIDUMS > SOLIDUM

SOLIDUS same as > SLASH

SOLILOQUY n speech made by a person while alone, esp in a play

SOLING > SOLE

SOLION n amplifier used in chemistry

SOLIONS > SOLION

SOLIPED n animal whose hooves are not cloven

SOLIPEDS > SOLIPED

SOLIPSISM n doctrine that the self is the only thing known to exist

SOLIPSIST > SOLIPSISM

SOLIQUID n semi-solid, semi-liquid solution

SOLIQUIDS > SOLIQUID

SOLITAIRE n game for one person played with pegs set in a board

SOLITARY adj alone, single ▷ n hermit

SOLITO adv musical instruction meaning play in usual manner

SOLITON n type of isolated particle-like wave

SOLITONS > SOLITON

SOLITUDE n state of being alone

SOLITUDES > SOLITUDE

SOLIVE n type of joist

SOLIVES > SOLIVE

SOLLAR n archaic word meaning attic ▷ vb put in a sollar

SOLLARED > SOLLAR

SOLLARING > SOLLAR

SOLLARS > SOLLAR

SOLLER same as > SOLLAR

SOLLERET n protective covering for the foot consisting of riveted plates of armour

SOLLERETS > SOLLERET

SOLLERS > SOLLER

SOLLICKER n something very large

SOLO n music for one performer ▷ adj done alone ▷ adv by oneself, alone ▷ vb undertake a venture alone

SOLOED > SOLO

SOLOES > SOLO

SOLOING > SOLO

SOLOIST n person who performs a solo

SOLOISTIC > SOLOIST

SOLOISTS > SOLOIST

SOLON n US congressperson

SOLONCHAK n type of intrazonal soil of arid regions with a greyish surface crust

SOLONETS same as > SOLONETZ

SOLONETZ n type of intrazonal soil with a high saline content characterized by leaching

SOLONS > SOLON

SOLOS > SOLO

SOLPUGID n venomous arachnid

SOLPUGIDS > SOLPUGID

SOLS > SOL

SOLSTICE n either the shortest (in winter) or longest (in summer) day of the year

SOLSTICES > SOLSTICE

SOLUBLE adj able to be dissolved ▷ n soluble substance

SOLUBLES > SOLUBLE

SOLUBLY > SOLUBLE

SOLUM n upper layers of the soil profile

SOLUMS > SOLUM

SOLUNAR adj relating to sun and moon

SOLUS n advert printed or published separately from others

SOLUSES > SOLUS

SOLUTAL adj relating to a solute

SOLUTE n substance in a solution that is dissolved ▷ adj loose or unattached

SOLUTES > SOLUTE

SOLUTION n answer to a problem

SOLUTIONS > SOLUTION

SOLUTIVE adj dissolving ▷ n solvent or laxative

SOLUTIVES > SOLUTIVE

SOLVABLE adj capable of being solved

SOLVATE vb undergo, cause to undergo, or partake in solvation

SOLVATED > SOLVATE

SOLVATES > SOLVATE

SOLVATING > SOLVATE

SOLVATION n type of chemical process

SOLVE vb find the answer to (a problem)

SOLVED > SOLVE

SOLVENCY n ability to pay all debts

SOLVENT adj having enough money to pay one's debts ▷ n liquid capable of dissolving other substances

SOLVENTLY > SOLVENT

SOLVENTS > SOLVENT

SOLVER > SOLVE

SOLVERS > SOLVE

SOLVES > SOLVE

SOLVING > SOLVE

SOM n currency of Kyrgyzstan and Uzbekistan

SOMA n body of an organism as distinct from the germ cells

SOMAN n compound developed as a nerve gas

SOMANS > SOMAN

SOMAS > SOMA

SOMASCOPE n instrument for inspecting internal organs

SOMATA > SOMA

SOMATIC adj of the body, as distinct from the mind

SOMATISM n materialism

SOMATISMS > SOMATISM

SOMATIST > SOMATISM

SOMATISTS > SOMATISM

SOMBER adj (in the US) sombre ▷ vb (in the US) make sombre

SOMBERED > SOMBER

SOMBERER > SOMBER

SOMBEREST > SOMBER

SOMBERING > SOMBER

SOMBERLY > SOMBER

SOMBERS > SOMBER

SOMBRE adj dark, gloomy ▷ vb make sombre

SOMBRED > SOMBRE

SOMBRELY > SOMBRE

SOMBRER > SOMBRE

SOMBRERO n wide-brimmed Mexican hat

SOMBREROS > SOMBRERO

SOMBRES > SOMBRE

SOMBREST > SOMBRE

SOMBRING > SOMBRE

SOMBROUS > SOMBRE

SOME pron certain unknown or unspecified people or things ▷ adv approximately

SOMEBODY pron some person ▷ n important person

SOMEDAY adv at some unspecified time in the future

SOMEDEAL adv to some extent ▷ n some part of something

SOMEDEALS > SOMEDEAL

SOMEDELE same as > SOMEDEAL

SOMEGATE adv Scots word meaning somehow

SOMEHOW adv in some unspecified way

SOMEONE pron somebody ▷ n significant or important person

SOMEONES > SOMEONE

SOMEPLACE adv in, at, or to some unspecified place or region

SOMERSET n somersault

SOMERSETS > SOMERSET

SOMETHING pron unknown or unspecified thing or amount ▷ n impressive or important person or thing

SOMETIME adv at some unspecified time ▷ adj former

SOMETIMES adv from time to time, now and then

SOMEWAY adv in some unspecified manner

SOMEWAYS same as > SOMEWAY

SOMEWHAT adv some extent, rather ▷ n vague amount

SOMEWHATS > SOMEWHAT

SOMEWHEN adv at some time

SOMEWHERE adv in, to, or at some unspecified or unknown place

SOMEWHILE adv sometimes

SOMEWHY adv for some reason

SOMEWISE adv in some way or to some degree

SOMITAL > SOMITE

SOMITE n segment of mesoderm in vertebrate embryos

SOMITES > SOMITE

SOMITIC > SOMITE

SOMMELIER n wine steward in a restaurant or hotel

SOMNIAL adj of dreams

SOMNIATE vb dream

SOMNIATED > SOMNIATE

SOMNIATES > SOMNIATE

SOMNIFIC adj inducing sleep

SOMNOLENT adj drowsy

SOMONI n monetary unit of Tajikistan

SOMONIS > SOMONI

SOMS > SOM

SOMY > SOM

SON n male offspring

SONANCE > SONANT

SONANCES > SONANT

SONANCIES > SONANT

SONANCY > SONANT

SONANT n voiced sound able to form a syllable or syllable nucleus ▷ adj denoting a voiced sound like this

SONANTAL > SONANT

SONANTIC > SONANT

SONANTS > SONANT

SONAR n device for detecting underwater objects by the reflection of sound waves

SONARMAN n sonar operator

SONARMEN > SONARMAN

SONARS > SONAR

SONATA n piece of music in several movements for one instrument

SONATAS > SONATA

SONATINA n short sonata

SONATINAS > SONATINA

SONATINE same as > SONATINA

SONCE n Scots word meaning good luck

SONCES > SONCE

SONDAGE n deep trial trench for inspecting stratigraphy

SONDAGES > SONDAGE

SONDE n rocket, balloon, or probe used for observing in the upper atmosphere

SONDELI n Indian shrew

SONDELIS > SONDELI

SONDER n yacht category

SONDERS > SONDER

SONDES > SONDE

SONE n subjective unit of loudness

SONERI n Indian cloth of gold

SONERIS > SONERI

SONES > SONE

SONG n music for the voice

SONGBIRD n any bird with a musical call

SONGBIRDS > SONGBIRD

SONGBOOK n book of songs

SONGBOOKS > SONGBOOK

SONGCRAFT n art of songwriting

SONGFEST n event with many songs

SONGFESTS > SONGFEST

SONGFUL adj tuneful

SONGFULLY > SONGFUL

SONGKOK n (in Malaysia and Indonesia) a kind of oval brimless hat, resembling a skull

SONGKOKS > SONGKOK

SONGLESS > SONG

SONGLIKE > SONG

SONGMAN n singer

SONGMEN > SONGMAN

SONGOLOLO n kind of millipede

SONGS > SONG

SONGSHEET n piece of paper with the words to a song on it

SONGSMITH n person who writes songs

SONGSTER n singer

SONGSTERS > SONGSTER

SONHOOD > SON

SONHOODS > SON

SONIC adj of or producing sound

SONICALLY > SONIC

SONICATE vb subject to sound waves

SONICATED > SONICATE

SONICATES > SONICATE

SONICATOR > SONICATE

SONICS n study of mechanical vibrations in matter

SONLESS > SON

SONLIER > SONLY

SONLIEST > SONLY

SONLIKE > SON

SONLY adj like a son

SONNE same as > SON

SONNES > SONNE

SONNET *n* fourteen-line poem ▷ *vb* compose sonnets

SONNETARY > SONNET

SONNETED > SONNET

SONNETEER *n* writer of sonnets

SONNETING > SONNET

SONNETISE *same as* > SONNETIZE

SONNETIZE *vb* write sonnets

SONNETS > SONNET

SONNETTED > SONNET

SONNIES > SONNY

SONNY *n* term of address to a boy

SONOBUOY *n* buoy equipped to detect underwater noises and transmit them by radio

SONOBUOYS > SONOBUOY

SONOGRAM *n* three-dimensional representation of a sound signal

SONOGRAMS > SONOGRAM

SONOGRAPH *n* device for scanning sound

SONOMETER *same as* > MONOCHORD

SONORANT *n* type of frictionless continuant or nasal

SONORANTS > SONORANT

SONORITY > SONOROUS

SONOROUS *adj* (of sound) deep or resonant

SONOVOX *n* device used to alter sound of human voice in music recordings

SONOVOXES > SONOVOX

SONS > SON

SONSE *same as* > SONCE

SONSES > SONSE

SONSHIP > SON

SONSHIPS > SON

SONSIE *same as* > SONSY

SONSIER > SONSY

SONSIEST > SONSY

SONSY *adj* plump

SONTAG *n* type of knitted women's cape

SONTAGS > SONTAG

SONTIES *n* Shakespearian oath

SOOCHONG *same as* > SOUCHONG

SOOCHONGS > SOOCHONG

SOOEY *interj* call used to summon pigs

SOOGEE *vb* clean a ship using a special solution

SOOGEED > SOOGEE

SOOGEEING > SOOGEE

SOOGEES > SOOGEE

SOOGIE *same as* > SOOGEE

SOOGIED > SOOGIE

SOOGIEING > SOOGIE

SOOGIES > SOOGIE

SOOJEY *same as* > SOOGEE

SOOJEYS > SOOJEY

SOOK *n* baby ▷ *vb* suck

SOOKED > SOOK

SOOKIER > SOOKY

SOOKIEST > SOOKY

SOOKING > SOOK

SOOKS > SOOK

SOOKY *adj* tending to complain peevishly

SOOL *vb* incite (a dog) to attack

SOOLE *same as* > SOOL

SOOLED > SOOL

SOOLER *n* person who incites a dog to attack

SOOLERS > SOOLER

SOOLES > SOOLE

SOOLING > SOOL

SOOLS > SOOL

SOOM *Scots word for* > SWIM

SOOMED > SOOM

SOOMING > SOOM

SOOMS > SOOM

SOON *adv* in a short time

SOONER *adv* rather ▷ *n* idler or shirker

SOONERS > SOONER

SOONEST *adv* as soon as possible

SOONISH *adj* somewhat soon

SOOP *Scots word for* > SWEEP

SOOPED > SOOP

SOOPING > SOOP

SOOPINGS > SOOP

SOOPS > SOOP

SOOPSTAKE *adv* sweeping up all stakes

SOOT *n* black powder formed by the incomplete burning of an organic substance ▷ *vb* cover with soot

SOOTE *n* sweet

SOOTED > SOOT

SOOTERKIN *n* mythical black afterbirth of Dutch women that was believed to result from their warming themselves on stoves

SOOTES > SOOT

SOOTFLAKE *n* speck of soot

SOOTH *n* truth or reality ▷ *adj* true or real

SOOTHE *vb* make calm

SOOTHED > SOOTHE

SOOTHER *vb* flatter

SOOTHERED > SOOTHE

SOOTHERS > SOOTHER

SOOTHES > SOOTHE

SOOTHEST > SOOTHE

SOOTHFAST *adj* truthful

SOOTHFUL *adj* truthful

SOOTHING *adj* having a calming, assuaging, or relieving effect

SOOTHINGS > SOOTHING

SOOTHLICH *adv* truly

SOOTHLY > SOOTH

SOOTHS > SOOTH

SOOTHSAID > SOOTHSAY

SOOTHSAY *vb* predict the future

SOOTHSAYS > SOOTHSAY

SOOTIER > SOOTY

SOOTIEST > SOOTY

SOOTILY > SOOTY

SOOTINESS > SOOTY

SOOTING *n* state of becoming covered with soot

SOOTINGS > SOOTING

SOOTLESS > SOOT

SOOTS > SOOT

SOOTY *adj* covered with soot

SOP *n* concession to pacify someone ▷ *vb* mop up or absorb (liquid)

SOPAPILLA *n* Mexican deep-fried pastry

SOPH *shortened form of* > SOPHOMORE

SOPHERIC > SOPHERIM

SOPHERIM *n* Jewish scribes

SOPHIES > SOPHY

SOPHISM *n* argument that seems reasonable but is actually false and misleading

SOPHISMS > SOPHISM

SOPHIST *n* person who uses clever but invalid arguments

SOPHISTER *n* (esp formerly) a second-year undergraduate at certain British universities

SOPHISTIC *adj* of or relating to sophists or sophistry

SOPHISTRY *n* clever but invalid argument

SOPHISTS > SOPHIST

SOPHOMORE *n* student in second year at college

SOPHS > SOPH

SOPHY *n* title of the Persian monarchs

SOPITE *vb* lull to sleep

SOPITED > SOPITE

SOPITES > SOPITE

SOPITING > SOPITE

SOPOR *n* abnormally deep sleep

SOPORIFIC *adj* causing sleep ▷ *n* drug that causes sleep

SOPOROSE *adj* sleepy

SOPOROUS *same as* > SOPOROSE

SOPORS > SOPOR

SOPPED > SOP

SOPPIER > SOPPY

SOPPIEST > SOPPY

SOPPILY > SOPPY

SOPPINESS > SOPPY

SOPPING > SOP

SOPPINGS > SOP

SOPPY *adj* over-sentimental

SOPRA *adv* musical instruction meaning above

SOPRANI > SOPRANO

SOPRANINI > SOPRANINO

SOPRANINO *n* instrument with the highest possible pitch in a family of instruments

SOPRANIST *n* soprano

SOPRANO *n* singer with the highest female or boy's voice ▷ *adj* of a musical instrument that is the highest or second highest pitched in its family

SOPRANOS > SOPRANO

SOPS > SOP

SORA *n* North American rail with a yellow bill

SORAGE *n* first year in hawk's life

SORAGES > SORAGE

SORAL > SORUS

SORAS > SORA

SORB *n* any of various related trees, esp the mountain ash ▷ *vb* absorb or adsorb

SORBABLE > SORB

SORBARIA *n* Asian shrub

SORBARIAS > SORBARIA

SORBATE *n* salt of sorbic acid

SORBATES > SORBATE

SORBED > SORB

SORBENT > SORB

SORBENTS > SORB

SORBET *same as* > SHERBET

SORBETS > SORBET

SORBIC > SORB

SORBING > SORB

SORBITAN *n* any of a group of compounds derived from sorbitol

SORBITANS > SORBITAN

SORBITE *n* mineral found in steel

SORBITES > SORBITE

SORBITIC > SORBITE

SORBITISE *same as* > SORBITIZE

SORBITIZE *vb* turn metal into form containing sorbite

SORBITOL *n* white water-soluble crystalline alcohol with a sweet taste

SORBITOLS > SORBITOL

SORBO *n* as in *sorbo rubber* spongy form of rubber

SORBOSE *n* sugar derived from the berries of the mountain ash

SORBOSES > SORBOSE

SORBS > SORB

SORBUS *n* rowan or related tree

SORBUSES > SORBUS

SORCERER *n* magician

SORCERERS > SORCERER

SORCERESS *same as* > SORCERER

SORCERIES > SORCERY

SORCEROUS > SORCERY

SORCERY *n* witchcraft or magic

SORD *n* flock of mallard ducks ▷ *vb* ascend in flight

SORDA *n* deaf woman

SORDED > SORD

SORDES *pl n* dark incrustations on the lips and teeth of patients with prolonged fever

SORDID *adj* dirty, squalid

SORDIDER > SORDID

SORDIDEST > SORDID

SORDIDLY > SORDID

SORDINE *same as* > SORDINO

SORDINES > SORDINE

SORDING > SORD

SORDINI > SORDINO

SORDINO *n* mute for a stringed or brass musical instrument

SORDO *n* deaf man

SORDOR *n* sordidness

SORDORS > SORDOR

SORDS > SORD

SORE *adj* painful ▷ *n* painful area on the body ▷ *adv* greatly ▷ *vb* make sore

SORED > SORE

SOREDIA > SOREDIUM

SOREDIAL > SOREDIUM

SOREDIATE > SOREDIUM

SOREDIUM n organ of vegetative reproduction in lichens
SOREE same as > SORA
SOREES > SOREE
SOREHEAD n peevish or disgruntled person
SOREHEADS > SOREHEAD
SOREHON n old Irish feudal right
SOREHONS > SOREHON
SOREL variant of > SORREL
SORELL same as > SORREL
SORELLS > SORELL
SORELS > SOREL
SORELY adv greatly
SORENESS > SORE
SORER > SORE
SORES > SORE
SOREST > SORE
SOREX n shrew or related animal
SOREXES > SOREX
SORGHO same as > SORGO
SORGHOS > SORGHO
SORGHUM n kind of grass cultivated for grain
SORGHUMS > SORGHUM
SORGO n any of several varieties of sorghum that have watery sweet juice
SORGOS > SORGO
SORI > SORUS
SORICINE adj of or resembling a shrew
SORICOID same as > SORICINE
SORING > SORE
SORINGS > SORE
SORITES n type of syllogism in which only the final conclusion is stated
SORITIC > SORITES
SORITICAL > SORITES
SORN vb obtain food, etc, from another person by presuming on his or her generosity
SORNED > SORN
SORNER > SORN
SORNERS > SORN
SORNING > SORN
SORNINGS > SORN
SORNS > SORN
SOROBAN n Japanese abacus
SOROBANS > SOROBAN
SOROCHE n altitude sickness
SOROCHES > SOROCHE
SORORAL adj of sister
SORORALLY > SORORAL
SORORATE n custom in some societies of a widower marrying his deceased wife's younger sister
SORORATES > SORORATE
SORORIAL same as > SORORAL
SORORISE same as > SORORIZE
SORORISED > SORORISE
SORORISES > SORORISE
SORORITY n society for female students
SORORIZE vb socialize in sisterly way
SORORIZED > SORORIZE
SORORIZES > SORORIZE

SOROSES > SOROSIS
SOROSIS n fleshy multiple fruit
SOROSISES > SOROSIS
SORPTTON n process in which one substance takes up or holds another
SORPTIONS > SORPTION
SORPTIVE > SORPTION
SORRA Irish word for > SORROW
SORRAS > SORRA
SORREL n bitter-tasting plant
SORRELS > SORREL
SORRIER > SORRY
SORRIEST > SORRY
SORRILY > SORRY
SORRINESS > SORRY
SORROW n grief or sadness ▷ vb grieve
SORROWED > SORROW
SORROWER > SORROW
SORROWERS > SORROW
SORROWFUL > SORROW
SORROWING > SORROW
SORROWS > SORROW
SORRY adj feeling pity or regret ▷ interj exclamation expressing apology or asking someone to repeat what he or she has said
SORRYISH > SORRY
SORT n group all sharing certain qualities or characteristics ▷ vb arrange according to kind
SORTA adv phonetic representation of 'sort of'
SORTABLE > SORT
SORTABLY > SORT
SORTAL n type of logical or linguistic concept
SORTALS > SORTAL
SORTANCE n suitableness
SORTANCES > SORTANCE
SORTATION n act of sorting
SORTED interj exclamation of satisfaction, approval, etc ▷ adj having been corrected or made ready
SORTER > SORT
SORTERS > SORT
SORTES pl n divination by opening book at random
SORTIE n relatively short return trip ▷ vb make a sortie
SORTIED > SORTIE
SORTIEING > SORTIE
SORTIES > SORTIE
SORTILEGE n act or practice of divination by drawing lots
SORTILEGY same as > SORTILEGE
SORTING > SORT
SORTINGS > SORT
SORTITION n act of casting lots
SORTMENT n assortment
SORTMENTS > SORTMENT
SORTS > SORT
SORUS n cluster of sporangia on the undersurface of certain fern leaves
SOS > SO

SOSATIE n skewer of curried meat pieces
SOSATIES > SOSATIE
SOSS vb make dirty or muddy
SOSSED > SOSS
SOSSES > SOSS
SOSSING > SOSS
SOSSINGS > SOSS
SOSTENUTI > SOSTENUTO
SOSTENUTO adv to be performed in a smooth sustained manner
SOT n habitual drunkard ▷ adv indeed: used to contradict a negative statement ▷ vb be a drunkard
SOTERIAL adj of salvation
SOTH archaic variant of > SOOTH
SOTHS > SOTH
SOTOL n American plant related to agave
SOTOLS > SOTOL
SOTS > SOT
SOTTED > SOT
SOTTEDLY > SOT
SOTTING > SOT
SOTTINGS > SOT
SOTTISH > SOT
SOTTISHLY > SOT
SOTTISIER n collection of jokes
SOU n former French coin
SOUARI n tree of tropical America
SOUARIS > SOUARI
SOUBISE n purée of onions mixed into a thick white sauce and served over eggs, fish, etc
SOUBISES > SOUBISE
SOUBRETTE n minor female role in comedy, often that of a pert maid
SOUCAR n Indian banker
SOUCARS > SOUCAR
SOUCE same as > SOUSE
SOUCED > SOUCE
SOUCES > SOUCE
SOUCHONG n black tea with large leaves
SOUCHONGS > SOUCHONG
SOUCING > SOUCE
SOUCT > SOUCE
SOUDAN obsolete variaint of > SULTAN
SOUDANS > SOUDAN
SOUFFLE n light fluffy dish made with beaten egg whites ▷ adj made light and puffy
SOUFFLED > SOUFFLE
SOUFFLEED > SOUFFLE
SOUFFLES > SOUFFLE
SOUGH vb (of the wind) make a sighing sound ▷ n soft continuous murmuring sound
SOUGHED > SOUGH
SOUGHING > SOUGH
SOUGHS > SOUGH
SOUGHT > SEEK
SOUK same as > SOOK
SOUKED > SOUK
SOUKING > SOUK
SOUKOUS n style of African popular music

SOUKOUSES > SOUKOUS
SOUKS > SOUK
SOUL n spiritual and immortal part of a human being
SOULDAN same as > SOLDAN
SOULDANS > SOULDAN
SOULDIER same as > SOLDIER
SOULDIERS > SOULDIER
SOULED adj having soul
SOULFUL adj full of emotion
SOULFULLY > SOULFUL
SOULLESS adj lacking human qualities, mechanical
SOULLIKE adj resembling a soul
SOULMATE n person with whom one has most affinity
SOULMATES > SOULMATE
SOULS > SOUL
SOULSTER n soul music singer
SOULSTERS > SOULSTER
SOUM vb decide how many animals can graze particular pasture
SOUMED > SOUM
SOUMING > SOUM
SOUMINGS > SOUM
SOUMS > SOUM
SOUND n something heard, noise ▷ vb make or cause to make a sound ▷ adj in good condition ▷ adv soundly
SOUNDABLE > SOUND
SOUNDBAR n long, slender speaker
SOUNDBARS > SOUNDBAR
SOUNDBITE n short pithy sentence or phrase extracted from a longer speech
SOUNDBOX n resonating chamber of the hollow body of a violin, guitar, etc
SOUNDCARD n component giving computer sound effects
SOUNDED > SOUND
SOUNDER n device formerly used to convert electric signals into sounds
SOUNDERS > SOUNDER
SOUNDEST > SOUND
SOUNDING adj resounding
SOUNDINGS > SOUNDING
SOUNDLESS adj extremely still or silent
SOUNDLY > SOUND
SOUNDMAN n sound recorder in television crew
SOUNDMEN > SOUNDMAN
SOUNDNESS > SOUND
SOUNDPOST n small post on guitars, violins, etc, that joins the front surface to the back and allows the whole body of the instrument to vibrate
SOUNDS > SOUND
SOUP n liquid food made from meat, vegetables, etc ▷ vb give soup to
SOUPCON n small amount
SOUPCONS > SOUPCON
SOUPED > SOUP

s

SOUPER n person dispensing soup
SOUPERS > SOUPER
SOUPFIN n Pacific requiem shark valued for its fins
SOUPFINS > SOUPFIN
SOUPIER > SOUPY
SOUPIEST > SOUPY
SOUPILY adv in a soupy manner
SOUPINESS n quality of being soupy
SOUPING > SOUP
SOUPLE same as > SUPPLE
SOUPLED > SOUPLE
SOUPLES > SOUPLE
SOUPLESS > SOUP
SOUPLIKE > SOUP
SOUPLING > SOUPLE
SOUPS > SOUP
SOUPSPOON n spoon for eating soup
SOUPY adj having the appearance or consistency of soup
SOUR adj sharp-tasting ▷ vb make or become sour
SOURBALL n tart-flavoured boiled sweet
SOURBALLS > SOURBALL
SOURCE n origin or starting point ▷ vb establish a supplier of (a product, etc)
SOURCED > SOURCE
SOURCEFUL adj offering useful things
SOURCES > SOURCE
SOURCING > SOURCE
SOURCINGS > SOURCE
SOURDINE n soft stop on an organ or harmonium
SOURDINES > SOURDINE
SOURDOUGH adj (of bread) made with fermented dough used as a leaven ▷ n (in Western US, Canada, and Alaska) an old-time prospector or pioneer
SOURED > SOUR
SOURER > SOUR
SOUREST > SOUR
SOURGUM n tree of eastern N America
SOURGUMS > SOURGUM
SOURING > SOUR
SOURINGS > SOUR
SOURISH > SOUR
SOURISHLY > SOUR
SOURLY > SOUR
SOURNESS > SOUR
SOUROCK n Scots word for sorrel plant
SOUROCKS > SOUROCK
SOURPUSS n person who is always gloomy, pessimistic, or bitter
SOURS > SOUR
SOURSE same as > SOURCE
SOURSES > SOURSE
SOURSOP n small West Indian tree
SOURSOPS > SOURSOP
SOURVELD n grazing field with long coarse grass
SOURVELDS > SOURVELD
SOURWOOD n sorrel tree
SOURWOODS > SOURWOOD

SOUS > SOU
SOUSE vb plunge (something) into liquid ▷ n liquid used in pickling
SOUSED > SOUSE
SOUSER n person who frequently gets drunk
SOUSERS > SOUSER
SOUSES > SOUSE
SOUSING > SOUSE
SOUSINGS > SOUSE
SOUSLIK same as > SUSLIK
SOUSLIKS > SOUSLIK
SOUT same as > SOOT
SOUTACHE n narrow braid used as a decorative trimming
SOUTACHES > SOUTACHE
SOUTANE n Roman Catholic priest's cassock
SOUTANES > SOUTANE
SOUTAR same as > SOUTER
SOUTARS > SOUTAR
SOUTENEUR n pimp
SOUTER n shoemaker or cobbler
SOUTERLY > SOUTER
SOUTERS > SOUTER
SOUTH n direction towards the South Pole, opposite north ▷ adj in the south ▷ adv in, to, or towards the south ▷ vb turn south
SOUTHEAST adv (in or to) direction between south and east ▷ n point of the compass or the direction midway between south and east ▷ adj of or denoting the southeastern part of a specified country, area, etc
SOUTHED > SOUTH
SOUTHER n strong wind or storm from the south ▷ vb turn south
SOUTHERED > SOUTHER
SOUTHERLY adj of or in the south ▷ adv towards the south ▷ n wind from the south
SOUTHERN adj situated in or towards the south ▷ n southerner
SOUTHERNS > SOUTHERN
SOUTHERS > SOUTHER
SOUTHING n movement, deviation, or distance covered in a southerly direction
SOUTHINGS > SOUTHING
SOUTHLAND n southern part of country
SOUTHMOST adj situated or occurring farthest south
SOUTHPAW n left-handed person, esp a boxer ▷ adj left-handed
SOUTHPAWS > SOUTHPAW
SOUTHRON n southerner
SOUTHRONS > SOUTHRON
SOUTHS > SOUTH
SOUTHSAID > SOUTHSAY
SOUTHSAY same as > SOOTHSAY
SOUTHSAYS > SOUTHSAY
SOUTHWARD adv towards the south

SOUTHWEST adv (in or to) direction between south and west ▷ n point of the compass or the direction midway between west and south ▷ adj of or denoting the southwestern part of a specified country, area, etc
SOUTIE same as > SOUTPIEL
SOUTIES > SOUTIE
SOUTPIEL n South African derogatory slang for an English-speaking South African
SOUTPIELS > SOUTPIEL
SOUTS > SOUT
SOUVENIR n keepsake, memento ▷ vb steal or keep (something, esp a small article) for one's own use
SOUVENIRS > SOUVENIR
SOUVLAKI same as > SOUVLAKIA
SOUVLAKIA n Greek dish of kebabs, esp made with lamb
SOUVLAKIS > SOUVLAKI
SOV shortening of > SOVEREIGN
SOVENANCE n memory
SOVEREIGN n king or queen ▷ adj (of a state) independent
SOVIET n formerly, elected council in the USSR ▷ adj of the former USSR
SOVIETIC > SOVIET
SOVIETISE same as > SOVIETIZE
SOVIETISM n principle or practice of government through soviets
SOVIETIST > SOVIETISM
SOVIETIZE vb bring (a country, person, etc) under Soviet control or influence
SOVIETS > SOVIET
SOVKHOZ n large mechanized farm in former USSR
SOVKHOZES > SOVKHOZ
SOVKHOZY > SOVKHOZ
SOVRAN literary word for > SOVEREIGN
SOVRANLY > SOVRAN
SOVRANS > SOVRAN
SOVRANTY > SOVRAN
SOVS > SOV
SOW vb scatter or plant (seed) in or on (the ground) ▷ n female adult pig
SOWABLE > SOW
SOWANS same as > SOWENS
SOWAR n Indian cavalryman
SOWARREE n Indian mounted escort
SOWARREES > SOWARREE
SOWARRIES > SOWARRY
SOWARRY same as > SOWARREE
SOWARS > SOWAR
SOWBACK another name for > HOGBACK
SOWBACKS > SOWBACK
SOWBELLY n salt pork from pig's belly
SOWBREAD n S European primulaceous plant
SOWBREADS > SOWBREAD

SOWBUG n (in N America) woodlouse
SOWBUGS > SOWBUG
SOWCAR same as > SOUCAR
SOWCARS > SOWCAR
SOWCE same as > SOUSE
SOWCED > SOWCE
SOWCES > SOWCE
SOWCING > SOWCE
SOWDER same as > SAWDER
SOWDERS > SOWDER
SOWED > SOW
SOWENS n pudding made from oatmeal husks steeped and boiled
SOWER > SOW
SOWERS > SOW
SOWF same as > SOWTH
SOWFED > SOWF
SOWFF same as > SOWTH
SOWFFED > SOWFF
SOWFFING > SOWFF
SOWFFS > SOWFF
SOWFING > SOWF
SOWFS > SOWF
SOWING > SOW
SOWINGS > SOW
SOWL same as > SOLE
SOWLE same as > SOLE
SOWLED > SOWL
SOWLES > SOWLE
SOWLING > SOWL
SOWLS > SOWL
SOWM same as > SOUM
SOWMED > SOWM
SOWMING > SOWM
SOWMS > SOWM
SOWN > SOW
SOWND vb wield
SOWNDED > SOWND
SOWNDING > SOWND
SOWNDS > SOWND
SOWNE same as > SOUND
SOWNES > SOWNE
SOWP n spoonful ▷ vb soak
SOWPED > SOWP
SOWPING > SOWP
SOWPS > SOWP
SOWS > SOW
SOWSE same as > SOUSE
SOWSED > SOWSE
SOWSES > SOWSE
SOWSING > SOWSE
SOWSSE same as > SOUSE
SOWSSED > SOWSSE
SOWSSES > SOWSSE
SOWSSING > SOWSSE
SOWTER same as > SOUTER
SOWTERS > SOWTER
SOWTH vb Scots word meaning whistle
SOWTHED > SOWTH
SOWTHING > SOWTH
SOWTHS > SOWTH
SOX pl n informal spelling of 'socks'
SOY n soya bean
SOYA n plant whose edible bean is used for food and as a source of oil
SOYAS > SOYA
SOYBEAN n soya bean
SOYBEANS > SOYBEAN
SOYBURGER n burger made with soya bean
SOYLE n body ▷ vb elucidate

s

SOYLED > SOYLE
SOYLES > SOYLE
SOYLING > SOYLE
SOYMEAL n foodstuff made from soybeans
SOYMEALS > SOYMEAL
SOYMILK n milk substitute made from soya
SOYMILKS > SOYMILK
SOYS > SOY
SOYUZ n Russian spacecraft
SOYUZES > SOYUZ
SOZ interj (slang) sorry
SOZIN n form of protein
SOZINE same as > SOZIN
SOZINES > SOZINE
SOZINS > SOZIN
SOZZLE vb make wet
SOZZLED adj drunk
SOZZLES > SOZZLE
SOZZLIER > SOZZLY
SOZZLIEST > SOZZLY
SOZZLING > SOZZLE
SOZZLY adj wet
SPA n resort with a mineral-water spring ▷ vb visit a spa
SPACE n unlimited expanse in which all objects exist and move ▷ vb place at intervals
SPACEBAND n device on a linecaster for evening up the spaces between words
SPACED > SPACE
SPACELAB n laboratory in space where scientific experiments are performed
SPACELABS > SPACELAB
SPACELESS adj having no limits in space
SPACEMAN n person who travels in space
SPACEMEN > SPACEMAN
SPACEPORT n base equipped to launch, maintain, and test spacecraft
SPACER n piece of material used to create or maintain a space between two things
SPACERS > SPACER
SPACES > SPACE
SPACESHIP n (in science fiction) a spacecraft used for travel between planets and galaxies
SPACESUIT n sealed pressurized suit worn by an astronaut
SPACETIME n four-dimensional continuum having three spatial coordinates and one time coordinate
SPACEWALK n instance of floating and manoeuvring in space, outside but attached by a lifeline to a spacecraft ▷ vb float and manoeuvre in space while outside but attached to a spacecraft
SPACEWARD adv into space
SPACEY adj vague and dreamy
SPACIAL same as > SPATIAL
SPACIALLY > SPACIAL
SPACIER > SPACEY

SPACIEST > SPACEY
SPACINESS > SPACEY
SPACING n arrangement of letters, words, etc, on a page in order to achieve legibility
SPACINGS > SPACING
SPACIOUS adj having a large capacity or area
SPACKLE vb fill holes in plaster
SPACKLED > SPACKLE
SPACKLES > SPACKLE
SPACKLING > SPACKLE
SPACY same as > SPACEY
SPADASSIN n swordsman
SPADE n tool for digging
SPADED > SPADE
SPADEFEET > SPADEFOOT
SPADEFISH n type of spiny-finned food fish
SPADEFOOT n type of toad
SPADEFUL n amount spade will hold
SPADEFULS > SPADEFUL
SPADELIKE > SPADE
SPADEMAN n man who works with spade
SPADEMEN > SPADEMAN
SPADER > SPADE
SPADERS > SPADE
SPADES > SPADE
SPADESMAN same as > SPADEMAN
SPADESMEN > SPADEMAN
SPADEWORK n hard preparatory work
SPADGER n sparrow
SPADGERS > SPADGER
SPADICES > SPADIX
SPADILLE n (in ombre and quadrille) the ace of spades
SPADILLES > SPADILLE
SPADILLIO same as > SPADILLE
SPADILLO same as > SPADILLE
SPADILLOS > SPADILLO
SPADING > SPADE
SPADIX n spike of small flowers on a fleshy stem
SPADIXES > SPADIX
SPADO n neutered animal
SPADOES > SPADO
SPADONES > SPADO
SPADOS > SPADO
SPADROON n type of sword
SPADROONS > SPADROON
SPAE vb foretell (the future)
SPAED > SPAE
SPAEING > SPAE
SPAEINGS > SPAE
SPAEMAN n man who can supposedly foretell the future
SPAEMEN > SPAEMAN
SPAER > SPAE
SPAERS > SPAE
SPAES > SPAE
SPAETZLE n German noodle dish
SPAETZLES > SPAETZLE
SPAEWIFE n woman who can supposedly foretell the future
SPAEWIVES > SPAEWIFE
SPAG vb (of a cat) to scratch (a person) with the claws

SPAGERIC same as > SPAGYRIC
SPAGGED > SPAG
SPAGGING > SPAG
SPAGHETTI n pasta in the form of long strings
SPAGIRIC same as > SPAGYRIC
SPAGIRIST n an alchemist
SPAGS > SPAG
SPAGYRIC adj of or relating to alchemy ▷ n alchemist
SPAGYRICS > SPAGYRIC
SPAGYRIST > SPAGYRIC
SPAHEE same as > SPAHI
SPAHEES > SPAHEE
SPAHI n (formerly) an irregular cavalryman in the Turkish armed forces
SPAHIS > SPAHI
SPAIL Scots word for > SPALL
SPAILS > SPAIL
SPAIN variant of > SPANE
SPAINED > SPAIN
SPAING > SPA
SPAINGS > SPA
SPAINING > SPAIN
SPAINS > SPAIN
SPAIRGE Scots word for > SPARGE
SPAIRGED > SPAIRGE
SPAIRGES > SPAIRGE
SPAIRGING > SPAIRGE
SPAIT same as > SPATE
SPAITS > SPAIT
SPAKE past tense of > SPEAK
SPALD same as > SPAULD
SPALDEEN n ball used in street game
SPALDEENS > SPALDEEN
SPALDS > SPALD
SPALE Scots word for > SPALL
SPALES > SPALE
SPALL n splinter or chip of ore, rock, or stone ▷ vb split or cause to split into such fragments
SPALLABLE > SPALL
SPALLE same as > SPAULD
SPALLED > SPALL
SPALLER > SPALL
SPALLERS > SPALL
SPALLES > SPALLE
SPALLING > SPALL
SPALLINGS > SPALL
SPALLS > SPALL
SPALPEEN n itinerant seasonal labourer
SPALPEENS > SPALPEEN
SPALT vb split
SPALTED > SPALT
SPALTING > SPALT
SPALTS > SPALT
SPAM vb send unsolicited e-mail simultaneously to a number of newsgroups on the internet ▷ n unsolicited electronic mail or text messages sent in this way
SPAMBOT n computer program that sends spam
SPAMBOTS > SPAMBOT
SPAMMED > SPAM
SPAMMER > SPAM
SPAMMERS > SPAM
SPAMMIE n love bite
SPAMMIER > SPAMMY

SPAMMIES > SPAMMIE
SPAMMIEST > SPAMMY
SPAMMING > SPAM
SPAMMINGS > SPAM
SPAMMY adj bland
SPAMS > SPAM
SPAN n space between two points ▷ vb stretch or extend across
SPANAEMIA n lack of red corpuscles in blood
SPANAEMIC > SPANAEMIA
SPANCEL n length of rope for hobbling an animal ▷ vb hobble (an animal) with a loose rope
SPANCELED > SPANCEL
SPANCELS > SPANCEL
SPANDEX n type of synthetic stretch fabric made from polyurethane fibre
SPANDEXED adj wearing spandex
SPANDEXES > SPANDEX
SPANDREL n triangular surface bounded by the outer curve of an arch and the adjacent wall
SPANDRELS > SPANDREL
SPANDRIL same as > SPANDREL
SPANDRILS > SPANDRIL
SPANE vb Scots word meaning wean
SPANED > SPANE
SPANES > SPANE
SPANG adv exactly, firmly, or straight ▷ vb dash
SPANGED > SPANG
SPANGHEW vb throw in air
SPANGHEWS > SPANGHEW
SPANGING > SPANG
SPANGLE n small shiny metallic ornament ▷ vb decorate with spangles
SPANGLED > SPANGLE
SPANGLER > SPANGLE
SPANGLERS > SPANGLE
SPANGLES > SPANGLE
SPANGLET n little spangle
SPANGLETS > SPANGLET
SPANGLIER > SPANGLE
SPANGLING > SPANGLE
SPANGLY > SPANGLE
SPANGS > SPANG
SPANIEL n dog with long ears and silky hair
SPANIELS > SPANIEL
SPANING > SPANE
SPANK vb slap with the open hand, on the buttocks or legs ▷ n such a slap
SPANKED > SPANK
SPANKER n fore-and-aft sail or a mast that is aftermost in a sailing vessel
SPANKERS > SPANKER
SPANKING adj outstandingly fine or smart ▷ n series of spanks, usually as a punishment for children
SPANKINGS > SPANKING
SPANKS > SPANK
SPANLESS adj impossible to span
SPANNED > SPAN
SPANNER n tool for gripping and turning a nut or bolt

SPANNERS > SPANNER
SPANNING > SPAN
SPANS > SPAN
SPANSPEK *n* cantaloupe melon
SPANSPEKS > SPANSPEK
SPANSULE *n* modified-release capsule of a drug
SPANSULES > SPANSULE
SPANWORM *n* larva of a type of moth
SPANWORMS > SPANWORM
SPAR *n* pole used as a ship's mast, boom, or yard ▷ *vb* box or fight using light blows for practice
SPARABLE *n* small nail with no head, used for fixing the soles and heels of shoes
SPARABLES > SPARABLE
SPARAXIS *n* type of plant with dainty spikes of star-shaped purple, red, or orange flowers
SPARD > SPARE
SPARE *adj* extra ▷ *n* duplicate kept in case of damage or loss ▷ *vb* refrain from punishing or harming
SPAREABLE > SPARE
SPARED > SPARE
SPARELESS *adj* merciless
SPARELY > SPARE
SPARENESS > SPARE
SPARER > SPARE
SPARERIB *n* cut of pork ribs with most of the meat trimmed off
SPARERIBS > SPARERIB
SPARERS > SPARE
SPARES > SPARE
SPAREST > SPARE
SPARGE *vb* sprinkle or scatter (something)
SPARGED > SPARGE
SPARGER > SPARGE
SPARGERS > SPARGE
SPARGES > SPARGE
SPARGING > SPARGE
SPARID *n* type of marine percoid fish ▷ *adj* of or belonging to this family of fish
SPARIDS > SPARID
SPARING *adj* economical
SPARINGLY > SPARING
SPARK *n* fiery particle thrown out from a fire or caused by friction ▷ *vb* give off sparks
SPARKE *n* weapon
SPARKED > SPARK
SPARKER > SPARK
SPARKERS > SPARK
SPARKES > SPARKE
SPARKIE *n* electrician
SPARKIER > SPARKY
SPARKIES > SPARKIE
SPARKIEST > SPARKY
SPARKILY > SPARKY
SPARKING > SPARK
SPARKISH > SPARK
SPARKLE *vb* glitter with many points of light ▷ *n* sparkling points of light
SPARKLED > SPARKLE
SPARKLER *n* hand-held firework that emits sparks

SPARKLERS > SPARKLER
SPARKLES > SPARKLE
SPARKLESS > SPARK
SPARKLET *n* little spark
SPARKLETS > SPARKLET
SPARKLIER > SPARKLY
SPARKLIES > SPARKLY
SPARKLING *adj* (of wine or mineral water) slightly fizzy
SPARKLY *adj* sparkling ▷ *n* sparkling thing
SPARKPLUG *n* device in an engine that ignites the fuel
SPARKS *n* electrician
SPARKY *adj* lively
SPARLIKE > SPAR
SPARLING *n* European smelt
SPARLINGS > SPARLING
SPAROID *same as* > SPARID
SPAROIDS > SPAROID
SPARRE *same as* > SPAR
SPARRED > SPAR
SPARRER > SPAR
SPARRERS > SPAR
SPARRES > SPARRE
SPARRIER > SPARRY
SPARRIEST > SPARRY
SPARRING > SPAR
SPARRINGS > SPAR
SPARROW *n* small brownish bird
SPARROWS > SPARROW
SPARRY *adj* (of minerals) containing, relating to, or resembling spar
SPARS > SPAR
SPARSE *adj* thinly scattered
SPARSEDLY > SPARSE
SPARSELY > SPARSE
SPARSER > SPARSE
SPARSEST > SPARSE
SPARSITY > SPARSE
SPART *n* esparto
SPARTAN *adj* strict and austere ▷ *n* disciplined or brave person
SPARTANS > SPARTAN
SPARTEINE *n* viscous oily alkaloid extracted from the broom plant and lupin seeds
SPARTERIE *n* things made from esparto
SPARTH *n* type of battle-axe
SPARTHE *same as* > SPARTH
SPARTHES > SPARTHE
SPARTHS > SPARTH
SPARTICLE *n* hypothetical elementary particle thought to have been produced in the Big Bang
SPARTINA *n* grass growing in salt marshes
SPARTINAS > SPARTINA
SPARTS > SPART
SPAS > SPA
SPASM *n* involuntary muscular contraction ▷ *vb* go into spasm
SPASMATIC > SPASM
SPASMED > SPASM
SPASMIC > SPASM
SPASMING > SPASM
SPASMODIC *adj* occurring in spasms
SPASMS > SPASM

SPASTIC *n* offensive slang for a person with cerebral palsy ▷ *adj* affected by spasms
SPASTICS > SPASTIC
SPAT *vb* have a quarrel
SPATE *n* large number of things happening within a period of time
SPATES > SPATE
SPATFALL *n* mass of larvae on sea bed
SPATFALLS > SPATFALL
SPATHAL > SPATHE
SPATHE *n* large sheathlike leaf enclosing a flower cluster
SPATHED > SPATHE
SPATHES > SPATHE
SPATHIC *adj* (of minerals) resembling spar
SPATHOSE *same as* > SPATHIC
SPATIAL *adj* of or in space
SPATIALLY > SPATIAL
SPATLESE *n* type of German wine, usu white
SPATLESEN > SPATLESE
SPATLESES > SPATLESE
SPATS > SPAT
SPATTED > SPAT
SPATTEE *n* type of gaiter
SPATTEES > SPATTEE
SPATTER *vb* scatter or be scattered in drops over (something) ▷ *n* spattering sound
SPATTERED > SPATTER
SPATTERS > SPATTER
SPATTING > SPAT
SPATULA *n* utensil with a broad flat blade for spreading or stirring
SPATULAR > SPATULA
SPATULAS > SPATULA
SPATULATE *adj* shaped like a spatula
SPATULE *n* spatula
SPATULES > SPATULE
SPATZLE *same as* > SPAETZLE
SPATZLES > SPATZLE
SPAUL *same as* > SPAULD
SPAULD *n* shoulder
SPAULDS > SPAULD
SPAULS > SPAUL
SPAVIE *Scots variant of* > SPAVIN
SPAVIES > SPAVIE
SPAVIET *adj* Scots word meaning spavined
SPAVIN *n* enlargement of the hock of a horse by a bony growth
SPAVINED *adj* affected with spavin
SPAVINS > SPAVIN
SPAW *same as* > SPA
SPAWL *vb* spit
SPAWLED > SPAWL
SPAWLING > SPAWL
SPAWLS > SPAWL
SPAWN *n* jelly-like mass of eggs of fish, frogs, or molluscs ▷ *vb* (of fish, frogs, or molluscs) lay eggs
SPAWNED > SPAWN

SPAWNER > SPAWN
SPAWNERS > SPAWN
SPAWNIER > SPAWNY
SPAWNIEST > SPAWNY
SPAWNING > SPAWN
SPAWNINGS > SPAWN
SPAWNS > SPAWN
SPAWNY *adj* like spawn
SPAWS > SPAW
SPAY *vb* remove the ovaries from (a female animal)
SPAYAD *n* male deer
SPAYADS > SPAYAD
SPAYD *same as* > SPAYAD
SPAYDS > SPAYD
SPAYED > SPAY
SPAYING > SPAY
SPAYS > SPAY
SPAZ *vb* offensive slang meaning lose self-control
SPAZA *adj* as in *spaza shop* South African slang for a small shop in a township
SPAZZ *same as* > SPAZ
SPAZZED > SPAZ
SPAZZES > SPAZ
SPAZZING > SPAZ
SPEAK *vb* say words, talk
SPEAKABLE > SPEAK
SPEAKEASY *n* place where alcoholic drink was sold illegally during Prohibition
SPEAKER *n* person who speaks, esp at a formal occasion
SPEAKERS > SPEAKER
SPEAKING > SPEAK
SPEAKINGS > SPEAK
SPEAKOUT *n* firm or brave statement of one's beliefs
SPEAKOUTS > SPEAKOUT
SPEAKS > SPEAK
SPEAL *same as* > SPULE
SPEALS > SPEAL
SPEAN *same as* > SPANE
SPEANED > SPEAN
SPEANING > SPEAN
SPEANS > SPEAN
SPEAR *n* weapon consisting of a long shaft with a sharp point ▷ *vb* pierce with or as if with a spear
SPEARED > SPEAR
SPEARER > SPEAR
SPEARERS > SPEAR
SPEARFISH *another name for* > MARLIN
SPEARGUN *n* device for shooting spears underwater
SPEARGUNS > SPEARGUN
SPEARHEAD *vb* lead (an attack or campaign) ▷ *n* leading force in an attack or campaign
SPEARIER > SPEAR
SPEARIEST > SPEAR
SPEARING *n* act of spearing
SPEARINGS > SPEARING
SPEARLIKE > SPEAR
SPEARMAN *n* soldier armed with a spear
SPEARMEN > SPEARMAN
SPEARMINT *n* type of mint
SPEARS > SPEAR
SPEARWORT *n* any of several Eurasian ranunculaceous plants

S

SPEARY > SPEAR
SPEAT *same as* > SPATE
SPEATS > SPEAT
SPEC *vb* set specifications
SPECCED > SPEC
SPECCIER > SPECCY
SPECCIES > SPECCY
SPECCIEST > SPECCY
SPECCING > SPEC
SPECCY *n* person wearing spectacles ▷ *adj* wearing spectacles
SPECIAL *adj* distinguished from others of its kind ▷ *n* product, programme, etc which is only available at a certain time ▷ *vb* advertise and sell (an item) at a reduced price
SPECIALER > SPECIAL
SPECIALLY > SPECIAL
SPECIALS > SPECIAL
SPECIALTY *n* special interest or skill
SPECIATE *vb* form or develop into a new biological species
SPECIATED > SPECIATE
SPECIATES > SPECIATE
SPECIE *n* coins as distinct from paper money
SPECIES *n* group of plants or animals that are related closely enough to interbreed naturally
SPECIFIC *adj* particular, definite ▷ *n* drug used to treat a particular disease
SPECIFICS > SPECIFIC
SPECIFIED > SPECIFY
SPECIFIER > SPECIFY
SPECIFIES > SPECIFY
SPECIFY *vb* refer to or state specifically
SPECIMEN *n* individual or part typifying a whole
SPECIMENS > SPECIMEN
SPECIOUS *adj* apparently true, but actually false
SPECK *n* small spot or particle ▷ *vb* mark with specks or spots
SPECKED > SPECK
SPECKIER > SPECKY
SPECKIES > SPECKY
SPECKIEST > SPECKY
SPECKING > SPECK
SPECKLE *n* small spot ▷ *vb* mark with speckles
SPECKLED > SPECKLE
SPECKLES > SPECKLE
SPECKLESS > SPECK
SPECKLING > SPECKLE
SPECKS > SPECK
SPECKY *same as* > SPECCY
SPECS *pl n* spectacles
SPECT *vb* expect
SPECTACLE *n* strange, interesting, or ridiculous sight
SPECTATE *vb* watch
SPECTATED > SPECTATE
SPECTATES > SPECTATE
SPECTATOR *n* person viewing anything, onlooker
SPECTED > SPECT
SPECTER *same as* > SPECTRE

SPECTERS > SPECTER
SPECTING > SPECT
SPECTRA > SPECTRUM
SPECTRAL *adj* of or like a spectre
SPECTRE *n* ghost
SPECTRES > SPECTRE
SPECTRIN *n* any one of a class of fibrous proteins found in the membranes of red blood cells
SPECTRINS > SPECTRIN
SPECTRUM *n* range of different colours, radio waves, etc in order of their wavelengths
SPECTRUMS > SPECTRUM
SPECTS > SPECT
SPECULA > SPECULUM
SPECULAR *adj* of, relating to, or having the properties of a mirror
SPECULATE *vb* guess, conjecture
SPECULUM *n* medical instrument for examining body cavities
SPECULUMS > SPECULUM
SPED > SPEED
SPEECH *n* act, power, or manner of speaking ▷ *vb* make a speech
SPEECHED > SPEECH
SPEECHES > SPEECH
SPEECHFUL > SPEECH
SPEECHIFY *vb* make speeches, esp boringly
SPEECHING > SPEECH
SPEED *n* swiftness ▷ *vb* go quickly
SPEEDBALL *n* mixture of heroin with amphetamine or cocaine
SPEEDBOAT *n* light fast motorboat
SPEEDED > SPEED
SPEEDER > SPEED
SPEEDERS > SPEED
SPEEDFUL > SPEED
SPEEDIER > SPEEDY
SPEEDIEST > SPEEDY
SPEEDILY > SPEEDY
SPEEDING > SPEED
SPEEDINGS > SPEED
SPEEDLESS > SPEED
SPEEDO *n* speedometer
SPEEDOS > SPEEDO
SPEEDREAD *vb* read very quickly
SPEEDS > SPEED
SPEEDSTER *n* fast car, esp a sports model
SPEEDUP *n* acceleration
SPEEDUPS > SPEEDUP
SPEEDWALK *n* an endless conveyor belt or moving walkway used to transport standing persons from place to place
SPEEDWAY *n* track for motorcycle racing
SPEEDWAYS > SPEEDWAY
SPEEDWELL *n* plant with small blue flowers
SPEEDY *adj* prompt
SPEEL *n* splinter of wood ▷ *vb* Scots word meaning climb

SPEELED > SPEEL
SPEELER > SPEEL
SPEELERS > SPEEL
SPEELING > SPEEL
SPEELS > SPEEL
SPEER *same as* > SPEIR
SPEERED > SPEER
SPEERING > SPEER
SPEERINGS > SPEER
SPEERS > SPEER
SPEIL *dialect word for* > CLIMB
SPEILED > SPEIL
SPEILING > SPEIL
SPEILS > SPEIL
SPEIR *vb* ask
SPEIRED > SPEIR
SPEIRING > SPEIR
SPEIRINGS > SPEIR
SPEIRS > SPEIR
SPEISE *same as* > SPEISS
SPEISES > SPEISE
SPEISS *n* compounds formed when ores containing arsenic or antimony are smelted
SPEISSES > SPEISS
SPEK *n* bacon, fat, or fatty pork used for larding venison or other game
SPEKBOOM *n* South African shrub
SPEKBOOMS > SPEKBOOM
SPEKS > SPEK
SPELAEAN *adj* of, found in, or inhabiting caves
SPELD *vb* Scots word meaning spread
SPELDED > SPELD
SPELDER *same as* > SPELD
SPELDERED > SPELDER
SPELDERS > SPELDER
SPELDIN *n* fish split and dried
SPELDING *same as* > SPELDIN
SPELDINGS > SPELDING
SPELDINS > SPELDIN
SPELDRIN *same as* > SPELDIN
SPELDRING *same as* > SPELDIN
SPELDRINS > SPELDRIN
SPELDS > SPELD
SPELEAN *same as* > SPELAEAN
SPELK *n* splinter of wood
SPELKS > SPELK
SPELL *vb* give in correct order the letters that form (a word) ▷ *n* formula of words supposed to have magic power
SPELLABLE > SPELL
SPELLBIND *vb* cause to be spellbound
SPELLDOWN *n* spelling competition
SPELLED > SPELL
SPELLER *n* person who spells words in the manner specified
SPELLERS > SPELLER
SPELLFUL *adj* magical
SPELLICAN *same as* > SPILLIKIN
SPELLING > SPELL

SPELLINGS > SPELL
SPELLS > SPELL
SPELT *n* wheat variety
SPELTER *n* impure zinc, usually containing about 3 per cent of lead and other impurities
SPELTERS > SPELTER
SPELTS > SPELT
SPELTZ *n* wheat variety
SPELTZES > SPELTZ
SPELUNK *vb* explore caves
SPELUNKED > SPELUNK
SPELUNKER *n* person whose hobby is the exploration and study of caves
SPELUNKS > SPELUNK
SPENCE *n* larder or pantry
SPENCER *n* short fitted coat or jacket
SPENCERS > SPENCER
SPENCES > SPENCE
SPEND *vb* pay out (money)
SPENDABLE > SPEND
SPENDALL *n* spendthrift
SPENDALLS > SPENDALL
SPENDER *n* person who spends money in a manner specified
SPENDERS > SPENDER
SPENDIER > SPENDY
SPENDIEST > SPENDY
SPENDING > SPEND
SPENDINGS > SPEND
SPENDS > SPEND
SPENDY *adj* expensive
SPENSE *same as* > SPENCE
SPENSES > SPENSE
SPENT > SPEND
SPEOS *n* (esp in ancient Egypt) a temple or tomb cut into a rock face
SPEOSES > SPEOS
SPERLING *same as* > SPARLING
SPERLINGS > SPERLING
SPERM *n* male reproductive cell
SPERMARIA *pl n* spermaries
SPERMARY *n* any organ in which sperm are produced
SPERMATIA *pl n* male reproductive cells in red algae and some fungi
SPERMATIC *adj* of or relating to spermatozoa
SPERMATID *n* any of four immature male gametes that are formed from a spermatocyte
SPERMIC *same as* > SPERMATIC
SPERMINE *n* colourless basic water-soluble amine
SPERMINES > SPERMINE
SPERMOUS *same as* > SPERMATIC
SPERMS > SPERM
SPERRE *vb* bolt
SPERRED > SPERRE
SPERRES > SPERRE
SPERRING > SPERRE
SPERSE *vb* disperse
SPERSED > SPERSE
SPERSES > SPERSE
SPERSING > SPERSE

SPERST > SPERSE

SPERTHE *same as* > SPARTH

SPERTHES > SPERTHE

SPET *same as* > SPIT

SPETCH *n* piece of animal skin

SPETCHED > SPETCH

SPETCHES > SPETCH

SPETCHING > SPETCH

SPETS > SPET

SPETSNAZ *n* Soviet intelligence force

SPETTING > SPET

SPETZNAZ *same as* > SPETSNAZ

SPEUG *n* Scots word for sparrow

SPEUGS > SPEUG

SPEW *vb* vomit ▷ *n* something ejected from the mouth

SPEWED > SPEW

SPEWER > SPEW

SPEWERS > SPEW

SPEWIER > SPEWY

SPEWIEST > SPEWY

SPEWINESS > SPEWY

SPEWING > SPEW

SPEWS > SPEW

SPEWY *adj* marshy

SPHACELUS *n* death of living tissue

SPHAER *same as* > SPHERE

SPHAERE *same as* > SPHERE

SPHAERES > SPHAERE

SPHAERITE *n* aluminium phosphate

SPHAERS > SPHAER

SPHAGNOUS > SPHAGNUM

SPHAGNUM *n* moss found in bogs

SPHAGNUMS > SPHAGNUM

SPHAIREE *n* game resembling tennis played with wooden bats and a perforated plastic ball

SPHAIREES > SPHAIREE

SPHEAR *same as* > SPHERE

SPHEARE *same as* > SPHERE

SPHEARES > SPHEARE

SPHEARS > SPHEAR

SPHENDONE *n* ancient Greek headband

SPHENE *n* brown, yellow, green, or grey lustrous mineral

SPHENES > SPHENE

SPHENIC *adj* having the shape of a wedge

SPHENODON *technical name for the* > TUATARA

SPHENOID *adj* wedge-shaped ▷ *n* wedge-shaped thing

SPHENOIDS > SPHENOID

SPHERAL *adj* of or shaped like a sphere

SPHERE *n* perfectly round solid object ▷ *vb* surround or encircle

SPHERED > SPHERE

SPHERES > SPHERE

SPHERIC *same as* > SPHERICAL

SPHERICAL *adj* shaped like a sphere

SPHERICS *n* geometry and trigonometry of figures on the surface of a sphere

SPHERIER > SPHERY

SPHERIEST > SPHERY

SPHERING > SPHERE

SPHEROID *n* solid figure that is almost but not exactly a sphere

SPHEROIDS > SPHEROID

SPHERULAR > SPHERULE

SPHERULE *n* very small sphere or globule

SPHERULES > SPHERULE

SPHERY *adj* resembling a sphere

SPHINCTER *n* ring of muscle which controls the opening and closing of a hollow organ

SPHINGES > SPHINX

SPHINGID *n* hawk moth

SPHINGIDS > SPHINGID

SPHINX *n* huge statue built by the ancient Egyptians

SPHINXES > SPHINX

SPHYGMIC *adj* of or relating to the pulse

SPHYGMOID *adj* resembling the pulse

SPHYGMUS *n* person's pulse

SPHYNX *n* breed of cat

SPHYNXES > SPHYNX

SPIAL *n* observation

SPIALS > SPIAL

SPIC *n* offensive term for a Spanish-speaking person

SPICA *n* spiral bandage formed by a series of overlapping figure-of-eight turns

SPICAE > SPICA

SPICAS > SPICA

SPICATE *adj* having, arranged in, or relating to spikes

SPICATED *same as* > SPICATE

SPICCATO *n* style of playing a stringed instrument in which the bow bounces lightly off the strings

SPICCATOS > SPICCATO

SPICE *n* aromatic substance used as flavouring ▷ *vb* flavour with spices

SPICEBUSH *n* North American lauraceous shrub

SPICED > SPICE

SPICELESS > SPICE

SPICER > SPICE

SPICERIES > SPICERY

SPICERS > SPICE

SPICERY *n* spices collectively

SPICES > SPICE

SPICEY *same as* > SPICY

SPICIER > SPICY

SPICIEST > SPICY

SPICILEGE *n* anthology

SPICILY > SPICY

SPICINESS > SPICY

SPICING > SPICE

SPICK *adj* neat and clean ▷ *n* offensive term for a Spanish-speaking person

SPICKER > SPICK

SPICKEST > SPICK

SPICKNEL *same as* > SPIGNEL

SPICKNELS > SPICKNEL

SPICKS > SPICK

SPICS > SPIC

SPICULA *same as* > SPICULUM

SPICULAE > SPICULA

SPICULAR > SPICULUM

SPICULATE > SPICULE

SPICULE *n* small slender pointed structure or crystal

SPICULES > SPICULE

SPICULUM *same as* > SPICULE

SPICY *adj* flavoured with spices

SPIDE *n* insulting Irish word for a young working-class man who dresses in casual sports clothes

SPIDER *n* small eight-legged creature which spins a web to catch insects for food ▷ *vb* follow internet links to gather information

SPIDERED > SPIDER

SPIDERIER > SPIDERY

SPIDERING > SPIDER

SPIDERISH > SPIDER

SPIDERMAN *n* person who erects the steel structure of a building

SPIDERMEN > SPIDERMAN

SPIDERS > SPIDER

SPIDERWEB *n* spider's web

SPIDERY *adj* thin and angular like a spider's legs

SPIDES > SPIDE

SPIE *same as* > SPY

SPIED > SPY

SPIEGEL *n* manganese-rich pig iron

SPIEGELS > SPIEGEL

SPIEL *n* speech made to persuade someone to do something ▷ *vb* deliver a prepared spiel

SPIELED > SPIEL

SPIELER > SPIEL

SPIELERS > SPIEL

SPIELING > SPIEL

SPIELS > SPIEL

SPIER *variant of* > SPEIR

SPIERED > SPIER

SPIERING > SPIER

SPIERS > SPIER

SPIES > SPY

SPIF *n* postage stamp perforated with the initials of a firm to avoid theft by employees

SPIFF *vb* make smart

SPIFFED > SPIFF

SPIFFIED > SPIFFY

SPIFFIER > SPIFFY

SPIFFIES > SPIFFY

SPIFFIEST > SPIFFY

SPIFFILY > SPIFFY

SPIFFING *adj* excellent

SPIFFS > SPIFF

SPIFFY *adj* smart ▷ *n* smart thing or person ▷ *vb* smarten

SPIFFYING > SPIFFY

SPIFS > SPIF

SPIGHT *same as* > SPITE

SPIGHTED > SPIGHT

SPIGHTING > SPIGHT

SPIGHTS > SPIGHT

SPIGNEL *n* European umbelliferous plant

SPIGNELS > SPIGNEL

SPIGOT *n* stopper for, or tap fitted to, a cask

SPIGOTS > SPIGOT

SPIK *same as* > SPIC

SPIKE *n* sharp point ▷ *vb* put spikes on

SPIKED > SPIKE

SPIKEFISH *n* large sea fish

SPIKELET *n* unit of a grass inflorescence

SPIKELETS > SPIKELET

SPIKELIKE > SPIKE

SPIKENARD *n* fragrant Indian plant with rose-purple flowers

SPIKER > SPIKE

SPIKERIES > SPIKERY

SPIKERS > SPIKE

SPIKERY *n* High-Church Anglicanism

SPIKES > SPIKE

SPIKEY *same as* > SPIKY

SPIKIER > SPIKY

SPIKIEST > SPIKY

SPIKILY > SPIKY

SPIKINESS > SPIKY

SPIKING > SPIKE

SPIKS > SPIK

SPIKY *adj* resembling a spike

SPILE *n* heavy timber stake or pile ▷ *vb* provide or support with a spile

SPILED > SPILE

SPILES > SPILE

SPILIKIN *same as* > SPILLIKIN

SPILIKINS > SPILIKIN

SPILING > SPILE

SPILINGS > SPILE

SPILITE *n* type of igneous rock

SPILITES > SPILITE

SPILITIC > SPILITE

SPILL *vb* pour from or as if from a container ▷ *n* fall

SPILLABLE > SPILL

SPILLAGE *n* instance or the process of spilling

SPILLAGES > SPILLAGE

SPILLED > SPILL

SPILLER > SPILL

SPILLERS > SPILL

SPILLIKIN *n* thin strip of wood, cardboard, or plastic used in spillikins

SPILLING > SPILL

SPILLINGS > SPILL

SPILLOVER *n* act of spilling over

SPILLS > SPILL

SPILLWAY *n* channel that carries away surplus water, as from a dam

SPILLWAYS > SPILLWAY

SPILOSITE *n* form of slate

SPILT > SPILL

SPILTH *n* something spilled

SPILTHS > SPILTH

SPIM *n* spam sent and received via an instant-messaging system

SPIMMER n person who sends spam via an instant-messaging system

SPIMMERS > SPIMMER

SPIMMING n the sending of spam via an instant-messaging system

SPIMMINGS > SPIMMING

SPIMS > SPIM

SPIN vb revolve or cause to revolve rapidly ▷ n revolving motion

SPINA n spine

SPINACENE n type of vaccine

SPINACH n dark green leafy vegetable

SPINACHES > SPINACH

SPINACHY adj tasting of spinach

SPINAE > SPINA

SPINAGE same as > SPINACH

SPINAGES > SPINAGE

SPINAL adj of the spine ▷ n anaesthetic administered in the spine

SPINALLY > SPINAL

SPINALS > SPINAL

SPINAR n fast-spinning star

SPINARAMA n evasive move in ice hockey

SPINARS > SPINAR

SPINAS > SPINA

SPINATE adj having a spine

SPINDLE n rotating rod that acts as an axle ▷ vb form into a spindle or equip with spindles

SPINDLED > SPINDLE

SPINDLER > SPINDLE

SPINDLERS > SPINDLE

SPINDLES > SPINDLE

SPINDLIER > SPINDLY

SPINDLING adj long and slender, esp disproportionately so ▷ n spindling person or thing

SPINDLY adj long, slender, and frail

SPINDRIFT n spray blown up from the sea

SPINE n backbone

SPINED > SPINE

SPINEL n any of a group of hard glassy minerals of variable colour

SPINELESS adj lacking courage

SPINELIKE > SPINE

SPINELLE same as > SPINEL

SPINELLES > SPINELLE

SPINELS > SPINEL

SPINES > SPINE

SPINET n small harpsichord

SPINETS > SPINET

SPINETTE same as > SPINET

SPINETTES > SPINETTE

SPINIER > SPINY

SPINIEST > SPINY

SPINIFEX n coarse spiny Australian grass

SPINIFORM adj like a thorn

SPININESS > SPINY

SPINK n finch ▷ vb (of a finch) chirp

SPINKED > SPINK

SPINKING > SPINK

SPINKS > SPINK

SPINLESS > SPIN

SPINNAKER n large sail on a racing yacht

SPINNER n bowler who makes the ball change direction when it bounces

SPINNERET n organ through which silk threads come out of a spider

SPINNERS > SPINNER

SPINNERY n spinning mill

SPINNET same as > SPINET

SPINNETS > SPINNET

SPINNEY n small wood

SPINNEYS > SPINNEY

SPINNIER > SPINNY

SPINNIES > SPINNY

SPINNIEST > SPINNY

SPINNING > SPIN

SPINNINGS > SPIN

SPINNY adj crazy

SPINODE another name for > CUSP

SPINODES > SPINODE

SPINOFF n development derived incidentally from an existing enterprise

SPINOFFS > SPINOFF

SPINONE n as in Italian spinone wiry-coated gun dog

SPINONI > SPINONE

SPINOR n type of mathematical object

SPINORS > SPINOR

SPINOSE adj (esp of plants) bearing many spines

SPINOSELY > SPINOSE

SPINOSITY > SPINOSE

SPINOUS adj resembling a spine or thorn

SPINOUT n spinning skid that causes a car to run off the road

SPINOUTS > SPINOUT

SPINS > SPIN

SPINSTER n unmarried woman

SPINSTERS > SPINSTER

SPINTEXT n preacher

SPINTEXTS > SPINTEXT

SPINTO n lyrical singing voice

SPINTOS > SPINTO

SPINULA n small spine

SPINULAE > SPINULA

SPINULATE adj like a spine

SPINULE n very small spine, thorn, or prickle

SPINULES > SPINULE

SPINULOSE > SPINULE

SPINULOUS > SPINULE

SPINY adj covered with spines

SPIRACLE n small blowhole for breathing through, such as that of a whale

SPIRACLES > SPIRACLE

SPIRACULA pl n spiracles

SPIRAEA n plant with small white or pink flowers

SPIRAEAS > SPIRAEA

SPIRAL n continuous curve formed by a point winding about a central axis ▷ vb move in a spiral ▷ adj having the form of a spiral

SPIRALED > SPIRAL

SPIRALING > SPIRAL

SPIRALISM n ascent in spiral structure

SPIRALIST > SPIRALISM

SPIRALITY > SPIRAL

SPIRALLED > SPIRAL

SPIRALLY > SPIRAL

SPIRALS > SPIRAL

SPIRANT n fricative consonant

SPIRANTS > SPIRANT

SPIRASTER n part of living sponge

SPIRATED adj twisted in spiral

SPIRATION n breathing

SPIRE n pointed part of a steeple ▷ vb assume the shape of a spire

SPIREA same as > SPIRAEA

SPIREAS > SPIREA

SPIRED > SPIRE

SPIRELESS > SPIRE

SPIRELET another name for > FLECHE

SPIRELETS > SPIRELET

SPIREM same as > SPIREME

SPIREME n tangled mass of chromatin threads

SPIREMES > SPIREME

SPIREMS > SPIREM

SPIRES > SPIRE

SPIREWISE > SPIRE

SPIRIC n type of curve

SPIRICS > SPIRIC

SPIRIER > SPIRE

SPIRIEST > SPIRE

SPIRILLA > SPIRILLUM

SPIRILLAR > SPIRILLUM

SPIRILLUM n any bacterium having a curved or spirally twisted rodlike body

SPIRING > SPIRE

SPIRIT n nonphysical aspect of a person concerned with profound thoughts ▷ vb carry away mysteriously

SPIRITED adj lively

SPIRITFUL > SPIRIT

SPIRITING > SPIRIT

SPIRITISM n belief that the spirits of the dead can communicate with the living

SPIRITIST > SPIRITISM

SPIRITOSO adv to be played in a spirited or animated manner

SPIRITOUS adj high-spirited

SPIRITS > SPIRIT

SPIRITUAL adj relating to the spirit ▷ n type of religious folk song originating among Black slaves in America

SPIRITUEL adj having a refined and lively mind or wit

SPIRITUS n spirit

SPIRITY adj spirited

SPIRLING same as > SPARLING

SPIRLINGS > SPIRLING

SPIROGRAM n record made by spirograph

SPIROGYRA n green freshwater plant that floats on the surface of ponds and ditches

SPIROID adj resembling a spiral or displaying a spiral form

SPIRT same as > SPURT

SPIRTED > SPIRT

SPIRTING > SPIRT

SPIRTLE same as > SPURTLE

SPIRTLES > SPIRTLE

SPIRTS > SPIRT

SPIRULA n tropical cephalopod mollusc

SPIRULAE > SPIRULA

SPIRULAS > SPIRULA

SPIRULINA n type of cyanobacterium processed as a source of nutrients

SPIRY > SPIRE

SPIT vb eject (saliva or food) from the mouth ▷ n saliva

SPITAL n obsolete word for hospital

SPITALS > SPITAL

SPITBALL n small missile made from chewed paper ▷ vb make suggestions

SPITBALLS > SPITBALL

SPITCHER adj doomed ▷ vb be doomed

SPITCHERS > SPITCHER

SPITE n deliberate nastiness ▷ vb annoy or hurt from spite

SPITED > SPITE

SPITEFUL adj full of or motivated by spite

SPITES > SPITE

SPITFIRE n person with a fiery temper

SPITFIRES > SPITFIRE

SPITING > SPITE

SPITS > SPIT

SPITTED > SPIT

SPITTEN > SPIT

SPITTER > SPIT

SPITTERS > SPIT

SPITTIER > SPITTY

SPITTIEST > SPITTY

SPITTING > SPIT

SPITTINGS > SPIT

SPITTLE n fluid produced in the mouth, saliva

SPITTLES > SPITTLE

SPITTLIER > SPITTLY

SPITTLY adj covered with spittle

SPITTOON n bowl to spit into

SPITTOONS > SPITTOON

SPITTY adj covered with saliva

SPITZ n stockily built dog with a tightly curled tail

SPITZES > SPITZ

SPIV n smartly dressed man who makes a living by shady dealings

SPIVS > SPIV

SPIVVERY n behaviour of spivs

SPIVVIER > SPIV

SPIVVIEST > SPIV
SPIVVISH *adj* characteristic of a spiv
SPIVVY > SPIV
SPLAKE *n* type of hybrid trout bred by Canadian zoologists
SPLAKES > SPLAKE
SPLASH *vb* scatter liquid on (something) ▷ *n* splashing sound
SPLASHED > SPLASH
SPLASHER *n* anything used for protection against splashes
SPLASHERS > SPLASHER
SPLASHES > SPLASH
SPLASHIER > SPLASHY
SPLASHILY > SPLASHY
SPLASHING > SPLASH
SPLASHY *adj* having irregular marks
SPLAT *n* wet slapping sound ▷ *vb* make wet slapping sound
SPLATCH *vb* splash
SPLATCHED > SPLATCH
SPLATCHES > SPLATCH
SPLATS > SPLAT
SPLATTED > SPLAT
SPLATTER *n* splash ▷ *vb* splash (something or someone) with small blobs
SPLATTERS > SPLATTER
SPLATTING > SPLAT
SPLAY *vb* spread out, with ends spreading in different directions ▷ *adj* spread out ▷ *n* surface of a wall that forms an oblique angle to the main flat surfaces
SPLAYED > SPLAY
SPLAYFEET > SPLAYFOOT
SPLAYFOOT *n* foot of which the toes are spread out
SPLAYING > SPLAY
SPLAYS > SPLAY
SPLEEN *n* abdominal organ which filters bacteria from the blood
SPLEENFUL *adj* bad-tempered or irritable
SPLEENIER > SPLEEN
SPLEENISH > SPLEEN
SPLEENS > SPLEEN
SPLEENY > SPLEEN
SPLENDENT *adj* shining brightly
SPLENDID *adj* excellent
SPLENDOR *same as* > SPLENDOUR
SPLENDORS > SPLENDOR
SPLENDOUR *n* state or quality of being splendid
SPLENETIC *adj* spiteful or irritable ▷ *n* spiteful or irritable person
SPLENIA > SPLENIUM
SPLENIAL > SPLENIUS
SPLENIC *adj* of, relating to, or in the spleen
SPLENII > SPLENIUS
SPLENITIS *n* inflammation of the spleen
SPLENIUM *n* structure in brain
SPLENIUMS > SPLENIUM

SPLENIUS *n* either of two flat muscles situated at the back of the neck
SPLENT *same as* > SPLINT
SPLENTS > SPLENT
SPLEUCHAN *n* pouch for tobacco
SPLICE *vb* join by interweaving or overlapping ends
SPLICED > SPLICE
SPLICER > SPLICE
SPLICERS > SPLICE
SPLICES > SPLICE
SPLICING > SPLICE
SPLICINGS > SPLICING
SPLIFF *n* cannabis, used as a drug
SPLIFFS > SPLIFF
SPLINE *n* type of narrow key around a shaft that fits into a corresponding groove ▷ *vb* provide (a shaft, part, etc) with splines
SPLINED > SPLINE
SPLINES > SPLINE
SPLINING > SPLINE
SPLINT *n* rigid support for a broken bone ▷ *vb* apply a splint to (a broken arm, etc)
SPLINTED > SPLINT
SPLINTER *n* thin sharp piece broken off, esp from wood ▷ *vb* break into fragments
SPLINTERS > SPLINTER
SPLINTERY *adj* liable to produce or break into splinters
SPLINTING > SPLINT
SPLINTS > SPLINT
SPLISH *vb* splash
SPLISHED > SPLISH
SPLISHES > SPLISH
SPLISHING > SPLISH
SPLIT *vb* break into separate pieces ▷ *n* splitting
SPLITS > SPLIT
SPLITTED > SPLIT
SPLITTER > SPLIT
SPLITTERS > SPLIT
SPLITTING *n* Freudian psychological defence mechanism
SPLITTISM *n* advocation of separatism from a larger body
SPLITTIST *n* person who advocates separatism from a larger body
SPLODGE *n* large uneven spot or stain ▷ *vb* mark (something) with a splodge or splodges
SPLODGED > SPLODGE
SPLODGES > SPLODGE
SPLODGIER > SPLODGE
SPLODGILY > SPLODGE
SPLODGING > SPLODGE
SPLODGY > SPLODGE
SPLOG *n* spam blog
SPLOGS > SPLOG
SPLOOSH *vb* splash or cause to splash about uncontrollably ▷ *n* instance or sound of splooshing
SPLOOSHED > SPLOOSH

SPLOOSHES > SPLOOSH
SPLORE *n* revel
SPLORES > SPLORE
SPLOSH *vb* scatter (liquid) vigorously about in blobs ▷ *n* instance or sound of sploshing
SPLOSHED > SPLOSH
SPLOSHES > SPLOSH
SPLOSHING > SPLOSH
SPLOTCH *vb* splash, daub
SPLOTCHED > SPLOTCH
SPLOTCHES > SPLOTCH
SPLOTCHY > SPLOTCH
SPLURGE *vb* spend money extravagantly ▷ *n* bout of extravagance
SPLURGED > SPLURGE
SPLURGER > SPLURGE
SPLURGERS > SPLURGE
SPLURGES > SPLURGE
SPLURGIER > SPLURGE
SPLURGING > SPLURGE
SPLURGY > SPLURGE
SPLURT *vb* gush out
SPLURTED > SPLURT
SPLURTING > SPLURT
SPLURTS > SPLURT
SPLUTTER *vb* utter with spitting or choking sounds ▷ *n* spluttering
SPLUTTERS > SPLUTTER
SPLUTTERY *adj* spluttering
SPOD *adj* boring, unattractive, or overly studious
SPODDIER > SPOD
SPODDIEST > SPOD
SPODDY > SPOD
SPODE *n* type of English china or porcelain
SPODES > SPODE
SPODIUM *n* black powder
SPODIUMS > SPODIUM
SPODOGRAM *n* ash from plant used in studying it
SPODOSOL *n* ashy soil
SPODOSOLS > SPODOSOL
SPODS > SPOD
SPODUMENE *n* greyish-white, green, or lilac pyroxene mineral
SPOFFISH *adj* officious
SPOFFY *same as* > SPOFFISH
SPOIL *vb* damage
SPOILABLE > SPOIL
SPOILAGE *n* amount of material that has been spoilt
SPOILAGES > SPOILAGE
SPOILED > SPOIL
SPOILER *n* device on an aircraft or car to increase drag
SPOILERS > SPOILER
SPOILFIVE *n* card game for two or more players with five cards each
SPOILFUL *adj* taking spoils
SPOILING > SPOIL
SPOILS > SPOIL
SPOILSMAN *n* person who shares in the spoils of office or advocates the spoils system
SPOILSMEN > SPOILSMAN
SPOILT > SPOIL

SPOKE *n* radial member of a wheel ▷ *vb* equip with spokes
SPOKED > SPOKE
SPOKEN > SPEAK
SPOKES > SPOKE
SPOKESMAN *n* person chosen to speak on behalf of a group
SPOKESMEN > SPOKESMAN
SPOKEWISE > SPEAK
SPOKING > SPOKE
SPOLIATE *less common word for* > DESPOIL
SPOLIATED > SPOLIATE
SPOLIATES > SPOLIATE
SPOLIATOR > SPOLIATE
SPONDAIC *adj* of, relating to, or consisting of spondees ▷ *n* spondaic line
SPONDAICS > SPONDAIC
SPONDEE *n* metrical foot of two long syllables
SPONDEES > SPONDEE
SPONDULIX *n* money
SPONDYL *n* vertebra
SPONDYLS > SPONDYL
SPONGE *n* sea animal with a porous absorbent skeleton ▷ *vb* wipe with a sponge
SPONGEBAG *n* small bag for holding toiletries when travelling
SPONGED > SPONGE
SPONGEING *same as* > SPONGING
SPONGEOUS *adj* spongy
SPONGER *n* person who sponges on others
SPONGERS > SPONGER
SPONGES > SPONGE
SPONGIER > SPONGY
SPONGIEST > SPONGY
SPONGILY > SPONGY
SPONGIN *n* fibrous horny protein in sponges
SPONGING > SPONGE
SPONGINS > SPONGIN
SPONGIOSE > SPONGE
SPONGIOUS > SPONGE
SPONGOID > SPONGE
SPONGY *adj* of or resembling a sponge
SPONSAL *n* marriage
SPONSALIA *n* marriage ceremony
SPONSIBLE *adj* responsible
SPONSING *same as* > SPONSON
SPONSINGS > SPONSING
SPONSION *n* act or process of becoming surety
SPONSIONS > SPONSION
SPONSON *n* outboard support for a gun enabling it to fire fore and aft
SPONSONS > SPONSON
SPONSOR *n* person who promotes something ▷ *vb* act as a sponsor for
SPONSORED > SPONSOR
SPONSORS > SPONSOR
SPONTOON *n* infantry weapon used in the 18th and 19th centuries
SPONTOONS > SPONTOON

SPOOF n mildly satirical parody ▷ vb fool (a person) with a trick or deception
SPOOFED > SPOOF
SPOOFER > SPOOF
SPOOFERS > SPOOF
SPOOFERY n SPOOF
SPOOFIER > SPOOFY
SPOOFIEST > SPOOFY
SPOOFING > SPOOF
SPOOFINGS > SPOOF
SPOOFS > SPOOF
SPOOFY > SPOOF
SPOOK n ghost ▷ vb frighten
SPOOKED > SPOOK
SPOOKERY n spooky events
SPOOKIER > SPOOKY
SPOOKIEST > SPOOKY
SPOOKILY > SPOOKY
SPOOKING > SPOOK
SPOOKISH > SPOOK
SPOOKS > SPOOK
SPOOKY adj ghostly or eerie
SPOOL n cylinder round which something can be wound ▷ vb wind or be wound onto a spool or reel
SPOOLED > SPOOL
SPOOLER > SPOOL
SPOOLERS > SPOOL
SPOOLING > SPOOL
SPOOLINGS > SPOOL
SPOOLS > SPOOL
SPOOM vb sail fast before wind
SPOOMED > SPOOM
SPOOMING > SPOOM
SPOOMS > SPOOM
SPOON n shallow bowl attached to a handle for eating, stirring, or serving food ▷ vb lift with a spoon
SPOONBAIT n type of lure used in angling
SPOONBILL n wading bird of warm regions with a long flat bill
SPOONED > SPOON
SPOONER n person who engages in spooning
SPOONERS > SPOONER
SPOONEY same as > SPOONY
SPOONEYS > SPOONEY
SPOONFED adj having been given someone else's opinions
SPOONFUL n amount that a spoon is able to hold
SPOONFULS > SPOONFUL
SPOONHOOK n type of fishing lure
SPOONIER > SPOONY
SPOONIES > SPOONY
SPOONIEST > SPOONY
SPOONILY > SPOONY
SPOONING > SPOON
SPOONLIKE adj like a spoon
SPOONS > SPOON
SPOONSFUL > SPOONFUL
SPOONWAYS adv like spoons
SPOONWISE same as > SPOONWAYS
SPOONWORM n type of small marine worm with a spoonlike proboscis
SPOONY adj foolishly or stupidly in love ▷ vb fool or silly person, esp one in love

SPOOR n trail of an animal ▷ vb track (an animal) by following its trail
SPOORED > SPOOR
SPOORER > SPOOR
SPOORERS > SPOOR
SPOORING > SPOOR
SPOORS > SPOOR
SPOOT n razor shell
SPOOTS > SPOOT
SPORADIC adj intermittent, scattered
SPORAL > SPORE
SPORANGIA pl n organs in fungi in which asexual spores are produced
SPORE n minute reproductive body of some plants ▷ vb produce, carry, or release spores
SPORED > SPORE
SPORELIKE adj like a spore
SPORES > SPORE
SPORICIDE n substance killing spores
SPORIDESM n group of spores
SPORIDIA > SPORIDIUM
SPORIDIAL > SPORIDIUM
SPORIDIUM n type of spore
SPORING > SPORE
SPORK n spoon-shaped piece of cutlery with tines like a fork
SPORKS > SPORK
SPOROCARP n specialized leaf branch in certain aquatic ferns that encloses the sori
SPOROCYST n thick-walled rounded structure produced by sporozoan protozoans
SPOROCYTE n diploid cell that divides by meiosis to produce four haploid spores
SPOROGENY n process of spore formation in plants and animals
SPOROGONY n process in sporozoans by which sporozoites are formed
SPOROID adj of or like a spore
SPOROPHYL n leaf in ferns that bears the sporangia
SPOROZOA n class of microscopic creature
SPOROZOAL > SPOROZOA
SPOROZOAN n type of parasitic protozoan
SPOROZOIC > SPOROZOA
SPOROZOON same as > SPOROZOAN
SPORRAN n pouch worn in front of a kilt
SPORRANS > SPORRAN
SPORT n activity for pleasure, competition, or exercise ▷ vb wear proudly
SPORTABLE adj playful
SPORTANCE n playing
SPORTBIKE n type of high-performance motorcycle
SPORTCOAT n sports jacket
SPORTED > SPORT
SPORTER > SPORT
SPORTERS > SPORT
SPORTFUL > SPORT

SPORTIER > SPORTY
SPORTIES > SPORTY
SPORTIEST > SPORTY
SPORTIF adj sporty ▷ n sporty person
SPORTIFS > SPORTIF
SPORTILY > SPORTY
SPORTING adj of sport
SPORTIVE adj playful
SPORTLESS > SPORT
SPORTS adj of or used in sports ▷ n meeting held at a school or college for competitions in athletic events
SPORTSMAN n person who plays sports
SPORTSMEN > SPORTSMAN
SPORTY adj (of a person) interested in sport ▷ n young person who takes an interest in sport and fitness
SPORULAR > SPORULE
SPORULATE vb produce spores, esp by multiple fission
SPORULE n spore, esp a very small spore
SPORULES > SPORULE
SPOSH n slush
SPOSHES > SPOSH
SPOSHIER > SPOSH
SPOSHIEST > SPOSH
SPOSHY > SPOSH
SPOT n small mark on a surface ▷ vb notice
SPOTLESS adj absolutely clean
SPOTLIGHT n powerful light illuminating a small area ▷ vb draw attention to
SPOTLIT > SPOTLIGHT
SPOTS > SPOT
SPOTTABLE > SPOT
SPOTTED > SPOT
SPOTTER n person who notes numbers or types of trains or planes
SPOTTERS > SPOTTER
SPOTTIE n young deer of up to three months of age
SPOTTIER > SPOTTY
SPOTTIES > SPOTTIE
SPOTTIEST > SPOTTY
SPOTTILY > SPOTTY
SPOTTING > SPOT
SPOTTINGS > SPOT
SPOTTY adj with spots
SPOUSAGE n marriage
SPOUSAGES > SPOUSAGE
SPOUSAL n marriage ceremony ▷ adj of or relating to marriage
SPOUSALLY > SPOUSAL
SPOUSALS > SPOUSAL
SPOUSE n person to whom one is married ▷ vb marry
SPOUSED > SPOUSE
SPOUSES > SPOUSE
SPOUSING > SPOUSE
SPOUT vb pour out in a stream or jet ▷ n projecting tube or lip for pouring liquids
SPOUTED > SPOUT
SPOUTER > SPOUT
SPOUTERS > SPOUT
SPOUTIER > SPOUT

SPOUTIEST > SPOUT
SPOUTING n rainwater downpipe on the outside of a building
SPOUTINGS > SPOUTING
SPOUTLESS > SPOUT
SPOUTS > SPOUT
SPOUTY > SPOUT
SPRACK adj vigorous
SPRACKLE vb clamber
SPRACKLED > SPRACKLE
SPRACKLES > SPRACKLE
SPRAD > SPREAD
SPRADDLE n disease of fowl preventing them from standing
SPRADDLED adj affected by spraddle
SPRADDLES > SPRADDLE
SPRAG n device used to prevent a vehicle from running backwards on an incline ▷ vb use sprag to prevent vehicle from moving
SPRAGGED > SPRAG
SPRAGGING > SPRAG
SPRAGS > SPRAG
SPRAID vb chapped
SPRAIN vb injure (a joint) by a sudden twist ▷ n such an injury
SPRAINED > SPRAIN
SPRAINING > SPRAIN
SPRAINS > SPRAIN
SPRAINT n piece of otter's dung
SPRAINTS > SPRAINT
SPRANG n branch
SPRANGLE vb sprawl
SPRANGLED > SPRANGLE
SPRANGLES > SPRANGLE
SPRANGS > SPRANG
SPRAT n small sea fish
SPRATS > SPRAT
SPRATTLE vb scramble
SPRATTLED > SPRATTLE
SPRATTLES > SPRATTLE
SPRAUCHLE same as > SPRACKLE
SPRAUNCY adj smart
SPRAWL vb lie or sit with the limbs spread out ▷ n part of a city that has spread untidily over a large area
SPRAWLED > SPRAWL
SPRAWLER > SPRAWL
SPRAWLERS > SPRAWL
SPRAWLIER > SPRAWL
SPRAWLING > SPRAWL
SPRAWLS > SPRAWL
SPRAWLY > SPRAWL
SPRAY n (device for producing) fine drops of liquid ▷ vb scatter in fine drops
SPRAYED > SPRAY
SPRAYER > SPRAY
SPRAYERS > SPRAY
SPRAYEY > SPRAY
SPRAYIER > SPRAY
SPRAYIEST > SPRAY
SPRAYING > SPRAY
SPRAYINGS > SPRAY
SPRAYS > SPRAY
SPREAD vb open out or be displayed to the fullest extent ▷ n spreading ▷ adj

extended or stretched out, esp to the fullest extent

SPREADER n machine or device used for scattering bulk materials over a relatively wide area

SPREADERS > SPREADER

SPREADING > SPREAD

SPREADS > SPREAD

SPREAGH n cattle raid

SPREAGHS > SPREAGH

SPREATHE vb chap

SPREATHED adj sore

SPREATHES > SPREATHE

SPREAZE same as > SPREATHE

SPREAZED same as > SPREATHED

SPREAZES > SPREAZE

SPREAZING > SPREAZE

SPRECHERY n theft of cattle

SPRECKLED adj speckled

SPRED same as > SPREAD

SPREDD same as > SPREAD

SPREDDE same as > SPREAD

SPREDDEN > SPREDDE

SPREDDES > SPREDDE

SPREDDING > SPREDDE

SPREDDS > SPREDD

SPREDS > SPRED

SPREE n session of overindulgence, usu in drinking or spending money ▷ vb go on a spree

SPREED > SPREE

SPREEING > SPREE

SPREES > SPREE

SPREETHE same as > SPREATHE

SPREETHED > SPREETHE

SPREETHES > SPREETHE

SPREEZE same as > SPREATHE

SPREEZED > SPREEZE

SPREEZES > SPREEZE

SPREEZING > SPREEZE

SPREKELIA n bulbous plant grown for its striking crimson or white pendent flowers

SPRENT adj sprinkled ▷ vb leap forward in an agile manner

SPRENTED > SPRENT

SPRENTING > SPRENT

SPRENTS > SPRENT

SPREW same as > SPRUE

SPREWS > SPREW

SPRIER > SPRY

SPRIEST > SPRY

SPRIG n twig or shoot ▷ vb fasten or secure with sprigs

SPRIGGED > SPRIG

SPRIGGER > SPRIG

SPRIGGERS > SPRIG

SPRIGGIER > SPRIG

SPRIGGING > SPRIG

SPRIGGY > SPRIG

SPRIGHT same as > SPRITE

SPRIGHTED > SPRIGHT

SPRIGHTLY adj lively and brisk ▷ adv in a lively manner

SPRIGHTS > SPRIGHT

SPRIGS > SPRIG

SPRIGTAIL n species of duck

SPRING vb move suddenly upwards or forwards in a single motion, jump ▷ n season between winter and summer

SPRINGAL n young man

SPRINGALD same as > SPRINGAL

SPRINGALS > SPRINGAL

SPRINGBOK n S African antelope

SPRINGE n type of snare for catching small wild animals or birds ▷ vb set such a snare

SPRINGED > SPRINGE

SPRINGER n small spaniel

SPRINGERS > SPRINGER

SPRINGES > SPRINGE

SPRINGIER > SPRINGY

SPRINGILY > SPRINGY

SPRINGING > SPRING

SPRINGLE same as > SPRINGE

SPRINGLES > SPRINGE

SPRINGLET n small spring

SPRINGS > SPRING

SPRINGY adj elastic

SPRINKLE vb scatter (liquid or powder) in tiny drops or particles over (something) ▷ n act or an instance of sprinkling or a quantity that is sprinkled

SPRINKLED > SPRINKLE

SPRINKLER n device with small holes that is attached to a garden hose or watering can and used to spray water

SPRINKLES > SPRINKLE

SPRINT n short race run at top speed ▷ vb run a short distance at top speed

SPRINTED > SPRINT

SPRINTER > SPRINT

SPRINTERS > SPRINT

SPRINTING > SPRINT

SPRINTS > SPRINT

SPRIT n small spar set diagonally across a sail to extend it

SPRITE n elf

SPRITEFUL adj lively

SPRITELY same as > SPRIGHTLY

SPRITES > SPRITE

SPRITS > SPRIT

SPRITSAIL n sail extended by a sprit

SPRITZ vb spray liquid

SPRITZED > SPRITZ

SPRITZER n tall drink of wine and soda water

SPRITZERS > SPRITZER

SPRITZES > SPRITZ

SPRITZIER > SPRITZY

SPRITZIG adj (of wine) sparkling ▷ n sparkling wine

SPRITZIGS > SPRITZIG

SPRITZING > SPRITZ

SPRITZY adj fizzy

SPROCKET n wheel with teeth on the rim, that drives or is driven by a chain

SPROCKETS > SPROCKET

SPROD n young salmon

SPRODS > SPROD

SPROG n child

SPROGLET n small child

SPROGLETS > SPROGLET

SPROGS > SPROG

SPRONG > SPRING

SPROUT vb put forth shoots ▷ n shoot

SPROUTED > SPROUT

SPROUTING > SPROUT

SPROUTS > SPROUT

SPRUCE n kind of fir ▷ adj neat and smart

SPRUCED > SPRUCE

SPRUCELY > SPRUCE

SPRUCER > SPRUCE

SPRUCES > SPRUCE

SPRUCEST > SPRUCE

SPRUCIER > SPRUCE

SPRUCIEST > SPRUCE

SPRUCING > SPRUCE

SPRUCY > SPRUCE

SPRUE n vertical channel in a mould

SPRUES > SPRUE

SPRUG n sparrow

SPRUGS > SPRUG

SPRUIK vb speak in public (used esp of a showman or salesman)

SPRUIKED > SPRUIK

SPRUIKER > SPRUIK

SPRUIKERS > SPRUIK

SPRUIKING > SPRUIK

SPRUIKS > SPRUIK

SPRUIT n small tributary stream or watercourse

SPRUITS > SPRUIT

SPRUNG > SPRING

SPRUSH Scots form of > SPRUCE

SPRUSHED > SPRUSH

SPRUSHES > SPRUSH

SPRUSHING > SPRUSH

SPRY adj active or nimble

SPRYER > SPRY

SPRYEST > SPRY

SPRYLY > SPRY

SPRYNESS > SPRY

SPUD n potato ▷ vb remove (bark) or eradicate (weeds) with a spud

SPUDDED > SPUD

SPUDDER same as > SPUD

SPUDDERS > SPUDDER

SPUDDIER > SPUDDY

SPUDDIEST > SPUDDY

SPUDDING > SPUD

SPUDDINGS > SPUD

SPUDDLE n feeble movement

SPUDDLES > SPUDDLE

SPUDDY adj short and fat

SPUDGEL n bucket on a long handle

SPUDGELS > SPUDGEL

SPUDS > SPUD

SPUE same as > SPEW

SPUED > SPUE

SPUEING > SPUE

SPUER > SPUE

SPUERS > SPUE

SPUES > SPUE

SPUG same as > SPUGGY

SPUGGIES > SPUGGY

SPUGGY n house sparrow

SPUGS > SPUG

SPUILZIE vb plunder

SPUILZIED > SPUILZIE

SPUILZIES > SPUILZIE

SPUING > SPUE

SPULE Scots word for > SHOULDER

SPULES > SPULE

SPULYE same as > SPUILZIE

SPULYED > SPULYE

SPULYEING > SPULYE

SPULYES > SPULYE

SPULYIE same as > SPUILZIE

SPULYIED > SPULYIE

SPULYIES > SPULYIE

SPULZIE same as > SPUILZIE

SPULZIED > SPULZIE

SPULZIES > SPULZIE

SPUMANTE n Italian sparkling wine

SPUMANTES > SPUMANTE

SPUME vb froth ▷ n foam or froth on the sea

SPUMED > SPUME

SPUMES > SPUME

SPUMIER > SPUMY

SPUMIEST > SPUMY

SPUMING > SPUME

SPUMONE n creamy Italian ice cream

SPUMONES > SPUMONE

SPUMONI same as > SPUMONE

SPUMONIS > SPUMONI

SPUMOUS > SPUME

SPUMY > SPUME

SPUN > SPIN

SPUNGE same as > SPONGE

SPUNGES > SPUNGE

SPUNK n courage, spirit ▷ vb catch fire

SPUNKED > SPUNK

SPUNKIE n will-o'-the-wisp

SPUNKIER > SPUNK

SPUNKIES > SPUNKIE

SPUNKIEST > SPUNK

SPUNKILY > SPUNK

SPUNKING > SPUNK

SPUNKS > SPUNK

SPUNKY > SPUNK

SPUNYARN n small stuff made from rope yarns twisted together

SPUNYARNS > SPUNYARN

SPUR n stimulus or incentive ▷ vb urge on, incite (someone)

SPURDOG n the dogfish

SPURDOGS > SPURDOG

SPURGALL vb prod with spur

SPURGALLS > SPURGALL

SPURGE n plant with milky sap

SPURGES > SPURGE

SPURIAE n type of bird feathers

SPURIOUS adj not genuine

SPURLESS > SPUR

SPURLIKE adj like a spur

SPURLING same as > SPARLING

SPURLINGS > SPURLING

SPURN vb reject with scorn ▷ n instance of spurning

SPURNE vb spur

SPURNED > SPURN
SPURNER > SPURN
SPURNERS > SPURN
SPURNES > SPURNE
SPURNING > SPURN
SPURNINGS > SPURN
SPURNS > SPURN
SPURRED > SPUR
SPURRER > SPUR
SPURRERS > SPUR
SPURREY *n* any of several low-growing European plants
SPURREYS > SPURREY
SPURRIER *n* maker of spurs
SPURRIERS > SPURRIER
SPURRIES > SPURRY
SPURRIEST > SPURRY
SPURRING > SPUR
SPURRINGS > SPUR
SPURRY *n* spurrey ▷ *adj* resembling a spur
SPURS > SPUR
SPURT *vb* gush or cause to gush out in a jet ▷ *n* short sudden burst of activity or speed
SPURTED > SPURT
SPURTER > SPURT
SPURTERS > SPURT
SPURTING > SPURT
SPURTLE *n* wooden spoon for stirring porridge
SPURTLES > SPURTLE
SPURTS > SPURT
SPURWAY *n* path used by riders
SPURWAYS > SPURWAY
SPUTA > SPUTUM
SPUTNIK *n* early Soviet artificial satellite
SPUTNIKS > SPUTNIK
SPUTTER *n* splutter ▷ *vb* splutter
SPUTTERED > SPUTTER
SPUTTERER > SPUTTER
SPUTTERS > SPUTTER
SPUTTERY *adj* sputtering
SPUTUM *n* mass of spittle ejected from the mouth
SPUTUMS > SPUTUM
SPY *n* person employed to obtain secret information ▷ *vb* act as a spy
SPYAL *n* spy
SPYALS > SPYAL
SPYCAM *n* camera used for covert surveillance
SPYCAMS > SPYCAM
SPYGLASS *n* small telescope
SPYHOLE *n* small hole in a door, etc through which one may watch secretly
SPYHOLES > SPYHOLE
SPYING > SPY
SPYINGS > SPY
SPYMASTER *n* person who controls spy network
SPYPLANE *n* military aeroplane used to spy on enemy
SPYPLANES > SPYPLANE
SPYRE *same as* **>** SPIRE
SPYRES > SPYRE
SPYWARE *n* software used to gain information about a computer user

SPYWARES > SPYWARE
SQUAB *n* young bird yet to leave the nest ▷ *adj* (of birds) recently hatched and still unfledged ▷ *vb* fall
SQUABASH *vb* crush
SQUABBED > SQUAB
SQUABBER > SQUAB
SQUABBEST > SQUAB
SQUABBIER > SQUAB
SQUABBING > SQUAB
SQUABBISH > SQUAB
SQUABBLE *n* petty or noisy quarrel ▷ *vb* quarrel over a small matter
SQUABBLED > SQUABBLE
SQUABBLER > SQUABBLE
SQUABBLES > SQUABBLE
SQUABBY > SQUAB
SQUABS > SQUAB
SQUACCO *n* S European heron
SQUACCOS > SQUACCO
SQUAD *n* small group of people working or training together ▷ *vb* set up squads
SQUADDED > SQUAD
SQUADDIE *n* private soldier
SQUADDIES > SQUADDY
SQUADDING > SQUAD
SQUADDY *same as* **>** SQUADDIE
SQUADOOSH *n* (US slang) nothing
SQUADRON *n* division of an air force, fleet, or cavalry regiment ▷ *vb* assign to squadrons
SQUADRONE *n* former Scottish political party
SQUADRONS > SQUADRON
SQUADS > SQUAD
SQUAIL *vb* throw sticks at
SQUAILED > SQUAIL
SQUAILER > SQUAIL
SQUAILERS > SQUAIL
SQUAILING > SQUAIL
SQUAILS > SQUAIL
SQUALENE *n* terpene first found in the liver of sharks
SQUALENES > SQUALENE
SQUALID *adj* dirty and unpleasant
SQUALIDER > SQUALID
SQUALIDLY > SQUALID
SQUALL *n* sudden strong wind ▷ *vb* cry noisily, yell
SQUALLED > SQUALL
SQUALLER > SQUALL
SQUALLERS > SQUALL
SQUALLIER > SQUALL
SQUALLING > SQUALL
SQUALLISH > SQUALL
SQUALLS > SQUALL
SQUALLY > SQUALL
SQUALOID *adj* of or like a shark
SQUALOR *n* disgusting dirt and filth
SQUALORS > SQUALOR
SQUAMA *n* scale or scalelike structure
SQUAMAE > SQUAMA
SQUAMATE > SQUAMA
SQUAMATES > SQUAMA
SQUAME *same as* **>** SQUAMA
SQUAMELLA *n* small scale

SQUAMES > SQUAME
SQUAMOSAL *n* thin platelike paired bone in the skull of vertebrates ▷ *adj* of or relating to this bone
SQUAMOSE *same as* **>** SQUAMOUS
SQUAMOUS *adj* (of epithelium) consisting of one or more layers of flat platelike cells
SQUAMULA *same as* **>** SQUAMELLA
SQUAMULAS > SQUAMULA
SQUAMULE *same as* **>** SQUAMELLA
SQUAMULES > SQUAMULE
SQUANDER *vb* waste (money or resources) ▷ *n* extravagance or dissipation
SQUANDERS > SQUANDER
SQUARE *n* geometric figure with four equal sides and four right angles ▷ *adj* square in shape ▷ *vb* multiply (a number) by itself ▷ *adv* squarely, directly
SQUARED > SQUARE
SQUARELY *adv* in a direct way
SQUARER > SQUARE
SQUARERS > SQUARE
SQUARES > SQUARE
SQUAREST > SQUARE
SQUARIAL *n* type of square dish for receiving satellite television
SQUARIALS > SQUARIAL
SQUARING > SQUARE
SQUARINGS > SQUARE
SQUARISH > SQUARE
SQUARK *n* hypothetical boson partner of a quark
SQUARKS > SQUARK
SQUARROSE *adj* having a rough surface
SQUARSON *n* clergyman who is also landowner
SQUARSONS > SQUARSON
SQUASH *vb* crush flat ▷ *n* sweet fruit drink diluted with water
SQUASHED > SQUASH
SQUASHER > SQUASH
SQUASHERS > SQUASH
SQUASHES > SQUASH
SQUASHIER > SQUASHY
SQUASHILY > SQUASHY
SQUASHING > SQUASH
SQUASHY *adj* soft and easily squashed
SQUAT *vb* crouch with the knees bent and the weight on the feet ▷ *n* place where squatters live ▷ *adj* short and broad
SQUATLY > SQUAT
SQUATNESS > SQUAT
SQUATS > SQUAT
SQUATTED > SQUAT
SQUATTER *n* illegal occupier of unused premises ▷ *vb* splash along
SQUATTERS > SQUATTER
SQUATTEST > SQUAT
SQUATTIER > SQUATTY
SQUATTILY > SQUATTY

SQUATTING *n* act of squatting
SQUATTLE *vb* squat
SQUATTLED > SQUATTLE
SQUATTLES > SQUATTLE
SQUATTY *adj* short and broad
SQUAW *n* offensive term for a Native American woman
SQUAWBUSH *n* American shrub
SQUAWFISH *n* North American minnow
SQUAWK *n* loud harsh cry ▷ *vb* utter a squawk
SQUAWKED > SQUAWK
SQUAWKER > SQUAWK
SQUAWKERS > SQUAWK
SQUAWKIER > SQUAWK
SQUAWKING > SQUAWK
SQUAWKS > SQUAWK
SQUAWKY > SQUAWK
SQUAWMAN *n* offensive term for a White man married to a Native American woman
SQUAWMEN > SQUAWMAN
SQUAWROOT *n* North American parasitic plant
SQUAWS > SQUAW
SQUEAK *n* short shrill cry or sound ▷ *vb* make or utter a squeak
SQUEAKED > SQUEAK
SQUEAKER > SQUEAK
SQUEAKERS > SQUEAK
SQUEAKERY > SQUEAK
SQUEAKIER > SQUEAK
SQUEAKILY > SQUEAK
SQUEAKING > SQUEAK
SQUEAKS > SQUEAK
SQUEAKY > SQUEAK
SQUEAL *n* long shrill cry or sound ▷ *vb* make or utter a squeal
SQUEALED > SQUEAL
SQUEALER > SQUEAL
SQUEALERS > SQUEAL
SQUEALING > SQUEAL
SQUEALS > SQUEAL
SQUEAMISH *adj* easily sickened or shocked
SQUEEGEE *n* tool with a rubber blade for clearing water from a surface ▷ *vb* remove (water or other liquid) from (something) by use of a squeegee
SQUEEGEED > SQUEEGEE
SQUEEGEES > SQUEEGEE
SQUEEZE *vb* grip or press firmly ▷ *n* squeezing
SQUEEZED > SQUEEZE
SQUEEZER > SQUEEZE
SQUEEZERS > SQUEEZE
SQUEEZES > SQUEEZE
SQUEEZIER > SQUEEZE
SQUEEZING > SQUEEZE
SQUEEZY > SQUEEZE
SQUEG *vb* oscillate
SQUEGGED > SQUEG
SQUEGGER > SQUEG
SQUEGGERS > SQUEG
SQUEGGING > SQUEG
SQUEGS > SQUEG
SQUELCH *vb* make a wet sucking sound, as by walking through mud ▷ *n* squelching sound

SQUELCHED > SQUELCH
SQUELCHER > SQUELCH
SQUELCHES > SQUELCH
SQUELCHY > SQUELCH
SQUIB n small firework that hisses before exploding
SQUIBBED > SQUIB
SQUIBBER n (in baseball) ground ball that becomes a base hit
SQUIBBERS > SQUIBBER
SQUIBBING > SQUIB
SQUIBS > SQUIB
SQUID n sea creature with tentacles ▷ vb (of a parachute) to assume an elongated shape
SQUIDDED > SQUID
SQUIDDING > SQUID
SQUIDGE vb squash
SQUIDGED > SQUIDGE
SQUIDGES > SQUIDGE
SQUIDGIER > SQUIDGY
SQUIDGING > SQUIDGE
SQUIDGY adj soft, moist, and squashy
SQUIDLIKE adj like a squid
SQUIDS > SQUID
SQUIER same as > SQUIRE
SQUIERS > SQUIER
SQUIFF same as > SQUIFFY
SQUIFFED same as > SQUIFFY
SQUIFFER n concertina
SQUIFFERS > SQUIFFER
SQUIFFIER > SQUIFFY
SQUIFFY adj slightly drunk
SQUIGGLE n wavy line ▷ vb wriggle
SQUIGGLED > SQUIGGLE
SQUIGGLER > SQUIGGLE
SQUIGGLES > SQUIGGLE
SQUIGGLY > SQUIGGLE
SQUILGEE same as > SQUEEGEE
SQUILGEED > SQUILGEE
SQUILGEES > SQUILGEE
SQUILL n Mediterranean plant of the lily family
SQUILLA n type of mantis shrimp
SQUILLAE > SQUILLA
SQUILLAS > SQUILLA
SQUILLION n extremely large but unspecified number, quantity, or amount
SQUILLS > SQUILL
SQUINANCY same as > QUINSY
SQUINCH n small arch across an internal corner of a tower ▷ vb squeeze
SQUINCHED > SQUINCH
SQUINCHES > SQUINCH
SQUINIED > SQUINY
SQUINIES > SQUINY
SQUINNIED > SQUINNY
SQUINNIER > SQUINNY
SQUINNIES > SQUINNY
SQUINNY vb squint ▷ adj squint
SQUINT vb have eyes which face in different directions ▷ n squinting condition of the eye ▷ adj crooked
SQUINTED > SQUINT
SQUINTER > SQUINT

SQUINTERS > SQUINT
SQUINTEST > SQUINT
SQUINTIER > SQUINT
SQUINTING > SQUINT
SQUINTS > SQUINT
SQUINTY > SQUINT
SQUINY same as > SQUINNY
SQUINYING > SQUINY
SQUIRAGE n body of squires
SQUIRAGES > SQUIRAGE
SQUIRALTY same as > SQUIRAGE
SQUIRARCH n person who believes in government by squires
SQUIRE n country gentleman, usu the main landowner in a community ▷ vb (of a man) escort (a woman)
SQUIREAGE same as > SQUIRAGE
SQUIRED > SQUIRE
SQUIREDOM > SQUIRE
SQUIREEN n petty squire
SQUIREENS > SQUIREEN
SQUIRELY > SQUIRE
SQUIRES > SQUIRE
SQUIRESS n wife of squire
SQUIRING > SQUIRE
SQUIRISH > SQUIRE
SQUIRL n decorative flourish in handwriting
SQUIRLS > SQUIRL
SQUIRM vb wriggle, writhe ▷ n wriggling movement
SQUIRMED > SQUIRM
SQUIRMER > SQUIRM
SQUIRMERS > SQUIRM
SQUIRMIER > SQUIRMY
SQUIRMING > SQUIRM
SQUIRMS > SQUIRM
SQUIRMY adj moving with a wriggling motion
SQUIRR same as > SKIRR
SQUIRRED > SQUIRR
SQUIRREL n small bushy-tailed tree-living animal ▷ vb store for future use
SQUIRRELS > SQUIRREL
SQUIRRELY adj like a squirrel
SQUIRRING > SQUIRR
SQUIRRS > SQUIRR
SQUIRT vb force (a liquid) or (of a liquid) be forced out of a narrow opening ▷ n jet of liquid
SQUIRTED > SQUIRT
SQUIRTER > SQUIRT
SQUIRTERS > SQUIRT
SQUIRTING > SQUIRT
SQUIRTS > SQUIRT
SQUISH n soft squelching sound ▷ vb crush (something) with a soft squelching sound
SQUISHED > SQUISH
SQUISHES > SQUISH
SQUISHIER > SQUISHY
SQUISHING > SQUISH
SQUISHY adj soft and yielding to the touch
SQUIT n insignificant person
SQUITCH n couch grass
SQUITCHES > SQUITCH

SQUITS > SQUIT
SQUITTERS pl n slang word for diarrhoea
SQUIZ n look or glance, esp an inquisitive one
SQUIZZES > SQUIZ
SQUOOSH vb squash
SQUOOSHED > SQUOOSH
SQUOOSHES > SQUOOSH
SQUOOSHY > SQUOOSH
SQUUSH same as > SQUOOSH
SQUUSHED > SQUUSH
SQUUSHES > SQUUSH
SQUUSHING > SQUUSH
SRADDHA n Hindu offering to ancestor
SRADDHAS > SRADDHA
SRADHA same as > SRADDHA
SRADHAS > SRADHA
SRI n title of respect used when addressing a Hindu
SRIRACHA n type of spicy sauce
SRIRACHAS > SRIRACHA
SRIS > SRI
ST interj exclamation to attract attention
STAB vb pierce with something pointed ▷ n instance of stabbing
STABBED > STAB
STABBER > STAB
STABBERS > STAB
STABBING > STAB
STABBINGS > STAB
STABILATE n preserved collection of tiny animals
STABILE n stationary abstract construction, usually of wire, metal, wood, etc ▷ adj fixed
STABILES > STABILE
STABILISE same as > STABILIZE
STABILITY n quality of being stable
STABILIZE vb make or become stable
STABLE n building in which horses are kept ▷ vb put or keep (a horse) in a stable ▷ adj firmly fixed or established
STABLEBOY n boy or man who works in a stable
STABLED > STABLE
STABLEMAN same as > STABLEBOY
STABLEMEN > STABLEMAN
STABLER n stable owner
STABLERS > STABLER
STABLES > STABLE
STABLEST > STABLE
STABLING n stable buildings or accommodation
STABLINGS > STABLING
STABLISH archaic variant of > ESTABLISH
STABLY > STABLE
STABS > STAB
STACATION n holiday spent at home, rather than travelling
STACCATI > STACCATO
STACCATO adv with the notes sharply separated ▷ adj consisting of short

abrupt sounds ▷ n staccato note
STACCATOS > STACCATO
STACHYS n type of plant of the genus which includes lamb's ears and betony
STACHYSES > STACHYS
STACK n ordered pile ▷ vb pile in a stack
STACKABLE > STACK
STACKED > STACK
STACKER > STACK
STACKERS > STACK
STACKET n fence of wooden posts
STACKETS > STACKET
STACKING n arrangement of aircraft traffic in busy flight lanes
STACKINGS > STACKING
STACKLESS > STACK
STACKROOM n area of library where books are not on open shelves
STACKS > STACK
STACKUP n number of aircraft waiting to land
STACKUPS > STACKUP
STACKYARD n place where livestock are kept
STACTE n one of several sweet-smelling spices used in incense
STACTES > STACTE
STADDA n type of saw
STADDAS > STADDA
STADDLE n type of support or prop
STADDLES > STADDLE
STADE same as > STADIUM
STADES > STADE
STADIA n instrument used in surveying
STADIAL n stage in development of glacier
STADIALS > STADIAL
STADIAS > STADIA
STADIUM n sports arena with tiered seats for spectators
STADIUMS > STADIUM
STAFF n people employed in an organization ▷ vb supply with personnel
STAFFAGE n ornamentation in work of art
STAFFAGES > STAFFAGE
STAFFED > STAFF
STAFFER n member of staff, esp, in journalism, of editorial staff
STAFFERS > STAFFER
STAFFING n act of hiring employees
STAFFINGS > STAFFING
STAFFMAN n person who holds the levelling staff when a survey is being made
STAFFMEN > STAFFMAN
STAFFROOM n common room for teachers
STAFFS > STAFF
STAG n adult male deer ▷ adv without a female escort ▷ vb apply for (shares) with the intention of selling them for quick profit

STAGE n step or period of development ▷ vb put (a play) on stage
STAGEABLE > STAGE
STAGED > STAGE
STAGEFUL n amount that can appear on stage
STAGEFULS > STAGEFUL
STAGEHAND n person who moves props and scenery on a stage
STAGEHEAD n part of a fishing stage which extends into the water
STAGELIKE > STAGE
STAGER n person of experience
STAGERIES > STAGERY
STAGERS > STAGER
STAGERY n theatrical effects or techniques
STAGES > STAGE
STAGETTE n young unmarried professional woman
STAGETTES > STAGETTE
STAGEY same as > STAGY
STAGGARD n male red deer in the fourth year of life
STAGGARDS > STAGGARD
STAGGART same as > STAGGARD
STAGGARTS > STAGGART
STAGGED > STAG
STAGGER vb walk unsteadily ▷ n staggering
STAGGERED > STAGGER
STAGGERER > STAGGER
STAGGERS n disease of horses and other domestic animals that causes staggering
STAGGERY adj tending to stagger
STAGGIE n little stag
STAGGIER > STAG
STAGGIES > STAGGIE
STAGGIEST > STAG
STAGGING > STAG
STAGGY > STAG
STAGHORN n type of fern with fronds that resemble antlers
STAGHORNS > STAGHORN
STAGHOUND n breed of hound similar in appearance to the foxhound but larger
STAGIER > STAGY
STAGIEST > STAGY
STAGILY > STAGY
STAGINESS > STAGY
STAGING n temporary support used in building
STAGINGS > STAGING
STAGNANCE > STAGNANT
STAGNANCY > STAGNANT
STAGNANT adj (of water or air) stale from not moving
STAGNATE vb be stagnant
STAGNATED > STAGNATE
STAGNATES > STAGNATE
STAGS > STAG
STAGY adj too theatrical or dramatic
STAID adj sedate, serious, and rather dull
STAIDER > STAID

STAIDEST > STAID
STAIDLY > STAID
STAIDNESS > STAID
STAIG Scots variant of > STAG
STAIGS > STAIG
STAIN vb discolour, mark ▷ n discoloration or mark
STAINABLE > STAIN
STAINED > STAIN
STAINER > STAIN
STAINERS > STAIN
STAINING > STAIN
STAININGS > STAIN
STAINLESS adj resistant to discoloration, esp discoloration resulting from corrosion ▷ n stainless steel
STAINS > STAIN
STAIR n one step in a flight of stairs
STAIRCASE n flight of stairs with a handrail or banisters ▷ vb buy different houses in the same building
STAIRED adj having stairs
STAIRFOOT n place at foot of stairs
STAIRHEAD n top of a flight of stairs
STAIRLESS > STAIR
STAIRLIFT n wall-mounted lifting device to carry person up stairs
STAIRLIKE > STAIR
STAIRS pl n flight of steps between floors, usu indoors
STAIRSTEP n one of the steps in a staircase
STAIRWAY n staircase
STAIRWAYS > STAIRWAY
STAIRWELL n vertical shaft in a building that contains a staircase
STAIRWISE adv by steps
STAIRWORK n unseen plotting
STAITH same as > STAITHE
STAITHE n wharf
STAITHES > STAITHE
STAITHS > STAITH
STAKE n pointed stick or post driven into the ground as a support or marker ▷ vb support or mark out with stakes
STAKED > STAKE
STAKEOUT n police surveillance of an area or house ▷ vb keep an area or house under surveillance
STAKEOUTS > STAKEOUT
STAKER n person who marks off an area with stakes
STAKERS > STAKER
STAKES > STAKE
STAKING > STAKE
STALACTIC adj relating to the masses of calcium carbonate hanging from the roofs of limestone caves
STALAG n German prisoner-of-war camp
STALAGMA n stalagmite
STALAGMAS > STALAGMA
STALAGS > STALAG
STALE adj not fresh ▷ vb make or become stale ▷ n urine of horses or cattle

STALED > STALE
STALELY > STALE
STALEMATE n (in chess) position in which any of a player's moves would put their king in check, resulting in a draw ▷ vb subject to a stalemate
STALENESS > STALE
STALER > STALE
STALES > STALE
STALEST > STALE
STALING > STALE
STALK n plant's stem ▷ vb follow or approach stealthily
STALKED > STALK
STALKER > STALK
STALKERS > STALK
STALKIER > STALKY
STALKIEST > STALKY
STALKILY > STALKY
STALKING > STALK
STALKINGS > STALK
STALKLESS > STALK
STALKLIKE > STALK
STALKO n idle gentleman
STALKOES > STALKO
STALKOS > STALKO
STALKS > STALK
STALKY adj like a stalk
STALL n small stand for the display and sale of goods ▷ vb (of a motor vehicle or engine) stop accidentally
STALLAGE n rent paid for market stall
STALLAGES > STALLAGE
STALLED > STALL
STALLING > STALL
STALLINGS > STALL
STALLION n uncastrated male horse
STALLIONS > STALLION
STALLMAN n keeper of a stall
STALLMEN > STALLMAN
STALLS > STALL
STALWART adj strong and sturdy ▷ n stalwart person
STALWARTS > STALWART
STALWORTH n stalwart person
STAMEN n pollen-producing part of a flower
STAMENED adj having stamen
STAMENS > STAMEN
STAMINA n enduring energy and strength
STAMINAL > STAMINA
STAMINAS > STAMINA
STAMINATE adj (of plants) having stamens, esp having stamens but no carpels
STAMINEAL adj having a stamen
STAMINODE n stamen that produces no pollen
STAMINODY n development of any of various plant organs into stamens
STAMINOID adj like a stamen
STAMMEL n coarse woollen cloth in former use for undergarments
STAMMELS > STAMMEL

STAMMER vb speak or say with involuntary pauses or repetition of syllables ▷ n tendency to stammer
STAMMERED > STAMMER
STAMMERER > STAMMER
STAMMERS > STAMMER
STAMNOI > STAMNOS
STAMNOS n ancient Greek jar
STAMP n piece of gummed paper stuck to an envelope or parcel ▷ vb bring (one's foot) down forcefully
STAMPED > STAMP
STAMPEDE n sudden rush of frightened animals or of a crowd ▷ vb (cause to) take part in a stampede
STAMPEDED > STAMPEDE
STAMPEDER > STAMPEDE
STAMPEDES > STAMPEDE
STAMPEDO same as > STAMPEDE
STAMPEDOS > STAMPEDO
STAMPER > STAMP
STAMPERS > STAMP
STAMPING > STAMP
STAMPINGS > STAMP
STAMPLESS > STAMP
STAMPS > STAMP
STANCE n attitude
STANCES > STANCE
STANCH vb stem the flow of (a liquid, esp blood) ▷ adj loyal and dependable
STANCHED > STANCH
STANCHEL same as > STANCHION
STANCHELS > STANCHEL
STANCHER > STANCH
STANCHERS > STANCH
STANCHES > STANCH
STANCHEST > STANCH
STANCHING > STANCH
STANCHION n upright bar used as a support ▷ vb provide or support with a stanchion or stanchions
STANCHLY > STANCH
STANCK adj faint
STAND vb be in, rise to, or place in an upright position ▷ n stall for the sale of goods
STANDARD n level of quality ▷ adj usual, regular, or average
STANDARDS > STANDARD
STANDAWAY adj erect
STANDBY n person or thing that is ready for use
STANDBYS > STANDBY
STANDDOWN n return to normal after alert
STANDEE n person who stands
STANDEES > STANDEE
STANDEN > STAND
STANDER > STAND
STANDERS > STAND
STANDFAST n reliable person or thing
STANDGALE same as > STANIEL
STANDING > STAND
STANDINGS > STAND
STANDISH n stand, usually of metal, for pens, ink bottles, etc

STANDOFF n act or an instance of standing off or apart ▷ vb stay at a distance

STANDOFFS > STANDOFF

STANDOUT n distinctive or outstanding person or thing

STANDOUTS > STANDOUT

STANDOVER n threatening or intimidating act

STANDPAT n (in poker) refusal to change one's card

STANDPIPE n tap attached to a water main to provide a public water supply

STANDS > STAND

STANDUP n comedian who performs solo

STANDUPS > STANDUP

STANE Scot word for > STONE

STANED > STANE

STANES > STANE

STANG vb sting

STANGED > STANG

STANGING > STANG

STANGS > STANG

STANHOPE n light one-seater carriage with two or four wheels

STANHOPES > STANHOPE

STANIEL n kestrel

STANIELS > STANIEL

STANINE n scale of nine levels

STANINES > STANINE

STANING > STANE

STANK vb dam

STANKED > STANK

STANKING > STANK

STANKS > STANK

STANNARY n place or region where tin is mined or worked

STANNATE n salt of stannic acid

STANNATES > STANNATE

STANNATOR n member of old Cornish parliament

STANNEL same as > STANIEL

STANNELS > STANNEL

STANNIC adj of or containing tin, esp in the tetravalent state

STANNITE n grey metallic mineral

STANNITES > STANNITE

STANNOUS adj of or containing tin, esp in the divalent state

STANNUM n tin (the metal)

STANNUMS > STANNUM

STANOL n drug taken to prevent heart disease

STANOLS > STANOL

STANYEL same as > STANIEL

STANYELS > STANYEL

STANZA n verse of a poem

STANZAED > STANZA

STANZAIC > STANZA

STANZAS > STANZA

STANZE same as > STANZA

STANZES > STANZE

STANZO same as > STANZA

STANZOES > STANZO

STANZOS > STANZO

STAP same as > STOP

STAPEDES > STAPES

STAPEDIAL > STAPES

STAPEDII > STAPEDIUS

STAPEDIUS n muscle in the stapes

STAPELIA n fleshy cactus-like leafless African plant

STAPELIAS > STAPELIA

STAPES n stirrup-shaped bone in the middle ear of mammals

STAPH n staphylococcus

STAPHS > STAPH

STAPLE n U-shaped piece of metal used to fasten papers ▷ vb fasten with staples ▷ adj of prime importance

STAPLED > STAPLE

STAPLER n small device for fastening papers together

STAPLERS > STAPLER

STAPLES > STAPLE

STAPLING n as in stomach stapling surgical treatment for obesity

STAPLINGS > STAPLING

STAPPED > STAP

STAPPING > STAP

STAPPLE same as > STOPPLE

STAPPLES > STAPPLE

STAPS > STAP

STAR n hot gaseous mass in space, visible in the night sky as a point of light ▷ vb feature or be featured as a star ▷ adj leading, famous

STARAGEN n tarragon

STARAGENS > STARAGEN

STARBOARD n right-hand side of a ship, when facing forward ▷ adj of or on this side ▷ vb turn or be turned towards the starboard

STARBURST n pattern of rays or lines radiating from a light source

STARCH n carbohydrate forming the main food element in bread, potatoes, etc ▷ vb stiffen (fabric) with starch ▷ adj (of a person) formal

STARCHED > STARCH

STARCHER > STARCH

STARCHERS > STARCH

STARCHES > STARCH

STARCHIER > STARCHY

STARCHILY > STARCHY

STARCHING > STARCH

STARCHY adj containing starch

STARDOM n status of a star in the entertainment or sports world

STARDOMS > STARDOM

STARDRIFT n regular movement of stars

STARDUST n dusty material found between the stars

STARDUSTS > STARDUST

STARE vb look or gaze fixedly (at) ▷ n fixed gaze

STARED > STARE

STARER > STARE

STARERS > STARE

STARES > STARE

STARETS n Russian holy man

STARETSES > STARETS

STARETZ same as > STARETS

STARETZES > STARETZ

STARFISH n star-shaped sea creature

STARFRUIT n tree with edible yellow fruit which is star-shaped on cross section

STARGAZE vb observe the stars

STARGAZED > STARGAZE

STARGAZER > STARGAZE

STARGAZES > STARGAZE

STARGAZEY adj as in stargazey pie Cornish fish pie

STARING > STARE

STARINGLY > STARE

STARINGS > STARE

STARK adj harsh, unpleasant, and plain ▷ adv completely ▷ vb stiffen

STARKED > STARK

STARKEN vb become or make stark

STARKENED > STARKEN

STARKENS > STARKEN

STARKER > STARK

STARKERS adj completely naked

STARKEST > STARK

STARKING > STARK

STARKLY > STARK

STARKNESS > STARK

STARKS > STARK

STARLESS > STAR

STARLET n young actress presented as a future star

STARLETS > STARLET

STARLIGHT n light that comes from the stars ▷ adj of or like starlight

STARLIKE > STAR

STARLING n songbird with glossy black speckled feathers

STARLINGS > STARLING

STARLIT same as > STARLIGHT

STARN same as > STERN

STARNED > STARN

STARNIE n Scots word for little star

STARNIES > STARNIE

STARNING > STARN

STARNOSE n American mole with starlike nose

STARNOSES > STARNOSE

STARNS > STARN

STAROSTA n headman of Russian village

STAROSTAS > STAROSTA

STAROSTY n estate of Polish nobleman

STARR n (in Judaism) release from a debt

STARRED > STAR

STARRIER > STARRY

STARRIEST > STARRY

STARRILY > STARRY

STARRING > STAR

STARRINGS > STARE

STARRS > STARR

STARRY adj full of or like stars

STARS > STAR

STARSHINE n starlight

STARSHIP n spacecraft in science fiction

STARSHIPS > STARSHIP

STARSPOT n dark patch on surface of star

STARSPOTS > STARSPOT

STARSTONE n precious stone reflecting light in starlike pattern

START vb take the first step, begin ▷ n first part of something

STARTED > START

STARTER n first course of a meal

STARTERS > STARTER

STARTFUL adj tending to start

STARTING > START

STARTINGS > START

STARTISH same as > STARTFUL

STARTLE vb slightly surprise or frighten

STARTLED > STARTLE

STARTLER > STARTLE

STARTLERS > STARTLE

STARTLES > STARTLE

STARTLIER > STARTLY

STARTLING adj causing surprise or fear

STARTLISH adj easily startled

STARTLY adj (of a horse) prone to starting

STARTS > START

STARTSY > STARETS

STARTUP n business enterprise that has been launched recently

STARTUPS > STARTUP

STARVE vb die or suffer or cause to die or suffer from hunger

STARVED > STARVE

STARVER > STARVE

STARVERS > STARVE

STARVES > STARVE

STARVING > STARVE

STARVINGS > STARVE

STARWORT n plant with star-shaped flowers

STARWORTS > STARWORT

STASES > STASIS

STASH vb store in a secret place ▷ n secret store

STASHED > STASH

STASHES > STASH

STASHIE same as > STUSHIE

STASHIES > STASHIE

STASHING > STASH

STASIDION n stall in Greek church

STASIMA > STASIMON

STASIMON n ode sung in Greek tragedy

STASIS n stagnation in the normal flow of bodily fluids

STAT n statistic

STATABLE > STATE

STATAL adj of a federal state

STATANT adj (of an animal) in profile with all four feet on the ground

STATE n condition of a person or thing ▷ adj of or

concerning the State ▷ *vb* express in words

STATEABLE > STATE

STATED *adj* (esp of a sum) determined by agreement

STATEDLY > STATED

STATEHOOD > STATE

STATELESS *adj* not belonging to any country

STATELET *n* small state

STATELETS > STATELET

STATELIER > STATELY

STATELILY > STATELY

STATELY *adj* dignified or grand ▷ *adv* in a stately manner

STATEMENT *n* something stated ▷ *vb* assess (a pupil) with regard to his or her special educational needs

STATER *n* any of various usually silver coins of ancient Greece

STATEROOM *n* private cabin on a ship

STATERS > STATER

STATES > STATE

STATESIDE *adv* of, in, to, or towards the US

STATESMAN *n* experienced and respected political leader

STATESMEN > STATESMAN

STATEWIDE *adj* throughout a state

STATIC *adj* stationary or inactive ▷ *n* crackling sound or speckled picture caused by interference in radio or TV reception

STATICAL > STATIC

STATICE *n* plant name formerly used for both thrift and sea lavender

STATICES > STATICE

STATICKY *adj* characterized by static

STATICS *n* study of the forces producing a state of equilibrium

STATIM *adv* right away

STATIN *n* type of drug that lowers the levels of low-density lipoproteins in the blood

STATING > STATE

STATINS > STATIN

STATION *n* place where trains stop for passengers ▷ *vb* assign (someone) to a particular place

STATIONAL > STATION

STATIONED > STATION

STATIONER *n* dealer in stationery

STATIONS > STATION

STATISM *n* theory or practice of concentrating economic and political power in the state

STATISMS > STATISM

STATIST *n* advocate of statism ▷ *adj* of, characteristic of, advocating, or relating to statism

STATISTIC *n* numerical fact collected and classified systematically

STATISTS > STATIST

STATIVE *adj* denoting a verb describing a state rather than an activity, act, or event ▷ *n* stative verb

STATIVES > STATIVE

STATOCYST *n* organ of balance in some invertebrates

STATOLITH *n* any of the granules of calcium carbonate occurring in a statocyst

STATOR *n* stationary part of a rotary machine or device

STATORS > STATOR

STATS > STAT

STATTO *n* person preoccupied with the facts and figures of a subject

STATTOS > STATTO

STATUA *same as* > STATUE

STATUARY *n* statues collectively ▷ *adj* of, relating to, or suitable for statues

STATUAS > STATUA

STATUE *n* large sculpture of a human or animal figure

STATUED *adj* decorated with or portrayed in a statue or statues

STATUES > STATUE

STATUETTE *n* small statue

STATURE *n* person's height

STATURED *adj* having stature

STATURES > STATURE

STATUS *n* social position

STATUSES > STATUS

STATUSIER > STATUSY

STATUSY *adj* conferring or having status

STATUTE *n* written law

STATUTES > STATUTE

STATUTORY *adj* required or authorized by law

STAUMREL *n* stupid person

STAUMRELS > STAUMREL

STAUN *Scot word for* > STAND

STAUNCH *same as* > STANCH

STAUNCHED > STAUNCH

STAUNCHER > STAUNCH

STAUNCHES > STAUNCH

STAUNCHLY > STAUNCH

STAUNING > STAUN

STAUNS > STAUN

STAVE *same as* > STAFF

STAVED > STAVE

STAVES > STAVE

STAVING > STAVE

STAVUDINE *n* drug used to treat HIV

STAW *Scots form of* > STALL

STAWED > STAW

STAWING > STAW

STAWS > STAW

STAY *vb* remain in a place or condition ▷ *n* period of staying in a place

STAYAWAY *n* strike in South Africa

STAYAWAYS > STAYAWAY

STAYED > STAY

STAYER *n* person or thing that stays

STAYERS > STAYER

STAYING > STAY

STAYLESS *adj* with no stays or support

STAYMAKER *n* corset maker

STAYNE *same as* > STAIN

STAYNED > STAYNE

STAYNES > STAYNE

STAYNING > STAYNE

STAYRE *same as* > STAIR

STAYRES > STAYRE

STAYS *pl n* old-fashioned corsets with bones in them

STAYSAIL *n* sail fastened on a stay

STAYSAILS > STAYSAIL

STEAD *n* place or function that should be taken by another ▷ *vb* help or benefit

STEADED > STEAD

STEADFAST *adj* firm, determined

STEADIED > STEADY

STEADIER > STEADY

STEADIERS > STEADY

STEADIES > STEADY

STEADIEST > STEADY

STEADILY > STEADY

STEADING *n* farmstead

STEADINGS > STEADING

STEADS > STEAD

STEADY *adj* not shaky or wavering ▷ *vb* make steady ▷ *adv* in a steady manner

STEADYING > STEADY

STEAK *n* thick slice of meat, esp beef

STEAKETTE *n* thin minced beef patty

STEAKS > STEAK

STEAL *vb* take unlawfully or without permission

STEALABLE > STEAL

STEALAGE *n* theft

STEALAGES > STEALAGE

STEALE *n* handle

STEALED > STEAL

STEALER *n* person who steals something

STEALERS > STEALER

STEALES > STEALE

STEALING > STEAL

STEALINGS > STEAL

STEALS > STEAL

STEALT > STEAL

STEALTH *n* moving carefully and quietly ▷ *adj* (of technology) able to render an aircraft almost invisible to radar ▷ *vb* approach undetected

STEALTHED > STEALTH

STEALTHS > STEALTH

STEALTHY *adj* characterized by great caution, secrecy, etc

STEAM *n* vapour into which water changes when boiled ▷ *vb* give off steam

STEAMBOAT *n* boat powered by a steam engine

STEAMED > STEAM

STEAMER *n* steam-propelled ship ▷ *vb* travel by steamer

STEAMERED > STEAMER

STEAMERS > STEAMER

STEAMIE *n* public wash house

STEAMIER > STEAMY

STEAMIES > STEAMIE

STEAMIEST > STEAMY

STEAMILY > STEAMY

STEAMING *adj* very hot ▷ *n* robbery by a large gang of youths

STEAMINGS > STEAMING

STEAMPUNK *n* subgenre of science fiction set in Victorian times

STEAMROLL *vb* crush (opposition) by overpowering force

STEAMS > STEAM

STEAMSHIP *n* ship powered by steam engines

STEAMY *adj* full of steam

STEAN *n* earthenware vessel

STEANE *same as* > STEEN

STEANED > STEANE

STEANES > STEANE

STEANING > STEANE

STEANINGS > STEANE

STEANS > STEAN

STEAPSIN *n* pancreatic lipase

STEAPSINS > STEAPSIN

STEAR *same as* > STEER

STEARAGE *same as* > STEERAGE

STEARAGES > STEARAGE

STEARATE *n* any salt or ester of stearic acid

STEARATES > STEARATE

STEARD > STEAR

STEARE *same as* > STEER

STEARED > STEARE

STEARES > STEARE

STEARIC *adj* of or relating to suet or fat

STEARIN *n* colourless crystalline ester of glycerol and stearic acid

STEARINE *same as* > STEARIN

STEARINES > STEARINE

STEARING > STEAR

STEARINS > STEARIN

STEARS > STEAR

STEARSMAN *same as* > STEERSMAN

STEARSMEN > STEARSMAN

STEATITE *same as* > SOAPSTONE

STEATITES > STEATITE

STEATITIC > STEATITE

STEATOMA *n* tumour of sebaceous gland

STEATOMAS > STEATOMA

STEATOSES > STEATOSIS

STEATOSIS *n* abnormal accumulation of fat

STED *same as* > STEAD

STEDD *same as* > STEAD

STEDDE *same as* > STEAD

STEDDED > STED

STEDDES > STEDDE

STEDDIED > STEDDY

STEDDIES > STEDDY

STEDDING > STED

STEDDS > STEDD

STEDDY *same as* > STEADY

STEDDYING > STEDDY

STEDE *same as* > STEAD

STEDED > STEDE

STEDES > STEDE

STEDFAST *same as* > STEADFAST

STEDING > STEDE
STEDS > STED
STEED same as > STEAD
STEEDED > STEED
STEEDIED > STEEDY
STEEDIES > STEEDY
STEEDING > STEED
STEEDLIKE > STEED
STEEDS > STEED
STEEDY same as > STEADY
STEEDYING > STEEDY
STEEK vb Scots word meaning shut
STEEKED > STEEK
STEEKING > STEEK
STEEKIT > STEEK
STEEKS > STEEK
STEEL n hard malleable alloy of iron and carbon ▷ vb prepare (oneself) for something unpleasant
STEELBOW n material lent to tenant by landlord
STEELBOWS > STEELBOW
STEELD > STEEL
STEELED > STEEL
STEELHEAD n silvery North Pacific variety of the rainbow trout
STEELIE n steel ball bearing used as marble
STEELIER > STEEL
STEELIES > STEELIE
STEELIEST > STEELIE
STEELING > STEEL
STEELINGS > STEEL
STEELMAN n person working in steel industry
STEELMEN > STEELMAN
STEELS pl n shares and bonds of steel companies
STEELWARE n things made of steel
STEELWORK n frame, foundation, building, or article made of steel
STEELY > STEEL
STEELYARD n portable balance consisting of a pivoted bar with two unequal arms
STEEM variant of > ESTEEM
STEEMED > STEEM
STEEMING > STEEM
STEEMS > STEEM
STEEN vb line with stone
STEENBOK n small antelope of central and southern Africa
STEENBOKS > STEENBOK
STEENBRAS n variety of sea bream
STEENBUCK same as > STEENBOK
STEENED > STEEN
STEENING > STEEN
STEENINGS > STEEN
STEENKIRK n type of cravat
STEENS > STEEN
STEEP adj sloping sharply ▷ vb soak or be soaked in liquid ▷ n instance or the process of steeping
STEEPED > STEEP
STEEPEN vb become steep or steeper
STEEPENED > STEEPEN

STEEPENS > STEEPEN
STEEPER > STEEP
STEEPERS > STEEP
STEEPEST > STEEP
STEEPEUP adj very steep
STEEPIER > STEEPY
STEEPIEST > STEEPY
STEEPING > STEEP
STEEPISH > STEEP
STEEPLE same as > SPIRE
STEEPLED > STEEPLE
STEEPLES > STEEPLE
STEEPLING adj going up on a steep trajectory
STEEPLY > STEEP
STEEPNESS > STEEP
STEEPS > STEEP
STEEPUP adj very steep
STEEPY same as > STEEP
STEER vb direct the course of (a vehicle or ship) ▷ n castrated male ox
STEERABLE > STEER
STEERAGE n cheapest accommodation on a passenger ship
STEERAGES > STEERAGE
STEERED > STEER
STEERER > STEER
STEERERS > STEER
STEERIER > STEERY
STEERIES > STEERY
STEERIEST > STEERY
STEERING > STEER
STEERINGS > STEER
STEERLING n young steer
STEERS > STEER
STEERSMAN n person who steers a vessel
STEERSMEN > STEERSMAN
STEERY n commotion ▷ adj busy or bustling
STEEVE n spar having a pulley block at one end ▷ vb stow (cargo) securely in the hold of a ship
STEEVED > STEEVE
STEEVELY > STEEVE
STEEVER > STEEVE
STEEVES > STEEVE
STEEVEST > STEEVE
STEEVING > STEEVE
STEEVINGS > STEEVE
STEGNOSES > STEGNOSIS
STEGNOSIS n constriction of bodily pores
STEGNOTIC n medicine that stops bleeding
STEGODON n mammal of Pliocene to Pleistocene times, similar to the mastodon
STEGODONS > STEGODON
STEGODONT same as > STEGODON
STEGOMYIA former name for > AEDES
STEGOSAUR n quadrupedal herbivorous dinosaur
STEIL same as > STEAL
STEILS > STEIL
STEIN same as > STEEN
STEINBOCK another name for > IBEX
STEINBOK same as > STEENBOK
STEINBOKS > STEINBOK

STEINED > STEIN
STEINING > STEIN
STEININGS > STEIN
STEINKIRK same as > STEENKIRK
STEINS > STEIN
STELA same as > STELE
STELAE > STELA
STELAI > STELA
STELAR > STELE
STELE n upright stone slab or column decorated with figures or inscriptions
STELENE > STELE
STELES > STELE
STELIC > STELE
STELL n shelter for cattle or sheep built on moorland or hillsides ▷ vb position or place
STELLA n star or something star-shaped
STELLAR adj of stars
STELLAS > STELLA
STELLATE adj resembling a star in shape
STELLATED same as > STELLATE
STELLED > STELL
STELLERID n starfish
STELLIFY vb change or be changed into a star
STELLING > STELL
STELLIO n as in stellio lizard type of lizard
STELLION n Mediterranean lizard
STELLIONS > STELLION
STELLITE n alloy containing cobalt, chromium, carbon, tungsten, and molybdenum
STELLITES > STELLITE
STELLS > STELL
STELLULAR adj displaying or abounding in small stars
STEM vb stop (the flow of something) ▷ n main axis of a plant, which bears the leaves, axillary buds, and flowers
STEMBOK same as > STEENBOK
STEMBOKS > STEMBOK
STEMBUCK same as > STEENBOK
STEMBUCKS > STEMBUCK
STEME same as > STEAM
STEMED > STEME
STEMES > STEME
STEMHEAD n head of the stem of a vessel
STEMHEADS > STEMHEAD
STEMING > STEME
STEMLESS > STEM
STEMLET n little stem
STEMLETS > STEMLET
STEMLIKE > STEM
STEMMA n family tree
STEMMAS > STEMMA
STEMMATA > STEMMA
STEMMATIC > STEMMA
STEMME archaic variant of > STEM
STEMMED > STEM
STEMMER > STEM
STEMMERS > STEM

STEMMERY n tobacco factory
STEMMES > STEMME
STEMMIER > STEMMY
STEMMIEST > STEMMY
STEMMING > STEM
STEMMINGS > STEM
STEMMY adj (of wine) young and raw
STEMPEL n timber support
STEMPELS > STEMPEL
STEMPLE same as > STEMPEL
STEMPLES > STEMPLE
STEMS > STEM
STEMSON n curved timber at the bow of a wooden vessel
STEMSONS > STEMSON
STEMWARE n collective term for glasses, goblets, etc with stems
STEMWARES > STEMWARE
STEN vb stride
STENCH n foul smell ▷ vb cause to smell
STENCHED > STENCH
STENCHES > STENCH
STENCHFUL > STENCH
STENCHIER > STENCH
STENCHING > STENCH
STENCHY > STENCH
STENCIL n thin sheet through which ink passes to form a pattern on the surface below ▷ vb make (a pattern) with a stencil
STENCILED > STENCIL
STENCILER > STENCIL
STENCILS > STENCIL
STEND vb Scots word meaning bound
STENDED > STEND
STENDING > STEND
STENDS > STEND
STENGAH same as > STINGER
STENGAHS > STENGAH
STENLOCK n fish of northern seas
STENLOCKS > STENLOCK
STENNED > STEN
STENNING > STEN
STENO n stenographer
STENOBATH n stenobathic organism
STENOKIES > STENOKY
STENOKOUS adj able to live in narrow range of environments
STENOKY n survival dependent on conditions remaining within a narrow range of variables
STENOPAIC adj having a narrow opening
STENOS > STENO
STENOSED adj abnormally contracted
STENOSES > STENOSIS
STENOSING adj causing or characterized by stenosis
STENOSIS n abnormal narrowing of a bodily canal or passage
STENOTIC > STENOSIS
STENOTYPE n machine with a keyboard for recording

S

speeches in a phonetic shorthand

STENOTYPY n form of shorthand in which alphabetic combinations are used to represent groups of sounds or short common words

STENS > STEN

STENT n surgical implant used to keep an artery open ▷ vb assess

STENTED > STENT

STENTING > STENT

STENTOR n person with an unusually loud voice

STENTORS > STENTOR

STENTOUR n tax assessor

STENTOURS > STENTOUR

STENTS > STENT

STEP vb move and set down the foot, as when walking ▷ n stepping

STEPBAIRN Scots word for > STEPCHILD

STEPCHILD n stepson or stepdaughter

STEPDAD n stepfather

STEPDADS > STEPDAD

STEPDAME n woman married to one's father

STEPDAMES > STEPDAME

STEPHANE n ancient Greek headdress

STEPHANES > STEPHANE

STEPLESS adj without steps

STEPLIKE > STEP

STEPMOM n stepmother

STEPMOMS > STEPMOM

STEPNEY n spare wheel

STEPNEYS > STEPNEY

STEPOVER n (in football) instance of raising the foot over the ball as a feint

STEPOVERS > STEPOVER

STEPPE n extensive grassy plain usually without trees

STEPPED > STEP

STEPPER n person who or animal that steps, esp a horse or a dancer

STEPPERS > STEPPER

STEPPES > STEPPE

STEPPING > STEP

STEPS > STEP

STEPSON n son of one's spouse by an earlier relationship

STEPSONS > STEPSON

STEPSTOOL n stool able to be used as step

STEPT > STEP

STEPWISE adj arranged in the manner of or resembling steps ▷ adv with the form or appearance of steps

STERADIAN n SI unit of solid angle

STERANE n any of a class of hydrocarbons found in crude oils

STERANES > STERANE

STERCORAL adj relating to excrement

STERCULIA n dietary fibre used as a food stabilizer and denture adhesive

STERE n unit used to measure volumes of stacked timber

STEREO n stereophonic record player ▷ adj feeding two loudspeakers through separate channels ▷ vb make stereophonic

STEREOED > STEREO

STEREOING > STEREO

STEREOME n tissue of a plant that provides mechanical support

STEREOMES > STEREOME

STEREOS > STEREO

STERES > STERE

STERIC adj of or caused by the spatial arrangement of atoms in a molecule

STERICAL same as > STERIC

STERIGMA n minute stalk bearing a spore or chain of spores in certain fungi

STERIGMAS > STERIGMA

STERILANT n any substance or agent used in sterilization

STERILE adj free from germs

STERILELY > STERILE

STERILISE same as > STERILIZE

STERILITY > STERILE

STERILIZE vb make sterile

STERLET n small sturgeon of N Asia and E Europe

STERLETS > STERLET

STERLING n British money system ▷ adj genuine and reliable

STERLINGS > STERLING

STERN adj severe, strict ▷ n rear part of a ship ▷ vb row boat backward

STERNA > STERNUM

STERNAGE n sterns

STERNAGES > STERNAGE

STERNAL > STERNUM

STERNEBRA n part of breastbone

STERNED > STERN

STERNER > STERN

STERNEST > STERN

STERNFAST n rope for securing boat at stern

STERNING > STERN

STERNITE n part of an arthropod

STERNITES > STERNITE

STERNITIC > STERNITE

STERNLY > STERN

STERNMOST adj farthest to the stern

STERNNESS > STERN

STERNPORT n opening in stern of ship

STERNPOST n main upright timber or structure at the stern of a vessel

STERNS > STERN

STERNSON n timber bolted to the sternpost and keelson at the stern of a wooden vessel

STERNSONS > STERNSON

STERNUM n long flat bone to which most of the ribs are attached

STERNUMS > STERNUM

STERNWARD adv towards the stern

STERNWAY n movement of a vessel sternforemost

STERNWAYS > STERNWAY

STEROID n organic compound containing a carbon ring system

STEROIDAL > STEROID

STEROIDS > STEROID

STEROL n natural insoluble alcohol such as cholesterol and ergosterol

STEROLS > STEROL

STERTOR n laborious or noisy breathing

STERTORS > STERTOR

STERVE same as > STARVE

STERVED > STERVE

STERVES > STERVE

STERVING > STERVE

STET interj instruction to ignore an alteration previously made ▷ vb indicate to a printer that deleted matter is to be kept ▷ n mark indicating that deleted matter is to be kept

STETS > STET

STETSON n cowboy hat

STETSONS > STETSON

STETTED > STET

STETTING > STET

STEVEDORE n person who loads and unloads ships ▷ vb load or unload (a ship, ship's cargo, etc)

STEVEN n voice

STEVENS > STEVEN

STEVIA n any of a genus of plant with sweet leaves

STEVIAS > STEVIA

STEW n food cooked slowly in a closed pot ▷ vb cook slowly in a closed pot

STEWABLE > STEW

STEWARD n person who looks after passengers on a ship or aircraft ▷ vb act as a steward (of)

STEWARDED > STEWARD

STEWARDRY n office of steward

STEWARDS > STEWARD

STEWARTRY variant of > STEWARDRY

STEWBUM n drunkard

STEWBUMS > STEWBUM

STEWED adj (of food) cooked by stewing

STEWER > STEW

STEWERS > STEW

STEWIER > STEW

STEWIEST > STEW

STEWING > STEW

STEWINGS > STEW

STEWPAN n pan used for making stew

STEWPANS > STEWPAN

STEWPOND n fishpond

STEWPONDS > STEWPOND

STEWPOT n pot used for making stew

STEWPOTS > STEWPOT

STEWS > STEW

STEWY > STEW

STEY adj (Scots) steep ▷ n ladder

STEYER > STEY

STEYEST > STEY

STEYS > STEY

STHENIA n abnormal strength

STHENIAS > STHENIA

STHENIC adj abounding in energy or bodily strength

STIBBLE Scots form of > STUBBLE

STIBBLER n horse allowed to eat stubble

STIBBLERS > STIBBLE

STIBBLES > STIBBLE

STIBIAL > STIBIUM

STIBINE n colourless slightly soluble poisonous gas

STIBINES > STIBINE

STIBIUM obsolete name for > ANTIMONY

STIBIUMS > STIBIUM

STIBNITE n soft greyish mineral

STIBNITES > STIBNITE

STICCADO n type of xylophone

STICCADOS > STICCADO

STICCATO same as > STICCADO

STICCATOS > STICCATO

STICH n line of poetry

STICHARIA pl n priest's robes of the Greek Church

STICHERA > STICHERON

STICHERON n short hymn in the Greek Church

STICHIC > STICH

STICHIDIA pl n seaweed branches

STICHOI > STICHOS

STICHOS n line of poem

STICHS > STICH

STICK n long thin piece of wood ▷ vb push (a pointed object) into (something)

STICKABLE > STICK

STICKBALL n form of baseball played in the street

STICKED > STICK

STICKER n adhesive label or sign ▷ vb put stickers on

STICKERED > STICKER

STICKERS > STICKER

STICKFUL > STICK

STICKFULS > STICK

STICKIE n notepaper with an adhesive strip

STICKIED > STICKY

STICKIER > STICKY

STICKIES > STICKIE

STICKIEST > STICKY

STICKILY > STICKY

STICKING > STICK

STICKINGS > STICK

STICKIT Scots form of > STUCK

STICKJAW n stodgy food

STICKJAWS > STICKJAW

STICKLE vb dispute stubbornly, esp about minor points

STICKLED > STICKLE

STICKLER n person who insists on something

STICKLERS > STICKLER

STICKLES > STICKLE

STICKLIKE > STICK

STICKLING n act of making insistent demands

STICKMAN n human figure drawn in thin strokes

STICKMEN > STICKMAN

STICKOUT n conspicuous person or thing

STICKOUTS > STICKOUT

STICKPIN n tiepin

STICKPINS > STICKPIN

STICKS > STICK

STICKSEED n type of Eurasian and North American plant

STICKUM n adhesive

STICKUMS > STICKUM

STICKUP n robbery at gun-point

STICKUPS > STICKUP

STICKWEED n any of several plants that have clinging fruits or seeds, esp the ragweed

STICKWORK n use of stick in hockey

STICKY adj covered with an adhesive substance ▷ vb make sticky ▷ n inquisitive look or stare

STICKYING > STICKY

STICTION n frictional force to be overcome to set one object in motion when it is in contact with another

STICTIONS > STICTION

STIDDIE same as > STITHY

STIDDIED > STIDDIE

STIDDIES > STIDDIE

STIE same as > STY

STIED > STY

STIES > STY

STIEVE same as > STEEVE

STIEVELY > STIEVE

STIEVER > STIEVE

STIEVEST > STIEVE

STIFF adj not easily bent or moved ▷ n loser or failure ▷ adv completely or utterly ▷ vb fail completely

STIFFED > STIFF

STIFFEN vb make or become stiff

STIFFENED > STIFFEN

STIFFENER > STIFFEN

STIFFENS > STIFFEN

STIFFER > STIFF

STIFFEST > STIFF

STIFFIE n vulgar word for an erection of the penis

STIFFIES > STIFFIE

STIFFING > STIFF

STIFFISH > STIFF

STIFFLY > STIFF

STIFFNESS > STIFF

STIFFS > STIFF

STIFFWARE n computer software that is hard to modify

STIFFY n vulgar word for an erection of the penis

STIFLE vb suppress ▷ n joint in the hind leg of a horse, dog, etc

STIFLED > STIFLE

STIFLER > STIFLE

STIFLERS > STIFLE

STIFLES > STIFLE

STIFLING adj uncomfortably hot and stuffy

STIFLINGS > STIFLING

STIGMA n mark of social disgrace

STIGMAL adj of part of insect wing

STIGMAS > STIGMA

STIGMATA > STIGMA

STIGMATIC adj relating to or having a stigma or stigmata ▷ n person marked with the stigmata

STIGME n dot in Greek punctuation

STIGMES > STIGME

STILB n unit of luminance

STILBENE n colourless or slightly yellow crystalline hydrocarbon used in the manufacture of dyes

STILBENES > STILBENE

STILBITE n white or yellow zeolite mineral

STILBITES > STILBITE

STILBS > STILB

STILE same as > STYLE

STILED > STILE

STILES > STILE

STILET same as > STYLET

STILETS > STILET

STILETTO n small narrow dagger ▷ vb stab with a stiletto

STILETTOS > STILETTO

STILING > STILE

STILL adv now or in the future as before ▷ adj motionless ▷ n calmness; apparatus for distillation ▷ vb make still

STILLAGE n frame or stand for keeping things off the ground, such as casks in a brewery

STILLAGES > STILLAGE

STILLBORN adj born dead ▷ n stillborn fetus or baby

STILLED > STILL

STILLER > STILL

STILLERS > STILL

STILLEST > STILL

STILLIER > STILLY

STILLIEST > STILLY

STILLING > STILL

STILLINGS > STILL

STILLION n stand for cask

STILLIONS > STILLION

STILLMAN n someone involved in the operation of a still

STILLMEN > STILLMAN

STILLNESS > STILL

STILLROOM n room in which distilling is carried out

STILLS > STILL

STILLSON n type of wrench

STILLSONS > STILLSON

STILLY adv quietly or calmly ▷ adj still, quiet, or calm

STILT n either of a pair of long poles with footrests for walking raised from the

ground ▷ vb raise or place on or as if on stilts

STILTBIRD n long-legged wading bird

STILTED adj stiff and formal in manner

STILTEDLY > STILTED

STILTER > STILT

STILTERS > STILT

STILTIER > STILT

STILTIEST > STILT

STILTING > STILT

STILTINGS > STILT

STILTISH > STILT

STILTLIKE adj like a stilt

STILTS > STILT

STILTY > STILT

STIM n very small amount

STIME same as > STYME

STIMED > STIME

STIMES > STIME

STIMIE same as > STYMIE

STIMIED > STIMIE

STIMIES > STIMIE

STIMING > STIME

STIMS > STIM

STIMULANT n something, such as a drug, that acts as a stimulus ▷ adj stimulating

STIMULATE vb act as a stimulus (on)

STIMULI > STIMULUS

STIMULUS n something that rouses a person or thing to activity

STIMY same as > STYMIE

STIMYING > STIMY

STING vb (of certain animals or plants) wound by injecting with poison ▷ n wound or pain caused by or as if by stinging

STINGAREE popular name for > STINGRAY

STINGBULL n spiny fish

STINGE n stingy or miserly person

STINGED > STING

STINGER n person, plant, animal, etc, that stings or hurts

STINGERS > STINGER

STINGES > STINGE

STINGFISH same as > STINGBULL

STINGIER > STINGY

STINGIES > STINGY

STINGIEST > STINGY

STINGILY > STINGY

STINGING > STING

STINGINGS > STING

STINGLESS > STING

STINGO n strong alcohol

STINGOS > STINGO

STINGRAY n flatfish capable of inflicting painful wounds

STINGRAYS > STINGRAY

STINGS > STING

STINGY adj mean or miserly ▷ n stinging nettle

STINK n strong unpleasant smell ▷ vb give off a strong unpleasant smell

STINKARD n smelly person

STINKARDS > STINKARD

STINKBIRD same as > HOATZIN

STINKBUG n type of insect that releases an unpleasant odour

STINKBUGS > STINKBUG

STINKER n difficult or unpleasant person or thing

STINKEROO n bad or contemptible person or thing

STINKERS > STINKER

STINKHORN n type of fungus with an offensive odour

STINKIER > STINKY

STINKIEST > STINKY

STINKING > STINK

STINKO adj drunk

STINKPOT n thing that stinks

STINKPOTS > STINKPOT

STINKS > STINK

STINKWEED n plant that has a disagreeable smell when bruised

STINKWOOD n any of various trees having offensive-smelling wood

STINKY adj having a foul smell

STINT vb be miserly with (something) ▷ n allotted amount of work

STINTED > STINT

STINTEDLY > STINT

STINTER > STINT

STINTERS > STINT

STINTIER > STINT

STINTIEST > STINT

STINTING > STINT

STINTINGS > STINT

STINTLESS > STINT

STINTS > STINT

STINTY > STINT

STIPA n variety of grass

STIPAS > STIPA

STIPE n stalk in plants that bears reproductive structures

STIPED same as > STIPITATE

STIPEL n small paired leaflike structure at the base of certain leaflets

STIPELS > STIPEL

STIPEND n regular allowance or salary

STIPENDS > STIPEND

STIPES n second maxillary segment in insects and crustaceans

STIPIFORM > STIPES

STIPITATE adj possessing or borne on the end of a stipe

STIPITES > STIPES

STIPPLE vb paint, draw, or engrave using dots ▷ n technique of stippling

STIPPLED > STIPPLE

STIPPLER > STIPPLE

STIPPLERS > STIPPLE

STIPPLES > STIPPLE

STIPPLING > STIPPLE

STIPULAR > STIPULE

STIPULARY > STIPULE

STIPULATE vb specify as a condition of an agreement ▷ adj (of a plant) having stipules

S

STIPULE n small paired usually leaflike outgrowth occurring at the base of a leaf or its stalk
STIPULED > STIPULE
STIPULES > STIPULE
STIR vb mix up (a liquid) by moving a spoon etc around in it ▷ n stirring
STIRABOUT n kind of porridge originally made in Ireland
STIRE same as > STEER
STIRED > STIRE
STIRES > STIRE
STIRING > STIRE
STIRK n heifer of 6 to 12 months old
STIRKS > STIRK
STIRLESS > STIR
STIRP same as > STIRPS
STIRPES > STIRPS
STIRPS n line of descendants from an ancestor
STIRRA same as > SIRRA
STIRRABLE > STIR
STIRRAH same as > SIRRAH
STIRRAHS > STIRRAH
STIRRAS > STIRRA
STIRRE same as > STEER
STIRRED > STIR
STIRRER n person who deliberately causes trouble
STIRRERS > STIRRER
STIRRES > STIRRE
STIRRING > STIR
STIRRINGS > STIR
STIRRUP n metal loop attached to a saddle for supporting a rider's foot
STIRRUPS > STIRRUP
STIRS > STIR
STISHIE same as > STUSHIE
STISHIES > STISHIE
STITCH n link made by drawing thread through material with a needle ▷ vb sew
STITCHED > STITCH
STITCHER > STITCH
STITCHERS > STITCH
STITCHERY n needlework, esp modern embroidery
STITCHES > STITCH
STITCHING > STITCH
STITHIED > STITHY
STITHIES > STITHY
STITHY n forge or anvil ▷ vb forge on an anvil
STITHYING > STITHY
STIVE vb stifle
STIVED > STIVE
STIVER n former Dutch coin
STIVERS > STIVER
STIVES > STIVE
STIVIER > STIVY
STIVIEST > STIVY
STIVING > STIVE
STIVY adj stuffy
STOA n covered walk that has a colonnade on one or both sides
STOAE > STOA
STOAI > STOA
STOAS > STOA

STOAT n small mammal of the weasel family
STOATS > STOAT
STOB same as > STAB
STOBBED > STOB
STOBBING > STOB
STOBIE adj as in stobie pole steel and concrete pole for supporting electricity wires
STOBS > STOB
STOCCADO n fencing thrust
STOCCADOS > STOCCADO
STOCCATA same as > STOCCADO
STOCCATAS > STOCCATA
STOCIOUS same as > STOTIOUS
STOCK n total amount of goods available for sale in a shop ▷ adj kept in stock, standard ▷ vb keep for sale or future use
STOCKADE n enclosure or barrier made of stakes ▷ vb surround with a stockade
STOCKADED > STOCKADE
STOCKADES > STOCKADE
STOCKAGE n livestock put to graze on crops
STOCKAGES > STOCKAGE
STOCKCAR n car that has been strengthened for a form of racing in which the cars often collide
STOCKCARS > STOCKCAR
STOCKED > STOCK
STOCKER > STOCK
STOCKERS > STOCK
STOCKFISH n fish, such as cod or haddock, cured by splitting and drying in the air
STOCKHORN n type of obsolete woodwind instrument made from an animal horn
STOCKIER > STOCKY
STOCKIEST > STOCKY
STOCKILY > STOCKY
STOCKINET n machine-knitted elastic fabric
STOCKING n close-fitting covering for the foot and leg
STOCKINGS > STOCKING
STOCKISH adj stupid or dull
STOCKIST n dealer who stocks a particular product
STOCKISTS > STOCKIST
STOCKLESS > STOCK
STOCKLIST n list of items in stock
STOCKLOCK n lock that is enclosed in a wooden case
STOCKMAN n man engaged in the rearing or care of farm livestock, esp cattle
STOCKMEN > STOCKMAN
STOCKPILE vb store a large quantity of (something) for future use ▷ n accumulated store
STOCKPOT n pot in which stock for soup is made
STOCKPOTS > STOCKPOT
STOCKROOM n room in which a stock of goods is kept in a shop or factory
STOCKS pl n instrument of punishment in which an offender was locked

STOCKTAKE vb take stock
STOCKTOOK > STOCKTAKE
STOCKWORK n group of veins in mine
STOCKY adj (of a person) broad and sturdy
STOCKYARD n yard where farm animals are sold
STODGE n heavy starchy food ▷ vb stuff (oneself or another) with food
STODGED > STODGE
STODGER n dull person
STODGERS > STODGER
STODGES > STODGE
STODGIER > STODGY
STODGIEST > STODGY
STODGILY > STODGY
STODGING > STODGE
STODGY adj (of food) heavy and starchy
STOEP n verandah
STOEPS > STOEP
STOGEY same as > STOGY
STOGEYS > STOGEY
STOGIE same as > STOGY
STOGIES > STOGY
STOGY n any long cylindrical inexpensive cigar
STOIC n person who suffers hardship without showing his or her feelings ▷ adj suffering hardship without showing one's feelings
STOICAL adj suffering great difficulties without showing one's feelings
STOICALLY > STOICAL
STOICISM n indifference to pleasure and pain
STOICISMS > STOICISM
STOICS > STOIC
STOIT vb bounce
STOITED > STOIT
STOITER vb stagger
STOITERED > STOITER
STOITERS > STOITER
STOITING > STOIT
STOITS > STOIT
STOKE vb feed and tend (a fire or furnace)
STOKED adj very pleased
STOKEHOLD n hold for a ship's boilers
STOKEHOLE n hole in a furnace through which it is stoked
STOKER n person employed to tend a furnace on a ship or train powered by steam
STOKERS > STOKER
STOKES n cgs unit of kinematic viscosity
STOKESIA n American flowering plant
STOKESIAS > STOKESIA
STOKING > STOKE
STOKVEL n (in S Africa) informal savings pool or syndicate
STOKVELS > STOKVEL
STOLE n long scarf or shawl
STOLED adj wearing a stole
STOLEN > STEAL
STOLES > STOLE
STOLID adj showing little emotion or interest

STOLIDER > STOLID
STOLIDEST > STOLID
STOLIDITY > STOLID
STOLIDLY > STOLID
STOLLEN n rich sweet bread containing nuts, raisins, etc
STOLLENS > STOLLEN
STOLN > STEAL
STOLON n long horizontal stem that grows along the surface of the soil
STOLONATE adj having a stolon
STOLONIC > STOLON
STOLONS > STOLON
STOLPORT n airport for short take-off aircraft
STOLPORTS > STOLPORT
STOMA n pore in a plant leaf that controls the passage of gases
STOMACH n organ in the body which digests food ▷ vb put up with
STOMACHAL n stomach medication
STOMACHED > STOMACH
STOMACHER n decorative V-shaped panel of stiff material worn over the chest and stomach
STOMACHIC adj stimulating gastric activity ▷ n stomachic medicine
STOMACHS > STOMACH
STOMACHY adj having a large belly
STOMACK n as in have a stomack (in E Africa) be pregnant
STOMACKS > STOMACK
STOMAL > STOMA
STOMAS > STOMA
STOMATA > STOMA
STOMATAL adj of, relating to, or possessing stomata or a stoma
STOMATE n opening on leaf through which water evaporates
STOMATES > STOMATE
STOMATIC adj of or relating to a mouth or mouthlike part
STOMATOUS same as > STOMATAL
STOMIA > STOMIUM
STOMIUM n part of the sporangium of ferns that ruptures to release the spores
STOMIUMS > STOMIUM
STOMODAEA > STOMODEUM
STOMODEA > STOMODEUM
STOMODEAL > STOMODEUM
STOMODEUM n oral cavity of a vertebrate embryo
STOMP vb tread heavily ▷ n rhythmic stamping jazz dance
STOMPED > STOMP
STOMPER n song with a strong beat
STOMPERS > STOMPER
STOMPIE n cigarette butt
STOMPIER > STOMPY
STOMPIES > STOMPIE
STOMPIEST > STOMPY

STOMPING > STOMP

STOMPS > STOMP

STOMPY adj (of music) encouraging stomping of the feet

STONABLE > STONE

STOND same as **>** STAND

STONDS > STOND

STONE n material of which rocks are made ▷ vb throw stones at

STONEABLE > STONE

STONEBOAT n type of sleigh used for moving rocks from fields

STONECAST n short distance

STONECHAT n songbird that has black feathers and a reddish-brown breast

STONECROP n type of plant with fleshy leaves and red, yellow, or white flowers

STONECUT n (print made from) a carved block of stone

STONECUTS > STONECUT

STONED > STONE

STONEFISH n venomous tropical marine scorpaenid fish

STONEFLY n type of insect whose larvae are aquatic

STONEHAND n type of compositor

STONELESS > STONE

STONELIKE > STONE

STONEN adj of stone

STONER n device for removing stones from fruit

STONERAG n type of lichen

STONERAGS > STONERAG

STONERAW same as **>** STONERAG

STONERAWS > STONERAW

STONERN same as **>** STONEN

STONERS > STONER

STONES > STONE

STONESHOT n stone's throw

STONEWALL vb obstruct or hinder discussion

STONEWARE n hard kind of pottery fired at a very high temperature ▷ adj made of stoneware

STONEWASH vb wash with stones to give worn appearance

STONEWORK n part of a building made of stone

STONEWORT n any of various green algae which grow in brackish or fresh water

STONEY same as **>** STONY

STONG > STING

STONIED > STONY

STONIER > STONY

STONIES > STONY

STONIEST > STONY

STONILY > STONY

STONINESS > STONY

STONING > STONE

STONINGS > STONE

STONISH same as **>** ASTONISH

STONISHED > STONISH

STONISHES > STONISH

STONK vb bombard (soldiers, buildings, etc) with artillery ▷ n concentrated bombardment

STONKED > STONK

STONKER vb destroy

STONKERED adj completely exhausted or beaten

STONKERS > STONKER

STONKING > STONK

STONKS > STONK

STONN same as **>** STUN

STONNE same as **>** STUN

STONNED > STONNE

STONNES > STONNE

STONNING > STONN

STONNS > STONN

STONY adj of or like stone ▷ vb astonish

STONYING > STONY

STOOD > STAND

STOODEN > STAND

STOOGE n actor who feeds lines to a comedian ▷ vb act as a stooge

STOOGED > STOOGE

STOOGES > STOOGE

STOOGING > STOOGE

STOOK n number of sheaves set upright in a field to dry ▷ vb set up (sheaves) in stooks

STOOKED > STOOK

STOOKER > STOOK

STOOKERS > STOOK

STOOKIE n stucco

STOOKIES > STOOKIE

STOOKING n act of stooking

STOOKINGS > STOOKING

STOOKS > STOOK

STOOL n chair without arms or back ▷ vb (of a plant) send up shoots from the base of the stem

STOOLBALL n game resembling cricket played by girls

STOOLED > STOOL

STOOLIE n police informer

STOOLIES > STOOLIE

STOOLING > STOOL

STOOLS > STOOL

STOOLY n (US) informant for the police

STOOP vb bend forward and downward

STOOPBALL n American street game

STOOPE same as **>** STOUP

STOOPED > STOOP

STOOPER > STOOP

STOOPERS > STOOP

STOOPES > STOOPE

STOOPING > STOOP

STOOPS > STOOP

STOOR same as **>** STOUR

STOORS > STOOR

STOOSHIE same as **>** STUSHIE

STOOSHIES > STOOSHIE

STOOZE vb borrow money cheaply and invest it to make a profit

STOOZED > STOOZE

STOOZER n person who stoozes

STOOZERS > STOOZER

STOOZES > STOOZE

STOOZING > STOOZE

STOOZINGS > STOOZING

STOP vb cease or cause to cease from doing (something) ▷ n stopping or being stopped

STOPBAND n band of frequencies stopped by a filter

STOPBANDS > STOPBAND

STOPBANK n embankment to prevent flooding

STOPBANKS > STOPBANK

STOPCOCK n valve to control or stop the flow of fluid in a pipe

STOPCOCKS > STOPCOCK

STOPE n steplike excavation made in a mine to extract ore ▷ vb mine (ore, etc) by cutting stopes

STOPED > STOPE

STOPER n drill used in mining

STOPERS > STOPER

STOPES > STOPE

STOPGAP n temporary substitute

STOPGAPS > STOPGAP

STOPING n process by which country rock is broken up and engulfed by magma

STOPINGS > STOPING

STOPLESS > STOP

STOPLIGHT n red light on a traffic signal indicating that vehicles coming towards it should stop

STOPOFF n break in a journey

STOPOFFS > STOPOFF

STOPOVER n short break in a journey ▷ vb make a stopover

STOPOVERS > STOPOVER

STOPPABLE > STOP

STOPPAGE n act of stopping something or the state of being stopped

STOPPAGES > STOPPAGE

STOPPED > STOP

STOPPER n plug for closing a bottle etc ▷ vb close or fit with a stopper

STOPPERED > STOPPER

STOPPERS > STOPPER

STOPPING > STOP

STOPPINGS > STOP

STOPPLE same as **>** STOPPER

STOPPLED > STOPPLE

STOPPLES > STOPPLE

STOPPLING > STOPPLE

STOPS > STOP

STOPT > STOP

STOPWATCH n watch which can be stopped instantly for exact timing of a sporting event

STOPWORD n common word not used in computer search engines

STOPWORDS > STOPWORD

STORABLE > STORE

STORABLES > STORE

STORAGE n storing

STORAGES > STORAGE

STORAX n type of tree or shrub with white flowers

STORAXES > STORAX

STORE vb collect and keep (things) for future use ▷ n shop

STORECARD n charge card specific to one chain of shops

STORED > STORE

STOREMAN n man looking after storeroom

STOREMEN > STOREMAN

STORER > STORE

STOREROOM n room in which things are stored

STORERS > STORE

STORES pl n supply of food and essentials for a journey

STORESHIP n ship carrying naval stores

STOREWIDE adj throughout stores

STOREY n floor or level of a building

STOREYED adj having a storey or storeys

STOREYS > STOREY

STORGE n affection

STORGES > STORGE

STORIATED adj decorated with flowers or animals

STORIED > STORY

STORIES > STORY

STORIETTE n short story

STORING > STORE

STORK n large wading bird

STORKS > STORK

STORM n violent weather with wind, rain, or snow ▷ vb attack or capture (a place) suddenly

STORMBIRD n petrel

STORMCOCK n mistle thrush

STORMED > STORM

STORMER n outstanding example of its kind

STORMERS > STORMER

STORMFUL > STORM

STORMIER > STORMY

STORMIEST > STORMY

STORMILY > STORMY

STORMING adj characterized by or displaying dynamism, speed, and energy

STORMINGS > STORM

STORMLESS > STORM

STORMLIKE > STORM

STORMS > STORM

STORMY adj characterized by storms

STORNELLI > STORNELLO

STORNELLO n type of Italian poem

STORY n narration of a chain of events ▷ vb decorate with scenes from history

STORYBOOK n book containing stories for children ▷ adj better or happier than in real life

STORYETTE n short story

STORYING > STORY

STORYINGS > STORY

STORYLESS adj without a story

STORYLINE n plot of a book, film, play, etc

STORYTIME n time set aside for reading stories aloud

STOSS adj (of the side of a hill) facing the onward flow of a glacier ▷ n hillside facing glacier flow

STOSSES > STOSS

STOT n bullock ▷ vb bounce or cause to bounce

STOTIN n former monetary unit of Slovenia

STOTINKA n monetary unit of Bulgaria, worth one hundredth of a lev

STOTINKAS > STOTINKA

STOTINKI > STOTINKA

STOTINOV > STOTIN

STOTINS > STOTIN

STOTIOUS adj drunk

STOTS > STOT

STOTT same as > STOT

STOTTED > STOT

STOTTER same as > STOT

STOTTERED > STOTTER

STOTTERS > STOTTER

STOTTIE n wedge of bread cut from a flat round loaf

STOTTIES > STOTTIE

STOTTING > STOT

STOTTS > STOTT

STOTTY same as > STOTTIE

STOUN same as > STUN

STOUND n short while ▷ vb ache

STOUNDED > STOUND

STOUNDING > STOUND

STOUNDS > STOUND

STOUNING > STOUN

STOUNS > STOUN

STOUP n small basin for holy water

STOUPS > STOUP

STOUR n turmoil or conflict

STOURE same as > STOUR

STOURES > STOURE

STOURIE same as > STOURY

STOURIER > STOURY

STOURIEST > STOURY

STOURS > STOUR

STOURY adj dusty

STOUSH vb hit or punch (someone) ▷ n fighting or violence

STOUSHED > STOUSH

STOUSHES > STOUSH

STOUSHIE same as > STUSHIE

STOUSHIES > STOUSHIE

STOUSHING > STOUSH

STOUT adj fat ▷ n strong dark beer

STOUTEN vb make or become stout

STOUTENED > STOUTEN

STOUTENS > STOUTEN

STOUTER > STOUT

STOUTEST > STOUT

STOUTH n Scots word meaning theft

STOUTHS > STOUTH

STOUTISH > STOUT

STOUTLY > STOUT

STOUTNESS > STOUT

STOUTS > STOUT

STOVAINE n anaesthetic drug

STOVAINES > STOVAINE

STOVE n apparatus for cooking or heating ▷ vb process (ceramics, metalwork, etc) by heating in a stove

STOVED > STOVE

STOVEPIPE n pipe that takes fumes and smoke away from a stove

STOVER n fodder

STOVERS > STOVER

STOVES > STOVE

STOVETOP US word for > HOB

STOVETOPS > STOVETOP

STOVEWOOD n wood cut for use in a stove

STOVIES pl n potatoes stewed with onions

STOVING > STOVE

STOVINGS > STOVE

STOW vb pack or store

STOWABLE > STOW

STOWAGE n space or charge for stowing goods

STOWAGES > STOWAGE

STOWAWAY n person who hides on a ship or aircraft in order to travel free ▷ vb travel in such a way

STOWAWAYS > STOWAWAY

STOWDOWN n packing of ship's hold

STOWDOWNS > STOWDOWN

STOWED > STOW

STOWER > STOW

STOWERS > STOW

STOWING > STOW

STOWINGS > STOW

STOWLINS adv stealthily

STOWN > STEAL

STOWND same as > STOUND

STOWNDED > STOWND

STOWNDING > STOWND

STOWNDS > STOWND

STOWNLINS same as > STOWLINS

STOWP same as > STOUP

STOWPS > STOWP

STOWRE same as > STOUR

STOWRES > STOWRE

STOWS > STOW

STRABISM n abnormal alignment of one or both eyes

STRABISMS > STRABISM

STRACK vb archaic past tense form of strike

STRAD n violin made by Stradivarius

STRADDLE vb have one leg or part on each side of (something) ▷ n act or position of straddling

STRADDLED > STRADDLE

STRADDLER > STRADDLE

STRADDLES > STRADDLE

STRADIOT n Venetian cavalryman

STRADIOTS > STRADIOT

STRADS > STRAD

STRAE Scots form of > STRAW

STRAES > STRAE

STRAFE vb attack (an enemy) with machine guns

from the air ▷ n act or instance of strafing

STRAFED > STRAFE

STRAFER > STRAFE

STRAFERS > STRAFE

STRAFES > STRAFE

STRAFF same as > STRAFE

STRAFFED > STRAFF

STRAFFING > STRAFF

STRAFFS > STRAFF

STRAFING n act of strafing

STRAFINGS > STRAFING

STRAG n straggler

STRAGGLE vb go or spread in a rambling or irregular way

STRAGGLED > STRAGGLE

STRAGGLER > STRAGGLE

STRAGGLES > STRAGGLE

STRAGGLY > STRAGGLE

STRAGS > STRAG

STRAICHT Scots word for > STRAIGHT

STRAIGHT adj not curved or crooked ▷ adv in a straight line ▷ n straight part, esp of a racetrack ▷ vb tighten

STRAIGHTS > STRAIGHT

STRAIK Scots word for > STROKE

STRAIKED > STRAIK

STRAIKING > STRAIK

STRAIKS > STRAIK

STRAIN vb subject to mental tension ▷ n tension or tiredness

STRAINED adj not natural, forced

STRAINER n sieve

STRAINERS > STRAINER

STRAINING > STRAIN

STRAINS > STRAIN

STRAINT n pressure

STRAINTS > STRAINT

STRAIT n narrow channel connecting two areas of sea ▷ adj (of spaces, etc) affording little room ▷ vb tighten

STRAITED > STRAIT

STRAITEN vb embarrass or distress, esp financially

STRAITENS > STRAITEN

STRAITER > STRAIT

STRAITEST > STRAIT

STRAITING > STRAIT

STRAITLY > STRAIT

STRAITS > STRAIT

STRAK vb archaic past tense form of strike

STRAKE n curved metal plate forming part of the metal rim on a wooden wheel

STRAKED adj having a strake

STRAKES > STRAKE

STRAMACON same as > STRAMAZON

STRAMASH n uproar ▷ vb destroy

STRAMAZON n downward fencing stroke

STRAMMEL same as > STRUMMEL

STRAMMELS > STRAMMEL

STRAMONY n former asthma medicine made from the dried leaves and flowers of the thorn apple

STRAMP Scots variant of > TRAMP

STRAMPED > STRAMP

STRAMPING > STRAMP

STRAMPS > STRAMP

STRAND vb run aground ▷ n shore

STRANDED > STRAND

STRANDER > STRAND

STRANDERS > STRAND

STRANDING > STRAND

STRANDS > STRAND

STRANG dialect variant of > STRONG

STRANGE adj odd or unusual ▷ n odd or unfamiliar person or thing

STRANGELY > STRANGE

STRANGER n person who is not known or is new to a place or experience

STRANGERS > STRANGER

STRANGES > STRANGE

STRANGEST > STRANGE

STRANGLE vb kill by squeezing the throat

STRANGLED > STRANGLE

STRANGLER n person or thing that strangles

STRANGLES n acute bacterial disease of horses

STRANGURY n painful excretion of urine caused by muscular spasms of the urinary tract

STRAP n strip of flexible material for lifting or holding in place ▷ vb fasten with a strap or straps

STRAPHANG vb travel standing on public transport

STRAPHUNG > STRAPHANG

STRAPLESS adj (of women's clothes) without straps over the shoulders

STRAPLIKE adj like a strap

STRAPLINE n subheading in a newspaper or magazine article or in any advertisement

STRAPPADO n system of torture in which a victim was hoisted by a rope tied to the wrists ▷ vb subject to strappado

STRAPPED > STRAP

STRAPPER n strapping person

STRAPPERS > STRAPPER

STRAPPIER > STRAPPY

STRAPPING > STRAP

STRAPPY adj having straps

STRAPS > STRAP

STRAPWORT n plant with leaves like straps

STRASS another word for > PASTE

STRASSES > STRASS

STRATA > STRATUM

STRATAGEM n clever plan, trick

STRATAL > STRATUM

STRATAS > STRATUM

STRATEGIC adj advantageous

STRATEGY n overall plan

STRATH n flat river valley

STRATHS > STRATH
STRATI > STRATUS
STRATIFY vb form or be formed in layers or strata
STRATONIC adj of army
STRATOSE adj formed in strata
STRATOUS adj of stratus
STRATUM n layer, esp of rock
STRATUMS > STRATUM
STRATUS n grey layer cloud
STRATUSES > STRATUS
STRAUCHT Scots word for > STRETCH
STRAUCHTS > STRAUCHT
STRAUGHT same as > STRAUCHT
STRAUGHTS > STRAUGHT
STRAUNGE same as > STRANGE
STRAVAGE same as > STRAVAIG
STRAVAGED > STRAVAGE
STRAVAGES > STRAVAGE
STRAVAIG vb wander aimlessly
STRAVAIGS > STRAVAIG
STRAW n dried stalks of grain ▷ vb spread around
STRAWED > STRAW
STRAWEN adj of straw
STRAWHAT adj of summer dramatic performance
STRAWIER > STRAWY
STRAWIEST > STRAWY
STRAWING > STRAW
STRAWLESS > STRAW
STRAWLIKE > STRAW
STRAWN > STREW
STRAWS > STRAW
STRAWWORM n aquatic larva of a caddis fly
STRAWY adj containing straw, or like straw in colour or texture
STRAY vb wander ▷ adj having strayed ▷ n stray animal
STRAYED > STRAY
STRAYER > STRAY
STRAYERS > STRAY
STRAYING > STRAY
STRAYINGS > STRAY
STRAYLING n stray
STRAYS > STRAY
STRAYVE vb wander aimlessly
STRAYVED > STRAYVE
STRAYVES > STRAYVE
STRAYVING > STRAYVE
STREAK n long band of contrasting colour or substance ▷ vb mark with streaks
STREAKED > STREAK
STREAKER > STREAK
STREAKERS > STREAK
STREAKIER > STREAKY
STREAKILY > STREAKY
STREAKING > STREAK
STREAKS > STREAK
STREAKY adj marked with streaks
STREAM n small river ▷ vb flow steadily
STREAMBED n bottom of stream

STREAMED > STREAM
STREAMER n strip of coloured paper that unrolls when tossed
STREAMERS > STREAMER
STREAMIER > STREAMY
STREAMING > STREAM
STREAMLET > STREAM
STREAMS > STREAM
STREAMY adj (of an area, land, etc) having many streams
STREEK Scots word for > STRETCH
STREEKED > STREEK
STREEKER > STREEK
STREEKERS > STREEK
STREEKING > STREEK
STREEKS > STREEK
STREEL vb trail
STREELED > STREEL
STREELING > STREEL
STREELS > STREEL
STREET n public road, usu lined with buildings ▷ vb lay out a street or streets
STREETAGE n toll charged for using a street
STREETBOY n boy living on the street
STREETCAR n tram
STREETED > STREET
STREETFUL n amount of people or things a street can hold
STREETIER > STREETY
STREETING > STREET
STREETS > STREET
STREETY adj of streets
STREIGHT same as > STRAIT
STREIGHTS > STREIGHT
STREIGNE same as > STRAIN
STREIGNED > STREIGNE
STREIGNES > STREIGNE
STRELITZ n former Russian soldier
STRELITZI > STRELITZ
STRENE same as > STRAIN
STRENES > STRENE
STRENGTH n quality of being strong
STRENGTHS > STRENGTH
STRENUITY > STRENUOUS
STRENUOUS adj requiring great energy or effort
STREP n streptococcus
STREPENT adj noisy
STREPS > STREP
STRESS n tension or strain ▷ vb emphasize
STRESSED > STRESS
STRESSES > STRESS
STRESSFUL > STRESS
STRESSIER > STRESSY
STRESSING > STRESS
STRESSOR n event, experience, etc, that causes stress
STRESSORS > STRESSOR
STRESSY adj characterized by stress
STRETCH vb extend or be extended ▷ n stretching
STRETCHED > STRETCH

STRETCHER n frame covered with canvas on which an injured person is carried ▷ vb transport (a sick or injured person) on a stretcher
STRETCHES > STRETCH
STRETCHY adj characterized by elasticity
STRETTA same as > STRETTO
STRETTAS > STRETTA
STRETTE > STRETTA
STRETTI > STRETTO
STRETTO n (in a fugue) the close overlapping of two parts or voices
STRETTOS > STRETTO
STREUSEL n crumbly topping for rich pastries
STREUSELS > STREUSEL
STREW vb scatter (things) over a surface
STREWAGE > STREW
STREWAGES > STREW
STREWED > STREW
STREWER > STREW
STREWERS > STREW
STREWING > STREW
STREWINGS > STREW
STREWMENT n strewing
STREWN > STREW
STREWS > STREW
STREWTH interj expression of surprise or alarm
STRIA n scratch or groove on the surface of a rock crystal
STRIAE > STRIA
STRIATA > STRIATUM
STRIATAL adj relating to the corpus striatum in the brain
STRIATE adj marked with striae ▷ vb mark with striae
STRIATED adj having a pattern of scratches or grooves
STRIATES > STRIATE
STRIATING > STRIATE
STRIATION same as > STRIA
STRIATUM n part of brain
STRIATUMS > STRIATUM
STRIATURE n way something is striated
STRICH n screech owl
STRICHES > STRICH
STRICK n any bast fibres preparatory to being made into slivers
STRICKEN adj seriously affected by disease, grief, pain, etc
STRICKLE n board used for sweeping off excess material in a container ▷ vb level, form, or sharpen with a strickle
STRICKLED > STRICKLE
STRICKLES > STRICKLE
STRICKS > STRICK
STRICT adj stern or severe
STRICTER > STRICT
STRICTEST > STRICT
STRICTION n act of restricting

STRICTISH > STRICT
STRICTLY > STRICT
STRICTURE n severe criticism
STRIDDEN > STRIDE
STRIDDLE same as > STRADDLE
STRIDDLED > STRIDDLE
STRIDDLES > STRIDDLE
STRIDE vb walk with long steps ▷ n long step
STRIDENCE > STRIDENT
STRIDENCY > STRIDENT
STRIDENT adj loud and harsh
STRIDER > STRIDE
STRIDERS > STRIDE
STRIDES > STRIDE
STRIDING > STRIDE
STRIDLING adv astride
STRIDOR n high-pitched whistling sound made during respiration
STRIDORS > STRIDOR
STRIFE n conflict, quarrelling
STRIFEFUL > STRIFE
STRIFES > STRIFE
STRIFT n struggle
STRIFTS > STRIFT
STRIG vb remove stalk from
STRIGA same as > STRIA
STRIGAE > STRIGA
STRIGATE adj streaked
STRIGGED > STRIG
STRIGGING > STRIG
STRIGIL n curved blade used to scrape the body after bathing
STRIGILS > STRIGIL
STRIGINE adj of or like owl
STRIGOSE adj bearing stiff hairs or bristles
STRIGS > STRIG
STRIKABLE adj capable of being struck
STRIKE vb cease work as a protest ▷ n stoppage of work as a protest
STRIKEOUT n dismissal in baseball due to three successive failures to hit the ball
STRIKER n striking worker
STRIKERS > STRIKER
STRIKES > STRIKE
STRIKING > STRIKE
STRIKINGS > STRIKE
STRIM vb cut (grass) using an electric trimmer
STRIMMED > STRIM
STRIMMING > STRIM
STRIMS > STRIM
STRINE n informal name for Australian English
STRINES > STRINE
STRING n thin cord used for tying ▷ vb provide with a string or strings
STRINGED adj (of a musical instrument) having strings that are plucked or played with a bow
STRINGENT adj strictly controlled or enforced
STRINGER n journalist retained by a newspaper to

S

cover a particular town or area

STRINGERS > STRINGER

STRINGIER > STRINGY

STRINGILY > STRINGY

STRINGING > STRING

STRINGS > STRING

STRINGY *adj* like string

STRINKLE *Scots variant of* > SPRINKLE

STRINKLED > STRINKLE

STRINKLES > STRINKLE

STRIP *vb* take (the covering or clothes) off ▷ *n* act of stripping

STRIPE *n* long narrow band of contrasting colour or substance ▷ *vb* mark (something) with stripes

STRIPED *adj* marked or decorated with stripes

STRIPER *n* officer who has a stripe or stripes on his or her uniform

STRIPERS > STRIPER

STRIPES > STRIPE

STRIPEY *same as* > STRIPY

STRIPIER > STRIPY

STRIPIEST > STRIPY

STRIPING > STRIPE

STRIPINGS > STRIPE

STRIPLING *n* youth

STRIPPED > STRIP

STRIPPER *n* device or substance for removing paint etc

STRIPPERS > STRIPPER

STRIPPING > STRIP

STRIPS > STRIP

STRIPT > STRIP

STRIPY *adj* marked by or with stripes

STRIVE *vb* make a great effort

STRIVED > STRIVE

STRIVEN > STRIVE

STRIVER > STRIVE

STRIVERS > STRIVE

STRIVES > STRIVE

STRIVING > STRIVE

STRIVINGS > STRIVE

STROAM *vb* wander

STROAMED > STROAM

STROAMING > STROAM

STROAMS > STROAM

STROBE *n* high intensity flashing beam of light ▷ *vb* give the appearance of slow motion by using a strobe

STROBED > STROBE

STROBES > STROBE

STROBIC *adj* spinning or appearing to spin

STROBIL *n* scaly multiple fruit

STROBILA *n* body of a tapeworm, consisting of a string of similar segments

STROBILAE > STROBILA

STROBILAR > STROBILA

STROBILE *same as* > STROBILUS

STROBILES > STROBILE

STROBILI > STROBILUS

STROBILS > STROBIL

STROBILUS *technical name for* > CONE

STROBING > STROBE

STROBINGS > STROBE

STRODDLE *same as* > STRADDLE

STRODDLED > STRODDLE

STRODDLES > STRODDLE

STRODE > STRIDE

STRODLE *same as* > STRADDLE

STRODLED > STRODLE

STRODLES > STRODLE

STRODLING > STRODLE

STROKABLE *adj* appearing pleasant to stroke

STROKE *vb* touch or caress lightly with the hand ▷ *n* light touch or caress with the hand

STROKED > STROKE

STROKEN > STRIKE

STROKER > STROKE

STROKERS > STROKE

STROKES > STROKE

STROKING > STROKE

STROKINGS > STROKE

STROLL *vb* walk in a leisurely manner ▷ *n* leisurely walk

STROLLED > STROLL

STROLLER *n* chair-shaped carriage for a baby

STROLLERS > STROLLER

STROLLING > STROLL

STROLLS > STROLL

STROMA *n* gel-like matrix of chloroplasts and certain cells

STROMAL > STROMA

STROMATA > STROMA

STROMATIC > STROMA

STROMB *n* shellfish like a whelk

STROMBS > STROMB

STROMBUS *same as* > STROMB

STROND *same as* > STRAND

STRONDS > STROND

STRONG *adj* having physical power

STRONGARM *adj* involving physical force

STRONGBOX *n* box in which valuables are locked for safety

STRONGER > STRONG

STRONGEST > STRONG

STRONGISH > STRONG

STRONGLY > STRONG

STRONGMAN *n* performer, esp one in a circus, who performs feats of strength

STRONGMEN > STRONGMAN

STRONGYL *same as* > STRONGYLE

STRONGYLE *n* type of parasitic worm chiefly occurring in the intestines of horses

STRONGYLS > STRONGYL

STRONTIA > STRONTIUM

STRONTIAN *n* type of white mineral

STRONTIAS > STRONTIA

STRONTIC > STRONTIUM

STRONTIUM *n* silvery-white metallic element

STROOK > STRIKE

STROOKE *n* stroke

STROOKEN *same as* > STRICKEN

STROOKES > STROOKE

STROP *n* leather strap for sharpening razors ▷ *vb* sharpen (a razor, etc) on a strop

STROPHE *n* movement made by chorus during a choral ode

STROPHES > STROPHE

STROPHIC *adj* of, relating to, or employing a strophe or strophes

STROPHOID *n* type of curve on graph

STROPHULI *pl n* skin inflammations seen primarily on small children

STROPPED > STROP

STROPPER > STROP

STROPPERS > STROP

STROPPIER > STROPPY

STROPPILY > STROPPY

STROPPING > STROP

STROPPY *adj* angry or awkward

STROPS > STROP

STROSSERS *same as* > TROUSERS

STROUD *n* coarse woollen fabric

STROUDING *n* woolly material for making strouds

STROUDS > STROUD

STROUP *Scots word for* > SPOUT

STROUPACH *n* cup of tea

STROUPAN *same as* > STROUPACH

STROUPANS > STROUPAN

STROUPS > STROUP

STROUT *vb* bulge

STROUTED > STROUT

STROUTING > STROUT

STROUTS > STROUT

STROVE > STRIVE

STROW *archaic variant of* > STREW

STROWED > STROW

STROWER > STROW

STROWERS > STROW

STROWING > STROW

STROWINGS > STROW

STROWN > STROW

STROWS > STROW

STROY *archaic variant of* > DESTROY

STROYED > STROY

STROYER > STROY

STROYERS > STROY

STROYING > STROY

STROYS > STROY

STRUCK > STRIKE

STRUCKEN *same as* > STRICKEN

STRUCTURE *n* complex construction ▷ *vb* give a structure to

STRUDEL *n* thin sheet of filled dough rolled up and baked

STRUDELS > STRUDEL

STRUGGLE *vb* work, strive, or make one's way with difficulty ▷ *n* striving

STRUGGLED > STRUGGLE

STRUGGLER > STRUGGLE

STRUGGLES > STRUGGLE

STRUM *vb* play (a guitar, etc) by sweeping the thumb across the strings

STRUMA *n* abnormal enlargement of the thyroid gland

STRUMAE > STRUMA

STRUMAS > STRUMA

STRUMATIC > STRUMA

STRUMITIS *n* inflammation of thyroid gland

STRUMMED > STRUM

STRUMMEL *n* straw

STRUMMELS > STRUMMEL

STRUMMER > STRUM

STRUMMERS > STRUM

STRUMMING > STRUM

STRUMOSE > STRUMA

STRUMOUS > STRUMA

STRUMPET *n* prostitute ▷ *vb* turn into a strumpet

STRUMPETS > STRUMPET

STRUMS > STRUM

STRUNG > STRING

STRUNT *Scots word for* > STRUT

STRUNTED > STRUNT

STRUNTING > STRUNT

STRUNTS > STRUNT

STRUT *vb* walk pompously, swagger ▷ *n* bar supporting a structure

STRUTS > STRUT

STRUTTED > STRUT

STRUTTER > STRUT

STRUTTERS > STRUT

STRUTTING > STRUT

STRYCHNIA *n* strychnine

STRYCHNIC *adj* of, relating to, or derived from strychnine

STUB *n* short piece left after use ▷ *vb* strike (the toe) painfully against an object

STUBBED > STUB

STUBBIE *same as* > STUBBY

STUBBIER > STUBBY

STUBBIES > STUBBY

STUBBIEST > STUBBY

STUBBILY > STUBBY

STUBBING > STUB

STUBBLE *n* short stalks of grain left in a field after reaping

STUBBLED *adj* having the stubs of stalks left after a crop has been cut and harvested

STUBBLES > STUBBLE

STUBBLIER > STUBBLE

STUBBLY > STUBBLE

STUBBORN *adj* refusing to agree or give in ▷ *vb* make stubborn

STUBBORNS > STUBBORN

STUBBY *adj* short and broad ▷ *n* small bottle of beer

STUBS > STUB

STUCCO *n* plaster used for coating or decorating walls ▷ *vb* apply stucco to (a building)

STUCCOED > STUCCO

STUCCOER > STUCCO

STUCCOERS > STUCCO

STUCCOES > STUCCO

STUCCOING > STUCCO

STUCCOS > STUCCO

STUCK n thrust

STUCKS > STUCK

STUD n small piece of metal attached to a surface for decoration ▷ vb set with studs

STUDBOOK n written record of the pedigree of a purebred stock, esp of racehorses

STUDBOOKS > STUDBOOK

STUDDED > STUD

STUDDEN > STAND

STUDDIE Scots word for > ANVIL

STUDDIES > STUDDIE

STUDDING > STUD

STUDDINGS > STUD

STUDDLE n post

STUDDLES > STUDDLE

STUDE vb past tense and past participle of staun (Scots form of stand)

STUDENT n person who studies a subject, esp at university

STUDENTRY n body of students

STUDENTS > STUDENT

STUDENTY adj denoting the characteristics believed typical of a student

STUDFARM n farm where horses are bred

STUDFARMS > STUDFARM

STUDFISH n American minnow

STUDHORSE another word for > STALLION

STUDIED adj carefully practised

STUDIEDLY > STUDIED

STUDIER > STUDY

STUDIERS > STUDY

STUDIES > STUDY

STUDIO n workroom of an artist or photographer

STUDIOS > STUDIO

STUDIOUS adj fond of study

STUDLIER > STUDLY

STUDLIEST > STUDLY

STUDLIKE adj like a stud

STUDLY adj strong and virile

STUDS > STUD

STUDWORK n work decorated with studs

STUDWORKS > STUDWORK

STUDY vb be engaged in learning (a subject) ▷ n act or process of studying

STUDYING > STUDY

STUFF n substance or material ▷ vb pack, cram, or fill completely

STUFFED > STUFF

STUFFER > STUFF

STUFFERS > STUFF

STUFFIER > STUFFY

STUFFIEST > STUFFY

STUFFILY > STUFFY

STUFFING n seasoned mixture with which food is stuffed

STUFFINGS > STUFFING

STUFFLESS > STUFF

STUFFS > STUFF

STUFFY adj lacking fresh air

STUGGIER > STUGGY

STUGGIEST > STUGGY

STUGGY adj stout

STUIVER same as > STIVER

STUIVERS > STUIVER

STUKKEND adj South African slang for broken or wrecked

STULL n timber prop or platform in a stope

STULLS > STULL

STULM n shaft

STULMS > STULM

STULTIFY vb dull (the mind) by boring routine

STUM n partly fermented wine added to fermented wine as a preservative ▷ vb preserve (wine) by adding stum

STUMBLE vb trip and nearly fall ▷ n stumbling

STUMBLED > STUMBLE

STUMBLER > STUMBLE

STUMBLERS > STUMBLE

STUMBLES > STUMBLE

STUMBLIER > STUMBLY

STUMBLING > STUMBLE

STUMBLY adj tending to stumble

STUMER n forgery or cheat

STUMERS > STUMER

STUMM same as > SHTOOM

STUMMED > STUM

STUMMEL n bowl of a smoker's pipe

STUMMELS > STUMMEL

STUMMING > STUM

STUMP n base of a tree left when the main trunk has been cut away ▷ vb baffle

STUMPAGE n standing timber or its value

STUMPAGES > STUMPAGE

STUMPED > STUMP

STUMPER > STUMP

STUMPERS > STUMP

STUMPIER > STUMPY

STUMPIES > STUMPY

STUMPIEST > STUMPY

STUMPILY > STUMPY

STUMPING > STUMP

STUMPINGS > STUMPING

STUMPS > STUMP

STUMPWORK n type of embroidery featuring raised figures, padded with cotton wool or hair

STUMPY adj short and thick ▷ n stumpy thing

STUMS > STUM

STUN vb shock or overwhelm ▷ n state or effect of being stunned

STUNG > STING

STUNK > STINK

STUNKARD adj sulky

STUNNED > STUN

STUNNER n beautiful person or thing

STUNNERS > STUNNER

STUNNING > STUN

STUNNINGS > STUN

STUNS > STUN

STUNSAIL n type of light auxiliary sail

STUNSAILS > STUNSAIL

STUNT vb prevent or impede the growth of ▷ n acrobatic or dangerous action

STUNTED > STUNT

STUNTING > STUNT

STUNTMAN n person who performs dangerous acts in a film, etc in place of an actor

STUNTMEN > STUNTMAN

STUNTS > STUNT

STUPA n domed edifice housing Buddhist or Jain relics

STUPAS > STUPA

STUPE n hot damp cloth applied to the body to relieve pain ▷ vb treat with a stupe

STUPED > STUPE

STUPEFIED > STUPEFY

STUPEFIER > STUPEFY

STUPEFIES > STUPEFY

STUPEFY vb make insensitive or lethargic

STUPENT adj astonished

STUPES > STUPE

STUPID adj lacking intelligence ▷ n stupid person

STUPIDER > STUPID

STUPIDEST > STUPID

STUPIDITY n quality or state of being stupid

STUPIDLY > STUPID

STUPIDS > STUPID

STUPING > STUPE

STUPOR n dazed or unconscious state

STUPOROUS > STUPOR

STUPORS > STUPOR

STUPRATE vb ravish

STUPRATED > STUPRATE

STUPRATES > STUPRATE

STURDIED > STURDY

STURDIER > STURDY

STURDIES > STURDY

STURDIEST > STURDY

STURDILY > STURDY

STURDY adj healthy and robust ▷ n disease of sheep

STURE same as > STOOR

STURGEON n fish from which caviar is obtained

STURGEONS > STURGEON

STURMER n type of eating apple with pale green skin

STURMERS > STURMER

STURNINE > STURNUS

STURNOID > STURNUS

STURNUS n bird of starling family

STURNUSES > STURNUS

STURT vb bother

STURTED > STURT

STURTING > STURT

STURTS > STURT

STUSHIE n commotion, rumpus, or row

STUSHIES > STUSHIE

STUTTER vb speak with repetition of initial consonants ▷ n tendency to stutter

STUTTERED > STUTTER

STUTTERER > STUTTER

STUTTERS > STUTTER

STY vb climb

STYE n inflammation at the base of an eyelash

STYED > STYE

STYES > STYE

STYGIAN adj dark, gloomy, or hellish

STYING > STY

STYLAR > STYLUS

STYLATE adj having style

STYLE n shape or design ▷ vb shape or design

STYLEBOOK n book containing rules of punctuation, etc, for the use of writers, editors, and printers

STYLED > STYLE

STYLEE same as > STYLE

STYLEES > STYLEE

STYLELESS > STYLE

STYLER > STYLE

STYLERS > STYLE

STYLES > STYLE

STYLET n wire to stiffen a flexible cannula or catheter

STYLETS > STYLET

STYLI > STYLUS

STYLIE adj fashion-conscious

STYLIER > STYLIE

STYLIEST > STYLIE

STYLIFORM adj shaped like a stylus or bristle

STYLING > STYLE

STYLINGS > STYLE

STYLISE same as > STYLIZE

STYLISED > STYLISE

STYLISER > STYLISE

STYLISERS > STYLISE

STYLISES > STYLISE

STYLISH adj smart, elegant, and fashionable

STYLISHLY > STYLISH

STYLISING > STYLISE

STYLIST n hairdresser

STYLISTIC adj of literary or artistic style

STYLISTS > STYLIST

STYLITE n one of a class of recluses who in ancient times lived on the top of high pillars

STYLITES > STYLITE

STYLITIC > STYLITE

STYLITISM > STYLITE

STYLIZE vb cause to conform to an established stylistic form

STYLIZED > STYLIZE

STYLIZER > STYLIZE

STYLIZERS > STYLIZE

STYLIZES > STYLIZE

STYLIZING > STYLIZE

STYLO n type of fountain pen

STYLOBATE n continuous horizontal course of masonry that supports a colonnade

STYLOID adj resembling a stylus ▷ n spiny growth

STYLOIDS > STYLOID

STYLOLITE n any of the small striated columnar or irregular structures within the strata of some limestones

S

STYLOPES > STYLOPS
STYLOPID *n* type of parasitic insect
STYLOPIDS > STYLOPID
STYLOPISE *same as* **>** STYLOPIZE
STYLOPIZE *vb* (of a stylops) to parasitize (a host)
STYLOPS *n* type of insect that lives as a parasite in other insects
STYLOS > STYLO
STYLUS *n* needle-like device on a record player
STYLUSES > STYLUS
STYME *vb* peer
STYMED > STYME
STYMES > STYME
STYMIE *vb* hinder or thwart
STYMIED > STYMY
STYMIEING > STYMIE
STYMIES > STYMY
STYMING > STYME
STYMY *same as* **>** STYMIE
STYMYING > STYMY
STYPSIS *n* action, application, or use of a styptic
STYPSISES > STYPSIS
STYPTIC *adj* (drug) used to stop bleeding ▷ *n* styptic drug
STYPTICAL > STYPTIC
STYPTICS > STYPTIC
STYRAX *n* type of tropical or subtropical tree
STYRAXES > STYRAX
STYRE *same as* **>** STIR
STYRED > STYRE
STYRENE *n* colourless flammable liquid
STYRENES > STYRENE
STYRES > STYRE
STYRING > STYRE
STYROFOAM *n* tradename for a light expanded polystyrene plastic
STYTE *vb* bounce
STYTED > STYTE
STYTES > STYTE
STYTING > STYTE
SUABILITY > SUABLE
SUABLE *adj* liable to be sued in a court
SUABLY > SUABLE
SUASIBLE > SUASION
SUASION *n* persuasion
SUASIONS > SUASION
SUASIVE > SUASION
SUASIVELY > SUASION
SUASORY > SUASION
SUAVE *adj* smooth and sophisticated in manner
SUAVELY > SUAVE
SUAVENESS > SUAVE
SUAVER > SUAVE
SUAVEST > SUAVE
SUAVITIES > SUAVE
SUAVITY > SUAVE
SUB *n* subeditor ▷ *vb* act as a substitute
SUBA *n* shepherd's cloak
SUBABBOT *n* abbot who is subordinate to another abbot
SUBABBOTS > SUBABBOT

SUBACID *adj* (esp of some fruits) moderately acid or sour
SUBACIDLY > SUBACID
SUBACRID *adj* slightly acrid
SUBACT *vb* subdue
SUBACTED > SUBACT
SUBACTING > SUBACT
SUBACTION > SUBACT
SUBACTS > SUBACT
SUBACUTE *adj* intermediate between acute and chronic
SUBADAR *n* chief native officer of a company of Indian soldiers in the British service
SUBADARS > SUBADAR
SUBADULT *n* animal not quite at adult stage
SUBADULTS > SUBADULT
SUBAERIAL *adj* in open air
SUBAGENCY *n* agency employed by larger agency
SUBAGENT *n* agent who is subordinate to another agent
SUBAGENTS > SUBAGENT
SUBAH *same as* **>** SUBADAR
SUBAHDAR *same as* **>** SUBADAR
SUBAHDARS > SUBAHDAR
SUBAHDARY *n* office of subahdar
SUBAHS > SUBAH
SUBAHSHIP > SUBAH
SUBALAR *adj* below a wing
SUBALPINE *adj* situated in or relating to the regions at the foot of mountains
SUBALTERN *n* British army officer below the rank of captain ▷ *adj* of inferior position or rank
SUBAPICAL *adj* below an apex
SUBAQUA *adj* of or relating to underwater sport
SUBARCTIC *adj* of or relating to latitudes immediately south of the Arctic Circle
SUBAREA *n* area within a larger area
SUBAREAS > SUBAREA
SUBARID *adj* receiving slightly more rainfall than arid regions
SUBAS > SUBA
SUBASTRAL *adj* terrestrial
SUBATOM *n* part of an atom
SUBATOMIC *adj* of or being one of the particles which make up an atom
SUBATOMS > SUBATOM
SUBAUDIO *adj* (of sound) low frequency
SUBAURAL *adj* below the ear
SUBAXIAL *adj* below an axis of the body
SUBBASAL > SUBBASE
SUBBASE *same as* **>** SUBBASS
SUBBASES > SUBBASE
SUBBASIN *n* geographical basin within larger basin
SUBBASINS > SUBBASIN
SUBBASS *another name for* **>** BOURDON

SUBBASSES > SUBBASS
SUBBED > SUB
SUBBIE *n* subcontractor
SUBBIES > SUBBIE
SUBBING > SUB
SUBBINGS > SUB
SUBBLOCK *n* part of mathematical matrix
SUBBLOCKS > SUBBLOCK
SUBBRANCH *n* branch within another branch
SUBBREED *n* breed within a larger breed
SUBBREEDS > SUBBREED
SUBBUREAU *n* bureau subordinate to the main bureau
SUBBY *same as* **>** SUBBIE
SUBCANTOR *n* deputy to a cantor
SUBCASTE *n* subdivision of a caste
SUBCASTES > SUBCASTE
SUBCAUDAL *adj* below a tail
SUBCAUSE *n* factor less important than a cause
SUBCAUSES > SUBCAUSE
SUBCAVITY *n* cavity within a larger cavity
SUBCELL *n* cell within a larger cell
SUBCELLAR *n* cellar below another cellar
SUBCELLS > SUBCELL
SUBCENTER *n* secondary center
SUBCENTRE *same as* **>** SUBCENTER
SUBCHASER *n* anti-submarine warship
SUBCHIEF *n* chief below the main chief
SUBCHIEFS > SUBCHIEF
SUBCHORD *n* part of a curve
SUBCHORDS > SUBCHORD
SUBCLAIM *n* claim that is part of a larger claim
SUBCLAIMS > SUBCLAIM
SUBCLAN *n* clan within a larger clan
SUBCLANS > SUBCLAN
SUBCLASS *n* principal subdivision of a class ▷ *vb* assign to a subclass
SUBCLAUSE *n* subordinate section of a larger clause in a document
SUBCLERK *n* clerk who is subordinate to another clerk
SUBCLERKS > SUBCLERK
SUBCLIMAX *n* community in which development has been arrested before climax has been attained
SUBCODE *n* computer tag identifying data
SUBCODES > SUBCODE
SUBCOLONY *n* colony established by existing colony
SUBCONSUL *n* assistant to a consul
SUBCOOL *vb* make colder
SUBCOOLED > SUBCOOL
SUBCOOLS > SUBCOOL
SUBCORTEX *n* matter of the brain situated beneath the cerebral cortex

SUBCOSTA *n* vein in insect wing
SUBCOSTAE > SUBCOSTA
SUBCOSTAL *adj* below the rib
SUBCOUNTY *n* division of a county
SUBCRUST *n* secondary crust below main crust
SUBCRUSTS > SUBCRUST
SUBCULT *n* cult within larger cult
SUBCULTS > SUBCULT
SUBCUTES > SUBCUTIS
SUBCUTIS *n* layer of tissue beneath outer skin
SUBDEACON *n* cleric who assists at High Mass
SUBDEALER *n* dealer who buys from other dealer
SUBDEAN *n* deputy of dean
SUBDEANS > SUBDEAN
SUBDEB *n* young woman who is not yet a debutante
SUBDEBS > SUBDEB
SUBDEPOT *n* depot within a larger depot
SUBDEPOTS > SUBDEPOT
SUBDEPUTY *n* assistant to a deputy
SUBDERMAL *adj* below the skin
SUBDEW *same as* **>** SUBDUE
SUBDEWED > SUBDEW
SUBDEWING > SUBDEW
SUBDEWS > SUBDEW
SUBDIVIDE *vb* divide (a part of something) into smaller parts
SUBDOLOUS *adj* clever
SUBDORSAL *adj* situated close to the back
SUBDUABLE > SUBDUE
SUBDUABLY > SUBDUE
SUBDUAL > SUBDUE
SUBDUALS > SUBDUE
SUBDUCE *vb* withdraw
SUBDUCED > SUBDUCE
SUBDUCES > SUBDUCE
SUBDUCING > SUBDUCE
SUBDUCT *vb* draw or turn (the eye, etc) downwards
SUBDUCTED > SUBDUCT
SUBDUCTS > SUBDUCT
SUBDUE *vb* overcome
SUBDUED *adj* cowed, passive, or shy
SUBDUEDLY > SUBDUED
SUBDUER > SUBDUE
SUBDUERS > SUBDUE
SUBDUES > SUBDUE
SUBDUING > SUBDUE
SUBDUPLE *adj* in proportion of one to two
SUBDURAL *adj* between the dura mater and the arachnoid
SUBDWARF *n* star smaller than a dwarf star
SUBDWARFS > SUBDWARF
SUBECHO *n* echo resonating more quietly than another echo
SUBECHOES > SUBECHO
SUBEDAR *same as* **>** SUBADAR
SUBEDARS > SUBEDAR

SUBEDIT *vb* edit and correct (written or printed material)
SUBEDITED > SUBEDIT
SUBEDITOR *n* person who checks and edits text for a newspaper or magazine
SUBEDITS > SUBEDIT
SUBENTIRE *adj* slightly indented
SUBENTRY *n* entry within another entry
SUBEPOCH *n* epoch within another epoch
SUBEPOCHS > SUBEPOCH
SUBEQUAL *adj* not quite equal
SUBER *n* cork
SUBERATE *n* salt of suberic acid
SUBERATES > SUBERATE
SUBERECT *adj* not quite erect
SUBEREOUS *same as* > SUBEROSE
SUBERIC *same as* > SUBEROSE
SUBERIN *n* fatty or waxy substance that is present in the walls of cork cells
SUBERINS > SUBERIN
SUBERISE *same as* > SUBERIZE
SUBERISED > SUBERISE
SUBERISES > SUBERISE
SUBERIZE *vb* impregnate (cell walls) with suberin during the formation of corky tissue
SUBERIZED > SUBERIZE
SUBERIZES > SUBERIZE
SUBEROSE *adj* relating to, resembling, or consisting of cork
SUBEROUS *same as* > SUBEROSE
SUBERS > SUBER
SUBFAMILY *n* taxonomic group that is a subdivision of a family
SUBFEU *vb* grant feu to vassal
SUBFEUED > SUBFEU
SUBFEUING > SUBFEU
SUBFEUS > SUBFEU
SUBFIELD *n* subdivision of a field
SUBFIELDS > SUBFIELD
SUBFILE *n* file within another file
SUBFILES > SUBFILE
SUBFIX *n* suffix
SUBFIXES > SUBFIX
SUBFLOOR *n* rough floor that forms a base for a finished floor
SUBFLOORS > SUBFLOOR
SUBFLUID *adj* viscous
SUBFOLDER *n* subdivision of a folder
SUBFOSSIL *n* something partly fossilized
SUBFRAME *n* frame on which car body is built
SUBFRAMES > SUBFRAME
SUBFUSC *adj* devoid of brightness or appeal ▷ *n* (at Oxford University) formal academic dress

SUBFUSCS > SUBFUSC
SUBFUSK *same as* > SUBFUSC
SUBFUSKS > SUBFUSK
SUBGENERA > SUBGENUS
SUBGENRE *n* genre within a larger genre
SUBGENRES > SUBGENRE
SUBGENUS *n* taxonomic group that is a subdivision of a genus but of higher rank than a species
SUBGOAL *n* secondary goal
SUBGOALS > SUBGOAL
SUBGRADE *n* ground beneath a roadway or pavement
SUBGRADES > SUBGRADE
SUBGRAPH *n* graph sharing vertices of other graph
SUBGRAPHS > SUBGRAPH
SUBGROUP *n* small group that is part of a larger group
SUBGROUPS > SUBGROUP
SUBGUM *n* Chinese dish
SUBGUMS > SUBGUM
SUBHA *n* string of beads used in praying and meditating
SUBHAS > SUBHA
SUBHEAD *n* heading of a subsection in a printed work
SUBHEADS > SUBHEAD
SUBHEDRAL *adj* with some characteristics of crystal
SUBHUMAN *adj* less than human
SUBHUMANS > SUBHUMAN
SUBHUMID *adj* not wet enough for trees to grow
SUBIDEA *n* secondary idea
SUBIDEAS > SUBIDEA
SUBIMAGO *n* first winged stage of the mayfly
SUBIMAGOS > SUBIMAGO
SUBINCISE *vb* perform subincision
SUBINDEX *same as* > SUBSCRIPT
SUBINFEUD *vb* grant by feudal tenant to further tenant
SUBITEM *n* item that is less important than another item
SUBITEMS > SUBITEM
SUBITISE *same as* > SUBITIZE
SUBITISED > SUBITISE
SUBITISES > SUBITISE
SUBITIZE *vb* perceive the number of (a group of items) at a glance and without counting
SUBITIZED > SUBITIZE
SUBITIZES > SUBITIZE
SUBITO *adv* (preceding or following a dynamic marking, etc) suddenly
SUBJACENT *adj* forming a foundation
SUBJECT *n* person or thing being dealt with or studied ▷ *adj* being under the rule of a monarch or government ▷ *vb* cause to undergo
SUBJECTED > SUBJECT
SUBJECTS > SUBJECT

SUBJOIN *vb* add or attach at the end of something spoken, written, etc
SUBJOINED > SUBJOIN
SUBJOINS > SUBJOIN
SUBJUGATE *vb* bring (a group of people) under one's control
SUBLATE *vb* deny
SUBLATED > SUBLATE
SUBLATES > SUBLATE
SUBLATING > SUBLATE
SUBLATION > SUBLATE
SUBLEASE *n* lease of property made by a person who is a lessee of that property ▷ *vb* grant a sublease of (property)
SUBLEASED > SUBLEASE
SUBLEASES > SUBLEASE
SUBLESSEE > SUBLEASE
SUBLESSOR > SUBLEASE
SUBLET *vb* rent out (property rented from someone else) ▷ *n* sublease
SUBLETHAL *adj* not strong enough to kill
SUBLETS > SUBLET
SUBLETTER > SUBLET
SUBLEVEL *n* subdivision of a level
SUBLEVELS > SUBLEVEL
SUBLIMATE *vb* direct the energy of (a strong desire) into socially acceptable activities ▷ *n* material obtained when a substance is sublimed ▷ *adj* exalted or purified
SUBLIME *adj* of high moral, intellectual, or spiritual value ▷ *vb* change from a solid to a vapour without first melting
SUBLIMED > SUBLIME
SUBLIMELY > SUBLIME
SUBLIMER > SUBLIME
SUBLIMERS > SUBLIME
SUBLIMES > SUBLIME
SUBLIMEST > SUBLIME
SUBLIMING > SUBLIME
SUBLIMISE *same as* > SUBLIMIZE
SUBLIMIT *n* limit on a subcategory
SUBLIMITS > SUBLIMIT
SUBLIMITY > SUBLIME
SUBLIMIZE *vb* make sublime
SUBLINE *n* secondary headline
SUBLINEAR *adj* beneath a line
SUBLINES > SUBLINE
SUBLOT *n* subdivision of a lot
SUBLOTS > SUBLOT
SUBLUNAR *same as* > SUBLUNARY
SUBLUNARY *adj* situated between the moon and the earth
SUBLUNATE *adj* almost crescent-shaped
SUBLUXATE *vb* partially dislocate
SUBMAN *n* primitive form of human
SUBMARINE *n* vessel which can operate below the

surface of the sea ▷ *adj* below the surface of the sea ▷ *vb* slide beneath seatbelt in car crash
SUBMARKET *n* specialized market within larger market
SUBMATRIX *n* part of matrix
SUBMEN > SUBMAN
SUBMENTA > SUBMENTUM
SUBMENTAL *adj* situated beneath the chin
SUBMENTUM *n* base of insect lip
SUBMENU *n* further list of options within computer menu
SUBMENUS > SUBMENU
SUBMERGE *vb* put or go below the surface of water or other liquid
SUBMERGED *adj* (of plants or plant parts) growing beneath the surface of the water
SUBMERGES > SUBMERGE
SUBMERSE *same as* > SUBMERGE
SUBMERSED *same as* > SUBMERGED
SUBMERSES > SUBMERSE
SUBMICRON *n* object only visible through a powerful microscope
SUBMISS *adj* docile
SUBMISSLY *adv* submissively
SUBMIT *vb* surrender
SUBMITS > SUBMIT
SUBMITTAL > SUBMIT
SUBMITTED > SUBMIT
SUBMITTER > SUBMIT
SUBMUCOSA *n* connective tissue beneath a mucous membrane
SUBMUCOUS > SUBMUCOSA
SUBNASAL *adj* beneath nose
SUBNET *n* part of network
SUBNETS > SUBNET
SUBNEURAL *adj* beneath a nerve centre
SUBNICHE *n* subdivision of a niche
SUBNICHES > SUBNICHE
SUBNIVEAL *adj* beneath the snow
SUBNIVEAN *same as* > SUBNIVEAL
SUBNODAL *adj* below the level of a node
SUBNORMAL *adj* less than normal ▷ *n* subnormal person
SUBNUCLEI *pl n* plural of subnucleus, secondary nucleus
SUBOCEAN *adj* beneath the ocean
SUBOCTAVE *n* octave below another
SUBOCULAR *adj* below the eye
SUBOFFICE *n* office that is subordinate to another office
SUBOPTIC *adj* below the eye
SUBORAL *adj* not quite oral
SUBORDER *n* taxonomic group that is a subdivision of an order

SUBORDERS > SUBORDER
SUBORN *vb* bribe or incite (a person) to commit a wrongful act
SUBORNED > SUBORN
SUBORNER > SUBORN
SUBORNERS > SUBORN
SUBORNING > SUBORN
SUBORNS > SUBORN
SUBOSCINE *adj* belonging to a subfamily of birds
SUBOVAL *adj* not quite oval
SUBOVATE *adj* almost egg-shaped
SUBOXIDE *n* oxide of an element containing less oxygen than the common oxide formed by the element
SUBOXIDES > SUBOXIDE
SUBPANEL *n* panel that is part of larger panel
SUBPANELS > SUBPANEL
SUBPAR *adj* not up to standard
SUBPART *n* part within another part
SUBPARTS > SUBPART
SUBPENA *same as* > SUBPOENA
SUBPENAED > SUBPENA
SUBPENAS > SUBPENA
SUBPERIOD *n* subdivision of a time period
SUBPHASE *n* subdivision of a phase
SUBPHASES > SUBPHASE
SUBPHYLA > SUBPHYLUM
SUBPHYLAR > SUBPHYLUM
SUBPHYLUM *n* taxonomic group that is a subdivision of a phylum
SUBPLOT *n* secondary plot in a novel, play, or film
SUBPLOTS > SUBPLOT
SUBPOENA *n* writ requiring a person to appear before a law court ▷ *vb* summon (someone) with a subpoena
SUBPOENAS > SUBPOENA
SUBPOLAR *adj* of the areas south of the Arctic and north of the Antarctic
SUBPOTENT *adj* not at full strength
SUBPRIME *n* loan made to a borrower with a poor credit rating
SUBPRIMES > SUBPRIME
SUBPRIOR *n* monk junior to a prior
SUBPRIORS > SUBPRIOR
SUBPUBIC *adj* beneath the pubic bone
SUBRACE *n* race of people considered to be inferior
SUBRACES > SUBRACE
SUBREGION *n* subdivision of a region, esp a zoogeographical or ecological region
SUBRENT *n* rent paid to renter who rents to another ▷ *vb* rent out (a property that is already rented)
SUBRENTED > SUBRENT
SUBRENTS > SUBRENT
SUBRING *n* mathematical ring that is a subset of another ring

SUBRINGS > SUBRING
SUBROGATE *vb* put (one person or thing) in the place of another in respect of a right or claim
SUBRULE *n* rule within another rule
SUBRULES > SUBRULE
SUBS > SUB
SUBSACRAL *adj* below the sacrum
SUBSALE *n* sale carried out within the process of a larger sale
SUBSALES > SUBSALE
SUBSAMPLE *vb* take further sample from existing sample
SUBSCALE *n* scale within a scale
SUBSCALES > SUBSCALE
SUBSCHEMA *n* part of computer database used by an individual
SUBSCRIBE *vb* pay (a subscription)
SUBSCRIPT *adj* (character) printed below the line ▷ *n* subscript character
SUBSEA *adj* undersea
SUBSECIVE *adj* left over
SUBSECT *n* sect within a larger sect
SUBSECTOR *n* subdivision of sector
SUBSECTS > SUBSECT
SUBSELLIA *pl n* ledges underneath the hinged seats in a church
SUBSENSE *n* definition that is a division of a wider definition
SUBSENSES > SUBSENSE
SUBSERE *n* secondary sere arising when the progress of a sere has been interrupted
SUBSERES > SUBSERE
SUBSERIES *n* series within a larger series
SUBSERVE *vb* be helpful or useful to
SUBSERVED > SUBSERVE
SUBSERVES > SUBSERVE
SUBSET *n* mathematical set contained within a larger set
SUBSETS > SUBSET
SUBSHAFT *n* secondary shaft in a mine
SUBSHAFTS > SUBSHAFT
SUBSHELL *n* part of a shell of an atom
SUBSHELLS > SUBSHELL
SUBSHRUB *n* small bushy plant that is woody except for the tips of the branches
SUBSHRUBS > SUBSHRUB
SUBSIDE *vb* become less intense
SUBSIDED > SUBSIDE
SUBSIDER > SUBSIDE
SUBSIDERS > SUBSIDE
SUBSIDES > SUBSIDE
SUBSIDIES > SUBSIDY
SUBSIDING > SUBSIDE
SUBSIDISE *same as* > SUBSIDIZE
SUBSIDIZE *vb* help financially
SUBSIDY *n* financial aid

SUBSIST *vb* manage to live
SUBSISTED > SUBSIST
SUBSISTER > SUBSIST
SUBSISTS > SUBSIST
SUBSITE *n* location within a website
SUBSITES > SUBSITE
SUBSIZAR *n* type of undergraduate at Cambridge
SUBSIZARS > SUBSIZAR
SUBSKILL *n* element of a wider skill
SUBSKILLS > SUBSKILL
SUBSOCIAL *adj* lacking a complex or definite social structure
SUBSOIL *n* earth just below the surface soil ▷ *vb* plough (land) to a depth below the normal ploughing level
SUBSOILED > SUBSOIL
SUBSOILER > SUBSOIL
SUBSOILS > SUBSOIL
SUBSOLAR *adj* (of a point on the earth) directly below the sun
SUBSONG *n* subdued form of birdsong modified from the full territorial song
SUBSONGS > SUBSONG
SUBSONIC *adj* moving at a speed less than that of sound
SUBSPACE *n* part of a mathematical matrix
SUBSPACES > SUBSPACE
SUBSTAGE *n* part of a microscope below the stage
SUBSTAGES > SUBSTAGE
SUBSTANCE *n* physical composition of something
SUBSTATE *n* subdivision of state
SUBSTATES > SUBSTATE
SUBSTORM *n* disturbance in the magnetic field of a planet
SUBSTORMS > SUBSTORM
SUBSTRACT *same as* > SUBTRACT
SUBSTRATA *pl n* layers lying underneath other layers
SUBSTRATE *n* substance upon which an enzyme acts
SUBSTRUCT *vb* build as a foundation
SUBSTYLAR > SUBSTYLE
SUBSTYLE *n* line on a dial
SUBSTYLES > SUBSTYLE
SUBSULTUS *n* abnormal twitching
SUBSUME *vb* include (an idea, case, etc) under a larger classification or group
SUBSUMED > SUBSUME
SUBSUMES > SUBSUME
SUBSUMING > SUBSUME
SUBSYSTEM *n* system operating within a larger system
SUBTACK *Scots word for* > SUBLEASE
SUBTACKS > SUBTACK
SUBTALAR *adj* beneath the ankle-bone
SUBTASK *n* task that is part of a larger task
SUBTASKS > SUBTASK
SUBTAXA > SUBTAXON

SUBTAXON *n* supplementary piece of identifying information in plant or animal scientific name
SUBTAXONS > SUBTAXON
SUBTEEN *n* young person who has not yet become a teenager
SUBTEENS > SUBTEEN
SUBTENANT *n* person who rents property from a tenant
SUBTEND *vb* be opposite (an angle or side)
SUBTENDED > SUBTEND
SUBTENDS > SUBTEND
SUBTENSE *n* line that subtends
SUBTENSES > SUBTENSE
SUBTENURE *n* tenancy given by another tenant
SUBTEST *n* test that is part of larger test
SUBTESTS > SUBTEST
SUBTEXT *n* underlying theme in a piece of writing
SUBTEXTS > SUBTEXT
SUBTHEME *n* secondary theme
SUBTHEMES > SUBTHEME
SUBTIDAL *adj* below the level of low tide
SUBTIL *same as* > SUBTLE
SUBTILE *rare spelling of* > SUBTLE
SUBTILELY > SUBTILE
SUBTILER > SUBTILE
SUBTILEST > SUBTILE
SUBTILIN *n* antibiotic drug
SUBTILINS > SUBTILIN
SUBTILISE *same as* > SUBTILIZE
SUBTILITY > SUBTILE
SUBTILIZE *vb* bring to a purer state
SUBTILTY > SUBTILE
SUBTITLE *n* secondary title of a book ▷ *vb* provide with a subtitle or subtitles
SUBTITLED > SUBTITLE
SUBTITLES > SUBTITLE
SUBTLE *adj* not immediately obvious
SUBTLER > SUBTLE
SUBTLEST > SUBTLE
SUBTLETY *n* fine distinction
SUBTLY > SUBTLE
SUBTONE *n* subdivision of a tone
SUBTONES > SUBTONE
SUBTONIC *n* seventh degree of a major or minor scale
SUBTONICS > SUBTONIC
SUBTOPIA *n* suburban development that encroaches on rural areas
SUBTOPIAN > SUBTOPIA
SUBTOPIAS > SUBTOPIA
SUBTOPIC *n* topic within a larger topic
SUBTOPICS > SUBTOPIC
SUBTORRID *same as* > SUBTROPIC
SUBTOTAL *n* total made up by a column of figures, forming part of the total made up by a larger group ▷ *vb* work out a subtotal for (a group)

SUBTOTALS > SUBTOTAL
SUBTRACT vb take (one number or quantity) from another
SUBTRACTS > SUBTRACT
SUBTRADE n (in N America) specialist hired by a building contractor
SUBTRADES > SUBTRADE
SUBTREND n minor trend
SUBTRENDS > SUBTREND
SUBTRIBE n tribe within a larger tribe
SUBTRIBES > SUBTRIBE
SUBTRIST adj slightly sad
SUBTROPIC adj relating to the region lying between the tropics and the temperate lands
SUBTRUDE vb intrude stealthily
SUBTRUDED > SUBTRUDE
SUBTRUDES > SUBTRUDE
SUBTUNIC adj below membrane ▷ n garment worn under a tunic
SUBTUNICS > SUBTUNIC
SUBTWEET vb post a negative tweet about someone without naming them
SUBTWEETS > SUBTWEET
SUBTYPE n secondary or subordinate type or genre
SUBTYPES > SUBTYPE
SUBUCULA n ancient Roman man's undergarment
SUBUCULAS > SUBUCULA
SUBULATE adj (esp of plant parts) tapering to a point
SUBUNIT n distinct part or component of something larger
SUBUNITS > SUBUNIT
SUBURB n residential area on the outskirts of a city
SUBURBAN adj mildly derogatory term for inhabiting a suburb ▷ n mildly derogatory term for a person who lives in a suburb
SUBURBANS > SUBURBAN
SUBURBED > SUBURB
SUBURBIA n suburbs and their inhabitants
SUBURBIAS > SUBURBIA
SUBURBS > SUBURB
SUBURSINE adj of a bear subspecies
SUBVASSAL n vassal of a vassal
SUBVENE vb happen in such a way as to be of assistance
SUBVENED > SUBVENE
SUBVENES > SUBVENE
SUBVENING > SUBVENE
SUBVERSAL > SUBVERT
SUBVERSE same as
   > SUBVERT
SUBVERSED > SUBVERSE
SUBVERSES > SUBVERSE
SUBVERST > SUBVERSE
SUBVERT vb overthrow the authority of
SUBVERTED > SUBVERT
SUBVERTER > SUBVERT
SUBVERTS > SUBVERT

SUBVICAR n assistant to a vicar
SUBVICARS > SUBVICAR
SUBVIRAL adj of, caused by, or denoting a part of the structure of a virus
SUBVIRUS n organism smaller than a virus
SUBVISUAL adj not visible to the naked eye
SUBVOCAL adj formed in mind without being spoken aloud
SUBWARDEN n assistant to a warden
SUBWAY n passage under a road or railway ▷ vb travel by subway
SUBWAYED > SUBWAY
SUBWAYING > SUBWAY
SUBWAYS > SUBWAY
SUBWOOFER n loudspeaker for very low tones
SUBWORLD n underworld
SUBWORLDS > SUBWORLD
SUBWRITER n person carrying out writing tasks for other writer
SUBZERO adj lower than zero
SUBZONAL > SUBZONE
SUBZONE n subdivision of a zone
SUBZONES > SUBZONE
SUCCADE n piece of candied fruit
SUCCADES > SUCCADE
SUCCAH same as **>** SUKKAH
SUCCAHS > SUCCAH
SUCCEDENT adj following ▷ n successor
SUCCEED vb accomplish an aim
SUCCEEDED > SUCCEED
SUCCEEDER > SUCCEED
SUCCEEDS > SUCCEED
SUCCENTOR n deputy of the precentor of a cathedral that has retained its statutes from pre-Reformation days
SUCCES French word for
   > SUCCESS
SUCCESS n achievement of something attempted
SUCCESSES > SUCCESS
SUCCESSOR n person who succeeds someone in a position
SUCCI > SUCCUS
SUCCINATE n any salt or ester of succinic acid
SUCCINCT adj brief and clear
SUCCINIC adj of, relating to, or obtained from amber
SUCCINITE n type of amber
SUCCINYL n constituent of succinic acid
SUCCINYLS > SUCCINYL
SUCCISE adj ending abruptly, as if cut off
SUCCOR same as **>** SUCCOUR
SUCCORED > SUCCOR
SUCCORER > SUCCOR
SUCCORERS > SUCCOR
SUCCORIES > SUCCORY
SUCCORING > SUCCOR

SUCCORS > SUCCOR
SUCCORY another name for
   > CHICORY
SUCCOS same as **>** SUCCOTH
SUCCOSE > SUCCUS
SUCCOT same as **>** SUKKOTH
SUCCOTASH n mixture of cooked sweet corn kernels and lima beans, served as a vegetable
SUCCOTH variant of
   > SUKKOTH
SUCCOUR n help in distress ▷ vb give aid to (someone in time of difficulty)
SUCCOURED > SUCCOUR
SUCCOURER > SUCCOUR
SUCCOURS > SUCCOUR
SUCCOUS > SUCCUS
SUCCUBA same as
   > SUCCUBUS
SUCCUBAE > SUCCUBA
SUCCUBAS > SUCCUBA
SUCCUBI > SUCCUBUS
SUCCUBINE > SUCCUBUS
SUCCUBOUS adj having the leaves arranged so that the upper margin of each leaf is covered by the lower margin of the next leaf along
SUCCUBUS n female demon believed to have sex with sleeping men
SUCCULENT adj juicy and delicious ▷ n succulent plant
SUCCUMB vb give way (to something overpowering)
SUCCUMBED > SUCCUMB
SUCCUMBER > SUCCUMB
SUCCUMBS > SUCCUMB
SUCCURSAL adj (esp of a religious establishment) subsidiary ▷ n subsidiary establishment
SUCCUS n fluid
SUCCUSS vb shake (a patient) to detect the sound of fluid in a cavity
SUCCUSSED > SUCCUSS
SUCCUSSES > SUCCUSS
SUCH adj of the kind specified ▷ pron such things
SUCHLIKE pron such or similar things ▷ n such or similar things ▷ adj of such a kind
SUCHLIKES > SUCHLIKE
SUCHNESS > SUCH
SUCHWISE > SUCH
SUCK vb draw (liquid or air) into the mouth ▷ n sucking
SUCKED > SUCK
SUCKEN Scots word for
   > DISTRICT
SUCKENER n tenant
SUCKENERS > SUCKENER
SUCKENS > SUCKEN
SUCKER n person who is easily deceived or swindled ▷ vb strip off the suckers from (a plant)
SUCKERED > SUCKER
SUCKERING > SUCKER
SUCKERS > SUCKER
SUCKET same as **>** SUCCADE
SUCKETS > SUCKET

SUCKFISH n type of spiny-finned marine fish
SUCKHOLE n sycophant ▷ vb behave in a sycophantic manner
SUCKHOLED > SUCKHOLE
SUCKHOLES > SUCKHOLE
SUCKIER > SUCKY
SUCKIEST > SUCKY
SUCKINESS n state of inferiority
SUCKING adj not yet weaned
SUCKINGS > SUCKING
SUCKLE vb feed at the breast
SUCKLED > SUCKLE
SUCKLER > SUCKLE
SUCKLERS > SUCKLE
SUCKLES > SUCKLE
SUCKLESS > SUCK
SUCKLING n unweaned baby or young animal
SUCKLINGS > SUCKLING
SUCKS interj expression of disappointment
SUCKY adj despicable
SUCRALOSE n artificial sweetener
SUCRASE another name for
   > INVERTASE
SUCRASES > SUCRASE
SUCRE n former standard monetary unit of Ecuador
SUCRES > SUCRE
SUCRIER n small container for sugar at table
SUCRIERS > SUCRIER
SUCROSE same as **>** SUGAR
SUCROSES > SUCROSE
SUCTION n sucking ▷ vb subject to suction
SUCTIONAL > SUCTION
SUCTIONED > SUCTION
SUCTIONS > SUCTION
SUCTORIAL adj specialized for sucking or adhering
SUCTORIAN n microscopic creature
SUCURUJU n anaconda
SUCURUJUS > SUCURUJU
SUD singular of **>** SUDS
SUDAMEN n small cavity in the skin
SUDAMENS > SUDAMEN
SUDAMINA > SUDAMEN
SUDAMINAL > SUDAMEN
SUDARIA > SUDARIUM
SUDARIES > SUDARY
SUDARIUM n room in a Roman bathhouse where sweating is induced by heat
SUDARY same as
   > SUDARIUM
SUDATE vb sweat
SUDATED > SUDATE
SUDATES > SUDATE
SUDATING > SUDATE
SUDATION > SUDATE
SUDATIONS > SUDATE
SUDATORIA same as
   > SUDARIA
SUDATORY > SUDATE
SUDD n floating masses of reeds and weeds on the White Nile
SUDDEN adj done or occurring quickly and unexpectedly

SUDDENLY adv quickly and without warning

SUDDENS > SUDDEN

SUDDENTY n suddenness

SUDDER n supreme court in India

SUDDERS > SUDDER

SUDDS > SUDD

SUDOKU n type of puzzle in which numbers must be arranged in a grid according to certain rules

SUDOKUS > SUDOKU

SUDOR technical name for > SWEAT

SUDORAL > SUDOR

SUDORIFIC adj (drug) causing sweating ▷ n drug that causes sweating

SUDOROUS > SUDOR

SUDORS > SUDOR

SUDS pl n froth of soap and water, lather ▷ vb wash in suds

SUDSED > SUDS

SUDSER n soap opera

SUDSERS > SUDSER

SUDSES > SUDS

SUDSIER > SUDS

SUDSIEST > SUDS

SUDSING > SUDS

SUDSLESS > SUDS

SUDSY > SUDS

SUE vb start legal proceedings against

SUEABLE > SUE

SUED > SUE

SUEDE n leather with a velvety finish on one side ▷ vb give a suede finish to

SUEDED > SUEDE

SUEDELIKE adj like suede

SUEDES > SUEDE

SUEDETTE n imitation suede fabric

SUEDETTES > SUEDETTE

SUEDING > SUEDE

SUENT adj smooth

SUER > SUE

SUERS > SUE

SUES > SUE

SUET n hard fat obtained from sheep and cattle

SUETE n southeasterly wind in Cape Breton Island

SUETES > SUETE

SUETIER > SUET

SUETIEST > SUET

SUETS > SUET

SUETTIER > SUET

SUETTIEST > SUET

SUETTY > SUET

SUETY > SUET

SUFFARI same as > SAFARI

SUFFARIS > SUFFARI

SUFFECT adj additional ▷ n additional consul in ancient Rome

SUFFECTS > SUFFECT

SUFFER vb undergo or be subjected to

SUFFERED > SUFFER

SUFFERER > SUFFER

SUFFERERS > SUFFER

SUFFERING n pain, misery, or loss experienced by a person who suffers

SUFFERS > SUFFER

SUFFETE n official in ancient Carthage

SUFFETES > SUFFETE

SUFFICE vb be enough for a purpose

SUFFICED > SUFFICE

SUFFICER > SUFFICE

SUFFICERS > SUFFICE

SUFFICES > SUFFICE

SUFFICING > SUFFICE

SUFFIX n letters added to the end of a word to form another word ▷ vb add (letters) to the end of a word to form another word

SUFFIXAL > SUFFIX

SUFFIXED > SUFFIX

SUFFIXES > SUFFIX

SUFFIXING > SUFFIX

SUFFIXION > SUFFIX

SUFFLATE archaic word for > INFLATE

SUFFLATED > SUFFLATE

SUFFLATES > SUFFLATE

SUFFOCATE vb kill or be killed by deprivation of oxygen

SUFFRAGAN n bishop appointed to assist an archbishop ▷ adj (of any bishop of a diocese) subordinate to and assisting the superior archbishop

SUFFRAGE n right to vote in public elections

SUFFRAGES > SUFFRAGE

SUFFUSE vb spread through or over (something)

SUFFUSED > SUFFUSE

SUFFUSES > SUFFUSE

SUFFUSING > SUFFUSE

SUFFUSION > SUFFUSE

SUFFUSIVE > SUFFUSE

SUG vb sell a product while pretending to conduct market research

SUGAN n straw rope

SUGANS > SUGAN

SUGAR n carbohydrate used to sweeten food and drinks ▷ vb sweeten or cover with sugar

SUGARALLY n liquorice

SUGARBUSH n area covered in sugar maple trees

SUGARCANE n coarse grass that yields sugar

SUGARCOAT vb cover with sugar

SUGARED adj made sweeter or more appealing with or as with sugar

SUGARER > SUGAR

SUGARERS > SUGAR

SUGARIER > SUGARY

SUGARIEST > SUGARY

SUGARING n method of removing unwanted body hair

SUGARINGS > SUGARING

SUGARLESS > SUGAR

SUGARLIKE > SUGAR

SUGARLOAF n large conical mass of unrefined sugar

SUGARPLUM n crystallized plum

SUGARS > SUGAR

SUGARY adj of, like, or containing sugar

SUGGED > SUG

SUGGEST vb put forward (an idea) for consideration

SUGGESTED > SUGGEST

SUGGESTER > SUGGEST

SUGGESTS > SUGGEST

SUGGING n practice of selling products under the pretence of conducting market research

SUGGINGS > SUGGING

SUGH same as > SOUGH

SUGHED > SUGH

SUGHING > SUGH

SUGHS > SUGH

SUGO n Italian pasta sauce

SUGOS > SUGO

SUGS > SUG

SUHUR n meal eaten before sunrise by Muslims fasting during Ramadan

SUHURS > SUHUR

SUI adj of itself

SUICIDAL adj liable to commit suicide

SUICIDE n killing oneself intentionally ▷ vb commit suicide

SUICIDED > SUICIDE

SUICIDES > SUICIDE

SUICIDING > SUICIDE

SUID n pig or related animal

SUIDIAN > SUID

SUIDIANS > SUID

SUIDS > SUID

SUILLINE adj of or like a pig

SUING > SUE

SUINGS > SUE

SUINT n water-soluble substance found in the fleece of sheep

SUINTS > SUINT

SUIPLAP n South African slang for a drunkard

SUIPLAPS > SUIPLAP

SUIT n set of clothes designed to be worn together ▷ vb be appropriate for

SUITABLE adj appropriate or proper

SUITABLY > SUITABLE

SUITCASE n portable travelling case for clothing

SUITCASES > SUITCASE

SUITE n set of connected rooms in a hotel

SUITED > SUIT

SUITER n piece of luggage for carrying suits and dresses

SUITERS > SUITER

SUITES > SUITE

SUITING n fabric used for suits

SUITINGS > SUITING

SUITLIKE > SUIT

SUITOR n man who is courting someone ▷ vb act as a suitor

SUITORED > SUITOR

SUITORING > SUITOR

SUITORS > SUITOR

SUITRESS n female suitor

SUITS > SUIT

SUIVANTE n lady's maid

SUIVANTES > SUIVANTE

SUIVEZ vb musical direction meaning follow

SUJEE same as > SOOGEE

SUJEES > SUJEE

SUK same as > SUQ

SUKH same as > SUQ

SUKHS > SUKH

SUKIYAKI n Japanese dish consisting of sliced meat and vegetables

SUKIYAKIS > SUKIYAKI

SUKKAH n structure in which orthodox Jews eat and sleep during Sukkoth

SUKKAHS > SUKKAH

SUKKOS same as > SUKKOTH

SUKKOT same as > SUKKOTH

SUKKOTH n eight-day Jewish harvest festival

SUKS > SUK

SUKUK n financial certificate conforming to Islam lending principles

SUKUKS > SUKUK

SULCAL > SULCUS

SULCALISE same as > SULCALIZE

SULCALIZE vb furrow

SULCATE adj marked with longitudinal parallel grooves

SULCATED same as > SULCATE

SULCATION > SULCATE

SULCI > SULCUS

SULCUS n linear groove, furrow, or slight depression

SULDAN same as > SULTAN

SULDANS > SULDAN

SULFA same as > SULPHA

SULFAS > SULFA

SULFATASE n type of enzyme

SULFATE same as > SULPHATE

SULFATED > SULFATE

SULFATES > SULFATE

SULFATIC adj relating to sulphate

SULFATING > SULFATE

SULFATION > SULFATE

SULFID same as > SULPHIDE

SULFIDE same as > SULPHIDE

SULFIDES > SULFIDE

SULFIDS > SULFID

SULFINYL same as > SULPHINYL

SULFINYLS > SULFINYL

SULFITE same as > SULPHITE

SULFITES > SULFITE

SULFITIC > SULFITE

SULFO same as > SULPHONIC

SULFONATE n salt or ester of sulphonic acid

SULFONE same as > SULPHONE

SULFONES > SULFONE

SULFONIC > SULFONE

SULFONIUM n one of a type of salts

SULFONYL same as > SULPHURYL**

SULFONYLS > SULFONYL
SULFOXIDE n compound containing sulphur
SULFUR variant of > SULPHUR
SULFURATE vb treat with sulphur
SULFURED > SULFUR
SULFURET same as > SULPHURET
SULFURETS > SULFURET
SULFURIC > SULFUR
SULFURIER > SULFURY
SULFURING > SULFUR
SULFURISE variant of > SULFURIZE
SULFURIZE vb combine or treat with sulphur
SULFUROUS adj resembling sulphur
SULFURS > SULFUR
SULFURY adj containing sulfur
SULFURYL same as > SULPHURYL
SULFURYLS > SULFURYL
SULK vb be silent and sullen because of resentment or bad temper ▷ n resentful or sullen mood
SULKED > SULK
SULKER same as > SULK
SULKERS > SULKER
SULKIER > SULKY
SULKIES > SULKY
SULKIEST > SULKY
SULKILY > SULKY
SULKINESS > SULKY
SULKING > SULK
SULKS > SULK
SULKY adj moody or silent because of anger or resentment ▷ n light two-wheeled vehicle for one person
SULLAGE n filth or waste, esp sewage
SULLAGES > SULLAGE
SULLEN adj unwilling to talk or be sociable ▷ n sullen mood
SULLENER > SULLEN
SULLENEST > SULLEN
SULLENLY > SULLEN
SULLENS > SULLEN
SULLIABLE > SULLY
SULLIED > SULLY
SULLIES > SULLY
SULLY vb ruin (someone's reputation) ▷ n stain
SULLYING > SULLY
SULPH n amphetamine sulphate
SULPHA n any of a group of sulphonamides that prevent the growth of bacteria
SULPHAS > SULPHA
SULPHATE n salt or ester of sulphuric acid ▷ vb treat with a sulphate or convert into a sulphate
SULPHATED > SULPHATE
SULPHATES > SULPHATE
SULPHATIC > SULPHATE
SULPHID same as > SULPHIDE

SULPHIDE n compound of sulphur with another element
SULPHIDES > SULPHIDE
SULPHIDS > SULPHID
SULPHINYL another term for > THIONYL
SULPHITE n salt or ester of sulphurous acid
SULPHITES > SULPHITE
SULPHITIC > SULPHITE
SULPHONE n type of organic compound
SULPHONES > SULPHONE
SULPHONIC adj as in sulphonic acid type of strong organic acid
SULPHONYL same as > SULPHURYL
SULPHS > SULPH
SULPHUR n pale yellow nonmetallic element ▷ vb treat with sulphur
SULPHURED > SULPHUR
SULPHURET vb treat or combine with sulphur
SULPHURIC > SULPHUR
SULPHURS > SULPHUR
SULPHURY adj containing sulphur
SULPHURYL n particular chemical divalent group
SULTAN n sovereign of a Muslim country
SULTANA n kind of raisin
SULTANAS > SULTANA
SULTANATE n territory of a sultan
SULTANESS same as > SULTANA
SULTANIC > SULTAN
SULTANS > SULTAN
SULTRIER > SULTRY
SULTRIEST > SULTRY
SULTRILY > SULTRY
SULTRY adj (of weather or climate) hot and humid
SULU n type of sarong worn in Fiji
SULUS > SULU
SUM n result of addition, total ▷ vb add or form a total of (something)
SUMAC same as > SUMACH
SUMACH n type of temperate or subtropical shrub or small tree
SUMACHS > SUMACH
SUMACS > SUMAC
SUMATRA n violent storm blowing from the direction of Sumatra
SUMATRAS > SUMATRA
SUMBITCH n son of a bitch
SUMI n type of black ink used in Japan
SUMIS > SUMI
SUMLESS adj uncountable
SUMMA n compendium of theology, philosophy, or canon law
SUMMABLE > SUM
SUMMAE > SUMMA
SUMMAND n number or quantity forming part of a sum
SUMMANDS > SUMMAND

SUMMAR Scots variant of > SUMMER
SUMMARIES > SUMMARY
SUMMARILY > SUMMARY
SUMMARISE same as > SUMMARIZE
SUMMARIST > SUMMARIZE
SUMMARIZE vb make or be a summary of (something)
SUMMARY n brief account giving the main points of something ▷ adj done quickly, without formalities
SUMMAS > SUMMA
SUMMAT pron something ▷ n impressive or important person or thing
SUMMATE vb add up
SUMMATED > SUMMATE
SUMMATES > SUMMATE
SUMMATING > SUMMATE
SUMMATION n summary
SUMMATIVE > SUMMATION
SUMMATS > SUMMAT
SUMMED > SUM
SUMMER n warmest season of the year ▷ vb spend the summer (at a place)
SUMMERED > SUMMER
SUMMERIER > SUMMER
SUMMERING > SUMMER
SUMMERLY adj like summer
SUMMERS > SUMMER
SUMMERSET n somersault
SUMMERY > SUMMER
SUMMING > SUM
SUMMINGS > SUM
SUMMIST n writer of summae
SUMMISTS > SUMMIST
SUMMIT n top of a mountain or hill ▷ vb reach summit
SUMMITAL > SUMMIT
SUMMITED > SUMMIT
SUMMITEER n person who participates in a summit conference
SUMMITING > SUMMIT
SUMMITRY n practice of conducting international negotiations by summit conferences
SUMMITS > SUMMIT
SUMMON vb order (someone) to come
SUMMONED > SUMMON
SUMMONER > SUMMON
SUMMONERS > SUMMON
SUMMONING > SUMMON
SUMMONS n command summoning someone ▷ vb order (someone) to appear in court
SUMMONSED > SUMMONS
SUMMONSES > SUMMONS
SUMO n Japanese style of wrestling
SUMOIST > SUMO
SUMOISTS > SUMO
SUMOS > SUMO
SUMOTORI n sumo wrestler
SUMOTORIS > SUMOTORI
SUMP n container in an internal-combustion engine into which oil can drain
SUMPH n stupid person
SUMPHISH > SUMPH

SUMPHS > SUMPH
SUMPIT n Malay blowpipe
SUMPITAN same as > SUMPIT
SUMPITANS > SUMPITAN
SUMPITS > SUMPIT
SUMPS > SUMP
SUMPSIMUS n correct form of expression
SUMPTER n packhorse, mule, or other beast of burden
SUMPTERS > SUMPTER
SUMPTUARY adj controlling expenditure or extravagant use of resources
SUMPTUOUS adj lavish, magnificent
SUMPWEED n American weed
SUMPWEEDS > SUMPWEED
SUMS > SUM
SUMY pl n the monetary units of Uzbekistan
SUN n star around which the earth and other planets revolve ▷ vb expose (oneself) to the sun's rays
SUNBACK adj (of dress) cut low at back
SUNBAKE vb sunbathe, esp in order to become tanned ▷ n period of sunbaking
SUNBAKED adj (esp of roads, etc) dried or cracked by the sun's heat
SUNBAKES > SUNBAKE
SUNBAKING > SUNBAKE
SUNBATH n exposure of the body to the sun to get a suntan
SUNBATHE vb lie in the sunshine in order to get a suntan
SUNBATHED > SUNBATHE
SUNBATHER > SUNBATHE
SUNBATHES > SUNBATHE
SUNBATHS > SUNBATH
SUNBEAM n ray of sun
SUNBEAMED > SUNBEAM
SUNBEAMS > SUNBEAM
SUNBEAMY adj full of sunbeams
SUNBEAT adj exposed to sun
SUNBEATEN same as > SUNBEAT
SUNBED n machine for giving an artificial tan
SUNBEDS > SUNBED
SUNBELT n southern states of the US
SUNBELTS > SUNBELT
SUNBERRY n red fruit like the blackberry
SUNBIRD n type of small songbird with a bright plumage in the males
SUNBIRDS > SUNBIRD
SUNBLIND n blind that shades a room from the sun's glare
SUNBLINDS > SUNBLIND
SUNBLOCK n cream applied to the skin to protect it from the sun's rays
SUNBLOCKS > SUNBLOCK
SUNBONNET n hat that shades the face and neck from the sun

SUNBOW n bow of colours produced when sunlight shines through spray

SUNBOWS > SUNBOW

SUNBRIGHT adj bright as the sun

SUNBURN n painful reddening of the skin caused by overexposure to the sun ▷ vb become sunburnt

SUNBURNED > SUNBURN

SUNBURNS > SUNBURN

SUNBURNT > SUNBURN

SUNBURST n burst of sunshine, as through a break in the clouds

SUNBURSTS > SUNBURST

SUNCARE n use of products in protecting skin from the sun

SUNCARES > SUNCARE

SUNCHOKE n Jerusalem artichoke

SUNCHOKES > SUNCHOKE

SUNDAE n ice cream topped with fruit etc

SUNDAES > SUNDAE

SUNDARI n Indian tree

SUNDARIS > SUNDARI

SUNDECK n upper open deck on a passenger ship

SUNDECKS > SUNDECK

SUNDER vb break apart

SUNDERED > SUNDER

SUNDERER > SUNDER

SUNDERERS > SUNDER

SUNDERING > SUNDER

SUNDERS > SUNDER

SUNDEW n type of bog plant with leaves covered in sticky hairs

SUNDEWS > SUNDEW

SUNDIAL n device showing the time by means of a pointer that casts a shadow

SUNDIALS > SUNDIAL

SUNDOG n small rainbow or halo near the horizon

SUNDOGS > SUNDOG

SUNDOWN same as > SUNSET

SUNDOWNED > SUNDOWN

SUNDOWNER n tramp, esp one who seeks food and lodging at sundown when it is too late to work

SUNDOWNS > SUNDOWN

SUNDRA same as > SUNDARI

SUNDRAS > SUNDRA

SUNDRESS n strapped dress worn in hot weather

SUNDRI same as > SUNDARI

SUNDRIES > SUNDRY

SUNDRILY > SUNDRY

SUNDRIS > SUNDRI

SUNDROPS pl n any of various American primroses

SUNDRY adj several, various

SUNFAST adj not fading in sunlight

SUNFISH n large sea fish with a rounded body

SUNFISHES > SUNFISH

SUNFLOWER n tall plant with large golden flowers

SUNG > SING

SUNGAR same as > SANGAR

SUNGARS > SUNGAR

SUNGAZER n person who practises sungazing

SUNGAZERS > SUNGAZER

SUNGAZING n staring directly at the sun

SUNGLASS n convex lens used to focus the sun's rays and thus produce heat or ignition

SUNGLOW n pinkish glow often seen in the sky before sunrise or after sunset

SUNGLOWS > SUNGLOW

SUNGREBE another name for > FINFOOT

SUNGREBES > SUNGREBE

SUNHAT n hat that shades the face and neck from the sun

SUNHATS > SUNHAT

SUNI n S African dwarf antelope

SUNIS > SUNI

SUNK n bank or pad

SUNKEN adj unhealthily hollow

SUNKER n rock (partially) submerged in shallow water

SUNKERS > SUNKER

SUNKET n something good to eat

SUNKETS > SUNKET

SUNKIE n little stool

SUNKIES > SUNKIE

SUNKS > SUNK

SUNLAMP n lamp that generates ultraviolet rays

SUNLAMPS > SUNLAMP

SUNLAND n sunny area

SUNLANDS > SUNLAND

SUNLESS adj without sun or sunshine

SUNLESSLY > SUNLESS

SUNLIGHT n light that comes from the sun

SUNLIGHTS > SUNLIGHT

SUNLIKE > SUN

SUNLIT > SUNLIGHT

SUNN n leguminous plant of the East Indies

SUNNA n body of traditional Islamic law

SUNNAH same as > SUNNA

SUNNAHS > SUNNAH

SUNNAS > SUNNA

SUNNED > SUN

SUNNIER > SUNNY

SUNNIES pl n pair of sunglasses

SUNNIEST > SUNNY

SUNNILY > SUNNY

SUNNINESS > SUNNY

SUNNING > SUN

SUNNS > SUNN

SUNNY adj full of or exposed to sunlight

SUNPORCH n porch for sunbathing on

SUNPROOF > SUN

SUNRAY n ray of light from the sun

SUNRAYS > SUNRAY

SUNRISE n daily appearance of the sun above the horizon

SUNRISES > SUNRISE

SUNRISING same as > SUNRISE

SUNROOF n panel in the roof of a car that opens to let in air

SUNROOFS > SUNROOF

SUNROOM n room or glass-enclosed porch designed to display beautiful views

SUNROOMS > SUNROOM

SUNS > SUN

SUNSCALD n sun damage on tomato plants

SUNSCALDS > SUNSCALD

SUNSCREEN n cream or lotion applied to exposed skin to protect it from the ultraviolet rays of the sun

SUNSEEKER n person looking for sunny weather

SUNSET vb phase out

SUNSETS > SUNSET

SUNSETTED > SUNSET

SUNSHADE n anything used to shade people from the sun, such as a parasol or awning

SUNSHADES > SUNSHADE

SUNSHINE n light and warmth from the sun

SUNSHINES > SUNSHINE

SUNSHINY adj sunny

SUNSPECS pl n sunglasses

SUNSPOT n dark patch appearing temporarily on the sun's surface

SUNSPOTS > SUNSPOT

SUNSTAR n type of starfish with up to 13 arms

SUNSTARS > SUNSTAR

SUNSTONE n type of translucent feldspar with reddish-gold speckles

SUNSTONES > SUNSTONE

SUNSTROKE n illness caused by prolonged exposure to intensely hot sunlight

SUNSTRUCK adj suffering from sunstroke

SUNSUIT n child's outfit consisting of a brief top and shorts or a short skirt

SUNSUITS > SUNSUIT

SUNTAN n browning of the skin caused by exposure to the sun

SUNTANNED > SUNTAN

SUNTANS > SUNTAN

SUNTRAP n very sunny sheltered place

SUNTRAPS > SUNTRAP

SUNUP same as > SUNRISE

SUNUPS > SUNUP

SUNWARD same as > SUNWARDS

SUNWARDS adv towards the sun

SUNWISE adv moving in the same direction as the sun

SUP same as > SUPINE

SUPAWN same as > SUPPAWN

SUPAWNS > SUPAWN

SUPE n superintendent

SUPER adj excellent ▷ n superannuation ▷ interj enthusiastic expression of approval or assent ▷ vb work as superintendent

SUPERABLE adj able to be surmounted or overcome

SUPERABLY > SUPERABLE

SUPERADD vb add (something) to something that has already been added

SUPERADDS > SUPERADD

SUPERATE vb overcome

SUPERATED > SUPERATE

SUPERATES > SUPERATE

SUPERATOM n cluster of atoms behaving like a single atom

SUPERB adj excellent, impressive, or splendid

SUPERBAD adj exceptionally bad

SUPERBANK n bank that owns other banks

SUPERBER > SUPERB

SUPERBEST > SUPERB

SUPERBIKE n high-performance motorcycle

SUPERBITY > SUPERB

SUPERBLY > SUPERB

SUPERBOLD adj exceptionally bold

SUPERBOMB n large bomb

SUPERBRAT n exceptionally unpleasant child

SUPERBUG n bacterium resistant to antibiotics

SUPERBUGS > SUPERBUG

SUPERCAR n very expensive fast or powerful car with a centrally located engine

SUPERCARS > SUPERCAR

SUPERCEDE former variant of > SUPERSEDE

SUPERCELL n unusually large storm cell

SUPERCHIC adj highly chic

SUPERCITY n very large city

SUPERCLUB n large and important club

SUPERCOIL vb form a complex coil

SUPERCOLD adj very cold

SUPERCOOL vb cool or be cooled to a temperature below that at which freezing or crystallization should occur

SUPERCOP n high-ranking police officer

SUPERCOPS > SUPERCOP

SUPERCOW n dairy cow that produces a very high milk yield

SUPERCOWS > SUPERCOW

SUPERCUTE adj very cute

SUPERED > SUPER

SUPEREGO n that part of the unconscious mind that governs ideas about what is right and wrong

SUPEREGOS > SUPEREGO

SUPERETTE n small store or dairy laid out along the lines of a supermarket

SUPERFAN n very devoted fan

SUPERFANS > SUPERFAN

SUPERFARM n very large farm

SUPERFAST adj very fast

SUPERFINE adj of exceptional fineness or quality

SUPERFIRM adj very firm

SUPERFIT *adj* highly fit

SUPERFIX *n* linguistic feature distinguishing the meaning of one word from another

SUPERFLUX *n* superfluity

SUPERFLY *adj* pretentiously flamboyant

SUPERFOOD *n* food thought to be beneficial to health

SUPERFUND *n* large fund

SUPERFUSE *vb* pour or be poured so as to cover something

SUPERGENE *n* cluster of genes

SUPERGLUE *n* extremely strong and quick-drying glue ▷ *vb* fix with superglue

SUPERGOOD *adj* very good

SUPERGUN *n* large powerful gun

SUPERGUNS > SUPERGUN

SUPERHARD *adj* extremely hard

SUPERHEAT *vb* heat (a vapour, esp steam) to a temperature above its saturation point for a given pressure

SUPERHERO *n* any of various comic-strip characters with superhuman abilities or magical powers

SUPERHET *n* type of radio receiver

SUPERHETS > SUPERHET

SUPERHIGH *adj* extremely high

SUPERHIT *n* very popular hit

SUPERHITS > SUPERHIT

SUPERHIVE *n* upper part of beehive

SUPERHOT *adj* very hot

SUPERHYPE *n* exaggerated hype

SUPERING > SUPER

SUPERIOR *adj* greater in quality, quantity, or merit ▷ *n* person of greater rank or status

SUPERIORS > SUPERIOR

SUPERJET *n* supersonic aircraft

SUPERJETS > SUPERJET

SUPERJOCK *n* very athletic person

SUPERLAIN > SUPERLIE

SUPERLAY > SUPERLIE

SUPERLIE *vb* lie above

SUPERLIES > SUPERLIE

SUPERLOAD *n* variable weight on a structure

SUPERLONG *adj* very long

SUPERLOO *n* automated public toilet

SUPERLOOS > SUPERLOO

SUPERMALE *former name for* > METAMALE

SUPERMAN *n* man with great physical or mental powers

SUPERMART *n* large self-service store selling food and household supplies

SUPERMAX *n* jail or other facility having the very highest levels of security

SUPERMEN > SUPERMAN

SUPERMIND *n* very powerful brain

SUPERMINI *n* small car, usually a hatchback, that is economical to run but has a high level of performance

SUPERMOM *n* very capable and busy mother

SUPERMOMS > SUPERMOM

SUPERMOON *n* occasion when the perigee coincides with a full moon

SUPERMOTO *n* form of motorcycle racing over part-tarmac and part-dirt circuits

SUPERNAL *adj* of or from the world of the divine

SUPERNATE *n* liquid lying above a sediment ▷ *vb* float on (a surface)

SUPERNOVA *n* star that explodes and briefly becomes exceptionally bright

SUPERPIMP *n* pimp controlling many prostitutes

SUPERPLUS *n* surplus

SUPERPORT *n* large port

SUPERPOSE *vb* transpose (the coordinates of one geometric figure) to coincide with those of another

SUPERPRO *n* person regarded as a real professional

SUPERPROS > SUPERPRO

SUPERRACE *n* important race

SUPERREAL *adj* surreal

SUPERRICH *adj* exceptionally wealthy

SUPERROAD *n* very large road

SUPERS > SUPER

SUPERSAFE *adj* very safe

SUPERSALE *n* large sale

SUPERSALT *n* acid salt

SUPERSAUR *n* very large dinosaur

SUPERSEDE *vb* replace, supplant

SUPERSELL *vb* sell in very large numbers

SUPERSET *n* set containing all the members of another set plus other members

SUPERSETS > SUPERSET

SUPERSEX *n* in genetics, type of sterile organism

SUPERSHOW *n* very impressive show

SUPERSIZE *vb* make larger

SUPERSOFT *adj* very soft

SUPERSOLD > SUPERSELL

SUPERSPY *n* highly accomplished spy

SUPERSTAR *n* very famous entertainer or sportsperson

SUPERSTUD *n* highly virile man

SUPERTAX *n* extra tax on incomes above a certain level

SUPERTHIN *adj* very thin

SUPERTRAM *n* type of tram with greater capacity and speed than conventional trams

SUPERUSER *n* type of administration-level account in a computing system

SUPERVENE *vb* occur as an unexpected development

SUPERVISE *vb* watch over to direct or check

SUPERWAIF *n* very young and very thin supermodel

SUPERWAVE *n* large wave

SUPERWEED *n* hybrid plant that contains genes for herbicide resistance

SUPERWIDE *n* very wide lens

SUPERWIFE *n* highly accomplished wife

SUPES > SUPE

SUPINATE *vb* turn (the hand and forearm) so that the palm faces up or forwards

SUPINATED > SUPINATE

SUPINATES > SUPINATE

SUPINATOR *n* muscle of the forearm that can produce the motion of supination

SUPINE *adj* lying flat on one's back ▷ *n* noun form derived from a verb in Latin

SUPINELY > SUPINE

SUPINES > SUPINE

SUPLEX *n* type of wrestling hold

SUPLEXES > SUPLEX

SUPPAWN *n* kind of porridge

SUPPAWNS > SUPPAWN

SUPPEAGO *same as* > SERPIGO

SUPPED > SUP

SUPPER *n* light evening meal ▷ *vb* eat supper

SUPPERED > SUPPER

SUPPERING > SUPPER

SUPPERS > SUPPER

SUPPING > SUP

SUPPLANT *vb* take the place of, oust

SUPPLANTS > SUPPLANT

SUPPLE *adj* (of a person) moving and bending easily and gracefully ▷ *vb* make or become supple

SUPPLED > SUPPLE

SUPPLELY *same as* > SUPPLY

SUPPLER > SUPPLE

SUPPLES > SUPPLE

SUPPLEST > SUPPLE

SUPPLIAL *n* instance of supplying

SUPPLIALS > SUPPLIAL

SUPPLIANT *n* person who requests humbly

SUPPLICAT *n* university petition

SUPPLIED > SUPPLY

SUPPLIER > SUPPLY

SUPPLIERS > SUPPLY

SUPPLIES > SUPPLY

SUPPLING > SUPPLE

SUPPLY *vb* provide with something required ▷ *n* supplying ▷ *adj* acting as a temporary substitute ▷ *adv* in a supple manner

SUPPLYING > SUPPLY

SUPPORT *vb* bear the weight of ▷ *n* supporting

SUPPORTED > SUPPORT

SUPPORTER *n* person who supports a team, principle, etc

SUPPORTS > SUPPORT

SUPPOSAL *n* supposition

SUPPOSALS > SUPPOSAL

SUPPOSE *vb* presume to be true

SUPPOSED *adj* presumed to be true without proof, doubtful

SUPPOSER > SUPPOSE

SUPPOSERS > SUPPOSE

SUPPOSES > SUPPOSE

SUPPOSING > SUPPOSE

SUPPRESS *vb* put an end to

SUPPURATE *vb* (of a wound etc) produce pus

SUPRA *adv* above, esp referring to earlier parts of a book etc

SUPREMA > SUPREMUM

SUPREMACY *n* supreme power

SUPREME *adj* highest in authority, rank, or degree ▷ *n* rich sauce made with a base of veal or chicken stock

SUPREMELY > SUPREME

SUPREMER > SUPREME

SUPREMES > SUPREME

SUPREMEST > SUPREME

SUPREMITY *n* supremeness

SUPREMO *n* person in overall authority

SUPREMOS > SUPREMO

SUPREMUM *n* (in maths) smallest quantity greater than or equal to each of a set or subset

SUPREMUMS > SUPREMUM

SUPS > SUP

SUQ *n* open-air marketplace

SUQS > SUQ

SUR *prep* above

SURA *n* any of the 114 chapters of the Koran

SURAH *n* twill-weave fabric of silk or rayon, used for dresses, blouses, etc

SURAHS > SURAH

SURAL *adj* of or relating to the calf of the leg

SURAMIN *n* drug used in treating sleeping sickness

SURAMINS > SURAMIN

SURANCE *same as* > ASSURANCE

SURANCES > SURANCE

SURAS > SURA

SURAT *n* cotton fabric from Surat in India

SURATS > SURAT

SURBAHAR *n* Indian string instrument

SURBAHARS > SURBAHAR

SURBASE *n* uppermost part, such as a moulding, of a pedestal, base, or skirting

SURBASED *adj* having a surbase

SURBASES > SURBASE

SURBATE *vb* make feet sore through walking

SURBATED > SURBATE

SURBATES > SURBATE

SURBATING > SURBATE
SURBED vb put something on its edge
SURBEDDED > SURBED
SURBEDS > SURBED
SURBET > SURBATE
SURCEASE n cessation or intermission ▷ vb desist from (some action)
SURCEASED > SURCEASE
SURCEASES > SURCEASE
SURCHARGE n additional charge ▷ vb charge (someone) an additional sum or tax
SURCINGLE n girth for a horse which goes around the body, used esp with a racing saddle ▷ vb put a surcingle on or over (a horse)
SURCOAT n tunic worn by a knight over their armour
SURCOATS > SURCOAT
SURCULI > SURCULUS
SURCULOSE adj (of a plant) bearing suckers
SURCULUS n sucker on plant
SURD n number that cannot be expressed in whole numbers ▷ adj of or relating to a surd
SURDITIES > SURDITY
SURDITY n deafness
SURDS > SURD
SURE adj free from uncertainty or doubt ▷ interj certainly ▷ vb archaic form of sewer
SURED > SURE
SUREFIRE adj certain to succeed
SURELY adv it must be true that
SURENESS > SURE
SURER > SURE
SURES > SURE
SUREST > SURE
SURETIED > SURETY
SURETIES > SURETY
SURETY n person who takes responsibility for the fulfilment of another's obligation ▷ vb be surety for
SURETYING > SURETY
SURF n foam caused by waves breaking on the shore ▷ vb take part in surfing
SURFABLE > SURF
SURFACE n outside or top of an object ▷ vb become apparent
SURFACED > SURFACE
SURFACER > SURFACE
SURFACERS > SURFACE
SURFACES > SURFACE
SURFACING > SURFACE
SURFBIRD n American shore bird
SURFBIRDS > SURFBIRD
SURFBOARD n long smooth board used in surfing
SURFBOAT n boat with a high bow and stern and flotation chambers
SURFBOATS > SURFBOAT
SURFED > SURF
SURFEIT n excessive amount ▷ vb supply or feed excessively

SURFEITED > SURFEIT
SURFEITER > SURFEIT
SURFEITS > SURFEIT
SURFER > SURFING
SURFERS > SURFING
SURFFISH n fish of American coastal seas
SURFICIAL adj superficial
SURFIE n young person whose main interest is in surfing
SURFIER > SURF
SURFIES > SURFIE
SURFIEST > SURF
SURFING n sport of riding on a board on the crest of a wave
SURFINGS > SURFING
SURFLIKE > SURF
SURFMAN n sailor skilled in sailing through surf
SURFMEN > SURFMAN
SURFPERCH n type of marine fish of North American Pacific coastal waters
SURFRIDE vb ride on surf
SURFRIDER > SURFRIDE
SURFRIDES > SURFRIDE
SURFRODE > SURFRIDE
SURFS > SURF
SURFSIDE adj next to the sea
SURFY > SURF
SURGE n sudden powerful increase ▷ vb increase suddenly
SURGED > SURGE
SURGEFUL > SURGE
SURGELESS > SURGE
SURGENT > SURGE
SURGEON n doctor who specializes in surgery
SURGEONCY n office, duties, or position of a surgeon, esp in the army or navy
SURGEONS > SURGEON
SURGER > SURGE
SURGERIES > SURGERY
SURGERS > SURGE
SURGERY n treatment in which the patient's body is cut open in order to treat the affected part
SURGES > SURGE
SURGICAL adj involving or used in surgery
SURGIER > SURGE
SURGIEST > SURGE
SURGING > SURGE
SURGINGS > SURGE
SURGY > SURGE
SURICATE n type of meerkat
SURICATES > SURICATE
SURIMI n blended seafood product made from precooked fish
SURIMIS > SURIMI
SURING > SURE
SURLIER > SURLY
SURLIEST > SURLY
SURLILY > SURLY
SURLINESS > SURLY
SURLOIN same as > SIRLOIN
SURLOINS > SURLOIN

SURLY adj ill-tempered and rude
SURMASTER n deputy headmaster
SURMISAL > SURMISE
SURMISALS > SURMISE
SURMISE n guess, conjecture ▷ vb guess (something) from incomplete or uncertain evidence
SURMISED > SURMISE
SURMISER > SURMISE
SURMISERS > SURMISE
SURMISES > SURMISE
SURMISING > SURMISE
SURMOUNT vb overcome (a problem)
SURMOUNTS > SURMOUNT
SURMULLET n red mullet
SURNAME n family name ▷ vb furnish with or call by a surname
SURNAMED > SURNAME
SURNAMER > SURNAME
SURNAMERS > SURNAME
SURNAMES > SURNAME
SURNAMING > SURNAME
SURPASS vb be greater than or superior to
SURPASSED > SURPASS
SURPASSER > SURPASS
SURPASSES > SURPASS
SURPLICE n loose white robe worn by members of the clergy and choristers
SURPLICED > SURPLICE
SURPLICES > SURPLICE
SURPLUS n amount left over in excess of what is required ▷ adj extra ▷ vb be left over in excess of what is required
SURPLUSED > SURPLUS
SURPLUSES > SURPLUS
SURPRINT vb print (additional matter) over something already printed ▷ n marks, printed matter, etc, that have been surprinted
SURPRINTS > SURPRINT
SURPRISAL > SURPRISE
SURPRISE n unexpected event ▷ vb cause to feel amazement or wonder
SURPRISED > SURPRISE
SURPRISER > SURPRISE
SURPRISES > SURPRISE
SURPRIZE same as > SURPRISE
SURPRIZED > SURPRIZE
SURPRIZES > SURPRIZE
SURQUEDRY n arrogance
SURQUEDY same as > SURQUEDRY
SURRA n tropical febrile disease of animals
SURRAS > SURRA
SURREAL adj bizarre ▷ n atmosphere or qualities evoked by surrealism
SURREALLY > SURREAL
SURREALS > SURREAL
SURREBUT vb give evidence to support the surrebutter
SURREBUTS > SURREBUT

SURREINED adj (of horse) ridden too much
SURREJOIN vb reply to legal rejoinder
SURRENDER vb give oneself up ▷ n surrendering
SURRENDRY same as > SURRENDER
SURREY n light four-wheeled horse-drawn carriage
SURREYS > SURREY
SURROGACY > SURROGATE
SURROGATE n substitute ▷ adj acting as a substitute ▷ vb put in another's position as a deputy, substitute, etc
SURROUND vb be, come, or place all around (a person or thing) ▷ n border or edging
SURROUNDS > SURROUND
SURROYAL n high point on stag's horns
SURROYALS > SURROYAL
SURTAX n extra tax on incomes above a certain level ▷ vb assess for liability to surtax
SURTAXED > SURTAX
SURTAXES > SURTAX
SURTAXING > SURTAX
SURTITLE n printed translation of the libretto of an opera in a language foreign to the audience
SURTITLES pl n brief translations of the text of an opera or play projected above the stage
SURTOUT n man's overcoat resembling a frock coat
SURTOUTS > SURTOUT
SURUCUCU n South American snake
SURUCUCUS > SURUCUCU
SURVEIL same as > SURVEILLE
SURVEILED > SURVEIL
SURVEILLE vb observe closely
SURVEILS > SURVEIL
SURVEY vb view or consider in a general way ▷ n surveying
SURVEYAL > SURVEY
SURVEYALS > SURVEY
SURVEYED > SURVEY
SURVEYING n practice of measuring altitudes, angles, and distances on the land surface so that they can be accurately plotted on a map
SURVEYOR n person whose occupation is to survey land or buildings
SURVEYORS > SURVEYOR
SURVEYS > SURVEY
SURVIEW vb survey
SURVIEWED > SURVIEW
SURVIEWS > SURVIEW
SURVIVAL n condition of having survived ▷ adj of, relating to, or assisting the act of surviving
SURVIVALS > SURVIVAL
SURVIVE vb continue to live or exist after (a difficult experience)
SURVIVED > SURVIVE

SURVIVER same as
> SURVIVOR
SURVIVERS > SURVIVER
SURVIVES > SURVIVE
SURVIVING > SURVIVE
SURVIVOR n person or thing
that survives
SURVIVORS > SURVIVOR
SUS same as > SUSS
SUSCEPTOR n sponsor
SUSCITATE vb excite
SUSED > SUS
SUSES > SUS
SUSHI n Japanese dish of
small cakes of cold rice with a
topping of raw fish
SUSHIS > SUSHI
SUSING > SUS
SUSLIK n central Eurasian
ground squirrel
SUSLIKS > SUSLIK
SUSPECT vb believe
(someone) to be guilty
without having any proof
▷ adj not to be trusted ▷ n
person who is suspected
SUSPECTED > SUSPECT
SUSPECTER > SUSPECT
SUSPECTS > SUSPECT
SUSPENCE same as
> SUSPENSE
SUSPEND vb hang from a
high place
SUSPENDED > SUSPEND
SUSPENDER n elastic strap
for holding up women's
stockings
SUSPENDS > SUSPEND
SUSPENS same as
> SUSPENSE
SUSPENSE n state of
uncertainty while awaiting
news, an event, etc
SUSPENSER n film that
creates a feeling of suspense
SUSPENSES > SUSPENSE
SUSPENSOR n ligament or
muscle that holds a part in
position
SUSPICION n feeling of not
trusting a person or thing
SUSPIRE vb sigh or utter
with a sigh
SUSPIRED > SUSPIRE
SUSPIRES > SUSPIRE
SUSPIRING > SUSPIRE
SUSS vb attempt to work out
(a situation, etc), using one's
intuition ▷ n sharpness of
mind
SUSSED > SUSS
SUSSES > SUSS
SUSSING > SUSS
SUSTAIN vb maintain or
prolong ▷ n prolongation of
a note, by playing technique
or electronics
SUSTAINED > SUSTAIN
SUSTAINER n rocket engine
that maintains the velocity
of a space vehicle after the
booster has been jettisoned
SUSTAINS > SUSTAIN
SUSTINENT adj sustaining
SUSU n (in the Caribbean)
savings fund shared by
friends
SUSURRANT > SUSURRATE

SUSURRATE vb make a soft
rustling sound
SUSURROUS adj full of
murmuring sounds
SUSURRUS > SUSURRATE
SUSUS > SUSU
SUTILE adj involving sewing
SUTLER n merchant who
accompanied an army in
order to sell provisions
SUTLERIES > SUTLER
SUTLERS > SUTLER
SUTLERY > SUTLER
SUTOR n cobbler
SUTORIAL > SUTOR
SUTORIAN > SUTOR
SUTORS > SUTOR
SUTRA n Sanskrit sayings or
collections of sayings
SUTRAS > SUTRA
SUTTA n Buddhist scripture
SUTTAS > SUTTA
SUTTEE n custom whereby a
widow burnt herself on her
husband's funeral pyre
SUTTEEISM > SUTTEE
SUTTEES > SUTTEE
SUTTLE vb work as a sutler
SUTTLED > SUTTLE
SUTTLES > SUTTLE
SUTTLETIE same as
> SUBTLETY
SUTTLING > SUTTLE
SUTTLY > SUBTLE
SUTURAL > SUTURE
SUTURALLY > SUTURE
SUTURE n stitch joining the
edges of a wound ▷ vb join
(the edges of a wound, etc)
by means of sutures
SUTURED > SUTURE
SUTURES > SUTURE
SUTURING > SUTURE
SUZERAIN n state or
sovereign with limited
authority over another
self-governing state
SUZERAINS > SUZERAIN
SVARAJ same as > SWARAJ
SVARAJES > SVARAJ
SVASTIKA same as
> SWASTIKA
SVASTIKAS > SVASTIKA
SVEDBERG n unit used in
physics
SVEDBERGS > SVEDBERG
SVELTE adj attractively or
gracefully slim
SVELTELY > SVELTE
SVELTER > SVELTE
SVELTEST > SVELTE
SWAB n small piece of cotton
wool used to apply
medication, clean a wound,
etc ▷ vb clean (a wound)
with a swab
SWABBED > SWAB
SWABBER n person who uses
a swab
SWABBERS > SWABBER
SWABBIE same as > SWABBY
SWABBIES > SWABBY
SWABBING > SWAB
SWABBY n seaman
SWABS > SWAB
SWACHH adj (in Indian
English) clean

SWACK adj flexible ▷ vb strike
SWACKED > SWACK
SWACKING > SWACK
SWACKS > SWACK
SWAD n loutish person
SWADDIE same as > SWADDY
SWADDIES > SWADDY
SWADDLE vb wrap (a baby) in
swaddling clothes ▷ n
swaddling clothes
SWADDLED > SWADDLE
SWADDLER > SWADDLE
SWADDLERS > SWADDLE
SWADDLES > SWADDLE
SWADDLING > SWADDLE
SWADDY n private soldier
SWADS > SWAD
SWAG n stolen property ▷ vb
sway from side to side
SWAGE n shaped tool or die
used in forming cold metal by
hammering ▷ vb form
(metal) with a swage
SWAGED > SWAGE
SWAGER > SWAGE
SWAGERS > SWAGE
SWAGES > SWAGE
SWAGGED > SWAG
SWAGGER vb walk or behave
arrogantly ▷ n arrogant walk
or manner ▷ adj elegantly
fashionable
SWAGGERED > SWAGGER
SWAGGERER > SWAGGER
SWAGGERS > SWAGGER
SWAGGIE same as
> SWAGGER
SWAGGIES > SWAGGIE
SWAGGING > SWAG
SWAGING > SWAGE
SWAGMAN n tramp who
carries their belongings in a
bundle on their back
SWAGMEN > SWAGMAN
SWAGS > SWAG
SWAGSHOP n shop selling
cheap goods
SWAGSHOPS > SWAGSHOP
SWAGSMAN same as
> SWAGMAN
SWAGSMEN > SWAGSMAN
SWAIL same as > SWALE
SWAILS > SWAIL
SWAIN n suitor
SWAINING n acting as suitor
SWAININGS > SWAINING
SWAINISH > SWAIN
SWAINS > SWAIN
SWALE n moist depression in
a tract of land ▷ vb sway
SWALED > SWALE
SWALES > SWALE
SWALIER > SWALE
SWALIEST > SWALE
SWALING > SWALE
SWALINGS > SWALE
SWALLET n hole where
water goes underground
SWALLETS > SWALLET
SWALLIES > SWALLY
SWALLOW vb cause to pass
down one's throat ▷ n
swallowing
SWALLOWED > SWALLOW
SWALLOWER > SWALLOW
SWALLOWS > SWALLOW
SWALLY n alcoholic drink

SWALY > SWALE
SWAM > SWIM
SWAMI n Hindu religious
teacher
SWAMIES > SWAMI
SWAMIS > SWAMI
SWAMP n watery area of land,
bog ▷ vb cause (a boat) to fill
with water and sink
SWAMPED > SWAMP
SWAMPER n person who lives
or works in a swampy region
SWAMPERS > SWAMPER
SWAMPIER > SWAMP
SWAMPIEST > SWAMP
SWAMPING > SWAMP
SWAMPISH > SWAMP
SWAMPLAND n permanently
waterlogged area
SWAMPLESS > SWAMP
SWAMPS > SWAMP
SWAMPY > SWAMP
SWAMY same as > SWAMI
SWAN n large usu white water
bird with a long graceful neck
▷ vb wander about idly
SWANG > SWING
SWANHERD n person who
herds swans
SWANHERDS > SWANHERD
SWANK vb show off or boast
▷ n showing off or boasting
SWANKED > SWANK
SWANKER > SWANK
SWANKERS > SWANK
SWANKEST > SWANK
SWANKEY same as > SWANKY
SWANKEYS > SWANKEY
SWANKIE same as > SWANKY
SWANKIER > SWANKY
SWANKIES > SWANKY
SWANKIEST > SWANKY
SWANKILY > SWANKY
SWANKING > SWANK
SWANKPOT same as > SWANK
SWANKPOTS > SWANKPOT
SWANKS > SWANK
SWANKY adj expensive and
showy, stylish ▷ n lively
person
SWANLIKE > SWAN
SWANNED > SWAN
SWANNERY n place where
swans are kept and bred
SWANNIE n (in NZ) type of
all-weather heavy woollen
shirt
SWANNIER > SWANNY
SWANNIES > SWANNIE
SWANNIEST > SWANNY
SWANNING > SWAN
SWANNINGS > SWAN
SWANNY adj swanlike
SWANPAN n Chinese abacus
SWANPANS > SWANPAN
SWANS > SWAN
SWANSDOWN n fine soft
feathers of a swan
SWANSKIN n skin of a swan
with the feathers attached
SWANSKINS > SWANSKIN
SWANSONG n beautiful song
fabled to be sung by a swan
before it dies
SWANSONGS > SWANSONG
SWAP vb exchange
(something) for something
else ▷ n exchange

SWAPFILE n computer file which provides space for transferred programs

SWAPFILES > SWAPFILE

SWAPPABLE adj capable of being swapped

SWAPPED > SWAP

SWAPPER > SWAP

SWAPPERS > SWAP

SWAPPING > SWAP

SWAPPINGS > SWAP

SWAPS > SWAP

SWAPT > SWAP

SWAPTION another name for > SWAP

SWAPTIONS > SWAPTION

SWARAJ n (in British India) self-government

SWARAJES > SWARAJ

SWARAJISM > SWARAJ

SWARAJIST > SWARAJ

SWARD n stretch of short grass ▷ vb cover or become covered with grass

SWARDED > SWARD

SWARDIER > SWARDY

SWARDIEST > SWARDY

SWARDING > SWARD

SWARDS > SWARD

SWARDY adj covered with sward

SWARE > SWEAR

SWARF n material removed by cutting tools in the machining of metals, stone, etc ▷ vb faint

SWARFED > SWARF

SWARFING > SWARF

SWARFS > SWARF

SWARM n large group of bees or other insects ▷ vb move in a swarm

SWARMED > SWARM

SWARMER > SWARM

SWARMERS > SWARM

SWARMING > SWARM

SWARMINGS > SWARM

SWARMS > SWARM

SWART adj swarthy

SWARTH same as > SWART

SWARTHIER > SWARTHY

SWARTHILY > SWARTHY

SWARTHS > SWARTH

SWARTHY adj dark-complexioned

SWARTIER > SWARTY

SWARTIEST > SWARTY

SWARTNESS > SWART

SWARTY adj swarthy

SWARVE same as > SWARF

SWARVED > SWARF

SWARVES > SWARF

SWARVING > SWARF

SWASH n rush of water up a beach following each break of the waves ▷ vb wash or move with noisy splashing

SWASHED > SWASH

SWASHER n braggart

SWASHERS > SWASHER

SWASHES > SWASH

SWASHIER > SWASHY

SWASHIEST > SWASHY

SWASHING > SWASH

SWASHINGS > SWASH

SWASHWORK n type of work done on a lathe

SWASHY adj slushy

SWASTICA same as > SWASTIKA

SWASTICAS > SWASTICA

SWASTIKA n symbol used as the emblem of Nazi Germany

SWASTIKAS > SWASTIKA

SWAT vb strike or hit sharply ▷ n swatter

SWATCH n sample of cloth

SWATCHES > SWATCH

SWATH n width of one sweep of a scythe or of the blade of a mowing machine

SWATHABLE > SWATHE

SWATHE vb bandage or wrap completely ▷ n bandage or wrapping

SWATHED > SWATHE

SWATHER > SWATHE

SWATHERS > SWATHE

SWATHES > SWATHE

SWATHIER > SWATH

SWATHIEST > SWATH

SWATHING n act of enveloping (with a garment, bandage, etc)

SWATHINGS > SWATHING

SWATHS > SWATH

SWATHY > SWATH

SWATS > SWAT

SWATTED > SWAT

SWATTER n device for killing insects ▷ vb splash

SWATTERED > SWATTER

SWATTERS > SWATTER

SWATTIER same as > SWOTTIER

SWATTIEST same as > SWOTTIEST

SWATTING > SWAT

SWATTINGS > SWAT

SWATTY same as > SWOTTY

SWAY vb swing to and fro or from side to side ▷ n power or influence

SWAYABLE > SWAY

SWAYBACK n abnormal sagging in the spine of older horses

SWAYBACKS > SWAYBACK

SWAYED > SWAY

SWAYER > SWAY

SWAYERS > SWAY

SWAYFUL > SWAY

SWAYING > SWAY

SWAYINGS > SWAY

SWAYL same as > SWEAL

SWAYLED > SWAYL

SWAYLING > SWAYL

SWAYLINGS > SWAYL

SWAYLS > SWAYL

SWAYS > SWAY

SWAZZLE n small metal instrument used to produce a shrill voice

SWAZZLES > SWAZZLE

SWEAL vb scorch

SWEALED > SWEAL

SWEALING > SWEAL

SWEALINGS > SWEAL

SWEALS > SWEAL

SWEAR vb use obscene or blasphemous language

SWEARD same as > SWORD

SWEARDS > SWEARD

SWEARER > SWEAR

SWEARERS > SWEAR

SWEARIER > SWEARY

SWEARIEST > SWEARY

SWEARING > SWEAR

SWEARINGS > SWEAR

SWEARS > SWEAR

SWEARWORD n word considered obscene or blasphemous

SWEARY adj using swear-words

SWEAT n salty liquid given off through the pores of the skin ▷ vb have sweat coming through the pores

SWEATBAND n strip of cloth tied around the forehead or wrist to absorb sweat

SWEATBOX n device for causing tobacco leaves, fruit, or hides to sweat

SWEATED adj made by exploited labour

SWEATER n (woollen) garment for the upper part of the body

SWEATERED adj wearing a sweater

SWEATERS > SWEATER

SWEATIER > SWEATY

SWEATIEST > SWEATY

SWEATILY > SWEATY

SWEATING > SWEAT

SWEATINGS > SWEAT

SWEATLESS > SWEAT

SWEATS > SWEAT

SWEATSHOP n place where employees work long hours in poor conditions for low pay

SWEATSUIT n knitted suit worn by athletes for training

SWEATY adj covered with sweat

SWEDE n kind of turnip

SWEDES > SWEDE

SWEDGER n Scots dialect word for sweet

SWEDGERS > SWEDGER

SWEE vb sway

SWEED > SWEE

SWEEING > SWEE

SWEEL same as > SWEAL

SWEELED > SWEEL

SWEELING > SWEEL

SWEELS > SWEEL

SWEENEY n police flying squad

SWEENEYS > SWEENEY

SWEENIES > SWEENY

SWEENY n wasting of the shoulder muscles of a horse

SWEEP vb remove dirt from (a floor) with a broom ▷ n sweeping

SWEEPBACK n rearward inclination of a component or surface

SWEEPER n device used to sweep carpets

SWEEPERS > SWEEPER

SWEEPIER > SWEEP

SWEEPIEST > SWEEP

SWEEPING > SWEEP

SWEEPINGS pl n debris, litter, or refuse

SWEEPS > SWEEP

SWEEPY > SWEEP

SWEER variant of > SWEIR

SWEERED > SWEER

SWEERING > SWEER

SWEERS > SWEER

SWEERT variant of > SWEER

SWEES > SWEE

SWEET adj tasting of or like sugar ▷ n shaped piece of food consisting mainly of sugar ▷ vb sweeten

SWEETCORN n variety of maize, the kernels of which are eaten when young

SWEETED > SWEET

SWEETEN vb make (food or drink) sweet or sweeter

SWEETENED > SWEETEN

SWEETENER n sweetening agent that does not contain sugar

SWEETENS > SWEETEN

SWEETER > SWEET

SWEETEST > SWEET

SWEETFISH n small Japanese fish

SWEETIE n lovable person

SWEETIES > SWEETIE

SWEETING n variety of sweet apple

SWEETINGS > SWEETING

SWEETISH > SWEET

SWEETLIP n type of Australian fish with big lips

SWEETLIPS > SWEETLIP

SWEETLY > SWEET

SWEETMAN n (in the Caribbean) a man kept by a woman

SWEETMEAL adj (of biscuits) sweet and wholemeal

SWEETMEAT n sweet delicacy such as a small cake

SWEETMEN > SWEETMAN

SWEETNESS > SWEET

SWEETS > SWEET

SWEETSHOP n shop selling confectionery

SWEETSOP n small West Indian tree

SWEETSOPS > SWEETSOP

SWEETVELD n grazing field with high-quality grass

SWEETWOOD n tropical tree

SWEETY same as > SWEETIE

SWEIR vb swear ▷ adj lazy

SWEIRED > SWEIR

SWEIRER > SWEIR

SWEIREST > SWEIR

SWEIRING > SWEIR

SWEIRNESS > SWEIR

SWEIRS > SWEIR

SWEIRT variant of > SWEIR

SWELCHIE n whirlpool in Orkney

SWELCHIES > SWELCHIE

SWELL vb expand or increase ▷ n swelling or being swollen ▷ adj excellent or fine

SWELLDOM n fashionable society

SWELLDOMS > SWELLDOM

SWELLED > SWELL

SWELLER > SWELL

SWELLERS > SWELL

SWELLEST > SWELL

SWELLFISH *popular name for* > PUFFER
SWELLHEAD *n* conceited person
SWELLING > SWELL
SWELLINGS > SWELL
SWELLISH > SWELL
SWELLS > SWELL
SWELT *vb* die
SWELTED > SWELT
SWELTER *vb* feel uncomfortably hot ▷ *n* hot and uncomfortable condition
SWELTERED > SWELTER
SWELTERS > SWELTER
SWELTING > SWELT
SWELTRIER > SWELTRY
SWELTRY *adj* sultry
SWELTS > SWELT
SWEPT > SWEEP
SWEPTBACK *adj* (of an aircraft wing) having the leading edge inclined backwards towards the rear
SWEPTWING *adj* (of an aircraft) having wings swept backwards
SWERF *same as* > SWARF
SWERFED > SWERF
SWERFING > SWERF
SWERFS > SWERF
SWERVABLE > SWERVE
SWERVE *vb* turn aside from a course sharply or suddenly ▷ *n* swerving
SWERVED > SWERVE
SWERVER > SWERVE
SWERVERS > SWERVE
SWERVES > SWERVE
SWERVING > SWERVE
SWERVINGS > SWERVE
SWEVEN *n* vision or dream
SWEVENS > SWEVEN
SWEY *same as* > SWEE
SWEYED > SWEY
SWEYING > SWEY
SWEYS > SWEY
SWIDDEN *n* area of land where slash-and-burn techniques have been used
SWIDDENS > SWIDDEN
SWIES > SWY
SWIFT *adj* moving or able to move quickly ▷ *n* fast-flying bird with pointed wings ▷ *adv* swiftly or quickly ▷ *vb* make tight
SWIFTED > SWIFT
SWIFTER *n* line run around the ends of capstan bars
SWIFTERS > SWIFTER
SWIFTEST > SWIFT
SWIFTIE *n* trick, ruse, or deception
SWIFTIES > SWIFTY
SWIFTING > SWIFT
SWIFTLET *n* type of small Asian swift
SWIFTLETS > SWIFTLET
SWIFTLY > SWIFT
SWIFTNESS > SWIFT
SWIFTS > SWIFT
SWIFTY *same as* > SWIFTIE
SWIG *n* large mouthful of drink ▷ *vb* drink in large mouthfuls

SWIGGED > SWIG
SWIGGER > SWIG
SWIGGERS > SWIG
SWIGGING > SWIG
SWIGS > SWIG
SWILE *n* seal (the marine animal)
SWILER *n* (in Newfoundland) a seal hunter
SWILERS > SWILER
SWILES > SWILE
SWILING *n* practice of hunting seals
SWILINGS > SWILING
SWILL *vb* drink greedily ▷ *n* sloppy mixture containing waste food, fed to pigs
SWILLED > SWILL
SWILLER > SWILL
SWILLERS > SWILL
SWILLING > SWILL
SWILLINGS > SWILL
SWILLS > SWILL
SWIM *vb* move along in water by movements of the limbs ▷ *n* act or period of swimming
SWIMMABLE > SWIM
SWIMMER > SWIM
SWIMMERET *n* any of the small paired appendages on the abdomen of crustaceans
SWIMMERS *pl n* swimming costume
SWIMMIER > SWIMMY
SWIMMIEST > SWIMMY
SWIMMILY > SWIMMY
SWIMMING > SWIM
SWIMMINGS > SWIM
SWIMMY *adj* dizzy
SWIMS > SWIM
SWIMSUIT *n* woman's swimming garment that leaves the arms and legs bare
SWIMSUITS > SWIMSUIT
SWIMWEAR *n* swimming costumes
SWIMWEARS > SWIMWEAR
SWINDGE *same as* > SWINGE
SWINDGED > SWINDGE
SWINDGES > SWINDGE
SWINDGING > SWINDGE
SWINDLE *vb* cheat (someone) out of money ▷ *n* instance of swindling
SWINDLED > SWINDLE
SWINDLER > SWINDLE
SWINDLERS > SWINDLE
SWINDLES > SWINDLE
SWINDLING > SWINDLE
SWINE *n* contemptible person
SWINEHERD *n* person who looks after pigs
SWINEHOOD > SWINE
SWINELIKE > SWINE
SWINEPOX *n* acute infectious viral disease of pigs
SWINERIES > SWINERY
SWINERY *n* pig farm
SWINES > SWINE
SWING *vb* move to and fro, sway ▷ *n* swinging
SWINGARM *n* main part of the rear suspension on a motorcycle

SWINGARMS > SWINGARM
SWINGBEAT *n* type of modern dance music that combines soul, rhythm and blues, and hip-hop
SWINGBIN *n* rubbish bin with a lid that swings shut after being opened
SWINGBINS > SWINGBIN
SWINGBOAT *n* piece of fairground equipment consisting of a boat-shaped carriage for swinging in
SWINGBY *n* act of spacecraft passing close to planet
SWINGBYS > SWINGBY
SWINGE *vb* beat, flog, or punish
SWINGED > SWINGE
SWINGEING > SWINGE
SWINGER *n* person regarded as being modern and lively
SWINGERS > SWINGER
SWINGES > SWINGE
SWINGIER > SWINGY
SWINGIEST > SWINGY
SWINGING *adj* lively and modern
SWINGINGS > SWING
SWINGISM *n* former resistance to use of agricultural machines
SWINGISMS > SWINGISM
SWINGLE *n* flat-bladed wooden instrument used for beating and scraping flax ▷ *vb* use a swingle on
SWINGLED > SWINGLE
SWINGLES > SWINGLE
SWINGLING > SWINGLE
SWINGMAN *n* musician specializing in swing music
SWINGMEN > SWINGMAN
SWINGS > SWING
SWINGTAIL *n* as in *swingtail cargo aircraft* kind of cargo aircraft
SWINGTREE *n* crossbar in a horse's harness
SWINGY *adj* lively and modern
SWINISH > SWINE
SWINISHLY > SWINE
SWINK *vb* toil or drudge ▷ *n* toil or drudgery
SWINKED > SWINK
SWINKER > SWINK
SWINKERS > SWINK
SWINKING > SWINK
SWINKS > SWINK
SWINNEY *variant of* > SWEENY
SWINNEYS > SWINNEY
SWIPE *vb* strike (at) with a sweeping blow ▷ *n* hard blow
SWIPED > SWIPE
SWIPER > SWIPE
SWIPERS > SWIPE
SWIPES *pl n* beer, esp when poor or weak
SWIPEY *adj* drunk
SWIPIER > SWIPEY
SWIPIEST > SWIPEY
SWIPING > SWIPE
SWIPLE *same as* > SWIPPLE
SWIPLES > SWIPLE

SWIPPLE *n* part of a flail that strikes the grain
SWIPPLES > SWIPPLE
SWIRE *n* neck
SWIRES > SWIRE
SWIRL *vb* turn with a whirling motion ▷ *n* whirling motion
SWIRLED > SWIRL
SWIRLIER > SWIRL
SWIRLIEST > SWIRL
SWIRLING > SWIRL
SWIRLS > SWIRL
SWIRLY > SWIRL
SWISH *vb* move with a whistling or hissing sound ▷ *n* whistling or hissing sound ▷ *adj* fashionable, smart
SWISHED > SWISH
SWISHER > SWISH
SWISHERS > SWISH
SWISHES > SWISH
SWISHEST > SWISH
SWISHIER > SWISHY
SWISHIEST > SWISHY
SWISHING > SWISH
SWISHINGS > SWISH
SWISHY *adj* moving with a swishing sound
SWISS *n* type of muslin
SWISSES > SWISS
SWISSING *n* method of treating cloth
SWISSINGS > SWISSING
SWITCH *n* device for opening and closing an electric circuit ▷ *vb* change abruptly
SWITCHED > SWITCH
SWITCHEL *n* type of beer
SWITCHELS > SWITCHEL
SWITCHER > SWITCH
SWITCHERS > SWITCH
SWITCHES > SWITCH
SWITCHIER > SWITCH
SWITCHING > SWITCH
SWITCHMAN *n* person who operates railway points
SWITCHMEN > SWITCHMAN
SWITCHY > SWITCH
SWITH *adv* swiftly
SWITHE *same as* > SWITH
SWITHER *vb* hesitate or be indecisive ▷ *n* state of hesitation or uncertainty
SWITHERED > SWITHER
SWITHERS > SWITHER
SWITHLY > SWITH
SWITS *same as* > SWITCH
SWITSES > SWITS
SWIVE *vb* have sexual intercourse with (a person)
SWIVED > SWIVE
SWIVEL *vb* turn on a central point ▷ *n* coupling device that allows an attached object to turn freely
SWIVELED > SWIVEL
SWIVELING > SWIVEL
SWIVELLED > SWIVEL
SWIVELS > SWIVEL
SWIVES > SWIVE
SWIVET *n* nervous state
SWIVETS > SWIVET
SWIVING > SWIVE
SWIZ *n* swindle or disappointment

SWIZZ same as > SWIZ
SWIZZED > SWIZZ
SWIZZES > SWIZZ
SWIZZING > SWIZZ
SWIZZLE vb cheat or con ▷ n act of cheating or conning
SWIZZLED > SWIZZLE
SWIZZLER > SWIZZLE
SWIZZLERS > SWIZZLE
SWIZZLES > SWIZZLE
SWIZZLING > SWIZZLE
SWOB less common word for > SWAB
SWOBBED > SWOB
SWOBBER > SWOB
SWOBBERS > SWOB
SWOBBING > SWOB
SWOBS > SWOB
SWOFFER > SWOFFING
SWOFFERS > SWOFFING
SWOFFING n sport of saltwater fly-fishing
SWOFFINGS > SWOFFING
SWOLE adj muscular from weight training
SWOLER > SWOLE
SWOLEST > SWOLE
SWOLLEN > SWELL
SWOLLENLY > SWELL
SWOLN > SWELL
SWOON n faint ▷ vb faint because of shock or strong emotion
SWOONED > SWOON
SWOONER > SWOON
SWOONERS > SWOON
SWOONIER > SWOONY
SWOONIEST > SWOONY
SWOONING > SWOON
SWOONINGS > SWOON
SWOONS > SWOON
SWOONY adj romantic
SWOOP vb sweep down or pounce on suddenly ▷ n swooping
SWOOPED > SWOOP
SWOOPER > SWOOP
SWOOPERS > SWOOP
SWOOPIER > SWOOP
SWOOPIEST > SWOOP
SWOOPING > SWOOP
SWOOPS > SWOOP
SWOOPY > SWOOP
SWOOSH vb make a swirling or rustling sound when moving or pouring out ▷ n swirling or rustling sound or movement
SWOOSHED > SWOOSH
SWOOSHES > SWOOSH
SWOOSHING > SWOOSH
SWOP same as > SWAP
SWOPPABLE same as > SWAPPABLE
SWOPPED > SWOP
SWOPPER > SWOP
SWOPPERS > SWOP
SWOPPING > SWOP
SWOPPINGS > SWOP
SWOPS > SWOP
SWOPT > SWOP
SWORD n weapon with a long sharp blade ▷ vb bear a sword
SWORDBILL n South American hummingbird

SWORDED > SWORD
SWORDER n fighter with sword
SWORDERS > SWORDER
SWORDFERN n type of fern with long thin fronds
SWORDFISH n large fish with a very long upper jaw
SWORDING > SWORD
SWORDLESS > SWORD
SWORDLIKE > SWORD
SWORDMAN same as > SWORDSMAN
SWORDMEN > SWORDMAN
SWORDPLAY n action or art of fighting with a sword
SWORDS > SWORD
SWORDSMAN n person skilled in the use of a sword
SWORDSMEN > SWORDSMAN
SWORDTAIL n type of small freshwater fish of Central America
SWORE > SWEAR
SWORN > SWEAR
SWOT vb study (a subject) intensively ▷ n person who studies hard ·
SWOTS > SWOT
SWOTTED > SWOT
SWOTTER same as > SWOT
SWOTTERS > SWOTTER
SWOTTIER > SWOTTY
SWOTTIEST > SWOTTY
SWOTTING > SWOT
SWOTTINGS > SWOT
SWOTTY adj given to studying hard, esp to the exclusion of other activities
SWOUN same as > SWOON
SWOUND same as > SWOON
SWOUNDED > SWOUND
SWOUNDING > SWOUND
SWOUNDS less common spelling of > ZOUNDS
SWOUNE same as > SWOON
SWOUNED > SWOUNE
SWOUNES > SWOUNE
SWOUNING > SWOUNE
SWOUNS > SWOUN
SWOWND same as > SWOON
SWOWNDS > SWOWND
SWOWNE same as > SWOON
SWOWNES > SWOWNE
SWOZZLE same as > SWAZZLE
SWOZZLES > SWOZZLE
SWUM > SWIM
SWUNG > SWING
SWY n Australian gambling game involving two coins
SYBARITE n lover of luxury ▷ adj luxurious
SYBARITES > SYBARITE
SYBARITIC > SYBARITE
SYBBE same as > SIB
SYBBES > SYBBE
SYBIL same as > SIBYL
SYBILS > SYBIL
SYBO n spring onion
SYBOE same as > SYBO
SYBOES > SYBOE
SYBOTIC adj of a swineherd
SYBOTISM > SYBOTIC
SYBOTISMS > SYBOTIC
SYBOW same as > SYBO

SYBOWS > SYBOW
SYCAMINE n mulberry tree mentioned in the Bible, thought to be the black mulberry
SYCAMINES > SYCAMINE
SYCAMORE n tree with five-pointed leaves and two-winged fruits
SYCAMORES > SYCAMORE
SYCE n (formerly, in India) a servant employed to look after horses, etc
SYCEE n silver ingots formerly used as a medium of exchange in China
SYCEES > SYCEE
SYCES > SYCE
SYCOMORE same as > SYCAMORE
SYCOMORES > SYCOMORE
SYCON n type of sponge
SYCONIA > SYCONIUM
SYCONIUM n fleshy fruit of the fig
SYCONOID adj of or like a sycon
SYCONS > SYCON
SYCOPHANT n person who uses flattery to win favour from people with power or influence
SYCOSES > SYCOSIS
SYCOSIS n chronic inflammation of the hair follicles
SYE vb strain
SYED > SYE
SYEING > SYE
SYEN same as > SCION
SYENITE n light-coloured coarse-grained plutonic igneous rock
SYENITES > SYENITE
SYENITIC > SYENITE
SYENS > SYEN
SYES > SYE
SYKE same as > SIKE
SYKER adv surely
SYKES > SYKE
SYLI n Finnish unit of volume
SYLIS > SYLI
SYLLABARY n table or list of syllables
SYLLABI > SYLLABUS
SYLLABIC adj of or relating to syllables ▷ n syllabic consonant
SYLLABICS > SYLLABIC
SYLLABIFY vb divide (a word) into syllables
SYLLABISE same as > SYLLABIZE
SYLLABISM n use of a writing system consisting of characters for syllables
SYLLABIZE vb divide into syllables
SYLLABLE n part of a word pronounced as a unit
SYLLABLED > SYLLABLE
SYLLABLES > SYLLABLE
SYLLABUB n dessert of beaten cream, sugar, and wine
SYLLABUBS > SYLLABUB

SYLLABUS n list of subjects for a course of study
SYLLEPSES > SYLLEPSIS
SYLLEPSIS n (in grammar or rhetoric) the use of a single sentence construction in which a verb, adjective, etc is made to cover two syntactical functions
SYLLEPTIC > SYLLEPSIS
SYLLOGE n collection or summary
SYLLOGES > SYLLOGE
SYLLOGISE same as > SYLLOGIZE
SYLLOGISM n form of logical reasoning consisting of two premises and a conclusion
SYLLOGIST > SYLLOGISM
SYLLOGIZE vb reason or infer by using syllogisms
SYLPH n slender graceful girl or woman
SYLPHIC > SYLPH
SYLPHID n little sylph
SYLPHIDE same as > SYLPHID
SYLPHIDES > SYLPHIDE
SYLPHIDS > SYLPHID
SYLPHIER > SYLPH
SYLPHIEST > SYLPH
SYLPHINE > SYLPH
SYLPHISH > SYLPH
SYLPHLIKE > SYLPH
SYLPHS > SYLPH
SYLPHY > SYLPH
SYLVA n trees growing in a particular region
SYLVAE > SYLVA
SYLVAN adj relating to woods and trees ▷ n inhabitant of the woods, esp a spirit
SYLVANER n German variety of grape
SYLVANERS > SYLVANER
SYLVANITE n silver-white mineral
SYLVANS > SYLVAN
SYLVAS > SYLVA
SYLVATIC adj growing, living, or occurring in a wood or beneath a tree
SYLVIA n songbird
SYLVIAS > SYLVIA
SYLVIINE > SYLVIA
SYLVIN same as > SYLVITE
SYLVINE same as > SYLVITE
SYLVINES > SYLVINE
SYLVINITE n rock containing sylvine
SYLVINS > SYLVIN
SYLVITE n soluble colourless, white, or coloured mineral
SYLVITES > SYLVITE
SYMAR same as > CYMAR
SYMARS > SYMAR
SYMBION same as > SYMBIONT
SYMBIONS > SYMBION
SYMBIONT n organism living in a state of symbiosis
SYMBIONTS > SYMBIONT
SYMBIOSES > SYMBIOSIS

SYMBIOSIS n close association of two species living together to their mutual benefit
SYMBIOT same as > SYMBIONT
SYMBIOTE same as > SYMBIONT
SYMBIOTES > SYMBIOTE
SYMBIOTIC > SYMBIOSIS
SYMBIOTS > SYMBIOT
SYMBOL n sign or thing that stands for something else ▷ vb be a symbol
SYMBOLE same as > CYMBAL
SYMBOLED > SYMBOL
SYMBOLES > SYMBOLE
SYMBOLIC adj of or relating to a symbol or symbols
SYMBOLICS n study of beliefs
SYMBOLING > SYMBOL
SYMBOLISE same as > SYMBOLIZE
SYMBOLISM n representation of something by symbols
SYMBOLIST n person who uses or can interpret symbols ▷ adj of, relating to, or characterizing symbolism or symbolists
SYMBOLIZE vb be a symbol of
SYMBOLLED > SYMBOL
SYMBOLOGY n use, study, or interpretation of symbols
SYMBOLS > SYMBOL
SYMITAR same as > SCIMITAR
SYMITARE same as > SCIMITAR
SYMITARES > SYMITARE
SYMITARS > SYMITAR
SYMMETRAL > SYMMETRY
SYMMETRIC adj (of a disease) affecting both sides of the body
SYMMETRY n state of having two halves that are mirror images of each other
SYMPATHIN n substance released at certain sympathetic nerve endings
SYMPATHY n compassion for someone's pain or distress
SYMPATICO adj nice
SYMPATRIC adj (of biological speciation or species) existing in the same geographical areas
SYMPATRY n existing of organisms together without interbreeding
SYMPETALY n quality of having petals that are united
SYMPHILE n insect that lives in the nests of social insects and is fed and reared by the inmates
SYMPHILES > SYMPHILE
SYMPHILY n presence of different kinds of animal in ants' nests
SYMPHONIC > SYMPHONY
SYMPHONY n composition for orchestra, with several movements

SYMPHYSES > SYMPHYSIS
SYMPHYSIS n growing together of parts or structures
SYMPHYTIC > SYMPHYSIS
SYMPLAST n continuous system of protoplasts, linked by plasmodesmata and bounded by the cell wall
SYMPLASTS > SYMPLAST
SYMPLOCE n word repetition in successive clauses
SYMPLOCES > SYMPLOCE
SYMPODIA > SYMPODIUM
SYMPODIAL > SYMPODIUM
SYMPODIUM n main axis of growth in the grapevine and similar plants
SYMPOSIA > SYMPOSIUM
SYMPOSIAC adj of, suitable for, or occurring at a symposium
SYMPOSIAL > SYMPOSIUM
SYMPOSIUM n conference for discussion of a particular topic
SYMPTOM n sign indicating the presence of an illness
SYMPTOMS > SYMPTOM
SYMPTOSES > SYMPTOSIS
SYMPTOSIS n wasting condition
SYMPTOTIC > SYMPTOSIS
SYN Scots word for > SINCE
SYNAGOG same as > SYNAGOGUE
SYNAGOGAL > SYNAGOGUE
SYNAGOGS > SYNAGOG
SYNAGOGUE n Jewish place of worship and religious instruction
SYNALEPHA n elision of vowels in speech
SYNANDRIA pl n peculiar bunchings of stamens
SYNANGIA > SYNANGIUM
SYNANGIUM n junction between arteries
SYNANON n type of therapy given to drug addicts
SYNANONS > SYNANON
SYNANTHIC > SYNANTHY
SYNANTHY n abnormal joining between flowers
SYNAPHEA n continuity in metre of verses of poem
SYNAPHEAS > SYNAPHEA
SYNAPHEIA same as > SYNAPHEA
SYNAPSE n gap where nerve impulses pass between two nerve cells ▷ vb create a synapse
SYNAPSED > SYNAPSE
SYNAPSES > SYNAPSIS
SYNAPSID n prehistoric mammal-like reptile
SYNAPSIDS > SYNAPSID
SYNAPSING > SYNAPSE
SYNAPSIS n association in pairs of homologous chromosomes at the start of meiosis
SYNAPTASE n type of enzyme
SYNAPTE n litany in Greek Orthodox Church

SYNAPTES > SYNAPTE
SYNAPTIC adj of or relating to a synapse
SYNARCHY n joint rule
SYNASTRY n coincidence of astrological influences
SYNAXARIA pl n readings in the Greek Orthodox Church
SYNAXES > SYNAXIS
SYNAXIS n early Christian meeting
SYNBIOTIC n synthesis of prebiotic bacteria and one or more probiotics, used in food products
SYNC n synchronization ▷ vb synchronize
SYNCARP n fleshy multiple fruit
SYNCARPS > SYNCARP
SYNCARPY n quality of consisting of united carpels
SYNCED > SYNC
SYNCH same as > SYNC
SYNCHED > SYNCH
SYNCHING > SYNCH
SYNCHRO n type of electrical device
SYNCHRONY n state of being synchronous
SYNCHROS > SYNCHRO
SYNCHS > SYNCH
SYNCHYSES > SYNCHYSIS
SYNCHYSIS n muddled meaning
SYNCING > SYNC
SYNCLINAL > SYNCLINE
SYNCLINE n downward slope of stratified rock
SYNCLINES > SYNCLINE
SYNCOM n communications satellite in stationary orbit
SYNCOMS > SYNCOM
SYNCOPAL > SYNCOPE
SYNCOPATE vb stress the weak beats in (a rhythm) instead of the strong ones
SYNCOPE n omission of one or more sounds or letters from the middle of a word
SYNCOPES > SYNCOPE
SYNCOPIC > SYNCOPE
SYNCOPTIC > SYNCOPE
SYNCRETIC adj of the tendency of languages to reduce their use of inflection
SYNCS > SYNC
SYNCYTIA > SYNCYTIUM
SYNCYTIAL > SYNCYTIUM
SYNCYTIUM n mass of cytoplasm containing many nuclei and enclosed in a cell membrane
SYND same as > SYNE
SYNDACTYL adj (of certain animals) having two or more digits growing fused together ▷ n animal with this arrangement of digits
SYNDED > SYND
SYNDESES > SYNDESIS
SYNDESIS n use of syndetic constructions
SYNDET n synthetic detergent
SYNDETIC adj denoting a grammatical construction in which two clauses are connected by a conjunction

SYNDETON n syndetic construction
SYNDETONS > SYNDETON
SYNDETS > SYNDET
SYNDIC n business or legal agent of some institutions
SYNDICAL adj relating to the theory that syndicates of workers should seize the means of production
SYNDICATE n group of people or firms undertaking a joint business project ▷ vb publish (material) in several newspapers
SYNDICS > SYNDIC
SYNDING > SYND
SYNDINGS > SYND
SYNDROME n combination of symptoms indicating a particular disease
SYNDROMES > SYNDROME
SYNDROMIC > SYNDROME
SYNDS > SYND
SYNE vb rinse ▷ n rinse ▷ adv since
SYNECHIA n abnormality of the eye
SYNECHIAS > SYNECHIA
SYNECIOUS adj having male and female organs together on a branch
SYNECTIC > SYNECTICS
SYNECTICS n method of identifying and solving problems that depends on creative thinking
SYNED > SYNE
SYNEDRIA > SYNEDRION
SYNEDRIAL > SYNEDRION
SYNEDRION n assembly of judges
SYNEDRIUM same as > SYNEDRION
SYNERESES > SYNERESIS
SYNERESIS n process in which a gel contracts on standing and exudes liquid
SYNERGIA same as > SYNERGY
SYNERGIAS > SYNERGIA
SYNERGIC > SYNERGY
SYNERGID n type of cell in embryo
SYNERGIDS > SYNERGID
SYNERGIES > SYNERGY
SYNERGISE same as > SYNERGIZE
SYNERGISM same as > SYNERGY
SYNERGIST n drug, muscle, etc, that increases the action of another ▷ adj of or relating to synergism
SYNERGIZE vb act in synergy
SYNERGY n collective effect that is greater than the sum of individual effects
SYNES > SYNE
SYNESES > SYNESIS
SYNESIS n grammatical construction in which the form of a word is conditioned by the meaning
SYNESISES > SYNESIS
SYNFUEL n synthetic fuel
SYNFUELS > SYNFUEL

S

SYNGAMIC > SYNGAMY
SYNGAMIES > SYNGAMY
SYNGAMOUS > SYNGAMY
SYNGAMY n reproduction involving the fusion of male and female gametes
SYNGAS n mixture of carbon monoxide and hydrogen
SYNGASES > SYNGAS
SYNGASSES > SYNGAS
SYNGENEIC adj with identical genes
SYNGENIC same as > SYNGENEIC
SYNGRAPH n document signed by several parties
SYNGRAPHS > SYNGRAPH
SYNING > SYNE
SYNIZESES > SYNIZESIS
SYNIZESIS n contraction of two vowels originally belonging to separate syllables into a single syllable
SYNKARYA > SYNKARYON
SYNKARYON n nucleus of a fertilized egg
SYNOD n church council
SYNODAL adj of or relating to a synod ▷ n money paid to a bishop by less senior members of the clergy at a synod
SYNODALS > SYNODAL
SYNODIC adj involving conjunction of the same star, planet, or satellite
SYNODICAL > SYNOD
SYNODS > SYNOD
SYNODSMAN n layman at synod
SYNODSMEN > SYNODSMAN
SYNOECETE same as > SYNOEKETE
SYNOECISE same as > SYNOECIZE
SYNOECISM n union
SYNOECIZE vb unite
SYNOEKETE n insect that lives in the nests of social insects without receiving any attentions from the inmates
SYNOICOUS variant of > SYNECIOUS
SYNONYM n word with the same meaning as another
SYNONYME same as > SYNONYM
SYNONYMES > SYNONYME
SYNONYMIC > SYNONYM
SYNONYMS > SYNONYM
SYNONYMY n study of synonyms
SYNOPSES > SYNOPSIS
SYNOPSIS n summary or outline
SYNOPSISE same as > SYNOPSIZE
SYNOPSIZE vb make a synopsis of

SYNOPTIC adj of or relating to a synopsis ▷ n any of the three synoptic Gospels
SYNOPTICS > SYNOPTIC
SYNOPTIST > SYNOPTIC
SYNOVIA n clear thick fluid that lubricates the body joints
SYNOVIAL adj of or relating to the synovia
SYNOVIAS > SYNOVIA
SYNOVITIC > SYNOVITIS
SYNOVITIS n inflammation of the membrane surrounding a joint
SYNROC n titanium-ceramic substance that can incorporate nuclear waste in its crystals
SYNROCS > SYNROC
SYNTACTIC adj relating to or determined by syntax
SYNTAGM same as > SYNTAGMA
SYNTAGMA n syntactic unit or a word or phrase forming a syntactic unit
SYNTAGMAS > SYNTAGMA
SYNTAGMIC > SYNTAGMA
SYNTAGMS > SYNTAGM
SYNTAN n synthetic tanning substance
SYNTANS > SYNTAN
SYNTAX n way in which words are arranged to form phrases and sentences
SYNTAXES > SYNTAX
SYNTECTIC > SYNTEXIS
SYNTENIC > SYNTENY
SYNTENIES > SYNTENY
SYNTENY n presence of two or more genes on the same chromosome
SYNTEXIS n liquefaction
SYNTH n type of electrophonic musical instrument operated by a keyboard and pedals
SYNTHASE n enzyme that catalyses a synthesis process
SYNTHASES > SYNTHASE
SYNTHESES > SYNTHESIS
SYNTHESIS n combination of objects or ideas into a whole
SYNTHETIC adj (of a substance) made artificially ▷ n synthetic substance or material
SYNTHON n molecule used in synthesis
SYNTHONS > SYNTHON
SYNTHPOP n pop music using synthesizers
SYNTHPOPS > SYNTHPOP
SYNTHRONI pl n combined thrones for bishops and their subordinates
SYNTHS > SYNTH
SYNTONE n person who is syntonic

SYNTONES > SYNTONE
SYNTONIC adj emotionally in harmony with one's environment
SYNTONIES > SYNTONY
SYNTONIN n substance in muscle
SYNTONINS > SYNTONIN
SYNTONISE same as > SYNTONIZE
SYNTONIZE vb make frequencies match
SYNTONOUS same as > SYNTONIC
SYNTONY n matching of frequencies
SYNTYPE n original specimen by which a new species is described
SYNTYPES > SYNTYPE
SYNURA n variety of microbe
SYNURAE > SYNURA
SYPE same as > SIPE
SYPED > SYPE
SYPES > SYPE
SYPH shortening of > SYPHILIS
SYPHER vb lap (a chamfered edge) in order to form a flush surface
SYPHERED > SYPHER
SYPHERING > SYPHER
SYPHERS > SYPHER
SYPHILIS n serious sexually transmitted disease
SYPHILISE same as > SYPHILIZE
SYPHILIZE vb infect with syphilis
SYPHILOID > SYPHILIS
SYPHILOMA n tumour or gumma caused by infection with syphilis
SYPHON same as > SIPHON
SYPHONAGE n action of a syphon
SYPHONAL same as > SIPHONAL
SYPHONED > SYPHON
SYPHONIC same as > SIPHONIC
SYPHONING > SYPHON
SYPHONS > SYPHON
SYPHS > SYPH
SYPING > SYPE
SYRAH n type of French red wine
SYRAHS > SYRAH
SYREN same as > SIREN
SYRENS > SYREN
SYRETTE n small disposable syringe
SYRETTES > SYRETTE
SYRINGA n mock orange or lilac
SYRINGAS > SYRINGA
SYRINGE n device for withdrawing or injecting fluids ▷ vb wash out or inject with a syringe
SYRINGEAL > SYRINX

SYRINGED > SYRINGE
SYRINGES > SYRINX
SYRINGING > SYRINGE
SYRINX n vocal organ of a bird
SYRINXES > SYRINX
SYRPHIAN same as > SYRPHID
SYRPHIANS > SYRPHIAN
SYRPHID n type of fly
SYRPHIDS > SYRPHID
SYRTES > SYRTIS
SYRTIS n area of quicksand
SYRUP n solution of sugar in water ▷ vb bring to the consistency of syrup
SYRUPED > SYRUP
SYRUPIER > SYRUPY
SYRUPIEST > SYRUPY
SYRUPING > SYRUP
SYRUPLIKE > SYRUP
SYRUPS > SYRUP
SYRUPY adj thick and sweet
SYSADMIN n computer system administrator
SYSADMINS > SYSADMIN
SYSOP n person who runs a system or network
SYSOPS > SYSOP
SYSSITIA n ancient Spartan communal meal
SYSSITIAS > SYSSITIA
SYSTALTIC adj (esp of the action of the heart) characterized by alternate contractions and dilations
SYSTEM n method or set of methods
SYSTEMED adj having system
SYSTEMIC adj affecting the entire animal or body ▷ n systemic pesticide, fungicide, etc
SYSTEMICS > SYSTEMIC
SYSTEMISE same as > SYSTEMIZE
SYSTEMIZE vb give a system to
SYSTEMS > SYSTEM
SYSTOLE n regular contraction of the heart as it pumps blood
SYSTOLES > SYSTOLE
SYSTOLIC > SYSTOLE
SYSTYLE n building with different types of columns
SYSTYLES > SYSTYLE
SYTHE same as > SITH
SYTHES > SYTHE
SYVER n street drain or the grating over it
SYVERS > SYVER
SYZYGAL > SYZYGY
SYZYGETIC > SYZYGY
SYZYGIAL > SYZYGY
SYZYGIES > SYZYGY
SYZYGY n position of a celestial body when sun, earth, and the body are in line

Tt

TA interj thank you ▷ n thank you

TAAL n language: usually, by implication, Afrikaans

TAALS > TAAL

TAATA child's word for **>** FATHER

TAATAS > TAATA

TAB n small flap or projecting label ▷ vb supply with a tab

TABANID n stout-bodied fly

TABANIDS > TABANID

TABARD n short sleeveless tunic decorated with a coat of arms, worn in medieval times

TABARDED adj wearing a tabard

TABARDS > TABARD

TABARET n hard-wearing fabric of silk or similar cloth with stripes of satin or moire

TABARETS > TABARET

TABASHEER n dried bamboo sap, used medicinally

TABASHIR same as **>** TABASHEER

TABASHIRS > TABASHIR

TABBED > TAB

TABBIED > TABBY

TABBIER > TABBY

TABBIES > TABBY

TABBIEST > TABBY

TABBINET same as **>** TABINET

TABBINETS > TABBINET

TABBING n act of supplying with tabs

TABBINGS > TABBING

TABBIS n silken cloth

TABBISES > TABBIS

TABBOULEH n kind of Middle Eastern salad made with cracked wheat, mint, parsley, and usually cucumber

TABBOULI same as **>** TABBOULEH

TABBOULIS > TABBOULI

TABBY vb make (a material) appear wavy ▷ n female domestic cat ▷ adj brindled

TABBYHOOD n spinsterhood

TABBYING > TABBY

TABEFIED > TABEFY

TABEFIES > TABEFY

TABEFY vb emaciate or become emaciated

TABEFYING > TABEFY

TABELLION n scribe or notary authorized by the Roman Empire

TABER old variant of **>** TABOR

TABERD same as **>** TABARD

TABERDAR n holder of a scholarship at Queen's College, Oxford

TABERDARS > TABERDAR

TABERDS > TABERD

TABERED > TABER

TABERING > TABER

TABERS > TABER

TABES n wasting of a bodily organ or part

TABESCENT adj progressively emaciating

TABETIC > TABES

TABETICS > TABES

TABI n thick-soled Japanese sock, worn with sandals

TABID adj emaciated

TABINET n type of tabbied fabric

TABINETS > TABINET

TABIS > TABI

TABLA n one of a pair of Indian drums played with the hands

TABLAS > TABLA

TABLATURE n any of a number of forms of musical notation, esp for playing the lute, consisting of letters and signs indicating rhythm and fingering

TABLE n piece of furniture with a flat top supported by legs ▷ vb submit (a motion) for discussion by a meeting

TABLEAU n silent motionless group arranged to represent some scene

TABLEAUS > TABLEAU

TABLEAUX > TABLEAU

TABLED > TABLE

TABLEFUL > TABLE

TABLEFULS > TABLE

TABLELAND n high plateau

TABLELESS > TABLE

TABLEMAT n small mat used for protecting the surface of a table from hot dishes

TABLEMATE n someone with whom one shares a table

TABLEMATS > TABLEMAT

TABLES > TABLE

TABLESFUL > TABLE

TABLESIDE adj (of cooking) performed beside the table of a diner

TABLET n medicinal pill ▷ vb make (something) into a tablet

TABLETED > TABLET

TABLETING > TABLET

TABLETOP n upper surface of a table

TABLETOPS > TABLETOP

TABLETS > TABLET

TABLETTED > TABLET

TABLEWARE n articles such as dishes, plates, knives, forks, etc, used at meals

TABLEWISE adv in the form of a table

TABLIER n (formerly) part of a dress resembling an apron

TABLIERS > TABLIER

TABLING > TABLE

TABLINGS > TABLE

TABLOID n small-sized newspaper with many photographs

TABLOIDS > TABLOID

TABLOIDY adj characteristic of a tabloid newspaper; trashy

TABOGGAN same as **>** TOBOGGAN

TABOGGANS > TABOGGAN

TABOO n prohibition resulting from religious or social conventions ▷ adj forbidden by a taboo ▷ vb place under a taboo

TABOOED > TABOO

TABOOING > TABOO

TABOOLEY variant of **>** TABBOULEH

TABOOLEYS > TABOOLEY

TABOOS > TABOO

TABOR vb play the tabor

TABORED > TABOR

TABORER > TABOR

TABORERS > TABOR

TABORET n low stool, originally in the shape of a drum

TABORETS > TABORET

TABORIN same as **>** TABORET

TABORINE same as **>** TABOURIN

TABORINES > TABORINE

TABORING > TABOR

TABORINS > TABORIN

TABORS > TABOR

TABOULEH variant of **>** TABBOULEH

TABOULEHS > TABOULEH

TABOULI same as **>** TABBOULEH

TABOULIS > TABOULI

TABOUR same as **>** TABOR

TABOURED > TABOUR

TABOURER > TABOUR

TABOURERS > TABOUR

TABOURET same as **>** TABORET

TABOURETS > TABOURET

TABOURIN same as **>** TABORET

TABOURING > TABOUR

TABOURINS > TABOURIN

TABOURS > TABOUR

TABRERE same as **>** TABOR

TABRERES > TABRERE

TABRET n smaller version of a tabor

TABRETS > TABRET

TABS > TAB

TABU same as **>** TABOO

TABUED > TABU

TABUING > TABU

TABULA n tablet for writing on

TABULABLE > TABULATE

TABULAE > TABULA

TABULAR adj arranged in a table

TABULARLY > TABULAR

TABULATE vb arrange (information) in a table ▷ adj having a flat surface

TABULATED > TABULATE

TABULATES > TABULATE

TABULATOR n key on a typewriter or word processor that sets stops so that data can be arranged and presented in columns

TABULI variant of **>** TABBOULEH

TABULIS > TABULI

TABUN n organic compound used as a lethal nerve gas

TABUNS > TABUN

TABUS > TABU

TACAHOUT n abnormal outgrowth on the tamarisk plant

TACAHOUTS > TACAHOUT

TACAMAHAC n any of several strong-smelling resinous gums obtained from certain trees, used in making ointments, incense, etc

TACAN n electronic ultrahigh-frequency navigation system for aircraft

TACANS > TACAN

TACE same as **>** TASSET

TACES > TACE

TACET n musical direction indicating that an

instrument or singer does not take part

TACH n device for measuring speed

TACHE n buckle, clasp, or hook

TACHES > TACHE

TACHINA n as in tachina fly bristly fly

TACHINID n type of fly

TACHINIDS > TACHINID

TACHISM same as > TACHISME

TACHISME n type of action painting evolved in France

TACHISMES > TACHISME

TACHISMS > TACHISM

TACHIST > TACHISM

TACHISTE > TACHISME

TACHISTES > TACHISME

TACHISTS > TACHIST

TACHO same as > TACHOGRAM

TACHOGRAM n graphical record of readings

TACHOS > TACHO

TACHS > TACH

TACHYLITE same as > TACHYLYTE

TACHYLYTE n black basaltic glass often found on the edges of intrusions of basalt

TACHYON n hypothetical elementary particle

TACHYONIC > TACHYON

TACHYONS > TACHYON

TACHYPNEA n abnormally rapid breathing

TACIT adj implied but not spoken

TACITLY > TACIT

TACITNESS > TACIT

TACITURN adj habitually uncommunicative

TACK n short nail with a large head ▷ vb fasten with tacks

TACKBOARD n noticeboard

TACKED > TACK

TACKER > TACK

TACKERS > TACK

TACKET n nail, esp a hobnail

TACKETIER > TACKETY

TACKETS > TACKET

TACKETY adj studded with tackets

TACKEY same as > TACKY

TACKIER > TACKY

TACKIES pl n tennis shoes or plimsolls

TACKIEST > TACKY

TACKIFIED > TACKIFY

TACKIFIER > TACKIFY

TACKIFIES > TACKIFY

TACKIFY vb give (eg rubber) a sticky feel

TACKILY > TACKY

TACKINESS > TACKY

TACKING > TACK

TACKINGS > TACK

TACKLE vb deal with (a task) ▷ n act of tackling an opposing player

TACKLED > TACKLE

TACKLER > TACKLE

TACKLERS > TACKLE

TACKLES > TACKLE

TACKLESS > TACK

TACKLING > TACKLE

TACKLINGS > TACKLE

TACKS > TACK

TACKSMAN n leaseholder, esp a tenant in the Highlands who sublets

TACKSMEN > TACKSMAN

TACKY adj slightly sticky

TACMAHACK same as > TACAMAHAC

TACNODE n point at which two branches of a curve have a common tangent

TACNODES > TACNODE

TACO n tortilla fried until crisp, served with a filling

TACONITE n fine-grained sedimentary rock

TACONITES > TACONITE

TACOS > TACO

TACRINE n drug used to treat Alzheimer's disease

TACRINES > TACRINE

TACT n skill in avoiding giving offence

TACTFUL > TACT

TACTFULLY > TACT

TACTIC n method or plan to achieve an end

TACTICAL adj of or employing tactics

TACTICIAN > TACTICS

TACTICITY n quality of regularity in the arrangement of repeated units within a polymer chain

TACTICS n art of directing military forces in battle

TACTILE adj of or having the sense of touch

TACTILELY > TACTILE

TACTILIST n artist whose work strives to appeal to the sense of touch

TACTILITY > TACTILE

TACTION n act of touching

TACTIONS > TACTION

TACTISM another word for > TAXIS

TACTISMS > TACTISM

TACTLESS > TACT

TACTS > TACT

TACTUAL adj caused by touch

TACTUALLY > TACTUAL

TAD n small bit or piece

TADALAFIL n drug used to treat erectile dysfunction

TADDIE short for > TADPOLE

TADDIES > TADDIE

TADPOLE n limbless tailed larva of a frog or toad

TADPOLES > TADPOLE

TADS > TAD

TAE Scots form of the verb > TOE

TAED > TAE

TAEDIUM archaic spelling of > TEDIUM

TAEDIUMS > TAEDIUM

TAEING > TAE

TAEKWONDO n Korean martial art

TAEL n unit of weight, used in the Far East

TAELS > TAEL

TAENIA n (in ancient Greece) a narrow fillet or headband for the hair

TAENIAE > TAENIA

TAENIAS > TAENIA

TAENIASES > TAENIASIS

TAENIASIS n infestation with tapeworms

TAENIATE adj ribbon-like

TAENIOID adj ribbon-like

TAENITE n nickel-iron alloy found in meteorites

TAENITES > TAENITE

TAES > TAE

TAFFAREL same as > TAFFRAIL

TAFFARELS > TAFFAREL

TAFFEREL same as > TAFFRAIL

TAFFERELS > TAFFEREL

TAFFETA n shiny silk or rayon fabric

TAFFETAS same as > TAFFETA

TAFFETIER > TAFFETY

TAFFETY adj made of taffeta

TAFFIA same as > TAFIA

TAFFIAS > TAFFIA

TAFFIES > TAFFY

TAFFRAIL n rail at the back of a ship or boat

TAFFRAILS > TAFFRAIL

TAFFY same as > TOFFEE

TAFIA n type of rum, esp from Guyana or the Caribbean

TAFIAS > TAFIA

TAG n label bearing information ▷ vb attach a tag to

TAGALONG n one who trails behind, esp uninvited; a hanger-on

TAGALONGS > TAGALONG

TAGAREEN n junk shop

TAGAREENS > TAGAREEN

TAGBOARD n sturdy form of cardboard

TAGBOARDS > TAGBOARD

TAGETES n any of a genus of plants with yellow or orange flowers

TAGGANT n microscopic material added to substance to identify it

TAGGANTS > TAGGANT

TAGGED > TAG

TAGGEE n one who has been made to wear a tag

TAGGEES > TAGGEE

TAGGER n one who marks with a tag

TAGGERS > TAGGER

TAGGIER > TAGGY

TAGGIEST > TAGGY

TAGGING > TAG

TAGGINGS > TAG

TAGGY adj (of wool, hair, etc) matted

TAGHAIRM n form of divination once practised in the Highlands of Scotland

TAGHAIRMS > TAGHAIRM

TAGINE n large, heavy N African cooking pot with a conical lid

TAGINES > TAGINE

TAGLESS adj having no tag

TAGLIKE adj resembling a tag

TAGLINE n funny line of a joke

TAGLINES > TAGLINE

TAGLIONI n type of coat

TAGLIONIS > TAGLIONI

TAGMA n distinct region of the body of an arthropod

TAGMATA > TAGMA

TAGMEME n class of speech elements all of which may fulfil the same grammatical role

TAGMEMES > TAGMEME

TAGMEMIC > TAGMEME

TAGMEMICS > TAGMEME

TAGRAG same as > RAGTAG

TAGRAGS > TAGRAG

TAGS > TAG

TAGUAN n nocturnal flying squirrel of the East Indies

TAGUANS > TAGUAN

TAHA n type of South African bird

TAHAS > TAHA

TAHINA same as > TAHINI

TAHINAS > TAHINA

TAHINI n paste made from ground sesame seeds

TAHINIS > TAHINI

TAHR n goatlike mammal of mountainous regions of S and SW Asia

TAHRS > TAHR

TAHSIL n administrative division of a zila in certain states in India

TAHSILDAR n officer in charge of the collection of revenues, etc, in a tahsil

TAHSILS > TAHSIL

TAI n type of sea bream

TAIAHA n carved weapon in the form of a staff, now used in Māori ceremonial oratory

TAIAHAS > TAIAHA

TAIG n derogatory term for a Roman Catholic

TAIGA n belt of coniferous forest

TAIGAS > TAIGA

TAIGLACH same as > TEIGLACH

TAIGLE vb entangle or impede

TAIGLED > TAIGLE

TAIGLES > TAIGLE

TAIGLING > TAIGLE

TAIGS > TAIG

TAIHOA vb in New Zealand English, wait

TAIHOAED > TAIHOA

TAIHOAING > TAIHOA

TAIHOAS > TAIHOA

TAIKO n large Japanese drum

TAIKONAUT n astronaut from the People's Republic of China

TAIKOS > TAIKO

TAIL n rear part of an animal's body, usu forming a flexible appendage ▷ adj at the rear ▷ vb follow (someone) secretly

TAILARD n one having a tail
TAILARDS > TAILARD
TAILBACK n queue of traffic stretching back from an obstruction
TAILBACKS > TAILBACK
TAILBOARD n removable or hinged rear board on a truck etc
TAILBONE nontechnical name for **> COCCYX**
TAILBONES > TAILBONE
TAILCOAT n man's black coat with a tapering tail
TAILCOATS > TAILCOAT
TAILED > TAIL
TAILENDER n (in cricket) the batter last in the batting order
TAILER n one that tails
TAILERON n aileron located on the tailplane of an aircraft
TAILERONS > TAILERON
TAILERS > TAILER
TAILFAN n fanned structure at the hind end of a lobster
TAILFANS > TAILFAN
TAILFIN n decorative projection at the back of a car
TAILFINS > TAILFIN
TAILFLIES > TAILFLY
TAILFLY n in angling, the lowest fly on a wet-fly cast
TAILGATE n door at the rear of a hatchback vehicle ▷ vb drive very close behind (a vehicle)
TAILGATED > TAILGATE
TAILGATER > TAILGATE
TAILGATES > TAILGATE
TAILHOOK n hook on an aircraft that catches a braking cable
TAILHOOKS > TAILHOOK
TAILING n part of a beam, rafter, projecting brick or stone, etc, embedded in a wall
TAILINGS pl n waste left over after milling processes
TAILLAMP n rear light
TAILLAMPS > TAILLAMP
TAILLE n (in France before 1789) a tax levied by a king or overlord on his subjects
TAILLES > TAILLE
TAILLESS > TAIL
TAILLEUR n woman's suit
TAILLEURS > TAILLEUR
TAILLIE n (in law) the limitation of an estate or interest to a person and the heirs of their body
TAILLIES > TAILLIE
TAILLIGHT same as **>** TAILLAMP
TAILLIKE adj resembling a tail
TAILOR n person who makes men's clothes ▷ vb cut or style (a garment) to specific requirements
TAILORED > TAILOR
TAILORESS n female tailor
TAILORING > TAILOR
TAILORS > TAILOR

TAILPIECE n piece added at the end of something, for example a report
TAILPIPE vb attach an object, esp a tin can, to the tail of an animal
TAILPIPED > TAILPIPE
TAILPIPES > TAILPIPE
TAILPLANE n small stabilizing wing at the rear of an aircraft
TAILRACE n channel that carries water away from a water wheel, turbine, etc
TAILRACES > TAILRACE
TAILS adv with the side of a coin that does not have a portrait of a head on it uppermost
TAILSKID n runner under the tail of an aircraft
TAILSKIDS > TAILSKID
TAILSLIDE n backwards descent of an aeroplane after stalling while in an upward trajectory
TAILSPIN n uncontrolled spinning dive of an aircraft ▷ vb go into a tailspin
TAILSPINS > TAILSPIN
TAILSPUN > TAILSPIN
TAILSTOCK n casting that slides on the bed of a lathe in alignment with the headstock and is locked in position to support the free end of a workpiece
TAILWATER n water flowing in a tailrace
TAILWHEEL n wheel fitted to the rear of a vehicle, esp the landing wheel under the tail of an aircraft
TAILWIND n wind coming from the rear
TAILWINDS > TAILWIND
TAILYE same as **>** TAILLIE
TAILYES > TAILYE
TAILZIE same as **>** TAILLIE
TAILZIES > TAILZIE
TAIN n tinfoil used in backing mirrors
TAINS > TAIN
TAINT vb spoil with a small amount of decay or other bad quality ▷ n something that taints
TAINTED > TAINT
TAINTING > TAINT
TAINTLESS > TAINT
TAINTS > TAINT
TAINTURE n contamination; staining
TAINTURES > TAINTURE
TAIPAN n large poisonous Australian snake
TAIPANS > TAIPAN
TAIRA same as **>** TAYRA
TAIRAS > TAIRA
TAIS > TAI
TAISCH n (in Scotland) apparition of a person whose death is imminent
TAISCHES > TAISCH
TAISH same as **>** TAISCH
TAISHES > TAISH
TAIT same as **>** TATE

TAITS > TAIT
TAIVER same as **>** TAVER
TAIVERED > TAIVER
TAIVERING > TAIVER
TAIVERS > TAIVER
TAIVERT adj Scots word meaning confused or bewildered
TAJ n tall conical cap worn as a mark of distinction by Muslims
TAJES > TAJ
TAJINE same as **>** TAGINE
TAJINES > TAJINE
TAK Scots variant spelling of **>** TAKE
TAKA n standard monetary unit of Bangladesh, divided into 100 paise
TAKABLE > TAKE
TAKAHE n very rare flightless New Zealand bird
TAKAHES > TAKAHE
TAKAMAKA same as **>** TACAMAHAC
TAKAMAKAS > TAKAMAKA
TAKAS > TAKA
TAKE vb remove from a place ▷ n one of a series of recordings from which the best will be used
TAKEABLE > TAKE
TAKEAWAY adj (of food) sold for consumption away from the premises ▷ n shop or restaurant selling meals for eating elsewhere
TAKEAWAYS > TAKEAWAY
TAKEDOWN n disassembly
TAKEDOWNS > TAKEDOWN
TAKEN > TAKE
TAKEOFF n act or process of making an aircraft airborne
TAKEOFFS > TAKEOFF
TAKEOUT n shop or restaurant that sells such food
TAKEOUTS > TAKEOUT
TAKEOVER n act of taking control of a company by buying a large number of its shares
TAKEOVERS > TAKEOVER
TAKER n person who agrees to take something that is offered
TAKERS > TAKER
TAKES > TAKE
TAKEUP n claiming or acceptance of something that is due or available
TAKEUPS > TAKEUP
TAKHI n type of wild Mongolian horse
TAKHIS > TAKHI
TAKI same as **>** TAKHI
TAKIER > TAKY
TAKIEST > TAKY
TAKIN n bovid mammal of mountainous regions of S Asia
TAKING > TAKE
TAKINGLY > TAKE
TAKINGS > TAKE
TAKINS > TAKIN
TAKIS > TAKI
TAKKIES > TAKKY

TAKKY n (S Africa) plimsoll
TAKS > TAK
TAKY adj appealing
TALA n standard monetary unit of Samoa, divided into 100 sene
TALAK same as **>** TALAQ
TALAKS > TALAK
TALANT old variant of **>** TALON
TALANTS > TALANT
TALAPOIN n smallest of the guenon monkeys
TALAPOINS > TALAPOIN
TALAQ n Muslim form of divorce
TALAQS > TALAQ
TALAR n ankle-length robe
TALARIA pl n winged sandals, such as those worn by Hermes
TALARS > TALAR
TALAS > TALA
TALAUNT old variant of **>** TALON
TALAUNTS > TALAUNT
TALAYOT n ancient Balearic stone tower
TALAYOTS > TALAYOT
TALBOT n ancient breed of large hound
TALBOTS > TALBOT
TALBOTYPE n early type of photographic process (invented by W H Fox Talbot) or a photograph produced using it
TALC n talcum powder ▷ vb apply talc to ▷ adj of, or relating to, talc
TALCED > TALC
TALCIER > TALCY
TALCIEST > TALCY
TALCING > TALC
TALCKED > TALC
TALCKIER > TALCKY
TALCKIEST > TALCKY
TALCKING > TALC
TALCKY same as **>** TALCY
TALCOSE > TALC
TALCOUS > TALC
TALCS > TALC
TALCUM n white, grey, brown, or pale green mineral ▷ vb apply talcum to
TALCUMED > TALCUM
TALCUMING > TALCUM
TALCUMS > TALCUM
TALCY adj like, containing, or covered in talc
TALE n story
TALEA n rhythmic pattern in certain mediaeval choral compositions
TALEAE > TALEA
TALEFUL adj having many tales
TALEGALLA n brush turkey, of New Guinea and Australia
TALEGGIO n Italian cheese
TALEGGIOS > TALEGGIO
TALENT n natural ability
TALENTED > TALENT
TALENTS > TALENT
TALER same as **>** THALER
TALERS > TALER

TALES n group of persons summoned to fill vacancies on a jury panel
TALESMAN > TALES
TALESMEN > TALES
TALEYSIM > TALLITH
TALI > TALUS
TALIGRADE adj (of mammals) walking on the outer side of the foot
TALION n principle of making punishment correspond to the crime
TALIONIC adj of or relating to talion
TALIONS > TALION
TALIPAT same as **>** TALIPOT
TALIPATS > TALIPAT
TALIPED adj having a club foot ▷ n club-footed person
TALIPEDS > TALIPED
TALIPES n congenital deformity of the foot by which it is twisted in any of various positions
TALIPOT n palm tree of the East Indies
TALIPOTS > TALIPOT
TALISMAN n object believed to have magic power
TALISMANS > TALISMAN
TALK vb express ideas or feelings by means of speech ▷ n speech or lecture
TALKABLE > TALK
TALKATHON n epic bout of discussion or speechifying
TALKATIVE adj fond of talking
TALKBACK n broadcast in which telephone comments or questions from the public are transmitted live
TALKBACKS > TALKBACK
TALKBOX n voice box
TALKBOXES > TALKBOX
TALKED > TALK
TALKER > TALK
TALKERS > TALK
TALKFEST n lengthy discussion
TALKFESTS > TALKFEST
TALKIE n early film with a soundtrack
TALKIER > TALKY
TALKIES > TALKIE
TALKIEST > TALKY
TALKINESS n quality or condition of being talky
TALKING n speech; the act of speaking
TALKINGS > TALKING
TALKS > TALK
TALKTIME n length of time a mobile phone can be used before its battery runs out
TALKTIMES > TALKTIME
TALKY adj containing too much dialogue or inconsequential talk
TALL adj higher than average
TALLAGE n tax levied on Crown lands and royal towns ▷ vb levy a tax (upon)
TALLAGED > TALLAGE
TALLAGES > TALLAGE

TALLAGING > TALLAGE
TALLAISIM > TALLITH
TALLAT same as **>** TALLET
TALLATS > TALLAT
TALLBOY n high chest of drawers
TALLBOYS > TALLBOY
TALLENT n plenty
TALLENTS > TALLENT
TALLER > TALL
TALLEST > TALL
TALLET n loft
TALLETS > TALLET
TALLGRASS n long grass in North American prairie
TALLIABLE adj taxable
TALLIATE vb levy a tax
TALLIATED > TALLIATE
TALLIATES > TALLIATE
TALLIED > TALLY
TALLIER > TALLY
TALLIERS > TALLY
TALLIES > TALLY
TALLIS variant of **>** TALLITH
TALLISES > TALLIS
TALLISH adj quite tall
TALLISIM > TALLIS
TALLIT variant of **>** TALLITH
TALLITES > TALLIT
TALLITH n shawl worn by Jewish males during religious services
TALLITHES > TALLITH
TALLITHIM > TALLITH
TALLITHS > TALLITH
TALLITIM > TALLIT
TALLITOT > TALLIT
TALLITOTH > TALLITH
TALLITS > TALLIT
TALLNESS > TALL
TALLOL n oily liquid used for making soaps, lubricants, etc
TALLOLS > TALLOL
TALLOT same as **>** TALLET
TALLOTS > TALLOT
TALLOW n hard animal fat used to make candles ▷ vb cover or smear with tallow
TALLOWED > TALLOW
TALLOWIER > TALLOWY
TALLOWING > TALLOW
TALLOWISH > TALLOW
TALLOWS > TALLOW
TALLOWY adj like tallow
TALLS > TALL
TALLY vb (of two things) correspond ▷ n record of a debt or score
TALLYHO n cry to encourage hounds when the quarry is sighted ▷ vb make the cry of tallyho
TALLYHOED > TALLYHO
TALLYHOES > TALLYHO
TALLYHOS > TALLYHO
TALLYING > TALLY
TALLYMAN n scorekeeper or recorder
TALLYMEN > TALLYMAN
TALLYSHOP n shop that allows customers to pay in instalments
TALMA n short cloak
TALMAS > TALMA

TALMUD n primary source of Jewish religious law, consisting of the Mishnah and the Gemara
TALMUDIC > TALMUD
TALMUDISM > TALMUD
TALMUDS > TALMUD
TALON n bird's hooked claw
TALONED > TALON
TALONS > TALON
TALOOKA same as **>** TALUK
TALOOKAS > TALOOKA
TALPA n sebaceous cyst
TALPAE > TALPA
TALPAS > TALPA
TALUK n subdivision of a district
TALUKA same as **>** TALUK
TALUKAS > TALUKA
TALUKDAR n person in charge of a taluk
TALUKDARS > TALUKDAR
TALUKS > TALUK
TALUS n bone of the ankle that articulates with the leg bones to form the ankle joint
TALUSES > TALUS
TALWEG same as **>** THALWEG
TALWEGS > TALWEG
TAM n type of hat
TAMABLE > TAME
TAMAL same as **>** TAMALE
TAMALE n Mexican dish of minced meat wrapped in maize husks and steamed
TAMALES > TAMALE
TAMALS > TAMAL
TAMANDU same as **>** TAMANDUA
TAMANDUA n small arboreal edentate mammal
TAMANDUAS > TAMANDUA
TAMANDUS > TAMANDU
TAMANOIR n anteater
TAMANOIRS > TAMANOIR
TAMANU n poon tree
TAMANUS > TAMANU
TAMARA n powder consisting of cloves, cinnamon, fennel, coriander, etc
TAMARACK n North American larch
TAMARACKS > TAMARACK
TAMARAO same as **>** TAMARAU
TAMARAOS > TAMARAO
TAMARAS > TAMARA
TAMARAU n small rare member of a cattle tribe in the Philippines
TAMARAUS > TAMARAU
TAMARI n Japanese variety of soy sauce
TAMARILLO n shrub with a red oval edible fruit
TAMARIN n small monkey of South and Central America
TAMARIND n tropical tree
TAMARINDS > TAMARIND
TAMARINS > TAMARIN
TAMARIS > TAMARI
TAMARISK n evergreen shrub with slender branches and feathery flower clusters
TAMARISKS > TAMARISK
TAMASHA n (in India) a show
TAMASHAS > TAMASHA

TAMBAC same as **>** TOMBAC
TAMBACS > TAMBAC
TAMBAK same as **>** TOMBAK
TAMBAKS > TAMBAK
TAMBALA n unit of Malawian currency
TAMBALAS > TAMBALA
TAMBER same as **>** TIMBRE
TAMBERS > TAMBER
TAMBOUR n embroidery frame consisting of two hoops ▷ vb embroider (fabric or a design) on a tambour
TAMBOURA n stringed instrument used in Indian music
TAMBOURAS > TAMBOURA
TAMBOURED > TAMBOUR
TAMBOURER n one who embroiders on a tambour
TAMBOURIN n 18th-century Provençal folk dance
TAMBOURS > TAMBOUR
TAMBUR n old Turkish stringed instrument
TAMBURA n Middle-Eastern stringed instrument with a long neck
TAMBURAS > TAMBURA
TAMBURIN n Spenserian form of 'tambourine'
TAMBURINS > TAMBURIN
TAMBURS > TAMBUR
TAME adj (of animals) brought under human control ▷ vb make tame
TAMEABLE > TAME
TAMED > TAME
TAMEIN n Burmese skirt
TAMEINS > TAMEIN
TAMELESS > TAME
TAMELY > TAME
TAMENESS > TAME
TAMER > TAME
TAMERS > TAME
TAMES > TAME
TAMEST > TAME
TAMIN n thin woollen fabric
TAMINE same as **>** TAMIN
TAMINES > TAMINE
TAMING n act of making (something) tame
TAMINGS > TAMING
TAMINS > TAMIN
TAMIS same as **>** TAMMY
TAMISE n type of thin cloth
TAMISES > TAMIS
TAMMAR n small scrub wallaby
TAMMARS > TAMMAR
TAMMIE n short for tam-o'shanter, a traditional Scottish hat
TAMMIED > TAMMY
TAMMIES > TAMMIE
TAMMY n glazed woollen or mixed fabric ▷ vb strain (sauce, soup, etc) through a tammy
TAMMYING > TAMMY
TAMOXIFEN n drug that antagonizes the action of oestrogen and is used to treat breast cancer and some types of infertility in women
TAMP vb pack down by repeated taps

TAMPALA n Asian plant, eaten as food
TAMPALAS > TAMPALA
TAMPAN n biting mite
TAMPANS > TAMPAN
TAMPED > TAMP
TAMPER vb interfere ▷ n person or thing that tamps
TAMPERED > TAMPER
TAMPERER > TAMPER
TAMPERERS > TAMPER
TAMPERING > TAMPER
TAMPERS > TAMPER
TAMPING adj very angry ▷ n act or instance of tamping
TAMPINGS > TAMPING
TAMPION n plug placed in a gun's muzzle to keep out moisture and dust
TAMPIONS > TAMPION
TAMPON n plug of cotton wool inserted into a wound or body cavity to absorb blood ▷ vb use a tampon
TAMPONADE > TAMPON
TAMPONAGE > TAMPON
TAMPONED > TAMPON
TAMPONING > TAMPON
TAMPONS > TAMPON
TAMPS > TAMP
TAMS > TAM
TAMWORTH n any of a hardy rare breed of long-bodied reddish pigs
TAMWORTHS > TAMWORTH
TAN n brown coloration of the skin from exposure to sunlight ▷ vb (of skin) go brown from exposure to sunlight ▷ adj yellowish-brown
TANA n small Madagascan lemur
TANADAR n commanding officer of an Indian police station
TANADARS > TANADAR
TANAGER n American songbird with a short thick bill
TANAGERS > TANAGER
TANAGRA n type of tanager
TANAGRAS > TANAGRA
TANAGRINE adj of or relating to the tanager
TANAISTE n deputy prime minister of the Republic of Ireland
TANAISTES > TANAISTE
TANALISED adj having been treated with the trademarked timber preservative Tanalith
TANALIZED same as > TANALISED
TANAS > TANA
TANBARK n bark of certain trees, esp the oak and hemlock, used as a source of tannin
TANBARKS > TANBARK
TANDEM n bicycle for two riders, one behind the other
TANDEMS > TANDEM
TANDOOR n type of Indian clay oven
TANDOORI adj (of food) cooked in an Indian clay oven

▷ n Indian method of cooking meat or vegetables on a spit in a clay oven
TANDOORIS > TANDOORI
TANDOORS > TANDOOR
TANE old Scottish variant of > TAKEN
TANG n strong taste or smell ▷ vb cause to ring
TANGA n triangular loincloth worn by indigenous peoples in tropical America
TANGAS > TANGA
TANGED > TANG
TANGELO n hybrid produced by crossing a tangerine tree with a grapefruit tree
TANGELOS > TANGELO
TANGENCE n touching
TANGENCES > TANGENCE
TANGENCY > TANGENT
TANGENT n line that touches a curve without intersecting it
TANGENTAL > TANGENT
TANGENTS > TANGENT
TANGERINE n small orange-like fruit of an Asian citrus tree ▷ adj reddish-orange
TANGHIN n poison formerly used in Madagascar to determine the guilt of crime suspects
TANGHININ n active ingredient in tanghin
TANGHINS > TANGHIN
TANGI n Māori funeral ceremony
TANGIBLE adj able to be touched ▷ n tangible thing or asset
TANGIBLES > TANGIBLE
TANGIBLY > TANGIBLE
TANGIE n water spirit of Orkney, appearing as a figure draped in seaweed, or as a seahorse
TANGIER > TANGY
TANGIES > TANGIE
TANGIEST > TANGY
TANGINESS > TANGY
TANGING > TANG
TANGIS > TANGI
TANGLE n confused mass or situation ▷ vb twist together in a tangle
TANGLED > TANGLE
TANGLER > TANGLE
TANGLERS > TANGLE
TANGLES > TANGLE
TANGLIER > TANGLE
TANGLIEST > TANGLE
TANGLING n act or condition of tangling
TANGLINGS > TANGLING
TANGLY > TANGLE
TANGO n S American dance ▷ vb dance a tango
TANGOED > TANGO
TANGOES > TANGO
TANGOING > TANGO
TANGOIST > TANGO
TANGOISTS > TANGO
TANGOLIKE > TANGO
TANGOS > TANGO
TANGRAM n type of Chinese puzzle

TANGRAMS > TANGRAM
TANGS > TANG
TANGUN n small and sturdy Tibetan pony
TANGUNS > TANGUN
TANGY adj having a pungent, fresh, or briny flavour or aroma
TANH n hyperbolic tangent
TANHS > TANH
TANIST n heir apparent of a Celtic chieftain
TANISTRY > TANIST
TANISTS > TANIST
TANIWHA n mythical Māori monster that lives in water
TANIWHAS > TANIWHA
TANK n container for liquids or gases ▷ vb put or keep in a tank
TANKA n Japanese verse form consisting of five lines
TANKAGE n capacity or contents of a tank or tanks
TANKAGES > TANKAGE
TANKARD n large beer-mug, often with a hinged lid
TANKARDS > TANKARD
TANKAS > TANKA
TANKED > TANK
TANKER n ship or truck for carrying liquid in bulk ▷ vb transport by means of a tanker
TANKERED > TANKER
TANKERING > TANKER
TANKERS > TANKER
TANKFUL n quantity contained in a tank
TANKFULS > TANKFUL
TANKIA n type of boat used in Canton
TANKIAS > TANKIA
TANKIES > TANKY
TANKING n heavy defeat
TANKINGS > TANKING
TANKINI n swimming costume consisting of a camisole top and bikini briefs
TANKINIS > TANKINI
TANKLESS > TANK
TANKLIKE > TANK
TANKS > TANK
TANKSHIP same as > TANKER
TANKSHIPS > TANKSHIP
TANKY n die-hard communist
TANLING n suntanned person
TANLINGS > TANLING
TANNA n Indian police station or army base
TANNABLE > TAN
TANNAGE n act or process of tanning
TANNAGES > TANNAGE
TANNAH same as > TANNA
TANNAHS > TANNAH
TANNAS > TANNA
TANNATE n any salt or ester of tannic acid
TANNATES > TANNATE
TANNED > TAN
TANNER > TAN
TANNERIES > TANNERY
TANNERS > TAN

TANNERY n place where hides are tanned
TANNEST > TAN
TANNIC adj of, containing, or produced from tannin or tannic acid
TANNIE n in S Africa, title of respect used to refer to an elderly woman
TANNIES > TANNIE
TANNIN n vegetable substance used in tanning
TANNING > TAN
TANNINGS > TAN
TANNINS > TANNIN
TANNISH > TAN
TANNOY n sound-amplifying apparatus used as a public-address system ▷ vb announce (something) using a Tannoy system
TANNOYED > TANNOY
TANNOYING > TANNOY
TANNOYS > TANNOY
TANOREXIC n person obsessed with maintaining a tan
TANREC same as > TENREC
TANRECS > TANREC
TANS > TAN
TANSIES > TANSY
TANSY n yellow-flowered plant
TANTALATE n any of various salts of tantalic acid formed when the pentoxide of tantalum dissolves in an alkali
TANTALIC adj of or containing tantalum, esp in the pentavalent state
TANTALISE same as > TANTALIZE
TANTALISM > TANTALISE
TANTALITE n heavy brownish mineral consisting of a tantalum oxide of iron and manganese in orthorhombic crystalline form
TANTALIZE vb torment by showing but withholding something desired
TANTALOUS adj of or containing tantalum in the trivalent state
TANTALUM n hard greyish-white metallic element
TANTALUMS > TANTALUM
TANTALUS n case in which bottles of drink are locked with their contents tantalizingly visible
TANTARA n blast, as on a trumpet or horn
TANTARARA same as > TANTARA
TANTARAS > TANTARA
TANTI adj old word for worthwhile
TANTIES > TANTY
TANTIVIES > TANTIVY
TANTIVY adv at full speed ▷ interj hunting cry, esp at full gallop
TANTO adv too much ▷ n type of Japanese sword

t

TANTONIES > TANTONY
TANTONY *n* runt
TANTOS > TANTO
TANTRA *n* sacred books of Tantrism
TANTRAS > TANTRA
TANTRIC > TANTRA
TANTRISM *n* teaching of tantra
TANTRISMS > TANTRISM
TANTRIST *n* person who practises or teaches tantrism
TANTRISTS > TANTRIST
TANTRUM *n* childish outburst of temper
TANTRUMS > TANTRUM
TANTY *n* tantrum
TANUKI *n* animal similar to a raccoon, found in Japan
TANUKIS > TANUKI
TANYARD *n* part of a tannery
TANYARDS > TANYARD
TANZANITE *n* blue gemstone
TAO *n* (in Confucian philosophy) the correct course of action
TAONGA *n* treasure
TAONGAS > TAONGA
TAOS > TAO
TAP *vb* knock lightly and usu repeatedly ▷ *n* light knock
TAPA *n* inner bark of the paper mulberry
TAPACOLO *n* small bird of Chile and Argentina
TAPACOLOS > TAPACOLO
TAPACULO *same as* > TAPACOLO
TAPACULOS > TAPACULO
TAPADERA *n* leather covering for the stirrup on an American saddle
TAPADERAS > TAPADERA
TAPADERO *same as* > TAPADERA
TAPADEROS > TAPADERO
TAPALO *n* Latin American scarf, often patterned and brightly coloured
TAPALOS > TAPALO
TAPAS *pl n* (in Spanish cookery) light snacks or appetizers
TAPE *n* narrow long strip of material ▷ *vb* (formerly) record on magnetic tape
TAPEABLE > TAPE
TAPED > TAPE
TAPELESS > TAPE
TAPELIKE > TAPE
TAPELINE *n* tape used for measuring and fitting garments
TAPELINES > TAPELINE
TAPEN *adj* made of tape
TAPENADE *n* savoury paste made from capers, olives, and anchovies, with olive oil and lemon juice
TAPENADES > TAPENADE
TAPER > TAPE
TAPERED > TAPE
TAPERER > TAPE
TAPERERS > TAPE
TAPERING > TAPE
TAPERINGS > TAPE

TAPERNESS *n* state or quality of being tapered
TAPERS > TAPE
TAPERWISE *adv* in the manner of a taper
TAPES > TAPE
TAPESTRY *n* fabric decorated with coloured woven designs ▷ *vb* portray in tapestry
TAPET *n* example of tapestry ▷ *vb* decorate with tapestries
TAPETA > TAPETUM
TAPETAL > TAPETUM
TAPETED > TAPET
TAPETI *n* forest rabbit of Brazil
TAPETING > TAPET
TAPETIS > TAPETI
TAPETS > TAPET
TAPETUM *n* layer of nutritive cells that surrounds developing spore cells
TAPETUMS > TAPETUM
TAPEWORM *n* long flat parasitic worm living in the intestines of vertebrates
TAPEWORMS > TAPEWORM
TAPHOLE *n* hole in a furnace for running off molten metal or slag
TAPHOLES > TAPHOLE
TAPHONOMY *n* study of the processes affecting an organism after death that result in its fossilization
TAPHOUSE *n* inn or bar
TAPHOUSES > TAPHOUSE
TAPING *n* act of taping
TAPINGS > TAPING
TAPIOCA *n* beadlike starch made from cassava root
TAPIOCAS > TAPIOCA
TAPIR *n* piglike mammal of tropical America and SE Asia, with a long snout
TAPIROID > TAPIR
TAPIROIDS > TAPIROID
TAPIRS > TAPIR
TAPIS *n* tapestry or carpeting
TAPISES > TAPIS
TAPIST *n* person who records printed matter in an audio format
TAPISTS > TAPIST
TAPLASH *n* dregs of beer
TAPLASHES > TAPLASH
TAPLESS *adj* without a tap
TAPPA *same as* > TAPA
TAPPABLE > TAP
TAPPAS > TAPPA
TAPPED > TAP
TAPPER *n* person who taps
TAPPERS > TAPPER
TAPPET *n* short steel rod in an engine, transferring motion from one part to another
TAPPETS > TAPPET
TAPPICE *vb* hide
TAPPICED > TAPPICE
TAPPICES > TAPPICE
TAPPICING > TAPPICE
TAPPING > TAP
TAPPINGS > TAP
TAPPIT *adj* crested; topped

TAPROOM *n* public bar in a hotel or pub
TAPROOMS > TAPROOM
TAPROOT *n* main root of a plant, growing straight down
TAPROOTED > TAPROOT
TAPROOTS > TAPROOT
TAPS > TAP
TAPSMAN *n* old word for a barman
TAPSMEN > TAPSMAN
TAPSTER *n* barman
TAPSTERS > TAPSTER
TAPSTRESS > TAPSTER
TAPSTRIES > TAPSTRY
TAPSTRY *adj* relating to tapestry ▷ *n* taproom in a public house
TAPU *adj* sacred ▷ *n* Māori religious or superstitious restriction on something ▷ *vb* put a tapu on something
TAPUED > TAPU
TAPUING > TAPU
TAPUS > TAPU
TAQUERIA *n* restaurant specializing in tacos
TAQUERIAS > TAQUERIA
TAR *n* thick black liquid distilled from coal etc ▷ *vb* coat with tar
TARA *same as* > TARO
TARABISH *n* type of card game
TARAIRE *n* type of New Zealand tree
TARAIRES > TARAIRE
TARAKIHI *n* common edible sea fish of New Zealand waters
TARAKIHIS > TARAKIHI
TARAMA *n* cod roe
TARAMAS > TARAMA
TARAMEA *n* variety of New Zealand speargrass
TARAMEAS > TARAMEA
TARAND *n* northern animal of legend, now supposed to have been the reindeer
TARANDS > TARAND
TARANTARA *same as* > TANTARA
TARANTAS *same as* > TARANTASS
TARANTASS *n* large horse-drawn four-wheeled Russian carriage without springs
TARANTISM *n* nervous disorder marked by uncontrollable bodily movement, widespread in S Italy during the 15th to 17th centuries: popularly thought to be caused by the bite of a tarantula
TARANTIST > TARANTISM
TARANTULA *n* large hairy spider with a poisonous bite
TARAS > TARA
TARAXACUM *n* perennial plant with dense heads of small yellow flowers and seeds with a feathery attachment
TARBOGGIN *same as* > TOBOGGAN

TARBOOSH *n* brimless cap formerly worn by Muslim men
TARBOUCHE *same as* > TARBOOSH
TARBOUSH *same as* > TARBOOSH
TARBOY *n* boy who applies tar to the skin of sheep cut during shearing
TARBOYS > TARBOY
TARBUSH *same as* > TARBOOSH
TARBUSHES > TARBUSH
TARCEL *same as* > TERCEL
TARCELS > TARCEL
TARDIED > TARDY
TARDIER > TARDY
TARDIES > TARDY
TARDIEST > TARDY
TARDILY > TARDY
TARDINESS > TARDY
TARDIVE *adj* tending to develop late
TARDO *adj* (of music) slow; to be played slowly
TARDY *adj* slow or late ▷ *vb* delay or impede (something or someone)
TARDYING > TARDY
TARDYON *n* particle travelling more slowly than the speed of light
TARDYONS > TARDYON
TARE *n* weight of the wrapping or container of goods ▷ *vb* weigh (a package, etc) in order to calculate the amount of tare
TARED > TARE
TARES > TARE
TARGA *n* as in *targa top* denotes removable hard roof on a car
TARGAS > TARGA
TARGE *vb* interrogate
TARGED > TARGE
TARGES > TARGE
TARGET *n* object or person a missile is aimed at ▷ *vb* aim or direct
TARGETED > TARGET
TARGETEER *n* soldier armed with a small round shield
TARGETING *n* act of targeting
TARGETS > TARGET
TARGING > TARGE
TARIFF *n* tax levied on imports ▷ *vb* impose punishment for a criminal offence
TARIFFED > TARIFF
TARIFFING > TARIFF
TARIFFS > TARIFF
TARING > TARE
TARINGS > TARE
TARLATAN *n* open-weave cotton fabric, used for stiffening garments
TARLATANS > TARLATAN
TARLETAN *same as* > TARLATAN
TARLETANS > TARLETAN
TARMAC *See also* > MACADAM
TARMACKED > TARMAC
TARMACS > TARMAC

TARN n small mountain lake

TARNAL adj damned ▷ adv extremely

TARNALLY > TARNAL

TARNATION euphemism for > DAMNATION

TARNISH vb make or become stained or less bright ▷ n discoloration or blemish

TARNISHED > TARNISH

TARNISHER > TARNISH

TARNISHES > TARNISH

TARNS > TARN

TARO n plant with a large edible rootstock

TAROC old variant of > TAROT

TAROCS > TAROC

TAROK old variant of > TAROT

TAROKS > TAROK

TAROS > TARO

TAROT n special pack of cards used mainly in fortune-telling ▷ adj relating to tarot cards

TAROTS > TAROT

TARP informal word for > TARPAULIN

TARPAN n European wild horse common in prehistoric times

TARPANS > TARPAN

TARPAPER n paper coated or impregnated with tar

TARPAPERS > TARPAPER

TARPAULIN n (sheet of) heavy waterproof fabric

TARPON n large silvery clupeoid game fish found in warm Atlantic waters

TARPONS > TARPON

TARPS > TARP

TARRAGON n aromatic herb

TARRAGONS > TARRAGON

TARRAS same as > TRASS

TARRASES > TARRAS

TARRE vb old word meaning to provoke or goad

TARRED > TAR

TARRES > TARRE

TARRIANCE archaic word for > DELAY

TARRIED > TARRY

TARRIER > TARRY

TARRIERS > TARRY

TARRIES > TARRY

TARRIEST > TARRY

TARRINESS > TAR

TARRING > TAR

TARRINGS > TAR

TARROCK n seabird

TARROCKS > TARROCK

TARROW vb exhibit reluctance

TARROWED > TARROW

TARROWING > TARROW

TARROWS > TARROW

TARRY vb linger or delay ▷ adj covered in or resembling tar

TARRYING > TARRY

TARS > TAR

TARSAL adj of the tarsus or tarsi ▷ n tarsal bone

TARSALGIA n pain in the tarsus

TARSALS > TARSAL

TARSEAL n bitumen surface of a road

TARSEALS > TARSEAL

TARSEL same as > TERCEL

TARSELS > TARSEL

TARSI > TARSUS

TARSIA another term for > INTARSIA

TARSIAS > TARSIA

TARSIER n small nocturnal primate of the E Indies

TARSIERS > TARSIER

TARSIOID adj resembling a tarsier ▷ n type of fossil

TARSIOIDS > TARSIOID

TARSIPED n generic term for a number of marsupials

TARSIPEDS > TARSIPED

TARSUS n bones of the heel and ankle collectively

TART n pie or flan with a sweet filling ▷ adj sharp or bitter ▷ vb (of food, drink, etc) become tart (sour)

TARTAN n design of straight lines crossing at right angles

TARTANA n small Mediterranean sailing boat

TARTANAS > TARTANA

TARTANE same as > TARTANA

TARTANED > TARTAN

TARTANES > TARTANE

TARTANRY n excessive use of Scottish imagery to produce a distorted sentimental view of Scotland

TARTANS > TARTAN

TARTAR n hard deposit on the teeth

TARTARE n mayonnaise sauce mixed with hard-boiled egg yolks, herbs, etc

TARTARES > TARTARE

TARTARIC adj of or derived from tartar or tartaric acid

TARTARISE same as > TARTARIZE

TARTARIZE vb impregnate or treat with tartar or tartar emetic

TARTARLY adj resembling a tartar

TARTAROUS adj consisting of, containing, or resembling tartar

TARTARS > TARTAR

TARTED > TART

TARTER > TART

TARTEST > TART

TARTIER > TARTY

TARTIEST > TARTY

TARTILY > TARTY

TARTINE n slice of bread with butter or jam spread on it

TARTINES > TARTINE

TARTINESS > TARTY

TARTING > TART

TARTISH > TART

TARTISHLY > TART

TARTLET n individual pastry case with a filling of fruit or other sweet or savoury mixture

TARTLETS > TARTLET

TARTLY > TART

TARTNESS > TART

TARTRATE n any salt or ester of tartaric acid

TARTRATED adj being in the form of a tartrate

TARTRATES > TARTRATE

TARTS > TART

TARTUFE same as > TARTUFFE

TARTUFES > TARTUFE

TARTUFFE n person who hypocritically pretends to be deeply pious

TARTUFFES > TARTUFFE

TARTUFI > TARTUFO

TARTUFO n Italian mousse-like chocolate dessert

TARTUFOS > TARTUFO

TARTY adj provocative in a cheap and bawdy way

TARWEED n resinous Californian plant

TARWEEDS > TARWEED

TARWHINE n bream of E Australia, silver in colour with gold streaks

TARWHINES > TARWHINE

TARZAN n man with great physical strength

TARZANS > TARZAN

TAS > TA

TASAR same as > TUSSORE

TASARS > TASAR

TASBIH n form of Islamic prayer

TASBIHS > TASBIH

TASE vb stun with a taser gun

TASED > TASE

TASER vb use a taser stun gun on (someone)

TASERED > TASER

TASERING > TASER

TASERS > TASER

TASES > TASE

TASH vb stain or besmirch

TASHED > TASH

TASHES > TASH

TASHING > TASH

TASIMETER n device for measuring small temperature changes. It depends on the changes of pressure resulting from expanding or contracting solids

TASIMETRY > TASIMETER

TASING > TASE

TASK n piece of work to be done ▷ vb give someone a task to do

TASKBAR n area of computer screen showing what programs are running

TASKBARS > TASKBAR

TASKED > TASK

TASKER > TASK

TASKERS > TASK

TASKING > TASK

TASKINGS > TASK

TASKLESS > TASK

TASKS > TASK

TASKWORK n hard or unpleasant work

TASKWORKS > TASKWORK

TASLET same as > TASSET

TASLETS > TASLET

TASS n cup, goblet, or glass

TASSA n type of Indian kettledrum **TASSAS** > TASSA

TASSE same as > TASSET

TASSEL n decorative fringed knot of threads ▷ vb adorn with a tassel or tassels

TASSELED > TASSEL

TASSELIER > TASSELY

TASSELING > TASSEL

TASSELL same as > TASSEL

TASSELLED > TASSEL

TASSELLS > TASSELL

TASSELLY adj adorned with tassels

TASSELS > TASSEL

TASSELY adj decorated with tassels

TASSES > TASSE

TASSET n piece of armour to protect the thigh

TASSETS > TASSET

TASSIE same as > TASS

TASSIES > TASSIE

TASSO n spicy cured pork cut into strips

TASSOS > TASSO

TASSWAGE vb assuage

TASTABLE > TASTE

TASTE n sense by which the flavour of a substance is distinguished ▷ vb distinguish the taste of (a substance)

TASTEABLE > TASTE

TASTED > TASTE

TASTEFUL adj having or showing good taste

TASTELESS adj bland or insipid

TASTER n person employed to test the quality of food or drink by tasting it

TASTERS > TASTER

TASTES > TASTE

TASTEVIN n small shallow cup for wine tasting

TASTEVINS > TASTEVIN

TASTIER > TASTY

TASTIEST > TASTY

TASTILY > TASTY

TASTINESS > TASTY

TASTING > TASTE

TASTINGS > TASTE

TASTY adj pleasantly flavoured

TAT n tatty or tasteless article(s) ▷ vb make (something) by tatting

TATAHASH n stew containing potatoes and cheap cuts of meat

TATAMI n thick rectangular mat of woven straw

TATAMIS > TATAMI

TATAR n brutal person

TATARS > TATAR

TATE n small tuft of fibre

TATER n potato

TATERS > TATER

TATES > TATE

TATH vb (of cattle) to defecate

TATHATA n (in Buddhism) ultimate nature of things

TATHATAS > TATHATA

TATHED > TATH

TATHING > TATH

TATHS > TATH

TATIE same as > TATTIE

TATIES > TATIE

TATLER old variant of > TATTLER

TATLERS > TATLER

TATOU n armadillo

TATOUAY n large armadillo of South America

TATOUAYS > TATOUAY

TATOUS > TATOU

TATS > TAT

TATSOI n variety of Chinese cabbage

TATSOIS > TATSOI

TATT same as > TAT

TATTED > TAT

TATTER vb make or become torn

TATTERED > TATTER

TATTERIER > TATTERY

TATTERING > TATTER

TATTERS > TATTER

TATTERY adj ragged

TATTIE Scot or dialect word for > POTATO

TATTIER > TATTY

TATTIES > TATTIE

TATTIEST > TATTY

TATTILY > TATTY

TATTINESS > TATTY

TATTING > TAT

TATTINGS > TAT

TATTLE n gossip or chatter ▷ vb gossip or chatter

TATTLED > TATTLE

TATTLER n person who tattles

TATTLERS > TATTLER

TATTLES > TATTLE

TATTLING > TATTLE

TATTLINGS > TATTLE

TATTOO n pattern made on the body by pricking the skin and staining it with indelible inks ▷ vb make such a pattern on the skin

TATTOOED > TATTOO

TATTOOER > TATTOO

TATTOOERS > TATTOO

TATTOOING > TATTOO

TATTOOIST > TATTOO

TATTOOS > TATTOO

TATTOW old variant of > TATTOO

TATTOWED > TATTOW

TATTOWING > TATTOW

TATTOWS > TATTOW

TATTS > TATT

TATTY adj worn out, shabby, tawdry, or unkempt

TATU old variant of > TATTOO

TATUED > TATU

TATUING > TATU

TATUS > TATU

TAU n 19th letter in the Greek alphabet

TAUBE n type of obsolete German aeroplane

TAUBES > TAUBE

TAUGHT > TEACH

TAUHINU New Zealand name for > POPLAR

TAUHINUS > TAUHINU

TAUHOU same as > SILVEREYE

TAUHOUS > TAUHOU

TAUIWI n Māori term for the non-Māori people of New Zealand

TAUIWIS > TAUIWI

TAULD vb old Scots variant of told

TAUNT vb tease with jeers ▷ n jeering remark ▷ adj (of the mast or masts of a sailing vessel) unusually tall

TAUNTED > TAUNT

TAUNTER > TAUNT

TAUNTERS > TAUNT

TAUNTING > TAUNT

TAUNTINGS > TAUNT

TAUNTS > TAUNT

TAUON n negatively charged elementary particle

TAUONS > TAUON

TAUPATA n New Zealand shrub or tree

TAUPATAS > TAUPATA

TAUPE adj brownish-grey ▷ n brownish-grey colour

TAUPES > TAUPE

TAUPIE same as > TAWPIE

TAUPIES > TAUPIE

TAUREAN adj born under or characteristic of Taurus

TAURIC same as > TAUREAN

TAURIFORM adj in the form of a bull

TAURINE adj of, relating to, or resembling a bull ▷ n substance obtained from the bile of animals

TAURINES > TAURINE

TAUS > TAU

TAUT adj drawn tight ▷ vb Scots word meaning to tangle

TAUTAUG same as > TAUTOG

TAUTAUGS > TAUTAUG

TAUTED > TAUT

TAUTEN vb make or become taut

TAUTENED > TAUTEN

TAUTENING > TAUTEN

TAUTENS > TAUTEN

TAUTER > TAUT

TAUTEST > TAUT

TAUTING > TAUT

TAUTIT adj Scots word meaning tangled

TAUTLY > TAUT

TAUTNESS > TAUT

TAUTOG n large dark-coloured wrasse, used as a food fish

TAUTOGS > TAUTOG

TAUTOLOGY n use of words which merely repeat something already stated

TAUTOMER n either of the two forms of a chemical compound that exhibits tautomerism

TAUTOMERS > TAUTOMER

TAUTONYM n taxonomic name in which the generic and specific components are the same

TAUTONYMS > TAUTONYM

TAUTONYMY > TAUTONYM

TAUTS > TAUT

TAV n 23rd and last letter in the Hebrew alphabet

TAVA n thick Indian frying pan

TAVAH variant of > TAVA

TAVAHS > TAVAH

TAVAS > TAVA

TAVER vb wander about

TAVERED > TAVER

TAVERING > TAVER

TAVERN n pub

TAVERNA n Greek restaurant

TAVERNAS > TAVERNA

TAVERNER n keeper of a tavern

TAVERNERS > TAVERNER

TAVERNS > TAVERN

TAVERS > TAVER

TAVERT adj bewildered or confused

TAVS > TAV

TAW vb convert skins into leather

TAWA n tall timber tree from New Zealand

TAWAI n New Zealand beech

TAWAIS > TAWAI

TAWAS > TAWA

TAWDRIER > TAWDRY

TAWDRIES > TAWDRY

TAWDRIEST > TAWDRY

TAWDRILY > TAWDRY

TAWDRY adj cheap, showy, and of poor quality ▷ n gaudy finery of poor quality

TAWED > TAW

TAWER > TAW

TAWERIES > TAWERY

TAWERS > TAW

TAWERY n place where tawing is carried out

TAWHAI same as > TAWAI

TAWHAIS > TAWHAI

TAWHIRI n small New Zealand tree with wavy green glossy leaves

TAWHIRIS > TAWHIRI

TAWIE adj easily persuaded or managed

TAWIER > TAWIE

TAWIEST > TAWIE

TAWING > TAW

TAWINGS > TAW

TAWNEY same as > TAWNY

TAWNEYS > TAWNEY

TAWNIER > TAWNY

TAWNIES > TAWNY

TAWNIEST > TAWNY

TAWNILY > TAWNY

TAWNINESS > TAWNY

TAWNY adj yellowish-brown ▷ n light brown to brownish-orange colour

TAWPIE n foolish or maladroit girl

TAWPIES > TAWPIE

TAWS same as > TAWSE

TAWSE n leather strap with one end cut into thongs ▷ vb punish (someone) with or as if with a tawse

TAWSED > TAWSE

TAWSES > TAWSE

TAWSING > TAWSE

TAWT same as > TAUT

TAWTED > TAWT

TAWTIE > TAWT

TAWTIER > TAWT

TAWTIEST > TAWT

TAWTING > TAWT

TAWTS > TAWT

TAX n compulsory payment levied by a government on income, property, etc to raise revenue ▷ vb levy a tax on

TAXA > TAXON

TAXABLE adj capable of being taxed ▷ n person, income, property, etc, that is subject to tax

TAXABLES > TAXABLE

TAXABLY > TAXABLE

TAXACEOUS adj relating to a family of coniferous trees that includes the yews

TAXAMETER old variant of > TAXIMETER

TAXATION n levying of taxes

TAXATIONS > TAXATION

TAXATIVE > TAXATION

TAXED > TAX

TAXEME n any element of speech that may differentiate meaning

TAXEMES > TAXEME

TAXEMIC > TAXEME

TAXER > TAX

TAXERS > TAX

TAXES > TAX

TAXI n car with a driver that may be hired ▷ vb (of an aircraft) run along the ground

TAXIARCH n soldier in charge of a Greek taxis

TAXIARCHS > TAXIARCH

TAXICAB same as > TAXI

TAXICABS > TAXICAB

TAXIDERMY n art of stuffing and mounting animal skins to give them a lifelike appearance

TAXIED > TAXI

TAXIES > TAXI

TAXIING > TAXI

TAXIMAN n taxi driver

TAXIMEN > TAXIMAN

TAXIMETER n meter fitted to a taxi to register the fare, based on the length of the journey

TAXING adj demanding, onerous

TAXINGLY > TAXING

TAXINGS > TAX

TAXIPLANE n aircraft that is available for hire

TAXIS n movement of a cell or organism in response to an external stimulus

TAXISES > TAXIS

TAXITE n type of volcanic rock

TAXITES > TAXITE

TAXITIC > TAXITE

TAXIWAY n marked path along which aircraft taxi to or from a runway, parking area, etc

TAXIWAYS > TAXIWAY

TAXLESS > TAX

TAXMAN n collector of taxes

TAXMEN > TAXMAN

TAXOL n trademarked anti-cancer drug

TAXOLS > TAXOL

TAXON n any taxonomic group or rank

TAXONOMER > TAXONOMY

TAXONOMIC > TAXONOMY

TAXONOMY n classification of plants and animals into groups

TAXONS > TAXON

TAXOR > TAX

TAXORS > TAX

TAXPAID adj having had the applicable tax paid already

TAXPAYER n person or organization that pays taxes

TAXPAYERS > TAXPAYER

TAXPAYING > TAXPAYER

TAXUS n genus of conifers

TAXWISE adv regarding tax

TAXYING > TAXI

TAY Irish dialect word for > TEA

TAYASSUID n peccary

TAYBERRY n hybrid shrub produced by crossing a blackberry, raspberry, and loganberry

TAYRA n large arboreal mammal of Central and South America

TAYRAS > TAYRA

TAYS > TAY

TAZZA n cup with a shallow bowl and a circular foot

TAZZAS > TAZZA

TAZZE > TAZZA

TCHICK vb make a clicking noise with the tongue

TCHICKED > TCHICK

TCHICKING > TCHICK

TCHICKS > TCHICK

TCHOTCHKE n trinket

TE n (in tonic sol-fa) seventh degree of any major scale

TEA n drink made from infusing the dried leaves of an Asian bush in boiling water ▷ vb take tea

TEABAG n porous bag of tea leaves for infusion

TEABAGS > TEABAG

TEABERRY n berry of the wintergreen

TEABOARD n tea tray

TEABOARDS > TEABOARD

TEABOWL n small bowl used (instead of a teacup) for serving tea

TEABOWLS > TEABOWL

TEABOX n box for storing tea

TEABOXES > TEABOX

TEABREAD n loaf-shaped cake with dried fruit which has been steeped in tea before baking

TEABREADS > TEABREAD

TEACAKE n flat bun, usually eaten toasted and buttered

TEACAKES > TEACAKE

TEACART n trolley from which tea is served

TEACARTS > TEACART

TEACH vb tell or show (someone) how to do something

TEACHABLE > TEACH

TEACHABLY > TEACH

TEACHER n person who teaches, esp in a school

TEACHERLY adj like a teacher

TEACHERS > TEACHER

TEACHES > TEACH

TEACHIE old form of > TETCHY

TEACHING > TEACH

TEACHINGS > TEACH

TEACHLESS adj unable to be taught

TEACUP n cup out of which tea may be drunk

TEACUPFUL n amount a teacup will hold, about four fluid ounces

TEACUPS > TEACUP

TEAD old word for > TORCH

TEADE same as > TEAD

TEADES > TEADE

TEADS > TEAD

TEAED > TEA

TEAGLE vb raise or hoist using a tackle

TEAGLED > TEAGLE

TEAGLES > TEAGLE

TEAGLING > TEAGLE

TEAHOUSE n restaurant, esp in Japan or China, where tea and light refreshments are served

TEAHOUSES > TEAHOUSE

TEAING > TEA

TEAK n very hard wood of an E Indian tree

TEAKETTLE n kettle for boiling water to make tea

TEAKS > TEAK

TEAKWOOD another word for > TEAK

TEAKWOODS > TEAKWOOD

TEAL n kind of small duck

TEALIGHT n small candle

TEALIGHTS > TEALIGHT

TEALIKE adj resembling tea

TEALS > TEAL

TEAM n group of people forming one side in a game ▷ vb make or cause to make a team

TEAMAKER n person or thing that makes tea

TEAMAKERS > TEAMAKER

TEAMED > TEAM

TEAMER > TEAM

TEAMERS > TEAM

TEAMING > TEAM

TEAMINGS > TEAM

TEAMMATE n fellow member of a team

TEAMMATES > TEAMMATE

TEAMS > TEAM

TEAMSTER n commercial vehicle driver

TEAMSTERS > TEAMSTER

TEAMWISE adv in respect of a team; in the manner of a team

TEAMWORK n cooperative work by a team

TEAMWORKS > TEAMWORK

TEAPOT n container for making and serving tea

TEAPOTS > TEAPOT

TEAPOY n small table or stand with a tripod base

TEAPOYS > TEAPOY

TEAR n drop of fluid appearing in and falling from the eye ▷ vb rip a hole in ▷ vb shed tears

TEARABLE > TEAR

TEARAWAY n wild or unruly person

TEARAWAYS > TEARAWAY

TEARDOWN n demolition; disassembly

TEARDOWNS > TEARDOWN

TEARDROP same as > TEAR

TEARDROPS > TEARDROP

TEARED > TEAR

TEARER > TEAR

TEARERS > TEAR

TEARFUL adj weeping or about to weep

TEARFULLY > TEARFUL

TEARGAS n gas or vapour that makes the eyes smart and water ▷ vb deploy teargas against

TEARGASES > TEARGAS

TEARIER > TEARY

TEARIEST > TEARY

TEARILY > TEARY

TEARINESS > TEARY

TEARING > TEAR

TEARLESS > TEAR

TEARLIKE adj like a tear

TEAROOM same as > TEASHOP

TEAROOMS > TEAROOM

TEARS > TEAR

TEARSHEET n page in a newspaper or periodical that is cut or perforated so that it can be easily torn out

TEARSTAIN n stain or streak left by tears

TEARSTRIP n part of packaging torn to open it

TEARY adj characterized by, covered with, or secreting tears

TEAS > TEA

TEASABLE > TEASE

TEASE vb make fun of (someone) in a provoking or playful way ▷ n person who teases

TEASED > TEASE

TEASEL n plant with prickly leaves and flowers ▷ vb tease (a fabric)

TEASELED > TEASEL

TEASELER > TEASEL

TEASELERS > TEASEL

TEASELING > TEASEL

TEASELLED > TEASEL

TEASELLER > TEASEL

TEASELS > TEASEL

TEASER n annoying or difficult problem

TEASERS > TEASER

TEASES > TEASE

TEASHOP n restaurant where tea and light refreshments are served

TEASHOPS > TEASHOP

TEASING > TEASE

TEASINGLY > TEASE

TEASINGS > TEASE

TEASPOON n small spoon for stirring tea

TEASPOONS > TEASPOON

TEAT n nipple of a breast or udder

TEATASTER n person assessing teas by tasting them

TEATED > TEAT

TEATIME n late afternoon

TEATIMES > TEATIME

TEATS > TEAT

TEAWARE n implements for brewing and serving tea

TEAWARES > TEAWARE

TEAZE old variant of > TEASE

TEAZED > TEAZE

TEAZEL same as > TEASEL

TEAZELED > TEAZEL

TEAZELING > TEAZEL

TEAZELLED > TEAZEL

TEAZELS > TEAZEL

TEAZES > TEAZE

TEAZING > TEAZE

TEAZLE same as > TEASEL

TEAZLED > TEAZLE

TEAZLES > TEAZLE

TEAZLING > TEAZLE

TEBBAD n sandstorm

TEBBADS > TEBBAD

TEBIBYTE n 2^{40} bytes

TEBIBYTES > TEBIBYTE

TEC short for > DETECTIVE

TECH n technical college

TECHED adj showing slight insanity

TECHIE n person who is skilled in the use of technology ▷ adj relating to or skilled in the use of technology

TECHIER > TECHY

TECHIES > TECHIE

TECHIEST > TECHY

TECHILY > TECHY

TECHINESS > TECHY

TECHNIC another word for > TECHNIQUE

TECHNICAL adj of or specializing in industrial, practical, or mechanical arts and applied sciences ▷ n small armed military truck

TECHNICS n study or theory of industry and industrial arts

TECHNIKON n technical college

TECHNIQUE n method or skill used for a particular task

TECHNO n type of electronic dance music with a very fast beat

TECHNOID n technician

TECHNOIDS > TECHNOID

TECHNOPOP n pop music sharing certain features with techno

TECHNOS > TECHNO

TECHS > TECH

TECHY same as > TECHIE

TECKEL n dachshund

TECKELS > TECKEL

TECS > TEC

TECTA > TECTUM

TECTAL > TECTUM

TECTIFORM adj in the form of a roof

TECTITE same as
> TEKTITE

TECTITES > TECTITE

TECTONIC adj denoting or relating to construction or building

TECTONICS n study of the earth's crust and the forces affecting it

TECTONISM > TECTONIC

TECTORIAL adj as in tectorial membrane membrane in the inner ear that covers the organ of Corti

TECTRICES > TECTRIX

TECTRIX another name for
> COVERT

TECTUM n any roof-like structure in the body

TECTUMS > TECTUM

TED vb shake out (hay), so as to dry it

TEDDED > TED

TEDDER n machine equipped with a series of small rotating forks for tedding hay

TEDDERED > TEDDER

TEDDERING > TEDDER

TEDDERS > TEDDER

TEDDIE same as > TEDDY

TEDDIES > TEDDY

TEDDING > TED

TEDDY n teddy bear

TEDIER > TEDY

TEDIEST > TEDY

TEDIOSITY > TEDIOUS

TEDIOUS adj causing fatigue or boredom

TEDIOUSLY > TEDIOUS

TEDISOME old Scottish variant of > TEDIOUS

TEDIUM n monotony

TEDIUMS > TEDIUM

TEDS > TED

TEDY same as > TEDIOUS

TEE n small peg from which a golf ball can be played at the start of each hole ▷ vb position (the ball) ready for striking, on or as if on a tee

TEED > TEE

TEEING > TEE

TEEK adj in Indian English, well

TEEL same as > SESAME

TEELS > TEEL

TEEM vb be full of

TEEMED > TEEM

TEEMER > TEEM

TEEMERS > TEEM

TEEMFUL > TEEM

TEEMING > TEEM

TEEMINGLY > TEEM

TEEMLESS > TEEM

TEEMS > TEEM

TEEN n teenager ▷ vb set alight

TEENAGE adj (of a person) aged between 13 and 19 ▷ n this period of time

TEENAGED adj (of a person) aged between 13 and 19

TEENAGER n person aged between 13 and 19

TEENAGERS > TEENAGER

TEENAGES > TEENAGE

TEEND same as > TIND

TEENDED > TEEND

TEENDING > TEEND

TEENDOM n state of being a teenager

TEENDOMS > TEENDOM

TEENDS > TEEND

TEENE n affliction or woe

TEENED > TEEN

TEENER > TEEN

TEENERS > TEEN

TEENES > TEENE

TEENFUL adj troublesome or harmful

TEENIER > TEENY

TEENIEST > TEENY

TEENING > TEEN

TEENS > TEEN

TEENSIER > TEENSY

TEENSIEST > TEENSY

TEENSY same as > TEENY

TEENTIER > TEENTY

TEENTIEST > TEENTY

TEENTSIER > TEENTSY

TEENTSY same as > TEENY

TEENTY same as > TEENY

TEENY adj extremely small

TEENYBOP adj of or relating to a young teenager who avidly follows fashions in music and clothes

TEEPEE same as > TEPEE

TEEPEES > TEEPEE

TEER vb smear; daub

TEERED > TEER

TEERING > TEER

TEERS > TEER

TEES > TEE

TEETER vb wobble or move unsteadily

TEETERED > TEETER

TEETERING > TEETER

TEETERS > TEETER

TEETH > TOOTH

TEETHE vb (of a baby) grow his or her first teeth

TEETHED > TEETHE

TEETHER n object for an infant to bite on during teething

TEETHERS > TEETHER

TEETHES > TEETHE

TEETHING > TEETHE

TEETHINGS > TEETHING

TEETHLESS > TEETH

TEETOTAL adj drinking no alcohol ▷ vb advocate total abstinence from alcohol

TEETOTALS > TEETOTAL

TEETOTUM n spinning top bearing letters of the alphabet on its four sides

TEETOTUMS > TEETOTUM

TEEVEE n television

TEEVEES > TEEVEE

TEF n annual grass, of NE Africa, grown for its grain

TEFF same as > TEF

TEFFS > TEFF

TEFILLAH n either of the pair of blackened square cases worn by Jewish men during weekday morning prayers

TEFILLIN > TEFILLAH

TEFLON n substance used in nonstick cooking vessels

TEFLONS > TEFLON

TEFS > TEF

TEG n two-year-old sheep

TEGG same as > TEG

TEGGS > TEGG

TEGMEN n either of the leathery forewings of the cockroach and related insects

TEGMENTA > TEGMENTUM

TEGMENTAL > TEGMENTUM

TEGMENTUM n one of the hard protective sometimes hairy or resinous specialized leaves surrounding the buds of certain plants

TEGMINA > TEGMEN

TEGMINAL > TEGMEN

TEGS > TEG

TEGU n large South American lizard

TEGUA n type of moccasin

TEGUAS > TEGUA

TEGUEXIN same as > TEGU

TEGUEXINS > TEGUEXIN

TEGULA n one of a pair of coverings of the forewings of certain insects

TEGULAE > TEGULA

TEGULAR adj of, relating to, or resembling a tile or tiles

TEGULARLY > TEGULAR

TEGULATED adj overlapping in the manner of roof tiles

TEGUMEN same as > TEGMEN

TEGUMENT n protective layer around an ovule

TEGUMENTS > TEGUMENT

TEGUMINA > TEGUMEN

TEGUS > TEGU

TEHR same as > TAHR

TEHRS > TEHR

TEHSIL n administrative region in some S Asian countries

TEHSILDAR n person who administrates a tehsil

TEHSILS > TEHSIL

TEIGLACH pl n morsels of dough boiled in honey, eaten as a dessert

TEIID n member of the Teiidae family of lizards

TEIIDS > TEIID

TEIL n lime tree

TEILS > TEIL

TEIN n monetary unit of Kazakhstan

TEIND Scot and northern English word for > TITHE

TEINDED > TEIND

TEINDING > TEIND

TEINDS > TEIND

TEINS > TEIN

TEKKIE variant of > TECHIE

TEKKIES > TEKKIE

TEKNONYMY n practice of naming a child after his or her parent

TEKTITE n small dark glassy object found in several areas around the world

TEKTITES > TEKTITE

TEKTITIC > TEKTITE

TEL same as > TELL

TELA n any delicate tissue or weblike structure

TELAE > TELA

TELAMON n column in the form of a male figure

TELAMONES > TELAMON

TELAMONS > TELAMON

TELARY adj capable of spinning a web

TELCO n telecommunications company

TELCOS > TELCO

TELD same as > TAULD

TELE same as > TELLY

TELECAST vb broadcast by television ▷ n television broadcast

TELECASTS > TELECAST

TELECHIR n robot arm controlled by a human operator

TELECHIRS > TELECHIR

TELECINE n apparatus for producing a television signal from cinematograph film

TELECINES > TELECINE

TELECOM n telecommunications

TELECOMM n telecommunication

TELECOMMS > TELECOMM

TELECOMS same as
> TELECOM

TELECON n (short for) teleconference

TELECONS > TELECON

TELECOPY n message or document sent by fax

TELEDU n badger of SE Asia and Indonesia

TELEDUS > TELEDU

TELEFAX another word for
> FAX

TELEFAXED > TELEFAX

TELEFAXES > TELEFAX

TELEFILM n film made for TV

TELEFILMS > TELEFILM

TELEGA n rough four-wheeled cart used in Russia

TELEGAS > TELEGA

TELEGENIC adj having or showing a pleasant television image

TELEGONIC > TELEGONY

TELEGONY n supposed influence of a previous sire on offspring borne by a female to other sires

TELEGRAM n formerly, a message sent by telegraph ▷ vb send a telegram

TELEGRAMS > TELEGRAM

TELEGRAPH n formerly, a system for sending messages over a distance along a cable ▷ vb communicate by telegraph

TELEMAN n noncommissioned officer in the US navy

TELEMARK n turn in which one ski is placed far forward of the other and turned gradually inwards ▷ vb perform a telemark turn

TELEMARKS > TELEMARK

TELEMATIC adj of, or relating to, the branch of

science concerned with the use of technological devices to transmit information over long distances

TELEMEN > TELEMAN

TELEMETER *n* any device for recording or measuring a distant event and transmitting the data to a receiver or observer ▷ *vb* obtain and transmit (data) from a distant source, esp from a spacecraft

TELEMETRY *n* use of electronic devices to record or measure a distant event and transmit the data to a receiver

TELEOLOGY *n* belief that all things have a predetermined purpose

TELEONOMY *n* condition of having a fundamental purpose

TELEOSAUR *n* type of crocodile from the Jurassic period

TELEOST *n* bony fish with rayed fins and a swim bladder ▷ *adj* of, relating to, or belonging to this type of fish

TELEOSTS > TELEOST

TELEPATH *n* person who is telepathic ▷ *vb* practise telepathy

TELEPATHS > TELEPATH

TELEPATHY *n* direct communication between minds

TELEPHEME *n* any message sent by telephone

TELEPHONE *n* device for transmitting sound over a distance along wires ▷ *vb* call or talk to (a person) by telephone ▷ *adj* of or using a telephone

TELEPHONY *n* system of telecommunications for the transmission of speech or other sounds

TELEPHOTO *n* short for telephoto lens: a compound camera lens that produces a magnified image of distant objects

TELEPIC *n* feature-length film made for television

TELEPICS > TELEPIC

TELEPLAY *n* play written for television

TELEPLAYS > TELEPLAY

TELEPOINT *n* system providing a place where a cordless telephone can be connected to a telephone network

TELEPORT *vb* (in science fiction) to transport (a person or object) across a distance instantaneously

TELEPORTS > TELEPORT

TELEPRINT *vb* print (a message) with a teleprinter

TELERAN *n* electronic navigational aid

TELERANS > TELERAN

TELERGIC > TELERGY

TELERGIES > TELERGY

TELERGY *n* name for the form of energy supposedly transferred during telepathy

TELEROBOT *n* remote-controlled robot

TELES > TELE

TELESALE > TELESALES

TELESALES *n* selling of a product or service by telephone

TELESCOPE *n* optical instrument for magnifying distant objects ▷ *vb* shorten

TELESCOPY *n* branch of astronomy concerned with the use and design of telescopes

TELESEME *n* old-fashioned electric signalling system

TELESEMES > TELESEME

TELESES > TELESIS

TELESHOP *vb* buy goods by telephone or internet

TELESHOPS > TELESHOP

TELESIS *n* purposeful use of natural and social processes to obtain specific social goals

TELESM *n* talisman

TELESMS > TELESM

TELESTIC *adj* relating to a hierophant

TELESTICH *n* short poem in which the last letters of each successive line form a word

TELESTICS *n* ancient pseudoscientific art of animating statues, idols, etc, or causing them to be inhabited by a deity

TELETEX *n* international means of communicating text between a variety of terminals

TELETEXES > TELETEX

TELETEXT *n* system which shows information and news on television screens

TELETEXTS > TELETEXT

TELETHON *n* lengthy television programme to raise charity funds, etc

TELETHONS > TELETHON

TELETRON *n* system for showing enlarged televisual images, eg in sports stadiums

TELETRONS > TELETRON

TELETYPE *vb* send typed message by telegraph

TELETYPED > TELETYPE

TELETYPES > TELETYPE

TELEVIEW *vb* watch television

TELEVIEWS > TELEVIEW

TELEVISE *vb* broadcast on television

TELEVISED > TELEVISE

TELEVISER > TELEVISE

TELEVISES > TELEVISE

TELEVISOR *n* apparatus through which one transmits or receives televisual images

TELEWORK *vb* work from home, communicating by computer, telephone etc

TELEWORKS > TELEWORK

TELEX *n* (formerly) international communication service using teleprinters ▷ *vb* (formerly) transmit by telex

TELEXED > TELEX

TELEXES > TELEX

TELEXING > TELEX

TELFER *n* overhead transport system

TELFERAGE *n* overhead transport system in which an electrically driven truck runs along a single rail or cable, the load being suspended in a separate car beneath

TELFERED > TELFER

TELFERIC > TELFER

TELFERING > TELFER

TELFERS > TELFER

TELFORD *n* road built using a method favoured by Thomas Telford

TELFORDS > TELFORD

TELIA > TELIUM

TELIAL > TELIUM

TELIC *adj* directed or moving towards some goal

TELICALLY > TELIC

TELICITY *n* quality of being telic

TELIUM *n* spore-producing body of some rust fungi in which the teliospores are formed

TELL *vb* make known in words ▷ *n* large mound resulting from the accumulation of rubbish

TELLABLE > TELL

TELLAR *same as* > TILLER

TELLARED > TELLAR

TELLARING > TELLAR

TELLARS > TELLAR

TELLEN *same as* > TELLIN

TELLENS > TELLEN

TELLER *n* narrator ▷ *vb* (of a plant) to produce tillers

TELLERED > TELLER

TELLERING > TELLER

TELLERS > TELLER

TELLIES > TELLY

TELLIN *n* slim marine bivalve molluscs that live in intertidal sand

TELLING > TELL

TELLINGLY > TELL

TELLINGS > TELL

TELLINOID > TELLIN

TELLINS > TELLIN

TELLS > TELL

TELLTALE *n* person who reveals secrets ▷ *adj* revealing

TELLTALES > TELLTALE

TELLURAL *adj* of or relating to the earth

TELLURATE *n* any salt or ester of telluric acid

TELLURIAN *same as* > TELLURION

TELLURIC *adj* of, relating to, or originating on or in the earth or soil

TELLURIDE *n* any compound of tellurium, esp one formed between

tellurium and a more electropositive element or group

TELLURION *n* instrument that shows how day and night and the seasons result from the tilt of the earth, its rotation on its axis, and its revolution around the sun

TELLURISE *same as* > TELLURIZE

TELLURITE *n* any salt or ester of tellurous acid

TELLURIUM *n* brittle silvery-white nonmetallic element

TELLURIZE *vb* mix or combine with tellurium

TELLUROUS *adj* of or containing tellurium, esp in a low valence state

TELLUS *n* earth

TELLUSES > TELLUS

TELLY *n* television

TELLYS > TELLY

TELNET *n* system allowing remote access to other computers on the same network ▷ *vb* use a telnet system

TELNETED > TELNET

TELNETING > TELNET

TELNETS > TELNET

TELNETTED > TELNET

TELOGEN *n* phase of hair growth

TELOGENS > TELOGEN

TELOI > TELOS

TELOME *n* fundamental unit of a plant's structure

TELOMERE *n* either of the ends of a chromosome

TELOMERES > TELOMERE

TELOMES > TELOME

TELOMIC > TELOME

TELOPHASE *n* final stage of mitosis, during which a set of chromosomes is present at each end of the cell and a nuclear membrane forms around each, producing two new nuclei

TELOS *n* objective; ultimate purpose

TELOTAXES > TELOTAXIS

TELOTAXIS *n* movement of an organism in response to one particular stimulus, overriding any response to other stimuli present

TELPHER *same as* > TELFERAGE

TELPHERED > TELPHER

TELPHERIC > TELPHER

TELPHERS > TELPHER

TELS > TEL

TELSON *n* segment of the body of crustaceans and arachnids

TELSONIC > TELSON

TELSONS > TELSON

TELT *same as* > TAULD

TEMAZEPAM *n* sedative in the form of a gel-like capsule

TEMBLOR *n* earthquake or earth tremor

TEMBLORES > TEMBLOR

TEMBLORS > TEMBLOR

TEME *old variant of* > TEAM

TEMED > TEME

TEMENE > TEMENOS

TEMENOS *n* sacred area, esp one surrounding a temple

TEMERITY *n* boldness or audacity

TEMEROUS > TEMERITY

TEMES > TEME

TEMP *same as* **>** TEMPORARY

TEMPED > TEMP

TEMPEH *n* fermented soya beans

TEMPEHS > TEMPEH

TEMPER *n* outburst of anger ▷ *vb* make less extreme

TEMPERA *n* painting medium for powdered pigments

TEMPERAS > TEMPERA

TEMPERATE *adj* (of climate) not extreme ▷ *vb* temper

TEMPERED *adj* having the frequency differences between notes adjusted in accordance with the system of equal temperament

TEMPERER > TEMPER

TEMPERERS > TEMPER

TEMPERING > TEMPER

TEMPERS > TEMPER

TEMPEST *n* violent storm ▷ *vb* agitate or disturb violently

TEMPESTED > TEMPEST

TEMPESTS > TEMPEST

TEMPI > TEMPO

TEMPING *n* act of temping

TEMPINGS > TEMPING

TEMPLAR *n* lawyer who has chambers in the Inner or Middle Temple in London

TEMPLARS > TEMPLAR

TEMPLATE *n* pattern used to cut out shapes accurately

TEMPLATES > TEMPLATE

TEMPLE *n* building for worship

TEMPLED > TEMPLE

TEMPLES > TEMPLE

TEMPLET *same as* **>** TEMPLATE

TEMPLETS > TEMPLET

TEMPO *n* rate or pace

TEMPORAL *adj* of time ▷ *n* any body part relating to or near the temple or temples

TEMPORALS > TEMPORAL

TEMPORARY *adj* lasting only for a short time ▷ *n* person, esp a secretary or other office worker, employed on a temporary basis

TEMPORE *adv* in the time of

TEMPORISE *same as* **>** TEMPORIZE

TEMPORIZE *vb* gain time by negotiation or evasiveness

TEMPOS > TEMPO

TEMPS > TEMP

TEMPT *vb* entice (a person) to do something wrong

TEMPTABLE > TEMPT

TEMPTED > TEMPT

TEMPTER > TEMPT

TEMPTERS > TEMPT

TEMPTING *adj* attractive or inviting

TEMPTINGS > TEMPTING

TEMPTRESS *n* woman who sets out to allure someone

TEMPTS > TEMPT

TEMPURA *n* Japanese dish of seafood or vegetables dipped in batter and deep-fried

TEMPURAS > TEMPURA

TEMS *same as* **>** TEMSE

TEMSE *vb* sieve

TEMSED > TEMSE

TEMSES > TEMSE

TEMSING > TEMSE

TEMULENCE *n* drunkenness

TEMULENCY *same as* **>** TEMULENCE

TEMULENT > TEMULENCE

TEN *n* one more than nine

TENABLE *adj* able to be upheld or maintained

TENABLY > TENABLE

TENACE *n* holding of two nonconsecutive high cards of a suit, such as the ace and queen

TENACES > TENACE

TENACIOUS *adj* holding fast

TENACITY > TENACIOUS

TENACULA > TENACULUM

TENACULUM *n* surgical or dissecting instrument for grasping and holding parts, consisting of a slender hook mounted in a handle

TENAIL *same as* **>** TENAILLE

TENAILLE *n* low outwork in the main ditch between two bastions

TENAILLES > TENAILLE

TENAILLON *n* outwork shoring up a ravelin

TENAILS > TENAIL

TENANCIES > TENANCY

TENANCY *n* temporary possession of property owned by somebody else

TENANT *n* person who rents land or a building ▷ *vb* hold (land or property) as a tenant

TENANTED > TENANT

TENANTING > TENANT

TENANTRY *n* tenants collectively

TENANTS > TENANT

TENCH *n* freshwater game fish of the carp family

TENCHES > TENCH

TEND *vb* be inclined

TENDANCE *n* care and attention

TENDANCES > TENDANCE

TENDED > TEND

TENDENCE *same as* **>** TENDENCY

TENDENCES > TENDENCE

TENDENCY *n* inclination to act in a certain way

TENDENZ *same as* **>** TENDENCY

TENDENZEN > TENDENZ

TENDER *adj* not tough ▷ *vb* offer ▷ *n* such an offer

TENDERED > TENDER

TENDERER > TENDER

TENDERERS > TENDER

TENDEREST > TENDER

TENDERING > TENDER

TENDERISE *same as* **>** TENDERIZE

TENDERIZE *vb* soften (meat) by pounding or treatment with a special substance

TENDERLY > TENDER

TENDERS > TENDER

TENDING > TEND

TENDINOUS *adj* of, relating to, possessing, or resembling tendons

TENDON *n* strong tissue attaching a muscle to a bone

TENDONS > TENDON

TENDRE *n* care

TENDRES > TENDRE

TENDRESSE *n* feeling of love; tenderness

TENDRIL *n* slender stem by which a climbing plant clings

TENDRILED > TENDRIL

TENDRILLY *adj* of or similar to a tendril

TENDRILS > TENDRIL

TENDRON *n* shoot

TENDRONS > TENDRON

TENDS > TEND

TENDU *n* position in ballet

TENDUS > TENDU

TENE *same as* **>** TEEN

TENEBRAE *n* darkness

TENEBRIO *n* type of small mealworm

TENEBRIOS > TENEBRIO

TENEBRISM *n* school, style, or method of painting, adopted chiefly by 17th-century Spanish and Neapolitan painters, esp Caravaggio, characterized by large areas of dark colours, usually relieved with a shaft of light

TENEBRIST > TENEBRISM

TENEBRITY *n* darkness; gloominess

TENEBROSE *same as* **>** TENEBROUS

TENEBROUS *adj* gloomy, shadowy, or dark

TENEMENT *n* (esp in Scotland or the US) building divided into several flats

TENEMENTS > TENEMENT

TENENDA > TENENDUM

TENENDUM *n* part of a deed that specifies the terms of tenure

TENENDUMS > TENENDUM

TENES > TENE

TENESI *n* monetary unit of Turkmenistan

TENESMIC > TENESMUS

TENESMUS *n* bowel disorder

TENET *n* doctrine or belief

TENETS > TENET

TENFOLD *n* one tenth

TENFOLDS > TENFOLD

TENGE *n* standard monetary unit of Kazakhstan

TENGES > TENGE

TENIA *same as* **>** TAENIA

TENIACIDE *n* substance, esp a drug, that kills tapeworms

TENIAE > TENIA

TENIAFUGE *same as* **>** TENIACIDE

TENIAS > TENIA

TENIASES > TENIASIS

TENIASIS *same as* **>** TAENIASIS

TENIOID > TENIA

TENNE *n* tawny colour

TENNER *n* ten-pound note

TENNERS > TENNER

TENNES > TENNE

TENNESI *same as* **>** TENESI

TENNIES > TENNY

TENNIS *n* game in which players use rackets to hit a ball back and forth over a net

TENNISES > TENNIS

TENNIST *n* tennis player

TENNISTS > TENNIST

TENNO *n* formal title of the Japanese emperor

TENNOS > TENNO

TENNY *same as* **>** TENNE

TENON *n* projecting end on a piece of wood fitting into a slot in another ▷ *vb* form a tenon on (a piece of wood)

TENONED > TENON

TENONER > TENON

TENONERS > TENON

TENONING > TENON

TENONS > TENON

TENOR *n* (singer with) the second highest male voice ▷ *adj* (of a voice or instrument) between alto and baritone

TENORINI > TENORINO

TENORINO *n* high tenor

TENORIST *n* musician playing any tenor instrument

TENORISTS > TENORIST

TENORITE *n* black mineral found in copper deposits

TENORITES > TENORITE

TENORLESS > TENOR

TENORMAN *n* person who plays tenor saxophone

TENORMEN > TENORMAN

TENOROON *n* tenor bassoon

TENOROONS > TENOROON

TENORS > TENOR

TENOTOMY *n* surgical division of a tendon

TENOUR *old variant of* **>** TENOR

TENOURS > TENOUR

TENPENCE *n* sum of money equivalent to ten pennies

TENPENCES > TENPENCE

TENPENNY *adj* (of a nail) three inches in length

TENPIN *n* one of the pins used in tenpin bowling

TENPINNER *n* player of tenpin bowling

TENPINS > TENPIN

TENREC *n* small mammal resembling hedgehogs or shrews

TENRECS > TENREC

TENS > TEN

TENSE *adj* emotionally strained ▷ *vb* make or become tense ▷ *n* form of a verb showing the time of action

TENSED > TENSE
TENSELESS > TENSE
TENSELY > TENSE
TENSENESS > TENSE
TENSER > TENSE
TENSES > TENSE
TENSEST > TENSE
TENSIBLE adj capable of being stretched
TENSIBLY > TENSIBLE
TENSILE adj of tension
TENSILELY > TENSILE
TENSILITY > TENSILE
TENSING > TENSE
TENSION n hostility or suspense ▷ vb tighten
TENSIONAL > TENSION
TENSIONED > TENSION
TENSIONER > TENSION
TENSIONS > TENSION
TENSITIES > TENSITY
TENSITY rare word for > TENSION
TENSIVE adj of or causing tension or strain
TENSON n type of French lyric poem
TENSONS > TENSON
TENSOR n any muscle that can cause a part to become firm or tense
TENSORIAL > TENSOR
TENSORS > TENSOR
TENT n portable canvas shelter ▷ vb camp in a tent
TENTACLE n flexible organ of many invertebrates, used for grasping, feeding, etc
TENTACLED > TENTACLE
TENTACLES > TENTACLE
TENTACULA > TENTACLE
TENTAGE n tents collectively
TENTAGES > TENTAGE
TENTATION n method of achieving the correct adjustment of a mechanical device by a series of trials
TENTATIVE adj provisional or experimental ▷ n investigative attempt
TENTED > TENT
TENTER > TENT
TENTERED > TENT
TENTERING > TENT
TENTERS > TENT
TENTFUL n number of people or objects that can fit in a tent
TENTFULS > TENTFUL
TENTH n number ten in a series ▷ adj coming after the ninth in numbering or counting order, position, time, etc
TENTHLY same as > TENTH
TENTHS > TENTH
TENTIE adj wary
TENTIER > TENTIE
TENTIEST > TENTIE
TENTIGO n morbid preoccupation with sex
TENTIGOS > TENTIGO
TENTING > TENT
TENTINGS > TENT
TENTLESS > TENT
TENTLIKE > TENT
TENTMAKER n maker of tents

TENTORIA > TENTORIUM
TENTORIAL > TENTORIUM
TENTORIUM n tough membrane covering the upper part of the cerebellum
TENTPOLE n film whose high earnings offset the cost of less profitable ones
TENTPOLES > TENTPOLE
TENTS > TENT
TENTWISE adv in the manner of a tent
TENTY same as > TENTIE
TENUE n deportment
TENUES > TENUIS
TENUIOUS same as > TENUOUS
TENUIS n (in the grammar of classical Greek) any of the voiceless stops
TENUITIES > TENUOUS
TENUITY > TENUOUS
TENUOUS adj slight or flimsy
TENUOUSLY > TENUOUS
TENURABLE > TENURE
TENURE n (period of) the holding of an office or position ▷ vb assign a tenured position to
TENURED adj having tenure of office
TENURES > TENURE
TENURIAL > TENURE
TENURING > TENURE
TENUTI > TENUTO
TENUTO adv (of a note) to be held for or beyond its full time value ▷ vb note sustained thus
TENUTOS > TENUTO
TENZON same as > TENSON
TENZONS > TENZON
TEOCALLI n any of various truncated pyramids built by the Aztecs as bases for their temples
TEOCALLIS > TEOCALLI
TEOPAN n enclosure surrounding a teocalli
TEOPANS > TEOPAN
TEOSINTE n tall Central American annual grass
TEOSINTES > TEOSINTE
TEPA n type of tree native to South America
TEPACHE n type of Mexican soft drink
TEPACHES > TEPACHE
TEPAL n subdivisions of a perianth
TEPALS > TEPAL
TEPAS > TEPA
TEPEE n cone-shaped tent, formerly used by Native Americans
TEPEES > TEPEE
TEPEFIED > TEPEFY
TEPEFIES > TEPEFY
TEPEFY vb make or become tepid
TEPEFYING > TEPEFY
TEPHIGRAM n chart depicting variations in atmospheric conditions relative to altitude
TEPHILLAH same as > TEFILLAH

TEPHILLIN > TEPHILLAH
TEPHRA n solid matter ejected during a volcanic eruption
TEPHRAS > TEPHRA
TEPHRITE n variety of basalt
TEPHRITES > TEPHRITE
TEPHRITIC > TEPHRITE
TEPHROITE n manganese silicate
TEPID adj slightly warm
TEPIDARIA pl n in Ancient Rome, the warm rooms of the baths
TEPIDER > TEPID
TEPIDEST > TEPID
TEPIDITY > TEPID
TEPIDLY > TEPID
TEPIDNESS > TEPID
TEPOY same as > TEAPOY
TEPOYS > TEPOY
TEQUILA n Mexican alcoholic drink
TEQUILAS > TEQUILA
TEQUILLA same as > TEQUILA
TEQUILLAS > TEQUILLA
TERABYTE n large unit of computer memory
TERABYTES > TERABYTE
TERAFLOP n large unit of computer processing speed
TERAFLOPS > TERAFLOP
TERAGLIN n edible marine fish of Australia which has fine scales and is blue in colour
TERAGLINS > TERAGLIN
TERAHERTZ n large unit of electrical frequency
TERAI n felt hat with a wide brim worn in subtropical regions
TERAIS > TERAI
TERAKIHI same as > TARAKIHI
TERAKIHIS > TERAKIHI
TERAMETER n 10^{12} metres
TERAOHM n unit of resistance
TERAOHMS > TERAOHM
TERAPH n household god or image venerated by ancient Semitic peoples
TERAPHIM > TERAPH
TERAPHIMS > TERAPH
TERAS n monstrosity; teratism
TERATA > TERAS
TERATISM n malformed animal or human, esp in the fetal stage
TERATISMS > TERATISM
TERATOGEN n any substance, organism, or process that causes malformations in a fetus
TERATOID adj resembling a monster
TERATOMA n tumour or group of tumours composed of tissue foreign to the site of growth
TERATOMAS > TERATOMA
TERAWATT n unit of power equal to one million megawatts

TERAWATTS > TERAWATT
TERBIA n amorphous white insoluble powder
TERBIAS > TERBIA
TERBIC > TERBIUM
TERBIUM n rare metallic element
TERBIUMS > TERBIUM
TERCE n third of the seven canonical hours of the divine office
TERCEL n male falcon or hawk, esp as used in falconry
TERCELET same as > TERCEL
TERCELETS > TERCELET
TERCELS > TERCEL
TERCES > TERCE
TERCET n group of three lines of verse that rhyme together
TERCETS > TERCET
TERCIO n regiment of Spanish or Italian infantry
TERCIOS > TERCIO
TEREBENE n mixture of hydrocarbons prepared from oil of turpentine and sulphuric acid
TEREBENES > TEREBENE
TEREBIC adj as in terebic acid white crystalline carboxylic acid produced by the action of nitric acid on turpentine
TEREBINTH n small anacardiaceous tree with winged leafstalks and clusters of small flowers, and yielding a turpentine
TEREBRA n ancient Roman device used for boring holes in defensive walls
TEREBRAE > TEREBRA
TEREBRANT n type of hymenopterous insect
TEREBRAS > TEREBRA
TEREBRATE adj (of animals, esp insects) having a boring or penetrating organ, such as a sting ▷ vb bore
TEREDINES > TEREDO
TEREDO n marine mollusc that bores into and destroys submerged timber
TEREDOS > TEREDO
TEREFA same as > TREF
TEREFAH same as > TREF
TEREK n type of sandpiper
TEREKS > TEREK
TERES n shoulder muscle
TERESES > TERES
TERETE adj (esp of plant parts) smooth and usually cylindrical and tapering
TERETES > TERETE
TERF old variant of > TURF
TERFE old variant of > TURF
TERFES > TERFE
TERFS > TERF
TERGA > TERGUM
TERGAL > TERGUM
TERGITE n constituent part of a tergum
TERGITES > TERGITE
TERGUM n cuticular plate covering the dorsal surface of a body segment of an arthropod

t

TERIYAKI *adj* basted with soy sauce and rice wine and broiled over an open fire ▷ *n* dish prepared in this way

TERIYAKIS > TERIYAKI

TERM *n* word or expression ▷ *vb* name or designate

TERMAGANT *n* unpleasant and bad-tempered woman

TERMED > TERM

TERMER *same as* **>** TERMOR

TERMERS > TERMER

TERMINAL *adj* (of an illness) ending in death ▷ *n* place where people or vehicles begin or end a journey

TERMINALS > TERMINAL

TERMINATE *vb* bring or come to an end

TERMINER *n* person or thing that limits or determines

TERMINERS > TERMINER

TERMING > TERM

TERMINI > TERMINUS

TERMINISM *n* philosophical theory

TERMINIST > TERMINISM

TERMINUS *n* railway or bus station at the end of a line

TERMITARY *n* termite nest

TERMITE *n* white antlike insect that destroys timber

TERMITES > TERMITE

TERMITIC > TERMITE

TERMLESS *adj* without limit or boundary

TERMLIES > TERMLY

TERMLY *n* publication issued once a term

TERMOR *n* person who holds an estate for a term of years or until he or she dies

TERMORS > TERMOR

TERMS > TERM

TERMTIME *n* time during a term, esp a school or university term

TERMTIMES > TERMTIME

TERN *n* gull-like sea bird with a forked tail and pointed wings

TERNAL > TERN

TERNARIES > TERNARY

TERNARY *adj* consisting of three parts ▷ *n* group of three

TERNATE *adj* (esp of a leaf) consisting of three leaflets or other parts

TERNATELY > TERNATE

TERNE *n* alloy of lead containing tin and antimony ▷ *vb* coat with this alloy

TERNED > TERNE

TERNES > TERNE

TERNING > TERNE

TERNION *n* group of three

TERNIONS > TERNION

TERNS > TERN

TERPENE *n* unsaturated hydrocarbon found in the essential oils of many plants

TERPENES > TERPENE

TERPENIC > TERPENE

TERPENOID > TERPENE

TERPINE *n* type of expectorant

TERPINEOL *n* terpene alcohol with an odour of lilac, present in several essential oils

TERPINES > TERPINE

TERPINOL *same as* **>** TERPINEOL

TERPINOLS > TERPINOL

TERRA *n* (in legal contexts) earth or land

TERRACE *n* row of houses built as one block ▷ *vb* form into or provide with a terrace

TERRACED > TERRACE

TERRACES > TERRACE

TERRACING *n* series of terraces, esp one dividing a slope into a steplike system of flat narrow fields

TERRAE > TERRA

TERRAFORM *vb* engage in planetary engineering to enhance the capacity of an extraterrestrial planetary environment to sustain life

TERRAIN *same as* **>** TERRANE

TERRAINS > TERRAIN

TERRAMARA *n* neolithic Italian pile-dwelling

TERRAMARE > TERRAMARA

TERRANE *n* series of rock formations

TERRANES > TERRANE

TERRAPIN *n* small turtle-like reptile

TERRAPINS > TERRAPIN

TERRARIA > TERRARIUM

TERRARIUM *n* enclosed container for small plants or animals

TERRAS *same as* **>** TRASS

TERRASES > TERRAS

TERRASSE *n* paved area alongside a café

TERRASSES > TERRASSE

TERRAZZO *n* floor of marble chips set in mortar and polished

TERRAZZOS > TERRAZZO

TERREEN *old variant of* **>** TUREEN

TERREENS > TERREEN

TERRELLA *n* magnetic globe designed to simulate and demonstrate the earth's magnetic fields

TERRELLAS > TERRELLA

TERRENE *adj* of or relating to the earth ▷ *n* land

TERRENELY > TERRENE

TERRENES > TERRENE

TERRET *n* ring on a harness saddle through which the reins are passed

TERRETS > TERRET

TERRIBLE *adj* very serious ▷ *n* something terrible

TERRIBLES > TERRIBLE

TERRIBLY *adv* in a terrible manner

TERRICOLE *n* plant or animal living on land

TERRIER *n* any of various breeds of small active dog

TERRIERS > TERRIER

TERRIES > TERRY

TERRIFIC *adj* great or intense

TERRIFIED > TERRIFY

TERRIFIER > TERRIFY

TERRIFIES > TERRIFY

TERRIFY *vb* fill with fear

TERRINE *n* earthenware dish with a lid

TERRINES > TERRINE

TERRIT *same as* **>** TERRET

TERRITORY *n* district

TERRITS > TERRIT

TERROIR *n* combination of factors that gives a wine its distinctive character

TERROIRS > TERROIR

TERROR *n* great fear

TERRORFUL > TERROR

TERRORISE *same as* **>** TERRORIZE

TERRORISM *n* use of violence and intimidation to achieve political ends

TERRORIST *n* person who employs terror or terrorism, esp as a political weapon

TERRORIZE *vb* force or oppress by fear or violence

TERRORS > TERROR

TERRY *n* fabric with small loops covering both sides

TERSE *adj* neat and concise

TERSELY > TERSE

TERSENESS > TERSE

TERSER > TERSE

TERSEST > TERSE

TERSION *n* action of rubbing off or wiping

TERSIONS > TERSION

TERTIA *same as* **>** TERCIO

TERTIAL *same as* **>** TERTIARY

TERTIALS > TERTIAL

TERTIAN *adj* (of a fever or the symptoms of a disease) occurring every other day ▷ *n* tertian fever or symptoms

TERTIANS > TERTIAN

TERTIARY *adj* third in degree, order, etc ▷ *n* any of the tertiary feathers

TERTIAS > TERTIA

TERTIUM *adj* as in *tertium quid* unknown or indefinite thing related in some way to two known or definite things, but distinct from both

TERTIUS *n* third (in a group)

TERTIUSES > TERTIUS

TERTS *n* card game using 32 cards

TERVALENT *same as* **>** TRIVALENT

TERYLENE *n* tradename for a synthetic polyester fibre based on terephthalic acid

TERYLENES > TERYLENE

TERZETTA *n* tercet

TERZETTAS > TERZETTA

TERZETTI > TERZETTO

TERZETTO *n* trio, esp a vocal one

TERZETTOS > TERZETTO

TES > TE

TESLA *n* derived SI unit of magnetic flux density

TESLAS > TESLA

TESSELATE *vb* cover with small tiles

TESSELLA *n* little tessera

TESSELLAE > TESSELLA

TESSELLAR *adj* of or relating to tessellae

TESSERA *n* small square tile used in mosaics

TESSERACT *n* cube inside another cube

TESSERAE > TESSERA

TESSERAL > TESSERA

TESSITURA *n* general pitch level of a piece of vocal music

TESSITURE > TESSITURA

TEST *vb* try out to ascertain the worth, capability, or endurance of ▷ *n* critical examination

TESTA *n* hard outer layer of a seed

TESTABLE > TEST

TESTACEAN *n* microscopic animal with hard shell

TESTACIES > TESTATE

TESTACY > TESTATE

TESTAE > TESTA

TESTAMENT *n* proof or tribute

TESTAMUR *n* certificate proving an examination has been passed

TESTAMURS > TESTAMUR

TESTATA > TESTATUM

TESTATE *adj* having left a valid will ▷ *n* person who dies and leaves a legally valid will

TESTATES > TESTATE

TESTATION > TESTATOR

TESTATOR *n* maker of a will

TESTATORS > TESTATOR

TESTATRIX *same as* **>** TESTATOR

TESTATUM *n* part of a purchase deed

TESTATUMS > TESTATUM

TESTCROSS *vb* subject to a testcross, a genetic test for ascertaining whether an individual is homozygous or heterozygous

TESTE *n* witness

TESTED > TEST

TESTEE *n* person subjected to a test

TESTEES > TESTEE

TESTER *n* person or thing that tests or is used for testing

TESTERN *vb* give (someone) a teston

TESTERNED > TESTERN

TESTERNS > TESTERN

TESTERS > TESTER

TESTES > TESTIS

TESTICLE *n* either of the two male reproductive glands

TESTICLES > TESTICLE

TESTIER > TESTY

TESTIEST > TESTY

TESTIFIED > TESTIFY

TESTIFIER > TESTIFY

TESTIFIES > TESTIFY

TESTIFY *vb* give evidence under oath

TESTILY > TESTY

TESTIMONY n declaration of truth or fact ▷ vb testify

TESTINESS > TESTY

TESTING > TEST

TESTINGS > TEST

TESTIS same as > TESTICLE

TESTON n French silver coin of the 16th century

TESTONS > TESTON

TESTOON same as > TESTON

TESTOONS > TESTOON

TESTRIL same as > TESTRILL

TESTRILL n sixpence

TESTRILLS > TESTRILL

TESTRILS > TESTRIL

TESTS > TEST

TESTUDO n protective cover used by the ancient Roman army

TESTUDOS > TESTUDO

TESTY adj irritable or touchy

TET same as > TETH

TETANAL > TETANUS

TETANIC adj of, relating to, or producing tetanus ▷ n tetanic drug or agent

TETANICAL > TETANUS

TETANICS > TETANIC

TETANIES > TETANY

TETANISE same as > TETANIZE

TETANISED > TETANISE

TETANISES > TETANISE

TETANIZE vb induce tetanus in (a muscle)

TETANIZED > TETANIZE

TETANIZES > TETANIZE

TETANOID > TETANUS

TETANUS n acute infectious disease producing muscular spasms and convulsions

TETANUSES > TETANUS

TETANY n abnormal increase in the excitability of nerves and muscles

TETCHED same as > TECHED

TETCHIER > TETCHY

TETCHIEST > TETCHY

TETCHILY > TETCHY

TETCHY adj cross and irritable

TETE n elaborate hairstyle

TETES > TETE

TETH n ninth letter of the Hebrew alphabet

TETHER n rope or chain for tying an animal to a spot ▷ vb tie up with rope

TETHERED > TETHER

TETHERING > TETHER

TETHERS > TETHER

TETHS > TETH

TETOTUM same as > TEETOTUM

TETOTUMS > TETOTUM

TETRA n brightly coloured tropical freshwater fish

TETRACID adj (of a base) capable of reacting with four molecules of a monobasic acid

TETRACIDS > TETRACID

TETRACT n sponge spicule with four rays

TETRACTS > TETRACT

TETRAD n group or series of four

TETRADIC > TETRAD

TETRADITE n person who believes that the number four has supernatural significance

TETRADS > TETRAD

TETRAGON n figure with four angles and four sides

TETRAGONS > TETRAGON

TETRAGRAM n any word of four letters

TETRALOGY n series of four related works

TETRAMER n four-molecule polymer

TETRAMERS > TETRAMER

TETRAPLA n book containing versions of the same text in four languages

TETRAPLAS > TETRAPLA

TETRAPOD n any vertebrate that has four limbs

TETRAPODS > TETRAPOD

TETRAPODY n metrical unit consisting of four feet

TETRARCH n ruler of one fourth of a country

TETRARCHS > TETRARCH

TETRARCHY > TETRARCH

TETRAS > TETRA

TETRAXON n four-pointed spicule

TETRAXONS > TETRAXON

TETRI n currency unit of Georgia

TETRIS > TETRI

TETRODE n electronic valve having four electrodes

TETRODES > TETRODE

TETRONAL n sedative drug

TETRONALS > TETRONAL

TETROSE n type of sugar

TETROSES > TETROSE

TETROXID same as > TETROXIDE

TETROXIDE n any oxide that contains four oxygen atoms per molecule

TETROXIDS > TETROXID

TETRYL n yellow crystalline explosive solid used in detonators

TETRYLS > TETRYL

TETS > TET

TETTER n blister or pimple ▷ vb cause a tetter to erupt (on)

TETTERED > TETTER

TETTERING > TETTER

TETTEROUS > TETTER

TETTERS > TETTER

TETTIX n cicada

TETTIXES > TETTIX

TEUCH Scots variant of > TOUGH

TEUCHAT Scots variant of > TEWIT

TEUCHATS > TEUCHAT

TEUCHER > TEUCH

TEUCHEST > TEUCH

TEUCHTER n in Scotland, derogatory word used by Lowlanders for a Highlander

TEUCHTERS > TEUCHTER

TEUGH same as > TEUCH

TEUGHER > TEUGH

TEUGHEST > TEUGH

TEUGHLY > TEUGH

TEUTONISE same as > TEUTONIZE

TEUTONIZE vb make or become German or Germanic

TEVATRON n machine used in nuclear research

TEVATRONS > TEVATRON

TEW vb work hard

TEWART same as > TUART

TEWARTS > TEWART

TEWED > TEW

TEWEL n horse's rectum

TEWELS > TEWEL

TEWHIT same as > TEWIT

TEWHITS > TEWHIT

TEWING > TEW

TEWIT n lapwing

TEWITS > TEWIT

TEWS > TEW

TEX n unit of weight used to measure yarn density

TEXAS n structure on the upper deck of a paddle-steamer

TEXASES > TEXAS

TEXES > TEX

TEXT n main body of a book as distinct from illustrations etc ▷ vb send a text message to (someone)

TEXTBOOK n standard book on a particular subject ▷ adj perfect

TEXTBOOKS > TEXTBOOK

TEXTED > TEXT

TEXTER n person who communicates by text messaging

TEXTERS > TEXTER

TEXTILE n fabric or cloth, esp woven ▷ adj of (the making of) fabrics

TEXTILES > TEXTILE

TEXTING > TEXT

TEXTINGS > TEXTING

TEXTISM n word typically used in a text message

TEXTISMS > TEXTISM

TEXTLESS > TEXT

TEXTONYM n one of two or more words that can be created by pressing the same combination of numbers on a mobile phone

TEXTONYMS > TEXTONYM

TEXTORIAL adj of or relating to weaving or weavers

TEXTPHONE n phone designed to translate speech into text and vice versa

TEXTS > TEXT

TEXTSPEAK n jargon and abbreviations typically used by frequent senders of text messages

TEXTUAL adj of, based on, or relating to, a text or texts

TEXTUALLY > TEXTUAL

TEXTUARY adj of, relating to, or contained in a text ▷ n textual critic

TEXTURAL > TEXTURE

TEXTURE n structure, feel, or consistency ▷ vb give a distinctive texture to (something)

TEXTURED > TEXTURE

TEXTURES > TEXTURE

TEXTURING n process of giving a rough or grainy texture to

TEXTURISE same as > TEXTURIZE

TEXTURIZE vb texture

TEXTUROUS adj having texture

THACK Scots word for > THATCH

THACKED > THACK

THACKING > THACK

THACKS > THACK

THAE Scots word for > THOSE

THAGI same as > THUGGEE

THAGIS > THAGI

THAIM Scots variant of > THEM

THAIRM n catgut

THAIRMS > THAIRM

THALAMI > THALAMUS

THALAMIC > THALAMUS

THALAMUS n mass of grey matter at the base of the brain

THALASSIC adj of or relating to the sea

THALE n as in thale cress cruciferous wall plant

THALER n former German, Austrian, or Swiss silver coin

THALERS > THALER

THALI n meal consisting of several small dishes accompanied by rice, bread, etc

THALIAN adj of or relating to comedy

THALIS > THALI

THALLI > THALLUS

THALLIC adj of or containing thallium

THALLINE n type of chemical used in medicine

THALLINES > THALLINE

THALLIOUS > THALLIUM

THALLIUM n highly toxic metallic element

THALLIUMS > THALLIUM

THALLOID > THALLUS

THALLOUS adj of or containing thallium, esp in the monovalent state

THALLUS n undifferentiated vegetative body of algae, fungi, and lichens

THALLUSES > THALLUS

THALWEG n longitudinal outline of a riverbed from source to mouth

THALWEGS > THALWEG

THAN prep used to introduce the second element of a comparison ▷ n old variant of "then" (that time)

THANA same as > TANA

THANADAR same as > TANADAR

THANADARS > THANADAR

THANAGE n state of being a thane

THANAGES > THANAGE
THANAH same as **>** TANA
THANAHS > THANAH
THANAS > THANA
THANATISM n belief that the soul ceases to exist when the body dies
THANATIST > THANATISM
THANATOID adj like death
THANATOS n Greek personification of death
THANE n Anglo-Saxon or medieval Scottish nobleman
THANEDOM > THANE
THANEDOMS > THANE
THANEHOOD > THANE
THANES > THANE
THANESHIP > THANE
THANG n thing
THANGKA n (in Tibetan Buddhism) a religious painting on a scroll
THANGKAS > THANGKA
THANGS > THANG
THANK vb express gratitude to
THANKED > THANK
THANKEE interj thank you
THANKER > THANK
THANKERS > THANK
THANKFUL adj grateful
THANKING > THANK
THANKINGS > THANK
THANKIT adj as in be thankit thank God
THANKLESS adj unrewarding or unappreciated
THANKS pl n words of gratitude ▷ interj polite expression of gratitude
THANKYOU n conventional expression of gratitude
THANKYOUS > THANKYOU
THANNA same as **>** TANA
THANNAH same as **>** TANA
THANNAHS > THANNAH
THANNAS > THANNA
THANS > THAN
THANX interj (coll.) thank you
THAR same as **>** TAHR
THARM n stomach
THARMS > THARM
THARS > THAR
THAT pron used to refer to something already mentioned or familiar, or further away
THATAWAY adv that way
THATCH n roofing material of reeds or straw ▷ vb roof (a house) with reeds or straw
THATCHED > THATCH
THATCHER > THATCH
THATCHERS > THATCH
THATCHES > THATCH
THATCHIER > THATCH
THATCHING > THATCH
THATCHT old variant of **>** THATCHED
THATCHY > THATCH
THATNESS n state or quality of being 'that'
THAUMATIN n type of natural sweetener
THAW vb make or become unfrozen ▷ n thawing

THAWED > THAW
THAWER > THAW
THAWERS > THAW
THAWIER > THAWY
THAWIEST > THAWY
THAWING > THAW
THAWINGS > THAW
THAWLESS > THAW
THAWS > THAW
THAWY adj tending to thaw
THE determiner definite article, used before a noun
THEACEOUS adj relating to a family of evergreen trees and shrubs of tropical and warm regions, which includes the tea plant
THEANDRIC adj both divine and human
THEANINE n amino acid found in tea leaves
THEANINES > THEANINE
THEARCHIC > THEARCHY
THEARCHY n rule or government by God or gods
THEATER same as **>** THEATRE
THEATERS > THEATER
THEATRAL adj of or relating to the theatre
THEATRE n place where plays etc are performed
THEATRES > THEATRE
THEATRIC adj of or relating to the theatre
THEATRICS n art of staging plays
THEAVE n young ewe
THEAVES > THEAVE
THEBAINE n poisonous white crystalline alkaloid, found in opium but without opioid actions
THEBAINES > THEBAINE
THEBE n monetary unit of Botswana
THEBES > THEBE
THECA n enclosing organ, cell, or spore case
THECAE > THECA
THECAL > THECA
THECATE > THECA
THECODONT adj (of mammals and certain reptiles) having teeth that grow in sockets ▷ n extinct reptile
THEE pron refers to the person addressed ▷ vb use the word "thee"
THEED > THEE
THEEING > THEE
THEEK Scots variant of **>** THATCH
THEEKED > THEEK
THEEKING > THEEK
THEEKS > THEEK
THEELIN trade name for **>** ESTRONE
THEELINS > THEELIN
THEELOL n estriol
THEELOLS > THEELOL
THEES > THEE
THEFT n act or an instance of stealing
THEFTLESS > THEFT
THEFTS > THEFT

THEFTUOUS adj tending to commit theft
THEGITHER Scots variant of **>** TOGETHER
THEGN same as **>** THANE
THEGNLIER > THEGNLY
THEGNLY adj like a thegn
THEGNS > THEGN
THEIC n person who drinks excessive amounts of tea
THEICS > THEIC
THEIN old variant of **>** THANE
THEINE another name for **>** CAFFEINE
THEINES > THEINE
THEINS > THEIN
THEIR determiner of, belonging to, or associated in some way with them
THEIRS pron something belonging to them
THEIRSELF pron dialect form of themselves: reflexive form of they or them
THEISM n belief in a God or gods
THEISMS > THEISM
THEIST > THEISM
THEISTIC > THEISM
THEISTS > THEISM
THELEMENT n old contraction of "the element"
THELF n old contraction of "the element"
THELITIS n inflammation of the nipple
THELVES > THELF
THELYTOKY n type of reproduction resulting in female offspring only
THEM pron refers to people or things other than the speaker or those addressed
THEMA n theme
THEMATA > THEMA
THEMATIC adj of, relating to, or consisting of a theme or themes ▷ n thematic vowel
THEMATICS > THEMATIC
THEMATISE same as **>** THEMATIZE
THEMATIZE vb make thematic
THEME n main idea or subject being discussed ▷ vb design, decorate, arrange, etc, in accordance with a theme
THEMED > THEME
THEMELESS > THEME
THEMES > THEME
THEMING > THEME
THEMSELF pron reflexive form of one, whoever, anybody
THEN adv at that time ▷ pron that time ▷ adj existing or functioning at that time ▷ n that time
THENABOUT adv around then
THENAGE old variant of **>** THANAGE
THENAGES > THENAGE
THENAL adj of or relating to the thenar
THENAR n palm of the hand ▷ adj of or relating to the

palm or the region at the base of the thumb
THENARS > THENAR
THENCE adv from that place or time
THENS > THEN
THEOCON n person who believes that religion should play a greater role in politics
THEOCONS > THEOCON
THEOCRACY n government by a god or priests
THEOCRASY n mingling into one of deities or divine attributes previously regarded as distinct
THEOCRAT > THEOCRACY
THEOCRATS > THEOCRACY
THEODICY n branch of theology concerned with defending the attributes of God
THEOGONIC > THEOGONY
THEOGONY n origin and descent of the gods
THEOLOG same as **>** THEOLOGUE
THEOLOGER n theologian
THEOLOGIC > THEOLOGY
THEOLOGS > THEOLOG
THEOLOGUE n theologian
THEOLOGY n study of religions and religious beliefs
THEOMACHY n battle among the gods or against them
THEOMANCY n divination or prophecy by an oracle or by people directly inspired by a god
THEOMANIA n religious madness, esp when it takes the form of believing oneself to be a god
THEONOMY n state of being governed by God
THEOPATHY n religious emotion engendered by the contemplation of or meditation upon God
THEOPHAGY n sacramental eating of a god
THEOPHANY n manifestation of a deity to human beings in a form that, though visible, is not necessarily material
THEORBIST > THEORBO
THEORBO n obsolete form of the lute, having two necks
THEORBOS > THEORBO
THEOREM n proposition that can be proved by reasoning
THEOREMIC > THEOREM
THEOREMS > THEOREM
THEORETIC adj of, or based on, a theory
THEORIC n theory; conjecture
THEORICS > THEORIC
THEORIES > THEORY
THEORIQUE same as **>** THEORIC
THEORISE same as **>** THEORIZE
THEORISED > THEORISE
THEORISER > THEORISE
THEORISES > THEORISE
THEORIST n originator of a theory

THEORISTS > THEORIST
THEORIZE *vb* form theories, speculate
THEORIZED > THEORIZE
THEORIZER > THEORIZE
THEORIZES > THEORIZE
THEORY *n* set of ideas to explain something
THEOSOPH *n* proponent of theosophy
THEOSOPHS > THEOSOPH
THEOSOPHY *n* religious or philosophical system claiming to be based on intuitive insight into the divine nature
THEOTOKOI > THEOTOKOS
THEOTOKOS *n* mother of God
THEOW *n* slave in Anglo-Saxon Britain
THEOWS > THEOW
THERALITE *n* type of igneous rock
THERAPIES > THERAPY
THERAPISE *same as* > THERAPIZE
THERAPIST *n* person skilled in a particular type of therapy
THERAPIZE *vb* subject to therapy
THERAPSID *n* extinct reptile: considered to be the ancestors of mammals
THERAPY *n* curing treatment
THERBLIG *n* basic unit of work in an industrial process
THERBLIGS > THERBLIG
THERE *adv* in or to that place ▷ *n* that place
THEREAT *adv* at that point or time
THEREAWAY *adv* in that direction
THEREBY *adv* by that means
THEREFOR *adv* for this, that, or it
THEREFORE *adv* consequently, that being so
THEREFROM *adv* from that or there
THEREIN *adv* in or into that place or thing
THEREINTO *adv* into that place, circumstance, etc
THEREMIN *n* musical instrument played by moving the hands through electromagnetic fields
THEREMINS > THEREMIN
THERENESS *n* quality of having existence
THEREOF *adv* of or concerning that or it
THEREON *archaic word for* > THEREUPON
THEREOUT *another word for* > THEREFROM
THERES > THERE
THERETO *adv* that or it
THEREUNTO *adv* to that
THEREUPON *adv* immediately after that
THEREWITH *adv* with or in addition to that

THERIAC *n* ointment or potion used as an antidote to a poison
THERIACA *same as* > THERIAC
THERIACAL > THERIAC
THERIACAS > THERIACA
THERIACS > THERIAC
THERIAN *n* animal of the class Theria, a subclass of mammals
THERIANS > THERIAN
THERM *n* unit of measurement of heat ▷ *n* public bath
THERMAE *pl n* public baths or hot springs, esp in ancient Greece or Rome
THERMAL *adj* of heat ▷ *n* rising current of warm air
THERMALLY > THERMAL
THERMALS > THERMAL
THERME *old variant of* > THERM
THERMEL *n* type of thermometer using thermoelectric current
THERMELS > THERMEL
THERMES > THERME
THERMETTE *n* device, used outdoors, for boiling water rapidly
THERMIC *same as* > THERMAL
THERMICAL *same as* > THERMAL
THERMIDOR *adj* as in *lobster thermidor* dish of cooked lobster
THERMION *n* electron or ion emitted by a body at high temperature
THERMIONS > THERMION
THERMIT *variant of* > THERMITE
THERMITE *adj* as in *thermite process* process for reducing metallic oxides
THERMITES > THERMITE
THERMITS > THERMIT
THERMOS *n* trademark for a stoppered vacuum flask
THERMOSES > THERMOS
THERMOSET *n* material (esp a synthetic plastic or resin) that hardens permanently after one application of heat and pressure
THERMOTIC *adj* of or because of heat
THERMS > THERM
THEROID *adj* of, relating to, or resembling a beast
THEROLOGY *n* study of mammals
THEROPOD *n* bipedal carnivorous saurischian dinosaur with strong hind legs and grasping hands
THEROPODS > THEROPOD
THESAURAL > THESAURUS
THESAURI > THESAURUS
THESAURUS *n* book containing lists of synonyms and related words
THESE *determiner* form of this used before a plural noun

THESES > THESIS
THESIS *n* written work submitted for a degree
THESP *short for* > THESPIAN
THESPIAN *adj* of or relating to drama and the theatre ▷ *n* actor or actress
THESPIANS > THESPIAN
THESPS > THESP
THETA *n* eighth letter of the Greek alphabet
THETAS > THETA
THETCH *old variant spelling of* > THATCH
THETCHED > THETCH
THETCHES > THETCH
THETCHING > THETCH
THETE *n* member of the lowest order of freeman in ancient Athens
THETES > THETE
THETHER *old variant of* > THITHER
THETIC *adj* (in classical prosody) of, bearing, or relating to a metrical stress
THETICAL *another word for* > THETIC
THETRI *n* currency unit of Georgia
THETRIS > THETRI
THEURGIC > THEURGY
THEURGIES > THEURGY
THEURGIST > THEURGY
THEURGY *n* intervention of a divine or supernatural agency in the affairs of human beings
THEW *n* muscle, esp if strong or well-developed
THEWED *adj* strong; muscular
THEWES > THEW
THEWIER > THEW
THEWIEST > THEW
THEWLESS > THEW
THEWS > THEW
THEWY > THEW
THEY *pron* people or things other than the speaker or people addressed
THIAMIN *same as* > THIAMINE
THIAMINE *n* vitamin found in the outer coat of rice and other grains
THIAMINES > THIAMINE
THIAMINS > THIAMIN
THIASUS *n* people gathered to sing and dance in honour of a god
THIASUSES > THIASUS
THIAZIDE *n* diuretic drug
THIAZIDES > THIAZIDE
THIAZIN *same as* > THIAZINE
THIAZINE *n* organic compound containing a ring system composed of four carbon atoms, a sulphur atom, and a nitrogen atom
THIAZINES > THIAZINE
THIAZINS > THIAZIN
THIAZOL *same as* > THIAZOLE
THIAZOLE *n* colourless liquid with a pungent smell

THIAZOLES > THIAZOLE
THIAZOLS > THIAZOL
THIBET *n* coloured woollen cloth
THIBETS > THIBET
THIBLE *n* stick for stirring porridge
THIBLES > THIBLE
THICK *adj* of great or specified extent from one side to the other ▷ *vb* thicken
THICKED > THICK
THICKEN *vb* make or become thick or thicker
THICKENED > THICKEN
THICKENER > THICKEN
THICKENS > THICKEN
THICKER > THICK
THICKEST > THICK
THICKET *n* dense growth of small trees
THICKETED *adj* covered in thicket
THICKETS > THICKET
THICKETY *adj* covered in thickets
THICKHEAD *n* insulting word for a stupid person
THICKIE *same as* > THICKO
THICKIES > THICKY
THICKING > THICK
THICKISH > THICK
THICKLEAF *n* succulent plant with sessile or short-stalked fleshy leaves
THICKLY > THICK
THICKNESS *n* state of being thick
THICKO *n* insulting word for a stupid person
THICKOES > THICKO
THICKOS > THICKO
THICKS > THICK
THICKSET *adj* stocky in build
THICKSETS > THICKSET
THICKSKIN *n* insensitive person
THICKY *same as* > THICKO
THIEF *n* person who steals
THIEFLIKE *adj* like a thief
THIEVE *vb* steal
THIEVED > THIEVE
THIEVERY > THIEVE
THIEVES > THIEVE
THIEVING *adj* given to stealing other people's possessions
THIEVINGS > THIEVING
THIEVISH > THIEF
THIG *vb* beg
THIGGED > THIG
THIGGER > THIG
THIGGERS > THIG
THIGGING > THIG
THIGGINGS > THIG
THIGGIT *Scots inflection of* > THIG
THIGH *n* upper part of the human leg
THIGHBONE *same as* > FEMUR
THIGHED *adj* having thighs
THIGHS > THIGH
THIGS > THIG
THILK *pron* that same

THILL another word for
> SHAFT
THILLER n horse that goes between the thills of a cart
THILLERS > THILLER
THILLS > THILL
THIMBLE n cap protecting the end of the finger when sewing ▷ vb use a thimble
THIMBLED > THIMBLE
THIMBLES > THIMBLE
THIMBLING > THIMBLE
THIN adj not thick ▷ vb make or become thin ▷ adv in order to produce something thin
THINCLAD n track-and-field athlete
THINCLADS > THINCLAD
THINDOWN n reduction in the amount of particles of very high energy penetrating the earth's atmosphere
THINDOWNS > THINDOWN
THINE adj of or associated with you (thou) ▷ pron something belonging to you (thou)
THING n material object
THINGAMY n person or thing the name of which is unknown
THINGHOOD n existence; state or condition of being a thing
THINGIER > THINGY
THINGIES > THINGY
THINGIEST > THINGY
THINGNESS n state of being a thing
THINGO n object whose name is unknown
THINGOS > THINGO
THINGS > THING
THINGUMMY n person or thing the name of which is unknown, temporarily forgotten, or deliberately overlooked
THINGY adj existing in reality; actual
THINK vb consider, judge, or believe
THINKABLE adj able to be conceived or considered
THINKABLY > THINKABLE
THINKER > THINK
THINKERS > THINK
THINKING > THINK
THINKINGS > THINK
THINKS > THINK
THINLY > THIN
THINNED > THIN
THINNER > THIN
THINNERS > THIN
THINNESS > THIN
THINNEST > THIN
THINNING > THIN
THINNINGS > THIN
THINNISH > THIN
THINS > THIN
THIO adj of, or relating to, sulphur
THIOFURAN another name for
> THIOPHEN
THIOL n any of a class of sulphur-containing organic compounds

THIOLIC > THIOL
THIOLS > THIOL
THIONATE n any salt or ester of thionic acid
THIONATES > THIONATE
THIONIC adj of, relating to, or containing sulphur
THIONIN same as
> THIONINE
THIONINE n crystalline derivative of thiazine used as a violet dye to stain microscope specimens
THIONINES > THIONINE
THIONINS > THIONIN
THIONYL n the divalent group SO
THIONYLS > THIONYL
THIOPHEN n colourless liquid heterocyclic compound found in the benzene fraction of coal tar
THIOPHENE same as
> THIOPHEN
THIOPHENS > THIOPHEN
THIOPHIL adj having an attraction to sulphur
THIOTEPA n drug used in chemotherapy
THIOTEPAS > THIOTEPA
THIOUREA n white water-soluble crystalline substance with a bitter taste
THIOUREAS > THIOUREA
THIR Scots word for > THESE
THIRAM n antifungal agent
THIRAMS > THIRAM
THIRD adj of number three in a series ▷ n one of three equal parts ▷ vb divide (something) by three
THIRDED > THIRD
THIRDHAND adv from the second of two intermediaries
THIRDING > THIRD
THIRDINGS > THIRD
THIRDLY > THIRD
THIRDS > THIRD
THIRDSMAN n intermediary
THIRDSMEN > THIRDSMAN
THIRL vb bore or drill
THIRLAGE n obligation imposed upon tenants requiring them to have their grain ground at a specified mill
THIRLAGES > THIRLAGE
THIRLED > THIRL
THIRLING > THIRL
THIRLS > THIRL
THIRST n desire to drink ▷ vb feel thirst
THIRSTED > THIRST
THIRSTER > THIRST
THIRSTERS > THIRSTER
THIRSTFUL > THIRST
THIRSTIER > THIRSTY
THIRSTILY > THIRSTY
THIRSTING > THIRST
THIRSTS > THIRST
THIRSTY adj feeling a desire to drink
THIRTEEN n three and ten
THIRTEENS > THIRTEEN
THIRTIES > THIRTY
THIRTIETH adj being the ordinal number of thirty in

counting order, position, time, etc: often written 30th ▷ n one of 30 approximately equal parts of something
THIRTY n three times ten
THIRTYISH adj around thirty years of age
THIS pron used to refer to a thing or person nearby, just mentioned, or about to be mentioned ▷ adj used to refer to the present time
THISAWAY adv this way
THISNESS n state or quality of being this
THISTLE n prickly plant with dense flower heads
THISTLES > THISTLE
THISTLIER > THISTLE
THISTLY > THISTLE
THITHER adv or towards that place
THITHERTO adv until that time
THIVEL same as > THIBLE
THIVELS > THIVEL
THLIPSES > THLIPSIS
THLIPSIS n compression, esp of part of the body
THO short for > THOUGH
THOFT n bench (in a boat) upon which a rower sits
THOFTS > THOFT
THOLE n wooden pin set in the side of a rowing boat to serve as a fulcrum for rowing ▷ vb bear or put up with
THOLED > THOLE
THOLEIITE n type of volcanic rock
THOLEPIN same as > THOLE
THOLEPINS > THOLEPIN
THOLES > THOLE
THOLI > THOLUS
THOLING > THOLE
THOLOBATE n structure supporting a dome
THOLOI > THOLOS
THOLOS n beehive-shaped tomb associated with Mycenaean Greece
THOLUS n domed tomb
THON Scot word for > YON
THONDER Scot word for
> YONDER
THONG n thin strip of leather etc ▷ vb decorate with a thong or thongs
THONGED adj fastened with a thong
THONGIER > THONGY
THONGIEST > THONGY
THONGING > THONG
THONGS > THONG
THONGY adj resembling a thong
THORACAL another word for
> THORACIC
THORACES > THORAX
THORACIC adj of, near, or relating to the thorax
THORAX n part of the body between the neck and the abdomen
THORAXES > THORAX
THORIA n insoluble white powder

THORIAS > THORIA
THORIC > THORIUM
THORITE n yellow, brownish, or black radioactive mineral
THORITES > THORITE
THORIUM n radioactive metallic element
THORIUMS > THORIUM
THORN n prickle on a plant ▷ vb jag or prick (something) as if with a thorn
THORNBACK n European ray with a row of spines along the back and tail
THORNBILL n South American hummingbird
THORNBIRD n small S American bird
THORNBUSH n tree, shrub, or bush with thorns
THORNED > THORN
THORNIER > THORNY
THORNIEST > THORNY
THORNILY > THORNY
THORNING > THORN
THORNLESS > THORN
THORNLIKE > THORN
THORNS > THORN
THORNSET adj set with thorns
THORNTAIL n tropical hummingbird
THORNTREE n tree with thorns
THORNY adj covered with thorns
THORO (nonstandard) variant spelling of > THOROUGH
THORON n radioisotope of radon that is a decay product of thorium
THORONS > THORON
THOROUGH adj complete ▷ n passage
THOROUGHS > THOROUGH
THORP n small village
THORPE same as > THORP
THORPES > THORPE
THORPS > THORP
THOSE determiner form of that used before a plural noun
THOTHER pron old contraction of the other
THOU pron used when talking to one person ▷ n one thousandth of an inch ▷ vb use the word thou
THOUED > THOU
THOUGH adv nevertheless
THOUGHT > THINK
THOUGHTED adj with thoughts
THOUGHTEN adj convinced
THOUGHTS > THINK
THOUING > THOU
THOUS > THOU
THOUSAND n ten hundred ▷ adj amounting to a thousand ▷ determiner amounting to a thousand
THOUSANDS > THOUSAND
THOWEL old variant of
> THOLE
THOWELS > THOWEL
THOWL old variant of > THOLE

THOWLESS *adj* lacking in vigour

THOWLS > THOWL

THRAE *same as* > FRAE

THRAIPING *n* thrashing

THRALDOM *same as* > THRALL

THRALDOMS > THRALDOM

THRALL *n* state of being in the power of another person ▷ *vb* enslave or dominate

THRALLDOM *same as* > THRALL

THRALLED > THRALL

THRALLING > THRALL

THRALLS > THRALL

THRANG *n* throng ▷ *vb* throng ▷ *adj* crowded

THRANGED > THRANG

THRANGING > THRANG

THRANGS > THRANG

THRAPPLE *n* throat or windpipe ▷ *vb* throttle

THRAPPLED > THRAPPLE

THRAPPLES > THRAPPLE

THRASH *vb* beat, esp with a stick or whip ▷ *n* party

THRASHED > THRASH

THRASHER *same as* > THRESHER

THRASHERS > THRASHER

THRASHES > THRASH

THRASHIER > THRASHY

THRASHING *n* severe beating

THRASHY *adj* relating to thrash punk

THRASONIC *adj* bragging or boastful

THRAVE *n* twenty-four sheaves of corn

THRAVES > THRAVE

THRAW *vb* twist (something); make something thrawn

THRAWARD *adj* contrary or stubborn

THRAWART *same as* > THRAWARD

THRAWED > THRAW

THRAWING > THRAW

THRAWN *adj* crooked or twisted

THRAWNLY > THRAWN

THRAWS > THRAW

THREAD *n* fine strand or yarn ▷ *vb* pass thread through

THREADED > THREAD

THREADEN *adj* made of thread

THREADER > THREAD

THREADERS > THREAD

THREADFIN *n* spiny-finned tropical marine fish

THREADIER > THREADY

THREADING > THREAD

THREADS *slang word for* > CLOTHES

THREADY *adj* of, relating to, or resembling a thread or threads

THREAP *vb* scold

THREAPED > THREAP

THREAPER > THREAP

THREAPERS > THREAP

THREAPING > THREAP

THREAPIT *variant past participle of* > THREAP

THREAPS > THREAP

THREAT *n* declaration of intent to harm

THREATED > THREAT

THREATEN *vb* make or be a threat to

THREATENS > THREATEN

THREATFUL > THREAT

THREATING > THREAT

THREATS > THREAT

THREAVE *same as* > THRAVE

THREAVES > THREAVE

THREE *n* one more than two

THREEFOLD *adv* (having) three times as many or as much ▷ *adj* having three times as many or as much

THREENESS *n* state or quality of being three

THREEP *same as* > THREAP

THREEPEAT *n* third consecutive win of a particular sporting championship ▷ *vb* win a sporting championship for the third consecutive time

THREEPED > THREEP

THREEPER > THREAP

THREEPERS > THREAP

THREEPING > THREEP

THREEPIT *variant past participle of* > THREEP

THREEQUEL *n* third instalment in a series of films, books, plays, etc

THREES > THREE

THREESOME *n* group of three

THRENE *n* dirge; threnody

THRENES > THRENE

THRENETIC > THRENE

THRENODE *same as* > THRENODY

THRENODES > THRENODE

THRENODIC > THRENODY

THRENODY *n* lament for the dead

THRENOS *n* threnody; lamentation

THRENOSES > THRENOS

THREONINE *n* essential amino acid that occurs in certain proteins

THRESH *vb* beat (wheat etc) to separate the grain from the husks and straw ▷ *n* act of threshing

THRESHED > THRESH

THRESHEL *n* flail

THRESHELS > THRESHEL

THRESHER *n* large shark of tropical and temperate seas

THRESHERS > THRESHER

THRESHES > THRESH

THRESHING > THRESH

THRESHOLD *n* bar forming the bottom of a doorway

THRETTIES > THRETTY

THRETTY *nonstandard variant of* > THIRTY

THREW > THROW

THRICE *adv* three times

THRID *old variant of* > THREAD

THRIDACE *n* sedative made from lettuce juice

THRIDACES > THRIDACE

THRIDDED > THRID

THRIDDING > THRID

THRIDS > THRID

THRIFT *n* wisdom and caution with money

THRIFTIER > THRIFTY

THRIFTILY > THRIFTY

THRIFTS > THRIFT

THRIFTY *adj* not wasteful with money

THRILL *n* sudden feeling of excitement ▷ *vb* (cause to) feel a thrill

THRILLANT *another word for* > THRILLING

THRILLED > THRILL

THRILLER *n* book, film, etc with an atmosphere of mystery or suspense

THRILLERS > THRILLER

THRILLIER > THRILLY

THRILLING *adj* very exciting or stimulating

THRILLS > THRILL

THRILLY *adj* causing thrills

THRIMSA *same as* > THRYMSA

THRIMSAS > THRIMSA

THRIP *same as* > THRIPS

THRIPS *n* small slender-bodied insect with piercing mouthparts that feeds on plant sap

THRIPSES > THRIPS

THRISSEL *Scots variant of* > THISTLE

THRISSELS > THRISSEL

THRIST *old variant of* > THIRST

THRISTED > THRIST

THRISTING > THRIST

THRISTLE *Scots variant of* > THISTLE

THRISTLES > THRISTLE

THRISTS > THRIST

THRISTY > THRIST

THRIVE *vb* flourish or prosper

THRIVED > THRIVE

THRIVEN > THRIVE

THRIVER > THRIVE

THRIVERS > THRIVE

THRIVES > THRIVE

THRIVING > THRIVE

THRIVINGS > THRIVE

THRO *same as* > THROUGH

THROAT *n* passage from the mouth and nose to the stomach and lungs ▷ *vb* vocalize in the throat

THROATED > THROAT

THROATIER > THROATY

THROATILY > THROATY

THROATING > THROAT

THROATS > THROAT

THROATY *adj* (of the voice) hoarse

THROB *vb* pulsate repeatedly ▷ *n* throbbing

THROBBED > THROB

THROBBER > THROB

THROBBERS > THROB

THROBBING > THROB

THROBLESS > THROB

THROBS > THROB

THROE *n* pang or pain ▷ *vb* endure throes

THROED > THROE

THROEING > THROE

THROES *pl n* violent pangs or pains

THROMBI > THROMBUS

THROMBIN *n* enzyme that acts on fibrinogen in blood, causing it to clot

THROMBINS > THROMBIN

THROMBOSE *vb* become or affect with a thrombus

THROMBUS *n* clot of coagulated blood that remains at the site of its formation

THRONE *n* ceremonial seat of a monarch or bishop ▷ *vb* place or be placed on a throne

THRONED > THRONE

THRONES > THRONE

THRONG *vb* crowd ▷ *n* great number of people or things crowded together ▷ *adj* busy

THRONGED > THRONG

THRONGFUL > THRONG

THRONGING > THRONG

THRONGS > THRONG

THRONING > THRONE

THRONNER *n* person who is good at doing odd jobs

THRONNERS > THRONNER

THROPPLE *vb* strangle or choke

THROPPLED > THROPPLE

THROPPLES > THROPPLE

THROSTLE *n* song thrush

THROSTLES > THROSTLE

THROTTLE *n* device controlling the amount of fuel entering an engine ▷ *vb* control the flow of fluid in an engine by using the throttle

THROTTLED > THROTTLE

THROTTLER > THROTTLE

THROTTLES > THROTTLE

THROUGH *prep* from end to end or side to side of ▷ *adj* finished

THROUGHLY *adv* thoroughly

THROVE > THRIVE

THROW *vb* hurl through the air ▷ *n* throwing

THROWABLE *adj* capable of being thrown

THROWAWAY *adj* done or said casually ▷ *vb* get rid of or discard ▷ *n* handbill or advertisement distributed in a public place

THROWBACK *n* person or thing that reverts to an earlier type ▷ *vb* remind someone of (something he or she said or did previously) in order to upset him or her

THROWDOWN *n* challenge to a physical or artistic competition

THROWE *old variant of* > THROE

THROWER > THROW

THROWERS > THROW

THROWES > THROWE

THROWING > THROW

THROWINGS > THROW

THROWN > THROW

THROWOVER n material placed over an object for decoration or protection

THROWS > THROW

THROWSTER n person who twists silk or other fibres into yarn

THRU same as **>** THROUGH

THRUM vb strum rhythmically but without expression ▷ n in textiles, unwoven ends of warp thread

THRUMMED > THRUM

THRUMMER > THRUM

THRUMMERS > THRUM

THRUMMIER > THRUMMY

THRUMMING > THRUM

THRUMMY adj made of thrums

THRUMS > THRUM

THRUPENNY n twelve-sided British coin of nickel-brass, valued at three old pence, obsolete since 1971

THRUPUT n quantity of raw material or information processed in a given period

THRUPUTS > THRUPUT

THRUSH n brown songbird

THRUSHES > THRUSH

THRUST vb push forcefully ▷ n forceful stab

THRUSTED > THRUST

THRUSTER n person or thing that thrusts

THRUSTERS > THRUSTER

THRUSTFUL > THRUST

THRUSTING > THRUST

THRUSTOR variant of **>** THRUSTER

THRUSTORS > THRUSTOR

THRUSTS > THRUST

THRUTCH n narrow, fast-moving stream ▷ vb thrust

THRUTCHED > THRUTCH

THRUTCHES > THRUTCH

THRUWAY n thoroughfare

THRUWAYS > THRUWAY

THRYMSA n gold coin used in Anglo-Saxon England

THRYMSAS > THRYMSA

THUD n dull heavy sound ▷ vb make such a sound

THUDDED > THUD

THUDDING n act of thudding

THUDDINGS > THUDDING

THUDS > THUD

THUG n violent man, esp a criminal

THUGGEE n methods and practices of the thugs of India

THUGGEES > THUGGEE

THUGGERY > THUG

THUGGISH > THUG

THUGGISM > THUG

THUGGISMS > THUG

THUGGO n tough and violent person

THUGGOS > THUGGO

THUGS > THUG

THUJA n coniferous tree of North America and East Asia

THUJAS > THUJA

THULIA n oxide of thulium

THULIAS > THULIA

THULITE n rose-coloured zoisite sometimes incorporated into jewellery

THULITES > THULITE

THULIUM n malleable ductile silvery-grey element

THULIUMS > THULIUM

THUMB n short thick finger set apart from the others ▷ vb touch or handle with the thumb

THUMBED > THUMB

THUMBHOLE n hole for putting the thumb into

THUMBIER > THUMBY

THUMBIEST > THUMBY

THUMBING > THUMB

THUMBKIN n thumbscrew

THUMBKINS n thumbscrew

THUMBLESS > THUMB

THUMBLIKE > THUMB

THUMBLING n extremely small person

THUMBNAIL n nail of the thumb ▷ adj concise and brief

THUMBNUT n nut with projections enabling it to be turned by the thumb and forefinger

THUMBNUTS > THUMBNUT

THUMBPOT n tiny flowerpot

THUMBPOTS > THUMBPOT

THUMBS > THUMB

THUMBTACK n short tack with a broad smooth head for fastening papers to a drawing board, etc

THUMBY adj clumsy; uncoordinated

THUMP n (sound of) a dull heavy blow ▷ vb strike heavily

THUMPED > THUMP

THUMPER > THUMP

THUMPERS > THUMP

THUMPING adj huge or excessive

THUMPS > THUMP

THUNDER n loud noise accompanying lightning ▷ vb rumble with thunder

THUNDERED > THUNDER

THUNDERER > THUNDER

THUNDERS > THUNDER

THUNDERY > THUNDER

THUNDROUS > THUNDER

THUNK another word for **>** THUD

THUNKED > THUNK

THUNKING > THUNK

THUNKS > THUNK

THURIBLE same as **>** CENSER

THURIBLES > THURIBLE

THURIFER n person appointed to carry the censer at religious ceremonies

THURIFERS > THURIFER

THURIFIED > THURIFY

THURIFIES > THURIFY

THURIFY vb burn incense near or before an altar, shrine, etc

THURL same as **>** THIRL

THURLS > THURL

THUS adv in this manner ▷ n aromatic gum resin

THUSES > THUS

THUSLY adv in such a way; thus

THUSNESS n state or quality of being thus

THUSWISE adj in this way; thus

THUYA same as **>** THUJA

THUYAS > THUYA

THWACK n whack ▷ vb beat with something flat ▷ interj exclamation imitative of this sound

THWACKED > THWACK

THWACKER > THWACK

THWACKERS > THWACK

THWACKING > THWACK

THWACKS > THWACK

THWAITE n piece of land cleared from forest or reclaimed from wasteland

THWAITES > THWAITE

THWART vb foil or frustrate ▷ n seat across a boat ▷ adj passing or being situated across ▷ adv across

THWARTED > THWART

THWARTER > THWART

THWARTERS > THWART

THWARTING > THWART

THWARTLY > THWART

THWARTS > THWART

THY adj of or associated with you (thou) ▷ determiner belonging to or associated in some way with you (thou)

THYINE adj of relating to the sandarac tree

THYLACINE n extinct doglike Tasmanian marsupial

THYLAKOID n small membranous sac within a chloroplast

THYLOSE old variant of **>** TYLOSIS

THYLOSES > THYLOSIS

THYLOSIS same as **>** TYLOSIS

THYME n aromatic herb

THYMES > THYME

THYMEY > THYME

THYMI > THYMUS

THYMIC adj of or relating to the thymus

THYMIDINE n crystalline nucleoside of thymine, found in DNA

THYMIER > THYME

THYMIEST > THYME

THYMINE n white crystalline pyrimidine base found in DNA

THYMINES > THYMINE

THYMOCYTE n lymphocyte found in the thymus

THYMOL n substance obtained from thyme

THYMOLS > THYMOL

THYMOMA n type of tumour

THYMOMAS > THYMOMA

THYMOMATA > THYMOMA

THYMOSIN n hormone secreted by the thymus

THYMOSINS > THYMOSIN

THYMUS n small gland at the base of the neck

THYMUSES > THYMUS

THYMY > THYME

THYRATRON n gas-filled tube that has three electrodes and can be switched between an 'off' state and an 'on' state. It has been superseded, except for application involving high-power switching, by the thyristor

THYREOID same as **>** THYROID

THYREOIDS > THYREOID

THYRISTOR n any of a group of semiconductor devices, such as the silicon-controlled rectifier, that can be switched between two states

THYROID n gland in the neck controlling body growth ▷ adj of or relating to the thyroid gland

THYROIDAL > THYROID

THYROIDS > THYROID

THYROXIN same as **>** THYROXINE

THYROXINE n principal hormone produced by the thyroid gland

THYROXINS > THYROXIN

THYRSE n type of inflorescence, occurring in the lilac and grape

THYRSES > THYRSE

THYRSI > THYRSUS

THYRSOID > THYRSE

THYRSUS same as **>** THYRSE

THYSELF pron reflexive form of thou

TI same as **>** TE

TIAN n traditional French vegetable stew or earthenware dish it is cooked in

TIANS > TIAN

TIAR same as **>** TIARA

TIARA n semicircular jewelled headdress

TIARAED > TIARA

TIARAS > TIARA

TIARS > TIAR

TIBIA n inner bone of the lower leg

TIBIAE > TIBIA

TIBIAL > TIBIA

TIBIALES > TIBIALIS

TIBIALIS n muscle in the calf of the leg

TIBIAS > TIBIA

TIC n spasmodic muscular twitch

TICAL n former standard monetary unit of Thailand

TICALS > TICAL

TICCA adj acquired for temporary use in exchange for payment

TICCED > TIC

TICCING > TIC

TICE vb tempt or allure; entice

TICED > TICE

TICES > TICE

TICH same as **>** TITCH

TICHES > TICH

TICHIER > TICHY

TICHIEST > TICHY

TICHY same as > .TITCHY

TICING > TICE

TICK n mark used to check off or indicate the correctness of something ▷ vb mark with a tick

TICKED > TICK

TICKEN same as > TICKING

TICKENS > TICKEN

TICKER n heart

TICKERS > TICKER

TICKET n card or paper entitling the holder to admission, travel, etc ▷ vb attach or issue a ticket to

TICKETED > TICKET

TICKETING > TICKET

TICKETS pl n death or ruin

TICKEY n former South African threepenny piece

TICKEYS > TICKEY

TICKIES > TICKY

TICKING n strong material for mattress covers

TICKINGS > TICKING

TICKLACE n (in Newfoundland) a kittiwake

TICKLACES > TICKLACE

TICKLE vb touch or stroke (a person) to produce laughter ▷ n tickling

TICKLEASS n informal name for a kittiwake

TICKLED > TICKLE

TICKLER n difficult or delicate problem

TICKLERS > TICKLER

TICKLES > TICKLE

TICKLIER > TICKLE

TICKLIEST > TICKLE

TICKLING > TICKLE

TICKLINGS > TICKLE

TICKLISH adj sensitive to tickling

TICKLY > TICKLE

TICKS > TICK

TICKSEED another name for > COREOPSIS

TICKSEEDS > TICKSEED

TICKTACK n sound made by a clock ▷ vb make a ticking sound

TICKTACKS > TICKTACK

TICKTOCK n ticking sound made by a clock ▷ vb make a ticking sound

TICKTOCKS > TICKTOCK

TICKY same as > TICKEY

TICS > TIC

TICTAC same as > TICKTACK

TICTACKED > TICTAC

TICTACS > TICTAC

TICTOC same as > TICKTOCK

TICTOCKED > TICTOC

TICTOCS > TICTOC

TID n girl

TIDAL adj (of a river, lake, or sea) having tides

TIDALLY > TIDAL

TIDBIT same as > TITBIT

TIDBITS > TIDBIT

TIDDIER > TIDDY

TIDDIES > TIDDY

TIDDIEST > TIDDY

TIDDLE vb busy oneself with inconsequential tasks

TIDDLED > TIDDLE

TIDDLER n very small fish

TIDDLERS > TIDDLER

TIDDLES > TIDDLE

TIDDLEY same as > TIDDLY

TIDDLEYS > TIDDLEY

TIDDLIER > TIDDLY

TIDDLIES > TIDDLY

TIDDLIEST > TIDDLY

TIDDLING > TIDDLE

TIDDLY adj tiny ▷ n alcoholic beverage

TIDDY n four of trumps in the card game gleek

TIDE n rise and fall of the sea caused by the gravitational pull of the sun and moon ▷ vb carry or be carried with or as if with the tide

TIDED > TIDE

TIDELAND n land between high-water and low-water marks

TIDELANDS > TIDELAND

TIDELESS > TIDE

TIDELIKE > TIDE

TIDELINE n high-water mark left by the retreating tide

TIDELINES > TIDELINE

TIDEMARK n mark left by the highest or lowest point of a tide

TIDEMARKS > TIDEMARK

TIDEMILL n watermill powered by the force of the tide

TIDEMILLS > TIDEMILL

TIDERIP same as > RIPTIDE

TIDERIPS > TIDERIP

TIDES > TIDE

TIDESMAN n customs official at a port

TIDESMEN > TIDESMAN

TIDEWATER n water that advances and recedes with the tide

TIDEWAVE n undulation of the earth's water levels as the tide moves around it

TIDEWAVES > TIDEWAVE

TIDEWAY n strong tidal current or its channel, esp the tidal part of a river

TIDEWAYS > TIDEWAY

TIDIED > TIDY

TIDIER > TIDY

TIDIERS > TIDY

TIDIES > TIDY

TIDIEST > TIDY

TIDILY > TIDY

TIDINESS > TIDY

TIDING > TIDE

TIDINGS pl n news

TIDIVATE same as > TITIVATE

TIDIVATED > TITIVATE

TIDIVATES > TITIVATE

TIDS > TID

TIDY adj neat and orderly ▷ vb put in order ▷ n small container for odds and ends

TIDYING > TIDY

TIDYTIPS n herb with flowers resembling those of the daisy

TIE vb fasten or be fastened with string, rope, etc ▷ n long narrow piece of material worn knotted round the neck

TIEBACK n length of cord, ribbon, or other fabric used for tying a curtain to one side

TIEBACKS > TIEBACK

TIEBREAK n deciding game in drawn match

TIEBREAKS > TIEBREAK

TIECLASP n clip, often ornamental, which holds a tie in place against a shirt

TIECLASPS > TIECLASP

TIED > TIE

TIEING same as > TIE

TIELESS > TIE

TIEPIN n ornamental pin used to pin the two ends of a tie to a shirt

TIEPINS > TIEPIN

TIER n one of a set of rows placed one above and behind the other ▷ vb be or arrange in tiers

TIERCE same as > TERCE

TIERCED adj (of a shield) divided into three sections of similar size but different colour

TIERCEL same as > TERCEL

TIERCELET another name for > TERCEL

TIERCELS > TIERCEL

TIERCERON n (in Gothic architecture) a type of rib on a vault

TIERCES > TIERCE

TIERCET same as > TERCET

TIERCETS > TIERCET

TIERED > TIER

TIERING > TIER

TIERS > TIER

TIES > TIE

TIETAC n fastener for holding a tie in place

TIETACK same as > TIETAC

TIETACKS > TIETACK

TIETACS > TIETAC

TIFF n petty quarrel ▷ vb have or be in a tiff

TIFFANIES > TIFFANY

TIFFANY n sheer fine gauzy fabric

TIFFED > TIFF

TIFFIN n (in India) a light meal, esp at midday ▷ vb take tiffin

TIFFINED > TIFFIN

TIFFING > TIFF

TIFFINGS > TIFF

TIFFINING > TIFFIN

TIFFINS > TIFFIN

TIFFS > TIFF

TIFO n organized fan display during a football match

TIFOS > TIFO

TIFOSI > TIFOSO

TIFOSO n fanatical fan (esp an Italian F1 fan)

TIFOSOS > TIFOSO

TIFT Scots variant of > TIFF

TIFTED > TIFT

TIFTING > TIFT

TIFTS > TIFT

TIG n child's game

TIGE n trunk of an architectural column

TIGER n large yellow-and-black striped Asian cat

TIGEREYE n golden brown silicified variety of crocidolite, used as an ornamental stone

TIGEREYES > TIGEREYE

TIGERIER > TIGERY

TIGERIEST > TIGERY

TIGERISH > TIGER

TIGERISM n arrogant and showy manner

TIGERISMS > TIGERISM

TIGERLIER > TIGERLY

TIGERLIKE adj resembling a tiger

TIGERLY adj of or like a tiger

TIGERS > TIGER

TIGERWOOD n striped wood used in cabinetmaking

TIGERY adj like a tiger

TIGES > TIGE

TIGGED > TIG

TIGGER vb damage beyond repair by tinkering

TIGGERED > TIGGER

TIGGERING > TIGGER

TIGGERS > TIGGER

TIGGING > TIG

TIGHT adj stretched or drawn taut ▷ adv in a close, firm, or secure way

TIGHTASS n slang word for an excessively self-controlled person

TIGHTEN vb make or become tight or tighter

TIGHTENED > TIGHTEN

TIGHTENER > TIGHTEN

TIGHTENS > TIGHTEN

TIGHTER > TIGHT

TIGHTEST > TIGHT

TIGHTISH > TIGHT

TIGHTKNIT adj closely integrated

TIGHTLY > TIGHT

TIGHTNESS > TIGHT

TIGHTROPE n rope stretched taut on which acrobats perform

TIGHTS pl n one-piece clinging garment covering the body from the waist to the feet

TIGHTWAD n stingy person

TIGHTWADS > TIGHTWAD

TIGHTWIRE n wire tightrope

TIGLIC adj as in tiglic acid syrupy liquid or crystalline colourless unsaturated carboxylic acid

TIGLON same as > TIGON

TIGLONS > TIGLON

TIGNON n type of cloth headdress

TIGNONS > TIGNON

TIGON n hybrid offspring of a male tiger and a female lion

TIGONS > TIGON

SECTION 1: Words between 2 and 9 letters in length

TIGRESS n female tiger

TIGRESSES > TIGRESS

TIGRIDIA n type of tropical American plant

TIGRIDIAS > TIGRIDIA

TIGRINE adj of, characteristic of, or resembling a tiger

TIGRISH > TIGER

TIGRISHLY > TIGER

TIGROID adj resembling a tiger

TIGS > TIG

TIK n South African slang term for crystal meth

TIKA same as > TIKKA

TIKANGA n Māori ways or customs

TIKANGAS > TIKANGA

TIKAS > TIKA

TIKE same as > TYKE

TIKES > TIKE

TIKI n small carving of a grotesque person worn as a pendant ▷ vb take a scenic tour around an area

TIKIED > TIKI

TIKIING > TIKI

TIKINAGAN n Native American device allowing an infant to be carried on someone's back

TIKIS > TIKI

TIKKA adj marinated in spices and dry-roasted ▷ n act of marking a tikka on the forehead

TIKKAS > TIKKA

TIKOLOSHE same as > TOKOLOSHE

TIKS > TIK

TIKTAALIK n extinct species thought to be a missing link between water and land animals

TIL another name for > SESAME

TILAK n coloured spot or mark worn by Hindus

TILAKS > TILAK

TILAPIA n type of fish

TILAPIAS > TILAPIA

TILBURIES > TILBURY

TILBURY n light two-wheeled horse-drawn open carriage

TILDE n mark used in Spanish to indicate pronunciation

TILDES > TILDE

TILE n flat piece of ceramic, plastic, etc used to cover a roof, floor, or wall ▷ vb cover with tiles

TILED > TILE

TILEFISH n large brightly coloured deep-sea percoid food fish

TILELIKE adj like a tile

TILER > TILE

TILERIES > TILERY

TILERS > TILE

TILERY n place where tiles are produced

TILES > TILE

TILING n tiles collectively

TILINGS > TILING

TILL prep until ▷ vb cultivate (land) ▷ n drawer for money, usu in a cash register

TILLABLE > TILL

TILLAGE n act, process, or art of tilling

TILLAGES > TILLAGE

TILLED > TILL

TILLER n on boats, a handle fixed to the top of a rudderpost to serve as a lever in steering ▷ vb use a tiller

TILLERED > TILLER

TILLERING n (of a plant) the production of shoots

TILLERMAN n one working a tiller

TILLERMEN > TILLERMAN

TILLERS > TILLER

TILLICUM n (in the Pacific Northwest) a friend

TILLICUMS > TILLICUM

TILLIER > TILL

TILLIEST > TILL

TILLING > TILL

TILLINGS > TILL

TILLITE n rock formed from hardened till

TILLITES > TILLITE

TILLS > TILL

TILLY > TILL

TILS > TIL

TILT vb slant at an angle ▷ n slope

TILTABLE > TILT

TILTED > TILT

TILTER > TILT

TILTERS > TILT

TILTH n (condition of) land that has been tilled

TILTHS > TILTH

TILTING > TILT

TILTINGS > TILT

TILTMETER n instrument for measuring the tilt of the earth's surface

TILTROTOR n aircraft with rotors that can be tilted

TILTS > TILT

TILTYARD n (formerly) an enclosed area for tilting

TILTYARDS > TILTYARD

TIMARAU same as > TAMARAU

TIMARAUS > TIMARAU

TIMARIOT n one holding a fief in feudal Turkey

TIMARIOTS > TIMARIOT

TIMBAL n type of kettledrum

TIMBALE n mixture of meat, fish, etc, in a rich sauce

TIMBALES > TIMBALE

TIMBALS > TIMBAL

TIMBER n wood as a building material ▷ adj made out of timber ▷ vb provide with timbers ▷ interj lumberjack's shouted warning when a tree is about to fall

TIMBERED adj made of or containing timber or timbers

TIMBERIER > TIMBERY

TIMBERING n timbers collectively

TIMBERMAN n any of various longicorn beetles that have destructive wood-eating larvae

TIMBERMEN > TIMBERMAN

TIMBERS > TIMBER

TIMBERY adj like timber

TIMBO n Amazonian vine from which a useful insecticide can be derived

TIMBOS > TIMBO

TIMBRAL adj relating to timbre

TIMBRE n distinctive quality of sound of a voice or instrument

TIMBREL n tambourine

TIMBRELS > TIMBREL

TIMBRES > TIMBRE

TIME n past, present, and future as a continuous whole ▷ vb note the time taken by

TIMEBOMB n bomb containing a timing mechanism that determines the time it will detonate

TIMEBOMBS > TIMEBOMB

TIMECARD n card used with a time clock

TIMECARDS > TIMECARD

TIMED > TIME

TIMEFRAME n period of time within which certain events are scheduled to occur

TIMELESS adj unaffected by time

TIMELIER > TIMELY

TIMELIEST > TIMELY

TIMELINE n graphic representation showing the passage of time as a line

TIMELINES > TIMELINE

TIMELY adj at the appropriate time ▷ adv at the right or an appropriate time

TIMENOGUY n taut rope on a ship

TIMEOUS adj in good time

TIMEOUSLY > TIMEOUS

TIMEOUT n in sport, interruption in play during which players rest, etc

TIMEOUTS > TIMEOUT

TIMEPASS n way of passing the time ▷ vb pass the time

TIMEPIECE n watch or clock

TIMER n device for measuring time

TIMERS > TIMER

TIMES > TIME

TIMESAVER n something that saves time

TIMESCALE n period of time within which events occur or are due to occur

TIMESHARE n time-shared property

TIMESHIFT vb enable the viewing of a programme later than its original broadcast

TIMESTAMP vb (of a computer) add a record of the date and time of an event to (data)

TIMETABLE n plan showing the times when something takes place, the departure and arrival times of trains or

buses, etc ▷ vb set a time when a particular thing should be done

TIMEWORK n work paid for by the length of time taken, esp by the hour or the day

TIMEWORKS > TIMEWORK

TIMEWORN adj showing the adverse effects of overlong use or of old age

TIMID adj easily frightened

TIMIDER > TIMID

TIMIDEST > TIMID

TIMIDITY > TIMID

TIMIDLY > TIMID

TIMIDNESS > TIMID

TIMING n ability to judge when to do or say something so as to make the best effect

TIMINGS > TIMING

TIMIST n one concerned with time

TIMISTS > TIMIST

TIMOCRACY n political unit or system in which possession of property serves as the first requirement for participation in government

TIMOLOL n relaxant medicine used (for example) to reduce blood pressure

TIMOLOLS > TIMOLOL

TIMON n apparatus by which a vessel is steered

TIMONEER n helmsman; tillerman

TIMONEERS > TIMONEER

TIMONS > TIMON

TIMOROUS adj timid

TIMORSOME adj timorous; timid

TIMOTHIES > TIMOTHY

TIMOTHY n perennial grass of temperate regions

TIMOUS same as > TIMEOUS

TIMOUSLY > TIMOUS

TIMPANA n traditional Maltese baked pasta and pastry dish

TIMPANAS > TIMPANA

TIMPANI pl n set of kettledrums

TIMPANIST > TIMPANI

TIMPANO n kettledrum

TIMPANUM same as > TYMPANUM

TIMPANUMS > TIMPANUM

TIMPS same as > TIMPANI

TIN n soft metallic element ▷ vb put (food) into tins

TINA n (slang) crystal meth

TINAJA n large jar for cooling water

TINAJAS > TINAJA

TINAMOU n type of bird of Central and S America

TINAMOUS > TINAMOU

TINAS > TINA

TINCAL another name for > BORAX

TINCALS > TINCAL

TINCHEL n in Scotland, a circle of deer hunters who gradually close in on their quarry

TINCHELS > TINCHEL

TINCT vb tint ▷ adj tinted or coloured
TINCTED > TINCT
TINCTING > TINCT
TINCTS > TINCT
TINCTURE n medicinal extract in a solution of alcohol ▷ vb give a tint or colour to
TINCTURED > TINCTURE
TINCTURES > TINCTURE
TIND vb set alight
TINDAL n petty officer
TINDALS > TINDAL
TINDED > TIND
TINDER n dry easily burning material used to start a fire
TINDERBOX n formerly, small box for tinder, esp one fitted with a flint and steel
TINDERIER > TINDERY
TINDERS > TINDER
TINDERY adj like tinder
TINDING > TIND
TINDS > TIND
TINE n prong of a fork or antler ▷ vb lose
TINEA n any fungal skin disease, esp ringworm
TINEAL > TINEA
TINEAS > TINEA
TINED > TINE
TINEID n type of moth of the family which includes the clothes moths
TINEIDS > TINEID
TINES > TINE
TINFOIL n paper-thin sheet of metal, used for wrapping foodstuffs
TINFOILS > TINFOIL
TINFUL n contents of a tin or the amount a tin will hold
TINFULS > TINFUL
TING same as > THING
TINGE n slight tint ▷ vb give a slight tint or trace to
TINGED > TINGE
TINGEING > TINGE
TINGES > TINGE
TINGING > TINGE
TINGLE n prickling or stinging sensation ▷ vb feel a mild prickling or stinging sensation, as from cold or excitement
TINGLED > TINGLE
TINGLER > TINGLE
TINGLERS > TINGLE
TINGLES > TINGLE
TINGLIER > TINGLY
TINGLIEST > TINGLY
TINGLING > TINGLE
TINGLINGS > TINGLE
TINGLISH adj exciting
TINGLY > TINGLE
TINGS > TING
TINGUAITE n type of igneous rock
TINHORN n cheap pretentious person ▷ adj cheap and showy
TINHORNS > TINHORN
TINIER > TINY
TINIES pl n small children
TINIEST > TINY
TINILY > TINY

TININESS > TINY
TINING > TINE
TINK vb make short sound like a bell
TINKED > TINK
TINKER n (formerly) travelling mender of pots and pans ▷ vb fiddle with (an engine etc) in an attempt to repair it
TINKERED > TINKER
TINKERER > TINKER
TINKERERS > TINKER
TINKERING > TINKER
TINKERMAN n football coach who continually changes the team line-up or formation between games
TINKERMEN > TINKERMAN
TINKERS > TINKER
TINKERTOY n children's construction set
TINKING > TINK
TINKLE vb ring with a high tinny sound like a small bell ▷ n this sound or action
TINKLED > TINKLE
TINKLER same as > TINKER
TINKLERS > TINKLER
TINKLES > TINKLE
TINKLIER > TINKLE
TINKLIEST > TINKLE
TINKLING > TINKLE
TINKLINGS > TINKLE
TINKLY > TINKLE
TINKS > TINK
TINLIKE > TIN
TINMAN n one who works with tin or tin plate
TINMEN > TINMAN
TINNED > TIN
TINNER n tin miner
TINNERS > TINNER
TINNIE same as > TINNY
TINNIER > TINNY
TINNIES > TINNY
TINNIEST > TINNY
TINNILY > TINNY
TINNINESS > TINNY
TINNING > TIN
TINNINGS > TIN
TINNITUS n ringing or hissing sensation in one or both ears
TINNY adj (of sound) thin and metallic ▷ n can of beer
TINPLATE n thin steel sheet coated with tin ▷ vb coat (a metal or object) with a layer of tin
TINPLATED > TINPLATE
TINPLATES > TINPLATE
TINPOT adj worthless or unimportant ▷ n pot made of tin
TINPOTS > TINPOT
TINS > TIN
TINSEL n decorative metallic strips or threads ▷ adj made of or decorated with tinsel ▷ vb decorate with or as if with tinsel
TINSELED > TINSEL
TINSELIER > TINSELY
TINSELING > TINSEL
TINSELLED > TINSEL
TINSELLY adj adorned with tinsel

TINSELRY n tinsel-like material
TINSELS > TINSEL
TINSELY adj (US) like tinsel
TINSEY old variant of > TINSEL
TINSEYS > TINSEY
TINSMITH n person who works with tin or tin plate
TINSMITHS > TINSMITH
TINSNIPS n metal cutters
TINSTONE n black or brown stone
TINSTONES > TINSTONE
TINT n (pale) shade of a colour ▷ vb give a tint to
TINTACK n tin-plated tack
TINTACKS > TINTACK
TINTED > TINT
TINTER > TINT
TINTERS > TINT
TINTIER > TINTY
TINTIEST > TINTY
TINTINESS > TINTY
TINTING > TINT
TINTINGS > TINT
TINTLESS > TINT
TINTOOKIE n in informal Australian English, fawning or servile person
TINTS > TINT
TINTY adj having many tints
TINTYPE another name for > FERROTYPE
TINTYPES > TINTYPE
TINWARE n objects made of tin plate
TINWARES > TINWARE
TINWORK n objects made of tin
TINWORKS n place where tin is mined, smelted, or rolled
TINY adj very small
TIP n narrow or pointed end of anything ▷ vb put a tip on
TIPCART n cart that can be tipped to empty out its contents
TIPCARTS > TIPCART
TIPCAT n game in which a piece of wood is tipped in the air with a stick
TIPCATS > TIPCAT
TIPI variant spelling of > TEPEE
TIPIS > TIPI
TIPLESS > TIP
TIPOFF n warning or hint, esp given confidentially
TIPOFFS > TIPOFF
TIPPABLE > TIP
TIPPED > TIP
TIPPEE n person who receives a tip, esp regarding share prices
TIPPEES > TIPPEE
TIPPER n person who gives or leaves a tip
TIPPERS > TIPPER
TIPPET n fur cape for the shoulders
TIPPETS > TIPPET
TIPPIER > TIPPY
TIPPIEST > TIPPY
TIPPING > TIP
TIPPINGS > TIP

TIPPLE vb drink alcohol habitually, esp in small quantities ▷ n alcoholic drink
TIPPLED > TIPPLE
TIPPLER > TIPPLE
TIPPLERS > TIPPLE
TIPPLES > TIPPLE
TIPPLING > TIPPLE
TIPPY adj extremely fashionable or stylish
TIPPYTOE same as > TIPTOE
TIPPYTOED > TIPPYTOE
TIPPYTOES > TIPPYTOE
TIPS > TIP
TIPSHEET n list of advice or instructions
TIPSHEETS > TIPSHEET
TIPSIER > TIPSY
TIPSIEST > TIPSY
TIPSIFIED > TIPSIFY
TIPSIFIES > TIPSIFY
TIPSIFY vb make tipsy
TIPSILY > TIPSY
TIPSINESS > TIPSY
TIPSTAFF n court official
TIPSTAFFS > TIPSTAFF
TIPSTAVES > TIPSTAFF
TIPSTER n person who sells tips about races
TIPSTERS > TIPSTER
TIPSTOCK n detachable section of a gunstock, usually gripped by the left hand of the user
TIPSTOCKS > TIPSTOCK
TIPSY adj slightly drunk
TIPT > TIP
TIPTOE vb walk quietly with the heels off the ground
TIPTOED > TIPTOE
TIPTOEING > TIPTOE
TIPTOES > TIPTOE
TIPTOP adj of the highest quality or condition ▷ adv of the highest quality or condition ▷ n best in quality
TIPTOPS > TIPTOP
TIPTRONIC n type of gearbox that has both automatic and manual options
TIPULA n crane fly
TIPULAS > TIPULA
TIPUNA n ancestor
TIPUNAS > TIPUNA
TIRADE n long angry speech
TIRADES > TIRADE
TIRAGE n drawing of wine from a barrel prior to bottling
TIRAGES > TIRAGE
TIRAMISU n Italian coffee-flavoured dessert
TIRAMISUS > TIRAMISU
TIRASSE n mechanism in an organ connecting two pedals
TIRASSES > TIRASSE
TIRE vb reduce the energy of, as by exertion
TIRED adj exhausted
TIREDER > TIRED
TIREDEST > TIRED
TIREDLY > TIRED
TIREDNESS > TIRED

t

TIRELESS adj energetic and determined

TIRELING n fatigued person or animal

TIRELINGS > TIRELING

TIREMAKER same as > TYREMAKER

TIRES > TIRE

TIRESOME adj boring and irritating

TIREWOMAN n an obsolete term for lady's maid

TIREWOMEN > TIREWOMAN

TIRING > TIRE

TIRINGS > TIRE

TIRITI n another name for the Treaty of Waitangi

TIRITIS > TIRITI

TIRL vb turn

TIRLED > TIRL

TIRLING > TIRL

TIRLS > TIRL

TIRO same as > TYRO

TIROES > TIRO

TIRONIC variant of > TYRONIC

TIROS > TIRO

TIRR vb strip or denude

TIRRED > TIRR

TIRRING > TIRR

TIRRIT n panic; scare

TIRRITS > TIRRIT

TIRRIVEE n outburst of bad temper; rumpus

TIRRIVEES > TIRRIVEE

TIRRIVIE same as > TIRRIVEE

TIRRIVIES > TIRRIVIE

TIRRS > TIRR

TIS > TI

TISANE n infusion of dried or fresh leaves or flowers

TISANES > TISANE

TISICK n splutter; cough

TISICKS > TISICK

TISSUAL adj relating to tissue

TISSUE n substance of an animal body or plant ▷ vb weave into tissue

TISSUED > TISSUE

TISSUES > TISSUE

TISSUEY adj like tissue

TISSUIER > TISSUEY

TISSUIEST > TISSUEY

TISSUING > TISSUE

TISSULAR adj relating to tissue

TISWAS n state of anxiety or excitement

TISWASES > TISWAS

TIT n any of various small songbirds ▷ vb jerk or tug

TITAN n person who is huge, strong, or very important

TITANATE n any salt or ester of titanic acid

TITANATES > TITANATE

TITANESS n woman who is huge, strong, or very important

TITANIA > TITANIUM

TITANIAS > TITANIA

TITANIC adj huge or very important

TITANIS n large predatory flightless prehistoric bird

TITANISES > TITANIS

TITANISM n titanic power

TITANISMS > TITANISM

TITANITE another name for > SPHENE

TITANITES > TITANITE

TITANIUM n strong light metallic element used to make alloys

TITANIUMS > TITANIUM

TITANOUS adj of or containing titanium, esp in the trivalent state

TITANS > TITAN

TITBIT n tasty piece of food

TITBITS > TITBIT

TITCH n small person

TITCHES > TITCH

TITCHIE same as > TITCHY

TITCHIER > TITCHY

TITCHIEST > TITCHY

TITCHY adj very small

TITE adj immediately

TITELY adv immediately

TITER same as > TITRE

TITERS > TITER

TITFER n hat

TITFERS > TITFER

TITHABLE adj (until 1936) liable to pay tithes

TITHE n esp formerly, one tenth of one's income or produce paid to the church as a tax ▷ vb charge or pay a tithe

TITHED > TITHE

TITHER > TITHE

TITHERS > TITHE

TITHES > TITHE

TITHING > TITHE

TITHINGS > TITHING

TITHONIA n Central American herb with flowers resembling sunflowers

TITHONIAS > TITHONIA

TITI n small omnivorous monkey

TITIAN n reddish gold colour

TITIANS > TITIAN

TITILLATE vb excite or stimulate pleasurably

TITIS > TITI

TITIVATE vb smarten up

TITIVATED > TITIVATE

TITIVATES > TITIVATE

TITIVATOR > TITIVATE

TITLARK another name for > PIPIT

TITLARKS > TITLARK

TITLE n name of a book, film, etc ▷ vb give a title to

TITLED adj aristocratic

TITLELESS > TITLE

TITLER n one who writes titles

TITLERS > TITLER

TITLES > TITLE

TITLIKE adj like a tit

TITLING > TITLE

TITLINGS > TITLE

TITLIST n titleholder

TITLISTS > TITLIST

TITMAN n (of pigs) the runt of a litter

TITMEN > TITMAN

TITMICE > TITMOUSE

TITMOSE old spelling of > TITMOUSE

TITMOUSE n any small active songbird

TITOKI n New Zealand evergreen tree with a spreading crown and glossy green leaves

TITOKIS > TITOKI

TITRABLE > TITRATE

TITRANT n solution in a titration that is added to a measured quantity of another solution

TITRANTS > TITRANT

TITRATE vb measure the volume or concentration of (a solution) by titration

TITRATED > TITRATE

TITRATES > TITRATE

TITRATING > TITRATE

TITRATION n operation in which a measured amount of one solution is added to a known quantity of another solution until the reaction between the two is complete

TITRATOR n device used to perform titration

TITRATORS > TITRATOR

TITRE n concentration of a solution as determined by titration

TITRES > TITRE

TITS > TIT

TITTED > TIT

TITTER vb laugh in a suppressed way ▷ n suppressed laugh

TITTERED > TITTER

TITTERER > TITTER

TITTERERS > TITTER

TITTERING > TITTER

TITTERS > TITTER

TITTIE n dialect word for a sister or young woman

TITTIES > TITTIE

TITTING > TIT

TITTISH adj testy

TITTIVATE same as > TITIVATE

TITTLE n very small amount ▷ vb chatter; tattle

TITTLEBAT n child's name for the stickleback fish

TITTLED > TITTLE

TITTLES > TITTLE

TITTLING > TITTLE

TITTUP vb prance or frolic ▷ n caper

TITTUPED > TITTUP

TITTUPIER > TITTUPY

TITTUPING > TITTUP

TITTUPPED > TITTUP

TITTUPPY same as > TITTUPY

TITTUPS > TITTUP

TITTUPY adj sprightly; lively

TITTY same as > TITTIE

TITUBANCY n act of staggering

TITUBANT adj staggering

TITUBATE vb stagger

TITUBATED > TITUBATE

TITUBATES > TITUBATE

TITULAR adj in name only ▷ n bearer of a title

TITULARLY > TITULAR

TITULARS > TITULAR

TITULARY same as > TITULAR

TITULE same as > TITLE

TITULED > TITULE

TITULES > TITULE

TITULI > TITULUS

TITULING > TITULE

TITULUS n sign attached to the top of the cross during crucifixion

TITUP same as > TITTUP

TITUPED > TITUP

TITUPIER > TITUPY

TITUPIEST > TITUPY

TITUPING > TITUP

TITUPPED > TITUP

TITUPPING > TITUP

TITUPS > TITUP

TITUPY same as > TITTUPY

TIVY same as > TANTIVY

TIX pl n tickets

TIYIN n monetary unit of Uzbekistan and Kyrgyzstan

TIYINS > TIYIN

TIYN same as > TIYIN

TIYNS > TIYN

TIZ n state of confusion

TIZES > TIZ

TIZWAS same as > TISWAS

TIZWASES > TIZWAS

TIZZ same as > TIZZY

TIZZES > TIZZ

TIZZIES > TIZZY

TIZZY n confused or agitated state

TJANTING n pen-like tool used in batik for applying molten wax to fabric

TJANTINGS > TJANTING

TMESES > TMESIS

TMESIS n interpolation of a word between the parts of a compound word

TO prep indicating movement towards, equality or comparison, etc ▷ adv a closed position

TOAD n animal like a large frog

TOADEATER rare word for > TOADY

TOADFISH n spiny-finned fish with a wide mouth

TOADFLAX n plant with narrow leaves and yellow-orange flowers

TOADGRASS another name for > TOADRUSH

TOADIED > TOADY

TOADIES > TOADY

TOADISH > TOAD

TOADLESS adj having no toads

TOADLET n small toad

TOADLETS > TOADLET

TOADLIKE > TOAD

TOADRUSH n annual rush growing in damp lowlands

TOADS > TOAD

TOADSTONE n amygdaloidal basalt occurring in the limestone regions of Derbyshire

TOADSTOOL n poisonous fungus like a mushroom

TOADY n ingratiating person ▷ vb be ingratiating
TOADYING n act of toadying
TOADYINGS > TOADYING
TOADYISH > TOADY
TOADYISM > TOADY
TOADYISMS > TOADY
TOAST n sliced bread browned by heat ▷ vb brown (bread) by heat
TOASTED > TOAST
TOASTER > TOAST
TOASTERS > TOAST
TOASTIE same as > TOASTY
TOASTIER > TOASTY
TOASTIES > TOASTY
TOASTIEST > TOASTY
TOASTING > TOAST
TOASTINGS > TOAST
TOASTS > TOAST
TOASTY n toasted sandwich ▷ adj tasting or smelling like toast
TOAZE variant spelling of > TOZE
TOAZED > TOAZE
TOAZES > TOAZE
TOAZING > TOAZE
TOBACCO n plant with large leaves dried for smoking
TOBACCOES > TOBACCO
TOBACCOS > TOBACCO
TOBIES > TOBY
TOBOGGAN n narrow sledge for sliding over snow ▷ vb ride a toboggan
TOBOGGANS > TOBOGGAN
TOBOGGIN variant spelling of > TOBOGGAN
TOBOGGINS > TOBOGGIN
TOBY n water stopcock at the boundary of a street and house section
TOC n in communications code, signal for letter t
TOCCATA n rapid piece of music for a keyboard instrument
TOCCATAS > TOCCATA
TOCCATE > TOCCATA
TOCCATINA n short toccata
TOCHER n dowry ▷ vb give a dowry to
TOCHERED > TOCHER
TOCHERING > TOCHER
TOCHERS > TOCHER
TOCK n sound made by a clock ▷ vb (of a clock) make such a sound
TOCKED > TOCK
TOCKIER > TOCKY
TOCKIEST > TOCKY
TOCKING > TOCK
TOCKLEY n slang word for a penis
TOCKLEYS > TOCKLEY
TOCKS > TOCK
TOCKY adj muddy
TOCO n punishment
TOCOLOGY n branch of medicine concerned with childbirth
TOCOS > TOCO
TOCS > TOC
TOCSIN n warning signal
TOCSINS > TOCSIN
TOD n unit of weight, used for wool, etc ▷ vb produce a tod

TODAY n this day ▷ adv on this day
TODAYS > TODAY
TODDE same as > TOD
TODDED > TOD
TODDES > TODDE
TODDIES > TODDY
TODDING > TOD
TODDLE vb walk with short unsteady steps ▷ n act or an instance of toddling
TODDLED > TODDLE
TODDLER n child beginning to walk
TODDLERS > TODDLER
TODDLES > TODDLE
TODDLING > TODDLE
TODDY n sweetened drink of spirits and hot water
TODGER n vulgar word for a penis
TODGERS > TODGER
TODIES > TODY
TODS > TOD
TODY n small bird of the Caribbean
TOE n digit of the foot ▷ vb touch or kick with the toe
TOEA n monetary unit of Papua New Guinea
TOEAS > TOEA
TOEBIE n South African slang for sandwich
TOEBIES > TOEBIE
TOECAP n strengthened covering for the toe of a shoe
TOECAPS > TOECAP
TOECLIP n clip on a bicycle pedal for the toes
TOECLIPS > TOECLIP
TOED > TOE
TOEHOLD n small space on a mountain for supporting the toe of the foot in climbing
TOEHOLDS > TOEHOLD
TOEIER > TOEY
TOEIEST > TOEY
TOEING > TOE
TOELESS adj not having toes
TOELIKE > TOE
TOENAIL n thin hard clear plate covering part of the upper surface of the end of each toe ▷ vb join (beams) by driving nails obliquely
TOENAILED > TOENAIL
TOENAILS > TOENAIL
TOEPIECE n part of a shoe that covers the toes
TOEPIECES > TOEPIECE
TOEPLATE n metal reinforcement of the part of the sole of a shoe or boot underneath the toes
TOEPLATES > TOEPLATE
TOERAG n contemptible person
TOERAGGER same as > TOERAG
TOERAGS > TOERAG
TOES > TOE
TOESHOE n ballet pump with padded toes
TOESHOES > TOESHOE
TOETOE same as > TOITOI
TOETOES > TOETOE

TOEY adj (of a person) nervous or anxious
TOFF n well-dressed or upper-class person
TOFFEE n chewy sweet made of boiled sugar
TOFFEES > TOFFEE
TOFFIER > TOFFY
TOFFIES > TOFFY
TOFFIEST > TOFFY
TOFFISH adj belonging to or characteristic of the upper class
TOFFS adj like a toff
TOFFY same as > TOFFEE
TOFORE prep before
TOFT n homestead
TOFTS > TOFT
TOFU n soft food made from soya-bean curd
TOFUS > TOFU
TOFUTTI n tradename for nondairy, soya-based food products
TOFUTTIS > TOFUTTI
TOG n unit for measuring the insulating power of duvets ▷ vb dress oneself
TOGA n garment worn by citizens of ancient Rome ▷ vb wear a toga
TOGAE > TOGA
TOGAED > TOGA
TOGAS > TOGA
TOGATE adj clad in a toga
TOGATED same as > TOGATE
TOGAVIRUS n one of family of viruses
TOGE old variant of > TOGA
TOGED > TOGE
TOGES > TOGE
TOGETHER adv in company ▷ adj organized
TOGGED > TOG
TOGGER vb play football ▷ n football player
TOGGERED > TOGGER
TOGGERIES > TOGGERY
TOGGERING > TOGGER
TOGGERS > TOGGER
TOGGERY n clothes
TOGGING > TOG
TOGGLE n small bar-shaped button inserted through a loop for fastening ▷ vb supply or fasten with a toggle or toggles
TOGGLED > TOGGLE
TOGGLER > TOGGLE
TOGGLERS > TOGGLE
TOGGLES > TOGGLE
TOGGLING > TOGGLE
TOGROG n unit of currency in Mongolia
TOGROGS > TOGROG
TOGS > TOG
TOGUE n large North American freshwater game fish
TOGUES > TOGUE
TOHEROA n large edible mollusc of New Zealand
TOHEROAS > TOHEROA
TOHO n (to a hunting dog) an instruction to stop
TOHOS > TOHO
TOHUNGA n Māori priest

TOHUNGAS > TOHUNGA
TOIL n hard work ▷ vb work hard
TOILE n transparent linen or cotton fabric
TOILED > TOIL
TOILER > TOIL
TOILERS > TOIL
TOILES > TOILE
TOILET n bowl connected to a drain for receiving and disposing of urine and faeces ▷ vb go to the toilet
TOILETED > TOILET
TOILETING n act of using a toilet
TOILETRY n object or cosmetic used to clean or groom oneself
TOILETS > TOILET
TOILETTE same as > TOILET
TOILETTES > TOILETTE
TOILFUL same as > TOILSOME
TOILFULLY > TOILFUL
TOILINET n type of fabric with a woollen weft and a cotton or silk warp
TOILINETS > TOILINET
TOILING > TOIL
TOILINGS > TOIL
TOILLESS > TOIL
TOILS > TOIL
TOILSOME adj requiring hard work
TOILWORN adj fatigued, wearied by work
TOING n as in toing and froing state of going back and forth
TOINGS > TOING
TOISE n obsolete French unit of length roughly equal to 2m
TOISEACH n ancient Celtic nobleman
TOISEACHS > TOISEACH
TOISECH same as > TOISEACH
TOISECHS > TOISECH
TOISES > TOISE
TOISON n fleece
TOISONS > TOISON
TOIT vb walk or move in an unsteady manner, as from old age
TOITED > TOIT
TOITING > TOIT
TOITOI n tall grasses with feathery fronds
TOITOIS > TOITOI
TOITS > TOIT
TOKAMAK n reactor used in thermonuclear experiments
TOKAMAKS > TOKAMAK
TOKAY n small gecko of S and SE Asia, having a retractile claw at the tip of each digit
TOKAYS > TOKAY
TOKE n draw on a cannabis cigarette ▷ vb take a draw on a cannabis cigarette
TOKED > TOKE
TOKEN n sign or symbol ▷ adj nominal or slight
TOKENED > TOKEN
TOKENING > TOKEN

TOKENISM n policy of making only a token effort, esp to comply with a law
TOKENISMS > TOKENISM
TOKENS > TOKEN
TOKER > TOKE
TOKERS > TOKE
TOKES > TOKE
TOKING > TOKE
TOKO same as > TOCO
TOKOLOGY same as > TOCOLOGY
TOKOLOSHE n (in Bantu folklore) a malevolent mythical manlike animal of short stature
TOKOLOSHI variant of > TOKOLOSHE
TOKOMAK variant spelling of > TOKAMAK
TOKOMAKS > TOKOMAK
TOKONOMA n recess off a living room
TOKONOMAS > TOKONOMA
TOKOS > TOKO
TOKOTOKO n ceremonial carved Māori walking stick
TOKOTOKOS > TOKOTOKO
TOKTOKKIE n large South African beetle
TOLA n unit of weight, used in India
TOLAN n white crystalline derivative of acetylene
TOLANE same as > TOLAN
TOLANES > TOLANE
TOLANS > TOLAN
TOLAR n standard monetary unit of Slovenia
TOLARJEV > TOLAR
TOLARJI > TOLAR
TOLARS > TOLAR
TOLAS > TOLA
TOLBOOTH same as > TOLLBOOTH
TOLBOOTHS > TOLBOOTH
TOLD > TELL
TOLE same as > TOLL
TOLED > TOLE
TOLEDO n type of sword originally made in Toledo
TOLEDOS > TOLEDO
TOLERABLE adj bearable
TOLERABLY > TOLERABLE
TOLERANCE n acceptance of other people's rights to their own opinions or actions
TOLERANT adj able to tolerate the beliefs, actions, opinions, etc, of others
TOLERATE vb allow to exist or happen
TOLERATED > TOLERATE
TOLERATES > TOLERATE
TOLERATOR > TOLERATE
TOLES > TOLE
TOLEWARE n enamelled or lacquered metal ware, usually gilded
TOLEWARES > TOLEWARE
TOLIDIN same as > TOLIDINE
TOLIDINE n compound used in dyeing and chemical analysis
TOLIDINES > TOLIDINE
TOLIDINS > TOLIDIN

TOLING > TOLE
TOLINGS > TOLE
TOLL vb ring (a bell) slowly and regularly ▷ n instance of tolling
TOLLABLE > TOLL
TOLLAGE same as > TOLL
TOLLAGES > TOLLAGE
TOLLBAR n bar blocking passage of a thoroughfare, raised on payment of a toll
TOLLBARS > TOLLBAR
TOLLBOOTH n booth or kiosk at which a toll is collected
TOLLDISH n dish used to measure out the portion of grain given to a miller as payment for their work
TOLLED > TOLL
TOLLER > TOLL
TOLLERS > TOLLER
TOLLEY n large shooting marble used in a game of marbles
TOLLEYS > TOLLEY
TOLLGATE n gate across a toll road or bridge at which travellers must pay
TOLLGATED > TOLLGATE
TOLLGATES > TOLLGATE
TOLLHOUSE n small house at a tollgate occupied by a toll collector
TOLLIE same as > TOLLY
TOLLIES > TOLLY
TOLLING > TOLL
TOLLINGS > TOLL
TOLLMAN n man who collects tolls
TOLLMEN > TOLLMAN
TOLLS > TOLL
TOLLWAY n road on which users must pay tolls to travel
TOLLWAYS > TOLLWAY
TOLLY n castrated calf
TOLSEL n tolbooth
TOLSELS > TOLSEL
TOLSEY n tolbooth
TOLSEYS > TOLSEY
TOLT n type of obsolete English writ
TOLTER vb struggle or move with difficulty, as in mud
TOLTERED > TOLTER
TOLTERING > TOLTER
TOLTERS > TOLTER
TOLTS > TOLT
TOLU n sweet-smelling balsam obtained from a South American tree
TOLUATE n any salt or ester of any of the three isomeric forms of toluic acid
TOLUATES > TOLUATE
TOLUENE n colourless volatile flammable liquid obtained from petroleum and coal tar
TOLUENES > TOLUENE
TOLUIC adj as in toluic acid white crystalline derivative of toluene
TOLUID n white crystalline derivative of glycocoll
TOLUIDE variant of > TOLUID

TOLUIDES > TOLUIDE
TOLUIDIDE n chemical deriving from toluene
TOLUIDIN n type of dye
TOLUIDINE n compound used in dye production
TOLUIDINS > TOLUIDIN
TOLUIDS > TOLUID
TOLUOL another name for > TOLUENE
TOLUOLE another name for > TOLUENE
TOLUOLES > TOLUOLE
TOLUOLS > TOLUOL
TOLUS > TOLU
TOLUYL n any of three groups derived from a toluic acid
TOLUYLS > TOLUYL
TOLYL n type of monovalent radical
TOLYLS > TOLYL
TOLZEY n tolbooth
TOLZEYS > TOLZEY
TOM n male cat ▷ adj (of an animal) male ▷ vb prostitute oneself
TOMAHAWK n fighting axe of the Native Americans
TOMAHAWKS > TOMAHAWK
TOMALLEY n fat from a lobster, eaten as a delicacy
TOMALLEYS > TOMALLEY
TOMAN n gold coin formerly issued in Persia
TOMANS > TOMAN
TOMATILLO n Mexican plant bearing edible berries of the same name
TOMATO n red fruit used in salads and as a vegetable
TOMATOES > TOMATO
TOMATOEY adj tasting of tomato
TOMATOIER > TOMATOEY
TOMB n grave
TOMBAC n any of various brittle alloys containing copper and zinc
TOMBACK variant spelling of > TOMBAC
TOMBACKS > TOMBACK
TOMBACS > TOMBAC
TOMBAK same as > TOMBAC
TOMBAKS > TOMBAK
TOMBAL adj like or relating to a tomb
TOMBED > TOMB
TOMBIC adj of or relating to tombs
TOMBING > TOMB
TOMBLESS > TOMB
TOMBLIKE > TOMB
TOMBOC n weapon
TOMBOCS > TOMBOC
TOMBOLA n lottery with tickets drawn from a revolving drum
TOMBOLAS > TOMBOLA
TOMBOLO n narrow bar linking a small island with another island or the mainland
TOMBOLOS > TOMBOLO
TOMBOY n girl who acts or dresses like a boy
TOMBOYISH > TOMBOY

TOMBOYS > TOMBOY
TOMBS > TOMB
TOMBSTONE n gravestone
TOMCAT n male cat ▷ vb (of a man) to be promiscuous
TOMCATS > TOMCAT
TOMCATTED > TOMCAT
TOMCOD n small fish resembling the cod
TOMCODS > TOMCOD
TOME n large heavy book
TOMENTA > TOMENTUM
TOMENTOSE > TOMENTUM
TOMENTOUS > TOMENTUM
TOMENTUM n feltlike covering of downy hairs on leaves and other plant parts
TOMES > TOME
TOMFOOL n fool ▷ vb act the fool
TOMFOOLED > TOMFOOL
TOMFOOLS > TOMFOOL
TOMIA > TOMIUM
TOMIAL > TOMIUM
TOMIUM n sharp edge of a bird's beak
TOMMED > TOM
TOMMIED > TOMMY
TOMMIES > TOMMY
TOMMING > TOM
TOMMY n private in the British Army ▷ vb (formerly) to exploit workers by paying them in goods rather than in money
TOMMYCOD n type of cod
TOMMYCODS > TOMMYCOD
TOMMYING > TOMMY
TOMMYROT n utter nonsense
TOMMYROTS > TOMMYROT
TOMO n shaft formed by the action of water on limestone or volcanic rock
TOMOGRAM n X-ray photograph of a selected plane section of a solid object
TOMOGRAMS > TOMOGRAM
TOMOGRAPH n device for making tomograms
TOMORROW n (on) the day after today ▷ adv on the day after today
TOMORROWS > TOMORROW
TOMOS > TOMO
TOMPION same as > TAMPION
TOMPIONS > TOMPION
TOMPON same as > TAMPON
TOMPONED > TOMPON
TOMPONING > TOMPON
TOMPONS > TOMPON
TOMPOT adj as in tompot blenny variety of blenny with tentacles over its eyes
TOMS > TOM
TOMTIT n small European bird that eats insects and seeds
TOMTITS > TOMTIT
TON n unit of weight
TONAL adj written in a key
TONALITE n igneous rock found in the Italian Alps
TONALITES > TONALITE
TONALITIC adj relating to or consisting of tonalite**

t

TONALITY n presence of a musical key in a composition

TONALLY > TONAL

TONANT adj very loud

TONDI > TONDO

TONDINI > TONDINO

TONDINO n small tondo

TONDINOS > TONDINO

TONDO n circular easel painting or relief carving

TONDOS > TONDO

TONE n sound with reference to its pitch, volume, etc ▷ vb harmonize (with)

TONEARM same as > PICKUP

TONEARMS > TONEARM

TONED > TONE

TONELESS adj having no tone

TONEME n phoneme that is distinguished from another phoneme only by its tone

TONEMES > TONEME

TONEMIC > TONEME

TONEPAD n keypad used to transmit information

TONEPADS > TONEPAD

TONER n cosmetic applied to the skin to reduce oiliness

TONERS > TONER

TONES > TONE

TONETIC adj (of a language) distinguishing words by tone as well as by other sounds

TONETICS pl n area of linguistics concentrating on the use of tone to distinguish words semantically

TONETTE n small musical instrument resembling a recorder

TONETTES > TONETTE

TONEY variant spelling of > TONY

TONG vb gather or seize with tongs ▷ n (formerly) a Chinese secret society

TONGA n light two-wheeled vehicle used in rural areas of India

TONGAS > TONGA

TONGED > TONG

TONGER n one who uses tongs to gather oysters

TONGERS > TONGER

TONGING > TONG

TONGMAN another word for > TONGER

TONGMEN > TONGMAN

TONGS pl n large pincers for grasping and lifting

TONGSTER n tong member

TONGSTERS > TONGSTER

TONGUE n muscular organ in the mouth, used in speaking and tasting ▷ vb use the tongue

TONGUED > TONGUE

TONGUELET n small tongue

TONGUES > TONGUE

TONGUING > TONGUE

TONGUINGS > TONGUE

TONIC n medicine to improve body tone ▷ adj invigorating

TONICALLY > TONIC

TONICITY n state, condition, or quality of being tonic

TONICS > TONIC

TONIER > TONY

TONIES > TONY

TONIEST > TONY

TONIFIED > TONIFY

TONIFIES > TONIFY

TONIFY vb give tone to

TONIFYING > TONIFY

TONIGHT n the night or evening of this day ▷ adv in or during the night or evening of this day

TONIGHTS > TONIGHT

TONING > TONE

TONINGS > TONE

TONISH > TON

TONISHLY > TON

TONITE n explosive used in quarrying

TONITES > TONITE

TONK vb strike with a heavy blow

TONKA n as in tonka bean tall leguminous tree of tropical America

TONKED > TONK

TONKER > TONK

TONKERS > TONK

TONKING > TONK

TONKS > TONK

TONLET n skirt of a suit of armour, consisting of overlapping metal bands

TONLETS > TONLET

TONNAG n type of (usually tartan) shawl

TONNAGE n weight capacity of a ship

TONNAGES > TONNAGE

TONNAGS > TONNAG

TONNE same as > TON

TONNEAU n detachable cover to protect the rear part of an open car

TONNEAUS > TONNEAU

TONNEAUX > TONNEAU

TONNELL old spelling of > TUNNEL

TONNELLS > TONNELL

TONNER n something that weighs one ton

TONNERS > TONNER

TONNES > TONNE

TONNISH > TON

TONNISHLY > TON

TONOMETER n instrument for measuring the pitch of a sound, esp one consisting of a set of tuning forks

TONOMETRY > TONOMETER

TONOPLAST n membrane enclosing a vacuole in a plant cell

TONS > TON

TONSIL n small gland in the throat

TONSILAR > TONSIL

TONSILLAR > TONSIL

TONSILS > TONSIL

TONSOR n barber

TONSORIAL adj of a barber or their trade

TONSORS > TONSOR

TONSURE n shaving of all or the top of the head as a religious or monastic practice ▷ vb shave the head of

TONSURED > TONSURE

TONSURES > TONSURE

TONSURING > TONSURE

TONTINE n type of annuity scheme

TONTINER n subscriber to a tontine

TONTINERS > TONTINER

TONTINES > TONTINE

TONUS n normal tension of a muscle at rest

TONUSES > TONUS

TONY adj stylish or distinctive ▷ n stylish or distinctive person

TOO adv also, as well

TOOART variant spelling of > TUART

TOOARTS > TOOART

TOODLE vb tootle

TOODLED > TOODLE

TOODLES > TOODLE

TOODLING > TOODLE

TOOK > TAKE

TOOL n implement used by hand ▷ vb work on with a tool

TOOLBAG n bag for storing or carrying tools

TOOLBAGS > TOOLBAG

TOOLBAR n row or column of selectable buttons displayed on a computer screen

TOOLBARS > TOOLBAR

TOOLBOX n box for storing or carrying tools

TOOLBOXES > TOOLBOX

TOOLCASE n case for tools

TOOLCASES > TOOLCASE

TOOLCHEST n chest for tools

TOOLED > TOOL

TOOLER > TOOL

TOOLERS > TOOL

TOOLHEAD n adjustable attachment for a machine tool that holds the tool in position

TOOLHEADS > TOOLHEAD

TOOLHOUSE another word for > TOOLSHED

TOOLIE n adult who gatecrashes social events for school leavers

TOOLIES > TOOLIE

TOOLING n any decorative work done with a tool

TOOLINGS > TOOLING

TOOLKIT n set of tools designed to be used together or for a particular purpose

TOOLKITS > TOOLKIT

TOOLLESS adj having no tools

TOOLMAKER n person who makes tools

TOOLMAN n person who works with tools

TOOLMEN > TOOLMAN

TOOLPUSH n worker who directs the drilling on an oil rig

TOOLROOM n room, as in a machine shop, where tools are made or stored

TOOLROOMS > TOOLROOM

TOOLS > TOOL

TOOLSET n set of tools associated with a computer application

TOOLSETS > TOOLSET

TOOLSHED n small shed used for storing tools

TOOLSHEDS > TOOLSHED

TOOLTIP n temporary window containing information about a tool on a computer application

TOOLTIPS > TOOLTIP

TOOM vb empty (something) ▷ adj empty

TOOMED > TOOM

TOOMER > TOOM

TOOMEST > TOOM

TOOMING > TOOM

TOOMS > TOOM

TOON n large tree of the East Indies and Australia

TOONIE n Canadian two-dollar coin

TOONIES > TOONIE

TOONS > TOON

TOORIE n tassel or bobble on a bonnet

TOORIES > TOORIE

TOOSHIE adj angry

TOOSHIER > TOOSHIE

TOOSHIEST > TOOSHIE

TOOT n short hooting sound ▷ vb (cause to) make such a sound

TOOTED > TOOT

TOOTER > TOOT

TOOTERS > TOOT

TOOTH n bonelike projection in the jaws of most vertebrates for biting and chewing

TOOTHACHE n pain in or near a tooth

TOOTHCOMB n comb with fine teeth set closely together

TOOTHED adj having a tooth or teeth

TOOTHFISH n as in Patagonian toothfish Chilean sea bass

TOOTHFUL n little (esp alcoholic) drink

TOOTHFULS > TOOTHFUL

TOOTHIER > TOOTHY

TOOTHIEST > TOOTHY

TOOTHILY > TOOTHY

TOOTHING > TOOTH

TOOTHINGS > TOOTH

TOOTHLESS > TOOTH

TOOTHLIKE > TOOTH

TOOTHPICK n small stick for removing scraps of food from between the teeth

TOOTHS > TOOTH

TOOTHSOME adj delicious or appetizing in appearance, flavour, or smell

TOOTHWASH n tooth-cleaning liquid

TOOTHWORT n parasitic plant

t

TOOTHY *adj* having or showing numerous, large, or prominent teeth

TOOTING > TOOT

TOOTLE *vb* hoot softly or repeatedly ▷ *n* soft hoot or series of hoots

TOOTLED > TOOTLE

TOOTLER > TOOTLE

TOOTLERS > TOOTLE

TOOTLES > TOOTLE

TOOTLING > TOOTLE

TOOTS *Scots version of* > TUT

TOOTSED > TOOTS

TOOTSES > TOOTS

TOOTSIE *same as* > TOOTSY

TOOTSIES > TOOTSY

TOOTSING > TOOTS

TOOTSY *same as* > TOOTS

TOP *n* highest point or part ▷ *adj* at or of the top ▷ *vb* form a top on

TOPALGIA *n* pain restricted to a particular spot: a neurotic or hysterical symptom

TOPALGIAS > TOPALGIA

TOPARCH *n* ruler of a small state or realm

TOPARCHS > TOPARCH

TOPARCHY > TOPARCH

TOPAZ *n* semiprecious stone in various colours

TOPAZES > TOPAZ

TOPAZINE *adj* like topaz

TOPCOAT *n* overcoat

TOPCOATS > TOPCOAT

TOPCROSS *n* class of hybrid

TOPE *vb* drink alcohol regularly ▷ *n* small European shark

TOPECTOMY *n* (formerly) the surgical removal of part of the cerebral cortex to relieve certain psychiatric disorders

TOPED > TOPE

TOPEE *n* lightweight hat worn in tropical countries

TOPEES > TOPEE

TOPEK *same as* > TUPIK

TOPEKS > TOPEK

TOPER > TOPE

TOPERS > TOPE

TOPES > TOPE

TOPFLIGHT *adj* superior or excellent quality; outstanding

TOPFUL *variant spelling of* > TOPFULL

TOPFULL *adj* full to the top

TOPH *n* variety of sandstone

TOPHE *variant spelling of* > TOPH

TOPHES > TOPHE

TOPHI > TOPHUS

TOPHS > TOPH

TOPHUS *n* deposit of sodium urate in the helix of the ear or surrounding a joint

TOPI *same as* > TOPEE

TOPIARIAN > TOPIARY

TOPIARIES > TOPIARY

TOPIARIST > TOPIARY

TOPIARY *n* art of trimming trees and bushes into decorative shapes ▷ *adj* of or relating to topiary

TOPIC *n* subject of a conversation, book, etc

TOPICAL *adj* relating to current events ▷ *n* type of anaesthetic

TOPICALLY > TOPICAL

TOPICALS > TOPICAL

TOPICS > TOPIC

TOPING > TOPE

TOPIS > TOPI

TOPKICK *n* (formerly) sergeant

TOPKICKS > TOPKICK

TOPKNOT *n* crest, tuft, decorative bow, etc, on the top of the head

TOPKNOTS > TOPKNOT

TOPLESS *adj* having no top

TOPLINE *vb* headline; be the main focus of a newspaper story

TOPLINED > TOPLINE

TOPLINER > TOPLINE

TOPLINERS > TOPLINE

TOPLINES > TOPLINE

TOPLINING > TOPLINE

TOPLOFTY *adj* haughty or pretentious

TOPMAKER *n* wool dealer

TOPMAKERS > TOPMAKER

TOPMAKING > TOPMAKER

TOPMAN *n* sailor positioned in the rigging of the topsail

TOPMAST *n* mast next above a lower mast on a sailing vessel

TOPMASTS > TOPMAST

TOPMEN > TOPMAN

TOPMINNOW *n* small American freshwater cyprinodont fish

TOPMOST *adj* highest or best

TOPNOTCH *adj* excellent

TOPO *n* picture of a mountain with details of climbing routes superimposed on it

TOPOGRAPH *n* type of X-ray photograph

TOPOI > TOPO

TOPOLOGIC > TOPOLOGY

TOPOLOGY *n* geometry of the properties of a shape which are unaffected by continuous distortion

TOPOMETRY *n* measurement of the surface features of a region

TOPONYM *n* name of a place

TOPONYMAL > TOPONYMY

TOPONYMIC > TOPONYMY

TOPONYMS > TOPONYM

TOPONYMY *n* study of place names

TOPOS > TOPO

TOPOTYPE *n* specimen plant or animal taken from an area regarded as the typical habitat

TOPOTYPES > TOPOTYPE

TOPPED > TOP

TOPPER *n* top hat

TOPPERS > TOPPER

TOPPIER > TOPPY

TOPPIEST > TOPPY

TOPPING > TOP

TOPPINGLY > TOP

TOPPINGS > TOP

TOPPLE *vb* (cause to) fall over

TOPPLED > TOPPLE

TOPPLES > TOPPLE

TOPPLING > TOPPLE

TOPPY *adj* (of audio reproduction) having too many high-frequency sounds

TOPRAIL *n* top rail on something such as a piece of furniture

TOPRAILS > TOPRAIL

TOPS > TOP

TOPSAIL *n* square sail carried on a yard set on a topmast

TOPSAILS > TOPSAIL

TOPSCORE *vb* score the highest in a sports match or competition

TOPSCORED > TOPSCORE

TOPSCORES > TOPSCORE

TOPSIDE *n* lean cut of beef from the thigh

TOPSIDER *n* person in charge

TOPSIDERS > TOPSIDER

TOPSIDES > TOPSIDE

TOPSMAN *n* chief drover

TOPSMEN > TOPSMAN

TOPSOIL *n* surface layer of soil ▷ *vb* spread topsoil on (land)

TOPSOILED > TOPSOIL

TOPSOILS > TOPSOIL

TOPSPIN *n* spin imparted to make a ball bounce or travel exceptionally far, high, or quickly

TOPSPINS > TOPSPIN

TOPSTITCH *vb* stitch a line the outside of a garment, running close to a seam

TOPSTONE *n* stone forming the top of something

TOPSTONES > TOPSTONE

TOPWATER *adj* floating on the top of the water

TOPWORK *vb* graft shoots or twigs onto the main branches of (a tree)

TOPWORKED > TOPWORK

TOPWORKS > TOPWORK

TOQUE *same as* > TUQUE

TOQUES > TOQUE

TOQUET *same as* > TOQUE

TOQUETS > TOQUET

TOQUILLA *another name for* > JIPIJAPA

TOQUILLAS > TOQUILLA

TOR *n* high rocky hill

TORA *variant spelling of* > TORAH

TORAH *n* whole body of traditional Jewish teaching

TORAHS > TORAH

TORAN *n* (in Indian architecture) an archway

TORANA *same as* > TORAN

TORANAS > TORANA

TORANS > TORAN

TORAS > TORA

TORBANITE *n* type of oil shale

TORC *same as* > TORQUE

TORCH *n* small portable battery-powered lamp ▷ *vb* deliberately set (a building) on fire

TORCHABLE > TORCH

TORCHED > TORCH

TORCHER > TORCH

TORCHERE *n* tall narrow stand for holding a candelabrum

TORCHERES > TORCHERE

TORCHERS > TORCH

TORCHES > TORCH

TORCHIER *n* standing lamp with a bowl for casting light upwards

TORCHIERE *same as* > TORCHIER

TORCHIERS > TORCHIER

TORCHIEST > TORCHY

TORCHING > TORCH

TORCHINGS > TORCH

TORCHLIKE > TORCH

TORCHLIT *adj* lit by torches

TORCHON *n* coarse linen or cotton lace with a simple openwork pattern

TORCHONS > TORCHON

TORCHWOOD *n* rutaceous tree or shrub of Florida and the Caribbean, with hard resinous wood used for torches

TORCHY *adj* sentimental; maudlin; characteristic of a torch song

TORCS > TORC

TORCULAR *n* tourniquet

TORCULARS > TORCULAR

TORDION *n* old triple-time dance for two people

TORDIONS > TORDION

TORE *same as* > TORUS

TOREADOR *n* bullfighter

TOREADORS > TOREADOR

TORERO *n* bullfighter, esp one on foot

TOREROS > TORERO

TORES > TORE

TOREUTIC > TOREUTICS

TOREUTICS *n* art of making detailed ornamental reliefs, esp in metal, by embossing and chasing

TORGOCH *n* type of char

TORGOCHS > TORGOCH

TORI > TORUS

TORIC *adj* of, relating to, or having the form of a torus

TORICS > TORIC

TORIES > TORY

TORII *n* gateway, esp one at the entrance to a Japanese Shinto temple

TORMENT *vb* cause (someone) great suffering ▷ *n* great suffering

TORMENTA > TORMENTUM

TORMENTED > TORMENT

TORMENTER *same as* > TORMENTOR

TORMENTIL *n* creeping plant with yellow four-petalled flowers

TORMENTOR *n* person or thing that torments

TORMENTS > TORMENT

TORMENTUM *n* type of Roman catapult

TORMINA *n* complaints
TORMINAL > TORMINA
TORMINOUS > TORMINA
TORN > TEAR
TORNADE *same as* > TORNADO
TORNADES > TORNADE
TORNADIC > TORNADO
TORNADO *n* violent whirlwind
TORNADOES > TORNADO
TORNADOS > TORNADO
TORNILLO *n* shrub found in Mexico and some southwestern states of the US
TORNILLOS > TORNILLO
TORO *n* bull
TOROID *n* surface generated by rotating a closed plane curve about a coplanar line that does not intersect it
TOROIDAL > TOROID
TOROIDS > TOROID
TOROS > TORO
TOROSE *adj* (of a cylindrical part) having irregular swellings
TOROSITY > TOROSE
TOROT > TORAH
TOROTH > TORAH
TOROUS *same as* > TOROSE
TORPEDO *n* self-propelled underwater missile ▷ *vb* attack or destroy with or as if with torpedoes
TORPEDOED > TORPEDO
TORPEDOER > TORPEDO
TORPEDOES > TORPEDO
TORPEDOS > TORPEDO
TORPEFIED > TORPEFY
TORPEFIES > TORPEFY
TORPEFY *n* make torpid
TORPID *adj* sluggish and inactive
TORPIDITY > TORPID
TORPIDLY > TORPID
TORPIDS *n* series of boat races held at Oxford University
TORPITUDE *another word for* > TORPOR
TORPOR *n* torpid state
TORPORS > TORPOR
TORQUATE > TORQUES
TORQUATED > TORQUES
TORQUE *n* force causing rotation ▷ *vb* apply torque to (something)
TORQUED > TORQUE
TORQUER > TORQUE
TORQUERS > TORQUE
TORQUES *n* distinctive band of hair, feathers, skin, or colour around the neck of an animal
TORQUESES > TORQUES
TORQUEY *adj* providing torque
TORQUIER > TORQUEY
TORQUIEST > TORQUEY
TORQUING > TORQUE
TORR *n* unit of pressure
TORREFIED > TORREFY
TORREFIES > TORREFY
TORREFY *vb* dry (ores, etc) by subjection to intense heat

TORRENT *n* rushing stream ▷ *adj* like or relating to a torrent
TORRENTS > TORRENT
TORRET *same as* > TERRET
TORRETS > TORRET
TORRID *adj* very hot and dry
TORRIDER > TORRID
TORRIDEST > TORRID
TORRIDITY > TORRID
TORRIDLY > TORRID
TORRIFIED > TORRIFY
TORRIFIES > TORRIFY
TORRIFY *same as* > TORREFY
TORRS > TORR
TORS > TOR
TORSADE *n* ornamental twist or twisted cord, as on hats
TORSADES > TORSADE
TORSE *same as* > TORSO
TORSEL *n* wooden beam along the top of a wall
TORSELS > TORSEL
TORSES > TORSE
TORSI > TORSO
TORSION *n* twisting of a part by equal forces being applied at both ends but in opposite directions
TORSIONAL > TORSION
TORSIONS > TORSION
TORSIVE *adj* twisted
TORSK *n* fish with a single long dorsal fin
TORSKS > TORSK
TORSO *n* trunk of the human body
TORSOS > TORSO
TORT *n* civil wrong or injury for which damages may be claimed
TORTA *n* (in mining) a flat circular pile of silver ore
TORTAS > TORTA
TORTE *n* rich cake, originating in Austria
TORTELLI *pl n* type of stuffed pasta
TORTELLIS > TORTELLI
TORTEN > TORTE
TORTES > TORTE
TORTIE *n* tortoiseshell cat
TORTIES > TORTIE
TORTILE *adj* twisted or coiled
TORTILITY > TORTILE
TORTILLA *n* thin Mexican pancake
TORTILLAS > TORTILLA
TORTILLON *another word for* > STUMP
TORTIOUS *adj* having the nature of or involving a tort
TORTIVE *adj* twisted
TORTOISE *n* slow-moving land reptile with a dome-shaped shell
TORTOISES > TORTOISE
TORTONI *n* rich ice cream often flavoured with sherry
TORTONIS > TORTONI
TORTRICES > TORTRIX
TORTRICID *n* type of small moth of the family which includes the codling moth

TORTRIX *n* type of moth
TORTRIXES > TORTRIX
TORTS > TORT
TORTUOUS *adj* winding or twisting
TORTURE *vb* cause (someone) severe pain or mental anguish ▷ *n* severe physical or mental pain
TORTURED > TORTURE
TORTURER > TORTURE
TORTURERS > TORTURE
TORTURES > TORTURE
TORTURING > TORTURE
TORTUROUS > TORTURE
TORULA *n* any of various species of fungal microorganisms
TORULAE > TORULA
TORULAS > TORULA
TORULI > TORULUS
TORULIN *n* vitamin found in yeast
TORULINS > TORULIN
TORULOSE *adj* (of something cylindrical) alternately swollen and pinched along its length
TORULOSES > TORULOSIS
TORULOSIS *n* infection by one of the torula
TORULUS *n* socket in an insect's head in which its antenna is attached
TORUS *n* large convex moulding approximately semicircular in cross section
TORUSES > TORUS
TORY *n* conservative or reactionary person ▷ *adj* conservative or reactionary
TOSA *n* large reddish dog, originally bred for fighting
TOSAS > TOSA
TOSE *same as* > TOZE
TOSED > TOSE
TOSES > TOSE
TOSH *n* nonsense ▷ *vb* tidy or trim
TOSHACH *n* military leader of a clan
TOSHACHS > TOSHACH
TOSHED > TOSH
TOSHER > TOSH
TOSHERS > TOSH
TOSHES > TOSH
TOSHIER > TOSHY
TOSHIEST > TOSHY
TOSHING > TOSH
TOSHY *adj* neat; trim
TOSING > TOSE
TOSS *vb* throw lightly ▷ *n* tossing
TOSSED > TOSS
TOSSEN *old past participle of* > TOSS
TOSSER *n* slang for a stupid or despicable person
TOSSERS > TOSSER
TOSSES > TOSS
TOSSIER > TOSSY
TOSSIEST > TOSSY
TOSSILY > TOSSY
TOSSING > TOSS
TOSSINGS > TOSS
TOSSPOT *n* habitual drinker
TOSSPOTS > TOSSPOT

TOSSUP *n* instance of tossing up a coin
TOSSUPS > TOSSUP
TOSSY *adj* impudent
TOST *old past participle of* > TOSS
TOSTADA *n* crispy deep-fried tortilla topped with meat, cheese, and refried beans
TOSTADAS > TOSTADA
TOSTADO *same as* > TOSTADA
TOSTADOS > TOSTADO
TOSTONE *n* Mexican dish of fried plantains
TOSTONES > TOSTONE
TOT *n* small child ▷ *vb* total
TOTABLE > TOTE
TOTAL *n* whole, esp a sum of parts ▷ *adj* complete ▷ *vb* amount to
TOTALED > TOTAL
TOTALING > TOTAL
TOTALISE *same as* > TOTALIZE
TOTALISED > TOTALISE
TOTALISER > TOTALISE
TOTALISES > TOTALISE
TOTALISM *n* practice of a one-party state that regulates every area of life
TOTALISMS > TOTALISM
TOTALIST > TOTALISM
TOTALISTS > TOTALISM
TOTALITY *n* whole amount
TOTALIZE *vb* combine or make into a total
TOTALIZED > TOTALIZE
TOTALIZER > TOTALIZE
TOTALIZES > TOTALIZE
TOTALLED > TOTAL
TOTALLING > TOTAL
TOTALLY > TOTAL
TOTALS > TOTAL
TOTANUS *another name for* > REDSHANK
TOTANUSES > TOTANUS
TOTAQUINE *n* mixture of quinine and other alkaloids derived from cinchona bark, used as a substitute for quinine in treating malaria
TOTARA *n* tall coniferous forest tree of New Zealand
TOTARAS > TOTARA
TOTE *vb* carry (a gun etc) ▷ *n* act of or an instance of toting
TOTEABLE > TOTE
TOTED > TOTE
TOTEM *n* tribal badge or emblem
TOTEMIC > TOTEM
TOTEMISM *n* belief in kinship of groups or individuals having a common totem
TOTEMISMS > TOTEMISM
TOTEMIST > TOTEMISM
TOTEMISTS > TOTEMISM
TOTEMITE > TOTEMISM
TOTEMITES > TOTEMITE
TOTEMS > TOTEM
TOTER > TOTE
TOTERS > TOTE
TOTES > TOTE
TOTHER *n* other ▷ *adj* the other
TOTHERS > TOTHER

t

TOTIENT n quantity of numbers less than, and sharing no common factors with, a number

TOTIENTS > TOTIENT

TOTING > TOTE

TOTITIVE n number less than, and having no common factors with, a given number

TOTITIVES > TOTITIVE

TOTS > TOT

TOTTED > TOT

TOTTER vb move unsteadily ▷ n act or an instance of tottering

TOTTERED > TOTTER

TOTTERER > TOTTER

TOTTERERS > TOTTER

TOTTERIER > TOTTERY

TOTTERING > TOTTER

TOTTERS > TOTTER

TOTTERY adj tending to totter

TOTTIE adj very small

TOTTIER > TOTTY

TOTTIES > TOTTY

TOTTIEST > TOTTY

TOTTING > TOT

TOTTINGS > TOT

TOTTRING adj Shakespearian word referring to ragged cloth or clothing

TOTTY n small child ▷ adj very small

TOUCAN n tropical American bird with a large bill

TOUCANET n type of small toucan

TOUCANETS > TOUCAN

TOUCANS > TOUCAN

TOUCH vb come into contact with ▷ n sense by which an object's qualities are perceived when they come into contact with part of the body ▷ adj of a non-contact version of a particular sport

TOUCHABLE > TOUCH

TOUCHABLY adv in a touchable manner

TOUCHBACK n play in which the ball is put down by a player behind their own goal line when the ball has been put across the goal line by an opponent

TOUCHDOWN n moment at which a landing aircraft or spacecraft comes into contact with the landing surface ▷ vb (of an aircraft or spacecraft) to land

TOUCHE interj acknowledgment a remark or witty reply

TOUCHED adj emotionally moved

TOUCHER > TOUCH

TOUCHERS > TOUCH

TOUCHES > TOUCH

TOUCHHOLE n hole in the breech of early cannon and firearms through which the charge was ignited

TOUCHIER > TOUCHY

TOUCHIEST > TOUCHY

TOUCHILY > TOUCHY

TOUCHING adj emotionally moving ▷ prep relating to or concerning

TOUCHINGS > TOUCH

TOUCHLESS > TOUCH

TOUCHLINE n sideline of the pitch in some games

TOUCHMARK n maker's mark stamped on pewter objects

TOUCHPAD n part of laptop computer functioning like mouse

TOUCHPADS > TOUCHPAD

TOUCHTONE adj of or relating to a telephone dialling system in which each of the buttons pressed generates a tone of a different pitch, which is transmitted to the exchange

TOUCHUP n renovation or retouching, as of a painting

TOUCHUPS > TOUCHUP

TOUCHWOOD n something, esp dry wood, used as tinder

TOUCHY adj easily offended

TOUGH adj strong or resilient ▷ n rough violent person

TOUGHED > TOUGH

TOUGHEN vb make or become tough or tougher

TOUGHENED > TOUGHEN

TOUGHENER > TOUGHEN

TOUGHENS > TOUGHEN

TOUGHER > TOUGH

TOUGHEST > TOUGH

TOUGHIE n person who is tough

TOUGHIES > TOUGHIE

TOUGHING > TOUGH

TOUGHISH > TOUGH

TOUGHLY > TOUGH

TOUGHNESS n quality or an instance of being tough

TOUGHS > TOUGH

TOUGHY same as **>** TOUGHIE

TOUK same as **>** TUCK

TOUKED > TOUK

TOUKING > TOUK

TOUKS > TOUK

TOULADI same as **>** TULADI

TOULADIS > TOULADI

TOUN n town

TOUNS > TOUN

TOUPEE n small wig

TOUPEED adj wearing a toupee

TOUPEES > TOUPEE

TOUPET same as **>** TOUPEE

TOUPETS > TOUPET

TOUPIE n round boneless smoked ham

TOUPIES > TOUPIE

TOUR n journey visiting places of interest along the way ▷ vb make a tour (of)

TOURACO n brightly coloured crested arboreal African bird

TOURACOS > TOURACO

TOURED > TOUR

TOURER n large open car with a folding top

TOURERS > TOURER

TOURIE same as **>** TOORIE

TOURIES > TOURIE

TOURING > TOUR

TOURINGS > TOUR

TOURISM n tourist travel as an industry

TOURISMS > TOURISM

TOURIST n person travelling for pleasure ▷ adj of or relating to tourists or tourism

TOURISTA variant of **>** TOURIST

TOURISTAS > TOURISTA

TOURISTED adj busy with tourists

TOURISTIC > TOURIST

TOURISTS > TOURIST

TOURISTY adj informal term for full of tourists or tourist attractions

TOURNEDOS n thick round steak of beef

TOURNEY n knightly tournament ▷ vb engage in a tourney

TOURNEYED > TOURNEY

TOURNEYER > TOURNEY

TOURNEYS > TOURNEY

TOURNURE n outline or contour

TOURNURES > TOURNURE

TOURS > TOUR

TOURTIERE n type of meat pie

TOUSE vb tangle, ruffle, or disarrange; treat roughly

TOUSED > TOUSE

TOUSER > TOUSE

TOUSERS > TOUSE

TOUSES > TOUSE

TOUSIER > TOUSY

TOUSIEST > TOUSY

TOUSING > TOUSE

TOUSINGS > TOUSE

TOUSLE vb make (hair or clothes) ruffled and untidy ▷ n disorderly, tangled, or rumpled state

TOUSLED > TOUSLE

TOUSLES > TOUSLE

TOUSLING > TOUSLE

TOUSTIE adj irritable; testy

TOUSTIER > TOUSTIE

TOUSTIEST > TOUSTIE

TOUSY adj tousled

TOUT vb seek business in a persistent manner ▷ n person who sells tickets for a popular event at inflated prices

TOUTED > TOUT

TOUTER > TOUT

TOUTERS > TOUT

TOUTIE adj childishly irritable or sullen

TOUTIER > TOUTIE

TOUTIEST > TOUTIE

TOUTING > TOUT

TOUTON n deep-fried round of bread dough

TOUTONS > TOUTON

TOUTS > TOUT

TOUZE variant spelling of **>** TOUSE

TOUZED > TOUZE

TOUZES > TOUZE

TOUZIER > TOUZY

TOUZIEST > TOUZY

TOUZING > TOUZE

TOUZLE rare spelling of **>** TOUSLE

TOUZLED > TOUZLE

TOUZLES > TOUZLE

TOUZLING > TOUZLE

TOUZY variant spelling of **>** TOUSY

TOVARICH same as **>** TOVARISCH

TOVARISCH n comrade: a term of address

TOVARISH same as **>** TOVARISCH

TOW vb drag, esp by means of a rope ▷ n towing

TOWABLE > TOW

TOWAGE n charge made for towing

TOWAGES > TOWAGE

TOWARD same as **>** TOWARDS

TOWARDLY adj compliant

TOWARDS prep in the direction of

TOWAWAY n vehicle which has been towed away

TOWAWAYS > TOWAWAY

TOWBAR n metal bar on a car for towing vehicles

TOWBARS > TOWBAR

TOWBOAT n another word for tug (the boat)

TOWBOATS > TOWBOAT

TOWED > TOW

TOWEL n cloth for drying things ▷ vb dry or wipe with a towel

TOWELED > TOWEL

TOWELETTE n paper towel

TOWELHEAD n offensive term for someone who wears a turban

TOWELING > TOWEL

TOWELINGS > TOWEL

TOWELLED > TOWEL

TOWELLING n material used for making towels

TOWELS > TOWEL

TOWER n tall structure, often forming part of a larger building ▷ vb rise like a tower

TOWERED adj having a tower or towers

TOWERIER > TOWERY

TOWERIEST > TOWERY

TOWERING adj very tall or impressive

TOWERLESS adj not having a tower

TOWERLIKE adj like a tower

TOWERS > TOWER

TOWERY adj with towers

TOWHEAD n person with blond or yellowish hair

TOWHEADED adj having blonde or yellowish hair

TOWHEADS > TOWHEAD

TOWHEE n N American brownish-coloured sparrow

TOWHEES > TOWHEE

TOWIE n truck used for towing

TOWIER > TOW

TOWIES > TOWIE

TOWIEST > TOW

TOWING > TOW

TOWINGS > TOW

SECTION 1: Words between 2 and 9 letters in length

TOWKAY n sir
TOWKAYS > TOWKAY
TOWLINE same as > TOWROPE
TOWLINES > TOWLINE
TOWMON same as > TOWMOND
TOWMOND n old word for year
TOWMONDS > TOWMOND
TOWMONS > TOWMON
TOWMONT same as > TOWMOND
TOWMONTS > TOWMONT
TOWN n group of buildings larger than a village
TOWNEE same as > TOWNIE
TOWNEES > TOWNEE
TOWNFOLK same as > TOWNSFOLK
TOWNHALL adj of a variety of the Asian plant moschatel
TOWNHOME another word for > TOWNHOUSE
TOWNHOMES > TOWNHOME
TOWNHOUSE n terraced house in an urban area, esp a fashionable one, often having the main living room on the first floor with an integral garage on the ground floor
TOWNIE n resident of a town
TOWNIER > TOWNY
TOWNIES > TOWNY
TOWNIEST > TOWNY
TOWNISH > TOWN
TOWNLAND n division of land of various sizes
TOWNLANDS > TOWNLAND
TOWNLESS > TOWN
TOWNLET n small town
TOWNLETS > TOWNLET
TOWNLIER > TOWNLY
TOWNLIEST > TOWNLY
TOWNLING n person who lives in a town
TOWNLINGS > TOWNLING
TOWNLY adj characteristic of a town
TOWNS > TOWN
TOWNSCAPE n view of an urban scene
TOWNSFOLK n people of a town
TOWNSHIP n small town
TOWNSHIPS > TOWNSHIP
TOWNSITE n site of a town
TOWNSITES > TOWNSITE
TOWNSKIP n old term for a mischievous and roguish child who frequents city streets
TOWNSKIPS > TOWNSKIP
TOWNSMAN n inhabitant of a town
TOWNSMEN > TOWNSMAN
TOWNWARD adv in the direction of the town
TOWNWEAR n clothes suitable for wearing while pursuing activities usually associated with towns
TOWNWEARS > TOWNWEAR
TOWNY adj characteristic of a town
TOWPATH n path beside a canal or river
TOWPATHS > TOWPATH

TOWPLANE n aeroplane that tows gliders
TOWPLANES > TOWPLANE
TOWROPE n rope or cable used for towing a vehicle or vessel
TOWROPES > TOWROPE
TOWS > TOW
TOWSACK n sack made from tow
TOWSACKS > TOWSACK
TOWSE same as > TOUSE
TOWSED > TOWSE
TOWSER > TOWSE
TOWSERS > TOWSE
TOWSES > TOWSE
TOWSIER > TOWSY
TOWSIEST > TOWSY
TOWSING > TOWSE
TOWSY same as > TOUSY
TOWT vb sulk
TOWTED > TOWT
TOWTING > TOWT
TOWTS > TOWT
TOWY > TOW
TOWZE same as > TOUSE
TOWZED > TOWZE
TOWZES > TOWZE
TOWZIER > TOWZY
TOWZIEST > TOWZY
TOWZING > TOWZE
TOWZY same as > TOUSY
TOXAEMIA n blood poisoning
TOXAEMIAS > TOXAEMIA
TOXAEMIC > TOXAEMIA
TOXAPHENE n amber waxy solid with a pleasant pine odour, consisting of chlorinated terpenes, esp chlorinated camphene: used as an insecticide
TOXEMIA same as > TOXAEMIA
TOXEMIAS > TOXEMIA
TOXEMIC > TOXAEMIA
TOXIC adj poisonous ▷ n toxic substance
TOXICAL adj toxic
TOXICALLY > TOXIC
TOXICANT n toxic substance ▷ adj poisonous
TOXICANTS > TOXICANT
TOXICITY n degree of strength of a poison
TOXICOSES > TOXICOSIS
TOXICOSIS n any disease or condition caused by poisoning
TOXICS > TOXIC
TOXIGENIC adj producing poison
TOXIN n poison of bacterial origin
TOXINE nonstandard variant spelling of > TOXIN
TOXINES > TOXINE
TOXINS > TOXIN
TOXOCARA n parasitic worm infesting the intestines of cats and dogs
TOXOCARAL adj relating to toxocara
TOXOCARAS > TOXOCARA
TOXOID n toxin that has been treated to reduce its toxicity

TOXOIDS > TOXOID
TOXOPHILY n archer
TOY n something designed to be played with ▷ adj designed to be played with ▷ vb play, fiddle, or flirt
TOYBOX n box for toys
TOYBOXES > TOYBOX
TOYCHEST n chest for toys
TOYCHESTS > TOYCHEST
TOYED > TOY
TOYER > TOY
TOYERS > TOY
TOYETIC adj (of a film or television franchise) able to generate revenue via spin-off toys
TOYING > TOY
TOYINGS > TOY
TOYISH adj resembling a toy
TOYISHLY > TOYISH
TOYLAND n toy industry
TOYLANDS > TOYLAND
TOYLESOME old spelling of > TOILSOME
TOYLESS > TOY
TOYLIKE > TOY
TOYLSOM old spelling of > TOILSOME
TOYMAN n man who sells toys
TOYMEN > TOYMAN
TOYO n Japanese straw-like material made out of rice paper and used to make hats
TOYON n shrub related to the rose
TOYONS > TOYON
TOYOS > TOYO
TOYS > TOY
TOYSHOP n shop selling toys
TOYSHOPS > TOYSHOP
TOYSOME adj playful
TOYTOWN adj having an unreal and picturesque appearance ▷ n place with an unreal and picturesque appearance
TOYTOWNS > TOYTOWN
TOYWOMAN n woman who sells toys
TOYWOMEN > TOYWOMAN
TOZE vb tease out; (of wool, etc) card
TOZED > TOZE
TOZES > TOZE
TOZIE n type of shawl
TOZIES > TOZIE
TOZING > TOZE
TRABEATE same as > TRABEATED
TRABEATED adj constructed with horizontal beams as opposed to arches
TRABECULA n any of various rod-shaped structures that divide organs into separate chambers
TRABS pl n training shoes
TRACE vb locate or work out (the cause of something) ▷ n track left by something
TRACEABLE > TRACE
TRACEABLY > TRACE
TRACED > TRACE
TRACELESS > TRACE

TRACER n projectile which leaves a visible trail
TRACERIED > TRACERY
TRACERIES > TRACERY
TRACERS > TRACER
TRACERY n pattern of interlacing lines
TRACES > TRACE
TRACEUR n parkour participant
TRACEURS > TRACEUR
TRACHEA n windpipe
TRACHEAE > TRACHEA
TRACHEAL > TRACHEA
TRACHEARY adj using tracheae to breathe
TRACHEAS > TRACHEA
TRACHEATE > TRACHEA
TRACHEID n element of xylem tissue
TRACHEIDE same as > TRACHEID
TRACHEIDS > TRACHEID
TRACHEOLE n small trachea found in some insects
TRACHINUS n weever fish
TRACHITIS n another spelling of tracheitis (inflammation of the trachea)
TRACHLE vb (of hair, clothing, etc) make untidy
TRACHLED > TRACHLE
TRACHLES > TRACHLE
TRACHLING > TRACHLE
TRACHOMA n chronic contagious disease of the eye
TRACHOMAS > TRACHOMA
TRACHYTE n light-coloured fine-grained volcanic rock
TRACHYTES > TRACHYTE
TRACHYTIC adj (of the texture of certain igneous rocks) characterized by a parallel arrangement of crystals, which mark the flow of the lava when still molten
TRACING n traced copy
TRACINGS > TRACING
TRACK n rough road or path ▷ vb follow the trail or path of
TRACKABLE > TRACK
TRACKAGE n collective term for railway tracks
TRACKAGES > TRACKAGE
TRACKBALL n device consisting of a small ball, mounted in a cup, which can be rotated to move the cursor around the screen
TRACKBED n foundation on which railway tracks are laid
TRACKBEDS > TRACKBED
TRACKED > TRACK
TRACKER > TRACK
TRACKERS > TRACK
TRACKIE adj resembling or forming part of a tracksuit
TRACKIES pl n loose-fitting trousers with elasticated cuffs
TRACKING n act or process of following something or someone
TRACKINGS > TRACKING

TRACKLESS adj having or leaving no trace or trail

TRACKMAN n workman who lays and maintains railway track

TRACKMEN > TRACKMAN

TRACKPAD same as **>** TOUCHPAD

TRACKPADS > TRACKPAD

TRACKROAD another word for **>** TOWPATH

TRACKS > TRACK

TRACKSIDE n area alongside a track

TRACKSUIT n warm loose-fitting suit worn by athletes etc, esp during training

TRACKWAY n path or track

TRACKWAYS > TRACKWAY

TRACT n wide area ▷ vb track

TRACTABLE adj easy to manage or control

TRACTABLY > TRACTABLE

TRACTATE n short tract

TRACTATES > TRACTATE

TRACTATOR n person who writes tracts

TRACTED > TRACT

TRACTILE adj capable of being drawn out

TRACTING > TRACT

TRACTION n pulling, esp by engine power

TRACTIONS > TRACTION

TRACTIVE > TRACTION

TRACTOR n motor vehicle with large rear wheels for pulling farm machinery

TRACTORS > TRACTOR

TRACTRIX n (in geometry) type of curve

TRACTS > TRACT

TRACTUS n anthem sung in some RC masses

TRACTUSES > TRACTUS

TRAD n traditional jazz, as revived in the 1950s

TRADABLE > TRADE

TRADE n buying, selling, or exchange of goods ▷ vb buy and sell ▷ adj intended for or available only to people in industry or business

TRADEABLE > TRADE

TRADED > TRADE

TRADEFUL adj (of shops, for example) full of trade

TRADELESS > TRADE

TRADEMARK n (legally registered) name or symbol used by a firm to distinguish its goods ▷ vb label with a trademark

TRADENAME n name used by a trade to refer to a commodity, service, etc

TRADEOFF n exchange, esp as a compromise

TRADEOFFS > TRADEOFF

TRADER n person who engages in trade

TRADERS > TRADER

TRADES > TRADE

TRADESMAN n skilled worker

TRADESMEN > TRADESMAN

TRADIE n tradesperson

TRADIES > TRADIE

TRADING > TRADE

TRADINGS > TRADE

TRADITION n handing down of customs and beliefs through generations

TRADITIVE adj traditional

TRADITOR n Christian who betrayed fellow Christians at the time of the Roman persecutions

TRADITORS > TRADITOR

TRADS > TRAD

TRADUCE vb slander

TRADUCED > TRADUCE

TRADUCER > TRADUCE

TRADUCERS > TRADUCE

TRADUCES > TRADUCE

TRADUCIAN > TRADUCE

TRADUCING > TRADUCE

TRAFFIC n vehicles coming and going on a road ▷ vb trade

TRAFFICKY adj (of a street, area, town, etc) busy with motor vehicles

TRAFFICS > TRAFFIC

TRAGAL > TRAGUS

TRAGEDIAN n person who acts in or writes tragedies

TRAGEDIES > TRAGEDY

TRAGEDY n shocking or sad event

TRAGELAPH n mythical animal: a cross between a goat and a stag

TRAGI > TRAGUS

TRAGIC adj of or like a tragedy ▷ n tragedian

TRAGICAL same as **>** TRAGIC

TRAGICS > TRAGIC

TRAGOPAN n pheasant of S and SE Asia

TRAGOPANS > TRAGOPAN

TRAGULE n mouse deer

TRAGULES > TRAGULE

TRAGULINE adj like or characteristic of a tragule

TRAGUS n fleshy projection that partially covers the entrance to the external ear

TRAHISON n treason

TRAHISONS > TRAHISON

TRAIK vb trudge; trek with difficulty

TRAIKED > TRAIK

TRAIKING > TRAIK

TRAIKIT > TRAIK

TRAIKS > TRAIK

TRAIL n path, track, or road ▷ vb drag along the ground

TRAILABLE adj capable of being trailed

TRAILED > TRAIL

TRAILER n vehicle designed to be towed by another vehicle ▷ vb use a trailer to advertise (something)

TRAILERED > TRAILER

TRAILERS > TRAILER

TRAILHEAD n place where a trail begins

TRAILING adj (of a plant) having a long stem which spreads over the ground or hangs loosely

TRAILLESS adj without trail

TRAILS > TRAIL

TRAILSIDE adj beside a trail

TRAIN vb instruct in a skill ▷ n line of railway coaches or wagons drawn by an engine

TRAINABLE > TRAIN

TRAINBAND n company of English militia from the 16th to the 18th century

TRAINED > TRAIN

TRAINEE n person being trained ▷ adj (of a person) undergoing training

TRAINEES > TRAINEE

TRAINER n person who trains an athlete or sportsperson

TRAINERS pl n shoes in the style of those used for sports training

TRAINFUL n quantity of people or cargo that would be capable of filling a train

TRAINFULS > TRAINFUL

TRAINING n process of bringing a person to an agreed standard of proficiency by instruction

TRAININGS > TRAINING

TRAINLESS > TRAIN

TRAINLOAD n quantity of people or cargo sufficient to fill a train

TRAINMAN n man who works on a train

TRAINMEN > TRAINMAN

TRAINS > TRAIN

TRAINWAY n railway track; channel in a built-up area through which a train passes

TRAINWAYS > TRAINWAY

TRAIPSE vb walk wearily ▷ n long or tiring walk

TRAIPSED > TRAIPSE

TRAIPSES > TRAIPSE

TRAIPSING > TRAIPSE

TRAIT n characteristic feature

TRAITOR n person guilty of treason or treachery

TRAITORLY adj of or characteristic of a traitor

TRAITORS > TRAITOR

TRAITRESS > TRAITOR

TRAITS > TRAIT

TRAJECT vb transport or transmit

TRAJECTED > TRAJECT

TRAJECTS > TRAJECT

TRAM same as **>** TRAMWAY

TRAMCAR same as **>** TRAM

TRAMCARS > TRAMCAR

TRAMEL variant spelling of **>** TRAMMEL

TRAMELED > TRAMEL

TRAMELING > TRAMEL

TRAMELL variant spelling of **>** TRAMMEL

TRAMELLED > TRAMELL

TRAMELLS > TRAMELL

TRAMELS > TRAMEL

TRAMLESS > TRAM

TRAMLINE n tracks on which a tram runs

TRAMLINED adj having tramlines

TRAMLINES > TRAMLINE

TRAMMED > TRAM

TRAMMEL n hindrance to free action or movement ▷ vb hinder or restrain

TRAMMELED > TRAMMEL

TRAMMELER > TRAMMEL

TRAMMELS > TRAMMEL

TRAMMIE n conductor or driver of a tram

TRAMMIES > TRAMMIE

TRAMMING > TRAM

TRAMP vb travel on foot, hike ▷ n homeless person who travels on foot

TRAMPED > TRAMP

TRAMPER n person who tramps

TRAMPERS > TRAMPER

TRAMPET variant spelling of **>** TRAMPETTE

TRAMPETS > TRAMPET

TRAMPETTE n small trampoline

TRAMPIER > TRAMPY

TRAMPIEST > TRAMPY

TRAMPING > TRAMP

TRAMPINGS > TRAMP

TRAMPISH > TRAMP

TRAMPLE vb tread on and crush ▷ n action or sound of trampling

TRAMPLED > TRAMPLE

TRAMPLER > TRAMPLE

TRAMPLERS > TRAMPLE

TRAMPLES > TRAMPLE

TRAMPLING > TRAMPLE

TRAMPOLIN n variant of trampoline: a tough canvass sheet suspended by springs from a frame, used by acrobats, gymnasts, etc

TRAMPS > TRAMP

TRAMPY adj like or characteristic of a tramp

TRAMROAD same as **>** TRAMWAY

TRAMROADS > TRAMROAD

TRAMS > TRAM

TRAMWAY same as **>** TRAMLINE

TRAMWAYS > TRAMWAY

TRANCE n unconscious or dazed state ▷ vb put into or as into a trance

TRANCED > TRANCE

TRANCEDLY > TRANCE

TRANCES > TRANCE

TRANCEY adj (of music) characteristic of the trance sub-genre

TRANCHE n portion of something large

TRANCHES > TRANCHE

TRANCHET n stone age cutting tool

TRANCHETS > TRANCHET

TRANCIER > TRANCEY

TRANCIEST > TRANCEY

TRANCING > TRANCE

TRANECT n ferry

TRANECTS > TRANECT

TRANGAM n bauble or trinket

TRANGAMS > TRANGAM

TRANGLE n (in heraldry) a small fesse

TRANGLES > TRANGLE

TRANK n tranquillizer ▷ vb administer a tranquillizer

TRANKED > TRANK

TRANKING > TRANK

TRANKS > TRANK

TRANKUM same as **>** TRANGAM

TRANKUMS > TRANKUM

TRANNIE n transistor radio

TRANNIES > TRANNY

TRANNY same as **>** TRANNIE

TRANQ same as **>** TRANK

TRANQS > TRANQ

TRANQUIL adj calm and quiet

TRANS n short form of translation

TRANSACT vb conduct or negotiate (a business deal)

TRANSACTS > TRANSACT

TRANSAXLE n combined axle and gearbox

TRANSCEND vb rise above

TRANSCODE vb convert (digital computer data) from one format to another

TRANSDUCE vb change one form of energy to another

TRANSE n way through; passage

TRANSECT n sample strip of land used to monitor plant distribution and animal populations ▷ vb cut or divide crossways

TRANSECTS > TRANSECT

TRANSENNA n screen around a shrine

TRANSEPT n either of the two shorter wings of a cross-shaped church

TRANSEPTS > TRANSEPT

TRANSES > TRANSE

TRANSEUNT adj (of a mental act) causing effects outside the mind

TRANSFARD old past participle of **>** TRANSFER

TRANSFECT vb transfer genetic material isolated from a cell or virus into another cell

TRANSFER vb move or send from one person or place to another ▷ n transferring

TRANSFERS > TRANSFER

TRANSFIX vb astound or stun

TRANSFIXT > TRANSFIX

TRANSFORM vb change the shape or character of ▷ n result of a mathematical transformation

TRANSFUSE vb give a transfusion to

TRANSGENE n gene that is transferred from an organism of one species to an organism of another species by genetic engineering

TRANSHIP same as **>** TRANSSHIP

TRANSHIPS > TRANSHIP

TRANSHUME vb (of livestock) move to suitable grazing grounds according to the season

TRANSIENT same as **>** TRANSEUNT

TRANSIRE n document allowing goods to pass through customs

TRANSIRES > TRANSIRE

TRANSIT n passage or conveyance of goods or people ▷ vb make transit

TRANSITED > TRANSIT

TRANSITS > TRANSIT

TRANSLATE vb turn from one language into another

TRANSMAN n transgender man

TRANSMEN > TRANSMAN

TRANSMEW old variant of **>** TRANSMUTE

TRANSMEWS > TRANSMEW

TRANSMIT vb pass (something) from one person or place to another

TRANSMITS > TRANSMIT

TRANSMOVE vb change the form, character, or substance of

TRANSMUTE vb change the form or nature of

TRANSOM n horizontal bar across a window

TRANSOMED > TRANSOM

TRANSOMS > TRANSOM

TRANSONIC adj of or relating to conditions when travelling at or near the speed of sound

TRANSPIRE vb become known

TRANSPORT vb convey from one place to another ▷ n business or system of transporting

TRANSPOSE vb interchange two things ▷ n matrix resulting from interchanging the rows and columns of a given matrix

TRANSSHIP vb transfer or be transferred from one ship or vehicle to another

TRANSUDE vb (of a fluid) ooze or pass through interstices, pores, or small holes

TRANSUDED > TRANSUDE

TRANSUDES > TRANSUDE

TRANSUME vb make an official transcription of

TRANSUMED > TRANSUME

TRANSUMES > TRANSUME

TRANSUMPT n official transcription

TRANSVEST vb wear clothes traditionally associated with the opposite sex

TRANT vb travel from place to place selling goods

TRANTED > TRANT

TRANTER > TRANT

TRANTERS > TRANT

TRANTING > TRANT

TRANTS > TRANT

TRAP n device for catching animals ▷ vb catch

TRAPAN same as **>** TREPAN

TRAPANNED > TRAPAN

TRAPANNER > TRAPAN

TRAPANS > TRAPAN

TRAPBALL n obsolete ball game

TRAPBALLS > TRAPBALL

TRAPDOOR n door in floor or roof

TRAPDOORS > TRAPDOOR

TRAPE same as **>** TRAIPSE

TRAPED > TRAPE

TRAPES same as **>** TRAIPSE

TRAPESED > TRAPES

TRAPESES > TRAPES

TRAPESING > TRAPES

TRAPEZE n horizontal bar suspended from two ropes, used by circus acrobats ▷ vb swing on a trapeze

TRAPEZED > TRAPEZE

TRAPEZES > TRAPEZE

TRAPEZIA > TRAPEZIUM

TRAPEZIAL > TRAPEZIUM

TRAPEZII > TRAPEZIUS

TRAPEZING > TRAPEZE

TRAPEZIST n trapeze artist

TRAPEZIUM same as **>** TRAPEZOID

TRAPEZIUS n either of two flat triangular muscles, one covering each side of the back and shoulders, that rotate the shoulder blades

TRAPEZOID same as **>** TRAPEZIUM

TRAPFALL n trapdoor that opens under the feet

TRAPFALLS > TRAPFALL

TRAPING > TRAPE

TRAPLIKE > TRAP

TRAPLINE n line of traps

TRAPLINES > TRAPLINE

TRAPNEST n nest that holds the eggs of a single hen

TRAPNESTS > TRAPNEST

TRAPPEAN adj of, relating to, or consisting of igneous rock, esp a basalt

TRAPPED > TRAP

TRAPPER n person who traps animals for their fur

TRAPPERS > TRAPPER

TRAPPIER > TRAPPY

TRAPPIEST > TRAPPY

TRAPPING > TRAP

TRAPPINGS pl n accessories that symbolize an office or position

TRAPPOSE adj of or relating to traprock

TRAPPOUS same as **>** TRAPPOSE

TRAPPY adj having many traps

TRAPROCK another name for **>** TRAP

TRAPROCKS > TRAPROCK

TRAPS > TRAP

TRAPSE vb traipse

TRAPSED > TRAPSE

TRAPSES > TRAPSE

TRAPSING > TRAPSE

TRAPT old past participle of **>** TRAP

TRAPUNTO n type of quilting that is only partly padded in a design

TRAPUNTOS > TRAPUNTO

TRASH n anything worthless ▷ vb attack or destroy maliciously

TRASHCAN n dustbin

TRASHCANS > TRASHCAN

TRASHED > TRASH

TRASHER > TRASH

TRASHERS > TRASH

TRASHERY > TRASH

TRASHES > TRASH

TRASHIER > TRASHY

TRASHIEST > TRASHY

TRASHILY > TRASHY

TRASHING > TRASH

TRASHMAN another name for **>** BINMAN

TRASHMEN > TRASHMAN

TRASHTRIE n trash

TRASHY adj cheap, worthless, or badly made

TRASS n variety of the volcanic rock tuff

TRASSES > TRASS

TRAT n type of fishing line holding a series of baited hooks

TRATS > TRAT

TRATT short for **>** TRATTORIA

TRATTORIA n Italian restaurant

TRATTORIE > TRATTORIA

TRATTS > TRATT

TRAUCHLE n work or a task that is tiring, monotonous, and lengthy ▷ vb walk or work slowly and wearily

TRAUCHLED adj exhausted by long hard work or concern

TRAUCHLES > TRAUCHLE

TRAUMA n emotional shock

TRAUMAS > TRAUMA

TRAUMATA > TRAUMA

TRAUMATIC > TRAUMA

TRAVAIL n labour or toil ▷ vb suffer or labour painfully

TRAVAILED > TRAVAIL

TRAVAILS > TRAVAIL

TRAVE n stout wooden cage in which difficult horses are shod

TRAVEL vb go from one place to another, through an area, or for a specified distance ▷ n act if travelling, esp as a tourist

TRAVELED same as **>** TRAVELLED

TRAVELER same as **>** TRAVELLER

TRAVELERS > TRAVELER

TRAVELING > TRAVEL

TRAVELLED adj having experienced or undergone much travelling

TRAVELLER n person who makes a journey or travels a lot

TRAVELOG n film, lecture, or brochure on travel

TRAVELOGS > TRAVELOG

TRAVELS > TRAVEL

TRAVERSAL > TRAVERSE

TRAVERSE vb pass or go over

TRAVERSED > TRAVERSE

TRAVERSER > TRAVERSE
TRAVERSES > TRAVERSE
TRAVERTIN n porous rock
TRAVES > TRAVE
TRAVESTY n grotesque imitation or mockery ▷ vb make or be a travesty of
TRAVIS same as > TREVISS
TRAVISES > TRAVIS
TRAVOIS n sledge used for dragging logs
TRAVOISE same as > TRAVOIS
TRAVOISES > TRAVOISE
TRAWL n net dragged at deep levels behind a fishing boat ▷ vb fish with such a net
TRAWLED > TRAWL
TRAWLER n trawling boat
TRAWLERS > TRAWLER
TRAWLEY same as > TROLLEY
TRAWLEYS > TRAWLEY
TRAWLING > TRAWL
TRAWLINGS > TRAWL
TRAWLNET n large net used by trawlers
TRAWLNETS > TRAWLNET
TRAWLS > TRAWL
TRAY n flat board, usu with a rim, for carrying things
TRAYBAKE n flat cake which is baked in a tray and cut into small squares
TRAYBAKES > TRAYBAKE
TRAYBIT n threepenny bit
TRAYBITS > TRAYBIT
TRAYCLOTH n cloth for covering a tray
TRAYF adj not prepared according to Jewish law
TRAYFUL n as many or as much as will fit on a tray
TRAYFULS > TRAYFUL
TRAYNE old spelling of > TRAIN
TRAYNED > TRAYNE
TRAYNES > TRAYNE
TRAYNING > TRAYNE
TRAYS > TRAY
TRAZODONE n drug used to treat depression
TREACHER n traitor; treacherous person
TREACHERS > TREACHER
TREACHERY n wilful betrayal
TREACHOUR same as > TREACHER
TREACLE n thick dark syrup produced when sugar is refined ▷ vb add treacle to
TREACLED > TREACLE
TREACLES > TREACLE
TREACLIER > TREACLE
TREACLING > TREACLE
TREACLY > TREACLE
TREAD vb set one's foot on ▷ n way of walking or dancing
TREADED > TREAD
TREADER > TREAD
TREADERS > TREAD
TREADING > TREAD
TREADINGS > TREAD
TREADLE n lever worked by the foot to turn a wheel ▷ vb

work (a machine) with a treadle
TREADLED > TREADLE
TREADLER > TREADLE
TREADLERS > TREADLE
TREADLES > TREADLE
TREADLESS adj (of a tyre, for example) having no tread
TREADLING > TREADLE
TREADMILL n cylinder turned by treading on steps projecting from it
TREADS > TREAD
TREAGUE n agreement to stop fighting
TREAGUES > TREAGUE
TREASON n betrayal of one's sovereign or country
TREASONS > TREASON
TREASURE n collection of wealth, esp gold or jewels ▷ vb prize or cherish
TREASURED > TREASURE
TREASURER n official in charge of funds
TREASURES > TREASURE
TREASURY n storage place for treasure
TREAT vb deal with or regard in a certain manner ▷ n pleasure, entertainment, etc given or paid for by someone else
TREATABLE > TREAT
TREATED > TREAT
TREATER > TREAT
TREATERS > TREAT
TREATIES > TREATY
TREATING > TREAT
TREATINGS > TREAT
TREATISE n formal piece of writing on a particular subject
TREATISES > TREATISE
TREATMENT n medical care
TREATS > TREAT
TREATY n signed contract between states
TREBBIANO n grape used to make wine
TREBLE adj triple ▷ n (singer with or part for) a soprano voice ▷ vb increase three times
TREBLED > TREBLE
TREBLES > TREBLE
TREBLIER > TREBLY
TREBLIEST > TREBLY
TREBLING n act of trebling
TREBLINGS > TREBLING
TREBLY adj (of music) tinny
TREBUCHET n large medieval siege engine for hurling missiles consisting of a sling on a pivoted wooden arm set in motion by the fall of a weight
TREBUCKET same as > TREBUCHET
TRECENTO n 14th century, esp with reference to Italian art and literature
TRECENTOS > TRECENTO
TRECK same as > TREK
TRECKED > TRECK
TRECKING > TRECK
TRECKS > TRECK

TREDDLE variant spelling of > TREADLE
TREDDLED > TREDDLE
TREDDLES > TREDDLE
TREDDLING > TREDDLE
TREDILLE same as > TREDRILLE
TREDILLES > TREDILLE
TREDRILLE n card game for three players
TREE n large perennial plant with a woody trunk
TREED > TREE
TREEHOUSE n house built in tree
TREEING > TREE
TREELAWN n narrow band of grass between a road and a pavement, usually planted with trees
TREELAWNS > TREELAWN
TREELESS > TREE
TREELIKE > TREE
TREELINE n line marking the altitude above which trees will not grow
TREELINES > TREELINE
TREEN adj made of wood ▷ n art of making treenware
TREENAIL n dowel used for pinning planks or timbers together
TREENAILS > TREENAIL
TREENS > TREEN
TREENWARE n dishes and other household utensils made of wood, as by pioneers in North America
TREES > TREE
TREESHIP n state of being a tree
TREESHIPS > TREESHIP
TREETOP n top of a tree
TREETOPS > TREETOP
TREEWARE n reading materials that are printed on paper as opposed to a digital format
TREEWARES > TREEWARE
TREEWAX n yellowish wax secreted by an oriental scale insect
TREEWAXES > TREEWAX
TREF adj in Judaism, ritually unfit to be eaten
TREFA same as > TREF
TREFAH same as > TREF
TREFOIL n plant, such as clover, with a three-lobed leaf
TREFOILED > TREFOIL
TREFOILS > TREFOIL
TREGETOUR n juggler
TREGGINGS pl n thick close-fitting leggings
TREHALA n edible sugary substance from the cocoon of an Asian weevil
TREHALAS > TREHALA
TREHALOSE n white crystalline disaccharide that occurs in yeast and certain fungi
TREIF same as > TREF
TREIFA same as > TREF
TREILLAGE n latticework
TREILLE another word for > TRELLIS

TREILLES > TREILLE
TREK n long difficult journey, esp on foot ▷ vb make such a journey
TREKKED > TREK
TREKKER > TREK
TREKKERS > TREK
TREKKING n as in pony trekking the act of riding ponies cross-country
TREKKINGS > TREKKING
TREKS > TREK
TRELLIS n framework of horizontal and vertical strips of wood ▷ vb interweave (strips of wood, etc) to make a trellis
TRELLISED > TRELLIS
TRELLISES > TRELLIS
TREM n lever for producing a tremolo on a guitar
TREMA n mark placed over vowel to indicate it is to be pronounced separately
TREMAS > TREMA
TREMATIC adj relating to the gills
TREMATODE n parasitic flatworm
TREMATOID > TREMATODE
TREMBLANT adj (of jewels) set in such a way that they shake when the wearer moves
TREMBLE vb shake or quiver ▷ n trembling
TREMBLED > TREMBLE
TREMBLER n device that vibrates to make or break an electrical circuit
TREMBLERS > TREMBLER
TREMBLES n disease of cattle and sheep
TREMBLIER > TREMBLE
TREMBLING > TREMBLE
TREMBLOR n earth tremor
TREMBLORS > TREMBLOR
TREMBLY > TREMBLE
TREMIE n metal hopper and pipe used to distribute freshly mixed concrete underwater
TREMIES > TREMIE
TREMOLANT another word for > TREMOLO
TREMOLITE n white or pale green mineral of the amphibole group consisting of calcium magnesium silicate
TREMOLO n quivering effect in singing or playing
TREMOLOS > TREMOLO
TREMOR n involuntary shaking ▷ vb tremble
TREMORED > TREMOR
TREMORING > TREMOR
TREMOROUS > TREMOR
TREMORS > TREMOR
TREMS > TREM
TREMULANT n device on an organ by which the wind stream is made to fluctuate in intensity producing a tremolo effect
TREMULATE vb produce a tremulous sound
TREMULOUS adj trembling, as from fear or excitement

t

TRENAIL *same as*
> TREENAIL

TRENAILS > TRENAIL

TRENCH *n* long narrow ditch,
esp one used as a shelter in
war ▷ *adj* of or involving
military trenches ▷ *vb* make
a trench in (a place)

TRENCHAND *old variant of*
> TRENCHANT

TRENCHANT *adj* incisive

TRENCHARD *same as*
> TRENCHER

TRENCHED > TRENCH

TRENCHER *n* wooden plate
for serving food

TRENCHERS > TRENCHER

TRENCHES > TRENCH

TRENCHING > TRENCH

TREND *n* general tendency or
direction ▷ *vb* take a certain
trend

TRENDED > TREND

TRENDIER > TRENDY

TRENDIES > TRENDY

TRENDIEST > TRENDY

TRENDIFY *vb* render
fashionable

TRENDILY > TRENDY

TRENDING > TREND

TRENDOID *n* follower of
trends

TRENDOIDS > TRENDOID

TRENDS > TREND

TRENDY *n* consciously
fashionable person ▷ *adj*
consciously fashionable

TRENDYISM > TRENDY

TRENISE *n* one of the
figures in a quadrille

TRENISES > TRENISE

TRENTAL *n* mass said in
remembrance of a person 30
days after his or her death

TRENTALS > TRENTAL

TREPAN *same as*
> TREPHINE

TREPANG *n* any of various
large sea cucumbers

TREPANGS > TREPANG

TREPANNED > TREPAN

TREPANNER > TREPAN

TREPANS > TREPAN

TREPHINE *n* surgical
instrument for removing
circular sections of bone ▷ *vb*
remove a circular section of
bone from

TREPHINED > TREPHINE

TREPHINER > TREPHINE

TREPHINES > TREPHINE

TREPID *adj* trembling

TREPIDANT *adj* trembling

TREPONEMA *n* anaerobic
spirochaete bacterium that
causes syphilis

TREPONEME *same as*
> TREPONEMA

TRES *adj* very

TRESPASS *vb* go onto
another's property without
permission ▷ *n* act of
trespassing

TRESS *n* lock of hair, esp a
long lock of woman's hair
▷ *vb* arrange in tresses

TRESSED *adj* having a tress
or tresses as specified

TRESSEL *variant spelling of*
> TRESTLE

TRESSELS > TRESSEL

TRESSES > TRESS

TRESSIER > TRESS

TRESSIEST > TRESS

TRESSING > TRESS

TRESSOUR *same as*
> TRESSURE

TRESSOURS > TRESSOUR

TRESSURE *n* narrow inner
border on a shield, usually
decorated with fleurs-de-lys

TRESSURED > TRESSURE

TRESSURES > TRESSURE

TRESSY > TRESS

TREST *old variant of*
> TRESTLE

TRESTLE *n* board fixed on
pairs of spreading legs, used
as a support

TRESTLES > TRESTLE

TRESTS > TREST

TRET *n* (formerly) allowance
granted for waste due to
transportation

TRETINOIN *n* retinoid drug
used to treat certain skin
conditions

TRETS > TRET

TREVALLY *n* any of
various food and game
fishes

TREVALLYS > TREVALLY

TREVET *same as* > TRIVET

TREVETS > TREVET

TREVIS *variant spelling of*
> TREVISS

TREVISES > TREVIS

TREVISS *n* partition in a
stable for keeping animals
apart

TREVISSES > TREVISS

TREW *old variant spelling of*
> TRUE

TREWS *pl n* close-fitting
tartan trousers

TREWSMAN *n* Highlander

TREWSMEN > TREWSMAN

TREY *n* any card or dice
throw with three spots

TREYBIT *same as*
> TRAYBIT

TREYBITS > TREYBIT

TREYF *adj* not prepared
according to Jewish law

TREYFA *same as* > TREYF

TREYS > TREY

TREZ *same as* > TREY

TREZES > TREZ

TRIABLE *adj* liable to be
tried judicially

TRIAC *n* device for
regulating the amount of
electric current allowed to
reach a circuit

TRIACID *adj* (of a base)
capable of reacting with
three molecules of a
monobasic acid

TRIACIDS > TRIACID

TRIACS > TRIAC

TRIACT *adj* having three
rays ▷ *n* sponge spicule with
three rays

TRIACTINE *same as*
> TRIACT

TRIACTOR *n* type of bet

TRIACTORS > TRIACTOR

TRIACTS > TRIACT

TRIAD *n* group of three

TRIADIC *n* something that
has the characteristics of a
triad

TRIADICS > TRIADIC

TRIADISM > TRIAD

TRIADISMS > TRIAD

TRIADIST > TRIAD

TRIADISTS > TRIAD

TRIADS > TRIAD

TRIAGE *n* sorting
emergency patients into
categories of priority ▷ *vb*
sort (patients) into
categories of priority

TRIAGED > TRIAGE

TRIAGES > TRIAGE

TRIAGING > TRIAGE

TRIAL *n* investigation of a
case before a judge ▷ *vb* test
or try out

TRIALED > TRIAL

TRIALING > TRIAL

TRIALISM *n* belief that
humans consist of body,
soul, and spirit

TRIALISMS > TRIALISM

TRIALIST *same as*
> TRIALLIST

TRIALISTS > TRIALIST

TRIALITY > TRIALISM

TRIALLED > TRIAL

TRIALLING > TRIAL

TRIALLIST *n* person who
takes part in a competition

TRIALOGUE *n* dialogue
between three people

TRIALS > TRIAL

TRIALWARE *n* computer
software that can be used
without charge for a limited
evaluation period

TRIANGLE *n* geometric
figure with three sides

TRIANGLED > TRIANGLE

TRIANGLES > TRIANGLE

TRIAPSAL *adj* (of a church)
having three apses

TRIARCH *n* one of three
rulers of a triarchy

TRIARCHS > TRIARCH

TRIARCHY *n* government by
three people

TRIASSIC *adj* of, denoting,
or formed in the first period
of the Mesozoic era

TRIATHLON *n* athletic
contest in which each
athlete competes in three
different events: swimming,
cycling, and running

TRIATIC *n* rope between a
ship's mastheads

TRIATICS > TRIATIC

TRIATOMIC *adj* a molecule
having three atoms

TRIAXIAL *adj* having three
axes ▷ *n* sponge spicule with
three axes

TRIAXIALS > TRIAXIAL

TRIAXON *another name for*
> TRIAXIAL

TRIAXONS > TRIAXON

TRIAZIN *same as*
> TRIAZINE

TRIAZINE *n* any of three
azines that contain three
nitrogen atoms in their
molecules

TRIAZINES > TRIAZINE

TRIAZINS > TRIAZIN

TRIAZOLE *n* heterocyclic
compound

TRIAZOLES > TRIAZOLE

TRIAZOLIC > TRIAZOLE

TRIBADE *n* lesbian, esp one
who practises tribadism

TRIBADES > TRIBADE

TRIBADIC > TRIBADE

TRIBADIES > TRIBADY

TRIBADISM *n* lesbian
practice in which one
partner lies on top of the
other and simulates the male
role in heterosexual
intercourse

TRIBADY *another word for*
> TRIBADISM

TRIBAL *adj* of or denoting a
tribe or tribes ▷ *n* member of
a tribal community

TRIBALISM *n* loyalty to a
tribe

TRIBALIST > TRIBALISM

TRIBALLY > TRIBAL

TRIBALS > TRIBAL

TRIBASIC *adj* (of an acid)
containing three replaceable
hydrogen atoms in the
molecule

TRIBBLE *n* frame for drying
paper

TRIBBLES > TRIBBLE

TRIBE *n* group of clans or
families believed to have a
common ancestor

TRIBELESS > TRIBE

TRIBES > TRIBE

TRIBESMAN *n* member of a
tribe

TRIBESMEN > TRIBESMAN

TRIBLET *n* spindle or
mandrel used in making
rings, tubes, etc

TRIBLETS > TRIBLET

TRIBOLOGY *n* study of
friction, lubrication, and
wear between moving
surfaces

TRIBRACH *n* metrical foot of
three short syllables

TRIBRACHS > TRIBRACH

TRIBULATE *vb* trouble

TRIBUNAL *n* board
appointed to inquire into a
specific matter

TRIBUNALS > TRIBUNAL

TRIBUNARY > TRIBUNE

TRIBUNATE *n* office or rank
of a tribune

TRIBUNE *n* people's
representative, esp in
ancient Rome

TRIBUNES > TRIBUNE

TRIBUTARY *n* stream or
river flowing into a larger one
▷ *adj* (of a stream or river)
flowing into a larger one

TRIBUTE *n* sign of respect or
admiration

TRIBUTER *n* miner

TRIBUTERS > TRIBUTER

TRIBUTES > TRIBUTE

t

SECTION 1: Words between 2 and 9 letters in length

TRICAR n car with three wheels

TRICARS > TRICAR

TRICE n moment ▷ vb haul up or secure

TRICED > TRICE

TRICEP same as > TRICEPS

TRICEPS n muscle at the back of the upper arm

TRICEPSES > TRICEPS

TRICERION n candlestick with three arms

TRICES > TRICE

TRICHINA n parasitic nematode worm

TRICHINAE > TRICHINA

TRICHINAL > TRICHINA

TRICHINAS > TRICHINA

TRICHITE n any of various needle-shaped crystals that occur in some glassy volcanic rocks

TRICHITES > TRICHITE

TRICHITIC > TRICHITE

TRICHOID adj resembling a hair

TRICHOME n any hairlike outgrowth from the surface of a plant

TRICHOMES > TRICHOME

TRICHOMIC > TRICHOME

TRICHORD n musical instrument with three strings

TRICHORDS > TRICHORD

TRICHOSES > TRICHOSIS

TRICHOSIS n any abnormal condition or disease of the hair

TRICHROIC n state of having three colours

TRICHROME adj three-coloured

TRICING > TRICE

TRICITIES > TRICITY

TRICITY n area that comprises three adjoining cities

TRICK n deceitful or cunning action or plan ▷ vb cheat or deceive

TRICKED > TRICK

TRICKER > TRICK

TRICKERS > TRICK

TRICKERY n practice or an instance of using tricks

TRICKIE Scots form of > TRICKY

TRICKIER > TRICKY

TRICKIEST > TRICKY

TRICKILY > TRICKY

TRICKING > TRICK

TRICKINGS > TRICK

TRICKISH same as > TRICKY

TRICKLE vb (cause to) flow in a thin stream or drops ▷ n gradual flow

TRICKLED > TRICKLE

TRICKLES > TRICKLE

TRICKLESS > TRICK

TRICKLET n tiny trickle

TRICKLETS > TRICKLET

TRICKLIER > TRICKLE

TRICKLING > TRICKLE

TRICKLY > TRICKLE

TRICKS > TRICK

TRICKSIER > TRICKSY

TRICKSILY > TRICKSY

TRICKSOME adj full of tricks

TRICKSTER n person who deceives or plays tricks

TRICKSY adj playing tricks habitually

TRICKY adj difficult, needing careful handling

TRICLAD n type of worm having a tripartite intestine

TRICLADS > TRICLAD

TRICLINIA n plural of triclinium: in Ancient Rome, reclining couch

TRICLINIC adj relating to or belonging to the crystal system characterized by three unequal axes, no pair of which are perpendicular

TRICLOSAN n drug used to treat skin infections

TRICOLOR same as > TRICOLOUR

TRICOLORS > TRICOLOR

TRICOLOUR n three-coloured striped flag ▷ adj having or involving three colours

TRICORN n cocked hat with opposing brims turned back and caught in three places ▷ adj having three horns or corners

TRICORNE same as > TRICORN

TRICORNES > TRICORNE

TRICORNS > TRICORN

TRICOT n thin rayon or nylon fabric knitted or resembling knitting, used for dresses, etc

TRICOTINE n twill-weave woollen fabric resembling gabardine

TRICOTS > TRICOT

TRICROTIC adj (of the pulse) having a tracing characterized by three elevations with each beat

TRICTRAC n game similar to backgammon

TRICTRACS > TRICTRAC

TRICUSPID adj having three points, cusps, or segments ▷ n tooth having three cusps

TRICYCLE n three-wheeled cycle ▷ vb ride a tricycle

TRICYCLED > TRICYCLE

TRICYCLER > TRICYCLE

TRICYCLES > TRICYCLE

TRICYCLIC adj (of a chemical compound) containing three rings in the molecular structure ▷ n antidepressant drug having a tricyclic molecular structure

TRIDACNA n giant clam

TRIDACNAS > TRIDACNA

TRIDACTYL adj having three digits on one hand or foot

TRIDARN n sideboard with three levels

TRIDARNS > TRIDARN

TRIDE old spelling of the past tense of > TRY

TRIDENT n three-pronged spear ▷ adj having three prongs

TRIDENTAL adj having three prongs, teeth, etc

TRIDENTED adj having three prongs

TRIDENTS > TRIDENT

TRIDUAN adj three days long

TRIDUUM n period of three days for prayer before a feast

TRIDUUMS > TRIDUUM

TRIDYMITE n form of silica

TRIE old spelling of > TRY

TRIECIOUS adj (of a plant) having male, female, and hermaphroditic flowers

TRIED > TRY

TRIELLA n bet on the winners of three nominated horse races

TRIELLAS > TRIELLA

TRIENE n chemical compound containing three double bonds

TRIENES > TRIENE

TRIENNIA > TRIENNIUM

TRIENNIAL adj happening every three years ▷ n event occurring every three years

TRIENNIUM n period or cycle of three years

TRIENS n Byzantine gold coin worth one third of a solidus

TRIENTES > TRIENS

TRIER n person or thing that tries

TRIERARCH n citizen responsible for fitting out a state trireme, esp in Athens

TRIERS > TRIER

TRIES > TRY

TRIETERIC adj occurring once every two years

TRIETHYL adj consisting of three groups of ethyls

TRIFACIAL adj relating to the trigeminal nerve

TRIFECTA n form of betting in which the punter selects the first three place-winners in a horse race in the correct order

TRIFECTAS > TRIFECTA

TRIFF adj terrific; very good indeed

TRIFFER > TRIFF

TRIFFEST > TRIFF

TRIFFIC adj terrific; very good indeed

TRIFFID n fictional plant that could kill humans

TRIFFIDS > TRIFFID

TRIFFIDY adj resembling a triffid

TRIFID adj divided or split into three parts or lobes

TRIFLE n insignificant thing or amount ▷ vb deal (with) as if worthless

TRIFLED > TRIFLE

TRIFLER > TRIFLE

TRIFLERS > TRIFLE

TRIFLES > TRIFLE

TRIFLING adj insignificant

TRIFLINGS > TRIFLE

TRIFOCAL adj having three focuses

TRIFOCALS pl n glasses that have trifocal lenses

TRIFOLD less common word for > TRIPLE

TRIFOLIA > TRIFOLIUM

TRIFOLIES > TRIFOLY

TRIFOLIUM n leguminous plant with leaves divided into three leaflets and dense heads of small white, yellow, red, or purple flowers

TRIFOLY same as > TREFOIL

TRIFORIA > TRIFORIUM

TRIFORIAL > TRIFORIUM

TRIFORIUM n arcade above the arches of the nave, choir, or transept of a church

TRIFORM adj having three parts

TRIFORMED same as > TRIFORM

TRIG adj neat or spruce ▷ vb make or become spruce

TRIGAMIES > TRIGAMY

TRIGAMIST > TRIGAMY

TRIGAMOUS > TRIGAMY

TRIGAMY n condition of having three spouses

TRIGEMINI pl n facial nerves

TRIGGED > TRIG

TRIGGER n small lever releasing a catch on a gun or machine ▷ vb set (an action or process) in motion

TRIGGERED > TRIGGER

TRIGGERS > TRIGGER

TRIGGEST > TRIG

TRIGGING > TRIG

TRIGLOT n person who can speak three languages

TRIGLOTS > TRIGLOT

TRIGLY > TRIG

TRIGLYPH n stone block in a Doric frieze, having three vertical channels

TRIGLYPHS > TRIGLYPH

TRIGNESS > TRIG

TRIGO n wheat field

TRIGON n (in classical Greece or Rome) a triangular harp or lyre

TRIGONAL adj triangular

TRIGONIC > TRIGON

TRIGONOUS adj (of stems, seeds, and similar parts) having a triangular cross section

TRIGONS > TRIGON

TRIGOS > TRIGO

TRIGRAM n three-letter inscription

TRIGRAMS > TRIGRAM

TRIGRAPH n combination of three letters used to represent a single speech sound

TRIGRAPHS > TRIGRAPH

TRIGS > TRIG

TRIGYNIAN adj relating to the Trigynia order of plants

TRIGYNOUS adj (of a plant) having three pistils

TRIHEDRA > TRIHEDRON

TRIHEDRAL *adj* having or formed by three plane faces meeting at a point ▷ *n* figure formed by the intersection of three lines in different planes

TRIHEDRON *n* figure determined by the intersection of three planes

TRIHYBRID *n* hybrid that differs from its parents in three genetic traits

TRIHYDRIC *adj* (of an alcohol or similar compound) containing three hydroxyl groups

TRIJET *n* jet with three engines

TRIJETS > TRIJET

TRIJUGATE *adj* in three pairs

TRIJUGOUS *same as* > TRIJUGATE

TRIKE *n* tricycle

TRIKES > TRIKE

TRILBIED *adj* wearing a trilby

TRILBIES > TRILBY

TRILBY *n* soft felt hat

TRILBYS > TRILBY

TRILD *old past tense of* > TRILL

TRILEMMA *n* quandary posed by three alternative courses of action

TRILEMMAS > TRILEMMA

TRILINEAR *adj* consisting of, bounded by, or relating to three lines

TRILITH *same as* > TRILITHON

TRILITHIC > TRILITHON

TRILITHON *n* structure consisting of two upright stones with a third placed across the top, such as those of Stonehenge

TRILITHS > TRILITH

TRILL *n* rapid alternation between two notes ▷ *vb* play or sing a trill

TRILLED > TRILL

TRILLER > TRILL

TRILLERS > TRILL

TRILLING > TRILL

TRILLINGS > TRILL

TRILLION *n* one million million ▷ *adj* amounting to a trillion

TRILLIONS > TRILLION

TRILLIUM *n* plant of Asia and North America

TRILLIUMS > TRILLIUM

TRILLO *n* (in music) a trill

TRILLOES > TRILLO

TRILLS > TRILL

TRILOBAL > TRILOBE

TRILOBATE *adj* (esp of a leaf) consisting of or having three lobes or parts

TRILOBE *n* three-lobed thing

TRILOBED *adj* having three lobes

TRILOBES > TRILOBE

TRILOBITE *n* small prehistoric sea animal

TRILOGIES > TRILOGY

TRILOGY *n* series of three related books, plays, etc

TRIM *adj* neat and smart ▷ *vb* cut or prune into good shape ▷ *n* decoration

TRIMARAN *n* three-hulled boat

TRIMARANS > TRIMARAN

TRIMER *n* polymer or a molecule of a polymer consisting of three identical monomers

TRIMERIC > TRIMER

TRIMERISM > TRIMER

TRIMEROUS *adj* (of plants) having parts arranged in groups of three

TRIMERS > TRIMER

TRIMESTER *n* period of three months

TRIMETER *n* verse line consisting of three metrical feet ▷ *adj* designating such a line

TRIMETERS > TRIMETER

TRIMETHYL *adj* having three methyl groups

TRIMETRIC *adj* of, relating to, or consisting of a trimeter or trimeters

TRIMIX *n* gas mixture of nitrogen, helium and oxygen used by deep-sea divers

TRIMIXES > TRIMIX

TRIMLY > TRIM

TRIMMED > TRIM

TRIMMER > TRIM

TRIMMERS > TRIM

TRIMMEST > TRIM

TRIMMING > TRIM

TRIMMINGS > TRIM

TRIMNESS > TRIM

TRIMORPH *n* substance, esp a mineral, that exists in three distinct forms

TRIMORPHS > TRIMORPH

TRIMOTOR *n* vehicle with three motors

TRIMOTORS > TRIMOTOR

TRIMPHONE *n* type of phone designed in the 1960s

TRIMPOT *n* small instrument for adjusting resistance or voltage

TRIMPOTS > TRIMPOT

TRIMS > TRIM

TRIMTAB *n* small control surface to enable the pilot to balance an aircraft

TRIMTABS > TRIMTAB

TRIN *n* triplet

TRINAL > TRINE

TRINARY *adj* made up of three parts

TRINDLE *vb* move heavily on (or as if on) wheels

TRINDLED > TRINDLE

TRINDLES > TRINDLE

TRINDLING > TRINDLE

TRINE *n* aspect of 120° between two planets, an orb of 8° being allowed ▷ *adj* of or relating to a trine ▷ *vb* put in a trine aspect

TRINED > TRINE

TRINES > TRINE

TRINGLE *n* slim rod

TRINGLES > TRINGLE

TRINING > TRINE

TRINITIES > TRINITY

TRINITRIN *n* pale yellow viscous explosive liquid substance made from glycerol and nitric and sulphuric acids

TRINITY *n* group of three

TRINKET *n* small or worthless ornament or piece of jewellery ▷ *vb* ornament with trinkets

TRINKETED > TRINKET

TRINKETER > TRINKET

TRINKETRY > TRINKET

TRINKETS > TRINKET

TRINKUM *n* trinket or bauble

TRINKUMS > TRINKUM

TRINODAL *adj* having three nodes

TRINOMIAL *adj* consisting of or relating to three terms ▷ *n* polynomial consisting of three terms

TRINS > TRIN

TRIO *n* group of three

TRIODE *n* electronic valve having three electrodes, a cathode, an anode, and a grid

TRIODES > TRIODE

TRIOL *n* any of a class of alcohols that have three hydroxyl groups per molecule

TRIOLEIN *n* naturally occurring glyceride of oleic acid, found in fats and oils

TRIOLEINS > TRIOLEIN

TRIOLET *n* verse form of eight lines

TRIOLETS > TRIOLET

TRIOLS > TRIOL

TRIONES *pl n* seven stars of the constellation Ursa Major

TRIONYM *another name for* > TRINOMIAL

TRIONYMAL > TRIONYM

TRIONYMS > TRIONYM

TRIOR *old form of* > TRIER

TRIORS > TRIOR

TRIOS > TRIO

TRIOSE *n* simple monosaccharide produced by the oxidation of glycerol

TRIOSES > TRIOSE

TRIOXID *same as* > TRIOXIDE

TRIOXIDE *n* any oxide that contains three oxygen atoms per molecule

TRIOXIDES > TRIOXIDE

TRIOXIDS > TRIOXID

TRIOXYGEN *technical name for* > OXYGEN

TRIP *n* journey to a place and back, esp for pleasure ▷ *vb* (cause to) stumble

TRIPACK *n* pack of three

TRIPACKS > TRIPACK

TRIPART *adj* composed of three parts

TRIPE *n* stomach of a cow used as food

TRIPEDAL *adj* having three feet

TRIPERIES > TRIPERY

TRIPERY *n* place where tripe is prepared

TRIPES > TRIPE

TRIPEY > TRIPE

TRIPHASE *adj* having three phases

TRIPHONE *n* group of three phonemes

TRIPHONES > TRIPHONE

TRIPIER > TRIPE

TRIPIEST > TRIPE

TRIPITAKA *n* three collections of books making up the Buddhist canon of scriptures

TRIPLANE *n* aeroplane having three wings arranged one above the other

TRIPLANES > TRIPLANE

TRIPLE *adj* having three parts ▷ *vb* increase three times ▷ *n* something that is, or contains, three times as much as normal

TRIPLED > TRIPLE

TRIPLES > TRIPLE

TRIPLET *n* one of three babies born at one birth

TRIPLETS > TRIPLET

TRIPLEX *n* building divided into three separate dwellings ▷ *vb* separate into three parts

TRIPLEXED > TRIPLEX

TRIPLEXES > TRIPLEX

TRIPLIED > TRIPLY

TRIPLIES > TRIPLY

TRIPLING > TRIPLE

TRIPLINGS > TRIPLE

TRIPLITE *n* brownish-red phosphate

TRIPLITES > TRIPLITE

TRIPLOID *adj* having or relating to three times the haploid number of chromosomes ▷ *n* triploid organism

TRIPLOIDS > TRIPLOID

TRIPLOIDY *n* triploid state

TRIPLY *vb* give a reply to a duply

TRIPLYING > TRIPLY

TRIPMAN *n* man working on a trip

TRIPMEN > TRIPMAN

TRIPMETER *n* vehicle instrument displaying the distance travelled on a trip

TRIPOD *n* three-legged stand, stool, etc

TRIPODAL > TRIPOD

TRIPODIC > TRIPOD

TRIPODIES > TRIPODY

TRIPODS > TRIPOD

TRIPODY *n* metrical unit consisting of three feet

TRIPOLI *n* lightweight porous siliceous rock

TRIPOLIS > TRIPOLI

TRIPOS *n* final examinations for an honours degree at Cambridge University

TRIPOSES > TRIPOS

TRIPPANT *adj* (in heraldry) in the process of tripping

TRIPPED > TRIP

TRIPPER *n* tourist

TRIPPERS > TRIPPER

TRIPPERY *adj* like a tripper

TRIPPET n any mechanism that strikes or is struck at regular intervals, as by a cam

TRIPPETS > TRIPPET

TRIPPIER > TRIPPY

TRIPPIEST > TRIPPY

TRIPPING > TRIP

TRIPPINGS > TRIP

TRIPPLE vb canter

TRIPPLED > TRIPPLE

TRIPPLER > TRIPPLE

TRIPPLERS > TRIPPLE

TRIPPLES > TRIPPLE

TRIPPLING > TRIPPLE

TRIPPY adj suggestive of or resembling the effect produced by a hallucinogenic drug

TRIPS > TRIP

TRIPSES > TRIPSIS

TRIPSIS n act of kneading the body to promote circulation, suppleness, etc

TRIPTAN n drug used to treat migraine

TRIPTANE n colourless highly flammable liquid

TRIPTANES > TRIPTANE

TRIPTANS > TRIPTAN

TRIPTOTE n word that has only three cases

TRIPTOTES > TRIPTOTE

TRIPTYCA variant of > TRIPTYCH

TRIPTYCAS > TRIPTYCA

TRIPTYCH n painting or carving on three hinged panels, often forming an altarpiece

TRIPTYCHS > TRIPTYCH

TRIPTYQUE n customs permit for the temporary importation of a motor vehicle

TRIPUDIA > TRIPUDIUM

TRIPUDIUM n ancient religious dance

TRIPWIRE n wire that activates a trap, mine, etc, when tripped over

TRIPWIRES > TRIPWIRE

TRIPY > TRIPE

TRIQUETRA n ornament in the shape of three intersecting ellipses roughly forming a triangle

TRIRADIAL adj having or consisting of three rays or radiating branches

TRIREME n ancient Greek warship with three rows of oars on each side

TRIREMES > TRIREME

TRISAGION n old hymn

TRISCELE variant spelling of > TRISKELE

TRISCELES > TRISCELE

TRISECT vb divide into three parts, esp three equal parts

TRISECTED > TRISECT

TRISECTOR > TRISECT

TRISECTS > TRISECT

TRISEME n metrical foot of a length equal to three short syllables

TRISEMES > TRISEME

TRISEMIC > TRISEME

TRISERIAL adj arranged in three rows or series

TRISHAW another name for > RICKSHAW

TRISHAWS > TRISHAW

TRISKELE n three-limbed symbol

TRISKELES > TRISKELE

TRISKELIA n plural of singular triskelion: three-limbed symbol

TRISMIC > TRISMUS

TRISMUS n state of being unable to open the mouth

TRISMUSES > TRISMUS

TRISODIUM adj containing three sodium atoms

TRISOME n chromosome occurring three times (rather than twice) in a cell

TRISOMES > TRISOME

TRISOMIC > TRISOMY

TRISOMICS n study of trisomy

TRISOMIES > TRISOMY

TRISOMY n condition of having one chromosome represented three times

TRIST variant spelling of > TRISTE

TRISTATE adj (of a digital computer chip) having high, low, and floating output states

TRISTE adj sad

TRISTESSE n sadness

TRISTEZA n disease affecting citrus trees

TRISTEZAS > TRISTEZA

TRISTFUL same as > TRISTE

TRISTICH n poem, stanza, or strophe that consists of three lines

TRISTICHS > TRISTICH

TRISUL n trident symbol of Siva

TRISULA same as > TRISUL

TRISULAS > TRISULA

TRISULS > TRISUL

TRITANOPE n person who cannot distinguish the colour blue

TRITE adj (of a remark or idea) commonplace and unoriginal ▷ n (on a lyre) the third string from the highest in pitch

TRITELY > TRITE

TRITENESS > TRITE

TRITER > TRITE

TRITES > TRITE

TRITEST > TRITE

TRITHEISM n belief in three gods, esp in the Trinity as consisting of three distinct gods

TRITHEIST > TRITHEISM

TRITHING n tripartition

TRITHINGS > TRITHING

TRITIATE vb replace normal hydrogen atoms in (a compound) by those of tritium

TRITIATED > TRITIATE

TRITIATES > TRITIATE

TRITICAL n trite; hackneyed

TRITICALE n fertile hybrid cereal

TRITICISM n something trite

TRITICUM n type of cereal grass of the genus which includes the wheats

TRITICUMS > TRITICUM

TRITIDE n tritium compound

TRITIDES > TRITIDE

TRITIUM n radioactive isotope of hydrogen

TRITIUMS > TRITIUM

TRITOMA another name for > KNIPHOFIA

TRITOMAS > TRITOMA

TRITON n any of various chiefly tropical marine gastropod molluscs

TRITONE n musical interval consisting of three whole tones

TRITONES > TRITONE

TRITONIA n type of plant with typically scarlet or orange flowers

TRITONIAS > TRITONIA

TRITONS > TRITON

TRITURATE vb grind or rub into a fine powder or pulp ▷ n powder or pulp resulting from this grinding

TRIUMPH n (happiness caused by) victory or success ▷ vb be victorious or successful

TRIUMPHAL adj celebrating a triumph

TRIUMPHED > TRIUMPH

TRIUMPHER > TRIUMPH

TRIUMPHS > TRIUMPH

TRIUMVIR n (esp in ancient Rome) a member of a triumvirate

TRIUMVIRI > TRIUMVIR

TRIUMVIRS > TRIUMVIR

TRIUMVIRY n triumvirate

TRIUNE adj constituting three things in one ▷ n group of three

TRIUNES > TRIUNE

TRIUNITY > TRIUNE

TRIVALENT adj having a valency of three

TRIVALVE n animal having three valves

TRIVALVED adj having three valves

TRIVALVES > TRIVALVE

TRIVET n metal stand for a pot or kettle

TRIVETS > TRIVET

TRIVIA pl n trivial things or details

TRIVIAL adj of little importance

TRIVIALLY > TRIVIAL

TRIVIUM n (in medieval learning) the lower division of the seven liberal arts

TRIVIUMS > TRIVIUM

TRIWEEKLY adv every three weeks ▷ n triweekly publication

TRIZONAL > TRIZONE

TRIZONE n area comprising three zones

TRIZONES > TRIZONE

TROAD same as > TROD

TROADE same as > TROD

TROADES > TROADE

TROADS > TROAD

TROAK old form of > TRUCK

TROAKED > TROAK

TROAKING > TROAK

TROAKS > TROAK

TROAT vb (of a rutting buck) to call or bellow

TROATED > TROAT

TROATING > TROAT

TROATS > TROAT

TROCAR n surgical instrument for removing fluid from bodily cavities

TROCARS > TROCAR

TROCHAIC adj of, relating to, or consisting of trochees ▷ n verse composed of trochees

TROCHAICS > TROCHAIC

TROCHAL adj shaped like a wheel

TROCHAR old variant spelling of > TROCAR

TROCHARS > TROCHAR

TROCHE another name for > LOZENGE

TROCHEE n metrical foot of one long and one short syllable

TROCHEES > TROCHEE

TROCHES > TROCHE

TROCHI > TROCHUS

TROCHIL same as > TROCHILUS

TROCHILI > TROCHILUS

TROCHILIC adj relating to the movement of a hummingbird's wings

TROCHILS > TROCHIL

TROCHILUS n any of several Old World warblers

TROCHISCI n plural of trochiscus, a kind of lozenge

TROCHISK another word for > TROCHE

TROCHISKS > TROCHISK

TROCHITE n joint of a crinoid

TROCHITES > TROCHITE

TROCHLEA n any bony or cartilaginous part with a grooved surface

TROCHLEAE > TROCHLEA

TROCHLEAR n as in trochlear nerve either one of the fourth pair of cranial nerves, which supply the superior oblique muscle of the eye

TROCHLEAS > TROCHLEA

TROCHOID n curve described by a fixed point on the radius or extended radius of a circle as the circle rolls along a straight line ▷ adj rotating about a central axis

TROCHOIDS > TROCHOID

TROCHUS n hoop (used in exercise)

TROCHUSES > TROCHUS

TROCK same as > TRUCK

TROCKED > TROCK

TROCKEN adj dry (used of wine)

TROCKING > TROCK

TROCKS > TROCK

TROD vb past participle of tread ▷ n path

TRODDEN > TREAD

TRODE same as > TROD

TRODES > TRODE

TRODS > TROD

TROELIE same as > TROOLIE

TROELIES > TROELIE

TROELY same as > TROOLIE

TROFFER n fixture for holding and reflecting light from a fluorescent tube

TROFFERS > TROFFER

TROG vb walk, esp aimlessly or heavily

TROGGED > TROG

TROGGING > TROG

TROGGS n loyalty; fidelity

TROGON n bird of tropical and subtropical America, Africa, and Asia

TROGONS > TROGON

TROGS > TROG

TROIKA n Russian vehicle drawn by three horses abreast

TROIKAS > TROIKA

TROILISM n sexual activity involving three people

TROILISMS > TROILISM

TROILIST > TROILISM

TROILISTS > TROILISM

TROILITE n iron sulphide present in most meteorites

TROILITES > TROILITE

TROILUS n type of large butterfly

TROILUSES > TROILUS

TROIS Scots form of > TROY

TROJAN n bug inserted into a computer program

TROJANS > TROJAN

TROKE same as > TRUCK

TROKED > TROKE

TROKES > TROKE

TROKING > TROKE

TROLAND n unit of light intensity in the eye

TROLANDS > TROLAND

TROLL n giant or dwarf in Scandinavian folklore ▷ vb fish by dragging a lure through the water

TROLLED > TROLL

TROLLER > TROLL

TROLLERS > TROLL

TROLLEY n small wheeled table for food and drink ▷ vb transport on a trolley

TROLLEYED > TROLLEY

TROLLEYS pl n men's underpants

TROLLIED > TROLLY

TROLLIES > TROLLY

TROLLING > TROLL

TROLLINGS > TROLL

TROLLISH adj like a troll

TROLLIUS n plant with globe-shaped flowers

TROLLOP n promiscuous or slovenly woman ▷ vb behave like a trollop

TROLLOPED > TROLLOP

TROLLOPEE n loose dress or gown

TROLLOPS > TROLLOP

TROLLOPY adj like a trollop

TROLLS > TROLL

TROLLY same as > TROLLEY

TROLLYING > TROLLY

TROMBONE n brass musical instrument with a sliding tube

TROMBONES > TROMBONE

TROMINO n shape made from three squares, each joined to the next along one full side

TROMINOES > TROMINO

TROMINOS > TROMINO

TROMMEL n revolving cylindrical sieve used to screen crushed ore

TROMMELS > TROMMEL

TROMP vb trample

TROMPE n apparatus for supplying the blast of air in a forge

TROMPED > TROMP

TROMPES > TROMPE

TROMPING > TROMP

TROMPS > TROMP

TRON n public weighing machine

TRONA n greyish mineral that occurs in salt deposits

TRONAS > TRONA

TRONC n pool into which waiters, waitresses, hotel workers, etc, pay their tips

TRONCS > TRONC

TRONE same as > TRON

TRONES > TRONE

TRONK n jail

TRONKS > TRONK

TRONS > TRON

TROOLIE n large palm leaf

TROOLIES > TROOLIE

TROOP n large group ▷ vb move in a crowd

TROOPED > TROOP

TROOPER n cavalry soldier

TROOPERS > TROOPER

TROOPIAL same as > TROUPIAL

TROOPIALS > TROOPIAL

TROOPING > TROOP

TROOPS > TROOP

TROOPSHIP n ship used to transport military personnel

TROOSTITE n reddish or greyish mineral that is a variety of willemite in which some of the zinc is replaced by manganese

TROOZ same as > TREWS

TROP adv too, too much

TROPAEOLA n plural of singular tropaeolum (a garden plant)

TROPARIA > TROPARION

TROPARION n short hymn

TROPE n figure of speech ▷ vb use tropes

TROPED > TROPE

TROPEOLIN n type of dye

TROPES > TROPE

TROPHESY n disorder of the nerves relating to nutrition

TROPHI pl n collective term for the mandibles and other parts of an insect's mouth

TROPHIC adj of or relating to nutrition

TROPHIED > TROPHY

TROPHIES > TROPHY

TROPHY n cup, shield, etc given as a prize ▷ adj regraded as a highly desirable symbol of wealth or success ▷ vb award a trophy to (someone)

TROPHYING > TROPHY

TROPIC n either of two lines of latitude at 23½°N or 23½°S

TROPICAL adj of or in the tropics ▷ n tropical thing or place

TROPICALS > TROPICAL

TROPICS > TROPIC

TROPIN n adrenal androgen

TROPINE n white crystalline poisonous alkaloid

TROPINES > TROPINE

TROPING > TROPE

TROPINS > TROPIN

TROPISM n tendency of a plant or animal to turn in response to an external stimulus

TROPISMS > TROPISM

TROPIST > TROPISM

TROPISTIC > TROPISM

TROPISTS > TROPISM

TROPOLOGY n use of figurative language in speech or writing

TROPONIN n muscle-tissue protein involved in the controlling of muscle contraction

TROPONINS > TROPONIN

TROPPO adv too much ▷ adj mentally affected by a tropical climate

TROSSERS old form of > TROUSERS

TROT vb (of a horse) move at a medium pace, lifting the feet in diagonal pairs ▷ n act of trotting

TROTH n pledge of devotion, esp a betrothal ▷ vb promise to marry (someone)

TROTHED > TROTH

TROTHFUL > TROTH

TROTHING > TROTH

TROTHLESS > TROTH

TROTHS > TROTH

TROTLINE n line suspended across a stream to which shorter hooked and baited lines are attached

TROTLINES > TROTLINE

TROTS > TROT

TROTTED > TROT

TROTTER n pig's foot

TROTTERS > TROTTER

TROTTING > TROT

TROTTINGS > TROT

TROTTOIR n pavement

TROTTOIRS > TROTTOIR

TROTYL n yellow solid used chiefly as a high explosive

TROTYLS > TROTYL

TROU pl n trousers

TROUBLE n (cause of) distress or anxiety ▷ vb (cause to) worry

TROUBLED > TROUBLE

TROUBLER > TROUBLE

TROUBLERS > TROUBLE

TROUBLES > TROUBLE

TROUBLING > TROUBLE

TROUBLOUS adj unsettled or agitated

TROUCH n rubbish

TROUCHES > TROUCH

TROUGH n long open container, esp for animals' food or water ▷ vb eat, consume, or take greedily

TROUGHED > TROUGH

TROUGHING n as in troughing and peaking reaching the lowest and highest levels in a range

TROUGHS > TROUGH

TROULE old variant of > TROLL

TROULED > TROULE

TROULES > TROULE

TROULING > TROULE

TROUNCE vb defeat utterly

TROUNCED > TROUNCE

TROUNCER > TROUNCE

TROUNCERS > TROUNCE

TROUNCES > TROUNCE

TROUNCING > TROUNCE

TROUPE n company of performers ▷ vb (esp of actors) to move or travel in a group

TROUPED > TROUPE

TROUPER n member of a troupe

TROUPERS > TROUPER

TROUPES > TROUPE

TROUPIAL n any of various American orioles

TROUPIALS > TROUPIAL

TROUPING > TROUPE

TROUSE pl n close-fitting breeches worn in Ireland

TROUSER vb take (something, esp money), often surreptitiously or unlawfully

TROUSERED > TROUSERS

TROUSERS pl n two-legged outer garment with legs reaching usu to the ankles

TROUSES > TROUSE

TROUSSEAU n bride's collection of clothing etc for her marriage

TROUT n game fish related to the salmon ▷ vb fish for trout

TROUTER > TROUT

TROUTERS > TROUT

TROUTFUL adj (of a body of water) full of trout

TROUTIER > TROUT

TROUTIEST > TROUT

TROUTING > TROUT

TROUTINGS > TROUT

TROUTLESS > TROUT

TROUTLET n small trout

TROUTLETS > TROUTLET

TROUTLIKE adj like a trout

TROUTLING n small trout

TROUTS > TROUT

TROUTY > TROUT

TROUVERE n poet of N France during the 12th and 13th centuries

TROUVERES > TROUVERE

t

SECTION 1: Words between 2 and 9 letters in length

TROUVEUR *same as* > TROUVERE

TROUVEURS > TROUVEUR

TROVE *n* as in *treasure-trove* valuable articles found hidden in the earth

TROVER *n* act of assuming proprietary rights over goods or property belonging to another

TROVERS > TROVER

TROVES > TROVE

TROW *vb* think, believe, or trust

TROWED > TROW

TROWEL *n* hand tool with a wide blade ▷ *vb* use a trowel on (plaster, soil, etc)

TROWELED > TROWEL

TROWELER > TROWEL

TROWELERS > TROWEL

TROWELING > TROWEL

TROWELLED > TROWEL

TROWELLER > TROWEL

TROWELS > TROWEL

TROWING > TROW

TROWS > TROW

TROWSERS *old spelling of* > TROUSERS

TROWTH *variant spelling of* > TROTH

TROWTHS > TROWTH

TROY *n* system of weights used for precious metals and gemstones

TROYS > TROY

TRUANCIES > TRUANT

TRUANCY > TRUANT

TRUANT *n* pupil who stays away from school without permission ▷ *adj* being or relating to a truant ▷ *vb* play truant

TRUANTED > TRUANT

TRUANTING *n* act of playing truant

TRUANTLY > TRUANT

TRUANTRY > TRUANT

TRUANTS > TRUANT

TRUCAGE *n* art forgery

TRUCAGES > TRUCAGE

TRUCE *n* temporary agreement to stop fighting ▷ *vb* make a truce

TRUCED > TRUCE

TRUCELESS > TRUCE

TRUCES > TRUCE

TRUCHMAN *n* interpreter; translator

TRUCHMANS > TRUCHMAN

TRUCHMEN > TRUCHMAN

TRUCIAL > TRUCE

TRUCING > TRUCE

TRUCK *n* railway goods wagon ▷ *vb* exchange (goods); barter

TRUCKABLE > TRUCK

TRUCKAGE *n* conveyance of cargo by truck

TRUCKAGES > TRUCKAGE

TRUCKED > TRUCK

TRUCKER *n* truck driver

TRUCKERS > TRUCKER

TRUCKFUL *n* amount of something that can be conveyed in a truck

TRUCKFULS > TRUCKFUL

TRUCKIE *n* truck driver

TRUCKIES > TRUCKIE

TRUCKING *n* transportation of goods by lorry

TRUCKINGS > TRUCKING

TRUCKLE *vb* yield weakly or give in ▷ *n* small wheel

TRUCKLED > TRUCKLE

TRUCKLER > TRUCKLE

TRUCKLERS > TRUCKLE

TRUCKLES > TRUCKLE

TRUCKLINE *n* organisation that conveys freight by truck

TRUCKLING > TRUCKLE

TRUCKLOAD *n* amount carried by a truck

TRUCKMAN *n* truck driver

TRUCKMEN > TRUCKMAN

TRUCKS > TRUCK

TRUCKSTOP *n* place providing fuel, oil, and often service facilities for truck drivers

TRUCULENT *adj* aggressively defiant

TRUDGE *vb* walk heavily or wearily ▷ *n* long tiring walk

TRUDGED > TRUDGE

TRUDGEN *n* type of swimming stroke

TRUDGENS > TRUDGEN

TRUDGEON *nonstandard variant of* > TRUDGEN

TRUDGEONS > TRUDGEON

TRUDGER > TRUDGE

TRUDGERS > TRUDGE

TRUDGES > TRUDGE

TRUDGING > TRUDGE

TRUDGINGS > TRUDGE

TRUE *adj* in accordance with facts

TRUEBLUE *n* staunch royalist or Conservative

TRUEBLUES > TRUEBLUE

TRUEBORN *adj* being such by birth

TRUEBRED *adj* thoroughbred

TRUED > TRUE

TRUEING > TRUE

TRUELOVE *n* person that one loves

TRUELOVES > TRUELOVE

TRUEMAN *n* honest person

TRUEMEN > TRUEMAN

TRUENESS > TRUE

TRUEPENNY *n* truthful person

TRUER > TRUE

TRUES > TRUE

TRUEST > TRUE

TRUFFE *rare word for* > TRUFFLE

TRUFFES > TRUFFE

TRUFFLE *n* edible underground fungus ▷ *vb* hunt for truffles

TRUFFLED > TRUFFLE

TRUFFLES > TRUFFLE

TRUFFLING > TRUFFLE

TRUG *n* long shallow basket used by gardeners

TRUGO *n* game similar to croquet

TRUGOS > TRUGO

TRUGS > TRUG

TRUING > TRUE

TRUISM *n* self-evident truth

TRUISMS > TRUISM

TRUISTIC > TRUISM

TRULL *n* prostitute

TRULLS > TRULL

TRULY *adv* in a true manner

TRUMEAU *n* section of a wall or pillar between two openings

TRUMEAUX > TRUMEAU

TRUMP *adj* (in card games) of the suit outranking the others ▷ *vb* play a trump card on (another card)

TRUMPED > TRUMP

TRUMPERY *n* something useless or worthless ▷ *adj* useless or worthless

TRUMPET *n* valved brass instrument with a flared tube ▷ *vb* proclaim loudly

TRUMPETED > TRUMPET

TRUMPETER *n* person who plays the trumpet, esp one whose duty it is to play fanfares, signals, etc

TRUMPETS > TRUMPET

TRUMPING > TRUMP

TRUMPINGS > TRUMP

TRUMPLESS > TRUMP

TRUMPS > TRUMP

TRUNCAL *adj* of or relating to the trunk

TRUNCATE *vb* cut short ▷ *adj* cut short

TRUNCATED *adj* (of a cone, pyramid, prism, etc) having an apex or end removed by a plane intersection that is usually nonparallel to the base

TRUNCATES > TRUNCATE

TRUNCHEON *n* club formerly carried by a policeman ▷ *vb* beat with a truncheon

TRUNDLE *vb* move heavily on wheels ▷ *n* act or an instance of trundling

TRUNDLED > TRUNDLE

TRUNDLER *n* golf or shopping trolley

TRUNDLERS > TRUNDLER

TRUNDLES > TRUNDLE

TRUNDLING > TRUNDLE

TRUNK *n* main stem of a tree ▷ *vb* lop or truncate

TRUNKED > TRUNK

TRUNKFISH *n* tropical fish, having the body encased in bony plates with openings for the fins, eyes, mouth, etc

TRUNKFUL > TRUNK

TRUNKFULS > TRUNK

TRUNKING *n* cables that take a common route through an exchange building linking ranks of selectors

TRUNKINGS > TRUNKING

TRUNKLESS > TRUNK

TRUNKLIKE *adj* like a trunk

TRUNKS *pl n* shorts worn by a man for swimming

TRUNKWORK *n* clandestine action of visiting someone in a trunk

TRUNNEL *same as* > TREENAIL

TRUNNELS > TRUNNEL

TRUNNION *n* one of a pair of coaxial projections attached to opposite sides of a cannon

TRUNNIONS > TRUNNION

TRUQUAGE *variant of* > TRUCAGE

TRUQUAGES > TRUQUAGE

TRUQUEUR *n* art forger

TRUQUEURS > TRUQUEUR

TRUSS *vb* tie or bind up ▷ *n* device for holding a hernia, etc in place

TRUSSED > TRUSS

TRUSSER > TRUSS

TRUSSERS > TRUSS

TRUSSES > TRUSS

TRUSSING *n* system of trusses, esp for strengthening or reinforcing a structure

TRUSSINGS > TRUSSING

TRUST *vb* believe in and rely on ▷ *n* confidence in the truth, reliability, etc of a person or thing ▷ *adj* of or relating to a trust or trusts

TRUSTABLE > TRUST

TRUSTED > TRUST

TRUSTEE *n* person holding property on another's behalf ▷ *vb* act as a trustee

TRUSTEED > TRUSTEE

TRUSTEES > TRUSTEE

TRUSTER > TRUST

TRUSTERS > TRUST

TRUSTFUL *adj* inclined to trust others

TRUSTIER > TRUSTY

TRUSTIES > TRUSTY

TRUSTIEST > TRUSTY

TRUSTILY > TRUSTY

TRUSTING *same as* > TRUSTFUL

TRUSTLESS *adj* untrustworthy

TRUSTOR *n* person who sets up a trust

TRUSTORS > TRUSTOR

TRUSTS > TRUST

TRUSTY *adj* faithful or reliable ▷ *n* trustworthy convict to whom special privileges are granted

TRUTH *n* state of being true

TRUTHER *n* person who does not believe official accounts of the 9/11 attacks on the US

TRUTHERS > TRUTHER

TRUTHFUL *adj* honest

TRUTHIER > TRUTHY

TRUTHIEST > TRUTHY

TRUTHLESS > TRUTH

TRUTHLIKE *n* truthful

TRUTHS > TRUTH

TRUTHY *adj* truthful

TRY *vb* make an effort or attempt ▷ *n* attempt or effort

TRYE *adj* very good; select

TRYER *variant of* > TRIER

TRYERS > TRYER

TRYING > TRY

TRYINGLY > TRY

TRYINGS > TRY

TRYKE *variant spelling of* > TRIKE**

TRYKES > TRYKE

TRYMA n drupe produced by the walnut and similar plants

TRYMATA > TRYMA

TRYOUT n trial or test, as of an athlete or actor

TRYOUTS > TRYOUT

TRYP n parasitic protozoan

TRYPAN modifier as in trypan blue dye used for staining cells in biological research

TRYPS > TRYP

TRYPSIN n enzyme occurring in pancreatic juice

TRYPSINS > TRYPSIN

TRYPTIC > TRYPSIN

TRYSAIL n small fore-and-aft sail on a sailing vessel

TRYSAILS > TRYSAIL

TRYST n arrangement to meet ▷ vb meet at or arrange a tryst

TRYSTE variant spelling of > TRYST

TRYSTED > TRYST

TRYSTER > TRYST

TRYSTERS > TRYST

TRYSTES > TRYSTE

TRYSTING > TRYST

TRYSTS > TRYST

TRYWORKS n furnace for rendering blubber

TSADDIK variant of > ZADDIK

TSADDIKIM > TSADDIK

TSADDIKS > TSADDIK

TSADDIQ variant of > ZADDIK

TSADDIQIM > TSADDIQ

TSADDIQS > TSADDIQ

TSADE variant spelling of > SADHE

TSADES > TSADE

TSADI variant of > SADHE

TSADIK same as > ZADDIK

TSADIKS > TSADIK

TSADIS > TSADI

TSAMBA n Tibetan dish made from roasted barley and tea

TSAMBAS > TSAMBA

TSANTSA n shrunken head of an enemy kept as a trophy

TSANTSAS > TSANTSA

TSAR n Russian emperor

TSARDOM > TSAR

TSARDOMS > TSAR

TSAREVICH n tsar's son

TSAREVNA n daughter of a Russian tsar

TSAREVNAS > TSAREVNA

TSARINA n wife of a Russian tsar

TSARINAS > TSARINA

TSARISM n system of government by a tsar

TSARISMS > TSARISM

TSARIST > TSARISM

TSARISTS > TSARISM

TSARITSA same as > TSARINA

TSARITSAS > TSARITSA

TSARITZA variant spelling of > TSARITZA

TSARITZAS > TSARITZA

TSARS > TSAR

TSATSKE variant of > TCHOTCHKE

TSATSKES > TSATSKE

TSESSEBE South African variant of > SASSABY

TSESSEBES > TSESSEBE

TSETSE n any of various bloodsucking African flies

TSETSES > TSETSE

TSIGANE variant of > TZIGANE

TSIGANES > TSIGANE

TSIMMES variant spelling of > TZIMMES

TSITSITH n tassels or fringes of thread attached to the four corners of the tallith

TSK vb utter the sound "tsk", usu in disapproval

TSKED > TSK

TSKING > TSK

TSKS > TSK

TSKTSK same as > TSK

TSKTSKED > TSKTSK

TSKTSKING > TSKTSK

TSKTSKS > TSKTSK

TSOORIS variant of > TSURIS

TSORES variant of > TSURIS

TSORIS variant of > TSURIS

TSORRISS variant of > TSURIS

TSOTSI n (in South Africa) Black street thug or gang member

TSOTSIS > TSOTSI

TSOURIS variant of > TSURIS

TSOURISES > TSOURIS

TSUBA n sword guard of a Japanese sword

TSUBAS > TSUBA

TSUBO n unit of area

TSUBOS > TSUBO

TSUNAMI n tidal wave, usu caused by an earthquake under the sea

TSUNAMIC > TSUNAMI

TSUNAMIS > TSUNAMI

TSURIS n grief or strife

TSURISES > TSURIS

TSUTSUMU n Japanese art of wrapping gifts

TSUTSUMUS > TSUTSUMU

TUAN n lord

TUANS > TUAN

TUART n eucalyptus tree of Australia

TUARTS > TUART

TUATARA n large lizard-like New Zealand reptile

TUATARAS > TUATARA

TUATERA variant spelling of > TUATARA

TUATERAS > TUATERA

TUATH n territory of an ancient Irish tribe

TUATHS > TUATH

TUATUA n edible marine bivalve of New Zealand waters

TUATUAS > TUATUA

TUB n open, usu round container ▷ vb wash (oneself or another) in a tub

TUBA n valved low-pitched brass instrument

TUBAE > TUBA

TUBAGE n insertion of a tube

TUBAGES > TUBAGE

TUBAIST > TUBA

TUBAISTS > TUBA

TUBAL adj of or relating to a tube

TUBAR another word for > TUBULAR

TUBAS > TUBA

TUBATE less common word for > TUBULAR

TUBBABLE > TUB

TUBBED > TUB

TUBBER > TUB

TUBBERS > TUB

TUBBIER > TUBBY

TUBBIEST > TUBBY

TUBBINESS > TUBBY

TUBBING > TUB

TUBBINGS > TUB

TUBBISH adj fat

TUBBY adj (of a person) short and fat

TUBE n hollow cylinder

TUBECTOMY n excision of the Fallopian tubes

TUBED > TUBE

TUBEFUL n quantity (of something) that a tube can hold

TUBEFULS > TUBEFUL

TUBELESS adj without a tube

TUBELIKE adj resembling a tube

TUBENOSE n seabird with tubular nostrils on its beak

TUBENOSES > TUBENOSE

TUBER n fleshy underground root of a plant such as a potato

TUBERCLE n small rounded swelling

TUBERCLED adj having tubercles

TUBERCLES > TUBERCLE

TUBERCULA n plural of tuberculum (another name for "tubercle")

TUBERCULE variant of > TUBERCLE

TUBEROID adj resembling a tuber ▷ n fleshy root resembling a tuber

TUBEROIDS > TUBEROID

TUBEROSE same as > TUBEROUS

TUBEROSES > TUBEROSE

TUBEROUS adj (of plants) forming, bearing, or resembling a tuber or tubers

TUBERS > TUBER

TUBES > TUBE

TUBEWELL n type of water well

TUBEWELLS > TUBEWELL

TUBEWORK n collective term for tubes or tubing

TUBEWORKS > TUBEWORK

TUBEWORM n undersea worm

TUBEWORMS > TUBEWORM

TUBFAST n period of fasting and sweating in a tub, intended as a cure for disease

TUBFASTS > TUBFAST

TUBFISH another name for > GURNARD

TUBFISHES > TUBFISH

TUBFUL n amount a tub will hold

TUBFULS > TUBFUL

TUBICOLAR adj tube-dwelling

TUBICOLE n tube-dwelling creature

TUBICOLES > TUBICOLE

TUBIFEX n type of small reddish freshwater worm

TUBIFEXES > TUBIFEX

TUBIFICID n type of threadlike annelid worm

TUBIFORM same as > TUBULAR

TUBING n length of tube

TUBINGS > TUBING

TUBIST > TUBA

TUBISTS > TUBA

TUBLIKE > TUB

TUBS > TUB

TUBULAR adj of or shaped like a tube ▷ n type of tyre

TUBULARLY > TUBULAR

TUBULARS > TUBULAR

TUBULATE vb form or shape into a tube

TUBULATED > TUBULATE

TUBULATES > TUBULATE

TUBULATOR > TUBULATE

TUBULE n any small tubular structure

TUBULES > TUBULE

TUBULIN n protein forming the basis of microtubules

TUBULINS > TUBULIN

TUBULOSE adj tube-shaped; consisting of tubes

TUBULOUS adj tube-shaped

TUBULURE n tube leading into a retort or other receptacle

TUBULURES > TUBULURE

TUCHIS n buttocks

TUCHISES > TUCHIS

TUCHUN n (formerly) a Chinese military governor or warlord

TUCHUNS > TUCHUN

TUCHUS same as > TUCHIS

TUCHUSES > TUCHUS

TUCK vb push or fold into a small space ▷ n stitched fold

TUCKAHOE n type of edible root

TUCKAHOES > TUCKAHOE

TUCKAMORE n Newfoundland spruce tree bent by winds

TUCKBOX n box used for carrying food to school

TUCKBOXES > TUCKBOX

TUCKED > TUCK

TUCKER n food ▷ vb weary or tire completely

TUCKERBAG n in Australia, bag or box used for carrying food

TUCKERBOX same as > TUCKERBAG

TUCKERED > TUCKER

TUCKERING > TUCKER

TUCKERS > TUCKER

TUCKET n flourish on a trumpet

TUCKETS > TUCKET
TUCKING n act of tucking
TUCKINGS > TUCKING
TUCKS > TUCK
TUCKSHOP n shop, esp one in or near a school, where food such as cakes and sweets are sold
TUCKSHOPS > TUCKSHOP
TUCOTUCO n colonial burrowing South American rodent
TUCOTUCOS > TUCOTUCO
TUCUTUCO variant spelling of > TUCOTUCO
TUCUTUCOS > TUCUTUCO
TUCUTUCU same as > TUCOTUCO
TUCUTUCUS > TUCUTUCU
TUFA n porous rock formed as a deposit from springs
TUFACEOUS > TUFA
TUFAS > TUFA
TUFF n porous rock formed from volcanic dust or ash
TUFFE old form of > TUFT
TUFFES > TUFFE
TUFFET n small mound or seat
TUFFETS > TUFFET
TUFFS > TUFF
TUFOLI n type of tubular pasta
TUFOLIS > TUFOLI
TUFT n bunch of feathers, grass, hair, etc held or growing together at the base ▷ vb provide or decorate with a tuft or tufts
TUFTED adj having a tuft or tufts
TUFTER > TUFT
TUFTERS > TUFT
TUFTIER > TUFT
TUFTIEST > TUFT
TUFTILY > TUFT
TUFTING > TUFT
TUFTINGS > TUFT
TUFTS > TUFT
TUFTY > TUFT
TUG vb pull hard ▷ n hard pull
TUGBOAT same as > TUG
TUGBOATS > TUGBOAT
TUGGED > TUG
TUGGER > TUG
TUGGERS > TUG
TUGGING > TUG
TUGGINGLY > TUG
TUGGINGS > TUG
TUGHRA n Turkish Sultan's official emblem
TUGHRAS > TUGHRA
TUGHRIK same as > TUGRIK
TUGHRIKS > TUGHRIK
TUGLESS > TUG
TUGRA variant of > TUGHRA
TUGRAS > TUGRA
TUGRIK n standard monetary unit of Mongolia
TUGRIKS > TUGRIK
TUGS > TUG
TUI n New Zealand honeyeater that mimics human speech and the songs of other birds
TUILE n type of almond-flavoured dessert biscuit

TUILES > TUILE
TUILLE n (in a suit of armour) hanging plate protecting the thighs
TUILLES > TUILLE
TUILLETTE n little tuille
TUILYIE vb fight
TUILYIED > TUILYIE
TUILYIES > TUILYIE
TUILZIE variant form of > TUILYIE
TUILZIED > TUILZIE
TUILZIES > TUILZIE
TUINA n form of massage originating in China
TUINAS > TUINA
TUIS > TUI
TUISM n practice of putting the interests of another before one's own
TUISMS > TUISM
TUITION n instruction, esp received individually or in a small group
TUITIONAL > TUITION
TUITIONS > TUITION
TUKTOO same as > TUKTU
TUKTOOS > TUKTOO
TUKTU (in Canada) another name for > CARIBOU
TUKTUS > TUKTU
TULADI n large trout found in Canada and northern US
TULADIS > TULADI
TULAREMIA n infectious disease of rodents
TULAREMIC > TULAREMIA
TULBAN old form of > TURBAN
TULBANS > TULBAN
TULCHAN n skin of a calf placed next to a cow to induce it to give milk
TULCHANS > TULCHAN
TULE n type of bulrush found in California
TULES > TULE
TULIP n plant with bright cup-shaped flowers
TULIPANT n turban
TULIPANTS > TULIPANT
TULIPLIKE > TULIP
TULIPS > TULIP
TULIPWOOD n light soft wood of the tulip tree, used in making furniture and veneer
TULLE n fine net fabric of silk etc
TULLES > TULLE
TULLIBEE n cisco of the Great Lakes of Canada
TULLIBEES > TULLIBEE
TULPA n being or object created through willpower and visualization techniques
TULPAS > TULPA
TULSI n type of basil
TULSIS > TULSI
TULWAR n Indian sabre
TULWARS > TULWAR
TUM informal or childish word for > STOMACH
TUMBLE vb (cause to) fall, esp awkwardly or violently ▷ n fall
TUMBLEBUG n type of beetle
TUMBLED > TUMBLE

TUMBLER n stemless drinking glass
TUMBLERS > TUMBLER
TUMBLES > TUMBLE
TUMBLESET n somersault
TUMBLING > TUMBLE
TUMBLINGS > TUMBLING
TUMBREL n farm cart for carrying manure
TUMBRELS > TUMBREL
TUMBRIL same as > TUMBREL
TUMBRILS > TUMBRIL
TUMEFIED > TUMEFY
TUMEFIES > TUMEFY
TUMEFY vb make or become tumid
TUMEFYING > TUMEFY
TUMESCE vb swell
TUMESCED > TUMESCE
TUMESCENT adj swollen or becoming swollen
TUMESCES > TUMESCE
TUMESCING > TUMESCE
TUMID adj (of an organ or part of the body) enlarged or swollen
TUMIDITY > TUMID
TUMIDLY > TUMID
TUMIDNESS > TUMID
TUMMIES > TUMMY
TUMMLER n entertainer employed to encourage audience participation
TUMMLERS > TUMMLER
TUMMY n stomach
TUMOR same as > TUMOUR
TUMORAL > TUMOUR
TUMORLIKE > TUMOUR
TUMOROUS > TUMOUR
TUMORS > TUMOR
TUMOUR n abnormal growth in or on the body
TUMOURS > TUMOUR
TUMP n small mound or clump ▷ vb make a tump around
TUMPED > TUMP
TUMPHIES > TUMPHY
TUMPHY n dolt; fool
TUMPIER > TUMP
TUMPIEST > TUMP
TUMPING > TUMP
TUMPLINE n band strung across the forehead or chest and attached to a pack in order to support it
TUMPLINES > TUMPLINE
TUMPS > TUMP
TUMPY > TUMP
TUMS > TUM
TUMSHIE n turnip
TUMSHIES > TUMSHIE
TUMULAR adj of, relating to, or like a mound
TUMULARY same as > TUMULAR
TUMULI > TUMULUS
TUMULOSE adj abounding in small hills or mounds
TUMULOUS same as > TUMULOSE
TUMULT n uproar or commotion ▷ vb stir up a commotion
TUMULTED > TUMULT
TUMULTING > TUMULT

TUMULTS > TUMULT
TUMULUS n burial mound
TUMULUSES > TUMULUS
TUN n large beer cask ▷ vb put into or keep in tuns
TUNA n large marine food fish
TUNABLE adj able to be tuned
TUNABLY > TUNABLE
TUNAS > TUNA
TUNBELLY n large round belly
TUND vb beat; strike
TUNDED > TUND
TUNDING > TUND
TUNDISH n type of funnel
TUNDISHES > TUNDISH
TUNDRA n vast treeless Arctic region with permanently frozen subsoil
TUNDRAS > TUNDRA
TUNDS > TUND
TUNDUN n wooden instrument used by Australian Aborigines in religious rites
TUNDUNS > TUNDUN
TUNE n (pleasing) sequence of musical notes ▷ vb adjust (a musical instrument) so that it is in tune
TUNEABLE same as > TUNABLE
TUNEABLY > TUNEABLE
TUNEAGE n music
TUNEAGES > TUNEAGE
TUNED > TUNE
TUNEFUL adj having a pleasant tune
TUNEFULLY > TUNEFUL
TUNELESS adj having no melody or tune
TUNER n part of a radio or television receiver for selecting channels
TUNERS > TUNER
TUNES > TUNE
TUNESMITH n composer of light or popular music and songs
TUNEUP n adjustments made to an engine to improve its performance
TUNEUPS > TUNEUP
TUNG n fast-drying oil obtained from the seeds of a central Asian tree
TUNGS > TUNG
TUNGSTATE n salt of tungstic acid
TUNGSTEN n greyish-white metal
TUNGSTENS > TUNGSTEN
TUNGSTIC adj of or containing tungsten, esp in a high valence state
TUNGSTITE n yellow earthy rare secondary mineral that consists of tungsten oxide and occurs with tungsten ores
TUNGSTOUS adj of or containing tungsten in a low valence state
TUNIC n close-fitting jacket forming part of some uniforms

TUNICA *n* tissue forming a layer or covering of an organ or part

TUNICAE > TUNICA

TUNICATE *n* minute primitive marine chordate animal ▷ *adj* of, relating to this animal ▷ *vb* wear a tunic

TUNICATED > TUNICATE

TUNICATES > TUNICATE

TUNICIN *n* cellulose-like substance found in tunicates

TUNICINS > TUNICIN

TUNICKED *adj* wearing a tunic

TUNICLE *n* vestment worn at High Mass and other religious ceremonies

TUNICLES > TUNICLE

TUNICS > TUNIC

TUNIER *same as >* TUNY

TUNIEST > TUNY

TUNING *n* set of pitches to which the open strings of a guitar, violin, etc, are tuned

TUNINGS > TUNING

TUNKET *n* hell

TUNKETS > TUNKET

TUNNAGE *same as >* TONNAGE

TUNNAGES > TUNNAGE

TUNNED > TUN

TUNNEL *n* underground passage ▷ *vb* make a tunnel (through)

TUNNELED > TUNNEL

TUNNELER > TUNNEL

TUNNELERS > TUNNEL

TUNNELING > TUNNEL

TUNNELLED > TUNNEL

TUNNELLER > TUNNEL

TUNNELS > TUNNEL

TUNNIES > TUNNY

TUNNING > TUN

TUNNINGS > TUN

TUNNY *same as >* TUNA

TUNS > TUN

TUNY *adj* having an easily discernable melody

TUP *n* male sheep ▷ *vb* cause (a ram) to mate with a ewe

TUPEK *same as >* TUPIK

TUPEKS > TUPEK

TUPELO *n* large tree of deep swamps and rivers of the southern US

TUPELOS > TUPELO

TUPIK *n* tent of seal or caribou skin used for shelter by Inuit people in summer

TUPIKS > TUPIK

TUPLE *n* row of values in a relational database

TUPLES > TUPLE

TUPPED > TUP

TUPPENCE *same as >* TWOPENCE

TUPPENCES > TUPPENCE

TUPPENNY *same as >* TWOPENNY

TUPPING *n* act of sheep mating

TUPPINGS > TUPPING

TUPS > TUP

TUPTOWING *n* study of Greek grammar

TUPUNA *same as >* TIPUNA

TUPUNAS > TUPUNA

TUQUE *n* knitted cap with a long tapering end

TUQUES > TUQUE

TURACIN *n* red pigment found in touraco feathers

TURACINS > TURACIN

TURACO *same as >* TOURACO

TURACOS > TURACO

TURACOU *variant of >* TOURACO

TURACOUS > TURACOU

TURBAN *n* Muslim, Hindu, or Sikh man's head covering

TURBAND *old variant of >* TURBAN

TURBANDS > TURBAND

TURBANED > TURBAN

TURBANNED > TURBAN

TURBANS > TURBAN

TURBANT *old variant of >* TURBAN

TURBANTS > TURBANT

TURBARIES > TURBARY

TURBARY *n* land where peat or turf is cut or has been cut

TURBETH *variant of >* TURPETH

TURBETHS > TURBETH

TURBID *adj* muddy, not clear

TURBIDITE *n* sediment deposited by a turbidity current

TURBIDITY > TURBID

TURBIDLY > TURBID

TURBINAL *same as >* TURBINATE

TURBINALS > TURBINAL

TURBINATE *adj* of or relating to any of the thin scroll-shaped bones situated on the walls of the nasal passages ▷ *n* turbinate bone

TURBINE *n* machine or generator driven by gas, water, etc turning blades

TURBINED *adj* having a turbine

TURBINES > TURBINE

TURBIT *n* crested breed of domestic pigeon

TURBITH *variant of >* TURPETH

TURBITHS > TURBITH

TURBITS > TURBIT

TURBO *n* compressor in an engine

TURBOCAR *n* car driven by a gas turbine

TURBOCARS > TURBOCAR

TURBOFAN *n* engine in which a fan driven by a turbine forces air rearwards to increase thrust

TURBOFANS > TURBOFAN

TURBOJET *n* gas turbine in which the exhaust gases provide the propulsive thrust to drive an aircraft

TURBOJETS > TURBOJET

TURBOND *old variant of >* TURBAN

TURBONDS > TURBOND

TURBOPROP *n* gas turbine for driving an aircraft propeller

TURBOS > TURBO

TURBOT *n* large European edible flatfish

TURBOTS > TURBOT

TURBULENT *adj* involving a lot of sudden changes and conflicting elements

TURCOPOLE *n* lightly armed and highly mobile class of Crusader

TURD *n* slang word for a piece of excrement

TURDINE *adj* of, relating to, or characteristic of thrushes

TURDION *variant of >* TORDION

TURDIONS > TURDION

TURDOID *same as >* TURDINE

TURDS > TURD

TURDUCKEN *n* turkey stuffed with duck stuffed with chicken

TUREEN *n* serving dish for soup

TUREENS > TUREEN

TURF *n* short thick even grass ▷ *vb* cover with turf

TURFED > TURF

TURFEN *adj* made of turf

TURFGRASS *n* grass grown for lawns

TURFIER > TURFY

TURFIEST > TURFY

TURFINESS > TURFY

TURFING > TURF

TURFINGS > TURF

TURFITE *same as >* TURFMAN

TURFITES > TURFITE

TURFLESS > TURF

TURFLIKE > TURF

TURFMAN *n* person devoted to horse racing

TURFMEN > TURFMAN

TURFS > TURF

TURFSKI *n* ski down a grassy hill on skis modified with integral wheels

TURFSKIS > TURFSKI

TURFY *adj* of, covered with, or resembling turf

TURGENCY > TURGENT

TURGENT *obsolete word for >* TURGID

TURGENTLY > TURGENT

TURGID *adj* (of language) pompous

TURGIDER > TURGID

TURGIDEST > TURGID

TURGIDITY > TURGID

TURGIDLY > TURGID

TURGITE *n* red or black mineral consisting of hydrated ferric oxide

TURGITES > TURGITE

TURGOR *n* normal rigid state of a cell

TURGORS > TURGOR

TURION *n* perennating bud produced by many aquatic plants

TURIONS > TURION

TURISTA *n* traveller's diarrhoea

TURISTAS > TURISTA

TURK *n* obsolete derogatory term for a violent, brutal, or domineering person

TURKEY *n* large bird bred for food

TURKEYS > TURKEY

TURKIES *old form of >* TURQUOISE

TURKIESES > TURKIES

TURKIS *old form of >* TURQUOISE

TURKISES > TURKIS

TURKOIS *old form of >* TURQUOISE

TURKOISES > TURKOIS

TURKS > TURK

TURLOUGH *n* seasonal lake or pond

TURLOUGHS > TURLOUGH

TURM *n* troop of horsemen

TURME *variant of >* TURM

TURMERIC *n* yellow spice obtained from the root of an Asian plant

TURMERICS > TURMERIC

TURMES > TURME

TURMOIL *n* agitation or confusion ▷ *vb* make or become turbulent

TURMOILED > TURMOIL

TURMOILS > TURMOIL

TURMS > TURM

TURN *vb* change the position or direction (of) ▷ *n* turning

TURNABLE > TURN

TURNABOUT *n* act of turning so as to face a different direction

TURNAGAIN *n* revolution

TURNBACK *n* one who turns back (from a challenge, for example)

TURNBACKS > TURNBACK

TURNCOAT *n* person who deserts one party or cause to join another

TURNCOATS > TURNCOAT

TURNCOCK *n* (formerly) official employed to turn on the water for the mains supply

TURNCOCKS > TURNCOCK

TURNDOWN *adj* capable of being or designed to be folded or doubled down ▷ *n* instance of turning down

TURNDOWNS > TURNDOWN

TURNDUN *another name for >* TUNDUN

TURNDUNS > TURNDUN

TURNED > TURN

TURNER *n* person or thing that turns

TURNERIES > TURNERY

TURNERS > TURNER

TURNERY *n* objects made on a lathe

TURNHALL *n* building in which gymnastics is taught and practised

TURNHALLS > TURNHALL

TURNING *n* road or path leading off a main route

TURNINGS > TURNING

TURNIP *n* root vegetable with orange or white flesh ▷ *vb* sow (a field) with turnips

TURNIPED > TURNIP

TURNIPIER > TURNIPY

t

SECTION 1: Words between 2 and 9 letters in length

TURNIPING > TURNIP
TURNIPS > TURNIP
TURNIPY *adj* like a turnip
TURNKEY *n* jailer ▷ *adj* denoting a project in which a single contractor has responsibility for the complete job
TURNKEYS > TURNKEY
TURNOFF *n* road or other way branching off from the main
TURNOFFS > TURNOFF
TURNON *n* something sexually exciting
TURNONS > TURNON
TURNOUT *n* number of people appearing at a gathering
TURNOUTS > TURNOUT
TURNOVER *n* total sales made by a business over a certain period
TURNOVERS > TURNOVER
TURNPIKE *n* road where a toll is collected at barriers
TURNPIKES > TURNPIKE
TURNROUND *n* act or process in which a ship, aircraft, etc, unloads passengers and freight at end of a trip and reloads for next trip
TURNS > TURN
TURNSKIN *n* old name for a werewolf
TURNSKINS > TURNSKIN
TURNSOLE *n* any of various plants having flowers that are said to turn towards the sun
TURNSOLES > TURNSOLE
TURNSPIT *n* servant whose job was to turn the spit on which meat was roasting
TURNSPITS > TURNSPIT
TURNSTILE *n* revolving gate for admitting one person at a time
TURNSTONE *n* shore bird
TURNT *adj* intoxicated
TURNTABLE *n* revolving platform
TURNUP *n* the turned-up fold at the bottom of some trouser legs
TURNUPS > TURNUP
TUROPHILE *n* person who loves cheese
TURPETH *n* convolvulaceous plant of the East Indies, having roots with purgative properties
TURPETHS > TURPETH
TURPITUDE *n* wickedness
TURPS *n* colourless, flammable liquid
TURQUOIS *variant of* **>** TURQUOISE
TURQUOISE *adj* blue-green ▷ *n* blue-green precious stone
TURR *n* Newfoundland name for the guillemot
TURRET *n* small tower
TURRETED *adj* having or resembling a turret or turrets
TURRETS > TURRET
TURRIBANT *old variant of* **>** TURBAN

TURRICAL *adj* of, relating to, or resembling a turret
TURRS > TURR
TURTLE *n* sea tortoise
TURTLED > TURTLE
TURTLER > TURTLE
TURTLERS > TURTLE
TURTLES > TURTLE
TURTLING > TURTLE
TURTLINGS > TURTLE
TURVES > TURF
TUSCHE *n* substance used in lithography for drawing the design
TUSCHES > TUSCHE
TUSH *interj* exclamation of disapproval or contempt ▷ *n* small tusk ▷ *vb* utter the interjection "tush"
TUSHED > TUSH
TUSHERIES > TUSHERY
TUSHERY *n* use of affectedly archaic language in novels, etc
TUSHES > TUSH
TUSHIE *n* pair of buttocks
TUSHIES > TUSHIE
TUSHING > TUSH
TUSHKAR *variant of* **>** TUSKAR
TUSHKARS > TUSHKAR
TUSHKER *variant of* **>** TUSKAR
TUSHKERS > TUSHKER
TUSHY *variant of* **>** TUSHIE
TUSK *n* long pointed tooth of an elephant, walrus, etc ▷ *vb* stab, tear, or gore with the tusks
TUSKAR *n* peat-cutting spade
TUSKARS > TUSKAR
TUSKED > TUSK
TUSKER *n* any animal with prominent tusks, esp a wild boar or elephant
TUSKERS > TUSKER
TUSKIER > TUSK
TUSKIEST > TUSK
TUSKING > TUSK
TUSKINGS > TUSK
TUSKLESS > TUSK
TUSKLIKE > TUSK
TUSKS > TUSK
TUSKY > TUSK
TUSSAC *modifier* as in *tussac grass* kind of grass
TUSSAH *same as* **>** TUSSORE
TUSSAHS > TUSSAH
TUSSAL > TUSSIS
TUSSAR *variant of* **>** TUSSORE
TUSSARS > TUSSAR
TUSSEH *variant of* **>** TUSSORE
TUSSEHS > TUSSEH
TUSSER *same as* **>** TUSSORE
TUSSERS > TUSSER
TUSSES > TUSSIS
TUSSIS *technical name for a* **>** COUGH
TUSSISES > TUSSIS
TUSSIVE > TUSSIS
TUSSLE *vb* fight or scuffle ▷ *n* energetic fight, struggle, or argument
TUSSLED > TUSSLE

TUSSLES > TUSSLE
TUSSLING > TUSSLE
TUSSOCK *n* tuft of grass
TUSSOCKED *adj* having tussocks
TUSSOCKS > TUSSOCK
TUSSOCKY *adj* covered with tussocks
TUSSOR *variant of* **>** TUSSORE
TUSSORE *n* strong coarse brownish Indian silk
TUSSORES > TUSSORE
TUSSORS > TUSSOR
TUSSUCK *variant of* **>** TUSSOCK
TUSSUCKS > TUSSUCK
TUSSUR *variant of* **>** TUSSORE
TUSSURS > TUSSUR
TUT *interj* exclamation of mild disapproval, or surprise ▷ *vb* express disapproval by the exclamation of "tut-tut". ▷ *n* payment system based on measurable work done
TUTANIA *n* alloy of low melting point used mostly for decorative purposes
TUTANIAS > TUTANIA
TUTEE *n* one who is tutored, esp in a university
TUTEES > TUTEE
TUTELAGE *n* instruction or guidance, esp by a tutor
TUTELAGES > TUTELAGE
TUTELAR *same as* **>** TUTELARY
TUTELARS > TUTELAR
TUTELARY *adj* having the role of guardian or protector ▷ *n* tutelary person, deity, or saint
TUTENAG *n* zinc alloy
TUTENAGS > TUTENAG
TUTIORISM *n* (in Roman Catholic moral theology) the doctrine that in cases of moral doubt it is best to follow the safer course or that in agreement with the law
TUTIORIST > TUTIORISM
TUTMAN *n* one who does tutwork
TUTMEN > TUTMAN
TUTOR *n* person teaching individuals or small groups ▷ *vb* act as a tutor to
TUTORAGE > TUTOR
TUTORAGES > TUTOR
TUTORED > TUTOR
TUTORESS *n* female tutor
TUTORIAL *n* period of instruction with a tutor ▷ *adj* of or relating to a tutor
TUTORIALS > TUTORIAL
TUTORING > TUTOR
TUTORINGS > TUTOR
TUTORISE *variant spelling of* **>** TUTORIZE
TUTORISED > TUTORISE
TUTORISES > TUTORISE
TUTORISM > TUTOR
TUTORISMS > TUTOR
TUTORIZE *vb* tutor
TUTORIZED > TUTOR

TUTORIZES > TUTORIZE
TUTORS > TUTOR
TUTORSHIP > TUTOR
TUTOYED *adj* addressed in a familiar way
TUTOYER *vb* speak to someone on familiar terms
TUTOYERED > TUTOYER
TUTOYERS > TUTOYER
TUTRESS *same as* **>** TUTORESS
TUTRESSES > TUTRESS
TUTRICES > TUTRIX
TUTRIX *n* female tutor; tutoress
TUTRIXES > TUTRIX
TUTS *Scots version of* **>** TUT
TUTSAN *n* woodland shrub of Europe and W Asia
TUTSANS > TUTSAN
TUTSED > TUTS
TUTSES > TUTS
TUTSING > TUTS
TUTTED > TUT
TUTTI *adv* to be performed by the whole orchestra or choir ▷ *n* piece of tutti music
TUTTIES > TUTTY
TUTTING > TUT
TUTTINGS > TUT
TUTTIS > TUTTI
TUTTY *n* finely powdered impure zinc oxide
TUTU *n* short stiff skirt worn by ballerinas
TUTUED *adj* wearing tutu
TUTUS > TUTU
TUTWORK *n* work paid using a tut system
TUTWORKER > TUTWORK
TUTWORKS > TUTWORK
TUX *short for* **>** TUXEDO
TUXEDO *n* dinner jacket
TUXEDOED *adj* wearing a tuxedo
TUXEDOES > TUXEDO
TUXEDOS > TUXEDO
TUXES > TUX
TUYER *variant of* **>** TUYERE
TUYERE *n* water-cooled nozzle through which air is blown into a cupola, blast furnace, or forge
TUYERES > TUYERE
TUYERS > TUYER
TUZZ *n* tuft or clump of hair
TUZZES > TUZZ
TWA *Scots word for* **>** TWO
TWADDLE *n* silly or pretentious talk or writing ▷ *vb* talk or write in a silly or pretentious way
TWADDLED > TWADDLE
TWADDLER > TWADDLE
TWADDLERS > TWADDLE
TWADDLES > TWADDLE
TWADDLIER > TWADDLE
TWADDLING > TWADDLE
TWADDLY > TWADDLE
TWAE *same as* **>** TWA
TWAES > TWAE
TWAFALD *Scots variant of* **>** TWOFOLD
TWAIN *n* two
TWAINS > TWAIN
TWAITE *n* herring-like food fish

TWAITES > TWAITE

TWAL n twelve

TWALPENNY n shilling

TWALS > TWAL

TWANG n sharp ringing sound ▷ vb (cause to) make a twang

TWANGED > TWANG

TWANGER > TWANG

TWANGERS > TWANG

TWANGIER > TWANG

TWANGIEST > TWANG

TWANGING > TWANG

TWANGINGS > TWANG

TWANGLE vb make a continuous loose twanging sound

TWANGLED > TWANGLE

TWANGLER > TWANGLE

TWANGLERS > TWANGLE

TWANGLES > TWANGLE

TWANGLING > TWANGLE

TWANGS > TWANG

TWANGY > TWANG

TWANK vb make a sharply curtailed twang

TWANKAY n variety of Chinese green tea

TWANKAYS > TWANKAY

TWANKED > TWANK

TWANKIES > TWANKY

TWANKING > TWANK

TWANKS > TWANK

TWANKY same as **>** TWANKAY

TWAS > TWA

TWASOME same as **>** TWOSOME

TWASOMES > TWASOME

TWAT vb hit or strike violently

TWATS > TWAT

TWATTED > TWAT

TWATTING > TWAT

TWATTLE rare word for **>** TWADDLE

TWATTLED > TWATTLE

TWATTLER > TWATTLE

TWATTLERS > TWATTLE

TWATTLES > TWATTLE

TWATTLING > TWATTLE

TWAY old variant of **>** TWAIN

TWAYBLADE n type of orchid

TWAYS > TWAY

TWEAK vb pinch or twist sharply ▷ n instance of tweaking

TWEAKED > TWEAK

TWEAKER n engineer's small screwdriver

TWEAKERS > TWEAKER

TWEAKIER > TWEAK

TWEAKIEST > TWEAK

TWEAKING > TWEAK

TWEAKINGS > TWEAK

TWEAKS > TWEAK

TWEAKY > TWEAK

TWEE adj too sentimental, sweet, or pretty

TWEED n thick woollen cloth

TWEEDIER > TWEEDY

TWEEDIEST > TWEEDY

TWEEDILY adv in a manner characteristic of upper-class people who live in the country

TWEEDLE vb improvise aimlessly on a musical instrument

TWEEDLED > TWEEDLE

TWEEDLER > TWEEDLE

TWEEDLERS > TWEEDLE

TWEEDLES > TWEEDLE

TWEEDLING > TWEEDLE

TWEEDS > TWEED

TWEEDY adj of or made of tweed

TWEEL variant of **>** TWILL

TWEELED > TWEEL

TWEELING > TWEEL

TWEELS > TWEEL

TWEELY > TWEE

TWEEN same as **>** BETWEEN

TWEENAGE adj (of a child) between about eight and fourteen years old

TWEENAGER n child of approximately eight to fourteen years of age

TWEENER same as **>** TWEENAGER

TWEENERS > TWEENER

TWEENESS > TWEE

TWEENIE same as **>** TWEENY

TWEENIES > TWEENY

TWEENS > TWEEN

TWEENY n maid who assists both cook and housemaid

TWEEP n person who uses Twitter

TWEEPLE pl n people who communicate via the Twitter website

TWEEPS > TWEEP

TWEER variant of **>** TWIRE

TWEERED > TWEER

TWEERING > TWEER

TWEERS > TWEER

TWEEST > TWEE

TWEET vb chirp ▷ interj imitation of the thin chirping sound made by small birds

TWEETABLE adj (of a message) short enough to be posted on Twitter

TWEETED > TWEET

TWEETER n loudspeaker reproducing high-frequency sounds

TWEETERS > TWEETER

TWEETING > TWEET

TWEETS > TWEET

TWEETUP n online meeting of individuals arranged on the social networking website Twitter

TWEETUPS > TWEETUP

TWEEZE vb take hold of or pluck (hair, small objects, etc) with or as if with tweezers

TWEEZED > TWEEZE

TWEEZER same as **>** TWEEZERS

TWEEZERS pl n small pincer-like tool

TWEEZES > TWEEZE

TWEEZING > TWEEZE

TWELFTH n number twelve in a series ▷ adj of or being number twelve in a series

TWELFTHLY adv after the eleventh person, position, event, etc

TWELFTHS > TWELFTH

TWELVE n two more than ten

TWELVEMO another word for **>** DUODECIMO

TWELVEMOS > TWELVEMO

TWELVES > TWELVE

TWENTIES > TWENTY

TWENTIETH adj coming after the nineteenth in numbering or counting order, position, time, etc ▷ n one of 20 approximately equal parts of something

TWENTY n two times ten

TWENTYISH adj around 20

TWERK vb dance provocatively by moving the hips rapidly back and forth

TWERKED > TWERK

TWERKING n type of dance involving rapid hip movement

TWERKINGS > TWERKING

TWERKS > TWERK

TWERP n silly person

TWERPIER > TWERP

TWERPIEST > TWERP

TWERPS > TWERP

TWERPY > TWERP

TWIBIL same as **>** TWIBILL

TWIBILL n mattock with a blade shaped like an adze at one end and like an axe at the other

TWIBILLS > TWIBILL

TWIBILS > TWIBIL

TWICE adv two times

TWICER n someone who does something twice

TWICERS > TWICER

TWICHILD n person in his or her dotage

TWIDDLE vb fiddle or twirl in an idle way ▷ n act or instance of twiddling

TWIDDLED > TWIDDLE

TWIDDLER > TWIDDLE

TWIDDLERS > TWIDDLE

TWIDDLES > TWIDDLE

TWIDDLIER > TWIDDLE

TWIDDLING > TWIDDLE

TWIDDLY > TWIDDLE

TWIER variant of **>** TUYERE

TWIERS > TWIER

TWIFOLD variant of **>** TWOFOLD

TWIFORKED adj having two forks; bifurcate

TWIFORMED adj having two forms

TWIG n small branch or shoot ▷ vb realize or understand

TWIGGED > TWIG

TWIGGEN adj made of twigs

TWIGGER > TWIG

TWIGGERS > TWIG

TWIGGIER > TWIGGY

TWIGGIEST > TWIGGY

TWIGGING > TWIG

TWIGGY adj of or relating to a twig or twigs

TWIGHT old variant of **>** TWIT

TWIGHTED > TWIGHT

TWIGHTING > TWIGHT

TWIGHTS > TWIGHT

TWIGLESS > TWIG

TWIGLET n small twig

TWIGLETS > TWIGLET

TWIGLIKE > TWIG

TWIGLOO n temporary shelter made from twigs, branches, leaves, etc

TWIGLOOS > TWIGLOO

TWIGS > TWIG

TWIGSOME adj covered with twigs; twiggy

TWILIGHT n soft dim light just after sunset ▷ adj of or relating to the period towards the end of the day

TWILIGHTS > TWILIGHT

TWILIT > TWILIGHT

TWILL n fabric woven to produce parallel ridges ▷ adj of a weave in which the weft yarns are worked around two or more warp yarns ▷ vb weave in this fashion

TWILLED > TWILL

TWILLIES > TWILLY

TWILLING > TWILL

TWILLINGS > TWILL

TWILLS > TWILL

TWILLY n machine having revolving spikes for opening and cleaning raw textile fibres

TWILT variant of **>** QUILT

TWILTED > TWILT

TWILTING > TWILT

TWILTS > TWILT

TWIN n one of a pair, esp of two children born at one birth ▷ vb pair or be paired

TWINBERRY n creeping wooden plant

TWINBORN adj born as a twin

TWINE n string or cord ▷ vb twist or coil round

TWINED > TWINE

TWINER > TWINE

TWINERS > TWINE

TWINES > TWINE

TWINGE n sudden sharp pain or emotional pang ▷ vb have or cause to have a twinge

TWINGED > TWINGE

TWINGEING > TWINGE

TWINGES > TWINGE

TWINGING > TWINGE

TWINIER > TWINE

TWINIEST > TWINE

TWINIGHT adj (of a baseball double-header) held in the late afternoon and evening

TWINING > TWINE

TWININGLY > TWINE

TWININGS > TWINE

TWINJET n jet aircraft with two engines

TWINJETS > TWINJET

TWINK n white correction fluid for deleting written text ▷ vb twinkle

TWINKED > TWINK

TWINKIE n stupid person

TWINKIES > TWINKIE

TWINKING > TWINK

TWINKLE vb shine brightly but intermittently ▷ n flickering brightness

TWINKLED > TWINKLE

TWINKLER > TWINKLE

TWINKLERS > TWINKLE

TWINKLES > TWINKLE

TWINKLIER > TWINKLY
TWINKLING n very short time
TWINKLY adj sparkling
TWINKS > TWINK
TWINKY n stupid person
TWINLING old name for > TWIN
TWINLINGS > TWINLING
TWINNED > TWIN
TWINNING > TWIN
TWINNINGS > TWIN
TWINS > TWIN
TWINSET n matching jumper and cardigan
TWINSETS > TWINSET
TWINSHIP n condition of being a twin or twins
TWINSHIPS > TWIN
TWINTER n animal that is 2 years old
TWINTERS > TWINTER
TWINY > TWINE
TWIRE vb look intently at with (or as if with) difficulty
TWIRED > TWIRE
TWIRES > TWIRE
TWIRING > TWIRE
TWIRL vb turn or spin around quickly ▷ n whirl or twist
TWIRLED > TWIRL
TWIRLER > TWIRL
TWIRLERS > TWIRL
TWIRLIER > TWIRL
TWIRLIEST > TWIRL
TWIRLING > TWIRL
TWIRLS > TWIRL
TWIRLY > TWIRL
TWIRP same as > TWERP
TWIRPIER > TWIRP
TWIRPIEST > TWIRP
TWIRPS > TWIRP
TWIRPY > TWIRP
TWISCAR variant of > TUSKAR
TWISCARS > TWISCAR
TWIST vb turn out of the natural position ▷ n twisting
TWISTABLE > TWIST
TWISTED > TWIST
TWISTER n swindler
TWISTERS > TWISTER
TWISTIER > TWIST
TWISTIEST > TWIST
TWISTING > TWIST
TWISTINGS > TWIST
TWISTOR n variable corresponding to the coordinates of a point in space and time
TWISTORS > TWISTOR
TWISTS > TWIST
TWISTY > TWIST
TWIT vb poke fun at (someone) ▷ n foolish person
TWITCH vb move spasmodically ▷ n nervous muscular spasm
TWITCHED > TWITCH
TWITCHER n bird-watcher who tries to spot as many rare varieties as possible
TWITCHERS > TWITCHER
TWITCHES > TWITCH
TWITCHIER > TWITCHY
TWITCHILY > TWITCHY

TWITCHING > TWITCH
TWITCHY adj nervous, worried, and ill-at-ease
TWITE n N European finch with a brown streaked plumage
TWITES > TWITE
TWITS > TWIT
TWITTED > TWIT
TWITTEN n narrow alleyway
TWITTENS > TWITTEN
TWITTER vb (of birds) utter chirping sounds ▷ n act or sound of twittering
TWITTERED > TWITTER
TWITTERER > TWITTER
TWITTERS > TWITTER
TWITTERY adj making a chirping sound
TWITTING > TWIT
TWITTINGS > TWIT
TWITTISH adj silly; foolish
TWIXT same as > BETWIXT
TWIZZLE vb spin around
TWIZZLED > TWIZZLE
TWIZZLES > TWIZZLE
TWIZZLING > TWIZZLE
TWO n one more than one
TWOCCER > TWOCCING
TWOCCERS > TWOCCING
TWOCCING n act of breaking into a motor vehicle and driving it away
TWOCCINGS > TWOCCING
TWOCKER > TWOCCING
TWOCKERS > TWOCCING
TWOCKING same as > TWOCCING
TWOCKINGS > TWOCKING
TWOER n (in a game) something that scores two
TWOERS > TWOER
TWOFER n single ticket allowing the buyer entrance to two events
TWOFERS > TWOFER
TWOFOLD adj having twice as many or as much ▷ adv by twice as many or as much ▷ n folding piece of theatrical scenery
TWOFOLDS > TWOFOLD
TWONESS n state or condition of being two
TWONESSES > TWONESS
TWONIE same as > TOONIE
TWONIES > TWONIE
TWOONIE variant of > TOONIE
TWOONIES > TWOONIE
TWOPENCE n sum of two pennies
TWOPENCES > TWOPENCE
TWOPENNY adj cheap or tawdry
TWOS > TWO
TWOSEATER n vehicle providing seats for two people
TWOSOME n group of two people
TWOSOMES > TWOSOME
TWOSTROKE adj relating to or designating an internal-combustion engine whose piston makes two strokes for every explosion

TWP adj stupid
TWYER same as > TUYERE
TWYERE variant of > TUYERE
TWYERES > TWYERE
TWYERS > TWYER
TWYFOLD adj twofold
TYCHISM n theory that chance is an objective reality at work in the universe
TYCHISMS > TYCHISM
TYCOON n powerful wealthy businessperson; shogun
TYCOONATE n office or rule of a tycoon
TYCOONERY > TYCOON
TYCOONS > TYCOON
TYDE old variant of the past participle of > TIE
TYE n trough used in mining to separate valuable material from dross ▷ vb (in mining) isolate valuable material from dross using a tye
TYED > TYE
TYEE n large northern Pacific salmon
TYEES > TYEE
TYEING > TYE
TYER > TYE
TYERS > TYE
TYES > TYE
TYG n mug with two handles
TYGS > TYG
TYIN variant of > TYIYN
TYING > TIE
TYIYN n money unit of Kyrgyzstan
TYIYNS > TYIYN
TYKE n dog
TYKES > TYKE
TYKISH > TYKE
TYLECTOMY n excision of a breast tumour
TYLER variant of > TILER
TYLERS > TYLER
TYLOPOD n mammal with padded feet, such as a camel or llama
TYLOPODS > TYLOPOD
TYLOSES > TYLOSIS
TYLOSIN n broad spectrum antibiotic
TYLOSINS > TYLOSIN
TYLOSIS n bladder-like outgrowth from certain cells in woody tissue
TYLOTE n knobbed sponge spicule
TYLOTES > TYLOTE
TYMBAL same as > TIMBAL
TYMBALS > TYMBAL
TYMP n blast furnace outlet through which molten metal flows
TYMPAN same as > TYMPANUM
TYMPANA > TYMPANUM
TYMPANAL adj relating to the tympanum
TYMPANI same as > TIMPANI
TYMPANIC adj of, relating to, or having a tympanum ▷ n part of the temporal bone in the mammalian skull that surrounds the auditory canal

TYMPANICS > TYMPANIC
TYMPANIES > TYMPANY
TYMPANIST > TIMPANI
TYMPANO > TYMPANI
TYMPANS > TYMPAN
TYMPANUM n cavity of the middle ear
TYMPANUMS > TYMPANUM
TYMPANY n distention of the abdomen
TYMPS > TYMP
TYND variant of > TIND
TYNDE variant of > TIND
TYNE variant of > TINE
TYNED variant of > TYNE
TYNES > TYNE
TYNING > TYNE
TYPABLE > TYPE
TYPAL rare word for > TYPICAL
TYPE n class or category ▷ vb print with a typewriter or word processor
TYPEABLE > TYPE
TYPEBAR n one of the bars in a typewriter that carry the type and are operated by keys
TYPEBARS > TYPEBAR
TYPECASE n compartmental tray for storing printer's type
TYPECASES > TYPECASE
TYPECAST vb continually cast (an actor or actress) in similar roles
TYPECASTS > TYPECAST
TYPED > TYPE
TYPEFACE n style of the type
TYPEFACES > TYPEFACE
TYPES > TYPE
TYPESET vb set (text for printing) in type
TYPESETS > TYPESET
TYPESTYLE another word for > TYPEFACE
TYPEWRITE vb write by means of a typewriter
TYPEWROTE > TYPEWRITE
TYPEY variant of > TYPY
TYPHLITIC > TYPHLITIS
TYPHLITIS n inflammation of the caecum
TYPHOID adj of or relating to typhoid fever
TYPHOIDAL > TYPHOID
TYPHOIDIN n culture of dead typhoid bacillus for injection into the skin to test for typhoid fever
TYPHOIDS > TYPHOID
TYPHON n whirlwind
TYPHONIAN > TYPHON
TYPHONIC > TYPHOON
TYPHONS > TYPHON
TYPHOON n violent tropical storm
TYPHOONS > TYPHOON
TYPHOSE adj relating to typhoid
TYPHOUS > TYPHUS
TYPHUS n infectious feverish disease
TYPHUSES > TYPHUS
TYPIC same as > TYPICAL
TYPICAL adj true to type, characteristic

TYPICALLY > TYPICAL
TYPIER > TYPY
TYPIEST > TYPY
TYPIFIED > TYPIFY
TYPIFIER > TYPIFY
TYPIFIERS > TYPIFY
TYPIFIES > TYPIFY
TYPIFY *vb* be typical of
TYPIFYING > TYPIFY
TYPING *n* work or activity of using a typewriter or word processor
TYPINGS > TYPING
TYPIST *n* person who types with a typewriter or word processor
TYPISTS > TYPIST
TYPO *n* typographical error
TYPOGRAPH *n* person skilled in the art of composing type and printing from it
TYPOLOGIC > TYPOLOGY
TYPOLOGY *n* study of types
TYPOMANIA *n* obsession with typology
TYPOS > TYPO
TYPP *n* unit of thickness of yarn
TYPPS > TYPP
TYPTO *vb* learn Greek conjugations
TYPTOED > TYPTO
TYPTOING > TYPTO
TYPTOS > TYPTO
TYPY *adj* (of an animal) typifying the breed
TYRAMINE *n* colourless crystalline amine derived from phenol

TYRAMINES > TYRAMINE
TYRAN *vb* act as a tyrant
TYRANED > TYRAN
TYRANING > TYRAN
TYRANNE *variant of* > TYRAN
TYRANNED > TYRANNE
TYRANNES > TYRANNE
TYRANNESS *n* female tyrant
TYRANNIC > TYRANNY
TYRANNIES > TYRANNY
TYRANNING > TYRANNE
TYRANNIS *n* tyrannical government
TYRANNISE *same as* > TYRANNIZE
TYRANNIZE *vb* exert power (over) oppressively or cruelly
TYRANNOUS > TYRANNY
TYRANNY *n* tyrannical rule
TYRANS > TYRAN
TYRANT *n* oppressive or cruel ruler ▷ *vb* act the tyrant
TYRANTED > TYRANT
TYRANTING > TYRANT
TYRANTS > TYRANT
TYRE *n* rubber ring, usu inflated, over the rim of a vehicle's wheel to grip the road ▷ *vb* fit a tyre or tyres to (a wheel, vehicle, etc)
TYRED > TYRE
TYRELESS > TYRE
TYREMAKER *n* one who makes tyres
TYRES > TYRE
TYRING > TYRE
TYRO *n* novice or beginner
TYROCIDIN *n* antibiotic
TYROES > TYRO

TYRONES > TYRO
TYRONIC > TYRO
TYROPITA *n* Greek cheese pie
TYROPITAS > TYROPITA
TYROPITTA *n* Greek cheese pie
TYROS > TYRO
TYROSINE *n* aromatic nonessential amino acid
TYROSINES > TYROSINE
TYSTIE *n* black guillemot
TYSTIES > TYSTIE
TYTE *variant spelling of* > TITE
TYTHE *variant of* > TITHE
TYTHED > TYTHE
TYTHES > TYTHE
TYTHING > TYTHE
TZADDI *same as* > SADHE
TZADDIK *variant of* > ZADDIK
TZADDIKIM > TZADDIK
TZADDIKS > TZADDIK
TZADDIQ *variant of* > ZADDIK
TZADDIQIM > TZADDIQ
TZADDIQS > TZADDIQ
TZADDIS > TZADDI
TZADIK *same as* > ZADDIK
TZADIKS > TZADIK
TZAR *same as* > TSAR
TZARDOM > TZAR
TZARDOMS > TZAR
TZAREVNA *variant of* > TSAREVNA
TZAREVNAS > TZAREVNA
TZARINA *variant of* > TSARINA

TZARINAS > TZARINA
TZARISM *variant of* > TSARISM
TZARISMS > TZARISM
TZARIST > TZARISM
TZARISTS > TZARISM
TZARITZA *variant of* > TSARITSA
TZARITZAS > TZARITZA
TZARS > TZAR
TZATZIKI *n* Greek dip made from yogurt, chopped cucumber, and mint
TZATZIKIS > TZATZIKI
TZEDAKAH *n* charitable donations as a Jewish moral obligation
TZEDAKAHS > TZEDAKAH
TZETSE *variant of* > TSETSE
TZETSES > TZETSE
TZETZE *variant of* > TSETSE
TZETZES > TZETZE
TZIGANE *n* type of Gypsy music
TZIGANES > TZIGANE
TZIGANIES > TZIGANY
TZIGANY *variant of* > TZIGANE
TZIMMES *n* traditional Jewish stew
TZITZIS *variant of* > TSITSITH
TZITZIT *variant of* > TSITSITH
TZITZITH *variant of* > TSITSITH
TZURIS *variant of* > TSURIS
TZURISES > TZURIS

Uu

UAKARI n type of monkey
UAKARIS > UAKARI
UBEROUS adj abundant
UBERTIES > UBERTY
UBERTY n abundance
UBIETIES > UBIETY
UBIETY n condition of being in a particular place
UBIQUE adv everywhere
UBIQUITIN n type of polypeptide
UBIQUITY n state of apparently being everywhere at once; omnipresence
UBUNTU n quality of compassion and humanity
UBUNTUS > UBUNTU
UCKERS n type of naval game
UDAL n form of freehold possession of land used in Orkney and Shetland
UDALLER n person possessing a udal
UDALLERS > UDALLER
UDALS > UDAL
UDDER n large baglike milk-producing gland of cows, sheep, or goats
UDDERED > UDDER
UDDERFUL n capacity of an udder
UDDERFULS > UDDERFUL
UDDERLESS > UDDER
UDDERS > UDDER
UDO n stout perennial plant of Japan and China
UDOMETER n archaic term for an instrument for measuring rainfall or snowfall
UDOMETERS > UDOMETER
UDOMETRIC > UDOMETER
UDOMETRY > UDOMETER
UDON n (in Japanese cookery) large noodles made of wheat flour
UDONS > UDON
UDOS > UDO
UDS interj God's or God save
UEY n u-turn
UEYS > UEY
UFO n flying saucer
UFOLOGIES > UFOLOGY
UFOLOGIST > UFOLOGY
UFOLOGY n study of UFOs
UFOS > UFO
UG vb hate
UGALI n type of stiff porridge
UGALIS > UGALI
UGGED > UG
UGGING > UG

UGH interj exclamation of disgust ▷ n sound made to indicate disgust
UGHS > UGH
UGLIED > UGLY
UGLIER > UGLY
UGLIES > UGLY
UGLIEST > UGLY
UGLIFIED > UGLIFY
UGLIFIER > UGLIFY
UGLIFIERS > UGLIFY
UGLIFIES > UGLIFY
UGLIFY vb make or become ugly or more ugly
UGLIFYING > UGLIFY
UGLILY > UGLY
UGLINESS > UGLY
UGLY adj of unpleasant appearance ▷ vb make ugly
UGLYING > UGLY
UGS > UG
UGSOME adj loathsome
UH interj used to express hesitation
UHLAN n member of a body of lancers first employed in the Polish army
UHLANS > UHLAN
UHURU n national independence
UHURUS > UHURU
UILLEAN adj as in uillean pipes bagpipes developed in Ireland
UILLEANN same as **>** UILLEAN
UINTAHITE same as **>** UINTAITE
UINTAITE n variety of asphalt
UINTAITES > UINTAITE
UITLANDER n foreigner
UJAMAA n communally organized village in Tanzania
UJAMAAS > UJAMAA
UKASE n (in imperial Russia) a decree from the tsar
UKASES > UKASE
UKE short form of **>** UKULELE
UKELELE same as **>** UKULELE
UKELELES > UKELELE
UKES > UKE
UKULELE n small guitar with four strings
UKULELES > UKULELE
ULAMA n body of Muslim scholars or religious leaders
ULAMAS > ULAMA
ULAN same as **>** UHLAN
ULANS > ULAN

ULCER n open sore on the surface of the skin or mucous membrane. ▷ vb make or become ulcerous
ULCERATE vb make or become ulcerous
ULCERATED > ULCERATE
ULCERATES > ULCERATE
ULCERED > ULCER
ULCERING > ULCER
ULCEROUS adj of, like, or characterized by ulcers
ULCERS > ULCER
ULE n rubber tree
ULEMA same as **>** ULAMA
ULEMAS > ULEMA
ULES > ULE
ULEX n variety of shrub
ULEXES > ULEX
ULEXITE n type of mineral
ULEXITES > ULEXITE
ULICES > ULEX
ULICON same as **>** EULACHON
ULICONS > ULICON
ULIGINOSE same as **>** ULIGINOUS
ULIGINOUS adj marshy
ULIKON same as **>** EULACHON
ULIKONS > ULIKON
ULITIS n gingivitis
ULITISES > ULITIS
ULLAGE n volume by which a liquid container falls short of being full ▷ vb create ullage in
ULLAGED > ULLAGE
ULLAGES > ULLAGE
ULLAGING > ULLAGE
ULLING n process of filling
ULLINGS > ULLING
ULMACEOUS adj relating to the family of deciduous trees and shrubs which includes the elms
ULMIN n substance found in decaying vegetation
ULMINS > ULMIN
ULNA n inner and longer of the two bones of the human forearm
ULNAD adv towards the ulna
ULNAE > ULNA
ULNAR > ULNA
ULNARE n bone in the wrist
ULNARIA > ULNARE
ULNAS > ULNA
ULOSES > ULOSIS
ULOSIS n formation of a scar
ULOTRICHY n state of having woolly or curly hair

ULPAN n Israeli study centre
ULPANIM > ULPAN
ULSTER n man's heavy double-breasted overcoat
ULSTERED adj wearing an ulster
ULSTERS > ULSTER
ULTERIOR adj (of an aim, reason, etc) concealed or hidden
ULTIMA n final syllable of a word
ULTIMACY > ULTIMATE
ULTIMAS > ULTIMA
ULTIMATA > ULTIMATUM
ULTIMATE adj final in a series or process ▷ n most significant, highest, furthest, or greatest thing ▷ vb end
ULTIMATED > ULTIMATE
ULTIMATES > ULTIMATE
ULTIMATUM n final warning stating that action will be taken unless certain conditions are met
ULTIMO adv in or during the previous month
ULTION n vengeance
ULTIONS > ULTION
ULTISOL n reddish-yellow acid soil
ULTISOLS > ULTISOL
ULTRA n person who has extreme or immoderate beliefs or opinions ▷ adj extreme or immoderate, esp in beliefs or opinions
ULTRACHIC adj extremely chic
ULTRACOLD adj extremely cold
ULTRACOOL adj extremely cool
ULTRADRY adj extremely dry
ULTRAFAST adj extremely fast
ULTRAFINE adj extremely fine
ULTRAHEAT vb sterilize through extreme heat treatment
ULTRAHIGH adj as in ultrahigh frequency radio-frequency band or radio frequency lying between 3000 and 300 megahertz
ULTRAHIP adj extremely trendy
ULTRAHOT adj extremely hot
ULTRAISM n extreme philosophy, belief, or action

ULTRAISMS > ULTRAISM

ULTRAIST > ULTRAISM

ULTRAISTS > ULTRAISM

ULTRALEFT *n* extreme political Left ▷ *adj* of the extreme political Left or extremely radical

ULTRALOW *adj* extremely low

ULTRAPOSH *adj* extremely posh

ULTRAPURE *adj* extremely pure

ULTRARARE *adj* extremely rare

ULTRARED *obsolete word for* > INFRARED

ULTRAREDS > ULTRARED

ULTRARICH *adj* extremely rich

ULTRAS > ULTRA

ULTRASAFE *adj* extremely safe

ULTRASLOW *adj* extremely slow

ULTRASOFT *adj* extremely soft

ULTRATHIN *adj* extremely thin

ULTRATINY *adj* extremely small

ULTRAWIDE *adj* extremely wide

ULU *n* type of knife

ULULANT > ULULATE

ULULATE *vb* howl or wail

ULULATED > ULULATE

ULULATES > ULULATE

ULULATING > ULULATE

ULULATION > ULULATE

ULUS > ULU

ULVA *n* genus of seaweed

ULVAS > ULVA

ULYIE *Scots variant of* > OIL

ULYIES > ULYIE

ULZIE *Scots variant of* > OIL

ULZIES > ULZIE

UM *interj* representation of a common sound made when hesitating in speech ▷ *vb* hesitate while speaking

UMAMI *n* savoury flavour

UMAMIS > UMAMI

UMANGITE *n* type of mineral

UMANGITES > UMANGITE

UMBEL *n* umbrella-like flower cluster

UMBELED *same as* > UMBELLED

UMBELLAR > UMBEL

UMBELLATE > UMBEL

UMBELLED *adj* having umbels

UMBELLET *same as* > UMBELLULE

UMBELLETS > UMBELLET

UMBELLULE *n* any of the small secondary umbels that make up a compound umbel

UMBELS > UMBEL

UMBELULE *n* secondary umbel

UMBELULES > UMBELULE

UMBER *adj* dark brown to reddish-brown ▷ *n* type of dark brown earth containing ferric oxide (rust) ▷ *vb* stain with umber

UMBERED > UMBER

UMBERIER > UMBERY

UMBERIEST > UMBERY

UMBERING > UMBER

UMBERS > UMBER

UMBERY *adj* like umber

UMBILICAL *adj* of the navel

UMBILICI > UMBILICUS

UMBILICUS *n* navel

UMBLE *adj* as in *umble pie* (formerly) a pie made from the heart, entrails, etc, of a deer

UMBLES *another term for* > NUMBLES

UMBO *n* small hump projecting from the centre of the cap in certain mushrooms

UMBONAL > UMBO

UMBONATE > UMBO

UMBONES > UMBO

UMBONIC > UMBO

UMBOS > UMBO

UMBRA *n* shadow, esp the shadow cast by the moon onto the earth during a solar eclipse

UMBRACULA *pl n* umbrella-like structures

UMBRAE > UMBRA

UMBRAGE *n* displeasure or resentment ▷ *vb* shade

UMBRAGED > UMBRAGE

UMBRAGES > UMBRAGE

UMBRAGING > UMBRAGE

UMBRAL > UMBRA

UMBRAS > UMBRA

UMBRATED *adj* shown in a faint manner

UMBRATIC > UMBRA

UMBRATILE *adj* shadowy ▷ *n* person who spends their time in the shade or shadows

UMBRE *same as* > UMBRETTE

UMBREL *n* umbrella

UMBRELLA *n* portable device used for protection against rain ▷ *adj* containing many different organizations

UMBRELLAS > UMBRELLA

UMBRELLO *same as* > UMBRELLA

UMBRELLOS > UMBRELLO

UMBRELS > UMBREL

UMBRERE *n* helmet visor

UMBRERES > UMBRERE

UMBRES > UMBRE

UMBRETTE *n* African wading bird

UMBRETTES > UMBRETTE

UMBRIERE *same as* > UMBRERE

UMBRIERES > UMBRIERE

UMBRIL *same as* > UMBRERE

UMBRILS > UMBRIL

UMBROSE *same as* > UMBROUS

UMBROUS *adj* shady

UME *n* sour Japanese fruit

UMEBOSHI *n* dried and pickled ume

UMEBOSHIS > UMEBOSHI

UMES > UME

UMFAZI *n* African married woman

UMFAZIS > UMFAZI

UMIAC *variant of* > UMIAK

UMIACK *variant of* > UMIAK

UMIACKS > UMIACK

UMIACS > UMIAC

UMIAK *n* Inuit boat made of skins

UMIAKS > UMIAK

UMIAQ *same as* > UMIAK

UMIAQS > UMIAQ

UMLAUT *n* mark (¨) placed over a vowel, esp in German, to indicate a change in its sound ▷ *vb* modify by umlaut

UMLAUTED > UMLAUT

UMLAUTING > UMLAUT

UMLAUTS > UMLAUT

UMLUNGU *n* White man: used esp as a term of address

UMLUNGUS > UMLUNGU

UMM *same as* > UM

UMMA *n* Muslim community

UMMAH *same as* > UMMA

UMMAHS > UMMAH

UMMAS > UMMA

UMMED > UM

UMMING > UM

UMP *short for* > UMPIRE

UMPED > UMP

UMPH *same as* > HUMPH

UMPHS > UMPH

UMPIE *informal word for* > UMPIRE

UMPIES > UMPY

UMPING > UMP

UMPIRAGE > UMPIRE

UMPIRAGES > UMPIRE

UMPIRE *n* official who rules on the playing of a game ▷ *vb* act as umpire in (a game)

UMPIRED > UMPIRE

UMPIRES > UMPIRE

UMPIRING > UMPIRE

UMPS > UMP

UMPTEEN *adj* very many

UMPTEENTH *n* latest in a tediously long series

UMPTIER > UMPTY

UMPTIEST > UMPTY

UMPTIETH *same as* > UMPTEENTH

UMPTY *adj* very many

UMPY *same as* > UMPIE

UMQUHILE *adv* formerly

UMRA *n* pilgrimage to Mecca that can be made at any time of the year

UMRAH *same as* > UMRA

UMRAHS > UMRAH

UMRAS > UMRA

UMS > UM

UMTEENTH *same as* > UMPTEENTH

UMU *n* type of oven

UMUS > UMU

UMWELT *n* environmental factors that affect the behaviour of an animal or individual

UMWELTS > UMWELT

UMWHILE *same as* > UMQUHILE

UN *pron* spelling of 'one' intended to reflect a dialectal or informal pronunciation

UNABASHED *adj* not ashamed or embarrassed

UNABATED *adv* without any reduction in force ▷ *adj* not losing any original force or violence

UNABATING *adj* not growing less in strength

UNABETTED *adj* without assistance

UNABIDING *adj* not lasting

UNABJURED *adj* not denied

UNABLE *adj* lacking the necessary power, ability, or authority (to do something)

UNABORTED *adj* not aborted

UNABRADED *adj* not eroded

UNABUSED *adj* not abused

UNABUSIVE *adj* not abusive

UNACCRUED *adj* not accrued

UNACCUSED *adj* not charged with wrongdoing

UNACERBIC *adj* not acerbic

UNACHING *adj* not aching

UNACIDIC *adj* not acidic

UNACTABLE *adj* unable to be acted

UNACTED *adj* not acted or performed

UNACTIVE *adj* inactive ▷ *vb* make (a person) inactive

UNACTIVED > UNACTIVE

UNACTIVES > UNACTIVE

UNADAPTED *adj* not adapted

UNADDED *adj* not added

UNADEPT *adj* not adept ▷ *n* person who is not adept

UNADEPTLY > UNADEPT

UNADEPTS > UNADEPT

UNADMIRED *adj* not admired

UNADOPTED *adj* (of a road) not maintained by a local authority

UNADORED *adj* not adored

UNADORNED *adj* not decorated

UNADULT *adj* not mature

UNADVISED *adj* rash or unwise

UNAFRAID *adj* not frightened or nervous

UNAGED *adj* not old

UNAGEING *adj* not ageing

UNAGILE *adj* not agile

UNAGING *same as* > UNAGEING

UNAGREED *adj* not agreed

UNAI *same as* > UNAU

UNAIDABLE *adj* unable to be helped

UNAIDED *adv* without any help or assistance ▷ *adj* not having received any help

UNAIDEDLY > UNAIDED

UNAIMED *adj* not aimed or specifically targeted

UNAIRED *adj* not aired

UNAIS > UNAI

UNAKIN *adj* not related

UNAKING *Shakespearean form of* > UNACHING

UNAKITE *n* type of mineral

UNAKITES > UNAKITE

UNALARMED *adj* not alarmed

UNALERTED *adj* not alerted

UNALIGNED *adj* not aligned

UNALIKE adj not similar

UNALIST n priest holding only one benefice

UNALISTS > UNALIST

UNALIVE adj unaware

UNALLAYED adj not allayed

UNALLEGED adj not alleged

UNALLIED adj not allied

UNALLOWED adj not allowed

UNALLOYED adj not spoiled by being mixed with anything else

UNALTERED adj not altered

UNAMASSED adj not amassed

UNAMAZED adj not greatly surprised

UNAMENDED adj not amended

UNAMERCED adj not amerced

UNAMIABLE adj not amiable

UNAMUSED adj not entertained, diverted, or laughing

UNAMUSING adj not entertaining

UNANCHOR vb remove anchor

UNANCHORS > UNANCHOR

UNANELED adj not having received extreme unction

UNANIMITY > UNANIMOUS

UNANIMOUS adj in complete agreement

UNANNEXED adj not annexed

UNANNOYED adj not annoyed

UNANXIOUS adj not anxious

UNAPPAREL vb undress

UNAPPLIED adj not applied

UNAPT adj not suitable or qualified

UNAPTLY > UNAPT

UNAPTNESS > UNAPT

UNARCHED adj not arched

UNARGUED adj not debated

UNARISEN adj not having risen

UNARM less common word for **>** DISARM

UNARMED adj without weapons

UNARMING > UNARM

UNARMORED adj without armour

UNARMS > UNARM

UNAROUSED adj not aroused

UNARRAYED adj not arrayed

UNARTFUL adj not artful

UNARY adj consisting of, or affecting, a single element or component

UNASHAMED adj not embarrassed, esp when doing something some people might find offensive

UNASKED adv without being asked to do something ▷ adj (of a question) not asked, although sometimes implied

UNASSAYED adj untried

UNASSUMED adj not assumed

UNASSURED adj insecure

UNATONED adj not atoned for

UNATTIRED adj unclothed

UNATTUNED adj unaccustomed

UNAU n two-toed sloth

UNAUDITED adj not having been audited

UNAUS > UNAU

UNAVENGED adj not avenged

UNAVERAGE adj not average

UNAVERTED adj not averted

UNAVOIDED adj not avoided

UNAVOWED adj not openly admitted

UNAWAKE adj not awake

UNAWAKED adj not aroused

UNAWARDED adj not awarded

UNAWARE adj not aware or conscious ▷ adv by surprise

UNAWARELY > UNAWARE

UNAWARES adv by surprise

UNAWED adj not awed

UNAWESOME adj not awesome

UNAXED adj not axed

UNBACKED adj (of a book, chair, etc) not having a back

UNBAFFLED adj not baffled

UNBAG vb take out of a bag

UNBAGGED > UNBAG

UNBAGGING > UNBAG

UNBAGS > UNBAG

UNBAITED adj not baited

UNBAKED adj not having been baked

UNBALANCE vb upset the equilibrium or balance of ▷ n imbalance or instability

UNBALE vb remove from bale

UNBALED > UNBALE

UNBALES > UNBALE

UNBALING > UNBALE

UNBAN vb stop banning or permit again

UNBANDAGE vb remove bandage from

UNBANDED adj not fastened with a band

UNBANKED adj not having been banked

UNBANNED > UNBAN

UNBANNING n act of permitting again

UNBANS > UNBAN

UNBAPTISE same as **>** UNBAPTIZE

UNBAPTIZE vb remove the effect of baptism

UNBAR vb take away a bar or bars from

UNBARBED adj without barbs

UNBARE vb expose

UNBARED > UNBARE

UNBARES > UNBARE

UNBARING > UNBARE

UNBARK vb strip bark from

UNBARKED > UNBARK

UNBARKING > UNBARK

UNBARKS > UNBARK

UNBARRED > UNBAR

UNBARRING > UNBAR

UNBARS > UNBAR

UNBASED adj not having a base

UNBASHFUL adj not shy

UNBASTED adj not basted

UNBATED adj (of a sword, lance, etc) not covered with a protective button

UNBATHED adj unwashed

UNBE vb make non-existent

UNBEAR vb release (horse) from the bearing rein

UNBEARDED adj not having a beard

UNBEARED > UNBEAR

UNBEARING > UNBEAR

UNBEARS > UNBEAR

UNBEATEN adj having suffered no defeat

UNBED vb remove from bed

UNBEDDED > UNBED

UNBEDDING > UNBED

UNBEDS > UNBED

UNBEEN > UNBE

UNBEGET vb deprive of existence

UNBEGETS > UNBEGET

UNBEGGED adj not obtained by begging

UNBEGOT adj unbegotten

UNBEGUILE vb undeceive

UNBEGUN adj not commenced

UNBEING n non-existence

UNBEINGS > UNBEING

UNBEKNOWN adv without the knowledge (of a person) ▷ adj not known (to)

UNBELIEF n disbelief or rejection of belief

UNBELIEFS > UNBELIEF

UNBELIEVE vb disbelieve

UNBELOVED adj unhappy in love

UNBELT vb unbuckle the belt of (a garment)

UNBELTED > UNBELT

UNBELTING > UNBELT

UNBELTS > UNBELT

UNBEMUSED adj not bemused

UNBEND vb become less strict or more informal in one's attitudes or behaviour

UNBENDED > UNBEND

UNBENDING adj rigid or inflexible

UNBENDS > UNBEND

UNBENIGN adj not benign

UNBENT adj not bent or bowed

UNBEREFT adj not bereft

UNBERUFEN adj not called for

UNBESEEM vb be unbefitting to

UNBESEEMS > UNBESEEM

UNBESPEAK vb annul

UNBESPOKE adj not bespoken

UNBIAS vb free from prejudice

UNBIASED adj not having or showing prejudice or favouritism

UNBIASES > UNBIAS

UNBIASING n act or process of making unbiased

UNBIASSED same as **>** UNBIASED

UNBIASSES > UNBIAS

UNBID same as **>** UNBIDDEN

UNBIDDEN adj not ordered or asked

UNBIGOTED adj not bigoted

UNBILLED adj not having been billed

UNBIND vb set free from bonds or chains

UNBINDING > UNBIND

UNBINDS > UNBIND

UNBISHOP vb remove from the position of bishop

UNBISHOPS > UNBISHOP

UNBITT vb remove (cable) from the bitts

UNBITTED > UNBITT

UNBITTEN adj not having been bitten

UNBITTER adj not bitter

UNBITTING > UNBITT

UNBITTS > UNBITT

UNBLAMED vb not blamed

UNBLENDED adj not blended

UNBLENT same as **>** UNBLENDED

UNBLESS vb deprive of a blessing

UNBLESSED adj deprived of blessing

UNBLESSES > UNBLESS

UNBLEST same as **>** UNBLESSED

UNBLIND vb rid of blindness

UNBLINDED > UNBLIND

UNBLINDS > UNBLIND

UNBLOCK vb remove a blockage from

UNBLOCKED > UNBLOCK

UNBLOCKS > UNBLOCK

UNBLOODED adj not bloodied

UNBLOODY adj not covered with blood

UNBLOTTED adj not blotted

UNBLOWED same as **>** UNBLOWN

UNBLOWN adj (of a flower) still in the bud

UNBLUNTED adj not blunted

UNBLURRED adj not blurred

UNBOARDED adj not boarded

UNBOBBED adj not bobbed

UNBODIED adj having no body

UNBODING adj having no presentiment

UNBOILED adj not boiled

UNBOLT vb unfasten a bolt of (a door)

UNBOLTED adj (of grain, meal, or flour) not sifted

UNBOLTING > UNBOLT

UNBOLTS > UNBOLT

UNBONDED adj not bonded

UNBONE vb remove bone from

UNBONED adj (of meat, fish, etc) not having had the bones removed

UNBONES > UNBONE

UNBONING > UNBONE

UNBONNET vb remove the bonnet from

UNBONNETS > UNBONNET

UNBOOKED adj not reserved

UNBOOKISH adj not studious

UNBOOT *vb* remove boots from

UNBOOTED > UNBOOT

UNBOOTING > UNBOOT

UNBOOTS > UNBOOT

UNBORE *adj* unborn

UNBORN *adj* not yet born

UNBORNE *adj* not borne

UNBOSOM *vb* relieve (oneself) of (secrets or feelings) by telling someone

UNBOSOMED > UNBOSOM

UNBOSOMER > UNBOSOM

UNBOSOMS > UNBOSOM

UNBOTTLE *vb* allow out of bottle

UNBOTTLED > UNBOTTLE

UNBOTTLES > UNBOTTLE

UNBOUGHT *adj* not purchased

UNBOUNCY *adj* not bouncy

UNBOUND *adj* (of a book) not bound within a cover

UNBOUNDED *adj* having no boundaries or limits

UNBOWED *adj* not giving in or submitting

UNBOWING *adj* not bowing

UNBOX *vb* empty a box

UNBOXED > UNBOX

UNBOXES > UNBOX

UNBOXING > UNBOX

UNBRACE *vb* remove tension or strain from

UNBRACED > UNBRACE

UNBRACES > UNBRACE

UNBRACING > UNBRACE

UNBRAID *vb* remove braids from

UNBRAIDED > UNBRAID

UNBRAIDS > UNBRAID

UNBRAKE *vb* stop reducing speed by releasing brake

UNBRAKED > UNBRAKE

UNBRAKES > UNBRAKE

UNBRAKING > UNBRAKE

UNBRANDED *adj* not having a brand name

UNBRASTE *archaic past form of* > UNBRACE

UNBRED *adj* not taught or instructed

UNBREECH *vb* remove breech from

UNBRIDGED *adj* not spanned by a bridge

UNBRIDLE *vb* remove the bridle from (a horse)

UNBRIDLED *adj* (of feelings or behaviour) not controlled in any way

UNBRIDLES > UNBRIDLE

UNBRIEFED *adj* not instructed

UNBRIGHT *adj* not bright

UNBRIZZED *same as* > UNBRUISED

UNBROILED *adj* not broiled

UNBROKE *same as* > UNBROKEN

UNBROKEN *adj* complete or whole

UNBROWNED *adj* not browned

UNBRUISED *adj* not bruised

UNBRUSED *same as* > UNBRUISED

UNBRUSHED *adj* not brushed

UNBUCKLE *vb* undo the buckle or buckles of

UNBUCKLED > UNBUCKLE

UNBUCKLES > UNBUCKLE

UNBUDDED *adj* not having buds

UNBUDGING *adj* not moving

UNBUILD *vb* destroy

UNBUILDS > UNBUILD

UNBUILT > UNBUILD

UNBULKIER > UNBULKY

UNBULKY *adj* not bulky

UNBUNDLE *vb* separate (hardware from software) for sales purposes

UNBUNDLED > UNBUNDLE

UNBUNDLER > UNBUNDLE

UNBUNDLES > UNBUNDLE

UNBURDEN *vb* relieve (one's mind or oneself) of a worry by confiding in someone

UNBURDENS > UNBURDEN

UNBURIED > UNBURY

UNBURIES > UNBURY

UNBURNED *same as* > UNBURNT

UNBURNT *adj* not burnt

UNBURROW *vb* remove from a burrow

UNBURROWS > UNBURROW

UNBURTHEN *same as* > UNBURDEN

UNBURY *vb* unearth

UNBURYING > UNBURY

UNBUSIED > UNBUSY

UNBUSIER > UNBUSY

UNBUSIES > UNBUSY

UNBUSIEST > UNBUSY

UNBUSTED *adj* unbroken

UNBUSY *adj* not busy ▷ *vb* make less busy

UNBUSYING > UNBUSY

UNBUTTON *vb* undo by unfastening the buttons of (a garment)

UNBUTTONS > UNBUTTON

UNCAGE *vb* release from a cage

UNCAGED *adj* at liberty

UNCAGES > UNCAGE

UNCAGING > UNCAGE

UNCAKE *vb* remove compacted matter from

UNCAKED > UNCAKE

UNCAKES > UNCAKE

UNCAKING > UNCAKE

UNCALLED *adj* not called

UNCANDID *adj* not frank

UNCANDLED *adj* not illuminated by candle

UNCANDOR *n* lack of candor

UNCANDORS > UNCANDOR

UNCANDOUR *n* lack of candour

UNCANNED *adj* not canned

UNCANNIER > UNCANNY

UNCANNILY > UNCANNY

UNCANNY *adj* weird or mysterious

UNCANONIC *adj* unclerical

UNCAP *vb* remove a cap or top from (a container)

UNCAPABLE *same as* > INCAPABLE

UNCAPE *vb* remove the cape from

UNCAPED > UNCAPE

UNCAPES > UNCAPE

UNCAPING > UNCAPE

UNCAPPED > UNCAP

UNCAPPING > UNCAP

UNCAPS > UNCAP

UNCARDED *adj* not carded

UNCARED *adj* as in *uncared for* not cared (for)

UNCAREFUL *adj* careless

UNCARING *adj* thoughtless

UNCART *vb* remove from a cart

UNCARTED > UNCART

UNCARTING > UNCART

UNCARTS > UNCART

UNCARVED *adj* not carved

UNCASE *vb* display

UNCASED > UNCASE

UNCASES > UNCASE

UNCASHED *adj* not cashed

UNCASING > UNCASE

UNCASKED *adj* removed from a cask

UNCAST *adj* not cast ▷ *vb* undo the process of casting

UNCASTED > UNCAST

UNCASTING > UNCAST

UNCASTS > UNCAST

UNCATCHY *adj* not catchy

UNCATE *same as* > UNCINATE

UNCATERED *adj* not catered

UNCAUGHT *adj* not caught

UNCAUSED *adj* not brought into existence by any cause

UNCE *same as* > OUNCE

UNCEASING *adj* continuing without a break

UNCEDED *adj* not ceded

UNCERTAIN *adj* not able to be accurately known or predicted

UNCES > UNCE

UNCESSANT *same as* > INCESSANT

UNCHAIN *vb* remove a chain or chains from

UNCHAINED > UNCHAIN

UNCHAINS > UNCHAIN

UNCHAIR *vb* unseat from chair

UNCHAIRED > UNCHAIR

UNCHAIRS > UNCHAIR

UNCHANCY *adj* unlucky, ill-omened, or dangerous

UNCHANGED *adj* remaining the same

UNCHARGE *vb* unload

UNCHARGED *adj* (of land or other property) not subject to a charge

UNCHARGES > UNCHARGE

UNCHARIER > UNCHARY

UNCHARITY *n* lack of charity

UNCHARM *vb* disenchant

UNCHARMED *adj* not charmed

UNCHARMS > UNCHARM

UNCHARNEL *vb* exhume

UNCHARRED *adj* not charred

UNCHARTED *adj* (of an area of sea or land) not having had a map made of it, esp because it is unexplored

UNCHARY *adj* not cautious

UNCHASTE *adj* not chaste

UNCHASTER > UNCHASTE

UNCHECK *vb* remove check mark from

UNCHECKED *adj* not prevented from continuing or growing ▷ *adv* without being stopped or hindered

UNCHECKS > UNCHECK

UNCHEERED *adj* miserable

UNCHEWED *adj* not chewed

UNCHIC *adj* not chic

UNCHICLY > UNCHIC

UNCHILD *vb* deprive of children

UNCHILDED > UNCHILD

UNCHILDS > UNCHILD

UNCHILLED *adj* not chilled

UNCHOKE *vb* unblock

UNCHOKED > UNCHOKE

UNCHOKES > UNCHOKE

UNCHOKING > UNCHOKE

UNCHOSEN *adj* not chosen

UNCHRISOM *adj* unchristened

UNCHURCH *vb* excommunicate

UNCI > UNCUS

UNCIA *n* twelfth part

UNCIAE > UNCIA

UNCIAL *adj* of a writing style used in manuscripts of the third to ninth centuries ▷ *n* uncial letter or manuscript

UNCIALLY > UNCIAL

UNCIALS > UNCIAL

UNCIFORM *adj* having the shape of a hook ▷ *n* any hook-shaped structure or part, esp a small bone of the wrist

UNCIFORMS > UNCIFORM

UNCINAL *same as* > UNCINATE

UNCINARIA *same as* > HOOKWORM

UNCINATE *adj* shaped like a hook

UNCINATED > UNCINATE

UNCINI > UNCINUS

UNCINUS *n* small hooked structure

UNCIPHER *vb* decode

UNCIPHERS > UNCIPHER

UNCITED *adj* not quoted

UNCIVIL *adj* impolite, rude or bad-mannered

UNCIVILLY > UNCIVIL

UNCLAD *adj* having no clothes on

UNCLAIMED *adj* not having been claimed

UNCLAMP *vb* remove clamp from

UNCLAMPED > UNCLAMP

UNCLAMPS > UNCLAMP

UNCLARITY *adj* lack of clarity

UNCLASP *vb* unfasten the clasp of (something)

UNCLASPED > UNCLASP

UNCLASPS > UNCLASP

UNCLASSED *adj* not divided into classes

UNCLASSY *adj* not classy

UNCLAWED *adj* not clawed

UNCLE *n* brother of one's father or mother ▷ *vb* refer to as uncle

U

UNCLEAN adj lacking moral, spiritual, or physical cleanliness
UNCLEANED adj not cleaned
UNCLEANER > UNCLEAN
UNCLEANLY adv in an unclean manner ▷ adj characterized by an absence of cleanliness
UNCLEAR adj confusing or hard to understand
UNCLEARED adj not cleared
UNCLEARER > UNCLEAR
UNCLEARLY > UNCLEAR
UNCLED > UNCLE
UNCLEFT adj not cleft
UNCLENCH vb relax from a clenched position
UNCLES > UNCLE
UNCLESHIP n position of an uncle
UNCLEW vb undo
UNCLEWED > UNCLEW
UNCLEWING > UNCLEW
UNCLEWS > UNCLEW
UNCLICHED adj not cliched
UNCLIMBED adj not climbed
UNCLINCH same as **>** UNCLENCH
UNCLING > UNCLE
UNCLIP vb remove clip from
UNCLIPPED > UNCLIP
UNCLIPS > UNCLIP
UNCLIPT archaic past form of **>** UNCLIP
UNCLOAK vb remove cloak from
UNCLOAKED > UNCLOAK
UNCLOAKS > UNCLOAK
UNCLOG vb remove an obstruction from (a drain, etc)
UNCLOGGED > UNCLOG
UNCLOGS > UNCLOG
UNCLONED adj not cloned
UNCLOSE vb open or cause to open
UNCLOSED > UNCLOSE
UNCLOSES > UNCLOSE
UNCLOSING > UNCLOSE
UNCLOTHE vb take off garments from
UNCLOTHED > UNCLOTHE
UNCLOTHES > UNCLOTHE
UNCLOUD vb clear clouds from
UNCLOUDED > UNCLOUD
UNCLOUDS > UNCLOUD
UNCLOUDY adj not cloudy
UNCLOVEN adj not cleaved
UNCLOYED adj not cloyed
UNCLOYING adj not cloying
UNCLUTCH vb open from tight grip
UNCLUTTER vb tidy and straighten up
UNCO adj unfamiliar or strange ▷ n remarkable person or thing
UNCOATED adj not covered with a layer
UNCOATING n process whereby a virus exposes its genome in order to replicate
UNCOBBLED adj not cobbled
UNCOCK vb remove from a cocked position

UNCOCKED > UNCOCK
UNCOCKING > UNCOCK
UNCOCKS > UNCOCK
UNCODED adj not coded
UNCOER > UNCO
UNCOERCED adj unforced
UNCOES > UNCO
UNCOEST > UNCO
UNCOFFIN vb take out of a coffin
UNCOFFINS > UNCOFFIN
UNCOIL vb unwind or untwist
UNCOILED > UNCOIL
UNCOILING > UNCOIL
UNCOILS > UNCOIL
UNCOINED adj (of a metal) not made into coin
UNCOLORED adj not coloured
UNCOLT vb divest of a horse
UNCOLTED > UNCOLT
UNCOLTING > UNCOLT
UNCOLTS > UNCOLT
UNCOMBED adj not combed
UNCOMBINE vb break apart
UNCOMELY adj not attractive
UNCOMFIER > UNCOMFY
UNCOMFY adj not comfortable
UNCOMIC adj not comical
UNCOMMON adj not happening or encountered often
UNCONCERN n apathy or indifference
UNCONFINE vb remove restrictions from
UNCONFORM adj dissimilar
UNCONFUSE vb remove confusion from
UNCONGEAL vb become liquid again
UNCOOKED adj raw
UNCOOL adj unsophisticated
UNCOOLED adj not cooled
UNCOPE vb unmuzzle
UNCOPED > UNCOPE
UNCOPES > UNCOPE
UNCOPING > UNCOPE
UNCORD vb release from cords
UNCORDED > UNCORD
UNCORDIAL adj unfriendly
UNCORDING > UNCORD
UNCORDS > UNCORD
UNCORK vb remove the cork from (a bottle)
UNCORKED > UNCORK
UNCORKING > UNCORK
UNCORKS > UNCORK
UNCORRUPT adj not corrupt
UNCOS > UNCO
UNCOSTLY adj inexpensive
UNCOUNTED adj unable to be counted
UNCOUPLE vb disconnect or become disconnected
UNCOUPLED > UNCOUPLE
UNCOUPLER > UNCOUPLE
UNCOUPLES > UNCOUPLE
UNCOURTLY adj not courtly
UNCOUTH adj lacking in good manners, refinement, or grace
UNCOUTHER > UNCOUTH

UNCOUTHLY > UNCOUTH
UNCOVER vb reveal or disclose
UNCOVERED adj not covered
UNCOVERS > UNCOVER
UNCOWL vb remove hood from
UNCOWLED > UNCOWL
UNCOWLING > UNCOWL
UNCOWLS > UNCOWL
UNCOY adj not modest
UNCOYNED same as **>** UNCOINED
UNCRACKED adj not cracked
UNCRATE vb remove from a crate
UNCRATED > UNCRATE
UNCRATES > UNCRATE
UNCRATING > UNCRATE
UNCRAZIER > UNCRAZY
UNCRAZY adj not crazy
UNCREASED adj not creased
UNCREATE vb unmake
UNCREATED > UNCREATE
UNCREATES > UNCREATE
UNCREWED adj not crewed
UNCROPPED adj not cropped
UNCROSS vb cease to cross
UNCROSSED > UNCROSS
UNCROSSES > UNCROSS
UNCROWDED adj (of a confined space, area, etc) not containing too many people or things
UNCROWN vb take the crown from
UNCROWNED adj having the powers, but not the title, of royalty
UNCROWNS > UNCROWN
UNCRUDDED adj uncurdled
UNCRUMPLE vb remove creases from
UNCRUSHED adj not crushed
UNCTION n act of anointing with oil in sacramental ceremonies
UNCTIONS > UNCTION
UNCTUOUS adj pretending to be kind and concerned
UNCUFF vb remove handcuffs from
UNCUFFED > UNCUFF
UNCUFFING > UNCUFF
UNCUFFS > UNCUFF
UNCULLED adj not culled
UNCURABLE same as **>** INCURABLE
UNCURABLY > UNCURABLE
UNCURB vb remove curbs from (a horse)
UNCURBED > UNCURB
UNCURBING > UNCURB
UNCURBS > UNCURB
UNCURDLED adj not curdled
UNCURED adj not cured
UNCURIOUS adj not curious
UNCURL vb move or cause to move out of a curled or rolled up position
UNCURLED > UNCURL
UNCURLING > UNCURL
UNCURLS > UNCURL
UNCURRENT adj not current
UNCURSE vb remove curse from
UNCURSED > UNCURSE

UNCURSES > UNCURSE
UNCURSING > UNCURSE
UNCURTAIN vb reveal
UNCURVED adj not curved
UNCUS n hooked part or process, as in the human cerebrum
UNCUT adj not shortened or censored
UNCUTE adj not cute
UNCYNICAL adj not cynical
UNDAM vb free from a dam
UNDAMAGED adj not spoilt or damaged
UNDAMMED > UNDAM
UNDAMMING > UNDAM
UNDAMNED adj not damned
UNDAMPED adj (of an oscillating system) having unrestricted motion
UNDAMS > UNDAM
UNDARING adj not daring
UNDASHED adj not dashed
UNDATABLE adj not able to be dated
UNDATE vb remove date from
UNDATED adj (of a manuscript, letter, etc) not having an identifying date
UNDATES > UNDATE
UNDATING > UNDATE
UNDAUNTED adj not put off, discouraged, or beaten
UNDAWNING adj not dawning
UNDAZZLE vb recover from a daze
UNDAZZLED > UNDAZZLE
UNDAZZLES > UNDAZZLE
UNDE same as **>** UNDEE
UNDEAD adj alive
UNDEAF vb restore hearing to
UNDEAFED > UNDEAF
UNDEAFING > UNDEAF
UNDEAFS > UNDEAF
UNDEALT adj not dealt (with)
UNDEAR adj not dear
UNDEBASED adj not debased
UNDEBATED adj not debated
UNDECAGON n polygon having eleven sides
UNDECAYED adj not rotten
UNDECEIVE vb reveal the truth to (someone previously misled or deceived)
UNDECENT same as **>** INDECENT
UNDECIDED adj not having made up one's mind
UNDECIMAL adj based on the number 11
UNDECK vb remove decorations from
UNDECKED > UNDECK
UNDECKING > UNDECK
UNDECKS > UNDECK
UNDEE adj wavy
UNDEEDED adj not transferred by deed
UNDEFACED adj not spoilt
UNDEFIDE same as **>** UNDEFIED
UNDEFIED adj not challenged

UNDEFILED *adj* not defiled

UNDEFINED *adj* not defined or made clear

UNDEIFIED > UNDEIFY

UNDEIFIES > UNDEIFY

UNDEIFY *vb* strip of the status of a deity

UNDELAYED *adj* not delayed

UNDELETE *vb* restore (a deleted computer file or text)

UNDELETED *adj* not deleted, or restored after being deleted

UNDELETES > UNDELETE

UNDELIGHT *n* absence of delight

UNDELUDED *adj* not deluded

UNDENIED *adj* not denied

UNDENTED *adj* not dented

UNDER *adv* indicating movement to or position beneath the underside or base ▷ *prep* less than

UNDERACT *vb* play (a role) without adequate emphasis

UNDERACTS > UNDERACT

UNDERAGE *adj* below the required or standard age ▷ *n* shortfall

UNDERAGED *adj* not old enough

UNDERAGES > UNDERAGE

UNDERARM *adj* denoting a style of throwing in which the hand is swung below shoulder level ▷ *adv* in an underarm style ▷ *n* armpit

UNDERARMS > UNDERARM

UNDERATE > UNDEREAT

UNDERBAKE *vb* bake insufficiently

UNDERBEAR *vb* endure

UNDERBID *vb* submit a bid lower than that of (others)

UNDERBIDS > UNDERBID

UNDERBIT > UNDERBITE

UNDERBITE *vb* use insufficient acid in etching

UNDERBODY *n* underpart of a body, as of an animal or motor vehicle

UNDERBORE > UNDERBEAR

UNDERBOSS *n* person who is second in command

UNDERBRED *adj* of impure stock

UNDERBRIM *n* part of a hat

UNDERBUD *vb* produce fewer buds than expected

UNDERBUDS > UNDERBUD

UNDERBUSH *n* undergrowth or underbrush

UNDERBUY *vb* buy (stock in trade) in amounts lower than required

UNDERBUYS > UNDERBUY

UNDERCARD *n* event supporting a main event

UNDERCART *n* aircraft undercarriage

UNDERCAST *vb* cast beneath

UNDERCLAD *adj* not wearing enough clothes

UNDERCLAY *n* grey or whitish clay rock containing fossilized plant roots and occurring beneath coal

seams. When used as a refractory, it is known as fireclay

UNDERCLUB *vb* use a golf club that will not hit the ball as far as required

UNDERCOAT *n* coat of paint applied before the final coat ▷ *vb* apply an undercoat to a surface

UNDERCOOK *vb* cook for too short a time or at too low a temperature

UNDERCOOL *vb* cool insufficiently

UNDERCUT *vb* charge less than (a competitor) to obtain trade ▷ *n* act or an instance of cutting underneath

UNDERCUTS > UNDERCUT

UNDERDAKS *pl n* underpants

UNDERDECK *n* lower deck of a vessel

UNDERDID > UNDERDO

UNDERDO *vb* do (something) inadequately

UNDERDOER > UNDERDO

UNDERDOES > UNDERDO

UNDERDOG *n* person or team in a weak or underprivileged position

UNDERDOGS > UNDERDOG

UNDERDONE *adj* not cooked enough

UNDERDOSE *vb* give insufficient dose

UNDERDRAW *vb* sketch the subject before painting it on the same surface

UNDERDREW > UNDERDRAW

UNDEREAT *vb* not eat enough

UNDEREATS > UNDEREAT

UNDERFED > UNDERFEED

UNDERFEED *vb* give too little food to ▷ *n* apparatus by which fuel, etc, is supplied from below

UNDERFELT *n* thick felt laid under a carpet to increase insulation

UNDERFIRE *vb* bake insufficiently

UNDERFISH *vb* catch fewer fish than the permitted maximum amount

UNDERFLOW *n* undercurrent

UNDERFONG *vb* receive

UNDERFOOT *adv* under the feet

UNDERFUND *vb* provide insufficient funding

UNDERFUR *n* layer of dense soft fur occurring beneath the outer coarser fur in certain mammals

UNDERFURS > UNDERFUR

UNDERGIRD *vb* strengthen or reinforce by passing a rope, cable, or chain around the underside of (an object, load, etc)

UNDERGIRT > UNDERGIRD

UNDERGO *vb* experience, endure, or sustain

UNDERGOD *n* subordinate god

UNDERGODS > UNDERGOD

UNDERGOER > UNDERGO

UNDERGOES > UNDERGO

UNDERGONE > UNDERGO

UNDERGOWN *n* gown worn under another article of clothing

UNDERGRAD *n* person studying for a first degree; undergraduate

UNDERHAIR *n* lower layer of animal's hair

UNDERHAND *vb* throw with the arm kept below the level of the shoulder

UNDERHEAT *vb* heat insufficiently

UNDERHUNG *adj* (of the lower jaw) projecting beyond the upper jaw

UNDERIVED *adj* not derived

UNDERJAW *n* lower jaw

UNDERJAWS > UNDERJAW

UNDERKEEP *vb* suppress

UNDERKEPT > UNDERKEEP

UNDERKILL *n* less force than is needed to defeat enemy

UNDERKING *n* ruler subordinate to a king

UNDERLAID *adj* laid underneath

UNDERLAIN > UNDERLIE

UNDERLAP *vb* project under the edge of

UNDERLAPS > UNDERLAP

UNDERLAY *n* felt or rubber laid beneath a carpet to increase insulation and resilience ▷ *vb* place (something) under or beneath

UNDERLAYS > UNDERLAY

UNDERLEAF *n* (in liverworts) any of the leaves forming a row on the underside of the stem: usually smaller than the two rows of lateral leaves and sometimes absent

UNDERLET *vb* let for a price lower than expected or justified

UNDERLETS > UNDERLET

UNDERLIE *vb* lie or be placed under

UNDERLIER > UNDERLIE

UNDERLIES > UNDERLIE

UNDERLINE *vb* draw a line under ▷ *n* line underneath, esp under written matter

UNDERLING *n* subordinate

UNDERLIP *n* lower lip

UNDERLIPS > UNDERLIP

UNDERLIT *adj* lit from beneath

UNDERLOAD *vb* load incompletely

UNDERMAN *vb* supply with insufficient staff ▷ *n* subordinate man

UNDERMANS > UNDERMAN

UNDERMEN > UNDERMAN

UNDERMINE *vb* weaken gradually

UNDERMOST *adj* being the furthest under ▷ *adv* in the lowest place

UNDERN *n* time between sunrise and noon

UNDERNOTE *n* undertone

UNDERNS > UNDERN

UNDERPAD *n* layer of soft foam laid under carpeting

UNDERPADS > UNDERPAD

UNDERPAID *adj* not paid as much as the job deserves

UNDERPART *n* lower part or underside of something such as an animal

UNDERPASS *n* section of a road that passes under another road or a railway line

UNDERPAY *vb* pay someone insufficiently

UNDERPAYS > UNDERPAY

UNDERPEEP *vb* peep under

UNDERPIN *vb* give strength or support to

UNDERPINS > UNDERPIN

UNDERPLAY *vb* achieve (an effect) by deliberate lack of emphasis

UNDERPLOT *n* subsidiary plot in a literary or dramatic work

UNDERPROP *vb* prop up from beneath

UNDERRAN > UNDERRUN

UNDERRATE *vb* underestimate

UNDERRIPE *adj* not quite ripe

UNDERRUN *vb* run beneath

UNDERRUNS > UNDERRUN

UNDERSAID > UNDERSAY

UNDERSAY *vb* say by way of response

UNDERSAYS > UNDERSAY

UNDERSEA *adv* below the surface of the sea

UNDERSEAL *n* coating of tar etc applied to the underside of a motor vehicle to prevent corrosion ▷ *vb* apply such a coating to a motor vehicle

UNDERSEAS *same as* > UNDERSEA

UNDERSELF *n* subconscious or person within

UNDERSELL *vb* sell at a price lower than that of another seller

UNDERSET *n* ocean undercurrent ▷ *vb* support from underneath

UNDERSETS > UNDERSET

UNDERSHOT *adj* (of the lower jaw) projecting beyond the upper jaw

UNDERSIDE *n* bottom or lower surface

UNDERSIGN *vb* sign the bottom (of a document)

UNDERSIZE *adj* smaller than normal

UNDERSKY *n* lower sky

UNDERSOIL *another word for* > SUBSOIL

UNDERSOLD > UNDERSELL

UNDERSONG *n* accompanying secondary melody

UNDERSOW *vb* sow a later-growing crop on already-seeded land

UNDERSOWN > UNDERSOW
UNDERSOWS > UNDERSOW
UNDERSPIN n backspin
UNDERTAKE vb agree or commit oneself to (something) or to do (something)
UNDERTANE Shakespearean past participle of > UNDERTAKE
UNDERTAX vb tax insufficiently
UNDERTIME n time spent by an employee at work in non-work-related activities like socializing, surfing the internet, making personal telephone calls, etc
UNDERTINT n slight, subdued, or delicate tint
UNDERTONE n quiet tone of voice
UNDERTOOK past tense of > UNDERTAKE
UNDERTOW n strong undercurrent flowing in a different direction from the surface current
UNDERTOWS > UNDERTOW
UNDERUSE vb use less than normal
UNDERUSED > UNDERUSE
UNDERUSES > UNDERUSE
UNDERVEST another name for > VEST
UNDERVOTE n vote cast but invalid
UNDERWAY adj in progress ▷ adv in progress
UNDERWEAR n clothing worn under the outer garments and next to the skin
UNDERWENT past tense of > UNDERGO
UNDERWING n hind wing of an insect, esp when covered by the forewing
UNDERWIRE vb support with wire underneath
UNDERWIT n half-wit
UNDERWITS > UNDERWIT
UNDERWOOD n small trees, bushes, ferns, etc growing beneath taller trees in a wood or forest
UNDERWOOL n lower layer of an animal's coat
UNDERWORK vb do less work than expected
UNDESERT n lack of worth
UNDESERTS > UNDESERT
UNDESERVE vb fail to deserve
UNDESIRED adj not desired
UNDEVOUT adj not devout
UNDID > UNDO
UNDIES pl n underwear, esp women's
UNDIGHT vb remove
UNDIGHTS > UNDIGHT
UNDIGNIFY vb divest of dignity
UNDILUTED adj (of a liquid) not having any water added to it
UNDIMMED adj (of eyes, light, etc) still bright or shining

UNDINE n female water spirit
UNDINES > UNDINE
UNDINISM n obsession with water
UNDINISMS > UNDINISM
UNDINTED adj not dinted
UNDIPPED adj not dipped
UNDIVIDED adj total and whole-hearted
UNDIVINE adj not divine
UNDO vb open, unwrap ▷ n instance of undoing something
UNDOABLE adj impossible
UNDOCILE adj not docile
UNDOCK vb take out of a dock
UNDOCKED > UNDOCK
UNDOCKING > UNDOCK
UNDOCKS > UNDOCK
UNDOER > UNDO
UNDOERS > UNDO
UNDOES > UNDO
UNDOING n cause of someone's downfall
UNDOINGS > UNDOING
UNDONE adj not done or completed
UNDOOMED adj not doomed
UNDOS > UNDO
UNDOTTED adj not dotted
UNDOUBLE vb stretch out
UNDOUBLED > UNDOUBLE
UNDOUBLES > UNDOUBLE
UNDOUBTED adj certain or indisputable
UNDOWERED adj not dowered
UNDRAINED adj not drained
UNDRAPE vb remove drapery from
UNDRAPED > UNDRAPE
UNDRAPES > UNDRAPE
UNDRAPING > UNDRAPE
UNDRAW vb open (curtains)
UNDRAWING > UNDRAW
UNDRAWN > UNDRAW
UNDRAWS > UNDRAW
UNDREADED adj not feared
UNDREAMED adj not thought of or imagined
UNDREAMT same as > UNDREAMED
UNDRESS vb take off clothes from (oneself or another) ▷ n partial or complete nakedness ▷ adj characterized by or requiring informal or normal working dress or uniform
UNDRESSED adj partially or completely naked
UNDRESSES > UNDRESS
UNDREST same as > UNDRESSED
UNDREW > UNDRAW
UNDRIED adj not dried
UNDRILLED adj not drilled
UNDRIVEN adj not driven
UNDROSSY adj pure
UNDROWNED adj not drowned
UNDRUNK adj not drunk
UNDUBBED adj (of a film, etc) not dubbed
UNDUE adj greater than is reasonable; excessive

UNDUG adj not having been dug
UNDULANCE > UNDULANT
UNDULANCY > UNDULANT
UNDULANT adj resembling waves
UNDULAR > UNDULATE
UNDULATE vb move in waves ▷ adj having a wavy or rippled appearance, margin, or form
UNDULATED > UNDULATE
UNDULATES > UNDULATE
UNDULATOR > UNDULATE
UNDULLED adj not dulled
UNDULOSE same as > UNDULOUS
UNDULOUS adj undulate
UNDULY adv excessively
UNDUTEOUS same as > UNDUTIFUL
UNDUTIFUL adj not dutiful
UNDY same as > UNDEE
UNDYED adj not dyed
UNDYING adj never ending, eternal
UNDYINGLY > UNDYING
UNDYNAMIC adj not dynamic
UNEAGER adj nonchalant
UNEAGERLY > UNEAGER
UNEARED adj not ploughed
UNEARNED adj not deserved
UNEARTH vb reveal or discover by searching
UNEARTHED > UNEARTH
UNEARTHLY adj ghostly or eerie
UNEARTHS > UNEARTH
UNEASE > UNEASY
UNEASES > UNEASY
UNEASIER > UNEASY
UNEASIEST > UNEASY
UNEASILY > UNEASY
UNEASY adj (of a person) anxious or apprehensive
UNEATABLE adj (of food) so rotten or unattractive as to be unfit to eat
UNEATEN adj (of food) not having been consumed
UNEATH adv not easily
UNEATHES > UNEATH
UNEDGE vb take the edge off
UNEDGED > UNEDGE
UNEDGES > UNEDGE
UNEDGING > UNEDGE
UNEDIBLE variant of > INEDIBLE
UNEDITED adj not edited
UNEFFACED adj not destroyed
UNELATED adj not elated
UNELECTED adj not elected
UNEMPTIED adj not emptied
UNENDED adj without end
UNENDING adj not showing any signs of ever stopping
UNENDOWED adj not endowed
UNENGAGED adj not engaged
UNENJOYED adj not enjoyed
UNENSURED adj not ensured
UNENTERED adj not having been entered previously

UNENVIED adj not envied
UNENVIOUS adj not envious
UNENVYING adj not envying
UNEQUABLE adj unstable
UNEQUAL adj not equal in quantity, size, rank, value, etc ▷ n person who is not equal
UNEQUALED adj (in US English) not equalled
UNEQUALLY > UNEQUAL
UNEQUALS > UNEQUAL
UNERASED adj not rubbed out
UNEROTIC adj not erotic
UNERRING adj never mistaken, consistently accurate
UNERUPTED adj (of a volcano) not having erupted
UNESPIED adj unnoticed
UNESSAYED adj untried
UNESSENCE vb deprive of being
UNETH same as > UNEATH
UNETHICAL adj morally wrong
UNEVADED adj not evaded
UNEVEN adj not level or flat
UNEVENER > UNEVEN
UNEVENEST > UNEVEN
UNEVENLY > UNEVEN
UNEVOLVED adj not evolved
UNEXALTED adj not exalted
UNEXCITED adj not aroused to pleasure, interest, agitation, etc
UNEXCUSED adj not excused
UNEXOTIC adj not exotic
UNEXPERT same as > INEXPERT
UNEXPIRED adj not having expired
UNEXPOSED adj not having been exhibited or brought to public notice
UNEXTINCT adj not extinct
UNEXTREME adj not extreme
UNEYED adj unseen
UNFABLED adj not fictitious
UNFACETED adj not faceted
UNFACT n event or thing not provable
UNFACTS > UNFACT
UNFADABLE adj incapable of fading
UNFADED adj not faded
UNFADING adj not fading
UNFAILING adj continuous or reliable
UNFAIR adj not right, fair, or just ▷ vb disfigure
UNFAIRED > UNFAIR
UNFAIRER > UNFAIR
UNFAIREST > UNFAIR
UNFAIRING > UNFAIR
UNFAIRLY > UNFAIR
UNFAIRS > UNFAIR
UNFAITH n lack of faith
UNFAITHS > UNFAITH
UNFAKED adj not faked
UNFALLEN adj not fallen
UNFAMED adj not famous
UNFAMOUS adj not famous
UNFANCIED > UNFANCY
UNFANCIER > UNFANCY

UNFANCY *vb* consider (a sportsperson or team) unlikely to win or succeed ▷ *adj* not fancy

UNFANNED *adj* not fanned

UNFASTEN *vb* undo, untie, or open or become undone, untied, or opened

UNFASTENS > UNFASTEN

UNFAULTY *adj* not faulty

UNFAVORED *adj* (in US English) not favoured

UNFAZABLE *adj* not capable of being fazed

UNFAZED *adj* not disconcerted

UNFEARED *adj* unafraid

UNFEARFUL *adj* not scared

UNFEARING *adj* having no fear

UNFED *adj* not fed

UNFEED *adj* unpaid

UNFEELING *adj* without sympathy

UNFEIGNED *adj* not feigned

UNFELLED *adj* not cut down

UNFELT *adj* not felt

UNFELTED *adj* not felted

UNFENCE *vb* remove a fence from

UNFENCED *adj* not enclosed by a fence

UNFENCES > UNFENCE

UNFENCING > UNFENCE

UNFERTILE *same as* > INFERTILE

UNFETTER *vb* release from fetters, bonds, etc

UNFETTERS > UNFETTER

UNFEUDAL *adj* not feudal

UNFEUED *adj* not feued

UNFIGURED *adj* not numbered

UNFILDE *archaic form of* > UNFILED

UNFILED *adj* not filed

UNFILIAL *adj* not filial

UNFILLED *adj* (of a container, receptacle, etc) not having become or been made full

UNFILMED *adj* not filmed

UNFINE *adj* not fine

UNFIRED *adj* not fired

UNFIRM *adj* soft or unsteady

UNFISHED *adj* not used for fishing

UNFIT *adj* unqualified or unsuitable ▷ *vb* make unfit

UNFITLY *adv* in an unfit way

UNFITNESS > UNFIT

UNFITS > UNFIT

UNFITTED *adj* unsuitable

UNFITTER > UNFIT

UNFITTEST > UNFIT

UNFITTING *adj* not fitting

UNFIX *vb* unfasten, detach, or loosen

UNFIXED *adj* not fixed

UNFIXES > UNFIX

UNFIXING > UNFIX

UNFIXITY *n* instability

UNFIXT *variant of* > UNFIXED

UNFLAPPED *adj* not agitated or excited

UNFLASHY *adj* not flashy

UNFLAWED *adj* perfect

UNFLEDGED *adj* (of a young bird) not having developed adult feathers

UNFLESH *vb* remove flesh from

UNFLESHED > UNFLESH

UNFLESHES > UNFLESH

UNFLESHLY *adj* immaterial

UNFLEXED *adj* unbent

UNFLOORED *adj* without flooring

UNFLUSH *vb* lose the colour caused by flushing

UNFLUSHED > UNFLUSH

UNFLUSHES > UNFLUSH

UNFLUTED *adj* not fluted

UNFLYABLE *adj* unable to be flown

UNFOCUSED *adj* blurry

UNFOILED *adj* not thwarted

UNFOLD *vb* open or spread out from a folded state

UNFOLDED > UNFOLD

UNFOLDER > UNFOLD

UNFOLDERS > UNFOLD

UNFOLDING > UNFOLD

UNFOLDS > UNFOLD

UNFOLLOW *vb* stop following a person on a social networking site

UNFOLLOWS > UNFOLLOW

UNFOND *adj* not fond

UNFONDLY *adv* in an unfond manner

UNFOOL *vb* undeceive

UNFOOLED > UNFOOL

UNFOOLING > UNFOOL

UNFOOLS > UNFOOL

UNFOOTED *adj* untrodden

UNFORBID *adj* archaic word meaning unforbidden

UNFORCED *adj* not forced or having been forced

UNFORGED *adj* genuine

UNFORGOT *adj* archaic word meaning unforgotten

UNFORKED *adj* not forked

UNFORM *vb* make formless

UNFORMAL *same as* > INFORMAL

UNFORMED *adj* in an early stage of development

UNFORMING > UNFORM

UNFORMS > UNFORM

UNFORTUNE *n* misfortune

UNFOUGHT *adj* not fought

UNFOUND *adj* not found

UNFOUNDED *adj* not based on facts or evidence

UNFRAMED *adj* not framed

UNFRANKED *adj* not franked

UNFRAUGHT *adj* not fraught

UNFREE *vb* remove freedom from

UNFREED > UNFREE

UNFREEDOM *n* lack of freedom

UNFREEING > UNFREE

UNFREEMAN *n* person who is not a freeman

UNFREEMEN > UNFREEMAN

UNFREES > UNFREE

UNFREEZE *vb* thaw or cause to thaw

UNFREEZES > UNFREEZE

UNFRETTED *adj* not worried

UNFRIEND *vb* remove someone from one's list of friends on a social networking site

UNFRIENDS > UNFRIEND

UNFROCK *vb* deprive (a priest in holy orders) of his or her priesthood

UNFROCKED > UNFROCK

UNFROCKS > UNFROCK

UNFROZE > UNFREEZE

UNFROZEN > UNFREEZE

UNFUELLED *adj* not fuelled

UNFUMED *adj* not fumigated

UNFUNDED *adj* not funded

UNFUNNIER > UNFUNNY

UNFUNNILY *adv* in an unfunny manner

UNFUNNY *adj* not funny

UNFURL *vb* unroll or unfold

UNFURLED > UNFURL

UNFURLING > UNFURL

UNFURLS > UNFURL

UNFURNISH *vb* clear

UNFURRED *adj* not adorned with fur

UNFUSED *adj* not fused

UNFUSSED *adj* not fussed

UNFUSSIER > UNFUSSY

UNFUSSILY > UNFUSSY

UNFUSSY *adj* not characterized by overelaborate detail

UNGAG *vb* restore freedom of speech to

UNGAGGED > UNGAG

UNGAGGING > UNGAG

UNGAGS > UNGAG

UNGAIN *adj* inconvenient

UNGAINFUL > UNGAIN

UNGAINLY *adj* lacking grace when moving ▷ *adv* clumsily

UNGALLANT *adj* not gallant

UNGALLED *adj* not annoyed

UNGARBED *adj* undressed

UNGARBLED *adj* clear

UNGATED *adj* without gate

UNGAUGED *adj* not measured

UNGAZED *adj* as in *ungazed at/ungazed upon* not gazed (at or upon)

UNGAZING *adj* not gazing

UNGEAR *vb* disengage

UNGEARED > UNGEAR

UNGEARING > UNGEAR

UNGEARS > UNGEAR

UNGELDED *adj* not gelded

UNGENIAL *adj* unfriendly

UNGENTEEL *adj* impolite

UNGENTLE *adj* not gentle

UNGENTLER > UNGENTLE

UNGENTLY > UNGENTLE

UNGENUINE *adj* false

UNGERMANE *adj* inappropriate

UNGET *vb* get rid of

UNGETS > UNGET

UNGETTING > UNGET

UNGHOSTED *adj* not ghostwritten

UNGHOSTLY *adj* not ghostly

UNGIFTED *adj* not talented

UNGILD *vb* remove gilding from

UNGILDED > UNGILD

UNGILDING > UNGILD

UNGILDS > UNGILD

UNGILT > UNGILD

UNGIRD *vb* remove belt from

UNGIRDED > UNGIRD

UNGIRDING > UNGIRD

UNGIRDS > UNGIRD

UNGIRT *adj* not belted

UNGIRTH *vb* release from a girth

UNGIRTHED > UNGIRTH

UNGIRTHS > UNGIRTH

UNGIVING *adj* inflexible

UNGLAD *adj* not glad

UNGLAZED *adj* not glazed

UNGLITZY *adj* not glitzy

UNGLOSSED *adj* not glossed

UNGLOVE *vb* remove glove(s)

UNGLOVED > UNGLOVE

UNGLOVES > UNGLOVE

UNGLOVING > UNGLOVE

UNGLUE *vb* remove adhesive from

UNGLUED > UNGLUE

UNGLUES > UNGLUE

UNGLUING > UNGLUE

UNGOD *vb* remove status of being a god from

UNGODDED > UNGOD

UNGODDING > UNGOD

UNGODLIER > UNGODLY

UNGODLIKE *adj* not godlike

UNGODLILY > UNGODLY

UNGODLY *adj* unreasonable or outrageous

UNGODS > UNGOD

UNGORD *same as* > UNGORED

UNGORED *adj* not gored

UNGORGED *same as* > UNGORED

UNGOT *same as* > UNGOTTEN

UNGOTTEN *adj* not obtained or won

UNGOWN *vb* remove gown (from)

UNGOWNED > UNGOWN

UNGOWNING > UNGOWN

UNGOWNS > UNGOWN

UNGRACED *adj* not graced

UNGRADED *adj* not graded

UNGRASSED *adj* not covered with grass

UNGRAVELY *adv* Shakespearian word meaning not in a serious or solemn manner

UNGRAZED *adj* not grazed

UNGREASED *adj* not greased

UNGREEDY *adj* not greedy

UNGREEN *adj* not environmentally friendly

UNGREENER > UNGREEN

UNGROOMED *adj* not groomed

UNGROUND *adj* not crushed

UNGROUP *vb* separate from a group

UNGROUPED *adj* not placed in a group

UNGROUPS > UNGROUP

UNGROWN *adj* not fully developed

UNGRUDGED *adj* not grudged

UNGUAL *adj* of, relating to, or affecting the fingernails or toenails

UNGUARD vb expose (to attack)
UNGUARDED adj not protected
UNGUARDS > UNGUARD
UNGUENT n ointment
UNGUENTA > UNGUENTUM
UNGUENTS > UNGUENT
UNGUENTUM same as > UNGUENT
UNGUES > UNGUIS
UNGUESSED adj unexpected
UNGUIDED adj not having a flight path controlled internally or externally
UNGUIFORM adj shaped like a nail or claw
UNGUILTY adj innocent
UNGUINOUS adj fatty
UNGUIS n nail, claw, or hoof, or the part of the digit giving rise to it
UNGULA n truncated cone, cylinder, etc
UNGULAE > UNGULA
UNGULAR > UNGULA
UNGULATE n hoofed mammal
UNGULATES > UNGULATE
UNGULED adj hoofed
UNGUM vb remove adhesive from
UNGUMMED > UNGUM
UNGUMMING > UNGUM
UNGUMS > UNGUM
UNGYVE vb release from shackles
UNGYVED > UNGYVE
UNGYVES > UNGYVE
UNGYVING > UNGYVE
UNHABLE same as > UNABLE
UNHACKED adj not hacked
UNHAILED adj not hailed
UNHAIR vb remove the hair from (a hide)
UNHAIRED > UNHAIR
UNHAIRER > UNHAIR
UNHAIRERS > UNHAIR
UNHAIRING > UNHAIR
UNHAIRS > UNHAIR
UNHALLOW vb desecrate
UNHALLOWS > UNHALLOW
UNHALSED adj not hailed
UNHALVED adj not divided in half
UNHAND vb release from one's grasp
UNHANDED > UNHAND
UNHANDIER > UNHANDY
UNHANDILY > UNHANDY
UNHANDING > UNHAND
UNHANDLED adj not handled
UNHANDS > UNHAND
UNHANDY adj not skilful with one's hands
UNHANG vb take down from hanging position
UNHANGED adj not executed by hanging
UNHANGING > UNHANG
UNHANGS > UNHANG
UNHAPPEN vb become as though never having happened
UNHAPPENS > UNHAPPEN
UNHAPPIED > UNHAPPY
UNHAPPIER > UNHAPPY

UNHAPPIES > UNHAPPY
UNHAPPILY > UNHAPPY
UNHAPPY adj sad or depressed ▷ vb make unhappy
UNHARBOUR vb force out of shelter
UNHARDIER > UNHARDY
UNHARDY adj fragile
UNHARMED adj not hurt or damaged in any way
UNHARMFUL adj not harmful
UNHARMING adj not capable of harming
UNHARNESS vb remove the harness from (a horse, etc)
UNHARRIED adj not harried
UNHASP vb unfasten
UNHASPED > UNHASP
UNHASPING > UNHASP
UNHASPS > UNHASP
UNHASTIER > UNHASTY
UNHASTING adj not rushing
UNHASTY adj not speedy
UNHAT vb doff one's hat
UNHATCHED adj (of an egg) not having broken to release the fully developed young
UNHATS > UNHAT
UNHATTED > UNHAT
UNHATTING > UNHAT
UNHAUNTED adj not haunted
UNHEAD vb remove the head from
UNHEADED adj not having a heading
UNHEADING > UNHEAD
UNHEADS > UNHEAD
UNHEAL vb expose
UNHEALED adj not having healed physically, mentally, or emotionally
UNHEALING adj not healing
UNHEALS > UNHEAL
UNHEALTH n illness
UNHEALTHS > UNHEALTH
UNHEALTHY adj likely to cause poor health
UNHEARD adj not listened to
UNHEARSE vb remove from a hearse
UNHEARSED > UNHEARSE
UNHEARSES > UNHEARSE
UNHEART vb discourage
UNHEARTED > UNHEART
UNHEARTS > UNHEART
UNHEATED adj not having been warmed up
UNHEDGED adj unprotected
UNHEEDED adj noticed but ignored
UNHEEDFUL adj not heedful
UNHEEDIER > UNHEEDY
UNHEEDILY adv carelessly
UNHEEDING adj not heeding
UNHEEDY adj not heedful
UNHELE same as > UNHEAL
UNHELED > UNHELE
UNHELES > UNHELE
UNHELING > UNHELE
UNHELM vb remove the helmet of (oneself or another)
UNHELMED > UNHELM
UNHELMING > UNHELM
UNHELMS > UNHELM

UNHELPED adj without help
UNHELPFUL adj doing nothing to improve a situation
UNHEMMED adj not hemmed
UNHEPPEN adj awkward
UNHEROIC adj not heroic
UNHERST archaic past form of > UNHEARSE
UNHEWN adj not hewn
UNHIDDEN adj not hidden
UNHINGE vb derange or unbalance (a person or his or her mind)
UNHINGED > UNHINGE
UNHINGES > UNHINGE
UNHINGING > UNHINGE
UNHIP adj not at all fashionable or up to date
UNHIPPER > UNHIP
UNHIPPEST > UNHIP
UNHIRABLE adj not fit to be hired
UNHIRED adj not hired
UNHITCH vb unfasten or detach
UNHITCHED > UNHITCH
UNHITCHES > UNHITCH
UNHIVE vb remove from a hive
UNHIVED > UNHIVE
UNHIVES > UNHIVE
UNHIVING > UNHIVE
UNHOARD vb remove from a hoard
UNHOARDED > UNHOARD
UNHOARDS > UNHOARD
UNHOLIER > UNHOLY
UNHOLIEST > UNHOLY
UNHOLILY > UNHOLY
UNHOLPEN same as > UNHELPED
UNHOLSTER vb remove (a gun) from a holster
UNHOLY adj immoral or wicked
UNHOMELY adj not homely
UNHONEST same as > DISHONEST
UNHONORED adj not honoured
UNHOOD vb remove hood from
UNHOODED > UNHOOD
UNHOODING > UNHOOD
UNHOODS > UNHOOD
UNHOOK vb unfasten the hooks of (a garment)
UNHOOKED > UNHOOK
UNHOOKING > UNHOOK
UNHOOKS > UNHOOK
UNHOOP vb remove hoop(s) from
UNHOOPED > UNHOOP
UNHOOPING > UNHOOP
UNHOOPS > UNHOOP
UNHOPED adj unhoped-for
UNHOPEFUL adj not hopeful
UNHORSE vb knock or throw from a horse
UNHORSED > UNHORSE
UNHORSES > UNHORSE
UNHORSING > UNHORSE
UNHOSTILE adj not hostile
UNHOUSE vb remove from a house
UNHOUSED > UNHOUSE

UNHOUSES > UNHOUSE
UNHOUSING > UNHOUSE
UNHUMAN adj inhuman or not human
UNHUMANLY > UNHUMAN
UNHUMBLED adj not humbled
UNHUNG > UNHANG
UNHUNTED adj not hunted
UNHURRIED adj done at a leisurely pace, without any rush or anxiety
UNHURT adj not injured in an accident, attack, etc
UNHURTFUL adj not hurtful
UNHUSK vb remove the husk from
UNHUSKED > UNHUSK
UNHUSKING > UNHUSK
UNHUSKS > UNHUSK
UNI n (in informal English) university
UNIALGAL adj containing only one species of alga
UNIAXIAL adj (esp of plants) having an unbranched main axis
UNIBODIES > UNIBODY
UNIBODY adj of a vehicle in which the frame and body are one unit ▷ n vehicle in which the frame and body are one unit
UNIBROW n informal word for eyebrows that meet above the nose
UNIBROWS > UNIBROW
UNICA > UNICUM
UNICED adj not iced
UNICITIES > UNICITY
UNICITY n oneness
UNICOLOR same as > UNICOLOUR
UNICOLOUR adj of one colour
UNICOM n designated radio frequency at some airports
UNICOMS > UNICOM
UNICORN n imaginary horselike creature with one horn growing from its forehead
UNICORNS > UNICORN
UNICUM n unique example or specimen
UNICYCLE n one-wheeled vehicle driven by pedals, used in a circus ▷ vb ride a unicycle
UNICYCLED > UNICYCLE
UNICYCLES > UNICYCLE
UNIDEAED adj not having ideas
UNIDEAL adj not ideal
UNIFACE n type of tool
UNIFACES > UNIFACE
UNIFIABLE > UNIFY
UNIFIC adj unifying
UNIFIED > UNIFY
UNIFIER > UNIFY
UNIFIERS > UNIFY
UNIFIES > UNIFY
UNIFILAR adj composed of, having, or using only one wire, thread, filament, etc
UNIFORM n special set of clothes for the members of an organization ▷ adj regular

and even throughout, unvarying ▷ *vb* fit out (a body of soldiers, etc) with uniforms

UNIFORMED > UNIFORM
UNIFORMER > UNIFORM
UNIFORMLY > UNIFORM
UNIFORMS > UNIFORM
UNIFY *vb* make or become one
UNIFYING > UNIFY
UNIFYINGS > UNIFY
UNIGNITED *adj* not ignited
UNIJUGATE *adj* (of a compound leaf) having only one pair of leaflets
UNILINEAL *same as* **>** UNILINEAR
UNILINEAR *adj* developing in a progressive sequence
UNILLUMED *adj* not illuminated
UNILOBAR *adj* having one lobe
UNILOBED *same as* **>** UNILOBAR
UNIMBUED *adj* not imbued
UNIMODAL *adj* having or involving one mode
UNIMPEDED *adj* not stopped or disrupted by anything
UNIMPOSED *adj* not imposed
UNINCITED *adj* unprovoked
UNINDEXED *adj* not indexed
UNINJURED *adj* not having sustained any injury
UNINSTAL *same as* **>** UNINSTALL
UNINSTALL *vb* remove from a computer system
UNINSTALS > UNINSTAL
UNINSURED *adj* not covered by insurance
UNINURED *adj* unaccustomed
UNINVITED *adj* not having been asked ▷ *adv* without having been asked
UNINVOKED *adj* not invoked
UNION *n* act of uniting or being united ▷ *adj* of a trade union
UNIONISE *same as* **>** UNIONIZE
UNIONISED > UNIONISE
UNIONISER > UNIONISE
UNIONISES > UNIONISE
UNIONISM *n* principles of trade unions
UNIONISMS > UNIONISM
UNIONIST *n* member or supporter of a trade union ▷ *adj* of or relating to union or unionism, esp trade unionism
UNIONISTS > UNIONIST
UNIONIZE *vb* organize (workers) into a trade union
UNIONIZED > UNIONIZE
UNIONIZER > UNIONIZE
UNIONIZES > UNIONIZE
UNIONS > UNION
UNIPAROUS *adj* (of certain animals) producing a single offspring at each birth
UNIPED *n* person or thing with one foot

UNIPEDS > UNIPED
UNIPLANAR *adj* situated in one plane
UNIPOD *n* one-legged support, as for a camera
UNIPODS > UNIPOD
UNIPOLAR *adj* of, concerned with, or having a single magnetic or electric pole
UNIPOTENT *adj* able to form only one type of cell
UNIQUE *adj* being the only one of a particular type ▷ *n* person or thing that is unique
UNIQUELY > UNIQUE
UNIQUER > UNIQUE
UNIQUES > UNIQUE
UNIQUEST > UNIQUE
UNIRAMOSE *same as* **>** UNIRAMOUS
UNIRAMOUS *adj* (esp of the appendages of crustaceans) consisting of a single branch
UNIRONED *adj* not ironed
UNIRONIC *adj* not ironic
UNIS > UNI
UNISERIAL *adj* in or relating to a single series
UNISEX *adj* designed for use by both sexes ▷ *n* condition of seeming not to belong obviously either to one sex or the other
UNISEXES > UNISEX
UNISEXUAL *adj* of one sex only
UNISIZE *adj* in one size only
UNISON *n* complete agreement
UNISONAL > UNISON
UNISONANT > UNISON
UNISONOUS > UNISON
UNISONS > UNISON
UNISSUED *adj* not issued
UNIT *n* single undivided entity or whole
UNITAGE > UNIT
UNITAGES > UNIT
UNITAL > UNIT
UNITARD *n* all-in-one skintight suit
UNITARDS > UNITARD
UNITARIAN *n* supporter of unity or centralization ▷ *adj* of or relating to unity or centralization
UNITARILY > UNITARY
UNITARITY *n* quality of being unitary
UNITARY *adj* consisting of a single undivided whole
UNITE *vb* make or become an integrated whole ▷ *n* English gold coin minted in the Stuart period
UNITED *adj* produced by two or more people or things in combination
UNITEDLY > UNITED
UNITER > UNITE
UNITERS > UNITE
UNITES > UNITE
UNITIES > UNITY
UNITING > UNITE
UNITINGS > UNITE
UNITION *n* joining

UNITIONS > UNITION
UNITISE *same as* **>** UNITIZE
UNITISED > UNITISE
UNITISER *same as* **>** UNITIZER
UNITISERS > UNITISER
UNITISES > UNITISE
UNITISING > UNITISE
UNITIVE *adj* tending to unite or capable of uniting
UNITIVELY > UNITIVE
UNITIZE *vb* convert (an investment trust) into a unit trust
UNITIZED > UNITIZE
UNITIZER *n* person or thing that arranges units into batches
UNITIZERS > UNITIZER
UNITIZES > UNITIZE
UNITIZING > UNITIZE
UNITRUST *n* type of income-producing trust fund
UNITRUSTS > UNITRUST
UNITS > UNIT
UNITY *n* state of being one
UNIVALENT *adj* (of a chromosome during meiosis) not paired with its homologue
UNIVALVE *adj* relating to a mollusc shell that consists of a single piece (valve) ▷ *n* gastropod mollusc or its shell
UNIVALVED > UNIVALVE
UNIVALVES > UNIVALVE
UNIVERSAL *adj* of or typical of the whole of mankind or of nature ▷ *n* something which exists or is true in all places and all situations
UNIVERSE *n* whole of all existing matter, energy, and space
UNIVERSES > UNIVERSE
UNIVOCAL *adj* unambiguous or unmistakable ▷ *n* word or term that has only one meaning
UNIVOCALS > UNIVOCAL
UNJADED *adj* not jaded
UNJAM *vb* remove blockage from
UNJAMMED > UNJAM
UNJAMMING > UNJAM
UNJAMS > UNJAM
UNJEALOUS *adj* not jealous
UNJOINED *adj* not joined
UNJOINT *vb* disjoint
UNJOINTED > UNJOINT
UNJOINTS > UNJOINT
UNJOYFUL *adj* not joyful
UNJOYOUS *adj* not joyous
UNJUDGED *adj* not judged
UNJUST *adj* not fair or just
UNJUSTER > UNJUST
UNJUSTEST > UNJUST
UNJUSTLY > UNJUST
UNKED *adj* alien
UNKEELED *adj* without a keel
UNKEMPT *adj* (of the hair) not combed
UNKEMPTLY > UNKEMPT
UNKEND *same as* **>** UNKENNED

UNKENNED *adj* unknown
UNKENNEL *vb* release from a kennel
UNKENNELS > UNKENNEL
UNKENT *same as* **>** UNKENNED
UNKEPT *adj* not kept
UNKET *same as* **>** UNKED
UNKID *same as* **>** UNKED
UNKIND *adj* unsympathetic or cruel
UNKINDER > UNKIND
UNKINDEST > UNKIND
UNKINDLED *adj* not kindled
UNKINDLY > UNKIND
UNKING *vb* strip of sovereignty
UNKINGED > UNKING
UNKINGING > UNKING
UNKINGLY *adj* not kingly
UNKINGS > UNKING
UNKINK *vb* straighten out
UNKINKED > UNKINK
UNKINKING > UNKINK
UNKINKS > UNKINK
UNKISS *vb* cancel (a previous action) with a kiss
UNKISSED *adj* not kissed
UNKISSES > UNKISS
UNKISSING > UNKISS
UNKNELLED *adj* not tolled
UNKNIGHT *vb* strip of knighthood
UNKNIGHTS > UNKNIGHT
UNKNIT *vb* make or become undone, untied, or unravelled
UNKNITS > UNKNIT
UNKNITTED > UNKNIT
UNKNOT *vb* disentangle or undo a knot or knots in
UNKNOTS > UNKNOT
UNKNOTTED > UNKNOT
UNKNOWING *adj* unaware or ignorant
UNKNOWN *adj* not known ▷ *n* unknown person, quantity, or thing
UNKNOWNS > UNKNOWN
UNKOSHER *adj* not conforming to Jewish religious law
UNLABELED *adj* not labelled
UNLABORED *adj* not laboured
UNLACE *vb* loosen or undo the lacing of (shoes, garments, etc)
UNLACED *adj* not laced
UNLACES > UNLACE
UNLACING > UNLACE
UNLADE *less common word for* **>** UNLOAD
UNLADED > UNLADE
UNLADEN *adj* not laden
UNLADES > UNLADE
UNLADING > UNLADE
UNLADINGS > UNLADE
UNLAID > UNLAY
UNLASH *vb* untie or unfasten
UNLASHED > UNLASH
UNLASHES > UNLASH
UNLASHING > UNLASH
UNLAST *archaic variant of* **>** UNLACED
UNLASTE *archaic variant of* **>** UNLACED

U

SECTION 1: Words between 2 and 9 letters in length

UNLATCH vb open or unfasten or come open or unfastened by the lifting or release of a latch
UNLATCHED > UNLATCH
UNLATCHES > UNLATCH
UNLAW vb penalize
UNLAWED > UNLAW
UNLAWFUL adj not permitted by law
UNLAWING > UNLAW
UNLAWS > UNLAW
UNLAY vb untwist (a rope or cable) to separate its strands
UNLAYING > UNLAY
UNLAYS > UNLAY
UNLEAD vb strip off lead
UNLEADED adj (of petrol) containing less tetraethyl lead ▷ n petrol containing a reduced amount of tetraethyl lead
UNLEADEDS > UNLEADED
UNLEADING > UNLEAD
UNLEADS > UNLEAD
UNLEAL adj treacherous
UNLEARN vb try to forget something learnt or to discard accumulated knowledge
UNLEARNED same as
> UNLEARNT
UNLEARNS > UNLEARN
UNLEARNT adj denoting knowledge or skills innately present rather than learnt
UNLEASED adj not leased
UNLEASH vb set loose or cause (something bad)
UNLEASHED > UNLEASH
UNLEASHES > UNLEASH
UNLED adj not led
UNLESS conj except under the circumstances that ▷ prep except
UNLET adj not rented
UNLETHAL adj not deadly
UNLETTED adj unimpeded
UNLEVEL adj not level ▷ vb make unbalanced
UNLEVELED > UNLEVEL
UNLEVELS > UNLEVEL
UNLEVIED adj not levied
UNLICH Spenserian form of
> UNLIKE
UNLICKED adj not licked
UNLID vb remove lid from
UNLIDDED > UNLID
UNLIDDING > UNLID
UNLIDS > UNLID
UNLIGHTED adj not lit
UNLIKABLE adj not likable
UNLIKE adj dissimilar or different ▷ prep not like or typical of ▷ n person or thing that is unlike another
UNLIKED adj not liked
UNLIKELY adj improbable
UNLIKES > UNLIKE
UNLIMBER vb disengage (a gun) from its limber
UNLIMBERS > UNLIMBER
UNLIME vb detach
UNLIMED > UNLIME
UNLIMES > UNLIME
UNLIMING > UNLIME

UNLIMITED adj apparently endless
UNLINE vb remove the lining from
UNLINEAL adj not lineal
UNLINED adj not having any lining
UNLINES > UNLINE
UNLINING > UNLINE
UNLINK vb undo the link or links between
UNLINKED > UNLINK
UNLINKING > UNLINK
UNLINKS > UNLINK
UNLISTED adj not entered on a list
UNLIT adj (of a fire, cigarette, etc) not lit and therefore not burning
UNLIVABLE adj not fit for living in
UNLIVE vb live so as to nullify, undo, or live down (past events or times)
UNLIVED > UNLIVE
UNLIVELY adj lifeless
UNLIVES > UNLIVE
UNLIVING > UNLIVE
UNLOAD vb remove (cargo) from (a ship, truck, or plane)
UNLOADED > UNLOAD
UNLOADER > UNLOAD
UNLOADERS > UNLOAD
UNLOADING > UNLOAD
UNLOADS > UNLOAD
UNLOBED adj without lobes
UNLOCATED adj not located
UNLOCK vb unfasten (a lock or door)
UNLOCKED adj not locked
UNLOCKING > UNLOCK
UNLOCKS > UNLOCK
UNLOGICAL same as
> ILLOGICAL
UNLOOKED adj not looked (at)
UNLOOSE vb set free or release
UNLOOSED > UNLOOSE
UNLOOSEN same as
> UNLOOSE
UNLOOSENS > UNLOOSEN
UNLOOSES > UNLOOSE
UNLOOSING > UNLOOSE
UNLOPPED adj not chopped off
UNLORD vb remove from position of being lord
UNLORDED > UNLORD
UNLORDING > UNLORD
UNLORDLY adv not in a lordlike manner
UNLORDS > UNLORD
UNLOSABLE adj unable to be lost
UNLOST adj not lost
UNLOVABLE adj too unpleasant or unattractive to be loved
UNLOVE vb stop loving
UNLOVED adj not loved by anyone
UNLOVELY adj unpleasant in appearance or character
UNLOVES > UNLOVE
UNLOVING adj not feeling or showing love and affection

UNLUCKIER > UNLUCKY
UNLUCKILY > UNLUCKY
UNLUCKY adj having bad luck, unfortunate
UNLYRICAL adj not lyrical
UNMACHO adj not macho
UNMADE adj (of a bed) with the bedclothes not smoothed and tidied
UNMAILED adj not sent by post
UNMAIMED adj not injured
UNMAKABLE adj unable to be made
UNMAKE vb undo or destroy
UNMAKER > UNMAKE
UNMAKERS > UNMAKE
UNMAKES > UNMAKE
UNMAKING > UNMAKE
UNMAKINGS > UNMAKE
UNMAN vb cause to lose courage or nerve
UNMANACLE vb release from manacles
UNMANAGED adj not managed
UNMANFUL adj unmanly
UNMANLIER > UNMANLY
UNMANLIKE adj not worthy of a man
UNMANLY adj not masculine
UNMANNED adj having no personnel or crew
UNMANNING > UNMAN
UNMANNISH adj not mannish
UNMANS > UNMAN
UNMANTLE vb remove mantle from
UNMANTLED > UNMANTLE
UNMANTLES > UNMANTLE
UNMANURED adj not treated with manure
UNMAPPED adj not charted
UNMARD same as
> UNMARRED
UNMARKED adj having no signs of damage or injury
UNMARRED adj not married
UNMARRIED adj not married
UNMARRIES > UNMARRY
UNMARRY vb divorce
UNMASK vb remove the mask or disguise from
UNMASKED > UNMASK
UNMASKER > UNMASK
UNMASKERS > UNMASK
UNMASKING > UNMASK
UNMASKS > UNMASK
UNMATCHED adj not equalled or surpassed
UNMATED adj not mated
UNMATTED adj not matted
UNMATURED adj not matured
UNMEANING adj having no meaning
UNMEANT adj unintentional
UNMEEK adj not submissive
UNMEET adj not meet
UNMEETLY > UNMEET
UNMELLOW adj not mellow
UNMELTED adj not melted
UNMENDED adj not mended
UNMERITED adj not merited or deserved
UNMERRIER > UNMERRY

UNMERRY adj not merry
UNMESH vb release from mesh
UNMESHED > UNMESH
UNMESHES > UNMESH
UNMESHING > UNMESH
UNMET adj unfulfilled
UNMETED adj unmeasured
UNMETERED adj not metered
UNMEW vb release from confinement
UNMEWED > UNMEW
UNMEWING > UNMEW
UNMEWS > UNMEW
UNMILKED adj not milked
UNMILLED adj not milled
UNMINDED adj disregarded
UNMINDFUL adj careless, heedless, or forgetful
UNMINED adj not mined
UNMINGLE vb separate
UNMINGLED > UNMINGLE
UNMINGLES > UNMINGLE
UNMIRIER > UNMIRY
UNMIRIEST > UNMIRY
UNMIRY adj not swampy
UNMISSED adj unnoticed
UNMITER same as
> UNMITRE
UNMITERED > UNMITER
UNMITERS > UNMITER
UNMITRE vb divest of a mitre
UNMITRED > UNMITRE
UNMITRES > UNMITRE
UNMITRING > UNMITRE
UNMIX vb separate
UNMIXABLE adj incapable of being mixed
UNMIXED > UNMIX
UNMIXEDLY > UNMIXED
UNMIXES > UNMIX
UNMIXING > UNMIX
UNMIXT same as > UNMIX
UNMOANED adj unmourned
UNMODISH adj passé
UNMOLD same as > UNMOULD
UNMOLDED > UNMOLD
UNMOLDING > UNMOLD
UNMOLDS > UNMOLD
UNMOLTEN adj not molten
UNMONEYED adj poor
UNMONIED same as
> UNMONEYED
UNMOOR vb weigh the anchor or drop the mooring of (a vessel)
UNMOORED > UNMOOR
UNMOORING > UNMOOR
UNMOORS > UNMOOR
UNMORAL adj outside morality
UNMORALLY > UNMORAL
UNMORTISE vb release from mortise
UNMOTIVED adj without motive
UNMOULD vb change shape of
UNMOULDED > UNMOULD
UNMOULDS > UNMOULD
UNMOUNT vb dismount
UNMOUNTED > UNMOUNT
UNMOUNTS > UNMOUNT
UNMOURNED adj not mourned

u

UNMOVABLE *adj* not movable

UNMOVABLY > UNMOVABLE

UNMOVED *adj* not affected by emotion, indifferent

UNMOVEDLY > UNMOVED

UNMOVING *adj* still and motionless

UNMOWN *adj* not mown

UNMUFFLE *vb* remove a muffle or muffles from

UNMUFFLED > UNMUFFLE

UNMUFFLES > UNMUFFLE

UNMUSICAL *adj* (of a person) unable to appreciate or play music

UNMUZZLE *vb* take the muzzle off (a dog, etc)

UNMUZZLED > UNMUZZLE

UNMUZZLES > UNMUZZLE

UNNAIL *vb* unfasten by removing nails

UNNAILED > UNNAIL

UNNAILING > UNNAIL

UNNAILS > UNNAIL

UNNAMABLE *adj* that cannot or must not be named

UNNAMED *adj* not mentioned by name

UNNANELD *same as* **>** UNANELED

UNNATIVE *adj* not native ▷ *vb* no longer be a native of a place

UNNATIVES > UNNATIVE

UNNATURAL *adj* strange and frightening because not usual

UNNEATH *adj* archaic word for underneath

UNNEEDED *adj* not needed

UNNEEDFUL *adj* not needful

UNNERVE *vb* cause to lose courage, confidence, or self-control

UNNERVED > UNNERVE

UNNERVES > UNNERVE

UNNERVING > UNNERVE

UNNEST *vb* remove from a nest

UNNESTED > UNNEST

UNNESTING > UNNEST

UNNESTS > UNNEST

UNNETHES *same as* **>** UNNEATH

UNNETTED *adj* not having or not enclosed in a net

UNNOBLE *vb* strip of nobility

UNNOBLED > UNNOBLE

UNNOBLES > UNNOBLE

UNNOBLING > UNNOBLE

UNNOISIER > UNNOISY

UNNOISY *adj* quiet

UNNOTED *adj* not noted

UNNOTICED *adj* without being seen or noticed

UNNUANCED *adj* without nuances

UNOAKED *adj* (of wine) not matured in an oak barrel

UNOBEYED *adj* not obeyed

UNOBVIOUS *adj* unapparent

UNOFFERED *adj* not offered

UNOFTEN *adv* infrequently

UNOILED *adj* not lubricated with oil

UNOPEN *adj* not open

UNOPENED *adj* closed, barred, or sealed

UNOPPOSED *adj* not opposed

UNORDER *vb* cancel an order

UNORDERED *adj* not ordered

UNORDERLY *adj* not orderly or disorderly

UNORDERS > UNORDER

UNORNATE *same as* **>** INORNATE

UNOWED *same as* **>** UNOWNED

UNOWNED *adj* not owned

UNPACED *adj* without the aid of a pacemaker

UNPACK *vb* remove the contents of (a suitcase, trunk, etc)

UNPACKED > UNPACK

UNPACKER > UNPACK

UNPACKERS > UNPACK

UNPACKING > UNPACK

UNPACKS > UNPACK

UNPADDED *adj* not padded

UNPAGED *adj* (of a book) having no page numbers

UNPAID *adj* without a salary or wage

UNPAINED *adj* not suffering pain

UNPAINFUL *adj* painless

UNPAINT *vb* remove paint from

UNPAINTED > UNPAINT

UNPAINTS > UNPAINT

UNPAIRED *adj* not paired up

UNPALSIED *adj* not affected with palsy

UNPANEL *vb* unsaddle

UNPANELS > UNPANEL

UNPANGED *adj* without pain or sadness

UNPANNEL *same as* **>** UNPANEL

UNPANNELS > UNPANNEL

UNPAPER *vb* remove paper from

UNPAPERED > UNPAPER

UNPAPERS > UNPAPER

UNPARED *adj* not pared

UNPARTED *adj* not parted

UNPARTIAL *same as* **>** IMPARTIAL

UNPATCHED *adj* not patched

UNPATHED *adj* not having a path

UNPAVED *adj* not covered in paving

UNPAY *vb* undo

UNPAYABLE *adj* incapable of being paid

UNPAYING > UNPAY

UNPAYS > UNPAY

UNPEELED *adj* not peeled

UNPEERED *adj* unparalleled

UNPEG *vb* remove the peg or pegs from, esp to unfasten

UNPEGGED > UNPEG

UNPEGGING > UNPEG

UNPEGS > UNPEG

UNPEN *vb* release from a pen

UNPENNED > UNPEN

UNPENNIED *adj* not having pennies

UNPENNING > UNPEN

UNPENS > UNPEN

UNPENT *archaic past form of* **>** UNPEN

UNPEOPLE *vb* empty of people

UNPEOPLED > UNPEOPLE

UNPEOPLES > UNPEOPLE

UNPERCH *vb* remove from a perch

UNPERCHED > UNPERCH

UNPERCHES > UNPERCH

UNPERFECT *same as* **>** IMPERFECT

UNPERPLEX *vb* remove confusion from

UNPERSON *n* person whose existence is officially denied or ignored

UNPERSONS > UNPERSON

UNPERVERT *vb* free (someone) from perversion

UNPICK *vb* undo (the stitches) of (a piece of sewing)

UNPICKED *adj* (of knitting, sewing, etc) having been unravelled or picked out

UNPICKING > UNPICK

UNPICKS > UNPICK

UNPIERCED *adj* not pierced

UNPILE *vb* remove from a pile

UNPILED > UNPILE

UNPILES > UNPILE

UNPILING > UNPILE

UNPILOTED *adj* unguided

UNPIN *vb* remove a pin or pins from

UNPINKED *adj* not decorated with a perforated pattern

UNPINKT *same as* **>** UNPINKED

UNPINNED > UNPIN

UNPINNING > UNPIN

UNPINS > UNPIN

UNPITIED *adj* not pitied

UNPITIFUL *adj* pitiless

UNPITTED *adj* not having had pits removed

UNPITYING *adj* not pitying

UNPLACE *same as* **>** DISPLACE

UNPLACED *adj* not given or put in a particular place

UNPLACES > UNPLACE

UNPLACING > UNPLACE

UNPLAGUED *adj* not plagued

UNPLAINED *adj* unmourned

UNPLAIT *vb* remove plaits from

UNPLAITED > UNPLAIT

UNPLAITS > UNPLAIT

UNPLANKED *adj* not planked

UNPLANNED *adj* not intentional or deliberate

UNPLANTED *adj* not planted

UNPLAYED *adj* not played

UNPLEASED *adj* not pleased or displeased

UNPLEATED *adj* not pleated

UNPLEDGED *adj* not pledged

UNPLIABLE *adj* not easily bent

UNPLIABLY > UNPLIABLE

UNPLIANT *adj* not pliant

UNPLOWED *adj* not ploughed

UNPLUCKED *adj* not plucked

UNPLUG *vb* disconnect (a piece of electrical equipment)

UNPLUGGED *adj* using acoustic rather than electric instruments

UNPLUGS > UNPLUG

UNPLUMB *vb* remove lead from

UNPLUMBED *adj* not measured

UNPLUMBS > UNPLUMB

UNPLUME *vb* remove feathers from

UNPLUMED > UNPLUME

UNPLUMES > UNPLUME

UNPLUMING > UNPLUME

UNPOETIC *adj* not poetic

UNPOINTED *adj* not pointed

UNPOISED *adj* not poised

UNPOISON *vb* extract poison from

UNPOISONS > UNPOISON

UNPOLICED *adj* without police control

UNPOLISH *vb* remove polish from

UNPOLITE *same as* **>** IMPOLITE

UNPOLITIC *another word for* **>** IMPOLITIC

UNPOLLED *adj* not included in an opinion poll

UNPOPE *vb* strip of popedom

UNPOPED > UNPOPE

UNPOPES > UNPOPE

UNPOPING > UNPOPE

UNPOPULAR *adj* generally disliked or disapproved of

UNPOSED *adj* not posed

UNPOSTED *adj* not sent by post

UNPOTABLE *adj* undrinkable

UNPOTTED *adj* not planted in a pot

UNPOURED *adj* not poured

UNPOWERED *adj* not powered

UNPRAISE *vb* withhold praise from

UNPRAISED > UNPRAISE

UNPRAISES > UNPRAISE

UNPRAY *vb* withdraw (a prayer)

UNPRAYED > UNPRAY

UNPRAYING > UNPRAY

UNPRAYS > UNPRAY

UNPREACH *vb* retract (a sermon)

UNPRECISE *same as* **>** IMPRECISE

UNPREDICT *vb* retract (a previous prediction)

UNPREPARE *vb* make unprepared

UNPRESSED *adj* not pressed

UNPRETTY *adj* unattractive

UNPRICED *adj* having no fixed or marked price

UNPRIEST *vb* strip of priesthood

UNPRIESTS > UNPRIEST

UNPRIMED *adj* not primed

UNPRINTED *adj* not printed

UNPRISON *vb* release from prison

UNPRISONS > UNPRISON

UNPRIZED adj not treasured
UNPROBED adj not examined
UNPROP vb remove support from
UNPROPER same as > IMPROPER
UNPROPPED > UNPROP
UNPROPS > UNPROP
UNPROVED adj not having been established as true, valid, or possible
UNPROVEN adj not established as true by evidence or demonstration
UNPROVIDE vb fail to supply requirements for
UNPROVOKE vb remove provocation from
UNPRUNED adj not pruned
UNPUCKER vb remove wrinkles from
UNPUCKERS > UNPUCKER
UNPULLED adj not pulled
UNPURE same as > IMPURE
UNPURELY > UNPURE
UNPURGED adj not purged
UNPURSE vb relax (lips) from pursed position
UNPURSED > UNPURSE
UNPURSES > UNPURSE
UNPURSING > UNPURSE
UNPURSUED adj not followed
UNPUZZLE vb figure out
UNPUZZLED > UNPUZZLE
UNPUZZLES > UNPUZZLE
UNQUAKING adj not quaking
UNQUALIFY vb disqualify
UNQUEEN vb depose from the position of queen
UNQUEENED > UNQUEEN
UNQUEENLY adv not in a queenlike manner
UNQUEENS > UNQUEEN
UNQUELLED adj not quelled
UNQUIET adj anxious or uneasy ▷ n state of unrest ▷ vb disquiet
UNQUIETED > UNQUIET
UNQUIETER > UNQUIET
UNQUIETLY > UNQUIET
UNQUIETS > UNQUIET
UNQUOTE interj expression used to indicate the end of a quotation ▷ vb close (a quotation), esp in printing
UNQUOTED > UNQUOTE
UNQUOTES > UNQUOTE
UNQUOTING > UNQUOTE
UNRACED adj not raced
UNRACKED adj not stretched
UNRAISED adj not raised
UNRAKE vb unearth through raking
UNRAKED adj not raked
UNRAKES > UNRAKE
UNRAKING > UNRAKE
UNRANKED adj not ranked
UNRATED adj not rated
UNRAVAGED adj not ravaged
UNRAVEL vb reduce (something knitted or woven) to separate strands
UNRAVELED > UNRAVEL
UNRAVELS > UNRAVEL
UNRAZED adj not razed
UNRAZORED adj unshaven

UNREACHED adj not reached
UNREAD adj (of a book or article) not yet read
UNREADIER > UNREADY
UNREADILY > UNREADY
UNREADY adj not ready or prepared
UNREAL adj (as if) existing only in the imagination
UNREALISE same as > UNREALIZE
UNREALISM n abstractionism
UNREALITY n quality or state of being unreal, fanciful, or impractical
UNREALIZE vb make unreal
UNREALLY > UNREAL
UNREAPED adj not reaped
UNREASON n irrationality or madness ▷ vb deprive of reason
UNREASONS > UNREASON
UNREAVE vb unwind
UNREAVED > UNREAVE
UNREAVES > UNREAVE
UNREAVING > UNREAVE
UNREBATED adj not refunded
UNREBUKED adj not rebuked
UNRECKED adj disregarded
UNRED same as > UNREAD
UNREDREST adj not redressed
UNREDUCED adj not reduced
UNREDY same as > UNREADY
UNREEL vb unwind from a reel
UNREELED > UNREEL
UNREELER n machine that unwinds something from a reel
UNREELERS > UNREELER
UNREELING > UNREEL
UNREELS > UNREEL
UNREEVE vb withdraw (a rope) from a block, thimble, etc
UNREEVED > UNREEVE
UNREEVES > UNREEVE
UNREEVING > UNREEVE
UNREFINED adj (of substances such as petroleum, ores, and sugar) not processed into a pure or usable form
UNREFUTED adj not refuted
UNREIN vb free from reins
UNREINED > UNREIN
UNREINING > UNREIN
UNREINS > UNREIN
UNRELATED adj not connected with each other
UNRELAXED adj not relaxed
UNREMOVED adj not removed
UNRENEWED adj not renewed
UNRENT adj not torn
UNRENTED adj not rented
UNREPAID adj not repaid
UNREPAIR less common word for > DISREPAIR
UNREPAIRS > UNREPAIR
UNRESERVE n candour
UNREST n rebellious state of discontent

UNRESTED adj not rested
UNRESTFUL adj restless
UNRESTING adj not resting
UNRESTS > UNREST
UNRETIRE vb resume work after retiring
UNRETIRED > UNRETIRE
UNRETIRES > UNRETIRE
UNREVISED adj not revised
UNREVOKED adj not revoked
UNRHYMED adj not rhymed
UNRIBBED adj not ribbed
UNRID adj unridden
UNRIDABLE adj not capable of being ridden
UNRIDDEN adj not or never ridden
UNRIDDLE vb solve or puzzle out
UNRIDDLED > UNRIDDLE
UNRIDDLER > UNRIDDLE
UNRIDDLES > UNRIDDLE
UNRIDGED adj not ridged
UNRIFLED adj (of a firearm or its bore) not rifled
UNRIG vb strip (a vessel) of standing and running rigging
UNRIGGED > UNRIG
UNRIGGING > UNRIG
UNRIGHT n wrong ▷ adj not right or fair ▷ vb make wrong
UNRIGHTED > UNRIGHT
UNRIGHTS > UNRIGHT
UNRIGS > UNRIG
UNRIMED same as > UNRHYMED
UNRINGED adj not having or wearing a ring
UNRINSED adj not rinsed
UNRIP vb rip open
UNRIPE adj not fully matured
UNRIPELY > UNRIPE
UNRIPENED same as > UNRIPE
UNRIPER > UNRIPE
UNRIPEST > UNRIPE
UNRIPPED > UNRIP
UNRIPPING > UNRIP
UNRIPS > UNRIP
UNRISEN adj not risen
UNRIVALED adj (in US English) matchless or unrivalled
UNRIVEN adj not torn apart
UNRIVET vb remove rivets from
UNRIVETED > UNRIVET
UNRIVETS > UNRIVET
UNROASTED adj not roasted
UNROBE same as > DISROBE
UNROBED > UNROBE
UNROBES > UNROBE
UNROBING > UNROBE
UNROLL vb open out or unwind (something rolled or coiled)
UNROLLED > UNROLL
UNROLLING > UNROLL
UNROLLS > UNROLL
UNROOF vb remove the roof from
UNROOFED > UNROOF
UNROOFING > UNROOF
UNROOFS > UNROOF
UNROOST vb remove from a perch

UNROOSTED > UNROOST
UNROOSTS > UNROOST
UNROOT less common word for > UPROOT
UNROOTED > UNROOT
UNROOTING > UNROOT
UNROOTS > UNROOT
UNROPE vb release from a rope
UNROPED > UNROPE
UNROPES > UNROPE
UNROPING > UNROPE
UNROSINED adj not coated with rosin
UNROTTED adj not rotted
UNROTTEN adj not rotten
UNROUGED adj not coloured with rouge
UNROUGH adj not rough
UNROUND vb release (lips) from a rounded position
UNROUNDED adj articulated with the lips spread
UNROUNDS > UNROUND
UNROUSED adj not roused
UNROVE > UNREEVE
UNROVEN > UNREEVE
UNROYAL adj not royal
UNROYALLY > UNROYAL
UNRUBBED adj not rubbed
UNRUDE adj not rude
UNRUFFE same as > UNROUGH
UNRUFFLE vb calm
UNRUFFLED adj calm and unperturbed
UNRUFFLES > UNRUFFLE
UNRULE n lack of authority
UNRULED adj not ruled
UNRULES > UNRULE
UNRULIER > UNRULY
UNRULIEST > UNRULY
UNRULY adj difficult to control or organize
UNRUMPLED adj neat
UNRUSHED adj unhurried
UNRUSTED adj not rusted
UNS > UN
UNSADDLE vb remove the saddle from (a horse)
UNSADDLED > UNSADDLE
UNSADDLES > UNSADDLE
UNSAFE adj dangerous
UNSAFELY > UNSAFE
UNSAFER > UNSAFE
UNSAFEST > UNSAFE
UNSAFETY n lack of safety
UNSAID adj not said or expressed
UNSAILED adj not sailed
UNSAINED adj not blessed
UNSAINT vb remove status of being a saint from
UNSAINTED > UNSAINT
UNSAINTLY adj not saintly
UNSAINTS > UNSAINT
UNSALABLE adj not capable of being sold
UNSALABLY > UNSALABLE
UNSALTED adj not seasoned, preserved, or treated with salt
UNSALUTED adj not saluted
UNSAMPLED adj not sampled
UNSAPPED adj not undermined

UNSASHED *adj* not furnished with a sash

UNSATABLE *adj* not able to be sated; insatiable

UNSATED *adj* not sated

UNSATIATE *adj* insatiable

UNSATING *adj* not satisfying

UNSAVED *adj* not saved

UNSAVORY *same as* > UNSAVOURY

UNSAVOURY *adj* distasteful or objectionable

UNSAW > UNSEE

UNSAWED *same as* > UNSAWN

UNSAWN *adj* not cut with a saw

UNSAY *vb* retract or withdraw (something said or written)

UNSAYABLE *adj* that cannot be said

UNSAYING > UNSAY

UNSAYS > UNSAY

UNSCALE *same as* > DESCALE

UNSCALED > UNSCALE

UNSCALES > UNSCALE

UNSCALING > UNSCALE

UNSCANNED *adj* not scanned

UNSCARIER > UNSCARY

UNSCARRED *adj* not scarred

UNSCARY *adj* not scary

UNSCATHED *adj* not harmed or injured

UNSCENTED *adj* not filled or impregnated with odour or fragrance

UNSCOURED *adj* not scoured

UNSCREW *vb* loosen (a screw or lid) by turning it

UNSCREWED > UNSCREW

UNSCREWS > UNSCREW

UNSCYTHED *adj* not cut with a scythe

UNSEAL *vb* remove or break the seal of

UNSEALED > UNSEAL

UNSEALING > UNSEAL

UNSEALS > UNSEAL

UNSEAM *vb* open or undo the seam of

UNSEAMED > UNSEAM

UNSEAMING > UNSEAM

UNSEAMS > UNSEAM

UNSEARED *adj* not seared

UNSEASON *vb* affect unfavourably

UNSEASONS > UNSEASON

UNSEAT *vb* throw or displace from a seat or saddle

UNSEATED > UNSEAT

UNSEATING > UNSEAT

UNSEATS > UNSEAT

UNSECRET *adj* not secret ▷ *vb* inform or make aware

UNSECRETS > UNSECRET

UNSECULAR *adj* not secular

UNSECURED *adj* (of a loan, etc) secured only against general assets and not against a specific asset

UNSEDUCED *adj* not seduced

UNSEE *vb* undo the act of seeing something

UNSEEABLE *adj* not able to be seen

UNSEEDED *adj* not given a top player's position in the opening rounds of a tournament

UNSEEING *adj* not noticing or looking at anything

UNSEEL *vb* undo seeling

UNSEELED > UNSEEL

UNSEELIE *pl n* evil malevolent fairies ▷ *adj* of or belonging to the unseelie

UNSEELING > UNSEEL

UNSEELS > UNSEEL

UNSEEMING *adj* unseemly

UNSEEMLY *adj* not according to expected standards of behaviour ▷ *adv* in an unseemly manner

UNSEEN *adj* hidden or invisible ▷ *adv* without being seen ▷ *n* passage given to students for translation without them having seen it in advance

UNSEENS > UNSEEN

UNSEES > UNSEE

UNSEIZED *adj* not seized

UNSELDOM *adv* frequently

UNSELF *vb* remove self-centredness from ▷ *n* lack of self

UNSELFED > UNSELF

UNSELFING > UNSELF

UNSELFISH *adj* concerned about other people's wishes and needs rather than one's own

UNSELFS > UNSELF

UNSELL *vb* speak unfavourably and off-puttingly of (something or someone)

UNSELLING > UNSELL

UNSELLS > UNSELL

UNSELVES > UNSELF

UNSENSE *vb* remove sense from

UNSENSED > UNSENSE

UNSENSES > UNSENSE

UNSENSING > UNSENSE

UNSENT *adj* not sent

UNSERIOUS *adj* not serious

UNSERVED *adj* not served

UNSET *adj* not yet solidified or firm ▷ *vb* displace

UNSETS > UNSET

UNSETTING > UNSET

UNSETTLE *vb* change or become changed from a fixed or settled condition

UNSETTLED *adj* lacking order or stability

UNSETTLES > UNSETTLE

UNSEVERED *adj* not severed

UNSEW *vb* undo stitching of

UNSEWED > UNSEW

UNSEWING > UNSEW

UNSEWN > UNSEW

UNSEWS > UNSEW

UNSEX *vb* deprive (a person) of the attributes of his or her sex

UNSEXED > UNSEX

UNSEXES > UNSEX

UNSEXIER > UNSEXY

UNSEXIEST > UNSEXY

UNSEXILY *adv* in an unsexy manner

UNSEXING > UNSEX

UNSEXIST *adj* not sexist

UNSEXUAL *adj* not sexual

UNSEXY *adj* not exciting or attractive

UNSHACKLE *vb* release from shackles

UNSHADED *adj* not shaded

UNSHADOW *vb* remove shadow from

UNSHADOWS > UNSHADOW

UNSHAKED *same as* > UNSHAKEN

UNSHAKEN *adj* (of faith or feelings) not having been weakened

UNSHALE *vb* expose

UNSHALED > UNSHALE

UNSHALES > UNSHALE

UNSHALING > UNSHALE

UNSHAMED *same as* > UNASHAMED

UNSHAPE *vb* make shapeless

UNSHAPED > UNSHAPE

UNSHAPELY *adj* not shapely

UNSHAPEN *adj* having no definite shape

UNSHAPES > UNSHAPE

UNSHAPING > UNSHAPE

UNSHARED *adj* not shared

UNSHARP *adj* not sharp

UNSHAVED *adj* not shaved

UNSHAVEN *adj* having a stubbled chin

UNSHEATHE *vb* pull (a weapon) from a sheath

UNSHED *adj* not shed

UNSHELL *vb* remove from a shell

UNSHELLED > UNSHELL

UNSHELLS > UNSHELL

UNSHENT *adj* undamaged

UNSHEWN *adj* unshown

UNSHIFT *vb* release the shift key on a keyboard

UNSHIFTED > UNSHIFT

UNSHIFTS > UNSHIFT

UNSHIP *vb* be or cause to be unloaded, discharged, or disembarked from a ship

UNSHIPPED > UNSHIP

UNSHIPS > UNSHIP

UNSHIRTED *adj* not wearing a shirt

UNSHOCKED *adj* not shocked

UNSHOD *adj* not wearing shoes

UNSHOE *vb* remove shoes from

UNSHOED *same as* > UNSHOD

UNSHOEING > UNSHOE

UNSHOES > UNSHOE

UNSHOOT *Shakespearean variant of* > UNSHOUT

UNSHOOTED > UNSHOOT

UNSHOOTS > UNSHOOT

UNSHORN *adj* not cut

UNSHOT *adj* not shot ▷ *vb* remove shot from

UNSHOTS > UNSHOT

UNSHOTTED > UNSHOT

UNSHOUT *vb* revoke (an earlier statement) by shouting a contrary one

UNSHOUTED > UNSHOUT

UNSHOUTS > UNSHOUT

UNSHOWIER > UNSHOWY

UNSHOWN *adj* not shown

UNSHOWY *adj* not showy

UNSHRIVED *same as* > UNSHRIVEN

UNSHRIVEN *adj* not shriven

UNSHROUD *vb* uncover

UNSHROUDS > UNSHROUD

UNSHRUBD *adj* not having shrubs

UNSHRUNK *adj* not shrunk

UNSHUNNED *adj* not shunned

UNSHUT *vb* open

UNSHUTS > UNSHUT

UNSHUTTER *vb* remove shutters from

UNSICKER *adj* unsettled

UNSICKLED *adj* not cut with a sickle

UNSIFTED *adj* not strained

UNSIGHING *adj* not lamented

UNSIGHT *vb* obstruct vision of

UNSIGHTED *adj* not sighted

UNSIGHTLY *adj* unpleasant to look at

UNSIGHTS > UNSIGHT

UNSIGNED *adj* (of a letter etc) anonymous

UNSILENT *adj* not silent

UNSIMILAR *adj* not similar

UNSINEW *vb* weaken

UNSINEWED > UNSINEW

UNSINEWS > UNSINEW

UNSINFUL *adj* without sin

UNSISTING *adj* Shakespearean term, possibly meaning insisting

UNSIZABLE *adj* of inadequate size

UNSIZED *adj* not made or sorted according to size

UNSKILFUL *adj* lacking dexterity or proficiency

UNSKILLED *adj* not having or requiring any special skill or training

UNSKIMMED *adj* not skimmed

UNSKINNED *adj* not skinned

UNSLAIN *adj* not killed

UNSLAKED *adj* not slaked

UNSLICED *adj* not sliced

UNSLICK *adj* not slick

UNSLING *vb* remove or release from a slung position

UNSLINGS > UNSLING

UNSLUICE *vb* let flow

UNSLUICED > UNSLUICE

UNSLUICES > UNSLUICE

UNSLUNG > UNSLING

UNSMART *adj* not smart

UNSMILING *adj* not wearing or assuming a smile

UNSMITTEN *adj* not smitten

UNSMOKED *adj* not smoked

UNSMOOTH *vb* roughen

UNSMOOTHS > UNSMOOTH

UNSMOTE *same as* > UNSMITTEN

UNSNAG *vb* remove snags from

UNSNAGGED > UNSNAG

UNSNAGS > UNSNAG

u

UNSNAP *vb* unfasten (the snap or catch) of (something)
UNSNAPPED > UNSNAP
UNSNAPS > UNSNAP
UNSNARL *vb* free from a snarl or tangle
UNSNARLED > UNSNARL
UNSNARLS > UNSNARL
UNSNECK *vb* unlatch
UNSNECKED > UNSNECK
UNSNECKS > UNSNECK
UNSNUFFED *adj* not snuffed
UNSOAKED *adj* not soaked
UNSOAPED *adj* not rubbed with soap
UNSOBER *adj* not sober ▷ *vb* make unrefined in manners
UNSOBERED > UNSOBER
UNSOBERLY > UNSOBER
UNSOBERS > UNSOBER
UNSOCIAL *adj* avoiding the company of other people
UNSOCKET *vb* remove from a socket
UNSOCKETS > UNSOCKET
UNSOD *same as* > UNSODDEN
UNSODDEN *adj* not soaked
UNSOFT *adj* hard
UNSOILED *adj* not soiled
UNSOLACED *adj* not comforted
UNSOLD *adj* not sold
UNSOLDER *vb* remove soldering from
UNSOLDERS > UNSOLDER
UNSOLEMN *adj* unceremonious
UNSOLID *adj* not solid
UNSOLIDLY > UNSOLID
UNSOLVED *adj* not having been solved or explained
UNSONCY *same as* > UNSONSY
UNSONSIE *same as* > UNSONSY
UNSONSIER > UNSONSY
UNSONSY *adj* unfortunate
UNSOOTE *adj* not sweet
UNSOOTHED *adj* not soothed
UNSORTED *adj* not sorted
UNSOUGHT *adj* not sought after
UNSOUL *vb* cause to be soulless
UNSOULED > UNSOUL
UNSOULING > UNSOUL
UNSOULS > UNSOUL
UNSOUND *adj* unhealthy or unstable
UNSOUNDED *adj* not sounded
UNSOUNDER > UNSOUND
UNSOUNDLY > UNSOUND
UNSOURCED *adj* without a source
UNSOURED *adj* not soured
UNSOWED *same as* > UNSOWN
UNSOWN *adj* not sown
UNSPAR *vb* open
UNSPARED *adj* not spared
UNSPARING *adj* very generous
UNSPARRED > UNSPAR
UNSPARS > UNSPAR
UNSPEAK *obsolete word for* > UNSAY
UNSPEAKS > UNSPEAK

UNSPED *adj* not achieved
UNSPELL *vb* release from a spell
UNSPELLED > UNSPELL
UNSPELLS > UNSPELL
UNSPENT *adj* not spent
UNSPHERE *vb* remove from its, one's, etc, sphere or place
UNSPHERED > UNSPHERE
UNSPHERES > UNSPHERE
UNSPIDE *same as* > UNSPIED
UNSPIED *adj* unnoticed
UNSPILLED *same as* > UNSPILT
UNSPILT *adj* not spilt
UNSPLIT *adj* not split
UNSPOILED *adj* not damaged or harmed
UNSPOILT *same as* > UNSPOILED
UNSPOKE > UNSPEAK
UNSPOKEN *adj* not openly expressed
UNSPOOL *vb* unwind from spool
UNSPOOLED > UNSPOOL
UNSPOOLS > UNSPOOL
UNSPOTTED *adj* without spots or stains
UNSPRAYED *adj* not sprayed
UNSPRUNG *adj* without springs
UNSPUN *adj* not spun
UNSQUARED *adj* not made into a square shape
UNSTABLE *adj* lacking stability or firmness
UNSTABLER > UNSTABLE
UNSTABLY > UNSTABLE
UNSTACK *vb* remove from a stack
UNSTACKED > UNSTACK
UNSTACKS > UNSTACK
UNSTAGED *adj* not staged
UNSTAID *adj* not staid
UNSTAINED *adj* not stained
UNSTALKED *adj* without a stalk
UNSTAMPED *adj* not stamped
UNSTARCH *vb* remove starch from
UNSTARRED *adj* not marked with a star
UNSTARRY *adj* not resembling or characteristic of a star from the entertainment world
UNSTATE *vb* deprive of state
UNSTATED *adj* not having been articulated or uttered
UNSTATES > UNSTATE
UNSTATING > UNSTATE
UNSTAYED *adj* unhindered
UNSTAYING *adj* nonstop
UNSTEADY *adj* not securely fixed ▷ *vb* make unsteady
UNSTEEL *vb* make (the heart, feelings, etc) more gentle or compassionate
UNSTEELED > UNSTEEL
UNSTEELS > UNSTEEL
UNSTEMMED *adj* without a stem
UNSTEP *vb* remove (a mast) from its step

UNSTEPPED > UNSTEP
UNSTEPS > UNSTEP
UNSTERILE *adj* not free from living, esp pathogenic, microorganisms
UNSTICK *vb* free or loosen (something stuck)
UNSTICKS > UNSTICK
UNSTIFFEN *vb* remove the stiffness from
UNSTIFLED *adj* not suppressed
UNSTILLED *adj* not reduced
UNSTINTED *adj* not stinted
UNSTIRRED *adj* not stirred
UNSTITCH *vb* remove stitching from
UNSTOCK *vb* remove stock from
UNSTOCKED *adj* without stock
UNSTOCKS > UNSTOCK
UNSTONED *adj* not stoned
UNSTOP *vb* remove the stop or stopper from
UNSTOPPED *adj* not obstructed or stopped up
UNSTOPPER *vb* unplug
UNSTOPS > UNSTOP
UNSTOW *vb* remove from storage
UNSTOWED > UNSTOW
UNSTOWING > UNSTOW
UNSTOWS > UNSTOW
UNSTRAP *vb* undo the straps fastening (something) in position
UNSTRAPS > UNSTRAP
UNSTRESS *n* weak syllable ▷ *vb* become less stressed
UNSTRING *vb* remove the strings of
UNSTRINGS > UNSTRING
UNSTRIP *vb* strip
UNSTRIPED *adj* (esp of smooth muscle) not having stripes
UNSTRIPS > UNSTRIP
UNSTRUCK *adj* not struck
UNSTRUNG *adj* emotionally distressed
UNSTUCK *adj* freed from being stuck, glued, fastened, etc
UNSTUDIED *adj* natural or spontaneous
UNSTUFFED *adj* not stuffed
UNSTUFFY *adj* well-ventilated
UNSTUFT *same as* > UNSTUFFED
UNSTUNG *adj* not stung
UNSTYLISH *adj* unfashionable
UNSUBDUED *adj* not subdued
UNSUBJECT *adj* not subject ▷ *vb* remove from subjugation
UNSUBTLE *adj* not subtle
UNSUBTLER > UNSUBTLE
UNSUBTLY > UNSUBTLE
UNSUCCESS *n* failure
UNSUCKED *adj* not sucked
UNSUIT *vb* make unsuitable
UNSUITED *adj* not appropriate for a particular task or situation

UNSUITING > UNSUIT
UNSUITS > UNSUIT
UNSULLIED *adj* (of a reputation, etc) not stained or tarnished
UNSUMMED *adj* not calculated
UNSUNG *adj* not acclaimed or honoured
UNSUNK *adj* not sunken
UNSUNNED *adj* not subjected to sunlight
UNSUNNIER > UNSUNNY
UNSUNNY *adj* not sunny
UNSUPPLE *adj* rigid
UNSURE *adj* lacking assurance or self-confidence
UNSURED *adj* not assured
UNSURELY > UNSURE
UNSURER > UNSURE
UNSUREST > UNSURE
UNSUSPECT *adj* not open to suspicion
UNSWADDLE *same as* > UNSWATHE
UNSWATHE *vb* unwrap
UNSWATHED > UNSWATHE
UNSWATHES > UNSWATHE
UNSWAYED *adj* not swayed
UNSWEAR *vb* retract or revoke (a sworn oath)
UNSWEARS > UNSWEAR
UNSWEET *adj* not sweet
UNSWEPT *adj* not swept
UNSWOLLEN *adj* not swollen
UNSWORE > UNSWEAR
UNSWORN > UNSWEAR
UNTACK *vb* remove saddle and harness, etc, from
UNTACKED > UNTACK
UNTACKING > UNTACK
UNTACKLE *vb* remove tackle from
UNTACKLED > UNTACKLE
UNTACKLES > UNTACKLE
UNTACKS > UNTACK
UNTACTFUL *adj* not tactful
UNTAGGED *adj* without a label
UNTAILED *adj* tailless
UNTAINTED *adj* not tarnished, contaminated, or polluted
UNTAKEN *adj* not taken
UNTAMABLE *adj* (of an animal or person) not capable of being tamed, subdued, or made obedient
UNTAMABLY > UNTAMABLE
UNTAME *vb* undo the taming of
UNTAMED *adj* not brought under human control
UNTAMES > UNTAME
UNTAMING > UNTAME
UNTANGLE *vb* free from tangles or confusion
UNTANGLED > UNTANGLE
UNTANGLES > UNTANGLE
UNTANNED *adj* not tanned
UNTAPPED *adj* not yet used
UNTARRED *adj* not coated with tar
UNTASTED *adj* not tasted
UNTAUGHT *adj* without training or education
UNTAX *vb* stop taxing

UNTAXABLE adj not taxable
UNTAXED adj not subject to taxation
UNTAXES > UNTAX
UNTAXING > UNTAX
UNTEACH vb cause to disbelieve (teaching)
UNTEACHES > UNTEACH
UNTEAM vb disband a team
UNTEAMED > UNTEAM
UNTEAMING > UNTEAM
UNTEAMS > UNTEAM
UNTEMPER vb soften
UNTEMPERS > UNTEMPER
UNTEMPTED adj not tempted
UNTENABLE adj (of a theory, idea, etc) incapable of being defended
UNTENABLY > UNTENABLE
UNTENANT vb remove (a tenant)
UNTENANTS > UNTENANT
UNTENDED adj not cared for or attended to
UNTENDER adj not tender
UNTENT vb remove from a tent
UNTENTED > UNTENT
UNTENTIER > UNTENTY
UNTENTING > UNTENT
UNTENTS > UNTENT
UNTENTY adj inattentive
UNTENURED adj not having tenure
UNTESTED adj not having been tested or examined
UNTETHER vb untie
UNTETHERS > UNTETHER
UNTHANKED adj not thanked
UNTHATCH vb remove the thatch from
UNTHAW same as **>** THAW
UNTHAWED adj not thawed
UNTHAWING > UNTHAW
UNTHAWS > UNTHAW
UNTHINK vb reverse one's opinion about
UNTHINKS > UNTHINK
UNTHOUGHT > UNTHINK
UNTHREAD vb draw out the thread or threads from (a needle, etc)
UNTHREADS > UNTHREAD
UNTHRIFT n unthrifty person
UNTHRIFTS > UNTHRIFT
UNTHRIFTY adj careless with money
UNTHRONE less common word for **>** DETHRONE
UNTHRONED > UNTHRONE
UNTHRONES > UNTHRONE
UNTIDIED > UNTIDY
UNTIDIER > UNTIDY
UNTIDIES > UNTIDY
UNTIDIEST > UNTIDY
UNTIDILY > UNTIDY
UNTIDY adj messy and disordered **▷** vb make untidy
UNTIDYING > UNTIDY
UNTIE vb open or free (something that is tied)
UNTIED > UNTIE
UNTIEING > UNTIE
UNTIES > UNTIE

UNTIL prep in or throughout the period before
UNTILE vb strip tiles from
UNTILED > UNTILE
UNTILES > UNTILE
UNTILING > UNTILE
UNTILLED adj not tilled
UNTILTED adj not tilted
UNTIMED adj not timed
UNTIMELY adj occurring before the expected or normal time **▷** adv prematurely or inopportunely
UNTIMEOUS same as **>** UNTIMELY
UNTIN vb remove tin from
UNTINGED adj not tinged
UNTINNED > UNTIN
UNTINNING > UNTIN
UNTINS > UNTIN
UNTIPPED adj not tipped
UNTIRABLE adj not able to be fatigued
UNTIRED adj not tired
UNTIRING adj continuing without declining in strength
UNTITLED adj without a title
UNTO prep to
UNTOILING adj not labouring
UNTOLD adj incapable of description
UNTOMB vb exhume
UNTOMBED > UNTOMB
UNTOMBING > UNTOMB
UNTOMBS > UNTOMB
UNTONED adj not toned
UNTOOLED adj not tooled
UNTOOTHED adj not toothed
UNTORN adj not torn
UNTOUCHED adj not changed, moved, or affected
UNTOWARD adj causing misfortune or annoyance
UNTRACE vb remove traces from
UNTRACED adj not traced
UNTRACES > UNTRACE
UNTRACING > UNTRACE
UNTRACK vb remove from track
UNTRACKED adj not tracked
UNTRACKS > UNTRACK
UNTRADED adj not traded
UNTRAINED adj without formal or adequate training or education
UNTRAPPED adj not trapped
UNTREAD vb retrace (a course, path, etc)
UNTREADED > UNTREAD
UNTREADS > UNTREAD
UNTREATED adj (of an illness, etc) not having been dealt with
UNTRENDY adj not trendy
UNTRESSED adj not having a tress
UNTRIDE same as **>** UNTRIED
UNTRIED adj not yet used, done, or tested
UNTRIM vb deprive of elegance or adornment
UNTRIMMED > UNTRIM

UNTRIMS > UNTRIM
UNTROD > UNTREAD
UNTRODDEN > UNTREAD
UNTRUE adj incorrect or false
UNTRUER > UNTRUE
UNTRUEST > UNTRUE
UNTRUISM n something that is false
UNTRUISMS > UNTRUISM
UNTRULY > UNTRUE
UNTRUSS vb release from or as if from a truss
UNTRUSSED > UNTRUSS
UNTRUSSER n person who untrusses
UNTRUSSES > UNTRUSS
UNTRUST n mistrust
UNTRUSTED adj not trusted
UNTRUSTS > UNTRUST
UNTRUSTY adj not trusty
UNTRUTH n statement that is not true, lie
UNTRUTHS > UNTRUTH
UNTUCK vb become or cause to become loose or not tucked in
UNTUCKED > UNTUCK
UNTUCKING > UNTUCK
UNTUCKS > UNTUCK
UNTUFTED adj not having tufts
UNTUMBLED adj not tumbled
UNTUNABLE adj not tuneful
UNTUNABLY > UNTUNABLE
UNTUNE vb make out of tune
UNTUNED > UNTUNE
UNTUNEFUL adj not tuneful
UNTUNES > UNTUNE
UNTUNING > UNTUNE
UNTURBID adj clear
UNTURF vb remove turf from
UNTURFED > UNTURF
UNTURFING > UNTURF
UNTURFS > UNTURF
UNTURN vb turn in a reverse direction
UNTURNED adj not turned
UNTURNING > UNTURN
UNTURNS > UNTURN
UNTUTORED adj without formal education
UNTWILLED adj not twilled
UNTWINE vb untwist, unravel, and separate
UNTWINED > UNTWINE
UNTWINES > UNTWINE
UNTWINING > UNTWINE
UNTWIST vb twist apart and loosen
UNTWISTED > UNTWIST
UNTWISTS > UNTWIST
UNTYING > UNTIE
UNTYINGS > UNTIE
UNTYPABLE adj incapable of being typed
UNTYPICAL adj not representative or characteristic of a particular type, person, etc
UNUNBIUM n chemical element
UNUNBIUMS > UNUNBIUM
UNUNITED adj separated
UNUNUNIUM n chemical element
UNURGED adj not urged

UNUSABLE adj not in good enough condition to be used
UNUSABLY > UNUSABLE
UNUSED adj not being or never having been used
UNUSEFUL adj useless
UNUSHERED adj not escorted
UNUSUAL adj uncommon or extraordinary
UNUSUALLY > UNUSUAL
UNUTTERED adj not uttered
UNVAIL same as **>** UNVEIL
UNVAILE same as **>** UNVEIL
UNVAILED > UNVAIL
UNVAILES > UNVAIL
UNVAILING > UNVAIL
UNVAILS > UNVAIL
UNVALUED adj not appreciated or valued
UNVARIED adj not varied
UNVARYING adj always staying the same
UNVEIL vb ceremonially remove the cover from (a new picture, plaque, etc)
UNVEILED > UNVEIL
UNVEILER n person who removes a veil
UNVEILERS > UNVEILER
UNVEILING n ceremony involving the removal of a veil covering a statue
UNVEILS > UNVEIL
UNVEINED adj without veins
UNVENTED adj not vented
UNVERSED adj not versed
UNVESTED adj not vested
UNVETTED adj not thoroughly examined
UNVEXED adj not annoyed
UNVEXT same as **>** UNVEXED
UNVIABLE adj not capable of succeeding, esp financially
UNVIEWED adj not viewed
UNVIRTUE n state of having no virtue
UNVIRTUES > UNVIRTUE
UNVISITED adj not visited
UNVISOR vb remove visor from
UNVISORED > UNVISOR
UNVISORS > UNVISOR
UNVITAL adj not vital
UNVIZARD same as **>** UNVISOR
UNVIZARDS > UNVIZARD
UNVOCAL adj not vocal
UNVOICE vb pronounce without vibration of the vocal cords
UNVOICED adj not expressed or spoken
UNVOICES > UNVOICE
UNVOICING > UNVOICE
UNVULGAR adj not vulgar
UNWAGED adj (of a person) not having a paid job
UNWAISTED adj not waisted
UNWAKED same as **>** UNWAKENED
UNWAKENED adj not roused from sleep
UNWALLED adj not surrounded by walls
UNWANING adj not waning
UNWANTED adj not wanted or welcome

U

UNWARDED adj not warded
UNWARE same as > UNAWARE
UNWARELY > UNWARE
UNWARES same as
> UNAWARES
UNWARIE same as > UNWARY
UNWARIER > UNWARY
UNWARIEST > UNWARY
UNWARILY > UNWARY
UNWARLIKE adj not warlike
UNWARMED adj not warmed
UNWARNED adj not warned
UNWARPED adj not warped
UNWARY adj not careful or cautious and therefore likely to be harmed
UNWASHED adj not washed
UNWASHEDS > UNWASHED
UNWASHEN same as
> UNWASHED
UNWASTED adj not wasted
UNWASTING adj not wasting
UNWATCHED adj (of an automatic device, such as a beacon) not manned
UNWATER vb dry out
UNWATERED > UNWATER
UNWATERS > UNWATER
UNWATERY adj not watery
UNWAXED adj not treated with wax
UNWAYED adj having no routes
UNWEAL n ill or sorrow
UNWEALS > UNWEAL
UNWEANED adj not weaned
UNWEAPON vb disarm
UNWEAPONS > UNWEAPON
UNWEARIED adj not abating or tiring
UNWEARIER > UNWEARY
UNWEARIES > UNWEARY
UNWEARY adj not weary ▷ vb refresh or energize
UNWEAVE vb undo (weaving)
UNWEAVES > UNWEAVE
UNWEAVING > UNWEAVE
UNWEBBED adj not webbed
UNWED adj not wed
UNWEDDED adj not wedded
UNWEEDED adj not weeded
UNWEENED adj unknown
UNWEETING same as
> UNWITTING
UNWEIGHED adj (of quantities purchased, etc) not measured for weight
UNWEIGHT vb remove weight from
UNWEIGHTS > UNWEIGHT
UNWELCOME adj unpleasant and unwanted
UNWELDED adj not welded
UNWELDY same as
> UNWIELDY
UNWELL adj not healthy, ill
UNWEPT adj not wept for or lamented
UNWET adj not wet
UNWETTED same as > UNWET
UNWHIPPED adj not whipped
UNWHIPT same as
> UNWHIPPED
UNWHITE adj not white
UNWIELDLY same as
> UNWIELDY

UNWIELDY adj too heavy, large, or awkward to be easily handled
UNWIFELY adj not like a wife
UNWIGGED adj without a wig
UNWILFUL adj complaisant
UNWILL vb will the reversal of (something that has already occurred)
UNWILLED adj not intentional
UNWILLING adj reluctant
UNWILLS > UNWILL
UNWIND vb relax after a busy or tense time
UNWINDER > UNWIND
UNWINDERS > UNWIND
UNWINDING > UNWIND
UNWINDS > UNWIND
UNWINGED adj without wings
UNWINKING adj vigilant
UNWIPED adj not wiped
UNWIRE vb remove wiring from
UNWIRED > UNWIRE
UNWIRES > UNWIRE
UNWIRING > UNWIRE
UNWISDOM n imprudence
UNWISDOMS > UNWISDOM
UNWISE adj foolish
UNWISELY > UNWISE
UNWISER > UNWISE
UNWISEST > UNWISE
UNWISH vb retract or revoke (a wish)
UNWISHED adj not desired
UNWISHES > UNWISH
UNWISHFUL adj not wishful
UNWISHING > UNWISH
UNWIST adj unknown
UNWIT vb divest of wit
UNWITCH vb release from witchcraft
UNWITCHED > UNWITCH
UNWITCHES > UNWITCH
UNWITS > UNWIT
UNWITTED > UNWIT
UNWITTIER > UNWITTY
UNWITTILY > UNWITTY
UNWITTING adj not intentional
UNWITTY adj not clever and amusing
UNWIVE vb remove a wife from
UNWIVED > UNWIVE
UNWIVES > UNWIVE
UNWIVING > UNWIVE
UNWOMAN vb remove womanly qualities from
UNWOMANED > UNWOMAN
UNWOMANLY adj not womanly
UNWOMANS > UNWOMAN
UNWON adj not won
UNWONT adj unaccustomed
UNWONTED adj out of the ordinary
UNWOODED adj not wooded
UNWOOED adj not wooed
UNWORDED adj not expressed in words
UNWORK vb destroy (work previously done)
UNWORKED adj not worked

UNWORKING > UNWORK
UNWORKS > UNWORK
UNWORLDLY adj not concerned with material values or pursuits
UNWORMED adj not rid of worms
UNWORN adj not having deteriorated through use or age
UNWORRIED adj not bothered or perturbed
UNWORTH n lack of value
UNWORTHS > UNWORTH
UNWORTHY adj not deserving or worthy
UNWOUND past tense and past participle of > UNWIND
UNWOUNDED adj not wounded
UNWOVE > UNWEAVE
UNWOVEN > UNWEAVE
UNWRAP vb remove the wrapping from (something)
UNWRAPPED > UNWRAP
UNWRAPS > UNWRAP
UNWREAKED adj unavenged
UNWREATHE vb untwist from a wreathed shape
UNWRINKLE vb remove wrinkles from
UNWRITE vb cancel (what has been written)
UNWRITES > UNWRITE
UNWRITING > UNWRITE
UNWRITTEN adj not printed or in writing
UNWROTE > UNWRITE
UNWROUGHT adj not worked
UNWRUNG adj not twisted
UNYEANED adj not having given birth
UNYIELDED adj not yielded
UNYOKE vb release (an animal, etc) from a yoke
UNYOKED > UNYOKE
UNYOKES > UNYOKE
UNYOKING > UNYOKE
UNYOUNG adj not young
UNZEALOUS adj unenthusiastic
UNZIP vb unfasten the zip of (a garment)
UNZIPPED > UNZIP
UNZIPPING > UNZIP
UNZIPS > UNZIP
UNZONED adj not divided into zones
UP adv indicating movement to or position at a higher place ▷ adj of a high or higher position ▷ vb increase or raise
UPADAISY same as
> UPSADAISY
UPAITHRIC adj without a roof
UPALONG n location away from a place
UPALONGS > UPALONG
UPAS n large Javan tree with whitish bark and poisonous milky sap
UPASES > UPAS
UPBEAR vb sustain
UPBEARER > UPBEAR
UPBEARERS > UPBEAR

UPBEARING > UPBEAR
UPBEARS > UPBEAR
UPBEAT adj cheerful and optimistic ▷ n unaccented beat
UPBEATS > UPBEAT
UPBIND vb bind up
UPBINDING > UPBIND
UPBINDS > UPBIND
UPBLEW > UPBLOW
UPBLOW vb inflate
UPBLOWING > UPBLOW
UPBLOWN > UPBLOW
UPBLOWS > UPBLOW
UPBOIL vb boil up
UPBOILED > UPBOIL
UPBOILING > UPBOIL
UPBOILS > UPBOIL
UPBORE > UPBEAR
UPBORNE adj held up
UPBOUND adj travelling upwards
UPBOUNDEN same as
> UPBOUND
UPBOW n stroke of the bow from its tip to its nut on a stringed instrument
UPBOWS > UPBOW
UPBRAID vb scold or reproach
UPBRAIDED > UPBRAID
UPBRAIDER > UPBRAID
UPBRAIDS > UPBRAID
UPBRAST same as
> UPBURST
UPBRAY vb shame
UPBRAYED > UPBRAY
UPBRAYING > UPBRAY
UPBRAYS > UPBRAY
UPBREAK vb escape upwards
UPBREAKS > UPBREAK
UPBRING vb rear
UPBRINGS > UPBRING
UPBROKE > UPBREAK
UPBROKEN > UPBREAK
UPBROUGHT > UPBRING
UPBUILD vb build up
UPBUILDER > UPBUILD
UPBUILDS > UPBUILD
UPBUILT > UPBUILD
UPBURNING adj burning upwards
UPBURST vb burst upwards
UPBURSTS > UPBURST
UPBY same as > UPBYE
UPBYE adv yonder
UPCAST n material cast or thrown up ▷ adj directed or thrown upwards ▷ vb throw or cast up
UPCASTING > UPCAST
UPCASTS > UPCAST
UPCATCH vb catch up
UPCATCHES > UPCATCH
UPCAUGHT > UPCATCH
UPCHEER vb cheer up
UPCHEERED > UPCHEER
UPCHEERS > UPCHEER
UPCHUCK vb vomit
UPCHUCKED > UPCHUCK
UPCHUCKS > UPCHUCK
UPCLIMB vb ascend
UPCLIMBED > UPCLIMB
UPCLIMBS > UPCLIMB
UPCLOSE vb close up

UPCLOSED > UPCLOSE
UPCLOSES > UPCLOSE
UPCLOSING > UPCLOSE
UPCOAST adv up the coast
UPCOIL vb make into a coil
UPCOILED > UPCOIL
UPCOILING > UPCOIL
UPCOILS > UPCOIL
UPCOME vb come up
UPCOMES > UPCOME
UPCOMING adj coming soon
UPCOUNTRY adj of or from
the interior of a country
▷ adv towards or in the
interior of a country ▷ n
interior part of a region or
country
UPCOURT adv up basketball
court
UPCURL vb curl up
UPCURLED > UPCURL
UPCURLING > UPCURL
UPCURLS > UPCURL
UPCURVE vb curve upwards
UPCURVED > UPCURVE
UPCURVES > UPCURVE
UPCURVING > UPCURVE
UPCYCLE vb recycle a
disposable product into an
object of greater value
UPCYCLED > UPCYCLE
UPCYCLES > UPCYCLE
UPCYCLING > UPCYCLE
UPDART vb dart upwards
UPDARTED > UPDART
UPDARTING > UPDART
UPDARTS > UPDART
UPDATABLE adj capable of
being updated
UPDATE vb bring up to date
▷ n act of updating or
something that is updated
UPDATED > UPDATE
UPDATER > UPDATE
UPDATERS > UPDATE
UPDATES > UPDATE
UPDATING > UPDATE
UPDIVE vb leap upwards
UPDIVED > UPDIVE
UPDIVES > UPDIVE
UPDIVING > UPDIVE
UPDO n type of hairstyle
UPDOMING n expansion of a
rock upwards into a dome
shape
UPDOMINGS > UPDOMING
UPDOS > UPDO
UPDOVE > UPDIVE
UPDRAFT n upwards air
current
UPDRAFTS > UPDRAFT
UPDRAG vb drag up
UPDRAGGED > UPDRAG
UPDRAGS > UPDRAG
UPDRAUGHT n upward
movement of air or other
gas
UPDRAW vb draw up
UPDRAWING > UPDRAW
UPDRAWN > UPDRAW
UPDRAWS > UPDRAW
UPDREW > UPDRAW
UPDRIED > UPDRY
UPDRIES > UPDRY
UPDRY vb dry up
UPDRYING > UPDRY

UPEND vb turn or set
(something) on its end
UPENDED > UPEND
UPENDING > UPEND
UPENDS > UPEND
UPFIELD adj in sport, away
from the defending team's
goal
UPFILL vb fill up
UPFILLED > UPFILL
UPFILLING > UPFILL
UPFILLS > UPFILL
UPFLING vb throw upwards
UPFLINGS > UPFLING
UPFLOW vb flow upwards
UPFLOWED > UPFLOW
UPFLOWING > UPFLOW
UPFLOWS > UPFLOW
UPFLUNG > UPFLING
UPFOLD vb fold up
UPFOLDED > UPFOLD
UPFOLDING > UPFOLD
UPFOLDS > UPFOLD
UPFOLLOW vb follow
UPFOLLOWS > UPFOLLOW
UPFRONT adj open and frank
▷ adv (of money) paid out at
the beginning of a business
arrangement
UPFURL vb roll up
UPFURLED > UPFURL
UPFURLING > UPFURL
UPFURLS > UPFURL
UPGANG n climb
UPGANGS > UPGANG
UPGATHER vb draw together
UPGATHERS > UPGATHER
UPGAZE vb gaze upwards
UPGAZED > UPGAZE
UPGAZES > UPGAZE
UPGAZING > UPGAZE
UPGIRD vb support or hold
up
UPGIRDED > UPGIRD
UPGIRDING > UPGIRD
UPGIRDS > UPGIRD
UPGIRT same as **>** UPGIRD
UPGIRTED > UPGIRT
UPGIRTING > UPGIRT
UPGIRTS > UPGIRT
UPGO vb ascend
UPGOES > UPGO
UPGOING > UPGO
UPGOINGS > UPGO
UPGONE > UPGO
UPGRADE vb promote (a
person or job) to a higher
rank
UPGRADED > UPGRADE
UPGRADER > UPGRADE
UPGRADERS > UPGRADE
UPGRADES > UPGRADE
UPGRADING > UPGRADE
UPGREW > UPGROW
UPGROW vb grow up
UPGROWING > UPGROW
UPGROWN > UPGROW
UPGROWS > UPGROW
UPGROWTH n process of
developing or growing
upwards
UPGROWTHS > UPGROWTH
UPGUSH vb flow upwards
UPGUSHED > UPGUSH
UPGUSHES > UPGUSH
UPGUSHING > UPGUSH

UPHAND adj lifted by hand
UPHANG vb hang up
UPHANGING > UPHANG
UPHANGS > UPHANG
UPHAUD Scots variant of
> UPHOLD
UPHAUDING > UPHAUD
UPHAUDS > UPHAUD
UPHEAP vb heap or pile up
UPHEAPED > UPHEAP
UPHEAPING > UPHEAP
UPHEAPS > UPHEAP
UPHEAVAL n strong,
sudden, or violent
disturbance
UPHEAVALS > UPHEAVAL
UPHEAVE vb heave or rise
upwards
UPHEAVED > UPHEAVE
UPHEAVER > UPHEAVE
UPHEAVERS > UPHEAVE
UPHEAVES > UPHEAVE
UPHEAVING > UPHEAVE
UPHELD > UPHOLD
UPHILD archaic past form of
> UPHOLD
UPHILL adj sloping or
leading upwards ▷ adv up a
slope ▷ n difficulty
UPHILLS > UPHILL
UPHOARD vb hoard up
UPHOARDED > UPHOARD
UPHOARDS > UPHOARD
UPHOIST vb raise
UPHOISTED > UPHOIST
UPHOISTS > UPHOIST
UPHOLD vb maintain or
defend against opposition
UPHOLDER > UPHOLD
UPHOLDERS > UPHOLD
UPHOLDING > UPHOLD
UPHOLDS > UPHOLD
UPHOLSTER vb fit (a chair or
sofa) with padding, springs,
and covering
UPHOORD vb heap up
UPHOORDED > UPHOORD
UPHOORDS > UPHOORD
UPHOVE > UPHEAVE
UPHROE variant spelling of
> EUPHROE
UPHROES > UPHROE
UPHUDDEN > UPHAUD
UPHUNG > UPHANG
UPHURL vb throw upwards
UPHURLED > UPHURL
UPHURLING > UPHURL
UPHURLS > UPHURL
UPJET vb stream upwards
UPJETS > UPJET
UPJETTED > UPJET
UPJETTING > UPJET
UPKEEP n act, process, or
cost of keeping something in
good repair
UPKEEPS > UPKEEP
UPKNIT vb bind
UPKNITS > UPKNIT
UPKNITTED > UPKNIT
UPLAID > UPLAY
UPLAND adj of or in an area of
high or relatively high
ground ▷ n area of high or
relatively high ground
UPLANDER n person hailing
from the uplands

UPLANDERS > UPLANDER
UPLANDISH > UPLAND
UPLANDS > UPLAND
UPLAY vb stash
UPLAYING > UPLAY
UPLAYS > UPLAY
UPLEAD vb lead upwards
UPLEADING > UPLEAD
UPLEADS > UPLEAD
UPLEAN vb lean on
something
UPLEANED > UPLEAN
UPLEANING > UPLEAN
UPLEANS > UPLEAN
UPLEANT > UPLEAN
UPLEAP vb jump upwards
UPLEAPED > UPLEAP
UPLEAPING > UPLEAP
UPLEAPS > UPLEAP
UPLEAPT > UPLEAP
UPLED > UPLEAD
UPLIFT vb raise or lift up ▷ n
act or process of improving
moral, social, or cultural
conditions
UPLIFTED > UPLIFT
UPLIFTER > UPLIFT
UPLIFTERS > UPLIFT
UPLIFTING adj acting to
raise moral, spiritual,
cultural, etc, levels
UPLIFTS > UPLIFT
UPLIGHT n lamp or wall
light designed or positioned
to cast its light upwards ▷ vb
light in an upward direction
UPLIGHTED > UPLIGHT
UPLIGHTER n lamp or wall
light designed or positioned
to cast its light upwards
UPLIGHTS > UPLIGHT
UPLINK n transmitter that
sends signals up to a
communications satellite
▷ vb send (data) to a
communications satellite
UPLINKED > UPLINK
UPLINKING > UPLINK
UPLINKS > UPLINK
UPLIT > UPLIGHT
UPLOAD vb transfer (data or
a program) into the memory
of another computer
UPLOADED > UPLOAD
UPLOADING > UPLOAD
UPLOADS > UPLOAD
UPLOCK vb lock up
UPLOCKED > UPLOCK
UPLOCKING > UPLOCK
UPLOCKS > UPLOCK
UPLOOK vb look up
UPLOOKED > UPLOOK
UPLOOKING > UPLOOK
UPLOOKS > UPLOOK
UPLYING adj raised
UPMADE > UPMAKE
UPMAKE vb make up
UPMAKER > UPMAKE
UPMAKERS > UPMAKE
UPMAKES > UPMAKE
UPMAKING > UPMAKE
UPMAKINGS > UPMAKE
UPMANSHIP n one-
upmanship
UPMARKET adj expensive
and of superior quality ▷ vb
make something upmarket

u

UPMARKETS > UPMARKET

UPMOST another word for > UPPERMOST

UPO prep upon

UPON prep on

UPPED > UP

UPPER adj higher or highest in physical position, wealth, rank, or status ▷ n part of a shoe above the sole

UPPERCASE adj capitalized ▷ vb capitalize or print in capitals

UPPERCUT n short swinging upward punch delivered to the chin ▷ vb hit (an opponent) with an uppercut

UPPERCUTS > UPPERCUT

UPPERMOST adj highest in position, power, or importance ▷ adv in or into the highest place or position

UPPERPART n highest part

UPPERS > UPPER

UPPILE vb pile up

UPPILED > UPPILE

UPPILES > UPPILE

UPPILING > UPPILE

UPPING > UP

UPPINGS > UP

UPPISH adj snobbish, arrogant, or presumptuous

UPPISHLY > UPPISH

UPPITIER > UPPITY

UPPITIEST > UPPITY

UPPITY adj snobbish, arrogant, or presumptuous

UPPROP vb support

UPPROPPED > UPPROP

UPPROPS > UPPROP

UPRAISE vb lift up

UPRAISED > UPRAISE

UPRAISER > UPRAISE

UPRAISERS > UPRAISE

UPRAISES > UPRAISE

UPRAISING > UPRAISE

UPRAN > UPRUN

UPRATE vb raise the value, rate, or size of, upgrade

UPRATED > UPRATE

UPRATES > UPRATE

UPRATING > UPRATE

UPREACH vb reach up

UPREACHED > UPREACH

UPREACHES > UPREACH

UPREAR vb lift up

UPREARED > UPREAR

UPREARING > UPREAR

UPREARS > UPREAR

UPREST n uprising

UPRESTS > UPREST

UPRIGHT adj vertical or erect ▷ adv vertically or in an erect position ▷ n vertical support, such as a post ▷ vb make upright

UPRIGHTED > UPRIGHT

UPRIGHTLY > UPRIGHT

UPRIGHTS > UPRIGHT

UPRISAL > UPRISE

UPRISALS > UPRISE

UPRISE vb rise up

UPRISEN > UPRISE

UPRISER > UPRISE

UPRISERS > UPRISE

UPRISES > UPRISE

UPRISING n rebellion or revolt

UPRISINGS > UPRISING

UPRIST same as > UPREST

UPRISTS > UPRIST

UPRIVER adv towards or near the source of a river ▷ n area located upstream

UPRIVERS > UPRIVER

UPROAR n disturbance characterized by loud noise and confusion ▷ vb cause an uproar

UPROARED > UPROAR

UPROARING > UPROAR

UPROARS > UPROAR

UPROLL vb roll up

UPROLLED > UPROLL

UPROLLING > UPROLL

UPROLLS > UPROLL

UPROOT vb pull up by or as if by the roots

UPROOTAL > UPROOT

UPROOTALS > UPROOT

UPROOTED > UPROOT

UPROOTER > UPROOT

UPROOTERS > UPROOT

UPROOTING > UPROOT

UPROOTS > UPROOT

UPROSE > UPRISE

UPROUSE vb rouse or stir up

UPROUSED > UPROUSE

UPROUSES > UPROUSE

UPROUSING > UPROUSE

UPRUN vb run up

UPRUNNING > UPRUN

UPRUNS > UPRUN

UPRUSH n upward rush, as of consciousness ▷ vb rush upwards

UPRUSHED > UPRUSH

UPRUSHES > UPRUSH

UPRUSHING > UPRUSH

UPRYST same as > UPREST

UPS > UP

UPSADAISY interj expression of reassurance often uttered when someone stumbles or is lifted up

UPSCALE adj of or for the upper end of an economic or social scale ▷ vb upgrade

UPSCALED > UPSCALE

UPSCALES > UPSCALE

UPSCALING > UPSCALE

UPSEE n drunken revel

UPSEES > UPSEE

UPSELL vb persuade a customer to buy a more expensive or additional item

UPSELLING > UPSELL

UPSELLS > UPSELL

UPSEND vb send up

UPSENDING > UPSEND

UPSENDS > UPSEND

UPSENT > UPSEND

UPSET adj emotionally or physically disturbed or distressed ▷ vb tip over ▷ n unexpected defeat or reversal

UPSETS > UPSET

UPSETTER > UPSET

UPSETTERS > UPSET

UPSETTING > UPSET

UPSEY same as > UPSEE

UPSEYS > UPSEY

UPSHIFT vb move up (a gear)

UPSHIFTED > UPSHIFT

UPSHIFTS > UPSHIFT

UPSHOOT vb shoot upwards

UPSHOOTS > UPSHOOT

UPSHOT n final result or conclusion

UPSHOTS > UPSHOT

UPSIDE n upper surface or part

UPSIDES > UPSIDE

UPSIES > UPSY

UPSILON n 20th letter in the Greek alphabet

UPSILONS > UPSILON

UPSITTING n sitting up of a woman after childbirth

UPSIZE vb increase in size

UPSIZED > UPSIZE

UPSIZES > UPSIZE

UPSIZING > UPSIZE

UPSKILL vb improve the aptitude for work of (a person)

UPSKILLED > UPSKILL

UPSKILLS > UPSKILL

UPSKIRT n photo of a woman's exposed underwear taken without her consent ▷ adj indicating a such a photo

UPSKIRTS > UPSKIRT

UPSLOPE adv up a or the slope ▷ n upward slope

UPSLOPES > UPSLOPE

UPSOAR vb soar up

UPSOARED > UPSOAR

UPSOARING > UPSOAR

UPSOARS > UPSOAR

UPSOLD > UPSELL

UPSPAKE > UPSPEAK

UPSPEAK vb speak with rising intonation

UPSPEAKS > UPSPEAK

UPSPEAR vb grow upwards in a spear-like manner

UPSPEARED > UPSPEAR

UPSPEARS > UPSPEAR

UPSPOKE > UPSPEAK

UPSPOKEN > UPSPEAK

UPSPRANG > UPSPRING

UPSPRING vb spring up or come into existence ▷ n leap forwards or upwards

UPSPRINGS > UPSPRING

UPSPRUNG > UPSPRING

UPSTAGE adj at the back half of the stage ▷ vb draw attention to oneself from (someone else) ▷ adv on, at, or to the rear of the stage ▷ n back half of the stage

UPSTAGED > UPSTAGE

UPSTAGER > UPSTAGE

UPSTAGERS > UPSTAGE

UPSTAGES > UPSTAGE

UPSTAGING > UPSTAGE

UPSTAIR same as > UPSTAIRS

UPSTAIRS adv to or on an upper floor of a building ▷ n upper floor ▷ adj situated on an upper floor

UPSTAND vb rise

UPSTANDS > UPSTAND

UPSTARE vb stare upwards

UPSTARED > UPSTARE

UPSTARES > UPSTARE

UPSTARING > UPSTARE

UPSTART n person who has risen suddenly to a position of power and behaves arrogantly ▷ vb start up, as in surprise, etc

UPSTARTED > UPSTART

UPSTARTS > UPSTART

UPSTATE adv towards, in, from, or relating to the outlying or northern sections of a state ▷ n outlying, esp northern, sections of a state

UPSTATER > UPSTATE

UPSTATERS > UPSTATE

UPSTATES > UPSTATE

UPSTAY vb support

UPSTAYED > UPSTAY

UPSTAYING > UPSTAY

UPSTAYS > UPSTAY

UPSTEP n type of vocal intonation

UPSTEPPED > UPSTEP

UPSTEPS > UPSTEP

UPSTIR vb stir up ▷ n commotion

UPSTIRRED > UPSTIR

UPSTIRS > UPSTIR

UPSTOOD > UPSTAND

UPSTREAM adj in or towards the higher part of a stream ▷ vb stream upwards

UPSTREAMS > UPSTREAM

UPSTROKE n upward stroke or movement, as of a pen or brush

UPSTROKES > UPSTROKE

UPSURGE n rapid rise or swell ▷ vb surge up

UPSURGED > UPSURGE

UPSURGES > UPSURGE

UPSURGING > UPSURGE

UPSWARM vb rise or send upwards in a swarm

UPSWARMED > UPSWARM

UPSWARMS > UPSWARM

UPSWAY vb swing in the air

UPSWAYED > UPSWAY

UPSWAYING > UPSWAY

UPSWAYS > UPSWAY

UPSWEEP n curve or sweep upwards ▷ vb sweep, curve, or brush or be swept, curved, or brushed upwards

UPSWEEPS > UPSWEEP

UPSWELL vb swell up or cause to swell up

UPSWELLED > UPSWELL

UPSWELLS > UPSWELL

UPSWEPT > UPSWEEP

UPSWING n recovery period in the trade cycle ▷ vb swing or move up

UPSWINGS > UPSWING

UPSWOLLEN > UPSWELL

UPSWUNG > UPSWING

UPSY same as > UPSEE

UPTA same as > UPTER

UPTAK same as > UPTAKE

UPTAKE n numbers taking up something such as an offer or the act of taking it up ▷ vb take up

UPTAKEN > UPTAKE

UPTAKES > UPTAKE

UPTAKING > UPTAKE

UPTAKS > UPTAK

UPTALK *n* style of speech in which every sentence ends with a rising tone ▷ *vb* talk in this manner
UPTALKED > UPTALK
UPTALKING > UPTALK
UPTALKS > UPTALK
UPTEAR *vb* tear up
UPTEARING > UPTEAR
UPTEARS > UPTEAR
UPTEMPO *adj* fast ▷ *n* uptempo piece
UPTEMPOS > UPTEMPO
UPTER *adj* of poor quality
UPTHREW > UPTHROW
UPTHROW *n* upward movement of rocks on one side of a fault plane relative to rocks on the other side ▷ *vb* throw upwards
UPTHROWN > UPTHROW
UPTHROWS > UPTHROW
UPTHRUST *n* upward push
UPTHRUSTS > UPTHRUST
UPTHUNDER *vb* make a noise like thunder
UPTICK *n* rise or increase
UPTICKS > UPTICK
UPTIE *vb* tie up
UPTIED > UPTIE
UPTIES > UPTIE
UPTIGHT *adj* nervously tense, irritable, or angry
UPTIGHTER > UPTIGHT
UPTILT *vb* tilt up
UPTILTED > UPTILT
UPTILTING > UPTILT
UPTILTS > UPTILT
UPTIME *n* time during which a machine, such as a computer, actually operates
UPTIMES > UPTIME
UPTITLING *n* practice of conferring grandiose job titles to employees performing relatively menial jobs
UPTOOK > UPTAKE
UPTORE > UPTEAR
UPTORN > UPTEAR
UPTOSS *vb* throw upwards
UPTOSSED > UPTOSS
UPTOSSES > UPTOSS
UPTOSSING > UPTOSS
UPTOWN *adv* towards, in, or relating to some part of a town that is away from the centre ▷ *n* such a part of town, esp a residential part
UPTOWNER > UPTOWN
UPTOWNERS > UPTOWN
UPTOWNS > UPTOWN
UPTRAIN *vb* train up
UPTRAINED > UPTRAIN
UPTRAINS > UPTRAIN
UPTREND *n* upward trend
UPTRENDS > UPTREND
UPTRILLED *adj* trilled high
UPTURN *n* upward trend or improvement ▷ *vb* turn or cause to turn over or upside down
UPTURNED > UPTURN
UPTURNING > UPTURN
UPTURNS > UPTURN
UPTYING > UPTIE
UPVALUE *vb* raise the value of

UPVALUED > UPVALUE
UPVALUES > UPVALUE
UPVALUING > UPVALUE
UPVOTE *vb* publicly approve of a social media post
UPVOTED > UPVOTE
UPVOTES > UPVOTE
UPVOTING > UPVOTE
UPWAFT *vb* waft upwards
UPWAFTED > UPWAFT
UPWAFTING > UPWAFT
UPWAFTS > UPWAFT
UPWARD *same as* > UPWARDS
UPWARDLY > UPWARD
UPWARDS *adv* from a lower to a higher place, level, condition, etc
UPWELL *vb* well up
UPWELLED > UPWELL
UPWELLING > UPWELL
UPWELLS > UPWELL
UPWENT > UPGO
UPWHIRL *vb* spin upwards
UPWHIRLED > UPWHIRL
UPWHIRLS > UPWHIRL
UPWIND *adv* into or against the wind ▷ *adj* going against the wind ▷ *vb* wind up
UPWINDING > UPWIND
UPWINDS > UPWIND
UPWOUND > UPWIND
UPWRAP *vb* wrap up
UPWRAPS > UPWRAP
UPWROUGHT *adj* wrought up
UR *interj* hesitant utterance used to fill gaps in talking
URACHI > URACHUS
URACHUS *n* cord of tissue connected to the bladder
URACHUSES > URACHUS
URACIL *n* pyrimidine present in all living cells
URACILS > URACIL
URAEI > URAEUS
URAEMIA *n* accumulation of waste products in the blood
URAEMIAS > URAEMIA
URAEMIC > URAEMIA
URAEUS *n* sacred serpent of ancient Egypt
URAEUSES > URAEUS
URALI *n* type of plant
URALIS > URALI
URALITE *n* mineral that replaces pyroxene in some rocks
URALITES > URALITE
URALITIC > URALITE
URALITISE *same as* > URALITIZE
URALITIZE *vb* turn into uralite
URANIA *n* uranium dioxide
URANIAN *adj* heavenly
URANIAS > URANIA
URANIC *adj* of or containing uranium, esp in a high valence state
URANIDE *n* any element having an atomic number greater than that of protactinium
URANIDES > URANIDE
URANIN *n* type of alkaline substance
URANINITE *n* blackish heavy radioactive mineral

consisting of uranium oxide in cubic crystalline form together with radium, lead, helium, etc: occurs in coarse granite
URANINS > URANIN
URANISCI > URANISCUS
URANISCUS *n* palate
URANISM *n* homosexuality
URANISMS > URANISM
URANITE *n* any of various minerals containing uranium, esp torbernite or autunite
URANITES > URANITE
URANITIC > URANITE
URANIUM *n* radioactive silvery-white metallic element
URANIUMS > URANIUM
URANOLOGY *n* study of the universe and planets
URANOUS *adj* of or containing uranium, esp in a low valence state
URANYL *n* type of divalent ion
URANYLIC > URANYL
URANYLS > URANYL
URAO *n* type of mineral
URAOS > URAO
URARE *same as* > URALI
URARES > URARE
URARI *same as* > URALI
URARIS > URARI
URASE *same as* > UREASE
URASES > URASE
URATE *n* any salt or ester of uric acid
URATES > URATE
URATIC > URATE
URB *n* urban area
URBAN *adj* of or living in a city or town
URBANE *adj* characterized by courtesy, elegance, and sophistication
URBANELY > URBANE
URBANER > URBANE
URBANEST > URBANE
URBANISE *same as* > URBANIZE
URBANISED > URBANISE
URBANISES > URBANISE
URBANISM *n* character of city life
URBANISMS > URBANISM
URBANIST *n* person who studies towns and cities
URBANISTS > URBANIST
URBANITE *n* resident of an urban community
URBANITES > URBANITE
URBANITY *n* quality of being urbane
URBANIZE *vb* make (a rural area) more industrialized and urban
URBANIZED > URBANIZE
URBANIZES > URBANIZE
URBEX *n* short for urban exploration, the hobby of exploring derelict urban structures
URBEXES > URBEX
URBIA *n* urban area
URBIAS > URBIA

URBS > URB
URCEOLATE *adj* shaped like an urn or pitcher
URCEOLI > URCEOLUS
URCEOLUS *n* organ of a plant
URCHIN *n* mischievous child
URCHINS > URCHIN
URD *n* type of plant with edible seeds
URDE *adj* (in heraldry) having points
URDEE *same as* > URDE
URDS > URD
URDY *n* heraldic line pattern
URE *same as* > AUROCHS
UREA *n* white soluble crystalline compound found in urine
UREAL > UREA
UREAS > UREA
UREASE *n* enzyme that converts urea to ammonium carbonate
UREASES > UREASE
UREDIA > UREDIUM
UREDIAL > UREDIUM
UREDINE > UREDO
UREDINES > UREDO
UREDINIA > UREDINIUM
UREDINIAL > UREDINIUM
UREDINIUM *same as* > UREDIUM
UREDINOUS > UREDO
UREDIUM *n* spore-producing body of some rust fungi in which uredospores are formed
UREDO *less common name for* > URTICARIA
UREDOS > UREDO
UREDOSORI *pl n* spore-producing bodies of some rust fungi in which uredospores are formed; uredia
UREIC > UREA
UREIDE *n* any of a class of organic compounds derived from urea
UREIDES > UREIDE
UREMIA *same as* > URAEMIA
UREMIAS > UREMIA
UREMIC > UREMIA
URENA *n* plant genus
URENAS > URENA
URENT *adj* burning
UREOTELIC *adj* excreting urea
URES > URE
URESES > URESIS
URESIS *n* urination
URETER *n* tube that conveys urine from the kidney to the bladder
URETERAL > URETER
URETERIC > URETER
URETERS > URETER
URETHAN *same as* > URETHANE
URETHANE *n* short for the synthetic material polyurethane ▷ *vb* treat with urethane
URETHANED > URETHANE
URETHANES > URETHANE
URETHANS > URETHAN

URETHRA n canal that carries urine from the bladder out of the body

URETHRAE > URETHRA

URETHRAL > URETHRA

URETHRAS > URETHRA

URETIC adj of or relating to the urine

URGE n strong impulse, inner drive, or yearning ▷ vb plead with or press (a person to do something)

URGED > URGE

URGENCE > URGENT

URGENCES > URGENT

URGENCIES > URGENT

URGENCY > URGENT

URGENT adj requiring speedy action or attention

URGENTLY > URGENT

URGER > URGE

URGERS > URGE

URGES > URGE

URGING > URGE

URGINGLY > URGE

URGINGS > URGE

URIAL n type of sheep

URIALS > URIAL

URIC adj of or derived from urine

URICASE n type of enzyme

URICASES > URICASE

URIDINE n nucleoside present in all living cells in a combined form, esp in RNA

URIDINES > URIDINE

URIDYLIC adj as in uridylic acid nucleotide consisting of uracil, ribose, and a phosphate group

URINAL n sanitary fitting used by men for urination

URINALS > URINAL

URINANT adj having the head downwards

URINARIES > URINARY

URINARY adj of urine or the organs that secrete and pass urine ▷ n reservoir for urine

URINATE vb discharge urine

URINATED > URINATE

URINATES > URINATE

URINATING > URINATE

URINATION > URINATE

URINATIVE > URINATE

URINATOR > URINATE

URINATORS > URINATE

URINE n pale yellow fluid passed as waste from the body ▷ vb urinate

URINED > URINE

URINEMIA same as > UREMIA

URINEMIAS > URINEMIA

URINEMIC > URINEMIA

URINES > URINE

URINING > URINE

URINOLOGY same as > UROLOGY

URINOSE same as > URINOUS

URINOUS adj of, resembling, or containing urine

URITE n part of the abdomen

URITES > URITE

URMAN n forest

URMANS > URMAN

URN n vase used as a container for the ashes of the dead ▷ vb put in an urn

URNAL > URN

URNED > URN

URNFIELD n cemetery full of individual cremation urns ▷ adj characterized by cremation in urns

URNFIELDS > URNFIELD

URNFUL n capacity of an urn

URNFULS > URNFUL

URNING n homosexual man

URNINGS > URNING

URNLIKE > URN

URNS > URN

UROBILIN n brownish pigment found in faeces and sometimes in urine

UROBILINS > UROBILIN

UROBORIC adj of or like a uroboros

UROBOROS same as > OUROBOROS

UROCHORD n notochord of a larval tunicate, typically confined to the tail region

UROCHORDS > UROCHORD

UROCHROME n yellowish pigment that colours urine

URODELAN > URODELE

URODELANS > URODELAN

URODELE n amphibian of the order which includes the salamanders and newts

URODELES > URODELE

URODELOUS > URODELE

UROGENOUS adj producing or derived from urine

UROGRAM n X-ray of the urinary tract

UROGRAMS > UROGRAM

UROGRAPHY n branch of radiology concerned with X-ray examination of the kidney and associated structures

UROKINASE n biochemical catalyst

UROLAGNIA n sexual arousal involving urination

UROLITH n calculus in the urinary tract

UROLITHIC > UROLITH

UROLITHS > UROLITH

UROLOGIC > UROLOGY

UROLOGIES > UROLOGY

UROLOGIST > UROLOGY

UROLOGY n branch of medicine concerned with the urinary system and its diseases

UROMERE n part of the abdomen

UROMERES > UROMERE

UROPOD n paired appendage forms part of the tailfan in lobsters

UROPODAL > UROPOD

UROPODOUS > UROPOD

UROPODS > UROPOD

UROPYGIA > UROPYGIUM

UROPYGIAL > UROPYGIUM

UROPYGIUM n hindmost part of a bird's body, from which the tail feathers grow

UROSCOPIC > UROSCOPY

UROSCOPY n examination of the urine

UROSES > UROSIS

UROSIS n urinary disease

UROSOME n abdomen of arthropods

UROSOMES > UROSOME

UROSTEGE n part of a serpent's tail

UROSTEGES > UROSTEGE

UROSTOMY n type of urinary surgery

UROSTYLE n bony rod forming the last segment of the vertebral column of frogs and toads

UROSTYLES > UROSTYLE

URP dialect word for > VOMIT

URPED > URP

URPING > URP

URPS > URP

URSA n she-bear

URSAE > URSA

URSID n meteor

URSIDS > URSID

URSIFORM adj bear-shaped or bearlike in form

URSINE adj of or like a bear

URSON n type of porcupine

URSONS > URSON

URTEXT n earliest form of a text

URTEXTE same as > URTEXTS

URTEXTS > URTEXT

URTICA n type of nettle

URTICANT n something that causes itchiness and irritation

URTICANTS > URTICANT

URTICARIA n skin condition characterized by the formation of itchy red or whitish raised patches, usually caused by an allergy

URTICAS > URTICA

URTICATE adj characterized by the presence of weals ▷ vb sting

URTICATED > URTICATE

URTICATES > URTICATE

URUBU n type of bird

URUBUS > URUBU

URUS another name for the > AUROCHS

URUSES > URUS

URUSHIOL n poisonous pale yellow liquid occurring in poison ivy and the lacquer tree

URUSHIOLS > URUSHIOL

URVA n Indian mongoose

URVAS > URVA

US pron refers to the speaker or writer and another person or other people

USABILITY > USABLE

USABLE adj able to be used

USABLY > USABLE

USAGE n regular or constant use

USAGER n person who has the use of something in trust

USAGERS > USAGER

USAGES > USAGE

USANCE n period of time permitted for the redemption of foreign bills of exchange

USANCES > USANCE

USAUNCE same as > USANCE

USAUNCES > USAUNCE

USE vb put into service or action ▷ n using or being used

USEABLE same as > USABLE

USEABLY > USABLE

USED adj second-hand

USEFUL adj able to be used advantageously or for several different purposes ▷ n odd-jobman or general factotum

USEFULLY > USEFUL

USEFULS > USEFUL

USELESS adj having no practical use

USELESSLY > USELESS

USER n continued exercise, use, or enjoyment of a right, esp in property

USERNAME n name given by computer user to gain access

USERNAMES > USERNAME

USERS > USER

USES > USE

USHER n official who shows people to their seats, as in a church ▷ vb conduct or escort

USHERED > USHER

USHERESS n female usher

USHERETTE n female assistant in a cinema who shows people to their seats

USHERING > USHER

USHERINGS > USHER

USHERS > USHER

USHERSHIP > USHER

USING > USE

USNEA n type of lichen

USNEAS > USNEA

USQUABAE n whisky

USQUABAES > USQUABAE

USQUE n whisky

USQUEBAE same as > USQUABAE

USQUEBAES > USQUEBAE

USQUES > USQUE

USTION n burning

USTIONS > USTION

USTULATE adj charred ▷ vb give a charred appearance to

USTULATED > USTULATE

USTULATES > USTULATE

USUAL adj of the most normal, frequent, or regular type ▷ n ordinary or commonplace events

USUALLY adv most often, in most cases

USUALNESS > USUAL

USUALS > USUAL

USUCAPION n method of acquiring property

USUCAPT > USUCAPION

USUCAPTED > USUCAPION

USUCAPTS > USUCAPION

USUFRUCT n right to use and derive profit from a piece of property belonging to another

USUFRUCTS > USUFRUCT
USURE vb be involved in usury
USURED > USURE
USURER n person who lends funds at an exorbitant rate of interest
USURERS > USURER
USURES > USURE
USURESS n female usurer
USURESSES > USURESS
USURIES > USURY
USURING > USURE
USURIOUS > USURY
USUROUS > USURY
USURP vb seize (a position or power) without authority
USURPED > USURP
USURPEDLY > USURP
USURPER > USURP
USURPERS > USURP
USURPING > USURP
USURPINGS > USURP
USURPS > USURP
USURY n practice of lending money at an extremely high rate of interest
USWARD adv towards us
USWARDS same as > USWARD
UT n syllable used in the fixed system of solmization for the note C
UTA n side-blotched lizard
UTAS n eighth day of a festival
UTASES > UTAS
UTE same as > UTILITY
UTENSIL n tool or container for practical use
UTENSILS > UTENSIL
UTERI > UTERUS

UTERINE adj of or affecting the womb
UTERITIS n inflammation of the womb
UTEROTOMY n surgery on the uterus
UTERUS n womb
UTERUSES > UTERUS
UTES > UTE
UTILE n W African tree
UTILES > UTILE
UTILIDOR n above-ground insulated casing for pipes in permafrost regions
UTILIDORS > UTILIDOR
UTILISE same as > UTILIZE
UTILISED > UTILISE
UTILISER > UTILISE
UTILISERS > UTILISE
UTILISES > UTILISE
UTILISING > UTILISE
UTILITIES > UTILITY
UTILITY n usefulness ▷ adj designed for use rather than beauty
UTILIZE vb make practical use of
UTILIZED > UTILIZE
UTILIZER > UTILIZE
UTILIZERS > UTILIZE
UTILIZES > UTILIZE
UTILIZING > UTILIZE
UTIS n uproar
UTISES > UTIS
UTMOST n the greatest possible degree or amount ▷ adj of the greatest possible degree or amount
UTMOSTS > UTMOST
UTOPIA n real or imaginary

society, place, state, etc, considered to be perfect or ideal
UTOPIAN adj of or relating to a perfect or ideal existence ▷ n idealistic social reformer
UTOPIANS > UTOPIAN
UTOPIAS > UTOPIA
UTOPIAST > UTOPIA
UTOPIASTS > UTOPIA
UTOPISM > UTOPIA
UTOPISMS > UTOPIA
UTOPIST > UTOPIA
UTOPISTIC > UTOPIA
UTOPISTS > UTOPIA
UTRICLE n larger of the two parts of the membranous labyrinth of the internal ear
UTRICLES > UTRICLE
UTRICULAR > UTRICLE
UTRICULI > UTRICULUS
UTRICULUS same as > UTRICLE
UTS > UT
UTTER vb express (something) in sounds or words ▷ adj total or absolute
UTTERABLE > UTTER
UTTERANCE n something uttered
UTTERED > UTTER
UTTERER > UTTER
UTTERERS > UTTER
UTTEREST > UTTER
UTTERING > UTTER
UTTERINGS > UTTER
UTTERLESS > UTTER
UTTERLY adv extremely
UTTERMOST same as > UTMOST
UTTERNESS > UTTER

UTTERS > UTTER
UTU n reward
UTUS > UTU
UVA n grape or fruit resembling this
UVAE > UVA
UVAROVITE n emerald-green garnet found in chromium deposits: consists of calcium chromium silicate
UVAS > UVA
UVEA n part of the eyeball consisting of the iris, ciliary body, and choroid
UVEAL > UVEA
UVEAS > UVEA
UVEITIC > UVEITIS
UVEITIS n inflammation of the uvea
UVEITISES > UVEITIS
UVEOUS > UVEA
UVULA n small fleshy part of the soft palate that hangs in the back of the throat
UVULAE > UVULA
UVULAR adj of or relating to the uvula ▷ n uvular consonant
UVULARLY > UVULAR
UVULARS > UVULAR
UVULAS > UVULA
UVULITIS n inflammation of the uvula
UXORIAL adj of or relating to a wife
UXORIALLY > UXORIAL
UXORICIDE n act of killing one's wife
UXORIOUS adj excessively fond of or dependent on one's wife

Vv

VAC vb clean with a vacuum cleaner
VACANCE n vacant period
VACANCES > VACANCE
VACANCIES > VACANCY
VACANCY n unfilled job
VACANT adj (of a toilet, room, etc) unoccupied
VACANTLY > VACANT
VACATABLE > VACATE
VACATE vb cause (something) to be empty by leaving
VACATED > VACATE
VACATES > VACATE
VACATING > VACATE
VACATION n time when universities and law courts are closed ▷ vb take a vacation
VACATIONS > VACATION
VACATUR n annulment
VACATURS > VACATUR
VACCINA same as > VACCINIA
VACCINAL adj of or relating to vaccine or vaccination
VACCINAS > VACCINA
VACCINATE vb inject with a vaccine
VACCINE n substance designed to make a person immune to a disease
VACCINEE n person who has been vaccinated
VACCINEES > VACCINEE
VACCINES > VACCINE
VACCINIA technical name for > COWPOX
VACCINIAL > VACCINIA
VACCINIAS > VACCINIA
VACCINIUM n shrub genus
VACHERIN n soft cheese made from cows' milk
VACHERINS > VACHERIN
VACILLANT adj indecisive
VACILLATE vb keep changing one's mind or opinions
VACKED > VAC
VACKING > VAC
VACS > VAC
VACUA > VACUUM
VACUATE vb empty
VACUATED > VACUATE
VACUATES > VACUATE
VACUATING > VACUATE
VACUATION > VACUATE
VACUIST n person believing in the existence of vacuums in nature
VACUISTS > VACUIST

VACUITIES > VACUITY
VACUITY n absence of intelligent thought or ideas
VACUOLAR > VACUOLE
VACUOLATE > VACUOLE
VACUOLE n fluid-filled cavity in the cytoplasm of a cell
VACUOLES > VACUOLE
VACUOUS adj not expressing intelligent thought
VACUOUSLY > VACUOUS
VACUUM n empty space from which all or most air or gas has been removed ▷ vb clean with a vacuum cleaner
VACUUMED > VACUUM
VACUUMING > VACUUM
VACUUMS > VACUUM
VADE vb fade
VADED > VADE
VADES > VADE
VADING > VADE
VADOSE adj of or derived from water occurring above the water table
VAE same as > VOE
VAES > VAE
VAG n vagrant ▷ vb arrest someone for vagrancy
VAGABOND n person with no fixed home, esp a beggar
VAGABONDS > VAGABOND
VAGAL adj of, relating to, or affecting the vagus nerve
VAGALLY > VAGAL
VAGARIES > VAGARY
VAGARIOUS adj characterized or caused by vagaries
VAGARISH > VAGARY
VAGARY n unpredictable change
VAGGED > VAG
VAGGING > VAG
VAGI > VAGUS
VAGILE adj able to move freely
VAGILITY > VAGILE
VAGINA n (in female mammals) passage from the womb to the external genitals
VAGINAE > VAGINA
VAGINAL > VAGINA
VAGINALLY > VAGINA
VAGINANT adj sheathing
VAGINAS > VAGINA
VAGINATE adj (esp of plant parts) having a sheath
VAGINATED > VAGINATE
VAGINITIS n inflammation of the vagina

VAGINOSES > VAGINOSIS
VAGINOSIS n bacterial vaginal infection
VAGINULA n little sheath
VAGINULAE > VAGINULA
VAGINULE same as > VAGINULA
VAGINULES > VAGINULE
VAGITUS n new-born baby's cry
VAGITUSES > VAGITUS
VAGOTOMY n surgical division of the vagus nerve
VAGOTONIA n pathological overactivity of the vagus nerve
VAGOTONIC > VAGOTONIA
VAGRANCY n state or condition of being a vagrant
VAGRANT n person with no settled home ▷ adj wandering
VAGRANTLY > VAGRANT
VAGRANTS > VAGRANT
VAGROM same as > VAGRANT
VAGS > VAG
VAGUE adj not clearly explained ▷ vb wander
VAGUED > VAGUE
VAGUELY > VAGUE
VAGUENESS > VAGUE
VAGUER > VAGUE
VAGUES > VAGUE
VAGUEST > VAGUE
VAGUING > VAGUE
VAGUISH adj rather vague
VAGUS n tenth cranial nerve, which supplies the heart, lungs, and viscera
VAHANA n vehicle
VAHANAS > VAHANA
VAHINE n Polynesian woman
VAHINES > VAHINE
VAIL vb lower (something, such as a weapon), esp as a sign of deference or submission
VAILED > VAIL
VAILING > VAIL
VAILS > VAIL
VAIN adj excessively proud, esp of one's appearance
VAINER > VAIN
VAINESSE n vainness
VAINESSES > VAINESSE
VAINEST > VAIN
VAINGLORY n boastfulness or vanity
VAINLY > VAIN
VAINNESS > VAIN
VAIR n fur used to trim robes in the Middle Ages

VAIRE adj of Russian squirrel fur
VAIRIER > VAIR
VAIRIEST > VAIR
VAIRS > VAIR
VAIRY > VAIR
VAIVODE n European ruler
VAIVODES > VAIVODE
VAJAZZLE vb decorate the female genitals with jewellery
VAJAZZLED > VAJAZZLE
VAJAZZLES > VAJAZZLE
VAKAS n Armenian priestly garment
VAKASES > VAKAS
VAKASS n priest's cloak with a metal breastplate
VAKASSES > VAKASS
VAKEEL n ambassador
VAKEELS > VAKEEL
VAKIL same as > VAKEEL
VAKILS > VAKIL
VALANCE n piece of drapery round the edge of a bed ▷ vb provide with a valance
VALANCED > VALANCE
VALANCES > VALANCE
VALANCING > VALANCE
VALE n valley ▷ sentence substitute farewell
VALENCE same as > VALENCY
VALENCES > VALENCE
VALENCIA n type of fabric
VALENCIAS > VALENCIA
VALENCIES > VALENCY
VALENCY n power of an atom to make molecular bonds
VALENTINE n (person to whom one sends) a romantic card on Saint Valentine's Day, 14th February
VALERATE n salt of valeric acid
VALERATES > VALERATE
VALERIAN n herb used as a sedative
VALERIANS > VALERIAN
VALERIC adj of, relating to, or derived from valerian
VALES > VALE
VALET n man's personal male servant ▷ vb act as a valet (for)
VALETA n old-time dance in triple time
VALETAS > VALETA
VALETE n farewell
VALETED > VALET
VALETES > VALETE

v

VALETING > VALET
VALETINGS > VALET
VALETS > VALET
VALGOID > VALGUS
VALGOUS same as > VALGUS
VALGUS adj denoting a deformity of a limb ▷ n abnormal position of a limb
VALGUSES > VALGUS
VALI n Turkish civil governor
VALIANCE > VALIANT
VALIANCES > VALIANT
VALIANCY > VALIANT
VALIANT adj brave or courageous ▷ n brave person
VALIANTLY > VALIANT
VALIANTS > VALIANT
VALID adj soundly reasoned
VALIDATE vb make valid
VALIDATED > VALIDATE
VALIDATES > VALIDATE
VALIDATOR n person who validates
VALIDER > VALID
VALIDEST > VALID
VALIDITY > VALID
VALIDLY > VALID
VALIDNESS > VALID
VALINE n essential amino acid
VALINES > VALINE
VALIS > VALI
VALISE n small suitcase
VALISES > VALISE
VALIUM n as in valium picnic refers to a day on the New York Stock Exchange when business is slow
VALIUMS > VALIUM
VALKYR variant of > VALKYRIE
VALKYRIE n Norse maiden who collects dead warriors to take to Valhalla
VALKYRIES > VALKYRIE
VALKYRS > VALKYR
VALLAR adj pertaining to a rampart ▷ n gold Roman crown awarded to the first soldier who broke into the enemy's camp
VALLARIES > VALLARY
VALLARS > VALLAR
VALLARY n Roman circular gold crown
VALLATE adj surrounded with a wall
VALLATION n act or process of building fortifications
VALLECULA n any of various natural depressions or crevices
VALLEY n low area between hills, often with a river running through it
VALLEYED adj having a valley
VALLEYS > VALLEY
VALLHUND n Swedish breed of dog
VALLHUNDS > VALLHUND
VALLONIA same as > VALONIA
VALLONIAS > VALLONIA
VALLUM n Roman rampart or earthwork
VALLUMS > VALLUM

VALONEA same as > VALONIA
VALONEAS > VALONEA
VALONIA n acorn cups and unripe acorns of a particular oak
VALONIAS > VALONIA
VALOR same as > VALOUR
VALORISE same as > VALORIZE
VALORISED > VALORISE
VALORISES > VALORISE
VALORIZE vb fix and maintain an artificial price for (a commodity) by governmental action
VALORIZED > VALORIZE
VALORIZES > VALORIZE
VALOROUS > VALOUR
VALORS > VALOR
VALOUR n bravery ▷ n courageous person
VALOURS > VALOUR
VALPROATE n medicament derived from valproic acid
VALPROIC adj as in valproic acid synthetic crystalline compound, used as an anticonvulsive
VALSE another word for > WALTZ
VALSED > VALSE
VALSES > VALSE
VALSING > VALSE
VALUABLE adj having great worth ▷ n valuable article of personal property, esp jewellery
VALUABLES > VALUABLE
VALUABLY > VALUABLE
VALUATE vb value or evaluate
VALUATED > VALUATE
VALUATES > VALUATE
VALUATING > VALUATE
VALUATION n assessment of worth
VALUATOR n person who estimates the value of objects, paintings, etc
VALUATORS > VALUATOR
VALUE n importance, usefulness ▷ vb assess the worth or desirability of
VALUED > VALUE
VALUELESS adj having or possessing no value
VALUER > VALUE
VALUERS > VALUE
VALUES > VALUE
VALUING > VALUE
VALUTA n value of one currency in terms of its exchange rate with another
VALUTAS > VALUTA
VALVAL same as > VALVULAR
VALVAR same as > VALVULAR
VALVASSOR same as > VAVASOR
VALVATE adj furnished with a valve or valves
VALVE n device to control the movement of fluid through a pipe ▷ vb provide with a valve
VALVED > VALVE

VALVELESS > VALVE
VALVELET same as > VALVULE
VALVELETS > VALVELET
VALVELIKE > VALVE
VALVES > VALVE
VALVING > VALVE
VALVULA same as > VALVULE
VALVULAE > VALVULA
VALVULAR adj of or having valves
VALVULE n small valve or a part resembling one
VALVULES > VALVULE
VAMBRACE n piece of armour used to protect the arm
VAMBRACED > VAMBRACE
VAMBRACES > VAMBRACE
VAMOOSE vb leave a place hurriedly
VAMOOSED > VAMOOSE
VAMOOSES > VAMOOSE
VAMOOSING > VAMOOSE
VAMOSE same as > VAMOOSE
VAMOSED > VAMOSE
VAMOSES > VAMOSE
VAMOSING > VAMOSE
VAMP n attractive woman who exploits men ▷ vb exploit (a man) in the fashion of a vamp
VAMPED > VAMP
VAMPER > VAMP
VAMPERS > VAMP
VAMPIER > VAMP
VAMPIEST > VAMP
VAMPING > VAMP
VAMPINGS > VAMP
VAMPIRE n (in folklore) corpse that rises at night to drink the blood of the living ▷ vb assail
VAMPIRED > VAMPIRE
VAMPIRES > VAMPIRE
VAMPIRIC > VAMPIRE
VAMPIRING > VAMPIRE
VAMPIRISE same as > VAMPIRIZE
VAMPIRISH > VAMPIRE
VAMPIRISM n belief in the existence of vampires
VAMPIRIZE vb suck blood from
VAMPISH > VAMP
VAMPISHLY > VAMP
VAMPLATE n piece of metal mounted on a lance to protect the hand
VAMPLATES > VAMPLATE
VAMPS > VAMP
VAMPY > VAMP
VAN n motor vehicle for transporting goods ▷ vb send in a van
VANADATE n any salt or ester of a vanadic acid
VANADATES > VANADATE
VANADIATE same as > VANADATE
VANADIC adj of or containing vanadium, esp in a trivalent or pentavalent state
VANADIUM n metallic element, used in steel

VANADIUMS > VANADIUM
VANADOUS adj of or containing vanadium
VANASPATI n hydrogenated vegetable fat commonly used in India as a substitute for butter
VANDA n type of orchid
VANDAL n person who deliberately damages property
VANDALIC > VANDAL
VANDALISE same as > VANDALIZE
VANDALISH > VANDAL
VANDALISM n wanton or deliberate destruction caused by a vandal or an instance of such destruction
VANDALIZE vb cause damage to (personal or public property) deliberately
VANDALS > VANDAL
VANDAS > VANDA
VANDYKE n short pointed beard ▷ vb cut with deep zigzag indentations
VANDYKED > VANDYKE
VANDYKES > VANDYKE
VANDYKING > VANDYKE
VANE n flat blade on a rotary device such as a weathercock or propeller
VANED > VANE
VANELESS > VANE
VANES > VANE
VANESSA n type of butterfly
VANESSAS > VANESSA
VANESSID n type of butterfly ▷ adj relating to this butterfly
VANESSIDS > VANESSID
VANG n type of rope or tackle on a sailing ship
VANGS > VANG
VANGUARD n unit of soldiers leading an army
VANGUARDS > VANGUARD
VANILLA n seed pod of a tropical climbing orchid, used for flavouring ▷ adj flavoured with vanilla
VANILLAS > VANILLA
VANILLIC adj of, resembling, containing, or derived from vanilla or vanillin
VANILLIN n white crystalline aldehyde found in vanilla
VANILLINS > VANILLIN
VANISH vb disappear suddenly or mysteriously ▷ n second and weaker of the two vowels in a falling diphthong
VANISHED > VANISH
VANISHER > VANISH
VANISHERS > VANISH
VANISHES > VANISH
VANISHING > VANISH
VANITAS n type of Dutch painting
VANITASES > VANITAS
VANITIED adj with vanity units or mirrors
VANITIES > VANITY
VANITORY n vanity unit

V

VANITY n (display of) excessive pride

VANLIKE adj like a van

VANLOAD n amount van will carry

VANLOADS > VANLOAD

VANMAN n man in control of a van

VANMEN > VANMAN

VANNED > VAN

VANNER n horse used to pull delivery vehicles

VANNERS > VANNER

VANNING > VAN

VANNINGS > VAN

VANPOOL n van-sharing group

VANPOOLS > VANPOOL

VANQUISH vb defeat (someone) utterly

VANS > VAN

VANT archaic word for > VANGUARD

VANTAGE n state, position, or opportunity offering advantage ▷ vb benefit

VANTAGED > VANTAGE

VANTAGES > VANTAGE

VANTAGING > VANTAGE

VANTBRACE n armour for the arm

VANTBRASS > VAMBRACE

VANTS > VANT

VANWARD adv in or towards the front

VAPE vb inhale nicotine vapour (from an electronic cigarette)

VAPED > VAPE

VAPER n one who inhales nicotine vapour from an electronic cigarette

VAPERS > VAPER

VAPES > VAPE

VAPID adj lacking character, dull

VAPIDER > VAPID

VAPIDEST > VAPID

VAPIDITY > VAPID

VAPIDLY > VAPID

VAPIDNESS > VAPID

VAPING n the practice of inhaling nicotine vapour (from an electronic cigarette)

VAPINGS > VAPING

VAPOR same as > VAPOUR

VAPORABLE > VAPOR

VAPORED > VAPOR

VAPORER > VAPOR

VAPORERS > VAPOR

VAPORETTI > VAPORETTO

VAPORETTO n steam-powered passenger boat, as used on the canals in Venice

VAPORIER > VAPORY

VAPORIEST > VAPORY

VAPORIFIC adj producing, causing, or tending to produce vapour

VAPORING > VAPOR

VAPORINGS > VAPOR

VAPORISE same as > VAPORIZE

VAPORISED > VAPORISE

VAPORISER same as > VAPORIZER

VAPORISES > VAPORISE

VAPORISH > VAPOR

VAPORIZE vb change into a vapour

VAPORIZED > VAPORIZE

VAPORIZER n substance that vaporizes or a device that causes vaporization

VAPORIZES > VAPORIZE

VAPORLESS > VAPOR

VAPORLIKE > VAPOR

VAPOROUS same as > VAPORIFIC

VAPORS > VAPOR

VAPORWARE n new software that has not yet been produced

VAPORY same as > VAPOURY

VAPOUR n moisture suspended in air as steam or mist ▷ vb evaporate

VAPOURED > VAPOUR

VAPOURER > VAPOUR

VAPOURERS > VAPOUR

VAPOURIER > VAPOURY

VAPOURING > VAPOUR

VAPOURISH > VAPOUR

VAPOUROUS adj like vapour

VAPOURS > VAPOUR

VAPOURY adj full of vapours

VAPULATE vb strike

VAPULATED > VAPULATE

VAPULATES > VAPULATE

VAQUERO n cattle-hand

VAQUEROS > VAQUERO

VAR n unit of reactive power of an alternating current

VARA n unit of length used in Spain, Portugal, and South America

VARACTOR n semiconductor diode that acts as a voltage-dependent capacitor

VARACTORS > VARACTOR

VARAN n type of lizard

VARANS > VARAN

VARAS > VARA

VARDIES > VARDY

VARDY n verdict

VARE n rod

VAREC n ash obtained from kelp

VARECH same as > VAREC

VARECHS > VARECH

VARECS > VAREC

VARENYKY pl n Ukrainian stuffed dumplings

VARES > VARE

VAREUSE n type of coat

VAREUSES > VAREUSE

VARGUENO n type of Spanish cabinet

VARGUENOS > VARGUENO

VARIA n collection or miscellany, esp of literary works

VARIABLE adj not always the same, changeable ▷ n something that is subject to variation

VARIABLES > VARIABLE

VARIABLY > VARIABLE

VARIANCE n act of varying

VARIANCES > VARIANCE

VARIANT adj differing from a standard or type ▷ n something that differs from a standard or type

VARIANTS > VARIANT

VARIAS > VARIA

VARIATE n random variable or a numerical value taken by it ▷ vb vary

VARIATED > VARIATE

VARIATES > VARIATE

VARIATING > VARIATE

VARIATION n something presented in a slightly different form

VARIATIVE > VARIATE

VARICEAL adj relating to a varix

VARICELLA n chickenpox

VARICES > VARIX

VARICOID same as > CIRSOID

VARICOSE adj of or resulting from varicose veins

VARICOSED same as > VARICOSE

VARICOSES > VARICOSIS

VARICOSIS n any condition characterized by distension of the veins

VARIED > VARY

VARIEDLY > VARY

VARIEGATE vb alter the appearance of, esp by adding different colours

VARIER n person who varies

VARIERS > VARIER

VARIES > VARY

VARIETAL adj of or forming a variety, esp a biological variety ▷ n wine labelled with the name of the grape from which it is pressed

VARIETALS > VARIETAL

VARIETIES > VARIETY

VARIETY n state of being diverse or various

VARIFOCAL adj gradated to permit any length of vision between near and distant ▷ n lens of this type

VARIFORM adj varying in form or shape

VARIOLA n smallpox

VARIOLAR > VARIOLA

VARIOLAS > VARIOLA

VARIOLATE vb inoculate with the smallpox virus ▷ adj marked or pitted with or as if with the scars of smallpox

VARIOLE n any of the rounded masses that make up the rock variolite

VARIOLES > VARIOLE

VARIOLITE n type of basic igneous rock

VARIOLOID adj resembling smallpox ▷ n mild form of smallpox occurring in persons with partial immunity

VARIOLOUS adj relating to or resembling smallpox

VARIORUM adj containing notes by various scholars or critics or various versions of the text ▷ n edition or text of this kind

VARIORUMS > VARIORUM

VARIOUS adj of several kinds

VARIOUSLY > VARIOUS

VARISCITE n green secondary mineral

VARISIZED adj of different sizes

VARISTOR n type of semiconductor device

VARISTORS > VARISTOR

VARITYPE vb produce (copy) on a Varityper ▷ n copy produced on a Varityper

VARITYPED > VARITYPE

VARITYPES > VARITYPE

VARIX n tortuous dilated vein

VARLET n menial servant

VARLETESS n female varlet

VARLETRY n varlets collectively

VARLETS > VARLET

VARLETTO same as > VARLET

VARLETTOS > VARLETTO

VARMENT same as > VARMINT

VARMENTS > VARMENT

VARMINT n irritating or obnoxious person or animal

VARMINTS > VARMINT

VARNA n any of the four Hindu castes

VARNAS > VARNA

VARNISH n solution of oil and resin, put on a surface to make it hard and glossy ▷ vb apply varnish to

VARNISHED > VARNISH

VARNISHER > VARNISH

VARNISHES > VARNISH

VARNISHY adj like varnish

VAROOM same as > VROOM

VAROOMED same as > VAROOM

VAROOMING same as > VAROOM

VAROOMS same as > VAROOM

VARROA n small parasite

VARROAS > VARROA

VARS > VAR

VARSAL adj universal

VARSITIES > VARSITY

VARSITY n university

VARTABED n position in the Armenian church

VARTABEDS > VARTABED

VARUS adj denoting a deformity of a limb ▷ n abnormal position of a limb

VARUSES > VARUS

VARVE n typically thin band of sediment deposited annually in glacial lakes

VARVED adj having layers of sedimentary deposit

VARVEL n piece of falconry equipment

VARVELLED adj having varvels

VARVELS > VARVEL

VARVES > VARVE

VARY vb change

VARYING > VARY

VARYINGLY > VARY

VARYINGS > VARY

VAS n vessel or tube that carries a fluid

VASA > VAS

VASAL > VAS

VASCULA > VASCULUM
VASCULAR *adj* relating to vessels
VASCULUM *n* metal box used by botanists in the field for carrying botanical specimens
VASCULUMS > VASCULUM
VASE *n* ornamental jar, esp for flowers
VASECTOMY *n* removal of part of the vas deferens
VASEFUL *n* contents of a vase
VASEFULS > VASEFUL
VASELIKE > VASE
VASELINE *n* translucent gelatinous substance obtained from petroleum ▷ *vb* apply vaseline to
VASELINED > VASELINE
VASELINES > VASELINE
VASES > VASE
VASIFORM > VAS
VASOMOTOR *adj* (of a drug, agent, nerve, etc) affecting the diameter of blood vessels
VASOSPASM *n* sudden contraction of a blood vessel
VASOTOCIN *n* chemical found in birds, reptiles, and some amphibians
VASOTOMY *n* surgery on the vas deferens
VASOVAGAL *adj* relating to blood vessels and the vagus nerve
VASSAIL *archaic variant of* > VASSAL
VASSAILS > VASSAIL
VASSAL *n* man given land by a lord in return for military service ▷ *adj* of or relating to a vassal ▷ *vb* vassalize
VASSALAGE *n* condition of being a vassal or the obligations to which a vassal was liable
VASSALESS > VASSAL
VASSALISE *same as* > VASSALIZE
VASSALIZE *vb* make a vassal of
VASSALLED > VASSAL
VASSALRY *n* vassalage
VASSALS > VASSAL
VAST *adj* extremely large ▷ *n* immense or boundless space
VASTER > VAST
VASTEST > VAST
VASTIDITY *n* vastness
VASTIER > VASTY
VASTIEST > VASTY
VASTITIES > VAST
VASTITUDE *n* condition or quality of being vast
VASTITY > VAST
VASTLY > VAST
VASTNESS > VAST
VASTS > VAST
VASTY *archaic or poetic word for* > VAST
VAT *n* large container for liquids ▷ *vb* place, store, or treat in a vat
VATABLE *adj* subject to VAT
VATFUL *n* amount enough to fill a vat

VATFULS > VATFUL
VATIC *adj* of, relating to, or characteristic of a prophet
VATICAL *same as* > VATIC
VATICIDE *n* murder of a prophet
VATICIDES > VATICIDE
VATICINAL *adj* foretelling or prophesying
VATMAN *n* Customs and Excise employee
VATMEN > VATMAN
VATS > VAT
VATTED > VAT
VATTER *n* person who works with vats; blender
VATTERS > VATTER
VATTING > VAT
VATU *n* standard monetary unit of Vanuatu
VATUS > VATU
VAU *same as* > VAV
VAUCH *vb* move fast
VAUCHED > VAUCH
VAUCHES > VAUCH
VAUCHING > VAUCH
VAUDOO *same as* > VOODOO
VAUDOOS > VAUDOO
VAUDOUX *same as* > VOODOO
VAULT *n* secure room for storing valuables ▷ *vb* jump over (something) by resting one's hand(s) on it
VAULTAGE *n* group of vaults
VAULTAGES > VAULTAGE
VAULTED > VAULT
VAULTER > VAULT
VAULTERS > VAULT
VAULTIER > VAULTY
VAULTIEST > VAULTY
VAULTING *n* arrangement of ceiling vaults in a building ▷ *adj* excessively confident
VAULTINGS > VAULTING
VAULTLIKE > VAULT
VAULTS > VAULT
VAULTY *adj* arched
VAUNCE *same as* > ADVANCE
VAUNCED > VAUNCE
VAUNCES > VAUNCE
VAUNCING > VAUNCE
VAUNT *vb* describe or display (success or possessions) boastfully ▷ *n* boast
VAUNTAGE *archaic variant of* > VANTAGE
VAUNTAGES > VAUNTAGE
VAUNTED > VAUNT
VAUNTER > VAUNT
VAUNTERS > VAUNT
VAUNTERY *n* bravado
VAUNTFUL > VAUNT
VAUNTIE *same as* > VAUNTY
VAUNTIER > VAUNTY
VAUNTIEST > VAUNT
VAUNTING > VAUNT
VAUNTINGS > VAUNT
VAUNTS > VAUNT
VAUNTY *adj* proud
VAURIEN *n* rascal
VAURIENS > VAURIEN
VAUS > VAU
VAUT *same as* > VAULT
VAUTE *same as* > VAULT
VAUTED > VAUTE
VAUTES > VAUTE

VAUTING > VAUTE
VAUTS > VAUT
VAV *n* sixth letter of the Hebrew alphabet
VAVASOR *n* (in feudal society) vassal who also has their own vassals
VAVASORS > VAVASOR
VAVASORY *n* lands held by a vavasor
VAVASOUR *same as* > VAVASOR
VAVASOURS > VAVASOUR
VAVASSOR *same as* > VAVASOR
VAVASSORS > VAVASSOR
VAVS > VAV
VAW *same as* > VAV
VAWARD *n* vanguard
VAWARDS > VAWARD
VAWNTIE > VAUNT
VAWNTIER > VAWNTIE
VAWNTIEST > VAWNTIE
VAWS > VAW
VAWTE *same as* > VAULT
VAWTED > VAWTE
VAWTES > VAWTE
VAWTING > VAWTE
VAX *n* vaccination
VAXES > VAX
VEAL *n* calf meat ▷ *vb* rear (calves) for use as veal
VEALE *Spenserian word for* > VEIL
VEALED > VEAL
VEALER *n* young bovine animal of up to 14 months old grown for veal
VEALERS > VEALER
VEALES > VEALE
VEALIER > VEAL
VEALIEST > VEAL
VEALING > VEAL
VEALS > VEAL
VEALY > VEAL
VECTOR *n* quantity that has size and direction, such as force ▷ *vb* direct or guide (a pilot) by directions transmitted by radio
VECTORED > VECTOR
VECTORIAL > VECTOR
VECTORING > VECTOR
VECTORISE *same as* > VECTORIZE
VECTORIZE *vb* computing term
VECTORS > VECTOR
VEDALIA *n* Australian ladybird which is a pest of citrus fruits
VEDALIAS > VEDALIA
VEDETTE *n* small patrol vessel
VEDETTES > VEDETTE
VEDUTA *n* painting of a town or city
VEDUTAS > VEDUTA
VEDUTE > VEDUTA
VEDUTISTA *n* artist who creates vedutas
VEDUTISTE > VEDUTISTA
VEDUTISTI > VEDUTISTA
VEE *n* letter 'v'
VEEJAY *n* video jockey
VEEJAYS > VEEJAY
VEENA *same as* > VINA

VEENAS > VEENA
VEEP *n* vice president
VEEPEE *n* vice president
VEEPEES > VEEPEE
VEEPS > VEEP
VEER *vb* change direction suddenly ▷ *n* change of course or direction
VEERED > VEER
VEERIES > VEERY
VEERING > VEER
VEERINGLY > VEER
VEERINGS > VEER
VEERS > VEER
VEERY *n* tawny brown North American thrush
VEES > VEE
VEG *n* vegetable or vegetables ▷ *vb* relax
VEGA *n* tobacco plantation
VEGAN *n* person who eats no meat, fish, eggs, or dairy products ▷ *adj* suitable for a vegan
VEGANIC *adj* farmed without the use of animal products or byproducts
VEGANISM > VEGAN
VEGANISMS > VEGAN
VEGANS > VEGAN
VEGAS > VEGA
VEGELATE *n* type of chocolate
VEGELATES > VEGELATE
VEGEMITE *n* informal Australian word for a child
VEGEMITES > VEGEMITE
VEGES > VEG
VEGETABLE *n* edible plant ▷ *adj* of or like plants or vegetables
VEGETABLY *adj* full of vegetables
VEGETAL *adj* of or relating to plant life ▷ *n* vegetable
VEGETALLY > VEGETAL
VEGETALS > VEGETAL
VEGETANT *adj* causing growth or vegetation-like
VEGETATE *vb* live a dull boring life with no mental stimulation
VEGETATED > VEGETATE
VEGETATES > VEGETATE
VEGETE *adj* lively
VEGETIST *n* vegetable cultivator or enthusiast
VEGETISTS > VEGETIST
VEGETIVE *adj* dull or passive ▷ *n* vegetable
VEGETIVES > VEGETIVE
VEGGED > VEG
VEGGES > VEG
VEGGIE *n* vegetable ▷ *adj* vegetarian
VEGGIER > VEGGIE
VEGGIES > VEGGIE
VEGGIEST > VEGGIE
VEGGING > VEG
VEGIE *n* vegetable ▷ *adj* vegetarian
VEGIER > VEGIE
VEGIES > VEGIE
VEGIEST > VEGIE
VEGO *adj* vegetarian ▷ *n* vegetarian
VEGOS > VEGO**

V

VEHEMENCE > VEHEMENT
VEHEMENCY > VEHEMENT
VEHEMENT adj expressing strong feelings
VEHICLE n machine for carrying people or objects
VEHICLES > VEHICLE
VEHICULAR > VEHICLE
VEHM n type of medieval German court
VEHME > VEHM
VEHMIC > VEHM
VEHMIQUE > VEHM
VEIL n piece of thin cloth covering the head or face ▷ vb cover with or as if with a veil
VEILED adj disguised
VEILEDLY > VEILED
VEILER > VEIL
VEILERS > VEIL
VEILIER > VEIL
VEILIEST > VEIL
VEILING n veil or the fabric used for veils
VEILINGS > VEILING
VEILLESS > VEIL
VEILLEUSE n small night-light
VEILLIKE > VEIL
VEILS > VEIL
VEILY > VEIL
VEIN n tube that takes blood to the heart ▷ vb diffuse over or cause to diffuse over in streaked patterns
VEINAL > VEIN
VEINED > VEIN
VEINER n wood-carving tool
VEINERS > VEINER
VEINIER > VEIN
VEINIEST > VEIN
VEINING n pattern or network of veins or streaks
VEININGS > VEINING
VEINLESS > VEIN
VEINLET n any small vein or venule
VEINLETS > VEINLET
VEINLIKE > VEIN
VEINOUS > VEIN
VEINS > VEIN
VEINSTONE another word for > GANGUE
VEINSTUFF another word for > GANGUE
VEINULE less common spelling of > VENULE
VEINULES > VEINULE
VEINULET same as > VEINLET
VEINULETS > VEINULET
VEINY > VEIN
VELA > VELUM
VELAMEN n thick layer of dead cells that covers the aerial roots of certain orchids
VELAMINA > VELAMEN
VELAR adj of, relating to, or attached to a velum ▷ n velar sound
VELARIA > VELARIUM
VELARIC > VELAR
VELARISE same as > VELARIZE
VELARISED > VELARISE
VELARISES > VELARISE

VELARIUM n awning used to protect the audience in ancient Roman theatres and amphitheatres
VELARIZE vb supplement the pronunciation of (a speech sound) with articulation at the soft palate
VELARIZED > VELARIZE
VELARIZES > VELARIZE
VELARS > VELAR
VELATE adj having or covered with velum
VELATED same as > VELATE
VELATURA n overglaze
VELATURAS > VELATURA
VELCRO n tradename for a fastening of two strips of nylon fabric pressed together
VELCROS > VELCRO
VELD n high grassland in southern Africa
VELDS > VELD
VELDSKOEN n leather ankle boot
VELDT same as > VELD
VELDTS > VELDT
VELE same as > VEIL
VELES > VELE
VELETA same as > VALETA
VELETAS > VELETA
VELIGER n free-swimming larva of many molluscs
VELIGERS > VELIGER
VELITES pl n light-armed troops in ancient Rome, drawn from the poorer classes
VELL n salted calf's stomach, used in cheese making
VELLEITY n weakest level of desire or volition
VELLENAGE n (in Medieval Europe) status of being a villein
VELLET n velvet
VELLETS > VELLET
VELLICATE vb twitch, pluck, or pinch
VELLON n silver and copper alloy used in old Spanish coins
VELLONS > VELLON
VELLS > VELL
VELLUM n fine calfskin parchment ▷ adj made of or resembling vellum
VELLUMS > VELLUM
VELLUS n as in vellus hair short fine unpigmented hair covering the human body
VELOCE adv to be played rapidly
VELOCITY n speed of movement in a given direction
VELODROME n arena with a banked track for cycle racing
VELOUR n fabric similar to velvet
VELOURS same as > VELOUR
VELOUTE n rich white sauce or soup made from stock, egg yolks, and cream
VELOUTES > VELOUTE
VELOUTINE n type of velvety fabric

VELSKOEN n type of shoe
VELSKOENS > VELSKOEN
VELUM n any of various membranous structures
VELURE n velvet or a similar fabric ▷ vb cover with velure
VELURED > VELURE
VELURES > VELURE
VELURING > VELURE
VELVERET n type of velvet-like fabric
VELVERETS > VELVERET
VELVET n fabric with a thick soft pile ▷ vb cover with velvet
VELVETED > VELVET
VELVETEEN n cotton velvet
VELVETIER > VELVET
VELVETING > VELVET
VELVETS > VELVET
VELVETY > VELVET
VENA n vein in the body
VENAE > VENA
VENAL adj easily bribed
VENALITY > VENAL
VENALLY > VENAL
VENATIC adj of, relating to, or used in hunting
VENATICAL same as > VENATIC
VENATION n arrangement of the veins in a leaf or in the wing of an insect
VENATIONS > VENATION
VENATOR n hunter
VENATORS > VENATOR
VEND vb sell
VENDABLE > VEND
VENDABLES > VEND
VENDACE n either of two small whitefish occurring in lakes in Scotland and NW England
VENDACES > VENDACE
VENDAGE n vintage
VENDAGES > VENDAGE
VENDANGE same as > VENDAGE
VENDANGES > VENDANGE
VENDED > VEND
VENDEE n person to whom something, esp real property, is sold
VENDEES > VENDEE
VENDER same as > VENDOR
VENDERS > VENDER
VENDETTA n long-lasting quarrel between people in which they attempt to harm each other
VENDETTAS > VENDETTA
VENDEUSE n female salesperson
VENDEUSES > VENDEUSE
VENDIBLE adj saleable or marketable ▷ n saleable object
VENDIBLES > VENDIBLE
VENDIBLY > VENDIBLE
VENDING > VEND
VENDINGS > VEND
VENDIS same as > VENDACE
VENDISES > VENDIS
VENDISS same as > VENDACE
VENDISSES > VENDIS
VENDITION > VEND

VENDOR n person who sells goods such as newspapers or hamburgers from a stall or cart
VENDORS > VENDOR
VENDS > VEND
VENDU n derogatory name for an anglified Quebecois
VENDUE n public sale
VENDUES > VENDUE
VENDUS > VENDU
VENEER n thin layer of wood etc covering a cheaper material ▷ vb cover (a surface) with a veneer
VENEERED > VENEER
VENEERER > VENEER
VENEERERS > VENEER
VENEERING n material used as veneer or a veneered surface
VENEERS > VENEER
VENEFIC adj having poisonous effects
VENEFICAL same as > VENEFIC
VENENATE vb poison
VENENATED > VENENATE
VENENATES > VENENATE
VENENE n medicine from snake venom
VENENES > VENENE
VENENOSE adj poisonous
VENERABLE adj worthy of deep respect
VENERABLY > VENERABLE
VENERATE vb hold (a person) in deep respect
VENERATED > VENERATE
VENERATES > VENERATE
VENERATOR > VENERATE
VENEREAL adj of or involving the genitals
VENEREAN n sex addict
VENEREANS > VENEREAN
VENEREOUS adj libidinous
VENERER n hunter
VENERERS > VENERER
VENERIES > VENERY
VENERY n pursuit of sexual gratification
VENETIAN n Venetian blind
VENETIANS > VENETIAN
VENEWE same as > VENUE
VENEWES > VENEWE
VENEY n thrust
VENEYS > VENEY
VENGE vb avenge
VENGEABLE > VENGE
VENGEABLY > VENGE
VENGEANCE n revenge
VENGED > VENGE
VENGEFUL adj wanting revenge
VENGEMENT > VENGE
VENGER > VENGE
VENGERS > VENGE
VENGES > VENGE
VENGING > VENGE
VENIAL adj (of a sin or fault) easily forgiven
VENIALITY > VENIAL
VENIALLY > VENIAL
VENIDIUM n genus of flowering plants
VENIDIUMS > VENIDIUM

VENIN n any of the poisonous constituents of animal venoms
VENINE same as > VENIN
VENINES > VENINE
VENINS > VENIN
VENIRE n list from which jurors are selected
VENIREMAN n person summoned for jury service
VENIREMEN > VENIREMAN
VENIRES > VENIRE
VENISON n deer meat
VENISONS > VENISON
VENITE n musical setting for the 95th psalm
VENITES > VENITE
VENNEL n lane
VENNELS > VENNEL
VENOGRAM n X-ray of a vein
VENOGRAMS > VENOGRAM
VENOLOGY n study of veins
VENOM n malice or spite ▷ vb poison
VENOMED > VENOM
VENOMER > VENOM
VENOMERS > VENOM
VENOMING > VENOM
VENOMLESS > VENOM
VENOMOUS > VENOM
VENOMS > VENOM
VENOSE adj having veins
VENOSITY n excessive quantity of blood in the venous system or in an organ or part
VENOUS adj of veins
VENOUSLY > VENOUS
VENT n outlet releasing fumes or fluid ▷ vb express (an emotion) freely
VENTAGE n small opening
VENTAGES > VENTAGE
VENTAIL n (in medieval armour) a covering for the lower part of the face
VENTAILE same as > VENTAIL
VENTAILES > VENTAILE
VENTAILS > VENTAIL
VENTANA n window
VENTANAS > VENTANA
VENTAYLE same as > VENTAIL
VENTAYLES > VENTAYLE
VENTED > VENT
VENTER > VENT
VENTERS > VENT
VENTIDUCT n air pipe
VENTIFACT n pebble that has been shaped by wind-blown sand
VENTIGE same as > VENTAGE
VENTIGES > VENTIGE
VENTIL n valve on a musical instrument
VENTILATE vb let fresh air into
VENTILS > VENTIL
VENTING > VENT
VENTINGS > VENT
VENTLESS > VENT
VENTOSE adj full of wind ▷ n apparatus sometimes used to assist the delivery of a baby

VENTOSES > VENTOSE
VENTOSITY n flatulence
VENTOUSE n ventose
VENTOUSES > VENTOUSE
VENTRAL adj relating to the front of the body ▷ n ventral fin
VENTRALLY > VENTRAL
VENTRALS > VENTRAL
VENTRE same as > VENTURE
VENTRED > VENTRE
VENTRES > VENTRE
VENTRICLE n cavity in an organ such as the heart
VENTRING > VENTRE
VENTRINGS > VENTRE
VENTROUS > VENTRE
VENTS > VENT
VENTURE n risky undertaking, esp in business ▷ vb do something risky
VENTURED > VENTURE
VENTURER > VENTURE
VENTURERS > VENTURE
VENTURES > VENTURE
VENTURI n tube used to control the flow of fluid
VENTURING > VENTURE
VENTURIS > VENTURI
VENTUROUS adj adventurous
VENUE n place where an organized gathering is held
VENUES > VENUE
VENULAR > VENULE
VENULE n any of the small branches of a vein
VENULES > VENULE
VENULOSE > VENULE
VENULOUS > VENULE
VENUS n type of marine bivalve mollusc
VENUSES > VENUS
VENVILLE n type of parish tenure
VENVILLES > VENVILLE
VERA adj as in aloe vera plant substance used in skin and hair preparations
VERACIOUS adj habitually truthful
VERACITY n truthfulness
VERANDA n porch or portico along the outside of a building
VERANDAED > VERANDA
VERANDAH same as > VERANDA
VERANDAHS > VERANDAH
VERANDAS > VERANDA
VERAPAMIL n calcium-channel blocker used in the treatment of some types of irregular heart rhythm
VERATRIA same as > VERATRINE
VERATRIAS > VERATRIA
VERATRIN same as > VERATRINE
VERATRINE n white poisonous mixture obtained from the seeds of sabadilla
VERATRINS > VERATRIN
VERATRUM n genus of herbs
VERATRUMS > VERATRUM
VERB n word that expresses the idea of action, happening, or being

VERBAL adj spoken ▷ n abuse or invective ▷ vb implicate (someone) in a crime by quoting alleged admission of guilt in court
VERBALISE same as > VERBALIZE
VERBALISM n exaggerated emphasis on the importance of words
VERBALIST n person who deals with words alone, rather than facts, ideas, feeling, etc
VERBALITY > VERBAL
VERBALIZE vb express (something) in words
VERBALLED > VERBAL
VERBALLY > VERBAL
VERBALS > VERBAL
VERBARIAN n inventor of words
VERBASCUM See > MULLEIN
VERBATIM adj word for word ▷ adv using exactly the same words
VERBENA n plant with sweet-smelling flowers
VERBENAS > VERBENA
VERBERATE vb lash
VERBIAGE n excessive use of words
VERBIAGES > VERBIAGE
VERBICIDE n person who destroys a word
VERBID n any nonfinite form of a verb or any nonverbal word derived from a verb
VERBIDS > VERBID
VERBIFIED > VERBIFY
VERBIFIES > VERBIFY
VERBIFY another word for > VERBALIZE
VERBILE n person who is best stimulated by words
VERBILES > VERBILE
VERBING n use of nouns as verbs
VERBINGS > VERBING
VERBLESS > VERB
VERBOSE adj speaking at tedious length
VERBOSELY > VERBOSE
VERBOSER > VERBOSE
VERBOSEST > VERBOSE
VERBOSITY > VERBOSE
VERBOTEN adj forbidden
VERBS > VERB
VERD n as in verd antique dark green mottled impure variety of serpentine marble
VERDANCY > VERDANT
VERDANT adj covered in green vegetation
VERDANTLY > VERDANT
VERDELHO n type of grape
VERDELHOS > VERDELHO
VERDERER n officer responsible for the maintenance of law and order in the royal forests
VERDERERS > VERDERER
VERDEROR same as > VERDERER
VERDERORS > VERDEROR
VERDET n type of verdigris
VERDETS > VERDET

VERDICT n decision of a jury
VERDICTS > VERDICT
VERDIGRIS n green film on copper, brass, or bronze
VERDIN n small W North American tit having grey plumage with a yellow head
VERDINS > VERDIN
VERDIT same as > VERDICT
VERDITE n type of rock used in jewellery
VERDITER n blue-green pigment made from copper
VERDITERS > VERDITER
VERDITES > VERDITE
VERDITS > VERDIT
VERDOY n floral or leafy shield decoration
VERDOYS > VERDOY
VERDURE n flourishing green vegetation
VERDURED > VERDURE
VERDURES > VERDURE
VERDUROUS > VERDURE
VERECUND adj shy or modest
VERGE n grass border along a road ▷ vb move in a specified direction
VERGED > VERGE
VERGENCE n inward or outward turning movement of the eyes in convergence or divergence
VERGENCES > VERGENCE
VERGENCY adj inclination
VERGER n church caretaker
VERGERS > VERGER
VERGES > VERGE
VERGING > VERGE
VERGLAS n thin film of ice on rock
VERGLASES > VERGLAS
VERIDIC same as > VERIDICAL
VERIDICAL adj truthful
VERIER > VERY
VERIEST > VERY
VERIFIED > VERIFY
VERIFIER > VERIFY
VERIFIERS > VERIFY
VERIFIES > VERIFY
VERIFY vb check the truth or accuracy of
VERIFYING > VERIFY
VERILY adv in truth
VERISM n extreme naturalism in art or literature
VERISMO n school of composition that originated in Italian opera
VERISMOS > VERISMO
VERISMS > VERISM
VERIST > VERISM
VERISTIC > VERISM
VERISTS > VERISM
VERITABLE adj rightly called, without exaggeration
VERITABLY > VERITABLE
VERITAS n truth
VERITATES > VERITAS
VERITE adj involving a high degree of realism or naturalism ▷ n this kind of realism in film
VERITES > VERITE
VERITIES > VERITY

VERITY n true statement or principle

VERJUICE n acid juice of unripe grapes, apples, or crab apples ▷ vb make sour

VERJUICED > VERJUICE

VERJUICES > VERJUICE

VERJUS n acid juice of unripe grapes, apples, or crab apples

VERJUSES > VERJUS

VERKLEMPT adj emotional

VERKRAMP adj bigoted or illiberal

VERLAN n variety of French slang in which the syllables are inverted

VERLANS > VERLAN

VERLIG adj enlightened

VERLIGTE n (during apartheid) a White political liberal

VERLIGTES > VERLIGTE

VERMAL > VERMIS

VERMEIL n gilded silver, bronze, or other metal, used esp in the 19th century ▷ vb decorate with vermeil ▷ adj vermilion

VERMEILED > VERMEIL

VERMEILLE variant of > VERMEIL

VERMEILS > VERMEIL

VERMELL same as > VERMEIL

VERMELLS > VERMELL

VERMES > VERMIS

VERMIAN > VERMIS

VERMICIDE n any substance used to kill worms

VERMICULE n small worm

VERMIFORM adj shaped like a worm

VERMIFUGE n any drug or agent able to destroy or expel intestinal worms

VERMIL same as > VERMEIL

VERMILIES > VERMILY

VERMILION adj orange-red ▷ n mercuric sulphide, used as an orange-red pigment

VERMILLED > VERMIL

VERMILS > VERMIL

VERMILY > VERMEIL

VERMIN pl n animals, esp insects and rodents, that spread disease or cause damage

VERMINATE vb breed vermin

VERMINED adj plagued with vermin

VERMINIER > VERMINY

VERMINOUS adj relating to, infested with, or suggestive of vermin

VERMINS > VERMIN

VERMINY adj full of vermin

VERMIS n middle lobe connecting the two halves of the cerebellum

VERMOULU adj worm-eaten

VERMOUTH n wine flavoured with herbs

VERMOUTHS > VERMOUTH

VERMUTH same as > VERMOUTH

VERMUTHS > VERMUTH

VERNACLE same as > VERNICLE

VERNACLES > VERNACLE

VERNAL adj occurring in spring

VERNALISE same as > VERNALIZE

VERNALITY > VERNAL

VERNALIZE vb subject (ungerminated or germinating seeds) to low temperatures

VERNALLY > VERNAL

VERNANT > VERNAL

VERNATION n way in which leaves are arranged in the bud

VERNICLE n veronica

VERNICLES > VERNICLE

VERNIER n movable scale on a measuring instrument for taking readings in fractions

VERNIERS > VERNIER

VERNIX n white substance covering the skin of a foetus

VERNIXES > VERNIX

VERONAL n long-acting barbiturate used medicinally

VERONALS > VERONAL

VERONICA n plant with small blue, pink, or white flowers

VERONICAS > VERONICA

VERONIQUE adj (of a dish) garnished with seedless white grapes

VERQUERE n type of backgammon game

VERQUERES > VERQUERE

VERQUIRE variant of > VERQUERE

VERQUIRES > VERQUIRE

VERRA Scot word for > VERY

VERREL n ferrule

VERRELS > VERREL

VERREY same as > VAIR

VERRINE n starter, dessert, or other dish served in a glass

VERRINES > VERRINE

VERRUCA n wart, usu on the foot

VERRUCAE > VERRUCA

VERRUCAS > VERRUCA

VERRUCOSE adj covered with warts

VERRUCOUS same as > VERRUCOSE

VERRUGA same as > VERRUCA

VERRUGAS > VERRUGA

VERRY same as > VAIR

VERS n verse

VERSAL n embellished letter

VERSALS > VERSAL

VERSANT n side or slope of a mountain or mountain range

VERSANTS > VERSANT

VERSATILE adj having many skills or uses

VERSE n group of lines forming part of a song or poem ▷ vb write verse

VERSED adj thoroughly knowledgeable (about)

VERSELET n small verse

VERSELETS > VERSELET

VERSEMAN n man who writes verse

VERSEMEN > VERSEMAN

VERSER n versifier

VERSERS > VERSER

VERSES > VERSE

VERSET n short, often sacred, verse

VERSETS > VERSET

VERSICLE n short verse

VERSICLES > VERSICLE

VERSIFIED > VERSIFY

VERSIFIER > VERSIFY

VERSIFIES > VERSIFY

VERSIFORM adj changing in form

VERSIFY vb write in verse

VERSIN same as > VERSINE

VERSINE n mathematical term

VERSINES > VERSINE

VERSING > VERSE

VERSINGS > VERSE

VERSINS > VERSIN

VERSION n form of something, with some differences from other forms ▷ vb keep track of the changes made to a computer file at different stages

VERSIONAL > VERSION

VERSIONED > VERSION

VERSIONER n translator

VERSIONS > VERSION

VERSO n left-hand page of a book

VERSOS > VERSO

VERST n unit of length used in Russia

VERSTE same as > VERST

VERSTES > VERSTE

VERSTS > VERST

VERSUS prep in opposition to or in contrast with

VERSUTE adj cunning

VERT n right to cut green wood in a forest ▷ vb turn

VERTEBRA n one of the bones that form the spine

VERTEBRAE > VERTEBRA

VERTEBRAL > VERTEBRA

VERTEBRAS > VERTEBRA

VERTED > VERT

VERTEX n point on a geometric figure where the sides form an angle

VERTEXES > VERTEX

VERTICAL adj straight up and down ▷ n vertical direction

VERTICALS > VERTICAL

VERTICES > VERTEX

VERTICIL n circular arrangement of parts about an axis, esp leaves around a stem

VERTICILS > VERTICIL

VERTICITY n ability to turn

VERTIGO n dizziness, usu when looking down from a high place

VERTIGOES > VERTIGO

VERTIGOS > VERTIGO

VERTING > VERT

VERTIPORT n type of airport

VERTISOL n type of clayey soil

VERTISOLS > VERTISOL

VERTS > VERT

VERTU same as > VIRTU

VERTUE same as > VIRTU

VERTUES > VERTUE

VERTUOUS > VERTU

VERTUS > VERTU

VERVAIN n plant with spikes of blue, purple, or white flowers

VERVAINS > VERVAIN

VERVE n enthusiasm or liveliness

VERVEL same as > VARVEL

VERVELLED > VERVEL

VERVELS > VERVEL

VERVEN same as > VERVAIN

VERVENS > VERVEN

VERVES > VERVE

VERVET n variety of a South African guenon monkey

VERVETS > VERVET

VERY adv more than usually, extremely ▷ adj absolute, exact

VESICA n bladder

VESICAE > VESICA

VESICAL adj of or relating to a vesica, esp the urinary bladder

VESICANT n any substance that causes blisters ▷ adj acting as a vesicant

VESICANTS > VESICANT

VESICAS > VESICA

VESICATE vb blister

VESICATED > VESICATE

VESICATES > VESICATE

VESICLE n sac or small cavity, esp one containing fluid

VESICLES > VESICLE

VESICULA n vesicle

VESICULAE > VESICULA

VESICULAR > VESICLE

VESPA n type of wasp

VESPAS > VESPA

VESPER n evening prayer, service, or hymn

VESPERAL n liturgical book containing the prayers, psalms, and hymns used at vespers

VESPERALS > VESPERAL

VESPERS pl n service of evening prayer

VESPIARY n nest or colony of social wasps or hornets

VESPID n insect of the family that includes the common wasp and hornet ▷ adj of or belonging to this family

VESPIDS > VESPID

VESPINE adj of, relating to, or resembling a wasp or wasps

VESPOID adj like a wasp

VESSAIL archaic variant of > VESSEL

VESSAILS > VESSAIL

VESSEL n container or ship ▷ adj contained in a vessel

VESSELED > VESSEL

VESSELS > VESSEL

VEST n undergarment worn on the top half of the body ▷ vb give (authority) to (someone)

VESTA n short friction match, usually of wood

VESTAL adj pure, chaste ▷ n chaste woman

VESTALLY > VESTAL

VESTALS > VESTAL

VESTAS > VESTA

VESTED adj having an existing right to the immediate or future possession of property

VESTEE n person having a vested interest in something

VESTEES > VESTEE

VESTIARY n room for storing clothes or dressing in, such as a vestry ▷ adj of or relating to clothes

VESTIBULA > VESTIBULE

VESTIBULE n small entrance hall

VESTIGE n small amount or trace

VESTIGES > VESTIGE

VESTIGIA > VESTIGIUM

VESTIGIAL adj remaining after a larger or more important thing has gone

VESTIGIUM n trace

VESTIMENT same as > VESTMENT

VESTING > VEST

VESTINGS > VEST

VESTITURE n investiture

VESTLESS > VEST

VESTLIKE > VEST

VESTMENT n garment or robe, esp one denoting office, authority, or rank

VESTMENTS > VESTMENT

VESTRAL > VESTRY

VESTRIES > VESTRY

VESTRY n room in a church used as an office by the priest or minister

VESTRYMAN n member of a church vestry

VESTRYMEN > VESTRYMAN

VESTS > VEST

VESTURAL > VESTURE

VESTURE n garment or something that seems like a garment ▷ vb clothe

VESTURED > VESTURE

VESTURER n person in charge of church vestments

VESTURERS > VESTURER

VESTURES > VESTURE

VESTURING > VESTURE

VESUVIAN n match for lighting cigars

VESUVIANS > VESUVIAN

VET vb check the suitability of ▷ n military veteran

VETCH n climbing plant with a beanlike fruit used as fodder

VETCHES > VETCH

VETCHIER > VETCHY

VETCHIEST > VETCHY

VETCHLING n type of climbing plant

VETCHY adj consisting of vetches

VETERAN n person with long experience in a particular activity ▷ adj long-serving

VETERANS > VETERAN

VETIVER n tall hairless grass of tropical and subtropical Asia

VETIVERS > VETIVER

VETIVERT n oil from the vetiver

VETIVERTS > VETIVERT

VETKOEK n South African cake

VETKOEKS > VETKOEK

VETO n official power to cancel a proposal ▷ vb enforce a veto against

VETOED > VETO

VETOER > VETO

VETOERS > VETO

VETOES > VETO

VETOING > VETO

VETOLESS > VETO

VETS > VET

VETTED > VET

VETTER > VET

VETTERS > VET

VETTING n as in positive vetting checking a person's background to assess their suitability of an important post

VETTINGS > VETTING

VETTURA n Italian mode of transport

VETTURAS > VETTURA

VETTURINI > VETTURINO

VETTURINO n person who drives a vettura

VEX vb frustrate, annoy

VEXATION n something annoying

VEXATIONS > VEXATION

VEXATIOUS adj vexing

VEXATORY > VEX

VEXED adj annoyed and puzzled

VEXEDLY > VEXED

VEXEDNESS > VEXED

VEXER > VEX

VEXERS > VEX

VEXES > VEX

VEXIL same as > VEXILLUM

VEXILLA > VEXILLUM

VEXILLAR > VEXILLUM

VEXILLARY > VEXILLUM

VEXILLATE > VEXILLUM

VEXILLUM n vane of a feather

VEXILS > VEXIL

VEXING > VEX

VEXINGLY > VEX

VEXINGS > VEX

VEXT same as > VEXED

VEZIR same as > VIZIER

VEZIRS > VEZIR

VIA prep by way of ▷ n road

VIABILITY > VIABLE

VIABLE adj able to be put into practice

VIABLY > VIABLE

VIADUCT n bridge over a valley

VIADUCTS > VIADUCT

VIAE > VIA

VIAL n small bottle for liquids ▷ vb put into a vial

VIALED > VIAL

VIALFUL > VIAL

VIALFULS > VIAL

VIALING > VIAL

VIALLED > VIAL

VIALLING > VIAL

VIALS > VIAL

VIAMETER n device to measure distance travelled

VIAMETERS > VIAMETER

VIAND n type of food, esp a delicacy

VIANDS > VIAND

VIAS > VIA

VIATIC same as > VIATICAL

VIATICA > VIATICUM

VIATICAL adj of a road or a journey ▷ n purchase of a terminal patient's life assurance policy so that he or she may make use of the proceeds

VIATICALS > VIATICAL

VIATICUM n Holy Communion given to a person who is dying or in danger of death

VIATICUMS > VIATICUM

VIATOR n traveller

VIATORES > VIATOR

VIATORIAL adj pertaining to travelling

VIATORS > VIATOR

VIBE n feeling or flavour of the kind specified

VIBES pl n vibrations

VIBEX n mark under the skin

VIBEY adj lively and vibrant

VIBICES > VIBEX

VIBIER > VIBEY

VIBIEST > VIBEY

VIBIST n person who plays a vibraphone in a jazz band or group

VIBISTS > VIBIST

VIBRACULA pl n bristle-like polyps in certain bryozoans

VIBRAHARP n type of percussion instrument

VIBRANCE n vibrancy

VIBRANCES > VIBRANCE

VIBRANCY > VIBRANT

VIBRANT adj vigorous in appearance, energetic ▷ n trilled or rolled speech sound

VIBRANTLY > VIBRANT

VIBRANTS > VIBRANT

VIBRATE vb move back and forth rapidly

VIBRATED > VIBRATE

VIBRATES > VIBRATE

VIBRATILE > VIBRATE

VIBRATING > VIBRATE

VIBRATION n vibrating

VIBRATIVE > VIBRATE

VIBRATO n rapid fluctuation in the pitch of a note

VIBRATOR n device that produces vibratory motion

VIBRATORS > VIBRATOR

VIBRATORY > VIBRATE

VIBRATOS > VIBRATO

VIBRIO n curved or spiral rodlike bacterium

VIBRIOID > VIBRIO

VIBRION same as > VIBRIO

VIBRIONIC > VIBRIO

VIBRIONS > VIBRION

VIBRIOS > VIBRIO

VIBRIOSES > VIBRIOSIS

VIBRIOSIS n bacterial disease

VIBRISSA n any of the bristle-like sensitive hairs on the face of many mammals

VIBRISSAE > VIBRISSA

VIBRISSAL > VIBRISSA

VIBRONIC adj of, concerned with, or involving both electronic and vibrational energy levels of a molecule

VIBS pl n type of climbing shoes

VIBURNUM n subtropical shrub with white flowers and berry-like fruits

VIBURNUMS > VIBURNUM

VICAR n member of the clergy in charge of a parish

VICARAGE n vicar's house

VICARAGES > VICARAGE

VICARATE same as > VICARIATE

VICARATES > VICARATE

VICARESS n rank of nun

VICARIAL adj of or relating to a vicar, vicars, or a vicariate

VICARIANT n any of several closely related species, etc, each of which exists in a separate geographical area

VICARIATE n office, rank, or authority of a vicar

VICARIES > VICARY

VICARIOUS adj felt indirectly by imagining what another person experiences

VICARLIER > VICARLY

VICARLY adj like a vicar

VICARS > VICAR

VICARSHIP same as > VICARIATE

VICARY n office of a vicar

VICE n immoral or evil habit or action ▷ adj serving in place of ▷ vb grip (something) with or as if with a vice ▷ prep instead of

VICED > VICE

VICEGERAL adj of or relating to a person who deputizes for another

VICELESS > VICE

VICELIKE > VICE

VICENARY adj relating to or consisting of 20

VICENNIAL adj occurring every 20 years

VICEREGAL adj of a viceroy

VICEREINE n wife of a viceroy

VICEROY n governor of a colony who represents the monarch

VICEROYS > VICEROY

VICES > VICE

VICESIMAL same as > VIGESIMAL

VICHIES > VICHY

VICHY n French mineral water

VICIATE same as > VITIATE

VICIATED > VICIATE
VICIATES > VICIATE
VICIATING > VICIATE
VICINAGE n residents of a particular neighbourhood
VICINAGES > VICINAGE
VICINAL adj neighbouring
VICING > VICE
VICINITY n surrounding area
VICIOSITY same as > VITIOSITY
VICIOUS adj cruel and violent
VICIOUSLY > VICIOUS
VICOMTE n French nobleman
VICOMTES > VICOMTE
VICTIM n person or thing harmed or killed
VICTIMISE same as > VICTIMIZE
VICTIMIZE vb punish unfairly
VICTIMS > VICTIM
VICTOR n person who has defeated an opponent, esp in war or in sport
VICTORESS same as > VICTRESS
VICTORIA n large sweet plum, red and yellow in colour
VICTORIAS > VICTORIA
VICTORIES > VICTORY
VICTORINE n woman's article of clothing
VICTORS > VICTOR
VICTORY n winning of a battle or contest
VICTRESS n female victor
VICTRIX same as > VICTRESS
VICTRIXES > VICTRIX
VICTROLA n gramophone
VICTROLAS > VICTROLA
VICTUAL vb supply with or obtain victuals
VICTUALED > VICTUAL
VICTUALER > VICTUAL
VICTUALS pl n food and drink
VICUGNA same as > VICUNA
VICUGNAS > VICUGNA
VICUNA n S American animal like the llama
VICUNAS > VICUNA
VID same as > VIDEO
VIDALIA n type of sweet onion
VIDALIAS > VIDALIA
VIDAME n French nobleman
VIDAMES > VIDAME
VIDE interj look
VIDELICET adv namely: used to specify items
VIDENDA > VIDENDUM
VIDENDUM n that which is to be seen
VIDEO vb record (a TV programme or event) on video ▷ adj relating to or used in producing television images ▷ n recording and showing of films and events
VIDEOCAM n camera for recording video footage

VIDEOCAMS > VIDEOCAM
VIDEODISC variant of > VIDEODISK
VIDEODISK n (formerly) disk on which information is stored in digital form
VIDEOED > VIDEO
VIDEOFIT n computer-generated picture of a person sought by the police
VIDEOFITS > VIDEOFIT
VIDEOGRAM n audiovisual recording
VIDEOING > VIDEO
VIDEOLAND n world of television and televised images
VIDEOS > VIDEO
VIDEOTAPE vb (formerly) record (a TV programme) on video tape
VIDEOTEX n information system that displays data from a distant computer on a screen
VIDEOTEXT n means of representing on a TV screen information that is held in a computer
VIDETTE same as > VEDETTE
VIDETTES > VIDETTE
VIDICON n small television camera tube used in closed-circuit television
VIDICONS > VIDICON
VIDIMUS n inspection
VIDIMUSES > VIDIMUS
VIDIOT n person who watches a lot of low-quality television
VIDIOTS > VIDIOT
VIDS > VID
VIDSCREEN n video screen
VIDUAGE n widows collectively
VIDUAGES > VIDUAGE
VIDUAL adj widowed
VIDUITIES > VIDUITY
VIDUITY n widowhood
VIDUOUS adj empty
VIE vb compete (with someone)
VIED > VIE
VIELLE n stringed musical instrument
VIELLES > VIELLE
VIENNA n as in vienna loaf, vienna steak associated with Vienna
VIER > VIE
VIERS > VIE
VIES > VIE
VIEW n opinion or belief ▷ vb think of (something) in a particular way
VIEWABLE > VIEW
VIEWBOOK n promotional booklet for a college or university
VIEWBOOKS > VIEWBOOK
VIEWDATA n interactive form of videotext
VIEWDATAS > VIEWDATA
VIEWED > VIEW
VIEWER n person who watches television
VIEWERS > VIEWER

VIEWIER > VIEWY
VIEWIEST > VIEWY
VIEWINESS > VIEWY
VIEWING n act of watching television
VIEWINGS > VIEWING
VIEWLESS adj (of windows, etc) not affording a view
VIEWLY adj pleasant on the eye
VIEWPHONE n videophone
VIEWPOINT n person's attitude towards something
VIEWPORT n viewable area on a computer display
VIEWPORTS > VIEWPORT
VIEWS > VIEW
VIEWSHED n natural environment visible from a specific point
VIEWSHEDS > VIEWSHED
VIEWY adj having fanciful opinions or ideas
VIFDA same as > VIVDA
VIFDAS > VIFDA
VIFF vb (of an aircraft) change direction abruptly
VIFFED > VIFF
VIFFING > VIFF
VIFFS > VIFF
VIG n interest on a loan that is paid to a moneylender
VIGA n rafter
VIGAS > VIGA
VIGESIMAL adj relating to or based on the number 20
VIGIA n navigational hazard whose existence has not been confirmed
VIGIAS > VIGIA
VIGIL n night-time period of staying awake to look after a sick person, pray, etc
VIGILANCE n careful attention
VIGILANT adj watchful in case of danger
VIGILANTE n person who takes it upon himself or herself to enforce the law
VIGILS > VIGIL
VIGNERON n person who grows grapes for winemaking
VIGNERONS > VIGNERON
VIGNETTE n small illustration placed at the beginning or end of a chapter or book ▷ vb portray in a vignette
VIGNETTED > VIGNETTE
VIGNETTER n device used in printing vignettes
VIGNETTES > VIGNETTE
VIGOR same as > VIGOUR
VIGORISH n type of commission
VIGORO n women's game similar to cricket
VIGOROS > VIGORO
VIGOROSO adv in music, emphatically
VIGOROUS adj having physical or mental energy
VIGORS > VIGOR
VIGOUR n physical or mental energy

VIGOURS > VIGOUR
VIGS > VIG
VIHARA n type of Buddhist temple
VIHARAS > VIHARA
VIHUELA n obsolete plucked stringed instrument of Spain
VIHUELAS > VIHUELA
VIKING n Dane, Norwegian, or Swede who raided by sea between the 8th and 11th centuries
VIKINGISM > VIKING
VIKINGS > VIKING
VILAYET n major administrative division of Turkey
VILAYETS > VILAYET
VILD same as > VILE
VILDE same as > VILE
VILDLY > VILD
VILDNESS > VILD
VILE adj very wicked
VILELY > VILE
VILENESS > VILE
VILER > VILE
VILEST > VILE
VILIACO n coward
VILIACOES > VILIACO
VILIACOS > VILIACO
VILIAGO same as > VILIACO
VILIAGOES > VILIAGO
VILIAGOS > VILIAGO
VILIFIED > VILIFY
VILIFIER > VILIFY
VILIFIERS > VILIFY
VILIFIES > VILIFY
VILIFY vb attack the character of
VILIFYING > VILIFY
VILIPEND vb treat or regard with contempt
VILIPENDS > VILIPEND
VILL n township
VILLA n large house with gardens
VILLADOM > VILLA
VILLADOMS > VILLA
VILLAE > VILLA
VILLAGE n small group of houses in a country area
VILLAGER n inhabitant of a village ▷ adj backward, unsophisticated, or illiterate
VILLAGERS > VILLAGER
VILLAGERY n villages
VILLAGES > VILLAGE
VILLAGEY adj of or like a village
VILLAGIER > VILLAGEY
VILLAGIO same as > VILIACO
VILLAGIOS > VILLAGIO
VILLAGREE variant of > VILLAGERY
VILLAIN n wicked person
VILLAINS > VILLAIN
VILLAINY n evil or vicious behaviour
VILLAN same as > VILLEIN
VILLANAGE > VILLAN
VILLANIES > VILLANY
VILLANOUS > VILLAIN
VILLANS > VILLAN
VILLANY same as > VILLAINY

VILLAR > VILL

VILLAS > VILLA

VILLATIC adj of or relating to a villa, village, or farm

VILLEIN n peasant bound in service to their lord

VILLEINS > VILLEIN

VILLI > VILLUS

VILLIACO n coward

VILLIACOS > VILLIACO

VILLIAGO same as > VILIACO

VILLIAGOS > VILLIAGO

VILLIFORM adj having the form of a villus or a series of villi

VILLOSE same as > VILLOUS

VILLOSITY n state of being villous

VILLOUS adj (of plant parts) covered with long hairs

VILLOUSLY > VILLOUS

VILLS > VILL

VILLUS n one of the finger-like projections in the small intestine of many vertebrates

VIM n force, energy

VIMANA n Indian mythological chariot of the gods

VIMANAS > VIMANA

VIMEN n long flexible shoot that occurs in certain plants

VIMINA > VIMEN

VIMINAL > VIMEN

VIMINEOUS adj having, producing, or resembling long flexible shoots

VIMS > VIM

VIN n French wine

VINA n stringed musical instrument related to the sitar

VINACEOUS adj of, relating to, or containing wine

VINAL n type of manmade fibre

VINALS > VINAL

VINAS > VINA

VINASSE n residue left in a still after distilling spirits, esp brandy

VINASSES > VINASSE

VINCA n type of trailing plant with blue flowers

VINCAS > VINCA

VINCIBLE adj capable of being defeated or overcome

VINCIBLY > VINCIBLE

VINCULA > VINCULUM

VINCULAR adj of or like a vinculum

VINCULUM n horizontal line drawn above a group of mathematical terms

VINCULUMS > VINCULUM

VINDALOO n type of very hot Indian curry

VINDALOOS > VINDALOO

VINDEMIAL adj relating to a grape harvest

VINDICATE vb clear (someone) of guilt

VINE n climbing plant, esp one producing grapes ⊳ vb form like a vine

VINEAL adj relating to wines

VINED > VINE

VINEGAR n acid liquid made from wine, beer, or cider ⊳ vb apply vinegar to

VINEGARED > VINEGAR

VINEGARS > VINEGAR

VINEGARY adj containing vinegar

VINELESS > VINE

VINELIKE > VINE

VINER n vinedresser

VINERIES > VINERY

VINERS > VINER

VINERY n hothouse for growing grapes

VINES > VINE

VINEW vb become mouldy

VINEWED > VINEW

VINEWING > VINEW

VINEWS > VINEW

VINEYARD n plantation of grape vines

VINEYARDS > VINEYARD

VINIC adj of, relating to, or contained in wine

VINIER > VINE

VINIEST > VINE

VINIFERA n species of vine

VINIFERAS > VINIFERA

VINIFIED > VINIFY

VINIFIES > VINIFY

VINIFY vb convert into wine

VINIFYING > VINIFY

VINING > VINE

VINO n wine

VINOLENT adj drunken

VINOLOGY n scientific study of vines

VINOS > VINO

VINOSITY n distinctive and essential quality and flavour of wine

VINOUS adj of or characteristic of wine

VINOUSLY > VINOUS

VINS > VIN

VINT vb sell (wine)

VINTAGE n wine from a particular harvest of grapes ⊳ adj best and most typical ⊳ vb gather (grapes) or make (wine)

VINTAGED > VINTAGE

VINTAGER n grape harvester

VINTAGERS > VINTAGER

VINTAGES > VINTAGE

VINTAGING > VINTAGE

VINTED > VINT

VINTING > VINT

VINTNER n dealer in wine

VINTNERS > VINTNER

VINTRIES > VINTRY

VINTRY n place where wine is sold

VINTS > VINT

VINY > VINE

VINYL n type of plastic, used in mock leather and records ⊳ adj of or containing a particular group of atoms

VINYLIC > VINYL

VINYLS > VINYL

VIOL n early stringed instrument preceding the violin

VIOLA n stringed instrument lower in pitch than a violin

VIOLABLE > VIOLATE

VIOLABLY > VIOLATE

VIOLAS > VIOLA

VIOLATE vb break (a law or agreement) ⊳ adj violated or dishonoured

VIOLATED > VIOLATE

VIOLATER > VIOLATE

VIOLATERS > VIOLATE

VIOLATES > VIOLATE

VIOLATING > VIOLATE

VIOLATION > VIOLATE

VIOLATIVE > VIOLATE

VIOLATOR > VIOLATE

VIOLATORS > VIOLATE

VIOLD archaic or poetic past form of > VIAL

VIOLENCE n use of physical force, usu intended to cause injury or destruction

VIOLENCES > VIOLENCE

VIOLENT adj using physical force with the intention of causing injury ⊳ vb coerce

VIOLENTED > VIOLENT

VIOLENTLY > VIOLENT

VIOLENTS > VIOLENT

VIOLER n person who plays the viol

VIOLERS > VIOLER

VIOLET n plant with bluish-purple flowers ⊳ adj bluish-purple

VIOLETS > VIOLET

VIOLIN n small four-stringed musical instrument played with a bow

VIOLINIST n person who plays the violin

VIOLINS > VIOLIN

VIOLIST n person who plays the viola

VIOLISTS > VIOLIST

VIOLONE n double-bass member of the viol family

VIOLONES > VIOLONE

VIOLS > VIOL

VIOMYCIN n type of antibiotic

VIOMYCINS > VIOMYCIN

VIOSTEROL n type of vitamin

VIPASSANA n type of meditative practice in Buddhism

VIPER n poisonous snake

VIPERFISH n predatory deep-sea fish

VIPERINE same as > VIPEROUS

VIPERISH same as > VIPEROUS

VIPERLIKE adj like a viper

VIPEROUS adj of, relating to, or resembling a viper

VIPERS > VIPER

VIRAEMIA n condition in which virus particles circulate and reproduce in the bloodstream

VIRAEMIAS > VIRAEMIA

VIRAEMIC > VIRAEMIA

VIRAGO n aggressive woman

VIRAGOES > VIRAGO

VIRAGOISH > VIRAGO

VIRAGOS > VIRAGO

VIRAL adj of or caused by a virus ⊳ n video, image, etc that spreads quickly on the internet

VIRALITY n the state of being viral

VIRALLY > VIRAL

VIRALS > VIRAL

VIRANDA same as > VERANDA

VIRANDAS > VIRANDA

VIRANDO same as > VERANDA

VIRANDOS > VIRANDO

VIRE vb turn

VIRED > VIRE

VIRELAI same as > VIRELAY

VIRELAIS > VIRELAI

VIRELAY n old French verse form

VIRELAYS > VIRELAY

VIREMENT n administrative transfer of funds from one part of a budget to another

VIREMENTS > VIREMENT

VIREMIA same as > VIRAEMIA

VIREMIAS > VIREMIA

VIREMIC > VIREMIA

VIRENT adj green

VIREO n American songbird

VIREONINE > VIREO

VIREOS > VIREO

VIRES > VIRE

VIRESCENT adj greenish or becoming green

VIRETOT n as in on the viretot in a rush

VIRETOTS > VIRETOT

VIRGA n wisps of rain or snow that evaporate before reaching the earth

VIRGAE > VIRGA

VIRGAS > VIRGA

VIRGATE adj long, straight, and thin ⊳ n obsolete measure of land area

VIRGATES > VIRGATE

VIRGE n rod

VIRGER n rod-bearer

VIRGERS > VIRGER

VIRGES > VIRGE

VIRGIN n person, esp a woman, who has not had sexual intercourse ⊳ adj not having had sexual intercourse ⊳ vb behave like a virgin

VIRGINAL adj like a virgin ⊳ n early keyboard instrument like a small harpsichord

VIRGINALS > VIRGINAL

VIRGINED > VIRGIN

VIRGINIA n type of flue-cured tobacco grown originally in Virginia

VIRGINIAS > VIRGINIA

VIRGINING > VIRGIN

VIRGINITY n condition or fact of being a virgin

V

VIRGINIUM former name for > FRANCIUM
VIRGINLY > VIRGIN
VIRGINS > VIRGIN
VIRGULATE adj rod-shaped or rodlike
VIRGULE another name for > SLASH
VIRGULES > VIRGULE
VIRICIDAL > VIRICIDE
VIRICIDE n substance that destroys viruses
VIRICIDES > VIRICIDE
VIRID adj verdant
VIRIDIAN n green pigment consisting of a hydrated form of chromic oxide
VIRIDIANS > VIRIDIAN
VIRIDITE n greenish mineral
VIRIDITES > VIRIDITE
VIRIDITY n quality or state of being green
VIRILE adj having traditional male characteristics
VIRILELY > VIRILE
VIRILISE same as > VIRILIZE
VIRILISED > VIRILISE
VIRILISES > VIRILISE
VIRILISM n development in a woman of male secondary sex characteristics
VIRILISMS > VIRILISM
VIRILITY > VIRILE
VIRILIZE vb cause male characteristics to appear in female
VIRILIZED > VIRILIZE
VIRILIZES > VIRILIZE
VIRILOCAL adj living with or near the husband's family
VIRING > VIRE
VIRINO n entity postulated to be the causative agent of BSE
VIRINOS > VIRINO
VIRION n virus in infective form, consisting of an RNA particle within a protein covering
VIRIONS > VIRION
VIRL same as > FERRULE
VIRLS > VIRL
VIROGENE n type of viral gene
VIROGENES > VIROGENE
VIROID n any of various infective RNA particles
VIROIDS > VIROID
VIROLOGIC > VIROLOGY
VIROLOGY n study of viruses
VIROSE adj poisonous
VIROSES > VIROSIS
VIROSIS n viral disease
VIROUS same as > VIROSE
VIRTU n taste or love for curios or works of fine art
VIRTUAL adj having the effect but not the form of
VIRTUALLY adv practically, almost
VIRTUE n moral goodness
VIRTUES > VIRTUE
VIRTUOSA n female virtuoso

VIRTUOSAS > VIRTUOSA
VIRTUOSE > VIRTUOSA
VIRTUOSI > VIRTUOSO
VIRTUOSIC > VIRTUOSO
VIRTUOSO n person with impressive esp musical skill ⊳ adj showing exceptional skill or brilliance
VIRTUOSOS > VIRTUOSO
VIRTUOUS adj morally good
VIRTUS > VIRTU
VIRUCIDAL > VIRUCIDE
VIRUCIDE same as > VIRICIDE
VIRUCIDES > VIRUCIDE
VIRULENCE n quality of being virulent
VIRULENCY same as > VIRULENCE
VIRULENT adj extremely bitter or hostile
VIRUS n microorganism that causes disease in humans, animals, and plants
VIRUSES > VIRUS
VIRUSLIKE > VIRUS
VIRUSOID n small plant virus
VIRUSOIDS > VIRUSOID
VIS n power, force, or strength
VISA n permission to enter a country, shown by a stamp on the passport ⊳ vb enter a visa into (a passport)
VISAED > VISA
VISAGE n face
VISAGED > VISAGE
VISAGES > VISAGE
VISAGIST same as > VISAGISTE
VISAGISTE n person who designs and applies face make-up
VISAGISTS > VISAGIST
VISAING > VISA
VISARD same as > VIZARD
VISARDS > VISARD
VISAS > VISA
VISCACHA n South American rodent
VISCACHAS > VISCACHA
VISCARIA n type of perennial plant
VISCARIAS > VISCARIA
VISCERA pl n large abdominal organs
VISCERAL adj instinctive
VISCERATE vb disembowel
VISCID adj sticky
VISCIDITY > VISCID
VISCIDLY > VISCID
VISCIN n sticky substance found on plants
VISCINS > VISCIN
VISCOID adj (of a fluid) somewhat viscous
VISCOIDAL same as > VISCOID
VISCOSE same as > VISCOUS
VISCOSES > VISCOSE
VISCOSITY n state of being viscous
VISCOUNT n British nobleman ranking between an earl and a baron

VISCOUNTS > VISCOUNT
VISCOUNTY > VISCOUNT
VISCOUS adj thick and sticky
VISCOUSLY > VISCOUS
VISCUM n shrub genus
VISCUMS > VISCUM
VISCUS n internal organ
VISE vb advise or award a visa to ⊳ n (in US English) vice
VISED > VISE
VISEED > VISE
VISEING > VISE
VISELIKE > VICE
VISES > VISE
VISHING n telephone scam used to gain access to credit card numbers or bank details
VISHINGS > VISHING
VISIBLE adj able to be seen ⊳ n visible item of trade
VISIBLES > VISIBLE
VISIBLY > VISIBLE
VISIE same as > VIZY
VISIED > VISIE
VISIEING > VISIE
VISIER > VISIE
VISIERS > VISIE
VISIES > VISIE
VISILE n person best stimulated by vision
VISILES > VISILE
VISING > VISE
VISION n ability to see ⊳ vb see or show in or as if in a vision
VISIONAL adj of, relating to, or seen in a vision, apparition, etc
VISIONARY adj showing foresight ⊳ n visionary person
VISIONED > VISION
VISIONER n visionary
VISIONERS > VISIONER
VISIONING > VISION
VISIONIST n type of visionary
VISIONS > VISION
VISIT vb go or come to see ⊳ n instance of visiting
VISITABLE > VISIT
VISITANT n ghost or apparition ⊳ adj paying a visit
VISITANTS > VISITANT
VISITATOR n official visitor
VISITE n type of cape
VISITED > VISIT
VISITEE n person who is visited
VISITEES > VISITEE
VISITER variant of > VISITOR
VISITERS > VISITER
VISITES > VISITE
VISITING > VISIT
VISITINGS > VISIT
VISITOR n person who visits a person or place
VISITORS > VISITOR
VISITRESS n female visitor
VISITS > VISIT
VISIVE adj visual
VISNE n neighbourhood
VISNES > VISNE

VISNOMIE same as > VISNOMY
VISNOMIES > VISNOMY
VISNOMY n method of judging character from facial features
VISON n type of mink
VISONS > VISON
VISOR n transparent part of a helmet that pulls down over the face ⊳ vb cover, provide, or protect with a visor
VISORED > VISOR
VISORING > VISOR
VISORLESS > VISOR
VISORS > VISOR
VISTA n (beautiful) extensive view ⊳ vb make into vistas
VISTAED > VISTA
VISTAING > VISTA
VISTAL > VISTA
VISTALESS > VISTA
VISTAS > VISTA
VISTO same as > VISTA
VISTOS > VISTO
VISUAL adj done by or used in seeing ⊳ n sketch to show the proposed layout of an advertisement
VISUALISE same as > VISUALIZE
VISUALIST n visualiser
VISUALITY > VISUAL
VISUALIZE vb form a mental image of
VISUALLY > VISUAL
VISUALS > VISUAL
VITA n curriculum vitae
VITACEOUS adj of a family of flowering plants that includes the grapevine
VITAE > VITA
VITAL adj essential or highly important ⊳ n bodily organs that are necessary to maintain life
VITALISE same as > VITALIZE
VITALISED > VITALISE
VITALISER > VITALISE
VITALISES > VITALISE
VITALISM n philosophical doctrine that the phenomena of life cannot be explained in purely mechanical terms
VITALISMS > VITALISM
VITALIST > VITALISM
VITALISTS > VITALISM
VITALITY n physical or mental energy
VITALIZE vb fill with life or vitality
VITALIZED > VITALIZE
VITALIZER > VITALIZE
VITALIZES > VITALIZE
VITALLY > VITAL
VITALNESS > VITAL
VITALS > VITAL
VITAMER n type of chemical
VITAMERS > VITAMER
VITAMIN n one of a group of substances that are essential in the diet

VITAMINE same as > VITAMIN
VITAMINES > VITAMINE
VITAMINIC > VITAMIN
VITAMINS > VITAMIN
VITAS > VITA
VITASCOPE n early type of film projector
VITATIVE adj fond of life
VITE adv musical direction
VITELLARY n location within an egg where the yolk is formed
VITELLI > VITELLUS
VITELLIN n phosphoprotein that is the major protein in egg yolk
VITELLINE adj of or relating to the yolk of an egg
VITELLINS > VITELLIN
VITELLUS n yolk of an egg
VITESSE n speed
VITESSES > VITESSE
VITEX n type of herb
VITEXES > VITEX
VITIABLE > VITIATE
VITIATE vb spoil the effectiveness of
VITIATED > VITIATE
VITIATES > VITIATE
VITIATING > VITIATE
VITIATION > VITIATE
VITIATOR > VITIATE
VITIATORS > VITIATE
VITICETA > VITICETUM
VITICETUM n place where vines are cultivated
VITICIDE n vine killer
VITICIDES > VITICIDE
VITILIGO n area of skin that is white from albinism or loss of melanin pigmentation
VITILIGOS > VITILIGO **VITIOSITY** n viciousness
VITIOUS adj mistaken
VITRAGE n light fabric
VITRAGES > VITRAGE
VITRAIL n stained glass
VITRAIN n type of coal
VITRAINS > VITRAIN
VITRAUX > VITRAIL
VITREOUS adj like or made from glass
VITREUM n vitreous body
VITREUMS > VITREUM
VITRIC adj of, relating to, resembling, or having the nature of glass
VITRICS n glassware
VITRIFIED > VITRIFY
VITRIFIES > VITRIFY
VITRIFORM adj having the form or appearance of glass
VITRIFY vb change or be changed into glass or a glassy substance
VITRINE n glass display case or cabinet for works of art, curios, etc
VITRINES > VITRINE
VITRIOL n language expressing bitterness and hatred ▷ vb attack or injure with or as if with vitriol
VITRIOLED > VITRIOL

VITRIOLIC adj (of language) severely bitter or harsh
VITRIOLS > VITRIOL
VITRO n as in in vitro glass
VITTA n tubelike cavity containing oil that occurs in the fruits of certain plants
VITTAE > VITTA
VITTATE > VITTA
VITTLE obsolete or dialect spelling of > VICTUAL
VITTLED > VITTLE
VITTLES obsolete or dialect spelling of > VICTUALS
VITTLING > VITTLE
VITULAR same as > VITULINE
VITULINE adj of or resembling a calf or veal
VIVA interj long live (a person or thing) ▷ n examination in the form of an interview ▷ vb examine (a candidate) in a spoken interview
VIVACE adv in a lively manner ▷ n piece of music to be performed in this way
VIVACES > VIVACE
VIVACIOUS adj full of energy and enthusiasm
VIVACITY n quality of being vivacious
VIVAED > VIVA
VIVAING > VIVA
VIVAMENTE adv in a lively manner
VIVANDIER n sutler
VIVARIA > VIVARIUM
VIVARIES > VIVARY
VIVARIUM n place where animals are kept in natural conditions
VIVARIUMS > VIVARIUM
VIVARY same as > VIVARIUM
VIVAS > VIVA
VIVAT interj long live ▷ n expression of acclamation
VIVATS > VIVAT
VIVDA n method of drying meat
VIVDAS > VIVDA
VIVE interj long live
VIVELY adv in a lively manner
VIVENCIES > VIVENCY
VIVENCY n physical or mental energy
VIVER n fish pond
VIVERRA n civet genus
VIVERRAS > VIVERRA
VIVERRID > VIVERRINE
VIVERRIDS > VIVERRINE
VIVERRINE n type of mammal of Eurasia and Africa ▷ adj of this family of mammals
VIVERS > VIVER
VIVES n disease found in horses
VIVIANITE n type of mineral
VIVID adj very bright
VIVIDER > VIVID
VIVIDEST > VIVID
VIVIDITY > VIVID

VIVIDLY > VIVID
VIVIDNESS > VIVID
VIVIFIC adj giving life
VIVIFIED > VIVIFY
VIVIFIER > VIVIFY
VIVIFIERS > VIVIFY
VIVIFIES > VIVIFY
VIVIFY vb animate, inspire
VIVIFYING > VIVIFY
VIVIPARA n animals that produce offspring that develop as embryos within the female parent
VIVIPARY n act of giving birth producing offspring that have developed as embryos
VIVISECT vb subject (an animal) to vivisection
VIVISECTS > VIVISECT
VIVO adv with life and vigour
VIVRES n provisions
VIXEN n female fox
VIXENISH > VIXEN
VIXENLY > VIXEN
VIXENS > VIXEN
VIZAMENT n consultation
VIZAMENTS > VIZAMENT
VIZARD n means of disguise ▷ vb conceal by means of a disguise
VIZARDED > VIZARD
VIZARDING > VIZARD
VIZARDS > VIZARD
VIZCACHA same as > VISCACHA
VIZCACHAS > VIZCACHA
VIZIED > VIZY
VIZIER n high official in certain Muslim countries
VIZIERATE n position, rank, or authority of a vizier
VIZIERIAL > VIZIER
VIZIERS > VIZIER
VIZIES > VIZY
VIZIR same as > VIZIER
VIZIRATE > VIZIR
VIZIRATES > VIZIR
VIZIRIAL > VIZIR
VIZIRS > VIZIR
VIZIRSHIP > VIZIR
VIZOR same as > VISOR
VIZORED > VIZOR
VIZORING > VIZOR
VIZORLESS > VIZOR
VIZORS > VIZOR
VIZSLA n breed of Hungarian hunting dog
VIZSLAS > VIZSLA
VIZY vb look
VIZYING > VIZY
VIZZIE same as > VIZY
VIZZIED > VIZZIE
VIZZIEING > VIZZIE
VIZZIES > VIZZIE
VLEI n area of low marshy ground
VLEIS > VLEI
VLIES > VLY
VLOG n video weblog ▷ vb make and upload a vlog
VLOGGED > VLOG
VLOGGER n person who keeps a video blog
VLOGGERS > VLOGGER

VLOGGING n action of keeping a video blog
VLOGGINGS > VLOGGING
VLOGS > VLOG
VLY same as > VLEI
VOAR n spring
VOARS > VOAR
VOCAB n vocabulary
VOCABLE n word regarded simply as a sequence of letters or spoken sounds ▷ adj capable of being uttered
VOCABLES > VOCABLE
VOCABLY > VOCABLE
VOCABS > VOCAB
VOCABULAR > VOCABLE
VOCAL adj relating to the voice ▷ n piece of jazz or pop music that is sung
VOCALESE n style of jazz singing
VOCALESES > VOCALESE
VOCALIC adj of, relating to, or containing a vowel or vowels
VOCALICS n non-verbal aspects of voice
VOCALION n type of musical instrument
VOCALIONS > VOCALION
VOCALISE same as > VOCALIZE
VOCALISED > VOCALISE
VOCALISER > VOCALISE
VOCALISES > VOCALISE
VOCALISM n exercise of the voice, as in singing or speaking
VOCALISMS > VOCALISM
VOCALIST n singer
VOCALISTS > VOCALIST
VOCALITY > VOCAL
VOCALIZE vb express with the voice
VOCALIZED > VOCALIZE
VOCALIZER > VOCALIZE
VOCALIZES > VOCALIZE
VOCALLY > VOCAL
VOCALNESS > VOCAL
VOCALS > VOCAL
VOCATION n profession or trade
VOCATIONS > VOCATION
VOCATIVE n (in some languages) case of nouns used when addressing a person ▷ adj relating to, used in, or characterized by calling
VOCATIVES > VOCATIVE
VOCES > VOX
VOCODER n type of synthesizer that uses the human voice as an oscillator
VOCODERED adj synthesized by a vocoder
VOCODERS > VOCODER
VOCULAR > VOCULE
VOCULE n faint noise made when articulating certain sounds
VOCULES > VOCULE
VODCAST vb podcast with video
VODCASTED > VODCAST
VODCASTER > VODCAST

VODCASTS > VODCAST

VODDIES > VODDY

VODDY n vodka

VODKA n (Russian) spirit distilled from potatoes or grain

VODKAS > VODKA

VODOU variant of > VOODOO

VODOUN same as > VODUN

VODOUNS > VODOUN

VODOUS > VODOU

VODUN n voodoo

VODUNS > VODUN

VOE n (in Orkney and Shetland) a small bay or narrow creek

VOEMA n vigour or energy

VOEMAS > VOEMA

VOERTSAK variant of > VOETSEK

VOERTSEK variant of > VOETSEK

VOES > VOE

VOETSAK same as > VOETSEK

VOETSEK interj S African offensive expression of rejection

VOG n air pollution caused by volcanic dust

VOGIE adj conceited

VOGIER > VOGIE

VOGIEST > VOGIE

VOGS > VOG

VOGUE n popular style ▷ adj popular or fashionable ▷ vb bring into vogue

VOGUED > VOGUE

VOGUEING n dance style of the late 1980s

VOGUEINGS > VOGUEING

VOGUER > VOGUE

VOGUERS > VOGUE

VOGUES > VOGUE

VOGUEY > VOGUE

VOGUIER > VOGUE

VOGUIEST > VOGUE

VOGUING same as > VOGUEING

VOGUINGS > VOGUING

VOGUISH > VOGUE

VOGUISHLY > VOGUE

VOICE n (quality of) sound made when speaking or singing ▷ vb express verbally

VOICED adj articulated with accompanying vibration of the vocal cords

VOICEFUL > VOICE

VOICELESS adj without a voice

VOICEMAIL n facility of leaving recorded message by telephone

VOICEOVER n spoken commentary by unseen narrator on film

VOICER > VOICE

VOICERS > VOICE

VOICES > VOICE

VOICING > VOICE

VOICINGS > VOICE

VOID adj not legally binding ▷ n feeling of deprivation ▷ vb make invalid

VOIDABLE adj capable of being voided

VOIDANCE n annulment, as of a contract

VOIDANCES > VOIDANCE

VOIDED adj (of a design) with a hole in the centre of the same shape as the design

VOIDEE n light meal eaten before bed

VOIDEES > VOIDEE

VOIDER > VOID

VOIDERS > VOID

VOIDING > VOID

VOIDINGS > VOID

VOIDNESS > VOID

VOIDS > VOID

VOILA interj word used to express satisfaction

VOILE n light semitransparent fabric

VOILES > VOILE

VOIP n voice over internet protocol

VOIPS > VOIP

VOISINAGE n district or neighbourhood

VOITURE n type of vehicle

VOITURES > VOITURE

VOITURIER n driver of a voiture

VOIVODE n type of military leader

VOIVODES > VOIVODE

VOL n heraldic wings

VOLA n palm of hand or sole of foot

VOLABLE adj quick-witted

VOLAE > VOLA

VOLAGE adj changeable

VOLANT adj in a flying position

VOLANTE n Spanish horse carriage

VOLANTES > VOLANTE

VOLAR adj of or relating to the palm of the hand or the sole of the foot

VOLARIES > VOLARY

VOLARY n large bird enclosure

VOLATIC adj flying ▷ n creature with wings

VOLATICS > VOLATIC

VOLATILE adj liable to sudden change, esp in behaviour ▷ n volatile substance

VOLATILES > VOLATILE

VOLCANIAN same as > VOLCANIC

VOLCANIC adj of or relating to volcanoes

VOLCANICS n types of rock

VOLCANISE same as > VOLCANIZE

VOLCANISM n processes that result in the formation of volcanoes

VOLCANIST n person who studies volcanoes

VOLCANIZE vb subject to the effects of or change by volcanic heat

VOLCANO n mountain with a vent through which lava is ejected

VOLCANOES > VOLCANO

VOLCANOS > VOLCANO

VOLE n small rodent ▷ vb win by taking all the tricks in a deal

VOLED > VOLE

VOLELIKE adj like a vole

VOLENS adj as in nolens volens whether willing or unwilling

VOLERIES > VOLERY

VOLERY same as > VOLARY

VOLES > VOLE

VOLET n type of veil

VOLETS > VOLET

VOLING > VOLE

VOLITANT adj flying or moving about rapidly

VOLITATE vb flutter

VOLITATED > VOLITATE

VOLITATES > VOLITATE

VOLITIENT > VOLITION

VOLITION n ability to decide things for oneself

VOLITIONS > VOLITION

VOLITIVE adj of, relating to, or emanating from the will ▷ n (in some languages) a verb form or mood used to express a wish or desire

VOLITIVES > VOLITIVE

VOLK n people or nation, esp the nation of Afrikaners

VOLKS > VOLK

VOLKSLIED n German folk song

VOLKSRAAD n Boer assembly in South Africa in the 19th century

VOLLEY n simultaneous discharge of ammunition ▷ vb discharge (ammunition) in a volley

VOLLEYED > VOLLEY

VOLLEYER > VOLLEY

VOLLEYERS > VOLLEY

VOLLEYING > VOLLEY

VOLLEYS > VOLLEY

VOLOST n (in the former Soviet Union) a rural soviet

VOLOSTS > VOLOST

VOLPINO n Italian breed of dog

VOLPINOS > VOLPINO

VOLPLANE vb glide in an aeroplane

VOLPLANED > VOLPLANE

VOLPLANES > VOLPLANE

VOLS > VOL

VOLT n unit of electric potential ▷ vb (in fencing) make a quick movement to avoid a thrust

VOLTA n quick-moving Italian dance

VOLTAGE n electric potential difference expressed in volts

VOLTAGES > VOLTAGE

VOLTAIC adj producing an electric current

VOLTAISM another name for > GALVANISM

VOLTAISMS > VOLTAISM

VOLTE same as > VOLT

VOLTED > VOLT

VOLTES > VOLTE

VOLTI n musical direction meaning turn the page

VOLTIGEUR n French infantry member

VOLTING > VOLT

VOLTINISM n number of annual broods of an animal

VOLTIS > VOLTI

VOLTMETER n instrument for measuring voltage

VOLTS > VOLT

VOLUBIL same as > VOLUBLE

VOLUBLE adj talking easily and at length

VOLUBLY > VOLUBLE

VOLUCRINE adj relating to birds

VOLUME n size of the space occupied by something ▷ vb billow or surge in volume

VOLUMED > VOLUME

VOLUMES > VOLUME

VOLUMETER n any instrument for measuring the volume of a solid, liquid, or gas

VOLUMETRY n act of measuring by volume

VOLUMINAL > VOLUME

VOLUMING > VOLUME

VOLUMISE same as > VOLUMIZE

VOLUMISED > VOLUMISE

VOLUMISER same as > VOLUMIZER

VOLUMISES > VOLUMISE

VOLUMIST n author

VOLUMISTS > VOLUMIST

VOLUMIZE vb create volume in something

VOLUMIZED > VOLUMIZE

VOLUMIZER n product used to give extra body to hair

VOLUMIZES > VOLUMIZE

VOLUNTARY adj done by choice ▷ n organ solo in a church service

VOLUNTEER n person who offers voluntarily to do something ▷ vb offer one's services

VOLUSPA n Icelandic mythological poem

VOLUSPAS > VOLUSPA

VOLUTE n spiral or twisting turn, form, or object ▷ adj having the form of a volute

VOLUTED > VOLUTE

VOLUTES > VOLUTE

VOLUTIN n granular substance found in cells

VOLUTINS > VOLUTIN

VOLUTION n rolling, revolving, or spiral form or motion

VOLUTIONS > VOLUTION

VOLUTOID > VOLUTE

VOLVA n cup-shaped structure that sheathes the base of the stalk of certain mushrooms

VOLVAE > VOLVA

VOLVAS > VOLVA

VOLVATE > VOLVA

VOLVE vb turn over

VOLVED > VOLVE

VOLVES > VOLVE

VOLVING > VOLVE

VOLVOX n freshwater protozoan

VOLVOXES > VOLVOX
VOLVULI > VOLVULUS
VOLVULUS n abnormal twisting of the intestines causing obstruction
VOM vb vomit
VOMER n thin flat bone separating the nasal passages in mammals
VOMERINE > VOMER
VOMERS > VOMER
VOMICA n pus-containing cavity
VOMICAE > VOMICA
VOMICAS > VOMICA
VOMIT vb eject (the contents of the stomach) through the mouth ▷ n matter vomited
VOMITED > VOMIT
VOMITER > VOMIT
VOMITERS > VOMIT
VOMITIER > VOMITY
VOMITIEST > VOMITY
VOMITING > VOMIT
VOMITINGS > VOMIT
VOMITIVE same as > VOMITORY
VOMITIVES > VOMITIVE
VOMITO n form of yellow fever
VOMITORIA n entrances in an amphitheatre
VOMITORY adj causing vomiting ▷ n vomitory agent
VOMITOS > VOMITO
VOMITOUS adj arousing feelings of disgust
VOMITS > VOMIT
VOMITUS n matter that has been vomited
VOMITUSES > VOMITUS
VOMITY adj resembling or smelling of vomit
VOMMED > VOM
VOMMING > VOM
VOMS > VOM
VONGOLE pl n (in Italian cookery) clams
VOODOO n religion involving ancestor worship and witchcraft ▷ adj of or relating to voodoo ▷ vb affect by or as if by the power of voodoo
VOODOOED > VOODOO
VOODOOING > VOODOO
VOODOOISM same as > VOODOO
VOODOOIST > VOODOO
VOODOOS > VOODOO
VOORKAMER n front room of a house
VOORSKOT n (in South Africa) advance payment made to a farmer for crops
VOORSKOTS > VOORSKOT
VOR vb (in dialect) warn
VORACIOUS adj craving great quantities of food
VORACITY > VORACIOUS
VORAGO n chasm
VORAGOES > VORAGO
VORAGOS > VORAGO
VORANT adj devouring
VORLAGE n skiing position
VORLAGES > VORLAGE

VORPAL adj sharp
VORRED > VOR
VORRING > VOR
VORS > VOR
VORTEX n whirlpool
VORTEXES > VORTEX
VORTICAL > VORTEX
VORTICES > VORTEX
VORTICISM n art movement in 20th-century England
VORTICIST > VORTICISM
VORTICITY n rotational spin in a fluid
VORTICOSE adj rotating quickly
VOSTRO adj as in vostro account bank account held by a foreign bank with a British bank
VOTABLE > VOTE
VOTARESS n female votary
VOTARIES > VOTARY
VOTARIST variant of > VOTARY
VOTARISTS > VOTARIST
VOTARY n person dedicated to religion or to a cause ▷ adj ardently devoted to the services or worship of God
VOTE n choice made by a participant in a shared decision ▷ vb make a choice by a vote
VOTEABLE > VOTE
VOTED > VOTE
VOTEEN n devotee
VOTEENS > VOTEEN
VOTELESS > VOTE
VOTER n person who can or does vote
VOTERS > VOTER
VOTES > VOTE
VOTING > VOTE
VOTINGS > VOTE
VOTIVE adj done or given to fulfil a vow ▷ n votive offering
VOTIVELY > VOTIVE
VOTIVES > VOTIVE
VOTRESS > VOTARESS
VOTRESSES > VOTRESS
VOUCH vb give personal assurance ▷ n act of vouching
VOUCHED > VOUCH
VOUCHEE n person summoned to court to defend a title
VOUCHEES > VOUCHEE
VOUCHER n ticket used instead of money to buy specified goods ▷ vb summon someone to court as a vouchee
VOUCHERED > VOUCHER
VOUCHERS > VOUCHER
VOUCHES > VOUCH
VOUCHING > VOUCH
VOUCHSAFE vb give, entrust
VOUDON variant of > VOODOO
VOUDONS > VOUDON
VOUDOU same as > VOODOO
VOUDOUED > VOUDOU
VOUDOUING > VOUDOU
VOUDOUN variant of > VOODOO

VOUDOUNS > VOUDOUN
VOUDOUS > VOUDOU
VOUGE n form of pike used by foot soldiers in the 14th century and later
VOUGES > VOUGE
VOULGE n type of medieval weapon
VOULGES > VOULGE
VOULU adj deliberate
VOUSSOIR n wedge-shaped stone or brick that is used with others to construct an arch
VOUSSOIRS > VOUSSOIR
VOUTSAFE same as > VOUCHSAFE
VOUTSAFED > VOUTSAFE
VOUTSAFES > VOUTSAFE
VOUVRAY n dry white French wine
VOUVRAYS > VOUVRAY
VOW n solemn and binding promise ▷ vb promise solemnly
VOWED > VOW
VOWEL n speech sound made without obstructing the flow of breath ▷ vb say as a vowel
VOWELED adj having vowels
VOWELISE same as > VOWELIZE
VOWELISED > VOWELISE
VOWELISES > VOWELISE
VOWELIZE vb mark the vowel points in (a Hebrew word or text)
VOWELIZED > VOWELIZE
VOWELIZES > VOWELIZE
VOWELLED > VOWEL
VOWELLESS > VOWEL
VOWELLIER > VOWELLY
VOWELLING > VOWEL
VOWELLY adj marked by vowels
VOWELS > VOWEL
VOWER > VOW
VOWERS > VOW
VOWESS n nun
VOWESSES > VOWESS
VOWING > VOW
VOWLESS > VOW
VOWS > VOW
VOX n voice or sound
VOXEL n term used in computing imaging
VOXELS > VOXEL
VOYAGE n long journey by sea or in space ▷ vb make a voyage
VOYAGED > VOYAGE
VOYAGER > VOYAGE
VOYAGERS > VOYAGE
VOYAGES > VOYAGE
VOYAGEUR n French canoeman who transported furs from trading posts in .N America
VOYAGEURS > VOYAGEUR
VOYAGING n act of voyaging
VOYAGINGS > VOYAGING
VOYEUR n person abnormally interested in other people's distress
VOYEURISM > VOYEUR

VOYEURS > VOYEUR
VOZHD n Russian leader
VOZHDS > VOZHD
VRAIC n type of seaweed
VRAICKER n person who gathers vraic
VRAICKERS > VRAICKER
VRAICKING n act of gathering vraic
VRAICS > VRAIC
VRIL n life force
VRILS > VRIL
VROOM interj exclamation imitative of a car engine revving up ▷ vb move noisily and at high speed
VROOMED > VROOM
VROOMING > VROOM
VROOMS > VROOM
VROT adj South African slang for rotten
VROU n Afrikaner woman, esp a married woman
VROUS > VROU
VROUW n woman
VROUWS > VROUW
VROW same as > VROUW
VROWS > VROW
VRYSTATER n (in S Africa) inhabitant of the Free State, esp one who is White
VUG n small cavity in a rock or vein, usually lined with crystals
VUGG same as > VUG
VUGGIER > VUG
VUGGIEST > VUG
VUGGS > VUGG
VUGGY > VUG
VUGH same as > VUG
VUGHIER > VUGH
VUGHIEST > VUGH
VUGHS > VUGH
VUGHY > VUG
VUGS > VUG
VUGULAR adj relating to vugs
VULCAN n blacksmith
VULCANIAN adj of or relating to a volcanic eruption
VULCANIC same as > VOLCANIC
VULCANISE same as > VULCANIZE
VULCANISM same as > VOLCANISM
VULCANIST same as > VOLCANIST
VULCANITE n vulcanized rubber
VULCANIZE vb strengthen (rubber) by treating it with sulphur
VULCANS > VULCAN
VULGAR adj showing lack of good taste, decency, or refinement ▷ n common and ignorant person
VULGARER > VULGAR
VULGAREST > VULGAR
VULGARIAN n vulgar (rich) person
VULGARISE same as > VULGARIZE
VULGARISM n coarse word or phrase

V

VULGARITY n condition of being vulgar

VULGARIZE vb make vulgar or too common

VULGARLY > VULGAR

VULGARS > VULGAR

VULGATE n commonly recognized text or version ▷ adj generally accepted

VULGATES > VULGATE

VULGO adv generally

VULGUS n the common people

VULGUSES > VULGUS

VULN vb wound

VULNED > VULN

VULNERARY adj of, relating to, or used to heal a wound ▷ n vulnerary drug or agent

VULNERATE vb wound

VULNING > VULN

VULNS > VULN

VULPICIDE n person who kills foxes

VULPINE adj of or like a fox

VULPINISM > VULPINE

VULPINITE n type of granular anhydrite

VULSELLA n forceps

VULSELLAE > VULSELLA

VULSELLUM variant of > VULSELLA

VULTURE n large bird that feeds on the flesh of dead animals

VULTURES > VULTURE

VULTURINE adj of, relating to, or resembling a vulture

VULTURISH > VULTURE

VULTURISM n greed

VULTURN n type of turkey

VULTURNS > VULTURN

VULTUROUS same as > VULTURINE

VULVA n female external genitals

VULVAE > VULVA

VULVAL > VULVA

VULVAR > VULVA

VULVAS > VULVA

VULVATE > VULVA

VULVIFORM > VULVA

VULVITIS n inflammation of the vulva

VUM vb swear

VUMMED > VUM

VUMMING > VUM

VUMS > VUM

VUTTIER > VUTTY

VUTTIEST > VUTTY

VUTTY adj dirty

VUVUZELA n South African instrument blown by football fans

VUVUZELAS > VUVUZELA

VYING > VIE

VYINGLY > VIE

VYINGS > VIE

Ww

WAAC n (formerly) member of the Women's Auxiliary Army Corp

WAACS > WAAC

WAAH interj interjection used to express wailing

WAB n skin web between the digits of certain animals

WABAIN same as > OUABAIN

WABAINS > WABAIN

WABBIT adj weary

WABBLE same as > WOBBLE

WABBLED > WABBLE

WABBLER > WABBLE

WABBLERS > WABBLE

WABBLES > WABBLE

WABBLIER > WABBLE

WABBLIEST > WABBLE

WABBLING > WABBLE

WABBLY > WABBLE

WABOOM another word for > WAGENBOOM

WABOOMS > WABOOM

WABS > WAB

WABSTER Scots form of > WEBSTER

WABSTERS > WABSTER

WACK n friend ▷ adj bad or inferior

WACKE n any of various soft earthy rocks that resemble or are derived from basaltic rocks

WACKED adj exhausted

WACKER same as > WACK

WACKERS > WACKER

WACKES > WACKE

WACKEST > WACK

WACKIER > WACKY

WACKIEST > WACKY

WACKILY > WACKY

WACKINESS > WACKY

WACKO adj mad or eccentric ▷ n mad or eccentric person

WACKOES > WACKO

WACKOS > WACKO

WACKS > WACK

WACKY adj eccentric or funny

WACONDA n supernatural force in Sioux belief

WACONDAS > WACONDA

WAD n black earthy ore of manganese ▷ n small mass of soft material ▷ vb form (something) into a wad

WADABLE > WADE

WADD same as > WAD

WADDED > WAD

WADDER > WAD

WADDERS > WAD

WADDIE same as > WADDY

WADDIED > WADDY

WADDIES > WADDY

WADDING > WAD

WADDINGS > WAD

WADDLE vb walk with short swaying steps ▷ n swaying walk

WADDLED > WADDLE

WADDLER > WADDLE

WADDLERS > WADDLE

WADDLES > WADDLE

WADDLIER > WADDLE

WADDLIEST > WADDLE

WADDLING > WADDLE

WADDLY > WADDLE

WADDS > WADD

WADDY n heavy wooden club used by Australian Aborigines ▷ vb hit with a waddy

WADDYING > WADDY

WADE vb walk with difficulty through water or mud ▷ n act or an instance of wading

WADEABLE > WADE

WADED > WADE

WADER n long-legged water bird

WADERS pl n long waterproof boots which completely cover the legs

WADES > WADE

WADGE n large or roughly cut portion

WADGES > WADGE

WADI n (in N Africa and Arabia) river which is dry except in the wet season

WADIES > WADY

WADING > WADE

WADINGS > WADE

WADIS > WADI

WADMAAL same as > WADMAL

WADMAALS > WADMAAL

WADMAL n coarse thick woollen fabric, formerly woven for outer garments

WADMALS > WADMAL

WADMEL same as > WADMAL

WADMELS > WADMEL

WADMOL same as > WADMAL

WADMOLL same as > WADMAL

WADMOLLS > WADMOLL

WADMOLS > WADMOL

WADS > WAD

WADSET vb pledge or mortgage

WADSETS > WADSET

WADSETT same as > WADSET

WADSETTED > WADSET

WADSETTER > WADSET

WADSETTS > WADSETT

WADT same as > WAD

WADTS > WADT

WADY same as > WADI

WAE old form of > WOE

WAEFUL old form of > WOEFUL

WAENESS n sorrow

WAENESSES > WAENESS

WAES > WAE

WAESOME adj sorrowful

WAESUCK interj alas

WAESUCKS interj alas

WAFER n thin crisp biscuit ▷ vb seal, fasten, or attach with a wafer

WAFERED > WAFER

WAFERIER > WAFERY

WAFERIEST > WAFERY

WAFERING > WAFER

WAFERS > WAFER

WAFERY adj like wafer; thin

WAFF n gust or puff of air ▷ vb flutter or cause to flutter

WAFFED > WAFF

WAFFIE n person regarded as having little worth to society

WAFFIES > WAFFIE

WAFFING > WAFF

WAFFLE vb speak or write in a vague wordy way ▷ n vague wordy talk or writing

WAFFLED > WAFFLE

WAFFLER > WAFFLE

WAFFLERS > WAFFLE

WAFFLES > WAFFLE

WAFFLIER > WAFFLE

WAFFLIEST > WAFFLE

WAFFLING > WAFFLE

WAFFLINGS > WAFFLE

WAFFLY > WAFFLE

WAFFS > WAFF

WAFT vb drift or carry gently through the air ▷ n something wafted

WAFTAGE > WAFT

WAFTAGES > WAFT

WAFTED > WAFT

WAFTER n device that causes a draught

WAFTERS > WAFTER

WAFTING > WAFT

WAFTINGS > WAFT

WAFTS > WAFT

WAFTURE n act of wafting or waving

WAFTURES > WAFTURE

WAG vb move rapidly from side to side ▷ n wagging movement

WAGE n payment for work done, esp when paid weekly ▷ vb engage in (an activity)

WAGED > WAGE

WAGELESS > WAGE

WAGENBOOM n S African tree

WAGER vb bet on the outcome of something ▷ n bet on the outcome of an event or activity

WAGERED > WAGER

WAGERER > WAGER

WAGERERS > WAGER

WAGERING n act of wagering

WAGERINGS > WAGERING

WAGERS > WAGER

WAGES > WAGE

WAGGA n blanket or bed covering made out of sacks stitched together

WAGGAS > WAGGA

WAGGED > WAG

WAGGER > WAG

WAGGERIES > WAGGERY

WAGGERS > WAG

WAGGERY n quality of being humorous

WAGGING > WAG

WAGGISH adj jocular or humorous

WAGGISHLY > WAGGISH

WAGGLE vb move with a rapid shaking or wobbling motion ▷ n rapid shaking or wobbling motion

WAGGLED > WAGGLE

WAGGLER n float only the bottom of which is attached to the fishing line

WAGGLERS > WAGGLER

WAGGLES > WAGGLE

WAGGLIER > WAGGLE

WAGGLIEST > WAGGLE

WAGGLING > WAGGLE

WAGGLY > WAGGLE

WAGGON same as > WAGON

WAGGONED > WAGGON

WAGGONER same as > WAGONER

WAGGONERS > WAGGONER

WAGGONING > WAGGON

WAGGONS > WAGGON

WAGHALTER n person likely to be hanged

WAGING > WAGE

WAGMOIRE obsolete word for > QUAGMIRE

WAGMOIRES > WAGMOIRE

WAGON n four-wheeled vehicle for heavy loads ▷ vb transport by wagon

WAGONAGE n money paid for transport by wagon

WAGONAGES > WAGONAGE

WAGONED > WAGON

WAGONER n person who drives a wagon

WAGONERS > WAGONER

WAGONETTE n light four-wheeled horse-drawn vehicle with two lengthwise seats facing each other behind a crosswise driver's seat

WAGONFUL > WAGON

WAGONFULS > WAGON

WAGONING > WAGON

WAGONLESS > WAGON

WAGONLOAD n load that is or can be carried by a wagon

WAGONS > WAGON

WAGS > WAG

WAGSOME another word for > WAGGISH

WAGTAIL n small long-tailed bird

WAGTAILS > WAGTAIL

WAGYU n Japanese breed of beef cattle

WAGYUS > WAGYU

WAHCONDA n supreme being

WAHCONDAS > WAHCONDA

WAHINE n Māori woman, esp a wife

WAHINES > WAHINE

WAHOO n food and game fish of tropical seas

WAHOOS > WAHOO

WAI n in New Zealand, water

WAIATA n Māori song

WAIATAS > WAIATA

WAID > WEIGH

WAIDE > WEIGH

WAIF n young person who is, or seems, homeless or neglected ▷ vb treat as a waif

WAIFED > WAIF

WAIFING > WAIF

WAIFISH > WAIF

WAIFLIKE > WAIF

WAIFS > WAIF

WAIFT n piece of lost property found by someone other than the owner

WAIFTS > WAIFT

WAIL vb cry out in pain or misery ▷ n mournful cry

WAILED > WAIL

WAILER > WAIL

WAILERS > WAIL

WAILFUL > WAIL

WAILFULLY > WAIL

WAILING > WAIL

WAILINGLY > WAIL

WAILINGS > WAIL

WAILS > WAIL

WAILSOME > WAIL

WAIN vb transport ▷ n farm wagon

WAINAGE n carriages, etc, for transportation of goods

WAINAGES > WAINAGE

WAINED > WAIN

WAINING > WAIN

WAINS > WAIN

WAINSCOT n wooden lining of the lower part of the walls of a room ▷ vb line (a wall of a room) with a wainscot

WAINSCOTS > WAINSCOT

WAIR vb spend

WAIRED > WAIR

WAIRING > WAIR

WAIRS > WAIR

WAIRSH variant spelling of > WERSH

WAIRSHER > WAIRSH

WAIRSHEST > WAIRSH

WAIRUA n in New Zealand, spirit or soul

WAIRUAS > WAIRUA

WAIS > WAI

WAIST n part of the trunk between the ribs and the hips

WAISTBAND n band of material sewn on to the waist of a garment to strengthen it

WAISTBELT n belt

WAISTCOAT n sleeveless garment which buttons up the front, usu worn over a shirt and under a jacket

WAISTED adj having a waist or waistlike part

WAISTER n sailor performing menial duties

WAISTERS > WAISTER

WAISTING n act of wasting

WAISTINGS > WAISTING

WAISTLESS > WAIST

WAISTLINE n (size of) the waist of a person or garment

WAISTS > WAIST

WAIT vb remain inactive in expectation (of something) ▷ n act or period of waiting

WAITE old form of > WAIT

WAITED > WAIT

WAITER n person who serves in a restaurant etc ▷ vb serve at table

WAITERAGE n service

WAITERED > WAITER

WAITERING n act of serving at table

WAITERS > WAITER

WAITES > WAITE

WAITING > WAIT

WAITINGLY > WAIT

WAITINGS > WAIT

WAITLIST n waiting list

WAITLISTS > WAITLIST

WAITRESS n woman who serves people with food and drink in a restaurant ▷ vb work as a waitress

WAITRON n waiter or waitress

WAITRONS > WAITRON

WAITS > WAIT

WAITSTAFF n waiters and waitresses collectively

WAIVE vb refrain from enforcing (a law, right, etc)

WAIVED > WAIVE

WAIVER n act or instance of voluntarily giving up a claim, right, etc

WAIVERS > WAIVER

WAIVES > WAIVE

WAIVING > WAIVE

WAIVODE same as > VOIVODE

WAIVODES > WAIVODE

WAIWODE same as > VOIVODE

WAIWODES > WAIWODE

WAKA n Māori canoe

WAKAME n edible seaweed

WAKAMES > WAKAME

WAKANDA n supernatural quality in Native American belief system

WAKANDAS > WAKANDA

WAKANE n type of seaweed

WAKANES > WAKANE

WAKAS > WAKA

WAKE vb rouse from sleep or inactivity ▷ n vigil beside a body the night before the funeral

WAKEBOARD n short surfboard for a rider towed behind a motorboat ▷ vb ride a wakeboard

WAKED > WAKE

WAKEFUL adj unable to sleep

WAKEFULLY > WAKEFUL

WAKELESS adj (of sleep) deep or unbroken

WAKEMAN n watchman

WAKEMEN > WAKEMAN

WAKEN vb wake

WAKENED > WAKEN

WAKENER > WAKEN

WAKENERS > WAKEN

WAKENING > WAKEN

WAKENINGS > WAKEN

WAKENS > WAKEN

WAKER > WAKE

WAKERIFE adj watchful

WAKERS > WAKE

WAKES > WAKE

WAKF same as > WAQF

WAKFS > WAKF

WAKIKI n Melanesian shell currency

WAKIKIS > WAKIKI

WAKING > WAKE

WAKINGS > WAKE

WALD Scots form of > WELD

WALDFLUTE n organ flute stop

WALDGRAVE n (in medieval Germany) an officer with jurisdiction over a royal forest

WALDHORN n organ reed stop

WALDHORNS > WALDHORN

WALDO n gadget for manipulating objects by remote control

WALDOES > WALDO

WALDOS > WALDO

WALDRAPP n type of ibis

WALDRAPPS > WALDRAPP

WALDS > WALD

WALE same as > WEAL

WALED > WALE

WALER > WALE

WALERS > WALE

WALES > WALE

WALI same as > VALI

WALIE adj robust or strong

WALIER > WALY

WALIES > WALY

WALIEST > WALY

WALING > WALE

WALIS > WALI

WALISE same as > VALISE

WALISES > WALISE

WAIWODES > WAIWODE

WALK vb move on foot with at least one foot always on the ground ▷ n short journey on foot, usu for pleasure

WALKABLE > WALK

WALKABOUT n informal walk among the public by royalty etc

WALKATHON n long walk done, esp for charity

WALKAWAY n easily achieved victory

WALKAWAYS > WALKAWAY

WALKED > WALK

WALKER n person who walks

WALKERS > WALKER

WALKIES pl n as in go walkies a walk

WALKING adj (of a person) considered to possess the qualities of something inanimate as specified ▷ n act of walking

WALKINGS > WALKING

WALKMILL same as > WAULKMILL

WALKMILLS > WALKMILL

WALKOUT n strike

WALKOUTS > WALKOUT

WALKOVER n easy victory

WALKOVERS > WALKOVER

WALKS > WALK

WALKUP n building with stairs to upper floors

WALKUPS > WALKUP

WALKWAY n path designed for use by pedestrians

WALKWAYS > WALKWAY

WALKYRIE variant of > VALKYRIE

WALKYRIES > WALKYRIE

WALL n structure of brick, stone, etc used to enclose, divide, or support ▷ vb enclose or seal with a wall or walls

WALLA same as > WALLAH

WALLABA n type of S American tree

WALLABAS > WALLABA

WALLABIES > WALLABY

WALLABY n marsupial like a small kangaroo

WALLAH n person involved with or in charge of a specified thing

WALLAHS > WALLAH

WALLAROO n large stocky Australian kangaroo of rocky regions

WALLAROOS > WALLAROO

WALLAS > WALLA

WALLBOARD n thin board made of materials, such as compressed wood fibres or gypsum plaster, between stiff paper, and used to cover walls, partitions, etc

WALLCHART n chart on wall

WALLED > WALL

WALLER > WALL

WALLERS > WALL

WALLET n small folding case for paper money, documents, etc

WALLETS > WALLET

WALLEY n type of jump in figure skating

WALLEYE n fish with large staring eyes
WALLEYED > WALLEYE
WALLEYES > WALLEYE
WALLEYS > WALLEY
WALLFISH n snail
WALLIE same as > WALLY
WALLIER > WALLY
WALLIES > WALLY
WALLIEST > WALLY
WALLING > WALL
WALLINGS > WALL
WALLOP vb hit hard ▷ n hard blow
WALLOPED > WALLOP
WALLOPER n person or thing that wallops
WALLOPERS > WALLOPER
WALLOPING n thrashing ▷ adj large or great
WALLOPS > WALLOP
WALLOW vb revel in an emotion ▷ n act or instance of wallowing
WALLOWED > WALLOW
WALLOWER > WALLOW
WALLOWERS > WALLOW
WALLOWING > WALLOW
WALLOWS > WALLOW
WALLPAPER n decorative paper to cover interior walls ▷ vb cover (walls) with wallpaper
WALLS > WALL
WALLSEND n type of coal
WALLSENDS > WALLSEND
WALLWORT n type of plant
WALLWORTS > WALLWORT
WALLY n stupid person ▷ adj fine, pleasing, or splendid
WALLYBALL n ball game played on court
WALLYDRAG n worthless person or animal
WALNUT n edible nut with a wrinkled shell ▷ adj made from the wood of a walnut tree
WALNUTS > WALNUT
WALRUS n large sea mammal with long tusks
WALRUSES > WALRUS
WALTIER > WALTY
WALTIEST > WALTY
WALTY adj (of a ship) likely to roll over
WALTZ n ballroom dance ▷ vb dance a waltz
WALTZED > WALTZ
WALTZER n person who waltzes
WALTZERS > WALTZER
WALTZES > WALTZ
WALTZING > WALTZ
WALTZINGS > WALTZ
WALTZLIKE > WALTZ
WALY same as > WALLY
WAMBENGER another name for > TUAN
WAMBLE vb move unsteadily ▷ n unsteady movement
WAMBLED > WAMBLE
WAMBLES > WAMBLE
WAMBLIER > WAMBLE
WAMBLIEST > WAMBLE
WAMBLING > WAMBLE
WAMBLINGS > WAMBLE

WAMBLY > WAMBLE
WAME n belly, abdomen, or womb
WAMED > WAME
WAMEFOU Scots variant of > WAMEFUL
WAMEFOUS > WAMEFOU
WAMEFUL n bellyful
WAMEFULS > WAMEFUL
WAMES > WAME
WAMMUL n dog
WAMMULS > WAMMUL
WAMMUS same as > WAMUS
WAMMUSES > WAMMUS
WAMPEE n type of Asian fruit tree
WAMPEES > WAMPEE
WAMPISH vb wave
WAMPISHED > WAMPISH
WAMPISHES > WAMPISH
WAMPUM n shells woven together, formerly used by Native Americans for money
WAMPUMS > WAMPUM
WAMPUS same as > WAMUS
WAMPUSES > WAMPUS
WAMUS n type of cardigan or jacket
WAMUSES > WAMUS
WAN adj pale and sickly looking ▷ vb make or become wan
WANCHANCY adj infelicitous
WAND n thin rod, esp one used in performing magic tricks
WANDER vb move about without a definite destination or aim ▷ n act or instance of wandering
WANDERED > WANDER
WANDERER > WANDER
WANDERERS > WANDER
WANDERING > WANDER
WANDEROO n macaque of India and Sri Lanka
WANDEROOS > WANDEROO
WANDERS > WANDER
WANDLE adj supple ▷ vb walk haltingly
WANDLED > WANDLE
WANDLES > WANDLE
WANDLIKE > WAND
WANDLING > WANDLE
WANDOO n eucalyptus tree of W Australia, having white bark and durable wood
WANDOOS > WANDOO
WANDS > WAND
WANE vb decrease gradually in size or strength
WANED > WANE
WANES > WANE
WANEY > WANE
WANG n cheekbone
WANGAN same as > WANIGAN
WANGANS > WANGAN
WANGLE vb get by devious methods ▷ n act or an instance of wangling
WANGLED > WANGLE
WANGLER > WANGLE
WANGLERS > WANGLE
WANGLES > WANGLE
WANGLING > WANGLE
WANGLINGS > WANGLE
WANGS > WANG
WANGUN same as > WANIGAN

WANGUNS > WANGUN
WANHOPE n delusion
WANHOPES > WANHOPE
WANIER > WANY
WANIEST > WANY
WANIGAN n provisions for camp
WANIGANS > WANIGAN
WANING > WANE
WANINGS > WANE
WANION n vehemence
WANIONS > WANION
WANK vb vulgar slang word for masturbate ▷ n instance of masturbating ▷ adj bad, useless, or worthless
WANKED > WANK
WANKER n vulgar slang word for a worthless person
WANKERS > WANKER
WANKIER > WANKY
WANKIEST > WANKY
WANKING > WANK
WANKLE adj unstable
WANKS > WANK
WANKSTA n slang word for a person who acts like a gangster but is not involved in crime
WANKSTAS > WANKSTA
WANKY adj slang word for pretentious
WANLE same as > WANDLE
WANLY > WAN
WANNA vb spelling of 'want to' intended to reflect a dialectal or informal pronunciation
WANNABE adj wanting to be, or be like, a particular person or thing ▷ n person who wants to be, or be like, a particular person or thing
WANNABEE same as > WANNABE
WANNABEES > WANNABEE
WANNABES > WANNABE
WANNED > WAN
WANNEL same as > WANDLE
WANNER > WAN
WANNESS > WAN
WANNESSES > WAN
WANNEST > WAN
WANNIGAN same as > WANIGAN
WANNIGANS > WANIGAN
WANNING > WAN
WANNION same as > WANION
WANNIONS > WANNION
WANNISH adj rather wan
WANS > WAN
WANT vb need or long for ▷ n act or instance of wanting
WANTAGE n shortage
WANTAGES > WANTAGE
WANTAWAY n footballer who wants to transfer to another club
WANTAWAYS > WANTAWAY
WANTED > WANT
WANTER > WANT
WANTERS > WANT
WANTHILL n molehill
WANTHILLS > WANTHILL
WANTIES > WANTY
WANTING adj lacking ▷ prep without

WANTON adj without motive, provocation, or justification ▷ n playful or capricious person ▷ vb squander or waste
WANTONED > WANTON
WANTONER > WANTON
WANTONERS > WANTON
WANTONEST > WANTON
WANTONING > WANTON
WANTONISE same as > WANTONIZE
WANTONIZE vb behave wantonly
WANTONLY > WANTON
WANTONS > WANTON
WANTS > WANT
WANTY adj belt
WANWORDY adj without merit
WANWORTH n inexpensive purchase
WANWORTHS > WANWORTH
WANY > WANE
WANZE vb wane
WANZED > WANZE
WANZES > WANZE
WANZING > WANZE
WAP vb strike
WAPENSHAW n showing of weapons
WAPENTAKE n subdivision of certain shires or counties, esp in the Midlands and North of England
WAPINSHAW same as > WAPENSHAW
WAPITI n large N American deer
WAPITIS > WAPITI
WAPPED > WAP
WAPPEND adj tired
WAPPER vb blink
WAPPERED > WAPPER
WAPPERING > WAPPER
WAPPERS > WAPPER
WAPPING > WAP
WAPS > WAP
WAQF n endowment in Muslim law
WAQFS > WAQF
WAR n fighting between nations ▷ adj of, like, or caused by war ▷ vb conduct a war
WARAGI n Ugandan alcoholic drink made from bananas
WARAGIS > WARAGI
WARATAH n Australian shrub with crimson flowers
WARATAHS > WARATAH
WARB n dirty or insignificant person
WARBIER > WARB
WARBIEST > WARB
WARBIRD n vintage military aeroplane
WARBIRDS > WARBIRD
WARBLE vb sing in a trilling voice ▷ n act or an instance of warbling
WARBLED > WARBLE
WARBLER n any of various small songbirds
WARBLERS > WARBLER
WARBLES > WARBLE

W

WARBLIER > WARBLY

WARBLIEST > WARBLY

WARBLING > WARBLE

WARBLINGS > WARBLE

WARBLY adj said in a quavering manner

WARBONNET n headband with trailing feathers worn by certain Native American warriors

WARBOT n any robot or unmanned vehicle or device designed for and used in warfare

WARBOTS > WARBOT

WARBS > WARB

WARBY > WARB

WARCRAFT n skill in warfare

WARCRAFTS > WARCRAFT

WARD n room in a hospital for patients needing a similar kind of care ▷ vb guard or protect

WARDCORN n payment of corn

WARDCORNS > WARDCORN

WARDED > WARD

WARDEN n person in charge of a building and its occupants ▷ vb act as a warden

WARDENED > WARDEN

WARDENING > WARDEN

WARDENRY > WARDEN

WARDENS > WARDEN

WARDER vb guard ▷ n prison officer

WARDERED > WARDER

WARDERING > WARDER

WARDERS > WARDER

WARDIAN n as in wardian case type of glass container for housing delicate plants

WARDING > WARD

WARDINGS > WARD

WARDLESS > WARD

WARDMOTE n assembly of the citizens or liverymen of an area

WARDMOTES > WARDMOTE

WARDOG n veteran warrior

WARDOGS > WARDOG

WARDRESS n female officer in charge of prisoners in a jail

WARDROBE n cupboard for hanging clothes in

WARDROBED > WARDROBE

WARDROBER n person in charge of someone's wardrobe

WARDROBES > WARDROBE

WARDROOM n officers' quarters on a warship

WARDROOMS > WARDROOM

WARDROP obsolete form of > WARDROBE

WARDROPS > WARDROP

WARDS > WARD

WARDSHIP n state of being a ward

WARDSHIPS > WARDSHIP

WARE n articles of a specified type or material ▷ vb spend or squander

WARED > WARE

WAREHOU n any of several edible saltwater New Zealand fish

WAREHOUS > WAREHOU

WAREHOUSE n building for storing goods prior to sale or distribution ▷ vb store or place in a warehouse, esp a bonded warehouse

WARELESS adj careless

WAREROOM n storeroom

WAREROOMS > WAREROOM

WARES pl n goods for sale

WAREZ pl n illegally copied computer software

WARFARE vb engage in war ▷ n fighting or hostilities

WARFARED > WARFARE

WARFARER > WARFARE

WARFARERS > WARFARE

WARFARES > WARFARE

WARFARIN n crystalline compound, used as a medical anticoagulant

WARFARING > WARFARE

WARFARINS > WARFARIN

WARGAME vb engage in simulated military conflicts

WARGAMED > WARGAME

WARGAMER n person who takes part in wargames

WARGAMERS > WARGAMER

WARGAMES > WARGAME

WARGAMING n activity of playing war games

WARHABLE adj able to fight in war

WARHEAD n explosive front part of a missile

WARHEADS > WARHEAD

WARHORSE n (formerly) a horse used in battle

WARHORSES > WARHORSE

WARIBASHI n pair of disposable chopsticks

WARIER > WARY

WARIEST > WARY

WARILY > WARY

WARIMENT n caution

WARIMENTS > WARIMENT

WARINESS > WARY

WARING > WARE

WARISON n (esp formerly) a bugle note used as an order to a military force to attack

WARISONS > WARISON

WARK Scots form of > WORK

WARKED > WARK

WARKING > WARK

WARKS > WARK

WARLESS > WAR

WARLIKE adj of or relating to war

WARLING n one who is not liked

WARLINGS > WARLING

WARLOCK n man who practises black magic

WARLOCKRY n witchcraft

WARLOCKS > WARLOCK

WARLORD n military leader of a nation or part of a nation

WARLORDS > WARLORD

WARM adj moderately hot ▷ vb make or become warm ▷ n warm place or area

WARMAKER n one who wages war

WARMAKERS > WARMAKER

WARMAN n one experienced in warfare

WARMBLOOD n type of horse

WARMED > WARM

WARMEN > WARMAN

WARMER > WARM

WARMERS > WARM

WARMEST > WARM

WARMING > WARM

WARMINGS > WARM

WARMISH > WARM

WARMIST n person who believes global warming results from human activity

WARMISTS > WARMIST

WARMLY > WARM

WARMNESS > WARM

WARMONGER n person who encourages war

WARMOUTH n type of fish

WARMOUTHS > WARMOUTH

WARMS > WARM

WARMTH n mild heat

WARMTHS > WARMTH

WARMUP n preparatory exercise routine

WARMUPS > WARMUP

WARN vb make aware of possible danger or harm

WARNED > WARN

WARNER > WARN

WARNERS > WARN

WARNING n something that warns ▷ adj giving or serving as a warning

WARNINGLY > WARNING

WARNINGS > WARNING

WARNS > WARN

WARP vb twist out of shape ▷ n state of being warped

WARPAGE > WARP

WARPAGES > WARP

WARPAINT n paint used to decorate the face and body before battle

WARPAINTS > WARPAINT

WARPATH n route taken by Native Americans on a warlike expedition

WARPATHS > WARPATH

WARPED > WARP

WARPER > WARP

WARPERS > WARP

WARPING > WARP

WARPINGS > WARP

WARPLANE n any aircraft designed for and used in warfare

WARPLANES > WARPLANE

WARPOWER n ability to wage war

WARPOWERS > WARPOWER

WARPS > WARP

WARPWISE adv (weaving) in the direction of the warp

WARRAGAL same as > WARRIGAL

WARRAGALS > WARRAGAL

WARRAGLE same as > WARRIGAL

WARRAGLES > WARRAGLE

WARRAGUL same as > WARRIGAL

WARRAGULS > WARRAGUL

WARRAN same as > WARRANT

WARRAND same as > WARRANT

WARRANDED > WARRAND

WARRANDS > WARRAND

WARRANED > WARRAN

WARRANING > WARRAN

WARRANS > WARRAN

WARRANT n (document giving) official authorization ▷ vb make necessary

WARRANTED > WARRANT

WARRANTEE n person to whom a warranty is given

WARRANTER > WARRANT

WARRANTOR n person or company that provides a warranty

WARRANTS > WARRANT

WARRANTY n (document giving) a guarantee

WARRAY vb wage war on

WARRAYED > WARRAY

WARRAYING > WARRAY

WARRAYS > WARRAY

WARRE same as > WAR

WARRED > WAR

WARREN n series of burrows in which rabbits live

WARRENER n gamekeeper or keeper of a warren

WARRENERS > WARRENER

WARRENS > WARREN

WARREY same as > WARRAY

WARREYED > WARREY

WARREYING > WARREY

WARREYS > WARREY

WARRIGAL n dingo ▷ adj wild

WARRIGALS > WARRIGAL

WARRING > WAR

WARRIOR n person who fights in a war

WARRIORS > WARRIOR

WARRISON same as > WARISON

WARRISONS > WARRISON

WARS > WAR

WARSAW n type of grouper fish

WARSAWS > WARSAW

WARSHIP n ship designed and equipped for naval combat

WARSHIPS > WARSHIP

WARSLE dialect word for > WRESTLE

WARSLED > WARSLE

WARSLER > WARSLE

WARSLERS > WARSLE

WARSLES > WARSLE

WARSLING > WARSLE

WARST obsolete form of > WORST

WARSTLE dialect form of > WRESTLE

WARSTLED > WARSTLE

WARSTLER > WARSTLE

WARSTLERS > WARSTLE

WARSTLES > WARSTLE

WARSTLING > WARSTLE

WART n small hard growth on the skin

WARTED > WART

WARTHOG n wild African pig with wartlike lumps on the face

WARTHOGS > WARTHOG

WARTIER > WART

WARTIEST > WART

WARTIME *n* time of war ▷ *adj* of or in a time of war

WARTIMES > WARTIME

WARTLESS > WART

WARTLIKE > WART

WARTS > WART

WARTWEED *n* type of plant

WARTWEEDS > WARTWEED

WARTWORT *another word for* > WARTWEED

WARTWORTS > WARTWORT

WARTY > WART

WARWOLF *n* Roman engine of war

WARWOLVES > WARWOLF

WARWORK *n* work contributing to war effort

WARWORKS > WARWORK

WARWORN *adj* worn down by war

WARY *adj* watchful or cautious

WARZONE *n* area where a war is taking place or there is some other violent conflict

WARZONES > WARZONE

WAS *vb* form of the past tense of *be*

WASABI *n* Japanese cruciferous plant cultivated for its thick green pungent root

WASABIS > WASABI

WASE *n* pad to relieve pressure of load carried on head

WASES > WASE

WASH *vb* clean (oneself, clothes, etc) with water and usu soap ▷ *n* act or process of washing

WASHABLE *n* thing that can be washed ▷ *adj* (esp of fabrics or clothes) capable of being washed without deteriorating

WASHABLES > WASHABLE

WASHAWAY *another word for* > WASHOUT

WASHAWAYS > WASHAWAY

WASHBAG *n* small bag for carrying toiletries when travelling

WASHBAGS > WASHBAG

WASHBALL *n* ball of soap

WASHBALLS > WASHBALL

WASHBASIN *n* basin for washing the face and hands

WASHBOARD *n* board having a surface, usually of corrugated metal, on which esp formerly, clothes were scrubbed

WASHBOWL *same as* > WASHBASIN

WASHBOWLS > WASHBOWL

WASHCLOTH *n* small piece of cloth used to wash the face and hands

WASHDAY *n* day on which clothes and linen are washed, often the same day each week

WASHDAYS > WASHDAY

WASHDOWN *n* the act of washing (oneself or something) down

WASHDOWNS > WASHDOWN

WASHED > WASH

WASHEN > WASH

WASHER *n* ring put under a nut or bolt or in a tap as a seal ▷ *vb* fit with a washer

WASHERED > WASHER

WASHERIES > WASHERY

WASHERING > WASHER

WASHERMAN *n* man who washes clothes for a living

WASHERMEN > WASHERMAN

WASHERS > WASHER

WASHERY *n* plant where liquid is used to remove dirt from a mineral

WASHES > WASH

WASHFAST *adj* not fading when washed

WASHHAND *n* as in *washhand basin, washhand stand* for the washing of hands

WASHHOUSE *n* (formerly) building in which laundry was done

WASHIER > WASHY

WASHIEST > WASHY

WASHILY > WASHY

WASHIN *n* increase in the angle of attack of an aircraft wing towards the wing tip

WASHINESS > WASHY

WASHING *n* clothes to be washed

WASHINGS > WASHING

WASHINS > WASHIN

WASHLAND *n* frequently flooded plain

WASHLANDS > WASHLAND

WASHOUT *n* complete failure

WASHOUTS > WASHOUT

WASHPOT *n* pot for washing things in

WASHPOTS > WASHPOT

WASHRAG *same as* > WASHCLOTH

WASHRAGS > WASHRAG

WASHROOM *n* toilet

WASHROOMS > WASHROOM

WASHSTAND *n* piece of furniture designed to hold a basin for washing the face and hands in

WASHTUB *n* tub or large container used for washing anything, esp clothes

WASHTUBS > WASHTUB

WASHUP *n* outcome of a process

WASHUPS > WASHUP

WASHWIPE *n* windscreen spray-cleaning mechanism

WASHWIPES > WASHWIPE

WASHWOMAN *n* woman who washes clothes for a living

WASHWOMEN > WASHWOMAN

WASHY *adj* overdiluted or weak

WASM *n* obsolete belief; an out-of-fashion 'ism'

WASMS > WASM

WASP *n* stinging insect with a slender black-and-yellow striped body

WASPIE *n* tight-waisted corset

WASPIER > WASP

WASPIES > WASPIE

WASPIEST > WASP

WASPILY > WASP

WASPINESS > WASP

WASPISH *adj* bad-tempered

WASPISHLY > WASPISH

WASPLIKE > WASP

WASPNEST *n* nest of wasps

WASPNESTS > WASPNEST

WASPS > WASP

WASPY > WASP

WASSAIL *n* formerly, festivity when much drinking took place ▷ *vb* drink health of (a person) at a wassail

WASSAILED > WASSAIL

WASSAILER > WASSAIL

WASSAILRY > WASSAIL

WASSAILS > WASSAIL

WASSERMAN *n* man-shaped sea monster

WASSERMEN > WASSERMAN

WASSUP *sentence substitute* what is happening?

WAST *singular form of the past tense of* > BE

WASTABLE > WASTE

WASTAGE *n* loss by wear or waste

WASTAGES > WASTAGE

WASTE *vb* use pointlessly or thoughtlessly ▷ *n* act of wasting or state of being wasted ▷ *adj* rejected as worthless or surplus to requirements

WASTEBIN *n* bin for rubbish

WASTEBINS > WASTEBIN

WASTED > WASTE

WASTEFUL *adj* extravagant

WASTEL *n* fine bread or cake

WASTELAND *n* barren or desolate area of land

WASTELOT *n* piece of waste ground in a city

WASTELOTS > WASTELOT

WASTELS > WASTEL

WASTENESS > WASTE

WASTER *vb* waste ▷ *n* layabout

WASTERED > WASTER

WASTERFUL *Scots variant of* > WASTEFUL

WASTERIE *same as* > WASTERY

WASTERIES > WASTERIE

WASTERING > WASTER

WASTERS > WASTER

WASTERY *n* extravagance

WASTES > WASTE

WASTEWAY *n* open ditch

WASTEWAYS > WASTEWAY

WASTEWEIR *another name for* > SPILLWAY

WASTFULL *obsolete form of* > WASTEFUL

WASTING *adj* reducing the vitality and strength of the body

WASTINGLY > WASTING

WASTINGS > WASTE

WASTNESS *same as* > WASTENESS

WASTREL *n* lazy or worthless person

WASTRELS > WASTREL

WASTRIE *same as* > WASTERY

WASTRIES > WASTRIE

WASTRIFE *n* wastefulness

WASTRIFES > WASTRIFE

WASTRY *n* wastefulness

WASTS > WAST

WAT *adj* wet

WATAP *n* stringy thread made by Native Americans from the roots of conifers

WATAPE *same as* > WATAP

WATAPES > WATAPE

WATAPS > WATAP

WATCH *vb* look at closely ▷ *n* portable timepiece for the wrist or pocket

WATCHA *interj* greeting meaning 'what are you?'

WATCHABLE *adj* interesting, enjoyable, or entertaining

WATCHBAND *n* watch strap

WATCHBOX *n* sentry's box

WATCHCASE *n* protective case for a watch, generally of metal such as gold, silver, brass, or gunmetal

WATCHCRY *n* slogan used to rally support

WATCHDOG *n* dog kept to guard property

WATCHDOGS > WATCHDOG

WATCHED > WATCH

WATCHER *n* person who watches

WATCHERS > WATCHER

WATCHES > WATCH

WATCHET *n* shade of blue

WATCHETS > WATCHET

WATCHEYE *n* eye with a light-coloured iris

WATCHEYES > WATCHEYE

WATCHFUL *adj* vigilant or alert

WATCHING > WATCH

WATCHLIST *n* list of things to be monitored

WATCHMAN *n* man employed to guard a building or property

WATCHMEN > WATCHMAN

WATCHOUT *n* lookout

WATCHOUTS > WATCHOUT

WATCHWORD *n* word or phrase that sums up the attitude of a particular group

WATE > WIT

WATER *n* clear colourless tasteless liquid that falls as rain and forms rivers etc ▷ *vb* put water on or into

WATERAGE *n* transportation of cargo by means of ships, or the charges for such transportation

WATERAGES > WATERAGE

WATERBED *n* watertight mattress filled with water

WATERBEDS > WATERBED

WATERBIRD *n* any aquatic bird

WATERBUCK *n* any of various antelopes of the swampy areas of Africa, having long curved ridged horns

WATERBUS *n* boat offering regular transport service

WATERDOG *n* dog trained to hunt in water

WATERDOGS > WATERDOG

W

WATERED > WATER
WATERER > WATER
WATERERS > WATER
WATERFALL n place where the waters of a river drop vertically
WATERFOWL n bird that swims on water, such as a duck or swan
WATERGATE n gate opening onto a stretch of water
WATERHEAD n source of river
WATERHEN another name for > GALLINULE
WATERHENS > WATERHEN
WATERHOLE n hole in which water collects
WATERIER > WATERY
WATERIEST > WATERY
WATERILY > WATERY
WATERING > WATER
WATERINGS > WATER
WATERISH > WATER
WATERJET n jet of water
WATERJETS > WATERJET
WATERLEAF n carved column design
WATERLESS > WATER
WATERLILY n any of various aquatic plants having large leaves and showy flowers that float on the surface of the water
WATERLINE n level to which a ship's hull will be immersed when afloat
WATERLOG vb flood with water
WATERLOGS > WATERLOG
WATERLOO n total defeat
WATERLOOS > WATERLOO
WATERMAN n skilled boatman
WATERMARK n faint translucent design in a sheet of paper ▷ vb mark (paper) with a watermark
WATERMEN > WATERMAN
WATERMILL n mill driven by water
WATERPOX n chickenpox
WATERS > WATER
WATERSHED n important period or factor serving as a dividing line
WATERSIDE n area of land beside a river or lake
WATERSKI vb ski on water towed behind motorboat
WATERSKIS > WATERSKI
WATERWAY n river, canal, or other navigable channel used as a means of travel or transport
WATERWAYS > WATERWAY
WATERWEED n any of various weedy aquatic plants
WATERWORK n machinery, etc for storing, purifying, and distributing water
WATERWORN adj worn smooth by the action or passage of water
WATERY adj of, like, or containing water
WATERZOOI n type of Flemish stew

WATS > WAT
WATT n unit of power
WATTAGE n electrical power expressed in watts
WATTAGES > WATTAGE
WATTAPE same as > WATAP
WATTAPES > WATTAPE
WATTER > WAT
WATTEST > WAT
WATTHOUR n unit of energy equal to the power of one watt operating for an hour
WATTHOURS > WATTHOUR
WATTLE n branches woven over sticks to make a fence ▷ adj made of, formed by, or covered with wattle ▷ vb construct from wattle
WATTLED > WATTLE
WATTLES > WATTLE
WATTLESS > WATT
WATTLING > WATTLE
WATTLINGS > WATTLE
WATTMETER n meter for measuring electric power in watts
WATTS > WATT
WAUCHT same as > WAUGHT
WAUCHTED > WAUCHT
WAUCHTING > WAUCHT
WAUCHTS > WAUCHT
WAUFF same as > WAFF
WAUFFED > WAUFF
WAUFFING > WAUFF
WAUFFS > WAUFF
WAUGH vb bark
WAUGHED > WAUGH
WAUGHING > WAUGH
WAUGHS > WAUGH
WAUGHT vb drink in large amounts
WAUGHTED > WAUGHT
WAUGHTING > WAUGHT
WAUGHTS > WAUGHT
WAUK vb full (cloth)
WAUKED > WAUK
WAUKER > WAUK
WAUKERS > WAUK
WAUKING > WAUK
WAUKMILL same as > WAULKMILL
WAUKMILLS > WAUKMILL
WAUKRIFE variant of > WAKERIFE
WAUKS > WAUK
WAUL vb cry or wail plaintively like a cat
WAULED > WAUL
WAULING > WAUL
WAULINGS > WAUL
WAULK same as > WAUK
WAULKED > WAULK
WAULKER > WAULK
WAULKERS > WAULK
WAULKING > WAULK
WAULKMILL n cloth-fulling mill
WAULKS > WAULK
WAULS > WAUL
WAUR obsolete form of > WAR
WAURED > WAUR
WAURING > WAUR
WAURS > WAUR
WAURST > WAUR
WAVE vb move the hand to and fro as a greeting or signal ▷ n moving ridge on water

WAVEBAND n range of wavelengths or frequencies used for a particular type of radio transmission
WAVEBANDS > WAVEBAND
WAVED > WAVE
WAVEFORM n shape of the graph of a wave or oscillation obtained by plotting the value of some changing quantity against time
WAVEFORMS > WAVEFORM
WAVEFRONT n surface associated with a propagating wave and passing through all points in the wave that have the same phase
WAVEGUIDE n solid rod of dielectric or a hollow metal tube, usually of rectangular cross section, used as a path to guide microwaves
WAVELESS > WAVE
WAVELET n small wave
WAVELETS > WAVELET
WAVELIKE > WAVE
WAVELLITE n greyish-white, yellow, or brown mineral
WAVEMETER n instrument for measuring the frequency or wavelength of radio waves
WAVEOFF n signal or instruction to an aircraft not to land
WAVEOFFS > WAVEOFF
WAVER vb hesitate or be irresolute ▷ n act or an instance of wavering
WAVERED > WAVER
WAVERER > WAVER
WAVERERS > WAVER
WAVERIER > WAVERY
WAVERIEST > WAVERY
WAVERING > WAVER
WAVERINGS > WAVER
WAVEROUS same as > WAVERY
WAVERS > WAVER
WAVERY adj lacking firmness
WAVES > WAVE
WAVESHAPE another word for > WAVEFORM
WAVESON n goods floating on waves after shipwreck
WAVESONS > WAVESON
WAVETABLE n table of recorded sound waves used in certain types of synthesizers
WAVEY n snow goose or other wild goose
WAVEYS > WAVEY
WAVICLE n origin of wave
WAVICLES > WAVICLE
WAVIER > WAVY
WAVIES > WAVY
WAVIEST > WAVY
WAVILY > WAVY
WAVINESS > WAVY
WAVING > WAVE
WAVINGS > WAVE
WAVY adj having curves ▷ n snow goose or other wild goose
WAW another name for > VAV
WAWA n speech ▷ vb speak

WAWAED > WAWA
WAWAING > WAWA
WAWAS > WAWA
WAWE same as > WAW
WAWES > WAWE
WAWL same as > WAUL
WAWLED > WAWL
WAWLING > WAWL
WAWLINGS > WAWL
WAWLS > WAWL
WAWS > WAW
WAX n solid shiny fatty or oily substance used for sealing, making candles, etc ▷ vb coat or polish with wax
WAXABLE > WAX
WAXBERRY n waxy fruit of the wax myrtle or the snowberry
WAXBILL n any of various chiefly African finchlike weaverbirds
WAXBILLS > WAXBILL
WAXCLOTH another name for > OILCLOTH
WAXCLOTHS > WAXCLOTH
WAXED > WAX
WAXEN adj made of or like wax
WAXER > WAX
WAXERS > WAX
WAXES > WAX
WAXEYE n small New Zealand bird
WAXEYES > WAXEYE
WAXFLOWER n any of various plants with waxy flowers
WAXIER > WAXY
WAXIEST > WAXY
WAXILY > WAXY
WAXINESS > WAXY
WAXING > WAX
WAXINGS > WAX
WAXLIKE > WAX
WAXPLANT n climbing shrub of E Asia and Australia
WAXPLANTS > WAXPLANT
WAXWEED n type of wild flower
WAXWEEDS > WAXWEED
WAXWING n type of songbird
WAXWINGS > WAXWING
WAXWORK n lifelike wax model of a (famous) person
WAXWORKER > WAXWORK
WAXWORKS > WAXWORK
WAXWORM n wax moth larva
WAXWORMS > WAXWORM
WAXY adj resembling wax in colour, appearance, or texture
WAY n manner or method ▷ vb travel
WAYANG n type of Indonesian performance with dancers or puppets
WAYANGS > WAYANG
WAYBACK n area in the rear of a vehicle
WAYBACKS > WAYBACK
WAYBILL n document stating the nature, origin, and destination of goods being transported
WAYBILLS > WAYBILL
WAYBOARD n thin geological seam separating larger strata

WAYBOARDS > WAYBOARD
WAYBREAD n plantain
WAYBREADS > WAYBREAD
WAYED > WAY
WAYFARE vb travel
WAYFARED > WAYFARE
WAYFARER n traveller
WAYFARERS > WAYFARER
WAYFARES > WAYFARE
WAYFARING > WAYFARE
WAYGOING n leaving
WAYGOINGS > WAYGOING
WAYGONE adj travel-weary
WAYGOOSE same as
  > WAYZGOOSE
WAYGOOSES > WAYGOOSE
WAYING > WAY
WAYLAID > WAYLAY
WAYLAY vb lie in wait for and
  accost or attack
WAYLAYER > WAYLAY
WAYLAYERS > WAYLAY
WAYLAYING > WAYLAY
WAYLAYS > WAYLAY
WAYLEAVE n access to
  property granted by a
  landowner for payment
WAYLEAVES > WAYLEAVE
WAYLEGGO interj away here!
  let go!
WAYLESS > WAY
WAYMARK n symbol or
  signpost marking the route
  of a footpath ▷ vb mark out
  with waymarks
WAYMARKED > WAYMARK
WAYMARKS > WAYMARK
WAYMENT vb express grief
WAYMENTED > WAYMENT
WAYMENTS > WAYMENT
WAYPOINT n stopping point
  on route
WAYPOINTS > WAYPOINT
WAYPOST n signpost
WAYPOSTS > WAYPOST
WAYS > WAY
WAYSIDE n side of a road
WAYSIDES > WAYSIDE
WAYWARD adj erratic, selfish,
  or stubborn
WAYWARDLY > WAYWARD
WAYWISER n device for
  measuring distance
WAYWISERS > WAYWISER
WAYWODE n Slavonic
  governor
WAYWODES > WAYWODE
WAYWORN adj worn or tired
  by travel
WAYZGOOSE n works outing
  made annually by a printing
  house
WAZ same as > WAZZ
WAZIR another word for
  > VIZIER
WAZIRS > WAZIR
WAZOO n slang word for
  person's bottom
WAZOOS > WAZOO
WAZZ vb urinate ▷ n act of
  urinating
WAZZED > WAZZ
WAZZES > WAZZ
WAZZING > WAZZ
WAZZOCK n foolish or
  annoying person
WAZZOCKS > WAZZOCK

WE pron speaker or writer and
  one or more others
WEAK adj lacking strength
WEAKEN vb make or become
  weak
WEAKENED > WEAKEN
WEAKENER > WEAKEN
WEAKENERS > WEAKEN
WEAKENING n act of
  weakening
WEAKENS > WEAKEN
WEAKER > WEAK
WEAKEST > WEAK
WEAKFISH n any of several
  sea trouts
WEAKISH > WEAK
WEAKISHLY > WEAK
WEAKLIER > WEAKLY
WEAKLIEST > WEAKLY
WEAKLING n feeble person
  or animal
WEAKLINGS > WEAKLING
WEAKLY adv feebly ▷ adj
  weak or sickly
WEAKNESS n being weak
WEAKON n subatomic
  particle
WEAKONS > WEAKON
WEAKSIDE n (in basketball)
  side of court away from ball
WEAKSIDES > WEAKSIDE
WEAL n raised mark left on
  the skin by a blow
WEALD n open or forested
  country
WEALDS > WEALD
WEALS > WEAL
WEALSMAN n statesman
WEALSMEN > WEALSMAN
WEALTH n state of being rich
WEALTHIER > WEALTHY
WEALTHILY > WEALTHY
WEALTHS > WEALTH
WEALTHY adj possessing
  wealth
WEAMB same as > WAME
WEAMBS > WEAMB
WEAN vb accustom (a baby or
  young mammal) to food
  other than mother's milk
WEANED > WEAN
WEANEL n recently weaned
  child or animal
WEANELS > WEANEL
WEANER n person or thing
  that weans
WEANERS > WEANER
WEANING > WEAN
WEANINGS > WEAN
WEANLING n child or young
  animal recently weaned
WEANLINGS > WEANLING
WEANS > WEAN
WEAPON vb arm ▷ n object
  used in fighting
WEAPONED > WEAPON
WEAPONEER n person
  associated with the use or
  maintenance of weapons,
  esp nuclear weapons ▷ vb
  supply with weapons
WEAPONING > WEAPON
WEAPONISE same as
  > WEAPONIZE
WEAPONIZE vb adapt (a
  chemical, bacillus, etc) in
  such a way that it can be
  used as a weapon

WEAPONRY n weapons
  collectively
WEAPONS > WEAPON
WEAR vb have on the body as
  clothing or ornament ▷ n
  clothes suitable for a
  particular time or purpose
WEARABLE adj suitable for
  wear or able to be worn ▷ n
  any garment that can be
  worn
WEARABLES > WEARABLE
WEARED > WEAR
WEARER > WEAR
WEARERS > WEAR
WEARIED > WEARY
WEARIER > WEARY
WEARIES > WEARY
WEARIEST > WEARY
WEARIFUL same as
  > WEARISOME
WEARILESS adj not wearied
  or able to be wearied
WEARILY > WEARY
WEARINESS > WEARY
WEARING adj tiring ▷ n act
  of wearing
WEARINGLY > WEARING
WEARINGS > WEAR
WEARISH adj withered
WEARISOME adj tedious
WEARPROOF adj resistant to
  damage from normal wear
  or usage
WEARS > WEAR
WEARY adj tired or exhausted
  ▷ vb make or become weary
WEARYING > WEARY
WEASAND former name for the
  > TRACHEA
WEASANDS > WEASAND
WEASEL n small carnivorous
  mammal with a long body
  and short legs ▷ vb use
  ambiguous language to
  avoid speaking directly or
  honestly
WEASELED > WEASEL
WEASELER > WEASEL
WEASELERS > WEASEL
WEASELIER > WEASELY
WEASELING > WEASEL
WEASELLED > WEASEL
WEASELLER > WEASEL
WEASELLY adj devious,
  cunning
WEASELS > WEASEL
WEASELY adj devious,
  cunning
WEASON Scots form of
  > WEASAND
WEASONS > WEASON
WEATHER n day-to-day
  atmospheric conditions of a
  place ▷ vb (cause to) be
  affected by the weather
WEATHERED adj affected by
  exposure to the action of the
  weather
WEATHERER > WEATHER
WEATHERLY adj (of a sailing
  vessel) making very little
  leeway when close-hauled,
  even in a stiff breeze
WEATHERS > WEATHER
WEAVE vb make (fabric) by
  interlacing (yarn) on a loom

WEAVED > WEAVE
WEAVER n person who
  weaves, esp as a means of
  livelihood
WEAVERS > WEAVER
WEAVES > WEAVE
WEAVING > WEAVE
WEAVINGS > WEAVE
WEAZAND same as
  > WEASAND
WEAZANDS > WEAZAND
WEAZEN same as > WIZEN
WEAZENED > WEAZEN
WEAZENING > WEAZEN
WEAZENS > WEAZEN
WEB n net spun by a spider
  ▷ vb cover with or as if with a
  web
WEBAPP n application
  program that is accessed on
  the internet
WEBAPPS > WEBAPP
WEBBED > WEB
WEBBIE n person who is well
  versed in the use of the World
  Wide Web
WEBBIER > WEBBY
WEBBIES > WEBBIE
WEBBIEST > WEBBY
WEBBING n anything that
  forms a web
WEBBINGS > WEBBING
WEBBY adj of, relating to,
  resembling, or consisting of
  a web
WEBCAM n camera that
  transmits images over the
  internet
WEBCAMS > WEBCAM
WEBCAST n broadcast of an
  event over the internet ▷ vb
  make such a broadcast
WEBCASTED > WEBCAST
WEBCASTER > WEBCAST
WEBCASTS > WEBCAST
WEBCHAT vb exchange
  messages via the internet
WEBCHATS > WEBCHAT
WEBER n SI unit of magnetic
  flux
WEBERS > WEBER
WEBFED adj (of printing
  press) printing from rolls of
  paper
WEBFEET > WEBFOOT
WEBFOOT n foot having the
  toes connected by folds of
  skin
WEBFOOTED > WEBFOOT
WEBHEAD n person who uses
  the internet a lot
WEBHEADS > WEBHEAD
WEBIFIED > WEBIFY
WEBIFIES > WEBIFY
WEBIFY vb convert
  (information) for display on
  the internet
WEBIFYING > WEBIFY
WEBINAR n interactive
  seminar conducted over the
  World Wide Web
WEBINARS > WEBINAR
WEBISODE n episode (of a
  television series) intended
  for on-line viewing
WEBISODES > WEBISODE
WEBLESS > WEB

W

WEBLIKE > WEB

WEBLISH n shorthand form of English that is used in text messaging, chat rooms, etc

WEBLISHES > WEBLISH

WEBLOG n person's online journal

WEBLOGGER > WEBLOG

WEBLOGS > WEBLOG

WEBMAIL n system of electronic mail accessed mail via the internet

WEBMAILS > WEBMAIL

WEBMASTER n person responsible for the administration of a website on the World Wide Web

WEBPAGE n page on website

WEBPAGES > WEBPAGE

WEBRING n group of websites organized in a circular structure

WEBRINGS > WEBRING

WEBS > WEB

WEBSITE n group of connected pages on the World Wide Web

WEBSITES > WEBSITE

WEBSPACE n storage space on a web server

WEBSPACES > WEBSPACE

WEBSTER archaic word for > WEAVER

WEBSTERS > WEBSTER

WEBWHEEL n wheel containing a plate or web instead of spokes

WEBWHEELS > WEBWHEEL

WEBWORK n work done using the World Wide Web

WEBWORKS > WEBWORK

WEBWORM n type of caterpillar

WEBWORMS > WEBWORM

WEBZINE n magazine published on the internet

WEBZINES > WEBZINE

WECHT n agricultural tool ▷ vb winnow (corn)

WECHTED > WECHT

WECHTING > WECHT

WECHTS > WECHT

WED vb marry

WEDDED > WED

WEDDER dialect form of > WEATHER

WEDDERED > WEDDER

WEDDERING > WEDDER

WEDDERS > WEDDER

WEDDING > WED

WEDDINGS > WEDDING

WEDEL variant of > WEDELN

WEDELED > WEDEL

WEDELING > WEDEL

WEDELN n succession of high-speed turns performed in skiing ▷ vb perform a wedeln

WEDELNED > WEDELN

WEDELNING > WEDELN

WEDELNS > WEDELN

WEDELS > WEDEL

WEDGE n piece of material thick at one end and thin at the other ▷ vb fasten or split with a wedge

WEDGED > WEDGE

WEDGELIKE > WEDGE

WEDGES > WEDGE

WEDGEWISE adv in manner of a wedge

WEDGIE n wedge-heeled shoe

WEDGIER > WEDGE

WEDGIES > WEDGIE

WEDGIEST > WEDGE

WEDGING > WEDGE

WEDGINGS > WEDGE

WEDGY > WEDGE

WEDLOCK n marriage

WEDLOCKS > WEDLOCK

WEDS > WED

WEE adj small or short ▷ n instance of urinating ▷ vb urinate

WEED n plant growing where undesired ▷ vb clear of weeds

WEEDBED n body of water having lots of weeds

WEEDBEDS > WEEDBED

WEEDED > WEED

WEEDER > WEED

WEEDERIES > WEEDERY

WEEDERS > WEED

WEEDERY n weed-ridden area

WEEDHEAD n habitual user of marijuana

WEEDHEADS > WEEDHEAD

WEEDICIDE n weed-killer

WEEDIER > WEEDY

WEEDIEST > WEEDY

WEEDILY > WEEDY

WEEDINESS > WEEDY

WEEDING > WEED

WEEDINGS > WEED

WEEDLESS > WEED

WEEDLIKE > WEED

WEEDLINE n edge of a weedbed

WEEDLINES > WEEDLINE

WEEDS pl n widow's mourning clothes

WEEDY adj (of a person) thin and weak

WEEING > WEE

WEEJUNS pl n moccasin-style shoes for casual wear

WEEK n period of seven days, esp one beginning on a Sunday ▷ adv seven days before or after a specified day

WEEKDAY n any day of the week except Saturday or Sunday

WEEKDAYS > WEEKDAY

WEEKE same as > WICK

WEEKEND n Saturday and Sunday ▷ vb spend or pass a weekend

WEEKENDED > WEEKEND

WEEKENDER n person spending a weekend holiday in a place, esp habitually

WEEKENDS adv at the weekend, esp regularly or during every weekend

WEEKES > WEEKE

WEEKLIES > WEEKLY

WEEKLONG adj lasting a week

WEEKLY adv happening, done, etc once a week ▷ n

newspaper or magazine published once a week ▷ adj happening once a week or every week

WEEKNIGHT n evening or night of a weekday

WEEKS > WEEK

WEEL Scot word for > WELL

WEELS > WEEL

WEEM n underground home

WEEMS > WEEM

WEEN vb think or imagine (something)

WEENED > WEEN

WEENIE adj very small ▷ n wiener

WEENIER > WEENY

WEENIES > WEENIE

WEENIEST > WEENY

WEENING > WEEN

WEENS > WEEN

WEENSIER > WEENSY

WEENSIEST > WEENSY

WEENSY same as > WEENY

WEENY adj very small

WEEP vb shed tears ▷ n spell of weeping

WEEPER n person who weeps, esp a hired mourner

WEEPERS > WEEPER

WEEPHOLE n small drain hole in wall

WEEPHOLES > WEEPHOLE

WEEPIE same as > WEEPY

WEEPIER > WEEPY

WEEPIES > WEEPY

WEEPIEST > WEEPY

WEEPILY > WEEPY

WEEPINESS > WEEPY

WEEPING adj (of plants) having slender hanging branches

WEEPINGLY > WEEPING

WEEPINGS > WEEPING

WEEPS > WEEP

WEEPY adj liable to cry ▷ n sentimental film or book

WEER > WEE

WEES > WEE

WEEST > WEE

WEET dialect form of > WET

WEETE same as > WIT

WEETED > WEETE

WEETEN same as > WIT

WEETER > WEET

WEETEST > WEET

WEETING > WEET

WEETINGLY > WEET

WEETLESS obsolete variant of > WITLESS

WEETS > WEET

WEEVER n type of small fish

WEEVERS > WEEVER

WEEVIL n small beetle that eats grain etc

WEEVILED same as > WEEVILLED

WEEVILIER > WEEVILY

WEEVILLED adj weevil-ridden

WEEVILLY adj full of weevils

WEEVILS > WEEVIL

WEEVILY adj full of weevils

WEEWEE vb urinate

WEEWEED > WEEWEE

WEEWEEING > WEEWEE

WEEWEES > WEEWEE

WEFT n cross threads in weaving ▷ vb form weft

WEFTAGE n texture

WEFTAGES > WEFTAGE

WEFTE n forsaken child

WEFTED > WEFT

WEFTES > WEFTE

WEFTING > WEFT

WEFTS > WEFT

WEFTWISE adv in the direction of the weft

WEID n sudden illness

WEIDS > WEID

WEIGELA n type of shrub

WEIGELAS > WEIGELA

WEIGELIA same as > WEIGELA

WEIGELIAS > WEIGELIA

WEIGH vb have a specified weight

WEIGHABLE > WEIGH

WEIGHAGE n duty paid for weighing goods

WEIGHAGES > WEIGHAGE

WEIGHED > WEIGH

WEIGHER > WEIGH

WEIGHERS > WEIGH

WEIGHING > WEIGH

WEIGHINGS > WEIGH

WEIGHMAN n person responsible for weighing goods

WEIGHMEN > WEIGHMAN

WEIGHS > WEIGH

WEIGHT n heaviness of an object ▷ vb add weight to

WEIGHTAGE same as > WEIGHTING

WEIGHTED > WEIGHT

WEIGHTER > WEIGHT

WEIGHTERS > WEIGHT

WEIGHTIER > WEIGHTY

WEIGHTILY > WEIGHTY

WEIGHTING n extra allowance paid in special circumstances

WEIGHTS > WEIGHT

WEIGHTY adj important or serious

WEIL n whirlpool

WEILS > WEIL

WEINER same as > WIENER

WEINERS > WEINER

WEIR vb ward off ▷ n river dam

WEIRD adj strange or bizarre ▷ vb warn beforehand

WEIRDED > WEIRD

WEIRDER > WEIRD

WEIRDEST > WEIRD

WEIRDIE same as > WEIRDO

WEIRDIES > WEIRDIE

WEIRDING > WEIRD

WEIRDLY > WEIRD

WEIRDNESS > WEIRD

WEIRDO n peculiar person

WEIRDOES > WEIRDO

WEIRDOS > WEIRDO

WEIRDS > WEIRD

WEIRDY n weird person

WEIRED > WEIR

WEIRING > WEIR

WEIRS > WEIR

WEISE same as > WISE

WEISED > WEISE

WEISES > WEISE

WEISING > WEISE

WEIZE same as **>** WISE

WEIZED > WEIZE

WEIZES > WEIZE

WEIZING > WEIZE

WEKA n flightless New Zealand rail

WEKAS > WEKA

WELAWAY same as **>** WELLAWAY

WELCH same as **>** WELSH

WELCHED > WELCH

WELCHER > WELCH

WELCHERS > WELCH

WELCHES > WELCH

WELCHING > WELCH

WELCOME vb greet with pleasure ▷ n kindly greeting ▷ adj received gladly

WELCOMED > WELCOME

WELCOMELY > WELCOME

WELCOMER > WELCOME

WELCOMERS > WELCOME

WELCOMES > WELCOME

WELCOMING > WELCOME

WELD vb join (pieces of metal or plastic) by softening with heat ▷ n welded joint

WELDABLE > WELD

WELDED > WELD

WELDER > WELD

WELDERS > WELD

WELDING > WELD

WELDINGS > WELD

WELDLESS > WELD

WELDMENT n unit composed of welded pieces

WELDMENTS > WELDMENT

WELDMESH n type of fencing consisting of wire mesh reinforced by welding

WELDOR > WELD

WELDORS > WELDOR

WELDS > WELD

WELFARE n wellbeing

WELFARES > WELFARE

WELFARISM n policies or attitudes associated with a welfare state

WELFARIST > WELFARISM

WELFARITE n (US) person who is on welfare

WELK vb wither; dry up

WELKE obsolete form of **>** WELK

WELKED > WELK

WELKES > WELKE

WELKIN n sky, heavens, or upper air

WELKING > WELK

WELKINS > WELKIN

WELKS > WELK

WELKT adj twisted

WELL adv satisfactorily ▷ adj in good health ▷ interj exclamation of surprise, interrogation, etc ▷ n hole sunk into the earth to reach water, oil, or gas ▷ vb flow upwards or outwards

WELLADAY interj alas

WELLADAYS interj alas

WELLANEAR interj alas

WELLAWAY interj alas

WELLAWAYS interj alas

WELLBEING n state of being well, happy, or prosperous

WELLBORN adj having been born into a wealthy family

WELLCURB n stone surround at top of well

WELLCURBS > WELLCURB

WELLDOER n moral person

WELLDOERS > WELLDOER

WELLED > WELL

WELLHEAD n source of a well or stream

WELLHEADS > WELLHEAD

WELLHOLE n well shaft

WELLHOLES > WELLHOLE

WELLHOUSE n housing for well

WELLIE n wellington boot

WELLIES > WELLY

WELLING > WELL

WELLINGS > WELL

WELLNESS n state of being in good physical and mental health

WELLS > WELL

WELLSITE n site of well

WELLSITES > WELLSITE

WELLY n energy or commitment

WELS n type of catfish

WELSH vb fail to pay a debt or fulfil an obligation

WELSHED > WELSH

WELSHER > WELSH

WELSHERS > WELSH

WELSHES > WELSH

WELSHING > WELSH

WELT same as **>** WEAL

WELTED > WELT

WELTER n jumbled mass ▷ vb roll about, writhe, or wallow

WELTERED > WELTER

WELTERING > WELTER

WELTERS > WELTER

WELTING > WELT

WELTINGS > WELT

WELTS > WELT

WEM same as **>** WAME

WEMB same as **>** WAME

WEMBS > WEMB

WEMS > WEM

WEN n cyst on the scalp

WENA pron South African word for you

WENCH n young woman ▷ vb frequent the company of prostitutes

WENCHED > WENCH

WENCHER > WENCH

WENCHERS > WENCH

WENCHES > WENCH

WENCHING > WENCH

WEND vb go or travel

WENDED > WEND

WENDIGO n evil spirit or cannibal

WENDIGOES > WENDIGO

WENDIGOS > WENDIGO

WENDING > WEND

WENDS > WEND

WENGE n type of tree found in central and West Africa

WENGES > WENGE

WENNIER > WEN

WENNIEST > WEN

WENNISH > WEN

WENNY > WEN

WENS > WEN

WENT n path

WENTS > WENT

WEPT > WEEP

WERE vb form of the past tense of be

WEREGILD same as **>** WERGILD

WEREGILDS > WEREGILD

WEREWOLF n (in folklore) person who can turn into a wolf

WERGELD same as **>** WERGILD

WERGELDS > WERGELD

WERGELT same as **>** WERGELD

WERGELTS > WERGELT

WERGILD n price set on a person's life, to be paid as compensation by their slayer

WERGILDS > WERGILD

WERNERITE another name for **>** SCAPOLITE

WERO n challenge made by an armed Māori warrior to a visitor to a marae

WEROS > WERO

WERRIS slang word for **>** URINATION

WERRISES > WERRIS

WERSH adj tasteless

WERSHER > WERSH

WERSHEST > WERSH

WERT singular form of the past tense of **>** BE

WERWOLF same as **>** WEREWOLF

WERWOLVES > WERWOLF

WESAND same as **>** WEASAND

WESANDS > WESAND

WESKIT informal word for **>** WAISTCOAT

WESKITS > WESKIT

WESSAND same as **>** WEASAND

WESSANDS > WESSAND

WEST n part of the horizon where the sun sets ▷ adj in the west ▷ adv in, to, or towards the west ▷ vb move in westerly direction

WESTABOUT adv in, to, or towards the west

WESTBOUND adj going towards the west

WESTED > WEST

WESTER vb move or appear to move towards the west ▷ n strong wind or storm from the west

WESTERED > WESTER

WESTERING > WESTER

WESTERLY adj of or in the west ▷ adv towards the west ▷ n wind blowing from the west

WESTERN adj of or in the west ▷ n film or story about cowboys in the western US

WESTERNER n person from the west of a country or area

WESTERNS > WESTERN

WESTERS > WESTER

WESTIE n insulting word for a young working-class person from the western suburbs of Sydney

WESTIES > WESTIE

WESTING n movement, deviation, or distance covered in a westerly direction

WESTINGS > WESTING

WESTLIN Scots word for **>** WESTERN

WESTLINS adv to or in west

WESTMOST adj most western

WESTS > WEST

WESTWARD adv towards the west ▷ n westward part or direction ▷ adj moving, facing, or situated in the west

WESTWARDS same as **>** WESTWARD

WET adj covered or soaked with water or another liquid ▷ n moisture or rain ▷ vb make wet

WETA n type of wingless insect

WETAS > WETA

WETBACK n offensive word for a Mexican labourer who enters the US illegally

WETBACKS > WETBACK

WETHER n male sheep

WETHERS > WETHER

WETLAND n area of marshy land

WETLANDS > WETLAND

WETLY > WET

WETNESS n the state of being wet

WETNESSES > WET

WETPROOF adj waterproof

WETS > WET

WETSUIT n body suit for diving

WETSUITS > WETSUIT

WETTABLE > WET

WETTED > WET

WETTER > WET

WETTERS > WET

WETTEST > WET

WETTIE n wetsuit

WETTIES > WETTIE

WETTING > WET

WETTINGS > WET

WETTISH > WET

WETWARE n humorous term for the brain

WETWARES > WETWARE

WEX obsolete form of **>** WAX

WEXE obsolete form of **>** WAX

WEXED > WEX

WEXES > WEX

WEXING > WEX

WEY n measurement of weight

WEYARD obsolete form of **>** WEIRD

WEYS > WEY

WEYWARD obsolete form of **>** WEIRD

WEZAND obsolete form of **>** WEASAND

WEZANDS > WEZAND

WHA Scot word for **>** WHO

WHACK vb strike with a resounding blow ▷ n such a blow

WHACKED > WHACK

WHACKER > WHACK

WHACKER > WHACK

W

WHACKERS > WHACK
WHACKIER > WHACKY
WHACKIEST > WHACKY
WHACKING adj huge ▷ n severe beating ▷ adv extremely
WHACKINGS > WHACKING
WHACKO n mad person
WHACKOES > WHACKO
WHACKOS > WHACKO
WHACKS > WHACK
WHACKY variant spelling of > WACKY
WHAE same as > WHA
WHAISLE Scots form of > WHEEZE
WHAISLED > WHAISLE
WHAISLES > WHAISLE
WHAISLING > WHAISLE
WHAIZLE same as > WHAISLE
WHAIZLED > WHAIZLE
WHAIZLES > WHAIZLE
WHAIZLING > WHAIZLE
WHAKAIRO n art of carving
WHAKAIROS > WHAKAIRO
WHAKAPAPA n genealogy
WHALE n large fish-shaped sea mammal ▷ vb hunt for whales
WHALEBACK n something shaped like the back of a whale
WHALEBOAT n narrow boat from 20 to 30 feet long having a sharp prow and stern, formerly used in whaling
WHALEBONE n horny substance hanging from the upper jaw of toothless whales
WHALED > WHALE
WHALELIKE > WHALE
WHALEMAN n person employed in whaling
WHALEMEN > WHALEMAN
WHALER n ship or person involved in whaling
WHALERIES > WHALERY
WHALERS > WHALER
WHALERY n whaling
WHALES > WHALE
WHALING n hunting of whales for food and oil ▷ adv extremely
WHALINGS > WHALING
WHALLY adj (of eyes) with light-coloured irises
WHAM interj expression indicating suddenness or forcefulness ▷ n forceful blow or impact ▷ vb strike or cause to strike with great force
WHAMMED > WHAM
WHAMMIES > WHAMMY
WHAMMING > WHAM
WHAMMO n sound of a sudden collision
WHAMMOS > WHAMMO
WHAMMY n devastating setback
WHAMO same as > WHAMMO
WHAMPLE n strike
WHAMPLES > WHAMPLE
WHAMS > WHAM

WHANAU n (in Māori societies) a family, esp an extended family
WHANAUS > WHANAU
WHANG vb strike or be struck so as to cause a resounding noise ▷ n resounding noise produced by a heavy blow
WHANGAM n imaginary creature
WHANGAMS > WHANGAM
WHANGED > WHANG
WHANGEE n tall woody grass grown for its stems, which are used for bamboo canes
WHANGEES > WHANGEE
WHANGING > WHANG
WHANGS > WHANG
WHAP same as > WHOP
WHAPPED > WHAP
WHAPPER same as > WHOPPER
WHAPPERS > WHAPPER
WHAPPING > WHAP
WHAPS > WHAP
WHARE n Māori hut or dwelling place
WHARENUI n (in New Zealand) meeting house
WHARENUIS > WHARENUI
WHAREPUNI n (in a Māori community) a tall carved building used as a guesthouse
WHARES > WHARE
WHARF n platform at a harbour for loading and unloading ships ▷ vb put (goods, etc) on a wharf
WHARFAGE n accommodation for ships at wharves
WHARFAGES > WHARFAGE
WHARFED > WHARF
WHARFIE n person employed to load and unload ships
WHARFIES > WHARFIE
WHARFING > WHARF
WHARFINGS > WHARF
WHARFS > WHARF
WHARVE n wooden disc or wheel on a shaft serving as a flywheel or pulley
WHARVES > WHARVE
WHAT pron which thing ▷ interj exclamation of anger, surprise, etc ▷ adv in which way, how much ▷ n part; portion
WHATA n building on stilts or a raised platform for storing provisions
WHATAS > WHATA
WHATCHA interj greeting meaning 'what are you?'
WHATEN adj what; what kind of
WHATEVER pron everything or anything that ▷ determiner intensive form of what
WHATEVS interj whatever
WHATNA another word for > WHATEN
WHATNESS n what something is
WHATNOT n similar unspecified thing

WHATNOTS > WHATNOT
WHATS > WHAT
WHATSIS US form of > WHATSIT
WHATSISES > WHATSIS
WHATSIT n person or thing the name of which is temporarily forgotten
WHATSITS > WHATSIT
WHATSO adj of whatever kind
WHATTEN same as > WHATEN
WHAUP n curlew
WHAUPS > WHAUP
WHAUR Scot word for > WHERE
WHAURS > WHAUR
WHEAL same as > WEAL
WHEALS > WHEAL
WHEAR obsolete variant of > WHERE
WHEARE obsolete variant of > WHERE
WHEAT n grain used in making flour, bread, and pasta
WHEATEAR n small songbird
WHEATEARS > WHEATEAR
WHEATEN n type of dog ▷ adj made of the grain or flour of wheat
WHEATENS > WHEATEN
WHEATGERM n vitamin-rich embryo of the wheat kernel
WHEATIER > WHEATY
WHEATIEST > WHEATY
WHEATLAND n region where wheat is grown
WHEATLESS > WHEAT
WHEATLIKE adj like wheat
WHEATMEAL n brown, but not wholemeal, flour
WHEATS > WHEAT
WHEATWORM n parasitic nematode worm that forms galls in the seeds of wheat
WHEATY adj having a wheat-like taste
WHEE interj exclamation of joy, thrill, etc
WHEECH vb move quickly
WHEECHED > WHEECH
WHEECHING > WHEECH
WHEECHS > WHEECH
WHEEDLE vb coax or cajole
WHEEDLED > WHEEDLE
WHEEDLER > WHEEDLE
WHEEDLERS > WHEEDLE
WHEEDLES > WHEEDLE
WHEEDLING > WHEEDLE
WHEEL n disc that revolves on an axle ▷ vb push or pull (something with wheels)
WHEELBASE n distance between a vehicle's front and back axles
WHEELED adj having or equipped with a wheel or wheels
WHEELER n horse or other draught animal nearest the wheel
WHEELERS > WHEELER
WHEELIE n manoeuvre on a bike in which the front wheel is raised off the ground
WHEELIER > WHEELY
WHEELIES > WHEELIE
WHEELIEST > WHEELY

WHEELING > WHEEL
WHEELINGS > WHEEL
WHEELLESS adj having no wheels
WHEELMAN n helmsman
WHEELMEN > WHEELMAN
WHEELS > WHEEL
WHEELSMAN same as > WHEELMAN
WHEELSMEN > WHEELSMAN
WHEELSPIN n rotation of a wheel when it is not achieving any grip on a surface
WHEELWORK n arrangement of wheels in a machine, esp a train of gears
WHEELY adj resembling a wheel
WHEEN n few
WHEENGE Scots form of > WHINGE
WHEENGED > WHEENGE
WHEENGES > WHEENGE
WHEENGING > WHEENGE
WHEENS > WHEEN
WHEEP vb fly quickly and lightly
WHEEPED > WHEEP
WHEEPING > WHEEP
WHEEPLE vb whistle weakly
WHEEPLED > WHEEPLE
WHEEPLES > WHEEPLE
WHEEPLING > WHEEPLE
WHEEPS > WHEEP
WHEESH vb silence (a person, noise, etc) or be silenced
WHEESHED > WHEESH
WHEESHES > WHEESH
WHEESHING > WHEESH
WHEESHT same as > WHEESH
WHEESHTED > WHEESHT
WHEESHTS > WHEESHT
WHEEZE vb breathe with a hoarse whistling noise ▷ n wheezing sound
WHEEZED > WHEEZE
WHEEZER > WHEEZE
WHEEZERS > WHEEZE
WHEEZES > WHEEZE
WHEEZIER > WHEEZE
WHEEZIEST > WHEEZE
WHEEZILY > WHEEZE
WHEEZING > WHEEZE
WHEEZINGS > WHEEZE
WHEEZLE vb make hoarse breathing sound
WHEEZLED > WHEEZLE
WHEEZLES > WHEEZLE
WHEEZLING > WHEEZLE
WHEEZY > WHEEZE
WHEFT same as > WAFT
WHEFTS > WHEFT
WHELK n edible snail-like shellfish
WHELKED adj having or covered with whelks
WHELKIER > WHELK
WHELKIEST > WHELK
WHELKS > WHELK
WHELKY > WHELK
WHELM vb engulf entirely with or as if with water
WHELMED > WHELM
WHELMING > WHELM
WHELMS > WHELM

WHELP n pup or cub ▷ vb (of an animal) give birth

WHELPED > WHELP

WHELPING > WHELP

WHELPLESS > WHELP

WHELPS > WHELP

WHEMMLE vb overturn

WHEMMLED > WHEMMLE

WHEMMLES > WHEMMLE

WHEMMLING > WHEMMLE

WHEN adv at what time? ▷ pron at which time ▷ n question of when

WHENAS conj while; inasmuch as

WHENCE n point of origin ▷ adv from what place or source ▷ pron from what place, cause, or origin

WHENCES > WHENCE

WHENCEVER adv out of whatsoever place, cause or origin

WHENEVER adv at whatever time

WHENS > WHEN

WHENUA n land

WHENUAS > WHENUA

WHENWE n White immigrant to South Africa from Zimbabwe

WHENWES > WHENWE

WHERE adv in, at, or to what place? ▷ pron in, at, or to which place ▷ n question as to the position, direction, or destination of something

WHEREAS n testimonial introduced by whereas

WHEREASES > WHEREAS

WHEREAT adv at or to which place

WHEREBY pron by which ▷ adv how? by what means?

WHEREFOR adv for which ▷ n explanation or reason

WHEREFORE adv why ▷ n explanation or reason

WHEREFORS > WHEREFOR

WHEREFROM adv from what or where? whence? ▷ pron from which place

WHEREIN adv in what place or respect? ▷ pron in which place or thing

WHEREINTO adv into what place? ▷ pron into which place

WHERENESS n state of having a place

WHEREOF adv of what or which person or thing? ▷ pron of which person or thing

WHEREON adv on what thing or place? ▷ pron on which thing, place, etc

WHEREOUT adv out of which

WHERES > WHERE

WHERESO adv in or to unspecified place

WHERETO adv towards what (place, end, etc)? ▷ pron to which

WHEREUNTO same as > WHERETO

WHEREUPON adv upon what?

WHEREVER adv at whatever place ▷ pron at, in, or to every place or point which

WHEREWITH pron with or by which ▷ adv with what?

WHERRET vb strike (someone) a blow ▷ n blow, esp a slap on the face

WHERRETED > WHERRET

WHERRETS > WHERRET

WHERRIED > WHERRY

WHERRIES > WHERRY

WHERRIT vb worry or cause to worry

WHERRITED > WHERRIT

WHERRITS > WHERRIT

WHERRY n any of certain kinds of half-decked commercial boats ▷ vb travel in a wherry

WHERRYING > WHERRY

WHERRYMAN > WHERRY

WHERRYMEN > WHERRY

WHERVE same as > WHARVE

WHERVES > WHERVE

WHET vb sharpen (a tool) ▷ n act of whetting

WHETHER conj used to introduce any indirect question

WHETS > WHET

WHETSTONE n stone for sharpening tools

WHETTED > WHET

WHETTER > WHET

WHETTERS > WHET

WHETTING > WHET

WHEUGH same as > WHEW

WHEUGHED > WHEUGH

WHEUGHING > WHEUGH

WHEUGHS > WHEUGH

WHEW interj exclamation expressing relief, delight, etc ▷ vb express relief

WHEWED > WHEW

WHEWING > WHEW

WHEWS > WHEW

WHEY n watery liquid that separates from the curd when milk is clotted

WHEYEY > WHEY

WHEYFACE n pale bloodless face

WHEYFACED > WHEYFACE

WHEYFACES > WHEYFACE

WHEYIER > WHEY

WHEYIEST > WHEY

WHEYISH > WHEY

WHEYLIKE > WHEY

WHEYS > WHEY

WHICH pron used to request or refer to a choice from different possibilities ▷ adj used with a noun in requesting that a particular thing is further identified or distinguished

WHICHEVER pron any out of several ▷ determiner any (one, two, etc, out of several)

WHICKER vb (of a horse) to whinny or neigh

WHICKERED > WHICKER

WHICKERS > WHICKER

WHID vb move quickly

WHIDAH same as > WHYDAH

WHIDAHS > WHIDAH

WHIDDED > WHID

WHIDDER vb move with force

WHIDDERED > WHIDDER

WHIDDERS > WHIDDER

WHIDDING > WHID

WHIDS > WHID

WHIFF n puff of air or odour ▷ vb come, convey, or go in whiffs

WHIFFED > WHIFF

WHIFFER > WHIFF

WHIFFERS > WHIFF

WHIFFET n insignificant person

WHIFFETS > WHIFFET

WHIFFIER > WHIFFY

WHIFFIEST > WHIFFY

WHIFFING > WHIFF

WHIFFINGS > WHIFF

WHIFFLE vb think or behave in an erratic or unpredictable way

WHIFFLED > WHIFFLE

WHIFFLER n person who whiffles

WHIFFLERS > WHIFFLER

WHIFFLERY n frivolity

WHIFFLES > WHIFFLE

WHIFFLING > WHIFFLE

WHIFFS > WHIFF

WHIFFY adj smelly

WHIFT n brief emission of air

WHIFTS > WHIFT

WHIG vb go quickly

WHIGGED > WHIG

WHIGGING > WHIG

WHIGS > WHIG

WHILE n period of time

WHILED > WHILE

WHILERE adv a while ago

WHILES adv at times

WHILEVER conj as long as

WHILING > WHILE

WHILK archaic and dialect word for > WHICH

WHILLIED > WHILLY

WHILLIES > WHILLY

WHILLY vb influence by flattery

WHILLYING > WHILLY

WHILLYWHA variant of > WHILLY

WHILOM adv formerly ▷ adj one-time

WHILST same as > WHILE

WHIM n sudden fancy ▷ vb have a whim

WHIMBERRY n whortleberry

WHIMBREL n small European curlew with a striped head

WHIMBRELS > WHIMBREL

WHIMMED > WHIM

WHIMMIER > WHIMMY

WHIMMIEST > WHIMMY

WHIMMING > WHIM

WHIMMY adj having whims

WHIMPER vb cry in a soft whining way ▷ n soft plaintive whine

WHIMPERED > WHIMPER

WHIMPERER > WHIMPER

WHIMPERS > WHIMPER

WHIMPLE same as > WIMPLE

WHIMPLED > WHIMPLE

WHIMPLES > WHIMPLE

WHIMPLING > WHIMPLE

WHIMS > WHIM

WHIMSEY same as > WHIMSY

WHIMSEYS > WHIMSEY

WHIMSICAL adj unusual, playful, and fanciful

WHIMSIED > WHIMSY

WHIMSIER > WHIMSY

WHIMSIES > WHIMSY

WHIMSIEST > WHIMSY

WHIMSILY > WHIMSY

WHIMSY n capricious idea ▷ adj quaint, comical, or unusual

WHIN n gorse

WHINBERRY same as > WHIMBERRY

WHINCHAT n type of songbird

WHINCHATS > WHINCHAT

WHINE n high-pitched plaintive cry ▷ vb make such a sound

WHINED > WHINE

WHINER > WHINE

WHINERS > WHINE

WHINES > WHINE

WHINEY same as > WHINY

WHINGDING same as > WINGDING

WHINGE vb complain ▷ n complaint

WHINGED > WHINGE

WHINGEING > WHINGE

WHINGER > WHINGE

WHINGERS > WHINGE

WHINGES > WHINGE

WHINGIER > WHINGY

WHINGIEST > WHINGY

WHINGING > WHINGE

WHINGY adj complaining peevishly, whining

WHINIARD same as > WHINYARD

WHINIARDS > WHINIARD

WHINIER > WHINY

WHINIEST > WHINY

WHININESS > WHINY

WHINING > WHINE

WHININGLY > WHINE

WHININGS > WHINE

WHINNIED > WHINNY

WHINNIER > WHINNY

WHINNIES > WHINNY

WHINNIEST > WHINNY

WHINNY vb neigh softly ▷ n soft neigh ▷ adj covered in whin

WHINNYING > WHINNY

WHINS > WHIN

WHINSTONE n any dark hard fine-grained rock, such as basalt

WHINY adj high-pitched and plaintive

WHINYARD n sword

WHINYARDS > WHINYARD

WHIO n New Zealand mountain duck with blue plumage

WHIOS > WHIO

WHIP n cord attached to a handle, used for beating animals or people ▷ vb strike with a whip, strap, or cane

WHIPBIRD n any of several birds having a whistle ending in a whipcrack note

WHIPBIRDS > WHIPBIRD

WHIPCAT n tailor

WHIPCATS > WHIPCAT

WHIPCORD n strong worsted or cotton fabric with a diagonally ribbed surface

WHIPCORDS > WHIPCORD

WHIPCORDY adj whipcord-like

WHIPCRACK n sound made by a whip

WHIPJACK n beggar imitating a sailor

WHIPJACKS > WHIPJACK

WHIPLASH n quick lash of a whip

WHIPLESS adj without a whip

WHIPLIKE > WHIP

WHIPPED > WHIP

WHIPPER > WHIP

WHIPPERS > WHIP

WHIPPET n racing dog like a small greyhound

WHIPPETS > WHIPPET

WHIPPIER > WHIPPY

WHIPPIEST > WHIPPY

WHIPPING > WHIP

WHIPPINGS > WHIP

WHIPPIT n small canister of nitrous oxide

WHIPPITS > WHIPPIT

WHIPPY adj springy

WHIPRAY n stingray

WHIPRAYS > WHIPRAY

WHIPS > WHIP

WHIPSAW n any saw with a flexible blade, such as a bandsaw ▷ vb saw with a whipsaw

WHIPSAWED > WHIPSAW

WHIPSAWN > WHIPSAW

WHIPSAWS > WHIPSAW

WHIPSNAKE n thin snake like leather whip

WHIPSTAFF n ship's steering bar

WHIPSTALL n stall in which an aircraft goes into a nearly vertical climb, pauses, slips backwards momentarily, and drops suddenly with its nose down

WHIPSTER n insignificant but pretentious or cheeky person, esp a young one

WHIPSTERS > WHIPSTER

WHIPSTOCK n handle of a whip

WHIPT old past tense of > WHIP

WHIPTAIL n type of lizard

WHIPTAILS > WHIPTAIL

WHIPWORM n parasitic worm living in the intestines of mammals

WHIPWORMS > WHIPWORM

WHIR n prolonged soft swish or buzz ▷ vb make or cause to make a whir

WHIRL vb spin or revolve ▷ n whirling movement

WHIRLBAT n thing moved with a whirl

WHIRLBATS > WHIRLBAT

WHIRLED > WHIRL

WHIRLER > WHIRL

WHIRLERS > WHIRL

WHIRLIER > WHIRLY

WHIRLIES pl n illness induced by excessive use of alcohol

WHIRLIEST > WHIRLY

WHIRLIGIG same as > WINDMILL

WHIRLING > WHIRL

WHIRLINGS > WHIRL

WHIRLPOOL n strong circular current of water

WHIRLS > WHIRL

WHIRLWIND n column of air whirling violently upwards in a spiral ▷ adj much quicker than normal

WHIRLY adj characterized by whirling

WHIRR same as > WHIR

WHIRRA interj exclamation of sorrow or deep concern

WHIRRED > WHIR

WHIRRET vb strike with sharp blow

WHIRRETED > WHIRRET

WHIRRETS > WHIRRET

WHIRRIED > WHIRRY

WHIRRIER > WHIRRY

WHIRRIES > WHIRRY

WHIRRIEST > WHIRRY

WHIRRING > WHIR

WHIRRINGS > WHIR

WHIRRS > WHIRR

WHIRRY vb move quickly ▷ adj characteristic of a whir

WHIRRYING > WHIRRY

WHIRS > WHIR

WHIRTLE same as > WORTLE

WHIRTLES > WHIRTLE

WHISH less common word for > SWISH

WHISHED > WHISH

WHISHES > WHISH

WHISHING > WHISH

WHISHT interj hush!, be quiet! ▷ adj silent or still ▷ vb make or become silent

WHISHTED > WHISHT

WHISHTING > WHISHT

WHISHTS > WHISHT

WHISK vb move or remove quickly ▷ n quick movement

WHISKED > WHISK

WHISKER n any of the long stiff hairs on the face of a cat or other mammal

WHISKERED adj having whiskers

WHISKERS > WHISKER

WHISKERY adj having whiskers

WHISKET same as > WISKET

WHISKETS > WHISKET

WHISKEY n Irish or American whisky

WHISKEYS > WHISKEY

WHISKIES > WHISKY

WHISKING > WHISK

WHISKS > WHISK

WHISKY n spirit distilled from fermented cereals

WHISPER vb speak softly, without vibration of the vocal cords ▷ n soft voice

WHISPERED > WHISPER

WHISPERER n person or thing that whispers

WHISPERS > WHISPER

WHISPERY adj like a whisper

WHISS vb hiss

WHISSED > WHISS

WHISSES > WHISS

WHISSING > WHISS

WHIST same as > WHISHT

WHISTED > WHIST

WHISTING > WHIST

WHISTLE vb produce a shrill sound ▷ n whistling sound

WHISTLED > WHISTLE

WHISTLER n person or thing that whistles

WHISTLERS > WHISTLER

WHISTLES > WHISTLE

WHISTLING > WHISTLE

WHISTS > WHIST

WHIT n smallest particle

WHITE adj of the colour of snow ▷ n colour of snow

WHITEBAIT n small edible fish

WHITEBASS n type of fish

WHITEBEAM n type of tree

WHITECAP n wave with a white broken crest

WHITECAPS > WHITECAP

WHITECOAT n person who wears a white coat

WHITECOMB n fungal disease infecting the combs of certain fowls

WHITED adj as in whited sepulchre hypocrite

WHITEDAMP n mixture of poisonous gases, mainly carbon monoxide, occurring in coal mines

WHITEFACE n white stage make-up

WHITEFISH n type of fish

WHITEFLY n tiny whitish insect that is harmful to greenhouse plants

WHITEHEAD n type of pimple with a white head

WHITELIST n list of e-mail contacts from whom messages are regarded as acceptable by the user ▷ vb put (an email contact) on a whitelist

WHITELY > WHITE

WHITEN vb make or become white or whiter

WHITENED > WHITEN

WHITENER n substance that makes something white or whiter

WHITENERS > WHITENER

WHITENESS > WHITE

WHITENING > WHITEN

WHITENS > WHITEN

WHITEOUT n atmospheric condition in which blizzards or low clouds make it very difficult to see

WHITEOUTS > WHITEOUT

WHITEPOT n custard or milk pudding

WHITEPOTS > WHITEPOT

WHITER > WHITE

WHITES pl n white clothes, as worn for playing cricket

WHITEST > WHITE

WHITETAIL n type of deer

WHITEWALL n pneumatic tyre having white sidewalls

WHITEWARE n white ceramics

WHITEWASH n substance for whitening walls ▷ vb cover with whitewash

WHITEWING n type of bird

WHITEWOOD n light-coloured wood often prepared for staining

WHITEY same as > WHITY

WHITEYS > WHITEY

WHITHER same as > WUTHER

WHITHERED > WHITHER

WHITHERS > WHITHER

WHITIER > WHITY

WHITIES > WHITY

WHITIEST > WHITY

WHITING n edible sea fish

WHITINGS > WHITING

WHITISH > WHITE

WHITLING n type of trout

WHITLINGS > WHITLING

WHITLOW n inflamed sore on a finger or toe, esp round a nail

WHITLOWS > WHITLOW

WHITRACK n weasel or stoat

WHITRACKS > WHITRACK

WHITRET same as > WHITTRET

WHITRETS > WHITRET

WHITRICK n dialect word for a male weasel

WHITRICKS > WHITRICK

WHITS > WHIT

WHITSTER n person who whitens clothes

WHITSTERS > WHITSTER

WHITTAW same as > WHITTAWER

WHITTAWER n person who treats leather

WHITTAWS > WHITTAW

WHITTER variant spelling of > WITTER

WHITTERED > WHITTER

WHITTERS > WHITTER

WHITTLE vb cut or carve (wood) with a knife ▷ n knife, esp a large one

WHITTLED > WHITTLE

WHITTLER > WHITTLE

WHITTLERS > WHITTLE

WHITTLES > WHITTLE

WHITTLING > WHITTLE

WHITTRET n male weasel

WHITTRETS > WHITTRET

WHITY adj of a white colour ▷ n derogatory term for a White person

WHIZ same as > WHIZZ

WHIZBANG n small-calibre shell

WHIZBANGS > WHIZBANG

WHIZZ vb make a loud buzzing sound ▷ n loud buzzing sound

WHIZZBANG same as > WHIZBANG

WHIZZED > WHIZZ

WHIZZER > WHIZZ

WHIZZERS > WHIZZ
WHIZZES > WHIZZ
WHIZZIER > WHIZZY
WHIZZIEST > WHIZZY
WHIZZING > WHIZZ
WHIZZINGS > WHIZZ
WHIZZO same as > WHIZZY
WHIZZY adj using sophisticated technology
WHO pron which person
WHOA interj command used to stop or slow down
WHODUNIT same as > WHODUNNIT
WHODUNITS > WHODUNIT
WHODUNNIT n detective story, play, or film
WHOEVER pron any person who
WHOLE adj containing all the elements or parts ▷ n complete thing or system
WHOLEFOOD n food that has been processed as little as possible ▷ adj of or relating to wholefood
WHOLEMEAL adj (of flour) made from the whole wheat grain
WHOLENESS > WHOLE
WHOLES > WHOLE
WHOLESALE adv dealing by selling goods in large quantities to retailers ▷ n business of selling goods in large quantities and at lower prices to retailers for resale
WHOLESOME adj physically or morally beneficial
WHOLISM same as > HOLISM
WHOLISMS > WHOLISM
WHOLIST same as > HOLIST
WHOLISTIC same as > HOLISTIC
WHOLISTS > WHOLIST
WHOLLY adv completely or totally
WHOLPHIN n whale-dolphin hybrid
WHOLPHINS > WHOLPHIN
WHOM pron objective form of who
WHOMBLE same as > WHEMMLE
WHOMBLED > WHOMBLE
WHOMBLES > WHOMBLE
WHOMBLING > WHOMBLE
WHOMEVER pron objective form of whoever
WHOMMLE same as > WHEMMLE
WHOMMLED > WHOMMLE
WHOMMLES > WHOMMLE
WHOMMLING > WHOMMLE
WHOMP vb strike; thump
WHOMPED > WHOMP
WHOMPING > WHOMP
WHOMPS > WHOMP
WHOMSO pron whom; whomever
WHOOBUB same as > HUBBUB
WHOOBUBS > WHOOBUB
WHOOF same as > WOOF
WHOOFED > WHOOF
WHOOFING > WHOOF
WHOOFS > WHOOF

WHOOMP n sudden loud sound
WHOOMPH same as > WHOOMP
WHOOMPHS > WHOOMPH
WHOOMPS > WHOOMP
WHOONGA n narcotic smoked as a recreational drug in S Africa
WHOONGAS > WHOONGA
WHOOP n shout or cry to express excitement ▷ vb emit a whoop
WHOOPED > WHOOP
WHOOPEE n cry of joy
WHOOPEES > WHOOPEE
WHOOPER n type of swan
WHOOPERS > WHOOPER
WHOOPIE same as > WHOOPEE
WHOOPIES > WHOOPIE
WHOOPING > WHOOP
WHOOPINGS > WHOOPING
WHOOPLA n commotion; fuss
WHOOPLAS > WHOOPLA
WHOOPS interj exclamation of surprise or of apology
WHOOPSIE n animal excrement
WHOOPSIES > WHOOPSIE
WHOOSH n hissing or rushing sound ▷ vb make or move with a hissing or rushing sound
WHOOSHED > WHOOSH
WHOOSHES > WHOOSH
WHOOSHING > WHOOSH
WHOOSIS n thingamajig
WHOOSISES > WHOOSIS
WHOOT obsolete variant of > HOOT
WHOOTED > WHOOT
WHOOTING > WHOOT
WHOOTS > WHOOT
WHOP vb strike, beat, or thrash
WHOPPED > WHOP
WHOPPER n anything unusually large
WHOPPERS > WHOPPER
WHOPPING n beating as punishment ▷ adj unusually large ▷ adv extremely
WHOPPINGS > WHOPPING
WHOPS > WHOP
WHORE n old-fashioned word for a prostitute ▷ vb be or act as a prostitute
WHORED > WHORE
WHOREDOM n old-fashioned word for a state of being a prostitute
WHOREDOMS > WHOREDOM
WHORES > WHORE
WHORESON n archaic, derogatory word for a person who is illegitimate by birth ▷ adj vile or hateful
WHORESONS > WHORESON
WHORING n act of whoring
WHORINGS > WHORING
WHORISH > WHORE
WHORISHLY > WHORE
WHORL n ring of leaves or petals ▷ vb form a whorl or whorls
WHORLBAT same as > WHIRLBAT

WHORLBATS > WHORLBAT
WHORLED > WHORL
WHORLING > WHORL
WHORLS > WHORL
WHORT n small shrub bearing blackish edible sweet berries
WHORTLE n whortleberry
WHORTLES > WHORTLE
WHORTS > WHORT
WHOSE pron of whom or of which ▷ determiner of whom or of which
WHOSESO adj possessive form of whoso
WHOSEVER pron belonging to whoever
WHOSIS n thingamajig
WHOSISES > WHOSIS
WHOSIT n object or person whose name is not known
WHOSITS > WHOSIT
WHOSO archaic word for > WHOEVER
WHOSOEVER same as > WHOEVER
WHOT obsolete variant of > HOT
WHOW interj wow ▷ vb to wow
WHOWED > WHOW
WHOWING > WHOW
WHOWS > WHOW
WHUMMLE same as > WHEMMLE
WHUMMLED > WHUMMLE
WHUMMLES > WHUMMLE
WHUMMLING > WHUMMLE
WHUMP vb make a dull thud ▷ n dull thud
WHUMPED > WHUMP
WHUMPING > WHUMP
WHUMPS > WHUMP
WHUNSTANE Scots variant of > WHINSTONE
WHUP vb defeat totally
WHUPPED > WHUP
WHUPPING > WHUP
WHUPPINGS > WHUPPING
WHUPS > WHUP
WHY adv for what reason ▷ pron because of which ▷ n reason, purpose, or cause of something
WHYDA same as > WHYDAH
WHYDAH n type of black African bird
WHYDAHS > WHYDAH
WHYDAS > WHYDA
WHYDUNIT same as > WHYDUNNIT
WHYDUNITS > WHYDUNIT
WHYDUNNIT n novel, film, etc, concerned with the motives of the criminal rather than his or her identity
WHYEVER adv for whatever reason
WHYS > WHY
WIBBLE vb wobble
WIBBLED > WIBBLE
WIBBLES > WIBBLE
WIBBLING > WIBBLE
WICCA n cult or practice of witchcraft
WICCAN n member of wicca
WICCANS > WICCAN
WICCAS > WICCA
WICE Scots form of > WISE
WICH n variant of wych

WICHES > WICH
WICK n cord through a lamp or candle which carries fuel to the flame ▷ adj lively or active ▷ vb (of a material) draw in (water, fuel, etc)
WICKAPE same as > WICOPY
WICKAPES > WICKAPE
WICKED adj morally bad ▷ n wicked person
WICKEDER > WICKED
WICKEDEST > WICKED
WICKEDLY > WICKED
WICKEDS > WICKED
WICKEN same as > QUICKEN
WICKENS > WICKEN
WICKER adj made of woven cane ▷ n slender flexible twig or shoot, esp of willow
WICKERED > WICKER
WICKERS > WICKER
WICKET n set of three cricket stumps and two bails
WICKETS > WICKET
WICKIES > WICKY
WICKING > WICK
WICKINGS > WICK
WICKIUP n crude shelter made of brushwood, mats, or grass and having an oval frame
WICKIUPS > WICKIUP
WICKLESS > WICK
WICKS > WICK
WICKTHING n creeping animal, such as a woodlouse
WICKY same as > QUICKEN
WICKYUP same as > WICKIUP
WICKYUPS > WICKYUP
WICOPIES > WICOPY
WICOPY n any of various North American trees, shrubs, or herbaceous plants
WIDDER same as > WIDOW
WIDDERS > WIDDER
WIDDIE same as > WIDDY
WIDDIES > WIDDY
WIDDLE vb urinate ▷ n urine
WIDDLED > WIDDLE
WIDDLES > WIDDLE
WIDDLING > WIDDLE
WIDDY vb rope made of twigs
WIDE adj large from side to side ▷ adv the full extent ▷ n (in cricket) a ball outside a batsman's reach
WIDEAWAKE n hat with a low crown and a very wide brim
WIDEBAND n wide bandwidth transmission medium ▷ adj capable of transmitting on a wide bandwidth
WIDEBANDS > WIDEBAND
WIDEBODY n aircraft with a wide fuselage
WIDELY > WIDE
WIDEN vb make or become wider
WIDENED > WIDEN
WIDENER > WIDEN
WIDENERS > WIDEN
WIDENESS > WIDE
WIDENING n act of widening
WIDENINGS > WIDENING

W

WIDENS > WIDEN
WIDEOUT n (in American football) player who catches passes from the quarterback
WIDEOUTS > WIDEOUT
WIDER > WIDE
WIDES > WIDE
WIDEST > WIDE
WIDGEON same as **>** WIGEON
WIDGEONS > WIDGEON
WIDGET n any small device, the name of which is unknown or forgotten
WIDGETS > WIDGET
WIDGIE n female larrikin or bodgie
WIDGIES > WIDGIE
WIDISH > WIDE
WIDOW n woman whose spouse is dead and who has not remarried ▷ vb cause to become a widow
WIDOWBIRD n whydah
WIDOWED > WIDOW
WIDOWER n man whose spouse is dead and who has not remarried
WIDOWERED > WIDOWER
WIDOWERS > WIDOWER
WIDOWHOOD > WIDOW
WIDOWING > WIDOW
WIDOWMAN n widower
WIDOWMEN > WIDOWMAN
WIDOWS > WIDOW
WIDTH n distance from side to side
WIDTHS > WIDTH
WIDTHWAY adj across the width
WIDTHWAYS same as **>** WIDTHWISE
WIDTHWISE adv in the direction of the width
WIEL same as **>** WEEL
WIELD vb hold and use (a weapon)
WIELDABLE > WIELD
WIELDED > WIELD
WIELDER > WIELD
WIELDERS > WIELD
WIELDIER > WIELDY
WIELDIEST > WIELDY
WIELDING > WIELD
WIELDLESS adj unwieldy
WIELDS > WIELD
WIELDY adj easily handled, used, or managed
WIELS > WIEL
WIENER n kind of smoked beef or pork sausage, similar to a frankfurter
WIENERS > WIENER
WIENIE same as **>** WIENER
WIENIES > WIENIE
WIFE n woman to whom one is married ▷ vb marry
WIFED > WIFE
WIFEDOM n state of being a wife
WIFEDOMS > WIFEDOM
WIFEHOOD > WIFE
WIFEHOODS > WIFE
WIFELESS > WIFE
WIFELIER > WIFE
WIFELIEST > WIFE
WIFELIKE > WIFE
WIFELY > WIFE

WIFES > WIFE
WIFEY n wife
WIFEYS > WIFEY
WIFIE n woman
WIFIES > WIFIE
WIFING > WIFE
WIFTIER > WIFTY
WIFTIEST > WIFTY
WIFTY adj scatterbrained
WIG n artificial head of hair ▷ vb furnish with a wig
WIGAN n stiff fabric
WIGANS > WIGAN
WIGEON n duck found in marshland
WIGEONS > WIGEON
WIGGA same as **>** WIGGER
WIGGAS > WIGGA
WIGGED > WIG
WIGGER n derogatory term for a White youth who adopts Black youth culture
WIGGERIES > WIGGERY
WIGGERS > WIGGER
WIGGERY n wigs
WIGGIER > WIGGY
WIGGIEST > WIGGY
WIGGING > WIG
WIGGINGS > WIG
WIGGLE vb move jerkily from side to side ▷ n wiggling movement
WIGGLED > WIGGLE
WIGGLER > WIGGLE
WIGGLERS > WIGGLE
WIGGLES > WIGGLE
WIGGLIER > WIGGLE
WIGGLIEST > WIGGLE
WIGGLING > WIGGLE
WIGGLY > WIGGLE
WIGGY adj eccentric
WIGHT vb blame ▷ n human being ▷ adj strong and brave
WIGHTED > WIGHT
WIGHTING > WIGHT
WIGHTLY adv swiftly
WIGHTS > WIGHT
WIGLESS > WIG
WIGLET n small wig
WIGLETS > WIGLET
WIGLIKE > WIG
WIGMAKER n person who makes wigs
WIGMAKERS > WIGMAKER
WIGS > WIG
WIGWAG vb move (something) back and forth ▷ n system of communication by flag semaphore
WIGWAGGED > WIGWAG
WIGWAGGER > WIGWAG
WIGWAGS > WIGWAG
WIGWAM n Native American's tent
WIGWAMS > WIGWAM
WIKI n website consisting mainly of user-generated content
WIKIALITY n version of facts which is agreed to be true, but which may not actually be true
WIKIS > WIKI
WIKIUP same as **>** WICKIUP
WIKIUPS > WIKIUP

WILCO interj expression indicating that the message just received will be complied with
WILD same as **>** WIELD
WILDCARD n person given entry to competition without qualifying
WILDCARDS > WILDCARD
WILDCAT n European wild animal like a large domestic cat ▷ adj risky and financially unsound ▷ vb drill for petroleum or natural gas in an area having no known reserves
WILDCATS > WILDCAT
WILDED > WILD
WILDER vb lead or be led astray
WILDERED > WILDER
WILDERING > WILDER
WILDERS > WILDER
WILDEST > WILD
WILDFIRE n highly flammable material, such as Greek fire, formerly used in warfare
WILDFIRES > WILDFIRE
WILDFOWL n wild bird that is hunted for sport or food
WILDFOWLS > WILDFOWL
WILDGRAVE same as **>** WALDGRAVE
WILDING n uncultivated plant
WILDINGS > WILDING
WILDISH > WILD
WILDLAND n land which has not been cultivated
WILDLANDS > WILDLAND
WILDLIFE n wild animals and plants collectively
WILDLIFES > WILDLIFE
WILDLING same as **>** WILDING
WILDLINGS > WILDLING
WILDLY > WILD
WILDMAN n man who lives in the wild
WILDMEN > WILDMAN
WILDNESS > WILD
WILDS > WILD
WILDWOOD n wood or forest growing in a natural uncultivated state
WILDWOODS > WILDWOOD
WILE n trickery, cunning, or craftiness ▷ vb lure, beguile, or entice
WILED > WILE
WILEFUL adj deceitful
WILES > WILE
WILFUL adj headstrong or obstinate
WILFULLY > WILFUL
WILGA n small drought-resistant tree of Australia
WILGAS > WILGA
WILI n spirit
WILIER > WILY
WILIEST > WILY
WILILY > WILY
WILINESS > WILY
WILING > WILE
WILIS > WILI
WILJA same as **>** WILTJA

WILJAS > WILJA
WILL vb used as an auxiliary to form the future tense or to indicate intention, ability, or expectation ▷ n strong determination
WILLABLE adj able to be wished or determined by the will
WILLED adj having a will as specified
WILLEMITE n secondary mineral consisting of zinc silicate
WILLER > WILL
WILLERS > WILL
WILLEST > WILL
WILLET n large American shore bird
WILLETS > WILLET
WILLEY same as **>** WILLY
WILLEYED > WILLEY
WILLEYING > WILLEY
WILLEYS > WILLEY
WILLFUL same as **>** WILFUL
WILLFULLY > WILLFUL
WILLIAM n as in sweet william flowering plant
WILLIAMS > WILLIAM
WILLIE n informal word for a penis
WILLIED > WILLY
WILLIES > WILLY
WILLING adj ready or inclined (to do something)
WILLINGER > WILLING
WILLINGLY > WILLING
WILLIWAU same as **>** WILLIWAW
WILLIWAUS > WILLIWAU
WILLIWAW n sudden strong gust of cold wind blowing offshore from a mountainous coast
WILLIWAWS > WILLIWAW
WILLOW n tree with thin flexible branches ▷ vb open and clean (fibres) with rotating spikes
WILLOWED > WILLOW
WILLOWER n willow
WILLOWERS > WILLOWER
WILLOWIER > WILLOWY
WILLOWING > WILLOW
WILLOWISH > WILLOW
WILLOWS > WILLOW
WILLOWY adj slender and graceful
WILLPOWER n ability to control oneself and one's actions
WILLS > WILL
WILLY vb clean in a willowing-machine
WILLYARD adj timid
WILLYART same as **>** WILLYARD
WILLYING > WILLY
WILLYWAW same as **>** WILLIWAW
WILLYWAWS > WILLYWAW
WILT vb (cause to) become limp or lose strength ▷ n act of wilting or state of becoming wilted
WILTED > WILT
WILTING > WILT

WILTJA n Aboriginal shelter
WILTJAS >WILTJA
WILTS >WILT
WILY adj crafty or sly
WIMBLE n any of a number of hand tools used for boring holes ▷ vb bore (a hole) with or as if with a wimble
WIMBLED >WIMBLE
WIMBLES >WIMBLE
WIMBLING >WIMBLE
WIMBREL same as >WHIMBREL
WIMBRELS >WIMBREL
WIMMIN n common intentional misspelling of 'women'
WIMP n feeble ineffectual person ▷ vb as in wimp out fail to complete something through fear
WIMPED >WIMP
WIMPIER >WIMP
WIMPIEST >WIMP
WIMPINESS >WIMP
WIMPING >WIMP
WIMPISH >WIMP
WIMPISHLY >WIMP
WIMPLE n garment framing the face, worn by medieval women and now by nuns ▷ vb ripple or cause to ripple or undulate
WIMPLED >WIMPLE
WIMPLES >WIMPLE
WIMPLING >WIMPLE
WIMPS >WIMP
WIMPY >WIMP
WIN vb come first in (a competition, fight, etc) ▷ n victory, esp in a game
WINCE vb draw back, as if in pain ▷ n wincing
WINCED >WINCE
WINCER >WINCE
WINCERS >WINCE
WINCES >WINCE
WINCEY n plain- or twill-weave cloth
WINCEYS >WINCEY
WINCH n machine for lifting or hauling using a cable or chain wound round a drum ▷ vb lift or haul using a winch
WINCHED >WINCH
WINCHER >WINCH
WINCHERS >WINCH
WINCHES >WINCH
WINCHING >WINCH
WINCHMAN n man who operates winch
WINCHMEN >WINCHMAN
WINCING >WINCE
WINCINGLY adv while wincing or in a wincing manner
WINCINGS >WINCE
WINCOPIPE n type of plant
WIND n current of air ▷ vb render short of breath
WINDABLE n able to be wound
WINDAC same as >WINDAS
WINDACS >WINDAC
WINDAGE n deflection of a projectile as a result of the effect of the wind

WINDAGES >WINDAGE
WINDAS n windlass
WINDASES >WINDAS
WINDBAG n person who talks much but uninterestingly
WINDBAGS >WINDBAG
WINDBELL n light bell made to be sounded by wind
WINDBELLS >WINDBELL
WINDBILL n bill of exchange cosigned by a guarantor
WINDBILLS >WINDBILL
WINDBLAST n strong gust of wind
WINDBLOW n trees uprooted by wind
WINDBLOWN adj blown about by the wind
WINDBLOWS >WINDBLOW
WINDBORNE adj (of plant seeds, etc) borne on the wind
WINDBOUND adj (of a sailing vessel) prevented from sailing by an unfavourable wind
WINDBREAK n fence or line of trees providing shelter from the wind
WINDBURN n irritation and redness of the skin caused by exposure to wind
WINDBURNS >WINDBURN
WINDBURNT >WINDBURN
WINDCHILL n chilling effect of wind and low temperature
WINDED >WIND
WINDER n person or device that winds, as an engine for hoisting the cages in a mine shaft
WINDERS >WINDER
WINDFALL n unexpected good luck
WINDFALLS >WINDFALL
WINDFLAW n squall
WINDFLAWS >WINDFLAW
WINDGALL n soft swelling in the area of the fetlock joint of a horse
WINDGALLS >WINDGALL
WINDGUN n air gun
WINDGUNS >WINDGUN
WINDHOVER dialect name for >KESTREL
WINDIER >WINDY
WINDIEST >WINDY
WINDIGO same as >WENDIGO
WINDIGOES >WINDIGO
WINDIGOS >WINDIGO
WINDILY >WINDY
WINDINESS >WINDY
WINDING >WIND
WINDINGLY >WINDING
WINDINGS >WIND
WINDLASS n winch worked by a crank ▷ vb raise or haul (a weight, etc) by means of a windlass
WINDLE vb wind something round continuously
WINDLED >WINDLE
WINDLES >WINDLE
WINDLESS >WIND
WINDLING >WINDLE
WINDLINGS >WINDLE

WINDLOAD n force on a structure from wind
WINDLOADS >WINDLOAD
WINDMILL n machine for grinding or pumping driven by sails turned by the wind ▷ vb move or cause to move like the arms of a windmill
WINDMILLS >WINDMILL
WINDOCK same as >WINNOCK
WINDOCKS >WINDOCK
WINDORE n window
WINDORES >WINDORE
WINDOW n opening in a wall to let in light or air ▷ vb furnish with windows
WINDOWED >WINDOW
WINDOWIER >WINDOWY
WINDOWING >WINDOW
WINDOWS >WINDOW
WINDOWY adj having many windows
WINDPACK n snow that has been compacted by the wind
WINDPACKS >WINDPACK
WINDPIPE n tube linking the throat and the lungs
WINDPIPES >WINDPIPE
WINDPROOF adj not penetrable by wind ▷ vb make windproof
WINDRING adj winding
WINDROW n long low ridge or line of hay or a similar crop ▷ vb put (hay or a similar crop) into windrows
WINDROWED >WINDROW
WINDROWER >WINDROW
WINDROWS >WINDROW
WINDS >WIND
WINDSAIL n sail rigged as an air scoop over a hatch or companionway
WINDSAILS >WINDSAIL
WINDSES pl n ventilation shafts within mines
WINDSHAKE n crack between the annual rings in wood
WINDSHIP n ship propelled by wind
WINDSHIPS >WINDSHIP
WINDSLAB n crust formed on soft snow by the wind
WINDSLABS >WINDSLAB
WINDSOCK n cloth cone on a mast at an airfield to indicate wind direction
WINDSOCKS >WINDSOCK
WINDSTORM n storm consisting of violent winds
WINDSURF vb sail standing on a board equipped with a mast, sail, and boom
WINDSURFS >WINDSURF
WINDSWEPT adj exposed to the wind
WINDTHROW n uprooting of trees by wind
WINDTIGHT adj impenetrable by wind
WINDUP n prank or hoax
WINDUPS >WINDUP
WINDWARD n direction from which the wind is blowing ▷ adj of or in the direction from which the wind blows ▷ adv towards the wind

WINDWARDS adv in the direction of the wind
WINDWAY n part of wind instrument
WINDWAYS >WINDWAY
WINDY adj denoting a time or conditions in which there is a strong wind
WINE n alcoholic drink made from fermented grapes ▷ adj of a dark purplish-red colour ▷ vb give wine to
WINEBERRY another name for >MAKO
WINED >WINE
WINEGLASS n glass for wine, usually with a small bowl on a stem with a flared base
WINELESS >WINE
WINEMAKER n maker of wine
WINEPRESS n any equipment used for squeezing the juice from grapes in order to make wine
WINERIES >WINERY
WINERY n place where wine is made
WINES >WINE
WINESAP n variety of apple
WINESAPS >WINESAP
WINESHOP n shop where wine is sold
WINESHOPS >WINESHOP
WINESKIN n skin of a sheep or goat sewn up and used as a holder for wine
WINESKINS >WINESKIN
WINESOP n old word for an alcoholic
WINESOPS >WINESOP
WINEY adj having the taste or qualities of wine
WING n one of the limbs or organs of a bird, insect, or bat that are used for flying ▷ vb fly
WINGBACK n football position
WINGBACKS >WINGBACK
WINGBEAT n complete cycle of moving the wing by a bird in flight
WINGBEATS >WINGBEAT
WINGBOW n distinctive band of colour marking the wing of a bird
WINGBOWS >WINGBOW
WINGCHAIR n chair with forward projections from back
WINGDING n noisy lively party or festivity
WINGDINGS >WINGDING
WINGE same as >WHINGE
WINGED adj furnished with wings
WINGEDLY >WINGED
WINGEING >WINGE
WINGER n player positioned on a wing
WINGERS >WINGER
WINGES >WINGE
WINGIER >WINGY
WINGIEST >WINGY
WINGING >WING

W

WINGLESS adj having no wings or vestigial wings

WINGLET n small wing

WINGLETS > WINGLET

WINGLIKE > WING

WINGMAN n player in the wing position in Australian Rules

WINGMEN > WINGMAN

WINGNUT n nut with projections for gripping with the thumb and finger

WINGNUTS > WINGNUT

WINGOVER n manoeuvre for reversing the direction of flight of an aircraft

WINGOVERS > WINGOVER

WINGS > WING

WINGSPAN n distance between the wing tips of an aircraft, bird, or insect

WINGSPANS > WINGSPAN

WINGSUIT n type of skydiving suit

WINGSUITS > WINGSUIT

WINGTIP n outermost edge of a wing

WINGTIPS > WINGTIP

WINGY adj having wings

WINIER > WINY

WINIEST > WINY

WINING > WINE

WINISH > WINE

WINK vb close and open (an eye) quickly as a signal ▷ n winking

WINKED > WINK

WINKER n person or thing that winks

WINKERS > WINKER

WINKING > WINK

WINKINGLY > WINK

WINKINGS > WINK

WINKLE n shellfish with a spiral shell ▷ vb extract or prise out

WINKLED > WINKLE

WINKLER n one who forces a person or thing out

WINKLERS > WINKLER

WINKLES > WINKLE

WINKLING > WINKLE

WINKS > WINK

WINLESS adj not having won anything

WINN n penny

WINNA vb will not

WINNABLE > WIN

WINNARD n heron

WINNARDS > WINNARD

WINNED > WIN

WINNER n person or thing that wins

WINNERS > WINNER

WINNING adj (of a person) charming, attractive, etc

WINNINGLY > WINNING

WINNINGS > WIN

WINNLE n machine for winding thread or yarn

WINNLES > WINNLE

WINNOCK n window

WINNOCKS > WINNOCK

WINNOW vb separate (chaff) from (grain) ▷ n device for winnowing

WINNOWED > WINNOW

WINNOWER > WINNOW

WINNOWERS > WINNOW

WINNOWING > WINNOW

WINNOWS > WINNOW

WINNS > WINN

WINO n destitute person who habitually drinks cheap wine

WINOES > WINO

WINOS > WINO

WINS > WIN

WINSEY same as > WINCEY

WINSEYS > WINSEY

WINSOME adj charming or winning

WINSOMELY > WINSOME

WINSOMER > WINSOME

WINSOMEST > WINSOME

WINTER n coldest season ▷ vb spend the winter

WINTERED > WINTER

WINTERER > WINTER

WINTERERS > WINTER

WINTERFED vb past tense of 'winterfeed' (to feed (livestock) in winter when the grazing is not rich enough)

WINTERIER > WINTERY

WINTERING > WINTER

WINTERISE same as > WINTERIZE

WINTERISH > WINTER

WINTERIZE vb prepare (a house, car, etc) to withstand winter conditions

WINTERLY adj like winter

WINTERS > WINTER

WINTERY same as > WINTRY

WINTLE vb reel; stagger

WINTLED > WINTLE

WINTLES > WINTLE

WINTLING > WINTLE

WINTRIER > WINTRY

WINTRIEST > WINTRY

WINTRILY > WINTRY

WINTRY adj of or like winter

WINY same as > WINEY

WINZE n steeply inclined shaft, as for ventilation between levels

WINZES > WINZE

WIPE vb clean or dry by rubbing ▷ n act of wiping

WIPEABLE adj able to be wiped

WIPED > WIPE

WIPEOUT n instance of wiping out

WIPEOUTS > WIPEOUT

WIPER n any piece of cloth, such as a handkerchief, towel, etc, used for wiping

WIPERS > WIPER

WIPES > WIPE

WIPING > WIPE

WIPINGS > WIPE

WIPPEN n part of hammer action in piano

WIPPENS > WIPPEN

WIRABLE adj that can be wired

WIRE n thin flexible strand of metal ▷ vb fasten with wire

WIRED adj excited or nervous

WIREDRAW vb convert (metal) into wire by drawing through successively smaller dies

WIREDRAWN > WIREDRAW

WIREDRAWS > WIREDRAW

WIREDREW > WIREDRAW

WIREFRAME n visual representation of the structure of a web page

WIREGRASS n fine variety of grass

WIREHAIR n type of terrier

WIREHAIRS > WIREHAIR

WIRELESS adj (of a computer network) connected by radio rather than by cables or fibre optics ▷ n old-fashioned name for radio ▷ vb send by wireless

WIRELIKE > WIRE

WIRELINE n telegraph or telephone line

WIRELINES > WIRELINE

WIREMAN n person who installs and maintains electric wiring, cables, etc

WIREMEN > WIREMAN

WIREPHOTO n facsimile of a photograph transmitted electronically via a telephone system

WIRER n person who sets or uses wires to snare rabbits and similar animals

WIRERS > WIRER

WIRES > WIRE

WIRETAP vb obtain information secretly via telegraph or telephone

WIRETAPS > WIRETAP

WIREWAY n tube for electric wires

WIREWAYS > WIREWAY

WIREWORK n functional or decorative work made of wire

WIREWORKS n factory where wire or articles of wire are made

WIREWORM n destructive wormlike beetle larva

WIREWORMS > WIREWORM

WIREWOVE adj woven out of wire

WIRIER > WIRY

WIRIEST > WIRY

WIRILDA n SE Australian acacia tree with edible seeds

WIRILDAS > WIRILDA

WIRILY > WIRY

WIRINESS > WIRY

WIRING n system of wires ▷ adj used in wiring

WIRINGS > WIRING

WIRRA interj exclamation of sorrow or deep concern

WIRRAH n Australian saltwater fish with bright blue spots

WIRRAHS > WIRRAH

WIRRICOW same as > WORRICOW

WIRRICOWS > WIRRICOW

WIRY adj lean and tough

WIS vb know or suppose (something)

WISARD obsolete spelling of > WIZARD

WISARDS > WISARD

WISDOM n good sense and judgment

WISDOMS > WISDOM

WISE vb guide ▷ adj having wisdom ▷ n manner

WISEACRE n person who wishes to seem wise

WISEACRES > WISEACRE

WISEASS n person who thinks he or she is being witty or clever

WISEASSES > WISEASS

WISECRACK n clever, sometimes unkind, remark ▷ vb make a wisecrack

WISED > WISE

WISEGUY n person who wants to seem clever

WISEGUYS > WISEGUY

WISELIER > WISE

WISELIEST > WISE

WISELING n one who claims to be wise

WISELINGS > WISELING

WISELY > WISE

WISENESS > WISE

WISENT n European bison

WISENTS > WISENT

WISER > WISE

WISES > WISE

WISEST > WISE

WISEWOMAN n witch

WISEWOMEN > WISEWOMAN

WISH vb want or desire ▷ n expression of a desire

WISHA interj expression of surprise

WISHBONE n V-shaped bone above the breastbone of a fowl

WISHBONES > WISHBONE

WISHED > WISH

WISHER > WISH

WISHERS > WISH

WISHES > WISH

WISHFUL adj too optimistic

WISHFULLY > WISHFUL

WISHING > WISH

WISHINGS > WISH

WISHLESS > WISH

WISHT variant of > WHISHT

WISING > WISE

WISKET n basket

WISKETS > WISKET

WISP n light delicate streak ▷ vb move or act like a wisp

WISPED > WISP

WISPIER > WISPY

WISPIEST > WISPY

WISPILY > WISPY

WISPINESS > WISPY

WISPING > WISP

WISPISH > WISP

WISPLIKE > WISP

WISPS > WISP

WISPY adj thin, fine, or delicate

WISS vb urinate

WISSED > WIS

WISSES > WIS

WISSING > WIS

WIST vb know

WISTARIA same as > WISTERIA

WISTARIAS > WISTARIA

WISTED > WIST

WISTERIA n climbing shrub with blue or purple flowers

WISTERIAS > WISTERIA
WISTFUL adj sadly longing
WISTFULLY > WISTFUL
WISTING > WIST
WISTITI n marmoset
WISTITIS > WISTITI
WISTLY adv intently
WISTS > WIST
WIT vb detect ▷ n ability to use words or ideas in a clever and amusing way
WITAN n Anglo-Saxon assembly that met to counsel the king
WITANS > WITAN
WITBLITS n illegally distilled strong alcoholic drink
WITCH n person, usu female, who practises (black) magic ▷ vb cause or change by or as if by witchcraft
WITCHED > WITCH
WITCHEN n rowan tree
WITCHENS > WITCHEN
WITCHERY n practice of witchcraft
WITCHES > WITCH
WITCHETTY n edible larva of certain Australian moths and beetles
WITCHHOOD > WITCH
WITCHIER > WITCHY
WITCHIEST > WITCHY
WITCHING adj relating to or appropriate for witchcraft ▷ n witchcraft
WITCHINGS > WITCHING
WITCHKNOT n knot in hair
WITCHLIKE > WITCH
WITCHWEED n type of plant that is a serious pest of grain crops in parts of Africa and Asia
WITCHY adj like a witch
WITE vb blame
WITED > WITE
WITELESS adj witless
WITES > WITE
WITGAT n type of S African tree
WITGATS > WITGAT
WITH prep indicating presence alongside, possession, means of performance, characteristic manner, etc ▷ n division between flues in chimney
WITHAL adv as well
WITHDRAW vb take or move out or away
WITHDRAWN adj unsociable
WITHDRAWS > WITHDRAW
WITHDREW past tense of > WITHDRAW
WITHE n strong flexible twig suitable for binding things together ▷ vb bind with withes
WITHED > WITHE
WITHER vb wilt or dry up
WITHERED > WITHER
WITHERER > WITHER
WITHERS > WITHER
WITHERING > WITHER
WITHERITE n white, grey, or yellowish mineral

WITHEROD n American shrub
WITHERODS > WITHEROD
WITHERS pl n ridge between a horse's shoulder blades
WITHES > WITHE
WITHHAULT > WITHHOLD
WITHHELD > WITHHOLD
WITHHOLD vb refrain from giving
WITHHOLDS > WITHHOLD
WITHIER > WITHY
WITHIES > WITHY
WITHIEST > WITHY
WITHIN adv in or inside ▷ prep in or inside ▷ n something that is within
WITHING > WITHE
WITHINS > WITHIN
WITHOUT prep not accompanied by, using, or having ▷ adv outside ▷ n person who is without
WITHOUTEN obsolete form of > WITHOUT
WITHOUTS > WITHOUT
WITHS > WITH
WITHSTAND vb oppose or resist successfully
WITHSTOOD > WITHSTAND
WITHWIND n bindweed
WITHWINDS > WITHWIND
WITHY n willow tree, esp an osier ▷ adj (of people) tough and agile
WITHYWIND same as > WITHWIND
WITING > WITE
WITLESS adj foolish
WITLESSLY > WITLESS
WITLING n person who thinks themself witty
WITLINGS > WITLING
WITLOOF n chicory
WITLOOFS > WITLOOF
WITNESS n person who has seen something happen ▷ vb see at first hand
WITNESSED > WITNESS
WITNESSER > WITNESS
WITNESSES > WITNESS
WITNEY n type of blanket; heavy cloth
WITNEYS > WITNEY
WITS > WIT
WITTED adj having wit
WITTER vb chatter pointlessly or at unnecessary length ▷ n pointless chat
WITTERED > WITTER
WITTERING > WITTER
WITTERS > WITTER
WITTICISM n witty remark
WITTIER > WITTY
WITTIEST > WITTY
WITTILY > WITTY
WITTINESS > WITTY
WITTING adj deliberate ▷ n act of becoming aware
WITTINGLY > WITTING
WITTINGS > WITTING
WITTOL n man who tolerates his wife's unfaithfulness
WITTOLLY > WITTOL
WITTOLS > WITTOL

WITTY adj clever and amusing
WITWALL n golden oriole
WITWALLS > WITWALL
WITWANTON vb be disrespectfully witty
WIVE vb marry (a woman)
WIVED > WIVE
WIVEHOOD obsolete variant of > WIFEHOOD
WIVEHOODS > WIVEHOOD
WIVER another word for > WIVERN
WIVERN same as > WYVERN
WIVERNS > WIVERN
WIVERS > WIVER
WIVES > WIFE
WIVING > WIVE
WIZ shortened form of > WIZARD
WIZARD n magician ▷ adj superb
WIZARDER > WIZARD
WIZARDEST > WIZARD
WIZARDLY adj like a wizard
WIZARDRY n magic or sorcery
WIZARDS > WIZARD
WIZEN vb make or become shrivelled ▷ n archaic word for 'weasand' (the gullet) ▷ adj wizened
WIZENED adj shrivelled or wrinkled
WIZENER > WIZEN
WIZENEST > WIZEN
WIZENING > WIZEN
WIZENS > WIZEN
WIZES > WIZ
WIZIER same as > VIZIER
WIZIERS > WIZIER
WIZZEN same as > WIZEN
WIZZENS > WIZZEN
WIZZES > WIZ
WO archaic spelling of > WOE
WOAD n blue dye obtained from a plant
WOADED adj coloured blue with woad
WOADS > WOAD
WOADWAX n small Eurasian leguminous shrub
WOADWAXEN n small leguminous shrub with yellow flowers producing a yellow dye
WOADWAXES > WOADWAX
WOAH same as > WHOA
WOALD same as > WELD
WOALDS > WOALD
WOBBEGONG n Australian shark with brown-and-white skin
WOBBLE vb move unsteadily ▷ n wobbling movement or sound
WOBBLED > WOBBLE
WOBBLER > WOBBLE
WOBBLERS > WOBBLE
WOBBLES > WOBBLE
WOBBLIER > WOBBLY
WOBBLIES > WOBBLY
WOBBLIEST > WOBBLY
WOBBLING > WOBBLE
WOBBLINGS > WOBBLE
WOBBLY adj unsteady ▷ n temper tantrum

WOBEGONE same as > WOEBEGONE
WOCK same as > WOK
WOCKS > WOCK
WODGE n thick lump or chunk
WODGES > WODGE
WOE n grief
WOEBEGONE adj looking miserable
WOEFUL adj extremely sad
WOEFULLER > WOEFUL
WOEFULLY > WOEFUL
WOENESS > WOE
WOENESSES > WOE
WOES > WOE
WOESOME adj woeful
WOF n fool
WOFS > WOF
WOFUL same as > WOEFUL
WOFULLER > WOFUL
WOFULLEST > WOFUL
WOFULLY > WOFUL
WOFULNESS > WOFUL
WOG n offensive word for a foreigner, esp one who is not White ▷ n Australian slang word for any flu-like illness
WOGGISH > WOG
WOGGLE n ring of leather through which a Scout neckerchief is threaded
WOGGLES > WOGGLE
WOGS > WOG
WOIWODE same as > VOIVODE
WOIWODES > WOIWODE
WOJUS adj (Irish) of a poor quality
WOK n bowl-shaped Chinese cooking pan, used for stir-frying
WOKE adj alert to social and political injustice
WOKEN > WAKE
WOKER > WOKE
WOKEST > WOKE
WOKKA modifier as in wokka board piece of fibreboard used as a musical instrument
WOKS > WOK
WOLD same as > WELD
WOLDS > WOLD
WOLF n wild predatory canine mammal ▷ vb eat ravenously
WOLFBERRY n type of shrub
WOLFED > WOLF
WOLFER same as > WOLVER
WOLFERS > WOLF
WOLFFISH n type of large northern deep-sea fish with large sharp teeth
WOLFHOUND n very large breed of dog
WOLFING > WOLF
WOLFINGS > WOLF
WOLFISH > WOLF
WOLFISHLY > WOLF
WOLFKIN n young wolf
WOLFKINS > WOLFKIN
WOLFLIKE > WOLF
WOLFLING n young wolf
WOLFLINGS > WOLFLING
WOLFRAM another name for > TUNGSTEN
WOLFRAMS > WOLFRAM
WOLFS > WOLF

w

WOLFSBANE n type of poisonous plant with yellow hoodlike flowers
WOLFSKIN n skin of wolf used for clothing, etc
WOLFSKINS > WOLFSKIN
WOLLIES > WOLLY
WOLLY n pickled cucumber or olive
WOLVE vb hunt for wolves
WOLVED > WOLVE
WOLVER n person who hunts wolves
WOLVERENE same as > WOLVERINE
WOLVERINE n carnivorous mammal of Arctic regions
WOLVERS > WOLVER
WOLVES > WOLF
WOLVING > WOLVE
WOLVINGS > WOLVE
WOLVISH same as > WOLFISH
WOLVISHLY > WOLVISH
WOMAN n adult human female ▷ adj female ▷ vb provide with a woman or women
WOMANED > WOMAN
WOMANHOOD n state of being a woman
WOMANING > WOMAN
WOMANISE same as > WOMANIZE
WOMANISED > WOMANISE
WOMANISER > WOMANISE
WOMANISES > WOMANISE
WOMANISH adj effeminate
WOMANISM n feminism among Black women
WOMANISMS > WOMANISM
WOMANIST > WOMANISM
WOMANISTS > WOMANISM
WOMANIZE vb (of a man) to indulge in many casual affairs with women
WOMANIZED > WOMANIZE
WOMANIZER > WOMANIZE
WOMANIZES > WOMANIZE
WOMANKIND n all women considered as a group
WOMANLESS > WOMAN
WOMANLIER > WOMANLY
WOMANLIKE adj like a woman
WOMANLY adj having qualities traditionally associated with a woman
WOMANNED > WOMAN
WOMANNESS > WOMAN
WOMANNING > WOMAN
WOMANS > WOMAN
WOMB vb enclose ▷ n hollow organ in female mammals where babies develop
WOMBAT n small heavily built burrowing Australian marsupial
WOMBATS > WOMBAT
WOMBED > WOMB
WOMBIER > WOMBY
WOMBIEST > WOMBY
WOMBING > WOMB
WOMBLIKE > WOMB
WOMBS > WOMB
WOMBY adj hollow; spacious
WOMEN > WOMAN
WOMENFOLK pl n women collectively

WOMENKIND same as > WOMANKIND
WOMERA same as > WOOMERA
WOMERAS > WOMERA
WOMMERA same as > WOOMERA
WOMMERAS > WOMMERA
WOMMIT n foolish person
WOMMITS > WOMMIT
WOMYN same as > WOMAN
WON n standard monetary unit of North Korea ▷ vb live or dwell
WONDER vb be curious about ▷ n wonderful thing ▷ adj spectacularly successful
WONDERED > WONDER
WONDERER > WONDER
WONDERERS > WONDER
WONDERFUL adj very fine
WONDERING > WONDER
WONDERKID n informal word for an exceptionally successful young person
WONDEROUS obsolete variant of > WONDROUS
WONDERS > WONDER
WONDRED adj splendid
WONDROUS adj wonderful
WONGA n money
WONGAS > WONGA
WONGI vb talk informally
WONGIED > WONGI
WONGIING > WONGI
WONGIS > WONGI
WONING > WON
WONINGS > WON
WONK n person who is obsessively interested in a specified subject
WONKERIES > WONKERY
WONKERY n activities of a wonk
WONKIER > WONKY
WONKIEST > WONKY
WONKILY adv in a wonky manner
WONKINESS n state of being wonky
WONKISH adj like a wonk
WONKS > WONK
WONKY adj shaky or unsteady
WONNED > WON
WONNER > WON
WONNERS > WON
WONNING > WON
WONNINGS > WON
WONS > WON
WONT adj accustomed ▷ n custom ▷ vb become or cause to become accustomed
WONTED adj accustomed or habituated (to doing something)
WONTEDLY > WONTED
WONTING > WONT
WONTLESS > WONT
WONTON n dumpling filled with spiced minced pork
WONTONS > WONTON
WONTS > WONT
WOO vb seek the love or affection of
WOOABLE adj able to be wooed
WOOBUT same as > WOUBIT

WOOBUTS > WOOBUT
WOOD n substance trees are made of, used in carpentry and as fuel ▷ adj made of or using wood ▷ vb (of land) plant with trees
WOODBIN n box for firewood
WOODBIND same as > WOODBINE
WOODBINDS > WOODBIND
WOODBINE n honeysuckle
WOODBINES > WOODBINE
WOODBINS > WOODBIN
WOODBLOCK n hollow block of wood used as a percussion instrument
WOODBORER n type of beetle whose larvae bore into and damage wood
WOODBOX n box for firewood
WOODBOXES > WOODBOX
WOODCHAT n European and N African songbird
WOODCHATS > WOODCHAT
WOODCHIP n textured wallpaper
WOODCHIPS > WOODCHIP
WOODCHOP n wood-chopping competition, esp at a show
WOODCHOPS > WOODCHOP
WOODCHUCK n N American marmot with coarse reddish-brown fur
WOODCOCK n game bird
WOODCOCKS > WOODCOCK
WOODCRAFT n ability and experience in matters concerned with living in a wood or forest
WOODCUT n (print made from) an engraved block of wood
WOODCUTS > WOODCUT
WOODED adj covered with trees
WOODEN adj made of wood ▷ vb fell or kill (a person or animal)
WOODENED > WOODEN
WOODENER > WOODEN
WOODENEST > WOODEN
WOODENING > WOODEN
WOODENLY > WOODEN
WOODENS > WOODEN
WOODENTOP n dull, foolish, or unintelligent person
WOODFERN n type of evergreen fern
WOODFERNS > WOODFERN
WOODFREE adj (of paper) made from pulp that has been treated to remove impurities
WOODGRAIN n grain in wood
WOODHEN another name for > WEKA
WOODHENS > WOODHEN
WOODHOLE n store area for wood
WOODHOLES > WOODHOLE
WOODHORSE n frame for holding wood being sawn
WOODHOUSE n shed for firewood
WOODIE n gallows rope
WOODIER > WOODY
WOODIES > WOODIE

WOODIEST > WOODY
WOODINESS > WOODY
WOODING > WOOD
WOODLAND n forest ▷ adj living in woods
WOODLANDS > WOODLAND
WOODLARK n type of Old World lark
WOODLARKS > WOODLARK
WOODLESS > WOOD
WOODLICE > WOODLOUSE
WOODLORE n woodcraft skills
WOODLORES > WOODLORE
WOODLOT n area restricted to the growing of trees
WOODLOTS > WOODLOT
WOODLOUSE n small insect-like creature with many legs
WOODMAN same as > WOODSMAN
WOODMEAL n sawdust powder
WOODMEALS > WOODMEAL
WOODMEN > WOODMAN
WOODMICE > WOODMOUSE
WOODMOUSE n field mouse
WOODNESS > WOOD
WOODNOTE n natural musical note or song, like that of a wild bird
WOODNOTES > WOODNOTE
WOODPILE n heap of firewood
WOODPILES > WOODPILE
WOODPRINT another name for > WOODCUT
WOODRAT n pack-rat
WOODRATS > WOODRAT
WOODREEVE n steward responsible for wood
WOODROOF same as > WOODRUFF
WOODROOFS > WOODROOF
WOODRUFF n plant with small sweet-smelling white flowers and sweet-smelling leaves
WOODRUFFS > WOODRUFF
WOODRUSH n plant with grasslike leaves and small brown flowers
WOODS pl n closely packed trees forming a forest or wood
WOODSCREW n metal screw that tapers to a point so that it can be driven into wood by a screwdriver
WOODSHED n small outbuilding where firewood, garden tools, etc, are stored
WOODSHEDS > WOODSHED
WOODSHOCK n type of bird
WOODSIA n type of small fern with tufted rhizomes and wiry fronds
WOODSIAS > WOODSIA
WOODSIER > WOODSY
WOODSIEST > WOODSY
WOODSKIN n canoe made of bark
WOODSKINS > WOODSKIN
WOODSMAN n person who lives in a wood or who is skilled at woodwork or carving

w

WOODSMEN > WOODSMAN

WOODSMOKE n smoke produced by burning wood

WOODSPITE n green woodpecker

WOODSTONE n type of stone resembling wood

WOODSTOVE n wood-burning stove

WOODSY adj of, reminiscent of, or connected with woods

WOODTONE n colour matching that of wood

WOODTONES > WOODTONE

WOODWALE n green woodpecker

WOODWALES > WOODWALE

WOODWARD n person in charge of a forest or wood

WOODWARDS > WOODWARD

WOODWASP n large wasplike insect

WOODWASPS > WOODWASP

WOODWAX same as > WOODWAXEN

WOODWAXEN same as > WOADWAXEN

WOODWAXES > WOODWAX

WOODWIND n type of wind instrument made of wood ▷ adj of or denoting a type of wind instrument, such as the oboe

WOODWINDS > WOODWIND

WOODWORK n parts of a room or building made of wood

WOODWORKS > WOODWORK

WOODWORM n insect larva that bores into wood

WOODWORMS > WOODWORM

WOODWOSE n hairy wildman of the woods

WOODWOSES > WOODWOSE

WOODY adj (of a plant) having a very hard stem

WOODYARD n place where timber is cut and stored

WOODYARDS > WOODYARD

WOOED > WOO

WOOER > WOO

WOOERS > WOO

WOOF vb (of dogs) bark

WOOFED > WOOF

WOOFER n loudspeaker reproducing low-frequency sounds

WOOFERS > WOOFER

WOOFIER > WOOFY

WOOFIEST > WOOFY

WOOFING > WOOF

WOOFS > WOOF

WOOFTAH same as > WOOFTER

WOOFTAHS > WOOFTAH

WOOFTER n offensive term for a homosexual man

WOOFTERS > WOOFTER

WOOFY adj with close, dense texture

WOOHOO interj expression of joy, approval, etc

WOOING > WOO

WOOINGLY > WOO

WOOINGS > WOO

WOOL n soft hair of sheep, goats, etc

WOOLD vb wind (rope)

WOOLDED > WOOLD

WOOLDER n stick for winding rope

WOOLDERS > WOOLDER

WOOLDING > WOOLD

WOOLDINGS > WOOLD

WOOLDS > WOOLD

WOOLED same as > WOOLLED

WOOLEN same as > WOOLLEN

WOOLENS > WOOLEN

WOOLER same as > WOOLDER

WOOLERS > WOOLER

WOOLFAT same as > LANOLIN

WOOLFATS > WOOLFAT

WOOLFELL n skin of a sheep or similar animal with the fleece still attached

WOOLFELLS > WOOLFELL

WOOLHAT n hat made of wool

WOOLHATS > WOOLHAT

WOOLIE n wool garment

WOOLIER > WOOLY

WOOLIES > WOOLY

WOOLIEST > WOOLY

WOOLILY > WOOLY

WOOLINESS > WOOLY

WOOLLED adj (of animals) having wool

WOOLLEN adj relating to or consisting partly or wholly of wool ▷ n garment or piece of cloth made of wool

WOOLLENS > WOOLLEN

WOOLLIER > WOOLLY

WOOLLIES > WOOLLY

WOOLLIEST > WOOLLY

WOOLLIKE > WOOL

WOOLLILY > WOOLLY

WOOLLY adj of or like wool ▷ n knitted woollen garment

WOOLMAN n wool trader

WOOLMEN > WOOLMAN

WOOLPACK n cloth or canvas wrapping used to pack a bale of wool

WOOLPACKS > WOOLPACK

WOOLS > WOOL

WOOLSACK n sack containing or intended to contain wool

WOOLSACKS > WOOLSACK

WOOLSEY n cotton and wool blend

WOOLSEYS > WOOLSEY

WOOLSHED n large building in which sheep shearing takes place

WOOLSHEDS > WOOLSHED

WOOLSKIN n sheepskin with wool still on

WOOLSKINS > WOOLSKIN

WOOLWARD adv with woollen side touching the skin

WOOLWORK n embroidery with wool

WOOLWORKS > WOOLWORK

WOOLY same as > WOOLLY

WOOMERA n notched stick used by Australian Aborigines to aid the propulsion of a spear

WOOMERANG same as > WOOMERA

WOOMERAS > WOOMERA

WOON same as > WON

WOONED > WOON

WOONERF n (in the Netherlands) road primarily for cyclists and pedestrians

WOONERFS > WOONERF

WOONING > WOON

WOONS > WOON

WOOPIE n well-off older person

WOOPIES > WOOPIE

WOOPS vb (esp of small child) vomit

WOOPSED > WOOPS

WOOPSES > WOOPS

WOOPSING > WOOPS

WOOPY n well-off older person

WOORALI less common name for > CURARE

WOORALIS > WOORALI

WOORARA same as > WOURALI

WOORARAS > WOORARA

WOORARI same as > WOURALI

WOORARIS > WOORARI

WOOS > WOO

WOOSE same as > WUSS

WOOSEL same as > OUZEL

WOOSELL same as > OUZEL

WOOSELLS > WOOSELL

WOOSELS > WOOSEL

WOOSES > WOOSE

WOOSH same as > WHOOSH

WOOSHED > WOOSH

WOOSHES > WOOSH

WOOSHING > WOOSH

WOOT interj (esp used by players in online games) shout of joy, victory, etc

WOOTZ n Middle-Eastern steel

WOOTZES > WOOTZ

WOOZIER > WOOZY

WOOZIEST > WOOZY

WOOZILY > WOOZY

WOOZINESS > WOOZY

WOOZY adj weak, dizzy, and confused

WOP vb strike, beat, or thrash

WOPPED > WOP

WOPPING > WOP

WOPS > WOP

WORCESTER n type of woollen fabric

WORD n smallest single meaningful unit of speech or writing ▷ vb express in words

WORDAGE n words considered collectively, esp a quantity of words

WORDAGES > WORDAGE

WORDBOOK n book containing words, usually with their meanings

WORDBOOKS > WORDBOOK

WORDBOUND adj unable to find words to express something

WORDBREAK n point at which a word is divided when it runs over from one line of print to the next

WORDCOUNT n count of words in a document

WORDED > WORD

WORDGAME n any game involving the formation, discovery, or alteration of a word or words

WORDGAMES > WORDGAME

WORDIE n person who loves words

WORDIER > WORDY

WORDIES > WORDIE

WORDIEST > WORDY

WORDILY > WORDY

WORDINESS > WORDY

WORDING n choice and arrangement of words

WORDINGS > WORDING

WORDISH adj talkative

WORDLESS adj inarticulate or silent

WORDLORE n knowledge about words

WORDLORES > WORDLORE

WORDPLAY n verbal wit based on the meanings and ambiguities of words

WORDPLAYS > WORDPLAY

WORDS > WORD

WORDSMITH n person skilled in using words

WORDWRAP n word-processing function that shifts a word at the end of a line to a new line to keep within preset margins

WORDWRAPS > WORDWRAP

WORDY adj using too many words

WORE > WEAR

WORK n physical or mental effort directed to making or doing something ▷ adj of or for work ▷ vb (cause to) do work

WORKABLE adj able to operate efficiently

WORKABLY > WORKABLE

WORKADAY n working day ▷ adj ordinary

WORKADAYS > WORKADAY

WORKBAG n container for implements, tools, or materials

WORKBAGS > WORKBAG

WORKBENCH n heavy table at which a craftsman or mechanic works

WORKBOAT n boat used for tasks

WORKBOATS > WORKBOAT

WORKBOOK n exercise book or textbook used for study, esp a textbook with spaces for answers

WORKBOOKS > WORKBOOK

WORKBOOT n type of sturdy leather boot

WORKBOOTS > WORKBOOT

WORKBOX same as > WORKBAG

WORKBOXES > WORKBOX

WORKDAY another word for > WORKADAY

WORKDAYS > WORKDAY

WORKED adj made or decorated with evidence of workmanship

WORKER n person who works in a specified way

WORKERIST n supporter of working-class politics

W

WORKERS > WORKER

WORKFARE n scheme under which unemployed people are required to do community work or undergo job training in return for social-security payments

WORKFARES > WORKFARE

WORKFLOW n rate of progress of work

WORKFLOWS > WORKFLOW

WORKFOLK pl n working people, esp labourers on a farm

WORKFOLKS same as > WORKFOLK

WORKFORCE n total number of workers

WORKFUL adj hardworking

WORKGIRL n young female manual worker

WORKGIRLS > WORKGIRL

WORKGROUP n collection of networked computers

WORKHORSE n person or thing that does a lot of dull or routine work

WORKHOUR n time set aside for work

WORKHOURS > WORKHOUR

WORKHOUSE n (in England, formerly) institution where the poor were given food and lodgings in return for work

WORKING n operation or mode of operation of something ▷ adj relating to or concerned with a person or thing that works

WORKINGS > WORKING

WORKLESS > WORK

WORKLOAD n amount of work to be done, esp in a specified period

WORKLOADS > WORKLOAD

WORKMAN n manual worker

WORKMANLY adj appropriate to or befitting a good workman

WORKMATE n person who works with another person

WORKMATES > WORKMATE

WORKMEN > WORKMAN

WORKOUT n session of physical exercise for training or fitness

WORKOUTS > WORKOUT

WORKPIECE n piece of metal or other material that is in the process of being worked on or made or has actually been cut or shaped by a hand tool or machine

WORKPLACE n place, such as a factory or office, where people work

WORKPRINT n unfinished print of cinema film

WORKROOM n room in which work, usually manual labour, is done

WORKROOMS > WORKROOM

WORKS > WORK

WORKSAFE adj (of an internet link) suitable for viewing in the workplace

WORKSHEET n sheet of paper containing exercises to be completed by a student

WORKSHOP n room or building for a manufacturing process ▷ vb perform (a play) with no costumes, set, or musical accompaniment

WORKSHOPS > WORKSHOP

WORKSHY adj not inclined to work

WORKSITE n area where work is done

WORKSITES > WORKSITE

WORKSOME adj hardworking

WORKSONG n song sung while doing physical work

WORKSONGS > WORKSONG

WORKSPACE n area set aside for work

WORKTABLE n table at which writing, sewing, or other work may be done

WORKTOP n surface used for food preparation

WORKTOPS > WORKTOP

WORKUP n medical examination

WORKUPS > WORKUP

WORKWEAR n clothes, such as overalls, as worn for work in a factory, shop, etc

WORKWEARS > WORKWEAR

WORKWEEK n number of hours or days in a week actually or officially allocated to work

WORKWEEKS > WORKWEEK

WORKWOMAN n female manual worker

WORKWOMEN > WORKWOMAN

WORLD n planet earth ▷ adj of the whole world

WORLDBEAT n popular music from outside western mainstream

WORLDED adj incorporating worlds

WORLDER n person who belongs to a specified class or domain

WORLDERS > WORLDER

WORLDIE n world-class performance, achievement, person, etc

WORLDIES > WORLDIE

WORLDLIER > WORLDLY

WORLDLING n person who is primarily concerned with worldly matters or material things

WORLDLY adj not spiritual ▷ adv in a worldly manner

WORLDS > WORLD

WORLDVIEW n comprehensive view of human life and the universe

WORLDWIDE adj applying or extending throughout the world

WORM n small limbless invertebrate animal ▷ vb rid of worms

WORMCAST n coil of earth excreted by a burrowing worm

WORMCASTS > WORMCAST

WORMED > WORM

WORMER > WORM

WORMERIES > WORMERY

WORMERS > WORM

WORMERY n piece of apparatus in which worms are kept for study

WORMFLIES > WORMFLY

WORMFLY n type of lure dressed on a double hook

WORMGEAR n gear with screw thread

WORMGEARS > WORMGEAR

WORMHOLE n hole made by a worm in timber, plants, or fruit

WORMHOLED > WORMHOLE

WORMHOLES > WORMHOLE

WORMIER > WORMY

WORMIEST > WORMY

WORMIL n burrowing larva of type of fly

WORMILS > WORMIL

WORMINESS > WORMY

WORMING > WORM

WORMISH > WORM

WORMLIKE > WORM

WORMROOT n plant used to cure worms

WORMROOTS > WORMROOT

WORMS n disease caused by parasitic worms living in the intestines

WORMSEED n any of various plants used to treat worm infestation

WORMSEEDS > WORMSEED

WORMWHEEL n wheel of a wormgear

WORMWOOD n bitter plant

WORMWOODS > WORMWOOD

WORMY adj infested with or eaten by worms

WORN > WEAR

WORNNESS n quality or condition of being worn

WORRAL n type of lizard

WORRALS > WORRAL

WORREL same as > WORRAL

WORRELS > WORREL

WORRICOW n frightening creature

WORRICOWS > WORRICOW

WORRIED > WORRY

WORRIEDLY > WORRY

WORRIER > WORRY

WORRIERS > WORRY

WORRIES > WORRY

WORRIMENT n anxiety or the trouble that causes it

WORRISOME adj causing worry

WORRIT vb tease or worry

WORRITED > WORRIT

WORRITING > WORRIT

WORRITS > WORRIT

WORRY vb (cause to) be anxious or uneasy ▷ n (cause of) anxiety or concern

WORRYCOW same as > WORRICOW

WORRYCOWS > WORRYCOW

WORRYGUTS n person who tends to worry, esp about insignificant matters

WORRYING > WORRY

WORRYINGS > WORRY

WORRYWART same as > WORRYGUTS

WORSE vb defeat

WORSED > WORSE

WORSEN vb make or grow worse

WORSENED > WORSEN

WORSENESS n state or condition of being worse

WORSENING n act of worsening

WORSENS > WORSEN

WORSER archaic or nonstandard word for > WORSE

WORSES > WORSE

WORSET n worsted fabric

WORSETS > WORSET

WORSHIP vb show religious devotion to ▷ n act or instance of worshipping

WORSHIPED > WORSHIP

WORSHIPER n worshipper

WORSHIPS > WORSHIP

WORSING > WORSE

WORST n worst thing ▷ vb defeat

WORSTED n type of woollen yarn or fabric

WORSTEDS > WORSTED

WORSTING > WORST

WORSTS > WORST

WORT n any of various plants formerly used to cure diseases

WORTH prep having a value of ▷ n value or price ▷ vb happen or betide

WORTHED > WORTH

WORTHFUL adj worthy

WORTHIED > WORTHY

WORTHIER > WORTHY

WORTHIES > WORTHY

WORTHIEST > WORTHY

WORTHILY > WORTHY

WORTHING > WORTH

WORTHLESS adj without value or usefulness

WORTHS > WORTH

WORTHY adj deserving admiration or respect ▷ n notable person ▷ vb make worthy

WORTHYING > WORTHY

WORTLE n plate with holes for drawing wire through

WORTLES > WORTLE

WORTS > WORT

WOS > WO

WOSBIRD n illegitimate child

WOSBIRDS > WOSBIRD

WOST vb wit, to know

WOT vb wit, to know

WOTCHA same as > WOTCHER

WOTCHER sentence substitute slang term of greeting

WOTS > WOT

WOTTED > WOT

WOTTEST > WOT

WOTTETH > WOT

WOTTING > WOT

WOUBIT n type of caterpillar

WOUBITS > WOUBIT

WOULD > WILL

WOULDEST same as > WOULDST

WOULDS same as > WOULDST

WOULDST singular form of the past tense of > WILL

WOUND vb injure ▷ n injury

WOUNDABLE > WOUND

WOUNDED adj suffering from wounds

WOUNDEDLY > WOUNDED

WOUNDER > WOUND

WOUNDERS > WOUND

WOUNDIER > WOUNDY

WOUNDIEST > WOUNDY

WOUNDILY > WOUNDY

WOUNDING > WOUND

WOUNDINGS > WOUND

WOUNDLESS > WOUND

WOUNDS > WOUND

WOUNDWORT n type of plant formerly used for dressing wounds

WOUNDY adj extreme

WOURALI n plant from which curare is obtained

WOURALIS > WOURALI

WOVE > WEAVE

WOVEN n article made from woven cloth

WOVENS > WOVEN

WOW interj exclamation of astonishment ▷ n astonishing person or thing ▷ vb be a great success with

WOWED > WOW

WOWEE stronger form of > WOW

WOWF adj mad

WOWFER > WOWF

WOWFEST > WOWF

WOWING > WOW

WOWS > WOW

WOWSER n puritanical person

WOWSERS > WOWSER

WOX > WAX

WOXEN > WAX

WRACK n seaweed ▷ vb strain or shake (something) violently

WRACKED > WRACK

WRACKFUL n ruinous

WRACKING > WRACK

WRACKS > WRACK

WRAITH n ghost

WRAITHS > WRAITH

WRANG Scot word for > WRONG

WRANGED > WRANG

WRANGING > WRANG

WRANGLE vb argue noisily ▷ n noisy argument

WRANGLED > WRANGLE

WRANGLER n one who wrangles

WRANGLERS > WRANGLER

WRANGLES > WRANGLE

WRANGLING > WRANGLE

WRANGS > WRANG

WRAP vb fold (something) round (a person or thing) so as to cover ▷ n garment wrapped round the shoulders

WRAPOVER adj (of a garment) worn wrapped round the body and fastened so that the open edges overlap ▷ n such a garment

WRAPOVERS > WRAPOVER

WRAPPAGE n material for wrapping

WRAPPAGES > WRAPPAGE

WRAPPED > WRAP

WRAPPER vb cover with wrapping ▷ n cover for a product

WRAPPERED > WRAPPER

WRAPPERS > WRAPPER

WRAPPING > WRAP

WRAPPINGS > WRAP

WRAPROUND same as > WRAPOVER

WRAPS > WRAP

WRAPT same as > RAPT

WRASSE n colourful sea fish

WRASSES > WRASSE

WRASSLE same as > WRESTLE

WRASSLED > WRASSLE

WRASSLES > WRASSLE

WRASSLING > WRASSLE

WRAST same as > WREST

WRASTED > WRAST

WRASTING > WRAST

WRASTLE same as > WRESTLE

WRASTLED > WRASTLE

WRASTLES > WRASTLE

WRASTLING > WRASTLE

WRASTS > WRAST

WRATE > WRITE

WRATH n intense anger ▷ adj incensed ▷ vb make angry

WRATHED > WRATH

WRATHFUL adj full of wrath

WRATHIER > WRATHY

WRATHIEST > WRATHY

WRATHILY > WRATHY

WRATHING > WRATH

WRATHLESS > WRATH

WRATHS > WRATH

WRATHY same as > WRATHFUL

WRAWL vb howl

WRAWLED > WRAWL

WRAWLING > WRAWL

WRAWLS > WRAWL

WRAXLE vb wrestle

WRAXLED > WRAXLE

WRAXLES > WRAXLE

WRAXLING > WRAXLE

WRAXLINGS > WRAXLE

WREAK vb inflict (vengeance, etc) or cause (chaos, etc)

WREAKED > WREAK

WREAKER > WREAK

WREAKERS > WREAK

WREAKFUL adj seeking revenge

WREAKING > WREAK

WREAKLESS adj unrevengeful

WREAKS > WREAK

WREATH n twisted ring or band of flowers or leaves used as a memorial or tribute

WREATHE vb form into or take the form of a wreath by twisting together

WREATHED > WREATHE

WREATHEN adj twisted into a wreath

WREATHER > WREATHE

WREATHERS > WREATHE

WREATHES > WREATHE

WREATHIER > WREATHY

WREATHING > WREATHE

WREATHS > WREATH

WREATHY adj twisted into wreath

WRECK vb destroy ▷ n remains of something that has been destroyed or badly damaged

WRECKAGE n wrecked remains

WRECKAGES > WRECKAGE

WRECKED > WRECK

WRECKER n formerly, person who lured ships onto the rocks in order to plunder them

WRECKERS > WRECKER

WRECKFISH n large sea perch

WRECKFUL adj causing wreckage

WRECKING > WRECK

WRECKINGS > WRECK

WRECKS > WRECK

WREN n small brown songbird

WRENCH vb twist or pull violently ▷ n violent twist or pull

WRENCHED > WRENCH

WRENCHER > WRENCH

WRENCHERS > WRENCH

WRENCHES > WRENCH

WRENCHING > WRENCH

WRENS > WREN

WRENTIT n type of long-tailed North American bird

WRENTITS > WRENTIT

WREST vb twist violently ▷ n act or an instance of wresting

WRESTED > WREST

WRESTER > WREST

WRESTERS > WREST

WRESTING > WREST

WRESTLE vb fight by grappling with an opponent ▷ n act of wrestling

WRESTLED > WRESTLE

WRESTLER > WRESTLE

WRESTLERS > WRESTLE

WRESTLES > WRESTLE

WRESTLING n sport in which each contestant tries to overcome the other either by throwing or pinning him or her to the ground or by forcing a submission

WRESTS > WREST

WRETCH n despicable person

WRETCHED adj miserable or unhappy

WRETCHES > WRETCH

WRETHE same as > WREATHE

WRETHED > WRETHE

WRETHES > WRETHE

WRETHING > WRETHE

WRICK variant spelling (chiefly Brit) of > RICK

WRICKED > WRICK

WRICKING > WRICK

WRICKS > WRICK

WRIED > WRY

WRIER > WRY

WRIES > WRY

WRIEST > WRY

WRIGGLE vb move with a twisting action ▷ n wriggling movement

WRIGGLED > WRIGGLE

WRIGGLER > WRIGGLE

WRIGGLERS > WRIGGLE

WRIGGLES > WRIGGLE

WRIGGLIER > WRIGGLE

WRIGGLING > WRIGGLE

WRIGGLY > WRIGGLE

WRIGHT n maker

WRIGHTS > WRIGHT

WRING vb twist, esp to squeeze liquid out of

WRINGED > WRING

WRINGER same as > MANGLE

WRINGERS > WRINGER

WRINGING > WRING

WRINGS > WRING

WRINKLE n slight crease, esp one in the skin due to age ▷ vb make or become slightly creased

WRINKLED > WRINKLE

WRINKLES > WRINKLE

WRINKLIE n derogatory word for an old person

WRINKLIER > WRINKLE

WRINKLIES pl n derogatory word for old people

WRINKLING > WRINKLE

WRINKLY > WRINKLE

WRIST n joint between the hand and the arm ▷ vb hit an object with a twist of the wrist

WRISTBAND n band around the wrist, esp one attached to a watch or forming part of a long sleeve

WRISTED > WRIST

WRISTER n type of shot in hockey

WRISTERS > WRISTER

WRISTIER > WRISTY

WRISTIEST > WRISTY

WRISTING > WRIST

WRISTLET n band or bracelet worn around the wrist

WRISTLETS > WRISTLET

WRISTLOCK n wrestling hold in which a wrestler seizes their opponent's wrist and exerts pressure against the joints of their hand, arm, or shoulder

WRISTS > WRIST

WRISTY adj characterized by considerable movement of the wrist

WRIT n written legal command

WRITABLE > WRITE

WRITATIVE adj inclined to write a lot

WRITE vb mark paper etc with symbols or words

WRITEABLE > WRITE

WRITEDOWN n reduction in the estimated value of an asset

WRITEOFF n uncollectible debt that is cancelled

WRITEOFFS > WRITEOFF

WRITER n author

WRITERESS n female writer

WRITERLY adj of or characteristic of a writer

WRITERS > WRITER

WRITES > WRITE

WRITHE vb twist or squirm in or as if in pain ▷ n act or an instance of writhing

WRITHED > WRITHE
WRITHEN adj twisted
WRITHER > WRITHE
WRITHERS > WRITHE
WRITHES > WRITHE
WRITHING > WRITHE
WRITHINGS > WRITHE
WRITHLED adj wrinkled
WRITING > WRITE
WRITINGS > WRITE
WRITS > WRIT
WRITTEN > WRITE
WRIZLED adj wrinkled
WROATH n unforeseen trouble
WROATHS > WROATH
WROKE > WREAK
WROKEN > WREAK
WRONG adj incorrect or mistaken ▷ adv in a wrong manner ▷ n something immoral or unjust ▷ vb treat unjustly
WRONGDOER n person who acts immorally or illegally
WRONGED > WRONG
WRONGER > WRONG
WRONGERS > WRONG
WRONGEST > WRONG
WRONGFUL adj unjust or illegal
WRONGING > WRONG
WRONGLY > WRONG
WRONGNESS > WRONG
WRONGOUS adj unfair
WRONGS > WRONG
WROOT obsolete form of > ROOT
WROOTED > WROOT
WROOTING > WROOT
WROOTS > WROOT

WROTE > WRITE
WROTH adj angry
WROTHFUL same as > WRATHFUL
WROUGHT adj (of metals) shaped by hammering or beating
WRUNG > WRING
WRY adj drily humorous ▷ vb twist or contort
WRYBILL n New Zealand plover whose bill is bent to one side
WRYBILLS > WRYBILL
WRYER > WRY
WRYEST > WRY
WRYING > WRY
WRYLY > WRY
WRYNECK n woodpecker that has a habit of twisting its neck round
WRYNECKS > WRYNECK
WRYNESS > WRY
WRYNESSES > WRY
WRYTHEN adj twisted
WUD Scots form of > WOOD
WUDDED > WUD
WUDDIES > WUDDY
WUDDING > WUD
WUDDY n loop at the end of a rope
WUDJULA n Australian word for a non-Aboriginal person
WUDJULAS > WUDJULA
WUDS > WUD
WUDU n practice of ritual washing before daily prayer
WUDUS > WUDU
WUKKAS pl n Australian taboo slang expression for no problems

WULFENITE n yellow, orange, red, or grey lustrous secondary mineral
WULL obsolete form of > WILL
WILLED > WULL
WULLING > WULL
WULLS > WULL
WUNNER same as > ONER
WUNNERS > WUNNER
WURLEY n Aboriginal hut
WURLEYS > WURLEY
WURLIE same as > WURLEY
WURLIES > WURLIE
WURST n large sausage, esp of a type made in Germany, Austria, etc
WURSTS > WURST
WURTZITE n zinc sulphide
WURTZITES > WURTZITE
WURZEL n root
WURZELS > WURZEL
WUS n casual term of address
WUSES > WUS
WUSHU n Chinese martial arts
WUSHUS > WUSHU
WUSS n feeble person
WUSSES > WUSS
WUSSIER > WUSSY
WUSSIES > WUSSY
WUSSIEST > WUSSY
WUSSY adj feeble ▷ n feeble person
WUTHER vb (of wind) blow and roar
WUTHERED > WUTHER
WUTHERING adj (of a wind) blowing strongly with a roaring sound
WUTHERS > WUTHER

WUXIA n Chinese fiction concerning the adventures of sword-wielding heroes
WUXIAS > WUXIA
WUZ vb nonstandard spelling of was
WUZZLE vb mix up
WUZZLED > WUZZLE
WUZZLES > WUZZLE
WUZZLING > WUZZLE
WYANDOTTE n heavy American breed of domestic fowl
WYCH n type of tree having flexible branches
WYCHES > WYCH
WYE n y-shaped pipe
WYES > WYE
WYLE vb entice
WYLED > WYLE
WYLES > WYLE
WYLIECOAT n petticoat
WYLING > WYLE
WYN n rune equivalent to English 'w'
WYND n narrow lane or alley
WYNDS > WYND
WYNN same as > WYN
WYNNS > WYNN
WYNS > WYN
WYSIWYG adj denoting a computer screen display showing exactly what will print out
WYTE vb blame
WYTED > WYTE
WYTES > WYTE
WYTING > WYTE
WYVERN n heraldic beast
WYVERNS > WYVERN

Xx

XANTHAM n acacia gum

XANTHAMS > XANTHAM

XANTHAN same as > XANTHAM

XANTHANS > XANTHAN

XANTHATE n any salt or ester of xanthic acid

XANTHATES > XANTHATE

XANTHEIN n soluble part of the yellow pigment that is found in the cell sap of some flowers

XANTHEINS > XANTHEIN

XANTHENE n yellowish crystalline heterocyclic compound used as a fungicide

XANTHENES > XANTHENE

XANTHIC adj of, containing, or derived from xanthic acid

XANTHIN n any of a group of yellow or orange carotene derivatives

XANTHINE n crystalline compound found in urine, blood, certain plants, and certain animal tissues

XANTHINES > XANTHINE

XANTHINS > XANTHIN

XANTHISM n condition of skin, fur, or feathers in which yellow coloration predominates

XANTHISMS > XANTHISM

XANTHOMA n presence in the skin of fatty yellow or brownish plaques or nodules

XANTHOMAS > XANTHOMA

XANTHONE n crystalline compound

XANTHONES > XANTHONE

XANTHOUS adj of, relating to, or designating races with yellowish hair and a light complexion

XANTHOXYL n South American plant

XEBEC n small three-masted Mediterranean vessel

XEBECS > XEBEC

XED adj having a cross against

XENIA n influence of pollen upon the form of the fruit developing after pollination

XENIAL > XENIA

XENIAS > XENIA

XENIC adj denoting the presence of bacteria

XENIUM n diplomatic gift

XENOBLAST n type of mineral deposit

XENOCRYST n crystal included within an igneous rock as the magma cooled but not formed from it

XENOGAMY n fertilization by the fusion of male and female gametes from different individuals of the same species

XENOGENIC adj relating to the supposed production of offspring completely unlike either parent

XENOGENY n offspring unlike either parent

XENOGRAFT n tissue graft obtained from a donor of a different species from the recipient

XENOLITH n fragment of rock differing in origin, composition, structure, etc, from the igneous rock enclosing it

XENOLITHS > XENOLITH

XENOMANIA n passion for foreign things

XENOMENIA n menstruation from unusual orifices

XENON n colourless odourless gas found in very small quantities in the air

XENONS > XENON

XENOPHILE n person who likes foreigners or things foreign

XENOPHOBE n person who hates or fears foreigners or strangers

XENOPHOBY n hatred or fear of foreigners or strangers

XENOPHYA pl n parts of shell or skeleton formed by foreign bodies

XENOPUS n African frog

XENOPUSES > XENOPUS

XENOTIME n yellow-brown mineral

XENOTIMES > XENOTIME

XENURINE adj relating to a type of armadillo ▷ n type of armadillo

XENURINES > XENURINE

XERAFIN n Indian coin

XERAFINS > XERAFIN

XERANSES > XERANSIS

XERANSIS n gradual loss of tissue moisture

XERANTIC > XERANSIS

XERAPHIN same as > XERAFIN

XERAPHINS > XERAPHIN

XERARCH adj (of a sere) having its origin in a dry habitat

XERASIA n dryness of the hair

XERASIAS > XERASIA

XERIC adj of, relating to, or growing in dry conditions

XERICALLY > XERIC

XERISCAPE n landscape designed to conserve water ▷ vb landscape (an area) so that it needs little water

XEROCHASY n release of seeds or pollen on drying

XERODERMA n any abnormal dryness of the skin as the result of diminished secretions from the sweat or sebaceous glands

XEROMA n excessive dryness of the cornea

XEROMAS > XEROMA

XEROMATA > XEROMA

XEROMORPH n xerophilous plant

XEROPHAGY n fasting by eating only dry food

XEROPHILE n plant or animal which likes living in dry surroundings

XEROPHILY > XEROPHILE

XEROPHYTE n xerophilous plant, such as a cactus

XEROSERE n sere that originates in dry surroundings

XEROSERES > XEROSERE

XEROSES > XEROSIS

XEROSIS n abnormal dryness of bodily tissues, esp the skin, eyes, or mucous membranes

XEROSTOMA n abnormal lack of saliva; dryness of the mouth

XEROTES same as > XEROSIS

XEROTIC > XEROSIS

XEROX n trade name for a machine employing a xerographic copying process ▷ vb produce a copy (of a document, etc) using such a machine

XEROXED > XEROX

XEROXES > XEROX

XEROXING > XEROX

XERUS n ground squirrel

XERUSES > XERUS

XI n 14th letter in the Greek alphabet

XIPHOID adj shaped like a sword ▷ n part of the sternum

XIPHOIDAL > XIPHOID

XIPHOIDS > XIPHOID

XIPHOPAGI n Siamese twins joined at the lower sternum

XIS > XI

XOANA > XOANON

XOANON n primitive image of a god supposed to have fallen from heaven

XRAY n code word for the letter X

XRAYS > XRAY

XU n Vietnamese currency unit

XYLAN n yellow polysaccharide consisting of xylose units

XYLANS > XYLAN

XYLEM n plant tissue that conducts water and minerals from the roots to all other parts

XYLEMS > XYLEM

XYLENE n type of hydrocarbon

XYLENES > XYLENE

XYLENOL n synthetic resin made from xylene

XYLENOLS > XYLENOL

XYLIC > XYLEM

XYLIDIN same as > XYLIDINE

XYLIDINE n mixture of six isomeric amines derived from xylene and used in dyes

XYLIDINES > XYLIDINE

XYLIDINS > XYLIDIN

XYLITOL n crystalline alcohol used as sweetener

XYLITOLS > XYLITOL

XYLOCARP n fruit, such as a coconut, having a hard woody pericarp

XYLOCARPS > XYLOCARP

XYLOGEN same as > XYLEM

XYLOGENS > XYLOGEN

XYLOGRAPH n engraving in wood ▷ vb print (a design, illustration, etc) from a wood engraving

XYLOID adj of, relating to, or resembling wood

XYLOIDIN n type of explosive

XYLOIDINE same as > XYLOIDIN

XYLOIDINS > XYLOIDIN

XYLOL another name (not in technical usage) for > XYLENE

X

XYLOLOGY *n* study of the composition of wood

XYLOLS > XYLOL

XYLOMA *n* hard growth in fungi

XYLOMAS > XYLOMA

XYLOMATA > XYLOMA

XYLOMETER *n* device for measuring the specific gravity of wood

XYLONIC *adj* denoting an acid formed from xylose

XYLONITE *n* type of plastic

XYLONITES > XYLONITE

XYLOPHAGE *n* creature that eats wood

XYLOPHONE *n* musical instrument made of a row of wooden bars played with hammers

XYLORIMBA *n* large xylophone with an extended range of five octaves

XYLOSE *n* white crystalline sugar found in wood and straw

XYLOSES > XYLOSE

XYLOTOMY *n* preparation of sections of wood for examination by microscope

XYLYL *n* group of atoms

XYLYLS > XYLYL

XYST *n* long portico, esp one used in ancient Greece for athletics

XYSTER *n* surgical instrument for scraping bone

XYSTERS > XYSTER

XYSTI > XYSTUS

XYSTOI > XYSTOS

XYSTOS *same as* > XYST

XYSTS > XYST

XYSTUS *same as* > XYST

YA *n* type of Asian pear **YAAR** *n* in informal Indian English, a friend

YAARS > YAAR

YABA *n* informal word for 'yet another bloody acronym'

YABAS > YABA

YABBA *n* form of methamphetamine

YABBAS > YABBA

YABBER *vb* talk or jabber ▷ *n* talk or jabber

YABBERED > YABBER

YABBERING > YABBER

YABBERS > YABBER

YABBIE *same as* > YABBY

YABBIED > YABBY

YABBIES > YABBY

YABBY *n* small freshwater crayfish ▷ *vb* go out to catch yabbies

YABBYING > YABBY

YACCA *n* Australian plant with a woody stem

YACCAS > YACCA

YACHT *n* large boat with sails or an engine ▷ *vb* sail in a yacht

YACHTED > YACHT

YACHTER > YACHT

YACHTERS > YACHT

YACHTIE *n* yachtsman

YACHTIES > YACHTIE

YACHTING *n* sport or practice of navigating a yacht

YACHTINGS > YACHTING

YACHTMAN *same as* > YACHTSMAN

YACHTMEN > YACHTMAN

YACHTS > YACHT

YACHTSMAN *n* person who sails a yacht

YACHTSMEN > YACHTSMAN

YACK *same as* > YAK

YACKA *same as* > YACCA

YACKAS > YACKA

YACKED > YACK

YACKER *same as* > YAKKA

YACKERS > YACKER

YACKING > YACK

YACKS > YACK

YAD *n* hand-held pointer used for reading the sefer torah

YADS > YAD

YAE *same as* > AE

YAFF *vb* bark

YAFFED > YAFF

YAFFING > YAFF

YAFFLE *n* woodpecker with a green back and wings

YAFFLES > YAFFLE

YAFFS > YAFF

YAG *n* artificial crystal

YAGE *n* tropical vine of the Amazon region

YAGER *same as* > JAEGER

YAGERS > YAGER

YAGES > YAGE

YAGGER *n* pedlar

YAGGERS > YAGGER

YAGI *n* type of highly directional aerial

YAGIS > YAGI

YAGS > YAG

YAH *interj* exclamation of derision or disgust ▷ *n* affected upper-class person

YAHOO *n* crude coarse person

YAHOOISM > YAHOO

YAHOOISMS > YAHOO

YAHOOS > YAHOO

YAHRZEIT *n* (in Judaism) the anniversary of the death of a close relative

YAHRZEITS > YAHRZEIT

YAHS > YAH

YAIRD *Scots form of* > YARD

YAIRDS > YAIRD

YAK *n* Tibetan ox with long shaggy hair ▷ *vb* talk continuously about unimportant matters

YAKHDAN *n* box for carrying ice on a pack animal

YAKHDANS > YAKHDAN

YAKIMONO *n* grilled food

YAKIMONOS > YAKIMONO

YAKITORI *n* Japanese dish consisting of small pieces of chicken skewered and grilled

YAKITORIS > YAKITORI

YAKKA *n* work

YAKKAS > YAKKA

YAKKED > YAK

YAKKER *same as* > YAKKA

YAKKERS > YAKKER

YAKKING > YAK

YAKOW *n* animal bred from a male yak and a domestic cow

YAKOWS > YAKOW

YAKS > YAK

YAKUZA *n* Japanese criminal organization

YALD *adj* vigorous

YALE *n* mythical beast with the body of an antelope (or similar animal) and swivelling horns

YALES > YALE

YAM *n* tropical root vegetable

YAMALKA *same as* > YARMULKE

YAMALKAS > YAMALKA

YAMEN *n* (in imperial China) the office or residence of a public official

YAMENS > YAMEN

YAMMER *vb* whine in a complaining manner ▷ *n* yammering sound

YAMMERED > YAMMER

YAMMERER > YAMMER

YAMMERERS > YAMMER

YAMMERING > YAMMER

YAMMERS > YAMMER

YAMPIES > YAMPY

YAMPY *n* foolish person

YAMS > YAM

YAMULKA *same as* > YARMULKE

YAMULKAS > YAMULKA

YAMUN *same as* > YAMEN

YAMUNS > YAMUN

YANG *n* (in Chinese philosophy) one of two complementary principles maintaining harmony in the universe

YANGS > YANG

YANK *vb* pull or jerk suddenly ▷ *n* sudden pull or jerk

YANKED > YANK

YANKEE *n* code word for the letter Y

YANKEES > YANKEE

YANKER > YANK

YANKERS > YANK

YANKIE *n* impudent woman

YANKIES > YANKIE

YANKING > YANK

YANKS > YANK

YANQUI *n* slang word for American

YANQUIS > YANQUI

YANTRA *n* diagram used in meditation

YANTRAS > YANTRA

YAOURT *n* yoghurt

YAOURTS > YAOURT

YAP *vb* bark with a high-pitched sound ▷ *n* high-pitched bark ▷ *interj* imitation or representation of the sound of a dog yapping

YAPOCK *same as* > YAPOK

YAPOCKS > YAPOCK

YAPOK *n* type of opossum

YAPOKS > YAPOK

YAPON *same as* > YAUPON

YAPONS > YAPON

YAPP *n* type of book binding

YAPPED > YAP

YAPPER > YAP

YAPPERS > YAP

YAPPIE *n* young aspiring professional

YAPPIER > YAP

YAPPIES > YAPPIE

YAPPIEST > YAP

YAPPING *n* act of yapping

YAPPINGLY > YAP

YAPPINGS > YAPPING

YAPPS > YAPP

YAPPY > YAP

YAPS > YAP

YAPSTER > YAP

YAPSTERS > YAP

YAQONA *n* Polynesian shrub

YAQONAS > YAQONA

YAR *adj* nimble

YARAK *n* fit condition for hunting

YARAKS > YARAK

YARCO *n* insulting word for a young working-class person who wears casual sports clothes

YARCOS > YARCO

YARD *n* unit of length ▷ *vb* draft (animals), esp to a saleyard

YARDAGE *n* length measured in yards

YARDAGES > YARDAGE

YARDANG *n* ridge formed by wind erosion

YARDANGS > YARDANG

YARDARM *n* outer end of a ship's yard

YARDARMS > YARDARM

YARDBIRD *n* inexperienced, untrained, or clumsy soldier, esp one employed on menial duties

YARDBIRDS > YARDBIRD

YARDED > YARD

YARDER *n* one who drafts animals to a sale yard

YARDERS > YARDER

YARDING *n* group of animals displayed for sale

YARDINGS > YARDING

YARDLAND *n* archaic unit of land

YARDLANDS > YARDLAND

YARDLIGHT *n* light hanging on a pole, used to light a yard

YARDMAN *n* farm overseer

YARDMEN > YARDMAN

YARDS > YARD

YARDSTICK *n* standard against which to judge other people or things

YARDWAND *same as* > YARDSTICK

YARDWANDS > YARDWAND

YARDWORK n garden work
YARDWORKS > YARDWORK
YARE adj ready, brisk, or eager ▷ adv readily or eagerly
YARELY > YARE
YARER > YARE
YAREST > YARE
YARFA n peat
YARFAS > YARFA
YARK vb make ready
YARKED > YARK
YARKING > YARK
YARKS > YARK
YARMELKE same as > YARMULKE
YARMELKES > YARMELKE
YARMULKA same as > YARMULKE
YARMULKAS > YARMULKA
YARMULKE n skullcap worn by Jewish men
YARMULKES > YARMULKE
YARN n thread used for knitting or making cloth ▷ vb thread with yarn
YARNED > YARN
YARNER > YARN
YARNERS > YARN
YARNING > YARN
YARNS > YARN
YARPHA n peat
YARPHAS > YARPHA
YARR n wild white flower ▷ vb growl or snarl
YARRAMAN n horse
YARRAMANS > YARRAMAN
YARRAMEN > YARRAMAN
YARRAN n type of small hardy tree of inland Australia
YARRANS > YARRAN
YARRED > YARR
YARRING > YARR
YARROW n wild plant with flat clusters of white flowers
YARROWS > YARROW
YARRS > YARR
YARTA Shetland word for > HEART
YARTAS > YARTA
YARTO same as > YARTA
YARTOS > YARTO
YAS > YA
YASHMAC same as > YASHMAK
YASHMACS > YASHMAC
YASHMAK n veil worn by a Muslim woman in public
YASHMAKS > YASHMAK
YASMAK same as > YASHMAK
YASMAKS > YASMAK
YATAGAN same as > YATAGHAN
YATAGANS > YATAGAN
YATAGHAN n Turkish sword with a curved single-edged blade
YATAGHANS > YATAGHAN
YATE n type of small eucalyptus tree yielding a very hard timber
YATES > YATE
YATTER vb talk at length ▷ n continuous chatter
YATTERED > YATTER
YATTERING > YATTER
YATTERS > YATTER
YAUD Scots word for > MARE

YAUDS > YAUD
YAULD adj alert, spritely, or nimble
YAUP variant spelling of > YAWP
YAUPED > YAUP
YAUPER > YAUP
YAUPERS > YAUP
YAUPING > YAUP
YAUPON n southern US evergreen holly shrub
YAUPONS > YAUPON
YAUPS > YAUP
YAUTIA n Caribbean plant cultivated for its edible leaves and underground stems
YAUTIAS > YAUTIA
YAW vb (of an aircraft or ship) turn to one side or from side to side while moving ▷ n act or movement of yawing
YAWED > YAW
YAWEY > YAWS
YAWIER > YAWY
YAWIEST > YAWY
YAWING > YAW
YAWL n two-masted sailing boat ▷ vb howl, weep, or scream harshly
YAWLED > YAWL
YAWLING > YAWL
YAWLS > YAWL
YAWMETER n instrument for measuring an aircraft's yaw
YAWMETERS > YAWMETER
YAWN vb open the mouth wide and take in air deeply, often when sleepy or bored ▷ n act of yawning
YAWNED > YAWN
YAWNER > YAWN
YAWNERS > YAWN
YAWNIER > YAWN
YAWNIEST > YAWN
YAWNING > YAWN
YAWNINGLY > YAWN
YAWNINGS > YAWN
YAWNS > YAWN
YAWNSOME adj boring
YAWNY > YAWN
YAWP vb gape or yawn, esp audibly ▷ n shout, bark, yelp, or cry
YAWPED > YAWP
YAWPER > YAWP
YAWPERS > YAWP
YAWPING > YAWP
YAWPINGS > YAWP
YAWPS > YAWP
YAWS n infectious tropical skin disease
YAWY adj having or resembling yaws
YAY interj exclamation indicating approval or triumph ▷ n cry of approval
YAYS > YAY
YBET archaic past participle of > BEAT
YBLENT archaic past participle of > BLEND
YBORE archaic past participle of > BEAR
YBOUND archaic past participle of > BIND

YBOUNDEN archaic past participle of > BIND
YBRENT archaic past participle of > BURN
YCLAD archaic past participle of > CLOTHE
YCLED archaic past participle of > CLOTHE
YCLEEPE archaic form of > CLEPE
YCLEEPED > YCLEEPE
YCLEEPES > YCLEEPE
YCLEEPING > YCLEEPE
YCLEPED same as > YCLEPT
YCLEPT adj having the name of
YCOND archaic past participle of > CON
YDRAD archaic past participle of > DREAD
YDRED archaic past participle of > DREAD
YE pron you ▷ adj the
YEA interj yes ▷ adv indeed or truly ▷ n cry of agreement
YEAD vb proceed
YEADING > YEAD
YEADS > YEAD
YEAH n positive affirmation
YEAHS > YEAH
YEALDON n fuel
YEALDONS > YEALDON
YEALING n person of the same age as oneself
YEALINGS > YEALING
YEALM vb prepare for thatching
YEALMED > YEALM
YEALMING > YEALM
YEALMS > YEALM
YEAN vb (of a sheep or goat) to give birth to (offspring)
YEANED > YEAN
YEANING > YEAN
YEANLING n young of a goat or sheep
YEANLINGS > YEANLING
YEANS > YEAN
YEAR n time taken for the earth to make one revolution around the sun, about 365 days
YEARBOOK n reference book published annually containing details of the previous year's events
YEARBOOKS > YEARBOOK
YEARD vb bury
YEARDED > YEARD
YEARDING > YEARD
YEARDS > YEARD
YEAREND n end of the year
YEARENDS > YEAREND
YEARLIES > YEARLY
YEARLING n animal between one and two years old ▷ adj being a year old
YEARLINGS > YEARLING
YEARLONG adj throughout a whole year
YEARLY adv every year or once a year ▷ adj occurring, done, or appearing once a year or every year ▷ n publication, event, etc, that occurs once a year

YEARN vb want (something) very much
YEARNED > YEARN
YEARNER > YEARN
YEARNERS > YEARN
YEARNING n intense or overpowering longing, desire, or need
YEARNINGS > YEARNING
YEARNS > YEARN
YEARS > YEAR
YEAS > YEA
YEASAYER n person who usually agrees with proposals
YEASAYERS > YEASAYER
YEAST n fungus used to make bread rise ▷ vb froth or foam
YEASTED > YEAST
YEASTIER > YEASTY
YEASTIEST > YEASTY
YEASTILY > YEASTY
YEASTING > YEAST
YEASTLESS > YEAST
YEASTLIKE > YEAST
YEASTS > YEAST
YEASTY adj of, resembling, or containing yeast
YEBO interj yes
YECCH same as > YECH
YECCHS > YECCH
YECH n expression of disgust
YECHIER > YECHY
YECHIEST > YECHY
YECHS > YECH
YECHY > YECH
YEDE same as > YEAD
YEDES > YEDE
YEDING > YEDE
YEED same as > YEAD
YEEDING > YEED
YEEDS > YEED
YEELIN n person of the same age as oneself
YEELINS > YEELIN
YEESH interj interjection used to express frustration
YEGG n burglar or safe-breaker
YEGGMAN same as > YEGG
YEGGMEN > YEGGMAN
YEGGS > YEGG
YEH same as > YEAH
YELD adj (of an animal) barren or too young to bear young
YELDRING n yellowhammer (bird)
YELDRINGS > YELDRING
YELDROCK same as > YELDRING
YELDROCKS > YELDROCK
YELK n yolk of an egg
YELKS > YELK
YELL vb shout or scream in a loud or piercing way ▷ n loud cry of pain, anger, or fear
YELLED > YELL
YELLER > YELL
YELLERS > YELL
YELLING > YELL
YELLINGS > YELL
YELLOCH vb yell
YELLOCHED > YELLOCH
YELLOCHS > YELLOCH**

YELLOW n colour of gold, a lemon, etc ▷ adj of this colour ▷ vb make or become yellow

YELLOWED > YELLOW

YELLOWER > YELLOW

YELLOWEST > YELLOW

YELLOWFIN n type of tuna

YELLOWIER > YELLOW

YELLOWING > YELLOW

YELLOWISH > YELLOW

YELLOWLY > YELLOW

YELLOWS n any of various fungal or viral diseases of plants

YELLOWY > YELLOW

YELLS > YELL

YELM same as > YEALM

YELMED > YELM

YELMING > YELM

YELMS > YELM

YELP n short sudden cry ▷ vb utter a sharp or high-pitched cry of pain

YELPED > YELP

YELPER > YELP

YELPERS > YELP

YELPING > YELP

YELPINGS > YELP

YELPS > YELP

YELT n young sow

YELTS > YELT

YEMMER southwest English form of > EMBER

YEMMERS > YEMMER

YEN n monetary unit of Japan ▷ vb have a longing

YENNED > YEN

YENNING > YEN

YENS > YEN

YENTA n meddlesome woman

YENTAS > YENTA

YENTE same as > YENTA

YENTES > YENTE

YEOMAN n farmer owning and farming their own land

YEOMANLY adj of, relating to, or like a yeoman ▷ adv in a yeomanly manner, as in being brave, staunch, or loyal

YEOMANRY n yeomen

YEOMEN > YEOMAN

YEOW interj interjection used to express pain

YEP n affirmative statement

YEPS > YEP

YER adj (coll.) your; you

YERBA n stimulating South American drink made from dried leaves

YERBAS > YERBA

YERD vb bury

YERDED > YERD

YERDING > YERD

YERDS > YERD

YERK vb tighten stitches

YERKED > YERK

YERKING > YERK

YERKS > YERK

YERSINIA n plague bacterium

YERSINIAE > YERSINIA

YERSINIAS > YERSINIA

YES interj expresses consent, agreement, or approval or answer or vote of yes ▷ vb reply in the affirmative

YESES > YES

YESHIVA n traditional Jewish school

YESHIVAH same as > YESHIVA

YESHIVAHS > YESHIVAH

YESHIVAS > YESHIVA

YESHIVOT > YESHIVA

YESHIVOTH > YESHIVA

YESK vb hiccup

YESKED > YESK

YESKING > YESK

YESKS > YESK

YESSED > YES

YESSES > YES

YESSING > YES

YESSIR interj expression of assent to a man

YESSIREE interj expression of assent

YESSUM interj expression of assent to a woman

YEST archaic form of > YEAST

YESTER adj of or relating to yesterday

YESTERDAY n the day before today ▷ adv on or during the day before today

YESTEREVE n yesterday evening

YESTERN same as > YESTER

YESTREEN n yesterday evening

YESTREENS > YESTREEN

YESTS > YEST

YESTY archaic form of > YEASTY

YET adv up until then or now

YETI n large legendary manlike creature alleged to inhabit the Himalayan Mountains

YETIS > YETI

YETT n gate or door

YETTIE n young, entrepreneurial, and technology-based (person)

YETTIES > YETTIE

YETTS > YETT

YEUK vb itch

YEUKED > YEUK

YEUKIER > YEUKY

YEUKIEST > YEUKY

YEUKING > YEUK

YEUKS > YEUK

YEUKY > YEUK

YEVE vb give

YEVEN > YEVE

YEVES > YEVE

YEVING > YEVE

YEW n evergreen tree with needle-like leaves and red berries

YEWEN adj made of yew

YEWS > YEW

YEX vb hiccup

YEXED > YEX

YEXES > YEX

YEXING > YEX

YEZ interj yes

YFERE adv together ▷ n friend or associate

YFERES > YFERE

YGLAUNST archaic past participle of > GLANCE

YGO archaic past participle of > GO

YGOE archaic past participle of > GO

YIBBLES adv perhaps

YICKER vb squeal or squeak

YICKERED > YICKER

YICKERING > YICKER

YICKERS > YICKER

YID n offensive word for a Jew

YIDAKI n long wooden wind instrument played by the Aboriginal peoples of Arnhem Land

YIDAKIS > YIDAKI

YIDS > YID

YIELD vb produce or bear ▷ n amount produced

YIELDABLE > YIELD

YIELDED > YIELD

YIELDER > YIELD

YIELDERS > YIELD

YIELDING adj submissive

YIELDINGS > YIELD

YIELDS > YIELD

YIKE n argument, squabble, or fight ▷ vb argue, squabble, or fight

YIKED > YIKE

YIKES interj expression of surprise, fear, or alarm

YIKING > YIKE

YIKKER vb squeal or squeak

YIKKERED > YIKKER

YIKKERING > YIKKER

YIKKERS > YIKKER

YILL n ale ▷ vb entertain with ale

YILLED > YILL

YILLING > YILL

YILLS > YILL

YIN Scots word for > ONE

YINCE Scots form of > ONCE

YINDIE n person who combines a lucrative career with non-mainstream tastes

YINDIES > YINDIE

YINGYANG n two opposing but complementary principles in Chinese philosophy

YINGYANGS > YINGYANG

YINS > YIN

YIP vb emit a high-pitched bark

YIPE same as > YIPES

YIPES interj expression of surprise, fear, or alarm

YIPPED > YIP

YIPPEE interj exclamation of joy or pleasure

YIPPER n golfer who suffers from a failure of nerve

YIPPERS > YIPPER

YIPPIE n young person sharing hippy ideals

YIPPIES > YIPPIE

YIPPING > YIP

YIPPY same as > YIPPIE

YIPS > YIP

YIRD vb bury

YIRDED > YIRD

YIRDING > YIRD

YIRDS > YIRD

YIRK same as > YERK

YIRKED > YIRK

YIRKING > YIRK

YIRKS > YIRK

YIRR vb snarl, growl, or yell

YIRRED > YIRR

YIRRING > YIRR

YIRRS > YIRR

YIRTH n earth

YIRTHS > YIRTH

YITE n European bunting with a yellowish head and body and brown streaked wings and tail

YITES > YITE

YITIE same as > YITE

YITIES > YITIE

YITTEN adj frightened

YLEM n original matter from which the basic elements are said to have been formed

YLEMS > YLEM

YLIKE Spenserian form of > ALIKE

YLKE archaic spelling of > ILK

YLKES > YLKE

YMOLT Spenserian past participle of > MELT

YMOLTEN Spenserian past participle of > MELT

YMPE Spenserian form of > IMP

YMPES > YMPE

YMPING > YMPE

YMPT > YMPE

YNAMBU n South American bird

YNAMBUS > YNAMBU

YO interj expression used as a greeting

YOB n bad-mannered aggressive youth

YOBBERIES > YOBBERY

YOBBERY n behaviour typical of aggressive surly youths

YOBBIER > YOBBY

YOBBIEST > YOBBY

YOBBISH adj typical of aggressive surly youths

YOBBISHLY > YOBBISH

YOBBISM > YOB

YOBBISMS > YOB

YOBBO same as > YOB

YOBBOES > YOBBO

YOBBOS > YOBBO

YOBBY adj like a yob

YOBS > YOB

YOCK vb chuckle

YOCKED > YOCK

YOCKING > YOCK

YOCKS > YOCK

YOD n tenth letter in the Hebrew alphabet

YODE > YEAD

YODEL vb sing with abrupt changes between a normal and a falsetto voice ▷ n act or sound of yodelling

YODELED > YODEL

YODELER > YODEL

YODELERS > YODEL

YODELING > YODELLING

YODELINGS > YODELING

YODELLED > YODEL

YODELLER > YODEL

YODELLERS > YODEL

YODELLING n type of singing traditional in Switzerland

YODELS > YODEL

YODH same as > YOD

YODHS > YODH
YODLE variant spelling of > YODEL
YODLED > YODLE
YODLER > YODLE
YODLERS > YODLE
YODLES > YODLE
YODLING > YODLE
YODS > YOD
YOGA n Hindu method of exercise and discipline
YOGAS > YOGA
YOGEE same as > YOGI
YOGEES > YOGEE
YOGH n character used in Old and Middle English to represent a palatal fricative
YOGHOURT variant form of > YOGURT
YOGHOURTS > YOGHOURT
YOGHS > YOGH
YOGHURT same as > YOGURT
YOGHURTS > YOGHURT
YOGI n person who practises yoga
YOGIC > YOGA
YOGIN same as > YOGI
YOGINI > YOGI
YOGINIS > YOGI
YOGINS > YOGIN
YOGIS > YOGI
YOGISM > YOGI
YOGISMS > YOGI
YOGOURT same as > YOGURT
YOGOURTS > YOGOURT
YOGURT n slightly sour custard-like food made from milk that has had bacteria added
YOGURTS > YOGURT
YOHIMBE n bark used in herbal medicine
YOHIMBES > YOHIMBE
YOHIMBINE n alkaloid found in the bark of a tropical African tree
YOICK vb urge on foxhounds
YOICKED > YOICK
YOICKING > YOICK
YOICKS interj cry used by huntsmen to urge on the hounds ▷ vb urge on foxhounds
YOICKSED > YOICKS
YOICKSES > YOICKS
YOICKSING > YOICKS
YOJAN n Indian unit of distance
YOJANA same as > YOJAN
YOJANAS > YOJANA
YOJANS > YOJAN
YOK vb chuckle
YOKE n wooden bar put across the necks of two animals to hold them together ▷ vb put a yoke on
YOKED > YOKE
YOKEL n simple person who lives in the country
YOKELESS > YOKE
YOKELISH > YOKEL
YOKELS > YOKEL
YOKEMATE n colleague
YOKEMATES > YOKEMATE
YOKER vb spit
YOKERED > YOKER
YOKERING > YOKER

YOKERS > YOKE
YOKES > YOKE
YOKING > YOKE
YOKINGS > YOKE
YOKKED > YOK
YOKKING > YOK
YOKOZUNA n grand champion sumo wrestler
YOKOZUNAS > YOKOZUNA
YOKS > YOK
YOKUL Shetland word for > YES
YOLD archaic past participle of > YIELD
YOLDRING n yellowhammer (bird)
YOLDRINGS > YOLDRING
YOLK n yellow part of an egg that provides food for the developing embryo
YOLKED > YOLK
YOLKIER > YOLK
YOLKIEST > YOLK
YOLKLESS > YOLK
YOLKS > YOLK
YOLKY > YOLK
YOM n day
YOMIM > YOM
YOMP vb walk or trek laboriously
YOMPED > YOMP
YOMPING > YOMP
YOMPS > YOMP
YON adj that or those over there ▷ adv yonder ▷ pron that person or thing
YOND same as > YON
YONDER adv over there ▷ adj situated over there ▷ determiner being at a distance, either within view or as if within view ▷ n person
YONDERLY > YONDER
YONDERS > YONDER
YONI n female genitalia
YONIC adj resembling a vulva
YONIS > YONI
YONKER same as > YOUNKER
YONKERS > YONKER
YONKS pl n very long time
YONNIE n stone
YONNIES > YONNIE
YONT same as > YON
YOOF n non-standard spelling of youth
YOOFS > YOOF
YOOP n sob
YOOPS > YOOP
YOPPER n young person employed on a former UK government training programme
YOPPERS > YOPPER
YORE n time long past ▷ adv in the past
YORES > YORE
YORK vb bowl or try to bowl (a batsman) by pitching the ball under or just beyond the bat
YORKED > YORK
YORKER n ball that pitches just under the bat
YORKERS > YORKER
YORKIE n Yorkshire terrier

YORKIES > YORKIE
YORKING > YORK
YORKS > YORK
YORLING n as in yellow yorling yellowhammer
YORLINGS > YORLING
YORP vb shout
YORPED > YORP
YORPING > YORP
YORPS > YORP
YOTTABYTE n very large unit of computer memory
YOU pron person or people addressed ▷ n personality of the person being addressed
YOUK vb itch
YOUKED > YOUK
YOUKING > YOUK
YOUKS > YOUK
YOUNG adj in an early stage of life or growth ▷ n young people in general; offspring
YOUNGER > YOUNG
YOUNGERS n young people
YOUNGEST > YOUNG
YOUNGISH > YOUNG
YOUNGLING n young person, animal, or plant
YOUNGLY adv youthfully
YOUNGNESS > YOUNG
YOUNGS > YOUNG
YOUNGSTER n young person
YOUNGTH n youth
YOUNGTHLY adj youthful
YOUNGTHS > YOUNGTH
YOUNKER n young man
YOUNKERS > YOUNKER
YOUPON same as > YAUPON
YOUPONS > YOUPON
YOUR adj of, belonging to, or associated with you
YOURN dialect form of > YOURS
YOURS pron something belonging to you
YOURSELF pron reflexive form of you
YOURT same as > YURT
YOURTS > YOURT
YOUS pron refers to more than one person including the person or persons addressed but not the speaker
YOUSE same as > YOUS
YOUTH n time of being young
YOUTHEN vb render more youthful-seeming
YOUTHENED > YOUTHEN
YOUTHENS > YOUTHEN
YOUTHFUL adj vigorous or active
YOUTHHEAD same as > YOUTHHOOD
YOUTHHOOD n youth
YOUTHIER > YOUTHY
YOUTHIEST > YOUTHY
YOUTHLESS > YOUTH
YOUTHLY adv young
YOUTHS > YOUTH
YOUTHSOME archaic variant of > YOUTHFUL
YOUTHY Scots word for > YOUNG
YOW vb howl
YOWE Scot word for > EWE
YOWED > YOW

YOWES > YOWE
YOWIE n legendary Australian apelike creature
YOWIES > YOWIE
YOWING > YOW
YOWL n loud mournful cry ▷ vb produce a loud mournful wail or cry
YOWLED > YOWL
YOWLER > YOWL
YOWLERS > YOWL
YOWLEY n yellowhammer (bird)
YOWLEYS > YOWLEY
YOWLING > YOWL
YOWLINGS > YOWL
YOWLS > YOWL
YOWS > YOW
YOWZA interj exclamation of enthusiasm
YPERITE n mustard gas
YPERITES > YPERITE
YPIGHT archaic past participle of > PITCH
YPLAST archaic past participle of > PLACE
YPLIGHT archaic past participle of > PLIGHT
YPSILOID > YPSILON
YPSILON same as > UPSILON
YPSILONS > YPSILON
YRAPT Spenserian form of > RAPT
YRAVISHED archaic past participle of > RAVISH
YRENT archaic past participle of > REND
YRIVD archaic past participle of > RIVE
YRNEH n unit of reciprocal inductance
YRNEHS > YRNEH
YSAME Spenserian word for > TOGETHER
YSHEND Spenserian form of > SHEND
YSHENDING > YSHEND
YSHENDS > YSHEND
YSHENT > YSHEND
YSLAKED archaic past participle of > SLAKE
YTOST archaic past participle of > TOSS
YTTERBIA n colourless hygroscopic substance used in certain alloys and ceramics
YTTERBIAS > YTTERBIA
YTTERBIC > YTTERBIUM
YTTERBITE n rare mineral
YTTERBIUM n soft silvery element
YTTERBOUS > YTTERBIUM
YTTRIA n insoluble solid used mainly in incandescent mantles
YTTRIAS > YTTRIA
YTTRIC > YTTRIUM
YTTRIOUS > YTTRIUM
YTTRIUM n silvery metallic element used in various alloys
YTTRIUMS > YTTRIUM
YU n jade
YUAN n standard monetary unit of the People's Republic of China

YUANS > YUAN

YUCA *same as* **>** YUCCA

YUCAS > YUCA

YUCCA *n* tropical plant with spikes of white leaves

YUCCAS > YUCCA

YUCCH *interj* expression of disgust

YUCH *interj* expression of disgust

YUCK *interj* exclamation indicating contempt, dislike, or disgust ▷ *vb* chuckle

YUCKED > YUCK

YUCKER > YUCK

YUCKERS > YUCK

YUCKIER > YUCKY

YUCKIEST > YUCKY

YUCKINESS > YUCKY

YUCKING > YUCK

YUCKO *adj* disgusting ▷ *interj* exclamation of disgust

YUCKS > YUCK

YUCKY *adj* disgusting, nasty

YUFT *n* Russia leather

YUFTS > YUFT

YUG *same as* **>** YUGA

YUGA *n* (in Hindu cosmology) one of the four ages of mankind

YUGARIE *variant spelling of*

> EUGARIE

YUGARIES > YUGARIE

YUGAS > YUGA

YUGS > YUG

YUK *same as* **>** YUCK

YUKATA *n* light kimono

YUKATAS > YUKATA

YUKE *vb* itch

YUKED > YUKE

YUKES > YUKE

YUKIER > YUKY

YUKIEST > YUKY

YUKING > YUKE

YUKKED > YUK

YUKKIER > YUKKY

YUKKIEST > YUKKY

YUKKING > YUK

YUKKY *same as* **>** YUCKY

YUKO *n* score of five points in judo

YUKOS > YUKO

YUKS > YUK

YUKY *adj* itchy

YULAN *n* Chinese magnolia with white flowers

YULANS > YULAN

YULE *n* Christmas

YULES > YULE

YULETIDE *n* Christmas season

YULETIDES > YULETIDE

YUM *interj* expression of delight

YUMBERRY *n* purple-red edible fruit of an E Asian tree

YUMMIER > YUMMY

YUMMIES > YUMMY

YUMMIEST > YUMMY

YUMMINESS > YUMMY

YUMMO *adj* tasty ▷ *interj* exclamation of delight or approval

YUMMY *adj* delicious ▷ *interj* exclamation indicating pleasure or delight ▷ *n* delicious food item

YUMP *vb* leave the ground when driving over a ridge

YUMPED > YUMP

YUMPIE *n* young upwardly mobile person

YUMPIES > YUMPIE

YUMPING > YUMP

YUMPS > YUMP

YUNX *n* wryneck

YUNXES > YUNX

YUP *n* informal affirmative statement

YUPON *same as* **>** YAUPON

YUPONS > YUPON

YUPPIE *n* young highly paid professional person ▷ *adj*

typical of or reflecting the values of yuppies

YUPPIEDOM > YUPPIE

YUPPIEISH > YUPPIE

YUPPIES > YUPPY

YUPPIFIED > YUPPIFY

YUPPIFIES > YUPPIFY

YUPPIFY *vb* make yuppie in nature

YUPPY *same as* **>** YUPPIE

YUPPYDOM *n* state of being a yuppie

YUPPYDOMS > YUPPYDOM

YUPS > YUP

YUPSTER *same as* **>** YINDIE

YUPSTERS > YUPSTER

YURT *n* circular tent consisting of a framework of poles covered with felt or skins

YURTA *same as* **>** YURT

YURTAS > YURTA

YURTS > YURT

YUS > YU

YUTZ *n* Yiddish word meaning fool

YUTZES > YUTZ

YUZU *n* type of citrus fruit

YUZUS > YUZU

YWIS *adv* certainly

YWROKE *archaic past participle of* **>** WREAK

Zz

ZA n pizza

ZABAIONE n light foamy dessert

ZABAIONES > ZABAIONE

ZABAJONE same as > ZABAIONE

ZABAJONES > ZABAJONE

ZABETA n tariff

ZABETAS > ZABETA

ZABRA n small sailing vessel

ZABRAS > ZABRA

ZABTIEH n Turkish police officer

ZABTIEHS > ZABTIEH

ZACATON n coarse grass

ZACATONS > ZACATON

ZACK n Australian five-cent piece

ZACKS > ZACK

ZADDICK adj righteous ▷ n Hasidic Jewish spiritual leader

ZADDICKS > ZADDICK

ZADDIK n Hasidic Jewish leader

ZADDIKIM > ZADDIK

ZADDIKS > ZADDIK

ZAFFAR same as > ZAFFER

ZAFFARS > ZAFFAR

ZAFFER n impure cobalt oxide, used to impart a blue colour to enamels

ZAFFERS > ZAFFER

ZAFFIR same as > ZAFFER

ZAFFIRS > ZAFFIR

ZAFFRE same as > ZAFFER

ZAFFRES > ZAFFRE

ZAFTIG adj ripe or curvaceous

ZAG vb change direction sharply

ZAGGED > ZAG

ZAGGING > ZAG

ZAGS > ZAG

ZAIBATSU n group or combine comprising a few wealthy families that controls industry, business, and finance in Japan

ZAIBATSUS > ZAIBATSU

ZAIDA n grandfather

ZAIDAS > ZAIDA

ZAIDEH same as > ZAIDA

ZAIDEHS > ZAIDEH

ZAIDIES > ZAIDY

ZAIDY same as > ZAIDA

ZAIKAI n Japanese business community

ZAIKAIS > ZAIKAI

ZAIRE n currency used in the former Zaire

ZAIRES > ZAIRE

ZAITECH n investment in financial markets by a company to supplement its main income

ZAITECHS > ZAITECH

ZAKAT n annual tax on Muslims to aid the poor in the Muslim community

ZAKATS > ZAKAT

ZAKOUSKA > ZAKOUSKI

ZAKOUSKI same as > ZAKUSKI

ZAKUSKA > ZAKUSKI

ZAKUSKI pl n hors d'oeuvres, consisting of tiny open sandwiches

ZAMAN n tropical tree

ZAMANG same as > ZAMAN

ZAMANGS > ZAMANG

ZAMANS > ZAMAN

ZAMARRA n sheepskin coat

ZAMARRAS > ZAMARRA

ZAMARRO same as > ZAMARRA

ZAMARROS > ZAMARRO

ZAMBO n offensive word for a Black person

ZAMBOMBA n drum-like musical instrument

ZAMBOMBAS > ZAMBOMBA

ZAMBOORAK n small swivel-mounted cannon

ZAMBOS > ZAMBO

ZAMBUCK n St John ambulance attendant

ZAMBUCKS > ZAMBUCK

ZAMBUK same as > ZAMBUCK

ZAMBUKS > ZAMBUK

ZAMIA n type of plant of tropical and subtropical America

ZAMIAS > ZAMIA

ZAMINDAR n (in India) the owner of an agricultural estate

ZAMINDARI n (in India) a large agricultural estate

ZAMINDARS > ZAMINDAR

ZAMINDARY same as > ZAMINDARI

ZAMOUSE n West African buffalo

ZAMOUSES > ZAMOUSE

ZAMPOGNA n Italian bagpipes

ZAMPOGNAS > ZAMPOGNA

ZAMPONE n sausage made from pig's trotters

ZAMPONI > ZAMPONE

ZAMZAWED adj (of tea) having been left in the pot to stew

ZANAMIVIR n drug used to treat influenza

ZANANA same as > ZENANA

ZANANAS > ZANANA

ZANDER n European freshwater pikeperch, valued as a food fish

ZANDERS > ZANDER

ZANELLA n twill fabric

ZANELLAS > ZANELLA

ZANIED > ZANY

ZANIER > ZANY

ZANIES > ZANY

ZANIEST > ZANY

ZANILY > ZANY

ZANINESS > ZANY

ZANJA n irrigation canal

ZANJAS > ZANJA

ZANJERO n irrigation supervisor

ZANJEROS > ZANJERO

ZANTE n type of wood

ZANTES > ZANTE

ZANTEWOOD n wood of the zante tree

ZANTHOXYL variant spelling of > XANTHOXYL

ZANY adj comical in an endearing way ▷ n clown or buffoon who imitated other performers ▷ vb clown

ZANYING > ZANY

ZANYISH > ZANY

ZANYISM > ZANY

ZANYISMS > ZANY

ZANZA same as > ZANZE

ZANZAS > ZANZA

ZANZE n African musical instrument

ZANZES > ZANZE

ZAP vb move quickly ▷ n energy, vigour, or pep ▷ interj exclamation used to express sudden or swift action

ZAPATA adj (of a moustache) drooping

ZAPATEADO n Spanish dance with stamping and very fast footwork

ZAPATEO n Cuban folk dance

ZAPATEOS > ZAPATEO

ZAPOTILLA n shoe

ZAPPED > ZAP

ZAPPER n remote control for a television etc

ZAPPERS > ZAPPER

ZAPPIER > ZAPPY

ZAPPIEST > ZAPPY

ZAPPING > ZAP

ZAPPY adj energetic

ZAPS > ZAP

ZAPTIAH same as > ZAPTIEH

ZAPTIAHS > ZAPTIAH

ZAPTIEH n Turkish police officer

ZAPTIEHS > ZAPTIEH

ZARAPE n blanket-like shawl

ZARAPES > ZARAPE

ZARATITE n green amorphous mineral

ZARATITES > ZARATITE

ZAREBA n stockade or enclosure of thorn bushes around a village or campsite

ZAREBAS > ZAREBA

ZAREEBA same as > ZAREBA

ZAREEBAS > ZAREEBA

ZARF n (esp in the Middle East) a holder, usually ornamental, for a hot coffee cup

ZARFS > ZARF

ZARI n thread made from fine gold or silver wire

ZARIBA same as > ZAREBA

ZARIBAS > ZARIBA

ZARIS > ZARI

ZARNEC n sulphide of arsenic

ZARNECS > ZARNEC

ZARNICH same as > ZARNEC

ZARNICHS > ZARNICH

ZARZUELA n type of Spanish vaudeville or operetta, usually satirical in nature

ZARZUELAS > ZARZUELA

ZAS > ZA

ZASTRUGA variant spelling of > SASTRUGA

ZASTRUGI > ZASTRUGA

ZATI n type of macaque

ZATIS > ZATI

ZAX n tool for cutting roofing slate

ZAXES > ZAX

ZAYIN n seventh letter of the Hebrew alphabet

ZAYINS > ZAYIN

ZAZEN n deep meditation undertaken whilst sitting upright with legs crossed

ZAZENS > ZAZEN

ZE pron gender-neutral pronoun

ZEA n corn silk

ZEAL n great enthusiasm or eagerness

ZEALANT archaic variant of > ZEALOT

ZEALANTS > ZEALANT

ZEALFUL > ZEAL

ZEALLESS > ZEAL

ZEALOT n fanatic or extreme enthusiast

ZEALOTISM > ZEALOT

ZEALOTRY n extreme or excessive zeal or devotion

ZEALOTS > ZEALOT

ZEALOUS adj extremely eager or enthusiastic

ZEALOUSLY > ZEALOUS

ZEALS > ZEAL

ZEAS > ZEA

ZEATIN n cytokinin derived from corn

ZEATINS > ZEATIN

ZEBEC variant spelling of > XEBEC

ZEBECK same as > ZEBEC

ZEBECKS > ZEBECK

ZEBECS > ZEBEC

ZEBRA n black-and-white striped African animal of the horse family

ZEBRAFISH n striped tropical fish

ZEBRAIC adj like a zebra

ZEBRANO n type of striped wood

ZEBRANOS > ZEBRANO

ZEBRAS > ZEBRA

ZEBRASS n offspring of a male zebra and a female ass

ZEBRASSES > ZEBRASS

ZEBRAWOOD n tree yielding striped hardwood used in cabinetwork

ZEBRINA n trailing herbaceous plant

ZEBRINAS > ZEBRINA

ZEBRINE > ZEBRA

ZEBRINES > ZEBRA

ZEBRINNY n offspring of a male horse and a female zebra

ZEBROID > ZEBRA

ZEBRULA n offspring of a male zebra and a female horse

ZEBRULAS > ZEBRULA

ZEBRULE same as > ZEBRULA

ZEBRULES > ZEBRULE

ZEBU n Asian ox with a humped back and long horns

ZEBUB n large African fly

ZEBUBS > ZEBUB

ZEBUS > ZEBU

ZECCHIN same as > ZECCHINO

ZECCHINE same as > ZECCHINO

ZECCHINES > ZECCHINE

ZECCHINI > ZECCHINO

ZECCHINO n former gold coin

ZECCHINOS > ZECCHINO

ZECCHINS > ZECCHIN

ZECHIN same as > ZECCHINO

ZECHINS > ZECHIN

ZED n British and New Zealand spoken form of the letter z

ZEDA n grandfather

ZEDAS > ZEDA

ZEDOARIES > ZEDOARY

ZEDOARY n dried rhizome of a tropical Asian plant

ZEDS > ZED

ZEE the US word for > ZED

ZEES > ZEE

ZEIN n protein occurring in maize

ZEINS > ZEIN

ZEITGEBER n agent or event that sets or resets the biological clock

ZEITGEIST n spirit or attitude of a specific time or period

ZEK n Soviet prisoner

ZEKS > ZEK

ZEL n Turkish cymbal

ZELANT alternative form of > ZEALANT

ZELANTS > ZELANT

ZELATOR same as > ZELATRIX

ZELATORS > ZELATOR

ZELATRICE same as > ZELATRIX

ZELATRIX n nun who monitors the behaviour of younger nuns

ZELKOVA n type of elm tree

ZELKOVAS > ZELKOVA

ZELOSO adv with zeal

ZELOTYPIA n morbid zeal

ZELS > ZEL

ZEMINDAR same as > ZAMINDAR

ZEMINDARI > ZEMINDAR

ZEMINDARS > ZEMINDAR

ZEMINDARY n jurisdiction of a zemindar

ZEMSTVA > ZEMSTVO

ZEMSTVO n council in Tsarist Russia

ZEMSTVOS > ZEMSTVO

ZEN n calm meditative state

ZENAIDA n dove

ZENAIDAS > ZENAIDA

ZENANA n part of Muslim or Hindu home reserved for women and girls

ZENANAS > ZENANA

ZENDIK n unbeliever or heretic

ZENDIKS > ZENDIK

ZENDO n place where Zen Buddhists study

ZENDOS > ZENDO

ZENITH n highest point of success or power

ZENITHAL > ZENITH

ZENITHS > ZENITH

ZENS > ZEN

ZEOLITE n any of a large group of glassy secondary minerals

ZEOLITES > ZEOLITE

ZEOLITIC > ZEOLITE

ZEP n type of long sandwich

ZEPHYR n soft gentle breeze

ZEPHYRS > ZEPHYR

ZEPPELIN n large cylindrical airship

ZEPPELINS > ZEPPELIN

ZEPPOLE n Italian fritter

ZEPPOLES > ZEPPOLE

ZEPPOLI > ZEPPOLE

ZEPS > ZEP

ZERDA n fennec

ZERDAS > ZERDA

ZEREBA same as > ZAREBA

ZEREBAS > ZEREBA

ZERIBA same as > ZAREBA

ZERIBAS > ZERIBA

ZERK n grease fitting

ZERKS > ZERK

ZERO n (symbol representing) the number 0 ▷ adj having no measurable quantity or size ▷ vb adjust (an instrument or scale) so as to read zero ▷ determiner no (thing) at all

ZEROED > ZERO

ZEROES > ZERO

ZEROING > ZERO

ZEROS > ZERO

ZEROTH adj denoting a term in a series that precedes the term otherwise regarded as the first term

ZERUMBET n plant stem used as stimulant and condiment

ZERUMBETS > ZERUMBET

ZEST n enjoyment or excitement ▷ vb give flavour, interest, or piquancy to

ZESTED > ZEST

ZESTER n kitchen utensil used to scrape fine shreds of peel from citrus fruits

ZESTERS > ZESTER

ZESTFUL > ZEST

ZESTFULLY > ZEST

ZESTIER > ZEST

ZESTIEST > ZEST

ZESTILY > ZEST

ZESTINESS n quality of being zesty

ZESTING > ZEST

ZESTLESS > ZEST

ZESTS > ZEST

ZESTY > ZEST

ZETA n sixth letter in the Greek alphabet

ZETAS > ZETA

ZETETIC adj proceeding by inquiry ▷ n investigation

ZETETICS > ZETETIC

ZETTABYTE n 10^{21} or 2^{70} bytes

ZEUGMA n figure of speech in which a word is used with two words although appropriate to only one of them

ZEUGMAS > ZEUGMA

ZEUGMATIC > ZEUGMA

ZEUXITE n ferriferous mineral

ZEUXITES > ZEUXITE

ZEX n tool for cutting roofing slate

ZEXES > ZEX

ZEZE n stringed musical instrument

ZEZES > ZEZE

ZHO same as > ZO

ZHOMO n female zho

ZHOMOS > ZHOMO

ZHOOSH vb make more exciting or attractive

ZHOOSHED > ZHOOSH

ZHOOSHES > ZHOOSH

ZHOOSHING > ZHOOSH

ZHOS > ZHO

ZIBELINE n sable or the fur of this animal ▷ adj of, relating to, or resembling a sable

ZIBELINES > ZIBELINE

ZIBELLINE same as > ZIBELINE

ZIBET n large civet of S and SE Asia

ZIBETH same as > ZIBET

ZIBETHS > ZIBETH

ZIBETS > ZIBET

ZIFF n beard

ZIFFIUS n sea monster

ZIFFIUSES > ZIFFIUS

ZIFFS > ZIFF

ZIG same as > ZAG

ZIGAN n gypsy

ZIGANKA n Russian dance

ZIGANKAS > ZIGANKA

ZIGANS > ZIGAN

ZIGGED > ZIG

ZIGGING > ZIG

ZIGGURAT n (in ancient Mesopotamia) a temple in the shape of a pyramid

ZIGGURATS > ZIGGURAT

ZIGS > ZIG

ZIGZAG n line or course having sharp turns in alternating directions ▷ vb move in a zigzag ▷ adj formed in or proceeding in a zigzag ▷ adv in a zigzag manner

ZIGZAGGED > ZIGZAG

ZIGZAGGER > ZIGZAG

ZIGZAGGY adj having sharp turns

ZIGZAGS > ZIGZAG

ZIKKURAT same as > ZIGGURAT

ZIKKURATS > ZIKKURAT

ZIKURAT same as > ZIGGURAT

ZIKURATS > ZIKURAT

ZILA n administrative district in India

ZILAS > ZILA

ZILCH n nothing

ZILCHES > ZILCH

ZILL n finger cymbal

ZILLA same as > ZILA

ZILLAH same as > ZILA

ZILLAHS > ZILLAH

ZILLAS > ZILLA

ZILLION n extremely large but unspecified number

ZILLIONS > ZILLION

ZILLIONTH > ZILLION

ZILLS > ZILL

ZIMB same as > ZEBUB

ZIMBI n cowrie shell used as money

ZIMBIS > ZIMBI

ZIMBS > ZIMB

ZIMOCCA n bath sponge

ZIMOCCAS > ZIMOCCA

ZIN short form of > ZINFANDEL

ZINC n bluish-white metallic element ▷ vb coat with zinc

ZINCATE n any of a class of salts derived from the amphoteric hydroxide of zinc

ZINCATES > ZINCATE

ZINCED > ZINC

Z

ZINCIC > ZINC
ZINCIER > ZINC
ZINCIEST > ZINC
ZINCIFIED > ZINCIFY
ZINCIFIES > ZINCIFY
ZINCIFY vb coat with zinc
ZINCING > ZINC
ZINCITE n red or yellow mineral
ZINCITES > ZINCITE
ZINCKED > ZINC
ZINCKIER > ZINC
ZINCKIEST > ZINC
ZINCKIFY same as > ZINCIFY
ZINCKING > ZINC
ZINCKY > ZINC
ZINCO n printing plate made from zincography
ZINCODE n positive electrode
ZINCODES > ZINCODE
ZINCOID > ZINC
ZINCOS > ZINCO
ZINCOUS > ZINC
ZINCS > ZINC
ZINCY > ZINC
ZINDABAD interj long live: used as part of a slogan in India, Pakistan, etc
ZINE n magazine or fanzine
ZINEB n organic insecticide
ZINEBS > ZINEB
ZINES > ZINE
ZINFANDEL n type of Californian wine
ZING n quality in something that makes it lively or interesting ▷ vb make or move with or as if with a high-pitched buzzing sound
ZINGANI > ZINGANO
ZINGANO n gypsy
ZINGARA n female Italian gypsy
ZINGARE > ZINGARA
ZINGARI > ZINGARO
ZINGARO n Italian gypsy
ZINGED > ZING
ZINGEL n small freshwater perch
ZINGELS > ZINGEL
ZINGER > ZING
ZINGERS > ZING
ZINGIBER n ginger plant
ZINGIBERS > ZINGIBER
ZINGIER > ZINGY
ZINGIEST > ZINGY
ZINGING > ZING
ZINGS > ZING
ZINGY adj vibrant
ZINKE n cornett
ZINKED > ZINC
ZINKENITE n steel-grey metallic mineral consisting of a sulphide of lead and antimony
ZINKES > ZINKE
ZINKIER > ZINC
ZINKIEST > ZINC
ZINKIFIED > ZINCIFY
ZINKIFIES > ZINKIFY
ZINKIFY vb coat with zinc
ZINKING > ZINC
ZINKY > ZINC

ZINNIA n plant of tropical and subtropical America
ZINNIAS > ZINNIA
ZINS > ZIN
ZIP same as > ZIPPER
ZIPLESS > ZIP
ZIPLINE n cable used for transportation across a river, gorge, etc
ZIPLINES > ZIPLINE
ZIPLOCK adj fastened with interlocking plastic strips ▷ vb seal (a ziplock storage bag)
ZIPLOCKED > ZIPLOCK
ZIPLOCKS > ZIPLOCK
ZIPOLA n nothing
ZIPOLAS > ZIPOLA
ZIPPED > ZIP
ZIPPER n fastening device operating by means of two rows of metal or plastic teeth ▷ vb fasten with a zipper
ZIPPERED adj provided or fastened with a zip
ZIPPERING > ZIPPER
ZIPPERS > ZIPPER
ZIPPIER > ZIPPY
ZIPPIEST > ZIPPY
ZIPPILY adv in a zippy manner
ZIPPINESS n quality of being zippy
ZIPPING > ZIP
ZIPPO n nothing
ZIPPOS > ZIPPO
ZIPPY adj full of energy
ZIPS > ZIP
ZIPTOP adj (of a bag) closed with a zipper
ZIPWIRE same as > ZIPLINE
ZIPWIRES > ZIPWIRE
ZIRAM n industrial fungicide
ZIRAMS > ZIRAM
ZIRCALLOY n alloy of zirconium containing small amounts of tin, chromium, and nickel. It is used in pressurized-water reactors
ZIRCALOY same as > ZIRCALLOY
ZIRCALOYS > ZIRCALOY
ZIRCON n mineral used as a gemstone and in industry
ZIRCONIA n white oxide of zirconium, used as a pigment for paints, a catalyst, and an abrasive
ZIRCONIAS > ZIRCONIA
ZIRCONIC > ZIRCONIUM
ZIRCONIUM n greyish-white metallic element that is resistant to corrosion
ZIRCONS > ZIRCON
ZIT n spot or pimple
ZITE same as > ZITI
ZITHER n musical instrument consisting of strings stretched over a flat box
ZITHERIST > ZITHER
ZITHERN same as > ZITHER
ZITHERNS > ZITHERN
ZITHERS > ZITHER
ZITI n type of pasta
ZITIS > ZITI

ZITS > ZIT
ZIZ same as > ZIZZ
ZIZANIA n aquatic grass
ZIZANIAS > ZIZANIA
ZIZEL n chipmunk
ZIZELS > ZIZEL
ZIZIT same as > ZIZITH
ZIZITH variant spelling of > TSITSITH
ZIZYPHUS n jujube tree
ZIZZ n short sleep ▷ vb take a short sleep, snooze
ZIZZED > ZIZZ
ZIZZES > ZIZZ
ZIZZING > ZIZZ
ZIZZLE vb sizzle
ZIZZLED > ZIZZLE
ZIZZLES > ZIZZLE
ZIZZLING > ZIZZLE
ZLOTE > ZLOTY
ZLOTIES > ZLOTY
ZLOTY n monetary unit of Poland
ZLOTYCH same as > ZLOTY
ZLOTYS > ZLOTY
ZO n Tibetan breed of cattle
ZOA > ZOON
ZOAEA same as > ZOEA
ZOAEAE > ZOAEA
ZOAEAS > ZOAEA
ZOARIA > ZOARIUM
ZOARIAL > ZOARIUM
ZOARIUM n colony of zooids
ZOBO same as > ZO
ZOBOS > ZOBO
ZOBU same as > ZO
ZOBUS > ZOBU
ZOCALO n plaza in Mexico
ZOCALOS > ZOCALO
ZOCCO n plinth
ZOCCOLO same as > ZOCCO
ZOCCOLOS > ZOCCOLO
ZOCCOS > ZOCCO
ZODIAC n imaginary belt in the sky within which the sun, moon, and planets appear to move
ZODIACAL > ZODIAC
ZODIACS > ZODIAC
ZOEA n free-swimming larva of a crab or related crustacean
ZOEAE > ZOEA
ZOEAL > ZOEA
ZOEAS > ZOEA
ZOECHROME same as > ZOETROPE
ZOECIA > ZOECIUM
ZOECIUM same as > ZOOECIUM
ZOEFORM > ZOEA
ZOETIC adj pertaining to life
ZOETROPE n cylinder-shaped toy with a sequence of pictures on its inner surface which produce an illusion of animation when it is rotated
ZOETROPES > ZOETROPE
ZOETROPIC > ZOETROPE
ZOFTIG adj ripe or curvaceous
ZOIATRIA n veterinary surgery
ZOIATRIAS > ZOIATRIA
ZOIATRICS n veterinary surgery

ZOIC adj relating to or having animal life
ZOISITE n grey, brown, or pink mineral
ZOISITES > ZOISITE
ZOISM n belief in magical animal powers
ZOISMS > ZOISM
ZOIST > ZOISM
ZOISTS > ZOISM
ZOL n South African slang for a cannabis cigarette
ZOLPIDEM n drug used to treat insomnia
ZOLPIDEMS > ZOLPIDEM
ZOLS > ZOL
ZOMBI same as > ZOMBIE
ZOMBIE n corpse that has been reanimated by a supernatural spirit
ZOMBIES > ZOMBIE
ZOMBIFIED > ZOMBIFY
ZOMBIFIES > ZOMBIFY
ZOMBIFY vb turn into a zombie
ZOMBIISM > ZOMBIE
ZOMBIISMS > ZOMBIE
ZOMBIS > ZOMBI
ZOMBOID adj like a zombie
ZOMBORUK n small swivel-mounted cannon
ZOMBORUKS > ZOMBORUK
ZONA n zone or belt
ZONAE > ZONA
ZONAL adj of, relating to, or of the nature of a zone
ZONALLY > ZONAL
ZONARY same as > ZONAL
ZONATE adj marked with, divided into, or arranged in zones
ZONATED same as > ZONATE
ZONATION n arrangement in zones
ZONATIONS > ZONATION
ZONDA n South American wind
ZONDAS > ZONDA
ZONE n area with particular features or properties ▷ vb divide into zones
ZONED > ZONE
ZONELESS > ZONE
ZONER n something which divides other things into zones
ZONERS > ZONER
ZONES > ZONE
ZONETIME n standard time of the time zone in which a ship is located at sea
ZONETIMES > ZONETIME
ZONING > ZONE
ZONINGS > ZONE
ZONK vb strike resoundingly
ZONKED > ZONK
ZONKING > ZONK
ZONKS > ZONK
ZONOID adj resembling a zone ▷ n finite vector sum of line segments
ZONOIDS > ZONOID
ZONULA n small zone or belt
ZONULAE > ZONULA
ZONULAR > ZONULE
ZONULAS > ZONULA

ZONULE n small zone, band, or area

ZONULES > ZONULE

ZONULET n small belt

ZONULETS > ZONULET

ZONURE n lizard with ringed tail

ZONURES > ZONURE

ZOO n place where live animals are kept for show

ZOOBIOTIC adj parasitic on or living in association with an animal

ZOOBLAST n animal cell

ZOOBLASTS > ZOOBLAST

ZOOCHORE n plant with the spores or seeds dispersed by animals

ZOOCHORES > ZOOCHORE

ZOOCHORY > ZOOCHORE

ZOOCYTIA > ZOOCYTIUM

ZOOCYTIUM n outer sheath of some social infusorians

ZOOEA same as **>** ZOEA

ZOOEAE > ZOOEA

ZOOEAL > ZOOEA

ZOOEAS > ZOOEA

ZOOECIA > ZOOECIUM

ZOOECIUM n part of a polyzoan colony that houses the feeding zooids

ZOOEY > ZOO

ZOOGAMETE n gamete that can move independently

ZOOGAMIES > ZOOGAMY

ZOOGAMOUS > ZOOGAMY

ZOOGAMY n reproduction involving zoosperm

ZOOGENIC adj produced from animals

ZOOGENIES > ZOOGENY

ZOOGENOUS same as **>** ZOOGENIC

ZOOGENY n doctrine of formation of animals

ZOOGLEA same as **>** ZOOGLOEA

ZOOGLEAE > ZOOGLEA

ZOOGLEAL > ZOOGLEA

ZOOGLEAS > ZOOGLEA

ZOOGLOEA n mass of bacteria adhering together by a jelly-like substance derived from their cell walls

ZOOGLOEAE > ZOOGLOEA

ZOOGLOEAL > ZOOGLOEA

ZOOGLOEAS > ZOOGLOEA

ZOOGLOEIC > ZOOGLOEA

ZOOGONIES > ZOOGONY

ZOOGONOUS > ZOOGONY

ZOOGONY same as **>** ZOOGENY

ZOOGRAFT n animal tissue grafted onto a human body

ZOOGRAFTS > ZOOGRAFT

ZOOGRAPHY n branch of zoology concerned with the description of animals

ZOOID n any independent animal body, such as an individual of a coral colony

ZOOIDAL > ZOOID

ZOOIDS > ZOOID

ZOOIER > ZOO

ZOOIEST > ZOO

ZOOKEEPER n person who cares for animals in a zoo

ZOOKS short form of **>** GADZOOKS

ZOOLATER > ZOOLATRY

ZOOLATERS > ZOOLATRY

ZOOLATRIA same as **>** ZOOLATRY

ZOOLATRY n worship of animals

ZOOLITE n fossilized animal

ZOOLITES > ZOOLITE

ZOOLITH n fossilized animal

ZOOLITHIC > ZOOLITH

ZOOLITHS > ZOOLITH

ZOOLITIC > ZOOLITE

ZOOLOGIC > ZOOLOGY

ZOOLOGIES > ZOOLOGY

ZOOLOGIST > ZOOLOGY

ZOOLOGY n study of animals

ZOOM vb move or rise very rapidly ▷ n sound or act of zooming

ZOOMABLE adj capable of being viewed at various levels of magnification

ZOOMANCY n divination through observing the actions of animals

ZOOMANIA n extreme or excessive devotion to animals

ZOOMANIAS > ZOOMANIA

ZOOMANTIC > ZOOMANCY

ZOOMED > ZOOM

ZOOMETRIC > ZOOMETRY

ZOOMETRY n study of the relative size of the different parts of an animal or animals

ZOOMING > ZOOM

ZOOMORPH n representation of an animal form

ZOOMORPHS > ZOOMORPH

ZOOMORPHY > ZOOMORPH

ZOOMS > ZOOM

ZOON vb zoom ▷ n zooid

ZOONAL > ZOON

ZOONED > ZOON

ZOONIC adj concerning animals

ZOONING > ZOON

ZOONITE n segment of an articulated animal

ZOONITES > ZOONITE

ZOONITIC > ZOONITE

ZOONOMIA same as **>** ZOONOMY

ZOONOMIAS > ZOONOMIA

ZOONOMIC > ZOONOMY

ZOONOMIES > ZOONOMY

ZOONOMIST > ZOONOMY

ZOONOMY n science of animal life

ZOONOSES > ZOONOSIS

ZOONOSIS n any infection or disease that is transmitted to humans from lower vertebrates

ZOONOTIC > ZOONOSIS

ZOONS > ZOON

ZOOPATHY n science of animal diseases

ZOOPERAL > ZOOPERY

ZOOPERIES > ZOOPERY

ZOOPERIST > ZOOPERY

ZOOPERY n experimentation on animals

ZOOPHAGAN n carnivore

ZOOPHAGY n eating other animals

ZOOPHILE n person who is devoted to animals and their protection

ZOOPHILES > ZOOPHILE

ZOOPHILIA n condition in which a person has a sexual attraction to animals

ZOOPHILIC > ZOOPHILE

ZOOPHILY same as **>** ZOOPHILIA

ZOOPHOBE > ZOOPHOBIA

ZOOPHOBES > ZOOPHOBIA

ZOOPHOBIA n unusual or morbid dread of animals

ZOOPHORI > ZOOPHORUS

ZOOPHORIC > ZOOPHORUS

ZOOPHORUS n frieze with animal figures

ZOOPHYTE n any animal resembling a plant, such as a sea anemone

ZOOPHYTES > ZOOPHYTE

ZOOPHYTIC > ZOOPHYTE

ZOOPLASTY n surgical transplantation to humans of animal tissues

ZOOS > ZOO

ZOOSCOPIC > ZOOSCOPY

ZOOSCOPY n condition causing hallucinations of animals

ZOOSPERM n gamete that can move independently

ZOOSPERMS > ZOOSPERM

ZOOSPORE n asexual spore of some algae and fungi that moves by means of flagella

ZOOSPORES > ZOOSPORE

ZOOSPORIC > ZOOSPORE

ZOOSTEROL n any of a group of animal sterols, such as cholesterol

ZOOT n as in zoot suit man's suit consisting of baggy trousers and a long jacket

ZOOTAXIES > ZOOTAXY

ZOOTAXY n science of the classification of animals

ZOOTECHNY n science of breeding animals

ZOOTHECIA n outer layers of certain protozoans

ZOOTHEISM n treatment of an animal as a god

ZOOTHOME n group of zooids

ZOOTHOMES > ZOOTHOME

ZOOTIER > ZOOTY

ZOOTIEST > ZOOTY

ZOOTOMIC > ZOOTOMY

ZOOTOMIES > ZOOTOMY

ZOOTOMIST > ZOOTOMY

ZOOTOMY n branch of zoology concerned with the dissection and anatomy of animals

ZOOTOXIC > ZOOTOXIN

ZOOTOXIN n toxin, such as snake venom, that is produced by an animal

ZOOTOXINS > ZOOTOXIN

ZOOTROPE same as **>** ZOETROPE

ZOOTROPES > ZOOTROPE

ZOOTROPHY n nourishment of animals

ZOOTY adj showy

ZOOTYPE n animal figure used as a symbol

ZOOTYPES > ZOOTYPE

ZOOTYPIC > ZOOTYPE

ZOOZOO n wood pigeon

ZOOZOOS > ZOOZOO

ZOPILOTE n small American vulture

ZOPILOTES > ZOPILOTE

ZOPPA adj syncopated

ZOPPO same as **>** ZOPPA

ZORBING n activity of travelling downhill inside a large air-cushioned hollow ball

ZORBINGS > ZORBING

ZORBONAUT n person who engages in the activity of zorbing

ZORGITE n copper-lead selenide

ZORGITES > ZORGITE

ZORI n Japanese sandal

ZORIL same as **>** ZORILLA

ZORILLA n skunk-like African musteline mammal having a long black-and-white coat

ZORILLAS > ZORILLA

ZORILLE same as **>** ZORILLA

ZORILLES > ZORILLE

ZORILLO same as **>** ZORILLE

ZORILLOS > ZORILLO

ZORILS > ZORIL

ZORINO n skunk fur

ZORINOS > ZORINO

ZORIS > ZORI

ZORRO n hoary fox

ZORROS > ZORRO

ZOS > ZO

ZOSTER n shingles; herpes zoster

ZOSTERS > ZOSTER

ZOUAVE n (formerly) member of a body of French infantry composed of Algerian recruits

ZOUAVES > ZOUAVE

ZOUK n style of dance music that combines African and Latin American rhythms

ZOUKS > ZOUK

ZOUNDS interj mild oath indicating surprise or indignation

ZOWEE same as **>** ZOWIE

ZOWIE interj expression of pleasurable surprise

ZOYSIA n type of grass with short stiffly pointed leaves, often used for lawns

ZOYSIAS > ZOYSIA

ZUCCHETTI > ZUCCHETTO

ZUCCHETTO n small round skullcap worn by clergymen and varying in colour according to the rank of the wearer

ZUCCHINI n courgette

ZUCCHINIS > ZUCCHINI

ZUCHETTA same as **>** ZUCCHETTO

ZUCHETTAS > ZUCHETTA

ZUCHETTO same as **>** ZUCCHETTO

Z

ZUCHETTOS > ZUCHETTO
ZUFFOLI > ZUFFOLO
ZUFFOLO same as > ZUFOLO
ZUFOLI > ZUFOLO
ZUFOLO n small flute
ZUFOLOS > ZUFOLO
ZUGZWANG n (in chess) position in which one player can move only with loss or severe disadvantage ▷ vb manoeuvre (one's opponent) into a zugzwang
ZUGZWANGS > ZUGZWANG
ZULU n (in the NATO phonetic alphabet) used to represent z
ZULUS > ZULU
ZUMBOORUK n small swivel-mounted cannon
ZUPA n confederation of Serbian villages
ZUPAN n head of a zupa
ZUPANS > ZUPAN
ZUPAS > ZUPA
ZUPPA n Italian soup
ZUPPAS > ZUPPA
ZURF same as > ZARF
ZURFS > ZURF
ZUZ n ancient Hebrew silver coin
ZUZIM > ZUZ
ZUZZIM > ZUZ
ZWANZIGER n silver coin formerly used in Southern Germany and Austria until the end of the 19th century
ZWIEBACK n small type of rusk

ZWIEBACKS > ZWIEBACK
ZYDECO n type of Black Cajun music
ZYDECOS > ZYDECO
ZYGA > ZYGON
ZYGAENID adj of the burnet moth genus
ZYGAENOID same as > ZYGAENID
ZYGAL > ZYGON
ZYGANTRA > ZYGANTRUM
ZYGANTRUM n vertebral articulation in snakes and some lizards
ZYGOCACTI n branching cactuses
ZYGODONT adj possessing paired molar cusps
ZYGOID same as > DIPLOID
ZYGOMA n slender arch of bone on each side of the skull of mammals
ZYGOMAS > ZYGOMA
ZYGOMATA > ZYGOMA
ZYGOMATIC adj of or relating to the zygoma
ZYGON n brain fissure
ZYGOPHYTE n plant that reproduces by means of zygospores
ZYGOSE > ZYGOSIS
ZYGOSES > ZYGOSIS
ZYGOSIS n direct transfer of DNA between two cells that are temporarily joined
ZYGOSITY > ZYGOSIS
ZYGOSPERM same as > ZYGOSPORE

ZYGOSPORE n thick-walled spore formed from the zygote of some fungi and algae
ZYGOTE n fertilized egg cell
ZYGOTENE n second stage of the prophase of meiosis
ZYGOTENES > ZYGOTENE
ZYGOTES > ZYGOTE
ZYGOTIC > ZYGOTE
ZYLONITE variant spelling of > XYLONITE
ZYLONITES > ZYLONITE
ZYMASE n mixture of enzymes that is obtained as an extract from yeast and ferments sugars
ZYMASES > ZYMASE
ZYME n ferment
ZYMES > ZYME
ZYMIC > ZYME
ZYMITE n priest who uses leavened bread during communion
ZYMITES > ZYMITE
ZYMOGEN n any of various inactive precursors of enzymes activated by a kinase
ZYMOGENE same as > ZYMOGEN
ZYMOGENES > ZYMOGENE
ZYMOGENIC adj of, or relating to a zymogen
ZYMOGENS > ZYMOGEN
ZYMOGRAM n band of electrophoretic medium showing a pattern of enzymes following

electrophoresis
ZYMOGRAMS > ZYMOGRAM
ZYMOID adj relating to a ferment
ZYMOLOGIC > ZYMOLOGY
ZYMOLOGY n chemistry of fermentation
ZYMOLYSES > ZYMOLYSIS
ZYMOLYSIS n process of fermentation
ZYMOLYTIC > ZYMOLYSIS
ZYMOME n glutinous substance that is insoluble in alcohol
ZYMOMES > ZYMOME
ZYMOMETER n instrument for estimating the degree of fermentation
ZYMOSAN n insoluble carbohydrate found in yeast
ZYMOSANS > ZYMOSAN
ZYMOSES > ZYMOSIS
ZYMOSIS same as > ZYMOLYSIS
ZYMOTIC adj of, relating to, or causing fermentation ▷ n disease
ZYMOTICS > ZYMOTIC
ZYMURGIES > ZYMURGY
ZYMURGY n study of fermentation processes
ZYTHUM n Ancient Egyptian beer
ZYTHUMS > ZYTHUM
ZYZZYVA n American weevil
ZYZZYVAS > ZYZZYVA
ZZZ n informal word for sleep
ZZZS > ZZZ

Improving Your SCRABBLE™ Game

Barry Grossman

CONTENTS

1 Two- and three-letter words

A major part of improving your Scrabble game consists of having a large armoury of useful words at your disposal. You may think the longer the word you know is, the more useful it will be, as it's likely to score more. However, in fact, the key to a good Scrabble vocabulary is a good knowledge of short words, particularly words of two and three letters.

Short words are, of course, invaluable for helping you complete a game and to use difficult letters. They have another great use, which can really help you boost your score. You can use short words to join or 'hook' the word you want to play on to the board, by playing parallel to another word. You will usually make more than one word each turn and so make a higher score than just by crossing over another word. Look at the two different ways of playing on the two boards shown here.

High-scoring play
Adding the letters **F**, **A**, **R**, **E** to **TEAM** gives you a score of 25.

Low-scoring play
Adding the letters **F**, **A**, **R**, **E** to **TEAM** to give **AFTER** gives you a score of 8.

Notice that the high-scoring play has scored 17 more points than the low-scoring play. This score was only possible because of the word **FA** (think musical scales).

Two-letter words

Here is the first, essential thing you have to know to improve your game: *know all the allowable two-letter words*. There are 127 of them in *Collins Official Scrabble Words*, but to make the list more manageable, you can divide them into three groups:

- The ones you already know.
- The ones you already know, but may not have realized were words.
- The ones you probably don't know.

Commonly known two-letter words

Here are the words you most likely know and which will appear in most dictionaries:

AH	AM	AN	AS	AT	AX	AY
BE	BY					
DO						
EH						
GO						
HA	HE	HI	HO			
ID	IF	IN	IS	IT		
LA	LO					
MA	ME	MY				
NO						
OF	OH	ON	OR	OX		
PA						
SO						
TO						
UP	US					
WE						
YE						

Less well-known two-letter words

There are then a good selection of words that you probably know but were unsure whether they were allowable Scrabble words. As we enter less familiar areas, it is useful to know the meaning of the special words you use, not least so you can convince those you are playing with that the words are for real.

Contracted words

AD	advertisement
BI	bisexual
MO	moment
OP	operation
PO	chamberpot
RE	regarding
TA	thank you

Exclamations and interjections

BO	exclamation used to startle or surprise someone
ER	sound made when hesitating in speech
EW	expression of disgust
HM	sound made to express hesitation or doubt
MM	expression of enjoyment of taste or smell
OI	shout to attract attention
OK	expression of approval
OW	exclamation of pain
SH	exclamation to request silence or quiet
ST	used to attract attention
UH, UM, UR	used to express hesitation or uncertainty in speech
YO	used as a greeting

Then there are letters of the alphabet when spelt out. At the end of the list are some names for some Greek letters.

Letters of the alphabet

AR	letter **R**
EF	letter **F**
EL	letter **L** or an abbreviated version of **ELEVATED RAILWAY**, as in Chicago
EM	letter **M** or a standard unit of measurement in typography
EN	letter **N** or a unit of measurement that is half an em
ES	letter **S**
EX	letter **X** or a preposition meaning not including or an informal name for a former husband or wife
PE	letter **P** or the 17th letter of the Hebrew alphabet
TE	letter **T** or the seventh degree of any major scale
MU, **NU**, **PI** and **XI** are all Greek letters	

Unfamiliar two-letter words

The third group of words will be less familiar, but, as a result, likely to be very useful once you have remembered them. They are listed below, and then some explanations follow.

AA	AB	AE	AG	AI	AL
BA	BO				
CH					
DA	DE	DI			
EA	ED	EE	ET		
FA	FE	FY			
GI	GU				
IO					
JA	JO				
KA	KI	KO	KY		
LI					
MI					
NA	NE	NY			
OB	OD	OE	OM	OO	OS
OU					
QI					
SI					
TI					
UG	UN	UT			
WO					
XU					
YU					
ZA	ZE	ZO			

If all this looks a bit gobbledygookish, you may be surprised to know that even some of these are more familiar to you than you might realise:

- An **AB** is an abdominal muscle, as in toning up your abs and your pecs.
- **OM** is what Hindus and Buddhists chant as part of their prayers.
- **AA** is a word from Hawaiian, meaning a rough volcanic rock. Its opposite, smooth volcanic rock, is called **PAHOEHOE**.
- **ZO** is a Tibetan cross-breed of a yak and a cow, also spelt **ZHO**, **DZO**, **DZHO** or **DSO**, useful Scrabble words every man-jack of them.

Just to help you along, here are a list of meanings for the rest of them.

AE	one
AG	agriculture
AI	shaggy-coated slow-moving South American animal
AL	Asian shrub or tree
BA	Ancient Egyptian symbol for the soul
BO	exclamation used to startle or surprise someone
CH	obsolete form of I
DA	Burmese knife
DE	of, from
DI	plural of **DEUS** (god)
EA	river
ED	editor
EE	eye (*Scots*)
ET	ate (*dialect*)
FA	fourth degree of any major scale (*music*)
FE	*variant of* Hebrew letter **PE**
FY	exclamation of disapproval
GI	loose-fitting white suit worn in judo and karate
GU	type of violin used in Shetland
IO	exclamation of triumph
JA	yes (*in South Africa*)
JO	sweetheart (*Scots*)
KA	(in ancient Egypt) a spirit dwelling as a vital force in a person
KI	vital energy
KO	traditional digging tool (*in New Zealand*)
KY	cows (*Scots*)
LI	Chinese measurement of distance
MI	third degree of any major scale (*music*)
NA	no (*Scots*)
NE	nor
NY	near
OB	expression of opposition
OD	hypothetical force formerly thought to be responsible for many natural phenomena
OE	grandchild

OO	wool (*Scots*)
OS	mouthlike opening
OU	man, chap
QI	vital life force (*in Oriental medicine and martial arts*)
SI	seventh degree of any major scale (*music*)
TI	seventh degree of any major scale (*music*)
UG	to hate
UN	one
UT	the note C
WO	woe
XU	Vietnamese currency unit
YU	jade
ZA	pizza
ZE	gender-neutral pronoun

JOE	sweetheart (*Scots*)
RAJ	British government in India before 1947
TAJ	tall conical cap

Containing Q
QAT	evergreen shrubs
QIN	a Chinese stringed instrument
QIS	plural of **QI** (*vital life force*)
QUA	in the capacity of
SUQ	open-air market place, e.g. in North Africa

Containing X
DEX	dextroamphetamine
DOX	publish someone's personal information on the internet
GOX	gaseous oxygen
HOX	to hamstring
KEX	any of several umbelliferous plants
LUX	unit of illumination
RAX	to stretch or extend
REX	king
VAX	vaccination
VOX	voice
WEX	wax
WOX	wax
XED	having a cross against
XIS	plural of **XI** (*Greek alphabet letter*)
ZAX	tool for cutting roof slate

Have a look back at the two-letter words every so often as you're going through the book. Once you're happy with the first few groups (i.e. the common ones, the contractions, the interjections and the letters), have a real go at mastering the unusual ones. They really are the essential first step to improving your game.

Three-letter words
But it doesn't end there. **Three-letter words are almost as important as the twos** for helping you build up your moves – and there are a lot more of them. Unless you have a lot of time and aptitude to study lists, or have a photographic memory, it will take you a few months to get to grips fully with the threes. Take them gradually, starting with the ones containing **J**, **Q**, **X** and **Z**. You won't need to know all of them before your game starts to improve.

Here are some of the most useful threes:

Containing J
AJI	type of spicy pepper
GJU	type of violin used in Shetland
JAP	to splash
JEE	mild exclamation of surprise
JIZ	wig

Containing Z
You can remember some of the **Z**-threes in sets of two and three:
BEZ	part of a deer's horn
BIZ	business
CAZ	casual
COZ, CUZ	cousin
FEZ	tasselled cap
FIZ	fizz
MIZ	misery
MOZ	hex
SAZ	Middle Eastern stringed instrument
SEZ	informal spelling of 'says'
ZEN	calm meditative state
ZEP	type of long sandwich
ZIG, ZAG	to change direction sharply

Other useful Z-threes

ADZ	tool with cutting blade at right angles to the handle
DZO	Tibetan breed of cattle
JIZ	wig
TIZ	state of confusion
YEZ	yes
ZAX	tool for cutting roof slate
ZOA	independent animal bodies (*plural of* **ZOON**)
ZOS	plural of **ZO** (*Tibetan breed of cattle*)

These lists are not exhaustive, but they will get you started. You won't always be able to fit in a **QUIVER**, a **ZEBRA** or an **ANNEX**, so you need to know a good selection of these shorter words to help you play your high-scoring letters – preferably for a more than face-value score.

Threes containing awkward letters

Other useful three-letter words are those that can help you get rid of awkward letters like **U** and **V**, or which allow you to use excess vowels. You should try to remember:

AIA	female servant, usually Indian or Malay
AUA	yellow-eye mullet (*Māori*)
AUE	Māori exclamation of pain or astonishment
AYU	small Japanese fish
EAU	river
UME	sour Japanese fruit
UVA	grape
VAU, VAV	sixth letter of the Hebrew alphabet

Threes as 'hooks'

By 'hooks', we mean words which can be formed by adding one letter at the beginning or end of another word. Threes which are

hooks of frequently used twos can be very helpful. You'll find that you play **ZO** fairly often now that you know it, which is why it's especially good to know **AZO**, **DZO** and **ZOA** – so that you can add the extra letter to an already-played **ZO**, making another word at right angles while you're doing it.

The lists of useful **J**, **Q**, **X** and **Z** words above have been compiled partly with hooks in mind. Here are a few more commonly played twos with the threes you can make from them:

AA:	AAH	AAL	AAS	BAA
	CAA	FAA	MAA	
CH:	ACH	CHA	CHE	CHI
	ECH	ICH	OCH	
HM:	HMM	OHM		
KY:	KYE	KYU	SKY	

By now, you're no doubt wondering what these odd-looking words mean. As with the twos, some are more familiar than you might realize – **BAA** and **MAA** are the cries of a sheep and a goat respectively, **CHA** is tea, **ACH** and **OCH** are what you say in Scotland when you're surprised, **HMM** is what you say if you're puzzled, and **AAS** is the plural of the rough volcanic rock **AA**. Here are some more meanings:

AAH	to exclaim in pleasure
AAL	Asian shrub or tree
CAA	to call (*Scots*)
FAA	to fall (*Scots*)
CHE	dialect form of I
CHI	22nd letter of the Greek alphabet
ECH, ICH	to eke out
KYE	Korean fundraising meeting
KYU	in judo, one of the five grades for inexperienced competitors
OHM	unit of electrical resistance

Scrabble facts – The only letter which does not feature in any two-letter word is **V**. *There are no twos ending in* **C**, **J**, **Q** *or* **Z**.

Don't worry about meanings

A word of advice – don't get too hung-up on meanings. It's a familiar, plaintive cry when someone new to a Scrabble club has an unfamiliar word played against them: 'What does that mean?'. It only adds to their bafflement when, as often as not, the answer comes back, 'I don't know'. It comes back to what has been said before – it's not knowing lots of words that wins you games, it's knowing the right words.

Experienced players build up a stockpile of words that they know will prove useful to them again and again. Sometimes the words have interesting meanings which can help you remember them. But often it's just another fish or plant, or a word Shakespeare used, and which has lain, dusty and unloved, at the back of the cupboard of English words ever since. Until, that is, Scrabble players came along, blew the dust off and started using it. Some of the meanings worth knowing are given in this book, but there is no rule that says you have to know the meaning of every word you play and, at the risk of incurring the wrath of the purists,

I would suggest that it's very often all right just to know the word because it's good for Scrabble and not to worry about the meaning.

Another reason it is not *de rigueur* to ask about meanings during a game is that you might seem to be fishing for useful information, such as whether the word is a noun, verb or adjective, and therefore whether you can put an **S** or some other letter after it. The time to ask about meanings is after a game, not during it.

> **Scrabble tip** – *You can get rid of excess* **I**s *and* **U**s *with* **IWI** *(a Māori tribe),* **ULU** *(type of knife) and* **UTU** *(a reward). You can then use hooks to turn them into* **KIWI**, **ZULU** *and* **TUTU**.

When you are ready, you can find complete lists of three-letter words on the internet. In the meantime, you will be doing fine if you learn the twos and make a start on the threes highlighted in this chapter. You'll soon wonder how you ever managed to play without **AIA**, **AUA**, **WEX** or **WOX**.

2 Dealing with J, Q, X and Z

Many players don't like to pick 'the big tiles' – **J**, **Q**, **X** and **Z**. They think that because there are fewer words in which to play them, they'll be hard to get rid of, and perhaps will even end up on their rack at the end of the game, costing them a handful of points. This is wrong. The big tiles are, *usually*, good tiles to pick.

The big tiles
You have already seen the two-letter words and some of the threes containing **J**, **Q**, **X** and **Z**. Right away you have an armoury of words that will help play these tiles.

Your rack: **D E I K L Q U**

Get points with short words
The good thing about these small words is that they may well help you play a big tile for a worthwhile score. Remind yourself of the twos containing 'the big four':

JA	JO			
QI				
AX	EX	XI	OX	XU
ZA	ZE	ZO		

Have a look at the section of a board in play opposite.

You could play **QUITE** using the **T** on the board, scoring 16. But with your new-found knowledge of **QI**, you can play **QI** both ways, slotting in another two-letter word, **ID**, as well for a very healthy 65 points.

In a similar way, how would you score more than 60 points with the board and rack at the top of the facing page?

You should see right away that the Triple Letter square is the one which is going to pay the dividend. Playing the **J** alone to make **JO** scores 25. But can you play a word downwards as well to get the **J** tripled again? **JO** doesn't fit in this case because you can't have **OTE**, but there's no problem with **ATE**.

Playing **QI** scores 65 points.

So play **JA** downwards, also making **JO** and **ATE**, and you're getting somewhere – 53 points for doing very little. Even better, add the **P** to the end of **JA** making **JAP**, turning **LATE** into **PLATE**, and you've bagged yourself another 10 – 63 for the move which is shown on the right-hand column.

Always be on the lookout for these small but profitable moves when you have one of the big tiles. The **X**, which forms two-letter words with all the vowels (**AX EX XI OX XU**), is particularly useful for this tactic.

Your rack: **A D F I J O P**

Playing **JAP** scores 63.

Get points with longer words

Another great way to get big scores with the big tiles is to look for 'double-letter–double-word' slots, or, even better, 'triple-letter–double-word' or 'double-letter–triple-word'. It works like this. Remember that if one of the letters in your word covers a Premium *Letter* square, and another covers a Premium *Word* square, the appropriate letter is doubled or tripled before the whole word. So it's another way of making a letter count for a mighty *six times* its face value. You need to make sure that it's a high-scoring tile that gets the six-times treatment.

Look at the situation on the board shown opposite. On your rack you have **E E I N O S** plus one of the big tiles. Can you see where you could get your big tile doubled then redoubled, or doubled then tripled, or tripled then doubled, if it was a **J**, a **Q** or a **Z**?

Of course, you need to think here of rather longer words than the two- and three-letter ones we have been using up to now. There are plenty of common five- and six-letter words, even with the big tiles in them, and none of the words you are looking for here is unusual. The four boards at the top of the next page show you some possible solutions.

With a rack of **E E I N O S** plus a **J**, **Q** or **Z**, there are opportunities for multiple scores.

Score with J, Q, X or Z on the Triple Word square

If no such opportunities present themselves when you have a big tile, you can often get a good score simply by mopping up a handy Triple Word square.

Look at the position on the board shown at the bottom of the next page. Ordinarily it wouldn't be worth much to use this Triple Word square. Low-scoring tiles will not score

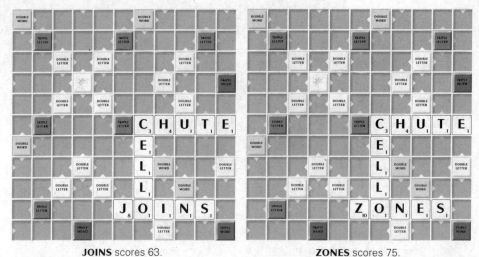

JOINS scores 63.

ZONES scores 75.

QUINS scores 48.

SNEEZE scores 75.

much and, if the left-hand row is usable all the way to the top or bottom, you could be opening a good place for your opponent to play their seven tiles for a high-scoring bonus. But if you can slot in **JET**, **QAT** or **ZIT**, you pocket a handy 30 or 36 points, and you would be very unlucky if your opponent was ready to move in with an eight-letter word beginning or ending with the high-scoring tile you have provided. If your opponent does use the high-scorer to make a word that isn't a 50-point bonus, it would be most unlikely to score as many as yours just has. It would quite likely score no more than 12 or 14 points – a big net profit for you.

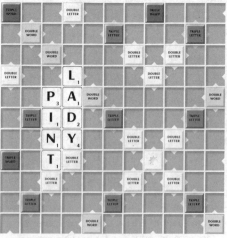

On this board use the Triple Word square for a high-score.

Useful four- and five-letter words with J, Q, X and Z

JOCO	relaxed
JUGA	plural of **JUGUM**, part of an insect's forewing
JORAM	large drinking bowl
JORUM	large drinking bowl
AFLAJ	plural of **FALAJ**
FALAJ	water channel
NDUJA	spicy pork paste
AQUA	water
QAPIK	monetary unit of Azerbaijan
QUATE	fortune
QUINE	a young, unmarried woman (*Scots*)
TRANQ	tranquiliser
IXIA	southern African plant
PREX	US college president
URBEX	urban exploration
EXOME	part of the genome
FLEXI	flexitime
SOREX	a shrew or related animal
XENIA	influence of pollen upon the form of the fruit that develops
ZEDA	grandfather
ZEIN	protein occurring in maize
ZILA	administrative district in India
YOWZA	exclamation of enthusiasm
ZAIRE	currency used in the former Zaire

But the big tiles aren't always good

There are times when you don't want to pull one of these high-scorers out of the bag: when you're close to a bonus, and, sometimes, when you're close to the end of a game.

Breaking up a bonus word

If you have six low-scoring tiles, well balanced between vowels and consonants, and with not too many duplicates, you should be well on your way to making a seven-letter bonus word. Picking **J**, **Q**, **X** or **Z** at that stage just screws the whole thing up, unless you're lucky enough to pick, say, a **Z** to a rack of **A E I N S T**,

which you can then arrange into **ZANIEST**. Usually you just have to play the high-scorer as quickly as possible for a low score, such as using the **Z** to make **ZO** for 11 points.

Pulling out a **Q** in such circumstances can be a real challenge. You need to know that there are some words that use a **Q** without a **U**, many of Arabic origin. Here are some examples of allowed words:

QI	vital life force (*in Oriental medicine and martial arts*)
QAT	white-flowered evergreen shrub
QADI	judge in a Muslim country
QAID	chief
QOPH	19th letter of the Hebrew alphabet
WAQF	religious or charitable endowment
FAQIR	Muslim who spurns worldly possessions
QANAT	underground irrigation channel
QIBLA	direction of Mecca
TALAQ	Muslim form of divorce

Sometimes you are faced with the dilemma of whether to break up your promising combination (**A E I N S T** or whatever) for the sake of getting around 20 points for your high scorer rather than about 11 or so. How much easier if you had drawn an **R** for **RETAINS** or **G** for **SEATING**.

At the end of a game

The other time you may not want to see a big tile arriving on your rack is towards the end of the game. It depends on whether there is somewhere to play it for at least 20 points or so. If there is, it can win you a close game. If not, you either have to play it off for what you can (possibly giving your opponent a chance to play out and leave you with the rest of your letters on your rack), or conversely, get rid of the rest of your letters for whatever you can and perhaps be stuck with the biggie. In some cases, if the board is blocked, you might not be able to get rid of it at all.

3 Using the S

Although **S** is only worth one point, it's much more valuable than you might think, because it can help you form seven-letter words and score 50 bonus points.

If you look at a game played between two good club players, and one between two less experienced players, a few differences will quickly be obvious.

- The stronger players will have played plenty of those unusual two- and three-letter words we have already looked at.
- There will be more parallel plays, resulting in solid blocks of tiles, rather than words which criss-cross through each other.
- There will be more seven- and eight-letter words played for 50-point bonuses.

This chapter will focus on the third of these, and in particular, how to use four of the six best tiles in the set – the four **S**s.

Why is the S so useful?
Look around you and come up with the first few words that come into your head. You might think of **CHAIR**, **TABLE**, **BOOK**, **SIT** and **READ**. Depending on who's in the room with you, you could come up with **MAN**, **WOMAN**, **HUSBAND**, **WIFE**, **BOY**, **GIRL**.

And what does every one of those words have in common? Yes, you can put an **S** at the end of all of them. Even **MAN** (he mans the lifeboat), **WOMAN** (to staff with women) and **WIFE** (to become a wife or take a wife) are verbs which can have **S** after them (or 'take an **S**', as Scrabble players tend to say). In fact, nearly every noun and verb in the English language can take an **S**. Many of the smaller words take **S**, and not always because of their status as a noun or verb – **DI** is a noun but is plural already (plural of **DEUS**, a god), but you can have **DIS**, teenage slang meaning to disrespect.

> **Scrabble tip** – *Some unexpected words that take an **S** (i.e. they can have an **S** put at the end of them):*
> **EROTIC ERRATIC MALTED PRY TELLY TRILBY WICKED**

Even a lot of words that end in **S** take an **S** – **PRINCES** (to give **PRINCESS**), **POSSES** (to give **POSSESS**), **BRAS** (to give **BRASS**), **NEEDLES** (to give **NEEDLESS**) and indeed **DIS** (to give **DISS**, to treat with contempt). **ZEBRAS** can become **ZEBRASS** (a cross between a zebra and an ass), and if you're ever in a game where **DEADLINE** is played, then someone makes it **DEADLINES**, you could well and truly flabbergast your opponent by turning that into **DEADLINESS**.

> **Scrabble facts** – *Don't forget that there are four **S** tiles in a set, so there's a reasonably high chance that you'll get one at some point in the game.*

Using your S
The relevance of all this to the **S** on your Scrabble rack is twofold. Firstly, if you can make a six-letter word with the other six letters, the chances are you'll be able to stick an **S** on the end of it and you've got a seven-letter word. So you've only got six letters to worry about manipulating. That means, assuming no blanks or duplicates, you only have 720 different ways to arrange your tiles which, while it might sound quite a lot, is a lot easier than the 5,040 ways you can arrange seven different tiles.

Of course, you may have a seven-letter word with an **S** in it, but the **S** isn't at the end. For example, with a rack of **I L N O R S T**, it may only be after coming up with wrong 'uns like *litrons* and *trinols* that you finally sniff out

A good board for playing an **S**.

Using the **S** to get down **WRITS** scores 44.

NOSTRIL. However, it's worth putting your **S** at the end of the rack and thinking around the other six to start with, and only if that fails should you need to be more imaginative.

Secondly, once you've found your bonus word, you have a high chance of being able to fit it in. What can match the desolation of working out a splendid seven and then not being able to get it down? But with all those other words already on the board, most of them taking an **S**, you will usually have a couple of positions onto which you can hook your brilliant bonus.

It is worth stressing that you should not necessarily hang onto an **S** until you can get a bonus with it. Its usefulness for hooking means you can often get a good score without using it in a bonus word. Watch especially for positions where you can get two words doubled with the addition of an **S**. Look at the board above with a Double Word square next to **FIRM**.

If you have an **S** in this position, you should be looking to make whatever word you can with it, and use it to turn **FIRM** into **FIRMS**. If you can get a high-scorer on the Double Letter square, so much the better. Something like **WRITS**, coming down to also make **FIRMS**, would score 44 (see above).

To summarize, the S can:

- Allow you to play a word, hooking an existing word, and thus scoring for both.
- Increase your chance of finding a seven-letter word.
- Taking 1 and 2 together, it can increase your chance of finding a playable position for your seven-letter word.

You should expect to score at least 20 for an **S**, preferably more than 25.

The two Ss problem

If one **S** is good, it follows that two on your rack at the same time must be twice as good. Right? Wrong!

Why? Well, quite simply, two of anything on your rack tends to weaken it (leaving aside blanks, which we'll come to in the next chapter). It's all to do with those different combinations again – you have far fewer separate ways of arranging your letters if you have a duplicate.

Two **E**s are usually alright, because **E** is such a common letter in English. And two **S**s are certainly better than some other duplicates; the dreaded duplicate **V** or **U** are real killers.

But a second **S** has basically lost its advantage of being an **S** – its essential 'essness' (no, not a valid word). If you put one **S** to one side, hoping to make a word with the other six letters, and then stick the **S** at the end of it to make a seven, what has happened is that your second **S** has turned into just another letter. You're not really very likely to pick the letters for **ZEBRASS**, and your opponent would be amazed if you got all four **S**s for **POSSESS**.

As it happens, the most common initial letter for a word in this book is **S**, and by quite a long way. So yes, there are lots of words, many of them seven- and eight-letter words, that begin and end with an **S**. Then there are armies of words ending in –**ISES** and –**ISTS**. So it's far from impossible to get a bonus word with two **S**s. It's just not twice as easy as getting one with one **S**.

Generally, the thing to do with a duplicate **S** is play one, hooking it onto a word already on the board, making another word at the same time, preferably using your higher-scoring tiles – you should be getting the hang of it by now – and then you're still left with one **S** and your lower-scoring tiles with which, fingers crossed, to get a bonus next time.

S at the beginning

As well as being an 'end hook' (going on the end of a word), the **S** is frequently also a 'front hook', which means that it can be placed at the front of a word to form another word. You can often put an **S** at the front of words beginning with:

> **C:** **(S)CAM, (S)CAMP, (S)CABBY, (S)CANNER, (S)CURRIED,** and many more, including unusual words like **(S)CAMEL** and **(S)COPULATE**.
>
> **H:** **(S)HOD, (S)HALL, (S)HATTER, (S)HEATH, (S)HELLFIRE** and, more surprisingly, **(S)HADDOCK** and **(S)HOOKS**.

> **L:** **(S)LAP, (S)LINK, (S)LOUGH, (S)LIPPY, (S)LIGHTLY** and nice words like **(S)LOWDOWN** and **(S)LAUGHTER**.
>
> **P:** **(S)PUD, (S)PRAY, (S)PRINT, (S)PRIEST, (S)PLATTER** and the more unexpected **(S)PINK** and **(S)PROD**.
>
> **T:** **(S)TRAP, (S)TANNIC, (S)TICKER, (S)TAKEOUT** and **TATUS**, the plural of an old spelling of tattoo, converts rather pleasingly into **STATUS**.

Scrabble facts – Here are the meanings of some of the more surprising words that can be formed by adding an **S** at the start.

S-CAMEL	Shakespearian word of uncertain meaning
S-COPULATE	of or like the small tufts of dense hair on the legs of some spiders
S-DEIGN	old form of disdain
S-GRAFFITI	ceramic objects that are decorated with patterns incised in to the top layer of the glaze to reveal parts of the ground
S-HADDOCK	edible yellow fruit that is a bit like a grapefruit
S-HOOK	set of parts ready for assembly
S-PINK	finch
S-PROD	young salmon

Words beginning with **M, N, W** and even **Q** are also good to check for **S** front-hooks. And of course, like most other consonants, it will often go before a word starting with a vowel (**S-ADDER, S-EVEN, S-IRE, S-ODIUM, S-UNDRESS**). Add in exotica like **S-DEIGN** and **S-GRAFFITI** and you might almost start to think an **S** was as likely to go before a word as after it. It is, however, its power as an end hook that makes the **S** such a potent weapon to have on your rack.

4 Using the blank

Sometimes a very inexperienced player will feel hard done by when they pick the blank, because it doesn't score anything. Wrong, wrong, wrong!

If you pick a blank, your heart should leap like a March hare on a trampoline. So long as there is an opening on the board somewhere, a blank should set you on your way to being able to play a bonus word, maybe not immediately, but reasonably soon.

Why? It's those combinations again. The larger the number of different ways you can form your rack into seven letters, the more likely it is that one of them will be a seven-letter word. We've already noted that a straightforward rack of seven different letters can be arranged 5,040 different ways. But six different letters plus a blank can be arranged in a massive 115,920 ways, counting the blank as each possible letter in each separate position. That's 23 times as many; picking a blank is like having 23 tickets in the lottery instead of just one.

> **Scrabble facts** – *Don't forget that the blank has no value, whatever letter it is standing in for.*

How to use the blank

You could try painstakingly working your way through all 115,920 combinations to find if you have a seven-letter word. At, say, 10 seconds per combination, that would take about 13½ days, assuming you don't stop for sleeping, eating or other essentials. Your opponent may get a tad restless. Happily, your brain will automatically shut out consideration of the vast number of these combinations that are obviously fruitless. In addition, the following will help you work at the challenge:

1 If some of your letters form a useful combination such as **–ING** or **–ATE**, put the blank with the other letters and see if any words suggest themselves. **G H I L N R ?** (**?** represents a blank) might look a bit of a mishmash. But make it **H L R ? + I N G** and it should immediately resolve itself into **HURLING**.

2 If there are no such handy combinations on your rack, go through the alphabet, making the blank each letter in turn. **D F I M N U ?** may not immediately look like anything, but once you try making the blank an **L**, **MINDFUL** might pop into your head.

3 Perhaps the blank will become the last letter in one of those useful combinations. **G H I L R U ?** also makes **HURLING**, even though you can't immediately isolate **–ING**.

4 You may be able to save a bit of time and mental energy by eliminating several possibilities for the blank:

- If you have five consonants, one vowel and a blank, the blank is almost certainly going to have to be a vowel if you are using it to make a seven-letter word.

- More obviously, with five bonus-friendly tiles (i.e. mainly one-pointers with a good vowel–consonant balance) plus a blank and a **Q**, there's really only one letter you need to think about making the blank. If you don't have a **U**, that's almost certainly what the blank is going to have to be if you are going for a bonus.

Play your blank with care

You must avoid the ultimate Scrabble crime of wasting your blank for a low score. Don't just stick it into a four- or five-letter word for a few points, even if you can't see anything else.

Hold onto the blank and get rid of some of your more awkward tiles, even for a lower score this time round, and some bonus possibilities ought to start revealing themselves within one or two moves.

In club and tournament Scrabble, the blank will rarely be played other than in a bonus move, unless the blank is picked right at the end of the game, when it may be too late to knock the rest of the rack into shape or there may be nowhere to play a bonus.

You may also be able to use the blank to get a move as good as a bonus, even if not an actual one. Remember we talked about getting a **J**, **Q**, **X** or **Z** on a Premium Letter square, at the same time as getting the word on a Premium Word square. Such a move can easily score 60–70 points or more, and could be well worth using a blank for.

> *Scrabble tip* – *Do you ever feel the blank in the Scrabble bag? Mattel produce special tile sets for tournaments where every tile is smooth.*

As a general rule, you should be looking to score at least 50 for a blank.

Two blanks

Even some quite experienced club players claim to dislike getting two blanks at the same time. The mesmerizingly high number of different combinations that can be made throws some people into confusion, and they say they 'just can't think', or even, appropriately enough, 'go blank'. This is a bit like people who say that being rich doesn't make you happy. It may be true, but you wouldn't mind giving it a try anyway.

The fact is that with two blanks you should be well on your way to making a bonus, unless the board is extremely blocked. If you find a double blank difficult to cope with, try thinking of one of them as the most useful letter it could be (bearing in mind your other five tiles) if it was not a blank. With a rack of, say, **A A C I P ? ?**, given that you have three vowels, at least one of your blanks is going to be a consonant. So think of it as one of those one-point, bonus-friendly consonants like **N** or **T**, and words like **CAPTAIN** and **CAPITAL** should soon start suggesting themselves to you. If you have **H O R T X ? ?**, make the rack more manageable by calling one blank an **E**, and **EXHORTS** suddenly becomes much easier to find.

However, with a rack like that, you may be able to play your **X**, perhaps with one of the blanks, for around 40 points, and still have a good chance of the bonus next turn. Unless you can play **EXHORTS** (or whatever) for a real stonker of a score – I would suggest at least 80 – a rack with lots of goodies like that should be good for two high scores.

Never change a blank

Above all, never change a blank. Why give your opponent the chance of picking it later? The only possible time you might want to try breaking that rule is if you are over 100 behind, and thus need two bonuses to come back. You could try putting a blank back in the hope of picking it later and getting bonuses with both of them. But this is an unwise tactic – particularly as by changing you waste a turn and fall even further behind.

SECTION 2:
Words between 10 and 15 letters in length

A

AARDWOLVES	ABHORRENCES	ABOLISHMENT	ABRIDGABLE	ABSOLVABLE
ABACTERIAL	ABHORRENCIES	ABOLISHMENTS	ABRIDGEABLE	ABSOLVENTS
ABACTINALLY	ABHORRENCY	ABOLITIONAL	ABRIDGEMENT	ABSOLVITOR
ABANDONEDLY	ABHORRENTLY	ABOLITIONARY	ABRIDGEMENTS	ABSOLVITORS
ABANDONEES	ABHORRENTLY	ABOLITIONISM	ABRIDGMENT	ABSORBABILITIES
ABANDONERS	ABHORRINGS	ABOLITIONISMS	ABRIDGMENTS	ABSORBABILITY
ABANDONING	ABIOGENESES	ABOLITIONIST	ABROGATING	ABSORBABLE
ABANDONMENT	ABIOGENESIS	ABOLITIONISTS	ABROGATION	ABSORBANCE
ABANDONMENTS	ABIOGENETIC	ABOLITIONS	ABROGATIONS	ABSORBANCES
ABANDONWARE	ABIOGENETICALLY	ABOMINABLE	ABROGATIVE	ABSORBANCIES
ABANDONWARES	ABIOGENICALLY	ABOMINABLENESS	ABROGATORS	ABSORBANCY
ABASEMENTS	ABIOGENIST	ABOMINABLY	ABRUPTIONS	ABSORBANTS
ABASHMENTS	ABIOGENISTS	ABOMINATED	ABRUPTNESS	ABSORBATES
ABATEMENTS	ABIOLOGICAL	ABOMINATES	ABRUPTNESSES	ABSORBEDLY
ABBOTSHIPS	ABIOTICALLY	ABOMINATING	ABSCESSING	ABSORBEFACIENT
ABBREVIATE	ABIOTROPHIC	ABOMINATION	ABSCINDING	ABSORBEFACIENTS
ABBREVIATED	ABIOTROPHIES	ABOMINATIONS	ABSCISSINS	ABSORBENCIES
ABBREVIATES	ABIOTROPHY	ABOMINATOR	ABSCISSION	ABSORBENCY
ABBREVIATING	ABIRRITANT	ABOMINATORS	ABSCISSIONS	ABSORBENTS
ABBREVIATION	ABIRRITANTS	ABONDANCES	ABSCONDENCE	ABSORBINGLY
ABBREVIATIONS	ABIRRITATE	ABONNEMENT	ABSCONDENCES	ABSORPTANCE
ABBREVIATOR	ABIRRITATED	ABONNEMENTS	ABSCONDERS	ABSORPTANCES
ABBREVIATORS	ABIRRITATES	ABORIGINAL	ABSCONDING	ABSORPTIOMETER
ABBREVIATORY	ABIRRITATING	ABORIGINALISM	ABSCONDINGS	ABSORPTIOMETERS
ABBREVIATURE	ABITURIENT	ABORIGINALISMS	ABSEILINGS	ABSORPTION
ABBREVIATURES	ABITURIENTS	ABORIGINALITIES	ABSENTEEISM	ABSORPTIONS
ABCOULOMBS	ABJECTIONS	ABORIGINALITY	ABSENTEEISMS	ABSORPTIVE
ABDICATING	ABJECTNESS	ABORIGINALLY	ABSENTMINDED	ABSORPTIVENESS
ABDICATION	ABJECTNESSES	ABORIGINALS	ABSENTMINDEDLY	ABSORPTIVITIES
ABDICATIONS	ABJOINTING	ABORIGINES	ABSINTHIATED	ABSORPTIVITY
ABDICATIVE	ABJUNCTION	ABORTICIDE	ABSINTHISM	ABSQUATULATE
ABDICATORS	ABJUNCTIONS	ABORTICIDES	ABSINTHISMS	ABSQUATULATED
ABDOMINALLY	ABJURATION	ABORTIFACIENT	ABSOLUTELY	ABSQUATULATES
ABDOMINALS	ABJURATIONS	ABORTIFACIENTS	ABSOLUTENESS	ABSQUATULATING
ABDOMINOPLASTY	ABLACTATION	ABORTIONAL	ABSOLUTENESSES	ABSTAINERS
ABDOMINOUS	ABLACTATIONS	ABORTIONIST	ABSOLUTEST	ABSTAINING
ABDUCENTES	ABLATITIOUS	ABORTIONISTS	ABSOLUTION	ABSTEMIOUS
ABDUCTIONS	ABLATIVELY	ABORTIVELY	ABSOLUTIONS	ABSTEMIOUSLY
ABDUCTORES	ABLUTIONARY	ABORTIVENESS	ABSOLUTISE	ABSTEMIOUSNESS
ABECEDARIAN	ABLUTOMANE	ABORTIVENESSES	ABSOLUTISED	ABSTENTION
ABECEDARIANS	ABLUTOMANES	ABORTUARIES	ABSOLUTISES	ABSTENTIONISM
ABERDEVINE	ABNEGATING	ABOVEBOARD	ABSOLUTISING	ABSTENTIONISMS
ABERDEVINES	ABNEGATION	ABOVEGROUND	ABSOLUTISM	ABSTENTIONIST
ABERNETHIES	ABNEGATIONS	ABRACADABRA	ABSOLUTISMS	ABSTENTIONISTS
ABERRANCES	ABNEGATORS	ABRACADABRAS	ABSOLUTIST	ABSTENTIONS
ABERRANCIES	ABNORMALISM	ABRANCHIAL	ABSOLUTISTIC	ABSTENTIOUS
ABERRANTLY	ABNORMALISMS	ABRANCHIATE	ABSOLUTISTS	ABSTERGENT
ABERRATING	ABNORMALITIES	ABRASIVELY	ABSOLUTIVE	ABSTERGENTS
ABERRATION	ABNORMALITY	ABRASIVENESS	ABSOLUTIVES	ABSTERGING
ABERRATIONAL	ABNORMALLY	ABRASIVENESSES	ABSOLUTIZE	ABSTERSION
ABERRATIONS	ABNORMITIES	ABREACTING	ABSOLUTIZED	ABSTERSIONS
ABEYANCIES	ABODEMENTS	ABREACTION	ABSOLUTIZES	ABSTERSIVE
ABHOMINABLE	ABOLISHABLE	ABREACTIONS	ABSOLUTIZING	ABSTERSIVES
ABHORRENCE	ABOLISHERS	ABREACTIVE	ABSOLUTORY	ABSTINENCE

ABSTINENCES
ABSTINENCIES
ABSTINENCY
ABSTINENTLY
ABSTRACTABLE
ABSTRACTED
ABSTRACTEDLY
ABSTRACTEDNESS
ABSTRACTER
ABSTRACTERS
ABSTRACTEST
ABSTRACTING
ABSTRACTION
ABSTRACTIONAL
ABSTRACTIONISM
ABSTRACTIONISMS
ABSTRACTIONIST
ABSTRACTIONISTS
ABSTRACTIONS
ABSTRACTIVE
ABSTRACTIVELY
ABSTRACTIVES
ABSTRACTLY
ABSTRACTNESS
ABSTRACTNESSES
ABSTRACTOR
ABSTRACTORS
ABSTRICTED
ABSTRICTING
ABSTRICTION
ABSTRICTIONS
ABSTRUSELY
ABSTRUSENESS
ABSTRUSENESSES
ABSTRUSEST
ABSTRUSITIES
ABSTRUSITY
ABSURDISMS
ABSURDISTS
ABSURDITIES
ABSURDNESS
ABSURDNESSES
ABUNDANCES
ABUNDANCIES
ABUNDANTLY
ABUSIVENESS
ABUSIVENESSES
ABYSSOPELAGIC
ACADEMICAL
ACADEMICALISM
ACADEMICALISMS
ACADEMICALLY
ACADEMICALS
ACADEMICIAN
ACADEMICIANS
ACADEMICISM
ACADEMICISMS
ACADEMISMS
ACADEMISTS
ACALCULIAS
ACALEPHANS
ACANACEOUS
ACANTHACEOUS
ACANTHOCEPHALAN
ACANTHUSES
ACARICIDAL
ACARICIDES

ACARIDEANS
ACARIDIANS
ACARIDOMATIA
ACARIDOMATIUM
ACARODOMATIA
ACARODOMATIUM
ACAROLOGIES
ACAROLOGIST
ACAROLOGISTS
ACAROPHILIES
ACAROPHILY
ACARPELLOUS
ACARPELOUS
ACATALECTIC
ACATALECTICS
ACATALEPSIES
ACATALEPSY
ACATALEPTIC
ACATALEPTICS
ACATAMATHESIA
ACATAMATHESIAS
ACATHISIAS
ACAULESCENT
ACCEDENCES
ACCELERABLE
ACCELERANDO
ACCELERANDOS
ACCELERANT
ACCELERANTS
ACCELERATE
ACCELERATED
ACCELERATES
ACCELERATING
ACCELERATINGLY
ACCELERATION
ACCELERATIONS
ACCELERATIVE
ACCELERATOR
ACCELERATORS
ACCELERATORY
ACCELEROMETER
ACCELEROMETERS
ACCENSIONS
ACCENTLESS
ACCENTUALITIES
ACCENTUALITY
ACCENTUALLY
ACCENTUATE
ACCENTUATED
ACCENTUATES
ACCENTUATING
ACCENTUATION
ACCENTUATIONS
ACCEPTABILITIES
ACCEPTABILITY
ACCEPTABLE
ACCEPTABLENESS
ACCEPTABLY
ACCEPTANCE
ACCEPTANCES
ACCEPTANCIES
ACCEPTANCY
ACCEPTANTS
ACCEPTATION
ACCEPTATIONS
ACCEPTEDLY
ACCEPTILATION

ACCEPTILATIONS
ACCEPTINGLY
ACCEPTINGNESS
ACCEPTINGNESSES
ACCEPTIVITIES
ACCEPTIVITY
ACCESSARIES
ACCESSARILY
ACCESSARINESS
ACCESSARINESSES
ACCESSIBILITIES
ACCESSIBILITY
ACCESSIBLE
ACCESSIBLENESS
ACCESSIBLY
ACCESSIONAL
ACCESSIONED
ACCESSIONING
ACCESSIONS
ACCESSORIAL
ACCESSORIES
ACCESSORII
ACCESSORILY
ACCESSORINESS
ACCESSORINESSES
ACCESSORISE
ACCESSORISED
ACCESSORISES
ACCESSORISING
ACCESSORIUS
ACCESSORIZE
ACCESSORIZED
ACCESSORIZES
ACCESSORIZING
ACCIACCATURA
ACCIACCATURAS
ACCIACCATURE
ACCIDENCES
ACCIDENTAL
ACCIDENTALISM
ACCIDENTALISMS
ACCIDENTALITIES
ACCIDENTALITY
ACCIDENTALLY
ACCIDENTALNESS
ACCIDENTALS
ACCIDENTED
ACCIDENTLY
ACCIDENTOLOGIES
ACCIDENTOLOGY
ACCIPITERS
ACCIPITRAL
ACCIPITRINE
ACCIPITRINES
ACCLAIMERS
ACCLAIMING
ACCLAMATION
ACCLAMATIONS
ACCLAMATORY
ACCLIMATABLE
ACCLIMATATION
ACCLIMATATIONS
ACCLIMATED
ACCLIMATES
ACCLIMATING
ACCLIMATION
ACCLIMATIONS

ACCLIMATISABLE
ACCLIMATISATION
ACCLIMATISE
ACCLIMATISED
ACCLIMATISER
ACCLIMATISERS
ACCLIMATISES
ACCLIMATISING
ACCLIMATIZABLE
ACCLIMATIZATION
ACCLIMATIZE
ACCLIMATIZED
ACCLIMATIZER
ACCLIMATIZERS
ACCLIMATIZES
ACCLIMATIZING
ACCLIVITIES
ACCLIVITOUS
ACCOASTING
ACCOLADING
ACCOMMODABLE
ACCOMMODATE
ACCOMMODATED
ACCOMMODATES
ACCOMMODATING
ACCOMMODATINGLY
ACCOMMODATION
ACCOMMODATIONAL
ACCOMMODATIONS
ACCOMMODATIVE
ACCOMMODATOR
ACCOMMODATORS
ACCOMPANIED
ACCOMPANIER
ACCOMPANIERS
ACCOMPANIES
ACCOMPANIMENT
ACCOMPANIMENTS
ACCOMPANIST
ACCOMPANISTS
ACCOMPANYING
ACCOMPANYIST
ACCOMPANYISTS
ACCOMPLICE
ACCOMPLICES
ACCOMPLISH
ACCOMPLISHABLE
ACCOMPLISHED
ACCOMPLISHER
ACCOMPLISHERS
ACCOMPLISHES
ACCOMPLISHING
ACCOMPLISHMENT
ACCOMPLISHMENTS
ACCOMPTABLE
ACCOMPTANT
ACCOMPTANTS
ACCOMPTING
ACCORAGING
ACCORDABLE
ACCORDANCE
ACCORDANCES
ACCORDANCIES
ACCORDANCY
ACCORDANTLY
ACCORDINGLY
ACCORDIONIST

ACCORDIONISTS
ACCORDIONS
ACCOSTABLE
ACCOUCHEMENT
ACCOUCHEMENTS
ACCOUCHEUR
ACCOUCHEURS
ACCOUCHEUSE
ACCOUCHEUSES
ACCOUNTABILITY
ACCOUNTABLE
ACCOUNTABLENESS
ACCOUNTABLY
ACCOUNTANCIES
ACCOUNTANCY
ACCOUNTANT
ACCOUNTANTS
ACCOUNTANTSHIP
ACCOUNTANTSHIPS
ACCOUNTING
ACCOUNTINGS
ACCOUPLEMENT
ACCOUPLEMENTS
ACCOURAGED
ACCOURAGES
ACCOURAGING
ACCOURTING
ACCOUSTREMENT
ACCOUSTREMENTS
ACCOUTERED
ACCOUTERING
ACCOUTERMENT
ACCOUTERMENTS
ACCOUTREMENT
ACCOUTREMENTS
ACCOUTRING
ACCREDITABLE
ACCREDITATION
ACCREDITATIONS
ACCREDITED
ACCREDITING
ACCRESCENCE
ACCRESCENCES
ACCRESCENT
ACCRETIONARY
ACCRETIONS
ACCRUEMENT
ACCRUEMENTS
ACCUBATION
ACCUBATIONS
ACCULTURAL
ACCULTURATE
ACCULTURATED
ACCULTURATES
ACCULTURATING
ACCULTURATION
ACCULTURATIONAL
ACCULTURATIONS
ACCULTURATIVE
ACCUMBENCIES
ACCUMBENCY
ACCUMULABLE
ACCUMULATE
ACCUMULATED
ACCUMULATES
ACCUMULATING
ACCUMULATION

ACCUMULATIONS	ACETONITRILES	ACIDIMETRIC	ACQUIGHTING	ACROPHOBICS
ACCUMULATIVE	ACETONURIA	ACIDIMETRICAL	ACQUIRABILITIES	ACROPHONETIC
ACCUMULATIVELY	ACETONURIAS	ACIDIMETRICALLY	ACQUIRABILITY	ACROPHONIC
ACCUMULATOR	ACETOPHENETIDIN	ACIDIMETRIES	ACQUIRABLE	ACROPHONIES
ACCUMULATORS	ACETYLATED	ACIDIMETRY	ACQUIREMENT	ACROPOLISES
ACCURACIES	ACETYLATES	ACIDNESSES	ACQUIREMENTS	ACROSPIRES
ACCURATELY	ACETYLATING	ACIDOMETER	ACQUISITION	ACROSTICAL
ACCURATENESS	ACETYLATION	ACIDOMETERS	ACQUISITIONAL	ACROSTICALLY
ACCURATENESSES	ACETYLATIONS	ACIDOPHILE	ACQUISITIONS	ACROTERIAL
ACCURSEDLY	ACETYLATIVE	ACIDOPHILES	ACQUISITIVE	ACROTERION
ACCURSEDNESS	ACETYLCHOLINE	ACIDOPHILIC	ACQUISITIVELY	ACROTERIUM
ACCURSEDNESSES	ACETYLCHOLINES	ACIDOPHILOUS	ACQUISITIVENESS	ACRYLAMIDE
ACCUSATION	ACETYLENES	ACIDOPHILS	ACQUISITOR	ACRYLAMIDES
ACCUSATIONS	ACETYLENIC	ACIDOPHILUS	ACQUISITORS	ACRYLONITRILE
ACCUSATIVAL	ACETYLIDES	ACIDOPHILUSES	ACQUITMENT	ACRYLONITRILES
ACCUSATIVE	ACETYLSALICYLIC	ACIDULATED	ACQUITMENTS	ACTABILITIES
ACCUSATIVELY	ACHAENIUMS	ACIDULATES	ACQUITTALS	ACTABILITY
ACCUSATIVES	ACHAENOCARP	ACIDULATING	ACQUITTANCE	ACTINICALLY
ACCUSATORIAL	ACHAENOCARPS	ACIDULATION	ACQUITTANCED	ACTINIFORM
ACCUSATORY	ACHALASIAS	ACIDULATIONS	ACQUITTANCES	ACTINOBACILLI
ACCUSEMENT	ACHIEVABLE	ACIERATING	ACQUITTANCING	ACTINOBACILLUS
ACCUSEMENTS	ACHIEVEMENT	ACIERATION	ACQUITTERS	ACTINOBIOLOGIES
ACCUSINGLY	ACHIEVEMENTS	ACIERATIONS	ACQUITTING	ACTINOBIOLOGY
ACCUSTOMARY	ACHINESSES	ACINACEOUS	ACRIDITIES	ACTINOCHEMISTRY
ACCUSTOMATION	ACHLAMYDEOUS	ACINACIFORM	ACRIDNESSES	ACTINOLITE
ACCUSTOMATIONS	ACHLORHYDRIA	ACINETOBACTER	ACRIFLAVIN	ACTINOLITES
ACCUSTOMED	ACHLORHYDRIAS	ACINETOBACTERS	ACRIFLAVINE	ACTINOMERE
ACCUSTOMEDNESS	ACHLORHYDRIC	ACKNOWLEDGE	ACRIFLAVINES	ACTINOMERES
ACCUSTOMING	ACHONDRITE	ACKNOWLEDGEABLE	ACRIFLAVINS	ACTINOMETER
ACCUSTREMENT	ACHONDRITES	ACKNOWLEDGEABLY	ACRIMONIES	ACTINOMETERS
ACCUSTREMENTS	ACHONDRITIC	ACKNOWLEDGED	ACRIMONIOUS	ACTINOMETRIC
ACEPHALOUS	ACHONDROPLASIA	ACKNOWLEDGEDLY	ACRIMONIOUSLY	ACTINOMETRICAL
ACERACEOUS	ACHONDROPLASIAS	ACKNOWLEDGEMENT	ACRIMONIOUSNESS	ACTINOMETRIES
ACERBATING	ACHONDROPLASTIC	ACKNOWLEDGER	ACRITARCHS	ACTINOMETRY
ACERBICALLY	ACHROMATIC	ACKNOWLEDGERS	ACROAMATIC	ACTINOMORPHIC
ACERBITIES	ACHROMATICALLY	ACKNOWLEDGES	ACROAMATICAL	ACTINOMORPHIES
ACERVATELY	ACHROMATICITIES	ACKNOWLEDGING	ACROBATICALLY	ACTINOMORPHOUS
ACERVATION	ACHROMATICITY	ACKNOWLEDGMENT	ACROBATICS	ACTINOMORPHY
ACERVATIONS	ACHROMATIN	ACKNOWLEDGMENTS	ACROBATISM	ACTINOMYCES
ACESCENCES	ACHROMATINS	ACOELOMATE	ACROBATISMS	ACTINOMYCETE
ACESCENCIES	ACHROMATISATION	ACOELOMATES	ACROCARPOUS	ACTINOMYCETES
ACETABULAR	ACHROMATISE	ACOLOUTHIC	ACROCENTRIC	ACTINOMYCETOUS
ACETABULUM	ACHROMATISED	ACOLOUTHITE	ACROCENTRICS	ACTINOMYCIN
ACETABULUMS	ACHROMATISES	ACOLOUTHITES	ACROCYANOSES	ACTINOMYCINS
ACETALDEHYDE	ACHROMATISING	ACOLOUTHOS	ACROCYANOSIS	ACTINOMYCOSES
ACETALDEHYDES	ACHROMATISM	ACOLOUTHOSES	ACRODROMOUS	ACTINOMYCOSIS
ACETAMIDES	ACHROMATISMS	ACONITINES	ACROGENOUS	ACTINOMYCOTIC
ACETAMINOPHEN	ACHROMATIZATION	ACOTYLEDON	ACROGENOUSLY	ACTINOPODS
ACETAMINOPHENS	ACHROMATIZE	ACOTYLEDONOUS	ACROLITHIC	ACTINOTHERAPIES
ACETANILID	ACHROMATIZED	ACOTYLEDONS	ACROMEGALIC	ACTINOTHERAPY
ACETANILIDE	ACHROMATIZES	ACOUSTICAL	ACROMEGALICS	ACTINOURANIUM
ACETANILIDES	ACHROMATIZING	ACOUSTICALLY	ACROMEGALIES	ACTINOURANIUMS
ACETANILIDS	ACHROMATOPSIA	ACOUSTICIAN	ACROMEGALY	ACTINOZOAN
ACETAZOLAMIDE	ACHROMATOPSIAS	ACOUSTICIANS	ACRONICALLY	ACTINOZOANS
ACETAZOLAMIDES	ACHROMATOUS	ACQUAINTANCE	ACRONYCALLY	ACTIONABLE
ACETIFICATION	ACICLOVIRS	ACQUAINTANCES	ACRONYCHAL	ACTIONABLY
ACETIFICATIONS	ACICULATED	ACQUAINTED	ACRONYCHALLY	ACTIONISTS
ACETIFIERS	ACIDANTHERA	ACQUAINTING	ACRONYMANIA	ACTIONLESS
ACETIFYING	ACIDANTHERAS	ACQUIESCED	ACRONYMANIAS	ACTIVATING
ACETOACETIC	ACIDICALLY	ACQUIESCENCE	ACRONYMICALLY	ACTIVATION
ACETOMETER	ACIDIFIABLE	ACQUIESCENCES	ACRONYMOUS	ACTIVATIONS
ACETOMETERS	ACIDIFICATION	ACQUIESCENT	ACROPARESTHESIA	ACTIVATORS
ACETONAEMIA	ACIDIFICATIONS	ACQUIESCENTLY	ACROPETALLY	ACTIVENESS
ACETONAEMIAS	ACIDIFIERS	ACQUIESCENTS	ACROPHOBES	ACTIVENESSES
ACETONEMIA	ACIDIFYING	ACQUIESCES	ACROPHOBIA	ACTIVISING
ACETONEMIAS	ACIDIMETER	ACQUIESCING	ACROPHOBIAS	ACTIVISTIC
ACETONITRILE	ACIDIMETERS	ACQUIESCINGLY	ACROPHOBIC	ACTIVITIES

ACTIVIZING	ADDITAMENT	ADIATHERMANCIES	ADMINISTRATED	ADORABLENESSES
ACTOMYOSIN	ADDITAMENTS	ADIATHERMANCY	ADMINISTRATES	ADORATIONS
ACTOMYOSINS	ADDITIONAL	ADIATHERMANOUS	ADMINISTRATING	ADORNMENTS
ACTORLIEST	ADDITIONALITIES	ADIATHERMIC	ADMINISTRATION	ADPRESSING
ACTRESSIER	ADDITIONALITY	ADIPOCERES	ADMINISTRATIONS	ADRENALECTOMIES
ACTRESSIEST	ADDITIONALLY	ADIPOCEROUS	ADMINISTRATIVE	ADRENALECTOMY
ACTUALISATION	ADDITITIOUS	ADIPOCYTES	ADMINISTRATOR	ADRENALINE
ACTUALISATIONS	ADDITIVELY	ADIPOSITIES	ADMINISTRATORS	ADRENALINES
ACTUALISED	ADDITIVITIES	ADJACENCES	ADMINISTRATRIX	ADRENALINS
ACTUALISES	ADDITIVITY	ADJACENCIES	ADMIRABILITIES	ADRENALISED
ACTUALISING	ADDLEMENTS	ADJACENTLY	ADMIRABILITY	ADRENALIZED
ACTUALISTS	ADDLEPATED	ADJECTIVAL	ADMIRABLENESS	ADRENERGIC
ACTUALITES	ADDRESSABILITY	ADJECTIVALLY	ADMIRABLENESSES	ADRENERGICALLY
ACTUALITIES	ADDRESSABLE	ADJECTIVELY	ADMIRALSHIP	ADRENOCEPTOR
ACTUALIZATION	ADDRESSEES	ADJECTIVES	ADMIRALSHIPS	ADRENOCEPTORS
ACTUALIZATIONS	ADDRESSERS	ADJOURNING	ADMIRALTIES	ADRENOCHROME
ACTUALIZED	ADDRESSING	ADJOURNMENT	ADMIRANCES	ADRENOCHROMES
ACTUALIZES	ADDRESSINGS	ADJOURNMENTS	ADMIRATION	ADRENOCORTICAL
ACTUALIZING	ADDRESSORS	ADJUDGEMENT	ADMIRATIONS	ADRIAMYCIN
ACTUARIALLY	ADDUCEABLE	ADJUDGEMENTS	ADMIRATIVE	ADRIAMYCINS
ACTUATIONS	ADDUCTIONS	ADJUDGMENT	ADMIRAUNCE	ADROITNESS
ACUMINATED	ADELANTADO	ADJUDGMENTS	ADMIRAUNCES	ADROITNESSES
ACUMINATES	ADELANTADOS	ADJUDICATE	ADMIRINGLY	ADSCITITIOUS
ACUMINATING	ADEMPTIONS	ADJUDICATED	ADMISSIBILITIES	ADSCITITIOUSLY
ACUMINATION	ADENECTOMIES	ADJUDICATES	ADMISSIBILITY	ADSCRIPTION
ACUMINATIONS	ADENECTOMY	ADJUDICATING	ADMISSIBLE	ADSCRIPTIONS
ACUPRESSURE	ADENITISES	ADJUDICATION	ADMISSIBLENESS	ADSORBABILITIES
ACUPRESSURES	ADENOCARCINOMA	ADJUDICATIONS	ADMISSIONS	ADSORBABILITY
ACUPUNCTURAL	ADENOCARCINOMAS	ADJUDICATIVE	ADMITTABLE	ADSORBABLE
ACUPUNCTURE	ADENOHYPOPHYSES	ADJUDICATOR	ADMITTANCE	ADSORBATES
ACUPUNCTURES	ADENOHYPOPHYSIS	ADJUDICATORS	ADMITTANCES	ADSORBENTS
ACUPUNCTURIST	ADENOIDECTOMIES	ADJUDICATORY	ADMITTEDLY	ADSORPTION
ACUPUNCTURISTS	ADENOIDECTOMY	ADJUNCTION	ADMIXTURES	ADSORPTIONS
ACUTENESSES	ADENOMATOUS	ADJUNCTIONS	ADMONISHED	ADSORPTIVE
ACYCLOVIRS	ADENOPATHIES	ADJUNCTIVE	ADMONISHER	ADULARESCENCE
ACYLATIONS	ADENOPATHY	ADJUNCTIVELY	ADMONISHERS	ADULARESCENCES
ADACTYLOUS	ADENOSINES	ADJURATION	ADMONISHES	ADULARESCENT
ADAMANCIES	ADENOVIRAL	ADJURATIONS	ADMONISHING	ADULATIONS
ADAMANTEAN	ADENOVIRUS	ADJURATORY	ADMONISHINGLY	ADULTERANT
ADAMANTINE	ADENOVIRUSES	ADJUSTABILITIES	ADMONISHMENT	ADULTERANTS
ADAPTABILITIES	ADENYLATES	ADJUSTABILITY	ADMONISHMENTS	ADULTERATE
ADAPTABILITY	ADEPTNESSES	ADJUSTABLE	ADMONITION	ADULTERATED
ADAPTABLENESS	ADEQUACIES	ADJUSTABLY	ADMONITIONS	ADULTERATES
ADAPTABLENESSES	ADEQUATELY	ADJUSTMENT	ADMONITIVE	ADULTERATING
ADAPTATION	ADEQUATENESS	ADJUSTMENTAL	ADMONITORILY	ADULTERATION
ADAPTATIONAL	ADEQUATENESSES	ADJUSTMENTS	ADMONITORS	ADULTERATIONS
ADAPTATIONALLY	ADEQUATIVE	ADJUTANCIES	ADMONITORY	ADULTERATOR
ADAPTATIONS	ADHERENCES	ADJUVANCIES	ADNOMINALS	ADULTERATORS
ADAPTATIVE	ADHERENTLY	ADMEASURED	ADOLESCENCE	ADULTERERS
ADAPTEDNESS	ADHESIONAL	ADMEASUREMENT	ADOLESCENCES	ADULTERESS
ADAPTEDNESSES	ADHESIVELY	ADMEASUREMENTS	ADOLESCENT	ADULTERESSES
ADAPTIVELY	ADHESIVENESS	ADMEASURES	ADOLESCENTLY	ADULTERIES
ADAPTIVENESS	ADHESIVENESSES	ADMEASURING	ADOLESCENTS	ADULTERINE
ADAPTIVENESSES	ADHIBITING	ADMINICLES	ADOPTABILITIES	ADULTERINES
ADAPTIVITIES	ADHIBITION	ADMINICULAR	ADOPTABILITY	ADULTERIZE
ADAPTIVITY	ADHIBITIONS	ADMINICULATE	ADOPTIANISM	ADULTERISED
ADAPTOGENIC	ADHOCRACIES	ADMINICULATED	ADOPTIANISMS	ADULTERISES
ADAPTOGENS	ADIABATICALLY	ADMINICULATES	ADOPTIANIST	ADULTERISING
ADDERBEADS	ADIABATICS	ADMINICULATING	ADOPTIANISTS	ADULTERIZE
ADDERSTONE	ADIACTINIC	ADMINISTER	ADOPTIONISM	ADULTERIZED
ADDERSTONES	ADIAPHORISM	ADMINISTERED	ADOPTIONISMS	ADULTERIZES
ADDERWORTS	ADIAPHORISMS	ADMINISTERING	ADOPTIONIST	ADULTERIZING
ADDICTEDNESS	ADIAPHORIST	ADMINISTERS	ADOPTIONISTS	ADULTEROUS
ADDICTEDNESSES	ADIAPHORISTIC	ADMINISTRABLE	ADOPTIVELY	ADULTEROUSLY
ADDICTIONS	ADIAPHORISTS	ADMINISTRANT	ADORABILITIES	ADULTESCENT
ADDICTIVENESS	ADIAPHORON	ADMINISTRANTS	ADORABILITY	ADULTESCENTS
ADDICTIVENESSES	ADIAPHOROUS	ADMINISTRATE	ADORABLENESS	ADULTHOODS

ADULTNESSES	ADVERTENCE	AEROACOUSTICS	AEROMETERS	AESTHESIOGENIC
ADULTRESSES	ADVERTENCES	AEROBALLISTICS	AEROMETRIC	AESTHESIOGENS
ADUMBRATED	ADVERTENCIES	AEROBATICS	AEROMETRIES	AESTHETICAL
ADUMBRATES	ADVERTENCY	AEROBICALLY	AEROMODELLING	AESTHETICALLY
ADUMBRATING	ADVERTENTLY	AEROBICISE	AEROMODELLINGS	AESTHETICIAN
ADUMBRATION	ADVERTISED	AEROBICISED	AEROMOTORS	AESTHETICIANS
ADUMBRATIONS	ADVERTISEMENT	AEROBICISES	AERONAUTIC	AESTHETICISE
ADUMBRATIVE	ADVERTISEMENTS	AEROBICISING	AERONAUTICAL	AESTHETICISED
ADUMBRATIVELY	ADVERTISER	AEROBICIST	AERONAUTICALLY	AESTHETICISES
ADUNCITIES	ADVERTISERS	AEROBICISTS	AERONAUTICS	AESTHETICISING
ADVANCEMENT	ADVERTISES	AEROBICIZE	AERONEUROSES	AESTHETICISM
ADVANCEMENTS	ADVERTISING	AEROBICIZED	AERONEUROSIS	AESTHETICISMS
ADVANCINGLY	ADVERTISINGS	AEROBICIZES	AERONOMERS	AESTHETICIST
ADVANTAGEABLE	ADVERTIZED	AEROBICIZING	AERONOMICAL	AESTHETICISTS
ADVANTAGED	ADVERTIZEMENT	AEROBIOLOGICAL	AERONOMIES	AESTHETICIZE
ADVANTAGEOUS	ADVERTIZEMENTS	AEROBIOLOGIES	AERONOMIST	AESTHETICIZED
ADVANTAGEOUSLY	ADVERTIZER	AEROBIOLOGIST	AERONOMISTS	AESTHETICIZES
ADVANTAGES	ADVERTIZERS	AEROBIOLOGISTS	AEROPAUSES	AESTHETICIZING
ADVANTAGING	ADVERTIZES	AEROBIOLOGY	AEROPHAGIA	AESTHETICS
ADVECTIONS	ADVERTIZING	AEROBIONTS	AEROPHAGIAS	AESTIVATED
ADVENTITIA	ADVERTIZINGS	AEROBIOSES	AEROPHAGIES	AESTIVATES
ADVENTITIAL	ADVERTORIAL	AEROBIOSIS	AEROPHOBES	AESTIVATING
ADVENTITIAS	ADVERTORIALS	AEROBIOTIC	AEROPHOBIA	AESTIVATION
ADVENTITIOUS	ADVISABILITIES	AEROBIOTICALLY	AEROPHOBIAS	AESTIVATIONS
ADVENTITIOUSLY	ADVISABILITY	AEROBRAKED	AEROPHOBIC	AESTIVATOR
ADVENTIVES	ADVISABLENESS	AEROBRAKES	AEROPHONES	AESTIVATORS
ADVENTURED	ADVISABLENESSES	AEROBRAKING	AEROPHORES	AETHEREALITIES
ADVENTUREFUL	ADVISATORY	AEROBRAKINGS	AEROPHYTES	AETHEREALITY
ADVENTURER	ADVISEDNESS	AEROBUSSES	AEROPLANES	AETHEREALLY
ADVENTURERS	ADVISEDNESSES	AERODIGESTIVE	AEROPLANKTON	AETHRIOSCOPE
ADVENTURES	ADVISEMENT	AERODONETICS	AEROPLANKTONS	AETHRIOSCOPES
ADVENTURESOME	ADVISEMENTS	AERODROMES	AEROPULSES	AETIOLOGICAL
ADVENTURESS	ADVISERSHIP	AERODYNAMIC	AEROSCOPES	AETIOLOGICALLY
ADVENTURESSES	ADVISERSHIPS	AERODYNAMICAL	AEROSHELLS	AETIOLOGIES
ADVENTURING	ADVISORATE	AERODYNAMICALLY	AEROSIDERITE	AETIOLOGIST
ADVENTURINGS	ADVISORATES	AERODYNAMICIST	AEROSIDERITES	AETIOLOGISTS
ADVENTURISM	ADVISORIES	AERODYNAMICISTS	AEROSOLISATION	AFFABILITIES
ADVENTURISMS	ADVOCACIES	AERODYNAMICS	AEROSOLISATIONS	AFFABILITY
ADVENTURIST	ADVOCATING	AEROELASTIC	AEROSOLISE	AFFECTABILITIES
ADVENTURISTIC	ADVOCATION	AEROELASTICIAN	AEROSOLISED	AFFECTABILITY
ADVENTURISTS	ADVOCATIONS	AEROELASTICIANS	AEROSOLISES	AFFECTABLE
ADVENTUROUS	ADVOCATIVE	AEROELASTICITY	AEROSOLISING	AFFECTATION
ADVENTUROUSLY	ADVOCATORS	AEROEMBOLISM	AEROSOLIZATION	AFFECTATIONS
ADVENTUROUSNESS	ADVOCATORY	AEROEMBOLISMS	AEROSOLIZATIONS	AFFECTEDLY
ADVERBIALISE	ADVOUTRERS	AEROGENERATOR	AEROSOLIZE	AFFECTEDNESS
ADVERBIALISED	ADVOUTRIES	AEROGENERATORS	AEROSOLIZED	AFFECTEDNESSES
ADVERBIALISES	AECIDIOSPORE	AEROGRAMME	AEROSOLIZES	AFFECTINGLY
ADVERBIALISING	AECIDIOSPORES	AEROGRAMMES	AEROSOLIZING	AFFECTIONAL
ADVERBIALIZE	AECIDOSPORE	AEROGRAPHIES	AEROSPACES	AFFECTIONALLY
ADVERBIALIZED	AECIDOSPORES	AEROGRAPHS	AEROSPHERE	AFFECTIONATE
ADVERBIALIZES	AECIOSPORE	AEROGRAPHY	AEROSPHERES	AFFECTIONATELY
ADVERBIALIZING	AECIOSPORES	AEROHYDROPLANE	AEROSPIKES	AFFECTIONED
ADVERBIALLY	AEDILESHIP	AEROHYDROPLANES	AEROSTATIC	AFFECTIONING
ADVERBIALS	AEDILESHIPS	AEROLITHOLOGIES	AEROSTATICAL	AFFECTIONLESS
ADVERGAMING	AEOLIPILES	AEROLITHOLOGY	AEROSTATICS	AFFECTIONS
ADVERGAMINGS	AEOLIPYLES	AEROLOGICAL	AEROSTATION	AFFECTIVELY
ADVERSARIA	AEOLOTROPIC	AEROLOGIES	AEROSTATIONS	AFFECTIVENESS
ADVERSARIAL	AEOLOTROPIES	AEROLOGIST	AEROSTRUCTURE	AFFECTIVENESSES
ADVERSARIES	AEOLOTROPY	AEROLOGISTS	AEROSTRUCTURES	AFFECTIVITIES
ADVERSARINESS	AEPYORNISES	AEROMAGNETIC	AEROTACTIC	AFFECTIVITY
ADVERSARINESSES	AERENCHYMA	AEROMANCIES	AEROTRAINS	AFFECTLESS
ADVERSATIVE	AERENCHYMAS	AEROMECHANIC	AEROTROPIC	AFFECTLESSNESS
ADVERSATIVELY	AERENCHYMATOUS	AEROMECHANICAL	AEROTROPISM	AFFEERMENT
ADVERSATIVES	AERIALISTS	AEROMECHANICS	AEROTROPISMS	AFFEERMENTS
ADVERSENESS	AERIALITIES	AEROMEDICAL	AERUGINOUS	AFFENPINSCHER
ADVERSENESSES	AERIFICATION	AEROMEDICINE	AESTHESIAS	AFFENPINSCHERS
ADVERSITIES	AERIFICATIONS	AEROMEDICINES	AESTHESIOGEN	AFFERENTLY

AFFETTUOSO
AFFIANCING
AFFICIONADO
AFFICIONADOS
AFFIDAVITS
AFFILIABLE
AFFILIATED
AFFILIATES
AFFILIATING
AFFILIATION
AFFILIATIONS
AFFINITIES
AFFINITIVE
AFFIRMABLE
AFFIRMANCE
AFFIRMANCES
AFFIRMANTS
AFFIRMATION
AFFIRMATIONS
AFFIRMATIVE
AFFIRMATIVELY
AFFIRMATIVES
AFFIRMATORY
AFFIRMINGLY
AFFIXATION
AFFIXATIONS
AFFIXMENTS
AFFIXTURES
AFFLATIONS
AFFLATUSES
AFFLICTERS
AFFLICTING
AFFLICTINGS
AFFLICTION
AFFLICTIONS
AFFLICTIVE
AFFLICTIVELY
AFFLUENCES
AFFLUENCIES
AFFLUENTIAL
AFFLUENTIALS
AFFLUENTLY
AFFLUENTNESS
AFFLUENTNESSES
AFFLUENZAS
AFFLUXIONS
AFFOORDING
AFFORCEMENT
AFFORCEMENTS
AFFORDABILITIES
AFFORDABILITY
AFFORDABLE
AFFORDABLY
AFFORESTABLE
AFFORESTATION
AFFORESTATIONS
AFFORESTED
AFFORESTING
AFFRANCHISE
AFFRANCHISED
AFFRANCHISEMENT
AFFRANCHISES
AFFRANCHISING
AFFRAPPING
AFFREIGHTMENT
AFFREIGHTMENTS
AFFRICATED

AFFRICATES
AFFRICATING
AFFRICATION
AFFRICATIONS
AFFRICATIVE
AFFRICATIVES
AFFRIGHTED
AFFRIGHTEDLY
AFFRIGHTEN
AFFRIGHTENED
AFFRIGHTENING
AFFRIGHTENS
AFFRIGHTFUL
AFFRIGHTING
AFFRIGHTMENT
AFFRIGHTMENTS
AFFRONTING
AFFRONTINGLY
AFFRONTINGS
AFFRONTIVE
AFICIONADA
AFICIONADAS
AFICIONADO
AFICIONADOS
AFLATOXINS
AFOREMENTIONED
AFORETHOUGHT
AFORETHOUGHTS
AFRORMOSIA
AFRORMOSIAS
AFTERBIRTH
AFTERBIRTHS
AFTERBODIES
AFTERBRAIN
AFTERBRAINS
AFTERBURNER
AFTERBURNERS
AFTERBURNING
AFTERBURNINGS
AFTERBURNS
AFTERCARES
AFTERCLAPS
AFTERDAMPS
AFTERDECKS
AFTEREFFECT
AFTEREFFECTS
AFTEREYEING
AFTEREYING
AFTERGAMES
AFTERGLOWS
AFTERGRASS
AFTERGRASSES
AFTERGROWTH
AFTERGROWTHS
AFTERGUARD
AFTERGUARDS
AFTERHEATS
AFTERIMAGE
AFTERIMAGES
AFTERLIFES
AFTERLIVES
AFTERMARKET
AFTERMARKETS
AFTERMASTS
AFTERMATHS
AFTERNOONS
AFTERPAINS

AFTERPARTIES
AFTERPARTY
AFTERPEAKS
AFTERPIECE
AFTERPIECES
AFTERSALES
AFTERSENSATION
AFTERSENSATIONS
AFTERSHAFT
AFTERSHAFTS
AFTERSHAVE
AFTERSHAVES
AFTERSHOCK
AFTERSHOCKS
AFTERSHOWS
AFTERSUPPER
AFTERSUPPERS
AFTERSWARM
AFTERSWARMS
AFTERTASTE
AFTERTASTES
AFTERTHOUGHT
AFTERTHOUGHTS
AFTERTIMES
AFTERTREATMENT
AFTERTREATMENTS
AFTERWARDS
AFTERWORDS
AFTERWORLD
AFTERWORLDS
AGALACTIAS
AGALMATOLITE
AGALMATOLITES
AGAMICALLY
AGAMOGENESES
AGAMOGENESIS
AGAMOGENETIC
AGAMOGONIES
AGAMOSPERMIES
AGAMOSPERMY
AGAPANTHUS
AGAPANTHUSES
AGARICACEOUS
AGATEWARES
AGATHODAIMON
AGATHODAIMONS
AGEDNESSES
AGELESSNESS
AGELESSNESSES
AGENDALESS
AGENTIVITIES
AGENTIVITY
AGFLATIONS
AGGIORNAMENTI
AGGIORNAMENTO
AGGIORNAMENTOS
AGGLOMERATE
AGGLOMERATED
AGGLOMERATES
AGGLOMERATING
AGGLOMERATION
AGGLOMERATIONS
AGGLOMERATIVE
AGGLUTINABILITY
AGGLUTINABLE
AGGLUTINANT
AGGLUTINANTS

AGGLUTINATE
AGGLUTINATED
AGGLUTINATES
AGGLUTINATING
AGGLUTINATION
AGGLUTINATIONS
AGGLUTINATIVE
AGGLUTININ
AGGLUTININS
AGGLUTINOGEN
AGGLUTINOGENIC
AGGLUTINOGENS
AGGRADATION
AGGRADATIONS
AGGRANDISE
AGGRANDISED
AGGRANDISEMENT
AGGRANDISEMENTS
AGGRANDISER
AGGRANDISERS
AGGRANDISES
AGGRANDISING
AGGRANDIZE
AGGRANDIZED
AGGRANDIZEMENT
AGGRANDIZEMENTS
AGGRANDIZER
AGGRANDIZERS
AGGRANDIZES
AGGRANDIZING
AGGRAVATED
AGGRAVATES
AGGRAVATING
AGGRAVATINGLY
AGGRAVATION
AGGRAVATIONS
AGGREGATED
AGGREGATELY
AGGREGATENESS
AGGREGATENESSES
AGGREGATES
AGGREGATING
AGGREGATION
AGGREGATIONAL
AGGREGATIONS
AGGREGATIVE
AGGREGATIVELY
AGGREGATOR
AGGREGATORS
AGGRESSING
AGGRESSION
AGGRESSIONS
AGGRESSIVE
AGGRESSIVELY
AGGRESSIVENESS
AGGRESSIVITIES
AGGRESSIVITY
AGGRESSORS
AGGRIEVEDLY
AGGRIEVEMENT
AGGRIEVEMENTS
AGGRIEVING
AGILENESSES
AGISTMENTS
AGITATEDLY
AGITATIONAL
AGITATIONS

AGNATICALLY
AGNOIOLOGIES
AGNOIOLOGY
AGNOLOTTIS
AGNOSTICISM
AGNOSTICISMS
AGONISEDLY
AGONISINGLY
AGONISTICAL
AGONISTICALLY
AGONISTICS
AGONIZEDLY
AGONIZINGLY
AGONOTHETES
AGORAPHOBE
AGORAPHOBES
AGORAPHOBIA
AGORAPHOBIAS
AGORAPHOBIC
AGORAPHOBICS
AGRAMMATICAL
AGRANULOCYTE
AGRANULOCYTES
AGRANULOCYTOSES
AGRANULOCYTOSIS
AGRANULOSES
AGRANULOSIS
AGRARIANISM
AGRARIANISMS
AGREEABILITIES
AGREEABILITY
AGREEABLENESS
AGREEABLENESSES
AGREEMENTS
AGREGATION
AGREGATIONS
AGRIBUSINESS
AGRIBUSINESSES
AGRIBUSINESSMAN
AGRIBUSINESSMEN
AGRICHEMICAL
AGRICHEMICALS
AGRICULTURAL
AGRICULTURALIST
AGRICULTURALLY
AGRICULTURE
AGRICULTURES
AGRICULTURIST
AGRICULTURISTS
AGRIFOODSTUFFS
AGRIMONIES
AGRIOLOGIES
AGRIPRODUCT
AGRIPRODUCTS
AGRITOURISM
AGRITOURISMS
AGRITOURIST
AGRITOURISTS
AGROBIOLOGICAL
AGROBIOLOGIES
AGROBIOLOGIST
AGROBIOLOGISTS
AGROBIOLOGY
AGROBUSINESS
AGROBUSINESSES
AGROCHEMICAL
AGROCHEMICALS

AGRODOLCES
AGROFORESTER
AGROFORESTERS
AGROFORESTRIES
AGROFORESTRY
AGROINDUSTRIAL
AGROINDUSTRIES
AGROINDUSTRY
AGROLOGICAL
AGROLOGIES
AGROLOGIST
AGROLOGISTS
AGRONOMIAL
AGRONOMICAL
AGRONOMICALLY
AGRONOMICS
AGRONOMIES
AGRONOMIST
AGRONOMISTS
AGROSTEMMA
AGROSTEMMAS
AGROSTEMMATA
AGROSTOLOGIC
AGROSTOLOGICAL
AGROSTOLOGIES
AGROSTOLOGIST
AGROSTOLOGISTS
AGROSTOLOGY
AGROTERRORISM
AGROTERRORISMS
AGROTOURISM
AGROTOURISMS
AGROTOURIST
AGROTOURISTS
AGRYPNOTIC
AGRYPNOTICS
AGTERSKOTS
AGUARDIENTE
AGUARDIENTES
AHISTORICAL
AHORSEBACK
AHURUHURUS
AICHMOPHOBIA
AICHMOPHOBIAS
AIGUILLETTE
AIGUILLETTES
AILANTHUSES
AILOUROPHILE
AILOUROPHILES
AILOUROPHILIA
AILOUROPHILIAS
AILOUROPHILIC
AILOUROPHOBE
AILOUROPHOBES
AILOUROPHOBIA
AILOUROPHOBIAS
AILOUROPHOBIC
AILUROPHILE
AILUROPHILES
AILUROPHILIA
AILUROPHILIAS
AILUROPHILIC
AILUROPHOBE
AILUROPHOBES
AILUROPHOBIA
AILUROPHOBIAS
AILUROPHOBIC

AIMLESSNESS
AIMLESSNESSES
AIRBALLING
AIRBOARDING
AIRBOARDINGS
AIRBRUSHED
AIRBRUSHES
AIRBRUSHING
AIRBURSTED
AIRBURSTING
AIRCOACHES
AIRCRAFTMAN
AIRCRAFTMEN
AIRCRAFTSMAN
AIRCRAFTSMEN
AIRCRAFTSWOMAN
AIRCRAFTSWOMEN
AIRCRAFTWOMAN
AIRCRAFTWOMEN
AIRDROPPED
AIRDROPPING
AIRFREIGHT
AIRFREIGHTED
AIRFREIGHTING
AIRFREIGHTS
AIRINESSES
AIRLESSNESS
AIRLESSNESSES
AIRLIFTING
AIRMAILING
AIRMANSHIP
AIRMANSHIPS
AIRPROOFED
AIRPROOFING
AIRSICKNESS
AIRSICKNESSES
AIRSTREAMS
AIRSTRIKES
AIRTIGHTNESS
AIRTIGHTNESSES
AIRWORTHIER
AIRWORTHIEST
AIRWORTHINESS
AIRWORTHINESSES
AITCHBONES
AKATHISIAS
AKOLOUTHOS
AKOLOUTHOSES
AKOLUTHOSES
ALABAMINES
ALABANDINE
ALABANDINES
ALABANDITE
ALABANDITES
ALABASTERS
ALABASTRINE
ALABLASTER
ALABLASTERS
ALACRITIES
ALACRITOUS
ALARMINGLY
ALBARELLOS
ALBATROSSES
ALBERTITES
ALBESCENCE
ALBESCENCES
ALBESPINES

ALBESPYNES
ALBINESSES
ALBINISTIC
ALBINOISMS
ALBITISING
ALBITIZING
ALBUGINEOUS
ALBUMBLATT
ALBUMBLATTER
ALBUMBLATTS
ALBUMENISE
ALBUMENISED
ALBUMENISES
ALBUMENISING
ALBUMENIZE
ALBUMENIZED
ALBUMENIZES
ALBUMENIZING
ALBUMINATE
ALBUMINATES
ALBUMINISE
ALBUMINISED
ALBUMINISES
ALBUMINISING
ALBUMINIZE
ALBUMINIZED
ALBUMINIZES
ALBUMINIZING
ALBUMINOID
ALBUMINOIDS
ALBUMINOUS
ALBUMINURIA
ALBUMINURIAS
ALBUMINURIC
ALBUTEROLS
ALCAICERIA
ALCAICERIAS
ALCARRAZAS
ALCATRASES
ALCHEMICAL
ALCHEMICALLY
ALCHEMISED
ALCHEMISES
ALCHEMISING
ALCHEMISTIC
ALCHEMISTICAL
ALCHEMISTS
ALCHEMIZED
ALCHEMIZES
ALCHEMIZING
ALCHERINGA
ALCHERINGAS
ALCOHOLICALLY
ALCOHOLICITIES
ALCOHOLICITY
ALCOHOLICS
ALCOHOLISATION
ALCOHOLISATIONS
ALCOHOLISE
ALCOHOLISED
ALCOHOLISES
ALCOHOLISING
ALCOHOLISM
ALCOHOLISMS
ALCOHOLIZATION
ALCOHOLIZATIONS
ALCOHOLIZE

ALCOHOLIZED
ALCOHOLIZES
ALCOHOLIZING
ALCOHOLOMETER
ALCOHOLOMETERS
ALCOHOLOMETRIES
ALCOHOLOMETRY
ALCYONARIAN
ALCYONARIANS
ALDERFLIES
ALDERMANIC
ALDERMANITIES
ALDERMANITY
ALDERMANLIER
ALDERMANLIEST
ALDERMANLIKE
ALDERMANLY
ALDERMANRIES
ALDERMANRY
ALDERMANSHIP
ALDERMANSHIPS
ALDERWOMAN
ALDERWOMEN
ALDOHEXOSE
ALDOHEXOSES
ALDOLISATION
ALDOLISATIONS
ALDOLIZATION
ALDOLIZATIONS
ALDOPENTOSE
ALDOPENTOSES
ALDOSTERONE
ALDOSTERONES
ALDOSTERONISM
ALDOSTERONISMS
ALEATORIES
ALEBENCHES
ALECTRYONS
ALEGGEAUNCE
ALEGGEAUNCES
ALEMBICATED
ALEMBICATION
ALEMBICATIONS
ALEMBROTHS
ALERTNESSES
ALEXANDERS
ALEXANDERSES
ALEXANDRINE
ALEXANDRINES
ALEXANDRITE
ALEXANDRITES
ALEXIPHARMAKON
ALEXIPHARMAKONS
ALEXIPHARMIC
ALEXIPHARMICS
ALEXITHYMIA
ALEXITHYMIAS
ALFILARIAS
ALFILERIAS
ALGAECIDES
ALGARROBAS
ALGARROBOS
ALGEBRAICAL
ALGEBRAICALLY
ALGEBRAIST
ALGEBRAISTS
ALGIDITIES

ALGIDNESSES
ALGOLAGNIA
ALGOLAGNIAC
ALGOLAGNIACS
ALGOLAGNIAS
ALGOLAGNIC
ALGOLAGNIST
ALGOLAGNISTS
ALGOLOGICAL
ALGOLOGICALLY
ALGOLOGIES
ALGOLOGIST
ALGOLOGISTS
ALGOMETERS
ALGOMETRIES
ALGOPHOBIA
ALGOPHOBIAS
ALGORISMIC
ALGORITHMIC
ALGORITHMICALLY
ALGORITHMS
ALIENABILITIES
ALIENABILITY
ALIENATING
ALIENATION
ALIENATIONS
ALIENATORS
ALIENNESSES
ALIGHTMENT
ALIGHTMENTS
ALIGNMENTS
ALIKENESSES
ALIMENTARY
ALIMENTATION
ALIMENTATIONS
ALIMENTATIVE
ALIMENTING
ALIMENTIVENESS
ALINEATION
ALINEATIONS
ALINEMENTS
ALISMACEOUS
ALITERACIES
ALITERATES
ALIVENESSES
ALIZARINES
ALKAHESTIC
ALKALESCENCE
ALKALESCENCES
ALKALESCENCIES
ALKALESCENCY
ALKALESCENT
ALKALIFIED
ALKALIFIES
ALKALIFYING
ALKALIMETER
ALKALIMETERS
ALKALIMETRIC
ALKALIMETRIES
ALKALIMETRY
ALKALINISATION
ALKALINISATIONS
ALKALINISE
ALKALINISED
ALKALINISES
ALKALINISING
ALKALINITIES

ALKALINITY	ALLERGENICITY	ALLOMETRIES	ALMANDINES	ALSTROEMERIAS
ALKALINIZATION	ALLERGISTS	ALLOMORPHIC	ALMANDITES	ALTALTISSIMO
ALKALINIZATIONS	ALLETHRINS	ALLOMORPHISM	ALMIGHTIER	ALTALTISSIMOS
ALKALINIZE	ALLEVIANTS	ALLOMORPHISMS	ALMIGHTIEST	ALTARPIECE
ALKALINIZED	ALLEVIATED	ALLOMORPHS	ALMIGHTILY	ALTARPIECES
ALKALINIZES	ALLEVIATES	ALLONYMOUS	ALMIGHTINESS	ALTAZIMUTH
ALKALINIZING	ALLEVIATING	ALLOPATHIC	ALMIGHTINESSES	ALTAZIMUTHS
ALKALISABLE	ALLEVIATION	ALLOPATHICALLY	ALMONDIEST	ALTERABILITIES
ALKALISERS	ALLEVIATIONS	ALLOPATHIES	ALMONDITES	ALTERABILITY
ALKALISING	ALLEVIATIVE	ALLOPATHIST	ALMSGIVERS	ALTERATION
ALKALIZABLE	ALLEVIATOR	ALLOPATHISTS	ALMSGIVING	ALTERATIONS
ALKALIZERS	ALLEVIATORS	ALLOPATRIC	ALMSGIVINGS	ALTERATIVE
ALKALIZING	ALLEVIATORY	ALLOPATRICALLY	ALMSHOUSES	ALTERATIVES
ALKALOIDAL	ALLHALLOND	ALLOPATRIES	ALMUCANTAR	ALTERCATED
ALKYLATING	ALLHALLOWEN	ALLOPHANES	ALMUCANTARS	ALTERCATES
ALKYLATION	ALLHALLOWN	ALLOPHONES	ALOESWOODS	ALTERCATING
ALKYLATIONS	ALLHOLLOWN	ALLOPHONIC	ALOGICALLY	ALTERCATION
ALLANTOIDAL	ALLIACEOUS	ALLOPLASMIC	ALONENESSES	ALTERCATIONS
ALLANTOIDES	ALLICHOLIES	ALLOPLASMS	ALONGSHORE	ALTERCATIVE
ALLANTOIDS	ALLIGARTAS	ALLOPLASTIC	ALONGSHOREMAN	ALTERITIES
ALLANTOINS	ALLIGATING	ALLOPOLYPLOID	ALONGSHOREMEN	ALTERNANCE
ALLANTOISES	ALLIGATION	ALLOPOLYPLOIDS	ALOOFNESSES	ALTERNANCES
ALLARGANDO	ALLIGATIONS	ALLOPOLYPLOIDY	ALOPECOIDS	ALTERNANTS
ALLAYMENTS	ALLIGATORS	ALLOPURINOL	ALPARGATAS	ALTERNATED
ALLEGATION	ALLINEATION	ALLOPURINOLS	ALPENGLOWS	ALTERNATELY
ALLEGATIONS	ALLINEATIONS	ALLOSAURUS	ALPENHORNS	ALTERNATES
ALLEGEANCE	ALLITERATE	ALLOSAURUSES	ALPENSTOCK	ALTERNATIM
ALLEGEANCES	ALLITERATED	ALLOSTERIC	ALPENSTOCKS	ALTERNATING
ALLEGIANCE	ALLITERATES	ALLOSTERICALLY	ALPESTRINE	ALTERNATION
ALLEGIANCES	ALLITERATING	ALLOSTERIES	ALPHABETARIAN	ALTERNATIONS
ALLEGIANTS	ALLITERATION	ALLOTETRAPLOID	ALPHABETARIANS	ALTERNATIVE
ALLEGORICAL	ALLITERATIONS	ALLOTETRAPLOIDS	ALPHABETED	ALTERNATIVELY
ALLEGORICALLY	ALLITERATIVE	ALLOTETRAPLOIDY	ALPHABETIC	ALTERNATIVENESS
ALLEGORICALNESS	ALLITERATIVELY	ALLOTHEISM	ALPHABETICAL	ALTERNATIVES
ALLEGORIES	ALLNIGHTER	ALLOTHEISMS	ALPHABETICALLY	ALTERNATOR
ALLEGORISATION	ALLNIGHTERS	ALLOTMENTS	ALPHABETIFORM	ALTERNATORS
ALLEGORISATIONS	ALLOANTIBODIES	ALLOTRIOMORPHIC	ALPHABETING	ALTIGRAPHS
ALLEGORISE	ALLOANTIBODY	ALLOTROPES	ALPHABETISATION	ALTIMETERS
ALLEGORISED	ALLOANTIGEN	ALLOTROPIC	ALPHABETISE	ALTIMETRICAL
ALLEGORISER	ALLOANTIGENS	ALLOTROPICALLY	ALPHABETISED	ALTIMETRICALLY
ALLEGORISERS	ALLOCARPIES	ALLOTROPIES	ALPHABETISER	ALTIMETRIES
ALLEGORISES	ALLOCATABLE	ALLOTROPISM	ALPHABETISERS	ALTIPLANOS
ALLEGORISING	ALLOCATING	ALLOTROPISMS	ALPHABETISES	ALTISONANT
ALLEGORIST	ALLOCATION	ALLOTROPOUS	ALPHABETISING	ALTISSIMOS
ALLEGORISTS	ALLOCATIONS	ALLOTTERIES	ALPHABETIZATION	ALTITONANT
ALLEGORIZATION	ALLOCATORS	ALLOTYPICALLY	ALPHABETIZE	ALTITUDINAL
ALLEGORIZATIONS	ALLOCHEIRIA	ALLOTYPIES	ALPHABETIZED	ALTITUDINARIAN
ALLEGORIZE	ALLOCHEIRIAS	ALLOWABILITIES	ALPHABETIZER	ALTITUDINARIANS
ALLEGORIZED	ALLOCHIRIA	ALLOWABILITY	ALPHABETIZERS	ALTITUDINOUS
ALLEGORIZER	ALLOCHIRIAS	ALLOWABLENESS	ALPHABETIZES	ALTOCUMULI
ALLEGORIZERS	ALLOCHTHONOUS	ALLOWABLENESSES	ALPHABETIZING	ALTOCUMULUS
ALLEGORIZES	ALLOCUTION	ALLOWABLES	ALPHAMERIC	ALTOGETHER
ALLEGORIZING	ALLOCUTIONS	ALLOWANCED	ALPHAMERICAL	ALTOGETHERS
ALLEGRETTO	ALLODYNIAS	ALLOWANCES	ALPHAMERICALLY	ALTORUFFLED
ALLEGRETTOS	ALLOGAMIES	ALLOWANCING	ALPHAMETIC	ALTOSTRATI
ALLELOMORPH	ALLOGAMOUS	ALLUREMENT	ALPHAMETICS	ALTOSTRATUS
ALLELOMORPHIC	ALLOGENEIC	ALLUREMENTS	ALPHANUMERIC	ALTRICIALS
ALLELOMORPHISM	ALLOGRAFTED	ALLURINGLY	ALPHANUMERICAL	ALTRUISTIC
ALLELOMORPHISMS	ALLOGRAFTING	ALLUSIVELY	ALPHANUMERICS	ALTRUISTICALLY
ALLELOMORPHS	ALLOGRAFTS	ALLUSIVENESS	ALPHASORTED	ALUMINATES
ALLELOPATHIC	ALLOGRAPHIC	ALLUSIVENESSES	ALPHASORTING	ALUMINIDES
ALLELOPATHIES	ALLOGRAPHS	ALLWEATHER	ALPHASORTS	ALUMINIFEROUS
ALLELOPATHY	ALLOIOSTROPHOS	ALLWEATHERS	ALPHATESTED	ALUMINISED
ALLELUIAHS	ALLOMERISM	ALLYCHOLLIES	ALPHATESTING	ALUMINISES
ALLEMANDES	ALLOMERISMS	ALLYCHOLLY	ALPHATESTS	ALUMINISING
ALLERGENIC	ALLOMEROUS	ALMACANTAR	ALPHOSISES	ALUMINIUMS
ALLERGENICITIES	ALLOMETRIC	ALMACANTARS	ALSTROEMERIA	ALUMINIZED

a

ALUMINIZES	AMBERGRISES	AMBUSHMENTS	AMINOPHENAZONE	AMORTISEMENTS
ALUMINIZING	AMBERJACKS	AMEBOCYTES	AMINOPHENAZONES	AMORTISING
ALUMINOSILICATE	AMBIDENTATE	AMELIORABLE	AMINOPHENOL	AMORTIZABLE
ALUMINOSITIES	AMBIDEXTER	AMELIORANT	AMINOPHENOLS	AMORTIZATION
ALUMINOSITY	AMBIDEXTERITIES	AMELIORANTS	AMINOPHYLLINE	AMORTIZATIONS
ALUMINOTHERMIES	AMBIDEXTERITY	AMELIORATE	AMINOPHYLLINES	AMORTIZEMENT
ALUMINOTHERMY	AMBIDEXTEROUS	AMELIORATED	AMINOPTERIN	AMORTIZEMENTS
ALUMSTONES	AMBIDEXTERS	AMELIORATES	AMINOPTERINS	AMORTIZING
ALVEOLARLY	AMBIDEXTROUS	AMELIORATING	AMINOPYRINE	AMOURETTES
ALVEOLATION	AMBIDEXTROUSLY	AMELIORATION	AMINOPYRINES	AMOXICILLIN
ALVEOLATIONS	AMBIGUITIES	AMELIORATIONS	AMINOTOLUENE	AMOXICILLINS
ALVEOLITIS	AMBIGUOUSLY	AMELIORATIVE	AMINOTOLUENES	AMOXYCILLIN
ALVEOLITISES	AMBIGUOUSNESS	AMELIORATOR	AMISSIBILITIES	AMOXYCILLINS
ALYCOMPAINE	AMBIGUOUSNESSES	AMELIORATORS	AMISSIBILITY	AMPACITIES
ALYCOMPAINES	AMBILATERAL	AMELIORATORY	AMITOTICALLY	AMPELOGRAPHIES
AMAKWEREKWERE	AMBIOPHONIES	AMELOBLAST	AMITRIPTYLINE	AMPELOGRAPHY
AMALGAMATE	AMBIOPHONY	AMELOBLASTS	AMITRIPTYLINES	AMPELOPSES
AMALGAMATED	AMBISEXUAL	AMELOGENESES	AMITRYPTYLINE	AMPELOPSIS
AMALGAMATES	AMBISEXUALITIES	AMELOGENESIS	AMITRYPTYLINES	AMPELOPSISES
AMALGAMATING	AMBISEXUALITY	AMENABILITIES	AMMOCOETES	AMPEROMETRIC
AMALGAMATION	AMBISEXUALS	AMENABILITY	AMMONIACAL	AMPERSANDS
AMALGAMATIONS	AMBISONICS	AMENABLENESS	AMMONIACUM	AMPERZANDS
AMALGAMATIVE	AMBITIONED	AMENABLENESSES	AMMONIACUMS	AMPHETAMINE
AMALGAMATOR	AMBITIONING	AMENAUNCES	AMMONIATED	AMPHETAMINES
AMALGAMATORS	AMBITIONLESS	AMENDATORY	AMMONIATES	AMPHIARTHROSES
AMANTADINE	AMBITIOUSLY	AMENDMENTS	AMMONIATING	AMPHIARTHROSIS
AMANTADINES	AMBITIOUSNESS	AMENORRHEA	AMMONIATION	AMPHIASTER
AMANUENSES	AMBITIOUSNESSES	AMENORRHEAS	AMMONIATIONS	AMPHIASTERS
AMANUENSIS	AMBIVALENCE	AMENORRHEIC	AMMONIFICATION	AMPHIBIANS
AMARACUSES	AMBIVALENCES	AMENORRHOEA	AMMONIFICATIONS	AMPHIBIOTIC
AMARANTACEOUS	AMBIVALENCIES	AMENORRHOEAS	AMMONIFIED	AMPHIBIOUS
AMARANTHACEOUS	AMBIVALENCY	AMENTACEOUS	AMMONIFIES	AMPHIBIOUSLY
AMARANTHINE	AMBIVALENT	AMENTIFEROUS	AMMONIFYING	AMPHIBIOUSNESS
AMARANTINE	AMBIVALENTLY	AMERCEABLE	AMMONOLYSES	AMPHIBLASTIC
AMARANTINS	AMBIVERSION	AMERCEMENT	AMMONOLYSIS	AMPHIBLASTULA
AMARYLLIDACEOUS	AMBIVERSIONS	AMERCEMENTS	AMMOPHILOUS	AMPHIBLASTULAE
AMARYLLIDS	AMBLYGONITE	AMERCIABLE	AMMUNITION	AMPHIBOLES
AMARYLLISES	AMBLYGONITES	AMERCIAMENT	AMMUNITIONED	AMPHIBOLIC
AMASSMENTS	AMBLYOPIAS	AMERCIAMENTS	AMMUNITIONING	AMPHIBOLIES
AMATEURISH	AMBOCEPTOR	AMERICIUMS	AMMUNITIONS	AMPHIBOLITE
AMATEURISHLY	AMBOCEPTORS	AMETABOLIC	AMNESTYING	AMPHIBOLITES
AMATEURISHNESS	AMBOSEXUAL	AMETABOLISM	AMNIOCENTESES	AMPHIBOLOGICAL
AMATEURISM	AMBROSIALLY	AMETABOLISMS	AMNIOCENTESIS	AMPHIBOLOGIES
AMATEURISMS	AMBROTYPES	AMETABOLOUS	AMNIOTOMIES	AMPHIBOLOGY
AMATEURSHIP	AMBULACRAL	AMETHYSTINE	AMOBARBITAL	AMPHIBOLOUS
AMATEURSHIPS	AMBULACRUM	AMETROPIAS	AMOBARBITALS	AMPHIBRACH
AMATIVENESS	AMBULANCEMAN	AMIABILITIES	AMOEBIASES	AMPHIBRACHIC
AMATIVENESSES	AMBULANCEMEN	AMIABILITY	AMOEBIASIS	AMPHIBRACHS
AMATORIALLY	AMBULANCES	AMIABLENESS	AMOEBIFORM	AMPHICHROIC
AMATORIOUS	AMBULANCEWOMAN	AMIABLENESSES	AMOEBOCYTE	AMPHICHROMATIC
AMAZEBALLS	AMBULANCEWOMEN	AMIANTHINE	AMOEBOCYTES	AMPHICOELOUS
AMAZEDNESS	AMBULATING	AMIANTHOID	AMONTILLADO	AMPHICTYON
AMAZEDNESSES	AMBULATION	AMIANTHOIDAL	AMONTILLADOS	AMPHICTYONIC
AMAZEMENTS	AMBULATIONS	AMIANTHUSES	AMORALISMS	AMPHICTYONIES
AMAZONIANS	AMBULATORIES	AMIANTUSES	AMORALISTS	AMPHICTYONS
AMAZONITES	AMBULATORILY	AMICABILITIES	AMORALITIES	AMPHICTYONY
AMAZONSTONE	AMBULATORS	AMICABILITY	AMOROSITIES	AMPHIDENTATE
AMAZONSTONES	AMBULATORY	AMICABLENESS	AMOROUSNESS	AMPHIDIPLOID
AMBAGITORY	AMBULETTES	AMICABLENESSES	AMOROUSNESSES	AMPHIDIPLOIDIES
AMBASSADOR	AMBUSCADED	AMINOACETIC	AMORPHISMS	AMPHIDIPLOIDS
AMBASSADORIAL	AMBUSCADER	AMINOACIDURIA	AMORPHOUSLY	AMPHIDIPLOIDY
AMBASSADORS	AMBUSCADERS	AMINOACIDURIAS	AMORPHOUSNESS	AMPHIGASTRIA
AMBASSADORSHIP	AMBUSCADES	AMINOBENZOIC	AMORPHOUSNESSES	AMPHIGASTRIUM
AMBASSADORSHIPS	AMBUSCADING	AMINOBUTENE	AMORTISABLE	AMPHIGORIC
AMBASSADRESS	AMBUSCADOES	AMINOBUTENES	AMORTISATION	AMPHIGORIES
AMBASSADRESSES	AMBUSCADOS	AMINOPEPTIDASE	AMORTISATIONS	AMPHIGOURI
AMBASSAGES	AMBUSHMENT	AMINOPEPTIDASES	AMORTISEMENT	AMPHIGOURIS

AMPHIMACER
AMPHIMACERS
AMPHIMICTIC
AMPHIMIXES
AMPHIMIXIS
AMPHIOXUSES
AMPHIPATHIC
AMPHIPHILE
AMPHIPHILES
AMPHIPHILIC
AMPHIPLOID
AMPHIPLOIDIES
AMPHIPLOIDS
AMPHIPLOIDY
AMPHIPODOUS
AMPHIPROSTYLAR
AMPHIPROSTYLE
AMPHIPROSTYLES
AMPHIPROTIC
AMPHISBAENA
AMPHISBAENAE
AMPHISBAENAS
AMPHISBAENIC
AMPHISCIAN
AMPHISCIANS
AMPHISTOMATAL
AMPHISTOMATIC
AMPHISTOMOUS
AMPHISTYLAR
AMPHISTYLARS
AMPHITHEATER
AMPHITHEATERS
AMPHITHEATRAL
AMPHITHEATRE
AMPHITHEATRES
AMPHITHEATRIC
AMPHITHEATRICAL
AMPHITHECIA
AMPHITHECIUM
AMPHITRICHA
AMPHITRICHOUS
AMPHITROPOUS
AMPHOLYTES
AMPHOTERIC
AMPICILLIN
AMPICILLINS
AMPLENESSES
AMPLEXICAUL
AMPLEXUSES
AMPLIATION
AMPLIATIONS
AMPLIATIVE
AMPLIDYNES
AMPLIFIABLE
AMPLIFICATION
AMPLIFICATIONS
AMPLIFIERS
AMPLIFYING
AMPLITUDES
AMPLOSOMES
AMPULLACEAL
AMPULLACEOUS
AMPULLOSITIES
AMPULLOSITY
AMPUTATING
AMPUTATION
AMPUTATIONS

AMPUTATORS
AMRITATTVA
AMRITATTVAS
AMSINCKIAS
AMUSEMENTS
AMUSINGNESS
AMUSINGNESSES
AMUSIVENESS
AMUSIVENESSES
AMYGDALACEOUS
AMYGDALATE
AMYGDALINE
AMYGDALINS
AMYGDALOID
AMYGDALOIDAL
AMYGDALOIDS
AMYLACEOUS
AMYLOBARBITONE
AMYLOBARBITONES
AMYLOIDOSES
AMYLOIDOSIS
AMYLOLYSES
AMYLOLYSIS
AMYLOLYTIC
AMYLOPECTIN
AMYLOPECTINS
AMYLOPLAST
AMYLOPLASTS
AMYLOPSINS
AMYOTONIAS
AMYOTROPHIC
AMYOTROPHIES
AMYOTROPHY
ANABANTIDS
ANABAPTISE
ANABAPTISED
ANABAPTISES
ANABAPTISING
ANABAPTISM
ANABAPTISMS
ANABAPTIST
ANABAPTISTIC
ANABAPTISTS
ANABAPTIZE
ANABAPTIZED
ANABAPTIZES
ANABAPTIZING
ANABLEPSES
ANABOLISMS
ANABOLITES
ANABOLITIC
ANABRANCHES
ANACARDIACEOUS
ANACARDIUM
ANACARDIUMS
ANACATHARSES
ANACATHARSIS
ANACATHARTIC
ANACATHARTICS
ANACHARISES
ANACHORISM
ANACHORISMS
ANACHRONIC
ANACHRONICAL
ANACHRONICALLY
ANACHRONISM
ANACHRONISMS

ANACHRONISTIC
ANACHRONOUS
ANACHRONOUSLY
ANACLASTIC
ANACOLUTHA
ANACOLUTHIA
ANACOLUTHIAS
ANACOLUTHIC
ANACOLUTHICALLY
ANACOLUTHON
ANACOLUTHONS
ANACOUSTIC
ANACREONTIC
ANACREONTICALLY
ANACREONTICS
ANACRUSTIC
ANADIPLOSES
ANADIPLOSIS
ANADROMOUS
ANADYOMENE
ANAEMICALLY
ANAEROBICALLY
ANAEROBIONT
ANAEROBIONTS
ANAEROBIOSES
ANAEROBIOSIS
ANAEROBIOTIC
ANAEROBIUM
ANAESTHESES
ANAESTHESIA
ANAESTHESIAS
ANAESTHESIOLOGY
ANAESTHESIS
ANAESTHETIC
ANAESTHETICALLY
ANAESTHETICS
ANAESTHETISE
ANAESTHETISED
ANAESTHETISES
ANAESTHETISING
ANAESTHETIST
ANAESTHETISTS
ANAESTHETIZE
ANAESTHETIZED
ANAESTHETIZES
ANAESTHETIZING
ANAGENESES
ANAGENESIS
ANAGLYPHIC
ANAGLYPHICAL
ANAGLYPHIES
ANAGLYPTIC
ANAGLYPTICAL
ANAGNORISES
ANAGNORISIS
ANAGOGICAL
ANAGOGICALLY
ANAGRAMMATIC
ANAGRAMMATICAL
ANAGRAMMATISE
ANAGRAMMATISED
ANAGRAMMATISES
ANAGRAMMATISING
ANAGRAMMATISM
ANAGRAMMATISMS
ANAGRAMMATIST
ANAGRAMMATISTS

ANAGRAMMATIZE
ANAGRAMMATIZED
ANAGRAMMATIZES
ANAGRAMMATIZING
ANAGRAMMED
ANAGRAMMER
ANAGRAMMERS
ANAGRAMMING
ANALEMMATA
ANALEMMATIC
ANALEPTICS
ANALGESIAS
ANALGESICS
ANALGETICS
ANALOGICAL
ANALOGICALLY
ANALOGISED
ANALOGISES
ANALOGISING
ANALOGISMS
ANALOGISTS
ANALOGIZED
ANALOGIZES
ANALOGIZING
ANALOGOUSLY
ANALOGOUSNESS
ANALOGOUSNESSES
ANALPHABET
ANALPHABETE
ANALPHABETES
ANALPHABETIC
ANALPHABETICS
ANALPHABETISM
ANALPHABETISMS
ANALPHABETS
ANALYSABILITIES
ANALYSABILITY
ANALYSABLE
ANALYSANDS
ANALYSATION
ANALYSATIONS
ANALYTICAL
ANALYTICALLY
ANALYTICITIES
ANALYTICITY
ANALYZABILITIES
ANALYZABILITY
ANALYZABLE
ANALYZATION
ANALYZATIONS
ANAMNESTIC
ANAMNESTICALLY
ANAMNIOTES
ANAMNIOTIC
ANAMORPHIC
ANAMORPHISM
ANAMORPHISMS
ANAMORPHOSCOPE
ANAMORPHOSCOPES
ANAMORPHOSES
ANAMORPHOSIS
ANAMORPHOUS
ANANDAMIDE
ANANDAMIDES
ANAPAESTIC
ANAPAESTICAL
ANAPESTICS

ANAPHORESES
ANAPHORESIS
ANAPHORICAL
ANAPHORICALLY
ANAPHRODISIA
ANAPHRODISIAC
ANAPHRODISIACS
ANAPHRODISIAS
ANAPHYLACTIC
ANAPHYLACTOID
ANAPHYLAXES
ANAPHYLAXIES
ANAPHYLAXIS
ANAPHYLAXY
ANAPLASIAS
ANAPLASMOSES
ANAPLASMOSIS
ANAPLASTIC
ANAPLASTIES
ANAPLEROSES
ANAPLEROSIS
ANAPLEROTIC
ANAPTYCTIC
ANAPTYCTICAL
ANARCHICAL
ANARCHICALLY
ANARCHISED
ANARCHISES
ANARCHISING
ANARCHISMS
ANARCHISTIC
ANARCHISTICALLY
ANARCHISTS
ANARCHIZED
ANARCHIZES
ANARCHIZING
ANARTHRIAS
ANARTHROUS
ANARTHROUSLY
ANARTHROUSNESS
ANASARCOUS
ANASTIGMAT
ANASTIGMATIC
ANASTIGMATISM
ANASTIGMATISMS
ANASTIGMATS
ANASTOMOSE
ANASTOMOSED
ANASTOMOSES
ANASTOMOSING
ANASTOMOSIS
ANASTOMOTIC
ANASTROPHE
ANASTROPHES
ANASTROZOLE
ANASTROZOLES
ANATHEMATA
ANATHEMATICAL
ANATHEMATICALS
ANATHEMATISE
ANATHEMATISED
ANATHEMATISES
ANATHEMATISING
ANATHEMATIZE
ANATHEMATIZED
ANATHEMATIZES
ANATHEMATIZING

a

ANATOMICAL	ANDROCENTRISM	ANEMOMETRY	ANGIOSARCOMA	ANGULARNESS
ANATOMICALLY	ANDROCENTRISMS	ANEMOPHILIES	ANGIOSARCOMAS	ANGULARNESSES
ANATOMISATION	ANDROCEPHALOUS	ANEMOPHILOUS	ANGIOSARCOMATA	ANGULATING
ANATOMISATIONS	ANDROCLINIA	ANEMOPHILY	ANGIOSPERM	ANGULATION
ANATOMISED	ANDROCLINIUM	ANEMOPHOBIA	ANGIOSPERMAL	ANGULATIONS
ANATOMISER	ANDRODIOECIOUS	ANEMOPHOBIAS	ANGIOSPERMOUS	ANGUSTIFOLIATE
ANATOMISERS	ANDRODIOECISM	ANEMOSCOPE	ANGIOSPERMS	ANGUSTIROSTRATE
ANATOMISES	ANDRODIOECISMS	ANEMOSCOPES	ANGIOSTOMATOUS	ANGWANTIBO
ANATOMISING	ANDROECIAL	ANENCEPHALIA	ANGIOSTOMOUS	ANGWANTIBOS
ANATOMISTS	ANDROECIUM	ANENCEPHALIAS	ANGIOTENSIN	ANHARMONIC
ANATOMIZATION	ANDROGENESES	ANENCEPHALIC	ANGIOTENSINS	ANHEDONIAS
ANATOMIZATIONS	ANDROGENESIS	ANENCEPHALIES	ANGISHORES	ANHELATION
ANATOMIZED	ANDROGENETIC	ANENCEPHALY	ANGLEBERRIES	ANHELATIONS
ANATOMIZER	ANDROGENIC	ANESTHESIA	ANGLEBERRY	ANHIDROSES
ANATOMIZERS	ANDROGENOUS	ANESTHESIAS	ANGLEDOZER	ANHIDROSIS
ANATOMIZES	ANDROGYNES	ANESTHESIOLOGY	ANGLEDOZERS	ANHIDROTIC
ANATOMIZING	ANDROGYNIES	ANESTHETIC	ANGLERFISH	ANHIDROTICS
ANATROPIES	ANDROGYNOPHORE	ANESTHETICALLY	ANGLERFISHES	ANHUNGERED
ANATROPOUS	ANDROGYNOPHORES	ANESTHETICS	ANGLESITES	ANHYDRASES
ANCESTORED	ANDROGYNOUS	ANESTHETISATION	ANGLETWITCH	ANHYDRIDES
ANCESTORIAL	ANDROLOGIES	ANESTHETISE	ANGLETWITCHES	ANHYDRITES
ANCESTORING	ANDROLOGIST	ANESTHETISED	ANGLEWORMS	ANICONISMS
ANCESTRALLY	ANDROLOGISTS	ANESTHETISES	ANGLICISATION	ANICONISTS
ANCESTRALS	ANDROMEDAS	ANESTHETISING	ANGLICISATIONS	ANILINCTUS
ANCESTRESS	ANDROMEDOTOXIN	ANESTHETIST	ANGLICISED	ANILINCTUSES
ANCESTRESSES	ANDROMEDOTOXINS	ANESTHETISTS	ANGLICISES	ANILINGUSES
ANCESTRIES	ANDROMONOECIOUS	ANESTHETIZATION	ANGLICISING	ANIMADVERSION
ANCHORAGES	ANDROMONOECISM	ANESTHETIZE	ANGLICISMS	ANIMADVERSIONS
ANCHORESSES	ANDROMONOECISMS	ANESTHETIZED	ANGLICISTS	ANIMADVERT
ANCHORETIC	ANDROPAUSE	ANESTHETIZES	ANGLICIZATION	ANIMADVERTED
ANCHORETICAL	ANDROPAUSES	ANESTHETIZING	ANGLICIZATIONS	ANIMADVERTER
ANCHORETTE	ANDROPHORE	ANEUPLOIDIES	ANGLICIZED	ANIMADVERTERS
ANCHORETTES	ANDROPHORES	ANEUPLOIDS	ANGLICIZES	ANIMADVERTING
ANCHORITES	ANDROSPHINGES	ANEUPLOIDY	ANGLICIZING	ANIMADVERTS
ANCHORITIC	ANDROSPHINX	ANEURISMAL	ANGLIFYING	ANIMALCULA
ANCHORITICAL	ANDROSPHINXES	ANEURISMALLY	ANGLISTICS	ANIMALCULAR
ANCHORITICALLY	ANDROSTERONE	ANEURISMATIC	ANGLOMANIA	ANIMALCULE
ANCHORLESS	ANDROSTERONES	ANEURYSMAL	ANGLOMANIAC	ANIMALCULES
ANCHORPEOPLE	ANECDOTAGE	ANEURYSMALLY	ANGLOMANIACS	ANIMALCULISM
ANCHORPERSON	ANECDOTAGES	ANEURYSMATIC	ANGLOMANIAS	ANIMALCULISMS
ANCHORPERSONS	ANECDOTALISM	ANFRACTUOSITIES	ANGLOPHILE	ANIMALCULIST
ANCHORWOMAN	ANECDOTALISMS	ANFRACTUOSITY	ANGLOPHILES	ANIMALCULISTS
ANCHORWOMEN	ANECDOTALIST	ANFRACTUOUS	ANGLOPHILIA	ANIMALCULUM
ANCHOVETAS	ANECDOTALISTS	ANGASHORES	ANGLOPHILIAS	ANIMALIERS
ANCHOVETTA	ANECDOTALLY	ANGELFISHES	ANGLOPHILIC	ANIMALISATION
ANCHOVETTAS	ANECDOTICAL	ANGELHOODS	ANGLOPHILS	ANIMALISATIONS
ANCHYLOSED	ANECDOTICALLY	ANGELICALLY	ANGLOPHOBE	ANIMALISED
ANCHYLOSES	ANECDOTIST	ANGELOLATRIES	ANGLOPHOBES	ANIMALISES
ANCHYLOSING	ANECDOTISTS	ANGELOLATRY	ANGLOPHOBIA	ANIMALISING
ANCHYLOSIS	ANELASTICITIES	ANGELOLOGIES	ANGLOPHOBIAC	ANIMALISMS
ANCHYLOTIC	ANELASTICITY	ANGELOLOGIST	ANGLOPHOBIACS	ANIMALISTIC
ANCIENTEST	ANEMICALLY	ANGELOLOGISTS	ANGLOPHOBIAS	ANIMALISTS
ANCIENTNESS	ANEMOCHORE	ANGELOLOGY	ANGLOPHOBIC	ANIMALITIES
ANCIENTNESSES	ANEMOCHORES	ANGELOPHANIES	ANGLOPHONE	ANIMALIZATION
ANCIENTRIES	ANEMOCHOROUS	ANGELOPHANY	ANGLOPHONES	ANIMALIZATIONS
ANCILLARIES	ANEMOGRAMS	ANGIOCARPOUS	ANGLOPHONIC	ANIMALIZED
ANCIPITOUS	ANEMOGRAPH	ANGIOGENESES	ANGOPHORAS	ANIMALIZES
ANCYLOSTOMIASES	ANEMOGRAPHIC	ANGIOGENESIS	ANGOSTURAS	ANIMALIZING
ANCYLOSTOMIASIS	ANEMOGRAPHIES	ANGIOGENIC	ANGRINESSES	ANIMALLIKE
ANDALUSITE	ANEMOGRAPHS	ANGIOGRAMS	ANGUIFAUNA	ANIMATEDLY
ANDALUSITES	ANEMOGRAPHY	ANGIOGRAPHIC	ANGUIFAUNAE	ANIMATENESS
ANDANTINOS	ANEMOLOGIES	ANGIOGRAPHIES	ANGUIFAUNAS	ANIMATENESSES
ANDOUILLES	ANEMOMETER	ANGIOGRAPHY	ANGUILLIFORM	ANIMATEURS
ANDOUILLETTE	ANEMOMETERS	ANGIOLOGIES	ANGUIPEDES	ANIMATINGLY
ANDOUILLETTES	ANEMOMETRIC	ANGIOMATOUS	ANGUISHING	ANIMATIONS
ANDRADITES	ANEMOMETRICAL	ANGIOPLASTIES	ANGULARITIES	ANIMATISMS
ANDROCENTRIC	ANEMOMETRIES	ANGIOPLASTY	ANGULARITY	ANIMATISTS

ANIMATRONIC
ANIMATRONICALLY
ANIMATRONICS
ANIMOSITIES
ANISEIKONIA
ANISEIKONIAS
ANISEIKONIC
ANISOCERCAL
ANISODACTYL
ANISODACTYLOUS
ANISODACTYLS
ANISOGAMIES
ANISOGAMOUS
ANISOMERIC
ANISOMEROUS
ANISOMETRIC
ANISOMETROPIA
ANISOMETROPIAS
ANISOMETROPIC
ANISOMORPHIC
ANISOPHYLLIES
ANISOPHYLLOUS
ANISOPHYLLY
ANISOTROPIC
ANISOTROPICALLY
ANISOTROPIES
ANISOTROPISM
ANISOTROPISMS
ANISOTROPY
ANKLEBONES
ANKYLOSAUR
ANKYLOSAURS
ANKYLOSAURUS
ANKYLOSAURUSES
ANKYLOSING
ANKYLOSTOMIASES
ANKYLOSTOMIASIS
ANNABERGITE
ANNABERGITES
ANNALISING
ANNALISTIC
ANNALIZING
ANNEALINGS
ANNELIDANS
ANNEXATION
ANNEXATIONAL
ANNEXATIONISM
ANNEXATIONISMS
ANNEXATIONIST
ANNEXATIONISTS
ANNEXATIONS
ANNEXMENTS
ANNIHILABLE
ANNIHILATE
ANNIHILATED
ANNIHILATES
ANNIHILATING
ANNIHILATION
ANNIHILATIONISM
ANNIHILATIONS
ANNIHILATIVE
ANNIHILATOR
ANNIHILATORS
ANNIHILATORY
ANNIVERSARIES
ANNIVERSARY
ANNOTATABLE

ANNOTATING
ANNOTATION
ANNOTATIONS
ANNOTATIVE
ANNOTATORS
ANNOUNCEMENT
ANNOUNCEMENTS
ANNOUNCERS
ANNOUNCING
ANNOYANCES
ANNOYINGLY
ANNUALISED
ANNUALISES
ANNUALISING
ANNUALIZED
ANNUALIZES
ANNUALIZING
ANNUITANTS
ANNUITISED
ANNUITISES
ANNUITISING
ANNUITIZED
ANNUITIZES
ANNUITIZING
ANNULARITIES
ANNULARITY
ANNULATION
ANNULATIONS
ANNULLABLE
ANNULMENTS
ANNUNCIATE
ANNUNCIATED
ANNUNCIATES
ANNUNCIATING
ANNUNCIATION
ANNUNCIATIONS
ANNUNCIATIVE
ANNUNCIATOR
ANNUNCIATORS
ANNUNCIATORY
ANNUNTIATE
ANNUNTIATED
ANNUNTIATES
ANNUNTIATING
ANODICALLY
ANODISATION
ANODISATIONS
ANODIZATION
ANODIZATIONS
ANODONTIAS
ANOESTROUS
ANOINTINGS
ANOINTMENT
ANOINTMENTS
ANOMALISTIC
ANOMALISTICAL
ANOMALISTICALLY
ANOMALOUSLY
ANOMALOUSNESS
ANOMALOUSNESSES
ANONACEOUS
ANONYMISED
ANONYMISES
ANONYMISING
ANONYMITIES
ANONYMIZED
ANONYMIZES

ANONYMIZING
ANONYMOUSLY
ANONYMOUSNESS
ANONYMOUSNESSES
ANOPHELINE
ANOPHELINES
ANORECTICS
ANOREXIGENIC
ANORTHITES
ANORTHITIC
ANORTHOSITE
ANORTHOSITES
ANORTHOSITIC
ANOTHERGUESS
ANOVULANTS
ANOVULATION
ANOVULATIONS
ANOVULATORY
ANOXAEMIAS
ANSAPHONES
ANSWERABILITIES
ANSWERABILITY
ANSWERABLE
ANSWERABLENESS
ANSWERABLY
ANSWERLESS
ANSWERPHONE
ANSWERPHONES
ANTAGONISABLE
ANTAGONISATION
ANTAGONISATIONS
ANTAGONISE
ANTAGONISED
ANTAGONISES
ANTAGONISING
ANTAGONISM
ANTAGONISMS
ANTAGONIST
ANTAGONISTIC
ANTAGONISTS
ANTAGONIZABLE
ANTAGONIZATION
ANTAGONIZATIONS
ANTAGONIZE
ANTAGONIZED
ANTAGONIZES
ANTAGONIZING
ANTALKALIES
ANTALKALINE
ANTALKALINES
ANTALKALIS
ANTAPHRODISIAC
ANTAPHRODISIACS
ANTARTHRITIC
ANTARTHRITICS
ANTASTHMATIC
ANTASTHMATICS
ANTEBELLUM
ANTECEDENCE
ANTECEDENCES
ANTECEDENT
ANTECEDENTLY
ANTECEDENTS
ANTECEDING
ANTECESSOR
ANTECESSORS
ANTECHAMBER

ANTECHAMBERS
ANTECHAPEL
ANTECHAPELS
ANTECHOIRS
ANTEDATING
ANTEDATINGS
ANTEDILUVIAL
ANTEDILUVIALLY
ANTEDILUVIAN
ANTEDILUVIANS
ANTEMERIDIAN
ANTEMORTEM
ANTEMUNDANE
ANTENATALLY
ANTENATALS
ANTENNIFEROUS
ANTENNIFORM
ANTENNULAR
ANTENNULES
ANTENUPTIAL
ANTENUPTIALS
ANTEORBITAL
ANTEPENDIA
ANTEPENDIUM
ANTEPENDIUMS
ANTEPENULT
ANTEPENULTIMA
ANTEPENULTIMAS
ANTEPENULTIMATE
ANTEPENULTS
ANTEPOSITION
ANTEPOSITIONS
ANTEPRANDIAL
ANTERIORITIES
ANTERIORITY
ANTERIORLY
ANTEROGRADE
ANTEVERSION
ANTEVERSIONS
ANTEVERTED
ANTEVERTING
ANTHELICES
ANTHELIONS
ANTHELIXES
ANTHELMINTHIC
ANTHELMINTHICS
ANTHELMINTIC
ANTHELMINTICS
ANTHEMISES
ANTHEMWISE
ANTHERIDIA
ANTHERIDIAL
ANTHERIDIUM
ANTHEROZOID
ANTHEROZOIDS
ANTHEROZOOID
ANTHEROZOOIDS
ANTHERSMUT
ANTHERSMUTS
ANTHOCARPOUS
ANTHOCARPS
ANTHOCHLORE
ANTHOCHLORES
ANTHOCYANIN
ANTHOCYANINS
ANTHOCYANS
ANTHOLOGICAL

ANTHOLOGIES
ANTHOLOGISE
ANTHOLOGISED
ANTHOLOGISER
ANTHOLOGISERS
ANTHOLOGISES
ANTHOLOGISING
ANTHOLOGIST
ANTHOLOGISTS
ANTHOLOGIZE
ANTHOLOGIZED
ANTHOLOGIZER
ANTHOLOGIZERS
ANTHOLOGIZES
ANTHOLOGIZING
ANTHOMANIA
ANTHOMANIAC
ANTHOMANIACS
ANTHOMANIAS
ANTHOPHILOUS
ANTHOPHORE
ANTHOPHORES
ANTHOPHYLLITE
ANTHOPHYLLITES
ANTHOTAXIES
ANTHOXANTHIN
ANTHOXANTHINS
ANTHOZOANS
ANTHRACENE
ANTHRACENES
ANTHRACITE
ANTHRACITES
ANTHRACITIC
ANTHRACNOSE
ANTHRACNOSES
ANTHRACOID
ANTHRACOSES
ANTHRACOSIS
ANTHRACYCLINE
ANTHRACYCLINES
ANTHRANILATE
ANTHRANILATES
ANTHRANILIC
ANTHRAQUINONE
ANTHRAQUINONES
ANTHROPICAL
ANTHROPOBIOLOGY
ANTHROPOCENTRIC
ANTHROPOGENESES
ANTHROPOGENESIS
ANTHROPOGENETIC
ANTHROPOGENIC
ANTHROPOGENIES
ANTHROPOGENY
ANTHROPOGONIES
ANTHROPOGONY
ANTHROPOGRAPHY
ANTHROPOID
ANTHROPOIDAL
ANTHROPOIDS
ANTHROPOLATRIES
ANTHROPOLATRY
ANTHROPOLOGICAL
ANTHROPOLOGIES
ANTHROPOLOGIST
ANTHROPOLOGISTS
ANTHROPOLOGY

ANTHROPOMETRIC	ANTIBACTERIALS	ANTICIPATORY	ANTIDIARRHEAL	ANTIFREEZES
ANTHROPOMETRIES	ANTIBALLISTIC	ANTICISING	ANTIDIARRHEALS	ANTIFRICTION
ANTHROPOMETRIST	ANTIBARBARUS	ANTICIVISM	ANTIDIARRHOEAL	ANTIFUNGAL
ANTHROPOMETRY	ANTIBARBARUSES	ANTICIVISMS	ANTIDIARRHOEALS	ANTIFUNGALS
ANTHROPOMORPH	ANTIBARYON	ANTICIZING	ANTIDILUTION	ANTIGAMBLING
ANTHROPOMORPHIC	ANTIBARYONS	ANTICLASSICAL	ANTIDIURETIC	ANTIGENICALLY
ANTHROPOMORPHS	ANTIBILIOUS	ANTICLASTIC	ANTIDIURETICS	ANTIGENICITIES
ANTHROPOPATHIC	ANTIBILLBOARD	ANTICLERICAL	ANTIDOGMATIC	ANTIGENICITY
ANTHROPOPATHIES	ANTIBIOSES	ANTICLERICALISM	ANTIDOTALLY	ANTIGLOBULIN
ANTHROPOPATHISM	ANTIBIOSIS	ANTICLERICALS	ANTIDOTING	ANTIGLOBULINS
ANTHROPOPATHY	ANTIBIOTIC	ANTICLIMACTIC	ANTIDROMIC	ANTIGOVERNMENT
ANTHROPOPHAGI	ANTIBIOTICALLY	ANTICLIMACTICAL	ANTIDROMICALLY	ANTIGRAVITIES
ANTHROPOPHAGIC	ANTIBIOTICS	ANTICLIMAX	ANTIDUMPING	ANTIGRAVITY
ANTHROPOPHAGIES	ANTIBLACKISM	ANTICLIMAXES	ANTIDUMPINGS	ANTIGROPELOES
ANTHROPOPHAGITE	ANTIBLACKISMS	ANTICLINAL	ANTIECONOMIC	ANTIGROPELOS
ANTHROPOPHAGOUS	ANTIBODIES	ANTICLINALS	ANTIEDUCATIONAL	ANTIGROWTH
ANTHROPOPHAGUS	ANTIBOURGEOIS	ANTICLINES	ANTIEGALITARIAN	ANTIGUERRILLA
ANTHROPOPHAGY	ANTIBOYCOTT	ANTICLINORIA	ANTIELECTRON	ANTIHALATION
ANTHROPOPHOBIA	ANTIBURGLAR	ANTICLINORIUM	ANTIELECTRONS	ANTIHALATIONS
ANTHROPOPHOBIAS	ANTIBURGLARY	ANTICLOCKWISE	ANTIELITES	ANTIHELICES
ANTHROPOPHOBIC	ANTIBUSERS	ANTICLOTTING	ANTIELITISM	ANTIHELIXES
ANTHROPOPHOBICS	ANTIBUSINESS	ANTICOAGULANT	ANTIELITISMS	ANTIHELMINTHIC
ANTHROPOPHUISM	ANTIBUSING	ANTICOAGULANTS	ANTIELITIST	ANTIHELMINTHICS
ANTHROPOPHUISMS	ANTICAKING	ANTICODONS	ANTIELITISTS	ANTIHEROES
ANTHROPOPHYTE	ANTICANCER	ANTICOINCIDENCE	ANTIEMETIC	ANTIHEROIC
ANTHROPOPHYTES	ANTICAPITALISM	ANTICOLLISION	ANTIEMETICS	ANTIHEROINE
ANTHROPOPSYCHIC	ANTICAPITALISMS	ANTICOLONIAL	ANTIENTROPIC	ANTIHEROINES
ANTHROPOSOPHIC	ANTICAPITALIST	ANTICOLONIALISM	ANTIEPILEPSY	ANTIHERPES
ANTHROPOSOPHIES	ANTICAPITALISTS	ANTICOLONIALIST	ANTIEPILEPTIC	ANTIHIJACK
ANTHROPOSOPHIST	ANTICARCINOGEN	ANTICOLONIALS	ANTIEPILEPTICS	ANTIHISTAMINE
ANTHROPOSOPHY	ANTICARCINOGENS	ANTICOMMERCIAL	ANTIEROTIC	ANTIHISTAMINES
ANTHROPOTOMIES	ANTICARIES	ANTICOMMUNISM	ANTIESTROGEN	ANTIHISTAMINIC
ANTHROPOTOMY	ANTICATALYST	ANTICOMMUNISMS	ANTIESTROGENS	ANTIHISTAMINICS
ANTHURIUMS	ANTICATALYSTS	ANTICOMMUNIST	ANTIEVOLUTION	ANTIHISTORICAL
ANTIABORTION	ANTICATHODE	ANTICOMMUNISTS	ANTIEVOLUTIONS	ANTIHOMOSEXUAL
ANTIABORTIONIST	ANTICATHODES	ANTICOMPETITIVE	ANTIFAMILY	ANTIHUMANISM
ANTIACADEMIC	ANTICATHOLIC	ANTICONSUMER	ANTIFASCISM	ANTIHUMANISMS
ANTIADITIS	ANTICELLULITE	ANTICONVULSANT	ANTIFASCISMS	ANTIHUMANISTIC
ANTIADITISES	ANTICENSORSHIP	ANTICONVULSANTS	ANTIFASCIST	ANTIHUNTER
ANTIAGGRESSION	ANTICHLORISTIC	ANTICONVULSIVE	ANTIFASCISTS	ANTIHUNTERS
ANTIAIRCRAFT	ANTICHLORS	ANTICONVULSIVES	ANTIFASHION	ANTIHUNTING
ANTIAIRCRAFTS	ANTICHOICE	ANTICORPORATE	ANTIFASHIONABLE	ANTIHYDROGEN
ANTIALCOHOL	ANTICHOICER	ANTICORROSION	ANTIFASHIONS	ANTIHYDROGENS
ANTIALCOHOLISM	ANTICHOICERS	ANTICORROSIONS	ANTIFATIGUE	ANTIHYSTERIC
ANTIALCOHOLISMS	ANTICHOLESTEROL	ANTICORROSIVE	ANTIFEBRILE	ANTIHYSTERICS
ANTIALLERGENIC	ANTICHOLINERGIC	ANTICORROSIVES	ANTIFEBRILES	ANTIJACOBIN
ANTIANDROGEN	ANTICHRIST	ANTICORRUPTION	ANTIFEDERALIST	ANTIJACOBINS
ANTIANDROGENS	ANTICHRISTIAN	ANTICREATIVE	ANTIFEDERALISTS	ANTIJAMMING
ANTIANEMIA	ANTICHRISTIANLY	ANTICRUELTY	ANTIFEMALE	ANTIJAMMINGS
ANTIANXIETY	ANTICHRISTS	ANTICULTURAL	ANTIFEMININE	ANTIKICKBACK
ANTIAPARTHEID	ANTICHTHONES	ANTICYCLONE	ANTIFEMINISM	ANTIKNOCKS
ANTIAPHRODISIAC	ANTICHURCH	ANTICYCLONES	ANTIFEMINISMS	ANTILEGOMENA
ANTIARMOUR	ANTICIGARETTE	ANTICYCLONIC	ANTIFEMINIST	ANTILEPROSY
ANTIARRHYTHMIC	ANTICIPANT	ANTIDANDRUFF	ANTIFEMINISTS	ANTILEPTON
ANTIARRHYTHMICS	ANTICIPANTS	ANTIDAZZLE	ANTIFERROMAGNET	ANTILEPTONS
ANTIARTHRITIC	ANTICIPATABLE	ANTIDEFAMATION	ANTIFERTILITY	ANTILEUKEMIC
ANTIARTHRITICS	ANTICIPATE	ANTIDEMOCRATIC	ANTIFILIBUSTER	ANTILIBERAL
ANTIARTHRITIS	ANTICIPATED	ANTIDEPRESSANT	ANTIFILIBUSTERS	ANTILIBERALISM
ANTIASTHMA	ANTICIPATES	ANTIDEPRESSANTS	ANTIFOAMING	ANTILIBERALISMS
ANTIASTHMATIC	ANTICIPATING	ANTIDEPRESSION	ANTIFOGGING	ANTILIBERALS
ANTIASTHMATICS	ANTICIPATION	ANTIDERIVATIVE	ANTIFORECLOSURE	ANTILIBERTARIAN
ANTIAUTHORITY	ANTICIPATIONS	ANTIDERIVATIVES	ANTIFOREIGN	ANTILIFERS
ANTIAUXINS	ANTICIPATIVE	ANTIDESICCANT	ANTIFOREIGNER	ANTILITERATE
ANTIBACCHII	ANTICIPATIVELY	ANTIDESICCANTS	ANTIFORMALIST	ANTILITTER
ANTIBACCHIUS	ANTICIPATOR	ANTIDEVELOPMENT	ANTIFOULING	ANTILITTERING
ANTIBACKLASH	ANTICIPATORILY	ANTIDIABETIC	ANTIFOULINGS	ANTILOGARITHM
ANTIBACTERIAL	ANTICIPATORS	ANTIDIABETICS	ANTIFREEZE	ANTILOGARITHMIC

ANTILOGARITHMS	ANTIMONOPOLISTS	ANTIPATHISTS	ANTIQUARIANISMS	ANTISECRECY
ANTILOGICAL	ANTIMONOPOLY	ANTIPERIODIC	ANTIQUARIANS	ANTISEGREGATION
ANTILOGIES	ANTIMONOUS	ANTIPERIODICS	ANTIQUARIES	ANTISEIZURE
ANTILOGOUS	ANTIMONYLS	ANTIPERISTALSES	ANTIQUARKS	ANTISENTIMENTAL
ANTILOPINE	ANTIMOSQUITO	ANTIPERISTALSIS	ANTIQUATED	ANTISEPALOUS
ANTILYNCHING	ANTIMUSICAL	ANTIPERISTALTIC	ANTIQUATEDNESS	ANTISEPARATIST
ANTIMACASSAR	ANTIMUSICS	ANTIPERISTASES	ANTIQUATES	ANTISEPARATISTS
ANTIMACASSARS	ANTIMUTAGEN	ANTIPERISTASIS	ANTIQUATING	ANTISEPSES
ANTIMAGNETIC	ANTIMUTAGENS	ANTIPERSONNEL	ANTIQUATION	ANTISEPSIS
ANTIMALARIA	ANTIMYCINS	ANTIPERSPIRANT	ANTIQUATIONS	ANTISEPTIC
ANTIMALARIAL	ANTIMYCOTIC	ANTIPERSPIRANTS	ANTIQUENESS	ANTISEPTICALLY
ANTIMALARIALS	ANTINARRATIVE	ANTIPESTICIDE	ANTIQUENESSES	ANTISEPTICISE
ANTIMANAGEMENT	ANTINARRATIVES	ANTIPETALOUS	ANTIQUIEST	ANTISEPTICISED
ANTIMARIJUANA	ANTINATIONAL	ANTIPHLOGISTIC	ANTIQUITARIAN	ANTISEPTICISES
ANTIMARKET	ANTINATIONALIST	ANTIPHLOGISTICS	ANTIQUITARIANS	ANTISEPTICISING
ANTIMARKETEER	ANTINATURAL	ANTIPHONAL	ANTIQUITIES	ANTISEPTICISM
ANTIMARKETEERS	ANTINATURE	ANTIPHONALLY	ANTIRABIES	ANTISEPTICISMS
ANTIMASQUE	ANTINAUSEA	ANTIPHONALS	ANTIRACHITIC	ANTISEPTICIZE
ANTIMASQUES	ANTINEOPLASTIC	ANTIPHONARIES	ANTIRACHITICS	ANTISEPTICIZED
ANTIMATERIALISM	ANTINEOPLASTICS	ANTIPHONARY	ANTIRACISM	ANTISEPTICIZES
ANTIMATERIALIST	ANTINEPHRITIC	ANTIPHONER	ANTIRACISMS	ANTISEPTICIZING
ANTIMATTER	ANTINEPHRITICS	ANTIPHONERS	ANTIRACIST	ANTISEPTICS
ANTIMATTERS	ANTINEPOTISM	ANTIPHONIC	ANTIRACISTS	ANTISERUMS
ANTIMECHANIST	ANTINEUTRINO	ANTIPHONICAL	ANTIRADARS	ANTISEXIST
ANTIMECHANISTS	ANTINEUTRINOS	ANTIPHONICALLY	ANTIRADICAL	ANTISEXISTS
ANTIMERGER	ANTINEUTRON	ANTIPHONIES	ANTIRADICALISM	ANTISEXUAL
ANTIMERISM	ANTINEUTRONS	ANTIPHRASES	ANTIRADICALISMS	ANTISEXUALITIES
ANTIMERISMS	ANTINOISES	ANTIPHRASIS	ANTIRATIONAL	ANTISEXUALITY
ANTIMETABOLE	ANTINOMIAN	ANTIPHRASTIC	ANTIRATIONALISM	ANTISEXUALS
ANTIMETABOLES	ANTINOMIANISM	ANTIPHRASTICAL	ANTIRATIONALIST	ANTISHAKES
ANTIMETABOLIC	ANTINOMIANISMS	ANTIPIRACY	ANTIRATIONALITY	ANTISHOCKS
ANTIMETABOLITE	ANTINOMIANS	ANTIPLAGUE	ANTIREALISM	ANTISHOPLIFTING
ANTIMETABOLITES	ANTINOMICAL	ANTIPLAQUE	ANTIREALISMS	ANTISLAVERY
ANTIMETATHESES	ANTINOMICALLY	ANTIPLEASURE	ANTIREALIST	ANTISMOKER
ANTIMETATHESIS	ANTINOMIES	ANTIPOACHING	ANTIREALISTS	ANTISMOKERS
ANTIMICROBIAL	ANTINOVELIST	ANTIPODALS	ANTIRECESSION	ANTISMOKING
ANTIMICROBIALS	ANTINOVELISTS	ANTIPODEAN	ANTIREFLECTION	ANTISMUGGLING
ANTIMILITARISM	ANTINOVELS	ANTIPODEANS	ANTIREFLECTIVE	ANTISOCIAL
ANTIMILITARISMS	ANTINUCLEAR	ANTIPOETIC	ANTIREFORM	ANTISOCIALISM
ANTIMILITARIST	ANTINUCLEARIST	ANTIPOLICE	ANTIREGULATORY	ANTISOCIALISMS
ANTIMILITARISTS	ANTINUCLEARISTS	ANTIPOLITICAL	ANTIREJECTION	ANTISOCIALIST
ANTIMILITARY	ANTINUCLEON	ANTIPOLITICS	ANTIRELIGION	ANTISOCIALISTS
ANTIMISSILE	ANTINUCLEONS	ANTIPOLLUTION	ANTIRELIGIONS	ANTISOCIALITIES
ANTIMISSILES	ANTINUKERS	ANTIPOLLUTIONS	ANTIRELIGIOUS	ANTISOCIALITY
ANTIMITOTIC	ANTIOBESITY	ANTIPOPULAR	ANTIREPUBLICAN	ANTISOCIALLY
ANTIMITOTICS	ANTIOBSCENITY	ANTIPORNOGRAPHY	ANTIREPUBLICANS	ANTISOCIALS
ANTIMNEMONIC	ANTIODONTALGIC	ANTIPORTER	ANTIRETROVIRAL	ANTISPASMODIC
ANTIMNEMONICS	ANTIODONTALGICS	ANTIPORTERS	ANTIRETROVIRALS	ANTISPASMODICS
ANTIMODERN	ANTIOESTROGEN	ANTIPOVERTY	ANTIRHEUMATIC	ANTISPASTIC
ANTIMODERNIST	ANTIOESTROGENS	ANTIPREDATOR	ANTIRHEUMATICS	ANTISPASTICS
ANTIMODERNISTS	ANTIOXIDANT	ANTIPRIESTLY	ANTIRITUALISM	ANTISPASTS
ANTIMONARCHICAL	ANTIOXIDANTS	ANTIPROGRESSIVE	ANTIRITUALISMS	ANTISPECULATION
ANTIMONARCHIST	ANTIOZONANT	ANTIPROTON	ANTIROMANTIC	ANTISPECULATIVE
ANTIMONARCHISTS	ANTIOZONANTS	ANTIPROTONS	ANTIROMANTICISM	ANTISPENDING
ANTIMONATE	ANTIPARALLEL	ANTIPRURITIC	ANTIROMANTICS	ANTISTATIC
ANTIMONATES	ANTIPARALLELS	ANTIPRURITICS	ANTIROYALIST	ANTISTATICS
ANTIMONIAL	ANTIPARASITIC	ANTIPSYCHIATRY	ANTIROYALISTS	ANTISTORIES
ANTIMONIALS	ANTIPARASITICS	ANTIPSYCHOTIC	ANTIRRHINUM	ANTISTRESS
ANTIMONIATE	ANTIPARTICLE	ANTIPSYCHOTICS	ANTIRRHINUMS	ANTISTRIKE
ANTIMONIATES	ANTIPARTICLES	ANTIPYRESES	ANTISATELLITE	ANTISTROPHE
ANTIMONIDE	ANTIPARTIES	ANTIPYRESIS	ANTISCIANS	ANTISTROPHES
ANTIMONIDES	ANTIPASTOS	ANTIPYRETIC	ANTISCIENCE	ANTISTROPHIC
ANTIMONIES	ANTIPATHETIC	ANTIPYRETICS	ANTISCIENCES	ANTISTROPHON
ANTIMONIOUS	ANTIPATHETICAL	ANTIPYRINE	ANTISCIENTIFIC	ANTISTROPHONS
ANTIMONITE	ANTIPATHIC	ANTIPYRINES	ANTISCORBUTIC	ANTISTUDENT
ANTIMONITES	ANTIPATHIES	ANTIQUARIAN	ANTISCORBUTICS	ANTISTYLES
ANTIMONOPOLIST	ANTIPATHIST	ANTIQUARIANISM	ANTISCRIPTURAL	ANTISUBMARINE

ANTISUBSIDY
ANTISUBVERSION
ANTISUBVERSIVE
ANTISUICIDE
ANTISYMMETRIC
ANTISYPHILITIC
ANTISYPHILITICS
ANTISYZYGIES
ANTISYZYGY
ANTITAKEOVER
ANTITARNISH
ANTITECHNOLOGY
ANTITERRORISM
ANTITERRORISMS
ANTITERRORIST
ANTITERRORISTS
ANTITHALIAN
ANTITHEISM
ANTITHEISMS
ANTITHEIST
ANTITHEISTIC
ANTITHEISTS
ANTITHEORETICAL
ANTITHESES
ANTITHESIS
ANTITHETIC
ANTITHETICAL
ANTITHETICALLY
ANTITHROMBIN
ANTITHROMBINS
ANTITHROMBOTIC
ANTITHROMBOTICS
ANTITHYROID
ANTITOBACCO
ANTITOXINS
ANTITRADES
ANTITRADITIONAL
ANTITRAGUS
ANTITRANSPIRANT
ANTITRINITARIAN
ANTITRUSTER
ANTITRUSTERS
ANTITUBERCULAR
ANTITUBERCULOUS
ANTITUMORAL
ANTITUMORS
ANTITUMOUR
ANTITUMOURAL
ANTITUSSIVE
ANTITUSSIVES
ANTITYPHOID
ANTITYPICAL
ANTITYPICALLY
ANTIUNIVERSITY
ANTIVAXERS
ANTIVAXXER
ANTIVAXXERS
ANTIVENENE
ANTIVENENES
ANTIVENINS
ANTIVENOMS
ANTIVIOLENCE
ANTIVIRALS
ANTIVIRUSES
ANTIVITAMIN
ANTIVITAMINS
ANTIVIVISECTION

ANTIWELFARE
ANTIWHALING
ANTIWORLDS
ANTIWRINKLE
ANTONINIANUS
ANTONINIANUSES
ANTONOMASIA
ANTONOMASIAS
ANTONOMASTIC
ANTONYMIES
ANTONYMOUS
ANTRORSELY
ANTSINESSES
ANUCLEATED
ANXIOLYTIC
ANXIOLYTICS
ANXIOUSNESS
ANXIOUSNESSES
ANYTHINGARIAN
ANYTHINGARIANS
ANYWHITHER
AORISTICALLY
AORTITISES
AORTOGRAPHIC
AORTOGRAPHIES
AORTOGRAPHY
APAGOGICAL
APAGOGICALLY
APARTHEIDS
APARTHOTEL
APARTHOTELS
APARTMENTAL
APARTMENTS
APARTNESSES
APATHATONS
APATHETICAL
APATHETICALLY
APATOSAURS
APATOSAURUS
APATOSAURUSES
APERIODICALLY
APERIODICITIES
APERIODICITY
APERITIVES
APERTNESSES
APFELSTRUDEL
APFELSTRUDELS
APHAERESES
APHAERESIS
APHAERETIC
APHANIPTEROUS
APHELANDRA
APHELANDRAS
APHELIOTROPIC
APHELIOTROPISM
APHELIOTROPISMS
APHETICALLY
APHETISING
APHETIZING
APHIDICIDE
APHIDICIDES
APHORISERS
APHORISING
APHORISTIC
APHORISTICALLY
APHORIZERS
APHORIZING

APHRODISIA
APHRODISIAC
APHRODISIACAL
APHRODISIACS
APHRODISIAS
APHRODITES
APICULTURAL
APICULTURE
APICULTURES
APICULTURIST
APICULTURISTS
APIOLOGIES
APISHNESSES
APITHERAPIES
APITHERAPY
APLACENTAL
APLANATICALLY
APLANATISM
APLANATISMS
APLANOGAMETE
APLANOGAMETES
APLANOSPORE
APLANOSPORES
APOAPSIDES
APOCALYPSE
APOCALYPSES
APOCALYPTIC
APOCALYPTICAL
APOCALYPTICALLY
APOCALYPTICISM
APOCALYPTICISMS
APOCALYPTISM
APOCALYPTISMS
APOCALYPTIST
APOCALYPTISTS
APOCARPIES
APOCARPOUS
APOCATASTASES
APOCATASTASIS
APOCHROMAT
APOCHROMATIC
APOCHROMATISM
APOCHROMATISMS
APOCHROMATS
APOCOPATED
APOCOPATES
APOCOPATING
APOCOPATION
APOCOPATIONS
APOCRYPHAL
APOCRYPHALLY
APOCRYPHALNESS
APOCRYPHON
APOCYNACEOUS
APOCYNTHION
APOCYNTHIONS
APODEICTIC
APODEICTICAL
APODEICTICALLY
APODICTICAL
APODICTICALLY
APODYTERIUM
APODYTERIUMS
APOENZYMES
APOGAMOUSLY
APOGEOTROPIC
APOGEOTROPISM

APOGEOTROPISMS
APOLAUSTIC
APOLAUSTICS
APOLIPOPROTEIN
APOLIPOPROTEINS
APOLITICAL
APOLITICALITIES
APOLITICALITY
APOLITICALLY
APOLITICISM
APOLITICISMS
APOLLONIAN
APOLLONICON
APOLLONICONS
APOLOGETIC
APOLOGETICAL
APOLOGETICALLY
APOLOGETICS
APOLOGISED
APOLOGISER
APOLOGISERS
APOLOGISES
APOLOGISING
APOLOGISTS
APOLOGIZED
APOLOGIZER
APOLOGIZERS
APOLOGIZES
APOLOGIZING
APOMICTICAL
APOMICTICALLY
APOMORPHIA
APOMORPHIAS
APOMORPHINE
APOMORPHINES
APONEUROSES
APONEUROSIS
APONEUROTIC
APOPEMPTIC
APOPEMPTICS
APOPHENIAS
APOPHLEGMATIC
APOPHLEGMATICS
APOPHONIES
APOPHTHEGM
APOPHTHEGMATIC
APOPHTHEGMATISE
APOPHTHEGMATIST
APOPHTHEGMATIZE
APOPHTHEGMS
APOPHYLLITE
APOPHYLLITES
APOPHYSATE
APOPHYSEAL
APOPHYSIAL
APOPLECTIC
APOPLECTICAL
APOPLECTICALLY
APOPLECTICS
APOPLEXIES
APOPLEXING
APOPROTEIN
APOPROTEINS
APOSEMATIC
APOSEMATICALLY
APOSIOPESES
APOSIOPESIS

APOSIOPETIC
APOSPORIES
APOSPOROUS·
APOSTACIES
APOSTASIES
APOSTATICAL
APOSTATISE
APOSTATISED
APOSTATISES
APOSTATISING
APOSTATIZE
APOSTATIZED
APOSTATIZES
APOSTATIZING
APOSTILLES
APOSTLESHIP
APOSTLESHIPS
APOSTOLATE
APOSTOLATES
APOSTOLICAL
APOSTOLICALLY
APOSTOLICISM
APOSTOLICISMS
APOSTOLICITIES
APOSTOLICITY
APOSTOLISE
APOSTOLISED
APOSTOLISES
APOSTOLISING
APOSTOLIZE
APOSTOLIZED
APOSTOLIZES
APOSTOLIZING
APOSTROPHE
APOSTROPHES
APOSTROPHIC
APOSTROPHISE
APOSTROPHISED
APOSTROPHISES
APOSTROPHISING
APOSTROPHIZE
APOSTROPHIZED
APOSTROPHIZES
APOSTROPHIZING
APOSTROPHUS
APOSTROPHUSES
APOTHECARIES
APOTHECARY
APOTHECIAL
APOTHECIUM
APOTHEGMATIC
APOTHEGMATICAL
APOTHEGMATISE
APOTHEGMATISED
APOTHEGMATISES
APOTHEGMATISING
APOTHEGMATIST
APOTHEGMATISTS
APOTHEGMATIZE
APOTHEGMATIZED
APOTHEGMATIZES
APOTHEGMATIZING
APOTHEOSES
APOTHEOSIS
APOTHEOSISE
APOTHEOSISED
APOTHEOSISES

APOTHEOSISING
APOTHEOSIZE
APOTHEOSIZED
APOTHEOSIZES
APOTHEOSIZING
APOTROPAIC
APOTROPAICALLY
APOTROPAISM
APOTROPAISMS
APOTROPOUS
APPALLINGLY
APPALOOSAS
APPARATCHIK
APPARATCHIKI
APPARATCHIKS
APPARATUSES
APPARELING
APPARELLED
APPARELLING
APPARELMENT
APPARELMENTS
APPARENCIES
APPARENTLY
APPARENTNESS
APPARENTNESSES
APPARITION
APPARITIONAL
APPARITIONS
APPARITORS
APPARTEMENT
APPARTEMENTS
APPASSIONATO
APPEACHING
APPEACHMENT
APPEACHMENTS
APPEALABILITIES
APPEALABILITY
APPEALABLE
APPEALINGLY
APPEALINGNESS
APPEALINGNESSES
APPEARANCE
APPEARANCES
APPEASABLE
APPEASEMENT
APPEASEMENTS
APPEASINGLY
APPELLANTS
APPELLATION
APPELLATIONAL
APPELLATIONS
APPELLATIVE
APPELLATIVELY
APPELLATIVES
APPENDAGES
APPENDANTS
APPENDECTOMIES
APPENDECTOMY
APPENDENTS
APPENDICECTOMY
APPENDICES
APPENDICITIS
APPENDICITISES
APPENDICLE
APPENDICLES
APPENDICULAR
APPENDICULARIAN

APPENDICULATE
APPENDIXES
APPERCEIVE
APPERCEIVED
APPERCEIVES
APPERCEIVING
APPERCEPTION
APPERCEPTIONS
APPERCEPTIVE
APPERCIPIENT
APPERTAINANCE
APPERTAINANCES
APPERTAINED
APPERTAINING
APPERTAINMENT
APPERTAINMENTS
APPERTAINS
APPERTINENT
APPERTINENTS
APPETEEZEMENT
APPETEEZEMENTS
APPETENCES
APPETENCIES
APPETISEMENT
APPETISEMENTS
APPETISERS
APPETISING
APPETISINGLY
APPETITION
APPETITIONS
APPETITIVE
APPETIZERS
APPETIZING
APPETIZINGLY
APPLAUDABLE
APPLAUDABLY
APPLAUDERS
APPLAUDING
APPLAUDINGLY
APPLAUSIVE
APPLAUSIVELY
APPLECARTS
APPLEDRAIN
APPLEDRAINS
APPLEJACKS
APPLERINGIE
APPLERINGIES
APPLESAUCE
APPLESAUCES
APPLETINIS
APPLIANCES
APPLICABILITIES
APPLICABILITY
APPLICABLE
APPLICABLENESS
APPLICABLY
APPLICANTS
APPLICATION
APPLICATIONS
APPLICATIVE
APPLICATIVELY
APPLICATOR
APPLICATORS
APPLICATORY
APPLIQUEING
APPOGGIATURA
APPOGGIATURAS

APPOGGIATURE
APPOINTEES
APPOINTERS
APPOINTING
APPOINTIVE
APPOINTMENT
APPOINTMENTS
APPOINTORS
APPORTIONABLE
APPORTIONED
APPORTIONER
APPORTIONERS
APPORTIONING
APPORTIONMENT
APPORTIONMENTS
APPORTIONS
APPOSITELY
APPOSITENESS
APPOSITENESSES
APPOSITION
APPOSITIONAL
APPOSITIONS
APPOSITIVE
APPOSITIVELY
APPOSITIVES
APPRAISABLE
APPRAISALS
APPRAISEES
APPRAISEMENT
APPRAISEMENTS
APPRAISERS
APPRAISING
APPRAISINGLY
APPRAISIVE
APPRAISIVELY
APPRECIABLE
APPRECIABLY
APPRECIATE
APPRECIATED
APPRECIATES
APPRECIATING
APPRECIATION
APPRECIATIONS
APPRECIATIVE
APPRECIATIVELY
APPRECIATOR
APPRECIATORILY
APPRECIATORS
APPRECIATORY
APPREHENDED
APPREHENDING
APPREHENDS
APPREHENSIBLE
APPREHENSIBLY
APPREHENSION
APPREHENSIONS
APPREHENSIVE
APPREHENSIVELY
APPRENTICE
APPRENTICED
APPRENTICEHOOD
APPRENTICEHOODS
APPRENTICEMENT
APPRENTICEMENTS
APPRENTICES
APPRENTICESHIP
APPRENTICESHIPS

APPRENTICING
APPRESSING
APPRESSORIA
APPRESSORIUM
APPRISINGS
APPRIZINGS
APPROACHABILITY
APPROACHABLE
APPROACHED
APPROACHES
APPROACHING
APPROBATED
APPROBATES
APPROBATING
APPROBATION
APPROBATIONS
APPROBATIVE
APPROBATORY
APPROPINQUATE
APPROPINQUATED
APPROPINQUATES
APPROPINQUATING
APPROPINQUATION
APPROPINQUE
APPROPINQUED
APPROPINQUES
APPROPINQUING
APPROPINQUITIES
APPROPINQUITY
APPROPRIABLE
APPROPRIACIES
APPROPRIACY
APPROPRIATE
APPROPRIATED
APPROPRIATELY
APPROPRIATENESS
APPROPRIATES
APPROPRIATING
APPROPRIATION
APPROPRIATIONS
APPROPRIATIVE
APPROPRIATOR
APPROPRIATORS
APPROVABLE
APPROVABLY
APPROVANCE
APPROVANCES
APPROVINGLY
APPROXIMAL
APPROXIMATE
APPROXIMATED
APPROXIMATELY
APPROXIMATES
APPROXIMATING
APPROXIMATION
APPROXIMATIONS
APPROXIMATIVE
APPROXIMEETING
APPROXIMEETINGS
APPULSIVELY
APPURTENANCE
APPURTENANCES
APPURTENANT
APPURTENANTS
APRICATING
APRICATION
APRICATIONS

APRIORISMS
APRIORISTS
APRIORITIES
APSIDIOLES
APTERYGIAL
APTITUDINAL
APTITUDINALLY
AQUABATICS
AQUABOARDS
AQUACEUTICAL
AQUACEUTICALS
AQUACULTURAL
AQUACULTURE
AQUACULTURES
AQUACULTURIST
AQUACULTURISTS
AQUADROMES
AQUAEROBICS
AQUAFARMED
AQUAFARMING
AQUAFARMINGS
AQUAFITNESS
AQUAFITNESSES
AQUAFORTIS
AQUAFORTISES
AQUAFORTIST
AQUAFORTISTS
AQUALEATHER
AQUALEATHERS
AQUAMANALE
AQUAMANALES
AQUAMANILE
AQUAMANILES
AQUAMARINE
AQUAMARINES
AQUANAUTICS
AQUAPHOBES
AQUAPHOBIA
AQUAPHOBIAS
AQUAPHOBIC
AQUAPHOBICS
AQUAPLANED
AQUAPLANER
AQUAPLANERS
AQUAPLANES
AQUAPLANING
AQUAPLANINGS
AQUAPORINS
AQUARELLES
AQUARELLIST
AQUARELLISTS
AQUARIISTS
AQUAROBICS
AQUASCAPES
AQUATICALLY
AQUATINTAS
AQUATINTED
AQUATINTER
AQUATINTERS
AQUATINTING
AQUATINTIST
AQUATINTISTS
AQUICULTURAL
AQUICULTURE
AQUICULTURES
AQUICULTURIST
AQUICULTURISTS

AQUIFEROUS
AQUIFOLIACEOUS
AQUILEGIAS
AQUILINITIES
AQUILINITY
ARABESQUED
ARABESQUES
ARABICISATION
ARABICISATIONS
ARABICISED
ARABICISES
ARABICISING
ARABICIZATION
ARABICIZATIONS
ARABICIZED
ARABICIZES
ARABICIZING
ARABILITIES
ARABINOSES
ARABINOSIDE
ARABINOSIDES
ARABISATION
ARABISATIONS
ARABIZATION
ARABIZATIONS
ARACHIDONIC
ARACHNIDAN
ARACHNIDANS
ARACHNOIDAL
ARACHNOIDITIS
ARACHNOIDITISES
ARACHNOIDS
ARACHNOLOGICAL
ARACHNOLOGIES
ARACHNOLOGIST
ARACHNOLOGISTS
ARACHNOLOGY
ARACHNOPHOBE
ARACHNOPHOBES
ARACHNOPHOBIA
ARACHNOPHOBIAS
ARACHNOPHOBIC
ARACHNOPHOBICS
ARAEOMETER
ARAEOMETERS
ARAEOMETRIC
ARAEOMETRICAL
ARAEOMETRIES
ARAEOMETRY
ARAEOSTYLE
ARAEOSTYLES
ARAEOSYSTYLE
ARAEOSYSTYLES
ARAGONITES
ARAGONITIC
ARALIACEOUS
ARAUCARIAN
ARAUCARIAS
ARBALESTER
ARBALESTERS
ARBALISTER
ARBALISTERS
ARBITRABLE
ARBITRAGED
ARBITRAGER
ARBITRAGERS
ARBITRAGES

ARBITRAGEUR
ARBITRAGEURS
ARBITRAGING
ARBITRAMENT
ARBITRAMENTS
ARBITRARILY
ARBITRARINESS
ARBITRARINESSES
ARBITRATED
ARBITRATES
ARBITRATING
ARBITRATION
ARBITRATIONAL
ARBITRATIONS
ARBITRATIVE
ARBITRATOR
ARBITRATORS
ARBITRATRICES
ARBITRATRIX
ARBITRATRIXES
ARBITREMENT
ARBITREMENTS
ARBITRESSES
ARBITRIUMS
ARBLASTERS
ARBORACEOUS
ARBOREALLY
ARBORESCENCE
ARBORESCENCES
ARBORESCENT
ARBORETUMS
ARBORICULTURAL
ARBORICULTURE
ARBORICULTURES
ARBORICULTURIST
ARBORISATION
ARBORISATIONS
ARBORISING
ARBORIZATION
ARBORIZATIONS
ARBORIZING
ARBORVITAE
ARBORVITAES
ARBOVIRUSES
ARBUSCULAR
ARCANENESS
ARCANENESSES
ARCCOSINES
ARCHAEBACTERIA
ARCHAEBACTERIUM
ARCHAEOBOTANIES
ARCHAEOBOTANIST
ARCHAEOBOTANY
ARCHAEOLOGICAL
ARCHAEOLOGIES
ARCHAEOLOGIST
ARCHAEOLOGISTS
ARCHAEOLOGY
ARCHAEOMETRIC
ARCHAEOMETRIES
ARCHAEOMETRIST
ARCHAEOMETRISTS
ARCHAEOMETRY
ARCHAEOPTERYX
ARCHAEOPTERYXES
ARCHAEORNIS
ARCHAEORNISES

ARCHAEOZOOLOGY
ARCHAEZOOLOGIES
ARCHAEZOOLOGY
ARCHAICALLY
ARCHAICISM
ARCHAICISMS
ARCHAISERS
ARCHAISING
ARCHAISTIC
ARCHAIZERS
ARCHAIZING
ARCHANGELIC
ARCHANGELS
ARCHBISHOP
ARCHBISHOPRIC
ARCHBISHOPRICS
ARCHBISHOPS
ARCHDEACON
ARCHDEACONRIES
ARCHDEACONRY
ARCHDEACONS
ARCHDIOCESAN
ARCHDIOCESE
ARCHDIOCESES
ARCHDRUIDS
ARCHDUCHESS
ARCHDUCHESSES
ARCHDUCHIES
ARCHDUKEDOM
ARCHDUKEDOMS
ARCHEGONIA
ARCHEGONIAL
ARCHEGONIATE
ARCHEGONIATES
ARCHEGONIUM
ARCHENEMIES
ARCHENTERA
ARCHENTERIC
ARCHENTERON
ARCHENTERONS
ARCHEOASTRONOMY
ARCHEOBOTANIES
ARCHEOBOTANIST
ARCHEOBOTANISTS
ARCHEOBOTANY
ARCHEOLOGICAL
ARCHEOLOGICALLY
ARCHEOLOGIES
ARCHEOLOGIST
ARCHEOLOGISTS
ARCHEOLOGY
ARCHEOMAGNETISM
ARCHEOMETRIES
ARCHEOMETRY
ARCHEOZOOLOGIES
ARCHEOZOOLOGIST
ARCHEOZOOLOGY
ARCHERESSES
ARCHERFISH
ARCHERFISHES
ARCHESPORE
ARCHESPORES
ARCHESPORIA
ARCHESPORIAL
ARCHESPORIUM
ARCHETYPAL
ARCHETYPALLY

ARCHETYPES
ARCHETYPICAL
ARCHETYPICALLY
ARCHFIENDS
ARCHGENETHLIAC
ARCHGENETHLIACS
ARCHICARPS
ARCHIDIACONAL
ARCHIDIACONATE
ARCHIDIACONATES
ARCHIEPISCOPACY
ARCHIEPISCOPAL
ARCHIEPISCOPATE
ARCHILOWES
ARCHIMAGES
ARCHIMANDRITE
ARCHIMANDRITES
ARCHIPELAGIAN
ARCHIPELAGIC
ARCHIPELAGO
ARCHIPELAGOES
ARCHIPELAGOS
ARCHIPHONEME
ARCHIPHONEMES
ARCHIPLASM
ARCHIPLASMIC
ARCHIPLASMS
ARCHITECTED
ARCHITECTING
ARCHITECTONIC
ARCHITECTONICS
ARCHITECTS
ARCHITECTURAL
ARCHITECTURALLY
ARCHITECTURE
ARCHITECTURES
ARCHITRAVE
ARCHITRAVED
ARCHITRAVES
ARCHITYPES
ARCHIVISTS
ARCHIVOLTS
ARCHNESSES
ARCHOLOGIES
ARCHONSHIP
ARCHONSHIPS
ARCHONTATE
ARCHONTATES
ARCHOPLASM
ARCHOPLASMIC
ARCHOPLASMS
ARCHOSAURIAN
ARCHOSAURIANS
ARCHOSAURS
ARCHPRIEST
ARCHPRIESTHOOD
ARCHPRIESTHOODS
ARCHPRIESTS
ARCHPRIESTSHIP
ARCHPRIESTSHIPS
ARCHRIVALS
ARCHSTONES
ARCMINUTES
ARCOGRAPHS
ARCOLOGIES
ARCSECONDS
ARCTANGENT

ARCTANGENTS
ARCTICALLY
ARCTOPHILE
ARCTOPHILES
ARCTOPHILIA
ARCTOPHILIAS
ARCTOPHILIES
ARCTOPHILIST
ARCTOPHILISTS
ARCTOPHILS
ARCTOPHILY
ARCUATIONS
ARCUBALIST
ARCUBALISTS
ARDUOUSNESS
ARDUOUSNESSES
ARECOLINES
AREFACTION
AREFACTIONS
ARENACEOUS
ARENATIONS
ARENICOLOUS
AREOCENTRIC
AREOGRAPHIC
AREOGRAPHIES
AREOGRAPHY
AREOLATION
AREOLATIONS
AREOLOGIES
AREOMETERS
AREOMETRIES
AREOSTYLES
AREOSYSTILE
AREOSYSTILES
ARFVEDSONITE
ARFVEDSONITES
ARGENTIFEROUS
ARGENTINES
ARGENTITES
ARGILLACEOUS
ARGILLIFEROUS
ARGILLITES
ARGILLITIC
ARGONAUTIC
ARGUMENTATION
ARGUMENTATIONS
ARGUMENTATIVE
ARGUMENTATIVELY
ARGUMENTIVE
ARGUMENTUM
ARGUMENTUMS
ARGUTENESS
ARGUTENESSES
ARGYRODITE
ARGYRODITES
ARHATSHIPS
ARHYTHMIAS
ARIBOFLAVINOSES
ARIBOFLAVINOSIS
ARIDNESSES
ARISTOCRACIES
ARISTOCRACY
ARISTOCRAT
ARISTOCRATIC
ARISTOCRATICAL
ARISTOCRATISM
ARISTOCRATISMS

ARISTOCRATS	ARRAGONITES	ARTERIALLY	ARTIFICERS	ASCENSIONAL
ARISTOLOCHIA	ARRAGONITIC	ARTERIOGRAM	ARTIFICIAL	ASCENSIONIST
ARISTOLOCHIAS	ARRAIGNERS	ARTERIOGRAMS	ARTIFICIALISE	ASCENSIONISTS
ARISTOLOGIES	ARRAIGNING	ARTERIOGRAPHIC	ARTIFICIALISED	ASCENSIONS
ARISTOLOGY	ARRAIGNINGS	ARTERIOGRAPHIES	ARTIFICIALISES	ASCERTAINABLE
ARISTOTLES	ARRAIGNMENT	ARTERIOGRAPHY	ARTIFICIALISING	ASCERTAINABLY
ARITHMETIC	ARRAIGNMENTS	ARTERIOLAR	ARTIFICIALITIES	ASCERTAINED
ARITHMETICAL	ARRANGEABLE	ARTERIOLES	ARTIFICIALITY	ASCERTAINING
ARITHMETICALLY	ARRANGEMENT	ARTERIOTOMIES	ARTIFICIALIZE	ASCERTAINMENT
ARITHMETICIAN	ARRANGEMENTS	ARTERIOTOMY	ARTIFICIALIZED	ASCERTAINMENTS
ARITHMETICIANS	ARRAYMENTS	ARTERIOVENOUS	ARTIFICIALIZES	ASCERTAINS
ARITHMETICS	ARREARAGES	ARTERITIDES	ARTIFICIALIZING	ASCETICALLY
ARITHMOMANIA	ARRESTABLE	ARTERITISES	ARTIFICIALLY	ASCETICISM
ARITHMOMANIAS	ARRESTANTS	ARTFULNESS	ARTIFICIALNESS	ASCETICISMS
ARITHMOMETER	ARRESTATION	ARTFULNESSES	ARTILLERIES	ASCITITIOUS
ARITHMOMETERS	ARRESTATIONS	ARTHRALGIA	ARTILLERIST	ASCLEPIADACEOUS
ARITHMOPHOBIA	ARRESTINGLY	ARTHRALGIAS	ARTILLERISTS	ASCLEPIADS
ARITHMOPHOBIAS	ARRESTMENT	ARTHRALGIC	ARTILLERYMAN	ASCLEPIASES
ARMADILLOS	ARRESTMENTS	ARTHRECTOMIES	ARTILLERYMEN	ASCOCARPIC
ARMAMENTARIA	ARRHENOTOKIES	ARTHRECTOMY	ARTINESSES	ASCOGONIUM
ARMAMENTARIUM	ARRHENOTOKY	ARTHRITICALLY	ARTIODACTYL	ASCOMYCETE
ARMAMENTARIUMS	ARRHYTHMIA	ARTHRITICS	ARTIODACTYLOUS	ASCOMYCETES
ARMATURING	ARRHYTHMIAS	ARTHRITIDES	ARTIODACTYLS	ASCOMYCETOUS
ARMIGEROUS	ARRHYTHMIC	ARTHRITISES	ARTISANSHIP	ASCORBATES
ARMILLARIA	ARRIVANCES	ARTHRODESES	ARTISANSHIPS	ASCOSPORES
ARMILLARIAS	ARRIVANCIES	ARTHRODESIS	ARTISTICAL	ASCOSPORIC
ARMIPOTENCE	ARRIVEDERCI	ARTHRODIAE	ARTISTICALLY	ASCRIBABLE
ARMIPOTENCES	ARRIVISMES	ARTHRODIAL	ARTISTRIES	ASCRIPTION
ARMIPOTENT	ARRIVISTES	ARTHROGRAPHIES	ARTLESSNESS	ASCRIPTIONS
ARMISTICES	ARROGANCES	ARTHROGRAPHY	ARTLESSNESSES	ASCRIPTIVE
ARMLOCKING	ARROGANCIES	ARTHROMERE	ARTMAKINGS	ASEPTICALLY
ARMORIALLY	ARROGANTLY	ARTHROMERES	ARTOCARPUS	ASEPTICISE
ARMOURLESS	ARROGATING	ARTHROMERIC	ARTOCARPUSES	ASEPTICISED
AROMATASES	ARROGATION	ARTHROPATHIES	ARTSINESSES	ASEPTICISES
AROMATHERAPIES	ARROGATIONS	ARTHROPATHY	ARUNDINACEOUS	ASEPTICISING
AROMATHERAPIST	ARROGATIVE	ARTHROPLASTIES	ARVICOLINE	ASEPTICISM
AROMATHERAPISTS	ARROGATORS	ARTHROPLASTY	ARYBALLOID	ASEPTICISMS
AROMATHERAPY	ARRONDISSEMENT	ARTHROPODAL	ARYBALLOSES	ASEPTICIZE
AROMATICALLY	ARRONDISSEMENTS	ARTHROPODAN	ARYTAENOID	ASEPTICIZED
AROMATICITIES	ARROWGRASS	ARTHROPODOUS	ARYTAENOIDS	ASEPTICIZES
AROMATICITY	ARROWGRASSES	ARTHROPODS	ARYTENOIDAL	ASEPTICIZING
AROMATISATION	ARROWHEADS	ARTHROSCOPE	ARYTENOIDS	ASEXUALITIES
AROMATISATIONS	ARROWROOTS	ARTHROSCOPES	ASAFETIDAS	ASEXUALITY
AROMATISED	ARROWWOODS	ARTHROSCOPIC	ASAFOETIDA	ASHAMEDNESS
AROMATISES	ARROWWORMS	ARTHROSCOPIES	ASAFOETIDAS	ASHAMEDNESSES
AROMATISING	ARSENIATES	ARTHROSCOPY	ASARABACCA	ASHINESSES
AROMATIZATION	ARSENICALS	ARTHROSPORE	ASARABACCAS	ASHLARINGS
AROMATIZATIONS	ARSENOPYRITE	ARTHROSPORES	ASBESTIFORM	ASHLERINGS
AROMATIZED	ARSENOPYRITES	ARTHROSPORIC	ASBESTOSES	ASHRAMITES
AROMATIZES	ARSMETRICK	ARTHROSPOROUS	ASBESTOSIS	ASININITIES
AROMATIZING	ARSMETRICKS	ARTICHOKES	ASBESTUSES	ASKEWNESSES
ARPEGGIATE	ARSPHENAMINE	ARTICULABLE	ASCARIASES	ASPARAGINASE
ARPEGGIATED	ARSPHENAMINES	ARTICULACIES	ASCARIASIS	ASPARAGINASES
ARPEGGIATES	ARTEFACTUAL	ARTICULACY	ASCENDABLE	ASPARAGINE
ARPEGGIATING	ARTEMISIAS	ARTICULATE	ASCENDANCE	ASPARAGINES
ARPEGGIATION	ARTEMISININ	ARTICULATED	ASCENDANCES	ASPARAGUSES
ARPEGGIATIONS	ARTEMISININS	ARTICULATELY	ASCENDANCIES	ASPARTAMES
ARPEGGIONE	ARTERIALISATION	ARTICULATENESS	ASCENDANCY	ASPARTATES
ARPEGGIONES	ARTERIALISE	ARTICULATES	ASCENDANTLY	ASPECTABLE
ARPILLERAS	ARTERIALISED	ARTICULATING	ASCENDANTS	ASPERATING
ARQUEBUSADE	ARTERIALISES	ARTICULATION	ASCENDENCE	ASPERGATION
ARQUEBUSADES	ARTERIALISING	ARTICULATIONS	ASCENDENCES	ASPERGATIONS
ARQUEBUSES	ARTERIALIZATION	ARTICULATIVE	ASCENDENCIES	ASPERGILLA
ARQUEBUSIER	ARTERIALIZE	ARTICULATOR	ASCENDENCY	ASPERGILLI
ARQUEBUSIERS	ARTERIALIZED	ARTICULATORS	ASCENDENTS	ASPERGILLOSES
ARRACACHAS	ARTERIALIZES	ARTICULATORY	ASCENDEURS	ASPERGILLOSIS
ARRAGONITE	ARTERIALIZING	ARTIFACTUAL	ASCENDIBLE	ASPERGILLS

ASPERGILLUM
ASPERGILLUMS
ASPERGILLUS
ASPERITIES
ASPERSIONS
ASPERSIVELY
ASPERSOIRS
ASPERSORIA
ASPERSORIES
ASPERSORIUM
ASPERSORIUMS
ASPHALTERS
ASPHALTING
ASPHALTITE
ASPHALTITES
ASPHALTUMS
ASPHERICAL
ASPHETERISE
ASPHETERISED
ASPHETERISES
ASPHETERISING
ASPHETERISM
ASPHETERISMS
ASPHETERIZE
ASPHETERIZED
ASPHETERIZES
ASPHETERIZING
ASPHYXIANT
ASPHYXIANTS
ASPHYXIATE
ASPHYXIATED
ASPHYXIATES
ASPHYXIATING
ASPHYXIATION
ASPHYXIATIONS
ASPHYXIATOR
ASPHYXIATORS
ASPHYXYING
ASPIDISTRA
ASPIDISTRAS
ASPIRATING
ASPIRATION
ASPIRATIONAL
ASPIRATIONS
ASPIRATORS
ASPIRATORY
ASPIRINGLY
ASPIRINGNESS
ASPIRINGNESSES
ASPLANCHNIC
ASPLENIUMS
ASPORTATION
ASPORTATIONS
ASSAFETIDA
ASSAFETIDAS
ASSAFOETIDA
ASSAFOETIDAS
ASSAGAIING
ASSAILABLE
ASSAILANTS
ASSAILMENT
ASSAILMENTS
ASSASSINATE
ASSASSINATED
ASSASSINATES
ASSASSINATING
ASSASSINATION

ASSASSINATIONS
ASSASSINATOR
ASSASSINATORS
ASSAULTERS
ASSAULTING
ASSAULTIVE
ASSAULTIVELY
ASSAULTIVENESS
ASSEGAAIED
ASSEGAAIING
ASSEGAIING
ASSEMBLAGE
ASSEMBLAGES
ASSEMBLAGIST
ASSEMBLAGISTS
ASSEMBLANCE
ASSEMBLANCES
ASSEMBLAUNCE
ASSEMBLAUNCES
ASSEMBLERS
ASSEMBLIES
ASSEMBLING
ASSEMBLYMAN
ASSEMBLYMEN
ASSEMBLYWOMAN
ASSEMBLYWOMEN
ASSENTANEOUS
ASSENTATION
ASSENTATIONS
ASSENTATOR
ASSENTATORS
ASSENTIENT
ASSENTIENTS
ASSENTINGLY
ASSENTIVENESS
ASSENTIVENESSES
ASSERTABLE
ASSERTEDLY
ASSERTIBLE
ASSERTIONS
ASSERTIVELY
ASSERTIVENESS
ASSERTIVENESSES
ASSERTORIC
ASSESSABLE
ASSESSMENT
ASSESSMENTS
ASSESSORIAL
ASSESSORSHIP
ASSESSORSHIPS
ASSEVERATE
ASSEVERATED
ASSEVERATES
ASSEVERATING
ASSEVERATINGLY
ASSEVERATION
ASSEVERATIONS
ASSEVERATIVE
ASSEVERING
ASSIBILATE
ASSIBILATED
ASSIBILATES
ASSIBILATING
ASSIBILATION
ASSIBILATIONS
ASSIDUITIES
ASSIDUOUSLY

ASSIDUOUSNESS
ASSIDUOUSNESSES
ASSIGNABILITIES
ASSIGNABILITY
ASSIGNABLE
ASSIGNABLY
ASSIGNATION
ASSIGNATIONS
ASSIGNMENT
ASSIGNMENTS
ASSIMILABILITY
ASSIMILABLE
ASSIMILABLY
ASSIMILATE
ASSIMILATED
ASSIMILATES
ASSIMILATING
ASSIMILATION
ASSIMILATIONISM
ASSIMILATIONIST
ASSIMILATIONS
ASSIMILATIVE
ASSIMILATIVELY
ASSIMILATOR
ASSIMILATORS
ASSIMILATORY
ASSISTANCE
ASSISTANCES
ASSISTANTS
ASSISTANTSHIP
ASSISTANTSHIPS
ASSOCIABILITIES
ASSOCIABILITY
ASSOCIABLE
ASSOCIATED
ASSOCIATES
ASSOCIATESHIP
ASSOCIATESHIPS
ASSOCIATING
ASSOCIATION
ASSOCIATIONAL
ASSOCIATIONISM
ASSOCIATIONISMS
ASSOCIATIONIST
ASSOCIATIONISTS
ASSOCIATIONS
ASSOCIATIVE
ASSOCIATIVELY
ASSOCIATIVITIES
ASSOCIATIVITY
ASSOCIATOR
ASSOCIATORS
ASSOCIATORY
ASSOILMENT
ASSOILMENTS
ASSOILZIED
ASSOILZIEING
ASSOILZIES
ASSONANCES
ASSONANTAL
ASSONATING
ASSORTATIVE
ASSORTATIVELY
ASSORTEDNESS
ASSORTEDNESSES
ASSORTMENT
ASSORTMENTS

ASSUAGEMENT
ASSUAGEMENTS
ASSUAGINGS
ASSUBJUGATE
ASSUBJUGATED
ASSUBJUGATES
ASSUBJUGATING
ASSUEFACTION
ASSUEFACTIONS
ASSUETUDES
ASSUMABILITIES
ASSUMABILITY
ASSUMINGLY
ASSUMPSITS
ASSUMPTION
ASSUMPTIONS
ASSUMPTIVE
ASSUMPTIVELY
ASSURANCES
ASSUREDNESS
ASSUREDNESSES
ASSURGENCIES
ASSURGENCY
ASSYTHMENT
ASSYTHMENTS
ASTACOLOGICAL
ASTACOLOGIES
ASTACOLOGIST
ASTACOLOGISTS
ASTACOLOGY
ASTARBOARD
ASTATICALLY
ASTATICISM
ASTATICISMS
ASTEREOGNOSES
ASTEREOGNOSIS
ASTERIATED
ASTERIDIAN
ASTERIDIANS
ASTERISKED
ASTERISKING
ASTERISKLESS
ASTEROIDAL
ASTEROIDEAN
ASTEROIDEANS
ASTHENOPIA
ASTHENOPIAS
ASTHENOPIC
ASTHENOSPHERE
ASTHENOSPHERES
ASTHENOSPHERIC
ASTHMATICAL
ASTHMATICALLY
ASTHMATICS
ASTIGMATIC
ASTIGMATICALLY
ASTIGMATICS
ASTIGMATISM
ASTIGMATISMS
ASTOMATOUS
ASTONISHED
ASTONISHES
ASTONISHING
ASTONISHINGLY
ASTONISHMENT
ASTONISHMENTS
ASTOUNDING

ASTOUNDINGLY
ASTOUNDMENT
ASTOUNDMENTS
ASTRACHANS
ASTRAGALUS
ASTRAKHANS
ASTRANTIAS
ASTRAPHOBIA
ASTRAPHOBIAS
ASTRAPHOBIC
ASTRAPOPHOBIA
ASTRAPOPHOBIAS
ASTRICTING
ASTRICTION
ASTRICTIONS
ASTRICTIVE
ASTRICTIVELY
ASTRINGENCE
ASTRINGENCES
ASTRINGENCIES
ASTRINGENCY
ASTRINGENT
ASTRINGENTLY
ASTRINGENTS
ASTRINGERS
ASTRINGING
ASTROBIOLOGIES
ASTROBIOLOGIST
ASTROBIOLOGISTS
ASTROBIOLOGY
ASTROBLEME
ASTROBLEMES
ASTROBOTANIES
ASTROBOTANY
ASTROCHEMISTRY
ASTROCOMPASS
ASTROCOMPASSES
ASTROCYTES
ASTROCYTIC
ASTROCYTOMA
ASTROCYTOMAS
ASTROCYTOMATA
ASTRODOMES
ASTRODYNAMICIST
ASTRODYNAMICS
ASTROFELLS
ASTROGEOLOGIES
ASTROGEOLOGIST
ASTROGEOLOGISTS
ASTROGEOLOGY
ASTROHATCH
ASTROHATCHES
ASTROLABES
ASTROLATRIES
ASTROLATRY
ASTROLOGER
ASTROLOGERS
ASTROLOGIC
ASTROLOGICAL
ASTROLOGICALLY
ASTROLOGIES
ASTROLOGIST
ASTROLOGISTS
ASTROMETRIC
ASTROMETRICAL
ASTROMETRIES
ASTROMETRY

ASTRONAUTIC	ASYNERGIES	ATONALISTS	ATTESTATION	ATTRIBUTES
ASTRONAUTICAL	ASYNTACTIC	ATONALITIES	ATTESTATIONS	ATTRIBUTING
ASTRONAUTICALLY	ASYSTOLISM	ATONEMENTS	ATTESTATIVE	ATTRIBUTION
ASTRONAUTICS	ASYSTOLISMS	ATONICITIES	ATTESTATOR	ATTRIBUTIONAL
ASTRONAUTS	ATACAMITES	ATORVASTATIN	ATTESTATORS	ATTRIBUTIONS
ASTRONAVIGATION	ATARACTICS	ATORVASTATINS	ATTICISING	ATTRIBUTIVE
ASTRONAVIGATOR	ATAVISTICALLY	ATRABILIAR	ATTICIZING	ATTRIBUTIVELY
ASTRONAVIGATORS	ATCHIEVING	ATRABILIOUS	ATTIREMENT	ATTRIBUTIVENESS
ASTRONOMER	ATELECTASES	ATRABILIOUSNESS	ATTIREMENTS	ATTRIBUTIVES
ASTRONOMERS	ATELECTASIS	ATRACURIUM	ATTITUDINAL	ATTRIBUTOR
ASTRONOMIC	ATELECTATIC	ATRACURIUMS	ATTITUDINALLY	ATTRIBUTORS
ASTRONOMICAL	ATELEIOSES	ATRAMENTAL	ATTITUDINARIAN	ATTRISTING
ASTRONOMICALLY	ATELEIOSIS	ATRAMENTOUS	ATTITUDINARIANS	ATTRITIONAL
ASTRONOMIES	ATHANASIES	ATROCIOUSLY	ATTITUDINISE	ATTRITIONS
ASTRONOMISE	ATHEISTICAL	ATROCIOUSNESS	ATTITUDINISED	ATTRITTING
ASTRONOMISED	ATHEISTICALLY	ATROCIOUSNESSES	ATTITUDINISER	ATTUITIONAL
ASTRONOMISES	ATHEMATICALLY	ATROCITIES	ATTITUDINISERS	ATTUITIONS
ASTRONOMISING	ATHENAEUMS	ATROPHYING	ATTITUDINISES	ATTUITIVELY
ASTRONOMIZE	ATHEOLOGICAL	ATTACHABLE	ATTITUDINISING	ATTUNEMENT
ASTRONOMIZED	ATHEOLOGIES	ATTACHMENT	ATTITUDINISINGS	ATTUNEMENTS
ASTRONOMIZES	ATHEORETICAL	ATTACHMENTS	ATTITUDINIZE	ATYPICALITIES
ASTRONOMIZING	ATHERMANCIES	ATTACKABLE	ATTITUDINIZED	ATYPICALITY
ASTROPHELS	ATHERMANCY	ATTAINABILITIES	ATTITUDINIZER	ATYPICALLY
ASTROPHOBIA	ATHERMANOUS	ATTAINABILITY	ATTITUDINIZERS	AUBERGINES
ASTROPHOBIAS	ATHEROGENESES	ATTAINABLE	ATTITUDINIZES	AUBERGISTE
ASTROPHOBIC	ATHEROGENESIS	ATTAINABLENESS	ATTITUDINIZING	AUBERGISTES
ASTROPHOTOGRAPH	ATHEROGENIC	ATTAINDERS	ATTITUDINIZINGS	AUBRIETIAS
ASTROPHYSICAL	ATHEROMATA	ATTAINMENT	ATTOLASERS	AUCTIONARY
ASTROPHYSICALLY	ATHEROMATOUS	ATTAINMENTS	ATTOLLENTS	AUCTIONEER
ASTROPHYSICIST	ATHEROSCLEROSES	ATTAINTING	ATTOMETERS	AUCTIONEERED
ASTROPHYSICISTS	ATHEROSCLEROSIS	ATTAINTMENT	ATTOMETRES	AUCTIONEERING
ASTROPHYSICS	ATHEROSCLEROTIC	ATTAINTMENTS	ATTOPHYSICS	AUCTIONEERS
ASTROSPHERE	ATHETISING	ATTAINTURE	ATTORNEYDOM	AUCTIONING
ASTROSPHERES	ATHETIZING	ATTAINTURES	ATTORNEYDOMS	AUDACIOUSLY
ASTROTOURISM	ATHLEISURE	ATTEMPERED	ATTORNEYED	AUDACIOUSNESS
ASTROTOURISMS	ATHLEISURES	ATTEMPERING	ATTORNEYING	AUDACIOUSNESSES
ASTROTOURIST	ATHLETICALLY	ATTEMPERMENT	ATTORNEYISM	AUDACITIES
ASTROTOURISTS	ATHLETICISM	ATTEMPERMENTS	ATTORNEYISMS	AUDIBILITIES
ASTROTURFER	ATHLETICISMS	ATTEMPTABILITY	ATTORNEYSHIP	AUDIBILITY
ASTROTURFERS	ATHROCYTES	ATTEMPTABLE	ATTORNEYSHIPS	AUDIBLENESS
ASTROTURFING	ATHROCYTOSES	ATTEMPTERS	ATTORNMENT	AUDIBLENESSES
ASTROTURFINGS	ATHROCYTOSIS	ATTEMPTING	ATTORNMENTS	AUDIENCIAS
ASTUCIOUSLY	ATHWARTSHIP	ATTENDANCE	ATTOSECOND	AUDIOBOOKS
ASTUCITIES	ATHWARTSHIPS	ATTENDANCES	ATTOSECONDS	AUDIOCASSETTE
ASTUTENESS	ATMOLOGIES	ATTENDANCIES	ATTOTESLAS	AUDIOCASSETTES
ASTUTENESSES	ATMOLOGIST	ATTENDANCY	ATTRACTABLE	AUDIOGENIC
ASYMMETRIC	ATMOLOGISTS	ATTENDANTS	ATTRACTANCE	AUDIOGRAMS
ASYMMETRICAL	ATMOLYSING	ATTENDEMENT	ATTRACTANCES	AUDIOGRAPH
ASYMMETRICALLY	ATMOLYZING	ATTENDEMENTS	ATTRACTANCIES	AUDIOGRAPHS
ASYMMETRIES	ATMOMETERS	ATTENDINGS	ATTRACTANCY	AUDIOLOGIC
ASYMPTOMATIC	ATMOMETRIES	ATTENDMENT	ATTRACTANT	AUDIOLOGICAL
ASYMPTOTES	ATMOSPHERE	ATTENDMENTS	ATTRACTANTS	AUDIOLOGICALLY
ASYMPTOTIC	ATMOSPHERED	ATTENTIONAL	ATTRACTERS	AUDIOLOGIES
ASYMPTOTICAL	ATMOSPHERES	ATTENTIONS	ATTRACTING	AUDIOLOGIST
ASYMPTOTICALLY	ATMOSPHERIC	ATTENTIVELY	ATTRACTINGLY	AUDIOLOGISTS
ASYNARTETE	ATMOSPHERICAL	ATTENTIVENESS	ATTRACTION	AUDIOMETER
ASYNARTETES	ATMOSPHERICALLY	ATTENTIVENESSES	ATTRACTIONS	AUDIOMETERS
ASYNARTETIC	ATMOSPHERICS	ATTENUANTS	ATTRACTIVE	AUDIOMETRIC
ASYNCHRONIES	ATOMICALLY	ATTENUATED	ATTRACTIVELY	AUDIOMETRICALLY
ASYNCHRONISM	ATOMICITIES	ATTENUATES	ATTRACTIVENESS	AUDIOMETRICIAN
ASYNCHRONISMS	ATOMISATION	ATTENUATING	ATTRACTORS	AUDIOMETRICIANS
ASYNCHRONOUS	ATOMISATIONS	ATTENUATION	ATTRAHENTS	AUDIOMETRIES
ASYNCHRONOUSLY	ATOMISTICAL	ATTENUATIONS	ATTRAPPING	AUDIOMETRIST
ASYNCHRONY	ATOMISTICALLY	ATTENUATOR	ATTRIBUTABLE	AUDIOMETRISTS
ASYNDETICALLY	ATOMIZATION	ATTENUATORS	ATTRIBUTED	AUDIOMETRY
ASYNDETONS	ATOMIZATIONS	ATTESTABLE	ATTRIBUTER	AUDIOPHILE
ASYNERGIAS	ATONALISMS	ATTESTANTS	ATTRIBUTERS	AUDIOPHILES

AUDIOPHILS	AUSTENITIC	AUTOBAHNEN	AUTODROMES	AUTOMAKERS
AUDIOTAPED	AUSTERENESS	AUTOBIOGRAPHER	AUTOECIOUS	AUTOMATABLE
AUDIOTAPES	AUSTERENESSES	AUTOBIOGRAPHERS	AUTOECIOUSLY	AUTOMATICAL
AUDIOTAPING	AUSTERITIES	AUTOBIOGRAPHIC	AUTOECISMS	AUTOMATICALLY
AUDIOTYPING	AUSTRALITE	AUTOBIOGRAPHIES	AUTOEROTIC	AUTOMATICITIES
AUDIOTYPINGS	AUSTRALITES	AUTOBIOGRAPHY	AUTOEROTICISM	AUTOMATICITY
AUDIOTYPIST	AUSTRINGER	AUTOBODIES	AUTOEROTICISMS	AUTOMATICS
AUDIOTYPISTS	AUSTRINGERS	AUTOBUSSES	AUTOEROTISM	AUTOMATING
AUDIOVISUAL	AUTARCHICAL	AUTOCATALYSE	AUTOEROTISMS	AUTOMATION
AUDIOVISUALLY	AUTARCHIES	AUTOCATALYSED	AUTOEXPOSURE	AUTOMATIONS
AUDIOVISUALS	AUTARCHIST	AUTOCATALYSES	AUTOEXPOSURES	AUTOMATISATION
AUDIPHONES	AUTARCHISTS	AUTOCATALYSING	AUTOFLARES	AUTOMATISATIONS
AUDITIONED	AUTARKICAL	AUTOCATALYSIS	AUTOFOCUSES	AUTOMATISE
AUDITIONER	AUTARKISTS	AUTOCATALYTIC	AUTOGAMIES	AUTOMATISED
AUDITIONERS	AUTECOLOGIC	AUTOCATALYZE	AUTOGAMOUS	AUTOMATISES
AUDITIONING	AUTECOLOGICAL	AUTOCATALYZED	AUTOGENESES	AUTOMATISING
AUDITORIAL	AUTECOLOGIES	AUTOCATALYZES	AUTOGENESIS	AUTOMATISM
AUDITORIES	AUTECOLOGY	AUTOCATALYZING	AUTOGENETIC	AUTOMATISMS
AUDITORILY	AUTEURISMS	AUTOCEPHALIC	AUTOGENICS	AUTOMATIST
AUDITORIUM	AUTEURISTS	AUTOCEPHALIES	AUTOGENIES	AUTOMATISTS
AUDITORIUMS	AUTHENTICAL	AUTOCEPHALOUS	AUTOGENOUS	AUTOMATIZATION
AUDITORSHIP	AUTHENTICALLY	AUTOCEPHALY	AUTOGENOUSLY	AUTOMATIZATIONS
AUDITORSHIPS	AUTHENTICATE	AUTOCHANGER	AUTOGRAFTED	AUTOMATIZE
AUDITRESSES	AUTHENTICATED	AUTOCHANGERS	AUTOGRAFTING	AUTOMATIZED
AUGMENTABLE	AUTHENTICATES	AUTOCHTHON	AUTOGRAFTS	AUTOMATIZES
AUGMENTATION	AUTHENTICATING	AUTOCHTHONAL	AUTOGRAPHED	AUTOMATIZING
AUGMENTATIONS	AUTHENTICATION	AUTOCHTHONES	AUTOGRAPHIC	AUTOMATONS
AUGMENTATIVE	AUTHENTICATIONS	AUTOCHTHONIC	AUTOGRAPHICAL	AUTOMATOUS
AUGMENTATIVELY	AUTHENTICATOR	AUTOCHTHONIES	AUTOGRAPHICALLY	AUTOMETERS
AUGMENTATIVES	AUTHENTICATORS	AUTOCHTHONISM	AUTOGRAPHIES	AUTOMOBILE
AUGMENTERS	AUTHENTICITIES	AUTOCHTHONISMS	AUTOGRAPHING	AUTOMOBILED
AUGMENTING	AUTHENTICITY	AUTOCHTHONOUS	AUTOGRAPHS	AUTOMOBILES
AUGMENTORS	AUTHIGENIC	AUTOCHTHONOUSLY	AUTOGRAPHY	AUTOMOBILIA
AUGURSHIPS	AUTHORCRAFT	AUTOCHTHONS	AUTOGRAVURE	AUTOMOBILING
AUGUSTNESS	AUTHORCRAFTS	AUTOCHTHONY	AUTOGRAVURES	AUTOMOBILISM
AUGUSTNESSES	AUTHORESSES	AUTOCLAVED	AUTOGUIDES	AUTOMOBILISMS
AURALITIES	AUTHORINGS	AUTOCLAVES	AUTOHYPNOSES	AUTOMOBILIST
AUREATENESS	AUTHORISABLE	AUTOCLAVING	AUTOHYPNOSIS	AUTOMOBILISTS
AUREATENESSES	AUTHORISATION	AUTOCOMPLETE	AUTOHYPNOTIC	AUTOMOBILITIES
AURICULARLY	AUTHORISATIONS	AUTOCOMPLETES	AUTOIMMUNE	AUTOMOBILITY
AURICULARS	AUTHORISED	AUTOCOPROPHAGY	AUTOIMMUNITIES	AUTOMORPHIC
AURICULATE	AUTHORISER	AUTOCORRECT	AUTOIMMUNITY	AUTOMORPHICALLY
AURICULATED	AUTHORISERS	AUTOCORRECTS	AUTOINFECTION	AUTOMORPHISM
AURICULATELY	AUTHORISES	AUTOCORRELATION	AUTOINFECTIONS	AUTOMORPHISMS
AURIFEROUS	AUTHORISING	AUTOCRACIES	AUTOINOCULATION	AUTOMOTIVE
AURISCOPES	AUTHORISMS	AUTOCRATIC	AUTOIONISATION	AUTONOMICAL
AURISCOPIC	AUTHORITARIAN	AUTOCRATICAL	AUTOIONISATIONS	AUTONOMICALLY
AUSCULTATE	AUTHORITARIANS	AUTOCRATICALLY	AUTOIONIZATION	AUTONOMICS
AUSCULTATED	AUTHORITATIVE	AUTOCRIMES	AUTOIONIZATIONS	AUTONOMIES
AUSCULTATES	AUTHORITATIVELY	AUTOCRITIQUE	AUTOJUMBLE	AUTONOMIST
AUSCULTATING	AUTHORITIES	AUTOCRITIQUES	AUTOJUMBLES	AUTONOMISTS
AUSCULTATION	AUTHORIZABLE	AUTOCROSSES	AUTOKINESES	AUTONOMOUS
AUSCULTATIONS	AUTHORIZATION	AUTOCUTIES	AUTOKINESIS	AUTONOMOUSLY
AUSCULTATIVE	AUTHORIZATIONS	AUTOCYCLES	AUTOKINETIC	AUTONYMOUS
AUSCULTATOR	AUTHORIZED	AUTODESTRUCT	AUTOLATRIES	AUTOPHAGIA
AUSCULTATORS	AUTHORIZER	AUTODESTRUCTED	AUTOLOADED	AUTOPHAGIAS
AUSCULTATORY	AUTHORIZERS	AUTODESTRUCTING	AUTOLOADING	AUTOPHAGIES
AUSFORMING	AUTHORIZES	AUTODESTRUCTIVE	AUTOLOGIES	AUTOPHAGOUS
AUSFORMINGS	AUTHORIZING	AUTODESTRUCTS	AUTOLOGOUS	AUTOPHANOUS
AUSLANDERS	AUTHORLESS	AUTODIALED	AUTOLYSATE	AUTOPHOBIA
AUSPICATED	AUTHORSHIP	AUTODIALING	AUTOLYSATES	AUTOPHOBIAS
AUSPICATES	AUTHORSHIPS	AUTODIALLED	AUTOLYSING	AUTOPHOBIES
AUSPICATING	AUTISTICALLY	AUTODIALLING	AUTOLYSINS	AUTOPHONIES
AUSPICIOUS	AUTOALLOGAMIES	AUTODIDACT	AUTOLYZATE	AUTOPHYTES
AUSPICIOUSLY	AUTOALLOGAMY	AUTODIDACTIC	AUTOLYZATES	AUTOPHYTIC
AUSPICIOUSNESS	AUTOANTIBODIES	AUTODIDACTICISM	AUTOLYZING	AUTOPHYTICALLY
AUSTENITES	AUTOANTIBODY	AUTODIDACTS	AUTOMAGICALLY	AUTOPILOTS

AUTOPISTAS	AUTOSUGGESTIVE	AUXOTROPHS	AVICULTURIST	AXIOLOGIST
AUTOPLASTIC	AUTOSUGGESTS	AUXOTROPHY	AVICULTURISTS	AXIOLOGISTS
AUTOPLASTIES	AUTOTELLER	AVAILABILITIES	AVIDNESSES	AXIOMATICAL
AUTOPLASTY	AUTOTELLERS	AVAILABILITY	AVISANDUMS	AXIOMATICALLY
AUTOPOINTS	AUTOTETRAPLOID	AVAILABLENESS	AVISEMENTS	AXIOMATICS
AUTOPOLYPLOID	AUTOTETRAPLOIDS	AVAILABLENESSES	AVITAMINOSES	AXIOMATISATION
AUTOPOLYPLOIDS	AUTOTETRAPLOIDY	AVAILINGLY	AVITAMINOSIS	AXIOMATISATIONS
AUTOPOLYPLOIDY	AUTOTHEISM	AVALANCHED	AVITAMINOTIC	AXIOMATISE
AUTOPSISTS	AUTOTHEISMS	AVALANCHES	AVIZANDUMS	AXIOMATISED
AUTOPSYING	AUTOTHEIST	AVALANCHING	AVOCATIONAL	AXIOMATISES
AUTOPTICAL	AUTOTHEISTS	AVALEMENTS	AVOCATIONALLY	AXIOMATISING
AUTOPTICALLY	AUTOTIMERS	AVANTURINE	AVOCATIONS	AXIOMATIZATION
AUTORADIOGRAM	AUTOTOMIES	AVANTURINES	AVOIDANCES	AXIOMATIZATIONS
AUTORADIOGRAMS	AUTOTOMISE	AVARICIOUS	AVOIRDUPOIS	AXIOMATIZE
AUTORADIOGRAPH	AUTOTOMISED	AVARICIOUSLY	AVOIRDUPOISES	AXIOMATIZED
AUTORADIOGRAPHS	AUTOTOMISES	AVARICIOUSNESS	AVOPARCINS	AXIOMATIZES
AUTORADIOGRAPHY	AUTOTOMISING	AVASCULARITIES	AVOUCHABLE	AXIOMATIZING
AUTOREPLIES	AUTOTOMIZE	AVASCULARITY	AVOUCHMENT	AXISYMMETRIC
AUTOREVERSE	AUTOTOMIZED	AVENACEOUS	AVOUCHMENTS	AXISYMMETRICAL
AUTOREVERSES	AUTOTOMIZES	AVENGEMENT	AVOUTERERS	AXISYMMETRIES
AUTORICKSHAW	AUTOTOMIZING	AVENGEMENTS	AVOWABLENESS	AXISYMMETRY
AUTORICKSHAWS	AUTOTOMOUS	AVENGERESS	AVOWABLENESSES	AXOLEMMATA
AUTOROTATE	AUTOTOXAEMIA	AVENGERESSES	AVUNCULARITIES	AXONOMETRIC
AUTOROTATED	AUTOTOXAEMIAS	AVENTAILES	AVUNCULARITY	AXONOMETRIES
AUTOROTATES	AUTOTOXEMIA	AVENTURINE	AVUNCULARLY	AXONOMETRY
AUTOROTATING	AUTOTOXEMIAS	AVENTURINES	AVUNCULATE	AXOPLASMIC
AUTOROTATION	AUTOTOXINS	AVENTURINS	AVUNCULATES	AYAHUASCAS
AUTOROTATIONS	AUTOTRANSFORMER	AVERAGENESS	AVVOGADORE	AYAHUASCOS
AUTOROUTES	AUTOTRANSFUSION	AVERAGENESSES	AVVOGADORES	AYATOLLAHS
AUTOSAVING	AUTOTROPHIC	AVERAGINGS	AWAKENINGS	AYUNTAMIENTO
AUTOSCHEDIASM	AUTOTROPHICALLY	AVERRUNCATE	AWARENESSES	AYUNTAMIENTOS
AUTOSCHEDIASMS	AUTOTROPHIES	AVERRUNCATED	AWAYNESSES	AYURVEDICS
AUTOSCHEDIASTIC	AUTOTROPHS	AVERRUNCATES	AWELESSNESS	AZATHIOPRINE
AUTOSCHEDIAZE	AUTOTROPHY	AVERRUNCATING	AWELESSNESSES	AZATHIOPRINES
AUTOSCHEDIAZED	AUTOTYPIES	AVERRUNCATION	AWESOMENESS	AZEDARACHS
AUTOSCHEDIAZES	AUTOTYPING	AVERRUNCATIONS	AWESOMENESSES	AZEOTROPES
AUTOSCHEDIAZING	AUTOTYPOGRAPHY	AVERRUNCATOR	AWESTRICKEN	AZEOTROPIC
AUTOSCOPIC	AUTOWINDER	AVERRUNCATORS	AWESTRIKES	AZEOTROPIES
AUTOSCOPIES	AUTOWINDERS	AVERSENESS	AWESTRIKING	AZIDOTHYMIDINE
AUTOSEXING	AUTOWORKER	AVERSENESSES	AWFULNESSES	AZIDOTHYMIDINES
AUTOSEXINGS	AUTOWORKERS	AVERSIVELY	AWKWARDEST	AZIMUTHALLY
AUTOSOMALLY	AUTOXIDATION	AVERSIVENESS	AWKWARDISH	AZOBENZENE
AUTOSPORES	AUTOXIDATIONS	AVERSIVENESSES	AWKWARDNESS	AZOBENZENES
AUTOSPORTS	AUTUMNALLY	AVERTIMENT	AWKWARDNESSES	AZOOSPERMIA
AUTOSTABILITIES	AUTUMNIEST	AVERTIMENTS	AXENICALLY	AZOOSPERMIAS
AUTOSTABILITY	AUXANOMETER	AVGOLEMONO	AXEROPHTHOL	AZOOSPERMIC
AUTOSTRADA	AUXANOMETERS	AVGOLEMONOS	AXEROPHTHOLS	AZOTAEMIAS
AUTOSTRADAS	AUXILIARIES	AVIANISING	AXIALITIES	AZOTOBACTER
AUTOSTRADE	AUXOCHROME	AVIANIZING	AXILLARIES	AZOTOBACTERS
AUTOSUGGEST	AUXOCHROMES	AVIATRESSES	AXINOMANCIES	AZYGOSPORE
AUTOSUGGESTED	AUXOMETERS	AVIATRICES	AXINOMANCY	AZYGOSPORES
AUTOSUGGESTING	AUXOSPORES	AVIATRIXES	AXIOLOGICAL	
AUTOSUGGESTION	AUXOTROPHIC	AVICULTURE	AXIOLOGICALLY	
AUTOSUGGESTIONS	AUXOTROPHIES	AVICULTURES	AXIOLOGIES	

B

BAALEBATIM
BABACOOTES
BABBITRIES
BABBITTING
BABBITTRIES
BABBLATIVE
BABBLEMENT
BABBLEMENTS
BABELESQUE
BABESIASES
BABESIASIS
BABESIOSES
BABESIOSIS
BABINGTONITE
BABINGTONITES
BABIROUSSA
BABIROUSSAS
BABIRUSSAS
BABOONERIES
BABYCCINOS
BABYDADDIES
BABYPROOFED
BABYPROOFING
BABYPROOFS
BABYSITTING
BACCALAUREAN
BACCALAUREATE
BACCALAUREATES
BACCHANALIA
BACCHANALIAN
BACCHANALIANISM
BACCHANALIANS
BACCHANALS
BACCHANTES
BACCIFEROUS
BACCIVOROUS
BACHARACHS
BACHELORDOM
BACHELORDOMS
BACHELORETTE
BACHELORETTES
BACHELORHOOD
BACHELORHOODS
BACHELORISM
BACHELORISMS
BACHELORSHIP
BACHELORSHIPS
BACILLAEMIA
BACILLAEMIAS
BACILLEMIA
BACILLEMIAS
BACILLICIDE
BACILLICIDES
BACILLIFORM

BACILLURIA
BACILLURIAS
BACITRACIN
BACITRACINS
BACKACTERS
BACKBENCHER
BACKBENCHERS
BACKBENCHES
BACKBITERS
BACKBITING
BACKBITINGS
BACKBITTEN
BACKBLOCKER
BACKBLOCKERS
BACKBLOCKS
BACKBOARDS
BACKBONELESS
BACKBREAKER
BACKBREAKERS
BACKBREAKING
BACKBURNED
BACKBURNING
BACKCASTING
BACKCHANNEL
BACKCHANNELS
BACKCHATTED
BACKCHATTING
BACKCHECKED
BACKCHECKING
BACKCHECKS
BACKCLOTHS
BACKCOMBED
BACKCOMBING
BACKCOUNTRIES
BACKCOUNTRY
BACKCOURTMAN
BACKCOURTMEN
BACKCOURTS
BACKCROSSED
BACKCROSSES
BACKCROSSING
BACKDATING
BACKDRAFTS
BACKDRAUGHT
BACKDRAUGHTS
BACKDROPPED
BACKDROPPING
BACKFIELDS
BACKFILLED
BACKFILLING
BACKFILLINGS
BACKFIRING
BACKFISCHES
BACKFITTED

BACKFITTING
BACKFITTINGS
BACKFLIPPED
BACKFLIPPING
BACKFLIPPINGS
BACKGAMMON
BACKGAMMONED
BACKGAMMONING
BACKGAMMONS
BACKGROUND
BACKGROUNDED
BACKGROUNDER
BACKGROUNDERS
BACKGROUNDING
BACKGROUNDS
BACKHANDED
BACKHANDEDLY
BACKHANDEDNESS
BACKHANDER
BACKHANDERS
BACKHANDING
BACKHAULED
BACKHAULING
BACKHOEING
BACKHOUSES
BACKLASHED
BACKLASHER
BACKLASHERS
BACKLASHES
BACKLASHING
BACKLIGHTED
BACKLIGHTING
BACKLIGHTS
BACKLINERS
BACKLISTED
BACKLISTING
BACKLOADED
BACKLOADING
BACKLOGGED
BACKLOGGING
BACKMARKER
BACKMARKERS
BACKPACKED
BACKPACKER
BACKPACKERS
BACKPACKING
BACKPACKINGS
BACKPEDALED
BACKPEDALING
BACKPEDALLED
BACKPEDALLING
BACKPEDALS
BACKPIECES
BACKPLANES

BACKPLATES
BACKRONYMS
BACKRUSHES
BACKSCATTER
BACKSCATTERED
BACKSCATTERING
BACKSCATTERINGS
BACKSCATTERS
BACKSCRATCH
BACKSCRATCHED
BACKSCRATCHER
BACKSCRATCHERS
BACKSCRATCHES
BACKSCRATCHING
BACKSCRATCHINGS
BACKSETTING
BACKSHEESH
BACKSHEESHED
BACKSHEESHES
BACKSHEESHING
BACKSHISHED
BACKSHISHES
BACKSHISHING
BACKSHORES
BACKSIGHTS
BACKSLAPPED
BACKSLAPPER
BACKSLAPPERS
BACKSLAPPING
BACKSLASHES
BACKSLIDDEN
BACKSLIDER
BACKSLIDERS
BACKSLIDES
BACKSLIDING
BACKSLIDINGS
BACKSPACED
BACKSPACER
BACKSPACERS
BACKSPACES
BACKSPACING
BACKSPEERED
BACKSPEERING
BACKSPEERS
BACKSPEIRED
BACKSPEIRING
BACKSPEIRS
BACKSPLASH
BACKSPLASHES
BACKSPLITS
BACKSTABBED
BACKSTABBER
BACKSTABBERS
BACKSTABBING

BACKSTABBINGS
BACKSTAGES
BACKSTAIRS
BACKSTALLED
BACKSTALLING
BACKSTALLS
BACKSTAMPED
BACKSTAMPING
BACKSTAMPS
BACKSTARTING
BACKSTARTINGS
BACKSTITCH
BACKSTITCHED
BACKSTITCHES
BACKSTITCHING
BACKSTOPPED
BACKSTOPPING
BACKSTORIES
BACKSTRAPS
BACKSTREET
BACKSTREETS
BACKSTRETCH
BACKSTRETCHES
BACKSTROKE
BACKSTROKED
BACKSTROKES
BACKSTROKING
BACKSWIMMER
BACKSWIMMERS
BACKSWINGS
BACKSWORDMAN
BACKSWORDMEN
BACKSWORDS
BACKSWORDSMAN
BACKSWORDSMEN
BACKTRACKED
BACKTRACKING
BACKTRACKINGS
BACKTRACKS
BACKVELDER
BACKVELDERS
BACKWARDATION
BACKWARDATIONS
BACKWARDLY
BACKWARDNESS
BACKWARDNESSES
BACKWASHED
BACKWASHES
BACKWASHING
BACKWATERS
BACKWINDED
BACKWINDING
BACKWOODSIER
BACKWOODSIEST

BACKWOODSMAN	BADDERLOCK	BALDICOOTS	BALLOTTEMENTS	BANDICOOTED
BACKWOODSMEN	BADDERLOCKS	BALDMONEYS	BALLPLAYER	BANDICOOTING
BACKWOODSY	BADGERLIER	BALDNESSES	BALLPLAYERS	BANDICOOTS
BACKWORKER	BADGERLIEST	BALECTIONS	BALLPOINTS	BANDINESSES
BACKWORKERS	BADINAGING	BALEFULNESS	BALLSINESS	BANDITRIES
BACTERAEMIA	BADINERIES	BALEFULNESSES	BALLSINESSES	BANDLEADER
BACTERAEMIAS	BADMINTONS	BALIBUNTAL	BALLYHOOED	BANDLEADERS
BACTERAEMIC	BADMOUTHED	BALIBUNTALS	BALLYHOOING	BANDMASTER
BACTEREMIA	BADMOUTHING	BALKANISATION	BALLYRAGGED	BANDMASTERS
BACTEREMIAS	BAFFLEGABS	BALKANISATIONS	BALLYRAGGING	BANDOBASTS
BACTEREMIC	BAFFLEMENT	BALKANISED	BALMACAANS	BANDOBUSTS
BACTERIALLY	BAFFLEMENTS	BALKANISES	BALMINESSES	BANDOLEERED
BACTERIALS	BAFFLINGLY	BALKANISING	BALMORALITIES	BANDOLEERS
BACTERICIDAL	BAGASSOSES	BALKANIZATION	BALMORALITY	BANDOLEONS
BACTERICIDALLY	BAGASSOSIS	BALKANIZATIONS	BALNEARIES	BANDOLEROS
BACTERICIDE	BAGATELLES	BALKANIZED	BALNEATION	BANDOLIERED
BACTERICIDES	BAGGINESSES	BALKANIZES	BALNEATIONS	BANDOLIERS
BACTERIOCIN	BAGPIPINGS	BALKANIZING	BALNEOLOGICAL	BANDOLINED
BACTERIOCINS	BAGSWINGER	BALKINESSES	BALNEOLOGIES	BANDOLINES
BACTERIOID	BAGSWINGERS	BALLABILES	BALNEOLOGIST	BANDOLINING
BACTERIOIDS	BAHUVRIHIS	BALLADEERED	BALNEOLOGISTS	BANDONEONS
BACTERIOLOGIC	BAIGNOIRES	BALLADEERING	BALNEOLOGY	BANDONIONS
BACTERIOLOGICAL	BAILIESHIP	BALLADEERS	BALNEOTHERAPIES	BANDPASSES
BACTERIOLOGIES	BAILIESHIPS	BALLADINES	BALNEOTHERAPY	BANDSAWING
BACTERIOLOGIST	BAILIFFSHIP	BALLADISTS	BALSAMIEST	BANDSHELLS
BACTERIOLOGISTS	BAILIFFSHIPS	BALLADMONGER	BALSAMIFEROUS	BANDSPREADING
BACTERIOLOGY	BAILIWICKS	BALLADMONGERS	BALSAMINACEOUS	BANDSPREADINGS
BACTERIOLYSES	BAILLIAGES	BALLADRIES	BALSAWOODS	BANDSTANDS
BACTERIOLYSIN	BAILLIESHIP	BALLANTING	BALTHASARS	BANDURISTS
BACTERIOLYSINS	BAILLIESHIPS	BALLANWRASSE	BALTHAZARS	BANDWAGONS
BACTERIOLYSIS	BAIRNLIEST	BALLANWRASSES	BALUSTERED	BANDWIDTHS
BACTERIOLYTIC	BAISEMAINS	BALLASTERS	BALUSTRADE	BANEBERRIES
BACTERIOPHAGE	BAITFISHES	BALLASTING	BALUSTRADED	BANEFULNESS
BACTERIOPHAGES	BAJILLIONS	BALLBREAKER	BALUSTRADES	BANEFULNESSES
BACTERIOPHAGIC	BAKEAPPLES	BALLBREAKERS	BALZARINES	BANGBELLIES
BACTERIOPHAGIES	BAKEBOARDS	BALLCARRIER	BAMBOOZLED	BANGSRINGS
BACTERIOPHAGOUS	BAKEHOUSES	BALLCARRIERS	BAMBOOZLEMENT	BANISHMENT
BACTERIOPHAGY	BAKESTONES	BALLERINAS	BAMBOOZLEMENTS	BANISHMENTS
BACTERIOSES	BAKHSHISHED	BALLETICALLY	BAMBOOZLER	BANISTERED
BACTERIOSIS	BAKHSHISHES	BALLETOMANE	BAMBOOZLERS	BANJOLELES
BACTERIOSTASES	BAKHSHISHING	BALLETOMANES	BAMBOOZLES	BANJULELES
BACTERIOSTASIS	BAKSHEESHED	BALLETOMANIA	BAMBOOZLING	BANKABILITIES
BACTERIOSTAT	BAKSHEESHES	BALLETOMANIAS	BANALISATION	BANKABILITY
BACTERIOSTATIC	BAKSHEESHING	BALLFIELDS	BANALISATIONS	BANKERLIER
BACTERIOSTATS	BAKSHISHED	BALLFLOWER	BANALISING	BANKERLIEST
BACTERIOTOXIN	BAKSHISHES	BALLFLOWERS	BANALITIES	BANKROLLED
BACTERIOTOXINS	BAKSHISHING	BALLHANDLING	BANALIZATION	BANKROLLER
BACTERISATION	BALACLAVAS	BALLHANDLINGS	BANALIZATIONS	BANKROLLERS
BACTERISATIONS	BALALAIKAS	BALLHAWKED	BANALIZING	BANKROLLING
BACTERISED	BALANCEABLE	BALLHAWKING	BANCASSURANCE	BANKRUPTCIES
BACTERISES	BALANCINGS	BALLICATTER	BANCASSURANCES	BANKRUPTCY
BACTERISING	BALANITISES	BALLICATTERS	BANCASSURER	BANKRUPTED
BACTERIURIA	BALAYAGING	BALLISTICALLY	BANCASSURERS	BANKRUPTING
BACTERIURIAS	BALBRIGGAN	BALLISTICS	BANDAGINGS	BANNERALLS
BACTERIZATION	BALBRIGGANS	BALLISTITE	BANDALORES	BANNERETTE
BACTERIZATIONS	BALBUTIENT	BALLISTITES	BANDBRAKES	BANNERETTES
BACTERIZED	BALCONETTE	BALLISTOSPORE	BANDEIRANTE	BANNISTERS
BACTERIZES	BALCONETTES	BALLISTOSPORES	BANDEIRANTES	BANQUETEER
BACTERIZING	BALDACHINO	BALLOCKSED	BANDELIERS	BANQUETEERS
BACTEROIDS	BALDACHINOS	BALLOCKSES	BANDERILLA	BANQUETERS
BACTERURIA	BALDACHINS	BALLOCKSING	BANDERILLAS	BANQUETING
BACTERURIAS	BALDAQUINS	BALLOONING	BANDERILLERO	BANQUETINGS
BACULIFORM	BALDERDASH	BALLOONINGS	BANDERILLEROS	BANQUETTES
BACULOVIRUS	BALDERDASHES	BALLOONIST	BANDEROLES	BANTAMWEIGHT
BACULOVIRUSES	BALDERLOCKS	BALLOONISTS	BANDERSNATCH	BANTAMWEIGHTS
BADDELEYITE	BALDERLOCKSES	BALLOTINGS	BANDERSNATCHES	BANTERINGLY
BADDELEYITES	BALDHEADED	BALLOTTEMENT	BANDFISHES	BANTERINGS

BANTINGISM	BAREHANDING	BAROSCOPIC	BASALTINES	BASTARDISE
BANTINGISMS	BAREHEADED	BAROTITISES	BASALTWARE	BASTARDISED
BAPHOMETIC	BARELEGGED	BAROTRAUMA	BASALTWARES	BASTARDISES
BAPTISMALLY	BARENESSES	BAROTRAUMAS	BASEBALLER	BASTARDISING
BAPTISTERIES	BARESTHESIA	BAROTRAUMATA	BASEBALLERS	BASTARDISM
BAPTISTERY	BARESTHESIAS	BARPERSONS	BASEBOARDS	BASTARDISMS
BAPTISTRIES	BARGAINERS	BARQUANTINE	BASEBURNER	BASTARDIZATION
BARACHOISES	BARGAINING	BARQUANTINES	BASEBURNERS	BASTARDIZATIONS
BARAESTHESIA	BARGAININGS	BARQUENTINE	BASELESSLY	BASTARDIZE
BARAESTHESIAS	BARGANDERS	BARQUENTINES	BASELESSNESS	BASTARDIZED
BARAGOUINS	BARGEBOARD	BARQUETTES	BASELESSNESSES	BASTARDIZES
BARASINGAS	BARGEBOARDS	BARRACKERS	BASELINERS	BASTARDIZING
BARASINGHA	BARGEMASTER	BARRACKING	BASEMENTLESS	BASTARDLIER
BARASINGHAS	BARGEMASTERS	BARRACKINGS	BASENESSES	BASTARDLIEST
BARATHRUMS	BARGEPOLES	BARRACOONS	BASEPLATES	BASTARDRIES
BARBARESQUE	BARHOPPING	BARRACOUTA	BASERUNNER	BASTINADED
BARBARIANISM	BARIATRICS	BARRACOUTAS	BASERUNNERS	BASTINADES
BARBARIANISMS	BARKANTINE	BARRACUDAS	BASERUNNING	BASTINADING
BARBARIANS	BARKANTINES	BARRAMUNDA	BASERUNNINGS	BASTINADOED
BARBARICALLY	BARKEEPERS	BARRAMUNDAS	BASHAWISMS	BASTINADOES
BARBARISATION	BARKENTINE	BARRAMUNDI	BASHAWSHIP	BASTINADOING
BARBARISATIONS	BARKENTINES	BARRAMUNDIES	BASHAWSHIPS	BASTNAESITE
BARBARISED	BARLEYCORN	BARRAMUNDIS	BASHFULLER	BASTNAESITES
BARBARISES	BARLEYCORNS	BARRASWAYS	BASHFULLEST	BASTNASITE
BARBARISING	BARMBRACKS	BARRATRIES	BASHFULNESS	BASTNASITES
BARBARISMS	BARMINESSES	BARRATROUS	BASHFULNESSES	BATFOWLERS
BARBARITIES	BARMITSVAH	BARRATROUSLY	BASHIBAZOUK	BATFOWLING
BARBARIZATION	BARMITSVAHS	BARRELAGES	BASHIBAZOUKS	BATFOWLINGS
BARBARIZATIONS	BARMITZVAH	BARRELFULS	BASICITIES	BATHETICALLY
BARBARIZED	BARMITZVAHS	BARRELHEAD	BASICRANIAL	BATHHOUSES
BARBARIZES	BARNBOARDS	BARRELHEADS	BASIDIOCARP	BATHMITSVAH
BARBARIZING	BARNBRACKS	BARRELHOUSE	BASIDIOCARPS	BATHMITSVAHS
BARBAROUSLY	BARNSBREAKING	BARRELHOUSES	BASIDIOMYCETE	BATHMITZVAH
BARBAROUSNESS	BARNSBREAKINGS	BARRELLING	BASIDIOMYCETES	BATHMITZVAHS
BARBAROUSNESSES	BARNSTORMED	BARRELSFUL	BASIDIOMYCETOUS	BATHMIZVAH
BARBASCOES	BARNSTORMER	BARRENNESS	BASIDIOSPORE	BATHMIZVAHS
BARBASTELLE	BARNSTORMERS	BARRENNESSES	BASIDIOSPORES	BATHOCHROME
BARBASTELLES	BARNSTORMING	BARRENWORT	BASIDIOSPOROUS	BATHOCHROMES
BARBASTELS	BARNSTORMINGS	BARRENWORTS	BASIFICATION	BATHOCHROMIC
BARBECUERS	BARNSTORMS	BARRETRIES	BASIFICATIONS	BATHOLITES
BARBECUING	BAROCEPTOR	BARRETROUS	BASILICONS	BATHOLITHIC
BARBELLATE	BAROCEPTORS	BARRETROUSLY	BASIPETALLY	BATHOLITHS
BARBEQUING	BARODYNAMICS	BARRETTERS	BASKETBALL	BATHOLITIC
BARBERRIES	BAROGNOSES	BARRICADED	BASKETBALLS	BATHOMETER
BARBERSHOP	BAROGNOSIS	BARRICADER	BASKETFULS	BATHOMETERS
BARBERSHOPS	BAROGRAPHIC	BARRICADERS	BASKETLIKE	BATHOMETRIC
BARBITONES	BAROGRAPHS	BARRICADES	BASKETRIES	BATHOMETRICALLY
BARBITURATE	BAROMETERS	BARRICADING	BASKETSFUL	BATHOMETRIES
BARBITURATES	BAROMETRIC	BARRICADOED	BASKETWEAVE	BATHOMETRY
BARBITURIC	BAROMETRICAL	BARRICADOES	BASKETWEAVER	BATHOPHILOUS
BARBOTINES	BAROMETRICALLY	BARRICADOING	BASKETWEAVERS	BATHOPHOBIA
BARCAROLES	BAROMETRIES	BARRICADOS	BASKETWEAVES	BATHOPHOBIAS
BARCAROLLE	BAROMETZES	BARRIERING	BASKETWORK	BATHWATERS
BARCAROLLES	BARONESSES	BARRISTERIAL	BASKETWORKS	BATHYBIUSES
BARDOLATER	BARONETAGE	BARRISTERS	BASMITZVAH	BATHYGRAPHIC
BARDOLATERS	BARONETAGES	BARRISTERSHIP	BASMITZVAHS	BATHYGRAPHICAL
BARDOLATRIES	BARONETCIES	BARRISTERSHIPS	BASOPHILES	BATHYLIMNETIC
BARDOLATROUS	BARONETESS	BARROWFULS	BASOPHILIA	BATHYLITES
BARDOLATRY	BARONETESSES	BARTENDERS	BASOPHILIAS	BATHYLITHIC
BAREBACKED	BARONETICAL	BARTENDING	BASOPHILIC	BATHYLITHS
BAREBACKING	BAROPHILES	BARTENDINGS	BASSETTING	BATHYLITIC
BAREBACKINGS	BAROPHILIC	BARTIZANED	BASSNESSES	BATHYMETER
BAREFACEDLY	BAROPHORESES	BARYCENTRE	BASSOONIST	BATHYMETERS
BAREFACEDNESS	BAROPHORESIS	BARYCENTRES	BASSOONISTS	BATHYMETRIC
BAREFACEDNESSES	BARORECEPTOR	BARYCENTRIC	BASTARDIES	BATHYMETRICAL
BAREFOOTED	BARORECEPTORS	BARYSPHERE	BASTARDISATION	BATHYMETRICALLY
BAREHANDED	BAROSCOPES	BARYSPHERES	BASTARDISATIONS	BATHYMETRIES

b

BATHYMETRY	BAULKINGLY	BEASTLINESSES	BECUDGELED	BEEFSTEAKS
BATHYPELAGIC	BAULKLINES	BEATBOXERS	BECUDGELING	BEEKEEPERS
BATHYSCAPE	BAVARDAGES	BEATBOXING	BECUDGELLED	BEEKEEPING
BATHYSCAPES	BAVAROISES	BEATBOXINGS	BECUDGELLING	BEEKEEPINGS
BATHYSCAPH	BAWDINESSES	BEATIFICAL	BEDABBLING	BEERINESSES
BATHYSCAPHE	BAWDYHOUSE	BEATIFICALLY	BEDAGGLING	BEESWAXING
BATHYSCAPHES	BAWDYHOUSES	BEATIFICATION	BEDARKENED	BEESWINGED
BATHYSCAPHS	BAYBERRIES	BEATIFICATIONS	BEDARKENING	BEETLEBRAIN
BATHYSPHERE	BAYNODDIES	BEATIFYING	BEDAZZLEMENT	BEETLEBRAINED
BATHYSPHERES	BAYONETING	BEATITUDES	BEDAZZLEMENTS	BEETLEBRAINS
BATMITZVAH	BAYONETTED	BEAUJOLAIS	BEDAZZLING	BEETLEHEAD
BATMITZVAHS	BAYONETTING	BEAUJOLAISES	BEDCHAMBER	BEETLEHEADED
BATOLOGICAL	BAZILLIONS	BEAUMONTAGE	BEDCHAMBERS	BEETLEHEADS
BATOLOGIES	BEACHBALLS	BEAUMONTAGES	BEDCLOTHES	BEETMASTER
BATOLOGIST	BEACHCOMBED	BEAUMONTAGUE	BEDCOVERING	BEETMASTERS
BATOLOGISTS	BEACHCOMBER	BEAUMONTAGUES	BEDCOVERINGS	BEETMISTER
BATONNIERS	BEACHCOMBERS	BEAUTEOUSLY	BEDEAFENED	BEETMISTERS
BATRACHIAN	BEACHCOMBING	BEAUTEOUSNESS	BEDEAFENING	BEFINGERED
BATRACHIANS	BEACHCOMBINGS	BEAUTEOUSNESSES	BEDEHOUSES	BEFINGERING
BATRACHOPHOBIA	BEACHCOMBS	BEAUTICIAN	BEDELLSHIP	BEFITTINGLY
BATRACHOPHOBIAS	BEACHFRONT	BEAUTICIANS	BEDELLSHIPS	BEFLAGGING
BATRACHOPHOBIC	BEACHFRONTS	BEAUTIFICATION	BEDELSHIPS	BEFLECKING
BATSMANSHIP	BEACHGOERS	BEAUTIFICATIONS	BEDEVILING	BEFLOWERED
BATSMANSHIPS	BEACHHEADS	BEAUTIFIED	BEDEVILLED	BEFLOWERING
BATTAILOUS	BEACHWEARS	BEAUTIFIER	BEDEVILLING	BEFLUMMING
BATTALIONS	BEADBLASTED	BEAUTIFIERS	BEDEVILMENT	BEFOREHAND
BATTEILANT	BEADBLASTER	BEAUTIFIES	BEDEVILMENTS	BEFORETIME
BATTELLING	BEADBLASTERS	BEAUTIFULLER	BEDFELLOWS	BEFORTUNED
BATTEMENTS	BEADBLASTING	BEAUTIFULLEST	BEDIAPERED	BEFORTUNES
BATTENINGS	BEADBLASTS	BEAUTIFULLY	BEDIAPERING	BEFORTUNING
BATTERINGS	BEADHOUSES	BEAUTIFULNESS	BEDIGHTING	BEFOULMENT
BATTILLING	BEADINESSES	BEAUTIFULNESSES	BEDIMMINGS	BEFOULMENTS
BATTINESSES	BEADLEDOMS	BEAUTIFYING	BEDIMPLING	BEFRETTING
BATTLEAXES	BEADLEHOOD	BEAVERBOARD	BEDIRTYING	BEFRIENDED
BATTLEBUSES	BEADLEHOODS	BEAVERBOARDS	BEDIZENING	BEFRIENDER
BATTLEBUSSES	BEADLESHIP	BEBEERINES	BEDIZENMENT	BEFRIENDERS
BATTLEDOOR	BEADLESHIPS	BEBLOODING	BEDIZENMENTS	BEFRIENDING
BATTLEDOORS	BEADSWOMAN	BEBLUBBERED	BEDLAMISMS	BEFRINGING
BATTLEDORE	BEADSWOMEN	BECARPETED	BEDLAMITES	BEFUDDLEMENT
BATTLEDORES	BEAKERFULS	BECARPETING	BEDPRESSER	BEFUDDLEMENTS
BATTLEDRESS	BEAMINESSES	BECCACCIAS	BEDPRESSERS	BEFUDDLING
BATTLEDRESSES	BEANFEASTS	BECCAFICOS	BEDRAGGLED	BEGGARDOMS
BATTLEFIELD	BEANSPROUT	BECHALKING	BEDRAGGLES	BEGGARHOOD
BATTLEFIELDS	BEANSPROUTS	BECHANCING	BEDRAGGLING	BEGGARHOODS
BATTLEFRONT	BEANSTALKS	BECHARMING	BEDRENCHED	BEGGARLIER
BATTLEFRONTS	BEARABILITIES	BECKONINGLY	BEDRENCHES	BEGGARLIEST
BATTLEGROUND	BEARABILITY	BECKONINGS	BEDRENCHING	BEGGARLINESS
BATTLEGROUNDS	BEARABLENESS	BECLAMORED	BEDRIVELED	BEGGARLINESSES
BATTLEMENT	BEARABLENESSES	BECLAMORING	BEDRIVELING	BEGGARWEED
BATTLEMENTED	BEARBAITING	BECLAMOURED	BEDRIVELLED	BEGGARWEEDS
BATTLEMENTS	BEARBAITINGS	BECLAMOURING	BEDRIVELLING	BEGINNINGLESS
BATTLEPIECE	BEARBERRIES	BECLAMOURS	BEDROPPING	BEGINNINGS
BATTLEPIECES	BEARDEDNESS	BECLASPING	BEDRUGGING	BEGIRDLING
BATTLEPLANE	BEARDEDNESSES	BECLOAKING	BEDSITTERS	BEGLADDING
BATTLEPLANES	BEARDLESSNESS	BECLOGGING	BEDSITTING	BEGLAMORED
BATTLESHIP	BEARDLESSNESSES	BECLOTHING	BEDSPREADS	BEGLAMORING
BATTLESHIPS	BEARDTONGUE	BECLOUDING	BEDSPRINGS	BEGLAMOURED
BATTLESPACE	BEARDTONGUES	BECLOWNING	BEDWARFING	BEGLAMOURING
BATTLESPACES	BEARGRASSES	BECOMINGLY	BEDWARMERS	BEGLAMOURS
BATTLEWAGON	BEARHUGGED	BECOMINGNESS	BEDWETTERS	BEGLERBEGS
BATTLEWAGONS	BEARHUGGING	BECOMINGNESSES	BEECHDROPS	BEGLOOMING
BATTOLOGICAL	BEARISHNESS	BECOWARDED	BEECHMASTS	BEGRIMMING
BATTOLOGIES	BEARISHNESSES	BECOWARDING	BEECHWOODS	BEGROANING
BAUDRICKES	BEARNAISES	BECQUERELS	BEEFBURGER	BEGRUDGERIES
BAUDRONSES	BEASTHOODS	BECRAWLING	BEEFBURGERS	BEGRUDGERS
BAULKINESS	BEASTLIEST	BECROWDING	BEEFEATERS	BEGRUDGERY
BAULKINESSES	BEASTLINESS	BECRUSTING	BEEFINESSES	BEGRUDGING

BEGRUDGINGLY
BEGUILEMENT
BEGUILEMENTS
BEGUILINGLY
BEGUINAGES
BEHAPPENED
BEHAPPENING
BEHAVIORAL
BEHAVIORALLY
BEHAVIORISM
BEHAVIORISMS
BEHAVIORIST
BEHAVIORISTIC
BEHAVIORISTS
BEHAVIOURAL
BEHAVIOURALLY
BEHAVIOURISM
BEHAVIOURISMS
BEHAVIOURIST
BEHAVIOURISTIC
BEHAVIOURISTS
BEHAVIOURS
BEHEADINGS
BEHIGHTING
BEHINDHAND
BEHOLDINGS
BEINGNESSES
BEINNESSES
BEJABERSES
BEJEEZUSES
BEJESUITED
BEJESUITING
BEJEWELING
BEJEWELLED
BEJEWELLING
BEJUMBLING
BEKNIGHTED
BEKNIGHTING
BEKNOTTING
BELABORING
BELABOURED
BELABOURING
BELAMOURES
BELATEDNESS
BELATEDNESSES
BELEAGUERED
BELEAGUERING
BELEAGUERMENT
BELEAGUERMENTS
BELEAGUERS
BELEMNITES
BELGICISMS
BELIEFLESS
BELIEVABILITIES
BELIEVABILITY
BELIEVABLE
BELIEVABLY
BELIEVINGLY
BELIEVINGS
BELIQUORED
BELIQUORING
BELITTLEMENT
BELITTLEMENTS
BELITTLERS
BELITTLING
BELITTLINGLY
BELLADONNA

BELLADONNAS
BELLAMOURE
BELLAMOURES
BELLARMINE
BELLARMINES
BELLETRISM
BELLETRISMS
BELLETRIST
BELLETRISTIC
BELLETRISTICAL
BELLETRISTS
BELLETTRIST
BELLETTRISTS
BELLFLOWER
BELLFLOWERS
BELLFOUNDER
BELLFOUNDERS
BELLFOUNDRIES
BELLFOUNDRY
BELLHANGER
BELLHANGERS
BELLIBONES
BELLICOSELY
BELLICOSITIES
BELLICOSITY
BELLIGERATI
BELLIGERENCE
BELLIGERENCES
BELLIGERENCIES
BELLIGERENCY
BELLIGERENT
BELLIGERENTLY
BELLIGERENTS
BELLOCKING
BELLOWINGS
BELLWETHER
BELLWETHERS
BELLYACHED
BELLYACHER
BELLYACHERS
BELLYACHES
BELLYACHING
BELLYACHINGS
BELLYBANDS
BELLYBOATS
BELLYBUTTON
BELLYBUTTONS
BELLYFLOPPED
BELLYFLOPPING
BELLYFLOPS
BELOMANCIES
BELONGINGNESS
BELONGINGNESSES
BELONGINGS
BELOWDECKS
BELOWGROUND
BELOWSTAIRS
BELSHAZZAR
BELSHAZZARS
BELTCOURSE
BELTCOURSES
BELVEDERES
BEMADAMING
BEMADDENED
BEMADDENING
BEMEDALING
BEMEDALLED

BEMEDALLING
BEMINGLING
BEMOANINGS
BEMONSTERED
BEMONSTERING
BEMONSTERS
BEMOUTHING
BEMUDDLING
BEMUFFLING
BEMURMURED
BEMURMURING
BEMUSEMENT
BEMUSEMENTS
BEMUZZLING
BENCHERSHIP
BENCHERSHIPS
BENCHLANDS
BENCHMARKED
BENCHMARKING
BENCHMARKINGS
BENCHMARKS
BENCHWARMER
BENCHWARMERS
BENDINESSES
BENEDICITE
BENEDICITES
BENEDICTION
BENEDICTIONAL
BENEDICTIONALS
BENEDICTIONS
BENEDICTIVE
BENEDICTORY
BENEDICTUS
BENEDICTUSES
BENEFACTED
BENEFACTING
BENEFACTION
BENEFACTIONS
BENEFACTOR
BENEFACTORS
BENEFACTORY
BENEFACTRESS
BENEFACTRESSES
BENEFICENCE
BENEFICENCES
BENEFICENT
BENEFICENTIAL
BENEFICENTLY
BENEFICIAL
BENEFICIALLY
BENEFICIALNESS
BENEFICIALS
BENEFICIARIES
BENEFICIARY
BENEFICIATE
BENEFICIATED
BENEFICIATES
BENEFICIATING
BENEFICIATION
BENEFICIATIONS
BENEFICING
BENEFITERS
BENEFITING
BENEFITTED
BENEFITTING
BENEPLACITO
BENEVOLENCE

BENEVOLENCES
BENEVOLENT
BENEVOLENTLY
BENEVOLENTNESS
BENGALINES
BENIGHTEDLY
BENIGHTEDNESS
BENIGHTEDNESSES
BENIGHTENED
BENIGHTENING
BENIGHTENINGS
BENIGHTENS
BENIGHTERS
BENIGHTING
BENIGHTINGS
BENIGHTMENT
BENIGHTMENTS
BENIGNANCIES
BENIGNANCY
BENIGNANTLY
BENIGNITIES
BENTGRASSES
BENTHOPELAGIC
BENTHOSCOPE
BENTHOSCOPES
BENTONITES
BENTONITIC
BENUMBEDNESS
BENUMBEDNESSES
BENUMBINGLY
BENUMBMENT
BENUMBMENTS
BENZALDEHYDE
BENZALDEHYDES
BENZANTHRACENE
BENZANTHRACENES
BENZENECARBONYL
BENZENOIDS
BENZIDINES
BENZIMIDAZOLE
BENZIMIDAZOLES
BENZOAPYRENE
BENZOAPYRENES
BENZOCAINE
BENZOCAINES
BENZODIAZEPINE
BENZODIAZEPINES
BENZOFURAN
BENZOFURANS
BENZOLINES
BENZOPHENONE
BENZOPHENONES
BENZOQUINONE
BENZOQUINONES
BENZPYRENE
BENZPYRENES
BENZYLIDINE
BENZYLIDINES
BEPAINTING
BEPEARLING
BEPEPPERED
BEPEPPERING
BEPESTERED
BEPESTERING
BEPIMPLING
BEPLASTERED
BEPLASTERING

BEPLASTERS
BEPOMMELLED
BEPOMMELLING
BEPOWDERED
BEPOWDERING
BEPRAISING
BEQUEATHABLE
BEQUEATHAL
BEQUEATHALS
BEQUEATHED
BEQUEATHER
BEQUEATHERS
BEQUEATHING
BEQUEATHMENT
BEQUEATHMENTS
BERASCALED
BERASCALING
BERBERIDACEOUS
BERBERINES
BERBERISES
BEREAVEMENT
BEREAVEMENTS
BERGAMASKO
BERGAMASKOS
BERGAMASKS
BERGANDERS
BERGOMASKS
BERGSCHRUND
BERGSCHRUNDS
BERIBBONED
BERKELIUMS
BERRYFRUIT
BERRYFRUITS
BERSAGLIERE
BERSAGLIERI
BERSERKERS
BERTILLONAGE
BERTILLONAGES
BERYLLIOSES
BERYLLIOSIS
BERYLLIUMS
BESAINTING
BESCATTERED
BESCATTERING
BESCATTERS
BESCORCHED
BESCORCHES
BESCORCHING
BESCOURING
BESCRAWLED
BESCRAWLING
BESCREENED
BESCREENING
BESCRIBBLE
BESCRIBBLED
BESCRIBBLES
BESCRIBBLING
BESEECHERS
BESEECHING
BESEECHINGLY
BESEECHINGNESS
BESEECHINGS
BESEEMINGLY
BESEEMINGNESS
BESEEMINGNESSES
BESEEMINGS
BESEEMLIER

BESEEMLIEST	BESTIALISES	BETWEENBRAIN	BIBLIOMANIACAL	BICOMPONENT
BESETMENTS	BESTIALISING	BETWEENBRAINS	BIBLIOMANIACS	BICOMPONENTS
BESHADOWED	BESTIALISM	BETWEENITIES	BIBLIOMANIAS	BICONCAVITIES
BESHADOWING	BESTIALISMS	BETWEENITY	BIBLIOPEGIC	BICONCAVITY
BESHIVERED	BESTIALITIES	BETWEENNESS	BIBLIOPEGIES	BICONDITIONAL
BESHIVERING	BESTIALITY	BETWEENNESSES	BIBLIOPEGIST	BICONDITIONALS
BESHOUTING	BESTIALIZE	BETWEENTIME	BIBLIOPEGISTS	BICONVEXITIES
BESHREWING	BESTIALIZED	BETWEENTIMES	BIBLIOPEGY	BICONVEXITY
BESHROUDED	BESTIALIZES	BETWEENWHILES	BIBLIOPHAGIST	BICORNUATE
BESHROUDING	BESTIALIZING	BEVELLINGS	BIBLIOPHAGISTS	BICORPORATE
BESIEGEMENT	BESTIARIES	BEVELMENTS	BIBLIOPHIL	BICULTURAL
BESIEGEMENTS	BESTICKING	BEVOMITING	BIBLIOPHILE	BICULTURALISM
BESIEGINGLY	BESTILLING	BEWAILINGLY	BIBLIOPHILES	BICULTURALISMS
BESIEGINGS	BESTIRRING	BEWAILINGS	BIBLIOPHILIC	BICUSPIDATE
BESLAVERED	BESTORMING	BEWEARYING	BIBLIOPHILIES	BICUSPIDATES
BESLAVERING	BESTOWMENT	BEWELTERED	BIBLIOPHILISM	BICYCLICAL
BESLOBBERED	BESTOWMENTS	BEWHISKERED	BIBLIOPHILISMS	BICYCLISTS
BESLOBBERING	BESTRADDLE	BEWILDERED	BIBLIOPHILIST	BIDDABILITIES
BESLOBBERS	BESTRADDLED	BEWILDEREDLY	BIBLIOPHILISTIC	BIDDABILITY
BESLUBBERED	BESTRADDLES	BEWILDEREDNESS	BIBLIOPHILISTS	BIDDABLENESS
BESLUBBERING	BESTRADDLING	BEWILDERING	BIBLIOPHILS	BIDDABLENESSES
BESLUBBERS	BESTRAUGHT	BEWILDERINGLY	BIBLIOPHILY	BIDENTATED
BESMEARERS	BESTREAKED	BEWILDERMENT	BIBLIOPHOBIA	BIDIALECTAL
BESMEARING	BESTREAKING	BEWILDERMENTS	BIBLIOPHOBIAS	BIDIALECTALISM
BESMIRCHED	BESTREWING	BEWITCHERIES	BIBLIOPOLE	BIDIALECTALISMS
BESMIRCHES	BESTRIDABLE	BEWITCHERS	BIBLIOPOLES	BIDIRECTIONAL
BESMIRCHING	BESTRIDDEN	BEWITCHERY	BIBLIOPOLIC	BIDIRECTIONALLY
BESMOOTHED	BESTRIDING	BEWITCHING	BIBLIOPOLICAL	BIDONVILLE
BESMOOTHING	BESTROWING	BEWITCHINGLY	BIBLIOPOLIES	BIDONVILLES
BESMUDGING	BESTSELLER	BEWITCHMENT	BIBLIOPOLIST	BIENNIALLY
BESMUTCHED	BESTSELLERDOM	BEWITCHMENTS	BIBLIOPOLISTS	BIENSEANCE
BESMUTCHES	BESTSELLERDOMS	BEWORRYING	BIBLIOPOLY	BIENSEANCES
BESMUTCHING	BESTSELLERS	BEWRAPPING	BIBLIOTHECA	BIERKELLER
BESMUTTING	BESTSELLING	BHIKKHUNIS	BIBLIOTHECAE	BIERKELLERS
BESOOTHING	BESTUDDING	BIANNUALLY	BIBLIOTHECAL	BIERWURSTS
BESOTTEDLY	BESWARMING	BIANNULATE	BIBLIOTHECARIES	BIFACIALLY
BESOTTEDNESS	BETACAROTENE	BIASNESSES	BIBLIOTHECARY	BIFARIOUSLY
BESOTTEDNESSES	BETACAROTENES	BIATHLETES	BIBLIOTHECAS	BIFIDITIES
BESPANGLED	BETACYANIN	BIAURICULAR	BIBLIOTHERAPIES	BIFLAGELLATE
BESPANGLES	BETACYANINS	BIAURICULATE	BIBLIOTHERAPY	BIFOLIOLATE
BESPANGLING	BETATTERED	BIBLICALLY	BIBLIOTICS	BIFUNCTIONAL
BESPATTERED	BETATTERING	BIBLICISMS	BIBLIOTIST	BIFURCATED
BESPATTERING	BETHANKING	BIBLICISTS	BIBLIOTISTS	BIFURCATES
BESPATTERS	BETHANKITS	BIBLIOGRAPHER	BIBULOUSLY	BIFURCATING
BESPEAKING	BETHINKING	BIBLIOGRAPHERS	BIBULOUSNESS	BIFURCATION
BESPECKLED	BETHORNING	BIBLIOGRAPHIC	BIBULOUSNESSES	BIFURCATIONS
BESPECKLES	BETHRALLED	BIBLIOGRAPHICAL	BICAMERALISM	BIGAMOUSLY
BESPECKLING	BETHRALLING	BIBLIOGRAPHIES	BICAMERALISMS	BIGARREAUS
BESPECTACLED	BETHUMBING	BIBLIOGRAPHY	BICAMERALIST	BIGEMINIES
BESPEEDING	BETHUMPING	BIBLIOLATER	BICAMERALISTS	BIGFOOTING
BESPITTING	BETHWACKED	BIBLIOLATERS	BICAPSULAR	BIGGETIEST
BESPORTING	BETHWACKING	BIBLIOLATRIES	BICARBONATE	BIGGITIEST
BESPOTTEDNESS	BETOKENING	BIBLIOLATRIST	BICARBONATES	BIGHEADEDLY
BESPOTTEDNESSES	BETREADING	BIBLIOLATRISTS	BICARPELLARY	BIGHEADEDNESS
BESPOTTING	BETRIMMING	BIBLIOLATROUS	BICENTENARIES	BIGHEADEDNESSES
BESPOUSING	BETROTHALS	BIBLIOLATRY	BICENTENARY	BIGHEARTED
BESPOUTING	BETROTHEDS	BIBLIOLOGICAL	BICENTENNIAL	BIGHEARTEDLY
BESPREADING	BETROTHING	BIBLIOLOGIES	BICENTENNIALS	BIGHEARTEDNESS
BESPRINKLE	BETROTHMENT	BIBLIOLOGIST	BICEPHALOUS	BIGMOUTHED
BESPRINKLED	BETROTHMENTS	BIBLIOLOGISTS	BICHLORIDE	BIGNONIACEOUS
BESPRINKLES	BETTERINGS	BIBLIOLOGY	BICHLORIDES	BIGUANIDES
BESPRINKLING	BETTERMENT	BIBLIOMANCIES	BICHROMATE	BIJECTIONS
BESTAINING	BETTERMENTS	BIBLIOMANCY	BICHROMATED	BIJOUTERIE
BESTARRING	BETTERMOST	BIBLIOMANE	BICHROMATES	BIJOUTERIES
BESTEADING	BETTERNESS	BIBLIOMANES	BICKERINGS	BILATERALISM
BESTIALISE	BETTERNESSES	BIBLIOMANIA	BICOLLATERAL	BILATERALISMS
BESTIALISED	BETULACEOUS	BIBLIOMANIAC	BICOLOURED	BILATERALLY

BILBERRIES
BILDUNGSROMAN
BILDUNGSROMANS
BILECTIONS
BILESTONES
BILGEWATER
BILGEWATERS
BILHARZIAL
BILHARZIAS
BILHARZIASES
BILHARZIASIS
BILHARZIOSES
BILHARZIOSIS
BILIMBINGS
BILINGUALISM
BILINGUALISMS
BILINGUALLY
BILINGUALS
BILINGUIST
BILINGUISTS
BILIOUSNESS
BILIOUSNESSES
BILIRUBINS
BILIVERDIN
BILIVERDINS
BILLABONGS
BILLBOARDED
BILLBOARDING
BILLBOARDS
BILLETINGS
BILLFISHES
BILLINGSGATE
BILLINGSGATES
BILLIONAIRE
BILLIONAIRES
BILLIONTHS
BILLOWIEST
BILLOWINESS
BILLOWINESSES
BILLOWINGS
BILLPOSTER
BILLPOSTERS
BILLPOSTING
BILLPOSTINGS
BILLSTICKER
BILLSTICKERS
BILLSTICKING
BILLSTICKINGS
BILLYCOCKS
BILOCATION
BILOCATIONS
BILOCULATE
BIMANUALLY
BIMATERNAL
BIMESTRIAL
BIMESTRIALLY
BIMETALLIC
BIMETALLICS
BIMETALLISM
BIMETALLISMS
BIMETALLIST
BIMETALLISTIC
BIMETALLISTS
BIMILLENARIES
BIMILLENARY
BIMILLENNIA
BIMILLENNIAL

BIMILLENNIALS
BIMILLENNIUM
BIMILLENNIUMS
BIMODALITIES
BIMODALITY
BIMOLECULAR
BIMOLECULARLY
BIMONTHLIES
BIMORPHEMIC
BINATIONAL
BINAURALLY
BINDINGNESS
BINDINGNESSES
BINOCULARITIES
BINOCULARITY
BINOCULARLY
BINOCULARS
BINOMIALLY
BINOMINALS
BINTURONGS
BINUCLEATE
BINUCLEATED
BIOACCUMULATE
BIOACCUMULATED
BIOACCUMULATES
BIOACCUMULATING
BIOACCUMULATION
BIOACOUSTICS
BIOACTIVITIES
BIOACTIVITY
BIOAERATION
BIOAERATIONS
BIOAERONAUTICS
BIOARCHAEOLOGY
BIOASSAYED
BIOASSAYING
BIOASTRONAUTICS
BIOASTRONOMIES
BIOASTRONOMY
BIOAVAILABILITY
BIOAVAILABLE
BIOBANKING
BIOBANKINGS
BIOCATALYST
BIOCATALYSTS
BIOCATALYTIC
BIOCELLATE
BIOCENOLOGIES
BIOCENOLOGY
BIOCENOSES
BIOCENOSIS
BIOCENOTIC
BIOCHEMICAL
BIOCHEMICALLY
BIOCHEMICALS
BIOCHEMIST
BIOCHEMISTRIES
BIOCHEMISTRY
BIOCHEMISTS
BIOCLASTIC
BIOCLIMATIC
BIOCLIMATOLOGY
BIOCOENOLOGIES
BIOCOENOLOGY
BIOCOENOSES
BIOCOENOSIS
BIOCOENOTIC

BIOCOMPATIBLE
BIOCOMPUTING
BIOCOMPUTINGS
BIOCONTROL
BIOCONTROLS
BIOCONVERSION
BIOCONVERSIONS
BIODEGRADABLE
BIODEGRADABLES
BIODEGRADATION
BIODEGRADATIONS
BIODEGRADE
BIODEGRADED
BIODEGRADES
BIODEGRADING
BIODESTRUCTIBLE
BIODIESELS
BIODIVERSE
BIODIVERSITIES
BIODIVERSITY
BIODYNAMIC
BIODYNAMICAL
BIODYNAMICS
BIOECOLOGICAL
BIOECOLOGICALLY
BIOECOLOGIES
BIOECOLOGIST
BIOECOLOGISTS
BIOECOLOGY
BIOELECTRIC
BIOELECTRICAL
BIOELECTRICITY
BIOENERGETIC
BIOENERGETICS
BIOENERGIES
BIOENGINEER
BIOENGINEERED
BIOENGINEERING
BIOENGINEERINGS
BIOENGINEERS
BIOETHANOL
BIOETHANOLS
BIOETHICAL
BIOETHICIST
BIOETHICISTS
BIOFEEDBACK
BIOFEEDBACKS
BIOFLAVONOID
BIOFLAVONOIDS
BIOFOULERS
BIOFOULING
BIOFOULINGS
BIOFUELLED
BIOGENESES
BIOGENESIS
BIOGENETIC
BIOGENETICAL
BIOGENETICALLY
BIOGENETICS
BIOGEOCHEMICAL
BIOGEOCHEMICALS
BIOGEOCHEMISTRY
BIOGEOGRAPHER
BIOGEOGRAPHERS
BIOGEOGRAPHIC
BIOGEOGRAPHICAL
BIOGEOGRAPHIES

BIOGEOGRAPHY
BIOGRAPHED
BIOGRAPHEE
BIOGRAPHEES
BIOGRAPHER
BIOGRAPHERS
BIOGRAPHIC
BIOGRAPHICAL
BIOGRAPHICALLY
BIOGRAPHIES
BIOGRAPHING
BIOGRAPHISE
BIOGRAPHISED
BIOGRAPHISES
BIOGRAPHISING
BIOGRAPHIZE
BIOGRAPHIZED
BIOGRAPHIZES
BIOGRAPHIZING
BIOHACKERS
BIOHAZARDOUS
BIOHAZARDS
BIOINDUSTRIES
BIOINDUSTRY
BIOINFORMATICS
BIOLOGICAL
BIOLOGICALLY
BIOLOGICALS
BIOLOGISMS
BIOLOGISTIC
BIOLOGISTS
BIOLUMINESCENCE
BIOLUMINESCENT
BIOMAGNETICS
BIOMARKERS
BIOMATERIAL
BIOMATERIALS
BIOMATHEMATICAL
BIOMATHEMATICS
BIOMECHANICAL
BIOMECHANICALLY
BIOMECHANICS
BIOMEDICAL
BIOMEDICINE
BIOMEDICINES
BIOMETEOROLOGY
BIOMETRICAL
BIOMETRICALLY
BIOMETRICIAN
BIOMETRICIANS
BIOMETRICS
BIOMETRIES
BIOMIMETIC
BIOMIMETICS
BIOMIMICRIES
BIOMIMICRY
BIOMININGS
BIOMOLECULAR
BIOMOLECULE
BIOMOLECULES
BIOMORPHIC
BIONOMICALLY
BIONOMISTS
BIOPARENTS
BIOPESTICIDAL
BIOPESTICIDE
BIOPESTICIDES

BIOPHILIAS
BIOPHYSICAL
BIOPHYSICALLY
BIOPHYSICIST
BIOPHYSICISTS
BIOPHYSICS
BIOPIRACIES
BIOPIRATES
BIOPLASMIC
BIOPLASTIC
BIOPLASTICS
BIOPOIESES
BIOPOIESIS
BIOPOLYMER
BIOPOLYMERS
BIOPRINTING
BIOPRINTINGS
BIOPRIVACIES
BIOPRIVACY
BIOPROSPECTING
BIOPROSPECTINGS
BIOPSYCHOLOGIES
BIOPSYCHOLOGY
BIOREACTOR
BIOREACTORS
BIOREAGENT
BIOREAGENTS
BIOREGIONAL
BIOREGIONALISM
BIOREGIONALISMS
BIOREGIONALIST
BIOREGIONALISTS
BIOREGIONS
BIOREMEDIATION
BIOREMEDIATIONS
BIORHYTHMIC
BIORHYTHMICALLY
BIORHYTHMICS
BIORHYTHMS
BIOSAFETIES
BIOSATELLITE
BIOSATELLITES
BIOSCIENCE
BIOSCIENCES
BIOSCIENTIFIC
BIOSCIENTIST
BIOSCIENTISTS
BIOSCOPIES
BIOSENSORS
BIOSOCIALLY
BIOSPHERES
BIOSPHERIC
BIOSTATICALLY
BIOSTATICS
BIOSTATISTICAL
BIOSTATISTICIAN
BIOSTATISTICS
BIOSTRATIGRAPHY
BIOSTROMES
BIOSURGERIES
BIOSURGERY
BIOSYNTHESES
BIOSYNTHESIS
BIOSYNTHETIC
BIOSYSTEMATIC
BIOSYSTEMATICS
BIOSYSTEMATIST

BIOSYSTEMATISTS	BIRDDOGGINGS	BISYMMETRIC	BIZARRERIE	BLACKLISTED
BIOTECHNICAL	BIRDHOUSES	BISYMMETRICAL	BIZARRERIES	BLACKLISTER
BIOTECHNOLOGIES	BIRDLIMING	BISYMMETRICALLY	BLABBERING	BLACKLISTERS
BIOTECHNOLOGIST	RIRDSFOOTS	BISYMMETRIES	BLABBERMOUTH	BLACKLISTING
BIOTECHNOLOGY	BIRDWATCHED	BISYMMETRY	BLABBERMOUTHS	BLACKLISTINGS
BIOTELEMETRIC	BIRDWATCHER	BITARTRATE	BLACKAMOOR	BLACKLISTS
BIOTELEMETRIES	BIRDWATCHERS	BITARTRATES	BLACKAMOORS	BLACKMAILED
BIOTELEMETRY	BIRDWATCHES	BITCHERIES	BLACKBALLED	BLACKMAILER
BIOTERRORS	BIRDWATCHING	BITCHFESTS	BLACKBALLING	BLACKMAILERS
BIOTICALLY	BIRDWATCHINGS	BITCHINESS	BLACKBALLINGS	BLACKMAILING
BIOTURBATION	BIREFRINGENCE	BITCHINESSES	BLACKBALLS	BLACKMAILS
BIOTURBATIONS	BIREFRINGENCES	BITEPLATES	BLACKBANDS	BLACKNESSES
BIOWEAPONS	BIREFRINGENT	BITMAPPING	BLACKBERRIED	BLACKPOLLS
BIPARENTAL	BIROSTRATE	BITONALITIES	BLACKBERRIES	BLACKSMITH
BIPARENTALLY	BIRTHDATES	BITONALITY	BLACKBERRY	BLACKSMITHING
BIPARIETAL	BIRTHMARKS	BITSTREAMS	BLACKBERRYING	BLACKSMITHINGS
BIPARTISAN	BIRTHNAMES	BITTERBARK	BLACKBERRYINGS	BLACKSMITHS
BIPARTISANISM	BIRTHNIGHT	BITTERBARKS	BLACKBIRDED	BLACKSNAKE
BIPARTISANISMS	BIRTHNIGHTS	BITTERBRUSH	BLACKBIRDER	BLACKSNAKES
BIPARTISANSHIP	BIRTHPLACE	BITTERBRUSHES	BLACKBIRDERS	BLACKSPOTS
BIPARTISANSHIPS	BIRTHPLACES	BITTERCRESS	BLACKBIRDING	BLACKSTRAP
BIPARTITELY	BIRTHRATES	BITTERCRESSES	BLACKBIRDINGS	BLACKSTRAPS
BIPARTITION	BIRTHRIGHT	BITTERLING	BLACKBIRDS	BLACKTHORN
BIPARTITIONS	BIRTHRIGHTS	BITTERLINGS	BLACKBOARD	BLACKTHORNS
BIPEDALISM	BIRTHROOTS	BITTERNESS	BLACKBOARDS	BLACKTOPPED
BIPEDALISMS	BIRTHSTONE	BITTERNESSES	BLACKBODIES	BLACKTOPPING
BIPEDALITIES	BIRTHSTONES	BITTERNUTS	BLACKBUCKS	BLACKWASHED
BIPEDALITY	BIRTHWORTS	BITTERROOT	BLACKBUTTS	BLACKWASHES
BIPETALOUS	BISCUITIER	BITTERROOTS	BLACKCOCKS	BLACKWASHING
BIPINNARIA	BISCUITIEST	BITTERSWEET	BLACKCURRANT	BLACKWATER
BIPINNARIAS	BISECTIONAL	BITTERSWEETLY	BLACKCURRANTS	BLACKWATERS
BIPINNATELY	BISECTIONALLY	BITTERSWEETNESS	BLACKDAMPS	BLACKWOODS
BIPOLARISATION	BISECTIONS	BITTERSWEETS	BLACKENERS	BLADDERIER
BIPOLARISATIONS	BISECTRICES	BITTERWEED	BLACKENING	BLADDERIEST
BIPOLARISE	BISEXUALISM	BITTERWEEDS	BLACKENINGS	BLADDERLIKE
BIPOLARISED	BISEXUALISMS	BITTERWOOD	BLACKFACED	BLADDERNOSE
BIPOLARISES	BISEXUALITIES	BITTERWOODS	BLACKFACES	BLADDERNOSES
BIPOLARISING	BISEXUALITY	BITTINESSES	BLACKFELLA	BLADDERNUT
BIPOLARITIES	BISEXUALLY	BITUMINATE	BLACKFELLAS	BLADDERNUTS
BIPOLARITY	BISHOPBIRD	BITUMINATED	BLACKFISHES	BLADDERWORT
BIPOLARIZATION	BISHOPBIRDS	BITUMINATES	BLACKFLIES	BLADDERWORTS
BIPOLARIZATIONS	BISHOPDOMS	BITUMINATING	BLACKGAMES	BLADDERWRACK
BIPOLARIZE	BISHOPESSES	BITUMINISATION	BLACKGUARD	BLADDERWRACKS
BIPOLARIZED	BISHOPRICS	BITUMINISATIONS	BLACKGUARDED	BLADEWORKS
BIPOLARIZES	BISHOPWEED	BITUMINISE	BLACKGUARDING	BLAEBERRIES
BIPOLARIZING	BISHOPWEEDS	BITUMINISED	BLACKGUARDISM	BLAMABLENESS
BIPROPELLANT	BISMUTHINITE	BITUMINISES	BLACKGUARDISMS	BLAMABLENESSES
BIPROPELLANTS	BISMUTHINITES	BITUMINISING	BLACKGUARDLIER	BLAMEABLENESS
BIPYRAMIDAL	BISMUTHOUS	BITUMINIZATION	BLACKGUARDLIEST	BLAMEABLENESSES
BIPYRAMIDS	BISOCIATION	BITUMINIZATIONS	BLACKGUARDLY	BLAMEFULLY
BIQUADRATE	BISOCIATIONS	BITUMINIZE	BLACKGUARDS	BLAMEFULNESS
BIQUADRATES	BISOCIATIVE	BITUMINIZED	BLACKHANDER	BLAMEFULNESSES
BIQUADRATIC	BISPHENOLS	BITUMINIZES	BLACKHANDERS	BLAMELESSLY
BIQUADRATICS	BISPHOSPHONATE	BITUMINIZING	BLACKHEADED	BLAMELESSNESS
BIQUARTERLY	BISPHOSPHONATES	BITUMINOUS	BLACKHEADS	BLAMELESSNESSES
BIQUINTILE	BISSEXTILE	BIUNIQUENESS	BLACKHEART	BLAMESTORM
BIQUINTILES	BISSEXTILES	BIUNIQUENESSES	BLACKHEARTS	BLAMESTORMED
BIRACIALISM	BISTOURIES	BIVALENCES	BLACKISHLY	BLAMESTORMING
BIRACIALISMS	BISULFATES	BIVALENCIES	BLACKJACKED	BLAMESTORMINGS
BIRACIALLY	BISULFIDES	BIVALVULAR	BLACKJACKING	BLAMESTORMS
BIRADICALS	BISULFITES	BIVARIANTS	BLACKJACKS	BLAMEWORTHIER
BIRCHBARKS	BISULPHATE	BIVARIATES	BLACKLANDS	BLAMEWORTHIEST
BIRCHWOODS	BISULPHATES	BIVOUACKED	BLACKLEADED	BLAMEWORTHINESS
BIRDBRAINED	BISULPHIDE	BIVOUACKING	BLACKLEADING	BLAMEWORTHY
BIRDBRAINS	BISULPHIDES	BIWEEKLIES	BLACKLEADS	BLANCHISSEUSE
BIRDDOGGED	BISULPHITE	BIZARRENESS	BLACKLEGGED	BLANCHISSEUSES
BIRDDOGGING	BISULPHITES	BIZARRENESSES	BLACKLEGGING	

BLANCMANGE
BLANCMANGES
BLANDISHED
BLANDISHER
BLANDISHERS
BLANDISHES
BLANDISHING
BLANDISHMENT
BLANDISHMENTS
BLANDNESSES
BLANKETFLOWER
BLANKETFLOWERS
BLANKETIES
BLANKETING
BLANKETINGS
BLANKETLIKE
BLANKETWEED
BLANKETWEEDS
BLANKNESSES
BLANQUETTE
BLANQUETTES
BLARNEYING
BLASPHEMED
BLASPHEMER
BLASPHEMERS
BLASPHEMES
BLASPHEMIES
BLASPHEMING
BLASPHEMOUS
BLASPHEMOUSLY
BLASPHEMOUSNESS
BLASTEMATA
BLASTEMATIC
BLASTHOLES
BLASTMENTS
BLASTOCHYLE
BLASTOCHYLES
BLASTOCOEL
BLASTOCOELE
BLASTOCOELES
BLASTOCOELIC
BLASTOCOELS
BLASTOCYST
BLASTOCYSTS
BLASTODERM
BLASTODERMIC
BLASTODERMS
BLASTODISC
BLASTODISCS
BLASTOGENESES
BLASTOGENESIS
BLASTOGENETIC
BLASTOGENIC
BLASTOMATA
BLASTOMERE
BLASTOMERES
BLASTOMERIC
BLASTOMYCOSES
BLASTOMYCOSIS
BLASTOPORAL
BLASTOPORE
BLASTOPORES
BLASTOPORIC
BLASTOPORS
BLASTOSPHERE
BLASTOSPHERES
BLASTOSPORE

BLASTOSPORES
BLASTULATION
BLASTULATIONS
BLATANCIES
BLATHERERS
BLATHERING
BLATHERINGS
BLATHERSKITE
BLATHERSKITES
BLATTERING
BLAXPLOITATION
BLAXPLOITATIONS
BLAZONINGS
BLAZONRIES
BLEACHABLE
BLEACHERIES
BLEACHERITE
BLEACHERITES
BLEACHINGS
BLEAKNESSES
BLEARINESS
BLEARINESSES
BLEMISHERS
BLEMISHING
BLEMISHMENT
BLEMISHMENTS
BLENNIOIDS
BLENNORRHEA
BLENNORRHEAS
BLENNORRHOEA
BLENNORRHOEAS
BLEOMYCINS
BLEPHARISM
BLEPHARISMS
BLEPHARITIC
BLEPHARITIS
BLEPHARITISES
BLEPHAROPLAST
BLEPHAROPLASTS
BLEPHAROPLASTY
BLEPHAROSPASM
BLEPHAROSPASMS
BLESSEDEST
BLESSEDNESS
BLESSEDNESSES
BLETHERANSKATE
BLETHERANSKATES
BLETHERATION
BLETHERATIONS
BLETHERERS
BLETHERING
BLETHERINGS
BLETHERSKATE
BLETHERSKATES
BLIGHTINGLY
BLIGHTINGS
BLIMPERIES
BLIMPISHLY
BLIMPISHNESS
BLIMPISHNESSES
BLINDFISHES
BLINDFOLDED
BLINDFOLDING
BLINDFOLDS
BLINDINGLY
BLINDNESSES
BLINDSIDED

BLINDSIDES
BLINDSIDING
BLINDSIGHT
BLINDSIGHTS
BLINDSTOREY
BLINDSTOREYS
BLINDSTORIES
BLINDSTORY
BLINDWORMS
BLINGLISHES
BLINKERING
BLISSFULLY
BLISSFULNESS
BLISSFULNESSES
BLISTERIER
BLISTERIEST
BLISTERING
BLISTERINGLY
BLITHENESS
BLITHENESSES
BLITHERING
BLITHESOME
BLITHESOMELY
BLITHESOMENESS
BLITZKRIEG
BLITZKRIEGS
BLIZZARDED
BLIZZARDIER
BLIZZARDIEST
BLIZZARDING
BLIZZARDLY
BLOATEDNESS
BLOATEDNESSES
BLOATWARES
BLOCKADERS
BLOCKADING
BLOCKBOARD
BLOCKBOARDS
BLOCKBUSTED
BLOCKBUSTER
BLOCKBUSTERS
BLOCKBUSTING
BLOCKBUSTINGS
BLOCKBUSTS
BLOCKCHAIN
BLOCKCHAINS
BLOCKHEADED
BLOCKHEADEDLY
BLOCKHEADEDNESS
BLOCKHEADS
BLOCKHOLES
BLOCKHOUSE
BLOCKHOUSES
BLOCKINESS
BLOCKINESSES
BLOCKISHLY
BLOCKISHNESS
BLOCKISHNESSES
BLOCKSHIPS
BLOCKWORKS
BLOGGERATI
BLOGJACKING
BLOGJACKINGS
BLOGOSPHERE
BLOGOSPHERES
BLOGSTREAM
BLOGSTREAMS

BLOKARTING
BLOKARTINGS
BLOKEISHNESS
BLOKEISHNESSES
BLOKISHNESS
BLOKISHNESSES
BLONDENESS
BLONDENESSES
BLONDINING
BLONDNESSES
BLOODBATHS
BLOODCURDLING
BLOODCURDLINGLY
BLOODGUILT
BLOODGUILTIER
BLOODGUILTIEST
BLOODGUILTINESS
BLOODGUILTS
BLOODGUILTY
BLOODHOUND
BLOODHOUNDS
BLOODINESS
BLOODINESSES
BLOODLESSLY
BLOODLESSNESS
BLOODLESSNESSES
BLOODLETTER
BLOODLETTERS
BLOODLETTING
BLOODLETTINGS
BLOODLINES
BLOODLUSTS
BLOODMOBILE
BLOODMOBILES
BLOODROOTS
BLOODSHEDS
BLOODSPRENT
BLOODSTAIN
BLOODSTAINED
BLOODSTAINS
BLOODSTOCK
BLOODSTOCKS
BLOODSTONE
BLOODSTONES
BLOODSTREAM
BLOODSTREAMS
BLOODSUCKER
BLOODSUCKERS
BLOODSUCKING
BLOODTHIRSTIER
BLOODTHIRSTIEST
BLOODTHIRSTILY
BLOODTHIRSTY
BLOODWOODS
BLOODWORMS
BLOODWORTS
BLOOMERIES
BLOQUISTES
BLOSSOMIER
BLOSSOMIEST
BLOSSOMING
BLOSSOMINGS
BLOSSOMLESS
BLOTCHIEST
BLOTCHINESS
BLOTCHINESSES
BLOTCHINGS

BLOTTESQUE
BLOTTESQUES
BLOVIATING
BLOVIATION
BLOVIATIONS
BLOWFISHES
BLOWINESSES
BLOWSINESS
BLOWSINESSES
BLOWTORCHED
BLOWTORCHES
BLOWTORCHING
BLOWZINESS
BLOWZINESSES
BLUBBERERS
BLUBBERIER
BLUBBERIEST
BLUBBERING
BLUDGEONED
BLUDGEONER
BLUDGEONERS
BLUDGEONING
BLUEBEARDS
BLUEBERRIES
BLUEBLOODS
BLUEBONNET
BLUEBONNETS
BLUEBOTTLE
BLUEBOTTLES
BLUEBREAST
BLUEBREASTS
BLUEBUSHES
BLUEFISHES
BLUEGRASSES
BLUEISHNESS
BLUEISHNESSES
BLUEJACKET
BLUEJACKETS
BLUEJACKING
BLUEJACKINGS
BLUELINERS
BLUEMOUTHS
BLUENESSES
BLUEPOINTS
BLUEPRINTED
BLUEPRINTING
BLUEPRINTS
BLUESHIFTED
BLUESHIFTS
BLUESNARFING
BLUESNARFINGS
BLUESTOCKING
BLUESTOCKINGS
BLUESTONES
BLUETHROAT
BLUETHROATS
BLUETONGUE
BLUETONGUES
BLUFFNESSES
BLUISHNESS
BLUISHNESSES
BLUNDERBUSS
BLUNDERBUSSES
BLUNDERERS
BLUNDERING
BLUNDERINGLY
BLUNDERINGS

b

BLUNTHEADS	BODYBOARDED	BOLOMETERS	BONESETTER	BOOSTERISH
BLUNTNESSES	BODYBOARDING	BOLOMETRIC	BONESETTERS	BOOSTERISM
BLURREDNESS	BODYBOARDINGS	BOLOMETRICALLY	BONESHAKER	BOOSTERISMS
BLURREDNESSES	BODYBOARDS	BOLOMETRIES	BONESHAKERS	BOOTBLACKS
BLURRINESS	BODYBUILDER	BOLSHEVIKI	BONHOMMIES	BOOTLEGGED
BLURRINESSES	BODYBUILDERS	BOLSHEVIKS	BONILASSES	BOOTLEGGER
BLURRINGLY	BODYBUILDING	BOLSHEVISE	BONINESSES	BOOTLEGGERS
BLUSHINGLY	BODYBUILDINGS	BOLSHEVISED	BONKBUSTER	BOOTLEGGING
BLUSHLESSLY	BODYBUILDS	BOLSHEVISES	BONKBUSTERS	BOOTLEGGINGS
BLUSTERERS	BODYCHECKED	BOLSHEVISING	BONNIBELLS	BOOTLESSLY
BLUSTERIER	BODYCHECKING	BOLSHEVISM	BONNILASSE	BOOTLESSNESS
BLUSTERIEST	BODYCHECKS	BOLSHEVISMS	BONNILASSES	BOOTLESSNESSES
BLUSTERING	BODYGUARDED	BOLSHEVIZE	BONNINESSES	BOOTLICKED
BLUSTERINGLY	BODYGUARDING	BOLSHEVIZED	BONNYCLABBER	BOOTLICKER
BLUSTERINGS	BODYGUARDS	BOLSHEVIZES	BONNYCLABBERS	BOOTLICKERS
BLUSTEROUS	BODYSHAPER	BOLSHEVIZING	BOOBIALLAS	BOOTLICKING
BLUSTEROUSLY	BODYSHAPERS	BOLSTERERS	BOOBOISIES	BOOTLICKINGS
BLUTWURSTS	BODYSHELLS	BOLSTERING	BOOGALOOED	BOOTLOADER
BOARDINGHOUSE	BODYSNATCHER	BOLSTERINGS	BOOGALOOING	BOOTLOADERS
BOARDINGHOUSES	BODYSNATCHERS	BOMBACACEOUS	BOOKBINDER	BOOTMAKERS
BOARDROOMS	BODYSURFED	BOMBARDERS	BOOKBINDERIES	BOOTMAKING
BOARDSAILING	BODYSURFER	BOMBARDIER	BOOKBINDERS	BOOTMAKINGS
BOARDSAILINGS	BODYSURFERS	BOMBARDIERS	BOOKBINDERY	BOOTSTRAPPED
BOARDSAILOR	BODYSURFING	BOMBARDING	BOOKBINDING	BOOTSTRAPPING
BOARDSAILORS	BODYSURFINGS	BOMBARDMENT	BOOKBINDINGS	BOOTSTRAPS
BOARDWALKS	BODYWASHES	BOMBARDMENTS	BOOKCROSSING	BOOTYLICIOUS
BOARFISHES	BODYWORKER	BOMBARDONS	BOOKCROSSINGS	BOOZEHOUND
BOARHOUNDS	BODYWORKERS	BOMBASINES	BOOKENDING	BOOZEHOUNDS
BOARISHNESS	BOEREMUSIEK	BOMBASTERS	BOOKISHNESS	BOOZINESSES
BOARISHNESSES	BOEREMUSIEKS	BOMBASTICALLY	BOOKISHNESSES	BORAGINACEOUS
BOASTFULLY	BOEREWORSES	BOMBASTING	BOOKKEEPER	BORBORYGMAL
BOASTFULNESS	BOFFINIEST	BOMBAZINES	BOOKKEEPERS	BORBORYGMI
BOASTFULNESSES	BOGGINESSES	BOMBILATED	BOOKKEEPING	BORBORYGMIC
BOASTINGLY	BOGTROTTER	BOMBILATES	BOOKKEEPINGS	BORBORYGMUS
BOATBUILDER	BOGTROTTERS	BOMBILATING	BOOKLIGHTS	BORDEREAUX
BOATBUILDERS	BOGTROTTING	BOMBILATION	BOOKMAKERS	BORDERLAND
BOATBUILDING	BOGTROTTINGS	BOMBILATIONS	BOOKMAKING	BORDERLANDS
BOATBUILDINGS	BOGUSNESSES	BOMBINATED	BOOKMAKINGS	BORDERLESS
BOATHOUSES	BOHEMIANISM	BOMBINATES	BOOKMARKED	BORDERLINE
BOATLIFTED	BOHEMIANISMS	BOMBINATING	BOOKMARKER	BORDERLINES
BOATLIFTING	BOILERMAKER	BOMBINATION	BOOKMARKERS	BORDRAGING
BOATSWAINS	BOILERMAKERS	BOMBINATIONS	BOOKMARKING	BORDRAGINGS
BOBBEJAANS	BOILERMAKING	BOMBPROOFED	BOOKMOBILE	BORESCOPES
BOBBITTING	BOILERMAKINGS	BOMBPROOFING	BOOKMOBILES	BORGHETTOS
BOBBLEHEAD	BOILERPLATE	BOMBPROOFS	BOOKPLATES	BORINGNESS
BOBBLEHEADS	BOILERPLATED	BOMBSHELLS	BOOKSELLER	BORINGNESSES
BOBBYSOCKS	BOILERPLATES	BOMBSIGHTS	BOOKSELLERS	BOROHYDRIDE
BOBBYSOXER	BOILERPLATING	BONAMIASES	BOOKSELLING	BOROHYDRIDES
BOBBYSOXERS	BOILERSUIT	BONAMIASIS	BOOKSELLINGS	BOROSILICATE
BOBSLEDDED	BOILERSUITS	BONASSUSES	BOOKSHELVES	BOROSILICATES
BOBSLEDDER	BOISTEROUS	BONBONNIERE	BOOKSTALLS	BORROWINGS
BOBSLEDDERS	BOISTEROUSLY	BONBONNIERES	BOOKSTANDS	BOSBERAADS
BOBSLEDDING	BOISTEROUSNESS	BONDHOLDER	BOOKSTORES	BOSCHVARKS
BOBSLEDDINGS	BOKMAKIERIE	BONDHOLDERS	BOOMERANGED	BOSCHVELDS
BOBSLEIGHED	BOKMAKIERIES	BONDMANSHIP	BOOMERANGING	BOSKINESSES
BOBSLEIGHING	BOLDFACING	BONDMANSHIPS	BOOMERANGS	BOSSINESSES
BOBSLEIGHINGS	BOLDNESSES	BONDSERVANT	BOOMSLANGS	BOSSNAPPING
BOBSLEIGHS	BOLECTIONS	BONDSERVANTS	BOOMSTICKS	BOSSNAPPINGS
BOBTAILING	BOLIVIANOS	BONDSTONES	BOONDOGGLE	BOSSYBOOTS
BOBWEIGHTS	BOLLETRIES	BONDSWOMAN	BOONDOGGLED	BOTANICALLY
BOCCONCINI	BOLLOCKING	BONDSWOMEN	BOONDOGGLER	BOTANICALS
BODACIOUSLY	BOLLOCKINGS	BONEBLACKS	BOONDOGGLERS	BOTANISERS
BODDHISATTVA	BOLLOCKSED	BONEFISHES	BOONDOGGLES	BOTANISING
BODDHISATTVAS	BOLLOCKSES	BONEFISHING	BOONDOGGLING	BOTANIZERS
BODEGUEROS	BOLLOCKSING	BONEFISHINGS	BOONGARIES	BOTANIZING
BODHISATTVA	BOLOGNESES	BONEHEADED	BOORISHNESS	BOTANOMANCIES
BODHISATTVAS	BOLOGRAPHS	BONEHEADEDNESS	BOORISHNESSES	BOTANOMANCY

BOTCHERIES	BOUNTIFULLY	BOXKEEPERS	BRACKETINGS	BRAINWASHERS
BOTCHINESS	BOUNTIFULNESS	BOXWALLAHS	BRACKISHNESS	BRAINWASHES
BOTCHINESSES	BOUNTIFULNESSES	BOYCOTTERS	BRACKISHNESSES	BRAINWASHING
BOTHERATION	BOUNTYHEDS	BOYCOTTING	BRACTEATES	BRAINWASHINGS
BOTHERATIONS	BOUQUETIERE	BOYFRIENDS	BRACTEOLATE	BRAINWAVES
BOTHERSOME	BOUQUETIERES	BOYISHNESS	BRACTEOLES	BRAINWORKS
BOTRYOIDAL	BOURASQUES	BOYISHNESSES	BRADYCARDIA	BRAMBLIEST
BOTRYTISES	BOURBONISM	BOYSENBERRIES	BRADYCARDIAC	BRAMBLINGS
BOTTLEBRUSH	BOURBONISMS	BOYSENBERRY	BRADYCARDIAS	BRANCHERIES
BOTTLEBRUSHES	BOURGEOISE	BRAAIVLEIS	BRADYKINESIA	BRANCHIATE
BOTTLEFULS	BOURGEOISES	BRAAIVLEISES	BRADYKINESIAS	BRANCHIEST
BOTTLENECK	BOURGEOISIE	BRABBLEMENT	BRADYKININ	BRANCHINGS
BOTTLENECKED	BOURGEOISIES	BRABBLEMENTS	BRADYKININS	BRANCHIOPOD
BOTTLENECKING	BOURGEOISIFIED	BRACHIATED	BRADYPEPTIC	BRANCHIOPODS
BOTTLENECKS	BOURGEOISIFIES	BRACHIATES	BRADYPEPTICS	BRANCHIOSTEGAL
BOTTLENOSE	BOURGEOISIFY	BRACHIATING	BRADYSEISM	BRANCHLESS
BOTTLENOSES	BOURGEOISIFYING	BRACHIATION	BRADYSEISMS	BRANCHLETS
BOTTOMINGS	BOURGEONED	BRACHIATIONS	BRAGADISME	BRANCHLIKE
BOTTOMLAND	BOURGEONING	BRACHIATOR	BRAGADISMES	BRANCHLINE
BOTTOMLANDS	BOURGUIGNON	BRACHIATORS	BRAGGADOCIO	BRANCHLINES
BOTTOMLESS	BOURGUIGNONNE	BRACHIOCEPHALIC	BRAGGADOCIOS	BRANDERING
BOTTOMLESSLY	BOURGUIGNONNES	BRACHIOPOD	BRAGGADOCIOUS	BRANDISHED
BOTTOMLESSNESS	BOURGUIGNONS	BRACHIOPODS	BRAGGARTISM	BRANDISHER
BOTTOMMOST	BOUSINGKEN	BRACHIOSAURUS	BRAGGARTISMS	BRANDISHERS
BOTTOMNESS	BOUSINGKENS	BRACHIOSAURUSES	BRAGGARTLIER	BRANDISHES
BOTTOMNESSES	BOUSTROPHEDON	BRACHISTOCHRONE	BRAGGARTLIEST	BRANDISHING
BOTTOMRIES	BOUSTROPHEDONIC	BRACHYAXES	BRAGGARTLY	BRANDLINGS
BOTULINUMS	BOUSTROPHEDONS	BRACHYAXIS	BRAGGINGLY	BRANDRETHS
BOTULINUSES	BOUTIQUIER	BRACHYCEPHAL	BRAHMANISM	BRANFULNESS
BOUGAINVILIA	BOUTIQUIEST	BRACHYCEPHALIC	BRAHMANISMS	BRANFULNESSES
BOUGAINVILIAS	BOUTONNIERE	BRACHYCEPHALICS	BRAHMANIST	BRANGLINGS
BOUGAINVILLAEA	BOUTONNIERES	BRACHYCEPHALIES	BRAHMANISTS	BRANKURSINE
BOUGAINVILLAEAS	BOUVARDIAS	BRACHYCEPHALISM	BRAHMINISM	BRANKURSINES
BOUGAINVILLEA	BOVINITIES	BRACHYCEPHALOUS	BRAHMINISMS	BRANNIGANS
BOUGAINVILLEAS	BOWDLERISATION	BRACHYCEPHALS	BRAHMINIST	BRASHINESS
BOUILLABAISSE	BOWDLERISATIONS	BRACHYCEPHALY	BRAHMINISTS	BRASHINESSES
BOUILLABAISSES	BOWDLERISE	BRACHYCEROUS	BRAILLEWRITER	BRASHNESSES
BOUILLOTTE	BOWDLERISED	BRACHYDACTYL	BRAILLEWRITERS	BRASILEINS
BOUILLOTTES	BOWDLERISER	BRACHYDACTYLIC	BRAILLISTS	BRASSBOUND
BOULDERERS	BOWDLERISERS	BRACHYDACTYLIES	BRAINBOXES	BRASSERIES
BOULDERIER	BOWDLERISES	BRACHYDACTYLISM	BRAINCASES	BRASSFOUNDER
BOULDERIEST	BOWDLERISING	BRACHYDACTYLOUS	BRAINCHILD	BRASSFOUNDERS
BOULDERING	BOWDLERISM	BRACHYDACTYLY	BRAINCHILDREN	BRASSFOUNDING
BOULDERINGS	BOWDLERISMS	BRACHYDIAGONAL	BRAINFARTS	BRASSFOUNDINGS
BOULEVARDIER	BOWDLERIZATION	BRACHYDIAGONALS	BRAINFOODS	BRASSICACEOUS
BOULEVARDIERS	BOWDLERIZATIONS	BRACHYDOME	BRAININESS	BRASSIERES
BOULEVARDS	BOWDLERIZE	BRACHYDOMES	BRAININESSES	BRASSINESS
BOULEVERSEMENT	BOWDLERIZED	BRACHYGRAPHIES	BRAINLESSLY	BRASSINESSES
BOULEVERSEMENTS	BOWDLERIZER	BRACHYGRAPHY	BRAINLESSNESS	BRASSWARES
BOULLEWORK	BOWDLERIZERS	BRACHYLOGIES	BRAINLESSNESSES	BRATPACKER
BOULLEWORKS	BOWDLERIZES	BRACHYLOGOUS	BRAINPOWER	BRATPACKERS
BOUNCEDOWN	BOWDLERIZING	BRACHYLOGY	BRAINPOWERS	BRATTICING
BOUNCEDOWNS	BOWERBIRDS	BRACHYODONT	BRAINSICKLY	BRATTICINGS
BOUNCINESS	BOWERWOMAN	BRACHYPINAKOID	BRAINSICKNESS	BRATTINESS
BOUNCINESSES	BOWERWOMEN	BRACHYPINAKOIDS	BRAINSICKNESSES	BRATTINESSES
BOUNCINGLY	BOWHUNTERS	BRACHYPRISM	BRAINSTEMS	BRATTISHED
BOUNDARIES	BOWHUNTING	BRACHYPRISMS	BRAINSTORM	BRATTISHES
BOUNDEDNESS	BOWHUNTINGS	BRACHYPTERISM	BRAINSTORMED	BRATTISHING
BOUNDEDNESSES	BOWLINGUAL	BRACHYPTERISMS	BRAINSTORMER	BRATTISHINGS
BOUNDERISH	BOWLINGUALS	BRACHYPTEROUS	BRAINSTORMERS	BRATTLINGS
BOUNDLESSLY	BOWSTRINGED	BRACHYTHERAPIES	BRAINSTORMING	BRATWURSTS
BOUNDLESSNESS	BOWSTRINGING	BRACHYTHERAPY	BRAINSTORMINGS	BRAUNCHING
BOUNDLESSNESSES	BOWSTRINGS	BRACHYURAL	BRAINSTORMS	BRAUNSCHWEIGER
BOUNDNESSES	BOXBERRIES	BRACHYURAN	BRAINTEASER	BRAUNSCHWEIGERS
BOUNTEOUSLY	BOXERCISES	BRACHYURANS	BRAINTEASERS	BRAVADOING
BOUNTEOUSNESS	BOXHAULING	BRACHYUROUS	BRAINWASHED	BRAVENESSES
BOUNTEOUSNESSES	BOXINESSES	BRACKETING	BRAINWASHER	BRAVISSIMO

BRAWNINESS
BRAWNINESSES
BRAZENNESS
BRAZENNESSES
BRAZENRIES
BRAZIERIES
BRAZILEINS
BRAZILWOOD
BRAZILWOODS
BREADBASKET
BREADBASKETS
BREADBERRIES
BREADBERRY
BREADBOARD
BREADBOARDED
BREADBOARDING
BREADBOARDS
BREADBOXES
BREADCRUMB
BREADCRUMBED
BREADCRUMBING
BREADCRUMBS
BREADFRUIT
BREADFRUITS
BREADHEADS
BREADKNIFE
BREADKNIVES
BREADLINES
BREADROOMS
BREADROOTS
BREADSTICK
BREADSTICKS
BREADSTUFF
BREADSTUFFS
BREADTHWAYS
BREADTHWISE
BREADWINNER
BREADWINNERS
BREADWINNING
BREADWINNINGS
BREAKABLENESS
BREAKABLENESSES
BREAKABLES
BREAKAWAYS
BREAKBEATS
BREAKDANCE
BREAKDANCED
BREAKDANCER
BREAKDANCERS
BREAKDANCES
BREAKDANCING
BREAKDANCINGS
BREAKDOWNS
BREAKEVENS
BREAKFASTED
BREAKFASTER
BREAKFASTERS
BREAKFASTING
BREAKFASTS
BREAKFRONT
BREAKFRONTS
BREAKPOINT
BREAKPOINTS
BREAKTHROUGH
BREAKTHROUGHS
BREAKTIMES
BREAKWALLS

BREAKWATER
BREAKWATERS
BREASTBONE
BREASTBONES
BREASTFEED
BREASTFEEDING
BREASTFEEDINGS
BREASTFEEDS
BREASTPINS
BREASTPLATE
BREASTPLATES
BREASTPLOUGH
BREASTPLOUGHS
BREASTRAIL
BREASTRAILS
BREASTSTROKE
BREASTSTROKER
BREASTSTROKERS
BREASTSTROKES
BREASTSUMMER
BREASTSUMMERS
BREASTWORK
BREASTWORKS
BREATHABILITIES
BREATHABILITY
BREATHABLE
BREATHALYSE
BREATHALYSED
BREATHALYSER
BREATHALYSERS
BREATHALYSES
BREATHALYSING
BREATHALYZE
BREATHALYZED
BREATHALYZER
BREATHALYZERS
BREATHALYZES
BREATHALYZING
BREATHARIAN
BREATHARIANISM
BREATHARIANISMS
BREATHARIANS
BREATHIEST
BREATHINESS
BREATHINESSES
BREATHINGS
BREATHLESS
BREATHLESSLY
BREATHLESSNESS
BREATHTAKING
BREATHTAKINGLY
BRECCIATED
BRECCIATES
BRECCIATING
BRECCIATION
BRECCIATIONS
BREECHBLOCK
BREECHBLOCKS
BREECHCLOTH
BREECHCLOTHS
BREECHCLOUT
BREECHCLOUTS
BREECHINGS
BREECHLESS
BREECHLOADER
BREECHLOADERS
BREEZELESS

BREEZEWAYS
BREEZINESS
BREEZINESSES
BREMSSTRAHLUNG
BREMSSTRAHLUNGS
BRESSUMMER
BRESSUMMERS
BRETASCHES
BRETTICING
BREUNNERITE
BREUNNERITES
BREVETCIES
BREVETTING
BREVIARIES
BREVIPENNATE
BREWHOUSES
BREWMASTER
BREWMASTERS
BRIARROOTS
BRIARWOODS
BRICABRACS
BRICKCLAYS
BRICKEARTH
BRICKEARTHS
BRICKFIELD
BRICKFIELDER
BRICKFIELDERS
BRICKFIELDS
BRICKKILNS
BRICKLAYER
BRICKLAYERS
BRICKLAYING
BRICKLAYINGS
BRICKMAKER
BRICKMAKERS
BRICKMAKING
BRICKMAKINGS
BRICKSHAPED
BRICKWALLS
BRICKWORKS
BRICKYARDS
BRICOLAGES
BRICOLEURS
BRIDECAKES
BRIDEGROOM
BRIDEGROOMS
BRIDEMAIDEN
BRIDEMAIDENS
BRIDEMAIDS
BRIDESMAID
BRIDESMAIDS
BRIDEWEALTH
BRIDEWEALTHS
BRIDEWELLS
BRIDEZILLA
BRIDEZILLAS
BRIDGEABLE
BRIDGEBOARD
BRIDGEBOARDS
BRIDGEHEAD
BRIDGEHEADS
BRIDGELESS
BRIDGELIKE
BRIDGEWORK
BRIDGEWORKS
BRIDLEWAYS
BRIDLEWISE

BRIEFCASES
BRIEFNESSES
BRIERROOTS
BRIERWOODS
BRIGADIERS
BRIGANDAGE
BRIGANDAGES
BRIGANDINE
BRIGANDINES
BRIGANDRIES
BRIGANTINE
BRIGANTINES
BRIGHTENED
BRIGHTENER
BRIGHTENERS
BRIGHTENING
BRIGHTNESS
BRIGHTNESSES
BRIGHTSOME
BRIGHTWORK
BRIGHTWORKS
BRILLIANCE
BRILLIANCES
BRILLIANCIES
BRILLIANCY
BRILLIANTE
BRILLIANTED
BRILLIANTINE
BRILLIANTINED
BRILLIANTINES
BRILLIANTING
BRILLIANTLY
BRILLIANTNESS
BRILLIANTNESSES
BRILLIANTS
BRIMFULLNESS
BRIMFULLNESSES
BRIMFULNESS
BRIMFULNESSES
BRIMSTONES
BRIMSTONIER
BRIMSTONIEST
BRINELLING
BRINELLINGS
BRINGDOWNS
BRININESSES
BRINJARRIES
BRINKMANSHIP
BRINKMANSHIPS
BRINKSMANSHIP
BRINKSMANSHIPS
BRIOLETTES
BRIQUETTED
BRIQUETTES
BRIQUETTING
BRISKENING
BRISKNESSES
BRISTLECONE
BRISTLECONES
BRISTLELIKE
BRISTLETAIL
BRISTLETAILS
BRISTLIEST
BRISTLINESS
BRISTLINESSES
BRITANNIAS
BRITSCHKAS

BRITTANIAS
BRITTLENESS
BRITTLENESSES
BROADBANDS
BROADBEANS
BROADBILLS
BROADBRIMS
BROADBRUSH
BROADCASTED
BROADCASTER
BROADCASTERS
BROADCASTING
BROADCASTINGS
BROADCASTS
BROADCLOTH
BROADCLOTHS
BROADENERS
BROADENING
BROADLEAVED
BROADLEAVES
BROADLINES
BROADLOOMS
BROADNESSES
BROADPIECE
BROADPIECES
BROADSCALE
BROADSHEET
BROADSHEETS
BROADSIDED
BROADSIDES
BROADSIDING
BROADSWORD
BROADSWORDS
BROADTAILS
BROBDINGNAGIAN
BROCATELLE
BROCATELLES
BROCCOLINI
BROCCOLINIS
BROCHETTES
BROGUERIES
BROIDERERS
BROIDERIES
BROIDERING
BROIDERINGS
BROKENHEARTED
BROKENHEARTEDLY
BROKENNESS
BROKENNESSES
BROKERAGES
BROKERINGS
BROMEGRASS
BROMEGRASSES
BROMELAINS
BROMELIACEOUS
BROMELIADS
BROMEOSINS
BROMHIDROSES
BROMHIDROSIS
BROMIDROSES
BROMIDROSIS
BROMINATED
BROMINATES
BROMINATING
BROMINATION
BROMINATIONS
BROMINISMS

BROMOCRIPTINE	BROTHERLINESSES	BRYOPHYLLUM	BUHRSTONES	BULLYCIDES
BROMOCRIPTINES	BROUGHTASES	BRYOPHYLLUMS	BUILDDOWNS	BULLYRAGGED
BROMOFORMS	BROWALLIAS	BRYOPHYTES	BUIRDLIEST	BULLYRAGGING
BROMOURACIL	BROWBEATEN	BRYOPHYTIC	BULBIFEROUS	BULRUSHIER
BROMOURACILS	BROWBEATER	BUBBLEGUMS	BULBOSITIES	BULRUSHIEST
BRONCHIALLY	BROWBEATERS	BUBBLEHEAD	BULBOUSNESS	BULWADDEES
BRONCHIECTASES	BROWBEATING	BUBBLEHEADED	BULBOUSNESSES	BULWADDIES
BRONCHIECTASIS	BROWBEATINGS	BUBBLEHEADS	BULGINESSES	BULWARKING
BRONCHIOLAR	BROWNFIELD	BUBONOCELE	BULKHEADED	BUMBAILIFF
BRONCHIOLE	BROWNFIELDS	BUBONOCELES	BULKINESSES	BUMBAILIFFS
BRONCHIOLES	BROWNNESSES	BUCCANEERED	BULLBAITING	BUMBERSHOOT
BRONCHIOLITIS	BROWNNOSED	BUCCANEERING	BULLBAITINGS	BUMBERSHOOTS
BRONCHIOLITISES	BROWNNOSER	BUCCANEERINGS	BULLBRIERS	BUMBLEBEES
BRONCHITIC	BROWNNOSERS	BUCCANEERISH	BULLDOGGED	BUMBLEBERRIES
BRONCHITICS	BROWNNOSES	BUCCANEERS	BULLDOGGER	BUMBLEBERRY
BRONCHITIS	BROWNNOSING	BUCCANIERED	BULLDOGGERS	BUMBLEDOMS
BRONCHITISES	BROWNSHIRT	BUCCANIERING	BULLDOGGING	BUMBLINGLY
BRONCHODILATOR	BROWNSHIRTS	BUCCANIERS	BULLDOGGINGS	BUMFREEZER
BRONCHODILATORS	BROWNSTONE	BUCCINATOR	BULLDOZERS	BUMFREEZERS
BRONCHOGENIC	BROWNSTONES	BUCCINATORS	BULLDOZING	BUMFUZZLED
BRONCHOGRAPHIES	BROWRIDGES	BUCCINATORY	BULLETINED	BUMFUZZLES
BRONCHOGRAPHY	BROWSABLES	BUCELLASES	BULLETINING	BUMFUZZLING
BRONCHOSCOPE	BRUCELLOSES	BUCENTAURS	BULLETPROOF	BUMMALOTIS
BRONCHOSCOPES	BRUCELLOSIS	BUCKBOARDS	BULLETPROOFED	BUMPINESSES
BRONCHOSCOPIC	BRUGMANSIA	BUCKBRUSHES	BULLETPROOFING	BUMPKINISH
BRONCHOSCOPICAL	BRUGMANSIAS	BUCKETFULS	BULLETPROOFS	BUMPKINLIER
BRONCHOSCOPIES	BRUMMAGEMS	BUCKETINGS	BULLETRIES	BUMPKINLIEST
BRONCHOSCOPIST	BRUSCHETTA	BUCKETSFUL	BULLETWOOD	BUMPOLOGIES
BRONCHOSCOPISTS	BRUSCHETTAS	BUCKHOUNDS	BULLETWOODS	BUMPSADAISY
BRONCHOSCOPY	BRUSCHETTE	BUCKJUMPER	BULLFIGHTER	BUMPTIOUSLY
BRONCHOSPASM	BRUSHABILITIES	BUCKJUMPERS	BULLFIGHTERS	BUMPTIOUSNESS
BRONCHOSPASMS	BRUSHABILITY	BUCKJUMPING	BULLFIGHTING	BUMPTIOUSNESSES
BRONCHOSPASTIC	BRUSHBACKS	BUCKJUMPINGS	BULLFIGHTINGS	BUMSUCKERS
BRONCOBUSTER	BRUSHFIRES	BUCKLERING	BULLFIGHTS	BUMSUCKING
BRONCOBUSTERS	BRUSHLANDS	BUCKRAMING	BULLFINCHES	BUMSUCKINGS
BRONDYRONS	BRUSHMARKS	BUCKSHISHED	BULLHEADED	BUNBURYING
BRONTOBYTE	BRUSHSTROKE	BUCKSHISHES	BULLHEADEDLY	BUNCHBERRIES
BRONTOBYTES	BRUSHSTROKES	BUCKSHISHING	BULLHEADEDNESS	BUNCHBERRY
BRONTOSAUR	BRUSHWHEEL	BUCKSKINNED	BULLIONIST	BUNCHGRASS
BRONTOSAURS	BRUSHWHEELS	BUCKTHORNS	BULLIONISTS	BUNCHGRASSES
BRONTOSAURUS	BRUSHWOODS	BUCKTOOTHED	BULLISHNESS	BUNCHINESS
BRONTOSAURUSES	BRUSHWORKS	BUCKWHEATS	BULLISHNESSES	BUNCHINESSES
BRONZIFIED	BRUSQUENESS	BUCKYBALLS	BULLMASTIFF	BUNDOBUSTS
BRONZIFIES	BRUSQUENESSES	BUCKYTUBES	BULLMASTIFFS	BUNGALOIDS
BRONZIFYING	BRUSQUERIE	BUCOLICALLY	BULLNECKED	BUNGLESOME
BROODINESS	BRUSQUERIES	BUDGERIGAR	BULLOCKIER	BUNGLINGLY
BROODINESSES	BRUTALISATION	BUDGERIGARS	BULLOCKIES	BUNKHOUSES
BROODINGLY	BRUTALISATIONS	BUDGETEERS	BULLOCKIEST	BUOYANCIES
BROODMARES	BRUTALISED	BUDGETINGS	BULLOCKING	BUOYANTNESS
BROOKLIMES	BRUTALISES	BUDTENDERS	BULLROARER	BUOYANTNESSES
BROOKWEEDS	BRUTALISING	BUFFALOBERRIES	BULLROARERS	BUPIVACAINE
BROOMBALLER	BRUTALISMS	BUFFALOBERRY	BULLRUSHES	BUPIVACAINES
BROOMBALLERS	BRUTALISTS	BUFFALOFISH	BULLSHITTED	BUPRENORPHINE
BROOMBALLS	BRUTALITIES	BUFFALOFISHES	BULLSHITTER	BUPRENORPHINES
BROOMCORNS	BRUTALIZATION	BUFFALOING	BULLSHITTERS	BUPRESTIDS
BROOMRAPES	BRUTALIZATIONS	BUFFERINGS	BULLSHITTING	BUPROPIONS
BROOMSTAFF	BRUTALIZED	BUFFETINGS	BULLSHITTINGS	BURDENSOME
BROOMSTAFFS	BRUTALIZES	BUFFLEHEAD	BULLSNAKES	BUREAUCRACIES
BROOMSTICK	BRUTALIZING	BUFFLEHEADS	BULLTERRIER	BUREAUCRACY
BROOMSTICKS	BRUTENESSES	BUFFOONERIES	BULLTERRIERS	BUREAUCRAT
BROTHERHOOD	BRUTIFYING	BUFFOONERY	BULLWADDIE	BUREAUCRATESE
BROTHERHOODS	BRUTISHNESS	BUFFOONISH	BULLWADDIES	BUREAUCRATESES
BROTHERING	BRUTISHNESSES	BUFOTALINS	BULLWHACKED	BUREAUCRATIC
BROTHERLIER	BRYOLOGICAL	BUFOTENINE	BULLWHACKING	BUREAUCRATISE
BROTHERLIEST	BRYOLOGIES	BUFOTENINES	BULLWHACKS	BUREAUCRATISED
BROTHERLIKE	BRYOLOGIST	BUGGINESSES	BULLWHIPPED	BUREAUCRATISES
BROTHERLINESS	BRYOLOGISTS	BUGLEWEEDS	BULLWHIPPING	BUREAUCRATISING

BUREAUCRATISM	BURNISHERS	BUSHWALKER	BUTLERSHIP	BUTTONHOLD
BUREAUCRATISMS	BURNISHING	BUSHWALKERS	BUTLERSHIPS	BUTTONHOLDING
BUREAUCRATIST	BURNISHINGS	BUSHWALKING	BUTTERBALL	BUTTONHOLDS
BUREAUCRATISTS	BURNISHMENT	BUSHWALKINGS	BUTTERBALLS	BUTTONHOLE
BUREAUCRATIZE	BURNISHMENTS	BUSHWHACKED	BUTTERBURS	BUTTONHOLED
BUREAUCRATIZED	BURRAMUNDI	BUSHWHACKER	BUTTERCREAM	BUTTONHOLER
BUREAUCRATIZES	BURRAMUNDIS	BUSHWHACKERS	BUTTERCREAMS	BUTTONHOLERS
BUREAUCRATIZING	BURRAMYSES	BUSHWHACKING	BUTTERCUPS	BUTTONHOLES
BUREAUCRATS	BURRAWANGS	BUSHWHACKINGS	BUTTERDOCK	BUTTONHOLING
BURGEONING	BURRFISHES	BUSHWHACKS	BUTTERDOCKS	BUTTONHOOK
BURGLARIES	BURROWSTOWN	BUSINESSES	BUTTERFATS	BUTTONHOOKED
BURGLARING	BURROWSTOWNS	BUSINESSIER	BUTTERFINGERED	BUTTONHOOKING
BURGLARIOUS	BURRSTONES	BUSINESSIEST	BUTTERFINGERS	BUTTONHOOKS
BURGLARIOUSLY	BURSARSHIP	BUSINESSLIKE	BUTTERFISH	BUTTONIEST
BURGLARISE	BURSARSHIPS	BUSINESSMAN	BUTTERFISHES	BUTTONLESS
BURGLARISED	BURSERACEOUS	BUSINESSMEN	BUTTERFLIED	BUTTONMOULD
BURGLARISES	BURSICULATE	BUSINESSPEOPLE	BUTTERFLIES	BUTTONMOULDS
BURGLARISING	BURSITISES	BUSINESSPERSON	BUTTERFLYER	BUTTONWOOD
BURGLARIZE	BURTHENING	BUSINESSPERSONS	BUTTERFLYERS	BUTTONWOODS
BURGLARIZED	BURTHENSOME	BUSINESSWOMAN	BUTTERFLYFISH	BUTTRESSED
BURGLARIZES	BUSHBABIES	BUSINESSWOMEN	BUTTERFLYFISHES	BUTTRESSES
BURGLARIZING	BUSHBASHING	BUSTICATED	BUTTERFLYING	BUTTRESSING
BURGLARPROOF	BUSHBASHINGS	BUSTICATES	BUTTERIEST	BUTTSTOCKS
BURGOMASTER	BUSHCRAFTS	BUSTICATING	BUTTERINES	BUTYLATING
BURGOMASTERS	BUSHELFULS	BUSTINESSES	BUTTERINESS	BUTYLATION
BURGUNDIES	BUSHELLERS	BUSTLINGLY	BUTTERINESSES	BUTYLATIONS
BURLADEROS	BUSHELLING	BUSYBODIED	BUTTERLESS	BUTYRACEOUS
BURLESQUED	BUSHELLINGS	BUSYBODIES	BUTTERMILK	BUTYRALDEHYDE
BURLESQUELY	BUSHELWOMAN	BUSYBODYING	BUTTERMILKS	BUTYRALDEHYDES
BURLESQUER	BUSHELWOMEN	BUSYBODYINGS	BUTTERNUTS	BUTYROPHENONE
BURLESQUERS	BUSHFIGHTING	BUSYNESSES	BUTTERSCOTCH	BUTYROPHENONES
BURLESQUES	BUSHFIGHTINGS	BUTADIENES	BUTTERSCOTCHES	BUXOMNESSES
BURLESQUING	BUSHHAMMER	BUTCHERBIRD	BUTTERWEED	BUZZKILLER
BURLEYCUES	BUSHHAMMERS	BUTCHERBIRDS	BUTTERWEEDS	BUZZKILLERS
BURLINESSES	BUSHINESSES	BUTCHERERS	BUTTERWORT	BYPRODUCTS
BURNETTISE	BUSHMANSHIP	BUTCHERIES	BUTTERWORTS	BYSSACEOUS
BURNETTISED	BUSHMANSHIPS	BUTCHERING	BUTTINSKIES	BYSSINOSES
BURNETTISES	BUSHMASTER	BUTCHERINGS	BUTTINSKIS	BYSSINOSIS
BURNETTISING	BUSHMASTERS	BUTCHERLIER	BUTTOCKING	BYSTANDERS
BURNETTIZE	BUSHRANGER	BUTCHERLIEST	BUTTONBALL	BYTOWNITES
BURNETTIZED	BUSHRANGERS	BUTCHNESSES	BUTTONBALLS	
BURNETTIZES	BUSHRANGING	BUTENEDIOIC	BUTTONBUSH	
BURNETTIZING	BUSHRANGINGS	BUTEONINES	BUTTONBUSHES	
BURNISHABLE	BUSHWALKED	BUTLERAGES	BUTTONHELD	

C

CABALETTAS	CACOGENICS	CAFETERIAS	CALCEDONIO	CALEFACTORS
CABALISTIC	CACOGRAPHER	CAFETIERES	CALCEDONIOS	CALEFACTORY
CABALISTICAL	CACOGRAPHERS	CAFETORIUM	CALCEIFORM	CALEMBOURS
CABALLEROS	CACOGRAPHIC	CAFETORIUMS	CALCEOLARIA	CALENDARED
CABBAGETOWN	CACOGRAPHICAL	CAFFEINATED	CALCEOLARIAS	CALENDARER
CABBAGETOWNS	CACOGRAPHIES	CAFFEINISM	CALCEOLATE	CALENDARERS
CABBAGEWORM	CACOGRAPHY	CAFFEINISMS	CALCICOLES	CALENDARING
CABBAGEWORMS	CACOLOGIES	CAGEYNESSES	CALCICOLOUS	CALENDARISATION
CABBAGIEST	CACOMISTLE	CAGINESSES	CALCIFEROL	CALENDARISE
CABBALISMS	CACOMISTLES	CAGMAGGING	CALCIFEROLS	CALENDARISED
CABBALISTIC	CACOMIXLES	CAGYNESSES	CALCIFEROUS	CALENDARISES
CABBALISTICAL	CACONYMIES	CAILLEACHS	CALCIFICATION	CALENDARISING
CABBALISTS	CACOPHONIC	CAILLIACHS	CALCIFICATIONS	CALENDARIST
CABDRIVERS	CACOPHONICAL	CAINOGENESES	CALCIFUGAL	CALENDARISTS
CABINETMAKER	CACOPHONICALLY	CAINOGENESIS	CALCIFUGES	CALENDARIZATION
CABINETMAKERS	CACOPHONIES	CAINOGENETIC	CALCIFUGOUS	CALENDARIZE
CABINETMAKING	CACOPHONIOUS	CAIRNGORMS	CALCIFYING	CALENDARIZED
CABINETMAKINGS	CACOPHONOUS	CAJOLEMENT	CALCIGEROUS	CALENDARIZES
CABINETRIES	CACOPHONOUSLY	CAJOLEMENTS	CALCIMINED	CALENDARIZING
CABINETWORK	CACOTOPIAN	CAJOLERIES	CALCIMINES	CALENDERED
CABINETWORKS	CACOTOPIAS	CAJOLINGLY	CALCIMINING	CALENDERER
CABINMATES	CACOTROPHIES	CAKEWALKED	CALCINABLE	CALENDERERS
CABLECASTED	CACOTROPHY	CAKEWALKER	CALCINATION	CALENDERING
CABLECASTING	CACTACEOUS	CAKEWALKERS	CALCINATIONS	CALENDERINGS
CABLECASTS	CACTOBLASTES	CAKEWALKING	CALCINOSES	CALENDRERS
CABLEGRAMS	CACTOBLASTIS	CAKINESSES	CALCINOSIS	CALENDRICAL
CABLEVISION	CACUMINALS	CALABASHES	CALCITONIN	CALENDRIES
CABLEVISIONS	CACUMINOUS	CALABOGUSES	CALCITONINS	CALENDULAS
CABRIOLETS	CADASTRALLY	CALABOOSES	CALCSINTER	CALENTURES
CACAFUEGOS	CADAVERINE	CALABRESES	CALCSINTERS	CALESCENCE
CACCIATORA	CADAVERINES	CALAMANCOES	CALCULABILITIES	CALESCENCES
CACCIATORE	CADAVEROUS	CALAMANCOS	CALCULABILITY	CALFDOZERS
CACHAEMIAS	CADAVEROUSLY	CALAMANDER	CALCULABLE	CALIATOURS
CACHECTICAL	CADAVEROUSNESS	CALAMANDERS	CALCULABLY	CALIBRATED
CACHINNATE	CADDISFLIES	CALAMARIES	CALCULATED	CALIBRATER
CACHINNATED	CADDISHNESS	CALAMINING	CALCULATEDLY	CALIBRATERS
CACHINNATES	CADDISHNESSES	CALAMITIES	CALCULATEDNESS	CALIBRATES
CACHINNATING	CADDISWORM	CALAMITOUS	CALCULATES	CALIBRATING
CACHINNATION	CADDISWORMS	CALAMITOUSLY	CALCULATING	CALIBRATION
CACHINNATIONS	CADETSHIPS	CALAMITOUSNESS	CALCULATINGLY	CALIBRATIONS
CACHINNATORY	CADUCITIES	CALAMONDIN	CALCULATION	CALIBRATOR
CACHOLONGS	CAECILIANS	CALAMONDINS	CALCULATIONAL	CALIBRATORS
CACIQUISMS	CAECITISES	CALANDRIAS	CALCULATIONS	CALIDITIES
CACKERMANDER	CAENOGENESES	CALAVANCES	CALCULATIVE	CALIFORNIUM
CACKERMANDERS	CAENOGENESIS	CALAVERITE	CALCULATOR	CALIFORNIUMS
CACKLEBERRIES	CAENOGENETIC	CALAVERITES	CALCULATORS	CALIGINOSITIES
CACKLEBERRY	CAESALPINOID	CALCAREOUS	CALCULUSES	CALIGINOSITY
CACODAEMON	CAESAREANS	CALCAREOUSLY	CALEFACIENT	CALIGINOUS
CACODAEMONS	CAESARIANS	CALCARIFEROUS	CALEFACIENTS	CALIMOCHOS
CACODEMONIC	CAESARISMS	CALCARIFORM	CALEFACTION	CALIOLOGIES
CACODEMONS	CAESAROPAPISM	CALCEAMENTA	CALEFACTIONS	CALIPASHES
CACODOXIES	CAESAROPAPISMS	CALCEAMENTUM	CALEFACTIVE	CALIPERING
CACOEPISTIC	CAESPITOSE	CALCEATING	CALEFACTOR	CALIPHATES
CACOGASTRIC	CAESPITOSELY	CALCEDONIES	CALEFACTORIES	CALISTHENIC

CALISTHENICS	CALUMNIATING	CAMPAIGNED	CANCELLARIAL	CANDLEWOODS
CALLBOARDS	CALUMNIATION	CAMPAIGNER	CANCELLARIAN	CANDYFLOSS
CALLIATURE	CALUMNIATIONS	CAMPAIGNERS	CANCELLARIATE	CANDYFLOSSES
CALLIATURES	CALUMNIATOR	CAMPAIGNING	CANCELLARIATES	CANDYGRAMS
CALLIDITIES	CALUMNIATORS	CAMPANEROS	CANCELLATE	CANDYTUFTS
CALLIGRAMME	CALUMNIATORY	CAMPANIFORM	CANCELLATED	CANEBRAKES
CALLIGRAMMES	CALUMNIOUS	CAMPANILES	CANCELLATION	CANEFRUITS
CALLIGRAMS	CALUMNIOUSLY	CAMPANISTS	CANCELLATIONS	CANEPHORAS
CALLIGRAPHER	CALUMNYING	CAMPANOLOGER	CANCELLERS	CANEPHORES
CALLIGRAPHERS	CALVADOSES	CAMPANOLOGERS	CANCELLING	CANEPHORUS
CALLIGRAPHIC	CALVARIUMS	CAMPANOLOGICAL	CANCELLOUS	CANEPHORUSES
CALLIGRAPHICAL	CALYCANTHEMIES	CAMPANOLOGIES	CANCERATED	CANESCENCE
CALLIGRAPHIES	CALYCANTHEMY	CAMPANOLOGIST	CANCERATES	CANESCENCES
CALLIGRAPHIST	CALYCANTHUS	CAMPANOLOGISTS	CANCERATING	CANINITIES
CALLIGRAPHISTS	CALYCANTHUSES	CAMPANOLOGY	CANCERATION	CANISTERED
CALLIGRAPHY	CALYCIFORM	CAMPANULACEOUS	CANCERATIONS	CANISTERING
CALLIOPSIS	CALYCOIDEOUS	CAMPANULAR	CANCEROPHOBIA	CANISTERISATION
CALLIPASHES	CALYCULATE	CAMPANULAS	CANCEROPHOBIAS	CANISTERISE
CALLIPERED	CALYPSONIAN	CAMPANULATE	CANCEROUSLY	CANISTERISED
CALLIPERING	CALYPSONIANS	CAMPCRAFTS	CANCERPHOBIA	CANISTERISES
CALLIPYGEAN	CALYPTERAS	CAMPEADORS	CANCERPHOBIAS	CANISTERISING
CALLIPYGIAN	CALYPTRATE	CAMPESINOS	CANCIONERO	CANISTERIZATION
CALLIPYGOUS	CALYPTROGEN	CAMPESTRAL	CANCIONEROS	CANISTERIZE
CALLISTEMON	CALYPTROGENS	CAMPESTRIAN	CANCRIFORM	CANISTERIZED
CALLISTEMONS	CAMANACHDS	CAMPGROUND	CANCRIZANS	CANISTERIZES
CALLISTHENIC	CAMARADERIE	CAMPGROUNDS	CANDELABRA	CANISTERIZING
CALLISTHENICS	CAMARADERIES	CAMPHORACEOUS	CANDELABRAS	CANKEREDLY
CALLITHUMP	CAMARILLAS	CAMPHORATE	CANDELABRUM	CANKEREDNESS
CALLITHUMPIAN	CAMBERINGS	CAMPHORATED	CANDELABRUMS	CANKEREDNESSES
CALLITHUMPS	CAMBISTRIES	CAMPHORATES	CANDELILLA	CANKERIEST
CALLOSITIES	CAMCORDERS	CAMPHORATING	CANDELILLAS	CANKERWORM
CALLOUSING	CAMCORDING	CAMPIMETRIES	CANDESCENCE	CANKERWORMS
CALLOUSNESS	CAMELBACKS	CAMPIMETRY	CANDESCENCES	CANNABINOID
CALLOUSNESSES	CAMELEOPARD	CAMPINESSES	CANDESCENT	CANNABINOIDS
CALLOWNESS	CAMELEOPARDS	CAMPNESSES	CANDESCENTLY	CANNABINOL
CALLOWNESSES	CAMELHAIRS	CAMPODEIDS	CANDIDACIES	CANNABINOLS
CALMATIVES	CAMELOPARD	CAMPODEIFORM	CANDIDATES	CANNABISES
CALMNESSES	CAMELOPARDS	CAMPSHIRTS	CANDIDATESHIP	CANNELLINI
CALMODULIN	CAMERAPERSON	CAMPSTOOLS	CANDIDATESHIPS	CANNELLINIS
CALMODULINS	CAMERAPERSONS	CAMPYLOBACTER	CANDIDATURE	CANNELLONI
CALMSTANES	CAMERAPHONE	CAMPYLOBACTERS	CANDIDATURES	CANNELURES
CALMSTONES	CAMERAPHONES	CAMPYLOTROPOUS	CANDIDIASES	CANNIBALISATION
CALORESCENCE	CAMERATION	CAMSTEERIE	CANDIDIASIS	CANNIBALISE
CALORESCENCES	CAMERATIONS	CAMWHORING	CANDIDNESS	CANNIBALISED
CALORESCENT	CAMERAWOMAN	CANALBOATS	CANDIDNESSES	CANNIBALISES
CALORICALLY	CAMERAWOMEN	CANALICULAR	CANDLEBERRIES	CANNIBALISING
CALORICITIES	CAMERAWORK	CANALICULATE	CANDLEBERRY	CANNIBALISM
CALORICITY	CAMERAWORKS	CANALICULATED	CANDLEFISH	CANNIBALISMS
CALORIFICALLY	CAMERLENGO	CANALICULI	CANDLEFISHES	CANNIBALISTIC
CALORIFICATION	CAMERLENGOS	CANALICULUS	CANDLEHOLDER	CANNIBALIZATION
CALORIFICATIONS	CAMERLINGO	CANALISATION	CANDLEHOLDERS	CANNIBALIZE
CALORIFIER	CAMERLINGOS	CANALISATIONS	CANDLELIGHT	CANNIBALIZED
CALORIFIERS	CAMIKNICKERS	CANALISING	CANDLELIGHTED	CANNIBALIZES
CALORIMETER	CAMIKNICKS	CANALIZATION	CANDLELIGHTER	CANNIBALIZING
CALORIMETERS	CAMISADOES	CANALIZATIONS	CANDLELIGHTERS	CANNIBALLY
CALORIMETRIC	CAMORRISTA	CANALIZING	CANDLELIGHTS	CANNINESSES
CALORIMETRICAL	CAMORRISTI	CANCELABLE	CANDLENUTS	CANNISTERS
CALORIMETRIES	CAMORRISTS	CANCELATION	CANDLEPINS	CANNONADED
CALORIMETRY	CAMOUFLAGE	CANCELATIONS	CANDLEPOWER	CANNONADES
CALORISING	CAMOUFLAGEABLE	CANCELBOTS	CANDLEPOWERS	CANNONADING
CALORIZING	CAMOUFLAGED	CANCELEERED	CANDLESNUFFER	CANNONBALL
CALOTYPIST	CAMOUFLAGES	CANCELEERING	CANDLESNUFFERS	CANNONBALLED
CALOTYPISTS	CAMOUFLAGIC	CANCELEERS	CANDLESTICK	CANNONBALLING
CALUMNIABLE	CAMOUFLAGING	CANCELIERED	CANDLESTICKS	CANNONBALLS
CALUMNIATE	CAMOUFLETS	CANCELIERING	CANDLEWICK	CANNONEERS
CALUMNIATED	CAMOUFLEUR	CANCELIERS	CANDLEWICKS	CANNONIERS
CALUMNIATES	CAMOUFLEURS	CANCELLABLE	CANDLEWOOD	CANNONRIES

CANNULATED	CANTILLATED	CAPERNOITIE	CAPREOLATE	CARAMBOLAS
CANNULATES	CANTILLATES	CAPERNOITIES	CAPRICCIOS	CARAMBOLED
CANNULATING	CANTILLATING	CAPERNOITY	CAPRICCIOSO	CARAMBOLES
CANNULATION	CANTILLATION	CAPICOLLAS	CAPRICIOUS	CARAMBOLING
CANNULATIONS	CANTILLATIONS	CAPICOLLOS	CAPRICIOUSLY	CARAMELISATION
CANOEWOODS	CANTILLATORY	CAPILLACEOUS	CAPRICIOUSNESS	CARAMELISATIONS
CANONESSES	CANTINESSES	CAPILLAIRE	CAPRIFICATION	CARAMELISE
CANONICALLY	CANTONISATION	CAPILLAIRES	CAPRIFICATIONS	CARAMELISED
CANONICALS	CANTONISATIONS	CAPILLARIES	CAPRIFOILS	CARAMELISES
CANONICATE	CANTONISED	CAPILLARITIES	CAPRIFOLES	CARAMELISING
CANONICATES	CANTONISES	CAPILLARITY	CAPRIFOLIACEOUS	CARAMELIZATION
CANONICITIES	CANTONISING	CAPILLITIA	CAPRIFYING	CARAMELIZATIONS
CANONICITY	CANTONIZATION	CAPILLITIUM	CAPRIOLING	CARAMELIZE
CANONISATION	CANTONIZATIONS	CAPITALISATION	CAPROLACTAM	CARAMELIZED
CANONISATIONS	CANTONIZED	CAPITALISATIONS	CAPROLACTAMS	CARAMELIZES
CANONISERS	CANTONIZES	CAPITALISE	CAPRYLATES	CARAMELIZING
CANONISING	CANTONIZING	CAPITALISED	CAPSAICINS	CARAMELLED
CANONISTIC	CANTONMENT	CAPITALISES	CAPSIZABLE	CARAMELLING
CANONIZATION	CANTONMENTS	CAPITALISING	CAPSOMERES	CARANGOIDS
CANONIZATIONS	CANULATING	CAPITALISM	CAPSULATED	CARAPACIAL
CANONIZERS	CANULATION	CAPITALISMS	CAPSULATION	CARAVANCES
CANONIZING	CANULATIONS	CAPITALIST	CAPSULATIONS	CARAVANEER
CANOODLERS	CANVASBACK	CAPITALISTIC	CAPSULISED	CARAVANEERS
CANOODLING	CANVASBACKS	CAPITALISTS	CAPSULISES	CARAVANERS
CANOPHILIA	CANVASLIKE	CAPITALIZATION	CAPSULISING	CARAVANETTE
CANOPHILIAS	CANVASSERS	CAPITALIZATIONS	CAPSULIZED	CARAVANETTES
CANOPHILIST	CANVASSING	CAPITALIZE	CAPSULIZES	CARAVANING
CANOPHILISTS	CANVASSINGS	CAPITALIZED	CAPSULIZING	CARAVANINGS
CANOPHOBIA	CANYONEERS	CAPITALIZES	CAPTAINCIES	CARAVANNED
CANOPHOBIAS	CANYONINGS	CAPITALIZING	CAPTAINING	CARAVANNER
CANOROUSLY	CANZONETTA	CAPITATION	CAPTAINRIES	CARAVANNERS
CANOROUSNESS	CANZONETTAS	CAPITATIONS	CAPTAINSHIP	CARAVANNING
CANOROUSNESSES	CANZONETTE	CAPITATIVE	CAPTAINSHIPS	CARAVANNINGS
CANTABANKS	CAOUTCHOUC	CAPITELLUM	CAPTIONING	CARAVANSARAI
CANTABILES	CAOUTCHOUCS	CAPITOLIAN	CAPTIONLESS	CARAVANSARAIS
CANTALOUPE	CAPABILITIES	CAPITOLINE	CAPTIOUSLY	CARAVANSARIES
CANTALOUPES	CAPABILITY	CAPITULANT	CAPTIOUSNESS	CARAVANSARY
CANTALOUPS	CAPABLENESS	CAPITULANTS	CAPTIOUSNESSES	CARAVANSERAI
CANTANKEROUS	CAPABLENESSES	CAPITULARIES	CAPTIVANCE	CARAVANSERAIS
CANTANKEROUSLY	CAPACIOUSLY	CAPITULARLY	CAPTIVANCES	CARAVELLES
CANTATRICE	CAPACIOUSNESS	CAPITULARS	CAPTIVATED	CARBACHOLS
CANTATRICES	CAPACIOUSNESSES	CAPITULARY	CAPTIVATES	CARBAMATES
CANTATRICI	CAPACITANCE	CAPITULATE	CAPTIVATING	CARBAMAZEPINE
CANTERBURIES	CAPACITANCES	CAPITULATED	CAPTIVATINGLY	CARBAMAZEPINES
CANTERBURY	CAPACITATE	CAPITULATES	CAPTIVATION	CARBAMIDES
CANTERBURYS	CAPACITATED	CAPITULATING	CAPTIVATIONS	CARBAMIDINE
CANTHARIDAL	CAPACITATES	CAPITULATION	CAPTIVATOR	CARBAMIDINES
CANTHARIDES	CAPACITATING	CAPITULATIONS	CAPTIVATORS	CARBAMOYLS
CANTHARIDIAN	CAPACITATION	CAPITULATOR	CAPTIVAUNCE	CARBANIONS
CANTHARIDIC	CAPACITATIONS	CAPITULATORS	CAPTIVAUNCES	CARBAZOLES
CANTHARIDIN	CAPACITIES	CAPITULATORY	CAPTIVITIES	CARBIDOPAS
CANTHARIDINS	CAPACITIVE	CAPNOMANCIES	CAPTOPRILS	CARBIMAZOLE
CANTHARIDS	CAPACITIVELY	CAPNOMANCY	CARABINEER	CARBIMAZOLES
CANTHAXANTHIN	CAPACITORS	CAPOCCHIAS	CARABINEERS	CARBINEERS
CANTHAXANTHINE	CAPARISONED	CAPODASTRO	CARABINERO	CARBINIERS
CANTHAXANTHINES	CAPARISONING	CAPODASTROS	CARABINEROS	CARBOCYCLIC
CANTHAXANTHINS	CAPARISONS	CAPONIERES	CARABINERS	CARBOHYDRASE
CANTHITISES	CAPELLINES	CAPONISING	CARABINIER	CARBOHYDRASES
CANTICOING	CAPELLINIS	CAPONIZING	CARABINIERE	CARBOHYDRATE
CANTICOYED	CAPELLMEISTER	CAPOTASTOS	CARABINIERI	CARBOHYDRATES
CANTICOYING	CAPELLMEISTERS	CAPPARIDACEOUS	CARABINIERS	CARBOLATED
CANTILENAS	CAPERCAILLIE	CAPPELLETTI	CARACOLERS	CARBOLISED
CANTILEVER	CAPERCAILLIES	CAPPERNOITIES	CARACOLING	CARBOLISES
CANTILEVERED	CAPERCAILZIE	CAPPERNOITY	CARACOLLED	CARBOLISING
CANTILEVERING	CAPERCAILZIES	CAPPUCCINI	CARACOLLING	CARBOLIZED
CANTILEVERS	CAPERINGLY	CAPPUCCINO	CARAGEENAN	CARBOLIZES
CANTILLATE	CAPERNOITED	CAPPUCCINOS	CARAGEENANS	CARBOLIZING

CARBONACEOUS	CARBURETOR	CARDIOCENTESIS	CARFUFFLES	CARNOTITES
CARBONADES	CARBURETORS	CARDIOGENIC	CARFUFFLING	CAROLLINGS
CARBONADOED	CARBURETTED	CARDIOGRAM	CARHOPPING	CAROMELLED
CARBONADOES	CARBURETTER	CARDIOGRAMS	CARHOPPINGS	CAROMELLING
CARBONADOING	CARBURETTERS	CARDIOGRAPH	CARICATURA	CAROTENOID
CARBONADOS	CARBURETTING	CARDIOGRAPHER	CARICATURAL	CAROTENOIDS
CARBONARAS	CARBURETTOR	CARDIOGRAPHERS	CARICATURAS	CAROTINOID
CARBONATED	CARBURETTORS	CARDIOGRAPHIC	CARICATURE	CAROTINOIDS
CARBONATES	CARBURISATION	CARDIOGRAPHICAL	CARICATURED	CAROUSINGLY
CARBONATING	CARBURISATIONS	CARDIOGRAPHIES	CARICATURES	CAROUSINGS
CARBONATION	CARBURISED	CARDIOGRAPHS	CARICATURING	CARPACCIOS
CARBONATIONS	CARBURISES	CARDIOGRAPHY	CARICATURIST	CARPELLARY
CARBONATITE	CARBURISING	CARDIOLOGICAL	CARICATURISTS	CARPELLATE
CARBONATITES	CARBURIZATION	CARDIOLOGIES	CARILLONED	CARPELLATES
CARBONETTE	CARBURIZATIONS	CARDIOLOGIST	CARILLONING	CARPENTARIA
CARBONETTES	CARBURIZED	CARDIOLOGISTS	CARILLONIST	CARPENTARIAS
CARBONIFEROUS	CARBURIZES	CARDIOLOGY	CARILLONISTS	CARPENTERED
CARBONISATION	CARBURIZING	CARDIOMEGALIES	CARILLONNED	CARPENTERING
CARBONISATIONS	CARBYLAMINE	CARDIOMEGALY	CARILLONNEUR	CARPENTERS
CARBONISED	CARBYLAMINES	CARDIOMOTOR	CARILLONNEURS	CARPENTRIES
CARBONISER	CARCASSING	CARDIOMYOPATHY	CARILLONNING	CARPETBAGGED
CARBONISERS	CARCINOGEN	CARDIOPATHIES	CARIOGENIC	CARPETBAGGER
CARBONISES	CARCINOGENESES	CARDIOPATHY	CARIOSITIES	CARPETBAGGERIES
CARBONISING	CARCINOGENESIS	CARDIOPLEGIA	CARIOUSNESS	CARPETBAGGERS
CARBONIUMS	CARCINOGENIC	CARDIOPLEGIAS	CARIOUSNESSES	CARPETBAGGERY
CARBONIZATION	CARCINOGENICITY	CARDIOPULMONARY	CARJACKERS	CARPETBAGGING
CARBONIZATIONS	CARCINOGENS	CARDIOTHORACIC	CARJACKING	CARPETBAGGINGS
CARBONIZED	CARCINOIDS	CARDIOTONIC	CARJACKINGS	CARPETBAGS
CARBONIZER	CARCINOLOGICAL	CARDIOTONICS	CARMAGNOLE	CARPETINGS
CARBONIZERS	CARCINOLOGIES	CARDIOVASCULAR	CARMAGNOLES	CARPETLIKE
CARBONIZES	CARCINOLOGIST	CARDITISES	CARMELITES	CARPETMONGER
CARBONIZING	CARCINOLOGISTS	CARDOPHAGI	CARMINATIVE	CARPETMONGERS
CARBONLESS	CARCINOLOGY	CARDOPHAGUS	CARMINATIVES	CARPETWEED
CARBONNADE	CARCINOMAS	CARDPHONES	CARNAHUBAS	CARPETWEEDS
CARBONNADES	CARCINOMATA	CARDPLAYER	CARNALISED	CARPHOLOGIES
CARBONYLATE	CARCINOMATOID	CARDPLAYERS	CARNALISES	CARPHOLOGY
CARBONYLATED	CARCINOMATOSES	CARDPUNCHES	CARNALISING	CARPOGONIA
CARBONYLATES	CARCINOMATOSIS	CARDSHARPER	CARNALISMS	CARPOGONIAL
CARBONYLATING	CARCINOMATOUS	CARDSHARPERS	CARNALISTS	CARPOGONIUM
CARBONYLATION	CARCINOSARCOMA	CARDSHARPING	CARNALITIES	CARPOLOGICAL
CARBONYLATIONS	CARCINOSARCOMAS	CARDSHARPINGS	CARNALIZED	CARPOLOGIES
CARBONYLIC	CARCINOSES	CARDSHARPS	CARNALIZES	CARPOLOGIST
CARBOREXIC	CARCINOSIS	CARDUACEOUS	CARNALIZING	CARPOLOGISTS
CARBOREXICS	CARDAMINES	CAREENAGES	CARNALLING	CARPOMETACARPI
CARBOXYLASE	CARDBOARDIER	CAREERISMS	CARNALLITE	CARPOMETACARPUS
CARBOXYLASES	CARDBOARDIEST	CAREERISTS	CARNALLITES	CARPOOLERS
CARBOXYLATE	CARDBOARDS	CAREFREENESS	CARNAPTIOUS	CARPOOLING
CARBOXYLATED	CARDBOARDY	CAREFREENESSES	CARNAROLIS	CARPOOLINGS
CARBOXYLATES	CARDCASTLE	CAREFULLER	CARNASSIAL	CARPOPHAGOUS
CARBOXYLATING	CARDCASTLES	CAREFULLEST	CARNASSIALS	CARPOPHORE
CARBOXYLATION	CARDHOLDER	CAREFULNESS	CARNATIONED	CARPOPHORES
CARBOXYLATIONS	CARDHOLDERS	CAREFULNESSES	CARNATIONS	CARPOSPORE
CARBOXYLIC	CARDIALGIA	CAREGIVERS	CARNELIANS	CARPOSPORES
CARBUNCLED	CARDIALGIAS	CAREGIVING	CARNIFEXES	CARRAGEENAN
CARBUNCLES	CARDIALGIC	CAREGIVINGS	CARNIFICATION	CARRAGEENANS
CARBUNCULAR	CARDIALGIES	CARELESSLY	CARNIFICATIONS	CARRAGEENIN
CARBURATED	CARDIGANED	CARELESSNESS	CARNIFICIAL	CARRAGEENINS
CARBURATES	CARDINALATE	CARELESSNESSES	CARNIFYING	CARRAGEENS
CARBURATING	CARDINALATES	CARESSINGLY	CARNITINES	CARRAGHEEN
CARBURATION	CARDINALATIAL	CARESSINGS	CARNIVALESQUE	CARRAGHEENAN
CARBURATIONS	CARDINALITIAL	CARESSIVELY	CARNIVORES	CARRAGHEENANS
CARBURETED	CARDINALITIES	CARETAKERS	CARNIVORIES	CARRAGHEENIN
CARBURETER	CARDINALITY	CARETAKING	CARNIVOROUS	CARRAGHEENINS
CARBURETERS	CARDINALLY	CARETAKINGS	CARNIVOROUSLY	CARRAGHEENS
CARBURETING	CARDINALSHIP	CAREWORKER	CARNIVOROUSNESS	CARREFOURS
CARBURETION	CARDINALSHIPS	CAREWORKERS	CARNOSAURS	CARRIAGEABLE
CARBURETIONS	CARDIOCENTESES	CARFUFFLED	CARNOSITIES	CARRIAGEWAY

CARRIAGEWAYS
CARRITCHES
CARRIWITCHET
CARRIWITCHETS
CARRONADES
CARROTIEST
CARROTTOPPED
CARROTTOPS
CARROUSELS
CARRYBACKS
CARRYFORWARD
CARRYFORWARDS
CARRYOVERS
CARRYTALES
CARSHARING
CARSHARINGS
CARSICKNESS
CARSICKNESSES
CARTELISATION
CARTELISATIONS
CARTELISED
CARTELISES
CARTELISING
CARTELISMS
CARTELISTS
CARTELIZATION
CARTELIZATIONS
CARTELIZED
CARTELIZES
CARTELIZING
CARTHAMINE
CARTHAMINES
CARTHORSES
CARTILAGES
CARTILAGINOUS
CARTOGRAMS
CARTOGRAPHER
CARTOGRAPHERS
CARTOGRAPHIC
CARTOGRAPHICAL
CARTOGRAPHIES
CARTOGRAPHY
CARTOLOGICAL
CARTOLOGIES
CARTOMANCIES
CARTOMANCY
CARTONAGES
CARTONNAGE
CARTONNAGES
CARTOONIER
CARTOONIEST
CARTOONING
CARTOONINGS
CARTOONISH
CARTOONISHLY
CARTOONIST
CARTOONISTS
CARTOONLIKE
CARTOPHILE
CARTOPHILES
CARTOPHILIC
CARTOPHILIES
CARTOPHILIST
CARTOPHILISTS
CARTOPHILY
CARTOPPERS
CARTOUCHES

CARTRIDGES
CARTULARIES
CARTWHEELED
CARTWHEELER
CARTWHEELERS
CARTWHEELING
CARTWHEELS
CARTWRIGHT
CARTWRIGHTS
CARUNCULAR
CARUNCULATE
CARUNCULATED
CARUNCULOUS
CARVACROLS
CARYATIDAL
CARYATIDEAN
CARYATIDES
CARYATIDIC
CARYOPSIDES
CARYOPTERIS
CARYOPTERISES
CASCADURAS
CASCARILLA
CASCARILLAS
CASEATIONS
CASEBEARER
CASEBEARERS
CASEINATES
CASEINOGEN
CASEINOGENS
CASEMAKERS
CASEMENTED
CASEVACING
CASEWORKER
CASEWORKERS
CASHIERERS
CASHIERING
CASHIERINGS
CASHIERMENT
CASHIERMENTS
CASHMOBBING
CASHMOBBINGS
CASHPOINTS
CASHSPIELS
CASINGHEAD
CASINGHEADS
CASKSTANDS
CASSAREEPS
CASSATIONS
CASSEROLED
CASSEROLES
CASSEROLING
CASSIMERES
CASSINGLES
CASSIOPEIUM
CASSIOPEIUMS
CASSITERITE
CASSITERITES
CASSOLETTE
CASSOLETTES
CASSONADES
CASSOULETS
CASSOWARIES
CASSUMUNAR
CASSUMUNARS
CASTABILITIES
CASTABILITY

CASTANOSPERMINE
CASTELLANS
CASTELLATED
CASTELLATION
CASTELLATIONS
CASTELLUMS
CASTIGATED
CASTIGATES
CASTIGATING
CASTIGATION
CASTIGATIONS
CASTIGATOR
CASTIGATORS
CASTIGATORY
CASTOREUMS
CASTRAMETATION
CASTRAMETATIONS
CASTRATERS
CASTRATING
CASTRATION
CASTRATIONS
CASTRATORS
CASTRATORY
CASUALISATION
CASUALISATIONS
CASUALISED
CASUALISES
CASUALISING
CASUALISMS
CASUALIZATION
CASUALIZATIONS
CASUALIZED
CASUALIZES
CASUALIZING
CASUALNESS
CASUALNESSES
CASUALTIES
CASUARINAS
CASUISTICAL
CASUISTICALLY
CASUISTRIES
CATABOLICALLY
CATABOLISE
CATABOLISED
CATABOLISES
CATABOLISING
CATABOLISM
CATABOLISMS
CATABOLITE
CATABOLITES
CATABOLIZE
CATABOLIZED
CATABOLIZES
CATABOLIZING
CATACAUSTIC
CATACAUSTICS
CATACHRESES
CATACHRESIS
CATACHRESTIC
CATACHRESTICAL
CATACLASES
CATACLASIS
CATACLASMIC
CATACLASMS
CATACLASTIC
CATACLINAL
CATACLYSMAL

CATACLYSMIC
CATACLYSMICALLY
CATACLYSMS
CATACOUSTICS
CATACUMBAL
CATADIOPTRIC
CATADIOPTRICAL
CATADROMOUS
CATAFALCOES
CATAFALQUE
CATAFALQUES
CATALECTIC
CATALECTICS
CATALEPSIES
CATALEPTIC
CATALEPTICALLY
CATALEPTICS
CATALLACTIC
CATALLACTICALLY
CATALLACTICS
CATALOGERS
CATALOGING
CATALOGISE
CATALOGISED
CATALOGISES
CATALOGISING
CATALOGIZE
CATALOGIZED
CATALOGIZES
CATALOGIZING
CATALOGNES
CATALOGUED
CATALOGUER
CATALOGUERS
CATALOGUES
CATALOGUING
CATALOGUISE
CATALOGUISED
CATALOGUISES
CATALOGUISING
CATALOGUIST
CATALOGUISTS
CATALOGUIZE
CATALOGUIZED
CATALOGUIZES
CATALOGUIZING
CATALYSERS
CATALYSING
CATALYTICAL
CATALYTICALLY
CATALYZERS
CATALYZING
CATAMARANS
CATAMENIAL
CATAMOUNTAIN
CATAMOUNTAINS
CATAMOUNTS
CATANANCHE
CATANANCHES
CATAPHONIC
CATAPHONICS
CATAPHORAS
CATAPHORESES
CATAPHORESIS
CATAPHORETIC
CATAPHORIC
CATAPHORICALLY

CATAPHRACT
CATAPHRACTIC
CATAPHRACTS
CATAPHYLLARY
CATAPHYLLS
CATAPHYSICAL
CATAPLASIA
CATAPLASIAS
CATAPLASMS
CATAPLASTIC
CATAPLECTIC
CATAPLEXIES
CATAPULTED
CATAPULTIC
CATAPULTIER
CATAPULTIERS
CATAPULTING
CATARACTOUS
CATARHINES
CATARRHALLY
CATARRHINE
CATARRHINES
CATARRHOUS
CATASTASES
CATASTASIS
CATASTROPHE
CATASTROPHES
CATASTROPHIC
CATASTROPHISM
CATASTROPHISMS
CATASTROPHIST
CATASTROPHISTS
CATATONIAS
CATATONICALLY
CATATONICS
CATATONIES
CATCALLERS
CATCALLING
CATCHCRIES
CATCHFLIES
CATCHINESS
CATCHINESSES
CATCHLINES
CATCHMENTS
CATCHPENNIES
CATCHPENNY
CATCHPHRASE
CATCHPHRASES
CATCHPOLES
CATCHPOLLS
CATCHWATER
CATCHWATERS
CATCHWEEDS
CATCHWEIGHT
CATCHWORDS
CATECHESES
CATECHESIS
CATECHESISES
CATECHETIC
CATECHETICAL
CATECHETICALLY
CATECHETICS
CATECHISATION
CATECHISATIONS
CATECHISED
CATECHISER
CATECHISERS

CATECHISES	CATERWAULINGS	CATHOLYTES	CAUTIONARY	CELESTITES
CATECHISING	CATERWAULS	CATIONICALLY	CAUTIONERS	CELIBACIES
CATECHISINGS	CATFACINGS	CATLINITES	CAUTIONING	CELIBATARIAN
CATECHISMAL	CATFISHING	CATNAPPERS	CAUTIONRIES	CELIBATARIANS
CATECHISMS	CATHARISED	CATNAPPING	CAUTIOUSLY	CELLARAGES
CATECHISTIC	CATHARISES	CATOPTRICAL	CAUTIOUSNESS	CELLARETTE
CATECHISTICAL	CATHARISING	CATOPTRICS	CAUTIOUSNESSES	CELLARETTES
CATECHISTICALLY	CATHARIZED	CATTINESSES	CAVALCADED	CELLARISTS
CATECHISTS	CATHARIZES	CATTISHNESS	CAVALCADES	CELLARWAYS
CATECHIZATION	CATHARIZING	CATTISHNESSES	CAVALCADING	CELLBLOCKS
CATECHIZATIONS	CATHARTICAL	CAUCHEMARS	CAVALIERED	CELLENTANI
CATECHIZED	CATHARTICALLY	CAUCUSSING	CAVALIERING	CELLENTANIS
CATECHIZER	CATHARTICS	CAUCUSSINGS	CAVALIERISH	CELLIFEROUS
CATECHIZERS	CATHECTING	CAUDATIONS	CAVALIERISM	CELLOBIOSE
CATECHIZES	CATHEDRALS	CAUDILLISMO	CAVALIERISMS	CELLOBIOSES
CATECHIZING	CATHEDRATIC	CAUDILLISMOS	CAVALIERLY	CELLOIDINS
CATECHIZINGS	CATHEPSINS	CAULESCENT	CAVALLETTI	CELLOPHANE
CATECHOLAMINE	CATHETERISATION	CAULICOLOUS	CAVALRYMAN	CELLOPHANES
CATECHOLAMINES	CATHETERISE	CAULICULATE	CAVALRYMEN	CELLPHONES
CATECHUMEN	CATHETERISED	CAULICULUS	CAVEFISHES	CELLULARITIES
CATECHUMENAL	CATHETERISES	CAULICULUSES	CAVENDISHES	CELLULARITY
CATECHUMENATE	CATHETERISING	CAULIFLORIES	CAVERNICOLOUS	CELLULASES
CATECHUMENATES	CATHETERISM	CAULIFLOROUS	CAVERNOUSLY	CELLULATED
CATECHUMENICAL	CATHETERISMS	CAULIFLORY	CAVERNULOUS	CELLULIFEROUS
CATECHUMENISM	CATHETERIZATION	CAULIFLOWER	CAVILLATION	CELLULITES
CATECHUMENISMS	CATHETERIZE	CAULIFLOWERET	CAVILLATIONS	CELLULITIS
CATECHUMENS	CATHETERIZED	CAULIFLOWERETS	CAVILLINGS	CELLULITISES
CATECHUMENSHIP	CATHETERIZES	CAULIFLOWERS	CAVITATING	CELLULOIDS
CATECHUMENSHIPS	CATHETERIZING	CAULIGENOUS	CAVITATION	CELLULOLYTIC
CATEGOREMATIC	CATHETOMETER	CAUMSTANES	CAVITATIONS	CELLULOSES
CATEGORIAL	CATHETOMETERS	CAUMSTONES	CAVORTINGS	CELLULOSIC
CATEGORIALLY	CATHETUSES	CAUSABILITIES	CEANOTHUSES	CELLULOSICS
CATEGORICAL	CATHINONES	CAUSABILITY	CEASEFIRES	CELSITUDES
CATEGORICALLY	CATHIODERMIE	CAUSALGIAS	CEASELESSLY	CEMBALISTS
CATEGORICALNESS	CATHIODERMIES	CAUSALITIES	CEASELESSNESS	CEMENTATION
CATEGORIES	CATHODALLY	CAUSATIONAL	CEASELESSNESSES	CEMENTATIONS
CATEGORISATION	CATHODICAL	CAUSATIONISM	CEBADILLAS	CEMENTATORY
CATEGORISATIONS	CATHODICALLY	CAUSATIONISMS	CECUTIENCIES	CEMENTITES
CATEGORISE	CATHODOGRAPH	CAUSATIONIST	CECUTIENCY	CEMENTITIOUS
CATEGORISED	CATHODOGRAPHER	CAUSATIONISTS	CEDARBIRDS	CEMETERIES
CATEGORISES	CATHODOGRAPHERS	CAUSATIONS	CEDARWOODS	CENESTHESES
CATEGORISING	CATHODOGRAPHIES	CAUSATIVELY	CEDRELACEOUS	CENESTHESIA
CATEGORIST	CATHODOGRAPHS	CAUSATIVENESS	CEILOMETER	CENESTHESIAS
CATEGORISTS	CATHODOGRAPHY	CAUSATIVENESSES	CEILOMETERS	CENESTHESIS
CATEGORIZATION	CATHOLICALLY	CAUSATIVES	CELANDINES	CENESTHETIC
CATEGORIZATIONS	CATHOLICATE	CAUSELESSLY	CELEBRANTS	CENOBITICAL
CATEGORIZE	CATHOLICATES	CAUSELESSNESS	CELEBRATED	CENOGENESES
CATEGORIZED	CATHOLICISATION	CAUSELESSNESSES	CELEBRATEDNESS	CENOGENESIS
CATEGORIZES	CATHOLICISE	CAUSEWAYED	CELEBRATES	CENOGENETIC
CATEGORIZING	CATHOLICISED	CAUSEWAYING	CELEBRATING	CENOGENETICALLY
CATENACCIO	CATHOLICISES	CAUSTICALLY	CELEBRATION	CENOSPECIES
CATENACCIOS	CATHOLICISING	CAUSTICITIES	CELEBRATIONS	CENOTAPHIC
CATENARIAN	CATHOLICISM	CAUSTICITY	CELEBRATIVE	CENSORABLE
CATENARIES	CATHOLICISMS	CAUSTICNESS	CELEBRATOR	CENSORIOUS
CATENATING	CATHOLICITIES	CAUSTICNESSES	CELEBRATORS	CENSORIOUSLY
CATENATION	CATHOLICITY	CAUTERANTS	CELEBRATORY	CENSORIOUSNESS
CATENATIONS	CATHOLICIZATION	CAUTERISATION	CELEBREALITIES	CENSORSHIP
CATENULATE	CATHOLICIZE	CAUTERISATIONS	CELEBREALITY	CENSORSHIPS
CATERCORNER	CATHOLICIZED	CAUTERISED	CELEBRITIES	CENSURABILITIES
CATERCORNERED	CATHOLICIZES	CAUTERISES	CELEBUTANTE	CENSURABILITY
CATERESSES	CATHOLICIZING	CAUTERISING	CELEBUTANTES	CENSURABLE
CATERPILLAR	CATHOLICLY	CAUTERISMS	CELECOXIBS	CENSURABLENESS
CATERPILLARS	CATHOLICOI	CAUTERIZATION	CELERITIES	CENSURABLY
CATERWAULED	CATHOLICON	CAUTERIZATIONS	CELERYLIKE	CENTAUREAS
CATERWAULER	CATHOLICONS	CAUTERIZED	CELESTIALLY	CENTAURIAN
CATERWAULERS	CATHOLICOS	CAUTERIZES	CELESTIALS	CENTAURIES
CATERWAULING	CATHOLICOSES	CAUTERIZING	CELESTINES	CENTENARIAN

C

CENTENARIANISM	CENTRALIZATION	CENTUPLICATING	CERCOPITHECIDS	CERTIORARI
CENTENARIANISMS	CENTRALIZATIONS	CENTUPLICATION	CERCOPITHECOID	CERTIORARIS
CENTENARIANS	CENTRALIZE	CENTUPLICATIONS	CERCOPITHECOIDS	CERTITUDES
CENTENARIES	CENTRALIZED	CENTUPLING	CEREALISTS	CERULOPLASMIN
CENTENIERS	CENTRALIZER	CENTURIATION	CEREBELLAR	CERULOPLASMINS
CENTENNIAL	CENTRALIZERS	CENTURIATIONS	CEREBELLIC	CERUMINOUS
CENTENNIALLY	CENTRALIZES	CENTURIATOR	CEREBELLOUS	CERUSSITES
CENTENNIALS	CENTRALIZING	CENTURIATORS	CEREBELLUM	CERVELASES
CENTERBOARD	CENTREBOARD	CENTURIONS	CEREBELLUMS	CERVICITIS
CENTERBOARDS	CENTREBOARDS	CEPHALAGRA	CEREBRALISM	CERVICITISES
CENTEREDNESS	CENTREDNESS	CEPHALAGRAS	CEREBRALISMS	CERVICOGRAPHIES
CENTEREDNESSES	CENTREDNESSES	CEPHALALGIA	CEREBRALIST	CERVICOGRAPHY
CENTERFOLD	CENTREFOLD	CEPHALALGIAS	CEREBRALISTS	CESAREVICHES
CENTERFOLDS	CENTREFOLDS	CEPHALALGIC	CEREBRALLY	CESAREVICHES
CENTERINGS	CENTREINGS	CEPHALALGICS	CEREBRATED	CESAREVITCH
CENTERLESS	CENTRELESS	CEPHALEXIN	CEREBRATES	CESAREVITCHES
CENTERLINE	CENTRELINE	CEPHALEXINS	CEREBRATING	CESAREVNAS
CENTERLINES	CENTRELINES	CEPHALICALLY	CEREBRATION	CESAREWICH
CENTERPIECE	CENTREPIECE	CEPHALISATION	CEREBRATIONS	CESAREWICHES
CENTERPIECES	CENTREPIECES	CEPHALISATIONS	CEREBRIFORM	CESAREWITCH
CENTESIMAL	CENTRICALLY	CEPHALITIS	CEREBRITIS	CESAREWITCHES
CENTESIMALLY	CENTRICALNESS	CEPHALITISES	CEREBRITISES	CESPITOSELY
CENTESIMALS	CENTRICALNESSES	CEPHALIZATION	CEREBROSIDE	CESSATIONS
CENTESIMOS	CENTRICITIES	CEPHALIZATIONS	CEREBROSIDES	CESSIONARIES
CENTIGRADE	CENTRICITY	CEPHALOCELE	CEREBROSPINAL	CESSIONARY
CENTIGRADES	CENTRIFUGAL	CEPHALOCELES	CEREBROTONIA	CESTOIDEAN
CENTIGRAMME	CENTRIFUGALISE	CEPHALOCHORDATE	CEREBROTONIAS	CESTOIDEANS
CENTIGRAMMES	CENTRIFUGALISED	CEPHALOMETER	CEREBROTONIC	CETEOSAURUS
CENTIGRAMS	CENTRIFUGALISES	CEPHALOMETERS	CEREBROTONICS	CETEOSAURUSES
CENTILITER	CENTRIFUGALIZE	CEPHALOMETRIC	CEREBROVASCULAR	CETOLOGICAL
CENTILITERS	CENTRIFUGALIZED	CEPHALOMETRIES	CERECLOTHS	CETOLOGIES
CENTILITRE	CENTRIFUGALIZES	CEPHALOMETRY	CEREMONIAL	CETOLOGIST
CENTILITRES	CENTRIFUGALLY	CEPHALOPOD	CEREMONIALISM	CETOLOGISTS
CENTILLION	CENTRIFUGALS	CEPHALOPODAN	CEREMONIALISMS	CETRIMIDES
CENTILLIONS	CENTRIFUGATION	CEPHALOPODANS	CEREMONIALIST	CETUXIMABS
CENTILLIONTH	CENTRIFUGATIONS	CEPHALOPODIC	CEREMONIALISTS	CEVADILLAS
CENTILLIONTHS	CENTRIFUGE	CEPHALOPODOUS	CEREMONIALLY	CEYLANITES
CENTIMETER	CENTRIFUGED	CEPHALOPODS	CEREMONIALS	CEYLONITES
CENTIMETERS	CENTRIFUGENCE	CEPHALORIDINE	CEREMONIES	CHABAZITES
CENTIMETRE	CENTRIFUGENCES	CEPHALORIDINES	CEREMONIOUS	CHACONINES
CENTIMETRES	CENTRIFUGES	CEPHALOSPORIN	CEREMONIOUSLY	CHAENOMELES
CENTIMETRIC	CENTRIFUGING	CEPHALOSPORINS	CEREMONIOUSNESS	CHAENOMELESES
CENTIMORGAN	CENTRIOLES	CEPHALOTHIN	CERIFEROUS	CHAETIFEROUS
CENTIMORGANS	CENTRIPETAL	CEPHALOTHINS	CEROGRAPHIC	CHAETODONS
CENTINELLS	CENTRIPETALISM	CEPHALOTHORACES	CEROGRAPHICAL	CHAETOGNATH
CENTIPEDES	CENTRIPETALISMS	CEPHALOTHORACIC	CEROGRAPHIES	CHAETOGNATHS
CENTIPOISE	CENTRIPETALLY	CEPHALOTHORAX	CEROGRAPHIST	CHAETOPODS
CENTIPOISES	CENTROBARIC	CEPHALOTHORAXES	CEROGRAPHISTS	CHAFFERERS
CENTONATES	CENTROCLINAL	CEPHALOTOMIES	CEROGRAPHS	CHAFFERIES
CENTONELLS	CENTROIDAL	CEPHALOTOMY	CEROGRAPHY	CHAFFERING
CENTONISTS	CENTROLECITHAL	CERAMICIST	CEROMANCIES	CHAFFINCHES
CENTRALEST	CENTROMERE	CERAMICISTS	CEROPLASTIC	CHAFFINGLY
CENTRALISATION	CENTROMERES	CERAMOGRAPHIES	CEROPLASTICS	CHAGRINING
CENTRALISATIONS	CENTROMERIC	CERAMOGRAPHY	CERTAINEST	CHAGRINNED
CENTRALISE	CENTROSOME	CERARGYRITE	CERTAINTIES	CHAGRINNING
CENTRALISED	CENTROSOMES	CERARGYRITES	CERTIFIABLE	CHAINBRAKE
CENTRALISER	CENTROSOMIC	CERASTIUMS	CERTIFIABLY	CHAINBRAKES
CENTRALISERS	CENTROSPHERE	CERATITISES	CERTIFICATE	CHAINFALLS
CENTRALISES	CENTROSPHERES	CERATODUSES	CERTIFICATED	CHAINPLATE
CENTRALISING	CENTROSYMMETRIC	CERATOPSIAN	CERTIFICATES	CHAINPLATES
CENTRALISM	CENTUMVIRATE	CERATOPSIANS	CERTIFICATING	CHAINSAWED
CENTRALISMS	CENTUMVIRATES	CERATOPSID	CERTIFICATION	CHAINSAWING
CENTRALIST	CENTUMVIRI	CERATOPSIDS	CERTIFICATIONS	CHAINSHOTS
CENTRALISTIC	CENTUMVIRS	CERAUNOGRAPH	CERTIFICATORIES	CHAINSTITCH
CENTRALISTS	CENTUPLICATE	CERAUNOGRAPHS	CERTIFICATORY	CHAINSTITCHES
CENTRALITIES	CENTUPLICATED	CERCARIANS	CERTIFIERS	CHAINWHEEL
CENTRALITY	CENTUPLICATES	CERCOPITHECID	CERTIFYING	CHAINWHEELS

C

CHAINWORKS
CHAIRBACKS
CHAIRBORNE
CHAIRBOUND
CHAIRLIFTS
CHAIRMANED
CHAIRMANING
CHAIRMANNED
CHAIRMANNING
CHAIRMANSHIP
CHAIRMANSHIPS
CHAIRPERSON
CHAIRPERSONS
CHAIRWARMER
CHAIRWARMERS
CHAIRWOMAN
CHAIRWOMEN
CHAISELESS
CHAKALAKAS
CHALANNING
CHALAZIONS
CHALAZOGAMIC
CHALAZOGAMIES
CHALAZOGAMY
CHALCANTHITE
CHALCANTHITES
CHALCEDONIC
CHALCEDONIES
CHALCEDONY
CHALCEDONYX
CHALCEDONYXES
CHALCOCITE
CHALCOCITES
CHALCOGENIDE
CHALCOGENIDES
CHALCOGENS
CHALCOGRAPHER
CHALCOGRAPHERS
CHALCOGRAPHIC
CHALCOGRAPHICAL
CHALCOGRAPHIES
CHALCOGRAPHIST
CHALCOGRAPHISTS
CHALCOGRAPHY
CHALCOLITHIC
CHALCOPYRITE
CHALCOPYRITES
CHALICOTHERE
CHALICOTHERES
CHALKBOARD
CHALKBOARDS
CHALKFACES
CHALKINESS
CHALKINESSES
CHALKLANDS
CHALKMARKS
CHALKSTONE
CHALKSTONES
CHALKSTRIPE
CHALKSTRIPES
CHALLENGEABLE
CHALLENGED
CHALLENGER
CHALLENGERS
CHALLENGES
CHALLENGING
CHALLENGINGLY

CHALUMEAUS
CHALUMEAUX
CHALYBEATE
CHALYBEATES
CHALYBITES
CHAMAELEON
CHAMAELEONS
CHAMAEPHYTE
CHAMAEPHYTES
CHAMBERERS
CHAMBERHAND
CHAMBERHANDS
CHAMBERING
CHAMBERINGS
CHAMBERLAIN
CHAMBERLAINS
CHAMBERLAINSHIP
CHAMBERMAID
CHAMBERMAIDS
CHAMBERPOT
CHAMBERPOTS
CHAMBRANLE
CHAMBRANLES
CHAMELEONIC
CHAMELEONLIKE
CHAMELEONS
CHAMFERERS
CHAMFERING
CHAMFRAINS
CHAMOISING
CHAMOMILES
CHAMPAGNES
CHAMPAIGNS
CHAMPERTIES
CHAMPERTOUS
CHAMPIGNON
CHAMPIGNONS
CHAMPIONED
CHAMPIONESS
CHAMPIONESSES
CHAMPIONING
CHAMPIONSHIP
CHAMPIONSHIPS
CHAMPLEVES
CHANCELESS
CHANCELLERIES
CHANCELLERY
CHANCELLOR
CHANCELLORIES
CHANCELLORS
CHANCELLORSHIP
CHANCELLORSHIPS
CHANCELLORY
CHANCERIES
CHANCINESS
CHANCINESSES
CHANCROIDAL
CHANCROIDS
CHANDELIER
CHANDELIERED
CHANDELIERS
CHANDELLED
CHANDELLES
CHANDELLING
CHANDLERIES
CHANDLERING
CHANDLERINGS

CHANDLERLY
CHANGEABILITIES
CHANGEABILITY
CHANGEABLE
CHANGEABLENESS
CHANGEABLY
CHANGEAROUND
CHANGEAROUNDS
CHANGEFULLY
CHANGEFULNESS
CHANGEFULNESSES
CHANGELESS
CHANGELESSLY
CHANGELESSNESS
CHANGELING
CHANGELINGS
CHANGEOVER
CHANGEOVERS
CHANGEROUND
CHANGEROUNDS
CHANNELERS
CHANNELING
CHANNELISATION
CHANNELISATIONS
CHANNELISE
CHANNELISED
CHANNELISES
CHANNELISING
CHANNELIZATION
CHANNELIZATIONS
CHANNELIZE
CHANNELIZED
CHANNELIZES
CHANNELIZING
CHANNELLED
CHANNELLER
CHANNELLERS
CHANNELLING
CHANSONETTE
CHANSONETTES
CHANSONNIER
CHANSONNIERS
CHANTARELLE
CHANTARELLES
CHANTECLER
CHANTECLERS
CHANTERELLE
CHANTERELLES
CHANTEUSES
CHANTICLEER
CHANTICLEERS
CHANTINGLY
CHANTRESSES
CHANUKIAHS
CHAOLOGIES
CHAOLOGIST
CHAOLOGISTS
CHAOTICALLY
CHAPARAJOS
CHAPAREJOS
CHAPARRALS
CHAPATTIES
CHAPELRIES
CHAPERONAGE
CHAPERONAGES
CHAPERONED
CHAPERONES

CHAPERONING
CHAPFALLEN
CHAPLAINCIES
CHAPLAINCY
CHAPLAINRIES
CHAPLAINRY
CHAPLAINSHIP
CHAPLAINSHIPS
CHAPMANSHIP
CHAPMANSHIPS
CHAPPESSES
CHAPRASSIES
CHAPRASSIS
CHAPSTICKS
CHAPTALISATION
CHAPTALISATIONS
CHAPTALISE
CHAPTALISED
CHAPTALISES
CHAPTALISING
CHAPTALIZATION
CHAPTALIZATIONS
CHAPTALIZE
CHAPTALIZED
CHAPTALIZES
CHAPTALIZING
CHAPTERHOUSE
CHAPTERHOUSES
CHAPTERING
CHARABANCS
CHARACINOID
CHARACTERED
CHARACTERFUL
CHARACTERIES
CHARACTERING
CHARACTERISABLE
CHARACTERISE
CHARACTERISED
CHARACTERISER
CHARACTERISERS
CHARACTERISES
CHARACTERISING
CHARACTERISM
CHARACTERISMS
CHARACTERISTIC
CHARACTERISTICS
CHARACTERIZABLE
CHARACTERIZE
CHARACTERIZED
CHARACTERIZER
CHARACTERIZERS
CHARACTERIZES
CHARACTERIZING
CHARACTERLESS
CHARACTEROLOGY
CHARACTERS
CHARACTERY
CHARBROILED
CHARBROILER
CHARBROILERS
CHARBROILING
CHARBROILS
CHARCOALED
CHARCOALIER
CHARCOALIEST
CHARCOALING
CHARCUTERIE

CHARCUTERIES
CHARDONNAY
CHARDONNAYS
CHARGEABILITIES
CHARGEABILITY
CHARGEABLE
CHARGEABLENESS
CHARGEABLY
CHARGEBACK
CHARGEBACKS
CHARGEHAND
CHARGEHANDS
CHARGELESS
CHARGESHEET
CHARGESHEETS
CHARGRILLED
CHARGRILLING
CHARGRILLS
CHARINESSES
CHARIOTEER
CHARIOTEERED
CHARIOTEERING
CHARIOTEERS
CHARIOTING
CHARISMATA
CHARISMATIC
CHARISMATICS
CHARITABLE
CHARITABLENESS
CHARITABLY
CHARIVARIED
CHARIVARING
CHARIVARIS
CHARLADIES
CHARLATANIC
CHARLATANICAL
CHARLATANISM
CHARLATANISMS
CHARLATANISTIC
CHARLATANRIES
CHARLATANRY
CHARLATANS
CHARLESTON
CHARLESTONED
CHARLESTONING
CHARLESTONS
CHARLOTTES
CHARMEUSES
CHARMINGER
CHARMINGEST
CHARMINGLY
CHARMLESSLY
CHARMONIUM
CHAROSETHS
CHARREADAS
CHARTACEOUS
CHARTERERS
CHARTERING
CHARTERPARTIES
CHARTERPARTY
CHARTHOUSE
CHARTHOUSES
CHARTOGRAPHER
CHARTOGRAPHERS
CHARTOGRAPHIC
CHARTOGRAPHICAL
CHARTOGRAPHIES

CHARTOGRAPHY
CHARTREUSE
CHARTREUSES
CHARTULARIES
CHARTULARY
CHASEPORTS
CHASMOGAMIC
CHASMOGAMIES
CHASMOGAMOUS
CHASMOGAMY
CHASSEPOTS
CHASTENERS
CHASTENESS
CHASTENESSES
CHASTENING
CHASTENINGLY
CHASTENMENT
CHASTENMENTS
CHASTISABLE
CHASTISEMENT
CHASTISEMENTS
CHASTISERS
CHASTISING
CHASTITIES
CHATEAUBRIAND
CHATEAUBRIANDS
CHATELAINE
CHATELAINES
CHATELAINS
CHATOYANCE
CHATOYANCES
CHATOYANCIES
CHATOYANCY
CHATOYANTS
CHATTERATI
CHATTERBOX
CHATTERBOXES
CHATTERERS
CHATTERIER
CHATTERIEST
CHATTERING
CHATTERINGS
CHATTINESS
CHATTINESSES
CHAUDFROID
CHAUDFROIDS
CHAUFFEURED
CHAUFFEURING
CHAUFFEURS
CHAUFFEUSE
CHAUFFEUSED
CHAUFFEUSES
CHAUFFEUSING
CHAULMOOGRA
CHAULMOOGRAS
CHAULMUGRA
CHAULMUGRAS
CHAUNTRESS
CHAUNTRESSES
CHAUNTRIES
CHAUSSURES
CHAUTAUQUA
CHAUTAUQUAS
CHAUVINISM
CHAUVINISMS
CHAUVINIST
CHAUVINISTIC

CHAUVINISTS
CHAVENDERS'
CHAVTASTIC
CHAWBACONS
CHEAPENERS
CHEAPENING
CHEAPISHLY
CHEAPJACKS
CHEAPNESSES
CHEAPSHOTS
CHEAPSKATE
CHEAPSKATES
CHEATERIES
CHEATINGLY
CHECHAKOES
CHECHAQUOS
CHECKBOOKS
CHECKBOXES
CHECKCLERK
CHECKCLERKS
CHECKERBERRIES
CHECKERBERRY
CHECKERBLOOM
CHECKERBLOOMS
CHECKERBOARD
CHECKERBOARDS
CHECKERING
CHECKLATON
CHECKLATONS
CHECKLISTED
CHECKLISTING
CHECKLISTS
CHECKMARKED
CHECKMARKING
CHECKMARKS
CHECKMATED
CHECKMATES
CHECKMATING
CHECKPOINT
CHECKPOINTS
CHECKRAILS
CHECKREINS
CHECKROOMS
CHECKROWED
CHECKROWING
CHECKSTOPS
CHECKWEIGHER
CHECKWEIGHERS
CHEDDARIER
CHEDDARIEST
CHEECHAKOES
CHEECHAKOS
CHEECHALKO
CHEECHALKOES
CHEECHALKOS
CHEEKBONES
CHEEKINESS
CHEEKINESSES
CHEEKPIECE
CHEEKPIECES
CHEEKPOUCH
CHEEKPOUCHES
CHEEKTEETH
CHEEKTOOTH
CHEERFULLER
CHEERFULLEST
CHEERFULLY

CHEERFULNESS
CHEERFULNESSES
CHEERINESS
CHEERINESSES
CHEERINGLY
CHEERISHNESS
CHEERISHNESSES
CHEERLEADER
CHEERLEADERS
CHEERLEADING
CHEERLEADS
CHEERLESSLY
CHEERLESSNESS
CHEERLESSNESSES
CHEESEBOARD
CHEESEBOARDS
CHEESEBURGER
CHEESEBURGERS
CHEESECAKE
CHEESECAKES
CHEESECLOTH
CHEESECLOTHS
CHEESECUTTER
CHEESECUTTERS
CHEESEHOPPER
CHEESEHOPPERS
CHEESELIKE
CHEESEMITE
CHEESEMITES
CHEESEMONGER
CHEESEMONGERS
CHEESEPARER
CHEESEPARERS
CHEESEPARING
CHEESEPARINGS
CHEESEPRESS
CHEESEPRESSES
CHEESESTEAK
CHEESESTEAKS
CHEESETASTER
CHEESETASTERS
CHEESEVATS
CHEESEWIRE
CHEESEWIRES
CHEESEWOOD
CHEESEWOODS
CHEESEWRING
CHEESEWRINGS
CHEESINESS
CHEESINESSES
CHEILITISES
CHEIROMANCER
CHEIROMANCERS
CHEIROMANCIES
CHEIROMANCY
CHELASHIPS
CHELATABLE
CHELATIONS
CHELICERAE
CHELICERAL
CHELICERATE
CHELICERATES
CHELIFEROUS
CHELONIANS
CHELUVIATION
CHELUVIATIONS
CHEMAUTOTROPH

CHEMAUTOTROPHIC
CHEMAUTOTROPHS
CHEMIATRIC
CHEMICALLY
CHEMICKING
CHEMICKINGS
CHEMICOPHYSICAL
CHEMIOSMOSES
CHEMIOSMOSIS
CHEMIOSMOTIC
CHEMISETTE
CHEMISETTES
CHEMISORBED
CHEMISORBING
CHEMISORBS
CHEMISORPTION
CHEMISORPTIONS
CHEMISTRIES
CHEMITYPES
CHEMITYPIES
CHEMOATTRACTANT
CHEMOAUTOTROPH
CHEMOAUTOTROPHS
CHEMOAUTOTROPHY
CHEMOAUTROPH
CHEMOAUTROPHS
CHEMOCEPTOR
CHEMOCEPTORS
CHEMOKINES
CHEMOKINESES
CHEMOKINESIS
CHEMOLITHOTROPH
CHEMONASTIES
CHEMONASTY
CHEMOPREVENTION
CHEMOPSYCHIATRY
CHEMORECEPTION
CHEMORECEPTIONS
CHEMORECEPTIVE
CHEMORECEPTOR
CHEMORECEPTORS
CHEMOSMOSES
CHEMOSMOSIS
CHEMOSMOTIC
CHEMOSORBED
CHEMOSORBING
CHEMOSORBS
CHEMOSPHERE
CHEMOSPHERES
CHEMOSPHERIC
CHEMOSTATS
CHEMOSURGERIES
CHEMOSURGERY
CHEMOSURGICAL
CHEMOSYNTHESES
CHEMOSYNTHESIS
CHEMOSYNTHETIC
CHEMOTACTIC
CHEMOTACTICALLY
CHEMOTAXES
CHEMOTAXIS
CHEMOTAXISES
CHEMOTAXONOMIC
CHEMOTAXONOMIES
CHEMOTAXONOMIST
CHEMOTAXONOMY
CHEMOTHERAPIES

CHEMOTHERAPIST
CHEMOTHERAPISTS
CHEMOTHERAPY
CHEMOTROPIC
CHEMOTROPICALLY
CHEMOTROPISM
CHEMOTROPISMS
CHEMPADUKS
CHEMTRAILS
CHEMURGICAL
CHEMURGIES
CHENOPODIACEOUS
CHEONGSAMS
CHEQUEBOOK
CHEQUEBOOKS
CHEQUERBOARD
CHEQUERBOARDS
CHEQUERING
CHEQUERWISE
CHEQUERWORK
CHEQUERWORKS
CHERALITES
CHERIMOYAS
CHERIMOYER
CHERIMOYERS
CHERISHABLE
CHERISHERS
CHERISHING
CHERISHINGLY
CHERISHMENT
CHERISHMENTS
CHERMOULAS
CHERNOZEMIC
CHERNOZEMS
CHERRYLIKE
CHERRYSTONE
CHERRYSTONES
CHERSONESE
CHERSONESES
CHERUBICAL
CHERUBICALLY
CHERUBIMIC
CHERUBLIKE
CHERVONETS
CHESSBOARD
CHESSBOARDS
CHESSBOXING
CHESSBOXINGS
CHESSPIECE
CHESSPIECES
CHESSPLAYER
CHESSPLAYERS
CHESSYLITE
CHESSYLITES
CHESTERFIELD
CHESTERFIELDS
CHESTINESS
CHESTINESSES
CHEVALIERS
CHEVELURES
CHEVESAILE
CHEVESAILES
CHEVISANCE
CHEVISANCES
CHEVRETTES
CHEVROTAIN
CHEVROTAINS

CHEVROTINS	CHILDERMASES	CHINCHIEST	CHIROPRACTORS	CHLORENCHYMA
CHEWINESSES	CHILDHOODS	CHINCHILLA	CHIROPTERAN	CHLORENCHYMAS
CHIACKINGS	CHILDISHLY	CHINCHILLAS	CHIROPTERANS	CHLORHEXIDINE
CHIAREZZAS	CHILDISHNESS	CHINCOUGHS	CHIROPTEROUS	CHLORHEXIDINES
CHIAROSCURISM	CHILDISHNESSES	CHINKAPINS	CHIROPTERS	CHLORIDATE
CHIAROSCURISMS	CHILDLESSNESS	CHINKERINCHEE	CHIRPINESS	CHLORIDATED
CHIAROSCURIST	CHILDLESSNESSES	CHINKERINCHEES	CHIRPINESSES	CHLORIDATES
CHIAROSCURISTS	CHILDLIEST	CHINOISERIE	CHIRRUPERS	CHLORIDATING
CHIAROSCURO	CHILDLIKENESS	CHINOISERIES	CHIRRUPIER	CHLORIDISE
CHIAROSCUROS	CHILDLIKENESSES	CHINOVNIKS	CHIRRUPIEST	CHLORIDISED
CHIASMATIC	CHILDMINDER	CHINQUAPIN	CHIRRUPING	CHLORIDISES
CHIASTOLITE	CHILDMINDERS	CHINQUAPINS	CHIRURGEON	CHLORIDISING
CHIASTOLITES	CHILDMINDING	CHINSTRAPS	CHIRURGEONLY	CHLORIDIZE
CHIBOUQUES	CHILDMINDINGS	CHINTZIEST	CHIRURGEONS	CHLORIDIZED
CHICALOTES	CHILDNESSES	CHINWAGGED	CHIRURGERIES	CHLORIDIZES
CHICANERIES	CHILDPROOF	CHINWAGGING	CHIRURGERY	CHLORIDIZING
CHICANINGS	CHILDPROOFED	CHIONODOXA	CHIRURGICAL	CHLORIMETER
CHICCORIES	CHILDPROOFING	CHIONODOXAS	CHISELLERS	CHLORIMETERS
CHICKABIDDIES	CHILDPROOFS	CHIPBOARDS	CHISELLING	CHLORIMETRIC
CHICKABIDDY	CHILDRENSWEAR	CHIPMAKERS	CHISELLINGS	CHLORIMETRIES
CHICKADEES	CHILDRENSWEARS	CHIPOCHIAS	CHITARRONE	CHLORIMETRY
CHICKAREES	CHILIAGONS	CHIPOLATAS	CHITARRONI	CHLORINATE
CHICKENHEARTED	CHILIAHEDRA	CHIPPEREST	CHITCHATTED	CHLORINATED
CHICKENING	CHILIAHEDRON	CHIPPERING	CHITCHATTING	CHLORINATES
CHICKENPOX	CHILIAHEDRONS	CHIPPINESS	CHITTAGONG	CHLORINATING
CHICKENPOXES	CHILIARCHIES	CHIPPINESSES	CHITTAGONGS	CHLORINATION
CHICKENSHIT	CHILIARCHS	CHIQUICHIQUI	CHITTERING	CHLORINATIONS
CHICKENSHITS	CHILIARCHY	CHIQUICHIQUIS	CHITTERINGS	CHLORINATOR
CHICKLINGS	CHILIASTIC	CHIRAGRICAL	CHITTERLING	CHLORINATORS
CHICKORIES	CHILLAXING	CHIRALITIES	CHITTERLINGS	CHLORINISE
CHICKWEEDS	CHILLINESS	CHIRIMOYAS	CHIVALRESQUE	CHLORINISED
CHICNESSES	CHILLINESSES	CHIROGNOMIES	CHIVALRIES	CHLORINISES
CHIEFERIES	CHILLINGLY	CHIROGNOMIST	CHIVALROUS	CHLORINISING
CHIEFESSES	CHILLNESSES	CHIROGNOMISTS	CHIVALROUSLY	CHLORINITIES
CHIEFLINGS	CHILOPODAN	CHIROGNOMY	CHIVALROUSNESS	CHLORINITY
CHIEFSHIPS	CHILOPODANS	CHIROGRAPH	CHIVAREEING	CHLORINIZE
CHIEFTAINCIES	CHILOPODOUS	CHIROGRAPHER	CHIVARIING	CHLORINIZED
CHIEFTAINCY	CHILTEPINS	CHIROGRAPHERS	CHIWEENIES	CHLORINIZES
CHIEFTAINESS	CHIMAERISM	CHIROGRAPHIC	CHIYOGAMIS	CHLORINIZING
CHIEFTAINESSES	CHIMAERISMS	CHIROGRAPHICAL	CHLAMYDATE	CHLORITISATION
CHIEFTAINRIES	CHIMERICAL	CHIROGRAPHIES	CHLAMYDEOUS	CHLORITISATIONS
CHIEFTAINRY	CHIMERICALLY	CHIROGRAPHIST	CHLAMYDIAE	CHLORITIZATION
CHIEFTAINS	CHIMERICALNESS	CHIROGRAPHISTS	CHLAMYDIAL	CHLORITIZATIONS
CHIEFTAINSHIP	CHIMERISMS	CHIROGRAPHS	CHLAMYDIAS	CHLOROACETIC
CHIEFTAINSHIPS	CHIMICHANGA	CHIROGRAPHY	CHLAMYDOMONADES	CHLOROARGYRITE
CHIFFCHAFF	CHIMICHANGAS	CHIROLOGIES	CHLAMYDOMONAS	CHLOROBENZENE
CHIFFCHAFFS	CHIMNEYBOARD	CHIROLOGIST	CHLAMYDOSPORE	CHLOROBENZENES
CHIFFONADE	CHIMNEYBOARDS	CHIROLOGISTS	CHLAMYDOSPORES	CHLOROBROMIDE
CHIFFONADES	CHIMNEYBREAST	CHIROMANCER	CHLOANTHITE	CHLOROBROMIDES
CHIFFONIER	CHIMNEYBREASTS	CHIROMANCERS	CHLOANTHITES	CHLOROCALCITE
CHIFFONIERS	CHIMNEYING	CHIROMANCIES	CHLOASMATA	CHLOROCALCITES
CHIFFONNIER	CHIMNEYLIKE	CHIROMANCY	CHLORACETIC	CHLOROCRUORIN
CHIFFONNIERS	CHIMNEYPIECE	CHIROMANTIC	CHLORACNES	CHLOROCRUORINS
CHIFFONNIEST	CHIMNEYPIECES	CHIROMANTICAL	CHLORALISM	CHLORODYNE
CHIFFOROBE	CHIMNEYPOT	CHIRONOMER	CHLORALISMS	CHLORODYNES
CHIFFOROBES	CHIMNEYPOTS	CHIRONOMERS	CHLORALOSE	CHLOROETHENE
CHIHUAHUAS	CHIMPANZEE	CHIRONOMIC	CHLORALOSED	CHLOROETHENES
CHILBLAINED	CHIMPANZEES	CHIRONOMID	CHLORALOSES	CHLOROETHYLENE
CHILBLAINS	CHINABERRIES	CHIRONOMIDS	CHLORAMBUCIL	CHLOROETHYLENES
CHILDBEARING	CHINABERRY	CHIRONOMIES	CHLORAMBUCILS	CHLOROFORM
CHILDBEARINGS	CHINACHINA	CHIROPODIAL	CHLORAMINE	CHLOROFORMED
CHILDBIRTH	CHINACHINAS	CHIROPODIES	CHLORAMINES	CHLOROFORMER
CHILDBIRTHS	CHINAROOTS	CHIROPODIST	CHLORAMPHENICOL	CHLOROFORMERS
CHILDCARES	CHINAWARES	CHIROPODISTS	CHLORARGYRITE	CHLOROFORMING
CHILDCROWING	CHINCAPINS	CHIROPRACTIC	CHLORARGYRITES	CHLOROFORMIST
CHILDCROWINGS	CHINCHERINCHEE	CHIROPRACTICS	CHLORDANES	CHLOROFORMISTS
CHILDERMAS	CHINCHERINCHEES	CHIROPRACTOR	CHLORELLAS	CHLOROFORMS

CHLOROHYDRIN	CHOKECHERRY	CHONDROGENESIS	CHORIOALLANTOIS	CHROMATICITY
CHLOROHYDRINS	CHOKECOILS	CHONDROITIN	CHORIOCARCINOMA	CHROMATICNESS
CHLOROMETER	CHOKEDAMPS	CHONDROITINS	CHORISATION	CHROMATICNESSES
CHLOROMETERS	CHOKEHOLDS	CHONDROMAS	CHORISATIONS	CHROMATICS
CHLOROMETHANE	CHOLAEMIAS	CHONDROMATA	CHORISTERS	CHROMATIDS
CHLOROMETHANES	CHOLAGOGIC	CHONDROMATOSES	CHORIZATION	CHROMATINIC
CHLOROMETRIC	CHOLAGOGUE	CHONDROMATOSIS	CHORIZATIONS	CHROMATINS
CHLOROMETRIES	CHOLAGOGUES	CHONDROMATOUS	CHORIZONTIST	CHROMATIST
CHLOROMETRY	CHOLANGIOGRAM	CHONDROPHORE	CHORIZONTISTS	CHROMATISTS
CHLOROPHYL	CHOLANGIOGRAMS	CHONDROPHORES	CHORIZONTS	CHROMATOGRAM
CHLOROPHYLL	CHOLANGIOGRAPHY	CHONDROPHORINE	CHOROGRAPHER	CHROMATOGRAMS
CHLOROPHYLLOID	CHOLECALCIFEROL	CHONDROPHORINES	CHOROGRAPHERS	CHROMATOGRAPH
CHLOROPHYLLOUS	CHOLECYSTECTOMY	CHONDROSAMINE	CHOROGRAPHIC	CHROMATOGRAPHED
CHLOROPHYLLS	CHOLECYSTITIDES	CHONDROSAMINES	CHOROGRAPHICAL	CHROMATOGRAPHER
CHLOROPHYLS	CHOLECYSTITIS	CHONDROSKELETON	CHOROGRAPHIES	CHROMATOGRAPHIC
CHLOROPHYTUM	CHOLECYSTITISES	CHONDROSTIAN	CHOROGRAPHY	CHROMATOGRAPHS
CHLOROPHYTUMS	CHOLECYSTOKININ	CHONDROSTIANS	CHOROIDITIS	CHROMATOGRAPHY
CHLOROPICRIN	CHOLECYSTOSTOMY	CHONDRULES	CHOROIDITISES	CHROMATOID
CHLOROPICRINS	CHOLECYSTOTOMY	CHOPFALLEN	CHOROLOGICAL	CHROMATOLOGIES
CHLOROPLAST	CHOLECYSTS	CHOPHOUSES	CHOROLOGIES	CHROMATOLOGIST
CHLOROPLASTAL	CHOLELITHIASES	CHOPLOGICS	CHOROLOGIST	CHROMATOLOGISTS
CHLOROPLASTIC	CHOLELITHIASIS	CHOPPERING	CHOROLOGISTS	CHROMATOLOGY
CHLOROPLASTS	CHOLELITHS	CHOPPINESS	CHOROPLETH	CHROMATOLYSES
CHLOROPRENE	CHOLERICALLY	CHOPPINESSES	CHOROPLETHS	CHROMATOLYSIS
CHLOROPRENES	CHOLERICLY	CHOPSOCKIES	CHORUSMASTER	CHROMATOLYTIC
CHLOROQUIN	CHOLESTASES	CHOPSTICKS	CHORUSMASTERS	CHROMATOPHORE
CHLOROQUINE	CHOLESTASIS	CHORAGUSES	CHORUSSING	CHROMATOPHORES
CHLOROQUINES	CHOLESTATIC	CHORALISTS	CHOUCROUTE	CHROMATOPHORIC
CHLOROQUINS	CHOLESTERATE	CHORDAMESODERM	CHOUCROUTES	CHROMATOPHOROUS
CHLOROSISES	CHOLESTERATES	CHORDAMESODERMS	CHOULTRIES	CHROMATOPSIA
CHLOROTHIAZIDE	CHOLESTERIC	CHORDOPHONE	CHOUNTERED	CHROMATOPSIAS
CHLOROTHIAZIDES	CHOLESTERIN	CHORDOPHONES	CHOUNTERING	CHROMATOSPHERE
CHLORPICRIN	CHOLESTERINS	CHORDOPHONIC	CHOWDERHEAD	CHROMATOSPHERES
CHLORPICRINS	CHOLESTEROL	CHORDOTOMIES	CHOWDERHEADED	CHROMATYPE
CHLORPROMAZINE	CHOLESTEROLEMIA	CHORDOTOMY	CHOWDERHEADS	CHROMATYPES
CHLORPROMAZINES	CHOLESTEROLS	CHOREGRAPH	CHOWDERING	CHROMIDIUM
CHLORPROPAMIDE	CHOLESTYRAMINE	CHOREGRAPHED	CHOWHOUNDS	CHROMINANCE
CHLORPROPAMIDES	CHOLESTYRAMINES	CHOREGRAPHER	CHOWKIDARS	CHROMINANCES
CHLORTHALIDONE	CHOLIAMBIC	CHOREGRAPHERS	CHREMATIST	CHROMISING
CHLORTHALIDONES	CHOLIAMBICS	CHOREGRAPHIC	CHREMATISTIC	CHROMIZING
CHOANOCYTE	CHOLINERGIC	CHOREGRAPHIES	CHREMATISTICS	CHROMOCENTER
CHOANOCYTES	CHOLINERGICALLY	CHOREGRAPHING	CHREMATISTS	CHROMOCENTERS
CHOCAHOLIC	CHOLINESTERASE	CHOREGRAPHS	CHRESTOMATHIC	CHROMOCENTRE
CHOCAHOLICS	CHOLINESTERASES	CHOREGRAPHY	CHRESTOMATHICAL	CHROMOCENTRES
CHOCKABLOCK	CHOMOPHYTE	CHOREGUSES	CHRESTOMATHIES	CHROMODYNAMICS
CHOCKSTONE	CHOMOPHYTES	CHOREIFORM	CHRESTOMATHY	CHROMOGENIC
CHOCKSTONES	CHONDRICHTHYAN	CHOREODRAMA	CHRISMATION	CHROMOGENS
CHOCOHOLIC	CHONDRICHTHYANS	CHOREODRAMAS	CHRISMATIONS	CHROMOGRAM
CHOCOHOLICS	CHONDRIFICATION	CHOREOGRAPH	CHRISMATORIES	CHROMOGRAMS
CHOCOLATES	CHONDRIFIED	CHOREOGRAPHED	CHRISMATORY	CHROMOLIES
CHOCOLATEY	CHONDRIFIES	CHOREOGRAPHER	CHRISTCROSS	CHROMOMERE
CHOCOLATIER	CHONDRIFYING	CHOREOGRAPHERS	CHRISTCROSSES	CHROMOMERES
CHOCOLATIERS	CHONDRIOSOMAL	CHOREOGRAPHIC	CHRISTENED	CHROMOMERIC
CHOCOLATIEST	CHONDRIOSOME	CHOREOGRAPHIES	CHRISTENER	CHROMONEMA
CHOICENESS	CHONDRIOSOMES	CHOREOGRAPHING	CHRISTENERS	CHROMONEMAL
CHOICENESSES	CHONDRITES	CHOREOGRAPHS	CHRISTENING	CHROMONEMATA
CHOIRGIRLS	CHONDRITIC	CHOREOGRAPHY	CHRISTENINGS	CHROMONEMATIC
CHOIRMASTER	CHONDRITIS	CHOREOLOGIES	CHRISTIANIA	CHROMONEMIC
CHOIRMASTERS	CHONDRITISES	CHOREOLOGIST	CHRISTIANIAS	CHROMOPHIL
CHOIRSCREEN	CHONDROBLAST	CHOREOLOGISTS	CHRISTOPHANIES	CHROMOPHILIC
CHOIRSCREENS	CHONDROBLASTS	CHOREOLOGY	CHRISTOPHANY	CHROMOPHILS
CHOIRSTALL	CHONDROCRANIA	CHOREPISCOPAL	CHROMAFFIN	CHROMOPHOBE
CHOIRSTALLS	CHONDROCRANIUM	CHORIAMBIC	CHROMAKEYS	CHROMOPHOBES
CHOKEBERRIES	CHONDROCRANIUMS	CHORIAMBICS	CHROMATICALLY	CHROMOPHORE
CHOKEBERRY	CHONDROCYTE	CHORIAMBUS	CHROMATICISM	CHROMOPHORES
CHOKEBORES	CHONDROCYTES	CHORIAMBUSES	CHROMATICISMS	CHROMOPHORIC
CHOKECHERRIES	CHONDROGENESES	CHORIOALLANTOIC	CHROMATICITIES	CHROMOPHOROUS

CHROMOPLAST	CHRONOTHERAPIES	CHURCHIEST	CICATRIXES	CINEMATOGRAPHS
CHROMOPLASTS	CHRONOTHERAPY	CHURCHINGS	CICATRIZANT	CINEMATOGRAPHY
CHROMOPROTEIN	CHRONOTRON	CHURCHISMS	CICATRIZATION	CINEMICROGRAPHY
CHROMOPROTEINS	CHRONOTRONS	CHURCHLESS	CICATRIZATIONS	CINEPHILES
CHROMOSCOPE	CHRYSALIDAL	CHURCHLIER	CICATRIZED	CINEPLEXES
CHROMOSCOPES	CHRYSALIDES	CHURCHLIEST	CICATRIZER	CINERARIAS
CHROMOSOMAL	CHRYSALIDS	CHURCHLINESS	CICATRIZERS	CINERARIUM
CHROMOSOMALLY	CHRYSALISES	CHURCHLINESSES	CICATRIZES	CINERARIUMS
CHROMOSOME	CHRYSANTHEMUM	CHURCHMANLIER	CICATRIZING	CINERATION
CHROMOSOMES	CHRYSANTHEMUMS	CHURCHMANLIEST	CICERONEING	CINERATIONS
CHROMOSPHERE	CHRYSANTHS	CHURCHMANLY	CICHORACEOUS	CINERATORS
CHROMOSPHERES	CHRYSAROBIN	CHURCHMANSHIP	CICINNUSES	CINERITIOUS
CHROMOSPHERIC	CHRYSAROBINS	CHURCHMANSHIPS	CICISBEISM	CINGULATED
CHROMOTHERAPIES	CHRYSOBERYL	CHURCHPEOPLE	CICISBEISMS	CINNABARIC
CHROMOTHERAPY	CHRYSOBERYLS	CHURCHWARD	CICLATOUNS	CINNABARINE
CHROMOTYPE	CHRYSOCOLLA	CHURCHWARDEN	CICLOSPORIN	CINNAMONIC
CHROMOTYPES	CHRYSOCOLLAS	CHURCHWARDENS	CICLOSPORINS	CINNAMONIER
CHROMOXYLOGRAPH	CHRYSOCRACIES	CHURCHWARDS	CIGARETTES	CINNAMONIEST
CHRONAXIES	CHRYSOCRACY	CHURCHWAYS	CIGARILLOS	CINNARIZINE
CHRONICALLY	CHRYSOLITE	CHURCHWOMAN	CIGUATERAS	CINNARIZINES
CHRONICITIES	CHRYSOLITES	CHURCHWOMEN	CIGUATOXIN	CINQUECENTIST
CHRONICITY	CHRYSOLITIC	CHURCHYARD	CIGUATOXINS	CINQUECENTISTS
CHRONICLED	CHRYSOMELID	CHURCHYARDS	CILIATIONS	CINQUECENTO
CHRONICLER	CHRYSOMELIDS	CHURLISHLY	CIMETIDINE	CINQUECENTOS
CHRONICLERS	CHRYSOPHAN	CHURLISHNESS	CIMETIDINES	CINQUEFOIL
CHRONICLES	CHRYSOPHANS	CHURLISHNESSES	CINCHONACEOUS	CINQUEFOILS
CHRONICLING	CHRYSOPHILITE	CHURNALISM	CINCHONIDINE	CIPHERINGS
CHRONOBIOLOGIC	CHRYSOPHILITES	CHURNALISMS	CINCHONIDINES	CIPHERTEXT
CHRONOBIOLOGIES	CHRYSOPHYTE	CHURNMILKS	CINCHONINE	CIPHERTEXTS
CHRONOBIOLOGIST	CHRYSOPHYTES	CHURRIGUERESCO	CINCHONINES	CIPOLLINOS
CHRONOBIOLOGY	CHRYSOPRASE	CHURRIGUERESQUE	CINCHONINIC	CIPROFLOXACIN
CHRONOGRAM	CHRYSOPRASES	CHYLACEOUS	CINCHONISATION	CIPROFLOXACINS
CHRONOGRAMMATIC	CHRYSOTILE	CHYLIFEROUS	CINCHONISATIONS	CIRCASSIAN
CHRONOGRAMS	CHRYSOTILES	CHYLIFICATION	CINCHONISE	CIRCASSIANS
CHRONOGRAPH	CHUBBINESS	CHYLIFICATIONS	CINCHONISED	CIRCASSIENNE
CHRONOGRAPHER	CHUBBINESSES	CHYLIFYING	CINCHONISES	CIRCASSIENNES
CHRONOGRAPHERS	CHUCKAWALLA	CHYLOMICRON	CINCHONISING	CIRCENSIAL
CHRONOGRAPHIC	CHUCKAWALLAS	CHYLOMICRONS	CINCHONISM	CIRCENSIAN
CHRONOGRAPHIES	CHUCKHOLES	CHYMIFEROUS	CINCHONISMS	CIRCINATELY
CHRONOGRAPHS	CHUCKLEHEAD	CHYMIFICATION	CINCHONIZATION	CIRCUITEER
CHRONOGRAPHY	CHUCKLEHEADED	CHYMIFICATIONS	CINCHONIZATIONS	CIRCUITEERED
CHRONOLOGER	CHUCKLEHEADS	CHYMIFYING	CINCHONIZE	CIRCUITEERING
CHRONOLOGERS	CHUCKLESOME	CHYMISTRIES	CINCHONIZED	CIRCUITEERS
CHRONOLOGIC	CHUCKLINGLY	CHYMOTRYPSIN	CINCHONIZES	CIRCUITIES
CHRONOLOGICAL	CHUCKLINGS	CHYMOTRYPSINS	CINCHONIZING	CIRCUITING
CHRONOLOGICALLY	CHUCKWALLA	CHYMOTRYPTIC	CINCINNATE	CIRCUITOUS
CHRONOLOGIES	CHUCKWALLAS	CIBACHROME	CINCINNUSES	CIRCUITOUSLY
CHRONOLOGISE	CHUFFINESS	CIBACHROMES	CINCTURING	CIRCUITOUSNESS
CHRONOLOGISED	CHUFFINESSES	CICADELLID	CINDERIEST	CIRCUITRIES
CHRONOLOGISES	CHUGALUGGED	CICADELLIDS	CINEANGIOGRAPHY	CIRCULABLE
CHRONOLOGISING	CHUGALUGGING	CICATRICES	CINEMAGOER	CIRCULARISATION
CHRONOLOGIST	CHUMMINESS	CICATRICHULE	CINEMAGOERS	CIRCULARISE
CHRONOLOGISTS	CHUMMINESSES	CICATRICHULES	CINEMATHEQUE	CIRCULARISED
CHRONOLOGIZE	CHUNDERING	CICATRICIAL	CINEMATHEQUES	CIRCULARISER
CHRONOLOGIZED	CHUNDEROUS	CICATRICLE	CINEMATICALLY	CIRCULARISERS
CHRONOLOGIZES	CHUNKINESS	CICATRICLES	CINEMATISE	CIRCULARISES
CHRONOLOGIZING	CHUNKINESSES	CICATRICOSE	CINEMATISED	CIRCULARISING
CHRONOLOGY	CHUNNERING	CICATRICULA	CINEMATISES	CIRCULARITIES
CHRONOMETER	CHUNTERING	CICATRICULAS	CINEMATISING	CIRCULARITY
CHRONOMETERS	CHUPATTIES	CICATRISANT	CINEMATIZE	CIRCULARIZATION
CHRONOMETRIC	CHUPRASSIES	CICATRISATION	CINEMATIZED	CIRCULARIZE
CHRONOMETRICAL	CHURCHGOER	CICATRISATIONS	CINEMATIZES	CIRCULARIZED
CHRONOMETRIES	CHURCHGOERS	CICATRISED	CINEMATIZING	CIRCULARIZER
CHRONOMETRY	CHURCHGOING	CICATRISER	CINEMATOGRAPH	CIRCULARIZERS
CHRONOSCOPE	CHURCHGOINGS	CICATRISERS	CINEMATOGRAPHED	CIRCULARIZES
CHRONOSCOPES	CHURCHIANITIES	CICATRISES	CINEMATOGRAPHER	CIRCULARIZING
CHRONOSCOPIC	CHURCHIANITY	CICATRISING	CINEMATOGRAPHIC	CIRCULARLY

CIRCULARNESS	CIRCUMFORANEAN	CIRCUMSOLAR	CITIZENIZE	CLAIRAUDIENCES
CIRCULARNESSES	CIRCUMFORANEOUS	CIRCUMSPECT	CITIZENIZED	CLAIRAUDIENT
CIRCULATABLE	CIRCUMFUSE	CIRCUMSPECTION	CITIZENIZES	CLAIRAUDIENTLY
CIRCULATED	CIRCUMFUSED	CIRCUMSPECTIONS	CITIZENIZING	CLAIRAUDIENTS
CIRCULATES	CIRCUMFUSES	CIRCUMSPECTIVE	CITIZENLIER	CLAIRCOLLE
CIRCULATING	CIRCUMFUSILE	CIRCUMSPECTLY	CITIZENLIEST	CLAIRCOLLES
CIRCULATINGS	CIRCUMFUSING	CIRCUMSPECTNESS	CITIZENRIES	CLAIRSCHACH
CIRCULATION	CIRCUMFUSION	CIRCUMSTANCE	CITIZENSHIP	CLAIRSCHACHS
CIRCULATIONS	CIRCUMFUSIONS	CIRCUMSTANCED	CITIZENSHIPS	CLAIRVOYANCE
CIRCULATIVE	CIRCUMGYRATE	CIRCUMSTANCES	CITRICULTURE	CLAIRVOYANCES
CIRCULATOR	CIRCUMGYRATED	CIRCUMSTANCING	CITRICULTURES	CLAIRVOYANCIES
CIRCULATORS	CIRCUMGYRATES	CIRCUMSTANTIAL	CITRICULTURIST	CLAIRVOYANCY
CIRCULATORY	CIRCUMGYRATING	CIRCUMSTANTIALS	CITRICULTURISTS	CLAIRVOYANT
CIRCUMAMBAGES	CIRCUMGYRATION	CIRCUMSTANTIATE	CITRONELLA	CLAIRVOYANTLY
CIRCUMAMBAGIOUS	CIRCUMGYRATIONS	CIRCUMSTELLAR	CITRONELLAL	CLAIRVOYANTS
CIRCUMAMBIENCE	CIRCUMGYRATORY	CIRCUMVALLATE	CITRONELLALS	CLAMANCIES
CIRCUMAMBIENCES	CIRCUMINCESSION	CIRCUMVALLATED	CITRONELLAS	CLAMATORIAL
CIRCUMAMBIENCY	CIRCUMINSESSION	CIRCUMVALLATES	CITRONELLOL	CLAMBERERS
CIRCUMAMBIENT	CIRCUMJACENCIES	CIRCUMVALLATING	CITRONELLOLS	CLAMBERING
CIRCUMAMBIENTLY	CIRCUMJACENCY	CIRCUMVALLATION	CITRULLINE	CLAMJAMFRIES
CIRCUMAMBULATE	CIRCUMJACENT	CIRCUMVENT	CITRULLINES	CLAMJAMFRY
CIRCUMAMBULATED	CIRCUMLITTORAL	CIRCUMVENTED	CITRUSIEST	CLAMJAMPHRIE
CIRCUMAMBULATES	CIRCUMLOCUTE	CIRCUMVENTER	CITRUSSIER	CLAMJAMPHRIES
CIRCUMAMBULATOR	CIRCUMLOCUTED	CIRCUMVENTERS	CITRUSSIEST	CLAMMINESS
CIRCUMBENDIBUS	CIRCUMLOCUTES	CIRCUMVENTING	CITYFICATION	CLAMMINESSES
CIRCUMCENTER	CIRCUMLOCUTING	CIRCUMVENTION	CITYFICATIONS	CLAMOROUSLY
CIRCUMCENTERS	CIRCUMLOCUTION	CIRCUMVENTIONS	CITYSCAPES	CLAMOROUSNESS
CIRCUMCENTRE	CIRCUMLOCUTIONS	CIRCUMVENTIVE	CIVILIANISATION	CLAMOROUSNESSES
CIRCUMCENTRES	CIRCUMLOCUTORY	CIRCUMVENTOR	CIVILIANISE	CLAMOURERS
CIRCUMCIRCLE	CIRCUMLUNAR	CIRCUMVENTORS	CIVILIANISED	CLAMOURING
CIRCUMCIRCLES	CIRCUMMURE	CIRCUMVENTS	CIVILIANISES	CLAMPDOWNS
CIRCUMCISE	CIRCUMMURED	CIRCUMVOLUTION	CIVILIANISING	CLAMPERING
CIRCUMCISED	CIRCUMMURES	CIRCUMVOLUTIONS	CIVILIANIZATION	CLAMSHELLS
CIRCUMCISER	CIRCUMMURING	CIRCUMVOLUTORY	CIVILIANIZE	CLANDESTINE
CIRCUMCISERS	CIRCUMNAVIGABLE	CIRCUMVOLVE	CIVILIANIZED	CLANDESTINELY
CIRCUMCISES	CIRCUMNAVIGATE	CIRCUMVOLVED	CIVILIANIZES	CLANDESTINENESS
CIRCUMCISING	CIRCUMNAVIGATED	CIRCUMVOLVES	CIVILIANIZING	CLANDESTINITIES
CIRCUMCISION	CIRCUMNAVIGATES	CIRCUMVOLVING	CIVILISABLE	CLANDESTINITY
CIRCUMCISIONS	CIRCUMNAVIGATOR	CIRCUSIEST	CIVILISATION	CLANGBOXES
CIRCUMDUCE	CIRCUMNUTATE	CIRCUSSIER	CIVILISATIONAL	CLANGORING
CIRCUMDUCED	CIRCUMNUTATED	CIRCUSSIEST	CIVILISATIONS	CLANGOROUS
CIRCUMDUCES	CIRCUMNUTATES	CIRRHIPEDE	CIVILISERS	CLANGOROUSLY
CIRCUMDUCING	CIRCUMNUTATING	CIRRHIPEDES	CIVILISING	CLANGOURED
CIRCUMDUCT	CIRCUMNUTATION	CIRRHOTICS	CIVILITIES	CLANGOURING
CIRCUMDUCTED	CIRCUMNUTATIONS	CIRRIGRADE	CIVILIZABLE	CLANJAMFRAY
CIRCUMDUCTING	CIRCUMNUTATORY	CIRRIPEDES	CIVILIZATION	CLANJAMFRAYS
CIRCUMDUCTION	CIRCUMPOLAR	CIRROCUMULI	CIVILIZATIONAL	CLANKINGLY
CIRCUMDUCTIONS	CIRCUMPOSE	CIRROCUMULUS	CIVILIZATIONS	CLANNISHLY
CIRCUMDUCTORY	CIRCUMPOSED	CIRROSTRATI	CIVILIZERS	CLANNISHNESS
CIRCUMDUCTS	CIRCUMPOSES	CIRROSTRATIVE	CIVILIZING	CLANNISHNESSES
CIRCUMFERENCE	CIRCUMPOSING	CIRROSTRATUS	CIVILNESSES	CLANSWOMAN
CIRCUMFERENCES	CIRCUMPOSITION	CISGENDERED	CLABBERING	CLANSWOMEN
CIRCUMFERENTIAL	CIRCUMPOSITIONS	CISMONTANE	CLACKBOXES	CLAPBOARDED
CIRCUMFERENTOR	CIRCUMROTATE	CISPLATINS	CLACKDISHES	CLAPBOARDING
CIRCUMFERENTORS	CIRCUMROTATED	CISPONTINE	CLADISTICALLY	CLAPBOARDS
CIRCUMFLECT	CIRCUMROTATES	CISTACEOUS	CLADISTICS	CLAPBREADS
CIRCUMFLECTED	CIRCUMROTATING	CITATIONAL	CLADOCERAN	CLAPDISHES
CIRCUMFLECTING	CIRCUMSCISSILE	CITHARISTIC	CLADOCERANS	CLAPOMETER
CIRCUMFLECTS	CIRCUMSCRIBABLE	CITHARISTS	CLADOGENESES	CLAPOMETERS
CIRCUMFLEX	CIRCUMSCRIBE	CITIFICATION	CLADOGENESIS	CLAPPERBOARD
CIRCUMFLEXES	CIRCUMSCRIBED	CITIFICATIONS	CLADOGENETIC	CLAPPERBOARDS
CIRCUMFLEXION	CIRCUMSCRIBER	CITIZENESS	CLADOGRAMS	CLAPPERBOY
CIRCUMFLEXIONS	CIRCUMSCRIBERS	CITIZENESSES	CLADOPHYLL	CLAPPERBOYS
CIRCUMFLUENCE	CIRCUMSCRIBES	CITIZENISE	CLADOPHYLLS	CLAPPERCLAW
CIRCUMFLUENCES	CIRCUMSCRIBING	CITIZENISED	CLADOSPORIA	CLAPPERCLAWED
CIRCUMFLUENT	CIRCUMSCRIPTION	CITIZENISES	CLADOSPORIUM	CLAPPERCLAWER
CIRCUMFLUOUS	CIRCUMSCRIPTIVE	CITIZENISING	CLAIRAUDIENCE	CLAPPERCLAWERS

CLAPPERCLAWING	CLATTERIER	CLEARSTORIES	CLICKTIVISMS	CLINOMETRICAL
CLAPPERCLAWS	CLATTERIEST	CLEARSTORY	CLICKWRAPS	CLINOMETRIES
CLAPPERING	CLATTERING	CLEARWEEDS	CLIENTAGES	CLINOMETRY
CLAPPERINGS	CLATTERINGLY	CLEARWINGS	CLIENTELES	CLINOPINACOID
CLAPTRAPPERIES	CLAUCHTING	CLEAVABILITIES	CLIENTLESS	CLINOPINACOIDS
CLAPTRAPPERY	CLAUDICATION	CLEAVABILITY	CLIENTSHIP	CLINOPINAKOID
CLARABELLA	CLAUDICATIONS	CLEAVABLENESS	CLIENTSHIPS	CLINOPINAKOIDS
CLARABELLAS	CLAUGHTING	CLEAVABLENESSES	CLIFFHANGER	CLINOPYROXENE
CLARENDONS	CLAUSTRATION	CLEISTOGAMIC	CLIFFHANGERS	CLINOPYROXENES
CLARIBELLA	CLAUSTRATIONS	CLEISTOGAMIES	CLIFFHANGING	CLINOSTATS
CLARIBELLAS	CLAUSTROPHILIA	CLEISTOGAMOUS	CLIFFHANGINGS	CLINQUANTS
CLARICHORD	CLAUSTROPHILIAS	CLEISTOGAMOUSLY	CLIFFHANGS	CLINTONIAS
CLARICHORDS	CLAUSTROPHOBE	CLEISTOGAMY	CLIFFSIDES	CLIOMETRIC
CLARIFICATION	CLAUSTROPHOBES	CLEMATISES	CLIMACTERIC	CLIOMETRICAL
CLARIFICATIONS	CLAUSTROPHOBIA	CLEMENCIES	CLIMACTERICAL	CLIOMETRICIAN
CLARIFIERS	CLAUSTROPHOBIAS	CLEMENTINE	CLIMACTERICALLY	CLIOMETRICIANS
CLARIFYING	CLAUSTROPHOBIC	CLEMENTINES	CLIMACTERICS	CLIOMETRICS
CLARINETIST	CLAVATIONS	CLENBUTEROL	CLIMACTICAL	CLIOMETRIES
CLARINETISTS	CLAVECINIST	CLENBUTEROLS	CLIMACTICALLY	CLIPBOARDS
CLARINETTIST	CLAVECINISTS	CLEOPATRAS	CLIMATICAL	CLIPSHEARS
CLARINETTISTS	CLAVICEMBALO	CLEPSYDRAE	CLIMATICALLY	CLIPSHEETS
CLARIONETS	CLAVICEMBALOS	CLEPSYDRAS	CLIMATISED	CLIQUINESS
CLARIONING	CLAVICHORD	CLEPTOCRACIES	CLIMATISES	CLIQUINESSES
CLARTHEADS	CLAVICHORDIST	CLEPTOCRACY	CLIMATISING	CLIQUISHLY
CLASHINGLY	CLAVICHORDISTS	CLEPTOMANIA	CLIMATIZED	CLIQUISHNESS
CLASSICALISM	CLAVICHORDS	CLEPTOMANIAC	CLIMATIZES	CLIQUISHNESSES
CLASSICALISMS	CLAVICORNS	CLEPTOMANIACS	CLIMATIZING	CLISHMACLAVER
CLASSICALIST	CLAVICULAE	CLEPTOMANIAS	CLIMATOGRAPHIES	CLISHMACLAVERS
CLASSICALISTS	CLAVICULAR	CLERESTORIED	CLIMATOGRAPHY	CLISTOGAMIES
CLASSICALITIES	CLAVICULATE	CLERESTORIES	CLIMATOLOGIC	CLISTOGAMY
CLASSICALITY	CLAVICYTHERIA	CLERESTORY	CLIMATOLOGICAL	CLITICISED
CLASSICALLY	CLAVICYTHERIUM	CLERGIABLE	CLIMATOLOGIES	CLITICISES
CLASSICALNESS	CLAVIERIST	CLERGYABLE	CLIMATOLOGIST	CLITICISING
CLASSICALNESSES	CLAVIERISTIC	CLERGYWOMAN	CLIMATOLOGISTS	CLITICIZED
CLASSICALS	CLAVIERISTS	CLERGYWOMEN	CLIMATOLOGY	CLITICIZES
CLASSICISE	CLAVIGEROUS	CLERICALISM	CLIMATURES	CLITICIZING
CLASSICISED	CLAWHAMMER	CLERICALISMS	CLIMAXLESS	CLITORECTOMIES
CLASSICISES	CLAWHAMMERS	CLERICALIST	CLIMBDOWNS	CLITORECTOMY
CLASSICISING	CLAYMATION	CLERICALISTS	CLINANDRIA	CLITORIDECTOMY
CLASSICISM	CLAYMATIONS	CLERICALLY	CLINANDRIUM	CLITORIDES
CLASSICISMS	CLAYSTONES	CLERICATES	CLINCHINGLY	CLITORISES
CLASSICIST	CLAYTONIAS	CLERICITIES	CLINDAMYCIN	CLITTERING
CLASSICISTIC	CLEANABILITIES	CLERKESSES	CLINDAMYCINS	CLOACALINE
CLASSICISTS	CLEANABILITY	CLERKLIEST	CLINGFILMS	CLOACITISES
CLASSICIZE	CLEANHANDED	CLERKLINESS	CLINGFISHES	CLOAKROOMS
CLASSICIZED	CLEANLIEST	CLERKLINESSES	CLINGINESS	CLOBBERING
CLASSICIZES	CLEANLINESS	CLERKLINGS	CLINGINESSES	CLOCKFACES
CLASSICIZING	CLEANLINESSES	CLERKSHIPS	CLINGINGLY	CLOCKMAKER
CLASSIFIABLE	CLEANNESSES	CLEROMANCIES	CLINGINGNESS	CLOCKMAKERS
CLASSIFICATION	CLEANSABLE	CLEROMANCY	CLINGINGNESSES	CLOCKWORKS
CLASSIFICATIONS	CLEANSINGS	CLERUCHIAL	CLINGSTONE	CLODDISHLY
CLASSIFICATORY	CLEANSKINS	CLERUCHIAS	CLINGSTONES	CLODDISHNESS
CLASSIFIED	CLEANTECHS	CLERUCHIES	CLINGWRAPS	CLODDISHNESSES
CLASSIFIEDS	CLEARANCES	CLEVERALITIES	CLINICALLY	CLODHOPPER
CLASSIFIER	CLEARCOLED	CLEVERALITY	CLINICALNESS	CLODHOPPERS
CLASSIFIERS	CLEARCOLES	CLEVERDICK	CLINICALNESSES	CLODHOPPING
CLASSIFIES	CLEARCOLING	CLEVERDICKS	CLINICIANS	CLOFIBRATE
CLASSIFYING	CLEARCUTTING	CLEVERNESS	CLINKERING	CLOFIBRATES
CLASSINESS	CLEARCUTTINGS	CLEVERNESSES	CLINKSTONE	CLOGDANCES
CLASSINESSES	CLEARHEADED	CLIANTHUSES	CLINKSTONES	CLOGGINESS
CLASSLESSNESS	CLEARHEADEDLY	CLICKBAITS	CLINOCHLORE	CLOGGINESSES
CLASSLESSNESSES	CLEARHEADEDNESS	CLICKETING	CLINOCHLORES	CLOGMAKERS
CLASSMATES	CLEARINGHOUSE	CLICKJACKING	CLINODIAGONAL	CLOISONNAGE
CLASSROOMS	CLEARINGHOUSES	CLICKJACKINGS	CLINODIAGONALS	CLOISONNAGES
CLASSWORKS	CLEARNESSES	CLICKSTREAM	CLINOMETER	CLOISONNES
CLATHRATES	CLEARSKINS	CLICKSTREAMS	CLINOMETERS	CLOISTERED
CLATTERERS	CLEARSTORIED	CLICKTIVISM	CLINOMETRIC	CLOISTERER

CLOISTERERS	CLUBBABILITIES	COADMIRING	COASTGUARDMEN	COCHAIRMAN
CLOISTERING	CLUBBABILITY	COADMITTED	COASTGUARDS	COCHAIRMANSHIP
CLOISTRESS	CLUBBINESS	COADMITTING	COASTGUARDSMAN	COCHAIRMANSHIPS
CLOISTRESSES	CLUBBINESSES	COADUNATED	COASTGUARDSMEN	COCHAIRMEN
CLOMIPHENE	CLUBFOOTED	COADUNATES	COASTLANDS	COCHAIRPERSON
CLOMIPHENES	CLUBHAULED	COADUNATING	COASTLINES	COCHAIRPERSONS
CLONAZEPAM	CLUBHAULING	COADUNATION	COASTWARDS	COCHAIRWOMAN
CLONAZEPAMS	CLUBHOUSES	COADUNATIONS	COATDRESSES	COCHAIRWOMEN
CLONICITIES	CLUBMANSHIP	COADUNATIVE	COATIMUNDI	COCHAMPION
CLONIDINES	CLUBMANSHIPS	COAGENCIES	COATIMUNDIS	COCHAMPIONS
CLOSEDOWNS	CLUBMASTER	COAGULABILITIES	COATSTANDS	COCHINEALS
CLOSEFISTED	CLUBMASTERS	COAGULABILITY	COATTENDED	COCHLEARES
CLOSEHEADS	CLUBMOSSES	COAGULABLE	COATTENDING	COCHLEARIFORM
CLOSEMOUTHED	CLUBRUSHES	COAGULANTS	COATTESTED	COCHLEATED
CLOSENESSES	CLUMPERING	COAGULASES	COATTESTING	COCKABULLIES
CLOSESTOOL	CLUMPINESS	COAGULATED	COAUTHORED	COCKABULLY
CLOSESTOOLS	CLUMPINESSES	COAGULATES	COAUTHORING	COCKALEEKIE
CLOSETFULS	CLUMSINESS	COAGULATING	COAUTHORSHIP	COCKALEEKIES
CLOSTRIDIA	CLUMSINESSES	COAGULATION	COAUTHORSHIPS	COCKALORUM
CLOSTRIDIAL	CLUSTERIER	COAGULATIONS	COBALAMINS	COCKALORUMS
CLOSTRIDIAN	CLUSTERIEST	COAGULATIVE	COBALTIFEROUS	COCKAMAMIE
CLOSTRIDIUM	CLUSTERING	COAGULATOR	COBALTINES	COCKAMAMIER
CLOSTRIDIUMS	CLUSTERINGLY	COAGULATORS	COBALTITES	COCKAMAMIEST
CLOTHBOUND	CLUTCHIEST	COAGULATORY	COBBLERIES	COCKATEELS
CLOTHESHORSE	CLUTTERIER	COALESCENCE	COBBLESTONE	COCKATIELS
CLOTHESHORSES	CLUTTERIEST	COALESCENCES	COBBLESTONED	COCKATRICE
CLOTHESLINE	CLUTTERING	COALESCENT	COBBLESTONES	COCKATRICES
CLOTHESLINED	CLYPEIFORM	COALESCING	COBBLESTONING	COCKBILLED
CLOTHESLINES	CNIDARIANS	COALFIELDS	COBELLIGERENT	COCKBILLING
CLOTHESLINING	CNIDOBLAST	COALFISHES	COBELLIGERENTS	COCKCHAFER
CLOTHESPIN	CNIDOBLASTS	COALHOUSES	COBWEBBERIES	COCKCHAFERS
CLOTHESPINS	COACERVATE	COALIFICATION	COBWEBBERY	COCKCROWING
CLOTHESPRESS	COACERVATED	COALIFICATIONS	COBWEBBIER	COCKCROWINGS
CLOTHESPRESSES	COACERVATES	COALIFYING	COBWEBBIEST	COCKERNONIES
CLOTTERING	COACERVATING	COALITIONAL	COBWEBBING	COCKERNONY
CLOTTINESS	COACERVATION	COALITIONER	COCAINISATION	COCKEYEDLY
CLOTTINESSES	COACERVATIONS	COALITIONERS	COCAINISATIONS	COCKEYEDNESS
CLOUDBERRIES	COACHBUILDER	COALITIONISM	COCAINISED	COCKEYEDNESSES
CLOUDBERRY	COACHBUILDERS	COALITIONISMS	COCAINISES	COCKFIGHTING
CLOUDBURST	COACHBUILDING	COALITIONIST	COCAINISING	COCKFIGHTINGS
CLOUDBURSTS	COACHBUILDINGS	COALITIONISTS	COCAINISMS	COCKFIGHTS
CLOUDINESS	COACHBUILT	COALITIONS	COCAINISTS	COCKHORSES
CLOUDINESSES	COACHLINES	COALMASTER	COCAINIZATION	COCKIELEEKIE
CLOUDLANDS	COACHLOADS	COALMASTERS	COCAINIZATIONS	COCKIELEEKIES
CLOUDLESSLY	COACHROOFS	COALMINERS	COCAINIZED	COCKINESSES
CLOUDLESSNESS	COACHWHIPS	COANCHORED	COCAINIZES	COCKLEBOAT
CLOUDLESSNESSES	COACHWOODS	COANCHORING	COCAINIZING	COCKLEBOATS
CLOUDSCAPE	COACHWORKS	COANNEXING	COCAPTAINED	COCKLEBURS
CLOUDSCAPES	COACTIVELY	COAPPEARED	COCAPTAINING	COCKLEERTS
CLOUDTOWNS	COACTIVITIES	COAPPEARING	COCAPTAINS	COCKLESHELL
CLOVERGRASS	COACTIVITY	COAPTATION	COCARBOXYLASE	COCKLESHELLS
CLOVERGRASSES	COADAPTATION	COAPTATIONS	COCARBOXYLASES	COCKMATCHES
CLOVERIEST	COADAPTATIONS	COARCTATED	COCARCINOGEN	COCKNEYDOM
CLOVERLEAF	COADJACENCIES	COARCTATES	COCARCINOGENIC	COCKNEYDOMS
CLOVERLEAFS	COADJACENCY	COARCTATING	COCARCINOGENS	COCKNEYFICATION
CLOVERLEAVES	COADJACENT	COARCTATION	COCATALYST	COCKNEYFIED
CLOVERLIKE	COADJACENTS	COARCTATIONS	COCATALYSTS	COCKNEYFIES
CLOWNERIES	COADJUTANT	COARSENESS	COCCIDIANS	COCKNEYFYING
CLOWNFISHES	COADJUTANTS	COARSENESSES	COCCIDIOSES	COCKNEYISH
CLOWNISHLY	COADJUTORS	COARSENING	COCCIDIOSIS	COCKNEYISM
CLOWNISHNESS	COADJUTORSHIP	COASSISTED	COCCIDIOSTAT	COCKNEYISMS
CLOWNISHNESSES	COADJUTORSHIPS	COASSISTING	COCCIDIOSTATS	COCKNIFICATION
CLOXACILLIN	COADJUTRESS	COASSUMING	COCCIFEROUS	COCKNIFICATIONS
CLOXACILLINS	COADJUTRESSES	COASTEERING	COCCINEOUS	COCKNIFIED
CLOZAPINES	COADJUTRICES	COASTEERINGS	COCCOLITES	COCKNIFIES
CLUBABILITIES	COADJUTRIX	COASTGUARD	COCCOLITHS	COCKNIFYING
CLUBABILITY	COADJUTRIXES	COASTGUARDMAN	COCHAIRING	COCKROACHES

C

COCKSCOMBS	CODETERMINATION	COENAESTHESIAS	COEXISTENCE	COGNOSCENTE
COCKSFOOTS	CODEVELOPED	COENAESTHESIS	COEXISTENCES	COGNOSCENTI
COCKSINESS	CODEVELOPER	COENAMORED	COEXISTENT	COGNOSCIBLE
COCKSINESSES	CODEVELOPERS	COENAMORING	COEXISTING	COGNOSCING
COCKSUCKER	CODEVELOPING	COENAMOURED	COEXTENDED	COHABITANT
COCKSUCKERS	CODEVELOPS	COENAMOURING	COEXTENDING	COHABITANTS
COCKSURELY	CODICILLARY	COENAMOURS	COEXTENSION	COHABITATION
COCKSURENESS	CODICOLOGICAL	COENDURING	COEXTENSIONS	COHABITATIONS
COCKSURENESSES	CODICOLOGIES	COENENCHYMA	COEXTENSIVE	COHABITEES
COCKSWAINED	CODICOLOGY	COENENCHYMAS	COEXTENSIVELY	COHABITERS
COCKSWAINING	CODIFIABILITIES	COENENCHYMATA	COFAVORITE	COHABITING
COCKSWAINS	CODIFIABILITY	COENENCHYME	COFAVORITES	COHABITORS
COCKTAILED	CODIFIABLE	COENENCHYMES	COFEATURED	COHEIRESSES
COCKTAILING	CODIFICATION	COENESTHESES	COFEATURES	COHERENCES
COCKTEASER	CODIFICATIONS	COENESTHESIA	COFEATURING	COHERENCIES
COCKTEASERS	CODIRECTED	COENESTHESIAS	COFFEEHOUSE	COHERENTLY
COCKTHROWING	CODIRECTING	COENESTHESIS	COFFEEHOUSES	COHERITORS
COCKTHROWINGS	CODIRECTION	COENESTHETIC	COFFEEMAKER	COHESIBILITIES
COCKYLEEKIES	CODIRECTIONS	COENOBITES	COFFEEMAKERS	COHESIBILITY
COCKYLEEKY	CODIRECTOR	COENOBITIC	COFFEEPOTS	COHESIONLESS
COCOMPOSER	CODIRECTORS	COENOBITICAL	COFFERDAMS	COHESIVELY
COCOMPOSERS	CODISCOVER	COENOBITISM	COFFINITES	COHESIVENESS
COCONSCIOUS	CODISCOVERED	COENOBITISMS	COFINANCED	COHESIVENESSES
COCONSCIOUSES	CODISCOVERER	COENOCYTES	COFINANCES	COHIBITING
COCONSCIOUSNESS	CODISCOVERERS	COENOCYTIC	COFINANCING	COHIBITION
COCONSPIRATOR	CODISCOVERING	COENOSARCS	COFOUNDERS	COHIBITIONS
COCONSPIRATORS	CODISCOVERS	COENOSPECIES	COFOUNDING	COHIBITIVE
COCONUTTIER	CODOLOGIES	COENOSTEUM	COFUNCTION	COHOBATING
COCONUTTIEST	CODOMINANCE	COENOSTEUMS	COFUNCTIONS	COHOMOLOGICAL
COCOONERIES	CODOMINANCES	COENZYMATIC	COGENERATION	COHOMOLOGIES
COCOONINGS	CODOMINANT	COENZYMATICALLY	COGENERATIONS	COHOMOLOGY
COCOUNSELED	CODOMINANTS	COEQUALITIES	COGENERATOR	COHORTATIVE
COCOUNSELING	CODSWALLOP	COEQUALITY	COGENERATORS	COHORTATIVES
COCOUNSELLED	CODSWALLOPS	COEQUALNESS	COGITATING	COHOSTESSED
COCOUNSELLING	COECILIANS	COEQUALNESSES	COGITATINGLY	COHOSTESSES
COCOUNSELS	COEDUCATION	COEQUATING	COGITATION	COHOSTESSING
COCOZELLES	COEDUCATIONAL	COERCIMETER	COGITATIONS	COHOUSINGS
COCREATING	COEDUCATIONALLY	COERCIMETERS	COGITATIVE	COHYPONYMS
COCREATORS	COEDUCATIONS	COERCIONIST	COGITATIVELY	COIFFEUSES
COCULTIVATE	COEFFICIENT	COERCIONISTS	COGITATIVENESS	COIFFURING
COCULTIVATED	COEFFICIENTS	COERCIVELY	COGITATORS	COILABILITIES
COCULTIVATES	COELACANTH	COERCIVENESS	COGNATENESS	COILABILITY
COCULTIVATING	COELACANTHIC	COERCIVENESSES	COGNATENESSES	COINCIDENCE
COCULTIVATION	COELACANTHS	COERCIVITIES	COGNATIONS	COINCIDENCES
COCULTIVATIONS	COELANAGLYPHIC	COERCIVITY	COGNISABLE	COINCIDENCIES
COCULTURED	COELENTERA	COERECTING	COGNISABLY	COINCIDENCY
COCULTURES	COELENTERATE	COESSENTIAL	COGNISANCE	COINCIDENT
COCULTURING	COELENTERATES	COESSENTIALITY	COGNISANCES	COINCIDENTAL
COCURATING	COELENTERIC	COESSENTIALLY	COGNITIONAL	COINCIDENTALLY
COCURATORS	COELENTERON	COESSENTIALNESS	COGNITIONS	COINCIDENTLY
COCURRICULAR	COELENTERONS	COETANEOUS	COGNITIVELY	COINCIDING
COCUSWOODS	COELIOSCOPIES	COETANEOUSLY	COGNITIVISM	COINFECTED
CODEBREAKER	COELIOSCOPY	COETANEOUSNESS	COGNITIVISMS	COINFECTING
CODEBREAKERS	COELOMATES	COETERNALLY	COGNITIVITIES	COINFERRED
CODECLINATION	COELOMATIC	COETERNITIES	COGNITIVITY	COINFERRING
CODECLINATIONS	COELOSTATS	COETERNITY	COGNIZABLE	COINHERENCE
CODEFENDANT	COELUROSAUR	COEVALITIES	COGNIZABLY	COINHERENCES
CODEFENDANTS	COELUROSAURS	COEVOLUTION	COGNIZANCE	COINHERING
CODEPENDENCE	COEMBODIED	COEVOLUTIONARY	COGNIZANCES	COINHERITANCE
CODEPENDENCES	COEMBODIES	COEVOLUTIONS	COGNOMINAL	COINHERITANCES
CODEPENDENCIES	COEMBODYING	COEVOLVING	COGNOMINALLY	COINHERITOR
CODEPENDENCY	COEMPLOYED	COEXECUTOR	COGNOMINATE	COINHERITORS
CODEPENDENT	COEMPLOYING	COEXECUTORS	COGNOMINATED	COINSTANTANEITY
CODEPENDENTS	COEMPTIONS	COEXECUTRICES	COGNOMINATES	COINSTANTANEOUS
CODERIVING	COENACTING	COEXECUTRIX	COGNOMINATING	COINSURANCE
CODESIGNED	COENAESTHESES	COEXECUTRIXES	COGNOMINATION	COINSURANCES
CODESIGNING	COENAESTHESIA	COEXERTING	COGNOMINATIONS	COINSURERS

COINSURING
COINTERRED
COINTERRING
COINTREAUS
COINVENTED
COINVENTING
COINVENTOR
COINVENTORS
COINVESTED
COINVESTIGATOR
COINVESTIGATORS
COINVESTING
COINVESTOR
COINVESTORS
COKULORISES
COLATITUDE
COLATITUDES
COLCANNONS
COLCHICINE
COLCHICINES
COLCHICUMS
COLDBLOODS
COLDCOCKED
COLDCOCKING
COLDHEARTED
COLDHEARTEDLY
COLDHEARTEDNESS
COLDHOUSES
COLDNESSES
COLECTOMIES
COLEMANITE
COLEMANITES
COLEOPTERA
COLEOPTERAL
COLEOPTERAN
COLEOPTERANS
COLEOPTERIST
COLEOPTERISTS
COLEOPTERON
COLEOPTERONS
COLEOPTEROUS
COLEOPTERS
COLEOPTILE
COLEOPTILES
COLEORHIZA
COLEORHIZAE
COLEORRHIZA
COLEORRHIZAE
COLESTIPOL
COLESTIPOLS
COLICKIEST
COLICROOTS
COLICWEEDS
COLINEARITIES
COLINEARITY
COLIPHAGES
COLLABORATE
COLLABORATED
COLLABORATES
COLLABORATING
COLLABORATION
COLLABORATIONS
COLLABORATIVE
COLLABORATIVELY
COLLABORATIVES
COLLABORATOR

COLLABORATORS
COLLAGENASE
COLLAGENASES
COLLAGENIC
COLLAGENOUS
COLLAGISTS
COLLAPSABILITY
COLLAPSABLE
COLLAPSARS
COLLAPSIBILITY
COLLAPSIBLE
COLLAPSING
COLLARBONE
COLLARBONES
COLLARETTE
COLLARETTES
COLLARLESS
COLLARSTUD
COLLARSTUDS
COLLATABLE
COLLATERAL
COLLATERALISE
COLLATERALISED
COLLATERALISES
COLLATERALISING
COLLATERALITIES
COLLATERALITY
COLLATERALIZE
COLLATERALIZED
COLLATERALIZES
COLLATERALIZING
COLLATERALLY
COLLATERALS
COLLATIONS
COLLEAGUED
COLLEAGUES
COLLEAGUESHIP
COLLEAGUESHIPS
COLLEAGUING
COLLECTABLE
COLLECTABLES
COLLECTANEA
COLLECTEDLY
COLLECTEDNESS
COLLECTEDNESSES
COLLECTIBLE
COLLECTIBLES
COLLECTING
COLLECTINGS
COLLECTION
COLLECTIONS
COLLECTIVE
COLLECTIVELY
COLLECTIVENESS
COLLECTIVES
COLLECTIVISE
COLLECTIVISED
COLLECTIVISES
COLLECTIVISING
COLLECTIVISM
COLLECTIVISMS
COLLECTIVIST
COLLECTIVISTIC
COLLECTIVISTS
COLLECTIVITIES
COLLECTIVITY
COLLECTIVIZE

COLLECTIVIZED
COLLECTIVIZES
COLLECTIVIZING
COLLECTORATE
COLLECTORATES
COLLECTORS
COLLECTORSHIP
COLLECTORSHIPS
COLLEGIALISM
COLLEGIALISMS
COLLEGIALITIES
COLLEGIALITY
COLLEGIALLY
COLLEGIANER
COLLEGIANERS
COLLEGIANS
COLLEGIATE
COLLEGIATELY
COLLEGIATES
COLLEGIUMS
COLLEMBOLAN
COLLEMBOLANS
COLLEMBOLOUS
COLLENCHYMA
COLLENCHYMAS
COLLENCHYMATA
COLLENCHYMATOUS
COLLETERIAL
COLLICULUS
COLLIERIES
COLLIESHANGIE
COLLIESHANGIES
COLLIGATED
COLLIGATES
COLLIGATING
COLLIGATION
COLLIGATIONS
COLLIGATIVE
COLLIMATED
COLLIMATES
COLLIMATING
COLLIMATION
COLLIMATIONS
COLLIMATOR
COLLIMATORS
COLLINEARITIES
COLLINEARITY
COLLINEARLY
COLLINSIAS
COLLIQUABLE
COLLIQUANT
COLLIQUATE
COLLIQUATED
COLLIQUATES
COLLIQUATING
COLLIQUATION
COLLIQUATIONS
COLLIQUATIVE
COLLIQUESCENCE
COLLIQUESCENCES
COLLISIONAL
COLLISIONALLY
COLLISIONS
COLLOCATED
COLLOCATES
COLLOCATING
COLLOCATION

COLLOCATIONAL
COLLOCATIONS
COLLOCUTOR
COLLOCUTORS
COLLOCUTORY
COLLOCUTORY
COLLODIONS
COLLODIUMS
COLLOGUING
COLLOIDALITIES
COLLOIDALITY
COLLOIDALLY
COLLOQUIAL
COLLOQUIALISM
COLLOQUIALISMS
COLLOQUIALIST
COLLOQUIALISTS
COLLOQUIALITIES
COLLOQUIALITY
COLLOQUIALLY
COLLOQUIALNESS
COLLOQUIALS
COLLOQUIED
COLLOQUIES
COLLOQUING
COLLOQUISE
COLLOQUISED
COLLOQUISES
COLLOQUISING
COLLOQUIST
COLLOQUISTS
COLLOQUIUM
COLLOQUIUMS
COLLOQUIZE
COLLOQUIZED
COLLOQUIZES
COLLOQUIZING
COLLOQUYING
COLLOTYPES
COLLOTYPIC
COLLOTYPIES
COLLUCTATION
COLLUCTATIONS
COLLUSIONS
COLLUSIVELY
COLLUVIUMS
COLLYRIUMS
COLLYWOBBLES
COLOBOMATA
COLOCATING
COLOCYNTHS
COLOGARITHM
COLOGARITHMS
COLOMBARDS
COLONELCIES
COLONELLING
COLONELLINGS
COLONELSHIP
COLONELSHIPS
COLONIALISE
COLONIALISED
COLONIALISES
COLONIALISING
COLONIALISM
COLONIALISMS
COLONIALIST
COLONIALISTIC
COLONIALISTS

COLONIALIZE
COLONIALIZED
COLONIALIZES
COLONIALIZING
COLONIALLY
COLONIALNESS
COLONIALNESSES
COLONISABLE
COLONISATION
COLONISATIONIST
COLONISATIONS
COLONISERS
COLONISING
COLONITISES
COLONIZABLE
COLONIZATION
COLONIZATIONIST
COLONIZATIONS
COLONIZERS
COLONIZING
COLONNADED
COLONNADES
COLONOSCOPE
COLONOSCOPES
COLONOSCOPIES
COLONOSCOPY
COLOPHONIES
COLOQUINTIDA
COLOQUINTIDAS
COLORABILITIES
COLORABILITY
COLORABLENESS
COLORABLENESSES
COLORATION
COLORATIONS
COLORATURA
COLORATURAS
COLORATURE
COLORATURES
COLORBREED
COLORBREEDING
COLORBREEDS
COLORCASTED
COLORCASTING
COLORCASTS
COLORECTAL
COLORFASTNESS
COLORFASTNESSES
COLORFULLY
COLORFULNESS
COLORFULNESSES
COLORIMETER
COLORIMETERS
COLORIMETRIC
COLORIMETRICAL
COLORIMETRIES
COLORIMETRY
COLORISATION
COLORISATIONS
COLORISERS
COLORISING
COLORISTIC
COLORISTICALLY
COLORIZATION
COLORIZATIONS
COLORIZERS
COLORIZING

COLORLESSLY
COLORLESSNESS
COLORLESSNESSES
COLORPOINT
COLORPOINTS
COLORWASHED
COLORWASHES
COLORWASHING
COLOSSALLY
COLOSSEUMS
COLOSSUSES
COLOSTOMIES
COLOSTROUS
COLOSTRUMS
COLOTOMIES
COLOURABILITIES
COLOURABILITY
COLOURABLE
COLOURABLENESS
COLOURABLY
COLOURANTS
COLOURATION
COLOURATIONS
COLOURBRED
COLOURBREED
COLOURBREEDING
COLOURBREEDS
COLOURCAST
COLOURCASTED
COLOURCASTING
COLOURCASTS
COLOURFAST
COLOURFASTNESS
COLOURFULLY
COLOURFULNESS
COLOURFULNESSES
COLOURIEST
COLOURINGS
COLOURISATION
COLOURISATIONS
COLOURISED
COLOURISER
COLOURISERS
COLOURISES
COLOURISING
COLOURISMS
COLOURISTIC
COLOURISTICALLY
COLOURISTS
COLOURIZATION
COLOURIZATIONS
COLOURIZED
COLOURIZER
COLOURIZERS
COLOURIZES
COLOURIZING
COLOURLESS
COLOURLESSLY
COLOURLESSNESS
COLOURPOINT
COLOURPOINTS
COLOURWASH
COLOURWASHED
COLOURWASHES
COLOURWASHING
COLOURWAYS
COLPITISES

COLPORTAGE
COLPORTAGES
COLPORTEUR
COLPORTEURS
COLPOSCOPE
COLPOSCOPES
COLPOSCOPICAL
COLPOSCOPICALLY
COLPOSCOPIES
COLPOSCOPY
COLPOTOMIES
COLTISHNESS
COLTISHNESSES
COLTSFOOTS
COLUBRIADS
COLUBRIFORM
COLUMBARIA
COLUMBARIES
COLUMBARIUM
COLUMBATES
COLUMBINES
COLUMBITES
COLUMBIUMS
COLUMELLAE
COLUMELLAR
COLUMNARITIES
COLUMNARITY
COLUMNATED
COLUMNIATED
COLUMNIATION
COLUMNIATIONS
COLUMNISTIC
COLUMNISTS
COMANAGEMENT
COMANAGEMENTS
COMANAGERS
COMANAGING
COMANCHERO
COMANCHEROS
COMATOSELY
COMATULIDS
COMBATABLE
COMBATANTS
COMBATIVELY
COMBATIVENESS
COMBATIVENESSES
COMBATTING
COMBINABILITIES
COMBINABILITY
COMBINABLE
COMBINATION
COMBINATIONAL
COMBINATIONS
COMBINATIVE
COMBINATORIAL
COMBINATORIALLY
COMBINATORICS
COMBINATORY
COMBININGS
COMBRETUMS
COMBURGESS
COMBURGESSES
COMBUSTIBILITY
COMBUSTIBLE
COMBUSTIBLENESS
COMBUSTIBLES
COMBUSTIBLY

COMBUSTING
COMBUSTION
COMBUSTIONS
COMBUSTIOUS
COMBUSTIVE
COMBUSTIVES
COMBUSTORS
COMEDDLING
COMEDICALLY
COMEDIENNE
COMEDIENNES
COMEDIETTA
COMEDIETTAS
COMEDOGENIC
COMELINESS
COMELINESSES
COMESTIBLE
COMESTIBLES
COMETOGRAPHIES
COMETOGRAPHY
COMETOLOGIES
COMETOLOGY
COMEUPPANCE
COMEUPPANCES
COMFINESSES
COMFITURES
COMFORTABLE
COMFORTABLENESS
COMFORTABLY
COMFORTERS
COMFORTING
COMFORTINGLY
COMFORTLESS
COMFORTLESSLY
COMFORTLESSNESS
COMICALITIES
COMICALITY
COMICALNESS
COMICALNESSES
COMINGLING
COMITADJIS
COMITATIVE
COMITATIVES
COMITATUSES
COMMANDABLE
COMMANDANT
COMMANDANTS
COMMANDANTSHIP
COMMANDANTSHIPS
COMMANDEER
COMMANDEERED
COMMANDEERING
COMMANDEERS
COMMANDERIES
COMMANDERS
COMMANDERSHIP
COMMANDERSHIPS
COMMANDERY
COMMANDING
COMMANDINGLY
COMMANDMENT
COMMANDMENTS
COMMANDOES
COMMEASURABLE
COMMEASURE
COMMEASURED
COMMEASURES

COMMEASURING
COMMEMORABLE
COMMEMORATE
COMMEMORATED
COMMEMORATES
COMMEMORATING
COMMEMORATION
COMMEMORATIONAL
COMMEMORATIONS
COMMEMORATIVE
COMMEMORATIVELY
COMMEMORATIVES
COMMEMORATOR
COMMEMORATORS
COMMEMORATORY
COMMENCEMENT
COMMENCEMENTS
COMMENCERS
COMMENCING
COMMENDABLE
COMMENDABLENESS
COMMENDABLY
COMMENDAMS
COMMENDATION
COMMENDATIONS
COMMENDATOR
COMMENDATORS
COMMENDATORY
COMMENDERS
COMMENDING
COMMENSALISM
COMMENSALISMS
COMMENSALITIES
COMMENSALITY
COMMENSALLY
COMMENSALS
COMMENSURABLE
COMMENSURABLY
COMMENSURATE
COMMENSURATELY
COMMENSURATION
COMMENSURATIONS
COMMENTARIAL
COMMENTARIAT
COMMENTARIATS
COMMENTARIES
COMMENTARY
COMMENTATE
COMMENTATED
COMMENTATES
COMMENTATING
COMMENTATION
COMMENTATIONS
COMMENTATOR
COMMENTATORIAL
COMMENTATORS
COMMENTERS
COMMENTING
COMMENTORS
COMMERCIAL
COMMERCIALESE
COMMERCIALESES
COMMERCIALISE
COMMERCIALISED
COMMERCIALISES
COMMERCIALISING
COMMERCIALISM

COMMERCIALISMS
COMMERCIALIST
COMMERCIALISTIC
COMMERCIALISTS
COMMERCIALITIES
COMMERCIALITY
COMMERCIALIZE
COMMERCIALIZED
COMMERCIALIZES
COMMERCIALIZING
COMMERCIALLY
COMMERCIALS
COMMERCING
COMMERGING
COMMINATED
COMMINATES
COMMINATING
COMMINATION
COMMINATIONS
COMMINATIVE
COMMINATORY
COMMINGLED
COMMINGLES
COMMINGLING
COMMINUTED
COMMINUTES
COMMINUTING
COMMINUTION
COMMINUTIONS
COMMISERABLE
COMMISERATE
COMMISERATED
COMMISERATES
COMMISERATING
COMMISERATINGLY
COMMISERATION
COMMISERATIONS
COMMISERATIVE
COMMISERATIVELY
COMMISERATOR
COMMISERATORS
COMMISSAIRE
COMMISSAIRES
COMMISSARIAL
COMMISSARIAT
COMMISSARIATS
COMMISSARIES
COMMISSARS
COMMISSARY
COMMISSARYSHIP
COMMISSARYSHIPS
COMMISSION
COMMISSIONAIRE
COMMISSIONAIRES
COMMISSIONAL
COMMISSIONARY
COMMISSIONED
COMMISSIONER
COMMISSIONERS
COMMISSIONING
COMMISSIONS
COMMISSURAL
COMMISSURE
COMMISSURES
COMMITMENT
COMMITMENTS
COMMITTABLE

COMMITTALS
COMMITTEEMAN
COMMITTEEMEN
COMMITTEES
COMMITTEESHIP
COMMITTEESHIPS
COMMITTEEWOMAN
COMMITTEEWOMEN
COMMITTERS
COMMITTING
COMMIXTION
COMMIXTIONS
COMMIXTURE
COMMIXTURES
COMMODIFICATION
COMMODIFIED
COMMODIFIES
COMMODIFYING
COMMODIOUS
COMMODIOUSLY
COMMODIOUSNESS
COMMODITIES
COMMODITISE
COMMODITISED
COMMODITISES
COMMODITISING
COMMODITIZE
COMMODITIZED
COMMODITIZES
COMMODITIZING
COMMODORES
COMMONABLE
COMMONAGES
COMMONALITIES
COMMONALITY
COMMONALTIES
COMMONALTY
COMMONHOLD
COMMONHOLDS
COMMONINGS
COMMONNESS
COMMONNESSES
COMMONPLACE
COMMONPLACED
COMMONPLACENESS
COMMONPLACES
COMMONPLACING
COMMONSENSE
COMMONSENSIBLE
COMMONSENSICAL
COMMONWEAL
COMMONWEALS
COMMONWEALTH
COMMONWEALTHS
COMMORANTS
COMMORIENTES
COMMOTIONAL
COMMOTIONS
COMMUNALISATION
COMMUNALISE
COMMUNALISED
COMMUNALISER
COMMUNALISERS
COMMUNALISES
COMMUNALISING
COMMUNALISM
COMMUNALISMS

COMMUNALIST
COMMUNALISTIC
COMMUNALISTS
COMMUNALITIES
COMMUNALITY
COMMUNALIZATION
COMMUNALIZE
COMMUNALIZED
COMMUNALIZER
COMMUNALIZERS
COMMUNALIZES
COMMUNALIZING
COMMUNALLY
COMMUNARDS
COMMUNAUTAIRE
COMMUNAUTAIRES
COMMUNICABILITY
COMMUNICABLE
COMMUNICABLY
COMMUNICANT
COMMUNICANTS
COMMUNICATE
COMMUNICATED
COMMUNICATEE
COMMUNICATEES
COMMUNICATES
COMMUNICATING
COMMUNICATION
COMMUNICATIONAL
COMMUNICATIONS
COMMUNICATIVE
COMMUNICATIVELY
COMMUNICATOR
COMMUNICATORS
COMMUNICATORY
COMMUNINGS
COMMUNIONAL
COMMUNIONALLY
COMMUNIONS
COMMUNIQUE
COMMUNIQUES
COMMUNISATION
COMMUNISATIONS
COMMUNISED
COMMUNISES
COMMUNISING
COMMUNISMS
COMMUNISTIC
COMMUNISTICALLY
COMMUNISTS
COMMUNITAIRE
COMMUNITAIRES
COMMUNITARIAN
COMMUNITARIANS
COMMUNITIES
COMMUNIZATION
COMMUNIZATIONS
COMMUNIZED
COMMUNIZES
COMMUNIZING
COMMUTABILITIES
COMMUTABILITY
COMMUTABLE
COMMUTABLENESS
COMMUTATED
COMMUTATES
COMMUTATING

COMMUTATION
COMMUTATIONS
COMMUTATIVE
COMMUTATIVELY
COMMUTATIVITIES
COMMUTATIVITY
COMMUTATOR
COMMUTATORS
COMMUTINGS
COMONOMERS
COMORBIDITIES
COMORBIDITY
COMPACTEDLY
COMPACTEDNESS
COMPACTEDNESSES
COMPACTERS
COMPACTEST
COMPACTIBLE
COMPACTIFIED
COMPACTIFIES
COMPACTIFY
COMPACTIFYING
COMPACTING
COMPACTION
COMPACTIONS
COMPACTNESS
COMPACTNESSES
COMPACTORS
COMPACTURE
COMPACTURES
COMPAGINATE
COMPAGINATED
COMPAGINATES
COMPAGINATING
COMPAGINATION
COMPAGINATIONS
COMPANDERS
COMPANDING
COMPANDORS
COMPANIABLE
COMPANIONABLE
COMPANIONABLY
COMPANIONATE
COMPANIONED
COMPANIONHOOD
COMPANIONHOODS
COMPANIONING
COMPANIONLESS
COMPANIONS
COMPANIONSHIP
COMPANIONSHIPS
COMPANIONWAY
COMPANIONWAYS
COMPANYING
COMPARABILITIES
COMPARABILITY
COMPARABLE
COMPARABLENESS
COMPARABLY
COMPARATIST
COMPARATISTS
COMPARATIVE
COMPARATIVELY
COMPARATIVENESS
COMPARATIVES
COMPARATIVIST
COMPARATIVISTS

COMPARATOR
COMPARATORS
COMPARISON
COMPARISONS
COMPARTING
COMPARTMENT
COMPARTMENTAL
COMPARTMENTALLY
COMPARTMENTED
COMPARTMENTING
COMPARTMENTS
COMPASSABLE
COMPASSING
COMPASSINGS
COMPASSION
COMPASSIONABLE
COMPASSIONATE
COMPASSIONATED
COMPASSIONATELY
COMPASSIONATES
COMPASSIONATING
COMPASSIONED
COMPASSIONING
COMPASSIONLESS
COMPASSIONS
COMPATIBILITIES
COMPATIBILITY
COMPATIBLE
COMPATIBLENESS
COMPATIBLES
COMPATIBLY
COMPATRIOT
COMPATRIOTIC
COMPATRIOTISM
COMPATRIOTISMS
COMPATRIOTS
COMPEARANCE
COMPEARANCES
COMPEARANT
COMPEARANTS
COMPEARING
COMPEERING
COMPELLABLE
COMPELLABLY
COMPELLATION
COMPELLATIONS
COMPELLATIVE
COMPELLATIVES
COMPELLERS
COMPELLING
COMPELLINGLY
COMPENDIOUS
COMPENDIOUSLY
COMPENDIOUSNESS
COMPENDIUM
COMPENDIUMS
COMPENSABILITY
COMPENSABLE
COMPENSATE
COMPENSATED
COMPENSATES
COMPENSATING
COMPENSATION
COMPENSATIONAL
COMPENSATIONS
COMPENSATIVE
COMPENSATOR

COMPENSATORS
COMPENSATORY
COMPESCING
COMPETENCE
COMPETENCES
COMPETENCIES
COMPETENCY
COMPETENTLY
COMPETENTNESS
COMPETENTNESSES
COMPETITION
COMPETITIONS
COMPETITIVE
COMPETITIVELY
COMPETITIVENESS
COMPETITOR
COMPETITORS
COMPILATION
COMPILATIONS
COMPILATOR
COMPILATORS
COMPILATORY
COMPILEMENT
COMPILEMENTS
COMPLACENCE
COMPLACENCES
COMPLACENCIES
COMPLACENCY
COMPLACENT
COMPLACENTLY
COMPLAINANT
COMPLAINANTS
COMPLAINED
COMPLAINER
COMPLAINERS
COMPLAINING
COMPLAININGLY
COMPLAININGS
COMPLAINTS
COMPLAISANCE
COMPLAISANCES
COMPLAISANT
COMPLAISANTLY
COMPLANATE
COMPLANATION
COMPLANATIONS
COMPLEATED
COMPLEATING
COMPLECTED
COMPLECTING
COMPLEMENT
COMPLEMENTAL
COMPLEMENTALLY
COMPLEMENTARIES
COMPLEMENTARILY
COMPLEMENTARITY
COMPLEMENTARY
COMPLEMENTATION
COMPLEMENTED
COMPLEMENTING
COMPLEMENTISER
COMPLEMENTISERS
COMPLEMENTIZER
COMPLEMENTIZERS
COMPLEMENTS
COMPLETABLE
COMPLETEDNESS

COMPLETEDNESSES	COMPLIMENTED	COMPRADORES	COMPULSIVITIES	COMRADESHIP
COMPLETELY	COMPLIMENTER	COMPRADORS	COMPULSIVITY	COMRADESHIPS
COMPLETENESS	COMPLIMENTERS	COMPREHEND	COMPULSORIES	COMSTOCKER
COMPLETENESSES	COMPLIMENTING	COMPREHENDED	COMPULSORILY	COMSTOCKERIES
COMPLETERS	COMPLIMENTS	COMPREHENDIBLE	COMPULSORINESS	COMSTOCKERS
COMPLETEST	COMPLISHED	COMPREHENDING	COMPULSORY	COMSTOCKERY
COMPLETING	COMPLISHES	COMPREHENDS	COMPUNCTION	COMSTOCKISM
COMPLETION	COMPLISHING	COMPREHENSIBLE	COMPUNCTIONS	COMSTOCKISMS
COMPLETIONS	COMPLOTTED	COMPREHENSIBLY	COMPUNCTIOUS	CONACREISM
COMPLETIST	COMPLOTTER	COMPREHENSION	COMPUNCTIOUSLY	CONACREISMS
COMPLETISTS	COMPLOTTERS	COMPREHENSIONS	COMPURGATION	CONATIONAL
COMPLETIVE	COMPLOTTING	COMPREHENSIVE	COMPURGATIONS	CONCANAVALIN
COMPLETORIES	COMPLUVIUM	COMPREHENSIVELY	COMPURGATOR	CONCANAVALINS
COMPLETORY	COMPLUVIUMS	COMPREHENSIVES	COMPURGATORIAL	CONCATENATE
COMPLEXATION	COMPONENCIES	COMPREHENSIVISE	COMPURGATORS	CONCATENATED
COMPLEXATIONS	COMPONENCY	COMPREHENSIVIZE	COMPURGATORY	CONCATENATES
COMPLEXEDNESS	COMPONENTAL	COMPRESSED	COMPURSION	CONCATENATING
COMPLEXEDNESSES	COMPONENTIAL	COMPRESSEDLY	COMPURSIONS	CONCATENATION
COMPLEXEST	COMPONENTS	COMPRESSES	COMPUTABILITIES	CONCATENATIONS
COMPLEXIFIED	COMPORTANCE	COMPRESSIBILITY	COMPUTABILITY	CONCAVENESS
COMPLEXIFIES	COMPORTANCES	COMPRESSIBLE	COMPUTABLE	CONCAVENESSES
COMPLEXIFY	COMPORTING	COMPRESSIBLY	COMPUTANTS	CONCAVITIES
COMPLEXIFYING	COMPORTMENT	COMPRESSING	COMPUTATION	CONCEALABLE
COMPLEXING	COMPORTMENTS	COMPRESSION	COMPUTATIONAL	CONCEALERS
COMPLEXION	COMPOSEDLY	COMPRESSIONAL	COMPUTATIONALLY	CONCEALING
COMPLEXIONAL	COMPOSEDNESS	COMPRESSIONS	COMPUTATIONS	CONCEALINGLY
COMPLEXIONED	COMPOSEDNESSES	COMPRESSIVE	COMPUTATIVE	CONCEALMENT
COMPLEXIONLESS	COMPOSITED	COMPRESSIVELY	COMPUTATOR	CONCEALMENTS
COMPLEXIONS	COMPOSITELY	COMPRESSOR	COMPUTATORS	CONCEDEDLY
COMPLEXITIES	COMPOSITENESS	COMPRESSORS	COMPUTERATE	CONCEITEDLY
COMPLEXITY	COMPOSITENESSES	COMPRESSURE	COMPUTERDOM	CONCEITEDNESS
COMPLEXNESS	COMPOSITES	COMPRESSURES	COMPUTERDOMS	CONCEITEDNESSES
COMPLEXNESSES	COMPOSITING	COMPRIMARIO	COMPUTERESE	CONCEITFUL
COMPLEXOMETRIC	COMPOSITION	COMPRIMARIOS	COMPUTERESES	CONCEITING
COMPLEXONE	COMPOSITIONAL	COMPRINTED	COMPUTERISABLE	CONCEITLESS
COMPLEXONES	COMPOSITIONALLY	COMPRINTING	COMPUTERISATION	CONCEIVABILITY
COMPLEXUSES	COMPOSITIONS	COMPRISABLE	COMPUTERISE	CONCEIVABLE
COMPLIABLE	COMPOSITIVE	COMPRISALS	COMPUTERISED	CONCEIVABLENESS
COMPLIABLENESS	COMPOSITOR	COMPRISING	COMPUTERISES	CONCEIVABLY
COMPLIABLY	COMPOSITORIAL	COMPRIZING	COMPUTERISING	CONCEIVERS
COMPLIANCE	COMPOSITORS	COMPROMISE	COMPUTERIST	CONCEIVING
COMPLIANCES	COMPOSITOUS	COMPROMISED	COMPUTERISTS	CONCELEBRANT
COMPLIANCIES	COMPOSSIBILITY	COMPROMISER	COMPUTERITIS	CONCELEBRANTS
COMPLIANCY	COMPOSSIBLE	COMPROMISERS	COMPUTERITISES	CONCELEBRATE
COMPLIANTLY	COMPOSTABLE	COMPROMISES	COMPUTERIZABLE	CONCELEBRATED
COMPLIANTNESS	COMPOSTERS	COMPROMISING	COMPUTERIZATION	CONCELEBRATES
COMPLIANTNESSES	COMPOSTING	COMPROMISINGLY	COMPUTERIZE	CONCELEBRATING
COMPLICACIES	COMPOSTINGS	COMPROVINCIAL	COMPUTERIZED	CONCELEBRATION
COMPLICACY	COMPOSTURE	COMPTROLLED	COMPUTERIZES	CONCELEBRATIONS
COMPLICANT	COMPOSTURED	COMPTROLLER	COMPUTERIZING	CONCENTERED
COMPLICATE	COMPOSTURES	COMPTROLLERS	COMPUTERLESS	CONCENTERING
COMPLICATED	COMPOSTURING	COMPTROLLERSHIP	COMPUTERLIKE	CONCENTERS
COMPLICATEDLY	COMPOSURES	COMPTROLLING	COMPUTERNIK	CONCENTRATE
COMPLICATEDNESS	COMPOTATION	COMPTROLLS	COMPUTERNIKS	CONCENTRATED
COMPLICATES	COMPOTATIONS	COMPULSATIVE	COMPUTERPHOBE	CONCENTRATEDLY
COMPLICATING	COMPOTATIONSHIP	COMPULSATORY	COMPUTERPHOBES	CONCENTRATES
COMPLICATION	COMPOTATOR	COMPULSING	COMPUTERPHOBIA	CONCENTRATING
COMPLICATIONS	COMPOTATORS	COMPULSION	COMPUTERPHOBIAS	CONCENTRATION
COMPLICATIVE	COMPOTATORY	COMPULSIONIST	COMPUTERPHOBIC	CONCENTRATIONS
COMPLICITIES	COMPOTIERS	COMPULSIONISTS	COMPUTERPHOBICS	CONCENTRATIVE
COMPLICITLY	COMPOUNDABLE	COMPULSIONS	COMPUTINGS	CONCENTRATIVELY
COMPLICITOUS	COMPOUNDED	COMPULSITOR	COMPUTISTS	CONCENTRATOR
COMPLICITY	COMPOUNDER	COMPULSITORS	COMRADELIER	CONCENTRATORS
COMPLIMENT	COMPOUNDERS	COMPULSIVE	COMRADELIEST	CONCENTRED
COMPLIMENTAL	COMPOUNDING	COMPULSIVELY	COMRADELINESS	CONCENTRES
COMPLIMENTARILY	COMPOUNDINGS	COMPULSIVENESS	COMRADELINESSES	CONCENTRIC
COMPLIMENTARY	COMPRADORE	COMPULSIVES	COMRADERIES	CONCENTRICAL

C

CONCENTRICALLY
CONCENTRICITIES
CONCENTRICITY
CONCENTRING
CONCEPTACLE
CONCEPTACLES
CONCEPTION
CONCEPTIONAL
CONCEPTIONS
CONCEPTIOUS
CONCEPTIVE
CONCEPTUAL
CONCEPTUALISE
CONCEPTUALISED
CONCEPTUALISER
CONCEPTUALISERS
CONCEPTUALISES
CONCEPTUALISING
CONCEPTUALISM
CONCEPTUALISMS
CONCEPTUALIST
CONCEPTUALISTIC
CONCEPTUALISTS
CONCEPTUALITIES
CONCEPTUALITY
CONCEPTUALIZE
CONCEPTUALIZED
CONCEPTUALIZER
CONCEPTUALIZERS
CONCEPTUALIZES
CONCEPTUALIZING
CONCEPTUALLY
CONCEPTUSES
CONCERNANCIES
CONCERNANCY
CONCERNEDLY
CONCERNEDNESS
CONCERNEDNESSES
CONCERNING
CONCERNMENT
CONCERNMENTS
CONCERTANTE
CONCERTANTES
CONCERTANTI
CONCERTEDLY
CONCERTEDNESS
CONCERTEDNESSES
CONCERTGOER
CONCERTGOERS
CONCERTGOING
CONCERTGOINGS
CONCERTINA
CONCERTINAED
CONCERTINAING
CONCERTINAS
CONCERTING
CONCERTINI
CONCERTINIST
CONCERTINISTS
CONCERTINO
CONCERTINOS
CONCERTISE
CONCERTISED
CONCERTISES
CONCERTISING
CONCERTIZE
CONCERTIZED

CONCERTIZES
CONCERTIZING
CONCERTMASTER
CONCERTMASTERS
CONCERTMEISTER
CONCERTMEISTERS
CONCERTMISTRESS
CONCERTSTUCK
CONCERTSTUCKS
CONCESSIBLE
CONCESSION
CONCESSIONAIRE
CONCESSIONAIRES
CONCESSIONAL
CONCESSIONARIES
CONCESSIONARY
CONCESSIONER
CONCESSIONERS
CONCESSIONIST
CONCESSIONISTS
CONCESSIONNAIRE
CONCESSIONS
CONCESSIVE
CONCESSIVELY
CONCETTISM
CONCETTISMS
CONCETTIST
CONCETTISTS
CONCHIFEROUS
CONCHIFORM
CONCHIGLIE
CONCHIOLIN
CONCHIOLINS
CONCHITISES
CONCHOIDAL
CONCHOIDALLY
CONCHOLOGICAL
CONCHOLOGIES
CONCHOLOGIST
CONCHOLOGISTS
CONCHOLOGY
CONCIERGES
CONCILIABLE
CONCILIARLY
CONCILIARY
CONCILIATE
CONCILIATED
CONCILIATES
CONCILIATING
CONCILIATION
CONCILIATIONS
CONCILIATIVE
CONCILIATOR
CONCILIATORILY
CONCILIATORS
CONCILIATORY
CONCINNITIES
CONCINNITY
CONCINNOUS
CONCIPIENCIES
CONCIPIENCY
CONCIPIENT
CONCISENESS
CONCISENESSES
CONCISIONS
CONCLAMATION
CONCLAMATIONS

CONCLAVISM
CONCLAVISMS
CONCLAVIST
CONCLAVISTS
CONCLUDERS
CONCLUDING
CONCLUSION
CONCLUSIONARY
CONCLUSIONS
CONCLUSIVE
CONCLUSIVELY
CONCLUSIVENESS
CONCLUSORY
CONCOCTERS
CONCOCTING
CONCOCTION
CONCOCTIONS
CONCOCTIVE
CONCOCTORS
CONCOLORATE
CONCOLOROUS
CONCOMITANCE
CONCOMITANCES
CONCOMITANCIES
CONCOMITANCY
CONCOMITANT
CONCOMITANTLY
CONCOMITANTS
CONCORDANCE
CONCORDANCES
CONCORDANT
CONCORDANTLY
CONCORDATS
CONCORDIAL
CONCORDING
CONCORPORATE
CONCORPORATED
CONCORPORATES
CONCORPORATING
CONCOURSES
CONCREATED
CONCREATES
CONCREATING
CONCREMATION
CONCREMATIONS
CONCRESCENCE
CONCRESCENCES
CONCRESCENT
CONCRETELY
CONCRETENESS
CONCRETENESSES
CONCRETING
CONCRETION
CONCRETIONARY
CONCRETIONS
CONCRETISATION
CONCRETISATIONS
CONCRETISE
CONCRETISED
CONCRETISES
CONCRETISING
CONCRETISM
CONCRETISMS
CONCRETIST
CONCRETISTS
CONCRETIVE
CONCRETIVELY

CONCRETIZATION
CONCRETIZATIONS
CONCRETIZE
CONCRETIZED
CONCRETIZES
CONCRETIZING
CONCREWING
CONCUBINAGE
CONCUBINAGES
CONCUBINARIES
CONCUBINARY
CONCUBINES
CONCUBITANCIES
CONCUBITANCY
CONCUBITANT
CONCUBITANTS
CONCUPISCENCE
CONCUPISCENCES
CONCUPISCENT
CONCUPISCIBLE
CONCURRENCE
CONCURRENCES
CONCURRENCIES
CONCURRENCY
CONCURRENT
CONCURRENTLY
CONCURRENTS
CONCURRING
CONCURRINGLY
CONCUSSING
CONCUSSION
CONCUSSIONS
CONCUSSIVE
CONCYCLICALLY
CONDEMNABLE
CONDEMNABLY
CONDEMNATION
CONDEMNATIONS
CONDEMNATORY
CONDEMNERS
CONDEMNING
CONDEMNINGLY
CONDEMNORS
CONDENSABILITY
CONDENSABLE
CONDENSATE
CONDENSATED
CONDENSATES
CONDENSATING
CONDENSATION
CONDENSATIONAL
CONDENSATIONS
CONDENSERIES
CONDENSERS
CONDENSERY
CONDENSIBILITY
CONDENSIBLE
CONDENSING
CONDESCEND
CONDESCENDED
CONDESCENDENCE
CONDESCENDENCES
CONDESCENDING
CONDESCENDINGLY
CONDESCENDS
CONDESCENSION
CONDESCENSIONS

CONDIDDLED
CONDIDDLES
CONDIDDLING
CONDIGNNESS
CONDIGNNESSES
CONDIMENTAL
CONDIMENTED
CONDIMENTING
CONDIMENTS
CONDISCIPLE
CONDISCIPLES
CONDITIONABLE
CONDITIONAL
CONDITIONALITY
CONDITIONALLY
CONDITIONALS
CONDITIONATE
CONDITIONATED
CONDITIONATES
CONDITIONATING
CONDITIONED
CONDITIONER
CONDITIONERS
CONDITIONING
CONDITIONINGS
CONDITIONS
CONDOLATORY
CONDOLEMENT
CONDOLEMENTS
CONDOLENCE
CONDOLENCES
CONDOLINGLY
CONDOMINIA
CONDOMINIUM
CONDOMINIUMS
CONDONABLE
CONDONATION
CONDONATIONS
CONDOTTIERE
CONDOTTIERI
CONDUCEMENT
CONDUCEMENTS
CONDUCIBLE
CONDUCINGLY
CONDUCIVENESS
CONDUCIVENESSES
CONDUCTANCE
CONDUCTANCES
CONDUCTIBILITY
CONDUCTIBLE
CONDUCTIMETRIC
CONDUCTING
CONDUCTIOMETRIC
CONDUCTION
CONDUCTIONAL
CONDUCTIONS
CONDUCTIVE
CONDUCTIVELY
CONDUCTIVITIES
CONDUCTIVITY
CONDUCTOMETRIC
CONDUCTORIAL
CONDUCTORS
CONDUCTORSHIP
CONDUCTORSHIPS
CONDUCTRESS
CONDUCTRESSES

CONDUPLICATE	CONFESSIONALIST	CONFISCATABLE	CONFRATERNITIES	CONGLOBULATED
CONDUPLICATION	CONFESSIONALLY	CONFISCATE	CONFRATERNITY	CONGLOBULATES
CONDUPLICATIONS	CONFESSIONALS	CONFISCATED	CONFRERIES	CONGLOBULATING
CONDYLOMAS	CONFESSIONARIES	CONFISCATES	CONFRONTAL	CONGLOBULATION
CONDYLOMATA	CONFESSIONARY	CONFISCATING	CONFRONTALS	CONGLOBULATIONS
CONDYLOMATOUS	CONFESSIONS	CONFISCATION	CONFRONTATION	CONGLOMERATE
CONEFLOWER	CONFESSORESS	CONFISCATIONS	CONFRONTATIONAL	CONGLOMERATED
CONEFLOWERS	CONFESSORESSES	CONFISCATOR	CONFRONTATIONS	CONGLOMERATES
CONFABBING	CONFESSORS	CONFISCATORS	CONFRONTED	CONGLOMERATEUR
CONFABULAR	CONFESSORSHIP	CONFISCATORY	CONFRONTER	CONGLOMERATEURS
CONFABULATE	CONFESSORSHIPS	CONFISERIE	CONFRONTERS	CONGLOMERATIC
CONFABULATED	CONFIDANTE	CONFISERIES	CONFRONTING	CONGLOMERATING
CONFABULATES	CONFIDANTES	CONFISEURS	CONFRONTMENT	CONGLOMERATION
CONFABULATING	CONFIDANTS	CONFITEORS	CONFRONTMENTS	CONGLOMERATIONS
CONFABULATION	CONFIDENCE	CONFITURES	CONFUSABILITIES	CONGLOMERATIVE
CONFABULATIONS	CONFIDENCES	CONFLAGRANT	CONFUSABILITY	CONGLOMERATOR
CONFABULATOR	CONFIDENCIES	CONFLAGRATE	CONFUSABLE	CONGLOMERATORS
CONFABULATORS	CONFIDENCY	CONFLAGRATED	CONFUSABLES	CONGLUTINANT
CONFABULATORY	CONFIDENTIAL	CONFLAGRATES	CONFUSEDLY	CONGLUTINATE
CONFARREATE	CONFIDENTIALITY	CONFLAGRATING	CONFUSEDNESS	CONGLUTINATED
CONFARREATION	CONFIDENTIALLY	CONFLAGRATION	CONFUSEDNESSES	CONGLUTINATES
CONFARREATIONS	CONFIDENTLY	CONFLAGRATIONS	CONFUSIBLE	CONGLUTINATING
CONFECTING	CONFIDENTS	CONFLAGRATIVE	CONFUSIBLES	CONGLUTINATION
CONFECTION	CONFIDINGLY	CONFLATING	CONFUSINGLY	CONGLUTINATIONS
CONFECTIONARIES	CONFIDINGNESS	CONFLATION	CONFUSIONAL	CONGLUTINATIVE
CONFECTIONARY	CONFIDINGNESSES	CONFLATIONS	CONFUSIONS	CONGLUTINATOR
CONFECTIONER	CONFIGURATE	CONFLICTED	CONFUTABLE	CONGLUTINATORS
CONFECTIONERIES	CONFIGURATED	CONFLICTFUL	CONFUTATION	CONGRATTERS
CONFECTIONERS	CONFIGURATES	CONFLICTING	CONFUTATIONS	CONGRATULABLE
CONFECTIONERY	CONFIGURATING	CONFLICTINGLY	CONFUTATIVE	CONGRATULANT
CONFECTIONS	CONFIGURATION	CONFLICTION	CONFUTEMENT	CONGRATULANTS
CONFEDERACIES	CONFIGURATIONAL	CONFLICTIONS	CONFUTEMENTS	CONGRATULATE
CONFEDERACY	CONFIGURATIONS	CONFLICTIVE	CONGEALABLE	CONGRATULATED
CONFEDERAL	CONFIGURATIVE	CONFLICTORY	CONGEALABLENESS	CONGRATULATES
CONFEDERATE	CONFIGURATOR	CONFLICTUAL	CONGEALERS	CONGRATULATING
CONFEDERATED	CONFIGURATORS	CONFLUENCE	CONGEALING	CONGRATULATION
CONFEDERATES	CONFIGURED	CONFLUENCES	CONGEALMENT	CONGRATULATIONS
CONFEDERATING	CONFIGURES	CONFLUENTLY	CONGEALMENTS	CONGRATULATIVE
CONFEDERATION	CONFIGURING	CONFLUENTS	CONGELATION	CONGRATULATOR
CONFEDERATIONS	CONFINABLE	CONFOCALLY	CONGELATIONS	CONGRATULATORS
CONFEDERATIVE	CONFINEABLE	CONFORMABILITY	CONGENERIC	CONGRATULATORY
CONFERENCE	CONFINEDLY	CONFORMABLE	CONGENERICAL	CONGREEING
CONFERENCES	CONFINEDNESS	CONFORMABLENESS	CONGENERICS	CONGREETED
CONFERENCIER	CONFINEDNESSES	CONFORMABLY	CONGENEROUS	CONGREETING
CONFERENCIERS	CONFINELESS	CONFORMANCE	CONGENETIC	CONGREGANT
CONFERENCING	CONFINEMENT	CONFORMANCES	CONGENIALITIES	CONGREGANTS
CONFERENCINGS	CONFINEMENTS	CONFORMATION	CONGENIALITY	CONGREGATE
CONFERENTIAL	CONFIRMABILITY	CONFORMATIONAL	CONGENIALLY	CONGREGATED
CONFERMENT	CONFIRMABLE	CONFORMATIONS	CONGENIALNESS	CONGREGATES
CONFERMENTS	CONFIRMAND	CONFORMERS	CONGENIALNESSES	CONGREGATING
CONFERRABLE	CONFIRMANDS	CONFORMING	CONGENITAL	CONGREGATION
CONFERRALS	CONFIRMATION	CONFORMINGLY	CONGENITALLY	CONGREGATIONAL
CONFERREES	CONFIRMATIONAL	CONFORMISM	CONGENITALNESS	CONGREGATIONS
CONFERRENCE	CONFIRMATIONS	CONFORMISMS	CONGESTIBLE	CONGREGATIVE
CONFERRENCES	CONFIRMATIVE	CONFORMIST	CONGESTING	CONGREGATOR
CONFERRERS	CONFIRMATOR	CONFORMISTS	CONGESTION	CONGREGATORS
CONFERRING	CONFIRMATORS	CONFORMITIES	CONGESTIONS	CONGRESSED
CONFERVOID	CONFIRMATORY	CONFORMITY	CONGESTIVE	CONGRESSES
CONFERVOIDS	CONFIRMEDLY	CONFOUNDABLE	CONGIARIES	CONGRESSING
CONFESSABLE	CONFIRMEDNESS	CONFOUNDED	CONGLOBATE	CONGRESSIONAL
CONFESSANT	CONFIRMEDNESSES	CONFOUNDEDLY	CONGLOBATED	CONGRESSIONALLY
CONFESSANTS	CONFIRMEES	CONFOUNDEDNESS	CONGLOBATES	CONGRESSMAN
CONFESSEDLY	CONFIRMERS	CONFOUNDER	CONGLOBATING	CONGRESSMEN
CONFESSING	CONFIRMING	CONFOUNDERS	CONGLOBATION	CONGRESSPEOPLE
CONFESSION	CONFIRMINGS	CONFOUNDING	CONGLOBATIONS	CONGRESSPERSON
CONFESSIONAL	CONFIRMORS	CONFOUNDINGLY	CONGLOBING	CONGRESSPERSONS
CONFESSIONALISM	CONFISCABLE	CONFRATERNAL	CONGLOBULATE	CONGRESSWOMAN

CONGRESSWOMEN	CONJUNCTURE	CONNOISSEURS	CONSCRIPTING	CONSERVATIVE
CONGRUENCE	CONJUNCTURES	CONNOISSEURSHIP	CONSCRIPTION	CONSERVATIVELY
CONGRUENCES	CONJURATION	CONNOTATED	CONSCRIPTIONAL	CONSERVATIVES
CONGRUENCIES	CONJURATIONS	CONNOTATES	CONSCRIPTIONIST	CONSERVATIZE
CONGRUENCY	CONJURATOR	CONNOTATING	CONSCRIPTIONS	CONSERVATIZED
CONGRUENTLY	CONJURATORS	CONNOTATION	CONSCRIPTS	CONSERVATIZES
CONGRUITIES	CONJUREMENT	CONNOTATIONAL	CONSECRATE	CONSERVATIZING
CONGRUOUSLY	CONJUREMENTS	CONNOTATIONS	CONSECRATED	CONSERVATOIRE
CONGRUOUSNESS	CONJURINGS	CONNOTATIVE	CONSECRATEDNESS	CONSERVATOIRES
CONGRUOUSNESSES	CONLANGERS	CONNOTATIVELY	CONSECRATES	CONSERVATOR
CONICITIES	CONNASCENCE	CONNOTIVELY	CONSECRATING	CONSERVATORIA
CONIDIOPHORE	CONNASCENCES	CONNUBIALISM	CONSECRATION	CONSERVATORIAL
CONIDIOPHORES	CONNASCENCIES	CONNUBIALISMS	CONSECRATIONS	CONSERVATORIES
CONIDIOPHOROUS	CONNASCENCY	CONNUBIALITIES	CONSECRATIVE	CONSERVATORIUM
CONIDIOSPORE	CONNASCENT	CONNUBIALITY	CONSECRATOR	CONSERVATORIUMS
CONIDIOSPŌRES	CONNATENESS	CONNUBIALLY	CONSECRATORS	CONSERVATORS
CONIFEROUS	CONNATENESSES	CONNUMERATE	CONSECRATORY	CONSERVATORSHIP
CONIOLOGIES	CONNATIONS	CONNUMERATED	CONSECTANEOUS	CONSERVATORY
CONIROSTRAL	CONNATURAL	CONNUMERATES	CONSECTARIES	CONSERVATRICES
CONJECTING	CONNATURALISE	CONNUMERATING	CONSECTARY	CONSERVATRIX
CONJECTURABLE	CONNATURALISED	CONNUMERATION	CONSECUTION	CONSERVATRIXES
CONJECTURABLY	CONNATURALISES	CONNUMERATIONS	CONSECUTIONS	CONSERVERS
CONJECTURAL	CONNATURALISING	CONOIDALLY	CONSECUTIVE	CONSERVING
CONJECTURALLY	CONNATURALITIES	CONOIDICAL	CONSECUTIVELY	CONSIDERABLE
CONJECTURE	CONNATURALITY	CONOMINEES	CONSECUTIVENESS	CONSIDERABLES
CONJECTURED	CONNATURALIZE	CONOSCENTE	CONSENESCENCE	CONSIDERABLY
CONJECTURER	CONNATURALIZED	CONOSCENTI	CONSENESCENCES	CONSIDERANCE
CONJECTURERS	CONNATURALIZES	CONQUERABILITY	CONSENESCENCIES	CONSIDERANCES
CONJECTURES	CONNATURALIZING	CONQUERABLE	CONSENESCENCY	CONSIDERATE
CONJECTURING	CONNATURALLY	CONQUERABLENESS	CONSENSION	CONSIDERATELY
CONJOINERS	CONNATURALNESS	CONQUERERS	CONSENSIONS	CONSIDERATENESS
CONJOINING	CONNATURES	CONQUERESS	CONSENSUAL	CONSIDERATION
CONJOINTLY	CONNECTABLE	CONQUERESSES	CONSENSUALLY	CONSIDERATIONS
CONJUGABLE	CONNECTEDLY	CONQUERING	CONSENSUSES	CONSIDERATIVE
CONJUGALITIES	CONNECTEDNESS	CONQUERINGLY	CONSENTANEITIES	CONSIDERATIVELY
CONJUGALITY	CONNECTEDNESSES	CONQUERORS	CONSENTANEITY	CONSIDERED
CONJUGALLY	CONNECTERS	CONQUISTADOR	CONSENTANEOUS	CONSIDERER
CONJUGANTS	CONNECTIBLE	CONQUISTADORES	CONSENTANEOUSLY	CONSIDERERS
CONJUGATED	CONNECTING	CONQUISTADORS	CONSENTERS	CONSIDERING
CONJUGATELY	CONNECTION	CONSANGUINE	CONSENTIENCE	CONSIDERINGLY
CONJUGATENESS	CONNECTIONAL	CONSANGUINEOUS	CONSENTIENCES	CONSIGLIERE
CONJUGATENESSES	CONNECTIONISM	CONSANGUINITIES	CONSENTIENT	CONSIGLIERES
CONJUGATES	CONNECTIONISMS	CONSANGUINITY	CONSENTING	CONSIGLIERI
CONJUGATING	CONNECTIONS	CONSCIENCE	CONSENTINGLY	CONSIGNABLE
CONJUGATINGS	CONNECTIVE	CONSCIENCELESS	CONSEQUENCE	CONSIGNATION
CONJUGATION	CONNECTIVELY	CONSCIENCES	CONSEQUENCED	CONSIGNATIONS
CONJUGATIONAL	CONNECTIVES	CONSCIENTIOUS	CONSEQUENCES	CONSIGNATORIES
CONJUGATIONALLY	CONNECTIVITIES	CONSCIENTIOUSLY	CONSEQUENCING	CONSIGNATORY
CONJUGATIONS	CONNECTIVITY	CONSCIENTISE	CONSEQUENT	CONSIGNEES
CONJUGATIVE	CONNECTORS	CONSCIENTISED	CONSEQUENTIAL	CONSIGNERS
CONJUGATOR	CONNEXIONAL	CONSCIENTISES	CONSEQUENTIALLY	CONSIGNIFIED
CONJUGATORS	CONNEXIONS	CONSCIENTISING	CONSEQUENTLY	CONSIGNIFIES
CONJUNCTION	CONNIPTION	CONSCIENTIZE	CONSEQUENTS	CONSIGNIFY
CONJUNCTIONAL	CONNIPTIONS	CONSCIENTIZED	CONSERVABLE	CONSIGNIFYING
CONJUNCTIONALLY	CONNIVANCE	CONSCIENTIZES	CONSERVANCIES	CONSIGNING
CONJUNCTIONS	CONNIVANCES	CONSCIENTIZING	CONSERVANCY	CONSIGNMENT
CONJUNCTIVA	CONNIVANCIES	CONSCIONABILITY	CONSERVANT	CONSIGNMENTS
CONJUNCTIVAE	CONNIVANCY	CONSCIONABLE	CONSERVATION	CONSIGNORS
CONJUNCTIVAL	CONNIVENCE	CONSCIONABLY	CONSERVATIONAL	CONSILIENCE
CONJUNCTIVAS	CONNIVENCES	CONSCIOUSES	CONSERVATIONIST	CONSILIENCES
CONJUNCTIVE	CONNIVENCIES	CONSCIOUSLY	CONSERVATIONS	CONSILIENT
CONJUNCTIVELY	CONNIVENCY	CONSCIOUSNESS	CONSERVATISE	CONSIMILAR
CONJUNCTIVENESS	CONNIVENTLY	CONSCIOUSNESSES	CONSERVATISED	CONSIMILARITIES
CONJUNCTIVES	CONNIVERIES	CONSCRIBED	CONSERVATISES	CONSIMILARITY
CONJUNCTIVITIS	CONNIVINGLY	CONSCRIBES	CONSERVATISING	CONSIMILITIES
CONJUNCTLY	CONNIVINGS	CONSCRIBING	CONSERVATISM	CONSIMILITUDE
CONJUNCTURAL	CONNOISSEUR	CONSCRIPTED	CONSERVATISMS	CONSIMILITUDES

C

CONSIMILITY	CONSPICUOUSLY	CONSTITUTING	CONSTUPRATING	CONTABESCENCES
CONSISTENCE	CONSPICUOUSNESS	CONSTITUTION	CONSTUPRATION	CONTABESCENT
CONSISTENCES	CONSPIRACIES	CONSTITUTIONAL	CONSTUPRATIONS	CONTACTABLE
CONSISTENCIES	CONSPIRACY	CONSTITUTIONALS	CONSUBSIST	CONTACTEES
CONSISTENCY	CONSPIRANT	CONSTITUTIONIST	CONSUBSISTED	CONTACTING
CONSISTENT	CONSPIRANTS	CONSTITUTIONS	CONSUBSISTING	CONTACTLESS
CONSISTENTLY	CONSPIRATION	CONSTITUTIVE	CONSUBSISTS	CONTACTORS
CONSISTING	CONSPIRATIONAL	CONSTITUTIVELY	CONSUBSTANTIAL	CONTACTUAL
CONSISTORIAL	CONSPIRATIONS	CONSTITUTOR	CONSUBSTANTIATE	CONTACTUALLY
CONSISTORIAN	CONSPIRATOR	CONSTITUTORS	CONSUETUDE	CONTADINAS
CONSISTORIES	CONSPIRATORIAL	CONSTRAINABLE	CONSUETUDES	CONTADINOS
CONSISTORY	CONSPIRATORS	CONSTRAINED	CONSUETUDINARY	CONTAGIONIST
CONSOCIATE	CONSPIRATORY	CONSTRAINEDLY	CONSULAGES	CONTAGIONISTS
CONSOCIATED	CONSPIRATRESS	CONSTRAINER	CONSULATES	CONTAGIONS
CONSOCIATES	CONSPIRATRESSES	CONSTRAINERS	CONSULSHIP	CONTAGIOUS
CONSOCIATING	CONSPIRERS	CONSTRAINING	CONSULSHIPS	CONTAGIOUSLY
CONSOCIATION	CONSPIRING	CONSTRAINS	CONSULTABLE	CONTAGIOUSNESS
CONSOCIATIONAL	CONSPIRINGLY	CONSTRAINT	CONSULTANCIES	CONTAINABLE
CONSOCIATIONS	CONSPURCATION	CONSTRAINTS	CONSULTANCY	CONTAINERBOARD
CONSOLABLE	CONSPURCATIONS	CONSTRICTED	CONSULTANT	CONTAINERBOARDS
CONSOLATED	CONSTABLES	CONSTRICTING	CONSULTANTS	CONTAINERISE
CONSOLATES	CONSTABLESHIP	CONSTRICTION	CONSULTANTSHIP	CONTAINERISED
CONSOLATING	CONSTABLESHIPS	CONSTRICTIONS	CONSULTANTSHIPS	CONTAINERISES
CONSOLATION	CONSTABLEWICK	CONSTRICTIVE	CONSULTATION	CONTAINERISING
CONSOLATIONS	CONSTABLEWICKS	CONSTRICTIVELY	CONSULTATIONS	CONTAINERIZE
CONSOLATORIES	CONSTABULARIES	CONSTRICTOR	CONSULTATIVE	CONTAINERIZED
CONSOLATORY	CONSTABULARY	CONSTRICTORS	CONSULTATIVELY	CONTAINERIZES
CONSOLATRICES	CONSTANCIES	CONSTRICTS	CONSULTATORY	CONTAINERIZING
CONSOLATRIX	CONSTANTAN	CONSTRINGE	CONSULTEES	CONTAINERLESS
CONSOLATRIXES	CONSTANTANS	CONSTRINGED	CONSULTERS	CONTAINERPORT
CONSOLEMENT	CONSTANTLY	CONSTRINGENCE	CONSULTING	CONTAINERPORTS
CONSOLEMENTS	CONSTATATION	CONSTRINGENCES	CONSULTINGS	CONTAINERS
CONSOLIDATE	CONSTATATIONS	CONSTRINGENCIES	CONSULTIVE	CONTAINERSHIP
CONSOLIDATED	CONSTATING	CONSTRINGENCY	CONSULTORS	CONTAINERSHIPS
CONSOLIDATES	CONSTATIVE	CONSTRINGENT	CONSULTORY	CONTAINING
CONSOLIDATING	CONSTATIVES	CONSTRINGES	CONSUMABLE	CONTAINMENT
CONSOLIDATION	CONSTELLATE	CONSTRINGING	CONSUMABLES	CONTAINMENTS
CONSOLIDATIONS	CONSTELLATED	CONSTRUABILITY	CONSUMEDLY	CONTAMINABLE
CONSOLIDATIVE	CONSTELLATES	CONSTRUABLE	CONSUMERISM	CONTAMINANT
CONSOLIDATOR	CONSTELLATING	CONSTRUALS	CONSUMERISMS	CONTAMINANTS
CONSOLIDATORS	CONSTELLATION	CONSTRUCTABLE	CONSUMERIST	CONTAMINATE
CONSOLINGLY	CONSTELLATIONAL	CONSTRUCTED	CONSUMERISTIC	CONTAMINATED
CONSONANCE	CONSTELLATIONS	CONSTRUCTER	CONSUMERISTS	CONTAMINATES
CONSONANCES	CONSTELLATORY	CONSTRUCTERS	CONSUMERSHIP	CONTAMINATING
CONSONANCIES	CONSTERING	CONSTRUCTIBLE	CONSUMERSHIPS	CONTAMINATION
CONSONANCY	CONSTERNATE	CONSTRUCTING	CONSUMINGLY	CONTAMINATIONS
CONSONANTAL	CONSTERNATED	CONSTRUCTION	CONSUMINGS	CONTAMINATIVE
CONSONANTALLY	CONSTERNATES	CONSTRUCTIONAL	CONSUMMATE	CONTAMINATOR
CONSONANTLY	CONSTERNATING	CONSTRUCTIONISM	CONSUMMATED	CONTAMINATORS
CONSONANTS	CONSTERNATION	CONSTRUCTIONIST	CONSUMMATELY	CONTANGOED
CONSORTABLE	CONSTERNATIONS	CONSTRUCTIONS	CONSUMMATES	CONTANGOES
CONSORTERS	CONSTIPATE	CONSTRUCTIVE	CONSUMMATING	CONTANGOING
CONSORTIAL	CONSTIPATED	CONSTRUCTIVELY	CONSUMMATION	CONTEMNERS
CONSORTING	CONSTIPATES	CONSTRUCTIVISM	CONSUMMATIONS	CONTEMNIBLE
CONSORTISM	CONSTIPATING	CONSTRUCTIVISMS	CONSUMMATIVE	CONTEMNIBLY
CONSORTISMS	CONSTIPATION	CONSTRUCTIVIST	CONSUMMATOR	CONTEMNING
CONSORTIUM	CONSTIPATIONS	CONSTRUCTIVISTS	CONSUMMATORS	CONTEMNORS
CONSORTIUMS	CONSTITUENCIES	CONSTRUCTOR	CONSUMMATORY	CONTEMPERATION
CONSPECIFIC	CONSTITUENCY	CONSTRUCTORS	CONSUMPTION	CONTEMPERATIONS
CONSPECIFICS	CONSTITUENT	CONSTRUCTS	CONSUMPTIONS	CONTEMPERATURE
CONSPECTUITIES	CONSTITUENTLY	CONSTRUCTURE	CONSUMPTIVE	CONTEMPERATURES
CONSPECTUITY	CONSTITUENTS	CONSTRUCTURES	CONSUMPTIVELY	CONTEMPERED
CONSPECTUS	CONSTITUTE	CONSTRUERS	CONSUMPTIVENESS	CONTEMPERING
CONSPECTUSES	CONSTITUTED	CONSTRUING	CONSUMPTIVES	CONTEMPERS
CONSPICUITIES	CONSTITUTER	CONSTUPRATE	CONSUMPTIVITIES	CONTEMPLABLE
CONSPICUITY	CONSTITUTERS	CONSTUPRATED	CONSUMPTIVITY	CONTEMPLANT
CONSPICUOUS	CONSTITUTES	CONSTUPRATES	CONTABESCENCE	CONTEMPLANTS

CONTEMPLATE
CONTEMPLATED
CONTEMPLATES
CONTEMPLATING
CONTEMPLATION
CONTEMPLATIONS
CONTEMPLATIST
CONTEMPLATISTS
CONTEMPLATIVE
CONTEMPLATIVELY
CONTEMPLATIVES
CONTEMPLATOR
CONTEMPLATORS
CONTEMPORANEAN
CONTEMPORANEANS
CONTEMPORANEITY
CONTEMPORANEOUS
CONTEMPORARIES
CONTEMPORARILY
CONTEMPORARY
CONTEMPORISE
CONTEMPORISED
CONTEMPORISES
CONTEMPORISING
CONTEMPORIZE
CONTEMPORIZED
CONTEMPORIZES
CONTEMPORIZING
CONTEMPTIBILITY
CONTEMPTIBLE
CONTEMPTIBLY
CONTEMPTUOUS
CONTEMPTUOUSLY
CONTENDENT
CONTENDENTS
CONTENDERS
CONTENDING
CONTENDINGLY
CONTENDINGS
CONTENEMENT
CONTENEMENTS
CONTENTATION
CONTENTATIONS
CONTENTEDLY
CONTENTEDNESS
CONTENTEDNESSES
CONTENTING
CONTENTION
CONTENTIONS
CONTENTIOUS
CONTENTIOUSLY
CONTENTIOUSNESS
CONTENTLESS
CONTENTMENT
CONTENTMENTS
CONTERMINAL
CONTERMINALLY
CONTERMINANT
CONTERMINATE
CONTERMINOUS
CONTERMINOUSLY
CONTESSERATION
CONTESSERATIONS
CONTESTABILITY
CONTESTABLE
CONTESTABLENESS
CONTESTABLY

CONTESTANT
CONTESTANTS
CONTESTATION
CONTESTATIONS
CONTESTERS
CONTESTING
CONTESTINGLY
CONTEXTLESS
CONTEXTUAL
CONTEXTUALISE
CONTEXTUALISED
CONTEXTUALISES
CONTEXTUALISING
CONTEXTUALIZE
CONTEXTUALIZED
CONTEXTUALIZES
CONTEXTUALIZING
CONTEXTUALLY
CONTEXTURAL
CONTEXTURE
CONTEXTURES
CONTIGNATION
CONTIGNATIONS
CONTIGUITIES
CONTIGUITY
CONTIGUOUS
CONTIGUOUSLY
CONTIGUOUSNESS
CONTINENCE
CONTINENCES
CONTINENCIES
CONTINENCY
CONTINENTAL
CONTINENTALISM
CONTINENTALISMS
CONTINENTALIST
CONTINENTALISTS
CONTINENTALLY
CONTINENTALS
CONTINENTLY
CONTINENTS
CONTINGENCE
CONTINGENCES
CONTINGENCIES
CONTINGENCY
CONTINGENT
CONTINGENTLY
CONTINGENTS
CONTINUABLE
CONTINUALITIES
CONTINUALITY
CONTINUALLY
CONTINUALNESS
CONTINUALNESSES
CONTINUANCE
CONTINUANCES
CONTINUANT
CONTINUANTS
CONTINUATE
CONTINUATION
CONTINUATIONS
CONTINUATIVE
CONTINUATIVELY
CONTINUATIVES
CONTINUATOR
CONTINUATORS
CONTINUEDLY

CONTINUEDNESS
CONTINUEDNESSES
CONTINUERS
CONTINUING
CONTINUINGLY
CONTINUITIES
CONTINUITY
CONTINUOUS
CONTINUOUSLY
CONTINUOUSNESS
CONTINUUMS
CONTORNIATE
CONTORNIATES
CONTORTEDLY
CONTORTEDNESS
CONTORTEDNESSES
CONTORTING
CONTORTION
CONTORTIONAL
CONTORTIONATE
CONTORTIONED
CONTORTIONISM
CONTORTIONISMS
CONTORTIONIST
CONTORTIONISTIC
CONTORTIONISTS
CONTORTIONS
CONTORTIVE
CONTOURING
CONTRABAND
CONTRABANDISM
CONTRABANDISMS
CONTRABANDIST
CONTRABANDISTS
CONTRABANDS
CONTRABASS
CONTRABASSES
CONTRABASSI
CONTRABASSIST
CONTRABASSISTS
CONTRABASSO
CONTRABASSOON
CONTRABASSOONS
CONTRABASSOS
CONTRABBASSI
CONTRABBASSO
CONTRABBASSOS
CONTRACEPTION
CONTRACEPTIONS
CONTRACEPTIVE
CONTRACEPTIVES
CONTRACLOCKWISE
CONTRACTABILITY
CONTRACTABLE
CONTRACTABLY
CONTRACTED
CONTRACTEDLY
CONTRACTEDNESS
CONTRACTIBILITY
CONTRACTIBLE
CONTRACTIBLY
CONTRACTILE
CONTRACTILITIES
CONTRACTILITY
CONTRACTING
CONTRACTION
CONTRACTIONAL

CONTRACTIONARY
CONTRACTIONS
CONTRACTIVE
CONTRACTIVELY
CONTRACTIVENESS
CONTRACTOR
CONTRACTORS
CONTRACTUAL
CONTRACTUALLY
CONTRACTURAL
CONTRACTURE
CONTRACTURES
CONTRACYCLICAL
CONTRADANCE
CONTRADANCES
CONTRADICT
CONTRADICTABLE
CONTRADICTED
CONTRADICTER
CONTRADICTERS
CONTRADICTING
CONTRADICTION
CONTRADICTIONS
CONTRADICTIOUS
CONTRADICTIVE
CONTRADICTIVELY
CONTRADICTOR
CONTRADICTORIES
CONTRADICTORILY
CONTRADICTORS
CONTRADICTORY
CONTRADICTS
CONTRAFAGOTTI
CONTRAFAGOTTO
CONTRAFAGOTTOS
CONTRAFLOW
CONTRAFLOWS
CONTRAGESTION
CONTRAGESTIONS
CONTRAGESTIVE
CONTRAGESTIVES
CONTRAHENT
CONTRAHENTS
CONTRAINDICANT
CONTRAINDICANTS
CONTRAINDICATE
CONTRAINDICATED
CONTRAINDICATES
CONTRALATERAL
CONTRALTOS
CONTRANATANT
CONTRAOCTAVE
CONTRAOCTAVES
CONTRAPLEX
CONTRAPOSITION
CONTRAPOSITIONS
CONTRAPOSITIVE
CONTRAPOSITIVES
CONTRAPPOSTO
CONTRAPPOSTOS
CONTRAPROP
CONTRAPROPELLER
CONTRAPROPS
CONTRAPTION
CONTRAPTIONS
CONTRAPUNTAL
CONTRAPUNTALIST

CONTRAPUNTALLY
CONTRAPUNTIST
CONTRAPUNTISTS
CONTRARIAN
CONTRARIANS
CONTRARIED
CONTRARIES
CONTRARIETIES
CONTRARIETY
CONTRARILY
CONTRARINESS
CONTRARINESSES
CONTRARIOUS
CONTRARIOUSLY
CONTRARIOUSNESS
CONTRARIWISE
CONTRARYING
CONTRASEXUAL
CONTRASEXUALS
CONTRASTABLE
CONTRASTABLY
CONTRASTED
CONTRASTIER
CONTRASTIEST
CONTRASTING
CONTRASTINGLY
CONTRASTIVE
CONTRASTIVELY
CONTRATERRENE
CONTRAVALLATION
CONTRAVENE
CONTRAVENED
CONTRAVENER
CONTRAVENERS
CONTRAVENES
CONTRAVENING
CONTRAVENTION
CONTRAVENTIONS
CONTRAYERVA
CONTRAYERVAS
CONTRECOUP
CONTRECOUPS
CONTREDANCE
CONTREDANCES
CONTREDANSE
CONTREDANSES
CONTRETEMPS
CONTRIBUTABLE
CONTRIBUTARIES
CONTRIBUTARY
CONTRIBUTE
CONTRIBUTED
CONTRIBUTES
CONTRIBUTING
CONTRIBUTION
CONTRIBUTIONS
CONTRIBUTIVE
CONTRIBUTIVELY
CONTRIBUTOR
CONTRIBUTORIES
CONTRIBUTORS
CONTRIBUTORY
CONTRISTATION
CONTRISTATIONS
CONTRISTED
CONTRISTING
CONTRITELY

CONTRITENESS	CONVALESCENTLY	CONVERSATIONAL	CONVINCEMENT	COOPERATIONIST
CONTRITENESSES	CONVALESCENTS	CONVERSATIONISM	CONVINCEMENTS	COOPERATIONISTS
CONTRITION	CONVALESCES	CONVERSATIONIST	CONVINCERS	COOPERATIONS
CONTRITIONS	CONVALESCING	CONVERSATIONS	CONVINCIBLE	COOPERATIVE
CONTRITURATE	CONVECTING	CONVERSATIVE	CONVINCING	COOPERATIVELY
CONTRITURATED	CONVECTION	CONVERSAZIONE	CONVINCINGLY	COOPERATIVENESS
CONTRITURATES	CONVECTIONAL	CONVERSAZIONES	CONVINCINGNESS	COOPERATIVES
CONTRITURATING	CONVECTIONS	CONVERSAZIONI	CONVIVIALIST	COOPERATIVITIES
CONTRIVABLE	CONVECTIVE	CONVERSELY	CONVIVIALISTS	COOPERATIVITY
CONTRIVANCE	CONVECTORS	CONVERSERS	CONVIVIALITIES	COOPERATOR
CONTRIVANCES	CONVENABLE	CONVERSING	CONVIVIALITY	COOPERATORS
CONTRIVEMENT	CONVENANCE	CONVERSION	CONVIVIALLY	COOPERINGS
CONTRIVEMENTS	CONVENANCES	CONVERSIONAL	CONVOCATED	COOPTATION
CONTRIVERS	CONVENERSHIP	CONVERSIONARY	CONVOCATES	COOPTATIONS
CONTRIVING	CONVENERSHIPS	CONVERSIONS	CONVOCATING	COOPTATIVE
CONTROLLABILITY	CONVENIENCE	CONVERTAPLANE	CONVOCATION	COORDINANCE
CONTROLLABLE	CONVENIENCES	CONVERTAPLANES	CONVOCATIONAL	COORDINANCES
CONTROLLABLY	CONVENIENCIES	CONVERTEND	CONVOCATIONIST	COORDINATE
CONTROLLED	CONVENIENCY	CONVERTENDS	CONVOCATIONISTS	COORDINATED
CONTROLLER	CONVENIENT	CONVERTERS	CONVOCATIONS	COORDINATELY
CONTROLLERS	CONVENIENTLY	CONVERTIBILITY	CONVOCATIVE	COORDINATENESS
CONTROLLERSHIP	CONVENINGS	CONVERTIBLE	CONVOCATOR	COORDINATES
CONTROLLERSHIPS	CONVENORSHIP	CONVERTIBLENESS	CONVOCATORS	COORDINATING
CONTROLLING	CONVENORSHIPS	CONVERTIBLES	CONVOLUTED	COORDINATION
CONTROLMENT	CONVENTICLE	CONVERTIBLY	CONVOLUTEDLY	COORDINATIONS
CONTROLMENTS	CONVENTICLED	CONVERTING	CONVOLUTEDNESS	COORDINATIVE
CONTROULED	CONVENTICLER	CONVERTIPLANE	CONVOLUTELY	COORDINATOR
CONTROULING	CONVENTICLERS	CONVERTIPLANES	CONVOLUTES	COORDINATORS
CONTROVERSE	CONVENTICLES	CONVERTITE	CONVOLUTING	COPARCENARIES
CONTROVERSES	CONVENTICLING	CONVERTITES	CONVOLUTION	COPARCENARY
CONTROVERSIAL	CONVENTING	CONVERTIVE	CONVOLUTIONAL	COPARCENER
CONTROVERSIALLY	CONVENTION	CONVERTOPLANE	CONVOLUTIONARY	COPARCENERIES
CONTROVERSIES	CONVENTIONAL	CONVERTOPLANES	CONVOLUTIONS	COPARCENERS
CONTROVERSY	CONVENTIONALISE	CONVERTORS	CONVOLVING	COPARCENERY
CONTROVERT	CONVENTIONALISM	CONVEXEDLY	CONVOLVULACEOUS	COPARCENIES
CONTROVERTED	CONVENTIONALIST	CONVEXITIES	CONVOLVULI	COPARENTED
CONTROVERTER	CONVENTIONALITY	CONVEXNESS	CONVOLVULUS	COPARENTING
CONTROVERTERS	CONVENTIONALIZE	CONVEXNESSES	CONVOLVULUSES	COPARTNERED
CONTROVERTIBLE	CONVENTIONALLY	CONVEYABLE	CONVULSANT	COPARTNERIES
CONTROVERTIBLY	CONVENTIONALS	CONVEYANCE	CONVULSANTS	COPARTNERING
CONTROVERTING	CONVENTIONARY	CONVEYANCER	CONVULSIBLE	COPARTNERS
CONTROVERTIST	CONVENTIONEER	CONVEYANCERS	CONVULSING	COPARTNERSHIP
CONTROVERTISTS	CONVENTIONEERS	CONVEYANCES	CONVULSION	COPARTNERSHIPS
CONTROVERTS	CONVENTIONER	CONVEYANCING	CONVULSIONAL	COPARTNERY
CONTUBERNAL	CONVENTIONERS	CONVEYANCINGS	CONVULSIONARIES	COPATRIOTS
CONTUBERNYAL	CONVENTIONIST	CONVEYORISATION	CONVULSIONARY	COPAYMENTS
CONTUMACIES	CONVENTIONISTS	CONVEYORISE	CONVULSIONIST	COPERNICIUM
CONTUMACIOUS	CONVENTIONS	CONVEYORISED	CONVULSIONISTS	COPERNICIUMS
CONTUMACIOUSLY	CONVENTUAL	CONVEYORISES	CONVULSIONS	COPESETTIC
CONTUMACITIES	CONVENTUALLY	CONVEYORISING	CONVULSIVE	COPESTONES
CONTUMACITY	CONVENTUALS	CONVEYORIZATION	CONVULSIVELY	COPILOTING
CONTUMELIES	CONVERGENCE	CONVEYORIZE	CONVULSIVENESS	COPINGSTONE
CONTUMELIOUS	CONVERGENCES	CONVEYORIZED	COOKHOUSES	COPINGSTONES
CONTUMELIOUSLY	CONVERGENCIES	CONVEYORIZES	COOKSHACKS	COPIOUSNESS
CONTUNDING	CONVERGENCY	CONVEYORIZING	COOKSTOVES	COPIOUSNESSES
CONTUSIONED	CONVERGENT	CONVICINITIES	COOLHEADED	COPLAINTIFF
CONTUSIONS	CONVERGING	CONVICINITY	COOLHOUSES	COPLAINTIFFS
CONUNDRUMS	CONVERSABLE	CONVICTABLE	COOLINGNESS	COPLANARITIES
CONURBATION	CONVERSABLENESS	CONVICTIBLE	COOLINGNESSES	COPLANARITY
CONURBATIONS	CONVERSABLY	CONVICTING	COOLNESSES	COPLOTTING
CONVALESCE	CONVERSANCE	CONVICTION	COOMCEILED	COPLOTTINGS
CONVALESCED	CONVERSANCES	CONVICTIONAL	COONHOUNDS	COPOLYMERIC
CONVALESCENCE	CONVERSANCIES	CONVICTIONS	COOPERAGES	COPOLYMERISE
CONVALESCENCES	CONVERSANCY	CONVICTISM	COOPERATED	COPOLYMERISED
CONVALESCENCIES	CONVERSANT	CONVICTISMS	COOPERATES	COPOLYMERISES
CONVALESCENCY	CONVERSANTLY	CONVICTIVE	COOPERATING	COPOLYMERISING
CONVALESCENT	CONVERSATION	CONVICTIVELY	COOPERATION	COPOLYMERIZE

COPOLYMERIZED	COPROPRIETOR	CORALLOIDAL	CORESPONDENTS	CORNICULATE
COPOLYMERIZES	COPROPRIETORS	CORALLOIDS	CORFHOUSES	CORNICULUM
COPOLYMERIZING	COPROSPERITIES	CORALROOTS	CORIACEOUS	CORNICULUMS
COPOLYMERS	COPROSPERITY	CORALWORTS	CORIANDERS	CORNIFEROUS
COPPERASES	COPROSTEROL	CORBEILLES	CORINTHIANISE	CORNIFICATION
COPPERHEAD	COPROSTEROLS	CORBELINGS	CORINTHIANISED	CORNIFICATIONS
COPPERHEADS	COPSEWOODS	CORBELLING	CORINTHIANISES	CORNIFYING
COPPERIEST	COPUBLISHED	CORBELLINGS	CORINTHIANISING	CORNIGEROUS
COPPERINGS	COPUBLISHER	CORBICULAE	CORINTHIANIZE	CORNINESSES
COPPERPLATE	COPUBLISHERS	CORBICULATE	CORINTHIANIZED	CORNOPEANS
COPPERPLATES	COPUBLISHES	CORDECTOMIES	CORINTHIANIZES	CORNROWING
COPPERSKIN	COPUBLISHING	CORDECTOMY	CORINTHIANIZING	CORNSTALKS
COPPERSKINS	COPULATING	CORDELLING	CORIVALLED	CORNSTARCH
COPPERSMITH	COPULATION	CORDGRASSES	CORIVALLING	CORNSTARCHES
COPPERSMITHS	COPULATIONS	CORDIALISE	CORIVALRIES	CORNSTONES
COPPERWORK	COPULATIVE	CORDIALISED	CORIVALSHIP	CORNUCOPIA
COPPERWORKS	COPULATIVELY	CORDIALISES	CORIVALSHIPS	CORNUCOPIAN
COPPERWORM	COPULATIVES	CORDIALISING	CORKBOARDS	CORNUCOPIAS
COPPERWORMS	COPULATORY	CORDIALITIES	CORKBORERS	COROLLACEOUS
COPPICINGS	COPURIFIED	CORDIALITY	CORKINESSES	COROLLARIES
COPRAEMIAS	COPURIFIES	CORDIALIZE	CORKSCREWED	COROLLIFLORAL
COPRESENCE	COPURIFYING	CORDIALIZED	CORKSCREWING	COROLLIFLOROUS
COPRESENCES	COPYCATTED	CORDIALIZES	CORKSCREWS	COROLLIFORM
COPRESENTED	COPYCATTING	CORDIALIZING	CORMOPHYTE	COROMANDEL
COPRESENTING	COPYEDITED	CORDIALNESS	CORMOPHYTES	COROMANDELS
COPRESENTS	COPYEDITING	CORDIALNESSES	CORMOPHYTIC	CORONAGRAPH
COPRESIDENT	COPYFIGHTS	CORDIERITE	CORMORANTS	CORONAGRAPHS
COPRESIDENTS	COPYGRAPHS	CORDIERITES	CORNACEOUS	CORONARIES
COPRINCIPAL	COPYHOLDER	CORDILLERA	CORNBORERS	CORONATING
COPRINCIPALS	COPYHOLDERS	CORDILLERAN	CORNBRAIDED	CORONATION
COPRISONER	COPYLEFTED	CORDILLERAS	CORNBRAIDING	CORONATIONS
COPRISONERS	COPYLEFTING	CORDLESSES	CORNBRAIDS	CORONAVIRUS
COPROCESSING	COPYREADER	CORDOCENTESES	CORNBRANDIES	CORONAVIRUSES
COPROCESSINGS	COPYREADERS	CORDOCENTESIS	CORNBRANDY	CORONERSHIP
COPROCESSOR	COPYREADING	CORDONNETS	CORNBRASHES	CORONERSHIPS
COPROCESSORS	COPYREADINGS	CORDOTOMIES	CORNBREADS	CORONOGRAPH
COPRODUCED	COPYRIGHTABLE	CORDUROYED	CORNCOCKLE	CORONOGRAPHS
COPRODUCER	COPYRIGHTED	CORDUROYING	CORNCOCKLES	COROTATING
COPRODUCERS	COPYRIGHTER	CORDWAINER	CORNCRAKES	COROTATION
COPRODUCES	COPYRIGHTERS	CORDWAINERIES	CORNEITISES	COROTATIONS
COPRODUCING	COPYRIGHTING	CORDWAINERS	CORNELIANS	CORPORALES
COPRODUCTION	COPYRIGHTS	CORDWAINERY	CORNEMUSES	CORPORALITIES
COPRODUCTIONS	COPYTAKERS	CORDYLINES	CORNERBACK	CORPORALITY
COPRODUCTS	COPYWRITER	CORECIPIENT	CORNERBACKS	CORPORALLY
COPROLALIA	COPYWRITERS	CORECIPIENTS	CORNERINGS	CORPORALSHIP
COPROLALIAC	COPYWRITING	COREDEEMED	CORNERSTONE	CORPORALSHIPS
COPROLALIAS	COPYWRITINGS	COREDEEMING	CORNERSTONES	CORPORASES
COPROLITES	COQUELICOT	COREFERENTIAL	CORNERWAYS	CORPORATELY
COPROLITHS	COQUELICOTS	COREGONINE	CORNERWISE	CORPORATENESS
COPROLITIC	COQUETRIES	CORELATING	CORNETCIES	CORPORATENESSES
COPROLOGIES	COQUETTING	CORELATION	CORNETISTS	CORPORATES
COPROMOTER	COQUETTISH	CORELATIONS	CORNETTINI	CORPORATION
COPROMOTERS	COQUETTISHLY	CORELATIVE	CORNETTINO	CORPORATIONS
COPROPHAGAN	COQUETTISHNESS	CORELATIVES	CORNETTINOS	CORPORATISE
COPROPHAGANS	COQUIMBITE	CORELIGIONIST	CORNETTIST	CORPORATISED
COPROPHAGIC	COQUIMBITES	CORELIGIONISTS	CORNETTISTS	CORPORATISES
COPROPHAGIES	CORACIIFORM	COREOPSISES	CORNFIELDS	CORPORATISING
COPROPHAGIST	CORADICATE	COREPRESSOR	CORNFLAKES	CORPORATISM
COPROPHAGISTS	CORALBELLS	COREPRESSORS	CORNFLOURS	CORPORATISMS
COPROPHAGOUS	CORALBERRIES	COREQUISITE	CORNFLOWER	CORPORATIST
COPROPHAGY	CORALBERRY	COREQUISITES	CORNFLOWERS	CORPORATISTS
COPROPHILIA	CORALLACEOUS	CORESEARCHER	CORNHUSKER	CORPORATIVE
COPROPHILIAC	CORALLIFEROUS	CORESEARCHERS	CORNHUSKERS	CORPORATIVISM
COPROPHILIACS	CORALLIFORM	CORESIDENT	CORNHUSKING	CORPORATIVISMS
COPROPHILIAS	CORALLIGENOUS	CORESIDENTIAL	CORNHUSKINGS	CORPORATIZE
COPROPHILIC	CORALLINES	CORESIDENTS	CORNICHONS	CORPORATIZED
COPROPHILOUS	CORALLITES	CORESPONDENT	CORNICINGS	CORPORATIZES

CORPORATIZING	CORRELATIONAL	CORROSIVENESS	CORYNEBACTERIUM	COSMOLINING
CORPORATOR	CORRELATIONS	CORROSIVENESSES	CORYNEFORM	COSMOLOGIC
CORPORATORS	CORRELATIVE	CORROSIVES	CORYPHAEUS	COSMOLOGICAL
CORPOREALISE	CORRELATIVELY	CORRUGATED	CORYPHENES	COSMOLOGICALLY
CORPOREALISED	CORRELATIVENESS	CORRUGATES	COSCINOMANCIES	COSMOLOGIES
CORPOREALISES	CORRELATIVES	CORRUGATING	COSCINOMANCY	COSMOLOGIST
CORPOREALISING	CORRELATIVITIES	CORRUGATION	COSCRIPTED	COSMOLOGISTS
CORPOREALISM	CORRELATIVITY	CORRUGATIONS	COSCRIPTING	COSMONAUTICS
CORPOREALISMS	CORRELATOR	CORRUGATOR	COSEISMALS	COSMONAUTS
CORPOREALIST	CORRELATORS	CORRUGATORS	COSEISMICS	COSMOPLASTIC
CORPOREALISTS	CORRELIGIONIST	CORRUPTERS	COSENTIENT	COSMOPOLIS
CORPOREALITIES	CORRELIGIONISTS	CORRUPTEST	COSHERINGS	COSMOPOLISES
CORPOREALITY	CORREPTION	CORRUPTIBILITY	COSIGNATORIES	COSMOPOLITAN
CORPOREALIZE	CORREPTIONS	CORRUPTIBLE	COSIGNATORY	COSMOPOLITANISM
CORPOREALIZED	CORRESPOND	CORRUPTIBLENESS	COSIGNIFICATIVE	COSMOPOLITANS
CORPOREALIZES	CORRESPONDED	CORRUPTIBLY	COSINESSES	COSMOPOLITE
CORPOREALIZING	CORRESPONDENCE	CORRUPTING	COSMECEUTICAL	COSMOPOLITES
CORPOREALLY	CORRESPONDENCES	CORRUPTION	COSMECEUTICALS	COSMOPOLITIC
CORPOREALNESS	CORRESPONDENCY	CORRUPTIONIST	COSMETICAL	COSMOPOLITICAL
CORPOREALNESSES	CORRESPONDENT	CORRUPTIONISTS	COSMETICALLY	COSMOPOLITICS
CORPOREITIES	CORRESPONDENTLY	CORRUPTIONS	COSMETICIAN	COSMOPOLITISM
CORPOREITY	CORRESPONDENTS	CORRUPTIVE	COSMETICIANS	COSMOPOLITISMS
CORPORIFICATION	CORRESPONDING	CORRUPTIVELY	COSMETICISE	COSMORAMAS
CORPORIFIED	CORRESPONDINGLY	CORRUPTNESS	COSMETICISED	COSMORAMIC
CORPORIFIES	CORRESPONDS	CORRUPTNESSES	COSMETICISES	COSMOSPHERE
CORPORIFYING	CORRESPONSIVE	CORRUPTORS	COSMETICISING	COSMOSPHERES
CORPOSANTS	CORRIGENDA	CORSELETTE	COSMETICISM	COSMOTHEISM
CORPSELIKE	CORRIGENDUM	CORSELETTES	COSMETICISMS	COSMOTHEISMS
CORPULENCE	CORRIGENTS	CORSETIERE	COSMETICIZE	COSMOTHETIC
CORPULENCES	CORRIGIBILITIES	CORSETIERES	COSMETICIZED	COSMOTHETICAL
CORPULENCIES	CORRIGIBILITY	CORSETIERS	COSMETICIZES	COSMOTRONS
CORPULENCY	CORRIGIBLE	CORSETRIES	COSMETICIZING	COSPONSORED
CORPULENTLY	CORRIGIBLY	CORTICALLY	COSMETICOLOGIES	COSPONSORING
CORPUSCLES	CORRIVALLED	CORTICATED	COSMETICOLOGY	COSPONSORS
CORPUSCULAR	CORRIVALLING	CORTICATION	COSMETOLOGIES	COSPONSORSHIP
CORPUSCULARIAN	CORRIVALRIES	CORTICATIONS	COSMETOLOGIST	COSPONSORSHIPS
CORPUSCULARIANS	CORRIVALRY	CORTICOIDS	COSMETOLOGISTS	COSSETTING
CORPUSCULARITY	CORRIVALSHIP	CORTICOLOUS	COSMETOLOGY	COSTALGIAS
CORPUSCULE	CORRIVALSHIPS	CORTICOSTEROID	COSMICALLY	COSTARDMONGER
CORPUSCULES	CORROBORABLE	CORTICOSTEROIDS	COSMOCHEMICAL	COSTARDMONGERS
CORRALLING	CORROBORANT	CORTICOSTERONE	COSMOCHEMIST	COSTARRING
CORRASIONS	CORROBORATE	CORTICOSTERONES	COSMOCHEMISTRY	COSTEANING
CORRECTABLE	CORROBORATED	CORTICOTROPHIC	COSMOCHEMISTS	COSTEANINGS
CORRECTEST	CORROBORATES	CORTICOTROPHIN	COSMOCRATIC	COSTERMONGER
CORRECTIBLE	CORROBORATING	CORTICOTROPHINS	COSMOCRATS	COSTERMONGERS
CORRECTING	CORROBORATION	CORTICOTROPIC	COSMODROME	COSTIVENESS
CORRECTION	CORROBORATIONS	CORTICOTROPIN	COSMODROMES	COSTIVENESSES
CORRECTIONAL	CORROBORATIVE	CORTICOTROPINS	COSMOGENIC	COSTLESSLY
CORRECTIONER	CORROBORATIVELY	CORTISONES	COSMOGENIES	COSTLINESS
CORRECTIONERS	CORROBORATIVES	CORUSCATED	COSMOGONAL	COSTLINESSES
CORRECTIONS	CORROBORATOR	CORUSCATES	COSMOGONIC	COSTMARIES
CORRECTITUDE	CORROBORATORS	CORUSCATING	COSMOGONICAL	COSTOTOMIES
CORRECTITUDES	CORROBORATORY	CORUSCATION	COSMOGONIES	COSTUMERIES
CORRECTIVE	CORROBOREE	CORUSCATIONS	COSMOGONIST	COSTUMIERS
CORRECTIVELY	CORROBOREED	CORVETTING	COSMOGONISTS	COSTUMINGS
CORRECTIVES	CORROBOREEING	CORYBANTES	COSMOGRAPHER	COSURFACTANT
CORRECTNESS	CORROBOREES	CORYBANTIC	COSMOGRAPHERS	COSURFACTANTS
CORRECTNESSES	CORRODANTS	CORYBANTISM	COSMOGRAPHIC	COTANGENTIAL
CORRECTORS	CORRODENTS	CORYBANTISMS	COSMOGRAPHICAL	COTANGENTS
CORRECTORY	CORRODIBILITIES	CORYDALINE	COSMOGRAPHIES	COTELETTES
CORREGIDOR	CORRODIBILITY	CORYDALINES	COSMOGRAPHIST	COTEMPORANEOUS
CORREGIDORS	CORRODIBLE	CORYDALISES	COSMOGRAPHISTS	COTEMPORARY
CORRELATABLE	CORROSIBILITIES	CORYLOPSES	COSMOGRAPHY	COTENANCIES
CORRELATED	CORROSIBILITY	CORYLOPSIS	COSMOLATRIES	COTERMINOUS
CORRELATES	CORROSIBLE	CORYMBOSELY	COSMOLATRY	COTERMINOUSLY
CORRELATING	CORROSIONS	CORYNEBACTERIA	COSMOLINED	COTILLIONS
CORRELATION	CORROSIVELY	CORYNEBACTERIAL	COSMOLINES	COTONEASTER

COTONEASTERS
COTRANSDUCE
COTRANSDUCED
COTRANSDUCES
COTRANSDUCING
COTRANSDUCTION
COTRANSDUCTIONS
COTRANSFER
COTRANSFERS
COTRANSPORT
COTRANSPORTED
COTRANSPORTING
COTRANSPORTS
COTRUSTEES
COTTABUSES
COTTAGIEST
COTTAGINGS
COTTERLESS
COTTIERISM
COTTIERISMS
COTTONADES
COTTONIEST
COTTONMOUTH
COTTONMOUTHS
COTTONOCRACIES
COTTONOCRACY
COTTONSEED
COTTONSEEDS
COTTONTAIL
COTTONTAILS
COTTONWEED
COTTONWEEDS
COTTONWOOD
COTTONWOODS
COTURNIXES
COTYLEDONAL
COTYLEDONARY
COTYLEDONOID
COTYLEDONOUS
COTYLEDONS
COTYLIFORM
COTYLOIDAL
COTYLOIDALS
COTYLOSAUR
COTYLOSAURS
COUCHETTES
COUCHSURFING
COUCHSURFINGS
COULIBIACA
COULIBIACAS
COULIBIACS
COULOMBMETER
COULOMBMETERS
COULOMETER
COULOMETERS
COULOMETRIC
COULOMETRICALLY
COULOMETRIES
COULOMETRY
COUMARILIC
COUMARONES
COUNCILLOR
COUNCILLORS
COUNCILLORSHIP
COUNCILLORSHIPS
COUNCILMAN
COUNCILMANIC

COUNCILMEN
COUNCILORS
COUNCILORSHIP
COUNCILORSHIPS
COUNCILWOMAN
COUNCILWOMEN
COUNSELABLE
COUNSELEES
COUNSELING
COUNSELINGS
COUNSELLABLE
COUNSELLED
COUNSELLEE
COUNSELLEES
COUNSELLING
COUNSELLINGS
COUNSELLOR
COUNSELLORS
COUNSELLORSHIP
COUNSELLORSHIPS
COUNSELORS
COUNSELORSHIP
COUNSELORSHIPS
COUNTABILITIES
COUNTABILITY
COUNTBACKS
COUNTDOWNS
COUNTENANCE
COUNTENANCED
COUNTENANCER
COUNTENANCERS
COUNTENANCES
COUNTENANCING
COUNTERACT
COUNTERACTED
COUNTERACTING
COUNTERACTION
COUNTERACTIONS
COUNTERACTIVE
COUNTERACTIVELY
COUNTERACTS
COUNTERAGENT
COUNTERAGENTS
COUNTERARGUE
COUNTERARGUED
COUNTERARGUES
COUNTERARGUING
COUNTERARGUMENT
COUNTERASSAULT
COUNTERASSAULTS
COUNTERATTACK
COUNTERATTACKED
COUNTERATTACKER
COUNTERATTACKS
COUNTERBALANCE
COUNTERBALANCED
COUNTERBALANCES
COUNTERBASE
COUNTERBASES
COUNTERBID
COUNTERBIDDER
COUNTERBIDDERS
COUNTERBIDS
COUNTERBLAST
COUNTERBLASTS
COUNTERBLOCKADE
COUNTERBLOW

COUNTERBLOWS
COUNTERBLUFF
COUNTERBLUFFS
COUNTERBOND
COUNTERBONDS
COUNTERBORE
COUNTERBORED
COUNTERBORES
COUNTERBORING
COUNTERBRACE
COUNTERBRACED
COUNTERBRACES
COUNTERBRACING
COUNTERBUFF
COUNTERBUFFED
COUNTERBUFFING
COUNTERBUFFS
COUNTERCAMPAIGN
COUNTERCHANGE
COUNTERCHANGED
COUNTERCHANGES
COUNTERCHANGING
COUNTERCHARGE
COUNTERCHARGED
COUNTERCHARGES
COUNTERCHARGING
COUNTERCHARM
COUNTERCHARMED
COUNTERCHARMING
COUNTERCHARMS
COUNTERCHECK
COUNTERCHECKED
COUNTERCHECKING
COUNTERCHECKS
COUNTERCLAIM
COUNTERCLAIMANT
COUNTERCLAIMED
COUNTERCLAIMING
COUNTERCLAIMS
COUNTERCOUP
COUNTERCOUPS
COUNTERCRIES
COUNTERCRY
COUNTERCULTURAL
COUNTERCULTURE
COUNTERCULTURES
COUNTERCURRENT
COUNTERCURRENTS
COUNTERCYCLICAL
COUNTERDEMAND
COUNTERDEMANDS
COUNTERDRAW
COUNTERDRAWING
COUNTERDRAWN
COUNTERDRAWS
COUNTERDREW
COUNTEREFFORT
COUNTEREFFORTS
COUNTEREVIDENCE
COUNTEREXAMPLE
COUNTEREXAMPLES
COUNTERFACTUAL
COUNTERFACTUALS
COUNTERFECT
COUNTERFEISANCE
COUNTERFEIT
COUNTERFEITED

COUNTERFEITER
COUNTERFEITERS
COUNTERFEITING
COUNTERFEITINGS
COUNTERFEITLY
COUNTERFEITS
COUNTERFESAUNCE
COUNTERFIRE
COUNTERFIRES
COUNTERFLOW
COUNTERFLOWS
COUNTERFOIL
COUNTERFOILS
COUNTERFORCE
COUNTERFORCES
COUNTERFORT
COUNTERFORTS
COUNTERGLOW
COUNTERGLOWS
COUNTERGUERILLA
COUNTERIMAGE
COUNTERIMAGES
COUNTERING
COUNTERINSTANCE
COUNTERION
COUNTERIONS
COUNTERIRRITANT
COUNTERLIGHT
COUNTERLIGHTS
COUNTERMAN
COUNTERMAND
COUNTERMANDABLE
COUNTERMANDED
COUNTERMANDING
COUNTERMANDS
COUNTERMARCH
COUNTERMARCHED
COUNTERMARCHES
COUNTERMARCHING
COUNTERMARK
COUNTERMARKS
COUNTERMEASURE
COUNTERMEASURES
COUNTERMELODIES
COUNTERMELODY
COUNTERMEMO
COUNTERMEMOS
COUNTERMEN
COUNTERMINE
COUNTERMINED
COUNTERMINES
COUNTERMINING
COUNTERMOTION
COUNTERMOTIONS
COUNTERMOVE
COUNTERMOVED
COUNTERMOVEMENT
COUNTERMOVES
COUNTERMOVING
COUNTERMURE
COUNTERMURED
COUNTERMURES
COUNTERMURING
COUNTERMYTH
COUNTERMYTHS
COUNTEROFFER
COUNTEROFFERS

COUNTERORDER
COUNTERORDERED
COUNTERORDERING
COUNTERORDERS
COUNTERPACE
COUNTERPACES
COUNTERPANE
COUNTERPANES
COUNTERPART
COUNTERPARTIES
COUNTERPARTS
COUNTERPARTY
COUNTERPEISE
COUNTERPEISED
COUNTERPEISES
COUNTERPEISING
COUNTERPETITION
COUNTERPICKET
COUNTERPICKETED
COUNTERPICKETS
COUNTERPLAN
COUNTERPLANNED
COUNTERPLANNING
COUNTERPLANS
COUNTERPLAY
COUNTERPLAYED
COUNTERPLAYER
COUNTERPLAYERS
COUNTERPLAYING
COUNTERPLAYS
COUNTERPLEA
COUNTERPLEAD
COUNTERPLEADED
COUNTERPLEADING
COUNTERPLEADS
COUNTERPLEAS
COUNTERPLED
COUNTERPLOT
COUNTERPLOTS
COUNTERPLOTTED
COUNTERPLOTTING
COUNTERPLOY
COUNTERPLOYS
COUNTERPOINT
COUNTERPOINTED
COUNTERPOINTING
COUNTERPOINTS
COUNTERPOISE
COUNTERPOISED
COUNTERPOISES
COUNTERPOISING
COUNTERPOSE
COUNTERPOSED
COUNTERPOSES
COUNTERPOSING
COUNTERPOWER
COUNTERPOWERS
COUNTERPRESSURE
COUNTERPROJECT
COUNTERPROJECTS
COUNTERPROOF
COUNTERPROOFS
COUNTERPROPOSAL
COUNTERPROTEST
COUNTERPROTESTS
COUNTERPUNCH
COUNTERPUNCHED

COUNTERPUNCHER	COUNTERSTYLE	COUNTRYMAN	COVALENTLY	COZINESSES
COUNTERPUNCHERS	COUNTERSTYLES	COUNTRYMEN	COVARIANCE	CRABAPPLES
COUNTERPUNCHES	COUNTERSUBJECT	COUNTRYSEAT	COVARIANCES	CRABBEDNESS
COUNTERPUNCHING	COUNTERSUBJECTS	COUNTRYSEATS	COVARIANTS	CRABBEDNESSES
COUNTERQUESTION	COUNTERSUE	COUNTRYSIDE	COVARIATES	CRABBINESS
COUNTERRAID	COUNTERSUED	COUNTRYSIDES	COVARIATION	CRABBINESSES
COUNTERRAIDED	COUNTERSUES	COUNTRYWIDE	COVARIATIONS	CRABEATERS
COUNTERRAIDING	COUNTERSUING	COUNTRYWOMAN	COVELLINES	CRABGRASSES
COUNTERRAIDS	COUNTERSUIT	COUNTRYWOMEN	COVELLITES	CRABSTICKS
COUNTERRALLIED	COUNTERSUITS	COUNTSHIPS	COVENANTAL	CRACKAJACK
COUNTERRALLIES	COUNTERSUNK	COUPLEDOMS	COVENANTALLY	CRACKAJACKS
COUNTERRALLY	COUNTERTACTIC	COUPLEMENT	COVENANTED	CRACKBACKS
COUNTERRALLYING	COUNTERTACTICS	COUPLEMENTS	COVENANTEE	CRACKBERRIES
COUNTERREACTION	COUNTERTENDENCY	COUPONINGS	COVENANTEES	CRACKBERRY
COUNTERREFORM	COUNTERTENOR	COURAGEFUL	COVENANTER	CRACKBRAIN
COUNTERREFORMED	COUNTERTENORS	COURAGEOUS	COVENANTERS	CRACKBRAINED
COUNTERREFORMER	COUNTERTERROR	COURAGEOUSLY	COVENANTING	CRACKBRAINS
COUNTERREFORMS	COUNTERTERRORS	COURAGEOUSNESS	COVENANTOR	CRACKDOWNS
COUNTERRESPONSE	COUNTERTHREAT	COURANTOES	COVENANTORS	CRACKERJACK
COUNTERSANK	COUNTERTHREATS	COURBARILS	COVERALLED	CRACKERJACKS
COUNTERSCARP	COUNTERTHRUST	COURBETTES	COVERMOUNT	CRACKHEADS
COUNTERSCARPS	COUNTERTHRUSTS	COURGETTES	COVERMOUNTED	CRACKLEWARE
COUNTERSEAL	COUNTERTOP	COURIERING	COVERMOUNTING	CRACKLEWARES
COUNTERSEALED	COUNTERTOPS	COURSEBOOK	COVERMOUNTS	CRACKLIEST
COUNTERSEALING	COUNTERTRADE	COURSEBOOKS	COVERSINES	CRACKLINGS
COUNTERSEALS	COUNTERTRADED	COURSEWARE	COVERSLIPS	CRACOVIENNE
COUNTERSHADING	COUNTERTRADES	COURSEWARES	COVERTNESS	CRACOVIENNES
COUNTERSHADINGS	COUNTERTRADING	COURSEWORK	COVERTNESSES	CRADLESONG
COUNTERSHAFT	COUNTERTREND	COURSEWORKS	COVERTURES	CRADLESONGS
COUNTERSHAFTS	COUNTERTRENDS	COURTCRAFT	COVETINGLY	CRADLEWALK
COUNTERSHOT	COUNTERTYPE	COURTCRAFTS	COVETIVENESS	CRADLEWALKS
COUNTERSHOTS	COUNTERTYPES	COURTEOUSLY	COVETIVENESSES	CRAFTINESS
COUNTERSIGN	COUNTERVAIL	COURTEOUSNESS	COVETOUSLY	CRAFTINESSES
COUNTERSIGNED	COUNTERVAILABLE	COURTEOUSNESSES	COVETOUSNESS	CRAFTMANSHIP
COUNTERSIGNING	COUNTERVAILED	COURTESANS	COVETOUSNESSES	CRAFTMANSHIPS
COUNTERSIGNS	COUNTERVAILING	COURTESIED	COWARDICES	CRAFTSMANLIKE
COUNTERSINK	COUNTERVAILS	COURTESIES	COWARDLIER	CRAFTSMANLY
COUNTERSINKING	COUNTERVIEW	COURTESYING	COWARDLIEST	CRAFTSMANSHIP
COUNTERSINKS	COUNTERVIEWS	COURTEZANS	COWARDLINESS	CRAFTSMANSHIPS
COUNTERSNIPER	COUNTERVIOLENCE	COURTHOUSE	COWARDLINESSES	CRAFTSPEOPLE
COUNTERSNIPERS	COUNTERWEIGH	COURTHOUSES	COWARDRIES	CRAFTSPERSON
COUNTERSPELL	COUNTERWEIGHED	COURTIERISM	COWARDSHIP	CRAFTSPERSONS
COUNTERSPELLS	COUNTERWEIGHING	COURTIERISMS	COWARDSHIPS	CRAFTSWOMAN
COUNTERSPIES	COUNTERWEIGHS	COURTIERLIKE	COWBERRIES	CRAFTSWOMEN
COUNTERSPY	COUNTERWEIGHT	COURTIERLY	COWBOYINGS	CRAFTWORKS
COUNTERSPYING	COUNTERWEIGHTED	COURTLIEST	COWCATCHER	CRAGGEDNESS
COUNTERSPYINGS	COUNTERWEIGHTS	COURTLINESS	COWCATCHERS	CRAGGEDNESSES
COUNTERSTAIN	COUNTERWORD	COURTLINESSES	COWERINGLY	CRAGGINESS
COUNTERSTAINED	COUNTERWORDS	COURTLINGS	COWFEEDERS	CRAGGINESSES
COUNTERSTAINING	COUNTERWORK	COURTROOMS	COWFETERIA	CRAIGFLUKE
COUNTERSTAINS	COUNTERWORKED	COURTSHIPS	COWFETERIAS	CRAIGFLUKES
COUNTERSTATE	COUNTERWORKER	COURTSIDES	COWGRASSES	CRAKEBERRIES
COUNTERSTATED	COUNTERWORKERS	COURTYARDS	COWLSTAFFS	CRAKEBERRY
COUNTERSTATES	COUNTERWORKING	COUSCOUSES	COWLSTAVES	CRAMBOCLINK
COUNTERSTATING	COUNTERWORKS	COUSCOUSOU	COWPUNCHER	CRAMBOCLINKS
COUNTERSTEP	COUNTERWORLD	COUSCOUSOUS	COWPUNCHERS	CRAMOISIES
COUNTERSTEPS	COUNTERWORLDS	COUSINAGES	COXCOMBICAL	CRAMPBARKS
COUNTERSTRATEGY	COUNTESSES	COUSINHOOD	COXCOMBICALITY	CRAMPFISHES
COUNTERSTREAM	COUNTINGHOUSE	COUSINHOODS	COXCOMBICALLY	CRAMPONING
COUNTERSTREAMS	COUNTINGHOUSES	COUSINRIES	COXCOMBRIES	CRAMPONNED
COUNTERSTRICKEN	COUNTLESSLY	COUSINSHIP	COXCOMICAL	CRAMPONNING
COUNTERSTRIKE	COUNTLINES	COUSINSHIPS	COXINESSES	CRAMPONNINGS
COUNTERSTRIKES	COUNTRIFIED	COUTURIERE	COXSWAINED	CRANACHANS
COUNTERSTRIKING	COUNTROLLED	COUTURIERES	COXSWAINING	CRANBERRIES
COUNTERSTROKE	COUNTROLLING	COUTURIERS	COYISHNESS	CRANEFLIES
COUNTERSTROKES	COUNTRYFIED	COVALENCES	COYISHNESSES	CRANESBILL
COUNTERSTRUCK	COUNTRYISH	COVALENCIES	COYOTILLOS	CRANESBILLS

CRANIECTOMIES	CRASSULACEOUS	CREDENTIALLINGS	CREOSOTING	CRIMINALISTICS
CRANIECTOMY	CRATERIFORM	CREDENTIALS	CREPEHANGER	CRIMINALISTS
CRANIOCEREBRAL	CRATERINGS	CREDIBILITIES	CREPEHANGERS	CRIMINALITIES
CRANIOFACIAL	CRATERLESS	CREDIBILITY	CREPEHANGING	CRIMINALITY
CRANIOGNOMIES	CRATERLETS	CREDIBLENESS	CREPEHANGINGS	CRIMINALIZATION
CRANIOGNOMY	CRATERLIKE	CREDIBLENESSES	CREPINESSES	CRIMINALIZE
CRANIOLOGICAL	CRAUNCHABLE	CREDITABILITIES	CREPITATED	CRIMINALIZED
CRANIOLOGICALLY	CRAUNCHIER	CREDITABILITY	CREPITATES	CRIMINALIZES
CRANIOLOGIES	CRAUNCHIEST	CREDITABLE	CREPITATING	CRIMINALIZING
CRANIOLOGIST	CRAUNCHINESS	CREDITABLENESS	CREPITATION	CRIMINALLY
CRANIOLOGISTS	CRAUNCHINESSES	CREDITABLY	CREPITATIONS	CRIMINATED
CRANIOLOGY	CRAUNCHING	CREDITLESS	CREPITATIVE	CRIMINATES
CRANIOMETER	CRAVATTING	CREDITORSHIP	CREPITUSES	CRIMINATING
CRANIOMETERS	CRAVENNESS	CREDITORSHIPS	CREPOLINES	CRIMINATION
CRANIOMETRIC	CRAVENNESSES	CREDITWORTHIER	CREPUSCLES	CRIMINATIONS
CRANIOMETRICAL	CRAWDADDIES	CREDITWORTHIEST	CREPUSCULAR	CRIMINATIVE
CRANIOMETRIES	CRAWFISHED	CREDITWORTHY	CREPUSCULE	CRIMINATOR
CRANIOMETRIST	CRAWFISHES	CREDULITIES	CREPUSCULES	CRIMINATORS
CRANIOMETRISTS	CRAWFISHING	CREDULOUSLY	CREPUSCULOUS	CRIMINATORY
CRANIOMETRY	CRAWLINGLY	CREDULOUSNESS	CRESCENDOED	CRIMINOGENIC
CRANIOPAGI	CRAYFISHES	CREDULOUSNESSES	CRESCENDOES	CRIMINOLOGIC
CRANIOPAGUS	CRAYONISTS	CREEKSIDES	CRESCENDOING	CRIMINOLOGICAL
CRANIOSACRAL	CRAZINESSES	CREEPINESS	CRESCENDOS	CRIMINOLOGIES
CRANIOSCOPIES	CRAZYWEEDS	CREEPINESSES	CRESCENTADE	CRIMINOLOGIST
CRANIOSCOPIST	CREAKINESS	CREEPINGLY	CRESCENTADES	CRIMINOLOGISTS
CRANIOSCOPISTS	CREAKINESSES	CREEPMOUSE	CRESCENTED	CRIMINOLOGY
CRANIOSCOPY	CREAKINGLY	CREEPMOUSES	CRESCENTIC	CRIMINOUSNESS
CRANIOTOMIES	CREAMERIES	CREESHIEST	CRESCIVELY	CRIMINOUSNESSES
CRANIOTOMY	CREAMINESS	CREMAILLERE	CRESCOGRAPH	CRIMSONING
CRANKBAITS	CREAMINESSES	CREMAILLERES	CRESCOGRAPHS	CRIMSONNESS
CRANKCASES	CREAMPUFFS	CREMASTERS	CRESTFALLEN	CRIMSONNESSES
CRANKHANDLE	CREAMWARES	CREMATIONISM	CRESTFALLENLY	CRINGELING
CRANKHANDLES	CREASELESS	CREMATIONISMS	CRESTFALLENNESS	CRINGELINGS
CRANKINESS	CREASOTING	CREMATIONIST	CRETACEOUS	CRINGEWORTHIER
CRANKINESSES	CREATIANISM	CREMATIONISTS	CRETACEOUSES	CRINGEWORTHIEST
CRANKNESSES	CREATIANISMS	CREMATIONS	CRETACEOUSLY	CRINGEWORTHY
CRANKSHAFT	CREATININE	CREMATORIA	CRETINISED	CRINGINGLY
CRANKSHAFTS	CREATININES	CREMATORIAL	CRETINISES	CRINICULTURAL
CRANREUCHS	CREATIONAL	CREMATORIES	CRETINISING	CRINIGEROUS
CRAPEHANGER	CREATIONISM	CREMATORIUM	CRETINISMS	CRINKLEROOT
CRAPEHANGERS	CREATIONISMS	CREMATORIUMS	CRETINIZED	CRINKLEROOTS
CRAPEHANGING	CREATIONIST	CREMOCARPS	CRETINIZES	CRINKLIEST
CRAPEHANGINGS	CREATIONISTIC	CRENATIONS	CRETINIZING	CRINOIDEAN
CRAPSHOOTER	CREATIONISTS	CRENATURES	CRETINOIDS	CRINOIDEANS
CRAPSHOOTERS	CREATIVELY	CRENELATED	CREVASSING	CRINOLETTE
CRAPSHOOTS	CREATIVENESS	CRENELATES	CREWELISTS	CRINOLETTES
CRAPULENCE	CREATIVENESSES	CRENELATING	CREWELLERIES	CRINOLINED
CRAPULENCES	CREATIVITIES	CRENELATION	CREWELLERY	CRINOLINES
CRAPULENTLY	CREATIVITY	CRENELATIONS	CREWELLING	CRIPPLEDOM
CRAPULOSITIES	CREATORSHIP	CRENELLATE	CREWELLINGS	CRIPPLEDOMS
CRAPULOSITY	CREATORSHIPS	CRENELLATED	CREWELWORK	CRIPPLEWARE
CRAPULOUSLY	CREATRESSES	CRENELLATES	CREWELWORKS	CRIPPLEWARES
CRAPULOUSNESS	CREATRIXES	CRENELLATING	CRIBRATION	CRIPPLINGLY
CRAPULOUSNESSES	CREATUREHOOD	CRENELLATION	CRIBRATIONS	CRIPPLINGS
CRAQUELURE	CREATUREHOODS	CRENELLATIONS	CRIBRIFORM	CRISPATION
CRAQUELURES	CREATURELINESS	CRENELLING	CRICKETERS	CRISPATIONS
CRASHINGLY	CREATURELY	CRENULATED	CRICKETING	CRISPATURE
CRASHWORTHIER	CREATURESHIP	CRENULATION	CRICKETINGS	CRISPATURES
CRASHWORTHIEST	CREATURESHIPS	CRENULATIONS	CRIMEWAVES	CRISPBREAD
CRASHWORTHINESS	CREDENTIAL	CREOLISATION	CRIMINALESE	CRISPBREADS
CRASHWORTHY	CREDENTIALED	CREOLISATIONS	CRIMINALESES	CRISPENING
CRASSAMENTA	CREDENTIALING	CREOLISING	CRIMINALISATION	CRISPHEADS
CRASSAMENTUM	CREDENTIALINGS	CREOLIZATION	CRIMINALISE	CRISPINESS
CRASSITUDE	CREDENTIALISM	CREOLIZATIONS	CRIMINALISED	CRISPINESSES
CRASSITUDES	CREDENTIALISMS	CREOLIZING	CRIMINALISES	CRISPNESSES
CRASSNESSES	CREDENTIALLED	CREOPHAGIES	CRIMINALISING	CRISSCROSS
CRASSULACEAN	CREDENTIALLING	CREOPHAGOUS	CRIMINALIST	CRISSCROSSED

C

CRISSCROSSES	CROSSABILITY	CROSSPIECES	CRUISEWAYS	CRYOSCOPES
CRISSCROSSING	CROSSANDRA	CROSSROADS	CRUISEWEAR	CRYOSCOPIC
CRISTIFORM	CROSSANDRAS	CROSSRUFFED	CRUISEWEARS	CRYOSCOPIES
CRISTOBALITE	CROSSBANDED	CROSSRUFFING	CRUMBCLOTH	CRYOSTATIC
CRISTOBALITES	CROSSBANDING	CROSSRUFFS	CRUMBCLOTHS	CRYOSURGEON
CRITERIONS	CROSSBANDINGS	CROSSTALKS	CRUMBLIEST	CRYOSURGEONS
CRITERIUMS	CROSSBANDS	CROSSTREES	CRUMBLINESS	CRYOSURGERIES
CRITHIDIAL	CROSSBARRED	CROSSWALKS	CRUMBLINESSES	CRYOSURGERY
CRITHOMANCIES	CROSSBARRING	CROSSWINDS	CRUMBLINGS	CRYOSURGICAL
CRITHOMANCY	CROSSBARRINGS	CROSSWIRES	CRUMMINESS	CRYOTHERAPIES
CRITICALITIES	CROSSBEAMS	CROSSWORDS	CRUMMINESSES	CRYOTHERAPY
CRITICALITY	CROSSBEARER	CROSSWORTS	CRUMPLIEST	CRYPTAESTHESIA
CRITICALLY	CROSSBEARERS	CROTALARIA	CRUMPLINGS	CRYPTAESTHESIAS
CRITICALNESS	CROSSBENCH	CROTALARIAS	CRUNCHABLE	CRYPTAESTHETIC
CRITICALNESSES	CROSSBENCHER	CROTALISMS	CRUNCHIEST	CRYPTANALYSES
CRITICASTER	CROSSBENCHERS	CROTCHETED	CRUNCHINESS	CRYPTANALYSIS
CRITICASTERS	CROSSBENCHES	CROTCHETEER	CRUNCHINESSES	CRYPTANALYSTS
CRITICISABLE	CROSSBILLS	CROTCHETEERS	CRUNCHINGS	CRYPTANALYSTS
CRITICISED	CROSSBIRTH	CROTCHETIER	CRUSHABILITIES	CRYPTANALYTIC
CRITICISER	CROSSBIRTHS	CROTCHETIEST	CRUSHABILITY	CRYPTANALYTICAL
CRITICISERS	CROSSBITES	CROTCHETINESS	CRUSHINGLY	CRYPTARITHM
CRITICISES	CROSSBITING	CROTCHETINESSES	CRUSHPROOF	CRYPTARITHMS
CRITICISING	CROSSBITTEN	CROTONALDEHYDE	CRUSTACEAN	CRYPTESTHESIA
CRITICISINGLY	CROSSBONES	CROTONALDEHYDES	CRUSTACEANS	CRYPTESTHESIAS
CRITICISMS	CROSSBOWER	CROTONBUGS	CRUSTACEOUS	CRYPTESTHETIC
CRITICIZABLE	CROSSBOWERS	CROUPINESS	CRUSTATION	CRYPTICALLY
CRITICIZED	CROSSBOWMAN	CROUPINESSES	CRUSTATIONS	CRYPTOBIONT
CRITICIZER	CROSSBOWMEN	CROUSTADES	CRUSTINESS	CRYPTOBIONTS
CRITICIZERS	CROSSBREDS	CROWBARRED	CRUSTINESSES	CRYPTOBIOSES
CRITICIZES	CROSSBREED	CROWBARRING	CRUTCHINGS	CRYPTOBIOSIS
CRITICIZING	CROSSBREEDING	CROWBERRIES	CRYMOTHERAPIES	CRYPTOCLASTIC
CRITICIZINGLY	CROSSBREEDINGS	CROWDEDNESS	CRYMOTHERAPY	CRYPTOCOCCAL
CRITIQUING	CROSSBREEDS	CROWDEDNESSES	CRYOBIOLOGICAL	CRYPTOCOCCI
CROAKINESS	CROSSBUCKS	CROWDFUNDED	CRYOBIOLOGIES	CRYPTOCOCCOSES
CROAKINESSES	CROSSCHECK	CROWDFUNDING	CRYOBIOLOGIST	CRYPTOCOCCOSIS
CROCHETERS	CROSSCHECKED	CROWDFUNDINGS	CRYOBIOLOGISTS	CRYPTOCOCCUS
CROCHETING	CROSSCHECKING	CROWDFUNDS	CRYOBIOLOGY	CRYPTOCURRENCY
CROCHETINGS	CROSSCHECKS	CROWDSOURCE	CRYOCABLES	CRYPTOGAMIAN
CROCIDOLITE	CROSSCLAIM	CROWDSOURCED	CRYOCONITE	CRYPTOGAMIC
CROCIDOLITES	CROSSCLAIMS	CROWDSOURCES	CRYOCONITES	CRYPTOGAMIES
CROCKERIES	CROSSCOURT	CROWDSOURCING	CRYOGENICALLY	CRYPTOGAMIST
CROCODILES	CROSSCURRENT	CROWDSOURCINGS	CRYOGENICS	CRYPTOGAMISTS
CROCODILIAN	CROSSCURRENTS	CROWKEEPER	CRYOGENIES	CRYPTOGAMOUS
CROCODILIANS	CROSSCUTTING	CROWKEEPERS	CRYOGLOBULIN	CRYPTOGAMS
CROCOISITE	CROSSCUTTINGS	CROWNLANDS	CRYOGLOBULINS	CRYPTOGAMY
CROCOISITES	CROSSETTES	CROWNPIECE	CRYOHYDRATE	CRYPTOGENIC
CROCOSMIAS	CROSSFALLS	CROWNPIECES	CRYOHYDRATES	CRYPTOGRAM
CROISSANTS	CROSSFIELD	CROWNWORKS	CRYOMETERS	CRYPTOGRAMS
CROKINOLES	CROSSFIRES	CROWSTEPPED	CRYOMETRIC	CRYPTOGRAPH
CROOKBACKED	CROSSFISHES	CRUCIATELY	CRYOMETRIES	CRYPTOGRAPHER
CROOKBACKS	CROSSHAIRS	CRUCIFEROUS	CRYONICALLY	CRYPTOGRAPHERS
CROOKEDEST	CROSSHATCH	CRUCIFIERS	CRYOPHILIC	CRYPTOGRAPHIC
CROOKEDNESS	CROSSHATCHED	CRUCIFIXES	CRYOPHORUS	CRYPTOGRAPHICAL
CROOKEDNESSES	CROSSHATCHES	CRUCIFIXION	CRYOPHORUSES	CRYPTOGRAPHIES
CROOKERIES	CROSSHATCHING	CRUCIFIXIONS	CRYOPHYSICS	CRYPTOGRAPHIST
CROOKNECKS	CROSSHATCHINGS	CRUCIFORMLY	CRYOPHYTES	CRYPTOGRAPHISTS
CROPDUSTER	CROSSHEADS	CRUCIFORMS	CRYOPLANKTON	CRYPTOGRAPHS
CROPDUSTERS	CROSSJACKS	CRUCIFYING	CRYOPLANKTONS	CRYPTOGRAPHY
CROPDUSTING	CROSSLIGHT	CRUCIVERBAL	CRYOPRECIPITATE	CRYPTOLOGIC
CROPDUSTINGS	CROSSLIGHTS	CRUCIVERBALISM	CRYOPRESERVE	CRYPTOLOGICAL
CROQUANTES	CROSSLINGUISTIC	CRUCIVERBALISMS	CRYOPRESERVED	CRYPTOLOGIES
CROQUETING	CROSSNESSES	CRUCIVERBALIST	CRYOPRESERVES	CRYPTOLOGIST
CROQUETTES	CROSSOPTERYGIAN	CRUCIVERBALISTS	CRYOPRESERVING	CRYPTOLOGISTS
CROQUIGNOLE	CROSSOVERS	CRUDENESSES	CRYOPROBES	CRYPTOLOGY
CROQUIGNOLES	CROSSPATCH	CRUELNESSES	CRYOPROTECTANT	CRYPTOMERIA
CROREPATIS	CROSSPATCHES	CRUISERWEIGHT	CRYOPROTECTANTS	CRYPTOMERIAS
CROSSABILITIES	CROSSPIECE	CRUISERWEIGHTS	CRYOPROTECTIVE	CRYPTOMETER

CRYPTOMETERS	CRYSTALLOID	CULTIVATABLE	CUPELLATION	CURRANTIEST
CRYPTOMNESIA	CRYSTALLOIDAL	CULTIVATED	CUPELLATIONS	CURRAWONGS
CRYPTOMNESIAS	CRYSTALLOIDS	CULTIVATES	CUPFERRONS	CURREJONGS
CRYPTOMNESIC	CRYSTALLOMANCY	CULTIVATING	CUPHOLDERS	CURRENCIES
CRYPTONYMOUS	CTENOPHORAN	CULTIVATION	CUPIDINOUS	CURRENTNESS
CRYPTONYMS	CTENOPHORANS	CULTIVATIONS	CUPIDITIES	CURRENTNESSES
CRYPTOPHYTE	CTENOPHORE	CULTIVATOR	CUPRAMMONIUM	CURRICULAR
CRYPTOPHYTES	CTENOPHORES	CULTIVATORS	CUPRAMMONIUMS	CURRICULUM
CRYPTOPHYTIC	CUADRILLAS	CULTRIFORM	CUPRESSUSES	CURRICULUMS
CRYPTORCHID	CUBANELLES	CULTURABLE	CUPRIFEROUS	CURRIERIES
CRYPTORCHIDISM	CUBBYHOLES	CULTURALLY	CUPRONICKEL	CURRIJONGS
CRYPTORCHIDISMS	CUBICALNESS	CULTURELESS	CUPRONICKELS	CURRISHNESS
CRYPTORCHIDS	CUBICALNESSES	CULTURISTS	CUPULIFEROUS	CURRISHNESSES
CRYPTORCHISM	CUBICITIES	CULVERINEER	CURABILITIES	CURRYCOMBED
CRYPTORCHISMS	CUBISTICALLY	CULVERINEERS	CURABILITY	CURRYCOMBING
CRYPTOSPORIDIA	CUCKOLDING	CULVERTAGE	CURABLENESS	CURRYCOMBS
CRYPTOSPORIDIUM	CUCKOLDISE	CULVERTAGES	CURABLENESSES	CURSEDNESS
CRYPTOZOIC	CUCKOLDISED	CULVERTAILED	CURANDERAS	CURSEDNESSES
CRYPTOZOITE	CUCKOLDISES	CULVERTING	CURANDEROS	CURSELARIE
CRYPTOZOITES	CUCKOLDISING	CUMBERBUND	CURARISATION	CURSIVENESS
CRYPTOZOOLOGIES	CUCKOLDIZE	CUMBERBUNDS	CURARISATIONS	CURSIVENESSES
CRYPTOZOOLOGIST	CUCKOLDIZED	CUMBERLESS	CURARISING	CURSORINESS
CRYPTOZOOLOGY	CUCKOLDIZES	CUMBERMENT	CURARIZATION	CURSORINESSES
CRYSTALISABLE	CUCKOLDIZING	CUMBERMENTS	CURARIZATIONS	CURSTNESSES
CRYSTALISATION	CUCKOLDOMS	CUMBERSOME	CURARIZING	CURTAILERS
CRYSTALISATIONS	CUCKOLDRIES	CUMBERSOMELY	CURATESHIP	CURTAILING
CRYSTALISE	CUCKOOFLOWER	CUMBERSOMENESS	CURATESHIPS	CURTAILMENT
CRYSTALISED	CUCKOOFLOWERS	CUMBRANCES	CURATIVELY	CURTAILMENTS
CRYSTALISER	CUCKOOPINT	CUMBROUSLY	CURATIVENESS	CURTAINING
CRYSTALISERS	CUCKOOPINTS	CUMBROUSNESS	CURATIVENESSES	CURTAINLESS
CRYSTALISES	CUCULIFORM	CUMBROUSNESSES	CURATORIAL	CURTALAXES
CRYSTALISING	CUCULLATED	CUMMERBUND	CURATORSHIP	CURTATIONS
CRYSTALIZABLE	CUCULLATELY	CUMMERBUNDS	CURATORSHIPS	CURTILAGES
CRYSTALIZATION	CUCUMIFORM	CUMMINGTONITE	CURATRIXES	CURTNESSES
CRYSTALIZATIONS	CUCURBITACEOUS	CUMMINGTONITES	CURBSTONES	CURTSEYING
CRYSTALIZE	CUCURBITAL	CUMULATELY	CURCUMINES	CURVACEOUS
CRYSTALIZED	CUDDLESOME	CUMULATING	CURDINESSES	CURVACEOUSLY
CRYSTALIZER	CUDGELINGS	CUMULATION	CURETTAGES	CURVACEOUSNESS
CRYSTALIZERS	CUDGELLERS	CUMULATIONS	CURETTEMENT	CURVACIOUS
CRYSTALIZES	CUDGELLING	CUMULATIVE	CURETTEMENTS	CURVACIOUSLY
CRYSTALIZING	CUDGELLINGS	CUMULATIVELY	CURFUFFLED	CURVACIOUSNESS
CRYSTALLINE	CUFFUFFLES	CUMULATIVENESS	CURFUFFLES	CURVATIONS
CRYSTALLINES	CUIRASSIER	CUMULIFORM	CURFUFFLING	CURVATURES
CRYSTALLINITIES	CUIRASSIERS	CUMULOCIRRI	CURIALISMS	CURVEBALLED
CRYSTALLINITY	CUIRASSING	CUMULOCIRRUS	CURIALISTIC	CURVEBALLING
CRYSTALLISABLE	CUISINARTS	CUMULONIMBI	CURIALISTS	CURVEBALLS
CRYSTALLISATION	CUISINIERS	CUMULONIMBUS	CURIETHERAPIES	CURVEDNESS
CRYSTALLISE	CULICIFORM	CUMULONIMBUSES	CURIETHERAPY	CURVEDNESSES
CRYSTALLISED	CULINARIAN	CUMULOSTRATI	CURIOSITIES	CURVETTING
CRYSTALLISER	CULINARIANS	CUMULOSTRATUS	CURIOUSEST	CURVICAUDATE
CRYSTALLISERS	CULINARILY	CUNCTATION	CURIOUSNESS	CURVICOSTATE
CRYSTALLISES	CULLENDERS	CUNCTATIONS	CURIOUSNESSES	CURVIFOLIATE
CRYSTALLISING	CULMIFEROUS	CUNCTATIOUS	CURLICUING	CURVILINEAL
CRYSTALLITE	CULMINATED	CUNCTATIVE	CURLIEWURLIE	CURVILINEALLY
CRYSTALLITES	CULMINATES	CUNCTATORS	CURLIEWURLIES	CURVILINEAR
CRYSTALLITIC	CULMINATING	CUNCTATORY	CURLINESSES	CURVILINEARITY
CRYSTALLITIS	CULMINATION	CUNEIFORMS	CURLPAPERS	CURVILINEARLY
CRYSTALLITISES	CULMINATIONS	CUNNILINCTUS	CURMUDGEON	CURVINESSES
CRYSTALLIZABLE	CULPABILITIES	CUNNILINCTUSES	CURMUDGEONLIER	CURVIROSTRAL
CRYSTALLIZATION	CULPABILITY	CUNNILINGUS	CURMUDGEONLIEST	CUSHINESSES
CRYSTALLIZE	CULPABLENESS	CUNNILINGUSES	CURMUDGEONLY	CUSHIONETS
CRYSTALLIZED	CULPABLENESSES	CUNNINGEST	CURMUDGEONS	CUSHIONIER
CRYSTALLIZER	CULTISHNESS	CUNNINGNESS	CURMURRING	CUSHIONIEST
CRYSTALLIZERS	CULTISHNESSES	CUNNINGNESSES	CURMURRINGS	CUSHIONING
CRYSTALLIZES	CULTIVABILITIES	CUPBEARERS	CURNAPTIOUS	CUSHIONINGS
CRYSTALLIZING	CULTIVABILITY	CUPBOARDED	CURRAJONGS	CUSHIONLESS
CRYSTALLOGRAPHY	CULTIVABLE	CUPBOARDING	CURRANTIER	CUSPIDATED

CUSPIDATION	CYANOETHYLATED	CYBERSTALKERS	CYCLOOLEFINIC	CYMBALEERS
CUSPIDATIONS	CYANOETHYLATES	CYBERSTALKING	CYCLOOLEFINS	CYMBALISTS
CUSPIDORES	CYANOETHYLATING	CYBERSTALKINGS	CYCLOPAEDIA	CYMBIDIUMS
CUSSEDNESS	CYANOETHYLATION	CYBERTERRORISM	CYCLOPAEDIAS	CYMIFEROUS
CUSSEDNESSES	CYANOGENAMIDE	CYBERTERRORISMS	CYCLOPAEDIC	CYMOGRAPHIC
CUSTARDIER	CYANOGENAMIDES	CYBERTERRORIST	CYCLOPAEDIST	CYMOGRAPHS
CUSTARDIEST	CYANOGENESES	CYBERTERRORISTS	CYCLOPAEDISTS	CYMOPHANES
CUSTODIANS	CYANOGENESIS	CYBRARIANS	CYCLOPARAFFIN	CYMOPHANOUS
CUSTODIANSHIP	CYANOGENETIC	CYCADACEOUS	CYCLOPARAFFINS	CYMOTRICHIES
CUSTODIANSHIPS	CYANOGENIC	CYCADEOIDS	CYCLOPEDIA	CYMOTRICHOUS
CUSTODIERS	CYANOHYDRIN	CYCADOPHYTE	CYCLOPEDIAS	CYMOTRICHY
CUSTOMABLE	CYANOHYDRINS	CYCADOPHYTES	CYCLOPEDIC	CYNGHANEDD
CUSTOMARIES	CYANOMETER	CYCLAMATES	CYCLOPEDIST	CYNGHANEDDS
CUSTOMARILY	CYANOMETERS	CYCLANDELATE	CYCLOPEDISTS	CYNICALNESS
CUSTOMARINESS	CYANOPHYTE	CYCLANDELATES	CYCLOPENTADIENE	CYNICALNESSES
CUSTOMARINESSES	CYANOPHYTES	CYCLANTHACEOUS	CYCLOPENTANE	CYNOMOLGUS
CUSTOMHOUSE	CYANOTYPES	CYCLAZOCINE	CYCLOPENTANES	CYNOMOLGUSES
CUSTOMHOUSES	CYANURATES	CYCLAZOCINES	CYCLOPENTOLATE	CYNOPHILIA
CUSTOMISATION	CYATHIFORM	CYCLEPATHS	CYCLOPENTOLATES	CYNOPHILIAS
CUSTOMISATIONS	CYBERATHLETE	CYCLICALITIES	CYCLOPLEGIA	CYNOPHILIST
CUSTOMISED	CYBERATHLETES	CYCLICALITY	CYCLOPLEGIAS	CYNOPHILISTS
CUSTOMISER	CYBERATHLETICS	CYCLICALLY	CYCLOPLEGIC	CYNOPHOBIA
CUSTOMISERS	CYBERATTACK	CYCLICISMS	CYCLOPROPANE	CYNOPHOBIAS
CUSTOMISES	CYBERATTACKS	CYCLICITIES	CYCLOPROPANES	CYNOPODOUS
CUSTOMISING	CYBERBULLIES	CYCLISATION	CYCLORAMAS	CYPERACEOUS
CUSTOMIZATION	CYBERBULLY	CYCLISATIONS	CYCLORAMIC	CYPRINODONT
CUSTOMIZATIONS	CYBERBULLYING	CYCLIZATION	CYCLOSERINE	CYPRINODONTS
CUSTOMIZED	CYBERBULLYINGS	CYCLIZATIONS	CYCLOSERINES	CYPRINOIDS
CUSTOMIZER	CYBERCAFES	CYCLIZINES	CYCLOSPERMOUS	CYPRIPEDIA
CUSTOMIZERS	CYBERCASTS	CYCLOADDITION	CYCLOSPORIN	CYPRIPEDIUM
CUSTOMIZES	CYBERCHONDRIA	CYCLOADDITIONS	CYCLOSPORINE	CYPRIPEDIUMS
CUSTOMIZING	CYBERCHONDRIAC	CYCLOALIPHATIC	CYCLOSPORINES	CYPROHEPTADINE
CUSTOMSHOUSE	CYBERCHONDRIACS	CYCLOALKANE	CYCLOSPORINS	CYPROHEPTADINES
CUSTOMSHOUSES	CYBERCHONDRIAS	CYCLOALKANES	CYCLOSTOMATE	CYPROTERONE
CUSTUMARIES	CYBERCRIME	CYCLOBARBITONE	CYCLOSTOMATOUS	CYPROTERONES
CUTABILITIES	CYBERCRIMES	CYCLOBARBITONES	CYCLOSTOME	CYSTEAMINE
CUTABILITY	CYBERCRIMINAL	CYCLODEXTRIN	CYCLOSTOMES	CYSTEAMINES
CUTANEOUSLY	CYBERCRIMINALS	CYCLODEXTRINS	CYCLOSTOMOUS	CYSTECTOMIES
CUTCHERIES	CYBERNATED	CYCLODIALYSES	CYCLOSTYLE	CYSTECTOMY
CUTCHERRIES	CYBERNATES	CYCLODIALYSIS	CYCLOSTYLED	CYSTICERCI
CUTENESSES	CYBERNATING	CYCLODIENE	CYCLOSTYLES	CYSTICERCOID
CUTGRASSES	CYBERNATION	CYCLODIENES	CYCLOSTYLING	CYSTICERCOIDS
CUTINISATION	CYBERNATIONS	CYCLOGENESES	CYCLOTHYME	CYSTICERCOSES
CUTINISATIONS	CYBERNAUTS	CYCLOGENESIS	CYCLOTHYMES	CYSTICERCOSIS
CUTINISING	CYBERNETIC	CYCLOGIROS	CYCLOTHYMIA	CYSTICERCUS
CUTINIZATION	CYBERNETICAL	CYCLOGRAPH	CYCLOTHYMIAC	CYSTIDEANS
CUTINIZATIONS	CYBERNETICALLY	CYCLOGRAPHIC	CYCLOTHYMIACS	CYSTINOSES
CUTINIZING	CYBERNETICIAN	CYCLOGRAPHS	CYCLOTHYMIAS	CYSTINOSIS
CUTTHROATS	CYBERNETICIANS	CYCLOHEXANE	CYCLOTHYMIC	CYSTINURIA
CUTTLEBONE	CYBERNETICIST	CYCLOHEXANES	CYCLOTHYMICS	CYSTINURIAS
CUTTLEBONES	CYBERNETICISTS	CYCLOHEXANONE	CYCLOTOMIC	CYSTITIDES
CUTTLEFISH	CYBERNETICS	CYCLOHEXANONES	CYCLOTRONS	CYSTITISES
CUTTLEFISHES	CYBERPHOBIA	CYCLOHEXIMIDE	CYLINDERED	CYSTOCARPIC
CYANAMIDES	CYBERPHOBIAS	CYCLOHEXIMIDES	CYLINDERING	CYSTOCARPS
CYANIDATION	CYBERPHOBIC	CYCLOHEXYLAMINE	CYLINDRACEOUS	CYSTOCELES
CYANIDATIONS	CYBERPORNS	CYCLOIDALLY	CYLINDRICAL	CYSTOGENOUS
CYANIDINGS	CYBERPUNKS	CYCLOIDIAN	CYLINDRICALITY	CYSTOGRAPHIES
CYANOACETYLENE	CYBERSECURITIES	CYCLOIDIANS	CYLINDRICALLY	CYSTOGRAPHY
CYANOACETYLENES	CYBERSECURITY	CYCLOLITHS	CYLINDRICALNESS	CYSTOLITHIASES
CYANOACRYLATE	CYBERSEXES	CYCLOMETER	CYLINDRICITIES	CYSTOLITHIASIS
CYANOACRYLATES	CYBERSPACE	CYCLOMETERS	CYLINDRICITY	CYSTOLITHS
CYANOBACTERIA	CYBERSPACES	CYCLOMETRIES	CYLINDRIFORM	CYSTOSCOPE
CYANOBACTERIUM	CYBERSQUATTER	CYCLOMETRY	CYLINDRITE	CYSTOSCOPES
CYANOCOBALAMIN	CYBERSQUATTERS	CYCLONICAL	CYLINDRITES	CYSTOSCOPIC
CYANOCOBALAMINE	CYBERSQUATTING	CYCLONICALLY	CYLINDROID	CYSTOSCOPIES
CYANOCOBALAMINS	CYBERSQUATTINGS	CYCLONITES	CYLINDROIDS	CYSTOSCOPY
CYANOETHYLATE	CYBERSTALKER	CYCLOOLEFIN	CYMAGRAPHS	CYSTOSTOMIES

CYSTOSTOMY
CYSTOTOMIES
CYTOCHALASIN
CYTOCHALASINS
CYTOCHEMICAL
CYTOCHEMISTRIES
CYTOCHEMISTRY
CYTOCHROME
CYTOCHROMES
CYTODIAGNOSES
CYTODIAGNOSIS
CYTOGENESES
CYTOGENESIS
CYTOGENETIC

CYTOGENETICAL
CYTOGENETICALLY
CYTOGENETICIST
CYTOGENETICISTS
CYTOGENETICS
CYTOGENIES
CYTOKINESES
CYTOKINESIS
CYTOKINETIC
CYTOKININS
CYTOLOGICAL
CYTOLOGICALLY
CYTOLOGIES
CYTOLOGIST

CYTOLOGISTS
CYTOLYSINS
CYTOMEGALIC
CYTOMEGALOVIRUS
CYTOMEMBRANE
CYTOMEMBRANES
CYTOMETERS
CYTOMETRIC
CYTOMETRIES
CYTOPATHIC
CYTOPATHIES
CYTOPATHOGENIC
CYTOPATHOLOGIES
CYTOPATHOLOGY

CYTOPENIAS
CYTOPHILIC
CYTOPHOTOMETRIC
CYTOPHOTOMETRY
CYTOPLASMIC
CYTOPLASMICALLY
CYTOPLASMS
CYTOPLASTIC
CYTOPLASTS
CYTOSKELETAL
CYTOSKELETON
CYTOSKELETONS
CYTOSTATIC
CYTOSTATICALLY

CYTOSTATICS
CYTOTAXONOMIC
CYTOTAXONOMIES
CYTOTAXONOMIST
CYTOTAXONOMISTS
CYTOTAXONOMY
CYTOTECHNOLOGY
CYTOTOXICITIES
CYTOTOXICITY
CYTOTOXINS
CZAREVICHES
CZAREVITCH
CZAREVITCHES

C

D

DABBLINGLY	DALTONIANS	DANDYISHLY	DATAVEILLANCE	DEACIDIFIED
DACHSHUNDS	DALTONISMS	DANDYPRATS	DATAVEILLANCES	DEACIDIFIES
DACOITAGES	DAMAGEABILITIES	DANGERLESS	DATEDNESSES	DEACIDIFYING
DACQUOISES	DAMAGEABILITY	DANGEROUSLY	DATELINING	DEACONESSES
DACTYLICALLY	DAMAGEABLE	DANGEROUSNESS	DAUGHTERBOARD	DEACONHOOD
DACTYLIOGRAPHY	DAMAGINGLY	DANGEROUSNESSES	DAUGHTERBOARDS	DEACONHOODS
DACTYLIOLOGIES	DAMASCEENE	DANGLINGLY	DAUGHTERHOOD	DEACONRIES
DACTYLIOLOGY	DAMASCEENED	DANKNESSES	DAUGHTERHOODS	DEACONSHIP
DACTYLIOMANCIES	DAMASCEENES	DANNEBROGS	DAUGHTERLESS	DEACONSHIPS
DACTYLIOMANCY	DAMASCEENING	DANTHONIAS	DAUGHTERLIER	DEACTIVATE
DACTYLISTS	DAMASCENED	DAPPERLING	DAUGHTERLIEST	DEACTIVATED
DACTYLOGRAM	DAMASCENES	DAPPERLINGS	DAUGHTERLINESS	DEACTIVATES
DACTYLOGRAMS	DAMASCENING	DAPPERNESS	DAUGHTERLING	DEACTIVATING
DACTYLOGRAPHER	DAMASCENINGS	DAPPERNESSES	DAUGHTERLINGS	DEACTIVATION
DACTYLOGRAPHERS	DAMASKEENED	DAREDEVILRIES	DAUGHTERLY	DEACTIVATIONS
DACTYLOGRAPHIC	DAMASKEENING	DAREDEVILRY	DAUNDERING	DEACTIVATOR
DACTYLOGRAPHIES	DAMASKEENS	DAREDEVILS	DAUNOMYCIN	DEACTIVATORS
DACTYLOGRAPHY	DAMASKINED	DAREDEVILTRIES	DAUNOMYCINS	DEADENINGLY
DACTYLOLOGIES	DAMASKINING	DAREDEVILTRY	DAUNORUBICIN	DEADENINGS
DACTYLOLOGY	DAMASQUINED	DARINGNESS	DAUNORUBICINS	DEADHEADED
DACTYLOSCOPIES	DAMASQUINING	DARINGNESSES	DAUNTINGLY	DEADHEADING
DACTYLOSCOPY	DAMASQUINS	DARKNESSES	DAUNTLESSLY	DEADHOUSES
DAFFADOWNDILLY	DAMINOZIDE	DARLINGNESS	DAUNTLESSNESS	DEADLIFTED
DAFFINESSES	DAMINOZIDES	DARLINGNESSES	DAUNTLESSNESSES	DEADLIFTING
DAFFODILLIES	DAMNABILITIES	DARMSTADTIUM	DAUNTONING	DEADLIGHTS
DAFFODILLY	DAMNABILITY	DARMSTADTIUMS	DAUPHINESS	DEADLINESS
DAFTNESSES	DAMNABLENESS	DARNATIONS	DAUPHINESSES	DEADLINESSES
DAGGERBOARD	DAMNABLENESSES	DARNEDESTS	DAVENPORTS	DEADLINING
DAGGERBOARDS	DAMNATIONS	DARRAIGNED	DAWDLINGLY	DEADLOCKED
DAGGERLIKE	DAMNEDESTS	DARRAIGNES	DAWSONITES	DEADLOCKING
DAGUERREAN	DAMNIFICATION	DARRAIGNING	DAYCATIONS	DEADNESSES
DAGUERREOTYPE	DAMNIFICATIONS	DARRAIGNMENT	DAYCENTRES	DEADPANNED
DAGUERREOTYPED	DAMNIFYING	DARRAIGNMENTS	DAYDREAMED	DEADPANNER
DAGUERREOTYPER	DAMOISELLE	DARRAINING	DAYDREAMER	DEADPANNERS
DAGUERREOTYPERS	DAMOISELLES	DARRAYNING	DAYDREAMERS	DEADPANNING
DAGUERREOTYPES	DAMPCOURSE	DARTBOARDS	DAYDREAMIER	DEADSTOCKS
DAGUERREOTYPIES	DAMPCOURSES	DARTITISES	DAYDREAMIEST	DEADSTROKE
DAGUERREOTYPING	DAMPISHNESS	DASHBOARDS	DAYDREAMING	DEADWATERS
DAGUERREOTYPIST	DAMPISHNESSES	DASHLIGHTS	DAYDREAMINGS	DEADWEIGHT
DAGUERREOTYPY	DAMPNESSES	DASTARDIES	DAYDREAMLIKE	DEADWEIGHTS
DAHABEEAHS	DAMSELFISH	DASTARDLIER	DAYFLOWERS	DEAERATING
DAHABEEYAH	DAMSELFISHES	DASTARDLIEST	DAYLIGHTED	DEAERATION
DAHABEEYAHS	DAMSELFLIES	DASTARDLINESS	DAYLIGHTING	DEAERATIONS
DAHABIYAHS	DANCECORES	DASTARDLINESSES	DAYLIGHTINGS	DEAERATORS
DAHABIYEHS	DANCEHALLS	DASTARDNESS	DAYSAILERS	DEAFENINGLY
DAILINESSES	DANCEWEARS	DASTARDNESSES	DAYSAILING	DEAFENINGS
DAILYNESSES	DANDELIONS	DASYMETERS	DAYSAILORS	DEAFNESSES
DAINTINESS	DANDIFICATION	DASYPAEDAL	DAYSPRINGS	DEALATIONS
DAINTINESSES	DANDIFICATIONS	DASYPHYLLOUS	DAYWORKERS	DEALBATION
DAIRYMAIDS	DANDIFYING	DATABASING	DAZEDNESSES	DEALBATIONS
DAISYWHEEL	DANDIPRATS	DATABUSSES	DAZZLEMENT	DEALBREAKER
DAISYWHEELS	DANDRUFFIER	DATAGLOVES	DAZZLEMENTS	DEALBREAKERS
DALLIANCES	DANDRUFFIEST	DATAMATION	DAZZLINGLY	DEALERSHIP
DALMATIANS	DANDYFUNKS	DATAMATIONS	DEACIDIFICATION	DEALERSHIPS

DEALFISHES
DEALIGNING
DEALMAKERS
DEAMBULATORIES
DEAMBULATORY
DEAMINASES
DEAMINATED
DEAMINATES
DEAMINATING
DEAMINATION
DEAMINATIONS
DEAMINISATION
DEAMINISATIONS
DEAMINISED
DEAMINISES
DEAMINISING
DEAMINIZATION
DEAMINIZATIONS
DEAMINIZED
DEAMINIZES
DEAMINIZING
DEARBOUGHT
DEARNESSES
DEARTICULATE
DEARTICULATED
DEARTICULATES
DEARTICULATING
DEASPIRATE
DEASPIRATED
DEASPIRATES
DEASPIRATING
DEASPIRATION
DEASPIRATIONS
DEATHBLOWS
DEATHLESSLY
DEATHLESSNESS
DEATHLESSNESSES
DEATHLIEST
DEATHLINESS
DEATHLINESSES
DEATHTRAPS
DEATHWARDS
DEATHWATCH
DEATHWATCHES
DEATTRIBUTE
DEATTRIBUTED
DEATTRIBUTES
DEATTRIBUTING
DEBAGGINGS
DEBARCATION
DEBARCATIONS
DEBARKATION
DEBARKATIONS
DEBARMENTS
DEBARRASSED
DEBARRASSES
DEBARRASSING
DEBASEDNESS
DEBASEDNESSES
DEBASEMENT
DEBASEMENTS
DEBASINGLY
DEBATEABLE
DEBATEMENT
DEBATEMENTS
DEBATINGLY
DEBAUCHEDLY

DEBAUCHEDNESS
DEBAUCHEDNESSES
DEBAUCHEES
DEBAUCHERIES
DEBAUCHERS
DEBAUCHERY
DEBAUCHING
DEBAUCHMENT
DEBAUCHMENTS
DEBEARDING
DEBENTURED
DEBENTURES
DEBILITATE
DEBILITATED
DEBILITATES
DEBILITATING
DEBILITATION
DEBILITATIONS
DEBILITATIVE
DEBILITIES
DEBONAIRLY
DEBONAIRNESS
DEBONAIRNESSES
DEBONNAIRE
DEBOUCHING
DEBOUCHMENT
DEBOUCHMENTS
DEBOUCHURE
DEBOUCHURES
DEBRIDEMENT
DEBRIDEMENTS
DEBRIEFERS
DEBRIEFING
DEBRIEFINGS
DEBRUISING
DEBUGGINGS
DEBUTANTES
DECACHORDS
DECADENCES
DECADENCIES
DECADENTLY
DECAFFEINATE
DECAFFEINATED
DECAFFEINATES
DECAFFEINATING
DECAGONALLY
DECAGRAMME
DECAGRAMMES
DECAGYNIAN
DECAGYNOUS
DECAHEDRAL
DECAHEDRON
DECAHEDRONS
DECAHYDRATE
DECAHYDRATES
DECALCIFICATION
DECALCIFIED
DECALCIFIER
DECALCIFIERS
DECALCIFIES
DECALCIFYING
DECALCOMANIA
DECALCOMANIAS
DECALESCENCE
DECALESCENCES
DECALESCENT
DECALITERS

DECALITRES
DECALOGIST
DECALOGISTS
DECALOGUES
DECAMERONIC
DECAMEROUS
DECAMETERS
DECAMETHONIUM
DECAMETHONIUMS
DECAMETRES
DECAMETRIC
DECAMPMENT
DECAMPMENTS
DECANDRIAN
DECANDROUS
DECANEDIOIC
DECANICALLY
DECANTATED
DECANTATES
DECANTATING
DECANTATION
DECANTATIONS
DECAPITALISE
DECAPITALISED
DECAPITALISES
DECAPITALISING
DECAPITALIZE
DECAPITALIZED
DECAPITALIZES
DECAPITALIZING
DECAPITATE
DECAPITATED
DECAPITATES
DECAPITATING
DECAPITATION
DECAPITATIONS
DECAPITATOR
DECAPITATORS
DECAPODANS
DECAPODOUS
DECAPSULATE
DECAPSULATED
DECAPSULATES
DECAPSULATING
DECAPSULATION
DECAPSULATIONS
DECARBONATE
DECARBONATED
DECARBONATES
DECARBONATING
DECARBONATION
DECARBONATIONS
DECARBONATOR
DECARBONATORS
DECARBONISATION
DECARBONISE
DECARBONISED
DECARBONISER
DECARBONISERS
DECARBONISES
DECARBONISING
DECARBONIZATION
DECARBONIZE
DECARBONIZED
DECARBONIZER
DECARBONIZERS
DECARBONIZES

DECARBONIZING
DECARBOXYLASE
DECARBOXYLASES
DECARBOXYLATE
DECARBOXYLATED
DECARBOXYLATES
DECARBOXYLATING
DECARBOXYLATION
DECARBURATION
DECARBURATIONS
DECARBURISATION
DECARBURISE
DECARBURISED
DECARBURISES
DECARBURISING
DECARBURIZATION
DECARBURIZE
DECARBURIZED
DECARBURIZES
DECARBURIZING
DECARTELISE
DECARTELISED
DECARTELISES
DECARTELISING
DECARTELIZE
DECARTELIZED
DECARTELIZES
DECARTELIZING
DECASTERES
DECASTICHS
DECASTYLES
DECASUALISATION
DECASUALISE
DECASUALISED
DECASUALISES
DECASUALISING
DECASUALIZATION
DECASUALIZE
DECASUALIZED
DECASUALIZES
DECASUALIZING
DECASYLLABIC
DECASYLLABICS
DECASYLLABLE
DECASYLLABLES
DECATHLETE
DECATHLETES
DECATHLONS
DECAUDATED
DECAUDATES
DECAUDATING
DECEITFULLY
DECEITFULNESS
DECEITFULNESSES
DECEIVABILITIES
DECEIVABILITY
DECEIVABLE
DECEIVABLENESS
DECEIVABLY
DECEIVINGLY
DECEIVINGS
DECELERATE
DECELERATED
DECELERATES
DECELERATING
DECELERATION
DECELERATIONS

DECELERATOR
DECELERATORS
DECELEROMETER
DECELEROMETERS
DECELERONS
DECEMVIRAL
DECEMVIRATE
DECEMVIRATES
DECENARIES
DECENNARIES
DECENNIALLY
DECENNIALS
DECENNIUMS
DECENNOVAL
DECENTERED
DECENTERING
DECENTERINGS
DECENTNESS
DECENTNESSES
DECENTRALISE
DECENTRALISED
DECENTRALISES
DECENTRALISING
DECENTRALIST
DECENTRALISTS
DECENTRALIZE
DECENTRALIZED
DECENTRALIZES
DECENTRALIZING
DECENTRING
DECEPTIBILITIES
DECEPTIBILITY
DECEPTIBLE
DECEPTIONAL
DECEPTIONS
DECEPTIOUS
DECEPTIVELY
DECEPTIVENESS
DECEPTIVENESSES
DECEREBRATE
DECEREBRATED
DECEREBRATES
DECEREBRATING
DECEREBRATION
DECEREBRATIONS
DECEREBRISE
DECEREBRISED
DECEREBRISES
DECEREBRISING
DECEREBRIZE
DECEREBRIZED
DECEREBRIZES
DECEREBRIZING
DECERTIFICATION
DECERTIFIED
DECERTIFIES
DECERTIFYING
DECESSIONS
DECHEANCES
DECHLORINATE
DECHLORINATED
DECHLORINATES
DECHLORINATING
DECHLORINATION
DECHLORINATIONS
DECHRISTIANISE
DECHRISTIANISED

DECHRISTIANISES	DECIVILISES	DECOLLATES	DECOMMUNISE	DECONSTRUCTIONS
DECHRISTIANIZE	DECIVILISING	DECOLLATING	DECOMMUNISED	DECONSTRUCTIVE
DECHRISTIANIZED	DECIVILIZE	DECOLLATION	DECOMMUNISES	DECONSTRUCTOR
DECHRISTIANIZES	DECIVILIZED	DECOLLATIONS	DECOMMUNISING	DECONSTRUCTORS
DECIDABILITIES	DECIVILIZES	DECOLLATOR	DECOMMUNIZATION	DECONSTRUCTS
DECIDABILITY	DECIVILIZING	DECOLLATORS	DECOMMUNIZE	DECONTAMINANT
DECIDEDNESS	DECKCHAIRS	DECOLLETAGE	DECOMMUNIZED	DECONTAMINANTS
DECIDEDNESSES	DECKHOUSES	DECOLLETAGES	DECOMMUNIZES	DECONTAMINATE
DECIDUOUSLY	DECLAIMANT	DECOLLETES	DECOMMUNIZING	DECONTAMINATED
DECIDUOUSNESS	DECLAIMANTS	DECOLONISATION	DECOMPENSATE	DECONTAMINATES
DECIDUOUSNESSES	DECLAIMERS	DECOLONISATIONS	DECOMPENSATED	DECONTAMINATING
DECIGRAMME	DECLAIMING	DECOLONISE	DECOMPENSATES	DECONTAMINATION
DECIGRAMMES	DECLAIMINGS	DECOLONISED	DECOMPENSATING	DECONTAMINATIVE
DECILITERS	DECLAMATION	DECOLONISES	DECOMPENSATION	DECONTAMINATOR
DECILITRES	DECLAMATIONS	DECOLONISING	DECOMPENSATIONS	DECONTAMINATORS
DECILLIONS	DECLAMATORILY	DECOLONIZATION	DECOMPOSABILITY	DECONTEXTUALISE
DECILLIONTH	DECLAMATORY	DECOLONIZATIONS	DECOMPOSABLE	DECONTEXTUALIZE
DECILLIONTHS	DECLARABLE	DECOLONIZE	DECOMPOSED	DECONTROLLED
DECIMALISATION	DECLARANTS	DECOLONIZED	DECOMPOSER	DECONTROLLING
DECIMALISATIONS	DECLARATION	DECOLONIZES	DECOMPOSERS	DECONTROLS
DECIMALISE	DECLARATIONS	DECOLONIZING	DECOMPOSES	DECORATING
DECIMALISED	DECLARATIVE	DECOLORANT	DECOMPOSING	DECORATINGS
DECIMALISES	DECLARATIVELY	DECOLORANTS	DECOMPOSITE	DECORATION
DECIMALISING	DECLARATOR	DECOLORATE	DECOMPOSITES	DECORATIONS
DECIMALISM	DECLARATORILY	DECOLORATED	DECOMPOSITION	DECORATIVE
DECIMALISMS	DECLARATORS	DECOLORATES	DECOMPOSITIONS	DECORATIVELY
DECIMALIST	DECLARATORY	DECOLORATING	DECOMPOUND	DECORATIVENESS
DECIMALISTS	DECLAREDLY	DECOLORATION	DECOMPOUNDABLE	DECORATORS
DECIMALIZATION	DECLASSIFIABLE	DECOLORATIONS	DECOMPOUNDED	DECOROUSLY
DECIMALIZATIONS	DECLASSIFIED	DECOLORING	DECOMPOUNDING	DECOROUSNESS
DECIMALIZE	DECLASSIFIES	DECOLORISATION	DECOMPOUNDS	DECOROUSNESSES
DECIMALIZED	DECLASSIFY	DECOLORISATIONS	DECOMPRESS	DECORTICATE
DECIMALIZES	DECLASSIFYING	DECOLORISE	DECOMPRESSED	DECORTICATED
DECIMALIZING	DECLASSING	DECOLORISED	DECOMPRESSES	DECORTICATES
DECIMATING	DECLENSION	DECOLORISER	DECOMPRESSING	DECORTICATING
DECIMATION	DECLENSIONAL	DECOLORISERS	DECOMPRESSION	DECORTICATION
DECIMATIONS	DECLENSIONALLY	DECOLORISES	DECOMPRESSIONS	DECORTICATIONS
DECIMATORS	DECLENSIONS	DECOLORISING	DECOMPRESSIVE	DECORTICATOR
DECIMETERS	DECLINABLE	DECOLORIZATION	DECOMPRESSOR	DECORTICATORS
DECIMETRES	DECLINANTS	DECOLORIZATIONS	DECOMPRESSORS	DECOUPAGED
DECIMETRIC	DECLINATION	DECOLORIZE	DECONCENTRATE	DECOUPAGES
DECINORMAL	DECLINATIONAL	DECOLORIZED	DECONCENTRATED	DECOUPAGING
DECIPHERABILITY	DECLINATIONS	DECOLORIZER	DECONCENTRATES	DECOUPLERS
DECIPHERABLE	DECLINATOR	DECOLORIZERS	DECONCENTRATING	DECOUPLING
DECIPHERED	DECLINATORIES	DECOLORIZES	DECONCENTRATION	DECOUPLINGS
DECIPHERER	DECLINATORS	DECOLORIZING	DECONDITION	DECRASSIFIED
DECIPHERERS	DECLINATORY	DECOLOURED	DECONDITIONED	DECRASSIFIES
DECIPHERING	DECLINATURE	DECOLOURING	DECONDITIONING	DECRASSIFY
DECIPHERMENT	DECLINATURES	DECOLOURISATION	DECONDITIONS	DECRASSIFYING
DECIPHERMENTS	DECLINISTS	DECOLOURISE	DECONGESTANT	DECREASING
DECISIONAL	DECLINOMETER	DECOLOURISED	DECONGESTANTS	DECREASINGLY
DECISIONED	DECLINOMETERS	DECOLOURISES	DECONGESTED	DECREASINGS
DECISIONING	DECLIVITIES	DECOLOURISING	DECONGESTING	DECREEABLE
DECISIVELY	DECLIVITOUS	DECOLOURIZATION	DECONGESTION	DECREMENTAL
DECISIVENESS	DECLUTCHED	DECOLOURIZE	DECONGESTIONS	DECREMENTED
DECISIVENESSES	DECLUTCHES	DECOLOURIZED	DECONGESTIVE	DECREMENTING
DECISTERES	DECLUTCHING	DECOLOURIZES	DECONGESTS	DECREMENTS
DECITIZENISE	DECLUTTERED	DECOLOURIZING	DECONSECRATE	DECREPITATE
DECITIZENISED	DECLUTTERING	DECOMMISSION	DECONSECRATED	DECREPITATED
DECITIZENISES	DECLUTTERS	DECOMMISSIONED	DECONSECRATES	DECREPITATES
DECITIZENISING	DECOCTIBLE	DECOMMISSIONER	DECONSECRATING	DECREPITATING
DECITIZENIZE	DECOCTIONS	DECOMMISSIONERS	DECONSECRATION	DECREPITATION
DECITIZENIZED	DECOCTURES	DECOMMISSIONING	DECONSECRATIONS	DECREPITATIONS
DECITIZENIZES	DECOHERENCE	DECOMMISSIONS	DECONSTRUCT	DECREPITLY
DECITIZENIZING	DECOHERENCES	DECOMMITTED	DECONSTRUCTED	DECREPITNESS
DECIVILISE	DECOHERERS	DECOMMITTING	DECONSTRUCTING	DECREPITNESSES
DECIVILISED	DECOLLATED	DECOMMUNISATION	DECONSTRUCTION	DECREPITUDE

DECREPITUDES	DEDUCEMENTS	DEFEATISTS	DEFERVESCENCIES	DEFINITIVES
DECRESCENCE	DEDUCIBILITIES	DEFEATURED	DEFERVESCENCY	DEFINITIZE
DECRESCENCES	DEDUCIBILITY	DEFEATURES	DEFEUDALISE	DEFINITIZED
DECRESCENDO	DEDUCIBLENESS	DEFEATURING	DEFEUDALISED	DEFINITIZES
DECRESCENDOS	DEDUCIBLENESSES	DEFECATING	DEFEUDALISES	DEFINITIZING
DECRESCENT	DEDUCTIBILITIES	DEFECATION	DEFEUDALISING	DEFINITUDE
DECRETALIST	DEDUCTIBILITY	DEFECATIONS	DEFEUDALIZE	DEFINITUDES
DECRETALISTS	DEDUCTIBLE	DEFECATORS	DEFEUDALIZED	DEFLAGRABILITY
DECRETISTS	DEDUCTIBLES	DEFECTIBILITIES	DEFEUDALIZES	DEFLAGRABLE
DECRIMINALISE	DEDUCTIONS	DEFECTIBILITY	DEFEUDALIZING	DEFLAGRATE
DECRIMINALISED	DEDUCTIVELY	DEFECTIBLE	DEFIANTNESS	DEFLAGRATED
DECRIMINALISES	DEDUPLICATE	DEFECTIONIST	DEFIANTNESSES	DEFLAGRATES
DECRIMINALISING	DEDUPLICATED	DEFECTIONISTS	DEFIBRILLATE	DEFLAGRATING
DECRIMINALIZE	DEDUPLICATES	DEFECTIONS	DEFIBRILLATED	DEFLAGRATION
DECRIMINALIZED	DEDUPLICATING	DEFECTIVELY	DEFIBRILLATES	DEFLAGRATIONS
DECRIMINALIZES	DEDUPLICATION	DEFECTIVENESS	DEFIBRILLATING	DEFLAGRATOR
DECRIMINALIZING	DEDUPLICATIONS	DEFECTIVENESSES	DEFIBRILLATION	DEFLAGRATORS
DECROWNING	DEEJAYINGS	DEFECTIVES	DEFIBRILLATIONS	DEFLATIONARY
DECRUSTATION	DEEMSTERSHIP	DEFEMINISATION	DEFIBRILLATOR	DEFLATIONIST
DECRUSTATIONS	DEEMSTERSHIPS	DEFEMINISATIONS	DEFIBRILLATORS	DEFLATIONISTS
DECRYPTING	DEEPENINGS	DEFEMINISE	DEFIBRINATE	DEFLATIONS
DECRYPTION	DEEPFREEZE	DEFEMINISED	DEFIBRINATED	DEFLECTABLE
DECRYPTIONS	DEEPFREEZES	DEFEMINISES	DEFIBRINATES	DEFLECTING
DECUMBENCE	DEEPFREEZING	DEFEMINISING	DEFIBRINATING	DEFLECTION
DECUMBENCES	DEEPFROZEN	DEFEMINIZATION	DEFIBRINATION	DEFLECTIONAL
DECUMBENCIES	DEEPNESSES	DEFEMINIZATIONS	DEFIBRINATIONS	DEFLECTIONS
DECUMBENCY	DEEPWATERMAN	DEFEMINIZE	DEFIBRINISE	DEFLECTIVE
DECUMBENTLY	DEEPWATERMEN	DEFEMINIZED	DEFIBRINISED	DEFLECTORS
DECUMBITURE	DEERBERRIES	DEFEMINIZES	DEFIBRINISES	DEFLEXIONAL
DECUMBITURES	DEERGRASSES	DEFEMINIZING	DEFIBRINISING	DEFLEXIONS
DECUMULATION	DEERHOUNDS	DEFENCELESS	DEFIBRINIZE	DEFLEXURES
DECUMULATIONS	DEERSTALKER	DEFENCELESSLY	DEFIBRINIZED	DEFLOCCULANT
DECURIONATE	DEERSTALKERS	DEFENCELESSNESS	DEFIBRINIZES	DEFLOCCULANTS
DECURIONATES	DEERSTALKING	DEFENCEMAN	DEFIBRINIZING	DEFLOCCULATE
DECURRENCIES	DEERSTALKINGS	DEFENCEMEN	DEFICIENCE	DEFLOCCULATED
DECURRENCY	DEFACEABLE	DEFENDABLE	DEFICIENCES	DEFLOCCULATES
DECURRENTLY	DEFACEMENT	DEFENDANTS	DEFICIENCIES	DEFLOCCULATING
DECURSIONS	DEFACEMENTS	DEFENESTRATE	DEFICIENCY	DEFLOCCULATION
DECURSIVELY	DEFACINGLY	DEFENESTRATED	DEFICIENTLY	DEFLOCCULATIONS
DECURVATION	DEFAECATED	DEFENESTRATES	DEFICIENTNESS	DEFLORATED
DECURVATIONS	DEFAECATES	DEFENESTRATING	DEFICIENTNESSES	DEFLORATES
DECUSSATED	DEFAECATING	DEFENESTRATION	DEFICIENTS	DEFLORATING
DECUSSATELY	DEFAECATION	DEFENESTRATIONS	DEFILADING	DEFLORATION
DECUSSATES	DEFAECATIONS	DEFENSATIVE	DEFILEMENT	DEFLORATIONS
DECUSSATING	DEFAECATOR	DEFENSATIVES	DEFILEMENTS	DEFLOWERED
DECUSSATION	DEFAECATORS	DEFENSELESS	DEFILIATION	DEFLOWERER
DECUSSATIONS	DEFALCATED	DEFENSELESSLY	DEFILIATIONS	DEFLOWERERS
DEDICATEDLY	DEFALCATES	DEFENSELESSNESS	DEFINABILITIES	DEFLOWERING
DEDICATEES	DEFALCATING	DEFENSEMAN	DEFINABILITY	DEFLUXIONS
DEDICATING	DEFALCATION	DEFENSEMEN	DEFINEMENT	DEFOCUSING
DEDICATION	DEFALCATIONS	DEFENSIBILITIES	DEFINEMENTS	DEFOCUSSED
DEDICATIONAL	DEFALCATOR	DEFENSIBILITY	DEFINIENDA	DEFOCUSSES
DEDICATIONS	DEFALCATORS	DEFENSIBLE	DEFINIENDUM	DEFOCUSSING
DEDICATIVE	DEFAMATION	DEFENSIBLENESS	DEFINIENTIA	DEFOLIANTS
DEDICATORIAL	DEFAMATIONS	DEFENSIBLY	DEFINITELY	DEFOLIATED
DEDICATORS	DEFAMATORILY	DEFENSIVELY	DEFINITENESS	DEFOLIATES
DEDICATORY	DEFAMATORY	DEFENSIVENESS	DEFINITENESSES	DEFOLIATING
DEDIFFERENTIATE	DEFAULTERS	DEFENSIVENESSES	DEFINITION	DEFOLIATION
DEDRAMATISE	DEFAULTING	DEFENSIVES	DEFINITIONAL	DEFOLIATIONS
DEDRAMATISED	DEFEASANCE	DEFERENCES	DEFINITIONS	DEFOLIATOR
DEDRAMATISES	DEFEASANCED	DEFERENTIAL	DEFINITISE	DEFOLIATORS
DEDRAMATISING	DEFEASANCES	DEFERENTIALLY	DEFINITISED	DEFORCEMENT
DEDRAMATIZE	DEFEASIBILITIES	DEFERMENTS	DEFINITISES	DEFORCEMENTS
DEDRAMATIZED	DEFEASIBILITY	DEFERRABLE	DEFINITISING	DEFORCIANT
DEDRAMATIZES	DEFEASIBLE	DEFERRABLES	DEFINITIVE	DEFORCIANTS
DEDRAMATIZING	DEFEASIBLENESS	DEFERVESCENCE	DEFINITIVELY	DEFORCIATION
DEDUCEMENT	DEFEATISMS	DEFERVESCENCES	DEFINITIVENESS	DEFORCIATIONS

DEFORESTATION	DEGENERATED	DEGUSTATIONS	DEINDEXING	DELEGITIMISING
DEFORESTATIONS	DEGENERATELY	DEGUSTATORY	DEINDIVIDUATION	DELEGITIMIZE
DEFORESTED	DEGENERATENESS	DEHISCENCE	DEINDUSTRIALISE	DELEGITIMIZED
DEFORESTER	DEGENERATES	DEHISCENCES	DEINDUSTRIALIZE	DELEGITIMIZES
DEFORESTERS	DEGENERATING	DEHORTATION	DEINONYCHUS	DELEGITIMIZING
DEFORESTING	DEGENERATION	DEHORTATIONS	DEINONYCHUSES	DELETERIOUS
DEFORMABILITIES	DEGENERATIONIST	DEHORTATIVE	DEINOSAURS	DELETERIOUSLY
DEFORMABILITY	DEGENERATIONS	DEHORTATORY	DEINOTHERE	DELETERIOUSNESS
DEFORMABLE	DEGENERATIVE	DEHUMANISATION	DEINOTHERES	DELEVERAGE
DEFORMALISE	DEGENEROUS	DEHUMANISATIONS	DEINOTHERIA	DELEVERAGED
DEFORMALISED	DEGLACIATED	DEHUMANISE	DEINOTHERIUM	DELEVERAGES
DEFORMALISES	DEGLACIATION	DEHUMANISED	DEINOTHERIUMS	DELEVERAGING
DEFORMALISING	DEGLACIATIONS	DEHUMANISES	DEIONISATION	DELEVERAGINGS
DEFORMALIZE	DEGLAMORISATION	DEHUMANISING	DEIONISATIONS	DELFTWARES
DEFORMALIZED	DEGLAMORISE	DEHUMANIZATION	DEIONISERS	DELIBATING
DEFORMALIZES	DEGLAMORISED	DEHUMANIZATIONS	DEIONISING	DELIBATION
DEFORMALIZING	DEGLAMORISES	DEHUMANIZE	DEIONIZATION	DELIBATIONS
DEFORMATION	DEGLAMORISING	DEHUMANIZED	DEIONIZATIONS	DELIBERATE
DEFORMATIONAL	DEGLAMORIZATION	DEHUMANIZES	DEIONIZERS	DELIBERATED
DEFORMATIONS	DEGLAMORIZE	DEHUMANIZING	DEIONIZING	DELIBERATELY
DEFORMATIVE	DEGLAMORIZED	DEHUMIDIFIED	DEIPNOSOPHIST	DELIBERATENESS
DEFORMEDLY	DEGLAMORIZES	DEHUMIDIFIER	DEIPNOSOPHISTS	DELIBERATES
DEFORMEDNESS	DEGLAMORIZING	DEHUMIDIFIERS	DEISTICALLY	DELIBERATING
DEFORMEDNESSES	DEGLUTINATE	DEHUMIDIFIES	DEJECTEDLY	DELIBERATION
DEFORMITIES	DEGLUTINATED	DEHUMIDIFY	DEJECTEDNESS	DELIBERATIONS
DEFRAGGERS	DEGLUTINATES	DEHUMIDIFYING	DEJECTEDNESSES	DELIBERATIVE
DEFRAGGING	DEGLUTINATING	DEHYDRATED	DEJECTIONS	DELIBERATIVELY
DEFRAGGINGS	DEGLUTINATION	DEHYDRATER	DEKALITERS	DELIBERATOR
DEFRAGMENT	DEGLUTINATIONS	DEHYDRATERS	DEKALITRES	DELIBERATORS
DEFRAGMENTED	DEGLUTITION	DEHYDRATES	DEKALOGIES	DELICACIES
DEFRAGMENTING	DEGLUTITIONS	DEHYDRATING	DEKAMETERS	DELICATELY
DEFRAGMENTS	DEGLUTITIVE	DEHYDRATION	DEKAMETRES	DELICATENESS
DEFRAUDATION	DEGLUTITORY	DEHYDRATIONS	DEKAMETRIC	DELICATENESSES
DEFRAUDATIONS	DEGRADABILITIES	DEHYDRATOR	DELAMINATE	DELICATESSEN
DEFRAUDERS	DEGRADABILITY	DEHYDRATORS	DELAMINATED	DELICATESSENS
DEFRAUDING	DEGRADABLE	DEHYDROGENASE	DELAMINATES	DELICIOUSLY
DEFRAUDMENT	DEGRADATION	DEHYDROGENASES	DELAMINATING	DELICIOUSNESS
DEFRAUDMENTS	DEGRADATIONS	DEHYDROGENATE	DELAMINATION	DELICIOUSNESSES
DEFRAYABLE	DEGRADATIVE	DEHYDROGENATED	DELAMINATIONS	DELIGATION
DEFRAYMENT	DEGRADEDLY	DEHYDROGENATES	DELAPSIONS	DELIGATIONS
DEFRAYMENTS	DEGRADINGLY	DEHYDROGENATING	DELASSEMENT	DELIGHTEDLY
DEFREEZING	DEGRADINGNESS	DEHYDROGENATION	DELASSEMENTS	DELIGHTEDNESS
DEFRIENDED	DEGRADINGNESSES	DEHYDROGENISE	DELAYERING	DELIGHTEDNESSES
DEFRIENDING	DEGRANULATION	DEHYDROGENISED	DELAYERINGS	DELIGHTERS
DEFROCKING	DEGRANULATIONS	DEHYDROGENISES	DELAYINGLY	DELIGHTFUL
DEFROSTERS	DEGREASANT	DEHYDROGENISING	DELECTABILITIES	DELIGHTFULLY
DEFROSTING	DEGREASANTS	DEHYDROGENIZE	DELECTABILITY	DELIGHTFULNESS
DEFROSTINGS	DEGREASERS	DEHYDROGENIZED	DELECTABLE	DELIGHTING
DEFTNESSES	DEGREASING	DEHYDROGENIZES	DELECTABLENESS	DELIGHTLESS
DEFUELLING	DEGREASINGS	DEHYDROGENIZING	DELECTABLES	DELIGHTSOME
DEFUNCTION	DEGREELESS	DEHYDRORETINOL	DELECTABLY	DELIMITATE
DEFUNCTIONS	DEGRESSION	DEHYDRORETINOLS	DELECTATED	DELIMITATED
DEFUNCTIVE	DEGRESSIONS	DEHYPNOTISATION	DELECTATES	DELIMITATES
DEFUNCTNESS	DEGRESSIVE	DEHYPNOTISE	DELECTATING	DELIMITATING
DEFUNCTNESSES	DEGRESSIVELY	DEHYPNOTISED	DELECTATION	DELIMITATION
DEGARNISHED	DEGRINGOLADE	DEHYPNOTISES	DELECTATIONS	DELIMITATIONS
DEGARNISHES	DEGRINGOLADED	DEHYPNOTISING	DELEGACIES	DELIMITATIVE
DEGARNISHING	DEGRINGOLADES	DEHYPNOTIZATION	DELEGATEES	DELIMITERS
DEGAUSSERS	DEGRINGOLADING	DEHYPNOTIZE	DELEGATING	DELIMITING
DEGAUSSING	DEGRINGOLER	DEHYPNOTIZED	DELEGATION	DELINEABLE
DEGAUSSINGS	DEGRINGOLERED	DEHYPNOTIZES	DELEGATIONS	DELINEATED
DEGEARINGS	DEGRINGOLERING	DEHYPNOTIZING	DELEGATORS	DELINEATES
DEGENDERED	DEGRINGOLERS	DEICTICALLY	DELEGITIMATION	DELINEATING
DEGENDERING	DEGUSTATED	DEIFICATION	DELEGITIMATIONS	DELINEATION
DEGENERACIES	DEGUSTATES	DEIFICATIONS	DELEGITIMISE	DELINEATIONS
DEGENERACY	DEGUSTATING	DEINDEXATION	DELEGITIMISED	DELINEATIVE
DEGENERATE	DEGUSTATION	DEINDEXATIONS	DELEGITIMISES	DELINEATOR

DELINEATORS	DELUSTERING	DEMERGERING	DEMOCRACIES	DEMONETISES
DELINEAVIT	DELUSTRANT	DEMERITING	DEMOCRATIC	DEMONETISING
DELINQUENCIES	DELUSTRANTS	DEMERITORIOUS	DEMOCRATICAL	DEMONETIZATION
DELINQUENCY	DELUSTRING	DEMERITORIOUSLY	DEMOCRATICALLY	DEMONETIZATIONS
DELINQUENT	DEMAGNETISATION	DEMERSIONS	DEMOCRATIES	DEMONETIZE
DELINQUENTLY	DEMAGNETISE	DEMIBASTION	DEMOCRATIFIABLE	DEMONETIZED
DELINQUENTS	DEMAGNETISED	DEMIBASTIONS	DEMOCRATISATION	DEMONETIZES
DELIQUESCE	DEMAGNETISER	DEMICANTON	DEMOCRATISE	DEMONETIZING
DELIQUESCED	DEMAGNETISERS	DEMICANTONS	DEMOCRATISED	DEMONIACAL
DELIQUESCENCE	DEMAGNETISES	DEMIGODDESS	DEMOCRATISER	DEMONIACALLY
DELIQUESCENCES	DEMAGNETISING	DEMIGODDESSES	DEMOCRATISERS	DEMONIACISM
DELIQUESCENT	DEMAGNETIZATION	DEMIGRATION	DEMOCRATISES	DEMONIACISMS
DELIQUESCES	DEMAGNETIZE	DEMIGRATIONS	DEMOCRATISING	DEMONIANISM
DELIQUESCING	DEMAGNETIZED	DEMILITARISE	DEMOCRATIST	DEMONIANISMS
DELIQUIUMS	DEMAGNETIZER	DEMILITARISED	DEMOCRATISTS	DEMONICALLY
DELIRATION	DEMAGNETIZERS	DEMILITARISES	DEMOCRATIZATION	DEMONISATION
DELIRATIONS	DEMAGNETIZES	DEMILITARISING	DEMOCRATIZE	DEMONISATIONS
DELIRIFACIENT	DEMAGNETIZING	DEMILITARIZE	DEMOCRATIZED	DEMONISING
DELIRIFACIENTS	DEMAGOGICAL	DEMILITARIZED	DEMOCRATIZER	DEMONIZATION
DELIRIOUSLY	DEMAGOGICALLY	DEMILITARIZES	DEMOCRATIZERS	DEMONIZATIONS
DELIRIOUSNESS	DEMAGOGIES	DEMILITARIZING	DEMOCRATIZES	DEMONIZING
DELIRIOUSNESSES	DEMAGOGING	DEMIMONDAINE	DEMOCRATIZING	DEMONOCRACIES
DELITESCENCE	DEMAGOGISM	DEMIMONDAINES	DEMODULATE	DEMONOCRACY
DELITESCENCES	DEMAGOGISMS	DEMIMONDES	DEMODULATED	DEMONOLATER
DELITESCENT	DEMAGOGUED	DEMINERALISE	DEMODULATES	DEMONOLATERS
DELIVERABILITY	DEMAGOGUERIES	DEMINERALISED	DEMODULATING	DEMONOLATRIES
DELIVERABLE	DEMAGOGUERY	DEMINERALISER	DEMODULATION	DEMONOLATRY
DELIVERABLES	DEMAGOGUES	DEMINERALISERS	DEMODULATIONS	DEMONOLOGIC
DELIVERANCE	DEMAGOGUING	DEMINERALISES	DEMODULATOR	DEMONOLOGICAL
DELIVERANCES	DEMAGOGUISM	DEMINERALISING	DEMODULATORS	DEMONOLOGIES
DELIVERERS	DEMAGOGUISMS	DEMINERALIZE	DEMOGRAPHER	DEMONOLOGIST
DELIVERIES	DEMANDABLE	DEMINERALIZED	DEMOGRAPHERS	DEMONOLOGISTS
DELIVERING	DEMANDANTS	DEMINERALIZER	DEMOGRAPHIC	DEMONOLOGY
DELIVERYMAN	DEMANDINGLY	DEMINERALIZERS	DEMOGRAPHICAL	DEMONOMANIA
DELIVERYMEN	DEMANDINGNESS	DEMINERALIZES	DEMOGRAPHICALLY	DEMONOMANIAS
DELOCALISATION	DEMANDINGNESSES	DEMINERALIZING	DEMOGRAPHICS	DEMONSTRABILITY
DELOCALISATIONS	DEMANNINGS	DEMIPIQUES	DEMOGRAPHIES	DEMONSTRABLE
DELOCALISE	DEMANTOIDS	DEMIRELIEF	DEMOGRAPHIST	DEMONSTRABLY
DELOCALISED	DEMARCATED	DEMIRELIEFS	DEMOGRAPHISTS	DEMONSTRATE
DELOCALISES	DEMARCATES	DEMIREPDOM	DEMOGRAPHY	DEMONSTRATED
DELOCALISING	DEMARCATING	DEMIREPDOMS	DEMOISELLE	DEMONSTRATES
DELOCALIZATION	DEMARCATION	DEMISEMIQUAVER	DEMOISELLES	DEMONSTRATING
DELOCALIZATIONS	DEMARCATIONS	DEMISEMIQUAVERS	DEMOLISHED	DEMONSTRATION
DELOCALIZE	DEMARCATOR	DEMISSIONS	DEMOLISHER	DEMONSTRATIONAL
DELOCALIZED	DEMARCATORS	DEMISTINGS	DEMOLISHERS	DEMONSTRATIONS
DELOCALIZES	DEMARKATION	DEMITASSES	DEMOLISHES	DEMONSTRATIVE
DELOCALIZING	DEMARKATIONS	DEMIURGEOUS	DEMOLISHING	DEMONSTRATIVELY
DELPHICALLY	DEMARKETED	DEMIURGICAL	DEMOLISHMENT	DEMONSTRATIVES
DELPHINIUM	DEMARKETING	DEMIURGICALLY	DEMOLISHMENTS	DEMONSTRATOR
DELPHINIUMS	DEMATERIALISE	DEMIURGUSES	DEMOLITION	DEMONSTRATORS
DELPHINOID	DEMATERIALISED	DEMIVEGGES	DEMOLITIONIST	DEMONSTRATORY
DELPHINOIDS	DEMATERIALISES	DEMIVIERGE	DEMOLITIONISTS	DEMORALISATION
DELTIOLOGIES	DEMATERIALISING	DEMIVIERGES	DEMOLITIONS	DEMORALISATIONS
DELTIOLOGIST	DEMATERIALIZE	DEMIVOLTES	DEMOLOGIES	DEMORALISE
DELTIOLOGISTS	DEMATERIALIZED	DEMIWORLDS	DEMONESSES	DEMORALISED
DELTIOLOGY	DEMATERIALIZES	DEMOBILISATION	DEMONETARISE	DEMORALISER
DELTOIDEUS	DEMATERIALIZING	DEMOBILISATIONS	DEMONETARISED	DEMORALISERS
DELUDINGLY	DEMEANOURS	DEMOBILISE	DEMONETARISES	DEMORALISES
DELUNDUNGS	DEMEASNURE	DEMOBILISED	DEMONETARISING	DEMORALISING
DELUSIONAL	DEMEASNURES	DEMOBILISES	DEMONETARIZE	DEMORALISINGLY
DELUSIONARY	DEMENTATED	DEMOBILISING	DEMONETARIZED	DEMORALIZATION
DELUSIONIST	DEMENTATES	DEMOBILIZATION	DEMONETARIZES	DEMORALIZATIONS
DELUSIONISTS	DEMENTATING	DEMOBILIZATIONS	DEMONETARIZING	DEMORALIZE
DELUSIVELY	DEMENTEDLY	DEMOBILIZE	DEMONETISATION	DEMORALIZED
DELUSIVENESS	DEMENTEDNESS	DEMOBILIZED	DEMONETISATIONS	DEMORALIZER
DELUSIVENESSES	DEMENTEDNESSES	DEMOBILIZES	DEMONETISE	DEMORALIZERS
DELUSTERED	DEMERGERED	DEMOBILIZING	DEMONETISED	DEMORALIZES

DEMORALIZING	DENATIONALIZED	DENIGRATING	DENSITOMETRY	DEODORIZERS
DEMORALIZINGLY	DENATIONALIZES	DENIGRATION	DENTALISED	DEODORIZES
DEMOSCENES	DENATIONALIZING	DENIGRATIONS	DENTALISES	DEODORIZING
DEMOTICIST	DENATURALISE	DENIGRATIVE	DENTALISING	DEONTOLOGICAL
DEMOTICISTS	DENATURALISED	DENIGRATOR	DENTALITIES	DEONTOLOGIES
DEMOTIVATE	DENATURALISES	DENIGRATORS	DENTALIUMS	DEONTOLOGIST
DEMOTIVATED	DENATURALISING	DENIGRATORY	DENTALIZED	DEONTOLOGISTS
DEMOTIVATES	DENATURALIZE	DENISATION	DENTALIZES	DEONTOLOGY
DEMOTIVATING	DENATURALIZED	DENISATIONS	DENTALIZING	DEOPPILATE
DEMOTIVATION	DENATURALIZES	DENITRATED	DENTATIONS	DEOPPILATED
DEMOTIVATIONS	DENATURALIZING	DENITRATES	DENTICARES	DEOPPILATES
DEMOUNTABLE	DENATURANT	DENITRATING	DENTICULATE	DEOPPILATING
DEMOUNTING	DENATURANTS	DENITRATION	DENTICULATED	DEOPPILATION
DEMULCENTS	DENATURATION	DENITRATIONS	DENTICULATELY	DEOPPILATIONS
DEMULSIFICATION	DENATURATIONS	DENITRIFICATION	DENTICULATION	DEOPPILATIVE
DEMULSIFIED	DENATURING	DENITRIFICATOR	DENTICULATIONS	DEOPPILATIVES
DEMULSIFIER	DENATURISE	DENITRIFICATORS	DENTIFRICE	DEORBITING
DEMULSIFIERS	DENATURISED	DENITRIFIED	DENTIFRICES	DEOXIDATED
DEMULSIFIES	DENATURISES	DENITRIFIER	DENTIGEROUS	DEOXIDATES
DEMULSIFYING	DENATURISING	DENITRIFIERS	DENTILABIAL	DEOXIDATING
DEMULTIPLEXER	DENATURIZE	DENITRIFIES	DENTILINGUAL	DEOXIDATION
DEMULTIPLEXERS	DENATURIZED	DENITRIFYING	DENTILINGUALS	DEOXIDATIONS
DEMURENESS	DENATURIZES	DENIZATION	DENTIROSTRAL	DEOXIDISATION
DEMURENESSES	DENATURIZING	DENIZATIONS	DENTISTRIES	DEOXIDISATIONS
DEMURRABLE	DENAZIFICATION	DENIZENING	DENTITIONS	DEOXIDISED
DEMURRAGES	DENAZIFICATIONS	DENIZENSHIP	DENTURISMS	DEOXIDISER
DEMUTUALISATION	DENAZIFIED	DENIZENSHIPS	DENTURISTS	DEOXIDISERS
DEMUTUALISE	DENAZIFIES	DENOMINABLE	DENUCLEARISE	DEOXIDISES
DEMUTUALISED	DENAZIFYING	DENOMINATE	DENUCLEARISED	DEOXIDISING
DEMUTUALISES	DENDRACHATE	DENOMINATED	DENUCLEARISES	DEOXIDIZATION
DEMUTUALISING	DENDRACHATES	DENOMINATES	DENUCLEARISING	DEOXIDIZATIONS
DEMUTUALIZATION	DENDRIFORM	DENOMINATING	DENUCLEARIZE	DEOXIDIZED
DEMUTUALIZE	DENDRIMERS	DENOMINATION	DENUCLEARIZED	DEOXIDIZER
DEMUTUALIZED	DENDRITICAL	DENOMINATIONAL	DENUCLEARIZES	DEOXIDIZERS
DEMUTUALIZES	DENDRITICALLY	DENOMINATIONS	DENUCLEARIZING	DEOXIDIZES
DEMUTUALIZING	DENDROBIUM	DENOMINATIVE	DENUDATING	DEOXIDIZING
DEMYELINATE	DENDROBIUMS	DENOMINATIVELY	DENUDATION	DEOXYCORTONE
DEMYELINATED	DENDROGLYPH	DENOMINATIVES	DENUDATIONS	DEOXYCORTONES
DEMYELINATES	DENDROGLYPHS	DENOMINATOR	DENUDEMENT	DEOXYGENATE
DEMYELINATING	DENDROGRAM	DENOMINATORS	DENUDEMENTS	DEOXYGENATED
DEMYELINATION	DENDROGRAMS	DENOTATING	DENUMERABILITY	DEOXYGENATES
DEMYELINATIONS	DENDROIDAL	DENOTATION	DENUMERABLE	DEOXYGENATING
DEMYSTIFICATION	DENDROLATRIES	DENOTATIONS	DENUMERABLY	DEOXYGENATION
DEMYSTIFIED	DENDROLATRY	DENOTATIVE	DENUNCIATE	DEOXYGENATIONS
DEMYSTIFIES	DENDROLOGIC	DENOTATIVELY	DENUNCIATED	DEOXYGENISE
DEMYSTIFYING	DENDROLOGICAL	DENOTEMENT	DENUNCIATES	DEOXYGENISED
DEMYTHIFICATION	DENDROLOGIES	DENOTEMENTS	DENUNCIATING	DEOXYGENISES
DEMYTHIFIED	DENDROLOGIST	DENOUEMENT	DENUNCIATION	DEOXYGENISING
DEMYTHIFIES	DENDROLOGISTS	DENOUEMENTS	DENUNCIATIONS	DEOXYGENIZE
DEMYTHIFYING	DENDROLOGOUS	DENOUNCEMENT	DENUNCIATIVE	DEOXYGENIZED
DEMYTHOLOGISE	DENDROLOGY	DENOUNCEMENTS	DENUNCIATOR	DEOXYGENIZES
DEMYTHOLOGISED	DENDROMETER	DENOUNCERS	DENUNCIATORS	DEOXYGENIZING
DEMYTHOLOGISER	DENDROMETERS	DENOUNCING	DENUNCIATORY	DEOXYRIBOSE
DEMYTHOLOGISERS	DENDROPHIS	DENSENESSES	DEOBSTRUENT	DEOXYRIBOSES
DEMYTHOLOGISES	DENDROPHISES	DENSIFICATION	DEOBSTRUENTS	DEPAINTING
DEMYTHOLOGISING	DENEGATION	DENSIFICATIONS	DEODORANTS	DEPANNEURS
DEMYTHOLOGIZE	DENEGATIONS	DENSIFIERS	DEODORISATION	DEPARTEMENT
DEMYTHOLOGIZED	DENERVATED	DENSIFYING	DEODORISATIONS	DEPARTEMENTS
DEMYTHOLOGIZER	DENERVATES	DENSIMETER	DEODORISED	DEPARTINGS
DEMYTHOLOGIZERS	DENERVATING	DENSIMETERS	DEODORISER	DEPARTMENT
DEMYTHOLOGIZES	DENERVATION	DENSIMETRIC	DEODORISERS	DEPARTMENTAL
DEMYTHOLOGIZING	DENERVATIONS	DENSIMETRIES	DEODORISES	DEPARTMENTALISE
DENATIONALISE	DENIABILITIES	DENSIMETRY	DEODORISING	DEPARTMENTALISM
DENATIONALISED	DENIABILITY	DENSITOMETER	DEODORIZATION	DEPARTMENTALIZE
DENATIONALISES	DENIALISTS	DENSITOMETERS	DEODORIZATIONS	DEPARTMENTALLY
DENATIONALISING	DENIGRATED	DENSITOMETRIC	DEODORIZED	DEPARTMENTS
DENATIONALIZE	DENIGRATES	DENSITOMETRIES	DEODORIZER	DEPARTURES

d

DEPASTURED	DEPILATORY	DEPOSITARIES	DEPRESSIVES	DERATIONING
DEPASTURES	DEPLENISHED	DEPOSITARY	DEPRESSOMOTOR	DEREALISATION
DEPASTURING	DEPLENISHES	DEPOSITATION	DEPRESSOMOTORS	DEREALISATIONS
DEPAUPERATE	DEPLENISHING	DEPOSITATIONS	DEPRESSORS	DEREALIZATION
DEPAUPERATED	DEPLETABLE	DEPOSITING	DEPRESSURISE	DEREALIZATIONS
DEPAUPERATES	DEPLETIONS	DEPOSITION	DEPRESSURISED	DERECOGNISE
DEPAUPERATING	DEPLORABILITIES	DEPOSITIONAL	DEPRESSURISES	DERECOGNISED
DEPAUPERISE	DEPLORABILITY	DEPOSITIONS	DEPRESSURISING	DERECOGNISES
DEPAUPERISED	DEPLORABLE	DEPOSITIVE	DEPRESSURIZE	DERECOGNISING
DEPAUPERISES	DEPLORABLENESS	DEPOSITORIES	DEPRESSURIZED	DERECOGNITION
DEPAUPERISING	DEPLORABLY	DEPOSITORS	DEPRESSURIZES	DERECOGNITIONS
DEPAUPERIZE	DEPLORATION	DEPOSITORY	DEPRESSURIZING	DERECOGNIZE
DEPAUPERIZED	DEPLORATIONS	DEPRAVATION	DEPRIVABLE	DERECOGNIZED
DEPAUPERIZES	DEPLORINGLY	DEPRAVATIONS	DEPRIVATION	DERECOGNIZES
DEPAUPERIZING	DEPLOYABLE	DEPRAVEDLY	DEPRIVATIONS	DERECOGNIZING
DEPEINCTED	DEPLOYMENT	DEPRAVEDNESS	DEPRIVATIVE	DEREGISTER
DEPEINCTING	DEPLOYMENTS	DEPRAVEDNESSES	DEPRIVEMENT	DEREGISTERED
DEPENDABILITIES	DEPLUMATION	DEPRAVEMENT	DEPRIVEMENTS	DEREGISTERING
DEPENDABILITY	DEPLUMATIONS	DEPRAVEMENTS	DEPROGRAMED	DEREGISTERS
DEPENDABLE	DEPOLARISATION	DEPRAVINGLY	DEPROGRAMING	DEREGISTRATION
DEPENDABLENESS	DEPOLARISATIONS	DEPRAVITIES	DEPROGRAMME	DEREGISTRATIONS
DEPENDABLY	DEPOLARISE	DEPRECABLE	DEPROGRAMMED	DEREGULATE
DEPENDANCE	DEPOLARISED	DEPRECATED	DEPROGRAMMER	DEREGULATED
DEPENDANCES	DEPOLARISER	DEPRECATES	DEPROGRAMMERS	DEREGULATES
DEPENDANCIES	DEPOLARISERS	DEPRECATING	DEPROGRAMMES	DEREGULATING
DEPENDANCY	DEPOLARISES	DEPRECATINGLY	DEPROGRAMMING	DEREGULATION
DEPENDANTS	DEPOLARISING	DEPRECATION	DEPROGRAMS	DEREGULATIONS
DEPENDENCE	DEPOLARIZATION	DEPRECATIONS	DEPURATING	DEREGULATOR
DEPENDENCES	DEPOLARIZATIONS	DEPRECATIVE	DEPURATION	DEREGULATORS
DEPENDENCIES	DEPOLARIZE	DEPRECATIVELY	DEPURATIONS	DEREGULATORY
DEPENDENCY	DEPOLARIZED	DEPRECATOR	DEPURATIVE	DERELICTION
DEPENDENTLY	DEPOLARIZER	DEPRECATORILY	DEPURATIVES	DERELICTIONS
DEPENDENTS	DEPOLARIZERS	DEPRECATORS	DEPURATORS	DERELIGIONISE
DEPENDINGLY	DEPOLARIZES	DEPRECATORY	DEPURATORY	DERELIGIONISED
DEPEOPLING	DEPOLARIZING	DEPRECIABLE	DEPUTATION	DERELIGIONISES
DEPERSONALISE	DEPOLISHED	DEPRECIATE	DEPUTATIONS	DERELIGIONISING
DEPERSONALISED	DEPOLISHES	DEPRECIATED	DEPUTISATION	DERELIGIONIZE
DEPERSONALISES	DEPOLISHING	DEPRECIATES	DEPUTISATIONS	DERELIGIONIZED
DEPERSONALISING	DEPOLITICISE	DEPRECIATING	DEPUTISING	DERELIGIONIZES
DEPERSONALIZE	DEPOLITICISED	DEPRECIATINGLY	DEPUTIZATION	DERELIGIONIZING
DEPERSONALIZED	DEPOLITICISES	DEPRECIATION	DEPUTIZATIONS	DEREPRESSED
DEPERSONALIZES	DEPOLITICISING	DEPRECIATIONS	DEPUTIZING	DEREPRESSES
DEPERSONALIZING	DEPOLITICIZE	DEPRECIATIVE	DEQUEUEING	DEREPRESSING
DEPHLEGMATE	DEPOLITICIZED	DEPRECIATOR	DERACIALISE	DEREPRESSION
DEPHLEGMATED	DEPOLITICIZES	DEPRECIATORS	DERACIALISED	DEREPRESSIONS
DEPHLEGMATES	DEPOLITICIZING	DEPRECIATORY	DERACIALISES	DEREQUISITION
DEPHLEGMATING	DEPOLYMERISE	DEPREDATED	DERACIALISING	DEREQUISITIONED
DEPHLEGMATION	DEPOLYMERISED	DEPREDATES	DERACIALIZE	DEREQUISITIONS
DEPHLEGMATIONS	DEPOLYMERISES	DEPREDATING	DERACIALIZED	DERESTRICT
DEPHLEGMATOR	DEPOLYMERISING	DEPREDATION	DERACIALIZES	DERESTRICTED
DEPHLEGMATORS	DEPOLYMERIZE	DEPREDATIONS	DERACIALIZING	DERESTRICTING
DEPHLOGISTICATE	DEPOLYMERIZED	DEPREDATOR	DERACINATE	DERESTRICTION
DEPHOSPHORYLATE	DEPOLYMERIZES	DEPREDATORS	DERACINATED	DERESTRICTIONS
DEPICTIONS	DEPOLYMERIZING	DEPREDATORY	DERACINATES	DERESTRICTS
DEPICTURED	DEPOPULATE	DEPREHENDED	DERACINATING	DERIDINGLY
DEPICTURES	DEPOPULATED	DEPREHENDING	DERACINATION	DERISIVELY
DEPICTURING	DEPOPULATES	DEPREHENDS	DERACINATIONS	DERISIVENESS
DEPIGMENTATION	DEPOPULATING	DEPRESSANT	DERAIGNING	DERISIVENESSES
DEPIGMENTATIONS	DEPOPULATION	DEPRESSANTS	DERAIGNMENT	DERIVATING
DEPIGMENTED	DEPOPULATIONS	DEPRESSIBLE	DERAIGNMENTS	DERIVATION
DEPIGMENTING	DEPOPULATOR	DEPRESSING	DERAILLEUR	DERIVATIONAL
DEPIGMENTS	DEPOPULATORS	DEPRESSINGLY	DERAILLEURS	DERIVATIONIST
DEPILATING	DEPORTABLE	DEPRESSION	DERAILMENT	DERIVATIONISTS
DEPILATION	DEPORTATION	DEPRESSIONS	DERAILMENTS	DERIVATIONS
DEPILATIONS	DEPORTATIONS	DEPRESSIVE	DERANGEMENT	DERIVATISATION
DEPILATORIES	DEPORTMENT	DEPRESSIVELY	DERANGEMENTS	DERIVATISATIONS
DEPILATORS	DEPORTMENTS	DEPRESSIVENESS	DERATIONED	DERIVATISE

DERIVATISED	DESACRALISED	DESCRIPTION	DESEXUALISING	DESIRABLENESSES
DERIVATISES	DESACRALISES	DESCRIPTIONS	DESEXUALIZATION	DESIRABLES
DERIVATISING	DESACRALISING	DESCRIPTIVE	DESEXUALIZE	DESIRELESS
DERIVATIVE	DESACRALIZATION	DESCRIPTIVELY	DESEXUALIZED	DESIROUSLY
DERIVATIVELY	DESACRALIZE	DESCRIPTIVENESS	DESEXUALIZES	DESIROUSNESS
DERIVATIVENESS	DESACRALIZED	DESCRIPTIVISM	DESEXUALIZING	DESIROUSNESSES
DERIVATIVES	DESACRALIZES	DESCRIPTIVISMS	DESHABILLE	DESISTANCE
DERIVATIZATION	DESACRALIZING	DESCRIPTIVIST	DESHABILLES	DESISTANCES
DERIVATIZATIONS	DESAGREMENT	DESCRIPTOR	DESICCANTS	DESISTENCE
DERIVATIZE	DESAGREMENTS	DESCRIPTORS	DESICCATED	DESISTENCES
DERIVATIZED	DESALINATE	DESCRIVING	DESICCATES	DESKILLING
DERIVATIZES	DESALINATED	DESECRATED	DESICCATING	DESKILLINGS
DERIVATIZING	DESALINATES	DESECRATER	DESICCATION	DESMODIUMS
DERMABRASION	DESALINATING	DESECRATERS	DESICCATIONS	DESMODROMIC
DERMABRASIONS	DESALINATION	DESECRATES	DESICCATIVE	DESMOSOMAL
DERMAPLANING	DESALINATIONS	DESECRATING	DESICCATIVES	DESMOSOMES
DERMAPLANINGS	DESALINATOR	DESECRATION	DESICCATOR	DESNOODING
DERMAPTERAN	DESALINATORS	DESECRATIONS	DESICCATORS	DESOBLIGEANTE
DERMAPTERANS	DESALINISATION	DESECRATOR	DESIDERATA	DESOBLIGEANTES
DERMATITIDES	DESALINISATIONS	DESECRATORS	DESIDERATE	DESOLATELY
DERMATITIS	DESALINISE	DESEGREGATE	DESIDERATED	DESOLATENESS
DERMATITISES	DESALINISED	DESEGREGATED	DESIDERATES	DESOLATENESSES
DERMATOGEN	DESALINISES	DESEGREGATES	DESIDERATING	DESOLATERS
DERMATOGENS	DESALINISING	DESEGREGATING	DESIDERATION	DESOLATING
DERMATOGLYPHIC	DESALINIZATION	DESEGREGATION	DESIDERATIONS	DESOLATINGLY
DERMATOGLYPHICS	DESALINIZATIONS	DESEGREGATIONS	DESIDERATIVE	DESOLATION
DERMATOGRAPHIA	DESALINIZE	DESELECTED	DESIDERATIVES	DESOLATIONS
DERMATOGRAPHIAS	DESALINIZED	DESELECTING	DESIDERATUM	DESOLATORS
DERMATOGRAPHIC	DESALINIZES	DESELECTION	DESIDERIUM	DESOLATORY
DERMATOGRAPHIES	DESALINIZING	DESELECTIONS	DESIDERIUMS	DESORIENTE
DERMATOGRAPHY	DESALTINGS	DESENSITISATION	DESIGNABLE	DESORPTION
DERMATOLOGIC	DESATURATE	DESENSITISE	DESIGNATED	DESORPTIONS
DERMATOLOGICAL	DESATURATED	DESENSITISED	DESIGNATES	DESOXYRIBOSE
DERMATOLOGIES	DESATURATES	DESENSITISER	DESIGNATING	DESOXYRIBOSES
DERMATOLOGIST	DESATURATING	DESENSITISERS	DESIGNATION	DESPAIRERS
DERMATOLOGISTS	DESATURATION	DESENSITISES	DESIGNATIONS	DESPAIRFUL
DERMATOLOGY	DESATURATIONS	DESENSITISING	DESIGNATIVE	DESPAIRING
DERMATOMAL	DESCANTERS	DESENSITIZATION	DESIGNATOR	DESPAIRINGLY
DERMATOMES	DESCANTING	DESENSITIZE	DESIGNATORS	DESPATCHED
DERMATOMIC	DESCENDABLE	DESENSITIZED	DESIGNATORY	DESPATCHER
DERMATOMYOSITIS	DESCENDANT	DESENSITIZER	DESIGNEDLY	DESPATCHERS
DERMATOPHYTE	DESCENDANTS	DESENSITIZERS	DESIGNINGLY	DESPATCHES
DERMATOPHYTES	DESCENDENT	DESENSITIZES	DESIGNINGS	DESPATCHING
DERMATOPHYTIC	DESCENDENTS	DESENSITIZING	DESIGNLESS	DESPERADOES
DERMATOPHYTOSES	DESCENDERS	DESERPIDINE	DESIGNMENT	DESPERADOS
DERMATOPHYTOSIS	DESCENDEUR	DESERPIDINES	DESIGNMENTS	DESPERATELY
DERMATOPLASTIC	DESCENDEURS	DESERTIFICATION	DESILVERED	DESPERATENESS
DERMATOPLASTIES	DESCENDIBLE	DESERTIFIED	DESILVERING	DESPERATENESSES
DERMATOPLASTY	DESCENDING	DESERTIFIES	DESILVERISATION	DESPERATION
DERMATOSES	DESCENDINGS	DESERTIFYING	DESILVERISE	DESPERATIONS
DERMATOSIS	DESCENSION	DESERTIONS	DESILVERISED	DESPICABILITIES
DERMESTIDS	DESCENSIONAL	DESERTISATION	DESILVERISES	DESPICABILITY
DERMOGRAPHIES	DESCENSIONS	DESERTISATIONS	DESILVERISING	DESPICABLE
DERMOGRAPHY	DESCHOOLED	DESERTIZATION	DESILVERIZATION	DESPICABLENESS
DEROGATELY	DESCHOOLER	DESERTIZATIONS	DESILVERIZE	DESPICABLY
DEROGATING	DESCHOOLERS	DESERTLESS	DESILVERIZED	DESPIRITUALISE
DEROGATION	DESCHOOLING	DESERVEDLY	DESILVERIZES	DESPIRITUALISED
DEROGATIONS	DESCHOOLINGS	DESERVEDNESS	DESILVERIZING	DESPIRITUALISES
DEROGATIVE	DESCRAMBLE	DESERVEDNESSES	DESINENCES	DESPIRITUALIZE
DEROGATIVELY	DESCRAMBLED	DESERVINGLY	DESINENTIAL	DESPIRITUALIZED
DEROGATORILY	DESCRAMBLER	DESERVINGNESS	DESIPIENCE	DESPIRITUALIZES
DEROGATORINESS	DESCRAMBLERS	DESERVINGNESSES	DESIPIENCES	DESPISABLE
DEROGATORY	DESCRAMBLES	DESERVINGS	DESIPRAMINE	DESPISEDNESS
DERRICKING	DESCRAMBLING	DESEXUALISATION	DESIPRAMINES	DESPISEDNESSES
DERRINGERS	DESCRIBABLE	DESEXUALISE	DESIRABILITIES	DESPISEMENT
DESACRALISATION	DESCRIBERS	DESEXUALISED	DESIRABILITY	DESPISEMENTS
DESACRALISE	DESCRIBING	DESEXUALISES	DESIRABLENESS	DESPISINGLY

DESPITEFUL	DESTAINING	DESULFURIZER	DETERGENCIES	DETHRONEMENT
DESPITEFULLY	DESTEMPERED	DESULFURIZERS	DETERGENCY	DETHRONEMENTS
DESPITEFULNESS	DESTEMPERING	DESULFURIZES	DETERGENTS	DETHRONERS
DESPITEOUS	DESTEMPERS	DESULFURIZING	DETERIORATE	DETHRONING
DESPITEOUSLY	DESTINATED	DESULPHURATE	DETERIORATED	DETHRONINGS
DESPITEOUSNESS	DESTINATES	DESULPHURATED	DETERIORATES	DETHRONISE
DESPOILERS	DESTINATING	DESULPHURATES	DETERIORATING	DETHRONISED
DESPOILING	DESTINATION	DESULPHURATING	DETERIORATION	DETHRONISES
DESPOILINGS	DESTINATIONS	DESULPHURATION	DETERIORATIONS	DETHRONISING
DESPOILMENT	DESTITUTED	DESULPHURATIONS	DETERIORATIVE	DETHRONIZE
DESPOILMENTS	DESTITUTENESS	DESULPHURED	DETERIORISM	DETHRONIZED
DESPOLIATION	DESTITUTENESSES	DESULPHURING	DETERIORISMS	DETHRONIZES
DESPOLIATIONS	DESTITUTES	DESULPHURISE	DETERIORITIES	DETHRONIZING
DESPONDENCE	DESTITUTING	DESULPHURISED	DETERIORITY	DETONABILITIES
DESPONDENCES	DESTITUTION	DESULPHURISER	DETERMENTS	DETONABILITY
DESPONDENCIES	DESTITUTIONS	DESULPHURISERS	DETERMINABILITY	DETONATABLE
DESPONDENCY	DESTOCKING	DESULPHURISES	DETERMINABLE	DETONATING
DESPONDENT	DESTREAMED	DESULPHURISING	DETERMINABLY	DETONATION
DESPONDENTLY	DESTREAMING	DESULPHURIZE	DETERMINACIES	DETONATIONS
DESPONDING	DESTRESSED	DESULPHURIZED	DETERMINACY	DETONATIVE
DESPONDINGLY	DESTRESSES	DESULPHURIZER	DETERMINANT	DETONATORS
DESPONDINGS	DESTRESSING	DESULPHURIZERS	DETERMINANTAL	DETORSIONS
DESPOTATES	DESTROYABLE	DESULPHURIZES	DETERMINANTS	DETORTIONS
DESPOTICAL	DESTROYERS	DESULPHURIZING	DETERMINATE	DETOXICANT
DESPOTICALLY	DESTROYING	DESULPHURS	DETERMINATED	DETOXICANTS
DESPOTICALNESS	DESTRUCTED	DESULTORILY	DETERMINATELY	DETOXICATE
DESPOTISMS	DESTRUCTIBILITY	DESULTORINESS	DETERMINATENESS	DETOXICATED
DESPOTOCRACIES	DESTRUCTIBLE	DESULTORINESSES	DETERMINATES	DETOXICATES
DESPOTOCRACY	DESTRUCTING	DETACHABILITIES	DETERMINATING	DETOXICATING
DESPUMATED	DESTRUCTION	DETACHABILITY	DETERMINATION	DETOXICATION
DESPUMATES	DESTRUCTIONAL	DETACHABLE	DETERMINATIONS	DETOXICATIONS
DESPUMATING	DESTRUCTIONIST	DETACHABLY	DETERMINATIVE	DETOXIFICATION
DESPUMATION	DESTRUCTIONISTS	DETACHEDLY	DETERMINATIVELY	DETOXIFICATIONS
DESPUMATIONS	DESTRUCTIONS	DETACHEDNESS	DETERMINATIVES	DETOXIFIED
DESQUAMATE	DESTRUCTIVE	DETACHEDNESSES	DETERMINATOR	DETOXIFIES
DESQUAMATED	DESTRUCTIVELY	DETACHMENT	DETERMINATORS	DETOXIFYING
DESQUAMATES	DESTRUCTIVENESS	DETACHMENTS	DETERMINED	DETRACTING
DESQUAMATING	DESTRUCTIVES	DETAILEDLY	DETERMINEDLY	DETRACTINGLY
DESQUAMATION	DESTRUCTIVISM	DETAILEDNESS	DETERMINEDNESS	DETRACTINGS
DESQUAMATIONS	DESTRUCTIVISMS	DETAILEDNESSES	DETERMINER	DETRACTION
DESQUAMATIVE	DESTRUCTIVIST	DETAILINGS	DETERMINERS	DETRACTIONS
DESQUAMATORIES	DESTRUCTIVISTS	DETAINABLE	DETERMINES	DETRACTIVE
DESQUAMATORY	DESTRUCTIVITIES	DETAINMENT	DETERMINING	DETRACTIVELY
DESSERTSPOON	DESTRUCTIVITY	DETAINMENTS	DETERMINISM	DETRACTORS
DESSERTSPOONFUL	DESTRUCTOR	DETANGLERS	DETERMINISMS	DETRACTORY
DESSERTSPOONS	DESTRUCTORS	DETANGLING	DETERMINIST	DETRACTRESS
DESSIATINE	DESTRUCTOS	DETASSELED	DETERMINISTIC	DETRACTRESSES
DESSIATINES	DESUETUDES	DETASSELING	DETERMINISTS	DETRAINING
DESSIGNMENT	DESUGARING	DETASSELLED	DETERRABILITIES	DETRAINMENT
DESSIGNMENTS	DESULFURATE	DETASSELLING	DETERRABILITY	DETRAINMENTS
DESSYATINE	DESULFURATED	DETECTABILITIES	DETERRABLE	DETRAQUEES
DESSYATINES	DESULFURATES	DETECTABILITY	DETERRENCE	DETRIBALISATION
DESSYATINS	DESULFURATING	DETECTABLE	DETERRENCES	DETRIBALISE
DESTABILISATION	DESULFURATION	DETECTIBLE	DETERRENTLY	DETRIBALISED
DESTABILISE	DESULFURATIONS	DETECTIONS	DETERRENTS	DETRIBALISES
DESTABILISED	DESULFURED	DETECTIVELIKE	DETERSIONS	DETRIBALISING
DESTABILISER	DESULFURING	DETECTIVES	DETERSIVES	DETRIBALIZATION
DESTABILISERS	DESULFURISATION	DETECTIVIST	DETESTABILITIES	DETRIBALIZE
DESTABILISES	DESULFURISE	DETECTIVISTS	DETESTABILITY	DETRIBALIZED
DESTABILISING	DESULFURISED	DETECTOPHONE	DETESTABLE	DETRIBALIZES
DESTABILIZATION	DESULFURISER	DETECTOPHONES	DETESTABLENESS	DETRIBALIZING
DESTABILIZE	DESULFURISERS	DETECTORIST	DETESTABLY	DETRIMENTAL
DESTABILIZED	DESULFURISES	DETECTORISTS	DETESTATION	DETRIMENTALLY
DESTABILIZER	DESULFURISING	DETENTIONS	DETESTATIONS	DETRIMENTALS
DESTABILIZERS	DESULFURIZATION	DETENTISTS	DETHATCHED	DETRIMENTS
DESTABILIZES	DESULFURIZE	DETERGENCE	DETHATCHES	DETRITIONS
DESTABILIZING	DESULFURIZED	DETERGENCES	DETHATCHING	DETRITOVORE

d

DETRITOVORES	DEVASTATINGLY	DEVONPORTS	DIABOLICALLY	DIAGONALIZATION
DETRUNCATE	DEVASTATION	DEVOTEDNESS	DIABOLICALNESS	DIAGONALIZE
DETRUNCATED	DEVASTATIONS	DEVOTEDNESSES	DIABOLISED	DIAGONALIZED
DETRUNCATES	DEVASTATIVE	DEVOTEMENT	DIABOLISES	DIAGONALIZES
DETRUNCATING	DEVASTATOR	DEVOTEMENTS	DIABOLISING	DIAGONALIZING
DETRUNCATION	DEVASTATORS	DEVOTIONAL	DIABOLISMS	DIAGONALLY
DETRUNCATIONS	DEVASTAVIT	DEVOTIONALIST	DIABOLISTS	DIAGRAMING
DETRUSIONS	DEVASTAVITS	DEVOTIONALISTS	DIABOLIZED	DIAGRAMMABLE
DETUMESCENCE	DEVELOPABLE	DEVOTIONALITIES	DIABOLIZES	DIAGRAMMATIC
DETUMESCENCES	DEVELOPERS	DEVOTIONALITY	DIABOLIZING	DIAGRAMMATICAL
DETUMESCENT	DEVELOPING	DEVOTIONALLY	DIABOLOGIES	DIAGRAMMED
DEUTERAGONIST	DEVELOPMENT	DEVOTIONALNESS	DIABOLOLOGIES	DIAGRAMMING
DEUTERAGONISTS	DEVELOPMENTAL	DEVOTIONALS	DIABOLOLOGY	DIAGRAPHIC
DEUTERANOMALIES	DEVELOPMENTALLY	DEVOTIONIST	DIACATHOLICON	DIAHELIOTROPIC
DEUTERANOMALOUS	DEVELOPMENTS	DEVOTIONISTS	DIACATHOLICONS	DIAHELIOTROPISM
DEUTERANOMALY	DEVELOPPES	DEVOURINGLY	DIACAUSTIC	DIAKINESES
DEUTERANOPE	DEVERBATIVE	DEVOURMENT	DIACAUSTICS	DIAKINESIS
DEUTERANOPES	DEVERBATIVES	DEVOURMENTS	DIACHRONIC	DIALECTALLY
DEUTERANOPIA	DEVIANCIES	DEVOUTNESS	DIACHRONICALLY	DIALECTICAL
DEUTERANOPIAS	DEVIATIONISM	DEVOUTNESSES	DIACHRONIES	DIALECTICALLY
DEUTERANOPIC	DEVIATIONISMS	DEVVELLING	DIACHRONISM	DIALECTICIAN
DEUTERATED	DEVIATIONIST	DEWATERERS	DIACHRONISMS	DIALECTICIANS
DEUTERATES	DEVIATIONISTS	DEWATERING	DIACHRONISTIC	DIALECTICISM
DEUTERATING	DEVIATIONS	DEWATERINGS	DIACHRONOUS	DIALECTICISMS
DEUTERATION	DEVILESSES	DEWBERRIES	DIACHYLONS	DIALECTICS
DEUTERATIONS	DEVILFISHES	DEWINESSES	DIACHYLUMS	DIALECTOLOGICAL
DEUTERIDES	DEVILISHLY	DEXAMETHASONE	DIACODIONS	DIALECTOLOGIES
DEUTERIUMS	DEVILISHNESS	DEXAMETHASONES	DIACODIUMS	DIALECTOLOGIST
DEUTEROGAMIES	DEVILISHNESSES	DEXAMPHETAMINE	DIACONATES	DIALECTOLOGISTS
DEUTEROGAMIST	DEVILMENTS	DEXAMPHETAMINES	DIACONICON	DIALECTOLOGY
DEUTEROGAMISTS	DEVILSHIPS	DEXIOTROPIC	DIACONICONS	DIALLAGOID
DEUTEROGAMY	DEVILTRIES	DEXTERITIES	DIACOUSTIC	DIALOGICAL
DEUTEROPLASM	DEVILWOODS	DEXTEROUSLY	DIACOUSTICS	DIALOGICALLY
DEUTEROPLASMS	DEVIOUSNESS	DEXTEROUSNESS	DIACRITICAL	DIALOGISED
DEUTEROSCOPIC	DEVIOUSNESSES	DEXTEROUSNESSES	DIACRITICALLY	DIALOGISES
DEUTEROSCOPIES	DEVITALISATION	DEXTERWISE	DIACRITICS	DIALOGISING
DEUTEROSCOPY	DEVITALISATIONS	DEXTRALITIES	DIACTINISM	DIALOGISMS
DEUTEROSTOME	DEVITALISE	DEXTRALITY	DIACTINISMS	DIALOGISTIC
DEUTEROSTOMES	DEVITALISED	DEXTRANASE	DIADELPHOUS	DIALOGISTICAL
DEUTEROTOKIES	DEVITALISES	DEXTRANASES	DIADOCHIES	DIALOGISTS
DEUTEROTOKY	DEVITALISING	DEXTROCARDIA	DIADROMOUS	DIALOGITES
DEUTOPLASM	DEVITALIZATION	DEXTROCARDIAC	DIAGENESES	DIALOGIZED
DEUTOPLASMIC	DEVITALIZATIONS	DEXTROCARDIACS	DIAGENESIS	DIALOGIZES
DEUTOPLASMS	DEVITALIZE	DEXTROCARDIAS	DIAGENETIC	DIALOGIZING
DEUTOPLASTIC	DEVITALIZED	DEXTROGLUCOSE	DIAGENETICALLY	DIALOGUERS
DEVALORISATION	DEVITALIZES	DEXTROGLUCOSES	DIAGEOTROPIC	DIALOGUING
DEVALORISATIONS	DEVITALIZING	DEXTROGYRATE	DIAGEOTROPISM	DIALYPETALOUS
DEVALORISE	DEVITRIFICATION	DEXTROGYRE	DIAGEOTROPISMS	DIALYSABILITIES
DEVALORISED	DEVITRIFIED	DEXTROROTARY	DIAGNOSABILITY	DIALYSABILITY
DEVALORISES	DEVITRIFIES	DEXTROROTATION	DIAGNOSABLE	DIALYSABLE
DEVALORISING	DEVITRIFYING	DEXTROROTATIONS	DIAGNOSEABLE	DIALYSATES
DEVALORIZATION	DEVOCALISE	DEXTROROTATORY	DIAGNOSING	DIALYSATION
DEVALORIZATIONS	DEVOCALISED	DEXTRORSAL	DIAGNOSTIC	DIALYSATIONS
DEVALORIZE	DEVOCALISES	DEXTRORSELY	DIAGNOSTICAL	DIALYTICALLY
DEVALORIZED	DEVOCALISING	DEXTROUSLY	DIAGNOSTICALLY	DIALYZABILITIES
DEVALORIZES	DEVOCALIZE	DEXTROUSNESS	DIAGNOSTICIAN	DIALYZABILITY
DEVALORIZING	DEVOCALIZED	DEXTROUSNESSES	DIAGNOSTICIANS	DIALYZABLE
DEVALUATED	DEVOCALIZES	DEZINCKING	DIAGNOSTICS	DIALYZATES
DEVALUATES	DEVOCALIZING	DHARMSALAS	DIAGOMETER	DIALYZATION
DEVALUATING	DEVOICINGS	DHARMSHALA	DIAGOMETERS	DIALYZATIONS
DEVALUATION	DEVOLUTION	DHARMSHALAS	DIAGONALISABLE	DIAMAGNETIC
DEVALUATIONS	DEVOLUTIONARY	DIABETICAL	DIAGONALISATION	DIAMAGNETICALLY
DEVANAGARI	DEVOLUTIONIST	DIABETOGENIC	DIAGONALISE	DIAMAGNETISM
DEVANAGARIS	DEVOLUTIONISTS	DIABETOLOGIST	DIAGONALISED	DIAMAGNETISMS
DEVASTATED	DEVOLUTIONS	DIABETOLOGISTS	DIAGONALISES	DIAMAGNETS
DEVASTATES	DEVOLVEMENT	DIABLERIES	DIAGONALISING	DIAMANTIFEROUS
DEVASTATING	DEVOLVEMENTS	DIABOLICAL	DIAGONALIZABLE	DIAMANTINE

DIAMETRALLY	DIASTEMATA	DICHASIALLY	DICOUMAROL	DIESELIZATION
DIAMETRICAL	DIASTEMATIC	DICHLAMYDEOUS	DICOUMAROLS	DIESELIZATIONS
DIAMETRICALLY	DIASTEREOISOMER	DICHLORACETIC	DICROTISMS	DIESELIZED
DIAMONDBACK	DIASTEREOMER	DICHLORIDE	DICTATIONAL	DIESELIZES
DIAMONDBACKS	DIASTEREOMERIC	DICHLORIDES	DICTATIONS	DIESELIZING
DIAMONDIFEROUS	DIASTEREOMERS	DICHLOROBENZENE	DICTATORIAL	DIESELLING
DIAMONDING	DIASTROPHIC	DICHLOROETHANE	DICTATORIALLY	DIESELLINGS
DIAMORPHINE	DIASTROPHICALLY	DICHLOROETHANES	DICTATORIALNESS	DIESINKERS
DIAMORPHINES	DIASTROPHISM	DICHLOROMETHANE	DICTATORSHIP	DIESTRUSES
DIANTHUSES	DIASTROPHISMS	DICHLORVOS	DICTATORSHIPS	DIETARIANS
DIAPASONAL	DIATESSARON	DICHLORVOSES	DICTATRESS	DIETETICAL
DIAPASONIC	DIATESSARONS	DICHOGAMIC	DICTATRESSES	DIETETICALLY
DIAPAUSING	DIATHERMACIES	DICHOGAMIES	DICTATRICES	DIETHYLAMIDE
DIAPEDESES	DIATHERMACY	DICHOGAMOUS	DICTATRIXES	DIETHYLAMIDES
DIAPEDESIS	DIATHERMAL	DICHONDRAS	DICTATURES	DIETHYLAMINE
DIAPEDETIC	DIATHERMANCIES	DICHOTICALLY	DICTIONALLY	DIETHYLAMINES
DIAPERINGS	DIATHERMANCY	DICHOTOMIC	DICTIONARIES	DIETHYLENE
DIAPHANEITIES	DIATHERMANEITY	DICHOTOMIES	DICTIONARY	DIETHYLENES
DIAPHANEITY	DIATHERMANOUS	DICHOTOMISATION	DICTYOGENS	DIETICIANS
DIAPHANOMETER	DIATHERMIA	DICHOTOMISE	DICTYOPTERAN	DIETITIANS
DIAPHANOMETERS	DIATHERMIAS	DICHOTOMISED	DICTYOPTERANS	DIEZEUGMENON
DIAPHANOUS	DIATHERMIC	DICHOTOMISES	DICTYOSOME	DIEZEUGMENONS
DIAPHANOUSLY	DIATHERMIES	DICHOTOMISING	DICTYOSOMES	DIFFARREATION
DIAPHANOUSNESS	DIATHERMOUS	DICHOTOMIST	DICTYOSTELE	DIFFARREATIONS
DIAPHONIES	DIATOMACEOUS	DICHOTOMISTS	DICTYOSTELES	DIFFERENCE
DIAPHORASE	DIATOMICITIES	DICHOTOMIZATION	DICUMAROLS	DIFFERENCED
DIAPHORASES	DIATOMICITY	DICHOTOMIZE	DICYNODONT	DIFFERENCES
DIAPHORESES	DIATOMISTS	DICHOTOMIZED	DICYNODONTS	DIFFERENCIED
DIAPHORESIS	DIATOMITES	DICHOTOMIZES	DIDACTICAL	DIFFERENCIES
DIAPHORETIC	DIATONICALLY	DICHOTOMIZING	DIDACTICALLY	DIFFERENCING
DIAPHORETICS	DIATONICISM	DICHOTOMOUS	DIDACTICISM	DIFFERENCY
DIAPHOTOTROPIC	DIATONICISMS	DICHOTOMOUSLY	DIDACTICISMS	DIFFERENCYING
DIAPHOTOTROPIES	DIATRETUMS	DICHOTOMOUSNESS	DIDACTYLISM	DIFFERENTIA
DIAPHOTOTROPISM	DIATRIBIST	DICHROISCOPE	DIDACTYLISMS	DIFFERENTIABLE
DIAPHOTOTROPY	DIATRIBISTS	DICHROISCOPES	DIDACTYLOUS	DIFFERENTIAE
DIAPHRAGMAL	DIATROPISM	DICHROISCOPIC	DIDASCALIC	DIFFERENTIAL
DIAPHRAGMATIC	DIATROPISMS	DICHROISMS	DIDELPHIAN	DIFFERENTIALLY
DIAPHRAGMATITIS	DIAZEUCTIC	DICHROITES	DIDELPHIDS	DIFFERENTIALS
DIAPHRAGMED	DIAZOMETHANE	DICHROITIC	DIDELPHINE	DIFFERENTIATE
DIAPHRAGMING	DIAZOMETHANES	DICHROMATE	DIDELPHOUS	DIFFERENTIATED
DIAPHRAGMITIS	DIAZONIUMS	DICHROMATES	DIDGERIDOO	DIFFERENTIATES
DIAPHRAGMITISES	DIAZOTISATION	DICHROMATIC	DIDGERIDOOS	DIFFERENTIATING
DIAPHRAGMS	DIAZOTISATIONS	DICHROMATICISM	DIDJERIDOO	DIFFERENTIATION
DIAPHYSEAL	DIAZOTISED	DICHROMATICISMS	DIDJERIDOOS	DIFFERENTIATOR
DIAPHYSIAL	DIAZOTISES	DICHROMATICS	DIDJERIDUS	DIFFERENTIATORS
DIAPIRISMS	DIAZOTISING	DICHROMATISM	DIDRACHMAS	DIFFERENTLY
DIAPOPHYSES	DIAZOTIZATION	DICHROMATISMS	DIDYNAMIAN	DIFFERENTNESS
DIAPOPHYSIAL	DIAZOTIZATIONS	DICHROMATS	DIDYNAMIES	DIFFERENTNESSES
DIAPOPHYSIS	DIAZOTIZED	DICHROMISM	DIDYNAMOUS	DIFFICULTIES
DIAPOSITIVE	DIAZOTIZES	DICHROMISMS	DIECIOUSLY	DIFFICULTLY
DIAPOSITIVES	DIAZOTIZING	DICHROOSCOPE	DIECIOUSNESS	DIFFICULTY
DIAPYETICS	DIBASICITIES	DICHROOSCOPES	DIECIOUSNESSES	DIFFIDENCE
DIARCHICAL	DIBASICITY	DICHROOSCOPIC	DIEFFENBACHIA	DIFFIDENCES
DIARRHETIC	DIBENZOFURAN	DICHROSCOPE	DIEFFENBACHIAS	DIFFIDENTLY
DIARRHOEAL	DIBENZOFURANS	DICHROSCOPES	DIELECTRIC	DIFFORMITIES
DIARRHOEAS	DIBRANCHIATE	DICHROSCOPIC	DIELECTRICALLY	DIFFORMITY
DIARRHOEIC	DIBRANCHIATES	DICKCISSEL	DIELECTRICS	DIFFRACTED
DIARTHRODIAL	DIBROMIDES	DICKCISSELS	DIENCEPHALA	DIFFRACTING
DIARTHROSES	DICACITIES	DICKEYBIRD	DIENCEPHALIC	DIFFRACTION
DIARTHROSIS	DICACODYLS	DICKEYBIRDS	DIENCEPHALON	DIFFRACTIONS
DIASCORDIUM	DICARBOXYLIC	DICKYBIRDS	DIENCEPHALONS	DIFFRACTIVE
DIASCORDIUMS	DICARPELLARY	DICLINISMS	DIESELINGS	DIFFRACTIVELY
DIASKEUAST	DICASTERIES	DICOTYLEDON	DIESELISATION	DIFFRACTIVENESS
DIASKEUASTS	DICENTRICS	DICOTYLEDONOUS	DIESELISATIONS	DIFFRACTOMETER
DIASTALSES	DICEPHALISM	DICOTYLEDONS	DIESELISED	DIFFRACTOMETERS
DIASTALSIS	DICEPHALISMS	DICOUMARIN	DIESELISES	DIFFRACTOMETRIC
DIASTALTIC	DICEPHALOUS	DICOUMARINS	DIESELISING	DIFFRACTOMETRY

DIFFRANGIBILITY	DIGITORIUMS	DILATATIONS	DIMIDIATIONS	DIOPTOMETRIES
DIFFRANGIBLE	DIGITOXIGENIN	DILATATORS	DIMINISHABLE	DIOPTOMETRY
DIFFUSEDLY	DIGITOXIGENINS	DILATOMETER	DIMINISHED	DIOPTRICAL
DIFFUSEDNESS	DIGITOXINS	DILATOMETERS	DIMINISHES	DIOPTRICALLY
DIFFUSEDNESSES	DIGLADIATE	DILATOMETRIC	DIMINISHING	DIORISTICAL
DIFFUSENESS	DIGLADIATED	DILATOMETRIES	DIMINISHINGLY	DIORISTICALLY
DIFFUSENESSES	DIGLADIATES	DILATOMETRY	DIMINISHINGS	DIORTHOSES
DIFFUSIBILITIES	DIGLADIATING	DILATORILY	DIMINISHMENT	DIORTHOSIS
DIFFUSIBILITY	DIGLADIATION	DILATORINESS	DIMINISHMENTS	DIORTHOTIC
DIFFUSIBLE	DIGLADIATIONS	DILATORINESSES	DIMINUENDO	DIOSCOREACEOUS
DIFFUSIBLENESS	DIGLADIATOR	DILEMMATIC	DIMINUENDOES	DIOSGENINS
DIFFUSIONAL	DIGLADIATORS	DILETTANTE	DIMINUENDOS	DIOTHELETE
DIFFUSIONISM	DIGLOSSIAS	DILETTANTEISH	DIMINUTION	DIOTHELETES
DIFFUSIONISMS	DIGLYCERIDE	DILETTANTEISM	DIMINUTIONS	DIOTHELETIC
DIFFUSIONIST	DIGLYCERIDES	DILETTANTEISMS	DIMINUTIVAL	DIOTHELETICAL
DIFFUSIONISTS	DIGNIFICATION	DILETTANTES	DIMINUTIVE	DIOTHELISM
DIFFUSIONS	DIGNIFICATIONS	DILETTANTI	DIMINUTIVELY	DIOTHELISMS
DIFFUSIVELY	DIGNIFIEDLY	DILETTANTISH	DIMINUTIVENESS	DIOTHELITE
DIFFUSIVENESS	DIGNIFIEDNESS	DILETTANTISM	DIMINUTIVES	DIOTHELITES
DIFFUSIVENESSES	DIGNIFIEDNESSES	DILETTANTISMS	DIMORPHISM	DIOXONITRIC
DIFFUSIVITIES	DIGNIFYING	DILIGENCES	DIMORPHISMS	DIPEPTIDASE
DIFFUSIVITY	DIGNITARIES	DILIGENTLY	DIMORPHOUS	DIPEPTIDASES
DIFUNCTIONAL	DIGONEUTIC	DILLYDALLIED	DIMPLEMENT	DIPEPTIDES
DIFUNCTIONALS	DIGONEUTISM	DILLYDALLIES	DIMPLEMENTS	DIPETALOUS
DIGASTRICS	DIGONEUTISMS	DILLYDALLY	DINANDERIE	DIPHENHYDRAMINE
DIGESTANTS	DIGRAPHICALLY	DILLYDALLYING	DINANDERIES	DIPHENYLAMINE
DIGESTEDLY	DIGRESSERS	DILTIAZEMS	DINARCHIES	DIPHENYLAMINES
DIGESTIBILITIES	DIGRESSING	DILUCIDATE	DINGDONGED	DIPHENYLENE
DIGESTIBILITY	DIGRESSION	DILUCIDATED	DINGDONGING	DIPHENYLENIMINE
DIGESTIBLE	DIGRESSIONAL	DILUCIDATES	DINGINESSES	DIPHENYLKETONE
DIGESTIBLENESS	DIGRESSIONARY	DILUCIDATING	DINGLEBERRIES	DIPHENYLKETONES
DIGESTIBLY	DIGRESSIONS	DILUCIDATION	DINGLEBERRY	DIPHOSGENE
DIGESTIONAL	DIGRESSIVE	DILUCIDATIONS	DINITROBENZENE	DIPHOSGENES
DIGESTIONS	DIGRESSIVELY	DILUTABLES	DINITROBENZENES	DIPHOSPHATE
DIGESTIVELY	DIGRESSIVENESS	DILUTENESS	DINITROGEN	DIPHOSPHATES
DIGESTIVES	DIHYBRIDISM	DILUTENESSES	DINITROPHENOL	DIPHTHERIA
DIGITALINS	DIHYBRIDISMS	DILUTIONARY	DINITROPHENOLS	DIPHTHERIAL
DIGITALISATION	DIHYDROCODEINE	DILUVIALISM	DINNERLESS	DIPHTHERIAS
DIGITALISATIONS	DIHYDROCODEINES	DILUVIALISMS	DINNERTIME	DIPHTHERIC
DIGITALISE	DIHYDROGEN	DILUVIALIST	DINNERTIMES	DIPHTHERITIC
DIGITALISED	DIJUDICATE	DILUVIALISTS	DINNERWARE	DIPHTHERITIS
DIGITALISES	DIJUDICATED	DIMENHYDRINATE	DINNERWARES	DIPHTHERITISES
DIGITALISING	DIJUDICATES	DIMENHYDRINATES	DINOCERASES	DIPHTHEROID
DIGITALISM	DIJUDICATING	DIMENSIONAL	DINOFLAGELLATE	DIPHTHEROIDS
DIGITALISMS	DIJUDICATION	DIMENSIONALITY	DINOFLAGELLATES	DIPHTHONGAL
DIGITALIZATION	DIJUDICATIONS	DIMENSIONALLY	DINOMANIAS	DIPHTHONGALLY
DIGITALIZATIONS	DILACERATE	DIMENSIONED	DINOSAURIAN	DIPHTHONGED
DIGITALIZE	DILACERATED	DIMENSIONING	DINOSAURIC	DIPHTHONGIC
DIGITALIZED	DILACERATES	DIMENSIONLESS	DINOTHERES	DIPHTHONGING
DIGITALIZES	DILACERATING	DIMENSIONS	DINOTHERIA	DIPHTHONGISE
DIGITALIZING	DILACERATION	DIMERCAPROL	DINOTHERIUM	DIPHTHONGISED
DIGITATELY	DILACERATIONS	DIMERCAPROLS	DINOTHERIUMS	DIPHTHONGISES
DIGITATION	DILAPIDATE	DIMERISATION	DINOTURBATION	DIPHTHONGISING
DIGITATIONS	DILAPIDATED	DIMERISATIONS	DINOTURBATIONS	DIPHTHONGIZE
DIGITIFORM	DILAPIDATES	DIMERISING	DINUCLEOTIDE	DIPHTHONGIZED
DIGITIGRADE	DILAPIDATING	DIMERIZATION	DINUCLEOTIDES	DIPHTHONGIZES
DIGITIGRADES	DILAPIDATION	DIMERIZATIONS	DIOECIOUSLY	DIPHTHONGIZING
DIGITISATION	DILAPIDATIONS	DIMERIZING	DIOECIOUSNESS	DIPHTHONGS
DIGITISATIONS	DILAPIDATOR	DIMETHOATE	DIOECIOUSNESSES	DIPHYCERCAL
DIGITISERS	DILAPIDATORS	DIMETHOATES	DIOESTRUSES	DIPHYLETIC
DIGITISING	DILATABILITIES	DIMETHYLAMINE	DIOICOUSLY	DIPHYLLOUS
DIGITIZATION	DILATABILITY	DIMETHYLAMINES	DIOICOUSNESS	DIPHYODONT
DIGITIZATIONS	DILATABLENESS	DIMETHYLANILINE	DIOICOUSNESSES	DIPHYODONTS
DIGITIZERS	DILATABLENESSES	DIMIDIATED	DIOPHYSITE	DIPHYSITES
DIGITIZING	DILATANCIES	DIMIDIATES	DIOPHYSITES	DIPHYSITISM
DIGITONINS	DILATATION	DIMIDIATING	DIOPTOMETER	DIPHYSITISMS
DIGITORIUM	DILATATIONAL	DIMIDIATION	DIOPTOMETERS	DIPLEIDOSCOPE

DIPLEIDOSCOPES	DIPTEROSES	DISADORNED	DISAMENITY	DISARRANGEMENT
DIPLOBIONT	DIRECTEDNESS	DISADORNING	DISANALOGIES	DISARRANGEMENTS
DIPLOBIONTIC	DIRECTEDNESSES	DISADVANCE	DISANALOGOUS	DISARRANGES
DIPLOBIONTS	DIRECTIONAL	DISADVANCED	DISANALOGY	DISARRANGING
DIPLOBLASTIC	DIRECTIONALITY	DISADVANCES	DISANCHORED	DISARRAYED
DIPLOCARDIAC	DIRECTIONLESS	DISADVANCING	DISANCHORING	DISARRAYING
DIPLOCOCCAL	DIRECTIONS	DISADVANTAGE	DISANCHORS	DISARTICULATE
DIPLOCOCCI	DIRECTIVES	DISADVANTAGED	DISANIMATE	DISARTICULATED
DIPLOCOCCIC	DIRECTIVITIES	DISADVANTAGEOUS	DISANIMATED	DISARTICULATES
DIPLOCOCCUS	DIRECTIVITY	DISADVANTAGES	DISANIMATES	DISARTICULATING
DIPLODOCUS	DIRECTNESS	DISADVANTAGING	DISANIMATING	DISARTICULATION
DIPLODOCUSES	DIRECTNESSES	DISADVENTURE	DISANNEXED	DISARTICULATOR
DIPLOGENESES	DIRECTORATE	DISADVENTURES	DISANNEXES	DISARTICULATORS
DIPLOGENESIS	DIRECTORATES	DISADVENTUROUS	DISANNEXING	DISASSEMBLE
DIPLOIDIES	DIRECTORIAL	DISAFFECTED	DISANNULLED	DISASSEMBLED
DIPLOMACIES	DIRECTORIALLY	DISAFFECTEDLY	DISANNULLER	DISASSEMBLER
DIPLOMAING	DIRECTORIES	DISAFFECTEDNESS	DISANNULLERS	DISASSEMBLERS
DIPLOMATED	DIRECTORSHIP	DISAFFECTING	DISANNULLING	DISASSEMBLES
DIPLOMATES	DIRECTORSHIPS	DISAFFECTION	DISANNULLINGS	DISASSEMBLIES
DIPLOMATESE	DIRECTRESS	DISAFFECTIONATE	DISANNULMENT	DISASSEMBLING
DIPLOMATESES	DIRECTRESSES	DISAFFECTIONS	DISANNULMENTS	DISASSEMBLY
DIPLOMATIC	DIRECTRICE	DISAFFECTS	DISANOINTED	DISASSIMILATE
DIPLOMATICAL	DIRECTRICES	DISAFFILIATE	DISANOINTING	DISASSIMILATED
DIPLOMATICALLY	DIRECTRIXES	DISAFFILIATED	DISANOINTS	DISASSIMILATES
DIPLOMATICS	DIREFULNESS	DISAFFILIATES	DISAPPAREL	DISASSIMILATING
DIPLOMATING	DIREFULNESSES	DISAFFILIATING	DISAPPARELLED	DISASSIMILATION
DIPLOMATISE	DIREMPTING	DISAFFILIATION	DISAPPARELLING	DISASSIMILATIVE
DIPLOMATISED	DIREMPTION	DISAFFILIATIONS	DISAPPARELS	DISASSOCIATE
DIPLOMATISES	DIREMPTIONS	DISAFFIRMANCE	DISAPPEARANCE	DISASSOCIATED
DIPLOMATISING	DIRENESSES	DISAFFIRMANCES	DISAPPEARANCES	DISASSOCIATES
DIPLOMATIST	DIRIGIBILITIES	DISAFFIRMATION	DISAPPEARED	DISASSOCIATING
DIPLOMATISTS	DIRIGIBILITY	DISAFFIRMATIONS	DISAPPEARING	DISASSOCIATION
DIPLOMATIZE	DIRIGIBLES	DISAFFIRMED	DISAPPEARS	DISASSOCIATIONS
DIPLOMATIZED	DIRIGISMES	DISAFFIRMING	DISAPPLICATION	DISASTROUS
DIPLOMATIZES	DIRTINESSES	DISAFFIRMS	DISAPPLICATIONS	DISASTROUSLY
DIPLOMATIZING	DISABILITIES	DISAFFOREST	DISAPPLIED	DISATTIRED
DIPLOMATOLOGIES	DISABILITY	DISAFFORESTED	DISAPPLIES	DISATTIRES
DIPLOMATOLOGY	DISABLEMENT	DISAFFORESTING	DISAPPLYING	DISATTIRING
DIPLONEMAS	DISABLEMENTS	DISAFFORESTMENT	DISAPPOINT	DISATTRIBUTION
DIPLOPHASE	DISABLISMS	DISAFFORESTS	DISAPPOINTED	DISATTRIBUTIONS
DIPLOPHASES	DISABLISTS	DISAGGREGATE	DISAPPOINTEDLY	DISATTUNED
DIPLOSPEAK	DISABUSALS	DISAGGREGATED	DISAPPOINTING	DISATTUNES
DIPLOSPEAKS	DISABUSING	DISAGGREGATES	DISAPPOINTINGLY	DISATTUNING
DIPLOSTEMONOUS	DISACCHARID	DISAGGREGATING	DISAPPOINTMENT	DISAUTHORISE
DIPLOTENES	DISACCHARIDASE	DISAGGREGATION	DISAPPOINTMENTS	DISAUTHORISED
DIPNETTING	DISACCHARIDASES	DISAGGREGATIONS	DISAPPOINTS	DISAUTHORISES
DIPPERFULS	DISACCHARIDE	DISAGGREGATIVE	DISAPPROBATION	DISAUTHORISING
DIPPINESSES	DISACCHARIDES	DISAGREEABILITY	DISAPPROBATIONS	DISAUTHORIZE
DIPRIONIDIAN	DISACCHARIDS	DISAGREEABLE	DISAPPROBATIVE	DISAUTHORIZED
DIPROPELLANT	DISACCOMMODATE	DISAGREEABLES	DISAPPROBATORY	DISAUTHORIZES
DIPROPELLANTS	DISACCOMMODATED	DISAGREEABLY	DISAPPROPRIATE	DISAUTHORIZING
DIPROTODON	DISACCOMMODATES	DISAGREEING	DISAPPROPRIATED	DISAVAUNCE
DIPROTODONS	DISACCORDANT	DISAGREEMENT	DISAPPROPRIATES	DISAVAUNCED
DIPROTODONT	DISACCORDED	DISAGREEMENTS	DISAPPROVAL	DISAVAUNCES
DIPROTODONTID	DISACCORDING	DISALLOWABLE	DISAPPROVALS	DISAVAUNCING
DIPROTODONTIDS	DISACCORDS	DISALLOWANCE	DISAPPROVE	DISAVENTROUS
DIPROTODONTS	DISACCREDIT	DISALLOWANCES	DISAPPROVED	DISAVENTURE
DIPSOMANIA	DISACCREDITED	DISALLOWED	DISAPPROVER	DISAVENTURES
DIPSOMANIAC	DISACCREDITING	DISALLOWING	DISAPPROVERS	DISAVOUCHED
DIPSOMANIACAL	DISACCREDITS	DISALLYING	DISAPPROVES	DISAVOUCHES
DIPSOMANIACS	DISACCUSTOM	DISAMBIGUATE	DISAPPROVING	DISAVOUCHING
DIPSOMANIAS	DISACCUSTOMED	DISAMBIGUATED	DISAPPROVINGLY	DISAVOWABLE
DIPSWITCHES	DISACCUSTOMING	DISAMBIGUATES	DISARMAMENT	DISAVOWALS
DIPTERISTS	DISACCUSTOMS	DISAMBIGUATING	DISARMAMENTS	DISAVOWEDLY
DIPTEROCARP	DISACKNOWLEDGE	DISAMBIGUATION	DISARMINGLY	DISAVOWERS
DIPTEROCARPOUS	DISACKNOWLEDGED	DISAMBIGUATIONS	DISARRANGE	DISAVOWING
DIPTEROCARPS	DISACKNOWLEDGES	DISAMENITIES	DISARRANGED	DISBANDING

DISBANDMENT	DISCEPTATOR	DISCOBOLUS	DISCOMPOSED	DISCONTINUING
DISBANDMENTS	DISCEPTATORIAL	DISCOBOLUSES	DISCOMPOSEDLY	DISCONTINUITIES
DISBARKING	DISCEPTATORS	DISCOGRAPHER	DISCOMPOSES	DISCONTINUITY
DISBARMENT	DISCEPTING	DISCOGRAPHERS	DISCOMPOSING	DISCONTINUOUS
DISBARMENTS	DISCERNABLE	DISCOGRAPHIC	DISCOMPOSINGLY	DISCONTINUOUSLY
DISBARRING	DISCERNABLY	DISCOGRAPHICAL	DISCOMPOSURE	DISCOPHILE
DISBELIEFS	DISCERNERS	DISCOGRAPHIES	DISCOMPOSURES	DISCOPHILES
DISBELIEVE	DISCERNIBLE	DISCOGRAPHY	DISCOMYCETE	DISCOPHORAN
DISBELIEVED	DISCERNIBLY	DISCOLOGIES	DISCOMYCETES	DISCOPHORANS
DISBELIEVER	DISCERNING	DISCOLOGIST	DISCOMYCETOUS	DISCOPHOROUS
DISBELIEVERS	DISCERNINGLY	DISCOLOGISTS	DISCONCERT	DISCORDANCE
DISBELIEVES	DISCERNMENT	DISCOLORATION	DISCONCERTED	DISCORDANCES
DISBELIEVING	DISCERNMENTS	DISCOLORATIONS	DISCONCERTEDLY	DISCORDANCIES
DISBELIEVINGLY	DISCERPIBILITY	DISCOLORED	DISCONCERTING	DISCORDANCY
DISBENCHED	DISCERPIBLE	DISCOLORING	DISCONCERTINGLY	DISCORDANT
DISBENCHES	DISCERPING	DISCOLORMENT	DISCONCERTION	DISCORDANTLY
DISBENCHING	DISCERPTIBLE	DISCOLORMENTS	DISCONCERTIONS	DISCORDFUL
DISBENEFIT	DISCERPTION	DISCOLOURATION	DISCONCERTMENT	DISCORDING
DISBENEFITS	DISCERPTIONS	DISCOLOURATIONS	DISCONCERTMENTS	DISCORPORATE
DISBOSOMED	DISCERPTIVE	DISCOLOURED	DISCONCERTS	DISCORPORATED
DISBOSOMING	DISCHARGEABLE	DISCOLOURING	DISCONFIRM	DISCORPORATES
DISBOWELED	DISCHARGED	DISCOLOURMENT	DISCONFIRMATION	DISCORPORATING
DISBOWELING	DISCHARGEE	DISCOLOURMENTS	DISCONFIRMED	DISCOTHEQUE
DISBOWELLED	DISCHARGEES	DISCOLOURS	DISCONFIRMING	DISCOTHEQUES
DISBOWELLING	DISCHARGER	DISCOMBOBERATE	DISCONFIRMS	DISCOUNSEL
DISBRANCHED	DISCHARGERS	DISCOMBOBERATED	DISCONFORMABLE	DISCOUNSELLED
DISBRANCHES	DISCHARGES	DISCOMBOBERATES	DISCONFORMITIES	DISCOUNSELLING
DISBRANCHING	DISCHARGING	DISCOMBOBULATE	DISCONFORMITY	DISCOUNSELS
DISBUDDING	DISCHUFFED	DISCOMBOBULATED	DISCONNECT	DISCOUNTABLE
DISBURDENED	DISCHURCHED	DISCOMBOBULATES	DISCONNECTED	DISCOUNTED
DISBURDENING	DISCHURCHES	DISCOMEDUSAN	DISCONNECTEDLY	DISCOUNTENANCE
DISBURDENMENT	DISCHURCHING	DISCOMEDUSANS	DISCONNECTER	DISCOUNTENANCED
DISBURDENMENTS	DISCIPLESHIP	DISCOMFITED	DISCONNECTERS	DISCOUNTENANCES
DISBURDENS	DISCIPLESHIPS	DISCOMFITER	DISCONNECTING	DISCOUNTER
DISBURSABLE	DISCIPLINABLE	DISCOMFITERS	DISCONNECTION	DISCOUNTERS
DISBURSALS	DISCIPLINAL	DISCOMFITING	DISCONNECTIONS	DISCOUNTING
DISBURSEMENT	DISCIPLINANT	DISCOMFITS	DISCONNECTIVE	DISCOURAGE
DISBURSEMENTS	DISCIPLINANTS	DISCOMFITURE	DISCONNECTS	DISCOURAGEABLE
DISBURSERS	DISCIPLINARIAN	DISCOMFITURES	DISCONNEXION	DISCOURAGED
DISBURSING	DISCIPLINARIANS	DISCOMFORT	DISCONNEXIONS	DISCOURAGEMENT
DISBURTHEN	DISCIPLINARILY	DISCOMFORTABLE	DISCONSENT	DISCOURAGEMENTS
DISBURTHENED	DISCIPLINARITY	DISCOMFORTED	DISCONSENTED	DISCOURAGER
DISBURTHENING	DISCIPLINARIUM	DISCOMFORTING	DISCONSENTING	DISCOURAGERS
DISBURTHENS	DISCIPLINARIUMS	DISCOMFORTS	DISCONSENTS	DISCOURAGES
DISCALCEATE	DISCIPLINARY	DISCOMMEND	DISCONSOLATE	DISCOURAGING
DISCALCEATES	DISCIPLINE	DISCOMMENDABLE	DISCONSOLATELY	DISCOURAGINGLY
DISCANDERING	DISCIPLINED	DISCOMMENDATION	DISCONSOLATION	DISCOURING
DISCANDERINGS	DISCIPLINER	DISCOMMENDED	DISCONSOLATIONS	DISCOURSAL
DISCANDIED	DISCIPLINERS	DISCOMMENDING	DISCONTENT	DISCOURSED
DISCANDIES	DISCIPLINES	DISCOMMENDS	DISCONTENTED	DISCOURSER
DISCANDYING	DISCIPLING	DISCOMMISSION	DISCONTENTEDLY	DISCOURSERS
DISCANDYINGS	DISCIPLINING	DISCOMMISSIONED	DISCONTENTFUL	DISCOURSES
DISCANTERS	DISCIPULAR	DISCOMMISSIONS	DISCONTENTING	DISCOURSING
DISCANTING	DISCISSION	DISCOMMODE	DISCONTENTMENT	DISCOURSIVE
DISCAPACITATE	DISCISSIONS	DISCOMMODED	DISCONTENTMENTS	DISCOURTEISE
DISCAPACITATED	DISCLAIMED	DISCOMMODES	DISCONTENTS	DISCOURTEOUS
DISCAPACITATES	DISCLAIMER	DISCOMMODING	DISCONTIGUITIES	DISCOURTEOUSLY
DISCAPACITATING	DISCLAIMERS	DISCOMMODIOUS	DISCONTIGUITY	DISCOURTESIES
DISCARDABLE	DISCLAIMING	DISCOMMODIOUSLY	DISCONTIGUOUS	DISCOURTESY
DISCARDERS	DISCLAMATION	DISCOMMODITIES	DISCONTINUANCE	DISCOVERABLE
DISCARDING	DISCLAMATIONS	DISCOMMODITY	DISCONTINUANCES	DISCOVERED
DISCARDMENT	DISCLIMAXES	DISCOMMONED	DISCONTINUATION	DISCOVERER
DISCARDMENTS	DISCLOSERS	DISCOMMONING	DISCONTINUE	DISCOVERERS
DISCARNATE	DISCLOSING	DISCOMMONS	DISCONTINUED	DISCOVERIES
DISCEPTATION	DISCLOSURE	DISCOMMUNITIES	DISCONTINUER	DISCOVERING
DISCEPTATIONS	DISCLOSURES	DISCOMMUNITY	DISCONTINUERS	DISCOVERTURE
DISCEPTATIOUS	DISCOBOLOS	DISCOMPOSE	DISCONTINUES	DISCOVERTURES

DISCREDITABLE
DISCREDITABLY
DISCREDITED
DISCREDITING
DISCREDITS
DISCREETER
DISCREETEST
DISCREETLY
DISCREETNESS
DISCREETNESSES
DISCREPANCE
DISCREPANCES
DISCREPANCIES
DISCREPANCY
DISCREPANT
DISCREPANTLY
DISCRETELY
DISCRETENESS
DISCRETENESSES
DISCRETEST
DISCRETION
DISCRETIONAL
DISCRETIONALLY
DISCRETIONARILY
DISCRETIONARY
DISCRETIONS
DISCRETIVE
DISCRETIVELY
DISCRETIVES
DISCRIMINABLE
DISCRIMINABLY
DISCRIMINANT
DISCRIMINANTS
DISCRIMINATE
DISCRIMINATED
DISCRIMINATELY
DISCRIMINATES
DISCRIMINATING
DISCRIMINATION
DISCRIMINATIONS
DISCRIMINATIVE
DISCRIMINATOR
DISCRIMINATORS
DISCRIMINATORY
DISCROWNED
DISCROWNING
DISCULPATE
DISCULPATED
DISCULPATES
DISCULPATING
DISCUMBERED
DISCUMBERING
DISCUMBERS
DISCURSION
DISCURSIONS
DISCURSIST
DISCURSISTS
DISCURSIVE
DISCURSIVELY
DISCURSIVENESS
DISCURSORY
DISCURSUSES
DISCUSSABLE
DISCUSSANT
DISCUSSANTS
DISCUSSERS
DISCUSSIBLE

DISCUSSING
DISCUSSION
DISCUSSIONAL
DISCUSSIONS
DISCUSSIVE
DISCUSSIVES
DISCUTIENT
DISCUTIENTS
DISDAINFUL
DISDAINFULLY
DISDAINFULNESS
DISDAINING
DISEASEDNESS
DISEASEDNESSES
DISEASEFUL
DISECONOMIES
DISECONOMY
DISEMBARKATION
DISEMBARKATIONS
DISEMBARKED
DISEMBARKING
DISEMBARKMENT
DISEMBARKMENTS
DISEMBARKS
DISEMBARRASS
DISEMBARRASSED
DISEMBARRASSES
DISEMBARRASSING
DISEMBELLISH
DISEMBELLISHED
DISEMBELLISHES
DISEMBELLISHING
DISEMBITTER
DISEMBITTERED
DISEMBITTERING
DISEMBITTERS
DISEMBODIED
DISEMBODIES
DISEMBODIMENT
DISEMBODIMENTS
DISEMBODYING
DISEMBOGUE
DISEMBOGUED
DISEMBOGUEMENT
DISEMBOGUEMENTS
DISEMBOGUES
DISEMBOGUING
DISEMBOSOM
DISEMBOSOMED
DISEMBOSOMING
DISEMBOSOMS
DISEMBOWEL
DISEMBOWELED
DISEMBOWELLED
DISEMBOWELLING
DISEMBOWELMENT
DISEMBOWELMENTS
DISEMBOWELS
DISEMBRANGLE
DISEMBRANGLED
DISEMBRANGLES
DISEMBRANGLING
DISEMBROIL
DISEMBROILED
DISEMBROILING
DISEMBROILS

DISEMBURDEN
DISEMBURDENED
DISEMBURDENING
DISEMBURDENS
DISEMPLOYED
DISEMPLOYING
DISEMPLOYMENT
DISEMPLOYMENTS
DISEMPLOYS
DISEMPOWER
DISEMPOWERED
DISEMPOWERING
DISEMPOWERMENT
DISEMPOWERMENTS
DISEMPOWERS
DISEMVOWEL
DISEMVOWELLED
DISEMVOWELLING
DISEMVOWELS
DISENABLED
DISENABLEMENT
DISENABLEMENTS
DISENABLES
DISENABLING
DISENCHAIN
DISENCHAINED
DISENCHAINING
DISENCHAINS
DISENCHANT
DISENCHANTED
DISENCHANTER
DISENCHANTERS
DISENCHANTING
DISENCHANTINGLY
DISENCHANTMENT
DISENCHANTMENTS
DISENCHANTRESS
DISENCHANTS
DISENCLOSE
DISENCLOSED
DISENCLOSES
DISENCLOSING
DISENCUMBER
DISENCUMBERED
DISENCUMBERING
DISENCUMBERMENT
DISENCUMBERS
DISENCUMBRANCE
DISENCUMBRANCES
DISENDOWED
DISENDOWER
DISENDOWERS
DISENDOWING
DISENDOWMENT
DISENDOWMENTS
DISENFRANCHISE
DISENFRANCHISED
DISENFRANCHISES
DISENGAGED
DISENGAGEDNESS
DISENGAGEMENT
DISENGAGEMENTS
DISENGAGES
DISENGAGING
DISENNOBLE
DISENNOBLED
DISENNOBLES

DISENNOBLING
DISENROLLED
DISENROLLING
DISENROLLINGS
DISENSHROUD
DISENSHROUDED
DISENSHROUDING
DISENSHROUDS
DISENSLAVE
DISENSLAVED
DISENSLAVES
DISENSLAVING
DISENTAILED
DISENTAILING
DISENTAILMENT
DISENTAILMENTS
DISENTAILS
DISENTANGLE
DISENTANGLED
DISENTANGLEMENT
DISENTANGLES
DISENTANGLING
DISENTHRAL
DISENTHRALL
DISENTHRALLED
DISENTHRALLING
DISENTHRALLMENT
DISENTHRALLS
DISENTHRALMENT
DISENTHRALMENTS
DISENTHRALS
DISENTHRONE
DISENTHRONED
DISENTHRONES
DISENTHRONING
DISENTITLE
DISENTITLED
DISENTITLES
DISENTITLING
DISENTOMBED
DISENTOMBING
DISENTOMBS
DISENTRAIL
DISENTRAILED
DISENTRAILING
DISENTRAILS
DISENTRAIN
DISENTRAINED
DISENTRAINING
DISENTRAINMENT
DISENTRAINMENTS
DISENTRAINS
DISENTRANCE
DISENTRANCED
DISENTRANCEMENT
DISENTRANCES
DISENTRANCING
DISENTRAYLE
DISENTRAYLED
DISENTRAYLES
DISENTRAYLING
DISENTWINE
DISENTWINED
DISENTWINES
DISENTWINING
DISENVELOP
DISENVELOPED

DISENVELOPING
DISENVELOPS
DISENVIRON
DISENVIRONED
DISENVIRONING
DISENVIRONS
DISEPALOUS
DISEQUILIBRATE
DISEQUILIBRATED
DISEQUILIBRATES
DISEQUILIBRIA
DISEQUILIBRIUM
DISEQUILIBRIUMS
DISESPOUSE
DISESPOUSED
DISESPOUSES
DISESPOUSING
DISESTABLISH
DISESTABLISHED
DISESTABLISHES
DISESTABLISHING
DISESTEEMED
DISESTEEMING
DISESTEEMS
DISESTIMATION
DISESTIMATIONS
DISFAVORED
DISFAVORING
DISFAVOURED
DISFAVOURER
DISFAVOURERS
DISFAVOURING
DISFAVOURS
DISFEATURE
DISFEATURED
DISFEATUREMENT
DISFEATUREMENTS
DISFEATURES
DISFEATURING
DISFELLOWSHIP
DISFELLOWSHIPED
DISFELLOWSHIPS
DISFIGURATION
DISFIGURATIONS
DISFIGURED
DISFIGUREMENT
DISFIGUREMENTS
DISFIGURER
DISFIGURERS
DISFIGURES
DISFIGURING
DISFLESHED
DISFLESHES
DISFLESHING
DISFLUENCIES
DISFLUENCY
DISFORESTATION
DISFORESTATIONS
DISFORESTED
DISFORESTING
DISFORESTS
DISFORMING
DISFRANCHISE
DISFRANCHISED
DISFRANCHISES
DISFRANCHISING
DISFROCKED

d

DISFROCKING
DISFUNCTION
DISFUNCTIONAL
DISFUNCTIONS
DISFURNISH
DISFURNISHED
DISFURNISHES
DISFURNISHING
DISFURNISHMENT
DISFURNISHMENTS
DISGARNISH
DISGARNISHED
DISGARNISHES
DISGARNISHING
DISGARRISON
DISGARRISONED
DISGARRISONING
DISGARRISONS
DISGAVELLED
DISGAVELLING
DISGAVELLINGS
DISGESTING
DISGESTION
DISGESTIONS
DISGLORIFIED
DISGLORIFIES
DISGLORIFY
DISGLORIFYING
DISGORGEMENT
DISGORGEMENTS
DISGORGERS
DISGORGING
DISGOSPELLING
DISGOWNING
DISGRACEFUL
DISGRACEFULLY
DISGRACEFULNESS
DISGRACERS
DISGRACING
DISGRACIOUS
DISGRADATION
DISGRADATIONS
DISGRADING
DISGREGATION
DISGREGATIONS
DISGRUNTLE
DISGRUNTLED
DISGRUNTLEMENT
DISGRUNTLEMENTS
DISGRUNTLES
DISGRUNTLING
DISGUISABLE
DISGUISEDLY
DISGUISEDNESS
DISGUISEDNESSES
DISGUISELESS
DISGUISEMENT
DISGUISEMENTS
DISGUISERS
DISGUISING
DISGUISINGS
DISGUSTEDLY
DISGUSTEDNESS
DISGUSTEDNESSES
DISGUSTFUL
DISGUSTFULLY
DISGUSTFULNESS

DISGUSTING
DISGUSTINGLY
DISGUSTINGNESS
DISHABILITATE
DISHABILITATED
DISHABILITATES
DISHABILITATING
DISHABILITATION
DISHABILLE
DISHABILLES
DISHABITED
DISHABITING
DISHABLING
DISHALLOWED
DISHALLOWING
DISHALLOWS
DISHARMONIC
DISHARMONIES
DISHARMONIOUS
DISHARMONIOUSLY
DISHARMONISE
DISHARMONISED
DISHARMONISES
DISHARMONISING
DISHARMONIZE
DISHARMONIZED
DISHARMONIZES
DISHARMONIZING
DISHARMONY
DISHCLOTHS
DISHCLOUTS
DISHDASHAS
DISHDASHES
DISHEARTEN
DISHEARTENED
DISHEARTENING
DISHEARTENINGLY
DISHEARTENMENT
DISHEARTENMENTS
DISHEARTENS
DISHELMING
DISHERISON
DISHERISONS
DISHERITED
DISHERITING
DISHERITOR
DISHERITORS
DISHEVELED
DISHEVELING
DISHEVELLED
DISHEVELLING
DISHEVELMENT
DISHEVELMENTS
DISHOARDED
DISHOARDING
DISHONESTIES
DISHONESTLY
DISHONESTY
DISHONORABLE
DISHONORABLY
DISHONORARY
DISHONORED
DISHONORER
DISHONORERS
DISHONORING
DISHONOURABLE
DISHONOURABLY

DISHONOURED
DISHONOURER
DISHONOURERS
DISHONOURING
DISHONOURS
DISHORNING
DISHORSING
DISHOUSING
DISHTOWELS
DISHUMOURED
DISHUMOURING
DISHUMOURS
DISHWASHER
DISHWASHERS
DISHWATERS
DISILLUDED
DISILLUDES
DISILLUDING
DISILLUMINATE
DISILLUMINATED
DISILLUMINATES
DISILLUMINATING
DISILLUSION
DISILLUSIONARY
DISILLUSIONED
DISILLUSIONING
DISILLUSIONISE
DISILLUSIONISED
DISILLUSIONISES
DISILLUSIONIZE
DISILLUSIONIZED
DISILLUSIONIZES
DISILLUSIONMENT
DISILLUSIONS
DISILLUSIVE
DISIMAGINE
DISIMAGINED
DISIMAGINES
DISIMAGINING
DISIMMURED
DISIMMURES
DISIMMURING
DISIMPASSIONED
DISIMPRISON
DISIMPRISONED
DISIMPRISONING
DISIMPRISONMENT
DISIMPRISONS
DISIMPROVE
DISIMPROVED
DISIMPROVES
DISIMPROVING
DISINCARCERATE
DISINCARCERATED
DISINCARCERATES
DISINCENTIVE
DISINCENTIVES
DISINCLINATION
DISINCLINATIONS
DISINCLINE
DISINCLINED
DISINCLINES
DISINCLINING
DISINCLOSE
DISINCLOSED
DISINCLOSES
DISINCLOSING

DISINCORPORATE
DISINCORPORATED
DISINCORPORATES
DISINFECTANT
DISINFECTANTS
DISINFECTED
DISINFECTING
DISINFECTION
DISINFECTIONS
DISINFECTOR
DISINFECTORS
DISINFECTS
DISINFESTANT
DISINFESTANTS
DISINFESTATION
DISINFESTATIONS
DISINFESTED
DISINFESTING
DISINFESTS
DISINFLATION
DISINFLATIONARY
DISINFLATIONS
DISINFORMATION
DISINFORMATIONS
DISINFORMED
DISINFORMING
DISINFORMS
DISINGENUITIES
DISINGENUITY
DISINGENUOUS
DISINGENUOUSLY
DISINHERISON
DISINHERISONS
DISINHERIT
DISINHERITANCE
DISINHERITANCES
DISINHERITED
DISINHERITING
DISINHERITS
DISINHIBIT
DISINHIBITED
DISINHIBITING
DISINHIBITION
DISINHIBITIONS
DISINHIBITORY
DISINHIBITS
DISINHUMED
DISINHUMES
DISINHUMING
DISINTEGRABLE
DISINTEGRATE
DISINTEGRATED
DISINTEGRATES
DISINTEGRATING
DISINTEGRATION
DISINTEGRATIONS
DISINTEGRATIVE
DISINTEGRATOR
DISINTEGRATORS
DISINTEREST
DISINTERESTED
DISINTERESTEDLY
DISINTERESTING
DISINTERESTS
DISINTERMENT
DISINTERMENTS
DISINTERRED

DISINTERRING
DISINTHRAL
DISINTHRALLED
DISINTHRALLING
DISINTHRALLINGS
DISINTHRALS
DISINTOXICATE
DISINTOXICATED
DISINTOXICATES
DISINTOXICATING
DISINTOXICATION
DISINTRICATE
DISINTRICATED
DISINTRICATES
DISINTRICATING
DISINURING
DISINVENTED
DISINVENTING
DISINVENTS
DISINVESTED
DISINVESTING
DISINVESTITURE
DISINVESTITURES
DISINVESTMENT
DISINVESTMENTS
DISINVESTS
DISINVIGORATE
DISINVIGORATED
DISINVIGORATES
DISINVIGORATING
DISINVITED
DISINVITES
DISINVITING
DISINVOLVE
DISINVOLVED
DISINVOLVES
DISINVOLVING
DISJECTING
DISJECTION
DISJECTIONS
DISJOINABLE
DISJOINING
DISJOINTED
DISJOINTEDLY
DISJOINTEDNESS
DISJOINTING
DISJUNCTION
DISJUNCTIONS
DISJUNCTIVE
DISJUNCTIVELY
DISJUNCTIVES
DISJUNCTOR
DISJUNCTORS
DISJUNCTURE
DISJUNCTURES
DISLEAFING
DISLEAVING
DISLIKABLE
DISLIKEABLE
DISLIKEFUL
DISLIKENED
DISLIKENESS
DISLIKENESSES
DISLIKENING
DISLIMBING
DISLIMNING
DISLINKING

DISLOADING	DISNATURALIZED	DISPARAGINGLY	DISPERSIVE	DISPOSINGS
DISLOCATED	DISNATURALIZES	DISPARATELY	DISPERSIVELY	DISPOSITION
DISLOCATEDLY	DISNATURALIZING	DISPARATENESS	DISPERSIVENESS	DISPOSITIONAL
DISLOCATES	DISNATURED	DISPARATENESSES	DISPERSOID	DISPOSITIONED
DISLOCATING	DISNATURES	DISPARATES	DISPERSOIDS	DISPOSITIONS
DISLOCATION	DISNATURING	DISPARITIES	DISPIRITED	DISPOSITIVE
DISLOCATIONS	DISNESTING	DISPARKING	DISPIRITEDLY	DISPOSITIVELY
DISLODGEMENT	DISOBEDIENCE	DISPARTING	DISPIRITEDNESS	DISPOSITIVES
DISLODGEMENTS	DISOBEDIENCES	DISPASSION	DISPIRITING	DISPOSITOR
DISLODGING	DISOBEDIENT	DISPASSIONATE	DISPIRITINGLY	DISPOSITORS
DISLODGMENT	DISOBEDIENTLY	DISPASSIONATELY	DISPIRITMENT	DISPOSSESS
DISLODGMENTS	DISOBEYERS	DISPASSIONS	DISPIRITMENTS	DISPOSSESSED
DISLOIGNED	DISOBEYING	DISPATCHED	DISPITEOUS	DISPOSSESSES
DISLOIGNING	DISOBLIGATION	DISPATCHER	DISPITEOUSLY	DISPOSSESSING
DISLOYALLY	DISOBLIGATIONS	DISPATCHERS	DISPITEOUSNESS	DISPOSSESSION
DISLOYALTIES	DISOBLIGATORY	DISPATCHES	DISPLACEABLE	DISPOSSESSIONS
DISLOYALTY	DISOBLIGED	DISPATCHFUL	DISPLACEMENT	DISPOSSESSOR
DISLUSTRED	DISOBLIGEMENT	DISPATCHING	DISPLACEMENTS	DISPOSSESSORS
DISLUSTRES	DISOBLIGEMENTS	DISPATHIES	DISPLACERS	DISPOSSESSORY
DISLUSTRING	DISOBLIGES	DISPAUPERED	DISPLACING	DISPOSTING
DISMALITIES	DISOBLIGING	DISPAUPERING	DISPLANTATION	DISPOSURES
DISMALLEST	DISOBLIGINGLY	DISPAUPERISE	DISPLANTATIONS	DISPRAISED
DISMALNESS	DISOBLIGINGNESS	DISPAUPERISED	DISPLANTED	DISPRAISER
DISMALNESSES	DISOPERATION	DISPAUPERISES	DISPLANTING	DISPRAISERS
DISMANNING	DISOPERATIONS	DISPAUPERISING	DISPLAYABLE	DISPRAISES
DISMANTLED	DISORDERED	DISPAUPERIZE	DISPLAYERS	DISPRAISING
DISMANTLEMENT	DISORDEREDLY	DISPAUPERIZED	DISPLAYING	DISPRAISINGLY
DISMANTLEMENTS	DISORDEREDNESS	DISPAUPERIZES	DISPLEASANCE	DISPREADING
DISMANTLER	DISORDERING	DISPAUPERIZING	DISPLEASANCES	DISPREDDEN
DISMANTLERS	DISORDERLIES	DISPAUPERS	DISPLEASANT	DISPREDDING
DISMANTLES	DISORDERLINESS	DISPELLERS	DISPLEASANTED	DISPRINCED
DISMANTLING	DISORDERLY	DISPELLING	DISPLEASANTING	DISPRISONED
DISMANTLINGS	DISORDINATE	DISPENCING	DISPLEASANTS	DISPRISONING
DISMASKING	DISORDINATELY	DISPENDING	DISPLEASED	DISPRISONS
DISMASTING	DISORGANIC	DISPENSABILITY	DISPLEASEDLY	DISPRIVACIED
DISMASTMENT	DISORGANISATION	DISPENSABLE	DISPLEASEDNESS	DISPRIVILEGE
DISMASTMENTS	DISORGANISE	DISPENSABLENESS	DISPLEASES	DISPRIVILEGED
DISMAYEDNESS	DISORGANISED	DISPENSABLY	DISPLEASING	DISPRIVILEGES
DISMAYEDNESSES	DISORGANISER	DISPENSARIES	DISPLEASINGLY	DISPRIVILEGING
DISMAYFULLY	DISORGANISERS	DISPENSARY	DISPLEASINGNESS	DISPRIZING
DISMAYINGLY	DISORGANISES	DISPENSATION	DISPLEASURE	DISPROFESS
DISMAYLING	DISORGANISING	DISPENSATIONAL	DISPLEASURED	DISPROFESSED
DISMEMBERED	DISORGANIZATION	DISPENSATIONS	DISPLEASURES	DISPROFESSES
DISMEMBERER	DISORGANIZE	DISPENSATIVE	DISPLEASURING	DISPROFESSING
DISMEMBERERS	DISORGANIZED	DISPENSATIVELY	DISPLENISH	DISPROFITED
DISMEMBERING	DISORGANIZER	DISPENSATOR	DISPLENISHED	DISPROFITING
DISMEMBERMENT	DISORGANIZERS	DISPENSATORIES	DISPLENISHES	DISPROFITS
DISMEMBERMENTS	DISORGANIZES	DISPENSATORILY	DISPLENISHING	DISPROOVED
DISMEMBERS	DISORGANIZING	DISPENSATORS	DISPLENISHMENT	DISPROOVES
DISMISSALS	DISORIENTATE	DISPENSATORY	DISPLENISHMENTS	DISPROOVING
DISMISSIBLE	DISORIENTATED	DISPENSERS	DISPLODING	DISPROPERTIED
DISMISSING	DISORIENTATES	DISPENSING	DISPLOSION	DISPROPERTIES
DISMISSION	DISORIENTATING	DISPEOPLED	DISPLOSIONS	DISPROPERTY
DISMISSIONS	DISORIENTATION	DISPEOPLES	DISPLUMING	DISPROPERTYING
DISMISSIVE	DISORIENTATIONS	DISPEOPLING	DISPONDAIC	DISPROPORTION
DISMISSIVELY	DISORIENTED	DISPERMOUS	DISPONDEES	DISPROPORTIONAL
DISMISSORY	DISORIENTING	DISPERSALS	DISPONGING	DISPROPORTIONED
DISMOUNTABLE	DISORIENTS	DISPERSANT	DISPORTING	DISPROPORTIONS
DISMOUNTED	DISOWNMENT	DISPERSANTS	DISPORTMENT	DISPROPRIATE
DISMOUNTING	DISOWNMENTS	DISPERSEDLY	DISPORTMENTS	DISPROPRIATED
DISMUTATION	DISPARAGED	DISPERSEDNESS	DISPOSABILITIES	DISPROPRIATES
DISMUTATIONS	DISPARAGEMENT	DISPERSEDNESSES	DISPOSABILITY	DISPROPRIATING
DISNATURALISE	DISPARAGEMENTS	DISPERSERS	DISPOSABLE	DISPROVABLE
DISNATURALISED	DISPARAGER	DISPERSIBLE	DISPOSABLENESS	DISPROVALS
DISNATURALISES	DISPARAGERS	DISPERSING	DISPOSABLES	DISPROVERS
DISNATURALISING	DISPARAGES	DISPERSION	DISPOSEDLY	DISPROVIDE
DISNATURALIZE	DISPARAGING	DISPERSIONS	DISPOSINGLY	DISPROVIDED

d

DISPROVIDES	DISRELATIONS	DISSEMBLINGLY	DISSIDENCES	DISSOLUBLE
DISPROVIDING	DISRELISHED	DISSEMBLINGS	DISSIDENTLY	DISSOLUBLENESS
DISPROVING	DISRELISHES	DISSEMINATE	DISSIDENTS	DISSOLUTELY
DISPUNGING	DISRELISHING	DISSEMTNATED	DISSILIENCE	DISSOLUTENESS
DISPURSING	DISREMEMBER	DISSEMINATES	DISSILIENCES	DISSOLUTENESSES
DISPURVEYANCE	DISREMEMBERED	DISSEMINATING	DISSILIENT	DISSOLUTES
DISPURVEYANCES	DISREMEMBERING	DISSEMINATION	DISSIMILAR	DISSOLUTION
DISPURVEYED	DISREMEMBERS	DISSEMINATIONS	DISSIMILARITIES	DISSOLUTIONISM
DISPURVEYING	DISREPAIRS	DISSEMINATIVE	DISSIMILARITY	DISSOLUTIONISMS
DISPURVEYS	DISREPUTABILITY	DISSEMINATOR	DISSIMILARLY	DISSOLUTIONIST
DISPUTABILITIES	DISREPUTABLE	DISSEMINATORS	DISSIMILARS	DISSOLUTIONISTS
DISPUTABILITY	DISREPUTABLY	DISSEMINULE	DISSIMILATE	DISSOLUTIONS
DISPUTABLE	DISREPUTATION	DISSEMINULES	DISSIMILATED	DISSOLUTIVE
DISPUTABLENESS	DISREPUTATIONS	DISSENSION	DISSIMILATES	DISSOLVABILITY
DISPUTABLY	DISREPUTES	DISSENSIONS	DISSIMILATING	DISSOLVABLE
DISPUTANTS	DISRESPECT	DISSENSUSES	DISSIMILATION	DISSOLVABLENESS
DISPUTATION	DISRESPECTABLE	DISSENTERISH	DISSIMILATIONS	DISSOLVENT
DISPUTATIONS	DISRESPECTED	DISSENTERISM	DISSIMILATIVE	DISSOLVENTS
DISPUTATIOUS	DISRESPECTFUL	DISSENTERISMS	DISSIMILATORY	DISSOLVERS
DISPUTATIOUSLY	DISRESPECTFULLY	DISSENTERS	DISSIMILES	DISSOLVING
DISPUTATIVE	DISRESPECTING	DISSENTIENCE	DISSIMILITUDE	DISSOLVINGS
DISPUTATIVELY	DISRESPECTS	DISSENTIENCES	DISSIMILITUDES	DISSONANCE
DISPUTATIVENESS	DISROBEMENT	DISSENTIENCIES	DISSIMULATE	DISSONANCES
DISQUALIFIABLE	DISROBEMENTS	DISSENTIENCY	DISSIMULATED	DISSONANCIES
DISQUALIFIED	DISROOTING	DISSENTIENT	DISSIMULATES	DISSONANCY
DISQUALIFIER	DISRUPTERS	DISSENTIENTLY	DISSIMULATING	DISSONANTLY
DISQUALIFIERS	DISRUPTING	DISSENTIENTS	DISSIMULATION	DISSUADABLE
DISQUALIFIES	DISRUPTION	DISSENTING	DISSIMULATIONS	DISSUADERS
DISQUALIFY	DISRUPTIONS	DISSENTINGLY	DISSIMULATIVE	DISSUADING
DISQUALIFYING	DISRUPTIVE	DISSENTION	DISSIMULATOR	DISSUASION
DISQUANTITIED	DISRUPTIVELY	DISSENTIONS	DISSIMULATORS	DISSUASIONS
DISQUANTITIES	DISRUPTIVENESS	DISSENTIOUS	DISSIPABLE	DISSUASIVE
DISQUANTITY	DISRUPTORS	DISSEPIMENT	DISSIPATED	DISSUASIVELY
DISQUANTITYING	DISSATISFACTION	DISSEPIMENTAL	DISSIPATEDLY	DISSUASIVENESS
DISQUIETED	DISSATISFACTORY	DISSEPIMENTS	DISSIPATEDNESS	DISSUASIVES
DISQUIETEDLY	DISSATISFIED	DISSERTATE	DISSIPATER	DISSUASORIES
DISQUIETEDNESS	DISSATISFIEDLY	DISSERTATED	DISSIPATERS	DISSUASORY
DISQUIETEN	DISSATISFIES	DISSERTATES	DISSIPATES	DISSUNDERED
DISQUIETENED	DISSATISFY	DISSERTATING	DISSIPATING	DISSUNDERING
DISQUIETENING	DISSATISFYING	DISSERTATION	DISSIPATION	DISSUNDERS
DISQUIETENS	DISSAVINGS	DISSERTATIONAL	DISSIPATIONS	DISSYLLABIC
DISQUIETFUL	DISSEATING	DISSERTATIONIST	DISSIPATIVE	DISSYLLABIFIED
DISQUIETING	DISSECTIBLE	DISSERTATIONS	DISSIPATOR	DISSYLLABIFIES
DISQUIETINGLY	DISSECTING	DISSERTATIVE	DISSIPATORS	DISSYLLABIFY
DISQUIETIVE	DISSECTINGS	DISSERTATOR	DISSOCIABILITY	DISSYLLABIFYING
DISQUIETLY	DISSECTION	DISSERTATORS	DISSOCIABLE	DISSYLLABISM
DISQUIETNESS	DISSECTIONS	DISSERTING	DISSOCIABLENESS	DISSYLLABISMS
DISQUIETNESSES	DISSECTIVE	DISSERVICE	DISSOCIABLY	DISSYLLABLE
DISQUIETOUS	DISSECTORS	DISSERVICEABLE	DISSOCIALISE	DISSYLLABLES
DISQUIETUDE	DISSEISEES	DISSERVICES	DISSOCIALISED	DISSYMMETRIC
DISQUIETUDES	DISSEISING	DISSERVING	DISSOCIALISES	DISSYMMETRICAL
DISQUISITION	DISSEISINS	DISSEVERANCE	DISSOCIALISING	DISSYMMETRIES
DISQUISITIONAL	DISSEISORS	DISSEVERANCES	DISSOCIALITIES	DISSYMMETRY
DISQUISITIONARY	DISSEIZEES	DISSEVERATION	DISSOCIALITY	DISTAINING
DISQUISITIONS	DISSEIZING	DISSEVERATIONS	DISSOCIALIZE	DISTANCELESS
DISQUISITIVE	DISSEIZINS	DISSEVERED	DISSOCIALIZED	DISTANCING
DISQUISITORY	DISSEIZORS	DISSEVERING	DISSOCIALIZES	DISTANTNESS
DISRANKING	DISSELBOOM	DISSEVERMENT	DISSOCIALIZING	DISTANTNESSES
DISREGARDED	DISSELBOOMS	DISSEVERMENTS	DISSOCIATE	DISTASTEFUL
DISREGARDER	DISSEMBLANCE	DISSHEATHE	DISSOCIATED	DISTASTEFULLY
DISREGARDERS	DISSEMBLANCES	DISSHEATHED	DISSOCIATES	DISTASTEFULNESS
DISREGARDFUL	DISSEMBLED	DISSHEATHES	DISSOCIATING	DISTASTING
DISREGARDFULLY	DISSEMBLER	DISSHEATHING	DISSOCIATION	DISTELFINK
DISREGARDING	DISSEMBLERS	DISSHIVERED	DISSOCIATIONS	DISTELFINKS
DISREGARDS	DISSEMBLES	DISSHIVERING	DISSOCIATIVE	DISTEMPERATE
DISRELATED	DISSEMBLIES	DISSHIVERS	DISSOLUBILITIES	DISTEMPERATURE
DISRELATION	DISSEMBLING	DISSIDENCE	DISSOLUBILITY	DISTEMPERATURES

DISTEMPERED
DISTEMPERING
DISTEMPERS
DISTENDERS
DISTENDING
DISTENSIBILITY
DISTENSIBLE
DISTENSILE
DISTENSION
DISTENSIONS
DISTENSIVE
DISTENTION
DISTENTIONS
DISTHRONED
DISTHRONES
DISTHRONING
DISTHRONISE
DISTHRONISED
DISTHRONISES
DISTHRONISING
DISTHRONIZE
DISTHRONIZED
DISTHRONIZES
DISTHRONIZING
DISTICHOUS
DISTICHOUSLY
DISTILLABLE
DISTILLAND
DISTILLANDS
DISTILLATE
DISTILLATES
DISTILLATION
DISTILLATIONS
DISTILLATORY
DISTILLERIES
DISTILLERS
DISTILLERY
DISTILLING
DISTILLINGS
DISTILMENT
DISTILMENTS
DISTINCTER
DISTINCTEST
DISTINCTION
DISTINCTIONS
DISTINCTIVE
DISTINCTIVELY
DISTINCTIVENESS
DISTINCTIVES
DISTINCTLY
DISTINCTNESS
DISTINCTNESSES
DISTINCTURE
DISTINCTURES
DISTINGUEE
DISTINGUISH
DISTINGUISHABLE
DISTINGUISHABLY
DISTINGUISHED
DISTINGUISHER
DISTINGUISHERS
DISTINGUISHES
DISTINGUISHING
DISTINGUISHMENT
DISTORTEDLY
DISTORTEDNESS
DISTORTEDNESSES

DISTORTERS
DISTORTING
DISTORTION
DISTORTIONAL
DISTORTIONS
DISTORTIVE
DISTRACTABLE
DISTRACTED
DISTRACTEDLY
DISTRACTEDNESS
DISTRACTER
DISTRACTERS
DISTRACTIBILITY
DISTRACTIBLE
DISTRACTING
DISTRACTINGLY
DISTRACTION
DISTRACTIONS
DISTRACTIVE
DISTRACTIVELY
DISTRACTOR
DISTRACTORS
DISTRAINABLE
DISTRAINED
DISTRAINEE
DISTRAINEES
DISTRAINER
DISTRAINERS
DISTRAINING
DISTRAINMENT
DISTRAINMENTS
DISTRAINOR
DISTRAINORS
DISTRAINTS
DISTRAUGHT
DISTRAUGHTLY
DISTRESSED
DISTRESSER
DISTRESSERS
DISTRESSES
DISTRESSFUL
DISTRESSFULLY
DISTRESSFULNESS
DISTRESSING
DISTRESSINGLY
DISTRESSINGS
DISTRIBUEND
DISTRIBUENDS
DISTRIBUTABLE
DISTRIBUTARIES
DISTRIBUTARY
DISTRIBUTE
DISTRIBUTED
DISTRIBUTEE
DISTRIBUTEES
DISTRIBUTER
DISTRIBUTERS
DISTRIBUTES
DISTRIBUTING
DISTRIBUTION
DISTRIBUTIONAL
DISTRIBUTIONS
DISTRIBUTIVE
DISTRIBUTIVELY
DISTRIBUTIVES
DISTRIBUTIVITY
DISTRIBUTOR

DISTRIBUTORS
DISTRIBUTORSHIP
DISTRICTED
DISTRICTING
DISTRINGAS
DISTRINGASES
DISTROUBLE
DISTROUBLED
DISTROUBLES
DISTROUBLING
DISTRUSTED
DISTRUSTER
DISTRUSTERS
DISTRUSTFUL
DISTRUSTFULLY
DISTRUSTFULNESS
DISTRUSTING
DISTRUSTLESS
DISTURBANCE
DISTURBANCES
DISTURBANT
DISTURBANTS
DISTURBATIVE
DISTURBERS
DISTURBING
DISTURBINGLY
DISUBSTITUTED
DISULFATES
DISULFIDES
DISULFIRAM
DISULFIRAMS
DISULFOTON
DISULFOTONS
DISULPHATE
DISULPHATES
DISULPHIDE
DISULPHIDES
DISULPHURET
DISULPHURETS
DISULPHURIC
DISUNIONIST
DISUNIONISTS
DISUNITERS
DISUNITIES
DISUNITING
DISUTILITIES
DISUTILITY
DISVALUING
DISVOUCHED
DISVOUCHES
DISVOUCHING
DISWORSHIP
DISWORSHIPED
DISWORSHIPING
DISWORSHIPPED
DISWORSHIPPING
DISWORSHIPS
DISYLLABIC
DISYLLABIFIED
DISYLLABIFIES
DISYLLABIFY
DISYLLABIFYING
DISYLLABISM
DISYLLABISMS
DISYLLABLE
DISYLLABLES
DITCHDIGGER

DITCHDIGGERS
DITCHWATER
DITCHWATERS
DITHEISTIC
DITHEISTICAL
DITHELETES
DITHELETIC
DITHELETICAL
DITHELETISM
DITHELETISMS
DITHELISMS
DITHELITISM
DITHELITISMS
DITHERIEST
DITHERINGS
DITHIOCARBAMATE
DITHIOCARBAMIC
DITHIONATE
DITHIONATES
DITHIONITE
DITHIONITES
DITHIONOUS
DITHYRAMBIC
DITHYRAMBICALLY
DITHYRAMBIST
DITHYRAMBISTS
DITHYRAMBS
DITRANSITIVE
DITRANSITIVES
DITRIGLYPH
DITRIGLYPHIC
DITRIGLYPHS
DITROCHEAN
DITROCHEES
DITSINESSES
DITTANDERS
DITTOGRAPHIC
DITTOGRAPHIES
DITTOGRAPHY
DITTOLOGIES
DITZINESSES
DIURETICALLY
DIURETICALNESS
DIURNALIST
DIURNALISTS
DIUTURNITIES
DIUTURNITY
DIVAGATING
DIVAGATION
DIVAGATIONS
DIVALENCES
DIVALENCIES
DIVARICATE
DIVARICATED
DIVARICATELY
DIVARICATES
DIVARICATING
DIVARICATINGLY
DIVARICATION
DIVARICATIONS
DIVARICATOR
DIVARICATORS
DIVEBOMBED
DIVEBOMBING
DIVELLICATE
DIVELLICATED
DIVELLICATES

DIVELLICATING
DIVERGEMENT
DIVERGEMENTS
DIVERGENCE
DIVERGENCES
DIVERGENCIES
DIVERGENCY
DIVERGENTLY
DIVERGINGLY
DIVERSENESS
DIVERSENESSES
DIVERSIFIABLE
DIVERSIFICATION
DIVERSIFIED
DIVERSIFIER
DIVERSIFIERS
DIVERSIFIES
DIVERSIFORM
DIVERSIFYING
DIVERSIONAL
DIVERSIONARY
DIVERSIONIST
DIVERSIONISTS
DIVERSIONS
DIVERSITIES
DIVERTIBILITIES
DIVERTIBILITY
DIVERTIBLE
DIVERTICULA
DIVERTICULAR
DIVERTICULATE
DIVERTICULATED
DIVERTICULITIS
DIVERTICULOSES
DIVERTICULOSIS
DIVERTICULUM
DIVERTIMENTI
DIVERTIMENTO
DIVERTIMENTOS
DIVERTINGLY
DIVERTISEMENT
DIVERTISEMENTS
DIVERTISSEMENT
DIVERTISSEMENTS
DIVESTIBLE
DIVESTITURE
DIVESTITURES
DIVESTMENT
DIVESTMENTS
DIVESTURES
DIVIDEDNESS
DIVIDEDNESSES
DIVIDENDLESS
DIVINATION
DIVINATIONS
DIVINATORIAL
DIVINATORS
DIVINATORY
DIVINENESS
DIVINENESSES
DIVINERESS
DIVINERESSES
DIVINIFIED
DIVINIFIES
DIVINIFYING
DIVINISATION
DIVINISATIONS

DIVINISING	DOCTORATES	DODECAPHONISMS	DOLCELATTES	DOMESTICABLE
DIVINITIES	DOCTORATING	DODECAPHONIST	DOLCEMENTE	DOMESTICAL
DIVINIZATION	DOCTORESSES	DODECAPHONISTS	DOLEFULLER	DOMESTICALLY
DIVINIZATIONS	DOCTORINGS	DODECAPHONY	DOLEFULLEST	DOMESTICATE
DIVINIZING	DOCTORLESS	DODECASTYLE	DOLEFULNESS	DOMESTICATED
DIVISIBILITIES	DOCTORSHIP	DODECASTYLES	DOLEFULNESSES	DOMESTICATES
DIVISIBILITY	DOCTORSHIPS	DODECASYLLABIC	DOLESOMELY	DOMESTICATING
DIVISIBLENESS	DOCTRESSES	DODECASYLLABLE	DOLICHOCEPHAL	DOMESTICATION
DIVISIBLENESSES	DOCTRINAIRE	DODECASYLLABLES	DOLICHOCEPHALIC	DOMESTICATIONS
DIVISIONAL	DOCTRINAIRES	DODGEBALLS	DOLICHOCEPHALS	DOMESTICATIVE
DIVISIONALLY	DOCTRINAIRISM	DODGINESSES	DOLICHOCEPHALY	DOMESTICATOR
DIVISIONARY	DOCTRINAIRISMS	DOGARESSAS	DOLICHOSAURUS	DOMESTICATORS
DIVISIONISM	DOCTRINALITIES	DOGBERRIES	DOLICHOSAURUSES	DOMESTICISE
DIVISIONISMS	DOCTRINALITY	DOGBERRYISM	DOLICHOSES	DOMESTICISED
DIVISIONIST	DOCTRINALLY	DOGBERRYISMS	DOLICHURUS	DOMESTICISES
DIVISIONISTS	DOCTRINARIAN	DOGCATCHER	DOLICHURUSES	DOMESTICISING
DIVISIVELY	DOCTRINARIANISM	DOGCATCHERS	DOLLARBIRD	DOMESTICITIES
DIVISIVENESS	DOCTRINARIANS	DOGFIGHTING	DOLLARBIRDS	DOMESTICITY
DIVISIVENESSES	DOCTRINARISM	DOGFIGHTINGS	DOLLARFISH	DOMESTICIZE
DIVORCEABLE	DOCTRINARISMS	DOGGEDNESS	DOLLARFISHES	DOMESTICIZED
DIVORCEMENT	DOCTRINISM	DOGGEDNESSES	DOLLARISATION	DOMESTICIZES
DIVORCEMENTS	DOCTRINISMS	DOGGINESSES	DOLLARISATIONS	DOMESTICIZING
DIVULGATED	DOCTRINIST	DOGGISHNESS	DOLLARISED	DOMESTIQUE
DIVULGATER	DOCTRINISTS	DOGGISHNESSES	DOLLARISES	DOMESTIQUES
DIVULGATERS	DOCUDRAMAS	DOGGONEDER	DOLLARISING	DOMICILIARY
DIVULGATES	DOCUMENTABLE	DOGGONEDEST	DOLLARIZATION	DOMICILIATE
DIVULGATING	DOCUMENTAL	DOGLEGGING	DOLLARIZATIONS	DOMICILIATED
DIVULGATION	DOCUMENTALIST	DOGMATICAL	DOLLARIZED	DOMICILIATES
DIVULGATIONS	DOCUMENTALISTS	DOGMATICALLY	DOLLARIZES	DOMICILIATING
DIVULGATOR	DOCUMENTARIAN	DOGMATICALNESS	DOLLARIZING	DOMICILIATION
DIVULGATORS	DOCUMENTARIANS	DOGMATISATION	DOLLARLESS	DOMICILIATIONS
DIVULGEMENT	DOCUMENTARIES	DOGMATISATIONS	DOLLAROCRACIES	DOMICILING
DIVULGEMENTS	DOCUMENTARILY	DOGMATISED	DOLLAROCRACY	DOMINANCES
DIVULGENCE	DOCUMENTARISE	DOGMATISER	DOLLARSHIP	DOMINANCIES
DIVULGENCES	DOCUMENTARISED	DOGMATISERS	DOLLARSHIPS	DOMINANTLY
DIVULSIONS	DOCUMENTARISES	DOGMATISES	DOLLHOUSES	DOMINATING
DIZENMENTS	DOCUMENTARISING	DOGMATISING	DOLLINESSES	DOMINATINGLY
DIZZINESSES	DOCUMENTARIST	DOGMATISMS	DOLLISHNESS	DOMINATION
DIZZYINGLY	DOCUMENTARISTS	DOGMATISTS	DOLLISHNESSES	DOMINATIONS
DJELLABAHS	DOCUMENTARIZE	DOGMATIZATION	DOLLYBIRDS	DOMINATIVE
DOBSONFLIES	DOCUMENTARIZED	DOGMATIZATIONS	DOLOMITISATION	DOMINATORS
DOCENTSHIP	DOCUMENTARIZES	DOGMATIZED	DOLOMITISATIONS	DOMINATRICES
DOCENTSHIPS	DOCUMENTARIZING	DOGMATIZER	DOLOMITISE	DOMINATRIX
DOCHMIACAL	DOCUMENTARY	DOGMATIZERS	DOLOMITISED	DOMINATRIXES
DOCHMIUSES	DOCUMENTATION	DOGMATIZES	DOLOMITISES	DOMINEERED
DOCIBILITIES	DOCUMENTATIONAL	DOGMATIZING	DOLOMITISING	DOMINEERING
DOCIBILITY	DOCUMENTATIONS	DOGMATOLOGIES	DOLOMITIZATION	DOMINEERINGLY
DOCIBLENESS	DOCUMENTED	DOGMATOLOGY	DOLOMITIZATIONS	DOMINEERINGNESS
DOCIBLENESSES	DOCUMENTER	DOGNAPINGS	DOLOMITIZE	DOMINICKER
DOCILITIES	DOCUMENTERS	DOGNAPPERS	DOLOMITIZED	DOMINICKERS
DOCIMASIES	DOCUMENTING	DOGNAPPING	DOLOMITIZES	DOMINIQUES
DOCIMASTIC	DODDERIEST	DOGNAPPINGS	DOLOMITIZING	DONATARIES
DOCIMOLOGIES	DODDIPOLLS	DOGROBBERS	DOLORIFEROUS	DONATISTIC
DOCIMOLOGY	DODDYPOLLS	DOGSBODIED	DOLORIMETRIES	DONATISTICAL
DOCKISATION	DODECAGONAL	DOGSBODIES	DOLORIMETRY	DONATORIES
DOCKISATIONS	DODECAGONS	DOGSBODYING	DOLOROUSLY	DONENESSES
DOCKIZATION	DODECAGYNIAN	DOGSBODYINGS	DOLOROUSNESS	DONEPEZILS
DOCKIZATIONS	DODECAGYNOUS	DOGSLEDDED	DOLOROUSNESSES	DONKEYWORK
DOCKMASTER	DODECAHEDRA	DOGSLEDDER	DOLOSTONES	DONKEYWORKS
DOCKMASTERS	DODECAHEDRAL	DOGSLEDDERS	DOLPHINARIA	DONNICKERS
DOCKWALLOPER	DODECAHEDRON	DOGSLEDDING	DOLPHINARIUM	DONNISHNESS
DOCKWALLOPERS	DODECAHEDRONS	DOGSLEDDINGS	DOLPHINARIUMS	DONNISHNESSES
DOCKWORKER	DODECANDROUS	DOGTROTTED	DOLPHINETS	DONNYBROOK
DOCKWORKERS	DODECANOIC	DOGTROTTING	DOLPHINFISH	DONNYBROOKS
DOCQUETING	DODECAPHONIC	DOGWATCHES	DOLPHINFISHES	DONORSHIPS
DOCTORANDS	DODECAPHONIES	DOLABRIFORM	DOLTISHNESS	DOODLEBUGS
DOCTORATED	DODECAPHONISM	DOLCELATTE	DOLTISHNESSES	DOOHICKEYS

d

DOOHICKIES	DOSIMETRIST	DOWNFALLEN	DOWNWASHES	DRAINLAYER
DOOMSAYERS	DOSIMETRISTS	DOWNFORCES	DOWNZONING	DRAINLAYERS
DOOMSAYING	DOSIOLOGIES	DOWNGRADED	DOXOGRAPHER	DRAINPIPES
DOOMSAYINGS	DOSOLOGIES	DOWNGRADES	DOXOGRAPHERS	DRAKESTONE
DOOMSDAYER	DOSSHOUSES	DOWNGRADING	DOXOGRAPHIC	DRAKESTONES
DOOMSDAYERS	DOTARDLIER	DOWNHEARTED	DOXOGRAPHIES	DRAMATICAL
DOOMWATCHED	DOTARDLIEST	DOWNHEARTEDLY	DOXOGRAPHY	DRAMATICALLY
DOOMWATCHER	DOTCOMMERS	DOWNHEARTEDNESS	DOXOLOGICAL	DRAMATICISM
DOOMWATCHERS	DOTTINESSES	DOWNHILLER	DOXOLOGICALLY	DRAMATICISMS
DOOMWATCHES	DOUBLEHEADER	DOWNHILLERS	DOXOLOGIES	DRAMATISABLE
DOOMWATCHING	DOUBLEHEADERS	DOWNINESSES	DOXORUBICIN	DRAMATISATION
DOOMWATCHINGS	DOUBLENESS	DOWNLIGHTER	DOXORUBICINS	DRAMATISATIONS
DOORFRAMES	DOUBLENESSES	DOWNLIGHTERS	DOXYCYCLINE	DRAMATISED
DOORKEEPER	DOUBLESPEAK	DOWNLIGHTS	DOXYCYCLINES	DRAMATISER
DOORKEEPERS	DOUBLESPEAKER	DOWNLINKED	DOZINESSES	DRAMATISERS
DOORKNOCKED	DOUBLESPEAKERS	DOWNLINKING	DRABBINESS	DRAMATISES
DOORKNOCKER	DOUBLESPEAKS	DOWNLOADABLE	DRABBINESSES	DRAMATISING
DOORKNOCKERS	DOUBLETHINK	DOWNLOADED	DRABBLINGS	DRAMATISTS
DOORKNOCKING	DOUBLETHINKS	DOWNLOADING	DRABNESSES	DRAMATIZABLE
DOORKNOCKS	DOUBLETONS	DOWNLOADINGS	DRACONIANISM	DRAMATIZATION
DOORNBOOMS	DOUBLETREE	DOWNLOOKED	DRACONIANISMS	DRAMATIZATIONS
DOORPLATES	DOUBLETREES	DOWNPLAYED	DRACONICALLY	DRAMATIZED
DOORSTEPPED	DOUBTFULLY	DOWNPLAYING	DRACONISMS	DRAMATIZER
DOORSTEPPER	DOUBTFULNESS	DOWNRATING	DRACONITES	DRAMATIZERS
DOORSTEPPERS	DOUBTFULNESSES	DOWNREGULATION	DRACONTIASES	DRAMATIZES
DOORSTEPPING	DOUBTINGLY	DOWNREGULATIONS	DRACONTIASIS	DRAMATIZING
DOORSTEPPINGS	DOUBTLESSLY	DOWNRIGHTLY	DRACUNCULIASES	DRAMATURGE
DOORSTONES	DOUBTLESSNESS	DOWNRIGHTNESS	DRACUNCULIASIS	DRAMATURGES
DOPAMINERGIC	DOUBTLESSNESSES	DOWNRIGHTNESSES	DRACUNCULUS	DRAMATURGIC
DOPESHEETS	DOUCENESSES	DOWNRUSHES	DRACUNCULUSES	DRAMATURGICAL
DOPEYNESSES	DOUCEPERES	DOWNSCALED	DRAFTINESS	DRAMATURGICALLY
DOPINESSES	DOUCHEBAGS	DOWNSCALES	DRAFTINESSES	DRAMATURGIES
DOPPELGANGER	DOUGHBALLS	DOWNSCALING	DRAFTSMANSHIP	DRAMATURGIST
DOPPELGANGERS	DOUGHFACED	DOWNSHIFTED	DRAFTSMANSHIPS	DRAMATURGISTS
DOPPLERITE	DOUGHFACES	DOWNSHIFTER	DRAFTSPERSON	DRAMATURGS
DOPPLERITES	DOUGHINESS	DOWNSHIFTERS	DRAFTSPERSONS	DRAMATURGY
DORBEETLES	DOUGHINESSES	DOWNSHIFTING	DRAFTSWOMAN	DRAPABILITIES
DORKINESSES	DOUGHNUTLIKE	DOWNSHIFTINGS	DRAFTSWOMEN	DRAPABILITY
DORMANCIES	DOUGHNUTTED	DOWNSHIFTS	DRAGGINGLY	DRAPEABILITIES
DORMITIONS	DOUGHNUTTING	DOWNSIZERS	DRAGGLETAILED	DRAPEABILITY
DORMITIVES	DOUGHNUTTINGS	DOWNSIZING	DRAGHOUNDS	DRAPERYING
DORMITORIES	DOUGHTIEST	DOWNSIZINGS	DRAGONESSES	DRASTICALLY
DORONICUMS	DOUGHTINESS	DOWNSLIDES	DRAGONFLIES	DRATCHELLS
DORSIBRANCHIATE	DOUGHTINESSES	DOWNSLOPES	DRAGONHEAD	DRAUGHTBOARD
DORSIFEROUS	DOULOCRACIES	DOWNSPOUTS	DRAGONHEADS	DRAUGHTBOARDS
DORSIFIXED	DOULOCRACY	DOWNSTAGES	DRAGONISED	DRAUGHTERS
DORSIFLEXED	DOUPPIONIS	DOWNSTAIRS	DRAGONISES	DRAUGHTIER
DORSIFLEXES	DOURNESSES	DOWNSTAIRSES	DRAGONISING	DRAUGHTIEST
DORSIFLEXING	DOUROUCOULI	DOWNSTATER	DRAGONISMS	DRAUGHTILY
DORSIFLEXION	DOUROUCOULIS	DOWNSTATERS	DRAGONIZED	DRAUGHTINESS
DORSIFLEXIONS	DOVEISHNESS	DOWNSTATES	DRAGONIZES	DRAUGHTINESSES
DORSIGRADE	DOVEISHNESSES	DOWNSTREAM	DRAGONIZING	DRAUGHTING
DORSIVENTRAL	DOVETAILED	DOWNSTROKE	DRAGONLIKE	DRAUGHTMAN
DORSIVENTRALITY	DOVETAILING	DOWNSTROKES	DRAGONNADE	DRAUGHTMEN
DORSIVENTRALLY	DOVETAILINGS	DOWNSWINGS	DRAGONNADED	DRAUGHTPROOF
DORSOLATERAL	DOVISHNESS	DOWNTHROWS	DRAGONNADES	DRAUGHTPROOFED
DORSOLUMBAR	DOVISHNESSES	DOWNTOWNER	DRAGONNADING	DRAUGHTPROOFING
DORSOVENTRAL	DOWDINESSES	DOWNTOWNERS	DRAGONROOT	DRAUGHTPROOFS
DORSOVENTRALITY	DOWELLINGS	DOWNTRENDED	DRAGONROOTS	DRAUGHTSMAN
DORSOVENTRALLY	DOWFNESSES	DOWNTRENDING	DRAGOONAGE	DRAUGHTSMANSHIP
DORTINESSES	DOWITCHERS	DOWNTRENDS	DRAGOONAGES	DRAUGHTSMEN
DOSEMETERS	DOWNBURSTS	DOWNTRODDEN	DRAGOONING	DRAUGHTSPERSON
DOSIMETERS	DOWNCOMERS	DOWNTURNED	DRAGSTRIPS	DRAUGHTSPERSONS
DOSIMETRIC	DOWNCRYING	DOWNVOTING	DRAGSVILLE	DRAUGHTSWOMAN
DOSIMETRICIAN	DOWNDRAFTS	DOWNWARDLY	DRAGSVILLES	DRAUGHTSWOMEN
DOSIMETRICIANS	DOWNDRAUGHT	DOWNWARDNESS	DRAINBOARD	DRAWBRIDGE
DOSIMETRIES	DOWNDRAUGHTS	DOWNWARDNESSES	DRAINBOARDS	DRAWBRIDGES

DRAWERFULS
DRAWKNIVES
DRAWLINGLY
DRAWLINGNESS
DRAWLINGNESSES
DRAWNWORKS
DRAWPLATES
DRAWSHAVES
DRAWSTRING
DRAWSTRINGS
DRAYHORSES
DREADFULLY
DREADFULNESS
DREADFULNESSES
DREADLESSLY
DREADLESSNESS
DREADLESSNESSES
DREADLOCKED
DREADLOCKS
DREADNAUGHT
DREADNAUGHTS
DREADNOUGHT
DREADNOUGHTS
DREAMBOATS
DREAMERIES
DREAMFULLY
DREAMFULNESS
DREAMFULNESSES
DREAMHOLES
DREAMINESS
DREAMINESSES
DREAMINGLY
DREAMLANDS
DREAMLESSLY
DREAMLESSNESS
DREAMLESSNESSES
DREAMTIMES
DREAMWHILE
DREAMWHILES
DREAMWORLD
DREAMWORLDS
DREARIHEAD
DREARIHEADS
DREARIHOOD
DREARIHOODS
DREARIMENT
DREARIMENTS
DREARINESS
DREARINESSES
DREARISOME
DRECKSILLS
DREGGINESS
DREGGINESSES
DREIKANTER
DREIKANTERS
DRENCHINGS
DREPANIUMS
DRERIHEADS
DRESSGUARD
DRESSGUARDS
DRESSINESS
DRESSINESSES
DRESSMAKER
DRESSMAKERS
DRESSMAKES
DRESSMAKING
DRESSMAKINGS

DRIBBLIEST
DRIBBLINGS
DRICKSIEST
DRIFTINGLY
DRIFTWOODS
DRILLABILITIES
DRILLABILITY
DRILLHOLES
DRILLMASTER
DRILLMASTERS
DRILLSHIPS
DRILLSTOCK
DRILLSTOCKS
DRINKABILITIES
DRINKABILITY
DRINKABLENESS
DRINKABLENESSES
DRINKABLES
DRIPSTONES
DRIVABILITIES
DRIVABILITY
DRIVEABILITIES
DRIVEABILITY
DRIVELINES
DRIVELLERS
DRIVELLING
DRIVENNESS
DRIVENNESSES
DRIVERLESS
DRIVESHAFT
DRIVESHAFTS
DRIVETHROUGH
DRIVETHROUGHS
DRIVETRAIN
DRIVETRAINS
DRIZZLIEST
DRIZZLINGLY
DROICHIEST
DROLLERIES
DROLLNESSES
DROMEDARES
DROMEDARIES
DROMOPHOBIA
DROMOPHOBIAS
DRONISHNESS
DRONISHNESSES
DRONKVERDRIET
DROOLWORTHIER
DROOLWORTHIEST
DROOLWORTHY
DROOPINESS
DROOPINESSES
DROOPINGLY
DROPCLOTHS
DROPFORGED
DROPFORGES
DROPFORGING
DROPKICKER
DROPKICKERS
DROPLIGHTS
DROPPERFUL
DROPPERFULS
DROPPERSFUL
DROPSICALLY
DROPSONDES
DROPSTONES
DROSERACEOUS

DROSOMETER
DROSOMETERS
DROSOPHILA
DROSOPHILAE
DROSOPHILAS
DROSSINESS
DROSSINESSES
DROUGHTIER
DROUGHTIEST
DROUGHTINESS
DROUGHTINESSES
DROUTHIEST
DROUTHINESS
DROUTHINESSES
DROWSIHEAD
DROWSIHEADS
DROWSIHEDS
DROWSINESS
DROWSINESSES
DRUCKENNESS
DRUCKENNESSES
DRUDGERIES
DRUDGINGLY
DRUGMAKERS
DRUGSTORES
DRUIDESSES
DRUMBEATER
DRUMBEATERS
DRUMBEATING
DRUMBEATINGS
DRUMBLEDOR
DRUMBLEDORS
DRUMBLEDRANE
DRUMBLEDRANES
DRUMFISHES
DRUMSTICKS
DRUNKALOGUE
DRUNKALOGUES
DRUNKATHON
DRUNKATHONS
DRUNKENNESS
DRUNKENNESSES
DRUNKOMETER
DRUNKOMETERS
DRUPACEOUS
DRYASDUSTS
DRYBEATING
DRYOPITHECINE
DRYOPITHECINES
DRYSALTERIES
DRYSALTERS
DRYSALTERY
DRYWALLERS
DRYWALLING
DRYWALLINGS
DUALISTICALLY
DUATHLETES
DUBIOSITIES
DUBIOUSNESS
DUBIOUSNESSES
DUBITANCIES
DUBITATING
DUBITATION
DUBITATIONS
DUBITATIVE
DUBITATIVELY
DUCHESSING

DUCKBOARDS
DUCKSHOVED
DUCKSHOVER
DUCKSHOVERS
DUCKSHOVES
DUCKSHOVING
DUCKSHOVINGS
DUCKWALKED
DUCKWALKING
DUCTILENESS
DUCTILENESSES
DUCTILITIES
DUDENESSES
DUENNASHIP
DUENNASHIPS
DUFFERDOMS
DUFFERISMS
DUIKERBOKS
DUKKERIPEN
DUKKERIPENS
DULCAMARAS
DULCETNESS
DULCETNESSES
DULCIFICATION
DULCIFICATIONS
DULCIFLUOUS
DULCIFYING
DULCILOQUIES
DULCILOQUY
DULCIMORES
DULCITUDES
DULLNESSES
DULLSVILLE
DULLSVILLES
DULOCRACIES
DUMBFOUNDED
DUMBFOUNDER
DUMBFOUNDERED
DUMBFOUNDERING
DUMBFOUNDERS
DUMBFOUNDING
DUMBFOUNDS
DUMBLEDORE
DUMBLEDORES
DUMBNESSES
DUMBSIZING
DUMBSTRICKEN
DUMBSTRUCK
DUMBWAITER
DUMBWAITERS
DUMFOUNDED
DUMFOUNDER
DUMFOUNDERED
DUMFOUNDERING
DUMFOUNDERS
DUMFOUNDING
DUMMELHEAD
DUMMELHEADS
DUMMINESSES
DUMORTIERITE
DUMORTIERITES
DUMOSITIES
DUMPINESSES
DUMPISHNESS
DUMPISHNESSES
DUMPTRUCKS
DUNDERFUNK

DUNDERFUNKS
DUNDERHEAD
DUNDERHEADED
DUNDERHEADISM
DUNDERHEADISMS
DUNDERHEADS
DUNDERPATE
DUNDERPATES
DUNDREARIES
DUNGEONERS
DUNGEONING
DUNIEWASSAL
DUNIEWASSALS
DUNIWASSAL
DUNIWASSALS
DUNNIEWASSAL
DUNNIEWASSALS
DUNNIEWASSAL
DUNNIEWASSALS
DUODECENNIAL
DUODECILLION
DUODECILLIONS
DUODECIMAL
DUODECIMALLY
DUODECIMALS
DUODECIMOS
DUODENECTOMIES
DUODENECTOMY
DUODENITIS
DUODENITISES
DUOPOLISTIC
DUOPOLISTS
DUOPSONIES
DUPABILITIES
DUPABILITY
DUPLEXINGS
DUPLEXITIES
DUPLICABILITIES
DUPLICABILITY
DUPLICABLE
DUPLICANDS
DUPLICATED
DUPLICATELY
DUPLICATES
DUPLICATING
DUPLICATION
DUPLICATIONS
DUPLICATIVE
DUPLICATOR
DUPLICATORS
DUPLICATURE
DUPLICATURES
DUPLICIDENT
DUPLICITIES
DUPLICITOUS
DUPLICITOUSLY
DURABILITIES
DURABILITY
DURABLENESS
DURABLENESSES
DURALUMINIUM
DURALUMINIUMS
DURALUMINS
DURATIONAL
DURCHKOMPONIERT
DURCHKOMPONIRT
DURICRUSTS
DUROMETERS
DUSKINESSES

DUSKISHNESS
DUSKISHNESSES
DUSKNESSES
DUSTCLOTHS
DUSTCOVERS
DUSTINESSES
DUSTSHEETS
DUSTSTORMS
DUTEOUSNESS
DUTEOUSNESSES
DUTIABILITIES
DUTIABILITY
DUTIFULNESS
DUTIFULNESSES
DUUMVIRATE
DUUMVIRATES
DWARFISHLY
DWARFISHNESS
DWARFISHNESSES
DWARFNESSES
DWINDLEMENT
DWINDLEMENTS
DYADICALLY
DYARCHICAL
DYEABILITIES
DYEABILITY
DYINGNESSES
DYNAMETERS
DYNAMICALLY
DYNAMICIST
DYNAMICISTS
DYNAMISING
DYNAMISTIC

DYNAMITARD
DYNAMITARDS
DYNAMITERS
DYNAMITING
DYNAMIZING
DYNAMOELECTRIC
DYNAMOGENESES
DYNAMOGENESIS
DYNAMOGENIES
DYNAMOGENY
DYNAMOGRAPH
DYNAMOGRAPHS
DYNAMOMETER
DYNAMOMETERS
DYNAMOMETRIC
DYNAMOMETRICAL
DYNAMOMETRIES
DYNAMOMETRY
DYNAMOTORS
DYNASTICAL
DYNASTICALLY
DYNASTICISM
DYNASTICISMS
DYNORPHINS
DYOPHYSITE
DYOPHYSITES
DYOTHELETE
DYOTHELETES
DYOTHELETIC
DYOTHELETICAL
DYOTHELETISM
DYOTHELETISMS
DYOTHELISM

DYOTHELISMS
DYOTHELITE
DYOTHELITES
DYOTHELITIC
DYOTHELITICAL
DYSAESTHESIA
DYSAESTHESIAS
DYSAESTHETIC
DYSARTHRIA
DYSARTHRIAS
DYSBINDINS
DYSCALCULIA
DYSCALCULIAS
DYSCHROIAS
DYSCRASIAS
DYSCRASITE
DYSCRASITES
DYSENTERIC
DYSENTERIES
DYSFUNCTION
DYSFUNCTIONAL
DYSFUNCTIONS
DYSGENESES
DYSGENESIS
DYSGRAPHIA
DYSGRAPHIAS
DYSGRAPHIC
DYSGRAPHICS
DYSHARMONIC
DYSKINESIA
DYSKINESIAS
DYSKINETIC
DYSLECTICS

DYSLOGISTIC
DYSLOGISTICALLY
DYSMENORRHEA
DYSMENORRHEAL
DYSMENORRHEAS
DYSMENORRHEIC
DYSMENORRHOEA
DYSMENORRHOEAL
DYSMENORRHOEAS
DYSMENORRHOEIC
DYSMORPHIC
DYSMORPHOPHOBIA
DYSMORPHOPHOBIC
DYSPAREUNIA
DYSPAREUNIAS
DYSPATHETIC
DYSPATHIES
DYSPEPSIAS
DYSPEPSIES
DYSPEPTICAL
DYSPEPTICALLY
DYSPEPTICS
DYSPHAGIAS
DYSPHAGIES
DYSPHASIAS
DYSPHASICS
DYSPHEMISM
DYSPHEMISMS
DYSPHEMISTIC
DYSPHONIAS
DYSPHORIAS
DYSPLASIAS
DYSPLASTIC

DYSPRACTIC
DYSPRAXIAS
DYSPROSIUM
DYSPROSIUMS
DYSRHYTHMIA
DYSRHYTHMIAS
DYSRHYTHMIC
DYSRHYTHMICS
DYSSYNERGIA
DYSSYNERGIAS
DYSSYNERGIC
DYSSYNERGIES
DYSSYNERGY
DYSTELEOLOGICAL
DYSTELEOLOGIES
DYSTELEOLOGIST
DYSTELEOLOGISTS
DYSTELEOLOGY
DYSTHESIAS
DYSTHYMIAC
DYSTHYMIACS
DYSTHYMIAS
DYSTHYMICS
DYSTOPIANS
DYSTROPHIA
DYSTROPHIAS
DYSTROPHIC
DYSTROPHIES
DYSTROPHIN
DYSTROPHINS
DZIGGETAIS

E

EAGERNESSES
EAGLEHAWKS
EAGLESTONE
EAGLESTONES
EAGLEWOODS
EARBASHERS
EARBASHING
EARBASHINGS
EARLIERISE
EARLIERISED
EARLIERISES
EARLIERISING
EARLIERIZE
EARLIERIZED
EARLIERIZES
EARLIERIZING
EARLINESSES
EARLYWOODS
EARMARKING
EARNESTNESS
EARNESTNESSES
EARSPLITTING
EARTHBOUND
EARTHENWARE
EARTHENWARES
EARTHFALLS
EARTHFLAXES
EARTHINESS
EARTHINESSES
EARTHLIEST
EARTHLIGHT
EARTHLIGHTS
EARTHLINESS
EARTHLINESSES
EARTHLINGS
EARTHMOVER
EARTHMOVERS
EARTHMOVING
EARTHMOVINGS
EARTHQUAKE
EARTHQUAKED
EARTHQUAKES
EARTHQUAKING
EARTHRISES
EARTHSHAKER
EARTHSHAKERS
EARTHSHAKING
EARTHSHAKINGLY
EARTHSHATTERING
EARTHSHINE
EARTHSHINES
EARTHSTARS
EARTHWARDS
EARTHWAXES

EARTHWOLVES
EARTHWOMAN
EARTHWOMEN
EARTHWORKS
EARTHWORMS
EARWIGGIER
EARWIGGIEST
EARWIGGING
EARWIGGINGS
EARWITNESS
EARWITNESSES
EASEFULNESS
EASEFULNESSES
EASINESSES
EASSELGATE
EASSELWARD
EASTERLIES
EASTERLING
EASTERLINGS
EASTERMOST
EASTERNERS
EASTERNMOST
EASTWARDLY
EASYGOINGNESS
EASYGOINGNESSES
EAVESDRIPS
EAVESDROPPED
EAVESDROPPER
EAVESDROPPERS
EAVESDROPPING
EAVESDROPPINGS
EAVESDROPS
EAVESTROUGH
EAVESTROUGHS
EBIONISING
EBIONITISM
EBIONITISMS
EBIONIZING
EBOULEMENT
EBOULEMENTS
EBRACTEATE
EBRACTEOLATE
EBRILLADES
EBRIOSITIES
EBULLIENCE
EBULLIENCES
EBULLIENCIES
EBULLIENCY
EBULLIENTLY
EBULLIOMETER
EBULLIOMETERS
EBULLIOMETRIES
EBULLIOMETRY
EBULLIOSCOPE

EBULLIOSCOPES
EBULLIOSCOPIC
EBULLIOSCOPICAL
EBULLIOSCOPIES
EBULLIOSCOPY
EBULLITION
EBULLITIONS
EBURNATION
EBURNATIONS
EBURNIFICATION
EBURNIFICATIONS
ECARDINATE
ECBLASTESES
ECBLASTESIS
ECCALEOBION
ECCALEOBIONS
ECCENTRICAL
ECCENTRICALLY
ECCENTRICITIES
ECCENTRICITY
ECCENTRICS
ECCHYMOSED
ECCHYMOSES
ECCHYMOSIS
ECCHYMOTIC
ECCLESIARCH
ECCLESIARCHS
ECCLESIAST
ECCLESIASTIC
ECCLESIASTICAL
ECCLESIASTICISM
ECCLESIASTICS
ECCLESIASTS
ECCLESIOLATER
ECCLESIOLATERS
ECCLESIOLATRIES
ECCLESIOLATRY
ECCLESIOLOGICAL
ECCLESIOLOGIES
ECCLESIOLOGIST
ECCLESIOLOGISTS
ECCLESIOLOGY
ECCOPROTIC
ECCOPROTICS
ECCREMOCARPUS
ECCREMOCARPUSES
ECCRINOLOGIES
ECCRINOLOGY
ECDYSIASTS
ECHELONING
ECHEVERIAS
ECHIDNINES
ECHINACEAS
ECHINOCOCCI

ECHINOCOCCOSES
ECHINOCOCCOSIS
ECHINOCOCCUS
ECHINODERM
ECHINODERMAL
ECHINODERMATOUS
ECHINODERMS
ECHIUROIDS
ECHOCARDIOGRAM
ECHOCARDIOGRAMS
ECHOGRAPHIES
ECHOGRAPHS
ECHOGRAPHY
ECHOICALLY
ECHOLALIAS
ECHOLOCATION
ECHOLOCATIONS
ECHOPRAXES
ECHOPRAXIA
ECHOPRAXIAS
ECHOPRAXIS
ECHOVIRUSES
ECLAIRCISSEMENT
ECLAMPSIAS
ECLAMPSIES
ECLECTICALLY
ECLECTICISM
ECLECTICISMS
ECLIPSISES
ECLIPTICALLY
ECOCATASTROPHE
ECOCATASTROPHES
ECOCENTRIC
ECOCLIMATE
ECOCLIMATES
ECOFEMINISM
ECOFEMINISMS
ECOFEMINIST
ECOFEMINISTS
ECOFRIENDLIER
ECOFRIENDLIEST
ECOFRIENDLY
ECOLOGICAL
ECOLOGICALLY
ECOLOGISTS
ECOMMERCES
ECOMOVEMENT
ECOMOVEMENTS
ECOMUSEUMS
ECONOBOXES
ECONOMETER
ECONOMETERS
ECONOMETRIC
ECONOMETRICAL

ECONOMETRICALLY
ECONOMETRICIAN
ECONOMETRICIANS
ECONOMETRICS
ECONOMETRIST
ECONOMETRISTS
ECONOMICAL
ECONOMICALLY
ECONOMISATION
ECONOMISATIONS
ECONOMISED
ECONOMISER
ECONOMISERS
ECONOMISES
ECONOMISING
ECONOMISMS
ECONOMISTIC
ECONOMISTS
ECONOMIZATION
ECONOMIZATIONS
ECONOMIZED
ECONOMIZER
ECONOMIZERS
ECONOMIZES
ECONOMIZING
ECOPHOBIAS
ECOPHYSIOLOGIES
ECOPHYSIOLOGY
ECOREGIONS
ECOSPECIES
ECOSPECIFIC
ECOSPHERES
ECOSSAISES
ECOSYSTEMS
ECOTARIANISM
ECOTARIANISMS
ECOTARIANS
ECOTECTURE
ECOTECTURES
ECOTERRORISM
ECOTERRORISMS
ECOTERRORIST
ECOTERRORISTS
ECOTOURING
ECOTOURISM
ECOTOURISMS
ECOTOURIST
ECOTOURISTS
ECOTOXICOLOGIES
ECOTOXICOLOGIST
ECOTOXICOLOGY
ECOTYPICALLY
ECPHONESES
ECPHONESIS

ECPHRACTIC
ECPHRACTICS
ECRITOIRES
ECSTASISED
ECSTASISES
ECSTASISING
ECSTASIZED
ECSTASIZES
ECSTASIZING
ECSTASYING
ECSTATICALLY
ECTHLIPSES
ECTHLIPSIS
ECTOBLASTIC
ECTOBLASTS
ECTOCRINES
ECTODERMAL
ECTODERMIC
ECTOENZYME
ECTOENZYMES
ECTOGENESES
ECTOGENESIS
ECTOGENETIC
ECTOGENICALLY
ECTOGENIES
ECTOGENOUS
ECTOMORPHIC
ECTOMORPHIES
ECTOMORPHS
ECTOMORPHY
ECTOMYCORRHIZA
ECTOMYCORRHIZAE
ECTOMYCORRHIZAS
ECTOPARASITE
ECTOPARASITES
ECTOPARASITIC
ECTOPHYTES
ECTOPHYTIC
ECTOPICALLY
ECTOPLASMIC
ECTOPLASMS
ECTOPLASTIC
ECTOPROCTS
ECTOSARCOUS
ECTOTHERMIC
ECTOTHERMS
ECTOTROPHIC
ECTROPIONS
ECTROPIUMS
ECTYPOGRAPHIES
ECTYPOGRAPHY
ECUMENICAL
ECUMENICALISM
ECUMENICALISMS
ECUMENICALLY
ECUMENICISM
ECUMENICISMS
ECUMENICIST
ECUMENICISTS
ECUMENICITIES
ECUMENICITY
ECUMENISMS
ECUMENISTS
ECZEMATOUS
EDACIOUSLY
EDACIOUSNESS
EDACIOUSNESSES

EDAPHICALLY
EDAPHOLOGIES
EDAPHOLOGY
EDELWEISSES
EDENTULATE
EDENTULOUS
EDGINESSES
EDIBILITIES
EDIBLENESS
EDIBLENESSES
EDIFICATION
EDIFICATIONS
EDIFICATORY
EDIFYINGLY
EDITIONING
EDITORIALISE
EDITORIALISED
EDITORIALISER
EDITORIALISERS
EDITORIALISES
EDITORIALISING
EDITORIALIST
EDITORIALISTS
EDITORIALIZE
EDITORIALIZED
EDITORIALIZER
EDITORIALIZERS
EDITORIALIZES
EDITORIALIZING
EDITORIALLY
EDITORIALS
EDITORSHIP
EDITORSHIPS
EDITRESSES
EDRIOPHTHALMIAN
EDRIOPHTHALMIC
EDRIOPHTHALMOUS
EDUCABILITIES
EDUCABILITY
EDUCATABILITIES
EDUCATABILITY
EDUCATABLE
EDUCATEDNESS
EDUCATEDNESSES
EDUCATIONAL
EDUCATIONALIST
EDUCATIONALISTS
EDUCATIONALLY
EDUCATIONESE
EDUCATIONESES
EDUCATIONIST
EDUCATIONISTS
EDUCATIONS
EDUCEMENTS
EDULCORANT
EDULCORATE
EDULCORATED
EDULCORATES
EDULCORATING
EDULCORATION
EDULCORATIONS
EDULCORATIVE
EDULCORATOR
EDULCORATORS
EDUTAINMENT
EDUTAINMENTS
EELGRASSES

EERINESSES
EFFACEABLE
EFFACEMENT
EFFACEMENTS
EFFECTIBLE
EFFECTIVELY
EFFECTIVENESS
EFFECTIVENESSES
EFFECTIVES
EFFECTIVITIES
EFFECTIVITY
EFFECTLESS
EFFECTUALITIES
EFFECTUALITY
EFFECTUALLY
EFFECTUALNESS
EFFECTUALNESSES
EFFECTUATE
EFFECTUATED
EFFECTUATES
EFFECTUATING
EFFECTUATION
EFFECTUATIONS
EFFEMINACIES
EFFEMINACY
EFFEMINATE
EFFEMINATED
EFFEMINATELY
EFFEMINATENESS
EFFEMINATES
EFFEMINATING
EFFEMINISE
EFFEMINISED
EFFEMINISES
EFFEMINISING
EFFEMINIZE
EFFEMINIZED
EFFEMINIZES
EFFEMINIZING
EFFERENCES
EFFERENTLY
EFFERVESCE
EFFERVESCED
EFFERVESCENCE
EFFERVESCENCES
EFFERVESCENCIES
EFFERVESCENCY
EFFERVESCENT
EFFERVESCENTLY
EFFERVESCES
EFFERVESCIBLE
EFFERVESCING
EFFERVESCINGLY
EFFETENESS
EFFETENESSES
EFFICACIES
EFFICACIOUS
EFFICACIOUSLY
EFFICACIOUSNESS
EFFICACITIES
EFFICACITY
EFFICIENCE
EFFICIENCES
EFFICIENCIES
EFFICIENCY
EFFICIENTLY
EFFICIENTS

EFFIERCING
EFFIGURATE
EFFIGURATION
EFFIGURATIONS
EFFLEURAGE
EFFLEURAGED
EFFLEURAGES
EFFLEURAGING
EFFLORESCE
EFFLORESCED
EFFLORESCENCE
EFFLORESCENCES
EFFLORESCENT
EFFLORESCES
EFFLORESCING
EFFLUENCES
EFFLUVIUMS
EFFLUXIONS
EFFORTFULLY
EFFORTFULNESS
EFFORTFULNESSES
EFFORTLESS
EFFORTLESSLY
EFFORTLESSNESS
EFFRONTERIES
EFFRONTERY
EFFULGENCE
EFFULGENCES
EFFULGENTLY
EFFUSIOMETER
EFFUSIOMETERS
EFFUSIVELY
EFFUSIVENESS
EFFUSIVENESSES
EGALITARIAN
EGALITARIANISM
EGALITARIANISMS
EGALITARIANS
EGAREMENTS
EGGBEATERS
EGGHEADEDNESS
EGGHEADEDNESSES
EGLANDULAR
EGLANDULOSE
EGLANTINES
EGOCENTRIC
EGOCENTRICAL
EGOCENTRICALLY
EGOCENTRICITIES
EGOCENTRICITY
EGOCENTRICS
EGOCENTRISM
EGOCENTRISMS
EGOISTICAL
EGOISTICALLY
EGOMANIACAL
EGOMANIACALLY
EGOMANIACS
EGOSURFING
EGOTHEISMS
EGOTISTICAL
EGOTISTICALLY
EGREGIOUSLY
EGREGIOUSNESS
EGREGIOUSNESSES
EGRESSIONS
EGRESSIVES

EGURGITATE
EGURGITATED
EGURGITATES
EGURGITATING
EICOSANOID
EICOSANOIDS
EIDERDOWNS
EIDETICALLY
EIDOGRAPHS
EIGENFREQUENCY
EIGENFUNCTION
EIGENFUNCTIONS
EIGENMODES
EIGENTONES
EIGENVALUE
EIGENVALUES
EIGENVECTOR
EIGENVECTORS
EIGHTBALLS
EIGHTEENMO
EIGHTEENMOS
EIGHTEENTH
EIGHTEENTHLY
EIGHTEENTHS
EIGHTFOILS
EIGHTIETHS
EIGHTPENCE
EIGHTPENCES
EIGHTPENNY
EIGHTSCORE
EIGHTSCORES
EIGHTSOMES
EINSTEINIUM
EINSTEINIUMS
EIRENICALLY
EIRENICONS
EISTEDDFOD
EISTEDDFODAU
EISTEDDFODIC
EISTEDDFODS
EJACULATED
EJACULATES
EJACULATING
EJACULATION
EJACULATIONS
EJACULATIVE
EJACULATOR
EJACULATORS
EJACULATORY
EJECTAMENTA
EJECTIVELY
EJECTMENTS
EKISTICIAN
EKISTICIANS
ELABORATED
ELABORATELY
ELABORATENESS
ELABORATENESSES
ELABORATES
ELABORATING
ELABORATION
ELABORATIONS
ELABORATIVE
ELABORATOR
ELABORATORIES
ELABORATORS
ELABORATORY

ELAEAGNUSES	ELECTORSHIP	ELECTROFORM	ELECTROMOTOR	ELECTROTYPE
ELAEOLITES	ELECTORSHIPS	ELECTROFORMED	ELECTROMOTORS	ELECTROTYPED
ELAEOPTENE	ELECTRESSES	ELECTROFORMING	ELECTROMYOGRAM	ELECTROTYPER
ELAEOPTENES	ELECTRICAL	ELECTROFORMINGS	ELECTROMYOGRAMS	ELECTROTYPERS
ELAIOSOMES	ELECTRICALLY	ELECTROFORMS	ELECTROMYOGRAPH	ELECTROTYPES
ELASMOBRANCH	ELECTRICALS	ELECTROGEN	ELECTRONEGATIVE	ELECTROTYPIC
ELASMOBRANCHS	ELECTRICIAN	ELECTROGENESES	ELECTRONIC	ELECTROTYPIES
ELASMOSAUR	ELECTRICIANS	ELECTROGENESIS	ELECTRONICA	ELECTROTYPING
ELASMOSAURS	ELECTRICITIES	ELECTROGENIC	ELECTRONICALLY	ELECTROTYPIST
ELASTANCES	ELECTRICITY	ELECTROGENS	ELECTRONICAS	ELECTROTYPISTS
ELASTICALLY	ELECTRIFIABLE	ELECTROGILDING	ELECTRONICS	ELECTROTYPY
ELASTICATE	ELECTRIFICATION	ELECTROGILDINGS	ELECTRONVOLT	ELECTROVALENCE
ELASTICATED	ELECTRIFIED	ELECTROGRAM	ELECTRONVOLTS	ELECTROVALENCES
ELASTICATES	ELECTRIFIER	ELECTROGRAMS	ELECTROOSMOSES	ELECTROVALENCY
ELASTICATING	ELECTRIFIERS	ELECTROGRAPH	ELECTROOSMOSIS	ELECTROVALENT
ELASTICATION	ELECTRIFIES	ELECTROGRAPHIC	ELECTROOSMOTIC	ELECTROVALENTLY
ELASTICATIONS	ELECTRIFYING	ELECTROGRAPHIES	ELECTROPHILE	ELECTROWEAK
ELASTICISE	ELECTRIFYINGLY	ELECTROGRAPHS	ELECTROPHILES	ELECTROWINNING
ELASTICISED	ELECTRISATION	ELECTROGRAPHY	ELECTROPHILIC	ELECTROWINNINGS
ELASTICISES	ELECTRISATIONS	ELECTROING	ELECTROPHONE	ELECTUARIES
ELASTICISING	ELECTRISED	ELECTROJET	ELECTROPHONES	ELEDOISINS
ELASTICITIES	ELECTRISES	ELECTROJETS	ELECTROPHONIC	ELEEMOSYNARY
ELASTICITY	ELECTRISING	ELECTROKINETIC	ELECTROPHORESE	ELEGANCIES
ELASTICIZE	ELECTRIZATION	ELECTROKINETICS	ELECTROPHORESED	ELEGIACALLY
ELASTICIZED	ELECTRIZATIONS	ELECTROLESS	ELECTROPHORESES	ELEMENTALISM
ELASTICIZES	ELECTRIZED	ELECTROLIER	ELECTROPHORESIS	ELEMENTALISMS
ELASTICIZING	ELECTRIZES	ELECTROLIERS	ELECTROPHORETIC	ELEMENTALLY
ELASTICNESS	ELECTRIZING	ELECTROLOGIES	ELECTROPHORI	ELEMENTALS
ELASTICNESSES	ELECTROACOUSTIC	ELECTROLOGIST	ELECTROPHORUS	ELEMENTARILY
ELASTOMERIC	ELECTROACTIVE	ELECTROLOGISTS	ELECTROPHORUSES	ELEMENTARINESS
ELASTOMERS	ELECTROACTIVITY	ELECTROLOGY	ELECTROPLATE	ELEMENTARY
ELATEDNESS	ELECTROANALYSES	ELECTROLYSATION	ELECTROPLATED	ELEOPTENES
ELATEDNESSES	ELECTROANALYSIS	ELECTROLYSE	ELECTROPLATER	ELEPHANTIASES
ELATERITES	ELECTROANALYTIC	ELECTROLYSED	ELECTROPLATERS	ELEPHANTIASIC
ELATERIUMS	ELECTROBIOLOGY	ELECTROLYSER	ELECTROPLATES	ELEPHANTIASIS
ELBOWROOMS	ELECTROCAUTERY	ELECTROLYSERS	ELECTROPLATING	ELEPHANTINE
ELDERBERRIES	ELECTROCEMENT	ELECTROLYSES	ELECTROPLATINGS	ELEPHANTOID
ELDERBERRY	ELECTROCEMENTS	ELECTROLYSING	ELECTROPOLAR	ELEPIDOTES
ELDERCARES	ELECTROCHEMIC	ELECTROLYSIS	ELECTROPOP	ELEUTHERARCH
ELDERFLOWER	ELECTROCHEMICAL	ELECTROLYTE	ELECTROPOPS	ELEUTHERARCHS
ELDERFLOWERS	ELECTROCHEMIST	ELECTROLYTES	ELECTROPOSITIVE	ELEUTHERIAN
ELDERLINESS	ELECTROCHEMISTS	ELECTROLYTIC	ELECTROPUNCTURE	ELEUTHEROCOCCI
ELDERLINESSES	ELECTROCLASH	ELECTROLYTICS	ELECTRORECEPTOR	ELEUTHEROCOCCUS
ELDERSHIPS	ELECTROCLASHES	ELECTROLYZATION	ELECTRORHEOLOGY	ELEUTHERODACTYL
ELECAMPANE	ELECTROCULTURE	ELECTROLYZE	ELECTROSCOPE	ELEUTHEROMANIA
ELECAMPANES	ELECTROCULTURES	ELECTROLYZED	ELECTROSCOPES	ELEUTHEROMANIAS
ELECTABILITIES	ELECTROCUTE	ELECTROLYZER	ELECTROSCOPIC	ELEUTHEROPHOBIA
ELECTABILITY	ELECTROCUTED	ELECTROLYZERS	ELECTROSHOCK	ELEUTHEROPHOBIC
ELECTIONEER	ELECTROCUTES	ELECTROLYZES	ELECTROSHOCKS	ELEVATIONAL
ELECTIONEERED	ELECTROCUTING	ELECTROLYZING	ELECTROSONDE	ELEVATIONS
ELECTIONEERER	ELECTROCUTION	ELECTROMAGNET	ELECTROSONDES	ELEVENTHLY
ELECTIONEERERS	ELECTROCUTIONS	ELECTROMAGNETIC	ELECTROSTATIC	ELFISHNESS
ELECTIONEERING	ELECTROCYTE	ELECTROMAGNETS	ELECTROSTATICS	ELFISHNESSES
ELECTIONEERINGS	ELECTROCYTES	ELECTROMER	ELECTROSURGERY	ELICITABLE
ELECTIONEERS	ELECTRODEPOSIT	ELECTROMERIC	ELECTROSURGICAL	ELICITATION
ELECTIVELY	ELECTRODEPOSITS	ELECTROMERISM	ELECTROTECHNICS	ELICITATIONS
ELECTIVENESS	ELECTRODERMAL	ELECTROMERISMS	ELECTROTHERAPY	ELIGIBILITIES
ELECTIVENESSES	ELECTRODES	ELECTROMERS	ELECTROTHERMAL	ELIGIBILITY
ELECTIVITIES	ELECTRODIALYSES	ELECTROMETER	ELECTROTHERMIC	ELIMINABILITIES
ELECTIVITY	ELECTRODIALYSIS	ELECTROMETERS	ELECTROTHERMIES	ELIMINABILITY
ELECTORALLY	ELECTRODIALYTIC	ELECTROMETRIC	ELECTROTHERMY	ELIMINABLE
ELECTORATE	ELECTRODYNAMIC	ELECTROMETRICAL	ELECTROTINT	ELIMINANTS
ELECTORATES	ELECTRODYNAMICS	ELECTROMETRIES	ELECTROTINTS	ELIMINATED
ELECTORESS	ELECTROFISHING	ELECTROMETRY	ELECTROTONIC	ELIMINATES
ELECTORESSES	ELECTROFISHINGS	ELECTROMOTANCE	ELECTROTONUS	ELIMINATING
ELECTORIAL	ELECTROFLUOR	ELECTROMOTANCES	ELECTROTONUSES	ELIMINATION
ELECTORIALLY	ELECTROFLUORS	ELECTROMOTIVE		ELIMINATIONS

ELIMINATIVE
ELIMINATIVISM
ELIMINATIVISMS
ELIMINATOR
ELIMINATORS
ELIMINATORY
ELLIPSOGRAPH
ELLIPSOGRAPHS
ELLIPSOIDAL
ELLIPSOIDS
ELLIPTICAL
ELLIPTICALLY
ELLIPTICALNESS
ELLIPTICALS
ELLIPTICITIES
ELLIPTICITY
ELOCUTIONARY
ELOCUTIONIST
ELOCUTIONISTS
ELOCUTIONS
ELOIGNMENT
ELOIGNMENTS
ELOINMENTS
ELONGATING
ELONGATION
ELONGATIONS
ELOPEMENTS
ELOQUENCES
ELOQUENTLY
ELSEWHITHER
ELUCIDATED
ELUCIDATES
ELUCIDATING
ELUCIDATION
ELUCIDATIONS
ELUCIDATIVE
ELUCIDATOR
ELUCIDATORS
ELUCIDATORY
ELUCUBRATE
ELUCUBRATED
ELUCUBRATES
ELUCUBRATING
ELUCUBRATION
ELUCUBRATIONS
ELUSIVENESS
ELUSIVENESSES
ELUSORINESS
ELUSORINESSES
ELUTRIATED
ELUTRIATES
ELUTRIATING
ELUTRIATION
ELUTRIATIONS
ELUTRIATOR
ELUTRIATORS
ELUVIATING
ELUVIATION
ELUVIATIONS
ELVISHNESS
ELVISHNESSES
ELYTRIFORM
ELYTRIGEROUS
EMACIATING
EMACIATION
EMACIATIONS
EMALANGENI

EMANATIONAL
EMANATIONS
EMANATISTS
EMANCIPATE
EMANCIPATED
EMANCIPATES
EMANCIPATING
EMANCIPATION
EMANCIPATIONIST
EMANCIPATIONS
EMANCIPATIVE
EMANCIPATOR
EMANCIPATORS
EMANCIPATORY
EMANCIPIST
EMANCIPISTS
EMARGINATE
EMARGINATED
EMARGINATELY
EMARGINATES
EMARGINATING
EMARGINATION
EMARGINATIONS
EMASCULATE
EMASCULATED
EMASCULATES
EMASCULATING
EMASCULATION
EMASCULATIONS
EMASCULATIVE
EMASCULATOR
EMASCULATORS
EMASCULATORY
EMBALLINGS
EMBALMINGS
EMBALMMENT
EMBALMMENTS
EMBANKMENT
EMBANKMENTS
EMBARCADERO
EMBARCADEROS
EMBARCATION
EMBARCATIONS
EMBARGOING
EMBARKATION
EMBARKATIONS
EMBARKMENT
EMBARKMENTS
EMBARQUEMENT
EMBARQUEMENTS
EMBARRASSABLE
EMBARRASSED
EMBARRASSEDLY
EMBARRASSES
EMBARRASSING
EMBARRASSINGLY
EMBARRASSMENT
EMBARRASSMENTS
EMBARRINGS
EMBASEMENT
EMBASEMENTS
EMBASSADES
EMBASSADOR
EMBASSADORS
EMBASSAGES
EMBATTLEMENT
EMBATTLEMENTS

EMBATTLING
EMBAYMENTS
EMBEDDINGS
EMBEDMENTS
EMBELLISHED
EMBELLISHER
EMBELLISHERS
EMBELLISHES
EMBELLISHING
EMBELLISHINGLY
EMBELLISHMENT
EMBELLISHMENTS
EMBEZZLEMENT
EMBEZZLEMENTS
EMBEZZLERS
EMBEZZLING
EMBIGGENED
EMBIGGENING
EMBITTERED
EMBITTERER
EMBITTERERS
EMBITTERING
EMBITTERINGS
EMBITTERMENT
EMBITTERMENTS
EMBLAZONED
EMBLAZONER
EMBLAZONERS
EMBLAZONING
EMBLAZONMENT
EMBLAZONMENTS
EMBLAZONRIES
EMBLAZONRY
EMBLEMATIC
EMBLEMATICAL
EMBLEMATICALLY
EMBLEMATISE
EMBLEMATISED
EMBLEMATISES
EMBLEMATISING
EMBLEMATIST
EMBLEMATISTS
EMBLEMATIZE
EMBLEMATIZED
EMBLEMATIZES
EMBLEMATIZING
EMBLEMENTS
EMBLEMISED
EMBLEMISES
EMBLEMISING
EMBLEMIZED
EMBLEMIZES
EMBLEMIZING
EMBLOOMING
EMBLOSSOMED
EMBLOSSOMING
EMBLOSSOMS
EMBODIMENT
EMBODIMENTS
EMBOITEMENT
EMBOITEMENTS
EMBOLDENED
EMBOLDENER
EMBOLDENERS
EMBOLDENING
EMBOLECTOMIES
EMBOLECTOMY

EMBOLISATION
EMBOLISATIONS
EMBOLISING
EMBOLISMAL
EMBOLISMIC
EMBOLIZATION
EMBOLIZATIONS
EMBOLIZING
EMBONPOINT
EMBONPOINTS
EMBORDERED
EMBORDERING
EMBOSCATAS
EMBOSOMING
EMBOSSABLE
EMBOSSINGS
EMBOSSMENT
EMBOSSMENTS
EMBOTHRIUM
EMBOTHRIUMS
EMBOUCHURE
EMBOUCHURES
EMBOUNDING
EMBOURGEOISE
EMBOURGEOISED
EMBOURGEOISES
EMBOURGEOISING
EMBOWELING
EMBOWELLED
EMBOWELLING
EMBOWELMENT
EMBOWELMENTS
EMBOWERING
EMBOWERMENT
EMBOWERMENTS
EMBOWMENTS
EMBRACEABLE
EMBRACEMENT
EMBRACEMENTS
EMBRACEORS
EMBRACERIES
EMBRACINGLY
EMBRACINGNESS
EMBRACINGNESSES
EMBRAIDING
EMBRANCHMENT
EMBRANCHMENTS
EMBRANGLED
EMBRANGLEMENT
EMBRANGLEMENTS
EMBRANGLES
EMBRANGLING
EMBRASURED
EMBRASURES
EMBRAZURES
EMBREADING
EMBREATHED
EMBREATHES
EMBREATHING
EMBRITTLED
EMBRITTLEMENT
EMBRITTLEMENTS
EMBRITTLES
EMBRITTLING
EMBROCATED
EMBROCATES
EMBROCATING

EMBROCATION
EMBROCATIONS
EMBROGLIOS
EMBROIDERED
EMBROIDERER
EMBROIDERERS
EMBROIDERIES
EMBROIDERING
EMBROIDERS
EMBROIDERY
EMBROILERS
EMBROILING
EMBROILMENT
EMBROILMENTS
EMBROWNING
EMBRUEMENT
EMBRUEMENTS
EMBRYECTOMIES
EMBRYECTOMY
EMBRYOGENESES
EMBRYOGENESIS
EMBRYOGENETIC
EMBRYOGENIC
EMBRYOGENIES
EMBRYOGENY
EMBRYOLOGIC
EMBRYOLOGICAL
EMBRYOLOGICALLY
EMBRYOLOGIES
EMBRYOLOGIST
EMBRYOLOGISTS
EMBRYOLOGY
EMBRYONATE
EMBRYONATED
EMBRYONICALLY
EMBRYOPHYTE
EMBRYOPHYTES
EMBRYOTICALLY
EMBRYOTOMIES
EMBRYOTOMY
EMBRYULCIA
EMBRYULCIAS
EMENDATING
EMENDATION
EMENDATIONS
EMENDATORS
EMENDATORY
EMERGENCES
EMERGENCIES
EMERGENTLY
EMETICALLY
EMETOPHOBIA
EMETOPHOBIAS
EMICATIONS
EMIGRATING
EMIGRATION
EMIGRATIONAL
EMIGRATIONIST
EMIGRATIONISTS
EMIGRATIONS
EMIGRATORY
EMINENCIES
EMINENTIAL
EMISSARIES
EMISSIVITIES
EMISSIVITY
EMITTANCES

EMMARBLING	EMPATHETIC	EMPLECTUMS	ENABLEMENTS	ENCASEMENTS
EMMENAGOGIC	EMPATHETICALLY	EMPLONGING	ENACTMENTS	ENCASHABLE
EMMENAGOGUE	EMPATHICALLY	EMPLOYABILITIES	ENALAPRILS	ENCASHMENT
EMMENAGOGUES	EMPATHISED	EMPLOYABILITY	ENAMELINGS	ENCASHMENTS
EMMENOLOGIES	EMPATHISES	EMPLOYABLE	ENAMELISTS	ENCAUSTICALLY
EMMENOLOGY	EMPATHISING	EMPLOYABLES	ENAMELLERS	ENCAUSTICS
EMMETROPES	EMPATHISTS	EMPLOYMENT	ENAMELLING	ENCEPHALALGIA
EMMETROPIA	EMPATHIZED	EMPLOYMENTS	ENAMELLINGS	ENCEPHALALGIAS
EMMETROPIAS	EMPATHIZES	EMPOISONED	ENAMELLIST	ENCEPHALIC
EMMETROPIC	EMPATHIZING	EMPOISONING	ENAMELLISTS	ENCEPHALIN
EMOLLESCENCE	EMPATRONED	EMPOISONMENT	ENAMELWARE	ENCEPHALINE
EMOLLESCENCES	EMPATRONING	EMPOISONMENTS	ENAMELWARES	ENCEPHALINES
EMOLLIATED	EMPEACHING	EMPOLDERED	ENAMELWORK	ENCEPHALINS
EMOLLIATES	EMPENNAGES	EMPOLDERING	ENAMELWORKS	ENCEPHALITIC
EMOLLIATING	EMPEOPLING	EMPOVERISH	ENAMORADOS	ENCEPHALITIDES
EMOLLIENCE	EMPERISHED	EMPOVERISHED	ENAMOURING	ENCEPHALITIS
EMOLLIENCES	EMPERISHES	EMPOVERISHER	ENANTHEMAS	ENCEPHALITISES
EMOLLIENTS	EMPERISHING	EMPOVERISHERS	ENANTIODROMIA	ENCEPHALITOGEN
EMOLLITION	EMPERISING	EMPOVERISHES	ENANTIODROMIAS	ENCEPHALITOGENS
EMOLLITIONS	EMPERIZING	EMPOVERISHING	ENANTIODROMIC	ENCEPHALOCELE
EMOLUMENTAL	EMPERORSHIP	EMPOVERISHMENT	ENANTIOMER	ENCEPHALOCELES
EMOLUMENTARY	EMPERORSHIPS	EMPOVERISHMENTS	ENANTIOMERIC	ENCEPHALOGRAM
EMOLUMENTS	EMPHASISED	EMPOWERING	ENANTIOMERS	ENCEPHALOGRAMS
EMOTIONABLE	EMPHASISES	EMPOWERMENT	ENANTIOMORPH	ENCEPHALOGRAPH
EMOTIONALISE	EMPHASISING	EMPOWERMENTS	ENANTIOMORPHIC	ENCEPHALOGRAPHS
EMOTIONALISED	EMPHASIZED	EMPRESSEMENT	ENANTIOMORPHIES	ENCEPHALOGRAPHY
EMOTIONALISES	EMPHASIZES	EMPRESSEMENTS	ENANTIOMORPHISM	ENCEPHALOID
EMOTIONALISING	EMPHASIZING	EMPTINESSES	ENANTIOMORPHOUS	ENCEPHALOMA
EMOTIONALISM	EMPHATICAL	EMPURPLING	ENANTIOMORPHS	ENCEPHALOMAS
EMOTIONALISMS	EMPHATICALLY	EMPYREUMATA	ENANTIOMORPHY	ENCEPHALOMATA
EMOTIONALIST	EMPHATICALNESS	EMPYREUMATIC	ENANTIOPATHIES	ENCEPHALON
EMOTIONALISTIC	EMPHRACTIC	EMPYREUMATICAL	ENANTIOPATHY	ENCEPHALONS
EMOTIONALISTS	EMPHRACTICS	EMPYREUMATISE	ENANTIOSES	ENCEPHALOPATHIC
EMOTIONALITIES	EMPHYSEMAS	EMPYREUMATISED	ENANTIOSIS	ENCEPHALOPATHY
EMOTIONALITY	EMPHYSEMATOUS	EMPYREUMATISES	ENANTIOSTYLIES	ENCEPHALOTOMIES
EMOTIONALIZE	EMPHYSEMIC	EMPYREUMATISING	ENANTIOSTYLOUS	ENCEPHALOTOMY
EMOTIONALIZED	EMPHYSEMICS	EMPYREUMATIZE	ENANTIOSTYLY	ENCEPHALOUS
EMOTIONALIZES	EMPHYTEUSES	EMPYREUMATIZED	ENANTIOTROPIC	ENCHAINING
EMOTIONALIZING	EMPHYTEUSIS	EMPYREUMATIZES	ENANTIOTROPIES	ENCHAINMENT
EMOTIONALLY	EMPHYTEUTIC	EMPYREUMATIZING	ENANTIOTROPY	ENCHAINMENTS
EMOTIONLESS	EMPIECEMENT	EMULATIONS	ENARRATION	ENCHANTERS
EMOTIONLESSLY	EMPIECEMENTS	EMULATIVELY	ENARRATIONS	ENCHANTING
EMOTIONLESSNESS	EMPIERCING	EMULATRESS	ENARTHRODIAL	ENCHANTINGLY
EMOTIVENESS	EMPIGHTING	EMULATRESSES	ENARTHROSES	ENCHANTMENT
EMOTIVENESSES	EMPIRICALLY	EMULGENCES	ENARTHROSIS	ENCHANTMENTS
EMOTIVISMS	EMPIRICALNESS	EMULOUSNESS	ENCAMPMENT	ENCHANTRESS
EMOTIVITIES	EMPIRICALNESSES	EMULOUSNESSES	ENCAMPMENTS	ENCHANTRESSES
EMPACKETED	EMPIRICALS	EMULSIFIABLE	ENCANTHISES	ENCHARGING
EMPACKETING	EMPIRICISM	EMULSIFICATION	ENCAPSULATE	ENCHARMING
EMPALEMENT	EMPIRICISMS	EMULSIFICATIONS	ENCAPSULATED	ENCHEASONS
EMPALEMENTS	EMPIRICIST	EMULSIFIED	ENCAPSULATES	ENCHEERING
EMPANELING	EMPIRICISTS	EMULSIFIER	ENCAPSULATING	ENCHEIRIDIA
EMPANELLED	EMPIRICUTIC	EMULSIFIERS	ENCAPSULATION	ENCHEIRIDION
EMPANELLING	EMPLACEMENT	EMULSIFIES	ENCAPSULATIONS	ENCHEIRIDIONS
EMPANELMENT	EMPLACEMENTS	EMULSIFYING	ENCAPSULED	ENCHILADAS
EMPANELMENTS	EMPLASTERED	EMULSIONISE	ENCAPSULES	ENCHIRIDIA
EMPANOPLIED	EMPLASTERING	EMULSIONISED	ENCAPSULING	ENCHIRIDION
EMPANOPLIES	EMPLASTERS	EMULSIONISES	ENCARNALISE	ENCHIRIDIONS
EMPANOPLYING	EMPLASTICS	EMULSIONISING	ENCARNALISED	ENCHONDROMA
EMPARADISE	EMPLASTRON	EMULSIONIZE	ENCARNALISES	ENCHONDROMAS
EMPARADISED	EMPLASTRONS	EMULSIONIZED	ENCARNALISING	ENCHONDROMATA
EMPARADISES	EMPLASTRUM	EMULSIONIZES	ENCARNALIZE	ENCHONDROMATOUS
EMPARADISING	EMPLASTRUMS	EMULSIONIZING	ENCARNALIZED	ENCINCTURE
EMPARLAUNCE	EMPLEACHED	EMULSOIDAL	ENCARNALIZES	ENCINCTURED
EMPARLAUNCES	EMPLEACHES	EMUNCTIONS	ENCARNALIZING	ENCINCTURES
EMPASSIONATE	EMPLEACHING	EMUNCTORIES	ENCARPUSES	ENCINCTURING
EMPASSIONED	EMPLECTONS	ENABLEMENT	ENCASEMENT	ENCIPHERED

e

ENCIPHERER
ENCIPHERERS
ENCIPHERING
ENCIPHERMENT
ENCIPHERMENTS
ENCIRCLEMENT
ENCIRCLEMENTS
ENCIRCLING
ENCLASPING
ENCLITICALLY
ENCLOISTER
ENCLOISTERED
ENCLOISTERING
ENCLOISTERS
ENCLOSABLE
ENCLOSURES
ENCLOTHING
ENCLOUDING
ENCODEMENT
ENCODEMENTS
ENCOIGNURE
ENCOIGNURES
ENCOLOURED
ENCOLOURING
ENCOLPIONS
ENCOLPIUMS
ENCOMENDERO
ENCOMENDEROS
ENCOMIASTIC
ENCOMIASTICAL
ENCOMIASTICALLY
ENCOMIASTS
ENCOMIENDA
ENCOMIENDAS
ENCOMPASSED
ENCOMPASSES
ENCOMPASSING
ENCOMPASSMENT
ENCOMPASSMENTS
ENCOPRESES
ENCOPRESIS
ENCOPRETIC
ENCOUNTERED
ENCOUNTERER
ENCOUNTERERS
ENCOUNTERING
ENCOUNTERS
ENCOURAGED
ENCOURAGEMENT
ENCOURAGEMENTS
ENCOURAGER
ENCOURAGERS
ENCOURAGES
ENCOURAGING
ENCOURAGINGLY
ENCOURAGINGS
ENCRADLING
ENCREASING
ENCRIMSONED
ENCRIMSONING
ENCRIMSONS
ENCRINITAL
ENCRINITES
ENCRINITIC
ENCROACHED
ENCROACHER
ENCROACHERS

ENCROACHES
ENCROACHING
ENCROACHINGLY
ENCROACHMENT
ENCROACHMENTS
ENCRUSTATION
ENCRUSTATIONS
ENCRUSTING
ENCRUSTMENT
ENCRUSTMENTS
ENCRYPTING
ENCRYPTION
ENCRYPTIONS
ENCULTURATE
ENCULTURATED
ENCULTURATES
ENCULTURATING
ENCULTURATION
ENCULTURATIONS
ENCULTURATIVE
ENCUMBERED
ENCUMBERING
ENCUMBERINGLY
ENCUMBERMENT
ENCUMBERMENTS
ENCUMBRANCE
ENCUMBRANCER
ENCUMBRANCERS
ENCUMBRANCES
ENCURTAINED
ENCURTAINING
ENCURTAINS
ENCYCLICAL
ENCYCLICALS
ENCYCLOPAEDIA
ENCYCLOPAEDIAS
ENCYCLOPAEDIC
ENCYCLOPAEDICAL
ENCYCLOPAEDISM
ENCYCLOPAEDISMS
ENCYCLOPAEDIST
ENCYCLOPAEDISTS
ENCYCLOPEDIA
ENCYCLOPEDIAN
ENCYCLOPEDIAS
ENCYCLOPEDIC
ENCYCLOPEDICAL
ENCYCLOPEDISM
ENCYCLOPEDISMS
ENCYCLOPEDIST
ENCYCLOPEDISTS
ENCYSTATION
ENCYSTATIONS
ENCYSTMENT
ENCYSTMENTS
ENDAMAGEMENT
ENDAMAGEMENTS
ENDAMAGING
ENDAMOEBAE
ENDAMOEBAS
ENDAMOEBIC
ENDANGERED
ENDANGERER
ENDANGERERS
ENDANGERING
ENDANGERMENT
ENDANGERMENTS

ENDARCHIES
ENDARTERECTOMY
ENDEARINGLY
ENDEARINGNESS
ENDEARINGNESSES
ENDEARMENT
ENDEARMENTS
ENDEAVORED
ENDEAVORER
ENDEAVORERS
ENDEAVORING
ENDEAVOURED
ENDEAVOURER
ENDEAVOURERS
ENDEAVOURING
ENDEAVOURMENT
ENDEAVOURMENTS
ENDEAVOURS
ENDECAGONS
ENDEIXISES
ENDEMICALLY
ENDEMICITIES
ENDEMICITY
ENDEMIOLOGIES
ENDEMIOLOGY
ENDENIZENED
ENDENIZENING
ENDENIZENS
ENDERGONIC
ENDERMATIC
ENDERMICAL
ENDLESSNESS
ENDLESSNESSES
ENDOBIOTIC
ENDOBLASTIC
ENDOBLASTS
ENDOCARDIA
ENDOCARDIAC
ENDOCARDIAL
ENDOCARDITIC
ENDOCARDITIDES
ENDOCARDITIS
ENDOCARDITISES
ENDOCARDIUM
ENDOCARPAL
ENDOCARPIC
ENDOCENTRIC
ENDOCHONDRAL
ENDOCHYLOUS
ENDOCRANIA
ENDOCRANIAL
ENDOCRANIUM
ENDOCRINAL
ENDOCRINES
ENDOCRINIC
ENDOCRINOLOGIC
ENDOCRINOLOGIES
ENDOCRINOLOGIST
ENDOCRINOLOGY
ENDOCRINOPATHIC
ENDOCRINOPATHY
ENDOCRINOUS
ENDOCRITIC
ENDOCUTICLE
ENDOCUTICLES
ENDOCYTOSES
ENDOCYTOSIS

ENDOCYTOTIC
ENDODERMAL
ENDODERMIC
ENDODERMIS
ENDODERMISES
ENDODONTAL
ENDODONTIC
ENDODONTICALLY
ENDODONTICS
ENDODONTIST
ENDODONTISTS
ENDOENZYME
ENDOENZYMES
ENDOGAMIES
ENDOGAMOUS
ENDOGENIES
ENDOGENOUS
ENDOGENOUSLY
ENDOLITHIC
ENDOLYMPHATIC
ENDOLYMPHS
ENDOMETRIA
ENDOMETRIAL
ENDOMETRIOSES
ENDOMETRIOSIS
ENDOMETRITIS
ENDOMETRITISES
ENDOMETRIUM
ENDOMITOSES
ENDOMITOSIS
ENDOMITOTIC
ENDOMIXISES
ENDOMORPHIC
ENDOMORPHIES
ENDOMORPHISM
ENDOMORPHISMS
ENDOMORPHS
ENDOMORPHY
ENDOMYCORRHIZA
ENDONEURIA
ENDONEURIUM
ENDONUCLEASE
ENDONUCLEASES
ENDONUCLEOLYTIC
ENDOPARASITE
ENDOPARASITES
ENDOPARASITIC
ENDOPARASITISM
ENDOPARASITISMS
ENDOPEPTIDASE
ENDOPEPTIDASES
ENDOPEROXIDE
ENDOPEROXIDES
ENDOPHAGIES
ENDOPHAGOUS
ENDOPHITIC
ENDOPHYLLOUS
ENDOPHYTES
ENDOPHYTIC
ENDOPHYTICALLY
ENDOPLASMIC
ENDOPLASMS
ENDOPLASTIC
ENDOPLEURA
ENDOPLEURAS
ENDOPODITE
ENDOPODITES

ENDOPOLYPLOID
ENDOPOLYPLOIDY
ENDOPROCTS
ENDORADIOSONDE
ENDORADIOSONDES
ENDORHIZAL
ENDORPHINS
ENDORSABLE
ENDORSATION
ENDORSATIONS
ENDORSEMENT
ENDORSEMENTS
ENDOSCOPES
ENDOSCOPIC
ENDOSCOPICALLY
ENDOSCOPIES
ENDOSCOPIST
ENDOSCOPISTS
ENDOSKELETAL
ENDOSKELETON
ENDOSKELETONS
ENDOSMOMETER
ENDOSMOMETERS
ENDOSMOMETRIC
ENDOSMOSES
ENDOSMOSIS
ENDOSMOTIC
ENDOSMOTICALLY
ENDOSPERMIC
ENDOSPERMS
ENDOSPORES
ENDOSPOROUS
ENDOSTEALLY
ENDOSTOSES
ENDOSTOSIS
ENDOSTYLES
ENDOSULFAN
ENDOSULFANS
ENDOSYMBIONT
ENDOSYMBIONTS
ENDOSYMBIOSES
ENDOSYMBIOSIS
ENDOSYMBIOTIC
ENDOTHECIA
ENDOTHECIAL
ENDOTHECIUM
ENDOTHELIA
ENDOTHELIAL
ENDOTHELIOID
ENDOTHELIOMA
ENDOTHELIOMAS
ENDOTHELIOMATA
ENDOTHELIUM
ENDOTHERMAL
ENDOTHERMIC
ENDOTHERMICALLY
ENDOTHERMIES
ENDOTHERMISM
ENDOTHERMISMS
ENDOTHERMS
ENDOTHERMY
ENDOTOXINS
ENDOTRACHEAL
ENDOTROPHIC
ENDOWMENTS
ENDPLAYING
ENDUNGEONED

ENDUNGEONING	ENFREEDOMED	ENGULFMENT	ENLARGEMENTS	ENREGISTERING
ENDUNGEONS	ENFREEDOMING	ENGULFMENTS	ENLARGENED	ENREGISTERS
ENDURABILITIES	ENFREEDOMS	ENGULPHING	ENLARGENING	ENRHEUMING
ENDURABILITY	ENFREEZING	ENGYSCOPES	ENLEVEMENT	ENRICHMENT
ENDURABLENESS	ENGAGEMENT	ENHANCEMENT	ENLEVEMENTS	ENRICHMENTS
ENDURABLENESSES	ENGAGEMENTS	ENHANCEMENTS	ENLIGHTED	ENROLLMENT
ENDURANCES	ENGAGINGLY	ENHARMONIC	ENLIGHTENED	ENROLLMENTS
ENDURINGLY	ENGAGINGNESS	ENHARMONICAL	ENLIGHTENER	ENROLMENTS
ENDURINGNESS	ENGAGINGNESSES	ENHARMONICALLY	ENLIGHTENERS	ENROUGHING
ENDURINGNESSES	ENGARLANDED	ENHEARSING	ENLIGHTENING	ENROUNDING
ENERGETICAL	ENGARLANDING	ENHEARTENED	ENLIGHTENMENT	ENSAMPLING
ENERGETICALLY	ENGARLANDS	ENHEARTENING	ENLIGHTENMENTS	ENSANGUINATED
ENERGETICS	ENGARRISON	ENHEARTENS	ENLIGHTENS	ENSANGUINE
ENERGISATION	ENGARRISONED	ENHUNGERED	ENLIGHTING	ENSANGUINED
ENERGISATIONS	ENGARRISONING	ENHUNGERING	ENLISTMENT	ENSANGUINES
ENERGISERS	ENGARRISONS	ENHYDRITES	ENLISTMENTS	ENSANGUINING
ENERGISING	ENGENDERED	ENHYDRITIC	ENLIVENERS	ENSCHEDULE
ENERGIZATION	ENGENDERER	ENHYDROSES	ENLIVENING	ENSCHEDULED
ENERGIZATIONS	ENGENDERERS	ENHYPOSTASIA	ENLIVENMENT	ENSCHEDULES
ENERGIZERS	ENGENDERING	ENHYPOSTASIAS	ENLIVENMENTS	ENSCHEDULING
ENERGIZING	ENGENDERMENT	ENHYPOSTATIC	ENLUMINING	ENSCONCING
ENERGUMENS	ENGENDERMENTS	ENHYPOSTATISE	ENMESHMENT	ENSCROLLED
ENERVATING	ENGENDRURE	ENHYPOSTATISED	ENMESHMENTS	ENSCROLLING
ENERVATION	ENGENDRURES	ENHYPOSTATISES	ENNEAGONAL	ENSEPULCHRE
ENERVATIONS	ENGENDURES	ENHYPOSTATISING	ENNEAGRAMS	ENSEPULCHRED
ENERVATIVE	ENGINEERED	ENHYPOSTATIZE	ENNEAHEDRA	ENSEPULCHRES
ENERVATORS	ENGINEERING	ENHYPOSTATIZED	ENNEAHEDRAL	ENSEPULCHRING
ENFACEMENT	ENGINEERINGS	ENHYPOSTATIZES	ENNEAHEDRON	ENSERFMENT
ENFACEMENTS	ENGINERIES	ENHYPOSTATIZING	ENNEAHEDRONS	ENSERFMENTS
ENFEEBLEMENT	ENGIRDLING	ENIGMATICAL	ENNEANDRIAN	ENSHEATHED
ENFEEBLEMENTS	ENGLACIALLY	ENIGMATICALLY	ENNEANDROUS	ENSHEATHES
ENFEEBLERS	ENGLISHING	ENIGMATISE	ENNEASTYLE	ENSHEATHING
ENFEEBLING	ENGLOOMING	ENIGMATISED	ENNEATHLON	ENSHELLING
ENFELONING	ENGLUTTING	ENIGMATISES	ENNEATHLONS	ENSHELTERED
ENFEOFFING	ENGORGEMENT	ENIGMATISING	ENNOBLEMENT	ENSHELTERING
ENFEOFFMENT	ENGORGEMENTS	ENIGMATIST	ENNOBLEMENTS	ENSHELTERS
ENFEOFFMENTS	ENGOUEMENT	ENIGMATISTS	ENOKIDAKES	ENSHIELDED
ENFESTERED	ENGOUEMENTS	ENIGMATIZE	ENOKITAKES	ENSHIELDING
ENFETTERED	ENGOUMENTS	ENIGMATIZED	ENOLOGICAL	ENSHRINEES
ENFETTERING	ENGRAFFING	ENIGMATIZES	ENOLOGISTS	ENSHRINEMENT
ENFEVERING	ENGRAFTATION	ENIGMATIZING	ENORMITIES	ENSHRINEMENTS
ENFIERCING	ENGRAFTATIONS	ENIGMATOGRAPHY	ENORMOUSLY	ENSHRINING
ENFILADING	ENGRAFTING	ENJAMBEMENT	ENORMOUSNESS	ENSHROUDED
ENFLESHING	ENGRAFTMENT	ENJAMBEMENTS	ENORMOUSNESSES	ENSHROUDING
ENFLEURAGE	ENGRAFTMENTS	ENJAMBMENT	ENOUNCEMENT	ENSIGNCIES
ENFLEURAGES	ENGRAILING	ENJAMBMENTS	ENOUNCEMENTS	ENSIGNSHIP
ENFLOWERED	ENGRAILMENT	ENJOINDERS	ENPHYTOTIC	ENSIGNSHIPS
ENFLOWERING	ENGRAILMENTS	ENJOINMENT	ENQUEUEING	ENSILABILITIES
ENFOLDMENT	ENGRAINEDLY	ENJOINMENTS	ENQUIRATION	ENSILABILITY
ENFOLDMENTS	ENGRAINEDNESS	ENJOYABLENESS	ENQUIRATIONS	ENSILAGEING
ENFORCEABILITY	ENGRAINEDNESSES	ENJOYABLENESSES	ENRAGEMENT	ENSILAGING
ENFORCEABLE	ENGRAINERS	ENJOYMENTS	ENRAGEMENTS	ENSLAVEMENT
ENFORCEDLY	ENGRAINING	ENKEPHALIN	ENRANCKLED	ENSLAVEMENTS
ENFORCEMENT	ENGRAMMATIC	ENKEPHALINE	ENRANCKLES	ENSNAREMENT
ENFORCEMENTS	ENGRASPING	ENKEPHALINES	ENRANCKLING	ENSNAREMENTS
ENFORESTED	ENGRAVERIES	ENKEPHALINS	ENRAPTURED	ENSNARLING
ENFORESTING	ENGRAVINGS	ENKERNELLED	ENRAPTURES	ENSORCELED
ENFOULDERED	ENGRENAGES	ENKERNELLING	ENRAPTURING	ENSORCELING
ENFRAMEMENT	ENGRIEVING	ENKINDLERS	ENRAUNGING	ENSORCELLED
ENFRAMEMENTS	ENGROOVING	ENKINDLING	ENRAVISHED	ENSORCELLING
ENFRANCHISE	ENGROSSEDLY	ENLACEMENT	ENRAVISHES	ENSORCELLMENT
ENFRANCHISED	ENGROSSERS	ENLACEMENTS	ENRAVISHING	ENSORCELLMENTS
ENFRANCHISEMENT	ENGROSSING	ENLARGEABLE	ENREGIMENT	ENSORCELLS
ENFRANCHISER	ENGROSSINGLY	ENLARGEDLY	ENREGIMENTED	ENSOULMENT
ENFRANCHISERS	ENGROSSMENT	ENLARGEDNESS	ENREGIMENTING	ENSOULMENTS
ENFRANCHISES	ENGROSSMENTS	ENLARGEDNESSES	ENREGIMENTS	ENSPHERING
ENFRANCHISING	ENGUARDING	ENLARGEMENT	ENREGISTER	ENSTAMPING
			ENREGISTERED	

ENSTATITES
ENSTEEPING
ENSTRUCTURED
ENSWATHEMENT
ENSWATHEMENTS
ENSWATHING
ENSWEEPING
ENTABLATURE
ENTABLATURES
ENTABLEMENT
ENTABLEMENTS
ENTAILMENT
ENTAILMENTS
ENTAMOEBAE
ENTAMOEBAS
ENTANGLEMENT
ENTANGLEMENTS
ENTANGLERS
ENTANGLING
ENTELECHIES
ENTELLUSES
ENTENDERED
ENTENDERING
ENTERCHAUNGE
ENTERCHAUNGED
ENTERCHAUNGES
ENTERCHAUNGING
ENTERDEALE
ENTERDEALED
ENTERDEALES
ENTERDEALING
ENTERECTOMIES
ENTERECTOMY
ENTERITIDES
ENTERITISES
ENTEROBACTERIA
ENTEROBACTERIAL
ENTEROBACTERIUM
ENTEROBIASES
ENTEROBIASIS
ENTEROCELE
ENTEROCELES
ENTEROCENTESES
ENTEROCENTESIS
ENTEROCOCCAL
ENTEROCOCCI
ENTEROCOCCUS
ENTEROCOEL
ENTEROCOELE
ENTEROCOELES
ENTEROCOELIC
ENTEROCOELOUS
ENTEROCOELS
ENTEROCOLITIDES
ENTEROCOLITIS
ENTEROCOLITISES
ENTEROGASTRONE
ENTEROGASTRONES
ENTEROHEPATITIS
ENTEROKINASE
ENTEROKINASES
ENTEROLITH
ENTEROLITHS
ENTEROPATHIES
ENTEROPATHY
ENTEROPNEUST
ENTEROPNEUSTAL

ENTEROPNEUSTS
ENTEROPTOSES
ENTEROPTOSIS
ENTEROSTOMAL
ENTEROSTOMIES
ENTEROSTOMY
ENTEROTOMIES
ENTEROTOMY
ENTEROTOXIN
ENTEROTOXINS
ENTEROVIRAL
ENTEROVIRUS
ENTEROVIRUSES
ENTERPRISE
ENTERPRISED
ENTERPRISER
ENTERPRISERS
ENTERPRISES
ENTERPRISING
ENTERPRISINGLY
ENTERTAINED
ENTERTAINER
ENTERTAINERS
ENTERTAINING
ENTERTAININGLY
ENTERTAININGS
ENTERTAINMENT
ENTERTAINMENTS
ENTERTAINS
ENTERTAKEN
ENTERTAKES
ENTERTAKING
ENTERTISSUED
ENTHALPIES
ENTHRALDOM
ENTHRALDOMS
ENTHRALLED
ENTHRALLER
ENTHRALLERS
ENTHRALLING
ENTHRALLMENT
ENTHRALLMENTS
ENTHRALMENT
ENTHRALMENTS
ENTHRONEMENT
ENTHRONEMENTS
ENTHRONING
ENTHRONISATION
ENTHRONISATIONS
ENTHRONISE
ENTHRONISED
ENTHRONISES
ENTHRONISING
ENTHRONIZATION
ENTHRONIZATIONS
ENTHRONIZE
ENTHRONIZED
ENTHRONIZES
ENTHRONIZING
ENTHUSIASM
ENTHUSIASMS
ENTHUSIAST
ENTHUSIASTIC
ENTHUSIASTICAL
ENTHUSIASTS
ENTHYMEMATIC
ENTHYMEMATICAL

ENTHYMEMES
ENTICEABLE
ENTICEMENT
ENTICEMENTS
ENTICINGLY
ENTICINGNESS
ENTICINGNESSES
ENTIRENESS
ENTIRENESSES
ENTIRETIES
ENTITATIVE
ENTITLEMENT
ENTITLEMENTS
ENTOBLASTIC
ENTOBLASTS
ENTODERMAL
ENTODERMIC
ENTOILMENT
ENTOILMENTS
ENTOMBMENT
ENTOMBMENTS
ENTOMOFAUNA
ENTOMOFAUNAE
ENTOMOFAUNAS
ENTOMOLOGIC
ENTOMOLOGICAL
ENTOMOLOGICALLY
ENTOMOLOGIES
ENTOMOLOGISE
ENTOMOLOGISED
ENTOMOLOGISES
ENTOMOLOGISING
ENTOMOLOGIST
ENTOMOLOGISTS
ENTOMOLOGIZE
ENTOMOLOGIZED
ENTOMOLOGIZES
ENTOMOLOGIZING
ENTOMOLOGY
ENTOMOPHAGIES
ENTOMOPHAGOUS
ENTOMOPHAGY
ENTOMOPHILIES
ENTOMOPHILOUS
ENTOMOPHILY
ENTOMOSTRACAN
ENTOMOSTRACANS
ENTOMOSTRACOUS
ENTOPHYTAL
ENTOPHYTES
ENTOPHYTIC
ENTOPHYTOUS
ENTOPLASTRA
ENTOPLASTRAL
ENTOPLASTRON
ENTOPROCTS
ENTOURAGES
ENTRAILING
ENTRAINEMENT
ENTRAINEMENTS
ENTRAINERS
ENTRAINING
ENTRAINMENT
ENTRAINMENTS
ENTRAMMELED
ENTRAMMELING
ENTRAMMELLED

ENTRAMMELLING
ENTRAMMELS
ENTRANCEMENT
ENTRANCEMENTS
ENTRANCEWAY
ENTRANCEWAYS
ENTRANCING
ENTRANCINGLY
ENTRAPMENT
ENTRAPMENTS
ENTRAPPERS
ENTRAPPING
ENTREASURE
ENTREASURED
ENTREASURES
ENTREASURING
ENTREATABLE
ENTREATIES
ENTREATING
ENTREATINGLY
ENTREATINGS
ENTREATIVE
ENTREATMENT
ENTREATMENTS
ENTRECHATS
ENTRECOTES
ENTREMESSE
ENTREMESSES
ENTRENCHED
ENTRENCHER
ENTRENCHERS
ENTRENCHES
ENTRENCHING
ENTRENCHMENT
ENTRENCHMENTS
ENTREPRENEUR
ENTREPRENEURIAL
ENTREPRENEURS
ENTREPRENEUSE
ENTREPRENEUSES
ENTROPICALLY
ENTROPIONS
ENTROPIUMS
ENTRUSTING
ENTRUSTMENT
ENTRUSTMENTS
ENTWINEMENT
ENTWINEMENTS
ENTWISTING
ENUCLEATED
ENUCLEATES
ENUCLEATING
ENUCLEATION
ENUCLEATIONS
ENUMERABILITIES
ENUMERABILITY
ENUMERABLE
ENUMERATED
ENUMERATES
ENUMERATING
ENUMERATION
ENUMERATIONS
ENUMERATIVE
ENUMERATOR
ENUMERATORS
ENUNCIABLE
ENUNCIATED

ENUNCIATES
ENUNCIATING
ENUNCIATION
ENUNCIATIONS
ENUNCIATIVE
ENUNCIATIVELY
ENUNCIATOR
ENUNCIATORS
ENUNCIATORY
ENUREDNESS
ENUREDNESSES
ENUREMENTS
ENURESISES
ENVASSALLED
ENVASSALLING
ENVAULTING
ENVEIGLING
ENVELOPERS
ENVELOPING
ENVELOPMENT
ENVELOPMENTS
ENVENOMING
ENVENOMISATION
ENVENOMISATIONS
ENVENOMIZATION
ENVENOMIZATIONS
ENVERMEILED
ENVERMEILING
ENVERMEILS
ENVIABLENESS
ENVIABLENESSES
ENVIOUSNESS
ENVIOUSNESSES
ENVIRONICS
ENVIRONING
ENVIRONMENT
ENVIRONMENTAL
ENVIRONMENTALLY
ENVIRONMENTS
ENVISAGEMENT
ENVISAGEMENTS
ENVISAGING
ENVISIONED
ENVISIONING
ENVOYSHIPS
ENWALLOWED
ENWALLOWING
ENWHEELING
ENWRAPMENT
ENWRAPMENTS
ENWRAPPING
ENWRAPPINGS
ENWREATHED
ENWREATHES
ENWREATHING
ENZOOTICALLY
ENZYMATICALLY
ENZYMICALLY
ENZYMOLOGICAL
ENZYMOLOGIES
ENZYMOLOGIST
ENZYMOLOGISTS
ENZYMOLOGY
ENZYMOLYSES
ENZYMOLYSIS
ENZYMOLYTIC
EOHIPPUSES

SECTION 2: Words between 10 and 15 letters in length

EOSINOPHIL	EPIBLASTIC	EPIDIDYMIS	EPILEPTIFORM	EPIPHYTOTIC
EOSINOPHILE	EPICALYCES	EPIDIDYMITIS	EPILEPTOGENIC	EPIPHYTOTICS
EOSINOPHILES	EPICALYXES	EPIDIDYMITISES	EPILEPTOID	EPIPLASTRA
EOSINOPHILIA	EPICANTHIC	EPIDIORITE	EPILIMNION	EPIPLASTRAL
EOSINOPHILIAS	EPICANTHUS	EPIDIORITES	EPILIMNIONS	EPIPLASTRON
EOSINOPHILIC	EPICARDIAC	EPIDOSITES	EPILOBIUMS	EPIPOLISMS
EOSINOPHILOUS	EPICARDIAL	EPIDOTISATION	EPILOGISED	EPIROGENETIC
EOSINOPHILS	EPICARDIUM	EPIDOTISATIONS	EPILOGISES	EPIROGENIC
EPAGOMENAL	EPICARDIUMS	EPIDOTISED	EPILOGISING	EPIROGENIES
EPANADIPLOSES	EPICEDIANS	EPIDOTIZATION	EPILOGISTIC	EPIRRHEMAS
EPANADIPLOSIS	EPICENISMS	EPIDOTIZATIONS	EPILOGISTS	EPIRRHEMATA
EPANALEPSES	EPICENTERS	EPIDOTIZED	EPILOGIZED	EPIRRHEMATIC
EPANALEPSIS	EPICENTRAL	EPIGASTRIA	EPILOGIZES	EPISCOPACIES
EPANALEPTIC	EPICENTRES	EPIGASTRIAL	EPILOGIZING	EPISCOPACY
EPANAPHORA	EPICENTRUM	EPIGASTRIC	EPILOGUING	EPISCOPALIAN
EPANAPHORAL	EPICHEIREMA	EPIGASTRIUM	EPILOGUISE	EPISCOPALIANISM
EPANAPHORAS	EPICHEIREMAS	EPIGENESES	EPILOGUISED	EPISCOPALIANS
EPANODOSES	EPICHEIREMATA	EPIGENESIS	EPILOGUISES	EPISCOPALISM
EPANORTHOSES	EPICHLOROHYDRIN	EPIGENESIST	EPILOGUISING	EPISCOPALISMS
EPANORTHOSIS	EPICONDYLE	EPIGENESISTS	EPILOGUIZE	EPISCOPALLY
EPANORTHOTIC	EPICONDYLES	EPIGENETIC	EPILOGUIZED	EPISCOPANT
EPARCHATES	EPICONDYLITIS	EPIGENETICALLY	EPILOGUIZES	EPISCOPANTS
EPAULEMENT	EPICONDYLITISES	EPIGENETICIST	EPILOGUIZING	EPISCOPATE
EPAULEMENTS	EPICONTINENTAL	EPIGENETICISTS	EPIMELETIC	EPISCOPATED
EPAULETTED	EPICRANIUM	EPIGENETICS	EPIMERASES	EPISCOPATES
EPAULETTES	EPICRANIUMS	EPIGENISTS	EPIMERISED	EPISCOPATING
EPEIROGENESES	EPICUREANISM	EPIGENOMES	EPIMERISES	EPISCOPIES
EPEIROGENESIS	EPICUREANISMS	EPIGLOTTAL	EPIMERISING	EPISCOPISE
EPEIROGENETIC	EPICUREANS	EPIGLOTTIC	EPIMERISMS	EPISCOPISED
EPEIROGENIC	EPICURISED	EPIGLOTTIDES	EPIMERIZED	EPISCOPISES
EPEIROGENICALLY	EPICURISES	EPIGLOTTIS	EPIMERIZES	EPISCOPISING
EPEIROGENIES	EPICURISING	EPIGLOTTISES	EPIMERIZING	EPISCOPIZE
EPEIROGENY	EPICURISMS	EPIGNATHOUS	EPIMORPHIC	EPISCOPIZED
EPENCEPHALA	EPICURIZED	EPIGONISMS	EPIMORPHOSES	EPISCOPIZES
EPENCEPHALIC	EPICURIZES	EPIGRAMMATIC	EPIMORPHOSIS	EPISCOPIZING
EPENCEPHALON	EPICURIZING	EPIGRAMMATICAL	EPINASTICALLY	EPISEMATIC
EPENCEPHALONS	EPICUTICLE	EPIGRAMMATISE	EPINASTIES	EPISEPALOUS
EPENTHESES	EPICUTICLES	EPIGRAMMATISED	EPINEPHRIN	EPISIOTOMIES
EPENTHESIS	EPICUTICULAR	EPIGRAMMATISER	EPINEPHRINE	EPISIOTOMY
EPENTHETIC	EPICYCLICAL	EPIGRAMMATISERS	EPINEPHRINES	EPISODICAL
EPEOLATRIES	EPICYCLOID	EPIGRAMMATISES	EPINEPHRINS	EPISODICALLY
EPEXEGESES	EPICYCLOIDAL	EPIGRAMMATISING	EPINEURIAL	EPISOMALLY
EPEXEGESIS	EPICYCLOIDS	EPIGRAMMATISM	EPINEURIUM	EPISPASTIC
EPEXEGETIC	EPIDEICTIC	EPIGRAMMATISMS	EPINEURIUMS	EPISPASTICS
EPEXEGETICAL	EPIDEICTICAL	EPIGRAMMATIST	EPINICIONS	EPISTASIES
EPEXEGETICALLY	EPIDEMICAL	EPIGRAMMATISTS	EPINIKIANS	EPISTAXISES
EPHEBOPHILE	EPIDEMICALLY	EPIGRAMMATIZE	EPINIKIONS	EPISTEMICALLY
EPHEBOPHILES	EPIDEMICITIES	EPIGRAMMATIZED	EPIPELAGIC	EPISTEMICS
EPHEBOPHILIA	EPIDEMICITY	EPIGRAMMATIZER	EPIPETALOUS	EPISTEMOLOGICAL
EPHEBOPHILIAS	EPIDEMIOLOGIC	EPIGRAMMATIZERS	EPIPHANIES	EPISTEMOLOGIES
EPHEDRINES	EPIDEMIOLOGICAL	EPIGRAMMATIZES	EPIPHANOUS	EPISTEMOLOGIST
EPHEMERALITIES	EPIDEMIOLOGIES	EPIGRAMMATIZING	EPIPHENOMENA	EPISTEMOLOGISTS
EPHEMERALITY	EPIDEMIOLOGIST	EPIGRAPHED	EPIPHENOMENAL	EPISTEMOLOGY
EPHEMERALLY	EPIDEMIOLOGISTS	EPIGRAPHER	EPIPHENOMENALLY	EPISTERNAL
EPHEMERALNESS	EPIDEMIOLOGY	EPIGRAPHERS	EPIPHENOMENON	EPISTERNUM
EPHEMERALNESSES	EPIDENDRONE	EPIGRAPHIC	EPIPHONEMA	EPISTERNUMS
EPHEMERALS	EPIDENDRONES	EPIGRAPHICAL	EPIPHONEMAS	EPISTILBITE
EPHEMERIDES	EPIDENDRUM	EPIGRAPHICALLY	EPIPHRAGMS	EPISTILBITES
EPHEMERIDIAN	EPIDENDRUMS	EPIGRAPHIES	EPIPHYLLOUS	EPISTOLARIAN
EPHEMERIDS	EPIDERMISES	EPIGRAPHING	EPIPHYSEAL	EPISTOLARIANS
EPHEMERIST	EPIDERMOID	EPIGRAPHIST	EPIPHYSIAL	EPISTOLARIES
EPHEMERISTS	EPIDERMOLYSES	EPIGRAPHISTS	EPIPHYTICAL	EPISTOLARY
EPHEMERONS	EPIDERMOLYSIS	EPILATIONS	EPIPHYTICALLY	EPISTOLATORY
EPHEMEROPTERAN	EPIDIASCOPE	EPILEPSIES	EPIPHYTISM	EPISTOLERS
EPHEMEROPTERANS	EPIDIASCOPES	EPILEPTICAL	EPIPHYTISMS	EPISTOLETS
EPHEMEROUS	EPIDIDYMAL	EPILEPTICALLY	EPIPHYTOLOGIES	EPISTOLICAL
EPHORALTIES	EPIDIDYMIDES	EPILEPTICS	EPIPHYTOLOGY	EPISTOLISE

EPISTOLISED
EPISTOLISES
EPISTOLISING
EPISTOLIST
EPISTOLISTS
EPISTOLIZE
EPISTOLIZED
EPISTOLIZES
EPISTOLIZING
EPISTOLOGRAPHY
EPISTROPHE
EPISTROPHES
EPITAPHERS
EPITAPHIAL
EPITAPHIAN
EPITAPHING
EPITAPHIST
EPITAPHISTS
EPITAXIALLY
EPITHALAMIA
EPITHALAMIC
EPITHALAMION
EPITHALAMIUM
EPITHALAMIUMS
EPITHELIAL
EPITHELIALISE
EPITHELIALISED
EPITHELIALISES
EPITHELIALISING
EPITHELIALIZE
EPITHELIALIZED
EPITHELIALIZES
EPITHELIALIZING
EPITHELIOID
EPITHELIOMA
EPITHELIOMAS
EPITHELIOMATA
EPITHELIOMATOUS
EPITHELISATION
EPITHELISATIONS
EPITHELISE
EPITHELISED
EPITHELISES
EPITHELISING
EPITHELIUM
EPITHELIUMS
EPITHELIZATION
EPITHELIZATIONS
EPITHELIZE
EPITHELIZED
EPITHELIZES
EPITHELIZING
EPITHEMATA
EPITHERMAL
EPITHETICAL
EPITHETICALLY
EPITHETING
EPITHETONS
EPITHYMETIC
EPITOMICAL
EPITOMISATION
EPITOMISATIONS
EPITOMISED
EPITOMISER
EPITOMISERS
EPITOMISES
EPITOMISING

EPITOMISTS
EPITOMIZATION
EPITOMIZATIONS
EPITOMIZED
EPITOMIZER
EPITOMIZERS
EPITOMIZES
EPITOMIZING
EPITRACHELION
EPITRACHELIONS
EPITROCHOID
EPITROCHOIDS
EPIZEUXISES
EPIZOOTICALLY
EPIZOOTICS
EPIZOOTIES
EPIZOOTIOLOGIC
EPIZOOTIOLOGIES
EPIZOOTIOLOGY
EPONYCHIUM
EPONYCHIUMS
EPONYMOUSLY
EPOXIDATION
EPOXIDATIONS
EPOXIDISED
EPOXIDISES
EPOXIDISING
EPOXIDIZED
EPOXIDIZES
EPOXIDIZING
EPROUVETTE
EPROUVETTES
EPULATIONS
EPURATIONS
EQUABILITIES
EQUABILITY
EQUABLENESS
EQUABLENESSES
EQUALISATION
EQUALISATIONS
EQUALISERS
EQUALISING
EQUALITARIAN
EQUALITARIANISM
EQUALITARIANS
EQUALITIES
EQUALIZATION
EQUALIZATIONS
EQUALIZERS
EQUALIZING
EQUALNESSES
EQUANIMITIES
EQUANIMITY
EQUANIMOUS
EQUANIMOUSLY
EQUATABILITIES
EQUATABILITY
EQUATIONAL
EQUATIONALLY
EQUATORIAL
EQUATORIALLY
EQUATORIALS
EQUATORWARD
EQUESTRIAN
EQUESTRIANISM
EQUESTRIANISMS
EQUESTRIANS

EQUESTRIENNE
EQUESTRIENNES
EQUIANGULAR
EQUIANGULARITY
EQUIBALANCE
EQUIBALANCED
EQUIBALANCES
EQUIBALANCING
EQUICALORIC
EQUIDIFFERENT
EQUIDISTANCE
EQUIDISTANCES
EQUIDISTANT
EQUIDISTANTLY
EQUIFINALLY
EQUILATERAL
EQUILATERALLY
EQUILATERALS
EQUILIBRANT
EQUILIBRANTS
EQUILIBRATE
EQUILIBRATED
EQUILIBRATES
EQUILIBRATING
EQUILIBRATION
EQUILIBRATIONS
EQUILIBRATOR
EQUILIBRATORS
EQUILIBRATORY
EQUILIBRIA
EQUILIBRIST
EQUILIBRISTIC
EQUILIBRISTS
EQUILIBRITIES
EQUILIBRITY
EQUILIBRIUM
EQUILIBRIUMS
EQUIMOLECULAR
EQUIMULTIPLE
EQUIMULTIPLES
EQUINITIES
EQUINOCTIAL
EQUINOCTIALLY
EQUINOCTIALS
EQUINUMEROUS
EQUIPAGING
EQUIPARATE
EQUIPARATED
EQUIPARATES
EQUIPARATING
EQUIPARATION
EQUIPARATIONS
EQUIPARTITION
EQUIPARTITIONS
EQUIPMENTS
EQUIPOISED
EQUIPOISES
EQUIPOISING
EQUIPOLLENCE
EQUIPOLLENCES
EQUIPOLLENCIES
EQUIPOLLENCY
EQUIPOLLENT
EQUIPOLLENTLY
EQUIPOLLENTS
EQUIPONDERANCE
EQUIPONDERANCES

EQUIPONDERANCY
EQUIPONDERANT
EQUIPONDERATE
EQUIPONDERATED
EQUIPONDERATES
EQUIPONDERATING
EQUIPOTENT
EQUIPOTENTIAL
EQUIPOTENTIALS
EQUIPROBABILITY
EQUIPROBABLE
EQUISETACEOUS
EQUISETIFORM
EQUISETUMS
EQUITABILITIES
EQUITABILITY
EQUITABLENESS
EQUITABLENESSES
EQUITATION
EQUITATIONS
EQUIVALENCE
EQUIVALENCES
EQUIVALENCIES
EQUIVALENCY
EQUIVALENT
EQUIVALENTLY
EQUIVALENTS
EQUIVOCACIES
EQUIVOCACY
EQUIVOCALITIES
EQUIVOCALITY
EQUIVOCALLY
EQUIVOCALNESS
EQUIVOCALNESSES
EQUIVOCATE
EQUIVOCATED
EQUIVOCATES
EQUIVOCATING
EQUIVOCATINGLY
EQUIVOCATION
EQUIVOCATIONS
EQUIVOCATOR
EQUIVOCATORS
EQUIVOCATORY
EQUIVOQUES
ERADIATING
ERADIATION
ERADIATIONS
ERADICABLE
ERADICABLY
ERADICANTS
ERADICATED
ERADICATES
ERADICATING
ERADICATION
ERADICATIONS
ERADICATIVE
ERADICATOR
ERADICATORS
ERASABILITIES
ERASABILITY
ERASEMENTS
ERECTILITIES
ERECTILITY
ERECTNESSES
EREMACAUSES
EREMACAUSIS

EREMITICAL
EREMITISMS
EREMURUSES
ERETHISMIC
ERETHISTIC
ERGASTOPLASM
ERGASTOPLASMIC
ERGASTOPLASMS
ERGATANDROMORPH
ERGATANERS
ERGATIVITIES
ERGATIVITY
ERGATOCRACIES
ERGATOCRACY
ERGATOGYNE
ERGATOGYNES
ERGATOMORPH
ERGATOMORPHIC
ERGATOMORPHS
ERGODICITIES
ERGODICITY
ERGOGRAPHS
ERGOMANIAC
ERGOMANIACS
ERGOMANIAS
ERGOMETERS
ERGOMETRIC
ERGOMETRIES
ERGONOMICALLY
ERGONOMICS
ERGONOMIST
ERGONOMISTS
ERGONOVINE
ERGONOVINES
ERGOPHOBIA
ERGOPHOBIAS
ERGOSTEROL
ERGOSTEROLS
ERGOTAMINE
ERGOTAMINES
ERGOTISING
ERGOTIZING
ERICACEOUS
ERINACEOUS
ERIOMETERS
ERIOPHOROUS
ERIOPHORUM
ERIOPHORUMS
ERIOPHYIDS
ERIOSTEMON
ERIOSTEMONS
ERISTICALLY
ERODIBILITIES
ERODIBILITY
EROGENEITIES
EROGENEITY
EROSIONALLY
EROSIVENESS
EROSIVENESSES
EROSIVITIES
EROTICALLY
EROTICISATION
EROTICISATIONS
EROTICISED
EROTICISES
EROTICISING
EROTICISMS

EROTICISTS
EROTICIZATION
EROTICIZATIONS
EROTICIZED
EROTICIZES
EROTICIZING
EROTISATION
EROTISATIONS
EROTIZATION
EROTIZATIONS
EROTOGENIC
EROTOGENOUS
EROTOLOGICAL
EROTOLOGIES
EROTOLOGIST
EROTOLOGISTS
EROTOMANIA
EROTOMANIAC
EROTOMANIACS
EROTOMANIAS
EROTOPHOBIA
EROTOPHOBIAS
ERRANTRIES
ERRATICALLY
ERRATICISM
ERRATICISMS
ERRONEOUSLY
ERRONEOUSNESS
ERRONEOUSNESSES
ERUBESCENCE
ERUBESCENCES
ERUBESCENCIES
ERUBESCENCY
ERUBESCENT
ERUBESCITE
ERUBESCITES
ERUCTATING
ERUCTATION
ERUCTATIONS
ERUCTATIVE
ERUDITENESS
ERUDITENESSES
ERUDITIONS
ERUPTIONAL
ERUPTIVELY
ERUPTIVENESS
ERUPTIVENESSES
ERUPTIVITIES
ERUPTIVITY
ERVALENTAS
ERYSIPELAS
ERYSIPELASES
ERYSIPELATOUS
ERYSIPELOID
ERYSIPELOIDS
ERYTHEMATIC
ERYTHEMATOUS
ERYTHORBATE
ERYTHORBATES
ERYTHORBIC
ERYTHRAEMIA
ERYTHRAEMIAS
ERYTHREMIA
ERYTHREMIAS
ERYTHRINAS
ERYTHRISMAL
ERYTHRISMS

ERYTHRISTIC
ERYTHRITES
ERYTHRITIC
ERYTHRITOL
ERYTHRITOLS
ERYTHROBLAST
ERYTHROBLASTIC
ERYTHROBLASTS
ERYTHROCYTE
ERYTHROCYTES
ERYTHROCYTIC
ERYTHROMELALGIA
ERYTHROMYCIN
ERYTHROMYCINS
ERYTHRONIUM
ERYTHRONIUMS
ERYTHROPENIA
ERYTHROPENIAS
ERYTHROPHOBIA
ERYTHROPHOBIAS
ERYTHROPOIESES
ERYTHROPOIESIS
ERYTHROPOIETIC
ERYTHROPOIETIN
ERYTHROPOIETINS
ERYTHROPSIA
ERYTHROPSIAS
ERYTHROSIN
ERYTHROSINE
ERYTHROSINES
ERYTHROSINS
ESCABECHES
ESCADRILLE
ESCADRILLES
ESCALADERS
ESCALADING
ESCALADOES
ESCALATING
ESCALATION
ESCALATIONS
ESCALATORS
ESCALATORY
ESCALLONIA
ESCALLONIAS
ESCALLOPED
ESCALLOPING
ESCALOPING
ESCAMOTAGE
ESCAMOTAGES
ESCAPADOES
ESCAPELESS
ESCAPEMENT
ESCAPEMENTS
ESCAPOLOGIES
ESCAPOLOGIST
ESCAPOLOGISTS
ESCAPOLOGY
ESCARMOUCHE
ESCARMOUCHES
ESCARPMENT
ESCARPMENTS
ESCHAROTIC
ESCHAROTICS
ESCHATOLOGIC
ESCHATOLOGICAL
ESCHATOLOGIES
ESCHATOLOGIST

ESCHATOLOGISTS
ESCHATOLOGY
ESCHEATABLE
ESCHEATAGE
ESCHEATAGES
ESCHEATING
ESCHEATMENT
ESCHEATMENTS
ESCHEATORS
ESCHSCHOLTZIA
ESCHSCHOLTZIAS
ESCHSCHOLZIA
ESCHSCHOLZIAS
ESCLANDRES
ESCOPETTES
ESCORTAGES
ESCRIBANOS
ESCRITOIRE
ESCRITOIRES
ESCRITORIAL
ESCUTCHEON
ESCUTCHEONED
ESCUTCHEONS
ESEMPLASIES
ESEMPLASTIC
ESEMPLASTICALLY
ESOPHAGEAL
ESOPHAGITIDES
ESOPHAGITIS
ESOPHAGITISES
ESOPHAGOSCOPE
ESOPHAGOSCOPES
ESOPHAGOSCOPIES
ESOPHAGOSCOPY
ESOPHAGUSES
ESOTERICALLY
ESOTERICAS
ESOTERICISM
ESOTERICISMS
ESOTERICIST
ESOTERICISTS
ESOTERISMS
ESOTROPIAS
ESPADRILLE
ESPADRILLES
ESPAGNOLES
ESPAGNOLETTE
ESPAGNOLETTES
ESPALIERED
ESPALIERING
ESPECIALLY
ESPERANCES
ESPIEGLERIE
ESPIEGLERIES
ESPIONAGES
ESPLANADES
ESPRESSIVO
ESQUIRESSES
ESSAYETTES
ESSAYISTIC
ESSENTIALISE
ESSENTIALISED
ESSENTIALISES
ESSENTIALISING
ESSENTIALISM
ESSENTIALISMS
ESSENTIALIST

ESSENTIALISTS
ESSENTIALITIES
ESSENTIALITY
ESSENTIALIZE
ESSENTIALIZED
ESSENTIALIZES
ESSENTIALIZING
ESSENTIALLY
ESSENTIALNESS
ESSENTIALNESSES
ESSENTIALS
ESTABLISHABLE
ESTABLISHED
ESTABLISHER
ESTABLISHERS
ESTABLISHES
ESTABLISHING
ESTABLISHMENT
ESTABLISHMENTS
ESTAFETTES
ESTAMINETS
ESTANCIERO
ESTANCIEROS
ESTATESMAN
ESTATESMEN
ESTERIFICATION
ESTERIFICATIONS
ESTERIFIED
ESTERIFIES
ESTERIFYING
ESTERISATION
ESTERISATIONS
ESTERIZATION
ESTERIZATIONS
ESTHESIOGEN
ESTHESIOGENS
ESTHESISES
ESTHETICAL
ESTHETICALLY
ESTHETICIAN
ESTHETICIANS
ESTHETICISM
ESTHETICISMS
ESTIMABLENESS
ESTIMABLENESSES
ESTIMATING
ESTIMATION
ESTIMATIONS
ESTIMATIVE
ESTIMATORS
ESTIPULATE
ESTIVATING
ESTIVATION
ESTIVATIONS
ESTIVATORS
ESTOPPAGES
ESTRADIOLS
ESTRAMAZONE
ESTRAMAZONES
ESTRANGEDNESS
ESTRANGEDNESSES
ESTRANGELO
ESTRANGELOS
ESTRANGEMENT
ESTRANGEMENTS
ESTRANGERS
ESTRANGHELO

ESTRANGHELOS
ESTRANGING
ESTRAPADES
ESTREATING
ESTREPEMENT
ESTREPEMENTS
ESTRIBUTOR
ESTRIBUTORS
ESTRILDIDS
ESTROGENIC
ESTROGENICALLY
ESURIENCES
ESURIENCIES
ESURIENTLY
ETEPIMELETIC
ETERNALISATION
ETERNALISATIONS
ETERNALISE
ETERNALISED
ETERNALISES
ETERNALISING
ETERNALIST
ETERNALISTS
ETERNALITIES
ETERNALITY
ETERNALIZATION
ETERNALIZATIONS
ETERNALIZE
ETERNALIZED
ETERNALIZES
ETERNALIZING
ETERNALNESS
ETERNALNESSES
ETERNISATION
ETERNISATIONS
ETERNISING
ETERNITIES
ETERNIZATION
ETERNIZATIONS
ETERNIZING
ETHAMBUTOL
ETHAMBUTOLS
ETHANEDIOIC
ETHANEDIOL
ETHANEDIOLS
ETHANOATES
ETHANOLAMINE
ETHANOLAMINES
ETHEOSTOMINE
ETHEREALISATION
ETHEREALISE
ETHEREALISED
ETHEREALISES
ETHEREALISING
ETHEREALITIES
ETHEREALITY
ETHEREALIZATION
ETHEREALIZE
ETHEREALIZED
ETHEREALIZES
ETHEREALIZING
ETHEREALLY
ETHEREALNESS
ETHEREALNESSES
ETHERIFICATION
ETHERIFICATIONS
ETHERIFIED

ETHERIFIES	ETHNOMUSICOLOGY	EUCHROMATINS	EUMELANINS	EURHYTHMICS
ETHERIFYING	ETHNOSCIENCE	EUCRYPHIAS	EUNUCHISED	EURHYTHMIES
ETHERISATION	ETHNOSCIENCES	EUDAEMONIA	EUNUCHISES	EURHYTHMIST
ETHERISATIONS	ETHOLOGICAL	EUDAEMONIAS	EUNUCHISING	EURHYTHMISTS
ETHERISERS	ETHOLOGICALLY	EUDAEMONIC	EUNUCHISMS	EUROCHEQUE
ETHERISING	ETHOLOGIES	EUDAEMONICS	EUNUCHIZED	EUROCHEQUES
ETHERIZATION	ETHOLOGIST	EUDAEMONIES	EUNUCHIZES	EUROCREDIT
ETHERIZATIONS	ETHOLOGISTS	EUDAEMONISM	EUNUCHIZING	EUROCREDITS
ETHERIZERS	ETHOXYETHANE	EUDAEMONISMS	EUNUCHOIDISM	EUROCREEPS
ETHERIZING	ETHOXYETHANES	EUDAEMONIST	EUNUCHOIDISMS	EUROCURRENCIES
ETHEROMANIA	ETHYLAMINE	EUDAEMONISTIC	EUNUCHOIDS	EUROCURRENCY
ETHEROMANIAC	ETHYLAMINES	EUDAEMONISTICAL	EUONYMUSES	EURODEPOSIT
ETHEROMANIACS	ETHYLATING	EUDAEMONISTS	EUPATORIUM	EURODEPOSITS
ETHEROMANIAS	ETHYLATION	EUDAIMONISM	EUPATORIUMS	EURODOLLAR
ETHICALITIES	ETHYLATIONS	EUDAIMONISMS	EUPATRIDAE	EURODOLLARS
ETHICALITY	ETHYLBENZENE	EUDEMONIAS	EUPEPTICITIES	EUROMARKET
ETHICALNESS	ETHYLBENZENES	EUDEMONICS	EUPEPTICITY	EUROMARKETS
ETHICALNESSES	ETIOLATING	EUDEMONISM	EUPHAUSIACEAN	EUROPHILES
ETHICISING	ETIOLATION	EUDEMONISMS	EUPHAUSIACEANS	EUROPHILIA
ETHICIZING	ETIOLATIONS	EUDEMONIST	EUPHAUSIDS	EUROPHILIAS
ETHIONAMIDE	ETIOLOGICAL	EUDEMONISTIC	EUPHAUSIID	EUROPHOBIA
ETHIONAMIDES	ETIOLOGICALLY	EUDEMONISTICAL	EUPHAUSIIDS	EUROPHOBIAS
ETHIONINES	ETIOLOGIES	EUDEMONISTS	EUPHEMISED	EUROPHOBIC
ETHNARCHIES	ETIOLOGIST	EUDIALYTES	EUPHEMISER	EUROTERMINAL
ETHNICALLY	ETIOLOGISTS	EUDICOTYLEDON	EUPHEMISERS	EUROTERMINALS
ETHNICISMS	ETIQUETTES	EUDICOTYLEDONS	EUPHEMISES	EURYBATHIC
ETHNICITIES	ETONOGESTREL	EUDIOMETER	EUPHEMISING	EURYHALINE
ETHNOBIOLOGIES	ETONOGESTRELS	EUDIOMETERS	EUPHEMISMS	EURYOECIOUS
ETHNOBIOLOGY	ETOURDERIE	EUDIOMETRIC	EUPHEMISTIC	EURYPTERID
ETHNOBOTANICAL	ETOURDERIES	EUDIOMETRICAL	EUPHEMISTICALLY	EURYPTERIDS
ETHNOBOTANIES	ETRANGERES	EUDIOMETRICALLY	EUPHEMISTS	EURYPTEROID
ETHNOBOTANIST	ETYMOLOGICA	EUDIOMETRIES	EUPHEMIZED	EURYPTEROIDS
ETHNOBOTANISTS	ETYMOLOGICAL	EUDIOMETRY	EUPHEMIZER	EURYTHERMAL
ETHNOBOTANY	ETYMOLOGICALLY	EUGENECIST	EUPHEMIZERS	EURYTHERMIC
ETHNOCENTRIC	ETYMOLOGICON	EUGENECISTS	EUPHEMIZES	EURYTHERMOUS
ETHNOCENTRICITY	ETYMOLOGICUM	EUGENICALLY	EUPHEMIZING	EURYTHERMS
ETHNOCENTRISM	ETYMOLOGIES	EUGENICIST	EUPHONICAL	EURYTHMICAL
ETHNOCENTRISMS	ETYMOLOGISE	EUGENICISTS	EUPHONICALLY	EURYTHMICS
ETHNOCIDES	ETYMOLOGISED	EUGEOSYNCLINAL	EUPHONIOUS	EURYTHMIES
ETHNOGENIC	ETYMOLOGISES	EUGEOSYNCLINE	EUPHONIOUSLY	EURYTHMIST
ETHNOGENIES	ETYMOLOGISING	EUGEOSYNCLINES	EUPHONIOUSNESS	EURYTHMISTS
ETHNOGENIST	ETYMOLOGIST	EUGLENOIDS	EUPHONISED	EUSPORANGIATE
ETHNOGENISTS	ETYMOLOGISTS	EUGLOBULIN	EUPHONISES	EUSTATICALLY
ETHNOGRAPHER	ETYMOLOGIZE	EUGLOBULINS	EUPHONISING	EUSTRESSES
ETHNOGRAPHERS	ETYMOLOGIZED	EUHARMONIC	EUPHONISMS	EUTECTOIDS
ETHNOGRAPHIC	ETYMOLOGIZES	EUHEMERISE	EUPHONIUMS	EUTHANASED
ETHNOGRAPHICA	ETYMOLOGIZING	EUHEMERISED	EUPHONIZED	EUTHANASES
ETHNOGRAPHICAL	EUBACTERIA	EUHEMERISES	EUPHONIZES	EUTHANASIA
ETHNOGRAPHIES	EUBACTERIUM	EUHEMERISING	EUPHONIZING	EUTHANASIAS
ETHNOGRAPHY	EUCALYPTOL	EUHEMERISM	EUPHORBIACEOUS	EUTHANASIAST
ETHNOHISTORIAN	EUCALYPTOLE	EUHEMERISMS	EUPHORBIAS	EUTHANASIASTS
ETHNOHISTORIANS	EUCALYPTOLES	EUHEMERIST	EUPHORBIUM	EUTHANASIC
ETHNOHISTORIC	EUCALYPTOLS	EUHEMERISTIC	EUPHORBIUMS	EUTHANASIES
ETHNOHISTORICAL	EUCALYPTUS	EUHEMERISTS	EUPHORIANT	EUTHANASING
ETHNOHISTORIES	EUCALYPTUSES	EUHEMERIZE	EUPHORIANTS	EUTHANATISE
ETHNOHISTORY	EUCARYOTES	EUHEMERIZED	EUPHORICALLY	EUTHANATISED
ETHNOLINGUIST	EUCARYOTIC	EUHEMERIZES	EUPHRASIAS	EUTHANATISES
ETHNOLINGUISTIC	EUCHARISES	EUHEMERIZING	EUPHRASIES	EUTHANATISING
ETHNOLINGUISTS	EUCHARISTIC	EUKARYOTES	EUPHUISING	EUTHANATIZE
ETHNOLOGIC	EUCHLORINE	EUKARYOTIC	EUPHUISTIC	EUTHANATIZED
ETHNOLOGICAL	EUCHLORINES	EULOGISERS	EUPHUISTICAL	EUTHANATIZES
ETHNOLOGICALLY	EUCHLORINS	EULOGISING	EUPHUISTICALLY	EUTHANATIZING
ETHNOLOGIES	EUCHOLOGIA	EULOGISTIC	EUPHUIZING	EUTHANAZED
ETHNOLOGIST	EUCHOLOGIES	EULOGISTICAL	EUPLASTICS	EUTHANAZES
ETHNOLOGISTS	EUCHOLOGION	EULOGISTICALLY	EUPLOIDIES	EUTHANAZING
ETHNOMEDICINE	EUCHROMATIC	EULOGIZERS	EURHYTHMIC	EUTHANISED
ETHNOMEDICINES	EUCHROMATIN	EULOGIZING	EURHYTHMICAL	EUTHANISES

EUTHANISING	EVANGELISTARY	EVERDURING	EXACTNESSES	EXCEEDABLE
EUTHANIZED	EVANGELISTIC	EVERGLADES	EXACTRESSES	EXCEEDINGLY
EUTHANIZES	EVANGELISTS	EVERGREENS	EXAGGERATE	EXCELLENCE
EUTHANIZING	EVANGELIZATION	EVERLASTING	EXAGGERATED	EXCELLENCES
EUTHENISTS	EVANGELIZATIONS	EVERLASTINGLY	EXAGGERATEDLY	EXCELLENCIES
EUTHERIANS	EVANGELIZE	EVERLASTINGNESS	EXAGGERATEDNESS	EXCELLENCY
EUTHYROIDS	EVANGELIZED	EVERLASTINGS	EXAGGERATES	EXCELLENTLY
EUTRAPELIA	EVANGELIZER	EVERYDAYNESS	EXAGGERATING	EXCELSIORS
EUTRAPELIAS	EVANGELIZERS	EVERYDAYNESSES	EXAGGERATINGLY	EXCENTRICS
EUTRAPELIES	EVANGELIZES	EVERYPLACE	EXAGGERATION	EXCEPTANTS
EUTROPHICATION	EVANGELIZING	EVERYTHING	EXAGGERATIONS	EXCEPTIONABLE
EUTROPHICATIONS	EVANISHING	EVERYWHENCE	EXAGGERATIVE	EXCEPTIONABLY
EUTROPHIES	EVANISHMENT	EVERYWHERE	EXAGGERATOR	EXCEPTIONAL
EVACUATING	EVANISHMENTS	EVERYWHITHER	EXAGGERATORS	EXCEPTIONALISM
EVACUATION	EVANITIONS	EVERYWOMAN	EXAGGERATORY	EXCEPTIONALISMS
EVACUATIONS	EVAPORABILITIES	EVERYWOMEN	EXAHERTZES	EXCEPTIONALITY
EVACUATIVE	EVAPORABILITY	EVIDENCING	EXALBUMINOUS	EXCEPTIONALLY
EVACUATIVES	EVAPORABLE	EVIDENTIAL	EXALTATION	EXCEPTIONALNESS
EVACUATORS	EVAPORATED	EVIDENTIALLY	EXALTATIONS	EXCEPTIONALS
EVAGATIONS	EVAPORATES	EVIDENTIARY	EXALTEDNESS	EXCEPTIONS
EVAGINATED	EVAPORATING	EVILDOINGS	EXALTEDNESSES	EXCEPTIOUS
EVAGINATES	EVAPORATION	EVILNESSES	EXAMINABILITIES	EXCEPTLESS
EVAGINATING	EVAPORATIONS	EVINCEMENT	EXAMINABILITY	EXCERPTERS
EVAGINATION	EVAPORATIVE	EVINCEMENTS	EXAMINABLE	EXCERPTIBLE
EVAGINATIONS	EVAPORATOR	EVISCERATE	EXAMINANTS	EXCERPTING
EVALUATING	EVAPORATORS	EVISCERATED	EXAMINATES	EXCERPTINGS
EVALUATION	EVAPORIMETER	EVISCERATES	EXAMINATION	EXCERPTION
EVALUATIONS	EVAPORIMETERS	EVISCERATING	EXAMINATIONAL	EXCERPTIONS
EVALUATIVE	EVAPORITES	EVISCERATION	EXAMINATIONS	EXCERPTORS
EVALUATORS	EVAPORITIC	EVISCERATIONS	EXAMINATOR	EXCESSIVELY
EVANESCENCE	EVAPOROGRAPH	EVISCERATOR	EXAMINATORS	EXCESSIVENESS
EVANESCENCES	EVAPOROGRAPHS	EVISCERATORS	EXAMINERSHIP	EXCESSIVENESSES
EVANESCENT	EVAPOROMETER	EVITATIONS	EXAMINERSHIPS	EXCHANGEABILITY
EVANESCENTLY	EVAPOROMETERS	EVITERNALLY	EXANIMATION	EXCHANGEABLE
EVANESCING	EVASIVENESS	EVITERNITIES	EXANIMATIONS	EXCHANGEABLY
EVANGELARIUM	EVASIVENESSES	EVITERNITY	EXANTHEMAS	EXCHANGERS
EVANGELARIUMS	EVECTIONAL	EVOCATIONS	EXANTHEMATA	EXCHANGING
EVANGELIAR	EVENEMENTS	EVOCATIVELY	EXANTHEMATIC	EXCHEQUERED
EVANGELIARIES	EVENHANDED	EVOCATIVENESS	EXANTHEMATOUS	EXCHEQUERING
EVANGELIARION	EVENHANDEDLY	EVOCATIVENESSES	EXARATIONS	EXCHEQUERS
EVANGELIARIONS	EVENHANDEDNESS	EVOLUTIONAL	EXARCHATES	EXCIPIENTS
EVANGELIARIUM	EVENNESSES	EVOLUTIONARILY	EXARCHISTS	EXCISIONAL
EVANGELIARIUMS	EVENTFULLY	EVOLUTIONARY	EXASPERATE	EXCITABILITIES
EVANGELIARS	EVENTFULNESS	EVOLUTIONISM	EXASPERATED	EXCITABILITY
EVANGELIARY	EVENTFULNESSES	EVOLUTIONISMS	EXASPERATEDLY	EXCITABLENESS
EVANGELICAL	EVENTRATED	EVOLUTIONIST	EXASPERATER	EXCITABLENESSES
EVANGELICALISM	EVENTRATES	EVOLUTIONISTIC	EXASPERATERS	EXCITANCIES
EVANGELICALISMS	EVENTRATING	EVOLUTIONISTS	EXASPERATES	EXCITATION
EVANGELICALLY	EVENTRATION	EVOLUTIONS	EXASPERATING	EXCITATIONS
EVANGELICALNESS	EVENTRATIONS	EVOLVEMENT	EXASPERATINGLY	EXCITATIVE
EVANGELICALS	EVENTUALISE	EVOLVEMENTS	EXASPERATION	EXCITATORY
EVANGELICISM	EVENTUALISED	EVONYMUSES	EXASPERATIONS	EXCITEDNESS
EVANGELICISMS	EVENTUALISES	EVULGATING	EXASPERATIVE	EXCITEDNESSES
EVANGELIES	EVENTUALISING	EXACERBATE	EXASPERATOR	EXCITEMENT
EVANGELISATION	EVENTUALITIES	EXACERBATED	EXASPERATORS	EXCITEMENTS
EVANGELISATIONS	EVENTUALITY	EXACERBATES	EXCAMBIONS	EXCITINGLY
EVANGELISE	EVENTUALIZE	EXACERBATING	EXCAMBIUMS	EXCLAIMERS
EVANGELISED	EVENTUALIZED	EXACERBATION	EXCARNATED	EXCLAIMING
EVANGELISER	EVENTUALIZES	EXACERBATIONS	EXCARNATES	EXCLAMATION
EVANGELISERS	EVENTUALIZING	EXACERBESCENCE	EXCARNATING	EXCLAMATIONAL
EVANGELISES	EVENTUALLY	EXACERBESCENCES	EXCARNATION	EXCLAMATIONS
EVANGELISING	EVENTUATED	EXACTINGLY	EXCARNATIONS	EXCLAMATIVE
EVANGELISM	EVENTUATES	EXACTINGNESS	EXCAVATING	EXCLAMATIVES
EVANGELISMS	EVENTUATING	EXACTINGNESSES	EXCAVATION	EXCLAMATORILY
EVANGELIST	EVENTUATION	EXACTITUDE	EXCAVATIONAL	EXCLAMATORY
EVANGELISTARIES	EVENTUATIONS	EXACTITUDES	EXCAVATIONS	EXCLAUSTRATION
EVANGELISTARION	EVERBLOOMING	EXACTMENTS	EXCAVATORS	EXCLAUSTRATIONS

EXCLOSURES	EXCRETIONS	EXEMPLARILY	EXHEREDATIONS	EXODONTIST
EXCLUDABILITIES	EXCRETORIES	EXEMPLARINESS	EXHIBITERS	EXODONTISTS
EXCLUDABILITY	EXCRUCIATE	EXEMPLARINESSES	EXHIBITING	EXOENZYMES
EXCLUDABLE	EXCRUCIATED	EXEMPLARITIES	EXHIBITION	EXOERYTHROCYTIC
EXCLUDIBLE	EXCRUCIATES	EXEMPLARITY	EXHIBITIONER	EXOGENETIC
EXCLUSIONARY	EXCRUCIATING	EXEMPLIFIABLE	EXHIBITIONERS	EXOGENISMS
EXCLUSIONISM	EXCRUCIATINGLY	EXEMPLIFICATION	EXHIBITIONISM	EXOGENOUSLY
EXCLUSIONISMS	EXCRUCIATION	EXEMPLIFICATIVE	EXHIBITIONISMS	EXONERATED
EXCLUSIONIST	EXCRUCIATIONS	EXEMPLIFIED	EXHIBITIONIST	EXONERATES
EXCLUSIONISTS	EXCULPABLE	EXEMPLIFIER	EXHIBITIONISTIC	EXONERATING
EXCLUSIONS	EXCULPATED	EXEMPLIFIERS	EXHIBITIONISTS	EXONERATION
EXCLUSIVELY	EXCULPATES	EXEMPLIFIES	EXHIBITIONS	EXONERATIONS
EXCLUSIVENESS	EXCULPATING	EXEMPLIFYING	EXHIBITIVE	EXONERATIVE
EXCLUSIVENESSES	EXCULPATION	EXEMPTIONS	EXHIBITIVELY	EXONERATOR
EXCLUSIVES	EXCULPATIONS	EXENTERATE	EXHIBITORS	EXONERATORS
EXCLUSIVISM	EXCULPATORY	EXENTERATED	EXHIBITORY	EXONUCLEASE
EXCLUSIVISMS	EXCURSIONED	EXENTERATES	EXHILARANT	EXONUCLEASES
EXCLUSIVIST	EXCURSIONING	EXENTERATING	EXHILARANTS	EXONUMISTS
EXCLUSIVISTS	EXCURSIONISE	EXENTERATION	EXHILARATE	EXOPARASITE
EXCLUSIVITIES	EXCURSIONISED	EXENTERATIONS	EXHILARATED	EXOPARASITES
EXCLUSIVITY	EXCURSIONISES	EXEQUATURS	EXHILARATES	EXOPARASITIC
EXCOGITABLE	EXCURSIONISING	EXERCISABLE	EXHILARATING	EXOPEPTIDASE
EXCOGITATE	EXCURSIONIST	EXERCISERS	EXHILARATINGLY	EXOPEPTIDASES
EXCOGITATED	EXCURSIONISTS	EXERCISING	EXHILARATION	EXOPHAGIES
EXCOGITATES	EXCURSIONIZE	EXERCITATION	EXHILARATIONS	EXOPHAGOUS
EXCOGITATING	EXCURSIONIZED	EXERCITATIONS	EXHILARATIVE	EXOPHTHALMIA
EXCOGITATION	EXCURSIONIZES	EXERCYCLES	EXHILARATOR	EXOPHTHALMIAS
EXCOGITATIONS	EXCURSIONIZING	EXERGAMING	EXHILARATORS	EXOPHTHALMIC
EXCOGITATIVE	EXCURSIONS	EXERGAMINGS	EXHILARATORY	EXOPHTHALMOS
EXCOGITATOR	EXCURSIVELY	EXERTAINMENT	EXHORTATION	EXOPHTHALMOSES
EXCOGITATORS	EXCURSIVENESS	EXERTAINMENTS	EXHORTATIONS	EXOPHTHALMUS
EXCOMMUNICABLE	EXCURSIVENESSES	EXFILTRATE	EXHORTATIVE	EXOPHTHALMUSES
EXCOMMUNICATE	EXCURSUSES	EXFILTRATED	EXHORTATORY	EXOPLANETS
EXCOMMUNICATED	EXCUSABLENESS	EXFILTRATES	EXHUMATING	EXOPODITES
EXCOMMUNICATES	EXCUSABLENESSES	EXFILTRATING	EXHUMATION	EXOPODITIC
EXCOMMUNICATING	EXCUSATORY	EXFOLIANTS	EXHUMATIONS	EXORABILITIES
EXCOMMUNICATION	EXECRABLENESS	EXFOLIATED	EXIGENCIES	EXORABILITY
EXCOMMUNICATIVE	EXECRABLENESSES	EXFOLIATES	EXIGUITIES	EXORATIONS
EXCOMMUNICATOR	EXECRATING	EXFOLIATING	EXIGUOUSLY	EXORBITANCE
EXCOMMUNICATORS	EXECRATION	EXFOLIATION	EXIGUOUSNESS	EXORBITANCES
EXCOMMUNICATORY	EXECRATIONS	EXFOLIATIONS	EXIGUOUSNESSES	EXORBITANCIES
EXCOMMUNION	EXECRATIVE	EXFOLIATIVE	EXILEMENTS	EXORBITANCY
EXCOMMUNIONS	EXECRATIVELY	EXFOLIATOR	EXIMIOUSLY	EXORBITANT
EXCORIATED	EXECRATORS	EXFOLIATORS	EXISTENCES	EXORBITANTLY
EXCORIATES	EXECRATORY	EXHALATION	EXISTENTIAL	EXORBITATE
EXCORIATING	EXECUTABLE	EXHALATIONS	EXISTENTIALISM	EXORBITATED
EXCORIATION	EXECUTABLES	EXHAUSTEDLY	EXISTENTIALISMS	EXORBITATES
EXCORIATIONS	EXECUTANCIES	EXHAUSTERS	EXISTENTIALIST	EXORBITATING
EXCORTICATE	EXECUTANCY	EXHAUSTIBILITY	EXISTENTIALISTS	EXORCISERS
EXCORTICATED	EXECUTANTS	EXHAUSTIBLE	EXISTENTIALLY	EXORCISING
EXCORTICATES	EXECUTARIES	EXHAUSTING	EXISTENTIALS	EXORCISTIC
EXCORTICATING	EXECUTIONER	EXHAUSTINGLY	EXOBIOLOGICAL	EXORCISTICAL
EXCORTICATION	EXECUTIONERS	EXHAUSTION	EXOBIOLOGIES	EXORCIZERS
EXCORTICATIONS	EXECUTIONS	EXHAUSTIONS	EXOBIOLOGIST	EXORCIZING
EXCREMENTA	EXECUTIVELY	EXHAUSTIVE	EXOBIOLOGISTS	EXOSKELETAL
EXCREMENTAL	EXECUTIVES	EXHAUSTIVELY	EXOBIOLOGY	EXOSKELETON
EXCREMENTITIAL	EXECUTORIAL	EXHAUSTIVENESS	EXOCENTRIC	EXOSKELETONS
EXCREMENTITIOUS	EXECUTORSHIP	EXHAUSTIVITIES	EXOCUTICLE	EXOSPHERES
EXCREMENTS	EXECUTORSHIPS	EXHAUSTIVITY	EXOCUTICLES	EXOSPHERIC
EXCREMENTUM	EXECUTRESS	EXHAUSTLESS	EXOCYTOSED	EXOSPHERICAL
EXCRESCENCE	EXECUTRESSES	EXHAUSTLESSLY	EXOCYTOSES	EXOSPORIUM
EXCRESCENCES	EXECUTRICES	EXHAUSTLESSNESS	EXOCYTOSING	EXOSPOROUS
EXCRESCENCIES	EXECUTRIES	EXHEREDATE	EXOCYTOSIS	EXOTERICAL
EXCRESCENCY	EXECUTRIXES	EXHEREDATED	EXOCYTOTIC	EXOTERICALLY
EXCRESCENT	EXEGETICAL	EXHEREDATES	EXODERMISES	EXOTERICISM
EXCRESCENTIAL	EXEGETICALLY	EXHEREDATING	EXODONTIAS	EXOTERICISMS
EXCRESCENTLY	EXEGETISTS	EXHEREDATION	EXODONTICS	EXOTHERMAL

EXOTHERMALLY	EXPECTEDLY	EXPERIMENT	EXPLOITATION	EXPRESSIONIST
EXOTHERMIC	EXPECTEDNESS	EXPERIMENTAL	EXPLOITATIONS	EXPRESSIONISTIC
EXOTHERMICALLY	EXPECTEDNESSES	EXPERIMENTALISE	EXPLOITATIVE	EXPRESSIONISTS
EXOTHERMICITIES	EXPECTINGLY	EXPERIMENTALISM	EXPLOITATIVELY	EXPRESSIONLESS
EXOTHERMICITY	EXPECTINGS	EXPERIMENTALIST	EXPLOITERS	EXPRESSIONS
EXOTICALLY	EXPECTORANT	EXPERIMENTALIZE	EXPLOITING	EXPRESSIVE
EXOTICISED	EXPECTORANTS	EXPERIMENTALLY	EXPLOITIVE	EXPRESSIVELY
EXOTICISES	EXPECTORATE	EXPERIMENTATION	EXPLORATION	EXPRESSIVENESS
EXOTICISING	EXPECTORATED	EXPERIMENTATIVE	EXPLORATIONAL	EXPRESSIVITIES
EXOTICISMS	EXPECTORATES	EXPERIMENTED	EXPLORATIONIST	EXPRESSIVITY
EXOTICISTS	EXPECTORATING	EXPERIMENTER	EXPLORATIONISTS	EXPRESSMAN
EXOTICIZED	EXPECTORATION	EXPERIMENTERS	EXPLORATIONS	EXPRESSMEN
EXOTICIZES	EXPECTORATIONS	EXPERIMENTING	EXPLORATIVE	EXPRESSNESS
EXOTICIZING	EXPECTORATIVE	EXPERIMENTIST	EXPLORATIVELY	EXPRESSNESSES
EXOTICNESS	EXPECTORATIVES	EXPERIMENTISTS	EXPLORATORY	EXPRESSURE
EXOTICNESSES	EXPECTORATOR	EXPERIMENTS	EXPLOSIBLE	EXPRESSURES
EXOTROPIAS	EXPECTORATORS	EXPERTISED	EXPLOSIONS	EXPRESSWAY
EXPANDABILITIES	EXPEDIENCE	EXPERTISES	EXPLOSIVELY	EXPRESSWAYS
EXPANDABILITY	EXPEDIENCES	EXPERTISING	EXPLOSIVENESS	EXPROBRATE
EXPANDABLE	EXPEDIENCIES	EXPERTISMS	EXPLOSIVENESSES	EXPROBRATED
EXPANSIBILITIES	EXPEDIENCY	EXPERTIZED	EXPLOSIVES	EXPROBRATES
EXPANSIBILITY	EXPEDIENTIAL	EXPERTIZES	EXPONENTIAL	EXPROBRATING
EXPANSIBLE	EXPEDIENTIALLY	EXPERTIZING	EXPONENTIALLY	EXPROBRATION
EXPANSIBLY	EXPEDIENTLY	EXPERTNESS	EXPONENTIALS	EXPROBRATIONS
EXPANSIONAL	EXPEDIENTS	EXPERTNESSES	EXPONENTIATION	EXPROBRATIVE
EXPANSIONARY	EXPEDITATE	EXPIATIONS	EXPONENTIATIONS	EXPROBRATORY
EXPANSIONISM	EXPEDITATED	EXPIRATION	EXPORTABILITIES	EXPROMISSION
EXPANSIONISMS	EXPEDITATES	EXPIRATIONS	EXPORTABILITY	EXPROMISSIONS
EXPANSIONIST	EXPEDITATING	EXPIRATORY	EXPORTABLE	EXPROMISSOR
EXPANSIONISTIC	EXPEDITATION	EXPISCATED	EXPORTATION	EXPROMISSORS
EXPANSIONISTS	EXPEDITATIONS	EXPISCATES	EXPORTATIONS	EXPROPRIABLE
EXPANSIONS	EXPEDITELY	EXPISCATING	EXPOSEDNESS	EXPROPRIATE
EXPANSIVELY	EXPEDITERS	EXPISCATION	EXPOSEDNESSES	EXPROPRIATED
EXPANSIVENESS	EXPEDITING	EXPISCATIONS	EXPOSITING	EXPROPRIATES
EXPANSIVENESSES	EXPEDITION	EXPISCATORY	EXPOSITION	EXPROPRIATING
EXPANSIVITIES	EXPEDITIONARY	EXPLAINABLE	EXPOSITIONAL	EXPROPRIATION
EXPANSIVITY	EXPEDITIONS	EXPLAINERS	EXPOSITIONS	EXPROPRIATIONS
EXPATIATED	EXPEDITIOUS	EXPLAINING	EXPOSITIVE	EXPROPRIATOR
EXPATIATES	EXPEDITIOUSLY	EXPLANATION	EXPOSITIVELY	EXPROPRIATORS
EXPATIATING	EXPEDITIOUSNESS	EXPLANATIONS	EXPOSITORILY	EXPUGNABLE
EXPATIATION	EXPEDITIVE	EXPLANATIVE	EXPOSITORS	EXPUGNATION
EXPATIATIONS	EXPEDITORS	EXPLANATIVELY	EXPOSITORY	EXPUGNATIONS
EXPATIATIVE	EXPELLABLE	EXPLANATORILY	EXPOSITRESS	EXPULSIONS
EXPATIATOR	EXPELLANTS	EXPLANATORY	EXPOSITRESSES	EXPUNCTING
EXPATIATORS	EXPELLENTS	EXPLANTATION	EXPOSTULATE	EXPUNCTION
EXPATIATORY	EXPENDABILITIES	EXPLANTATIONS	EXPOSTULATED	EXPUNCTIONS
EXPATRIATE	EXPENDABILITY	EXPLANTING	EXPOSTULATES	EXPURGATED
EXPATRIATED	EXPENDABLE	EXPLETIVELY	EXPOSTULATING	EXPURGATES
EXPATRIATES	EXPENDABLES	EXPLETIVES	EXPOSTULATINGLY	EXPURGATING
EXPATRIATING	EXPENDABLY	EXPLICABLE	EXPOSTULATION	EXPURGATION
EXPATRIATION	EXPENDITURE	EXPLICABLY	EXPOSTULATIONS	EXPURGATIONS
EXPATRIATIONS	EXPENDITURES	EXPLICATED	EXPOSTULATIVE	EXPURGATOR
EXPATRIATISM	EXPENSIVELY	EXPLICATES	EXPOSTULATOR	EXPURGATORIAL
EXPATRIATISMS	EXPENSIVENESS	EXPLICATING	EXPOSTULATORS	EXPURGATORS
EXPECTABLE	EXPENSIVENESSES	EXPLICATION	EXPOSTULATORY	EXPURGATORY
EXPECTABLY	EXPERIENCE	EXPLICATIONS	EXPOSTURES	EXQUISITELY
EXPECTANCE	EXPERIENCEABLE	EXPLICATIVE	EXPOUNDERS	EXQUISITENESS
EXPECTANCES	EXPERIENCED	EXPLICATIVELY	EXPOUNDING	EXQUISITENESSES
EXPECTANCIES	EXPERIENCELESS	EXPLICATOR	EXPRESSAGE	EXQUISITES
EXPECTANCY	EXPERIENCER	EXPLICATORS	EXPRESSAGES	EXSANGUINATE
EXPECTANTLY	EXPERIENCERS	EXPLICATORY	EXPRESSERS	EXSANGUINATED
EXPECTANTS	EXPERIENCES	EXPLICITLY	EXPRESSIBLE	EXSANGUINATES
EXPECTATION	EXPERIENCING	EXPLICITNESS	EXPRESSING	EXSANGUINATING
EXPECTATIONAL	EXPERIENTIAL	EXPLICITNESSES	EXPRESSION	EXSANGUINATION
EXPECTATIONS	EXPERIENTIALISM	EXPLOITABLE	EXPRESSIONAL	EXSANGUINATIONS
EXPECTATIVE	EXPERIENTIALIST	EXPLOITAGE	EXPRESSIONISM	EXSANGUINE
EXPECTATIVES	EXPERIENTIALLY	EXPLOITAGES	EXPRESSIONISMS	EXSANGUINED

EXSANGUINEOUS	EXTENSIONALISMS	EXTERNALIZES	EXTRADITABLE	EXTRAVAGANCIES
EXSANGUINITIES	EXTENSIONALITY	EXTERNALIZING	EXTRADITED	EXTRAVAGANCY
EXSANGUINITY	EXTENSIONALLY	EXTERNALLY	EXTRADITES	EXTRAVAGANT
EXSANGUINOUS	EXTENSIONIST	EXTERNSHIP	EXTRADITING	EXTRAVAGANTLY
EXSCINDING	EXTENSIONISTS	EXTERNSHIPS	EXTRADITION	EXTRAVAGANZA
EXSECTIONS	EXTENSIONS	EXTEROCEPTIVE	EXTRADITIONS	EXTRAVAGANZAS
EXSERTIONS	EXTENSITIES	EXTEROCEPTOR	EXTRADOSES	EXTRAVAGATE
EXSICCANTS	EXTENSIVELY	EXTEROCEPTORS	EXTRADOTAL	EXTRAVAGATED
EXSICCATED	EXTENSIVENESS	EXTERRITORIAL	EXTRADURAL	EXTRAVAGATES
EXSICCATES	EXTENSIVENESSES	EXTERRITORIALLY	EXTRADURALS	EXTRAVAGATING
EXSICCATING	EXTENSIVISATION	EXTINCTING	EXTRAEMBRYONIC	EXTRAVAGATION
EXSICCATION	EXTENSIVIZATION	EXTINCTION	EXTRAFLORAL	EXTRAVAGATIONS
EXSICCATIONS	EXTENSOMETER	EXTINCTIONS	EXTRAFORANEOUS	EXTRAVASATE
EXSICCATIVE	EXTENSOMETERS	EXTINCTIVE	EXTRAGALACTIC	EXTRAVASATED
EXSICCATOR	EXTENUATED	EXTINCTURE	EXTRAHEPATIC	EXTRAVASATES
EXSICCATORS	EXTENUATES	EXTINCTURES	EXTRAJUDICIAL	EXTRAVASATING
EXSOLUTION	EXTENUATING	EXTINGUISH	EXTRAJUDICIALLY	EXTRAVASATION
EXSOLUTIONS	EXTENUATINGLY	EXTINGUISHABLE	EXTRALEGAL	EXTRAVASATIONS
EXSTIPULATE	EXTENUATINGS	EXTINGUISHANT	EXTRALEGALLY	EXTRAVASCULAR
EXSTROPHIES	EXTENUATION	EXTINGUISHANTS	EXTRALIMITAL	EXTRAVEHICULAR
EXSUFFLATE	EXTENUATIONS	EXTINGUISHED	EXTRALIMITARY	EXTRAVERSION
EXSUFFLATED	EXTENUATIVE	EXTINGUISHER	EXTRALINGUISTIC	EXTRAVERSIONS
EXSUFFLATES	EXTENUATIVES	EXTINGUISHERS	EXTRALITERARY	EXTRAVERSIVE
EXSUFFLATING	EXTENUATOR	EXTINGUISHES	EXTRALITIES	EXTRAVERSIVELY
EXSUFFLATION	EXTENUATORS	EXTINGUISHING	EXTRALOGICAL	EXTRAVERTED
EXSUFFLATIONS	EXTENUATORY	EXTINGUISHMENT	EXTRAMARITAL	EXTRAVERTING
EXSUFFLICATE	EXTERIORISATION	EXTINGUISHMENTS	EXTRAMARITALLY	EXTRAVERTLY
EXTEMPORAL	EXTERIORISE	EXTIRPABLE	EXTRAMETRICAL	EXTRAVERTS
EXTEMPORALLY	EXTERIORISED	EXTIRPATED	EXTRAMUNDANE	EXTREATING
EXTEMPORANEITY	EXTERIORISES	EXTIRPATES	EXTRAMURAL	EXTREMENESS
EXTEMPORANEOUS	EXTERIORISING	EXTIRPATING	EXTRAMURALLY	EXTREMENESSES
EXTEMPORARILY	EXTERIORITIES	EXTIRPATION	EXTRAMUSICAL	EXTREMISMS
EXTEMPORARINESS	EXTERIORITY	EXTIRPATIONS	EXTRANEITIES	EXTREMISTS
EXTEMPORARY	EXTERIORIZATION	EXTIRPATIVE	EXTRANEITY	EXTREMITIES
EXTEMPORES	EXTERIORIZE	EXTIRPATOR	EXTRANEOUS	EXTREMOPHILE
EXTEMPORISATION	EXTERIORIZED	EXTIRPATORS	EXTRANEOUSLY	EXTREMOPHILES
EXTEMPORISE	EXTERIORIZES	EXTIRPATORY	EXTRANEOUSNESS	EXTRICABLE
EXTEMPORISED	EXTERIORIZING	EXTOLLINGLY	EXTRANUCLEAR	EXTRICATED
EXTEMPORISER	EXTERIORLY	EXTOLMENTS	EXTRAORDINAIRE	EXTRICATES
EXTEMPORISERS	EXTERMINABLE	EXTORSIVELY	EXTRAORDINARIES	EXTRICATING
EXTEMPORISES	EXTERMINATE	EXTORTIONARY	EXTRAORDINARILY	EXTRICATION
EXTEMPORISING	EXTERMINATED	EXTORTIONATE	EXTRAORDINARY	EXTRICATIONS
EXTEMPORIZATION	EXTERMINATES	EXTORTIONATELY	EXTRAPOLATE	EXTRINSICAL
EXTEMPORIZE	EXTERMINATING	EXTORTIONER	EXTRAPOLATED	EXTRINSICALITY
EXTEMPORIZED	EXTERMINATION	EXTORTIONERS	EXTRAPOLATES	EXTRINSICALLY
EXTEMPORIZER	EXTERMINATIONS	EXTORTIONIST	EXTRAPOLATING	EXTRINSICALS
EXTEMPORIZERS	EXTERMINATIVE	EXTORTIONISTS	EXTRAPOLATION	EXTROPIANS
EXTEMPORIZES	EXTERMINATOR	EXTORTIONS	EXTRAPOLATIONS	EXTROVERSION
EXTEMPORIZING	EXTERMINATORS	EXTRABOLDS	EXTRAPOLATIVE	EXTROVERSIONS
EXTENDABILITIES	EXTERMINATORY	EXTRACANONICAL	EXTRAPOLATOR	EXTROVERSIVE
EXTENDABILITY	EXTERMINED	EXTRACELLULAR	EXTRAPOLATORS	EXTROVERSIVELY
EXTENDABLE	EXTERMINES	EXTRACELLULARLY	EXTRAPOLATORY	EXTROVERTED
EXTENDEDLY	EXTERMINING	EXTRACORPOREAL	EXTRAPOSED	EXTROVERTING
EXTENDEDNESS	EXTERNALISATION	EXTRACRANIAL	EXTRAPOSES	EXTROVERTLY
EXTENDEDNESSES	EXTERNALISE	EXTRACTABILITY	EXTRAPOSING	EXTROVERTS
EXTENDIBILITIES	EXTERNALISED	EXTRACTABLE	EXTRAPOSITION	EXTRUDABILITIES
EXTENDIBILITY	EXTERNALISES	EXTRACTANT	EXTRAPOSITIONS	EXTRUDABILITY
EXTENDIBLE	EXTERNALISING	EXTRACTANTS	EXTRAPYRAMIDAL	EXTRUDABLE
EXTENSIBILITIES	EXTERNALISM	EXTRACTIBLE	EXTRASENSORY	EXTRUSIBLE
EXTENSIBILITY	EXTERNALISMS	EXTRACTING	EXTRASOLAR	EXTRUSIONS
EXTENSIBLE	EXTERNALIST	EXTRACTION	EXTRASYSTOLE	EXTUBATING
EXTENSIBLENESS	EXTERNALISTS	EXTRACTIONS	EXTRASYSTOLES	EXUBERANCE
EXTENSIFICATION	EXTERNALITIES	EXTRACTIVE	EXTRATEXTUAL	EXUBERANCES
EXTENSIMETER	EXTERNALITY	EXTRACTIVELY	EXTRATROPICAL	EXUBERANCIES
EXTENSIMETERS	EXTERNALIZATION	EXTRACTIVES	EXTRAUTERINE	EXUBERANCY
EXTENSIONAL	EXTERNALIZE	EXTRACTORS	EXTRAVAGANCE	EXUBERANTLY
EXTENSIONALISM	EXTERNALIZED	EXTRACURRICULAR	EXTRAVAGANCES	EXUBERATED

e

EXUBERATES	EXULCERATIONS	EXURBANITES	EYEDNESSES	EYEPOPPERS
EXUBERATING	EXULTANCES	EXUVIATING	EYEDROPPER	EYESHADOWS
EXUDATIONS	EXULTANCIES	EXUVIATION	EYEDROPPERS	EYESTRAINS
EXULCERATE	EXULTANTLY	EXUVIATIONS	EYEGLASSES	EYESTRINGS
EXULCERATED	EXULTATION	EYEBALLING	EYELETEERS	EYEWITNESS
EXULCERATES	EXULTATIONS	EYEBRIGHTS	EYELETTING	EYEWITNESSED
EXULCERATING	EXULTINGLY	EYEBROWING	EYEOPENERS	EYEWITNESSES
EXULCERATION	EXURBANITE	EYEBROWLESS	EYEPATCHES	EYEWITNESSING

FABRICANTS
FABRICATED
FABRICATES
FABRICATING
FABRICATION
FABRICATIONS
FABRICATIVE
FABRICATOR
FABRICATORS
FABRICKING
FABRICKINGS
FABULATING
FABULATORS
FABULISING
FABULISTIC
FABULIZING
FABULOSITIES
FABULOSITY
FABULOUSLY
FABULOUSNESS
FABULOUSNESSES
FACEBOOKED
FACEBOOKING
FACECLOTHS
FACELESSNESS
FACELESSNESSES
FACELIFTED
FACELIFTING
FACEPALMED
FACEPALMING
FACEPLANTED
FACEPLANTING
FACEPLANTS
FACEPLATES
FACEPRINTS
FACETIMING
FACETIOUSLY
FACETIOUSNESS
FACETIOUSNESSES
FACEWORKER
FACEWORKERS
FACIALISTS
FACILENESS
FACILENESSES
FACILITATE
FACILITATED
FACILITATES
FACILITATING
FACILITATION
FACILITATIONS
FACILITATIVE
FACILITATOR
FACILITATORS
FACILITATORY

FACILITIES
FACINERIOUS
FACINOROUS
FACINOROUSNESS
FACSIMILED
FACSIMILEING
FACSIMILES
FACSIMILIST
FACSIMILISTS
FACTICITIES
FACTIONALISE
FACTIONALISED
FACTIONALISES
FACTIONALISING
FACTIONALISM
FACTIONALISMS
FACTIONALIST
FACTIONALISTS
FACTIONALIZE
FACTIONALIZED
FACTIONALIZES
FACTIONALIZING
FACTIONALLY
FACTIONARIES
FACTIONARY
FACTIONIST
FACTIONISTS
FACTIOUSLY
FACTIOUSNESS
FACTIOUSNESSES
FACTITIOUS
FACTITIOUSLY
FACTITIOUSNESS
FACTITIVELY
FACTORABILITIES
FACTORABILITY
FACTORABLE
FACTORAGES
FACTORIALLY
FACTORIALS
FACTORINGS
FACTORISATION
FACTORISATIONS
FACTORISED
FACTORISES
FACTORISING
FACTORIZATION
FACTORIZATIONS
FACTORIZED
FACTORIZES
FACTORIZING
FACTORSHIP
FACTORSHIPS
FACTORYLIKE

FACTSHEETS
FACTUALISM
FACTUALISMS
FACTUALIST
FACTUALISTIC
FACTUALISTS
FACTUALITIES
FACTUALITY
FACTUALNESS
FACTUALNESSES
FACULTATIVE
FACULTATIVELY
FACUNDITIES
FADDINESSES
FADDISHNESS
FADDISHNESSES
FADEDNESSES
FADELESSLY
FADOMETERS
FAGGOTIEST
FAGGOTINGS
FAGGOTRIES
FAGOTTISTS
FAINEANCES
FAINEANCIES
FAINEANTISE
FAINEANTISES
FAINNESSES
FAINTHEARTED
FAINTHEARTEDLY
FAINTINGLY
FAINTISHNESS
FAINTISHNESSES
FAINTNESSES
FAIRGROUND
FAIRGROUNDS
FAIRLEADER
FAIRLEADERS
FAIRNESSES
FAIRNITICKLE
FAIRNITICKLES
FAIRNITICLE
FAIRNITICLES
FAIRNYTICKLE
FAIRNYTICKLES
FAIRNYTICLE
FAIRNYTICLES
FAIRYFLOSS
FAIRYFLOSSES
FAIRYHOODS
FAIRYLANDS
FAITHCURES
FAITHFULLY
FAITHFULNESS

FAITHFULNESSES
FAITHLESSLY
FAITHLESSNESS
FAITHLESSNESSES
FAITHWORTHIER
FAITHWORTHIEST
FAITHWORTHINESS
FAITHWORTHY
FALANGISMS
FALANGISTS
FALCATIONS
FALCONIFORM
FALCONOIDS
FALCONRIES
FALDERALED
FALDERALING
FALDISTORIES
FALDISTORY
FALDSTOOLS
FALLACIOUS
FALLACIOUSLY
FALLACIOUSNESS
FALLALERIES
FALLALISHLY
FALLBOARDS
FALLFISHES
FALLIBILISM
FALLIBILISMS
FALLIBILIST
FALLIBILISTS
FALLIBILITIES
FALLIBILITY
FALLIBLENESS
FALLIBLENESSES
FALLOWNESS
FALLOWNESSES
FALSEFACES
FALSEHOODS
FALSENESSES
FALSEWORKS
FALSIDICAL
FALSIFIABILITY
FALSIFIABLE
FALSIFICATION
FALSIFICATIONS
FALSIFIERS
FALSIFYING
FALTERINGLY
FALTERINGS
FAMILIARISATION
FAMILIARISE
FAMILIARISED
FAMILIARISER
FAMILIARISERS

FAMILIARISES
FAMILIARISING
FAMILIARITIES
FAMILIARITY
FAMILIARIZATION
FAMILIARIZE
FAMILIARIZED
FAMILIARIZER
FAMILIARIZERS
FAMILIARIZES
FAMILIARIZING
FAMILIARLY
FAMILIARNESS
FAMILIARNESSES
FAMILISTIC
FAMISHMENT
FAMISHMENTS
FAMOUSNESS
FAMOUSNESSES
FANATICALLY
FANATICALNESS
FANATICALNESSES
FANATICISATION
FANATICISATIONS
FANATICISE
FANATICISED
FANATICISES
FANATICISING
FANATICISM
FANATICISMS
FANATICIZATION
FANATICIZATIONS
FANATICIZE
FANATICIZED
FANATICIZES
FANATICIZING
FANCIFULLY
FANCIFULNESS
FANCIFULNESSES
FANCIFYING
FANCINESSES
FANCYWORKS
FANDABIDOZI
FANDANGLES
FANDANGOES
FANFARADES
FANFARONADE
FANFARONADED
FANFARONADES
FANFARONADING
FANFARONAS
FANFOLDING
FANTABULOUS
FANTASISED

f

FANTASISER
FANTASISERS
FANTASISES
FANTASISING
FANTASISTS
FANTASIZED
FANTASIZER
FANTASIZERS
FANTASIZES
FANTASIZING
FANTASMALLY
FANTASMICALLY
FANTASQUES
FANTASTICAL
FANTASTICALITY
FANTASTICALLY
FANTASTICALNESS
FANTASTICATE
FANTASTICATED
FANTASTICATES
FANTASTICATING
FANTASTICATION
FANTASTICATIONS
FANTASTICISM
FANTASTICISMS
FANTASTICO
FANTASTICOES
FANTASTICS
FANTASTRIES
FANTASYING
FANTASYLAND
FANTASYLANDS
FANTOCCINI
FARADISATION
FARADISATIONS
FARADISERS
FARADISING
FARADIZATION
FARADIZATIONS
FARADIZERS
FARADIZING
FARANDINES
FARANDOLES
FARAWAYNESS
FARAWAYNESSES
FARBOROUGH
FARBOROUGHS
FARCEMEATS
FARCICALITIES
FARCICALITY
FARCICALLY
FARCICALNESS
FARCICALNESSES
FARCIFYING
FAREWELLED
FAREWELLING
FARFETCHEDNESS
FARINACEOUS
FARINOSELY
FARKLEBERRIES
FARKLEBERRY
FARMERESSES
FARMERETTE
FARMERETTES
FARMHOUSES
FARMSTEADS
FARMWORKER

FARMWORKERS
FARNARKELED
FARNARKELING
FARNARKELINGS
FARNARKELS
FARRAGINOUS
FARRANDINE
FARRANDINES
FARRIERIES
FARROWINGS
FARSIGHTED
FARSIGHTEDLY
FARSIGHTEDNESS
FARTHERMORE
FARTHERMOST
FARTHINGALE
FARTHINGALES
FARTHINGLAND
FARTHINGLANDS
FARTHINGLESS
FARTHINGSWORTH
FARTHINGSWORTHS
FASCIATELY
FASCIATION
FASCIATIONS
FASCICULAR
FASCICULARLY
FASCICULATE
FASCICULATED
FASCICULATELY
FASCICULATION
FASCICULATIONS
FASCICULES
FASCICULUS
FASCIITISES
FASCINATED
FASCINATEDLY
FASCINATES
FASCINATING
FASCINATINGLY
FASCINATION
FASCINATIONS
FASCINATIVE
FASCINATOR
FASCINATORS
FASCIOLIASES
FASCIOLIASIS
FASCISTICALLY
FASCITISES
FASHIONABILITY
FASHIONABLE
FASHIONABLENESS
FASHIONABLES
FASHIONABLY
FASHIONERS
FASHIONIER
FASHIONIEST
FASHIONING
FASHIONIST
FASHIONISTA
FASHIONISTAS
FASHIONISTS
FASHIONMONGER
FASHIONMONGERS
FASHIONMONGING
FASHIOUSNESS
FASHIOUSNESSES

FASTBALLER
FASTBALLERS
FASTENINGS
FASTIDIOUS
FASTIDIOUSLY
FASTIDIOUSNESS
FASTIGIATE
FASTIGIATED
FASTIGIUMS
FASTNESSES
FATALISTIC
FATALISTICALLY
FATALITIES
FATALNESSES
FATBRAINED
FATEFULNESS
FATEFULNESSES
FATHEADEDLY
FATHEADEDNESS
FATHEADEDNESSES
FATHERHOOD
FATHERHOODS
FATHERINGS
FATHERLAND
FATHERLANDS
FATHERLESS
FATHERLESSNESS
FATHERLIER
FATHERLIEST
FATHERLIKE
FATHERLINESS
FATHERLINESSES
FATHERSHIP
FATHERSHIPS
FATHOMABLE
FATHOMETER
FATHOMETERS
FATHOMLESS
FATHOMLESSLY
FATHOMLESSNESS
FATIDICALLY
FATIGABILITIES
FATIGABILITY
FATIGABLENESS
FATIGABLENESSES
FATIGATING
FATIGUABLE
FATIGUABLENESS
FATIGUELESS
FATIGUINGLY
FATISCENCE
FATISCENCES
FATSHEDERA
FATSHEDERAS
FATTENABLE
FATTENINGS
FATTINESSES
FATUOUSNESS
FATUOUSNESSES
FAUCETRIES
FAULCHIONS
FAULTFINDER
FAULTFINDERS
FAULTFINDING
FAULTFINDINGS
FAULTINESS
FAULTINESSES

FAULTLESSLY
FAULTLESSNESS
FAULTLESSNESSES
FAULTLINES
FAUNISTICALLY
FAUXBOURDON
FAUXBOURDONS
FAUXMANCES
FAVORABLENESS
FAVORABLENESSES
FAVOREDNESS
FAVOREDNESSES
FAVORINGLY
FAVORITISM
FAVORITISMS
FAVOURABLE
FAVOURABLENESS
FAVOURABLY
FAVOUREDNESS
FAVOUREDNESSES
FAVOURINGLY
FAVOURITES
FAVOURITISM
FAVOURITISMS
FAVOURLESS
FAWNINGNESS
FAWNINGNESSES
FAZENDEIRO
FAZENDEIROS
FEARFULLER
FEARFULLEST
FEARFULNESS
FEARFULNESSES
FEARLESSLY
FEARLESSNESS
FEARLESSNESSES
FEARMONGER
FEARMONGERING
FEARMONGERINGS
FEARMONGERS
FEARNAUGHT
FEARNAUGHTS
FEARNOUGHT
FEARNOUGHTS
FEARSOMELY
FEARSOMENESS
FEARSOMENESSES
FEASIBILITIES
FEASIBILITY
FEASIBLENESS
FEASIBLENESSES
FEATEOUSLY
FEATHERBED
FEATHERBEDDED
FEATHERBEDDING
FEATHERBEDDINGS
FEATHERBEDS
FEATHERBRAIN
FEATHERBRAINED
FEATHERBRAINS
FEATHEREDGE
FEATHEREDGED
FEATHEREDGES
FEATHEREDGING
FEATHERHEAD
FEATHERHEADED
FEATHERHEADS

FEATHERIER
FEATHERIEST
FEATHERINESS
FEATHERINESSES
FEATHERING
FEATHERINGS
FEATHERLESS
FEATHERLIGHT
FEATHERSTITCH
FEATHERSTITCHED
FEATHERSTITCHES
FEATHERWEIGHT
FEATHERWEIGHTS
FEATLINESS
FEATLINESSES
FEATURELESS
FEATURELESSNESS
FEATURETTE
FEATURETTES
FEBRICITIES
FEBRICULAS
FEBRICULES
FEBRIFACIENT
FEBRIFACIENTS
FEBRIFEROUS
FEBRIFUGAL
FEBRIFUGES
FEBRILITIES
FECKLESSLY
FECKLESSNESS
FECKLESSNESSES
FECULENCES
FECULENCIES
FECUNDATED
FECUNDATES
FECUNDATING
FECUNDATION
FECUNDATIONS
FECUNDATOR
FECUNDATORS
FECUNDATORY
FECUNDITIES
FEDERACIES
FEDERALESE
FEDERALESES
FEDERALISATION
FEDERALISATIONS
FEDERALISE
FEDERALISED
FEDERALISES
FEDERALISING
FEDERALISM
FEDERALISMS
FEDERALIST
FEDERALISTIC
FEDERALISTS
FEDERALIZATION
FEDERALIZATIONS
FEDERALIZE
FEDERALIZED
FEDERALIZES
FEDERALIZING
FEDERARIES
FEDERATING
FEDERATION
FEDERATIONS
FEDERATIVE

f

FEDERATIVELY	FELQUISTES	FERNITICKLES	FERROPRUSSIATES	FETICHISMS
FEDERATORS	FELSPATHIC	FERNITICLE	FERROSILICON	FETICHISTIC
FEEBLEMINDED	FELSPATHOID	FERNITICLES	FERROSILICONS	FETICHISTS
FEEBLEMINDEDLY	FELSPATHOIDS	FERNTICKLE	FERROSOFERRIC	FETICHIZED
FEEBLENESS	FELSPATHOSE	FERNTICKLED	FERROTYPED	FETICHIZES
FEEBLENESSES	FEMALENESS	FERNTICKLES	FERROTYPES	FETICHIZING
FEEDGRAINS	FEMALENESSES	FERNTICLED	FERROTYPING	FETIDITIES
FEEDINGSTUFF	FEMALITIES	FERNTICLES	FERRUGINEOUS	FETIDNESSES
FEEDINGSTUFFS	FEMETARIES	FERNYTICKLE	FERRUGINOUS	FETIPAROUS
FEEDSTOCKS	FEMINACIES	FERNYTICKLES	FERRYBOATS	FETISHISATION
FEEDSTUFFS	FEMINALITIES	FERNYTICLE	FERTIGATED	FETISHISATIONS
FEEDTHROUGH	FEMINALITY	FERNYTICLES	FERTIGATES	FETISHISED
FEEDTHROUGHS	FEMINEITIES	FEROCIOUSLY	FERTIGATING	FETISHISES
FEEDWATERS	FEMINILITIES	FEROCIOUSNESS	FERTIGATION	FETISHISING
FEELINGLESS	FEMINILITY	FEROCIOUSNESSES	FERTIGATIONS	FETISHISMS
FEELINGNESS	FEMININELY	FEROCITIES	FERTILENESS	FETISHISTIC
FEELINGNESSES	FEMININENESS	FERRANDINE	FERTILENESSES	FETISHISTICALLY
FEIGNEDNESS	FEMININENESSES	FERRANDINES	FERTILISABLE	FETISHISTS
FEIGNEDNESSES	FEMININISM	FERREDOXIN	FERTILISATION	FETISHIZATION
FEIGNINGLY	FEMININISMS	FERREDOXINS	FERTILISATIONS	FETISHIZATIONS
FEISTINESS	FEMININITIES	FERRELLING	FERTILISED	FETISHIZED
FEISTINESSES	FEMININITY	FERRETIEST	FERTILISER	FETISHIZES
FELDSCHARS	FEMINISATION	FERRETINGS	FERTILISERS	FETISHIZING
FELDSCHERS	FEMINISATIONS	FERRICYANIC	FERTILISES	FETOLOGIES
FELDSPATHIC	FEMINISING	FERRICYANIDE	FERTILISING	FETOLOGIST
FELDSPATHOID	FEMINISTIC	FERRICYANIDES	FERTILITIES	FETOLOGISTS
FELDSPATHOIDS	FEMINITIES	FERRICYANOGEN	FERTILIZABLE	FETOPROTEIN
FELDSPATHOSE	FEMINIZATION	FERRICYANOGENS	FERTILIZATION	FETOPROTEINS
FELDSPATHS	FEMINIZATIONS	FERRIFEROUS	FERTILIZATIONS	FETOSCOPES
FELICITATE	FEMINIZING	FERRIMAGNET	FERTILIZED	FETOSCOPIES
FELICITATED	FEMTOSECOND	FERRIMAGNETIC	FERTILIZER	FETTERLESS
FELICITATES	FEMTOSECONDS	FERRIMAGNETISM	FERTILIZERS	FETTERLOCK
FELICITATING	FENCELESSNESS	FERRIMAGNETISMS	FERTILIZES	FETTERLOCKS
FELICITATION	FENCELESSNESSES	FERRIMAGNETS	FERTILIZING	FETTUCCINE
FELICITATIONS	FENCELINES	FERROCENES	FERULACEOUS	FETTUCCINES
FELICITATOR	FENCEWIRES	FERROCHROME	FERVENCIES	FETTUCCINI
FELICITATORS	FENDERLESS	FERROCHROMES	FERVENTEST	FETTUCCINIS
FELICITIES	FENESTELLA	FERROCHROMIUM	FERVENTNESS	FETTUCINES
FELICITOUS	FENESTELLAE	FERROCHROMIUMS	FERVENTNESSES	FETTUCINIS
FELICITOUSLY	FENESTELLAS	FERROCONCRETE	FERVESCENT	FEUDALISATION
FELICITOUSNESS	FENESTRALS	FERROCONCRETES	FERVIDITIES	FEUDALISATIONS
FELINENESS	FENESTRATE	FERROCYANIC	FERVIDNESS	FEUDALISED
FELINENESSES	FENESTRATED	FERROCYANIDE	FERVIDNESSES	FEUDALISES
FELINITIES	FENESTRATES	FERROCYANIDES	FESCENNINE	FEUDALISING
FELLATIONS	FENESTRATING	FERROCYANOGEN	FESTILOGIES	FEUDALISMS
FELLATRICES	FENESTRATION	FERROCYANOGENS	FESTINATED	FEUDALISTIC
FELLATRIXES	FENESTRATIONS	FERROELECTRIC	FESTINATELY	FEUDALISTS
FELLFIELDS	FENNELFLOWER	FERROELECTRICS	FESTINATES	FEUDALITIES
FELLMONGER	FENNELFLOWERS	FERROGRAMS	FESTINATING	FEUDALIZATION
FELLMONGERED	FENUGREEKS	FERROGRAPHIES	FESTINATION	FEUDALIZATIONS
FELLMONGERIES	FEOFFMENTS	FERROGRAPHY	FESTINATIONS	FEUDALIZED
FELLMONGERING	FERACITIES	FERROMAGNESIAN	FESTIVALGOER	FEUDALIZES
FELLMONGERINGS	FERETORIES	FERROMAGNET	FESTIVALGOERS	FEUDALIZING
FELLMONGERS	FERMENTABILITY	FERROMAGNETIC	FESTIVENESS	FEUDATORIES
FELLMONGERY	FERMENTABLE	FERROMAGNETISM	FESTIVENESSES	FEUILLETES
FELLNESSES	FERMENTATION	FERROMAGNETISMS	FESTIVITIES	FEUILLETON
FELLOWSHIP	FERMENTATIONS	FERROMAGNETS	FESTOLOGIES	FEUILLETONISM
FELLOWSHIPED	FERMENTATIVE	FERROMANGANESE	FESTOONERIES	FEUILLETONISMS
FELLOWSHIPING	FERMENTATIVELY	FERROMANGANESES	FESTOONERY	FEUILLETONIST
FELLOWSHIPPED	FERMENTERS	FERROMOLYBDENUM	FESTOONING	FEUILLETONISTIC
FELLOWSHIPPING	FERMENTESCIBLE	FERRONICKEL	FESTSCHRIFT	FEUILLETONISTS
FELLOWSHIPS	FERMENTING	FERRONICKELS	FESTSCHRIFTEN	FEUILLETONS
FELLWALKER	FERMENTITIOUS	FERRONIERE	FESTSCHRIFTS	FEVERISHLY
FELLWALKERS	FERMENTIVE	FERRONIERES	FETCHINGLY	FEVERISHNESS
FELONIOUSLY	FERMENTORS	FERRONNIERE	FETICHISED	FEVERISHNESSES
FELONIOUSNESS	FERNALLIES	FERRONNIERES	FETICHISES	FEVEROUSLY
FELONIOUSNESSES	FERNITICKLE	FERROPRUSSIATE	FETICHISING	FEVERROOTS

FEVERWEEDS	FIBROLITES	FIDEICOMMISSUM	FILIBUSTERER	FINALIZATION
FEVERWORTS	FIBROMATOUS	FIDELISMOS	FILIBUSTERERS	FINALIZATIONS
FIANCAILLES	FIBROMYALGIA	FIDELISTAS	FILIBUSTERING	FINALIZERS
FIANCHETTI	FIBROMYALGIAS	FIDELITIES	FILIBUSTERINGS	FINALIZING
FIANCHETTO	FIBRONECTIN	FIDGETIEST	FILIBUSTERISM	FINANCIALIST
FIANCHETTOED	FIBRONECTINS	FIDGETINESS	FILIBUSTERISMS	FINANCIALISTS
FIANCHETTOES	FIBROSARCOMA	FIDGETINESSES	FILIBUSTEROUS	FINANCIALLY
FIANCHETTOING	FIBROSARCOMAS	FIDGETINGLY	FILIBUSTERS	FINANCIALS
FIANCHETTOS	FIBROSARCOMATA	FIDUCIALLY	FILICINEAN	FINANCIERED
FIBERBOARD	FIBROSITIS	FIDUCIARIES	FILIGRAINS	FINANCIERING
FIBERBOARDS	FIBROSITISES	FIDUCIARILY	FILIGRANES	FINANCIERS
FIBERFILLS	FIBROUSNESS	FIELDBOOTS	FILIGREEING	FINANCINGS
FIBERGLASS	FIBROUSNESSES	FIELDCRAFT	FILIOPIETISTIC	FINEABLENESS
FIBERGLASSED	FIBROVASCULAR	FIELDCRAFTS	FILIPENDULOUS	FINEABLENESSES
FIBERGLASSES	FICKLENESS	FIELDFARES	FILLAGREED	FINENESSES
FIBERGLASSING	FICKLENESSES	FIELDMOUSE	FILLAGREEING	FINESSINGS
FIBERISATION	FICTIONALISE	FIELDPIECE	FILLAGREES	FINGERBOARD
FIBERISATIONS	FICTIONALISED	FIELDPIECES	FILLESTERS	FINGERBOARDS
FIBERISING	FICTIONALISES	FIELDSTONE	FILLIPEENS	FINGERBOWL
FIBERIZATION	FICTIONALISING	FIELDSTONES	FILLISTERS	FINGERBOWLS
FIBERIZATIONS	FICTIONALITIES	FIELDSTRIP	FILMGOINGS	FINGERBREADTH
FIBERIZING	FICTIONALITY	FIELDSTRIPPED	FILMICALLY	FINGERBREADTHS
FIBERSCOPE	FICTIONALIZE	FIELDSTRIPPING	FILMINESSES	FINGERGLASS
FIBERSCOPES	FICTIONALIZED	FIELDSTRIPS	FILMMAKERS	FINGERGLASSES
FIBREBOARD	FICTIONALIZES	FIELDVOLES	FILMMAKING	FINGERGUARD
FIBREBOARDS	FICTIONALIZING	FIELDWARDS	FILMMAKINGS	FINGERGUARDS
FIBREFILLS	FICTIONALLY	FIELDWORKER	FILMOGRAPHIES	FINGERHOLD
FIBREGLASS	FICTIONEER	FIELDWORKERS	FILMOGRAPHY	FINGERHOLDS
FIBREGLASSED	FICTIONEERING	FIELDWORKS	FILMSETTER	FINGERHOLE
FIBREGLASSES	FICTIONEERINGS	FIENDISHLY	FILMSETTERS	FINGERHOLES
FIBREGLASSING	FICTIONEERS	FIENDISHNESS	FILMSETTING	FINGERINGS
FIBREOPTIC	FICTIONISATION	FIENDISHNESSES	FILMSETTINGS	FINGERLESS
FIBRESCOPE	FICTIONISATIONS	FIERCENESS	FILMSTRIPS	FINGERLIKE
FIBRESCOPES	FICTIONISE	FIERCENESSES	FILOPLUMES	FINGERLING
FIBRILLARY	FICTIONISED	FIERINESSES	FILOPODIUM	FINGERLINGS
FIBRILLATE	FICTIONISES	FIFTEENERS	FILOSELLES	FINGERMARK
FIBRILLATED	FICTIONISING	FIFTEENTHLY	FILOVIRUSES	FINGERMARKS
FIBRILLATES	FICTIONIST	FIFTEENTHS	FILTERABILITIES	FINGERNAIL
FIBRILLATING	FICTIONISTS	FIGHTBACKS	FILTERABILITY	FINGERNAILS
FIBRILLATION	FICTIONIZATION	FIGURABILITIES	FILTERABLE	FINGERPICK
FIBRILLATIONS	FICTIONIZATIONS	FIGURABILITY	FILTERABLENESS	FINGERPICKED
FIBRILLIFORM	FICTIONIZE	FIGURANTES	FILTHINESS	FINGERPICKING
FIBRILLINS	FICTIONIZED	FIGURATELY	FILTHINESSES	FINGERPICKINGS
FIBRILLOSE	FICTIONIZES	FIGURATION	FILTRABILITIES	FINGERPICKS
FIBRILLOUS	FICTIONIZING	FIGURATIONS	FILTRABILITY	FINGERPLATE
FIBRINOGEN	FICTITIOUS	FIGURATIVE	FILTRABLENESS	FINGERPLATES
FIBRINOGENIC	FICTITIOUSLY	FIGURATIVELY	FILTRABLENESSES	FINGERPOST
FIBRINOGENOUS	FICTITIOUSNESS	FIGURATIVENESS	FILTRATABLE	FINGERPOSTS
FIBRINOGENS	FICTIVENESS	FIGUREHEAD	FILTRATING	FINGERPRINT
FIBRINOIDS	FICTIVENESSES	FIGUREHEADS	FILTRATION	FINGERPRINTED
FIBRINOLYSES	FIDDIOUSED	FIGURELESS	FILTRATIONS	FINGERPRINTING
FIBRINOLYSIN	FIDDIOUSES	FIGUREWORK	FIMBRIATED	FINGERPRINTINGS
FIBRINOLYSINS	FIDDIOUSING	FIGUREWORKS	FIMBRIATES	FINGERPRINTS
FIBRINOLYSIS	FIDDLEBACK	FILAGGRINS	FIMBRIATING	FINGERSTALL
FIBRINOLYTIC	FIDDLEBACKS	FILAGREEING	FIMBRIATION	FINGERSTALLS
FIBRINOPEPTIDE	FIDDLEDEDEE	FILAMENTARY	FIMBRIATIONS	FINGERTIPS
FIBRINOPEPTIDES	FIDDLEDEEDEE	FILAMENTOUS	FIMBRILLATE	FINICALITIES
FIBROBLAST	FIDDLEHEAD	FILARIASES	FIMICOLOUS	FINICALITY
FIBROBLASTIC	FIDDLEHEADS	FILARIASIS	FINABLENESS	FINICALNESS
FIBROBLASTS	FIDDLENECK	FILATORIES	FINABLENESSES	FINICALNESSES
FIBROCARTILAGE	FIDDLENECKS	FILCHINGLY	FINAGLINGS	FINICKETIER
FIBROCARTILAGES	FIDDLESTICK	FILEFISHES	FINALISATION	FINICKETIEST
FIBROCEMENT	FIDDLESTICKS	FILIALNESS	FINALISATIONS	FINICKIEST
FIBROCEMENTS	FIDDLEWOOD	FILIALNESSES	FINALISERS	FINICKINESS
FIBROCYSTIC	FIDDLEWOODS	FILIATIONS	FINALISING	FINICKINESSES
FIBROCYTES	FIDEICOMMISSA	FILIBUSTER	FINALISTIC	FINICKINGS
FIBROLINES	FIDEICOMMISSARY	FILIBUSTERED	FINALITIES	FINISHINGS

FINITENESS	FIRSTLINGS	FLACCIDEST	FLAMEPROOFS	FLATLINERS
FINITENESSES	FIRSTNESSES	FLACCIDITIES	FLAMETHROWER	FLATLINING
FINNICKIER	FISCALISTS	FLACCIDITY	FLAMETHROWERS	FLATNESSES
FINNICKIEST	FISHABILITIES	FLACCIDNESS	FLAMINGOES	FLATPICKED
FINNOCHIOS	FISHABILITY	FLACCIDNESSES	FLAMINICAL	FLATPICKING
FINOCCHIOS	FISHBURGER	FLACKERIES	FLAMMABILITIES	FLATSCREEN
FIORATURAE	FISHBURGERS	FLACKERING	FLAMMABILITY	FLATSCREENS
FIREBALLER	FISHERFOLK	FLACKETING	FLAMMABLES	FLATSHARES
FIREBALLERS	FISHERWOMAN	FLAFFERING	FLAMMIFEROUS	FLATTENERS
FIREBALLING	FISHERWOMEN	FLAGELLANT	FLAMMULATED	FLATTENING
FIREBOARDS	FISHFINGER	FLAGELLANTISM	FLAMMULATION	FLATTERABLE
FIREBOMBED	FISHFINGERS	FLAGELLANTISMS	FLAMMULATIONS	FLATTERERS
FIREBOMBER	FISHIFYING	FLAGELLANTS	FLANCHINGS	FLATTERIES
FIREBOMBERS	FISHINESSES	FLAGELLATE	FLANCONADE	FLATTERING
FIREBOMBING	FISHMONGER	FLAGELLATED	FLANCONADES	FLATTERINGLY
FIREBOMBINGS	FISHMONGERS	FLAGELLATES	FLANGELESS	FLATTEROUS
FIREBRANDS	FISHPLATES	FLAGELLATING	FLANKERING	FLATTEROUSLY
FIREBREAKS	FISHTAILED	FLAGELLATION	FLANNELBOARD	FLATULENCE
FIREBRICKS	FISHTAILING	FLAGELLATIONS	FLANNELBOARDS	FLATULENCES
FIREBUSHES	FISHWIFELIER	FLAGELLATOR	FLANNELETS	FLATULENCIES
FIRECRACKER	FISHWIFELIEST	FLAGELLATORS	FLANNELETTE	FLATULENCY
FIRECRACKERS	FISHWIFELY	FLAGELLATORY	FLANNELETTES	FLATULENTLY
FIRECRESTS	FISHYBACKS	FLAGELLIFEROUS	FLANNELGRAPH	FLATWASHES
FIREDRAGON	FISSICOSTATE	FLAGELLIFORM	FLANNELGRAPHS	FLATWATERS
FIREDRAGONS	FISSILINGUAL	FLAGELLINS	FLANNELING	FLAUGHTERED
FIREDRAKES	FISSILITIES	FLAGELLOMANIA	FLANNELLED	FLAUGHTERING
FIREFANGED	FISSIONABILITY	FLAGELLOMANIAC	FLANNELLIER	FLAUGHTERS
FIREFANGING	FISSIONABLE	FLAGELLOMANIACS	FLANNELLIEST	FLAUGHTING
FIREFIGHTER	FISSIONABLES	FLAGELLOMANIAS	FLANNELLING	FLAUNCHING
FIREFIGHTERS	FISSIONING	FLAGELLUMS	FLANNELMOUTHED	FLAUNCHINGS
FIREFIGHTING	FISSIPALMATE	FLAGEOLETS	FLAPDOODLE	FLAUNTIEST
FIREFIGHTINGS	FISSIPARISM	FLAGGINESS	FLAPDOODLES	FLAUNTINESS
FIREFIGHTS	FISSIPARISMS	FLAGGINESSES	FLAPPERHOOD	FLAUNTINESSES
FIREFLOATS	FISSIPARITIES	FLAGGINGLY	FLAPPERHOODS	FLAUNTINGLY
FIREFLOODS	FISSIPARITY	FLAGITATED	FLAPPERISH	FLAVANONES
FIREGUARDS	FISSIPAROUS	FLAGITATES	FLAPTRACKS	FLAVESCENT
FIREHOUSES	FISSIPAROUSLY	FLAGITATING	FLAREBACKS	FLAVIVIRUS
FIRELIGHTER	FISSIPAROUSNESS	FLAGITATION	FLASHBACKED	FLAVIVIRUSES
FIRELIGHTERS	FISSIPEDAL	FLAGITATIONS	FLASHBACKING	FLAVONOIDS
FIRELIGHTS	FISSIPEDES	FLAGITIOUS	FLASHBACKS	FLAVOPROTEIN
FIREPLACED	FISSIROSTRAL	FLAGITIOUSLY	FLASHBANGS	FLAVOPROTEINS
FIREPLACES	FISTFIGHTS	FLAGITIOUSNESS	FLASHBOARD	FLAVOPURPURIN
FIREPOWERS	FISTICUFFED	FLAGRANCES	FLASHBOARDS	FLAVOPURPURINS
FIREPROOFED	FISTICUFFING	FLAGRANCIES	FLASHBULBS	FLAVORFULLY
FIREPROOFING	FISTICUFFS	FLAGRANTLY	FLASHCARDS	FLAVORIEST
FIREPROOFINGS	FITFULNESS	FLAGRANTNESS	FLASHCUBES	FLAVORINGS
FIREPROOFS	FITFULNESSES	FLAGRANTNESSES	FLASHFORWARD	FLAVORISTS
FIRESCAPED	FITTINGNESS	FLAGSTAFFS	FLASHFORWARDS	FLAVORLESS
FIRESCAPES	FITTINGNESSES	FLAGSTAVES	FLASHINESS	FLAVORSOME
FIRESCAPING	FIVEFINGER	FLAGSTICKS	FLASHINESSES	FLAVOURDYNAMICS
FIRESCAPINGS	FIVEFINGERS	FLAGSTONES	FLASHLAMPS	FLAVOURERS
FIRESCREEN	FIVEPENCES	FLAKINESSES	FLASHLIGHT	FLAVOURFUL
FIRESCREENS	FIXEDNESSES	FLAMBEEING	FLASHLIGHTS	FLAVOURFULLY
FIRESTONES	FIXTURELESS	FLAMBOYANCE	FLASHMOBBING	FLAVOURIER
FIRESTORMS	FIZGIGGING	FLAMBOYANCES	FLASHMOBBINGS	FLAVOURIEST
FIRETHORNS	FIZZENLESS	FLAMBOYANCIES	FLASHOVERS	FLAVOURING
FIRETRUCKS	FIZZINESSES	FLAMBOYANCY	FLASHPACKER	FLAVOURINGS
FIREWALLED	FLABBERGAST	FLAMBOYANT	FLASHPACKERS	FLAVOURIST
FIREWALLING	FLABBERGASTED	FLAMBOYANTE	FLASHPOINT	FLAVOURISTS
FIREWARDEN	FLABBERGASTING	FLAMBOYANTES	FLASHPOINTS	FLAVOURLESS
FIREWARDENS	FLABBERGASTS	FLAMBOYANTLY	FLASHTUBES	FLAVOURSOME
FIREWATERS	FLABBINESS	FLAMBOYANTS	FLATBREADS	FLAWLESSLY
FIRMAMENTAL	FLABBINESSES	FLAMEPROOF	FLATFISHES	FLAWLESSNESS
FIRMAMENTS	FLABELLATE	FLAMEPROOFED	FLATFOOTED	FLAWLESSNESSES
FIRMNESSES	FLABELLATION	FLAMEPROOFER	FLATFOOTING	FLEAHOPPER
FIRSTBORNS	FLABELLATIONS	FLAMEPROOFERS	FLATLANDER	FLEAHOPPERS
FIRSTFRUITS	FLABELLIFORM	FLAMEPROOFING	FLATLANDERS	FLECHETTES

FLECKERING	FLIMFLAMMER	FLOODLIGHTS	FLOWCHARTING	FLUORESCEINES
FLECTIONAL	FLIMFLAMMERIES	FLOODMARKS	FLOWCHARTINGS	FLUORESCEINS
FLECTIONLESS	FLIMFLAMMERS	FLOODPLAIN	FLOWCHARTS	FLUORESCENCE
FLEDGELING	FLIMFLAMMERY	FLOODPLAINS	FLOWERAGES	FLUORESCENCES
FLEDGELINGS	FLIMFLAMMING	FLOODTIDES	FLOWERBEDS	FLUORESCENT
FLEDGLINGS	FLIMSINESS	FLOODWALLS	FLOWERETTE	FLUORESCENTS
FLEECELESS	FLIMSINESSES	FLOODWATER	FLOWERETTES	FLUORESCER
FLEECHINGS	FLINCHINGLY	FLOODWATERS	FLOWERHORN	FLUORESCERS
FLEECHMENT	FLINCHINGS	FLOORBOARD	FLOWERIEST	FLUORESCES
FLEECHMENTS	FLINDERING	FLOORBOARDS	FLOWERINESS	FLUORESCING
FLEECINESS	FLINDERSIA	FLOORCLOTH	FLOWERINESSES	FLUORIDATE
FLEECINESSES	FLINDERSIAS	FLOORCLOTHS	FLOWERINGS	FLUORIDATED
FLEERINGLY	FLINTHEADS	FLOORDROBE	FLOWERLESS	FLUORIDATES
FLEETINGLY	FLINTIFIED	FLOORDROBES	FLOWERLIKE	FLUORIDATING
FLEETINGNESS	FLINTIFIES	FLOORHEADS	FLOWERPOTS	FLUORIDATION
FLEETINGNESSES	FLINTIFYING	FLOORSHOWS	FLOWINGNESS	FLUORIDATIONS
FLEETNESSES	FLINTINESS	FLOORWALKER	FLOWINGNESSES	FLUORIDISE
FLEHMENING	FLINTINESSES	FLOORWALKERS	FLOWMETERS	FLUORIDISED
FLEMISHING	FLINTLOCKS	FLOPHOUSES	FLOWSTONES	FLUORIDISES
FLEROVIUMS	FLIPBOARDS	FLOPPINESS	FLUCTUATED	FLUORIDISING
FLESHHOODS	FLIPCHARTS	FLOPPINESSES	FLUCTUATES	FLUORIDIZE
FLESHINESS	FLIPFLOPPED	FLOPTICALS	FLUCTUATING	FLUORIDIZED
FLESHINESSES	FLIPFLOPPING	FLORENTINE	FLUCTUATION	FLUORIDIZES
FLESHLIEST	FLIPPANCIES	FLORENTINES	FLUCTUATIONAL	FLUORIDIZING
FLESHLINESS	FLIPPANTLY	FLORESCENCE	FLUCTUATIONS	FLUORIMETER
FLESHLINESSES	FLIPPANTNESS	FLORESCENCES	FLUEGELHORN	FLUORIMETERS
FLESHLINGS	FLIPPANTNESSES	FLORESCENT	FLUEGELHORNS	FLUORIMETRIC
FLESHMENTS	FLIRTATION	FLORIATION	FLUENTNESS	FLUORIMETRIES
FLESHMONGER	FLIRTATIONS	FLORIATIONS	FLUENTNESSES	FLUORIMETRY
FLESHMONGERS	FLIRTATIOUS	FLORIBUNDA	FLUFFBALLS	FLUORINATE
FLESHWORMS	FLIRTATIOUSLY	FLORIBUNDAS	FLUFFINESS	FLUORINATED
FLETCHINGS	FLIRTATIOUSNESS	FLORICANES	FLUFFINESSES	FLUORINATES
FLEURETTES	FLIRTINGLY	FLORICULTURAL	FLUGELHORN	FLUORINATING
FLEXECUTIVE	FLITTERING	FLORICULTURE	FLUGELHORNIST	FLUORINATION
FLEXECUTIVES	FLITTERMICE	FLORICULTURES	FLUGELHORNISTS	FLUORINATIONS
FLEXIBILITIES	FLITTERMOUSE	FLORICULTURIST	FLUGELHORNS	FLUOROACETATE
FLEXIBILITY	FLOATABILITIES	FLORICULTURISTS	FLUIDEXTRACT	FLUOROACETATES
FLEXIBLENESS	FLOATABILITY	FLORIDEANS	FLUIDEXTRACTS	FLUOROCARBON
FLEXIBLENESSES	FLOATATION	FLORIDEOUS	FLUIDIFIED	FLUOROCARBONS
FLEXICURITIES	FLOATATIONS	FLORIDITIES	FLUIDIFIES	FLUOROCHROME
FLEXICURITY	FLOATBASES	FLORIDNESS	FLUIDIFYING	FLUOROCHROMES
FLEXIHOURS	FLOATINGLY	FLORIDNESSES	FLUIDISATION	FLUOROGRAPHIC
FLEXIONLESS	FLOATPLANE	FLORIFEROUS	FLUIDISATIONS	FLUOROGRAPHIES
FLEXITARIAN	FLOATPLANES	FLORIFEROUSNESS	FLUIDISERS	FLUOROGRAPHY
FLEXITARIANISM	FLOCCILLATION	FLORIGENIC	FLUIDISING	FLUOROMETER
FLEXITARIANISMS	FLOCCILLATIONS	FLORILEGIA	FLUIDITIES	FLUOROMETERS
FLEXITARIANS	FLOCCULANT	FLORILEGIUM	FLUIDIZATION	FLUOROMETRIC
FLEXITIMES	FLOCCULANTS	FLORISTICALLY	FLUIDIZATIONS	FLUOROMETRIES
FLEXOGRAPHIC	FLOCCULATE	FLORISTICS	FLUIDIZERS	FLUOROMETRY
FLEXOGRAPHIES	FLOCCULATED	FLORISTRIES	FLUIDIZING	FLUOROPHORE
FLEXOGRAPHY	FLOCCULATES	FLOSCULOUS	FLUIDNESSES	FLUOROPHORES
FLEXTIMERS	FLOCCULATING	FLOTATIONS	FLUKINESSES	FLUOROPHOSPHATE
FLEXUOUSLY	FLOCCULATION	FLOUNCIEST	FLUMMERIES	FLUOROSCOPE
FLIBBERTIGIBBET	FLOCCULATIONS	FLOUNCINGS	FLUMMOXING	FLUOROSCOPED
FLICHTERED	FLOCCULATOR	FLOUNDERED	FLUNITRAZEPAM	FLUOROSCOPES
FLICHTERING	FLOCCULATORS	FLOUNDERING	FLUNITRAZEPAMS	FLUOROSCOPIC
FLICKERIER	FLOCCULENCE	FLOURISHED	FLUNKEYDOM	FLUOROSCOPIES
FLICKERIEST	FLOCCULENCES	FLOURISHER	FLUNKEYDOMS	FLUOROSCOPING
FLICKERING	FLOCCULENCIES	FLOURISHERS	FLUNKEYISH	FLUOROSCOPIST
FLICKERINGLY	FLOCCULENCY	FLOURISHES	FLUNKEYISM	FLUOROSCOPISTS
FLICKERTAIL	FLOCCULENT	FLOURISHIER	FLUNKEYISMS	FLUOROSCOPY
FLICKERTAILS	FLOCCULENTLY	FLOURISHIEST	FLUNKYISMS	FLUOROTYPE
FLIGHTIEST	FLOODGATES	FLOURISHING	FLUORAPATITE	FLUOROTYPES
FLIGHTINESS	FLOODLIGHT	FLOURISHINGLY	FLUORAPATITES	FLUOROURACIL
FLIGHTINESSES	FLOODLIGHTED	FLOUTINGLY	FLUORESCED	FLUOROURACILS
FLIGHTLESS	FLOODLIGHTING	FLOUTINGSTOCK	FLUORESCEIN	FLUORSPARS
FLIMFLAMMED	FLOODLIGHTINGS	FLOUTINGSTOCKS	FLUORESCEINE	FLUOXETINE

FLUOXETINES
FLUPHENAZINE
FLUPHENAZINES
FLUSHNESSES
FLUSHWORKS
FLUSTEREDLY
FLUSTERIER
FLUSTERIEST
FLUSTERING
FLUSTERMENT
FLUSTERMENTS
FLUSTRATED
FLUSTRATES
FLUSTRATING
FLUSTRATION
FLUSTRATIONS
FLUTEMOUTH
FLUTEMOUTHS
FLUTTERBOARD
FLUTTERBOARDS
FLUTTERERS
FLUTTERIER
FLUTTERIEST
FLUTTERING
FLUTTERINGLY
FLUTTERINGS
FLUVIALIST
FLUVIALISTS
FLUVIATILE
FLUVIOMARINE
FLUVOXAMINE
FLUVOXAMINES
FLUXIONALLY
FLUXIONARY
FLUXIONIST
FLUXIONISTS
FLUXMETERS
FLYBLOWING
FLYBRIDGES
FLYCATCHER
FLYCATCHERS
FLYFISHERS
FLYPITCHER
FLYPITCHERS
FLYPITCHES
FLYPOSTERS
FLYPOSTING
FLYPOSTINGS
FLYRODDERS
FLYSCREENS
FLYSPECKED
FLYSPECKING
FLYSTRIKES
FLYSWATTER
FLYSWATTERS
FLYWEIGHTS
FOAMFLOWER
FOAMFLOWERS
FOAMINESSES
FOCALISATION
FOCALISATIONS
FOCALISING
FOCALIZATION
FOCALIZATIONS
FOCALIZING
FOCIMETERS
FOCOMETERS

FODDERINGS
FOEDERATUS
FOETATIONS
FOETICIDAL
FOETICIDES
FOETIDNESS
FOETIDNESSES
FOETIPAROUS
FOETOSCOPIES
FOETOSCOPY
FOGGINESSES
FOGRAMITES
FOGRAMITIES
FOILSWOMAN
FOILSWOMEN
FOISONLESS
FOLIACEOUS
FOLIATIONS
FOLIATURES
FOLKINESSES
FOLKISHNESS
FOLKISHNESSES
FOLKLORISH
FOLKLORIST
FOLKLORISTIC
FOLKLORISTS
FOLKSINESS
FOLKSINESSES
FOLKSINGER
FOLKSINGERS
FOLKSINGING
FOLKSINGINGS
FOLKSONOMIES
FOLKSONOMY
FOLKTRONICA
FOLKTRONICAS
FOLLICULAR
FOLLICULATE
FOLLICULATED
FOLLICULIN
FOLLICULINS
FOLLICULITIS
FOLLICULITISES
FOLLICULOSE
FOLLICULOUS
FOLLOWABLE
FOLLOWERSHIP
FOLLOWERSHIPS
FOLLOWINGS
FOLLOWSHIP
FOLLOWSHIPS
FOMENTATION
FOMENTATIONS
FONCTIONNAIRE
FONCTIONNAIRES
FONDLINGLY
FONDNESSES
FONTANELLE
FONTANELLES
FONTICULUS
FONTINALIS
FONTINALISES
FOODLESSNESS
FOODLESSNESSES
FOODSTUFFS
FOOLBEGGED
FOOLFISHES

FOOLHARDIER
FOOLHARDIEST
FOOLHARDILY
FOOLHARDINESS
FOOLHARDINESSES
FOOLHARDISE
FOOLHARDISES
FOOLHARDIZE
FOOLHARDIZES
FOOLISHEST
FOOLISHNESS
FOOLISHNESSES
FOOTBALLENE
FOOTBALLENES
FOOTBALLER
FOOTBALLERS
FOOTBALLING
FOOTBALLIST
FOOTBALLISTS
FOOTBOARDS
FOOTBRAKES
FOOTBREADTH
FOOTBREADTHS
FOOTBRIDGE
FOOTBRIDGES
FOOTCLOTHS
FOOTDRAGGER
FOOTDRAGGERS
FOOTDRAGGING
FOOTDRAGGINGS
FOOTFAULTED
FOOTFAULTING
FOOTFAULTS
FOOTGUARDS
FOOTLAMBERT
FOOTLAMBERTS
FOOTLESSLY
FOOTLESSNESS
FOOTLESSNESSES
FOOTLIGHTS
FOOTLOCKER
FOOTLOCKERS
FOOTNOTING
FOOTPLATEMAN
FOOTPLATEMEN
FOOTPLATES
FOOTPLATEWOMAN
FOOTPLATEWOMEN
FOOTPRINTS
FOOTSLOGGED
FOOTSLOGGER
FOOTSLOGGERS
FOOTSLOGGING
FOOTSLOGGINGS
FOOTSORENESS
FOOTSORENESSES
FOOTSTALKS
FOOTSTALLS
FOOTSTOCKS
FOOTSTONES
FOOTSTOOLED
FOOTSTOOLS
FOOTWEARIER
FOOTWEARIEST
FOPPISHNESS
FOPPISHNESSES
FORAMINATED

FORAMINIFER
FORAMINIFERA
FORAMINIFERAL
FORAMINIFERAN
FORAMINIFERANS
FORAMINIFEROUS
FORAMINIFERS
FORAMINOUS
FORBEARANCE
FORBEARANCES
FORBEARANT
FORBEARERS
FORBEARING
FORBEARINGLY
FORBIDDALS
FORBIDDANCE
FORBIDDANCES
FORBIDDENLY
FORBIDDERS
FORBIDDING
FORBIDDINGLY
FORBIDDINGNESS
FORBIDDINGS
FORCEDNESS
FORCEDNESSES
FORCEFULLY
FORCEFULNESS
FORCEFULNESSES
FORCEMEATS
FORCEPSLIKE
FORCIBILITIES
FORCIBILITY
FORCIBLENESS
FORCIBLENESSES
FORCIPATED
FORCIPATION
FORCIPATIONS
FOREARMING
FOREBITTER
FOREBITTERS
FOREBODEMENT
FOREBODEMENTS
FOREBODERS
FOREBODIES
FOREBODING
FOREBODINGLY
FOREBODINGNESS
FOREBODINGS
FOREBRAINS
FORECABINS
FORECADDIE
FORECADDIES
FORECARRIAGE
FORECARRIAGES
FORECASTABLE
FORECASTED
FORECASTER
FORECASTERS
FORECASTING
FORECASTINGS
FORECASTLE
FORECASTLES
FORECHECKED
FORECHECKER
FORECHECKERS
FORECHECKING
FORECHECKS

FORECHOSEN
FORECLOSABLE
FORECLOSED
FORECLOSES
FORECLOSING
FORECLOSURE
FORECLOSURES
FORECLOTHS
FORECOURSE
FORECOURSES
FORECOURTS
FOREDAMNED
FOREDATING
FOREDOOMED
FOREDOOMING
FOREFATHER
FOREFATHERLY
FOREFATHERS
FOREFEELING
FOREFEELINGLY
FOREFENDED
FOREFENDING
FOREFINGER
FOREFINGERS
FOREFRONTS
FOREGATHER
FOREGATHERED
FOREGATHERING
FOREGATHERS
FOREGLEAMS
FOREGOINGS
FOREGONENESS
FOREGONENESSES
FOREGROUND
FOREGROUNDED
FOREGROUNDING
FOREGROUNDS
FOREHANDED
FOREHANDEDLY
FOREHANDEDNESS
FOREHANDING
FOREHENTING
FOREHOOVES
FOREIGNERS
FOREIGNISM
FOREIGNISMS
FOREIGNNESS
FOREIGNNESSES
FOREJUDGED
FOREJUDGEMENT
FOREJUDGEMENTS
FOREJUDGES
FOREJUDGING
FOREJUDGMENT
FOREJUDGMENTS
FOREKNOWABLE
FOREKNOWING
FOREKNOWINGLY
FOREKNOWLEDGE
FOREKNOWLEDGES
FORELADIES
FORELAYING
FORELENDING
FORELIFTED
FORELIFTING
FORELOCKED
FORELOCKING

FOREMANSHIP	FORESIGHTLESS	FOREVERNESSES	FORLORNEST	FORMULARISING
FOREMANSHIPS	FORESIGHTS	FOREVOUCHED	FORLORNNESS	FORMULARISTIC
FOREMASTMAN	FORESIGNIFIED	FOREWARDED	FORLORNNESSES	FORMULARIZATION
FOREMASTMEN	FORESIGNIFIES	FOREWARDING	FORMABILITIES	FORMULARIZE
FOREMEANING	FORESIGNIFY	FOREWARNED	FORMABILITY	FORMULARIZED
FOREMENTIONED	FORESIGNIFYING	FOREWARNER	FORMALDEHYDE	FORMULARIZER
FOREMOTHER	FORESKIRTS	FOREWARNERS	FORMALDEHYDES	FORMULARIZERS
FOREMOTHERS	FORESLACKED	FOREWARNING	FORMALINES	FORMULARIZES
FORENIGHTS	FORESLACKING	FOREWARNINGLY	FORMALISABLE	FORMULARIZING
FORENSICALITIES	FORESLACKS	FOREWARNINGS	FORMALISATION	FORMULATED
FORENSICALITY	FORESLOWED	FOREWEIGHED	FORMALISATIONS	FORMULATES
FORENSICALLY	FORESLOWING	FOREWEIGHING	FORMALISED	FORMULATING
FOREORDAIN	FORESPEAKING	FOREWEIGHS	FORMALISER	FORMULATION
FOREORDAINED	FORESPEAKS	FORFAIRING	FORMALISERS	FORMULATIONS
FOREORDAINING	FORESPENDING	FORFAITERS	FORMALISES	FORMULATOR
FOREORDAINMENT	FORESPENDS	FORFAITING	FORMALISING	FORMULATORS
FOREORDAINMENTS	FORESPOKEN	FORFAITINGS	FORMALISMS	FORMULISED
FOREORDAINS	FORESTAGES	FORFEITABLE	FORMALISTIC	FORMULISES
FOREORDINATION	FORESTAIRS	FORFEITERS	FORMALISTICALLY	FORMULISING
FOREORDINATIONS	FORESTALLED	FORFEITING	FORMALISTS	FORMULISMS
FOREPASSED	FORESTALLER	FORFEITURE	FORMALITER	FORMULISTIC
FOREPAYMENT	FORESTALLERS	FORFEITURES	FORMALITIES	FORMULISTS
FOREPAYMENTS	FORESTALLING	FORFENDING	FORMALIZABLE	FORMULIZED
FOREPLANNED	FORESTALLINGS	FORFEUCHEN	FORMALIZATION	FORMULIZES
FOREPLANNING	FORESTALLMENT	FORFICULATE	FORMALIZATIONS	FORMULIZING
FOREPOINTED	FORESTALLMENTS	FORFOUGHEN	FORMALIZED	FORNICATED
FOREPOINTING	FORESTALLS	FORFOUGHTEN	FORMALIZER	FORNICATES
FOREPOINTS	FORESTALMENT	FORGATHERED	FORMALIZERS	FORNICATING
FOREQUARTER	FORESTALMENTS	FORGATHERING	FORMALIZES	FORNICATION
FOREQUARTERS	FORESTATION	FORGATHERS	FORMALIZING	FORNICATIONS
FOREREACHED	FORESTATIONS	FORGEABILITIES	FORMALNESS	FORNICATOR
FOREREACHES	FORESTAYSAIL	FORGEABILITY	FORMALNESSES	FORNICATORS
FOREREACHING	FORESTAYSAILS	FORGETFULLY	FORMAMIDES	FORNICATRESS
FOREREADING	FORESTLAND	FORGETFULNESS	FORMATIONAL	FORNICATRESSES
FOREREADINGS	FORESTLANDS	FORGETFULNESSES	FORMATIONS	FORSAKENLY
FORERUNNER	FORESTLESS	FORGETTABLE	FORMATIVELY	FORSAKENNESS
FORERUNNERS	FORESTRIES	FORGETTERIES	FORMATIVENESS	FORSAKENNESSES
FORERUNNING	FORESWEARING	FORGETTERS	FORMATIVENESSES	FORSAKINGS
FORESAYING	FORESWEARS	FORGETTERY	FORMATIVES	FORSLACKED
FORESEEABILITY	FORETASTED	FORGETTING	FORMATTERS	FORSLACKING
FORESEEABLE	FORETASTES	FORGETTINGLY	FORMATTING	FORSLOEING
FORESEEING	FORETASTING	FORGETTINGS	FORMATTINGS	FORSLOWING
FORESEEINGLY	FORETAUGHT	FORGIVABLE	FORMFITTING	FORSPEAKING
FORESHADOW	FORETEACHES	FORGIVABLY	FORMICARIA	FORSPENDING
FORESHADOWED	FORETEACHING	FORGIVENESS	FORMICARIES	FORSTERITE
FORESHADOWER	FORETELLER	FORGIVENESSES	FORMICARIUM	FORSTERITES
FORESHADOWERS	FORETELLERS	FORGIVINGLY	FORMICATED	FORSWEARER
FORESHADOWING	FORETELLING	FORGIVINGNESS	FORMICATES	FORSWEARERS
FORESHADOWINGS	FORETHINKER	FORGIVINGNESSES	FORMICATING	FORSWEARING
FORESHADOWS	FORETHINKERS	FORGOTTENNESS	FORMICATION	FORSWINKED
FORESHANKS	FORETHINKING	FORGOTTENNESSES	FORMICATIONS	FORSWINKING
FORESHEETS	FORETHINKS	FORHAILING	FORMIDABILITIES	FORSWORNNESS
FORESHEWED	FORETHOUGHT	FORHENTING	FORMIDABILITY	FORSWORNNESSES
FORESHEWING	FORETHOUGHTFUL	FORHOOIEING	FORMIDABLE	FORSYTHIAS
FORESHOCKS	FORETHOUGHTS	FORINSECAL	FORMIDABLENESS	FORTALICES
FORESHORES	FORETOKENED	FORISFAMILIATE	FORMIDABLY	FORTEPIANIST
FORESHORTEN	FORETOKENING	FORISFAMILIATED	FORMLESSLY	FORTEPIANISTS
FORESHORTENED	FORETOKENINGS	FORISFAMILIATES	FORMLESSNESS	FORTEPIANO
FORESHORTENING	FORETOKENS	FORJUDGING	FORMLESSNESSES	FORTEPIANOS
FORESHORTENINGS	FORETOPMAN	FORJUDGMENT	FORMULAICALLY	FORTHCOMES
FORESHORTENS	FORETOPMAST	FORJUDGMENTS	FORMULARIES	FORTHCOMING
FORESHOWED	FORETOPMASTS	FORKEDNESS	FORMULARISATION	FORTHCOMINGNESS
FORESHOWING	FORETOPMEN	FORKEDNESSES	FORMULARISE	FORTHGOING
FORESIGHTED	FORETRIANGLE	FORKINESSES	FORMULARISED	FORTHGOINGS
FORESIGHTEDLY	FORETRIANGLES	FORKLIFTED	FORMULARISER	FORTHINKING
FORESIGHTEDNESS	FOREVERMORE	FORKLIFTING	FORMULARISERS	FORTHOUGHT
FORESIGHTFUL	FOREVERNESS	FORLENDING	FORMULARISES	FORTHRIGHT

FORTHRIGHTLY	FOSSILIZABLE	FRACTALITY	FRAGMENTISED	FRANKFURTS
FORTHRIGHTNESS	FOSSILIZATION	FRACTIONAL	FRAGMENTISES	FRANKINCENSE
FORTHRIGHTS	FOSSILIZATIONS	FRACTIONALISE	FRAGMENTISING	FRANKINCENSES
FORTIFIABLE	FOSSILIZED	FRACTIONALISED	FRAGMENTIZE	FRANKLINITE
FORTIFICATION	FOSSILIZES	FRACTIONALISES	FRAGMENTIZED	FRANKLINITES
FORTIFICATIONS	FOSSILIZING	FRACTIONALISING	FRAGMENTIZES	FRANKNESSES
FORTIFIERS	FOSTERAGES	FRACTIONALISM	FRAGMENTIZING	FRANKPLEDGE
FORTIFYING	FOSTERINGS	FRACTIONALISMS	FRAGRANCED	FRANKPLEDGES
FORTIFYINGLY	FOSTERLING	FRACTIONALIST	FRAGRANCES	FRANSERIAS
FORTILAGES	FOSTERLINGS	FRACTIONALISTS	FRAGRANCIES	FRANTICALLY
FORTISSIMI	FOSTRESSES	FRACTIONALIZE	FRAGRANCING	FRANTICNESS
FORTISSIMO	FOTHERGILLA	FRACTIONALIZED	FRAGRANTLY	FRANTICNESSES
FORTISSIMOS	FOTHERGILLAS	FRACTIONALIZES	FRAGRANTNESS	FRATCHETIER
FORTISSISSIMO	FOUDROYANT	FRACTIONALIZING	FRAGRANTNESSES	FRATCHETIEST
FORTITUDES	FOUGHTIEST	FRACTIONALLY	FRAICHEURS	FRATCHIEST
FORTITUDINOUS	FOULBROODS	FRACTIONARY	FRAILNESSES	FRATERNALISM
FORTNIGHTLIES	FOULDERING	FRACTIONATE	FRAMBESIAS	FRATERNALISMS
FORTNIGHTLY	FOULMOUTHED	FRACTIONATED	FRAMBOESIA	FRATERNALLY
FORTNIGHTS	FOULNESSES	FRACTIONATES	FRAMBOESIAS	FRATERNISATION
FORTRESSED	FOUNDATION	FRACTIONATING	FRAMBOISES	FRATERNISATIONS
FORTRESSES	FOUNDATIONAL	FRACTIONATION	FRAMESHIFT	FRATERNISE
FORTRESSING	FOUNDATIONALLY	FRACTIONATIONS	FRAMESHIFTS	FRATERNISED
FORTRESSLIKE	FOUNDATIONARY	FRACTIONATOR	FRAMEWORKS	FRATERNISER
FORTUITIES	FOUNDATIONER	FRACTIONATORS	FRANCHISED	FRATERNISERS
FORTUITISM	FOUNDATIONERS	FRACTIONED	FRANCHISEE	FRATERNISES
FORTUITISMS	FOUNDATIONLESS	FRACTIONING	FRANCHISEES	FRATERNISING
FORTUITIST	FOUNDATIONS	FRACTIONISATION	FRANCHISEMENT	FRATERNITIES
FORTUITISTS	FOUNDERING	FRACTIONISE	FRANCHISEMENTS	FRATERNITY
FORTUITOUS	FOUNDEROUS	FRACTIONISED	FRANCHISER	FRATERNIZATION
FORTUITOUSLY	FOUNDLINGS	FRACTIONISES	FRANCHISERS	FRATERNIZATIONS
FORTUITOUSNESS	FOUNDRESSES	FRACTIONISING	FRANCHISES	FRATERNIZE
FORTUNATELY	FOUNTAINED	FRACTIONIZATION	FRANCHISING	FRATERNIZED
FORTUNATENESS	FOUNTAINHEAD	FRACTIONIZE	FRANCHISOR	FRATERNIZER
FORTUNATENESSES	FOUNTAINHEADS	FRACTIONIZED	FRANCHISORS	FRATERNIZERS
FORTUNATES	FOUNTAINING	FRACTIONIZES	FRANCISATION	FRATERNIZES
FORTUNELESS	FOUNTAINLESS	FRACTIONIZING	FRANCISATIONS	FRATERNIZING
FORTUNISED	FOURCHETTE	FRACTIONLET	FRANCISING	FRATRICIDAL
FORTUNISES	FOURCHETTES	FRACTIONLETS	FRANCIZATION	FRATRICIDE
FORTUNISING	FOURDRINIER	FRACTIOUSLY	FRANCIZATIONS	FRATRICIDES
FORTUNIZED	FOURDRINIERS	FRACTIOUSNESS	FRANCIZING	FRAUDFULLY
FORTUNIZES	FOURFOLDNESS	FRACTIOUSNESSES	FRANCOLINS	FRAUDSTERS
FORTUNIZING	FOURFOLDNESSES	FRACTOCUMULI	FRANCOMANIA	FRAUDULENCE
FORWANDERED	FOURPENCES	FRACTOCUMULUS	FRANCOMANIAS	FRAUDULENCES
FORWANDERING	FOURPENNIES	FRACTOGRAPHIES	FRANCOPHIL	FRAUDULENCIES
FORWANDERS	FOURPLEXES	FRACTOGRAPHY	FRANCOPHILE	FRAUDULENCY
FORWARDERS	FOURRAGERE	FRACTOSTRATI	FRANCOPHILES	FRAUDULENT
FORWARDEST	FOURRAGERES	FRACTOSTRATUS	FRANCOPHILS	FRAUDULENTLY
FORWARDING	FOURSCORTH	FRACTURABLE	FRANCOPHOBE	FRAUDULENTNESS
FORWARDINGS	FOURSQUARE	FRACTURERS	FRANCOPHOBES	FRAUGHTAGE
FORWARDNESS	FOURSQUARELY	FRACTURING	FRANCOPHOBIA	FRAUGHTAGES
FORWARDNESSES	FOURSQUARENESS	FRAGILENESS	FRANCOPHOBIAS	FRAUGHTEST
FORWARNING	FOURTEENER	FRAGILENESSES	FRANCOPHONE	FRAUGHTING
FORWASTING	FOURTEENERS	FRAGILITIES	FRANCOPHONES	FRAXINELLA
FORWEARIED	FOURTEENTH	FRAGMENTAL	FRANGIBILITIES	FRAXINELLAS
FORWEARIES	FOURTEENTHLY	FRAGMENTALLY	FRANGIBILITY	FREAKERIES
FORWEARYING	FOURTEENTHS	FRAGMENTARILY	FRANGIBLENESS	FREAKINESS
FOSCARNETS	FOVEOLATED	FRAGMENTARINESS	FRANGIBLENESSES	FREAKINESSES
FOSSICKERS	FOXBERRIES	FRAGMENTARY	FRANGIPANE	FREAKISHLY
FOSSICKING	FOXHUNTERS	FRAGMENTATE	FRANGIPANES	FREAKISHNESS
FOSSICKINGS	FOXHUNTING	FRAGMENTATED	FRANGIPANI	FREAKISHNESSES
FOSSILIFEROUS	FOXHUNTINGS	FRAGMENTATES	FRANGIPANIS	FRECKLIEST
FOSSILISABLE	FOXINESSES	FRAGMENTATING	FRANGIPANNI	FRECKLINGS
FOSSILISATION	FOXTROTTED	FRAGMENTATION	FRANKALMOIGN	FREEBASERS
FOSSILISATIONS	FOXTROTTING	FRAGMENTATIONS	FRANKALMOIGNS	FREEBASING
FOSSILISED	FOZINESSES	FRAGMENTED	FRANKFORTS	FREEBOARDS
FOSSILISES	FRABJOUSLY	FRAGMENTING	FRANKFURTER	FREEBOOTED
FOSSILISING	FRACTALITIES	FRAGMENTISE	FRANKFURTERS	FREEBOOTER

FREEBOOTERIES	FREEZINGLY	FRIEDCAKES	FRIZZLIEST	FROSTWORKS
FREEBOOTERS	FREIGHTAGE	FRIENDINGS	FRIZZLINESS	FROTHERIES
FREEBOOTERY	FREIGHTAGES	FRIENDLESS	FRIZZLINESSES	FROTHINESS
FREEBOOTIES	FREIGHTERS	FRIENDLESSNESS	FROGFISHES	FROTHINESSES
FREEBOOTING	FREIGHTING	FRIENDLIER	FROGGERIES	FROUGHIEST
FREEBOOTINGS	FREIGHTLESS	FRIENDLIES	FROGHOPPER	FROUZINESS
FREECOOLING	FREMESCENCE	FRIENDLIEST	FROGHOPPERS	FROUZINESSES
FREECOOLINGS	FREMESCENCES	FRIENDLILY	FROGMARCHED	FROWARDNESS
FREECYCLED	FREMESCENT	FRIENDLINESS	FROGMARCHES	FROWARDNESSES
FREECYCLES	FREMITUSES	FRIENDLINESSES	FROGMARCHING	FROWNINGLY
FREECYCLING	FRENCHIFICATION	FRIENDSHIP	FROGMOUTHS	FROWSINESS
FREEDIVERS	FRENCHIFIED	FRIENDSHIPS	FROGSPAWNS	FROWSINESSES
FREEDIVING	FRENCHIFIES	FRIEZELIKE	FROLICKERS	FROWSTIEST
FREEDIVINGS	FRENCHIFYING	FRIGATOONS	FROLICKIER	FROWSTINESS
FREEDWOMAN	FRENETICAL	FRIGHTENED	FROLICKIEST	FROWSTINESSES
FREEDWOMEN	FRENETICALLY	FRIGHTENER	FROLICKING	FROWZINESS
FREEGANISM	FRENETICISM	FRIGHTENERS	FROLICSOME	FROWZINESSES
FREEGANISMS	FRENETICISMS	FRIGHTENING	FROLICSOMELY	FROZENNESS
FREEHANDED	FRENETICNESS	FRIGHTENINGLY	FROLICSOMENESS	FROZENNESSES
FREEHANDEDLY	FRENETICNESSES	FRIGHTFULLY	FROMENTIES	FRUCTIFEROUS
FREEHANDEDNESS	FRENZIEDLY	FRIGHTFULNESS	FRONDESCENCE	FRUCTIFEROUSLY
FREEHEARTED	FREQUENCES	FRIGHTFULNESSES	FRONDESCENCES	FRUCTIFICATION
FREEHEARTEDLY	FREQUENCIES	FRIGHTSOME	FRONDESCENT	FRUCTIFICATIONS
FREEHOLDER	FREQUENTABLE	FRIGIDARIA	FRONDIFEROUS	FRUCTIFIED
FREEHOLDERS	FREQUENTATION	FRIGIDARIUM	FRONTAGERS	FRUCTIFIER
FREELANCED	FREQUENTATIONS	FRIGIDITIES	FRONTALITIES	FRUCTIFIERS
FREELANCER	FREQUENTATIVE	FRIGIDNESS	FRONTALITY	FRUCTIFIES
FREELANCERS	FREQUENTATIVES	FRIGIDNESSES	FRONTBENCHER	FRUCTIFYING
FREELANCES	FREQUENTED	FRIGORIFIC	FRONTBENCHERS	FRUCTIVOROUS
FREELANCING	FREQUENTER	FRIGORIFICO	FRONTCOURT	FRUCTUARIES
FREELOADED	FREQUENTERS	FRIGORIFICOS	FRONTCOURTS	FRUCTUATED
FREELOADER	FREQUENTEST	FRIKKADELS	FRONTENISES	FRUCTUATES
FREELOADERS	FREQUENTING	FRILLERIES	FRONTIERED	FRUCTUATING
FREELOADING	FREQUENTLY	FRILLINESS	FRONTIERING	FRUCTUATION
FREELOADINGS	FREQUENTNESS	FRILLINESSES	FRONTIERSMAN	FRUCTUATIONS
FREEMARTIN	FREQUENTNESSES	FRINGELESS	FRONTIERSMEN	FRUCTUOUSLY
FREEMARTINS	FRESCOINGS	FRINGELIKE	FRONTIERSWOMAN	FRUCTUOUSNESS
FREEMASONIC	FRESCOISTS	FRINGILLACEOUS	FRONTIERSWOMEN	FRUCTUOUSNESSES
FREEMASONRIES	FRESHENERS	FRINGILLID	FRONTISPIECE	FRUGALISTA
FREEMASONRY	FRESHENING	FRINGILLIFORM	FRONTISPIECED	FRUGALISTAS
FREEMASONS	FRESHERDOM	FRINGILLINE	FRONTISPIECES	FRUGALISTS
FREENESSES	FRESHERDOMS	FRIPONNERIE	FRONTISPIECING	FRUGALITIES
FREEPHONES	FRESHMANSHIP	FRIPONNERIES	FRONTLESSLY	FRUGALNESS
FREESHEETS	FRESHMANSHIPS	FRIPPERERS	FRONTLINES	FRUGALNESSES
FREESTANDING	FRESHNESSES	FRIPPERIES	FRONTLISTS	FRUGIFEROUS
FREESTONES	FRESHWATER	FRISKINESS	FRONTOGENESES	FRUGIVORES
FREESTYLED	FRESHWATERS	FRISKINESSES	FRONTOGENESIS	FRUGIVOROUS
FREESTYLER	FRETBOARDS	FRISKINGLY	FRONTOGENETIC	FRUITARIAN
FREESTYLERS	FRETFULNESS	FRITHBORHS	FRONTOLYSES	FRUITARIANISM
FREESTYLES	FRETFULNESSES	FRITHSOKEN	FRONTOLYSIS	FRUITARIANISMS
FREESTYLING	FRIABILITIES	FRITHSOKENS	FRONTPAGED	FRUITARIANS
FREESTYLINGS	FRIABILITY	FRITHSTOOL	FRONTPAGES	FRUITCAKES
FREETHINKER	FRIABLENESS	FRITHSTOOLS	FRONTPAGING	FRUITERERS
FREETHINKERS	FRIABLENESSES	FRITILLARIA	FRONTRUNNER	FRUITERESS
FREETHINKING	FRIARBIRDS	FRITILLARIAS	FRONTRUNNERS	FRUITERESSES
FREETHINKINGS	FRICANDEAU	FRITILLARIES	FRONTRUNNING	FRUITERIES
FREEWHEELED	FRICANDEAUS	FRITILLARY	FRONTRUNNINGS	FRUITFULLER
FREEWHEELER	FRICANDEAUX	FRITTERERS	FRONTWARDS	FRUITFULLEST
FREEWHEELERS	FRICANDOES	FRITTERING	FROSTBITES	FRUITFULLY
FREEWHEELING	FRICASSEED	FRIVOLITIES	FROSTBITING	FRUITFULNESS
FREEWHEELINGLY	FRICASSEEING	FRIVOLLERS	FROSTBITINGS	FRUITFULNESSES
FREEWHEELINGS	FRICASSEES	FRIVOLLING	FROSTBITTEN	FRUITINESS
FREEWHEELS	FRICATIVES	FRIVOLOUSLY	FROSTBOUND	FRUITINESSES
FREEWRITES	FRICTIONAL	FRIVOLOUSNESS	FROSTFISHES	FRUITLESSLY
FREEWRITING	FRICTIONALLY	FRIVOLOUSNESSES	FROSTINESS	FRUITLESSNESS
FREEWRITINGS	FRICTIONLESS	FRIZZINESS	FROSTINESSES	FRUITLESSNESSES
FREEWRITTEN	FRICTIONLESSLY	FRIZZINESSES	FROSTLINES	FRUITWOODS

FRUITWORMS
FRUMENTACEOUS
FRUMENTARIOUS
FRUMENTATION
FRUMENTATIONS
FRUMENTIES
FRUMPINESS
FRUMPINESSES
FRUMPISHLY
FRUMPISHNESS
FRUMPISHNESSES
FRUSEMIDES
FRUSTRATED
FRUSTRATER
FRUSTRATERS
FRUSTRATES
FRUSTRATING
FRUSTRATINGLY
FRUSTRATION
FRUSTRATIONS
FRUTESCENCE
FRUTESCENCES
FRUTESCENT
FRUTIFYING
FUCIVOROUS
FUCOXANTHIN
FUCOXANTHINS
FUGACIOUSLY
FUGACIOUSNESS
FUGACIOUSNESSES
FUGACITIES
FUGGINESSES
FUGITATION
FUGITATIONS
FUGITIVELY
FUGITIVENESS
FUGITIVENESSES
FUGITOMETER
FUGITOMETERS
FULFILLERS
FULFILLING
FULFILLINGS
FULFILLMENT
FULFILLMENTS
FULFILMENT
FULFILMENTS
FULGENCIES
FULGURATED
FULGURATES
FULGURATING
FULGURATION
FULGURATIONS
FULGURITES
FULIGINOSITIES
FULIGINOSITY
FULIGINOUS
FULIGINOUSLY

FULIGINOUSNESS
FULLBLOODS
FULLERENES
FULLERIDES
FULLERITES
FULLMOUTHED
FULLNESSES
FULMINANTS
FULMINATED
FULMINATES
FULMINATING
FULMINATION
FULMINATIONS
FULMINATOR
FULMINATORS
FULMINATORY
FULMINEOUS
FULSOMENESS
FULSOMENESSES
FUMATORIES
FUMATORIUM
FUMATORIUMS
FUMBLINGLY
FUMBLINGNESS
FUMBLINGNESSES
FUMIGATING
FUMIGATION
FUMIGATIONS
FUMIGATORS
FUMIGATORY
FUMITORIES
FUMOSITIES
FUNAMBULATE
FUNAMBULATED
FUNAMBULATES
FUNAMBULATING
FUNAMBULATION
FUNAMBULATIONS
FUNAMBULATOR
FUNAMBULATORS
FUNAMBULATORY
FUNAMBULISM
FUNAMBULISMS
FUNAMBULIST
FUNAMBULISTS
FUNCTIONAL
FUNCTIONALISM
FUNCTIONALISMS
FUNCTIONALIST
FUNCTIONALISTIC
FUNCTIONALISTS
FUNCTIONALITIES
FUNCTIONALITY
FUNCTIONALLY
FUNCTIONALS
FUNCTIONARIES
FUNCTIONARY

FUNCTIONATE
FUNCTIONATED
FUNCTIONATES
FUNCTIONATING
FUNCTIONED
FUNCTIONING
FUNCTIONLESS
FUNDAMENTAL
FUNDAMENTALISM
FUNDAMENTALISMS
FUNDAMENTALIST
FUNDAMENTALISTS
FUNDAMENTALITY
FUNDAMENTALLY
FUNDAMENTALNESS
FUNDAMENTALS
FUNDAMENTS
FUNDHOLDER
FUNDHOLDERS
FUNDHOLDING
FUNDHOLDINGS
FUNDRAISED
FUNDRAISER
FUNDRAISERS
FUNDRAISES
FUNDRAISING
FUNDRAISINGS
FUNEREALLY
FUNGIBILITIES
FUNGIBILITY
FUNGICIDAL
FUNGICIDALLY
FUNGICIDES
FUNGISTATIC
FUNGISTATICALLY
FUNGISTATS
FUNGOSITIES
FUNICULARS
FUNICULATE
FUNKINESSES
FUNNELFORM
FUNNELLING
FUNNINESSES
FURACIOUSNESS
FURACIOUSNESSES
FURACITIES
FURALDEHYDE
FURALDEHYDES
FURANOSIDE
FURANOSIDES
FURAZOLIDONE
FURAZOLIDONES
FURBEARERS
FURBELOWED
FURBELOWING
FURBISHERS
FURBISHING

FURCATIONS
FURCIFEROUS
FURFURACEOUS
FURFURACEOUSLY
FURFURALDEHYDE
FURFURALDEHYDES
FURFUROLES
FURIOSITIES
FURIOUSNESS
FURIOUSNESSES
FURLOUGHED
FURLOUGHING
FURMENTIES
FURNIMENTS
FURNISHERS
FURNISHING
FURNISHINGS
FURNISHMENT
FURNISHMENTS
FURNITURES
FUROSEMIDE
FUROSEMIDES
FURRIERIES
FURRINESSES
FURROWIEST
FURROWLESS
FURSHLUGGINER
FURTHCOMING
FURTHCOMINGS
FURTHERANCE
FURTHERANCES
FURTHERERS
FURTHERING
FURTHERMORE
FURTHERMOST
FURTHERSOME
FURTIVENESS
FURTIVENESSES
FURUNCULAR
FURUNCULOSES
FURUNCULOSIS
FURUNCULOUS
FUSHIONLESS
FUSIBILITIES
FUSIBILITY
FUSIBLENESS
FUSIBLENESSES
FUSILLADED
FUSILLADES
FUSILLADING
FUSILLATION
FUSILLATIONS
FUSIONISMS
FUSIONISTS
FUSIONLESS
FUSSBUDGET
FUSSBUDGETIER

FUSSBUDGETIEST
FUSSBUDGETS
FUSSBUDGETY
FUSSINESSES
FUSTANELLA
FUSTANELLAS
FUSTANELLE
FUSTANELLES
FUSTIANISE
FUSTIANISED
FUSTIANISES
FUSTIANISING
FUSTIANIST
FUSTIANISTS
FUSTIANIZE
FUSTIANIZED
FUSTIANIZES
FUSTIANIZING
FUSTIGATED
FUSTIGATES
FUSTIGATING
FUSTIGATION
FUSTIGATIONS
FUSTIGATOR
FUSTIGATORS
FUSTIGATORY
FUSTILARIAN
FUSTILARIANS
FUSTILIRIAN
FUSTILIRIANS
FUSTILLIRIAN
FUSTILLIRIANS
FUSTINESSES
FUSULINIDS
FUTILENESS
FUTILENESSES
FUTILITARIAN
FUTILITARIANISM
FUTILITARIANS
FUTILITIES
FUTURELESS
FUTURELESSNESS
FUTURISTIC
FUTURISTICALLY
FUTURISTICS
FUTURITIES
FUTURITION
FUTURITIONS
FUTUROLOGICAL
FUTUROLOGIES
FUTUROLOGIST
FUTUROLOGISTS
FUTUROLOGY
FUZZINESSES

G

GABAPENTIN	GALABIYAHS	GALLABIYEH	GALLOGLASSES	GALVANOSCOPIES
GABAPENTINS	GALACTAGOGUE	GALLABIYEHS	GALLONAGES	GALVANOSCOPY
GABARDINES	GALACTAGOGUES	GALLAMINES	GALLOPADED	GALVANOTROPIC
GABBINESSES	GALACTICOS	GALLANTEST	GALLOPADES	GALVANOTROPISM
GABBLEMENT	GALACTOMETER	GALLANTING	GALLOPADING	GALVANOTROPISMS
GABBLEMENTS	GALACTOMETERS	GALLANTNESS	GALLOWGLASS	GAMAHUCHED
GABBROITIC	GALACTOMETRIES	GALLANTNESSES	GALLOWGLASSES	GAMAHUCHES
GABERDINES	GALACTOMETRY	GALLANTRIES	GALLOWSNESS	GAMAHUCHING
GABERLUNZIE	GALACTOPHOROUS	GALLBLADDER	GALLOWSNESSES	GAMARUCHED
GABERLUNZIES	GALACTOPOIESES	GALLBLADDERS	GALLSICKNESS	GAMARUCHES
GABIONADES	GALACTOPOIESIS	GALLEASSES	GALLSICKNESSES	GAMARUCHING
GABIONAGES	GALACTOPOIETIC	GALLERISTS	GALLSTONES	GAMBADOING
GABIONNADE	GALACTOPOIETICS	GALLERYGOER	GALLUMPHED	GAMBOLLING
GABIONNADES	GALACTORRHEA	GALLERYGOERS	GALLUMPHING	GAMEBREAKER
GADGETEERS	GALACTORRHEAS	GALLERYING	GALLYGASKINS	GAMEBREAKERS
GADGETIEST	GALACTORRHOEA	GALLERYITE	GALRAVAGED	GAMEFISHES
GADGETRIES	GALACTORRHOEAS	GALLERYITES	GALRAVAGES	GAMEKEEPER
GADOLINITE	GALACTOSAEMIA	GALLIAMBIC	GALRAVAGING	GAMEKEEPERS
GADOLINITES	GALACTOSAEMIAS	GALLIAMBICS	GALRAVITCH	GAMEKEEPING
GADOLINIUM	GALACTOSAEMIC	GALLIARDISE	GALRAVITCHED	GAMEKEEPINGS
GADOLINIUMS	GALACTOSAMINE	GALLIARDISES	GALRAVITCHES	GAMENESSES
GADROONING	GALACTOSAMINES	GALLIASSES	GALRAVITCHING	GAMESMANSHIP
GADROONINGS	GALACTOSEMIA	GALLICISATION	GALUMPHERS	GAMESMANSHIPS
GADZOOKERIES	GALACTOSEMIAS	GALLICISATIONS	GALUMPHING	GAMESOMELY
GADZOOKERY	GALACTOSEMIC	GALLICISED	GALVANICAL	GAMESOMENESS
GAELICISED	GALACTOSES	GALLICISES	GALVANICALLY	GAMESOMENESSES
GAELICISES	GALACTOSIDASE	GALLICISING	GALVANISATION	GAMETANGIA
GAELICISING	GALACTOSIDASES	GALLICISMS	GALVANISATIONS	GAMETANGIAL
GAELICISMS	GALACTOSIDE	GALLICIZATION	GALVANISED	GAMETANGIUM
GAELICIZED	GALACTOSIDES	GALLICIZATIONS	GALVANISER	GAMETICALLY
GAELICIZES	GALACTOSYL	GALLICIZED	GALVANISERS	GAMETOCYTE
GAELICIZING	GALACTOSYLS	GALLICIZES	GALVANISES	GAMETOCYTES
GAILLARDIA	GALANTAMINE	GALLICIZING	GALVANISING	GAMETOGENESES
GAILLARDIAS	GALANTAMINES	GALLIGASKINS	GALVANISMS	GAMETOGENESIS
GAINFULNESS	GALANTINES	GALLIMAUFRIES	GALVANISTS	GAMETOGENIC
GAINFULNESSES	GALAVANTED	GALLIMAUFRY	GALVANIZATION	GAMETOGENIES
GAINGIVING	GALAVANTING	GALLINACEAN	GALVANIZATIONS	GAMETOGENOUS
GAINGIVINGS	GALDRAGONS	GALLINACEANS	GALVANIZED	GAMETOGENY
GAINLESSNESS	GALENGALES	GALLINACEOUS	GALVANIZER	GAMETOPHORE
GAINLESSNESSES	GALENICALS	GALLINAZOS	GALVANIZERS	GAMETOPHORES
GAINLINESS	GALEOPITHECINE	GALLINIPPER	GALVANIZES	GAMETOPHORIC
GAINLINESSES	GALEOPITHECOID	GALLINIPPERS	GALVANIZING	GAMETOPHYTE
GAINSAYERS	GALIMATIAS	GALLINULES	GALVANOMETER	GAMETOPHYTES
GAINSAYING	GALIMATIASES	GALLISISED	GALVANOMETERS	GAMETOPHYTIC
GAINSAYINGS	GALINGALES	GALLISISES	GALVANOMETRIC	GAMEYNESSES
GAINSHARING	GALIONGEES	GALLISISING	GALVANOMETRICAL	GAMIFICATION
GAINSHARINGS	GALIVANTED	GALLISIZED	GALVANOMETRIES	GAMIFICATIONS
GAINSTRIVE	GALIVANTING	GALLISIZES	GALVANOMETRY	GAMINERIES
GAINSTRIVED	GALLABEAHS	GALLISIZING	GALVANOPLASTIC	GAMINESQUE
GAINSTRIVEN	GALLABIAHS	GALLIVANTED	GALVANOPLASTIES	GAMINESSES
GAINSTRIVES	GALLABIEHS	GALLIVANTING	GALVANOPLASTY	GAMMERSTANG
GAINSTRIVING	GALLABIYAH	GALLIVANTS	GALVANOSCOPE	GAMMERSTANGS
GAINSTROVE	GALLABIYAHS	GALLIWASPS	GALVANOSCOPES	GAMMOCKING
GAITERLESS	GALLABIYAS	GALLOGLASS	GALVANOSCOPIC	GAMMONINGS

GAMOGENESES	GARGARISING	GASOMETERS	GASTROSCOPY	GEALOUSIES
GAMOGENESIS	GARGARISMS	GASOMETRIC	GASTROSOPH	GEANTICLINAL
GAMOGENETIC	GARGARIZED	GASOMETRICAL	GASTROSOPHER	GEANTICLINE
GAMOGENETICAL	GARGARIZES	GASOMETRIES	GASTROSOPHERS	GEANTICLINES
GAMOGENETICALLY	GARGARIZING	GASPEREAUS	GASTROSOPHIES	GEARCHANGE
GAMOPETALOUS	GARGOYLISM	GASPEREAUX	GASTROSOPHS	GEARCHANGES
GAMOPHYLLOUS	GARGOYLISMS	GASPINESSES	GASTROSOPHY	GEARSHIFTS
GAMOSEPALOUS	GARIBALDIS	GASSINESSES	GASTROSTOMIES	GEARSTICKS
GAMOTROPIC	GARISHNESS	GASTEROPOD	GASTROSTOMY	GEARWHEELS
GAMOTROPISM	GARISHNESSES	GASTEROPODOUS	GASTROTOMIES	GEEKINESSES
GAMOTROPISMS	GARLANDAGE	GASTEROPODS	GASTROTOMY	GEEKSPEAKS
GAMYNESSES	GARLANDAGES	GASTHAUSER	GASTROTRICH	GEFUFFLING
GANDERISMS	GARLANDING	GASTHAUSES	GASTROTRICHS	GEGENSCHEIN
GANGBANGED	GARLANDLESS	GASTIGHTNESS	GASTROVASCULAR	GEGENSCHEINS
GANGBANGER	GARLANDRIES	GASTIGHTNESSES	GASTRULATE	GEHLENITES
GANGBANGERS	GARLICKIER	GASTNESSES	GASTRULATED	GEITONOGAMIES
GANGBANGING	GARLICKIEST	GASTRAEUMS	GASTRULATES	GEITONOGAMOUS
GANGBOARDS	GARLICKING	GASTRALGIA	GASTRULATING	GEITONOGAMY
GANGBUSTER	GARMENTING	GASTRALGIAS	GASTRULATION	GELANDESPRUNG
GANGBUSTERS	GARMENTLESS	GASTRALGIC	GASTRULATIONS	GELANDESPRUNGS
GANGBUSTING	GARMENTURE	GASTRECTOMIES	GATECRASHED	GELATINATE
GANGBUSTINGS	GARMENTURES	GASTRECTOMY	GATECRASHER	GELATINATED
GANGLIATED	GARNETIFEROUS	GASTRITIDES	GATECRASHERS	GELATINATES
GANGLIFORM	GARNIERITE	GASTRITISES	GATECRASHES	GELATINATING
GANGLIONATED	GARNIERITES	GASTROCNEMII	GATECRASHING	GELATINATION
GANGLIONIC	GARNISHEED	GASTROCNEMIUS	GATEHOUSES	GELATINATIONS
GANGLIOSIDE	GARNISHEEING	GASTROCOLIC	GATEKEEPER	GELATINISATION
GANGLIOSIDES	GARNISHEEMENT	GASTRODUODENAL	GATEKEEPERS	GELATINISATIONS
GANGMASTER	GARNISHEEMENTS	GASTROENTERIC	GATEKEEPING	GELATINISE
GANGMASTERS	GARNISHEES	GASTROENTERITIC	GATEKEEPINGS	GELATINISED
GANGPLANKS	GARNISHERS	GASTROENTERITIS	GATHERABLE	GELATINISER
GANGRENING	GARNISHING	GASTROLITH	GATHERINGS	GELATINISERS
GANGRENOUS	GARNISHINGS	GASTROLITHS	GAUCHENESS	GELATINISES
GANGSHAGGED	GARNISHMENT	GASTROLOGER	GAUCHENESSES	GELATINISING
GANGSHAGGING	GARNISHMENTS	GASTROLOGERS	GAUCHERIES	GELATINIZATION
GANGSTERDOM	GARNISHORS	GASTROLOGICAL	GAUDEAMUSES	GELATINIZATIONS
GANGSTERDOMS	GARNISHRIES	GASTROLOGIES	GAUDINESSES	GELATINIZE
GANGSTERISH	GARNITURES	GASTROLOGIST	GAUFFERING	GELATINIZED
GANGSTERISM	GAROTTINGS	GASTROLOGISTS	GAUFFERINGS	GELATINIZER
GANGSTERISMS	GARRETEERS	GASTROLOGY	GAULEITERS	GELATINIZERS
GANGSTERLAND	GARRISONED	GASTROMANCIES	GAULTHERIA	GELATINIZES
GANGSTERLANDS	GARRISONING	GASTROMANCY	GAULTHERIAS	GELATINIZING
GANNETRIES	GARROTTERS	GASTRONOME	GAUNTLETED	GELATINOID
GANNISTERS	GARROTTING	GASTRONOMER	GAUNTLETING	GELATINOIDS
GANTELOPES	GARROTTINGS	GASTRONOMERS	GAUNTNESSES	GELATINOUS
GANTLETING	GARRULITIES	GASTRONOMES	GAUSSMETER	GELATINOUSLY
GAOLBREAKING	GARRULOUSLY	GASTRONOMIC	GAUSSMETERS	GELATINOUSNESS
GAOLBREAKS	GARRULOUSNESS	GASTRONOMICAL	GAUZINESSES	GELIDITIES
GAOLBROKEN	GARRULOUSNESSES	GASTRONOMICALLY	GAVELKINDS	GELIDNESSES
GAOLERESSES	GARRYOWENS	GASTRONOMICS	GAWKIHOODS	GELIGNITES
GARAGISTES	GASBAGGING	GASTRONOMIES	GAWKINESSES	GELLIFLOWRE
GARBAGEMAN	GASCONADED	GASTRONOMIST	GAWKISHNESS	GELLIFLOWRES
GARBAGEMEN	GASCONADER	GASTRONOMISTS	GAWKISHNESSES	GELSEMINES
GARBAGIEST	GASCONADERS	GASTRONOMY	GAYCATIONS	GELSEMININE
GARBOLOGIES	GASCONADES	GASTROPODAN	GAZEHOUNDS	GELSEMININES
GARBOLOGIST	GASCONADING	GASTROPODANS	GAZETTEERED	GELSEMIUMS
GARBOLOGISTS	GASCONISMS	GASTROPODOUS	GAZETTEERING	GEMEINSCHAFT
GARBURATOR	GASEOUSNESS	GASTROPODS	GAZETTEERISH	GEMEINSCHAFTEN
GARBURATORS	GASEOUSNESSES	GASTROPORN	GAZETTEERS	GEMEINSCHAFTS
GARDENFULS	GASHLINESS	GASTROPORNS	GAZILLIONAIRE	GEMFIBROZIL
GARDENINGS	GASHLINESSES	GASTROPUBS	GAZILLIONAIRES	GEMFIBROZILS
GARDENLESS	GASHOLDERS	GASTROSCOPE	GAZILLIONS	GEMINATELY
GARDEROBES	GASIFIABLE	GASTROSCOPES	GAZUMPINGS	GEMINATING
GARGANTUAN	GASIFICATION	GASTROSCOPIC	GAZUNDERED	GEMINATION
GARGANTUAS	GASIFICATIONS	GASTROSCOPIES	GAZUNDERER	GEMINATIONS
GARGARISED	GASLIGHTED	GASTROSCOPIST	GAZUNDERERS	GEMMACEOUS
GARGARISES	GASLIGHTING	GASTROSCOPISTS	GAZUNDERING	GEMMATIONS

GEMMIFEROUS
GEMMINESSES
GEMMIPAROUS
GEMMIPAROUSLY
GEMMOLOGICAL
GEMMOLOGIES
GEMMOLOGIST
GEMMOLOGISTS
GEMMULATION
GEMMULATIONS
GEMOLOGICAL
GEMOLOGIES
GEMOLOGIST
GEMOLOGISTS
GEMUTLICHKEIT
GEMUTLICHKEITS
GENDARMERIE
GENDARMERIES
GENDARMERY
GENDERISED
GENDERISES
GENDERISING
GENDERIZED
GENDERIZES
GENDERIZING
GENDERLESS
GENDERQUEER
GENDERQUEERS
GENEALOGIC
GENEALOGICAL
GENEALOGICALLY
GENEALOGIES
GENEALOGISE
GENEALOGISED
GENEALOGISES
GENEALOGISING
GENEALOGIST
GENEALOGISTS
GENEALOGIZE
GENEALOGIZED
GENEALOGIZES
GENEALOGIZING
GENECOLOGIES
GENECOLOGY
GENERALATE
GENERALATES
GENERALCIES
GENERALISABLE
GENERALISATION
GENERALISATIONS
GENERALISE
GENERALISED
GENERALISER
GENERALISERS
GENERALISES
GENERALISING
GENERALISM
GENERALISMS
GENERALISSIMO
GENERALISSIMOS
GENERALIST
GENERALISTS
GENERALITIES
GENERALITY
GENERALIZABLE
GENERALIZATION
GENERALIZATIONS

GENERALIZE
GENERALIZED
GENERALIZER
GENERALIZERS
GENERALIZES
GENERALIZING
GENERALLED
GENERALLING
GENERALNESS
GENERALNESSES
GENERALSHIP
GENERALSHIPS
GENERATING
GENERATION
GENERATIONAL
GENERATIONALLY
GENERATIONISM
GENERATIONISMS
GENERATIONS
GENERATIVE
GENERATORS
GENERATRICES
GENERATRIX
GENERICALLY
GENERICNESS
GENERICNESSES
GENEROSITIES
GENEROSITY
GENEROUSLY
GENEROUSNESS
GENEROUSNESSES
GENETHLIAC
GENETHLIACAL
GENETHLIACALLY
GENETHLIACON
GENETHLIACONS
GENETHLIACS
GENETHLIALOGIC
GENETHLIALOGIES
GENETHLIALOGY
GENETICALLY
GENETICIST
GENETICISTS
GENETOTROPHIC
GENETRICES
GENETRIXES
GENEVRETTE
GENEVRETTES
GENIALISED
GENIALISES
GENIALISING
GENIALITIES
GENIALIZED
GENIALIZES
GENIALIZING
GENIALNESS
GENIALNESSES
GENICULATE
GENICULATED
GENICULATELY
GENICULATES
GENICULATING
GENICULATION
GENICULATIONS
GENISTEINS
GENITALIAL
GENITIVALLY

GENITIVELY
GENITOURINARY
GENITRICES
GENITRIXES
GENLOCKING
GENLOCKINGS
GENOCIDAIRE
GENOCIDAIRES
GENOPHOBIA
GENOPHOBIAS
GENOTYPICAL
GENOTYPICALLY
GENOTYPICITIES
GENOTYPICITY
GENOTYPING
GENOUILLERE
GENOUILLERES
GENSDARMES
GENTAMICIN
GENTAMICINS
GENTEELEST
GENTEELISE
GENTEELISED
GENTEELISES
GENTEELISH
GENTEELISING
GENTEELISM
GENTEELISMS
GENTEELIZE
GENTEELIZED
GENTEELIZES
GENTEELIZING
GENTEELNESS
GENTEELNESSES
GENTIANACEOUS
GENTIANELLA
GENTIANELLAS
GENTILESSE
GENTILESSES
GENTILHOMME
GENTILISED
GENTILISES
GENTILISING
GENTILISMS
GENTILITIAL
GENTILITIAN
GENTILITIES
GENTILITIOUS
GENTILIZED
GENTILIZES
GENTILIZING
GENTILSHOMMES
GENTLEFOLK
GENTLEFOLKS
GENTLEHOOD
GENTLEHOODS
GENTLEMANHOOD
GENTLEMANHOODS
GENTLEMANLIER
GENTLEMANLIEST
GENTLEMANLIKE
GENTLEMANLINESS
GENTLEMANLY
GENTLEMANSHIP
GENTLEMANSHIPS
GENTLENESS
GENTLENESSE

GENTLENESSES
GENTLEPERSON
GENTLEPERSONS
GENTLEWOMAN
GENTLEWOMANLIER
GENTLEWOMANLY
GENTLEWOMEN
GENTRIFICATION
GENTRIFICATIONS
GENTRIFIED
GENTRIFIER
GENTRIFIERS
GENTRIFIES
GENTRIFYING
GENUFLECTED
GENUFLECTING
GENUFLECTION
GENUFLECTIONS
GENUFLECTOR
GENUFLECTORS
GENUFLECTS
GENUFLEXION
GENUFLEXIONS
GENUINENESS
GENUINENESSES
GEOBOTANIC
GEOBOTANICAL
GEOBOTANIES
GEOBOTANIST
GEOBOTANISTS
GEOCACHERS
GEOCACHING
GEOCACHINGS
GEOCARPIES
GEOCENTRIC
GEOCENTRICAL
GEOCENTRICALLY
GEOCENTRICISM
GEOCENTRICISMS
GEOCHEMICAL
GEOCHEMICALLY
GEOCHEMIST
GEOCHEMISTRIES
GEOCHEMISTRY
GEOCHEMISTS
GEOCHRONOLOGIC
GEOCHRONOLOGIES
GEOCHRONOLOGIST
GEOCHRONOLOGY
GEOCORONAE
GEOCORONAS
GEODEMOGRAPHICS
GEODESICAL
GEODESISTS
GEODETICAL
GEODETICALLY
GEODYNAMIC
GEODYNAMICAL
GEODYNAMICIST
GEODYNAMICISTS
GEODYNAMICS
GEOENGINEERING
GEOENGINEERINGS
GEOGNOSIES
GEOGNOSTIC
GEOGNOSTICAL
GEOGNOSTICALLY

GEOGRAPHER
GEOGRAPHERS
GEOGRAPHIC
GEOGRAPHICAL
GEOGRAPHICALLY
GEOGRAPHIES
GEOHYDROLOGIC
GEOHYDROLOGIES
GEOHYDROLOGIST
GEOHYDROLOGISTS
GEOHYDROLOGY
GEOLATRIES
GEOLINGUISTICS
GEOLOCATION
GEOLOCATIONS
GEOLOGIANS
GEOLOGICAL
GEOLOGICALLY
GEOLOGISED
GEOLOGISES
GEOLOGISING
GEOLOGISTS
GEOLOGIZED
GEOLOGIZES
GEOLOGIZING
GEOMAGNETIC
GEOMAGNETICALLY
GEOMAGNETISM
GEOMAGNETISMS
GEOMAGNETIST
GEOMAGNETISTS
GEOMANCERS
GEOMANCIES
GEOMECHANICS
GEOMEDICAL
GEOMEDICINE
GEOMEDICINES
GEOMETRICAL
GEOMETRICALLY
GEOMETRICIAN
GEOMETRICIANS
GEOMETRICS
GEOMETRIDS
GEOMETRIES
GEOMETRISATION
GEOMETRISATIONS
GEOMETRISE
GEOMETRISED
GEOMETRISES
GEOMETRISING
GEOMETRIST
GEOMETRISTS
GEOMETRIZATION
GEOMETRIZATIONS
GEOMETRIZE
GEOMETRIZED
GEOMETRIZES
GEOMETRIZING
GEOMORPHIC
GEOMORPHOGENIC
GEOMORPHOGENIES
GEOMORPHOGENIST
GEOMORPHOGENY
GEOMORPHOLOGIC
GEOMORPHOLOGIES
GEOMORPHOLOGIST
GEOMORPHOLOGY

GEOPHAGIAS
GEOPHAGIES
GEOPHAGISM
GEOPHAGISMS
GEOPHAGIST
GEOPHAGISTS
GEOPHAGOUS
GEOPHILOUS
GEOPHYSICAL
GEOPHYSICALLY
GEOPHYSICIST
GEOPHYSICISTS
GEOPHYSICS
GEOPOLITICAL
GEOPOLITICALLY
GEOPOLITICIAN
GEOPOLITICIANS
GEOPOLITICS
GEOPONICAL
GEOPRESSURED
GEORGETTES
GEOSCIENCE
GEOSCIENCES
GEOSCIENTIFIC
GEOSCIENTIST
GEOSCIENTISTS
GEOSPATIAL
GEOSPHERES
GEOSTATICS
GEOSTATIONARY
GEOSTRATEGIC
GEOSTRATEGICAL
GEOSTRATEGIES
GEOSTRATEGIST
GEOSTRATEGISTS
GEOSTRATEGY
GEOSTROPHIC
GEOSTROPHICALLY
GEOSYNCHRONOUS
GEOSYNCLINAL
GEOSYNCLINE
GEOSYNCLINES
GEOTACTICAL
GEOTACTICALLY
GEOTAGGING
GEOTECHNIC
GEOTECHNICAL
GEOTECHNICS
GEOTECHNOLOGIES
GEOTECHNOLOGY
GEOTECTONIC
GEOTECTONICALLY
GEOTECTONICS
GEOTEXTILE
GEOTEXTILES
GEOTHERMAL
GEOTHERMALLY
GEOTHERMIC
GEOTHERMOMETER
GEOTHERMOMETERS
GEOTROPICALLY
GEOTROPISM
GEOTROPISMS
GERANIACEOUS
GERATOLOGICAL
GERATOLOGIES
GERATOLOGIST

GERATOLOGISTS
GERATOLOGY
GERFALCONS
GERIATRICIAN
GERIATRICIANS
GERIATRICS
GERIATRIST
GERIATRISTS
GERMANDERS
GERMANENESS
GERMANENESSES
GERMANISATION
GERMANISATIONS
GERMANISED
GERMANISES
GERMANISING
GERMANITES
GERMANIUMS
GERMANIZATION
GERMANIZATIONS
GERMANIZED
GERMANIZES
GERMANIZING
GERMICIDAL
GERMICIDES
GERMINABILITIES
GERMINABILITY
GERMINABLE
GERMINALLY
GERMINATED
GERMINATES
GERMINATING
GERMINATION
GERMINATIONS
GERMINATIVE
GERMINATOR
GERMINATORS
GERMINESSES
GERMPLASMS
GERONTOCRACIES
GERONTOCRACY
GERONTOCRAT
GERONTOCRATIC
GERONTOCRATS
GERONTOLOGIC
GERONTOLOGICAL
GERONTOLOGIES
GERONTOLOGIST
GERONTOLOGISTS
GERONTOLOGY
GERONTOMORPHIC
GERONTOPHIL
GERONTOPHILE
GERONTOPHILES
GERONTOPHILIA
GERONTOPHILIAS
GERONTOPHILS
GERONTOPHOBE
GERONTOPHOBES
GERONTOPHOBIA
GERONTOPHOBIAS
GERRYMANDER
GERRYMANDERED
GERRYMANDERER
GERRYMANDERERS
GERRYMANDERING
GERRYMANDERINGS

GERRYMANDERS
GERUNDIVAL
GERUNDIVELY
GERUNDIVES
GESELLSCHAFT
GESELLSCHAFTEN
GESELLSCHAFTS
GESNERIADS
GESSAMINES
GESTALTISM
GESTALTISMS
GESTALTIST
GESTALTISTS
GESTATIONAL
GESTATIONS
GESTATORIAL
GESTICULANT
GESTICULATE
GESTICULATED
GESTICULATES
GESTICULATING
GESTICULATION
GESTICULATIONS
GESTICULATIVE
GESTICULATOR
GESTICULATORS
GESTICULATORY
GESTURALLY
GESUNDHEIT
GETTERINGS
GEWURZTRAMINER
GEWURZTRAMINERS
GEYSERITES
GHASTFULLY
GHASTLIEST
GHASTLINESS
GHASTLINESSES
GHASTNESSES
GHETTOISATION
GHETTOISATIONS
GHETTOISED
GHETTOISES
GHETTOISING
GHETTOIZATION
GHETTOIZATIONS
GHETTOIZED
GHETTOIZES
GHETTOIZING
GHOSTLIEST
GHOSTLINESS
GHOSTLINESSES
GHOSTWRITE
GHOSTWRITER
GHOSTWRITERS
GHOSTWRITES
GHOSTWRITING
GHOSTWRITTEN
GHOSTWROTE
GHOULISHLY
GHOULISHNESS
GHOULISHNESSES
GIANTESSES
GIANTHOODS
GIANTLIEST
GIANTSHIPS
GIARDIASES
GIARDIASIS

GIBBERELLIC
GIBBERELLIN
GIBBERELLINS
GIBBERINGS
GIBBERISHES
GIBBETTING
GIBBOSITIES
GIBBOUSNESS
GIBBOUSNESSES
GIDDINESSES
GIFTEDNESS
GIFTEDNESSES
GIFTWRAPPED
GIFTWRAPPING
GIFTWRAPPINGS
GIGACYCLES
GIGAHERTZES
GIGANTESQUE
GIGANTICALLY
GIGANTICIDE
GIGANTICIDES
GIGANTICNESS
GIGANTICNESSES
GIGANTISMS
GIGANTOLOGIES
GIGANTOLOGY
GIGANTOMACHIA
GIGANTOMACHIAS
GIGANTOMACHIES
GIGANTOMACHY
GIGGLESOME
GIGGLINGLY
GIGMANITIES
GILDSWOMAN
GILDSWOMEN
GILLFLIRTS
GILLIFLOWER
GILLIFLOWERS
GILLNETTED
GILLNETTER
GILLNETTERS
GILLNETTING
GILLRAVAGE
GILLRAVAGED
GILLRAVAGES
GILLRAVAGING
GILLRAVITCH
GILLRAVITCHED
GILLRAVITCHES
GILLRAVITCHING
GILLYFLOWER
GILLYFLOWERS
GILRAVAGED
GILRAVAGER
GILRAVAGERS
GILRAVAGES
GILRAVAGING
GILRAVITCH
GILRAVITCHED
GILRAVITCHES
GILRAVITCHING
GILSONITES
GIMBALLING
GIMCRACKERIES
GIMCRACKERY
GIMMICKIER
GIMMICKIEST

GIMMICKING
GIMMICKRIES
GINGELLIES
GINGERADES
GINGERBREAD
GINGERBREADED
GINGERBREADIER
GINGERBREADIEST
GINGERBREADS
GINGERBREADY
GINGERIEST
GINGERLIER
GINGERLIEST
GINGERLINESS
GINGERLINESSES
GINGERROOT
GINGERROOTS
GINGERSNAP
GINGERSNAPS
GINGIVECTOMIES
GINGIVECTOMY
GINGIVITIS
GINGIVITISES
GINGLIMOID
GIPSYHOODS
GIPSYWORTS
GIRANDOLAS
GIRANDOLES
GIRDLECAKE
GIRDLECAKES
GIRDLESCONE
GIRDLESCONES
GIRDLESTEAD
GIRDLESTEADS
GIRLFRIEND
GIRLFRIENDS
GIRLISHNESS
GIRLISHNESSES
GIRTHLINES
GISMOLOGIES
GITTARONES
GITTERNING
GIVENNESSES
GIZMOLOGIES
GLABRESCENT
GLABROUSNESS
GLABROUSNESSES
GLACIALIST
GLACIALISTS
GLACIATING
GLACIATION
GLACIATIONS
GLACIOLOGIC
GLACIOLOGICAL
GLACIOLOGIES
GLACIOLOGIST
GLACIOLOGISTS
GLACIOLOGY
GLADDENERS
GLADDENING
GLADFULNESS
GLADFULNESSES
GLADIATORIAL
GLADIATORIAN
GLADIATORS
GLADIATORSHIP
GLADIATORSHIPS

GLADIATORY	GLASSCUTTER	GLISTENING	GLORIFIABLE	GLUCOSURIC
GLADIOLUSES	GLASSCUTTERS	GLISTENINGLY	GLORIFICATION	GLUCURONIC
GLADNESSES	GLASSHOUSE	GLISTERING	GLORIFICATIONS	GLUCURONIDASE
GLADSOMELY	GLASSHOUSES	GLISTERINGLY	GLORIFIERS	GLUCURONIDASES
GLADSOMENESS	GLASSIFIED	GLITCHIEST	GLORIFYING	GLUCURONIDE
GLADSOMENESSES	GLASSIFIES	GLITTERAND	GLORIOUSLY	GLUCURONIDES
GLADSOMEST	GLASSIFYING	GLITTERATI	GLORIOUSNESS	GLUEYNESSES
GLADSTONES	GLASSINESS	GLITTERIER	GLORIOUSNESSES	GLUINESSES
GLADWRAPPED	GLASSINESSES	GLITTERIEST	GLOSSARIAL	GLUMACEOUS
GLADWRAPPING	GLASSMAKER	GLITTERING	GLOSSARIALLY	GLUMIFEROUS
GLAIKETNESS	GLASSMAKERS	GLITTERINGLY	GLOSSARIES	GLUMNESSES
GLAIKETNESSES	GLASSMAKING	GLITTERINGS	GLOSSARIST	GLUTAMATES
GLAIKITNESS	GLASSMAKINGS	GLITZINESS	GLOSSARISTS	GLUTAMINASE
GLAIKITNESSES	GLASSPAPER	GLITZINESSES	GLOSSATORS	GLUTAMINASES
GLAIRINESS	GLASSPAPERED	GLOATINGLY	GLOSSECTOMIES	GLUTAMINES
GLAIRINESSES	GLASSPAPERING	GLOBALISATION	GLOSSECTOMY	GLUTAMINIC
GLAMORISATION	GLASSPAPERS	GLOBALISATIONS	GLOSSEMATICS	GLUTARALDEHYDE
GLAMORISATIONS	GLASSWARES	GLOBALISED	GLOSSINESS	GLUTARALDEHYDES
GLAMORISED	GLASSWORKER	GLOBALISES	GLOSSINESSES	GLUTATHIONE
GLAMORISER	GLASSWORKERS	GLOBALISING	GLOSSINGLY	GLUTATHIONES
GLAMORISERS	GLASSWORKS	GLOBALISMS	GLOSSITISES	GLUTETHIMIDE
GLAMORISES	GLASSWORMS	GLOBALISTS	GLOSSODYNIA	GLUTETHIMIDES
GLAMORISING	GLASSWORTS	GLOBALIZATION	GLOSSODYNIAS	GLUTINOSITIES
GLAMORIZATION	GLASSYHEADED	GLOBALIZATIONS	GLOSSOGRAPHER	GLUTINOSITY
GLAMORIZATIONS	GLAUBERITE	GLOBALIZED	GLOSSOGRAPHERS	GLUTINOUSLY
GLAMORIZED	GLAUBERITES	GLOBALIZES	GLOSSOGRAPHICAL	GLUTINOUSNESS
GLAMORIZER	GLAUCESCENCE	GLOBALIZING	GLOSSOGRAPHIES	GLUTINOUSNESSES
GLAMORIZERS	GLAUCESCENCES	GLOBEFISHES	GLOSSOGRAPHY	GLUTTINGLY
GLAMORIZES	GLAUCESCENT	GLOBEFLOWER	GLOSSOLALIA	GLUTTONIES
GLAMORIZING	GLAUCOMATOUS	GLOBEFLOWERS	GLOSSOLALIAS	GLUTTONISE
GLAMOROUSLY	GLAUCONITE	GLOBESITIES	GLOSSOLALIST	GLUTTONISED
GLAMOROUSNESS	GLAUCONITES	GLOBETROTS	GLOSSOLALISTS	GLUTTONISES
GLAMOROUSNESSES	GLAUCONITIC	GLOBETROTTED	GLOSSOLARYNGEAL	GLUTTONISH
GLAMOURING	GLAUCOUSLY	GLOBETROTTER	GLOSSOLOGICAL	GLUTTONISING
GLAMOURISE	GLAUCOUSNESS	GLOBETROTTERS	GLOSSOLOGIES	GLUTTONIZE
GLAMOURISED	GLAUCOUSNESSES	GLOBETROTTING	GLOSSOLOGIST	GLUTTONIZED
GLAMOURISES	GLAZIERIES	GLOBETROTTINGS	GLOSSOLOGISTS	GLUTTONIZES
GLAMOURISING	GLAZINESSES	GLOBIGERINA	GLOSSOLOGY	GLUTTONIZING
GLAMOURIZE	GLEAMINGLY	GLOBIGERINAE	GLOTTIDEAN	GLUTTONOUS
GLAMOURIZED	GLEEFULNESS	GLOBIGERINAS	GLOTTOGONIC	GLUTTONOUSLY
GLAMOURIZES	GLEEFULNESSES	GLOBOSENESS	GLOTTOLOGIES	GLUTTONOUSNESS
GLAMOURIZING	GLEEMAIDEN	GLOBOSENESSES	GLOTTOLOGY	GLYCAEMIAS
GLAMOURLESS	GLEEMAIDENS	GLOBOSITIES	GLOVEBOXES	GLYCATIONS
GLAMOUROUS	GLEGNESSES	GLOBULARITIES	GLOWERINGLY	GLYCERALDEHYDE
GLAMOUROUSLY	GLEISATION	GLOBULARITY	GLOWSTICKS	GLYCERALDEHYDES
GLAMOUROUSNESS	GLEISATIONS	GLOBULARLY	GLUCINIUMS	GLYCERIDES
GLAMOURPUSS	GLEIZATION	GLOBULARNESS	GLUCOCORTICOID	GLYCERIDIC
GLAMOURPUSSES	GLEIZATIONS	GLOBULARNESSES	GLUCOCORTICOIDS	GLYCERINATE
GLANCINGLY	GLENDOVEER	GLOBULIFEROUS	GLUCOKINASE	GLYCERINATED
GLANDEROUS	GLENDOVEERS	GLOBULITES	GLUCOKINASES	GLYCERINATES
GLANDIFEROUS	GLENGARRIES	GLOCHIDIATE	GLUCONATES	GLYCERINATING
GLANDIFORM	GLIBNESSES	GLOCHIDIUM	GLUCONEOGENESES	GLYCERINES
GLANDULARLY	GLIDEPATHS	GLOCKENSPIEL	GLUCONEOGENESIS	GLYCOCOLLS
GLANDULIFEROUS	GLIMMERIER	GLOCKENSPIELS	GLUCONEOGENIC	GLYCOGENESES
GLANDULOUS	GLIMMERIEST	GLOMERATED	GLUCOPHORE	GLYCOGENESIS
GLANDULOUSLY	GLIMMERING	GLOMERATES	GLUCOPHORES	GLYCOGENETIC
GLARINESSES	GLIMMERINGLY	GLOMERATING	GLUCOPROTEIN	GLYCOGENIC
GLARINGNESS	GLIMMERINGS	GLOMERATION	GLUCOPROTEINS	GLYCOGENOLYSES
GLARINGNESSES	GLIOBLASTOMA	GLOMERATIONS	GLUCOSAMINE	GLYCOGENOLYSIS
GLASNOSTIAN	GLIOBLASTOMAS	GLOMERULAR	GLUCOSAMINES	GLYCOGENOLYTIC
GLASNOSTIC	GLIOBLASTOMATA	GLOMERULATE	GLUCOSIDAL	GLYCOLIPID
GLASSBLOWER	GLIOMATOSES	GLOMERULES	GLUCOSIDASE	GLYCOLIPIDS
GLASSBLOWERS	GLIOMATOSIS	GLOMERULUS	GLUCOSIDASES	GLYCOLYSES
GLASSBLOWING	GLIOMATOUS	GLOOMFULLY	GLUCOSIDES	GLYCOLYSIS
GLASSBLOWINGS	GLISSADERS	GLOOMINESS	GLUCOSIDIC	GLYCOLYTIC
GLASSCLOTH	GLISSADING	GLOOMINESSES	GLUCOSURIA	GLYCONEOGENESES
GLASSCLOTHS	GLISSANDOS	GLOOMSTERS	GLUCOSURIAS	GLYCONEOGENESIS

g

GLYCOPEPTIDE	GNOSTICISM	GODROONINGS	GONENESSES	GOOSENECKED
GLYCOPEPTIDES	GNOSTICISMS	GOFFERINGS	GONFALONIER	GOOSENECKS
GLYCOPHYTE	GNOTOBIOLOGICAL	GOGGLEBOXES	GONFALONIERS	GOOSINESSES
GLYCOPHYTES	GNOTOBIOLOGIES	GOITROGENIC	GONGORISTIC	GOPHERWOOD
GLYCOPHYTIC	GNOTOBIOLOGY	GOITROGENICITY	GONIATITES	GOPHERWOODS
GLYCOPROTEIN	GNOTOBIOSES	GOITROGENS	GONIATITOID	GORBELLIES
GLYCOPROTEINS	GNOTOBIOSIS	GOLDARNING	GONIATITOIDS	GORBLIMEYS
GLYCOSIDASE	GNOTOBIOTE	GOLDBEATER	GONIMOBLAST	GORBLIMIES
GLYCOSIDASES	GNOTOBIOTES	GOLDBEATERS	GONIMOBLASTS	GOREHOUNDS
GLYCOSIDES	GNOTOBIOTIC	GOLDBRICKED	GONIOMETER	GORGEOUSLY
GLYCOSIDIC	GNOTOBIOTICALLY	GOLDBRICKING	GONIOMETERS	GORGEOUSNESS
GLYCOSIDICALLY	GNOTOBIOTICS	GOLDBRICKS	GONIOMETRIC	GORGEOUSNESSES
GLYCOSURIA	GOALKEEPER	GOLDCRESTS	GONIOMETRICAL	GORGONEION
GLYCOSURIAS	GOALKEEPERS	GOLDENBERRIES	GONIOMETRICALLY	GORGONIANS
GLYCOSURIC	GOALKEEPING	GOLDENBERRY	GONIOMETRIES	GORGONISED
GLYCOSYLATE	GOALKEEPINGS	GOLDENEYES	GONIOMETRY	GORGONISES
GLYCOSYLATED	GOALKICKER	GOLDENNESS	GONIOSCOPE	GORGONISING
GLYCOSYLATES	GOALKICKERS	GOLDENNESSES	GONIOSCOPES	GORGONIZED
GLYCOSYLATING	GOALKICKING	GOLDENRODS	GONOCOCCAL	GORGONIZES
GLYCOSYLATION	GOALKICKINGS	GOLDENSEAL	GONOCOCCIC	GORGONIZING
GLYCOSYLATIONS	GOALMOUTHS	GOLDENSEALS	GONOCOCCOID	GORILLAGRAM
GLYOXALINE	GOALSCORER	GOLDFIELDS	GONOCOCCUS	GORILLAGRAMS
GLYOXALINES	GOALSCORERS	GOLDFINCHES	GONOPHORES	GORINESSES
GLYPHOGRAPH	GOALTENDER	GOLDFINNIES	GONOPHORIC	GORMANDISE
GLYPHOGRAPHER	GOALTENDERS	GOLDFISHES	GONOPHOROUS	GORMANDISED
GLYPHOGRAPHERS	GOALTENDING	GOLDILOCKS	GONORRHEAL	GORMANDISER
GLYPHOGRAPHIC	GOALTENDINGS	GOLDILOCKSES	GONORRHEAS	GORMANDISERS
GLYPHOGRAPHICAL	GOATFISHES	GOLDMINERS	GONORRHEIC	GORMANDISES
GLYPHOGRAPHIES	GOATISHNESS	GOLDSINNIES	GONORRHOEA	GORMANDISING
GLYPHOGRAPHS	GOATISHNESSES	GOLDSMITHERIES	GONORRHOEAL	GORMANDISINGS
GLYPHOGRAPHY	GOATSBEARD	GOLDSMITHERY	GONORRHOEAS	GORMANDISM
GLYPHOSATE	GOATSBEARDS	GOLDSMITHRIES	GONORRHOEIC	GORMANDISMS
GLYPHOSATES	GOATSUCKER	GOLDSMITHRY	GOODFELLAS	GORMANDIZE
GLYPTODONT	GOATSUCKERS	GOLDSMITHS	GOODFELLOW	GORMANDIZED
GLYPTODONTS	GOBBELINES	GOLDSPINKS	GOODFELLOWS	GORMANDIZER
GLYPTOGRAPHER	GOBBLEDEGOOK	GOLDSTICKS	GOODFELLOWSHIP	GORMANDIZERS
GLYPTOGRAPHERS	GOBBLEDEGOOKS	GOLDSTONES	GOODFELLOWSHIPS	GORMANDIZES
GLYPTOGRAPHIC	GOBBLEDYGOOK	GOLDTHREAD	GOODINESSES	GORMANDIZING
GLYPTOGRAPHICAL	GOBBLEDYGOOKS	GOLDTHREADS	GOODLIHEAD	GORMANDIZINGS
GLYPTOGRAPHIES	GOBSMACKED	GOLIARDERIES	GOODLIHEADS	GOSLARITES
GLYPTOGRAPHY	GOBSTOPPER	GOLIARDERY	GOODLINESS	GOSPELISED
GLYPTOTHECA	GOBSTOPPERS	GOLIARDIES	GOODLINESSES	GOSPELISES
GLYPTOTHECAE	GOCHUJANGS	GOLIATHISE	GOODLYHEAD	GOSPELISING
GMELINITES	GODAMNDEST	GOLIATHISED	GOODLYHEADS	GOSPELIZED
GNAPHALIUM	GODCHILDREN	GOLIATHISES	GOODNESSES	GOSPELIZES
GNAPHALIUMS	GODDAMMING	GOLIATHISING	GOODNIGHTS	GOSPELIZING
GNASHINGLY	GODDAMNDEST	GOLIATHIZE	GOODWILLED	GOSPELLERS
GNATCATCHER	GODDAMNEDEST	GOLIATHIZED	GOOEYNESSES	GOSPELLIER
GNATCATCHERS	GODDAMNING	GOLIATHIZES	GOOFINESSES	GOSPELLIEST
GNATHONICAL	GODDAUGHTER	GOLIATHIZING	GOOGLEWHACK	GOSPELLING
GNATHONICALLY	GODDAUGHTERS	GOLLIWOGGS	GOOGLEWHACKS	GOSPELLINGS
GNATHOSTOMATOUS	GODDESSHOOD	GOLOMYNKAS	GOOGOLPLEX	GOSPELLISE
GNATHOSTOME	GODDESSHOODS	GOLOPTIOUS	GOOGOLPLEXES	GOSPELLISED
GNATHOSTOMES	GODFATHERED	GOLUPTIOUS	GOOINESSES	GOSPELLISES
GNEISSITIC	GODFATHERING	GOMBEENISM	GOONEYBIRD	GOSPELLISING
GNETOPHYTE	GODFATHERS	GOMBEENISMS	GOONEYBIRDS	GOSPELLIZE
GNETOPHYTES	GODFORSAKEN	GONADECTOMIES	GOOPINESSES	GOSPELLIZED
GNOMICALLY	GODLESSNESS	GONADECTOMISED	GOOSANDERS	GOSPELLIZES
GNOMONICAL	GODLESSNESSES	GONADECTOMIZED	GOOSEBERRIES	GOSPELLIZING
GNOMONICALLY	GODLIKENESS	GONADECTOMY	GOOSEBERRY	GOSSAMERIER
GNOMONOLOGIES	GODLIKENESSES	GONADOTROPHIC	GOOSEFISHES	GOSSAMERIEST
GNOMONOLOGY	GODLINESSES	GONADOTROPHIN	GOOSEFLESH	GOSSIPIEST
GNOSEOLOGIES	GODMOTHERED	GONADOTROPHINS	GOOSEFLESHES	GOSSIPINGLY
GNOSEOLOGY	GODMOTHERING	GONADOTROPIC	GOOSEFOOTS	GOSSIPINGS
GNOSIOLOGIES	GODMOTHERS	GONADOTROPIN	GOOSEGRASS	GOSSIPMONGER
GNOSIOLOGY	GODPARENTS	GONADOTROPINS	GOOSEGRASSES	GOSSIPMONGERS
GNOSTICALLY	GODROONING	GONDOLIERS	GOOSEHERDS	GOSSIPPERS

GOSSIPPING	GRACIOSITIES	GRAMMATICASTER	GRANDNEPHEWS	GRANTSMANSHIP
GOSSIPRIES	GRACIOSITY	GRAMMATICASTERS	GRANDNESSES	GRANTSMANSHIPS
GOTHICALLY	GRACIOUSLY	GRAMMATICISE	GRANDNIECE	GRANULARITIES
GOTHICISED	GRACIOUSNESS	GRAMMATICISED	GRANDNIECES	GRANULARITY
GOTHICISES	GRACIOUSNESSES	GRAMMATICISES	GRANDPAPAS	GRANULARLY
GOTHICISING	GRADABILITIES	GRAMMATICISING	GRANDPARENT	GRANULATED
GOTHICISMS	GRADABILITY	GRAMMATICISM	GRANDPARENTAL	GRANULATER
GOTHICIZED	GRADABLENESS	GRAMMATICISMS	GRANDPARENTHOOD	GRANULATERS
GOTHICIZES	GRADABLENESSES	GRAMMATICIZE	GRANDPARENTS	GRANULATES
GOTHICIZING	GRADATIONAL	GRAMMATICIZED	GRANDSIRES	GRANULATING
GOURDINESS	GRADATIONALLY	GRAMMATICIZES	GRANDSTAND	GRANULATION
GOURDINESSES	GRADATIONED	GRAMMATICIZING	GRANDSTANDED	GRANULATIONS
GOURMANDISE	GRADATIONS	GRAMMATIST	GRANDSTANDER	GRANULATIVE
GOURMANDISED	GRADATORIES	GRAMMATISTS	GRANDSTANDERS	GRANULATOR
GOURMANDISES	GRADDANING	GRAMMATOLOGIES	GRANDSTANDING	GRANULATORS
GOURMANDISING	GRADELIEST	GRAMMATOLOGIST	GRANDSTANDINGS	GRANULIFEROUS
GOURMANDISM	GRADIENTER	GRAMMATOLOGISTS	GRANDSTANDS	GRANULIFORM
GOURMANDISMS	GRADIENTERS	GRAMMATOLOGY	GRANDSTOOD	GRANULITES
GOURMANDIZE	GRADIOMETER	GRAMOPHONE	GRANDUNCLE	GRANULITIC
GOURMANDIZED	GRADIOMETERS	GRAMOPHONES	GRANDUNCLES	GRANULITISATION
GOURMANDIZES	GRADUALISM	GRAMOPHONIC	GRANGERISATION	GRANULITIZATION
GOURMANDIZING	GRADUALISMS	GRAMOPHONICALLY	GRANGERISATIONS	GRANULOCYTE
GOUTINESSES	GRADUALIST	GRAMOPHONIES	GRANGERISE	GRANULOCYTES
GOUVERNANTE	GRADUALISTIC	GRAMOPHONIST	GRANGERISED	GRANULOCYTIC
GOUVERNANTES	GRADUALISTS	GRAMOPHONISTS	GRANGERISER	GRANULOMAS
GOVERNABILITIES	GRADUALITIES	GRAMOPHONY	GRANGERISERS	GRANULOMATA
GOVERNABILITY	GRADUALITY	GRANADILLA	GRANGERISES	GRANULOMATOUS
GOVERNABLE	GRADUALNESS	GRANADILLAS	GRANGERISING	GRANULOSES
GOVERNABLENESS	GRADUALNESSES	GRANDADDIES	GRANGERISM	GRANULOSIS
GOVERNALLS	GRADUATESHIP	GRANDAUNTS	GRANGERISMS	GRAPEFRUIT
GOVERNANCE	GRADUATESHIPS	GRANDBABIES	GRANGERIZATION	GRAPEFRUITS
GOVERNANCES	GRADUATING	GRANDCHILD	GRANGERIZATIONS	GRAPELOUSE
GOVERNANTE	GRADUATION	GRANDCHILDREN	GRANGERIZE	GRAPESEEDS
GOVERNANTES	GRADUATIONS	GRANDDADDIES	GRANGERIZED	GRAPESHOTS
GOVERNESSED	GRADUATORS	GRANDDADDY	GRANGERIZER	GRAPESTONE
GOVERNESSES	GRAECISING	GRANDDAUGHTER	GRANGERIZERS	GRAPESTONES
GOVERNESSIER	GRAECIZING	GRANDDAUGHTERS	GRANGERIZES	GRAPETREES
GOVERNESSIEST	GRAFFITIED	GRANDEESHIP	GRANGERIZING	GRAPEVINES
GOVERNESSING	GRAFFITIING	GRANDEESHIPS	GRANITELIKE	GRAPHEMICALLY
GOVERNESSY	GRAFFITING	GRANDFATHER	GRANITEWARE	GRAPHEMICS
GOVERNMENT	GRAFFITIST	GRANDFATHERED	GRANITEWARES	GRAPHICACIES
GOVERNMENTAL	GRAFFITISTS	GRANDFATHERING	GRANITIFICATION	GRAPHICACY
GOVERNMENTALISE	GRAINFIELD	GRANDFATHERLIER	GRANITIFORM	GRAPHICALLY
GOVERNMENTALISM	GRAINFIELDS	GRANDFATHERLY	GRANITISATION	GRAPHICALNESS
GOVERNMENTALIST	GRAININESS	GRANDFATHERS	GRANITISATIONS	GRAPHICALNESSES
GOVERNMENTALIZE	GRAININESSES	GRANDIFLORA	GRANITISED	GRAPHICNESS
GOVERNMENTALLY	GRALLATORIAL	GRANDIFLORAS	GRANITISES	GRAPHICNESSES
GOVERNMENTESE	GRALLOCHED	GRANDILOQUENCE	GRANITISING	GRAPHITISABLE
GOVERNMENTESES	GRALLOCHING	GRANDILOQUENCES	GRANITITES	GRAPHITISATION
GOVERNMENTS	GRAMERCIES	GRANDILOQUENT	GRANITIZATION	GRAPHITISATIONS
GOVERNORATE	GRAMICIDIN	GRANDILOQUENTLY	GRANITIZATIONS	GRAPHITISE
GOVERNORATES	GRAMICIDINS	GRANDILOQUOUS	GRANITIZED	GRAPHITISED
GOVERNORSHIP	GRAMINACEOUS	GRANDIOSELY	GRANITIZES	GRAPHITISES
GOVERNORSHIPS	GRAMINEOUS	GRANDIOSENESS	GRANITIZING	GRAPHITISING
GOWDSPINKS	GRAMINICOLOUS	GRANDIOSENESSES	GRANITOIDS	GRAPHITIZABLE
GOWPENFULS	GRAMINIVOROUS	GRANDIOSITIES	GRANIVORES	GRAPHITIZATION
GRACEFULLER	GRAMINOLOGIES	GRANDIOSITY	GRANIVOROUS	GRAPHITIZATIONS
GRACEFULLEST	GRAMINOLOGY	GRANDMAMAS	GRANNIEING	GRAPHITIZE
GRACEFULLY	GRAMMALOGUE	GRANDMAMMA	GRANODIORITE	GRAPHITIZED
GRACEFULNESS	GRAMMALOGUES	GRANDMAMMAS	GRANODIORITES	GRAPHITIZES
GRACEFULNESSES	GRAMMARIAN	GRANDMASTER	GRANODIORITIC	GRAPHITIZING
GRACELESSLY	GRAMMARIANS	GRANDMASTERS	GRANOLITHIC	GRAPHITOID
GRACELESSNESS	GRAMMARLESS	GRANDMOTHER	GRANOLITHICS	GRAPHOLECT
GRACELESSNESSES	GRAMMATICAL	GRANDMOTHERLIER	GRANOLITHS	GRAPHOLECTS
GRACILENESS	GRAMMATICALITY	GRANDMOTHERLY	GRANOPHYRE	GRAPHOLOGIC
GRACILENESSES	GRAMMATICALLY	GRANDMOTHERS	GRANOPHYRES	GRAPHOLOGICAL
GRACILITIES	GRAMMATICALNESS	GRANDNEPHEW	GRANOPHYRIC	GRAPHOLOGIES

GRAPHOLOGIST
GRAPHOLOGISTS
GRAPHOLOGY
GRAPHOMANIA
GRAPHOMANIAS
GRAPHOMOTOR
GRAPHOPHOBIA
GRAPHOPHOBIAS
GRAPINESSES
GRAPLEMENT
GRAPLEMENTS
GRAPPLINGS
GRAPTOLITE
GRAPTOLITES
GRAPTOLITIC
GRASPINGLY
GRASPINGNESS
GRASPINGNESSES
GRASSBIRDS
GRASSFINCH
GRASSFINCHES
GRASSHOOKS
GRASSHOPPER
GRASSHOPPERS
GRASSINESS
GRASSINESSES
GRASSLANDS
GRASSPLOTS
GRASSQUITS
GRASSROOTS
GRASSWRACK
GRASSWRACKS
GRATEFULLER
GRATEFULLEST
GRATEFULLY
GRATEFULNESS
GRATEFULNESSES
GRATICULATION
GRATICULATIONS
GRATICULES
GRATIFICATION
GRATIFICATIONS
GRATIFIERS
GRATIFYING
GRATIFYINGLY
GRATILLITIES
GRATILLITY
GRATINATED
GRATINATES
GRATINATING
GRATINEEING
GRATITUDES
GRATUITIES
GRATUITOUS
GRATUITOUSLY
GRATUITOUSNESS
GRATULATED
GRATULATES
GRATULATING
GRATULATION
GRATULATIONS
GRATULATORY
GRAUNCHERS
GRAUNCHING
GRAVADLAXES
GRAVEDIGGER
GRAVEDIGGERS

GRAVELLIER
GRAVELLIEST
GRAVELLING
GRAVENESSES
GRAVEOLENT
GRAVEROBBER
GRAVEROBBERS
GRAVESIDES
GRAVESITES
GRAVESTONE
GRAVESTONES
GRAVEYARDS
GRAVIDITIES
GRAVIDNESS
GRAVIDNESSES
GRAVIMETER
GRAVIMETERS
GRAVIMETRIC
GRAVIMETRICAL
GRAVIMETRICALLY
GRAVIMETRIES
GRAVIMETRY
GRAVIPERCEPTION
GRAVITASES
GRAVITATED
GRAVITATER
GRAVITATERS
GRAVITATES
GRAVITATING
GRAVITATION
GRAVITATIONAL
GRAVITATIONALLY
GRAVITATIONS
GRAVITATIVE
GRAVITINOS
GRAVITOMETER
GRAVITOMETERS
GRAYBEARDED
GRAYBEARDS
GRAYFISHES
GRAYHEADED
GRAYHOUNDS
GRAYLISTED
GRAYLISTING
GRAYNESSES
GRAYSTONES
GRAYWACKES
GRAYWATERS
GRAYWETHER
GRAYWETHERS
GREASEBALL
GREASEBALLS
GREASEBAND
GREASEBANDS
GREASEBUSH
GREASEBUSHES
GREASELESS
GREASEPAINT
GREASEPAINTS
GREASEPROOF
GREASEPROOFS
GREASEWOOD
GREASEWOODS
GREASINESS
GREASINESSES
GREATCOATED
GREATCOATS

GREATENING
GREATHEARTED
GREATHEARTEDLY
GREATNESSES
GRECIANISE
GRECIANISED
GRECIANISES
GRECIANISING
GRECIANIZE
GRECIANIZED
GRECIANIZES
GRECIANIZING
GREEDHEADS
GREEDINESS
GREEDINESSES
GREENBACKER
GREENBACKERS
GREENBACKISM
GREENBACKISMS
GREENBACKS
GREENBELTS
GREENBONES
GREENBOTTLE
GREENBOTTLES
GREENBRIER
GREENBRIERS
GREENCLOTH
GREENCLOTHS
GREENERIES
GREENFIELD
GREENFIELDS
GREENFINCH
GREENFINCHES
GREENFLIES
GREENGAGES
GREENGROCER
GREENGROCERIES
GREENGROCERS
GREENGROCERY
GREENHANDS
GREENHEADS
GREENHEART
GREENHEARTS
GREENHORNS
GREENHOUSE
GREENHOUSES
GREENISHNESS
GREENISHNESSES
GREENKEEPER
GREENKEEPERS
GREENLIGHT
GREENLIGHTED
GREENLIGHTING
GREENLIGHTS
GREENLINGS
GREENMAILED
GREENMAILER
GREENMAILERS
GREENMAILING
GREENMAILS
GREENNESSES
GREENOCKITE
GREENOCKITES
GREENROOMS
GREENSANDS
GREENSHANK
GREENSHANKS

GREENSICKNESS
GREENSICKNESSES
GREENSKEEPER
GREENSKEEPERS
GREENSOMES
GREENSPEAK
GREENSPEAKS
GREENSTICK
GREENSTONE
GREENSTONES
GREENSTUFF
GREENSTUFFS
GREENSWARD
GREENSWARDS
GREENWASHED
GREENWASHES
GREENWASHING
GREENWASHINGS
GREENWEEDS
GREENWINGS
GREENWOODS
GREGARIANISM
GREGARIANISMS
GREGARINES
GREGARINIAN
GREGARIOUS
GREGARIOUSLY
GREGARIOUSNESS
GREISENISATION
GREISENISATIONS
GREISENISE
GREISENISED
GREISENISES
GREISENISING
GREISENIZATION
GREISENIZATIONS
GREISENIZE
GREISENIZED
GREISENIZES
GREISENIZING
GREMOLATAS
GRENADIERS
GRENADILLA
GRENADILLAS
GRENADINES
GRESSORIAL
GRESSORIOUS
GREVILLEAS
GREWHOUNDS
GREWSOMEST
GREYBEARDED
GREYBEARDS
GREYHEADED
GREYHOUNDS
GREYLISTED
GREYLISTING
GREYNESSES
GREYSCALES
GREYSTONES
GREYWACKES
GREYWETHER
GREYWETHERS
GRIDDLEBREAD
GRIDDLEBREADS
GRIDDLECAKE
GRIDDLECAKES
GRIDIRONED

GRIDIRONING
GRIDLOCKED
GRIDLOCKING
GRIEVANCES
GRIEVINGLY
GRIEVOUSLY
GRIEVOUSNESS
GRIEVOUSNESSES
GRIFFINISH
GRIFFINISM
GRIFFINISMS
GRILLERIES
GRILLROOMS
GRILLSTEAK
GRILLSTEAKS
GRILLWORKS
GRIMACINGLY
GRIMALKINS
GRIMINESSES
GRIMLOOKED
GRIMNESSES
GRINDELIAS
GRINDERIES
GRINDHOUSE
GRINDHOUSES
GRINDINGLY
GRINDSTONE
GRINDSTONES
GRINNINGLY
GRIPPINGLY
GRISAILLES
GRISEOFULVIN
GRISEOFULVINS
GRISLINESS
GRISLINESSES
GRISTLIEST
GRISTLINESS
GRISTLINESSES
GRISTMILLS
GRITSTONES
GRITTINESS
GRITTINESSES
GRIVATIONS
GRIZZLIEST
GROANINGLY
GROATSWORTH
GROATSWORTHS
GROCETERIA
GROCETERIAS
GROGGERIES
GROGGINESS
GROGGINESSES
GROMMETING
GROOVELESS
GROOVELIKE
GROOVINESS
GROOVINESSES
GROSGRAINS
GROSSIERETE
GROSSIERETES
GROSSNESSES
GROSSULARITE
GROSSULARITES
GROSSULARS
GROTESQUELY
GROTESQUENESS
GROTESQUENESSES

g

GROTESQUER	GROUPUSCULE	GUARDEDNESSES	GUILLOTINERS	GUTTURALISES
GROTESQUERIE	GROUPUSCULES	GUARDHOUSE	GUILLOTINES	GUTTURALISING
GROTESQUERIES	GROUPWARES	GUARDHOUSES	GUILLOTINING	GUTTURALISM
GROTESQUERY	GROUPWORKS	GUARDIANSHIP	GUILTINESS	GUTTURALISMS
GROTESQUES	GROUSELIKE	GUARDIANSHIPS	GUILTINESSES	GUTTURALITIES
GROTESQUEST	GROVELINGLY	GUARDRAILS	GUILTLESSLY	GUTTURALITY
GROTTINESS	GROVELINGS	GUARDROOMS	GUILTLESSNESS	GUTTURALIZATION
GROTTINESSES	GROVELLERS	GUARDSHIPS	GUILTLESSNESSES	GUTTURALIZE
GROUCHIEST	GROVELLING	GUARISHING	GUITARFISH	GUTTURALIZED
GROUCHINESS	GROVELLINGLY	GUAYABERAS	GUITARFISHES	GUTTURALIZES
GROUCHINESSES	GROVELLINGS	GUBERNACULA	GUITARISTS	GUTTURALIZING
GROUNDAGES	GROWLERIES	GUBERNACULAR	GULLIBILITIES	GUTTURALLY
GROUNDBAIT	GROWLINESS	GUBERNACULUM	GULLIBILITY	GUTTURALNESS
GROUNDBAITED	GROWLINESSES	GUBERNATION	GULOSITIES	GUTTURALNESSES
GROUNDBAITING	GROWLINGLY	GUBERNATIONS	GUMMIFEROUS	GYMNASIARCH
GROUNDBAITS	GROWTHIEST	GUBERNATOR	GUMMINESSES	GYMNASIARCHS
GROUNDBREAKER	GROWTHINESS	GUBERNATORIAL	GUMMOSITIES	GYMNASIAST
GROUNDBREAKERS	GROWTHINESSES	GUBERNATORS	GUMSHIELDS	GYMNASIASTS
GROUNDBREAKING	GROWTHISTS	GUBERNIYAS	GUMSHOEING	GYMNASIUMS
GROUNDBREAKINGS	GRUBBINESS	GUDGEONING	GUMSUCKERS	GYMNASTICAL
GROUNDBURST	GRUBBINESSES	GUERDONERS	GUNCOTTONS	GYMNASTICALLY
GROUNDBURSTS	GRUBSTAKED	GUERDONING	GUNFIGHTER	GYMNASTICS
GROUNDEDLY	GRUBSTAKER	GUERILLAISM	GUNFIGHTERS	GYMNORHINAL
GROUNDFISH	GRUBSTAKERS	GUERILLAISMS	GUNFIGHTING	GYMNOSOPHIES
GROUNDFISHES	GRUBSTAKES	GUERRILLAISM	GUNFIGHTINGS	GYMNOSOPHIST
GROUNDHOGS	GRUBSTAKING	GUERRILLAISMS	GUNKHOLING	GYMNOSOPHISTS
GROUNDINGS	GRUBSTREET	GUERRILLAS	GUNMANSHIP	GYMNOSOPHS
GROUNDLESS	GRUDGELESS	GUERRILLERO	GUNMANSHIPS	GYMNOSOPHY
GROUNDLESSLY	GRUDGINGLY	GUERRILLEROS	GUNNERSHIP	GYMNOSPERM
GROUNDLESSNESS	GRUELINGLY	GUESSINGLY	GUNNERSHIPS	GYMNOSPERMIES
GROUNDLING	GRUELLINGLY	GUESSTIMATE	GUNNYSACKS	GYMNOSPERMOUS
GROUNDLINGS	GRUELLINGS	GUESSTIMATED	GUNPOWDERIER	GYMNOSPERMS
GROUNDMASS	GRUESOMELY	GUESSTIMATES	GUNPOWDERIEST	GYMNOSPERMY
GROUNDMASSES	GRUESOMENESS	GUESSTIMATING	GUNPOWDERS	GYNAECEUMS
GROUNDNUTS	GRUESOMENESSES	GUESSWORKS	GUNPOWDERY	GYNAECOCRACIES
GROUNDOUTS	GRUESOMEST	GUESTBOOKS	GUNRUNNERS	GYNAECOCRACY
GROUNDPLOT	GRUFFNESSES	GUESTENING	GUNRUNNING	GYNAECOCRATIC
GROUNDPLOTS	GRUMBLIEST	GUESTHOUSE	GUNRUNNINGS	GYNAECOLOGIC
GROUNDPROX	GRUMBLINGLY	GUESTHOUSES	GUNSLINGER	GYNAECOLOGICAL
GROUNDPROXES	GRUMBLINGS	GUESTIMATE	GUNSLINGERS	GYNAECOLOGIES
GROUNDSELL	GRUMMETING	GUESTIMATED	GUNSLINGING	GYNAECOLOGIST
GROUNDSELLS	GRUMNESSES	GUESTIMATES	GUNSLINGINGS	GYNAECOLOGISTS
GROUNDSELS	GRUMPINESS	GUESTIMATING	GUNSMITHING	GYNAECOLOGY
GROUNDSHARE	GRUMPINESSES	GUIDEBOOKS	GUNSMITHINGS	GYNAECOMAST
GROUNDSHARED	GRUMPISHLY	GUIDELINES	GURGITATION	GYNAECOMASTIA
GROUNDSHARES	GRUMPISHNESS	GUIDEPOSTS	GURGITATIONS	GYNAECOMASTIAS
GROUNDSHARING	GRUMPISHNESSES	GUIDESHIPS	GUSHINESSES	GYNAECOMASTIES
GROUNDSHEET	GRUNTINGLY	GUIDEWORDS	GUSSETINGS	GYNAECOMASTS
GROUNDSHEETS	GUACAMOLES	GUIDWILLIE	GUSTATIONS	GYNAECOMASTY
GROUNDSILL	GUACAMOLE	GUILDHALLS	GUSTATORILY	GYNANDRIES
GROUNDSILLS	GUACHAMOLE	GUILDSHIPS	GUSTINESSES	GYNANDRISM
GROUNDSKEEPER	GUACHAMOLES	GUILDSWOMAN	GUTBUCKETS	GYNANDRISMS
GROUNDSKEEPERS	GUACHAROES	GUILDSWOMEN	GUTLESSNESS	GYNANDROMORPH
GROUNDSMAN	GUANABANAS	GUILEFULLY	GUTLESSNESSES	GYNANDROMORPHIC
GROUNDSMEN	GUANAZOLOS	GUILEFULNESS	GUTSINESSES	GYNANDROMORPHS
GROUNDSPEED	GUANETHIDINE	GUILEFULNESSES	GUTTATIONS	GYNANDROMORPHY
GROUNDSPEEDS	GUANETHIDINES	GUILELESSLY	GUTTERBLOOD	GYNANDROUS
GROUNDSWELL	GUANIDINES	GUILELESSNESS	GUTTERBLOODS	GYNARCHIES
GROUNDSWELLS	GUANIFEROUS	GUILELESSNESSES	GUTTERIEST	GYNECOCRACIES
GROUNDWATER	GUANOSINES	GUILLEMETS	GUTTERINGS	GYNECOCRACY
GROUNDWATERS	GUARANTEED	GUILLEMOTS	GUTTERSNIPE	GYNECOCRATIC
GROUNDWOOD	GUARANTEEING	GUILLOCHED	GUTTERSNIPES	GYNECOLOGIC
GROUNDWOODS	GUARANTEES	GUILLOCHES	GUTTERSNIPISH	GYNECOLOGICAL
GROUNDWORK	GUARANTIED	GUILLOCHING	GUTTIFEROUS	GYNECOLOGIES
GROUNDWORKS	GUARANTIES	GUILLOTINE	GUTTURALISATION	GYNECOLOGIST
GROUPTHINK	GUARANTORS	GUILLOTINED	GUTTURALISE	GYNECOLOGISTS
GROUPTHINKS	GUARANTYING	GUILLOTINER	GUTTURALISED	GYNECOLOGY
	GUARDEDNESS			

GYNECOMASTIA
GYNECOMASTIAS
GYNIATRICS
GYNIATRIES
GYNIOLATRIES
GYNIOLATRY
GYNOCRACIES
GYNOCRATIC
GYNODIOECIOUS
GYNODIOECISM
GYNODIOECISMS
GYNOGENESES

GYNOGENESIS
GYNOGENETIC
GYNOMONOECIOUS
GYNOMONOECISM
GYNOMONOECISMS
GYNOPHOBES
GYNOPHOBIA
GYNOPHOBIAS
GYNOPHOBIC
GYNOPHOBICS
GYNOPHORES
GYNOPHORIC

GYNOSTEMIA
GYNOSTEMIUM
GYPSIFEROUS
GYPSOPHILA
GYPSOPHILAS
GYPSYHOODS
GYPSYWORTS
GYRATIONAL
GYRFALCONS
GYROCOMPASS
GYROCOMPASSES
GYROCOPTER

GYROCOPTERS
GYROFREQUENCIES
GYROFREQUENCY
GYROMAGNETIC
GYROMAGNETISM
GYROMAGNETISMS
GYROMANCIES
GYROPILOTS
GYROPLANES
GYROSCOPES
GYROSCOPIC
GYROSCOPICALLY

GYROSCOPICS
GYROSTABILISER
GYROSTABILISERS
GYROSTABILIZER
GYROSTABILIZERS
GYROSTATIC
GYROSTATICALLY
GYROSTATICS
GYROVAGUES

g

HAANEPOOTS	HACKNEYMEN	HAEMATOPOIESES	HAEMOPHILES	HAGIOGRAPHIES
HABERDASHER	HACKSAWING	HAEMATOPOIESIS	HAEMOPHILIA	HAGIOGRAPHIST
HABERDASHERIES	HACKTIVISM	HAEMATOPOIETIC	HAEMOPHILIAC	HAGIOGRAPHISTS
HABERDASHERS	HACKTIVISMS	HAEMATOSES	HAEMOPHILIACS	HAGIOGRAPHY
HABERDASHERY	HACKTIVIST	HAEMATOSIS	HAEMOPHILIAS	HAGIOLATER
HABERDINES	HACKTIVISTS	HAEMATOTHERMAL	HAEMOPHILIC	HAGIOLATERS
HABERGEONS	HACQUETONS	HAEMATOXYLIC	HAEMOPHILIOID	HAGIOLATRIES
HABILATORY	HADROSAURS	HAEMATOXYLIN	HAEMOPHOBIA	HAGIOLATROUS
HABILIMENT	HADROSAURUS	HAEMATOXYLINS	HAEMOPHOBIAS	HAGIOLATRY
HABILIMENTS	HADROSAURUSES	HAEMATOXYLON	HAEMOPOIESES	HAGIOLOGIC
HABILITATE	HAECCEITIES	HAEMATOXYLONS	HAEMOPOIESIS	HAGIOLOGICAL
HABILITATED	HAEMACHROME	HAEMATOZOA	HAEMOPOIETIC	HAGIOLOGIES
HABILITATES	HAEMACHROMES	HAEMATOZOON	HAEMOPROTEIN	HAGIOLOGIST
HABILITATING	HAEMACYTOMETER	HAEMATURIA	HAEMOPROTEINS	HAGIOLOGISTS
HABILITATION	HAEMACYTOMETERS	HAEMATURIAS	HAEMOPTYSES	HAGIOSCOPE
HABILITATIONS	HAEMAGGLUTINATE	HAEMATURIC	HAEMOPTYSIS	HAGIOSCOPES
HABILITATOR	HAEMAGGLUTININ	HAEMOCHROME	HAEMORRHAGE	HAGIOSCOPIC
HABILITATORS	HAEMAGGLUTININS	HAEMOCHROMES	HAEMORRHAGED	HAILSTONES
HABITABILITIES	HAEMAGOGUE	HAEMOCOELS	HAEMORRHAGES	HAILSTORMS
HABITABILITY	HAEMAGOGUES	HAEMOCONIA	HAEMORRHAGIC	HAIRBRAINED
HABITABLENESS	HAEMANGIOMA	HAEMOCONIAS	HAEMORRHAGING	HAIRBREADTH
HABITABLENESSES	HAEMANGIOMAS	HAEMOCYANIN	HAEMORRHAGINGS	HAIRBREADTHS
HABITATION	HAEMANGIOMATA	HAEMOCYANINS	HAEMORRHOID	HAIRBRUSHES
HABITATIONAL	HAEMATEINS	HAEMOCYTES	HAEMORRHOIDAL	HAIRCLOTHS
HABITATIONS	HAEMATEMESES	HAEMOCYTOMETER	HAEMORRHOIDS	HAIRCUTTER
HABITAUNCE	HAEMATEMESIS	HAEMOCYTOMETERS	HAEMOSIDERIN	HAIRCUTTERS
HABITAUNCES	HAEMATINIC	HAEMODIALYSER	HAEMOSIDERINS	HAIRCUTTING
HABITUALLY	HAEMATINICS	HAEMODIALYSERS	HAEMOSTASES	HAIRCUTTINGS
HABITUALNESS	HAEMATITES	HAEMODIALYSES	HAEMOSTASIA	HAIRDRESSER
HABITUALNESSES	HAEMATITIC	HAEMODIALYSIS	HAEMOSTASIAS	HAIRDRESSERS
HABITUATED	HAEMATOBLAST	HAEMODIALYZER	HAEMOSTASIS	HAIRDRESSING
HABITUATES	HAEMATOBLASTIC	HAEMODIALYZERS	HAEMOSTATIC	HAIRDRESSINGS
HABITUATING	HAEMATOBLASTS	HAEMODILUTION	HAEMOSTATICS	HAIRDRIERS
HABITUATION	HAEMATOCELE	HAEMODILUTIONS	HAEMOSTATS	HAIRDRYERS
HABITUATIONS	HAEMATOCELES	HAEMODYNAMIC	HAEMOTOXIC	HAIRINESSES
HABITUDINAL	HAEMATOCRIT	HAEMODYNAMICS	HAEMOTOXIN	HAIRLESSES
HACENDADOS	HAEMATOCRITS	HAEMOFLAGELLATE	HAEMOTOXINS	HAIRLESSNESS
HACIENDADO	HAEMATOCRYAL	HAEMOGLOBIN	HAGBERRIES	HAIRLESSNESSES
HACIENDADOS	HAEMATOGENESES	HAEMOGLOBINS	HAGBUTEERS	HAIRPIECES
HACKAMORES	HAEMATOGENESIS	HAEMOGLOBINURIA	HAGBUTTERS	HAIRSBREADTH
HACKBERRIES	HAEMATOGENETIC	HAEMOGLOBINURIC	HAGGADICAL	HAIRSBREADTHS
HACKBUTEER	HAEMATOGENIC	HAEMOLYMPH	HAGGADISTIC	HAIRSPLITTER
HACKBUTEERS	HAEMATOGENOUS	HAEMOLYMPHS	HAGGADISTS	HAIRSPLITTERS
HACKBUTTER	HAEMATOLOGIC	HAEMOLYSED	HAGGARDNESS	HAIRSPLITTING
HACKBUTTERS	HAEMATOLOGICAL	HAEMOLYSES	HAGGARDNESSES	HAIRSPLITTINGS
HACKERAZZI	HAEMATOLOGIES	HAEMOLYSIN	HAGGISHNESS	HAIRSPRAYS
HACKERAZZIS	HAEMATOLOGIST	HAEMOLYSING	HAGGISHNESSES	HAIRSPRING
HACKERAZZO	HAEMATOLOGISTS	HAEMOLYSINS	HAGIARCHIES	HAIRSPRINGS
HACKMATACK	HAEMATOLOGY	HAEMOLYSIS	HAGIOCRACIES	HAIRSTREAK
HACKMATACKS	HAEMATOLYSES	HAEMOLYTIC	HAGIOCRACY	HAIRSTREAKS
HACKNEYING	HAEMATOLYSIS	HAEMOLYZED	HAGIOGRAPHER	HAIRSTYLES
HACKNEYISM	HAEMATOMAS	HAEMOLYZES	HAGIOGRAPHERS	HAIRSTYLING
HACKNEYISMS	HAEMATOMATA	HAEMOLYZING	HAGIOGRAPHIC	HAIRSTYLINGS
HACKNEYMAN	HAEMATOPHAGOUS	HAEMOPHILE	HAGIOGRAPHICAL	HAIRSTYLIST

HAIRSTYLISTS
HAIRWEAVING
HAIRWEAVINGS
HAIRYBACKS
HALACHISTS
HALAKHISTS
HALBERDIER
HALBERDIERS
HALCYONIAN
HALENESSES
HALFENDEALE
HALFENDEALES
HALFHEARTED
HALFHEARTEDLY
HALFHEARTEDNESS
HALFNESSES
HALFPENNIES
HALFPENNYWORTH
HALFPENNYWORTHS
HALFSERIOUSLY
HALFTRACKS
HALFWITTED
HALFWITTEDLY
HALFWITTEDNESS
HALIEUTICS
HALIPLANKTON
HALIPLANKTONS
HALLALLING
HALLEFLINTA
HALLEFLINTAS
HALLELUIAH
HALLELUIAHS
HALLELUJAH
HALLELUJAHS
HALLMARKED
HALLMARKING
HALLOWEDNESS
HALLOWEDNESSES
HALLOYSITE
HALLOYSITES
HALLSTANDS
HALLUCINANT
HALLUCINANTS
HALLUCINATE
HALLUCINATED
HALLUCINATES
HALLUCINATING
HALLUCINATION
HALLUCINATIONAL
HALLUCINATIONS
HALLUCINATIVE
HALLUCINATOR
HALLUCINATORS
HALLUCINATORY
HALLUCINOGEN
HALLUCINOGENIC
HALLUCINOGENICS
HALLUCINOGENS
HALLUCINOSES
HALLUCINOSIS
HALOBIONTIC
HALOBIONTS
HALOBIOTIC
HALOCARBON
HALOCARBONS
HALOCLINES
HALOGENATE

HALOGENATED
HALOGENATES
HALOGENATING
HALOGENATION
HALOGENATIONS
HALOGENOID
HALOGENOUS
HALOGETONS
HALOMORPHIC
HALOPERIDOL
HALOPERIDOLS
HALOPHILES
HALOPHILIC
HALOPHILIES
HALOPHILOUS
HALOPHOBES
HALOPHYTES
HALOPHYTIC
HALOPHYTISM
HALOPHYTISMS
HALOTHANES
HALTERBREAK
HALTERBREAKING
HALTERBREAKS
HALTERBROKE
HALTERBROKEN
HALTERNECK
HALTERNECKS
HALTINGNESS
HALTINGNESSES
HAMADRYADES
HAMADRYADS
HAMADRYASES
HAMAMELIDACEOUS
HAMAMELISES
HAMANTASCH
HAMANTASCHEN
HAMARTHRITIS
HAMARTHRITISES
HAMARTIOLOGIES
HAMARTIOLOGY
HAMBURGERS
HAMESUCKEN
HAMESUCKENS
HAMFATTERED
HAMFATTERING
HAMFATTERS
HAMMERCLOTH
HAMMERCLOTHS
HAMMERHEAD
HAMMERHEADED
HAMMERHEADS
HAMMERINGS
HAMMERKOPS
HAMMERLESS
HAMMERLOCK
HAMMERLOCKS
HAMMERSTONE
HAMMERSTONES
HAMMERTOES
HAMMINESSES
HAMPEREDNESS
HAMPEREDNESSES
HAMSHACKLE
HAMSHACKLED
HAMSHACKLES
HAMSHACKLING

HAMSTRINGED
HAMSTRINGING
HAMSTRINGS
HANDBAGGED
HANDBAGGING
HANDBAGGINGS
HANDBALLED
HANDBALLER
HANDBALLERS
HANDBALLING
HANDBARROW
HANDBARROWS
HANDBASKET
HANDBASKETS
HANDBRAKES
HANDBREADTH
HANDBREADTHS
HANDCLASPS
HANDCRAFTED
HANDCRAFTING
HANDCRAFTS
HANDCRAFTSMAN
HANDCRAFTSMEN
HANDCUFFED
HANDCUFFING
HANDEDNESS
HANDEDNESSES
HANDFASTED
HANDFASTING
HANDFASTINGS
HANDFEEDING
HANDGLASSES
HANDICAPPED
HANDICAPPER
HANDICAPPERS
HANDICAPPING
HANDICRAFT
HANDICRAFTER
HANDICRAFTERS
HANDICRAFTS
HANDICRAFTSMAN
HANDICRAFTSMEN
HANDICUFFS
HANDINESSES
HANDIWORKS
HANDKERCHER
HANDKERCHERS
HANDKERCHIEF
HANDKERCHIEFS
HANDKERCHIEVES
HANDLANGER
HANDLANGERS
HANDLEABLE
HANDLEBARS
HANDLELESS
HANDLINERS
HANDMAIDEN
HANDMAIDENS
HANDPASSED
HANDPASSES
HANDPASSING
HANDPHONES
HANDPICKED
HANDPICKING
HANDPRESSES
HANDPRINTS
HANDSBREADTH

HANDSBREADTHS
HANDSELING
HANDSELLED
HANDSELLING
HANDSHAKES
HANDSHAKING
HANDSHAKINGS
HANDSOMELY
HANDSOMENESS
HANDSOMENESSES
HANDSOMEST
HANDSPIKES
HANDSPRING
HANDSPRINGS
HANDSTAFFS
HANDSTAMPED
HANDSTAMPING
HANDSTAMPS
HANDSTANDS
HANDSTAVES
HANDSTROKE
HANDSTROKES
HANDSTURNS
HANDTOWELS
HANDWHEELS
HANDWORKED
HANDWORKER
HANDWORKERS
HANDWRINGER
HANDWRINGERS
HANDWRITES
HANDWRITING
HANDWRITINGS
HANDWRITTEN
HANDWROUGHT
HANDYPERSON
HANDYPERSONS
HANDYWORKS
HANGABILITIES
HANGABILITY
HANGARAGES
HANKERINGS
HANSARDISE
HANSARDISED
HANSARDISES
HANSARDISING
HANSARDIZE
HANSARDIZED
HANSARDIZES
HANSARDIZING
HANSELLING
HANTAVIRUS
HANTAVIRUSES
HAPAXANTHIC
HAPAXANTHOUS
HAPHAZARDLY
HAPHAZARDNESS
HAPHAZARDNESSES
HAPHAZARDRIES
HAPHAZARDRY
HAPHAZARDS
HAPHTARAHS
HAPHTAROTH
HAPLESSNESS
HAPLESSNESSES
HAPLOBIONT
HAPLOBIONTIC

HAPLOBIONTS
HAPLOGRAPHIES
HAPLOGRAPHY
HAPLOIDIES
HAPLOLOGIC
HAPLOLOGIES
HAPLOSTEMONOUS
HAPLOTYPES
HAPPENCHANCE
HAPPENCHANCES
HAPPENINGS
HAPPENSTANCE
HAPPENSTANCES
HAPPINESSES
HAPTOGLOBIN
HAPTOGLOBINS
HAPTOTROPIC
HAPTOTROPISM
HAPTOTROPISMS
HARAMZADAS
HARAMZADIS
HARANGUERS
HARANGUING
HARASSEDLY
HARASSINGLY
HARASSINGS
HARASSMENT
HARASSMENTS
HARBINGERED
HARBINGERING
HARBINGERS
HARBORAGES
HARBORFULS
HARBORLESS
HARBORMASTER
HARBORMASTERS
HARBORSIDE
HARBOURAGE
HARBOURAGES
HARBOURERS
HARBOURFUL
HARBOURFULS
HARBOURING
HARBOURLESS
HARBOURSIDE
HARBOURSIDES
HARDBACKED
HARDBOARDS
HARDBODIES
HARDBOUNDS
HARDCOVERS
HARDENINGS
HARDFISTED
HARDGRASSES
HARDHANDED
HARDHANDEDNESS
HARDHEADED
HARDHEADEDLY
HARDHEADEDNESS
HARDHEARTED
HARDHEARTEDLY
HARDHEARTEDNESS
HARDIHEADS
HARDIHOODS
HARDIMENTS
HARDINESSES
HARDINGGRASS

HARDINGGRASSES	HARMONIUMS	HASENPFEFFERS	HAZARDOUSLY	HEADSTALLS
HARDLINERS	HARMONIZABLE	HASHEESHES	HAZARDOUSNESS	HEADSTANDS
HARDMOUTHED	HARMONIZATION	HASSOCKIER	HAZARDOUSNESSES	HEADSTICKS
HARDNESSES	HARMONIZATIONS	HASSOCKIEST	HAZARDRIES	HEADSTOCKS
HARDSCAPES	HARMONIZED	HASTEFULLY	HAZELWOODS	HEADSTONES
HARDSCRABBLE	HARMONIZER	HASTINESSES	HAZINESSES	HEADSTREAM
HARDSCRABBLES	HARMONIZERS	HATBRUSHES	HEADACHIER	HEADSTREAMS
HARDSTANDING	HARMONIZES	HATCHABILITIES	HEADACHIEST	HEADSTRONG
HARDSTANDINGS	HARMONIZING	HATCHABILITY	HEADBANGED	HEADSTRONGLY
HARDSTANDS	HARMONOGRAM	HATCHBACKS	HEADBANGING	HEADSTRONGNESS
HARDWAREMAN	HARMONOGRAMS	HATCHELING	HEADBANGINGS	HEADTEACHER
HARDWAREMEN	HARMONOGRAPH	HATCHELLED	HEADBOARDS	HEADTEACHERS
HARDWIRING	HARMONOGRAPHS	HATCHELLER	HEADBOROUGH	HEADWAITER
HARDWORKING	HARMONOMETER	HATCHELLERS	HEADBOROUGHS	HEADWAITERS
HAREBRAINED	HARMONOMETERS	HATCHELLING	HEADCHAIRS	HEADWATERS
HARELIPPED	HARMOSTIES	HATCHERIES	HEADCHEESE	HEADWORKER
HARESTAILS	HARMOTOMES	HATCHETIER	HEADCHEESES	HEADWORKERS
HARIOLATED	HARNESSERS	HATCHETIEST	HEADCLOTHS	HEALTHCARE
HARIOLATES	HARNESSING	HATCHETTITE	HEADCOUNTS	HEALTHCARES
HARIOLATING	HARNESSLESS	HATCHETTITES	HEADDRESSES	HEALTHFULLY
HARIOLATION	HARPOONEER	HATCHLINGS	HEADFISHES	HEALTHFULNESS
HARIOLATIONS	HARPOONEERS	HATCHMENTS	HEADFOREMOST	HEALTHFULNESSES
HARLEQUINADE	HARPOONERS	HATEFULNESS	HEADFRAMES	HEALTHIEST
HARLEQUINADES	HARPOONING	HATEFULNESSES	HEADGUARDS	HEALTHINESS
HARLEQUINED	HARPSICHORD	HATELESSNESS	HEADHUNTED	HEALTHINESSES
HARLEQUINING	HARPSICHORDIST	HATELESSNESSES	HEADHUNTER	HEALTHISMS
HARLEQUINS	HARPSICHORDISTS	HATEWORTHIER	HEADHUNTERS	HEALTHLESS
HARLOTRIES	HARPSICHORDS	HATEWORTHIEST	HEADHUNTING	HEALTHLESSNESS
HARMALINES	HARQUEBUSE	HATEWORTHY	HEADHUNTINGS	HEALTHSOME
HARMATTANS	HARQUEBUSES	HATINATORS	HEADINESSES	HEAPSTEADS
HARMDOINGS	HARQUEBUSIER	HATLESSNESS	HEADLEASES	HEARKENERS
HARMFULNESS	HARQUEBUSIERS	HATLESSNESSES	HEADLESSNESS	HEARKENING
HARMFULNESSES	HARQUEBUSS	HAUBERGEON	HEADLESSNESSES	HEARTACHES
HARMLESSLY	HARQUEBUSSES	HAUBERGEONS	HEADLIGHTS	HEARTBEATS
HARMLESSNESS	HARROWINGLY	HAUGHTIEST	HEADLINERS	HEARTBREAK
HARMLESSNESSES	HARROWINGS	HAUGHTINESS	HEADLINING	HEARTBREAKER
HARMOLODIC	HARROWMENT	HAUGHTINESSES	HEADMASTER	HEARTBREAKERS
HARMOLODICS	HARROWMENTS	HAUNTINGLY	HEADMASTERLIER	HEARTBREAKING
HARMONICAL	HARRUMPHED	HAUSFRAUEN	HEADMASTERLIEST	HEARTBREAKINGLY
HARMONICALLY	HARRUMPHING	HAUSSMANNISE	HEADMASTERLY	HEARTBREAKS
HARMONICAS	HARSHENING	HAUSSMANNISED	HEADMASTERS	HEARTBROKE
HARMONICHORD	HARSHNESSES	HAUSSMANNISES	HEADMASTERSHIP	HEARTBROKEN
HARMONICHORDS	HARTBEESES	HAUSSMANNISING	HEADMASTERSHIPS	HEARTBROKENLY
HARMONICIST	HARTBEESTS	HAUSSMANNIZE	HEADMISTRESS	HEARTBROKENNESS
HARMONICISTS	HARTEBEEST	HAUSSMANNIZED	HEADMISTRESSES	HEARTBURNING
HARMONICON	HARTEBEESTS	HAUSSMANNIZES	HEADMISTRESSIER	HEARTBURNINGS
HARMONICONS	HARTSHORNS	HAUSSMANNIZING	HEADMISTRESSY	HEARTBURNS
HARMONIOUS	HARUMPHING	HAUSTELLATE	HEADPEACES	HEARTENERS
HARMONIOUSLY	HARUSPICAL	HAUSTELLUM	HEADPHONES	HEARTENING
HARMONIOUSNESS	HARUSPICATE	HAUSTORIAL	HEADPIECES	HEARTENINGLY
HARMONIPHON	HARUSPICATED	HAUSTORIUM	HEADQUARTER	HEARTHRUGS
HARMONIPHONE	HARUSPICATES	HAVERSACKS	HEADQUARTERED	HEARTHSTONE
HARMONIPHONES	HARUSPICATING	HAVERSINES	HEADQUARTERING	HEARTHSTONES
HARMONIPHONS	HARUSPICATION	HAWFINCHES	HEADQUARTERS	HEARTIKINS
HARMONISABLE	HARUSPICATIONS	HAWKISHNESS	HEADREACHED	HEARTINESS
HARMONISATION	HARUSPICES	HAWKISHNESSES	HEADREACHES	HEARTINESSES
HARMONISATIONS	HARUSPICIES	HAWKSBEARD	HEADREACHING	HEARTLANDS
HARMONISED	HARVESTABLE	HAWKSBEARDS	HEADSCARVES	HEARTLESSLY
HARMONISER	HARVESTERS	HAWKSBILLS	HEADSHAKES	HEARTLESSNESS
HARMONISERS	HARVESTING	HAWSEHOLES	HEADSHEETS	HEARTLESSNESSES
HARMONISES	HARVESTINGS	HAWSEPIPES	HEADSHRINKER	HEARTLINGS
HARMONISING	HARVESTLESS	HAWTHORNIER	HEADSHRINKERS	HEARTRENDING
HARMONISTIC	HARVESTMAN	HAWTHORNIEST	HEADSPACES	HEARTRENDINGLY
HARMONISTICALLY	HARVESTMEN	HAYCATIONS	HEADSPRING	HEARTSEASE
HARMONISTS	HARVESTTIME	HAYMAKINGS	HEADSPRINGS	HEARTSEASES
HARMONIUMIST	HARVESTTIMES	HAZARDABLE	HEADSQUARE	HEARTSEEDS
HARMONIUMISTS	HASENPFEFFER	HAZARDIZES	HEADSQUARES	HEARTSICKNESS

HEARTSICKNESSES	HEBEPHRENIAC	HEFTINESSES	HELIOLATERS	HELLENISES
HEARTSINKS	HEBEPHRENIACS	HEGEMONIAL	HELIOLATRIES	HELLENISING
HEARTSOMELY	HEBEPHRENIAS	HEGEMONICAL	HELIOLATROUS	HELLENIZATION
HEARTSOMENESS	HEBEPHRENIC	HEGEMONIES	HELIOLATRY	HELLENIZATIONS
HEARTSOMENESSES	HEBEPHRENICS	HEGEMONISM	HELIOLITHIC	HELLENIZED
HEARTSORES	HEBETATING	HEGEMONISMS	HELIOLOGIES	HELLENIZES
HEARTSTRING	HEBETATION	HEGEMONIST	HELIOMETER	HELLENIZING
HEARTSTRINGS	HEBETATIONS	HEGEMONISTS	HELIOMETERS	HELLGRAMITE
HEARTTHROB	HEBETATIVE	HEGUMENIES	HELIOMETRIC	HELLGRAMITES
HEARTTHROBS	HEBETUDINOSITY	HEGUMENOSES	HELIOMETRICAL	HELLGRAMMITE
HEARTWARMING	HEBETUDINOUS	HEIGHTENED	HELIOMETRICALLY	HELLGRAMMITES
HEARTWATER	HEBRAISATION	HEIGHTENER	HELIOMETRIES	HELLHOUNDS
HEARTWATERS	HEBRAISATIONS	HEIGHTENERS	HELIOMETRY	HELLISHNESS
HEARTWOODS	HEBRAISING	HEIGHTENING	HELIOPAUSE	HELLISHNESSES
HEARTWORMS	HEBRAIZATION	HEIGHTISMS	HELIOPAUSES	HELLSCAPES
HEATEDNESS	HEBRAIZATIONS	HEINOUSNESS	HELIOPHILOUS	HELMETINGS
HEATEDNESSES	HEBRAIZING	HEINOUSNESSES	HELIOPHOBIC	HELMETLIKE
HEATHBERRIES	HECKELPHONE	HEKTOGRAMS	HELIOPHYTE	HELMINTHIASES
HEATHBERRY	HECKELPHONES	HELDENTENOR	HELIOPHYTES	HELMINTHIASIS
HEATHBIRDS	HECOGENINS	HELDENTENORS	HELIOSCIOPHYTE	HELMINTHIC
HEATHCOCKS	HECTICALLY	HELIACALLY	HELIOSCIOPHYTES	HELMINTHICS
HEATHENDOM	HECTOCOTYLI	HELIANTHEMUM	HELIOSCOPE	HELMINTHOID
HEATHENDOMS	HECTOCOTYLUS	HELIANTHEMUMS	HELIOSCOPES	HELMINTHOLOGIC
HEATHENESSE	HECTOGRAMME	HELIANTHUS	HELIOSCOPIC	HELMINTHOLOGIES
HEATHENESSES	HECTOGRAMMES	HELIANTHUSES	HELIOSPHERE	HELMINTHOLOGIST
HEATHENISE	HECTOGRAMS	HELIBUSSES	HELIOSPHERES	HELMINTHOLOGY
HEATHENISED	HECTOGRAPH	HELICHRYSUM	HELIOSTATIC	HELMINTHOUS
HEATHENISES	HECTOGRAPHED	HELICHRYSUMS	HELIOSTATS	HELMSMANSHIP
HEATHENISH	HECTOGRAPHIC	HELICITIES	HELIOTACTIC	HELMSMANSHIPS
HEATHENISHLY	HECTOGRAPHIES	HELICLINES	HELIOTAXES	HELOPHYTES
HEATHENISHNESS	HECTOGRAPHING	HELICOGRAPH	HELIOTAXIS	HELPFULNESS
HEATHENISING	HECTOGRAPHS	HELICOGRAPHS	HELIOTHERAPIES	HELPFULNESSES
HEATHENISM	HECTOGRAPHY	HELICOIDAL	HELIOTHERAPY	HELPLESSLY
HEATHENISMS	HECTOLITER	HELICOIDALLY	HELIOTROPE	HELPLESSNESS
HEATHENIZE	HECTOLITERS	HELICONIAS	HELIOTROPES	HELPLESSNESSES
HEATHENIZED	HECTOLITRE	HELICOPTED	HELIOTROPIC	HELVETIUMS
HEATHENIZES	HECTOLITRES	HELICOPTER	HELIOTROPICAL	HEMACHROME
HEATHENIZING	HECTOMETER	HELICOPTERED	HELIOTROPICALLY	HEMACHROMES
HEATHENNESS	HECTOMETERS	HELICOPTERING	HELIOTROPIES	HEMACYTOMETER
HEATHENNESSES	HECTOMETRE	HELICOPTERS	HELIOTROPIN	HEMACYTOMETERS
HEATHENRIES	HECTOMETRES	HELICOPTING	HELIOTROPINS	HEMAGGLUTINATE
HEATHERIER	HECTORINGLY	HELICTITES	HELIOTROPISM	HEMAGGLUTINATED
HEATHERIEST	HECTORINGS	HELIDROMES	HELIOTROPISMS	HEMAGGLUTINATES
HEATHFOWLS	HECTORISMS	HELILIFTED	HELIOTROPY	HEMAGGLUTININ
HEATHLANDS	HECTORSHIP	HELILIFTING	HELIOTYPED	HEMAGGLUTININS
HEATSTROKE	HECTORSHIPS	HELIOCENTRIC	HELIOTYPES	HEMAGOGUES
HEATSTROKES	HECTOSTERE	HELIOCENTRICISM	HELIOTYPIC	HEMANGIOMA
HEAVENLIER	HECTOSTERES	HELIOCENTRICITY	HELIOTYPIES	HEMANGIOMAS
HEAVENLIEST	HEDGEBILLS	HELIOCHROME	HELIOTYPING	HEMANGIOMATA
HEAVENLINESS	HEDGEHOPPED	HELIOCHROMES	HELIOZOANS	HEMATEMESES
HEAVENLINESSES	HEDGEHOPPER	HELIOCHROMIC	HELIPILOTS	HEMATEMESIS
HEAVENWARD	HEDGEHOPPERS	HELIOCHROMIES	HELISKIING	HEMATINICS
HEAVENWARDS	HEDGEHOPPING	HELIOCHROMY	HELISKIINGS	HEMATOBLAST
HEAVINESSES	HEDGEHOPPINGS	HELIOGRAMS	HELISPHERIC	HEMATOBLASTIC
HEAVYHEARTED	HEDONICALLY	HELIOGRAPH	HELISPHERICAL	HEMATOBLASTS
HEAVYHEARTEDLY	HEDONISTIC	HELIOGRAPHED	HELLACIOUS	HEMATOCELE
HEAVYWEIGHT	HEDONISTICALLY	HELIOGRAPHER	HELLACIOUSLY	HEMATOCELES
HEAVYWEIGHTS	HEDYPHANES	HELIOGRAPHERS	HELLBENDER	HEMATOCRIT
HEBDOMADAL	HEDYSARUMS	HELIOGRAPHIC	HELLBENDERS	HEMATOCRITS
HEBDOMADALLY	HEEDFULNESS	HELIOGRAPHICAL	HELLBROTHS	HEMATOCRYAL
HEBDOMADAR	HEEDFULNESSES	HELIOGRAPHIES	HELLDIVERS	HEMATOGENESES
HEBDOMADARIES	HEEDINESSES	HELIOGRAPHING	HELLEBORES	HEMATOGENESIS
HEBDOMADARS	HEEDLESSLY	HELIOGRAPHS	HELLEBORINE	HEMATOGENETIC
HEBDOMADARY	HEEDLESSNESS	HELIOGRAPHY	HELLEBORINES	HEMATOGENIC
HEBDOMADER	HEEDLESSNESSES	HELIOGRAVURE	HELLENISATION	HEMATOGENOUS
HEBDOMADERS	HEELPIECES	HELIOGRAVURES	HELLENISATIONS	HEMATOLOGIC
HEBEPHRENIA	HEELPLATES	HELIOLATER	HELLENISED	HEMATOLOGICAL

HEMATOLOGIES	HEMIOPSIAS	HEMOPHILIAS	HEPATECTOMIES	HEPTATHLONS
HEMATOLOGIST	HEMIPARASITE	HEMOPHILIC	HEPATECTOMISED	HEPTATONIC
HEMATOLOGISTS	HEMIPARASITES	HEMOPHILICS	HEPATECTOMIZED	HEPTAVALENT
HEMATOLOGY	HEMIPARASITIC	HEMOPHILIOID	HEPATECTOMY	HERALDICALLY
HEMATOLYSES	HEMIPLEGIA	HEMOPOIESES	HEPATICOLOGICAL	HERALDISTS
HEMATOLYSIS	HEMIPLEGIAS	HEMOPOIESIS	HEPATICOLOGIES	HERALDRIES
HEMATOMATA	HEMIPLEGIC	HEMOPOIETIC	HEPATICOLOGIST	HERALDSHIP
HEMATOPHAGOUS	HEMIPLEGICS	HEMOPROTEIN	HEPATICOLOGISTS	HERALDSHIPS
HEMATOPOIESES	HEMIPTERAL	HEMOPROTEINS	HEPATICOLOGY	HERBACEOUS
HEMATOPOIESIS	HEMIPTERAN	HEMOPTYSES	HEPATISATION	HERBACEOUSLY
HEMATOPOIETIC	HEMIPTERANS	HEMOPTYSIS	HEPATISATIONS	HERBALISMS
HEMATOPORPHYRIN	HEMIPTERON	HEMORRHAGE	HEPATISING	HERBALISTS
HEMATOTHERMAL	HEMIPTERONS	HEMORRHAGED	HEPATITIDES	HERBARIANS
HEMATOXYLIN	HEMIPTEROUS	HEMORRHAGES	HEPATITISES	HERBARIUMS
HEMATOXYLINS	HEMISPACES	HEMORRHAGIC	HEPATIZATION	HERBICIDAL
HEMATOZOON	HEMISPHERE	HEMORRHAGING	HEPATIZATIONS	HERBICIDALLY
HEMATURIAS	HEMISPHERES	HEMORRHAGINGS	HEPATIZING	HERBICIDES
HEMELYTRAL	HEMISPHERIC	HEMORRHOID	HEPATOCELLULAR	HERBIVORES
HEMELYTRON	HEMISPHERICAL	HEMORRHOIDAL	HEPATOCYTE	HERBIVORIES
HEMELYTRUM	HEMISPHEROID	HEMORRHOIDALS	HEPATOCYTES	HERBIVOROUS
HEMERALOPIA	HEMISPHEROIDAL	HEMORRHOIDS	HEPATOGENOUS	HERBIVOROUSLY
HEMERALOPIAS	HEMISPHEROIDS	HEMOSIDERIN	HEPATOLOGIES	HERBIVOROUSNESS
HEMERALOPIC	HEMISTICHAL	HEMOSIDERINS	HEPATOLOGIST	HERBOLOGIES
HEMEROCALLIS	HEMISTICHS	HEMOSTASES	HEPATOLOGISTS	HERBORISATION
HEMEROCALLISES	HEMITERPENE	HEMOSTASIA	HEPATOLOGY	HERBORISATIONS
HEMERYTHRIN	HEMITERPENES	HEMOSTASIAS	HEPATOMATA	HERBORISED
HEMERYTHRINS	HEMITROPAL	HEMOSTASIS	HEPATOMEGALIES	HERBORISES
HEMIACETAL	HEMITROPES	HEMOSTATIC	HEPATOMEGALY	HERBORISING
HEMIACETALS	HEMITROPIC	HEMOSTATICS	HEPATOPANCREAS	HERBORISTS
HEMIALGIAS	HEMITROPIES	HEMOTOXINS	HEPATOSCOPIES	HERBORIZATION
HEMIANOPIA	HEMITROPISM	HEMSTITCHED	HEPATOSCOPY	HERBORIZATIONS
HEMIANOPIAS	HEMITROPISMS	HEMSTITCHER	HEPATOTOXIC	HERBORIZED
HEMIANOPIC	HEMITROPOUS	HEMSTITCHERS	HEPATOTOXICITY	HERBORIZES
HEMIANOPSIA	HEMIZYGOUS	HEMSTITCHES	HEPHTHEMIMER	HERBORIZING
HEMIANOPSIAS	HEMOCHROMATOSES	HEMSTITCHING	HEPHTHEMIMERAL	HERCOGAMIES
HEMIANOPTIC	HEMOCHROMATOSIS	HENCEFORTH	HEPHTHEMIMERS	HERCOGAMOUS
HEMICELLULOSE	HEMOCHROME	HENCEFORWARD	HEPTACHLOR	HERCULESES
HEMICELLULOSES	HEMOCHROMES	HENCEFORWARDS	HEPTACHLORS	HERCYNITES
HEMICHORDATE	HEMOCONIAS	HENCHPERSON	HEPTACHORD	HEREABOUTS
HEMICHORDATES	HEMOCYANIN	HENCHPERSONS	HEPTACHORDS	HEREAFTERS
HEMICRANIA	HEMOCYANINS	HENCHWOMAN	HEPTADECANOIC	HEREDITABILITY
HEMICRANIAS	HEMOCYTOMETER	HENCHWOMEN	HEPTAGLOTS	HEREDITABLE
HEMICRYPTOPHYTE	HEMOCYTOMETERS	HENDECAGON	HEPTAGONAL	HEREDITABLY
HEMICRYSTALLINE	HEMODIALYSES	HENDECAGONAL	HEPTAGYNOUS	HEREDITAMENT
HEMICYCLES	HEMODIALYSIS	HENDECAGONS	HEPTAHEDRA	HEREDITAMENTS
HEMICYCLIC	HEMODIALYZER	HENDECAHEDRA	HEPTAHEDRAL	HEREDITARIAN
HEMIELYTRA	HEMODIALYZERS	HENDECAHEDRON	HEPTAHEDRON	HEREDITARIANISM
HEMIELYTRAL	HEMODILUTION	HENDECAHEDRONS	HEPTAHEDRONS	HEREDITARIANIST
HEMIELYTRON	HEMODILUTIONS	HENDECASYLLABIC	HEPTAMEROUS	HEREDITARIANS
HEMIHEDRAL	HEMODYNAMIC	HENDECASYLLABLE	HEPTAMETER	HEREDITARILY
HEMIHEDRIES	HEMODYNAMICALLY	HENDIADYSES	HEPTAMETERS	HEREDITARINESS
HEMIHEDRISM	HEMODYNAMICS	HENOTHEISM	HEPTAMETRICAL	HEREDITARY
HEMIHEDRISMS	HEMOFLAGELLATE	HENOTHEISMS	HEPTANDROUS	HEREDITIES
HEMIHEDRON	HEMOFLAGELLATES	HENOTHEIST	HEPTANGULAR	HEREDITIST
HEMIHEDRONS	HEMOGLOBIN	HENOTHEISTIC	HEPTAPODIC	HEREDITISTS
HEMIHYDRATE	HEMOGLOBINS	HENOTHEISTS	HEPTAPODIES	HEREINABOVE
HEMIHYDRATED	HEMOGLOBINURIA	HENPECKERIES	HEPTARCHAL	HEREINAFTER
HEMIHYDRATES	HEMOGLOBINURIAS	HENPECKERY	HEPTARCHIC	HEREINBEFORE
HEMIMETABOLOUS	HEMOGLOBINURIC	HENPECKING	HEPTARCHIES	HEREINBELOW
HEMIMORPHIC	HEMOLYMPHS	HEORTOLOGICAL	HEPTARCHIST	HERENESSES
HEMIMORPHIES	HEMOLYSING	HEORTOLOGIES	HEPTARCHISTS	HERESIARCH
HEMIMORPHISM	HEMOLYSINS	HEORTOLOGIST	HEPTASTICH	HERESIARCHS
HEMIMORPHISMS	HEMOLYZING	HEORTOLOGISTS	HEPTASTICHS	HERESIOGRAPHER
HEMIMORPHITE	HEMOPHILES	HEORTOLOGY	HEPTASYLLABIC	HERESIOGRAPHERS
HEMIMORPHITES	HEMOPHILIA	HEPARINISED	HEPTATHLETE	HERESIOGRAPHIES
HEMIMORPHY	HEMOPHILIAC	HEPARINIZED	HEPTATHLETES	HERESIOGRAPHY
HEMIONUSES	HEMOPHILIACS	HEPARINOID	HEPTATHLON	HERESIOLOGIES

HERESIOLOGIST	HEROICNESSES	HETEROCHROMATIC	HETEROGRAPHIES	HETEROSEXUAL
HERESIOLOGISTS	HEROICOMIC	HETEROCHROMATIN	HETEROGRAPHY	HETEROSEXUALITY
HERESIOLOGY	HEROICOMICAL	HETEROCHROMOUS	HETEROGYNOUS	HETEROSEXUALLY
HERESTHETIC	HEROINISMS	HETEROCHRONIC	HETEROKARYON	HETEROSEXUALS
HERESTHETICAL	HERONSHAWS	HETEROCHRONIES	HETEROKARYONS	HETEROSOCIAL
HERESTHETICIAN	HERPESVIRUS	HETEROCHRONISM	HETEROKARYOSES	HETEROSOCIALITY
HERESTHETICIANS	HERPESVIRUSES	HETEROCHRONISMS	HETEROKARYOSIS	HETEROSOMATOUS
HERESTHETICS	HERPETOFAUNA	HETEROCHRONOUS	HETEROKARYOTIC	HETEROSPECIFIC
HERETICALLY	HERPETOFAUNAE	HETEROCHRONY	HETEROKONT	HETEROSPECIFICS
HERETICATE	HERPETOFAUNAS	HETEROCLITE	HETEROKONTAN	HETEROSPORIES
HERETICATED	HERPETOLOGIC	HETEROCLITES	HETEROKONTS	HETEROSPOROUS
HERETICATES	HERPETOLOGICAL	HETEROCLITIC	HETEROLECITHAL	HETEROSPORY
HERETICATING	HERPETOLOGIES	HETEROCLITOUS	HETEROLOGIES	HETEROSTROPHIC
HERETOFORE	HERPETOLOGIST	HETEROCONT	HETEROLOGOUS	HETEROSTROPHIES
HERETOFORES	HERPETOLOGISTS	HETEROCONTS	HETEROLOGOUSLY	HETEROSTROPHY
HERETRICES	HERPETOLOGY	HETEROCYCLE	HETEROLOGY	HETEROSTYLED
HERETRIXES	HERRENVOLK	HETEROCYCLES	HETEROLYSES	HETEROSTYLIES
HERIOTABLE	HERRENVOLKS	HETEROCYCLIC	HETEROLYSIS	HETEROSTYLISM
HERITABILITIES	HERRIMENTS	HETEROCYCLICS	HETEROLYTIC	HETEROSTYLISMS
HERITABILITY	HERRINGBONE	HETEROCYST	HETEROMEROUS	HETEROSTYLOUS
HERITRESSES	HERRINGBONED	HETEROCYSTOUS	HETEROMORPHIC	HETEROSTYLY
HERITRICES	HERRINGBONES	HETEROCYSTS	HETEROMORPHIES	HETEROTACTIC
HERITRIXES	HERRINGBONING	HETERODACTYL	HETEROMORPHISM	HETEROTACTOUS
HERKOGAMIES	HERRINGERS	HETERODACTYLOUS	HETEROMORPHISMS	HETEROTAXES
HERMANDADS	HERRYMENTS	HETERODACTYLS	HETEROMORPHOUS	HETEROTAXIA
HERMAPHRODITE	HERSTORIES	HETERODONT	HETEROMORPHY	HETEROTAXIAS
HERMAPHRODITES	HESITANCES	HETERODOXIES	HETERONOMIES	HETEROTAXIC
HERMAPHRODITIC	HESITANCIES	HETERODOXY	HETERONOMOUS	HETEROTAXIES
HERMAPHRODITISM	HESITANTLY	HETERODUPLEX	HETERONOMOUSLY	HETEROTAXIS
HERMATYPIC	HESITATERS	HETERODUPLEXES	HETERONOMY	HETEROTAXY
HERMENEUTIC	HESITATING	HETERODYNE	HETERONORMATIVE	HETEROTHALLIC
HERMENEUTICAL	HESITATINGLY	HETERODYNED	HETERONYMOUS	HETEROTHALLIES
HERMENEUTICALLY	HESITATION	HETERODYNES	HETERONYMOUSLY	HETEROTHALLISM
HERMENEUTICS	HESITATIONS	HETERODYNING	HETERONYMS	HETEROTHALLISMS
HERMENEUTIST	HESITATIVE	HETEROECIOUS	HETEROOUSIAN	HETEROTHALLY
HERMENEUTISTS	HESITATORS	HETEROECISM	HETEROOUSIANS	HETEROTHERMAL
HERMETICAL	HESITATORY	HETEROECISMS	HETEROPHIL	HETEROTOPIA
HERMETICALLY	HESPERIDIA	HETEROFLEXIBLE	HETEROPHILE	HETEROTOPIAS
HERMETICISM	HESPERIDIN	HETEROFLEXIBLES	HETEROPHILES	HETEROTOPIC
HERMETICISMS	HESPERIDINS	HETEROGAMETE	HETEROPHILS	HETEROTOPIES
HERMETICITIES	HESPERIDIUM	HETEROGAMETES	HETEROPHONIES	HETEROTOPOUS
HERMETICITY	HESSONITES	HETEROGAMETIC	HETEROPHONY	HETEROTOPY
HERMETISMS	HETAERISMIC	HETEROGAMETIES	HETEROPHYLLIES	HETEROTROPH
HERMETISTS	HETAERISMS	HETEROGAMETY	HETEROPHYLLOUS	HETEROTROPHIC
HERMITAGES	HETAERISTIC	HETEROGAMIES	HETEROPHYLLY	HETEROTROPHIES
HERMITESSES	HETAERISTS	HETEROGAMOUS	HETEROPLASIA	HETEROTROPHS
HERMITICAL	HETAIRISMIC	HETEROGAMY	HETEROPLASIAS	HETEROTROPHY
HERMITICALLY	HETAIRISMS	HETEROGENEITIES	HETEROPLASTIC	HETEROTYPIC
HERMITISMS	HETAIRISTIC	HETEROGENEITY	HETEROPLASTIES	HETEROTYPICAL
HERMITRIES	HETAIRISTS	HETEROGENEOUS	HETEROPLASTY	HETEROUSIAN
HERNIATING	HETERARCHIES	HETEROGENEOUSLY	HETEROPLOID	HETEROUSIANS
HERNIATION	HETERARCHY	HETEROGENESES	HETEROPLOIDIES	HETEROZYGOSES
HERNIATIONS	HETERAUXESES	HETEROGENESIS	HETEROPLOIDS	HETEROZYGOSIS
HERNIORRHAPHIES	HETERAUXESIS	HETEROGENETIC	HETEROPLOIDY	HETEROZYGOSITY
HERNIORRHAPHY	HETEROAROMATIC	HETEROGENIC	HETEROPODS	HETEROZYGOTE
HERNIOTOMIES	HETEROATOM	HETEROGENIES	HETEROPOLAR	HETEROZYGOTES
HERNIOTOMY	HETEROATOMS	HETEROGENOUS	HETEROPOLARITY	HETEROZYGOUS
HEROICALLY	HETEROAUXIN	HETEROGENY	HETEROPTERAN	HETHERWARD
HEROICALNESS	HETEROAUXINS	HETEROGONIC	HETEROPTERANS	HETMANATES
HEROICALNESSES	HETEROBLASTIC	HETEROGONIES	HETEROPTEROUS	HETMANSHIP
HEROICISED	HETEROBLASTIES	HETEROGONOUS	HETEROSCEDASTIC	HETMANSHIPS
HEROICISES	HETEROBLASTY	HETEROGONOUSLY	HETEROSCIAN	HEULANDITE
HEROICISING	HETEROCARPOUS	HETEROGONY	HETEROSCIANS	HEULANDITES
HEROICIZED	HETEROCERCAL	HETEROGRAFT	HETEROSEXISM	HEURISTICALLY
HEROICIZES	HETEROCERCALITY	HETEROGRAFTS	HETEROSEXISMS	HEURISTICS
HEROICIZING	HETEROCERCIES	HETEROGRAPHIC	HETEROSEXIST	HEXACHLORETHANE
HEROICNESS	HETEROCERCY	HETEROGRAPHICAL	HETEROSEXISTS	HEXACHLORIDE

HEXACHLORIDES	HEXASTICHONS	HIERARCHICALLY	HIGHBALLING	HINDSHANKS
HEXACHLOROPHANE	HEXASTICHS	HIERARCHIES	HIGHBINDER	HINDSIGHTS
HEXACHLOROPHENE	HEXASTYLES	HIERARCHISE	HIGHBINDERS	HINTERLAND
HEXACHORDS	HEXATEUCHAL	HIERARCHISED	HIGHBLOODED	HINTERLANDS
HEXACOSANOIC	HEXATHLONS	HIERARCHISES	HIGHBROWED	HIPPEASTRUM
HEXACTINAL	HEXAVALENT	HIERARCHISING	HIGHBROWISM	HIPPEASTRUMS
HEXACTINELLID	HEXOBARBITAL	HIERARCHISM	HIGHBROWISMS	HIPPIATRIC
HEXACTINELLIDS	HEXOBARBITALS	HIERARCHISMS	HIGHBUSHES	HIPPIATRICS
HEXADACTYLIC	HEXOKINASE	HIERARCHIZE	HIGHCHAIRS	HIPPIATRIES
HEXADACTYLOUS	HEXOKINASES	HIERARCHIZED	HIGHERMOST	HIPPIATRIST
HEXADECANE	HEXOSAMINIDASE	HIERARCHIZES	HIGHFALUTIN	HIPPIATRISTS
HEXADECANES	HEXOSAMINIDASES	HIERARCHIZING	HIGHFALUTING	HIPPIEDOMS
HEXADECANOIC	HEXYLRESORCINOL	HIERATICAL	HIGHFALUTINGS	HIPPIENESS
HEXADECIMAL	HIBAKUSHAS	HIERATICALLY	HIGHFALUTINS	HIPPIENESSES
HEXADECIMALS	HIBERNACLE	HIERATICAS	HIGHFLIERS	HIPPINESSES
HEXADECYLS	HIBERNACLES	HIEROCRACIES	HIGHFLYERS	HIPPOCAMPAL
HEXAEMERIC	HIBERNACULA	HIEROCRACY	HIGHJACKED	HIPPOCAMPI
HEXAEMERON	HIBERNACULUM	HIEROCRATIC	HIGHJACKER	HIPPOCAMPUS
HEXAEMERONS	HIBERNATED	HIEROCRATICAL	HIGHJACKERS	HIPPOCENTAUR
HEXAFLUORIDE	HIBERNATES	HIEROCRATS	HIGHJACKING	HIPPOCENTAURS
HEXAFLUORIDES	HIBERNATING	HIERODULES	HIGHJACKINGS	HIPPOCRASES
HEXAGONALLY	HIBERNATION	HIERODULIC	HIGHLANDER	HIPPOCREPIAN
HEXAGRAMMOID	HIBERNATIONS	HIEROGLYPH	HIGHLANDERS	HIPPOCREPIANS
HEXAGRAMMOIDS	HIBERNATOR	HIEROGLYPHED	HIGHLIGHTED	HIPPODAMES
HEXAGYNIAN	HIBERNATORS	HIEROGLYPHIC	HIGHLIGHTER	HIPPODAMIST
HEXAGYNOUS	HIBERNICISATION	HIEROGLYPHICAL	HIGHLIGHTERS	HIPPODAMISTS
HEXAHEDRAL	HIBERNICISE	HIEROGLYPHICS	HIGHLIGHTING	HIPPODAMOUS
HEXAHEDRON	HIBERNICISED	HIEROGLYPHING	HIGHLIGHTS	HIPPODROME
HEXAHEDRONS	HIBERNICISES	HIEROGLYPHIST	HIGHNESSES	HIPPODROMES
HEXAHEMERIC	HIBERNICISING	HIEROGLYPHISTS	HIGHTAILED	HIPPODROMIC
HEXAHEMERON	HIBERNICIZATION	HIEROGLYPHS	HIGHTAILING	HIPPOGRIFF
HEXAHEMERONS	HIBERNICIZE	HIEROGRAMMAT	HIGHWAYMAN	HIPPOGRIFFS
HEXAHYDRATE	HIBERNICIZED	HIEROGRAMMATE	HIGHWAYMEN	HIPPOGRYPH
HEXAHYDRATED	HIBERNICIZES	HIEROGRAMMATES	HIGHWROUGHT	HIPPOGRYPHS
HEXAHYDRATES	HIBERNICIZING	HIEROGRAMMATIC	HIJACKINGS	HIPPOLOGIES
HEXAMERISM	HIBERNISATION	HIEROGRAMMATIST	HILARIOUSLY	HIPPOLOGIST
HEXAMERISMS	HIBERNISATIONS	HIEROGRAMMATS	HILARIOUSNESS	HIPPOLOGISTS
HEXAMEROUS	HIBERNISED	HIEROGRAMS	HILARIOUSNESSES	HIPPOMANES
HEXAMETERS	HIBERNISES	HIEROGRAPH	HILARITIES	HIPPOPHAGIES
HEXAMETHONIUM	HIBERNISING	HIEROGRAPHER	HILLBILLIES	HIPPOPHAGIST
HEXAMETHONIUMS	HIBERNIZATION	HIEROGRAPHERS	HILLCRESTS	HIPPOPHAGISTS
HEXAMETRAL	HIBERNIZATIONS	HIEROGRAPHIC	HILLINESSES	HIPPOPHAGOUS
HEXAMETRIC	HIBERNIZED	HIEROGRAPHICAL	HILLOCKIER	HIPPOPHAGY
HEXAMETRICAL	HIBERNIZES	HIEROGRAPHIES	HILLOCKIEST	HIPPOPHILE
HEXAMETRISE	HIBERNIZING	HIEROGRAPHS	HILLSLOPES	HIPPOPHILES
HEXAMETRISED	HIBISCUSES	HIEROGRAPHY	HILLWALKER	HIPPOPHOBE
HEXAMETRISES	HICCOUGHED	HIEROLATRIES	HILLWALKERS	HIPPOPHOBES
HEXAMETRISING	HICCOUGHING	HIEROLATRY	HILLWALKING	HIPPOPOTAMI
HEXAMETRIST	HICCUPIEST	HIEROLOGIC	HILLWALKINGS	HIPPOPOTAMIAN
HEXAMETRISTS	HICCUPPING	HIEROLOGICAL	HINDBERRIES	HIPPOPOTAMIC
HEXAMETRIZE	HIDALGOISH	HIEROLOGIES	HINDBRAINS	HIPPOPOTAMUS
HEXAMETRIZED	HIDALGOISM	HIEROLOGIST	HINDCASTED	HIPPOPOTAMUSES
HEXAMETRIZES	HIDALGOISMS	HIEROLOGISTS	HINDCASTING	HIPPURITES
HEXAMETRIZING	HIDDENITES	HIEROMANCIES	HINDERANCE	HIPPURITIC
HEXANDRIAN	HIDDENMOST	HIEROMANCY	HINDERANCES	HIPSTERISM
HEXANDROUS	HIDDENNESS	HIEROPHANT	HINDERINGLY	HIPSTERISMS
HEXANGULAR	HIDDENNESSES	HIEROPHANTIC	HINDERINGS	HIRCOCERVUS
HEXAPLARIAN	HIDEOSITIES	HIEROPHANTS	HINDERLAND	HIRCOCERVUSES
HEXAPLARIC	HIDEOUSNESS	HIEROPHOBIA	HINDERLANDS	HIRCOSITIES
HEXAPLOIDIES	HIDEOUSNESSES	HIEROPHOBIAS	HINDERLANS	HIRSELLING
HEXAPLOIDS	HIERACIUMS	HIEROPHOBIC	HINDERLINGS	HIRSELLINGS
HEXAPLOIDY	HIERACOSPHINGES	HIEROPHOBICS	HINDERLINS	HIRSUTENESS
HEXAPODIES	HIERACOSPHINX	HIEROSCOPIES	HINDERMOST	HIRSUTENESSES
HEXARCHIES	HIERACOSPHINXES	HIEROSCOPY	HINDFOREMOST	HIRSUTISMS
HEXASTICHAL	HIERARCHAL	HIERURGICAL	HINDQUARTER	HIRUDINEAN
HEXASTICHIC	HIERARCHIC	HIERURGIES	HINDQUARTERS	HIRUDINEANS
HEXASTICHON	HIERARCHICAL	HIGHBALLED	HINDRANCES	HIRUDINOID

HIRUDINOUS	HISTORICAL	HOBBYHORSE	HOLODISCUSES	HOMEOMORPHOUS
HISPANICISE	HISTORICALLY	HOBBYHORSED	HOLOENZYME	HOMEOMORPHS
HISPANICISED	HISTORICALNESS	HOBBYHORSES	HOLOENZYMES	HOMEOMORPHY
HISPANICISES	HISTORICISE	HOBBYHORSING	HOLOGAMIES	HOMEOPATHIC
HISPANICISING	HISTORICISED	HOBGOBLINISM	HOLOGRAPHED	HOMEOPATHICALLY
HISPANICISM	HISTORICISES	HOBGOBLINISMS	HOLOGRAPHER	HOMEOPATHIES
HISPANICISMS	HISTORICISING	HOBGOBLINRIES	HOLOGRAPHERS	HOMEOPATHIST
HISPANICIZE	HISTORICISM	HOBGOBLINRY	HOLOGRAPHIC	HOMEOPATHISTS
HISPANICIZED	HISTORICISMS	HOBGOBLINS	HOLOGRAPHICALLY	HOMEOPATHS
HISPANICIZES	HISTORICIST	HOBJOBBERS	HOLOGRAPHIES	HOMEOPATHY
HISPANICIZING	HISTORICISTS	HOBJOBBING	HOLOGRAPHING	HOMEOSTASES
HISPANIDAD	HISTORICITIES	HOBJOBBINGS	HOLOGRAPHS	HOMEOSTASIS
HISPANIDADS	HISTORICITY	HOBNAILING	HOLOGRAPHY	HOMEOSTATIC
HISPANIOLISE	HISTORICIZE	HOBNOBBERS	HOLOGYNIES	HOMEOTELEUTON
HISPANIOLISED	HISTORICIZED	HOBNOBBIER	HOLOHEDRAL	HOMEOTELEUTONS
HISPANIOLISES	HISTORICIZES	HOBNOBBIEST	HOLOHEDRISM	HOMEOTHERM
HISPANIOLISING	HISTORICIZING	HOBNOBBING	HOLOHEDRISMS	HOMEOTHERMAL
HISPANIOLIZE	HISTORIETTE	HOCHMAGANDIES	HOLOHEDRON	HOMEOTHERMIC
HISPANIOLIZED	HISTORIETTES	HOCHMAGANDY	HOLOHEDRONS	HOMEOTHERMIES
HISPANIOLIZES	HISTORIFIED	HODGEPODGE	HOLOMETABOLIC	HOMEOTHERMISM
HISPANIOLIZING	HISTORIFIES	HODGEPODGES	HOLOMETABOLISM	HOMEOTHERMISMS
HISPANISMS	HISTORIFYING	HODMANDODS	HOLOMETABOLISMS	HOMEOTHERMOUS
HISPIDITIES	HISTORIOGRAPHER	HODOGRAPHIC	HOLOMETABOLOUS	HOMEOTHERMS
HISTAMINASE	HISTORIOGRAPHIC	HODOGRAPHS	HOLOMORPHIC	HOMEOTHERMY
HISTAMINASES	HISTORIOGRAPHY	HODOMETERS	HOLOPHOTAL	HOMEOTYPIC
HISTAMINERGIC	HISTORIOLOGIES	HODOMETRIES	HOLOPHOTES	HOMEOTYPICAL
HISTAMINES	HISTORIOLOGY	HODOSCOPES	HOLOPHRASE	HOMEOWNERS
HISTAMINIC	HISTORISMS	HOGGISHNESS	HOLOPHRASES	HOMEOWNERSHIP
HISTIDINES	HISTORYING	HOGGISHNESSES	HOLOPHRASTIC	HOMEOWNERSHIPS
HISTIOCYTE	HISTRIONIC	HOIDENISHNESS	HOLOPHYTES	HOMEPLACES
HISTIOCYTES	HISTRIONICAL	HOIDENISHNESSES	HOLOPHYTIC	HOMEPORTED
HISTIOCYTIC	HISTRIONICALLY	HOJATOLESLAM	HOLOPHYTISM	HOMEPORTING
HISTIOLOGIES	HISTRIONICISM	HOJATOLESLAMS	HOLOPHYTISMS	HOMESCHOOL
HISTIOLOGY	HISTRIONICISMS	HOJATOLISLAM	HOLOPLANKTON	HOMESCHOOLED
HISTIOPHOROID	HISTRIONICS	HOJATOLISLAMS	HOLOPLANKTONS	HOMESCHOOLER
HISTOBLAST	HISTRIONISM	HOKEYNESSES	HOLOSTERIC	HOMESCHOOLERS
HISTOBLASTS	HISTRIONISMS	HOKEYPOKEY	HOLOTHURIAN	HOMESCHOOLING
HISTOCHEMICAL	HITCHHIKED	HOKEYPOKEYS	HOLOTHURIANS	HOMESCHOOLS
HISTOCHEMICALLY	HITCHHIKER	HOKINESSES	HOLSTERING	HOMESCREETCH
HISTOCHEMIST	HITCHHIKERS	HOKYPOKIES	HOLYSTONED	HOMESCREETCHES
HISTOCHEMISTRY	HITCHHIKES	HOLARCHIES	HOLYSTONES	HOMESHORING
HISTOCHEMISTS	HITCHHIKING	HOLDERBATS	HOLYSTONING	HOMESHORINGS
HISTOCOMPATIBLE	HITCHHIKINGS	HOLDERSHIP	HOMALOGRAPHIC	HOMESICKNESS
HISTOGENESES	HITHERMOST	HOLDERSHIPS	HOMALOIDAL	HOMESICKNESSES
HISTOGENESIS	HITHERSIDE	HOLIDAYERS	HOMEBIRTHS	HOMESOURCING
HISTOGENETIC	HITHERSIDES	HOLIDAYING	HOMEBODIES	HOMESOURCINGS
HISTOGENIC	HITHERWARD	HOLIDAYMAKER	HOMEBUYERS	HOMESTALLS
HISTOGENICALLY	HITHERWARDS	HOLIDAYMAKERS	HOMECOMERS	HOMESTANDS
HISTOGENIES	HOACTZINES	HOLINESSES	HOMECOMING	HOMESTEADED
HISTOGRAMS	HOARFROSTS	HOLISTICALLY	HOMECOMINGS	HOMESTEADER
HISTOLOGIC	HOARHOUNDS	HOLLANDAISE	HOMECRAFTS	HOMESTEADERS
HISTOLOGICAL	HOARINESSES	HOLLANDAISES	HOMELESSNESS	HOMESTEADING
HISTOLOGICALLY	HOARSENESS	HOLLOWARES	HOMELESSNESSES	HOMESTEADINGS
HISTOLOGIES	HOARSENESSES	HOLLOWNESS	HOMELINESS	HOMESTEADS
HISTOLOGIST	HOARSENING	HOLLOWNESSES	HOMELINESSES	HOMESTRETCH
HISTOLOGISTS	HOBBITRIES	HOLLOWWARE	HOMEMAKERS	HOMESTRETCHES
HISTOLYSES	HOBBLEBUSH	HOLLOWWARES	HOMEMAKING	HOMEWORKER
HISTOLYSIS	HOBBLEBUSHES	HOLLYHOCKS	HOMEMAKINGS	HOMEWORKERS
HISTOLYTIC	HOBBLEDEHOY	HOLOBENTHIC	HOMEOBOXES	HOMEWORKING
HISTOLYTICALLY	HOBBLEDEHOYDOM	HOLOBLASTIC	HOMEOMERIC	HOMEWORKINGS
HISTOPATHOLOGIC	HOBBLEDEHOYDOMS	HOLOBLASTICALLY	HOMEOMERIES	HOMEYNESSES
HISTOPATHOLOGY	HOBBLEDEHOYHOOD	HOLOCAINES	HOMEOMEROUS	HOMICIDALLY
HISTOPHYSIOLOGY	HOBBLEDEHOYISH	HOLOCAUSTAL	HOMEOMORPH	HOMILETICAL
HISTOPLASMOSES	HOBBLEDEHOYISM	HOLOCAUSTIC	HOMEOMORPHIC	HOMILETICALLY
HISTOPLASMOSIS	HOBBLEDEHOYISMS	HOLOCAUSTS	HOMEOMORPHIES	HOMILETICS
HISTORIANS	HOBBLEDEHOYS	HOLOCRYSTALLINE	HOMEOMORPHISM	HOMINESSES
HISTORIATED	HOBBLINGLY	HOLODISCUS	HOMEOMORPHISMS	HOMINISATION

h

HOMINISATIONS	HOMOGENEOUSNESS	HOMOMORPHIC	HOMOTHALLY	HONOURABILITY
HOMINISING	HOMOGENESES	HOMOMORPHIES	HOMOTHERMAL	HONOURABLE
HOMINIZATION	HOMOGENESIS	HOMOMORPHISM	HOMOTHERMIC	HONOURABLENESS
HOMINIZATIONS	HOMOGENETIC	HOMOMORPHISMS	HOMOTHERMIES	HONOURABLY
HOMINIZING	HOMOGENETICAL	HOMOMORPHOSES	HOMOTHERMOUS	HONOURLESS
HOMOBLASTIC	HOMOGENIES	HOMOMORPHOSIS	HOMOTHERMY	HOODEDNESS
HOMOBLASTIES	HOMOGENISATION	HOMOMORPHOUS	HOMOTONIES	HOODEDNESSES
HOMOBLASTY	HOMOGENISATIONS	HOMOMORPHS	HOMOTONOUS	HOODLUMISH
HOMOCENTRIC	HOMOGENISE	HOMOMORPHY	HOMOTRANSPLANT	HOODLUMISM
HOMOCENTRICALLY	HOMOGENISED	HOMONUCLEAR	HOMOTRANSPLANTS	HOODLUMISMS
HOMOCERCAL	HOMOGENISER	HOMONYMIES	HOMOTYPIES	HOODOOISMS
HOMOCERCIES	HOMOGENISERS	HOMONYMITIES	HOMOUSIANS	HOODWINKED
HOMOCHLAMYDEOUS	HOMOGENISES	HOMONYMITY	HOMOZYGOSES	HOODWINKER
HOMOCHROMATIC	HOMOGENISING	HOMONYMOUS	HOMOZYGOSIS	HOODWINKERS
HOMOCHROMATISM	HOMOGENIZATION	HOMONYMOUSLY	HOMOZYGOSITIES	HOODWINKING
HOMOCHROMATISMS	HOMOGENIZATIONS	HOMOOUSIAN	HOMOZYGOSITY	HOOFPRINTS
HOMOCHROMIES	HOMOGENIZE	HOMOOUSIANS	HOMOZYGOTE	HOOKCHECKS
HOMOCHROMOUS	HOMOGENIZED	HOMOPHILES	HOMOZYGOTES	HOOKEDNESS
HOMOCHROMY	HOMOGENIZER	HOMOPHOBES	HOMOZYGOTIC	HOOKEDNESSES
HOMOCYCLIC	HOMOGENIZERS	HOMOPHOBIA	HOMOZYGOUS	HOOLACHANS
HOMOCYSTEINE	HOMOGENIZES	HOMOPHOBIAS	HOMOZYGOUSLY	HOOLIGANISM
HOMOCYSTEINES	HOMOGENIZING	HOMOPHOBIC	HOMUNCULAR	HOOLIGANISMS
HOMOEOMERIC	HOMOGENOUS	HOMOPHONES	HOMUNCULES	HOOPSKIRTS
HOMOEOMERIES	HOMOGONIES	HOMOPHONIC	HOMUNCULUS	HOOTANANNIE
HOMOEOMEROUS	HOMOGONOUS	HOMOPHONICALLY	HONESTNESS	HOOTANANNIES
HOMOEOMERY	HOMOGONOUSLY	HOMOPHONIES	HONESTNESSES	HOOTANANNY
HOMOEOMORPH	HOMOGRAFTS	HOMOPHONOUS	HONEYBELLS	HOOTENANNIE
HOMOEOMORPHIC	HOMOGRAPHIC	HOMOPHYLIES	HONEYBUNCH	HOOTENANNIES
HOMOEOMORPHIES	HOMOGRAPHIES	HOMOPHYLLIC	HONEYBUNCHES	HOOTENANNY
HOMOEOMORPHISM	HOMOGRAPHS	HOMOPLASIES	HONEYCOMBED	HOOTNANNIE
HOMOEOMORPHISMS	HOMOGRAPHY	HOMOPLASMIES	HONEYCOMBING	HOOTNANNIES
HOMOEOMORPHOUS	HOMOIOMEROUS	HOMOPLASMY	HONEYCOMBINGS	HOOVERINGS
HOMOEOMORPHS	HOMOIOTHERM	HOMOPLASTIC	HONEYCOMBS	HOPEFULNESS
HOMOEOMORPHY	HOMOIOTHERMAL	HOMOPLASTICALLY	HONEYCREEPER	HOPEFULNESSES
HOMOEOPATH	HOMOIOTHERMIC	HOMOPLASTIES	HONEYCREEPERS	HOPELESSLY
HOMOEOPATHIC	HOMOIOTHERMIES	HOMOPLASTY	HONEYDEWED	HOPELESSNESS
HOMOEOPATHIES	HOMOIOTHERMS	HOMOPOLARITIES	HONEYEATER	HOPELESSNESSES
HOMOEOPATHIST	HOMOIOTHERMY	HOMOPOLARITY	HONEYEATERS	HOPLOLOGIES
HOMOEOPATHISTS	HOMOIOUSIAN	HOMOPOLYMER	HONEYGUIDE	HOPLOLOGIST
HOMOEOPATHS	HOMOIOUSIANS	HOMOPOLYMERIC	HONEYGUIDES	HOPLOLOGISTS
HOMOEOPATHY	HOMOLOGATE	HOMOPOLYMERS	HONEYMONTH	HOPPERCARS
HOMOEOSTASES	HOMOLOGATED	HOMOPTERAN	HONEYMONTHED	HOPPINESSES
HOMOEOSTASIS	HOMOLOGATES	HOMOPTERANS	HONEYMONTHING	HOPSACKING
HOMOEOSTATIC	HOMOLOGATING	HOMOPTEROUS	HONEYMONTHS	HOPSACKINGS
HOMOEOTELEUTON	HOMOLOGATION	HOMORGANIC	HONEYMOONED	HOPSCOTCHED
HOMOEOTELEUTONS	HOMOLOGATIONS	HOMOSCEDASTIC	HONEYMOONER	HOPSCOTCHES
HOMOEOTHERM	HOMOLOGICAL	HOMOSEXUAL	HONEYMOONERS	HOPSCOTCHING
HOMOEOTHERMAL	HOMOLOGICALLY	HOMOSEXUALISM	HONEYMOONING	HOREHOUNDS
HOMOEOTHERMIC	HOMOLOGIES	HOMOSEXUALISMS	HONEYMOONS	HORIATIKIS
HOMOEOTHERMOUS	HOMOLOGISE	HOMOSEXUALIST	HONEYSUCKER	HORIZONLESS
HOMOEOTHERMS	HOMOLOGISED	HOMOSEXUALISTS	HONEYSUCKERS	HORIZONTAL
HOMOEOTYPIC	HOMOLOGISER	HOMOSEXUALITIES	HONEYSUCKLE	HORIZONTALITIES
HOMOEOTYPICAL	HOMOLOGISERS	HOMOSEXUALITY	HONEYSUCKLED	HORIZONTALITY
HOMOEROTIC	HOMOLOGISES	HOMOSEXUALLY	HONEYSUCKLES	HORIZONTALLY
HOMOEROTICISM	HOMOLOGISING	HOMOSEXUALS	HONEYTRAPS	HORIZONTALNESS
HOMOEROTICISMS	HOMOLOGIZE	HOMOSOCIAL	HONORABILITIES	HORIZONTALS
HOMOEROTISM	HOMOLOGIZED	HOMOSOCIALITIES	HONORABILITY	HORMOGONIA
HOMOEROTISMS	HOMOLOGIZER	HOMOSOCIALITY	HONORABLENESS	HORMOGONIUM
HOMOGAMETIC	HOMOLOGIZERS	HOMOSPORIES	HONORABLENESSES	HORMONALLY
HOMOGAMIES	HOMOLOGIZES	HOMOSPOROUS	HONORARIES	HORMONELIKE
HOMOGAMOUS	HOMOLOGIZING	HOMOSTYLIES	HONORARILY	HORNBLENDE
HOMOGENATE	HOMOLOGOUMENA	HOMOTAXIAL	HONORARIUM	HORNBLENDES
HOMOGENATES	HOMOLOGOUS	HOMOTAXIALLY	HONORARIUMS	HORNBLENDIC
HOMOGENEITIES	HOMOLOGRAPHIC	HOMOTHALLIC	HONORIFICAL	HORNEDNESS
HOMOGENEITY	HOMOLOGUES	HOMOTHALLIES	HONORIFICALLY	HORNEDNESSES
HOMOGENEOUS	HOMOLOGUMENA	HOMOTHALLISM	HONORIFICS	HORNFELSES
HOMOGENEOUSLY	HOMOLOSINE	HOMOTHALLISMS	HONOURABILITIES	HORNFISHES

h

HORNINESSES
HORNLESSNESS
HORNLESSNESSES
HORNSTONES
HORNSWOGGLE
HORNSWOGGLED
HORNSWOGGLES
HORNSWOGGLING
HORNWRACKS
HORNYHEADS
HORNYWINKS
HOROGRAPHER
HOROGRAPHERS
HOROGRAPHIES
HOROGRAPHY
HOROLOGERS
HOROLOGICAL
HOROLOGIES
HOROLOGION
HOROLOGIONS
HOROLOGIST
HOROLOGISTS
HOROLOGIUM
HOROMETRICAL
HOROMETRIES
HOROSCOPES
HOROSCOPIC
HOROSCOPIES
HOROSCOPIST
HOROSCOPISTS
HORRENDOUS
HORRENDOUSLY
HORRENDOUSNESS
HORRIBLENESS
HORRIBLENESSES
HORRIDNESS
HORRIDNESSES
HORRIFICALLY
HORRIFICATION
HORRIFICATIONS
HORRIFYING
HORRIFYINGLY
HORRIPILANT
HORRIPILATE
HORRIPILATED
HORRIPILATES
HORRIPILATING
HORRIPILATION
HORRIPILATIONS
HORRISONANT
HORRISONOUS
HORSEBACKS
HORSEBEANS
HORSEBOXES
HORSEFEATHERS
HORSEFLESH
HORSEFLESHES
HORSEFLIES
HORSEHAIRS
HORSEHEADS
HORSEHIDES
HORSELAUGH
HORSELAUGHS
HORSELEECH
HORSELEECHES
HORSEMANSHIP
HORSEMANSHIPS

HORSEMEATS
HORSEMINTS
HORSEPLAYER
HORSEPLAYERS
HORSEPLAYS
HORSEPONDS
HORSEPOWER
HORSEPOWERS
HORSEPOXES
HORSERACES
HORSERADISH
HORSERADISHES
HORSESHITS
HORSESHOED
HORSESHOEING
HORSESHOEINGS
HORSESHOER
HORSESHOERS
HORSESHOES
HORSETAILS
HORSEWEEDS
HORSEWHIPPED
HORSEWHIPPER
HORSEWHIPPERS
HORSEWHIPPING
HORSEWHIPS
HORSEWOMAN
HORSEWOMEN
HORSINESSES
HORTATIONS
HORTATIVELY
HORTATORILY
HORTENSIAS
HORTICULTURAL
HORTICULTURALLY
HORTICULTURE
HORTICULTURES
HORTICULTURIST
HORTICULTURISTS
HOSANNAING
HOSPITABLE
HOSPITABLENESS
HOSPITABLY
HOSPITAGES
HOSPITALER
HOSPITALERS
HOSPITALES
HOSPITALISATION
HOSPITALISE
HOSPITALISED
HOSPITALISES
HOSPITALISING
HOSPITALIST
HOSPITALISTS
HOSPITALITIES
HOSPITALITY
HOSPITALIZATION
HOSPITALIZE
HOSPITALIZED
HOSPITALIZES
HOSPITALIZING
HOSPITALLER
HOSPITALLERS
HOSTELINGS
HOSTELLERS
HOSTELLING
HOSTELLINGS

HOSTELRIES
HOSTESSING
HOSTILITIES
HOTCHPOTCH
HOTCHPOTCHES
HOTDOGGERS
HOTDOGGING
HOTELLINGS
HOTFOOTING
HOTHEADEDLY
HOTHEADEDNESS
HOTHEADEDNESSES
HOTHOUSING
HOTHOUSINGS
HOTPRESSED
HOTPRESSES
HOTPRESSING
HOTTENTOTS
HOUGHMAGANDIE
HOUGHMAGANDIES
HOUNDFISHES
HOURGLASSES
HOURPLATES
HOUSEBOATER
HOUSEBOATERS
HOUSEBOATS
HOUSEBOUND
HOUSEBREAK
HOUSEBREAKER
HOUSEBREAKERS
HOUSEBREAKING
HOUSEBREAKINGS
HOUSEBREAKS
HOUSEBROKE
HOUSEBROKEN
HOUSECARLS
HOUSECLEAN
HOUSECLEANED
HOUSECLEANING
HOUSECLEANINGS
HOUSECLEANS
HOUSECOATS
HOUSECRAFT
HOUSECRAFTS
HOUSEDRESS
HOUSEDRESSES
HOUSEFATHER
HOUSEFATHERS
HOUSEFLIES
HOUSEFRONT
HOUSEFRONTS
HOUSEGUEST
HOUSEGUESTS
HOUSEHOLDER
HOUSEHOLDERS
HOUSEHOLDERSHIP
HOUSEHOLDS
HOUSEHUSBAND
HOUSEHUSBANDS
HOUSEKEEPER
HOUSEKEEPERS
HOUSEKEEPING
HOUSEKEEPINGS
HOUSEKEEPS
HOUSELEEKS
HOUSELESSNESS
HOUSELESSNESSES

HOUSELIGHTS
HOUSELINES
HOUSELINGS
HOUSELLING
HOUSELLINGS
HOUSEMAIDS
HOUSEMASTER
HOUSEMASTERS
HOUSEMATES
HOUSEMISTRESS
HOUSEMISTRESSES
HOUSEMOTHER
HOUSEMOTHERS
HOUSEPAINTER
HOUSEPAINTERS
HOUSEPARENT
HOUSEPARENTS
HOUSEPERSON
HOUSEPERSONS
HOUSEPLANT
HOUSEPLANTS
HOUSEROOMS
HOUSESITTING
HOUSEWARES
HOUSEWARMING
HOUSEWARMINGS
HOUSEWIFELIER
HOUSEWIFELIEST
HOUSEWIFELINESS
HOUSEWIFELY
HOUSEWIFERIES
HOUSEWIFERY
HOUSEWIFESHIP
HOUSEWIFESHIPS
HOUSEWIFESKEP
HOUSEWIFESKEPS
HOUSEWIFEY
HOUSEWIFIER
HOUSEWIFIEST
HOUSEWIVES
HOUSEWORKER
HOUSEWORKERS
HOUSEWORKS
HOUSEWRAPS
HOUSTONIAS
HOVERBOARD
HOVERBOARDS
HOVERCRAFT
HOVERCRAFTS
HOVERFLIES
HOVERINGLY
HOVERPORTS
HOVERTRAIN
HOVERTRAINS
HOWLROUNDS
HOWSOMDEVER
HOWSOMEVER
HOWTOWDIES
HOYDENHOOD
HOYDENHOODS
HOYDENISHNESS
HOYDENISHNESSES
HOYDENISMS
HUBRISTICALLY
HUCKABACKS
HUCKLEBERRIES
HUCKLEBERRY

HUCKLEBERRYING
HUCKLEBERRYINGS
HUCKLEBONE
HUCKLEBONES
HUCKSTERAGE
HUCKSTERAGES
HUCKSTERED
HUCKSTERESS
HUCKSTERESSES
HUCKSTERIES
HUCKSTERING
HUCKSTERISM
HUCKSTERISMS
HUCKSTRESS
HUCKSTRESSES
HUDIBRASTIC
HUFFINESSES
HUFFISHNESS
HUFFISHNESSES
HUGENESSES
HUGEOUSNESS
HUGEOUSNESSES
HULLABALLOO
HULLABALLOOS
HULLABALOO
HULLABALOOS
HUMANENESS
HUMANENESSES
HUMANHOODS
HUMANISATION
HUMANISATIONS
HUMANISERS
HUMANISING
HUMANISTIC
HUMANISTICALLY
HUMANITARIAN
HUMANITARIANISM
HUMANITARIANIST
HUMANITARIANS
HUMANITIES
HUMANIZATION
HUMANIZATIONS
HUMANIZERS
HUMANIZING
HUMANKINDS
HUMANNESSES
HUMBLEBEES
HUMBLEBRAG
HUMBLEBRAGGED
HUMBLEBRAGGING
HUMBLEBRAGS
HUMBLENESS
HUMBLENESSES
HUMBLESSES
HUMBLINGLY
HUMBUCKERS
HUMBUGGABLE
HUMBUGGERIES
HUMBUGGERS
HUMBUGGERY
HUMBUGGING
HUMDINGERS
HUMDRUMNESS
HUMDRUMNESSES
HUMDUDGEON
HUMDUDGEONS
HUMDURGEON

HUMDURGEONS	HUNCHBACKED	HYALOPHANES	HYDROBIOLOGIST	HYDROGENISE
HUMECTANTS	HUNCHBACKS	HYALOPLASM	HYDROBIOLOGISTS	HYDROGENISED
HUMECTATED	HUNDREDERS	HYALOPLASMIC	HYDROBIOLOGY	HYDROGENISES
HUMECTATES	HUNDREDFOLD	HYALOPLASMS	HYDROBROMIC	HYDROGENISING
HUMECTATING	HUNDREDFOLDS	HYALURONIC	HYDROCARBON	HYDROGENIZATION
HUMECTATION	HUNDREDORS	HYALURONIDASE	HYDROCARBONS	HYDROGENIZE
HUMECTATIONS	HUNDREDTHS	HYALURONIDASES	HYDROCASTS	HYDROGENIZED
HUMECTIVES	HUNDREDWEIGHT	HYBRIDISABLE	HYDROCELES	HYDROGENIZES
HUMGRUFFIAN	HUNDREDWEIGHTS	HYBRIDISATION	HYDROCELLULOSE	HYDROGENIZING
HUMGRUFFIANS	HUNGERINGLY	HYBRIDISATIONS	HYDROCELLULOSES	HYDROGENOLYSES
HUMGRUFFIN	HUNGRINESS	HYBRIDISED	HYDROCEPHALI	HYDROGENOLYSIS
HUMGRUFFINS	HUNGRINESSES	HYBRIDISER	HYDROCEPHALIC	HYDROGENOUS
HUMICOLOUS	HUNTIEGOWK	HYBRIDISERS	HYDROCEPHALICS	HYDROGEOLOGICAL
HUMIDIFICATION	HUNTIEGOWKED	HYBRIDISES	HYDROCEPHALIES	HYDROGEOLOGIES
HUMIDIFICATIONS	HUNTIEGOWKING	HYBRIDISING	HYDROCEPHALOID	HYDROGEOLOGIST
HUMIDIFIED	HUNTIEGOWKS	HYBRIDISMS	HYDROCEPHALOUS	HYDROGEOLOGISTS
HUMIDIFIER	HUNTRESSES	HYBRIDISTS	HYDROCEPHALUS	HYDROGEOLOGY
HUMIDIFIERS	HUNTSMANSHIP	HYBRIDITIES	HYDROCEPHALUSES	HYDROGRAPH
HUMIDIFIES	HUNTSMANSHIPS	HYBRIDIZABLE	HYDROCEPHALY	HYDROGRAPHER
HUMIDIFYING	HUPAITHRIC	HYBRIDIZATION	HYDROCHLORIC	HYDROGRAPHERS
HUMIDISTAT	HURLBARROW	HYBRIDIZATIONS	HYDROCHLORIDE	HYDROGRAPHIC
HUMIDISTATS	HURLBARROWS	HYBRIDIZED	HYDROCHLORIDES	HYDROGRAPHICAL
HUMIDITIES	HURRICANES	HYBRIDIZER	HYDROCHORE	HYDROGRAPHIES
HUMIDNESSES	HURRICANOES	HYBRIDIZERS	HYDROCHORES	HYDROGRAPHS
HUMIFICATION	HURRIEDNESS	HYBRIDIZES	HYDROCHORIC	HYDROGRAPHY
HUMIFICATIONS	HURRIEDNESSES	HYBRIDIZING	HYDROCODONE	HYDROKINETIC
HUMILIATED	HURRYINGLY	HYBRIDOMAS	HYDROCODONES	HYDROKINETICAL
HUMILIATES	HURTFULNESS	HYBRIDOMATA	HYDROCOLLOID	HYDROKINETICS
HUMILIATING	HURTFULNESSES	HYDANTOINS	HYDROCOLLOIDAL	HYDROLASES
HUMILIATINGLY	HURTLEBERRIES	HYDATHODES	HYDROCOLLOIDS	HYDROLOGIC
HUMILIATION	HURTLEBERRY	HYDATIDIFORM	HYDROCORAL	HYDROLOGICAL
HUMILIATIONS	HURTLESSLY	HYDNOCARPATE	HYDROCORALLINE	HYDROLOGICALLY
HUMILIATIVE	HURTLESSNESS	HYDNOCARPATES	HYDROCORALLINES	HYDROLOGIES
HUMILIATOR	HURTLESSNESSES	HYDNOCARPIC	HYDROCORALS	HYDROLOGIST
HUMILIATORS	HUSBANDAGE	HYDRAEMIAS	HYDROCORTISONE	HYDROLOGISTS
HUMILIATORY	HUSBANDAGES	HYDRAGOGUE	HYDROCORTISONES	HYDROLYSABLE
HUMILITIES	HUSBANDERS	HYDRAGOGUES	HYDROCRACK	HYDROLYSATE
HUMMELLERS	HUSBANDING	HYDRALAZINE	HYDROCRACKED	HYDROLYSATES
HUMMELLING	HUSBANDLAND	HYDRALAZINES	HYDROCRACKER	HYDROLYSATION
HUMMELLINGS	HUSBANDLANDS	HYDRANGEAS	HYDROCRACKERS	HYDROLYSATIONS
HUMMINGBIRD	HUSBANDLESS	HYDRARGYRAL	HYDROCRACKING	HYDROLYSED
HUMMINGBIRDS	HUSBANDLIER	HYDRARGYRIA	HYDROCRACKINGS	HYDROLYSER
HUMMOCKIER	HUSBANDLIEST	HYDRARGYRIAS	HYDROCRACKS	HYDROLYSERS
HUMMOCKIEST	HUSBANDLIKE	HYDRARGYRIC	HYDROCYANIC	HYDROLYSES
HUMMOCKING	HUSBANDMAN	HYDRARGYRISM	HYDRODYNAMIC	HYDROLYSING
HUMORALISM	HUSBANDMEN	HYDRARGYRISMS	HYDRODYNAMICAL	HYDROLYSIS
HUMORALISMS	HUSBANDRIES	HYDRARGYRUM	HYDRODYNAMICIST	HYDROLYTES
HUMORALIST	HUSHABYING	HYDRARGYRUMS	HYDRODYNAMICS	HYDROLYTIC
HUMORALISTS	HUSHPUPPIES	HYDRARTHROSES	HYDROELASTIC	HYDROLYTICALLY
HUMORESQUE	HUSKINESSES	HYDRARTHROSIS	HYDROELECTRIC	HYDROLYZABLE
HUMORESQUES	HYACINTHINE	HYDRASTINE	HYDROEXTRACTOR	HYDROLYZATE
HUMORISTIC	HYALINISATION	HYDRASTINES	HYDROEXTRACTORS	HYDROLYZATES
HUMORLESSLY	HYALINISATIONS	HYDRASTININE	HYDROFLUORIC	HYDROLYZATION
HUMORLESSNESS	HYALINISED	HYDRASTININES	HYDROFOILS	HYDROLYZATIONS
HUMORLESSNESSES	HYALINISES	HYDRASTINES	HYDROFORMING	HYDROLYZED
HUMOROUSLY	HYALINISING	HYDRATIONS	HYDROFORMINGS	HYDROLYZER
HUMOROUSNESS	HYALINIZATION	HYDRAULICALLY	HYDROGENASE	HYDROLYZERS
HUMOROUSNESSES	HYALINIZATIONS	HYDRAULICKED	HYDROGENASES	HYDROLYZES
HUMORSOMENESS	HYALINIZED	HYDRAULICKING	HYDROGENATE	HYDROLYZING
HUMORSOMENESSES	HYALINIZES	HYDRAULICKINGS	HYDROGENATED	HYDROMAGNETIC
HUMOURLESS	HYALINIZING	HYDRAULICS	HYDROGENATES	HYDROMAGNETICS
HUMOURLESSLY	HYALOMELAN	HYDRAZIDES	HYDROGENATING	HYDROMANCER
HUMOURLESSNESS	HYALOMELANE	HYDRAZINES	HYDROGENATION	HYDROMANCERS
HUMOURSOME	HYALOMELANES	HYDRICALLY	HYDROGENATIONS	HYDROMANCIES
HUMOURSOMENESS	HYALOMELANS	HYDROACOUSTICS	HYDROGENATOR	HYDROMANCY
HUMPBACKED	HYALONEMAS	HYDROBIOLOGICAL	HYDROGENATORS	HYDROMANIA
HUMPINESSES	HYALOPHANE	HYDROBIOLOGIES	HYDROGENISATION	HYDROMANIAS

HYDROMANTIC
HYDROMECHANICAL
HYDROMECHANICS
HYDROMEDUSA
HYDROMEDUSAE
HYDROMEDUSAN
HYDROMEDUSANS
HYDROMEDUSAS
HYDROMEDUSOID
HYDROMEDUSOIDS
HYDROMETALLURGY
HYDROMETEOR
HYDROMETEORS
HYDROMETER
HYDROMETERS
HYDROMETRIC
HYDROMETRICAL
HYDROMETRICALLY
HYDROMETRIES
HYDROMETRY
HYDROMORPHIC
HYDRONAUTS
HYDRONEPHROSES
HYDRONEPHROSIS
HYDRONEPHROTIC
HYDRONICALLY
HYDRONIUMS
HYDROPATHIC
HYDROPATHICAL
HYDROPATHICALLY
HYDROPATHICS
HYDROPATHIES
HYDROPATHIST
HYDROPATHISTS
HYDROPATHS
HYDROPATHY
HYDROPEROXIDE
HYDROPEROXIDES
HYDROPHANE
HYDROPHANES
HYDROPHANOUS
HYDROPHILE
HYDROPHILES
HYDROPHILIC
HYDROPHILICITY
HYDROPHILIES
HYDROPHILITE
HYDROPHILITES
HYDROPHILOUS
HYDROPHILY
HYDROPHOBIA
HYDROPHOBIAS
HYDROPHOBIC
HYDROPHOBICITY
HYDROPHOBOUS
HYDROPHONE
HYDROPHONES
HYDROPHYTE
HYDROPHYTES
HYDROPHYTIC
HYDROPHYTON
HYDROPHYTONS
HYDROPHYTOUS
HYDROPLANE
HYDROPLANED
HYDROPLANES
HYDROPLANING

HYDROPNEUMATIC
HYDROPOLYP
HYDROPOLYPS
HYDROPONIC
HYDROPONICALLY
HYDROPONICS
HYDROPOWER
HYDROPOWERS
HYDROPSIES
HYDROPULTS
HYDROQUINOL
HYDROQUINOLS
HYDROQUINONE
HYDROQUINONES
HYDROSCOPE
HYDROSCOPES
HYDROSCOPIC
HYDROSCOPICAL
HYDROSERES
HYDROSOLIC
HYDROSOMAL
HYDROSOMATA
HYDROSOMATOUS
HYDROSOMES
HYDROSPACE
HYDROSPACES
HYDROSPHERE
HYDROSPHERES
HYDROSPHERIC
HYDROSTATIC
HYDROSTATICAL
HYDROSTATICALLY
HYDROSTATICS
HYDROSTATS
HYDROSULPHATE
HYDROSULPHATES
HYDROSULPHIDE
HYDROSULPHIDES
HYDROSULPHITE
HYDROSULPHITES
HYDROSULPHURIC
HYDROSULPHUROUS
HYDROTACTIC
HYDROTAXES
HYDROTAXIS
HYDROTHECA
HYDROTHECAE
HYDROTHERAPIC
HYDROTHERAPIES
HYDROTHERAPIST
HYDROTHERAPISTS
HYDROTHERAPY
HYDROTHERMAL
HYDROTHERMALLY
HYDROTHORACES
HYDROTHORACIC
HYDROTHORAX
HYDROTHORAXES
HYDROTROPIC
HYDROTROPICALLY
HYDROTROPISM
HYDROTROPISMS
HYDROVANES
HYDROXIDES
HYDROXIUMS
HYDROXONIUM
HYDROXONIUMS

HYDROXYACETIC
HYDROXYAPATITE
HYDROXYAPATITES
HYDROXYBUTYRATE
HYDROXYCITRIC
HYDROXYLAMINE
HYDROXYLAMINES
HYDROXYLAPATITE
HYDROXYLASE
HYDROXYLASES
HYDROXYLATE
HYDROXYLATED
HYDROXYLATES
HYDROXYLATING
HYDROXYLATION
HYDROXYLATIONS
HYDROXYLIC
HYDROXYPROLINE
HYDROXYPROLINES
HYDROXYUREA
HYDROXYUREAS
HYDROXYZINE
HYDROXYZINES
HYDROZINCITE
HYDROZINCITES
HYDROZOANS
HYETOGRAPH
HYETOGRAPHIC
HYETOGRAPHICAL
HYETOGRAPHIES
HYETOGRAPHS
HYETOGRAPHY
HYETOLOGIES
HYETOMETER
HYETOMETERS
HYETOMETROGRAPH
HYGIENICALLY
HYGIENISTS
HYGRISTORS
HYGROCHASIES
HYGROCHASTIC
HYGROCHASY
HYGRODEIKS
HYGROGRAPH
HYGROGRAPHIC
HYGROGRAPHICAL
HYGROGRAPHS
HYGROLOGIES
HYGROMETER
HYGROMETERS
HYGROMETRIC
HYGROMETRICAL
HYGROMETRICALLY
HYGROMETRIES
HYGROMETRY
HYGROPHILE
HYGROPHILES
HYGROPHILOUS
HYGROPHOBE
HYGROPHOBES
HYGROPHYTE
HYGROPHYTES
HYGROPHYTIC
HYGROSCOPE
HYGROSCOPES
HYGROSCOPIC
HYGROSCOPICAL

HYGROSCOPICALLY
HYGROSCOPICITY
HYGROSTATS
HYLOGENESES
HYLOGENESIS
HYLOMORPHIC
HYLOMORPHISM
HYLOMORPHISMS
HYLOPATHISM
HYLOPATHISMS
HYLOPATHIST
HYLOPATHISTS
HYLOPHAGOUS
HYLOPHYTES
HYLOTHEISM
HYLOTHEISMS
HYLOTHEIST
HYLOTHEISTS
HYLOTOMOUS
HYLOZOICAL
HYLOZOISMS
HYLOZOISTIC
HYLOZOISTICALLY
HYLOZOISTS
HYMENAEANS
HYMENEALLY
HYMENOPHORE
HYMENOPHORES
HYMENOPLASTIES
HYMENOPLASTY
HYMENOPTERA
HYMENOPTERAN
HYMENOPTERANS
HYMENOPTERON
HYMENOPTERONS
HYMENOPTEROUS
HYMNODICAL
HYMNODISTS
HYMNOGRAPHER
HYMNOGRAPHERS
HYMNOGRAPHIES
HYMNOGRAPHY
HYMNOLOGIC
HYMNOLOGICAL
HYMNOLOGIES
HYMNOLOGIST
HYMNOLOGISTS
HYOPLASTRA
HYOPLASTRAL
HYOPLASTRON
HYOSCYAMINE
HYOSCYAMINES
HYOSCYAMUS
HYOSCYAMUSES
HYPABYSSAL
HYPABYSSALLY
HYPAESTHESIA
HYPAESTHESIAS
HYPAESTHESIC
HYPAETHRAL
HYPAETHRON
HYPAETHRONS
HYPALGESIA
HYPALGESIAS
HYPALGESIC
HYPALLACTIC
HYPALLAGES

HYPANTHIAL
HYPANTHIUM
HYPERACIDITIES
HYPERACIDITY
HYPERACTION
HYPERACTIONS
HYPERACTIVE
HYPERACTIVES
HYPERACTIVITIES
HYPERACTIVITY
HYPERACUITIES
HYPERACUITY
HYPERACUSES
HYPERACUSIS
HYPERACUTE
HYPERACUTENESS
HYPERADRENALISM
HYPERAEMIA
HYPERAEMIAS
HYPERAEMIC
HYPERAESTHESIA
HYPERAESTHESIAS
HYPERAESTHESIC
HYPERAESTHETIC
HYPERAGGRESSIVE
HYPERALERT
HYPERALGESIA
HYPERALGESIAS
HYPERALGESIC
HYPERAROUSAL
HYPERAROUSALS
HYPERAWARE
HYPERAWARENESS
HYPERBARIC
HYPERBARICALLY
HYPERBATIC
HYPERBATICALLY
HYPERBATON
HYPERBATONS
HYPERBOLAE
HYPERBOLAEON
HYPERBOLAEONS
HYPERBOLAS
HYPERBOLES
HYPERBOLIC
HYPERBOLICAL
HYPERBOLICALLY
HYPERBOLISE
HYPERBOLISED
HYPERBOLISES
HYPERBOLISING
HYPERBOLISM
HYPERBOLISMS
HYPERBOLIST
HYPERBOLISTS
HYPERBOLIZE
HYPERBOLIZED
HYPERBOLIZES
HYPERBOLIZING
HYPERBOLOID
HYPERBOLOIDAL
HYPERBOLOIDS
HYPERBOREAN
HYPERBOREANS
HYPERCALCAEMIA
HYPERCALCAEMIAS
HYPERCALCAEMIC

h

HYPERCALCEMIA	HYPEREXTENDED	HYPERMARKET	HYPERPLOIDS	HYPERSONICS
HYPERCALCEMIAS	HYPEREXTENDING	HYPERMARKETS	HYPERPLOIDY	HYPERSPACE
HYPERCALCEMIC	HYPEREXTENDS	HYPERMARTS	HYPERPNEAS	HYPERSPACES
HYPERCAPNIA	HYPEREXTENSION	HYPERMASCULINE	HYPERPNEIC	HYPERSPATIAL
HYPERCAPNIAS	HYPEREXTENSIONS	HYPERMEDIA	HYPERPNOEA	HYPERSTATIC
HYPERCAPNIC	HYPERFASTIDIOUS	HYPERMEDIAS	HYPERPNOEAS	HYPERSTHENE
HYPERCARBIA	HYPERFOCAL	HYPERMETABOLIC	HYPERPOLARISE	HYPERSTHENES
HYPERCARBIAS	HYPERFUNCTION	HYPERMETABOLISM	HYPERPOLARISED	HYPERSTHENIA
HYPERCATABOLISM	HYPERFUNCTIONAL	HYPERMETER	HYPERPOLARISES	HYPERSTHENIAS
HYPERCATALECTIC	HYPERFUNCTIONS	HYPERMETERS	HYPERPOLARISING	HYPERSTHENIC
HYPERCATALEXES	HYPERGAMIES	HYPERMETRIC	HYPERPOLARIZE	HYPERSTHENITE
HYPERCATALEXIS	HYPERGAMOUS	HYPERMETRICAL	HYPERPOLARIZED	HYPERSTHENITES
HYPERCAUTIOUS	HYPERGEOMETRIC	HYPERMETROPIA	HYPERPOLARIZES	HYPERSTIMULATE
HYPERCHARGE	HYPERGLYCAEMIA	HYPERMETROPIAS	HYPERPOLARIZING	HYPERSTIMULATED
HYPERCHARGED	HYPERGLYCAEMIAS	HYPERMETROPIC	HYPERPOWER	HYPERSTIMULATES
HYPERCHARGES	HYPERGLYCAEMIC	HYPERMETROPICAL	HYPERPOWERS	HYPERSTRESS
HYPERCHARGING	HYPERGLYCEMIA	HYPERMETROPIES	HYPERPRODUCER	HYPERSTRESSES
HYPERCIVILISED	HYPERGLYCEMIAS	HYPERMETROPY	HYPERPRODUCERS	HYPERSURFACE
HYPERCIVILIZED	HYPERGLYCEMIC	HYPERMILING	HYPERPRODUCTION	HYPERSURFACES
HYPERCOAGULABLE	HYPERGOLIC	HYPERMILINGS	HYPERPROSEXIA	HYPERTENSE
HYPERCOLOUR	HYPERGOLICALLY	HYPERMNESIA	HYPERPROSEXIAS	HYPERTENSION
HYPERCOLOURS	HYPERHIDROSES	HYPERMNESIAS	HYPERPYRETIC	HYPERTENSIONS
HYPERCOMPLEX	HYPERHIDROSIS	HYPERMNESIC	HYPERPYREXIA	HYPERTENSIVE
HYPERCONSCIOUS	HYPERICINS	HYPERMOBILITIES	HYPERPYREXIAL	HYPERTENSIVES
HYPERCORRECT	HYPERICUMS	HYPERMOBILITY	HYPERPYREXIAS	HYPERTEXTS
HYPERCORRECTION	HYPERIDROSES	HYPERMODERN	HYPERRATIONAL	HYPERTHERMAL
HYPERCORRECTLY	HYPERIDROSIS	HYPERMODERNISM	HYPERREACTIVE	HYPERTHERMIA
HYPERCRITIC	HYPERIMMUNE	HYPERMODERNISMS	HYPERREACTIVITY	HYPERTHERMIAS
HYPERCRITICAL	HYPERIMMUNISE	HYPERMODERNIST	HYPERREACTOR	HYPERTHERMIC
HYPERCRITICALLY	HYPERIMMUNISED	HYPERMODERNISTS	HYPERREACTORS	HYPERTHERMIES
HYPERCRITICISE	HYPERIMMUNISES	HYPERMUTABILITY	HYPERREALISM	HYPERTHERMY
HYPERCRITICISED	HYPERIMMUNISING	HYPERMUTABLE	HYPERREALISMS	HYPERTHYMIA
HYPERCRITICISES	HYPERIMMUNIZE	HYPERNATRAEMIA	HYPERREALIST	HYPERTHYMIAS
HYPERCRITICISM	HYPERIMMUNIZED	HYPERNATRAEMIAS	HYPERREALISTIC	HYPERTHYROID
HYPERCRITICISMS	HYPERIMMUNIZES	HYPERNOVAE	HYPERREALISTS	HYPERTHYROIDISM
HYPERCRITICIZE	HYPERIMMUNIZING	HYPERNOVAS	HYPERREALITIES	HYPERTHYROIDS
HYPERCRITICIZED	HYPERINFLATED	HYPERNYMIES	HYPERREALITY	HYPERTONIA
HYPERCRITICIZES	HYPERINFLATION	HYPEROPIAS	HYPERREALS	HYPERTONIAS
HYPERCRITICS	HYPERINFLATIONS	HYPEROREXIA	HYPERRESPONSIVE	HYPERTONIC
HYPERCUBES	HYPERINOSES	HYPEROREXIAS	HYPERROMANTIC	HYPERTONICITIES
HYPERDACTYL	HYPERINOSIS	HYPEROSMIA	HYPERROMANTICS	HYPERTONICITY
HYPERDACTYLIES	HYPERINOTIC	HYPEROSMIAS	HYPERSALINE	HYPERTROPHIC
HYPERDACTYLY	HYPERINSULINISM	HYPEROSTOSES	HYPERSALINITIES	HYPERTROPHICAL
HYPERDORIAN	HYPERINTENSE	HYPEROSTOSIS	HYPERSALINITY	HYPERTROPHIED
HYPERDULIA	HYPERINVOLUTION	HYPEROSTOSISES	HYPERSALIVATION	HYPERTROPHIES
HYPERDULIAS	HYPERIRRITABLE	HYPEROSTOTIC	HYPERSARCOMA	HYPERTROPHOUS
HYPERDULIC	HYPERKERATOSES	HYPEROXIDE	HYPERSARCOMAS	HYPERTROPHY
HYPERDULICAL	HYPERKERATOSIS	HYPEROXIDES	HYPERSARCOMATA	HYPERTROPHYING
HYPEREFFICIENT	HYPERKERATOTIC	HYPERPARASITE	HYPERSARCOSES	HYPERTYPICAL
HYPEREMESES	HYPERKINESES	HYPERPARASITES	HYPERSARCOSIS	HYPERURBANISM
HYPEREMESIS	HYPERKINESIA	HYPERPARASITIC	HYPERSECRETION	HYPERURBANISMS
HYPEREMETIC	HYPERKINESIAS	HYPERPARASITISM	HYPERSECRETIONS	HYPERURICAEMIA
HYPEREMIAS	HYPERKINESIS	HYPERPHAGIA	HYPERSENSITISE	HYPERURICAEMIAS
HYPEREMOTIONAL	HYPERKINETIC	HYPERPHAGIAS	HYPERSENSITISED	HYPERURICEMIA
HYPERENDEMIC	HYPERLINKED	HYPERPHAGIC	HYPERSENSITISES	HYPERURICEMIAS
HYPERENERGETIC	HYPERLINKING	HYPERPHRYGIAN	HYPERSENSITIVE	HYPERVELOCITIES
HYPERESTHESIA	HYPERLINKS	HYPERPHYSICAL	HYPERSENSITIZE	HYPERVELOCITY
HYPERESTHESIAS	HYPERLIPEMIA	HYPERPHYSICALLY	HYPERSENSITIZED	HYPERVENTILATE
HYPERESTHETIC	HYPERLIPEMIAS	HYPERPIGMENTED	HYPERSENSITIZES	HYPERVENTILATED
HYPEREUTECTIC	HYPERLIPEMIC	HYPERPITUITARY	HYPERSENSUAL	HYPERVENTILATES
HYPEREUTECTOID	HYPERLIPIDAEMIA	HYPERPLANE	HYPERSEXUAL	HYPERVIGILANCE
HYPEREXCITABLE	HYPERLIPIDEMIA	HYPERPLANES	HYPERSEXUALITY	HYPERVIGILANCES
HYPEREXCITED	HYPERLIPIDEMIAS	HYPERPLASIA	HYPERSOMNIA	HYPERVIGILANT
HYPEREXCITEMENT	HYPERLYDIAN	HYPERPLASIAS	HYPERSOMNIAS	HYPERVIRULENT
HYPEREXCRETION	HYPERMANIA	HYPERPLASTIC	HYPERSOMNOLENCE	HYPERVISCOSITY
HYPEREXCRETIONS	HYPERMANIAS	HYPERPLOID	HYPERSONIC	HYPESTHESIA
HYPEREXTEND	HYPERMANIC	HYPERPLOIDIES	HYPERSONICALLY	HYPESTHESIAS

HYPESTHESIC
HYPHENATED
HYPHENATES
HYPHENATING
HYPHENATION
HYPHENATIONS
HYPHENISATION
HYPHENISATIONS
HYPHENISED
HYPHENISES
HYPHENISING
HYPHENISMS
HYPHENIZATION
HYPHENIZATIONS
HYPHENIZED
HYPHENIZES
HYPHENIZING
HYPHENLESS
HYPNAGOGIC
HYPNOANALYSES
HYPNOANALYSIS
HYPNOANALYTIC
HYPNOBIRTHING
HYPNOBIRTHINGS
HYPNOGENESES
HYPNOGENESIS
HYPNOGENETIC
HYPNOGENIC
HYPNOGENIES
HYPNOGENOUS
HYPNOGOGIC
HYPNOIDISE
HYPNOIDISED
HYPNOIDISES
HYPNOIDISING
HYPNOIDIZE
HYPNOIDIZED
HYPNOIDIZES
HYPNOIDIZING
HYPNOLOGIC
HYPNOLOGICAL
HYPNOLOGIES
HYPNOLOGIST
HYPNOLOGISTS
HYPNOPAEDIA
HYPNOPAEDIAS
HYPNOPHOBIA
HYPNOPHOBIAS
HYPNOPOMPIC
HYPNOTHERAPIES
HYPNOTHERAPIST
HYPNOTHERAPISTS
HYPNOTHERAPY
HYPNOTICALLY
HYPNOTISABILITY
HYPNOTISABLE
HYPNOTISATION
HYPNOTISATIONS
HYPNOTISED
HYPNOTISER
HYPNOTISERS
HYPNOTISES
HYPNOTISING
HYPNOTISMS
HYPNOTISTIC
HYPNOTISTS
HYPNOTIZABILITY

HYPNOTIZABLE
HYPNOTIZATION
HYPNOTIZATIONS
HYPNOTIZED
HYPNOTIZER
HYPNOTIZERS
HYPNOTIZES
HYPNOTIZING
HYPOACIDITIES
HYPOACIDITY
HYPOAEOLIAN
HYPOALLERGENIC
HYPOBLASTIC
HYPOBLASTS
HYPOCALCAEMIA
HYPOCALCAEMIAS
HYPOCALCAEMIC
HYPOCALCEMIA
HYPOCALCEMIAS
HYPOCALCEMIC
HYPOCAUSTS
HYPOCENTER
HYPOCENTERS
HYPOCENTRAL
HYPOCENTRE
HYPOCENTRES
HYPOCHLORITE
HYPOCHLORITES
HYPOCHLOROUS
HYPOCHONDRIA
HYPOCHONDRIAC
HYPOCHONDRIACAL
HYPOCHONDRIACS
HYPOCHONDRIAS
HYPOCHONDRIASES
HYPOCHONDRIASIS
HYPOCHONDRIASM
HYPOCHONDRIASMS
HYPOCHONDRIAST
HYPOCHONDRIASTS
HYPOCHONDRIUM
HYPOCORISM
HYPOCORISMA
HYPOCORISMAS
HYPOCORISMS
HYPOCORISTIC
HYPOCORISTICAL
HYPOCOTYLOUS
HYPOCOTYLS
HYPOCRISIES
HYPOCRITES
HYPOCRITIC
HYPOCRITICAL
HYPOCRITICALLY
HYPOCRYSTALLINE
HYPOCYCLOID
HYPOCYCLOIDAL
HYPOCYCLOIDS
HYPODERMAL
HYPODERMAS
HYPODERMIC
HYPODERMICALLY
HYPODERMICS
HYPODERMIS
HYPODERMISES
HYPODIPLOID
HYPODIPLOIDIES

HYPODIPLOIDY
HYPODORIAN
HYPOEUTECTIC
HYPOEUTECTOID
HYPOGAEOUS
HYPOGASTRIA
HYPOGASTRIC
HYPOGASTRIUM
HYPOGENOUS
HYPOGLOSSAL
HYPOGLOSSALS
HYPOGLYCAEMIA
HYPOGLYCAEMIAS
HYPOGLYCAEMIC
HYPOGLYCEMIA
HYPOGLYCEMIAS
HYPOGLYCEMIC
HYPOGLYCEMICS
HYPOGNATHISM
HYPOGNATHISMS
HYPOGNATHOUS
HYPOGYNIES
HYPOGYNOUS
HYPOKALEMIA
HYPOKALEMIAS
HYPOKALEMIC
HYPOLIMNIA
HYPOLIMNION
HYPOLIMNIONS
HYPOLYDIAN
HYPOMAGNESAEMIA
HYPOMAGNESEMIA
HYPOMAGNESEMIAS
HYPOMANIAS
HYPOMANICS
HYPOMENORRHEA
HYPOMENORRHEAS
HYPOMENORRHOEA
HYPOMENORRHOEAS
HYPOMIXOLYDIAN
HYPOMORPHIC
HYPOMORPHS
HYPONASTIC
HYPONASTICALLY
HYPONASTIES
HYPONATRAEMIA
HYPONATRAEMIAS
HYPONITRITE
HYPONITRITES
HYPONITROUS
HYPONYMIES
HYPOPHARYNGES
HYPOPHARYNX
HYPOPHARYNXES
HYPOPHOSPHATE
HYPOPHOSPHATES
HYPOPHOSPHITE
HYPOPHOSPHITES
HYPOPHOSPHORIC
HYPOPHOSPHOROUS
HYPOPHRYGIAN
HYPOPHYGES
HYPOPHYSEAL
HYPOPHYSECTOMY
HYPOPHYSES
HYPOPHYSIAL
HYPOPHYSIS

HYPOPITUITARISM
HYPOPITUITARY
HYPOPLASIA
HYPOPLASIAS
HYPOPLASTIC
HYPOPLASTIES
HYPOPLASTRA
HYPOPLASTRON
HYPOPLASTY
HYPOPLOIDIES
HYPOPLOIDS
HYPOPLOIDY
HYPOPNOEAS
HYPOSENSITISE
HYPOSENSITISED
HYPOSENSITISES
HYPOSENSITISING
HYPOSENSITIZE
HYPOSENSITIZED
HYPOSENSITIZES
HYPOSENSITIZING
HYPOSPADIAS
HYPOSPADIASES
HYPOSTASES
HYPOSTASIS
HYPOSTASISATION
HYPOSTASISE
HYPOSTASISED
HYPOSTASISES
HYPOSTASISING
HYPOSTASIZATION
HYPOSTASIZE
HYPOSTASIZED
HYPOSTASIZES
HYPOSTASIZING
HYPOSTATIC
HYPOSTATICAL
HYPOSTATICALLY
HYPOSTATISATION
HYPOSTATISE
HYPOSTATISED
HYPOSTATISES
HYPOSTATISING
HYPOSTATIZATION
HYPOSTATIZE
HYPOSTATIZED
HYPOSTATIZES
HYPOSTATIZING
HYPOSTHENIA
HYPOSTHENIAS
HYPOSTHENIC
HYPOSTOMES
HYPOSTRESS
HYPOSTRESSES
HYPOSTROPHE
HYPOSTROPHES
HYPOSTYLES
HYPOSULPHATE
HYPOSULPHATES
HYPOSULPHITE
HYPOSULPHITES
HYPOSULPHURIC
HYPOSULPHUROUS
HYPOTACTIC
HYPOTENSION
HYPOTENSIONS
HYPOTENSIVE

HYPOTENSIVES
HYPOTENUSE
HYPOTENUSES
HYPOTHALAMI
HYPOTHALAMIC
HYPOTHALAMUS
HYPOTHECAE
HYPOTHECARY
HYPOTHECATE
HYPOTHECATED
HYPOTHECATES
HYPOTHECATING
HYPOTHECATION
HYPOTHECATIONS
HYPOTHECATOR
HYPOTHECATORS
HYPOTHENUSE
HYPOTHENUSES
HYPOTHERMAL
HYPOTHERMIA
HYPOTHERMIAS
HYPOTHERMIC
HYPOTHESES
HYPOTHESIS
HYPOTHESISE
HYPOTHESISED
HYPOTHESISER
HYPOTHESISERS
HYPOTHESISES
HYPOTHESISING
HYPOTHESIST
HYPOTHESISTS
HYPOTHESIZE
HYPOTHESIZED
HYPOTHESIZER
HYPOTHESIZERS
HYPOTHESIZING
HYPOTHETIC
HYPOTHETICAL
HYPOTHETICALLY
HYPOTHETISE
HYPOTHETISED
HYPOTHETISES
HYPOTHETISING
HYPOTHETIZE
HYPOTHETIZED
HYPOTHETIZES
HYPOTHETIZING
HYPOTHYMIA
HYPOTHYMIAS
HYPOTHYROID
HYPOTHYROIDISM
HYPOTHYROIDISMS
HYPOTHYROIDS
HYPOTONIAS
HYPOTONICITIES
HYPOTONICITY
HYPOTROCHOID
HYPOTROCHOIDS
HYPOTYPOSES
HYPOTYPOSIS
HYPOVENTILATION
HYPOXAEMIA
HYPOXAEMIAS
HYPOXAEMIC
HYPOXANTHINE

HYPOXANTHINES
HYPOXEMIAS
HYPSOCHROME
HYPSOCHROMES
HYPSOCHROMIC
HYPSOGRAPHIC
HYPSOGRAPHICAL
HYPSOGRAPHIES
HYPSOGRAPHY
HYPSOMETER
HYPSOMETERS
HYPSOMETRIC

HYPSOMETRICAL
HYPSOMETRICALLY
HYPSOMETRIES
HYPSOMETRIST
HYPSOMETRISTS
HYPSOMETRY
HYPSOPHOBE
HYPSOPHOBES
HYPSOPHOBIA
HYPSOPHOBIAS
HYPSOPHYLL
HYPSOPHYLLARY

HYPSOPHYLLS
HYRACOIDEAN
HYRACOIDEANS
HYSTERANTHOUS
HYSTERECTOMIES
HYSTERECTOMISE
HYSTERECTOMISED
HYSTERECTOMISES
HYSTERECTOMIZE
HYSTERECTOMIZED
HYSTERECTOMIZES
HYSTERECTOMY

HYSTERESES
HYSTERESIAL
HYSTERESIS
HYSTERETIC
HYSTERETICALLY
HYSTERICAL
HYSTERICALLY
HYSTERICKY
HYSTERITIS
HYSTERITISES
HYSTEROGENIC
HYSTEROGENIES

HYSTEROGENY
HYSTEROIDAL
HYSTEROMANIA
HYSTEROMANIAS
HYSTEROTOMIES
HYSTEROTOMY
HYSTRICOMORPH
HYSTRICOMORPHIC
HYSTRICOMORPHS

I

IAMBICALLY
IAMBOGRAPHER
IAMBOGRAPHERS
IATROCHEMICAL
IATROCHEMIST
IATROCHEMISTRY
IATROCHEMISTS
IATROGENIC
IATROGENICALLY
IATROGENICITIES
IATROGENICITY
IATROGENIES
IBUPROFENS
ICEBOATERS
ICEBOATING
ICEBOATINGS
ICEBREAKER
ICEBREAKERS
ICEBREAKING
ICEFISHING
ICHNEUMONS
ICHNOFOSSIL
ICHNOFOSSILS
ICHNOGRAPHIC
ICHNOGRAPHICAL
ICHNOGRAPHIES
ICHNOGRAPHY
ICHNOLITES
ICHNOLOGICAL
ICHNOLOGIES
ICHTHYOCOLLA
ICHTHYOCOLLAS
ICHTHYODORULITE
ICHTHYODORYLITE
ICHTHYOFAUNA
ICHTHYOFAUNAE
ICHTHYOFAUNAL
ICHTHYOFAUNAS
ICHTHYOIDAL
ICHTHYOIDS
ICHTHYOLATRIES
ICHTHYOLATROUS
ICHTHYOLATRY
ICHTHYOLITE
ICHTHYOLITES
ICHTHYOLITIC
ICHTHYOLOGIC
ICHTHYOLOGICAL
ICHTHYOLOGIES
ICHTHYOLOGIST
ICHTHYOLOGISTS
ICHTHYOLOGY
ICHTHYOPHAGIES
ICHTHYOPHAGIST

ICHTHYOPHAGISTS
ICHTHYOPHAGOUS
ICHTHYOPHAGY
ICHTHYOPSID
ICHTHYOPSIDAN
ICHTHYOPSIDANS
ICHTHYOPSIDS
ICHTHYORNIS
ICHTHYORNISES
ICHTHYOSAUR
ICHTHYOSAURI
ICHTHYOSAURIAN
ICHTHYOSAURIANS
ICHTHYOSAURS
ICHTHYOSAURUS
ICHTHYOSAURUSES
ICHTHYOSES
ICHTHYOSIS
ICHTHYOTIC
ICKINESSES
ICONICALLY
ICONICITIES
ICONIFYING
ICONOCLASM
ICONOCLASMS
ICONOCLAST
ICONOCLASTIC
ICONOCLASTS
ICONOGRAPHER
ICONOGRAPHERS
ICONOGRAPHIC
ICONOGRAPHICAL
ICONOGRAPHIES
ICONOGRAPHY
ICONOLATER
ICONOLATERS
ICONOLATRIES
ICONOLATROUS
ICONOLATRY
ICONOLOGICAL
ICONOLOGIES
ICONOLOGIST
ICONOLOGISTS
ICONOMACHIES
ICONOMACHIST
ICONOMACHISTS
ICONOMACHY
ICONOMATIC
ICONOMATICISM
ICONOMATICISMS
ICONOMETER
ICONOMETERS
ICONOMETRIES
ICONOMETRY

ICONOPHILISM
ICONOPHILISMS
ICONOPHILIST
ICONOPHILISTS
ICONOSCOPE
ICONOSCOPES
ICONOSTASES
ICONOSTASIS
ICOSAHEDRA
ICOSAHEDRAL
ICOSAHEDRON
ICOSAHEDRONS
ICOSANDRIAN
ICOSANDROUS
ICOSITETRAHEDRA
ICTERICALS
ICTERITIOUS
IDEALISATION
IDEALISATIONS
IDEALISERS
IDEALISING
IDEALISTIC
IDEALISTICALLY
IDEALITIES
IDEALIZATION
IDEALIZATIONS
IDEALIZERS
IDEALIZING
IDEALNESSES
IDEALOGIES
IDEALOGUES
IDEATIONAL
IDEATIONALLY
IDEMPOTENCIES
IDEMPOTENCY
IDEMPOTENT
IDEMPOTENTS
IDENTICALLY
IDENTICALNESS
IDENTICALNESSES
IDENTIFIABLE
IDENTIFIABLY
IDENTIFICATION
IDENTIFICATIONS
IDENTIFIED
IDENTIFIER
IDENTIFIERS
IDENTIFIES
IDENTIFYING
IDENTIKITS
IDENTITIES
IDEOGRAMIC
IDEOGRAMMATIC
IDEOGRAMMIC

IDEOGRAPHIC
IDEOGRAPHICAL
IDEOGRAPHICALLY
IDEOGRAPHIES
IDEOGRAPHS
IDEOGRAPHY
IDEOLOGICAL
IDEOLOGICALLY
IDEOLOGIES
IDEOLOGISE
IDEOLOGISED
IDEOLOGISES
IDEOLOGISING
IDEOLOGIST
IDEOLOGISTS
IDEOLOGIZE
IDEOLOGIZED
IDEOLOGIZES
IDEOLOGIZING
IDEOLOGUES
IDEOPHONES
IDEOPOLISES
IDEOPRAXIST
IDEOPRAXISTS
IDIOBLASTIC
IDIOBLASTS
IDIOGLOSSIA
IDIOGLOSSIAS
IDIOGRAPHIC
IDIOGRAPHS
IDIOLECTAL
IDIOLECTIC
IDIOMATICAL
IDIOMATICALLY
IDIOMATICALNESS
IDIOMATICNESS
IDIOMATICNESSES
IDIOMORPHIC
IDIOMORPHICALLY
IDIOMORPHISM
IDIOMORPHISMS
IDIOPATHIC
IDIOPATHICALLY
IDIOPATHIES
IDIOPHONES
IDIOPHONIC
IDIOPLASMATIC
IDIOPLASMIC
IDIOPLASMS
IDIORHYTHMIC
IDIORRHYTHMIC
IDIOSYNCRASIES
IDIOSYNCRASY
IDIOSYNCRATIC

IDIOSYNCRATICAL
IDIOTHERMOUS
IDIOTICALLY
IDIOTICALNESS
IDIOTICALNESSES
IDIOTICONS
IDLENESSES
IDOLATRESS
IDOLATRESSES
IDOLATRIES
IDOLATRISE
IDOLATRISED
IDOLATRISER
IDOLATRISERS
IDOLATRISES
IDOLATRISING
IDOLATRIZE
IDOLATRIZED
IDOLATRIZER
IDOLATRIZERS
IDOLATRIZES
IDOLATRIZING
IDOLATROUS
IDOLATROUSLY
IDOLATROUSNESS
IDOLISATION
IDOLISATIONS
IDOLIZATION
IDOLIZATIONS
IDOLOCLAST
IDOLOCLASTS
IDONEITIES
IDOXURIDINE
IDOXURIDINES
IDYLLICALLY
IFFINESSES
IGNESCENTS
IGNIMBRITE
IGNIMBRITES
IGNIPOTENT
IGNITABILITIES
IGNITABILITY
IGNITIBILITIES
IGNITIBILITY
IGNOBILITIES
IGNOBILITY
IGNOBLENESS
IGNOBLENESSES
IGNOMINIES
IGNOMINIOUS
IGNOMINIOUSLY
IGNOMINIOUSNESS
IGNORAMUSES
IGNORANCES

IGNORANTLY	ILLIMITATIONS	ILLUSTRATIVELY	IMINOUREAS	IMMEDIATISM
IGNORANTNESS	ILLIQUATION	ILLUSTRATOR	IMIPRAMINE	IMMEDIATISMS
IGNORANTNESSES	ILLIQUATIONS	ILLUSTRATORS	IMIPRAMINES	IMMEDICABLE
IGNORATION	ILLIQUIDITIES	ILLUSTRATORY	IMITABILITIES	IMMEDICABLENESS
IGNORATIONS	ILLIQUIDITY	ILLUSTRIOUS	IMITABILITY	IMMEDICABLY
IGUANODONS	ILLITERACIES	ILLUSTRIOUSLY	IMITABLENESS	IMMEMORIAL
ILEOSTOMIES	ILLITERACY	ILLUSTRIOUSNESS	IMITABLENESSES	IMMEMORIALLY
ILLAQUEABLE	ILLITERATE	ILLUSTRISSIMO	IMITANCIES	IMMENSENESS
ILLAQUEATE	ILLITERATELY	ILLUVIATED	IMITATIONAL	IMMENSENESSES
ILLAQUEATED	ILLITERATENESS	ILLUVIATES	IMITATIONS	IMMENSITIES
ILLAQUEATES	ILLITERATES	ILLUVIATING	IMITATIVELY	IMMENSURABILITY
ILLAQUEATING	ILLOCUTION	ILLUVIATION	IMITATIVENESS	IMMENSURABLE
ILLAQUEATION	ILLOCUTIONARY	ILLUVIATIONS	IMITATIVENESSES	IMMERGENCE
ILLAQUEATIONS	ILLOCUTIONS	IMAGINABLE	IMMACULACIES	IMMERGENCES
ILLATIVELY	ILLOGICALITIES	IMAGINABLENESS	IMMACULACY	IMMERITOUS
ILLAUDABLE	ILLOGICALITY	IMAGINABLY	IMMACULATE	IMMERSIBLE
ILLAUDABLY	ILLOGICALLY	IMAGINARIES	IMMACULATELY	IMMERSIONISM
ILLAWARRAS	ILLOGICALNESS	IMAGINARILY	IMMACULATENESS	IMMERSIONISMS
ILLEGALISATION	ILLOGICALNESSES	IMAGINARINESS	IMMANACLED	IMMERSIONIST
ILLEGALISATIONS	ILLUMINABLE	IMAGINARINESSES	IMMANACLES	IMMERSIONISTS
ILLEGALISE	ILLUMINANCE	IMAGINATION	IMMANACLING	IMMERSIONS
ILLEGALISED	ILLUMINANCES	IMAGINATIONAL	IMMANATION	IMMETHODICAL
ILLEGALISES	ILLUMINANT	IMAGINATIONS	IMMANATIONS	IMMETHODICALLY
ILLEGALISING	ILLUMINANTS	IMAGINATIVE	IMMANENCES	IMMIGRANCIES
ILLEGALITIES	ILLUMINATE	IMAGINATIVELY	IMMANENCIES	IMMIGRANCY
ILLEGALITY	ILLUMINATED	IMAGINATIVENESS	IMMANENTAL	IMMIGRANTS
ILLEGALIZATION	ILLUMINATES	IMAGINEERED	IMMANENTISM	IMMIGRATED
ILLEGALIZATIONS	ILLUMINATI	IMAGINEERING	IMMANENTISMS	IMMIGRATES
ILLEGALIZE	ILLUMINATING	IMAGINEERS	IMMANENTIST	IMMIGRATING
ILLEGALIZED	ILLUMINATINGLY	IMAGININGS	IMMANENTISTIC	IMMIGRATION
ILLEGALIZES	ILLUMINATION	IMAGINISTS	IMMANENTISTS	IMMIGRATIONAL
ILLEGALIZING	ILLUMINATIONAL	IMAGISTICALLY	IMMANENTLY	IMMIGRATIONS
ILLEGIBILITIES	ILLUMINATIONS	IMBALANCED	IMMANITIES	IMMIGRATOR
ILLEGIBILITY	ILLUMINATIVE	IMBALANCES	IMMANTLING	IMMIGRATORS
ILLEGIBLENESS	ILLUMINATO	IMBECILELY	IMMARCESCIBLE	IMMIGRATORY
ILLEGIBLENESSES	ILLUMINATOR	IMBECILICALLY	IMMARGINATE	IMMINENCES
ILLEGITIMACIES	ILLUMINATORS	IMBECILITIES	IMMATERIAL	IMMINENCIES
ILLEGITIMACY	ILLUMINERS	IMBECILITY	IMMATERIALISE	IMMINENTLY
ILLEGITIMATE	ILLUMINING	IMBIBITION	IMMATERIALISED	IMMINENTNESS
ILLEGITIMATED	ILLUMINISM	IMBIBITIONAL	IMMATERIALISES	IMMINENTNESSES
ILLEGITIMATELY	ILLUMINISMS	IMBIBITIONS	IMMATERIALISING	IMMINGLING
ILLEGITIMATES	ILLUMINIST	IMBITTERED	IMMATERIALISM	IMMINUTION
ILLEGITIMATING	ILLUMINISTS	IMBITTERING	IMMATERIALISMS	IMMINUTIONS
ILLEGITIMATION	ILLUSIONAL	IMBOLDENED	IMMATERIALIST	IMMISCIBILITIES
ILLEGITIMATIONS	ILLUSIONARY	IMBOLDENING	IMMATERIALISTS	IMMISCIBILITY
ILLIBERALISE	ILLUSIONED	IMBORDERED	IMMATERIALITIES	IMMISCIBLE
ILLIBERALISED	ILLUSIONISM	IMBORDERING	IMMATERIALITY	IMMISCIBLY
ILLIBERALISES	ILLUSIONISMS	IMBOSOMING	IMMATERIALIZE	IMMISERATION
ILLIBERALISING	ILLUSIONIST	IMBOWERING	IMMATERIALIZED	IMMISERATIONS
ILLIBERALISM	ILLUSIONISTIC	IMBRANGLED	IMMATERIALIZES	IMMISERISATION
ILLIBERALISMS	ILLUSIONISTS	IMBRANGLES	IMMATERIALIZING	IMMISERISATIONS
ILLIBERALITIES	ILLUSIVELY	IMBRANGLING	IMMATERIALLY	IMMISERISE
ILLIBERALITY	ILLUSIVENESS	IMBRICATED	IMMATERIALNESS	IMMISERISED
ILLIBERALIZE	ILLUSIVENESSES	IMBRICATELY	IMMATURELY	IMMISERISES
ILLIBERALIZED	ILLUSORILY	IMBRICATES	IMMATURENESS	IMMISERISING
ILLIBERALIZES	ILLUSORINESS	IMBRICATING	IMMATURENESSES	IMMISERIZATION
ILLIBERALIZING	ILLUSORINESSES	IMBRICATION	IMMATUREST	IMMISERIZATIONS
ILLIBERALLY	ILLUSTRATABLE	IMBRICATIONS	IMMATURITIES	IMMISERIZE
ILLIBERALNESS	ILLUSTRATE	IMBROCCATA	IMMATURITY	IMMISERIZED
ILLIBERALNESSES	ILLUSTRATED	IMBROCCATAS	IMMEASURABILITY	IMMISERIZES
ILLICITNESS	ILLUSTRATEDS	IMBROGLIOS	IMMEASURABLE	IMMISERIZING
ILLICITNESSES	ILLUSTRATES	IMBROWNING	IMMEASURABLY	IMMISSIONS
ILLIMITABILITY	ILLUSTRATING	IMBRUEMENT	IMMEASURED	IMMITIGABILITY
ILLIMITABLE	ILLUSTRATION	IMBRUEMENTS	IMMEDIACIES	IMMITIGABLE
ILLIMITABLENESS	ILLUSTRATIONAL	IMBUEMENTS	IMMEDIATELY	IMMITIGABLY
ILLIMITABLY	ILLUSTRATIONS	IMIDAZOLES	IMMEDIATENESS	IMMITTANCE
ILLIMITATION	ILLUSTRATIVE	IMINAZOLES	IMMEDIATENESSES	IMMITTANCES

IMMIXTURES	IMMOVABLENESSES	IMMUNOTHERAPIES	IMPASSIBILITY	IMPENITENTS
IMMOBILISATION	IMMOVABLES	IMMUNOTHERAPY	IMPASSIBLE	IMPERATIVAL
IMMOBILISATIONS	IMMOVEABILITIES	IMMUNOTOXIC	IMPASSIBLENESS	IMPERATIVE
IMMOBILISE	IMMOVEABILITY	IMMUNOTOXIN	IMPASSIBLY	IMPERATIVELY
IMMOBILISED	IMMOVEABLE	IMMUNOTOXINS	IMPASSIONATE	IMPERATIVENESS
IMMOBILISER	IMMOVEABLENESS	IMMUREMENT	IMPASSIONED	IMPERATIVES
IMMOBILISERS	IMMOVEABLES	IMMUREMENTS	IMPASSIONEDLY	IMPERATORIAL
IMMOBILISES	IMMOVEABLY	IMMUTABILITIES	IMPASSIONEDNESS	IMPERATORIALLY
IMMOBILISING	IMMUNIFACIENT	IMMUTABILITY	IMPASSIONING	IMPERATORS
IMMOBILISM	IMMUNISATION	IMMUTABLENESS	IMPASSIONS	IMPERATORSHIP
IMMOBILISMS	IMMUNISATIONS	IMMUTABLENESSES	IMPASSIVELY	IMPERATORSHIPS
IMMOBILITIES	IMMUNISERS	IMPACTIONS	IMPASSIVENESS	IMPERCEABLE
IMMOBILITY	IMMUNISING	IMPACTITES	IMPASSIVENESSES	IMPERCEIVABLE
IMMOBILIZATION	IMMUNITIES	IMPAINTING	IMPASSIVITIES	IMPERCEPTIBLE
IMMOBILIZATIONS	IMMUNIZATION	IMPAIRABLE	IMPASSIVITY	IMPERCEPTIBLY
IMMOBILIZE	IMMUNIZATIONS	IMPAIRINGS	IMPASTATION	IMPERCEPTION
IMMOBILIZED	IMMUNIZERS	IMPAIRMENT	IMPASTATIONS	IMPERCEPTIONS
IMMOBILIZER	IMMUNIZING	IMPAIRMENTS	IMPATIENCE	IMPERCEPTIVE
IMMOBILIZERS	IMMUNOASSAY	IMPALEMENT	IMPATIENCES	IMPERCEPTIVELY
IMMOBILIZES	IMMUNOASSAYABLE	IMPALEMENTS	IMPATIENTLY	IMPERCEPTIVITY
IMMOBILIZING	IMMUNOASSAYIST	IMPALPABILITIES	IMPEACHABILITY	IMPERCIPIENCE
IMMODERACIES	IMMUNOASSAYISTS	IMPALPABILITY	IMPEACHABLE	IMPERCIPIENCES
IMMODERACY	IMMUNOASSAYS	IMPALPABLE	IMPEACHERS	IMPERCIPIENT
IMMODERATE	IMMUNOBLOT	IMPALPABLY	IMPEACHING	IMPERCIPIENTLY
IMMODERATELY	IMMUNOBLOTS	IMPALUDISM	IMPEACHMENT	IMPERFECTER
IMMODERATENESS	IMMUNOBLOTTING	IMPALUDISMS	IMPEACHMENTS	IMPERFECTEST
IMMODERATION	IMMUNOBLOTTINGS	IMPANATION	IMPEARLING	IMPERFECTIBLE
IMMODERATIONS	IMMUNOCHEMICAL	IMPANATIONS	IMPECCABILITIES	IMPERFECTION
IMMODESTER	IMMUNOCHEMIST	IMPANELING	IMPECCABILITY	IMPERFECTIONS
IMMODESTEST	IMMUNOCHEMISTRY	IMPANELLED	IMPECCABLE	IMPERFECTIVE
IMMODESTIES	IMMUNOCHEMISTS	IMPANELLING	IMPECCABLY	IMPERFECTIVELY
IMMODESTLY	IMMUNOCOMPETENT	IMPANELMENT	IMPECCANCIES	IMPERFECTIVES
IMMOLATING	IMMUNOCOMPLEX	IMPANELMENTS	IMPECCANCY	IMPERFECTLY
IMMOLATION	IMMUNOCOMPLEXES	IMPANNELLED	IMPECUNIOSITIES	IMPERFECTNESS
IMMOLATIONS	IMMUNODEFICIENT	IMPANNELLING	IMPECUNIOSITY	IMPERFECTNESSES
IMMOLATORS	IMMUNODIAGNOSES	IMPARADISE	IMPECUNIOUS	IMPERFECTS
IMMOMENTOUS	IMMUNODIAGNOSIS	IMPARADISED	IMPECUNIOUSLY	IMPERFORABLE
IMMORALISM	IMMUNODIFFUSION	IMPARADISES	IMPECUNIOUSNESS	IMPERFORATE
IMMORALISMS	IMMUNOGENESES	IMPARADISING	IMPEDANCES	IMPERFORATED
IMMORALIST	IMMUNOGENESIS	IMPARIDIGITATE	IMPEDIMENT	IMPERFORATION
IMMORALISTS	IMMUNOGENETIC	IMPARIPINNATE	IMPEDIMENTA	IMPERFORATIONS
IMMORALITIES	IMMUNOGENETICAL	IMPARISYLLABIC	IMPEDIMENTAL	IMPERIALISE
IMMORALITY	IMMUNOGENETICS	IMPARITIES	IMPEDIMENTARY	IMPERIALISED
IMMORTALISATION	IMMUNOGENIC	IMPARKATION	IMPEDIMENTS	IMPERIALISES
IMMORTALISE	IMMUNOGENICALLY	IMPARKATIONS	IMPEDINGLY	IMPERIALISING
IMMORTALISED	IMMUNOGENICITY	IMPARLANCE	IMPEDITIVE	IMPERIALISM
IMMORTALISER	IMMUNOGENS	IMPARLANCES	IMPELLENTS	IMPERIALISMS
IMMORTALISERS	IMMUNOGLOBULIN	IMPARTABLE	IMPENDENCE	IMPERIALIST
IMMORTALISES	IMMUNOGLOBULINS	IMPARTATION	IMPENDENCES	IMPERIALISTIC
IMMORTALISING	IMMUNOLOGIC	IMPARTATIONS	IMPENDENCIES	IMPERIALISTS
IMMORTALITIES	IMMUNOLOGICAL	IMPARTIALITIES	IMPENDENCY	IMPERIALITIES
IMMORTALITY	IMMUNOLOGICALLY	IMPARTIALITY	IMPENETRABILITY	IMPERIALITY
IMMORTALIZATION	IMMUNOLOGIES	IMPARTIALLY	IMPENETRABLE	IMPERIALIZE
IMMORTALIZE	IMMUNOLOGIST	IMPARTIALNESS	IMPENETRABLY	IMPERIALIZED
IMMORTALIZED	IMMUNOLOGISTS	IMPARTIALNESSES	IMPENETRATE	IMPERIALIZES
IMMORTALIZER	IMMUNOLOGY	IMPARTIBILITIES	IMPENETRATED	IMPERIALIZING
IMMORTALIZERS	IMMUNOMODULATOR	IMPARTIBILITY	IMPENETRATES	IMPERIALLY
IMMORTALIZES	IMMUNOPATHOLOGY	IMPARTIBLE	IMPENETRATING	IMPERIALNESS
IMMORTALIZING	IMMUNOPHORESES	IMPARTIBLY	IMPENETRATION	IMPERIALNESSES
IMMORTALLY	IMMUNOPHORESIS	IMPARTMENT	IMPENETRATIONS	IMPERILING
IMMORTELLE	IMMUNOREACTION	IMPARTMENTS	IMPENITENCE	IMPERILLED
IMMORTELLES	IMMUNOREACTIONS	IMPASSABILITIES	IMPENITENCES	IMPERILLING
IMMOTILITIES	IMMUNOREACTIVE	IMPASSABILITY	IMPENITENCIES	IMPERILMENT
IMMOTILITY	IMMUNOSORBENT	IMPASSABLE	IMPENITENCY	IMPERILMENTS
IMMOVABILITIES	IMMUNOSORBENTS	IMPASSABLENESS	IMPENITENT	IMPERIOUSLY
IMMOVABILITY	IMMUNOSTIMULANT	IMPASSABLY	IMPENITENTLY	IMPERIOUSNESS
IMMOVABLENESS	IMMUNOSUPPRESS	IMPASSIBILITIES	IMPENITENTNESS	IMPERIOUSNESSES

IMPERISHABILITY	IMPETRATORS	IMPLICITIES	IMPOSSIBILIST	IMPREDICATIVE
IMPERISHABLE	IMPETRATORY	IMPLICITLY	IMPOSSIBILISTS	IMPREGNABILITY
IMPERISHABLES	IMPETUOSITIES	IMPLICITNESS	IMPOSSIBILITIES	IMPREGNABLE
IMPERISHABLY	IMPETUOSITY	IMPLICITNESSES	IMPOSSIBILITY	IMPREGNABLENESS
IMPERMANENCE	IMPETUOUSLY	IMPLODENTS	IMPOSSIBLE	IMPREGNABLY
IMPERMANENCES	IMPETUOUSNESS	IMPLORATION	IMPOSSTBLENESS	IMPREGNANT
IMPERMANENCIES	IMPETUOUSNESSES	IMPLORATIONS	IMPOSSIBLES	IMPREGNANTS
IMPERMANENCY	IMPICTURED	IMPLORATOR	IMPOSSIBLY	IMPREGNATABLE
IMPERMANENT	IMPIERCEABLE	IMPLORATORS	IMPOSTHUMATE	IMPREGNATE
IMPERMANENTLY	IMPIGNORATE	IMPLORATORY	IMPOSTHUMATED	IMPREGNATED
IMPERMEABILITY	IMPIGNORATED	IMPLORINGLY	IMPOSTHUMATES	IMPREGNATES
IMPERMEABLE	IMPIGNORATES	IMPLOSIONS	IMPOSTHUMATING	IMPREGNATING
IMPERMEABLENESS	IMPIGNORATING	IMPLOSIVELY	IMPOSTHUMATION	IMPREGNATION
IMPERMEABLY	IMPIGNORATION	IMPLOSIVES	IMPOSTHUMATIONS	IMPREGNATIONS
IMPERMISSIBLE	IMPIGNORATIONS	IMPLUNGING	IMPOSTHUME	IMPREGNATOR
IMPERMISSIBLY	IMPINGEMENT	IMPOCKETED	IMPOSTHUMED	IMPREGNATORS
IMPERSCRIPTIBLE	IMPINGEMENTS	IMPOCKETING	IMPOSTHUMES	IMPREGNING
IMPERSEVERANT	IMPIOUSNESS	IMPOLDERED	IMPOSTOROUS	IMPRESARIO
IMPERSISTENT	IMPIOUSNESSES	IMPOLDERING	IMPOSTROUS	IMPRESARIOS
IMPERSONAL	IMPISHNESS	IMPOLICIES	IMPOSTUMATE	IMPRESCRIPTIBLE
IMPERSONALISE	IMPISHNESSES	IMPOLITELY	IMPOSTUMATED	IMPRESCRIPTIBLY
IMPERSONALISED	IMPLACABILITIES	IMPOLITENESS	IMPOSTUMATES	IMPRESSERS
IMPERSONALISES	IMPLACABILITY	IMPOLITENESSES	IMPOSTUMATING	IMPRESSIBILITY
IMPERSONALISING	IMPLACABLE	IMPOLITEST	IMPOSTUMATION	IMPRESSIBLE
IMPERSONALITIES	IMPLACABLENESS	IMPOLITICAL	IMPOSTUMATIONS	IMPRESSING
IMPERSONALITY	IMPLACABLY	IMPOLITICALLY	IMPOSTUMED	IMPRESSION
IMPERSONALIZE	IMPLACENTAL	IMPOLITICLY	IMPOSTUMES	IMPRESSIONABLE
IMPERSONALIZED	IMPLANTABLE	IMPOLITICNESS	IMPOSTURES	IMPRESSIONAL
IMPERSONALIZES	IMPLANTATION	IMPOLITICNESSES	IMPOSTUROUS	IMPRESSIONALLY
IMPERSONALIZING	IMPLANTATIONS	IMPONDERABILIA	IMPOTENCES	IMPRESSIONISM
IMPERSONALLY	IMPLANTERS	IMPONDERABILITY	IMPOTENCIES	IMPRESSIONISMS
IMPERSONATE	IMPLANTING	IMPONDERABLE	IMPOTENTLY	IMPRESSIONIST
IMPERSONATED	IMPLAUSIBILITY	IMPONDERABLES	IMPOTENTNESS	IMPRESSIONISTIC
IMPERSONATES	IMPLAUSIBLE	IMPONDERABLY	IMPOTENTNESSES	IMPRESSIONISTS
IMPERSONATING	IMPLAUSIBLENESS	IMPONDEROUS	IMPOUNDABLE	IMPRESSIONS
IMPERSONATION	IMPLAUSIBLY	IMPORTABILITIES	IMPOUNDAGE	IMPRESSIVE
IMPERSONATIONS	IMPLEACHED	IMPORTABILITY	IMPOUNDAGES	IMPRESSIVELY
IMPERSONATOR	IMPLEACHES	IMPORTABLE	IMPOUNDERS	IMPRESSIVENESS
IMPERSONATORS	IMPLEACHING	IMPORTANCE	IMPOUNDING	IMPRESSMENT
IMPERTINENCE	IMPLEADABLE	IMPORTANCES	IMPOUNDMENT	IMPRESSMENTS
IMPERTINENCES	IMPLEADERS	IMPORTANCIES	IMPOUNDMENTS	IMPRESSURE
IMPERTINENCIES	IMPLEADING	IMPORTANCY	IMPOVERISH	IMPRESSURES
IMPERTINENCY	IMPLEDGING	IMPORTANTLY	IMPOVERISHED	IMPRIMATUR
IMPERTINENT	IMPLEMENTAL	IMPORTATION	IMPOVERISHER	IMPRIMATURS
IMPERTINENTLY	IMPLEMENTATION	IMPORTATIONS	IMPOVERISHERS	IMPRINTERS
IMPERTURBABLE	IMPLEMENTATIONS	IMPORTINGS	IMPOVERISHES	IMPRINTING
IMPERTURBABLY	IMPLEMENTED	IMPORTUNACIES	IMPOVERISHING	IMPRINTINGS
IMPERTURBATION	IMPLEMENTER	IMPORTUNACY	IMPOVERISHMENT	IMPRISONABLE
IMPERTURBATIONS	IMPLEMENTERS	IMPORTUNATE	IMPOVERISHMENTS	IMPRISONED
IMPERVIABILITY	IMPLEMENTING	IMPORTUNATELY	IMPOWERING	IMPRISONER
IMPERVIABLE	IMPLEMENTOR	IMPORTUNATENESS	IMPRACTICABLE	IMPRISONERS
IMPERVIABLENESS	IMPLEMENTORS	IMPORTUNED	IMPRACTICABLY	IMPRISONING
IMPERVIOUS	IMPLEMENTS	IMPORTUNELY	IMPRACTICAL	IMPRISONMENT
IMPERVIOUSLY	IMPLETIONS	IMPORTUNER	IMPRACTICALITY	IMPRISONMENTS
IMPERVIOUSNESS	IMPLEXIONS	IMPORTUNERS	IMPRACTICALLY	IMPROBABILITIES
IMPETICOSSED	IMPLEXUOUS	IMPORTUNES	IMPRACTICALNESS	IMPROBABILITY
IMPETICOSSES	IMPLICATED	IMPORTUNING	IMPRECATED	IMPROBABLE
IMPETICOSSING	IMPLICATES	IMPORTUNINGS	IMPRECATES	IMPROBABLENESS
IMPETIGINES	IMPLICATING	IMPORTUNITIES	IMPRECATING	IMPROBABLY
IMPETIGINOUS	IMPLICATION	IMPORTUNITY	IMPRECATION	IMPROBATION
IMPETRATED	IMPLICATIONAL	IMPOSINGLY	IMPRECATIONS	IMPROBATIONS
IMPETRATES	IMPLICATIONS	IMPOSINGNESS	IMPRECATORY	IMPROBITIES
IMPETRATING	IMPLICATIVE	IMPOSINGNESSES	IMPRECISELY	IMPROMPTUS
IMPETRATION	IMPLICATIVELY	IMPOSITION	IMPRECISENESS	IMPROPERER
IMPETRATIONS	IMPLICATIVENESS	IMPOSITIONS	IMPRECISENESSES	IMPROPEREST
IMPETRATIVE	IMPLICATURE	IMPOSSIBILISM	IMPRECISION	IMPROPERLY
IMPETRATOR	IMPLICATURES	IMPOSSIBILISMS	IMPRECISIONS	IMPROPERNESS

IMPROPERNESSES	IMPUISSANCE	INADVISABLY	INAUDIBILITIES	INCAPACITIES
IMPROPRIATE	IMPUISSANCES	INALIENABILITY	INAUDIBILITY	INCAPACITY
IMPROPRIATED	IMPUISSANT	INALIENABLE	INAUDIBLENESS	INCAPSULATE
IMPROPRIATES	IMPULSIONS	INALIENABLENESS	INAUDIBLENESSES	INCAPSULATED
IMPROPRIATING	IMPULSIVELY	INALIENABLY	INAUGURALS	INCAPSULATES
IMPROPRIATION	IMPULSIVENESS	INALTERABILITY	INAUGURATE	INCAPSULATING
IMPROPRIATIONS	IMPULSIVENESSES	INALTERABLE	INAUGURATED	INCAPSULATION
IMPROPRIATOR	IMPULSIVITIES	INALTERABLENESS	INAUGURATES	INCAPSULATIONS
IMPROPRIATORS	IMPULSIVITY	INALTERABLY	INAUGURATING	INCARCERATE
IMPROPRIETIES	IMPUNDULUS	INAMORATAS	INAUGURATION	INCARCERATED
IMPROPRIETY	IMPUNITIES	INAMORATOS	INAUGURATIONS	INCARCERATES
IMPROVABILITIES	IMPURENESS	INANENESSES	INAUGURATOR	INCARCERATING
IMPROVABILITY	IMPURENESSES	INANIMATELY	INAUGURATORS	INCARCERATION
IMPROVABLE	IMPURITIES	INANIMATENESS	INAUGURATORY	INCARCERATIONS
IMPROVABLENESS	IMPURPLING	INANIMATENESSES	INAURATING	INCARCERATOR
IMPROVABLY	IMPUTABILITIES	INANIMATION	INAUSPICIOUS	INCARCERATORS
IMPROVEMENT	IMPUTABILITY	INANIMATIONS	INAUSPICIOUSLY	INCARDINATE
IMPROVEMENTS	IMPUTABLENESS	INANITIONS	INAUTHENTIC	INCARDINATED
IMPROVIDENCE	IMPUTABLENESSES	INAPPARENT	INAUTHENTICITY	INCARDINATES
IMPROVIDENCES	IMPUTATION	INAPPARENTLY	INBOUNDING	INCARDINATING
IMPROVIDENT	IMPUTATIONS	INAPPEASABLE	INBREATHED	INCARDINATION
IMPROVIDENTLY	IMPUTATIVE	INAPPELLABLE	INBREATHES	INCARDINATIONS
IMPROVINGLY	IMPUTATIVELY	INAPPETENCE	INBREATHING	INCARNADINE
IMPROVISATE	INABILITIES	INAPPETENCES	INBREEDERS	INCARNADINED
IMPROVISATED	INABSTINENCE	INAPPETENCIES	INBREEDING	INCARNADINES
IMPROVISATES	INABSTINENCES	INAPPETENCY	INBREEDINGS	INCARNADINING
IMPROVISATING	INACCESSIBILITY	INAPPETENT	INBRINGING	INCARNATED
IMPROVISATION	INACCESSIBLE	INAPPLICABILITY	INBRINGINGS	INCARNATES
IMPROVISATIONAL	INACCESSIBLY	INAPPLICABLE	INBURSTING	INCARNATING
IMPROVISATIONS	INACCURACIES	INAPPLICABLY	INCALCULABILITY	INCARNATION
IMPROVISATOR	INACCURACY	INAPPOSITE	INCALCULABLE	INCARNATIONS
IMPROVISATORE	INACCURATE	INAPPOSITELY	INCALCULABLY	INCARVILLEA
IMPROVISATORES	INACCURATELY	INAPPOSITENESS	INCALESCENCE	INCARVILLEAS
IMPROVISATORI	INACCURATENESS	INAPPRECIABLE	INCALESCENCES	INCASEMENT
IMPROVISATORIAL	INACTIVATE	INAPPRECIABLY	INCALESCENT	INCASEMENTS
IMPROVISATORS	INACTIVATED	INAPPRECIATION	INCANDESCE	INCATENATE
IMPROVISATORY	INACTIVATES	INAPPRECIATIONS	INCANDESCED	INCATENATED
IMPROVISATRICE	INACTIVATING	INAPPRECIATIVE	INCANDESCENCE	INCATENATES
IMPROVISATRICES	INACTIVATION	INAPPREHENSIBLE	INCANDESCENCES	INCATENATING
IMPROVISATRIX	INACTIVATIONS	INAPPREHENSION	INCANDESCENCIES	INCATENATION
IMPROVISATRIXES	INACTIVELY	INAPPREHENSIONS	INCANDESCENCY	INCATENATIONS
IMPROVISED	INACTIVENESS	INAPPREHENSIVE	INCANDESCENT	INCAUTIONS
IMPROVISER	INACTIVENESSES	INAPPROACHABLE	INCANDESCENTLY	INCAUTIOUS
IMPROVISERS	INACTIVITIES	INAPPROACHABLY	INCANDESCENTS	INCAUTIOUSLY
IMPROVISES	INACTIVITY	INAPPROPRIATE	INCANDESCES	INCAUTIOUSNESS
IMPROVISING	INADAPTABLE	INAPPROPRIATELY	INCANDESCING	INCEDINGLY
IMPROVISOR	INADAPTATION	INAPTITUDE	INCANTATION	INCENDIARIES
IMPROVISORS	INADAPTATIONS	INAPTITUDES	INCANTATIONAL	INCENDIARISM
IMPROVVISATORE	INADAPTIVE	INAPTNESSES	INCANTATIONS	INCENDIARISMS
IMPROVVISATORES	INADEQUACIES	INARGUABLE	INCANTATOR	INCENDIARY
IMPROVVISATRICE	INADEQUACY	INARGUABLY	INCANTATORS	INCENDIVITIES
IMPRUDENCE	INADEQUATE	INARTICULACIES	INCANTATORY	INCENDIVITY
IMPRUDENCES	INADEQUATELY	INARTICULACY	INCAPABILITIES	INCENSATION
IMPRUDENTLY	INADEQUATENESS	INARTICULATE	INCAPABILITY	INCENSATIONS
IMPSONITES	INADEQUATES	INARTICULATELY	INCAPABLENESS	INCENSEMENT
IMPUDENCES	INADMISSIBILITY	INARTICULATES	INCAPABLENESSES	INCENSEMENTS
IMPUDENCIES	INADMISSIBLE	INARTICULATION	INCAPABLES	INCENSORIES
IMPUDENTLY	INADMISSIBLY	INARTICULATIONS	INCAPACIOUS	INCENTIVELY
IMPUDENTNESS	INADVERTENCE	INARTIFICIAL	INCAPACIOUSNESS	INCENTIVES
IMPUDENTNESSES	INADVERTENCES	INARTIFICIALLY	INCAPACITANT	INCENTIVISATION
IMPUDICITIES	INADVERTENCIES	INARTISTIC	INCAPACITANTS	INCENTIVISE
IMPUDICITY	INADVERTENCY	INARTISTICALLY	INCAPACITATE	INCENTIVISED
IMPUGNABLE	INADVERTENT	INATTENTION	INCAPACITATED	INCENTIVISES
IMPUGNATION	INADVERTENTLY	INATTENTIONS	INCAPACITATES	INCENTIVISING
IMPUGNATIONS	INADVISABILITY	INATTENTIVE	INCAPACITATING	INCENTIVIZATION
IMPUGNMENT	INADVISABLE	INATTENTIVELY	INCAPACITATION	INCENTIVIZE
IMPUGNMENTS	INADVISABLENESS	INATTENTIVENESS	INCAPACITATIONS	INCENTIVIZED

INCENTIVIZES	INCLINATION	INCOMMUTABLE	INCONSECUTIVE	INCORPORABLE
INCENTIVIZING	INCLINATIONAL	INCOMMUTABLY	INCONSECUTIVELY	INCORPORAL
INCEPTIONS	INCLINATIONS	INCOMPARABILITY	INCONSEQUENCE	INCORPORALL
INCEPTIVELY	INCLINATORIA	INCOMPARABLE	INCONSEQUENCES	INCORPORATE
INCEPTIVES	INCLINATORIUM	INCOMPARABLY	INCONSEQUENT	INCORPORATED
INCERTAINTIES	INCLINATORY	INCOMPARED	INCONSEQUENTIAL	INCORPORATES
INCERTAINTY	INCLININGS	INCOMPATIBILITY	INCONSEQUENTLY	INCORPORATING
INCERTITUDE	INCLINOMETER	INCOMPATIBLE	INCONSIDERABLE	INCORPORATION
INCERTITUDES	INCLINOMETERS	INCOMPATIBLES	INCONSIDERABLY	INCORPORATIONS
INCESSANCIES	INCLIPPING	INCOMPATIBLY	INCONSIDERATE	INCORPORATIVE
INCESSANCY	INCLOSABLE	INCOMPETENCE	INCONSIDERATELY	INCORPORATOR
INCESSANTLY	INCLOSURES	INCOMPETENCES	INCONSIDERATION	INCORPORATORS
INCESSANTNESS	INCLUDABLE	INCOMPETENCIES	INCONSISTENCE	INCORPOREAL
INCESSANTNESSES	INCLUDEDNESS	INCOMPETENCY	INCONSISTENCES	INCORPOREALITY
INCESTUOUS	INCLUDEDNESSES	INCOMPETENT	INCONSISTENCIES	INCORPOREALLY
INCESTUOUSLY	INCLUDIBLE	INCOMPETENTLY	INCONSISTENCY	INCORPOREITIES
INCESTUOUSNESS	INCLUSIONS	INCOMPETENTS	INCONSISTENT	INCORPOREITY
INCHARITABLE	INCLUSIVELY	INCOMPLETE	INCONSISTENTLY	INCORPSING
INCHOATELY	INCLUSIVENESS	INCOMPLETELY	INCONSOLABILITY	INCORRECTLY
INCHOATENESS	INCLUSIVENESSES	INCOMPLETENESS	INCONSOLABLE	INCORRECTNESS
INCHOATENESSES	INCLUSIVITIES	INCOMPLETION	INCONSOLABLY	INCORRECTNESSES
INCHOATING	INCLUSIVITY	INCOMPLETIONS	INCONSONANCE	INCORRIGIBILITY
INCHOATION	INCOAGULABLE	INCOMPLIANCE	INCONSONANCES	INCORRIGIBLE
INCHOATIONS	INCOERCIBLE	INCOMPLIANCES	INCONSONANT	INCORRIGIBLES
INCHOATIVE	INCOGITABILITY	INCOMPLIANCIES	INCONSONANTLY	INCORRIGIBLY
INCHOATIVELY	INCOGITABLE	INCOMPLIANCY	INCONSPICUOUS	INCORRODIBLE
INCHOATIVES	INCOGITANCIES	INCOMPLIANT	INCONSPICUOUSLY	INCORROSIBLE
INCIDENCES	INCOGITANCY	INCOMPLIANTLY	INCONSTANCIES	INCORRUPTED
INCIDENTAL	INCOGITANT	INCOMPOSED	INCONSTANCY	INCORRUPTIBLE
INCIDENTALLY	INCOGITATIVE	INCOMPOSITE	INCONSTANT	INCORRUPTIBLES
INCIDENTALNESS	INCOGNISABLE	INCOMPOSSIBLE	INCONSTANTLY	INCORRUPTIBLY
INCIDENTALS	INCOGNISANCE	INCOMPREHENSION	INCONSTRUABLE	INCORRUPTION
INCINERATE	INCOGNISANCES	INCOMPREHENSIVE	INCONSUMABLE	INCORRUPTIONS
INCINERATED	INCOGNISANT	INCOMPRESSIBLE	INCONSUMABLY	INCORRUPTIVE
INCINERATES	INCOGNITAS	INCOMPRESSIBLY	INCONTESTABLE	INCORRUPTLY
INCINERATING	INCOGNITOS	INCOMPUTABILITY	INCONTESTABLY	INCORRUPTNESS
INCINERATION	INCOGNIZABLE	INCOMPUTABLE	INCONTIGUOUS	INCORRUPTNESSES
INCINERATIONS	INCOGNIZANCE	INCOMPUTABLY	INCONTIGUOUSLY	INCRASSATE
INCINERATOR	INCOGNIZANCES	INCOMUNICADO	INCONTINENCE	INCRASSATED
INCINERATORS	INCOGNIZANT	INCONCEIVABLE	INCONTINENCES	INCRASSATES
INCIPIENCE	INCOHERENCE	INCONCEIVABLES	INCONTINENCIES	INCRASSATING
INCIPIENCES	INCOHERENCES	INCONCEIVABLY	INCONTINENCY	INCRASSATION
INCIPIENCIES	INCOHERENCIES	INCONCINNITIES	INCONTINENT	INCRASSATIONS
INCIPIENCY	INCOHERENCY	INCONCINNITY	INCONTINENTLY	INCRASSATIVE
INCIPIENTLY	INCOHERENT	INCONCINNOUS	INCONTROLLABLE	INCRASSATIVES
INCISIFORM	INCOHERENTLY	INCONCLUSION	INCONTROLLABLY	INCREASABLE
INCISIVELY	INCOHERENTNESS	INCONCLUSIONS	INCONVENIENCE	INCREASEDLY
INCISIVENESS	INCOHESIVE	INCONCLUSIVE	INCONVENIENCED	INCREASEFUL
INCISIVENESSES	INCOMBUSTIBLE	INCONCLUSIVELY	INCONVENIENCES	INCREASERS
INCISORIAL	INCOMBUSTIBLES	INCONDENSABLE	INCONVENIENCIES	INCREASING
INCITATION	INCOMBUSTIBLY	INCONDENSIBLE	INCONVENIENCING	INCREASINGLY
INCITATIONS	INCOMMENSURABLE	INCONDITELY	INCONVENIENCY	INCREASINGS
INCITATIVE	INCOMMENSURABLY	INCONFORMITIES	INCONVENIENT	INCREATELY
INCITATIVES	INCOMMENSURATE	INCONFORMITY	INCONVENIENTLY	INCREDIBILITIES
INCITEMENT	INCOMMISCIBLE	INCONGRUENCE	INCONVERSABLE	INCREDIBILITY
INCITEMENTS	INCOMMODED	INCONGRUENCES	INCONVERSANT	INCREDIBLE
INCITINGLY	INCOMMODES	INCONGRUENT	INCONVERTIBLE	INCREDIBLENESS
INCIVILITIES	INCOMMODING	INCONGRUENTLY	INCONVERTIBLY	INCREDIBLY
INCIVILITY	INCOMMODIOUS	INCONGRUITIES	INCONVINCIBLE	INCREDULITIES
INCLASPING	INCOMMODIOUSLY	INCONGRUITY	INCONVINCIBLY	INCREDULITY
INCLEMENCIES	INCOMMODITIES	INCONGRUOUS	INCOORDINATE	INCREDULOUS
INCLEMENCY	INCOMMODITY	INCONGRUOUSLY	INCOORDINATION	INCREDULOUSLY
INCLEMENTLY	INCOMMUNICABLE	INCONGRUOUSNESS	INCOORDINATIONS	INCREDULOUSNESS
INCLEMENTNESS	INCOMMUNICABLY	INCONSCIENT	INCORONATE	INCREMATED
INCLEMENTNESSES	INCOMMUNICADO	INCONSCIENTLY	INCORONATED	INCREMATES
INCLINABLE	INCOMMUNICATIVE	INCONSCIONABLE	INCORONATION	INCREMATING
INCLINABLENESS	INCOMMUTABILITY	INCONSCIOUS	INCORONATIONS	INCREMATION

INCREMATIONS
INCREMENTAL
INCREMENTALISM
INCREMENTALISMS
INCREMENTALIST
INCREMENTALISTS
INCREMENTALLY
INCREMENTALS
INCREMENTED
INCREMENTING
INCREMENTS
INCRESCENT
INCRETIONARY
INCRETIONS
INCRIMINATE
INCRIMINATED
INCRIMINATES
INCRIMINATING
INCRIMINATION
INCRIMINATIONS
INCRIMINATOR
INCRIMINATORS
INCRIMINATORY
INCROSSBRED
INCROSSBREDS
INCROSSBREED
INCROSSBREEDING
INCROSSBREEDS
INCROSSING
INCRUSTANT
INCRUSTANTS
INCRUSTATION
INCRUSTATIONS
INCRUSTING
INCRUSTMENT
INCRUSTMENTS
INCUBATING
INCUBATION
INCUBATIONAL
INCUBATIONS
INCUBATIVE
INCUBATORS
INCUBATORY
INCULCATED
INCULCATES
INCULCATING
INCULCATION
INCULCATIONS
INCULCATIVE
INCULCATOR
INCULCATORS
INCULCATORY
INCULPABILITIES
INCULPABILITY
INCULPABLE
INCULPABLENESS
INCULPABLY
INCULPATED
INCULPATES
INCULPATING
INCULPATION
INCULPATIONS
INCULPATIVE
INCULPATORY
INCUMBENCIES
INCUMBENCY
INCUMBENTLY

INCUMBENTS
INCUMBERED
INCUMBERING
INCUMBERINGLY
INCUMBRANCE
INCUMBRANCER
INCUMBRANCERS
INCUMBRANCES
INCUNABLES
INCUNABULA
INCUNABULAR
INCUNABULIST
INCUNABULISTS
INCUNABULUM
INCURABILITIES
INCURABILITY
INCURABLENESS
INCURABLENESSES
INCURABLES
INCURIOSITIES
INCURIOSITY
INCURIOUSLY
INCURIOUSNESS
INCURIOUSNESSES
INCURRABLE
INCURRENCE
INCURRENCES
INCURSIONS
INCURVATED
INCURVATES
INCURVATING
INCURVATION
INCURVATIONS
INCURVATURE
INCURVATURES
INCURVITIES
INDAGATING
INDAGATION
INDAGATIONS
INDAGATIVE
INDAGATORS
INDAGATORY
INDAPAMIDE
INDAPAMIDES
INDEBTEDNESS
INDEBTEDNESSES
INDECENCIES
INDECENTER
INDECENTEST
INDECENTLY
INDECIDUATE
INDECIDUOUS
INDECIPHERABLE
INDECIPHERABLY
INDECISION
INDECISIONS
INDECISIVE
INDECISIVELY
INDECISIVENESS
INDECLINABLE
INDECLINABLY
INDECOMPOSABLE
INDECOROUS
INDECOROUSLY
INDECOROUSNESS
INDECORUMS
INDEFATIGABLE

INDEFATIGABLY
INDEFEASIBILITY
INDEFEASIBLE
INDEFEASIBLY
INDEFECTIBILITY
INDEFECTIBLE
INDEFECTIBLY
INDEFENSIBILITY
INDEFENSIBLE
INDEFENSIBLY
INDEFINABILITY
INDEFINABLE
INDEFINABLENESS
INDEFINABLES
INDEFINABLY
INDEFINITE
INDEFINITELY
INDEFINITENESS
INDEFINITES
INDEHISCENCE
INDEHISCENCES
INDEHISCENT
INDELIBILITIES
INDELIBILITY
INDELIBLENESS
INDELIBLENESSES
INDELICACIES
INDELICACY
INDELICATE
INDELICATELY
INDELICATENESS
INDEMNIFICATION
INDEMNIFIED
INDEMNIFIER
INDEMNIFIERS
INDEMNIFIES
INDEMNIFYING
INDEMNITIES
INDEMONSTRABLE
INDEMONSTRABLY
INDENTATION
INDENTATIONS
INDENTIONS
INDENTURED
INDENTURES
INDENTURESHIP
INDENTURESHIPS
INDENTURING
INDEPENDENCE
INDEPENDENCES
INDEPENDENCIES
INDEPENDENCY
INDEPENDENT
INDEPENDENTLY
INDEPENDENTS
INDESCRIBABLE
INDESCRIBABLES
INDESCRIBABLY
INDESIGNATE
INDESTRUCTIBLE
INDESTRUCTIBLY
INDETECTABLE
INDETECTIBLE
INDETERMINABLE
INDETERMINABLY
INDETERMINACIES
INDETERMINACY

INDETERMINATE
INDETERMINATELY
INDETERMINATION
INDETERMINED
INDETERMINISM
INDETERMINISMS
INDETERMINIST
INDETERMINISTIC
INDETERMINISTS
INDEXATION
INDEXATIONS
INDEXICALS
INDEXTERITIES
INDEXTERITY
INDEXTROUS
INDICATABLE
INDICATING
INDICATION
INDICATIONAL
INDICATIONS
INDICATIVE
INDICATIVELY
INDICATIVES
INDICATORS
INDICATORY
INDICOLITE
INDICOLITES
INDICTABLE
INDICTABLY
INDICTIONAL
INDICTIONS
INDICTMENT
INDICTMENTS
INDIFFERENCE
INDIFFERENCES
INDIFFERENCIES
INDIFFERENCY
INDIFFERENT
INDIFFERENTISM
INDIFFERENTISMS
INDIFFERENTIST
INDIFFERENTISTS
INDIFFERENTLY
INDIFFERENTS
INDIGENCES
INDIGENCIES
INDIGENISATION
INDIGENISATIONS
INDIGENISE
INDIGENISED
INDIGENISES
INDIGENISING
INDIGENITIES
INDIGENITY
INDIGENIZATION
INDIGENIZATIONS
INDIGENIZE
INDIGENIZED
INDIGENIZES
INDIGENIZING
INDIGENOUS
INDIGENOUSLY
INDIGENOUSNESS
INDIGENTLY
INDIGESTED
INDIGESTIBILITY
INDIGESTIBLE

INDIGESTIBLES
INDIGESTIBLY
INDIGESTING
INDIGESTION
INDIGESTIONS
INDIGESTIVE
INDIGNANCE
INDIGNANCES
INDIGNANTLY
INDIGNATION
INDIGNATIONS
INDIGNIFIED
INDIGNIFIES
INDIGNIFYING
INDIGNITIES
INDIGOLITE
INDIGOLITES
INDIGOTINS
INDINAVIRS
INDIRECTION
INDIRECTIONS
INDIRECTLY
INDIRECTNESS
INDIRECTNESSES
INDIRUBINS
INDISCERNIBLE
INDISCERNIBLY
INDISCERPTIBLE
INDISCIPLINABLE
INDISCIPLINE
INDISCIPLINED
INDISCIPLINES
INDISCOVERABLE
INDISCREET
INDISCREETER
INDISCREETEST
INDISCREETLY
INDISCREETNESS
INDISCRETE
INDISCRETELY
INDISCRETENESS
INDISCRETION
INDISCRETIONARY
INDISCRETIONS
INDISCRIMINATE
INDISPENSABLE
INDISPENSABLES
INDISPENSABLY
INDISPOSED
INDISPOSEDNESS
INDISPOSES
INDISPOSING
INDISPOSITION
INDISPOSITIONS
INDISPUTABILITY
INDISPUTABLE
INDISPUTABLY
INDISSOCIABLE
INDISSOCIABLY
INDISSOLUBILITY
INDISSOLUBLE
INDISSOLUBLY
INDISSOLVABLE
INDISSUADABLE
INDISSUADABLY
INDISTINCT
INDISTINCTION

INDISTINCTIONS	INDOMITABLE	INDUSTRIOUS	INELOQUENCES	INEXECUTABLE
INDISTINCTIVE	INDOMITABLENESS	INDUSTRIOUSLY	INELOQUENT	INEXECUTION
INDISTINCTIVELY	INDOMITABLY	INDUSTRIOUSNESS	INELOQUENTLY	INEXECUTIONS
INDISTINCTLY	INDOPHENOL	INDUSTRYWIDE	INELUCTABILITY	INEXHAUSTED
INDISTINCTNESS	INDOPHENOLS	INDWELLERS	INELUCTABLE	INEXHAUSTIBLE
INDISTRIBUTABLE	INDORSABLE	INDWELLING	INELUCTABLY	INEXHAUSTIBLY
INDITEMENT	INDORSATION	INDWELLINGS	INELUDIBILITIES	INEXHAUSTIVE
INDITEMENTS	INDORSATIONS	INEARTHING	INELUDIBILITY	INEXISTANT
INDIVERTIBLE	INDORSEMENT	INEBRIANTS	INELUDIBLE	INEXISTENCE
INDIVERTIBLY	INDORSEMENTS	INEBRIATED	INELUDIBLY	INEXISTENCES
INDIVIDABLE	INDRAUGHTS	INEBRIATES	INENARRABLE	INEXISTENCIES
INDIVIDUAL	INDRENCHED	INEBRIATING	INEPTITUDE	INEXISTENCY
INDIVIDUALISE	INDRENCHES	INEBRIATION	INEPTITUDES	INEXISTENT
INDIVIDUALISED	INDRENCHING	INEBRIATIONS	INEPTNESSES	INEXORABILITIES
INDIVIDUALISER	INDUBITABILITY	INEBRIETIES	INEQUALITIES	INEXORABILITY
INDIVIDUALISERS	INDUBITABLE	INEDIBILITIES	INEQUALITY	INEXORABLE
INDIVIDUALISES	INDUBITABLENESS	INEDIBILITY	INEQUATION	INEXORABLENESS
INDIVIDUALISING	INDUBITABLY	INEDUCABILITIES	INEQUATIONS	INEXORABLY
INDIVIDUALISM	INDUCEMENT	INEDUCABILITY	INEQUIPOTENT	INEXPANSIBLE
INDIVIDUALISMS	INDUCEMENTS	INEDUCABLE	INEQUITABLE	INEXPECTANCIES
INDIVIDUALIST	INDUCIBILITIES	INEFFABILITIES	INEQUITABLENESS	INEXPECTANCY
INDIVIDUALISTIC	INDUCIBILITY	INEFFABILITY	INEQUITABLY	INEXPECTANT
INDIVIDUALISTS	INDUCTANCE	INEFFABLENESS	INEQUITIES	INEXPECTATION
INDIVIDUALITIES	INDUCTANCES	INEFFABLENESSES	INEQUIVALVE	INEXPECTATIONS
INDIVIDUALITY	INDUCTILITIES	INEFFACEABILITY	INEQUIVALVED	INEXPEDIENCE
INDIVIDUALIZE	INDUCTILITY	INEFFACEABLE	INERADICABILITY	INEXPEDIENCES
INDIVIDUALIZED	INDUCTIONAL	INEFFACEABLY	INERADICABLE	INEXPEDIENCIES
INDIVIDUALIZER	INDUCTIONS	INEFFECTIVE	INERADICABLY	INEXPEDIENCY
INDIVIDUALIZERS	INDUCTIVELY	INEFFECTIVELY	INERASABLE	INEXPEDIENT
INDIVIDUALIZES	INDUCTIVENESS	INEFFECTIVENESS	INERASABLY	INEXPEDIENTLY
INDIVIDUALIZING	INDUCTIVENESSES	INEFFECTUAL	INERASIBLE	INEXPENSIVE
INDIVIDUALLY	INDUCTIVITIES	INEFFECTUALITY	INERASIBLY	INEXPENSIVELY
INDIVIDUALS	INDUCTIVITY	INEFFECTUALLY	INERRABILITIES	INEXPENSIVENESS
INDIVIDUATE	INDULGENCE	INEFFECTUALNESS	INERRABILITY	INEXPERIENCE
INDIVIDUATED	INDULGENCED	INEFFICACIES	INERRABLENESS	INEXPERIENCED
INDIVIDUATES	INDULGENCES	INEFFICACIOUS	INERRABLENESSES	INEXPERIENCES
INDIVIDUATING	INDULGENCIES	INEFFICACIOUSLY	INERRANCIES	INEXPERTLY
INDIVIDUATION	INDULGENCING	INEFFICACITIES	INERTIALLY	INEXPERTNESS
INDIVIDUATIONS	INDULGENCY	INEFFICACITY	INERTNESSES	INEXPERTNESSES
INDIVIDUATOR	INDULGENTLY	INEFFICACY	INESCAPABLE	INEXPIABLE
INDIVIDUATORS	INDULGINGLY	INEFFICIENCIES	INESCAPABLY	INEXPIABLENESS
INDIVIDUUM	INDUMENTUM	INEFFICIENCY	INESCULENT	INEXPIABLY
INDIVISIBILITY	INDUMENTUMS	INEFFICIENT	INESCUTCHEON	INEXPLAINABLE
INDIVISIBLE	INDUPLICATE	INEFFICIENTLY	INESCUTCHEONS	INEXPLAINABLY
INDIVISIBLENESS	INDUPLICATED	INEFFICIENTS	INESSENTIAL	INEXPLICABILITY
INDIVISIBLES	INDUPLICATION	INEGALITARIAN	INESSENTIALITY	INEXPLICABLE
INDIVISIBLY	INDUPLICATIONS	INEGALITARIANS	INESSENTIALS	INEXPLICABLY
INDOCILITIES	INDURATING	INELABORATE	INESTIMABILITY	INEXPLICIT
INDOCILITY	INDURATION	INELABORATED	INESTIMABLE	INEXPLICITLY
INDOCTRINATE	INDURATIONS	INELABORATELY	INESTIMABLENESS	INEXPLICITNESS
INDOCTRINATED	INDURATIVE	INELABORATES	INESTIMABLY	INEXPRESSIBLE
INDOCTRINATES	INDUSTRIAL	INELABORATING	INEVITABILITIES	INEXPRESSIBLES
INDOCTRINATING	INDUSTRIALISE	INELASTICALLY	INEVITABILITY	INEXPRESSIBLY
INDOCTRINATION	INDUSTRIALISED	INELASTICITIES	INEVITABLE	INEXPRESSIVE
INDOCTRINATIONS	INDUSTRIALISES	INELASTICITY	INEVITABLENESS	INEXPRESSIVELY
INDOCTRINATOR	INDUSTRIALISING	INELEGANCE	INEVITABLES	INEXPUGNABILITY
INDOCTRINATORS	INDUSTRIALISM	INELEGANCES	INEVITABLY	INEXPUGNABLE
INDOLEACETIC	INDUSTRIALISMS	INELEGANCIES	INEXACTITUDE	INEXPUGNABLY
INDOLEBUTYRIC	INDUSTRIALIST	INELEGANCY	INEXACTITUDES	INEXPUNGIBLE
INDOLENCES	INDUSTRIALISTS	INELEGANTLY	INEXACTNESS	INEXTENDED
INDOLENCIES	INDUSTRIALIZE	INELIGIBILITIES	INEXACTNESSES	INEXTENSIBILITY
INDOLENTLY	INDUSTRIALIZED	INELIGIBILITY	INEXCITABLE	INEXTENSIBLE
INDOMETACIN	INDUSTRIALIZES	INELIGIBLE	INEXCUSABILITY	INEXTENSION
INDOMETACINS	INDUSTRIALIZING	INELIGIBLENESS	INEXCUSABLE	INEXTENSIONS
INDOMETHACIN	INDUSTRIALLY	INELIGIBLES	INEXCUSABLENESS	INEXTIRPABLE
INDOMETHACINS	INDUSTRIALS	INELIGIBLY	INEXCUSABLY	INEXTRICABILITY
INDOMITABILITY	INDUSTRIES	INELOQUENCE	INEXECRABLE	INEXTRICABLE

INEXTRICABLY
INFALLIBILISM
INFALLIBILISMS
INFALLIBILIST
INFALLIBILISTS
INFALLIBILITIES
INFALLIBILITY
INFALLIBLE
INFALLIBLENESS
INFALLIBLES
INFALLIBLY
INFAMISING
INFAMIZING
INFAMONISE
INFAMONISED
INFAMONISES
INFAMONISING
INFAMONIZE
INFAMONIZED
INFAMONIZES
INFAMONIZING
INFAMOUSLY
INFAMOUSNESS
INFAMOUSNESSES
INFANGTHIEF
INFANGTHIEFS
INFANTEERS
INFANTHOOD
INFANTHOODS
INFANTICIDAL
INFANTICIDE
INFANTICIDES
INFANTILISATION
INFANTILISE
INFANTILISED
INFANTILISES
INFANTILISING
INFANTILISM
INFANTILISMS
INFANTILITIES
INFANTILITY
INFANTILIZATION
INFANTILIZE
INFANTILIZED
INFANTILIZES
INFANTILIZING
INFANTRIES
INFANTRYMAN
INFANTRYMEN
INFARCTION
INFARCTIONS
INFATUATED
INFATUATEDLY
INFATUATES
INFATUATING
INFATUATION
INFATUATIONS
INFEASIBILITIES
INFEASIBILITY
INFEASIBLE
INFEASIBLENESS
INFECTANTS
INFECTIONS
INFECTIOUS
INFECTIOUSLY
INFECTIOUSNESS
INFECTIVELY

INFECTIVENESS
INFECTIVENESSES
INFECTIVITIES
INFECTIVITY
INFECUNDITIES
INFECUNDITY
INFEFTMENT
INFEFTMENTS
INFELICITIES
INFELICITOUS
INFELICITOUSLY
INFELICITY
INFEOFFING
INFERENCES
INFERENCING
INFERENCINGS
INFERENTIAL
INFERENTIALLY
INFERIORITIES
INFERIORITY
INFERIORLY
INFERNALITIES
INFERNALITY
INFERNALLY
INFERRABLE
INFERRIBLE
INFERTILELY
INFERTILITIES
INFERTILITY
INFESTANTS
INFESTATION
INFESTATIONS
INFEUDATION
INFEUDATIONS
INFIBULATE
INFIBULATED
INFIBULATES
INFIBULATING
INFIBULATION
INFIBULATIONS
INFIDELITIES
INFIDELITY
INFIELDERS
INFIELDSMAN
INFIELDSMEN
INFIGHTERS
INFIGHTING
INFIGHTINGS
INFILLINGS
INFILTRATE
INFILTRATED
INFILTRATES
INFILTRATING
INFILTRATION
INFILTRATIONS
INFILTRATIVE
INFILTRATOR
INFILTRATORS
INFINITANT
INFINITARY
INFINITATE
INFINITATED
INFINITATES
INFINITATING
INFINITELY
INFINITENESS
INFINITENESSES

INFINITESIMAL
INFINITESIMALLY
INFINITESIMALS
INFINITIES
INFINITIVAL
INFINITIVALLY
INFINITIVE
INFINITIVELY
INFINITIVES
INFINITUDE
INFINITUDES
INFIRMARER
INFIRMARERS
INFIRMARIAN
INFIRMARIANS
INFIRMARIES
INFIRMITIES
INFIRMNESS
INFIRMNESSES
INFIXATION
INFIXATIONS
INFLAMABLE
INFLAMINGLY
INFLAMMABILITY
INFLAMMABLE
INFLAMMABLENESS
INFLAMMABLES
INFLAMMABLY
INFLAMMATION
INFLAMMATIONS
INFLAMMATORILY
INFLAMMATORY
INFLATABLE
INFLATABLES
INFLATEDLY
INFLATEDNESS
INFLATEDNESSES
INFLATINGLY
INFLATIONARY
INFLATIONISM
INFLATIONISMS
INFLATIONIST
INFLATIONISTS
INFLATIONS
INFLATUSES
INFLECTABLE
INFLECTEDNESS
INFLECTEDNESSES
INFLECTING
INFLECTION
INFLECTIONAL
INFLECTIONALLY
INFLECTIONLESS
INFLECTIONS
INFLECTIVE
INFLECTORS
INFLEXIBILITIES
INFLEXIBILITY
INFLEXIBLE
INFLEXIBLENESS
INFLEXIBLY
INFLEXIONAL
INFLEXIONALLY
INFLEXIONLESS
INFLEXIONS
INFLEXURES
INFLICTABLE

INFLICTERS
INFLICTING
INFLICTION
INFLICTIONS
INFLICTIVE
INFLICTORS
INFLORESCENCE
INFLORESCENCES
INFLORESCENT
INFLOWINGS
INFLUENCEABLE
INFLUENCED
INFLUENCER
INFLUENCERS
INFLUENCES
INFLUENCING
INFLUENTIAL
INFLUENTIALLY
INFLUENTIALS
INFLUENZAL
INFLUENZAS
INFLUXIONS
INFOGRAPHIC
INFOGRAPHICS
INFOLDINGS
INFOLDMENT
INFOLDMENTS
INFOMANIAS
INFOMERCIAL
INFOMERCIALS
INFOPRENEURIAL
INFORMABLE
INFORMALITIES
INFORMALITY
INFORMALLY
INFORMANTS
INFORMATICIAN
INFORMATICIANS
INFORMATICS
INFORMATION
INFORMATIONAL
INFORMATIONALLY
INFORMATIONS
INFORMATISATION
INFORMATISE
INFORMATISED
INFORMATISES
INFORMATISING
INFORMATIVE
INFORMATIVELY
INFORMATIVENESS
INFORMATIZATION
INFORMATIZE
INFORMATIZED
INFORMATIZES
INFORMATIZING
INFORMATORILY
INFORMATORY
INFORMEDLY
INFORMIDABLE
INFORMINGLY
INFORTUNES
INFOSPHERE
INFOSPHERES
INFOTAINMENT
INFOTAINMENTS
INFRACOSTAL

INFRACTING
INFRACTION
INFRACTIONS
INFRACTORS
INFRAGRANT
INFRAHUMAN
INFRAHUMANS
INFRALAPSARIAN
INFRALAPSARIANS
INFRAMAXILLARY
INFRANGIBILITY
INFRANGIBLE
INFRANGIBLENESS
INFRANGIBLY
INFRAORBITAL
INFRAPOSED
INFRAPOSITION
INFRAPOSITIONS
INFRASONIC
INFRASOUND
INFRASOUNDS
INFRASPECIFIC
INFRASTRUCTURAL
INFRASTRUCTURE
INFRASTRUCTURES
INFREQUENCE
INFREQUENCES
INFREQUENCIES
INFREQUENCY
INFREQUENT
INFREQUENTLY
INFRINGEMENT
INFRINGEMENTS
INFRINGERS
INFRINGING
INFRUCTUOUS
INFRUCTUOUSLY
INFUNDIBULA
INFUNDIBULAR
INFUNDIBULATE
INFUNDIBULIFORM
INFUNDIBULUM
INFURIATED
INFURIATELY
INFURIATES
INFURIATING
INFURIATINGLY
INFURIATION
INFURIATIONS
INFUSCATED
INFUSIBILITIES
INFUSIBILITY
INFUSIBLENESS
INFUSIBLENESSES
INFUSIONISM
INFUSIONISMS
INFUSIONIST
INFUSIONISTS
INFUSORIAL
INFUSORIAN
INFUSORIANS
INFUSORIES
INGATHERED
INGATHERER
INGATHERERS
INGATHERING
INGATHERINGS

i

INGEMINATE	INGURGITATED	INHOSPITALITIES	INJOINTING	INNUMERABLENESS
INGEMINATED	INGURGITATES	INHOSPITALITY	INJUDICIAL	INNUMERABLY
INGEMINATES	INGURGITATING	INHUMANELY	INJUDICIALLY	INNUMERACIES
INGEMINATING	INGURGITATION	INHUMANEST	INJUDICIOUS	INNUMERACY
INGEMINATION	INGURGITATIONS	INHUMANITIES	INJUDICIOUSLY	INNUMERATE
INGEMINATIONS	INHABITABILITY	INHUMANITY	INJUDICIOUSNESS	INNUMERATES
INGENERATE	INHABITABLE	INHUMANNESS	INJUNCTING	INNUMEROUS
INGENERATED	INHABITANCE	INHUMANNESSES	INJUNCTION	INNUTRIENT
INGENERATES	INHABITANCES	INHUMATING	INJUNCTIONS	INNUTRITION
INGENERATING	INHABITANCIES	INHUMATION	INJUNCTIVE	INNUTRITIONS
INGENERATION	INHABITANCY	INHUMATIONS	INJUNCTIVELY	INNUTRITIOUS
INGENERATIONS	INHABITANT	INIMICALITIES	INJURIOUSLY	INOBEDIENCE
INGENIOUSLY	INHABITANTS	INIMICALITY	INJURIOUSNESS	INOBEDIENCES
INGENIOUSNESS	INHABITATION	INIMICALLY	INJURIOUSNESSES	INOBEDIENT
INGENIOUSNESSES	INHABITATIONS	INIMICALNESS	INJUSTICES	INOBEDIENTLY
INGENUITIES	INHABITERS	INIMICALNESSES	INKBERRIES	INOBSERVABLE
INGENUOUSLY	INHABITING	INIMICITIOUS	INKHOLDERS	INOBSERVANCE
INGENUOUSNESS	INHABITIVENESS	INIMITABILITIES	INKINESSES	INOBSERVANCES
INGENUOUSNESSES	INHABITORS	INIMITABILITY	INMARRIAGE	INOBSERVANT
INGESTIBLE	INHABITRESS	INIMITABLE	INMARRIAGES	INOBSERVANTLY
INGESTIONS	INHABITRESSES	INIMITABLENESS	INMIGRANTS	INOBSERVATION
INGLENEUKS	INHALATION	INIMITABLY	INNATENESS	INOBSERVATIONS
INGLENOOKS	INHALATIONAL	INIQUITIES	INNATENESSES	INOBTRUSIVE
INGLORIOUS	INHALATIONS	INIQUITOUS	INNAVIGABLE	INOBTRUSIVELY
INGLORIOUSLY	INHALATORIUM	INIQUITOUSLY	INNAVIGABLY	INOBTRUSIVENESS
INGLORIOUSNESS	INHALATORIUMS	INIQUITOUSNESS	INNERMOSTS	INOCCUPATION
INGRAFTATION	INHALATORS	INITIALERS	INNERNESSES	INOCCUPATIONS
INGRAFTATIONS	INHARMONIC	INITIALING	INNERSOLES	INOCULABILITIES
INGRAFTING	INHARMONICAL	INITIALISATION	INNERSPRING	INOCULABILITY
INGRAFTMENT	INHARMONICITIES	INITIALISATIONS	INNERVATED	INOCULABLE
INGRAFTMENTS	INHARMONICITY	INITIALISE	INNERVATES	INOCULANTS
INGRAINEDLY	INHARMONIES	INITIALISED	INNERVATING	INOCULATED
INGRAINEDNESS	INHARMONIOUS	INITIALISES	INNERVATION	INOCULATES
INGRAINEDNESSES	INHARMONIOUSLY	INITIALISING	INNERVATIONS	INOCULATING
INGRAINERS	INHAUSTING	INITIALISM	INNERWEARS	INOCULATION
INGRAINING	INHEARSING	INITIALISMS	INNKEEPERS	INOCULATIONS
INGRATEFUL	INHERENCES	INITIALIZATION	INNOCENCES	INOCULATIVE
INGRATIATE	INHERENCIES	INITIALIZATIONS	INNOCENCIES	INOCULATOR
INGRATIATED	INHERENTLY	INITIALIZE	INNOCENTER	INOCULATORS
INGRATIATES	INHERITABILITY	INITIALIZED	INNOCENTEST	INOCULATORY
INGRATIATING	INHERITABLE	INITIALIZES	INNOCENTLY	INODOROUSLY
INGRATIATINGLY	INHERITABLENESS	INITIALIZING	INNOCUITIES	INODOROUSNESS
INGRATIATION	INHERITABLY	INITIALLED	INNOCUOUSLY	INODOROUSNESSES
INGRATIATIONS	INHERITANCE	INITIALLER	INNOCUOUSNESS	INOFFENSIVE
INGRATIATORY	INHERITANCES	INITIALLERS	INNOCUOUSNESSES	INOFFENSIVELY
INGRATITUDE	INHERITING	INITIALLING	INNOMINABLE	INOFFENSIVENESS
INGRATITUDES	INHERITORS	INITIALNESS	INNOMINABLES	INOFFICIOUS
INGRAVESCENCE	INHERITRESS	INITIALNESSES	INNOMINATE	INOFFICIOUSLY
INGRAVESCENCES	INHERITRESSES	INITIATING	INNOVATING	INOFFICIOUSNESS
INGRAVESCENT	INHERITRICES	INITIATION	INNOVATION	INOPERABILITIES
INGREDIENT	INHERITRIX	INITIATIONS	INNOVATIONAL	INOPERABILITY
INGREDIENTS	INHERITRIXES	INITIATIVE	INNOVATIONIST	INOPERABLE
INGRESSION	INHIBITABLE	INITIATIVELY	INNOVATIONISTS	INOPERABLENESS
INGRESSIONS	INHIBITEDLY	INITIATIVES	INNOVATIONS	INOPERABLY
INGRESSIVE	INHIBITERS	INITIATORIES	INNOVATIVE	INOPERATIVE
INGRESSIVENESS	INHIBITING	INITIATORS	INNOVATIVELY	INOPERATIVENESS
INGRESSIVES	INHIBITION	INITIATORY	INNOVATIVENESS	INOPERCULATE
INGROOVING	INHIBITIONS	INITIATRESS	INNOVATORS	INOPERCULATES
INGROSSING	INHIBITIVE	INITIATRESSES	INNOVATORY	INOPPORTUNE
INGROUNDED	INHIBITORS	INITIATRICES	INNOXIOUSLY	INOPPORTUNELY
INGROUNDING	INHIBITORY	INITIATRIX	INNOXIOUSNESS	INOPPORTUNENESS
INGROWNNESS	INHOLDINGS	INITIATRIXES	INNOXIOUSNESSES	INOPPORTUNITIES
INGROWNNESSES	INHOMOGENEITIES	INJECTABLE	INNUENDOED	INOPPORTUNITY
INGULFMENT	INHOMOGENEITY	INJECTABLES	INNUENDOES	INORDINACIES
INGULFMENTS	INHOMOGENEOUS	INJECTANTS	INNUENDOING	INORDINACY
INGULPHING	INHOSPITABLE	INJECTIONS	INNUMERABILITY	INORDINATE
INGURGITATE	INHOSPITABLY	INJELLYING	INNUMERABLE	INORDINATELY

INORDINATENESS	INSALUBRITIES	INSELBERGS	INSINUATED	INSOULMENT
INORDINATION	INSALUBRITY	INSEMINATE	INSINUATES	INSOULMENTS
INORDINATIONS	INSALUTARY	INSEMINATED	INSINUATING	INSOURCING
INORGANICALLY	INSANENESS	INSEMINATES	INSINUATINGLY	INSOURCINGS
INORGANICS	INSANENESSES	INSEMINATING	INSINUATION	INSPANNING
INORGANISATION	INSANITARINESS	INSEMINATION	INSINUATIONS	INSPECTABLE
INORGANISATIONS	INSANITARY	INSEMINATIONS	INSINUATIVE	INSPECTING
INORGANISED	INSANITATION	INSEMINATOR	INSINUATOR	INSPECTINGLY
INORGANIZATION	INSANITATIONS	INSEMINATORS	INSINUATORS	INSPECTION
INORGANIZATIONS	INSANITIES	INSENSATELY	INSINUATORY	INSPECTIONAL
INORGANIZED	INSATIABILITIES	INSENSATENESS	INSIPIDEST	INSPECTIONS
INOSCULATE	INSATIABILITY	INSENSATENESSES	INSIPIDITIES	INSPECTIVE
INOSCULATED	INSATIABLE	INSENSIBILITIES	INSIPIDITY	INSPECTORAL
INOSCULATES	INSATIABLENESS	INSENSIBILITY	INSIPIDNESS	INSPECTORATE
INOSCULATING	INSATIABLY	INSENSIBLE	INSIPIDNESSES	INSPECTORATES
INOSCULATION	INSATIATELY	INSENSIBLENESS	INSIPIENCE	INSPECTORIAL
INOSCULATIONS	INSATIATENESS	INSENSIBLY	INSIPIENCES	INSPECTORS
INOSILICATE	INSATIATENESSES	INSENSITIVE	INSIPIENTLY	INSPECTORSHIP
INOSILICATES	INSATIETIES	INSENSITIVELY	INSISTENCE	INSPECTORSHIPS
INPATIENTS	INSCIENCES	INSENSITIVENESS	INSISTENCES	INSPHERING
INPAYMENTS	INSCONCING	INSENSITIVITIES	INSISTENCIES	INSPIRABLE
INPOURINGS	INSCRIBABLE	INSENSITIVITY	INSISTENCY	INSPIRATION
INQUIETING	INSCRIBABLENESS	INSENSUOUS	INSISTENTLY	INSPIRATIONAL
INQUIETUDE	INSCRIBERS	INSENTIENCE	INSISTINGLY	INSPIRATIONALLY
INQUIETUDES	INSCRIBING	INSENTIENCES	INSNAREMENT	INSPIRATIONISM
INQUILINES	INSCRIPTION	INSENTIENCIES	INSNAREMENTS	INSPIRATIONISMS
INQUILINIC	INSCRIPTIONAL	INSENTIENCY	INSOBRIETIES	INSPIRATIONIST
INQUILINICS	INSCRIPTIONS	INSENTIENT	INSOBRIETY	INSPIRATIONISTS
INQUILINISM	INSCRIPTIVE	INSEPARABILITY	INSOCIABILITIES	INSPIRATIONS
INQUILINISMS	INSCRIPTIVELY	INSEPARABLE	INSOCIABILITY	INSPIRATIVE
INQUILINITIES	INSCROLLED	INSEPARABLENESS	INSOCIABLE	INSPIRATOR
INQUILINITY	INSCROLLING	INSEPARABLES	INSOCIABLY	INSPIRATORS
INQUILINOUS	INSCRUTABILITY	INSEPARABLY	INSOLATING	INSPIRATORY
INQUINATED	INSCRUTABLE	INSEPARATE	INSOLATION	INSPIRINGLY
INQUINATES	INSCRUTABLENESS	INSERTABLE	INSOLATIONS	INSPIRITED
INQUINATING	INSCRUTABLY	INSERTIONAL	INSOLENCES	INSPIRITER
INQUINATION	INSCULPING	INSERTIONS	INSOLENTLY	INSPIRITERS
INQUINATIONS	INSCULPTURE	INSESSORIAL	INSOLIDITIES	INSPIRITING
INQUIRATION	INSCULPTURED	INSEVERABLE	INSOLIDITY	INSPIRITINGLY
INQUIRATIONS	INSCULPTURES	INSHEATHED	INSOLUBILISE	INSPIRITMENT
INQUIRENDO	INSCULPTURING	INSHEATHES	INSOLUBILISED	INSPIRITMENTS
INQUIRENDOS	INSECTARIA	INSHEATHING	INSOLUBILISES	INSPISSATE
INQUIRINGLY	INSECTARIES	INSHELLING	INSOLUBILISING	INSPISSATED
INQUIRITION	INSECTARIUM	INSHELTERED	INSOLUBILITIES	INSPISSATES
INQUISITION	INSECTARIUMS	INSHELTERING	INSOLUBILITY	INSPISSATING
INQUISITIONAL	INSECTICIDAL	INSHELTERS	INSOLUBILIZE	INSPISSATION
INQUISITIONIST	INSECTICIDALLY	INSHIPPING	INSOLUBILIZED	INSPISSATIONS
INQUISITIONISTS	INSECTICIDE	INSHRINEMENT	INSOLUBILIZES	INSPISSATOR
INQUISITIONS	INSECTICIDES	INSHRINEMENTS	INSOLUBILIZING	INSPISSATORS
INQUISITIVE	INSECTIFORM	INSHRINING	INSOLUBLENESS	INSTABILITIES
INQUISITIVELY	INSECTIFUGE	INSIDIOUSLY	INSOLUBLENESSES	INSTABILITY
INQUISITIVENESS	INSECTIFUGES	INSIDIOUSNESS	INSOLUBLES	INSTAGRAMMED
INQUISITOR	INSECTIONS	INSIDIOUSNESSES	INSOLVABILITIES	INSTAGRAMMING
INQUISITORIAL	INSECTIVORE	INSIGHTFUL	INSOLVABILITY	INSTAGRAMS
INQUISITORIALLY	INSECTIVORES	INSIGHTFULLY	INSOLVABLE	INSTALLANT
INQUISITORS	INSECTIVOROUS	INSIGNIFICANCE	INSOLVABLY	INSTALLANTS
INQUISITRESS	INSECTOLOGIES	INSIGNIFICANCES	INSOLVENCIES	INSTALLATION
INQUISITRESSES	INSECTOLOGIST	INSIGNIFICANCY	INSOLVENCY	INSTALLATIONS
INQUISITURIENT	INSECTOLOGISTS	INSIGNIFICANT	INSOLVENTS	INSTALLERS
INRUSHINGS	INSECTOLOGY	INSIGNIFICANTLY	INSOMNIACS	INSTALLING
INSALIVATE	INSECURELY	INSIGNIFICATIVE	INSOMNIOUS	INSTALLMENT
INSALIVATED	INSECURENESS	INSINCERELY	INSOMNOLENCE	INSTALLMENTS
INSALIVATES	INSECURENESSES	INSINCERER	INSOMNOLENCES	INSTALMENT
INSALIVATING	INSECUREST	INSINCEREST	INSOUCIANCE	INSTALMENTS
INSALIVATION	INSECURITIES	INSINCERITIES	INSOUCIANCES	INSTANCIES
INSALIVATIONS	INSECURITY	INSINCERITY	INSOUCIANT	INSTANCING
INSALUBRIOUS	INSELBERGE	INSINEWING	INSOUCIANTLY	INSTANTANEITIES

i

INSTANTANEITY	INSTRUCTION	INSUPPORTABLY	INTELLECTIVELY	INTENSIONALITY
INSTANTANEOUS	INSTRUCTIONAL	INSUPPRESSIBLE	INTELLECTS	INTENSIONALLY
INSTANTANEOUSLY	INSTRUCTIONS	INSUPPRESSIBLY	INTELLECTUAL	INTENSIONS
INSTANTIAL	INSTRUCTIVE	INSURABILITIES	INTELLECTUALISE	INTENSITIES
INSTANTIATE	INSTRUCTIVELY	INSURABILITY	INTELLECTUALISM	INTENSITTVE
INSTANTIATED	INSTRUCTIVENESS	INSURANCER	INTELLECTUALIST	INTENSITIVES
INSTANTIATES	INSTRUCTOR	INSURANCERS	INTELLECTUALITY	INTENSIVELY
INSTANTIATING	INSTRUCTORS	INSURANCES	INTELLECTUALIZE	INTENSIVENESS
INSTANTIATION	INSTRUCTORSHIP	INSURGENCE	INTELLECTUALLY	INTENSIVENESSES
INSTANTIATIONS	INSTRUCTORSHIPS	INSURGENCES	INTELLECTUALS	INTENSIVES
INSTANTNESS	INSTRUCTRESS	INSURGENCIES	INTELLIGENCE	INTENTIONAL
INSTANTNESSES	INSTRUCTRESSES	INSURGENCY	INTELLIGENCER	INTENTIONALITY
INSTARRING	INSTRUMENT	INSURGENTLY	INTELLIGENCERS	INTENTIONALLY
INSTATEMENT	INSTRUMENTAL	INSURGENTS	INTELLIGENCES	INTENTIONED
INSTATEMENTS	INSTRUMENTALISM	INSURMOUNTABLE	INTELLIGENT	INTENTIONS
INSTAURATION	INSTRUMENTALIST	INSURMOUNTABLY	INTELLIGENTIAL	INTENTNESS
INSTAURATIONS	INSTRUMENTALITY	INSURRECTION	INTELLIGENTLY	INTENTNESSES
INSTAURATOR	INSTRUMENTALLY	INSURRECTIONAL	INTELLIGENTSIA	INTERABANG
INSTAURATORS	INSTRUMENTALS	INSURRECTIONARY	INTELLIGENTSIAS	INTERABANGS
INSTIGATED	INSTRUMENTATION	INSURRECTIONISM	INTELLIGENTZIA	INTERACTANT
INSTIGATES	INSTRUMENTED	INSURRECTIONIST	INTELLIGENTZIAS	INTERACTANTS
INSTIGATING	INSTRUMENTING	INSURRECTIONS	INTELLIGIBILITY	INTERACTED
INSTIGATINGLY	INSTRUMENTS	INSUSCEPTIBLE	INTELLIGIBLE	INTERACTING
INSTIGATION	INSUBJECTION	INSUSCEPTIBLY	INTELLIGIBLY	INTERACTION
INSTIGATIONS	INSUBJECTIONS	INSUSCEPTIVE	INTEMERATE	INTERACTIONAL
INSTIGATIVE	INSUBORDINATE	INSUSCEPTIVELY	INTEMERATELY	INTERACTIONISM
INSTIGATOR	INSUBORDINATELY	INSWATHING	INTEMERATENESS	INTERACTIONISMS
INSTIGATORS	INSUBORDINATES	INSWINGERS	INTEMPERANCE	INTERACTIONIST
INSTILLATION	INSUBORDINATION	INTACTNESS	INTEMPERANCES	INTERACTIONISTS
INSTILLATIONS	INSUBSTANTIAL	INTACTNESSES	INTEMPERANT	INTERACTIONS
INSTILLERS	INSUBSTANTIALLY	INTAGLIATED	INTEMPERANTS	INTERACTIVE
INSTILLING	INSUFFERABLE	INTAGLIOED	INTEMPERATE	INTERACTIVELY
INSTILLMENT	INSUFFERABLY	INTAGLIOES	INTEMPERATELY	INTERACTIVITIES
INSTILLMENTS	INSUFFICIENCE	INTAGLIOING	INTEMPERATENESS	INTERACTIVITY
INSTILMENT	INSUFFICIENCES	INTANGIBILITIES	INTEMPESTIVE	INTERAGENCY
INSTILMENTS	INSUFFICIENCIES	INTANGIBILITY	INTEMPESTIVELY	INTERALLELIC
INSTINCTIVE	INSUFFICIENCY	INTANGIBLE	INTEMPESTIVITY	INTERALLIED
INSTINCTIVELY	INSUFFICIENT	INTANGIBLENESS	INTENDANCE	INTERAMBULACRA
INSTINCTIVITIES	INSUFFICIENTLY	INTANGIBLES	INTENDANCES	INTERAMBULACRAL
INSTINCTIVITY	INSUFFLATE	INTANGIBLY	INTENDANCIES	INTERAMBULACRUM
INSTINCTUAL	INSUFFLATED	INTEGRABILITIES	INTENDANCY	INTERANIMATION
INSTINCTUALLY	INSUFFLATES	INTEGRABILITY	INTENDANTS	INTERANIMATIONS
INSTITORIAL	INSUFFLATING	INTEGRABLE	INTENDEDLY	INTERANNUAL
INSTITUTED	INSUFFLATION	INTEGRALITIES	INTENDERED	INTERARCHED
INSTITUTER	INSUFFLATIONS	INTEGRALITY	INTENDERING	INTERARCHES
INSTITUTERS	INSUFFLATOR	INTEGRALLY	INTENDMENT	INTERARCHING
INSTITUTES	INSUFFLATORS	INTEGRANDS	INTENDMENTS	INTERATOMIC
INSTITUTING	INSULARISM	INTEGRANTS	INTENERATE	INTERBASIN
INSTITUTION	INSULARISMS	INTEGRATED	INTENERATED	INTERBEDDED
INSTITUTIONAL	INSULARITIES	INTEGRATES	INTENERATES	INTERBEDDING
INSTITUTIONALLY	INSULARITY	INTEGRATING	INTENERATING	INTERBEDDINGS
INSTITUTIONARY	INSULATING	INTEGRATION	INTENERATION	INTERBEHAVIOR
INSTITUTIONS	INSULATION	INTEGRATIONIST	INTENERATIONS	INTERBEHAVIORAL
INSTITUTIST	INSULATIONS	INTEGRATIONISTS	INTENSATED	INTERBEHAVIORS
INSTITUTISTS	INSULATORS	INTEGRATIONS	INTENSATES	INTERBEHAVIOUR
INSTITUTIVE	INSULINASE	INTEGRATIVE	INTENSATING	INTERBEHAVIOURS
INSTITUTIVELY	INSULINASES	INTEGRATOR	INTENSATIVE	INTERBLEND
INSTITUTOR	INSULSITIES	INTEGRATORS	INTENSATIVES	INTERBLENDED
INSTITUTORS	INSULTABLE	INTEGRITIES	INTENSENESS	INTERBLENDING
INSTREAMING	INSULTINGLY	INTEGUMENT	INTENSENESSES	INTERBLENDS
INSTREAMINGS	INSULTMENT	INTEGUMENTAL	INTENSIFICATION	INTERBOROUGH
INSTRESSED	INSULTMENTS	INTEGUMENTARY	INTENSIFIED	INTERBRAIN
INSTRESSES	INSUPERABILITY	INTEGUMENTS	INTENSIFIER	INTERBRAINS
INSTRESSING	INSUPERABLE	INTELLECTED	INTENSIFIERS	INTERBRANCH
INSTRUCTED	INSUPERABLENESS	INTELLECTION	INTENSIFIES	INTERBREED
INSTRUCTIBLE	INSUPERABLY	INTELLECTIONS	INTENSIFYING	INTERBREEDING
INSTRUCTING	INSUPPORTABLE	INTELLECTIVE	INTENSIONAL	INTERBREEDINGS

INTERBREEDS	INTERCLUSIONS	INTERCURRENCE	INTERFACES	INTERGRADE
INTERBROKER	INTERCLUSTER	INTERCURRENCES	INTERFACIAL	INTERGRADED
INTERCALAR	INTERCOASTAL	INTERCURRENT	INTERFACIALLY	INTERGRADES
INTERCALARILY	INTERCOLLEGIATE	INTERCURRENTLY	INTERFACING	INTERGRADIENT
INTERCALARY	INTERCOLLINE	INTERCURRENTS	INTERFACINGS	INTERGRADING
INTERCALATE	INTERCOLONIAL	INTERCUTTING	INTERFACULTY	INTERGRAFT
INTERCALATED	INTERCOLONIALLY	INTERDASHED	INTERFAITH	INTERGRAFTED
INTERCALATES	INTERCOLUMNAR	INTERDASHES	INTERFAMILIAL	INTERGRAFTING
INTERCALATING	INTERCOMMUNAL	INTERDASHING	INTERFAMILY	INTERGRAFTS
INTERCALATION	INTERCOMMUNE	INTERDEALER	INTERFASCICULAR	INTERGRANULAR
INTERCALATIONS	INTERCOMMUNED	INTERDEALERS	INTERFEMORAL	INTERGROUP
INTERCALATIVE	INTERCOMMUNES	INTERDEALING	INTERFERED	INTERGROUPS
INTERCAMPUS	INTERCOMMUNING	INTERDEALS	INTERFERENCE	INTERGROWING
INTERCASTE	INTERCOMMUNION	INTERDEALT	INTERFERENCES	INTERGROWN
INTERCEDED	INTERCOMMUNIONS	INTERDENTAL	INTERFERENTIAL	INTERGROWS
INTERCEDENT	INTERCOMMUNITY	INTERDENTALLY	INTERFERER	INTERGROWTH
INTERCEDER	INTERCOMPANY	INTERDEPEND	INTERFERERS	INTERGROWTHS
INTERCEDERS	INTERCOMPARE	INTERDEPENDED	INTERFERES	INTERINDIVIDUAL
INTERCEDES	INTERCOMPARED	INTERDEPENDENCE	INTERFERING	INTERINDUSTRY
INTERCEDING	INTERCOMPARES	INTERDEPENDENCY	INTERFERINGLY	INTERINFLUENCE
INTERCELLULAR	INTERCOMPARING	INTERDEPENDENT	INTERFEROGRAM	INTERINFLUENCED
INTERCENSAL	INTERCOMPARISON	INTERDEPENDING	INTERFEROGRAMS	INTERINFLUENCES
INTERCEPTED	INTERCONNECT	INTERDEPENDS	INTERFEROMETER	INTERINVOLVE
INTERCEPTER	INTERCONNECTED	INTERDIALECTAL	INTERFEROMETERS	INTERINVOLVED
INTERCEPTERS	INTERCONNECTING	INTERDICTED	INTERFEROMETRIC	INTERINVOLVES
INTERCEPTING	INTERCONNECTION	INTERDICTING	INTERFEROMETRY	INTERINVOLVING
INTERCEPTION	INTERCONNECTOR	INTERDICTION	INTERFERON	INTERIONIC
INTERCEPTIONS	INTERCONNECTORS	INTERDICTIONS	INTERFERONS	INTERIORISATION
INTERCEPTIVE	INTERCONNECTS	INTERDICTIVE	INTERFERTILE	INTERIORISE
INTERCEPTOR	INTERCONNEXION	INTERDICTIVELY	INTERFERTILITY	INTERIORISED
INTERCEPTORS	INTERCONNEXIONS	INTERDICTOR	INTERFIBER	INTERIORISES
INTERCEPTS	INTERCONVERSION	INTERDICTORS	INTERFIBRE	INTERIORISING
INTERCESSION	INTERCONVERT	INTERDICTORY	INTERFILED	INTERIORITIES
INTERCESSIONAL	INTERCONVERTED	INTERDICTS	INTERFILES	INTERIORITY
INTERCESSIONS	INTERCONVERTING	INTERDIFFUSE	INTERFILING	INTERIORIZATION
INTERCESSOR	INTERCONVERTS	INTERDIFFUSED	INTERFLOWED	INTERIORIZE
INTERCESSORIAL	INTERCOOLED	INTERDIFFUSES	INTERFLOWING	INTERIORIZED
INTERCESSORS	INTERCOOLER	INTERDIFFUSING	INTERFLOWS	INTERIORIZES
INTERCESSORY	INTERCOOLERS	INTERDIFFUSION	INTERFLUENCE	INTERIORIZING
INTERCHAIN	INTERCOOLING	INTERDIFFUSIONS	INTERFLUENCES	INTERIORLY
INTERCHAINED	INTERCOOLS	INTERDIGITAL	INTERFLUENT	INTERISLAND
INTERCHAINING	INTERCORPORATE	INTERDIGITATE	INTERFLUOUS	INTERJACENCIES
INTERCHAINS	INTERCORRELATE	INTERDIGITATED	INTERFLUVE	INTERJACENCY
INTERCHANGE	INTERCORRELATED	INTERDIGITATES	INTERFLUVES	INTERJACENT
INTERCHANGEABLE	INTERCORRELATES	INTERDIGITATING	INTERFLUVIAL	INTERJACULATE
INTERCHANGEABLY	INTERCORTICAL	INTERDIGITATION	INTERFOLDED	INTERJACULATED
INTERCHANGED	INTERCOSTAL	INTERDINED	INTERFOLDING	INTERJACULATES
INTERCHANGEMENT	INTERCOSTALLY	INTERDINES	INTERFOLDS	INTERJACULATING
INTERCHANGER	INTERCOSTALS	INTERDINING	INTERFOLIATE	INTERJACULATORY
INTERCHANGERS	INTERCOUNTRY	INTERDISTRICT	INTERFOLIATED	INTERJECTED
INTERCHANGES	INTERCOUNTY	INTERDIVISIONAL	INTERFOLIATES	INTERJECTING
INTERCHANGING	INTERCOUPLE	INTERDOMINION	INTERFOLIATING	INTERJECTION
INTERCHANNEL	INTERCOURSE	INTERELECTRODE	INTERFRATERNITY	INTERJECTIONAL
INTERCHAPTER	INTERCOURSES	INTERELECTRON	INTERFRETTED	INTERJECTIONARY
INTERCHAPTERS	INTERCRATER	INTERELECTRONIC	INTERFRONTAL	INTERJECTIONS
INTERCHURCH	INTERCROPPED	INTEREPIDEMIC	INTERFUSED	INTERJECTOR
INTERCIPIENT	INTERCROPPING	INTERESSED	INTERFUSES	INTERJECTORS
INTERCIPIENTS	INTERCROPS	INTERESSES	INTERFUSING	INTERJECTORY
INTERCLASS	INTERCROSS	INTERESSING	INTERFUSION	INTERJECTS
INTERCLAVICLE	INTERCROSSED	INTERESTED	INTERFUSIONS	INTERJECTURAL
INTERCLAVICLES	INTERCROSSES	INTERESTEDLY	INTERGALACTIC	INTERJOINED
INTERCLAVICULAR	INTERCROSSING	INTERESTEDNESS	INTERGENERATION	INTERJOINING
INTERCLUDE	INTERCRURAL	INTERESTING	INTERGENERIC	INTERJOINS
INTERCLUDED	INTERCULTURAL	INTERESTINGLY	INTERGLACIAL	INTERKINESES
INTERCLUDES	INTERCULTURALLY	INTERESTINGNESS	INTERGLACIALS	INTERKINESIS
INTERCLUDING	INTERCULTURE	INTERETHNIC	INTERGRADATION	INTERKNITS
INTERCLUSION	INTERCULTURES	INTERFACED	INTERGRADATIONS	INTERKNITTED

INTERKNITTING	INTERLOCKER	INTERMEDIUM	INTERNALNESS	INTERPELLATORS
INTERKNOTS	INTERLOCKERS	INTERMEDIUMS	INTERNALNESSES	INTERPENETRABLE
INTERKNOTTED	INTERLOCKING	INTERMEMBRANE	INTERNATIONAL	INTERPENETRANT
INTERKNOTTING	INTERLOCKS	INTERMENSTRUAL	INTERNATIONALLY	INTERPENETRATE
INTERLACED	INTERLOCUTION	INTERMENTS	INTERNATIONALS	INTERPENETRATED
INTERLACEDLY	INTERLOCUTIONS	INTERMESHED	INTERNECINE	INTERPENETRATES
INTERLACEMENT	INTERLOCUTOR	INTERMESHES	INTERNECIVE	INTERPERCEPTUAL
INTERLACEMENTS	INTERLOCUTORILY	INTERMESHING	INTERNEURAL	INTERPERMEATE
INTERLACES	INTERLOCUTORS	INTERMETALLIC	INTERNEURON	INTERPERMEATED
INTERLACING	INTERLOCUTORY	INTERMETALLICS	INTERNEURONAL	INTERPERMEATES
INTERLACUSTRINE	INTERLOCUTRESS	INTERMEZZI	INTERNEURONS	INTERPERMEATING
INTERLAMINAR	INTERLOCUTRICE	INTERMEZZO	INTERNISTS	INTERPERSONAL
INTERLAMINATE	INTERLOCUTRICES	INTERMEZZOS	INTERNMENT	INTERPERSONALLY
INTERLAMINATED	INTERLOCUTRIX	INTERMIGRATION	INTERNMENTS	INTERPETIOLAR
INTERLAMINATES	INTERLOCUTRIXES	INTERMIGRATIONS	INTERNODAL	INTERPHALANGEAL
INTERLAMINATING	INTERLOOPED	INTERMINABILITY	INTERNODES	INTERPHASE
INTERLAMINATION	INTERLOOPING	INTERMINABLE	INTERNODIAL	INTERPHASES
INTERLAPPED	INTERLOOPS	INTERMINABLY	INTERNSHIP	INTERPHONE
INTERLAPPING	INTERLOPED	INTERMINGLE	INTERNSHIPS	INTERPHONES
INTERLARDED	INTERLOPER	INTERMINGLED	INTERNUCLEAR	INTERPILASTER
INTERLARDING	INTERLOPERS	INTERMINGLES	INTERNUCLEON	INTERPILASTERS
INTERLARDS	INTERLOPES	INTERMINGLING	INTERNUCLEONIC	INTERPLANETARY
INTERLAYER	INTERLOPING	INTERMISSION	INTERNUCLEOTIDE	INTERPLANT
INTERLAYERED	INTERLUDED	INTERMISSIONS	INTERNUNCIAL	INTERPLANTED
INTERLAYERING	INTERLUDES	INTERMISSIVE	INTERNUNCIO	INTERPLANTING
INTERLAYERINGS	INTERLUDIAL	INTERMITOTIC	INTERNUNCIOS	INTERPLANTS
INTERLAYERS	INTERLUDING	INTERMITTED	INTEROBSERVER	INTERPLAYED
INTERLAYING	INTERLUNAR	INTERMITTENCE	INTEROCEAN	INTERPLAYING
INTERLEAVE	INTERLUNARY	INTERMITTENCES	INTEROCEANIC	INTERPLAYS
INTERLEAVED	INTERLUNATION	INTERMITTENCIES	INTEROCEPTION	INTERPLEAD
INTERLEAVES	INTERLUNATIONS	INTERMITTENCY	INTEROCEPTIONS	INTERPLEADED
INTERLEAVING	INTERMARGINAL	INTERMITTENT	INTEROCEPTIVE	INTERPLEADER
INTERLENDING	INTERMARRIAGE	INTERMITTENTLY	INTEROCEPTOR	INTERPLEADERS
INTERLENDS	INTERMARRIAGES	INTERMITTER	INTEROCEPTORS	INTERPLEADING
INTERLEUKIN	INTERMARRIED	INTERMITTERS	INTEROCULAR	INTERPLEADS
INTERLEUKINS	INTERMARRIES	INTERMITTING	INTEROFFICE	INTERPLEURAL
INTERLIBRARY	INTERMARRY	INTERMITTINGLY	INTEROPERABLE	INTERPLUVIAL
INTERLINEAL	INTERMARRYING	INTERMITTOR	INTEROPERATIVE	INTERPLUVIALS
INTERLINEALLY	INTERMATTED	INTERMITTORS	INTERORBITAL	INTERPOINT
INTERLINEAR	INTERMATTING	INTERMIXED	INTERORGAN	INTERPOINTS
INTERLINEARLY	INTERMAXILLA	INTERMIXES	INTEROSCULANT	INTERPOLABLE
INTERLINEARS	INTERMAXILLAE	INTERMIXING	INTEROSCULATE	INTERPOLAR
INTERLINEATE	INTERMAXILLARY	INTERMIXTURE	INTEROSCULATED	INTERPOLATE
INTERLINEATED	INTERMEDDLE	INTERMIXTURES	INTEROSCULATES	INTERPOLATED
INTERLINEATES	INTERMEDDLED	INTERMODAL	INTEROSCULATING	INTERPOLATER
INTERLINEATING	INTERMEDDLER	INTERMODULATION	INTEROSCULATION	INTERPOLATERS
INTERLINEATION	INTERMEDDLERS	INTERMOLECULAR	INTEROSSEAL	INTERPOLATES
INTERLINEATIONS	INTERMEDDLES	INTERMONTANE	INTEROSSEOUS	INTERPOLATING
INTERLINED	INTERMEDDLING	INTERMOUNTAIN	INTERPAGED	INTERPOLATION
INTERLINER	INTERMEDIA	INTERMUNDANE	INTERPAGES	INTERPOLATIONS
INTERLINERS	INTERMEDIACIES	INTERMURED	INTERPAGING	INTERPOLATIVE
INTERLINES	INTERMEDIACY	INTERMURES	INTERPANDEMIC	INTERPOLATOR
INTERLINGUA	INTERMEDIAL	INTERMURING	INTERPARIETAL	INTERPOLATORS
INTERLINGUAL	INTERMEDIARIES	INTERMUSCULAR	INTERPARISH	INTERPONED
INTERLINGUALLY	INTERMEDIARY	INTERNALISATION	INTERPAROCHIAL	INTERPONES
INTERLINGUAS	INTERMEDIATE	INTERNALISE	INTERPAROXYSMAL	INTERPONING
INTERLINING	INTERMEDIATED	INTERNALISED	INTERPARTICLE	INTERPOPULATION
INTERLININGS	INTERMEDIATELY	INTERNALISES	INTERPARTY	INTERPOSABLE
INTERLINKED	INTERMEDIATES	INTERNALISING	INTERPELLANT	INTERPOSAL
INTERLINKING	INTERMEDIATING	INTERNALITIES	INTERPELLANTS	INTERPOSALS
INTERLINKS	INTERMEDIATION	INTERNALITY	INTERPELLATE	INTERPOSED
INTERLOANS	INTERMEDIATIONS	INTERNALIZATION	INTERPELLATED	INTERPOSER
INTERLOBULAR	INTERMEDIATOR	INTERNALIZE	INTERPELLATES	INTERPOSERS
INTERLOCAL	INTERMEDIATORS	INTERNALIZED	INTERPELLATING	INTERPOSES
INTERLOCATION	INTERMEDIATORY	INTERNALIZES	INTERPELLATION	INTERPOSING
INTERLOCATIONS	INTERMEDIN	INTERNALIZING	INTERPELLATIONS	INTERPOSITION
INTERLOCKED	INTERMEDINS	INTERNALLY	INTERPELLATOR	INTERPOSITIONS

INTERPRETABLE	INTERROGATEE	INTERSPACED	INTERTRIBAL	INTERWEAVED
INTERPRETABLY	INTERROGATEES	INTERSPACES	INTERTRIGO	INTERWEAVEMENT
INTERPRETATE	INTERROGATES	INTERSPACING	INTERTRIGOS	INTERWEAVEMENTS
INTERPRETATED	INTERROGATING	INTERSPATIAL	INTERTROOP	INTERWEAVER
INTERPRETATES	INTERROGATINGLY	INTERSPATIALLY	INTERTROPICAL	INTERWEAVERS
INTERPRETATING	INTERROGATION	INTERSPECIES	INTERTWINE	INTERWEAVES
INTERPRETATION	INTERROGATIONAL	INTERSPECIFIC	INTERTWINED	INTERWEAVING
INTERPRETATIONS	INTERROGATIONS	INTERSPERSAL	INTERTWINEMENT	INTERWINDING
INTERPRETATIVE	INTERROGATIVE	INTERSPERSALS	INTERTWINEMENTS	INTERWINDS
INTERPRETED	INTERROGATIVELY	INTERSPERSE	INTERTWINES	INTERWORKED
INTERPRETER	INTERROGATIVES	INTERSPERSED	INTERTWINING	INTERWORKING
INTERPRETERS	INTERROGATOR	INTERSPERSEDLY	INTERTWININGLY	INTERWORKINGS
INTERPRETERSHIP	INTERROGATORIES	INTERSPERSES	INTERTWININGS	INTERWORKS
INTERPRETESS	INTERROGATORILY	INTERSPERSING	INTERTWIST	INTERWOUND
INTERPRETESSES	INTERROGATORS	INTERSPERSION	INTERTWISTED	INTERWOVEN
INTERPRETING	INTERROGATORY	INTERSPERSIONS	INTERTWISTING	INTERWREATHE
INTERPRETIVE	INTERROGEE	INTERSPINAL	INTERTWISTINGLY	INTERWREATHED
INTERPRETIVELY	INTERROGEES	INTERSPINOUS	INTERTWISTS	INTERWREATHES
INTERPRETRESS	INTERRUPTED	INTERSTADIAL	INTERUNION	INTERWREATHING
INTERPRETRESSES	INTERRUPTEDLY	INTERSTADIALS	INTERUNIONS	INTERWROUGHT
INTERPRETS	INTERRUPTER	INTERSTAGE	INTERUNIVERSITY	INTERZONAL
INTERPROVINCIAL	INTERRUPTERS	INTERSTATE	INTERURBAN	INTERZONES
INTERPROXIMAL	INTERRUPTIBLE	INTERSTATES	INTERVALES	INTESTACIES
INTERPSYCHIC	INTERRUPTING	INTERSTATION	INTERVALLEY	INTESTATES
INTERPUNCTION	INTERRUPTION	INTERSTELLAR	INTERVALLIC	INTESTINAL
INTERPUNCTIONS	INTERRUPTIONS	INTERSTELLARY	INTERVALLUM	INTESTINALLY
INTERPUNCTUATE	INTERRUPTIVE	INTERSTERILE	INTERVALLUMS	INTESTINES
INTERPUNCTUATED	INTERRUPTIVELY	INTERSTERILITY	INTERVALOMETER	INTHRALLED
INTERPUNCTUATES	INTERRUPTOR	INTERSTICE	INTERVALOMETERS	INTHRALLING
INTERPUPILLARY	INTERRUPTORS	INTERSTICES	INTERVARSITY	INTHRONING
INTERQUARTILE	INTERRUPTS	INTERSTIMULUS	INTERVEINED	INTIFADAHS
INTERRACIAL	INTERSCAPULAR	INTERSTITIAL	INTERVEINING	INTIFADEHS
INTERRACIALLY	INTERSCHOLASTIC	INTERSTITIALLY	INTERVEINS	INTIMACIES
INTERRADIAL	INTERSCHOOL	INTERSTITIALS	INTERVENED	INTIMATELY
INTERRADIALLY	INTERSCRIBE	INTERSTRAIN	INTERVENER	INTIMATENESS
INTERRADII	INTERSCRIBED	INTERSTRAND	INTERVENERS	INTIMATENESSES
INTERRADIUS	INTERSCRIBES	INTERSTRATIFIED	INTERVENES	INTIMATERS
INTERRADIUSES	INTERSCRIBING	INTERSTRATIFIES	INTERVENIENT	INTIMATING
INTERRAILED	INTERSECTED	INTERSTRATIFY	INTERVENING	INTIMATION
INTERRAILER	INTERSECTING	INTERSUBJECTIVE	INTERVENOR	INTIMATIONS
INTERRAILERS	INTERSECTION	INTERSYSTEM	INTERVENORS	INTIMIDATE
INTERRAILING	INTERSECTIONAL	INTERTANGLE	INTERVENTION	INTIMIDATED
INTERRAILS	INTERSECTIONS	INTERTANGLED	INTERVENTIONAL	INTIMIDATES
INTERRAMAL	INTERSECTS	INTERTANGLEMENT	INTERVENTIONISM	INTIMIDATING
INTERREGAL	INTERSEGMENT	INTERTANGLES	INTERVENTIONIST	INTIMIDATINGLY
INTERREGES	INTERSEGMENTAL	INTERTANGLING	INTERVENTIONS	INTIMIDATION
INTERREGIONAL	INTERSEGMENTS	INTERTARSAL	INTERVENTOR	INTIMIDATIONS
INTERREGNA	INTERSENSORY	INTERTENTACULAR	INTERVENTORS	INTIMIDATOR
INTERREGNAL	INTERSEPTAL	INTERTERMINAL	INTERVERTEBRAL	INTIMIDATORS
INTERREGNUM	INTERSERTAL	INTERTERMS	INTERVIEWED	INTIMIDATORY
INTERREGNUMS	INTERSERTED	INTERTEXTS	INTERVIEWEE	INTIMISTES
INTERRELATE	INTERSERTING	INTERTEXTUAL	INTERVIEWEES	INTIMITIES
INTERRELATED	INTERSERTS	INTERTEXTUALITY	INTERVIEWER	INTINCTION
INTERRELATEDLY	INTERSERVICE	INTERTEXTUALLY	INTERVIEWERS	INTINCTIONS
INTERRELATES	INTERSESSION	INTERTEXTURE	INTERVIEWING	INTITULING
INTERRELATING	INTERSESSIONS	INTERTEXTURES	INTERVIEWS	INTOLERABILITY
INTERRELATION	INTERSEXES	INTERTIDAL	INTERVILLAGE	INTOLERABLE
INTERRELATIONS	INTERSEXUAL	INTERTIDALLY	INTERVISIBILITY	INTOLERABLENESS
INTERRELIGIOUS	INTERSEXUALISM	INTERTILLAGE	INTERVISIBLE	INTOLERABLY
INTERRENAL	INTERSEXUALISMS	INTERTILLAGES	INTERVISITATION	INTOLERANCE
INTERROBANG	INTERSEXUALITY	INTERTILLED	INTERVITAL	INTOLERANCES
INTERROBANGS	INTERSEXUALLY	INTERTILLING	INTERVOCALIC	INTOLERANT
INTERROGABLE	INTERSEXUALS	INTERTILLS	INTERVOLVE	INTOLERANTLY
INTERROGANT	INTERSIDEREAL	INTERTISSUED	INTERVOLVED	INTOLERANTNESS
INTERROGANTS	INTERSOCIETAL	INTERTRAFFIC	INTERVOLVES	INTOLERANTS
INTERROGATE	INTERSOCIETY	INTERTRAFFICS	INTERVOLVING	INTOLERATION
INTERROGATED	INTERSPACE	INTERTRIAL	INTERWEAVE	INTOLERATIONS

i

INTONATING	INTRANSIGENCE	INTRICACIES	INTROVERSIVELY	INURBANELY
INTONATION	INTRANSIGENCES	INTRICATELY	INTROVERTED	INURBANITIES
INTONATIONAL	INTRANSIGENCIES	INTRICATENESS	INTROVERTING	INURBANITY
INTONATIONS	INTRANSIGENCY	INTRICATENESSES	INTROVERTIVE	INUREDNESS
INTONATORS	INTRANSIGENT	INTRIGANTE	INTROVERTS	INUREDNESSES
INTONINGLY	INTRANSIGENTISM	INTRIGANTES	INTRUDINGLY	INUREMENTS
INTORSIONS	INTRANSIGENTIST	INTRIGANTS	INTRUSIONAL	INURNMENTS
INTORTIONS	INTRANSIGENTLY	INTRIGUANT	INTRUSIONIST	INUSITATION
INTOXICABLE	INTRANSIGENTS	INTRIGUANTE	INTRUSIONISTS	INUSITATIONS
INTOXICANT	INTRANSITIVE	INTRIGUANTES	INTRUSIONS	INUTILITIES
INTOXICANTS	INTRANSITIVELY	INTRIGUANTS	INTRUSIVELY	INUTTERABLE
INTOXICATE	INTRANSITIVES	INTRIGUERS	INTRUSIVENESS	INVAGINABLE
INTOXICATED	INTRANSITIVITY	INTRIGUING	INTRUSIVENESSES	INVAGINATE
INTOXICATEDLY	INTRANSMISSIBLE	INTRIGUINGLY	INTRUSIVES	INVAGINATED
INTOXICATES	INTRANSMUTABLE	INTRINSICAL	INTRUSTING	INVAGINATES
INTOXICATING	INTRANUCLEAR	INTRINSICALITY	INTRUSTMENT	INVAGINATING
INTOXICATINGLY	INTRAOCULAR	INTRINSICALLY	INTRUSTMENTS	INVAGINATION
INTOXICATION	INTRAOCULARLY	INTRINSICALNESS	INTUBATING	INVAGINATIONS
INTOXICATIONS	INTRAPARIETAL	INTRINSICATE	INTUBATION	INVALIDATE
INTOXICATIVE	INTRAPARTUM	INTRODUCED	INTUBATIONS	INVALIDATED
INTOXICATOR	INTRAPERITONEAL	INTRODUCER	INTUITABLE	INVALIDATES
INTOXICATORS	INTRAPERSONAL	INTRODUCERS	INTUITIONAL	INVALIDATING
INTOXIMETER	INTRAPETIOLAR	INTRODUCES	INTUITIONALISM	INVALIDATION
INTOXIMETERS	INTRAPLATE	INTRODUCIBLE	INTUITIONALISMS	INVALIDATIONS
INTRACAPSULAR	INTRAPOPULATION	INTRODUCING	INTUITIONALIST	INVALIDATOR
INTRACARDIAC	INTRAPRENEUR	INTRODUCTION	INTUITIONALISTS	INVALIDATORS
INTRACARDIAL	INTRAPRENEURIAL	INTRODUCTIONS	INTUITIONALLY	INVALIDEST
INTRACARDIALLY	INTRAPRENEURS	INTRODUCTIVE	INTUITIONISM	INVALIDHOOD
INTRACAVITARY	INTRAPSYCHIC	INTRODUCTORILY	INTUITIONISMS	INVALIDHOODS
INTRACELLULAR	INTRASEXUAL	INTRODUCTORY	INTUITIONIST	INVALIDING
INTRACELLULARLY	INTRASPECIES	INTROFYING	INTUITIONISTS	INVALIDINGS
INTRACEREBRAL	INTRASPECIFIC	INTROGRESSANT	INTUITIONS	INVALIDISM
INTRACEREBRALLY	INTRASTATE	INTROGRESSANTS	INTUITIVELY	INVALIDISMS
INTRACOMPANY	INTRATELLURIC	INTROGRESSION	INTUITIVENESS	INVALIDITIES
INTRACRANIAL	INTRATHECAL	INTROGRESSIONS	INTUITIVENESSES	INVALIDITY
INTRACRANIALLY	INTRATHECALLY	INTROGRESSIVE	INTUITIVISM	INVALIDNESS
INTRACTABILITY	INTRATHORACIC	INTROITUSES	INTUITIVISMS	INVALIDNESSES
INTRACTABLE	INTRAUTERINE	INTROJECTED	INTUMESCED	INVALUABLE
INTRACTABLENESS	INTRAVASATION	INTROJECTING	INTUMESCENCE	INVALUABLENESS
INTRACTABLY	INTRAVASATIONS	INTROJECTION	INTUMESCENCES	INVALUABLY
INTRACUTANEOUS	INTRAVASCULAR	INTROJECTIONS	INTUMESCENCIES	INVARIABILITIES
INTRADERMAL	INTRAVASCULARLY	INTROJECTIVE	INTUMESCENCY	INVARIABILITY
INTRADERMALLY	INTRAVENOUS	INTROJECTS	INTUMESCENT	INVARIABLE
INTRADERMIC	INTRAVENOUSLY	INTROMISSIBLE	INTUMESCES	INVARIABLENESS
INTRADERMICALLY	INTRAVERSABLE	INTROMISSION	INTUMESCING	INVARIABLES
INTRADOSES	INTRAVITAL	INTROMISSIONS	INTURBIDATE	INVARIABLY
INTRAFALLOPIAN	INTRAVITALLY	INTROMISSIVE	INTURBIDATED	INVARIANCE
INTRAFASCICULAR	INTRAVITAM	INTROMITTED	INTURBIDATES	INVARIANCES
INTRAGALACTIC	INTRAZONAL	INTROMITTENT	INTURBIDATING	INVARIANCIES
INTRAGENIC	INTREATFULL	INTROMITTER	INTUSSUSCEPT	INVARIANCY
INTRAMEDULLARY	INTREATING	INTROMITTERS	INTUSSUSCEPTED	INVARIANTS
INTRAMERCURIAL	INTREATINGLY	INTROMITTING	INTUSSUSCEPTING	INVASIVELY
INTRAMOLECULAR	INTREATMENT	INTRORSELY	INTUSSUSCEPTION	INVASIVENESS
INTRAMUNDANE	INTREATMENTS	INTROSPECT	INTUSSUSCEPTIVE	INVASIVENESSES
INTRAMURAL	INTRENCHANT	INTROSPECTED	INTUSSUSCEPTS	INVEAGLING
INTRAMURALLY	INTRENCHED	INTROSPECTING	INTWINEMENT	INVECTIVELY
INTRAMURALS	INTRENCHER	INTROSPECTION	INTWINEMENTS	INVECTIVENESS
INTRAMUSCULAR	INTRENCHERS	INTROSPECTIONAL	INTWISTING	INVECTIVENESSES
INTRAMUSCULARLY	INTRENCHES	INTROSPECTIONS	INUMBRATED	INVECTIVES
INTRANASAL	INTRENCHING	INTROSPECTIVE	INUMBRATES	INVEIGHERS
INTRANASALLY	INTRENCHMENT	INTROSPECTIVELY	INUMBRATING	INVEIGHING
INTRANATIONAL	INTRENCHMENTS	INTROSPECTS	INUNCTIONS	INVEIGLEMENT
INTRANSIGEANCE	INTREPIDITIES	INTROSUSCEPTION	INUNDATING	INVEIGLEMENTS
INTRANSIGEANCES	INTREPIDITY	INTROVERSIBLE	INUNDATION	INVEIGLERS
INTRANSIGEANT	INTREPIDLY	INTROVERSION	INUNDATIONS	INVEIGLING
INTRANSIGEANTLY	INTREPIDNESS	INTROVERSIONS	INUNDATORS	INVENDIBILITIES
INTRANSIGEANTS	INTREPIDNESSES	INTROVERSIVE	INUNDATORY	INVENDIBILITY

INVENDIBLE	INVIGILATOR	INVOLUTELY	IRASCIBILITY	IRRATIONAL
INVENTABLE	INVIGILATORS	INVOLUTING	IRASCIBLENESS	IRRATIONALISE
INVENTIBLE	INVIGORANT	INVOLUTION	IRASCIBLENESSES	IRRATIONALISED
INVENTIONAL	INVIGORANTS	INVOLUTIONAL	IRATENESSES	IRRATIONALISES
INVENTIONLESS	INVIGORATE	INVOLUTIONS	IREFULNESS	IRRATIONALISING
INVENTIONS	INVIGORATED	INVOLVEDLY	IREFULNESSES	IRRATIONALISM
INVENTIVELY	INVIGORATES	INVOLVEMENT	IRENICALLY	IRRATIONALISMS
INVENTIVENESS	INVIGORATING	INVOLVEMENTS	IRENICISMS	IRRATIONALIST
INVENTIVENESSES	INVIGORATINGLY	INVULNERABILITY	IRENOLOGIES	IRRATIONALISTIC
INVENTORIABLE	INVIGORATION	INVULNERABLE	IRIDACEOUS	IRRATIONALISTS
INVENTORIAL	INVIGORATIONS	INVULNERABLY	IRIDECTOMIES	IRRATIONALITIES
INVENTORIALLY	INVIGORATIVE	INVULTUATION	IRIDECTOMY	IRRATIONALITY
INVENTORIED	INVIGORATIVELY	INVULTUATIONS	IRIDESCENCE	IRRATIONALIZE
INVENTORIES	INVIGORATOR	INWARDNESS	IRIDESCENCES	IRRATIONALIZED
INVENTORYING	INVIGORATORS	INWARDNESSES	IRIDESCENT	IRRATIONALIZES
INVENTRESS	INVINCIBILITIES	INWORKINGS	IRIDESCENTLY	IRRATIONALIZING
INVENTRESSES	INVINCIBILITY	INWRAPMENT	IRIDISATION	IRRATIONALLY
INVERACITIES	INVINCIBLE	INWRAPMENTS	IRIDISATIONS	IRRATIONALNESS
INVERACITY	INVINCIBLENESS	INWRAPPING	IRIDIZATION	IRRATIONALS
INVERITIES	INVINCIBLY	INWRAPPINGS	IRIDIZATIONS	IRREALISABLE
INVERNESSES	INVIOLABILITIES	INWREATHED	IRIDOCYTES	IRREALITIES
INVERSIONS	INVIOLABILITY	INWREATHES	IRIDOLOGIES	IRREALIZABLE
INVERTASES	INVIOLABLE	INWREATHING	IRIDOLOGIST	IRREBUTTABLE
INVERTEBRAL	INVIOLABLENESS	IODINATING	IRIDOLOGISTS	IRRECEPTIVE
INVERTEBRATE	INVIOLABLY	IODINATION	IRIDOSMINE	IRRECIPROCAL
INVERTEBRATES	INVIOLACIES	IODINATIONS	IRIDOSMINES	IRRECIPROCITIES
INVERTEDLY	INVIOLATED	IODISATION	IRIDOSMIUM	IRRECIPROCITY
INVERTIBILITIES	INVIOLATELY	IODISATIONS	IRIDOSMIUMS	IRRECLAIMABLE
INVERTIBILITY	INVIOLATENESS	IODIZATION	IRIDOTOMIES	IRRECLAIMABLY
INVERTIBLE	INVIOLATENESSES	IODIZATIONS	IRISATIONS	IRRECOGNISABLE
INVESTABLE	INVISIBILITIES	IODOMETRIC	IRKSOMENESS	IRRECOGNITION
INVESTIBLE	INVISIBILITY	IODOMETRICAL	IRKSOMENESSES	IRRECOGNITIONS
INVESTIGABLE	INVISIBLENESS	IODOMETRICALLY	IRONFISTED	IRRECOGNIZABLE
INVESTIGATE	INVISIBLENESSES	IODOMETRIES	IRONHANDED	IRRECONCILABLE
INVESTIGATED	INVISIBLES	IONICITIES	IRONHEARTED	IRRECONCILABLES
INVESTIGATES	INVITATION	IONISATION	IRONICALLY	IRRECONCILABLY
INVESTIGATING	INVITATIONAL	IONISATIONS	IRONICALNESS	IRRECONCILED
INVESTIGATION	INVITATIONALS	IONIZATION	IRONICALNESSES	IRRECONCILEMENT
INVESTIGATIONAL	INVITATIONS	IONIZATIONS	IRONMASTER	IRRECOVERABLE
INVESTIGATIONS	INVITATORIES	IONOPAUSES	IRONMASTERS	IRRECOVERABLY
INVESTIGATIVE	INVITATORY	IONOPHORES	IRONMONGER	IRRECUSABLE
INVESTIGATOR	INVITEMENT	IONOPHORESES	IRONMONGERIES	IRRECUSABLY
INVESTIGATORS	INVITEMENTS	IONOPHORESIS	IRONMONGERS	IRREDEEMABILITY
INVESTIGATORY	INVITINGLY	IONOSONDES	IRONMONGERY	IRREDEEMABLE
INVESTITIVE	INVITINGNESS	IONOSPHERE	IRONNESSES	IRREDEEMABLES
INVESTITURE	INVITINGNESSES	IONOSPHERES	IRONSMITHS	IRREDEEMABLY
INVESTITURES	INVOCATING	IONOSPHERIC	IRONSTONES	IRREDENTAS
INVESTMENT	INVOCATION	IONOSPHERICALLY	IRONWORKER	IRREDENTISM
INVESTMENTS	INVOCATIONAL	IONOTROPIC	IRONWORKERS	IRREDENTISMS
INVETERACIES	INVOCATIONS	IONOTROPIES	IRRADIANCE	IRREDENTIST
INVETERACY	INVOCATIVE	IONTOPHORESES	IRRADIANCES	IRREDENTISTS
INVETERATE	INVOCATORS	IONTOPHORESIS	IRRADIANCIES	IRREDUCIBILITY
INVETERATELY	INVOCATORY	IONTOPHORETIC	IRRADIANCY	IRREDUCIBLE
INVETERATENESS	INVOICINGS	IPECACUANHA	IRRADIATED	IRREDUCIBLENESS
INVIABILITIES	INVOLUCELLA	IPECACUANHAS	IRRADIATES	IRREDUCIBLY
INVIABILITY	INVOLUCELLATE	IPRATROPIUM	IRRADIATING	IRREDUCTIBILITY
INVIABLENESS	INVOLUCELLATED	IPRATROPIUMS	IRRADIATION	IRREDUCTION
INVIABLENESSES	INVOLUCELLUM	IPRINDOLES	IRRADIATIONS	IRREDUCTIONS
INVIDIOUSLY	INVOLUCELS	IPRONIAZID	IRRADIATIVE	IRREFLECTION
INVIDIOUSNESS	INVOLUCRAL	IPRONIAZIDS	IRRADIATOR	IRREFLECTIONS
INVIDIOUSNESSES	INVOLUCRATE	IPSELATERAL	IRRADIATORS	IRREFLECTIVE
INVIGILATE	INVOLUCRES	IPSILATERAL	IRRADICABLE	IRREFLEXION
INVIGILATED	INVOLUCRUM	IPSILATERALLY	IRRADICABLY	IRREFLEXIONS
INVIGILATES	INVOLUNTARILY	IRACUNDITIES	IRRADICATE	IRREFLEXIVE
INVIGILATING	INVOLUNTARINESS	IRACUNDITY	IRRADICATED	IRREFORMABILITY
INVIGILATION	INVOLUNTARY	IRACUNDULOUS	IRRADICATES	IRREFORMABLE
INVIGILATIONS	INVOLUTEDLY	IRASCIBILITIES	IRRADICATING	IRREFORMABLY

IRREFRAGABILITY	IRREPROVABLE	IRRUPTIONS	ISOCRACIES	ISOMERIZED
IRREFRAGABLE	IRREPROVABLY	IRRUPTIVELY	ISOCRYMALS	ISOMERIZES
IRREFRAGABLY	IRRESISTANCE	IRUKANDJIS	ISOCYANATE	ISOMERIZING
IRREFRANGIBLE	IRRESISTANCES	ISABELLINE	ISOCYANATES	ISOMETRICAL
IRREFRANGIBLY	IRRESISTIBILITY	ISABELLINES	ISOCYANIDE	ISOMETRICALLY
IRREFUTABILITY	IRRESISTIBLE	ISALLOBARIC	ISOCYANIDES	ISOMETRICS
IRREFUTABLE	IRRESISTIBLY	ISALLOBARS	ISODIAMETRIC	ISOMETRIES
IRREFUTABLENESS	IRRESOLUBILITY	ISAPOSTOLIC	ISODIAMETRICAL	ISOMETROPIA
IRREFUTABLY	IRRESOLUBLE	ISCHAEMIAS	ISODIAPHERE	ISOMETROPIAS
IRREGARDLESS	IRRESOLUBLY	ISCHURETIC	ISODIAPHERES	ISOMORPHIC
IRREGULARITIES	IRRESOLUTE	ISCHURETICS	ISODIMORPHIC	ISOMORPHICALLY
IRREGULARITY	IRRESOLUTELY	ISEIKONIAS	ISODIMORPHISM	ISOMORPHISM
IRREGULARLY	IRRESOLUTENESS	ISENTROPIC	ISODIMORPHISMS	ISOMORPHISMS
IRREGULARS	IRRESOLUTION	ISENTROPICALLY	ISODIMORPHOUS	ISOMORPHOUS
IRRELATION	IRRESOLUTIONS	ISINGLASSES	ISODONTALS	ISONIAZIDE
IRRELATIONS	IRRESOLVABILITY	ISLOMANIAS	ISODYNAMIC	ISONIAZIDES
IRRELATIVE	IRRESOLVABLE	ISMATICALNESS	ISODYNAMICS	ISONIAZIDS
IRRELATIVELY	IRRESOLVABLY	ISMATICALNESSES	ISOELECTRIC	ISONITRILE
IRRELATIVENESS	IRRESPECTIVE	ISOAGGLUTININ	ISOELECTRONIC	ISONITRILES
IRRELEVANCE	IRRESPECTIVELY	ISOAGGLUTININS	ISOENZYMATIC	ISOOCTANES
IRRELEVANCES	IRRESPIRABLE	ISOALLOXAZINE	ISOENZYMES	ISOPACHYTE
IRRELEVANCIES	IRRESPONSIBLE	ISOALLOXAZINES	ISOENZYMIC	ISOPACHYTES
IRRELEVANCY	IRRESPONSIBLES	ISOAMINILE	ISOFLAVONE	ISOPERIMETER
IRRELEVANT	IRRESPONSIBLY	ISOAMINILES	ISOFLAVONES	ISOPERIMETERS
IRRELEVANTLY	IRRESPONSIVE	ISOANTIBODIES	ISOGAMETES	ISOPERIMETRICAL
IRRELIEVABLE	IRRESPONSIVELY	ISOANTIBODY	ISOGAMETIC	ISOPERIMETRIES
IRRELIGION	IRRESTRAINABLE	ISOANTIGEN	ISOGENETIC	ISOPERIMETRY
IRRELIGIONIST	IRRESUSCITABLE	ISOANTIGENIC	ISOGEOTHERM	ISOPIESTIC
IRRELIGIONISTS	IRRESUSCITABLY	ISOANTIGENS	ISOGEOTHERMAL	ISOPIESTICALLY
IRRELIGIONS	IRRETENTION	ISOBARISMS	ISOGEOTHERMALS	ISOPLETHIC
IRRELIGIOUS	IRRETENTIONS	ISOBAROMETRIC	ISOGEOTHERMIC	ISOPLUVIAL
IRRELIGIOUSLY	IRRETENTIVE	ISOBILATERAL	ISOGEOTHERMICS	ISOPLUVIALS
IRRELIGIOUSNESS	IRRETENTIVENESS	ISOBUTANES	ISOGEOTHERMS	ISOPOLITIES
IRREMEABLE	IRRETRIEVABLE	ISOBUTENES	ISOGLOSSAL	ISOPRENALINE
IRREMEABLY	IRRETRIEVABLY	ISOBUTYLENE	ISOGLOSSES	ISOPRENALINES
IRREMEDIABLE	IRREVERENCE	ISOBUTYLENES	ISOGLOSSIC	ISOPRENOID
IRREMEDIABLY	IRREVERENCES	ISOCALORIC	ISOGLOTTAL	ISOPRENOIDS
IRREMISSIBILITY	IRREVERENT	ISOCARBOXAZID	ISOGLOTTIC	ISOPROPYLS
IRREMISSIBLE	IRREVERENTIAL	ISOCARBOXAZIDS	ISOGRAFTED	ISOPROTERENOL
IRREMISSIBLY	IRREVERENTLY	ISOCHASMIC	ISOGRAFTING	ISOPROTERENOLS
IRREMISSION	IRREVERSIBILITY	ISOCHEIMAL	ISOHYETALS	ISOPTERANS
IRREMISSIONS	IRREVERSIBLE	ISOCHEIMALS	ISOIMMUNISATION	ISOPTEROUS
IRREMISSIVE	IRREVERSIBLY	ISOCHEIMENAL	ISOIMMUNIZATION	ISOPYCNALS
IRREMOVABILITY	IRREVOCABILITY	ISOCHEIMENALS	ISOKINETIC	ISOPYCNICS
IRREMOVABLE	IRREVOCABLE	ISOCHEIMIC	ISOKONTANS	ISORHYTHMIC
IRREMOVABLENESS	IRREVOCABLENESS	ISOCHIMALS	ISOLABILITIES	ISOSEISMAL
IRREMOVABLY	IRREVOCABLY	ISOCHROMATIC	ISOLABILITY	ISOSEISMALS
IRRENOWNED	IRRIDENTAS	ISOCHROMOSOME	ISOLATABLE	ISOSEISMIC
IRREPAIRABLE	IRRIGATING	ISOCHROMOSOMES	ISOLATIONISM	ISOSEISMICS
IRREPARABILITY	IRRIGATION	ISOCHRONAL	ISOLATIONISMS	ISOSMOTICALLY
IRREPARABLE	IRRIGATIONAL	ISOCHRONALLY	ISOLATIONIST	ISOSPONDYLOUS
IRREPARABLENESS	IRRIGATIONS	ISOCHRONES	ISOLATIONISTS	ISOSPORIES
IRREPARABLY	IRRIGATIVE	ISOCHRONISE	ISOLATIONS	ISOSPOROUS
IRREPEALABILITY	IRRIGATORS	ISOCHRONISED	ISOLECITHAL	ISOSTACIES
IRREPEALABLE	IRRITABILITIES	ISOCHRONISES	ISOLEUCINE	ISOSTASIES
IRREPEALABLY	IRRITABILITY	ISOCHRONISING	ISOLEUCINES	ISOSTATICALLY
IRREPLACEABLE	IRRITABLENESS	ISOCHRONISM	ISOMAGNETIC	ISOSTEMONOUS
IRREPLACEABLY	IRRITABLENESSES	ISOCHRONISMS	ISOMAGNETICS	ISOSTHENURIA
IRREPLEVIABLE	IRRITANCIES	ISOCHRONIZE	ISOMERASES	ISOSTHENURIAS
IRREPLEVISABLE	IRRITATEDLY	ISOCHRONIZED	ISOMERISATION	ISOTENISCOPE
IRREPREHENSIBLE	IRRITATING	ISOCHRONIZES	ISOMERISATIONS	ISOTENISCOPES
IRREPREHENSIBLY	IRRITATINGLY	ISOCHRONIZING	ISOMERISED	ISOTHERALS
IRREPRESSIBLE	IRRITATION	ISOCHRONOUS	ISOMERISES	ISOTHERMAL
IRREPRESSIBLY	IRRITATIONS	ISOCHRONOUSLY	ISOMERISING	ISOTHERMALLY
IRREPROACHABLE	IRRITATIVE	ISOCHROOUS	ISOMERISMS	ISOTHERMALS
IRREPROACHABLY	IRRITATORS	ISOCLINALS	ISOMERIZATION	ISOTONICALLY
IRREPRODUCIBLE	IRROTATIONAL	ISOCLINICS	ISOMERIZATIONS	ISOTONICITIES

ISOTONICITY	ITALIANATE	ITALICISED	ITERATIVELY	ITINERANTLY
ISOTOPICALLY	ITALIANATED	ITALICISES	ITERATIVENESS	ITINERANTS
ISOTRETINOIN	ITALIANATES	ITALICISING	ITERATIVENESSES	ITINERARIES
ISOTRETINOINS	ITALIANATING	ITALICIZATION	ITEROPARITIES	ITINERATED
ISOTROPICALLY	ITALIANISE	ITALICIZATIONS	ITEROPARITY	ITINERATES
ISOTROPIES	ITALIANISED	ITALICIZED	ITEROPAROUS	ITINERATING
ISOTROPISM	ITALIANISES	ITALICIZES	ITHYPHALLI	ITINERATION
ISOTROPISMS	ITALIANISING	ITALICIZING	ITHYPHALLIC	ITINERATIONS
ISOTROPOUS	ITALIANIZE	ITCHINESSES	ITHYPHALLICS	IVERMECTIN
ISOXSUPRINE	ITALIANIZED	ITEMISATION	ITHYPHALLUS	IVERMECTINS
ISOXSUPRINES	ITALIANIZES	ITEMISATIONS	ITHYPHALLUSES	IVORYBILLS
ISPAGHULAS	ITALIANIZING	ITEMIZATION	ITINERACIES	IVORYWOODS
ITACOLUMITE	ITALICISATION	ITEMIZATIONS	ITINERANCIES	IZVESTIYAS
ITACOLUMITES	ITALICISATIONS	ITERATIONS	ITINERANCY	

J

j

JABBERINGLY	JACTITATION	JARGONIEST	JEISTIECOR	JETTISONABLE
JABBERINGS	JACTITATIONS	JARGONISATION	JEISTIECORS	JETTISONED
JABBERWOCK	JACULATING	JARGONISATIONS	JEJUNENESS	JETTISONING
JABBERWOCKIES	JACULATION	JARGONISED	JEJUNENESSES	JEWELFISHES
JABBERWOCKS	JACULATIONS	JARGONISES	JEJUNITIES	JEWELLERIES
JABBERWOCKY	JACULATORS	JARGONISING	JEJUNOSTOMIES	JEWELWEEDS
JABORANDIS	JACULATORY	JARGONISTIC	JEJUNOSTOMY	JICKAJOGGED
JABOTICABA	JADEDNESSES	JARGONISTS	JELLIFICATION	JICKAJOGGING
JABOTICABAS	JADISHNESS	JARGONIZATION	JELLIFICATIONS	JICKAJOGGINGS
JACARANDAS	JADISHNESSES	JARGONIZATIONS	JELLIFYING	JIGAJIGGED
JACKALLING	JAGDWURSTS	JARGONIZED	JELLYBEANS	JIGAJIGGING
JACKALOPES	JAGGEDNESS	JARGONIZES	JELLYFISHES	JIGAJOGGED
JACKANAPES	JAGGEDNESSES	JARGONIZING	JELLYGRAPH	JIGAJOGGING
JACKANAPESES	JAGGHERIES	JARLSBERGS	JELLYGRAPHED	JIGAMAREES
JACKAROOED	JAGHIRDARS	JAROVISING	JELLYGRAPHING	JIGGERMAST
JACKAROOING	JAGUARONDI	JAROVIZING	JELLYGRAPHS	JIGGERMASTS
JACKASSERIES	JAGUARONDIS	JASMONATES	JELLYROLLS	JIGGUMBOBS
JACKASSERY	JAGUARUNDI	JASPERIEST	JEMMINESSES	JILLFLIRTS
JACKBOOTED	JAGUARUNDIS	JASPERISED	JENNETINGS	JIMPNESSES
JACKBOOTING	JAILBREAKER	JASPERISES	JEOPARDERS	JIMSONWEED
JACKEROOED	JAILBREAKERS	JASPERISING	JEOPARDIED	JIMSONWEEDS
JACKEROOING	JAILBREAKING	JASPERIZED	JEOPARDIES	JINGOISTIC
JACKETLESS	JAILBREAKS	JASPERIZES	JEOPARDING	JINGOISTICALLY
JACKFISHES	JAILBROKEN	JASPERIZING	JEOPARDISE	JINRICKSHA
JACKFRUITS	JAILERESSES	JASPERWARE	JEOPARDISED	JINRICKSHAS
JACKHAMMER	JAILHOUSES	JASPERWARES	JEOPARDISES	JINRICKSHAW
JACKHAMMERED	JAILORESSES	JASPIDEOUS	JEOPARDISING	JINRICKSHAWS
JACKHAMMERING	JALOALLOFANE	JASPILITES	JEOPARDIZE	JINRIKISHA
JACKHAMMERS	JALOALLOFANES	JAUNDICING	JEOPARDIZED	JINRIKISHAS
JACKKNIFED	JAMAHIRIYA	JAUNTINESS	JEOPARDIZES	JINRIKSHAS
JACKKNIFES	JAMAHIRIYAS	JAUNTINESSES	JEOPARDIZING	JITTERBUGGED
JACKKNIFING	JAMBALAYAS	JAUNTINGLY	JEOPARDOUS	JITTERBUGGING
JACKKNIVES	JAMBOKKING	JAVELINING	JEOPARDOUSLY	JITTERBUGS
JACKLIGHTED	JAMBOLANAS	JAWBATIONS	JEOPARDYING	JITTERIEST
JACKLIGHTING	JAMBUSTERS	JAWBONINGS	JEQUERITIES	JITTERINESS
JACKLIGHTS	JANISARIES	JAWBREAKER	JEQUIRITIES	JITTERINESSES
JACKPLANES	JANISSARIES	JAWBREAKERS	JERFALCONS	JOBCENTRES
JACKPOTTED	JANITORIAL	JAWBREAKING	JERKINESSES	JOBERNOWLS
JACKPOTTING	JANITORSHIP	JAWBREAKINGLY	JERKINHEAD	JOBHOLDERS
JACKRABBIT	JANITORSHIPS	JAWCRUSHER	JERKINHEADS	JOBLESSNESS
JACKRABBITS	JANITRESSES	JAWCRUSHERS	JERKWATERS	JOBLESSNESSES
JACKROLLED	JANITRIXES	JAYHAWKERS	JERRYMANDER	JOBSEEKERS
JACKROLLING	JANIZARIAN	JAYWALKERS	JERRYMANDERED	JOBSWORTHS
JACKSCREWS	JANIZARIES	JAYWALKING	JERRYMANDERING	JOCKEYISMS
JACKSHAFTS	JANNEYINGS	JAYWALKINGS	JERRYMANDERS	JOCKEYSHIP
JACKSMELTS	JAPANISING	JAZZINESSES	JESSAMINES	JOCKEYSHIPS
JACKSMITHS	JAPANIZING	JEALOUSEST	JESSERANTS	JOCKSTRAPS
JACKSNIPES	JAPONAISERIE	JEALOUSHOOD	JESUITICAL	JOCKTELEGS
JACKSTAFFS	JAPONAISERIES	JEALOUSHOODS	JESUITICALLY	JOCOSENESS
JACKSTAVES	JARDINIERE	JEALOUSIES	JESUITISMS	JOCOSENESSES
JACKSTONES	JARDINIERES	JEALOUSING	JESUITRIES	JOCOSERIOUS
JACKSTRAWS	JARGONEERS	JEALOUSNESS	JETSTREAMS	JOCOSITIES
JACQUERIES	JARGONELLE	JEALOUSNESSES	JETTATURAS	JOCULARITIES
JACTATIONS	JARGONELLES	JEANSWEARS	JETTINESSES	JOCULARITY

JOCULATORS
JOCUNDITIES
JOCUNDNESS
JOCUNDNESSES
JOGTROTTED
JOGTROTTING
JOHANNESES
JOHNNYCAKE
JOHNNYCAKES
JOHNSONGRASS
JOHNSONGRASSES
JOINTEDNESS
JOINTEDNESSES
JOINTNESSES
JOINTRESSES
JOINTURESS
JOINTURESSES
JOINTURING
JOINTWEEDS
JOINTWORMS
JOKESMITHS
JOKINESSES
JOLIOTIUMS
JOLLEYINGS
JOLLIFICATION
JOLLIFICATIONS
JOLLIFYING
JOLLIMENTS
JOLLINESSES
JOLLYBOATS
JOLLYHEADS
JOLTERHEAD
JOLTERHEADS
JONNYCAKES
JOSEPHINITE
JOSEPHINITES
JOSTLEMENT
JOSTLEMENTS
JOUISANCES
JOURNALESE
JOURNALESES
JOURNALING

JOURNALINGS
JOURNALISATION
JOURNALISATIONS
JOURNALISE
JOURNALISED
JOURNALISER
JOURNALISERS
JOURNALISES
JOURNALISING
JOURNALISM
JOURNALISMS
JOURNALIST
JOURNALISTIC
JOURNALISTS
JOURNALIZATION
JOURNALIZATIONS
JOURNALIZE
JOURNALIZED
JOURNALIZER
JOURNALIZERS
JOURNALIZES
JOURNALIZING
JOURNALLED
JOURNALLING
JOURNALLINGS
JOURNEYERS
JOURNEYING
JOURNEYMAN
JOURNEYMEN
JOURNEYWORK
JOURNEYWORKS
JOUYSAUNCE
JOUYSAUNCES
JOVIALITIES
JOVIALNESS
JOVIALNESSES
JOVIALTIES
JOVYSAUNCE
JOVYSAUNCES
JOWLINESSES
JOYFULLEST
JOYFULNESS

JOYFULNESSES
JOYLESSNESS
JOYLESSNESSES
JOYOUSNESS
JOYOUSNESSES
JOYPOPPERS
JOYPOPPING
JOYRIDINGS
JUBILANCES
JUBILANCIES
JUBILANTLY
JUBILARIAN
JUBILARIANS
JUBILATING
JUBILATION
JUBILATIONS
JUDDERIEST
JUDGEMENTAL
JUDGEMENTALLY
JUDGEMENTS
JUDGESHIPS
JUDGMATICAL
JUDGMATICALLY
JUDGMENTAL
JUDGMENTALLY
JUDICATION
JUDICATIONS
JUDICATIVE
JUDICATORIAL
JUDICATORIES
JUDICATORS
JUDICATORY
JUDICATURE
JUDICATURES
JUDICIALLY
JUDICIARIES
JUDICIARILY
JUDICIOUSLY
JUDICIOUSNESS
JUDICIOUSNESSES
JUGGERNAUT
JUGGERNAUTS

JUGGLERIES
JUGGLINGLY
JUGLANDACEOUS
JUGULATING
JUGULATION
JUGULATIONS
JUICEHEADS
JUICINESSES
JULIENNING
JUMBLINGLY
JUMBOISING
JUMBOIZING
JUMHOURIYA
JUMHOURIYAS
JUMPINESSES
JUNCACEOUS
JUNCTIONAL
JUNEATINGS
JUNGLEGYMS
JUNGLELIKE
JUNIORATES
JUNIORITIES
JUNKERDOMS
JUNKETEERED
JUNKETEERING
JUNKETEERS
JUNKETINGS
JUNKETTERS
JUNKETTING
JUNKINESSES
JURIDICALLY
JURISCONSULT
JURISCONSULTS
JURISDICTION
JURISDICTIONAL
JURISDICTIONS
JURISDICTIVE
JURISPRUDENCE
JURISPRUDENCES
JURISPRUDENT
JURISPRUDENTIAL
JURISPRUDENTS

JURISTICAL
JURISTICALLY
JUSTICESHIP
JUSTICESHIPS
JUSTICIABILITY
JUSTICIABLE
JUSTICIALISM
JUSTICIALISMS
JUSTICIARIES
JUSTICIARS
JUSTICIARSHIP
JUSTICIARSHIPS
JUSTICIARY
JUSTIFIABILITY
JUSTIFIABLE
JUSTIFIABLENESS
JUSTIFIABLY
JUSTIFICATION
JUSTIFICATIONS
JUSTIFICATIVE
JUSTIFICATOR
JUSTIFICATORS
JUSTIFICATORY
JUSTIFIERS
JUSTIFYING
JUSTNESSES
JUVENESCENCE
JUVENESCENCES
JUVENESCENT
JUVENILELY
JUVENILENESS
JUVENILENESSES
JUVENILITIES
JUVENILITY
JUXTAPOSED
JUXTAPOSES
JUXTAPOSING
JUXTAPOSITION
JUXTAPOSITIONAL
JUXTAPOSITIONS

j

K

KABALISTIC
KABARAGOYA
KABARAGOYAS
KABBALISMS
KABBALISTIC
KABBALISTS
KABELJOUWS
KACHUMBERS
KADAITCHAS
KAFFEEKLATSCH
KAFFEEKLATSCHES
KAFFIRBOOM
KAFFIRBOOMS
KAHIKATEAS
KAHIKATOAS
KAIKAWAKAS
KAIKOMAKOS
KAILYAIRDS
KAINOGENESES
KAINOGENESIS
KAINOGENETIC
KAIROMONES
KAISERDOMS
KAISERISMS
KAISERSHIP
KAISERSHIPS
KAKISTOCRACIES
KAKISTOCRACY
KALAMKARIS
KALANCHOES
KALASHNIKOV
KALASHNIKOVS
KALEIDOPHONE
KALEIDOPHONES
KALEIDOSCOPE
KALEIDOSCOPES
KALEIDOSCOPIC
KALENDARED
KALENDARING
KALIPHATES
KALLIKREIN
KALLIKREINS
KALLITYPES
KALSOMINED
KALSOMINES
KALSOMINING
KAMELAUKION
KAMELAUKIONS
KAMERADING
KANAMYCINS
KANGAROOED
KANGAROOING
KANTIKOYED
KANTIKOYING

KAOLINISED
KAOLINISES
KAOLINISING
KAOLINITES
KAOLINIZED
KAOLINIZES
KAOLINIZING
KAOLINOSES
KAOLINOSIS
KAPELLMEISTER
KAPELLMEISTERS
KARABINERS
KARANGAING
KARATEISTS
KARMICALLY
KARSTIFICATION
KARSTIFICATIONS
KARSTIFIED
KARSTIFIES
KARSTIFYING
KARUHIRUHI
KARUHIRUHIS
KARYOGAMIC
KARYOGAMIES
KARYOGRAMS
KARYOKINESES
KARYOKINESIS
KARYOKINETIC
KARYOLOGIC
KARYOLOGICAL
KARYOLOGIES
KARYOLOGIST
KARYOLOGISTS
KARYOLYMPH
KARYOLYMPHS
KARYOLYSES
KARYOLYSIS
KARYOLYTIC
KARYOMAPPING
KARYOMAPPINGS
KARYOPLASM
KARYOPLASMIC
KARYOPLASMS
KARYOSOMES
KARYOTYPED
KARYOTYPES
KARYOTYPIC
KARYOTYPICAL
KARYOTYPICALLY
KARYOTYPING
KATABOLICALLY
KATABOLISM
KATABOLISMS

KATABOTHRON
KATABOTHRONS
KATADROMOUS
KATATHERMOMETER
KATAVOTHRON
KATAVOTHRONS
KATHAKALIS
KATHAREVOUSA
KATHAREVOUSAS
KATHAROMETER
KATHAROMETERS
KATZENJAMMER
KATZENJAMMERS
KAWANATANGA
KAWANATANGAS
KAZATSKIES
KAZILLIONS
KEELHALING
KEELHAULED
KEELHAULING
KEELHAULINGS
KEELIVINES
KEELYVINES
KEENNESSES
KEEPERLESS
KEEPERSHIP
KEEPERSHIPS
KEEPSAKIER
KEEPSAKIEST
KEESHONDEN
KEFUFFLING
KEKERENGUS
KELPFISHES
KELYPHITIC
KENNELLING
KENNETTING
KENOGENESES
KENOGENESIS
KENOGENETIC
KENOPHOBIA
KENOPHOBIAS
KENOTICIST
KENOTICISTS
KENSPECKLE
KENTLEDGES
KERATECTOMIES
KERATECTOMY
KERATINISATION
KERATINISATIONS
KERATINISE
KERATINISED
KERATINISES
KERATINISING

KERATINIZATION
KERATINIZATIONS
KERATINIZE
KERATINIZED
KERATINIZES
KERATINIZING
KERATINOPHILIC
KERATINOUS
KERATITIDES
KERATITISES
KERATOGENOUS
KERATOMATA
KERATOMETER
KERATOMETERS
KERATOPHYRE
KERATOPHYRES
KERATOPLASTIC
KERATOPLASTIES
KERATOPLASTY
KERATOTOMIES
KERATOTOMY
KERAUNOGRAPH
KERAUNOGRAPHS
KERBLOOEYS
KERBSTONES
KERCHIEFED
KERCHIEFING
KERCHIEVES
KERFUFFLED
KERFUFFLES
KERFUFFLING
KERMESITES
KERNELLIER
KERNELLIEST
KERNELLING
KERNICTERUS
KERNICTERUSES
KERNMANTEL
KERPLUNKED
KERPLUNKING
KERSANTITE
KERSANTITES
KERSEYMERE
KERSEYMERES
KERYGMATIC
KETCHUPIER
KETCHUPIEST
KETOACIDOSES
KETOACIDOSIS
KETOGENESES
KETOGENESIS
KETONAEMIA
KETONAEMIAS
KETONEMIAS

KETONURIAS
KETOSTEROID
KETOSTEROIDS
KETTLEBELL
KETTLEBELLS
KETTLEDRUM
KETTLEDRUMMER
KETTLEDRUMMERS
KETTLEDRUMS
KETTLEFULS
KETTLESTITCH
KETTLESTITCHES
KEYBOARDED
KEYBOARDER
KEYBOARDERS
KEYBOARDING
KEYBOARDINGS
KEYBOARDIST
KEYBOARDISTS
KEYBUTTONS
KEYLOGGERS
KEYLOGGING
KEYLOGGINGS
KEYPRESSES
KEYPUNCHED
KEYPUNCHER
KEYPUNCHERS
KEYPUNCHES
KEYPUNCHING
KEYSTONING
KEYSTROKED
KEYSTROKES
KEYSTROKING
KEYSTROKINGS
KEYWORKERS
KHALIFATES
KHANSAMAHS
KHEDIVATES
KHEDIVIATE
KHEDIVIATES
KHIDMUTGAR
KHIDMUTGARS
KHITMUTGAR
KHITMUTGARS
KHUSKHUSES
KIBBITZERS
KIBBITZING
KIBBUTZNIK
KIBBUTZNIKS
KICKABOUTS
KICKAROUND
KICKAROUNDS
KICKBOARDS
KICKBOXERS

KICKBOXING	KINDERGARTNER	KINGFISHER	KLEPTOCRATIC	KNOCKABOUTS
KICKBOXINGS	KINDERGARTNERS	KINGFISHERS	KLEPTOMANIA	KNOCKBACKS
KICKFLIPPED	KINDERSPIEL	KINGFISHES	KLEPTOMANIAC	KNOCKDOWNS
KICKFLIPPING	KINDERSPIELS	KINGLIHOOD	KLEPTOMANIACS	KNOCKWURST
KICKPLATES	KINDHEARTED	KINGLIHOODS	KLEPTOMANIAS	KNOCKWURSTS
KICKSHAWSES	KINDHEARTEDLY	KINGLINESS	KLETTERSCHUH	KNOTGRASSES
KICKSORTER	KINDHEARTEDNESS	KINGLINESSES	KLETTERSCHUHE	KNOTTINESS
KICKSORTERS	KINDLESSLY	KINGMAKERS	KLINOSTATS	KNOTTINESSES
KICKSTANDS	KINDLINESS	KINGSNAKES	KLIPSPRINGER	KNOWABLENESS
KICKSTARTED	KINDLINESSES	KINKINESSES	KLIPSPRINGERS	KNOWABLENESSES
KICKSTARTING	KINDNESSES	KINNIKINIC	KLONDIKERS	KNOWINGEST
KICKSTARTS	KINDREDNESS	KINNIKINICK	KLONDIKING	KNOWINGNESS
KIDDIEWINK	KINDREDNESSES	KINNIKINICKS	KLONDYKERS	KNOWINGNESSES
KIDDIEWINKIE	KINDREDSHIP	KINNIKINICS	KLONDYKING	KNOWLEDGABILITY
KIDDIEWINKIES	KINDREDSHIPS	KINNIKINNICK	KLOOCHMANS	KNOWLEDGABLE
KIDDIEWINKS	KINEMATICAL	KINNIKINNICKS	KLOOTCHMAN	KNOWLEDGABLY
KIDDISHNESS	KINEMATICALLY	KINTLEDGES	KLOOTCHMANS	KNOWLEDGEABLE
KIDDISHNESSES	KINEMATICS	KIRBIGRIPS	KLOOTCHMEN	KNOWLEDGEABLY
KIDDYWINKS	KINEMATOGRAPH	KIRKYAIRDS	KLUTZINESS	KNOWLEDGED
KIDNAPINGS	KINEMATOGRAPHER	KIRSCHWASSER	KLUTZINESSES	KNOWLEDGES
KIDNAPPEES	KINEMATOGRAPHIC	KIRSCHWASSERS	KNACKERIES	KNOWLEDGING
KIDNAPPERS	KINEMATOGRAPHS	KISSAGRAMS	KNACKERING	KNUBBLIEST
KIDNAPPING	KINEMATOGRAPHY	KISSOGRAMS	KNACKINESS	KNUCKLEBALL
KIDNAPPINGS	KINESCOPED	KISSPEPTIN	KNACKINESSES	KNUCKLEBALLER
KIDNEYLIKE	KINESCOPES	KISSPEPTINS	KNACKWURST	KNUCKLEBALLERS
KIDOLOGIES	KINESCOPING	KITCHENALIA	KNACKWURSTS	KNUCKLEBALLS
KIDOLOGIST	KINESIATRIC	KITCHENALIAS	KNAGGINESS	KNUCKLEBONE
KIDOLOGISTS	KINESIATRICS	KITCHENDOM	KNAGGINESSES	KNUCKLEBONES
KIESELGUHR	KINESIOLOGIES	KITCHENDOMS	KNAPSACKED	KNUCKLEDUSTER
KIESELGUHRS	KINESIOLOGIST	KITCHENERS	KNAVESHIPS	KNUCKLEDUSTERS
KIESELGURS	KINESIOLOGISTS	KITCHENETS	KNAVISHNESS	KNUCKLEHEAD
KIESERITES	KINESIOLOGY	KITCHENETTE	KNAVISHNESSES	KNUCKLEHEADED
KILDERKINS	KINESIPATH	KITCHENETTES	KNEEBOARDED	KNUCKLEHEADS
KILLIFISHES	KINESIPATHIC	KITCHENING	KNEEBOARDING	KNUCKLIEST
KILLIKINICK	KINESIPATHIES	KITCHENMAID	KNEEBOARDS	KOEKSISTER
KILLIKINICKS	KINESIPATHIST	KITCHENMAIDS	KNEECAPPED	KOEKSISTERS
KILOCALORIE	KINESIPATHISTS	KITCHENWARE	KNEECAPPING	KOHLRABIES
KILOCALORIES	KINESIPATHS	KITCHENWARES	KNEECAPPINGS	KOHUTUHUTU
KILOCURIES	KINESIPATHY	KITEBOARDS	KNEEPIECES	KOHUTUHUTUS
KILOCYCLES	KINESITHERAPIES	KITESURFER	KNEVELLING	KOLINSKIES
KILOGAUSSES	KINESITHERAPY	KITESURFERS	KNICKERBOCKER	KOLKHOZNIK
KILOGRAMME	KINESTHESES	KITESURFING	KNICKERBOCKERS	KOLKHOZNIKI
KILOGRAMMES	KINESTHESIA	KITESURFINGS	KNICKKNACK	KOLKHOZNIKS
KILOHERTZES	KINESTHESIAS	KITSCHIEST	KNICKKNACKS	KOMONDOROCK
KILOJOULES	KINESTHESIS	KITSCHIFIED	KNICKPOINT	KOMONDOROK
KILOLITERS	KINESTHETIC	KITSCHIFIES	KNICKPOINTS	KOMPROMATS
KILOLITRES	KINESTHETICALLY	KITSCHIFYING	KNIFEPOINT	KONIMETERS
KILOMETERS	KINETHEODOLITE	KITSCHNESS	KNIFEPOINTS	KONIOLOGIES
KILOMETRES	KINETHEODOLITES	KITSCHNESSES	KNIFERESTS	KONISCOPES
KILOMETRIC	KINETICALLY	KITTENIEST	KNIGHTAGES	KOOKABURRA
KILOMETRICAL	KINETICIST	KITTENISHLY	KNIGHTHEAD	KOOKABURRAS
KILOPARSEC	KINETICISTS	KITTENISHNESS	KNIGHTHEADS	KOOKINESSES
KILOPARSECS	KINETOCHORE	KITTENISHNESSES	KNIGHTHOOD	KOTAHITANGA
KILOPASCAL	KINETOCHORES	KITTIWAKES	KNIGHTHOODS	KOTAHITANGAS
KILOPASCALS	KINETOGRAPH	KIWIFRUITS	KNIGHTLESS	KOTTABOSES
KILOTONNES	KINETOGRAPHS	KIWISPORTS	KNIGHTLIER	KOTUKUTUKU
KIMBERLITE	KINETONUCLEI	KLANGFARBE	KNIGHTLIEST	KOTUKUTUKUS
KIMBERLITES	KINETONUCLEUS	KLANGFARBES	KNIGHTLINESS	KOULIBIACA
KINAESTHESES	KINETONUCLEUSES	KLEBSIELLA	KNIGHTLINESSES	KOULIBIACAS
KINAESTHESIA	KINETOPLAST	KLEBSIELLAS	KNIPHOFIAS	KOURBASHED
KINAESTHESIAS	KINETOPLASTS	KLEINHUISIE	KNOBBINESS	KOURBASHES
KINAESTHESIS	KINETOSCOPE	KLEINHUISIES	KNOBBINESSES	KOURBASHING
KINAESTHETIC	KINETOSCOPES	KLENDUSITIES	KNOBBLIEST	KOUSKOUSES
KINDERGARTEN	KINETOSOME	KLENDUSITY	KNOBKERRIE	KOWHAIWHAI
KINDERGARTENER	KINETOSOMES	KLEPHTISMS	KNOBKERRIES	KOWHAIWHAIS
KINDERGARTENERS	KINGCRAFTS	KLEPTOCRACIES	KNOBSTICKS	KRAKOWIAKS
KINDERGARTENS	KINGDOMLESS	KLEPTOCRACY	KNOCKABOUT	KRAUTROCKS

KREASOTING
KREMLINOLOGIES
KREMLINOLOGIST
KREMLINOLOGISTS
KREMLINOLOGY
KREOSOTING
KRIEGSPIEL
KRIEGSPIELS
KRIEGSSPIEL

KRIEGSSPIELS
KROMESKIES
KRUGERRAND
KRUGERRANDS
KRUMMHORNS
KRYOMETERS
KRYPTONITE
KRYPTONITES
KUMARAHOUS

KUMMERBUND
KUMMERBUNDS
KUNDALINIS
KURRASHING
KURCHATOVIUM
KURCHATOVIUMS
KURDAITCHA
KURDAITCHAS
KURFUFFLED

KURFUFFLES
KURFUFFLING
KURRAJONGS
KURTOSISES
KVETCHIEST
KVETCHINESS
KVETCHINESSES
KVETCHINGS
KWASHIORKOR

KWASHIORKORS
KYANISATION
KYANISATIONS
KYANIZATION
KYANTZATIONS
KYMOGRAPHIC
KYMOGRAPHIES
KYMOGRAPHS
KYMOGRAPHY

L

LABANOTATION
LABANOTATIONS
LABDACISMS
LABEFACTATION
LABEFACTATIONS
LABEFACTION
LABEFACTIONS
LABELLABLE
LABELLINGS
LABELLISTS
LABELMATES
LABIALISATION
LABIALISATIONS
LABIALISED
LABIALISES
LABIALISING
LABIALISMS
LABIALITIES
LABIALIZATION
LABIALIZATIONS
LABIALIZED
LABIALIZES
LABIALIZING
LABILITIES
LABIODENTAL
LABIODENTALS
LABIONASAL
LABIONASALS
LABIOVELAR
LABIOVELARS
LABORATORIES
LABORATORY
LABOREDNESS
LABOREDNESSES
LABORINGLY
LABORIOUSLY
LABORIOUSNESS
LABORIOUSNESSES
LABORSAVING
LABOUREDLY
LABOUREDNESS
LABOUREDNESSES
LABOURINGLY
LABOURISMS
LABOURISTS
LABOURITES
LABOURSAVING
LABOURSOME
LABRADOODLE
LABRADOODLES
LABRADORESCENT
LABRADORITE
LABRADORITES
LABYRINTHAL

LABYRINTHIAN
LABYRINTHIC
LABYRINTHICAL
LABYRINTHICALLY
LABYRINTHINE
LABYRINTHITIS
LABYRINTHITISES
LABYRINTHODONT
LABYRINTHODONTS
LABYRINTHS
LACCOLITES
LACCOLITHIC
LACCOLITHS
LACCOLITIC
LACEMAKERS
LACEMAKING
LACEMAKINGS
LACERABILITIES
LACERABILITY
LACERATING
LACERATION
LACERATIONS
LACERATIVE
LACERTIANS
LACERTILIAN
LACERTILIANS
LACERTINES
LACHRYMALS
LACHRYMARIES
LACHRYMARY
LACHRYMATION
LACHRYMATIONS
LACHRYMATOR
LACHRYMATORIES
LACHRYMATORS
LACHRYMATORY
LACHRYMOSE
LACHRYMOSELY
LACHRYMOSITIES
LACHRYMOSITY
LACINESSES
LACINIATED
LACINIATION
LACINIATIONS
LACKADAISICAL
LACKADAISICALLY
LACKADAISY
LACKLUSTER
LACKLUSTERS
LACKLUSTRE
LACKLUSTRES
LACONICALLY
LACONICISM
LACONICISMS

LACQUERERS
LACQUERING
LACQUERINGS
LACQUERWARE
LACQUERWARES
LACQUERWORK
LACQUERWORKS
LACQUEYING
LACRIMARIES
LACRIMATION
LACRIMATIONS
LACRIMATOR
LACRIMATORS
LACRIMATORY
LACRYMATOR
LACRYMATORS
LACRYMATORY
LACTALBUMIN
LACTALBUMINS
LACTARIANS
LACTATIONAL
LACTATIONALLY
LACTATIONS
LACTESCENCE
LACTESCENCES
LACTESCENT
LACTIFEROUS
LACTIFEROUSNESS
LACTIFLUOUS
LACTIVISMS
LACTIVISTS
LACTOBACILLI
LACTOBACILLUS
LACTOFLAVIN
LACTOFLAVINS
LACTOGENIC
LACTOGLOBULIN
LACTOGLOBULINS
LACTOMETER
LACTOMETERS
LACTOPROTEIN
LACTOPROTEINS
LACTOSCOPE
LACTOSCOPES
LACTOSURIA
LACTOSURIAS
LACTOVEGETARIAN
LACTULOSES
LACUNOSITIES
LACUNOSITY
LACUSTRINE
LADDERIEST
LADDERLIKE
LADDERPROOF

LADDISHNESS
LADDISHNESSES
LADIESWEAR
LADIESWEARS
LADYFINGER
LADYFINGERS
LADYFISHES
LADYLIKENESS
LADYLIKENESSES
LADYNESSES
LAEOTROPIC
LAEVIGATED
LAEVIGATES
LAEVIGATING
LAEVOGYRATE
LAEVOROTARY
LAEVOROTATION
LAEVOROTATIONS
LAEVOROTATORY
LAEVULOSES
LAGENIFORM
LAGERPHONE
LAGERPHONES
LAGGARDLIER
LAGGARDLIEST
LAGGARDNESS
LAGGARDNESSES
LAGNIAPPES
LAGOMORPHIC
LAGOMORPHOUS
LAGOMORPHS
LAICISATION
LAICISATIONS
LAICIZATION
LAICIZATIONS
LAIRDLIEST
LAIRDSHIPS
LAKEFRONTS
LAKESHORES
LALAPALOOZA
LALAPALOOZAS
LALLAPALOOZA
LALLAPALOOZAS
LALLATIONS
LALLYGAGGED
LALLYGAGGING
LAMASERAIS
LAMASERIES
LAMBASTING
LAMBDACISM
LAMBDACISMS
LAMBDOIDAL
LAMBENCIES
LAMBITIVES

LAMBREQUIN
LAMBREQUINS
LAMBRUSCOS
LAMBSWOOLS
LAMEBRAINED
LAMEBRAINS
LAMELLARLY
LAMELLATED
LAMELLATELY
LAMELLATION
LAMELLATIONS
LAMELLIBRANCH
LAMELLIBRANCHS
LAMELLICORN
LAMELLICORNS
LAMELLIFORM
LAMELLIROSTRAL
LAMELLIROSTRATE
LAMELLOSITIES
LAMELLOSITY
LAMENESSES
LAMENTABLE
LAMENTABLENESS
LAMENTABLY
LAMENTATION
LAMENTATIONS
LAMENTEDLY
LAMENTINGLY
LAMENTINGS
LAMESTREAM
LAMESTREAMS
LAMINARIAN
LAMINARIANS
LAMINARIAS
LAMINARINS
LAMINARISE
LAMINARISED
LAMINARISES
LAMINARISING
LAMINARIZE
LAMINARIZED
LAMINARIZES
LAMINARIZING
LAMINATING
LAMINATION
LAMINATIONS
LAMINATORS
LAMINECTOMIES
LAMINECTOMY
LAMINGTONS
LAMINITISES
LAMMERGEIER
LAMMERGEIERS
LAMMERGEYER

LAMMERGEYERS	LANDHOLDINGS	LANGUOROUS	LARRIKINISMS	LATERALIZE
LAMPADARIES	LANDLADIES	LANGUOROUSLY	LARVACEOUS	LATERALIZED
LAMPADEDROMIES	LANDLESSNESS	LANGUOROUSNESS	LARVICIDAL	LATERALIZES
LAMPADEDROMY	LANDLESSNESSES	LANIFEROUS	LARVICIDED	LATERALIZING
LAMPADEPHORIA	LANDLOCKED	LANIGEROUS	LARVICIDES	LATERALLED
LAMPADEPHORIAS	LANDLOPERS	LANKINESSES	LARVICIDING	LATERALLING
LAMPADISTS	LANDLORDISM	LANKNESSES	LARVIKITES	LATERBORNS
LAMPADOMANCIES	LANDLORDISMS	LANOSITIES	LARVIPAROUS	LATERIGRADE
LAMPADOMANCY	LANDLUBBER	LANSQUENET	LARYNGEALLY	LATERISATION
LAMPBLACKED	LANDLUBBERLY	LANSQUENETS	LARYNGEALS	LATERISATIONS
LAMPBLACKING	LANDLUBBERS	LANTERLOOS	LARYNGECTOMEE	LATERISING
LAMPBLACKS	LANDLUBBING	LANTERNING	LARYNGECTOMEES	LATERITIOUS
LAMPHOLDER	LANDMARKED	LANTERNIST	LARYNGECTOMIES	LATERIZATION
LAMPHOLDERS	LANDMARKING	LANTERNISTS	LARYNGECTOMISED	LATERIZATIONS
LAMPLIGHTER	LANDMASSES	LANTHANIDE	LARYNGECTOMIZED	LATERIZING
LAMPLIGHTERS	LANDMINING	LANTHANIDES	LARYNGECTOMY	LATEROVERSION
LAMPLIGHTS	LANDMININGS	LANTHANONS	LARYNGISMUS	LATEROVERSIONS
LAMPOONERIES	LANDOWNERS	LANTHANUMS	LARYNGISMUSES	LATESCENCE
LAMPOONERS	LANDOWNERSHIP	LANUGINOSE	LARYNGITIC	LATESCENCES
LAMPOONERY	LANDOWNERSHIPS	LANUGINOUS	LARYNGITIDES	LATHERIEST
LAMPOONING	LANDOWNING	LANUGINOUSNESS	LARYNGITIS	LATHYRISMS
LAMPOONIST	LANDOWNINGS	LANZKNECHT	LARYNGITISES	LATHYRITIC
LAMPOONISTS	LANDSCAPED	LANZKNECHTS	LARYNGOLOGIC	LATHYRUSES
LAMPROPHYRE	LANDSCAPER	LAODICEANS	LARYNGOLOGICAL	LATICIFEROUS
LAMPROPHYRES	LANDSCAPERS	LAPAROSCOPE	LARYNGOLOGIES	LATICIFERS
LAMPROPHYRIC	LANDSCAPES	LAPAROSCOPES	LARYNGOLOGIST	LATICLAVES
LAMPSHADES	LANDSCAPING	LAPAROSCOPIC	LARYNGOLOGISTS	LATIFUNDIA
LAMPSHELLS	LANDSCAPINGS	LAPAROSCOPIES	LARYNGOLOGY	LATIFUNDIO
LAMPSTANDS	LANDSCAPIST	LAPAROSCOPIST	LARYNGOPHONIES	LATIFUNDIOS
LANCEJACKS	LANDSCAPISTS	LAPAROSCOPISTS	LARYNGOPHONY	LATIFUNDIUM
LANCEOLATE	LANDSHARKS	LAPAROSCOPY	LARYNGOSCOPE	LATIMERIAS
LANCEOLATED	LANDSKIPPED	LAPAROTOMIES	LARYNGOSCOPES	LATINISATION
LANCEOLATELY	LANDSKIPPING	LAPAROTOMY	LARYNGOSCOPIC	LATINISATIONS
LANCEWOODS	LANDSKNECHT	LAPIDARIAN	LARYNGOSCOPIES	LATINISING
LANCINATED	LANDSKNECHTS	LAPIDARIES	LARYNGOSCOPIST	LATINITIES
LANCINATES	LANDSLIDDEN	LAPIDARIST	LARYNGOSCOPISTS	LATINIZATION
LANCINATING	LANDSLIDES	LAPIDARISTS	LARYNGOSCOPY	LATINIZATIONS
LANCINATION	LANDSLIDING	LAPIDATING	LARYNGOSPASM	LATINIZING
LANCINATIONS	LANDWAITER	LAPIDATION	LARYNGOSPASMS	LATIROSTRAL
LANDAMMANN	LANDWAITERS	LAPIDATIONS	LARYNGOTOMIES	LATIROSTRATE
LANDAMMANNS	LANDWASHES	LAPIDESCENCE	LARYNGOTOMY	LATISEPTATE
LANDAMMANS	LANGBEINITE	LAPIDESCENCES	LASCIVIOUS	LATITANCIES
LANDAULETS	LANGBEINITES	LAPIDESCENT	LASCIVIOUSLY	LATITATION
LANDAULETTE	LANGLAUFER	LAPIDICOLOUS	LASCIVIOUSNESS	LATITATIONS
LANDAULETTES	LANGLAUFERS	LAPIDIFICATION	LASERDISCS	LATITUDINAL
LANDBOARDING	LANGOSTINO	LAPIDIFICATIONS	LASERDISKS	LATITUDINALLY
LANDBOARDINGS	LANGOSTINOS	LAPIDIFIED	LASERWORTS	LATITUDINARIAN
LANDBOARDS	LANGOUSTES	LAPIDIFIES	LASSITUDES	LATITUDINARIANS
LANDDAMNED	LANGOUSTINE	LAPIDIFYING	LASTINGNESS	LATITUDINOUS
LANDDAMNES	LANGOUSTINES	LAPILLIFORM	LASTINGNESSES	LATRATIONS
LANDDAMNING	LANGRIDGES	LAPSTRAKES	LATCHSTRING	LATROCINIA
LANDDROSES	LANGSPIELS	LAPSTREAKS	LATCHSTRINGS	LATROCINIES
LANDDROSTS	LANGUAGELESS	LARCENISTS	LATECOMERS	LATROCINIUM
LANDFILLED	LANGUAGING	LARCENOUSLY	LATEENRIGGED	LATTERMATH
LANDFILLING	LANGUESCENT	LARCHWOODS	LATENESSES	LATTERMATHS
LANDFILLINGS	LANGUETTES	LARDACEOUS	LATENSIFICATION	LATTERMOST
LANDFORCES	LANGUIDNESS	LARDALITES	LATERALING	LATTICEWORK
LANDGRAVATE	LANGUIDNESSES	LARGEHEARTED	LATERALISATION	LATTICEWORKS
LANDGRAVATES	LANGUISHED	LARGEMOUTH	LATERALISATIONS	LATTICINGS
LANDGRAVES	LANGUISHER	LARGEMOUTHS	LATERALISE	LATTICINIO
LANDGRAVIATE	LANGUISHERS	LARGENESSES	LATERALISED	LAUDABILITIES
LANDGRAVIATES	LANGUISHES	LARGHETTOS	LATERALISES	LAUDABILITY
LANDGRAVINE	LANGUISHING	LARGITIONS	LATERALISING	LAUDABLENESS
LANDGRAVINES	LANGUISHINGLY	LARKINESSES	LATERALITIES	LAUDABLENESSES
LANDHOLDER	LANGUISHINGS	LARKISHNESS	LATERALITY	LAUDATIONS
LANDHOLDERS	LANGUISHMENT	LARKISHNESSES	LATERALIZATION	LAUDATIVES
LANDHOLDING	LANGUISHMENTS	LARRIKINISM	LATERALIZATIONS	LAUDATORIES

LAUGHABLENESS	LAWMONGERS	LEATHERETTE	LEGATORIAL	LEGITIMISED
LAUGHABLENESSES	LAWNMOWERS	LEATHERETTES	LEGENDARIES	LEGITIMISER
LAUGHINGLY	LAWRENCIUM	LEATHERGOODS	LEGENDARILY	LEGITIMISERS
LAUGHINGSTOCK	LAWRENCIUMS	LEATHERHEAD	LEGENDISED	LEGITIMISES
LAUGHINGSTOCKS	LAWYERINGS	LEATHERHEADS	LEGENDISES	LEGITIMISING
LAUGHLINES	LAWYERLIER	LEATHERIER	LEGENDISING	LEGITIMISM
LAUGHWORTHIER	LAWYERLIEST	LEATHERIEST	LEGENDISTS	LEGITIMISMS
LAUGHWORTHIEST	LAWYERLIKE	LEATHERINESS	LEGENDIZED	LEGITIMIST
LAUGHWORTHY	LAXATIVENESS	LEATHERINESSES	LEGENDIZES	LEGITIMISTIC
LAUNCEGAYE	LAXATIVENESSES	LEATHERING	LEGENDIZING	LEGITIMISTS
LAUNCEGAYES	LAYBACKING	LEATHERINGS	LEGENDRIES	LEGITIMIZATION
LAUNCHINGS	LAYMANISED	LEATHERJACKET	LEGERDEMAIN	LEGITIMIZATIONS
LAUNCHPADS	LAYMANISES	LEATHERJACKETS	LEGERDEMAINIST	LEGITIMIZE
LAUNDERERS	LAYMANISING	LEATHERLEAF	LEGERDEMAINISTS	LEGITIMIZED
LAUNDERETTE	LAYMANIZED	LEATHERLEAFS	LEGERDEMAINS	LEGITIMIZER
LAUNDERETTES	LAYMANIZES	LEATHERLEAVES	LEGERITIES	LEGITIMIZERS
LAUNDERING	LAYMANIZING	LEATHERLIKE	LEGGINESSES	LEGITIMIZES
LAUNDERINGS	LAYPERSONS	LEATHERNECK	LEGIBILITIES	LEGITIMIZING
LAUNDRESSES	LAZARETTES	LEATHERNECKS	LEGIBILITY	LEGLESSNESS
LAUNDRETTE	LAZARETTOS	LEATHERWOOD	LEGIBLENESS	LEGLESSNESSES
LAUNDRETTES	LAZINESSES	LEATHERWOODS	LEGIBLENESSES	LEGUMINOUS
LAUNDRYMAN	LEACHABILITIES	LEATHERWORK	LEGIONARIES	LEGWARMERS
LAUNDRYMEN	LEACHABILITY	LEATHERWORKS	LEGIONELLA	LEIOMYOMAS
LAUNDRYWOMAN	LEADENNESS	LEAVENINGS	LEGIONELLAE	LEIOMYOMATA
LAUNDRYWOMEN	LEADENNESSES	LEBENSRAUM	LEGIONELLAS	LEIOTRICHIES
LAURACEOUS	LEADERBOARD	LEBENSRAUMS	LEGIONNAIRE	LEIOTRICHOUS
LAURDALITE	LEADERBOARDS	LECHEROUSLY	LEGIONNAIRES	LEIOTRICHY
LAURDALITES	LEADERENES	LECHEROUSNESS	LEGISLATED	LEISHMANIA
LAUREATESHIP	LEADERETTE	LECHEROUSNESSES	LEGISLATES	LEISHMANIAE
LAUREATESHIPS	LEADERETTES	LECITHINASE	LEGISLATING	LEISHMANIAL
LAUREATING	LEADERLESS	LECITHINASES	LEGISLATION	LEISHMANIAS
LAUREATION	LEADERSHIP	LECTIONARIES	LEGISLATIONS	LEISHMANIASES
LAUREATIONS	LEADERSHIPS	LECTIONARY	LEGISLATIVE	LEISHMANIASIS
LAURELLING	LEADPLANTS	LECTISTERNIA	LEGISLATIVELY	LEISHMANIOSES
LAURUSTINE	LEADSCREWS	LECTISTERNIUM	LEGISLATIVES	LEISHMANIOSIS
LAURUSTINES	LEAFCUTTER	LECTISTERNIUMS	LEGISLATOR	LEISTERING
LAURUSTINUS	LEAFCUTTERS	LECTORATES	LEGISLATORIAL	LEISURABLE
LAURUSTINUSES	LEAFHOPPER	LECTORSHIP	LEGISLATORS	LEISURABLY
LAURVIKITE	LEAFHOPPERS	LECTORSHIPS	LEGISLATORSHIP	LEISURELIER
LAURVIKITES	LEAFINESSES	LECTOTYPES	LEGISLATORSHIPS	LEISURELIEST
LAVALIERES	LEAFLESSNESS	LECTRESSES	LEGISLATRESS	LEISURELINESS
LAVALLIERE	LEAFLESSNESSES	LECTURESHIP	LEGISLATRESSES	LEISURELINESSES
LAVALLIERES	LEAFLETEER	LECTURESHIPS	LEGISLATURE	LEISUREWEAR
LAVATIONAL	LEAFLETEERS	LECYTHIDACEOUS	LEGISLATURES	LEISUREWEARS
LAVATORIAL	LEAFLETERS	LECYTHISES	LEGITIMACIES	LEITMOTIFS
LAVATORIES	LEAFLETING	LEDERHOSEN	LEGITIMACY	LEITMOTIVS
LAVENDERED	LEAFLETTED	LEECHCRAFT	LEGITIMATE	LEMMATISATION
LAVENDERING	LEAFLETTING	LEECHCRAFTS	LEGITIMATED	LEMMATISATIONS
LAVERBREAD	LEAFSTALKS	LEERINESSES	LEGITIMATELY	LEMMATISED
LAVERBREADS	LEAGUERING	LEETSPEAKS	LEGITIMATENESS	LEMMATISES
LAVEROCKED	LEAKINESSES	LEFTWARDLY	LEGITIMATES	LEMMATISING
LAVEROCKING	LEANNESSES	LEGALISATION	LEGITIMATING	LEMMATIZATION
LAVISHMENT	LEAPFROGGED	LEGALISATIONS	LEGITIMATION	LEMMATIZATIONS
LAVISHMENTS	LEAPFROGGING	LEGALISERS	LEGITIMATIONS	LEMMATIZED
LAVISHNESS	LEARINESSES	LEGALISING	LEGITIMATISE	LEMMATIZES
LAVISHNESSES	LEARNABILITIES	LEGALISTIC	LEGITIMATISED	LEMMATIZING
LAVOLTAING	LEARNABILITY	LEGALISTICALLY	LEGITIMATISES	LEMMINGLIKE
LAWBREAKER	LEARNEDNESS	LEGALITIES	LEGITIMATISING	LEMNISCATE
LAWBREAKERS	LEARNEDNESSES	LEGALIZATION	LEGITIMATIZE	LEMNISCATES
LAWBREAKING	LEASEBACKS	LEGALIZATIONS	LEGITIMATIZED	LEMONFISHES
LAWBREAKINGS	LEASEHOLDER	LEGALIZERS	LEGITIMATIZES	LEMONGRASS
LAWFULNESS	LEASEHOLDERS	LEGALIZING	LEGITIMATIZING	LEMONGRASSES
LAWFULNESSES	LEASEHOLDS	LEGATARIES	LEGITIMATOR	LEMONWOODS
LAWGIVINGS	LEASTAWAYS	LEGATESHIP	LEGITIMATORS	LENGTHENED
LAWLESSNESS	LEATHERBACK	LEGATESHIPS	LEGITIMISATION	LENGTHENER
LAWLESSNESSES	LEATHERBACKS	LEGATIONARY	LEGITIMISATIONS	LENGTHENERS
LAWMAKINGS	LEATHERBOUND	LEGATISSIMO	LEGITIMISE	LENGTHENING

LENGTHIEST	LEPTODACTYL	LEUCOCIDINS	LEUKODERMAS	LEXICOLOGIST
LENGTHINESS	LEPTODACTYLOUS	LEUCOCRATIC	LEUKODERMIC	LEXICOLOGISTS
LENGTHINESSES	LEPTODACTYLS	LEUCOCYTES	LEUKODYSTROPHY	LEXICOLOGY
LENGTHSMAN	LEPTOKURTIC	LEUCOCYTHAEMIA	LEUKOPENIA	LEXIGRAPHIC
LENGTHSMEN	LEPTOPHOSES	LEUCOCYTHAEMIAS	LEUKOPENIAS	LEXIGRAPHICAL
LENGTHWAYS	LEPTOPHYLLOUS	LEUCOCYTIC	LEUKOPENIC	LEXIGRAPHTES
LENGTHWISE	LEPTORRHINE	LEUCOCYTOLYSES	LEUKOPLAKIA	LEXIGRAPHY
LENIENCIES	LEPTOSOMATIC	LEUCOCYTOLYSIS	LEUKOPLAKIAS	LEYLANDIIS
LENITIVELY	LEPTOSOMES	LEUCOCYTOPENIA	LEUKOPLAKIC	LHERZOLITE
LENOCINIUM	LEPTOSOMIC	LEUCOCYTOPENIAS	LEUKOPOIESES	LHERZOLITES
LENOCINIUMS	LEPTOSPIRAL	LEUCOCYTOSES	LEUKOPOIESIS	LIABILITIES
LENTAMENTE	LEPTOSPIRE	LEUCOCYTOSIS	LEUKOPOIETIC	LIABLENESS
LENTICELLATE	LEPTOSPIRES	LEUCOCYTOTIC	LEUKORRHEA	LIABLENESSES
LENTICULAR	LEPTOSPIROSES	LEUCODEPLETED	LEUKORRHEAL	LIBATIONAL
LENTICULARLY	LEPTOSPIROSIS	LEUCODERMA	LEUKORRHEAS	LIBATIONARY
LENTICULARS	LEPTOTENES	LEUCODERMAL	LEUKOTOMES	LIBECCHIOS
LENTICULES	LESBIANISM	LEUCODERMAS	LEUKOTOMIES	LIBELLANTS
LENTIGINES	LESBIANISMS	LEUCODERMIA	LEUKOTRIENE	LIBELLINGS
LENTIGINOSE	LESPEDEZAS	LEUCODERMIAS	LEUKOTRIENES	LIBELLOUSLY
LENTIGINOUS	LESSEESHIP	LEUCODERMIC	LEVANTINES	LIBELOUSLY
LENTISSIMO	LESSEESHIPS	LEUCOMAINE	LEVELHEADED	LIBERALISATION
LENTIVIRUS	LESSENINGS	LEUCOMAINES	LEVELHEADEDNESS	LIBERALISATIONS
LENTIVIRUSES	LESSONINGS	LEUCOPENIA	LEVELLINGS	LIBERALISE
LEONTIASES	LETHALITIES	LEUCOPENIAS	LEVELNESSES	LIBERALISED
LEONTIASIS	LETHARGICAL	LEUCOPENIC	LEVERAGING	LIBERALISER
LEONTOPODIUM	LETHARGICALLY	LEUCOPLAKIA	LEVIATHANS	LIBERALISERS
LEONTOPODIUMS	LETHARGIED	LEUCOPLAKIAS	LEVIGATING	LIBERALISES
LEOPARDESS	LETHARGIES	LEUCOPLAKIC	LEVIGATION	LIBERALISING
LEOPARDESSES	LETHARGISE	LEUCOPLAST	LEVIGATIONS	LIBERALISM
LEOPARDSKIN	LETHARGISED	LEUCOPLASTID	LEVIGATORS	LIBERALISMS
LEOPARDSKINS	LETHARGISES	LEUCOPLASTIDS	LEVIRATICAL	LIBERALIST
LEPIDODENDROID	LETHARGISING	LEUCOPLASTS	LEVIRATION	LIBERALISTIC
LEPIDODENDROIDS	LETHARGIZE	LEUCOPOIESES	LEVIRATIONS	LIBERALISTS
LEPIDOLITE	LETHARGIZED	LEUCOPOIESIS	LEVITATING	LIBERALITIES
LEPIDOLITES	LETHARGIZES	LEUCOPOIETIC	LEVITATION	LIBERALITY
LEPIDOMELANE	LETHARGIZING	LEUCORRHOEA	LEVITATIONAL	LIBERALIZATION
LEPIDOMELANES	LETHIFEROUS	LEUCORRHOEAL	LEVITATIONS	LIBERALIZATIONS
LEPIDOPTERA	LETROZOLES	LEUCORRHOEAS	LEVITATORS	LIBERALIZE
LEPIDOPTERAN	LETTERBOXED	LEUCOTOMES	LEVITICALLY	LIBERALIZED
LEPIDOPTERANS	LETTERBOXES	LEUCOTOMIES	LEVOROTARY	LIBERALIZER
LEPIDOPTERIST	LETTERBOXING	LEUKAEMIAS	LEVOROTATORY	LIBERALIZERS
LEPIDOPTERISTS	LETTERBOXINGS	LEUKAEMOGEN	LEWDNESSES	LIBERALIZES
LEPIDOPTEROLOGY	LETTERFORM	LEUKAEMOGENESES	LEXICALISATION	LIBERALIZING
LEPIDOPTERON	LETTERFORMS	LEUKAEMOGENESIS	LEXICALISATIONS	LIBERALNESS
LEPIDOPTERONS	LETTERHEAD	LEUKAEMOGENIC	LEXICALISE	LIBERALNESSES
LEPIDOPTEROUS	LETTERHEADS	LEUKAEMOGENS	LEXICALISED	LIBERATING
LEPIDOSIREN	LETTERINGS	LEUKEMOGEN	LEXICALISES	LIBERATION
LEPIDOSIRENS	LETTERLESS	LEUKEMOGENESES	LEXICALISING	LIBERATIONISM
LEPRECHAUN	LETTERPRESS	LEUKEMOGENESIS	LEXICALITIES	LIBERATIONISMS
LEPRECHAUNISH	LETTERPRESSES	LEUKEMOGENIC	LEXICALITY	LIBERATIONIST
LEPRECHAUNS	LETTERSETS	LEUKEMOGENS	LEXICALIZATION	LIBERATIONISTS
LEPRECHAWN	LETTERSPACING	LEUKOBLAST	LEXICALIZATIONS	LIBERATIONS
LEPRECHAWNS	LETTERSPACINGS	LEUKOBLASTS	LEXICALIZE	LIBERATORS
LEPROMATOUS	LEUCAEMIAS	LEUKOCIDIN	LEXICALIZED	LIBERATORY
LEPROSARIA	LEUCAEMOGEN	LEUKOCIDINS	LEXICALIZES	LIBERTARIAN
LEPROSARIUM	LEUCAEMOGENESES	LEUKOCYTES	LEXICALIZING	LIBERTARIANISM
LEPROSARIUMS	LEUCAEMOGENESIS	LEUKOCYTIC	LEXICOGRAPHER	LIBERTARIANISMS
LEPROSERIE	LEUCAEMOGENIC	LEUKOCYTOLYSES	LEXICOGRAPHERS	LIBERTARIANS
LEPROSERIES	LEUCAEMOGENS	LEUKOCYTOLYSIS	LEXICOGRAPHIC	LIBERTICIDAL
LEPROSITIES	LEUCHAEMIA	LEUKOCYTOPENIA	LEXICOGRAPHICAL	LIBERTICIDE
LEPROUSNESS	LEUCHAEMIAS	LEUKOCYTOPENIAS	LEXICOGRAPHIES	LIBERTICIDES
LEPROUSNESSES	LEUCITOHEDRA	LEUKOCYTOSES	LEXICOGRAPHIST	LIBERTINAGE
LEPTOCEPHALI	LEUCITOHEDRON	LEUKOCYTOSIS	LEXICOGRAPHISTS	LIBERTINAGES
LEPTOCEPHALIC	LEUCITOHEDRONS	LEUKOCYTOTIC	LEXICOGRAPHY	LIBERTINES
LEPTOCEPHALOUS	LEUCOBLAST	LEUKODEPLETED	LEXICOLOGICAL	LIBERTINISM
LEPTOCEPHALUS	LEUCOBLASTS	LEUKODERMA	LEXICOLOGICALLY	LIBERTINISMS
LEPTOCERCAL	LEUCOCIDIN	LEUKODERMAL	LEXICOLOGIES	LIBIDINALLY

LIBIDINIST
LIBIDINISTS
LIBIDINOSITIES
LIBIDINOSITY
LIBIDINOUS
LIBIDINOUSLY
LIBIDINOUSNESS
LIBRAIRIES
LIBRARIANS
LIBRARIANSHIP
LIBRARIANSHIPS
LIBRATIONAL
LIBRATIONS
LIBRETTIST
LIBRETTISTS
LICENSABLE
LICENSURES
LICENTIATE
LICENTIATES
LICENTIATESHIP
LICENTIATESHIPS
LICENTIATION
LICENTIATIONS
LICENTIOUS
LICENTIOUSLY
LICENTIOUSNESS
LICHANOSES
LICHENISMS
LICHENISTS
LICHENOLOGICAL
LICHENOLOGIES
LICHENOLOGIST
LICHENOLOGISTS
LICHENOLOGY
LICHTLYING
LICITNESSES
LICKERISHLY
LICKERISHNESS
LICKERISHNESSES
LICKPENNIES
LICKSPITTLE
LICKSPITTLES
LIDOCAINES
LIEBFRAUMILCH
LIEBFRAUMILCHS
LIENHOLDER
LIENHOLDERS
LIENTERIES
LIEUTENANCIES
LIEUTENANCY
LIEUTENANT
LIEUTENANTRIES
LIEUTENANTRY
LIEUTENANTS
LIEUTENANTSHIP
LIEUTENANTSHIPS
LIFEBLOODS
LIFEBOATMAN
LIFEBOATMEN
LIFEGUARDED
LIFEGUARDING
LIFEGUARDS
LIFEHACKED
LIFEHACKER
LIFEHACKERS
LIFEHACKING
LIFELESSLY

LIFELESSNESS
LIFELESSNESSES
LIFELIKENESS
LIFELIKENESSES
LIFEMANSHIP
LIFEMANSHIPS
LIFESAVERS
LIFESAVING
LIFESAVINGS
LIFESTYLER
LIFESTYLERS
LIFESTYLES
LIFEWORLDS
LIGAMENTAL
LIGAMENTARY
LIGAMENTOUS
LIGATURING
LIGHTBULBS
LIGHTENERS
LIGHTENING
LIGHTENINGS
LIGHTERAGE
LIGHTERAGES
LIGHTERING
LIGHTERMAN
LIGHTERMEN
LIGHTFACED
LIGHTFACES
LIGHTFASTNESS
LIGHTFASTNESSES
LIGHTHEARTED
LIGHTHEARTEDLY
LIGHTHOUSE
LIGHTHOUSEMAN
LIGHTHOUSEMEN
LIGHTHOUSES
LIGHTLYING
LIGHTNESSES
LIGHTNINGED
LIGHTNINGS
LIGHTPLANE
LIGHTPLANES
LIGHTPROOF
LIGHTSHIPS
LIGHTSOMELY
LIGHTSOMENESS
LIGHTSOMENESSES
LIGHTTIGHT
LIGHTWEIGHT
LIGHTWEIGHTS
LIGHTWOODS
LIGNICOLOUS
LIGNIFICATION
LIGNIFICATIONS
LIGNIFYING
LIGNIPERDOUS
LIGNIVOROUS
LIGNOCAINE
LIGNOCAINES
LIGNOCELLULOSE
LIGNOCELLULOSES
LIGNOCELLULOSIC
LIGNOSULFONATE
LIGNOSULFONATES
LIGULIFLORAL
LIGUSTRUMS
LIKABILITIES

LIKABILITY
LIKABLENESS
LIKABLENESSES
LIKEABILITIES
LIKEABILITY
LIKEABLENESS
LIKEABLENESSES
LIKELIHOOD
LIKELIHOODS
LIKELINESS
LIKELINESSES
LIKENESSES
LILANGENIS
LILIACEOUS
LILLIPUTIAN
LILLIPUTIANS
LILTINGNESS
LILTINGNESSES
LIMACIFORM
LIMACOLOGIES
LIMACOLOGIST
LIMACOLOGISTS
LIMACOLOGY
LIMBERNESS
LIMBERNESSES
LIMBURGITE
LIMBURGITES
LIMELIGHTED
LIMELIGHTER
LIMELIGHTERS
LIMELIGHTING
LIMELIGHTS
LIMERENCES
LIMESCALES
LIMESTONES
LIMEWASHES
LIMEWATERS
LIMICOLINE
LIMICOLOUS
LIMINESSES
LIMITABLENESS
LIMITABLENESSES
LIMITARIAN
LIMITARIANS
LIMITATION
LIMITATIONAL
LIMITATIONS
LIMITATIVE
LIMITEDNESS
LIMITEDNESSES
LIMITINGLY
LIMITLESSLY
LIMITLESSNESS
LIMITLESSNESSES
LIMITROPHE
LIMIVOROUS
LIMNOLOGIC
LIMNOLOGICAL
LIMNOLOGICALLY
LIMNOLOGIES
LIMNOLOGIST
LIMNOLOGISTS
LIMNOPHILOUS
LIMOUSINES
LIMPIDITIES
LIMPIDNESS
LIMPIDNESSES

LIMPNESSES
LINCOMYCIN
LINCOMYCINS
LINCRUSTAS
LINEALITIES
LINEAMENTAL
LINEAMENTS
LINEARISATION
LINEARISATIONS
LINEARISED
LINEARISES
LINEARISING
LINEARITIES
LINEARIZATION
LINEARIZATIONS
LINEARIZED
LINEARIZES
LINEARIZING
LINEATIONS
LINEBACKER
LINEBACKERS
LINEBACKING
LINEBACKINGS
LINEBREEDING
LINEBREEDINGS
LINECASTER
LINECASTERS
LINECASTING
LINECASTINGS
LINENFOLDS
LINEOLATED
LINERBOARD
LINERBOARDS
LINESCORES
LINGBERRIES
LINGERINGLY
LINGERINGS
LINGONBERRIES
LINGONBERRY
LINGUIFORM
LINGUISTER
LINGUISTERS
LINGUISTIC
LINGUISTICAL
LINGUISTICALLY
LINGUISTICIAN
LINGUISTICIANS
LINGUISTICS
LINGUISTRIES
LINGUISTRY
LINGULATED
LINISHINGS
LINKSLANDS
LINOLEATES
LINOTYPERS
LINOTYPING
LINTSTOCKS
LINTWHITES
LIONCELLES
LIONFISHES
LIONHEARTED
LIONHEARTEDNESS
LIONISATION
LIONISATIONS
LIONIZATION
LIONIZATIONS
LIPECTOMIES

LIPGLOSSES
LIPIDOPLAST
LIPIDOPLASTS
LIPOCHROME
LIPOCHROMES
LIPODYSTROPHIES
LIPODYSTROPHY
LIPOGENESES
LIPOGENESIS
LIPOGRAMMATIC
LIPOGRAMMATISM
LIPOGRAMMATISMS
LIPOGRAMMATIST
LIPOGRAMMATISTS
LIPOGRAPHIES
LIPOGRAPHY
LIPOMATOSES
LIPOMATOSIS
LIPOMATOUS
LIPOPHILIC
LIPOPLASTS
LIPOPROTEIN
LIPOPROTEINS
LIPOSCULPTURE
LIPOSCULPTURES
LIPOSUCKED
LIPOSUCKING
LIPOSUCTION
LIPOSUCTIONS
LIPOTROPIC
LIPOTROPIES
LIPOTROPIN
LIPOTROPINS
LIPPINESSES
LIPPITUDES
LIPREADERS
LIPREADING
LIPREADINGS
LIPSTICKED
LIPSTICKING
LIQUATIONS
LIQUEFACIENT
LIQUEFACIENTS
LIQUEFACTION
LIQUEFACTIONS
LIQUEFACTIVE
LIQUEFIABLE
LIQUEFIERS
LIQUEFYING
LIQUESCENCE
LIQUESCENCES
LIQUESCENCIES
LIQUESCENCY
LIQUESCENT
LIQUESCING
LIQUEURING
LIQUIDAMBAR
LIQUIDAMBARS
LIQUIDATED
LIQUIDATES
LIQUIDATING
LIQUIDATION
LIQUIDATIONISM
LIQUIDATIONISMS
LIQUIDATIONIST
LIQUIDATIONISTS
LIQUIDATIONS

LIQUIDATOR
LIQUIDATORS
LIQUIDIEST
LIQUIDISED
LIQUIDISER
LIQUIDISERS
LIQUIDISES
LIQUIDISING
LIQUIDITIES
LIQUIDIZED
LIQUIDIZER
LIQUIDIZERS
LIQUIDIZES
LIQUIDIZING
LIQUIDNESS
LIQUIDNESSES
LIQUIDUSES
LIQUIFACTION
LIQUIFACTIONS
LIQUIFACTIVE
LIQUIFIABLE
LIQUIFIERS
LIQUIFYING
LIQUORICES
LIQUORISHLY
LIQUORISHNESS
LIQUORISHNESSES
LIRIODENDRA
LIRIODENDRON
LIRIODENDRONS
LISSENCEPHALOUS
LISSOMENESS
LISSOMENESSES
LISSOMNESS
LISSOMNESSES
LISSOTRICHOUS
LISTENABILITIES
LISTENABILITY
LISTENABLE
LISTENERSHIP
LISTENERSHIPS
LISTENINGS
LISTERIOSES
LISTERIOSIS
LISTLESSLY
LISTLESSNESS
LISTLESSNESSES
LITENESSES
LITERACIES
LITERALISATION
LITERALISATIONS
LITERALISE
LITERALISED
LITERALISER
LITERALISERS
LITERALISES
LITERALISING
LITERALISM
LITERALISMS
LITERALIST
LITERALISTIC
LITERALISTS
LITERALITIES
LITERALITY
LITERALIZATION
LITERALIZATIONS
LITERALIZE

LITERALIZED
LITERALIZER
LITERALIZERS
LITERALIZES
LITERALIZING
LITERALNESS
LITERALNESSES
LITERARILY
LITERARINESS
LITERARINESSES
LITERARYISM
LITERARYISMS
LITERATELY
LITERATENESS
LITERATENESSES
LITERATION
LITERATIONS
LITERATORS
LITERATURE
LITERATURED
LITERATURES
LITEROSITIES
LITEROSITY
LITHENESSES
LITHESOMENESS
LITHESOMENESSES
LITHIFICATION
LITHIFICATIONS
LITHIFYING
LITHISTIDS
LITHOCHROMATIC
LITHOCHROMATICS
LITHOCHROMIES
LITHOCHROMY
LITHOCLAST
LITHOCLASTS
LITHOCYSTS
LITHODOMOUS
LITHOGENOUS
LITHOGLYPH
LITHOGLYPHS
LITHOGRAPH
LITHOGRAPHED
LITHOGRAPHER
LITHOGRAPHERS
LITHOGRAPHIC
LITHOGRAPHICAL
LITHOGRAPHIES
LITHOGRAPHING
LITHOGRAPHS
LITHOGRAPHY
LITHOLAPAXIES
LITHOLAPAXY
LITHOLATRIES
LITHOLATROUS
LITHOLATRY
LITHOLOGIC
LITHOLOGICAL
LITHOLOGICALLY
LITHOLOGIES
LITHOLOGIST
LITHOLOGISTS
LITHOMANCIES
LITHOMANCY
LITHOMARGE
LITHOMARGES
LITHOMETEOR

LITHOMETEORS
LITHONTHRYPTIC
LITHONTHRYPTICS
LITHONTRIPTIC
LITHONTRIPTICS
LITHONTRIPTIST
LITHONTRIPTISTS
LITHONTRIPTOR
LITHONTRIPTORS
LITHOPHAGOUS
LITHOPHANE
LITHOPHANES
LITHOPHILOUS
LITHOPHYSA
LITHOPHYSAE
LITHOPHYSE
LITHOPHYSES
LITHOPHYTE
LITHOPHYTES
LITHOPHYTIC
LITHOPONES
LITHOPRINT
LITHOPRINTS
LITHOSPERMUM
LITHOSPERMUMS
LITHOSPHERE
LITHOSPHERES
LITHOSPHERIC
LITHOSTATIC
LITHOTOMES
LITHOTOMIC
LITHOTOMICAL
LITHOTOMIES
LITHOTOMIST
LITHOTOMISTS
LITHOTOMOUS
LITHOTRIPSIES
LITHOTRIPSY
LITHOTRIPTER
LITHOTRIPTERS
LITHOTRIPTIC
LITHOTRIPTICS
LITHOTRIPTIST
LITHOTRIPTISTS
LITHOTRIPTOR
LITHOTRIPTORS
LITHOTRITE
LITHOTRITES
LITHOTRITIC
LITHOTRITICS
LITHOTRITIES
LITHOTRITISE
LITHOTRITISED
LITHOTRITISES
LITHOTRITISING
LITHOTRITIST
LITHOTRITISTS
LITHOTRITIZE
LITHOTRITIZED
LITHOTRITIZES
LITHOTRITIZING
LITHOTRITOR
LITHOTRITORS
LITHOTRITY
LITHOTYPES
LITIGATING
LITIGATION

LITIGATIONS
LITIGATORS
LITIGIOUSLY
LITIGIOUSNESS
LITIGIOUSNESSES
LITTERATEUR
LITTERATEURS
LITTERBAGS
LITTERBUGS
LITTERIEST
LITTERMATE
LITTERMATES
LITTLENECK
LITTLENECKS
LITTLENESS
LITTLENESSES
LITTLEWORTH
LITURGICAL
LITURGICALLY
LITURGIOLOGIES
LITURGIOLOGIST
LITURGIOLOGISTS
LITURGIOLOGY
LITURGISMS
LITURGISTIC
LITURGISTS
LIVABILITIES
LIVABILITY
LIVABLENESS
LIVABLENESSES
LIVEABILITIES
LIVEABILITY
LIVEABLENESS
LIVEABLENESSES
LIVEBLOGGED
LIVEBLOGGER
LIVEBLOGGERS
LIVEBLOGGING
LIVEBLOGGINGS
LIVELIHEAD
LIVELIHEADS
LIVELIHOOD
LIVELIHOODS
LIVELINESS
LIVELINESSES
LIVENESSES
LIVERISHLY
LIVERISHNESS
LIVERISHNESSES
LIVERLEAVES
LIVERMORIUM
LIVERMORIUMS
LIVERWORTS
LIVERWURST
LIVERWURSTS
LIVESTOCKS
LIVESTREAM
LIVESTREAMED
LIVESTREAMING
LIVESTREAMS
LIVETRAPPED
LIVETRAPPING
LIVIDITIES
LIVIDNESSES
LIVINGNESS
LIVINGNESSES
LIVRAISONS

LIXIVIATED
LIXIVIATES
LIXIVIATING
LIXIVIATION
LIXIVIATIONS
LOADMASTER
LOADMASTERS
LOADSAMONEY
LOADSAMONEYS
LOADSAMONIES
LOADSPACES
LOADSTONES
LOAMINESSES
LOANSHIFTS
LOATHEDNESS
LOATHEDNESSES
LOATHFULNESS
LOATHFULNESSES
LOATHINGLY
LOATHLIEST
LOATHLINESS
LOATHLINESSES
LOATHNESSES
LOATHSOMELY
LOATHSOMENESS
LOATHSOMENESSES
LOBECTOMIES
LOBLOLLIES
LOBOTOMIES
LOBOTOMISE
LOBOTOMISED
LOBOTOMISES
LOBOTOMISING
LOBOTOMIZE
LOBOTOMIZED
LOBOTOMIZES
LOBOTOMIZING
LOBSCOUSES
LOBSTERERS
LOBSTERING
LOBSTERINGS
LOBSTERLIKE
LOBSTERMAN
LOBSTERMEN
LOBTAILING
LOBTAILINGS
LOBULATION
LOBULATIONS
LOCALISABILITY
LOCALISABLE
LOCALISATION
LOCALISATIONS
LOCALISERS
LOCALISING
LOCALISTIC
LOCALITIES
LOCALIZABILITY
LOCALIZABLE
LOCALIZATION
LOCALIZATIONS
LOCALIZERS
LOCALIZING
LOCALNESSES
LOCATEABLE
LOCATIONAL
LOCATIONALLY
LOCKHOUSES

LOCKKEEPER
LOCKKEEPERS
LOCKMAKERS
LOCKSMITHERIES
LOCKSMITHERY
LOCKSMITHING
LOCKSMITHINGS
LOCKSMITHS
LOCKSTITCH
LOCKSTITCHED
LOCKSTITCHES
LOCKSTITCHING
LOCOMOBILE
LOCOMOBILES
LOCOMOBILITIES
LOCOMOBILITY
LOCOMOTING
LOCOMOTION
LOCOMOTIONS
LOCOMOTIVE
LOCOMOTIVELY
LOCOMOTIVENESS
LOCOMOTIVES
LOCOMOTIVITIES
LOCOMOTIVITY
LOCOMOTORS
LOCOMOTORY
LOCOPLANTS
LOCORESTIVE
LOCULAMENT
LOCULAMENTS
LOCULATION
LOCULATIONS
LOCULICIDAL
LOCUTIONARY
LOCUTORIES
LODESTONES
LODGEMENTS
LODGEPOLES
LOFTINESSES
LOGAGRAPHIA
LOGAGRAPHIAS
LOGANBERRIES
LOGANBERRY
LOGANIACEOUS
LOGAOEDICS
LOGARITHMIC
LOGARITHMICAL
LOGARITHMICALLY
LOGARITHMS
LOGGERHEAD
LOGGERHEADED
LOGGERHEADS
LOGICALITIES
LOGICALITY
LOGICALNESS
LOGICALNESSES
LOGICISING
LOGICIZING
LOGINESSES
LOGISTICAL
LOGISTICALLY
LOGISTICIAN
LOGISTICIANS
LOGJAMMING
LOGJAMMINGS
LOGNORMALITIES

LOGNORMALITY
LOGNORMALLY
LOGOCENTRISM
LOGOCENTRISMS
LOGODAEDALIC
LOGODAEDALIES
LOGODAEDALUS
LOGODAEDALUSES
LOGODAEDALY
LOGOGRAMMATIC
LOGOGRAPHER
LOGOGRAPHERS
LOGOGRAPHIC
LOGOGRAPHICAL
LOGOGRAPHICALLY
LOGOGRAPHIES
LOGOGRAPHS
LOGOGRAPHY
LOGOGRIPHIC
LOGOGRIPHS
LOGOMACHIES
LOGOMACHIST
LOGOMACHISTS
LOGOPAEDIC
LOGOPAEDICS
LOGOPEDICS
LOGOPHILES
LOGORRHEAS
LOGORRHEIC
LOGORRHOEA
LOGORRHOEAS
LOGOTHETES
LOGOTYPIES
LOGROLLERS
LOGROLLING
LOGROLLINGS
LOINCLOTHS
LOITERINGLY
LOITERINGS
LOLLAPALOOSA
LOLLAPALOOSAS
LOLLAPALOOZA
LOLLAPALOOZAS
LOLLOPIEST
LOLLYGAGGED
LOLLYGAGGING
LOMENTACEOUS
LONELINESS
LONELINESSES
LONENESSES
LONESOMELY
LONESOMENESS
LONESOMENESSES
LONGAEVOUS
LONGANIMITIES
LONGANIMITY
LONGANIMOUS
LONGBOARDS
LONGBOWMAN
LONGBOWMEN
LONGCLOTHS
LONGEVITIES
LONGHAIRED
LONGHEADED
LONGHEADEDNESS
LONGHOUSES
LONGICAUDATE

LONGICORNS
LONGINQUITIES
LONGINQUITY
LONGIPENNATE
LONGIROSTRAL
LONGITUDES
LONGITUDINAL
LONGITUDINALLY
LONGJUMPED
LONGJUMPING
LONGLEAVES
LONGLINERS
LONGLISTED
LONGLISTING
LONGNESSES
LONGPRIMER
LONGPRIMERS
LONGSHOREMAN
LONGSHOREMEN
LONGSHORING
LONGSHORINGS
LONGSIGHTED
LONGSIGHTEDNESS
LONGSOMELY
LONGSOMENESS
LONGSOMENESSES
LONGWEARING
LOOKALIKES
LOONINESSES
LOOPHOLING
LOOPINESSES
LOOSEBOXES
LOOSENESSES
LOOSENINGS
LOOSESTRIFE
LOOSESTRIFES
LOOYENWORK
LOOYENWORKS
LOPGRASSES
LOPHOBRANCH
LOPHOBRANCHIATE
LOPHOBRANCHS
LOPHOPHORATE
LOPHOPHORE
LOPHOPHORES
LOPSIDEDLY
LOPSIDEDNESS
LOPSIDEDNESSES
LOQUACIOUS
LOQUACIOUSLY
LOQUACIOUSNESS
LOQUACITIES
LORAZEPAMS
LORDLINESS
LORDLINESSES
LORDOLATRIES
LORDOLATRY
LORGNETTES
LORICATING
LORICATION
LORICATIONS
LORNNESSES
LOSABLENESS
LOSABLENESSES
LOSSMAKERS
LOSSMAKING
LOSTNESSES

LOTHNESSES
LOTUSLANDS
LOUDHAILER
LOUDHAILERS
LOUDMOUTHED
LOUDMOUTHS
LOUDNESSES
LOUDSPEAKER
LOUDSPEAKERS
LOUNDERING
LOUNDERINGS
LOUNGEWEAR
LOUNGEWEARS
LOUNGINGLY
LOUSEWORTS
LOUSINESSES
LOUTISHNESS
LOUTISHNESSES
LOVABILITIES
LOVABILITY
LOVABLENESS
LOVABLENESSES
LOVASTATIN
LOVASTATINS
LOVEABILITIES
LOVEABILITY
LOVEABLENESS
LOVEABLENESSES
LOVELESSLY
LOVELESSNESS
LOVELESSNESSES
LOVELIGHTS
LOVELIHEAD
LOVELIHEADS
LOVELINESS
LOVELINESSES
LOVELORNNESS
LOVELORNNESSES
LOVEMAKERS
LOVEMAKING
LOVEMAKINGS
LOVESICKNESS
LOVESICKNESSES
LOVESTRUCK
LOVEWORTHIER
LOVEWORTHIES
LOVEWORTHIEST
LOVEWORTHY
LOVINGNESS
LOVINGNESSES
LOWBALLING
LOWBALLINGS
LOWBROWISM
LOWBROWISMS
LOWERCASED
LOWERCASES
LOWERCASING
LOWERCLASSMAN
LOWERCLASSMEN
LOWERINGLY
LOWLANDERS
LOWLIGHTED
LOWLIGHTING
LOWLIHEADS
LOWLINESSES
LOWSENINGS
LOXODROMES

LOXODROMIC
LOXODROMICAL
LOXODROMICALLY
LOXODROMICS
LOXODROMIES
LOYALNESSES
LOZENGIEST
LUBBERLIER
LUBBERLIEST
LUBBERLINESS
LUBBERLINESSES
LUBRICANTS
LUBRICATED
LUBRICATES
LUBRICATING
LUBRICATION
LUBRICATIONAL
LUBRICATIONS
LUBRICATIVE
LUBRICATOR
LUBRICATORS
LUBRICIOUS
LUBRICIOUSLY
LUBRICITIES
LUBRICOUSLY
LUBRITORIA
LUBRITORIUM
LUBRITORIUMS
LUCIDITIES
LUCIDNESSES
LUCIFERASE
LUCIFERASES
LUCIFERINS
LUCIFEROUS
LUCIFUGOUS
LUCKENBOOTH
LUCKENBOOTHS
LUCKENGOWAN
LUCKENGOWANS
LUCKINESSES
LUCKLESSLY
LUCKLESSNESS
LUCKLESSNESSES
LUCKPENNIES
LUCRATIVELY
LUCRATIVENESS
LUCRATIVENESSES
LUCTATIONS
LUCUBRATED
LUCUBRATES
LUCUBRATING
LUCUBRATION
LUCUBRATIONS
LUCUBRATOR
LUCUBRATORS
LUCULENTLY
LUDICROUSLY
LUDICROUSNESS
LUDICROUSNESSES
LUETICALLY
LUFTMENSCH
LUFTMENSCHEN
LUGUBRIOUS
LUGUBRIOUSLY
LUGUBRIOUSNESS
LUKEWARMISH
LUKEWARMLY

LUKEWARMNESS
LUKEWARMNESSES
LUKEWARMTH
LUKEWARMTHS
LULLABYING
LUMBAGINOUS
LUMBERINGLY
LUMBERINGNESS
LUMBERINGNESSES
LUMBERINGS
LUMBERJACK
LUMBERJACKET
LUMBERJACKETS
LUMBERJACKS
LUMBERSOME
LUMBERSOMENESS
LUMBERYARD
LUMBERYARDS
LUMBOSACRAL
LUMBRICALES
LUMBRICALIS
LUMBRICALISES
LUMBRICALS
LUMBRICIFORM
LUMBRICOID
LUMBRICUSES
LUMINAIRES
LUMINANCES
LUMINARIAS
LUMINARIES
LUMINARISM
LUMINARISMS
LUMINARIST
LUMINARISTS
LUMINATION
LUMINATIONS
LUMINESCED
LUMINESCENCE
LUMINESCENCES
LUMINESCENT
LUMINESCÉS
LUMINESCING
LUMINIFEROUS
LUMINOSITIES
LUMINOSITY
LUMINOUSLY
LUMINOUSNESS
LUMINOUSNESSES
LUMISTEROL

LUMISTEROLS
LUMPECTOMIES
LUMPECTOMY
LUMPFISHES
LUMPINESSES
LUMPISHNESS
LUMPISHNESSES
LUMPSUCKER
LUMPSUCKERS
LUNARNAUTS
LUNATICALLY
LUNCHBOXES
LUNCHBREAK
LUNCHBREAKS
LUNCHEONED
LUNCHEONETTE
LUNCHEONETTES
LUNCHEONING
LUNCHMEATS
LUNCHPAILS
LUNCHROOMS
LUNCHTIMES
LUNGFISHES
LUNINESSES
LUNKHEADED
LURIDNESSES
LUSCIOUSLY
LUSCIOUSNESS
LUSCIOUSNESSES
LUSHNESSES
LUSKISHNESS
LUSKISHNESSES
LUSTERLESS
LUSTERWARE
LUSTERWARES
LUSTFULNESS
LUSTFULNESSES
LUSTIHEADS
LUSTIHOODS
LUSTINESSES
LUSTRATING
LUSTRATION
LUSTRATIONS
LUSTRATIVE
LUSTRELESS
LUSTREWARE
LUSTREWARES
LUSTROUSLY
LUSTROUSNESS

LUSTROUSNESSES
LUTEINISATION
LUTEINISATIONS
LUTEINISED
LUTEINISES
LUTEINISING
LUTEINIZATION
LUTEINIZATIONS
LUTEINIZED
LUTEINIZES
LUTEINIZING
LUTEOTROPHIC
LUTEOTROPHIN
LUTEOTROPHINS
LUTEOTROPIC
LUTEOTROPIN
LUTEOTROPINS
LUTESTRING
LUTESTRINGS
LUVVIEDOMS
LUXULIANITE
LUXULIANITES
LUXULLIANITE
LUXULLIANITES
LUXULYANITE
LUXULYANITES
LUXURIANCE
LUXURIANCES
LUXURIANCIES
LUXURIANCY
LUXURIANTLY
LUXURIATED
LUXURIATES
LUXURIATING
LUXURIATION
LUXURIATIONS
LUXURIOUSLY
LUXURIOUSNESS
LUXURIOUSNESSES
LYCANTHROPE
LYCANTHROPES
LYCANTHROPIC
LYCANTHROPIES
LYCANTHROPIST
LYCANTHROPISTS
LYCANTHROPY
LYCHNOSCOPE
LYCHNOSCOPES
LYCOPODIUM

LYCOPODIUMS
LYMPHADENITIS
LYMPHADENITISES
LYMPHADENOPATHY
LYMPHANGIAL
LYMPHANGIOGRAM
LYMPHANGIOGRAMS
LYMPHANGIOMA
LYMPHANGIOMAS
LYMPHANGIOMATA
LYMPHANGITIC
LYMPHANGITIDES
LYMPHANGITIS
LYMPHANGITISES
LYMPHATICALLY
LYMPHATICS
LYMPHOADENOMA
LYMPHOADENOMAS
LYMPHOADENOMATA
LYMPHOBLAST
LYMPHOBLASTIC
LYMPHOBLASTS
LYMPHOCYTE
LYMPHOCYTES
LYMPHOCYTIC
LYMPHOCYTOPENIA
LYMPHOCYTOSES
LYMPHOCYTOSIS
LYMPHOCYTOTIC
LYMPHOGRAM
LYMPHOGRAMS
LYMPHOGRANULOMA
LYMPHOGRAPHIC
LYMPHOGRAPHIES
LYMPHOGRAPHY
LYMPHOKINE
LYMPHOKINES
LYMPHOMATA
LYMPHOMATOID
LYMPHOMATOSES
LYMPHOMATOSIS
LYMPHOMATOUS
LYMPHOPENIA
LYMPHOPENIAS
LYMPHOPOIESES
LYMPHOPOIESIS
LYMPHOPOIETIC
LYMPHOSARCOMA
LYMPHOSARCOMAS

LYMPHOSARCOMATA
LYMPHOTROPHIC
LYOPHILISATION
LYOPHILISATIONS
LYOPHILISE
LYOPHILISED
LYOPHILISER
LYOPHILISERS
LYOPHILISES
LYOPHILISING
LYOPHILIZATION
LYOPHILIZATIONS
LYOPHILIZE
LYOPHILIZED
LYOPHILIZER
LYOPHILIZERS
LYOPHILIZES
LYOPHILIZING
LYOSORPTION
LYOSORPTIONS
LYRICALNESS
LYRICALNESSES
LYRICISING
LYRICIZING
LYSERGIDES
LYSIGENETIC
LYSIGENOUS
LYSIMETERS
LYSIMETRIC
LYSOGENICITIES
LYSOGENICITY
LYSOGENIES
LYSOGENISATION
LYSOGENISATIONS
LYSOGENISE
LYSOGENISED
LYSOGENISING
LYSOGENIZATION
LYSOGENIZATIONS
LYSOGENIZE
LYSOGENIZED
LYSOGENIZES
LYSOGENIZING
LYSOLECITHIN
LYSOLECITHINS
LYTHRACEOUS

I

M

MACABERESQUE	MACHINATED	MACROCOPIES	MACRONUCLEUS	MADERISATIONS
MACADAMIAS	MACHINATES	MACROCOSMIC	MACRONUCLEUSES	MADERISING
MACADAMISATION	MACHINATING	MACROCOSMICALLY	MACRONUTRIENT	MADERIZATION
MACADAMISATIONS	MACHINATION	MACROCOSMS	MACRONUTRIENTS	MADERIZATIONS
MACADAMISE	MACHINATIONS	MACROCYCLE	MACROPHAGE	MADERIZING
MACADAMISED	MACHINATOR	MACROCYCLES	MACROPHAGES	MADONNAISH
MACADAMISER	MACHINATORS	MACROCYCLIC	MACROPHAGIC	MADONNAWISE
MACADAMISERS	MACHINEABILITY	MACROCYSTS	MACROPHAGOUS	MADRASSAHS
MACADAMISES	MACHINEABLE	MACROCYTES	MACROPHOTOGRAPH	MADREPORAL
MACADAMISING	MACHINEGUN	MACROCYTIC	MACROPHYLA	MADREPORES
MACADAMIZATION	MACHINEGUNNED	MACROCYTOSES	MACROPHYLUM	MADREPORIAN
MACADAMIZATIONS	MACHINEGUNNING	MACROCYTOSIS	MACROPHYSICS	MADREPORIANS
MACADAMIZE	MACHINEGUNS	MACRODACTYL	MACROPHYTE	MADREPORIC
MACADAMIZED	MACHINELESS	MACRODACTYLIC	MACROPHYTES	MADREPORITE
MACADAMIZER	MACHINELIKE	MACRODACTYLIES	MACROPHYTIC	MADREPORITES
MACADAMIZERS	MACHINEMAN	MACRODACTYLOUS	MACROPINACOID	MADREPORITIC
MACADAMIZES	MACHINEMEN	MACRODACTYLS	MACROPINACOIDS	MADRIGALESQUE
MACADAMIZING	MACHINERIES	MACRODACTYLY	MACROPINAKOID	MADRIGALIAN
MACARISING	MACHINIMAS	MACRODIAGONAL	MACROPINAKOIDS	MADRIGALIST
MACARIZING	MACHININGS	MACRODIAGONALS	MACROPRISM	MADRIGALISTS
MACARONICALLY	MACHINISTS	MACRODOMES	MACROPRISMS	MADRILENES
MACARONICS	MACHMETERS	MACROECONOMIC	MACROPRUDENTIAL	MAELSTROMS
MACARONIES	MACHTPOLITIK	MACROECONOMICS	MACROPSIAS	MAENADICALLY
MACCARONIES	MACHTPOLITIKS	MACROEVOLUTION	MACROPTEROUS	MAENADISMS
MACCARONIS	MACINTOSHES	MACROEVOLUTIONS	MACROSCALE	MAFFICKERS
MACCHERONCINI	MACKINTOSH	MACROFAUNA	MACROSCALES	MAFFICKING
MACCHERONCINIS	MACKINTOSHES	MACROFAUNAE	MACROSCOPIC	MAFFICKINGS
MACCHIATOS	MACONOCHIE	MACROFAUNAS	MACROSCOPICALLY	MAGALOGUES
MACEBEARER	MACONOCHIES	MACROFLORA	MACROSOCIOLOGY	MAGAZINIST
MACEBEARERS	MACRENCEPHALIA	MACROFLORAE	MACROSPORANGIA	MAGAZINISTS
MACEDOINES	MACRENCEPHALIAS	MACROFLORAS	MACROSPORANGIUM	MAGDALENES
MACERANDUBA	MACRENCEPHALIES	MACROFOSSIL	MACROSPORE	MAGGOTIEST
MACERANDUBAS	MACRENCEPHALY	MACROFOSSILS	MACROSPORES	MAGGOTORIA
MACERATERS	MACROAGGREGATE	MACROGAMETE	MACROSTRUCTURAL	MAGGOTORIUM
MACERATING	MACROAGGREGATED	MACROGAMETES	MACROSTRUCTURE	MAGIANISMS
MACERATION	MACROAGGREGATES	MACROGLIAS	MACROSTRUCTURES	MAGISTERIAL
MACERATIONS	MACROBIOTA	MACROGLOBULIN	MACROZAMIA	MAGISTERIALLY
MACERATIVE	MACROBIOTAS	MACROGLOBULINS	MACROZAMIAS	MAGISTERIALNESS
MACERATORS	MACROBIOTE	MACROGRAPH	MACTATIONS	MAGISTERIES
MACHAIRODONT	MACROBIOTES	MACROGRAPHIC	MACULATING	MAGISTERIUM
MACHAIRODONTS	MACROBIOTIC	MACROGRAPHS	MACULATION	MAGISTERIUMS
MACHIAVELIAN	MACROBIOTICS	MACROLIDES	MACULATIONS	MAGISTRACIES
MACHIAVELIANS	MACROCARPA	MACROLOGIES	MACULATURE	MAGISTRACY
MACHIAVELLIAN	MACROCARPAS	MACROMARKETING	MACULATURES	MAGISTRALITIES
MACHIAVELLIANS	MACROCEPHALIA	MACROMARKETINGS	MADBRAINED	MAGISTRALITY
MACHICOLATE	MACROCEPHALIAS	MACROMERES	MADDENINGLY	MAGISTRALLY
MACHICOLATED	MACROCEPHALIC	MACROMOLECULAR	MADDENINGNESS	MAGISTRALS
MACHICOLATES	MACROCEPHALIES	MACROMOLECULE	MADDENINGNESSES	MAGISTRAND
MACHICOLATING	MACROCEPHALOUS	MACROMOLECULES	MADEFACTION	MAGISTRANDS
MACHICOLATION	MACROCEPHALY	MACROMOLES	MADEFACTIONS	MAGISTRATE
MACHICOLATIONS	MACROCLIMATE	MACROMUTATION	MADELEINES	MAGISTRATES
MACHINABILITIES	MACROCLIMATES	MACROMUTATIONS	MADEMOISELLE	MAGISTRATESHIP
MACHINABILITY	MACROCLIMATIC	MACRONUCLEAR	MADEMOISELLES	MAGISTRATESHIPS
MACHINABLE	MACROCODES	MACRONUCLEI	MADERISATION	MAGISTRATIC

MAGISTRATICAL	MAGNIFICENCES	MAINSPRING	MALACOPHILOUS	MALEDICTORY
MAGISTRATICALLY	MAGNIFICENT	MAINSPRINGS	MALACOPHILY	MALEFACTION
MAGISTRATURE	MAGNIFICENTLY	MAINSTAGES	MALACOPHYLLOUS	MALEFACTIONS
MAGISTRATURES	MAGNTFICENTNESS	MAINSTREAM	MALACOPTERYGIAN	MALEFACTOR
MAGMATISMS	MAGNIFICOES	MAINSTREAMED	MALACOSTRACAN	MALEFACTORS
MAGNALIUMS	MAGNIFICOS	MAINSTREAMING	MALACOSTRACANS	MALEFACTORY
MAGNANIMITIES	MAGNIFIERS	MAINSTREAMINGS	MALACOSTRACOUS	MALEFACTRESS
MAGNANIMITY	MAGNIFYING	MAINSTREAMS	MALADAPTATION	MALEFACTRESSES
MAGNANIMOUS	MAGNILOQUENCE	MAINSTREETING	MALADAPTATIONS	MALEFFECTS
MAGNANIMOUSLY	MAGNILOQUENCES	MAINSTREETINGS	MALADAPTED	MALEFICALLY
MAGNANIMOUSNESS	MAGNILOQUENT	MAINTAINABILITY	MALADAPTIVE	MALEFICENCE
MAGNATESHIP	MAGNILOQUENTLY	MAINTAINABLE	MALADAPTIVELY	MALEFICENCES
MAGNATESHIPS	MAGNITUDES	MAINTAINED	MALADDRESS	MALEFICENT
MAGNESITES	MAGNITUDINOUS	MAINTAINER	MALADDRESSES	MALEFICIAL
MAGNESIUMS	MAGNOLIACEOUS	MAINTAINERS	MALADJUSTED	MALENESSES
MAGNESSTONE	MAHARAJAHS	MAINTAINING	MALADJUSTIVE	MALENGINES
MAGNESSTONES	MAHARANEES	MAINTENANCE	MALADJUSTMENT	MALENTENDU
MAGNETICAL	MAHARISHIS	MAINTENANCED	MALADJUSTMENTS	MALENTENDUS
MAGNETICALLY	MAHATMAISM	MAINTENANCES	MALADMINISTER	MALEVOLENCE
MAGNETICIAN	MAHATMAISMS	MAINTENANCING	MALADMINISTERED	MALEVOLENCES
MAGNETICIANS	MAHLSTICKS	MAINTOPMAST	MALADMINISTERS	MALEVOLENT
MAGNETISABLE	MAHOGANIES	MAINTOPMASTS	MALADROITLY	MALEVOLENTLY
MAGNETISATION	MAIASAURAS	MAINTOPSAIL	MALADROITNESS	MALFEASANCE
MAGNETISATIONS	MAIDENHAIR	MAINTOPSAILS	MALADROITNESSES	MALFEASANCES
MAGNETISED	MAIDENHAIRS	MAISONETTE	MALADROITS	MALFEASANT
MAGNETISER	MAIDENHEAD	MAISONETTES	MALAGUENAS	MALFEASANTS
MAGNETISERS	MAIDENHEADS	MAISONNETTE	MALAGUETTA	MALFORMATION
MAGNETISES	MAIDENHOOD	MAISONNETTES	MALAGUETTAS	MALFORMATIONS
MAGNETISING	MAIDENHOODS	MAISTERDOME	MALAKATOONE	MALFUNCTION
MAGNETISMS	MAIDENLIER	MAISTERDOMES	MALAKATOONES	MALFUNCTIONED
MAGNETISTS	MAIDENLIEST	MAISTERING	MALAPERTLY	MALFUNCTIONING
MAGNETITES	MAIDENLIKE	MAISTRINGS	MALAPERTNESS	MALFUNCTIONINGS
MAGNETITIC	MAIDENLINESS	MAJESTICAL	MALAPERTNESSES	MALFUNCTIONS
MAGNETIZABLE	MAIDENLINESSES	MAJESTICALLY	MALAPPORTIONED	MALICIOUSLY
MAGNETIZATION	MAIDENWEED	MAJESTICALNESS	MALAPPROPRIATE	MALICIOUSNESS
MAGNETIZATIONS	MAIDENWEEDS	MAJESTICNESS	MALAPPROPRIATED	MALICIOUSNESSES
MAGNETIZED	MAIDISHNESS	MAJESTICNESSES	MALAPPROPRIATES	MALIGNANCE
MAGNETIZER	MAIDISHNESSES	MAJOLICAWARE	MALAPROPIAN	MALIGNANCES
MAGNETIZERS	MAIDSERVANT	MAJOLICAWARES	MALAPROPISM	MALIGNANCIES
MAGNETIZES	MAIDSERVANTS	MAJORDOMOS	MALAPROPISMS	MALIGNANCY
MAGNETIZING	MAIEUTICAL	MAJORETTES	MALAPROPIST	MALIGNANTLY
MAGNETOCHEMICAL	MAILABILITIES	MAJORETTING	MALAPROPISTS	MALIGNANTS
MAGNETOELECTRIC	MAILABILITY	MAJORETTINGS	MALAPROPOS	MALIGNITIES
MAGNETOGRAPH	MAILCOACHES	MAJORITAIRE	MALARIOLOGIES	MALIGNMENT
MAGNETOGRAPHS	MAILGRAMMED	MAJORITAIRES	MALARIOLOGIST	MALIGNMENTS
MAGNETOMETER	MAILGRAMMING	MAJORITARIAN	MALARIOLOGISTS	MALIMPRINTED
MAGNETOMETERS	MAILMERGED	MAJORITARIANISM	MALARIOLOGY	MALIMPRINTING
MAGNETOMETRIC	MAILMERGES	MAJORITARIANS	MALASSIMILATION	MALIMPRINTINGS
MAGNETOMETRIES	MAILMERGING	MAJORITIES	MALATHIONS	MALINGERED
MAGNETOMETRY	MAILPOUCHES	MAJORSHIPS	MALAXATING	MALINGERER
MAGNETOMOTIVE	MAILSHOTTED	MAJUSCULAR	MALAXATION	MALINGERERS
MAGNETOPAUSE	MAILSHOTTING	MAJUSCULES	MALAXATIONS	MALINGERIES
MAGNETOPAUSES	MAIMEDNESS	MAKEREADIES	MALAXATORS	MALINGERING
MAGNETOSPHERE	MAIMEDNESSES	MAKESHIFTS	MALCONFORMATION	MALLANDERS
MAGNETOSPHERES	MAINBRACES	MAKEWEIGHT	MALCONTENT	MALLEABILITIES
MAGNETOSPHERIC	MAINFRAMES	MAKEWEIGHTS	MALCONTENTED	MALLEABILITY
MAGNETOSTATIC	MAINLANDER	MAKUNOUCHI	MALCONTENTEDLY	MALLEABLENESS
MAGNETOSTATICS	MAINLANDERS	MAKUNOUCHIS	MALCONTENTS	MALLEABLENESSES
MAGNETRONS	MAINLINERS	MALABSORPTION	MALDEPLOYMENT	MALLEATING
MAGNIFIABLE	MAINLINING	MALABSORPTIONS	MALDEPLOYMENTS	MALLEATION
MAGNIFICAL	MAINLININGS	MALACHITES	MALDISTRIBUTION	MALLEATIONS
MAGNIFICALLY	MAINPERNOR	MALACOLOGICAL	MALEDICENT	MALLEIFORM
MAGNIFICAT	MAINPERNORS	MALACOLOGIES	MALEDICTED	MALLEMAROKING
MAGNIFICATION	MAINPRISED	MALACOLOGIST	MALEDICTING	MALLEMAROKINGS
MAGNIFICATIONS	MAINPRISES	MALACOLOGISTS	MALEDICTION	MALLEMUCKS
MAGNIFICATS	MAINPRISING	MALACOLOGY	MALEDICTIONS	MALLENDERS
MAGNIFICENCE	MAINSHEETS	MALACOPHILIES	MALEDICTIVE	MALLEOLUSES

MALLOPHAGOUS	MAMMOGRAMS	MANDUCATION	MANIFOLDED	MANSLAYERS
MALLOWPUFF	MAMMOGRAPH	MANDUCATIONS	MANIFOLDER	MANSONRIES
MALLOWPUFFS	MAMMOGRAPHIC	MANDUCATORY	MANIFOLDERS	MANSPLAINED
MALMSTONES	MAMMOGRAPHIES	MANDYLIONS	MANIFOLDING	MANSPLAINING
MALNOURISHED	MAMMOGRAPHS	MANEUVERABILITY	MANIFOLDLY	MANSPLAININGS
MALNUTRITION	MAMMOGRAPHY	MANEUVERABLE	MANIFOLDNESS	MANSPLAINS
MALNUTRITIONS	MAMMONISMS	MANEUVERED	MANIFOLDNESSES	MANSPREADING
MALOCCLUDED	MAMMONISTIC	MANEUVERER	MANIPULABILITY	MANSPREADINGS
MALOCCLUSION	MAMMONISTS	MANEUVERERS	MANIPULABLE	MANSPREADS
MALOCCLUSIONS	MAMMONITES	MANEUVERING	MANIPULARS	MANSUETUDE
MALODOROUS	MAMMOPLASTIES	MANEUVERINGS	MANIPULATABLE	MANSUETUDES
MALODOROUSLY	MAMMOPLASTY	MANFULLEST	MANIPULATE	MANTELLETTA
MALODOROUSNESS	MANAGEABILITIES	MANFULNESS	MANIPULATED	MANTELLETTAS
MALOLACTIC	MANAGEABILITY	MANFULNESSES	MANIPULATES	MANTELPIECE
MALONYLUREA	MANAGEABLE	MANGABEIRA	MANIPULATING	MANTELPIECES
MALONYLUREAS	MANAGEABLENESS	MANGABEIRAS	MANIPULATION	MANTELSHELF
MALPIGHIACEOUS	MANAGEABLY	MANGALSUTRA	MANIPULATIONS	MANTELSHELVES
MALPIGHIAS	MANAGEMENT	MANGALSUTRAS	MANIPULATIVE	MANTELTREE
MALPOSITION	MANAGEMENTAL	MANGANATES	MANIPULATIVELY	MANTELTREES
MALPOSITIONS	MANAGEMENTS	MANGANESES	MANIPULATIVES	MANTICALLY
MALPRACTICE	MANAGERESS	MANGANESIAN	MANIPULATOR	MANTICORAS
MALPRACTICES	MANAGERESSES	MANGANIFEROUS	MANIPULATORS	MANTICORES
MALPRACTITIONER	MANAGERIAL	MANGANITES	MANIPULATORY	MANTLETREE
MALPRESENTATION	MANAGERIALISM	MANGELWURZEL	MANLINESSES	MANTLETREES
MALTALENTS	MANAGERIALISMS	MANGELWURZELS	MANNEQUINS	MANTYHOSES
MALTINESSES	MANAGERIALIST	MANGEMANGE	MANNERISMS	MANUBRIUMS
MALTODEXTRIN	MANAGERIALISTS	MANGEMANGES	MANNERISTIC	MANUFACTORIES
MALTODEXTRINS	MANAGERIALLY	MANGETOUTS	MANNERISTICAL	MANUFACTORY
MALTREATED	MANAGERSHIP	MANGINESSES	MANNERISTICALLY	MANUFACTURABLE
MALTREATER	MANAGERSHIPS	MANGOLDWURZEL	MANNERISTS	MANUFACTURAL
MALTREATERS	MANCHESTER	MANGOLDWURZELS	MANNERLESS	MANUFACTURE
MALTREATING	MANCHESTERS	MANGOSTANS	MANNERLESSNESS	MANUFACTURED
MALTREATMENT	MANCHINEEL	MANGOSTEEN	MANNERLIER	MANUFACTURER
MALTREATMENTS	MANCHINEELS	MANGOSTEENS	MANNERLIEST	MANUFACTURERS
MALVACEOUS	MANCIPATED	MANGOUSTES	MANNERLINESS	MANUFACTURES
MALVERSATION	MANCIPATES	MANGULATED	MANNERLINESSES	MANUFACTURING
MALVERSATIONS	MANCIPATING	MANGULATES	MANNIFEROUS	MANUFACTURINGS
MALVOISIES	MANCIPATION	MANGULATING	MANNISHNESS	MANUMISSION
MAMAGUYING	MANCIPATIONS	MANHANDLED	MANNISHNESSES	MANUMISSIONS
MAMILLATED	MANCIPATORY	MANHANDLES	MANOEUVERED	MANUMITTED
MAMILLATION	MANDAMUSED	MANHANDLING	MANOEUVERING	MANUMITTER
MAMILLATIONS	MANDAMUSES	MANHATTANS	MANOEUVERS	MANUMITTERS
MAMILLIFORM	MANDAMUSING	MANHUNTERS	MANOEUVRABILITY	MANUMITTING
MAMMALIANS	MANDARINATE	MANIACALLY	MANOEUVRABLE	MANURANCES
MAMMALIFEROUS	MANDARINATES	MANICOTTIS	MANOEUVRED	MANUSCRIPT
MAMMALITIES	MANDARINES	MANICURING	MANOEUVRER	MANUSCRIPTS
MAMMALOGICAL	MANDARINIC	MANICURIST	MANOEUVRERS	MANZANILLA
MAMMALOGIES	MANDARINISM	MANICURISTS	MANOEUVRES	MANZANILLAS
MAMMALOGIST	MANDARINISMS	MANIFESTABLE	MANOEUVRING	MANZANITAS
MAMMALOGISTS	MANDATARIES	MANIFESTANT	MANOEUVRINGS	MAPMAKINGS
MAMMAPLASTIES	MANDATORIES	MANIFESTANTS	MANOMETERS	MAPPEMONDS
MAMMAPLASTY	MANDATORILY	MANIFESTATION	MANOMETRIC	MAQUILADORA
MAMMECTOMIES	MANDIBULAR	MANIFESTATIONAL	MANOMETRICAL	MAQUILADORAS
MAMMECTOMY	MANDIBULATE	MANIFESTATIONS	MANOMETRICALLY	MAQUILLAGE
MAMMETRIES	MANDIBULATED	MANIFESTATIVE	MANOMETRIES	MAQUILLAGES
MAMMIFEROUS	MANDIBULATES	MANIFESTED	MANORIALISM	MAQUISARDS
MAMMILLARIA	MANDILIONS	MANIFESTER	MANORIALISMS	MARABUNTAS
MAMMILLARIAS	MANDIOCCAS	MANIFESTERS	MANOSCOPIES	MARANATHAS
MAMMILLARY	MANDOLINES	MANIFESTIBLE	MANRIKIGUSARI	MARASCHINO
MAMMILLATE	MANDOLINIST	MANIFESTING	MANRIKIGUSARIS	MARASCHINOS
MAMMILLATED	MANDOLINISTS	MANIFESTLY	MANSCAPING	MARASMUSES
MAMMILLATION	MANDRAGORA	MANIFESTNESS	MANSCAPINGS	MARATHONER
MAMMILLATIONS	MANDRAGORAS	MANIFESTNESSES	MANSERVANT	MARATHONERS
MAMMILLIFORM	MANDUCABLE	MANIFESTOED	MANSIONARIES	MARATHONING
MAMMITIDES	MANDUCATED	MANIFESTOES	MANSIONARY	MARATHONINGS
MAMMOCKING	MANDUCATES	MANIFESTOING	MANSLAUGHTER	MARAUDINGS
MAMMOGENIC	MANDUCATING	MANIFESTOS	MANSLAUGHTERS	MARBELISED

m

MARBELISES	MARGINATION	MARLINSPIKE	MARSHLANDERS	MASCARPONES
MARBELISING	MARGINATIONS	MARLINSPIKES	MARSHLANDS	MASCULINELY
MARBELIZED	MARGRAVATE	MARLSTONES	MARSHLOCKS	MASCULINENESS
MARBELIZES	MARGRAVATES	MARMALADES	MARSHLOCKSES	MASCULINENESSES
MARBELIZING	MARGRAVIAL	MARMALISED	MARSHMALLOW	MASCULINES
MARBLEISED	MARGRAVIATE	MARMALISES	MARSHMALLOWIER	MASCULINISATION
MARBLEISES	MARGRAVIATES	MARMALISING	MARSHMALLOWIEST	MASCULINISE
MARBLEISING	MARGRAVINE	MARMALIZED	MARSHMALLOWS	MASCULINISED
MARBLEIZED	MARGRAVINES	MARMALIZES	MARSHMALLOWY	MASCULINISES
MARBLEIZES	MARGUERITA	MARMALIZING	MARSHWORTS	MASCULINISING
MARBLEIZING	MARGUERITAS	MARMARISED	MARSIPOBRANCH	MASCULINIST
MARBLEWOOD	MARGUERITE	MARMARISES	MARSIPOBRANCHS	MASCULINISTS
MARBLEWOODS	MARGUERITES	MARMARISING	MARSQUAKES	MASCULINITIES
MARCANTANT	MARIALITES	MARMARIZED	MARSUPIALIAN	MASCULINITY
MARCANTANTS	MARICULTURE	MARMARIZES	MARSUPIALIANS	MASCULINIZATION
MARCASITES	MARICULTURES	MARMARIZING	MARSUPIALS	MASCULINIZE
MARCASITICAL	MARICULTURIST	MARMAROSES	MARSUPIANS	MASCULINIZED
MARCATISSIMO	MARICULTURISTS	MARMAROSIS	MARTELLANDO	MASCULINIZES
MARCELLERS	MARIGRAPHS	MARMELISED	MARTELLANDOS	MASCULINIZING
MARCELLING	MARIHUANAS	MARMELISES	MARTELLATO	MASCULISTS
MARCESCENCE	MARIJUANAS	MARMELISING	MARTELLATOS	MASHGICHIM
MARCESCENCES	MARIMBAPHONE	MARMELIZED	MARTELLING	MASKALLONGE
MARCESCENT	MARIMBAPHONES	MARMELIZES	MARTENSITE	MASKALLONGES
MARCESCIBLE	MARIMBISTS	MARMELIZING	MARTENSITES	MASKALONGE
MARCHANTIA	MARINADING	MARMOREALLY	MARTENSITIC	MASKALONGES
MARCHANTIAS	MARINATING	MAROONINGS	MARTENSITICALLY	MASKANONGE
MARCHIONESS	MARINATION	MARPRELATE	MARTIALISM	MASKANONGES
MARCHIONESSES	MARINATIONS	MARPRELATED	MARTIALISMS	MASKINONGE
MARCHLANDS	MARIONBERRIES	MARPRELATES	MARTIALIST	MASKINONGES
MARCHPANES	MARIONBERRY	MARPRELATING	MARTIALISTS	MASKIROVKA
MARCONIGRAM	MARIONETTE	MARQUESSATE	MARTIALNESS	MASKIROVKAS
MARCONIGRAMS	MARIONETTES	MARQUESSATES	MARTIALNESSES	MASOCHISMS
MARCONIGRAPH	MARISCHALLED	MARQUESSES	MARTINETISH	MASOCHISTIC
MARCONIGRAPHED	MARISCHALLING	MARQUETERIE	MARTINETISM	MASOCHISTICALLY
MARCONIGRAPHING	MARISCHALS	MARQUETERIES	MARTINETISMS	MASOCHISTS
MARCONIGRAPHS	MARIVAUDAGE	MARQUETRIES	MARTINGALE	MASONICALLY
MARCONIING	MARIVAUDAGES	MARQUISATE	MARTINGALES	MASQUERADE
MARESCHALS	MARKEDNESS	MARQUISATES	MARTINGALS	MASQUERADED
MARGARINES	MARKEDNESSES	MARQUISETTE	MARTYRDOMS	MASQUERADER
MARGARITAS	MARKETABILITIES	MARQUISETTES	MARTYRISATION	MASQUERADERS
MARGARITES	MARKETABILITY	MARRIAGEABILITY	MARTYRISATIONS	MASQUERADES
MARGARITIC	MARKETABLE	MARRIAGEABLE	MARTYRISED	MASQUERADING
MARGARITIFEROUS	MARKETABLENESS	MARROWBONE	MARTYRISES	MASSACRERS
MARGENTING	MARKETABLY	MARROWBONES	MARTYRISING	MASSACRING
MARGHERITA	MARKETEERS	MARROWFATS	MARTYRIZATION	MASSAGISTS
MARGHERITAS	MARKETINGS	MARROWIEST	MARTYRIZATIONS	MASSARANDUBA
MARGINALIA	MARKETISATION	MARROWLESS	MARTYRIZED	MASSARANDUBAS
MARGINALISATION	MARKETISATIONS	MARROWSKIED	MARTYRIZES	MASSASAUGA
MARGINALISE	MARKETISED	MARROWSKIES	MARTYRIZING	MASSASAUGAS
MARGINALISED	MARKETISES	MARROWSKYING	MARTYROLOGIC	MASSERANDUBA
MARGINALISES	MARKETISING	MARSEILLES	MARTYROLOGICAL	MASSERANDUBAS
MARGINALISING	MARKETIZATION	MARSHALCIES	MARTYROLOGIES	MASSETERIC
MARGINALISM	MARKETIZATIONS	MARSHALERS	MARTYROLOGIST	MASSIFICATION
MARGINALISMS	MARKETIZED	MARSHALING	MARTYROLOGISTS	MASSIFICATIONS
MARGINALIST	MARKETIZES	MARSHALLED	MARTYROLOGY	MASSINESSES
MARGINALISTS	MARKETIZING	MARSHALLER	MARVELLERS	MASSIVENESS
MARGINALITIES	MARKETPLACE	MARSHALLERS	MARVELLING	MASSIVENESSES
MARGINALITY	MARKETPLACES	MARSHALLING	MARVELLOUS	MASSOTHERAPIES
MARGINALIZATION	MARKSMANSHIP	MARSHALLINGS	MARVELLOUSLY	MASSOTHERAPIST
MARGINALIZE	MARKSMANSHIPS	MARSHALSHIP	MARVELLOUSNESS	MASSOTHERAPISTS
MARGINALIZED	MARKSWOMAN	MARSHALSHIPS	MARVELOUSLY	MASSOTHERAPY
MARGINALIZES	MARKSWOMEN	MARSHBUCKS	MARVELOUSNESS	MASSPRIEST
MARGINALIZING	MARLACIOUS	MARSHELDER	MARVELOUSNESSES	MASSPRIESTS
MARGINALLY	MARLINESPIKE	MARSHELDERS	MARZIPANNED	MASSYMORES
MARGINATED	MARLINESPIKES	MARSHINESS	MARZIPANNING	MASTECTOMIES
MARGINATES	MARLINGSPIKE	MARSHINESSES	MASCARAING	MASTECTOMY
MARGINATING	MARLINGSPIKES	MARSHLANDER	MASCARPONE	MASTERATES

MASTERCLASS	MASTURBATIONS	MATHEMATIC	MATRIMONIES	MAXILLIPED
MASTERCLASSES	MASTURBATOR	MATHEMATICAL	MATRIOSHKA	MAXILLIPEDARY
MASTERDOMS	MASTURBATORS	MATHEMATICALLY	MATRIOSHKAS	MAXILLIPEDE
MASTERFULLY	MASTURBATORY	MATHEMATICIAN	MATRIOSHKI	MAXILLIPEDES
MASTERFULNESS	MATACHINAS	MATHEMATICIANS	MATROCLINAL	MAXILLIPEDS
MASTERFULNESSES	MATAGOURIS	MATHEMATICISE	MATROCLINIC	MAXILLOFACIAL
MASTERHOOD	MATCHBOARD	MATHEMATICISED	MATROCLINIES	MAXILLULAE
MASTERHOODS	MATCHBOARDING	MATHEMATICISES	MATROCLINOUS	MAXIMALIST
MASTERINGS	MATCHBOARDINGS	MATHEMATICISING	MATROCLINY	MAXIMALISTS
MASTERLESS	MATCHBOARDS	MATHEMATICISM	MATRONAGES	MAXIMAPHILIES
MASTERLIER	MATCHBOOKS	MATHEMATICISMS	MATRONHOOD	MAXIMAPHILY
MASTERLIEST	MATCHBOXES	MATHEMATICIZE	MATRONHOODS	MAXIMATION
MASTERLINESS	MATCHLESSLY	MATHEMATICIZED	MATRONISED	MAXIMATIONS
MASTERLINESSES	MATCHLESSNESS	MATHEMATICIZES	MATRONISES	MAXIMISATION
MASTERMIND	MATCHLESSNESSES	MATHEMATICIZING	MATRONISING	MAXIMISATIONS
MASTERMINDED	MATCHLOCKS	MATHEMATICS	MATRONIZED	MAXIMISERS
MASTERMINDING	MATCHMAKER	MATHEMATISATION	MATRONIZES	MAXIMISING
MASTERMINDS	MATCHMAKERS	MATHEMATISE	MATRONIZING	MAXIMIZATION
MASTERPIECE	MATCHMAKES	MATHEMATISED	MATRONLIER	MAXIMIZATIONS
MASTERPIECES	MATCHMAKING	MATHEMATISES	MATRONLIEST	MAXIMIZERS
MASTERSHIP	MATCHMAKINGS	MATHEMATISING	MATRONLINESS	MAXIMIZING
MASTERSHIPS	MATCHMARKED	MATHEMATIZATION	MATRONLINESSES	MAYFLOWERS
MASTERSINGER	MATCHMARKING	MATHEMATIZE	MATRONSHIP	MAYONNAISE
MASTERSINGERS	MATCHMARKS	MATHEMATIZED	MATRONSHIPS	MAYONNAISES
MASTERSTROKE	MATCHPLAYS	MATHEMATIZES	MATRONYMIC	MAYORALTIES
MASTERSTROKES	MATCHSTICK	MATHEMATIZING	MATRONYMICS	MAYORESSES
MASTERWORK	MATCHSTICKS	MATINESSES	MATROYSHKA	MAYORSHIPS
MASTERWORKS	MATCHWOODS	MATRESFAMILIAS	MATROYSHKAS	MAYSTERDOME
MASTERWORT	MATELASSES	MATRIARCHAL	MATRYOSHKA	MAYSTERDOMES
MASTERWORTS	MATELLASSE	MATRIARCHALISM	MATRYOSHKAS	MAZARINADE
MASTHEADED	MATELLASSES	MATRIARCHALISMS	MATRYOSHKI	MAZARINADES
MASTHEADING	MATELOTTES	MATRIARCHATE	MATSUTAKES	MAZEDNESSES
MASTHOUSES	MATERFAMILIAS	MATRIARCHATES	MATTAMORES	MAZINESSES
MASTICABLE	MATERFAMILIASES	MATRIARCHIC	MATTERIEST	MEADOWIEST
MASTICATED	MATERIALISATION	MATRIARCHIES	MATTERLESS	MEADOWLAND
MASTICATES	MATERIALISE	MATRIARCHS	MATTIFYING	MEADOWLANDS
MASTICATING	MATERIALISED	MATRIARCHY	MATTRASSES	MEADOWLARK
MASTICATION	MATERIALISER	MATRICIDAL	MATTRESSES	MEADOWLARKS
MASTICATIONS	MATERIALISERS	MATRICIDES	MATURATING	MEADOWSWEET
MASTICATOR	MATERIALISES	MATRICLINIC	MATURATION	MEADOWSWEETS
MASTICATORIES	MATERIALISING	MATRICLINOUS	MATURATIONAL	MEAGERNESS
MASTICATORS	MATERIALISM	MATRICULANT	MATURATIONS	MEAGERNESSES
MASTICATORY	MATERIALISMS	MATRICULANTS	MATURATIVE	MEAGRENESS
MASTIGOPHORAN	MATERIALIST	MATRICULAR	MATURENESS	MEAGRENESSES
MASTIGOPHORANS	MATERIALISTIC	MATRICULAS	MATURENESSES	MEALINESSES
MASTIGOPHORE	MATERIALISTICAL	MATRICULATE	MATURITIES	MEALYMOUTHED
MASTIGOPHORES	MATERIALISTS	MATRICULATED	MATUTINALLY	MEANDERERS
MASTIGOPHORIC	MATERIALITIES	MATRICULATES	MAUDLINISM	MEANDERING
MASTIGOPHOROUS	MATERIALITY	MATRICULATING	MAUDLINISMS	MEANDERINGLY
MASTITIDES	MATERIALIZATION	MATRICULATION	MAUDLINNESS	MEANDERINGS
MASTITISES	MATERIALIZE	MATRICULATIONS	MAUDLINNESSES	MEANINGFUL
MASTODONIC	MATERIALIZED	MATRICULATOR	MAULSTICKS	MEANINGFULLY
MASTODONTIC	MATERIALIZER	MATRICULATORS	MAUMETRIES	MEANINGFULNESS
MASTODONTS	MATERIALIZERS	MATRICULATORY	MAUNDERERS	MEANINGLESS
MASTODYNIA	MATERIALIZES	MATRIFOCAL	MAUNDERING	MEANINGLESSLY
MASTODYNIAS	MATERIALIZING	MATRIFOCALITIES	MAUNDERINGS	MEANINGLESSNESS
MASTOIDECTOMIES	MATERIALLY	MATRIFOCALITY	MAUSOLEUMS	MEANNESSES
MASTOIDECTOMY	MATERIALNESS	MATRILINEAL	MAVERICKED	MEANWHILES
MASTOIDITIDES	MATERIALNESSES	MATRILINEALLY	MAVERICKING	MEASLINESS
MASTOIDITIS	MATERNALISM	MATRILINEAR	MAVOURNEEN	MEASLINESSES
MASTOIDITISES	MATERNALISMS	MATRILINIES	MAVOURNEENS	MEASURABILITIES
MASTOPEXIES	MATERNALISTIC	MATRILOCAL	MAVOURNINS	MEASURABILITY
MASTURBATE	MATERNALLY	MATRILOCALITIES	MAWKISHNESS	MEASURABLE
MASTURBATED	MATERNITIES	MATRILOCALITY	MAWKISHNESSES	MEASURABLENESS
MASTURBATES	MATEYNESSES	MATRILOCALLY	MAWMETRIES	MEASURABLY
MASTURBATING	MATFELLONS	MATRIMONIAL	MAXIDRESSES	MEASUREDLY
MASTURBATION	MATGRASSES	MATRIMONIALLY	MAXILLARIES	MEASUREDNESS

MEASUREDNESSES	MEDEVACKING	MEDIEVALISMS	MEGALOBLASTS	MEIOTICALLY
MEASURELESS	MEDIAEVALISM	MEDIEVALIST	MEGALOCARDIA	MEITNERIUM
MEASURELESSLY	MEDIAEVALISMS	MEDIEVALISTIC	MEGALOCARDIAS	MEITNERIUMS
MEASURELESSNESS	MEDIAEVALIST	MEDIEVALISTS	MEGALOCEPHALIC	MEKOMETERS
MEASUREMENT	MEDIAEVALISTIC	MEDIEVALLY	MEGALOCEPHALIES	MELACONITE
MEASUREMENTS	MEDIAEVALISTS	MEDIOCRACIES	MEGALOCEPHALOUS	MELACONITES
MEASURINGS	MEDIAEVALLY	MEDIOCRACY	MEGALOCEPHALY	MELALEUCAS
MEATINESSES	MEDIAEVALS	MEDIOCRITIES	MEGALODONS	MELAMPODES
MEATLOAVES	MEDIAGENIC	MEDIOCRITY	MEGALOMANIA	MELANAEMIA
MEATPACKER	MEDIASTINA	MEDITATING	MEGALOMANIAC	MELANAEMIAS
MEATPACKERS	MEDIASTINAL	MEDITATION	MEGALOMANIACAL	MELANCHOLIA
MEATPACKING	MEDIASTINUM	MEDITATIONS	MEGALOMANIACS	MELANCHOLIAC
MEATPACKINGS	MEDIATENESS	MEDITATIVE	MEGALOMANIAS	MELANCHOLIACS
MEATSCREEN	MEDIATENESSES	MEDITATIVELY	MEGALOMANIC	MELANCHOLIAE
MEATSCREENS	MEDIATIONAL	MEDITATIVENESS	MEGALOPOLIS	MELANCHOLIAS
MEATSPACES	MEDIATIONS	MEDITATORS	MEGALOPOLISES	MELANCHOLIC
MECAMYLAMINE	MEDIATISATION	MEDITERRANEAN	MEGALOPOLITAN	MELANCHOLICALLY
MECAMYLAMINES	MEDIATISATIONS	MEDIUMISTIC	MEGALOPOLITANS	MELANCHOLICS
MECHANICAL	MEDIATISED	MEDIUMSHIP	MEGALOPSES	MELANCHOLIES
MECHANICALISM	MEDIATISES	MEDIUMSHIPS	MEGALOSAUR	MELANCHOLILY
MECHANICALISMS	MEDIATISING	MEDIVACING	MEGALOSAURI	MELANCHOLINESS
MECHANICALLY	MEDIATIZATION	MEDIVACKED	MEGALOSAURIAN	MELANCHOLIOUS
MECHANICALNESS	MEDIATIZATIONS	MEDIVACKING	MEGALOSAURIANS	MELANCHOLY
MECHANICALS	MEDIATIZED	MEDRESSEHS	MEGALOSAURS	MELANISATION
MECHANICIAN	MEDIATIZES	MEDULLATED	MEGALOSAURUS	MELANISATIONS
MECHANICIANS	MEDIATIZING	MEDULLOBLASTOMA	MEGANEWTON	MELANISING
MECHANISABLE	MEDIATORIAL	MEDUSIFORM	MEGANEWTONS	MELANISTIC
MECHANISATION	MEDIATORIALLY	MEEKNESSES	MEGAPARSEC	MELANIZATION
MECHANISATIONS	MEDIATORSHIP	MEERSCHAUM	MEGAPARSECS	MELANIZATIONS
MECHANISED	MEDIATORSHIPS	MEERSCHAUMS	MEGAPHONED	MELANIZING
MECHANISER	MEDIATRESS	MEETINGHOUSE	MEGAPHONES	MELANOBLAST
MECHANISERS	MEDIATRESSES	MEETINGHOUSES	MEGAPHONIC	MELANOBLASTS
MECHANISES	MEDIATRICES	MEETNESSES	MEGAPHONICALLY	MELANOCHROI
MECHANISING	MEDIATRIXES	MEFLOQUINE	MEGAPHONING	MELANOCHROIC
MECHANISMS	MEDICALISATION	MEFLOQUINES	MEGAPHYLLS	MELANOCHROOUS
MECHANISTIC	MEDICALISATIONS	MEGACEPHALIC	MEGAPIXELS	MELANOCYTE
MECHANISTICALLY	MEDICALISE	MEGACEPHALIES	MEGAPLEXES	MELANOCYTES
MECHANISTS	MEDICALISED	MEGACEPHALOUS	MEGAPROJECT	MELANOGENESES
MECHANIZABLE	MEDICALISES	MEGACEPHALY	MEGAPROJECTS	MELANOGENESIS
MECHANIZATION	MEDICALISING	MEGACHURCH	MEGAQUAKES	MELANOMATA
MECHANIZATIONS	MEDICALIZATION	MEGACHURCHES	MEGASCOPES	MELANOPHORE
MECHANIZED	MEDICALIZATIONS	MEGACITIES	MEGASCOPIC	MELANOPHORES
MECHANIZER	MEDICALIZE	MEGACORPORATION	MEGASCOPICALLY	MELANOSITIES
MECHANIZERS	MEDICALIZED	MEGACURIES	MEGASPORANGIA	MELANOSITY
MECHANIZES	MEDICALIZES	MEGACYCLES	MEGASPORANGIUM	MELANOSOME
MECHANIZING	MEDICALIZING	MEGADEATHS	MEGASPORES	MELANOSOMES
MECHANOCHEMICAL	MEDICAMENT	MEGAFARADS	MEGASPORIC	MELANOTROPIN
MECHANOMORPHISM	MEDICAMENTAL	MEGAFAUNAE	MEGASPOROPHYLL	MELANOTROPINS
MECHANORECEPTOR	MEDICAMENTALLY	MEGAFAUNAL	MEGASPOROPHYLLS	MELANTERITE
MECHANOTHERAPY	MEDICAMENTARY	MEGAFAUNAS	MEGASTORES	MELANTERITES
MECHATRONIC	MEDICAMENTED	MEGAFLORAE	MEGASTORMS	MELANURIAS
MECHATRONICS	MEDICAMENTING	MEGAFLORAS	MEGASTRUCTURE	MELAPHYRES
MECLIZINES	MEDICAMENTOUS	MEGAGAMETE	MEGASTRUCTURES	MELASTOMACEOUS
MECONOPSES	MEDICAMENTS	MEGAGAMETES	MEGATECHNOLOGY	MELASTOMES
MECONOPSIS	MEDICASTER	MEGAGAMETOPHYTE	MEGATHERES	MELATONINS
MEDAILLONS	MEDICASTERS	MEGAGAUSSES	MEGATHERIAN	MELIACEOUS
MEDALLIONED	MEDICATING	MEGAHERBIVORE	MEGATHRUST	MELICOTTON
MEDALLIONING	MEDICATION	MEGAHERBIVORES	MEGATONNAGE	MELICOTTONS
MEDALLIONS	MEDICATIONS	MEGAHERTZES	MEGATONNAGES	MELIORABLE
MEDALLISTS	MEDICATIVE	MEGAJOULES	MEGAVERTEBRATE	MELIORATED
MEDALPLAYS	MEDICINABLE	MEGAKARYOCYTE	MEGAVERTEBRATES	MELIORATES
MEDDLESOME	MEDICINALLY	MEGAKARYOCYTES	MEGAVITAMIN	MELIORATING
MEDDLESOMELY	MEDICINALS	MEGAKARYOCYTIC	MEGAVITAMINS	MELIORATION
MEDDLESOMENESS	MEDICINERS	MEGALITHIC	MEIOFAUNAE	MELIORATIONS
MEDDLINGLY	MEDICINING	MEGALITRES	MEIOFAUNAL	MELIORATIVE
MEDEVACING	MEDICOLEGAL	MEGALOBLAST	MEIOFAUNAS	MELIORATIVES
MEDEVACKED	MEDIEVALISM	MEGALOBLASTIC	MEIOSPORES	MELIORATOR

MELIORATORS	MEMBRANACEOUS	MENINGOCELE	MEPHITISMS	MERCURATED
MELIORISMS	MEMBRANEOUS	MENINGOCELES	MEPROBAMATE	MERCURATES
MELIORISTIC	MEMBRANOUS	MENINGOCOCCAL	MEPROBAMATES	MERCURATING
MELIORISTS	MEMBRANOUSLY	MENINGOCOCCI	MERBROMINS	MERCURATION
MELIORITIES	MEMOIRISMS	MENINGOCOCCIC	MERCANTILE	MERCURATIONS
MELIPHAGOUS	MEMOIRISTS	MENINGOCOCCUS	MERCANTILISM	MERCURIALISE
MELISMATIC	MEMORABILE	MENISCECTOMIES	MERCANTILISMS	MERCURIALISED
MELLIFEROUS	MEMORABILIA	MENISCECTOMY	MERCANTILIST	MERCURIALISES
MELLIFICATION	MEMORABILITIES	MENISCUSES	MERCANTILISTIC	MERCURIALISING
MELLIFICATIONS	MEMORABILITY	MENISPERMACEOUS	MERCANTILISTS	MERCURIALISM
MELLIFLUENCE	MEMORABLENESS	MENISPERMUM	MERCAPTANS	MERCURIALISMS
MELLIFLUENCES	MEMORABLENESSES	MENISPERMUMS	MERCAPTIDE	MERCURIALIST
MELLIFLUENT	MEMORANDUM	MENOLOGIES	MERCAPTIDES	MERCURIALISTS
MELLIFLUENTLY	MEMORANDUMS	MENOMINEES	MERCAPTOPURINE	MERCURIALITIES
MELLIFLUOUS	MEMORATIVE	MENOPAUSAL	MERCAPTOPURINES	MERCURIALITY
MELLIFLUOUSLY	MEMORIALISATION	MENOPAUSES	MERCENARIES	MERCURIALIZE
MELLIFLUOUSNESS	MEMORIALISE	MENOPAUSIC	MERCENARILY	MERCURIALIZED
MELLIPHAGOUS	MEMORIALISED	MENOPOLISES	MERCENARINESS	MERCURIALIZES
MELLIVOROUS	MEMORIALISER	MENORRHAGIA	MERCENARINESSES	MERCURIALIZING
MELLOPHONE	MEMORIALISERS	MENORRHAGIAS	MERCENARISM	MERCURIALLY
MELLOPHONES	MEMORIALISES	MENORRHAGIC	MERCENARISMS	MERCURIALNESS
MELLOTRONS	MEMORIALISING	MENORRHEAS	MERCERISATION	MERCURIALNESSES
MELLOWIEST	MEMORIALIST	MENORRHOEA	MERCERISATIONS	MERCURIALS
MELLOWNESS	MEMORIALISTS	MENORRHOEAS	MERCERISED	MERCURISED
MELLOWNESSES	MEMORIALIZATION	MENSCHIEST	MERCERISER	MERCURISES
MELLOWSPEAK	MEMORIALIZE	MENSERVANTS	MERCERISERS	MERCURISING
MELLOWSPEAKS	MEMORIALIZED	MENSTRUALLY	MERCERISES	MERCURIZED
MELOCOTONS	MEMORIALIZER	MENSTRUATE	MERCERISING	MERCURIZES
MELOCOTOON	MEMORIALIZERS	MENSTRUATED	MERCERIZATION	MERCURIZING
MELOCOTOONS	MEMORIALIZES	MENSTRUATES	MERCERIZATIONS	MERDIVOROUS
MELODICALLY	MEMORIALIZING	MENSTRUATING	MERCERIZED	MEREOLOGICAL
MELODIOUSLY	MEMORIALLY	MENSTRUATION	MERCERIZER	MEREOLOGIES
MELODIOUSNESS	MEMORISABLE	MENSTRUATIONS	MERCERIZERS	MERESTONES
MELODIOUSNESSES	MEMORISATION	MENSTRUOUS	MERCERIZES	MERETRICIOUS
MELODISERS	MEMORISATIONS	MENSTRUUMS	MERCERIZING	MERETRICIOUSLY
MELODISING	MEMORISERS	MENSURABILITIES	MERCHANDISE	MERGANSERS
MELODIZERS	MEMORISING	MENSURABILITY	MERCHANDISED	MERIDIONAL
MELODIZING	MEMORIZABLE	MENSURABLE	MERCHANDISER	MERIDIONALITIES
MELODRAMAS	MEMORIZATION	MENSURATION	MERCHANDISERS	MERIDIONALITY
MELODRAMATIC	MEMORIZATIONS	MENSURATIONAL	MERCHANDISES	MERIDIONALLY
MELODRAMATICS	MEMORIZERS	MENSURATIONS	MERCHANDISING	MERIDIONALS
MELODRAMATISE	MEMORIZING	MENSURATIVE	MERCHANDISINGS	MERISTEMATIC
MELODRAMATISED	MEMORIZINGS	MENTALESES	MERCHANDIZE	MERISTICALLY
MELODRAMATISES	MENACINGLY	MENTALISMS	MERCHANDIZED	MERITOCRACIES
MELODRAMATISING	MENADIONES	MENTALISTIC	MERCHANDIZER	MERITOCRACY
MELODRAMATIST	MENAGERIES	MENTALISTICALLY	MERCHANDIZERS	MERITOCRAT
MELODRAMATISTS	MENAQUINONE	MENTALISTS	MERCHANDIZES	MERITOCRATIC
MELODRAMATIZE	MENAQUINONES	MENTALITIES	MERCHANDIZING	MERITOCRATS
MELODRAMATIZED	MENARCHEAL	MENTATIONS	MERCHANDIZINGS	MERITORIOUS
MELODRAMATIZES	MENARCHIAL	MENTHACEOUS	MERCHANTABILITY	MERITORIOUSLY
MELODRAMATIZING	MENDACIOUS	MENTHOLATED	MERCHANTABLE	MERITORIOUSNESS
MELODRAMES	MENDACIOUSLY	MENTICIDES	MERCHANTED	MERMAIDENS
MELOMANIAC	MENDACIOUSNESS	MENTIONABLE	MERCHANTING	MEROBLASTIC
MELOMANIACS	MENDACITIES	MENTIONERS	MERCHANTINGS	MEROBLASTICALLY
MELOMANIAS	MENDELEVIUM	MENTIONING	MERCHANTLIKE	MEROGENESES
MELONGENES	MENDELEVIUMS	MENTONNIERE	MERCHANTMAN	MEROGENESIS
MELOXICAMS	MENDICANCIES	MENTONNIERES	MERCHANTMEN	MEROGENETIC
MELPHALANS	MENDICANCY	MENTORINGS	MERCHANTRIES	MEROGONIES
MELTABILITIES	MENDICANTS	MENTORSHIP	MERCHANTRY	MEROMORPHIC
MELTABILITY	MENDICITIES	MENTORSHIPS	MERCHILDREN	MEROMYOSIN
MELTINGNESS	MENINGIOMA	MENUISIERS	MERCIFULLY	MEROMYOSINS
MELTINGNESSES	MENINGIOMAS	MEPACRINES	MERCIFULNESS	MERONYMIES
MELTWATERS	MENINGIOMATA	MEPERIDINE	MERCIFULNESSES	MEROPIDANS
MELUNGEONS	MENINGITIC	MEPERIDINES	MERCIFYING	MEROPLANKTON
MEMBERLESS	MENINGITIDES	MEPHITICAL	MERCILESSLY	MEROPLANKTONS
MEMBERSHIP	MENINGITIS	MEPHITICALLY	MERCILESSNESS	MEROZOITES
MEMBERSHIPS	MENINGITISES	MEPHITISES	MERCILESSNESSES	MERPEOPLES

MERRIMENTS	MESOBENTHOSES	MESOTHORAXES	METACOMPUTINGS	METALLIZES
MERRINESSES	MESOBLASTIC	MESOTHORIUM	METAETHICAL	METALLIZING
MERRYMAKER	MESOBLASTS	MESOTHORIUMS	METAETHICS	METALLOCENE
MERRYMAKERS	MESOCEPHALIC	MESOTROPHIC	METAFEMALE	METALLOCENES
MERRYMAKING	MESOCEPHALICS	MESQUINERIE	METAFEMALES	METALLOGENETIC
MERRYMAKINGS	MESOCEPHALIES	MESQUINERIES	METAFICTION	METALLOGENIC
MERRYTHOUGHT	MESOCEPHALISM	MESSAGINGS	METAFICTIONAL	METALLOGENIES
MERRYTHOUGHTS	MESOCEPHALISMS	MESSALINES	METAFICTIONIST	METALLOGENY
MERVEILLEUSE	MESOCEPHALOUS	MESSEIGNEURS	METAFICTIONISTS	METALLOGRAPHER
MERVEILLEUSES	MESOCEPHALY	MESSENGERED	METAFICTIONS	METALLOGRAPHERS
MERVEILLEUX	MESOCRANIES	MESSENGERING	METAGALACTIC	METALLOGRAPHIC
MERVEILLEUXES	MESOCRATIC	MESSENGERS	METAGALAXIES	METALLOGRAPHIES
MESALLIANCE	MESOCYCLONE	MESSIAHSHIP	METAGALAXY	METALLOGRAPHIST
MESALLIANCES	MESOCYCLONES	MESSIAHSHIPS	METAGENESES	METALLOGRAPHY
MESATICEPHALIC	MESODERMAL	MESSIANICALLY	METAGENESIS	METALLOIDAL
MESATICEPHALIES	MESODERMIC	MESSIANISM	METAGENETIC	METALLOIDS
MESATICEPHALOUS	MESOGASTRIA	MESSIANISMS	METAGENETICALLY	METALLOPHONE
MESATICEPHALY	MESOGASTRIC	MESSINESSES	METAGNATHISM	METALLOPHONES
MESCALINES	MESOGASTRIUM	MESTRANOLS	METAGNATHISMS	METALLURGIC
MESCALISMS	MESOGLOEAS	METABISULPHITE	METAGNATHOUS	METALLURGICAL
MESDEMOISELLES	MESOGNATHIES	METABISULPHITES	METAGRABOLISE	METALLURGICALLY
MESENCEPHALA	MESOGNATHISM	METABOLICALLY	METAGRABOLISED	METALLURGIES
MESENCEPHALIC	MESOGNATHISMS	METABOLIES	METAGRABOLISES	METALLURGIST
MESENCEPHALON	MESOGNATHOUS	METABOLISABLE	METAGRABOLISING	METALLURGISTS
MESENCEPHALONS	MESOGNATHY	METABOLISE	METAGRABOLIZE	METALLURGY
MESENCHYMAL	MESOHIPPUS	METABOLISED	METAGRABOLIZED	METALMARKS
MESENCHYMATOUS	MESOHIPPUSES	METABOLISES	METAGRABOLIZES	METALSMITH
MESENCHYME	MESOKURTIC	METABOLISING	METAGRABOLIZING	METALSMITHS
MESENCHYMES	MESOMERISM	METABOLISM	METAGROBOLISE	METALWARES
MESENTERIAL	MESOMERISMS	METABOLISMS	METAGROBOLISED	METALWORKER
MESENTERIC	MESOMORPHIC	METABOLITE	METAGROBOLISES	METALWORKERS
MESENTERIES	MESOMORPHIES	METABOLITES	METAGROBOLISING	METALWORKING
MESENTERITIS	MESOMORPHISM	METABOLIZABLE	METAGROBOLIZE	METALWORKINGS
MESENTERITISES	MESOMORPHISMS	METABOLIZE	METAGROBOLIZED	METALWORKS
MESENTERON	MESOMORPHOUS	METABOLIZED	METAGROBOLIZES	METAMATERIAL
MESENTERONIC	MESOMORPHS	METABOLIZES	METAGROBOLIZING	METAMATERIALS
MESHUGAASEN	MESOMORPHY	METABOLIZING	METALANGUAGE	METAMATHEMATICS
MESHUGASEN	MESONEPHRIC	METABOLOME	METALANGUAGES	METAMERICALLY
MESHUGGENAH	MESONEPHROI	METABOLOMES	METALDEHYDE	METAMERISM
MESHUGGENAHS	MESONEPHROS	METABOLOMICS	METALDEHYDES	METAMERISMS
MESHUGGENEH	MESONEPHROSES	METABOTROPIC	METALEPSES	METAMICTISATION
MESHUGGENEHS	MESOPAUSES	METACARPAL	METALEPSIS	METAMICTIZATION
MESHUGGENER	MESOPELAGIC	METACARPALS	METALEPTIC	METAMORPHIC
MESHUGGENERS	MESOPHILES	METACARPUS	METALEPTICAL	METAMORPHICALLY
MESITYLENE	MESOPHILIC	METACENTER	METALHEADS	METAMORPHISM
MESITYLENES	MESOPHYLLIC	METACENTERS	METALINGUISTIC	METAMORPHISMS
MESMERICAL	MESOPHYLLOUS	METACENTRE	METALINGUISTICS	METAMORPHIST
MESMERICALLY	MESOPHYLLS	METACENTRES	METALISATION	METAMORPHISTS
MESMERISATION	MESOPHYTES	METACENTRIC	METALISATIONS	METAMORPHOSE
MESMERISATIONS	MESOPHYTIC	METACENTRICS	METALISING	METAMORPHOSED
MESMERISED	MESOSCAPHE	METACERCARIA	METALIZATION	METAMORPHOSES
MESMERISER	MESOSCAPHES	METACERCARIAE	METALIZATIONS	METAMORPHOSING
MESMERISERS	MESOSPHERE	METACERCARIAL	METALIZING	METAMORPHOSIS
MESMERISES	MESOSPHERES	METACERCARIAS	METALLICALLY	METAMORPHOUS
MESMERISING	MESOSPHERIC	METACHROMATIC	METALLIDING	METANALYSES
MESMERISMS	MESOTHELIA	METACHROMATISM	METALLIDINGS	METANALYSIS
MESMERISTS	MESOTHELIAL	METACHROMATISMS	METALLIFEROUS	METANARRATIVE
MESMERIZATION	MESOTHELIOMA	METACHRONISM	METALLINGS	METANARRATIVES
MESMERIZATIONS	MESOTHELIOMAS	METACHRONISMS	METALLISATION	METANEPHRIC
MESMERIZED	MESOTHELIOMATA	METACHROSES	METALLISATIONS	METANEPHROI
MESMERIZER	MESOTHELIUM	METACHROSIS	METALLISED	METANEPHROS
MESMERIZERS	MESOTHELIUMS	METACINNABARITE	METALLISES	METAPERIODIC
MESMERIZES	MESOTHERAPIES	METACOGNITION	METALLISING	METAPHASES
MESMERIZING	MESOTHERAPY	METACOGNITIONS	METALLISTS	METAPHORIC
MESNALTIES	MESOTHORACES	METACOMPUTER	METALLIZATION	METAPHORICAL
MESOAMERICAN	MESOTHORACIC	METACOMPUTERS	METALLIZATIONS	METAPHORICALLY
MESOBENTHOS	MESOTHORAX	METACOMPUTING	METALLIZED	METAPHORIST

METAPHORISTS	METASTASIZE	METEOROIDAL	METHODOLOGISTS	METRICISED
METAPHOSPHATE	METASTASIZED	METEOROIDS	METHODOLOGY	METRICISES
METAPHOSPHATES	METASTASIZES	METEOROLITE	METHOMANIA	METRICISING
METAPHOSPHORIC	METASTASIZING	METEOROLITES	METHOMANIAS	METRICISMS
METAPHRASE	METASTATIC	METEOROLOGIC	METHOTREXATE	METRICISTS
METAPHRASED	METASTATICALLY	METEOROLOGICAL	METHOTREXATES	METRICIZED
METAPHRASES	METATARSAL	METEOROLOGIES	METHOXIDES	METRICIZES
METAPHRASING	METATARSALS	METEOROLOGIST	METHOXYBENZENE	METRICIZING
METAPHRASIS	METATARSUS	METEOROLOGISTS	METHOXYBENZENES	METRIFICATION
METAPHRAST	METATHEORETICAL	METEOROLOGY	METHOXYCHLOR	METRIFICATIONS
METAPHRASTIC	METATHEORIES	METERSTICK	METHOXYCHLORS	METRIFIERS
METAPHRASTICAL	METATHEORY	METERSTICKS	METHOXYFLURANE	METRIFONATE
METAPHRASTS	METATHERIAN	METESTICKS	METHOXYFLURANES	METRIFONATES
METAPHYSIC	METATHERIANS	METESTROUS	METHYLAMINE	METRIFYING
METAPHYSICAL	METATHESES	METESTRUSES	METHYLAMINES	METRITISES
METAPHYSICALLY	METATHESIS	METFORMINS	METHYLASES	METROLOGIC
METAPHYSICIAN	METATHESISE	METHACRYLATE	METHYLATED	METROLOGICAL
METAPHYSICIANS	METATHESISED	METHACRYLATES	METHYLATES	METROLOGICALLY
METAPHYSICISE	METATHESISES	METHACRYLIC	METHYLATING	METROLOGIES
METAPHYSICISED	METATHESISING	METHADONES	METHYLATION	METROLOGIST
METAPHYSICISES	METATHESIZE	METHAEMOGLOBIN	METHYLATIONS	METROLOGISTS
METAPHYSICISING	METATHESIZED	METHAEMOGLOBINS	METHYLATOR	METROMANIA
METAPHYSICIST	METATHESIZES	METHAMPHETAMINE	METHYLATORS	METROMANIAS
METAPHYSICISTS	METATHESIZING	METHANAMIDE	METHYLCELLULOSE	METRONIDAZOLE
METAPHYSICIZE	METATHETIC	METHANAMIDES	METHYLDOPA	METRONIDAZOLES
METAPHYSICIZED	METATHETICAL	METHANATION	METHYLDOPAS	METRONOMES
METAPHYSICIZES	METATHETICALLY	METHANATIONS	METHYLENES	METRONOMIC
METAPHYSICIZING	METATHORACES	METHANOMETER	METHYLMERCURIES	METRONOMICAL
METAPHYSICS	METATHORACIC	METHANOMETERS	METHYLMERCURY	METRONOMICALLY
METAPLASES	METATHORAX	METHANOYLS	METHYLPHENIDATE	METRONYMIC
METAPLASIA	METATHORAXES	METHAQUALONE	METHYLPHENOL	METRONYMICS
METAPLASIAS	METATUNGSTIC	METHAQUALONES	METHYLPHENOLS	METROPLEXES
METAPLASIS	METAVANADIC	METHEDRINE	METHYLTHIONINE	METROPOLIS
METAPLASMIC	METAVERSES	METHEDRINES	METHYLTHIONINES	METROPOLISES
METAPLASMS	METAXYLEMS	METHEGLINS	METHYLXANTHINE	METROPOLITAN
METAPLASTIC	METECDYSES	METHEMOGLOBIN	METHYLXANTHINES	METROPOLITANATE
METAPOLITICAL	METECDYSIS	METHEMOGLOBINS	METHYSERGIDE	METROPOLITANISE
METAPOLITICS	METEMPIRIC	METHENAMINE	METHYSERGIDES	METROPOLITANISM
METAPROTEIN	METEMPIRICAL	METHENAMINES	METICULOSITIES	METROPOLITANIZE
METAPROTEINS	METEMPIRICALLY	METHICILLIN	METICULOSITY	METROPOLITANS
METAPSYCHIC	METEMPIRICISM	METHICILLINS	METICULOUS	METROPOLITICAL
METAPSYCHICAL	METEMPIRICISMS	METHINKETH	METICULOUSLY	METRORRHAGIA
METAPSYCHICS	METEMPIRICIST	METHIONINE	METICULOUSNESS	METRORRHAGIAS
METAPSYCHOLOGY	METEMPIRICISTS	METHIONINES	METOCLOPRAMIDE	METROSEXUAL
METARCHONS	METEMPIRICS	METHODICAL	METOCLOPRAMIDES	METROSEXUALS
METASEQUOIA	METEMPSYCHOSES	METHODICALLY	METOESTROUS	METROSTYLE
METASEQUOIAS	METEMPSYCHOSIS	METHODICALNESS	METOESTRUS	METROSTYLES
METASILICATE	METEMPSYCHOSIST	METHODISATION	METOESTRUSES	METTLESOME
METASILICATES	METENCEPHALA	METHODISATIONS	METONYMICAL	METTLESOMENESS
METASILICIC	METENCEPHALIC	METHODISED	METONYMICALLY	MEZCALINES
METASOMATA	METENCEPHALON	METHODISER	METONYMIES	MEZZALUNAS
METASOMATIC	METENCEPHALONS	METHODISERS	METOPOSCOPIC	MEZZANINES
METASOMATISM	METEORICALLY	METHODISES	METOPOSCOPICAL	MEZZOTINTED
METASOMATISMS	METEORISMS	METHODISING	METOPOSCOPIES	MEZZOTINTER
METASOMATOSES	METEORISTS	METHODISMS	METOPOSCOPIST	MEZZOTINTERS
METASOMATOSIS	METEORITAL	METHODISTIC	METOPOSCOPISTS	MEZZOTINTING
METASTABILITIES	METEORITES	METHODISTS	METOPOSCOPY	MEZZOTINTO
METASTABILITY	METEORITIC	METHODIZATION	METRALGIAS	MEZZOTINTOS
METASTABLE	METEORITICAL	METHODIZATIONS	METRESTICK	MEZZOTINTS
METASTABLES	METEORITICIST	METHODIZED	METRESTICKS	MIAROLITIC
METASTABLY	METEORITICISTS	METHODIZER	METRICALLY	MIASMATICAL
METASTASES	METEORITICS	METHODIZERS	METRICATED	MIASMATOUS
METASTASIS	METEOROGRAM	METHODIZES	METRICATES	MIASMICALLY
METASTASISE	METEOROGRAMS	METHODIZING	METRICATING	MICRIFYING
METASTASISED	METEOROGRAPH	METHODOLOGICAL	METRICATION	MICROAEROPHILE
METASTASISES	METEOROGRAPHIC	METHODOLOGIES	METRICATIONS	MICROAEROPHILES
METASTASISING	METEOROGRAPHS	METHODOLOGIST	METRICIANS	MICROAEROPHILIC

m

MICROAGGRESSION	MICROCIRCUITS	MICROFIBER	MICROINJECTING	MICRONISES
MICROAMPERE	MICROCLIMATE	MICROFIBERS	MICROINJECTION	MICRONISING
MICROAMPERES	MICROCLIMATES	MICROFIBRE	MICROINJECTIONS	MICRONIZATION
MICROANALYSES	MICROCLIMATIC	MICROFIBRES	MICROINJECTS	MICRONIZATIONS
MICROANALYSIS	MICROCLINE	MICROFIBRIL	MICROLIGHT	MICRONIZED
MICROANALYST	MICROCLINES	MICROFIBRILLAR	MICROLIGHTING	MICRONIZES
MICROANALYSTS	MICROCOCCAL	MICROFIBRILS	MICROLIGHTINGS	MICRONIZING
MICROANALYTIC	MICROCOCCI	MICROFICHE	MICROLIGHTS	MICRONUCLEI
MICROANALYTICAL	MICROCOCCUS	MICROFICHES	MICROLITER	MICRONUCLEUS
MICROANATOMICAL	MICROCODES	MICROFILAMENT	MICROLITERS	MICRONUCLEUSES
MICROANATOMIES	MICROCOMPONENT	MICROFILAMENTS	MICROLITES	MICRONUTRIENT
MICROANATOMY	MICROCOMPONENTS	MICROFILARIA	MICROLITHIC	MICRONUTRIENTS
MICROARRAY	MICROCOMPUTER	MICROFILARIAE	MICROLITHS	MICROORGANISM
MICROARRAYS	MICROCOMPUTERS	MICROFILARIAL	MICROLITIC	MICROORGANISMS
MICROBALANCE	MICROCOMPUTING	MICROFILING	MICROLITRE	MICROPARASITE
MICROBALANCES	MICROCOMPUTINGS	MICROFILINGS	MICROLITRES	MICROPARASITES
MICROBAROGRAPH	MICROCOPIED	MICROFILMABLE	MICROLOANS	MICROPARASITIC
MICROBAROGRAPHS	MICROCOPIES	MICROFILMED	MICROLOGIC	MICROPARTICLE
MICROBEADS	MICROCOPYING	MICROFILMER	MICROLOGICAL	MICROPARTICLES
MICROBEAMS	MICROCOPYINGS	MICROFILMERS	MICROLOGICALLY	MICROPARTIES
MICROBIOLOGIC	MICROCOSMIC	MICROFILMING	MICROLOGIES	MICROPARTY
MICROBIOLOGICAL	MICROCOSMICAL	MICROFILMS	MICROLOGIST	MICROPAYMENT
MICROBIOLOGIES	MICROCOSMICALLY	MICROFILTER	MICROLOGISTS	MICROPAYMENTS
MICROBIOLOGIST	MICROCOSMOS	MICROFILTERS	MICROLUCES	MICROPEGMATITE
MICROBIOLOGISTS	MICROCOSMOSES	MICROFLOPPIES	MICROLUXES	MICROPEGMATITES
MICROBIOLOGY	MICROCOSMS	MICROFLOPPY	MICROMANAGE	MICROPEGMATITIC
MICROBIOME	MICROCRACK	MICROFLORA	MICROMANAGED	MICROPHAGE
MICROBIOMES	MICROCRACKED	MICROFLORAE	MICROMANAGEMENT	MICROPHAGES
MICROBIOTA	MICROCRACKING	MICROFLORAL	MICROMANAGER	MICROPHAGOUS
MICROBIOTAS	MICROCRACKINGS	MICROFLORAS	MICROMANAGERS	MICROPHONE
MICROBLOGGER	MICROCRACKS	MICROFORMS	MICROMANAGES	MICROPHONES
MICROBLOGGERS	MICROCRYSTAL	MICROFOSSIL	MICROMANAGING	MICROPHONIC
MICROBLOGGING	MICROCRYSTALS	MICROFOSSILS	MICROMARKETING	MICROPHONICS
MICROBLOGGINGS	MICROCULTURAL	MICROFUNGI	MICROMARKETINGS	MICROPHOTOGRAPH
MICROBLOGS	MICROCULTURE	MICROFUNGUS	MICROMERES	MICROPHOTOMETER
MICROBREWER	MICROCULTURES	MICROFUNGUSES	MICROMESHES	MICROPHOTOMETRY
MICROBREWERIES	MICROCURIE	MICROGAMETE	MICROMETEORITE	MICROPHYLL
MICROBREWERS	MICROCURIES	MICROGAMETES	MICROMETEORITES	MICROPHYLLOUS
MICROBREWERY	MICROCYTES	MICROGAMETOCYTE	MICROMETEORITIC	MICROPHYLLS
MICROBREWING	MICROCYTIC	MICROGENERATION	MICROMETEOROID	MICROPHYSICAL
MICROBREWINGS	MICRODETECTION	MICROGLIAS	MICROMETEOROIDS	MICROPHYSICALLY
MICROBREWS	MICRODETECTIONS	MICROGRAMS	MICROMETER	MICROPHYSICIST
MICROBUBBLES	MICRODETECTOR	MICROGRANITE	MICROMETERS	MICROPHYSICISTS
MICROBURST	MICRODETECTORS	MICROGRANITES	MICROMETHOD	MICROPHYSICS
MICROBURSTS	MICRODISSECTION	MICROGRANITIC	MICROMETHODS	MICROPHYTE
MICROBUSES	MICRODONTOUS	MICROGRAPH	MICROMETRE	MICROPHYTES
MICROBUSSES	MICRODRIVE	MICROGRAPHED	MICROMETRES	MICROPHYTIC
MICROCAPSULE	MICRODRIVES	MICROGRAPHER	MICROMETRIC	MICROPIPET
MICROCAPSULES	MICRODRONE	MICROGRAPHERS	MICROMETRICAL	MICROPIPETS
MICROCARDS	MICRODRONES	MICROGRAPHIC	MICROMETRIES	MICROPIPETTE
MICROCASSETTE	MICROEARTHQUAKE	MICROGRAPHICS	MICROMETRY	MICROPIPETTES
MICROCASSETTES	MICROECONOMIC	MICROGRAPHIES	MICROMICROCURIE	MICROPLANKTON
MICROCELEBRITY	MICROECONOMICS	MICROGRAPHING	MICROMICROFARAD	MICROPLANKTONS
MICROCEPHAL	MICROELECTRODE	MICROGRAPHS	MICROMILLIMETRE	MICROPLASTIC
MICROCEPHALIC	MICROELECTRODES	MICROGRAPHY	MICROMINIATURE	MICROPLASTICS
MICROCEPHALICS	MICROELECTRONIC	MICROGRAVITIES	MICROMINIS	MICROPOLIS
MICROCEPHALIES	MICROELEMENT	MICROGRAVITY	MICROMOLAR	MICROPOLISES
MICROCEPHALOUS	MICROELEMENTS	MICROGREENS	MICROMOLES	MICROPORES
MICROCEPHALS	MICROEVOLUTION	MICROGROOVE	MICROMORPHOLOGY	MICROPOROSITIES
MICROCEPHALY	MICROEVOLUTIONS	MICROGROOVES	MICROMORTS	MICROPOROSITY
MICROCHEMICAL	MICROFARAD	MICROHABITAT	MICRONATION	MICROPOROUS
MICROCHEMISTRY	MICROFARADS	MICROHABITATS	MICRONATIONS	MICROPOWER
MICROCHIPPED	MICROFAUNA	MICROIMAGE	MICRONEEDLE	MICROPOWERS
MICROCHIPPING	MICROFAUNAE	MICROIMAGES	MICRONEEDLES	MICROPRINT
MICROCHIPS	MICROFAUNAL	MICROINCHES	MICRONISATION	MICROPRINTED
MICROCIRCUIT	MICROFAUNAS	MICROINJECT	MICRONISATIONS	MICROPRINTING
MICROCIRCUITRY	MICROFELSITIC	MICROINJECTED	MICRONISED	MICROPRINTINGS

MICROPRINTS	MICROSPORES	MIDDELSKOTS	MILITANTNESS	MILLESIMALS
MICROPRISM	MICROSPORIC	MIDDENSTEAD	MILITANTNESSES	MILLHOUSES
MICROPRISMS	MICROSPORIDIAN	MIDDENSTEADS	MILITARIES	MILLIAMPERE
MICROPROBE	MICROSPOROCYTE	MIDDLEBREAKER	MILITARILY	MILLIAMPERES
MICROPROBES	MICROSPOROCYTES	MIDDLEBREAKERS	MILITARISATION	MILLIARIES
MICROPROCESSING	MICROSPOROPHYLL	MIDDLEBROW	MILITARISATIONS	MILLICURIE
MICROPROCESSOR	MICROSPOROUS	MIDDLEBROWED	MILITARISE	MILLICURIES
MICROPROCESSORS	MICROSTATE	MIDDLEBROWISM	MILITARISED	MILLIDEGREE
MICROPROGRAM	MICROSTATES	MIDDLEBROWISMS	MILITARISES	MILLIDEGREES
MICROPROGRAMS	MICROSTOMATOUS	MIDDLEBROWS	MILITARISING	MILLIGRAMME
MICROPROJECTION	MICROSTOMOUS	MIDDLEBUSTER	MILITARISM	MILLIGRAMMES
MICROPROJECTOR	MICROSTRUCTURAL	MIDDLEBUSTERS	MILITARISMS	MILLIGRAMS
MICROPROJECTORS	MICROSTRUCTURE	MIDDLEMOST	MILITARIST	MILLIHENRIES
MICROPSIAS	MICROSTRUCTURES	MIDDLEWARE	MILITARISTIC	MILLIHENRY
MICROPTEROUS	MICROSURGEON	MIDDLEWARES	MILITARISTS	MILLIHENRYS
MICROPUBLISHER	MICROSURGEONS	MIDDLEWEIGHT	MILITARIZATION	MILLILAMBERT
MICROPUBLISHERS	MICROSURGERIES	MIDDLEWEIGHTS	MILITARIZATIONS	MILLILAMBERTS
MICROPUBLISHING	MICROSURGERY	MIDDLINGLY	MILITARIZE	MILLILITER
MICROPULSATION	MICROSURGICAL	MIDFIELDER	MILITARIZED	MILLILITERS
MICROPULSATIONS	MICROSWITCH	MIDFIELDERS	MILITARIZES	MILLILITRE
MICROPUMPS	MICROSWITCHES	MIDIBUSSES	MILITARIZING	MILLILITRES
MICROPUNCTURE	MICROTECHNIC	MIDINETTES	MILITATING	MILLILUCES
MICROPUNCTURES	MICROTECHNICS	MIDISKIRTS	MILITATION	MILLILUXES
MICROPYLAR	MICROTECHNIQUE	MIDLANDERS	MILITATIONS	MILLIMETER
MICROPYLES	MICROTECHNIQUES	MIDLATITUDE	MILITIAMAN	MILLIMETERS
MICROPYROMETER	MICROTECHNOLOGY	MIDLATITUDES	MILITIAMEN	MILLIMETRE
MICROPYROMETERS	MICROTOMES	MIDLITTORAL	MILKFISHES	MILLIMETRES
MICROQUAKE	MICROTOMIC	MIDLITTORALS	MILKINESSES	MILLIMICRON
MICROQUAKES	MICROTOMICAL	MIDNIGHTLY	MILKSHAKES	MILLIMICRONS
MICRORADIOGRAPH	MICROTOMIES	MIDRASHOTH	MILKSOPISM	MILLIMOLAR
MICROREADER	MICROTOMIST	MIDSAGITTAL	MILKSOPISMS	MILLIMOLES
MICROREADERS	MICROTOMISTS	MIDSECTION	MILKSOPPIER	MILLINERIES
MICROSATELLITE	MICROTONAL	MIDSECTIONS	MILKSOPPIEST	MILLIONAIRE
MICROSATELLITES	MICROTONALITIES	MIDSHIPMAN	MILKSOPPING	MILLIONAIRES
MICROSCALE	MICROTONALITY	MIDSHIPMATE	MILKTOASTS	MILLIONAIRESS
MICROSCALES	MICROTONALLY	MIDSHIPMATES	MILLBOARDS	MILLIONAIRESSES
MICROSCOPE	MICROTONES	MIDSHIPMEN	MILLEFEUILLE	MILLIONARY
MICROSCOPES	MICROTUBES	MIDSTORIES	MILLEFEUILLES	MILLIONFOLD
MICROSCOPIC	MICROTUBULAR	MIDSTREAMS	MILLEFIORI	MILLIONNAIRE
MICROSCOPICAL	MICROTUBULE	MIDSUMMERS	MILLEFIORIS	MILLIONNAIRES
MICROSCOPICALLY	MICROTUBULES	MIDWATCHES	MILLEFLEUR	MILLIONNAIRESS
MICROSCOPIES	MICROTUNNELLING	MIDWESTERN	MILLEFLEURS	MILLIONTHS
MICROSCOPIST	MICROVASCULAR	MIDWIFERIES	MILLENARIAN	MILLIOSMOL
MICROSCOPISTS	MICROVILLAR	MIDWINTERS	MILLENARIANISM	MILLIOSMOLS
MICROSCOPY	MICROVILLI	MIFEPRISTONE	MILLENARIANISMS	MILLIPEDES
MICROSECOND	MICROVILLOUS	MIFEPRISTONES	MILLENARIANS	MILLIPROBE
MICROSECONDS	MICROVILLUS	MIFFINESSES	MILLENARIES	MILLIPROBES
MICROSEISM	MICROVOLTS	MIGHTINESS	MILLENARISM	MILLIRADIAN
MICROSEISMIC	MICROWATTS	MIGHTINESSES	MILLENARISMS	MILLIRADIANS
MICROSEISMICAL	MICROWAVABLE	MIGMATITES	MILLENNIAL	MILLIROENTGEN
MICROSEISMICITY	MICROWAVEABLE	MIGNONETTE	MILLENNIALISM	MILLIROENTGENS
MICROSEISMS	MICROWAVED	MIGNONETTES	MILLENNIALISMS	MILLISECOND
MICROSITES	MICROWAVES	MIGRAINEUR	MILLENNIALIST	MILLISECONDS
MICROSKIRT	MICROWAVING	MIGRAINEURS	MILLENNIALISTS	MILLISIEVERT
MICROSKIRTS	MICROWIRES	MIGRAINOUS	MILLENNIALLY	MILLISIEVERTS
MICROSLEEP	MICROWORLD	MIGRATIONAL	MILLENNIALS	MILLIVOLTS
MICROSLEEPS	MICROWORLDS	MIGRATIONIST	MILLENNIANISM	MILLIWATTS
MICROSMATIC	MICROWRITER	MIGRATIONISTS	MILLENNIANISMS	MILLOCRACIES
MICROSOMAL	MICROWRITERS	MIGRATIONS	MILLENNIARISM	MILLOCRACY
MICROSOMES	MICRURGIES	MILDEWIEST	MILLENNIARISMS	MILLOCRATS
MICROSPECIES	MICTURATED	MILDNESSES	MILLENNIUM	MILLSCALES
MICROSPHERE	MICTURATES	MILEOMETER	MILLENNIUMS	MILLSTONES
MICROSPHERES	MICTURATING	MILEOMETERS	MILLEPEDES	MILLSTREAM
MICROSPHERICAL	MICTURITION	MILESTONES	MILLEPORES	MILLSTREAMS
MICROSPORANGIA	MICTURITIONS	MILITANCES	MILLERITES	MILLWHEELS
MICROSPORANGIUM	MIDDELMANNETJIE	MILITANCIES	MILLESIMAL	MILLWRIGHT
MICROSPORE	MIDDELSKOT	MILITANTLY	MILLESIMALLY	MILLWRIGHTS

MILOMETERS	MINERALOGISED	MINIMALISTIC	MIRACULOUSLY	MISANALYSES
MILQUETOAST	MINERALOGISES	MINIMALISTS	MIRACULOUSNESS	MISANALYSIS
MILQUETOASTS	MINERALOGISING	MINIMARKET	MIRANDISED	MISANDRIES
MIMEOGRAPH	MINERALOGIST	MINIMARKETS	MIRANDISES	MISANDRIST
MIMEOGRAPHED	MINERALOGISTS	MINTMAXING	MIRANDISING	MISANDRISTS
MIMEOGRAPHING	MINERALOGIZE	MINIMISATION	MIRANDIZED	MISANDROUS
MIMEOGRAPHS	MINERALOGIZED	MINIMISATIONS	MIRANDIZES	MISANTHROPE
MIMETICALLY	MINERALOGIZES	MINIMISERS	MIRANDIZING	MISANTHROPES
MIMIVIRUSES	MINERALOGIZING	MINIMISING	MIRIFICALLY	MISANTHROPIC
MIMMICKING	MINERALOGY	MINIMIZATION	MIRINESSES	MISANTHROPICAL
MIMOGRAPHER	MINESHAFTS	MINIMIZATIONS	MIRKINESSES	MISANTHROPIES
MIMOGRAPHERS	MINESTONES	MINIMIZERS	MIRRORINGS	MISANTHROPIST
MIMOGRAPHIES	MINESTRONE	MINIMIZING	MIRRORLIKE	MISANTHROPISTS
MIMOGRAPHY	MINESTRONES	MINIRUGBIES	MIRRORWISE	MISANTHROPOS
MIMOSACEOUS	MINESWEEPER	MINISCHOOL	MIRTHFULLY	MISANTHROPOSES
MINACIOUSLY	MINESWEEPERS	MINISCHOOLS	MIRTHFULNESS	MISANTHROPY
MINACITIES	MINESWEEPING	MINISCULES	MIRTHFULNESSES	MISAPPLICATION
MINATORIAL	MINESWEEPINGS	MINISERIES	MIRTHLESSLY	MISAPPLICATIONS
MINATORIALLY	MINEWORKER	MINISKIRTED	MIRTHLESSNESS	MISAPPLIED
MINATORILY	MINEWORKERS	MINISKIRTS	MIRTHLESSNESSES	MISAPPLIES
MINAUDERIE	MINGIMINGI	MINISTATES	MISACCEPTATION	MISAPPLYING
MINAUDERIES	MINGIMINGIS	MINISTERED	MISACCEPTATIONS	MISAPPRAISAL
MINAUDIERE	MINGINESSES	MINISTERIA	MISADAPTED	MISAPPRAISALS
MINAUDIERES	MINGLEMENT	MINISTERIAL	MISADAPTING	MISAPPRECIATE
MINCEMEATS	MINGLEMENTS	MINISTERIALIST	MISADDRESS	MISAPPRECIATED
MINDBLOWER	MINGLINGLY	MINISTERIALISTS	MISADDRESSED	MISAPPRECIATES
MINDBLOWERS	MINIATIONS	MINISTERIALLY	MISADDRESSES	MISAPPRECIATING
MINDEDNESS	MINIATURED	MINISTERING	MISADDRESSING	MISAPPRECIATION
MINDEDNESSES	MINIATURES	MINISTERIUM	MISADJUSTED	MISAPPRECIATIVE
MINDFULNESS	MINIATURING	MINISTERSHIP	MISADJUSTING	MISAPPREHEND
MINDFULNESSES	MINIATURISATION	MINISTERSHIPS	MISADJUSTS	MISAPPREHENDED
MINDLESSLY	MINIATURISE	MINISTRANT	MISADVENTURE	MISAPPREHENDING
MINDLESSNESS	MINIATURISED	MINISTRANTS	MISADVENTURED	MISAPPREHENDS
MINDLESSNESSES	MINIATURISES	MINISTRATION	MISADVENTURER	MISAPPREHENSION
MINDSCAPES	MINIATURISING	MINISTRATIONS	MISADVENTURERS	MISAPPREHENSIVE
MINDSHARES	MINIATURIST	MINISTRATIVE	MISADVENTURES	MISAPPROPRIATE
MINEFIELDS	MINIATURISTIC	MINISTRESS	MISADVENTUROUS	MISAPPROPRIATED
MINEHUNTER	MINIATURISTS	MINISTRESSES	MISADVERTENCE	MISAPPROPRIATES
MINEHUNTERS	MINIATURIZATION	MINISTRIES	MISADVERTENCES	MISARRANGE
MINELAYERS	MINIATURIZE	MINISTROKE	MISADVICES	MISARRANGED
MINELAYING	MINIATURIZED	MINISTROKES	MISADVISED	MISARRANGEMENT
MINELAYINGS	MINIATURIZES	MINISYSTEM	MISADVISEDLY	MISARRANGEMENTS
MINERALISABLE	MINIATURIZING	MINISYSTEMS	MISADVISEDNESS	MISARRANGES
MINERALISATION	MINIBIKERS	MINITOWERS	MISADVISES	MISARRANGING
MINERALISATIONS	MINIBREAKS	MINITRACKS	MISADVISING	MISARTICULATE
MINERALISE	MINIBUDGET	MINIVOLLEY	MISALIGNED	MISARTICULATED
MINERALISED	MINIBUDGETS	MINIVOLLEYS	MISALIGNING	MISARTICULATES
MINERALISER	MINIBUSSES	MINNESINGER	MISALIGNMENT	MISARTICULATING
MINERALISERS	MINICABBING	MINNESINGERS	MISALIGNMENTS	MISASSAYED
MINERALISES	MINICABBINGS	MINNICKING	MISALLEGED	MISASSAYING
MINERALISING	MINICALCULATOR	MINNOCKING	MISALLEGES	MISASSEMBLE
MINERALIST	MINICALCULATORS	MINORITAIRE	MISALLEGING	MISASSEMBLED
MINERALISTS	MINICASSETTE	MINORITAIRES	MISALLIANCE	MISASSEMBLES
MINERALIZABLE	MINICASSETTES	MINORITIES	MISALLIANCES	MISASSEMBLING
MINERALIZATION	MINICOMPUTER	MINORSHIPS	MISALLOCATE	MISASSIGNED
MINERALIZATIONS	MINICOMPUTERS	MINOXIDILS	MISALLOCATED	MISASSIGNING
MINERALIZE	MINICOURSE	MINSTRELSIES	MISALLOCATES	MISASSIGNS
MINERALIZED	MINICOURSES	MINSTRELSY	MISALLOCATING	MISASSUMED
MINERALIZER	MINIDISHES	MINUSCULAR	MISALLOCATION	MISASSUMES
MINERALIZERS	MINIDRESSES	MINUSCULES	MISALLOCATIONS	MISASSUMING
MINERALIZES	MINIFICATION	MINUTENESS	MISALLOTMENT	MISASSUMPTION
MINERALIZING	MINIFICATIONS	MINUTENESSES	MISALLOTMENTS	MISASSUMPTIONS
MINERALOGIC	MINIFLOPPIES	MIRABELLES	MISALLOTTED	MISATONING
MINERALOGICAL	MINIFLOPPY	MIRABILISES	MISALLOTTING	MISATTRIBUTE
MINERALOGICALLY	MINIMALISM	MIRACIDIAL	MISALLYING	MISATTRIBUTED
MINERALOGIES	MINIMALISMS	MIRACIDIUM	MISALTERED	MISATTRIBUTES
MINERALOGISE	MINIMALIST	MIRACULOUS	MISALTERING	MISATTRIBUTING

MISATTRIBUTION	MISCAPTIONS	MISCITATION	MISCONTENTING	MISDEVELOPS
MISATTRIBUTIONS	MISCARRIAGE	MISCITATIONS	MISCONTENTMENT	MISDEVOTION
MISAUNTERS	MISCARRIAGES	MISCLAIMED	MISCONTENTMENTS	MISDEVOTIONS
MISAVERRED	MISCARRIED	MISCLAIMING	MISCONTENTS	MISDIAGNOSE
MISAVERRING	MISCARRIES	MISCLASSED	MISCOOKING	MISDIAGNOSED
MISAWARDED	MISCARRYING	MISCLASSES	MISCOPYING	MISDIAGNOSES
MISAWARDING	MISCASTING	MISCLASSIFIED	MISCORRECT	MISDIAGNOSING
MISBALANCE	MISCATALOG	MISCLASSIFIES	MISCORRECTED	MISDIAGNOSIS
MISBALANCED	MISCATALOGED	MISCLASSIFY	MISCORRECTING	MISDIALING
MISBALANCES	MISCATALOGING	MISCLASSIFYING	MISCORRECTION	MISDIALLED
MISBALANCING	MISCATALOGS	MISCLASSING	MISCORRECTIONS	MISDIALLING
MISBECOMES	MISCEGENATE	MISCOINING	MISCORRECTS	MISDIETING
MISBECOMING	MISCEGENATED	MISCOLORED	MISCORRELATION	MISDIGHTED
MISBECOMINGNESS	MISCEGENATES	MISCOLORING	MISCORRELATIONS	MISDIGHTING
MISBEGINNING	MISCEGENATING	MISCOLOURED	MISCOUNSEL	MISDIRECTED
MISBEGOTTEN	MISCEGENATION	MISCOLOURING	MISCOUNSELLED	MISDIRECTING
MISBEHAVED	MISCEGENATIONAL	MISCOLOURS	MISCOUNSELLING	MISDIRECTION
MISBEHAVER	MISCEGENATIONS	MISCOMPREHEND	MISCOUNSELLINGS	MISDIRECTIONS
MISBEHAVERS	MISCEGENATOR	MISCOMPREHENDED	MISCOUNSELS	MISDIRECTS
MISBEHAVES	MISCEGENATORS	MISCOMPREHENDS	MISCOUNTED	MISDISTRIBUTION
MISBEHAVING	MISCEGENES	MISCOMPUTATION	MISCOUNTING	MISDIVIDED
MISBEHAVIOR	MISCEGENETIC	MISCOMPUTATIONS	MISCREANCE	MISDIVIDES
MISBEHAVIORS	MISCEGENIST	MISCOMPUTE	MISCREANCES	MISDIVIDING
MISBEHAVIOUR	MISCEGENISTS	MISCOMPUTED	MISCREANCIES	MISDIVISION
MISBEHAVIOURS	MISCEGINES	MISCOMPUTES	MISCREANCY	MISDIVISIONS
MISBELIEFS	MISCELLANARIAN	MISCOMPUTING	MISCREANTS	MISDOUBTED
MISBELIEVE	MISCELLANARIANS	MISCONCEIT	MISCREATED	MISDOUBTFUL
MISBELIEVED	MISCELLANEA	MISCONCEITED	MISCREATES	MISDOUBTING
MISBELIEVER	MISCELLANEOUS	MISCONCEITING	MISCREATING	MISDRAWING
MISBELIEVERS	MISCELLANEOUSLY	MISCONCEITS	MISCREATION	MISDRAWINGS
MISBELIEVES	MISCELLANIES	MISCONCEIVE	MISCREATIONS	MISDREADED
MISBELIEVING	MISCELLANIST	MISCONCEIVED	MISCREATIVE	MISDREADING
MISBESEEMED	MISCELLANISTS	MISCONCEIVER	MISCREATOR	MISDRIVING
MISBESEEMING	MISCELLANY	MISCONCEIVERS	MISCREATORS	MISEDITING
MISBESEEMS	MISCHALLENGE	MISCONCEIVES	MISCREAUNCE	MISEDUCATE
MISBESTOWAL	MISCHALLENGES	MISCONCEIVING	MISCREAUNCES	MISEDUCATED
MISBESTOWALS	MISCHANCED	MISCONCEPTION	MISCREDITED	MISEDUCATES
MISBESTOWED	MISCHANCEFUL	MISCONCEPTIONS	MISCREDITING	MISEDUCATING
MISBESTOWING	MISCHANCES	MISCONDUCT	MISCREDITS	MISEDUCATION
MISBESTOWS	MISCHANCIER	MISCONDUCTED	MISCUTTING	MISEDUCATIONS
MISBIASING	MISCHANCIEST	MISCONDUCTING	MISDEALERS	MISEMPHASES
MISBIASSED	MISCHANCING	MISCONDUCTS	MISDEALING	MISEMPHASIS
MISBIASSES	MISCHANNEL	MISCONJECTURE	MISDEEMFUL	MISEMPHASISE
MISBIASSING	MISCHANNELED	MISCONJECTURED	MISDEEMING	MISEMPHASISED
MISBILLING	MISCHANNELING	MISCONJECTURES	MISDEEMINGS	MISEMPHASISES
MISBINDING	MISCHANNELLED	MISCONJECTURING	MISDEFINED	MISEMPHASISING
MISBRANDED	MISCHANNELLING	MISCONNECT	MISDEFINES	MISEMPHASIZE
MISBRANDING	MISCHANNELS	MISCONNECTED	MISDEFINING	MISEMPHASIZED
MISBUILDING	MISCHANTER	MISCONNECTING	MISDEMEANANT	MISEMPHASIZES
MISBUTTONED	MISCHANTERS	MISCONNECTION	MISDEMEANANTS	MISEMPHASIZING
MISBUTTONING	MISCHARACTERISE	MISCONNECTIONS	MISDEMEANED	MISEMPLOYED
MISBUTTONS	MISCHARACTERIZE	MISCONNECTS	MISDEMEANING	MISEMPLOYING
MISCALCULATE	MISCHARGED	MISCONSTER	MISDEMEANOR	MISEMPLOYMENT
MISCALCULATED	MISCHARGES	MISCONSTERED	MISDEMEANORS	MISEMPLOYMENTS
MISCALCULATES	MISCHARGING	MISCONSTERING	MISDEMEANOUR	MISEMPLOYS
MISCALCULATING	MISCHIEFED	MISCONSTERS	MISDEMEANOURS	MISENROLLED
MISCALCULATION	MISCHIEFING	MISCONSTRUCT	MISDEMEANS	MISENROLLING
MISCALCULATIONS	MISCHIEVOUS	MISCONSTRUCTED	MISDESCRIBE	MISENROLLS
MISCALCULATOR	MISCHIEVOUSLY	MISCONSTRUCTING	MISDESCRIBED	MISENTERED
MISCALCULATORS	MISCHIEVOUSNESS	MISCONSTRUCTION	MISDESCRIBES	MISENTERING
MISCALLERS	MISCHMETAL	MISCONSTRUCTS	MISDESCRIBING	MISENTREAT
MISCALLING	MISCHMETALS	MISCONSTRUE	MISDESCRIPTION	MISENTREATED
MISCANTHUS	MISCHOICES	MISCONSTRUED	MISDESCRIPTIONS	MISENTREATING
MISCANTHUSES	MISCHOOSES	MISCONSTRUES	MISDESERTS	MISENTREATS
MISCAPTION	MISCHOOSING	MISCONSTRUING	MISDEVELOP	MISENTRIES
MISCAPTIONED	MISCIBILITIES	MISCONTENT	MISDEVELOPED	MISERABILISM
MISCAPTIONING	MISCIBILITY	MISCONTENTED	MISDEVELOPING	MISERABILISMS

MISERABILIST	MISGENDERS	MISINFORMATION	MISLUCKING	MISPAINTED
MISERABILISTS	MISGIVINGS	MISINFORMATIONS	MISMANAGED	MISPAINTING
MISERABLENESS	MISGOVERNANCE	MISINFORMED	MISMANAGEMENT	MISPARSING
MISERABLENESSES	MISGOVERNANCES	MISINFORMER	MISMANAGEMENTS	MISPARTING
MISERABLES	MISGOVERNAUNCE	MISINFORMERS	MISMANAGER	MISPATCHED
MISERABLISM	MISGOVERNAUNCES	MISINFORMING	MISMANAGERS	MISPATCHES
MISERABLISMS	MISGOVERNED	MISINFORMS	MISMANAGES	MISPATCHING
MISERABLIST	MISGOVERNING	MISINSTRUCT	MISMANAGING	MISPENNING
MISERABLISTS	MISGOVERNMENT	MISINSTRUCTED	MISMANNERS	MISPERCEIVE
MISERICORD	MISGOVERNMENTS	MISINSTRUCTING	MISMARKING	MISPERCEIVED
MISERICORDE	MISGOVERNOR	MISINSTRUCTION	MISMARRIAGE	MISPERCEIVES
MISERICORDES	MISGOVERNORS	MISINSTRUCTIONS	MISMARRIAGES	MISPERCEIVING
MISERICORDS	MISGOVERNS	MISINSTRUCTS	MISMARRIED	MISPERCEPTION
MISERLIEST	MISGRADING	MISINTELLIGENCE	MISMARRIES	MISPERCEPTIONS
MISERLINESS	MISGRAFTED	MISINTENDED	MISMARRYING	MISPERSUADE
MISERLINESSES	MISGRAFTING	MISINTENDING	MISMATCHED	MISPERSUADED
MISESTEEMED	MISGROWING	MISINTENDS	MISMATCHES	MISPERSUADES
MISESTEEMING	MISGROWTHS	MISINTERPRET	MISMATCHING	MISPERSUADING
MISESTEEMS	MISGUESSED	MISINTERPRETED	MISMATCHMENT	MISPERSUASION
MISESTIMATE	MISGUESSES	MISINTERPRETER	MISMATCHMENTS	MISPERSUASIONS
MISESTIMATED	MISGUESSING	MISINTERPRETERS	MISMATINGS	MISPHRASED
MISESTIMATES	MISGUGGLED	MISINTERPRETING	MISMEASURE	MISPHRASES
MISESTIMATING	MISGUGGLES	MISINTERPRETS	MISMEASURED	MISPHRASING
MISESTIMATION	MISGUGGLING	MISINTERRED	MISMEASUREMENT	MISPICKELS
MISESTIMATIONS	MISGUIDANCE	MISINTERRING	MISMEASUREMENTS	MISPLACEMENT
MISEVALUATE	MISGUIDANCES	MISJOINDER	MISMEASURES	MISPLACEMENTS
MISEVALUATED	MISGUIDEDLY	MISJOINDERS	MISMEASURING	MISPLACING
MISEVALUATES	MISGUIDEDNESS	MISJOINING	MISMEETING	MISPLANNED
MISEVALUATING	MISGUIDEDNESSES	MISJUDGEMENT	MISMETRING	MISPLANNING
MISEVALUATION	MISGUIDERS	MISJUDGEMENTS	MISNOMERED	MISPLANTED
MISEVALUATIONS	MISGUIDING	MISJUDGERS	MISNOMERING	MISPLANTING
MISFALLING	MISHALLOWED	MISJUDGING	MISNUMBERED	MISPLAYING
MISFARINGS	MISHANDLED	MISJUDGMENT	MISNUMBERING	MISPLEADED
MISFEASANCE	MISHANDLES	MISJUDGMENTS	MISNUMBERS	MISPLEADING
MISFEASANCES	MISHANDLING	MISKEEPING	MISOBSERVANCE	MISPLEADINGS
MISFEASORS	MISHANDLINGS	MISKENNING	MISOBSERVANCES	MISPLEASED
MISFEATURE	MISHANTERS	MISKICKING	MISOBSERVE	MISPLEASES
MISFEATURED	MISHAPPENED	MISKNOWING	MISOBSERVED	MISPLEASING
MISFEATURES	MISHAPPENING	MISKNOWLEDGE	MISOBSERVES	MISPOINTED
MISFEATURING	MISHAPPENS	MISKNOWLEDGES	MISOBSERVING	MISPOINTING
MISFEEDING	MISHAPPING	MISLABELED	MISOCAPNIC	MISPOISING
MISFEIGNED	MISHEARING	MISLABELING	MISOGAMIES	MISPOSITION
MISFEIGNING	MISHEGAASEN	MISLABELLED	MISOGAMIST	MISPOSITIONED
MISFIELDED	MISHGUGGLE	MISLABELLING	MISOGAMISTS	MISPOSITIONING
MISFIELDING	MISHGUGGLED	MISLABORED	MISOGYNIES	MISPOSITIONS
MISFITTING	MISHGUGGLES	MISLABORING	MISOGYNIST	MISPRAISED
MISFOCUSED	MISHGUGGLING	MISLABOURED	MISOGYNISTIC	MISPRAISES
MISFOCUSES	MISHITTING	MISLABOURING	MISOGYNISTICAL	MISPRAISING
MISFOCUSING	MISHMASHES	MISLABOURS	MISOGYNISTS	MISPRICING
MISFOCUSSED	MISHMOSHES	MISLEADERS	MISOGYNOUS	MISPRINTED
MISFOCUSSES	MISHUGASES	MISLEADING	MISOLOGIES	MISPRINTING
MISFOCUSSING	MISIDENTIFIED	MISLEADINGLY	MISOLOGIST	MISPRISING
MISFOLDING	MISIDENTIFIES	MISLEARNED	MISOLOGISTS	MISPRISION
MISFORMATION	MISIDENTIFY	MISLEARNING	MISONEISMS	MISPRISIONS
MISFORMATIONS	MISIDENTIFYING	MISLEEKING	MISONEISTIC	MISPRIZERS
MISFORMING	MISIMPRESSION	MISLIGHTED	MISONEISTS	MISPRIZING
MISFORTUNE	MISIMPRESSIONS	MISLIGHTING	MISORDERED	MISPROGRAM
MISFORTUNED	MISIMPROVE	MISLIKINGS	MISORDERING	MISPROGRAMED
MISFORTUNES	MISIMPROVED	MISLIPPENED	MISORIENTATION	MISPROGRAMING
MISFRAMING	MISIMPROVEMENT	MISLIPPENING	MISORIENTATIONS	MISPROGRAMMED
MISFUNCTION	MISIMPROVEMENTS	MISLIPPENS	MISORIENTED	MISPROGRAMMING
MISFUNCTIONED	MISIMPROVES	MISLOCATED	MISORIENTING	MISPROGRAMS
MISFUNCTIONING	MISIMPROVING	MISLOCATES	MISORIENTS	MISPRONOUNCE
MISFUNCTIONS	MISINFERRED	MISLOCATING	MISPACKAGE	MISPRONOUNCED
MISGAUGING	MISINFERRING	MISLOCATION	MISPACKAGED	MISPRONOUNCES
MISGENDERED	MISINFORMANT	MISLOCATIONS	MISPACKAGES	MISPRONOUNCING
MISGENDERING	MISINFORMANTS	MISLODGING	MISPACKAGING	MISPROPORTION

MISPROPORTIONED	MISSELLING	MISSTEERING	MISTRUSTED	MITOTICALLY
MISPROPORTIONS	MISSELLINGS	MISSTEPPED	MISTRUSTER	MITRAILLES
MISPUNCTUATE	MISSENDING	MISSTEPPING	MISTRUSTERS	MITRAILLEUR
MISPUNCTUATED	MISSENSING	MISSTOPPED	MISTRUSTFUL	MITRAILLEURS
MISPUNCTUATES	MISSETTING	MISSTOPPING	MISTRUSTFULLY	MITRAILLEUSE
MISPUNCTUATING	MISSHAPENLY	MISSTRICKEN	MISTRUSTFULNESS	MITRAILLEUSES
MISPUNCTUATION	MISSHAPENNESS	MISSTRIKES	MISTRUSTING	MITREWORTS
MISPUNCTUATIONS	MISSHAPENNESSES	MISSTRIKING	MISTRUSTINGLY	MITTIMUSES
MISQUOTATION	MISSHAPERS	MISSTYLING	MISTRUSTLESS	MIXABILITIES
MISQUOTATIONS	MISSHAPING	MISSUITING	MISTRYSTED	MIXABILITY
MISQUOTERS	MISSHEATHED	MISSUMMATION	MISTRYSTING	MIXEDNESSES
MISQUOTING	MISSILEERS	MISSUMMATIONS	MISTUTORED	MIXMASTERS
MISRAISING	MISSILEMAN	MISTAKABLE	MISTUTORING	MIXOBARBARIC
MISREADING	MISSILEMEN	MISTAKABLY	MISUNDERSTAND	MIXOLOGIES
MISREADINGS	MISSILERIES	MISTAKEABLE	MISUNDERSTANDS	MIXOLOGIST
MISRECKONED	MISSILRIES	MISTAKEABLY	MISUNDERSTOOD	MIXOLOGISTS
MISRECKONING	MISSIOLOGIES	MISTAKENLY	MISUTILISATION	MIXOLYDIAN
MISRECKONINGS	MISSIOLOGY	MISTAKENNESS	MISUTILISATIONS	MIXOTROPHIC
MISRECKONS	MISSIONARIES	MISTAKENNESSES	MISUTILIZATION	MIZENMASTS
MISRECOLLECTION	MISSIONARISE	MISTAKINGS	MISUTILIZATIONS	MIZZENMAST
MISRECORDED	MISSIONARISED	MISTEACHES	MISVALUING	MIZZENMASTS
MISRECORDING	MISSIONARISES	MISTEACHING	MISVENTURE	MIZZONITES
MISRECORDS	MISSIONARISING	MISTELLING	MISVENTURES	MNEMONICAL
MISREFERENCE	MISSIONARIZE	MISTEMPERED	MISVENTUROUS	MNEMONICALLY
MISREFERENCED	MISSIONARIZED	MISTEMPERING	MISVOCALISATION	MNEMONISTS
MISREFERENCES	MISSIONARIZES	MISTEMPERS	MISVOCALIZATION	MNEMOTECHNIC
MISREFERENCING	MISSIONARIZING	MISTENDING	MISWANDRED	MNEMOTECHNICS
MISREFERRED	MISSIONARY	MISTERMING	MISWEENING	MNEMOTECHNIST
MISREFERRING	MISSIONERS	MISTHINKING	MISWENDING	MNEMOTECHNISTS
MISREGARDED	MISSIONING	MISTHOUGHT	MISWORDING	MOBCASTING
MISREGARDING	MISSIONISATION	MISTHOUGHTS	MISWORDINGS	MOBCASTINGS
MISREGARDS	MISSIONISATIONS	MISTHROWING	MISWORSHIP	MOBILISABLE
MISREGISTER	MISSIONISE	MISTIGRISES	MISWORSHIPPED	MOBILISATION
MISREGISTERED	MISSIONISED	MISTIMINGS	MISWORSHIPPING	MOBILISATIONS
MISREGISTERING	MISSIONISER	MISTINESSES	MISWORSHIPPINGS	MOBILISERS
MISREGISTERS	MISSIONISERS	MISTITLING	MISWORSHIPS	MOBILISING
MISREGISTRATION	MISSIONISES	MISTLETOES	MISWRITING	MOBILITIES
MISRELATED	MISSIONISING	MISTOUCHED	MISWRITTEN	MOBILIZABLE
MISRELATES	MISSIONIZATION	MISTOUCHES	MITERWORTS	MOBILIZATION
MISRELATING	MISSIONIZATIONS	MISTOUCHING	MITHRADATIC	MOBILIZATIONS
MISRELATION	MISSIONIZE	MISTRACING	MITHRIDATE	MOBILIZERS
MISRELATIONS	MISSIONIZED	MISTRAINED	MITHRIDATES	MOBILIZING
MISRELYING	MISSIONIZER	MISTRAINING	MITHRIDATIC	MOBLOGGERS
MISREMEMBER	MISSIONIZERS	MISTRANSCRIBE	MITHRIDATISE	MOBOCRACIES
MISREMEMBERED	MISSIONIZES	MISTRANSCRIBED	MITHRIDATISED	MOBOCRATIC
MISREMEMBERING	MISSIONIZING	MISTRANSCRIBES	MITHRIDATISES	MOBOCRATICAL
MISREMEMBERS	MISSISHNESS	MISTRANSCRIBING	MITHRIDATISING	MOCHINESSES
MISRENDERED	MISSISHNESSES	MISTRANSLATE	MITHRIDATISM	MOCKERNUTS
MISRENDERING	MISSORTING	MISTRANSLATED	MITHRIDATISMS	MOCKINGBIRD
MISRENDERS	MISSOUNDED	MISTRANSLATES	MITHRIDATIZE	MOCKINGBIRDS
MISREPORTED	MISSOUNDING	MISTRANSLATING	MITHRIDATIZED	MOCKUMENTARIES
MISREPORTER	MISSPACING	MISTRANSLATION	MITHRIDATIZES	MOCKUMENTARY
MISREPORTERS	MISSPEAKING	MISTRANSLATIONS	MITHRIDATIZING	MODAFINILS
MISREPORTING	MISSPELLED	MISTRAYNED	MITIGATING	MODALISTIC
MISREPORTS	MISSPELLING	MISTREADING	MITIGATION	MODALITIES
MISREPRESENT	MISSPELLINGS	MISTREADINGS	MITIGATIONS	MODELLINGS
MISREPRESENTED	MISSPENDER	MISTREATED	MITIGATIVE	MODELLISTS
MISREPRESENTER	MISSPENDERS	MISTREATING	MITIGATIVES	MODERATELY
MISREPRESENTERS	MISSPENDING	MISTREATMENT	MITIGATORS	MODERATENESS
MISREPRESENTING	MISSTAMPED	MISTREATMENTS	MITIGATORY	MODERATENESSES
MISREPRESENTS	MISSTAMPING	MISTRESSED	MITOCHONDRIA	MODERATING
MISROUTEING	MISSTARTED	MISTRESSES	MITOCHONDRIAL	MODERATION
MISROUTING	MISSTARTING	MISTRESSING	MITOCHONDRION	MODERATIONS
MISSAYINGS	MISSTATEMENT	MISTRESSLESS	MITOGENETIC	MODERATISM
MISSEATING	MISSTATEMENTS	MISTRESSLIER	MITOGENICITIES	MODERATISMS
MISSEEMING	MISSTATING	MISTRESSLIEST	MITOGENICITY	MODERATORS
MISSEEMINGS	MISSTEERED	MISTRESSLY	MITOMYCINS	MODERATORSHIP

MODERATORSHIPS	MOITHERING	MOMENTOUSNESSES	MONEYLENDERS	MONOCARPOUS
MODERATRICES	MOLALITIES	MOMPRENEUR	MONEYLENDING	MONOCEROSES
MODERATRIX	MOLARITIES	MOMPRENEURS	MONEYLENDINGS	MONOCEROUS
MODERATRIXES	MOLASSESES	MONACHISMS	MONEYMAKER	MONOCHASIA
MODERNISATION	MOLDABILITIES	MONACHISTS	MONEYMAKERS	MONOCHASIAL
MODERNISATIONS	MOLDABILITY	MONACTINAL	MONEYMAKING	MONOCHASIUM
MODERNISED	MOLDAVITES	MONACTINES	MONEYMAKINGS	MONOCHLAMYDEOUS
MODERNISER	MOLDBOARDS	MONADELPHOUS	MONEYSPINNING	MONOCHLORIDE
MODERNISERS	MOLDINESSES	MONADICALLY	MONEYWORTS	MONOCHLORIDES
MODERNISES	MOLECATCHER	MONADIFORM	MONGERINGS	MONOCHORDS
MODERNISING	MOLECATCHERS	MONADISTIC	MONGOLISMS	MONOCHROIC
MODERNISMS	MOLECULARITIES	MONADNOCKS	MONGOLOIDS	MONOCHROICS
MODERNISTIC	MOLECULARITY	MONADOLOGIES	MONGRELISATION	MONOCHROMASIES
MODERNISTICALLY	MOLECULARLY	MONADOLOGY	MONGRELISATIONS	MONOCHROMASY
MODERNISTS	MOLENDINAR	MONANDRIES	MONGRELISE	MONOCHROMAT
MODERNITIES	MOLENDINARIES	MONANDROUS	MONGRELISED	MONOCHROMATE
MODERNIZATION	MOLENDINARS	MONANTHOUS	MONGRELISER	MONOCHROMATES
MODERNIZATIONS	MOLENDINARY	MONARCHALLY	MONGRELISERS	MONOCHROMATIC
MODERNIZED	MOLESTATION	MONARCHIAL	MONGRELISES	MONOCHROMATICS
MODERNIZER	MOLESTATIONS	MONARCHICAL	MONGRELISING	MONOCHROMATISM
MODERNIZERS	MOLIMINOUS	MONARCHICALLY	MONGRELISM	MONOCHROMATISMS
MODERNIZES	MOLLIFIABLE	MONARCHIES	MONGRELISMS	MONOCHROMATOR
MODERNIZING	MOLLIFICATION	MONARCHISE	MONGRELIZATION	MONOCHROMATORS
MODERNNESS	MOLLIFICATIONS	MONARCHISED	MONGRELIZATIONS	MONOCHROMATS
MODERNNESSES	MOLLIFIERS	MONARCHISES	MONGRELIZE	MONOCHROME
MODIFIABILITIES	MOLLIFYING	MONARCHISING	MONGRELIZED	MONOCHROMES
MODIFIABILITY	MOLLITIOUS	MONARCHISM	MONGRELIZER	MONOCHROMIC
MODIFIABLE	MOLLUSCANS	MONARCHISMS	MONGRELIZERS	MONOCHROMICAL
MODIFIABLENESS	MOLLUSCICIDAL	MONARCHIST	MONGRELIZES	MONOCHROMIES
MODIFICATION	MOLLUSCICIDE	MONARCHISTIC	MONGRELIZING	MONOCHROMIST
MODIFICATIONS	MOLLUSCICIDES	MONARCHISTS	MONGRELLIER	MONOCHROMISTS
MODIFICATIVE	MOLLUSCOID	MONARCHIZE	MONGRELLIEST	MONOCHROMY
MODIFICATORY	MOLLUSCOIDAL	MONARCHIZED	MONILIASES	MONOCLINAL
MODILLIONS	MOLLUSCOIDS	MONARCHIZES	MONILIASIS	MONOCLINALLY
MODISHNESS	MOLLUSCOUS	MONARCHIZING	MONILIFORM	MONOCLINALS
MODISHNESSES	MOLLUSKANS	MONASTERIAL	MONISTICAL	MONOCLINES
MODULABILITIES	MOLLYCODDLE	MONASTERIES	MONISTICALLY	MONOCLINIC
MODULABILITY	MOLLYCODDLED	MONASTICAL	MONITORIAL	MONOCLINISM
MODULARISED	MOLLYCODDLER	MONASTICALLY	MONITORIALLY	MONOCLINISMS
MODULARITIES	MOLLYCODDLERS	MONASTICISM	MONITORIES	MONOCLINOUS
MODULARITY	MOLLYCODDLES	MONASTICISMS	MONITORING	MONOCLONAL
MODULARIZED	MOLLYCODDLING	MONAURALLY	MONITORINGS	MONOCLONALS
MODULATING	MOLLYCODDLINGS	MONCHIQUITE	MONITORSHIP	MONOCOQUES
MODULATION	MOLLYHAWKS	MONCHIQUITES	MONITORSHIPS	MONOCOTYLEDON
MODULATIONS	MOLLYMAWKS	MONDEGREEN	MONITRESSES	MONOCOTYLEDONS
MODULATIVE	MOLOCHISED	MONDEGREENS	MONKEYGLAND	MONOCOTYLS
MODULATORS	MOLOCHISES	MONECIOUSLY	MONKEYISMS	MONOCRACIES
MODULATORY	MOLOCHISING	MONERGISMS	MONKEYPODS	MONOCRATIC
MOISTENERS	MOLOCHIZED	MONESTROUS	MONKEYPOTS	MONOCROPPED
MOISTENING	MOLOCHIZES	MONETARILY	MONKEYPOXES	MONOCROPPING
MOISTIFIED	MOLOCHIZING	MONETARISM	MONKEYSHINE	MONOCRYSTAL
MOISTIFIES	MOLYBDATES	MONETARISMS	MONKEYSHINES	MONOCRYSTALLINE
MOISTIFYING	MOLYBDENITE	MONETARIST	MONKFISHES	MONOCRYSTALS
MOISTNESSES	MOLYBDENITES	MONETARISTS	MONKISHNESS	MONOCULARLY
MOISTURELESS	MOLYBDENOSES	MONETISATION	MONKISHNESSES	MONOCULARS
MOISTURISE	MOLYBDENOSIS	MONETISATIONS	MONKSHOODS	MONOCULOUS
MOISTURISED	MOLYBDENOUS	MONETISING	MONOACIDIC	MONOCULTURAL
MOISTURISER	MOLYBDENUM	MONETIZATION	MONOAMINERGIC	MONOCULTURE
MOISTURISERS	MOLYBDENUMS	MONETIZATIONS	MONOAMINES	MONOCULTURES
MOISTURISES	MOLYBDOSES	MONETIZING	MONOATOMIC	MONOCYCLES
MOISTURISING	MOLYBDOSIS	MONEYBELTS	MONOBLEPSES	MONOCYCLIC
MOISTURIZE	MOMENTANEOUS	MONEYBOXES	MONOBLEPSIS	MONOCYTOID
MOISTURIZED	MOMENTARILY	MONEYCHANGER	MONOCARBOXYLIC	MONODACTYLOUS
MOISTURIZER	MOMENTARINESS	MONEYCHANGERS	MONOCARDIAN	MONODELPHIAN
MOISTURIZERS	MOMENTARINESSES	MONEYGRUBBING	MONOCARDIANS	MONODELPHIANS
MOISTURIZES	MOMENTOUSLY	MONEYGRUBBINGS	MONOCARPELLARY	MONODELPHIC
MOISTURIZING	MOMENTOUSNESS	MONEYLENDER	MONOCARPIC	MONODELPHOUS

MONODICALLY
MONODISPERSE
MONODRAMAS
MONODRAMATIC
MONOECIOUS
MONOECIOUSLY
MONOECISMS
MONOESTERS
MONOFILAMENT
MONOFILAMENTS
MONOGAMIES
MONOGAMIST
MONOGAMISTIC
MONOGAMISTS
MONOGAMOUS
MONOGAMOUSLY
MONOGAMOUSNESS
MONOGASTRIC
MONOGENEAN
MONOGENEANS
MONOGENESES
MONOGENESIS
MONOGENETIC
MONOGENICALLY
MONOGENIES
MONOGENISM
MONOGENISMS
MONOGENIST
MONOGENISTIC
MONOGENISTS
MONOGENOUS
MONOGLYCERIDE
MONOGLYCERIDES
MONOGONIES
MONOGRAMED
MONOGRAMING
MONOGRAMMATIC
MONOGRAMMED
MONOGRAMMER
MONOGRAMMERS
MONOGRAMMING
MONOGRAPHED
MONOGRAPHER
MONOGRAPHERS
MONOGRAPHIC
MONOGRAPHICAL
MONOGRAPHICALLY
MONOGRAPHIES
MONOGRAPHING
MONOGRAPHIST
MONOGRAPHISTS
MONOGRAPHS
MONOGRAPHY
MONOGYNIAN
MONOGYNIES
MONOGYNIST
MONOGYNISTS
MONOGYNOUS
MONOHYBRID
MONOHYBRIDS
MONOHYDRATE
MONOHYDRATED
MONOHYDRATES
MONOHYDRIC
MONOHYDROGEN
MONOHYDROXY
MONOICOUSLY

MONOLATERS
MONOLATRIES
MONOLATRIST
MONOLATRISTS
MONOLATROUS
MONOLAYERS
MONOLINGUAL
MONOLINGUALISM
MONOLINGUALISMS
MONOLINGUALS
MONOLINGUIST
MONOLINGUISTS
MONOLITHIC
MONOLITHICALLY
MONOLOGGED
MONOLOGGING
MONOLOGICAL
MONOLOGIES
MONOLOGISE
MONOLOGISED
MONOLOGISES
MONOLOGISING
MONOLOGIST
MONOLOGISTS
MONOLOGIZE
MONOLOGIZED
MONOLOGIZES
MONOLOGIZING
MONOLOGUED
MONOLOGUES
MONOLOGUING
MONOLOGUISE
MONOLOGUISED
MONOLOGUISES
MONOLOGUISING
MONOLOGUIST
MONOLOGUISTS
MONOLOGUIZE
MONOLOGUIZED
MONOLOGUIZES
MONOLOGUIZING
MONOMACHIA
MONOMACHIAS
MONOMACHIES
MONOMANIAC
MONOMANIACAL
MONOMANIACALLY
MONOMANIACS
MONOMANIAS
MONOMEROUS
MONOMETALLIC
MONOMETALLISM
MONOMETALLISMS
MONOMETALLIST
MONOMETALLISTS
MONOMETERS
MONOMETRIC
MONOMETRICAL
MONOMOLECULAR
MONOMOLECULARLY
MONOMORPHEMIC
MONOMORPHIC
MONOMORPHISM
MONOMORPHISMS
MONOMORPHOUS
MONOMYARIAN
MONOMYARIANS

MONONUCLEAR
MONONUCLEARS
MONONUCLEATE
MONONUCLEATED
MONONUCLEOSES
MONONUCLEOSIS
MONONUCLEOTIDE
MONONUCLEOTIDES
MONOPETALOUS
MONOPHAGIES
MONOPHAGOUS
MONOPHASES
MONOPHASIC
MONOPHOBIA
MONOPHOBIAS
MONOPHOBIC
MONOPHOBICS
MONOPHONIC
MONOPHONICALLY
MONOPHONIES
MONOPHOSPHATE
MONOPHOSPHATES
MONOPHTHONG
MONOPHTHONGAL
MONOPHTHONGISE
MONOPHTHONGISED
MONOPHTHONGISES
MONOPHTHONGIZE
MONOPHTHONGIZED
MONOPHTHONGIZES
MONOPHTHONGS
MONOPHYLETIC
MONOPHYLIES
MONOPHYLLOUS
MONOPHYODONT
MONOPHYODONTS
MONOPHYSITE
MONOPHYSITES
MONOPHYSITIC
MONOPHYSITISM
MONOPHYSITISMS
MONOPITCHES
MONOPLANES
MONOPLEGIA
MONOPLEGIAS
MONOPLEGIC
MONOPLEGICS
MONOPLOIDS
MONOPODIAL
MONOPODIALLY
MONOPODIAS
MONOPODIES
MONOPODIUM
MONOPOLIES
MONOPOLISATION
MONOPOLISATIONS
MONOPOLISE
MONOPOLISED
MONOPOLISER
MONOPOLISERS
MONOPOLISES
MONOPOLISING
MONOPOLISM
MONOPOLISMS
MONOPOLIST
MONOPOLISTIC
MONOPOLISTS

MONOPOLIZATION
MONOPOLIZATIONS
MONOPOLIZE
MONOPOLIZED
MONOPOLIZER
MONOPOLIZERS
MONOPOLIZES
MONOPOLIZING
MONOPRINTS
MONOPRIONIDIAN
MONOPROPELLANT
MONOPROPELLANTS
MONOPSONIES
MONOPSONIST
MONOPSONISTIC
MONOPSONISTS
MONOPTERAL
MONOPTEROI
MONOPTERON
MONOPTEROS
MONOPTEROSES
MONOPTOTES
MONOPULSES
MONORCHIDISM
MONORCHIDISMS
MONORCHIDS
MONORCHISM
MONORCHISMS
MONORHINAL
MONORHINES
MONORHYMED
MONORHYMES
MONOSACCHARIDE
MONOSACCHARIDES
MONOSATURATED
MONOSEMIES
MONOSEPALOUS
MONOSKIERS
MONOSKIING
MONOSKIINGS
MONOSODIUM
MONOSOMICS
MONOSOMIES
MONOSPACED
MONOSPECIFIC
MONOSPECIFICITY
MONOSPERMAL
MONOSPERMOUS
MONOSTABLE
MONOSTELES
MONOSTELIC
MONOSTELIES
MONOSTICHIC
MONOSTICHOUS
MONOSTICHS
MONOSTOMOUS
MONOSTROPHE
MONOSTROPHES
MONOSTROPHIC
MONOSTROPHICS
MONOSTYLAR
MONOSTYLOUS
MONOSYLLABIC
MONOSYLLABICITY
MONOSYLLABISM
MONOSYLLABISMS
MONOSYLLABLE

MONOSYLLABLES
MONOSYMMETRIC
MONOSYMMETRICAL
MONOSYMMETRIES
MONOSYMMETRY
MONOSYNAPTIC
MONOTASKED
MONOTASKING
MONOTASKINGS
MONOTELEPHONE
MONOTELEPHONES
MONOTERPENE
MONOTERPENES
MONOTHALAMIC
MONOTHALAMOUS
MONOTHECAL
MONOTHECOUS
MONOTHEISM
MONOTHEISMS
MONOTHEIST
MONOTHEISTIC
MONOTHEISTICAL
MONOTHEISTS
MONOTHELETE
MONOTHELETES
MONOTHELETIC
MONOTHELETICAL
MONOTHELETISM
MONOTHELETISMS
MONOTHELISM
MONOTHELISMS
MONOTHELITE
MONOTHELITES
MONOTHELITISM
MONOTHELITISMS
MONOTHERAPIES
MONOTHERAPY
MONOTOCOUS
MONOTONICALLY
MONOTONICITIES
MONOTONICITY
MONOTONIES
MONOTONING
MONOTONISE
MONOTONISED
MONOTONISES
MONOTONISING
MONOTONIZE
MONOTONIZED
MONOTONIZES
MONOTONIZING
MONOTONOUS
MONOTONOUSLY
MONOTONOUSNESS
MONOTREMATOUS
MONOTREMES
MONOTRICHIC
MONOTRICHOUS
MONOTROCHS
MONOUNSATURATE
MONOUNSATURATED
MONOUNSATURATES
MONOVALENCE
MONOVALENCES
MONOVALENCIES
MONOVALENCY
MONOVALENT

m

MONOXYLONS	MOONLIGHTING	MORDACITIES	MORPHOPHONOLOGY	MOSSTROOPERS
MONOXYLOUS	MOONLIGHTINGS	MORDANCIES	MORPHOSYNTAX	MOTETTISTS
MONOZYGOTIC	MOONLIGHTS	MORDANTING	MORPHOSYNTAXES	MOTHBALLED
MONOZYGOUS	MOONPHASES	MORENESSES	MORPHOTROPIC	MOTHBALLING
MONSEIGNEUR	MOONQUAKES	MORGANATIC	MORPHOTROPIES	MOTHERBOARD
MONSEIGNEURS	MOONRAKERS	MORGANATICALLY	MORPHOTROPY	MOTHERBOARDS
MONSIGNORI	MOONRAKING	MORGANITES	MORSELLING	MOTHERCRAFT
MONSIGNORIAL	MOONRAKINGS	MORGELLONS	MORSELLINGS	MOTHERCRAFTS
MONSIGNORS	MOONSCAPES	MORGENSTERN	MORTADELLA	MOTHERESES
MONSTERING	MOONSHINED	MORGENSTERNS	MORTADELLAS	MOTHERFUCKER
MONSTERINGS	MOONSHINER	MORIBUNDITIES	MORTADELLE	MOTHERFUCKERS
MONSTRANCE	MOONSHINERS	MORIBUNDITY	MORTALISED	MOTHERFUCKING
MONSTRANCES	MOONSHINES	MORIBUNDLY	MORTALISES	MOTHERHOOD
MONSTROSITIES	MOONSHINIER	MORIGERATE	MORTALISING	MOTHERHOODS
MONSTROSITY	MOONSHINIEST	MORIGERATED	MORTALITIES	MOTHERHOUSE
MONSTROUSLY	MOONSHINING	MORIGERATES	MORTALIZED	MOTHERHOUSES
MONSTROUSNESS	MOONSHININGS	MORIGERATING	MORTALIZES	MOTHERIEST
MONSTROUSNESSES	MOONSTONES	MORIGERATION	MORTALIZING	MOTHERINGS
MONSTRUOSITIES	MOONSTRICKEN	MORIGERATIONS	MORTARBOARD	MOTHERLAND
MONSTRUOSITY	MOONSTRIKE	MORIGEROUS	MORTARBOARDS	MOTHERLANDS
MONSTRUOUS	MOONSTRIKES	MORONICALLY	MORTARIEST	MOTHERLESS
MONTADALES	MOONSTRUCK	MORONITIES	MORTARLESS	MOTHERLESSNESS
MONTAGNARD	MOONWALKED	MOROSENESS	MORTCLOTHS	MOTHERLIER
MONTAGNARDS	MOONWALKER	MOROSENESSES	MORTGAGEABLE	MOTHERLIEST
MONTBRETIA	MOONWALKERS	MOROSITIES	MORTGAGEES	MOTHERLINESS
MONTBRETIAS	MOONWALKING	MORPHACTIN	MORTGAGERS	MOTHERLINESSES
MONTELIMAR	MOORBUZZARD	MORPHACTINS	MORTGAGING	MOTHERWORT
MONTELIMARS	MOORBUZZARDS	MORPHALLAXES	MORTGAGORS	MOTHERWORTS
MONTGOLFIER	MOOSEBIRDS	MORPHALLAXIS	MORTICIANS	MOTHPROOFED
MONTGOLFIERS	MOOSEHAIRS	MORPHEMICALLY	MORTIFEROUS	MOTHPROOFER
MONTHLINGS	MOOSEHIDES	MORPHEMICS	MORTIFEROUSNESS	MOTHPROOFERS
MONTICELLITE	MOOSEWOODS	MORPHINISM	MORTIFICATION	MOTHPROOFING
MONTICELLITES	MOOSEYARDS	MORPHINISMS	MORTIFICATIONS	MOTHPROOFS
MONTICOLOUS	MOOTNESSES	MORPHINOMANIA	MORTIFIERS	MOTILITIES
MONTICULATE	MOPINESSES	MORPHINOMANIAC	MORTIFYING	MOTIONISTS
MONTICULES	MOPISHNESS	MORPHINOMANIACS	MORTIFYINGLY	MOTIONLESS
MONTICULOUS	MOPISHNESSES	MORPHINOMANIAS	MORTIFYINGS	MOTIONLESSLY
MONTICULUS	MORALISATION	MORPHOGENESES	MORTUARIES	MOTIONLESSNESS
MONTICULUSES	MORALISATIONS	MORPHOGENESIS	MORULATION	MOTIVATING
MONTMORILLONITE	MORALISERS	MORPHOGENETIC	MORULATIONS	MOTIVATION
MONUMENTAL	MORALISING	MORPHOGENIC	MOSAICALLY	MOTIVATIONAL
MONUMENTALISE	MORALISINGS	MORPHOGENIES	MOSAICISMS	MOTIVATIONALLY
MONUMENTALISED	MORALISTIC	MORPHOGENS	MOSAICISTS	MOTIVATIONS
MONUMENTALISES	MORALISTICALLY	MORPHOGENY	MOSAICKING	MOTIVATIVE
MONUMENTALISING	MORALITIES	MORPHOGRAPHER	MOSAICKINGS	MOTIVATORS
MONUMENTALITIES	MORALIZATION	MORPHOGRAPHERS	MOSAICLIKE	MOTIVELESS
MONUMENTALITY	MORALIZATIONS	MORPHOGRAPHIES	MOSASAURUS	MOTIVELESSLY
MONUMENTALIZE	MORALIZERS	MORPHOGRAPHY	MOSBOLLETJIE	MOTIVELESSNESS
MONUMENTALIZED	MORALIZING	MORPHOLINE	MOSBOLLETJIES	MOTIVITIES
MONUMENTALIZES	MORALIZINGS	MORPHOLINES	MOSCHATELS	MOTOCROSSES
MONUMENTALIZING	MORASSIEST	MORPHOLINO	MOSCHIFEROUS	MOTONEURON
MONUMENTALLY	MORATORIUM	MORPHOLINOS	MOSCOVIUMS	MOTONEURONAL
MONUMENTED	MORATORIUMS	MORPHOLOGIC	MOSKONFYTS	MOTONEURONS
MONUMENTING	MORBIDEZZA	MORPHOLOGICAL	MOSQUITOES	MOTORBICYCLE
MONZONITES	MORBIDEZZAS	MORPHOLOGICALLY	MOSQUITOEY	MOTORBICYCLES
MONZONITIC	MORBIDITIES	MORPHOLOGIES	MOSQUITOFISH	MOTORBIKED
MOODINESSES	MORBIDNESS	MORPHOLOGIST	MOSQUITOFISHES	MOTORBIKES
MOONCALVES	MORBIDNESSES	MORPHOLOGISTS	MOSQUITOIER	MOTORBIKING
MOONCHILDREN	MORBIFEROUS	MORPHOLOGY	MOSQUITOIEST	MOTORBOATED
MOONCRAFTS	MORBIFICALLY	MORPHOMETRIC	MOSSBACKED	MOTORBOATER
MOONFISHES	MORBILLIFORM	MORPHOMETRICS	MOSSBLUITER	MOTORBOATERS
MOONFLOWER	MORBILLIVIRUS	MORPHOMETRIES	MOSSBLUITERS	MOTORBOATING
MOONFLOWERS	MORBILLIVIRUSES	MORPHOMETRY	MOSSBUNKER	MOTORBOATINGS
MOONINESSES	MORBILLOUS	MORPHOPHONEME	MOSSBUNKERS	MOTORBOATS
MOONLIGHTED	MORDACIOUS	MORPHOPHONEMES	MOSSINESSES	MOTORBUSES
MOONLIGHTER	MORDACIOUSLY	MORPHOPHONEMIC	MOSSPLANTS	MOTORBUSSES
MOONLIGHTERS	MORDACIOUSNESS	MORPHOPHONEMICS	MOSSTROOPER	MOTORCADED

MOTORCADES
MOTORCADING
MOTORCOACH
MOTORCOACHES
MOTORCYCLE
MOTORCYCLED
MOTORCYCLES
MOTORCYCLING
MOTORCYCLINGS
MOTORCYCLIST
MOTORCYCLISTS
MOTORHOMES
MOTORICALLY
MOTORISATION
MOTORISATIONS
MOTORISING
MOTORIZATION
MOTORIZATIONS
MOTORIZING
MOTORMOUTH
MOTORMOUTHS
MOTORSHIPS
MOTORTRUCK
MOTORTRUCKS
MOTOSCAFOS
MOUCHARABIES
MOUCHARABY
MOUDIEWART
MOUDIEWARTS
MOUDIEWORT
MOUDIEWORTS
MOUDIWARTS
MOUDIWORTS
MOULDABILITIES
MOULDABILITY
MOULDBOARD
MOULDBOARDS
MOULDERING
MOULDINESS
MOULDINESSES
MOULDWARPS
MOULDYWARP
MOULDYWARPS
MOUNDBIRDS
MOUNTAINBOARD
MOUNTAINBOARDER
MOUNTAINBOARDS
MOUNTAINED
MOUNTAINEER
MOUNTAINEERED
MOUNTAINEERING
MOUNTAINEERINGS
MOUNTAINEERS
MOUNTAINIER
MOUNTAINIEST
MOUNTAINOUS
MOUNTAINOUSLY
MOUNTAINOUSNESS
MOUNTAINSIDE
MOUNTAINSIDES
MOUNTAINTOP
MOUNTAINTOPS
MOUNTEBANK
MOUNTEBANKED
MOUNTEBANKERIES
MOUNTEBANKERY
MOUNTEBANKING

MOUNTEBANKINGS
MOUNTEBANKISM
MOUNTEBANKISMS
MOUNTEBANKS
MOUNTENANCE
MOUNTENANCES
MOUNTENAUNCE
MOUNTENAUNCES
MOURNFULLER
MOURNFULLEST
MOURNFULLY
MOURNFULNESS
MOURNFULNESSES
MOURNINGLY
MOURNIVALS
MOURVEDRES
MOUSEBIRDS
MOUSEOVERS
MOUSEPIECE
MOUSEPIECES
MOUSETAILS
MOUSETRAPPED
MOUSETRAPPING
MOUSETRAPPINGS
MOUSETRAPS
MOUSINESSES
MOUSQUETAIRE
MOUSQUETAIRES
MOUSSELIKE
MOUSSELINE
MOUSSELINES
MOUSTACHED
MOUSTACHES
MOUSTACHIAL
MOUSTACHIO
MOUSTACHIOED
MOUSTACHIOS
MOUTHBREATHER
MOUTHBREATHERS
MOUTHBREEDER
MOUTHBREEDERS
MOUTHBROODER
MOUTHBROODERS
MOUTHFEELS
MOUTHPARTS
MOUTHPIECE
MOUTHPIECES
MOUTHWASHES
MOUTHWATERING
MOUTHWATERINGLY
MOUVEMENTE
MOVABILITIES
MOVABILITY
MOVABLENESS
MOVABLENESSES
MOVEABILITIES
MOVEABILITY
MOVEABLENESS
MOVEABLENESSES
MOVELESSLY
MOVELESSNESS
MOVELESSNESSES
MOVIEGOERS
MOVIEGOING
MOVIEGOINGS
MOVIELANDS
MOVIEMAKER

MOVIEMAKERS
MOVIEMAKING
MOVIEMAKINGS
MOWBURNING
MOWBURNINGS
MOWDIEWART
MOWDIEWARTS
MOWDIEWORT
MOWDIEWORTS
MOXIBUSTION
MOXIBUSTIONS
MOYGASHELS
MOZZARELLA
MOZZARELLAS
MRIDAMGAMS
MRIDANGAMS
MUCEDINOUS
MUCHNESSES
MUCIDITIES
MUCIDNESSES
MUCIFEROUS
MUCILAGINOUS
MUCILAGINOUSLY
MUCINOGENS
MUCKAMUCKED
MUCKAMUCKING
MUCKAMUCKS
MUCKENDERS
MUCKINESSES
MUCKRAKERS
MUCKRAKING
MUCKRAKINGS
MUCKSPREAD
MUCKSPREADER
MUCKSPREADERS
MUCKSPREADING
MUCKSPREADS
MUCKSWEATS
MUCKYMUCKS
MUCOCUTANEOUS
MUCOLYTICS
MUCOMEMBRANOUS
MUCOPEPTIDE
MUCOPEPTIDES
MUCOPROTEIN
MUCOPROTEINS
MUCOPURULENT
MUCOSANGUINEOUS
MUCOSITIES
MUCOVISCIDOSES
MUCOVISCIDOSIS
MUCRONATED
MUCRONATION
MUCRONATIONS
MUDCAPPING
MUDCAPPINGS
MUDDINESSES
MUDDLEDNESS
MUDDLEDNESSES
MUDDLEHEAD
MUDDLEHEADED
MUDDLEHEADEDLY
MUDDLEHEADS
MUDDLEMENT
MUDDLEMENTS
MUDDLINGLY
MUDHOPPERS

MUDLARKING
MUDLOGGERS
MUDLOGGING
MUDLOGGINGS
MUDPUPPIES
MUDSKIPPER
MUDSKIPPERS
MUDSLINGER
MUDSLINGERS
MUDSLINGING
MUDSLINGINGS
MUFFETTEES
MUFFINEERS
MUGEARITES
MUGGINESSES
MUGWUMPERIES
MUGWUMPERY
MUGWUMPISH
MUGWUMPISM
MUGWUMPISMS
MUJAHEDDIN
MUJAHEDEEN
MUJAHIDEEN
MUKHABARAT
MUKHABARATS
MULATRESSES
MULATTRESS
MULATTRESSES
MULBERRIES
MULIEBRITIES
MULIEBRITY
MULISHNESS
MULISHNESSES
MULLAHISMS
MULLARKIES
MULLIGATAWNIES
MULLIGATAWNY
MULLIGRUBS
MULLIONING
MULLOCKIER
MULLOCKIEST
MULTANGULAR
MULTANIMOUS
MULTARTICULATE
MULTEITIES
MULTIACCESS
MULTIACCESSES
MULTIAGENCY
MULTIANGULAR
MULTIARMED
MULTIARTICULATE
MULTIAUTHOR
MULTIAXIAL
MULTIBARREL
MULTIBARRELED
MULTIBARRELLED
MULTIBARRELS
MULTIBILLION
MULTIBLADED
MULTIBRANCHED
MULTIBUILDING
MULTICAMERATE
MULTICAMPUS
MULTICAPITATE
MULTICARBON
MULTICASTS
MULTICAULINE

MULTICAUSAL
MULTICELLED
MULTICELLULAR
MULTICENTER
MULTICENTRAL
MULTICENTRE
MULTICENTRIC
MULTICHAIN
MULTICHAMBERED
MULTICHANNEL
MULTICHARACTER
MULTICIDES
MULTICIPITAL
MULTICLIENT
MULTICOATED
MULTICOLOR
MULTICOLORED
MULTICOLORS
MULTICOLOUR
MULTICOLOURED
MULTICOLOURS
MULTICOLUMN
MULTICOMPONENT
MULTICONDUCTOR
MULTICOPIES
MULTICOSTATE
MULTICOUNTY
MULTICOURSE
MULTICULTI
MULTICULTIS
MULTICULTURAL
MULTICULTURALLY
MULTICURIE
MULTICURRENCIES
MULTICURRENCY
MULTICUSPID
MULTICUSPIDATE
MULTICUSPIDS
MULTICYCLE
MULTICYCLES
MULTICYLINDER
MULTIDENTATE
MULTIDIALECTAL
MULTIDIGITATE
MULTIDISCIPLINE
MULTIDIVISIONAL
MULTIDOMAIN
MULTIELECTRODE
MULTIELEMENT
MULTIEMPLOYER
MULTIEMPLOYERS
MULTIENGINE
MULTIENGINED
MULTIENZYME
MULTIETHNIC
MULTIETHNICS
MULTIFACED
MULTIFACETED
MULTIFACTOR
MULTIFACTORIAL
MULTIFAMILIES
MULTIFAMILY
MULTIFARIOUS
MULTIFARIOUSLY
MULTIFIDLY
MULTIFIDOUS
MULTIFILAMENT

MULTIFILAMENTS	MULTIMEGAWATT	MULTIPLICATORS	MULTISTRANDED	MUMMERINGS
MULTIFLASH	MULTIMEGAWATTS	MULTIPLICITIES	MULTISTRIKE	MUMMICHOGS
MULTIFLORA	MULTIMEMBER	MULTIPLICITY	MULTISTRIKES	MUMMIFICATION
MULTIFLORAS	MULTIMETALLIC	MULTIPLIED	MULTISULCATE	MUMMIFICATIONS
MULTIFLOROUS	MULTIMETER	MULTIPLIER	MULTISYLLABIC	MUMMIFORMS
MULTIFOCAL	MULTIMETERS	MULTIPLIERS	MULTISYSTEM	MUMMIFYING
MULTIFOCALS	MULTIMILLENNIAL	MULTIPLIES	MULTITALENTED	MUMPISHNESS
MULTIFOILS	MULTIMILLION	MULTIPLYING	MULTITASKED	MUMPISHNESSES
MULTIFOLIATE	MULTIMODAL	MULTIPOINT	MULTITASKING	MUMPRENEUR
MULTIFOLIOLATE	MULTIMODES	MULTIPOLAR	MULTITASKINGS	MUMPRENEURS
MULTIFORMITIES	MULTIMOLECULAR	MULTIPOLARITIES	MULTITASKS	MUMPSIMUSES
MULTIFORMITY	MULTINATION	MULTIPOLARITY	MULTITERMINAL	MUMSINESSES
MULTIFORMS	MULTINATIONAL	MULTIPOLES	MULTITHREADING	MUNCHABLES
MULTIFREQUENCY	MULTINATIONALS	MULTIPOTENT	MULTITHREADINGS	MUNDANENESS
MULTIFUNCTION	MULTINOMIAL	MULTIPOTENTIAL	MULTITIERED	MUNDANENESSES
MULTIFUNCTIONAL	MULTINOMIALS	MULTIPOWER	MULTITONED	MUNDANITIES
MULTIGENES	MULTINOMINAL	MULTIPRESENCE	MULTITONES	MUNDIFICATION
MULTIGENIC	MULTINUCLEAR	MULTIPRESENCES	MULTITOOLS	MUNDIFICATIONS
MULTIGRADE	MULTINUCLEATE	MULTIPRESENT	MULTITOWERED	MUNDIFICATIVE
MULTIGRADES	MULTINUCLEATED	MULTIPROBLEM	MULTITRACK	MUNDIFICATIVES
MULTIGRAIN	MULTINUCLEOLAR	MULTIPROCESSING	MULTITRACKED	MUNDIFYING
MULTIGRAVIDA	MULTINUCLEOLATE	MULTIPROCESSOR	MULTITRACKING	MUNDUNGUSES
MULTIGRAVIDAE	MULTIORGASMIC	MULTIPROCESSORS	MULTITRACKS	MUNICIPALISE
MULTIGRAVIDAS	MULTIPACKS	MULTIPRODUCT	MULTITRILLION	MUNICIPALISED
MULTIGROUP	MULTIPANED	MULTIPRONGED	MULTITRILLIONS	MUNICIPALISES
MULTIHEADED	MULTIPARAE	MULTIPURPOSE	MULTITUDES	MUNICIPALISING
MULTIHOSPITAL	MULTIPARAMETER	MULTIRACIAL	MULTITUDINARY	MUNICIPALISM
MULTIHULLS	MULTIPARAS	MULTIRACIALISM	MULTITUDINOUS	MUNICIPALISMS
MULTIJUGATE	MULTIPARITIES	MULTIRACIALISMS	MULTITUDINOUSLY	MUNICIPALIST
MULTIJUGOUS	MULTIPARITY	MULTIRACIALLY	MULTIUNION	MUNICIPALISTS
MULTILANES	MULTIPAROUS	MULTIRAMIFIED	MULTIUTILITIES	MUNICIPALITIES
MULTILATERAL	MULTIPARTICLE	MULTIRANGE	MULTIUTILITY	MUNICIPALITY
MULTILATERALISM	MULTIPARTITE	MULTIREGIONAL	MULTIVALENCE	MUNICIPALIZE
MULTILATERALIST	MULTIPARTY	MULTIRELIGIOUS	MULTIVALENCES	MUNICIPALIZED
MULTILATERALLY	MULTIPARTYISM	MULTIROOMED	MULTIVALENCIES	MUNICIPALIZES
MULTILAYER	MULTIPARTYISMS	MULTISCIENCE	MULTIVALENCY	MUNICIPALIZING
MULTILAYERED	MULTIPEDES	MULTISCIENCES	MULTIVALENT	MUNICIPALLY
MULTILAYERS	MULTIPHASE	MULTISCREEN	MULTIVALENTS	MUNICIPALS
MULTILEVEL	MULTIPHASIC	MULTISCREENS	MULTIVARIABLE	MUNIFICENCE
MULTILEVELED	MULTIPHOTON	MULTISENSE	MULTIVARIATE	MUNIFICENCES
MULTILEVELLED	MULTIPICTURE	MULTISENSORY	MULTIVARIOUS	MUNIFICENT
MULTILINEAL	MULTIPIECE	MULTISEPTATE	MULTIVERSE	MUNIFICENTLY
MULTILINEAR	MULTIPISTON	MULTISERIAL	MULTIVERSES	MUNIFICENTNESS
MULTILINES	MULTIPLANE	MULTISERIATE	MULTIVERSITIES	MUNIFIENCE
MULTILINGUAL	MULTIPLANES	MULTISERVICE	MULTIVERSITY	MUNIFIENCES
MULTILINGUALISM	MULTIPLANT	MULTISIDED	MULTIVIBRATOR	MUNITIONED
MULTILINGUALLY	MULTIPLAYER	MULTISKILL	MULTIVIBRATORS	MUNITIONEER
MULTILINGUIST	MULTIPLAYERS	MULTISKILLED	MULTIVIOUS	MUNITIONEERS
MULTILINGUISTS	MULTIPLETS	MULTISKILLING	MULTIVITAMIN	MUNITIONER
MULTILOBATE	MULTIPLEXED	MULTISKILLINGS	MULTIVITAMINS	MUNITIONERS
MULTILOBED	MULTIPLEXER	MULTISKILLS	MULTIVOCAL	MUNITIONETTE
MULTILOBES	MULTIPLEXERS	MULTISONANT	MULTIVOCALS	MUNITIONETTES
MULTILOBULAR	MULTIPLEXES	MULTISOURCE	MULTIVOLTINE	MUNITIONING
MULTILOBULATE	MULTIPLEXING	MULTISPECIES	MULTIVOLUME	MURDERABILIA
MULTILOCATIONAL	MULTIPLEXINGS	MULTISPECTRAL	MULTIWARHEAD	MURDERBALL
MULTILOCULAR	MULTIPLEXOR	MULTISPEED	MULTIWAVELENGTH	MURDERBALLS
MULTILOCULATE	MULTIPLEXORS	MULTISPIRAL	MULTIWINDOW	MURDERESSES
MULTILOQUENCE	MULTIPLIABLE	MULTISPORT	MULTIWINDOWS	MURDEROUSLY
MULTILOQUENCES	MULTIPLICABLE	MULTISTAGE	MULTOCULAR	MURDEROUSNESS
MULTILOQUENT	MULTIPLICAND	MULTISTANDARD	MULTUNGULATE	MURDEROUSNESSES
MULTILOQUIES	MULTIPLICANDS	MULTISTATE	MULTUNGULATES	MURGEONING
MULTILOQUOUS	MULTIPLICATE	MULTISTEMMED	MUMBLEMENT	MURKINESSES
MULTILOQUY	MULTIPLICATES	MULTISTOREY	MUMBLEMENTS	MURMURATION
MULTIMANNED	MULTIPLICATION	MULTISTOREYS	MUMBLETYPEG	MURMURATIONS
MULTIMEDIA	MULTIPLICATIONS	MULTISTORIED	MUMBLETYPEGS	MURMURINGLY
MULTIMEDIAS	MULTIPLICATIVE	MULTISTORIES	MUMBLINGLY	MURMURINGS
MULTIMEGATON	MULTIPLICATOR	MULTISTORY	MUMCHANCES	MURMUROUSLY

MURTHERERS
MURTHERING
MUSCADELLE
MUSCADELLES
MUSCADINES
MUSCARDINE
MUSCARDINES
MUSCARINES
MUSCARINIC
MUSCATORIA
MUSCATORIUM
MUSCAVADOS
MUSCOLOGIES
MUSCOVADOS
MUSCOVITES
MUSCULARITIES
MUSCULARITY
MUSCULARLY
MUSCULATION
MUSCULATIONS
MUSCULATURE
MUSCULATURES
MUSCULOSKELETAL
MUSEOLOGICAL
MUSEOLOGIES
MUSEOLOGIST
MUSEOLOGISTS
MUSHINESSES
MUSHMOUTHS
MUSHROOMED
MUSHROOMER
MUSHROOMERS
MUSHROOMIER
MUSHROOMIEST
MUSHROOMING
MUSHROOMINGS
MUSICALISATION
MUSICALISATIONS
MUSICALISE
MUSICALISED
MUSICALISES
MUSICALISING
MUSICALITIES
MUSICALITY
MUSICALIZATION
MUSICALIZATIONS
MUSICALIZE
MUSICALIZED
MUSICALIZES
MUSICALIZING
MUSICALNESS
MUSICALNESSES
MUSICIANER
MUSICIANERS
MUSICIANLIER
MUSICIANLIEST
MUSICIANLY
MUSICIANSHIP
MUSICIANSHIPS
MUSICOLOGICAL
MUSICOLOGICALLY
MUSICOLOGIES
MUSICOLOGIST
MUSICOLOGISTS
MUSICOLOGY
MUSICOTHERAPIES
MUSICOTHERAPY

MUSKELLUNGE
MUSKELLUNGES
MUSKETEERS
MUSKETOONS
MUSKETRIES
MUSKINESSES
MUSKMELONS
MUSQUASHES
MUSQUETOON
MUSQUETOONS
MUSSELCRACKER
MUSSELCRACKERS
MUSSINESSES
MUSSITATED
MUSSITATES
MUSSITATING
MUSSITATION
MUSSITATIONS
MUSTACHIOED
MUSTACHIOS
MUSTARDIER
MUSTARDIEST
MUSTELINES
MUSTINESSES
MUTABILITIES
MUTABILITY
MUTABLENESS
MUTABLENESSES
MUTAGENESES
MUTAGENESIS
MUTAGENICALLY
MUTAGENICITIES
MUTAGENICITY
MUTAGENISE
MUTAGENISED
MUTAGENISES
MUTAGENISING
MUTAGENIZE
MUTAGENIZED
MUTAGENIZES
MUTAGENIZING
MUTATIONAL
MUTATIONALLY
MUTATIONIST
MUTATIONISTS
MUTENESSES
MUTESSARIF
MUTESSARIFAT
MUTESSARIFATS
MUTESSARIFS
MUTILATING
MUTILATION
MUTILATIONS
MUTILATIVE
MUTILATORS
MUTINEERED
MUTINEERING
MUTINOUSLY
MUTINOUSNESS
MUTINOUSNESSES
MUTOSCOPES
MUTTERATION
MUTTERATIONS
MUTTERINGLY
MUTTERINGS
MUTTONBIRD
MUTTONBIRDER

MUTTONBIRDERS
MUTTONBIRDS
MUTTONCHOPS
MUTTONFISH
MUTTONFISHES
MUTTONHEAD
MUTTONHEADED
MUTTONHEADS
MUTTONIEST
MUTUALISATION
MUTUALISATIONS
MUTUALISED
MUTUALISES
MUTUALISING
MUTUALISMS
MUTUALISTIC
MUTUALISTS
MUTUALITIES
MUTUALIZATION
MUTUALIZATIONS
MUTUALIZED
MUTUALIZES
MUTUALIZING
MUTUALNESS
MUTUALNESSES
MUZZINESSES
MYASTHENIA
MYASTHENIAS
MYASTHENIC
MYASTHENICS
MYCETOLOGIES
MYCETOLOGY
MYCETOMATA
MYCETOMATOUS
MYCETOPHAGOUS
MYCETOZOAN
MYCETOZOANS
MYCOBACTERIA
MYCOBACTERIAL
MYCOBACTERIUM
MYCOBIONTS
MYCODOMATIA
MYCODOMATIUM
MYCOFLORAE
MYCOFLORAS
MYCOLOGICAL
MYCOLOGICALLY
MYCOLOGIES
MYCOLOGIST
MYCOLOGISTS
MYCOPHAGIES
MYCOPHAGIST
MYCOPHAGISTS
MYCOPHAGOUS
MYCOPHILES
MYCOPLASMA
MYCOPLASMAL
MYCOPLASMAS
MYCOPLASMATA
MYCOPLASMOSES
MYCOPLASMOSIS
MYCORHIZAE
MYCORHIZAL
MYCORHIZAS
MYCORRHIZA
MYCORRHIZAE
MYCORRHIZAL

MYCORRHIZAS
MYCOTOXICOLOGY
MYCOTOXICOSES
MYCOTOXICOSIS
MYCOTOXINS
MYCOTOXOLOGIES
MYCOTOXOLOGY
MYCOTROPHIC
MYCOVIRUSES
MYDRIATICS
MYELENCEPHALA
MYELENCEPHALIC
MYELENCEPHALON
MYELENCEPHALONS
MYELINATED
MYELITIDES
MYELITISES
MYELOBLAST
MYELOBLASTIC
MYELOBLASTS
MYELOCYTES
MYELOCYTIC
MYELOFIBROSES
MYELOFIBROSIS
MYELOFIBROTIC
MYELOGENOUS
MYELOGRAMS
MYELOGRAPHIES
MYELOGRAPHY
MYELOMATOID
MYELOMATOUS
MYELOPATHIC
MYELOPATHIES
MYELOPATHY
MYIOPHILIES
MYIOPHILOUS
MYLOHYOIDS
MYLONITISATION
MYLONITISATIONS
MYLONITISE
MYLONITISED
MYLONITISES
MYLONITISING
MYLONITIZATION
MYLONITIZATIONS
MYLONITIZE
MYLONITIZED
MYLONITIZES
MYLONITIZING
MYOBLASTIC
MYOCARDIAL
MYOCARDIOGRAPH
MYOCARDIOGRAPHS
MYOCARDIOPATHY
MYOCARDITIS
MYOCARDITISES
MYOCARDIUM
MYOCLONUSES
MYOELECTRIC
MYOELECTRICAL
MYOFIBRILLAR
MYOFIBRILS
MYOFILAMENT
MYOFILAMENTS
MYOGLOBINS
MYOGRAPHIC
MYOGRAPHICAL

MYOGRAPHICALLY
MYOGRAPHIES
MYOGRAPHIST
MYOGRAPHISTS
MYOINOSITOL
MYOINOSITOLS
MYOLOGICAL
MYOLOGISTS
MYOMANCIES
MYOMECTOMIES
MYOMECTOMY
MYOPATHIES
MYOPHILIES
MYOPHILOUS
MYOPICALLY
MYOSITISES
MYOSOTISES
MYOSTATINS
MYRIADFOLD
MYRIADFOLDS
MYRIAPODAN
MYRIAPODOUS
MYRINGITIS
MYRINGITISES
MYRINGOSCOPE
MYRINGOSCOPES
MYRINGOTOMIES
MYRINGOTOMY
MYRIORAMAS
MYRIOSCOPE
MYRIOSCOPES
MYRISTICIVOROUS
MYRMECOCHORIES
MYRMECOCHORY
MYRMECOLOGIC
MYRMECOLOGICAL
MYRMECOLOGIES
MYRMECOLOGIST
MYRMECOLOGISTS
MYRMECOLOGY
MYRMECOPHAGOUS
MYRMECOPHILE
MYRMECOPHILES
MYRMECOPHILIES
MYRMECOPHILOUS
MYRMECOPHILY
MYRMIDONES
MYRMIDONIAN
MYROBALANS
MYRTACEOUS
MYSOPHOBIA
MYSOPHOBIAS
MYSTAGOGIC
MYSTAGOGICAL
MYSTAGOGICALLY
MYSTAGOGIES
MYSTAGOGUE
MYSTAGOGUES
MYSTAGOGUS
MYSTAGOGUSES
MYSTERIOUS
MYSTERIOUSLY
MYSTERIOUSNESS
MYSTICALLY
MYSTICALNESS
MYSTICALNESSES
MYSTICETES

m

SECTION 2: Words between 10 and 15 letters in length

MYSTICISMS
MYSTIFICATION
MYSTIFICATIONS
MYSTIFIERS
MYSTIFYING
MYSTIFYINGLY
MYTHICALLY
MYTHICISATION
MYTHICISATIONS
MYTHICISED
MYTHICISER
MYTHICISERS
MYTHICISES
MYTHICISING
MYTHICISMS
MYTHICISTS
MYTHICIZATION
MYTHICIZATIONS

MYTHICIZED
MYTHICIZER
MYTHICIZERS
MYTHICIZES
MYTHICIZING
MYTHMAKERS
MYTHMAKING
MYTHMAKINGS
MYTHOGENESES
MYTHOGENESIS
MYTHOGRAPHER
MYTHOGRAPHERS
MYTHOGRAPHIES
MYTHOGRAPHY
MYTHOLOGER
MYTHOLOGERS
MYTHOLOGIAN
MYTHOLOGIANS

MYTHOLOGIC
MYTHOLOGICAL
MYTHOLOGICALLY
MYTHOLOGIES
MYTHOLOGISATION
MYTHOLOGISE
MYTHOLOGISED
MYTHOLOGISER
MYTHOLOGISERS
MYTHOLOGISES
MYTHOLOGISING
MYTHOLOGIST
MYTHOLOGISTS
MYTHOLOGIZATION
MYTHOLOGIZE
MYTHOLOGIZED
MYTHOLOGIZER
MYTHOLOGIZERS

MYTHOLOGIZES
MYTHOLOGIZING
MYTHOMANES
MYTHOMANIA
MYTHOMANIAC
MYTHOMANIACS
MYTHOMANIAS
MYTHOPOEIA
MYTHOPOEIAS
MYTHOPOEIC
MYTHOPOEISM
MYTHOPOEISMS
MYTHOPOEIST
MYTHOPOEISTS
MYTHOPOESES
MYTHOPOESIS
MYTHOPOETIC
MYTHOPOETICAL

MYTHOPOETS
MYTILIFORM
MYXAMOEBAE
MYXAMOEBAS
MYXEDEMATOUS
MYXOEDEMAS
MYXOEDEMATOUS
MYXOEDEMIC
MYXOMATOSES
MYXOMATOSIS
MYXOMATOUS
MYXOMYCETE
MYXOMYCETES
MYXOMYCETOUS
MYXOVIRUSES

N

NABOBERIES
NABOBESSES
NACHTMAALS
NAFFNESSES
NAIFNESSES
NAILBITERS
NAILBRUSHES
NAISSANCES
NAIVENESSES
NAKEDNESSES
NALBUPHINE
NALBUPHINES
NALORPHINE
NALORPHINES
NALTREXONE
NALTREXONES
NAMAYCUSHES
NAMECHECKED
NAMECHECKING
NAMECHECKS
NAMELESSLY
NAMELESSNESS
NAMELESSNESSES
NAMEPLATES
NAMEWORTHIER
NAMEWORTHIEST
NAMEWORTHY
NANDROLONE
NANDROLONES
NANISATION
NANISATIONS
NANIZATION
NANIZATIONS
NANNOPLANKTON
NANNOPLANKTONS
NANOGRAMME
NANOGRAMMES
NANOGRASSES
NANOMATERIAL
NANOMATERIALS
NANOMETERS
NANOMETRES
NANOPARTICLE
NANOPARTICLES
NANOPHYSICS
NANOPLANKTON
NANOPLANKTONS
NANOPUBLISHING
NANOPUBLISHINGS
NANOSECOND
NANOSECONDS
NANOTECHNOLOGY
NANOTESLAS
NANOWORLDS

NAPHTHALENE
NAPHTHALENES
NAPHTHALIC
NAPHTHALIN
NAPHTHALINE
NAPHTHALINES
NAPHTHALINS
NAPHTHALISE
NAPHTHALISED
NAPHTHALISES
NAPHTHALISING
NAPHTHALIZE
NAPHTHALIZED
NAPHTHALIZES
NAPHTHALIZING
NAPHTHENES
NAPHTHENIC
NAPHTHYLAMINE
NAPHTHYLAMINES
NAPOLEONITE
NAPOLEONITES
NAPPINESSES
NAPRAPATHIES
NAPRAPATHY
NARCISSISM
NARCISSISMS
NARCISSIST
NARCISSISTIC
NARCISSISTS
NARCISSUSES
NARCOANALYSES
NARCOANALYSIS
NARCOCATHARSES
NARCOCATHARSIS
NARCOHYPNOSES
NARCOHYPNOSIS
NARCOLEPSIES
NARCOLEPSY
NARCOLEPTIC
NARCOLEPTICS
NARCOSYNTHESES
NARCOSYNTHESIS
NARCOTERRORISM
NARCOTERRORISMS
NARCOTERRORIST
NARCOTERRORISTS
NARCOTICALLY
NARCOTINES
NARCOTISATION
NARCOTISATIONS
NARCOTISED
NARCOTISES
NARCOTISING
NARCOTISMS

NARCOTISTS
NARCOTIZATION
NARCOTIZATIONS
NARCOTIZED
NARCOTIZES
NARCOTIZING
NARGHILIES
NARGHILLIES
NARGUILEHS
NARRATABLE
NARRATIONAL
NARRATIONS
NARRATIVELY
NARRATIVES
NARRATOLOGICAL
NARRATOLOGIES
NARRATOLOGIST
NARRATOLOGISTS
NARRATOLOGY
NARROWBAND
NARROWBANDS
NARROWCAST
NARROWCASTED
NARROWCASTING
NARROWCASTINGS
NARROWCASTS
NARROWINGS
NARROWNESS
NARROWNESSES
NASALISATION
NASALISATIONS
NASALISING
NASALITIES
NASALIZATION
NASALIZATIONS
NASALIZING
NASCENCIES
NASEBERRIES
NASOFRONTAL
NASOGASTRIC
NASOLACRYMAL
NASOPHARYNGEAL
NASOPHARYNGES
NASOPHARYNX
NASOPHARYNXES
NASTINESSES
NASTURTIUM
NASTURTIUMS
NATALITIAL
NATALITIES
NATATIONAL
NATATORIAL
NATATORIUM
NATATORIUMS

NATHELESSE
NATIONALISATION
NATIONALISE
NATIONALISED
NATIONALISER
NATIONALISERS
NATIONALISES
NATIONALISING
NATIONALISM
NATIONALISMS
NATIONALIST
NATIONALISTIC
NATIONALISTS
NATIONALITIES
NATIONALITY
NATIONALIZATION
NATIONALIZE
NATIONALIZED
NATIONALIZER
NATIONALIZERS
NATIONALIZES
NATIONALIZING
NATIONALLY
NATIONHOOD
NATIONHOODS
NATIONLESS
NATIONWIDE
NATIVENESS
NATIVENESSES
NATIVISTIC
NATIVITIES
NATRIURESES
NATRIURESIS
NATRIURESISES
NATRIURETIC
NATRIURETICS
NATROLITES
NATTERIEST
NATTERJACK
NATTERJACKS
NATTINESSES
NATURALISATION
NATURALISATIONS
NATURALISE
NATURALISED
NATURALISES
NATURALISING
NATURALISM
NATURALISMS
NATURALIST
NATURALISTIC
NATURALISTS
NATURALIZATION
NATURALIZATIONS

NATURALIZE
NATURALIZED
NATURALIZES
NATURALIZING
NATURALNESS
NATURALNESSES
NATURISTIC
NATUROPATH
NATUROPATHIC
NATUROPATHIES
NATUROPATHS
NATUROPATHY
NAUGAHYDES
NAUGHTIEST
NAUGHTINESS
NAUGHTINESSES
NAUMACHIAE
NAUMACHIAS
NAUMACHIES
NAUPLIIFORM
NAUSEATING
NAUSEATINGLY
NAUSEATION
NAUSEATIONS
NAUSEATIVE
NAUSEOUSLY
NAUSEOUSNESS
NAUSEOUSNESSES
NAUTICALLY
NAUTILOIDS
NAUTILUSES
NAVARCHIES
NAVELWORTS
NAVICULARE
NAVICULARES
NAVICULARS
NAVIGABILITIES
NAVIGABILITY
NAVIGABLENESS
NAVIGABLENESSES
NAVIGATING
NAVIGATION
NAVIGATIONAL
NAVIGATIONALLY
NAVIGATIONS
NAVIGATORS
NAYSAYINGS
NAZIFICATION
NAZIFICATIONS
NEANDERTAL
NEANDERTALER
NEANDERTALERS
NEANDERTALS
NEANDERTHAL

NEANDERTHALER	NECROBIOSES	NECTAREOUSNESS	NEGLIGENCE	NEMATOCIDAL
NEANDERTHALERS	NECROBIOSIS	NECTARIFEROUS	NEGLIGENCES	NEMATOCIDE
NEANDERTHALOID	NECROBIOTIC	NECTARINES	NEGLIGENTLY	NEMATOCIDES
NEANDERTHALS	NECROGRAPHER	NECTARIVOROUS	NEGLIGIBILITIES	NEMATOCYST
NEAPOLITAN	NECROGRAPHERS	NECTOCALYCES	NEGLIGIBILITY	NEMATOCYSTIC
NEAPOLITANS	NECROLATER	NECTOCALYX	NEGLIGIBLE	NEMATOCYSTS
NEARNESSES	NECROLATERS	NEEDCESSITIES	NEGLIGIBLENESS	NEMATODIRIASES
NEARSHORED	NECROLATRIES	NEEDCESSITY	NEGLIGIBLY	NEMATODIRIASIS
NEARSHORES	NECROLATRY	NEEDFULNESS	NEGOCIANTS	NEMATODIRUS
NEARSHORING	NECROLOGIC	NEEDFULNESSES	NEGOTIABILITIES	NEMATODIRUSES
NEARSIGHTED	NECROLOGICAL	NEEDINESSES	NEGOTIABILITY	NEMATOLOGICAL
NEARSIGHTEDLY	NECROLOGIES	NEEDLECORD	NEGOTIABLE	NEMATOLOGIES
NEARSIGHTEDNESS	NECROLOGIST	NEEDLECORDS	NEGOTIANTS	NEMATOLOGIST
NEARTHROSES	NECROLOGISTS	NEEDLECRAFT	NEGOTIATED	NEMATOLOGISTS
NEARTHROSIS	NECROMANCER	NEEDLECRAFTS	NEGOTIATES	NEMATOLOGY
NEATNESSES	NECROMANCERS	NEEDLEFISH	NEGOTIATING	NEMATOPHORE
NEBBISHERS	NECROMANCIES	NEEDLEFISHES	NEGOTIATION	NEMATOPHORES
NEBBISHIER	NECROMANCY	NEEDLEFULS	NEGOTIATIONS	NEMERTEANS
NEBBISHIEST	NECROMANIA	NEEDLELESS	NEGOTIATOR	NEMERTIANS
NEBENKERNS	NECROMANIAC	NEEDLELIKE	NEGOTIATORS	NEMERTINES
NEBUCHADNEZZAR	NECROMANIACS	NEEDLEPOINT	NEGOTIATORY	NEMOPHILAS
NEBUCHADNEZZARS	NECROMANIAS	NEEDLEPOINTED	NEGOTIATRESS	NEOANTHROPIC
NEBULISATION	NECROMANTIC	NEEDLEPOINTING	NEGOTIATRESSES	NEOARSPHENAMINE
NEBULISATIONS	NECROMANTICAL	NEEDLEPOINTS	NEGOTIATRICES	NEOCAPITALISM
NEBULISERS	NECROMANTICALLY	NEEDLESSLY	NEGOTIATRIX	NEOCAPITALISMS
NEBULISING	NECROPHAGOUS	NEEDLESSNESS	NEGOTIATRIXES	NEOCAPITALIST
NEBULIZATION	NECROPHILE	NEEDLESSNESSES	NEGRITUDES	NEOCAPITALISTS
NEBULIZATIONS	NECROPHILES	NEEDLESTICK	NEGROHEADS	NEOCLASSIC
NEBULIZERS	NECROPHILIA	NEEDLESTICKS	NEGROPHILE	NEOCLASSICAL
NEBULIZING	NECROPHILIAC	NEEDLEWOMAN	NEGROPHILES	NEOCLASSICISM
NEBULOSITIES	NECROPHILIACS	NEEDLEWOMEN	NEGROPHILISM	NEOCLASSICISMS
NEBULOSITY	NECROPHILIAS	NEEDLEWORK	NEGROPHILISMS	NEOCLASSICIST
NEBULOUSLY	NECROPHILIC	NEEDLEWORKER	NEGROPHILIST	NEOCLASSICISTS
NEBULOUSNESS	NECROPHILIES	NEEDLEWORKERS	NEGROPHILISTS	NEOCOLONIAL
NEBULOUSNESSES	NECROPHILISM	NEEDLEWORKS	NEGROPHILS	NEOCOLONIALISM
NECESSAIRE	NECROPHILISMS	NEESBERRIES	NEGROPHOBE	NEOCOLONIALISMS
NECESSAIRES	NECROPHILOUS	NEFARIOUSLY	NEGROPHOBES	NEOCOLONIALIST
NECESSARIAN	NECROPHILS	NEFARIOUSNESS	NEGROPHOBIA	NEOCOLONIALISTS
NECESSARIANISM	NECROPHILY	NEFARIOUSNESSES	NEGROPHOBIAS	NEOCONSERVATISM
NECESSARIANISMS	NECROPHOBE	NEGATIONAL	NEIGHBORED	NEOCONSERVATIVE
NECESSARIANS	NECROPHOBES	NEGATIONIST	NEIGHBORHOOD	NEOCORTEXES
NECESSARIES	NECROPHOBIA	NEGATIONISTS	NEIGHBORHOODS	NEOCORTICAL
NECESSARILY	NECROPHOBIAS	NEGATIVELY	NEIGHBORING	NEOCORTICES
NECESSARINESS	NECROPHOBIC	NEGATIVENESS	NEIGHBORLESS	NEODYMIUMS
NECESSARINESSES	NECROPHOROUS	NEGATIVENESSES	NEIGHBORLIER	NEOGENESES
NECESSITARIAN	NECROPOLEIS	NEGATIVING	NEIGHBORLIEST	NEOGENESIS
NECESSITARIANS	NECROPOLES	NEGATIVISM	NEIGHBORLINESS	NEOGENETIC
NECESSITATE	NECROPOLIS	NEGATIVISMS	NEIGHBORLY	NEOGOTHICS
NECESSITATED	NECROPOLISES	NEGATIVIST	NEIGHBOURED	NEOGRAMMARIAN
NECESSITATES	NECROPSIED	NEGATIVISTIC	NEIGHBOURHOOD	NEOGRAMMARIANS
NECESSITATING	NECROPSIES	NEGATIVISTS	NEIGHBOURHOODS	NEOLIBERAL
NECESSITATION	NECROPSYING	NEGATIVITIES	NEIGHBOURING	NEOLIBERALISM
NECESSITATIONS	NECROSCOPIC	NEGATIVITY	NEIGHBOURLESS	NEOLIBERALISMS
NECESSITATIVE	NECROSCOPICAL	NEGLECTABLE	NEIGHBOURLIER	NEOLIBERALS
NECESSITIED	NECROSCOPIES	NEGLECTEDNESS	NEIGHBOURLIEST	NEOLITHICS
NECESSITIES	NECROSCOPY	NEGLECTEDNESSES	NEIGHBOURLINESS	NEOLOGIANS
NECESSITOUS	NECROTISED	NEGLECTERS	NEIGHBOURLY	NEOLOGICAL
NECESSITOUSLY	NECROTISES	NEGLECTFUL	NEIGHBOURS	NEOLOGICALLY
NECESSITOUSNESS	NECROTISING	NEGLECTFULLY	NELUMBIUMS	NEOLOGISED
NECKCLOTHS	NECROTIZED	NEGLECTFULNESS	NEMATHELMINTH	NEOLOGISES
NECKERCHIEF	NECROTIZES	NEGLECTING	NEMATHELMINTHIC	NEOLOGISING
NECKERCHIEFS	NECROTIZING	NEGLECTINGLY	NEMATHELMINTHS	NEOLOGISMS
NECKERCHIEVES	NECROTOMIES	NEGLECTION	NEMATICIDAL	NEOLOGISTIC
NECKLACING	NECROTROPH	NEGLECTIONS	NEMATICIDE	NEOLOGISTICAL
NECKLACINGS	NECROTROPHIC	NEGLECTIVE	NEMATICIDES	NEOLOGISTICALLY
NECKPIECES	NECROTROPHS	NEGLECTORS	NEMATOBLAST	NEOLOGISTS
NECKVERSES	NECTAREOUS	NEGLIGEABLE	NEMATOBLASTS	NEOLOGIZED

NEOLOGIZES
NEOLOGIZING
NEONATALLY
NEONATICIDE
NEONATICIDES
NEONATOLOGIES
NEONATOLOGIST
NEONATOLOGISTS
NEONATOLOGY
NEONOMIANISM
NEONOMIANISMS
NEONOMIANS
NEOORTHODOX
NEOORTHODOXIES
NEOORTHODOXY
NEOPAGANISE
NEOPAGANISED
NEOPAGANISES
NEOPAGANISING
NEOPAGANISM
NEOPAGANISMS
NEOPAGANIZE
NEOPAGANIZED
NEOPAGANIZES
NEOPAGANIZING
NEOPHILIAC
NEOPHILIACS
NEOPHILIAS
NEOPHOBIAS
NEOPILINAS
NEOPLASIAS
NEOPLASTIC
NEOPLASTICISM
NEOPLASTICISMS
NEOPLASTICIST
NEOPLASTICISTS
NEOPLASTIES
NEOREALISM
NEOREALISMS
NEOREALIST
NEOREALISTIC
NEOREALISTS
NEOSTIGMINE
NEOSTIGMINES
NEOTEINIAS
NEOTERICAL
NEOTERICALLY
NEOTERICALS
NEOTERISED
NEOTERISES
NEOTERISING
NEOTERISMS
NEOTERISTS
NEOTERIZED
NEOTERIZES
NEOTERIZING
NEOTROPICS
NEOVITALISM
NEOVITALISMS
NEOVITALIST
NEOVITALISTS
NEPENTHEAN
NEPHALISMS
NEPHALISTS
NEPHELINES
NEPHELINIC
NEPHELINITE

NEPHELINITES
NEPHELINITIC
NEPHELITES
NEPHELOMETER
NEPHELOMETERS
NEPHELOMETRIC
NEPHELOMETRIES
NEPHELOMETRY
NEPHOGRAMS
NEPHOGRAPH
NEPHOGRAPHS
NEPHOLOGIC
NEPHOLOGICAL
NEPHOLOGIES
NEPHOLOGIST
NEPHOLOGISTS
NEPHOSCOPE
NEPHOSCOPES
NEPHRALGIA
NEPHRALGIAS
NEPHRALGIC
NEPHRALGIES
NEPHRECTOMIES
NEPHRECTOMISE
NEPHRECTOMISED
NEPHRECTOMISES
NEPHRECTOMISING
NEPHRECTOMIZE
NEPHRECTOMIZED
NEPHRECTOMIZES
NEPHRECTOMIZING
NEPHRECTOMY
NEPHRIDIAL
NEPHRIDIUM
NEPHRITICAL
NEPHRITICS
NEPHRITIDES
NEPHRITISES
NEPHROBLASTOMA
NEPHROBLASTOMAS
NEPHROLEPIS
NEPHROLEPISES
NEPHROLOGICAL
NEPHROLOGIES
NEPHROLOGIST
NEPHROLOGISTS
NEPHROLOGY
NEPHROPATHIC
NEPHROPATHIES
NEPHROPATHY
NEPHROPEXIES
NEPHROPEXY
NEPHROPTOSES
NEPHROPTOSIS
NEPHROSCOPE
NEPHROSCOPES
NEPHROSCOPIES
NEPHROSCOPY
NEPHROSTOME
NEPHROSTOMES
NEPHROTICS
NEPHROTOMIES
NEPHROTOMY
NEPHROTOXIC
NEPHROTOXICITY
NEPOTISTIC
NEPTUNIUMS

NERDINESSES
NERVATIONS
NERVATURES
NERVELESSLY
NERVELESSNESS
NERVELESSNESSES
NERVINESSES
NERVOSITIES
NERVOUSNESS
NERVOUSNESSES
NERVURATION
NERVURATIONS
NESCIENCES
NESHNESSES
NESSELRODE
NESSELRODES
NETBALLERS
NETHERLINGS
NETHERMORE
NETHERMORES
NETHERMOST
NETHERSTOCK
NETHERSTOCKS
NETHERWARD
NETHERWARDS
NETHERWORLD
NETHERWORLDS
NETIQUETTE
NETIQUETTES
NETMINDERS
NETSURFERS
NETSURFING
NETSURFINGS
NETTLELIKE
NETTLESOME
NETWORKERS
NETWORKING
NETWORKINGS
NEURALGIAS
NEURAMINIC
NEURAMINIDASE
NEURAMINIDASES
NEURASTHENIA
NEURASTHENIAC
NEURASTHENIACS
NEURASTHENIAS
NEURASTHENIC
NEURASTHENICS
NEURATIONS
NEURECTOMIES
NEURECTOMY
NEURILEMMA
NEURILEMMAL
NEURILEMMAS
NEURILITIES
NEURITIDES
NEURITISES
NEUROACTIVE
NEUROANATOMIC
NEUROANATOMICAL
NEUROANATOMIES
NEUROANATOMIST
NEUROANATOMISTS
NEUROANATOMY
NEUROBIOLOGICAL
NEUROBIOLOGIES
NEUROBIOLOGIST

NEUROBIOLOGISTS
NEUROBIOLOGY
NEUROBLAST
NEUROBLASTOMA
NEUROBLASTOMAS
NEUROBLASTOMATA
NEUROBLASTS
NEUROCHEMICAL
NEUROCHEMICALS
NEUROCHEMIST
NEUROCHEMISTRY
NEUROCHEMISTS
NEUROCHIPS
NEUROCOELE
NEUROCOELES
NEUROCOELS
NEUROCOGNITIVE
NEUROCOMPUTER
NEUROCOMPUTERS
NEUROCOMPUTING
NEUROCOMPUTINGS
NEURODIVERSITY
NEUROECTODERMAL
NEUROENDOCRINE
NEUROETHOLOGIES
NEUROETHOLOGY
NEUROFEEDBACK
NEUROFEEDBACKS
NEUROFIBRIL
NEUROFIBRILAR
NEUROFIBRILLAR
NEUROFIBRILLARY
NEUROFIBRILS
NEUROFIBROMA
NEUROFIBROMAS
NEUROFIBROMATA
NEUROGENESES
NEUROGENESIS
NEUROGENIC
NEUROGENICALLY
NEUROGLIAL
NEUROGLIAS
NEUROGRAMS
NEUROHORMONAL
NEUROHORMONE
NEUROHORMONES
NEUROHUMOR
NEUROHUMORAL
NEUROHUMORS
NEUROHUMOUR
NEUROHUMOURS
NEUROHYPNOLOGY
NEUROHYPOPHYSES
NEUROHYPOPHYSIS
NEUROLEMMA
NEUROLEMMAS
NEUROLEPTIC
NEUROLEPTICS
NEUROLINGUIST
NEUROLINGUISTIC
NEUROLINGUISTS
NEUROLOGIC
NEUROLOGICAL
NEUROLOGICALLY
NEUROLOGIES
NEUROLOGIST
NEUROLOGISTS

NEUROLYSES
NEUROLYSIS
NEUROMARKETING
NEUROMARKETINGS
NEUROMASTS
NEUROMATOUS
NEUROMOTOR
NEUROMUSCULAR
NEUROPATHIC
NEUROPATHICAL
NEUROPATHICALLY
NEUROPATHIES
NEUROPATHIST
NEUROPATHISTS
NEUROPATHOLOGIC
NEUROPATHOLOGY
NEUROPATHS
NEUROPATHY
NEUROPEPTIDE
NEUROPEPTIDES
NEUROPHYSIOLOGY
NEUROPLASM
NEUROPLASMS
NEUROPSYCHIATRY
NEUROPSYCHOLOGY
NEUROPTERA
NEUROPTERAN
NEUROPTERANS
NEUROPTERIST
NEUROPTERISTS
NEUROPTERON
NEUROPTERONS
NEUROPTEROUS
NEURORADIOLOGY
NEUROSCIENCE
NEUROSCIENCES
NEUROSCIENTIFIC
NEUROSCIENTIST
NEUROSCIENTISTS
NEUROSECRETION
NEUROSECRETIONS
NEUROSECRETORY
NEUROSENSORY
NEUROSPORA
NEUROSPORAS
NEUROSURGEON
NEUROSURGEONS
NEUROSURGERIES
NEUROSURGERY
NEUROSURGICAL
NEUROSURGICALLY
NEUROSYPHILIS
NEUROSYPHILISES
NEUROTICALLY
NEUROTICISM
NEUROTICISMS
NEUROTOMIES
NEUROTOMIST
NEUROTOMISTS
NEUROTOXIC
NEUROTOXICITIES
NEUROTOXICITY
NEUROTOXIN
NEUROTOXINS
NEUROTROPHIC
NEUROTROPHIES
NEUROTROPHY

NEUROTROPIC	NEWSINESSES	NICOTINISMS	NIGHTHAWKS	NINETEENTHS
NEUROTYPICAL	NEWSLETTER	NICROSILAL	NIGHTINGALE	NINETTETHS
NEUROVASCULAR	NEWSLETTERS	NICROSILALS	NIGHTINGALES	NINHYDRINS
NEURULATION	NEWSMAGAZINE	NICTATIONS	NIGHTLIFES	NINNYHAMMER
NEURULATIONS	NEWSMAGAZINES	NICTITATED	NIGHTLIVES	NINNYHAMMERS
NEURYPNOLOGIES	NEWSMAKERS	NICTITATES	NIGHTMARES	NIPCHEESES
NEURYPNOLOGY	NEWSMONGER	NICTITATING	NIGHTMARIER	NIPPERKINS
NEUTERINGS	NEWSMONGERS	NICTITATION	NIGHTMARIEST	NIPPINESSES
NEUTRALISATION	NEWSPAPERDOM	NICTITATIONS	NIGHTMARISH	NIPPLEWORT
NEUTRALISATIONS	NEWSPAPERDOMS	NIDAMENTAL	NIGHTMARISHLY	NIPPLEWORTS
NEUTRALISE	NEWSPAPERED	NIDAMENTUM	NIGHTMARISHNESS	NISBERRIES
NEUTRALISED	NEWSPAPERING	NIDDERINGS	NIGHTPIECE	NITPICKERS
NEUTRALISER	NEWSPAPERISM	NIDDERLING	NIGHTPIECES	NITPICKIER
NEUTRALISERS	NEWSPAPERISMS	NIDDERLINGS	NIGHTRIDER	NITPICKIEST
NEUTRALISES	NEWSPAPERMAN	NIDERLINGS	NIGHTRIDERS	NITPICKING
NEUTRALISING	NEWSPAPERMEN	NIDICOLOUS	NIGHTRIDING	NITPICKINGS
NEUTRALISM	NEWSPAPERS	NIDIFICATE	NIGHTRIDINGS	NITRAMINES
NEUTRALISMS	NEWSPAPERWOMAN	NIDIFICATED	NIGHTSCOPE	NITRANILINE
NEUTRALIST	NEWSPAPERWOMEN	NIDIFICATES	NIGHTSCOPES	NITRANILINES
NEUTRALISTIC	NEWSPEOPLE	NIDIFICATING	NIGHTSHADE	NITRATINES
NEUTRALISTS	NEWSPERSON	NIDIFICATION	NIGHTSHADES	NITRATIONS
NEUTRALITIES	NEWSPERSONS	NIDIFICATIONS	NIGHTSHIRT	NITRAZEPAM
NEUTRALITY	NEWSPRINTS	NIDIFUGOUS	NIGHTSHIRTS	NITRAZEPAMS
NEUTRALIZATION	NEWSREADER	NIDULATION	NIGHTSIDES	NITRIDINGS
NEUTRALIZATIONS	NEWSREADERS	NIDULATIONS	NIGHTSPOTS	NITRIFIABLE
NEUTRALIZE	NEWSSHEETS	NIFEDIPINE	NIGHTSTAND	NITRIFICATION
NEUTRALIZED	NEWSSTANDS	NIFEDIPINES	NIGHTSTANDS	NITRIFICATIONS
NEUTRALIZER	NEWSTRADES	NIFFNAFFED	NIGHTSTICK	NITRIFIERS
NEUTRALIZERS	NEWSWEEKLIES	NIFFNAFFING	NIGHTSTICKS	NITRIFYING
NEUTRALIZES	NEWSWEEKLY	NIFTINESSES	NIGHTTIDES	NITROBACTERIA
NEUTRALIZING	NEWSWORTHIER	NIGGARDING	NIGHTTIMES	NITROBACTERIUM
NEUTRALNESS	NEWSWORTHIEST	NIGGARDISE	NIGHTWALKER	NITROBENZENE
NEUTRALNESSES	NEWSWORTHINESS	NIGGARDISES	NIGHTWALKERS	NITROBENZENES
NEUTRETTOS	NEWSWORTHY	NIGGARDIZE	NIGHTWATCHMAN	NITROCELLULOSE
NEUTRINOLESS	NEWSWRITING	NIGGARDIZES	NIGHTWATCHMEN	NITROCELLULOSES
NEUTROPENIA	NEWSWRITINGS	NIGGARDLIER	NIGHTWEARS	NITROCHLOROFORM
NEUTROPENIAS	NEXTNESSES	NIGGARDLIEST	NIGRESCENCE	NITROCOTTON
NEUTROPHIL	NIACINAMIDE	NIGGARDLINESS	NIGRESCENCES	NITROCOTTONS
NEUTROPHILE	NIACINAMIDES	NIGGARDLINESSES	NIGRESCENT	NITROFURAN
NEUTROPHILES	NIAISERIES	NIGGERDOMS	NIGRIFYING	NITROFURANS
NEUTROPHILIC	NIALAMIDES	NIGGERHEAD	NIGRITUDES	NITROGELATIN
NEUTROPHILS	NIBBLINGLY	NIGGERHEADS	NIGROMANCIES	NITROGELATINE
NEVERMINDS	NICCOLITES	NIGGERIEST	NIGROMANCY	NITROGELATINES
NEVERTHELESS	NICENESSES	NIGGERISMS	NIGROSINES	NITROGELATINS
NEVERTHEMORE	NICKELIFEROUS	NIGGERLING	NIHILISTIC	NITROGENASE
NEWFANGLED	NICKELINES	NIGGERLINGS	NIHILITIES	NITROGENASES
NEWFANGLEDLY	NICKELISED	NIGGLINGLY	NIKETHAMIDE	NITROGENISATION
NEWFANGLEDNESS	NICKELISES	NIGHNESSES	NIKETHAMIDES	NITROGENISE
NEWFANGLENESS	NICKELISING	NIGHTBIRDS	NILPOTENTS	NITROGENISED
NEWFANGLENESSES	NICKELIZED	NIGHTBLIND	NIMBLENESS	NITROGENISES
NEWFANGLES	NICKELIZES	NIGHTCLASS	NIMBLENESSES	NITROGENISING
NEWISHNESS	NICKELIZING	NIGHTCLASSES	NIMBLESSES	NITROGENIZATION
NEWISHNESSES	NICKELLING	NIGHTCLOTHES	NIMBLEWITS	NITROGENIZE
NEWMARKETS	NICKELODEON	NIGHTCLUBBED	NIMBLEWITTED	NITROGENIZED
NEWSAGENCIES	NICKELODEONS	NIGHTCLUBBER	NIMBOSTRATI	NITROGENIZES
NEWSAGENCY	NICKERNUTS	NIGHTCLUBBERS	NIMBOSTRATUS	NITROGENIZING
NEWSAGENTS	NICKNAMERS	NIGHTCLUBBING	NIMBYNESSES	NITROGENOUS
NEWSBREAKS	NICKNAMING	NIGHTCLUBBINGS	NINCOMPOOP	NITROGLYCERIN
NEWSCASTER	NICKPOINTS	NIGHTCLUBS	NINCOMPOOPERIES	NITROGLYCERINE
NEWSCASTERS	NICKSTICKS	NIGHTDRESS	NINCOMPOOPERY	NITROGLYCERINES
NEWSCASTING	NICKUMPOOP	NIGHTDRESSES	NINCOMPOOPS	NITROGLYCERINS
NEWSCASTINGS	NICKUMPOOPS	NIGHTFALLS	NINEPENCES	NITROMETER
NEWSDEALER	NICOMPOOPS	NIGHTFARING	NINEPENNIES	NITROMETERS
NEWSDEALERS	NICOTIANAS	NIGHTFIRES	NINESCORES	NITROMETHANE
NEWSFLASHES	NICOTINAMIDE	NIGHTGEARS	NINETEENTH	NITROMETHANES
NEWSGROUPS	NICOTINAMIDES	NIGHTGLOWS	NINETEENTHLIES	NITROMETRIC
NEWSHOUNDS	NICOTINISM	NIGHTGOWNS	NINETEENTHLY	NITROPARAFFIN

NITROPARAFFINS	NOISEMAKERS	NOMOTHETICAL	NONAQUATIC	NONBROADCAST
NITROPHILOUS	NOISEMAKING	NONABRASIVE	NONAQUEOUS	NONBUILDING
NITROSAMINE	NOISEMAKINGS	NONABSORBABLE	NONARBITRARY	NONBURNABLE
NITROSAMINES	NOISINESSES	NONABSORBENT	NONARCHITECT	NONBUSINESS
NITROSATION	NOISOMENESS	NONABSORPTIVE	NONARCHITECTS	NONCABINET
NITROSATIONS	NOISOMENESSES	NONABSTRACT	NONARCHITECTURE	NONCALLABLE
NITROTOLUENE	NOMADICALLY	NONACADEMIC	NONARGUMENT	NONCALORIC
NITROTOLUENES	NOMADISATION	NONACADEMICS	NONARGUMENTS	NONCANCELABLE
NITWITTEDNESS	NOMADISATIONS	NONACCEPTANCE	NONARISTOCRATIC	NONCANCELLABLE
NITWITTEDNESSES	NOMADISING	NONACCEPTANCES	NONAROMATIC	NONCANCEROUS
NITWITTERIES	NOMADIZATION	NONACCIDENTAL	NONAROMATICS	NONCANDIDACIES
NITWITTERY	NOMADIZATIONS	NONACCOUNTABLE	NONARRIVAL	NONCANDIDACY
NOBBINESSES	NOMADIZING	NONACCREDITED	NONARRIVALS	NONCANDIDATE
NOBILESSES	NOMARCHIES	NONACCRUAL	NONARTISTIC	NONCANDIDATES
NOBILITATE	NOMENCLATIVE	NONACHIEVEMENT	NONARTISTS	NONCAPITAL
NOBILITATED	NOMENCLATOR	NONACHIEVEMENTS	NONASCETIC	NONCAPITALIST
NOBILITATES	NOMENCLATORIAL	NONACQUISITIVE	NONASCETICS	NONCAPITALISTS
NOBILITATING	NOMENCLATORS	NONACTINGS	NONASPIRIN	NONCARBOHYDRATE
NOBILITATION	NOMENCLATURAL	NONACTIONS	NONASSERTIVE	NONCARCINOGEN
NOBILITATIONS	NOMENCLATURE	NONACTIVATED	NONASSOCIATED	NONCARCINOGENIC
NOBILITIES	NOMENCLATURES	NONADAPTIVE	NONASTRONOMICAL	NONCARCINOGENS
NOBLENESSES	NOMENKLATURA	NONADDICTIVE	NONATHLETE	NONCARDIAC
NOBLEWOMAN	NOMENKLATURAS	NONADDICTS	NONATHLETES	NONCARRIER
NOBLEWOMEN	NOMINALISATION	NONADDITIVE	NONATHLETIC	NONCARRIERS
NOCHELLING	NOMINALISATIONS	NONADDITIVITIES	NONATTACHED	NONCELEBRATION
NOCICEPTIVE	NOMINALISE	NONADDITIVITY	NONATTACHMENT	NONCELEBRATIONS
NOCICEPTOR	NOMINALISED	NONADHESIVE	NONATTACHMENTS	NONCELEBRITIES
NOCICEPTORS	NOMINALISES	NONADIABATIC	NONATTENDANCE	NONCELEBRITY
NOCIRECEPTOR	NOMINALISING	NONADJACENT	NONATTENDANCES	NONCELLULAR
NOCIRECEPTORS	NOMINALISM	NONADMIRER	NONATTENDER	NONCELLULOSIC
NOCTAMBULATION	NOMINALISMS	NONADMIRERS	NONATTENDERS	NONCELLULOSICS
NOCTAMBULATIONS	NOMINALIST	NONADMISSION	NONATTRIBUTABLE	NONCENTRAL
NOCTAMBULISM	NOMINALISTIC	NONADMISSIONS	NONAUDITORY	NONCERTIFICATED
NOCTAMBULISMS	NOMINALISTS	NONAESTHETIC	NONAUTHORS	NONCERTIFIED
NOCTAMBULIST	NOMINALIZATION	NONAFFILIATED	NONAUTOMATED	NONCHALANCE
NOCTAMBULISTS	NOMINALIZATIONS	NONAFFLUENT	NONAUTOMATIC	NONCHALANCES
NOCTILUCAE	NOMINALIZE	NONAGENARIAN	NONAUTOMOTIVE	NONCHALANT
NOCTILUCAS	NOMINALIZED	NONAGENARIANS	NONAUTONOMOUS	NONCHALANTLY
NOCTILUCENCE	NOMINALIZES	NONAGESIMAL	NONAVAILABILITY	NONCHARACTER
NOCTILUCENCES	NOMINALIZING	NONAGESIMALS	NONBACTERIAL	NONCHARACTERS
NOCTILUCENT	NOMINATELY	NONAGGRESSION	NONBANKING	NONCHARISMATIC
NOCTILUCOUS	NOMINATING	NONAGGRESSIONS	NONBARBITURATE	NONCHARISMATICS
NOCTIVAGANT	NOMINATION	NONAGGRESSIVE	NONBARBITURATES	NONCHAUVINIST
NOCTIVAGANTS	NOMINATIONS	NONAGRICULTURAL	NONBEARING	NONCHAUVINISTS
NOCTIVAGATION	NOMINATIVAL	NONALCOHOLIC	NONBEHAVIORAL	NONCHEMICAL
NOCTIVAGATIONS	NOMINATIVALLY	NONALGEBRAIC	NONBEHAVIOURAL	NONCHEMICALS
NOCTIVAGOUS	NOMINATIVE	NONALIGNED	NONBELIEFS	NONCHROMOSOMAL
NOCTUARIES	NOMINATIVELY	NONALIGNMENT	NONBELIEVER	NONCHURCHED
NOCTURNALITIES	NOMINATIVES	NONALIGNMENTS	NONBELIEVERS	NONCHURCHES
NOCTURNALITY	NOMINATORS	NONALLELIC	NONBELLIGERENCY	NONCHURCHGOER
NOCTURNALLY	NOMOCRACIES	NONALLERGENIC	NONBELLIGERENT	NONCHURCHGOERS
NOCTURNALS	NOMOGENIES	NONALLERGIC	NONBELLIGERENTS	NONCHURCHING
NOCUOUSNESS	NOMOGRAPHER	NONALPHABETIC	NONBETTING	NONCIRCULAR
NOCUOUSNESSES	NOMOGRAPHERS	NONALUMINIUM	NONBINDING	NONCIRCULATING
NODALISING	NOMOGRAPHIC	NONALUMINUM	NONBIOGRAPHICAL	NONCITIZEN
NODALITIES	NOMOGRAPHICAL	NONAMBIGUOUS	NONBIOLOGICAL	NONCITIZENS
NODALIZING	NOMOGRAPHICALLY	NONANALYTIC	NONBIOLOGICALLY	NONCLANDESTINE
NODOSITIES	NOMOGRAPHIES	NONANATOMIC	NONBIOLOGIST	NONCLASSES
NODULATION	NOMOGRAPHS	NONANSWERED	NONBIOLOGISTS	NONCLASSICAL
NODULATIONS	NOMOGRAPHY	NONANSWERING	NONBONDING	NONCLASSIFIED
NOEMATICAL	NOMOLOGICAL	NONANSWERS	NONBOTANIST	NONCLASSROOM
NOEMATICALLY	NOMOLOGICALLY	NONANTAGONISTIC	NONBOTANISTS	NONCLERICAL
NOGOODNIKS	NOMOLOGIES	NONANTIBIOTIC	NONBREAKABLE	NONCLINICAL
NOISELESSLY	NOMOLOGIST	NONANTIBIOTICS	NONBREATHING	NONCLOGGING
NOISELESSNESS	NOMOLOGISTS	NONANTIGENIC	NONBREEDER	NONCOERCIVE
NOISELESSNESSES	NOMOTHETES	NONAPPEARANCE	NONBREEDERS	NONCOGNITIVE
NOISEMAKER	NOMOTHETIC	NONAPPEARANCES	NONBREEDING	NONCOGNITIVISM

NONCOGNITIVISMS
NONCOHERENT
NONCOINCIDENCE
NONCOINCIDENCES
NONCOLLECTOR
NONCOLLECTORS
NONCOLLEGE
NONCOLLEGIATE
NONCOLLINEAR
NONCOLORED
NONCOLORFAST
NONCOLOURED
NONCOLOURFAST
NONCOLOURS
NONCOMBATANT
NONCOMBATANTS
NONCOMBATIVE
NONCOMBUSTIBLE
NONCOMBUSTIBLES
NONCOMMERCIAL
NONCOMMISSIONED
NONCOMMITMENT
NONCOMMITMENTS
NONCOMMITTAL
NONCOMMITTALLY
NONCOMMITTALS
NONCOMMITTED
NONCOMMUNICANT
NONCOMMUNICANTS
NONCOMMUNIST
NONCOMMUNISTS
NONCOMMUNITY
NONCOMMUTATIVE
NONCOMPARABLE
NONCOMPATIBLE
NONCOMPETITION
NONCOMPETITIONS
NONCOMPETITIVE
NONCOMPETITOR
NONCOMPETITORS
NONCOMPLETION
NONCOMPLETIONS
NONCOMPLEX
NONCOMPLIANCE
NONCOMPLIANCES
NONCOMPLICATED
NONCOMPLYING
NONCOMPLYINGS
NONCOMPOSER
NONCOMPOSERS
NONCOMPOUND
NONCOMPRESSIBLE
NONCOMPUTER
NONCOMPUTERISED
NONCOMPUTERIZED
NONCONCEPTUAL
NONCONCERN
NONCONCERNS
NONCONCLUSION
NONCONCLUSIONS
NONCONCURRED
NONCONCURRENCE
NONCONCURRENCES
NONCONCURRENT
NONCONCURRING
NONCONCURS
NONCONDENSABLE

NONCONDITIONED
NONCONDUCTING
NONCONDUCTION
NONCONDUCTIONS
NONCONDUCTIVE
NONCONDUCTOR
NONCONDUCTORS
NONCONFERENCE
NONCONFIDENCE
NONCONFIDENCES
NONCONFIDENTIAL
NONCONFLICTING
NONCONFORM
NONCONFORMANCE
NONCONFORMANCES
NONCONFORMED
NONCONFORMER
NONCONFORMERS
NONCONFORMING
NONCONFORMINGS
NONCONFORMISM
NONCONFORMISMS
NONCONFORMIST
NONCONFORMISTS
NONCONFORMITIES
NONCONFORMITY
NONCONFORMS
NONCONGRUENT
NONCONJUGATED
NONCONNECTION
NONCONNECTIONS
NONCONSCIOUS
NONCONSECUTIVE
NONCONSENSUAL
NONCONSERVATION
NONCONSERVATIVE
NONCONSOLIDATED
NONCONSTANT
NONCONSTRUCTION
NONCONSTRUCTIVE
NONCONSUMER
NONCONSUMERS
NONCONSUMING
NONCONSUMPTION
NONCONSUMPTIONS
NONCONSUMPTIVE
NONCONTACT
NONCONTACTS
NONCONTAGIOUS
NONCONTEMPORARY
NONCONTIGUOUS
NONCONTINGENT
NONCONTINUOUS
NONCONTRACT
NONCONTRACTUAL
NONCONTRIBUTING
NONCONTRIBUTORY
NONCONTROLLABLE
NONCONTROLLED
NONCONTROLLING
NONCONVENTIONAL
NONCONVERTIBLE
NONCOOPERATION
NONCOOPERATIONS
NONCOOPERATIVE
NONCOOPERATOR
NONCOOPERATORS

NONCOPLANAR
NONCORPORATE
NONCORRELATION
NONCORRELATIONS
NONCORRODIBLE
NONCORRODING
NONCORROSIVE
NONCOUNTRIES
NONCOUNTRY
NONCOVERAGE
NONCOVERAGES
NONCREATIVE
NONCREATIVITIES
NONCREATIVITY
NONCREDENTIALED
NONCRIMINAL
NONCRIMINALS
NONCRITICAL
NONCROSSOVER
NONCROSSOVERS
NONCRUSHABLE
NONCRYSTALLINE
NONCULINARY
NONCULTIVATED
NONCULTIVATION
NONCULTIVATIONS
NONCULTURAL
NONCUMULATIVE
NONCURRENT
NONCUSTODIAL
NONCUSTOMER
NONCUSTOMERS
NONCYCLICAL
NONDANCERS
NONDEALERS
NONDECEPTIVE
NONDECISION
NONDECISIONS
NONDECREASING
NONDEDUCTIBLE
NONDEDUCTIVE
NONDEFENCE
NONDEFENSE
NONDEFERRABLE
NONDEFORMING
NONDEGENERATE
NONDEGRADABLE
NONDELEGATE
NONDELEGATES
NONDELIBERATE
NONDELINQUENT
NONDELINQUENTS
NONDELIVERIES
NONDELIVERY
NONDEMANDING
NONDEMANDS
NONDEMOCRATIC
NONDEPARTMENTAL
NONDEPENDENT
NONDEPENDENTS
NONDEPLETABLE
NONDEPLETING
NONDEPOSITION
NONDEPOSITIONS
NONDEPRESSED
NONDERIVATIVE
NONDESCRIPT

NONDESCRIPTIVE
NONDESCRIPTLY
NONDESCRIPTNESS
NONDESCRIPTS
NONDESTRUCTIVE
NONDETACHABLE
NONDEVELOPMENT
NONDEVELOPMENTS
NONDEVIANT
NONDIABETIC
NONDIABETICS
NONDIALYSABLE
NONDIALYZABLE
NONDIAPAUSING
NONDIDACTIC
NONDIFFUSIBLE
NONDIMENSIONAL
NONDIPLOMATIC
NONDIRECTED
NONDIRECTIONAL
NONDIRECTIVE
NONDISABLED
NONDISCLOSURE
NONDISCLOSURES
NONDISCOUNT
NONDISCURSIVE
NONDISJUNCTION
NONDISJUNCTIONS
NONDISPERSIVE
NONDISRUPTIVE
NONDISTINCTIVE
NONDIVERGENT
NONDIVERSIFIED
NONDIVIDING
NONDOCTORS
NONDOCTRINAIRE
NONDOCUMENTARY
NONDOGMATIC
NONDOMESTIC
NONDOMICILED
NONDOMINANT
NONDORMANT
NONDRAMATIC
NONDRINKER
NONDRINKERS
NONDRINKING
NONDRIVERS
NONDURABLE
NONDURABLES
NONEARNING
NONECONOMIC
NONECONOMIST
NONECONOMISTS
NONEDIBLES
NONEDITORIAL
NONEDUCATION
NONEDUCATIONAL
NONEFFECTIVE
NONEFFECTIVES
NONELASTIC
NONELECTED
NONELECTION
NONELECTIONS
NONELECTIVE
NONELECTRIC
NONELECTRICAL
NONELECTRICALS

NONELECTRICS
NONELECTROLYTE
NONELECTROLYTES
NONELECTRONIC
NONELEMENTARY
NONEMERGENCIES
NONEMERGENCY
NONEMOTIONAL
NONEMPHATIC
NONEMPIRICAL
NONEMPLOYEE
NONEMPLOYEES
NONEMPLOYMENT
NONEMPLOYMENTS
NONENCAPSULATED
NONENFORCEMENT
NONENFORCEMENTS
NONENGAGEMENT
NONENGAGEMENTS
NONENGINEERING
NONENTITIES
NONENTRIES
NONENZYMATIC
NONENZYMIC
NONEQUILIBRIA
NONEQUILIBRIUM
NONEQUILIBRIUMS
NONEQUIVALENCE
NONEQUIVALENCES
NONEQUIVALENT
NONESSENTIAL
NONESSENTIALS
NONESTABLISHED
NONESTERIFIED
NONESUCHES
NONETHELESS
NONETHICAL
NONETHNICS
NONEVALUATIVE
NONEVIDENCE
NONEVIDENCES
NONEXCLUSIVE
NONEXECUTIVE
NONEXECUTIVES
NONEXEMPTS
NONEXISTENCE
NONEXISTENCES
NONEXISTENT
NONEXISTENTIAL
NONEXISTENTS
NONEXPENDABLE
NONEXPERIMENTAL
NONEXPERTS
NONEXPLANATORY
NONEXPLOITATION
NONEXPLOITATIVE
NONEXPLOITIVE
NONEXPLOSIVE
NONEXPOSED
NONFACTORS
NONFACTUAL
NONFACULTIES
NONFACULTY
NONFAMILIAL
NONFAMILIES
NONFARMERS
NONFATTENING

NONFEASANCE
NONFEASANCES
NONFEDERAL
NONFEDERATED
NONFEEDING
NONFEMINIST
NONFEMINISTS
NONFERROUS
NONFICTION
NONFICTIONAL
NONFICTIONALLY
NONFICTIONS
NONFIGURATIVE
NONFILAMENTOUS
NONFILTERABLE
NONFINANCIAL
NONFISSIONABLE
NONFLAMMABILITY
NONFLAMMABLE
NONFLOWERING
NONFLUENCIES
NONFLUENCY
NONFLUORESCENT
NONFORFEITABLE
NONFORFEITURE
NONFORFEITURES
NONFREEZING
NONFRIVOLOUS
NONFULFILLMENT
NONFULFILLMENTS
NONFULFILMENT
NONFULFILMENTS
NONFUNCTIONAL
NONFUNCTIONING
NONGASEOUS
NONGENETIC
NONGENITAL
NONGEOMETRICAL
NONGLAMOROUS
NONGOLFERS
NONGONOCOCCAL
NONGOVERNMENT
NONGOVERNMENTAL
NONGRADUATE
NONGRADUATES
NONGRAMMATICAL
NONGRANULAR
NONGREGARIOUS
NONGROWING
NONGROWTHS
NONHAEMOLYTIC
NONHALOGENATED
NONHANDICAPPED
NONHAPPENING
NONHAPPENINGS
NONHARMONIC
NONHAZARDOUS
NONHEMOLYTIC
NONHEREDITARY
NONHIERARCHICAL
NONHISTONE
NONHISTORICAL
NONHOMOGENEITY
NONHOMOGENEOUS
NONHOMOLOGOUS
NONHOMOSEXUAL
NONHOMOSEXUALS

NONHORMONAL
NONHOSPITAL
NONHOSPITALISED
NONHOSPITALIZED
NONHOSTILE
NONHOUSING
NONHUNTERS
NONHUNTING
NONHYGROSCOPIC
NONHYSTERICAL
NONIDENTICAL
NONIDENTITIES
NONIDENTITY
NONIDEOLOGICAL
NONILLIONS
NONILLIONTH
NONILLIONTHS
NONIMITATIVE
NONIMMIGRANT
NONIMMIGRANTS
NONIMPACTS
NONIMPLICATION
NONIMPLICATIONS
NONIMPORTATION
NONIMPORTATIONS
NONINCLUSION
NONINCLUSIONS
NONINCREASING
NONINCUMBENT
NONINCUMBENTS
NONINDEPENDENCE
NONINDICTABLE
NONINDIGENOUS
NONINDIVIDUAL
NONINDIVIDUALS
NONINDUCTIVE
NONINDUSTRIAL
NONINDUSTRY
NONINFECTED
NONINFECTIOUS
NONINFECTIVE
NONINFESTED
NONINFLAMMABLE
NONINFLAMMATORY
NONINFLATIONARY
NONINFLECTIONAL
NONINFLUENCE
NONINFLUENCES
NONINFORMATION
NONINFORMATIONS
NONINFRINGEMENT
NONINITIAL
NONINITIATE
NONINITIATES
NONINSECTICIDAL
NONINSECTS
NONINSTALLMENT
NONINSTALLMENTS
NONINSTALMENT
NONINSTRUMENTAL
NONINSURANCE
NONINSURANCES
NONINSURED
NONINTEGRAL
NONINTEGRATED
NONINTELLECTUAL
NONINTERACTING

NONINTERACTIVE
NONINTERCOURSE
NONINTERCOURSES
NONINTEREST
NONINTERFERENCE
NONINTERSECTING
NONINTERVENTION
NONINTIMIDATING
NONINTOXICANT
NONINTOXICANTS
NONINTOXICATING
NONINTRUSIVE
NONINTUITIVE
NONINVASIVE
NONINVOLVED
NONINVOLVEMENT
NONINVOLVEMENTS
NONIONISING
NONIONIZING
NONIRRADIATED
NONIRRIGATED
NONIRRITANT
NONIRRITANTS
NONIRRITATING
NONJOINDER
NONJOINDERS
NONJOINERS
NONJUDGEMENTAL
NONJUDGMENTAL
NONJUDICIAL
NONJUSTICIABLE
NONKOSHERS
NONLADDERING
NONLANDOWNER
NONLANDOWNERS
NONLANGUAGE
NONLANGUAGES
NONLAWYERS
NONLEGUMES
NONLEGUMINOUS
NONLEXICAL
NONLIBRARIAN
NONLIBRARIANS
NONLIBRARY
NONLINEARITIES
NONLINEARITY
NONLINGUISTIC
NONLIQUIDS
NONLITERAL
NONLITERARY
NONLITERATE
NONLITERATES
NONLIVINGS
NONLOGICAL
NONLOGICALLY
NONLUMINOUS
NONMAGNETIC
NONMAINSTREAM
NONMALICIOUS
NONMALIGNANT
NONMALLEABLE
NONMANAGEMENT
NONMANAGERIAL
NONMANDATORY
NONMARITAL
NONMARKETS
NONMATERIAL

NONMATHEMATICAL
NONMATRICULATED
NONMEANINGFUL
NONMEASURABLE
NONMECHANICAL
NONMECHANISTIC
NONMEDICAL
NONMEETING
NONMEETINGS
NONMEMBERS
NONMEMBERSHIP
NONMEMBERSHIPS
NONMERCURIAL
NONMETALLIC
NONMETAMERIC
NONMETAPHORICAL
NONMETRICAL
NONMETROPOLITAN
NONMICROBIAL
NONMIGRANT
NONMIGRANTS
NONMIGRATORY
NONMILITANT
NONMILITANTS
NONMILITARY
NONMIMETIC
NONMINORITIES
NONMINORITY
NONMODERNS
NONMOLECULAR
NONMONETARIST
NONMONETARISTS
NONMONETARY
NONMONOGAMOUS
NONMORTALS
NONMOTILITIES
NONMOTILITY
NONMOTORISED
NONMOTORIZED
NONMUNICIPAL
NONMUSICAL
NONMUSICALS
NONMUSICIAN
NONMUSICIANS
NONMUTANTS
NONMYELINATED
NONMYSTICAL
NONNARRATIVE
NONNATIONAL
NONNATIONALS
NONNATIVES
NONNATURAL
NONNECESSITIES
NONNECESSITY
NONNEGATIVE
NONNEGLIGENT
NONNEGOTIABLE
NONNEGOTIABLES
NONNETWORK
NONNITROGENOUS
NONNORMATIVE
NONNUCLEAR
NONNUCLEATED
NONNUMERICAL
NONNUTRITIOUS
NONNUTRITIVE
NONOBJECTIVE

NONOBJECTIVISM
NONOBJECTIVISMS
NONOBJECTIVIST
NONOBJECTIVISTS
NONOBJECTIVITY
NONOBSCENE
NONOBSERVANCE
NONOBSERVANCES
NONOBSERVANT
NONOBVIOUS
NONOBVIOUSES
NONOCCUPATIONAL
NONOCCURRENCE
NONOCCURRENCES
NONOFFICIAL
NONOFFICIALS
NONOPERATIC
NONOPERATING
NONOPERATIONAL
NONOPERATIVE
NONOPTIMAL
NONORGANIC
NONORGASMIC
NONORTHODOX
NONOVERLAPPING
NONOXIDISING
NONOXIDIZING
NONPAPISTS
NONPARALLEL
NONPARAMETRIC
NONPARASITIC
NONPAREILS
NONPARENTS
NONPARITIES
NONPARTICIPANT
NONPARTICIPANTS
NONPARTIES
NONPARTISAN
NONPARTISANSHIP
NONPARTIZAN
NONPARTIZANSHIP
NONPASSERINE
NONPASSIVE
NONPATHOGENIC
NONPAYMENT
NONPAYMENTS
NONPECUNIARY
NONPERFORMANCE
NONPERFORMANCES
NONPERFORMER
NONPERFORMERS
NONPERFORMING
NONPERISHABLE
NONPERISHABLES
NONPERMANENT
NONPERMISSIVE
NONPERSISTENT
NONPERSONAL
NONPERSONS
NONPETROLEUM
NONPHILOSOPHER
NONPHILOSOPHERS
NONPHONEMIC
NONPHONETIC
NONPHOSPHATE
NONPHOTOGRAPHIC
NONPHYSICAL

n

NONPHYSICIAN	NONRECEIPT	NONRUMINANT	NONSPEECHES	NONTHINKING
NONPHYSICIANS	NONRECEIPTS	NONRUMINANTS	NONSPHERICAL	NONTHINKINGS
NONPLASTIC	NONRECIPROCAL	NONRUNNERS	NONSPORTING	NONTHREATENING
NONPLASTICS	NONRECOGNITION	NONSALABLE	NONSTAINING	NONTOBACCO
NONPLAYERS	NONRECOGNITIONS	NONSALEABLE	NONSTANDARD	NONTOTALITARIAN
NONPLAYING	NONRECOMBINANT	NONSAPONIFIABLE	NONSTAPLES	NONTRADING
NONPLUSING	NONRECOMBINANTS	NONSCHEDULED	NONSTARTER	NONTRADITIONAL
NONPLUSSED	NONRECOURSE	NONSCIENCE	NONSTARTERS	NONTRANSFERABLE
NONPLUSSES	NONRECOVERABLE	NONSCIENCES	NONSTATIONARY	NONTRANSITIVE
NONPLUSSING	NONRECURRENT	NONSCIENTIFIC	NONSTATISTICAL	NONTREATMENT .
NONPOISONOUS	NONRECURRING	NONSCIENTIST	NONSTATIVE	NONTREATMENTS
NONPOLARISABLE	NONRECYCLABLE	NONSCIENTISTS	NONSTATIVES	NONTRIVIAL
NONPOLARIZABLE	NONRECYCLABLES	NONSEASONAL	NONSTATUTORY	NONTROPICAL
NONPOLITICAL	NONREDUCING	NONSECRETOR	NONSTELLAR	NONTURBULENT
NONPOLITICALLY	NONREDUNDANT	NONSECRETORS	NONSTEROID	NONTYPICAL
NONPOLITICIAN	NONREFILLABLE	NONSECRETORY	NONSTEROIDAL	NONUNANIMOUS
NONPOLITICIANS	NONREFLECTING	NONSECRETS	NONSTEROIDS	NONUNIFORM
NONPOLLUTING	NONREFLECTIVE	NONSECTARIAN	NONSTORIES	NONUNIFORMITIES
NONPOPULAR	NONREFLEXIVE	NONSEDIMENTABLE	NONSTRATEGIC	NONUNIFORMITY
NONPORTABLE	NONREFUNDABLE	NONSEGREGATED	NONSTRIATED	NONUNIONISED
NONPOSSESSION	NONREGIMENTAL	NONSEGREGATION	NONSTRIKING	NONUNIONISM
NONPOSSESSIONS	NONREGULATED	NONSEGREGATIONS	NONSTRUCTURAL	NONUNIONISMS
NONPRACTICAL	NONREGULATION	NONSELECTED	NONSTRUCTURED	NONUNIONIST
NONPRACTICING	NONREIGNING	NONSELECTIVE	NONSTUDENT	NONUNIONISTS
NONPRACTISING	NONRELATIVE	NONSENSATIONAL	NONSTUDENTS '	NONUNIONIZED
NONPREGNANT	NONRELATIVES	NONSENSICAL	NONSUBJECT	NONUNIQUENESS
NONPREHENSILE	NONRELATIVISTIC	NONSENSICALITY	NONSUBJECTIVE	NONUNIQUENESSES
NONPRESCRIPTION	NONRELEVANT	NONSENSICALLY	NONSUBJECTS	NONUNIVERSAL
NONPRINTING	NONRELIGIOUS	NONSENSICALNESS	NONSUBSIDISED	NONUNIVERSITY
NONPROBLEM	NONRENEWABLE	NONSENSITIVE	NONSUBSIDIZED	NONUTILITARIAN
NONPROBLEMS	NONRENEWAL	NONSENSUOUS	NONSUCCESS	NONUTILITIES
NONPRODUCING	NONRENEWALS	NONSENTENCE	NONSUCCESSES	NONUTILITY
NONPRODUCTIVE	NONREPAYABLE	NONSENTENCES	NONSUITING	NONUTOPIAN
NONPRODUCTIVITY	NONREPRODUCTIVE	NONSEPTATE	NONSUPERVISORY	NONVALIDITIES
NONPROFESSIONAL	NONRESIDENCE	NONSEQUENTIAL	NONSUPPORT	NONVALIDITY
NONPROFESSORIAL	NONRESIDENCES	NONSERIALS	NONSUPPORTS	NONVANISHING
NONPROFITS	NONRESIDENCIES	NONSERIOUS	NONSURGICAL	NONVASCULAR
NONPROGRAM	NONRESIDENCY	NONSHRINKABLE	NONSWIMMER	NONVECTORS
NONPROGRAMMER	NONRESIDENT	NONSIGNERS	NONSWIMMERS	NONVEGETARIAN
NONPROGRAMMERS	NONRESIDENTIAL	NONSIGNIFICANT	NONSYLLABIC	NONVEGETARIANS
NONPROGRESSIVE	NONRESIDENTS	NONSIGNIFICANTS	NONSYLLABICS	NONVENEREAL
NONPROPRIETARY	NONRESISTANCE	NONSIMULTANEOUS	NONSYMBOLIC	NONVENOMOUS
NONPROSSED	NONRESISTANCES	NONSINKABLE	NONSYMMETRIC	NONVERBALLY
NONPROSSES	NONRESISTANT	NONSINUSOIDAL	NONSYMMETRICAL	NONVETERAN
NONPROSSING .	NONRESISTANTS	NONSKATERS	NONSYNCHRONOUS	NONVETERANS
NONPROTEIN	NONRESONANT	NONSKELETAL	NONSYSTEMATIC	NONVIEWERS
NONPSYCHIATRIC	NONRESPONDENT	NONSKILLED	NONSYSTEMIC	NONVINTAGE
NONPSYCHIATRIST	NONRESPONDENTS	NONSMOKERS	NONSYSTEMS .	NONVINTAGES
NONPSYCHOTIC	NONRESPONDER	NONSMOKING	NONTACTICAL	NONVIOLENCE
NONPUNITIVE	NONRESPONDERS	NONSOCIALIST	NONTALKERS	NONVIOLENCES
NONPURPOSIVE	NONRESPONSE	NONSOCIALISTS	NONTAXABLE	NONVIOLENT
NONQUANTIFIABLE	NONRESPONSES	NONSOLUTION	NONTEACHING	NONVIOLENTLY
NONQUANTITATIVE	NONRESPONSIVE	NONSOLUTIONS	NONTECHNICAL	NONVIRGINS
NONRACIALLY	NONRESTRICTED	NONSOLVENT	NONTEMPORAL	NONVISCOUS
NONRACISMS	NONRESTRICTIVE	NONSPATIAL	NONTENURED	NONVOCATIONAL
NONRADIOACTIVE	NONRETRACTILE	NONSPEAKER	NONTERMINAL	NONVOLATILE
NONRAILROAD	NONRETROACTIVE	NONSPEAKERS	NONTERMINALS	NONVOLCANIC
NONRANDOMNESS	NONRETURNABLE	NONSPEAKING	NONTERMINATING	NONVOLUNTARY
NONRANDOMNESSES	NONRETURNABLES	NONSPECIALIST	NONTEXTUAL	NONWINNING
NONRATIONAL	NONREUSABLE	NONSPECIALISTS	NONTHEATRICAL	NONWORKERS
NONREACTIVE	NONREVERSIBLE	NONSPECIFIC	NONTHEISMS	NONWORKING
NONREACTOR	NONRHOTICITIES	NONSPECIFICALLY	NONTHEISTIC	NONWRITERS
NONREACTORS	NONRHOTICITY	NONSPECIFICITY	NONTHEISTS	NONYELLOWING
NONREADERS	NONRIOTERS	NONSPECTACULAR	NONTHEOLOGICAL	NOODLEDOMS
NONREADING	NONRIOTING	NONSPECTRAL	NONTHEORETICAL	NOOGENESES
NONREADINGS	NONROTATING	NONSPECULAR	NONTHERAPEUTIC	NOOGENESIS
NONREALISTIC	NONROUTINE	NONSPECULATIVE	NONTHERMAL	NOOMETRIES

NOOSPHERES
NOOTROPICS
NORADRENALIN
NORADRENALINE
NORADRENALINES
NORADRENALINS
NORADRENERGIC
NORDICITIES
NOREPINEPHRINE
NOREPINEPHRINES
NORETHINDRONE
NORETHINDRONES
NORETHISTERONE
NORETHISTERONES
NORMALCIES
NORMALISABLE
NORMALISATION
NORMALISATIONS
NORMALISED
NORMALISER
NORMALISERS
NORMALISES
NORMALISING
NORMALITIES
NORMALIZABLE
NORMALIZATION
NORMALIZATIONS
NORMALIZED
NORMALIZER
NORMALIZERS
NORMALIZES
NORMALIZING
NORMATIVELY
NORMATIVENESS
NORMATIVENESSES
NORMOGLYCAEMIA
NORMOGLYCAEMIAS
NORMOGLYCAEMIC
NORMOGLYCEMIA
NORMOGLYCEMIAS
NORMOGLYCEMIC
NORMOTENSION
NORMOTENSIONS
NORMOTENSIVE
NORMOTENSIVES
NORMOTHERMIA
NORMOTHERMIAS
NORMOTHERMIC
NOROVIRUSES
NORSELLERS
NORSELLING
NORTHBOUND
NORTHCOUNTRYMAN
NORTHCOUNTRYMEN
NORTHEASTER
NORTHEASTERLIES
NORTHEASTERLY
NORTHEASTERN
NORTHEASTERS
NORTHEASTS
NORTHEASTWARD
NORTHEASTWARDLY
NORTHEASTWARDS
NORTHERING
NORTHERLIES
NORTHERLINESS
NORTHERLINESSES

NORTHERMOST
NORTHERNER
NORTHERNERS
NORTHERNISE
NORTHERNISED
NORTHERNISES
NORTHERNISING
NORTHERNISM
NORTHERNISMS
NORTHERNIZE
NORTHERNIZED
NORTHERNIZES
NORTHERNIZING
NORTHERNMOST
NORTHLANDS
NORTHWARDLY
NORTHWARDS
NORTHWESTER
NORTHWESTERLIES
NORTHWESTERLY
NORTHWESTERN
NORTHWESTERS
NORTHWESTS
NORTHWESTWARD
NORTHWESTWARDLY
NORTHWESTWARDS
NORTRIPTYLINE
NORTRIPTYLINES
NOSEBANDED
NOSEBLEEDING
NOSEBLEEDINGS
NOSEBLEEDS
NOSEDIVING
NOSEGUARDS
NOSEPIECES
NOSEWHEELS
NOSINESSES
NOSOCOMIAL
NOSOGRAPHER
NOSOGRAPHERS
NOSOGRAPHIC
NOSOGRAPHIES
NOSOGRAPHY
NOSOLOGICAL
NOSOLOGICALLY
NOSOLOGIES
NOSOLOGIST
NOSOLOGISTS
NOSOPHOBIA
NOSOPHOBIAS
NOSTALGIAS
NOSTALGICALLY
NOSTALGICS
NOSTALGIST
NOSTALGISTS
NOSTOLOGIC
NOSTOLOGICAL
NOSTOLOGIES
NOSTOMANIA
NOSTOMANIAS
NOSTOPATHIES
NOSTOPATHY
NOSTRADAMIC
NOTABILITIES
NOTABILITY
NOTABLENESS
NOTABLENESSES

NOTAPHILIC
NOTAPHILIES
NOTAPHILISM
NOTAPHILISMS
NOTAPHILIST
NOTAPHILISTS
NOTARIALLY
NOTARISATION
NOTARISATIONS
NOTARISING
NOTARIZATION
NOTARIZATIONS
NOTARIZING
NOTARYSHIP
NOTARYSHIPS
NOTATIONAL
NOTCHBACKS
NOTCHELING
NOTCHELLED
NOTCHELLING
NOTEBANDIS
NOTEDNESSES
NOTEPAPERS
NOTEWORTHIER
NOTEWORTHIEST
NOTEWORTHILY
NOTEWORTHINESS
NOTEWORTHY
NOTHINGARIAN
NOTHINGARIANISM
NOTHINGARIANS
NOTHINGISM
NOTHINGISMS
NOTHINGNESS
NOTHINGNESSES
NOTICEABILITIES
NOTICEABILITY
NOTICEABLE
NOTICEABLY
NOTICEBOARD
NOTICEBOARDS
NOTIFIABLE
NOTIFICATION
NOTIFICATIONS
NOTIONALIST
NOTIONALISTS
NOTIONALITIES
NOTIONALITY
NOTIONALLY
NOTIONISTS
NOTOCHORDAL
NOTOCHORDS
NOTODONTID
NOTODONTIDS
NOTONECTAL
NOTORIETIES
NOTORIOUSLY
NOTORIOUSNESS
NOTORIOUSNESSES
NOTORNISES
NOTOTHERIUM
NOTOTHERIUMS
NOTOUNGULATE
NOTOUNGULATES
NOTUNGULATE
NOTUNGULATES
NOTWITHSTANDING

NOTWORKING
NOTWORKINGS
NOUGATINES
NOUMENALISM
NOUMENALISMS
NOUMENALIST
NOUMENALISTS
NOUMENALITIES
NOUMENALITY
NOUMENALLY
NOURISHABLE
NOURISHERS
NOURISHING
NOURISHINGLY
NOURISHMENT
NOURISHMENTS
NOURITURES
NOURRITURE
NOURRITURES
NOUSELLING
NOVACULITE
NOVACULITES
NOVELETTES
NOVELETTISH
NOVELETTIST
NOVELETTISTS
NOVELISATION
NOVELISATIONS
NOVELISERS
NOVELISING
NOVELISTIC
NOVELISTICALLY
NOVELIZATION
NOVELIZATIONS
NOVELIZERS
NOVELIZING
NOVEMDECILLION
NOVEMDECILLIONS
NOVENARIES
NOVICEHOOD
NOVICEHOODS
NOVICESHIP
NOVICESHIPS
NOVICIATES
NOVITIATES
NOVOBIOCIN
NOVOBIOCINS
NOVOCAINES
NOVOCENTENARIES
NOVOCENTENARY
NOVODAMUSES
NOWCASTING
NOWCASTINGS
NOXIOUSNESS
NOXIOUSNESSES
NUBBINESSES
NUBIFEROUS
NUBIGENOUS
NUBILITIES
NUCIFEROUS
NUCIVOROUS
NUCLEARISATION
NUCLEARISATIONS
NUCLEARISE
NUCLEARISED
NUCLEARISES
NUCLEARISING

NUCLEARIZATION
NUCLEARIZATIONS
NUCLEARIZE
NUCLEARIZED
NUCLEARIZES
NUCLEARIZING
NUCLEATING
NUCLEATION
NUCLEATIONS
NUCLEATORS
NUCLEOCAPSID
NUCLEOCAPSIDS
NUCLEOLATE
NUCLEOLATED
NUCLEONICALLY
NUCLEONICS
NUCLEOPHILE
NUCLEOPHILES
NUCLEOPHILIC
NUCLEOPHILICITY
NUCLEOPLASM
NUCLEOPLASMATIC
NUCLEOPLASMIC
NUCLEOPLASMS
NUCLEOPROTEIN
NUCLEOPROTEINS
NUCLEOSIDE
NUCLEOSIDES
NUCLEOSOMAL
NUCLEOSOME
NUCLEOSOMES
NUCLEOSYNTHESES
NUCLEOSYNTHESIS
NUCLEOSYNTHETIC
NUCLEOTIDASE
NUCLEOTIDASES
NUCLEOTIDE
NUCLEOTIDES
NUDENESSES
NUDIBRANCH
NUDIBRANCHIATE
NUDIBRANCHIATES
NUDIBRANCHS
NUDICAUDATE
NUDICAULOUS
NUGATORINESS
NUGATORINESSES
NUGGETIEST
NUGGETTING
NUISANCERS
NULLIFICATION
NULLIFICATIONS
NULLIFIDIAN
NULLIFIDIANS
NULLIFIERS
NULLIFYING
NULLIPARAE
NULLIPARAS
NULLIPARITIES
NULLIPARITY
NULLIPAROUS
NULLIPORES
NULLNESSES
NUMBERABLE
NUMBERINGS
NUMBERLESS
NUMBERLESSLY

NUMBERLESSNESS	NUMINOUSES	NUNNISHNESS	NUTRACEUTICAL	NYCTINASTIES
NUMBERPLATE	NUMINOUSNESS	NUNNISHNESSES	NUTRACEUTICALS	NYCTINASTY
NUMBERPLATES	NUMINOUSNESSES	NUPTIALITIES	NUTRIGENETICS	NYCTITROPIC
NUMBFISHES	NUMTSMATIC	NUPTIALITY	NUTRIGENOMICS	NYCTITROPISM
NUMBNESSES	NUMISMATICALLY	NURSEHOUND	NUTRIMENTAL	NYCTITROPISMS
NUMBNUTSES	NUMISMATICS	NURSEHOUNDS	NUTRIMENTS	NYCTOPHOBIA
NUMBSKULLED	NUMISMATIST	NURSELINGS	NUTRITIONAL	NYCTOPHOBIAS
NUMBSKULLS	NUMISMATISTS	NURSEMAIDED	NUTRITIONALLY	NYCTOPHOBIC
NUMERABILITIES	NUMISMATOLOGIES	NURSEMAIDING	NUTRITIONARY	NYMPHAEACEOUS
NUMERABILITY	NUMISMATOLOGIST	NURSEMAIDS	NUTRITIONIST	NYMPHAEUMS
NUMERACIES	NUMISMATOLOGY	NURSERYMAID	NUTRITIONISTS	NYMPHALIDS
NUMERAIRES	NUMMULATED	NURSERYMAIDS	NUTRITIONS	NYMPHETTES
NUMERATING	NUMMULATION	NURSERYMAN	NUTRITIOUS	NYMPHLIEST
NUMERATION	NUMMULATIONS	NURSERYMEN	NUTRITIOUSLY	NYMPHOLEPSIES
NUMERATIONS	NUMMULINES	NURTURABLE	NUTRITIOUSNESS	NYMPHOLEPSY
NUMERATIVE	NUMMULITES	NURTURANCE	NUTRITIVELY	NYMPHOLEPT
NUMERATORS	NUMMULITIC	NURTURANCES	NUTRITIVES	NYMPHOLEPTIC
NUMERICALLY	NUMSKULLED	NUTATIONAL	NUTTINESSES	NYMPHOLEPTS
NUMEROLOGICAL	NUNCIATURE	NUTBUTTERS	NYCHTHEMERAL	NYMPHOMANIA
NUMEROLOGIES	NUNCIATURES	NUTCRACKER	NYCHTHEMERON	NYMPHOMANIAC
NUMEROLOGIST	NUNCUPATED	NUTCRACKERS	NYCHTHEMERONS	NYMPHOMANIACAL
NUMEROLOGISTS	NUNCUPATES	NUTGRASSES	NYCTAGINACEOUS	NYMPHOMANIACS
NUMEROLOGY	NUNCUPATING	NUTHATCHES	NYCTALOPES	NYMPHOMANIAS
NUMEROSITIES	NUNCUPATION	NUTJOBBERS	NYCTALOPIA	NYSTAGMOID
NUMEROSITY	NUNCUPATIONS	NUTMEGGIER	NYCTALOPIAS	NYSTAGMUSES
NUMEROUSLY	NUNCUPATIVE	NUTMEGGIEST	NYCTALOPIC	
NUMEROUSNESS	NUNCUPATORY	NUTMEGGING	NYCTANTHOUS	
NUMEROUSNESSES	NUNNATIONS	NUTPECKERS	NYCTINASTIC	

n

O

OAFISHNESS
OAFISHNESSES
OAKENSHAWS
OAKINESSES
OARSMANSHIP
OARSMANSHIPS
OASTHOUSES
OBBLIGATOS
OBCOMPRESSED
OBDURACIES
OBDURATELY
OBDURATENESS
OBDURATENESSES
OBDURATING
OBDURATION
OBDURATIONS
OBEDIENCES
OBEDIENTIAL
OBEDIENTIARIES
OBEDIENTIARY
OBEDIENTLY
OBEISANCES
OBEISANTLY
OBELISCOID
OBELISKOID
OBESENESSES
OBESOGENIC
OBFUSCATED
OBFUSCATES
OBFUSCATING
OBFUSCATION
OBFUSCATIONS
OBFUSCATORY
OBITUARIES
OBITUARIST
OBITUARISTS
OBJECTIFICATION
OBJECTIFIED
OBJECTIFIES
OBJECTIFYING
OBJECTIONABLE
OBJECTIONABLY
OBJECTIONS
OBJECTIVAL
OBJECTIVATE
OBJECTIVATED
OBJECTIVATES
OBJECTIVATING
OBJECTIVATION
OBJECTIVATIONS
OBJECTIVELY
OBJECTIVENESS
OBJECTIVENESSES
OBJECTIVES

OBJECTIVISE
OBJECTIVISED
OBJECTIVISES
OBJECTIVISING
OBJECTIVISM
OBJECTIVISMS
OBJECTIVIST
OBJECTIVISTIC
OBJECTIVISTS
OBJECTIVITIES
OBJECTIVITY
OBJECTIVIZE
OBJECTIVIZED
OBJECTIVIZES
OBJECTIVIZING
OBJECTLESS
OBJECTLESSNESS
OBJURATION
OBJURATIONS
OBJURGATED
OBJURGATES
OBJURGATING
OBJURGATION
OBJURGATIONS
OBJURGATIVE
OBJURGATOR
OBJURGATORS
OBJURGATORY
OBLANCEOLATE
OBLATENESS
OBLATENESSES
OBLATIONAL
OBLIGATELY
OBLIGATING
OBLIGATION
OBLIGATIONAL
OBLIGATIONS
OBLIGATIVE
OBLIGATORILY
OBLIGATORINESS
OBLIGATORS
OBLIGATORY
OBLIGEMENT
OBLIGEMENTS
OBLIGINGLY
OBLIGINGNESS
OBLIGINGNESSES
OBLIQUATION
OBLIQUATIONS
OBLIQUENESS
OBLIQUENESSES
OBLIQUITIES
OBLIQUITOUS
OBLITERATE

OBLITERATED
OBLITERATES
OBLITERATING
OBLITERATION
OBLITERATIONS
OBLITERATIVE
OBLITERATOR
OBLITERATORS
OBLIVIOUSLY
OBLIVIOUSNESS
OBLIVIOUSNESSES
OBLIVISCENCE
OBLIVISCENCES
OBMUTESCENCE
OBMUTESCENCES
OBMUTESCENT
OBNOXIOUSLY
OBNOXIOUSNESS
OBNOXIOUSNESSES
OBNUBILATE
OBNUBILATED
OBNUBILATES
OBNUBILATING
OBNUBILATION
OBNUBILATIONS
OBREPTIONS
OBREPTITIOUS
OBSCENENESS
OBSCENENESSES
OBSCENITIES
OBSCURANTIC
OBSCURANTISM
OBSCURANTISMS
OBSCURANTIST
OBSCURANTISTS
OBSCURANTS
OBSCURATION
OBSCURATIONS
OBSCUREMENT
OBSCUREMENTS
OBSCURENESS
OBSCURENESSES
OBSCURITIES
OBSECRATED
OBSECRATES
OBSECRATING
OBSECRATION
OBSECRATIONS
OBSEQUIOUS
OBSEQUIOUSLY
OBSEQUIOUSNESS
OBSERVABILITIES
OBSERVABILITY
OBSERVABLE

OBSERVABLENESS
OBSERVABLES
OBSERVABLY
OBSERVANCE
OBSERVANCES
OBSERVANCIES
OBSERVANCY
OBSERVANTLY
OBSERVANTS
OBSERVATION
OBSERVATIONAL
OBSERVATIONALLY
OBSERVATIONS
OBSERVATIVE
OBSERVATOR
OBSERVATORIES
OBSERVATORS
OBSERVATORY
OBSERVINGLY
OBSESSIONAL
OBSESSIONALLY
OBSESSIONIST
OBSESSIONISTS
OBSESSIONS
OBSESSIVELY
OBSESSIVENESS
OBSESSIVENESSES
OBSESSIVES
OBSIDIONAL
OBSIDIONARY
OBSIGNATED
OBSIGNATES
OBSIGNATING
OBSIGNATION
OBSIGNATIONS
OBSIGNATORY
OBSOLESCED
OBSOLESCENCE
OBSOLESCENCES
OBSOLESCENT
OBSOLESCENTLY
OBSOLESCES
OBSOLESCING
OBSOLETELY
OBSOLETENESS
OBSOLETENESSES
OBSOLETING
OBSOLETION
OBSOLETIONS
OBSOLETISM
OBSOLETISMS
OBSTETRICAL
OBSTETRICALLY
OBSTETRICIAN

OBSTETRICIANS
OBSTETRICS
OBSTINACIES
OBSTINATELY
OBSTINATENESS
OBSTINATENESSES
OBSTIPATION
OBSTIPATIONS
OBSTREPERATE
OBSTREPERATED
OBSTREPERATES
OBSTREPERATING
OBSTREPEROUS
OBSTREPEROUSLY
OBSTRICTION
OBSTRICTIONS
OBSTROPALOUS
OBSTROPULOUS
OBSTRUCTED
OBSTRUCTER
OBSTRUCTERS
OBSTRUCTING
OBSTRUCTINGLY
OBSTRUCTION
OBSTRUCTIONAL
OBSTRUCTIONALLY
OBSTRUCTIONISM
OBSTRUCTIONISMS
OBSTRUCTIONIST
OBSTRUCTIONISTS
OBSTRUCTIONS
OBSTRUCTIVE
OBSTRUCTIVELY
OBSTRUCTIVENESS
OBSTRUCTIVES
OBSTRUCTOR
OBSTRUCTORS
OBSTRUENTS
OBTAINABILITIES
OBTAINABILITY
OBTAINABLE
OBTAINMENT
OBTAINMENTS
OBTEMPERATE
OBTEMPERATED
OBTEMPERATES
OBTEMPERATING
OBTEMPERED
OBTEMPERING
OBTENTIONS
OBTESTATION
OBTESTATIONS
OBTRUDINGS
OBTRUNCATE

OBTRUNCATED
OBTRUNCATES
OBTRUNCATING
OBTRUSIONS
OBTRUSIVELY
OBTRUSIVENESS
OBTRUSIVENESSES
OBTUNDENTS
OBTUNDITIES
OBTURATING
OBTURATION
OBTURATIONS
OBTURATORS
OBTUSENESS
OBTUSENESSES
OBTUSITIES
OBUMBRATED
OBUMBRATES
OBUMBRATING
OBUMBRATION
OBUMBRATIONS
OBVENTIONS
OBVERSIONS
OBVIATIONS
OBVIOUSNESS
OBVIOUSNESSES
OBVOLUTION
OBVOLUTIONS
OBVOLUTIVE
OCCASIONAL
OCCASIONALISM
OCCASIONALISMS
OCCASIONALIST
OCCASIONALISTS
OCCASIONALITIES
OCCASIONALITY
OCCASIONALLY
OCCASIONED
OCCASIONER
OCCASIONERS
OCCASIONING
OCCIDENTAL
OCCIDENTALISE
OCCIDENTALISED
OCCIDENTALISES
OCCIDENTALISING
OCCIDENTALISM
OCCIDENTALISMS
OCCIDENTALIST
OCCIDENTALISTS
OCCIDENTALIZE
OCCIDENTALIZED
OCCIDENTALIZES
OCCIDENTALIZING
OCCIDENTALLY
OCCIDENTALS
OCCIPITALLY
OCCIPITALS
OCCLUDENTS
OCCLUSIONS
OCCLUSIVENESS
OCCLUSIVENESSES
OCCLUSIVES
OCCULTATION
OCCULTATIONS
OCCULTISMS
OCCULTISTS

OCCULTNESS
OCCULTNESSES
OCCUPANCES
OCCUPANCIES
OCCUPATING
OCCUPATION
OCCUPATIONAL
OCCUPATIONALLY
OCCUPATIONS
OCCUPATIVE
OCCURRENCE
OCCURRENCES
OCCURRENTS
OCEANARIUM
OCEANARIUMS
OCEANFRONT
OCEANFRONTS
OCEANGOING
OCEANOGRAPHER
OCEANOGRAPHERS
OCEANOGRAPHIC
OCEANOGRAPHICAL
OCEANOGRAPHIES
OCEANOGRAPHY
OCEANOLOGICAL
OCEANOLOGIES
OCEANOLOGIST
OCEANOLOGISTS
OCEANOLOGY
OCELLATION
OCELLATIONS
OCHLOCRACIES
OCHLOCRACY
OCHLOCRATIC
OCHLOCRATICAL
OCHLOCRATICALLY
OCHLOCRATS
OCHLOPHOBIA
OCHLOPHOBIAC
OCHLOPHOBIACS
OCHLOPHOBIAS
OCHLOPHOBIC
OCHLOPHOBICS
OCHRACEOUS
OCHROLEUCOUS
OCTACHORDAL
OCTACHORDS
OCTAGONALLY
OCTAHEDRAL
OCTAHEDRALLY
OCTAHEDRITE
OCTAHEDRITES
OCTAHEDRON
OCTAHEDRONS
OCTAMEROUS
OCTAMETERS
OCTANDRIAN
OCTANDROUS
OCTANEDIOIC
OCTANGULAR
OCTAPEPTIDE
OCTAPEPTIDES
OCTAPLOIDIES
OCTAPLOIDS
OCTAPLOIDY
OCTAPODIES
OCTARCHIES

OCTASTICHON
OCTASTICHONS
OCTASTICHOUS
OCTASTICHS
OCTASTROPHIC
OCTASTYLES
OCTAVALENT
OCTENNIALLY
OCTILLIONS
OCTILLIONTH
OCTILLIONTHS
OCTINGENARIES
OCTINGENARY
OCTINGENTENARY
OCTOCENTENARIES
OCTOCENTENARY
OCTODECILLION
OCTODECILLIONS
OCTODECIMO
OCTODECIMOS
OCTOGENARIAN
OCTOGENARIANS
OCTOGENARIES
OCTOGENARY
OCTOGYNOUS
OCTOHEDRON
OCTOHEDRONS
OCTONARIAN
OCTONARIANS
OCTONARIES
OCTONARIUS
OCTONOCULAR
OCTOPETALOUS
OCTOPLOIDS
OCTOPODANS
OCTOPODOUS
OCTOPUSHER
OCTOPUSHERS
OCTOPUSHES
OCTOSEPALOUS
OCTOSTICHOUS
OCTOSTYLES
OCTOSYLLABIC
OCTOSYLLABICS
OCTOSYLLABLE
OCTOSYLLABLES
OCTOTHORPS
OCTUPLICATE
OCTUPLICATES
OCULARISTS
OCULOMOTOR
ODALISQUES
ODDSMAKERS
ODIOUSNESS
ODIOUSNESSES
ODOMETRIES
ODONATISTS
ODONATOLOGIES
ODONATOLOGIST
ODONATOLOGISTS
ODONATOLOGY
ODONTALGIA
ODONTALGIAS
ODONTALGIC
ODONTALGIES
ODONTOBLAST
ODONTOBLASTIC

ODONTOBLASTS
ODONTOCETE
ODONTOCETES
ODONTOGENIC
ODONTOGENIES
ODONTOGENY
ODONTOGLOSSUM
ODONTOGLOSSUMS
ODONTOGRAPH
ODONTOGRAPHIES
ODONTOGRAPHS
ODONTOGRAPHY
ODONTOLITE
ODONTOLITES
ODONTOLOGIC
ODONTOLOGICAL
ODONTOLOGIES
ODONTOLOGIST
ODONTOLOGISTS
ODONTOLOGY
ODONTOMATA
ODONTOMATOUS
ODONTOPHOBIA
ODONTOPHOBIAS
ODONTOPHORAL
ODONTOPHORAN
ODONTOPHORANS
ODONTOPHORE
ODONTOPHORES
ODONTOPHOROUS
ODONTORHYNCHOUS
ODONTORNITHES
ODONTOSTOMATOUS
ODORIFEROUS
ODORIFEROUSLY
ODORIFEROUSNESS
ODORIMETRIES
ODORIMETRY
ODORIPHORE
ODORIPHORES
ODOROUSNESS
ODOROUSNESSES
OECOLOGICAL
OECOLOGICALLY
OECOLOGIES
OECOLOGIST
OECOLOGISTS
OECUMENICAL
OECUMENICALLY
OEDEMATOSE
OEDEMATOUS
OEDOMETERS
OENOLOGICAL
OENOLOGIES
OENOLOGIST
OENOLOGISTS
OENOMANCIES
OENOMANIAS
OENOMETERS
OENOPHILES
OENOPHILIES
OENOPHILIST
OENOPHILISTS
OENOTHERAS
OESOPHAGEAL
OESOPHAGITIS
OESOPHAGITISES

OESOPHAGOSCOPE
OESOPHAGOSCOPES
OESOPHAGOSCOPY
OESOPHAGUS
OESOPHAGUSES
OESTRADIOL
OESTRADIOLS
OESTROGENIC
OESTROGENICALLY
OESTROGENS
OFFENCEFUL
OFFENCELESS
OFFENDEDLY
OFFENDRESS
OFFENDRESSES
OFFENSELESS
OFFENSIVELY
OFFENSIVENESS
OFFENSIVENESSES
OFFENSIVES
OFFERTORIES
OFFHANDEDLY
OFFHANDEDNESS
OFFHANDEDNESSES
OFFICEHOLDER
OFFICEHOLDERS
OFFICERING
OFFICIALDOM
OFFICIALDOMS
OFFICIALESE
OFFICIALESES
OFFICIALISM
OFFICIALISMS
OFFICIALITIES
OFFICIALITY
OFFICIALLY
OFFICIALTIES
OFFICIALTY
OFFICIANTS
OFFICIARIES
OFFICIATED
OFFICIATES
OFFICIATING
OFFICIATION
OFFICIATIONS
OFFICIATOR
OFFICIATORS
OFFICINALLY
OFFICINALS
OFFICIOUSLY
OFFICIOUSNESS
OFFICIOUSNESSES
OFFISHNESS
OFFISHNESSES
OFFLOADING
OFFPRINTED
OFFPRINTING
OFFSADDLED
OFFSADDLES
OFFSADDLING
OFFSCOURING
OFFSCOURINGS
OFFSEASONS
OFFSETABLE
OFFSETTING
OFFSETTINGS
OFFSHORING

OFFSHORINGS
OFFSPRINGS
OFTENNESSES
OFTENTIMES
OGANESSONS
OILINESSES
OINOLOGIES
OLDFANGLED
OLEAGINOUS
OLEAGINOUSLY
OLEAGINOUSNESS
OLEANDOMYCIN
OLEANDOMYCINS
OLECRANONS
OLEIFEROUS
OLEOGRAPHIC
OLEOGRAPHIES
OLEOGRAPHS
OLEOGRAPHY
OLEOMARGARIN
OLEOMARGARINE
OLEOMARGARINES
OLEOMARGARINS
OLEOPHILIC
OLEORESINOUS
OLEORESINS
OLERACEOUS
OLFACTIBLE
OLFACTIONS
OLFACTOLOGIES
OLFACTOLOGIST
OLFACTOLOGISTS
OLFACTOLOGY
OLFACTOMETER
OLFACTOMETERS
OLFACTOMETRIES
OLFACTOMETRY
OLFACTORIES
OLFACTRONICS
OLIGAEMIAS
OLIGARCHAL
OLIGARCHIC
OLIGARCHICAL
OLIGARCHICALLY
OLIGARCHIES
OLIGOCHAETE
OLIGOCHAETES
OLIGOCHROME
OLIGOCHROMES
OLIGOCLASE
OLIGOCLASES
OLIGOCYTHAEMIA
OLIGOCYTHAEMIAS
OLIGODENDROCYTE
OLIGODENDROGLIA
OLIGOGENES
OLIGOMERIC
OLIGOMERISATION
OLIGOMERIZATION
OLIGOMEROUS
OLIGONUCLEOTIDE
OLIGOPEPTIDE
OLIGOPEPTIDES
OLIGOPHAGIES
OLIGOPHAGOUS
OLIGOPHAGY
OLIGOPOLIES

OLIGOPOLISTIC
OLIGOPSONIES
OLIGOPSONISTIC
OLIGOPSONY
OLIGOSACCHARIDE
OLIGOSPERMIA
OLIGOSPERMIAS
OLIGOTROPHIC
OLIGOTROPHIES
OLIGOTROPHY
OLIGURESES
OLIGURESIS
OLIGURETIC
OLINGUITOS
OLIVACEOUS
OLIVENITES
OLIVEWOODS
OLIVINITIC
OLOGOANING
OLOLIUQUIS
OMBROGENOUS
OMBROMETER
OMBROMETERS
OMBROPHILE
OMBROPHILES
OMBROPHILOUS
OMBROPHILS
OMBROPHOBE
OMBROPHOBES
OMBROPHOBOUS
OMBUDSMANSHIP
OMBUDSMANSHIPS
OMINOUSNESS
OMINOUSNESSES
OMISSIVENESS
OMISSIVENESSES
OMITTANCES
OMMATIDIAL
OMMATIDIUM
OMMATOPHORE
OMMATOPHORES
OMMATOPHOROUS
OMNIBENEVOLENCE
OMNIBENEVOLENT
OMNIBUSSES
OMNICOMPETENCE
OMNICOMPETENCES
OMNICOMPETENT
OMNIDIRECTIONAL
OMNIFARIOUS
OMNIFARIOUSLY
OMNIFARIOUSNESS
OMNIFEROUS
OMNIFICENCE
OMNIFICENCES
OMNIFICENT
OMNIFORMITIES
OMNIFORMITY
OMNIGENOUS
OMNIPARITIES
OMNIPARITY
OMNIPAROUS
OMNIPATIENT
OMNIPOTENCE
OMNIPOTENCES
OMNIPOTENCIES
OMNIPOTENCY

OMNIPOTENT
OMNIPOTENTLY
OMNIPOTENTS
OMNIPRESENCE
OMNIPRESENCES
OMNIPRESENT
OMNIRANGES
OMNISCIENCE
OMNISCIENCES
OMNISCIENT
OMNISCIENTLY
OMNISHAMBLES
OMNIVORIES
OMNIVOROUS
OMNIVOROUSLY
OMNIVOROUSNESS
OMOPHAGIAS
OMOPHAGIES
OMOPHAGOUS
OMOPHORION
OMOPLATOSCOPIES
OMOPLATOSCOPY
OMPHACITES
OMPHALOMANCIES
OMPHALOMANCY
OMPHALOSKEPSES
OMPHALOSKEPSIS
ONAGRACEOUS
ONBOARDING
ONBOARDINGS
ONCHOCERCIASES
ONCHOCERCIASIS
ONCOGENESES
ONCOGENESIS
ONCOGENETICIST
ONCOGENETICISTS
ONCOGENICITIES
ONCOGENICITY
ONCOGENOUS
ONCOLOGICAL
ONCOLOGIES
ONCOLOGIST
ONCOLOGISTS
ONCOLYTICS
ONCOMETERS
ONCORNAVIRUS
ONCORNAVIRUSES
ONCOTOMIES
ONCOVIRUSES
ONDOGRAPHS
ONEIRICALLY
ONEIROCRITIC
ONEIROCRITICAL
ONEIROCRITICISM
ONEIROCRITICS
ONEIRODYNIA
ONEIRODYNIAS
ONEIROLOGIES
ONEIROLOGY
ONEIROMANCER
ONEIROMANCERS
ONEIROMANCIES
ONEIROMANCY
ONEIROSCOPIES
ONEIROSCOPIST
ONEIROSCOPISTS
ONEIROSCOPY

ONEROUSNESS
ONEROUSNESSES
ONGOINGNESS
ONGOINGNESSES
ONIONSKINS
ONOCENTAUR
ONOCENTAURS
ONOMASIOLOGIES
ONOMASIOLOGY
ONOMASTICALLY
ONOMASTICIAN
ONOMASTICIANS
ONOMASTICON
ONOMASTICONS
ONOMASTICS
ONOMATOLOGIES
ONOMATOLOGIST
ONOMATOLOGISTS
ONOMATOLOGY
ONOMATOPOEIA
ONOMATOPOEIAS
ONOMATOPOEIC
ONOMATOPOESES
ONOMATOPOESIS
ONOMATOPOETIC
ONOMATOPOIESES
ONOMATOPOIESIS
ONSETTINGS
ONSHORINGS
ONSLAUGHTS
ONTOGENESES
ONTOGENESIS
ONTOGENETIC
ONTOGENETICALLY
ONTOGENICALLY
ONTOGENIES
ONTOLOGICAL
ONTOLOGICALLY
ONTOLOGIES
ONTOLOGIST
ONTOLOGISTS
ONYCHITISES
ONYCHOCRYPTOSES
ONYCHOCRYPTOSIS
ONYCHOMANCIES
ONYCHOMANCY
ONYCHOPHAGIES
ONYCHOPHAGIST
ONYCHOPHAGISTS
ONYCHOPHAGY
ONYCHOPHORAN
ONYCHOPHORANS
OOGAMOUSLY
OOJAMAFLIP
OOJAMAFLIPS
OOMPAHPAHS
OOPHORECTOMIES
OOPHORECTOMISE
OOPHORECTOMISED
OOPHORECTOMISES
OOPHORECTOMIZE
OOPHORECTOMIZED
OOPHORECTOMIZES
OOPHORECTOMY
OOPHORITIC
OOPHORITIS
OOPHORITISES

OOZINESSES
OPACIFIERS
OPACIFYING
OPALESCENCE
OPALESCENCES
OPALESCENT
OPALESCENTLY
OPALESCING
OPAQUENESS
OPAQUENESSES
OPEIDOSCOPE
OPEIDOSCOPES
OPENABILITIES
OPENABILITY
OPENHANDED
OPENHANDEDLY
OPENHANDEDNESS
OPENHEARTED
OPENHEARTEDLY
OPENHEARTEDNESS
OPENMOUTHED
OPENMOUTHEDLY
OPENMOUTHEDNESS
OPENNESSES
OPERABILITIES
OPERABILITY
OPERAGOERS
OPERAGOING
OPERAGOINGS
OPERATICALLY
OPERATIONAL
OPERATIONALISM
OPERATIONALISMS
OPERATIONALIST
OPERATIONALISTS
OPERATIONALLY
OPERATIONISM
OPERATIONISMS
OPERATIONIST
OPERATIONISTS
OPERATIONS
OPERATISED
OPERATISES
OPERATISING
OPERATIVELY
OPERATIVENESS
OPERATIVENESSES
OPERATIVES
OPERATIVITIES
OPERATIVITY
OPERATIZED
OPERATIZES
OPERATIZING
OPERATORLESS
OPERCULARS
OPERCULATE
OPERCULATED
OPERCULUMS
OPERETTIST
OPERETTISTS
OPEROSENESS
OPEROSENESSES
OPEROSITIES
OPHICALCITE
OPHICALCITES
OPHICLEIDE
OPHICLEIDES

OPHIDIARIA
OPHIDIARIUM
OPHIDTARIUMS
OPHIOLATER
OPHIOLATERS
OPHIOLATRIES
OPHIOLATROUS
OPHIOLATRY
OPHIOLITES
OPHIOLITIC
OPHIOLOGIC
OPHIOLOGICAL
OPHIOLOGIES
OPHIOLOGIST
OPHIOLOGISTS
OPHIOMORPH
OPHIOMORPHIC
OPHIOMORPHOUS
OPHIOMORPHS
OPHIOPHAGOUS
OPHIOPHILIST
OPHIOPHILISTS
OPHIUROIDS
OPHTHALMIA
OPHTHALMIAS
OPHTHALMIC
OPHTHALMIST
OPHTHALMISTS
OPHTHALMITIS
OPHTHALMITISES
OPHTHALMOLOGIC
OPHTHALMOLOGIES
OPHTHALMOLOGIST
OPHTHALMOLOGY
OPHTHALMOMETER
OPHTHALMOMETERS
OPHTHALMOMETRY
OPHTHALMOPHOBIA
OPHTHALMOPLEGIA
OPHTHALMOSCOPE
OPHTHALMOSCOPES
OPHTHALMOSCOPIC
OPHTHALMOSCOPY
OPINICUSES
OPINIONATE
OPINIONATED
OPINIONATEDLY
OPINIONATEDNESS
OPINIONATELY
OPINIONATES
OPINIONATING
OPINIONATIVE
OPINIONATIVELY
OPINIONATOR
OPINIONATORS
OPINIONIST
OPINIONISTS
OPISOMETER
OPISOMETERS
OPISTHOBRANCH
OPISTHOBRANCHS
OPISTHOCOELIAN
OPISTHOCOELOUS
OPISTHODOMOI
OPISTHODOMOS
OPISTHOGLOSSAL
OPISTHOGNATHISM

OPISTHOGNATHOUS
OPISTHOGRAPH
OPISTHOGRAPHIC
OPISTHOGRAPHIES
OPISTHOGRAPHS
OPISTHOGRAPHY
OPISTHOSOMA
OPISTHOSOMATA
OPISTHOTONIC
OPISTHOTONOS
OPISTHOTONOSES
OPOBALSAMS
OPODELDOCS
OPOPANAXES
OPOTHERAPIES
OPOTHERAPY
OPPIGNERATE
OPPIGNERATED
OPPIGNERATES
OPPIGNERATING
OPPIGNERATION
OPPIGNERATIONS
OPPIGNORATE
OPPIGNORATED
OPPIGNORATES
OPPIGNORATING
OPPIGNORATION
OPPIGNORATIONS
OPPILATING
OPPILATION
OPPILATIONS
OPPILATIVE
OPPONENCIES
OPPORTUNELY
OPPORTUNENESS
OPPORTUNENESSES
OPPORTUNISM
OPPORTUNISMS
OPPORTUNIST
OPPORTUNISTIC
OPPORTUNISTS
OPPORTUNITIES
OPPORTUNITY
OPPOSABILITIES
OPPOSABILITY
OPPOSELESS
OPPOSINGLY
OPPOSITELY
OPPOSITENESS
OPPOSITENESSES
OPPOSITION
OPPOSITIONAL
OPPOSITIONIST
OPPOSITIONISTS
OPPOSITIONLESS
OPPOSITIONS
OPPOSITIVE
OPPRESSING
OPPRESSINGLY
OPPRESSION
OPPRESSIONS
OPPRESSIVE
OPPRESSIVELY
OPPRESSIVENESS
OPPRESSORS
OPPROBRIOUS
OPPROBRIOUSLY

OPPROBRIOUSNESS
OPPROBRIUM
OPPROBRIUMS
OPPUGNANCIES
OPPUGNANCY
OPPUGNANTLY
OPPUGNANTS
OPSIMATHIES
OPSIOMETER
OPSIOMETERS
OPSOMANIAC
OPSOMANIACS
OPSOMANIAS
OPSONIFICATION
OPSONIFICATIONS
OPSONIFIED
OPSONIFIES
OPSONIFYING
OPSONISATION
OPSONISATIONS
OPSONISING
OPSONIZATION
OPSONIZATIONS
OPSONIZING
OPTATIVELY
OPTIMALISATION
OPTIMALISATIONS
OPTIMALISE
OPTIMALISED
OPTIMALISES
OPTIMALISING
OPTIMALITIES
OPTIMALITY
OPTIMALIZATION
OPTIMALIZATIONS
OPTIMALIZE
OPTIMALIZED
OPTIMALIZES
OPTIMALIZING
OPTIMISATION
OPTIMISATIONS
OPTIMISERS
OPTIMISING
OPTIMISTIC
OPTIMISTICAL
OPTIMISTICALLY
OPTIMIZATION
OPTIMIZATIONS
OPTIMIZERS
OPTIMIZING
OPTIONALITIES
OPTIONALITY
OPTIONALLY
OPTOACOUSTIC
OPTOELECTRONIC
OPTOELECTRONICS
OPTOKINETIC
OPTOLOGIES
OPTOLOGIST
OPTOLOGISTS
OPTOMETERS
OPTOMETRIC
OPTOMETRICAL
OPTOMETRIES
OPTOMETRIST
OPTOMETRISTS
OPTOPHONES

OPULENCIES
ORACULARITIES
ORACULARITY
ORACULARLY
ORACULARNESS
ORACULARNESSES
ORACULOUSLY
ORACULOUSNESS
ORACULOUSNESSES
ORANGEADES
ORANGERIES
ORANGEWOOD
ORANGEWOODS
ORANGUTANS
ORATORIANS
ORATORICAL
ORATORICALLY
ORATRESSES
ORBICULARES
ORBICULARIS
ORBICULARITIES
ORBICULARITY
ORBICULARLY
ORBICULATE
ORBICULATED
ORCHARDING
ORCHARDINGS
ORCHARDIST
ORCHARDISTS
ORCHARDMAN
ORCHARDMEN
ORCHESOGRAPHIES
ORCHESOGRAPHY
ORCHESTICS
ORCHESTRAL
ORCHESTRALIST
ORCHESTRALISTS
ORCHESTRALLY
ORCHESTRAS
ORCHESTRATE
ORCHESTRATED
ORCHESTRATER
ORCHESTRATERS
ORCHESTRATES
ORCHESTRATING
ORCHESTRATION
ORCHESTRATIONAL
ORCHESTRATIONS
ORCHESTRATOR
ORCHESTRATORS
ORCHESTRIC
ORCHESTRINA
ORCHESTRINAS
ORCHESTRION
ORCHESTRIONS
ORCHIDACEOUS
ORCHIDECTOMIES
ORCHIDECTOMY
ORCHIDEOUS
ORCHIDISTS
ORCHIDLIKE
ORCHIDOLOGIES
ORCHIDOLOGIST
ORCHIDOLOGISTS
ORCHIDOLOGY
ORCHIDOMANIA
ORCHIDOMANIAC

ORCHIDOMANIACS
ORCHIDOMANIAS
ORCHIECTOMIES
ORCHIECTOMY
ORCHITISES
ORDAINABLE
ORDAINMENT
ORDAINMENTS
ORDERLINESS
ORDERLINESSES
ORDINAIRES
ORDINANCES
ORDINARIER
ORDINARIES
ORDINARIEST
ORDINARILY
ORDINARINESS
ORDINARINESSES
ORDINATELY
ORDINATING
ORDINATION
ORDINATIONS
ORDONNANCE
ORDONNANCES
ORECCHIETTE
ORECCHIETTES
ORECCHIETTI
OREOGRAPHIC
OREOGRAPHICAL
OREOGRAPHICALLY
OREOGRAPHIES
OREOGRAPHY
OREOLOGICAL
OREOLOGIES
OREOLOGIST
OREOLOGISTS
OREPEARCHED
OREPEARCHES
OREPEARCHING
ORGANELLES
ORGANICALLY
ORGANICISM
ORGANICISMS
ORGANICIST
ORGANICISTIC
ORGANICISTS
ORGANICITIES
ORGANICITY
ORGANISABILITY
ORGANISABLE
ORGANISATION
ORGANISATIONAL
ORGANISATIONS
ORGANISERS
ORGANISING
ORGANISINGS
ORGANISMAL
ORGANISMALLY
ORGANISMIC
ORGANISMICALLY
ORGANISTRUM
ORGANISTRUMS
ORGANITIES
ORGANIZABILITY
ORGANIZABLE
ORGANIZATION
ORGANIZATIONAL

ORGANIZATIONS	ORIGINALITIES	ORNITHOSES	ORTHODROMIC	ORTHOPHOSPHATES
ORGANIZERS	ORIGINALITY	ORNITHOSIS	ORTHODROMICS	ORTHOPHOSPHORIC
ORGANIZING	ORIGINALLY	OROBANCHACEOUS	ORTHODROMIES	ORTHOPHYRE
ORGANIZINGS	ORIGINATED	OROGENESES	ORTHODROMY	ORTHOPHYRES
ORGANOCHLORINE	ORIGINATES	OROGENESIS	ORTHOEPICAL	ORTHOPHYRIC
ORGANOCHLORINES	ORIGINATING	OROGENETIC	ORTHOEPICALLY	ORTHOPINAKOID
ORGANOGENESES	ORIGINATION	OROGENETICALLY	ORTHOEPIES	ORTHOPINAKOIDS
ORGANOGENESIS	ORIGINATIONS	OROGENICALLY	ORTHOEPIST	ORTHOPNOEA
ORGANOGENETIC	ORIGINATIVE	OROGRAPHER	ORTHOEPISTS	ORTHOPNOEAS
ORGANOGENIES	ORIGINATIVELY	OROGRAPHERS	ORTHOGENESES	ORTHOPRAXES
ORGANOGENY	ORIGINATOR	OROGRAPHIC	ORTHOGENESIS	ORTHOPRAXIES
ORGANOGRAM	ORIGINATORS	OROGRAPHICAL	ORTHOGENETIC	ORTHOPRAXIS
ORGANOGRAMS	ORINASALLY	OROGRAPHICALLY	ORTHOGENIC	ORTHOPRAXY
ORGANOGRAPHIC	ORISMOLOGICAL	OROGRAPHIES	ORTHOGENICALLY	ORTHOPRISM
ORGANOGRAPHICAL	ORISMOLOGIES	OROLOGICAL	ORTHOGENICS	ORTHOPRISMS
ORGANOGRAPHIES	ORISMOLOGY	OROLOGICALLY	ORTHOGNATHIC	ORTHOPSYCHIATRY
ORGANOGRAPHIST	ORNAMENTAL	OROLOGISTS	ORTHOGNATHIES	ORTHOPTERA
ORGANOGRAPHISTS	ORNAMENTALLY	OROMAXILLARY	ORTHOGNATHISM	ORTHOPTERAN
ORGANOGRAPHY	ORNAMENTALS	OROPHARYNGEAL	ORTHOGNATHISMS	ORTHOPTERANS
ORGANOLEPTIC	ORNAMENTATION	OROPHARYNGES	ORTHOGNATHOUS	ORTHOPTERIST
ORGANOLOGICAL	ORNAMENTATIONS	OROPHARYNX	ORTHOGNATHY	ORTHOPTERISTS
ORGANOLOGIES	ORNAMENTED	OROPHARYNXES	ORTHOGONAL	ORTHOPTEROID
ORGANOLOGIST	ORNAMENTER	OROROTUNDITIES	ORTHOGONALISE	ORTHOPTEROIDS
ORGANOLOGISTS	ORNAMENTERS	OROROTUNDITY	ORTHOGONALISED	ORTHOPTEROLOGY
ORGANOLOGY	ORNAMENTING	OROTUNDITIES	ORTHOGONALISES	ORTHOPTERON
ORGANOMERCURIAL	ORNAMENTIST	OROTUNDITY	ORTHOGONALISING	ORTHOPTEROUS
ORGANOMETALLIC	ORNAMENTISTS	ORPHANAGES	ORTHOGONALITIES	ORTHOPTERS
ORGANOMETALLICS	ORNATENESS	ORPHANHOOD	ORTHOGONALITY	ORTHOPTICS
ORGANOPHOSPHATE	ORNATENESSES	ORPHANHOODS	ORTHOGONALIZE	ORTHOPTIST
ORGANOSOLS	ORNERINESS	ORPHANISMS	ORTHOGONALIZED	ORTHOPTISTS
ORGANOTHERAPIES	ORNERINESSES	ORPHARIONS	ORTHOGONALIZES	ORTHOPYROXENE
ORGANOTHERAPY	ORNITHICHNITE	ORPHEOREON	ORTHOGONALIZING	ORTHOPYROXENES
ORGANZINES	ORNITHICHNITES	ORPHEOREONS	ORTHOGONALLY	ORTHOREXIA
ORGASMICALLY	ORNITHINES	ORPHICALLY	ORTHOGRADE	ORTHOREXIAS
ORGASTICALLY	ORNITHISCHIAN	ORRISROOTS	ORTHOGRAPH	ORTHORHOMBIC
ORGIASTICALLY	ORNITHISCHIANS	ORTANIQUES	ORTHOGRAPHER	ORTHOSCOPE
ORICALCHES	ORNITHODELPHIAN	ORTHOBORATE	ORTHOGRAPHERS	ORTHOSCOPES
ORICHALCEOUS	ORNITHODELPHIC	ORTHOBORATES	ORTHOGRAPHIC	ORTHOSCOPIC
ORIENTALISE	ORNITHODELPHOUS	ORTHOBORIC	ORTHOGRAPHICAL	ORTHOSILICATE
ORIENTALISED	ORNITHOGALUM	ORTHOCAINE	ORTHOGRAPHIES	ORTHOSILICATES
ORIENTALISES	ORNITHOGALUMS	ORTHOCAINES	ORTHOGRAPHIST	ORTHOSILICIC
ORIENTALISING	ORNITHOLOGIC	ORTHOCENTER	ORTHOGRAPHISTS	ORTHOSTATIC
ORIENTALISM	ORNITHOLOGICAL	ORTHOCENTERS	ORTHOGRAPHS	ORTHOSTICHIES
ORIENTALISMS	ORNITHOLOGIES	ORTHOCENTRE	ORTHOGRAPHY	ORTHOSTICHOUS
ORIENTALIST	ORNITHOLOGIST	ORTHOCENTRES	ORTHOHYDROGEN	ORTHOSTICHY
ORIENTALISTS	ORNITHOLOGISTS	ORTHOCEPHALIC	ORTHOHYDROGENS	ORTHOTISTS
ORIENTALITIES	ORNITHOLOGY	ORTHOCEPHALIES	ORTHOMOLECULAR	ORTHOTONES
ORIENTALITY	ORNITHOMANCIES	ORTHOCEPHALOUS	ORTHOMORPHIC	ORTHOTONESES
ORIENTALIZE	ORNITHOMANCY	ORTHOCEPHALY	ORTHONORMAL	ORTHOTONESIS
ORIENTALIZED	ORNITHOMANTIC	ORTHOCHROMATIC	ORTHOPAEDIC	ORTHOTONIC
ORIENTALIZES	ORNITHOMORPH	ORTHOCHROMATISM	ORTHOPAEDICAL	ORTHOTOPIC
ORIENTALIZING	ORNITHOMORPHIC	ORTHOCLASE	ORTHOPAEDICALLY	ORTHOTROPIC
ORIENTALLY	ORNITHOMORPHS	ORTHOCLASES	ORTHOPAEDICS	ORTHOTROPIES
ORIENTATED	ORNITHOPHILIES	ORTHOCLASTIC	ORTHOPAEDIES	ORTHOTROPISM
ORIENTATES	ORNITHOPHILOUS	ORTHOCOUSINS	ORTHOPAEDIST	ORTHOTROPISMS
ORIENTATING	ORNITHOPHILY	ORTHODIAGONAL	ORTHOPAEDISTS	ORTHOTROPOUS
ORIENTATION	ORNITHOPHOBIA	ORTHODIAGONALS	ORTHOPAEDY	ORTHOTROPY
ORIENTATIONAL	ORNITHOPHOBIAS	ORTHODONTIA	ORTHOPEDIA	ORTHOTUNGSTIC
ORIENTATIONALLY	ORNITHOPOD	ORTHODONTIAS	ORTHOPEDIAS	ORTHOVANADIC
ORIENTATIONS	ORNITHOPODS	ORTHODONTIC	ORTHOPEDIC	ORYCTOLOGIES
ORIENTATOR	ORNITHOPTER	ORTHODONTICALLY	ORTHOPEDICAL	ORYCTOLOGY
ORIENTATORS	ORNITHOPTERS	ORTHODONTICS	ORTHOPEDICALLY	OSCILLATED
ORIENTEERED	ORNITHORHYNCHUS	ORTHODONTIST	ORTHOPEDICS	OSCILLATES
ORIENTEERING	ORNITHOSAUR	ORTHODONTISTS	ORTHOPEDIES	OSCILLATING
ORIENTEERINGS	ORNITHOSAURS	ORTHODOXES	ORTHOPEDIST	OSCILLATION
ORIENTEERS	ORNITHOSCOPIES	ORTHODOXIES	ORTHOPEDISTS	OSCILLATIONAL
ORIFLAMMES	ORNITHOSCOPY	ORTHODOXLY	ORTHOPHOSPHATE	OSCILLATIONS

o

OSCILLATIVE	OSTEOARTHRITIS	OSTRACTSABLE	OUTACHIEVED	OUTCALLING
OSCILLATOR	OSTEOARTHROSES	OSTRACISED	OUTACHIEVES	OUTCAPERED
OSCILLATORS	OSTEOARTHROSIS	OSTRACISER	OUTACHIEVING	OUTCAPERING
OSCILLATORY	OSTEOBLAST	OSTRACISERS	OUTARGUING	OUTCASTEING
OSCILLOGRAM	OSTEOBLASTIC	OSTRACISES	OUTBACKERS	OUTCASTING
OSCILLOGRAMS	OSTEOBLASTS	OSTRACISING	OUTBALANCE	OUTCATCHES
OSCILLOGRAPH	OSTEOCLASES	OSTRACISMS	OUTBALANCED	OUTCATCHING
OSCILLOGRAPHIC	OSTEOCLASIS	OSTRACIZABLE	OUTBALANCES	OUTCAVILED
OSCILLOGRAPHIES	OSTEOCLAST	OSTRACIZED	OUTBALANCING	OUTCAVILING
OSCILLOGRAPHS	OSTEOCLASTIC	OSTRACIZER	OUTBARGAIN	OUTCAVILLED
OSCILLOGRAPHY	OSTEOCLASTS	OSTRACIZERS	OUTBARGAINED	OUTCAVILLING
OSCILLOSCOPE	OSTEOCOLLA	OSTRACIZES	OUTBARGAINING	OUTCHARGED
OSCILLOSCOPES	OSTEOCOLLAS	OSTRACIZING	OUTBARGAINS	OUTCHARGES
OSCILLOSCOPIC	OSTEOCYTES	OSTRACODAN	OUTBARKING	OUTCHARGING
OSCITANCES	OSTEODERMAL	OSTRACODERM	OUTBARRING	OUTCHARMED
OSCITANCIES	OSTEODERMATOUS	OSTRACODERMS	OUTBAWLING	OUTCHARMING
OSCITANTLY	OSTEODERMIC	OSTRACODES	OUTBEAMING	OUTCHEATED
OSCITATING	OSTEODERMOUS	OSTRACODOUS	OUTBEGGING	OUTCHEATING
OSCITATION	OSTEODERMS	OSTREACEOUS	OUTBIDDERS	OUTCHIDDEN
OSCITATIONS	OSTEOFIBROSES	OSTREICULTURE	OUTBIDDING	OUTCHIDING
OSCULATING	OSTEOFIBROSIS	OSTREICULTURES	OUTBITCHED	OUTCLASSED
OSCULATION	OSTEOGENESES	OSTREICULTURIST	OUTBITCHES	OUTCLASSES
OSCULATIONS	OSTEOGENESIS	OSTREOPHAGE	OUTBITCHING	OUTCLASSING
OSCULATORIES	OSTEOGENETIC	OSTREOPHAGES	OUTBLAZING	OUTCLIMBED
OSCULATORY	OSTEOGENIC	OSTREOPHAGIES	OUTBLEATED	OUTCLIMBING
OSMETERIUM	OSTEOGENIES	OSTREOPHAGOUS	OUTBLEATING	OUTCOACHED
OSMIDROSES	OSTEOGENOUS	OSTREOPHAGY	OUTBLESSED	OUTCOACHES
OSMIDROSIS	OSTEOGRAPHIES	OSTRICHISM	OUTBLESSES	OUTCOACHING
OSMIRIDIUM	OSTEOGRAPHY	OSTRICHISMS	OUTBLESSING	OUTCOMPETE
OSMIRIDIUMS	OSTEOLOGICAL	OSTRICHLIKE	OUTBLOOMED	OUTCOMPETED
OSMOLALITIES	OSTEOLOGICALLY	OTHERGATES	OUTBLOOMING	OUTCOMPETES
OSMOLALITY	OSTEOLOGIES	OTHERGUESS	OUTBLUFFED	OUTCOMPETING
OSMOLARITIES	OSTEOLOGIST	OTHERNESSES	OUTBLUFFING	OUTCOOKING
OSMOLARITY	OSTEOLOGISTS	OTHERWHERE	OUTBLUSHED	OUTCOUNTED
OSMOMETERS	OSTEOMALACIA	OTHERWHILE	OUTBLUSHES	OUTCOUNTING
OSMOMETRIC	OSTEOMALACIAL	OTHERWHILES	OUTBLUSHING	OUTCRAFTIED
OSMOMETRICALLY	OSTEOMALACIAS	OTHERWORLD	OUTBLUSTER	OUTCRAFTIES
OSMOMETRIES	OSTEOMALACIC	OTHERWORLDISH	OUTBLUSTERED	OUTCRAFTYING
OSMOREGULATION	OSTEOMYELITIS	OTHERWORLDLIER	OUTBLUSTERING	OUTCRAWLED
OSMOREGULATIONS	OSTEOMYELITISES	OTHERWORLDLIEST	OUTBLUSTERS	OUTCRAWLING
OSMOREGULATORY	OSTEOPATHIC	OTHERWORLDLY	OUTBOASTED	OUTCROPPED
OSMOTICALLY	OSTEOPATHICALLY	OTHERWORLDS	OUTBOASTING	OUTCROPPING
OSMUNDINES	OSTEOPATHIES	OTIOSENESS	OUTBRAGGED	OUTCROPPINGS
OSSIFEROUS	OSTEOPATHIST	OTIOSENESSES	OUTBRAGGING	OUTCROSSED
OSSIFICATION	OSTEOPATHISTS	OTIOSITIES	OUTBRAVING	OUTCROSSES
OSSIFICATIONS	OSTEOPATHS	OTOLARYNGOLOGY	OUTBRAWLED	OUTCROSSING
OSSIFRAGAS	OSTEOPATHY	OTOLOGICAL	OUTBRAWLING	OUTCROSSINGS
OSSIFRAGES	OSTEOPETROSES	OTOLOGISTS	OUTBRAZENED	OUTCROWDED
OSSIVOROUS	OSTEOPETROSIS	OTOPLASTIES	OUTBRAZENING	OUTCROWDING
OSTEICHTHYAN	OSTEOPHYTE	OTORRHOEAS	OUTBRAZENS	OUTCROWING
OSTEICHTHYANS	OSTEOPHYTES	OTOSCLEROSES	OUTBREAKING	OUTCURSING
OSTEITIDES	OSTEOPHYTIC	OTOSCLEROSIS	OUTBREATHE	OUTDACIOUS
OSTEITISES	OSTEOPLASTIC	OTOSCOPIES	OUTBREATHED	OUTDANCING
OSTENSIBILITIES	OSTEOPLASTIES	OTOTOXICITIES	OUTBREATHES	OUTDATEDLY
OSTENSIBILITY	OSTEOPLASTY	OTOTOXICITY	OUTBREATHING	OUTDATEDNESS
OSTENSIBLE	OSTEOPOROSES	OTTERHOUND	OUTBREEDING	OUTDATEDNESSES
OSTENSIBLY	OSTEOPOROSIS	OTTERHOUNDS	OUTBREEDINGS	OUTDAZZLED
OSTENSIVELY	OSTEOPOROTIC	OTTRELITES	OUTBRIBING	OUTDAZZLES
OSTENSORIA	OSTEOSARCOMA	OUANANICHE	OUTBUILDING	OUTDAZZLING
OSTENSORIES	OSTEOSARCOMAS	OUANANICHES	OUTBUILDINGS	OUTDEBATED
OSTENSORIUM	OSTEOSARCOMATA	OUBLIETTES	OUTBULGING	OUTDEBATES
OSTENTATION	OSTEOSISES	OUGHTLINGS	OUTBULKING	OUTDEBATING
OSTENTATIONS	OSTEOTOMES	OUGHTNESSES	OUTBULLIED	OUTDELIVER
OSTENTATIOUS	OSTEOTOMIES	OUROBOROSES	OUTBULLIES	OUTDELIVERED
OSTENTATIOUSLY	OSTLERESSES	OUROLOGIES	OUTBULLYING	OUTDELIVERING
OSTEOARTHRITIC	OSTRACEANS	OUROSCOPIES	OUTBURNING	OUTDELIVERS
OSTEOARTHRITICS	OSTRACEOUS	OUTACHIEVE	OUTBURSTING	OUTDESIGNED

OUTDESIGNING
OUTDESIGNS
OUTDISTANCE
OUTDISTANCED
OUTDISTANCES
OUTDISTANCING
OUTDODGING
OUTDOORSIER
OUTDOORSIEST
OUTDOORSMAN
OUTDOORSMANSHIP
OUTDOORSMEN
OUTDRAGGED
OUTDRAGGING
OUTDRAWING
OUTDREAMED
OUTDREAMING
OUTDRESSED
OUTDRESSES
OUTDRESSING
OUTDRINKING
OUTDRIVING
OUTDROPPED
OUTDROPPING
OUTDUELING
OUTDUELLED
OUTDUELLING
OUTDWELLED
OUTDWELLING
OUTEARNING
OUTECHOING
OUTERCOATS
OUTERCOURSE
OUTERCOURSES
OUTERWEARS
OUTFABLING
OUTFANGTHIEF
OUTFANGTHIEVES
OUTFASTING
OUTFAWNING
OUTFEASTED
OUTFEASTING
OUTFEELING
OUTFENCING
OUTFIELDER
OUTFIELDERS
OUTFIGHTING
OUTFIGHTINGS
OUTFIGURED
OUTFIGURES
OUTFIGURING
OUTFINDING
OUTFISHING
OUTFITTERS
OUTFITTING
OUTFITTINGS
OUTFLANKED
OUTFLANKING
OUTFLASHED
OUTFLASHES
OUTFLASHING
OUTFLINGING
OUTFLOATED
OUTFLOATING
OUTFLOWING
OUTFLOWINGS
OUTFLUSHED

OUTFLUSHES
OUTFLUSHING
OUTFOOLING
OUTFOOTING
OUTFROWNED
OUTFROWNING
OUTFUMBLED
OUTFUMBLES
OUTFUMBLING
OUTGAINING
OUTGALLOPED
OUTGALLOPING
OUTGALLOPS
OUTGAMBLED
OUTGAMBLES
OUTGAMBLING
OUTGASSING
OUTGASSINGS
OUTGENERAL
OUTGENERALED
OUTGENERALING
OUTGENERALLED
OUTGENERALLING
OUTGENERALS
OUTGIVINGS
OUTGLARING
OUTGLEAMED
OUTGLEAMING
OUTGLITTER
OUTGLITTERED
OUTGLITTERING
OUTGLITTERS
OUTGLOWING
OUTGNAWING
OUTGOINGNESS
OUTGOINGNESSES
OUTGRINNED
OUTGRINNING
OUTGROSSED
OUTGROSSES
OUTGROSSING
OUTGROWING
OUTGROWTHS
OUTGUESSED
OUTGUESSES
OUTGUESSING
OUTGUIDING
OUTGUNNING
OUTGUSHING
OUTHANDLED
OUTHANDLES
OUTHANDLING
OUTHARBORS
OUTHAULERS
OUTHEARING
OUTHITTING
OUTHOMERED
OUTHOMERING
OUTHOWLING
OUTHUMORED
OUTHUMORING
OUTHUMOURED
OUTHUMOURING
OUTHUMOURS
OUTHUNTING
OUTHUSTLED
OUTHUSTLES

OUTHUSTLING
OUTINTRIGUE
OUTINTRIGUED
OUTINTRIGUES
OUTINTRIGUING
OUTJESTING
OUTJETTING
OUTJETTINGS
OUTJINXING
OUTJOCKEYED
OUTJOCKEYING
OUTJOCKEYS
OUTJUGGLED
OUTJUGGLES
OUTJUGGLING
OUTJUMPING
OUTJUTTING
OUTJUTTINGS
OUTKEEPING
OUTKICKING
OUTKILLING
OUTKISSING
OUTLANDERS
OUTLANDISH
OUTLANDISHLY
OUTLANDISHNESS
OUTLASHING
OUTLASTING
OUTLAUGHED
OUTLAUGHING
OUTLAUNCED
OUTLAUNCES
OUTLAUNCHED
OUTLAUNCHES
OUTLAUNCHING
OUTLAUNCING
OUTLAWRIES
OUTLEADING
OUTLEAPING
OUTLEARNED
OUTLEARNING
OUTLODGING
OUTLODGINGS
OUTLOOKING
OUTLUSTERED
OUTLUSTERING
OUTLUSTERS
OUTLUSTRED
OUTLUSTRES
OUTLUSTRING
OUTMANEUVER
OUTMANEUVERED
OUTMANEUVERING
OUTMANEUVERS
OUTMANIPULATE
OUTMANIPULATED
OUTMANIPULATES
OUTMANIPULATING
OUTMANNING
OUTMANOEUVRE
OUTMANOEUVRED
OUTMANOEUVRES
OUTMANOEUVRING
OUTMANTLED
OUTMANTLES
OUTMANTLING
OUTMARCHED

OUTMARCHES
OUTMARCHING
OUTMARRIAGE
OUTMARRIAGES
OUTMASTERED
OUTMASTERING
OUTMASTERS
OUTMATCHED
OUTMATCHES
OUTMATCHING
OUTMEASURE
OUTMEASURED
OUTMEASURES
OUTMEASURING
OUTMODEDLY
OUTMODEDNESS
OUTMODEDNESSES
OUTMUSCLED
OUTMUSCLES
OUTMUSCLING
OUTNIGHTED
OUTNIGHTING
OUTNUMBERED
OUTNUMBERING
OUTNUMBERS
OUTOFFICES
OUTORGANISE
OUTORGANISED
OUTORGANISES
OUTORGANISING
OUTORGANIZE
OUTORGANIZED
OUTORGANIZES
OUTORGANIZING
OUTPAINTED
OUTPAINTING
OUTPASSING
OUTPASSION
OUTPASSIONED
OUTPASSIONING
OUTPASSIONS
OUTPATIENT
OUTPATIENTS
OUTPEEPING
OUTPEERING
OUTPEOPLED
OUTPEOPLES
OUTPEOPLING
OUTPERFORM
OUTPERFORMED
OUTPERFORMING
OUTPERFORMS
OUTPITCHED
OUTPITCHES
OUTPITCHING
OUTPITYING
OUTPLACEMENT
OUTPLACEMENTS
OUTPLACERS
OUTPLACING
OUTPLANNED
OUTPLANNING
OUTPLAYING
OUTPLODDED
OUTPLODDING
OUTPLOTTED
OUTPLOTTING

OUTPOINTED
OUTPOINTING
OUTPOLITICK
OUTPOLITICKED
OUTPOLITICKING
OUTPOLITICKS
OUTPOLLING
OUTPOPULATE
OUTPOPULATED
OUTPOPULATES
OUTPOPULATING
OUTPORTERS
OUTPOURERS
OUTPOURING
OUTPOURINGS
OUTPOWERED
OUTPOWERING
OUTPRAYING
OUTPREACHED
OUTPREACHES
OUTPREACHING
OUTPREENED
OUTPREENING
OUTPRESSED
OUTPRESSES
OUTPRESSING
OUTPRICING
OUTPRIZING
OUTPRODUCE
OUTPRODUCED
OUTPRODUCES
OUTPRODUCING
OUTPROMISE
OUTPROMISED
OUTPROMISES
OUTPROMISING
OUTPSYCHED
OUTPSYCHING
OUTPULLING
OUTPUNCHED
OUTPUNCHES
OUTPUNCHING
OUTPURSUED
OUTPURSUES
OUTPURSUING
OUTPUSHING
OUTPUTTING
OUTQUARTERS
OUTQUOTING
OUTRAGEOUS
OUTRAGEOUSLY
OUTRAGEOUSNESS
OUTRAISING
OUTRANGING
OUTRANKING
OUTREACHED
OUTREACHES
OUTREACHING
OUTREADING
OUTREASONED
OUTREASONING
OUTREASONS
OUTREBOUND
OUTREBOUNDED
OUTREBOUNDING
OUTREBOUNDS
OUTRECKONED

OUTRECKONING	OUTSINNING	OUTSTRIDING	OUTVENOMING	OVERABOUNDS
OUTRECKONS	OUTSITTING	OUTSTRIKES	OUTVILLAIN	OVERABSTRACT
OUTRECUIDANCE	OUTSKATING	OUTSTRIKING	OUTVILLAINED	OVERABUNDANCE
OUTRECUIDANCES	OUTSLEEPING	OUTSTRIPPED	OUTVILLAINING	OVERABUNDANCES
OUTREDDENED	OUTSLICKED	OUTSTRIPPING	OUTVILLAINS	OVERABUNDANT
OUTREDDENING	OUTSLICKING	OUTSTRIVEN	OUTVOICING	OVERACCENTUATE
OUTREDDENS	OUTSMARTED	OUTSTRIVES	OUTWAITING	OVERACCENTUATED
OUTREDDING	OUTSMARTING	OUTSTRIVING	OUTWALKING	OVERACCENTUATES
OUTREDDINGS	OUTSMELLED	OUTSTROKES	OUTWARDNESS	OVERACHIEVE
OUTREIGNED	OUTSMELLING	OUTSTUDIED	OUTWARDNESSES	OVERACHIEVED
OUTREIGNING	OUTSMILING	OUTSTUDIES	OUTWARRING	OVERACHIEVEMENT
OUTRELIEFS	OUTSMOKING	OUTSTUDYING	OUTWASTING	OVERACHIEVER
OUTREPRODUCE	OUTSNORING	OUTSTUNTED	OUTWATCHED	OVERACHIEVERS
OUTREPRODUCED	OUTSOARING	OUTSTUNTING	OUTWATCHES	OVERACHIEVES
OUTREPRODUCES	OUTSOURCED	OUTSULKING	OUTWATCHING	OVERACHIEVING
OUTREPRODUCING	OUTSOURCES	OUTSUMMING	OUTWEARIED	OVERACTING
OUTRIDINGS	OUTSOURCING	OUTSWEARING	OUTWEARIES	OVERACTION
OUTRIGGERS	OUTSOURCINGS	OUTSWEEPING	OUTWEARING	OVERACTIONS
OUTRIGGING	OUTSPANNED	OUTSWEETEN	OUTWEARYING	OVERACTIVE
OUTRIGGINGS	OUTSPANNING	OUTSWEETENED	OUTWEEDING	OVERACTIVITIES
OUTRIGHTLY	OUTSPARKLE	OUTSWEETENING	OUTWEEPING	OVERACTIVITY
OUTRINGING	OUTSPARKLED	OUTSWEETENS	OUTWEIGHED	OVERADJUSTMENT
OUTRIVALED	OUTSPARKLES	OUTSWELLED	OUTWEIGHING	OVERADJUSTMENTS
OUTRIVALING	OUTSPARKLING	OUTSWELLING	OUTWELLING	OVERADVERTISE
OUTRIVALLED	OUTSPEAKING	OUTSWIMMING	OUTWHIRLED	OVERADVERTISED
OUTRIVALLING	OUTSPECKLE	OUTSWINGER	OUTWHIRLING	OVERADVERTISES
OUTROARING	OUTSPECKLES	OUTSWINGERS	OUTWICKING	OVERADVERTISING
OUTROCKING	OUTSPEEDED	OUTSWINGING	OUTWILLING	OVERADVERTIZE
OUTROLLING	OUTSPEEDING	OUTSWOLLEN	OUTWINDING	OVERADVERTIZED
OUTROOPERS	OUTSPELLED	OUTTALKING	OUTWINGING	OVERADVERTIZES
OUTROOTING	OUTSPELLING	OUTTASKING	OUTWINNING	OVERADVERTIZING
OUTRUNNERS	OUTSPENDING	OUTTELLING	OUTWISHING	OVERAGGRESSIVE
OUTRUNNING	OUTSPOKENLY	OUTTHANKED	OUTWITTING	OVERAMBITIOUS
OUTRUSHING	OUTSPOKENNESS	OUTTHANKING	OUTWORKERS	OVERAMPLIFIED
OUTSAILING	OUTSPOKENNESSES	OUTTHIEVED	OUTWORKING	OVERANALYSE
OUTSAVORED	OUTSPORTED	OUTTHIEVES	OUTWORTHED	OVERANALYSED
OUTSAVORING	OUTSPORTING	OUTTHIEVING	OUTWORTHING	OVERANALYSES
OUTSAVOURED	OUTSPREADING	OUTTHINKING	OUTWRESTED	OVERANALYSING
OUTSAVOURING	OUTSPREADS	OUTTHOUGHT	OUTWRESTING	OVERANALYSIS
OUTSAVOURS	OUTSPRINGING	OUTTHROBBED	OUTWRESTLE	OVERANALYTICAL
OUTSCHEMED	OUTSPRINGS	OUTTHROBBING	OUTWRESTLED	OVERANALYZE
OUTSCHEMES	OUTSPRINTED	OUTTHROWING	OUTWRESTLES	OVERANALYZED
OUTSCHEMING	OUTSPRINTING	OUTTHRUSTED	OUTWRESTLING	OVERANALYZES
OUTSCOLDED	OUTSPRINTS	OUTTHRUSTING	OUTWRITING	OVERANALYZING
OUTSCOLDING	OUTSTANDING	OUTTHRUSTS	OUTWRITTEN	OVERANXIETIES
OUTSCOOPED	OUTSTANDINGLY	OUTTONGUED	OUTWROUGHT	OVERANXIETY
OUTSCOOPING	OUTSTARING	OUTTONGUES	OUTYELLING	OVERANXIOUS
OUTSCORING	OUTSTARTED	OUTTONGUING	OUTYELPING	OVERAPPLICATION
OUTSCORNED	OUTSTARTING	OUTTOPPING	OUTYIELDED	OVERARCHED
OUTSCORNING	OUTSTATING	OUTTOWERED	OUTYIELDING	OVERARCHES
OUTSCREAMED	OUTSTATION	OUTTOWERING	OUVIRANDRA	OVERARCHING
OUTSCREAMING	OUTSTATIONS	OUTTRADING	OUVIRANDRAS	OVERARMING
OUTSCREAMS	OUTSTAYING	OUTTRAVELED	OVALBUMINS	OVERAROUSAL
OUTSELLING	OUTSTEERED	OUTTRAVELING	OVALNESSES	OVERAROUSALS
OUTSERVING	OUTSTEERING	OUTTRAVELLED	OVARIECTOMIES	OVERARRANGE
OUTSETTING	OUTSTEPPED	OUTTRAVELLING	OVARIECTOMISED	OVERARRANGED
OUTSETTINGS	OUTSTEPPING	OUTTRAVELS	OVARIECTOMIZED	OVERARRANGES
OUTSETTLEMENT	OUTSTRAINED	OUTTRICKED	OVARIECTOMY	OVERARRANGING
OUTSETTLEMENTS	OUTSTRAINING	OUTTRICKING	OVARIOTOMIES	OVERARTICULATE
OUTSHAMING	OUTSTRAINS	OUTTROTTED	OVARIOTOMIST	OVERARTICULATED
OUTSHINING	OUTSTRETCH	OUTTROTTING	OVARIOTOMISTS	OVERARTICULATES
OUTSHOOTING	OUTSTRETCHED	OUTTRUMPED	OVARIOTOMY	OVERASSERT
OUTSHOUTED	OUTSTRETCHES	OUTTRUMPING	OVARITIDES	OVERASSERTED
OUTSHOUTING	OUTSTRETCHING	OUTVALUING	OVARITISES	OVERASSERTING
OUTSIDERNESS	OUTSTRIDDEN	OUTVAUNTED	OVERABOUND	OVERASSERTION
OUTSIDERNESSES	OUTSTRIDED	OUTVAUNTING	OVERABOUNDED	OVERASSERTIONS
OUTSINGING	OUTSTRIDES	OUTVENOMED	OVERABOUNDING	OVERASSERTIVE

OVERASSERTS	OVERBRIMMING	OVERCHILLED	OVERCONCERN	OVERDEEPENING
OVERASSESSMENT	OVERBROWED	OVERCHILLING	OVERCONCERNED	OVERDELICATE
OVERASSESSMENTS	OVERBROWING	OVERCHILLS	OVERCONCERNING	OVERDEMANDING
OVERATTENTION	OVERBROWSE	OVERCIVILISED	OVERCONCERNS	OVERDEPENDENCE
OVERATTENTIONS	OVERBROWSED	OVERCIVILIZED	OVERCONFIDENCE	OVERDEPENDENCES
OVERATTENTIVE	OVERBROWSES	OVERCLAIMED	OVERCONFIDENCES	OVERDEPENDENT
OVERBAKING	OVERBROWSING	OVERCLAIMING	OVERCONFIDENT	OVERDESIGN
OVERBALANCE	OVERBRUTAL	OVERCLAIMS	OVERCONFIDENTLY	OVERDESIGNED
OVERBALANCED	OVERBUILDING	OVERCLASSES	OVERCONSCIOUS	OVERDESIGNING
OVERBALANCES	OVERBUILDS	OVERCLASSIFIED	OVERCONSTRUCT	OVERDESIGNS
OVERBALANCING	OVERBULKED	OVERCLASSIFIES	OVERCONSTRUCTED	OVERDETERMINED
OVERBEARING	OVERBULKING	OVERCLASSIFY	OVERCONSTRUCTS	OVERDEVELOP
OVERBEARINGLY	OVERBURDEN	OVERCLASSIFYING	OVERCONSUME	OVERDEVELOPED
OVERBEARINGNESS	OVERBURDENED	OVERCLEANED	OVERCONSUMED	OVERDEVELOPING
OVERBEATEN	OVERBURDENING	OVERCLEANING	OVERCONSUMES	OVERDEVELOPMENT
OVERBEATING	OVERBURDENS	OVERCLEANS	OVERCONSUMING	OVERDEVELOPS
OVERBEJEWELED	OVERBURDENSOME	OVERCLEARED	OVERCONSUMPTION	OVERDEVIATE
OVERBEJEWELLED	OVERBURNED	OVERCLEARING	OVERCONTROL	OVERDEVIATED
OVERBETTED	OVERBURNING	OVERCLEARS	OVERCONTROLLED	OVERDEVIATES
OVERBETTING	OVERBURTHEN	OVERCLEVER	OVERCONTROLLING	OVERDEVIATING
OVERBETTINGS	OVERBURTHENED	OVERCLOCKED	OVERCONTROLS	OVERDIAGNOSES
OVERBIDDEN	OVERBURTHENING	OVERCLOCKER	OVERCOOKED	OVERDIAGNOSIS
OVERBIDDER	OVERBURTHENS	OVERCLOCKERS	OVERCOOKING	OVERDILUTED
OVERBIDDERS	OVERBUSIED	OVERCLOCKING	OVERCOOLED	OVERDIRECT
OVERBIDDING	OVERBUSIES	OVERCLOCKINGS	OVERCOOLING	OVERDIRECTED
OVERBIDDINGS	OVERBUSYING	OVERCLOCKS	OVERCORRECT	OVERDIRECTING
OVERBILLED	OVERBUYING	OVERCLOUDED	OVERCORRECTED	OVERDIRECTS
OVERBILLING	OVERCALLED	OVERCLOUDING	OVERCORRECTING	OVERDISCOUNT
OVERBLANKET	OVERCALLING	OVERCLOUDS	OVERCORRECTION	OVERDISCOUNTED
OVERBLANKETS	OVERCANOPIED	OVERCLOYED	OVERCORRECTIONS	OVERDISCOUNTING
OVERBLEACH	OVERCANOPIES	OVERCLOYING	OVERCORRECTS	OVERDISCOUNTS
OVERBLEACHED	OVERCANOPY	OVERCLUBBED	OVERCOUNTED	OVERDIVERSITIES
OVERBLEACHES	OVERCANOPYING	OVERCLUBBING	OVERCOUNTING	OVERDIVERSITY
OVERBLEACHING	OVERCAPACITIES	OVERCOACHED	OVERCOUNTS	OVERDOCUMENT
OVERBLOUSE	OVERCAPACITY	OVERCOACHES	OVERCOVERED	OVERDOCUMENTED
OVERBLOUSES	OVERCAPITALISE	OVERCOACHING	OVERCOVERING	OVERDOCUMENTING
OVERBLOWING	OVERCAPITALISED	OVERCOATING	OVERCOVERS	OVERDOCUMENTS
OVERBOILED	OVERCAPITALISES	OVERCOATINGS	OVERCRAMMED	OVERDOMINANCE
OVERBOILING	OVERCAPITALIZE	OVERCOLORED	OVERCRAMMING	OVERDOMINANCES
OVERBOLDLY	OVERCAPITALIZED	OVERCOLORING	OVERCRAMMINGS	OVERDOMINANT
OVERBOOKED	OVERCAPITALIZES	OVERCOLORS	OVERCRAWED	OVERDOSAGE
OVERBOOKING	OVERCAREFUL	OVERCOLOUR	OVERCRAWING	OVERDOSAGES
OVERBOOKINGS	OVERCARRIED	OVERCOLOURED	OVERCREDULITIES	OVERDOSING
OVERBORROW	OVERCARRIES	OVERCOLOURING	OVERCREDULITY	OVERDRAFTS
OVERBORROWED	OVERCARRYING	OVERCOLOURS	OVERCREDULOUS	OVERDRAMATIC
OVERBORROWING	OVERCASTED	OVERCOMERS	OVERCRITICAL	OVERDRAMATISE
OVERBORROWS	OVERCASTING	OVERCOMING	OVERCROPPED	OVERDRAMATISED
OVERBOUGHT	OVERCASTINGS	OVERCOMMIT	OVERCROPPING	OVERDRAMATISES
OVERBOUNDED	OVERCATCHES	OVERCOMMITMENT	OVERCROWDED	OVERDRAMATISING
OVERBOUNDING	OVERCATCHING	OVERCOMMITMENTS	OVERCROWDING	OVERDRAMATIZE
OVERBOUNDS	OVERCAUGHT	OVERCOMMITS	OVERCROWDINGS	OVERDRAMATIZED
OVERBRAKED	OVERCAUTION	OVERCOMMITTED	OVERCROWDS	OVERDRAMATIZES
OVERBRAKES	OVERCAUTIONS	OVERCOMMITTING	OVERCROWED	OVERDRAMATIZING
OVERBRAKING	OVERCAUTIOUS	OVERCOMMUNICATE	OVERCROWING	OVERDRAUGHT
OVERBREATHING	OVERCAUTIOUSLY	OVERCOMPENSATE	OVERCULTIVATION	OVERDRAUGHTS
OVERBREATHINGS	OVERCENTRALISE	OVERCOMPENSATED	OVERCURING	OVERDRAWING
OVERBREEDING	OVERCENTRALISED	OVERCOMPENSATES	OVERCUTTING	OVERDRESSED
OVERBREEDS	OVERCENTRALISES	OVERCOMPLEX	OVERCUTTINGS	OVERDRESSES
OVERBRIDGE	OVERCENTRALIZE	OVERCOMPLIANCE	OVERDARING	OVERDRESSING
OVERBRIDGED	OVERCENTRALIZED	OVERCOMPLIANCES	OVERDECKED	OVERDRINKING
OVERBRIDGES	OVERCENTRALIZES	OVERCOMPLICATE	OVERDECKING	OVERDRINKS
OVERBRIDGING	OVERCHARGE	OVERCOMPLICATED	OVERDECORATE	OVERDRIVEN
OVERBRIEFED	OVERCHARGED	OVERCOMPLICATES	OVERDECORATED	OVERDRIVES
OVERBRIEFING	OVERCHARGES	OVERCOMPRESS	OVERDECORATES	OVERDRIVING
OVERBRIEFS	OVERCHARGING	OVERCOMPRESSED	OVERDECORATING	OVERDRYING
OVERBRIGHT	OVERCHARGINGS	OVERCOMPRESSES	OVERDECORATION	OVERDUBBED
OVERBRIMMED	OVERCHECKS	OVERCOMPRESSING	OVERDECORATIONS	OVERDUBBING

O

OVERDUSTED	OVERESTIMATING	OVERFAVORED	OVERFULFILLS	OVERGRAINING
OVERDUSTING	OVERESTIMATION	OVERFAVORING	OVERFULFILS	OVERGRAINS
OVERDYEING	OVERESTIMATIONS	OVERFAVORS	OVERFULLNESS	OVERGRASSED
OVEREAGERNESS	OVEREVALUATION	OVERFAVOUR	OVERFULLNESSES	OVERGRASSES
OVEREAGERNESSES	OVEREVALUATIONS	OVERFAVOURED	OVERFULNESS	OVERGRASSING
OVEREARNEST	OVEREXAGGERATE	OVERFAVOURING	OVERFULNESSES	OVERGRAZED
OVEREASIER	OVEREXAGGERATED	OVERFAVOURS	OVERFUNDED	OVERGRAZES
OVEREASIEST	OVEREXAGGERATES	OVERFEARED	OVERFUNDING	OVERGRAZING
OVEREATERS	OVEREXCITABLE	OVERFEARING	OVERFUNDINGS	OVERGRAZINGS
OVEREATING	OVEREXCITE	OVERFEEDING	OVERFUSSIER	OVERGREEDIER
OVEREATINGS	OVEREXCITED	OVERFEEDINGS	OVERFUSSIEST	OVERGREEDIEST
OVEREDITED	OVEREXCITEMENT	OVERFERTILISE	OVERGALLED	OVERGREEDY
OVEREDITING	OVEREXCITEMENTS	OVERFERTILISED	OVERGALLING	OVERGREENED
OVEREDUCATE	OVEREXCITES	OVERFERTILISES	OVERGANGING	OVERGREENING
OVEREDUCATED	OVEREXCITING	OVERFERTILISING	OVERGARMENT	OVERGREENS
OVEREDUCATES	OVEREXERCISE	OVERFERTILIZE	OVERGARMENTS	OVERGROUND
OVEREDUCATING	OVEREXERCISED	OVERFERTILIZED	OVERGEARED	OVERGROWING
OVEREDUCATION	OVEREXERCISES	OVERFERTILIZES	OVERGEARING	OVERGROWTH
OVEREDUCATIONS	OVEREXERCISING	OVERFERTILIZING	OVERGENERALISE	OVERGROWTHS
OVEREFFUSIVE	OVEREXERTED	OVERFILLED	OVERGENERALISED	OVERHAILED
OVEREGGING	OVEREXERTING	OVERFILLING	OVERGENERALISES	OVERHAILES
OVERELABORATE	OVEREXERTION	OVERFINENESS	OVERGENERALIZE	OVERHAILING
OVERELABORATED	OVEREXERTIONS	OVERFINENESSES	OVERGENERALIZED	OVERHALING
OVERELABORATES	OVEREXERTS	OVERFINISHED	OVERGENERALIZES	OVERHANDED
OVERELABORATING	OVEREXPAND	OVERFISHED	OVERGENEROSITY	OVERHANDING
OVERELABORATION	OVEREXPANDED	OVERFISHES	OVERGENEROUS	OVERHANDLE
OVEREMBELLISH	OVEREXPANDING	OVERFISHING	OVERGENEROUSLY	OVERHANDLED
OVEREMBELLISHED	OVEREXPANDS	OVERFISHINGS	OVERGETTING	OVERHANDLES
OVEREMBELLISHES	OVEREXPANSION	OVERFLIGHT	OVERGILDED	OVERHANDLING
OVEREMOTED	OVEREXPANSIONS	OVERFLIGHTS	OVERGILDING	OVERHANGING
OVEREMOTES	OVEREXPECTATION	OVERFLOODED	OVERGIRDED	OVERHAPPIER
OVEREMOTING	OVEREXPLAIN	OVERFLOODING	OVERGIRDING	OVERHAPPIEST
OVEREMOTIONAL	OVEREXPLAINED	OVERFLOODS	OVERGIVING	OVERHARVEST
OVEREMPHASES	OVEREXPLAINING	OVERFLOURISH	OVERGLAMORISE	OVERHARVESTED
OVEREMPHASIS	OVEREXPLAINS	OVERFLOURISHED	OVERGLAMORISED	OVERHARVESTING
OVEREMPHASISE	OVEREXPLICIT	OVERFLOURISHES	OVERGLAMORISES	OVERHARVESTS
OVEREMPHASISED	OVEREXPLOIT	OVERFLOURISHING	OVERGLAMORISING	OVERHASTES
OVEREMPHASISES	OVEREXPLOITED	OVERFLOWED	OVERGLAMORIZE	OVERHASTILY
OVEREMPHASISING	OVEREXPLOITING	OVERFLOWING	OVERGLAMORIZED	OVERHASTINESS
OVEREMPHASIZE	OVEREXPLOITS	OVERFLOWINGLY	OVERGLAMORIZES	OVERHASTINESSES
OVEREMPHASIZED	OVEREXPOSE	OVERFLOWINGS	OVERGLAMORIZING	OVERHATING
OVEREMPHASIZES	OVEREXPOSED	OVERFLUSHES	OVERGLANCE	OVERHAULED
OVEREMPHASIZING	OVEREXPOSES	OVERFLYING	OVERGLANCED	OVERHAULING
OVEREMPHATIC	OVEREXPOSING	OVERFOCUSED	OVERGLANCES	OVERHEAPED
OVEREMPLOYMENT	OVEREXPOSURE	OVERFOCUSES	OVERGLANCING	OVERHEAPING
OVEREMPLOYMENTS	OVEREXPOSURES	OVERFOCUSING	OVERGLAZED	OVERHEARING
OVERENAMORED	OVEREXTEND	OVERFOCUSSED	OVERGLAZES	OVERHEATED
OVERENAMOURED	OVEREXTENDED	OVERFOCUSSES	OVERGLAZING	OVERHEATING
OVERENCOURAGE	OVEREXTENDING	OVERFOCUSSING	OVERGLOOMED	OVERHEATINGS
OVERENCOURAGED	OVEREXTENDS	OVERFOLDED	OVERGLOOMING	OVERHENTING
OVERENCOURAGES	OVEREXTENSION	OVERFOLDING	OVERGLOOMS	OVERHITTING
OVERENCOURAGING	OVEREXTENSIONS	OVERFONDLY	OVERGOADED	OVERHOLDING
OVERENERGETIC	OVEREXTRACTION	OVERFONDNESS	OVERGOADING	OVERHOLIER
OVERENGINEER	OVEREXTRACTIONS	OVERFONDNESSES	OVERGOINGS	OVERHOLIEST
OVERENGINEERED	OVEREXTRAVAGANT	OVERFORWARD	OVERGORGED	OVERHOMOGENISE
OVERENGINEERING	OVEREXUBERANT	OVERFORWARDNESS	OVERGORGES	OVERHOMOGENISED
OVERENGINEERS	OVEREYEING	OVERFRAUGHT	OVERGORGING	OVERHOMOGENISES
OVERENROLLED	OVERFACILE	OVERFREEDOM	OVERGOVERN	OVERHOMOGENIZE
OVERENTERTAINED	OVERFALLEN	OVERFREEDOMS	OVERGOVERNED	OVERHOMOGENIZED
OVERENTHUSIASM	OVERFALLING	OVERFREELY	OVERGOVERNING	OVERHOMOGENIZES
OVERENTHUSIASMS	OVERFAMILIAR	OVERFREIGHT	OVERGOVERNS	OVERHONORED
OVEREQUIPPED	OVERFAMILIARITY	OVERFREIGHTING	OVERGRADED	OVERHONORING
OVEREQUIPPING	OVERFASTIDIOUS	OVERFREIGHTS	OVERGRADES	OVERHONORS
OVEREQUIPS	OVERFATIGUE	OVERFULFIL	OVERGRADING	OVERHONOUR
OVERESTIMATE	OVERFATIGUED	OVERFULFILL	OVERGRAINED	OVERHONOURED
OVERESTIMATED	OVERFATIGUES	OVERFULFILLED	OVERGRAINER	OVERHONOURING
OVERESTIMATES	OVERFATIGUING	OVERFULFILLING	OVERGRAINERS	OVERHONOURS

OVERHOPING	OVERKINDNESSES	OVERMANAGE	OVERNICENESSES	OVERPEOPLED
OVERHUNTED	OVERLABORED	OVERMANAGED	OVERNIGHTED	OVERPEOPLES
OVERHUNTING	OVERLABORING	OVERMANAGES	OVERNIGHTER	OVERPEOPLING
OVERHUNTINGS	OVERLABORS	OVERMANAGING	OVERNIGHTERS	OVERPERCHED
OVERHYPING	OVERLABOUR	OVERMANIES	OVERNIGHTING	OVERPERCHES
OVERIDEALISE	OVERLABOURED	OVERMANNED	OVERNIGHTS	OVERPERCHING
OVERIDEALISED	OVERLABOURING	OVERMANNERED	OVERNOURISH	OVERPERSUADE
OVERIDEALISES	OVERLABOURS	OVERMANNING	OVERNOURISHED	OVERPERSUADED
OVERIDEALISING	OVERLADING	OVERMANNINGS	OVERNOURISHES	OVERPERSUADES
OVERIDEALIZE	OVERLANDED	OVERMANTEL	OVERNOURISHING	OVERPERSUADING
OVERIDEALIZED	OVERLANDER	OVERMANTELS	OVERNUTRITION	OVERPERSUASION
OVERIDEALIZES	OVERLANDERS	OVERMASTED	OVERNUTRITIONS	OVERPERSUASIONS
OVERIDEALIZING	OVERLANDING	OVERMASTER	OVEROBVIOUS	OVERPESSIMISTIC
OVERIDENTIFIED	OVERLAPPED	OVERMASTERED	OVEROFFICE	OVERPICTURE
OVERIDENTIFIES	OVERLAPPING	OVERMASTERING	OVEROFFICED	OVERPICTURED
OVERIDENTIFY	OVERLARDED	OVERMASTERS	OVEROFFICES	OVERPICTURES
OVERIDENTIFYING	OVERLARDING	OVERMASTING	OVEROFFICING	OVERPICTURING
OVERIMAGINATIVE	OVERLAUNCH	OVERMATCHED	OVEROPERATE	OVERPITCHED
OVERIMPRESS	OVERLAUNCHED	OVERMATCHES	OVEROPERATED	OVERPITCHES
OVERIMPRESSED	OVERLAUNCHES	OVERMATCHING	OVEROPERATES	OVERPITCHING
OVERIMPRESSES	OVERLAUNCHING	OVERMATTER	OVEROPERATING	OVERPLACED
OVERIMPRESSING	OVERLAVISH	OVERMATTERS	OVEROPINIONATED	OVERPLAIDED
OVERINCLINED	OVERLAYING	OVERMATURE	OVEROPTIMISM	OVERPLAIDS
OVERINDULGE	OVERLAYINGS	OVERMATURITIES	OVEROPTIMISMS	OVERPLANNED
OVERINDULGED	OVERLEAPED	OVERMATURITY	OVEROPTIMIST	OVERPLANNING
OVERINDULGENCE	OVERLEAPING	OVERMEASURE	OVEROPTIMISTIC	OVERPLANNINGS
OVERINDULGENCES	OVERLEARNED	OVERMEASURED	OVEROPTIMISTS	OVERPLANTED
OVERINDULGENT	OVERLEARNING	OVERMEASURES	OVERORCHESTRATE	OVERPLANTING
OVERINDULGES	OVERLEARNS	OVERMEASURING	OVERORGANISE	OVERPLANTS
OVERINDULGING	OVERLEARNT	OVERMEDICATE	OVERORGANISED	OVERPLAYED
OVERINFLATE	OVERLEATHER	OVERMEDICATED	OVERORGANISES	OVERPLAYING
OVERINFLATED	OVERLEATHERS	OVERMEDICATES	OVERORGANISING	OVERPLOTTED
OVERINFLATES	OVERLEAVEN	OVERMEDICATING	OVERORGANIZE	OVERPLOTTING
OVERINFLATING	OVERLEAVENED	OVERMEDICATION	OVERORGANIZED	OVERPLOTTINGS
OVERINFLATION	OVERLEAVENING	OVERMEDICATIONS	OVERORGANIZES	OVERPLUSES
OVERINFLATIONS	OVERLEAVENS	OVERMELTED	OVERORGANIZING	OVERPLUSSES
OVERINFORM	OVERLENDING	OVERMELTING	OVERORNAMENT	OVERPLYING
OVERINFORMED	OVERLENGTH	OVERMERRIER	OVERORNAMENTED	OVERPOISED
OVERINFORMING	OVERLENGTHEN	OVERMERRIEST	OVERORNAMENTING	OVERPOISES
OVERINFORMS	OVERLENGTHENED	OVERMIGHTIER	OVERORNAMENTS	OVERPOISING
OVERINGENIOUS	OVERLENGTHENING	OVERMIGHTIEST	OVERPACKAGE	OVERPOPULATE
OVERINGENUITIES	OVERLENGTHENS	OVERMIGHTY	OVERPACKAGED	OVERPOPULATED
OVERINGENUITY	OVERLENGTHS	OVERMILKED	OVERPACKAGES	OVERPOPULATES
OVERINSISTENT	OVERLETTING	OVERMILKING	OVERPACKAGING	OVERPOPULATING
OVERINSURANCE	OVERLEVERAGED	OVERMINING	OVERPACKED	OVERPOPULATION
OVERINSURANCES	OVERLIGHTED	OVERMIXING	OVERPACKING	OVERPOPULATIONS
OVERINSURE	OVERLIGHTING	OVERMODEST	OVERPAINTED	OVERPOSTED
OVERINSURED	OVERLIGHTS	OVERMODESTLY	OVERPAINTING	OVERPOSTING
OVERINSURES	OVERLITERAL	OVERMOUNTED	OVERPAINTS	OVERPOTENT
OVERINSURING	OVERLITERARY	OVERMOUNTING	OVERPARTED	OVERPOWERED
OVERINTENSE	OVERLIVING	OVERMOUNTS	OVERPARTICULAR	OVERPOWERING
OVERINTENSITIES	OVERLOADED	OVERMUCHES	OVERPARTING	OVERPOWERINGLY
OVERINTENSITY	OVERLOADING	OVERMULTIPLIED	OVERPASSED	OVERPOWERS
OVERINVESTMENT	OVERLOCKED	OVERMULTIPLIES	OVERPASSES	OVERPRAISE
OVERINVESTMENTS	OVERLOCKER	OVERMULTIPLY	OVERPASSING	OVERPRAISED
OVERISSUANCE	OVERLOCKERS	OVERMULTIPLYING	OVERPAYING	OVERPRAISES
OVERISSUANCES	OVERLOCKING	OVERMULTITUDE	OVERPAYMENT	OVERPRAISING
OVERISSUED	OVERLOCKINGS	OVERMULTITUDED	OVERPAYMENTS	OVERPRECISE
OVERISSUES	OVERLOOKED	OVERMULTITUDES	OVERPEDALED	OVERPREPARATION
OVERISSUING	OVERLOOKER	OVERMULTITUDING	OVERPEDALING	OVERPREPARE
OVERJOYING	OVERLOOKERS	OVERMUSCLED	OVERPEDALLED	OVERPREPARED
OVERJUMPED	OVERLOOKING	OVERNAMING	OVERPEDALLING	OVERPREPARES
OVERJUMPING	OVERLORDED	OVERNETTED	OVERPEDALLINGS	OVERPREPARING
OVERKEEPING	OVERLORDING	OVERNETTING	OVERPEDALS	OVERPRESCRIBE
OVERKILLED	OVERLORDSHIP	OVERNETTINGS	OVERPEERED	OVERPRESCRIBED
OVERKILLING	OVERLORDSHIPS	OVERNICELY	OVERPEERING	OVERPRESCRIBES
OVERKINDNESS	OVERLOVING	OVERNICENESS	OVERPEOPLE	OVERPRESCRIBING

OVERPRESSED	OVERREACTED	OVERSAUCES	OVERSLEEVES	OVERSTIMULATION
OVERPRESSES	OVERREACTING	OVERSAUCING	OVERSLIPPED	OVERSTINKING
OVERPRESSING	OVERREACTION	OVERSAVING	OVERSLIPPING	OVERSTINKS
OVERPRESSURE	OVERREACTIONS	OVERSCALED	OVERSMOKED	OVERSTIRRED
OVERPRESSURES	OVERREACTS	OVERSCHUTCHT	OVERSMOKES	OVERSTIRRING
OVERPRICED	OVERREADING	OVERSCORED	OVERSMOKING	OVERSTOCKED
OVERPRICES	OVERRECKON	OVERSCORES	OVERSOAKED	OVERSTOCKING
OVERPRICING	OVERRECKONED	OVERSCORING	OVERSOAKING	OVERSTOCKS
OVERPRINTED	OVERRECKONING	OVERSCRUPULOUS	OVERSOLICITOUS	OVERSTOREY
OVERPRINTING	OVERRECKONS	OVERSCUTCHED	OVERSOWING	OVERSTOREYS
OVERPRINTS	OVERREDDED	OVERSECRETION	OVERSPECIALISE	OVERSTORIES
OVERPRIVILEGED	OVERREDDING	OVERSECRETIONS	OVERSPECIALISED	OVERSTRAIN
OVERPRIZED	OVERREFINE	OVERSEEDED	OVERSPECIALISES	OVERSTRAINED
OVERPRIZES	OVERREFINED	OVERSEEDING	OVERSPECIALIZE	OVERSTRAINING
OVERPRIZING	OVERREFINEMENT	OVERSEEING	OVERSPECIALIZED	OVERSTRAINS
OVERPROCESS	OVERREFINEMENTS	OVERSELLING	OVERSPECIALIZES	OVERSTRESS
OVERPROCESSED	OVERREFINES	OVERSENSITIVE	OVERSPECULATE	OVERSTRESSED
OVERPROCESSES	OVERREFINING	OVERSENSITIVITY	OVERSPECULATED	OVERSTRESSES
OVERPROCESSING	OVERREGULATE	OVERSERIOUS	OVERSPECULATES	OVERSTRESSING
OVERPRODUCE	OVERREGULATED	OVERSERIOUSLY	OVERSPECULATING	OVERSTRETCH
OVERPRODUCED	OVERREGULATES	OVERSERVICE	OVERSPECULATION	OVERSTRETCHED
OVERPRODUCES	OVERREGULATING	OVERSERVICED	OVERSPENDER	OVERSTRETCHES
OVERPRODUCING	OVERREGULATION	OVERSERVICES	OVERSPENDERS	OVERSTRETCHING
OVERPRODUCTION	OVERREGULATIONS	OVERSERVICING	OVERSPENDING	OVERSTREWED
OVERPRODUCTIONS	OVERRELIANCE	OVERSETTING	OVERSPENDINGS	OVERSTREWING
OVERPROGRAM	OVERRELIANCES	OVERSEWING	OVERSPENDS	OVERSTREWN
OVERPROGRAMED	OVERRENNING	OVERSHADED	OVERSPICED	OVERSTREWS
OVERPROGRAMING	OVERREPORT	OVERSHADES	OVERSPICES	OVERSTRIDDEN
OVERPROGRAMMED	OVERREPORTED	OVERSHADING	OVERSPICING	OVERSTRIDE
OVERPROGRAMMING	OVERREPORTING	OVERSHADOW	OVERSPILLED	OVERSTRIDES
OVERPROGRAMS	OVERREPORTS	OVERSHADOWED	OVERSPILLING	OVERSTRIDING
OVERPROMISE	OVERREPRESENTED	OVERSHADOWING	OVERSPILLS	OVERSTRIKE
OVERPROMISED	OVERRESPOND	OVERSHADOWS	OVERSPREAD	OVERSTRIKES
OVERPROMISES	OVERRESPONDED	OVERSHARED	OVERSPREADING	OVERSTRIKING
OVERPROMISING	OVERRESPONDING	OVERSHARES	OVERSPREADS	OVERSTRODE
OVERPROMOTE	OVERRESPONDS	OVERSHARING	OVERSTABILITIES	OVERSTRONG
OVERPROMOTED	OVERRIDDEN	OVERSHINES	OVERSTABILITY	OVERSTROOKE
OVERPROMOTES	OVERRIDERS	OVERSHINING	OVERSTAFFED	OVERSTRUCK
OVERPROMOTING	OVERRIDING	OVERSHIRTS	OVERSTAFFING	OVERSTRUCTURED
OVERPROOFS	OVERRIPENED	OVERSHOOTING	OVERSTAFFINGS	OVERSTRUNG
OVERPROPORTION	OVERRIPENESS	OVERSHOOTS	OVERSTAFFS	OVERSTUDIED
OVERPROPORTIONS	OVERRIPENESSES	OVERSHOWER	OVERSTAINED	OVERSTUDIES
OVERPROTECT	OVERRIPENING	OVERSHOWERED	OVERSTAINING	OVERSTUDYING
OVERPROTECTED	OVERRIPENS	OVERSHOWERING	OVERSTAINS	OVERSTUFFED
OVERPROTECTING	OVERROASTED	OVERSHOWERS	OVERSTANDING	OVERSTUFFING
OVERPROTECTION	OVERROASTING	OVERSIGHTS	OVERSTANDS	OVERSTUFFS
OVERPROTECTIONS	OVERROASTS	OVERSIMPLE	OVERSTARED	OVERSUBSCRIBE
OVERPROTECTIVE	OVERRUFFED	OVERSIMPLIFIED	OVERSTARES	OVERSUBSCRIBED
OVERPROTECTS	OVERRUFFING	OVERSIMPLIFIES	OVERSTARING	OVERSUBSCRIBES
OVERPUMPED	OVERRULERS	OVERSIMPLIFY	OVERSTATED	OVERSUBSCRIBING
OVERPUMPING	OVERRULING	OVERSIMPLIFYING	OVERSTATEMENT	OVERSUBTLE
OVERQUALIFIED	OVERRULINGS	OVERSIMPLISTIC	OVERSTATEMENTS	OVERSUBTLETIES
OVERRACKED	OVERRUNNER	OVERSIMPLY	OVERSTATES	OVERSUBTLETY
OVERRACKING	OVERRUNNERS	OVERSIZING	OVERSTATING	OVERSUDSED
OVERRAKING	OVERRUNNING	OVERSKATED	OVERSTAYED	OVERSUDSES
OVERRANKED	OVERSAILED	OVERSKATES	OVERSTAYER	OVERSUDSING
OVERRANKING	OVERSAILING	OVERSKATING	OVERSTAYERS	OVERSUPPED
OVERRASHLY	OVERSALTED	OVERSKIPPED	OVERSTAYING	OVERSUPPING
OVERRASHNESS	OVERSALTING	OVERSKIPPING	OVERSTEERED	OVERSUPPLIED
OVERRASHNESSES	OVERSANGUINE	OVERSKIRTS	OVERSTEERING	OVERSUPPLIES
OVERRATING	OVERSATURATE	OVERSLAUGH	OVERSTEERS	OVERSUPPLY
OVERRAUGHT	OVERSATURATED	OVERSLAUGHED	OVERSTEPPED	OVERSUPPLYING
OVERREACHED	OVERSATURATES	OVERSLAUGHING	OVERSTEPPING	OVERSUSPICIOUS
OVERREACHER	OVERSATURATING	OVERSLAUGHS	OVERSTIMULATE	OVERSWAYED
OVERREACHERS	OVERSATURATION	OVERSLEEPING	OVERSTIMULATED	OVERSWAYING
OVERREACHES	OVERSATURATIONS	OVERSLEEPS	OVERSTIMULATES	OVERSWEARING
OVERREACHING	OVERSAUCED	OVERSLEEVE	OVERSTIMULATING	OVERSWEARS

OVERSWEETEN	OVERTOPPED	OVERWARIEST	OVERWRESTLE	OXYACETYLENE
OVERSWEETENED	OVERTOPPING	OVERWARMED	OVERWRESTLED	OXYACETYLENES
OVERSWEETENING	OVERTOPPINGS	OVERWARMING	OVERWRESTLES	OXYCEPHALIC
OVERSWEETENS	OVERTOWERED	OVERWASHES	OVERWRESTLING	OXYCEPHALIES
OVERSWEETNESS	OVERTOWERING	OVERWATCHED	OVERWRESTS	OXYCEPHALOUS
OVERSWEETNESSES	OVERTOWERS	OVERWATCHES	OVERWRITES	OXYCEPHALY
OVERSWELLED	OVERTRADED	OVERWATCHING	OVERWRITING	OXYCODONES
OVERSWELLING	OVERTRADES	OVERWATERED	OVERWRITTEN	OXYGENASES
OVERSWELLS	OVERTRADING	OVERWATERING	OVERWROUGHT	OXYGENATED
OVERSWIMMING	OVERTRADINGS	OVERWATERS	OVERYEARED	OXYGENATES
OVERSWINGING	OVERTRAINED	OVERWEARIED	OVERYEARING	OXYGENATING
OVERSWINGS	OVERTRAINING	OVERWEARIES	OVERZEALOUS	OXYGENATION
OVERSWOLLEN	OVERTRAINS	OVERWEARING	OVERZEALOUSLY	OXYGENATIONS
OVERTAKING	OVERTREATED	OVERWEARYING	OVERZEALOUSNESS	OXYGENATOR
OVERTAKINGS	OVERTREATING	OVERWEATHER	OVIPARITIES	OXYGENATORS
OVERTALKATIVE	OVERTREATMENT	OVERWEATHERED	OVIPAROUSLY	OXYGENISED
OVERTALKED	OVERTREATMENTS	OVERWEATHERING	OVIPOSITED	OXYGENISER
OVERTALKING	OVERTREATS	OVERWEATHERS	OVIPOSITING	OXYGENISERS
OVERTASKED	OVERTRICKS	OVERWEENED	OVIPOSITION	OXYGENISES
OVERTASKING	OVERTRIMMED	OVERWEENING	OVIPOSITIONAL	OXYGENISING
OVERTAUGHT	OVERTRIMMING	OVERWEENINGLY	OVIPOSITIONS	OXYGENIZED
OVERTAXATION	OVERTRIPPED	OVERWEENINGNESS	OVIPOSITOR	OXYGENIZER
OVERTAXATIONS	OVERTRIPPING	OVERWEENINGS	OVIPOSITORS	OXYGENIZERS
OVERTAXING	OVERTRUMPED	OVERWEIGHED	OVIRAPTORS	OXYGENIZES
OVERTEACHES	OVERTRUMPING	OVERWEIGHING	OVOVIVIPARITIES	OXYGENIZING
OVERTEACHING	OVERTRUMPS	OVERWEIGHS	OVOVIVIPARITY	OXYGENLESS
OVERTEDIOUS	OVERTRUSTED	OVERWEIGHT	OVOVIVIPAROUS	OXYHAEMOGLOBIN
OVERTEEMED	OVERTRUSTING	OVERWEIGHTED	OVOVIVIPAROUSLY	OXYHAEMOGLOBINS
OVERTEEMING	OVERTRUSTS	OVERWEIGHTING	OVULATIONS	OXYHEMOGLOBIN
OVERTHINKING	OVERTURING	OVERWEIGHTS	OVULIFEROUS	OXYHEMOGLOBINS
OVERTHINKS	OVERTURNED	OVERWETTED	OWERLOUPEN	OXYHYDROGEN
OVERTHINNED	OVERTURNER	OVERWETTING	OWERLOUPING	OXYHYDROGENS
OVERTHINNING	OVERTURNERS	OVERWHELMED	OWERLOUPIT	OXYMORONIC
OVERTHOUGHT	OVERTURNING	OVERWHELMING	OWLISHNESS	OXYMORONICALLY
OVERTHROWER	OVERTYPING	OVERWHELMINGLY	OWLISHNESSES	OXYPHENBUTAZONE
OVERTHROWERS	OVERURGING	OVERWHELMINGS	OWNERSHIPS	OXYRHYNCHUS
OVERTHROWING	OVERUTILISATION	OVERWHELMS	OWRECOMING	OXYRHYNCHUSES
OVERTHROWN	OVERUTILISE	OVERWILIER	OXACILLINS	OXYSULPHIDE
OVERTHROWS	OVERUTILISED	OVERWILIEST	OXALACETATE	OXYSULPHIDES
OVERTHRUST	OVERUTILISES	OVERWINDED	OXALACETATES	OXYTETRACYCLINE
OVERTHRUSTS	OVERUTILISING	OVERWINDING	OXALOACETATE	OXYURIASES
OVERTHWART	OVERUTILIZATION	OVERWINGED	OXALOACETATES	OXYURIASIS
OVERTHWARTED	OVERUTILIZE	OVERWINGING	OXALOACETIC	OYSTERCATCHER
OVERTHWARTING	OVERUTILIZED	OVERWINTER	OXIDATIONAL	OYSTERCATCHERS
OVERTHWARTS	OVERUTILIZES	OVERWINTERED	OXIDATIONS	OYSTERINGS
OVERTIGHTEN	OVERUTILIZING	OVERWINTERING	OXIDATIVELY	OZOCERITES
OVERTIGHTENED	OVERVALUATION	OVERWINTERS	OXIDIMETRIC	OZOKERITES
OVERTIGHTENING	OVERVALUATIONS	OVERWISELY	OXIDIMETRIES	OZONATIONS
OVERTIGHTENS	OVERVALUED	OVERWITHHELD	OXIDIMETRY	OZONIFEROUS
OVERTIMELY	OVERVALUES	OVERWITHHOLD	OXIDISABLE	OZONISATION
OVERTIMERS	OVERVALUING	OVERWITHHOLDING	OXIDISATION	OZONISATIONS
OVERTIMING	OVERVEILED	OVERWITHHOLDS	OXIDISATIONS	OZONIZATION
OVERTIPPED	OVERVEILING	OVERWORKED	OXIDIZABLE	OZONIZATIONS
OVERTIPPING	OVERVIOLENT	OVERWORKING	OXIDIZATION	OZONOLYSES
OVERTIRING	OVERVOLTAGE	OVERWRAPPED	OXIDIZATIONS	OZONOLYSIS
OVERTNESSES	OVERVOLTAGES	OVERWRAPPING	OXIDOREDUCTASE	OZONOSPHERE
OVERTOILED	OVERVOTING	OVERWRESTED	OXIDOREDUCTASES	OZONOSPHERES
OVERTOILING	OVERWARIER	OVERWRESTING	OXIMETRIES	

O

P

PACEMAKERS
PACEMAKING
PACEMAKINGS
PACESETTER
PACESETTERS
PACESETTING
PACESETTINGS
PACHYCARPOUS
PACHYDACTYL
PACHYDACTYLOUS
PACHYDERMAL
PACHYDERMATOUS
PACHYDERMIA
PACHYDERMIAS
PACHYDERMIC
PACHYDERMOUS
PACHYDERMS
PACHYMENINGITIS
PACHYMETER
PACHYMETERS
PACHYSANDRA
PACHYSANDRAS
PACHYTENES
PACIFIABLE
PACIFICALLY
PACIFICATE
PACIFICATED
PACIFICATES
PACIFICATING
PACIFICATION
PACIFICATIONS
PACIFICATOR
PACIFICATORS
PACIFICATORY
PACIFICISM
PACIFICISMS
PACIFICIST
PACIFICISTS
PACIFISTIC
PACIFISTICALLY
PACKABILITIES
PACKABILITY
PACKAGINGS
PACKBOARDS
PACKCLOTHS
PACKETISED
PACKETISES
PACKETISING
PACKETIZED
PACKETIZES
PACKETIZING
PACKFRAMES
PACKHORSES
PACKINGHOUSE

PACKINGHOUSES
PACKNESSES
PACKSADDLE
PACKSADDLES
PACKSHEETS
PACKSTAFFS
PACKTHREAD
PACKTHREADS
PACLITAXEL
PACLITAXELS
PACTIONING
PADDLEBALL
PADDLEBALLS
PADDLEBOARD
PADDLEBOARDS
PADDLEBOAT
PADDLEBOATS
PADDLEFISH
PADDLEFISHES
PADDOCKING
PADDYMELON
PADDYMELONS
PADDYWACKED
PADDYWACKING
PADDYWACKS
PADDYWHACK
PADDYWHACKS
PADEMELONS
PADEREROES
PADLOCKING
PADRONISMS
PADYMELONS
PAEDAGOGIC
PAEDAGOGUE
PAEDAGOGUES
PAEDERASTIC
PAEDERASTIES
PAEDERASTS
PAEDERASTY
PAEDEUTICS
PAEDIATRIC
PAEDIATRICIAN
PAEDIATRICIANS
PAEDIATRICS
PAEDIATRIES
PAEDIATRIST
PAEDIATRISTS
PAEDOBAPTISM
PAEDOBAPTISMS
PAEDOBAPTIST
PAEDOBAPTISTS
PAEDODONTIC
PAEDODONTICS
PAEDOGENESES

PAEDOGENESIS
PAEDOGENETIC
PAEDOGENIC
PAEDOLOGICAL
PAEDOLOGIES
PAEDOLOGIST
PAEDOLOGISTS
PAEDOMORPHIC
PAEDOMORPHISM
PAEDOMORPHISMS
PAEDOMORPHOSES
PAEDOMORPHOSIS
PAEDOPHILE
PAEDOPHILES
PAEDOPHILIA
PAEDOPHILIAC
PAEDOPHILIACS
PAEDOPHILIAS
PAEDOPHILIC
PAEDOPHILICS
PAEDOTRIBE
PAEDOTRIBES
PAEDOTROPHIES
PAEDOTROPHY
PAGANISATION
PAGANISATIONS
PAGANISERS
PAGANISING
PAGANISTIC
PAGANISTICALLY
PAGANIZATION
PAGANIZATIONS
PAGANIZERS
PAGANIZING
PAGEANTRIES
PAGINATING
PAGINATION
PAGINATIONS
PAIDEUTICS
PAILLASSES
PAILLETTES
PAINFULLER
PAINFULLEST
PAINFULNESS
PAINFULNESSES
PAINKILLER
PAINKILLERS
PAINKILLING
PAINLESSLY
PAINLESSNESS
PAINLESSNESSES
PAINSTAKER
PAINSTAKERS
PAINSTAKING

PAINSTAKINGLY
PAINSTAKINGNESS
PAINSTAKINGS
PAINTBALLING
PAINTBALLINGS
PAINTBALLS
PAINTBOXES
PAINTBRUSH
PAINTBRUSHES
PAINTERLINESS
PAINTERLINESSES
PAINTINESS
PAINTINESSES
PAINTRESSES
PAINTWORKS
PAKIRIKIRI
PAKIRIKIRIS
PALACINKES
PALAEANTHROPIC
PALAEBIOLOGIES
PALAEBIOLOGIST
PALAEBIOLOGISTS
PALAEBIOLOGY
PALAEETHNOLOGY
PALAEOANTHROPIC
PALAEOBIOLOGIC
PALAEOBIOLOGIES
PALAEOBIOLOGIST
PALAEOBIOLOGY
PALAEOBOTANIC
PALAEOBOTANICAL
PALAEOBOTANIES
PALAEOBOTANIST
PALAEOBOTANISTS
PALAEOBOTANY
PALAEOCLIMATE
PALAEOCLIMATES
PALAEOCLIMATIC
PALAEOCRYSTIC
PALAEOCURRENT
PALAEOCURRENTS
PALAEOECOLOGIC
PALAEOECOLOGIES
PALAEOECOLOGIST
PALAEOECOLOGY
PALAEOETHNOLOGY
PALAEOGAEA
PALAEOGAEAS
PALAEOGEOGRAPHY
PALAEOGRAPHER
PALAEOGRAPHERS
PALAEOGRAPHIC
PALAEOGRAPHICAL
PALAEOGRAPHIES

PALAEOGRAPHIST
PALAEOGRAPHISTS
PALAEOGRAPHY
PALAEOLIMNOLOGY
PALAEOLITH
PALAEOLITHIC
PALAEOLITHS
PALAEOLOGIES
PALAEOLOGY
PALAEOMAGNETIC
PALAEOMAGNETISM
PALAEOMAGNETIST
PALAEONTOGRAPHY
PALAEONTOLOGIES
PALAEONTOLOGIST
PALAEONTOLOGY
PALAEOPATHOLOGY
PALAEOPEDOLOGY
PALAEOPHYTOLOGY
PALAEOSOLS
PALAEOTYPE
PALAEOTYPES
PALAEOTYPIC
PALAEOZOOLOGIES
PALAEOZOOLOGIST
PALAEOZOOLOGY
PALAESTRAE
PALAESTRAL
PALAESTRAS
PALAESTRIC
PALAESTRICAL
PALAFITTES
PALAGONITE
PALAGONITES
PALAMPORES
PALANKEENS
PALANQUINS
PALATABILITIES
PALATABILITY
PALATABLENESS
PALATABLENESSES
PALATALISATION
PALATALISATIONS
PALATALISE
PALATALISED
PALATALISES
PALATALISING
PALATALIZATION
PALATALIZATIONS
PALATALIZE
PALATALIZED
PALATALIZES
PALATALIZING
PALATIALLY

PALATIALNESS	PALINDROMICAL	PALMERWORMS	PANARITIUMS	PANEGYRISTS
PALATIALNESSES	PALINDROMIST	PALMETTOES	PANARTHRITIS	PANEGYRIZE
PALATINATE	PALINDROMISTS	PALMHOUSES	PANARTHRITISES	PANEGYRIZED
PALATINATES	PALINGENESES	PALMIFICATION	PANATELLAS	PANEGYRIZES
PALAVERERS	PALINGENESIA	PALMIFICATIONS	PANBROILED	PANEGYRIZING
PALAVERING	PALINGENESIAS	PALMIPEDES	PANBROILING	PANELLINGS
PALEACEOUS	PALINGENESIES	PALMISTERS	PANCHAYATS	PANELLISED
PALEMPORES	PALINGENESIS	PALMISTRIES	PANCHROMATIC	PANELLISTS
PALENESSES	PALINGENESIST	PALMITATES	PANCHROMATISM	PANELLIZED
PALEOBIOLOGIC	PALINGENESISTS	PALMPRINTS	PANCHROMATISMS	PANENTHEISM
PALEOBIOLOGICAL	PALINGENESY	PALOVERDES	PANCOSMISM	PANENTHEISMS
PALEOBIOLOGIES	PALINGENETIC	PALPABILITIES	PANCOSMISMS	PANENTHEIST
PALEOBIOLOGIST	PALINGENETICAL	PALPABILITY	PANCRATIAN	PANENTHEISTS
PALEOBIOLOGISTS	PALINODIES	PALPABLENESS	PANCRATIAST	PANESTHESIA
PALEOBIOLOGY	PALINOPIAS	PALPABLENESSES	PANCRATIASTS	PANESTHESIAS
PALEOBOTANIC	PALINOPSIA	PALPATIONS	PANCRATIST	PANETELLAS
PALEOBOTANICAL	PALINOPSIAS	PALPEBRATE	PANCRATISTS	PANETTONES
PALEOBOTANIES	PALISADING	PALPEBRATED	PANCRATIUM	PANFISHING
PALEOBOTANIST	PALISADOED	PALPEBRATES	PANCRATIUMS	PANFISHINGS
PALEOBOTANISTS	PALISADOES	PALPEBRATING	PANCREASES	PANGENESES
PALEOBOTANY	PALISADOING	PALPITATED	PANCREATECTOMY	PANGENESIS
PALEOECOLOGIC	PALISANDER	PALPITATES	PANCREATIC	PANGENETIC
PALEOECOLOGICAL	PALISANDERS	PALPITATING	PANCREATIN	PANGENETICALLY
PALEOECOLOGIES	PALLADIOUS	PALPITATION	PANCREATINS	PANGRAMMATIST
PALEOECOLOGIST	PALLADIUMS	PALPITATIONS	PANCREATITIDES	PANGRAMMATISTS
PALEOECOLOGISTS	PALLASITES	PALSGRAVES	PANCREATITIS	PANHANDLED
PALEOECOLOGY	PALLBEARER	PALSGRAVINE	PANCREATITISES	PANHANDLER
PALEOGEOGRAPHIC	PALLBEARERS	PALSGRAVINES	PANCREOZYMIN	PANHANDLERS
PALEOGEOGRAPHY	PALLESCENCE	PALTRINESS	PANCREOZYMINS	PANHANDLES
PALEOGRAPHER	PALLESCENCES	PALTRINESSES	PANCYTOPENIA	PANHANDLING
PALEOGRAPHERS	PALLESCENT	PALUDAMENT	PANCYTOPENIAS	PANHARMONICON
PALEOGRAPHIC	PALLETISATION	PALUDAMENTA	PANDAEMONIUM	PANHARMONICONS
PALEOGRAPHICAL	PALLETISATIONS	PALUDAMENTS	PANDAEMONIUMS	PANHELLENIC
PALEOGRAPHIES	PALLETISED	PALUDAMENTUM	PANDANACEOUS	PANHELLENION
PALEOGRAPHY	PALLETISER	PALUDAMENTUMS	PANDANUSES	PANHELLENIONS
PALEOLITHIC	PALLETISERS	PALUDICOLOUS	PANDATIONS	PANHELLENIUM
PALEOLITHS	PALLETISES	PALUDINOUS	PANDECTIST	PANHELLENIUMS
PALEOLOGIES	PALLETISING	PALUSTRIAN	PANDECTISTS	PANICKIEST
PALEOMAGNETIC	PALLETIZATION	PALUSTRINE	PANDEMONIAC	PANICMONGER
PALEOMAGNETISM	PALLETIZATIONS	PALYNOLOGIC	PANDEMONIACAL	PANICMONGERS
PALEOMAGNETISMS	PALLETIZED	PALYNOLOGICAL	PANDEMONIAN	PANICULATE
PALEOMAGNETIST	PALLETIZER	PALYNOLOGICALLY	PANDEMONIANS	PANICULATED
PALEOMAGNETISTS	PALLETIZERS	PALYNOLOGIES	PANDEMONIC	PANICULATELY
PALEONTOLOGIC	PALLETIZES	PALYNOLOGIST	PANDEMONIUM	PANIDIOMORPHIC
PALEONTOLOGICAL	PALLETIZING	PALYNOLOGISTS	PANDEMONIUMS	PANIFICATION
PALEONTOLOGIES	PALLIAMENT	PALYNOLOGY	PANDERESSES	PANIFICATIONS
PALEONTOLOGIST	PALLIAMENTS	PAMPELMOOSE	PANDERINGS	PANISLAMIST
PALEONTOLOGISTS	PALLIASSES	PAMPELMOOSES	PANDERISMS	PANJANDARUM
PALEONTOLOGY	PALLIATING	PAMPELMOUSE	PANDERMITE	PANJANDARUMS
PALEOPATHOLOGY	PALLIATION	PAMPELMOUSES	PANDERMITES	PANJANDRUM
PALEOZOOLOGICAL	PALLIATIONS	PAMPEREDNESS	PANDICULATION	PANJANDRUMS
PALEOZOOLOGIES	PALLIATIVE	PAMPEREDNESSES	PANDICULATIONS	PANLEUCOPENIA
PALEOZOOLOGIST	PALLIATIVELY	PAMPERINGS	PANDOWDIES	PANLEUCOPENIAS
PALEOZOOLOGISTS	PALLIATIVES	PAMPHLETED	PANDURATED	PANLEUKOPENIA
PALEOZOOLOGY	PALLIATORS	PAMPHLETEER	PANDURIFORM	PANLEUKOPENIAS
PALFRENIER	PALLIATORY	PAMPHLETEERED	PANEGOISMS	PANLOGISMS
PALFRENIERS	PALLIDITIES	PAMPHLETEERING	PANEGYRICA	PANMIXISES
PALIFICATION	PALLIDNESS	PAMPHLETEERINGS	PANEGYRICAL	PANNICULUS
PALIFICATIONS	PALLIDNESSES	PAMPHLETEERS	PANEGYRICALLY	PANNICULUSES
PALILALIAS	PALMACEOUS	PAMPHLETING	PANEGYRICON	PANNIKELLS
PALILLOGIES	PALMATIFID	PAMPOOTIES	PANEGYRICS	PANOMPHAEAN
PALIMONIES	PALMATIONS	PANACHAEAS	PANEGYRIES	PANOPHOBIA
PALIMPSEST	PALMATIPARTITE	PANAESTHESIA	PANEGYRISE	PANOPHOBIAS
PALIMPSESTS	PALMATISECT	PANAESTHESIAS	PANEGYRISED	PANOPHTHALMIA
PALINDROME	PALMCORDER	PANAESTHETISM	PANEGYRISES	PANOPHTHALMIAS
PALINDROMES	PALMCORDERS	PANAESTHETISMS	PANEGYRISING	PANOPHTHALMITIS
PALINDROMIC	PALMERWORM	PANARITIUM	PANEGYRIST	PANOPTICAL

PANOPTICALLY	PANTHERISII	PAPERBACKS	PARABLASTS	PARADOXICAL
PANOPTICON	PANTIHOSES	PAPERBARKS	PARABLEPSES	PARADOXICALITY
PANOPTICONS	PANTILINGS	PAPERBOARD	PARABLEPSIES	PARADOXICALLY
PANORAMICALLY	PANTISOCRACIES	PAPERBOARDS	PARABLEPSIS	PARADOXICALNESS
PANPHARMACON	PANTISOCRACY	PAPERBOUND	PARABLEPSY	PARADOXIDIAN
PANPHARMACONS	PANTISOCRAT	PAPERBOUNDS	PARABLEPTIC	PARADOXIES
PANPSYCHISM	PANTISOCRATIC	PAPERCLIPS	PARABOLANUS	PARADOXIST
PANPSYCHISMS	PANTISOCRATICAL	PAPERGIRLS	PARABOLANUSES	PARADOXISTS
PANPSYCHIST	PANTISOCRATIST	PAPERHANGER	PARABOLICAL	PARADOXOLOGIES
PANPSYCHISTIC	PANTISOCRATISTS	PAPERHANGERS	PARABOLICALLY	PARADOXOLOGY
PANPSYCHISTS	PANTISOCRATS	PAPERHANGING	PARABOLISATION	PARADOXURE
PANRADIOMETER	PANTOFFLES	PAPERHANGINGS	PARABOLISATIONS	PARADOXURES
PANRADIOMETERS	PANTOGRAPH	PAPERINESS	PARABOLISE	PARADOXURINE
PANSEXUALISM	PANTOGRAPHER	PAPERINESSES	PARABOLISED	PARADOXURINES
PANSEXUALISMS	PANTOGRAPHERS	PAPERKNIFE	PARABOLISES	PARADROPPED
PANSEXUALIST	PANTOGRAPHIC	PAPERKNIVES	PARABOLISING	PARADROPPING
PANSEXUALISTS	PANTOGRAPHICAL	PAPERMAKER	PARABOLIST	PARAENESES
PANSEXUALITIES	PANTOGRAPHIES	PAPERMAKERS	PARABOLISTS	PARAENESIS
PANSEXUALITY	PANTOGRAPHS	PAPERMAKING	PARABOLIZATION	PARAENETIC
PANSEXUALS	PANTOGRAPHY	PAPERMAKINGS	PARABOLIZATIONS	PARAENETICAL
PANSOPHICAL	PANTOMIMED	PAPERWARES	PARABOLIZE	PARAESTHESIA
PANSOPHICALLY	PANTOMIMES	PAPERWEIGHT	PARABOLIZED	PARAESTHESIAS
PANSOPHIES	PANTOMIMIC	PAPERWEIGHTS	PARABOLIZES	PARAESTHETIC
PANSOPHISM	PANTOMIMICAL	PAPERWORKS	PARABOLIZING	PARAFFINED
PANSOPHISMS	PANTOMIMICALLY	PAPETERIES	PARABOLOID	PARAFFINES
PANSOPHIST	PANTOMIMING	PAPILIONACEOUS	PARABOLOIDAL	PARAFFINIC
PANSOPHISTS	PANTOMIMIST	PAPILLATED	PARABOLOIDS	PARAFFINIER
PANSPERMATIC	PANTOMIMISTS	PAPILLIFEROUS	PARABRAKES	PARAFFINIEST
PANSPERMATISM	PANTOPHAGIES	PAPILLIFORM	PARACASEIN	PARAFFINING
PANSPERMATISMS	PANTOPHAGIST	PAPILLITIS	PARACASEINS	PARAFFINOID
PANSPERMATIST	PANTOPHAGISTS	PAPILLITISES	PARACENTESES	PARAGENESES
PANSPERMATISTS	PANTOPHAGOUS	PAPILLOMAS	PARACENTESIS	PARAGENESIA
PANSPERMIA	PANTOPHAGY	PAPILLOMATA	PARACETAMOL	PARAGENESIAS
PANSPERMIAS	PANTOPHOBIA	PAPILLOMATOSES	PARACETAMOLS	PARAGENESIS
PANSPERMIC	PANTOPHOBIAS	PAPILLOMATOSIS	PARACHRONISM	PARAGENETIC
PANSPERMIES	PANTOPRAGMATIC	PAPILLOMATOUS	PARACHRONISMS	PARAGENETICALLY
PANSPERMISM	PANTOPRAGMATICS	PAPILLOMAVIRUS	PARACHUTED	PARAGLIDED
PANSPERMISMS	PANTOSCOPE	PAPILLOTES	PARACHUTES	PARAGLIDER
PANSPERMIST	PANTOSCOPES	PAPILLULATE	PARACHUTIC	PARAGLIDERS
PANSPERMISTS	PANTOSCOPIC	PAPILLULES	PARACHUTING	PARAGLIDES
PANTAGAMIES	PANTOTHENATE	PAPISTICAL	PARACHUTINGS	PARAGLIDING
PANTAGRAPH	PANTOTHENATES	PAPISTICALLY	PARACHUTIST	PARAGLIDINGS
PANTAGRAPHS	PANTOTHENIC	PAPISTRIES	PARACHUTISTS	PARAGLOSSA
PANTALEONS	PANTOUFLES	PAPOVAVIRUS	PARACLETES	PARAGLOSSAE
PANTALETTED	PANTROPICAL	PAPOVAVIRUSES	PARACROSTIC	PARAGLOSSAL
PANTALETTES	PANTRYMAID	PAPPARDELLE	PARACROSTICS	PARAGLOSSATE
PANTALONES	PANTRYMAIDS	PAPPARDELLES	PARACYANOGEN	PARAGNATHISM
PANTALOONED	PANTSUITED	PAPRIKASES	PARACYANOGENS	PARAGNATHISMS
PANTALOONERIES	PANTYHOSES	PAPRIKASHES	PARADIDDLE	PARAGNATHOUS
PANTALOONERY	PANTYWAIST	PAPULATION	PARADIDDLED	PARAGNOSES
PANTALOONS	PANTYWAISTS	PAPULATIONS	PARADIDDLES	PARAGNOSIS
PANTDRESSES	PANZEROTTI	PAPULIFEROUS	PARADIDDLING	PARAGOGICAL
PANTECHNICON	PANZEROTTO	PAPYRACEOUS	PARADIGMATIC	PARAGOGICALLY
PANTECHNICONS	PANZEROTTOS	PAPYROLOGICAL	PARADIGMATICAL	PARAGOGUES
PANTHEISMS	PANZOOTICS	PAPYROLOGIES	PARADISAIC	PARAGONING
PANTHEISTIC	PAPALISING	PAPYROLOGIST	PARADISAICAL	PARAGONITE
PANTHEISTICAL	PAPALIZING	PAPYROLOGISTS	PARADISAICALLY	PARAGONITES
PANTHEISTICALLY	PAPAPRELATIST	PAPYROLOGY	PARADISEAN	PARAGRAMMATIST
PANTHEISTS	PAPAPRELATISTS	PARABAPTISM	PARADISIAC	PARAGRAMMATISTS
PANTHENOLS	PAPAVERACEOUS	PARABAPTISMS	PARADISIACAL	PARAGRAPHED
PANTHEOLOGIES	PAPAVERINE	PARABEMATA	PARADISIACALLY	PARAGRAPHER
PANTHEOLOGIST	PAPAVERINES	PARABEMATIC	PARADISIAL	PARAGRAPHERS
PANTHEOLOGISTS	PAPAVEROUS	PARABIOSES	PARADISIAN	PARAGRAPHIA
PANTHEOLOGY	PAPERBACKED	PARABIOSIS	PARADISICAL	PARAGRAPHIAS
PANTHERESS	PAPERBACKER	PARABIOTIC	PARADOCTOR	PARAGRAPHIC
PANTHERESSES	PAPERBACKERS	PARABIOTICALLY	PARADOCTORS	PARAGRAPHICAL
PANTHERINE	PAPERBACKING	PARABLASTIC	PARADOXERS	PARAGRAPHICALLY

PARAGRAPHING	PARALOGIAS	PARAMETRISING	PARAPHRASED	PARASITAEMIA
PARAGRAPHIST	PARALOGIES	PARAMETRIZATION	PARAPHRASER	PARASITAEMIAS
PARAGRAPHISTS	PARALOGISE	PARAMETRIZE	PARAPHRASERS	PARASITICAL
PARAGRAPHS	PARALOGISED	PARAMETRIZED	PARAPHRASES	PARASITICALLY
PARAHELIOTROPIC	PARALOGISES	PARAMETRIZES	PARAPHRASING	PARASITICALNESS
PARAHYDROGEN	PARALOGISING	PARAMETRIZING	PARAPHRAST	PARASITICIDAL
PARAHYDROGENS	PARALOGISM	PARAMILITARIES	PARAPHRASTIC	PARASITICIDE
PARAINFLUENZA	PARALOGISMS	PARAMILITARY	PARAPHRASTICAL	PARASITICIDES
PARAINFLUENZAS	PARALOGIST	PARAMNESIA	PARAPHRASTS	PARASITISATION
PARAJOURNALISM	PARALOGISTIC	PARAMNESIAS	PARAPHRAXES	PARASITISATIONS
PARAJOURNALISMS	PARALOGISTS	PARAMOECIA	PARAPHRAXIA	PARASITISE
PARAKEELYA	PARALOGIZE	PARAMOECIUM	PARAPHRAXIAS	PARASITISED
PARAKEELYAS	PARALOGIZED	PARAMORPHIC	PARAPHRAXIS	PARASITISES
PARAKELIAS	PARALOGIZES	PARAMORPHINE	PARAPHRENIA	PARASITISING
PARAKITING	PARALOGIZING	PARAMORPHINES	PARAPHRENIAS	PARASITISM
PARAKITINGS	PARALOGUES	PARAMORPHISM	PARAPHYSATE	PARASITISMS
PARALALIAS	PARALYMPIC	PARAMORPHISMS	PARAPHYSES	PARASITIZATION
PARALANGUAGE	PARALYMPICS	PARAMORPHOUS	PARAPHYSIS	PARASITIZATIONS
PARALANGUAGES	PARALYSATION	PARAMORPHS	PARAPINEAL	PARASITIZE
PARALDEHYDE	PARALYSATIONS	PARAMOUNCIES	PARAPLANNER	PARASITIZED
PARALDEHYDES	PARALYSERS	PARAMOUNCY	PARAPLANNERS	PARASITIZES
PARALEGALS	PARALYSING	PARAMOUNTCIES	PARAPLEGIA	PARASITIZING
PARALEIPOMENA	PARALYSINGLY	PARAMOUNTCY	PARAPLEGIAS	PARASITOID
PARALEIPOMENON	PARALYTICALLY	PARAMOUNTLY	PARAPLEGIC	PARASITOIDS
PARALEIPSES	PARALYTICS	PARAMOUNTS	PARAPLEGICS	PARASITOLOGIC
PARALEIPSIS	PARALYZATION	PARAMYLUMS	PARAPODIAL	PARASITOLOGICAL
PARALEXIAS	PARALYZATIONS	PARAMYXOVIRUS	PARAPODIUM	PARASITOLOGIES
PARALIMNION	PARALYZERS	PARAMYXOVIRUSES	PARAPOPHYSES	PARASITOLOGIST
PARALIMNIONS	PARALYZING	PARANEPHRIC	PARAPOPHYSIAL	PARASITOLOGISTS
PARALINGUISTIC	PARALYZINGLY	PARANEPHRINE	PARAPOPHYSIS	PARASITOLOGY
PARALINGUISTICS	PARAMAECIA	PARANEPHROSES	PARAPRAXES	PARASITOSES
PARALIPOMENA	PARAMAECIUM	PARANOEICS	PARAPRAXIS	PARASITOSIS
PARALIPOMENON	PARAMAGNET	PARANOIACS	PARAPRAXISES	PARASKIING
PARALIPSES	PARAMAGNETIC	PARANOICALLY	PARAPSYCHIC	PARASKIINGS
PARALIPSIS	PARAMAGNETISM	PARANOIDAL	PARAPSYCHICAL	PARASOMNIA
PARALLACTIC	PARAMAGNETISMS	PARANORMAL	PARAPSYCHISM	PARASOMNIAS
PARALLACTICAL	PARAMAGNETS	PARANORMALITIES	PARAPSYCHISMS	PARASPHENOID
PARALLACTICALLY	PARAMASTOID	PARANORMALITY	PARAPSYCHOLOGY	PARASPHENOIDS
PARALLAXES	PARAMASTOIDS	PARANORMALLY	PARAPSYCHOSES	PARASTATAL
PARALLELED	PARAMATTAS	PARANORMALS	PARAPSYCHOSIS	PARASTATALS
PARALLELEPIPED	PARAMECIUM	PARANTHELIA	PARAQUADRATE	PARASTICHIES
PARALLELEPIPEDA	PARAMECIUMS	PARANTHELION	PARAQUADRATES	PARASTICHOUS
PARALLELEPIPEDS	PARAMEDICAL	PARANTHROPUS	PARAQUITOS	PARASTICHY
PARALLELING	PARAMEDICALS	PARANTHROPUSES	PARARHYMES	PARASUICIDE
PARALLELINGS	PARAMEDICO	PARANYMPHS	PARAROSANILINE	PARASUICIDES
PARALLELISE	PARAMEDICOS	PARAPARESES	PARAROSANILINES	PARASYMBIONT
PARALLELISED	PARAMEDICS	PARAPARESIS	PARARTHRIA	PARASYMBIONTS
PARALLELISES	PARAMENSTRUA	PARAPARETIC	PARARTHRIAS	PARASYMBIOSES
PARALLELISING	PARAMENSTRUUM	PARAPENTES	PARASAILED	PARASYMBIOSIS
PARALLELISM	PARAMENSTRUUMS	PARAPENTING	PARASAILING	PARASYMBIOTIC
PARALLELISMS	PARAMETERISE	PARAPENTINGS	PARASAILINGS	PARASYMPATHETIC
PARALLELIST	PARAMETERISED	PARAPERIODIC	PARASCENDER	PARASYNAPSES
PARALLELISTIC	PARAMETERISES	PARAPHASIA	PARASCENDERS	PARASYNAPSIS
PARALLELISTS	PARAMETERISING	PARAPHASIAS	PARASCENDING	PARASYNAPTIC
PARALLELIZE	PARAMETERIZE	PARAPHASIC	PARASCENDINGS	PARASYNTHESES
PARALLELIZED	PARAMETERIZED	PARAPHERNALIA	PARASCENIA	PARASYNTHESIS
PARALLELIZES	PARAMETERIZES	PARAPHILIA	PARASCENIUM	PARASYNTHETA
PARALLELIZING	PARAMETERIZING	PARAPHILIAC	PARASCEVES	PARASYNTHETIC
PARALLELLED	PARAMETERS	PARAPHILIACS	PARASCIENCE	PARASYNTHETON
PARALLELLING	PARAMETRAL	PARAPHILIAS	PARASCIENCES	PARATACTIC
PARALLELLY	PARAMETRIC	PARAPHIMOSES	PARASELENAE	PARATACTICAL
PARALLELOGRAM	PARAMETRICAL	PARAPHIMOSIS	PARASELENE	PARATACTICALLY
PARALLELOGRAMS	PARAMETRICALLY	PARAPHONIA	PARASELENIC	PARATANIWHA
PARALLELOPIPED	PARAMETRISATION	PARAPHONIAS	PARASEXUAL	PARATANIWHAS
PARALLELOPIPEDA	PARAMETRISE	PARAPHONIC	PARASEXUALITIES	PARATHESES
PARALLELOPIPEDS	PARAMETRISED	PARAPHRASABLE	PARASEXUALITY	PARATHESIS
PARALLELWISE	PARAMETRISES	PARAPHRASE	PARASHIOTH	PARATHIONS

PARATHORMONE	PARENTHESIZING	PAROCHIALISE	PARSONAGES	PARTICULARISTS
PARATHORMONES	PARENTHETIC	PAROCHIALTSED	PARSONICAL	PARTICULARITIES
PARATHYROID	PARENTHETICAL	PAROCHIALISES	PARTAKINGS	PARTICULARITY
PARATHYROIDS	PARENTHETICALLY	PAROCHIALISING	PARTHENOCARPIC	PARTICULARTZE
PARATROOPER	PARENTHOOD	PAROCHIALISM	PARTHENOCARPIES	PARTICULARIZED
PARATROOPERS	PARENTHOODS	PAROCHIALISMS	PARTHENOCARPOUS	PARTICULARIZER
PARATROOPS	PARENTINGS	PAROCHIALITIES	PARTHENOCARPY	PARTICULARIZERS
PARATUNGSTIC	PARENTLESS	PAROCHIALITY	PARTHENOGENESES	PARTICULARIZES
PARATYPHOID	PARESTHESIA	PAROCHIALIZE	PARTHENOGENESIS	PARTICULARIZING
PARATYPHOIDS	PARESTHESIAS	PAROCHIALIZED	PARTHENOGENETIC	PARTICULARLY
PARAWALKER	PARESTHETIC	PAROCHIALIZES	PARTHENOSPORE	PARTICULARNESS
PARAWALKERS	PARFLECHES	PAROCHIALIZING	PARTHENOSPORES	PARTICULARS
PARBOILING	PARFLESHES	PAROCHIALLY	PARTIALISE	PARTICULATE
PARBREAKED	PARFOCALISE	PAROCHINES	PARTIALISED	PARTICULATES
PARBREAKING	PARFOCALISED	PARODISTIC	PARTIALISES	PARTISANLY
PARBUCKLED	PARFOCALISES	PAROECIOUS	PARTIALISING	PARTISANSHIP
PARBUCKLES	PARFOCALISING	PAROECISMS	PARTIALISM	PARTISANSHIPS
PARBUCKLING	PARFOCALITIES	PAROEMIACS	PARTIALISMS	PARTITIONED
PARCELLING	PARFOCALITY	PAROEMIOGRAPHER	PARTIALIST	PARTITIONER
PARCELWISE	PARFOCALIZE	PAROEMIOGRAPHY	PARTIALISTS	PARTITIONERS
PARCENARIES	PARFOCALIZED	PAROEMIOLOGIES	PARTIALITIES	PARTITIONING
PARCHEDNESS	PARFOCALIZES	PAROEMIOLOGY	PARTIALITY	PARTITIONIST
PARCHEDNESSES	PARFOCALIZING	PARONOMASIA	PARTIALIZE	PARTITIONISTS
PARCHEESIS	PARGASITES	PARONOMASIAS	PARTIALIZED	PARTITIONMENT
PARCHMENTIER	PARGETINGS	PARONOMASIES	PARTIALIZES	PARTITIONMENTS
PARCHMENTIEST	PARGETTERS	PARONOMASTIC	PARTIALIZING	PARTITIONS
PARCHMENTISE	PARGETTING	PARONOMASTICAL	PARTIALLED	PARTITIVELY
PARCHMENTISED	PARGETTINGS	PARONOMASY	PARTIALLING	PARTITIVES
PARCHMENTISES	PARGYLINES	PARONYCHIA	PARTIALNESS	PARTITURAS
PARCHMENTISING	PARHELIACAL	PARONYCHIAL	PARTIALNESSES	PARTIZANLY
PARCHMENTIZE	PARHELIONS	PARONYCHIAS	PARTIBILITIES	PARTIZANSHIP
PARCHMENTIZED	PARHYPATES	PARONYMIES	PARTIBILITY	PARTIZANSHIPS
PARCHMENTIZES	PARIPINNATE	PARONYMOUS	PARTICIPABLE	PARTNERING
PARCHMENTIZING	PARISCHANE	PARONYMOUSLY	PARTICIPANT	PARTNERINGS
PARCHMENTS	PARISCHANES	PAROTIDITIC	PARTICIPANTLY	PARTNERLESS
PARCHMENTY	PARISCHANS	PAROTIDITIS	PARTICIPANTS	PARTNERSHIP
PARCIMONIES	PARISHIONER	PAROTIDITISES	PARTICIPATE	PARTNERSHIPS
PARDALISES	PARISHIONERS	PAROTITIDES	PARTICIPATED	PARTRIDGEBERRY
PARDALOTES	PARISYLLABIC	PAROTITISES	PARTICIPATES	PARTRIDGES
PARDONABLE	PARKINSONIAN	PAROXETINE	PARTICIPATING	PARTURIENCIES
PARDONABLENESS	PARKINSONIANS	PAROXETINES	PARTICIPATION	PARTURIENCY
PARDONABLY	PARKINSONISM	PAROXYSMAL	PARTICIPATIONAL	PARTURIENT
PARDONINGS	PARKINSONISMS	PAROXYSMALLY	PARTICIPATIONS	PARTURIENTS
PARDONLESS	PARKLEAVES	PAROXYSMIC	PARTICIPATIVE	PARTURIFACIENT
PAREGORICS	PARLEMENTS	PAROXYTONE	PARTICIPATOR	PARTURIFACIENTS
PAREIDOLIA	PARLEYVOOED	PAROXYTONES	PARTICIPATORS	PARTURITION
PAREIDOLIAS	PARLEYVOOING	PAROXYTONIC	PARTICIPATORY	PARTURITIONS
PARENCEPHALA	PARLEYVOOS	PARQUETING	PARTICIPIAL	PARTYGOERS
PARENCEPHALON	PARLIAMENT	PARQUETRIES	PARTICIPIALLY	PARURETICS
PARENCHYMA	PARLIAMENTARIAN	PARQUETTED	PARTICIPIALS	PARVANIMITIES
PARENCHYMAL	PARLIAMENTARILY	PARQUETTING	PARTICIPLE	PARVANIMITY
PARENCHYMAS	PARLIAMENTARISM	PARRAKEETS	PARTICIPLES	PARVIFOLIATE
PARENCHYMATA	PARLIAMENTARY	PARRAMATTA	PARTICLEBOARD	PARVOLINES
PARENCHYMATOUS	PARLIAMENTING	PARRAMATTAS	PARTICLEBOARDS	PARVOVIRUS
PARENTAGES	PARLIAMENTINGS	PARRHESIAS	PARTICOLORED	PARVOVIRUSES
PARENTALLY	PARLIAMENTS	PARRICIDAL	PARTICOLOURED	PASIGRAPHIC
PARENTERAL	PARLOURMAID	PARRICIDES	PARTICULAR	PASIGRAPHICAL
PARENTERALLY	PARLOURMAIDS	PARRITCHES	PARTICULARISE	PASIGRAPHIES
PARENTHESES	PARLOUSNESS	PARROCKING	PARTICULARISED	PASIGRAPHY
PARENTHESIS	PARLOUSNESSES	PARROQUETS	PARTICULARISER	PASODOBLES
PARENTHESISE	PARMACITIE	PARROTFISH	PARTICULARISERS	PASQUEFLOWER
PARENTHESISED	PARMACITIES	PARROTFISHES	PARTICULARISES	PASQUEFLOWERS
PARENTHESISES	PARMIGIANA	PARROTIEST	PARTICULARISING	PASQUILANT
PARENTHESISING	PARMIGIANO	PARROTRIES	PARTICULARISM	PASQUILANTS
PARENTHESIZE	PARMIGIANOS	PARSIMONIES	PARTICULARISMS	PASQUILERS
PARENTHESIZED	PAROCCIPITAL	PARSIMONIOUS	PARTICULARIST	PASQUILLED
PARENTHESIZES	PAROCCIPITALS	PARSIMONIOUSLY	PARTICULARISTIC	PASQUILLING

PASQUINADE	PASSPORTED	PATCHOULIES	PATIENTEST	PATRISTICAL
PASQUINADED	PASSPORTING	PATCHOULIS	PATIENTING	PATRISTICALLY
PASQUINADER	PASTEBOARD	PATCHWORKED	PATINATING	PATRISTICISM
PASQUINADERS	PASTEBOARDS	PATCHWORKING	PATINATION	PATRISTICISMS
PASQUINADES	PASTEDOWNS	PATCHWORKS	PATINATIONS	PATRISTICS
PASQUINADING	PASTELISTS	PATELLECTOMIES	PATINISING	PATROCLINAL
PASSABLENESS	PASTELLIST	PATELLECTOMY	PATINIZING	PATROCLINIC
PASSABLENESSES	PASTELLISTS	PATELLIFORM	PATISSERIE	PATROCLINIES
PASSACAGLIA	PASTEURELLA	PATENTABILITIES	PATISSERIES	PATROCLINOUS
PASSACAGLIAS	PASTEURELLAE	PATENTABILITY	PATISSIERS	PATROCLINY
PASSAGEWAY	PASTEURELLAS	PATENTABLE	PATRESFAMILIAS	PATROLLERS
PASSAGEWAYS	PASTEURISATION	PATERCOVES	PATRIALISATION	PATROLLING
PASSAGEWORK	PASTEURISATIONS	PATEREROES	PATRIALISATIONS	PATROLOGICAL
PASSAGEWORKS	PASTEURISE	PATERFAMILIAS	PATRIALISE	PATROLOGIES
PASSALONGS	PASTEURISED	PATERFAMILIASES	PATRIALISED	PATROLOGIST
PASSAMENTED	PASTEURISER	PATERNALISM	PATRIALISES	PATROLOGISTS
PASSAMENTING	PASTEURISERS	PATERNALISMS	PATRIALISING	PATROLWOMAN
PASSAMENTS	PASTEURISES	PATERNALIST	PATRIALISM	PATROLWOMEN
PASSAMEZZO	PASTEURISING	PATERNALISTIC	PATRIALISMS	PATRONAGED
PASSAMEZZOS	PASTEURISM	PATERNALISTS	PATRIALITIES	PATRONAGES
PASSEMEASURE	PASTEURISMS	PATERNALLY	PATRIALITY	PATRONAGING
PASSEMEASURES	PASTEURIZATION	PATERNITIES	PATRIALIZATION	PATRONESSES
PASSEMENTED	PASTEURIZATIONS	PATERNOSTER	PATRIALIZATIONS	PATRONISATION
PASSEMENTERIE	PASTEURIZE	PATERNOSTERS	PATRIALIZE	PATRONISATIONS
PASSEMENTERIES	PASTEURIZED	PATHBREAKING	PATRIALIZED	PATRONISED
PASSEMENTING	PASTEURIZER	PATHETICAL	PATRIALIZES	PATRONISER
PASSEMENTS	PASTEURIZERS	PATHETICALLY	PATRIALIZING	PATRONISERS
PASSENGERS	PASTEURIZES	PATHFINDER	PATRIARCHAL	PATRONISES
PASSEPIEDS	PASTEURIZING	PATHFINDERS	PATRIARCHALISM	PATRONISING
PASSERIFORM	PASTICCIOS	PATHFINDING	PATRIARCHALISMS	PATRONISINGLY
PASSERINES	PASTICHEUR	PATHFINDINGS	PATRIARCHALLY	PATRONIZATION
PASSIBILITIES	PASTICHEURS	PATHLESSNESS	PATRIARCHATE	PATRONIZATIONS
PASSIBILITY	PASTINESSES	PATHLESSNESSES	PATRIARCHATES	PATRONIZED
PASSIBLENESS	PASTITSIOS	PATHOBIOLOGIES	PATRIARCHIES	PATRONIZER
PASSIBLENESSES	PASTNESSES	PATHOBIOLOGY	PATRIARCHISM	PATRONIZERS
PASSIFLORA	PASTORALES	PATHOGENES	PATRIARCHISMS	PATRONIZES
PASSIFLORACEOUS	PASTORALISM	PATHOGENESES	PATRIARCHS	PATRONIZING
PASSIFLORAS	PASTORALISMS	PATHOGENESIS	PATRIARCHY	PATRONIZINGLY
PASSIMETER	PASTORALIST	PATHOGENETIC	PATRIATING	PATRONLESS
PASSIMETERS	PASTORALISTS	PATHOGENIC	PATRIATION	PATRONLIER
PASSIONALS	PASTORALLY	PATHOGENICITIES	PATRIATIONS	PATRONLIEST
PASSIONARIES	PASTORALNESS	PATHOGENICITY	PATRICIANLY	PATRONYMIC
PASSIONARY	PASTORALNESSES	PATHOGENIES	PATRICIANS	PATRONYMICS
PASSIONATE	PASTORATES	PATHOGENOUS	PATRICIATE	PATROONSHIP
PASSIONATED	PASTORIUMS	PATHOGNOMIES	PATRICIATES	PATROONSHIPS
PASSIONATELY	PASTORLIER	PATHOGNOMONIC	PATRICIDAL	PATTERNING
PASSIONATENESS	PASTORLIEST	PATHOGNOMY	PATRICIDES	PATTERNINGS
PASSIONATES	PASTORSHIP	PATHOGRAPHIES	PATRICLINIC	PATTERNLESS
PASSIONATING	PASTORSHIPS	PATHOGRAPHY	PATRICLINOUS	PATTRESSES
PASSIONFLOWER	PASTOURELLE	PATHOLOGIC	PATRIFOCAL	PATULOUSLY
PASSIONFLOWERS	PASTOURELLES	PATHOLOGICAL	PATRIFOCALITIES	PATULOUSNESS
PASSIONING	PASTRYCOOK	PATHOLOGICALLY	PATRIFOCALITY	PATULOUSNESSES
PASSIONLESS	PASTRYCOOKS	PATHOLOGIES	PATRILINEAGE	PAUCILOQUENT
PASSIONLESSLY	PASTURABLE	PATHOLOGISE	PATRILINEAGES	PAUGHTIEST
PASSIONLESSNESS	PASTURAGES	PATHOLOGISED	PATRILINEAL	PAULOWNIAS
PASSIVATED	PASTURELAND	PATHOLOGISES	PATRILINEALLY	PAUNCHIEST
PASSIVATES	PASTURELANDS	PATHOLOGISING	PATRILINEAR	PAUNCHINESS
PASSIVATING	PASTURELESS	PATHOLOGIST	PATRILINEARLY	PAUNCHINESSES
PASSIVATION	PATAPHYSICS	PATHOLOGISTS	PATRILINIES	PAUPERDOMS
PASSIVATIONS	PATCHBOARD	PATHOLOGIZE	PATRILOCAL	PAUPERESSES
PASSIVENESS	PATCHBOARDS	PATHOLOGIZED	PATRILOCALLY	PAUPERISATION
PASSIVENESSES	PATCHCOCKE	PATHOLOGIZES	PATRIMONIAL	PAUPERISATIONS
PASSIVISMS	PATCHCOCKES	PATHOLOGIZING	PATRIMONIALLY	PAUPERISED
PASSIVISTS	PATCHERIES	PATHOPHOBIA	PATRIMONIES	PAUPERISES
PASSIVITIES	PATCHINESS	PATHOPHOBIAS	PATRIOTICALLY	PAUPERISING
PASSMENTED	PATCHINESSES	PATHOPHYSIOLOGY	PATRIOTISM	PAUPERISMS
PASSMENTING	PATCHOCKES	PATIBULARY	PATRIOTISMS	PAUPERIZATION

PAUPERIZATIONS	PEARMONGERS	PEDAGOGUES	PEDICULOSES	PELLETIZING
PAUPERIZED	PEARTNESSES	PEDAGOGUING	PEDICULOSIS	PELLICULAR
PAUPERIZES	PEASANTIER	PEDAGOGUISH	PEDICULOUS	PELLITORIES
PAUPERIZING	PEASANTIEST	PEDAGOGUISHNESS	PEDICURING	PELLUCIDITIES
PAUPIETTES	PEASANTRIES	PEDAGOGUISM	PEDICURIST	PELLUCIDITY
PAUSEFULLY	PEASHOOTER	PEDAGOGUISMS	PEDICURISTS	PELLUCIDLY
PAUSELESSLY	PEASHOOTERS	PEDALBOATS	PEDIMENTAL	PELLUCIDNESS
PAVEMENTED	PEASOUPERS	PEDALLINGS	PEDIMENTED	PELLUCIDNESSES
PAVEMENTING	PEBBLEDASH	PEDANTICAL	PEDIPALPUS	PELMANISMS
PAVILIONED	PEBBLEDASHED	PEDANTICALLY	PEDOGENESES	PELOLOGIES
PAVILIONING	PEBBLEDASHES	PEDANTICISE	PEDOGENESIS	PELOTHERAPIES
PAVONAZZOS	PEBBLEDASHING	PEDANTICISED	PEDOGENETIC	PELOTHERAPY
PAWKINESSES	PEBBLEWEAVE	PEDANTICISES	PEDOLOGICAL	PELTATIONS
PAWNBROKER	PEBBLEWEAVES	PEDANTICISING	PEDOLOGIES	PELTMONGER
PAWNBROKERS	PECCABILITIES	PEDANTICISM	PEDOLOGIST	PELTMONGERS
PAWNBROKING	PECCABILITY	PEDANTICISMS	PEDOLOGISTS	PELVIMETER
PAWNBROKINGS	PECCADILLO	PEDANTICIZE	PEDOMETERS	PELVIMETERS
PAWNTICKET	PECCADILLOES	PEDANTICIZED	PEDOPHILES	PELVIMETRIES
PAWNTICKETS	PECCADILLOS	PEDANTICIZES	PEDOPHILIA	PELVIMETRY
PAYCHEQUES	PECCANCIES	PEDANTICIZING	PEDOPHILIAC	PELYCOSAUR
PAYMASTERS	PECKERWOOD	PEDANTISED	PEDOPHILIACS	PELYCOSAURS
PAYNIMRIES	PECKERWOODS	PEDANTISES	PEDOPHILIAS	PEMPHIGOID
PAYSAGISTS	PECKISHNESS	PEDANTISING	PEDOPHILIC	PEMPHIGOIDS
PEABERRIES	PECKISHNESSES	PEDANTISMS	PEDOPHILICS	PEMPHIGOUS
PEACEABLENESS	PECTINACEOUS	PEDANTIZED	PEDUNCULAR	PEMPHIGUSES
PEACEABLENESSES	PECTINATED	PEDANTIZES	PEDUNCULATE	PENALISATION
PEACEFULLER	PECTINATELY	PEDANTIZING	PEDUNCULATED	PENALISATIONS
PEACEFULLEST	PECTINATION	PEDANTOCRACIES	PEDUNCULATION	PENALISING
PEACEFULLY	PECTINATIONS	PEDANTOCRACY	PEDUNCULATIONS	PENALITIES
PEACEFULNESS	PECTINESTERASE	PEDANTOCRAT	PEELGARLIC	PENALIZATION
PEACEFULNESSES	PECTINESTERASES	PEDANTOCRATIC	PEELGARLICS	PENALIZATIONS
PEACEKEEPER	PECTINEUSES	PEDANTOCRATS	PEERLESSLY	PENALIZING
PEACEKEEPERS	PECTISABLE	PEDANTRIES	PEERLESSNESS	PENANNULAR
PEACEKEEPING	PECTISATION	PEDDLERIES	PEERLESSNESSES	PENCILINGS
PEACEKEEPINGS	PECTISATIONS	PEDERASTIC	PEEVISHNESS	PENCILLERS
PEACELESSNESS	PECTIZABLE	PEDERASTIES	PEEVISHNESSES	PENCILLING
PEACELESSNESSES	PECTIZATION	PEDEREROES	PEGMATITES	PENCILLINGS
PEACEMAKER	PECTIZATIONS	PEDESTALED	PEGMATITIC	PENDENCIES
PEACEMAKERS	PECTOLITES	PEDESTALING	PEIRASTICALLY	PENDENTIVE
PEACEMAKING	PECTORALLY	PEDESTALLED	PEJORATING	PENDENTIVES
PEACEMAKINGS	PECTORILOQUIES	PEDESTALLING	PEJORATION	PENDICLERS
PEACETIMES	PECTORILOQUY	PEDESTRIAN	PEJORATIONS	PENDRAGONS
PEACHBLOWS	PECULATING	PEDESTRIANISE	PEJORATIVE	PENDRAGONSHIP
PEACHERINO	PECULATION	PEDESTRIANISED	PEJORATIVELY	PENDRAGONSHIPS
PEACHERINOS	PECULATIONS	PEDESTRIANISES	PEJORATIVES	PENDULATED
PEACHINESS	PECULATORS	PEDESTRIANISING	PELARGONIC	PENDULATES
PEACHINESSES	PECULIARISE	PEDESTRIANISM	PELARGONIUM	PENDULATING
PEACOCKERIES	PECULIARISED	PEDESTRIANISMS	PELARGONIUMS	PENDULOSITIES
PEACOCKERY	PECULIARISES	PEDESTRIANIZE	PELECYPODS	PENDULOSITY
PEACOCKIER	PECULIARISING	PEDESTRIANIZED	PELLAGRINS	PENDULOUSLY
PEACOCKIEST	PECULIARITIES	PEDESTRIANIZES	PELLAGROUS	PENDULOUSNESS
PEACOCKING	PECULIARITY	PEDESTRIANIZING	PELLETIFIED	PENDULOUSNESSES
PEACOCKISH	PECULIARIZE	PEDESTRIANS	PELLETIFIES	PENELOPISE
PEAKEDNESS	PECULIARIZED	PEDETENTOUS	PELLETIFYING	PENELOPISED
PEAKEDNESSES	PECULIARIZES	PEDIATRICIAN	PELLETISATION	PENELOPISES
PEAKINESSES	PECULIARIZING	PEDIATRICIANS	PELLETISATIONS	PENELOPISING
PEANUTTIER	PECULIARLY	PEDIATRICS	PELLETISED	PENELOPIZE
PEANUTTIEST	PECUNIARILY	PEDIATRIST	PELLETISER	PENELOPIZED
PEARLASHES	PEDAGOGICAL	PEDIATRISTS	PELLETISERS	PENELOPIZES
PEARLESCENCE	PEDAGOGICALLY	PEDICELLARIA	PELLETISES	PENELOPIZING
PEARLESCENCES	PEDAGOGICS	PEDICELLARIAE	PELLETISING	PENEPLAINS
PEARLESCENT	PEDAGOGIES	PEDICELLATE	PELLETIZATION	PENEPLANATION
PEARLINESS	PEDAGOGISM	PEDICULATE	PELLETIZATIONS	PENEPLANATIONS
PEARLINESSES	PEDAGOGISMS	PEDICULATED	PELLETIZED	PENEPLANES
PEARLWARES	PEDAGOGUED	PEDICULATES	PELLETIZER	PENETRABILITIES
PEARLWORTS	PEDAGOGUERIES	PEDICULATION	PELLETIZERS	PENETRABILITY
PEARMONGER	PEDAGOGUERY	PEDICULATIONS	PELLETIZES	PENETRABLE

PENETRABLENESS	PENNILESSNESS	PENTAGONAL	PENTECONTER	PEPTALKING
PENETRABLY	PENNILESSNESSES	PENTAGONALLY	PENTECONTERS	PEPTICITIES
PENETRALIA	PENNILLION	PENTAGONALS	PENTETERIC	PEPTIDASES
PENETRALIAN	PENNINITES	PENTAGRAMS	PENTHEMIMER	PEPTIDOGLYCAN
PENETRANCE	PENNONCELLE	PENTAGRAPH	PENTHEMIMERAL	PEPTIDOGLYCANS
PENETRANCES	PENNONCELLES	PENTAGRAPHS	PENTHEMIMERS	PEPTISABLE
PENETRANCIES	PENNONCELS	PENTAGYNIAN	PENTHOUSED	PEPTISATION
PENETRANCY	PENNYCRESS	PENTAGYNOUS	PENTHOUSES	PEPTISATIONS
PENETRANTS	PENNYCRESSES	PENTAHEDRA	PENTHOUSING	PEPTIZABLE
PENETRATED	PENNYLANDS	PENTAHEDRAL	PENTIMENTI	PEPTIZATION
PENETRATES	PENNYROYAL	PENTAHEDRON	PENTIMENTO	PEPTIZATIONS
PENETRATING	PENNYROYALS	PENTAHEDRONS	PENTLANDITE	PEPTONISATION
PENETRATINGLY	PENNYWEIGHT	PENTAHYDRATE	PENTLANDITES	PEPTONISATIONS
PENETRATION	PENNYWEIGHTS	PENTAHYDRATES	PENTOBARBITAL	PEPTONISED
PENETRATIONS	PENNYWHISTLE	PENTALOGIES	PENTOBARBITALS	PEPTONISER
PENETRATIVE	PENNYWHISTLES	PENTALPHAS	PENTOBARBITONE	PEPTONISERS
PENETRATIVELY	PENNYWINKLE	PENTAMERIES	PENTOBARBITONES	PEPTONISES
PENETRATIVENESS	PENNYWINKLES	PENTAMERISM	PENTOSANES	PEPTONISING
PENETRATOR	PENNYWORTH	PENTAMERISMS	PENTOSIDES	PEPTONIZATION
PENETRATORS	PENNYWORTHS	PENTAMEROUS	PENTOXIDES	PEPTONIZATIONS
PENETROMETER	PENNYWORTS	PENTAMETER	PENTSTEMON	PEPTONIZED
PENETROMETERS	PENOLOGICAL	PENTAMETERS	PENTSTEMONS	PEPTONIZER
PENFRIENDS	PENOLOGICALLY	PENTAMIDINE	PENTYLENES	PEPTONIZERS
PENGUINERIES	PENOLOGIES	PENTAMIDINES	PENULTIMAS	PEPTONIZES
PENGUINERY	PENOLOGIST	PENTANDRIAN	PENULTIMATE	PEPTONIZING
PENGUINRIES	PENOLOGISTS	PENTANDROUS	PENULTIMATELY	PERACIDITIES
PENHOLDERS	PENONCELLE	PENTANGLES	PENULTIMATES	PERACIDITY
PENICILLAMINE	PENONCELLES	PENTANGULAR	PENUMBROUS	PERADVENTURE
PENICILLAMINES	PENPUSHERS	PENTAPEPTIDE	PENURIOUSLY	PERADVENTURES
PENICILLATE	PENPUSHING	PENTAPEPTIDES	PENURIOUSNESS	PERAEOPODS
PENICILLATELY	PENPUSHINGS	PENTAPLOID	PENURIOUSNESSES	PERAMBULATE
PENICILLATION	PENSEROSOS	PENTAPLOIDIES	PEOPLEHOOD	PERAMBULATED
PENICILLATIONS	PENSIEROSO	PENTAPLOIDS	PEOPLEHOODS	PERAMBULATES
PENICILLIA	PENSILENESS	PENTAPLOIDY	PEOPLELESS	PERAMBULATING
PENICILLIFORM	PENSILENESSES	PENTAPODIC	PEPEROMIAS	PERAMBULATION
PENICILLIN	PENSILITIES	PENTAPODIES	PEPPERBOXES	PERAMBULATIONS
PENICILLINASE	PENSIONABLE	PENTAPOLIS	PEPPERCORN	PERAMBULATOR
PENICILLINASES	PENSIONARIES	PENTAPOLISES	PEPPERCORNIER	PERAMBULATORS
PENICILLINS	PENSIONARY	PENTAPOLITAN	PEPPERCORNIEST	PERAMBULATORY
PENICILLIUM	PENSIONEER	PENTAPRISM	PEPPERCORNS	PERBORATES
PENICILLIUMS	PENSIONERS	PENTAPRISMS	PEPPERCORNY	PERCALINES
PENICILLUS	PENSIONING	PENTAQUARK	PEPPERGRASS	PERCEIVABILITY
PENINSULAR	PENSIONLESS	PENTAQUARKS	PEPPERGRASSES	PERCEIVABLE
PENINSULARITIES	PENSIONNAT	PENTARCHICAL	PEPPERIDGE	PERCEIVABLY
PENINSULARITY	PENSIONNATS	PENTARCHIES	PEPPERIDGES	PERCEIVERS
PENINSULAS	PENSIVENESS	PENTASTICH	PEPPERIEST	PERCEIVING
PENINSULATE	PENSIVENESSES	PENTASTICHOUS	PEPPERINESS	PERCEIVINGS
PENINSULATED	PENSTEMONS	PENTASTICHS	PEPPERINESSES	PERCENTAGE
PENINSULATES	PENTABARBITAL	PENTASTYLE	PEPPERINGS	PERCENTAGES
PENINSULATING	PENTABARBITALS	PENTASTYLES	PEPPERMILL	PERCENTILE
PENISTONES	PENTACHORD	PENTASYLLABIC	PEPPERMILLS	PERCENTILES
PENITENCES	PENTACHORDS	PENTATEUCHAL	PEPPERMINT	PERCEPTIBILITY
PENITENCIES	PENTACRINOID	PENTATHLETE	PEPPERMINTIER	PERCEPTIBLE
PENITENTIAL	PENTACRINOIDS	PENTATHLETES	PEPPERMINTIEST	PERCEPTIBLY
PENITENTIALLY	PENTACTINAL	PENTATHLON	PEPPERMINTS	PERCEPTION
PENITENTIALS	PENTACYCLIC	PENTATHLONS	PEPPERMINTY	PERCEPTIONAL
PENITENTIARIES	PENTADACTYL	PENTATHLUM	PEPPERONIS	PERCEPTIONS
PENITENTIARY	PENTADACTYLE	PENTATHLUMS	PEPPERTREE	PERCEPTIVE
PENITENTLY	PENTADACTYLES	PENTATOMIC	PEPPERTREES	PERCEPTIVELY
PENMANSHIP	PENTADACTYLIC	PENTATONIC	PEPPERWORT	PERCEPTIVENESS
PENMANSHIPS	PENTADACTYLIES	PENTAVALENCE	PEPPERWORTS	PERCEPTIVITIES
PENNACEOUS	PENTADACTYLISM	PENTAVALENCES	PEPPINESSES	PERCEPTIVITY
PENNALISMS	PENTADACTYLISMS	PENTAVALENCIES	PEPSINATED	PERCEPTUAL
PENNATULACEOUS	PENTADACTYLOUS	PENTAVALENCY	PEPSINATES	PERCEPTUALLY
PENNATULAE	PENTADACTYLS	PENTAVALENT	PEPSINATING	PERCHERIES
PENNATULAS	PENTADACTYLY	PENTAZOCINE	PEPSINOGEN	PERCHERONS
PENNILESSLY	PENTADELPHOUS	PENTAZOCINES	PEPSINOGENS	PERCHLORATE

PERCHLORATES	PEREIOPODS	PERFOLIATIONS	PERICHORESES	PERIMORPHISMS
PERCHLORIC	PEREMPTORILY	PERFORABLE	PERICHORESIS	PERIMORPHOUS
PERCHLORIDE	PEREMPTORINESS	PERFORANSES	PERICHYLOUS	PERIMORPHS
PERCHLORIDES	PEREMPTORY	PERFORATED	PERICLASES	PERIMYSIUM
PERCHLOROETHENE	PERENNATED	PERFORATES	PERICLASTIC	PERINAEUMS
PERCIFORMS	PERENNATES	PERFORATING	PERICLINAL	PERINATALLY
PERCIPIENCE	PERENNATING	PERFORATION	PERICLINES	PERINEPHRIA
PERCIPIENCES	PERENNATION	PERFORATIONS	PERICLITATE	PERINEPHRIC
PERCIPIENCIES	PERENNATIONS	PERFORATIVE	PERICLITATED	PERINEPHRITIS
PERCIPIENCY	PERENNIALITIES	PERFORATOR	PERICLITATES	PERINEPHRITISES
PERCIPIENT	PERENNIALITY	PERFORATORS	PERICLITATING	PERINEPHRIUM
PERCIPIENTLY	PERENNIALLY	PERFORATORY	PERICRANIA	PERINEURAL
PERCIPIENTS	PERENNIALS	PERFORATUS	PERICRANIAL	PERINEURIA
PERCOCTING	PERENNIBRANCH	PERFORATUSES	PERICRANIUM	PERINEURIAL
PERCOIDEAN	PERENNIBRANCHS	PERFORMABILITY	PERICRANIUMS	PERINEURITIC
PERCOIDEANS	PERENNITIES	PERFORMABLE	PERICULOUS	PERINEURITIS
PERCOLABLE	PERESTROIKA	PERFORMANCE	PERICYCLES	PERINEURITISES
PERCOLATED	PERESTROIKAS	PERFORMANCES	PERICYCLIC	PERINEURIUM
PERCOLATES	PERFECTATION	PERFORMATIVE	PERICYNTHIA	PERIODATES
PERCOLATING	PERFECTATIONS	PERFORMATIVELY	PERICYNTHION	PERIODICAL
PERCOLATION	PERFECTERS	PERFORMATIVES	PERICYNTHIONS	PERIODICALIST
PERCOLATIONS	PERFECTEST	PERFORMATORY	PERIDERMAL	PERIODICALISTS
PERCOLATIVE	PERFECTIBILIAN	PERFORMERS	PERIDERMIC	PERIODICALLY
PERCOLATOR	PERFECTIBILIANS	PERFORMING	PERIDESMIA	PERIODICALS
PERCOLATORS	PERFECTIBILISM	PERFORMINGS	PERIDESMIUM	PERIODICITIES
PERCURRENT	PERFECTIBILISMS	PERFUMELESS	PERIDINIAN	PERIODICITY
PERCURSORY	PERFECTIBILIST	PERFUMERIES	PERIDINIANS	PERIODIDES
PERCUSSANT	PERFECTIBILISTS	PERFUMIERS	PERIDINIUM	PERIODISATION
PERCUSSING	PERFECTIBILITY	PERFUMIEST	PERIDINIUMS	PERIODISATIONS
PERCUSSION	PERFECTIBLE	PERFUNCTORILY	PERIDOTITE	PERIODISED
PERCUSSIONAL	PERFECTING	PERFUNCTORINESS	PERIDOTITES	PERIODISES
PERCUSSIONIST	PERFECTION	PERFUNCTORY	PERIDOTITIC	PERIODISING
PERCUSSIONISTS	PERFECTIONATE	PERFUSATES	PERIDROMES	PERIODIZATION
PERCUSSIONS	PERFECTIONATED	PERFUSIONIST	PERIEGESES	PERIODIZATIONS
PERCUSSIVE	PERFECTIONATES	PERFUSIONISTS	PERIEGESIS	PERIODIZED
PERCUSSIVELY	PERFECTIONATING	PERFUSIONS	PERIGASTRIC	PERIODIZES
PERCUSSIVENESS	PERFECTIONISM	PERGAMENEOUS	PERIGASTRITIS	PERIODIZING
PERCUSSORS	PERFECTIONISMS	PERGAMENTACEOUS	PERIGASTRITISES	PERIODONTAL
PERCUTANEOUS	PERFECTIONIST	PERGUNNAHS	PERIGENESES	PERIODONTALLY
PERCUTANEOUSLY	PERFECTIONISTIC	PERIASTRON	PERIGENESIS	PERIODONTIA
PERCUTIENT	PERFECTIONISTS	PERIASTRONS	PERIGLACIAL	PERIODONTIAS
PERCUTIENTS	PERFECTIONS	PERIBLASTS	PERIGONIAL	PERIODONTIC
PERDENDOSI	PERFECTIVE	PERICARDIA	PERIGONIUM	PERIODONTICALLY
PERDITIONABLE	PERFECTIVELY	PERICARDIAC	PERIGYNIES	PERIODONTICS
PERDITIONS	PERFECTIVENESS	PERICARDIAL	PERIGYNOUS	PERIODONTIST
PERDUELLION	PERFECTIVES	PERICARDIAN	PERIHELIAL	PERIODONTISTS
PERDUELLIONS	PERFECTIVITIES	PERICARDITIC	PERIHELION	PERIODONTITIS
PERDURABILITIES	PERFECTIVITY	PERICARDITIDES	PERIHEPATIC	PERIODONTITIDES
PERDURABILITY	PERFECTNESS	PERICARDITIS	PERIHEPATITIS	PERIODONTOLOGY
PERDURABLE	PERFECTNESSES	PERICARDITISES	PERIHEPATITISES	PERIONYCHIA
PERDURABLY	PERFECTORS	PERICARDIUM	PERIKARYAL	PERIONYCHIUM
PERDURANCE	PERFERVIDITIES	PERICARDIUMS	PERIKARYON	PERIOSTEAL
PERDURANCES	PERFERVIDITY	PERICARPIAL	PERILOUSLY	PERIOSTEUM
PERDURATION	PERFERVIDLY	PERICARPIC	PERILOUSNESS	PERIOSTITIC
PERDURATIONS	PERFERVIDNESS	PERICENTER	PERILOUSNESSES	PERIOSTITIDES
PEREGRINATE	PERFERVIDNESSES	PERICENTERS	PERILYMPHS	PERIOSTITIS
PEREGRINATED	PERFERVORS	PERICENTRAL	PERIMENOPAUSAL	PERIOSTITISES
PEREGRINATES	PERFERVOUR	PERICENTRE	PERIMENOPAUSE	PERIOSTRACUM
PEREGRINATING	PERFERVOURS	PERICENTRES	PERIMENOPAUSES	PERIOSTRACUMS
PEREGRINATION	PERFICIENT	PERICENTRIC	PERIMETERS	PERIPATETIC
PEREGRINATIONS	PERFICIENTS	PERICHAETIA	PERIMETRAL	PERIPATETICAL
PEREGRINATOR	PERFIDIOUS	PERICHAETIAL	PERIMETRIC	PERIPATETICALLY
PEREGRINATORS	PERFIDIOUSLY	PERICHAETIUM	PERIMETRICAL	PERIPATETICISM
PEREGRINATORY	PERFIDIOUSNESS	PERICHONDRAL	PERIMETRICALLY	PERIPATETICISMS
PEREGRINES	PERFLUOROCARBON	PERICHONDRIA	PERIMETRIES	PERIPATETICS
PEREGRINITIES	PERFOLIATE	PERICHONDRIAL	PERIMORPHIC	PERIPATUSES
PEREGRINITY	PERFOLIATION	PERICHONDRIUM	PERIMORPHISM	PERIPETEIA

PERIPETEIAN
PERIPETEIAS
PERIPETIAN
PERIPETIAS
PERIPETIES
PERIPHERAL
PERIPHERALITIES
PERIPHERALITY
PERIPHERALLY
PERIPHERALS
PERIPHERIC
PERIPHERICAL
PERIPHERIES
PERIPHONIC
PERIPHRASE
PERIPHRASED
PERIPHRASES
PERIPHRASING
PERIPHRASIS
PERIPHRASTIC
PERIPHRASTICAL
PERIPHYTIC
PERIPHYTON
PERIPHYTONS
PERIPLASMS
PERIPLASTS
PERIPLUSES
PERIPROCTS
PERIPTERAL
PERIPTERIES
PERISARCAL
PERISARCOUS
PERISCIANS
PERISCOPES
PERISCOPIC
PERISCOPICALLY
PERISELENIA
PERISELENIUM
PERISHABILITIES
PERISHABILITY
PERISHABLE
PERISHABLENESS
PERISHABLES
PERISHABLY
PERISHINGLY
PERISPERMAL
PERISPERMIC
PERISPERMS
PERISPOMENA
PERISPOMENON
PERISPOMENONS
PERISSODACTYL
PERISSODACTYLE
PERISSODACTYLES
PERISSODACTYLIC
PERISSODACTYLS
PERISSOLOGIES
PERISSOLOGY
PERISSOSYLLABIC
PERISTALITH
PERISTALITHS
PERISTALSES
PERISTALSIS
PERISTALTIC
PERISTALTICALLY
PERISTERITE
PERISTERITES

PERISTERONIC
PERISTOMAL
PERISTOMATIC
PERISTOMES
PERISTOMIAL
PERISTREPHIC
PERISTYLAR
PERISTYLES
PERITECTIC
PERITECTICS
PERITHECIA
PERITHECIAL
PERITHECIUM
PERITONAEA
PERITONAEAL
PERITONAEUM
PERITONAEUMS
PERITONEAL
PERITONEALLY
PERITONEOSCOPY
PERITONEUM
PERITONEUMS
PERITONITIC
PERITONITIS
PERITONITISES
PERITRACKS
PERITRICHA
PERITRICHOUS
PERITRICHOUSLY
PERITRICHS
PERITYPHLITIS
PERITYPHLITISES
PERIVITELLINE
PERIWIGGED
PERIWIGGING
PERIWINKLE
PERIWINKLES
PERJINKETY
PERJINKITIES
PERJINKITY
PERJURIOUS
PERJURIOUSLY
PERKINESSES
PERLEMOENS
PERLOCUTION
PERLOCUTIONARY
PERLOCUTIONS
PERLUSTRATE
PERLUSTRATED
PERLUSTRATES
PERLUSTRATING
PERLUSTRATION
PERLUSTRATIONS
PERMABEARS
PERMABULLS
PERMACULTURE
PERMACULTURES
PERMAFROST
PERMAFROSTS
PERMALINKS
PERMALLOYS
PERMANENCE
PERMANENCES
PERMANENCIES
PERMANENCY
PERMANENTLY
PERMANENTNESS

PERMANENTNESSES
PERMANENTS
PERMANGANATE
PERMANGANATES
PERMANGANIC
PERMEABILITIES
PERMEABILITY
PERMEABLENESS
PERMEABLENESSES
PERMEAMETER
PERMEAMETERS
PERMEANCES
PERMEATING
PERMEATION
PERMEATIONS
PERMEATIVE
PERMEATORS
PERMETHRIN
PERMETHRINS
PERMILLAGE
PERMILLAGES
PERMISSIBILITY
PERMISSIBLE
PERMISSIBLENESS
PERMISSIBLY
PERMISSION
PERMISSIONS
PERMISSIVE
PERMISSIVELY
PERMISSIVENESS
PERMITTANCE
PERMITTANCES
PERMITTEES
PERMITTERS
PERMITTING
PERMITTIVITIES
PERMITTIVITY
PERMUTABILITIES
PERMUTABILITY
PERMUTABLE
PERMUTABLENESS
PERMUTABLY
PERMUTATED
PERMUTATES
PERMUTATING
PERMUTATION
PERMUTATIONAL
PERMUTATIONS
PERNANCIES
PERNICIOUS
PERNICIOUSLY
PERNICIOUSNESS
PERNICKETIER
PERNICKETIEST
PERNICKETINESS
PERNICKETY
PERNOCTATE
PERNOCTATED
PERNOCTATES
PERNOCTATING
PERNOCTATION
PERNOCTATIONS
PERONEUSES
PERORATING
PERORATION
PERORATIONAL
PERORATIONS

PERORATORS
PEROVSKIAS
PEROVSKITE
PEROVSKITES
PEROXIDASE
PEROXIDASES
PEROXIDATION
PEROXIDATIONS
PEROXIDING
PEROXIDISE
PEROXIDISED
PEROXIDISES
PEROXIDISING
PEROXIDIZE
PEROXIDIZED
PEROXIDIZES
PEROXIDIZING
PEROXISOMAL
PEROXISOME
PEROXISOMES
PEROXYSULPHURIC
PERPENDICULAR
PERPENDICULARLY
PERPENDICULARS
PERPENDING
PERPETRABLE
PERPETRATE
PERPETRATED
PERPETRATES
PERPETRATING
PERPETRATION
PERPETRATIONS
PERPETRATOR
PERPETRATORS
PERPETUABLE
PERPETUALISM
PERPETUALISMS
PERPETUALIST
PERPETUALISTS
PERPETUALITIES
PERPETUALITY
PERPETUALLY
PERPETUALS
PERPETUANCE
PERPETUANCES
PERPETUATE
PERPETUATED
PERPETUATES
PERPETUATING
PERPETUATION
PERPETUATIONS
PERPETUATOR
PERPETUATORS
PERPETUITIES
PERPETUITY
PERPHENAZINE
PERPHENAZINES
PERPLEXEDLY
PERPLEXEDNESS
PERPLEXEDNESSES
PERPLEXERS
PERPLEXING
PERPLEXINGLY
PERPLEXITIES
PERPLEXITY
PERQUISITE
PERQUISITES

PERQUISITION
PERQUISITIONS
PERQUISITOR
PERQUISITORS
PERRUQUIER
PERRUQUIERS
PERSCRUTATION
PERSCRUTATIONS
PERSECUTED
PERSECUTEE
PERSECUTEES
PERSECUTES
PERSECUTING
PERSECUTION
PERSECUTIONS
PERSECUTIVE
PERSECUTOR
PERSECUTORS
PERSECUTORY
PERSEITIES
PERSELINES
PERSEVERANCE
PERSEVERANCES
PERSEVERANT
PERSEVERATE
PERSEVERATED
PERSEVERATES
PERSEVERATING
PERSEVERATION
PERSEVERATIONS
PERSEVERATIVE
PERSEVERATOR
PERSEVERATORS
PERSEVERED
PERSEVERES
PERSEVERING
PERSEVERINGLY
PERSICARIA
PERSICARIAS
PERSIENNES
PERSIFLAGE
PERSIFLAGES
PERSIFLEUR
PERSIFLEURS
PERSIMMONS
PERSISTENCE
PERSISTENCES
PERSISTENCIES
PERSISTENCY
PERSISTENT
PERSISTENTLY
PERSISTENTS
PERSISTERS
PERSISTING
PERSISTINGLY
PERSISTIVE
PERSNICKETIER
PERSNICKETIEST
PERSNICKETINESS
PERSNICKETY
PERSONABLE
PERSONABLENESS
PERSONABLY
PERSONAGES
PERSONALIA
PERSONALISATION
PERSONALISE

p

PERSONALISED	PERSPIRATION	PERVASIONS	PETHIDINES	PETROLOGIC
PERSONALISES	PERSPIRATIONS	PERVASIVELY	PETIOLATED	PETROLOGICAL
PERSONALISING	PERSPIRATORY	PERVASIVENESS	PETIOLULES	PETROLOGICALLY
PERSONALISM	PERSPIRIER	PERVASIVENESSES	PETITENESS	PETROLOGIES
PERSONALISMS	PERSPIRIEST	PERVERSELY	PETITENESSES	PETROLOGTST
PERSONALIST	PERSPIRING	PERVERSENESS	PETITIONARY	PETROLOGISTS
PERSONALISTIC	PERSPIRINGLY	PERVERSENESSES	PETITIONED	PETROMONEY
PERSONALISTS	PERSTRINGE	PERVERSEST	PETITIONER	PETROMONEYS
PERSONALITIES	PERSTRINGED	PERVERSION	PETITIONERS	PETROMONIES
PERSONALITY	PERSTRINGES	PERVERSIONS	PETITIONING	PETRONELLA
PERSONALIZATION	PERSTRINGING	PERVERSITIES	PETITIONINGS	PETRONELLAS
PERSONALIZE	PERSUADABILITY	PERVERSITY	PETITIONIST	PETROPHYSICAL
PERSONALIZED	PERSUADABLE	PERVERSIVE	PETITIONISTS	PETROPHYSICIST
PERSONALIZES	PERSUADERS	PERVERTEDLY	PETNAPINGS	PETROPHYSICISTS
PERSONALIZING	PERSUADING	PERVERTEDNESS	PETNAPPERS	PETROPHYSICS
PERSONALLY	PERSUASIBILITY	PERVERTEDNESSES	PETNAPPING	PETROPOUNDS
PERSONALTIES	PERSUASIBLE	PERVERTERS	PETNAPPINGS	PETROSTATE
PERSONALTY	PERSUASION	PERVERTIBLE	PETRICHORS	PETROSTATES
PERSONATED	PERSUASIONS	PERVERTING	PETRIFACTION	PETTEDNESS
PERSONATES	PERSUASIVE	PERVIATING	PETRIFACTIONS	PETTEDNESSES
PERSONATING	PERSUASIVELY	PERVICACIES	PETRIFACTIVE	PETTICHAPS
PERSONATINGS	PERSUASIVENESS	PERVICACIOUS	PETRIFICATION	PETTICHAPSES
PERSONATION	PERSUASIVES	PERVICACITIES	PETRIFICATIONS	PETTICOATED
PERSONATIONS	PERSUASORY	PERVICACITY	PETRIFIERS	PETTICOATS
PERSONATIVE	PERSULFATE	PERVIOUSLY	PETRIFYING	PETTIFOGGED
PERSONATOR	PERSULFATES	PERVIOUSNESS	PETRISSAGE	PETTIFOGGER
PERSONATORS	PERSULFURIC	PERVIOUSNESSES	PETRISSAGES	PETTIFOGGERIES
PERSONHOOD	PERSULPHATE	PESCATARIAN	PETROCHEMICAL	PETTIFOGGERS
PERSONHOODS	PERSULPHATES	PESCATARIANS	PETROCHEMICALLY	PETTIFOGGERY
PERSONIFIABLE	PERSULPHURIC	PESCETARIAN	PETROCHEMICALS	PETTIFOGGING
PERSONIFICATION	PERSWADING	PESCETARIANS	PETROCHEMIST	PETTIFOGGINGS
PERSONIFIED	PERTAINING	PESHMERGAS	PETROCHEMISTRY	PETTINESSES
PERSONIFIER	PERTINACIOUS	PESKINESSES	PETROCHEMISTS	PETTISHNESS
PERSONIFIERS	PERTINACIOUSLY	PESSIMISMS	PETROCURRENCIES	PETTISHNESSES
PERSONIFIES	PERTINACITIES	PESSIMISTIC	PETROCURRENCY	PETULANCES
PERSONIFYING	PERTINACITY	PESSIMISTICAL	PETRODOLLAR	PETULANCIES
PERSONISED	PERTINENCE	PESSIMISTICALLY	PETRODOLLARS	PETULANTLY
PERSONISES	PERTINENCES	PESSIMISTS	PETRODROME	PEWHOLDERS
PERSONISING	PERTINENCIES	PESTERINGLY	PETRODROMES	PEWTERIEST
PERSONIZED	PERTINENCY	PESTERMENT	PETROGENESES	PHACOLITES
PERSONIZES	PERTINENTLY	PESTERMENTS	PETROGENESIS	PHACOLITHS
PERSONIZING	PERTINENTS	PESTHOUSES	PETROGENETIC	PHAELONION
PERSONNELS	PERTNESSES	PESTICIDAL	PETROGENIES	PHAELONIONS
PERSONPOWER	PERTURBABLE	PESTICIDES	PETROGLYPH	PHAENOGAMIC
PERSONPOWERS	PERTURBABLY	PESTIFEROUS	PETROGLYPHIC	PHAENOGAMOUS
PERSPECTIVAL	PERTURBANCE	PESTIFEROUSLY	PETROGLYPHIES	PHAENOGAMS
PERSPECTIVE	PERTURBANCES	PESTIFEROUSNESS	PETROGLYPHS	PHAENOLOGIES
PERSPECTIVELY	PERTURBANT	PESTILENCE	PETROGLYPHY	PHAENOLOGY
PERSPECTIVES	PERTURBANTS	PESTILENCES	PETROGRAMS	PHAENOMENA
PERSPECTIVISM	PERTURBATE	PESTILENTIAL	PETROGRAPHER	PHAENOMENON
PERSPECTIVISMS	PERTURBATED	PESTILENTIALLY	PETROGRAPHERS	PHAENOTYPE
PERSPECTIVIST	PERTURBATES	PESTILENTLY	PETROGRAPHIC	PHAENOTYPED
PERSPECTIVISTS	PERTURBATING	PESTOLOGICAL	PETROGRAPHICAL	PHAENOTYPES
PERSPICACIOUS	PERTURBATION	PESTOLOGIES	PETROGRAPHIES	PHAENOTYPING
PERSPICACIOUSLY	PERTURBATIONAL	PESTOLOGIST	PETROGRAPHY	PHAEOMELANIN
PERSPICACITIES	PERTURBATIONS	PESTOLOGISTS	PETROLAGES	PHAEOMELANINS
PERSPICACITY	PERTURBATIVE	PETAHERTZES	PETROLATUM	PHAGEDAENA
PERSPICUITIES	PERTURBATOR	PETALIFEROUS	PETROLATUMS	PHAGEDAENAS
PERSPICUITY	PERTURBATORIES	PETALODIES	PETROLEOUS	PHAGEDAENIC
PERSPICUOUS	PERTURBATORS	PETALOMANIA	PETROLEUMS	PHAGEDENAS
PERSPICUOUSLY	PERTURBATORY	PETALOMANIAS	PETROLEURS	PHAGEDENIC
PERSPICUOUSNESS	PERTURBEDLY	PETAMETERS	PETROLEUSE	PHAGOCYTES
PERSPIRABLE	PERTURBERS	PETAMETRES	PETROLEUSES	PHAGOCYTIC
PERSPIRATE	PERTURBING	PETAURINES	PETROLHEAD	PHAGOCYTICAL
PERSPIRATED	PERTURBINGLY	PETAURISTS	PETROLHEADS	PHAGOCYTISE
PERSPIRATES	PERTUSIONS	PETCHARIES	PETROLIFEROUS	PHAGOCYTISED
PERSPIRATING	PERTUSSISES	PETERSHAMS	PETROLLING	PHAGOCYTISES

PHAGOCYTISING	PHANTASMAL	PHARYNGITISES	PHENOLOGICAL	PHENYLTHIOUREA
PHAGOCYTISM	PHANTASMALIAN	PHARYNGOLOGICAL	PHENOLOGICALLY	PHENYLTHIOUREAS
PHAGOCYTISMS	PHANTASMALITIES	PHARYNGOLOGIES	PHENOLOGIES	PHENYTOINS
PHAGOCYTIZE	PHANTASMALITY	PHARYNGOLOGIST	PHENOLOGIST	PHEROMONAL
PHAGOCYTIZED	PHANTASMALLY	PHARYNGOLOGISTS	PHENOLOGISTS	PHEROMONES
PHAGOCYTIZES	PHANTASMATA	PHARYNGOLOGY	PHENOLPHTHALEIN	PHIALIFORM
PHAGOCYTIZING	PHANTASMIC	PHARYNGOSCOPE	PHENOMENAL	PHILADELPHUS
PHAGOCYTOSE	PHANTASMICAL	PHARYNGOSCOPES	PHENOMENALISE	PHILADELPHUSES
PHAGOCYTOSED	PHANTASMICALLY	PHARYNGOSCOPIC	PHENOMENALISED	PHILANDERED
PHAGOCYTOSES	PHANTASTIC	PHARYNGOSCOPIES	PHENOMENALISES	PHILANDERER
PHAGOCYTOSING	PHANTASTICS	PHARYNGOSCOPY	PHENOMENALISING	PHILANDERERS
PHAGOCYTOSIS	PHANTASTRIES	PHARYNGOTOMIES	PHENOMENALISM	PHILANDERING
PHAGOCYTOTIC	PHANTASTRY	PHARYNGOTOMY	PHENOMENALISMS	PHILANDERINGS
PHAGOMANIA	PHANTASYING	PHASCOGALE	PHENOMENALIST	PHILANDERS
PHAGOMANIAC	PHANTOMATIC	PHASCOGALES	PHENOMENALISTIC	PHILANTHROPE
PHAGOMANIACS	PHANTOMISH	PHASEDOWNS	PHENOMENALISTS	PHILANTHROPES
PHAGOMANIAS	PHANTOMLIKE	PHASEOLINS	PHENOMENALITIES	PHILANTHROPIC
PHAGOPHOBIA	PHANTOSMES	PHATICALLY	PHENOMENALITY	PHILANTHROPICAL
PHAGOPHOBIAS	PHARISAICAL	PHEASANTRIES	PHENOMENALIZE	PHILANTHROPIES
PHAGOSOMES	PHARISAICALLY	PHEASANTRY	PHENOMENALIZED	PHILANTHROPIST
PHALANGEAL	PHARISAICALNESS	PHELLODERM	PHENOMENALIZES	PHILANTHROPISTS
PHALANGERS	PHARISAISM	PHELLODERMAL	PHENOMENALIZING	PHILANTHROPOID
PHALANGIDS	PHARISAISMS	PHELLODERMS	PHENOMENALLY	PHILANTHROPOIDS
PHALANGIST	PHARISEEISM	PHELLOGENETIC	PHENOMENAS	PHILANTHROPY
PHALANGISTS	PHARISEEISMS	PHELLOGENIC	PHENOMENISE	PHILATELIC
PHALANSTERIAN	PHARMACEUTIC	PHELLOGENS	PHENOMENISED	PHILATELICALLY
PHALANSTERIANS	PHARMACEUTICAL	PHELLOPLASTIC	PHENOMENISES	PHILATELIES
PHALANSTERIES	PHARMACEUTICALS	PHELLOPLASTICS	PHENOMENISING	PHILATELIST
PHALANSTERISM	PHARMACEUTICS	PHELONIONS	PHENOMENISM	PHILATELISTS
PHALANSTERISMS	PHARMACEUTIST	PHENACAINE	PHENOMENISMS	PHILAVERIES
PHALANSTERIST	PHARMACEUTISTS	PHENACAINES	PHENOMENIST	PHILHARMONIC
PHALANSTERISTS	PHARMACIES	PHENACETIN	PHENOMENISTS	PHILHARMONICS
PHALANSTERY	PHARMACIST	PHENACETINS	PHENOMENIZE	PHILHELLENE
PHALAROPES	PHARMACISTS	PHENACITES	PHENOMENIZED	PHILHELLENES
PHALLICALLY	PHARMACODYNAMIC	PHENAKISMS	PHENOMENIZES	PHILHELLENIC
PHALLICISM	PHARMACOGENOMIC	PHENAKISTOSCOPE	PHENOMENIZING	PHILHELLENISM
PHALLICISMS	PHARMACOGNOSIES	PHENAKITES	PHENOMENOLOGIES	PHILHELLENISMS
PHALLICIST	PHARMACOGNOSIST	PHENANTHRENE	PHENOMENOLOGIST	PHILHELLENIST
PHALLICISTS	PHARMACOGNOSTIC	PHENANTHRENES	PHENOMENOLOGY	PHILHELLENISTS
PHALLOCENTRIC	PHARMACOGNOSY	PHENARSAZINE	PHENOMENON	PHILHORSES
PHALLOCENTRISM	PHARMACOKINETIC	PHENARSAZINES	PHENOMENONS	PHILIPPICS
PHALLOCENTRISMS	PHARMACOLOGIC	PHENAZINES	PHENOTHIAZINE	PHILIPPINA
PHALLOCRAT	PHARMACOLOGICAL	PHENCYCLIDINE	PHENOTHIAZINES	PHILIPPINAS
PHALLOCRATIC	PHARMACOLOGIES	PHENCYCLIDINES	PHENOTYPED	PHILIPPINE
PHALLOCRATS	PHARMACOLOGIST	PHENETICIST	PHENOTYPES	PHILIPPINES
PHALLOIDIN	PHARMACOLOGISTS	PHENETICISTS	PHENOTYPIC	PHILISTIAS
PHALLOIDINS	PHARMACOLOGY	PHENETIDINE	PHENOTYPICAL	PHILISTINE
PHANEROGAM	PHARMACOPEIA	PHENETIDINES	PHENOTYPICALLY	PHILISTINES
PHANEROGAMIC	PHARMACOPEIAL	PHENETOLES	PHENOTYPING	PHILISTINISM
PHANEROGAMOUS	PHARMACOPEIAS	PHENFORMIN	PHENOXIDES	PHILISTINISMS
PHANEROGAMS	PHARMACOPOEIA	PHENFORMINS	PHENTOLAMINE	PHILLABEGS
PHANEROPHYTE	PHARMACOPOEIAL	PHENGOPHOBIA	PHENTOLAMINES	PHILLIBEGS
PHANEROPHYTES	PHARMACOPOEIAN	PHENGOPHOBIAS	PHENYLALANIN	PHILLIPSITE
PHANSIGARS	PHARMACOPOEIANS	PHENMETRAZINE	PHENYLALANINE	PHILLIPSITES
PHANTASIAST	PHARMACOPOEIAS	PHENMETRAZINES	PHENYLALANINES	PHILLUMENIES
PHANTASIASTS	PHARMACOPOEIC	PHENOBARBITAL	PHENYLALANINS	PHILLUMENIST
PHANTASIED	PHARMACOPOEIST	PHENOBARBITALS	PHENYLAMINE	PHILLUMENISTS
PHANTASIES	PHARMACOPOEISTS	PHENOBARBITONE	PHENYLAMINES	PHILLUMENY
PHANTASIME	PHARMACOPOLIST	PHENOBARBITONES	PHENYLBUTAZONE	PHILODENDRA
PHANTASIMES	PHARMACOPOLISTS	PHENOBARBS	PHENYLBUTAZONES	PHILODENDRON
PHANTASIMS	PHARMACOTHERAPY	PHENOCOPIES	PHENYLENES	PHILODENDRONS
PHANTASMAGORIA	PHARYNGALS	PHENOCRYST	PHENYLEPHRINE	PHILOGYNIES
PHANTASMAGORIAL	PHARYNGEAL	PHENOCRYSTIC	PHENYLEPHRINES	PHILOGYNIST
PHANTASMAGORIAS	PHARYNGEALS	PHENOCRYSTS	PHENYLKETONURIA	PHILOGYNISTS
PHANTASMAGORIC	PHARYNGITIC	PHENOLATED	PHENYLKETONURIC	PHILOGYNOUS
PHANTASMAGORIES	PHARYNGITIDES	PHENOLATES	PHENYLMETHYL	PHILOLOGER
PHANTASMAGORY	PHARYNGITIS	PHENOLATING	PHENYLMETHYLS	PHILOLOGERS

PHILOLOGIAN	PHLEBOLOGIES	PHONEMICISED	PHONOLITIC	PHOSPHOLIPASES
PHILOLOGIANS	PHLEBOLOGY	PHONEMICISES	PHONOLOGIC	PHOSPHOLIPID
PHILOLOGIC	PHLEBOSCLEROSES	PHONEMICISING	PHONOLOGICAL	PHOSPHOLIPIDS
PHILOLOGICAL	PHLEBOSCLEROSIS	PHONEMICIST	PHONOLOGICALLY	PHOSPHONIC
PHILOLOGICALLY	PHLEBOTOMIC	PHONEMICISTS	PHONOLOGIES	PHOSPHONIUM
PHILOLOGIES	PHLEBOTOMICAL	PHONEMICIZATION	PHONOLOGIST	PHOSPHONIUMS
PHILOLOGIST	PHLEBOTOMIES	PHONEMICIZE	PHONOLOGISTS	PHOSPHOPROTEIN
PHILOLOGISTS	PHLEBOTOMISE	PHONEMICIZED	PHONOMETER	PHOSPHOPROTEINS
PHILOLOGUE	PHLEBOTOMISED	PHONEMICIZES	PHONOMETERS	PHOSPHORATE
PHILOLOGUES	PHLEBOTOMISES	PHONEMICIZING	PHONOMETRIC	PHOSPHORATED
PHILOMATHIC	PHLEBOTOMISING	PHONENDOSCOPE	PHONOMETRICAL	PHOSPHORATES
PHILOMATHICAL	PHLEBOTOMIST	PHONENDOSCOPES	PHONOPHOBIA	PHOSPHORATING
PHILOMATHIES	PHLEBOTOMISTS	PHONETICAL	PHONOPHOBIAS	PHOSPHORES
PHILOMATHS	PHLEBOTOMIZE	PHONETICALLY	PHONOPHORE	PHOSPHORESCE
PHILOMATHY	PHLEBOTOMIZED	PHONETICIAN	PHONOPHORES	PHOSPHORESCED
PHILOMELAS	PHLEBOTOMIZES	PHONETICIANS	PHONOPORES	PHOSPHORESCENCE
PHILOPENAS	PHLEBOTOMIZING	PHONETICISATION	PHONOSCOPE	PHOSPHORESCENT
PHILOPOENA	PHLEBOTOMY	PHONETICISE	PHONOSCOPES	PHOSPHORESCES
PHILOPOENAS	PHLEGMAGOGIC	PHONETICISED	PHONOTACTIC	PHOSPHORESCING
PHILOSOPHASTER	PHLEGMAGOGICS	PHONETICISES	PHONOTACTICS	PHOSPHORET
PHILOSOPHASTERS	PHLEGMAGOGUE	PHONETICISING	PHONOTYPED	PHOSPHORETS
PHILOSOPHE	PHLEGMAGOGUES	PHONETICISM	PHONOTYPER	PHOSPHORETTED
PHILOSOPHER	PHLEGMASIA	PHONETICISMS	PHONOTYPERS	PHOSPHORIC
PHILOSOPHERESS	PHLEGMASIAS	PHONETICIST	PHONOTYPES	PHOSPHORISE
PHILOSOPHERS	PHLEGMATIC	PHONETICISTS	PHONOTYPIC	PHOSPHORISED
PHILOSOPHES	PHLEGMATICAL	PHONETICIZATION	PHONOTYPICAL	PHOSPHORISES
PHILOSOPHESS	PHLEGMATICALLY	PHONETICIZE	PHONOTYPIES	PHOSPHORISING
PHILOSOPHESSES	PHLEGMATICNESS	PHONETICIZED	PHONOTYPING	PHOSPHORISM
PHILOSOPHIC	PHLEGMIEST	PHONETICIZES	PHONOTYPIST	PHOSPHORISMS
PHILOSOPHICAL	PHLEGMONIC	PHONETICIZING	PHONOTYPISTS	PHOSPHORITE
PHILOSOPHICALLY	PHLEGMONOID	PHONETISATION	PHORMINGES	PHOSPHORITES
PHILOSOPHIES	PHLEGMONOUS	PHONETISATIONS	PHOSGENITE	PHOSPHORITIC
PHILOSOPHISE	PHLOGISTIC	PHONETISED	PHOSGENITES	PHOSPHORIZE
PHILOSOPHISED	PHLOGISTICATE	PHONETISES	PHOSPHATASE	PHOSPHORIZED
PHILOSOPHISER	PHLOGISTICATED	PHONETISING	PHOSPHATASES	PHOSPHORIZES
PHILOSOPHISERS	PHLOGISTICATES	PHONETISMS	PHOSPHATED	PHOSPHORIZING
PHILOSOPHISES	PHLOGISTICATING	PHONETISTS	PHOSPHATES	PHOSPHOROLYSES
PHILOSOPHISING	PHLOGISTON	PHONETIZATION	PHOSPHATIC	PHOSPHOROLYSIS
PHILOSOPHISINGS	PHLOGISTONS	PHONETIZATIONS	PHOSPHATIDE	PHOSPHOROLYTIC
PHILOSOPHISM	PHLOGOPITE	PHONETIZED	PHOSPHATIDES	PHOSPHOROSCOPE
PHILOSOPHISMS	PHLOGOPITES	PHONETIZES	PHOSPHATIDIC	PHOSPHOROSCOPES
PHILOSOPHIST	PHLORIZINS	PHONETIZING	PHOSPHATIDYL	PHOSPHOROUS
PHILOSOPHISTIC	PHLYCTAENA	PHONEYNESS	PHOSPHATIDYLS	PHOSPHORUS
PHILOSOPHISTS	PHLYCTAENAE	PHONEYNESSES	PHOSPHATING	PHOSPHORUSES
PHILOSOPHIZE	PHLYCTENAE	PHONICALLY	PHOSPHATISATION	PHOSPHORYL
PHILOSOPHIZED	PHOCOMELIA	PHONINESSES	PHOSPHATISE	PHOSPHORYLASE
PHILOSOPHIZER	PHOCOMELIAS	PHONMETERS	PHOSPHATISED	PHOSPHORYLASES
PHILOSOPHIZERS	PHOCOMELIC	PHONOCAMPTIC	PHOSPHATISES	PHOSPHORYLATE
PHILOSOPHIZES	PHOCOMELIES	PHONOCAMPTICS	PHOSPHATISING	PHOSPHORYLATED
PHILOSOPHIZING	PHOENIXISM	PHONOCARDIOGRAM	PHOSPHATIZATION	PHOSPHORYLATES
PHILOSOPHIZINGS	PHOENIXISMS	PHONOCHEMISTRY	PHOSPHATIZE	PHOSPHORYLATING
PHILOSOPHY	PHOENIXLIKE	PHONOFIDDLE	PHOSPHATIZED	PHOSPHORYLATION
PHILOXENIA	PHOLIDOSES	PHONOFIDDLES	PHOSPHATIZES	PHOSPHORYLATIVE
PHILOXENIAS	PHOLIDOSIS	PHONOGRAMIC	PHOSPHATIZING	PHOSPHORYLS
PHILTERING	PHONASTHENIA	PHONOGRAMICALLY	PHOSPHATURIA	PHOSPHURET
PHISNOMIES	PHONASTHENIAS	PHONOGRAMMIC	PHOSPHATURIAS	PHOSPHURETS
PHLEBECTOMIES	PHONATHONS	PHONOGRAMS	PHOSPHATURIC	PHOSPHURETTED
PHLEBECTOMY	PHONATIONS	PHONOGRAPH	PHOSPHENES	PHOTICALLY
PHLEBITIDES	PHONAUTOGRAPH	PHONOGRAPHER	PHOSPHIDES	PHOTOACTINIC
PHLEBITISES	PHONAUTOGRAPHIC	PHONOGRAPHERS	PHOSPHINES	PHOTOACTIVE
PHLEBOGRAM	PHONAUTOGRAPHS	PHONOGRAPHIC	PHOSPHITES	PHOTOAUTOTROPH
PHLEBOGRAMS	PHONECARDS	PHONOGRAPHIES	PHOSPHOCREATIN	PHOTOAUTOTROPHS
PHLEBOGRAPHIC	PHONEMATIC	PHONOGRAPHIST	PHOSPHOCREATINE	PHOTOBATHIC
PHLEBOGRAPHIES	PHONEMATICALLY	PHONOGRAPHISTS	PHOSPHOCREATINS	PHOTOBIOLOGIC
PHLEBOGRAPHY	PHONEMICALLY	PHONOGRAPHS	PHOSPHOKINASE	PHOTOBIOLOGICAL
PHLEBOLITE	PHONEMICISATION	PHONOGRAPHY	PHOSPHOKINASES	PHOTOBIOLOGIES
PHLEBOLITES	PHONEMICISE	PHONOLITES	PHOSPHOLIPASE	PHOTOBIOLOGIST

PHOTOBIOLOGISTS	PHOTOELECTRONS	PHOTOIONIZATION	PHOTOOXIDIZED	PHOTOSENSITIVE
PHOTOBIOLOGY	PHOTOEMISSION	PHOTOIONIZE	PHOTOOXIDIZES	PHOTOSENSITIZE
PHOTOBLOGGED	PHOTOEMISSIONS	PHOTOIONIZED	PHOTOOXIDIZING	PHOTOSENSITIZED
PHOTOBLOGGING	PHOTOEMISSIVE	PHOTOIONIZES	PHOTOPERIOD	PHOTOSENSITIZER
PHOTOBLOGS	PHOTOENGRAVE	PHOTOIONIZING	PHOTOPERIODIC	PHOTOSENSITIZES
PHOTOBOMBED	PHOTOENGRAVED	PHOTOJOURNALISM	PHOTOPERIODISM	PHOTOSENSOR
PHOTOBOMBING	PHOTOENGRAVER	PHOTOJOURNALIST	PHOTOPERIODISMS	PHOTOSENSORS
PHOTOBOMBS	PHOTOENGRAVERS	PHOTOKINESES	PHOTOPERIODS	PHOTOSETTER
PHOTOCALLS	PHOTOENGRAVES	PHOTOKINESIS	PHOTOPHASE	PHOTOSETTERS
PHOTOCARDS	PHOTOENGRAVING	PHOTOKINETIC	PHOTOPHASES	PHOTOSETTING
PHOTOCATALYSES	PHOTOENGRAVINGS	PHOTOLITHO	PHOTOPHILIC	PHOTOSETTINGS
PHOTOCATALYSIS	PHOTOEXCITATION	PHOTOLITHOGRAPH	PHOTOPHILIES	PHOTOSHOOT
PHOTOCATALYTIC	PHOTOEXCITED	PHOTOLITHOS	PHOTOPHILOUS	PHOTOSHOOTS
PHOTOCATHODE	PHOTOFINISHER	PHOTOLUMINESCE	PHOTOPHILS	PHOTOSHOPPED
PHOTOCATHODES	PHOTOFINISHERS	PHOTOLUMINESCED	PHOTOPHILY	PHOTOSHOPPING
PHOTOCELLS	PHOTOFINISHING	PHOTOLUMINESCES	PHOTOPHOBE	PHOTOSHOPS
PHOTOCHEMICAL	PHOTOFINISHINGS	PHOTOLYSABLE	PHOTOPHOBES	PHOTOSPHERE
PHOTOCHEMICALLY	PHOTOFISSION	PHOTOLYSED	PHOTOPHOBIA	PHOTOSPHERES
PHOTOCHEMIST	PHOTOFISSIONS	PHOTOLYSES	PHOTOPHOBIAS	PHOTOSPHERIC
PHOTOCHEMISTRY	PHOTOFLASH	PHOTOLYSING	PHOTOPHOBIC	PHOTOSTATED
PHOTOCHEMISTS	PHOTOFLASHES	PHOTOLYSIS	PHOTOPHONE	PHOTOSTATIC
PHOTOCHROMIC	PHOTOFLOOD	PHOTOLYTIC	PHOTOPHONES	PHOTOSTATING
PHOTOCHROMICS	PHOTOFLOODS	PHOTOLYTICALLY	PHOTOPHONIC	PHOTOSTATS
PHOTOCHROMIES	PHOTOFLUOROGRAM	PHOTOLYZABLE	PHOTOPHONIES	PHOTOSTATTED
PHOTOCHROMISM	PHOTOGELATIN	PHOTOLYZED	PHOTOPHONY	PHOTOSTATTING
PHOTOCHROMISMS	PHOTOGELATINE	PHOTOLYZES	PHOTOPHORE	PHOTOSYNTHATE
PHOTOCHROMY	PHOTOGENES	PHOTOLYZING	PHOTOPHORES	PHOTOSYNTHATES
PHOTOCOMPOSE	PHOTOGENIC	PHOTOMACHINE	PHOTOPHORESES	PHOTOSYNTHESES
PHOTOCOMPOSED	PHOTOGENICALLY	PHOTOMACHINES	PHOTOPHORESIS	PHOTOSYNTHESIS
PHOTOCOMPOSER	PHOTOGENIES	PHOTOMACROGRAPH	PHOTOPLAYS	PHOTOSYNTHESISE
PHOTOCOMPOSERS	PHOTOGEOLOGIC	PHOTOMAPPED	PHOTOPOLYMER	PHOTOSYNTHESIZE
PHOTOCOMPOSES	PHOTOGEOLOGICAL	PHOTOMAPPING	PHOTOPOLYMERS	PHOTOSYNTHETIC
PHOTOCOMPOSING	PHOTOGEOLOGIES	PHOTOMASKS	PHOTOPOSITIVE	PHOTOSYSTEM
PHOTOCONDUCTING	PHOTOGEOLOGIST	PHOTOMECHANICAL	PHOTOPRODUCT	PHOTOSYSTEMS
PHOTOCONDUCTION	PHOTOGEOLOGISTS	PHOTOMETER	PHOTOPRODUCTION	PHOTOTACTIC
PHOTOCONDUCTIVE	PHOTOGEOLOGY	PHOTOMETERS	PHOTOPRODUCTS	PHOTOTACTICALLY
PHOTOCONDUCTOR	PHOTOGLYPH	PHOTOMETRIC	PHOTOPSIAS	PHOTOTAXES
PHOTOCONDUCTORS	PHOTOGLYPHIC	PHOTOMETRICALLY	PHOTOPSIES	PHOTOTAXIES
PHOTOCOPIABLE	PHOTOGLYPHIES	PHOTOMETRIES	PHOTOREACTION	PHOTOTAXIS
PHOTOCOPIED	PHOTOGLYPHS	PHOTOMETRIST	PHOTOREACTIONS	PHOTOTELEGRAM
PHOTOCOPIER	PHOTOGLYPHY	PHOTOMETRISTS	PHOTOREACTIVE	PHOTOTELEGRAMS
PHOTOCOPIERS	PHOTOGRAMMETRIC	PHOTOMETRY	PHOTOREALISM	PHOTOTELEGRAPH
PHOTOCOPIES	PHOTOGRAMMETRY	PHOTOMICROGRAPH	PHOTOREALISMS	PHOTOTELEGRAPHS
PHOTOCOPYING	PHOTOGRAMS	PHOTOMONTAGE	PHOTOREALIST	PHOTOTELEGRAPHY
PHOTOCOPYINGS	PHOTOGRAPH	PHOTOMONTAGES	PHOTOREALISTIC	PHOTOTHERAPIES
PHOTOCURRENT	PHOTOGRAPHED	PHOTOMOSAIC	PHOTOREALISTS	PHOTOTHERAPY
PHOTOCURRENTS	PHOTOGRAPHER	PHOTOMOSAICS	PHOTORECEPTION	PHOTOTHERMAL
PHOTODEGRADABLE	PHOTOGRAPHERS	PHOTOMULTIPLIER	PHOTORECEPTIONS	PHOTOTHERMALLY
PHOTODETECTOR	PHOTOGRAPHIC	PHOTOMURAL	PHOTORECEPTIVE	PHOTOTHERMIC
PHOTODETECTORS	PHOTOGRAPHICAL	PHOTOMURALS	PHOTORECEPTOR	PHOTOTONIC
PHOTODIODE	PHOTOGRAPHIES	PHOTONASTIC	PHOTORECEPTORS	PHOTOTONUS
PHOTODIODES	PHOTOGRAPHING	PHOTONASTIES	PHOTOREDUCE	PHOTOTONUSES
PHOTODISKS	PHOTOGRAPHIST	PHOTONASTY	PHOTOREDUCED	PHOTOTOPOGRAPHY
PHOTODISSOCIATE	PHOTOGRAPHISTS	PHOTONEGATIVE	PHOTOREDUCES	PHOTOTOXIC
PHOTODUPLICATE	PHOTOGRAPHS	PHOTONEUTRON	PHOTOREDUCING	PHOTOTOXICITIES
PHOTODUPLICATED	PHOTOGRAPHY	PHOTONEUTRONS	PHOTOREDUCTION	PHOTOTOXICITY
PHOTODUPLICATES	PHOTOGRAVURE	PHOTONOVEL	PHOTOREDUCTIONS	PHOTOTRANSISTOR
PHOTODYNAMIC	PHOTOGRAVURES	PHOTONOVELS	PHOTOREFRACTIVE	PHOTOTROPE
PHOTODYNAMICS	PHOTOINDUCED	PHOTONUCLEAR	PHOTORESIST	PHOTOTROPES
PHOTOELASTIC	PHOTOINDUCTION	PHOTOOXIDATION	PHOTORESISTS	PHOTOTROPH
PHOTOELASTICITY	PHOTOINDUCTIONS	PHOTOOXIDATIONS	PHOTOSCANNED	PHOTOTROPHIC
PHOTOELECTRIC	PHOTOINDUCTIVE	PHOTOOXIDATIVE	PHOTOSCANNING	PHOTOTROPHS
PHOTOELECTRICAL	PHOTOIONISATION	PHOTOOXIDISE	PHOTOSCANS	PHOTOTROPIC
PHOTOELECTRODE	PHOTOIONISE	PHOTOOXIDISED	PHOTOSENSITISE	PHOTOTROPICALLY
PHOTOELECTRODES	PHOTOIONISED	PHOTOOXIDISES	PHOTOSENSITISED	PHOTOTROPIES
PHOTOELECTRON	PHOTOIONISES	PHOTOOXIDISING	PHOTOSENSITISER	PHOTOTROPISM
PHOTOELECTRONIC	PHOTOIONISING	PHOTOOXIDIZE	PHOTOSENSITISES	PHOTOTROPISMS

PHOTOTROPY
PHOTOTUBES
PHOTOTYPED
PHOTOTYPES
PHOTOTYPESET
PHOTOTYPESETS
PHOTOTYPESETTER
PHOTOTYPIC
PHOTOTYPICALLY
PHOTOTYPIES
PHOTOTYPING
PHOTOTYPOGRAPHY
PHOTOVOLTAIC
PHOTOVOLTAICS
PHOTOXYLOGRAPHY
PHOTOZINCOGRAPH
PHRAGMOPLAST
PHRAGMOPLASTS
PHRASELESS
PHRASEMAKER
PHRASEMAKERS
PHRASEMAKING
PHRASEMAKINGS
PHRASEMONGER
PHRASEMONGERING
PHRASEMONGERS
PHRASEOGRAM
PHRASEOGRAMS
PHRASEOGRAPH
PHRASEOGRAPHIC
PHRASEOGRAPHIES
PHRASEOGRAPHS
PHRASEOGRAPHY
PHRASEOLOGIC
PHRASEOLOGICAL
PHRASEOLOGIES
PHRASEOLOGIST
PHRASEOLOGISTS
PHRASEOLOGY
PHREAKINGS
PHREATOPHYTE
PHREATOPHYTES
PHREATOPHYTIC
PHRENESIAC
PHRENETICAL
PHRENETICALLY
PHRENETICNESS
PHRENETICNESSES
PHRENETICS
PHRENITIDES
PHRENITISES
PHRENOLOGIC
PHRENOLOGICAL
PHRENOLOGICALLY
PHRENOLOGIES
PHRENOLOGISE
PHRENOLOGISED
PHRENOLOGISES
PHRENOLOGISING
PHRENOLOGIST
PHRENOLOGISTS
PHRENOLOGIZE
PHRENOLOGIZED
PHRENOLOGIZES
PHRENOLOGIZING
PHRENOLOGY
PHRENSICAL

PHRENSYING
PHRONTISTERIES
PHRONTISTERY
PHTHALATES
PHTHALEINS
PHTHALOCYANIN
PHTHALOCYANINE
PHTHALOCYANINES
PHTHALOCYANINS
PHTHIRIASES
PHTHIRIASIS
PHTHISICAL
PHTHISICKY
PHYCOBILIN
PHYCOBILINS
PHYCOBIONT
PHYCOBIONTS
PHYCOCYANIN
PHYCOCYANINS
PHYCOCYANS
PHYCOERYTHRIN
PHYCOERYTHRINS
PHYCOLOGICAL
PHYCOLOGIES
PHYCOLOGIST
PHYCOLOGISTS
PHYCOMYCETE
PHYCOMYCETES
PHYCOMYCETOUS
PHYCOPHAEIN
PHYCOPHAEINS
PHYCOXANTHIN
PHYCOXANTHINS
PHYLACTERIC
PHYLACTERICAL
PHYLACTERIES
PHYLACTERY
PHYLARCHIES
PHYLAXISES
PHYLESISES
PHYLETICALLY
PHYLLARIES
PHYLLOCLAD
PHYLLOCLADE
PHYLLOCLADES
PHYLLOCLADS
PHYLLODIAL
PHYLLODIES
PHYLLODIUM
PHYLLOMANIA
PHYLLOMANIAS
PHYLLOPHAGOUS
PHYLLOPLANE
PHYLLOPLANES
PHYLLOPODS
PHYLLOQUINONE
PHYLLOQUINONES
PHYLLOSILICATE
PHYLLOSILICATES
PHYLLOSPHERE
PHYLLOSPHERES
PHYLLOTACTIC
PHYLLOTACTICAL
PHYLLOTAXES
PHYLLOTAXIES
PHYLLOTAXIS
PHYLLOTAXY

PHYLLOXERA
PHYLLOXERAE
PHYLLOXERAS
PHYLOGENESES
PHYLOGENESIS
PHYLOGENETIC
PHYLOGENIC
PHYLOGENIES
PHYSALISES
PHYSHARMONICA
PHYSHARMONICAS
PHYSIATRIC
PHYSIATRICAL
PHYSIATRICS
PHYSIATRIES
PHYSIATRIST
PHYSIATRISTS
PHYSICALISM
PHYSICALISMS
PHYSICALIST
PHYSICALISTIC
PHYSICALISTS
PHYSICALITIES
PHYSICALITY
PHYSICALLY
PHYSICALNESS
PHYSICALNESSES
PHYSICIANCIES
PHYSICIANCY
PHYSICIANER
PHYSICIANERS
PHYSICIANS
PHYSICIANSHIP
PHYSICIANSHIPS
PHYSICISMS
PHYSICISTS
PHYSICKING
PHYSICOCHEMICAL
PHYSIOCRACIES
PHYSIOCRACY
PHYSIOCRAT
PHYSIOCRATIC
PHYSIOCRATS
PHYSIOGNOMIC
PHYSIOGNOMICAL
PHYSIOGNOMIES
PHYSIOGNOMIST
PHYSIOGNOMISTS
PHYSIOGNOMY
PHYSIOGRAPHER
PHYSIOGRAPHERS
PHYSIOGRAPHIC
PHYSIOGRAPHICAL
PHYSIOGRAPHIES
PHYSIOGRAPHY
PHYSIOLATER
PHYSIOLATERS
PHYSIOLATRIES
PHYSIOLATRY
PHYSIOLOGIC
PHYSIOLOGICAL
PHYSIOLOGICALLY
PHYSIOLOGIES
PHYSIOLOGIST
PHYSIOLOGISTS
PHYSIOLOGUS
PHYSIOLOGUSES

PHYSIOLOGY
PHYSIOPATHOLOGY
PHYSIOTHERAPIES
PHYSIOTHERAPIST
PHYSIOTHERAPY
PHYSITHEISM
PHYSITHEISMS
PHYSITHEISTIC
PHYSOCLISTOUS
PHYSOSTIGMIN
PHYSOSTIGMINE
PHYSOSTIGMINES
PHYSOSTIGMINS
PHYSOSTOMOUS
PHYTOALEXIN
PHYTOALEXINS
PHYTOBENTHOS
PHYTOBENTHOSES
PHYTOCHEMICAL
PHYTOCHEMICALLY
PHYTOCHEMICALS
PHYTOCHEMIST
PHYTOCHEMISTRY
PHYTOCHEMISTS
PHYTOCHROME
PHYTOCHROMES
PHYTOESTROGEN
PHYTOESTROGENS
PHYTOFLAGELLATE
PHYTOGENESES
PHYTOGENESIS
PHYTOGENETIC
PHYTOGENETICAL
PHYTOGENIC
PHYTOGENIES
PHYTOGEOGRAPHER
PHYTOGEOGRAPHIC
PHYTOGEOGRAPHY
PHYTOGRAPHER
PHYTOGRAPHERS
PHYTOGRAPHIC
PHYTOGRAPHIES
PHYTOGRAPHY
PHYTOHORMONE
PHYTOHORMONES
PHYTOLITHS
PHYTOLOGICAL
PHYTOLOGICALLY
PHYTOLOGIES
PHYTOLOGIST
PHYTOLOGISTS
PHYTONADIONE
PHYTONADIONES
PHYTOPATHOGEN
PHYTOPATHOGENIC
PHYTOPATHOGENS
PHYTOPATHOLOGY
PHYTOPHAGIC
PHYTOPHAGIES
PHYTOPHAGOUS
PHYTOPHAGY
PHYTOPLANKTER
PHYTOPLANKTERS
PHYTOPLANKTON
PHYTOPLANKTONIC
PHYTOPLANKTONS
PHYTOSANITARY

PHYTOSOCIOLOGY
PHYTOSTEROL
PHYTOSTEROLS
PHYTOTHERAPIES
PHYTOTHERAPY
PHYTOTOMIES
PHYTOTOMIST
PHYTOTOMISTS
PHYTOTOXIC
PHYTOTOXICITIES
PHYTOTOXICITY
PHYTOTOXIN
PHYTOTOXINS
PHYTOTRONS
PIACULARITIES
PIACULARITY
PIANISSIMI
PIANISSIMO
PIANISSIMOS
PIANISSISSIMO
PIANISTICALLY
PIANOFORTE
PIANOFORTES
PIANOLISTS
PICADILLOS
PICANINNIES
PICARESQUE
PICARESQUES
PICAROONED
PICAROONING
PICAYUNISH
PICAYUNISHLY
PICAYUNISHNESS
PICCADILLIES
PICCADILLO
PICCADILLOES
PICCADILLOS
PICCADILLS
PICCADILLY
PICCALILLI
PICCALILLIS
PICCANINNIES
PICCANINNY
PICCOLOIST
PICCOLOISTS
PICHICIAGO
PICHICIAGOS
PICHICIEGO
PICHICIEGOS
PICHOLINES
PICKABACKED
PICKABACKING
PICKABACKS
PICKADILLIES
PICKADILLO
PICKADILLOES
PICKADILLOS
PICKADILLS
PICKADILLY
PICKANINNIES
PICKANINNY
PICKAPACKED
PICKAPACKING
PICKAPACKS
PICKAROONS
PICKBACKED
PICKBACKING

PICKEDNESS	PICTURISATION	PIGGYBACKS	PILLORISES	PINHOOKERS
PICKEDNESSES	PICTURISATIONS	PIGHEADEDLY	PILLORISING	PINKERTONS
PICKEERERS	PICTURISED	PIGHEADEDNESS	PILLORIZED	PINKINESSES
PICKEERING	PICTURISES	PIGHEADEDNESSES	PILLORIZES	PINKISHNESS
PICKELHAUBE	PICTURISING	PIGMENTARY	PILLORIZING	PINKISHNESSES
PICKELHAUBES	PICTURIZATION	PIGMENTATION	PILLORYING	PINKNESSES
PICKERELWEED	PICTURIZATIONS	PIGMENTATIONS	PILLOWCASE	PINNACLING
PICKERELWEEDS	PICTURIZED	PIGMENTING	PILLOWCASES	PINNATIFID
PICKETBOAT	PICTURIZES	PIGMENTOSA	PILLOWIEST	PINNATIFIDLY
PICKETBOATS	PICTURIZING	PIGMENTOSAS	PILLOWSLIP	PINNATIONS
PICKETINGS	PIDDLINGLY	PIGNERATED	PILLOWSLIPS	PINNATIPARTITE
PICKINESSES	PIDGINISATION	PIGNERATES	PILNIEWINKS	PINNATIPED
PICKPOCKET	PIDGINISATIONS	PIGNERATING	PILOCARPIN	PINNATISECT
PICKPOCKETED	PIDGINISED	PIGNERATION	PILOCARPINE	PINNIEWINKLE
PICKPOCKETING	PIDGINISES	PIGNERATIONS	PILOCARPINES	PINNIEWINKLES
PICKPOCKETS	PIDGINISING	PIGNORATED	PILOCARPINS	PINNIPEDES
PICKTHANKS	PIDGINIZATION	PIGNORATES	PILOSITIES	PINNIPEDIAN
PICNICKERS	PIDGINIZATIONS	PIGNORATING	PILOTFISHES	PINNIPEDIANS
PICNICKIER	PIDGINIZED	PIGNORATION	PILOTHOUSE	PINNULATED
PICNICKIEST	PIDGINIZES	PIGNORATIONS	PILOTHOUSES	PINNYWINKLE
PICNICKING	PIDGINIZING	PIGSCONCES	PIMPERNELS	PINNYWINKLES
PICOCURIES	PIECEMEALED	PIGSTICKED	PIMPLINESS	PINOCYTOSES
PICOFARADS	PIECEMEALING	PIGSTICKER	PIMPLINESSES	PINOCYTOSIS
PICOMETERS	PIECEMEALS	PIGSTICKERS	PIMPMOBILE	PINOCYTOTIC
PICOMETRES	PIECEWORKER	PIGSTICKING	PIMPMOBILES	PINOCYTOTICALLY
PICORNAVIRUS	PIECEWORKERS	PIGSTICKINGS	PINACOIDAL	PINPOINTED
PICORNAVIRUSES	PIECEWORKS	PIKEPERCHES	PINACOTHECA	PINPOINTING
PICOSECOND	PIEDMONTITE	PIKESTAFFS	PINACOTHECAE	PINPRICKED
PICOSECONDS	PIEDMONTITES	PIKESTAVES	PINAKOIDAL	PINPRICKING
PICOWAVING	PIEDNESSES	PILASTERED	PINAKOTHEK	PINSETTERS
PICQUETING	PIEMONTITE	PILEORHIZA	PINAKOTHEKS	PINSPOTTED
PICROCARMINE	PIEMONTITES	PILEORHIZAS	PINBALLING	PINSPOTTER
PICROCARMINES	PIEPOWDERS	PILFERABLE	PINCERLIKE	PINSPOTTERS
PICROTOXIN	PIERCEABLE	PILFERAGES	PINCHBECKS	PINSPOTTING
PICROTOXINS	PIERCINGLY	PILFERINGLY	PINCHCOCKS	PINSTRIPED
PICTARNIES	PIERCINGNESS	PILFERINGS	PINCHCOMMONS	PINSTRIPES
PICTOGRAMS	PIERCINGNESSES	PILFERPROOF	PINCHCOMMONSES	PINTADERAS
PICTOGRAPH	PIERRETTES	PILGARLICK	PINCHFISTS	PINTUCKING
PICTOGRAPHIC	PIETISTICAL	PILGARLICKS	PINCHINGLY	PINTUCKINGS
PICTOGRAPHIES	PIETISTICALLY	PILGARLICKY	PINCHPENNIES	PINWHEELED
PICTOGRAPHS	PIEZOCHEMISTRY	PILGARLICS	PINCHPENNY	PINWHEELING
PICTOGRAPHY	PIEZOELECTRIC	PILGRIMAGE	PINCHPOINT	PINWRENCHES
PICTORIALISE	PIEZOMAGNETIC	PILGRIMAGED	PINCHPOINTS	PIONEERING
PICTORIALISED	PIEZOMAGNETISM	PILGRIMAGER	PINCUSHION	PIOUSNESSES
PICTORIALISES	PIEZOMAGNETISMS	PILGRIMAGERS	PINCUSHIONS	PIPECLAYED
PICTORIALISING	PIEZOMETER	PILGRIMAGES	PINEALECTOMIES	PIPECLAYING
PICTORIALISM	PIEZOMETERS	PILGRIMAGING	PINEALECTOMISE	PIPEFISHES
PICTORIALISMS	PIEZOMETRIC	PILGRIMERS	PINEALECTOMISED	PIPEFITTER
PICTORIALIST	PIEZOMETRICALLY	PILGRIMING	PINEALECTOMISES	PIPEFITTERS
PICTORIALISTS	PIEZOMETRIES	PILGRIMISE	PINEALECTOMIZE	PIPEFITTING
PICTORIALIZE	PIEZOMETRY	PILGRIMISED	PINEALECTOMIZED	PIPEFITTINGS
PICTORIALIZED	PIFFERAROS	PILGRIMISES	PINEALECTOMIZES	PIPELINING
PICTORIALIZES	PIGEONHOLE	PILGRIMISING	PINEALECTOMY	PIPELININGS
PICTORIALIZING	PIGEONHOLED	PILGRIMIZE	PINEAPPLES	PIPERACEOUS
PICTORIALLY	PIGEONHOLER	PILGRIMIZED	PINFEATHER	PIPERAZINE
PICTORIALNESS	PIGEONHOLERS	PILGRIMIZES	PINFEATHERS	PIPERAZINES
PICTORIALNESSES	PIGEONHOLES	PILGRIMIZING	PINFOLDING	PIPERIDINE
PICTORIALS	PIGEONHOLING	PILIFEROUS	PINGRASSES	PIPERIDINES
PICTORICAL	PIGEONITES	PILLAGINGS	PINGUEFIED	PIPERONALS
PICTORICALLY	PIGEONRIES	PILLARISTS	PINGUEFIES	PIPESTONES
PICTUREGOER	PIGEONWING	PILLARLESS	PINGUEFYING	PIPINESSES
PICTUREGOERS	PIGEONWINGS	PILLICOCKS	PINGUIDITIES	PIPISTRELLE
PICTUREPHONE	PIGGINESSES	PILLIONING	PINGUIDITY	PIPISTRELLES
PICTUREPHONES	PIGGISHNESS	PILLIONIST	PINGUITUDE	PIPISTRELS
PICTURESQUE	PIGGISHNESSES	PILLIONISTS	PINGUITUDES	PIPIWHARAUROA
PICTURESQUELY	PIGGYBACKED	PILLIWINKS	PINHEADEDNESS	PIPIWHARAUROAS
PICTURESQUENESS	PIGGYBACKING	PILLORISED	PINHEADEDNESSES	PIPSISSEWA

PIPSISSEWAS	PITCHWOMAN	PLACENTATIONS	PLANCHETTES	PLANTSWOMEN
PIPSQUEAKS	PITCHWOMEN	PLACENTIFORM	PLANELOADS	PLANULIFORM
PIQUANCIES	PITEOUSNESS	PLACENTOLOGIES	PLANENESSES	PLAQUETTES
PIQUANTNESS	PITEOUSNESSES	PLACENTOLOGY	PLANESIDES	PLASMAGELS
PIQUANTNESSES	PITHECANTHROPI	PLACIDITIES	PLANETARIA	PLASMAGENE
PIRACETAMS	PITHECANTHROPUS	PLACIDNESS	PLANETARTES	PLASMAGENES
PIRATICALLY	PITHECOIDS	PLACIDNESSES	PLANETARIUM	PLASMAGENIC
PIRLICUING	PITHINESSES	PLACODERMS	PLANETARIUMS	PLASMALEMMA
PIROPLASMA	PITIABLENESS	PLAGIARIES	PLANETESIMAL	PLASMALEMMAS
PIROPLASMATA	PITIABLENESSES	PLAGIARISE	PLANETESIMALS	PLASMAPHERESES
PIROPLASMS	PITIFULLER	PLAGIARISED	PLANETICAL	PLASMAPHERESIS
PIROUETTED	PITIFULLEST	PLAGIARISER	PLANETLIKE	PLASMASOLS
PIROUETTER	PITIFULNESS	PLAGIARISERS	PLANETOIDAL	PLASMATICAL
PIROUETTERS	PITIFULNESSES	PLAGIARISES	PLANETOIDS	PLASMINOGEN
PIROUETTES	PITILESSLY	PLAGIARISING	PLANETOLOGICAL	PLASMINOGENS
PIROUETTING	PITILESSNESS	PLAGIARISM	PLANETOLOGIES	PLASMODESM
PISCATORIAL	PITILESSNESSES	PLAGIARISMS	PLANETOLOGIST	PLASMODESMA
PISCATORIALLY	PITTOSPORUM	PLAGIARIST	PLANETOLOGISTS	PLASMODESMAS
PISCATRIXES	PITTOSPORUMS	PLAGIARISTIC	PLANETOLOGY	PLASMODESMATA
PISCICOLOUS	PITUITARIES	PLAGIARISTS	PLANETWIDE	PLASMODESMS
PISCICULTURAL	PITUITRINS	PLAGIARIZE	PLANGENCIES	PLASMODIAL
PISCICULTURALLY	PITYRIASES	PLAGIARIZED	PLANGENTLY	PLASMODIUM
PISCICULTURE	PITYRIASIS	PLAGIARIZER	PLANIGRAMS	PLASMOGAMIES
PISCICULTURES	PITYROSPORUM	PLAGIARIZERS	PLANIGRAPH	PLASMOGAMY
PISCICULTURIST	PITYROSPORUMS	PLAGIARIZES	PLANIGRAPHIES	PLASMOLYSE
PISCICULTURISTS	PIWAKAWAKA	PLAGIARIZING	PLANIGRAPHS	PLASMOLYSED
PISCIFAUNA	PIWAKAWAKAS	PLAGIOCEPHALIES	PLANIGRAPHY	PLASMOLYSES
PISCIFAUNAE	PIXELATING	PLAGIOCEPHALY	PLANIMETER	PLASMOLYSING
PISCIFAUNAS	PIXELATION	PLAGIOCLASE	PLANIMETERS	PLASMOLYSIS
PISCIVORES	PIXELATIONS	PLAGIOCLASES	PLANIMETRIC	PLASMOLYTIC
PISCIVOROUS	PIXELLATED	PLAGIOCLASTIC	PLANIMETRICAL	PLASMOLYTICALLY
PISSASPHALT	PIXELLATES	PLAGIOCLIMAX	PLANIMETRICALLY	PLASMOLYZE
PISSASPHALTS	PIXELLATING	PLAGIOCLIMAXES	PLANIMETRIES	PLASMOLYZED
PISTACHIOS	PIXELLATION	PLAGIOSTOMATOUS	PLANIMETRY	PLASMOLYZES
PISTAREENS	PIXELLATIONS	PLAGIOSTOME	PLANISHERS	PLASMOLYZING
PISTILLARY	PIXILATING	PLAGIOSTOMES	PLANISHING	PLASMOSOMA
PISTILLATE	PIXILATION	PLAGIOSTOMOUS	PLANISPHERE	PLASMOSOMATA
PISTILLODE	PIXILATIONS	PLAGIOTROPIC	PLANISPHERES	PLASMOSOME
PISTILLODES	PIXILLATED	PLAGIOTROPISM	PLANISPHERIC	PLASMOSOMES
PISTOLEERS	PIXILLATES	PLAGIOTROPISMS	PLANKTONIC	PLASTERBOARD
PISTOLEROS	PIXILLATING	PLAGIOTROPOUS	PLANLESSLY	PLASTERBOARDS
PISTOLIERS	PIXILLATION	PLAGUELIKE	PLANLESSNESS	PLASTERERS
PISTOLLING	PIXILLATIONS	PLAGUESOME	PLANLESSNESSES	PLASTERIER
PITAPATTED	PIXINESSES	PLAINCHANT	PLANOBLAST	PLASTERIEST
PITAPATTING	PIZAZZIEST	PLAINCHANTS	PLANOBLASTS	PLASTERINESS
PITCHBENDS	PIZZAZZIER	PLAINCLOTHES	PLANOCONVEX	PLASTERINESSES
PITCHBLENDE	PIZZAZZIEST	PLAINCLOTHESMAN	PLANOGAMETE	PLASTERING
PITCHBLENDES	PIZZICATOS	PLAINCLOTHESMEN	PLANOGAMETES	PLASTERINGS
PITCHERFUL	PLACABILITIES	PLAINNESSES	PLANOGRAMS	PLASTERSTONE
PITCHERFULS	PLACABILITY	PLAINSONGS	PLANOGRAPHIC	PLASTERSTONES
PITCHERSFUL	PLACABLENESS	PLAINSPOKEN	PLANOGRAPHIES	PLASTERWORK
PITCHFORKED	PLACABLENESSES	PLAINSPOKENNESS	PLANOGRAPHY	PLASTERWORKS
PITCHFORKING	PLACARDING	PLAINSTANES	PLANOMETER	PLASTICALLY
PITCHFORKS	PLACATINGLY	PLAINSTONES	PLANOMETERS	PLASTICATED
PITCHINESS	PLACATIONS	PLAINTEXTS	PLANOMETRIC	PLASTICENE
PITCHINESSES	PLACEHOLDER	PLAINTIFFS	PLANOMETRICALLY	PLASTICENES
PITCHOMETER	PLACEHOLDERS	PLAINTIVELY	PLANOMETRIES	PLASTICINE
PITCHOMETERS	PLACEKICKED	PLAINTIVENESS	PLANOMETRY	PLASTICINES
PITCHPERSON	PLACEKICKER	PLAINTIVENESSES	PLANTAGINACEOUS	PLASTICISATION
PITCHPERSONS	PLACEKICKERS	PLAINTLESS	PLANTATION	PLASTICISATIONS
PITCHPINES	PLACEKICKING	PLAINWORKS	PLANTATIONS	PLASTICISE
PITCHPIPES	PLACEKICKS	PLAISTERED	PLANTIGRADE	PLASTICISED
PITCHPOLED	PLACELESSLY	PLAISTERING	PLANTIGRADES	PLASTICISER
PITCHPOLES	PLACEMENTS	PLANARIANS	PLANTLINGS	PLASTICISERS
PITCHPOLING	PLACENTALS	PLANARITIES	PLANTOCRACIES	PLASTICISES
PITCHSTONE	PLACENTATE	PLANATIONS	PLANTOCRACY	PLASTICISING
PITCHSTONES	PLACENTATION	PLANCHETTE	PLANTSWOMAN	PLASTICITIES

PLASTICITY	PLATINOCYANIDES	PLAYMAKERS	PLEIOMEROUS	PLETHYSMOGRAPH
PLASTICIZATION	PLATINOIDS	PLAYMAKING	PLEIOTAXIES	PLETHYSMOGRAPHS
PLASTICIZATIONS	PLATINOTYPE	PLAYMAKINGS	PLEIOTROPIC	PLETHYSMOGRAPHY
PLASTICIZE	PLATINOTYPES	PLAYREADER	PLEIOTROPIES	PLEURAPOPHYSES
PLASTICIZED	PLATITUDES	PLAYREADERS	PLEIOTROPISM	PLEURAPOPHYSIS
PLASTICIZER	PLATITUDINAL	PLAYSCHOOL	PLEIOTROPISMS	PLEURISIES
PLASTICIZERS	PLATITUDINARIAN	PLAYSCHOOLS	PLEIOTROPY	PLEURITICAL
PLASTICIZES	PLATITUDINISE	PLAYTHINGS	PLENARTIES	PLEURITICS
PLASTICIZING	PLATITUDINISED	PLAYWRIGHT	PLENILUNAR	PLEURITISES
PLASTICKIER	PLATITUDINISER	PLAYWRIGHTING	PLENILUNES	PLEUROCARPOUS
PLASTICKIEST	PLATITUDINISERS	PLAYWRIGHTINGS	PLENIPOTENCE	PLEUROCENTESES
PLASTIDIAL	PLATITUDINISES	PLAYWRIGHTS	PLENIPOTENCES	PLEUROCENTESIS
PLASTIDULE	PLATITUDINISING	PLAYWRITING	PLENIPOTENCIES	PLEURODONT
PLASTIDULES	PLATITUDINIZE	PLAYWRITINGS	PLENIPOTENCY	PLEURODONTS
PLASTILINA	PLATITUDINIZED	PLEADINGLY	PLENIPOTENT	PLEURODYNIA
PLASTILINAS	PLATITUDINIZER	PLEASANCES	PLENIPOTENTIAL	PLEURODYNIAS
PLASTINATION	PLATITUDINIZERS	PLEASANTER	PLENIPOTENTIARY	PLEURONIAS
PLASTINATIONS	PLATITUDINIZES	PLEASANTEST	PLENISHERS	PLEUROPNEUMONIA
PLASTIQUES	PLATITUDINIZING	PLEASANTLY	PLENISHING	PLEUROTOMIES
PLASTISOLS	PLATITUDINOUS	PLEASANTNESS	PLENISHINGS	PLEUROTOMY
PLASTOCYANIN	PLATITUDINOUSLY	PLEASANTNESSES	PLENISHMENT	PLEUSTONIC
PLASTOCYANINS	PLATONICALLY	PLEASANTRIES	PLENISHMENTS	PLEXIGLASS
PLASTOGAMIES	PLATONISMS	PLEASANTRY	PLENITUDES	PLEXIGLASSES
PLASTOGAMY	PLATOONING	PLEASINGLY	PLENITUDINOUS	PLEXIMETER
PLASTOMETER	PLATTELAND	PLEASINGNESS	PLENTEOUSLY	PLEXIMETERS
PLASTOMETERS	PLATTELANDS	PLEASINGNESSES	PLENTEOUSNESS	PLEXIMETRIC
PLASTOMETRIC	PLATTERFUL	PLEASURABILITY	PLENTEOUSNESSES	PLEXIMETRIES
PLASTOMETRIES	PLATTERFULS	PLEASURABLE	PLENTIFULLY	PLEXIMETRY
PLASTOMETRY	PLATTERSFUL	PLEASURABLENESS	PLENTIFULNESS	PLIABILITIES
PLASTOQUINONE	PLATYCEPHALIC	PLEASURABLY	PLENTIFULNESSES	PLIABILITY
PLASTOQUINONES	PLATYCEPHALOUS	PLEASUREFUL	PLENTITUDE	PLIABLENESS
PLATANACEOUS	PLATYFISHES	PLEASURELESS	PLENTITUDES	PLIABLENESSES
PLATEAUING	PLATYHELMINTH	PLEASURERS	PLEOCHROIC	PLIANTNESS
PLATEGLASS	PLATYHELMINTHIC	PLEASURING	PLEOCHROISM	PLIANTNESSES
PLATEGLASSES	PLATYHELMINTHS	PLEBEIANISE	PLEOCHROISMS	PLICATENESS
PLATELAYER	PLATYKURTIC	PLEBEIANISED	PLEOMORPHIC	PLICATENESSES
PLATELAYERS	PLATYPUSES	PLEBEIANISES	PLEOMORPHIES	PLICATIONS
PLATELAYING	PLATYRRHINE	PLEBEIANISING	PLEOMORPHISM	PLICATURES
PLATELAYINGS	PLATYRRHINES	PLEBEIANISM	PLEOMORPHISMS	PLODDINGLY
PLATEMAKER	PLATYRRHINIAN	PLEBEIANISMS	PLEOMORPHOUS	PLODDINGNESS
PLATEMAKERS	PLATYRRHINIANS	PLEBEIANIZE	PLEOMORPHY	PLODDINGNESSES
PLATEMAKING	PLAUDITORY	PLEBEIANIZED	PLEONASTES	PLOTLESSNESS
PLATEMAKINGS	PLAUSIBILITIES	PLEBEIANIZES	PLEONASTIC	PLOTLESSNESSES
PLATEMARKED	PLAUSIBILITY	PLEBEIANIZING	PLEONASTICAL	PLOTTERING
PLATEMARKING	PLAUSIBLENESS	PLEBEIANLY	PLEONASTICALLY	PLOTTINGLY
PLATEMARKS	PLAUSIBLENESSES	PLEBIFICATION	PLEONECTIC	PLOUGHABLE
PLATERESQUE	PLAYABILITIES	PLEBIFICATIONS	PLEONEXIAS	PLOUGHBACK
PLATFORMED	PLAYABILITY	PLEBIFYING	PLEROCERCOID	PLOUGHBACKS
PLATFORMER	PLAYACTING	PLEBISCITARY	PLEROCERCOIDS	PLOUGHBOYS
PLATFORMERS	PLAYACTINGS	PLEBISCITE	PLEROMATIC	PLOUGHGATE
PLATFORMING	PLAYACTORS	PLEBISCITES	PLEROPHORIA	PLOUGHGATES
PLATFORMINGS	PLAYBUSSES	PLECOPTERAN	PLEROPHORIAS	PLOUGHHEAD
PLATINIFEROUS	PLAYDOUGHS	PLECOPTERANS	PLEROPHORIES	PLOUGHHEADS
PLATINIRIDIUM	PLAYFELLOW	PLECOPTEROUS	PLEROPHORY	PLOUGHINGS
PLATINIRIDIUMS	PLAYFELLOWS	PLECTOGNATH	PLESIOSAUR	PLOUGHLAND
PLATINISATION	PLAYFIELDS	PLECTOGNATHIC	PLESIOSAURIAN	PLOUGHLANDS
PLATINISATIONS	PLAYFULNESS	PLECTOGNATHOUS	PLESIOSAURIANS	PLOUGHMANSHIP
PLATINISED	PLAYFULNESSES	PLECTOGNATHS	PLESIOSAURS	PLOUGHMANSHIPS
PLATINISES	PLAYGOINGS	PLECTOPTEROUS	PLESSIMETER	PLOUGHSHARE
PLATINISING	PLAYGROUND	PLEDGEABLE	PLESSIMETERS	PLOUGHSHARES
PLATINIZATION	PLAYGROUNDS	PLEINAIRISM	PLESSIMETRIC	PLOUGHSTAFF
PLATINIZATIONS	PLAYGROUPS	PLEINAIRISMS	PLESSIMETRIES	PLOUGHSTAFFS
PLATINIZED	PLAYHOUSES	PLEINAIRIST	PLESSIMETRY	PLOUGHTAIL
PLATINIZES	PLAYLEADER	PLEINAIRISTS	PLETHORICAL	PLOUGHTAILS
PLATINIZING	PLAYLEADERS	PLEIOCHASIA	PLETHORICALLY	PLOUGHWISE
PLATINOCYANIC	PLAYLISTED	PLEIOCHASIUM	PLETHYSMOGRAM	PLOUGHWRIGHT
PLATINOCYANIDE	PLAYLISTING	PLEIOMERIES	PLETHYSMOGRAMS	PLOUGHWRIGHTS

PLOUTERING	PLURISERIAL	PNEUMOGRAMS	PODOPHYLLINS	POINSETTIAS
PLOVERIEST	PLURISERIATE	PNEUMOGRAPH	PODOPHYLLUM	POINTEDNESS
PLOWMANSHIP	PLUSHINESS	PNEUMOGRAPHS	PODOPHYLLUMS	POINTEDNESSES
PLOWMANSHIPS	PLUSHINESSES	PNEUMOKONIOSES	PODOSPHERE	POINTELLES
PLOWSHARES	PLUSHNESSES	PNEUMOKONIOSIS	PODOSPHERES	POINTILLES
PLOWSTAFFS	PLUTOCRACIES	PNEUMONECTOMIES	PODSOLISATION	POINTILLISM
PLOWTERING	PLUTOCRACY	PNEUMONECTOMY	PODSOLISATIONS	POINTILLISME
PLOWWRIGHT	PLUTOCRATIC	PNEUMONIAS	PODSOLISED	POINTILLISMES
PLOWWRIGHTS	PLUTOCRATICAL	PNEUMONICS	PODSOLISES	POINTILLISMS
PLUCKINESS	PLUTOCRATICALLY	PNEUMONITIDES	PODSOLISING	POINTILLIST
PLUCKINESSES	PLUTOCRATS	PNEUMONITIS	PODSOLIZATION	POINTILLISTE
PLUGBOARDS	PLUTOLATRIES	PNEUMONITISES	PODSOLIZATIONS	POINTILLISTES
PLUGUGLIES	PLUTOLATRY	PNEUMONOLOGIES	PODSOLIZED	POINTILLISTIC
PLUMASSIER	PLUTOLOGIES	PNEUMONOLOGIST	PODSOLIZES	POINTILLISTS
PLUMASSIERS	PLUTOLOGIST	PNEUMONOLOGISTS	PODSOLIZING	POINTLESSLY
PLUMBAGINACEOUS	PLUTOLOGISTS	PNEUMONOLOGY	PODZOLISATION	POINTLESSNESS
PLUMBAGINOUS	PLUTONISMS	PNEUMOTHORACES	PODZOLISATIONS	POINTLESSNESSES
PLUMBERIES	PLUTONIUMS	PNEUMOTHORAX	PODZOLISED	POISONABLE
PLUMBIFEROUS	PLUTONOMIES	PNEUMOTHORAXES	PODZOLISES	POISONINGS
PLUMBISOLVENCY	PLUTONOMIST	POACHINESS	PODZOLISING	POISONOUSLY
PLUMBISOLVENT	PLUTONOMISTS	POACHINESSES	PODZOLIZATION	POISONOUSNESS
PLUMBNESSES	PLUVIOMETER	POCKETABLE	PODZOLIZATIONS	POISONOUSNESSES
PLUMBOSOLVENCY	PLUVIOMETERS	POCKETBIKE	PODZOLIZED	POISONWOOD
PLUMBOSOLVENT	PLUVIOMETRIC	POCKETBIKES	PODZOLIZES	POISONWOODS
PLUMDAMASES	PLUVIOMETRICAL	POCKETBOOK	PODZOLIZING	POKEBERRIES
PLUMIGEROUS	PLUVIOMETRIES	POCKETBOOKS	POENOLOGIES	POKELOGANS
PLUMMETING	PLUVIOMETRY	POCKETFULS	POETASTERIES	POKERISHLY
PLUMOSITIES	PLYOMETRIC	POCKETKNIFE	POETASTERING	POKERWORKS
PLUMPENING	PLYOMETRICS	POCKETKNIVES	POETASTERINGS	POKINESSES
PLUMPNESSES	PNEUMATHODE	POCKETLESS	POETASTERS	POLARIMETER
PLUMULACEOUS	PNEUMATHODES	POCKETPHONE	POETASTERY	POLARIMETERS
PLUMULARIAN	PNEUMATICAL	POCKETPHONES	POETASTRIES	POLARIMETRIC
PLUMULARIANS	PNEUMATICALLY	POCKETSFUL	POETICALLY	POLARIMETRIES
PLUNDERABLE	PNEUMATICITIES	POCKMANKIES	POETICALNESS	POLARIMETRY
PLUNDERAGE	PNEUMATICITY	POCKMANTIE	POETICALNESSES	POLARISABILITY
PLUNDERAGES	PNEUMATICS	POCKMANTIES	POETICISED	POLARISABLE
PLUNDERERS	PNEUMATOLOGICAL	POCKMARKED	POETICISES	POLARISATION
PLUNDERING	PNEUMATOLOGIES	POCKMARKING	POETICISING	POLARISATIONS
PLUNDEROUS	PNEUMATOLOGIST	POCKPITTED	POETICISMS	POLARISCOPE
PLUPERFECT	PNEUMATOLOGISTS	POCOCURANTE	POETICIZED	POLARISCOPES
PLUPERFECTS	PNEUMATOLOGY	POCOCURANTEISM	POETICIZES	POLARISCOPIC
PLURALISATION	PNEUMATOLYSES	POCOCURANTEISMS	POETICIZING	POLARISERS
PLURALISATIONS	PNEUMATOLYSIS	POCOCURANTES	POETICULES	POLARISING
PLURALISED	PNEUMATOLYTIC	POCOCURANTISM	POETRESSES	POLARITIES
PLURALISER	PNEUMATOMETER	POCOCURANTISMS	POGONOPHORAN	POLARIZABILITY
PLURALISERS	PNEUMATOMETERS	POCOCURANTIST	POGONOPHORANS	POLARIZABLE
PLURALISES	PNEUMATOMETRIES	POCOCURANTISTS	POGONOTOMIES	POLARIZATION
PLURALISING	PNEUMATOMETRY	POCULIFORM	POGONOTOMY	POLARIZATIONS
PLURALISMS	PNEUMATOPHORE	PODAGRICAL	POGROMISTS	POLARIZERS
PLURALISTIC	PNEUMATOPHORES	PODARGUSES	POHUTUKAWA	POLARIZING
PLURALISTICALLY	PNEUMECTOMIES	PODCASTERS	POHUTUKAWAS	POLAROGRAM
PLURALISTS	PNEUMECTOMY	PODCASTING	POIGNADOES	POLAROGRAMS
PLURALITIES	PNEUMOBACILLI	PODCASTINGS	POIGNANCES	POLAROGRAPH
PLURALIZATION	PNEUMOBACILLUS	PODGINESSES	POIGNANCIES	POLAROGRAPHIC
PLURALIZATIONS	PNEUMOCOCCAL	PODIATRIES	POIGNANTLY	POLAROGRAPHIES
PLURALIZED	PNEUMOCOCCI	PODIATRIST	POIKILITIC	POLAROGRAPHS
PLURALIZER	PNEUMOCOCCUS	PODIATRISTS	POIKILOCYTE	POLAROGRAPHY
PLURALIZERS	PNEUMOCONIOSES	PODOCONIOSES	POIKILOCYTES	POLEMARCHS
PLURALIZES	PNEUMOCONIOSIS	PODOCONIOSIS	POIKILOTHERM	POLEMICALLY
PLURALIZING	PNEUMOCONIOTIC	PODOLOGIES	POIKILOTHERMAL	POLEMICISE
PLURILITERAL	PNEUMOCONIOTICS	PODOLOGIST	POIKILOTHERMIC	POLEMICISED
PLURILOCULAR	PNEUMOCYSTIS	PODOLOGISTS	POIKILOTHERMIES	POLEMICISES
PLURIPARAE	PNEUMOCYSTISES	PODOPHTHALMOUS	POIKILOTHERMISM	POLEMICISING
PLURIPARAS	PNEUMODYNAMICS	PODOPHYLIN	POIKILOTHERMS	POLEMICIST
PLURIPOTENT	PNEUMOGASTRIC	PODOPHYLINS	POIKILOTHERMY	POLEMICISTS
PLURIPRESENCE	PNEUMOGASTRICS	PODOPHYLLI	POINCIANAS	POLEMICIZE
PLURIPRESENCES	PNEUMOGRAM	PODOPHYLLIN	POINSETTIA	POLEMICIZED

POLEMICIZES	POLLENISERS	POLYARTHRITIS	POLYCULTURES	POLYGLOTTS
POLEMICIZING	POLLENIZER	POLYARTHRITISES	POLYCYCLIC	POLYGONACEOUS
POLEMISING	POLLENIZERS	POLYATOMIC	POLYCYCLICS	POLYGONALLY
POLEMIZING	POLLENOSES	POLYAXIALS	POLYCYSTIC	POLYGONATUM
POLEMONIACEOUS	POLLENOSIS	POLYAXONIC	POLYCYTHAEMIA	POLYGONATUMS
POLEMONIUM	POLLICITATION	POLYBAGGED	POLYCYTHAEMIAS	POLYGONIES
POLEMONIUMS	POLLICITATIONS	POLYBAGGING	POLYCYTHEMIA	POLYGONUMS
POLIANITES	POLLINATED	POLYBASITE	POLYCYTHEMIAS	POLYGRAPHED
POLICEWOMAN	POLLINATES	POLYBASITES	POLYCYTHEMIC	POLYGRAPHER
POLICEWOMEN	POLLINATING	POLYBUTADIENE	POLYDACTYL	POLYGRAPHERS
POLICYHOLDER	POLLINATION	POLYBUTADIENES	POLYDACTYLIES	POLYGRAPHIC
POLICYHOLDERS	POLLINATIONS	POLYCARBONATE	POLYDACTYLISM	POLYGRAPHICALLY
POLICYMAKER	POLLINATOR	POLYCARBONATES	POLYDACTYLISMS	POLYGRAPHIES
POLICYMAKERS	POLLINATORS	POLYCARBOXYLATE	POLYDACTYLOUS	POLYGRAPHING
POLIOMYELITIDES	POLLINIFEROUS	POLYCARBOXYLIC	POLYDACTYLS	POLYGRAPHIST
POLIOMYELITIS	POLLINISED	POLYCARPELLARY	POLYDACTYLY	POLYGRAPHISTS
POLIOMYELITISES	POLLINISER	POLYCARPIC	POLYDAEMONISM	POLYGRAPHS
POLIORCETIC	POLLINISERS	POLYCARPIES	POLYDAEMONISMS	POLYGRAPHY
POLIORCETICS	POLLINISES	POLYCARPOUS	POLYDEMONISM	POLYGYNIAN
POLIOVIRUS	POLLINISING	POLYCENTRIC	POLYDEMONISMS	POLYGYNIES
POLIOVIRUSES	POLLINIZED	POLYCENTRICS	POLYDIPSIA	POLYGYNIST
POLISHABLE	POLLINIZER	POLYCENTRISM	POLYDIPSIAS	POLYGYNISTS
POLISHINGS	POLLINIZERS	POLYCENTRISMS	POLYDIPSIC	POLYGYNOUS
POLISHMENT	POLLINIZES	POLYCHAETE	POLYDISPERSE	POLYHALITE
POLISHMENTS	POLLINIZING	POLYCHAETES	POLYDISPERSITY	POLYHALITES
POLITBUROS	POLLINOSES	POLYCHAETOUS	POLYELECTROLYTE	POLYHEDRAL
POLITENESS	POLLINOSIS	POLYCHASIA	POLYEMBRYONATE	POLYHEDRIC
POLITENESSES	POLLTAKERS	POLYCHASIUM	POLYEMBRYONIC	POLYHEDRON
POLITESSES	POLLUCITES	POLYCHETES	POLYEMBRYONIES	POLYHEDRONS
POLITICALISE	POLLUSIONS	POLYCHETOUS	POLYEMBRYONY	POLYHEDROSES
POLITICALISED	POLLUTANTS	POLYCHLORINATED	POLYESTERS	POLYHEDROSIS
POLITICALISES	POLLUTEDLY	POLYCHLOROPRENE	POLYESTROUS	POLYHISTOR
POLITICALISING	POLLUTEDNESS	POLYCHOTOMIES	POLYETHENE	POLYHISTORIAN
POLITICALIZE	POLLUTEDNESSES	POLYCHOTOMOUS	POLYETHENES	POLYHISTORIANS
POLITICALIZED	POLLUTIONS	POLYCHOTOMY	POLYETHYLENE	POLYHISTORIC
POLITICALIZES	POLLYANNAISH	POLYCHREST	POLYETHYLENES	POLYHISTORIES
POLITICALIZING	POLLYANNAISM	POLYCHRESTS	POLYGALACEOUS	POLYHISTORS
POLITICALLY	POLLYANNAISMS	POLYCHROIC	POLYGAMIES	POLYHISTORY
POLITICASTER	POLLYANNAS	POLYCHROISM	POLYGAMISE	POLYHYBRID
POLITICASTERS	POLLYANNISH	POLYCHROISMS	POLYGAMISED	POLYHYBRIDS
POLITICIAN	POLONAISES	POLYCHROMATIC	POLYGAMISES	POLYHYDRIC
POLITICIANS	POLONISING	POLYCHROMATISM	POLYGAMISING	POLYHYDROXY
POLITICISATION	POLONIZING	POLYCHROMATISMS	POLYGAMIST	POLYIMIDES
POLITICISATIONS	POLTERGEIST	POLYCHROME	POLYGAMISTS	POLYISOPRENE
POLITICISE	POLTERGEISTS	POLYCHROMED	POLYGAMIZE	POLYISOPRENES
POLITICISED	POLTROONERIES	POLYCHROMES	POLYGAMIZED	POLYLEMMAS
POLITICISES	POLTROONERY	POLYCHROMIC	POLYGAMIZES	POLYLINGUAL
POLITICISING	POLVERINES	POLYCHROMIES	POLYGAMIZING	POLYLYSINE
POLITICIZATION	POLYACRYLAMIDE	POLYCHROMING	POLYGAMOUS	POLYLYSINES
POLITICIZATIONS	POLYACRYLAMIDES	POLYCHROMOUS	POLYGAMOUSLY	POLYMASTIA
POLITICIZE	POLYACTINAL	POLYCHROMY	POLYGENESES	POLYMASTIAS
POLITICIZED	POLYACTINE	POLYCISTRONIC	POLYGENESIS	POLYMASTIC
POLITICIZES	POLYACTINES	POLYCLINIC	POLYGENETIC	POLYMASTICS
POLITICIZING	POLYADELPHOUS	POLYCLINICS	POLYGENETICALLY	POLYMASTIES
POLITICKED	POLYALCOHOL	POLYCLONAL	POLYGENIES	POLYMASTISM
POLITICKER	POLYALCOHOLS	POLYCLONALS	POLYGENISM	POLYMASTISMS
POLITICKERS	POLYAMIDES	POLYCOTTON	POLYGENISMS	POLYMATHIC
POLITICKING	POLYAMINES	POLYCOTTONS	POLYGENIST	POLYMATHIES
POLITICKINGS	POLYAMORIES	POLYCOTYLEDON	POLYGENISTS	POLYMERASE
POLITICOES	POLYAMOROUS	POLYCOTYLEDONS	POLYGENOUS	POLYMERASES
POLITIQUES	POLYANDRIES	POLYCROTIC	POLYGLOTISM	POLYMERIDE
POLLARDING	POLYANDROUS	POLYCROTISM	POLYGLOTISMS	POLYMERIDES
POLLENATED	POLYANTHAS	POLYCROTISMS	POLYGLOTTAL	POLYMERIES
POLLENATES	POLYANTHUS	POLYCRYSTAL	POLYGLOTTIC	POLYMERISATION
POLLENATING	POLYANTHUSES	POLYCRYSTALLINE	POLYGLOTTISM	POLYMERISATIONS
POLLENIFEROUS	POLYARCHIES	POLYCRYSTALS	POLYGLOTTISMS	POLYMERISE
POLLENISER	POLYARTHRITIDES	POLYCULTURE	POLYGLOTTOUS	POLYMERISED

POLYMERISES	POLYPHYLLOUS	POLYTECHNIC	POMPHOLYGOUS	POPMOBILITY
POLYMERISING	POLYPHYODONT	POLYTECHNICAL	POMPHOLYXES	POPPERINGS
POLYMERISM	POLYPIDOMS	POLYTECHNICS	POMPOSITIES	POPPYCOCKS
POLYMERISMS	POLYPLOIDAL	POLYTENIES	POMPOUSNESS	POPPYHEADS
POLYMERIZATION	POLYPLOIDIC	POLYTHALAMOUS	POMPOUSNESSES	POPULARISATION
POLYMERIZATIONS	POLYPLOIDIES	POLYTHEISM	PONDERABILITIES	POPULARISATIONS
POLYMERIZE	POLYPLOIDS	POLYTHEISMS	PONDERABILITY	POPULARISE
POLYMERIZED	POLYPLOIDY	POLYTHEIST	PONDERABLE	POPULARISED
POLYMERIZES	POLYPODIES	POLYTHEISTIC	PONDERABLES	POPULARISER
POLYMERIZING	POLYPODOUS	POLYTHEISTICAL	PONDERABLY	POPULARISERS
POLYMEROUS	POLYPROPENE	POLYTHEISTS	PONDERANCE	POPULARISES
POLYMORPHIC	POLYPROPENES	POLYTHENES	PONDERANCES	POPULARISING
POLYMORPHICALLY	POLYPROPYLENE	POLYTOCOUS	PONDERANCIES	POPULARIST
POLYMORPHISM	POLYPROPYLENES	POLYTONALISM	PONDERANCY	POPULARITIES
POLYMORPHISMS	POLYPROTODONT	POLYTONALISMS	PONDERATED	POPULARITY
POLYMORPHOUS	POLYPROTODONTS	POLYTONALIST	PONDERATES	POPULARIZATION
POLYMORPHOUSLY	POLYPTYCHS	POLYTONALISTS	PONDERATING	POPULARIZATIONS
POLYMORPHS	POLYRHYTHM	POLYTONALITIES	PONDERATION	POPULARIZE
POLYMYOSITIS	POLYRHYTHMIC	POLYTONALITY	PONDERATIONS	POPULARIZED
POLYMYOSITISES	POLYRHYTHMS	POLYTONALLY	PONDERINGLY	POPULARIZER
POLYMYXINS	POLYRIBOSOMAL	POLYTROPHIC	PONDERMENT	POPULARIZERS
POLYNEURITIDES	POLYRIBOSOME	POLYTUNNEL	PONDERMENTS	POPULARIZES
POLYNEURITIS	POLYRIBOSOMES	POLYTUNNELS	PONDEROSAS	POPULARIZING
POLYNEURITISES	POLYSACCHARIDE	POLYTYPICAL	PONDEROSITIES	POPULATING
POLYNOMIAL	POLYSACCHARIDES	POLYTYPING	PONDEROSITY	POPULATION
POLYNOMIALISM	POLYSACCHAROSE	POLYUNSATURATE	PONDEROUSLY	POPULATIONAL
POLYNOMIALISMS	POLYSACCHAROSES	POLYUNSATURATED	PONDEROUSNESS	POPULATIONS
POLYNOMIALS	POLYSEMANT	POLYUNSATURATES	PONDEROUSNESSES	POPULISTIC
POLYNUCLEAR	POLYSEMANTS	POLYURETHAN	PONDOKKIES	POPULOUSLY
POLYNUCLEATE	POLYSEMIES	POLYURETHANE	PONEROLOGIES	POPULOUSNESS
POLYNUCLEOTIDE	POLYSEMOUS	POLYURETHANES	PONEROLOGY	POPULOUSNESSES
POLYNUCLEOTIDES	POLYSEPALOUS	POLYURETHANS	PONIARDING	PORBEAGLES
POLYOLEFIN	POLYSILOXANE	POLYVALENCE	PONTIANACS	PORCELAINEOUS
POLYOLEFINS	POLYSILOXANES	POLYVALENCES	PONTIANAKS	PORCELAINISE
POLYOMINOES	POLYSOMICS	POLYVALENCIES	PONTICELLO	PORCELAINISED
POLYOMINOS	POLYSOMIES	POLYVALENCY	PONTICELLOS	PORCELAINISES
POLYONYMIC	POLYSORBATE	POLYVALENT	PONTIFICAL	PORCELAINISING
POLYONYMIES	POLYSORBATES	POLYVINYLIDENE	PONTIFICALITIES	PORCELAINIZE
POLYONYMOUS	POLYSTICHOUS	POLYVINYLIDENES	PONTIFICALITY	PORCELAINIZED
POLYPARIES	POLYSTYLAR	POLYVINYLS	PONTIFICALLY	PORCELAINIZES
POLYPARIUM	POLYSTYLES	POLYWATERS	PONTIFICALS	PORCELAINIZING
POLYPEPTIDE	POLYSTYRENE	POLYZOARIA	PONTIFICATE	PORCELAINLIKE
POLYPEPTIDES	POLYSTYRENES	POLYZOARIAL	PONTIFICATED	PORCELAINOUS
POLYPEPTIDIC	POLYSULFIDE	POLYZOARIES	PONTIFICATES	PORCELAINS
POLYPETALOUS	POLYSULFIDES	POLYZOARIUM	PONTIFICATING	PORCELANEOUS
POLYPHAGIA	POLYSULPHIDE	POMATUMING	PONTIFICATION	PORCELLANEOUS
POLYPHAGIAS	POLYSULPHIDES	POMEGRANATE	PONTIFICATIONS	PORCELLANISE
POLYPHAGIES	POLYSYLLABIC	POMEGRANATES	PONTIFICATOR	PORCELLANISED
POLYPHAGOUS	POLYSYLLABICAL	POMICULTURE	PONTIFICATORS	PORCELLANISES
POLYPHARMACIES	POLYSYLLABICISM	POMICULTURES	PONTIFICES	PORCELLANISING
POLYPHARMACY	POLYSYLLABISM	POMIFEROUS	PONTIFYING	PORCELLANITE
POLYPHASIC	POLYSYLLABISMS	POMMELLING	PONTLEVISES	PORCELLANITES
POLYPHENOL	POLYSYLLABLE	POMOERIUMS	PONTONEERS	PORCELLANIZE
POLYPHENOLIC	POLYSYLLABLES	POMOLOGICAL	PONTONIERS	PORCELLANIZED
POLYPHENOLS	POLYSYLLOGISM	POMOLOGICALLY	PONTONNIER	PORCELLANIZES
POLYPHLOESBOEAN	POLYSYLLOGISMS	POMOLOGIES	PONTONNIERS	PORCELLANIZING
POLYPHLOISBIC	POLYSYNAPTIC	POMOLOGIST	PONTOONERS	PORCELLANOUS
POLYPHONES	POLYSYNDETON	POMOLOGISTS	PONTOONING	PORCHETTAS
POLYPHONIC	POLYSYNDETONS	POMOSEXUAL	PONYTAILED	PORCUPINES
POLYPHONICALLY	POLYSYNTHESES	POMOSEXUALS	POORHOUSES	PORCUPINIER
POLYPHONIES	POLYSYNTHESIS	POMPADOURED	POORMOUTHED	PORCUPINIEST
POLYPHONIST	POLYSYNTHESISM	POMPADOURS	POORMOUTHING	PORCUPINISH
POLYPHONISTS	POLYSYNTHESISMS	POMPELMOOSE	POORMOUTHS	PORIFERANS
POLYPHONOUS	POLYSYNTHETIC	POMPELMOOSES	POORNESSES	PORIFEROUS
POLYPHONOUSLY	POLYSYNTHETICAL	POMPELMOUS	POPLINETTE	PORINESSES
POLYPHOSPHORIC	POLYSYNTHETISM	POMPELMOUSE	POPLINETTES	PORISMATIC
POLYPHYLETIC	POLYSYNTHETISMS	POMPELMOUSES	POPMOBILITIES	PORISMATICAL

PORISTICAL	PORTEOUSES	POSSESSIONAL	POSTDIVORCE	POSTILIONS
PORKINESSES	PORTERAGES	POSSESSIONARY	POSTDOCTORAL	POSTILLATE
PORLOCKING	PORTERESSES	POSSESSIONATE	POSTDOCTORALS	POSTILLATED
PORNIFICATION	PORTERHOUSE	POSSESSIONATES	POSTDOCTORATE	POSTILLATES
PORNIFICATIONS	PORTERHOUSES	POSSESSIONED	POSTDOCTORATES	POSTILLATING
PORNOCRACIES	PORTFOLIOS	POSSESSIONLESS	POSTEDITING	POSTILLATION
PORNOCRACY	PORTHORSES	POSSESSIONS	POSTEDITINGS	POSTILLATIONS
PORNOGRAPHER	PORTHOUSES	POSSESSIVE	POSTELECTION	POSTILLATOR
PORNOGRAPHERS	PORTIONERS	POSSESSIVELY	POSTEMBRYONAL	POSTILLATORS
PORNOGRAPHIC	PORTIONING	POSSESSIVENESS	POSTEMBRYONIC	POSTILLERS
PORNOGRAPHIES	PORTIONIST	POSSESSIVES	POSTEMERGENCE	POSTILLING
PORNOGRAPHY	PORTIONISTS	POSSESSORS	POSTEMERGENCY	POSTILLION
PORNOTOPIA	PORTIONLESS	POSSESSORSHIP	POSTEPILEPTIC	POSTILLIONS
PORNOTOPIAN	PORTLINESS	POSSESSORSHIPS	POSTERIORITIES	POSTIMPACT
PORNOTOPIAS	PORTLINESSES	POSSESSORY	POSTERIORITY	POSTIMPERIAL
POROGAMIES	PORTMANTEAU	POSSIBILISM	POSTERIORLY	POSTINAUGURAL
POROMERICS	PORTMANTEAUS	POSSIBILISMS	POSTERIORS	POSTINDUSTRIAL
POROSCOPES	PORTMANTEAUX	POSSIBILIST	POSTERISATION	POSTINFECTION
POROSCOPIC	PORTMANTLE	POSSIBILISTS	POSTERISATIONS	POSTINJECTION
POROSCOPIES	PORTMANTLES	POSSIBILITIES	POSTERISED	POSTINOCULATION
POROSITIES	PORTMANTUA	POSSIBILITY	POSTERISES	POSTIRRADIATION
POROUSNESS	PORTMANTUAS	POSSIBLEST	POSTERISING	POSTISCHEMIC
POROUSNESSES	PORTOBELLO	POSTABORTION	POSTERITIES	POSTISOLATION
PORPENTINE	PORTOBELLOS	POSTACCIDENT	POSTERIZATION	POSTLANDING
PORPENTINES	PORTOLANOS	POSTADOLESCENT	POSTERIZATIONS	POSTLAPSARIAN
PORPHYRIAS	PORTRAITED	POSTADOLESCENTS	POSTERIZED	POSTLAUNCH
PORPHYRIES	PORTRAITING	POSTAMPUTATION	POSTERIZES	POSTLIBERATION
PORPHYRINS	PORTRAITIST	POSTAPOCALYPTIC	POSTERIZING	POSTLIMINARY
PORPHYRIOS	PORTRAITISTS	POSTARREST	POSTEROLATERAL	POSTLIMINIA
PORPHYRITE	PORTRAITURE	POSTATOMIC	POSTERUPTIVE	POSTLIMINIARY
PORPHYRITES	PORTRAITURES	POSTATTACK	POSTEXERCISE	POSTLIMINIES
PORPHYRITIC	PORTRAYABLE	POSTBELLUM	POSTEXILIAN	POSTLIMINIOUS
PORPHYROGENITE	PORTRAYALS	POSTBIBLICAL	POSTEXILIC	POSTLIMINIUM
PORPHYROGENITES	PORTRAYERS	POSTBOURGEOIS	POSTEXPERIENCE	POSTLIMINOUS
PORPHYROID	PORTRAYING	POSTBUSSES	POSTEXPOSURE	POSTLIMINY
PORPHYROIDS	PORTREEVES	POSTCAPITALIST	POSTFEMINISM	POSTLITERATE
PORPHYROPSIN	PORTRESSES	POSTCARDED	POSTFEMINISMS	POSTMARITAL
PORPHYROPSINS	PORTULACACEOUS	POSTCARDING	POSTFEMINIST	POSTMARKED
PORPHYROUS	PORTULACAS	POSTCARDLIKE	POSTFEMINISTS	POSTMARKING
PORPOISING	PORWIGGLES	POSTCLASSIC	POSTFIXING	POSTMASTECTOMY
PORRACEOUS	POSHNESSES	POSTCLASSICAL	POSTFLIGHT	POSTMASTER
PORRECTING	POSITIONAL	POSTCODING	POSTFORMED	POSTMASTERS
PORRECTION	POSITIONALLY	POSTCOITAL	POSTFORMING	POSTMASTERSHIP
PORRECTIONS	POSITIONED	POSTCOLLEGE	POSTFRACTURE	POSTMASTERSHIPS
PORRENGERS	POSITIONING	POSTCOLLEGIATE	POSTFREEZE	POSTMATING
PORRIDGIER	POSITIONINGS	POSTCOLONIAL	POSTGANGLIONIC	POSTMEDIEVAL
PORRIDGIEST	POSITIVELY	POSTCONCEPTION	POSTGLACIAL	POSTMENOPAUSAL
PORRIGINOUS	POSITIVENESS	POSTCONCERT	POSTGRADUATE	POSTMENSTRUAL
PORRINGERS	POSITIVENESSES	POSTCONQUEST	POSTGRADUATES	POSTMERIDIAN
PORTABELLA	POSITIVEST	POSTCONSONANTAL	POSTGRADUATION	POSTMIDNIGHT
PORTABELLAS	POSITIVISM	POSTCONVENTION	POSTGRADUATIONS	POSTMILLENARIAN
PORTABELLO	POSITIVISMS	POSTCOPULATORY	POSTHARVEST	POSTMILLENNIAL
PORTABELLOS	POSITIVIST	POSTCORONARY	POSTHASTES	POSTMISTRESS
PORTABILITIES	POSITIVISTIC	POSTCRANIAL	POSTHEATED	POSTMISTRESSES
PORTABILITY	POSITIVISTS	POSTCRANIALLY	POSTHEATING	POSTMODERN
PORTAMENTI	POSITIVITIES	POSTCRISIS	POSTHEMORRHAGIC	POSTMODERNISM
PORTAMENTO	POSITIVITY	POSTDATING	POSTHOLDER	POSTMODERNISMS
PORTAPACKS	POSITRONIUM	POSTDEADLINE	POSTHOLDERS	POSTMODERNIST
PORTATIVES	POSITRONIUMS	POSTDEBATE	POSTHOLIDAY	POSTMODERNISTS
PORTCULLIS	POSOLOGICAL	POSTDEBUTANTE	POSTHOLOCAUST	POSTMODERNS
PORTCULLISED	POSOLOGIES	POSTDELIVERY	POSTHORSES	POSTMODIFIED
PORTCULLISES	POSSESSABLE	POSTDEPRESSION	POSTHOSPITAL	POSTMODIFIES
PORTCULLISING	POSSESSEDLY	POSTDEVALUATION	POSTHOUSES	POSTMODIFY
PORTENDING	POSSESSEDNESS	POSTDILUVIAL	POSTHUMOUS	POSTMODIFYING
PORTENTOUS	POSSESSEDNESSES	POSTDILUVIAN	POSTHUMOUSLY	POSTMORTEM
PORTENTOUSLY	POSSESSING	POSTDILUVIANS	POSTHUMOUSNESS	POSTMORTEMS
PORTENTOUSNESS	POSSESSION	POSTDIVESTITURE	POSTHYPNOTIC	POSTNATALLY

POSTNEONATAL	POSTULANTS	POTENTIOMETRIES	POWELLIZES	PRAEMUNIRES
POSTNUPTIAL	POSTULANTSHIP	POTENTIOMETRY	POWELLIZING	PRAENOMENS
POSTOCULAR	POSTULANTSHIPS	POTENTISED	POWERBANDS	PRAENOMINA
POSTOCULARS	POSTULATED	POTENTISES	POWERBOATING	PRAENOMINAL
POSTOPERATIVE	POSTULATES	POTENTISING	POWERBOATINGS	PRAENOMINALLY
POSTOPERATIVELY	POSTULATING	POTENTIZED	POWERBOATS	PRAEPOSTOR
POSTORBITAL	POSTULATION	POTENTIZES	POWERBOATS	PRAEPOSTORS
POSTORGASMIC	POSTULATIONAL	POTENTIZING	POWERFULLY	PRAESIDIUM
POSTPARTUM	POSTULATIONALLY	POTENTNESS	POWERFULNESS	PRAESIDIUMS
POSTPERSON	POSTULATIONS	POTENTNESSES	POWERFULNESSES	PRAETORIAL
POSTPERSONS	POSTULATOR	POTHECARIES	POWERHOUSE	PRAETORIAN
POSTPOLLINATION	POSTULATORS	POTHERIEST	POWERHOUSES	PRAETORIANS
POSTPONABLE	POSTULATORY	POTHOLDERS	POWERLESSLY	PRAETORIUM
POSTPONEMENT	POSTULATUM	POTHOLINGS	POWERLESSNESS	PRAETORIUMS
POSTPONEMENTS	POSTURINGS	POTHUNTERS	POWERLESSNESSES	PRAETORSHIP
POSTPONENCE	POSTURISED	POTHUNTING	POWERLIFTER	PRAETORSHIPS
POSTPONENCES	POSTURISES	POTHUNTINGS	POWERLIFTERS	PRAGMATICAL
POSTPONERS	POSTURISING	POTICARIES	POWERLIFTING	PRAGMATICALITY
POSTPONING	POSTURISTS	POTICHOMANIA	POWERLIFTINGS	PRAGMATICALLY
POSTPOSING	POSTURIZED	POTICHOMANIAS	POWERPLAYS	PRAGMATICALNESS
POSTPOSITION	POSTURIZES	POTLATCHED	POWERTRAIN	PRAGMATICISM
POSTPOSITIONAL	POSTURIZING	POTLATCHES	POWERTRAINS	PRAGMATICISMS
POSTPOSITIONS	POSTVACCINAL	POTLATCHING	POWSOWDIES	PRAGMATICIST
POSTPOSITIVE	POSTVACCINATION	POTOMETERS	POXVIRUSES	PRAGMATICISTS
POSTPOSITIVELY	POSTVAGOTOMY	POTPOURRIS	POZZOLANAS	PRAGMATICS
POSTPOSITIVES	POSTVASECTOMY	POTSHOTTING	POZZOLANIC	PRAGMATISATION
POSTPRANDIAL	POSTVOCALIC	POTSHOTTINGS	POZZUOLANA	PRAGMATISATIONS
POSTPRIMARY	POSTWEANING	POTTERINGLY	POZZUOLANAS	PRAGMATISE
POSTPRISON	POSTWORKSHOP	POTTERINGS	PRACHARAKS	PRAGMATISED
POSTPRODUCTION	POTABILITIES	POTTINESSES	PRACTICABILITY	PRAGMATISER
POSTPRODUCTIONS	POTABILITY	POTTINGARS	PRACTICABLE	PRAGMATISERS
POSTPUBERTIES	POTABLENESS	POTTINGERS	PRACTICABLENESS	PRAGMATISES
POSTPUBERTY	POTABLENESSES	POTTYMOUTH	PRACTICABLY	PRAGMATISING
POSTPUBESCENT	POTAMOGETON	POTTYMOUTHS	PRACTICALISM	PRAGMATISM
POSTPUBESCENTS	POTAMOGETONS	POTWALLERS	PRACTICALISMS	PRAGMATISMS
POSTRECESSION	POTAMOLOGICAL	POULTERERS	PRACTICALIST	PRAGMATIST
POSTRETIREMENT	POTAMOLOGIES	POULTICING	PRACTICALISTS	PRAGMATISTIC
POSTRIDERS	POTAMOLOGIST	POULTROONE	PRACTICALITIES	PRAGMATISTS
POSTROMANTIC	POTAMOLOGISTS	POULTROONES	PRACTICALITY	PRAGMATIZATION
POSTROMANTICS	POTAMOLOGY	POULTRYMAN	PRACTICALLY	PRAGMATIZATIONS
POSTSCENIUM	POTASSIUMS	POULTRYMEN	PRACTICALNESS	PRAGMATIZE
POSTSCENIUMS	POTATOBUGS	POUNDCAKES	PRACTICALNESSES	PRAGMATIZED
POSTSCRIPT	POTBELLIED	POURBOIRES	PRACTICALS	PRAGMATIZER
POSTSCRIPTS	POTBELLIES	POURPARLER	PRACTICERS	PRAGMATIZERS
POSTSEASON	POTBOILERS	POURPARLERS	PRACTICIAN	PRAGMATIZES
POSTSEASONS	POTBOILING	POURPOINTS	PRACTICIANS	PRAGMATIZING
POSTSECONDARY	POTBOILINGS	POURSEWING	PRACTICING	PRAISEACHS
POSTSTIMULATION	POTENTATES	POURTRAHED	PRACTICKED	PRAISELESS
POSTSTIMULATORY	POTENTIALITIES	POURTRAICT	PRACTICKING	PRAISEWORTHIER
POSTSTIMULUS	POTENTIALITY	POURTRAICTS	PRACTICUMS	PRAISEWORTHIEST
POSTSTRIKE	POTENTIALLY	POURTRAYED	PRACTIQUES	PRAISEWORTHILY
POSTSURGICAL	POTENTIALS	POURTRAYING	PRACTISANT	PRAISEWORTHY
POSTSYNAPTIC	POTENTIARIES	POUSOWDIES	PRACTISANTS	PRAISINGLY
POSTSYNCED	POTENTIARY	POUSSETTED	PRACTISERS	PRALLTRILLER
POSTSYNCHRONISE	POTENTIATE	POUSSETTES	PRACTISING	PRALLTRILLERS
POSTSYNCHRONIZE	POTENTIATED	POUSSETTING	PRACTITIONER	PRANAYAMAS
POSTSYNCING	POTENTIATES	POUTASSOUS	PRACTITIONERS	PRANCINGLY
POSTTENSION	POTENTIATING	POUTHERING	PRACTOLOLS	PRANDIALLY
POSTTENSIONED	POTENTIATION	POWDERIEST	PRAEAMBLES	PRANKINGLY
POSTTENSIONING	POTENTIATIONS	POWDERINGS	PRAECOCIAL	PRANKISHLY
POSTTENSIONS	POTENTIATOR	POWDERLESS	PRAECORDIAL	PRANKISHNESS
POSTTRANSFUSION	POTENTIATORS	POWDERLIKE	PRAEDIALITIES	PRANKISHNESSES
POSTTRAUMATIC	POTENTILLA	POWELLISED	PRAEDIALITY	PRANKSTERS
POSTTREATMENT	POTENTILLAS	POWELLISES	PRAEFECTORIAL	PRASEODYMIUM
POSTTREATMENTS	POTENTIOMETER	POWELLISING	PRAELECTED	PRASEODYMIUMS
POSTULANCIES	POTENTIOMETERS	POWELLITES	PRAELECTING	PRATFALLEN
POSTULANCY	POTENTIOMETRIC	POWELLIZED	PRAELUDIUM	PRATFALLING
			PRAEMUNIRE	

PRATINCOLE	PREADOLESCENTS	PREBIOTICS	PRECEPTORS	PRECISIONIST
PRATINCOLES	PREADOPTED	PREBLESSED	PRECEPTORSHIP	PRECISIONISTS
PRATTLEBOX	PREADOPTING	PREBLESSES	PRECEPTORSHIPS	PRECISIONS
PRATTLEBOXES	PREAGRICULTURAL	PREBLESSING	PRECEPTORY	PRECLASSICAL
PRATTLEMENT	PREALLOTTED	PREBOARDED	PRECEPTRESS	PRECLEANED
PRATTLEMENTS	PREALLOTTING	PREBOARDING	PRECEPTRESSES	PRECLEANING
PRATTLINGLY	PREALTERED	PREBOILING	PRECESSING	PRECLEARANCE
PRAXEOLOGICAL	PREALTERING	PREBOOKING	PRECESSION	PRECLEARANCES
PRAXEOLOGIES	PREAMBLING	PREBREAKFAST	PRECESSIONAL	PRECLEARED
PRAXEOLOGY	PREAMBULARY	PREBUDGETS	PRECESSIONALLY	PRECLEARING
PRAXINOSCOPE	PREAMBULATE	PREBUILDING	PRECESSIONS	PRECLINICAL
PRAXINOSCOPES	PREAMBULATED	PREBUTTALS	PRECHARGED	PRECLINICALLY
PRAYERFULLY	PREAMBULATES	PRECALCULI	PRECHARGES	PRECLUDABLE
PRAYERFULNESS	PREAMBULATING	PRECALCULUS	PRECHARGING	PRECLUDING
PRAYERFULNESSES	PREAMBULATORY	PRECALCULUSES	PRECHECKED	PRECLUSION
PRAYERLESS	PREAMPLIFIER	PRECANCELED	PRECHECKING	PRECLUSIONS
PRAYERLESSLY	PREAMPLIFIERS	PRECANCELING	PRECHILLED	PRECLUSIVE
PRAYERLESSNESS	PREANAESTHETIC	PRECANCELLATION	PRECHILLING	PRECLUSIVELY
PREABSORBED	PREANAESTHETICS	PRECANCELLED	PRECHOOSES	PRECOCIALS
PREABSORBING	PREANESTHETIC	PRECANCELLING	PRECHOOSING	PRECOCIOUS
PREABSORBS	PREANNOUNCE	PRECANCELS	PRECHRISTIAN	PRECOCIOUSLY
PREACCUSED	PREANNOUNCED	PRECANCEROUS	PRECIEUSES	PRECOCIOUSNESS
PREACCUSES	PREANNOUNCES	PRECANCERS	PRECIOSITIES	PRECOCITIES
PREACCUSING	PREANNOUNCING	PRECAPITALIST	PRECIOSITY	PRECOGNISANT
PREACHABLE	PREAPPLIED	PRECARIATS	PRECIOUSES	PRECOGNISE
PREACHERSHIP	PREAPPLIES	PRECARIOUS	PRECIOUSLY	PRECOGNISED
PREACHERSHIPS	PREAPPLYING	PRECARIOUSLY	PRECIOUSNESS	PRECOGNISES
PREACHIEST	PREAPPOINT	PRECARIOUSNESS	PRECIOUSNESSES	PRECOGNISING
PREACHIFIED	PREAPPOINTED	PRECASTING	PRECIPICED	PRECOGNITION
PREACHIFIES	PREAPPOINTING	PRECAUTION	PRECIPICES	PRECOGNITIONS
PREACHIFYING	PREAPPOINTS	PRECAUTIONAL	PRECIPITABILITY	PRECOGNITIVE
PREACHIFYINGS	PREAPPROVE	PRECAUTIONARY	PRECIPITABLE	PRECOGNIZANT
PREACHINESS	PREAPPROVED	PRECAUTIONED	PRECIPITANCE	PRECOGNIZE
PREACHINESSES	PREAPPROVES	PRECAUTIONING	PRECIPITANCES	PRECOGNIZED
PREACHINGLY	PREAPPROVING	PRECAUTIONS	PRECIPITANCIES	PRECOGNIZES
PREACHINGS	PREARRANGE	PRECAUTIOUS	PRECIPITANCY	PRECOGNIZING
PREACHMENT	PREARRANGED	PRECEDENCE	PRECIPITANT	PRECOGNOSCE
PREACHMENTS	PREARRANGEMENT	PRECEDENCES	PRECIPITANTLY	PRECOGNOSCED
PREACQUAINT	PREARRANGEMENTS	PRECEDENCIES	PRECIPITANTNESS	PRECOGNOSCES
PREACQUAINTANCE	PREARRANGES	PRECEDENCY	PRECIPITANTS	PRECOGNOSCING
PREACQUAINTED	PREARRANGING	PRECEDENTED	PRECIPITATE	PRECOLLEGE
PREACQUAINTING	PREASSEMBLED	PRECEDENTIAL	PRECIPITATED	PRECOLLEGIATE
PREACQUAINTS	PREASSIGNED	PRECEDENTIALLY	PRECIPITATELY	PRECOLONIAL
PREACQUISITION	PREASSIGNING	PRECEDENTLY	PRECIPITATENESS	PRECOMBUSTION
PREADAMITE	PREASSIGNS	PRECEDENTS	PRECIPITATES	PRECOMBUSTIONS
PREADAMITES	PREASSURANCE	PRECENSORED	PRECIPITATING	PRECOMMITMENT
PREADAPTATION	PREASSURANCES	PRECENSORING	PRECIPITATION	PRECOMMITMENTS
PREADAPTATIONS	PREASSURED	PRECENSORS	PRECIPITATIONS	PRECOMPETITIVE
PREADAPTED	PREASSURES	PRECENTING	PRECIPITATIVE	PRECOMPOSE
PREADAPTING	PREASSURING	PRECENTORIAL	PRECIPITATOR	PRECOMPOSED
PREADAPTIVE	PREATTUNED	PRECENTORS	PRECIPITATORS	PRECOMPOSES
PREADJUSTED	PREATTUNES	PRECENTORSHIP	PRECIPITIN	PRECOMPOSING
PREADJUSTING	PREATTUNING	PRECENTORSHIPS	PRECIPITINOGEN	PRECOMPUTE
PREADJUSTS	PREAUDIENCE	PRECENTRESS	PRECIPITINOGENS	PRECOMPUTED
PREADMISSION	PREAUDIENCES	PRECENTRESSES	PRECIPITINS	PRECOMPUTER
PREADMISSIONS	PREAVERRED	PRECENTRICES	PRECIPITOUS	PRECOMPUTES
PREADMITTED	PREAVERRING	PRECENTRIX	PRECIPITOUSLY	PRECOMPUTING
PREADMITTING	PREAXIALLY	PRECENTRIXES	PRECIPITOUSNESS	PRECONCEIT
PREADMONISH	PREBENDARIES	PRECEPTIAL	PRECISENESS	PRECONCEITED
PREADMONISHED	PREBENDARY	PRECEPTIVE	PRECISENESSES	PRECONCEITING
PREADMONISHES	PREBIBLICAL	PRECEPTIVELY	PRECISIANISM	PRECONCEITS
PREADMONISHING	PREBIDDING	PRECEPTORAL	PRECISIANISMS	PRECONCEIVE
PREADMONITION	PREBIDDINGS	PRECEPTORATE	PRECISIANIST	PRECONCEIVED
PREADMONITIONS	PREBILLING	PRECEPTORATES	PRECISIANISTS	PRECONCEIVES
PREADOLESCENCE	PREBINDING	PRECEPTORIAL	PRECISIANS	PRECONCEIVING
PREADOLESCENCES	PREBIOLOGIC	PRECEPTORIALS	PRECISIONISM	PRECONCEPTION
PREADOLESCENT	PREBIOLOGICAL	PRECEPTORIES	PRECISIONISMS	PRECONCEPTIONS

PRECONCERT
PRECONCERTED
PRECONCERTEDLY
PRECONCERTING
PRECONCERTS
PRECONCILIAR
PRECONDEMN
PRECONDEMNED
PRECONDEMNING
PRECONDEMNS
PRECONDITION
PRECONDITIONED
PRECONDITIONING
PRECONDITIONS
PRECONISATION
PRECONISATIONS
PRECONISED
PRECONISES
PRECONISING
PRECONIZATION
PRECONIZATIONS
PRECONIZED
PRECONIZES
PRECONIZING
PRECONQUEST
PRECONSCIOUS
PRECONSCIOUSES
PRECONSCIOUSLY
PRECONSONANTAL
PRECONSTRUCT
PRECONSTRUCTED
PRECONSTRUCTING
PRECONSTRUCTION
PRECONSTRUCTS
PRECONSUME
PRECONSUMED
PRECONSUMES
PRECONSUMING
PRECONTACT
PRECONTACTS
PRECONTRACT
PRECONTRACTED
PRECONTRACTING
PRECONTRACTS
PRECONVENTION
PRECONVICTION
PRECONVICTIONS
PRECOOKERS
PRECOOKING
PRECOOLING
PRECOPULATORY
PRECORDIAL
PRECREASED
PRECREASES
PRECREASING
PRECRITICAL
PRECURRERS
PRECURSING
PRECURSIVE
PRECURSORS
PRECURSORY
PRECUTTING
PRECYCLING
PREDACEOUS
PREDACEOUSNESS
PREDACIOUS
PREDACIOUSNESS

PREDACITIES
PREDATIONS
PREDATISMS
PREDATORILY
PREDATORINESS
PREDATORINESSES
PREDECEASE
PREDECEASED
PREDECEASES
PREDECEASING
PREDECESSOR
PREDECESSORS
PREDEDUCTED
PREDEDUCTING
PREDEDUCTS
PREDEFINED
PREDEFINES
PREDEFINING
PREDEFINITION
PREDEFINITIONS
PREDELIVERIES
PREDELIVERY
PREDENTARY
PREDENTATE
PREDEPARTURE
PREDEPOSIT
PREDEPOSITED
PREDEPOSITING
PREDEPOSITS
PREDESIGNATE
PREDESIGNATED
PREDESIGNATES
PREDESIGNATING
PREDESIGNATION
PREDESIGNATIONS
PREDESIGNATORY
PREDESIGNED
PREDESIGNING
PREDESIGNS
PREDESTINABLE
PREDESTINARIAN
PREDESTINARIANS
PREDESTINATE
PREDESTINATED
PREDESTINATES
PREDESTINATING
PREDESTINATION
PREDESTINATIONS
PREDESTINATIVE
PREDESTINATOR
PREDESTINATORS
PREDESTINE
PREDESTINED
PREDESTINES
PREDESTINING
PREDESTINY
PREDETERMINABLE
PREDETERMINATE
PREDETERMINE
PREDETERMINED
PREDETERMINER
PREDETERMINERS
PREDETERMINES
PREDETERMINING
PREDETERMINISM
PREDETERMINISMS

PREDEVALUATION
PREDEVELOP
PREDEVELOPED
PREDEVELOPING
PREDEVELOPMENT
PREDEVELOPMENTS
PREDEVELOPS
PREDEVOTED
PREDEVOTES
PREDEVOTING
PREDIABETES
PREDIABETESES
PREDIABETIC
PREDIABETICS
PREDIALITIES
PREDIALITY
PREDICABILITIES
PREDICABILITY
PREDICABLE
PREDICABLENESS
PREDICABLES
PREDICAMENT
PREDICAMENTAL
PREDICAMENTS
PREDICANTS
PREDICATED
PREDICATES
PREDICATING
PREDICATION
PREDICATIONS
PREDICATIVE
PREDICATIVELY
PREDICATOR
PREDICATORS
PREDICATORY
PREDICTABILITY
PREDICTABLE
PREDICTABLENESS
PREDICTABLY
PREDICTERS
PREDICTING
PREDICTION
PREDICTIONS
PREDICTIVE
PREDICTIVELY
PREDICTORS
PREDIGESTED
PREDIGESTING
PREDIGESTION
PREDIGESTIONS
PREDIGESTS
PREDIKANTS
PREDILECTED
PREDILECTION
PREDILECTIONS
PREDINNERS
PREDISCHARGE
PREDISCOVERIES
PREDISCOVERY
PREDISPOSAL
PREDISPOSALS
PREDISPOSE
PREDISPOSED
PREDISPOSES
PREDISPOSING
PREDISPOSITION
PREDISPOSITIONS

PREDNISOLONE
PREDNISOLONES
PREDNISONE
PREDNISONES
PREDOCTORAL
PREDOMINANCE
PREDOMINANCES
PREDOMINANCIES
PREDOMINANCY
PREDOMINANT
PREDOMINANTLY
PREDOMINATE
PREDOMINATED
PREDOMINATELY
PREDOMINATES
PREDOMINATING
PREDOMINATION
PREDOMINATIONS
PREDOMINATOR
PREDOMINATORS
PREDOOMING
PREDRILLED
PREDRILLING
PREDYNASTIC
PREECLAMPSIA
PREECLAMPSIAS
PREECLAMPTIC
PREEDITING
PREELECTED
PREELECTING
PREELECTION
PREELECTRIC
PREEMBARGO
PREEMERGENCE
PREEMERGENT
PREEMINENCE
PREEMINENCES
PREEMINENT
PREEMINENTLY
PREEMPLOYMENT
PREEMPTING
PREEMPTION
PREEMPTIONS
PREEMPTIVE
PREEMPTIVELY
PREEMPTORS
PREENACTED
PREENACTING
PREENROLLMENT
PREERECTED
PREERECTING
PREESTABLISH
PREESTABLISHED
PREESTABLISHES
PREESTABLISHING
PREETHICAL
PREEXCITED
PREEXCITES
PREEXCITING
PREEXEMPTED
PREEXEMPTING
PREEXEMPTS
PREEXISTED
PREEXISTENCE
PREEXISTENCES
PREEXISTENT
PREEXISTING

PREEXPERIMENT
PREEXPOSED
PREEXPOSES
PREEXPOSING
PREFABBING
PREFABRICATE
PREFABRICATED
PREFABRICATES
PREFABRICATING
PREFABRICATION
PREFABRICATIONS
PREFABRICATOR
PREFABRICATORS
PREFASCIST
PREFATORIAL
PREFATORIALLY
PREFATORILY
PREFECTORIAL
PREFECTSHIP
PREFECTSHIPS
PREFECTURAL
PREFECTURE
PREFECTURES
PREFERABILITIES
PREFERABILITY
PREFERABLE
PREFERABLENESS
PREFERABLY
PREFERENCE
PREFERENCES
PREFERENTIAL
PREFERENTIALISM
PREFERENTIALIST
PREFERENTIALITY
PREFERENTIALLY
PREFERMENT
PREFERMENTS
PREFERRABLE
PREFERRERS
PREFERRING
PREFIGURATE
PREFIGURATED
PREFIGURATES
PREFIGURATING
PREFIGURATION
PREFIGURATIONS
PREFIGURATIVE
PREFIGURATIVELY
PREFIGURED
PREFIGUREMENT
PREFIGUREMENTS
PREFIGURES
PREFIGURING
PREFINANCE
PREFINANCED
PREFINANCES
PREFINANCING
PREFINANCINGS
PREFIXALLY
PREFIXIONS
PREFIXTURE
PREFIXTURES
PREFLIGHTED
PREFLIGHTING
PREFLIGHTS
PREFLORATION
PREFLORATIONS

PREFOCUSED
PREFOCUSES
PREFOCUSING
PREFOCUSSED
PREFOCUSSES
PREFOCUSSING
PREFOLIATION
PREFOLIATIONS
PREFORMATION
PREFORMATIONISM
PREFORMATIONIST
PREFORMATIONS
PREFORMATIVE
PREFORMATIVES
PREFORMATS
PREFORMATTED
PREFORMATTING
PREFORMING
PREFORMULATE
PREFORMULATED
PREFORMULATES
PREFORMULATING
PREFRANKED
PREFRANKING
PREFREEZES
PREFREEZING
PREFRESHMAN
PREFRESHMEN
PREFRONTAL
PREFRONTALS
PREFULGENT
PREFUNDING
PREGANGLIONIC
PREGENITAL
PREGLACIAL
PREGNABILITIES
PREGNABILITY
PREGNANCES
PREGNANCIES
PREGNANTLY
PREGNENOLONE
PREGNENOLONES
PREGROWTHS
PREGUIDING
PREGUSTATION
PREGUSTATIONS
PREHALLUCES
PREHANDLED
PREHANDLES
PREHANDLING
PREHARDENED
PREHARDENING
PREHARDENS
PREHARVEST
PREHARVESTS
PREHEADACHE
PREHEATERS
PREHEATING
PREHEMINENCE
PREHEMINENCES
PREHENDING
PREHENSIBLE
PREHENSILE
PREHENSILITIES
PREHENSILITY
PREHENSION
PREHENSIONS

PREHENSIVE
PREHENSORIAL
PREHENSORS
PREHENSORY
PREHISTORIAN
PREHISTORIANS
PREHISTORIC
PREHISTORICAL
PREHISTORICALLY
PREHISTORIES
PREHISTORY
PREHOLIDAY
PREHOMINID
PREHOMINIDS
PREIGNITION
PREIGNITIONS
PREIMPLANTATION
PREIMPOSED
PREIMPOSES
PREIMPOSING
PREINAUGURAL
PREINDUCTION
PREINDUSTRIAL
PREINFORMED
PREINFORMING
PREINFORMS
PREINSERTED
PREINSERTING
PREINSERTS
PREINTERVIEW
PREINTERVIEWED
PREINTERVIEWING
PREINTERVIEWS
PREINVASION
PREINVITED
PREINVITES
PREINVITING
PREJUDGEMENT
PREJUDGEMENTS
PREJUDGERS
PREJUDGING
PREJUDGMENT
PREJUDGMENTS
PREJUDICANT
PREJUDICATE
PREJUDICATED
PREJUDICATES
PREJUDICATING
PREJUDICATION
PREJUDICATIONS
PREJUDICATIVE
PREJUDICED
PREJUDICES
PREJUDICIAL
PREJUDICIALLY
PREJUDICIALNESS
PREJUDICING
PREJUDIZES
PREKINDERGARTEN
PRELAPSARIAN
PRELATESHIP
PRELATESHIPS
PRELATESSES
PRELATICAL
PRELATICALLY
PRELATIONS
PRELATISED

PRELATISES
PRELATISING
PRELATISMS
PRELATISTS
PRELATIZED
PRELATIZES
PRELATIZING
PRELATURES
PRELAUNCHED
PRELAUNCHES
PRELAUNCHING
PRELECTING
PRELECTION
PRELECTIONS
PRELECTORS
PRELEXICAL
PRELIBATION
PRELIBATIONS
PRELIMINARIES
PRELIMINARILY
PRELIMINARY
PRELIMITED
PRELIMITING
PRELINGUAL
PRELINGUALLY
PRELITERACIES
PRELITERACY
PRELITERARY
PRELITERATE
PRELITERATES
PRELOADING
PRELOCATED
PRELOCATES
PRELOCATING
PRELOGICAL
PRELUDIOUS
PRELUNCHEON
PRELUNCHEONS
PRELUSIONS
PRELUSIVELY
PRELUSORILY
PREMALIGNANT
PREMANDIBULAR
PREMANDIBULARS
PREMANUFACTURE
PREMANUFACTURED
PREMANUFACTURES
PREMARITAL
PREMARITALLY
PREMARKETED
PREMARKETING
PREMARKETS
PREMARRIAGE
PREMATURELY
PREMATURENESS
PREMATURENESSES
PREMATURES
PREMATURITIES
PREMATURITY
PREMAXILLA
PREMAXILLAE
PREMAXILLARIES
PREMAXILLARY
PREMAXILLAS
PREMEASURE
PREMEASURED
PREMEASURES

PREMEASURING
PREMEDICAL
PREMEDICALLY
PREMEDICATE
PREMEDICATED
PREMEDICATES
PREMEDICATING
PREMEDICATION
PREMEDICATIONS
PREMEDIEVAL
PREMEDITATE
PREMEDITATED
PREMEDITATEDLY
PREMEDITATES
PREMEDITATING
PREMEDITATION
PREMEDITATIONS
PREMEDITATIVE
PREMEDITATOR
PREMEDITATORS
PREMEIOTIC
PREMENOPAUSAL
PREMENSTRUAL
PREMENSTRUALLY
PREMIERING
PREMIERSHIP
PREMIERSHIPS
PREMIGRATION
PREMILLENARIAN
PREMILLENARIANS
PREMILLENNIAL
PREMILLENNIALLY
PREMILLENNIALS
PREMISSING
PREMODIFICATION
PREMODIFIED
PREMODIFIES
PREMODIFYING
PREMOISTEN
PREMOISTENED
PREMOISTENING
PREMOISTENS
PREMOLDING
PREMONISHED
PREMONISHES
PREMONISHING
PREMONISHMENT
PREMONISHMENTS
PREMONITION
PREMONITIONS
PREMONITIVE
PREMONITOR
PREMONITORILY
PREMONITORS
PREMONITORY
PREMOTIONS
PREMOULDED
PREMOULDING
PREMOVEMENT
PREMOVEMENTS
PREMUNITION
PREMUNITIONS
PREMYCOTIC
PRENATALLY
PRENEGOTIATE
PRENEGOTIATED
PRENEGOTIATES

PRENEGOTIATING
PRENEGOTIATION
PRENEGOTIATIONS
PRENOMINAL
PRENOMINALLY
PRENOMINATE
PRENOMINATED
PRENOMINATES
PRENOMINATING
PRENOMINATION
PRENOMINATIONS
PRENOTIFICATION
PRENOTIFIED
PRENOTIFIES
PRENOTIFYING
PRENOTIONS
PRENTICESHIP
PRENTICESHIPS
PRENTICING
PRENUMBERED
PRENUMBERING
PRENUMBERS
PRENUPTIAL
PRENUPTIALS
PREOBTAINED
PREOBTAINING
PREOBTAINS
PREOCCUPANCIES
PREOCCUPANCY
PREOCCUPANT
PREOCCUPANTS
PREOCCUPATE
PREOCCUPATED
PREOCCUPATES
PREOCCUPATING
PREOCCUPATION
PREOCCUPATIONS
PREOCCUPIED
PREOCCUPIES
PREOCCUPYING
PREOCULARS
PREOPENING
PREOPERATIONAL
PREOPERATIVE
PREOPERATIVELY
PREOPTIONS
PREORDAINED
PREORDAINING
PREORDAINMENT
PREORDAINMENTS
PREORDAINS
PREORDERED
PREORDERING
PREORDINANCE
PREORDINANCES
PREORDINATION
PREORDINATIONS
PREOVULATORY
PREPACKAGE
PREPACKAGED
PREPACKAGES
PREPACKAGING
PREPACKING
PREPARATION
PREPARATIONS
PREPARATIVE
PREPARATIVELY

PREPARATIVES	PREPOTENTLY	PREREQUIRE	PRESCIENCES	PRESENTISMS
PREPARATOR	PREPPINESS	PREREQUIRED	PRESCIENTIFIC	PRESENTIST
PREPARATORILY	PREPPINESSES	PREREQUIRES	PRESCIENTLY	PRESENTISTS
PREPARATORS	PREPRANDIAL	PREREQUIRING	PRESCINDED	PRESENTIVE
PREPARATORY	PREPREPARED	PREREQUISITE	PRESCINDENT	PRESENTIVENESS
PREPAREDLY	PREPRESIDENTIAL	PREREQUISITES	PRESCINDING	PRESENTIVES
PREPAREDNESS	PREPRESSES	PRERETIREMENT	PRESCISSION	PRESENTMENT
PREPAREDNESSES	PREPRICING	PREREVIEWED	PRESCISSIONS	PRESENTMENTS
PREPASTING	PREPRIMARIES	PREREVIEWING	PRESCORING	PRESENTNESS
PREPATELLAR	PREPRIMARY	PREREVIEWS	PRESCREENED	PRESENTNESSES
PREPAYABLE	PREPRINTED	PREREVISIONIST	PRESCREENING	PRESERVABILITY
PREPAYMENT	PREPRINTING	PREREVOLUTION	PRESCREENS	PRESERVABLE
PREPAYMENTS	PREPROCESS	PRERINSING	PRESCRIBED	PRESERVABLY
PREPENSELY	PREPROCESSED	PREROGATIVE	PRESCRIBER	PRESERVATION
PREPENSING	PREPROCESSES	PREROGATIVED	PRESCRIBERS	PRESERVATIONIST
PREPENSIVE	PREPROCESSING	PREROGATIVELY	PRESCRIBES	PRESERVATIONS
PREPERFORMANCE	PREPROCESSOR	PREROGATIVES	PRESCRIBING	PRESERVATIVE
PREPLACING	PREPROCESSORS	PREROMANTIC	PRESCRIBINGS	PRESERVATIVES
PREPLANNED	PREPRODUCTION	PREROMANTICS	PRESCRIPTIBLE	PRESERVATORIES
PREPLANNING	PREPRODUCTIONS	PRESAGEFUL	PRESCRIPTION	PRESERVATORY
PREPLANTING	PREPROFESSIONAL	PRESAGEFULLY	PRESCRIPTIONS	PRESERVERS
PREPOLLENCE	PREPROGRAM	PRESAGEMENT	PRESCRIPTIVE	PRESERVICE
PREPOLLENCES	PREPROGRAMED	PRESAGEMENTS	PRESCRIPTIVELY	PRESERVING
PREPOLLENCIES	PREPROGRAMING	PRESANCTIFIED	PRESCRIPTIVISM	PRESETTING
PREPOLLENCY	PREPROGRAMMED	PRESANCTIFIES	PRESCRIPTIVISMS	PRESETTLED
PREPOLLENT	PREPROGRAMMING	PRESANCTIFY	PRESCRIPTIVIST	PRESETTLEMENT
PREPOLLICES	PREPROGRAMMINGS	PRESANCTIFYING	PRESCRIPTIVISTS	PRESETTLES
PREPONDERANCE	PREPROGRAMS	PRESBYACOUSES	PRESCRIPTS	PRESETTLING
PREPONDERANCES	PREPSYCHEDELIC	PRESBYACOUSIS	PRESEASONS	PRESHAPING
PREPONDERANCIES	PREPUBERAL	PRESBYACUSES	PRESELECTED	PRESHIPPED
PREPONDERANCY	PREPUBERTAL	PRESBYACUSIS	PRESELECTING	PRESHIPPING
PREPONDERANT	PREPUBERTIES	PRESBYCOUSES	PRESELECTION	PRESHOWING
PREPONDERANTLY	PREPUBERTY	PRESBYCOUSIS	PRESELECTIONS	PRESHRINKING
PREPONDERATE	PREPUBESCENCE	PRESBYCUSES	PRESELECTOR	PRESHRINKS
PREPONDERATED	PREPUBESCENCES	PRESBYCUSIS	PRESELECTORS	PRESHRUNKEN
PREPONDERATELY	PREPUBESCENT	PRESBYOPES	PRESELECTS	PRESIDENCIES
PREPONDERATES	PREPUBESCENTS	PRESBYOPIA	PRESELLING	PRESIDENCY
PREPONDERATING	PREPUBLICATION	PRESBYOPIAS	PRESENSION	PRESIDENTESS
PREPONDERATION	PREPUBLICATIONS	PRESBYOPIC	PRESENSIONS	PRESIDENTESSES
PREPONDERATIONS	PREPUNCHED	PRESBYOPICS	PRESENTABILITY	PRESIDENTIAL
PREPORTION	PREPUNCHES	PRESBYOPIES	PRESENTABLE	PRESIDENTIALLY
PREPORTIONED	PREPUNCHING	PRESBYTERAL	PRESENTABLENESS	PRESIDENTS
PREPORTIONING	PREPUNCTUAL	PRESBYTERATE	PRESENTABLY	PRESIDENTSHIP
PREPORTIONS	PREPURCHASE	PRESBYTERATES	PRESENTATION	PRESIDENTSHIPS
PREPOSITION	PREPURCHASED	PRESBYTERIAL	PRESENTATIONAL	PRESIDIARY
PREPOSITIONAL	PREPURCHASES	PRESBYTERIALLY	PRESENTATIONISM	PRESIDIUMS
PREPOSITIONALLY	PREPURCHASING	PRESBYTERIALS	PRESENTATIONIST	PRESIFTING
PREPOSITIONS	PREQUALIFIED	PRESBYTERIAN	PRESENTATIONS	PRESIGNALED
PREPOSITIVE	PREQUALIFIES	PRESBYTERIANISE	PRESENTATIVE	PRESIGNALING
PREPOSITIVELY	PREQUALIFY	PRESBYTERIANISM	PRESENTEEISM	PRESIGNALLED
PREPOSITIVES	PREQUALIFYING	PRESBYTERIANIZE	PRESENTEEISMS	PRESIGNALLING
PREPOSITOR	PREREADING	PRESBYTERIANS	PRESENTEES	PRESIGNALS
PREPOSITORS	PRERECESSION	PRESBYTERIES	PRESENTENCE	PRESIGNIFIED
PREPOSSESS	PRERECORDED	PRESBYTERS	PRESENTENCED	PRESIGNIFIES
PREPOSSESSED	PRERECORDING	PRESBYTERSHIP	PRESENTENCES	PRESIGNIFY
PREPOSSESSES	PRERECORDS	PRESBYTERSHIPS	PRESENTENCING	PRESIGNIFYING
PREPOSSESSING	PREREGISTER	PRESBYTERY	PRESENTERS	PRESLAUGHTER
PREPOSSESSINGLY	PREREGISTERED	PRESBYTISM	PRESENTIAL	PRESLICING
PREPOSSESSION	PREREGISTERING	PRESBYTISMS	PRESENTIALITIES	PRESOAKING
PREPOSSESSIONS	PREREGISTERS	PRESCHEDULE	PRESENTIALITY	PRESOLVING
PREPOSTEROUS	PREREGISTRATION	PRESCHEDULED	PRESENTIALLY	PRESORTING
PREPOSTEROUSLY	PREREHEARSAL	PRESCHEDULES	PRESENTIENT	PRESPECIFIED
PREPOSTORS	PREREHEARSALS	PRESCHEDULING	PRESENTIMENT	PRESPECIFIES
PREPOTENCE	PRERELEASE	PRESCHOOLER	PRESENTIMENTAL	PRESPECIFY
PREPOTENCES	PRERELEASED	PRESCHOOLERS	PRESENTIMENTS	PRESPECIFYING
PREPOTENCIES	PRERELEASES	PRESCHOOLS	PRESENTING	PRESSBOARD
PREPOTENCY	PRERELEASING	PRESCIENCE	PRESENTISM	PRESSBOARDS

PRESSGANGS
PRESSINGLY
PRESSINGNESS
PRESSINGNESSES
PRESSMARKS
PRESSROOMS
PRESSURELESS
PRESSURING
PRESSURISATION
PRESSURISATIONS
PRESSURISE
PRESSURISED
PRESSURISER
PRESSURISERS
PRESSURISES
PRESSURISING
PRESSURIZATION
PRESSURIZATIONS
PRESSURIZE
PRESSURIZED
PRESSURIZER
PRESSURIZERS
PRESSURIZES
PRESSURIZING
PRESSWOMAN
PRESSWOMEN
PRESSWORKS
PRESTAMPED
PRESTAMPING
PRESTATION
PRESTATIONS
PRESTERILISE
PRESTERILISED
PRESTERILISES
PRESTERILISING
PRESTERILIZE
PRESTERILIZED
PRESTERILIZES
PRESTERILIZING
PRESTERNUM
PRESTERNUMS
PRESTIDIGITATOR
PRESTIGEFUL
PRESTIGIATOR
PRESTIGIATORS
PRESTIGIOUS
PRESTIGIOUSLY
PRESTIGIOUSNESS
PRESTISSIMO
PRESTISSIMOS
PRESTORAGE
PRESTORING
PRESTRESSED
PRESTRESSES
PRESTRESSING
PRESTRICTION
PRESTRICTIONS
PRESTRUCTURE
PRESTRUCTURED
PRESTRUCTURES
PRESTRUCTURING
PRESUMABLE
PRESUMABLY
PRESUMEDLY
PRESUMINGLY
PRESUMMITS
PRESUMPTION

PRESUMPTIONS
PRESUMPTIVE
PRESUMPTIVELY
PRESUMPTIVENESS
PRESUMPTUOUS
PRESUMPTUOUSLY
PRESUPPOSE
PRESUPPOSED
PRESUPPOSES
PRESUPPOSING
PRESUPPOSITION
PRESUPPOSITIONS
PRESURGERY
PRESURMISE
PRESURMISES
PRESURVEYED
PRESURVEYING
PRESURVEYS
PRESWEETEN
PRESWEETENED
PRESWEETENING
PRESWEETENS
PRESYMPTOMATIC
PRESYNAPTIC
PRESYNAPTICALLY
PRETASTING
PRETELEVISION
PRETELLING
PRETENCELESS
PRETENDANT
PRETENDANTS
PRETENDEDLY
PRETENDENT
PRETENDENTS
PRETENDERS
PRETENDERSHIP
PRETENDERSHIPS
PRETENDING
PRETENDINGLY
PRETENSELESS
PRETENSION
PRETENSIONED
PRETENSIONING
PRETENSIONLESS
PRETENSIONS
PRETENSIVE
PRETENTIOUS
PRETENTIOUSLY
PRETENTIOUSNESS
PRETERHUMAN
PRETERISTS
PRETERITENESS
PRETERITENESSES
PRETERITES
PRETERITION
PRETERITIONS
PRETERITIVE
PRETERMINAL
PRETERMINATION
PRETERMINATIONS
PRETERMISSION
PRETERMISSIONS
PRETERMITS
PRETERMITTED
PRETERMITTER
PRETERMITTERS
PRETERMITTING

PRETERNATURAL
PRETERNATURALLY
PRETERPERFECT
PRETERPERFECTS
PRETESTING
PRETEXTING
PRETEXTINGS
PRETHEATER
PRETHEATRE
PRETORIANS
PRETORSHIP
PRETORSHIPS
PRETOURNAMENT
PRETRAINED
PRETRAINING
PRETREATED
PRETREATING
PRETREATMENT
PRETREATMENTS
PRETRIMMED
PRETRIMMING
PRETTIFICATION
PRETTIFICATIONS
PRETTIFIED
PRETTIFIER
PRETTIFIERS
PRETTIFIES
PRETTIFYING
PRETTINESS
PRETTINESSES
PRETTYISMS
PRETZELLED
PRETZELLING
PREUNIFICATION
PREUNITING
PREUNIVERSITY
PREVAILERS
PREVAILING
PREVAILINGLY
PREVAILMENT
PREVAILMENTS
PREVALENCE
PREVALENCES
PREVALENCIES
PREVALENCY
PREVALENTLY
PREVALENTNESS
PREVALENTNESSES
PREVALENTS
PREVALUING
PREVARICATE
PREVARICATED
PREVARICATES
PREVARICATING
PREVARICATION
PREVARICATIONS
PREVARICATOR
PREVARICATORS
PREVENANCIES
PREVENANCY
PREVENIENCE
PREVENIENCES
PREVENIENT
PREVENIENTLY
PREVENTABILITY
PREVENTABLE
PREVENTABLY

PREVENTATIVE
PREVENTATIVES
PREVENTERS
PREVENTIBILITY
PREVENTIBLE
PREVENTIBLY
PREVENTING
PREVENTION
PREVENTIONS
PREVENTIVE
PREVENTIVELY
PREVENTIVENESS
PREVENTIVES
PREVIEWERS
PREVIEWING
PREVIOUSLY
PREVIOUSNESS
PREVIOUSNESSES
PREVISIONAL
PREVISIONARY
PREVISIONED
PREVISIONING
PREVISIONS
PREVISITED
PREVISITING
PREVOCALIC
PREVOCALICALLY
PREVOCATIONAL
PREWARMING
PREWARNING
PREWASHING
PREWEANING
PREWEIGHED
PREWEIGHING
PREWORKING
PREWRAPPED
PREWRAPPING
PREWRITING
PREWRITINGS
PREWRITTEN
PRICELESSLY
PRICELESSNESS
PRICELESSNESSES
PRICINESSES
PRICKLIEST
PRICKLINESS
PRICKLINESSES
PRICKLINGS
PRICKWOODS
PRIDEFULLY
PRIDEFULNESS
PRIDEFULNESSES
PRIESTCRAFT
PRIESTCRAFTS
PRIESTESSES
PRIESTHOOD
PRIESTHOODS
PRIESTLIER
PRIESTLIEST
PRIESTLIKE
PRIESTLINESS
PRIESTLINESSES
PRIESTLING
PRIESTLINGS
PRIESTSHIP
PRIESTSHIPS
PRIGGERIES

PRIGGISHLY
PRIGGISHNESS
PRIGGISHNESSES
PRIMAEVALLY
PRIMALITIES
PRIMAQUINE
PRIMAQUINES
PRIMARINESS
PRIMARINESSES
PRIMATESHIP
PRIMATESHIPS
PRIMATIALS
PRIMATICAL
PRIMATOLOGICAL
PRIMATOLOGIES
PRIMATOLOGIST
PRIMATOLOGISTS
PRIMATOLOGY
PRIMAVERAS
PRIMENESSES
PRIMEVALLY
PRIMIGENIAL
PRIMIGRAVIDA
PRIMIGRAVIDAE
PRIMIGRAVIDAS
PRIMIPARAE
PRIMIPARAS
PRIMIPARITIES
PRIMIPARITY
PRIMIPAROUS
PRIMITIVELY
PRIMITIVENESS
PRIMITIVENESSES
PRIMITIVES
PRIMITIVISM
PRIMITIVISMS
PRIMITIVIST
PRIMITIVISTIC
PRIMITIVISTS
PRIMITIVITIES
PRIMITIVITY
PRIMNESSES
PRIMOGENIAL
PRIMOGENIT
PRIMOGENITAL
PRIMOGENITARY
PRIMOGENITIVE
PRIMOGENITIVES
PRIMOGENITOR
PRIMOGENITORS
PRIMOGENITRICES
PRIMOGENITRIX
PRIMOGENITRIXES
PRIMOGENITS
PRIMOGENITURE
PRIMOGENITURES
PRIMORDIAL
PRIMORDIALISM
PRIMORDIALISMS
PRIMORDIALITIES
PRIMORDIALITY
PRIMORDIALLY
PRIMORDIALS
PRIMORDIUM
PRIMROSIER
PRIMROSIEST
PRIMROSING

PRIMULACEOUS	PRISMATOIDAL	PROBABILITY	PROCESSION	PROCTODAEA
PRIMULINES	PRISMATOIDS	PROBATIONAL	PROCESSIONAL	PROCTODAEAL
PRINCEDOMS	PRISMOIDAL	PROBATIONALLY	PROCESSIONALIST	PROCTODAEUM
PRINCEHOOD	PRISONMENT	PROBATIONARIES	PROCESSIONALLY	PROCTODAEUMS
PRINCEHOODS	PRISONMENTS	PROBATIONARY	PROCESSIONALS	PROCTODEAL
PRINCEKINS	PRISSINESS	PROBATIONER	PROCESSIONARIES	PROCTODEUM
PRINCELETS	PRISSINESSES	PROBATIONERS	PROCESSIONARY	PROCTODEUMS
PRINCELIER	PRISTINELY	PROBATIONERSHIP	PROCESSIONED	PROCTOLOGIC
PRINCELIEST	PRIVATDOCENT	PROBATIONS	PROCESSIONER	PROCTOLOGICAL
PRINCELIKE	PRIVATDOCENTS	PROBATIVELY	PROCESSIONERS	PROCTOLOGIES
PRINCELINESS	PRIVATDOZENT	PROBENECID	PROCESSIONING	PROCTOLOGIST
PRINCELINESSES	PRIVATDOZENTS	PROBENECIDS	PROCESSIONINGS	PROCTOLOGISTS
PRINCELING	PRIVATEERED	PROBIOTICS	PROCESSIONS	PROCTOLOGY
PRINCELINGS	PRIVATEERING	PROBLEMATIC	PROCESSORS	PROCTORAGE
PRINCESHIP	PRIVATEERINGS	PROBLEMATICAL	PROCESSUAL	PROCTORAGES
PRINCESHIPS	PRIVATEERS	PROBLEMATICALLY	PROCHRONISM	PROCTORIAL
PRINCESSES	PRIVATEERSMAN	PROBLEMATICS	PROCHRONISMS	PROCTORIALLY
PRINCESSLIER	PRIVATEERSMEN	PROBLEMIST	PROCIDENCE	PROCTORING
PRINCESSLIEST	PRIVATENESS	PROBLEMISTS	PROCIDENCES	PROCTORISE
PRINCESSLY	PRIVATENESSES	PROBOSCIDEAN	PROCLAIMANT	PROCTORISED
PRINCIFIED	PRIVATIONS	PROBOSCIDEANS	PROCLAIMANTS	PROCTORISES
PRINCIPALITIES	PRIVATISATION	PROBOSCIDES	PROCLAIMED	PROCTORISING
PRINCIPALITY	PRIVATISATIONS	PROBOSCIDIAN	PROCLAIMER	PROCTORIZE
PRINCIPALLY	PRIVATISED	PROBOSCIDIANS	PROCLAIMERS	PROCTORIZED
PRINCIPALNESS	PRIVATISER	PROBOSCISES	PROCLAIMING	PROCTORIZES
PRINCIPALNESSES	PRIVATISERS	PROBOULEUTIC	PROCLAMATION	PROCTORIZING
PRINCIPALS	PRIVATISES	PROBUSINESS	PROCLAMATIONS	PROCTORSHIP
PRINCIPALSHIP	PRIVATISING	PROCACIOUS	PROCLAMATORY	PROCTORSHIPS
PRINCIPALSHIPS	PRIVATISMS	PROCACITIES	PROCLITICS	PROCTOSCOPE
PRINCIPATE	PRIVATISTS	PROCAMBIAL	PROCLIVITIES	PROCTOSCOPES
PRINCIPATES	PRIVATIVELY	PROCAMBIUM	PROCLIVITY	PROCTOSCOPIC
PRINCIPIAL	PRIVATIVES	PROCAMBIUMS	PROCOELOUS	PROCTOSCOPIES
PRINCIPIUM	PRIVATIZATION	PROCAPITALIST	PROCONSULAR	PROCTOSCOPY
PRINCIPLED	PRIVATIZATIONS	PROCARBAZINE	PROCONSULATE	PROCUMBENT
PRINCIPLES	PRIVATIZED	PROCARBAZINES	PROCONSULATES	PROCURABLE
PRINCIPLING	PRIVATIZER	PROCARYONS	PROCONSULS	PROCURACIES
PRINTABILITIES	PRIVATIZERS	PROCARYOTE	PROCONSULSHIP	PROCURANCE
PRINTABILITY	PRIVATIZES	PROCARYOTES	PROCONSULSHIPS	PROCURANCES
PRINTABLENESS	PRIVATIZING	PROCARYOTIC	PROCRASTINATE	PROCURATION
PRINTABLENESSES	PRIVILEGED	PROCATHEDRAL	PROCRASTINATED	PROCURATIONS
PRINTERIES	PRIVILEGES	PROCATHEDRALS	PROCRASTINATES	PROCURATOR
PRINTHEADS	PRIVILEGING	PROCEDURAL	PROCRASTINATING	PROCURATORIAL
PRINTMAKER	PRIZEFIGHT	PROCEDURALLY	PROCRASTINATION	PROCURATORIES
PRINTMAKERS	PRIZEFIGHTER	PROCEDURALS	PROCRASTINATIVE	PROCURATORS
PRINTMAKING	PRIZEFIGHTERS	PROCEDURES	PROCRASTINATOR	PROCURATORSHIP
PRINTMAKINGS	PRIZEFIGHTING	PROCEEDERS	PROCRASTINATORS	PROCURATORSHIPS
PRINTWHEEL	PRIZEFIGHTINGS	PROCEEDING	PROCRASTINATORY	PROCURATORY
PRINTWHEELS	PRIZEFIGHTS	PROCEEDINGS	PROCREANTS	PROCUREMENT
PRINTWORKS	PRIZEWINNER	PROCELEUSMATIC	PROCREATED	PROCUREMENTS
PRIORESSES	PRIZEWINNERS	PROCELEUSMATICS	PROCREATES	PROCURESSES
PRIORITIES	PRIZEWINNING	PROCELLARIAN	PROCREATING	PROCUREURS
PRIORITISATION	PRIZEWOMAN	PROCELLARIANS	PROCREATION	PROCURINGS
PRIORITISATIONS	PRIZEWOMEN	PROCEPHALIC	PROCREATIONAL	PROCYONIDS
PRIORITISE	PROABORTION	PROCERCOID	PROCREATIONS	PRODIGALISE
PRIORITISED	PROACTIONS	PROCERCOIDS	PROCREATIVE	PRODIGALISED
PRIORITISES	PROAIRESES	PROCEREBRA	PROCREATIVENESS	PRODIGALISES
PRIORITISING	PROAIRESIS	PROCEREBRAL	PROCREATOR	PRODIGALISING
PRIORITIZATION	PROBABILIORISM	PROCEREBRUM	PROCREATORS	PRODIGALITIES
PRIORITIZATIONS	PROBABILIORISMS	PROCEREBRUMS	PROCRUSTEAN	PRODIGALITY
PRIORITIZE	PROBABILIORIST	PROCERITIES	PROCRYPSES	PRODIGALIZE
PRIORITIZED	PROBABILIORISTS	PROCESSABILITY	PROCRYPSIS	PRODIGALIZED
PRIORITIZES	PROBABILISM	PROCESSABLE	PROCRYPTIC	PRODIGALIZES
PRIORITIZING	PROBABILISMS	PROCESSERS	PROCRYPTICALLY	PRODIGALIZING
PRIORSHIPS	PROBABILIST	PROCESSIBILITY	PROCTALGIA	PRODIGALLY
PRISMATICAL	PROBABILISTIC	PROCESSIBLE	PROCTALGIAS	PRODIGIOSITIES
PRISMATICALLY	PROBABILISTS	PROCESSING	PROCTITIDES	PRODIGIOSITY
PRISMATOID	PROBABILITIES	PROCESSINGS	PROCTITISES	PRODIGIOUS

PRODIGIOUSLY	PROFITABILITIES	PROGNOSTICATE	PROHIBITIVE	PROLICIDES
PRODIGIOUSNESS	PROFITABILITY	PROGNOSTICATED	PROHIBITIVELY	PROLIFERATE
PRODITORIOUS	PROFITABLE	PROGNOSTICATES	PROHIBITIVENESS	PROLIFERATED
PRODNOSING	PROFITABLENESS	PROGNOSTICATING	PROHIBITOR	PROLIFERATES
PRODROMATA	PROFITABLY	PROGNOSTICATION	PROHIBITORS	PROLIFERATING
PRODUCEMENT	PROFITEERED	PROGNOSTICATIVE	PROHIBITORY	PROLIFERATION
PRODUCEMENTS	PROFITEERING	PROGNOSTICATOR	PROINSULIN	PROLIFERATIONS
PRODUCIBILITIES	PROFITEERINGS	PROGNOSTICATORS	PROINSULINS	PROLIFERATIVE
PRODUCIBILITY	PROFITEERS	PROGNOSTICS	PROJECTABLE	PROLIFEROUS
PRODUCIBLE	PROFITEROLE	PROGRADATION	PROJECTILE	PROLIFEROUSLY
PRODUCTIBILITY	PROFITEROLES	PROGRADATIONS	PROJECTILES	PROLIFICACIES
PRODUCTILE	PROFITINGS	PROGRADING	PROJECTING	PROLIFICACY
PRODUCTION	PROFITLESS	PROGRAMABLE	PROJECTINGS	PROLIFICAL
PRODUCTIONAL	PROFITLESSLY	PROGRAMERS	PROJECTION	PROLIFICALLY
PRODUCTIONS	PROFITWISE	PROGRAMING	PROJECTIONAL	PROLIFICATION
PRODUCTIVE	PROFLIGACIES	PROGRAMINGS	PROJECTIONIST	PROLIFICATIONS
PRODUCTIVELY	PROFLIGACY	PROGRAMMABILITY	PROJECTIONISTS	PROLIFICITIES
PRODUCTIVENESS	PROFLIGATE	PROGRAMMABLE	PROJECTIONS	PROLIFICITY
PRODUCTIVITIES	PROFLIGATELY	PROGRAMMABLES	PROJECTISATION	PROLIFICNESS
PRODUCTIVITY	PROFLIGATES	PROGRAMMATIC	PROJECTISATIONS	PROLIFICNESSES
PROEMBRYOS	PROFLUENCE	PROGRAMMED	PROJECTIVE	PROLIXIOUS
PROENZYMES	PROFLUENCES	PROGRAMMER	PROJECTIVELY	PROLIXITIES
PROESTRUSES	PROFOUNDER	PROGRAMMERS	PROJECTIVITIES	PROLIXNESS
PROFANATION	PROFOUNDEST	PROGRAMMES	PROJECTIVITY	PROLIXNESSES
PROFANATIONS	PROFOUNDLY	PROGRAMMING	PROJECTIZATION	PROLOCUTION
PROFANATORY	PROFOUNDNESS	PROGRAMMINGS	PROJECTIZATIONS	PROLOCUTIONS
PROFANENESS	PROFOUNDNESSES	PROGRESSED	PROJECTMENT	PROLOCUTOR
PROFANENESSES	PROFULGENT	PROGRESSES	PROJECTMENTS	PROLOCUTORS
PROFANITIES	PROFUNDITIES	PROGRESSING	PROJECTORS	PROLOCUTORSHIP
PROFASCIST	PROFUNDITY	PROGRESSION	PROJECTURE	PROLOCUTORSHIPS
PROFECTITIOUS	PROFUSENESS	PROGRESSIONAL	PROJECTURES	PROLOCUTRICES
PROFEMINIST	PROFUSENESSES	PROGRESSIONALLY	PROKARYONS	PROLOCUTRIX
PROFESSEDLY	PROFUSIONS	PROGRESSIONARY	PROKARYOTE	PROLOCUTRIXES
PROFESSING	PROGENITIVE	PROGRESSIONISM	PROKARYOTES	PROLOGISED
PROFESSION	PROGENITIVENESS	PROGRESSIONISMS	PROKARYOTIC	PROLOGISES
PROFESSIONAL	PROGENITOR	PROGRESSIONIST	PROKARYOTS	PROLOGISING
PROFESSIONALISE	PROGENITORIAL	PROGRESSIONISTS	PROLACTINS	PROLOGISTS
PROFESSIONALISM	PROGENITORS	PROGRESSIONS	PROLAMINES	PROLOGIZED
PROFESSIONALIST	PROGENITORSHIP	PROGRESSISM	PROLAPSING	PROLOGIZES
PROFESSIONALIZE	PROGENITORSHIPS	PROGRESSISMS	PROLAPSUSES	PROLOGIZING
PROFESSIONALLY	PROGENITRESS	PROGRESSIST	PROLATENESS	PROLOGUING
PROFESSIONALS	PROGENITRESSES	PROGRESSISTS	PROLATENESSES	PROLOGUISE
PROFESSIONS	PROGENITRICES	PROGRESSIVE	PROLATIONS	PROLOGUISED
PROFESSORATE	PROGENITRIX	PROGRESSIVELY	PROLEGOMENA	PROLOGUISES
PROFESSORATES	PROGENITRIXES	PROGRESSIVENESS	PROLEGOMENAL	PROLOGUISING
PROFESSORESS	PROGENITURE	PROGRESSIVES	PROLEGOMENARY	PROLOGUIZE
PROFESSORESSES	PROGENITURES	PROGRESSIVISM	PROLEGOMENON	PROLOGUIZED
PROFESSORIAL	PROGESTATIONAL	PROGRESSIVISMS	PROLEGOMENOUS	PROLOGUIZES
PROFESSORIALLY	PROGESTERONE	PROGRESSIVIST	PROLEPTICAL	PROLOGUIZING
PROFESSORIAT	PROGESTERONES	PROGRESSIVISTIC	PROLEPTICALLY	PROLONGABLE
PROFESSORIATE	PROGESTINS	PROGRESSIVISTS	PROLETARIAN	PROLONGATE
PROFESSORIATES	PROGESTOGEN	PROGRESSIVITIES	PROLETARIANISE	PROLONGATED
PROFESSORIATS	PROGESTOGENIC	PROGRESSIVITY	PROLETARIANISED	PROLONGATES
PROFESSORS	PROGESTOGENS	PROGYMNASIA	PROLETARIANISES	PROLONGATING
PROFESSORSHIP	PROGGINSES	PROGYMNASIUM	PROLETARIANISM	PROLONGATION
PROFESSORSHIPS	PROGLOTTIC	PROGYMNASIUMS	PROLETARIANISMS	PROLONGATIONS
PROFFERERS	PROGLOTTID	PROHIBITED	PROLETARIANIZE	PROLONGERS
PROFFERING	PROGLOTTIDEAN	PROHIBITER	PROLETARIANIZED	PROLONGING
PROFICIENCE	PROGLOTTIDES	PROHIBITERS	PROLETARIANIZES	PROLONGMENT
PROFICIENCES	PROGLOTTIDS	PROHIBITING	PROLETARIANNESS	PROLONGMENTS
PROFICIENCIES	PROGLOTTIS	PROHIBITION	PROLETARIANS	PROLUSIONS
PROFICIENCY	PROGNATHIC	PROHIBITIONARY	PROLETARIAT	PROMACHOSES
PROFICIENT	PROGNATHISM	PROHIBITIONISM	PROLETARIATE	PROMENADED
PROFICIENTLY	PROGNATHISMS	PROHIBITIONISMS	PROLETARIATES	PROMENADER
PROFICIENTS	PROGNATHOUS	PROHIBITIONIST	PROLETARIATS	PROMENADERS
PROFILINGS	PROGNOSING	PROHIBITIONISTS	PROLETARIES	PROMENADES
PROFILISTS	PROGNOSTIC	PROHIBITIONS	PROLICIDAL	PROMENADING

PROMETHAZINE	PRONEPHROSES	PROPAGANDIZING	PROPHYLAXES	PROPRANOLOL
PROMETHAZINES	PRONGBUCKS	PROPAGATED	PROPHYLAXIS	PROPRANOLOLS
PROMETHEUM	PRONGHORNS	PROPAGATES	PROPINQUITIES	PROPRETORS
PROMETHEUMS	PRONOMINAL	PROPAGATING	PROPINQUITY	PROPRIETARIES
PROMETHIUM	PRONOMINALISE	PROPAGATION	PROPIONATE	PROPRIETARILY
PROMETHIUMS	PRONOMINALISED	PROPAGATIONAL	PROPIONATES	PROPRIETARY
PROMILITARY	PRONOMINALISES	PROPAGATIONS	PROPITIABLE	PROPRIETIES
PROMINENCE	PRONOMINALISING	PROPAGATIVE	PROPITIATE	PROPRIETOR
PROMINENCES	PRONOMINALIZE	PROPAGATOR	PROPITIATED	PROPRIETORIAL
PROMINENCIES	PRONOMINALIZED	PROPAGATORS	PROPITIATES	PROPRIETORIALLY
PROMINENCY	PRONOMINALIZES	PROPAGULES	PROPITIATING	PROPRIETORS
PROMINENTLY	PRONOMINALIZING	PROPAGULUM	PROPITIATION	PROPRIETORSHIP
PROMINENTNESS	PRONOMINALLY	PROPANEDIOIC	PROPITIATIONS	PROPRIETORSHIPS
PROMINENTNESSES	PRONOUNCEABLE	PROPANONES	PROPITIATIOUS	PROPRIETRESS
PROMINENTS	PRONOUNCED	PROPAROXYTONE	PROPITIATIVE	PROPRIETRESSES
PROMISCUITIES	PRONOUNCEDLY	PROPAROXYTONES	PROPITIATOR	PROPRIETRICES
PROMISCUITY	PRONOUNCEMENT	PROPELLANT	PROPITIATORIES	PROPRIETRIX
PROMISCUOUS	PRONOUNCEMENTS	PROPELLANTS	PROPITIATORILY	PROPRIETRIXES
PROMISCUOUSLY	PRONOUNCER	PROPELLENT	PROPITIATORS	PROPRIOCEPTION
PROMISCUOUSNESS	PRONOUNCERS	PROPELLENTS	PROPITIATORY	PROPRIOCEPTIONS
PROMISEFUL	PRONOUNCES	PROPELLERS	PROPITIOUS	PROPRIOCEPTIVE
PROMISELESS	PRONOUNCING	PROPELLING	PROPITIOUSLY	PROPRIOCEPTOR
PROMISINGLY	PRONOUNCINGS	PROPELLINGS	PROPITIOUSNESS	PROPRIOCEPTORS
PROMISSIVE	PRONUCLEAR	PROPELLORS	PROPLASTID	PROPROCTOR
PROMISSORILY	PRONUCLEARIST	PROPELMENT	PROPLASTIDS	PROPROCTORS
PROMISSORS	PRONUCLEARISTS	PROPELMENTS	PROPODEONS	PROPUGNATION
PROMISSORY	PRONUCLEUS	PROPENDENT	PROPODEUMS	PROPUGNATIONS
PROMONARCHIST	PRONUCLEUSES	PROPENDING	PROPOLISES	PROPULSION
PROMONTORIES	PRONUNCIAMENTO	PROPENSELY	PROPONENTS	PROPULSIONS
PROMONTORY	PRONUNCIAMENTOS	PROPENSENESS	PROPORTION	PROPULSIVE
PROMOTABILITIES	PRONUNCIATION	PROPENSENESSES	PROPORTIONABLE	PROPULSORS
PROMOTABILITY	PRONUNCIATIONAL	PROPENSION	PROPORTIONABLY	PROPULSORY
PROMOTABLE	PRONUNCIATIONS	PROPENSIONS	PROPORTIONAL	PROPYLAEUM
PROMOTIONAL	PRONUNCIOS	PROPENSITIES	PROPORTIONALITY	PROPYLAMINE
PROMOTIONS	PROOEMIONS	PROPENSITY	PROPORTIONALLY	PROPYLAMINES
PROMOTIVENESS	PROOEMIUMS	PROPENSIVE	PROPORTIONALS	PROPYLENES
PROMOTIVENESSES	PROOFREADER	PROPERDINS	PROPORTIONATE	PROPYLITES
PROMPTBOOK	PROOFREADERS	PROPERISPOMENA	PROPORTIONATED	PROPYLITISATION
PROMPTBOOKS	PROOFREADING	PROPERISPOMENON	PROPORTIONATELY	PROPYLITISE
PROMPTINGS	PROOFREADINGS	PROPERNESS	PROPORTIONATES	PROPYLITISED
PROMPTITUDE	PROOFREADS	PROPERNESSES	PROPORTIONATING	PROPYLITISES
PROMPTITUDES	PROOFROOMS	PROPERTIED	PROPORTIONED	PROPYLITISING
PROMPTNESS	PROPAEDEUTIC	PROPERTIES	PROPORTIONING	PROPYLITIZATION
PROMPTNESSES	PROPAEDEUTICAL	PROPERTYING	PROPORTIONINGS	PROPYLITIZE
PROMPTUARIES	PROPAEDEUTICS	PROPERTYLESS	PROPORTIONLESS	PROPYLITIZED
PROMPTUARY	PROPAGABILITIES	PROPHECIES	PROPORTIONMENT	PROPYLITIZES
PROMPTURES	PROPAGABILITY	PROPHESIABLE	PROPORTIONMENTS	PROPYLITIZING
PROMULGATE	PROPAGABLE	PROPHESIED	PROPORTIONS	PRORATABLE
PROMULGATED	PROPAGABLENESS	PROPHESIER	PROPOSABLE	PRORATIONS
PROMULGATES	PROPAGANDA	PROPHESIERS	PROPOSITAE	PRORECTORS
PROMULGATING	PROPAGANDAS	PROPHESIES	PROPOSITION	PROROGATED
PROMULGATION	PROPAGANDISE	PROPHESYING	PROPOSITIONAL	PROROGATES
PROMULGATIONS	PROPAGANDISED	PROPHESYINGS	PROPOSITIONALLY	PROROGATING
PROMULGATOR	PROPAGANDISER	PROPHETESS	PROPOSITIONED	PROROGATION
PROMULGATORS	PROPAGANDISERS	PROPHETESSES	PROPOSITIONING	PROROGATIONS
PROMULGING	PROPAGANDISES	PROPHETHOOD	PROPOSITIONS	PROROGUING
PROMUSCIDATE	PROPAGANDISING	PROPHETHOODS	PROPOSITUS	PROSAICALLY
PROMUSCIDES	PROPAGANDISM	PROPHETICAL	PROPOUNDED	PROSAICALNESS
PROMYCELIA	PROPAGANDISMS	PROPHETICALLY	PROPOUNDER	PROSAICALNESSES
PROMYCELIAL	PROPAGANDIST	PROPHETICISM	PROPOUNDERS	PROSAICISM
PROMYCELIUM	PROPAGANDISTIC	PROPHETICISMS	PROPOUNDING	PROSAICISMS
PRONATIONS	PROPAGANDISTS	PROPHETISM	PROPOXYPHENE	PROSAICNESS
PRONATORES	PROPAGANDIZE	PROPHETISMS	PROPOXYPHENES	PROSAICNESSES
PRONENESSES	PROPAGANDIZED	PROPHETSHIP	PROPRAETOR	PROSATEURS
PRONEPHRIC	PROPAGANDIZER	PROPHETSHIPS	PROPRAETORIAL	PROSAUROPOD
PRONEPHROI	PROPAGANDIZERS	PROPHYLACTIC	PROPRAETORIAN	PROSAUROPODS
PRONEPHROS	PROPAGANDIZES	PROPHYLACTICS	PROPRAETORS	PROSCENIUM

PROSCENIUMS	PROSLAMBANOMENE	PROSTITUTED	PROTEINOUS	PROTOCHORDATES
PROSCIUTTI	PROSLAVERY	PROSTITUTES	PROTEINURIA	PROTOCOCCAL
PROSCIUTTO	PROSOBRANCH	PROSTITUTING	PROTEINURIAS	PROTOCOLED
PROSCIUTTOS	PROSOBRANCHS	PROSTITUTION	PROTENDING	PROTOCOLIC
PROSCRIBED	PROSODIANS	PROSTITUTIONS	PROTENSION	PROTOCOLING
PROSCRIBER	PROSODICAL	PROSTITUTOR	PROTENSIONS	PROTOCOLISE
PROSCRIBERS	PROSODICALLY	PROSTITUTORS	PROTENSITIES	PROTOCOLISED
PROSCRIBES	PROSODISTS	PROSTOMIAL	PROTENSITY	PROTOCOLISES
PROSCRIBING	PROSOPAGNOSIA	PROSTOMIUM	PROTENSIVE	PROTOCOLISING
PROSCRIPTION	PROSOPAGNOSIAS	PROSTRATED	PROTENSIVELY	PROTOCOLIST
PROSCRIPTIONS	PROSOPOGRAPHER	PROSTRATES	PROTEOCLASTIC	PROTOCOLISTS
PROSCRIPTIVE	PROSOPOGRAPHERS	PROSTRATING	PROTEOGLYCAN	PROTOCOLIZE
PROSCRIPTIVELY	PROSOPOGRAPHIES	PROSTRATION	PROTEOGLYCANS	PROTOCOLIZED
PROSCRIPTS	PROSOPOGRAPHY	PROSTRATIONS	PROTEOLYSE	PROTOCOLIZES
PROSECTING	PROSOPOPEIA	PROSYLLOGISM	PROTEOLYSED	PROTOCOLIZING
PROSECTORIAL	PROSOPOPEIAL	PROSYLLOGISMS	PROTEOLYSES	PROTOCOLLED
PROSECTORS	PROSOPOPEIAS	PROTACTINIUM	PROTEOLYSING	PROTOCOLLING
PROSECTORSHIP	PROSOPOPOEIA	PROTACTINIUMS	PROTEOLYSIS	PROTOCTIST
PROSECTORSHIPS	PROSOPOPOEIAL	PROTAGONISM	PROTEOLYTIC	PROTOCTISTS
PROSECUTABLE	PROSOPOPOEIAS	PROTAGONISMS	PROTEOLYTICALLY	PROTODERMS
PROSECUTED	PROSPECTED	PROTAGONIST	PROTEOMICS	PROTOGALAXIES
PROSECUTES	PROSPECTING	PROTAGONISTS	PROTERANDRIES	PROTOGALAXY
PROSECUTING	PROSPECTINGS	PROTAMINES	PROTERANDROUS	PROTOGENIC
PROSECUTION	PROSPECTION	PROTANDRIES	PROTERANDRY	PROTOGINES
PROSECUTIONS	PROSPECTIONS	PROTANDROUS	PROTEROGYNIES	PROTOGYNIES
PROSECUTOR	PROSPECTIVE	PROTANOMALIES	PROTEROGYNOUS	PROTOGYNOUS
PROSECUTORIAL	PROSPECTIVELY	PROTANOMALOUS	PROTEROGYNY	PROTOHISTORIAN
PROSECUTORS	PROSPECTIVENESS	PROTANOMALY	PROTERVITIES	PROTOHISTORIANS
PROSECUTRICES	PROSPECTIVES	PROTANOPES	PROTERVITY	PROTOHISTORIC
PROSECUTRIX	PROSPECTLESS	PROTANOPIA	PROTESTANT	PROTOHISTORIES
PROSECUTRIXES	PROSPECTOR	PROTANOPIAS	PROTESTANTS	PROTOHISTORY
PROSELYTED	PROSPECTORS	PROTANOPIC	PROTESTATION	PROTOHUMAN
PROSELYTES	PROSPECTUS	PROTEACEOUS	PROTESTATIONS	PROTOHUMANS
PROSELYTIC	PROSPECTUSES	PROTECTANT	PROTESTERS	PROTOLANGUAGE
PROSELYTING	PROSPERING	PROTECTANTS	PROTESTING	PROTOLANGUAGES
PROSELYTISATION	PROSPERITIES	PROTECTERS	PROTESTINGLY	PROTOLITHIC
PROSELYTISE	PROSPERITY	PROTECTING	PROTESTORS	PROTOMARTYR
PROSELYTISED	PROSPEROUS	PROTECTINGLY	PROTHALAMIA	PROTOMARTYRS
PROSELYTISER	PROSPEROUSLY	PROTECTION	PROTHALAMION	PROTOMORPHIC
PROSELYTISERS	PROSPEROUSNESS	PROTECTIONISM	PROTHALAMIUM	PROTONATED
PROSELYTISES	PROSTACYCLIN	PROTECTIONISMS	PROTHALLIA	PROTONATES
PROSELYTISING	PROSTACYCLINS	PROTECTIONIST	PROTHALLIAL	PROTONATING
PROSELYTISM	PROSTAGLANDIN	PROTECTIONISTS	PROTHALLIC	PROTONATION
PROSELYTISMS	PROSTAGLANDINS	PROTECTIONS	PROTHALLIUM	PROTONATIONS
PROSELYTIZATION	PROSTANTHERA	PROTECTIVE	PROTHALLOID	PROTONEMAL
PROSELYTIZE	PROSTANTHERAS	PROTECTIVELY	PROTHALLUS	PROTONEMATA
PROSELYTIZED	PROSTATECTOMIES	PROTECTIVENESS	PROTHALLUSES	PROTONEMATAL
PROSELYTIZER	PROSTATECTOMY	PROTECTIVES	PROTHETICALLY	PROTONOTARIAL
PROSELYTIZERS	PROSTATISM	PROTECTORAL	PROTHONOTARIAL	PROTONOTARIAT
PROSELYTIZES	PROSTATISMS	PROTECTORATE	PROTHONOTARIAT	PROTONOTARIATS
PROSELYTIZING	PROSTATITIS	PROTECTORATES	PROTHONOTARIATS	PROTONOTARIES
PROSEMINAR	PROSTATITISES	PROTECTORIAL	PROTHONOTARIES	PROTONOTARY
PROSEMINARS	PROSTERNUM	PROTECTORIES	PROTHONOTARY	PROTOPATHIC
PROSENCEPHALA	PROSTERNUMS	PROTECTORLESS	PROTHORACES	PROTOPATHIES
PROSENCEPHALIC	PROSTHESES	PROTECTORS	PROTHORACIC	PROTOPATHY
PROSENCEPHALON	PROSTHESIS	PROTECTORSHIP	PROTHORAXES	PROTOPHILIC
PROSENCHYMA	PROSTHETIC	PROTECTORSHIPS	PROTHROMBIN	PROTOPHLOEM
PROSENCHYMAS	PROSTHETICALLY	PROTECTORY	PROTHROMBINS	PROTOPHLOEMS
PROSENCHYMATA	PROSTHETICS	PROTECTRESS	PROTISTANS	PROTOPHYTE
PROSENCHYMATOUS	PROSTHETIST	PROTECTRESSES	PROTISTOLOGIES	PROTOPHYTES
PROSEUCHAE	PROSTHETISTS	PROTECTRICES	PROTISTOLOGIST	PROTOPHYTIC
PROSIFYING	PROSTHODONTIA	PROTECTRIX	PROTISTOLOGISTS	PROTOPLANET
PROSILIENCIES	PROSTHODONTIAS	PROTECTRIXES	PROTISTOLOGY	PROTOPLANETARY
PROSILIENCY	PROSTHODONTICS	PROTEIFORM	PROTOACTINIUM	PROTOPLANETS
PROSILIENT	PROSTHODONTIST	PROTEINACEOUS	PROTOACTINIUMS	PROTOPLASM
PROSIMIANS	PROSTHODONTISTS	PROTEINASE	PROTOAVISES	PROTOPLASMAL
PROSINESSES	PROSTITUTE	PROTEINASES	PROTOCHORDATE	PROTOPLASMATIC

PROTOPLASMIC	PROTUBERANCES	PROVINCIALISMS	PRURIENCIES	PSEUDOACID
PROTOPLASMS	PROTUBERANCIES	PROVINCIALIST	PRURIENTLY	PSEUDOACIDS
PROTOPLAST	PROTUBERANCY	PROVINCIALISTS	PRURIGINOUS	PSEUDOALLELE
PROTOPLASTIC	PROTUBERANT	PROVINCIALITIES	PRURITUSES	PSEUDOALLELES
PROTOPLASTS	PROTUBERANTLY	PROVINCIALITY	PRUSSIANISATION	PSEUDOARTHROSES
PROTOPORPHYRIN	PROTUBERATE	PROVINCIALIZE	PRUSSIANISE	PSEUDOARTHROSIS
PROTOPORPHYRINS	PROTUBERATED	PROVINCIALIZED	PRUSSIANISED	PSEUDOBULB
PROTOSPATAIRE	PROTUBERATES	PROVINCIALIZES	PRUSSIANISES	PSEUDOBULBS
PROTOSPATAIRES	PROTUBERATING	PROVINCIALIZING	PRUSSIANISING	PSEUDOCARP
PROTOSPATHAIRE	PROTUBERATION	PROVINCIALLY	PRUSSIANIZATION	PSEUDOCARPOUS
PROTOSPATHAIRES	PROTUBERATIONS	PROVINCIALS	PRUSSIANIZE	PSEUDOCARPS
PROTOSPATHARIUS	PROUDHEARTED	PROVIRUSES	PRUSSIANIZED	PSEUDOCIDE
PROTOSTARS	PROUDNESSES	PROVISIONAL	PRUSSIANIZES	PSEUDOCIDES
PROTOSTELE	PROUSTITES	PROVISIONALLY	PRUSSIANIZING	PSEUDOCLASSIC
PROTOSTELES	PROVABILITIES	PROVISIONALS	PRUSSIATES	PSEUDOCLASSICS
PROTOSTELIC	PROVABILITY	PROVISIONARIES	PSALIGRAPHIES	PSEUDOCODE
PROTOSTOME	PROVABLENESS	PROVISIONARY	PSALIGRAPHY	PSEUDOCODES
PROTOSTOMES	PROVABLENESSES	PROVISIONED	PSALMBOOKS	PSEUDOCOEL
PROTOTHERIAN	PROVANTING	PROVISIONER	PSALMODICAL	PSEUDOCOELOMATE
PROTOTHERIANS	PROVASCULAR	PROVISIONERS	PSALMODIES	PSEUDOCOELS
PROTOTROPH	PROVEABILITIES	PROVISIONING	PSALMODISE	PSEUDOCYESES
PROTOTROPHIC	PROVEABILITY	PROVISIONS	PSALMODISED	PSEUDOCYESIS
PROTOTROPHIES	PROVECTION	PROVISORILY	PSALMODISES	PSEUDOEPHEDRINE
PROTOTROPHS	PROVECTIONS	PROVITAMIN	PSALMODISING	PSEUDOGRAPH
PROTOTROPHY	PROVEDITOR	PROVITAMINS	PSALMODIST	PSEUDOGRAPHIES
PROTOTYPAL	PROVEDITORE	PROVOCABLE	PSALMODISTS	PSEUDOGRAPHS
PROTOTYPED	PROVEDITORES	PROVOCANTS	PSALMODIZE	PSEUDOGRAPHY
PROTOTYPES	PROVEDITORS	PROVOCATEUR	PSALMODIZED	PSEUDOLOGIA
PROTOTYPIC	PROVEDORES	PROVOCATEURS	PSALMODIZES	PSEUDOLOGIAS
PROTOTYPICAL	PROVENANCE	PROVOCATION	PSALMODIZING	PSEUDOLOGIES
PROTOTYPICALLY	PROVENANCES	PROVOCATIONS	PSALTERIAN	PSEUDOLOGUE
PROTOTYPING	PROVENDERED	PROVOCATIVE	PSALTERIES	PSEUDOLOGUES
PROTOXIDES	PROVENDERING	PROVOCATIVELY	PSALTERIUM	PSEUDOLOGY
PROTOXYLEM	PROVENDERS	PROVOCATIVENESS	PSALTRESSES	PSEUDOMARTYR
PROTOXYLEMS	PROVENIENCE	PROVOCATIVES	PSAMMOPHIL	PSEUDOMARTYRS
PROTOZOANS	PROVENIENCES	PROVOCATOR	PSAMMOPHILE	PSEUDOMEMBRANE
PROTOZOOLOGICAL	PROVENTRICULAR	PROVOCATORS	PSAMMOPHILES	PSEUDOMEMBRANES
PROTOZOOLOGIES	PROVENTRICULI	PROVOCATORY	PSAMMOPHILOUS	PSEUDOMONAD
PROTOZOOLOGIST	PROVENTRICULUS	PROVOKABLE	PSAMMOPHILS	PSEUDOMONADES
PROTOZOOLOGISTS	PROVERBIAL	PROVOKEMENT	PSAMMOPHYTE	PSEUDOMONADS
PROTOZOOLOGY	PROVERBIALISE	PROVOKEMENTS	PSAMMOPHYTES	PSEUDOMONAS
PROTOZOONS	PROVERBIALISED	PROVOKINGLY	PSAMMOPHYTIC	PSEUDOMORPH
PROTRACTED	PROVERBIALISES	PROVOLONES	PSELLISMUS	PSEUDOMORPHIC
PROTRACTEDLY	PROVERBIALISING	PROVOSTRIES	PSELLISMUSES	PSEUDOMORPHISM
PROTRACTEDNESS	PROVERBIALISM	PROVOSTSHIP	PSEPHOANALYSES	PSEUDOMORPHISMS
PROTRACTIBLE	PROVERBIALISMS	PROVOSTSHIPS	PSEPHOANALYSIS	PSEUDOMORPHOUS
PROTRACTILE	PROVERBIALIST	PROWLINGLY	PSEPHOLOGICAL	PSEUDOMORPHS
PROTRACTING	PROVERBIALISTS	PROXIMALLY	PSEPHOLOGICALLY	PSEUDOMUTUALITY
PROTRACTION	PROVERBIALIZE	PROXIMATELY	PSEPHOLOGIES	PSEUDONYMITIES
PROTRACTIONS	PROVERBIALIZED	PROXIMATENESS	PSEPHOLOGIST	PSEUDONYMITY
PROTRACTIVE	PROVERBIALIZES	PROXIMATENESSES	PSEPHOLOGISTS	PSEUDONYMOUS
PROTRACTOR	PROVERBIALIZING	PROXIMATION	PSEPHOLOGY	PSEUDONYMOUSLY
PROTRACTORS	PROVERBIALLY	PROXIMATIONS	PSEUDAESTHESIA	PSEUDONYMS
PROTREPTIC	PROVERBING	PROXIMITIES	PSEUDAESTHESIAS	PSEUDOPODAL
PROTREPTICAL	PROVIDABLE	PROZYMITES	PSEUDARTHROSES	PSEUDOPODIA
PROTREPTICS	PROVIDENCE	PRUDENTIAL	PSEUDARTHROSIS	PSEUDOPODIAL
PROTRUDABLE	PROVIDENCES	PRUDENTIALISM	PSEUDEPIGRAPH	PSEUDOPODIUM
PROTRUDENT	PROVIDENTIAL	PRUDENTIALISMS	PSEUDEPIGRAPHA	PSEUDOPODS
PROTRUDING	PROVIDENTIALLY	PRUDENTIALIST	PSEUDEPIGRAPHIC	PSEUDOPREGNANCY
PROTRUSIBLE	PROVIDENTLY	PRUDENTIALISTS	PSEUDEPIGRAPHON	PSEUDOPREGNANT
PROTRUSILE	PROVINCEWIDE	PRUDENTIALITIES	PSEUDEPIGRAPHS	PSEUDORANDOM
PROTRUSION	PROVINCIAL	PRUDENTIALITY	PSEUDEPIGRAPHY	PSEUDOSCALAR
PROTRUSIONS	PROVINCIALISE	PRUDENTIALLY	PSEUDERIES	PSEUDOSCALARS
PROTRUSIVE	PROVINCIALISED	PRUDENTIALS	PSEUDIMAGINES	PSEUDOSCIENCE
PROTRUSIVELY	PROVINCIALISES	PRUDISHNESS	PSEUDIMAGO	PSEUDOSCIENCES
PROTRUSIVENESS	PROVINCIALISING	PRUDISHNESSES	PSEUDIMAGOES	PSEUDOSCIENTIST
PROTUBERANCE	PROVINCIALISM	PRURIENCES	PSEUDIMAGOS	PSEUDOSCOPE

PSEUDOSCOPES	PSYCHOANALYZED	PSYCHOLOGISED	PSYCHOTHERAPIES	PUBLICATIONS
PSEUDOSCORPION	PSYCHOANALYZER	PSYCHOLOGISES	PSYCHOTHERAPIST	PUBLICISED
PSEUDOSCORPIONS	PSYCHOANALYZERS	PSYCHOLOGISING	PSYCHOTHERAPY	PUBLICISES
PSEUDOSOLUTION	PSYCHOANALYZES	PSYCHOLOGISM	PSYCHOTICALLY	PUBLICISING
PSEUDOSOLUTIONS	PSYCHOANALYZING	PSYCHOLOGISMS	PSYCHOTICISM	PUBLICISTS
PSEUDOSYMMETRY	PSYCHOBABBLE	PSYCHOLOGIST	PSYCHOTICISMS	PUBLICITIES
PSEUDOVECTOR	PSYCHOBABBLED	PSYCHOLOGISTIC	PSYCHOTICS	PUBLICIZED
PSEUDOVECTORS	PSYCHOBABBLER	PSYCHOLOGISTS	PSYCHOTOMIMETIC	PUBLICIZES
PSILANTHROPIC	PSYCHOBABBLERS	PSYCHOLOGIZE	PSYCHOTOXIC	PUBLICIZING
PSILANTHROPIES	PSYCHOBABBLES	PSYCHOLOGIZED	PSYCHOTROPIC	PUBLICNESS
PSILANTHROPISM	PSYCHOBABBLING	PSYCHOLOGIZES	PSYCHOTROPICS	PUBLICNESSES
PSILANTHROPISMS	PSYCHOBILLIES	PSYCHOLOGIZING	PSYCHROMETER	PUBLISHABLE
PSILANTHROPIST	PSYCHOBILLY	PSYCHOLOGY	PSYCHROMETERS	PUBLISHERS
PSILANTHROPISTS	PSYCHOBIOGRAPHY	PSYCHOMACHIA	PSYCHROMETRIC	PUBLISHING
PSILANTHROPY	PSYCHOBIOLOGIC	PSYCHOMACHIAS	PSYCHROMETRICAL	PUBLISHINGS
PSILOCYBIN	PSYCHOBIOLOGIES	PSYCHOMACHIES	PSYCHROMETRIES	PUBLISHMENT
PSILOCYBINS	PSYCHOBIOLOGIST	PSYCHOMACHY	PSYCHROMETRY	PUBLISHMENTS
PSILOMELANE	PSYCHOBIOLOGY	PSYCHOMETER	PSYCHROPHILIC	PUCCINIACEOUS
PSILOMELANES	PSYCHOCHEMICAL	PSYCHOMETERS	PTARMIGANS	PUCKERIEST
PSILOPHYTE	PSYCHOCHEMICALS	PSYCHOMETRIC	PTERANODON	PUCKEROOED
PSILOPHYTES	PSYCHOCHEMISTRY	PSYCHOMETRICAL	PTERANODONS	PUCKISHNESS
PSILOPHYTIC	PSYCHODELIA	PSYCHOMETRICIAN	PTERIDINES	PUCKISHNESSES
PSITTACINE	PSYCHODELIAS	PSYCHOMETRICS	PTERIDOLOGICAL	PUDDENINGS
PSITTACINES	PSYCHODELIC	PSYCHOMETRIES	PTERIDOLOGIES	PUDDINGIER
PSITTACOSES	PSYCHODELICALLY	PSYCHOMETRIST	PTERIDOLOGIST	PUDDINGIEST
PSITTACOSIS	PSYCHODRAMA	PSYCHOMETRISTS	PTERIDOLOGISTS	PUDGINESSES
PSITTACOTIC	PSYCHODRAMAS	PSYCHOMETRY	PTERIDOLOGY	PUDIBUNDITIES
PSORIATICS	PSYCHODRAMATIC	PSYCHOMOTOR	PTERIDOMANIA	PUDIBUNDITY
PSYCHAGOGUE	PSYCHODYNAMIC	PSYCHONEUROSES	PTERIDOMANIAS	PUDICITIES
PSYCHAGOGUES	PSYCHODYNAMICS	PSYCHONEUROSIS	PTERIDOPHILIST	PUERILISMS
PSYCHASTHENIA	PSYCHOGALVANIC	PSYCHONEUROTIC	PTERIDOPHILISTS	PUERILITIES
PSYCHASTHENIAS	PSYCHOGASES	PSYCHONEUROTICS	PTERIDOPHYTE	PUERPERALLY
PSYCHASTHENIC	PSYCHOGENESES	PSYCHONOMIC	PTERIDOPHYTES	PUERPERIUM
PSYCHASTHENICS	PSYCHOGENESIS	PSYCHONOMICS	PTERIDOPHYTIC	PUFFERFISH
PSYCHEDELIA	PSYCHOGENETIC	PSYCHOPATH	PTERIDOPHYTOUS	PUFFERFISHES
PSYCHEDELIAS	PSYCHOGENETICAL	PSYCHOPATHIC	PTERIDOSPERM	PUFFINESSES
PSYCHEDELIC	PSYCHOGENETICS	PSYCHOPATHICS	PTERIDOSPERMS	PUFFTALOONAS
PSYCHEDELICALLY	PSYCHOGENIC	PSYCHOPATHIES	PTERODACTYL	PUFTALOONAS
PSYCHEDELICS	PSYCHOGENICALLY	PSYCHOPATHIST	PTERODACTYLE	PUFTALOONIES
PSYCHIATER	PSYCHOGERIATRIC	PSYCHOPATHISTS	PTERODACTYLES	PUFTALOONS
PSYCHIATERS	PSYCHOGNOSES	PSYCHOPATHOLOGY	PTERODACTYLS	PUGGINESSES
PSYCHIATRIC	PSYCHOGNOSIS	PSYCHOPATHS	PTEROSAURIAN	PUGILISTIC
PSYCHIATRICAL	PSYCHOGNOSTIC	PSYCHOPATHY	PTEROSAURIANS	PUGILISTICAL
PSYCHIATRICALLY	PSYCHOGONIES	PSYCHOPHILIES	PTEROSAURS	PUGILISTICALLY
PSYCHIATRIES	PSYCHOGONY	PSYCHOPHILY	PTERYGIALS	PUGNACIOUS
PSYCHIATRIST	PSYCHOGRAM	PSYCHOPHYSICAL	PTERYGIUMS	PUGNACIOUSLY
PSYCHIATRISTS	PSYCHOGRAMS	PSYCHOPHYSICIST	PTERYGOIDS	PUGNACIOUSNESS
PSYCHIATRY	PSYCHOGRAPH	PSYCHOPHYSICS	PTERYLOGRAPHIC	PUGNACITIES
PSYCHICALLY	PSYCHOGRAPHIC	PSYCHOPOMP	PTERYLOGRAPHIES	PUISSANCES
PSYCHICISM	PSYCHOGRAPHICAL	PSYCHOPOMPS	PTERYLOGRAPHY	PUISSANTLY
PSYCHICISMS	PSYCHOGRAPHICS	PSYCHOSEXUAL	PTERYLOSES	PUISSAUNCE
PSYCHICIST	PSYCHOGRAPHIES	PSYCHOSEXUALITY	PTERYLOSIS	PUISSAUNCES
PSYCHICISTS	PSYCHOGRAPHS	PSYCHOSEXUALLY	PTOCHOCRACIES	PULCHRITUDE
PSYCHOACOUSTIC	PSYCHOGRAPHY	PSYCHOSOCIAL	PTOCHOCRACY	PULCHRITUDES
PSYCHOACOUSTICS	PSYCHOHISTORIAN	PSYCHOSOCIALLY	PTYALAGOGIC	PULCHRITUDINOUS
PSYCHOACTIVE	PSYCHOHISTORIES	PSYCHOSOCIOLOGY	PTYALAGOGUE	PULLULATED
PSYCHOANALYSE	PSYCHOHISTORY	PSYCHOSOMATIC	PTYALAGOGUES	PULLULATES
PSYCHOANALYSED	PSYCHOKINESES	PSYCHOSOMATICS	PTYALISING	PULLULATING
PSYCHOANALYSER	PSYCHOKINESIS	PSYCHOSOMIMETIC	PTYALIZING	PULLULATION
PSYCHOANALYSERS	PSYCHOKINETIC	PSYCHOSURGEON	PUBCRAWLER	PULLULATIONS
PSYCHOANALYSES	PSYCHOLINGUIST	PSYCHOSURGEONS	PUBCRAWLERS	PULMOBRANCH
PSYCHOANALYSING	PSYCHOLINGUISTS	PSYCHOSURGERIES	PUBERULENT	PULMOBRANCHIATE
PSYCHOANALYSIS	PSYCHOLOGIC	PSYCHOSURGERY	PUBERULOUS	PULMOBRANCHS
PSYCHOANALYST	PSYCHOLOGICAL	PSYCHOSURGICAL	PUBESCENCE	PULMONATES
PSYCHOANALYSTS	PSYCHOLOGICALLY	PSYCHOSYNTHESES	PUBESCENCES	PULMONOLOGIES
PSYCHOANALYTIC	PSYCHOLOGIES	PSYCHOSYNTHESIS	PUBLICALLY	PULMONOLOGIST
PSYCHOANALYZE	PSYCHOLOGISE	PSYCHOTECHNICS	PUBLICATION	PULMONOLOGISTS

PULMONOLOGY	PUNCHBOARD	PUPILLATED	PURPOSELESSNESS	PUTRIFICATION
PULPBOARDS	PUNCHBOARDS	PUPILLATES	PURPOSIVELY	PUTRIFICATIONS
PULPIFYING	PUNCHBOWLS	PUPILLATING	PURPOSIVENESS	PUTSCHISTS
PULPINESSES	PUNCHINELLO	PUPILSHIPS	PURPOSIVENESSES	PUTTYROOTS
PULPITEERED	PUNCHINELLOES	PUPIPAROUS	PURPRESTURE	PUZZLEDOMS
PULPITEERING	PUNCHINELLOS	PUPPETEERED	PURPRESTURES	PUZZLEHEADED
PULPITEERS	PUNCHINESS	PUPPETEERING	PURSERSHIP	PUZZLEMENT
PULPITRIES	PUNCHINESSES	PUPPETEERS	PURSERSHIPS	PUZZLEMENTS
PULPSTONES	PUNCHLINES	PUPPETLIKE	PURSINESSES	PUZZLINGLY
PULSATANCE	PUNCTATION	PUPPETRIES	PURSUANCES	PUZZOLANAS
PULSATANCES	PUNCTATIONS	PUPPYHOODS	PURSUANTLY	PYCNIDIOSPORE
PULSATILITIES	PUNCTATORS	PURBLINDLY	PURSUINGLY	PYCNIDIOSPORES
PULSATILITY	PUNCTILIOS	PURBLINDNESS	PURSUIVANT	PYCNOCONIDIA
PULSATILLA	PUNCTILIOUS	PURBLINDNESSES	PURSUIVANTS	PYCNOCONIDIUM
PULSATILLAS	PUNCTILIOUSLY	PURCHASABILITY	PURTENANCE	PYCNODYSOSTOSES
PULSATIONS	PUNCTILIOUSNESS	PURCHASABLE	PURTENANCES	PYCNODYSOSTOSIS
PULSATIVELY	PUNCTUALIST	PURCHASERS	PURULENCES	PYCNOGONID
PULSEBEATS	PUNCTUALISTS	PURCHASING	PURULENCIES	PYCNOGONIDS
PULSELESSNESS	PUNCTUALITIES	PURCHASINGS	PURULENTLY	PYCNOGONOID
PULSELESSNESSES	PUNCTUALITY	PURDONIUMS	PURVEYANCE	PYCNOGONOIDS
PULSIMETER	PUNCTUALLY	PUREBLOODS	PURVEYANCES	PYCNOMETER
PULSIMETERS	PUNCTUATED	PURENESSES	PUSCHKINIA	PYCNOMETERS
PULSOMETER	PUNCTUATES	PURGATIONS	PUSCHKINIAS	PYCNOMETRIC
PULSOMETERS	PUNCTUATING	PURGATIVELY	PUSHCHAIRS	PYCNOSOMES
PULTACEOUS	PUNCTUATION	PURGATIVES	PUSHFULNESS	PYCNOSPORE
PULTRUDING	PUNCTUATIONIST	PURGATORIAL	PUSHFULNESSES	PYCNOSPORES
PULTRUSION	PUNCTUATIONISTS	PURGATORIALLY	PUSHINESSES	PYCNOSTYLE
PULTRUSIONS	PUNCTUATIONS	PURGATORIAN	PUSHINGNESS	PYCNOSTYLES
PULVERABLE	PUNCTUATIVE	PURGATORIANS	PUSHINGNESSES	PYELITISES
PULVERATION	PUNCTUATOR	PURGATORIES	PUSILLANIMITIES	PYELOGRAMS
PULVERATIONS	PUNCTUATORS	PURIFICATION	PUSILLANIMITY	PYELOGRAPHIC
PULVERINES	PUNCTULATE	PURIFICATIONS	PUSILLANIMOUS	PYELOGRAPHIES
PULVERISABLE	PUNCTULATED	PURIFICATIVE	PUSILLANIMOUSLY	PYELOGRAPHY
PULVERISATION	PUNCTULATES	PURIFICATOR	PUSSYFOOTED	PYELONEPHRITIC
PULVERISATIONS	PUNCTULATING	PURIFICATORS	PUSSYFOOTER	PYELONEPHRITIS
PULVERISED	PUNCTULATION	PURIFICATORY	PUSSYFOOTERS	PYGARGUSES
PULVERISER	PUNCTULATIONS	PURISTICAL	PUSSYFOOTING	PYGOSTYLES
PULVERISERS	PUNCTURABLE	PURISTICALLY	PUSSYFOOTINGS	PYKNODYSOSTOSES
PULVERISES	PUNCTURATION	PURITANICAL	PUSSYFOOTS	PYKNODYSOSTOSIS
PULVERISING	PUNCTURATIONS	PURITANICALLY	PUSTULANTS	PYKNOMETER
PULVERIZABLE	PUNCTURERS	PURITANICALNESS	PUSTULATED	PYKNOMETERS
PULVERIZATION	PUNCTURING	PURITANISE	PUSTULATES	PYKNOSOMES
PULVERIZATIONS	PUNDIGRION	PURITANISED	PUSTULATING	PYLORECTOMIES
PULVERIZED	PUNDIGRIONS	PURITANISES	PUSTULATION	PYLORECTOMY
PULVERIZER	PUNDITRIES	PURITANISING	PUSTULATIONS	PYOGENESES
PULVERIZERS	PUNDONORES	PURITANISM	PUTANGITANGI	PYOGENESIS
PULVERIZES	PUNGENCIES	PURITANISMS	PUTANGITANGIS	PYORRHOEAL
PULVERIZING	PUNICACEOUS	PURITANIZE	PUTATIVELY	PYORRHOEAS
PULVERULENCE	PUNINESSES	PURITANIZED	PUTONGHUAS	PYORRHOEIC
PULVERULENCES	PUNISHABILITIES	PURITANIZES	PUTREFACIENT	PYRACANTHA
PULVERULENT	PUNISHABILITY	PURITANIZING	PUTREFACTION	PYRACANTHAS
PULVILISED	PUNISHABLE	PURLICUING	PUTREFACTIONS	PYRACANTHS
PULVILIZED	PUNISHINGLY	PURLOINERS	PUTREFACTIVE	PYRALIDIDS
PULVILLIFORM	PUNISHMENT	PURLOINING	PUTREFIABLE	PYRAMIDALLY
PULVILLING	PUNISHMENTS	PUROMYCINS	PUTREFIERS	PYRAMIDICAL
PULVILLIOS	PUNITIVELY	PURPLEHEART	PUTREFYING	PYRAMIDICALLY
PULVINATED	PUNITIVENESS	PURPLEHEARTS	PUTRESCENCE	PYRAMIDING
PULVINULES	PUNITIVENESSES	PURPLENESS	PUTRESCENCES	PYRAMIDION
PUMICATING	PUNKINESSES	PURPLENESSES	PUTRESCENT	PYRAMIDIONS
PUMMELLING	PUPIGEROUS	PURPORTEDLY	PUTRESCIBILITY	PYRAMIDIST
PUMMELLINGS	PUPILABILITIES	PURPORTING	PUTRESCIBLE	PYRAMIDISTS
PUMPERNICKEL	PUPILABILITY	PURPORTLESS	PUTRESCIBLES	PYRAMIDOLOGIES
PUMPERNICKELS	PUPILARITIES	PURPOSEFUL	PUTRESCINE	PYRAMIDOLOGIST
PUMPHOUSES	PUPILARITY	PURPOSEFULLY	PUTRESCINES	PYRAMIDOLOGISTS
PUMPKINSEED	PUPILLAGES	PURPOSEFULNESS	PUTRIDITIES	PYRAMIDOLOGY
PUMPKINSEEDS	PUPILLARITIES	PURPOSELESS	PUTRIDNESS	PYRAMIDONS
PUNCHBALLS	PUPILLARITY	PURPOSELESSLY	PUTRIDNESSES	PYRANOMETER

PYRANOMETERS	PYRITIZING	PYROGRAVURE	PYROMETERS	PYROTARTRATE
PYRANOSIDE	PYRITOHEDRA	PYROGRAVURES	PYROMETRIC	PYROTARTRATES
PYRANOSIDES	PYRITOHEDRAL	PYROKINESES	PYROMETRICAL	PYROTECHNIC
PYRARGYRITE	PYRITOHEDRON	PYROKINESIS	PYROMETRICALLY	PYROTECHNICAL
PYRARGYRITES	PYRITOHEDRONS	PYROLATERS	PYROMETRIES	PYROTECHNICALLY
PYRENEITES	PYROBALLOGIES	PYROLATRIES	PYROMORPHITE	PYROTECHNICIAN
PYRENOCARP	PYROBALLOGY	PYROLIGNEOUS	PYROMORPHITES	PYROTECHNICIANS
PYRENOCARPS	PYROCATECHIN	PYROLIGNIC	PYRONINOPHILIC	PYROTECHNICS
PYRENOMYCETOUS	PYROCATECHINS	PYROLISING	PYROPHOBIA	PYROTECHNIES
PYRETHRINS	PYROCATECHOL	PYROLIZING	PYROPHOBIAS	PYROTECHNIST
PYRETHROID	PYROCATECHOLS	PYROLOGIES	PYROPHOBIC	PYROTECHNISTS
PYRETHROIDS	PYROCERAMS	PYROLUSITE	PYROPHOBICS	PYROTECHNY
PYRETHRUMS	PYROCHEMICAL	PYROLUSITES	PYROPHONES	PYROVANADIC
PYRETOLOGIES	PYROCHEMICALLY	PYROLYSABLE	PYROPHORIC	PYROXENITE
PYRETOLOGY	PYROCLASTIC	PYROLYSATE	PYROPHOROUS	PYROXENITES
PYRETOTHERAPIES	PYROCLASTICS	PYROLYSATES	PYROPHORUS	PYROXENITIC
PYRETOTHERAPY	PYROCLASTS	PYROLYSERS	PYROPHORUSES	PYROXENOID
PYRGEOMETER	PYROELECTRIC	PYROLYSING	PYROPHOSPHATE	PYROXENOIDS
PYRGEOMETERS	PYROELECTRICITY	PYROLYTICALLY	PYROPHOSPHATES	PYROXYLINE
PYRHELIOMETER	PYROELECTRICS	PYROLYZABLE	PYROPHOSPHORIC	PYROXYLINES
PYRHELIOMETERS	PYROGALLATE	PYROLYZATE	PYROPHOTOGRAPH	PYROXYLINS
PYRHELIOMETRIC	PYROGALLATES	PYROLYZATES	PYROPHOTOGRAPHS	PYRRHICIST
PYRIDOXALS	PYROGALLIC	PYROLYZERS	PYROPHOTOGRAPHY	PYRRHICISTS
PYRIDOXAMINE	PYROGALLOL	PYROLYZING	PYROPHOTOMETER	PYRRHOTINE
PYRIDOXAMINES	PYROGALLOLS	PYROMAGNETIC	PYROPHOTOMETERS	PYRRHOTINES
PYRIDOXINE	PYROGENETIC	PYROMANCER	PYROPHOTOMETRY	PYRRHOTITE
PYRIDOXINES	PYROGENICITIES	PYROMANCERS	PYROPHYLLITE	PYRRHOTITES
PYRIDOXINS	PYROGENICITY	PYROMANCIES	PYROPHYLLITES	PYRRHULOXIA
PYRIMETHAMINE	PYROGENOUS	PYROMANIAC	PYROSCOPES	PYRRHULOXIAS
PYRIMETHAMINES	PYROGNOSTIC	PYROMANIACAL	PYROSTATIC	PYRROLIDINE
PYRIMIDINE	PYROGNOSTICS	PYROMANIACS	PYROSULFITE	PYRROLIDINES
PYRIMIDINES	PYROGRAPHER	PYROMANIAS	PYROSULFITES	PYTHOGENIC
PYRITHIAMINE	PYROGRAPHERS	PYROMANTIC	PYROSULPHATE	PYTHONESSES
PYRITHIAMINES	PYROGRAPHIC	PYROMERIDE	PYROSULPHATES	PYTHONOMORPH
PYRITIFEROUS	PYROGRAPHIES	PYROMERIDES	PYROSULPHURIC	PYTHONOMORPHS
PYRITISING	PYROGRAPHY	PYROMETALLURGY	PYROTARTARIC	

QABALISTIC	QUADRIENNIUMS	QUADRIVIAL	QUALIFICATIONS	QUARANTINES
QINGHAOSUS	QUADRIFARIOUS	QUADRIVIUM	QUALIFICATIVE	QUARANTINING
QUACKERIES	QUADRIFOLIATE	QUADRIVIUMS	QUALIFICATIVES	QUARENDENS
QUACKSALVER	QUADRIFORM	QUADROPHONIC	QUALIFICATOR	QUARENDERS
QUACKSALVERS	QUADRIGEMINAL	QUADROPHONICS	QUALIFICATORS	QUARRELERS
QUACKSALVING	QUADRIGEMINATE	QUADROPHONIES	QUALIFICATORY	QUARRELING
QUADCOPTER	QUADRIGEMINOUS	QUADROPHONY	QUALIFIEDLY	QUARRELINGS
QUADCOPTERS	QUADRILATERAL	QUADRUMANE	QUALIFIERS	QUARRELLED
QUADPLEXES	QUADRILATERALS	QUADRUMANES	QUALIFYING	QUARRELLER
QUADRAGENARIAN	QUADRILINGUAL	QUADRUMANOUS	QUALIFYINGS	QUARRELLERS
QUADRAGENARIANS	QUADRILITERAL	QUADRUMANS	QUALITATIVE	QUARRELLING
QUADRAGESIMAL	QUADRILITERALS	QUADRUMVIR	QUALITATIVELY	QUARRELLINGS
QUADRANGLE	QUADRILLED	QUADRUMVIRATE	QUALMISHLY	QUARRELLOUS
QUADRANGLES	QUADRILLER	QUADRUMVIRATES	QUALMISHNESS	QUARRELSOME
QUADRANGULAR	QUADRILLERS	QUADRUMVIRS	QUALMISHNESSES	QUARRELSOMELY
QUADRANGULARLY	QUADRILLES	QUADRUPEDAL	QUANDARIES	QUARRELSOMENESS
QUADRANTAL	QUADRILLING	QUADRUPEDS	QUANGOCRACIES	QUARRENDER
QUADRANTES	QUADRILLION	QUADRUPLED	QUANGOCRACY	QUARRENDERS
QUADRAPHONIC	QUADRILLIONS	QUADRUPLES	QUANTIFIABLE	QUARRIABLE
QUADRAPHONICS	QUADRILLIONTH	QUADRUPLET	QUANTIFICATION	QUARRINGTON
QUADRAPHONIES	QUADRILLIONTHS	QUADRUPLETS	QUANTIFICATIONS	QUARRINGTONS
QUADRAPHONY	QUADRILOCULAR	QUADRUPLEX	QUANTIFIED	QUARRYINGS
QUADRAPLEGIA	QUADRINGENARIES	QUADRUPLEXED	QUANTIFIER	QUARRYMASTER
QUADRAPLEGIAS	QUADRINGENARY	QUADRUPLEXES	QUANTIFIERS	QUARRYMASTERS
QUADRAPLEGIC	QUADRINOMIAL	QUADRUPLEXING	QUANTIFIES	QUARTATION
QUADRAPLEGICS	QUADRINOMIALS	QUADRUPLICATE	QUANTIFYING	QUARTATIONS
QUADRASONIC	QUADRIPARTITE	QUADRUPLICATED	QUANTISATION	QUARTERAGE
QUADRASONICS	QUADRIPARTITION	QUADRUPLICATES	QUANTISATIONS	QUARTERAGES
QUADRATICAL	QUADRIPHONIC	QUADRUPLICATING	QUANTISERS	QUARTERBACK
QUADRATICALLY	QUADRIPHONICS	QUADRUPLICATION	QUANTISING	QUARTERBACKED
QUADRATICS	QUADRIPLEGIA	QUADRUPLICITIES	QUANTITATE	QUARTERBACKING
QUADRATING	QUADRIPLEGIAS	QUADRUPLICITY	QUANTITATED	QUARTERBACKINGS
QUADRATRICES	QUADRIPLEGIC	QUADRUPLIES	QUANTITATES	QUARTERBACKS
QUADRATRIX	QUADRIPLEGICS	QUADRUPLING	QUANTITATING	QUARTERDECK
QUADRATRIXES	QUADRIPOLE	QUADRUPOLE	QUANTITATION	QUARTERDECKER
QUADRATURA	QUADRIPOLES	QUADRUPOLES	QUANTITATIONS	QUARTERDECKERS
QUADRATURE	QUADRIREME	QUAESITUMS	QUANTITATIVE	QUARTERDECKS
QUADRATURES	QUADRIREMES	QUAESTIONARIES	QUANTITATIVELY	QUARTERERS
QUADRATUSES	QUADRISECT	QUAESTIONARY	QUANTITIES	QUARTERFINAL
QUADRELLAS	QUADRISECTED	QUAESTORIAL	QUANTITIVE	QUARTERFINALIST
QUADRENNIA	QUADRISECTING	QUAESTORSHIP	QUANTITIVELY	QUARTERFINALS
QUADRENNIAL	QUADRISECTION	QUAESTORSHIPS	QUANTIVALENCE	QUARTERING
QUADRENNIALLY	QUADRISECTIONS	QUAESTUARIES	QUANTIVALENCES	QUARTERINGS
QUADRENNIALS	QUADRISECTS	QUAESTUARY	QUANTIVALENT	QUARTERLIES
QUADRENNIUM	QUADRISYLLABIC	QUAGGINESS	QUANTIZATION	QUARTERLIFE
QUADRENNIUMS	QUADRISYLLABICS	QUAGGINESSES	QUANTIZATIONS	QUARTERLIGHT
QUADRICEPS	QUADRISYLLABLE	QUAGMIRIER	QUANTIZERS	QUARTERLIGHTS
QUADRICEPSES	QUADRISYLLABLES	QUAGMIRIEST	QUANTIZING	QUARTERMASTER
QUADRICIPITAL	QUADRIVALENCE	QUAGMIRING	QUANTOMETER	QUARTERMASTERS
QUADRICONE	QUADRIVALENCES	QUAINTNESS	QUANTOMETERS	QUARTERMISTRESS
QUADRICONES	QUADRIVALENCIES	QUAINTNESSES	QUAQUAVERSAL	QUARTEROON
QUADRIENNIA	QUADRIVALENCY	QUAKINESSES	QUAQUAVERSALLY	QUARTEROONS
QUADRIENNIAL	QUADRIVALENT	QUALIFIABLE	QUARANTINE	QUARTERSAW
QUADRIENNIUM	QUADRIVALENTS	QUALIFICATION	QUARANTINED	QUARTERSAWED

QUARTERSAWING
QUARTERSAWN
QUARTERSAWS
QUARTERSTAFF
QUARTERSTAFFS
QUARTERSTAVES
QUARTETTES
QUARTODECIMAN
QUARTODECIMANS
QUARTZIEST
QUARTZIFEROUS
QUARTZITES
QUARTZITIC
QUASICRYSTAL
QUASICRYSTALS
QUASIPARTICLE
QUASIPARTICLES
QUASIPERIODIC
QUATERCENTENARY
QUATERNARIES
QUATERNARY
QUATERNATE
QUATERNION
QUATERNIONIST
QUATERNIONISTS
QUATERNIONS
QUATERNITIES
QUATERNITY
QUATORZAIN
QUATORZAINS
QUATREFEUILLE
QUATREFEUILLES
QUATREFOIL
QUATREFOILS
QUATTROCENTISM
QUATTROCENTISMS
QUATTROCENTIST
QUATTROCENTISTS
QUATTROCENTO
QUATTROCENTOS
QUAVERIEST
QUAVERINGLY
QUAVERINGS
QUEACHIEST
QUEASINESS
QUEASINESSES
QUEBRACHOS
QUEECHIEST
QUEENCAKES
QUEENCRAFT
QUEENCRAFTS
QUEENFISHES
QUEENHOODS
QUEENLIEST
QUEENLINESS

QUEENLINESSES
QUEENSHIPS
QUEENSIDES
QUEERCORES
QUEERITIES
QUEERNESSES
QUELQUECHOSE
QUELQUECHOSES
QUENCHABLE
QUENCHINGS
QUENCHLESS
QUENCHLESSLY
QUERCETINS
QUERCETUMS
QUERCITINS
QUERCITRON
QUERCITRONS
QUERIMONIES
QUERIMONIOUS
QUERIMONIOUSLY
QUERNSTONE
QUERNSTONES
QUERSPRUNG
QUERSPRUNGS
QUERULOUSLY
QUERULOUSNESS
QUERULOUSNESSES
QUERYINGLY
QUESADILLA
QUESADILLAS
QUESTINGLY
QUESTIONABILITY
QUESTIONABLE
QUESTIONABLY
QUESTIONARIES
QUESTIONARY
QUESTIONED
QUESTIONEE
QUESTIONEES
QUESTIONER
QUESTIONERS
QUESTIONING
QUESTIONINGLY
QUESTIONINGS
QUESTIONIST
QUESTIONISTS
QUESTIONLESS
QUESTIONLESSLY
QUESTIONNAIRE
QUESTIONNAIRES
QUESTORIAL
QUESTORSHIP
QUESTORSHIPS
QUESTRISTS
QUIBBLINGLY

QUIBBLINGS
QUICKBEAMS
QUICKENERS
QUICKENING
QUICKENINGS
QUICKLIMES
QUICKNESSES
QUICKSANDS
QUICKSILVER
QUICKSILVERED
QUICKSILVERIER
QUICKSILVERIEST
QUICKSILVERING
QUICKSILVERINGS
QUICKSILVERISH
QUICKSILVERS
QUICKSILVERY
QUICKSTEPPED
QUICKSTEPPING
QUICKSTEPS
QUICKTHORN
QUICKTHORNS
QUIDDANIED
QUIDDANIES
QUIDDANYING
QUIDDITATIVE
QUIDDITCHES
QUIDDITIES
QUIESCENCE
QUIESCENCES
QUIESCENCIES
QUIESCENCY
QUIESCENTLY
QUIETENERS
QUIETENING
QUIETENINGS
QUIETISTIC
QUIETNESSES
QUILLBACKS
QUILLWORKS
QUILLWORTS
QUINACRINE
QUINACRINES
QUINALBARBITONE
QUINAQUINA
QUINAQUINAS
QUINCENTENARIES
QUINCENTENARY
QUINCENTENNIAL
QUINCENTENNIALS
QUINCUNCIAL
QUINCUNCIALLY
QUINCUNXES
QUINCUNXIAL
QUINDECAGON

QUINDECAGONS
QUINDECAPLET
QUINDECAPLETS
QUINDECENNIAL
QUINDECENNIALS
QUINDECILLION
QUINDECILLIONS
QUINGENTENARIES
QUINGENTENARY
QUINIDINES
QUINOLINES
QUINOLONES
QUINQUAGENARIAN
QUINQUAGESIMAL
QUINQUECOSTATE
QUINQUEFARIOUS
QUINQUEFOLIATE
QUINQUENNIA
QUINQUENNIAD
QUINQUENNIADS
QUINQUENNIAL
QUINQUENNIALLY
QUINQUENNIALS
QUINQUENNIUM
QUINQUENNIUMS
QUINQUEPARTITE
QUINQUEREME
QUINQUEREMES
QUINQUEVALENCE
QUINQUEVALENCES
QUINQUEVALENCY
QUINQUEVALENT
QUINQUINAS
QUINQUIVALENCE
QUINQUIVALENCES
QUINQUIVALENCY
QUINQUIVALENT
QUINTESSENCE
QUINTESSENCES
QUINTESSENTIAL
QUINTESSENTIALS
QUINTETTES
QUINTILLION
QUINTILLIONS
QUINTILLIONTH
QUINTILLIONTHS
QUINTROONS
QUINTUPLED
QUINTUPLES
QUINTUPLET
QUINTUPLETS
QUINTUPLICATE
QUINTUPLICATED
QUINTUPLICATES
QUINTUPLICATING

QUINTUPLICATION
QUINTUPLIES
QUINTUPLING
QUIRISTERS
QUIRKINESS
QUIRKINESSES
QUISLINGISM
QUISLINGISMS
QUITCLAIMED
QUITCLAIMING
QUITCLAIMS
QUITTANCED
QUITTANCES
QUITTANCING
QUIVERFULS
QUIVERIEST
QUIVERINGLY
QUIVERINGS
QUIVERSFUL
QUIXOTICAL
QUIXOTICALLY
QUIXOTISMS
QUIXOTRIES
QUIZMASTER
QUIZMASTERS
QUIZZERIES
QUIZZICALITIES
QUIZZICALITY
QUIZZICALLY
QUIZZIFICATION
QUIZZIFICATIONS
QUIZZIFIED
QUIZZIFIES
QUIZZIFYING
QUIZZINESS
QUIZZINESSES
QUODLIBETARIAN
QUODLIBETARIANS
QUODLIBETIC
QUODLIBETICAL
QUODLIBETICALLY
QUODLIBETS
QUOTABILITIES
QUOTABILITY
QUOTABLENESS
QUOTABLENESSES
QUOTATIONS
QUOTATIOUS
QUOTATIVES
QUOTEWORTHIER
QUOTEWORTHIEST
QUOTEWORTHY
QUOTIDIANS
QUOTITIONS

R

RABATMENTS
RABATTEMENT
RABATTEMENTS
RABATTINGS
RABBINATES
RABBINICAL
RABBINICALLY
RABBINISMS
RABBINISTIC
RABBINISTS
RABBINITES
RABBITBRUSH
RABBITBRUSHES
RABBITFISH
RABBITFISHES
RABBITIEST
RABBITINGS
RABBITRIES
RABBLEMENT
RABBLEMENTS
RABIDITIES
RABIDNESSES
RACCAHOUTS
RACECOURSE
RACECOURSES
RACEGOINGS
RACEHORSES
RACEMATION
RACEMATIONS
RACEMISATION
RACEMISATIONS
RACEMISING
RACEMIZATION
RACEMIZATIONS
RACEMIZING
RACEMOSELY
RACEMOUSLY
RACETRACKER
RACETRACKERS
RACETRACKS
RACEWALKED
RACEWALKER
RACEWALKERS
RACEWALKING
RACEWALKINGS
RACHIOTOMIES
RACHIOTOMY
RACHISCHISES
RACHISCHISIS
RACHITIDES
RACHITISES
RACIALISED
RACIALISES
RACIALISING

RACIALISMS
RACIALISTIC
RACIALISTS
RACIALIZED
RACIALIZES
RACIALIZING
RACIATIONS
RACINESSES
RACKABONES
RACKETEERED
RACKETEERING
RACKETEERINGS
RACKETEERS
RACKETIEST
RACKETRIES
RACONTEURING
RACONTEURINGS
RACONTEURS
RACONTEUSE
RACONTEUSES
RACQUETBALL
RACQUETBALLS
RACQUETING
RACTOPAMINE
RACTOPAMINES
RADARSCOPE
RADARSCOPES
RADIALISATION
RADIALISATIONS
RADIALISED
RADIALISES
RADIALISING
RADIALITIES
RADIALIZATION
RADIALIZATIONS
RADIALIZED
RADIALIZES
RADIALIZING
RADIANCIES
RADIATIONAL
RADIATIONLESS
RADIATIONS
RADICALISATION
RADICALISATIONS
RADICALISE
RADICALISED
RADICALISES
RADICALISING
RADICALISM
RADICALISMS
RADICALISTIC
RADICALITIES
RADICALITY
RADICALIZATION

RADICALIZATIONS
RADICALIZE
RADICALIZED
RADICALIZES
RADICALIZING
RADICALNESS
RADICALNESSES
RADICATING
RADICATION
RADICATIONS
RADICCHIOS
RADICELLOSE
RADICICOLOUS
RADICIFORM
RADICIVOROUS
RADICULOSE
RADIESTHESIA
RADIESTHESIAS
RADIESTHESIST
RADIESTHESISTS
RADIESTHETIC
RADIOACTIVATE
RADIOACTIVATED
RADIOACTIVATES
RADIOACTIVATING
RADIOACTIVATION
RADIOACTIVE
RADIOACTIVELY
RADIOACTIVITIES
RADIOACTIVITY
RADIOAUTOGRAPH
RADIOAUTOGRAPHS
RADIOAUTOGRAPHY
RADIOBIOLOGIC
RADIOBIOLOGICAL
RADIOBIOLOGIES
RADIOBIOLOGIST
RADIOBIOLOGISTS
RADIOBIOLOGY
RADIOCARBON
RADIOCARBONS
RADIOCHEMICAL
RADIOCHEMICALLY
RADIOCHEMIST
RADIOCHEMISTRY
RADIOCHEMISTS
RADIOECOLOGIES
RADIOECOLOGY
RADIOELEMENT
RADIOELEMENTS
RADIOGENIC
RADIOGOLDS
RADIOGONIOMETER
RADIOGONIOMETRY

RADIOGRAMS
RADIOGRAPH
RADIOGRAPHED
RADIOGRAPHER
RADIOGRAPHERS
RADIOGRAPHIC
RADIOGRAPHIES
RADIOGRAPHING
RADIOGRAPHS
RADIOGRAPHY
RADIOIODINE
RADIOIODINES
RADIOISOTOPE
RADIOISOTOPES
RADIOISOTOPIC
RADIOLABEL
RADIOLABELED
RADIOLABELING
RADIOLABELLED
RADIOLABELLING
RADIOLABELS
RADIOLARIAN
RADIOLARIANS
RADIOLOCATION
RADIOLOCATIONAL
RADIOLOCATIONS
RADIOLOGIC
RADIOLOGICAL
RADIOLOGICALLY
RADIOLOGIES
RADIOLOGIST
RADIOLOGISTS
RADIOLUCENCIES
RADIOLUCENCY
RADIOLUCENT
RADIOLYSES
RADIOLYSIS
RADIOLYTIC
RADIOMETER
RADIOMETERS
RADIOMETRIC
RADIOMETRICALLY
RADIOMETRIES
RADIOMETRY
RADIOMICROMETER
RADIOMIMETIC
RADIONUCLIDE
RADIONUCLIDES
RADIOPACITIES
RADIOPACITY
RADIOPAGER
RADIOPAGERS
RADIOPAGING
RADIOPAGINGS

RADIOPAQUE
RADIOPHONE
RADIOPHONES
RADIOPHONIC
RADIOPHONICALLY
RADIOPHONICS
RADIOPHONIES
RADIOPHONIST
RADIOPHONISTS
RADIOPHONY
RADIOPHOSPHORUS
RADIOPHOTO
RADIOPHOTOS
RADIOPROTECTION
RADIOPROTECTIVE
RADIORESISTANT
RADIOSCOPE
RADIOSCOPES
RADIOSCOPIC
RADIOSCOPICALLY
RADIOSCOPIES
RADIOSCOPY
RADIOSENSITISE
RADIOSENSITISED
RADIOSENSITISES
RADIOSENSITIVE
RADIOSENSITIZE
RADIOSENSITIZED
RADIOSENSITIZES
RADIOSONDE
RADIOSONDES
RADIOSTRONTIUM
RADIOSTRONTIUMS
RADIOTELEGRAM
RADIOTELEGRAMS
RADIOTELEGRAPH
RADIOTELEGRAPHS
RADIOTELEGRAPHY
RADIOTELEMETER
RADIOTELEMETERS
RADIOTELEMETRIC
RADIOTELEMETRY
RADIOTELEPHONE
RADIOTELEPHONED
RADIOTELEPHONES
RADIOTELEPHONIC
RADIOTELEPHONY
RADIOTELETYPE
RADIOTELETYPES
RADIOTHERAPIES
RADIOTHERAPIST
RADIOTHERAPISTS
RADIOTHERAPY
RADIOTHERMIES

RADIOTHERMY	RAKISHNESS	RANGEFINDERS	RAREFIABLE	RATIONALISING
RADIOTHONS	RAKISHNESSES	RANGEFINDING	RAREFICATION	RATIONALISM
RADIOTHORIUM	RALLENTANDI	RANGEFINDINGS	RAREFICATIONAL	RATIONALISMS
RADIOTHORIUMS	RALLENTANDO	RANGELANDS	RAREFICATIONS	RATIONALIST
RADIOTOXIC	RALLENTANDOS	RANGERSHIP	RARENESSES	RATIONALISTIC
RADIOTRACER	RALLYCROSS	RANGERSHIPS	RASCAILLES	RATIONALISTS
RADIOTRACERS	RALLYCROSSES	RANGINESSES	RASCALDOMS	RATIONALITIES
RADULIFORM	RALLYINGLY	RANIVOROUS	RASCALISMS	RATIONALITY
RAFFINATES	RAMAPITHECINE	RANKNESSES	RASCALITIES	RATIONALIZABLE
RAFFINOSES	RAMAPITHECINES	RANKSHIFTED	RASCALLIER	RATIONALIZATION
RAFFISHNESS	RAMBLINGLY	RANKSHIFTING	RASCALLIEST	RATIONALIZE
RAFFISHNESSES	RAMBOUILLET	RANKSHIFTS	RASCALLION	RATIONALIZED
RAFFLESIAS	RAMBOUILLETS	RANSACKERS	RASCALLIONS	RATIONALIZER
RAFTERINGS	RAMBUNCTIOUS	RANSACKING	RASHNESSES	RATIONALIZERS
RAGAMUFFIN	RAMBUNCTIOUSLY	RANSACKINGS	RASPATORIES	RATIONALIZES
RAGAMUFFINS	RAMENTACEOUS	RANSHACKLE	RASPBERRIES	RATIONALIZING
RAGGAMUFFIN	RAMGUNSHOCH	RANSHACKLED	RASPINESSES	RATIONALLY
RAGGAMUFFINS	RAMIFICATION	RANSHACKLES	RASTAFARIAN	RATIONALNESS
RAGGEDIEST	RAMIFICATIONS	RANSHACKLING	RASTAFARIANS	RATIONALNESSES
RAGGEDNESS	RAMMISHNESS	RANSHAKLED	RASTAFARIS	RATIONINGS
RAGGEDNESSES	RAMMISHNESSES	RANSHAKLES	RASTERISED	RATTENINGS
RAGMATICAL	RAMOSITIES	RANSHAKLING	RASTERISES	RATTINESSES
RAGPICKERS	RAMPACIOUS	RANSOMABLE	RASTERISING	RATTLEBAGS
RAILBUSSES	RAMPAGEOUS	RANSOMLESS	RASTERIZED	RATTLEBOXES
RAILLERIES	RAMPAGEOUSLY	RANSOMWARE	RASTERIZES	RATTLEBRAIN
RAILROADED	RAMPAGEOUSNESS	RANSOMWARES	RASTERIZING	RATTLEBRAINED
RAILROADER	RAMPAGINGS	RANTERISMS	RATABILITIES	RATTLEBRAINS
RAILROADERS	RAMPALLIAN	RANTIPOLED	RATABILITY	RATTLEPODS
RAILROADING	RAMPALLIANS	RANTIPOLES	RATABLENESS	RATTLESNAKE
RAILROADINGS	RAMPANCIES	RANTIPOLING	RATABLENESSES	RATTLESNAKES
RAILWAYMAN	RAMPARTING	RANUNCULACEOUS	RATAPLANNED	RATTLETRAP
RAILWAYMEN	RAMPAUGING	RANUNCULUS	RATAPLANNING	RATTLETRAPS
RAILWORKER	RAMRODDING	RANUNCULUSES	RATATOUILLE	RATTLINGLY
RAILWORKERS	RAMSHACKLE	RAPACIOUSLY	RATATOUILLES	RATTOONING
RAINBOWIER	RANCELLING	RAPACIOUSNESS	RATBAGGERIES	RAUCOUSNESS
RAINBOWIEST	RANCHERIAS	RAPACIOUSNESSES	RATBAGGERY	RAUCOUSNESSES
RAINBOWLIKE	RANCHERIES	RAPACITIES	RATCHETING	RAUNCHIEST
RAINCHECKS	RANCHETTES	RAPIDITIES	RATEABILITIES	RAUNCHINESS
RAINFOREST	RANCHLANDS	RAPIDNESSES	RATEABILITY	RAUNCHINESSES
RAINFORESTS	RANCIDITIES	RAPIERLIKE	RATEABLENESS	RAUWOLFIAS
RAININESSES	RANCIDNESS	RAPPELLING	RATEABLENESSES	RAVAGEMENT
RAINMAKERS	RANCIDNESSES	RAPPELLINGS	RATEMETERS	RAVAGEMENTS
RAINMAKING	RANCOROUSLY	RAPPORTAGE	RATEPAYERS	RAVELLIEST
RAINMAKINGS	RANCOROUSNESS	RAPPORTAGES	RATHERIPES	RAVELLINGS
RAINPROOFED	RANCOROUSNESSES	RAPPORTEUR	RATHSKELLER	RAVELMENTS
RAINPROOFING	RANDINESSES	RAPPORTEURS	RATHSKELLERS	RAVENINGLY
RAINPROOFS	RANDOMISATION	RAPPROCHEMENT	RATIFIABLE	RAVENOUSLY
RAINSPOUTS	RANDOMISATIONS	RAPPROCHEMENTS	RATIFICATION	RAVENOUSNESS
RAINSQUALL	RANDOMISED	RAPSCALLION	RATIFICATIONS	RAVENOUSNESSES
RAINSQUALLS	RANDOMISER	RAPSCALLIONS	RATIOCINATE	RAVIGOTTES
RAINSTICKS	RANDOMISERS	RAPTATORIAL	RATIOCINATED	RAVISHINGLY
RAINSTORMS	RANDOMISES	RAPTNESSES	RATIOCINATES	RAVISHMENT
RAINWASHED	RANDOMISING	RAPTURELESS	RATIOCINATING	RAVISHMENTS
RAINWASHES	RANDOMIZATION	RAPTURISED	RATIOCINATION	RAWINSONDE
RAINWASHING	RANDOMIZATIONS	RAPTURISES	RATIOCINATIONS	RAWINSONDES
RAINWATERS	RANDOMIZED	RAPTURISING	RATIOCINATIVE	RAWMAISHES
RAISINIEST	RANDOMIZER	RAPTURISTS	RATIOCINATOR	RAYGRASSES
RAISONNEUR	RANDOMIZERS	RAPTURIZED	RATIOCINATORS	RAYLESSNESS
RAISONNEURS	RANDOMIZES	RAPTURIZES	RATIOCINATORY	RAYLESSNESSES
RAIYATWARI	RANDOMIZING	RAPTURIZING	RATIONALES	RAZMATAZES
RAIYATWARIS	RANDOMNESS	RAPTUROUSLY	RATIONALISABLE	RAZORBACKS
RAJAHSHIPS	RANDOMNESSES	RAPTUROUSNESS	RATIONALISATION	RAZORBILLS
RAJPRAMUKH	RANDOMWISE	RAPTUROUSNESSES	RATIONALISE	RAZORCLAMS
RAJPRAMUKHS	RANGATIRAS	RAREFACTION	RATIONALISED	RAZORFISHES
RAKEHELLIER	RANGATIRATANGA	RAREFACTIONAL	RATIONALISER	RAZZAMATAZZ
RAKEHELLIEST	RANGATIRATANGAS	RAREFACTIONS	RATIONALISERS	RAZZAMATAZZES
RAKESHAMES	RANGEFINDER	RAREFACTIVE	RATIONALISES	RAZZBERRIES

RAZZMATAZZ	REACTIVATION	REAFFIRMING	REANSWERING	REASONABLE
RAZZMATAZZES	REACTIVATIONS	REAFFIXING	REAPPARELED	REASONABLENESS
REABSORBED	REACTIVELY	REAFFOREST	REAPPARELING	REASONABLY
REABSORBING	REACTIVENESS	REAFFORESTATION	REAPPARELLED	REASONEDLY
REABSORPTION	REACTIVENESSES	REAFFORESTED	REAPPARELLING	REASONINGS
REABSORPTIONS	REACTIVITIES	REAFFORESTING	REAPPARELS	REASONLESS
REACCEDING	REACTIVITY	REAFFORESTS	REAPPEARANCE	REASONLESSLY
REACCELERATE	REACTUATED	REAGENCIES	REAPPEARANCES	REASSAILED
REACCELERATED	REACTUATES	REAGGREGATE	REAPPEARED	REASSAILING
REACCELERATES	REACTUATING	REAGGREGATED	REAPPEARING	REASSEMBLAGE
REACCELERATING	READABILITIES	REAGGREGATES	REAPPLICATION	REASSEMBLAGES
REACCENTED	READABILITY	REAGGREGATING	REAPPLICATIONS	REASSEMBLE
REACCENTING	READABLENESS	REAGGREGATION	REAPPLYING	REASSEMBLED
REACCEPTED	READABLENESSES	REAGGREGATIONS	REAPPOINTED	REASSEMBLES
REACCEPTING	READAPTATION	REALIGNING	REAPPOINTING	REASSEMBLIES
REACCESSION	READAPTATIONS	REALIGNMENT	REAPPOINTMENT	REASSEMBLING
REACCESSIONS	READAPTING	REALIGNMENTS	REAPPOINTMENTS	REASSEMBLY
REACCLAIMED	READDICTED	REALISABILITIES	REAPPOINTS	REASSERTED
REACCLAIMING	READDICTING	REALISABILITY	REAPPORTION	REASSERTING
REACCLAIMS	READDRESSED	REALISABLE	REAPPORTIONED	REASSERTION
REACCLIMATISE	READDRESSES	REALISABLY	REAPPORTIONING	REASSERTIONS
REACCLIMATISED	READDRESSING	REALISATION	REAPPORTIONMENT	REASSESSED
REACCLIMATISES	READERLIER	REALISATIONS	REAPPORTIONS	REASSESSES
REACCLIMATISING	READERLIEST	REALISTICALLY	REAPPRAISAL	REASSESSING
REACCLIMATIZE	READERSHIP	REALIZABILITIES	REAPPRAISALS	REASSESSMENT
REACCLIMATIZED	READERSHIPS	REALIZABILITY	REAPPRAISE	REASSESSMENTS
REACCLIMATIZES	READINESSES	REALIZABLE	REAPPRAISED	REASSIGNED
REACCLIMATIZING	READJUSTABLE	REALIZABLY	REAPPRAISEMENT	REASSIGNING
REACCREDIT	READJUSTED	REALIZATION	REAPPRAISEMENTS	REASSIGNMENT
REACCREDITATION	READJUSTER	REALIZATIONS	REAPPRAISER	REASSIGNMENTS
REACCREDITED	READJUSTERS	REALLOCATE	REAPPRAISERS	REASSORTED
REACCREDITING	READJUSTING	REALLOCATED	REAPPRAISES	REASSORTING
REACCREDITS	READJUSTMENT	REALLOCATES	REAPPRAISING	REASSORTMENT
REACCUSING	READJUSTMENTS	REALLOCATING	REAPPROPRIATE	REASSORTMENTS
REACCUSTOM	READMISSION	REALLOCATION	REAPPROPRIATED	REASSUMING
REACCUSTOMED	READMISSIONS	REALLOCATIONS	REAPPROPRIATES	REASSUMPTION
REACCUSTOMING	READMITTANCE	REALLOTMENT	REAPPROPRIATING	REASSUMPTIONS
REACCUSTOMS	READMITTANCES	REALLOTMENTS	REAPPROVED	REASSURANCE
REACQUAINT	READMITTED	REALLOTTED	REAPPROVES	REASSURANCES
REACQUAINTANCE	READMITTING	REALLOTTING	REAPPROVING	REASSURERS
REACQUAINTANCES	READOPTING	REALNESSES	REARGUARDS	REASSURING
REACQUAINTED	READOPTION	REALPOLITIK	REARGUMENT	REASSURINGLY
REACQUAINTING	READOPTIONS	REALPOLITIKER	REARGUMENTS	REASTINESS
REACQUAINTS	READORNING	REALPOLITIKERS	REARHORSES	REASTINESSES
REACQUIRED	READVANCED	REALPOLITIKS	REARMAMENT	REATTACHED
REACQUIRES	READVANCES	REALTERING	REARMAMENTS	REATTACHES
REACQUIRING	READVANCING	REAMENDING	REAROUSALS	REATTACHING
REACQUISITION	READVERTISE	REAMENDMENT	REAROUSING	REATTACHMENT
REACQUISITIONS	READVERTISED	REAMENDMENTS	REARRANGED	REATTACHMENTS
REACTANCES	READVERTISEMENT	REANALYSED	REARRANGEMENT	REATTACKED
REACTIONAL	READVERTISES	REANALYSES	REARRANGEMENTS	REATTACKING
REACTIONARIES	READVERTISING	REANALYSING	REARRANGER	REATTAINED
REACTIONARISM	READVERTIZE	REANALYSIS	REARRANGERS	REATTAINING
REACTIONARISMS	READVERTIZED	REANALYZED	REARRANGES	REATTEMPTED
REACTIONARIST	READVERTIZEMENT	REANALYZES	REARRANGING	REATTEMPTING
REACTIONARISTS	READVERTIZES	REANALYZING	REARRESTED	REATTEMPTS
REACTIONARY	READVERTIZING	REANIMATED	REARRESTING	REATTRIBUTE
REACTIONARYISM	READVISING	REANIMATES	REARTICULATE	REATTRIBUTED
REACTIONARYISMS	READYMADES	REANIMATING	REARTICULATED	REATTRIBUTES
REACTIONISM	REAEDIFIED	REANIMATION	REARTICULATES	REATTRIBUTING
REACTIONISMS	REAEDIFIES	REANIMATIONS	REARTICULATING	REATTRIBUTION
REACTIONIST	REAEDIFYED	REANNEXATION	REASCENDED	REATTRIBUTIONS
REACTIONISTS	REAEDIFYES	REANNEXATIONS	REASCENDING	REAUTHORISATION
REACTIVATE	REAEDIFYING	REANNEXING	REASCENSION	REAUTHORISE
REACTIVATED	REAFFIRMATION	REANOINTED	REASCENSIONS	REAUTHORISED
REACTIVATES	REAFFIRMATIONS	REANOINTING	REASONABILITIES	REAUTHORISES
REACTIVATING	REAFFIRMED	REANSWERED	REASONABILITY	REAUTHORISING

REAUTHORIZATION	REBUTTONING	RECAPPABLE	RECESSIONISTAS	RECIRCLING
REAUTHORIZE	RECALCITRANCE	RECAPTIONS	RECESSIONS	RECIRCULATE
REAUTHORIZED	RECALCITRANCES	RECAPTURED	RECESSIVELY	RECIRCULATED
REAUTHORIZES	RECALCITRANCIES	RECAPTURER	RECESSIVENESS	RECIRCULATES
REAUTHORIZING	RECALCITRANCY	RECAPTURERS	RECESSIVENESSES	RECIRCULATING
REAVAILING	RECALCITRANT	RECAPTURES	RECESSIVES	RECIRCULATION
REAWAKENED	RECALCITRANTS	RECAPTURING	RECHALLENGE	RECIRCULATIONS
REAWAKENING	RECALCITRATE	RECARPETED	RECHALLENGED	RECITALIST
REAWAKENINGS	RECALCITRATED	RECARPETING	RECHALLENGES	RECITALISTS
REBALANCED	RECALCITRATES	RECARRYING	RECHALLENGING	RECITATION
REBALANCES	RECALCITRATING	RECATALOGED	RECHANGING	RECITATIONIST
REBALANCING	RECALCITRATION	RECATALOGING	RECHANNELED	RECITATIONISTS
REBAPTISED	RECALCITRATIONS	RECATALOGS	RECHANNELING	RECITATIONS
REBAPTISES	RECALCULATE	RECATALOGUE	RECHANNELLED	RECITATIVE
REBAPTISING	RECALCULATED	RECATALOGUED	RECHANNELLING	RECITATIVES
REBAPTISMS	RECALCULATES	RECATALOGUES	RECHANNELS	RECITATIVI
REBAPTIZED	RECALCULATING	RECATALOGUING	RECHARGEABLE	RECITATIVO
REBAPTIZES	RECALCULATION	RECATCHING	RECHARGERS	RECITATIVOS
REBAPTIZING	RECALCULATIONS	RECAUTIONED	RECHARGING	RECKLESSLY
REBARBATIVE	RECALESCED	RECAUTIONING	RECHARTERED	RECKLESSNESS
REBARBATIVELY	RECALESCENCE	RECAUTIONS	RECHARTERING	RECKLESSNESSES
REBATEABLE	RECALESCENCES	RECEIPTING	RECHARTERS	RECKONINGS
REBATEMENT	RECALESCENT	RECEIPTORS	RECHARTING	RECLADDING
REBATEMENTS	RECALESCES	RECEIVABILITIES	RECHAUFFES	RECLAIMABLE
REBBETZINS	RECALESCING	RECEIVABILITY	RECHEATING	RECLAIMABLY
REBEGINNING	RECALIBRATE	RECEIVABLE	RECHECKING	RECLAIMANT
REBELLIONS	RECALIBRATED	RECEIVABLENESS	RECHIPPING	RECLAIMANTS
REBELLIOUS	RECALIBRATES	RECEIVABLES	RECHIPPINGS	RECLAIMERS
REBELLIOUSLY	RECALIBRATING	RECEIVERSHIP	RECHOOSING	RECLAIMING
REBELLIOUSNESS	RECALIBRATION	RECEIVERSHIPS	RECHOREOGRAPH	RECLAMATION
REBELLOWED	RECALIBRATIONS	RECEIVINGS	RECHOREOGRAPHED	RECLAMATIONS
REBELLOWING	RECALLABILITIES	RECEMENTED	RECHOREOGRAPHS	RECLASPING
REBIRTHERS	RECALLABILITY	RECEMENTING	RECHRISTEN	RECLASSIFIED
REBIRTHING	RECALLABLE	RECENSIONS	RECHRISTENED	RECLASSIFIES
REBIRTHINGS	RECALLMENT	RECENSORED	RECHRISTENING	RECLASSIFY
REBLENDING	RECALLMENTS	RECENSORING	RECHRISTENS	RECLASSIFYING
REBLOCHONS	RECALMENTS	RECENTNESS	RECHROMATOGRAPH	RECLEANING
REBLOOMERS	RECANALISATION	RECENTNESSES	RECIDIVISM	RECLIMBING
REBLOOMING	RECANALISATIONS	RECENTRIFUGE	RECIDIVISMS	RECLINABLE
REBLOSSOMED	RECANALISE	RECENTRIFUGED	RECIDIVIST	RECLINATION
REBLOSSOMING	RECANALISED	RECENTRIFUGES	RECIDIVISTIC	RECLINATIONS
REBLOSSOMS	RECANALISES	RECENTRIFUGING	RECIDIVISTS	RECLOSABLE
REBOARDING	RECANALISING	RECENTRING	RECIDIVOUS	RECLOTHING
REBOATIONS	RECANALIZATION	RECEPTACLE	RECIPIENCE	RECLUSENESS
REBORROWED	RECANALIZATIONS	RECEPTACLES	RECIPIENCES	RECLUSENESSES
REBORROWING	RECANALIZE	RECEPTACULA	RECIPIENCIES	RECLUSIONS
REBOTTLING	RECANALIZED	RECEPTACULAR	RECIPIENCY	RECLUSIVELY
REBOUNDERS	RECANALIZES	RECEPTACULUM	RECIPIENTS	RECLUSIVENESS
REBOUNDING	RECANALIZING	RECEPTIBILITIES	RECIPROCAL	RECLUSIVENESSES
REBOUNDINGS	RECANTATION	RECEPTIBILITY	RECIPROCALITIES	RECLUSORIES
REBRANCHED	RECANTATIONS	RECEPTIBLE	RECIPROCALITY	RECODIFICATION
REBRANCHES	RECAPITALISE	RECEPTIONIST	RECIPROCALLY	RECODIFICATIONS
REBRANCHING	RECAPITALISED	RECEPTIONISTS	RECIPROCALS	RECODIFIED
REBRANDING	RECAPITALISES	RECEPTIONS	RECIPROCANT	RECODIFIES
REBRANDINGS	RECAPITALISING	RECEPTIVELY	RECIPROCANTS	RECODIFYING
REBREEDING	RECAPITALIZE	RECEPTIVENESS	RECIPROCATE	RECOGNISABILITY
REBROADCAST	RECAPITALIZED	RECEPTIVENESSES	RECIPROCATED	RECOGNISABLE
REBROADCASTED	RECAPITALIZES	RECEPTIVITIES	RECIPROCATES	RECOGNISABLY
REBROADCASTING	RECAPITALIZING	RECEPTIVITY	RECIPROCATING	RECOGNISANCE
REBROADCASTS	RECAPITULATE	RECERTIFICATION	RECIPROCATION	RECOGNISANCES
REBUILDING	RECAPITULATED	RECERTIFIED	RECIPROCATIONS	RECOGNISANT
REBUILDINGS	RECAPITULATES	RECERTIFIES	RECIPROCATIVE	RECOGNISED
REBUKEFULLY	RECAPITULATING	RECERTIFYING	RECIPROCATOR	RECOGNISEE
REBUKINGLY	RECAPITULATION	RECESSIONAL	RECIPROCATORS	RECOGNISEES
REBUTMENTS	RECAPITULATIONS	RECESSIONALS	RECIPROCATORY	RECOGNISER
REBUTTABLE	RECAPITULATIVE	RECESSIONARY	RECIPROCITIES	RECOGNISERS
REBUTTONED	RECAPITULATORY	RECESSIONISTA	RECIPROCITY	RECOGNISES

RECOGNISING	RECOMMENCING	RECONCILABILITY	RECONQUERING	RECONVALESCENCE
RECOGNISOR	RECOMMENDABLE	RECONCILABLE	RECONQUERS	RECONVALESCENT
RECOGNISORS	RECOMMENDABLY	RECONCILABLY	RECONQUEST	RECONVALESCES
RECOGNITION	RECOMMENDATION	RECONCILED	RECONQUESTS	RECONVALESCING
RECOGNITIONS	RECOMMENDATIONS	RECONCILEMENT	RECONSECRATE	RECONVENED
RECOGNITIVE	RECOMMENDATORY	RECONCILEMENTS	RECONSECRATED	RECONVENES
RECOGNITORY	RECOMMENDED	RECONCILER	RECONSECRATES	RECONVENING
RECOGNIZABILITY	RECOMMENDER	RECONCILERS	RECONSECRATING	RECONVERSION
RECOGNIZABLE	RECOMMENDERS	RECONCILES	RECONSECRATION	RECONVERSIONS
RECOGNIZABLY	RECOMMENDING	RECONCILIATION	RECONSECRATIONS	RECONVERTED
RECOGNIZANCE	RECOMMENDS	RECONCILIATIONS	RECONSIDER	RECONVERTING
RECOGNIZANCES	RECOMMISSION	RECONCILIATORY	RECONSIDERATION	RECONVERTS
RECOGNIZANT	RECOMMISSIONED	RECONCILING	RECONSIDERED	RECONVEYANCE
RECOGNIZED	RECOMMISSIONING	RECONDENSATION	RECONSIDERING	RECONVEYANCES
RECOGNIZEE	RECOMMISSIONS	RECONDENSATIONS	RECONSIDERS	RECONVEYED
RECOGNIZEES	RECOMMITMENT	RECONDENSE	RECONSIGNED	RECONVEYING
RECOGNIZER	RECOMMITMENTS	RECONDENSED	RECONSIGNING	RECONVICTED
RECOGNIZERS	RECOMMITTAL	RECONDENSES	RECONSIGNS	RECONVICTING
RECOGNIZES	RECOMMITTALS	RECONDENSING	RECONSOLED	RECONVICTION
RECOGNIZING	RECOMMITTED	RECONDITELY	RECONSOLES	RECONVICTIONS
RECOGNIZOR	RECOMMITTING	RECONDITENESS	RECONSOLIDATE	RECONVICTS
RECOGNIZORS	RECOMPACTED	RECONDITENESSES	RECONSOLIDATED	RECONVINCE
RECOILLESS	RECOMPACTING	RECONDITION	RECONSOLIDATES	RECONVINCED
RECOINAGES	RECOMPACTS	RECONDITIONED	RECONSOLIDATING	RECONVINCES
RECOLLECTED	RECOMPENCE	RECONDITIONING	RECONSOLIDATION	RECONVINCING
RECOLLECTEDLY	RECOMPENCES	RECONDITIONS	RECONSOLING	RECORDABLE
RECOLLECTEDNESS	RECOMPENSABLE	RECONDUCTED	RECONSTITUENT	RECORDATION
RECOLLECTING	RECOMPENSE	RECONDUCTING	RECONSTITUENTS	RECORDATIONS
RECOLLECTION	RECOMPENSED	RECONDUCTS	RECONSTITUTABLE	RECORDERSHIP
RECOLLECTIONS	RECOMPENSER	RECONFERRED	RECONSTITUTE	RECORDERSHIPS
RECOLLECTIVE	RECOMPENSERS	RECONFERRING	RECONSTITUTED	RECORDINGS
RECOLLECTIVELY	RECOMPENSES	RECONFIGURATION	RECONSTITUTES	RECORDISTS
RECOLLECTS	RECOMPENSING	RECONFIGURE	RECONSTITUTING	RECOUNTALS
RECOLONISATION	RECOMPILATION	RECONFIGURED	RECONSTITUTION	RECOUNTERS
RECOLONISATIONS	RECOMPILATIONS	RECONFIGURES	RECONSTITUTIONS	RECOUNTING
RECOLONISE	RECOMPILED	RECONFIGURING	RECONSTRUCT	RECOUNTMENT
RECOLONISED	RECOMPILES	RECONFINED	RECONSTRUCTED	RECOUNTMENTS
RECOLONISES	RECOMPILING	RECONFINES	RECONSTRUCTIBLE	RECOUPABLE
RECOLONISING	RECOMPOSED	RECONFINING	RECONSTRUCTING	RECOUPLING
RECOLONIZATION	RECOMPOSES	RECONFIRMATION	RECONSTRUCTION	RECOUPMENT
RECOLONIZATIONS	RECOMPOSING	RECONFIRMATIONS	RECONSTRUCTIONS	RECOUPMENTS
RECOLONIZE	RECOMPOSITION	RECONFIRMED	RECONSTRUCTIVE	RECOURSING
RECOLONIZED	RECOMPOSITIONS	RECONFIRMING	RECONSTRUCTOR	RECOVERABILITY
RECOLONIZES	RECOMPRESS	RECONFIRMS	RECONSTRUCTORS	RECOVERABLE
RECOLONIZING	RECOMPRESSED	RECONNAISSANCE	RECONSTRUCTS	RECOVERABLENESS
RECOLORING	RECOMPRESSES	RECONNAISSANCES	RECONSULTED	RECOVEREES
RECOLOURED	RECOMPRESSING	RECONNECTED	RECONSULTING	RECOVERERS
RECOLOURING	RECOMPRESSION	RECONNECTING	RECONSULTS	RECOVERIES
RECOMBINANT	RECOMPRESSIONS	RECONNECTION	RECONTACTED	RECOVERING
RECOMBINANTS	RECOMPUTATION	RECONNECTIONS	RECONTACTING	RECOVERORS
RECOMBINATION	RECOMPUTATIONS	RECONNECTS	RECONTACTS	RECOWERING
RECOMBINATIONAL	RECOMPUTED	RECONNOISSANCE	RECONTAMINATE	RECREANCES
RECOMBINATIONS	RECOMPUTES	RECONNOISSANCES	RECONTAMINATED	RECREANCIES
RECOMBINED	RECOMPUTING	RECONNOITER	RECONTAMINATES	RECREANTLY
RECOMBINES	RECONCEIVE	RECONNOITERED	RECONTAMINATING	RECREATING
RECOMBINING	RECONCEIVED	RECONNOITERER	RECONTAMINATION	RECREATION
RECOMFORTED	RECONCEIVES	RECONNOITERERS	RECONTEXTUALISE	RECREATIONAL
RECOMFORTING	RECONCEIVING	RECONNOITERING	RECONTEXTUALIZE	RECREATIONALLY
RECOMFORTLESS	RECONCENTRATE	RECONNOITERS	RECONTINUE	RECREATIONIST
RECOMFORTS	RECONCENTRATED	RECONNOITRE	RECONTINUED	RECREATIONISTS
RECOMFORTURE	RECONCENTRATES	RECONNOITRED	RECONTINUES	RECREATIONS
RECOMFORTURES	RECONCENTRATING	RECONNOITRER	RECONTINUING	RECREATIVE
RECOMMENCE	RECONCENTRATION	RECONNOITRERS	RECONTOURED	RECREATIVELY
RECOMMENCED	RECONCEPTION	RECONNOITRES	RECONTOURING	RECREATORS
RECOMMENCEMENT	RECONCEPTIONS	RECONNOITRING	RECONTOURS	RECREMENTAL
RECOMMENCEMENTS	RECONCEPTUALISE	RECONNOITRINGS	RECONVALESCE	RECREMENTITIAL
RECOMMENCES	RECONCEPTUALIZE	RECONQUERED	RECONVALESCED	RECREMENTITIOUS

RECREMENTS
RECRIMINATE
RECRIMINATED
RECRIMINATES
RECRIMINATING
RECRIMINATION
RECRIMINATIONS
RECRIMINATIVE
RECRIMINATOR
RECRIMINATORS
RECRIMINATORY
RECROSSING
RECROWNING
RECRUDESCE
RECRUDESCED
RECRUDESCENCE
RECRUDESCENCES
RECRUDESCENCIES
RECRUDESCENCY
RECRUDESCENT
RECRUDESCES
RECRUDESCING
RECRUITABLE
RECRUITALS
RECRUITERS
RECRUITING
RECRUITINGS
RECRUITMENT
RECRUITMENTS
RECRYSTALLISE
RECRYSTALLISED
RECRYSTALLISES
RECRYSTALLISING
RECRYSTALLIZE
RECRYSTALLIZED
RECRYSTALLIZES
RECRYSTALLIZING
RECTANGLED
RECTANGLES
RECTANGULAR
RECTANGULARITY
RECTANGULARLY
RECTIFIABILITY
RECTIFIABLE
RECTIFICATION
RECTIFICATIONS
RECTIFIERS
RECTIFYING
RECTILINEAL
RECTILINEALLY
RECTILINEAR
RECTILINEARITY
RECTILINEARLY
RECTIPETALIES
RECTIPETALITIES
RECTIPETALITY
RECTIPETALY
RECTIROSTRAL
RECTISERIAL
RECTITISES
RECTITUDES
RECTITUDINOUS
RECTOCELES
RECTORATES
RECTORESSES
RECTORIALS
RECTORSHIP

RECTORSHIPS
RECTRESSES
RECTRICIAL
RECULTIVATE
RECULTIVATED
RECULTIVATES
RECULTIVATING
RECUMBENCE
RECUMBENCES
RECUMBENCIES
RECUMBENCY
RECUMBENTLY
RECUPERABLE
RECUPERATE
RECUPERATED
RECUPERATES
RECUPERATING
RECUPERATION
RECUPERATIONS
RECUPERATIVE
RECUPERATOR
RECUPERATORS
RECUPERATORY
RECURELESS
RECURRENCE
RECURRENCES
RECURRENCIES
RECURRENCY
RECURRENTLY
RECURRINGLY
RECURSIONS
RECURSIVELY
RECURSIVENESS
RECURSIVENESSES
RECURVIROSTRAL
RECUSANCES
RECUSANCIES
RECUSATION
RECUSATIONS
RECYCLABLE
RECYCLABLES
RECYCLATES
RECYCLEABLE
RECYCLEABLES
RECYCLINGS
RECYCLISTS
REDACTIONAL
REDACTIONS
REDACTORIAL
REDAMAGING
REDARGUING
REDBAITERS
REDBAITING
REDBELLIES
REDBREASTS
REDCURRANT
REDCURRANTS
REDDISHNESS
REDDISHNESSES
REDECIDING
REDECORATE
REDECORATED
REDECORATES
REDECORATING
REDECORATION
REDECORATIONS
REDECORATOR

REDECORATORS
REDECRAFTS
REDEDICATE
REDEDICATED
REDEDICATES
REDEDICATING
REDEDICATION
REDEDICATIONS
REDEEMABILITIES
REDEEMABILITY
REDEEMABLE
REDEEMABLENESS
REDEEMABLY
REDEEMLESS
REDEFEATED
REDEFEATING
REDEFECTED
REDEFECTING
REDEFINING
REDEFINITION
REDEFINITIONS
REDELIVERANCE
REDELIVERANCES
REDELIVERED
REDELIVERER
REDELIVERERS
REDELIVERIES
REDELIVERING
REDELIVERS
REDELIVERY
REDEMANDED
REDEMANDING
REDEMPTIBLE
REDEMPTION
REDEMPTIONAL
REDEMPTIONER
REDEMPTIONERS
REDEMPTIONS
REDEMPTIVE
REDEMPTIVELY
REDEMPTORY
REDEPLOYED
REDEPLOYING
REDEPLOYMENT
REDEPLOYMENTS
REDEPOSITED
REDEPOSITING
REDEPOSITS
REDESCENDED
REDESCENDING
REDESCENDS
REDESCRIBE
REDESCRIBED
REDESCRIBES
REDESCRIBING
REDESCRIPTION
REDESCRIPTIONS
REDESIGNED
REDESIGNING
REDETERMINATION
REDETERMINE
REDETERMINED
REDETERMINES
REDETERMINING
REDEVELOPED
REDEVELOPER
REDEVELOPERS

REDEVELOPING
REDEVELOPMENT
REDEVELOPMENTS
REDEVELOPS
REDIALLING
REDICTATED
REDICTATES
REDICTATING
REDIGESTED
REDIGESTING
REDIGESTION
REDIGESTIONS
REDIGRESSED
REDIGRESSES
REDIGRESSING
REDINGOTES
REDINTEGRATE
REDINTEGRATED
REDINTEGRATES
REDINTEGRATING
REDINTEGRATION
REDINTEGRATIONS
REDINTEGRATIVE
REDIRECTED
REDIRECTING
REDIRECTION
REDIRECTIONS
REDISBURSE
REDISBURSED
REDISBURSES
REDISBURSING
REDISCOUNT
REDISCOUNTABLE
REDISCOUNTED
REDISCOUNTING
REDISCOUNTS
REDISCOVER
REDISCOVERED
REDISCOVERER
REDISCOVERERS
REDISCOVERIES
REDISCOVERING
REDISCOVERS
REDISCOVERY
REDISCUSSED
REDISCUSSES
REDISCUSSING
REDISPLAYED
REDISPLAYING
REDISPLAYS
REDISPOSED
REDISPOSES
REDISPOSING
REDISPOSITION
REDISPOSITIONS
REDISSOLUTION
REDISSOLUTIONS
REDISSOLVE
REDISSOLVED
REDISSOLVES
REDISSOLVING
REDISTILLATION
REDISTILLATIONS
REDISTILLED
REDISTILLING
REDISTILLS
REDISTRIBUTE

REDISTRIBUTED
REDISTRIBUTES
REDISTRIBUTING
REDISTRIBUTION
REDISTRIBUTIONS
REDISTRIBUTIVE
REDISTRICT
REDISTRICTED
REDISTRICTING
REDISTRICTINGS
REDISTRICTS
REDIVIDING
REDIVISION
REDIVISIONS
REDIVORCED
REDIVORCES
REDIVORCING
REDLININGS
REDOLENCES
REDOLENCIES
REDOLENTLY
REDOUBLEMENT
REDOUBLEMENTS
REDOUBLERS
REDOUBLING
REDOUBTABLE
REDOUBTABLENESS
REDOUBTABLY
REDOUBTING
REDOUNDING
REDOUNDINGS
REDRAFTING
REDREAMING
REDRESSABLE
REDRESSALS
REDRESSERS
REDRESSIBLE
REDRESSING
REDRESSIVE
REDRESSORS
REDRILLING
REDRUTHITE
REDRUTHITES
REDSHIFTED
REDSHIRTED
REDSHIRTING
REDSTREAKS
REDUCIBILITIES
REDUCIBILITY
REDUCIBLENESS
REDUCIBLENESSES
REDUCTANTS
REDUCTASES
REDUCTIONAL
REDUCTIONISM
REDUCTIONISMS
REDUCTIONIST
REDUCTIONISTIC
REDUCTIONISTS
REDUCTIONS
REDUCTIVELY
REDUCTIVENESS
REDUCTIVENESSES
REDUCTIVES
REDUNDANCE
REDUNDANCES
REDUNDANCIES

r

REDUNDANCY	REENCOUNTERED	REEVALUATED	REFERENTIALLY	REFLEXIVES
REDUNDANTLY	REENCOUNTERING	REEVALUATES	REFERRABLE	REFLEXIVITIES
REDUPLICATE	REENCOUNTERS	REEVALUATING	REFERRIBLE	REFLEXIVITY
REDUPLICATED	REENDOWING	REEVALUATION	REFIGHTING	REFLEXOLOGICAL
REDUPLICATES	REENERGISE	REEVALUATIONS	REFIGURING	REFLEXOLOGIES
REDUPLICATING	REENERGISED	REEVESHIPS	REFILLABLE	REFLEXOLOGIST
REDUPLICATION	REENERGISES	REEXAMINATION	REFILTERED	REFLEXOLOGISTS
REDUPLICATIONS	REENERGISING	REEXAMINATIONS	REFILTERING	REFLEXOLOGY
REDUPLICATIVE	REENERGIZE	REEXAMINED	REFINANCED	REFLOATING
REDUPLICATIVELY	REENERGIZED	REEXAMINES	REFINANCES	REFLOODING
REEDIFYING	REENERGIZES	REEXAMINING	REFINANCING	REFLOWERED
REEDINESSES	REENERGIZING	REEXECUTED	REFINANCINGS	REFLOWERING
REEDITIONS	REENFORCED	REEXECUTES	REFINEDNESS	REFLOWERINGS
REEDUCATED	REENFORCES	REEXECUTING	REFINEDNESSES	REFLOWINGS
REEDUCATES	REENFORCING	REEXHIBITED	REFINEMENT	REFLUENCES
REEDUCATING	REENGAGEMENT	REEXHIBITING	REFINEMENTS	REFOCILLATE
REEDUCATION	REENGAGEMENTS	REEXHIBITS	REFINERIES	REFOCILLATED
REEDUCATIONS	REENGAGING	REEXPELLED	REFINISHED	REFOCILLATES
REEDUCATIVE	REENGINEER	REEXPELLING	REFINISHER	REFOCILLATING
REEFPOINTS	REENGINEERED	REEXPERIENCE	REFINISHERS	REFOCILLATION
REEJECTING	REENGINEERING	REEXPERIENCED	REFINISHES	REFOCILLATIONS
REELECTING	REENGINEERS	REEXPERIENCES	REFINISHING	REFOCUSING
REELECTION	REENGRAVED	REEXPERIENCING	REFITMENTS	REFOCUSSED
REELECTIONS	REENGRAVES	REEXPLAINED	REFITTINGS	REFOCUSSES
REELEVATED	REENGRAVING	REEXPLAINING	REFLAGGING	REFOCUSSING
REELEVATES	REENJOYING	REEXPLAINS	REFLATIONARY	REFORESTATION
REELEVATING	REENLARGED	REEXPLORED	REFLATIONS	REFORESTATIONS
REELIGIBILITIES	REENLARGES	REEXPLORES	REFLECTANCE	REFORESTED
REELIGIBILITY	REENLARGING	REEXPLORING	REFLECTANCES	REFORESTING
REELIGIBLE	REENLISTED	REEXPORTATION	REFLECTERS	REFORMABILITIES
REEMBARKED	REENLISTING	REEXPORTATIONS	REFLECTING	REFORMABILITY
REEMBARKING	REENLISTMENT	REEXPORTED	REFLECTINGLY	REFORMABLE
REEMBODIED	REENLISTMENTS	REEXPORTING	REFLECTION	REFORMADES
REEMBODIES	REENROLLED	REEXPOSING	REFLECTIONAL	REFORMADOES
REEMBODYING	REENROLLING	REEXPOSURE	REFLECTIONLESS	REFORMADOS
REEMBRACED	REENSLAVED	REEXPOSURES	REFLECTIONS	REFORMATES
REEMBRACES	REENSLAVES	REEXPRESSED	REFLECTIVE	REFORMATION
REEMBRACING	REENSLAVING	REEXPRESSES	REFLECTIVELY	REFORMATIONAL
REEMBROIDER	REENTERING	REEXPRESSING	REFLECTIVENESS	REFORMATIONIST
REEMBROIDERED	REENTHRONE	REFASHIONED	REFLECTIVITIES	REFORMATIONISTS
REEMBROIDERING	REENTHRONED	REFASHIONING	REFLECTIVITY	REFORMATIONS
REEMBROIDERS	REENTHRONES	REFASHIONMENT	REFLECTOGRAM	REFORMATIVE
REEMERGENCE	REENTHRONING	REFASHIONMENTS	REFLECTOGRAMS	REFORMATORIES
REEMERGENCES	REENTRANCE	REFASHIONS	REFLECTOGRAPH	REFORMATORY
REEMERGING	REENTRANCES	REFASTENED	REFLECTOGRAPHS	REFORMATTED
REEMISSION	REENTRANTS	REFASTENING	REFLECTOGRAPHY	REFORMATTING
REEMISSIONS	REEQUIPMENT	REFECTIONER	REFLECTOMETER	REFORMINGS
REEMITTING	REEQUIPMENTS	REFECTIONERS	REFLECTOMETERS	REFORMISMS
REEMPHASES	REEQUIPPED	REFECTIONS	REFLECTOMETRIES	REFORMISTS
REEMPHASIS	REEQUIPPING	REFECTORIAN	REFLECTOMETRY	REFORMULATE
REEMPHASISE	REERECTING	REFECTORIANS	REFLECTORISE	REFORMULATED
REEMPHASISED	REESCALATE	REFECTORIES	REFLECTORISED	REFORMULATES
REEMPHASISES	REESCALATED	REFEEDINGS	REFLECTORISES	REFORMULATING
REEMPHASISING	REESCALATES	REFEREEING	REFLECTORISING	REFORMULATION
REEMPHASIZE	REESCALATING	REFEREEINGS	REFLECTORIZE	REFORMULATIONS
REEMPHASIZED	REESCALATION	REFERENCED	REFLECTORIZED	REFORTIFICATION
REEMPHASIZES	REESCALATIONS	REFERENCER	REFLECTORIZES	REFORTIFIED
REEMPHASIZING	REESTABLISH	REFERENCERS	REFLECTORIZING	REFORTIFIES
REEMPLOYED	REESTABLISHED	REFERENCES	REFLECTORS	REFORTIFYING
REEMPLOYING	REESTABLISHES	REFERENCING	REFLEXIBILITIES	REFOULEMENT
REEMPLOYMENT	REESTABLISHING	REFERENCINGS	REFLEXIBILITY	REFOULEMENTS
REEMPLOYMENTS	REESTABLISHMENT	REFERENDARIES	REFLEXIBLE	REFOUNDATION
REENACTING	REESTIMATE	REFERENDARY	REFLEXIONAL	REFOUNDATIONS
REENACTMENT	REESTIMATED	REFERENDUM	REFLEXIONS	REFOUNDERS
REENACTMENTS	REESTIMATES	REFERENDUMS	REFLEXIVELY	REFOUNDING
REENACTORS	REESTIMATING	REFERENTIAL	REFLEXIVENESS	REFRACTABLE
REENCOUNTER	REEVALUATE	REFERENTIALITY	REFLEXIVENESSES	REFRACTARIES

REFRACTARY	REFUELLING	REGENTSHIPS	REGRETTABLE	REHOSPITALISED
REFRACTILE	REFUELLINGS	REGGAETONS	REGRETTABLY	REHOSPITALISES
REFRACTING	REFUGEEISM	REGIMENTAL	REGRETTERS	REHOSPITALISING
REFRACTION	REFUGEEISMS	REGIMENTALLY	REGRETTING	REHOSPITALIZE
REFRACTIONS	REFULGENCE	REGIMENTALS	REGRINDING	REHOSPITALIZED
REFRACTIVE	REFULGENCES	REGIMENTATION	REGROOMING	REHOSPITALIZES
REFRACTIVELY	REFULGENCIES	REGIMENTATIONS	REGROOVING	REHOSPITALIZING
REFRACTIVENESS	REFULGENCY	REGIMENTED	REGROUPING	REHOUSINGS
REFRACTIVITIES	REFULGENTLY	REGIMENTING	REGROUPINGS	REHUMANISE
REFRACTIVITY	REFUNDABILITIES	REGIONALISATION	REGUERDONED	REHUMANISED
REFRACTOMETER	REFUNDABILITY	REGIONALISE	REGUERDONING	REHUMANISES
REFRACTOMETERS	REFUNDABLE	REGIONALISED	REGUERDONS	REHUMANISING
REFRACTOMETRIC	REFUNDINGS	REGIONALISES	REGULARISATION	REHUMANIZE
REFRACTOMETRIES	REFUNDMENT	REGIONALISING	REGULARISATIONS	REHUMANIZED
REFRACTOMETRY	REFUNDMENTS	REGIONALISM	REGULARISE	REHUMANIZES
REFRACTORIES	REFURBISHED	REGIONALISMS	REGULARISED	REHUMANIZING
REFRACTORILY	REFURBISHER	REGIONALIST	REGULARISES	REHYDRATABLE
REFRACTORINESS	REFURBISHERS	REGIONALISTIC	REGULARISING	REHYDRATED
REFRACTORS	REFURBISHES	REGIONALISTS	REGULARITIES	REHYDRATES
REFRACTORY	REFURBISHING	REGIONALIZATION	REGULARITY	REHYDRATING
REFRACTURE	REFURBISHINGS	REGIONALIZE	REGULARIZATION	REHYDRATION
REFRACTURED	REFURBISHMENT	REGIONALIZED	REGULARIZATIONS	REHYDRATIONS
REFRACTURES	REFURBISHMENTS	REGIONALIZES	REGULARIZE	REHYPNOTISE
REFRACTURING	REFURNISHED	REGIONALIZING	REGULARIZED	REHYPNOTISED
REFRAINERS	REFURNISHES	REGIONALLY	REGULARIZES	REHYPNOTISES
REFRAINING	REFURNISHING	REGISSEURS	REGULARIZING	REHYPNOTISING
REFRAINMENT	REFUSENIKS	REGISTERABLE	REGULATING	REHYPNOTIZE
REFRAINMENTS	REFUTABILITIES	REGISTERED	REGULATION	REHYPNOTIZED
REFRANGIBILITY	REFUTABILITY	REGISTERER	REGULATIONS	REHYPNOTIZES
REFRANGIBLE	REFUTATION	REGISTERERS	REGULATIVE	REHYPNOTIZING
REFRANGIBLENESS	REFUTATIONS	REGISTERING	REGULATIVELY	REICHSMARK
REFREEZING	REGAINABLE	REGISTRABLE	REGULATORS	REICHSMARKS
REFRESHENED	REGAINMENT	REGISTRANT	REGULATORY	REIDENTIFIED
REFRESHENER	REGAINMENTS	REGISTRANTS	REGULISING	REIDENTIFIES
REFRESHENERS	REGALEMENT	REGISTRARIES	REGULIZING	REIDENTIFY
REFRESHENING	REGALEMENTS	REGISTRARS	REGURGITANT	REIDENTIFYING
REFRESHENS	REGALITIES	REGISTRARSHIP	REGURGITANTS	REIFICATION
REFRESHERS	REGALNESSES	REGISTRARSHIPS	REGURGITATE	REIFICATIONS
REFRESHFUL	REGARDABLE	REGISTRARY	REGURGITATED	REIFICATORY
REFRESHFULLY	REGARDFULLY	REGISTRATION	REGURGITATES	REIGNITING
REFRESHING	REGARDFULNESS	REGISTRATIONAL	REGURGITATING	REIGNITION
REFRESHINGLY	REGARDFULNESSES	REGISTRATIONS	REGURGITATION	REIGNITIONS
REFRESHMENT	REGARDLESS	REGISTRIES	REGURGITATIONS	REILLUMINE
REFRESHMENTS	REGARDLESSLY	REGLORIFIED	REHABILITANT	REILLUMINED
REFRIGERANT	REGARDLESSNESS	REGLORIFIES	REHABILITANTS	REILLUMINES
REFRIGERANTS	REGATHERED	REGLORIFYING	REHABILITATE	REILLUMING
REFRIGERATE	REGATHERING	REGLOSSING	REHABILITATED	REILLUMINING
REFRIGERATED	REGELATING	REGNANCIES	REHABILITATES .	REIMAGINED
REFRIGERATES	REGELATION	REGRAFTING	REHABILITATING	REIMAGINES
REFRIGERATING	REGELATIONS	REGRANTING	REHABILITATION	REIMAGINING
REFRIGERATION	REGENERABLE	REGRATINGS	REHABILITATIONS	REIMBURSABLE
REFRIGERATIONS	REGENERACIES	REGREDIENCE	REHABILITATIVE	REIMBURSED
REFRIGERATIVE	REGENERACY	REGREDIENCES	REHABILITATOR	REIMBURSEMENT
REFRIGERATOR	REGENERATE	REGREENING	REHABILITATORS	REIMBURSEMENTS
REFRIGERATORIES	REGENERATED	REGREETING	REHAMMERED	REIMBURSER
REFRIGERATORS	REGENERATELY	REGRESSING	REHAMMERING	REIMBURSERS
REFRIGERATORY	REGENERATENESS	REGRESSION	REHANDLING	REIMBURSES
REFRINGENCE	REGENERATES	REGRESSIONS	REHANDLINGS	REIMBURSING
REFRINGENCES	REGENERATING	REGRESSIVE	REHARDENED	REIMMERSED
REFRINGENCIES	REGENERATION	REGRESSIVELY	REHARDENING	REIMMERSES
REFRINGENCY	REGENERATIONS	REGRESSIVENESS	REHEARINGS	REIMMERSING
REFRINGENT	REGENERATIVE	REGRESSIVITIES	REHEARSALS	REIMPLANTATION
REFRINGING	REGENERATIVELY	REGRESSIVITY	REHEARSERS	REIMPLANTATIONS
REFRONTING	REGENERATOR	REGRESSORS	REHEARSING	REIMPLANTED
REFUELABLE	REGENERATORS	REGRETFULLY	REHEARSINGS	REIMPLANTING
REFUELINGS	REGENERATORY	REGRETFULNESS	REHEATINGS	REIMPLANTS
REFUELLABLE	REGENTSHIP	REGRETFULNESSES	REHOSPITALISE	REIMPORTATION

REIMPORTATIONS	REINHABITS	REINTEGRATES	REITERATION	RELABELLED
REIMPORTED	REINITIATE	REINTEGRATING	REITERATIONS	RELABELLING
REIMPORTER	REINITIATED	REINTEGRATION	REITERATIVE	RELACQUERED
REIMPORTERS	REINITIATES	REINTEGRATIONS	REITERATIVELY	RELACQUERING
REIMPORTING	REINITIATING	REINTEGRATIVE	REITERATIVES	RELACQUERS
REIMPOSING	REINJECTED	REINTERMENT	REJACKETED	RELANDSCAPE
REIMPOSITION	REINJECTING	REINTERMENTS	REJACKETING	RELANDSCAPED
REIMPOSITIONS	REINJECTION	REINTERPRET	REJECTABLE	RELANDSCAPES
REIMPRESSION	REINJECTIONS	REINTERPRETED	REJECTAMENTA	RELANDSCAPING
REIMPRESSIONS	REINJURIES	REINTERPRETING	REJECTIBLE	RELATEDNESS
REINCARNATE	REINJURING	REINTERPRETS	REJECTINGLY	RELATEDNESSES
REINCARNATED	REINNERVATE	REINTERRED	REJECTIONIST	RELATIONAL
REINCARNATES	REINNERVATED	REINTERRING	REJECTIONISTS	RELATIONALLY
REINCARNATING	REINNERVATES	REINTERROGATE	REJECTIONS	RELATIONISM
REINCARNATION	REINNERVATING	REINTERROGATED	REJIGGERED	RELATIONISMS
REINCARNATIONS	REINNERVATION	REINTERROGATES	REJIGGERING	RELATIONIST
REINCITING	REINNERVATIONS	REINTERROGATING	REJOICEFUL	RELATIONISTS
REINCORPORATE	REINOCULATE	REINTERROGATION	REJOICEMENT	RELATIONLESS
REINCORPORATED	REINOCULATED	REINTERVIEW	REJOICEMENTS	RELATIONSHIP
REINCORPORATES	REINOCULATES	REINTERVIEWED	REJOICINGLY	RELATIONSHIPS
REINCORPORATING	REINOCULATING	REINTERVIEWING	REJOICINGS	RELATIVELY
REINCORPORATION	REINOCULATION	REINTERVIEWS	REJOINDERS	RELATIVENESS
REINCREASE	REINOCULATIONS	REINTRODUCE	REJOINDURE	RELATIVENESSES
REINCREASED	REINSERTED	REINTRODUCED	REJOINDURES	RELATIVISATION
REINCREASES	REINSERTING	REINTRODUCES	REJONEADOR	RELATIVISATIONS
REINCREASING	REINSERTION	REINTRODUCING	REJONEADORA	RELATIVISE
REINCURRED	REINSERTIONS	REINTRODUCTION	REJONEADORAS	RELATIVISED
REINCURRING	REINSPECTED	REINTRODUCTIONS	REJONEADORES	RELATIVISES
REINDEXING	REINSPECTING	REINVADING	REJOURNING	RELATIVISING
REINDICTED	REINSPECTION	REINVASION	REJUGGLING	RELATIVISM
REINDICTING	REINSPECTIONS	REINVASIONS	REJUSTIFIED	RELATIVISMS
REINDICTMENT	REINSPECTS	REINVENTED	REJUSTIFIES	RELATIVIST
REINDICTMENTS	REINSPIRED	REINVENTING	REJUSTIFYING	RELATIVISTIC
REINDUCING	REINSPIRES	REINVENTION	REJUVENATE	RELATIVISTS
REINDUCTED	REINSPIRING	REINVENTIONS	REJUVENATED	RELATIVITIES
REINDUCTING	REINSPIRIT	REINVESTED	REJUVENATES	RELATIVITIST
REINDUSTRIALISE	REINSPIRITED	REINVESTIGATE	REJUVENATING	RELATIVITISTS
REINDUSTRIALIZE	REINSPIRITING	REINVESTIGATED	REJUVENATION	RELATIVITY
REINFECTED	REINSPIRITS	REINVESTIGATES	REJUVENATIONS	RELATIVIZATION
REINFECTING	REINSTALLATION	REINVESTIGATING	REJUVENATOR	RELATIVIZATIONS
REINFECTION	REINSTALLATIONS	REINVESTIGATION	REJUVENATORS	RELATIVIZE
REINFECTIONS	REINSTALLED	REINVESTING	REJUVENESCE	RELATIVIZED
REINFESTATION	REINSTALLING	REINVESTMENT	REJUVENESCED	RELATIVIZES
REINFESTATIONS	REINSTALLS	REINVESTMENTS	REJUVENESCENCE	RELATIVIZING
REINFLAMED	REINSTALMENT	REINVIGORATE	REJUVENESCENCES	RELAUNCHED
REINFLAMES	REINSTALMENTS	REINVIGORATED	REJUVENESCENT	RELAUNCHES
REINFLAMING	REINSTATED	REINVIGORATES	REJUVENESCES	RELAUNCHING
REINFLATED	REINSTATEMENT	REINVIGORATING	REJUVENESCING	RELAUNDERED
REINFLATES	REINSTATEMENTS	REINVIGORATION	REJUVENISE	RELAUNDERING
REINFLATING	REINSTATES	REINVIGORATIONS	REJUVENISED	RELAUNDERS
REINFLATION	REINSTATING	REINVIGORATOR	REJUVENISES	RELAXATION
REINFLATIONS	REINSTATION	REINVIGORATORS	REJUVENISING	RELAXATIONS
REINFORCEABLE	REINSTATIONS	REINVITING	REJUVENIZE	RELAXATIVE
REINFORCED	REINSTATOR	REINVOKING	REJUVENIZED	RELAXATIVES
REINFORCEMENT	REINSTATORS	REINVOLVED	REJUVENIZES	RELAXEDNESS
REINFORCEMENTS	REINSTITUTE	REINVOLVES	REJUVENIZING	RELAXEDNESSES
REINFORCER	REINSTITUTED	REINVOLVING	REKEYBOARD	RELEARNING
REINFORCERS	REINSTITUTES	REIOYNDURE	REKEYBOARDED	RELEASABLE
REINFORCES	REINSTITUTING	REIOYNDURES	REKEYBOARDING	RELEASEMENT
REINFORCING	REINSTITUTION	REISSUABLE	REKEYBOARDS	RELEASEMENTS
REINFORMED	REINSTITUTIONS	REISTAFELS	REKINDLING	RELEGATABLE
REINFORMING	REINSURANCE	REITERANCE	REKINDLINGS	RELEGATING
REINFUNDED	REINSURANCES	REITERANCES	REKNITTING	RELEGATION
REINFUNDING	REINSURERS	REITERATED	REKNITTINGS	RELEGATIONS
REINFUSING	REINSURING	REITERATEDLY	REKNOTTING	RELENTINGS
REINHABITED	REINTEGRATE	REITERATES	REKNOTTINGS	RELENTLESS
REINHABITING	REINTEGRATED	REITERATING	RELABELING	RELENTLESSLY

RELENTLESSNESS	RELISTENED	REMEASURED	REMISSIBLE	REMONSTRATIVE
RELENTMENT	RELISTENING	REMEASUREMENT	REMISSIBLENESS	REMONSTRATIVELY
RELENTMENTS	RELIVERING	REMEASUREMENTS	REMISSIBLY	REMONSTRATOR
RELETTERED	RELLISHING	REMEASURES	REMISSIONS	REMONSTRATORS
RELETTERING	RELOCATABLE	REMEASURING	REMISSIVELY	REMONSTRATORY
RELEVANCES	RELOCATEES	REMEDIABILITIES	REMISSNESS	REMONTANTS
RELEVANCIES	RELOCATING	REMEDIABILITY	REMISSNESSES	REMONTOIRE
RELEVANTLY	RELOCATION	REMEDIABLE	REMITMENTS	REMONTOIRES
RELIABILITIES	RELOCATIONS	REMEDIABLY	REMITTABLE	REMONTOIRS
RELIABILITY	RELOCATORS	REMEDIALLY	REMITTANCE	REMORALISATION
RELIABLENESS	RELUBRICATE	REMEDIATED	REMITTANCES	REMORALISATIONS
RELIABLENESSES	RELUBRICATED	REMEDIATES	REMITTENCE	REMORALISE
RELICENSED	RELUBRICATES	REMEDIATING	REMITTENCES	REMORALISED
RELICENSES	RELUBRICATING	REMEDIATION	REMITTENCIES	REMORALISES
RELICENSING	RELUBRICATION	REMEDIATIONS	REMITTENCY	REMORALISING
RELICENSURE	RELUBRICATIONS	REMEDILESS	REMITTENTLY	REMORALIZATION
RELICENSURES	RELUCTANCE	REMEDILESSLY	REMIXTURES	REMORALIZATIONS
RELICTIONS	RELUCTANCES	REMEDILESSNESS	REMOBILISATION	REMORALIZE
RELIEFLESS	RELUCTANCIES	REMEMBERABILITY	REMOBILISATIONS	REMORALIZED
RELIEVABLE	RELUCTANCY	REMEMBERABLE	REMOBILISE	REMORALIZES
RELIEVEDLY	RELUCTANTLY	REMEMBERABLY	REMOBILISED	REMORALIZING
RELIGHTING	RELUCTATED	REMEMBERED	REMOBILISES	REMORSEFUL
RELIGIEUSE	RELUCTATES	REMEMBERER	REMOBILISING	REMORSEFULLY
RELIGIEUSES	RELUCTATING	REMEMBERERS	REMOBILIZATION	REMORSEFULNESS
RELIGIONARIES	RELUCTATION	REMEMBERING	REMOBILIZATIONS	REMORSELESS
RELIGIONARY	RELUCTATIONS	REMEMBRANCE	REMOBILIZE	REMORSELESSLY
RELIGIONER	RELUCTIVITIES	REMEMBRANCER	REMOBILIZED	REMORSELESSNESS
RELIGIONERS	RELUCTIVITY	REMEMBRANCERS	REMOBILIZES	REMORTGAGE
RELIGIONISE	RELUMINING	REMEMBRANCES	REMOBILIZING	REMORTGAGED
RELIGIONISED	REMAILINGS	REMERCYING	REMODELERS	REMORTGAGES
RELIGIONISES	REMAINDERED	REMIGATING	REMODELING	REMORTGAGING
RELIGIONISING	REMAINDERING	REMIGATION	REMODELINGS	REMOTENESS
RELIGIONISM	REMAINDERMAN	REMIGATIONS	REMODELLED	REMOTENESSES
RELIGIONISMS	REMAINDERMEN	REMIGRATED	REMODELLER	REMOTIVATE
RELIGIONIST	REMAINDERS	REMIGRATES	REMODELLERS	REMOTIVATED
RELIGIONISTS	REMANDMENT	REMIGRATING	REMODELLING	REMOTIVATES
RELIGIONIZE	REMANDMENTS	REMIGRATION	REMODELLINGS	REMOTIVATING
RELIGIONIZED	REMANENCES	REMIGRATIONS	REMODIFIED	REMOTIVATION
RELIGIONIZES	REMANENCIES	REMILITARISE	REMODIFIES	REMOTIVATIONS
RELIGIONIZING	REMANUFACTURE	REMILITARISED	REMODIFYING	REMOULADES
RELIGIONLESS	REMANUFACTURED	REMILITARISES	REMOISTENED	REMOULDING
RELIGIOSELY	REMANUFACTURER	REMILITARISING	REMOISTENING	REMOUNTING
RELIGIOSITIES	REMANUFACTURERS	REMILITARIZE	REMOISTENS	REMOUNTINGS
RELIGIOSITY	REMANUFACTURES	REMILITARIZED	REMONETISATION	REMOVABILITIES
RELIGIOSOS	REMANUFACTURING	REMILITARIZES	REMONETISATIONS	REMOVABILITY
RELIGIOUSES	REMARKABILITIES	REMILITARIZING	REMONETISE	REMOVABLENESS
RELIGIOUSLY	REMARKABILITY	REMINERALISE	REMONETISED	REMOVABLENESSES
RELIGIOUSNESS	REMARKABLE	REMINERALISED	REMONETISES	REMOVALIST
RELIGIOUSNESSES	REMARKABLENESS	REMINERALISES	REMONETISING	REMOVALISTS
RELINQUISH	REMARKABLES	REMINERALISING	REMONETIZATION	REMOVEABLE
RELINQUISHED	REMARKABLY	REMINERALIZE	REMONETIZATIONS	REMOVEDNESS
RELINQUISHER	REMARKETED	REMINERALIZED	REMONETIZE	REMOVEDNESSES
RELINQUISHERS	REMARKETING	REMINERALIZES	REMONETIZED	REMUNERABILITY
RELINQUISHES	REMARRIAGE	REMINERALIZING	REMONETIZES	REMUNERABLE
RELINQUISHING	REMARRIAGES	REMINISCED	REMONETIZING	REMUNERATE
RELINQUISHMENT	REMARRYING	REMINISCENCE	REMONSTRANCE	REMUNERATED
RELINQUISHMENTS	REMASTERED	REMINISCENCES	REMONSTRANCES	REMUNERATES
RELIQUAIRE	REMASTERING	REMINISCENT	REMONSTRANT	REMUNERATING
RELIQUAIRES	REMATCHING	REMINISCENTIAL	REMONSTRANTLY	REMUNERATION
RELIQUARIES	REMATERIALISE	REMINISCENTLY	REMONSTRANTS	REMUNERATIONS
RELIQUEFIED	REMATERIALISED	REMINISCENTS	REMONSTRATE	REMUNERATIVE
RELIQUEFIES	REMATERIALISES	REMINISCER	REMONSTRATED	REMUNERATIVELY
RELIQUEFYING	REMATERIALISING	REMINISCERS	REMONSTRATES	REMUNERATOR
RELIQUIFIED	REMATERIALIZE	REMINISCES	REMONSTRATING	REMUNERATORS
RELIQUIFIES	REMATERIALIZED	REMINISCING	REMONSTRATINGLY	REMUNERATORY
RELIQUIFYING	REMATERIALIZES	REMISSIBILITIES	REMONSTRATION	REMURMURED
RELISHABLE	REMATERIALIZING	REMISSIBILITY	REMONSTRATIONS	REMURMURING

REMYTHOLOGISE	RENOMINATIONS	REOPERATING	REPAINTING	REPERTOIRE
REMYTHOLOGISED	RENORMALISATION	REOPERATION	REPAINTINGS	REPERTOIRES
REMYTHOLOGISES	RENORMALISE	REOPERATIONS	REPAIRABILITIES	REPERTORIAL
REMYTHOLOGISING	RENORMALISED	REOPPOSING	REPAIRABILITY	REPERTORIES
REMYTHOLOGIZE	RENORMALISES	REORCHESTRATE	REPAIRABLE	REPERUSALS
REMYTHOLOGIZED	RENORMALISING	REORCHESTRATED	REPANELING	REPERUSING
REMYTHOLOGIZES	RENORMALIZATION	REORCHESTRATES	REPANELLED	REPETITEUR
REMYTHOLOGIZING	RENORMALIZE	REORCHESTRATING	REPANELLING	REPETITEURS
RENAISSANCE	RENORMALIZED	REORCHESTRATION	REPAPERING	REPETITEUSE
RENAISSANCES	RENORMALIZES	REORDAINED	REPARABILITIES	REPETITEUSES
RENASCENCE	RENORMALIZING	REORDAINING	REPARABILITY	REPETITION
RENASCENCES	RENOSTERVELD	REORDERING	REPARATION	REPETITIONAL
RENATIONALISE	RENOSTERVELDS	REORDINATION	REPARATIONS	REPETITIONARY
RENATIONALISED	RENOTIFIED	REORDINATIONS	REPARATIVE	REPETITIONS
RENATIONALISES	RENOTIFIES	REORGANISATION	REPARATORY	REPETITIOUS
RENATIONALISING	RENOTIFYING	REORGANISATIONS	REPARTEEING	REPETITIOUSLY
RENATIONALIZE	RENOUNCEABLE	REORGANISE	REPARTITION	REPETITIOUSNESS
RENATIONALIZED	RENOUNCEMENT	REORGANISED	REPARTITIONED	REPETITIVE
RENATIONALIZES	RENOUNCEMENTS	REORGANISER	REPARTITIONING	REPETITIVELY
RENATIONALIZING	RENOUNCERS	REORGANISERS	REPARTITIONS	REPETITIVENESS
RENATURATION	RENOUNCING	REORGANISES	REPASSAGES	REPHOTOGRAPH
RENATURATIONS	RENOVASCULAR	REORGANISING	REPASTURES	REPHOTOGRAPHED
RENATURING	RENOVATING	REORGANIZATION	REPATCHING	REPHOTOGRAPHING
RENCONTRED	RENOVATION	REORGANIZATIONS	REPATRIATE	REPHOTOGRAPHS
RENCONTRES	RENOVATIONS	REORGANIZE	REPATRIATED	REPHRASING
RENCONTRING	RENOVATIVE	REORGANIZED	REPATRIATES	REPHRASINGS
RENCOUNTER	RENOVATORS	REORGANIZER	REPATRIATING	REPIGMENTED
RENCOUNTERED	RENSSELAERITE	REORGANIZERS	REPATRIATION	REPIGMENTING
RENCOUNTERING	RENSSELAERITES	REORGANIZES	REPATRIATIONS	REPIGMENTS
RENCOUNTERS	RENTABILITIES	REORGANIZING	REPATRIATOR	REPINEMENT
RENDERABLE	RENTABILITY	REORIENTATE	REPATRIATORS	REPINEMENTS
RENDERINGS	RENTALLERS	REORIENTATED	REPATTERNED	REPININGLY
RENDEZVOUS	RENUMBERED	REORIENTATES	REPATTERNING	REPLACEABILITY
RENDEZVOUSED	RENUMBERING	REORIENTATING	REPATTERNS	REPLACEABLE
RENDEZVOUSES	RENUNCIATE	REORIENTATION	REPAYMENTS	REPLACEMENT
RENDEZVOUSING	RENUNCIATES	REORIENTATIONS	REPEALABLE	REPLACEMENTS
RENDITIONED	RENUNCIATION	REORIENTED	REPEATABILITIES	REPLANNING
RENDITIONING	RENUNCIATIONS	REORIENTING	REPEATABILITY	REPLANTATION
RENDITIONS	RENUNCIATIVE	REOUTFITTED	REPEATABLE	REPLANTATIONS
RENEAGUING	RENUNCIATORY	REOUTFITTING	REPEATEDLY	REPLANTING
RENEGADING	RENVERSEMENT	REOVIRUSES	REPEATINGS	REPLASTERED
RENEGADOES	RENVERSEMENTS	REOXIDATION	REPECHAGES	REPLASTERING
RENEGATION	RENVERSING	REOXIDATIONS	REPELLANCE	REPLASTERS
RENEGATIONS	REOBJECTED	REOXIDISED	REPELLANCES	REPLEADERS
RENEGOTIABLE	REOBJECTING	REOXIDISES	REPELLANCIES	REPLEADING
RENEGOTIATE	REOBSERVED	REOXIDISING	REPELLANCY	REPLEDGING
RENEGOTIATED	REOBSERVES	REOXIDIZED	REPELLANTLY	REPLENISHABLE
RENEGOTIATES	REOBSERVING	REOXIDIZES	REPELLANTS	REPLENISHED
RENEGOTIATING	REOBTAINED	REOXIDIZING	REPELLENCE	REPLENISHER
RENEGOTIATION	REOBTAINING	REOXYGENATE	REPELLENCES	REPLENISHERS
RENEGOTIATIONS	REOCCUPATION	REOXYGENATED	REPELLENCIES	REPLENISHES
RENEWABILITIES	REOCCUPATIONS	REOXYGENATES	REPELLENCY	REPLENISHING
RENEWABILITY	REOCCUPIED	REOXYGENATING	REPELLENTLY	REPLENISHMENT
RENEWABLES	REOCCUPIES	REPACIFIED	REPELLENTS	REPLENISHMENTS
RENEWEDNESS	REOCCUPYING	REPACIFIES	REPELLINGLY	REPLETENESS
RENEWEDNESSES	REOCCURRED	REPACIFYING	REPENTANCE	REPLETENESSES
RENFORCING	REOCCURRENCE	REPACKAGED	REPENTANCES	REPLETIONS
RENITENCES	REOCCURRENCES	REPACKAGER	REPENTANTLY	REPLEVIABLE
RENITENCIES	REOCCURRING	REPACKAGERS	REPENTANTS	REPLEVINED
RENOGRAPHIC	REOFFENDED	REPACKAGES	REPENTINGLY	REPLEVINING
RENOGRAPHIES	REOFFENDER	REPACKAGING	REPEOPLING	REPLEVISABLE
RENOGRAPHY	REOFFENDERS	REPAGINATE	REPERCUSSED	REPLEVYING
RENOMINATE	REOFFENDING	REPAGINATED	REPERCUSSES	REPLICABILITIES
RENOMINATED	REOFFERING	REPAGINATES	REPERCUSSING	REPLICABILITY
RENOMINATES	REOPENINGS	REPAGINATING	REPERCUSSION	REPLICABLE
RENOMINATING	REOPERATED	REPAGINATION	REPERCUSSIONS	REPLICANTS
RENOMINATION	REOPERATES	REPAGINATIONS	REPERCUSSIVE	REPLICASES

REPLICATED	REPOSSESSION	REPRIEVERS	REPRODUCTIVELY	REPULSIVELY
REPLICATES	REPOSSESSIONS	REPRIEVING	REPRODUCTIVES	REPULSIVENESS
REPLICATING	REPOSSESSOR	REPRIMANDED	REPRODUCTIVITY	REPULSIVENESSES
REPLICATION	REPOSSESSORS	REPRIMANDING	REPROGRAMED	REPUNCTUATION
REPLICATIONS	REPOTTINGS	REPRIMANDS	REPROGRAMING	REPUNCTUATIONS
REPLICATIVE	REPOUSSAGE	REPRINTERS	REPROGRAMMABLE	REPURCHASE
REPLICATOR	REPOUSSAGES	REPRINTING	REPROGRAMME	REPURCHASED
REPLICATORS	REPOUSSOIR	REPRISTINATE	REPROGRAMMED	REPURCHASES
REPLOTTING	REPOUSSOIRS	REPRISTINATED	REPROGRAMMES	REPURCHASING
REPLOUGHED	REPOWERING	REPRISTINATES	REPROGRAMMING	REPURIFIED
REPLOUGHING	REPREEVING	REPRISTINATING	REPROGRAMS	REPURIFIES
REPLUMBING	REPREHENDABLE	REPRISTINATION	REPROGRAPHER	REPURIFYING
REPLUNGING	REPREHENDED	REPRISTINATIONS	REPROGRAPHERS	REPURPOSED
REPOINTING	REPREHENDER	REPRIVATISATION	REPROGRAPHIC	REPURPOSES
REPOINTINGS	REPREHENDERS	REPRIVATISE	REPROGRAPHICS	REPURPOSING
REPOLARISATION	REPREHENDING	REPRIVATISED	REPROGRAPHIES	REPURSUING
REPOLARISATIONS	REPREHENDS	REPRIVATISES	REPROGRAPHY	REPUTABILITIES
REPOLARISE	REPREHENSIBLE	REPRIVATISING	REPROOFING	REPUTABILITY
REPOLARISED	REPREHENSIBLY	REPRIVATIZATION	REPROVABLE	REPUTATION
REPOLARISES	REPREHENSION	REPRIVATIZE	REPROVINGLY	REPUTATIONAL
REPOLARISING	REPREHENSIONS	REPRIVATIZED	REPROVISION	REPUTATIONLESS
REPOLARIZATION	REPREHENSIVE	REPRIVATIZES	REPROVISIONED	REPUTATIONS
REPOLARIZATIONS	REPREHENSIVELY	REPRIVATIZING	REPROVISIONING	REPUTATIVE
REPOLARIZE	REPREHENSORY	REPROACHABLE	REPROVISIONS	REPUTATIVELY
REPOLARIZED	REPRESENTABLE	REPROACHABLY	REPTATIONS	REPUTELESS
REPOLARIZES	REPRESENTAMEN	REPROACHED	REPTILIANLY	REQUALIFIED
REPOLARIZING	REPRESENTAMENS	REPROACHER	REPTILIANS	REQUALIFIES
REPOLISHED	REPRESENTANT	REPROACHERS	REPTILIFEROUS	REQUALIFYING
REPOLISHES	REPRESENTANTS	REPROACHES	REPTILIFORM	REQUESTERS
REPOLISHING	REPRESENTATION	REPROACHFUL	REPTILIOUS	REQUESTING
REPOPULARISE	REPRESENTATIONS	REPROACHFULLY	REPTILOIDS	REQUESTORS
REPOPULARISED	REPRESENTATIVE	REPROACHFULNESS	REPUBLICAN	REQUICKENED
REPOPULARISES	REPRESENTATIVES	REPROACHING	REPUBLICANISE	REQUICKENING
REPOPULARISING	REPRESENTED	REPROACHINGLY	REPUBLICANISED	REQUICKENS
REPOPULARIZE	REPRESENTEE	REPROACHLESS	REPUBLICANISES	REQUIESCAT
REPOPULARIZED	REPRESENTEES	REPROBACIES	REPUBLICANISING	REQUIESCATS
REPOPULARIZES	REPRESENTER	REPROBANCE	REPUBLICANISM	REQUIGHTED
REPOPULARIZING	REPRESENTERS	REPROBANCES	REPUBLICANISMS	REQUIGHTING
REPOPULATE	REPRESENTING	REPROBATED	REPUBLICANIZE	REQUIRABLE
REPOPULATED	REPRESENTMENT	REPROBATER	REPUBLICANIZED	REQUIREMENT
REPOPULATES	REPRESENTMENTS	REPROBATERS	REPUBLICANIZES	REQUIREMENTS
REPOPULATING	REPRESENTOR	REPROBATES	REPUBLICANIZING	REQUIRINGS
REPOPULATION	REPRESENTORS	REPROBATING	REPUBLICANS	REQUISITELY
REPOPULATIONS	REPRESENTS	REPROBATION	REPUBLICATION	REQUISITENESS
REPORTABLE	REPRESSERS	REPROBATIONARY	REPUBLICATIONS	REQUISITENESSES
REPORTAGES	REPRESSIBILITY	REPROBATIONS	REPUBLISHED	REQUISITES
REPORTEDLY	REPRESSIBLE	REPROBATIVE	REPUBLISHER	REQUISITION
REPORTINGLY	REPRESSIBLY	REPROBATIVELY	REPUBLISHERS	REQUISITIONARY
REPORTINGS	REPRESSING	REPROBATOR	REPUBLISHES	REQUISITIONED
REPORTORIAL	REPRESSION	REPROBATORS	REPUBLISHING	REQUISITIONING
REPORTORIALLY	REPRESSIONIST	REPROBATORY	REPUDIABLE	REQUISITIONIST
REPOSEDNESS	REPRESSIONISTS	REPROCESSED	REPUDIATED	REQUISITIONISTS
REPOSEDNESSES	REPRESSIONS	REPROCESSES	REPUDIATES	REQUISITIONS
REPOSEFULLY	REPRESSIVE	REPROCESSING	REPUDIATING	REQUISITOR
REPOSEFULNESS	REPRESSIVELY	REPROCESSINGS	REPUDIATION	REQUISITORIES
REPOSEFULNESSES	REPRESSIVENESS	REPRODUCED	REPUDIATIONIST	REQUISITORS
REPOSITING	REPRESSORS	REPRODUCER	REPUDIATIONISTS	REQUISITORY
REPOSITION	REPRESSURISE	REPRODUCERS	REPUDIATIONS	REQUITABLE
REPOSITIONED	REPRESSURISED	REPRODUCES	REPUDIATIVE	REQUITEFUL
REPOSITIONING	REPRESSURISES	REPRODUCIBILITY	REPUDIATOR	REQUITELESS
REPOSITIONS	REPRESSURISING	REPRODUCIBLE	REPUDIATORS	REQUITEMENT
REPOSITORIES	REPRESSURIZE	REPRODUCIBLES	REPUGNANCE	REQUITEMENTS
REPOSITORS	REPRESSURIZED	REPRODUCIBLY	REPUGNANCES	REQUITTING
REPOSITORY	REPRESSURIZES	REPRODUCING	REPUGNANCIES	REQUOYLING
REPOSSESSED	REPRESSURIZING	REPRODUCTION	REPUGNANCY	RERADIATED
REPOSSESSES	REPRIEVABLE	REPRODUCTIONS	REPUGNANTLY	RERADIATES
REPOSSESSING	REPRIEVALS	REPRODUCTIVE	REPULSIONS	RERADIATING

RERADIATION	RESEARCHFUL	RESETTLING	RESISTENTS	RESOLVEDNESSES
RERADIATIONS	RESEARCHING	RESHAPINGS	RESISTIBILITIES	RESOLVENTS
RERAILINGS	RESEARCHIST	RESHARPENED	RESISTIBILITY	RESONANCES
REREADINGS	RESEARCHISTS	RESHARPENING	RESISTIBLE	RESONANTLY
REREBRACES	RESEASONED	RESHARPENS	RESISTIBLY	RESONATING
RERECORDED	RESEASONING	RESHINGLED	RESISTINGLY	RESONATION
RERECORDING	RESECTABILITIES	RESHINGLES	RESISTIVELY	RESONATIONS
REREDORTER	RESECTABILITY	RESHINGLING	RESISTIVENESS	RESONATORS
REREDORTERS	RESECTABLE	RESHIPMENT	RESISTIVENESSES	RESORBENCE
REREDOSSES	RESECTIONAL	RESHIPMENTS	RESISTIVITIES	RESORBENCES
REREGISTER	RESECTIONS	RESHIPPERS	RESISTIVITY	RESORCINAL
REREGISTERED	RESECURING	RESHIPPING	RESISTLESS	RESORCINOL
REREGISTERING	RESEGREGATE	RESHOOTING	RESISTLESSLY	RESORCINOLS
REREGISTERS	RESEGREGATED	RESHOWERED	RESISTLESSNESS	RESORPTION
REREGISTRATION	RESEGREGATES	RESHOWERING	RESITTINGS	RESORPTIONS
REREGISTRATIONS	RESEGREGATING	RESHOWINGS	RESITUATED	RESORPTIVE
REREGULATE	RESEGREGATION	RESHUFFLED	RESITUATES	RESOUNDING
REREGULATED	RESEGREGATIONS	RESHUFFLES	RESITUATING	RESOUNDINGLY
REREGULATES	RESEIZURES	RESHUFFLING	RESKETCHED	RESOURCEFUL
REREGULATING	RESELECTED	RESIDENCES	RESKETCHES	RESOURCEFULLY
REREGULATION	RESELECTING	RESIDENCIES	RESKETCHING	RESOURCEFULNESS
REREGULATIONS	RESELECTION	RESIDENTER	RESKILLING	RESOURCELESS
RERELEASED	RESELECTIONS	RESIDENTERS	RESKILLINGS	RESOURCING
RERELEASES	RESEMBLANCE	RESIDENTIAL	RESKINNING	RESOURCINGS
RERELEASING	RESEMBLANCES	RESIDENTIALLY	RESMELTING	RESPEAKING
REREMINDED	RESEMBLANT	RESIDENTIARIES	RESMOOTHED	RESPECIFIED
REREMINDING	RESEMBLERS	RESIDENTIARY	RESMOOTHING	RESPECIFIES
REREPEATED	RESEMBLING	RESIDENTSHIP	RESNATRONS	RESPECIFYING
REREPEATING	RESENSITISE	RESIDENTSHIPS	RESOCIALISATION	RESPECTABILISE
REREVIEWED	RESENSITISED	RESIDUALLY	RESOCIALISE	RESPECTABILISED
REREVIEWING	RESENSITISES	RESIGHTING	RESOCIALISED	RESPECTABILISES
REREVISING	RESENSITISING	RESIGNATION	RESOCIALISES	RESPECTABILITY
REROUTEING	RESENSITIZE	RESIGNATIONS	RESOCIALISING	RESPECTABILIZE
RESADDLING	RESENSITIZED	RESIGNEDLY	RESOCIALIZATION	RESPECTABILIZED
RESALEABLE	RESENSITIZES	RESIGNEDNESS	RESOCIALIZE	RESPECTABILIZES
RESALUTING	RESENSITIZING	RESIGNEDNESSES	RESOCIALIZED	RESPECTABLE
RESAMPLING	RESENTENCE	RESIGNMENT	RESOCIALIZES	RESPECTABLENESS
RESCHEDULE	RESENTENCED	RESIGNMENTS	RESOCIALIZING	RESPECTABLES
RESCHEDULED	RESENTENCES	RESILEMENT	RESOFTENED	RESPECTABLY
RESCHEDULES	RESENTENCING	RESILEMENTS	RESOFTENING	RESPECTANT
RESCHEDULING	RESENTFULLY	RESILIENCE	RESOLDERED	RESPECTERS
RESCHEDULINGS	RESENTFULNESS	RESILIENCES	RESOLDERING	RESPECTFUL
RESCHOOLED	RESENTFULNESSES	RESILIENCIES	RESOLIDIFIED	RESPECTFULLY
RESCHOOLING	RESENTINGLY	RESILIENCY	RESOLIDIFIES	RESPECTFULNESS
RESCINDABLE	RESENTMENT	RESILIENTLY	RESOLIDIFY	RESPECTING
RESCINDERS	RESENTMENTS	RESILVERED	RESOLIDIFYING	RESPECTIVE
RESCINDING	RESERPINES	RESILVERING	RESOLUBILITIES	RESPECTIVELY
RESCINDMENT	RESERVABLE	RESINATING	RESOLUBILITY	RESPECTIVENESS
RESCINDMENTS	RESERVATION	RESINIFEROUS	RESOLUBLENESS	RESPECTLESS
RESCISSIBLE	RESERVATIONIST	RESINIFICATION	RESOLUBLENESSES	RESPELLING
RESCISSION	RESERVATIONISTS	RESINIFICATIONS	RESOLUTELY	RESPELLINGS
RESCISSIONS	RESERVATIONS	RESINIFIED	RESOLUTENESS	RESPIRABILITIES
RESCISSORY	RESERVATORIES	RESINIFIES	RESOLUTENESSES	RESPIRABILITY
RESCREENED	RESERVATORY	RESINIFYING	RESOLUTEST	RESPIRABLE
RESCREENING	RESERVEDLY	RESINISING	RESOLUTION	RESPIRATION
RESCRIPTED	RESERVEDNESS	RESINIZING	RESOLUTIONER	RESPIRATIONAL
RESCRIPTING	RESERVEDNESSES	RESINOUSLY	RESOLUTIONERS	RESPIRATIONS
RESCRIPTION	RESERVICED	RESINOUSNESS	RESOLUTIONIST	RESPIRATOR
RESCRIPTIONS	RESERVICES	RESINOUSNESSES	RESOLUTIONISTS	RESPIRATORS
RESCULPTED	RESERVICING	RESIPISCENCE	RESOLUTIONS	RESPIRATORY
RESCULPTING	RESERVISTS	RESIPISCENCES	RESOLUTIVE	RESPIRITUALISE
RESEALABLE	RESERVOIRED	RESIPISCENCIES	RESOLVABILITIES	RESPIRITUALISED
RESEARCHABLE	RESERVOIRING	RESIPISCENCY	RESOLVABILITY	RESPIRITUALISES
RESEARCHED	RESERVOIRS	RESIPISCENT	RESOLVABLE	RESPIRITUALIZE
RESEARCHER	RESETTABLE	RESISTANCE	RESOLVABLENESS	RESPIRITUALIZED
RESEARCHERS	RESETTLEMENT	RESISTANCES	RESOLVEDLY	RESPIRITUALIZES
RESEARCHES	RESETTLEMENTS	RESISTANTS	RESOLVEDNESS	RESPIROLOGIES

RESPIROLOGIST	RESTARTABLE	RESTRAINERS	RESUPPLIED	RESYSTEMATISING
RESPIROLOGISTS	RESTARTERS	RESTRAINING	RESUPPLIES	RESYSTEMATIZE
RESPIROLOGY	RESTARTING	RESTRAININGS	RESUPPLYING	RESYSTEMATIZED
RESPIROMETER	RESTATEMENT	RESTRAINTS	RESURFACED	RESYSTEMATIZES
RESPIROMETERS	RESTATEMENTS	RESTRENGTHEN	RESURFACER	RESYSTEMATIZING
RESPIROMETRIC	RESTATIONED	RESTRENGTHENED	RESURFACERS	RETACKLING
RESPIROMETRIES	RESTATIONING	RESTRENGTHENING	RESURFACES	RETAILINGS
RESPIROMETRY	RESTATIONS	RESTRENGTHENS	RESURFACING	RETAILMENT
RESPITELESS	RESTAURANT	RESTRESSED	RESURGENCE	RETAILMENTS
RESPLENDED	RESTAURANTEUR	RESTRESSES	RESURGENCES	RETAILORED
RESPLENDENCE	RESTAURANTEURS	RESTRESSING	RESURRECTED	RETAILORING
RESPLENDENCES	RESTAURANTS	RESTRETCHED	RESURRECTING	RETAINABLE
RESPLENDENCIES	RESTAURATEUR	RESTRETCHES	RESURRECTION	RETAINERSHIP
RESPLENDENCY	RESTAURATEURS	RESTRETCHING	RESURRECTIONAL	RETAINERSHIPS
RESPLENDENT	RESTAURATION	RESTRICKEN	RESURRECTIONARY	RETAINMENT
RESPLENDENTLY	RESTAURATIONS	RESTRICTED	RESURRECTIONISE	RETAINMENTS
RESPLENDING	RESTEMMING	RESTRICTEDLY	RESURRECTIONISM	RETALIATED
RESPLICING	RESTFULLER	RESTRICTEDNESS	RESURRECTIONIST	RETALIATES
RESPLITTING	RESTFULLEST	RESTRICTING	RESURRECTIONIZE	RETALIATING
RESPONDENCE	RESTFULNESS	RESTRICTION	RESURRECTIONS	RETALIATION
RESPONDENCES	RESTFULNESSES	RESTRICTIONISM	RESURRECTIVE	RETALIATIONIST
RESPONDENCIES	RESTHARROW	RESTRICTIONISMS	RESURRECTOR	RETALIATIONISTS
RESPONDENCY	RESTHARROWS	RESTRICTIONIST	RESURRECTORS	RETALIATIONS
RESPONDENT	RESTIMULATE	RESTRICTIONISTS	RESURRECTS	RETALIATIVE
RESPONDENTIA	RESTIMULATED	RESTRICTIONS	RESURVEYED	RETALIATOR
RESPONDENTIAS	RESTIMULATES	RESTRICTIVE	RESURVEYING	RETALIATORS
RESPONDENTS	RESTIMULATING	RESTRICTIVELY	RESUSCITABLE	RETALIATORY
RESPONDERS	RESTIMULATION	RESTRICTIVENESS	RESUSCITANT	RETALLYING
RESPONDING	RESTIMULATIONS	RESTRICTIVES	RESUSCITANTS	RETARDANTS
RESPONSELESS	RESTITCHED	RESTRIKING	RESUSCITATE	RETARDATES
RESPONSERS	RESTITCHES	RESTRINGED	RESUSCITATED	RETARDATION
RESPONSIBILITY	RESTITCHING	RESTRINGEING	RESUSCITATES	RETARDATIONS
RESPONSIBLE	RESTITUTED	RESTRINGENT	RESUSCITATING	RETARDATIVE
RESPONSIBLENESS	RESTITUTES	RESTRINGENTS	RESUSCITATION	RETARDATORY
RESPONSIBLY	RESTITUTING	RESTRINGES	RESUSCITATIONS	RETARDMENT
RESPONSIONS	RESTITUTION	RESTRINGING	RESUSCITATIVE	RETARDMENTS
RESPONSIVE	RESTITUTIONISM	RESTRIVING	RESUSCITATOR	RETARGETED
RESPONSIVELY	RESTITUTIONISMS	RESTRUCTURE	RESUSCITATORS	RETARGETING
RESPONSIVENESS	RESTITUTIONIST	RESTRUCTURED	RESUSPENDED	RETEACHING
RESPONSORIAL	RESTITUTIONISTS	RESTRUCTURES	RESUSPENDING	RETELLINGS
RESPONSORIALS	RESTITUTIONS	RESTRUCTURING	RESUSPENDS	RETEMPERED
RESPONSORIES	RESTITUTIVE	RESTRUCTURINGS	RESVERATROL	RETEMPERING
RESPONSORS	RESTITUTOR	RESTUDYING	RESVERATROLS	RETENTIONIST
RESPONSORY	RESTITUTORS	RESTUFFING	RESWALLOWED	RETENTIONISTS
RESPONSUMS	RESTITUTORY	RESTUMPING	RESWALLOWING	RETENTIONS
RESPOOLING	RESTIVENESS	RESUBJECTED	RESWALLOWS	RETENTIVELY
RESPOTTING	RESTIVENESSES	RESUBJECTING	RESYNCHRONISE	RETENTIVENESS
RESPRAYING	RESTLESSLY	RESUBJECTS	RESYNCHRONISED	RETENTIVENESSES
RESPREADING	RESTLESSNESS	RESUBMISSION	RESYNCHRONISES	RETENTIVES
RESPRINGING	RESTLESSNESSES	RESUBMISSIONS	RESYNCHRONISING	RETENTIVITIES
RESPROUTED	RESTOCKING	RESUBMITTED	RESYNCHRONIZE	RETENTIVITY
RESPROUTING	RESTORABLE	RESUBMITTING	RESYNCHRONIZED	RETESTIFIED
RESSALDARS	RESTORABLENESS	RESULTANTLY	RESYNCHRONIZES	RETESTIFIES
RESSENTIMENT	RESTORATION	RESULTANTS	RESYNCHRONIZING	RETESTIFYING
RESSENTIMENTS	RESTORATIONISM	RESULTATIVE	RESYNTHESES	RETEXTURED
RESTABILISE	RESTORATIONISMS	RESULTATIVES	RESYNTHESIS	RETEXTURES
RESTABILISED	RESTORATIONIST	RESULTLESS	RESYNTHESISE	RETEXTURING
RESTABILISES	RESTORATIONISTS	RESULTLESSNESS	RESYNTHESISED	RETHINKERS
RESTABILISING	RESTORATIONS	RESUMMONED	RESYNTHESISES	RETHINKING
RESTABILIZE	RESTORATIVE	RESUMMONING	RESYNTHESISING	RETHINKINGS
RESTABILIZED	RESTORATIVELY	RESUMPTION	RESYNTHESIZE	RETHREADED
RESTABILIZES	RESTORATIVES	RESUMPTIONS	RESYNTHESIZED	RETHREADING
RESTABILIZING	RESTRAINABLE	RESUMPTIVE	RESYNTHESIZES	RETICELLAS
RESTABLING	RESTRAINED	RESUMPTIVELY	RESYNTHESIZING	RETICENCES
RESTACKING	RESTRAINEDLY	RESUPINATE	RESYSTEMATISE	RETICENCIES
RESTAFFING	RESTRAINEDNESS	RESUPINATION	RESYSTEMATISED	RETICENTLY
RESTAMPING	RESTRAINER	RESUPINATIONS	RESYSTEMATISES	RETICULARLY

RETICULARY	RETRACTING	RETROACTING	RETROMINGENCY	REUTILISES
RETICULATE	RETRACTION	RETROACTION	RETROMINGENT	REUTILISING
RETICULATED	RETRACTIONS	RETROACTIONS	RETROMINGENTS	REUTILIZATION
RETICULATELY	RETRACTIVE	RETROACTIVE	RETROPACKS	REUTILIZATIONS
RETICULATES	RETRACTIVELY	RETROACTIVELY	RETROPERITONEAL	REUTILIZED
RETICULATING	RETRACTORS	RETROACTIVENESS	RETROPHILIA	REUTILIZES
RETICULATION	RETRAINABLE	RETROACTIVITIES	RETROPHILIAC	REUTILIZING
RETICULATIONS	RETRAINEES	RETROACTIVITY	RETROPHILIACS	REUTTERING
RETICULOCYTE	RETRAINING	RETROBULBAR	RETROPHILIAS	REVACCINATE
RETICULOCYTES	RETRAININGS	RETROCEDED	RETROPULSION	REVACCINATED
RETICULUMS	RETRANSFER	RETROCEDENCE	RETROPULSIONS	REVACCINATES
RETIGHTENED	RETRANSFERRED	RETROCEDENCES	RETROPULSIVE	REVACCINATING
RETIGHTENING	RETRANSFERRING	RETROCEDENT	RETROREFLECTION	REVACCINATION
RETIGHTENS	RETRANSFERS	RETROCEDES	RETROREFLECTIVE	REVACCINATIONS
RETINACULA	RETRANSFORM	RETROCEDING	RETROREFLECTOR	REVALENTAS
RETINACULAR	RETRANSFORMED	RETROCESSION	RETROREFLECTORS	REVALIDATE
RETINACULUM	RETRANSFORMING	RETROCESSIONS	RETROROCKET	REVALIDATED
RETINALITE	RETRANSFORMS	RETROCESSIVE	RETROROCKETS	REVALIDATES
RETINALITES	RETRANSFUSE	RETROCHOIR	RETRORSELY	REVALIDATING
RETINISPORA	RETRANSFUSED	RETROCHOIRS	RETROSEXUAL	REVALIDATION
RETINISPORAS	RETRANSFUSES	RETROCOGNITION	RETROSEXUALS	REVALIDATIONS
RETINITIDES	RETRANSFUSING	RETROCOGNITIONS	RETROSPECT	REVALORISATION
RETINITISES	RETRANSLATE	RETRODICTED	RETROSPECTED	REVALORISATIONS
RETINOBLASTOMA	RETRANSLATED	RETRODICTING	RETROSPECTING	REVALORISE
RETINOBLASTOMAS	RETRANSLATES	RETRODICTION	RETROSPECTION	REVALORISED
RETINOPATHIES	RETRANSLATING	RETRODICTIONS	RETROSPECTIONS	REVALORISES
RETINOPATHY	RETRANSLATION	RETRODICTIVE	RETROSPECTIVE	REVALORISING
RETINOSCOPE	RETRANSLATIONS	RETRODICTS	RETROSPECTIVELY	REVALORIZATION
RETINOSCOPES	RETRANSMISSION	RETROENGINE	RETROSPECTIVES	REVALORIZATIONS
RETINOSCOPIC	RETRANSMISSIONS	RETROENGINES	RETROSPECTS	REVALORIZE
RETINOSCOPIES	RETRANSMIT	RETROFIRED	RETROUSSAGE	REVALORIZED
RETINOSCOPIST	RETRANSMITS	RETROFIRES	RETROUSSAGES	REVALORIZES
RETINOSCOPISTS	RETRANSMITTED	RETROFIRING	RETROVERSE	REVALORIZING
RETINOSCOPY	RETRANSMITTING	RETROFITTED	RETROVERSION	REVALUATED
RETINOSPORA	RETREADING	RETROFITTING	RETROVERSIONS	REVALUATES
RETINOSPORAS	RETREATANT	RETROFITTINGS	RETROVERTED	REVALUATING
RETINOTECTAL	RETREATANTS	RETROFLECTED	RETROVERTING	REVALUATION
RETIRACIES	RETREATERS	RETROFLECTION	RETROVERTS	REVALUATIONS
RETIREDNESS	RETREATING	RETROFLECTIONS	RETROVIRAL	REVAMPINGS
RETIREDNESSES	RETRENCHABLE	RETROFLEXED	RETROVIRUS	REVANCHISM
RETIREMENT	RETRENCHED	RETROFLEXES	RETROVIRUSES	REVANCHISMS
RETIREMENTS	RETRENCHES	RETROFLEXING	RETURNABILITIES	REVANCHIST
RETIRINGLY	RETRENCHING	RETROFLEXION	RETURNABILITY	REVANCHISTS
RETIRINGNESS	RETRENCHMENT	RETROFLEXIONS	RETURNABLE	REVARNISHED
RETIRINGNESSES	RETRENCHMENTS	RETROGRADATION	RETURNABLES	REVARNISHES
RETORSIONS	RETRIBUTED	RETROGRADATIONS	RETURNLESS	REVARNISHING
RETORTIONS	RETRIBUTES	RETROGRADE	RETWEETING	REVEALABILITIES
RETOTALING	RETRIBUTING	RETROGRADED	RETWISTING	REVEALABILITY
RETOTALLED	RETRIBUTION	RETROGRADELY	REUNIFICATION	REVEALABLE
RETOTALLING	RETRIBUTIONS	RETROGRADES	REUNIFICATIONS	REVEALINGLY
RETOUCHABLE	RETRIBUTIVE	RETROGRADING	REUNIFYING	REVEALINGNESS
RETOUCHERS	RETRIBUTIVELY	RETROGRESS	REUNIONISM	REVEALINGNESSES
RETOUCHING	RETRIBUTOR	RETROGRESSED	REUNIONISMS	REVEALINGS
RETOUCHINGS	RETRIBUTORS	RETROGRESSES	REUNIONIST	REVEALMENT
RETRACEABLE	RETRIBUTORY	RETROGRESSING	REUNIONISTIC	REVEALMENTS
RETRACEMENT	RETRIEVABILITY	RETROGRESSION	REUNIONISTS	REVEGETATE
RETRACEMENTS	RETRIEVABLE	RETROGRESSIONAL	REUNITABLE	REVEGETATED
RETRACKING	RETRIEVABLENESS	RETROGRESSIONS	REUPHOLSTER	REVEGETATES
RETRACTABILITY	RETRIEVABLY	RETROGRESSIVE	REUPHOLSTERED	REVEGETATING
RETRACTABLE	RETRIEVALS	RETROGRESSIVELY	REUPHOLSTERING	REVEGETATION
RETRACTATION	RETRIEVEMENT	RETROJECTED	REUPHOLSTERS	REVEGETATIONS
RETRACTATIONS	RETRIEVEMENTS	RETROJECTING	REUPTAKING	REVELATION
RETRACTIBILITY	RETRIEVERS	RETROJECTION	REUSABILITIES	REVELATIONAL
RETRACTIBLE	RETRIEVING	RETROJECTIONS	REUSABILITY	REVELATIONIST
RETRACTILE	RETRIEVINGS	RETROJECTS	REUTILISATION	REVELATIONISTS
RETRACTILITIES	RETRIMMING	RETROLENTAL	REUTILISATIONS	REVELATIONS
RETRACTILITY	RETROACTED	RETROMINGENCIES	REUTILISED	REVELATIVE

REVELATORS
REVELATORY
REVELLINGS
REVELMENTS
REVENDICATE
REVENDICATED
REVENDICATES
REVENDICATING
REVENDICATION
REVENDICATIONS
REVENGEFUL
REVENGEFULLY
REVENGEFULNESS
REVENGELESS
REVENGEMENT
REVENGEMENTS
REVENGINGLY
REVENGINGS
REVERBATORIES
REVERBATORY
REVERBERANT
REVERBERANTLY
REVERBERATE
REVERBERATED
REVERBERATES
REVERBERATING
REVERBERATION
REVERBERATIONS
REVERBERATIVE
REVERBERATOR
REVERBERATORIES
REVERBERATORS
REVERBERATORY
REVERENCED
REVERENCER
REVERENCERS
REVERENCES
REVERENCING
REVERENTIAL
REVERENTIALLY
REVERENTLY
REVERENTNESS
REVERENTNESSES
REVERIFIED
REVERIFIES
REVERIFYING
REVERSEDLY
REVERSELESS
REVERSIBILITIES
REVERSIBILITY
REVERSIBLE
REVERSIBLES
REVERSIBLY
REVERSINGS
REVERSIONAL
REVERSIONALLY
REVERSIONARIES
REVERSIONARY
REVERSIONER
REVERSIONERS
REVERSIONS
REVERSISES
REVERTANTS
REVERTIBLE
REVESTIARIES
REVESTIARY
REVESTRIES

REVETMENTS
REVIBRATED
REVIBRATES
REVIBRATING
REVICTUALED
REVICTUALING
REVICTUALLED
REVICTUALLING
REVICTUALS
REVIEWABLE
REVILEMENT
REVILEMENTS
REVILINGLY
REVINDICATE
REVINDICATED
REVINDICATES
REVINDICATING
REVINDICATION
REVINDICATIONS
REVIOLATED
REVIOLATES
REVIOLATING
REVISIONAL
REVISIONARY
REVISIONISM
REVISIONISMS
REVISIONIST
REVISIONISTS
REVISITANT
REVISITANTS
REVISITATION
REVISITATIONS
REVISITING
REVISUALISATION
REVISUALIZATION
REVITALISATION
REVITALISATIONS
REVITALISE
REVITALISED
REVITALISES
REVITALISING
REVITALIZATION
REVITALIZATIONS
REVITALIZE
REVITALIZED
REVITALIZES
REVITALIZING
REVIVABILITIES
REVIVABILITY
REVIVABILISM
REVIVALISMS
REVIVALIST
REVIVALISTIC
REVIVALISTS
REVIVEMENT
REVIVEMENTS
REVIVESCENCE
REVIVESCENCES
REVIVESCENCIES
REVIVESCENCY
REVIVESCENT
REVIVIFICATION
REVIVIFICATIONS
REVIVIFIED
REVIVIFIES
REVIVIFYING
REVIVINGLY

REVIVISCENCE
REVIVISCENCES
REVIVISCENCIES
REVIVISCENCY
REVIVISCENT
REVOCABILITIES
REVOCABILITY
REVOCABLENESS
REVOCABLENESSES
REVOCATION
REVOCATIONS
REVOCATORY
REVOKABILITIES
REVOKABILITY
REVOKEMENT
REVOKEMENTS
REVOLTINGLY
REVOLUTION
REVOLUTIONAL
REVOLUTIONARIES
REVOLUTIONARILY
REVOLUTIONARY
REVOLUTIONER
REVOLUTIONERS
REVOLUTIONISE
REVOLUTIONISED
REVOLUTIONISER
REVOLUTIONISERS
REVOLUTIONISES
REVOLUTIONISING
REVOLUTIONISM
REVOLUTIONISMS
REVOLUTIONIST
REVOLUTIONISTS
REVOLUTIONIZE
REVOLUTIONIZED
REVOLUTIONIZER
REVOLUTIONIZERS
REVOLUTIONIZES
REVOLUTIONIZING
REVOLUTIONS
REVOLVABLE
REVOLVABLY
REVOLVENCIES
REVOLVENCY
REVOLVINGLY
REVOLVINGS
REVULSIONARY
REVULSIONS
REVULSIVELY
REVULSIVES
REWAKENING
REWARDABLE
REWARDABLENESS
REWARDINGLY
REWARDLESS
REWATERING
REWEIGHING
REWIDENING
REWILDINGS
REWINDINGS
REWORDINGS
REWORKINGS
REWRAPPING
REWRITABLE
REWRITEABLE
RHABDOCOELE

RHABDOCOELES
RHABDOLITH
RHABDOLITHS
RHABDOMANCER
RHABDOMANCERS
RHABDOMANCIES
RHABDOMANCY
RHABDOMANTIST
RHABDOMANTISTS
RHABDOMERE
RHABDOMERES
RHABDOMYOMA
RHABDOMYOMAS
RHABDOMYOMATA
RHABDOSPHERE
RHABDOSPHERES
RHABDOVIRUS
RHABDOVIRUSES
RHACHIDIAL
RHACHILLAS
RHACHITISES
RHADAMANTHINE
RHAGADIFORM
RHAMNACEOUS
RHAMPHOTHECA
RHAMPHOTHECAE
RHAPONTICS
RHAPSODICAL
RHAPSODICALLY
RHAPSODIES
RHAPSODISE
RHAPSODISED
RHAPSODISES
RHAPSODISING
RHAPSODIST
RHAPSODISTIC
RHAPSODISTS
RHAPSODIZE
RHAPSODIZED
RHAPSODIZES
RHAPSODIZING
RHEOCHORDS
RHEOLOGICAL
RHEOLOGICALLY
RHEOLOGIES
RHEOLOGIST
RHEOLOGISTS
RHEOMETERS
RHEOMETRIC
RHEOMETRICAL
RHEOMETRIES
RHEOMORPHIC
RHEOMORPHISM
RHEOMORPHISMS
RHEOPHILES
RHEORECEPTOR
RHEORECEPTORS
RHEOSCOPES
RHEOSTATIC
RHEOTACTIC
RHEOTROPES
RHEOTROPIC
RHEOTROPISM
RHEOTROPISMS
RHETORICAL
RHETORICALLY
RHETORICIAN

RHETORICIANS
RHETORISED
RHETORISES
RHETORISING
RHETORIZED
RHETORIZES
RHETORIZING
RHEUMATEESE
RHEUMATEESES
RHEUMATICAL
RHEUMATICALLY
RHEUMATICKY
RHEUMATICS
RHEUMATISE
RHEUMATISES
RHEUMATISM
RHEUMATISMAL
RHEUMATISMS
RHEUMATIZE
RHEUMATIZES
RHEUMATOID
RHEUMATOIDALLY
RHEUMATOLOGICAL
RHEUMATOLOGIES
RHEUMATOLOGIST
RHEUMATOLOGISTS
RHEUMATOLOGY
RHIGOLENES
RHINENCEPHALA
RHINENCEPHALIC
RHINENCEPHALON
RHINENCEPHALONS
RHINESTONE
RHINESTONED
RHINESTONES
RHINITIDES
RHINITISES
RHINOCERICAL
RHINOCEROI
RHINOCEROS
RHINOCEROSES
RHINOCEROT
RHINOCEROTE
RHINOCEROTES
RHINOCEROTIC
RHINOLALIA
RHINOLALIAS
RHINOLITHS
RHINOLOGICAL
RHINOLOGIES
RHINOLOGIST
RHINOLOGISTS
RHINOPHONIA
RHINOPHONIAS
RHINOPHYMA
RHINOPHYMAS
RHINOPLASTIC
RHINOPLASTIES
RHINOPLASTY
RHINORRHAGIA
RHINORRHAGIAS
RHINORRHOEA
RHINORRHOEAL
RHINORRHOEAS
RHINOSCLEROMA
RHINOSCLEROMAS
RHINOSCLEROMATA

r

SECTION 2: Words between 10 and 15 letters in length

RHINOSCOPE	RHOICISSUSES	RHYTHMUSES	RIEBECKITES	RINKHALSES
RHINOSCOPES	RHOMBENCEPHALA	RHYTIDECTOMIES	RIFACIMENTI	RINSABILITIES
RHINOSCOPIC	RHOMBENCEPHALON	RHYTIDECTOMY	RIFACIMENTO	RINSABILITY
RHINOSCOPIES	RHOMBENPORPHYR	RHYTIDOMES	RIFACIMENTOS	RINSIBILITIES
RHINOSCOPY	RHOMBENPORPHYRS	RIBALDRIES	RIFAMPICIN	RINSIBILITY
RHINOTHECA	RHOMBENPORPHYRY	RIBATTUTAS	RIFAMPICINS	RINTHEREOUT
RHINOTHECAE	RHOMBOHEDRA	RIBAUDRIES	RIFAMYCINS	RINTHEREOUTS
RHINOVIRUS	RHOMBOHEDRAL	RIBAVIRINS	RIFENESSES	RIOTOUSNESS
RHINOVIRUSES	RHOMBOHEDRON	RIBBONFISH	RIFLEBIRDS	RIOTOUSNESSES
RHIPIDIONS	RHOMBOHEDRONS	RIBBONFISHES	RIGAMAROLE	RIPENESSES
RHIPIDIUMS	RHOMBOIDAL	RIBBONIEST	RIGAMAROLES	RIPIDOLITE
RHIZANTHOUS	RHOMBOIDEI	RIBBONLIKE	RIGHTABLENESS	RIPIDOLITES
RHIZOCARPIC	RHOMBOIDES	RIBBONRIES	RIGHTABLENESSES	RIPIENISTS
RHIZOCARPOUS	RHOMBOIDEUS	RIBBONWOOD	RIGHTENING	RIPPLINGLY
RHIZOCARPS	RHOMBPORPHYRIES	RIBBONWOODS	RIGHTEOUSLY	RIPRAPPING
RHIZOCAULS	RHOMBPORPHYRY	RIBGRASSES	RIGHTEOUSNESS	RIPSNORTER
RHIZOCEPHALAN	RHOPALISMS	RIBOFLAVIN	RIGHTEOUSNESSES	RIPSNORTERS
RHIZOCEPHALANS	RHOPALOCERAL	RIBOFLAVINE	RIGHTFULLY	RIPSNORTING
RHIZOCEPHALOUS	RHOPALOCEROUS	RIBOFLAVINES	RIGHTFULNESS	RIPSNORTINGLY
RHIZOCTONIA	RHOTACISED	RIBOFLAVINS	RIGHTFULNESSES	RISIBILITIES
RHIZOCTONIAS	RHOTACISES	RIBONUCLEASE	RIGHTNESSES	RISIBILITY
RHIZOGENETIC	RHOTACISING	RIBONUCLEASES	RIGHTSIZED	RISKINESSES
RHIZOGENIC	RHOTACISMS	RIBONUCLEIC	RIGHTSIZES	RISORGIMENTO
RHIZOGENOUS	RHOTACISTIC	RIBONUCLEOSIDE	RIGHTSIZING	RISORGIMENTOS
RHIZOMATOUS	RHOTACISTS	RIBONUCLEOSIDES	RIGHTSIZINGS	RISTRETTOS
RHIZOMORPH	RHOTACIZED	RIBONUCLEOTIDE	RIGHTWARDLY	RITARDANDI
RHIZOMORPHOUS	RHOTACIZES	RIBONUCLEOTIDES	RIGHTWARDS	RITARDANDO
RHIZOMORPHS	RHOTACIZING	RICEFIELDS	RIGIDIFICATION	RITARDANDOS
RHIZOPHAGOUS	RHOTICITIES	RICEGRASSES	RIGIDIFICATIONS	RITONAVIRS
RHIZOPHILOUS	RHUBARBIER	RICERCARES	RIGIDIFIED	RITORNELLE
RHIZOPHORE	RHUBARBIEST	RICERCATAS	RIGIDIFIES	RITORNELLES
RHIZOPHORES	RHUBARBING	RICHNESSES	RIGIDIFYING	RITORNELLI
RHIZOPLANE	RHUBARBINGS	RICINOLEIC	RIGIDISING	RITORNELLO
RHIZOPLANES	RHUMBATRON	RICKBURNER	RIGIDITIES	RITORNELLOS
RHIZOPODAN	RHUMBATRONS	RICKBURNERS	RIGIDIZING	RITORNELLS
RHIZOPODANS	RHYMESTERS	RICKETIEST	RIGIDNESSES	RITOURNELLE
RHIZOPODOUS	RHYNCHOCOEL	RICKETINESS	RIGMAROLES	RITOURNELLES
RHIZOPUSES	RHYNCHOCOELS	RICKETINESSES	RIGORISTIC	RITUALISATION
RHIZOSPHERE	RHYNCHODONT	RICKETTIER	RIGOROUSLY	RITUALISATIONS
RHIZOSPHERES	RHYNCHOPHORE	RICKETTIEST	RIGOROUSNESS	RITUALISED
RHIZOTOMIES	RHYNCHOPHORES	RICKETTSIA	RIGOROUSNESSES	RITUALISES
RHODAMINES	RHYNCHOPHOROUS	RICKETTSIAE	RIGSDALERS	RITUALISING
RHODANATES	RHYPAROGRAPHER	RICKETTSIAL	RIGWIDDIES	RITUALISMS
RHODANISED	RHYPAROGRAPHERS	RICKETTSIAS	RIGWOODIES	RITUALISTIC
RHODANISES	RHYPAROGRAPHIC	RICKSTANDS	RIJKSDAALER	RITUALISTICALLY
RHODANISING	RHYPAROGRAPHIES	RICKSTICKS	RIJKSDAALERS	RITUALISTS
RHODANIZED	RHYPAROGRAPHY	RICOCHETED	RIJSTAFELS	RITUALIZATION
RHODANIZES	RHYTHMICAL	RICOCHETING	RIJSTTAFEL	RITUALIZATIONS
RHODANIZING	RHYTHMICALLY	RICOCHETTED	RIJSTTAFELS	RITUALIZED
RHODOCHROSITE	RHYTHMICITIES	RICOCHETTING	RIMINESSES	RITUALIZES
RHODOCHROSITES	RHYTHMICITY	RIDABILITIES	RIMOSITIES	RITUALIZING
RHODODAPHNE	RHYTHMISATION	RIDABILITY	RINDERPEST	RITUXIMABS
RHODODAPHNES	RHYTHMISATIONS	RIDDLINGLY	RINDERPESTS	RITZINESSES
RHODODENDRA	RHYTHMISED	RIDERSHIPS	RINFORZANDO	RIVALESSES
RHODODENDRON	RHYTHMISES	RIDESHARING	RINGBARKED	RIVALISING
RHODODENDRONS	RHYTHMISING	RIDESHARINGS	RINGBARKING	RIVALITIES
RHODOLITES	RHYTHMISTS	RIDGEBACKS	RINGHALSES	RIVALIZING
RHODOMONTADE	RHYTHMIZATION	RIDGELINES	RINGLEADER	RIVALSHIPS
RHODOMONTADED	RHYTHMIZATIONS	RIDGELINGS	RINGLEADERS	RIVERBANKS
RHODOMONTADES	RHYTHMIZED	RIDGEPOLES	RINGLETIER	RIVERBOATS
RHODOMONTADING	RHYTHMIZES	RIDGETREES	RINGLETIEST	RIVERCRAFT
RHODONITES	RHYTHMIZING	RIDICULERS	RINGMASTER	RIVERCRAFTS
RHODOPHANE	RHYTHMLESS	RIDICULING	RINGMASTERS	RIVERFRONT
RHODOPHANES	RHYTHMOMETER	RIDICULOUS	RINGSIDERS	RIVERFRONTS
RHODOPSINS	RHYTHMOMETERS	RIDICULOUSLY	RINGSTANDS	RIVERHEADS
RHOEADINES	RHYTHMOPOEIA	RIDICULOUSNESS	RINGSTRAKED	RIVERSCAPE
RHOICISSUS	RHYTHMOPOEIAS	RIEBECKITE	RINGTOSSES	RIVERSCAPES

RIVERSIDES	ROCKSHAFTS	ROLLICKIER	RONTGENOSCOPY	ROTORCRAFTS
RIVERWALKS	ROCKSLIDES	ROLLICKIEST	RONTGENOTHERAPY	ROTOSCOPED
RIVERWARDS	ROCKSTEADIES	ROLLICKING	ROOFLESSNESS	ROTOSCOPES
RIVERWEEDS	ROCKSTEADY	ROLLICKINGS	ROOFLESSNESSES	ROTOSCOPING
RIVERWORTHIER	ROCKWATERS	ROLLOCKING	ROOFSCAPES	ROTOTILLED
RIVERWORTHIEST	RODENTICIDE	ROLLOCKINGS	ROOMINESSES	ROTOTILLER
RIVERWORTHINESS	RODENTICIDES	ROMANCICAL	ROOTEDNESS	ROTOTILLERS
RIVERWORTHY	RODFISHERS	ROMANCINGS	ROOTEDNESSES	ROTOTILLING
RIVETINGLY	RODFISHING	ROMANESCOS	ROOTINESSES	ROTOVATING
ROADABILITIES	RODFISHINGS	ROMANICITE	ROOTLESSNESS	ROTOVATORS
ROADABILITY	RODGERSIAS	ROMANICITES	ROOTLESSNESSES	ROTTENNESS
ROADBLOCKED	RODOMONTADE	ROMANISATION	ROOTSERVER	ROTTENNESSES
ROADBLOCKING	RODOMONTADED	ROMANISATIONS	ROOTSERVERS	ROTTENSTONE
ROADBLOCKS	RODOMONTADER	ROMANISING	ROOTSINESS	ROTTENSTONED
ROADCRAFTS	RODOMONTADERS	ROMANIZATION	ROOTSINESSES	ROTTENSTONES
ROADHEADER	RODOMONTADES	ROMANIZATIONS	ROOTSTALKS	ROTTENSTONING
ROADHEADERS	RODOMONTADING	ROMANIZING	ROOTSTOCKS	ROTTWEILER
ROADHOLDING	ROENTGENISATION	ROMANTICAL	ROPEDANCER	ROTTWEILERS
ROADHOLDINGS	ROENTGENISE	ROMANTICALITIES	ROPEDANCERS	ROTUNDITIES
ROADHOUSES	ROENTGENISED	ROMANTICALITY	ROPEDANCING	ROTUNDNESS
ROADMAKING	ROENTGENISES	ROMANTICALLY	ROPEDANCINGS	ROTUNDNESSES
ROADMAKINGS	ROENTGENISING	ROMANTICISATION	ROPEWALKER	ROUGHBACKS
ROADMENDER	ROENTGENIUM	ROMANTICISE	ROPEWALKERS	ROUGHCASTED
ROADMENDERS	ROENTGENIUMS	ROMANTICISED	ROPINESSES	ROUGHCASTER
ROADROLLER	ROENTGENIZATION	ROMANTICISES	ROQUEFORTS	ROUGHCASTERS
ROADROLLERS	ROENTGENIZE	ROMANTICISING	ROQUELAURE	ROUGHCASTING
ROADRUNNER	ROENTGENIZED	ROMANTICISM	ROQUELAURES	ROUGHCASTS
ROADRUNNERS	ROENTGENIZES	ROMANTICISMS	ROSANILINE	ROUGHDRIED
ROADSTEADS	ROENTGENIZING	ROMANTICIST	ROSANILINES	ROUGHDRIES
ROADWORTHIER	ROENTGENOGRAM	ROMANTICISTS	ROSANILINS	ROUGHDRYING
ROADWORTHIES	ROENTGENOGRAMS	ROMANTICIZATION	ROSEBUSHES	ROUGHENING
ROADWORTHIEST	ROENTGENOGRAPH	ROMANTICIZE	ROSEFINCHES	ROUGHHEWED
ROADWORTHINESS	ROENTGENOGRAPHS	ROMANTICIZED	ROSEFISHES	ROUGHHEWING
ROADWORTHY	ROENTGENOGRAPHY	ROMANTICIZES	ROSEMALING	ROUGHHOUSE
ROBERDSMAN	ROENTGENOLOGIC	ROMANTICIZING	ROSEMALINGS	ROUGHHOUSED
ROBERDSMEN	ROENTGENOLOGIES	ROMELDALES	ROSEMARIES	ROUGHHOUSES
ROBERTSMAN	ROENTGENOLOGIST	ROMPISHNESS	ROSETTINGS	ROUGHHOUSING
ROBERTSMEN	ROENTGENOLOGY	ROMPISHNESSES	ROSEWATERS	ROUGHHOUSINGS
ROBORATING	ROENTGENOPAQUE	RONDOLETTO	ROSINESSES	ROUGHNECKED
ROBOTICALLY	ROENTGENOSCOPE	RONDOLETTOS	ROSINWEEDS	ROUGHNECKING
ROBOTISATION	ROENTGENOSCOPES	RONTGENISATION	ROSMARINES	ROUGHNECKS
ROBOTISATIONS	ROENTGENOSCOPIC	RONTGENISATIONS	ROSTELLATE	ROUGHNESSES
ROBOTISING	ROENTGENOSCOPY	RONTGENISE	ROSTELLUMS	ROUGHRIDER
ROBOTIZATION	ROGUESHIPS	RONTGENISED	ROSTERINGS	ROUGHRIDERS
ROBOTIZATIONS	ROGUISHNESS	RONTGENISES	ROSTROCARINATE	ROULETTING
ROBOTIZING	ROGUISHNESSES	RONTGENISING	ROSTROCARINATES	ROUNCEVALS
ROBUSTIOUS	ROISTERERS	RONTGENIZATION	ROTACHUTES	ROUNDABOUT
ROBUSTIOUSLY	ROISTERING	RONTGENIZATIONS	ROTAMETERS	ROUNDABOUTATION
ROBUSTIOUSNESS	ROISTERINGS	RONTGENIZE	ROTAPLANES	ROUNDABOUTED
ROBUSTNESS	ROISTEROUS	RONTGENIZED	ROTATIONAL	ROUNDABOUTEDLY
ROBUSTNESSES	ROISTEROUSLY	RONTGENIZES	ROTATIVELY	ROUNDABOUTILITY
ROCAMBOLES	ROLLCOLLAR	RONTGENIZING	ROTAVATING	ROUNDABOUTING
ROCKABILLIES	ROLLCOLLARS	RONTGENOGRAM	ROTAVATORS	ROUNDABOUTLY
ROCKABILLY	ROLLERBALL	RONTGENOGRAMS	ROTAVIRUSES	ROUNDABOUTNESS
ROCKBURSTS	ROLLERBALLS	RONTGENOGRAPH	ROTGRASSES	ROUNDABOUTS
ROCKCRESSES	ROLLERBLADE	RONTGENOGRAPHS	ROTIFERANS	ROUNDARCHED
ROCKETEERS	ROLLERBLADED	RONTGENOGRAPHY	ROTIFEROUS	ROUNDBALLS
ROCKETRIES	ROLLERBLADER	RONTGENOLOGICAL	ROTISSERIE	ROUNDEDNESS
ROCKETSONDE	ROLLERBLADERS	RONTGENOLOGIES	ROTISSERIED	ROUNDEDNESSES
ROCKETSONDES	ROLLERBLADES	RONTGENOLOGIST	ROTISSERIEING	ROUNDELAYS
ROCKFISHES	ROLLERBLADING	RONTGENOLOGISTS	ROTISSERIES	ROUNDHANDS
ROCKHOPPER	ROLLERBLADINGS	RONTGENOLOGY	ROTOGRAPHED	ROUNDHEADED
ROCKHOPPERS	ROLLERCOASTER	RONTGENOPAQUE	ROTOGRAPHING	ROUNDHEADEDNESS
ROCKHOUNDING	ROLLERCOASTERED	RONTGENOSCOPE	ROTOGRAPHS	ROUNDHEELS
ROCKHOUNDINGS	ROLLERCOASTERS	RONTGENOSCOPES	ROTOGRAVURE	ROUNDHOUSE
ROCKHOUNDS	ROLLERDROME	RONTGENOSCOPIC	ROTOGRAVURES	ROUNDHOUSES
ROCKINESSES	ROLLERDROMES	RONTGENOSCOPIES	ROTORCRAFT	ROUNDNESSES

r

ROUNDTABLE
ROUNDTABLES
ROUNDTRIPPING
ROUNDTRIPPINGS
ROUNDTRIPS
ROUNDWOODS
ROUNDWORMS
ROUSEABOUT
ROUSEABOUTS
ROUSEDNESS
ROUSEDNESSES
ROUSEMENTS
ROUSSETTES
ROUSTABOUT
ROUSTABOUTS
ROUTEMARCH
ROUTEMARCHED
ROUTEMARCHES
ROUTEMARCHING
ROUTINEERS
ROUTINISATION
ROUTINISATIONS
ROUTINISED
ROUTINISES
ROUTINISING
ROUTINISMS
ROUTINISTS
ROUTINIZATION
ROUTINIZATIONS
ROUTINIZED
ROUTINIZES
ROUTINIZING
ROWANBERRIES
ROWANBERRY
ROWDINESSES
ROWDYDOWED
ROWDYDOWING
ROYALISING
ROYALISTIC
ROYALIZING
ROYALMASTS
ROYSTERERS
ROYSTERING
ROYSTEROUS
RUBBERIEST
RUBBERISED
RUBBERISES
RUBBERISING
RUBBERIZED

RUBBERIZES
RUBBERIZING
RUBBERLIKE
RUBBERNECK
RUBBERNECKED
RUBBERNECKER
RUBBERNECKERS
RUBBERNECKING
RUBBERNECKS
RUBBERWEAR
RUBBERWEARS
RUBBISHIER
RUBBISHIEST
RUBBISHING
RUBBISHLIER
RUBBISHLIEST
RUBBLEWORK
RUBBLEWORKS
RUBEFACIENT
RUBEFACIENTS
RUBEFACTION
RUBEFACTIONS
RUBELLITES
RUBESCENCE
RUBESCENCES
RUBIACEOUS
RUBICELLES
RUBICONING
RUBICUNDITIES
RUBICUNDITY
RUBIGINOSE
RUBIGINOUS
RUBRICALLY
RUBRICATED
RUBRICATES
RUBRICATING
RUBRICATION
RUBRICATIONS
RUBRICATOR
RUBRICATORS
RUBRICIANS
RUBYTHROAT
RUBYTHROATS
RUCTATIONS
RUDBECKIAS
RUDDERHEAD
RUDDERHEADS
RUDDERLESS
RUDDERPOST

RUDDERPOSTS
RUDDERSTOCK
RUDDERSTOCKS
RUDDINESSES
RUDENESSES
RUDIMENTAL
RUDIMENTALLY
RUDIMENTARILY
RUDIMENTARINESS
RUDIMENTARY
RUEFULNESS
RUEFULNESSES
RUFESCENCE
RUFESCENCES
RUFFIANING
RUFFIANISH
RUFFIANISM
RUFFIANISMS
RUGGEDISATION
RUGGEDISATIONS
RUGGEDISED
RUGGEDISES
RUGGEDISING
RUGGEDIZATION
RUGGEDIZATIONS
RUGGEDIZED
RUGGEDIZES
RUGGEDIZING.
RUGGEDNESS
RUGGEDNESSES
RUGOSITIES
RUINATIONS
RUINOUSNESS
RUINOUSNESSES
RULERSHIPS
RUMBLEDETHUMP
RUMBLEDETHUMPS
RUMBLEGUMPTION
RUMBLEGUMPTIONS
RUMBLINGLY
RUMBULLION
RUMBULLIONS
RUMBUNCTIOUS
RUMBUSTICAL
RUMBUSTIOUS
RUMBUSTIOUSLY
RUMBUSTIOUSNESS
RUMELGUMPTION
RUMELGUMPTIONS

RUMFUSTIAN
RUMFUSTIANS
RUMGUMPTION
RUMGUMPTIONS
RUMINANTLY
RUMINATING
RUMINATINGLY
RUMINATION
RUMINATIONS
RUMINATIVE
RUMINATIVELY
RUMINATORS
RUMLEGUMPTION
RUMLEGUMPTIONS
RUMMELGUMPTION
RUMMELGUMPTIONS
RUMMINESSES
RUMMISHING
RUMMLEGUMPTION
RUMMLEGUMPTIONS
RUMORMONGER
RUMORMONGERING
RUMORMONGERINGS
RUMORMONGERS
RUMRUNNERS
RUNAROUNDS
RUNECRAFTS
RUNNINESSES
RUNTINESSES
RUPESTRIAN
RUPICOLINE
RUPICOLOUS
RUPTURABLE
RUPTUREWORT
RUPTUREWORTS
RURALISATION
RURALISATIONS
RURALISING
RURALITIES
RURALIZATION
RURALIZATIONS
RURALIZING
RURALNESSES
RURIDECANAL
RUSHINESSES
RUSHLIGHTS
RUSSETIEST
RUSSETINGS
RUSSETTING

RUSSETTINGS
RUSSIFYING
RUSTBUCKET
RUSTBUCKETS
RUSTICALLY
RUSTICATED
RUSTICATES
RUSTICATING
RUSTICATINGS
RUSTICATION
RUSTICATIONS
RUSTICATOR
RUSTICATORS
RUSTICISED
RUSTICISES
RUSTICISING
RUSTICISMS
RUSTICITIES
RUSTICIZED
RUSTICIZES
RUSTICIZING
RUSTICWORK
RUSTICWORKS
RUSTINESSES
RUSTLINGLY
RUSTPROOFED
RUSTPROOFING
RUSTPROOFINGS
RUSTPROOFS
RUTHENIOUS
RUTHENIUMS
RUTHERFORD
RUTHERFORDIUM
RUTHERFORDIUMS
RUTHERFORDS
RUTHFULNESS
RUTHFULNESSES
RUTHLESSLY
RUTHLESSNESS
RUTHLESSNESSES
RUTTINESSES
RUTTISHNESS
RUTTISHNESSES
RYBAUDRYES
RYEGRASSES

r

S

SABADILLAS
SABBATARIAN
SABBATICAL
SABBATICALS
SABBATISED
SABBATISES
SABBATISING
SABBATISMS
SABBATIZED
SABBATIZES
SABBATIZING
SABERMETRICIAN
SABERMETRICIANS
SABERMETRICS
SABLEFISHES
SABOTAGING
SABRETACHE
SABRETACHES
SABREWINGS
SABULOSITIES
SABULOSITY
SABURRATION
SABURRATIONS
SACAHUISTA
SACAHUISTAS
SACAHUISTE
SACAHUISTES
SACCADICALLY
SACCHARASE
SACCHARASES
SACCHARATE
SACCHARATED
SACCHARATES
SACCHARIDE
SACCHARIDES
SACCHARIFEROUS
SACCHARIFIED
SACCHARIFIES
SACCHARIFY
SACCHARIFYING
SACCHARIMETER
SACCHARIMETERS
SACCHARIMETRIES
SACCHARIMETRY
SACCHARINE
SACCHARINELY
SACCHARINES
SACCHARINITIES
SACCHARINITY
SACCHARINS
SACCHARISATION
SACCHARISATIONS
SACCHARISE
SACCHARISED

SACCHARISES
SACCHARISING
SACCHARIZATION
SACCHARIZATIONS
SACCHARIZE
SACCHARIZED
SACCHARIZES
SACCHARIZING
SACCHAROID
SACCHAROIDAL
SACCHAROIDS
SACCHAROMETER
SACCHAROMETERS
SACCHAROMETRIES
SACCHAROMETRY
SACCHAROMYCES
SACCHAROMYCETES
SACCHAROSE
SACCHAROSES
SACCHARUMS
SACCULATED
SACCULATION
SACCULATIONS
SACCULIFORM
SACERDOTAL
SACERDOTALISE
SACERDOTALISED
SACERDOTALISES
SACERDOTALISING
SACERDOTALISM
SACERDOTALISMS
SACERDOTALIST
SACERDOTALISTS
SACERDOTALIZE
SACERDOTALIZED
SACERDOTALIZES
SACERDOTALIZING
SACERDOTALLY
SACHEMDOMS
SACHEMSHIP
SACHEMSHIPS
SACKCLOTHS
SACRALGIAS
SACRALISATION
SACRALISATIONS
SACRALISED
SACRALISES
SACRALISING
SACRALITIES
SACRALIZATION
SACRALIZATIONS
SACRALIZED
SACRALIZES
SACRALIZING

SACRAMENTAL
SACRAMENTALISM
SACRAMENTALISMS
SACRAMENTALIST
SACRAMENTALISTS
SACRAMENTALITY
SACRAMENTALLY
SACRAMENTALNESS
SACRAMENTALS
SACRAMENTARIAN
SACRAMENTARIANS
SACRAMENTARIES
SACRAMENTARY
SACRAMENTED
SACRAMENTING
SACRAMENTS
SACRARIUMS
SACREDNESS
SACREDNESSES
SACRIFICEABLE
SACRIFICED
SACRIFICER
SACRIFICERS
SACRIFICES
SACRIFICIAL
SACRIFICIALLY
SACRIFICING
SACRIFYING
SACRILEGES
SACRILEGIOUS
SACRILEGIOUSLY
SACRILEGIST
SACRILEGISTS
SACRISTANS
SACRISTIES
SACROCOCCYGEAL
SACROCOSTAL
SACROCOSTALS
SACROILIAC
SACROILIACS
SACROILIITIS
SACROILIITISES
SACROSANCT
SACROSANCTITIES
SACROSANCTITY
SACROSANCTNESS
SADDLEBACK
SADDLEBACKED
SADDLEBACKS
SADDLEBAGS
SADDLEBILL
SADDLEBILLS
SADDLEBOWS
SADDLEBRED

SADDLEBREDS
SADDLECLOTH
SADDLECLOTHS
SADDLELESS
SADDLERIES
SADDLEROOM
SADDLEROOMS
SADDLETREE
SADDLETREES
SADISTICALLY
SADOMASOCHISM
SADOMASOCHISMS
SADOMASOCHIST
SADOMASOCHISTIC
SADOMASOCHISTS
SAFECRACKER
SAFECRACKERS
SAFECRACKING
SAFECRACKINGS
SAFEGUARDED
SAFEGUARDING
SAFEGUARDS
SAFEKEEPING
SAFEKEEPINGS
SAFELIGHTS
SAFENESSES
SAFFLOWERS
SAFFRONIER
SAFFRONIEST
SAFRANINES
SAGACIOUSLY
SAGACIOUSNESS
SAGACIOUSNESSES
SAGACITIES
SAGANASHES
SAGAPENUMS
SAGEBRUSHES
SAGENESSES
SAGINATING
SAGINATION
SAGINATIONS
SAGITTALLY
SAGITTARIES
SAGITTIFORM
SAILBOARDED
SAILBOARDER
SAILBOARDERS
SAILBOARDING
SAILBOARDINGS
SAILBOARDS
SAILBOATER
SAILBOATERS
SAILBOATING
SAILBOATINGS

SAILCLOTHS
SAILFISHES
SAILMAKERS
SAILMAKING
SAILMAKINGS
SAILORINGS
SAILORLESS
SAILORLIER
SAILORLIEST
SAILORLIKE
SAILPLANED
SAILPLANER
SAILPLANERS
SAILPLANES
SAILPLANING
SAILPLANINGS
SAINTESSES
SAINTFOINS
SAINTHOODS
SAINTLIEST
SAINTLINESS
SAINTLINESSES
SAINTLINGS
SAINTPAULIA
SAINTPAULIAS
SAINTSHIPS
SALABILITIES
SALABILITY
SALABLENESS
SALABLENESSES
SALACIOUSLY
SALACIOUSNESS
SALACIOUSNESSES
SALACITIES
SALAMANDER
SALAMANDERS
SALAMANDRIAN
SALAMANDRIANS
SALAMANDRINE
SALAMANDROID
SALAMANDROIDS
SALANGANES
SALBUTAMOL
SALBUTAMOLS
SALEABILITIES
SALEABILITY
SALEABLENESS
SALEABLENESSES
SALERATUSES
SALESCLERK
SALESCLERKS
SALESGIRLS
SALESLADIES
SALESMANSHIP

SALESMANSHIPS	SALMONELLOSIS	SALUTIFEROUS	SANDALWOODS	SANGUINIVOROUS
SALESPEOPLE	SALMONIEST	SALVABILITIES	SANDARACHS	SANGUINOLENCIES
SALESPERSON	SALMONOIDS	SALVABILITY	SANDBAGGED	SANGUINOLENCY
SALESPERSONS	SALOMETERS	SALVABLENESS	SANDBAGGER	SANGUINOLENT
SALESROOMS	SALOPETTES	SALVABLENESSES	SANDBAGGERS	SANGUIVOROUS
SALESWOMAN	SALPIGLOSSES	SALVAGEABILITY	SANDBAGGING	SANITARIAN
SALESWOMEN	SALPIGLOSSIS	SALVAGEABLE	SANDBLASTED	SANITARIANISM
SALIAUNCES	SALPIGLOSSISES	SALVARSANS	SANDBLASTER	SANITARIANISMS
SALICACEOUS	SALPINGECTOMIES	SALVATIONAL	SANDBLASTERS	SANITARIANS
SALICETUMS	SALPINGECTOMY	SALVATIONISM	SANDBLASTING	SANITARIES
SALICIONAL	SALPINGIAN	SALVATIONISMS	SANDBLASTINGS	SANITARILY
SALICIONALS	SALPINGITIC	SALVATIONIST	SANDBLASTS	SANITARINESS
SALICORNIA	SALPINGITIS	SALVATIONISTS	SANDCASTLE	SANITARINESSES
SALICORNIAS	SALPINGITISES	SALVATIONS	SANDCASTLES	SANITARIST
SALICYLAMIDE	SALSOLACEOUS	SALVATORIES	SANDCRACKS	SANITARISTS
SALICYLAMIDES	SALSUGINOUS	SALVERFORM	SANDERLING	SANITARIUM
SALICYLATE	SALTARELLI	SALVIFICAL	SANDERLINGS	SANITARIUMS
SALICYLATED	SALTARELLO	SALVIFICALLY	SANDERSWOOD	SANITATING
SALICYLATES	SALTARELLOS	SALVINIACEOUS	SANDERSWOODS	SANITATION
SALICYLATING	SALTATIONISM	SAMARIFORM	SANDFISHES	SANITATIONIST
SALICYLISM	SALTATIONISMS	SAMARITANS	SANDGLASSES	SANITATIONISTS
SALICYLISMS	SALTATIONIST	SAMARSKITE	SANDGROPER	SANITATIONS
SALIENCIES	SALTATIONISTS	SAMARSKITES	SANDGROPERS	SANITISATION
SALIENTIAN	SALTATIONS	SAMENESSES	SANDGROUSE	SANITISATIONS
SALIENTIANS	SALTATORIAL	SAMEYNESSES	SANDGROUSES	SANITISERS
SALIFEROUS	SALTATORIOUS	SAMNITISES	SANDINESSES	SANITISING
SALIFIABLE	SALTBUSHES	SAMPLERIES	SANDLOTTER	SANITIZATION
SALIFICATION	SALTCELLAR	SANATORIUM	SANDLOTTERS	SANITIZATIONS
SALIFICATIONS	SALTCELLARS	SANATORIUMS	SANDPAINTING	SANITIZERS
SALIMETERS	SALTCHUCKER	SANBENITOS	SANDPAINTINGS	SANITIZING
SALIMETRIC	SALTCHUCKERS	SANCTIFIABLE	SANDPAPERED	SANITORIUM
SALIMETRIES	SALTCHUCKS	SANCTIFICATION	SANDPAPERIER	SANITORIUMS
SALINISATION	SALTFISHES	SANCTIFICATIONS	SANDPAPERIEST	SANNYASINS
SALINISATIONS	SALTIGRADE	SANCTIFIED	SANDPAPERING	SANSCULOTTE
SALINISING	SALTIGRADES	SANCTIFIEDLY	SANDPAPERINGS	SANSCULOTTERIE
SALINITIES	SALTIMBANCO	SANCTIFIER	SANDPAPERS	SANSCULOTTERIES
SALINIZATION	SALTIMBANCOS	SANCTIFIERS	SANDPAPERY	SANSCULOTTES
SALINIZATIONS	SALTIMBOCCA	SANCTIFIES	SANDPIPERS	SANSCULOTTIC
SALINIZING	SALTIMBOCCAS	SANCTIFYING	SANDSPOUTS	SANSCULOTTIDES
SALINOMETER	SALTINESSES	SANCTIFYINGLY	SANDSTONES	SANSCULOTTISH
SALINOMETERS	SALTIREWISE	SANCTIFYINGS	SANDSTORMS	SANSCULOTTISM
SALINOMETRIC	SALTISHNESS	SANCTIMONIES	SANDSUCKER	SANSCULOTTISMS
SALINOMETRIES	SALTISHNESSES	SANCTIMONIOUS	SANDSUCKERS	SANSCULOTTIST
SALINOMETRY	SALTNESSES	SANCTIMONIOUSLY	SANDWICHED	SANSCULOTTISTS
SALIVATING	SALTPETERS	SANCTIMONY	SANDWICHES	SANSEVIERIA
SALIVATION	SALTPETREMAN	SANCTIONABLE	SANDWICHING	SANSEVIERIAS
SALIVATIONS	SALTPETREMEN	SANCTIONED	SANENESSES	SANTALACEOUS
SALIVATORS	SALTPETRES	SANCTIONEER	SANGFROIDS	SANTOLINAS
SALLENDERS	SALTSHAKER	SANCTIONEERS	SANGUIFEROUS	SANTONICAS
SALLOWIEST	SALTSHAKERS	SANCTIONER	SANGUIFICATION	SAPANWOODS
SALLOWNESS	SALTWATERS	SANCTIONERS	SANGUIFICATIONS	SAPIDITIES
SALLOWNESSES	SALUBRIOUS	SANCTIONING	SANGUIFIED	SAPIDNESSES
SALLYPORTS	SALUBRIOUSLY	SANCTIONLESS	SANGUIFIES	SAPIENCIES
SALMAGUNDI	SALUBRIOUSNESS	SANCTITIES	SANGUIFYING	SAPIENTIAL
SALMAGUNDIES	SALUBRITIES	SANCTITUDE	SANGUINARIA	SAPIENTIALLY
SALMAGUNDIS	SALURETICS	SANCTITUDES	SANGUINARIAS	SAPINDACEOUS
SALMAGUNDY	SALUTARILY	SANCTUARIES	SANGUINARILY	SAPLESSNESS
SALMANASER	SALUTARINESS	SANCTUARISE	SANGUINARINESS	SAPLESSNESSES
SALMANASERS	SALUTARINESSES	SANCTUARISED	SANGUINARY	SAPODILLAS
SALMANAZAR	SALUTATION	SANCTUARISES	SANGUINELY	SAPOGENINS
SALMANAZARS	SALUTATIONAL	SANCTUARISING	SANGUINENESS	SAPONACEOUS
SALMONBERRIES	SALUTATIONS	SANCTUARIZE	SANGUINENESSES	SAPONACEOUSNESS
SALMONBERRY	SALUTATORIAN	SANCTUARIZED	SANGUINEOUS	SAPONARIAS
SALMONELLA	SALUTATORIANS	SANCTUARIZES	SANGUINEOUSNESS	SAPONIFIABLE
SALMONELLAE	SALUTATORIES	SANCTUARIZING	SANGUINING	SAPONIFICATION
SALMONELLAS	SALUTATORILY	SANDALLING	SANGUINITIES	SAPONIFICATIONS
SALMONELLOSES	SALUTATORY	SANDALWOOD	SANGUINITY	SAPONIFIED

SAPONIFIER	SARCOPHAGUSES	SATINETTAS	SAUERKRAUTS	SCAFFOLAGES
SAPONIFIERS	SARCOPLASM	SATINETTES	SAUNTERERS	SCAFFOLDAGE
SAPONIFIES	SARCOPLASMIC	SATINFLOWER	SAUNTERING	SCAFFOLDAGES
SAPONIFYING	SARCOPLASMS	SATINFLOWERS	SAUNTERINGLY	SCAFFOLDED
SAPOTACEOUS	SARCOSOMAL	SATINWOODS	SAUNTERINGS	SCAFFOLDER
SAPPANWOOD	SARCOSOMES	SATIRICALLY	SAURISCHIAN	SCAFFOLDERS
SAPPANWOODS	SARDONIANS	SATIRICALNESS	SAURISCHIANS	SCAFFOLDING
SAPPERMENT	SARDONICAL	SATIRICALNESSES	SAUROGNATHOUS	SCAFFOLDINGS
SAPPHIRINE	SARDONICALLY	SATIRISABLE	SAUROPODOUS	SCAGLIOLAS
SAPPHIRINES	SARDONICISM	SATIRISATION	SAUROPSIDAN	SCAITHLESS
SAPPINESSES	SARDONICISMS	SATIRISATIONS	SAUROPSIDANS	SCALABILITIES
SAPRAEMIAS	SARDONYXES	SATIRISERS	SAUROPTERYGIAN	SCALABILITY
SAPROBIONT	SARGASSOES	SATIRISING	SAUROPTERYGIANS	SCALABLENESS
SAPROBIONTS	SARGASSUMS	SATIRIZABLE	SAUSSURITE	SCALABLENESSES
SAPROBIOTIC	SARKINESSES	SATIRIZATION	SAUSSURITES	SCALARIFORM
SAPROBITIES	SARMENTACEOUS	SATIRIZATIONS	SAUSSURITIC	SCALARIFORMLY
SAPROGENIC	SARMENTOSE	SATIRIZERS	SAVABLENESS	SCALATIONS
SAPROGENICITIES	SARMENTOUS	SATIRIZING	SAVABLENESSES	SCALDBERRIES
SAPROGENICITY	SARPANCHES	SATISFACTION	SAVAGEDOMS	SCALDBERRY
SAPROGENOUS	SARRACENIA	SATISFACTIONS	SAVAGENESS	SCALDFISHES
SAPROLEGNIA	SARRACENIACEOUS	SATISFACTORILY	SAVAGENESSES	SCALDHEADS
SAPROLEGNIAS	SARRACENIAS	SATISFACTORY	SAVAGERIES	SCALDSHIPS
SAPROLITES	SARRUSOPHONE	SATISFIABLE	SAVEABLENESS	SCALEBOARD
SAPROLITIC	SARRUSOPHONES	SATISFICED	SAVEABLENESSES	SCALEBOARDS
SAPROPELIC	SARSAPARILLA	SATISFICER	SAVEGARDED	SCALENOHEDRA
SAPROPELITE	SARSAPARILLAS	SATISFICERS	SAVEGARDING	SCALENOHEDRON
SAPROPELITES	SARTORIALLY	SATISFICES	SAVINGNESS	SCALENOHEDRONS
SAPROPHAGOUS	SARTORIUSES	SATISFICING	SAVINGNESSES	SCALETAILS
SAPROPHYTE	SASKATOONS	SATISFICINGS	SAVORINESS	SCALEWORKS
SAPROPHYTES	SASQUATCHES	SATISFIERS	SAVORINESSES	SCALINESSES
SAPROPHYTIC	SASSAFRASES	SATISFYING	SAVOURIEST	SCALLAWAGS
SAPROPHYTICALLY	SASSARARAS	SATISFYINGLY	SAVOURINESS	SCALLOPERS
SAPROPHYTISM	SASSINESSES	SATURABILITIES	SAVOURINESSES	SCALLOPING
SAPROPHYTISMS	SASSOLITES	SATURABILITY	SAVOURLESS	SCALLOPINGS
SAPROTROPH	SASSYWOODS	SATURATERS	SAVVINESSES	SCALLOPINI
SAPROTROPHIC	SATANICALLY	SATURATING	SAWBONESES	SCALLOPINIS
SAPROTROPHS	SATANICALNESS	SATURATION	SAWDUSTIER	SCALLYWAGS
SAPSUCKERS	SATANICALNESSES	SATURATIONS	SAWDUSTIEST	SCALOGRAMS
SARABANDES	SATANITIES	SATURATORS	SAWDUSTING	SCALOPPINE
SARBACANES	SATANOLOGIES	SATURNALIA	SAWGRASSES	SCALOPPINES
SARCASTICALLY	SATANOLOGY	SATURNALIAN	SAWMILLERS	SCALOPPINI
SARCENCHYMATOUS	SATANOPHANIES	SATURNALIANLY	SAWTIMBERS	SCALPELLIC
SARCENCHYME	SATANOPHANY	SATURNALIAS	SAXICAVOUS	SCALPELLIFORM
SARCENCHYMES	SATANOPHOBIA	SATURNIIDS	SAXICOLINE	SCALPRIFORM
SARCOCARPS	SATANOPHOBIAS	SATURNINELY	SAXICOLOUS	SCAMBAITING
SARCOCOLLA	SATCHELFUL	SATURNINITIES	SAXIFRAGACEOUS	SCAMBAITINGS
SARCOCOLLAS	SATCHELFULS	SATURNINITY	SAXIFRAGES	SCAMBLINGLY
SARCOCYSTIS	SATCHELLED	SATURNISMS	SAXITOXINS	SCAMBLINGS
SARCOCYSTISES	SATCHELSFUL	SATURNISTS	SAXOPHONES	SCAMMONIATE
SARCOIDOSES	SATEDNESSES	SATYAGRAHA	SAXOPHONIC	SCAMMONIES
SARCOIDOSIS	SATELLITED	SATYAGRAHAS	SAXOPHONIST	SCAMPERERS
SARCOLEMMA	SATELLITES	SATYAGRAHI	SAXOPHONISTS	SCAMPERING
SARCOLEMMAL	SATELLITIC	SATYAGRAHIS	SCABBARDED	SCAMPERINGS
SARCOLEMMAS	SATELLITING	SATYRESQUE	SCABBARDING	SCAMPISHLY
SARCOLEMMATA	SATELLITISE	SATYRESSES	SCABBARDLESS	SCAMPISHNESS
SARCOLOGIES	SATELLITISED	SATYRIASES	SCABBEDNESS	SCAMPISHNESSES
SARCOMATOID	SATELLITISES	SATYRIASIS	SCABBEDNESSES	SCANDALING
SARCOMATOSES	SATELLITISING	SAUCEBOATS	SCABBINESS	SCANDALISATION
SARCOMATOSIS	SATELLITIUM	SAUCEBOXES	SCABBINESSES	SCANDALISATIONS
SARCOMATOUS	SATELLITIUMS	SAUCERFULS	SCABEROULOUS	SCANDALISE
SARCOMERES	SATELLITIZE	SAUCERLESS	SCABIOUSES	SCANDALISED
SARCOPENIA	SATELLITIZED	SAUCERLIKE	SCABRIDITIES	SCANDALISER
SARCOPENIAS	SATELLITIZES	SAUCINESSES	SCABRIDITY	SCANDALISERS
SARCOPHAGAL	SATELLITIZING	SAUCISSONS	SCABROUSLY	SCANDALISES
SARCOPHAGI	SATIABILITIES	SAUERBRATEN	SCABROUSNESS	SCANDALISING
SARCOPHAGOUS	SATIABILITY	SAUERBRATENS	SCABROUSNESSES	SCANDALIZATION
SARCOPHAGUS	SATIATIONS	SAUERKRAUT	SCAFFOLAGE	SCANDALIZATIONS

SCANDALIZE	SCARCEMENT	SCATURIENT	SCHEMATISE	SCHIZOGENESIS
SCANDALIZED	SCARCEMENTS	SCAVENGERED	SCHEMATISED	SCHIZOGENETIC
SCANDALIZER	SCARCENESS	SCAVENGERIES	SCHEMATISES	SCHIZOGENIC
SCANDALIZERS	SCARCENESSES	SCAVENGERING	SCHEMATISING	SCHIZOGNATHOUS
SCANDALIZES	SCARCITIES	SCAVENGERINGS	SCHEMATISM	SCHIZOGONIC
SCANDALIZING	SCARECROWS	SCAVENGERS	SCHEMATISMS	SCHIZOGONIES
SCANDALLED	SCAREHEADS	SCAVENGERY	SCHEMATIST	SCHIZOGONOUS
SCANDALLING	SCAREMONGER	SCAVENGING	SCHEMATISTS	SCHIZOGONY
SCANDALMONGER	SCAREMONGERING	SCAVENGINGS	SCHEMATIZATION	SCHIZOIDAL
SCANDALMONGERS	SCAREMONGERINGS	SCAZONTICS	SCHEMATIZATIONS	SCHIZOMYCETE
SCANDALOUS	SCAREMONGERS	SCELERATES	SCHEMATIZE	SCHIZOMYCETES
SCANDALOUSLY	SCAREWARES	SCENARISATION	SCHEMATIZED	SCHIZOMYCETIC
SCANDALOUSNESS	SCARFISHES	SCENARISATIONS	SCHEMATIZES	SCHIZOMYCETOUS
SCANSORIAL	SCARFSKINS	SCENARISED	SCHEMATIZING	SCHIZOPHRENE
SCANTINESS	SCARIFICATION	SCENARISES	SCHEMINGLY	SCHIZOPHRENES
SCANTINESSES	SCARIFICATIONS	SCENARISING	SCHEMOZZLE	SCHIZOPHRENETIC
SCANTITIES	SCARIFICATOR	SCENARISTS	SCHEMOZZLED	SCHIZOPHRENIA
SCANTLINGS	SCARIFICATORS	SCENARIZATION	SCHEMOZZLES	SCHIZOPHRENIAS
SCANTNESSES	SCARIFIERS	SCENARIZATIONS	SCHEMOZZLING	SCHIZOPHRENIC
SCAPEGALLOWS	SCARIFYING	SCENARIZED	SCHERZANDI	SCHIZOPHRENICS
SCAPEGALLOWSES	SCARIFYINGLY	SCENARIZES	SCHERZANDO	SCHIZOPHYCEOUS
SCAPEGOATED	SCARINESSES	SCENARIZING	SCHERZANDOS	SCHIZOPHYTE
SCAPEGOATING	SCARLATINA	SCENESHIFTER	SCHIAVONES	SCHIZOPHYTES
SCAPEGOATINGS	SCARLATINAL	SCENESHIFTERS	SCHILLERISATION	SCHIZOPHYTIC
SCAPEGOATISM	SCARLATINAS	SCENESTERS	SCHILLERISE	SCHIZOPODAL
SCAPEGOATISMS	SCARLETING	SCENICALLY	SCHILLERISED	SCHIZOPODOUS
SCAPEGOATS	SCARPERING	SCENOGRAPHER	SCHILLERISES	SCHIZOPODS
SCAPEGRACE	SCATHEFULNESS	SCENOGRAPHERS	SCHILLERISING	SCHIZOTHYMIA
SCAPEGRACES	SCATHEFULNESSES	SCENOGRAPHIC	SCHILLERIZATION	SCHIZOTHYMIAS
SCAPEMENTS	SCATHELESS	SCENOGRAPHICAL	SCHILLERIZE	SCHIZOTHYMIC
SCAPEWHEEL	SCATHINGLY	SCENOGRAPHIES	SCHILLERIZED	SCHIZZIEST
SCAPEWHEELS	SCATOLOGIC	SCENOGRAPHY	SCHILLERIZES	SCHLEMIELS
SCAPHOCEPHALI	SCATOLOGICAL	SCENTLESSNESS	SCHILLERIZING	SCHLEMIHLS
SCAPHOCEPHALIC	SCATOLOGIES	SCENTLESSNESSES	SCHILLINGS	SCHLEPPERS
SCAPHOCEPHALICS	SCATOLOGIST	SCEPTERING	SCHINDYLESES	SCHLEPPIER
SCAPHOCEPHALIES	SCATOLOGISTS	SCEPTERLESS	SCHINDYLESIS	SCHLEPPIEST
SCAPHOCEPHALISM	SCATOPHAGIES	SCEPTICALLY	SCHINDYLETIC	SCHLEPPING
SCAPHOCEPHALOUS	SCATOPHAGOUS	SCEPTICISM	SCHIPPERKE	SCHLIERENS
SCAPHOCEPHALUS	SCATOPHAGY	SCEPTICISMS	SCHIPPERKES	SCHLIMAZEL
SCAPHOCEPHALY	SCATTERABLE	SCEPTRELESS	SCHISMATIC	SCHLIMAZELS
SCAPHOPODS	SCATTERATION	SCEUOPHYLACIA	SCHISMATICAL	SCHLOCKERS
SCAPIGEROUS	SCATTERATIONS	SCEUOPHYLACIUM	SCHISMATICALLY	SCHLOCKEYS
SCAPOLITES	SCATTERBRAIN	SCEUOPHYLACIUMS	SCHISMATICALS	SCHLOCKIER
SCAPULARIES	SCATTERBRAINED	SCEUOPHYLAX	SCHISMATICS	SCHLOCKIEST
SCAPULATED	SCATTERBRAINS	SCEUOPHYLAXES	SCHISMATISE	SCHLUMBERGERA
SCAPULIMANCIES	SCATTEREDLY	SCHADENFREUDE	SCHISMATISED	SCHLUMBERGERAS
SCAPULIMANCY	SCATTERERS	SCHADENFREUDES	SCHISMATISES	SCHLUMPIER
SCAPULIMANTIC	SCATTERGOOD	SCHALSTEIN	SCHISMATISING	SCHLUMPIEST
SCAPULOMANCIES	SCATTERGOODS	SCHALSTEINS	SCHISMATIZE	SCHLUMPING
SCAPULOMANCY	SCATTERGRAM	SCHAPPEING	SCHISMATIZED	SCHMALTZES
SCAPULOMANTIC	SCATTERGRAMS	SCHATCHENS	SCHISMATIZES	SCHMALTZIER
SCARABAEAN	SCATTERGUN	SCHECHITAH	SCHISMATIZING	SCHMALTZIEST
SCARABAEANS	SCATTERGUNS	SCHECHITAHS	SCHISTOSITIES	SCHMALZIER
SCARABAEID	SCATTERIER	SCHECHITAS	SCHISTOSITY	SCHMALZIEST
SCARABAEIDS	SCATTERIEST	SCHECKLATON	SCHISTOSOMAL	SCHMEARING
SCARABAEIST	SCATTERING	SCHECKLATONS	SCHISTOSOME	SCHMECKERS
SCARABAEISTS	SCATTERINGLY	SCHEDULERS	SCHISTOSOMES	SCHMECKING
SCARABAEOID	SCATTERINGS	SCHEDULING	SCHISTOSOMIASES	SCHMEERING
SCARABAEOIDS	SCATTERLING	SCHEDULINGS	SCHISTOSOMIASIS	SCHMICKEST
SCARABAEUS	SCATTERLINGS	SCHEELITES	SCHIZAEACEOUS	SCHMOOSING
SCARABAEUSES	SCATTERMOUCH	SCHEFFLERA	SCHIZANTHUS	SCHMOOZERS
SCARABOIDS	SCATTERMOUCHES	SCHEFFLERAS	SCHIZANTHUSES	SCHMOOZIER
SCARAMOUCH	SCATTEROMETER	SCHEMATICAL	SCHIZOCARP	SCHMOOZIEST
SCARAMOUCHE	SCATTEROMETERS	SCHEMATICALLY	SCHIZOCARPIC	SCHMOOZING
SCARAMOUCHED	SCATTERSHOT	SCHEMATICS	SCHIZOCARPOUS	SCHMUCKIER
SCARAMOUCHES	SCATTINESS	SCHEMATISATION	SCHIZOCARPS	SCHMUCKIEST
SCARAMOUCHING	SCATTINESSES	SCHEMATISATIONS	SCHIZOGENESES	SCHMUCKING

SCHMUTTERS	SCHOOLMISTRESSY	SCINTILLATES	SCLEROMETRIC	SCOPTOPHILIAS
SCHNAPPERS	SCHOOLROOM	SCINTILLATING	SCLEROPHYLL	SCOPTOPHOBIA
SCHNAPPSES	SCHOOLROOMS	SCINTILLATINGLY	SCLEROPHYLLIES	SCOPTOPHOBIAS
SCHNAUZERS	SCHOOLTEACHER	SCINTILLATION	SCLEROPHYLLOUS	SCORBUTICALLY
SCHNITZELS	SCHOOLTEACHERS	SCINTILLATIONS	SCLEROPHYLLS	SCORCHINGLY
SCHNOODLES	SCHOOLTEACHING	SCINTILLATOR	SCLEROPHYLLY	SCORCHINGNESS
SCHNORKELED	SCHOOLTEACHINGS	SCINTILLATORS	SCLEROPROTEIN	SCORCHINGNESSES
SCHNORKELING	SCHOOLTIDE	SCINTILLISCAN	SCLEROPROTEINS	SCORCHINGS
SCHNORKELLED	SCHOOLTIDES	SCINTILLISCANS	SCLEROSING	SCORDATURA
SCHNORKELLING	SCHOOLTIME	SCINTILLOMETER	SCLEROTALS	SCORDATURAS
SCHNORKELS	SCHOOLTIMES	SCINTILLOMETERS	SCLEROTIAL	SCOREBOARD
SCHNORRERS	SCHOOLWARD	SCINTILLON	SCLEROTICS	SCOREBOARDS
SCHNORRING	SCHOOLWARDS	SCINTILLONS	SCLEROTINS	SCORECARDS
SCHNOZZLES	SCHOOLWORK	SCINTILLOSCOPE	SCLEROTIOID	SCOREKEEPER
SCHOLARCHS	SCHOOLWORKS	SCINTILLOSCOPES	SCLEROTISATION	SCOREKEEPERS
SCHOLARLIER	SCHOOLYARD	SCINTISCAN	SCLEROTISATIONS	SCORELINES
SCHOLARLIEST	SCHOOLYARDS	SCINTISCANNER	SCLEROTISE	SCORESHEET
SCHOLARLINESS	SCHORLACEOUS	SCINTISCANNERS	SCLEROTISED	SCORESHEETS
SCHOLARLINESSES	SCHORLOMITE	SCINTISCANS	SCLEROTISES	SCORIACEOUS
SCHOLARSHIP	SCHORLOMITES	SCIOLISTIC	SCLEROTISING	SCORIFICATION
SCHOLARSHIPS	SCHOTTISCHE	SCIOMACHIES	SCLEROTITIS	SCORIFICATIONS
SCHOLASTIC	SCHOTTISCHES	SCIOMANCER	SCLEROTITISES	SCORIFIERS
SCHOLASTICAL	SCHRECKLICH	SCIOMANCERS	SCLEROTIUM	SCORIFYING
SCHOLASTICALLY	SCHTUPPING	SCIOMANCIES	SCLEROTIZATION	SCORNFULLY
SCHOLASTICATE	SCHUSSBOOMER	SCIOMANTIC	SCLEROTIZATIONS	SCORNFULNESS
SCHOLASTICATES	SCHUSSBOOMERS	SCIOPHYTES	SCLEROTIZE	SCORNFULNESSES
SCHOLASTICISM	SCHVARTZES	SCIOPHYTIC	SCLEROTIZED	SCORODITES
SCHOLASTICISMS	SCHVITZING	SCIOSOPHIES	SCLEROTIZES	SCORPAENID
SCHOLASTICS	SCHWARMEREI	SCIRRHOSITIES	SCLEROTIZING	SCORPAENIDS
SCHOLIASTIC	SCHWARMEREIS	SCIRRHOSITY	SCLEROTOMIES	SCORPAENOID
SCHOLIASTS	SCHWARMERISCH	SCIRRHUSES	SCLEROTOMY	SCORPAENOIDS
SCHOOLBAGS	SCHWARTZES	SCISSIPARITIES	SCOFFINGLY	SCORPIOIDS
SCHOOLBOOK	SCHWARZLOT	SCISSIPARITY	SCOLDINGLY	SCORPIONIC
SCHOOLBOOKS	SCHWARZLOTS	SCISSORERS	SCOLECIFORM	SCORZONERA
SCHOOLBOYISH	SCIAENOIDS	SCISSORING	SCOLECITES	SCORZONERAS
SCHOOLBOYS	SCIAMACHIES	SCISSORTAIL	SCOLLOPING	SCOTODINIA
SCHOOLCHILD	SCIENTIFIC	SCISSORTAILS	SCOLOPACEOUS	SCOTODINIAS
SCHOOLCHILDREN	SCIENTIFICAL	SCISSORWISE	SCOLOPENDRA	SCOTOMATOUS
SCHOOLCRAFT	SCIENTIFICALLY	SCITAMINEOUS	SCOLOPENDRAS	SCOTOMETER
SCHOOLCRAFTS	SCIENTIFICITIES	SCLAUNDERS	SCOLOPENDRID	SCOTOMETERS
SCHOOLDAYS	SCIENTIFICITY	SCLEREIDES	SCOLOPENDRIDS	SCOUNDRELLIER
SCHOOLERIES	SCIENTISED	SCLERENCHYMA	SCOLOPENDRIFORM	SCOUNDRELLIEST
SCHOOLFELLOW	SCIENTISES	SCLERENCHYMAS	SCOLOPENDRINE	SCOUNDRELLY
SCHOOLFELLOWS	SCIENTISING	SCLERENCHYMATA	SCOLOPENDRIUM	SCOUNDRELS
SCHOOLGIRL	SCIENTISMS	SCLERIASES	SCOLOPENDRIUMS	SCOURGINGS
SCHOOLGIRLISH	SCIENTISTIC	SCLERIASIS	SCOLYTOIDS	SCOUTCRAFT
SCHOOLGIRLS	SCIENTISTS	SCLERITISES	SCOMBROIDS	SCOUTCRAFTS
SCHOOLGOING	SCIENTIZED	SCLEROCAULIES	SCOMFISHED	SCOUTHERED
SCHOOLGOINGS	SCIENTIZES	SCLEROCAULOUS	SCOMFISHES	SCOUTHERING
SCHOOLHOUSE	SCIENTIZING	SCLEROCAULY	SCOMFISHING	SCOUTHERINGS
SCHOOLHOUSES	SCINCOIDIAN	SCLERODERM	SCONCHEONS	SCOUTMASTER
SCHOOLINGS	SCINCOIDIANS	SCLERODERMA	SCOOTCHING	SCOUTMASTERS
SCHOOLKIDS	SCINDAPSUS	SCLERODERMAS	SCOOTERING	SCOWDERING
SCHOOLMAID	SCINDAPSUSES	SCLERODERMATA	SCOOTERIST	SCOWDERINGS
SCHOOLMAIDS	SCINTIGRAM	SCLERODERMATOUS	SCOOTERISTS	SCOWLINGLY
SCHOOLMARM	SCINTIGRAMS	SCLERODERMIA	SCOPELOIDS	SCOWTHERED
SCHOOLMARMISH	SCINTIGRAPHIC	SCLERODERMIAS	SCOPOLAMINE	SCOWTHERING
SCHOOLMARMS	SCINTIGRAPHIES	SCLERODERMIC	SCOPOLAMINES	SCRABBLERS
SCHOOLMASTER	SCINTIGRAPHY	SCLERODERMITE	SCOPOLINES	SCRABBLIER
SCHOOLMASTERED	SCINTILLAE	SCLERODERMITES	SCOPOPHILIA	SCRABBLIEST
SCHOOLMASTERING	SCINTILLANT	SCLERODERMOUS	SCOPOPHILIAC	SCRABBLING
SCHOOLMASTERISH	SCINTILLANTLY	SCLERODERMS	SCOPOPHILIACS	SCRABBLINGS
SCHOOLMASTERLY	SCINTILLAS	SCLEROMALACIA	SCOPOPHILIAS	SCRAGGEDNESS
SCHOOLMASTERS	SCINTILLASCOPE	SCLEROMALACIAS	SCOPOPHILIC	SCRAGGEDNESSES
SCHOOLMATE	SCINTILLASCOPES	SCLEROMATA	SCOPOPHOBIA	SCRAGGIEST
SCHOOLMATES	SCINTILLATE	SCLEROMETER	SCOPOPHOBIAS	SCRAGGINESS
SCHOOLMISTRESS	SCINTILLATED	SCLEROMETERS	SCOPTOPHILIA	SCRAGGINESSES

SCRAGGLIER	SCREAKINGS	SCRIMPINGS	SCROFULOUSNESS	SCRUTINISER
SCRAGGLIEST	SCREAMINGLY	SCRIMPNESS	SCROGGIEST	SCRUTINISERS
SCRAGGLING	SCREAMINGS	SCRIMPNESSES	SCROLLABLE	SCRUTINISES
SCRAICHING	SCREECHERS	SCRIMSHANDER	SCROLLINGS	SCRUTINISING
SCRAIGHING	SCREECHIER	SCRIMSHANDERED	SCROLLWISE	SCRUTINISINGLY
SCRAMBLERS	SCREECHIEST	SCRIMSHANDERING	SCROLLWORK	SCRUTINIZE
SCRAMBLING	SCREECHING	SCRIMSHANDERS	SCROLLWORKS	SCRUTINIZED
SCRAMBLINGLY	SCREEDINGS	SCRIMSHANDIED	SCROOCHING	SCRUTINIZER
SCRAMBLINGS	SCREENABLE	SCRIMSHANDIES	SCROOTCHED	SCRUTINIZERS
SCRANCHING	SCREENAGER	SCRIMSHANDY	SCROOTCHES	SCRUTINIZES
SCRANNIEST	SCREENAGERS	SCRIMSHANDYING	SCROOTCHING	SCRUTINIZING
SCRAPBOOKED	SCREENCAST	SCRIMSHANK	SCROPHULARIA	SCRUTINIZINGLY
SCRAPBOOKING	SCREENCASTS	SCRIMSHANKED	SCROPHULARIAS	SCRUTINOUS
SCRAPBOOKINGS	SCREENCRAFT	SCRIMSHANKER	SCROUNGERS	SCRUTINOUSLY
SCRAPBOOKS	SCREENCRAFTS	SCRIMSHANKERS	SCROUNGIER	SCRUTOIRES
SCRAPEGOOD	SCREENFULS	SCRIMSHANKING	SCROUNGIEST	SCUDDALERS
SCRAPEGOODS	SCREENINGS	SCRIMSHANKS	SCROUNGING	SCUFFLINGS
SCRAPEGUTS	SCREENLAND	SCRIMSHAWED	SCROUNGINGS	SCULDUDDERIES
SCRAPEPENNIES	SCREENLANDS	SCRIMSHAWING	SCROWDGING	SCULDUDDERY
SCRAPEPENNY	SCREENLIKE	SCRIMSHAWS	SCRUBBABLE	SCULDUDDRIES
SCRAPERBOARD	SCREENPLAY	SCRIMSHONER	SCRUBBIEST	SCULDUDDRY
SCRAPERBOARDS	SCREENPLAYS	SCRIMSHONERS	SCRUBBINESS	SCULDUGGERIES
SCRAPHEAPS	SCREENSAVER ·	SCRIPHOLDER	SCRUBBINESSES	SCULDUGGERY
SCRAPPAGES	SCREENSAVERS	SCRIPHOLDERS	SCRUBBINGS	SCULLERIES
SCRAPPIEST	SCREENSHOT	SCRIPOPHILE	SCRUBLANDS	SCULPTINGS
SCRAPPINESS	SCREENSHOTS	SCRIPOPHILES	SCRUBWOMAN	SCULPTRESS
SCRAPPINESSES	SCREENSHOTTED	SCRIPOPHILIES	SCRUBWOMEN	SCULPTRESSES
SCRAPPINGS	SCREENSHOTTING	SCRIPOPHILIST	SCRUFFIEST	SCULPTURAL
SCRAPYARDS	SCREENWRITER	SCRIPOPHILISTS	SCRUFFINESS	SCULPTURALLY
SCRATCHBACK	SCREENWRITERS	SCRIPOPHILY	SCRUFFINESSES	SCULPTURED
SCRATCHBACKS	SCREENWRITING	SCRIPPAGES	SCRUMDOWNS	SCULPTURES
SCRATCHBOARD	SCREENWRITINGS	SCRIPTORIA	SCRUMMAGED	SCULPTURESQUE
SCRATCHBOARDS	SCREEVINGS	SCRIPTORIAL	SCRUMMAGER	SCULPTURESQUELY
SCRATCHBUILD	SCREICHING	SCRIPTORIUM	SCRUMMAGERS	SCULPTURING
SCRATCHBUILDER	SCREIGHING	SCRIPTORIUMS	SCRUMMAGES	SCULPTURINGS
SCRATCHBUILDERS	SCREWBALLS	SCRIPTURAL	SCRUMMAGING	SCUMBERING
SCRATCHBUILDING	SCREWBEANS	SCRIPTURALISM	SCRUMMIEST	SCUMBLINGS
SCRATCHBUILDS	SCREWDRIVER	SCRIPTURALISMS	SCRUMPLING	SCUMFISHED
SCRATCHBUILT	SCREWDRIVERS	SCRIPTURALIST	SCRUMPOXES	SCUMFISHES
SCRATCHCARD	SCREWHEADS	SCRIPTURALISTS	SCRUMPTIOUS	SCUMFISHING
SCRATCHCARDS	SCREWINESS	SCRIPTURALLY	SCRUMPTIOUSLY	SCUNCHEONS
SCRATCHERS	SCREWINESSES	SCRIPTURES	SCRUMPTIOUSNESS	SCUNGILLIS
SCRATCHIER	SCREWWORMS	SCRIPTURISM	SCRUNCHEON	SCUNNERING
SCRATCHIES	SCRIBACIOUS	SCRIPTURISMS	SCRUNCHEONS	SCUPPERING
SCRATCHIEST	SCRIBACIOUSNESS	SCRIPTURIST	SCRUNCHIER	SCUPPERNONG
SCRATCHILY	SCRIBBLEMENT	SCRIPTURISTS	SCRUNCHIES	SCUPPERNONGS
SCRATCHINESS	SCRIBBLEMENTS	SCRIPTWRITER	SCRUNCHIEST	SCURFINESS
SCRATCHINESSES	SCRIBBLERS	SCRIPTWRITERS	SCRUNCHING	SCURFINESSES
SCRATCHING	SCRIBBLIER	SCRIPTWRITING	SCRUNCHINGS	SCURRILITIES
SCRATCHINGLY	SCRIBBLIEST	SCRIPTWRITINGS	SCRUNCHINS	SCURRILITY
SCRATCHINGS	SCRIBBLING	SCRITCHING	SCRUNCHION	SCURRILOUS
SCRATCHLESS	SCRIBBLINGLY	SCRITCHINGS	SCRUNCHIONS	SCURRILOUSLY
SCRATCHPLATE	SCRIBBLINGS	SCRIVEBOARD	SCRUNTIEST	SCURRILOUSNESS
SCRATCHPLATES	SCRIECHING	SCRIVEBOARDS	SCRUPLELESS	SCURRIOURS
SCRATTLING	SCRIEVEBOARD	SCRIVENERS	SCRUPULOSITIES	SCURVINESS
SCRAUCHING	SCRIEVEBOARDS	SCRIVENERSHIP	SCRUPULOSITY	SCURVINESSES
SCRAUGHING	SCRIGGLIER	SCRIVENERSHIPS	SCRUPULOUS	SCUTATIONS
SCRAVELING	SCRIGGLIEST	SCRIVENING	SCRUPULOUSLY	SCUTCHEONLESS
SCRAVELLED	SCRIGGLING	SCRIVENINGS	SCRUPULOUSNESS	SCUTCHEONS
SCRAVELLING	SCRIMMAGED	SCROBBLING	SCRUTABILITIES	SCUTCHINGS
SCRAWLIEST	SCRIMMAGER	SCROBICULAR	SCRUTABILITY	SCUTELLATE
SCRAWLINGLY	SCRIMMAGERS	SCROBICULATE	SCRUTATORS	SCUTELLATED
SCRAWLINGS	SCRIMMAGES	SCROBICULATED	SCRUTINEER	SCUTELLATION
SCRAWNIEST	SCRIMMAGING	SCROBICULE	SCRUTINEERS	SCUTELLATIONS
SCRAWNINESS	SCRIMPIEST	SCROBICULES	SCRUTINIES	SCUTTERING
SCRAWNINESSES	SCRIMPINESS	SCROFULOUS	SCRUTINISE	SCUTTLEBUTT
SCREAKIEST	SCRIMPINESSES	SCROFULOUSLY	SCRUTINISED	SCUTTLEBUTTS

SCUTTLEFUL
SCUTTLEFULS
SCUTTLINGS
SCUZZBALLS
SCYPHIFORM
SCYPHISTOMA
SCYPHISTOMAE
SCYPHISTOMAS
SCYPHOZOAN
SCYPHOZOANS
SCYTHELIKE
SDEIGNFULL
SDEIGNFULLY
SDRUCCIOLA
SEABEACHES
SEABORGIUM
SEABORGIUMS
SEABOTTLES
SEACHANGER
SEACHANGERS
SEACUNNIES
SEAFARINGS
SEAGRASSES
SEALIFTING
SEALPOINTS
SEAMANLIER
SEAMANLIEST
SEAMANLIKE
SEAMANSHIP
SEAMANSHIPS
SEAMINESSES
SEAMLESSLY
SEAMLESSNESS
SEAMLESSNESSES
SEAMSTRESS
SEAMSTRESSES
SEAMSTRESSIES
SEAMSTRESSY
SEANNACHIE
SEANNACHIES
SEAQUARIUM
SEAQUARIUMS
SEARCHABLE
SEARCHINGLY
SEARCHINGNESS
SEARCHINGNESSES
SEARCHINGS
SEARCHLESS
SEARCHLIGHT
SEARCHLIGHTS
SEAREDNESS
SEAREDNESSES
SEARNESSES
SEASICKEST
SEASICKNESS
SEASICKNESSES
SEASONABILITIES
SEASONABILITY
SEASONABLE
SEASONABLENESS
SEASONABLY
SEASONALITIES
SEASONALITY
SEASONALLY
SEASONALNESS
SEASONALNESSES
SEASONINGS

SEASONLESS
SEASTRANDS
SEAWEEDIER
SEAWEEDIEST
SEAWORTHIER
SEAWORTHIEST
SEAWORTHINESS
SEAWORTHINESSES
SEBIFEROUS
SEBORRHEAL
SEBORRHEAS
SEBORRHEIC
SEBORRHOEA
SEBORRHOEAL
SEBORRHOEAS
SEBORRHOEIC
SECERNENTS
SECERNMENT
SECERNMENTS
SECESSIONAL
SECESSIONISM
SECESSIONISMS
SECESSIONIST
SECESSIONISTS
SECESSIONS
SECLUDEDLY
SECLUDEDNESS
SECLUDEDNESSES
SECLUSIONIST
SECLUSIONISTS
SECLUSIONS
SECLUSIVELY
SECLUSIVENESS
SECLUSIVENESSES
SECOBARBITAL
SECOBARBITALS
SECONDARIES
SECONDARILY
SECONDARINESS
SECONDARINESSES
SECONDHAND
SECONDINGS
SECONDMENT
SECONDMENTS
SECRETAGES
SECRETAGOGIC
SECRETAGOGUE
SECRETAGOGUES
SECRETAIRE
SECRETAIRES
SECRETARIAL
SECRETARIAT
SECRETARIATE
SECRETARIATES
SECRETARIATS
SECRETARIES
SECRETARYSHIP
SECRETARYSHIPS
SECRETIONAL
SECRETIONARY
SECRETIONS
SECRETIVELY
SECRETIVENESS
SECRETIVENESSES
SECRETNESS
SECRETNESSES
SECRETORIES

SECTARIANISE
SECTARIANISED
SECTARIANISES
SECTARIANISING
SECTARIANISM
SECTARIANISMS
SECTARIANIZE
SECTARIANIZED
SECTARIANIZES
SECTARIANIZING
SECTARIANS
SECTILITIES
SECTIONALISE
SECTIONALISED
SECTIONALISES
SECTIONALISING
SECTIONALISM
SECTIONALISMS
SECTIONALIST
SECTIONALISTS
SECTIONALIZE
SECTIONALIZED
SECTIONALIZES
SECTIONALIZING
SECTIONALLY
SECTIONALS
SECTIONING
SECTIONISATION
SECTIONISATIONS
SECTIONISE
SECTIONISED
SECTIONISES
SECTIONISING
SECTIONIZATION
SECTIONIZATIONS
SECTIONIZE
SECTIONIZED
SECTIONIZES
SECTIONIZING
SECTORIALS
SECTORISATION
SECTORISATIONS
SECTORISED
SECTORISES
SECTORISING
SECTORIZATION
SECTORIZATIONS
SECTORIZED
SECTORIZES
SECTORIZING
SECULARISATION
SECULARISATIONS
SECULARISE
SECULARISED
SECULARISER
SECULARISERS
SECULARISES
SECULARISING
SECULARISM
SECULARISMS
SECULARIST
SECULARISTIC
SECULARISTS
SECULARITIES
SECULARITY
SECULARIZATION
SECULARIZATIONS

SECULARIZE
SECULARIZED
SECULARIZER
SECULARIZERS
SECULARIZES
SECULARIZING
SECUNDINES
SECUNDOGENITURE
SECURANCES
SECUREMENT
SECUREMENTS
SECURENESS
SECURENESSES
SECURIFORM
SECURITANS
SECURITIES
SECURITISATION
SECURITISATIONS
SECURITISE
SECURITISED
SECURITISES
SECURITISING
SECURITIZATION
SECURITIZATIONS
SECURITIZE
SECURITIZED
SECURITIZES
SECURITIZING
SECUROCRAT
SECUROCRATS
SEDATENESS
SEDATENESSES
SEDENTARILY
SEDENTARINESS
SEDENTARINESSES
SEDGELANDS
SEDIGITATED
SEDIMENTABLE
SEDIMENTARILY
SEDIMENTARY
SEDIMENTATION
SEDIMENTATIONS
SEDIMENTED
SEDIMENTING
SEDIMENTOLOGIC
SEDIMENTOLOGIES
SEDIMENTOLOGIST
SEDIMENTOLOGY
SEDIMENTOUS
SEDITIONARIES
SEDITIONARY
SEDITIOUSLY
SEDITIOUSNESS
SEDITIOUSNESSES
SEDUCEABLE
SEDUCEMENT
SEDUCEMENTS
SEDUCINGLY
SEDUCTIONS
SEDUCTIVELY
SEDUCTIVENESS
SEDUCTIVENESSES
SEDUCTRESS
SEDUCTRESSES
SEDULITIES
SEDULOUSLY
SEDULOUSNESS

SEDULOUSNESSES
SEECATCHES
SEECATCHIE
SEEDEATERS
SEEDINESSES
SEEDNESSES
SEEDSTOCKS
SEEMELESSE
SEEMINGNESS
SEEMINGNESSES
SEEMLIHEAD
SEEMLIHEADS
SEEMLIHEDS
SEEMLINESS
SEEMLINESSES
SEEMLYHEDS
SEERSUCKER
SEERSUCKERS
SEETHINGLY
SEGHOLATES
SEGMENTALLY
SEGMENTARY
SEGMENTATE
SEGMENTATION
SEGMENTATIONS
SEGMENTING
SEGREGABLE
SEGREGANTS
SEGREGATED
SEGREGATES
SEGREGATING
SEGREGATION
SEGREGATIONAL
SEGREGATIONIST
SEGREGATIONISTS
SEGREGATIONS
SEGREGATIVE
SEGREGATOR
SEGREGATORS
SEGUIDILLA
SEGUIDILLAS
SEIGNEURIAL
SEIGNEURIE
SEIGNEURIES
SEIGNIORAGE
SEIGNIORAGES
SEIGNIORALTIES
SEIGNIORALTY
SEIGNIORIAL
SEIGNIORIES
SEIGNIORSHIP
SEIGNIORSHIPS
SEIGNORAGE
SEIGNORAGES
SEIGNORIAL
SEIGNORIES
SEISMICALLY
SEISMICITIES
SEISMICITY
SEISMOGRAM
SEISMOGRAMS
SEISMOGRAPH
SEISMOGRAPHER
SEISMOGRAPHERS
SEISMOGRAPHIC
SEISMOGRAPHICAL
SEISMOGRAPHIES

SEISMOGRAPHS	SELFSAMENESS	SEMICARBAZONE	SEMIFINISHED	SEMIOTICIST
SEISMOGRAPHY	SELFSAMENESSES	SEMICARBAZONES	SEMIFITTED	SEMIOTICISTS
SEISMOLOGIC	SELLOTAPED	SEMICENTENNIAL	SEMIFLEXIBLE	SEMIOVIPAROUS
SEISMOLOGICAL	SELLOTAPES	SEMICENTENNIALS	SEMIFLUIDIC	SEMIPALMATE
SEISMOLOGICALLY	SELLOTAPING	SEMICHORUS	SEMIFLUIDITIES	SEMIPALMATED
SEISMOLOGIES	SELTZOGENE	SEMICHORUSES	SEMIFLUIDITY	SEMIPALMATION
SEISMOLOGIST	SELTZOGENES	SEMICIRCLE	SEMIFLUIDS	SEMIPALMATIONS
SEISMOLOGISTS	SELVEDGING	SEMICIRCLED	SEMIFORMAL	SEMIPARASITE
SEISMOLOGY	SEMAINIERS	SEMICIRCLES	SEMIFREDDI	SEMIPARASITES
SEISMOMETER	SEMANTEMES	SEMICIRCULAR	SEMIFREDDO	SEMIPARASITIC
SEISMOMETERS	SEMANTICAL	SEMICIRCULARLY	SEMIFREDDOS	SEMIPARASITISM
SEISMOMETRIC	SEMANTICALLY	SEMICIRQUE	SEMIGLOBES	SEMIPARASITISMS
SEISMOMETRICAL	SEMANTICIST	SEMICIRQUES	SEMIGLOBULAR	SEMIPELLUCID
SEISMOMETRIES	SEMANTICISTS	SEMICIVILISED	SEMIGLOSSES	SEMIPERIMETER
SEISMOMETRY	SEMANTIDES	SEMICIVILIZED	SEMIGROUPS	SEMIPERIMETERS
SEISMONASTIC	SEMANTRONS	SEMICLASSIC	SEMIHOBOES	SEMIPERMANENT
SEISMONASTIES	SEMAPHORED	SEMICLASSICAL	SEMILEGENDARY	SEMIPERMEABLE
SEISMONASTY	SEMAPHORES	SEMICLASSICS	SEMILETHAL	SEMIPLUMES
SEISMOSCOPE	SEMAPHORIC	SEMICOLONIAL	SEMILETHALS	SEMIPOLITICAL
SEISMOSCOPES	SEMAPHORICAL	SEMICOLONIALISM	SEMILIQUID	SEMIPOPULAR
SEISMOSCOPIC	SEMAPHORICALLY	SEMICOLONIES	SEMILIQUIDS	SEMIPORCELAIN
SELACHIANS	SEMAPHORING	SEMICOLONS	SEMILITERATE	SEMIPORCELAINS
SELAGINELLA	SEMASIOLOGICAL	SEMICOLONY	SEMILITERATES	SEMIPORNOGRAPHY
SELAGINELLAS	SEMASIOLOGIES	SEMICOMATOSE	SEMILOGARITHMIC	SEMIPOSTAL
SELDOMNESS	SEMASIOLOGIST	SEMICOMMERCIAL	SEMILUCENT	SEMIPOSTALS
SELDOMNESSES	SEMASIOLOGISTS	SEMICONDUCTING	SEMILUNATE	SEMIPRECIOUS
SELECTABLE	SEMASIOLOGY	SEMICONDUCTION	SEMILUSTROUS	SEMIPRIVATE
SELECTIONIST	SEMATOLOGIES	SEMICONDUCTIONS	SEMIMANUFACTURE	SEMIPUBLIC
SELECTIONISTS	SEMATOLOGY	SEMICONDUCTOR	SEMIMENSTRUAL	SEMIQUAVER
SELECTIONS	SEMBLABLES	SEMICONDUCTORS	SEMIMETALLIC	SEMIQUAVERS
SELECTIVELY	SEMBLANCES	SEMICONSCIOUS	SEMIMETALS	SEMIREFINED
SELECTIVENESS	SEMBLATIVE	SEMICONSCIOUSLY	SEMIMONASTIC	SEMIRELIGIOUS
SELECTIVENESSES	SEMEIOLOGIC	SEMICONSONANT	SEMIMONTHLIES	SEMIRETIRED
SELECTIVITIES	SEMEIOLOGICAL	SEMICONSONANTS	SEMIMONTHLY	SEMIRETIREMENT
SELECTIVITY	SEMEIOLOGIES	SEMICRYSTALLIC	SEMIMYSTICAL	SEMIRETIREMENTS
SELECTNESS	SEMEIOLOGIST	SEMICRYSTALLINE	SEMINALITIES	SEMIROUNDS
SELECTNESSES	SEMEIOLOGISTS	SEMICYLINDER	SEMINALITY	SEMISACRED
SELECTORATE	SEMEIOLOGY	SEMICYLINDERS	SEMINARIAL	SEMISECRET
SELECTORATES	SEMEIOTICALLY	SEMICYLINDRICAL	SEMINARIAN	SEMISEDENTARY
SELECTORIAL	SEMEIOTICIAN	SEMIDARKNESS	SEMINARIANS	SEMISHRUBBY
SELEGILINE	SEMEIOTICIANS	SEMIDARKNESSES	SEMINARIES	SEMISKILLED
SELEGILINES	SEMEIOTICS	SEMIDEIFIED	SEMINARIST	SEMISOLIDS
SELENIFEROUS	SEMELPARITIES	SEMIDEIFIES	SEMINARISTS	SEMISOLUSES
SELENOCENTRIC	SEMELPARITY	SEMIDEIFYING	SEMINATING	SEMISUBMERSIBLE
SELENODONT	SEMELPAROUS	SEMIDEPONENT	SEMINATION	SEMISYNTHETIC
SELENODONTS	SEMESTERED	SEMIDEPONENTS	SEMINATIONS	SEMITERETE
SELENOGRAPH	SEMESTERING	SEMIDESERT	SEMINATURAL	SEMITERRESTRIAL
SELENOGRAPHER	SEMESTERINGS	SEMIDESERTS	SEMINIFEROUS	SEMITONALLY
SELENOGRAPHERS	SEMESTRIAL	SEMIDETACHED	SEMINOMADIC	SEMITONICALLY
SELENOGRAPHIC	SEMIABSTRACT	SEMIDETACHEDS	SEMINOMADS	SEMITRAILER
SELENOGRAPHICAL	SEMIABSTRACTION	SEMIDIAMETER	SEMINOMATA	SEMITRAILERS
SELENOGRAPHIES	SEMIANGLES	SEMIDIAMETERS	SEMINUDITIES	SEMITRANSLUCENT
SELENOGRAPHIST	SEMIANNUAL	SEMIDIURNAL	SEMINUDITY	SEMITRANSPARENT
SELENOGRAPHISTS	SEMIANNUALLY	SEMIDIVINE	SEMIOCHEMICAL	SEMITROPIC
SELENOGRAPHS	SEMIAQUATIC	SEMIDOCUMENTARY	SEMIOCHEMICALS	SEMITROPICAL
SELENOGRAPHY	SEMIARBOREAL	SEMIDOMINANT	SEMIOFFICIAL	SEMITROPICS
SELENOLOGICAL	SEMIARIDITIES	SEMIDRIEST	SEMIOFFICIALLY	SEMITRUCKS
SELENOLOGIES	SEMIARIDITY	SEMIDRYING	SEMIOLOGIC	SEMIVITREOUS
SELENOLOGIST	SEMIAUTOMATED	SEMIDWARFS	SEMIOLOGICAL	SEMIVOCALIC
SELENOLOGISTS	SEMIAUTOMATIC	SEMIDWARVES	SEMIOLOGICALLY	SEMIVOWELS
SELENOLOGY	SEMIAUTOMATICS	SEMIELLIPTICAL	SEMIOLOGIES	SEMIWEEKLIES
SELFISHNESS	SEMIAUTONOMOUS	SEMIEMPIRICAL	SEMIOLOGIST	SEMIWEEKLY
SELFISHNESSES	SEMIBASEMENT	SEMIEVERGREEN	SEMIOLOGISTS	SEMIYEARLY
SELFLESSLY	SEMIBASEMENTS	SEMIFEUDAL	SEMIOPAQUE	SEMPERVIVUM
SELFLESSNESS	SEMIBREVES	SEMIFINALIST	SEMIOTICALLY	SEMPERVIVUMS
SELFLESSNESSES	SEMICARBAZIDE	SEMIFINALISTS	SEMIOTICIAN	SEMPITERNAL
SELFNESSES	SEMICARBAZIDES	SEMIFINALS	SEMIOTICIANS	SEMPITERNALLY

SEMPITERNITIES	SENSITIVITY	SENTIMENTALIZES	SEPTICEMIC	SEQUESTRUM
SEMPITERNITY	SENSITIZATION	SENTIMENTALLY	SEPTICIDAL	SEQUESTRUMS
SEMPITERNUM	SENSITIZATIONS	SENTIMENTS	SEPTICIDALLY	SERAPHICAL
SEMPITERNUMS	SENSITIZED	SENTINELED	SEPTICITIES	SERAPHICALLY
SEMPSTERING	SENSITIZER	SENTINELING	SEPTIFEROUS	SERAPHINES
SEMPSTERINGS	SENSITIZERS	SENTINELLED	SEPTIFRAGAL	SERASKIERATE
SEMPSTRESS	SENSITIZES	SENTINELLING	SEPTILATERAL	SERASKIERATES
SEMPSTRESSES	SENSITIZING	SEPALODIES	SEPTILLION	SERASKIERS
SEMPSTRESSING	SENSITOMETER	SEPARABILITIES	SEPTILLIONS	SERENADERS
SEMPSTRESSINGS	SENSITOMETERS	SEPARABILITY	SEPTILLIONTH	SERENADING
SENARMONTITE	SENSITOMETRIC	SEPARABLENESS	SEPTILLIONTHS	SERENATING
SENARMONTITES	SENSITOMETRIES	SEPARABLENESSES	SEPTIMOLES	SERENDIPITIES
SENATORIAL	SENSITOMETRY	SEPARATELY	SEPTIVALENT	SERENDIPITIST
SENATORIALLY	SENSOMOTOR	SEPARATENESS	SEPTUAGENARIAN	SERENDIPITISTS
SENATORIAN	SENSORIALLY	SEPARATENESSES	SEPTUAGENARIANS	SERENDIPITOUS
SENATORSHIP	SENSORIMOTOR	SEPARATING	SEPTUAGENARIES	SERENDIPITOUSLY
SENATORSHIPS	SENSORINEURAL	SEPARATION	SEPTUAGENARY	SERENDIPITY
SENECTITUDE	SENSORIUMS	SEPARATIONISM	SEPTUPLETS	SERENENESS
SENECTITUDES	SENSUALISATION	SEPARATIONISMS	SEPTUPLICATE	SERENENESSES
SENESCENCE	SENSUALISATIONS	SEPARATIONIST	SEPTUPLICATES	SERENITIES
SENESCENCES	SENSUALISE	SEPARATIONISTS	SEPTUPLING	SERGEANCIES
SENESCHALS	SENSUALISED	SEPARATIONS	SEPULCHERED	SERGEANTIES
SENESCHALSHIP	SENSUALISES	SEPARATISM	SEPULCHERING	SERGEANTSHIP
SENESCHALSHIPS	SENSUALISING	SEPARATISMS	SEPULCHERS	SERGEANTSHIPS
SENHORITAS	SENSUALISM	SEPARATIST	SEPULCHRAL	SERIALISATION
SENILITIES	SENSUALISMS	SEPARATISTIC	SEPULCHRALLY	SERIALISATIONS
SENIORITIES	SENSUALIST	SEPARATISTS	SEPULCHRED	SERIALISED
SENNACHIES	SENSUALISTIC	SEPARATIVE	SEPULCHRES	SERIALISES
SENSATIONAL	SENSUALISTS	SEPARATIVELY	SEPULCHRING	SERIALISING
SENSATIONALISE	SENSUALITIES	SEPARATIVENESS	SEPULCHROUS	SERIALISMS
SENSATIONALISED	SENSUALITY	SEPARATORIES	SEPULTURAL	SERIALISTS
SENSATIONALISES	SENSUALIZATION	SEPARATORS	SEPULTURED	SERIALITIES
SENSATIONALISM	SENSUALIZATIONS	SEPARATORY	SEPULTURES	SERIALIZATION
SENSATIONALISMS	SENSUALIZE	SEPARATRICES	SEPULTURING	SERIALIZATIONS
SENSATIONALIST	SENSUALIZED	SEPARATRIX	SEQUACIOUS	SERIALIZED
SENSATIONALISTS	SENSUALIZES	SEPARATUMS	SEQUACIOUSLY	SERIALIZES
SENSATIONALIZE	SENSUALIZING	SEPIOLITES	SEQUACIOUSNESS	SERIALIZING
SENSATIONALIZED	SENSUALNESS	SEPIOSTAIRE	SEQUACITIES	SERIATIONS
SENSATIONALIZES	SENSUALNESSES	SEPIOSTAIRES	SEQUELISED	SERICICULTURE
SENSATIONALLY	SENSUOSITIES	SEPTATIONS	SEQUELISES	SERICICULTURES
SENSATIONISM	SENSUOSITY	SEPTAVALENT	SEQUELISING	SERICICULTURIST
SENSATIONISMS	SENSUOUSLY	SEPTEMVIRATE	SEQUELIZED	SERICITISATION
SENSATIONIST	SENSUOUSNESS	SEPTEMVIRATES	SEQUELIZES	SERICITISATIONS
SENSATIONISTS	SENSUOUSNESSES	SEPTEMVIRI	SEQUELIZING	SERICITIZATION
SENSATIONLESS	SENTENCERS	SEPTEMVIRS	SEQUENCERS	SERICITIZATIONS
SENSATIONS	SENTENCING	SEPTENARIES	SEQUENCIES	SERICTERIA
SENSELESSLY	SENTENCINGS	SEPTENARII	SEQUENCING	SERICTERIUM
SENSELESSNESS	SENTENTIAE	SEPTENARIUS	SEQUENCINGS	SERICULTURAL
SENSELESSNESSES	SENTENTIAL	SEPTENDECILLION	SEQUENTIAL	SERICULTURE
SENSIBILIA	SENTENTIALLY	SEPTENNATE	SEQUENTIALITIES	SERICULTURES
SENSIBILITIES	SENTENTIOUS	SEPTENNATES	SEQUENTIALITY	SERICULTURIST
SENSIBILITY	SENTENTIOUSLY	SEPTENNIAL	SEQUENTIALLY	SERICULTURISTS
SENSIBLENESS	SENTENTIOUSNESS	SEPTENNIALLY	SEQUESTERED	SERIGRAPHER
SENSIBLENESSES	SENTENCES	SEPTENNIUM	SEQUESTERING	SERIGRAPHERS
SENSIBLEST	SENTIENCIES	SEPTENNIUMS	SEQUESTERS	SERIGRAPHIC
SENSITISATION	SENTIENTLY	SEPTENTRIAL	SEQUESTRABLE	SERIGRAPHIES
SENSITISATIONS	SENTIMENTAL	SEPTENTRION	SEQUESTRAL	SERIGRAPHS
SENSITISED	SENTIMENTALISE	SEPTENTRIONAL	SEQUESTRANT	SERIGRAPHY
SENSITISER	SENTIMENTALISED	SEPTENTRIONALLY	SEQUESTRANTS	SERINETTES
SENSITISERS	SENTIMENTALISES	SEPTENTRIONES	SEQUESTRATE	SERIOCOMIC
SENSITISES	SENTIMENTALISM	SEPTENTRIONS	SEQUESTRATED	SERIOCOMICAL
SENSITISING	SENTIMENTALISMS	SEPTICAEMIA	SEQUESTRATES	SERIOCOMICALLY
SENSITIVELY	SENTIMENTALIST	SEPTICAEMIAS	SEQUESTRATING	SERIOUSNESS
SENSITIVENESS	SENTIMENTALISTS	SEPTICAEMIC	SEQUESTRATION	SERIOUSNESSES
SENSITIVENESSES	SENTIMENTALITY	SEPTICALLY	SEQUESTRATIONS	SERJEANCIES
SENSITIVES	SENTIMENTALIZE	SEPTICEMIA	SEQUESTRATOR	SERJEANTIES
SENSITIVITIES	SENTIMENTALIZED	SEPTICEMIAS	SEQUESTRATORS	SERJEANTRIES

SERJEANTRY	SERPENTINITE	SERVITORIAL	SEXAGENARIAN	SHABRACQUES
SERJEANTSHIP	SERPENTINITES	SERVITORSHIP	SEXAGENARIANS	SHACKLEBONE
SERJEANTSHIPS	SERPENTINIZE	SERVITORSHIPS	SEXAGENARIES	SHACKLEBONES
SERMONEERS	SERPENTINIZED	SERVITRESS	SEXAGENARY	SHACKTOWNS
SERMONETTE	SERPENTINIZES	SERVITRESSES	SEXAGESIMAL	SHADBERRIES
SERMONETTES	SERPENTINIZING	SERVITUDES	SEXAGESIMALLY	SHADBUSHES
SERMONICAL	SERPENTINOUS	SERVOCONTROL	SEXAGESIMALS	SHADCHANIM
SERMONINGS	SERPENTISE	SERVOCONTROLS	SEXAHOLICS	SHADINESSES
SERMONISED	SERPENTISED	SERVOMECHANICAL	SEXANGULAR	SHADKHANIM
SERMONISER	SERPENTISES	SERVOMECHANISM	SEXANGULARLY	SHADOWBOXED
SERMONISERS	SERPENTISING	SERVOMECHANISMS	SEXAVALENT	SHADOWBOXES
SERMONISES	SERPENTIZE	SERVOMOTOR	SEXCAPADES	SHADOWBOXING
SERMONISING	SERPENTIZED	SERVOMOTORS	SEXCENTENARIES	SHADOWCAST
SERMONISINGS	SERPENTIZES	SESQUIALTER	SEXCENTENARY	SHADOWCASTED
SERMONIZED	SERPENTIZING	SESQUIALTERA	SEXDECILLION	SHADOWCASTING
SERMONIZER	SERPENTLIKE	SESQUIALTERAS	SEXDECILLIONS	SHADOWCASTINGS
SERMONIZERS	SERPENTRIES	SESQUIALTERS	SEXENNIALLY	SHADOWCASTS
SERMONIZES	SERPIGINES	SESQUICARBONATE	SEXENNIALS	SHADOWGRAPH
SERMONIZING	SERPIGINOUS	SESQUICENTENARY	SEXERCISES	SHADOWGRAPHIES
SERMONIZINGS	SERPIGINOUSLY	SESQUIOXIDE	SEXINESSES	SHADOWGRAPHS
SEROCONVERSION	SERPULITES	SESQUIOXIDES	SEXIVALENT	SHADOWGRAPHY
SEROCONVERSIONS	SERRADELLA	SESQUIPEDAL	SEXLESSNESS	SHADOWIEST
SEROCONVERT	SERRADELLAS	SESQUIPEDALIAN	SEXLESSNESSES	SHADOWINESS
SEROCONVERTED	SERRADILLA	SESQUIPEDALIANS	SEXLOCULAR	SHADOWINESSES
SEROCONVERTING	SERRADILLAS	SESQUIPEDALITY	SEXOLOGICAL	SHADOWINGS
SEROCONVERTS	SERRANOIDS	SESQUIPEDALS	SEXOLOGIES	SHADOWLESS
SERODIAGNOSES	SERRASALMO	SESQUIPLICATE	SEXOLOGIST	SHADOWLIKE
SERODIAGNOSIS	SERRASALMOS	SESQUISULPHIDE	SEXOLOGISTS	SHAGGEDNESS
SERODIAGNOSTIC	SERRATIONS	SESQUISULPHIDES	SEXPARTITE	SHAGGEDNESSES
SEROGROUPS	SERRATIROSTRAL	SESQUITERPENE	SEXPLOITATION	SHAGGINESS
SEROLOGICAL	SERRATULATE	SESQUITERPENES	SEXPLOITATIONS	SHAGGINESSES
SEROLOGICALLY	SERRATURES	SESQUITERTIA	SEXTARIUSES	SHAGGYMANE
SEROLOGIES	SERRATUSES	SESQUITERTIAS	SEXTILLION	SHAGGYMANES
SEROLOGIST	SERREFILES	SESSILITIES	SEXTILLIONS	SHAGREENED
SEROLOGISTS	SERRICORNS	SESSIONALLY	SEXTILLIONTH	SHAGTASTIC
SERONEGATIVE	SERRIEDNESS	SESTERTIUM	SEXTILLIONTHS	SHAHTOOSHES
SERONEGATIVITY	SERRIEDNESSES	SESTERTIUS	SEXTODECIMO	SHAKEDOWNS
SEROPOSITIVE	SERRULATED	SETACEOUSLY	SEXTODECIMOS	SHAKINESSES
SEROPOSITIVITY	SERRULATION	SETIFEROUS	SEXTONESSES	SHAKUHACHI
SEROPURULENT	SERRULATIONS	SETIGEROUS	SEXTONSHIP	SHAKUHACHIS
SEROSITIES	SERTULARIAN	SETTERWORT	SEXTONSHIPS	SHALLOWEST
SEROTAXONOMIES	SERTULARIANS	SETTERWORTS	SEXTUPLETS	SHALLOWING
SEROTAXONOMY	SERVANTHOOD	SETTLEABLE	SEXTUPLICATE	SHALLOWINGS
SEROTHERAPIES	SERVANTHOODS	SETTLEDNESS	SEXTUPLICATED	SHALLOWNESS
SEROTHERAPY	SERVANTING	SETTLEDNESSES	SEXTUPLICATES	SHALLOWNESSES
SEROTINIES	SERVANTLESS	SETTLEMENT	SEXTUPLICATING	SHAMANISMS
SEROTINOUS	SERVANTRIES	SETTLEMENTS	SEXTUPLIED	SHAMANISTIC
SEROTONERGIC	SERVANTSHIP	SEVENPENCE	SEXTUPLIES	SHAMANISTS
SEROTONINERGIC	SERVANTSHIPS	SEVENPENCES	SEXTUPLING	SHAMATEURISM
SEROTONINS	SERVEWARES	SEVENPENNIES	SEXTUPLYING	SHAMATEURISMS
SEROTYPING	SERVICEABILITY	SEVENPENNY	SEXUALISATION	SHAMATEURS
SEROTYPINGS	SERVICEABLE	SEVENTEENS	SEXUALISATIONS	SHAMBLIEST
SEROUSNESS	SERVICEABLENESS	SEVENTEENTH	SEXUALISED	SHAMBLINGS
SEROUSNESSES	SERVICEABLY	SEVENTEENTHLY	SEXUALISES	SHAMBOLICALLY
SERPENTIFORM	SERVICEBERRIES	SEVENTEENTHS	SEXUALISING	SHAMEFACED
SERPENTINE	SERVICEBERRY	SEVENTIETH	SEXUALISMS	SHAMEFACEDLY
SERPENTINED	SERVICELESS	SEVENTIETHS	SEXUALISTS	SHAMEFACEDNESS
SERPENTINELY	SERVICEMAN	SEVERABILITIES	SEXUALITIES	SHAMEFASTNESS
SERPENTINES	SERVICEMEN	SEVERABILITY	SEXUALIZATION	SHAMEFASTNESSES
SERPENTINIC	SERVICEWOMAN	SEVERALFOLD	SEXUALIZATIONS	SHAMEFULLY
SERPENTINING	SERVICEWOMEN	SEVERALTIES	SEXUALIZED	SHAMEFULNESS
SERPENTININGLY	SERVICINGS	SEVERANCES	SEXUALIZES	SHAMEFULNESSES
SERPENTININGS	SERVIETTES	SEVERENESS	SEXUALIZING	SHAMELESSLY
SERPENTINISE	SERVILENESS	SEVERENESSES	SFORZANDOS	SHAMELESSNESS
SERPENTINISED	SERVILENESSES	SEVERITIES	SHABBINESS	SHAMELESSNESSES
SERPENTINISES	SERVILISMS	SEWABILITIES	SHABBINESSES	SHAMEWORTHIER
SERPENTINISING	SERVILITIES	SEWABILITY	SHABRACQUE	SHAMEWORTHIEST

SHAMEWORTHY	SHARPSHOOTING	SHELDRAKES	SHERIFFALTY	SHIPBUILDER
SHAMIANAHS	SHARPSHOOTINGS	SHELFROOMS	SHERIFFDOM	SHIPBUILDERS
SHAMIYANAH	SHARPTAILS	SHELFTALKER	SHERIFFDOMS	SHIPBUILDING
SHAMIYANAHS	SHASHLICKS	SHELFTALKERS	SHERIFFSHIP	SHIPBUILDINGS
SHAMMASHIM	SHATOOSHES	SHELLACKED	SHERIFFSHIPS	SHIPFITTER
SHAMOISING	SHATTERERS	SHELLACKER	SHERLOCKED	SHIPFITTERS
SHAMPOOERS	SHATTERIER	SHELLACKERS	SHERLOCKING	SHIPLAPPED
SHAMPOOING	SHATTERIEST	SHELLACKING	SHEWBREADS	SHIPLAPPING
SHANACHIES	SHATTERING	SHELLACKINGS	SHIBBOLETH	SHIPLAPPINGS
SHANDRYDAN	SHATTERINGLY	SHELLBACKS	SHIBBOLETHS	SHIPMASTER
SHANDRYDANS	SHATTERPROOF	SHELLBARKS	SHIBUICHIS	SHIPMASTERS
SHANDYGAFF	SHAUCHLIER	SHELLBOUND	SHIDDUCHIM	SHIPOWNERS
SHANDYGAFFS	SHAUCHLIEST	SHELLCRACKER	SHIELDINGS	SHIPPOUNDS
SHANGHAIED	SHAUCHLING	SHELLCRACKERS	SHIELDLESS	SHIPWRECKED
SHANGHAIER	SHAVASANAS	SHELLDRAKE	SHIELDLIKE	SHIPWRECKING
SHANGHAIERS	SHAVELINGS	SHELLDRAKES	SHIELDLING	SHIPWRECKS
SHANGHAIING	SHAVETAILS	SHELLDUCKS	SHIELDLINGS	SHIPWRIGHT
SHANKBONES	SHEARLINGS	SHELLFIRES	SHIELDRAKE	SHIPWRIGHTS
SHANKPIECE	SHEARWATER	SHELLFISHERIES	SHIELDRAKES	SHIRETOWNS
SHANKPIECES	SHEARWATERS	SHELLFISHERY	SHIELDWALL	SHIRRALEES
SHANTYTOWN	SHEATFISHES	SHELLFISHES	SHIELDWALLS	SHIRTBANDS
SHANTYTOWNS	SHEATHBILL	SHELLINESS	SHIFTINESS	SHIRTDRESS
SHAPELESSLY	SHEATHBILLS	SHELLINESSES	SHIFTINESSES	SHIRTDRESSES
SHAPELESSNESS	SHEATHFISH	SHELLPROOF	SHIFTLESSLY	SHIRTFRONT
SHAPELESSNESSES	SHEATHFISHES	SHELLSHOCK	SHIFTLESSNESS	SHIRTFRONTED
SHAPELIEST	SHEATHIEST	SHELLSHOCKED	SHIFTLESSNESSES	SHIRTFRONTING
SHAPELINESS	SHEATHINGS	SHELLSHOCKS	SHIFTSTICK	SHIRTFRONTS
SHAPELINESSES	SHEATHLESS	SHELLWORKS	SHIFTSTICKS	SHIRTINESS
SHAPESHIFTER	SHEATHLIKE	SHELLYCOAT	SHIFTWORKS	SHIRTINESSES
SHAPESHIFTERS	SHEBAGGING	SHELLYCOATS	SHIGELLOSES	SHIRTLIFTER
SHAPESHIFTING	SHEBAGGINGS	SHELTERBELT	SHIGELLOSIS	SHIRTLIFTERS
SHAPESHIFTINGS	SHEBEENERS	SHELTERBELTS	SHIKARRING	SHIRTMAKER
SHAPEWEARS	SHEBEENING	SHELTERERS	SHILLABERS	SHIRTMAKERS
SHARAWADGI	SHEBEENINGS	SHELTERIER	SHILLALAHS	SHIRTSLEEVE
SHARAWADGIS	SHECHITAHS	SHELTERIEST	SHILLELAGH	SHIRTSLEEVED
SHARAWAGGI	SHECKLATON	SHELTERING	SHILLELAGHS	SHIRTSLEEVES
SHARAWAGGIS	SHECKLATONS	SHELTERINGS	SHILLELAHS	SHIRTTAILED
SHAREABILITIES	SHEEPBERRIES	SHELTERLESS	SHILLINGLESS	SHIRTTAILING
SHAREABILITY	SHEEPBERRY	SHEMOZZLED	SHILLINGSWORTH	SHIRTTAILS
SHARECROPPED	SHEEPCOTES	SHEMOZZLES	SHILLINGSWORTHS	SHIRTWAIST
SHARECROPPER	SHEEPFOLDS	SHEMOZZLING	SHILLYSHALLIED	SHIRTWAISTED
SHARECROPPERS	SHEEPHEADS	SHENANIGAN	SHILLYSHALLIER	SHIRTWAISTER
SHARECROPPING	SHEEPHERDER	SHENANIGANS	SHILLYSHALLIERS	SHIRTWAISTERS
SHARECROPPINGS	SHEEPHERDERS	SHEPHERDED	SHILLYSHALLIES	SHIRTWAISTS
SHARECROPS	SHEEPHERDING	SHEPHERDESS	SHILLYSHALLY	SHITCANNED
SHAREFARMER	SHEEPHERDINGS	SHEPHERDESSES	SHILLYSHALLYING	SHITCANNING
SHAREFARMERS	SHEEPISHLY	SHEPHERDING	SHIMMERIER	SHITHOUSES
SHAREHOLDER	SHEEPISHNESS	SHEPHERDINGS	SHIMMERIEST	SHITSTORMS
SHAREHOLDERS	SHEEPISHNESSES	SHEPHERDLESS	SHIMMERING	SHITTIMWOOD
SHAREHOLDING	SHEEPSHANK	SHEPHERDLING	SHIMMERINGLY	SHITTIMWOODS
SHAREHOLDINGS	SHEEPSHANKS	SHEPHERDLINGS	SHIMMERINGS	SHITTINESS
SHAREMILKER	SHEEPSHEAD	SHERARDISATION	SHIMOZZLES	SHITTINESSES
SHAREMILKERS	SHEEPSHEADS	SHERARDISATIONS	SHINGLIEST	SHIVAREEING
SHARENTING	SHEEPSHEARER	SHERARDISE	SHINGLINGS	SHIVERIEST
SHARENTINGS	SHEEPSHEARERS	SHERARDISED	SHINGUARDS	SHIVERINGLY
SHAREWARES	SHEEPSHEARING	SHERARDISES	SHININESSES	SHIVERINGS
SHARKSKINS	SHEEPSHEARINGS	SHERARDISING	SHININGNESS	SHLEMIEHLS
SHARKSUCKER	SHEEPSKINS	SHERARDIZATION	SHININGNESSES	SHLEMOZZLE
SHARKSUCKERS	SHEEPTRACK	SHERARDIZATIONS	SHINLEAVES	SHLEMOZZLED
SHARPBENDER	SHEEPTRACKS	SHERARDIZE	SHINNERIES	SHLEMOZZLES
SHARPBENDERS	SHEEPWALKS	SHERARDIZED	SHINNEYING	SHLEMOZZLING
SHARPENERS	SHEERNESSES	SHERARDIZES	SHINPLASTER	SHLEPPIEST
SHARPENING	SHEETROCKED	SHERARDIZING	SHINPLASTERS	SHLIMAZELS
SHARPENINGS	SHEETROCKING	SHEREEFIAN	SHINSPLINTS	SHLOCKIEST
SHARPNESSES	SHEETROCKS	SHERGOTTITE	SHIPBOARDS	SHLUMPIEST
SHARPSHOOTER	SHEIKHDOMS	SHERGOTTITES	SHIPBROKER	SHMALTZIER
SHARPSHOOTERS	SHELDDUCKS	SHERIFFALTIES	SHIPBROKERS	SHMALTZIEST

SHMOOZIEST	SHORELINES	SHOVELHEADS	SHRIMPLIKE	SIBILANCIES
SHMUCKIEST	SHORESIDES	SHOVELLERS	SHRINELIKE	SIBILANTLY
SHOALINESS	SHOREWARDS	SHOVELLING	SHRINKABLE	SIBILATING
SHOALINESSES	SHOREWEEDS	SHOVELNOSE	SHRINKAGES	SIBILATION
SHOALNESSES	SHORTARSES	SHOVELNOSES	SHRINKFLATION	SIBILATIONS
SHOCKABILITIES	SHORTBOARD	SHOVELSFUL	SHRINKFLATIONS	SIBILATORS
SHOCKABILITY	SHORTBOARDS	SHOWBIZZES	SHRINKINGLY	SIBILATORY
SHOCKHEADED	SHORTBREAD	SHOWBIZZIER	SHRINKPACK	SICCATIVES
SHOCKINGLY	SHORTBREADS	SHOWBIZZIEST	SHRINKPACKS	SICILIANAS
SHOCKINGNESS	SHORTCAKES	SHOWBOATED	SHRITCHING	SICILIANOS
SHOCKINGNESSES	SHORTCHANGE	SHOWBOATER	SHRIVELING	SICILIENNE
SHOCKPROOF	SHORTCHANGED	SHOWBOATERS	SHRIVELLED	SICILIENNES
SHOCKSTALL	SHORTCHANGER	SHOWBOATING	SHRIVELLING	SICKENINGLY
SHOCKSTALLS	SHORTCHANGERS	SHOWBREADS	SHROFFAGES	SICKENINGS
SHOCKUMENTARIES	SHORTCHANGES	SHOWCASING	SHROUDIEST	SICKERNESS
SHOCKUMENTARY	SHORTCHANGING	SHOWERHEAD	SHROUDINGS	SICKERNESSES
SHODDINESS	SHORTCOMING	SHOWERHEADS	SHROUDLESS	SICKISHNESS
SHODDINESSES	SHORTCOMINGS	SHOWERIEST	SHRUBBERIED	SICKISHNESSES
SHOEBLACKS	SHORTCRUST	SHOWERINESS	SHRUBBERIES	SICKLEBILL
SHOEBRUSHES	SHORTCUTTING	SHOWERINESSES	SHRUBBIEST	SICKLEBILLS
SHOEHORNED	SHORTENERS	SHOWERINGS	SHRUBBINESS	SICKLEMIAS
SHOEHORNING	SHORTENING	SHOWERLESS	SHRUBBINESSES	SICKLINESS
SHOEMAKERS	SHORTENINGS	SHOWERPROOF	SHRUBLANDS	SICKLINESSES
SHOEMAKING	SHORTFALLS	SHOWERPROOFED	SHTETELACH	SICKNESSES
SHOEMAKINGS	SHORTGOWNS	SHOWERPROOFING	SHTICKIEST	SICKNURSED
SHOESHINES	SHORTHAIRED	SHOWERPROOFINGS	SHTREIMELS	SICKNURSES
SHOESTRING	SHORTHAIRS	SHOWERPROOFS	SHUBUNKINS	SICKNURSING
SHOESTRINGS	SHORTHANDED	SHOWGROUND	SHUDDERIER	SICKNURSINGS
SHOGGLIEST	SHORTHANDS	SHOWGROUNDS	SHUDDERIEST	SIDDHUISMS
SHOGUNATES	SHORTHEADS	SHOWINESSES	SHUDDERING	SIDEARMERS
SHONGOLOLO	SHORTHORNS	SHOWJUMPED	SHUDDERINGLY	SIDEARMING
SHONGOLOLOS	SHORTLISTED	SHOWJUMPER	SHUDDERINGS	SIDEBOARDS
SHOOGIEING	SHORTLISTING	SHOWJUMPERS	SHUDDERSOME	SIDEBURNED
SHOOGLIEST	SHORTLISTS	SHOWJUMPING	SHUFFLEBOARD	SIDECHAIRS
SHOOTAROUND	SHORTNESSES	SHOWJUMPINGS	SHUFFLEBOARDS	SIDECHECKS
SHOOTAROUNDS	SHORTSHEET	SHOWMANCES	SHUFFLINGLY	SIDEDNESSES
SHOOTDOWNS	SHORTSHEETED	SHOWMANLIER	SHUFFLINGS	SIDEDRESSES
SHOPAHOLIC	SHORTSHEETING	SHOWMANLIEST	SHUNAMITISM	SIDELEVERS
SHOPAHOLICS	SHORTSHEETS	SHOWMANSHIP	SHUNAMITISMS	SIDELIGHTS
SHOPAHOLISM	SHORTSIGHTED	SHOWMANSHIPS	SHUNPIKERS	SIDELINERS
SHOPAHOLISMS	SHORTSIGHTEDLY	SHOWPIECES	SHUNPIKING	SIDELINING
SHOPBOARDS	SHORTSTOPS	SHOWPLACES	SHUNPIKINGS	SIDEPIECES
SHOPBREAKER	SHORTSWORD	SHOWROOMING	SHUTTERBUG	SIDERATING
SHOPBREAKERS	SHORTSWORDS	SHOWROOMINGS	SHUTTERBUGS	SIDERATION
SHOPBREAKING	SHORTWAVED	SHOWSTOPPER	SHUTTERING	SIDERATIONS
SHOPBREAKINGS	SHORTWAVES	SHOWSTOPPERS	SHUTTERINGS	SIDEREALLY
SHOPFITTER	SHORTWAVING	SHOWSTOPPING	SHUTTERLESS	SIDEROLITE
SHOPFITTERS	SHOTCRETES	SHREDDIEST	SHUTTLECOCK	SIDEROLITES
SHOPFRONTS	SHOTFIRERS	SHREDDINGS	SHUTTLECOCKED	SIDEROPENIA
SHOPHOUSES	SHOTGUNNED	SHREWDNESS	SHUTTLECOCKING	SIDEROPENIAS
SHOPKEEPER	SHOTGUNNER	SHREWDNESSES	SHUTTLECOCKS	SIDEROPHILE
SHOPKEEPERS	SHOTGUNNERS	SHREWISHLY	SHUTTLELESS	SIDEROPHILES
SHOPKEEPING	SHOTGUNNING	SHREWISHNESS	SHUTTLEWISE	SIDEROPHILIC
SHOPKEEPINGS	SHOTMAKERS	SHREWISHNESSES	SHYLOCKING	SIDEROPHILIN
SHOPLIFTED	SHOTMAKING	SHREWMOUSE	SIALAGOGIC	SIDEROPHILINS
SHOPLIFTER	SHOTMAKINGS	SHRIECHING	SIALAGOGUE	SIDEROSTAT
SHOPLIFTERS	SHOULDERED	SHRIEKIEST	SIALAGOGUES	SIDEROSTATIC
SHOPLIFTING	SHOULDERING	SHRIEKINGLY	SIALOGOGIC	SIDEROSTATS
SHOPLIFTINGS	SHOULDERINGS	SHRIEKINGS	SIALOGOGUE	SIDESADDLE
SHOPSOILED	SHOUTHERED	SHRIEVALTIES	SIALOGOGUES	SIDESADDLES
SHOPWALKER	SHOUTHERING	SHRIEVALTY	SIALOGRAMS	SIDESHOOTS
SHOPWALKERS	SHOUTINGLY	SHRILLIEST	SIALOGRAPHIES	SIDESLIPPED
SHOPWINDOW	SHOUTLINES	SHRILLINGS	SIALOGRAPHY	SIDESLIPPING
SHOPWINDOWS	SHOVELBOARD	SHRILLNESS	SIALOLITHS	SIDESPLITS
SHOREBIRDS	SHOVELBOARDS	SHRILLNESSES	SIALORRHOEA	SIDESPLITTING
SHOREFRONT	SHOVELFULS	SHRIMPIEST	SIALORRHOEAS	SIDESPLITTINGLY
SHOREFRONTS	SHOVELHEAD	SHRIMPINGS	SIBILANCES	SIDESTEPPED

SIDESTEPPER	SIGNALIZING	SILKOLINES	SIMILIZING	SINCERITIES
SIDESTEPPERS	SIGNALLERS	SILKSCREEN	SIMILLIMUM	SINCIPITAL
SIDESTEPPING	SIGNALLING	SILKSCREENED	SIMILLIMUMS	SINDONOLOGIES
SIDESTEPPINGS	SIGNALLINGS	SILKSCREENING	SIMONIACAL	SINDONOLOGIST
SIDESTREAM	SIGNALMENT	SILKSCREENS	SIMONIACALLY	SINDONOLOGISTS
SIDESTROKE	SIGNALMENTS	SILLIMANITE	SIMONISING	SINDONOLOGY
SIDESTROKES	SIGNATORIES	SILLIMANITES	SIMONIZING	SINDONOPHANIES
SIDESWIPED	SIGNATURES	SILLINESSES	SIMPERINGLY	SINDONOPHANY
SIDESWIPER	SIGNBOARDS	SILTATIONS	SIMPERINGS	SINECURISM
SIDESWIPERS	SIGNEURIES	SILTSTONES	SIMPLEMINDED	SINECURISMS
SIDESWIPES	SIGNIFIABLE	SILVERBACK	SIMPLEMINDEDLY	SINECURIST
SIDESWIPING	SIGNIFICANCE	SILVERBACKS	SIMPLENESS	SINECURISTS
SIDETABLES	SIGNIFICANCES	SILVERBERRIES	SIMPLENESSES	SINEWINESS
SIDETRACKED	SIGNIFICANCIES	SILVERBERRY	SIMPLESSES	SINEWINESSES
SIDETRACKING	SIGNIFICANCY	SILVERBILL	SIMPLETONS	SINFONIETTA
SIDETRACKS	SIGNIFICANT	SILVERBILLS	SIMPLICIAL	SINFONIETTAS
SIDEWHEELER	SIGNIFICANTLY	SILVEREYES	SIMPLICIALLY	SINFULNESS
SIDEWHEELERS	SIGNIFICANTS	SILVERFISH	SIMPLICIDENTATE	SINFULNESSES
SIDEWHEELS	SIGNIFICATE	SILVERFISHES	SIMPLICITER	SINGABLENESS
SIDEWINDER	SIGNIFICATES	SILVERHORN	SIMPLICITIES	SINGABLENESSES
SIDEWINDERS	SIGNIFICATION	SILVERHORNS	SIMPLICITY	SINGALONGS
SIEGECRAFT	SIGNIFICATIONS	SILVERIEST	SIMPLIFIABLE	SINGLEDOMS
SIEGECRAFTS	SIGNIFICATIVE	SILVERINESS	SIMPLIFICATION	SINGLEHOOD
SIEGEWORKS	SIGNIFICATIVELY	SILVERINESSES	SIMPLIFICATIONS	SINGLEHOODS
SIFFLEUSES	SIGNIFICATOR	SILVERINGS	SIMPLIFICATIVE	SINGLENESS
SIGHTLESSLY	SIGNIFICATORS	SILVERISED	SIMPLIFICATOR	SINGLENESSES
SIGHTLESSNESS	SIGNIFICATORY	SILVERISES	SIMPLIFICATORS	SINGLESTICK
SIGHTLESSNESSES	SIGNIFIEDS	SILVERISING	SIMPLIFIED	SINGLESTICKS
SIGHTLIEST	SIGNIFIERS	SILVERIZED	SIMPLIFIER	SINGLETONS
SIGHTLINES	SIGNIFYING	SILVERIZES	SIMPLIFIERS	SINGLETRACK
SIGHTLINESS	SIGNIFYINGS	SILVERIZING	SIMPLIFIES	SINGLETRACKS
SIGHTLINESSES	SIGNIORIES	SILVERLING	SIMPLIFYING	SINGLETREE
SIGHTSCREEN	SIGNORINAS	SILVERLINGS	SIMPLISTES	SINGLETREES
SIGHTSCREENS	SIGNPOSTED	SILVERPOINT	SIMPLISTIC	SINGSONGED
SIGHTSEEING	SIGNPOSTING	SILVERPOINTS	SIMPLISTICALLY	SINGSONGIER
SIGHTSEEINGS	SIGNPOSTINGS	SILVERSIDE	SIMULACRES	SINGSONGIEST
SIGHTSEERS	SIKORSKIES	SILVERSIDES	SIMULACRUM	SINGSONGING
SIGHTWORTHIER	SILDENAFIL	SILVERSKIN	SIMULACRUMS	SINGSPIELS
SIGHTWORTHIEST	SILDENAFILS	SILVERSKINS	SIMULATING	SINGULARISATION
SIGHTWORTHY	SILENTIARIES	SILVERSMITH	SIMULATION	SINGULARISE
SIGILLARIAN	SILENTIARY	SILVERSMITHING	SIMULATIONS	SINGULARISED
SIGILLARIANS	SILENTNESS	SILVERSMITHINGS	SIMULATIVE	SINGULARISES
SIGILLARID	SILENTNESSES	SILVERSMITHS	SIMULATIVELY	SINGULARISING
SIGILLARIDS	SILHOUETTE	SILVERTAIL	SIMULATORS	SINGULARISM
SIGILLATION	SILHOUETTED	SILVERTAILS	SIMULATORY	SINGULARISMS
SIGILLATIONS	SILHOUETTES	SILVERTIPS	SIMULCASTED	SINGULARIST
SIGMATIONS	SILHOUETTING	SILVERWARE	SIMULCASTING	SINGULARISTS
SIGMATISMS	SILHOUETTIST	SILVERWARES	SIMULCASTS	SINGULARITIES
SIGMATRONS	SILHOUETTISTS	SILVERWEED	SIMULTANEITIES	SINGULARITY
SIGMOIDALLY	SILICATING	SILVERWEEDS	SIMULTANEITY	SINGULARIZATION
SIGMOIDECTOMIES	SILICICOLOUS	SILVESTRIAN	SIMULTANEOUS	SINGULARIZE
SIGMOIDECTOMY	SILICIFEROUS	SILVICULTURAL	SIMULTANEOUSES	SINGULARIZED
SIGMOIDOSCOPE	SILICIFICATION	SILVICULTURALLY	SIMULTANEOUSLY	SINGULARIZES
SIGMOIDOSCOPES	SILICIFICATIONS	SILVICULTURE	SIMVASTATIN	SINGULARIZING
SIGMOIDOSCOPIC	SILICIFIED	SILVICULTURES	SIMVASTATINS	SINGULARLY
SIGMOIDOSCOPIES	SILICIFIES	SILVICULTURIST	SINANTHROPUS	SINGULARNESS
SIGMOIDOSCOPY	SILICIFYING	SILVICULTURISTS	SINANTHROPUSES	SINGULARNESSES
SIGNALINGS	SILICONISED	SILYMARINS	SINARCHISM	SINGULTUSES
SIGNALISATION	SILICONIZED	SIMAROUBACEOUS	SINARCHISMS	SINICISING
SIGNALISATIONS	SILICOTICS	SIMAROUBAS	SINARCHIST	SINICIZING
SIGNALISED	SILICULOSE	SIMARUBACEOUS	SINARCHISTS	SINISTERITIES
SIGNALISES	SILIQUACEOUS	SIMILARITIES	SINARQUISM	SINISTERITY
SIGNALISING	SILKALENES	SIMILARITY	SINARQUISMS	SINISTERLY
SIGNALIZATION	SILKALINES	SIMILATIVE	SINARQUIST	SINISTERNESS
SIGNALIZATIONS	SILKGROWER	SIMILISING	SINARQUISTS	SINISTERNESSES
SIGNALIZED	SILKGROWERS	SIMILITUDE	SINCERENESS	SINISTERWISE
SIGNALIZES	SILKINESSES	SIMILITUDES	SINCERENESSES	SINISTRALITIES

SINISTRALITY	SITIOPHOBIA	SKEPTICALNESS	SKINNINESSES	SKYWRITINGS
SINISTRALLY	SITIOPHOBIAS	SKEPTICALNESSES	SKINTIGHTER	SKYWRITTEN
SINISTRALS	SITOLOGIES	SKEPTICISM	SKINTIGHTEST	SLABBERERS
SINISTRODEXTRAL	SITOPHOBIA	SKEPTICISMS	SKINTIGHTS	SLABBERIER
SINISTRORSAL	SITOPHOBIAS	SKETCHABILITIES	SKIPPERING	SLABBERIEST
SINISTRORSALLY	SITOSTEROL	SKETCHABILITY	SKIPPERINGS	SLABBERING
SINISTRORSE	SITOSTEROLS	SKETCHABLE	SKIPPINGLY	SLABBINESS
SINISTRORSELY	SITUATIONAL	SKETCHBOOK	SKIRMISHED	SLABBINESSES
SINISTROUS	SITUATIONALLY	SKETCHBOOKS	SKIRMISHER	SLABSTONES
SINISTROUSLY	SITUATIONISM	SKETCHIEST	SKIRMISHERS	SLACKENERS
SINLESSNESS	SITUATIONISMS	SKETCHINESS	SKIRMISHES	SLACKENING
SINLESSNESSES	SITUATIONS	SKETCHINESSES	SKIRMISHING	SLACKENINGS
SINNINGIAS	SITUTUNGAS	SKETCHPADS	SKIRMISHINGS	SLACKLINING
SINOATRIAL	SITZKRIEGS	SKEUOMORPH	SKITTERIER	SLACKLININGS
SINOLOGICAL	SIXPENNIES	SKEUOMORPHIC	SKITTERIEST	SLACKNESSES
SINOLOGIES	SIXTEENERS	SKEUOMORPHISM	SKITTERING	SLACKTIVISM
SINOLOGIST	SIXTEENMOS	SKEUOMORPHISMS	SKITTISHLY	SLACKTIVISMS
SINOLOGISTS	SIXTEENTHLY	SKEUOMORPHS	SKITTISHNESS	SLACKTIVIST
SINOLOGUES	SIXTEENTHS	SKEWBACKED	SKITTISHNESSES	SLACKTIVISTS
SINSEMILLA	SIZABLENESS	SKEWNESSES	SKORDALIAS	SLACTIVISM
SINSEMILLAS	SIZABLENESSES	SKIAGRAPHS	SKREEGHING	SLACTIVISMS
SINTERABILITIES	SIZARSHIPS	SKIAMACHIES	SKREIGHING	SLACTIVIST
SINTERABILITY	SIZEABLENESS	SKIASCOPES	SKRIECHING	SLACTIVISTS
SINTERIEST	SIZEABLENESSES	SKIASCOPIES	SKRIEGHING	SLAISTERED
SINUATIONS	SIZINESSES	SKIBOBBERS	SKRIMMAGED	SLAISTERIES
SINUITISES	SIZZLINGLY	SKIBOBBING	SKRIMMAGES	SLAISTERING
SINUOSITIES	SJAMBOKING	SKIBOBBINGS	SKRIMMAGING	SLALOMISTS
SINUOUSNESS	SJAMBOKKED	SKIDDOOING	SKRIMSHANK	SLAMDANCED
SINUOUSNESSES	SJAMBOKKING	SKIDOOINGS	SKRIMSHANKED	SLAMDANCES
SINUPALLIAL	SKAITHLESS	SKIJORINGS	SKRIMSHANKER	SLAMDANCING
SINUPALLIATE	SKALDSHIPS	SKIJUMPERS	SKRIMSHANKERS	SLAMMAKINS
SINUSITISES	SKANKINESS	SKIKJORERS	SKRIMSHANKING	SLAMMERKIN
SINUSOIDAL	SKANKINESSES	SKIKJORING	SKRIMSHANKS	SLAMMERKINS
SINUSOIDALLY	SKATEBOARD	SKIKJORINGS	SKULDUDDERIES	SLANDERERS
SIPHONAGES	SKATEBOARDED	SKILFULNESS	SKULDUDDERY	SLANDERING
SIPHONOGAM	SKATEBOARDER	SKILFULNESSES	SKULDUGGERIES	SLANDEROUS
SIPHONOGAMIES	SKATEBOARDERS	SKILLCENTRE	SKULDUGGERY	SLANDEROUSLY
SIPHONOGAMS	SKATEBOARDING	SKILLCENTRES	SKULKINGLY	SLANDEROUSNESS
SIPHONOGAMY	SKATEBOARDINGS	SKILLESSNESS	SKULLDUGGERIES	SLANGINESS
SIPHONOPHORE	SKATEBOARDS	SKILLESSNESSES	SKULLDUGGERY	SLANGINESSES
SIPHONOPHORES	SKATEPARKS	SKILLFULLY	SKUMMERING	SLANGINGLY
SIPHONOPHOROUS	SKATEPUNKS	SKILLFULNESS	SKUNKBIRDS	SLANGUAGES
SIPHONOSTELE	SKEDADDLED	SKILLFULNESSES	SKUNKWEEDS	SLANTENDICULAR
SIPHONOSTELES	SKEDADDLER	SKILLIGALEE	SKUTTERUDITE	SLANTINDICULAR
SIPHONOSTELIC	SKEDADDLERS	SKILLIGALEES	SKUTTERUDITES	SLANTINGLY
SIPHUNCLES	SKEDADDLES	SKILLIGOLEE	SKYBRIDGES	SLANTINGWAYS
SIPUNCULID	SKEDADDLING	SKILLIGOLEES	SKYDIVINGS	SLAPDASHED
SIPUNCULIDS	SKELDERING	SKIMBOARDED	SKYJACKERS	SLAPDASHES
SIPUNCULOID	SKELETALLY	SKIMBOARDER	SKYJACKING	SLAPDASHING
SIPUNCULOIDS	SKELETOGENOUS	SKIMBOARDERS	SKYJACKINGS	SLAPHAPPIER
SIRENISING	SKELETONIC	SKIMBOARDING	SKYLARKERS	SLAPHAPPIEST
SIRENIZING	SKELETONISE	SKIMBOARDS	SKYLARKING	SLAPSTICKS
SIRONISING	SKELETONISED	SKIMMINGLY	SKYLARKINGS	SLASHFESTS
SIRONIZING	SKELETONISER	SKIMMINGTON	SKYLIGHTED	SLASHINGLY
SISERARIES	SKELETONISERS	SKIMMINGTONS	SKYROCKETED	SLATHERING
SISSINESSES	SKELETONISES	SKIMOBILED	SKYROCKETING	SLATINESSES
SISSYNESSES	SKELETONISING	SKIMOBILES	SKYROCKETS	SLATTERING
SISTERHOOD	SKELETONIZE	SKIMOBILING	SKYSCRAPER	SLATTERNLIER
SISTERHOODS	SKELETONIZED	SKIMPINESS	SKYSCRAPERS	SLATTERNLIEST
SISTERLESS	SKELETONIZER	SKIMPINESSES	SKYSURFERS	SLATTERNLINESS
SISTERLIER	SKELETONIZERS	SKIMPINGLY	SKYSURFING	SLATTERNLY
SISTERLIEST	SKELETONIZES	SKINFLICKS	SKYSURFINGS	SLAUGHTERABLE
SISTERLIKE	SKELETONIZING	SKINFLINTIER	SKYWATCHED	SLAUGHTERED
SISTERLINESS	SKELLOCHED	SKINFLINTIEST	SKYWATCHES	SLAUGHTERER
SISTERLINESSES	SKELLOCHING	SKINFLINTS	SKYWATCHING	SLAUGHTERERS
SITATUNGAS	SKELTERING	SKINFLINTY	SKYWRITERS	SLAUGHTERHOUSE
SITIOLOGIES	SKEPTICALLY	SKINNINESS	SKYWRITING	SLAUGHTERHOUSES

SLAUGHTERIES	SLENDERIZED	SLIPSTREAMS	SLUGGARDISING	SMALMINESS
SLAUGHTERING	SLENDERIZES	SLITHERIER	SLUGGARDIZE	SMALMINESSES
SLAUGHTERMAN	SLENDERIZING	SLITHERIEST	SLUGGARDIZED	SMARAGDINE
SLAUGHTERMEN	SLENDERNESS	SLITHERING	SLUGGARDIZES	SMARAGDITE
SLAUGHTEROUS	SLENDERNESSES	SLIVOVICAS	SLUGGARDIZING	SMARAGDITES
SLAUGHTEROUSLY	SLEUTHHOUND	SLIVOVICES	SLUGGARDLIER	SMARMINESS
SLAUGHTERS	SLEUTHHOUNDS	SLIVOVITZES	SLUGGARDLIEST	SMARMINESSES
SLAUGHTERY	SLEUTHINGS	SLIVOWITZES	SLUGGARDLINESS	SMARTARSED
SLAVEHOLDER	SLICKENERS	SLOBBERERS	SLUGGARDLY	SMARTARSES
SLAVEHOLDERS	SLICKENING	SLOBBERIER	SLUGGARDNESS	SMARTASSES
SLAVEHOLDING	SLICKENSIDE	SLOBBERIEST	SLUGGARDNESSES	SMARTENING
SLAVEHOLDINGS	SLICKENSIDED	SLOBBERING	SLUGGISHLY	SMARTINGLY
SLAVERINGLY	SLICKENSIDES	SLOBBISHNESS	SLUGGISHNESS	SMARTMOUTH
SLAVERINGS	SLICKNESSES	SLOBBISHNESSES	SLUGGISHNESSES	SMARTMOUTHS
SLAVISHNESS	SLICKROCKS	SLOCKDOLAGER	SLUGHORNES	SMARTNESSES
SLAVISHNESSES	SLICKSTERS	SLOCKDOLAGERS	SLUICEGATE	SMARTPHONE
SLAVOCRACIES	SLICKSTONE	SLOCKDOLIGER	SLUICEGATES	SMARTPHONES
SLAVOCRACY	SLICKSTONES	SLOCKDOLIGERS	SLUICELIKE	SMARTWATCH
SLAVOCRATS	SLIDDERIER	SLOCKDOLOGER	SLUICEWAYS	SMARTWATCHES
SLAVOPHILE	SLIDDERIEST	SLOCKDOLOGERS	SLUMBERERS	SMARTWEEDS
SLAVOPHILES	SLIDDERING	SLOCKENING	SLUMBERFUL	SMARTYPANTS
SLAVOPHILS	SLIDESHOWS	SLOEBUSHES	SLUMBERIER	SMASHEROOS
SLEAZEBAGS	SLIGHTINGLY	SLOETHORNS	SLUMBERIEST	SMASHINGLY
SLEAZEBALL	SLIGHTNESS	SLOGANEERED	SLUMBERING	SMASHMOUTH
SLEAZEBALLS	SLIGHTNESSES	SLOGANEERING	SLUMBERINGLY	SMATTERERS
SLEAZINESS	SLIMEBALLS	SLOGANEERINGS	SLUMBERINGS	SMATTERING
SLEAZINESSES	SLIMINESSES	SLOGANEERS	SLUMBERLAND	SMATTERINGLY
SLEDGEHAMMER	SLIMNASTICS	SLOGANISED	SLUMBERLANDS	SMATTERINGS
SLEDGEHAMMERED	SLIMNESSES	SLOGANISES	SLUMBERLESS	SMEARCASES
SLEDGEHAMMERING	SLIMPSIEST	SLOGANISING	SLUMBEROUS	SMEARINESS
SLEDGEHAMMERS	SLINGBACKS	SLOGANISINGS	SLUMBEROUSLY	SMEARINESSES
SLEECHIEST	SLINGSHOTS	SLOGANIZED	SLUMBEROUSNESS	SMELLINESS
SLEEKENING	SLINGSTONE	SLOGANIZES	SLUMBERSOME	SMELLINESSES
SLEEKNESSES	SLINGSTONES	SLOGANIZING	SLUMBROUSLY	SMELTERIES
SLEEKSTONE	SLINKINESS	SLOGANIZINGS	SLUMBROUSNESS	SMICKERING
SLEEKSTONES	SLINKINESSES	SLOMMOCKED	SLUMBROUSNESSES	SMICKERINGS
SLEEPINESS	SLINKSKINS	SLOMMOCKING	SLUMGULLION	SMIERCASES
SLEEPINESSES	SLINKWEEDS	SLOPESIDES	SLUMGULLIONS	SMIFLIGATE
SLEEPLESSLY	SLIPCOVERED	SLOPINGNESS	SLUMMOCKED	SMIFLIGATED
SLEEPLESSNESS	SLIPCOVERING	SLOPINGNESSES	SLUMMOCKING	SMIFLIGATES
SLEEPLESSNESSES	SLIPCOVERS	SLOPPINESS	SLUMPFLATION	SMIFLIGATING
SLEEPOVERS	SLIPDRESSES	SLOPPINESSES	SLUMPFLATIONARY	SMILACACEOUS
SLEEPSUITS	SLIPFORMED	SLOPWORKER	SLUMPFLATIONS	SMILINGNESS
SLEEPWALKED	SLIPFORMING	SLOPWORKERS	SLUNGSHOTS	SMILINGNESSES
SLEEPWALKER	SLIPNOOSES	SLOTHFULLY	SLUSHINESS	SMIRKINGLY
SLEEPWALKERS	SLIPPERIER	SLOTHFULNESS	SLUSHINESSES	SMITHCRAFT
SLEEPWALKING	SLIPPERIEST	SLOTHFULNESSES	SLUTCHIEST	SMITHCRAFTS
SLEEPWALKINGS	SLIPPERILY	SLOUCHIEST	SLUTTERIES	SMITHEREEN
SLEEPWALKS	SLIPPERINESS	SLOUCHINESS	SLUTTINESS	SMITHEREENED
SLEEPWEARS	SLIPPERINESSES	SLOUCHINESSES	SLUTTINESSES	SMITHEREENING
SLEEPYHEAD	SLIPPERING	SLOUCHINGLY	SLUTTISHLY	SMITHEREENS
SLEEPYHEADED	SLIPPERWORT	SLOUGHIEST	SLUTTISHNESS	SMITHERIES
SLEEPYHEADS	SLIPPERWORTS	SLOVENLIER	SLUTTISHNESSES	SMITHSONITE
SLEETINESS	SLIPPINESS	SLOVENLIEST	SMACKDOWNS	SMITHSONITES
SLEETINESSES	SLIPPINESSES	SLOVENLIKE	SMACKEROOS	SMOKEBOARD
SLEEVEHAND	SLIPSHEETED	SLOVENLINESS	SMACKHEADS	SMOKEBOARDS
SLEEVEHANDS	SLIPSHEETING	SLOVENLINESSES	SMALLCLOTHES	SMOKEBOXES
SLEEVELESS	SLIPSHEETS	SLOVENRIES	SMALLHOLDER	SMOKEBUSHES
SLEEVELETS	SLIPSHODDINESS	SLOWCOACHES	SMALLHOLDERS	SMOKEHOODS
SLEEVELIKE	SLIPSHODNESS	SLOWNESSES	SMALLHOLDING	SMOKEHOUSE
SLEIGHINGS	SLIPSHODNESSES	SLUBBERING	SMALLHOLDINGS	SMOKEHOUSES
SLENDEREST	SLIPSLOPPIER	SLUBBERINGLY	SMALLMOUTH	SMOKEJACKS
SLENDERISE	SLIPSLOPPIEST	SLUBBERINGS	SMALLMOUTHS	SMOKELESSLY
SLENDERISED	SLIPSLOPPY	SLUGGABEDS	SMALLNESSES	SMOKELESSNESS
SLENDERISES	SLIPSTREAM	SLUGGARDISE	SMALLPOXES	SMOKELESSNESSES
SLENDERISING	SLIPSTREAMED	SLUGGARDISED	SMALLSWORD	SMOKEPROOF
SLENDERIZE	SLIPSTREAMING	SLUGGARDISES	SMALLSWORDS	SMOKESCREEN

S

SMOKESCREENS	SNAPDRAGON	SNIPEFISHES	SNOWBOARDINGS	SOBERISING
SMOKESTACK	SNAPDRAGONS	SNIPERSCOPE	SNOWBOARDS	SOBERIZING
SMOKESTACKS	SNAPHANCES	SNIPERSCOPES	SNOWBRUSHES	SOBERNESSES
SMOKETIGHT	SNAPHAUNCE	SNIPPERSNAPPER	SNOWBUSHES	SOBERSIDED
SMOKINESSES	SNAPHAUNCES	SNIPPERSNAPPERS	SNOWCAPPED	SOBERSIDEDNESS
SMOLDERING	SNAPHAUNCH	SNIPPETIER	SNOWCLONES	SOBERSIDES
SMOOCHIEST	SNAPHAUNCHES	SNIPPETIEST	SNOWCOACHES	SOBOLIFEROUS
SMOOTHABLE	SNAPPERING	SNIPPETINESS	SNOWDRIFTS	SOBRIETIES
SMOOTHBORE	SNAPPINESS	SNIPPETINESSES	SNOWFIELDS	SOBRIQUETS
SMOOTHBORED	SNAPPINESSES	SNIPPINESS	SNOWFLAKES	SOCDOLAGER
SMOOTHBORES	SNAPPINGLY	SNIPPINESSES	SNOWFLECKS	SOCDOLAGERS
SMOOTHENED	SNAPPISHLY	SNITCHIEST	SNOWFLICKS	SOCDOLIGER
SMOOTHENING	SNAPPISHNESS	SNIVELIEST	SNOWGLOBES	SOCDOLIGERS
SMOOTHINGS	SNAPPISHNESSES	SNIVELINGS	SNOWINESSES	SOCDOLOGER
SMOOTHNESS	SNAPSHOOTER	SNIVELLERS	SNOWMAKERS	SOCDOLOGERS
SMOOTHNESSES	SNAPSHOOTERS	SNIVELLIER	SNOWMAKING	SOCIABILITIES
SMOOTHPATE	SNAPSHOOTING	SNIVELLIEST	SNOWMOBILE	SOCIABILITY
SMOOTHPATES	SNAPSHOOTINGS	SNIVELLING	SNOWMOBILED	SOCIABLENESS
SMORGASBORD	SNAPSHOTTED	SNIVELLINGS	SNOWMOBILER	SOCIABLENESSES
SMORGASBORDS	SNAPSHOTTING	SNOBBERIES	SNOWMOBILERS	SOCIALISABLE
SMORREBROD	SNARLINGLY	SNOBBISHLY	SNOWMOBILES	SOCIALISATION
SMORREBRODS	SNATCHIEST	SNOBBISHNESS	SNOWMOBILING	SOCIALISATIONS
SMOTHERERS	SNATCHINGLY	SNOBBISHNESSES	SNOWMOBILINGS	SOCIALISED
SMOTHERIER	SNATCHINGS	SNOBBOCRACIES	SNOWMOBILIST	SOCIALISER
SMOTHERIEST	SNAZZINESS	SNOBBOCRACY	SNOWMOBILISTS	SOCIALISERS
SMOTHERINESS	SNAZZINESSES	SNOBOCRACIES	SNOWMOULDS	SOCIALISES
SMOTHERINESSES	SNEAKBOXES	SNOBOCRACY	SNOWPLOUGH	SOCIALISING
SMOTHERING	SNEAKINESS	SNOBOGRAPHER	SNOWPLOUGHED	SOCIALISINGS
SMOTHERINGLY	SNEAKINESSES	SNOBOGRAPHERS	SNOWPLOUGHING	SOCIALISMS
SMOTHERINGS	SNEAKINGLY	SNOBOGRAPHIES	SNOWPLOUGHS	SOCIALISTIC
SMOULDERED	SNEAKINGNESS	SNOBOGRAPHY	SNOWPLOWED	SOCIALISTICALLY
SMOULDERING	SNEAKINGNESSES	SNOCOACHES	SNOWPLOWING	SOCIALISTS
SMOULDERINGLY	SNEAKISHLY	SNOLLYGOSTER	SNOWSCAPES	SOCIALITES
SMOULDERINGS	SNEAKISHNESS	SNOLLYGOSTERS	SNOWSHOEING	SOCIALITIES
SMOULDRIER	SNEAKISHNESSES	SNOOKERING	SNOWSHOEINGS	SOCIALIZABLE
SMOULDRIEST	SNEAKSBIES	SNOOPERSCOPE	SNOWSHOERS	SOCIALIZATION
SMUDGELESS	SNEERINGLY	SNOOPERSCOPES	SNOWSLIDES	SOCIALIZATIONS
SMUDGINESS	SNEESHINGS	SNOOTINESS	SNOWSNAKES	SOCIALIZED
SMUDGINESSES	SNEEZELESS	SNOOTINESSES	SNOWSTORMS	SOCIALIZER
SMUGGERIES	SNEEZEWEED	SNORKELERS	SNOWSURFING	SOCIALIZERS
SMUGGLINGS	SNEEZEWEEDS	SNORKELING	SNOWSURFINGS	SOCIALIZES
SMUGNESSES	SNEEZEWOOD	SNORKELINGS	SNOWTUBING	SOCIALIZING
SMUTCHIEST	SNEEZEWOODS	SNORKELLED	SNOWTUBINGS	SOCIALIZINGS
SMUTTINESS	SNEEZEWORT	SNORKELLER	SNUBBINESS	SOCIALNESS
SMUTTINESSES	SNEEZEWORTS	SNORKELLERS	SNUBBINESSES	SOCIALNESSES
SNACKETTES	SNICKERERS	SNORKELLING	SNUBBINGLY	SOCIATIONS
SNAGGLETEETH	SNICKERIER	SNORKELLINGS	SNUBNESSES	SOCIETALLY
SNAGGLETOOTH	SNICKERIEST	SNORTINGLY	SNUFFBOXES	SOCIOBIOLOGICAL
SNAGGLETOOTHED	SNICKERING	SNOTTERIES	SNUFFINESS	SOCIOBIOLOGIES
SNAILERIES	SNICKERSNEE	SNOTTERING	SNUFFINESSES	SOCIOBIOLOGIST
SNAILFISHES	SNICKERSNEED	SNOTTINESS	SNUFFLIEST	SOCIOBIOLOGISTS
SNAKEBIRDS	SNICKERSNEEING	SNOTTINESSES	SNUFFLINGS	SOCIOBIOLOGY
SNAKEBITES	SNICKERSNEES	SNOWBALLED	SNUGGERIES	SOCIOCULTURAL
SNAKEBITTEN	SNIDENESSES	SNOWBALLING	SNUGGLIEST	SOCIOCULTURALLY
SNAKEFISHES	SNIFFINESS	SNOWBERRIES	SNUGNESSES	SOCIOECONOMIC
SNAKEHEADS	SNIFFINESSES	SNOWBLADER	SOAPBERRIES	SOCIOGRAMS
SNAKEMOUTH	SNIFFINGLY	SNOWBLADERS	SOAPBOXING	SOCIOHISTORICAL
SNAKEMOUTHS	SNIFFISHLY	SNOWBLADES	SOAPDISHES	SOCIOLECTS
SNAKEROOTS	SNIFFISHNESS	SNOWBLADING	SOAPFISHES	SOCIOLINGUIST
SNAKESKINS	SNIFFISHNESSES	SNOWBLADINGS	SOAPFLAKES	SOCIOLINGUISTIC
SNAKESTONE	SNIFFLIEST	SNOWBLINKS	SOAPINESSES	SOCIOLINGUISTS
SNAKESTONES	SNIFTERING	SNOWBLOWER	SOAPOLALLIE	SOCIOLOGESE
SNAKEWEEDS	SNIGGERERS	SNOWBLOWERS	SOAPOLALLIES	SOCIOLOGESES
SNAKEWOODS	SNIGGERING	SNOWBOARDED	SOAPSTONES	SOCIOLOGIC
SNAKINESSES	SNIGGERINGLY	SNOWBOARDER	SOAPSUDSIER	SOCIOLOGICAL
SNAKISHNESS	SNIGGERINGS	SNOWBOARDERS	SOAPSUDSIEST	SOCIOLOGICALLY
SNAKISHNESSES	SNIGGLINGS	SNOWBOARDING	SOBERINGLY	SOCIOLOGIES

SOCIOLOGISM	SOLARISING	SOLICITOUS	SOLMISATION	SOMATOPLEURES
SOCIOLOGISMS	SOLARIZATION	SOLICITOUSLY	SOLMISATIONS	SOMATOPLEURIC
SOCIOLOGIST	SOLARIZATIONS	SOLICITOUSNESS	SOLMIZATION	SOMATOSENSORY
SOCIOLOGISTIC	SOLARIZING	SOLICITUDE	SOLMIZATIONS	SOMATOSTATIN
SOCIOLOGISTS	SOLDATESQUE	SOLICITUDES	SOLONCHAKS	SOMATOSTATINS
SOCIOMETRIC	SOLDERABILITIES	SOLIDARISM	SOLONETSES	SOMATOTENSIC
SOCIOMETRIES	SOLDERABILITY	SOLIDARISMS	SOLONETZES	SOMATOTONIA
SOCIOMETRIST	SOLDERABLE	SOLIDARIST	SOLONETZIC	SOMATOTONIAS
SOCIOMETRISTS	SOLDERINGS	SOLIDARISTIC	SOLONISATION	SOMATOTONIC
SOCIOMETRY	SOLDIERIES	SOLIDARISTS	SOLONISATIONS	SOMATOTONICS
SOCIOPATHIC	SOLDIERING	SOLIDARITIES	SOLONIZATION	SOMATOTROPHIC
SOCIOPATHIES	SOLDIERINGS	SOLIDARITY	SOLONIZATIONS	SOMATOTROPHIN
SOCIOPATHS	SOLDIERLIER	SOLIDATING	SOLSTITIAL	SOMATOTROPHINS
SOCIOPATHY	SOLDIERLIEST	SOLIDIFIABLE	SOLSTITIALLY	SOMATOTROPIC
SOCIOPOLITICAL	SOLDIERLIKE	SOLIDIFICATION	SOLUBILISATION	SOMATOTROPIN
SOCIORELIGIOUS	SOLDIERLINESS	SOLIDIFICATIONS	SOLUBILISATIONS	SOMATOTROPINE
SOCIOSEXUAL	SOLDIERLINESSES	SOLIDIFIED	SOLUBILISE	SOMATOTROPINES
SOCKDOLAGER	SOLDIERSHIP	SOLIDIFIER	SOLUBILISED	SOMATOTROPINS
SOCKDOLAGERS	SOLDIERSHIPS	SOLIDIFIERS	SOLUBILISES	SOMATOTYPE
SOCKDOLIGER	SOLECISING	SOLIDIFIES	SOLUBILISING	SOMATOTYPED
SOCKDOLIGERS	SOLECISTIC	SOLIDIFYING	SOLUBILITIES	SOMATOTYPES
SOCKDOLOGER	SOLECISTICAL	SOLIDITIES	SOLUBILITY	SOMATOTYPING
SOCKDOLOGERS	SOLECISTICALLY	SOLIDNESSES	SOLUBILIZATION	SOMBERNESS
SODALITIES	SOLECIZING	SOLIDUNGULATE	SOLUBILIZATIONS	SOMBERNESSES
SODBUSTERS	SOLEMNESSES	SOLIDUNGULATES	SOLUBILIZE	SOMBRENESS
SODDENNESS	SOLEMNIFICATION	SOLIDUNGULOUS	SOLUBILIZED	SOMBRENESSES
SODDENNESSES	SOLEMNIFIED	SOLIFIDIAN	SOLUBILIZES	SOMBRERITE
SODICITIES	SOLEMNIFIES	SOLIFIDIANISM	SOLUBILIZING	SOMBRERITES
SODOMISING	SOLEMNIFYING	SOLIFIDIANISMS	SOLUBLENESS	SOMEBODIES
SODOMITICAL	SOLEMNISATION	SOLIFIDIANS	SOLUBLENESSES	SOMEPLACES
SODOMITICALLY	SOLEMNISATIONS	SOLIFLUCTION	SOLUTIONAL	SOMERSAULT
SODOMIZING	SOLEMNISED	SOLIFLUCTIONS	SOLUTIONED	SOMERSAULTED
SOFTBALLER	SOLEMNISER	SOLIFLUXION	SOLUTIONING	SOMERSAULTING
SOFTBALLERS	SOLEMNISERS	SOLIFLUXIONS	SOLUTIONIST	SOMERSAULTS
SOFTBOUNDS	SOLEMNISES	SOLILOQUIES	SOLUTIONISTS	SOMERSETED
SOFTCOVERS	SOLEMNISING	SOLILOQUISE	SOLVABILITIES	SOMERSETING
SOFTENINGS	SOLEMNITIES	SOLILOQUISED	SOLVABILITY	SOMERSETTED
SOFTHEADED	SOLEMNIZATION	SOLILOQUISER	SOLVABLENESS	SOMERSETTING
SOFTHEADEDLY	SOLEMNIZATIONS	SOLILOQUISERS	SOLVABLENESSES	SOMESTHESIA
SOFTHEADEDNESS	SOLEMNIZED	SOLILOQUISES	SOLVATIONS	SOMESTHESIAS
SOFTHEARTED	SOLEMNIZER	SOLILOQUISING	SOLVENCIES	SOMESTHESIS
SOFTHEARTEDLY	SOLEMNIZERS	SOLILOQUIST	SOLVENTLESS	SOMESTHESISES
SOFTHEARTEDNESS	SOLEMNIZES	SOLILOQUISTS	SOLVOLYSES	SOMESTHETIC
SOFTNESSES	SOLEMNIZING	SOLILOQUIZE	SOLVOLYSIS	SOMETHINGS
SOFTSCAPES	SOLEMNNESS	SOLILOQUIZED	SOLVOLYTIC	SOMEWHENCE
SOFTSHELLS	SOLEMNNESSES	SOLILOQUIZER	SOMAESTHESIA	SOMEWHERES
SOGDOLAGER	SOLENESSES	SOLILOQUIZERS	SOMAESTHESIAS	SOMEWHILES
SOGDOLAGERS	SOLENETTES	SOLILOQUIZES	SOMAESTHESIS	SOMEWHITHER
SOGDOLIGER	SOLENODONS	SOLILOQUIZING	SOMAESTHESISES	SOMMELIERS
SOGDOLIGERS	SOLENOIDAL	SOLIPEDOUS	SOMAESTHETIC	SOMNAMBULANCE
SOGDOLOGER	SOLENOIDALLY	SOLIPSISMS	SOMASCOPES	SOMNAMBULANCES
SOGDOLOGERS	SOLEPLATES	SOLIPSISTIC	SOMATICALLY	SOMNAMBULANT
SOGGINESSES	SOLEPRINTS	SOLIPSISTICALLY	SOMATOGENIC	SOMNAMBULANTS
SOILINESSES	SOLFATARAS	SOLIPSISTS	SOMATOLOGIC	SOMNAMBULAR
SOJOURNERS	SOLFATARIC	SOLITAIRES	SOMATOLOGICAL	SOMNAMBULARY
SOJOURNING	SOLFEGGIOS	SOLITARIAN	SOMATOLOGICALLY	SOMNAMBULATE
SOJOURNINGS	SOLFERINOS	SOLITARIANS	SOMATOLOGIES	SOMNAMBULATED
SOJOURNMENT	SOLICITANT	SOLITARIES	SOMATOLOGIST	SOMNAMBULATES
SOJOURNMENTS	SOLICITANTS	SOLITARILY	SOMATOLOGISTS	SOMNAMBULATING
SOKEMANRIES	SOLICITATION	SOLITARINESS	SOMATOLOGY	SOMNAMBULATION
SOLACEMENT	SOLICITATIONS	SOLITARINESSES	SOMATOMEDIN	SOMNAMBULATIONS
SOLACEMENTS	SOLICITIES	SOLITUDINARIAN	SOMATOMEDINS	SOMNAMBULATOR
SOLANACEOUS	SOLICITING	SOLITUDINARIANS	SOMATOPLASM	SOMNAMBULATORS
SOLARIMETER	SOLICITINGS	SOLITUDINOUS	SOMATOPLASMS	SOMNAMBULE
SOLARIMETERS	SOLICITORS	SOLIVAGANT	SOMATOPLASTIC	SOMNAMBULES
SOLARISATION	SOLICITORSHIP	SOLIVAGANTS	SOMATOPLEURAL	SOMNAMBULIC
SOLARISATIONS	SOLICITORSHIPS	SOLLICKERS	SOMATOPLEURE	SOMNAMBULISM

SOMNAMBULISMS	SONOGRAPHY	SORENESSES	SOUPSPOONS	SOVEREIGNLY
SOMNAMBULIST	SONOMETERS	SORICIDENT	SOURCEBOOK	SOVEREIGNS
SOMNAMBULISTIC	SONORITIES	SORORIALLY	SOURCEBOOKS	SOVEREIGNTIES
SOMNAMBULISTS	SONOROUSLY	SORORICIDAL	SOURCELESS	SOVEREIGNTIST
SOMNIATING	SONOROUSNESS	SORORICIDE	SOURDELINE	SOVEREIGNTISTS
SOMNIATIVE	SONOROUSNESSES	SORORICIDES	SOURDELINES	SOVEREIGNTY
SOMNIATORY	SOOTERKINS	SORORISING	SOURDOUGHS	SOVIETISATION
SOMNIFACIENT	SOOTFLAKES	SORORITIES	SOURNESSES	SOVIETISATIONS
SOMNIFACIENTS	SOOTHERING	SORORIZING	SOURPUSSES	SOVIETISED
SOMNIFEROUS	SOOTHFASTLY	SORRINESSES	SOUSAPHONE	SOVIETISES
SOMNIFEROUSLY	SOOTHFASTNESS	SORROWFULLY	SOUSAPHONES	SOVIETISING
SOMNILOQUENCE	SOOTHFASTNESSES	SORROWFULNESS	SOUSAPHONIST	SOVIETISMS
SOMNILOQUENCES	SOOTHINGLY	SORROWFULNESSES	SOUSAPHONISTS	SOVIETISTIC
SOMNILOQUIES	SOOTHINGNESS	SORROWINGS	SOUTENEURS	SOVIETISTS
SOMNILOQUISE	SOOTHINGNESSES	SORROWLESS	SOUTERRAIN	SOVIETIZATION
SOMNILOQUISED	SOOTHSAYER	SORTATIONS	SOUTERRAINS	SOVIETIZATIONS
SOMNILOQUISES	SOOTHSAYERS	SORTILEGER	SOUTHBOUND	SOVIETIZED
SOMNILOQUISING	SOOTHSAYING	SORTILEGERS	SOUTHEASTER	SOVIETIZES
SOMNILOQUISM	SOOTHSAYINGS	SORTILEGES	SOUTHEASTERLIES	SOVIETIZING
SOMNILOQUISMS	SOOTINESSES	SORTILEGIES	SOUTHEASTERLY	SOVIETOLOGICAL
SOMNILOQUIST	SOPAIPILLA	SORTITIONS	SOUTHEASTERN	SOVIETOLOGIST
SOMNILOQUISTS	SOPAIPILLAS	SOSTENUTOS	SOUTHEASTERS	SOVIETOLOGISTS
SOMNILOQUIZE	SOPAPILLAS	SOTERIOLOGIC	SOUTHEASTS	SOVRANTIES
SOMNILOQUIZED	SOPHISTERS	SOTERIOLOGICAL	SOUTHEASTWARD	SOWBELLIES
SOMNILOQUIZES	SOPHISTICAL	SOTERIOLOGIES	SOUTHEASTWARDS	SOYBURGERS
SOMNILOQUIZING	SOPHISTICALLY	SOTERIOLOGY	SOUTHERING	SPACEBANDS
SOMNILOQUOUS	SOPHISTICATE	SOTTISHNESS	SOUTHERLIES	SPACEBORNE
SOMNILOQUY	SOPHISTICATED	SOTTISHNESSES	SOUTHERLINESS	SPACECRAFT
SOMNOLENCE	SOPHISTICATEDLY	SOTTISIERS	SOUTHERLINESSES	SPACECRAFTS
SOMNOLENCES	SOPHISTICATES	SOUBRETTES	SOUTHERMOST	SPACEFARING
SOMNOLENCIES	SOPHISTICATING	SOUBRETTISH	SOUTHERNER	SPACEFARINGS
SOMNOLENCY	SOPHISTICATION	SOUBRIQUET	SOUTHERNERS	SPACEFLIGHT
SOMNOLENTLY	SOPHISTICATIONS	SOUBRIQUETS	SOUTHERNISE	SPACEFLIGHTS
SOMNOLESCENT	SOPHISTICATOR	SOULDIERED	SOUTHERNISED	SPACEPLANE
SONGCRAFTS	SOPHISTICATORS	SOULDIERING	SOUTHERNISES	SPACEPLANES
SONGFULNESS	SOPHISTRIES	SOULFULNESS	SOUTHERNISING	SPACEPORTS
SONGFULNESSES	SOPHOMORES	SOULFULNESSES	SOUTHERNISM	SPACESHIPS
SONGLESSLY	SOPHOMORIC	SOULLESSLY	SOUTHERNISMS	SPACESUITS
SONGOLOLOS	SOPHOMORICAL	SOULLESSNESS	SOUTHERNIZE	SPACETIMES
SONGSHEETS	SOPORIFEROUS	SOULLESSNESSES	SOUTHERNIZED	SPACEWALKED
SONGSMITHS	SOPORIFEROUSLY	SOUNDALIKE	SOUTHERNIZES	SPACEWALKER
SONGSTRESS	SOPORIFICALLY	SOUNDALIKES	SOUTHERNIZING	SPACEWALKERS
SONGSTRESSES	SOPORIFICS	SOUNDBITES	SOUTHERNLY	SPACEWALKING
SONGWRITER	SOPPINESSES	SOUNDBOARD	SOUTHERNMOST	SPACEWALKS
SONGWRITERS	SOPRANINOS	SOUNDBOARDS	SOUTHERNNESS	SPACEWOMAN
SONGWRITING	SOPRANISTS	SOUNDBOXES	SOUTHERNNESSES	SPACEWOMEN
SONGWRITINGS	SORBABILITIES	SOUNDCARDS	SOUTHERNWOOD	SPACINESSES
SONICATING	SORBABILITY	SOUNDINGLY	SOUTHERNWOODS	SPACIOUSLY
SONICATION	SORBEFACIENT	SOUNDLESSLY	SOUTHLANDER	SPACIOUSNESS
SONICATIONS	SORBEFACIENTS	SOUNDLESSNESS	SOUTHLANDERS	SPACIOUSNESSES
SONICATORS	SORBITISATION	SOUNDLESSNESSES	SOUTHLANDS	SPADASSINS
SONIFEROUS	SORBITISATIONS	SOUNDNESSES	SOUTHSAYING	SPADEFISHES
SONNETEERING	SORBITISED	SOUNDPOSTS	SOUTHWARDLY	SPADEFOOTS
SONNETEERINGS	SORBITISES	SOUNDPROOF	SOUTHWARDS	SPADEWORKS
SONNETEERS	SORBITISING	SOUNDPROOFED	SOUTHWESTER	SPADICEOUS
SONNETISED	SORBITIZATION	SOUNDPROOFING	SOUTHWESTERLIES	SPADICIFLORAL
SONNETISES	SORBITIZATIONS	SOUNDPROOFINGS	SOUTHWESTERLY	SPADILLIOS
SONNETISING	SORBITIZED	SOUNDPROOFS	SOUTHWESTERN	SPAGHETTIFIED
SONNETIZED	SORBITIZES	SOUNDSCAPE	SOUTHWESTERS	SPAGHETTIFIES
SONNETIZES	SORBITIZING	SOUNDSCAPES	SOUTHWESTS	SPAGHETTIFY
SONNETIZING	SORCERESSES	SOUNDSTAGE	SOUTHWESTWARD	SPAGHETTIFYING
SONNETTING	SORDAMENTE	SOUNDSTAGES	SOUTHWESTWARDLY	SPAGHETTILIKE
SONOFABITCH	SORDIDNESS	SOUNDTRACK	SOUTHWESTWARDS	SPAGHETTINI
SONOGRAPHER	SORDIDNESSES	SOUNDTRACKED	SOUVENIRED	SPAGHETTINIS
SONOGRAPHERS	SOREHEADED	SOUNDTRACKING	SOUVENIRING	SPAGHETTIS
SONOGRAPHIES	SOREHEADEDLY	SOUNDTRACKS	SOUVLAKIAS	SPAGIRISTS
SONOGRAPHS	SOREHEADEDNESS	SOUPINESSES	SOVENANCES	SPAGYRICAL

SPAGYRICALLY
SPAGYRISTS
SPALLATION
SPALLATIONS
SPANAEMIAS
SPANAKOPITA
SPANAKOPITAS
SPANCELING
SPANCELLED
SPANCELLING
SPANGHEWED
SPANGHEWING
SPANGLIEST
SPANGLINGS
SPANIELLED
SPANIELLING
SPANIOLATE
SPANIOLATED
SPANIOLATES
SPANIOLATING
SPANIOLISE
SPANIOLISED
SPANIOLISES
SPANIOLISING
SPANIOLIZE
SPANIOLIZED
SPANIOLIZES
SPANIOLIZING
SPANKINGLY
SPANOKOPITA
SPANOKOPITAS
SPARAGMATIC
SPARAGRASS
SPARAGRASSES
SPARAXISES
SPARENESSES
SPARGANIUM
SPARGANIUMS
SPARINGNESS
SPARINGNESSES
SPARKISHLY
SPARKLEBERRIES
SPARKLEBERRY
SPARKLESSLY
SPARKLIEST
SPARKLINGLY
SPARKLINGS
SPARKPLUGGED
SPARKPLUGGING
SPARKPLUGS
SPARROWFART
SPARROWFARTS
SPARROWGRASS
SPARROWGRASSES
SPARROWHAWK
SPARROWHAWKS
SPARROWLIKE
SPARSENESS
SPARSENESSES
SPARSITIES
SPARTEINES
SPARTERIES
SPARTICLES
SPASMATICAL
SPASMODICAL
SPASMODICALLY
SPASMODIST

SPASMODISTS
SPASMOLYTIC
SPASMOLYTICS
SPASTICALLY
SPASTICITIES
SPASTICITY
SPATANGOID
SPATANGOIDS
SPATCHCOCK
SPATCHCOCKED
SPATCHCOCKING
SPATCHCOCKS
SPATHACEOUS
SPATHIPHYLLUM
SPATHIPHYLLUMS
SPATHULATE
SPATIALISATION
SPATIALISATIONS
SPATIALITIES
SPATIALITY
SPATIALIZATION
SPATIALIZATIONS
SPATIOTEMPORAL
SPATTERDASH
SPATTERDASHES
SPATTERDOCK
SPATTERDOCKS
SPATTERING
SPATTERWORK
SPATTERWORKS
SPEAKEASIES
SPEAKERINE
SPEAKERINES
SPEAKERPHONE
SPEAKERPHONES
SPEAKERSHIP
SPEAKERSHIPS
SPEAKINGLY
SPEARCARRIER
SPEARCARRIERS
SPEARFISHED
SPEARFISHES
SPEARFISHING
SPEARHEADED
SPEARHEADING
SPEARHEADS
SPEARMINTS
SPEARWORTS
SPECIALEST
SPECIALISATION
SPECIALISATIONS
SPECIALISE
SPECIALISED
SPECIALISER
SPECIALISERS
SPECIALISES
SPECIALISING
SPECIALISM
SPECIALISMS
SPECIALIST
SPECIALISTIC
SPECIALISTS
SPECIALITIES
SPECIALITY
SPECIALIZATION
SPECIALIZATIONS
SPECIALIZE

SPECIALIZED
SPECIALIZER
SPECIALIZERS
SPECIALIZES
SPECIALIZING
SPECIALLED
SPECIALLING
SPECIALNESS
SPECIALNESSES
SPECIALOGUE
SPECIALOGUES
SPECIALTIES
SPECIATING
SPECIATION
SPECIATIONAL
SPECIATIONS
SPECIESISM
SPECIESISMS
SPECIESIST
SPECIESISTS
SPECIFIABLE
SPECIFICAL
SPECIFICALLY
SPECIFICATE
SPECIFICATED
SPECIFICATES
SPECIFICATING
SPECIFICATION
SPECIFICATIONS
SPECIFICATIVE
SPECIFICATORY
SPECIFICITIES
SPECIFICITY
SPECIFIERS
SPECIFYING
SPECIOCIDE
SPECIOCIDES
SPECIOSITIES
SPECIOSITY
SPECIOUSLY
SPECIOUSNESS
SPECIOUSNESSES
SPECKLEDNESS
SPECKLEDNESSES
SPECKSIONEER
SPECKSIONEERS
SPECKTIONEER
SPECKTIONEERS
SPECTACLED
SPECTACLES
SPECTACULAR
SPECTACULARITY
SPECTACULARLY
SPECTACULARS
SPECTATING
SPECTATORIAL
SPECTATORS
SPECTATORSHIP
SPECTATORSHIPS
SPECTATRESS
SPECTATRESSES
SPECTATRICES
SPECTATRIX
SPECTATRIXES
SPECTINOMYCIN
SPECTINOMYCINS
SPECTRALITIES

SPECTRALITY
SPECTRALLY
SPECTRALNESS
SPECTRALNESSES
SPECTROGRAM
SPECTROGRAMS
SPECTROGRAPH
SPECTROGRAPHIC
SPECTROGRAPHIES
SPECTROGRAPHS
SPECTROGRAPHY
SPECTROLOGICAL
SPECTROLOGIES
SPECTROLOGY
SPECTROMETER
SPECTROMETERS
SPECTROMETRIC
SPECTROMETRIES
SPECTROMETRY
SPECTROSCOPE
SPECTROSCOPES
SPECTROSCOPIC
SPECTROSCOPICAL
SPECTROSCOPIES
SPECTROSCOPIST
SPECTROSCOPISTS
SPECTROSCOPY
SPECULARITIES
SPECULARITY
SPECULARLY
SPECULATED
SPECULATES
SPECULATING
SPECULATION
SPECULATIONS
SPECULATIST
SPECULATISTS
SPECULATIVE
SPECULATIVELY
SPECULATIVENESS
SPECULATOR
SPECULATORS
SPECULATORY
SPECULATRICE
SPECULATRICES
SPECULATRIX
SPECULATRIXES
SPEECHCRAFT
SPEECHCRAFTS
SPEECHFULNESS
SPEECHFULNESSES
SPEECHIFICATION
SPEECHIFIED
SPEECHIFIER
SPEECHIFIERS
SPEECHIFIES
SPEECHIFYING
SPEECHIFYINGS
SPEECHLESS
SPEECHLESSLY
SPEECHLESSNESS
SPEECHMAKER
SPEECHMAKERS
SPEECHMAKING
SPEECHMAKINGS
SPEECHWRITER
SPEECHWRITERS

SPEEDBALLED
SPEEDBALLING
SPEEDBALLINGS
SPEEDBALLS
SPEEDBOATING
SPEEDBOATINGS
SPEEDBOATS
SPEEDFREAK
SPEEDFREAKS
SPEEDFULLY
SPEEDINESS
SPEEDINESSES
SPEEDOMETER
SPEEDOMETERS
SPEEDREADING
SPEEDREADS
SPEEDSKATING
SPEEDSKATINGS
SPEEDSTERS
SPEEDWALKS
SPEEDWELLS
SPELAEOLOGICAL
SPELAEOLOGIES
SPELAEOLOGIST
SPELAEOLOGISTS
SPELAEOLOGY
SPELAEOTHEM
SPELAEOTHEMS
SPELDERING
SPELDRINGS
SPELEOLOGICAL
SPELEOLOGIES
SPELEOLOGIST
SPELEOLOGISTS
SPELEOLOGY
SPELEOTHEM
SPELEOTHEMS
SPELEOTHERAPIES
SPELEOTHERAPY
SPELLBINDER
SPELLBINDERS
SPELLBINDING
SPELLBINDINGLY
SPELLBINDS
SPELLBOUND
SPELLCHECK
SPELLCHECKED
SPELLCHECKER
SPELLCHECKERS
SPELLCHECKING
SPELLCHECKS
SPELLDOWNS
SPELLICANS
SPELLINGLY
SPELLSTOPT
SPELUNKERS
SPELUNKING
SPELUNKINGS
SPENDTHRIFT
SPENDTHRIFTS
SPERMACETI
SPERMACETIS
SPERMADUCT
SPERMADUCTS
SPERMAGONIA
SPERMAGONIUM
SPERMAPHYTE

SECTION 2: Words between 10 and 15 letters in length

S

SPERMAPHYTES
SPERMAPHYTIC
SPERMARIES
SPERMARIUM
SPERMATHECA
SPERMATHECAE
SPERMATHECAL
SPERMATHECAS
SPERMATIAL
SPERMATICAL
SPERMATICALLY
SPERMATICS
SPERMATIDS
SPERMATIUM
SPERMATOBLAST
SPERMATOBLASTIC
SPERMATOBLASTS
SPERMATOCELE
SPERMATOCELES
SPERMATOCIDAL
SPERMATOCIDE
SPERMATOCIDES
SPERMATOCYTE
SPERMATOCYTES
SPERMATOGENESES
SPERMATOGENESIS
SPERMATOGENETIC
SPERMATOGENIC
SPERMATOGENIES
SPERMATOGENOUS
SPERMATOGENY
SPERMATOGONIA
SPERMATOGONIAL
SPERMATOGONIUM
SPERMATOPHORAL
SPERMATOPHORE
SPERMATOPHORES
SPERMATOPHYTE
SPERMATOPHYTES
SPERMATOPHYTIC
SPERMATORRHEA
SPERMATORRHEAS
SPERMATORRHOEA
SPERMATORRHOEAS
SPERMATOTHECA
SPERMATOTHECAE
SPERMATOTHECAS
SPERMATOZOA
SPERMATOZOAL
SPERMATOZOAN
SPERMATOZOANS
SPERMATOZOIC
SPERMATOZOID
SPERMATOZOIDS
SPERMATOZOON
SPERMICIDAL
SPERMICIDE
SPERMICIDES
SPERMIDUCT
SPERMIDUCTS
SPERMIOGENESES
SPERMIOGENESIS
SPERMIOGENETIC
SPERMOGONE
SPERMOGONES
SPERMOGONIA
SPERMOGONIUM

SPERMOPHILE
SPERMOPHILES
SPERMOPHYTE
SPERMOPHYTES
SPERMOPHYTIC
SPERRYLITE
SPERRYLITES
SPESSARTINE
SPESSARTINES
SPESSARTITE
SPESSARTITES
SPETSNAZES
SPETZNAZES
SPEWINESSES
SPHACELATE
SPHACELATED
SPHACELATES
SPHACELATING
SPHACELATION
SPHACELATIONS
SPHACELUSES
SPHAERIDIA
SPHAERIDIUM
SPHAERITES
SPHAEROCRYSTAL
SPHAEROCRYSTALS
SPHAEROSIDERITE
SPHAGNICOLOUS
SPHAGNOLOGIES
SPHAGNOLOGIST
SPHAGNOLOGISTS
SPHAGNOLOGY
SPHAIRISTIKE
SPHAIRISTIKES
SPHALERITE
SPHALERITES
SPHENDONES
SPHENODONS
SPHENODONT
SPHENODONTS
SPHENOGRAM
SPHENOGRAMS
SPHENOIDAL
SPHENOPSID
SPHENOPSIDS
SPHERELESS
SPHERELIKE
SPHERICALITIES
SPHERICALITY
SPHERICALLY
SPHERICALNESS
SPHERICALNESSES
SPHERICITIES
SPHERICITY
SPHERISTERION
SPHERISTERIONS
SPHEROCYTE
SPHEROCYTES
SPHEROCYTOSES
SPHEROCYTOSIS
SPHEROIDAL
SPHEROIDALLY
SPHEROIDICALLY
SPHEROIDICITIES
SPHEROIDICITY
SPHEROIDISATION
SPHEROIDISE

SPHEROIDISED
SPHEROIDISES
SPHEROIDISING
SPHEROIDIZATION
SPHEROIDIZE
SPHEROIDIZED
SPHEROIDIZES
SPHEROIDIZING
SPHEROMETER
SPHEROMETERS
SPHEROPLAST
SPHEROPLASTS
SPHERULITE
SPHERULITES
SPHERULITIC
SPHINCTERAL
SPHINCTERIAL
SPHINCTERIC
SPHINCTERS
SPHINGOMYELIN
SPHINGOMYELINS
SPHINGOSINE
SPHINGOSINES
SPHINXLIKE
SPHRAGISTIC
SPHRAGISTICS
SPHYGMOGRAM
SPHYGMOGRAMS
SPHYGMOGRAPH
SPHYGMOGRAPHIC
SPHYGMOGRAPHIES
SPHYGMOGRAPHS
SPHYGMOGRAPHY
SPHYGMOLOGIES
SPHYGMOLOGY
SPHYGMOMETER
SPHYGMOMETERS
SPHYGMOPHONE
SPHYGMOPHONES
SPHYGMOSCOPE
SPHYGMOSCOPES
SPHYGMUSES
SPICEBERRIES
SPICEBERRY
SPICEBUSHES
SPICILEGES
SPICINESSES
SPICULATED
SPICULATION
SPICULATIONS
SPIDERIEST
SPIDERLIKE
SPIDERWEBS
SPIDERWOOD
SPIDERWOODS
SPIDERWORK
SPIDERWORKS
SPIDERWORT
SPIDERWORTS
SPIEGELEISEN
SPIEGELEISENS
SPIFFINESS
SPIFFINESSES
SPIFFLICATE
SPIFFLICATED
SPIFFLICATES
SPIFFLICATING

SPIFFLICATION
SPIFFLICATIONS
SPIFLICATE
SPIFLICATED
SPIFLICATES
SPIFLICATING
SPIFLICATION
SPIFLICATIONS
SPIKEFISHES
SPIKENARDS
SPIKINESSES
SPILLIKINS
SPILLOVERS
SPILOSITES
SPINACENES
SPINACEOUS
SPINACHIER
SPINACHIEST
SPINACHLIKE
SPINARAMAS
SPINDLELEGS
SPINDLESHANKS
SPINDLIEST
SPINDLINGS
SPINDRIFTS
SPINELESSLY
SPINELESSNESS
SPINELESSNESSES
SPINESCENCE
SPINESCENCES
SPINESCENT
SPINIFEROUS
SPINIFEXES
SPINIGEROUS
SPINIGRADE
SPINIGRADES
SPININESSES
SPINMEISTER
SPINMEISTERS
SPINNAKERS
SPINNERETS
SPINNERETTE
SPINNERETTES
SPINNERIES
SPINNERULE
SPINNERULES
SPINOSITIES
SPINSTERDOM
SPINSTERDOMS
SPINSTERHOOD
SPINSTERHOODS
SPINSTERIAL
SPINSTERIAN
SPINSTERISH
SPINSTERLIER
SPINSTERLIEST
SPINSTERLY
SPINSTERSHIP
SPINSTERSHIPS
SPINSTRESS
SPINSTRESSES
SPINTHARISCOPE
SPINTHARISCOPES
SPINULESCENT
SPINULIFEROUS
SPIRACULAR
SPIRACULATE

SPIRACULUM
SPIRALIFORM
SPIRALISER
SPIRALISERS
SPIRALISMS
SPIRALISTS
SPIRALITIES
SPIRALIZER
SPIRALIZERS
SPIRALLING
SPIRASTERS
SPIRATIONS
SPIRIFEROUS
SPIRILLOSES
SPIRILLOSIS
SPIRITEDLY
SPIRITEDNESS
SPIRITEDNESSES
SPIRITINGS
SPIRITISMS
SPIRITISTIC
SPIRITISTS
SPIRITLESS
SPIRITLESSLY
SPIRITLESSNESS
SPIRITOUSNESS
SPIRITOUSNESSES
SPIRITUALISE
SPIRITUALISED
SPIRITUALISER
SPIRITUALISERS
SPIRITUALISES
SPIRITUALISING
SPIRITUALISM
SPIRITUALISMS
SPIRITUALIST
SPIRITUALISTIC
SPIRITUALISTS
SPIRITUALITIES
SPIRITUALITY
SPIRITUALIZE
SPIRITUALIZED
SPIRITUALIZER
SPIRITUALIZERS
SPIRITUALIZES
SPIRITUALIZING
SPIRITUALLY
SPIRITUALNESS
SPIRITUALNESSES
SPIRITUALS
SPIRITUALTIES
SPIRITUALTY
SPIRITUELLE
SPIRITUOSITIES
SPIRITUOSITY
SPIRITUOUS
SPIRITUOUSNESS
SPIRITUSES
SPIRKETTING
SPIRKETTINGS
SPIROCHAETAEMIA
SPIROCHAETAL
SPIROCHAETE
SPIROCHAETES
SPIROCHAETOSES
SPIROCHAETOSIS
SPIROCHETAL

SPIROCHETE
SPIROCHETES
SPIROCHETOSES
SPIROCHETOSIS
SPIROGRAMS
SPIROGRAPH
SPIROGRAPHIC
SPIROGRAPHIES
SPIROGRAPHS
SPIROGRAPHY
SPIROGYRAS
SPIROMETER
SPIROMETERS
SPIROMETRIC
SPIROMETRIES
SPIROMETRY
SPIRONOLACTONE
SPIRONOLACTONES
SPIROPHORE
SPIROPHORES
SPIRULINAE
SPIRULINAS
SPISSITUDE
SPISSITUDES
SPITBALLED
SPITBALLING
SPITCHCOCK
SPITCHCOCKED
SPITCHCOCKING
SPITCHCOCKS
SPITCHERED
SPITCHERING
SPITEFULLER
SPITEFULLEST
SPITEFULLY
SPITEFULNESS
SPITEFULNESSES
SPITSTICKER
SPITSTICKERS
SPITTLEBUG
SPITTLEBUGS
SPITTLIEST
SPIVVERIES
SPLANCHNIC
SPLANCHNOCELE
SPLANCHNOCELES
SPLANCHNOLOGIES
SPLANCHNOLOGY
SPLASHBACK
SPLASHBACKS
SPLASHBOARD
SPLASHBOARDS
SPLASHDOWN
SPLASHDOWNS
SPLASHIEST
SPLASHINESS
SPLASHINESSES
SPLASHINGS
SPLASHPROOF
SPLATCHING
SPLATTERED
SPLATTERING
SPLATTERPUNK
SPLATTERPUNKS
SPLATTINGS
SPLAYFOOTED
SPLAYFOOTEDLY

SPLEENFULLY
SPLEENIEST
SPLEENLESS
SPLEENLIKE
SPLEENSTONE
SPLEENSTONES
SPLEENWORT
SPLEENWORTS
SPLENATIVE
SPLENDIDER
SPLENDIDEST
SPLENDIDIOUS
SPLENDIDLY
SPLENDIDNESS
SPLENDIDNESSES
SPLENDIDOUS
SPLENDIFEROUS
SPLENDIFEROUSLY
SPLENDOROUS
SPLENDOURS
SPLENDROUS
SPLENECTOMIES
SPLENECTOMISE
SPLENECTOMISED
SPLENECTOMISES
SPLENECTOMISING
SPLENECTOMIZE
SPLENECTOMIZED
SPLENECTOMIZES
SPLENECTOMIZING
SPLENECTOMY
SPLENETICAL
SPLENETICALLY
SPLENETICS
SPLENISATION
SPLENISATIONS
SPLENITISES
SPLENIUSES
SPLENIZATION
SPLENIZATIONS
SPLENOMEGALIES
SPLENOMEGALY
SPLEUCHANS
SPLINTERED
SPLINTERIER
SPLINTERIEST
SPLINTERING
SPLINTLIKE
SPLINTWOOD
SPLINTWOODS
SPLITTINGS
SPLITTISMS
SPLITTISTS
SPLODGIEST
SPLODGINESS
SPLODGINESSES
SPLOOSHING
SPLOTCHIER
SPLOTCHIEST
SPLOTCHILY
SPLOTCHINESS
SPLOTCHINESSES
SPLOTCHING
SPLURGIEST
SPLUTTERED
SPLUTTERER
SPLUTTERERS

SPLUTTERIER
SPLUTTERIEST
SPLUTTERING
SPLUTTERINGLY
SPLUTTERINGS
SPODOGRAMS
SPODOMANCIES
SPODOMANCY
SPODOMANTIC
SPODUMENES
SPOILFIVES
SPOILSPORT
SPOILSPORTS
SPOKESHAVE
SPOKESHAVES
SPOKESMANSHIP
SPOKESMANSHIPS
SPOKESPEOPLE
SPOKESPERSON
SPOKESPERSONS
SPOKESWOMAN
SPOKESWOMEN
SPOLIATING
SPOLIATION
SPOLIATIONS
SPOLIATIVE
SPOLIATORS
SPOLIATORY
SPONDAICAL
SPONDOOLICKS
SPONDULICKS
SPONDYLITIC
SPONDYLITICS
SPONDYLITIDES
SPONDYLITIS
SPONDYLITISES
SPONDYLOLYSES
SPONDYLOLYSIS
SPONDYLOSES
SPONDYLOSIS
SPONDYLOSISES
SPONDYLOUS
SPONGEABLE
SPONGEBAGS
SPONGELIKE
SPONGEWARE
SPONGEWARES
SPONGEWOOD
SPONGEWOODS
SPONGICOLOUS
SPONGIFORM
SPONGINESS
SPONGINESSES
SPONGIOBLAST
SPONGIOBLASTIC
SPONGIOBLASTS
SPONGOLOGIES
SPONGOLOGIST
SPONGOLOGISTS
SPONGOLOGY
SPONSIONAL
SPONSORIAL
SPONSORING
SPONSORSHIP
SPONSORSHIPS
SPONTANEITIES
SPONTANEITY

SPONTANEOUS
SPONTANEOUSLY
SPONTANEOUSNESS
SPOOFERIES
SPOOKERIES
SPOOKINESS
SPOOKINESSES
SPOONBAITS
SPOONBILLS
SPOONDRIFT
SPOONDRIFTS
SPOONERISM
SPOONERISMS
SPOONHOOKS
SPOONWORMS
SPORADICAL
SPORADICALLY
SPORADICALNESS
SPORANGIAL
SPORANGIOLA
SPORANGIOLE
SPORANGIOLES
SPORANGIOLUM
SPORANGIOPHORE
SPORANGIOPHORES
SPORANGIOSPORE
SPORANGIOSPORES
SPORANGIUM
SPORICIDAL
SPORICIDES
SPORIDESMS
SPOROCARPS
SPOROCYSTIC
SPOROCYSTS
SPOROCYTES
SPOROGENESES
SPOROGENESIS
SPOROGENIC
SPOROGENIES
SPOROGENOUS
SPOROGONIA
SPOROGONIAL
SPOROGONIC
SPOROGONIES
SPOROGONIUM
SPOROPHORE
SPOROPHORES
SPOROPHORIC
SPOROPHOROUS
SPOROPHYLL
SPOROPHYLLS
SPOROPHYLS
SPOROPHYTE
SPOROPHYTES
SPOROPHYTIC
SPOROPOLLENIN
SPOROPOLLENINS
SPOROTRICHOSES
SPOROTRICHOSIS
SPOROZOANS
SPOROZOITE
SPOROZOITES
SPORTABILITIES
SPORTABILITY
SPORTANCES
SPORTBIKES
SPORTCASTER

SPORTCASTERS
SPORTCOATS
SPORTFISHERMAN
SPORTFISHERMEN
SPORTFISHING
SPORTFISHINGS
SPORTFULLY
SPORTFULNESS
SPORTFULNESSES
SPORTINESS
SPORTINESSES
SPORTINGLY
SPORTIVELY
SPORTIVENESS
SPORTIVENESSES
SPORTSCAST
SPORTSCASTER
SPORTSCASTERS
SPORTSCASTS
SPORTSMANLIER
SPORTSMANLIEST
SPORTSMANLIKE
SPORTSMANLY
SPORTSMANSHIP
SPORTSMANSHIPS
SPORTSPEOPLE
SPORTSPERSON
SPORTSPERSONS
SPORTSWEAR
SPORTSWEARS
SPORTSWOMAN
SPORTSWOMEN
SPORTSWRITER
SPORTSWRITERS
SPORTSWRITING
SPORTSWRITINGS
SPORULATED
SPORULATES
SPORULATING
SPORULATION
SPORULATIONS
SPORULATIVE
SPOTLESSLY
SPOTLESSNESS
SPOTLESSNESSES
SPOTLIGHTED
SPOTLIGHTING
SPOTLIGHTS
SPOTTEDNESS
SPOTTEDNESSES
SPOTTINESS
SPOTTINESSES
SPOUSELESS
SPOYLEFULL
SPRACHGEFUHL
SPRACHGEFUHLS
SPRACKLING
SPRADDLING
SPRANGLING
SPRATTLING
SPRAUCHLED
SPRAUCHLES
SPRAUCHLING
SPRAUNCIER
SPRAUNCIEST
SPRAWLIEST
SPREADABILITIES

SPREADABILITY	SPRINKLING	SQUAMIFORM	SQUELCHIEST	STABILISATION
SPREADABLE	SPRINKLINGS	SQUAMOSALS	SQUELCHING	STABILISATIONS
SPREADEAGLED	SPRINTINGS	SQUAMOSELY	SQUELCHINGS	STABILISATOR
SPREADINGLY	SPRITEFULLY	SQUAMOSENESS	SQUETEAGUE	STABILISATORS
SPREADINGS	SPRITEFULNESS	SQUAMOSENESSES	SQUETEAGUES	STABILISED
SPREADSHEET	SPRITEFULNESSES	SQUAMOSITIES	SQUIBBINGS	STABILISER
SPREADSHEETS	SPRITELIER	SQUAMOSITY	SQUIDGIEST	STABILISERS
SPREAGHERIES	SPRITELIEST	SQUAMOUSLY	SQUIFFIEST	STABILISES
SPREAGHERY	SPRITSAILS	SQUAMOUSNESS	SQUIGGLERS	STABILISING
SPREATHING	SPRITZIEST	SQUAMOUSNESSES	SQUIGGLIER	STABILITIES
SPRECHERIES	SPROUTINGS	SQUAMULOSE	SQUIGGLIEST	STABILIZATION
SPRECHGESANG	SPRUCENESS	SQUANDERED	SQUIGGLING	STABILIZATIONS
SPRECHGESANGS	SPRUCENESSES	SQUANDERER	SQUILGEEING	STABILIZATOR
SPRECHSTIMME	SPRYNESSES	SQUANDERERS	SQUILLIONS	STABILIZATORS
SPRECHSTIMMES	SPUILZIEING	SQUANDERING	SQUINANCIES	STABILIZED
SPREETHING	SPULEBLADE	SQUANDERINGLY	SQUINCHING	STABILIZER
SPREKELIAS	SPULEBLADES	SQUANDERINGS	SQUINNIEST	STABILIZERS
SPRIGGIEST	SPULYIEING	SQUANDERMANIA	SQUINNYING	STABILIZES
SPRIGHTFUL	SPULZIEING	SQUANDERMANIAS	SQUINTIEST	STABILIZING
SPRIGHTFULLY	SPUMESCENCE	SQUAREHEAD	SQUINTINGLY	STABLEBOYS
SPRIGHTFULNESS	SPUMESCENCES	SQUAREHEADS	SQUINTINGS	STABLEMATE
SPRIGHTING	SPUMESCENT	SQUARENESS	SQUIRALITIES	STABLEMATES
SPRIGHTLESS	SPUNBONDED	SQUARENESSES	SQUIRALITY	STABLENESS
SPRIGHTLIER	SPUNKINESS	SQUAREWISE	SQUIRALTIES	STABLENESSES
SPRIGHTLIEST	SPUNKINESSES	SQUARISHLY	SQUIRARCHAL	STABLISHED
SPRIGHTLINESS	SPURGALLED	SQUARISHNESS	SQUIRARCHICAL	STABLISHES
SPRIGHTLINESSES	SPURGALLING	SQUARISHNESSES	SQUIRARCHIES	STABLISHING
SPRIGTAILS	SPURIOSITIES	SQUARSONAGE	SQUIRARCHS	STABLISHMENT
SPRINGALDS	SPURIOSITY	SQUARSONAGES	SQUIRARCHY	STABLISHMENTS
SPRINGBOARD	SPURIOUSLY	SQUASHABLE	SQUIREAGES	STACATIONS
SPRINGBOARDS	SPURIOUSNESS	SQUASHIEST	SQUIREARCH	STACCATISSIMO
SPRINGBOKS	SPURIOUSNESSES	SQUASHINESS	SQUIREARCHAL	STACKROOMS
SPRINGBUCK	SPUTTERERS	SQUASHINESSES	SQUIREARCHICAL	STACKYARDS
SPRINGBUCKS	SPUTTERIER	SQUATNESSES	SQUIREARCHIES	STACTOMETER
SPRINGEING	SPUTTERIEST	SQUATTERED	SQUIREARCHS	STACTOMETERS
SPRINGHAAS	SPUTTERING	SQUATTERING	SQUIREARCHY	STADDLESTONE
SPRINGHALT	SPUTTERINGLY	SQUATTIEST	SQUIREDOMS	STADDLESTONES
SPRINGHALTS	SPUTTERINGS	SQUATTINESS	SQUIREHOOD	STADHOLDER
SPRINGHASE	SPYCATCHER	SQUATTINESSES	SQUIREHOODS	STADHOLDERATE
SPRINGHEAD	SPYCATCHERS	SQUATTINGS	SQUIRELIKE	STADHOLDERATES
SPRINGHEADS	SPYGLASSES	SQUATTLING	SQUIRELING	STADHOLDERS
SPRINGHOUSE	SPYMASTERS	SQUATTOCRACIES	SQUIRELINGS	STADHOLDERSHIP
SPRINGHOUSES	SQUABASHED	SQUATTOCRACY	SQUIRESHIP	STADHOLDERSHIPS
SPRINGIEST	SQUABASHER	SQUAWBUSHES	SQUIRESHIPS	STADIOMETER
SPRINGINESS	SQUABASHERS	SQUAWFISHES	SQUIRESSES	STADIOMETERS
SPRINGINESSES	SQUABASHES	SQUAWKIEST	SQUIRMIEST	STADTHOLDER
SPRINGINGS	SQUABASHING	SQUAWKINGS	SQUIRMINGLY	STADTHOLDERATE
SPRINGKEEPER	SQUABBIEST	SQUAWROOTS	SQUIRRELED	STADTHOLDERATES
SPRINGKEEPERS	SQUABBLERS	SQUEAKERIES	SQUIRRELFISH	STADTHOLDERS
SPRINGLESS	SQUABBLING	SQUEAKIEST	SQUIRRELFISHES	STADTHOLDERSHIP
SPRINGLETS	SQUABBLINGS	SQUEAKINESS	SQUIRRELIER	STAFFRIDER
SPRINGLIKE	SQUADOOSHES	SQUEAKINESSES	SQUIRRELIEST	STAFFRIDERS
SPRINGTAIL	SQUADRONAL	SQUEAKINGLY	SQUIRRELING	STAFFROOMS
SPRINGTAILS	SQUADRONED	SQUEAKINGS	SQUIRRELLED	STAGECOACH
SPRINGTIDE	SQUADRONES	SQUEALINGS	SQUIRRELLIER	STAGECOACHES
SPRINGTIDES	SQUADRONING	SQUEAMISHLY	SQUIRRELLIEST	STAGECOACHING
SPRINGTIME	SQUAILINGS	SQUEAMISHNESS	SQUIRRELLING	STAGECOACHINGS
SPRINGTIMES	SQUALIDEST	SQUEAMISHNESSES	SQUIRRELLY	STAGECOACHMAN
SPRINGWATER	SQUALIDITIES	SQUEEGEEING	SQUIRTINGS	STAGECOACHMEN
SPRINGWATERS	SQUALIDITY	SQUEEZABILITIES	SQUISHIEST	STAGECRAFT
SPRINGWOOD	SQUALIDNESS	SQUEEZABILITY	SQUISHINESS	STAGECRAFTS
SPRINGWOODS	SQUALIDNESSES	SQUEEZABLE	SQUISHINESSES	STAGEHANDS
SPRINGWORT	SQUALLIEST	SQUEEZIEST	SQUOOSHIER	STAGEHEADS
SPRINGWORTS	SQUALLINGS	SQUEEZINGS	SQUOOSHIEST	STAGESTRUCK
SPRINKLERED	SQUAMATION	SQUEGGINGS	SQUOOSHING	STAGFLATION
SPRINKLERING	SQUAMATIONS	SQUELCHERS	STABBINGLY	STAGFLATIONARY
SPRINKLERS	SQUAMELLAS	SQUELCHIER	STABILATES	STAGFLATIONS

STAGGERBUSH
STAGGERBUSHES
STAGGERERS
STAGGERIER
STAGGERIEST
STAGGERING
STAGGERINGLY
STAGGERINGS
STAGHOUNDS
STAGINESSES
STAGNANCES
STAGNANCIES
STAGNANCIES
STAGNANTLY
STAGNATING
STAGNATION
STAGNATIONS
STAIDNESSES
STAINABILITIES
STAINABILITY
STAINLESSES
STAINLESSLY
STAINLESSNESS
STAINLESSNESSES
STAINPROOF
STAIRCASED
STAIRCASES
STAIRCASING
STAIRCASINGS
STAIRFOOTS
STAIRHEADS
STAIRLIFTS
STAIRSTEPPED
STAIRSTEPPING
STAIRSTEPS
STAIRWELLS
STAIRWORKS
STAKEHOLDER
STAKEHOLDERS
STAKHANOVISM
STAKHANOVISMS
STAKHANOVITE
STAKHANOVITES
STAKTOMETER
STAKTOMETERS
STALACTICAL
STALACTIFORM
STALACTITAL
STALACTITE
STALACTITED
STALACTITES
STALACTITIC
STALACTITICAL
STALACTITICALLY
STALACTITIFORM
STALACTITIOUS
STALAGMITE
STALAGMITES
STALAGMITIC
STALAGMITICAL
STALAGMITICALLY
STALAGMOMETER
STALAGMOMETERS
STALAGMOMETRIES
STALAGMOMETRY
STALEMATED
STALEMATES
STALEMATING

STALENESSES
STALKINESS
STALKINESSES
STALLENGER
STALLENGERS
STALLHOLDER
STALLHOLDERS
STALLINGER
STALLINGERS
STALLMASTER
STALLMASTERS
STALWARTLY
STALWARTNESS
STALWARTNESSES
STALWORTHS
STAMINEOUS
STAMINIFEROUS
STAMINODES
STAMINODIA
STAMINODIES
STAMINODIUM
STAMMERERS
STAMMERING
STAMMERINGLY
STAMMERINGS
STAMPEDERS
STAMPEDING
STAMPEDOED
STAMPEDOING
STANCHABLE
STANCHELLED
STANCHELLING
STANCHERED
STANCHERING
STANCHINGS
STANCHIONED
STANCHIONING
STANCHIONS
STANCHLESS
STANCHNESS
STANCHNESSES
STANDARDBRED
STANDARDBREDS
STANDARDISATION
STANDARDISE
STANDARDISED
STANDARDISER
STANDARDISERS
STANDARDISES
STANDARDISING
STANDARDIZATION
STANDARDIZE
STANDARDIZED
STANDARDIZER
STANDARDIZERS
STANDARDIZES
STANDARDIZING
STANDARDLESS
STANDARDLY
STANDDOWNS
STANDFASTS
STANDFIRST
STANDFIRSTS
STANDGALES
STANDISHES
STANDOFFISH
STANDOFFISHLY

STANDOFFISHNESS
STANDOVERS
STANDPATTER
STANDPATTERS
STANDPATTISM
STANDPATTISMS
STANDPIPES
STANDPOINT
STANDPOINTS
STANDSTILL
STANDSTILLS
STANNARIES
STANNATORS
STANNIFEROUS
STANNOTYPE
STANNOTYPES
STAPEDECTOMIES
STAPEDECTOMY
STAPEDIUSES
STAPHYLINE
STAPHYLINID
STAPHYLINIDS
STAPHYLITIS
STAPHYLITISES
STAPHYLOCOCCAL
STAPHYLOCOCCI
STAPHYLOCOCCIC
STAPHYLOCOCCUS
STAPHYLOMA
STAPHYLOMAS
STAPHYLOMATA
STAPHYLOPLASTIC
STAPHYLOPLASTY
STAPHYLORRHAPHY
STARBOARDED
STARBOARDING
STARBOARDS
STARBURSTS
STARCHEDLY
STARCHEDNESS
STARCHEDNESSES
STARCHIEST
STARCHINESS
STARCHINESSES
STARCHLIKE
STARDRIFTS
STARFISHED
STARFISHES
STARFLOWER
STARFLOWERS
STARFRUITS
STARFUCKER
STARFUCKERS
STARFUCKING
STARFUCKINGS
STARGAZERS
STARGAZING
STARGAZINGS
STARKENING
STARKNESSES
STARLIGHTED
STARLIGHTS
STARMONGER
STARMONGERS
STAROSTIES
STARRINESS
STARRINESSES

STARSHINES
STARSTONES
STARSTRUCK
STARTINGLY
STARTLEMENT
STARTLEMENTS
STARTLIEST
STARTLINGLY
STARTLINGS
STARVATION
STARVATIONS
STARVELING
STARVELINGS
STASIDIONS
STASIMORPHIES
STASIMORPHY
STATECRAFT
STATECRAFTS
STATEHOODS
STATEHOUSE
STATEHOUSES
STATELESSNESS
STATELESSNESSES
STATELIEST
STATELINESS
STATELINESSES
STATEMENTED
STATEMENTING
STATEMENTINGS
STATEMENTS
STATEROOMS
STATESMANLIER
STATESMANLIEST
STATESMANLIKE
STATESMANLY
STATESMANSHIP
STATESMANSHIPS
STATESPERSON
STATESPERSONS
STATESWOMAN
STATESWOMEN
STATICALLY
STATICKIER
STATICKIEST
STATIONARIES
STATIONARILY
STATIONARINESS
STATIONARY
STATIONERIES
STATIONERS
STATIONERY
STATIONING
STATIONMASTER
STATIONMASTERS
STATISTICAL
STATISTICALLY
STATISTICIAN
STATISTICIANS
STATISTICS
STATOBLAST
STATOBLASTS
STATOCYSTS
STATOLATRIES
STATOLATRY
STATOLITHIC
STATOLITHS
STATOSCOPE

STATOSCOPES
STATUARIES
STATUESQUE
STATUESQUELY
STATUESQUENESS
STATUETTES
STATUSIEST
STATUTABLE
STATUTABLY
STATUTORILY
STAUNCHABLE
STAUNCHERS
STAUNCHEST
STAUNCHING
STAUNCHINGS
STAUNCHLESS
STAUNCHNESS
STAUNCHNESSES
STAUROLITE
STAUROLITES
STAUROLITIC
STAUROSCOPE
STAUROSCOPES
STAUROSCOPIC
STAVESACRE
STAVESACRES
STAVUDINES
STAYCATION
STAYCATIONS
STAYMAKERS
STEADFASTLY
STEADFASTNESS
STEADFASTNESSES
STEADINESS
STEADINESSES
STEAKETTES
STEAKHOUSE
STEAKHOUSES
STEALINGLY
STEALTHFUL
STEALTHIER
STEALTHIEST
STEALTHILY
STEALTHINESS
STEALTHINESSES
STEALTHING
STEALTHINGS
STEAMBOATS
STEAMERING
STEAMFITTER
STEAMFITTERS
STEAMINESS
STEAMINESSES
STEAMPUNKS
STEAMROLLED
STEAMROLLER
STEAMROLLERED
STEAMROLLERING
STEAMROLLERS
STEAMROLLING
STEAMROLLS
STEAMSHIPS
STEAMTIGHT
STEAMTIGHTNESS
STEAROPTENE
STEAROPTENES
STEARSMATE

S

STEARSMATES	STEGANOGRAPHY	STENOGRAPHS	STERCORATES	STEREOTACTIC
STEATOCELE	STEGANOPOD	STENOGRAPHY	STERCORATING	STEREOTACTICAL
STEATOCELES	STEGANOPODOUS	STENOHALINE	STERCORICOLOUS	STEREOTAXES
STEATOLYSES	STEGANOPODS	STENOPAEIC	STERCULIACEOUS	STEREOTAXIA
STEATOLYSIS	STEGNOTICS	STENOPETALOUS	STERCULIAS	STEREOTAXIAS
STEATOMATOUS	STEGOCARPOUS	STENOPHAGOUS	STEREOACUITIES	STEREOTAXIC
STEATOPYGA	STEGOCEPHALIAN	STENOPHYLLOUS	STEREOACUITY	STEREOTAXICALLY
STEATOPYGAS	STEGOCEPHALIANS	STENOTHERM	STEREOBATE	STEREOTAXIS
STEATOPYGIA	STEGOCEPHALOUS	STENOTHERMAL	STEREOBATES	STEREOTOMIES
STEATOPYGIAS	STEGODONTS	STENOTHERMS	STEREOBATIC	STEREOTOMY
STEATOPYGIC	STEGOMYIAS	STENOTOPIC	STEREOBLIND	STEREOTROPIC
STEATOPYGOUS	STEGOPHILIST	STENOTROPIC	STEREOCARD	STEREOTROPISM
STEATORRHEA	STEGOPHILISTS	STENOTYPED	STEREOCARDS	STEREOTROPISMS
STEATORRHEAS	STEGOSAURIAN	STENOTYPER	STEREOCHEMICAL	STEREOTYPE
STEATORRHOEA	STEGOSAURIANS	STENOTYPERS	STEREOCHEMISTRY	STEREOTYPED
STEATORRHOEAS	STEGOSAURS	STENOTYPES	STEREOCHROME	STEREOTYPER
STEDFASTLY	STEGOSAURUS	STENOTYPIC	STEREOCHROMED	STEREOTYPERS
STEDFASTNESS	STEGOSAURUSES	STENOTYPIES	STEREOCHROMES	STEREOTYPES
STEDFASTNESSES	STEINBOCKS	STENOTYPING	STEREOCHROMIES	STEREOTYPIC
STEELHEADS	STEINKIRKS	STENOTYPIST	STEREOCHROMING	STEREOTYPICAL
STEELINESS	STELLARATOR	STENOTYPISTS	STEREOCHROMY	STEREOTYPICALLY
STEELINESSES	STELLARATORS	STENTMASTER	STEREOGNOSES	STEREOTYPIES
STEELMAKER	STELLATELY	STENTMASTERS	STEREOGNOSIS	STEREOTYPING
STEELMAKERS	STELLERIDAN	STENTORIAN	STEREOGRAM	STEREOTYPINGS
STEELMAKING	STELLERIDANS	STEPBAIRNS	STEREOGRAMS	STEREOTYPIST
STEELMAKINGS	STELLERIDS	STEPBROTHER	STEREOGRAPH	STEREOTYPISTS
STEELWARES	STELLIFEROUS	STEPBROTHERS	STEREOGRAPHED	STEREOTYPY
STEELWORKER	STELLIFIED	STEPCHILDREN	STEREOGRAPHIC	STEREOVISION
STEELWORKERS	STELLIFIES	STEPDANCER	STEREOGRAPHICAL	STEREOVISIONS
STEELWORKING	STELLIFORM	STEPDANCERS	STEREOGRAPHIES	STERICALLY
STEELWORKINGS	STELLIFYING	STEPDANCING	STEREOGRAPHING	STERIGMATA
STEELWORKS	STELLIFYINGS	STEPDANCINGS	STEREOGRAPHS	STERILANTS
STEELYARDS	STELLIONATE	STEPDAUGHTER	STEREOGRAPHY	STERILISABLE
STEENBRASES	STELLIONATES	STEPDAUGHTERS	STEREOISOMER	STERILISATION
STEENBUCKS	STELLULARLY	STEPFAMILIES	STEREOISOMERIC	STERILISATIONS
STEENKIRKS	STELLULATE	STEPFAMILY	STEREOISOMERISM	STERILISED
STEEPDOWNE	STEMMATOUS	STEPFATHER	STEREOISOMERS	STERILISER
STEEPEDOWNE	STEMMERIES	STEPFATHERS	STEREOISOMETRIC	STERILISERS
STEEPENING	STEMWINDER	STEPHANITE	STEREOLOGICAL	STERILISES
STEEPINESS	STEMWINDERS	STEPHANITES	STEREOLOGICALLY	STERILISING
STEEPINESSES	STENCHIEST	STEPHANOTIS	STEREOLOGIES	STERILITIES
STEEPLEBUSH	STENCILERS	STEPHANOTISES	STEREOLOGY	STERILIZABLE
STEEPLEBUSHES	STENCILING	STEPLADDER	STEREOMETER	STERILIZATION
STEEPLECHASE	STENCILINGS	STEPLADDERS	STEREOMETERS	STERILIZATIONS
STEEPLECHASED	STENCILLED	STEPMOTHER	STEREOMETRIC	STERILIZED
STEEPLECHASER	STENCILLER	STEPMOTHERLIER	STEREOMETRICAL	STERILIZER
STEEPLECHASERS	STENCILLERS	STEPMOTHERLIEST	STEREOMETRIES	STERILIZERS
STEEPLECHASES	STENCILLING	STEPMOTHERLY	STEREOMETRY	STERILIZES
STEEPLECHASING	STENCILLINGS	STEPMOTHERS	STEREOPHONIC	STERILIZING
STEEPLECHASINGS	STENOBATHIC	STEPPARENT	STEREOPHONIES	STERLINGLY
STEEPLEJACK	STENOBATHS	STEPPARENTING	STEREOPHONY	STERLINGNESS
STEEPLEJACKS	STENOCARDIA	STEPPARENTINGS	STEREOPSES	STERLINGNESSES
STEEPNESSES	STENOCARDIAS	STEPPARENTS	STEREOPSIS	STERNALGIA
STEERAGEWAY	STENOCHROME	STEPSISTER	STEREOPTICON	STERNALGIAS
STEERAGEWAYS	STENOCHROMES	STEPSISTERS	STEREOPTICONS	STERNALGIC
STEERLINGS	STENOCHROMIES	STEPSTOOLS	STEREOPTICS	STERNBOARD
STEERSMATE	STENOCHROMY	STERADIANS	STEREOREGULAR	STERNBOARDS
STEERSMATES	STENOGRAPH	STERCORACEOUS	STEREOSCOPE	STERNEBRAE
STEGANOGRAM	STENOGRAPHED	STERCORANISM	STEREOSCOPES	STERNFASTS
STEGANOGRAMS	STENOGRAPHER	STERCORANISMS	STEREOSCOPIC	STERNFOREMOST
STEGANOGRAPH	STENOGRAPHERS	STERCORANIST	STEREOSCOPICAL	STERNNESSES
STEGANOGRAPHER	STENOGRAPHIC	STERCORANISTS	STEREOSCOPIES	STERNOCOSTAL
STEGANOGRAPHERS	STENOGRAPHICAL	STERCORARIES	STEREOSCOPIST	STERNOTRIBE
STEGANOGRAPHIES	STENOGRAPHIES	STERCORARIOUS	STEREOSCOPISTS	STERNPORTS
STEGANOGRAPHIST	STENOGRAPHING	STERCORARY	STEREOSCOPY	STERNPOSTS
STEGANOGRAPHS	STENOGRAPHIST	STERCORATE	STEREOSONIC	STERNSHEET
	STENOGRAPHISTS	STERCORATED	STEREOSPECIFIC	STERNSHEETS

STERNUTATION
STERNUTATIONS
STERNUTATIVE
STERNUTATIVES
STERNUTATOR
STERNUTATORIES
STERNUTATORS
STERNUTATORY
STERNWARDS
STERNWORKS
STEROIDOGENESES
STEROIDOGENESIS
STEROIDOGENIC
STERTOROUS
STERTOROUSLY
STERTOROUSNESS
STETHOSCOPE
STETHOSCOPES
STETHOSCOPIC
STETHOSCOPIES
STETHOSCOPIST
STETHOSCOPISTS
STETHOSCOPY
STEVEDORED
STEVEDORES
STEVEDORING
STEVEDORINGS
STEVENGRAPH
STEVENGRAPHS
STEWARDESS
STEWARDESSES
STEWARDING
STEWARDRIES
STEWARDSHIP
STEWARDSHIPS
STEWARTRIES
STIACCIATO
STIACCIATOS
STIBIALISM
STIBIALISMS
STICCADOES
STICCATOES
STICHARION
STICHARIONS
STICHICALLY
STICHIDIUM
STICHOLOGIES
STICHOLOGY
STICHOMETRIC
STICHOMETRICAL
STICHOMETRIES
STICHOMETRY
STICHOMYTHIA
STICHOMYTHIAS
STICHOMYTHIC
STICHOMYTHIES
STICHOMYTHY
STICKABILITIES
STICKABILITY
STICKBALLS
STICKERING
STICKHANDLE
STICKHANDLED
STICKHANDLER
STICKHANDLERS
STICKHANDLES
STICKHANDLING

STICKHANDLINGS
STICKINESS
STICKINESSES
STICKLEADER
STICKLEADERS
STICKLEBACK
STICKLEBACKS
STICKLINGS
STICKSEEDS
STICKTIGHT
STICKTIGHTS
STICKWEEDS
STICKWORKS
STICKYBEAK
STICKYBEAKED
STICKYBEAKING
STICKYBEAKS
STIDDIEING
STIFFENERS
STIFFENING
STIFFENINGS
STIFFNESSES
STIFFWARES
STIFLINGLY
STIGMARIAN
STIGMARIANS
STIGMASTEROL
STIGMASTEROLS
STIGMATICAL
STIGMATICALLY
STIGMATICS
STIGMATIFEROUS
STIGMATISATION
STIGMATISATIONS
STIGMATISE
STIGMATISED
STIGMATISER
STIGMATISERS
STIGMATISES
STIGMATISING
STIGMATISM
STIGMATISMS
STIGMATIST
STIGMATISTS
STIGMATIZATION
STIGMATIZATIONS
STIGMATIZE
STIGMATIZED
STIGMATIZER
STIGMATIZERS
STIGMATIZES
STIGMATIZING
STIGMATOPHILIA
STIGMATOPHILIAS
STIGMATOPHILIST
STIGMATOSE
STILBESTROL
STILBESTROLS
STILBOESTROL
STILBOESTROLS
STILETTOED
STILETTOES
STILETTOING
STILLATORIES
STILLATORY
STILLBIRTH
STILLBIRTHS

STILLBORNS
STILLHOUSE
STILLHOUSES
STILLICIDE
STILLICIDES
STILLIFORM
STILLNESSES
STILLROOMS
STILPNOSIDERITE
STILTBIRDS
STILTEDNESS
STILTEDNESSES
STILTINESS
STILTINESSES
STIMPMETER
STIMPMETERS
STIMULABLE
STIMULANCIES
STIMULANCY
STIMULANTS
STIMULATED
STIMULATER
STIMULATERS
STIMULATES
STIMULATING
STIMULATINGLY
STIMULATION
STIMULATIONS
STIMULATIVE
STIMULATIVES
STIMULATOR
STIMULATORS
STIMULATORY
STINGAREES
STINGBULLS
STINGFISHES
STINGINESS
STINGINESSES
STINGINGLY
STINGINGNESS
STINGINGNESSES
STINKBIRDS
STINKEROOS
STINKHORNS
STINKINGLY
STINKINGNESS
STINKINGNESSES
STINKSTONE
STINKSTONES
STINKWEEDS
STINKWOODS
STINTEDNESS
STINTEDNESSES
STINTINGLY
STIPELLATE
STIPENDIARIES
STIPENDIARY
STIPENDIATE
STIPENDIATED
STIPENDIATES
STIPENDIATING
STIPITIFORM
STIPPLINGS
STIPULABLE
STIPULACEOUS
STIPULATED
STIPULATES

STIPULATING
STIPULATION
STIPULATIONS
STIPULATOR
STIPULATORS
STIPULATORY
STIRABOUTS
STIRPICULTURE
STIRPICULTURES
STIRRINGLY
STITCHCRAFT
STITCHCRAFTS
STITCHERIES
STITCHINGS
STITCHWORK
STITCHWORKS
STITCHWORT
STITCHWORTS
STOCCADOES
STOCHASTIC
STOCHASTICALLY
STOCKADING
STOCKBREEDER
STOCKBREEDERS
STOCKBREEDING
STOCKBREEDINGS
STOCKBROKER
STOCKBROKERAGE
STOCKBROKERAGES
STOCKBROKERS
STOCKBROKING
STOCKBROKINGS
STOCKFISHES
STOCKHOLDER
STOCKHOLDERS
STOCKHOLDING
STOCKHOLDINGS
STOCKHORNS
STOCKHORSE
STOCKHORSES
STOCKINESS
STOCKINESSES
STOCKINETS
STOCKINETTE
STOCKINETTES
STOCKINGED
STOCKINGER
STOCKINGERS
STOCKINGLESS
STOCKISHLY
STOCKISHNESS
STOCKISHNESSES
STOCKJOBBER
STOCKJOBBERIES
STOCKJOBBERS
STOCKJOBBERY
STOCKJOBBING
STOCKJOBBINGS
STOCKKEEPER
STOCKKEEPERS
STOCKLISTS
STOCKLOCKS
STOCKPILED
STOCKPILER
STOCKPILERS
STOCKPILES
STOCKPILING

STOCKPILINGS
STOCKPUNISHT
STOCKROOMS
STOCKROUTE
STOCKROUTES
STOCKTAKEN
STOCKTAKES
STOCKTAKING
STOCKTAKINGS
STOCKWORKS
STOCKYARDS
STODGINESS
STODGINESSES
STOECHIOLOGICAL
STOECHIOLOGIES
STOECHIOLOGY
STOECHIOMETRIC
STOECHIOMETRIES
STOECHIOMETRY
STOICALNESS
STOICALNESSES
STOICHEIOLOGIES
STOICHEIOLOGY
STOICHEIOMETRIC
STOICHEIOMETRY
STOICHIOLOGICAL
STOICHIOLOGIES
STOICHIOLOGY
STOICHIOMETRIC
STOICHIOMETRIES
STOICHIOMETRY
STOITERING
STOKEHOLDS
STOKEHOLES
STOLENWISE
STOLIDITIES
STOLIDNESS
STOLIDNESSES
STOLONIFEROUS
STOMACHACHE
STOMACHACHES
STOMACHALS
STOMACHERS
STOMACHFUL
STOMACHFULNESS
STOMACHFULS
STOMACHICAL
STOMACHICS
STOMACHIER
STOMACHIEST
STOMACHING
STOMACHLESS
STOMACHOUS
STOMATITIC
STOMATITIDES
STOMATITIS
STOMATITISES
STOMATODAEA
STOMATODAEUM
STOMATOGASTRIC
STOMATOLOGICAL
STOMATOLOGIES
STOMATOLOGIST
STOMATOLOGISTS
STOMATOLOGY
STOMATOPLASTIES
STOMATOPLASTY

STOMATOPOD
STOMATOPODS
STOMODAEAL
STOMODAEUM
STOMODAEUMS
STOMODEUMS
STONEBOATS
STONEBORER
STONEBORERS
STONEBRASH
STONEBRASHES
STONEBREAK
STONEBREAKER
STONEBREAKERS
STONEBREAKS
STONECASTS
STONECHATS
STONECROPS
STONECUTTER
STONECUTTERS
STONECUTTING
STONECUTTINGS
STONEFISHES
STONEFLIES
STONEGROUND
STONEHANDS
STONEHORSE
STONEHORSES
STONELESSNESS
STONELESSNESSES
STONEMASON
STONEMASONRIES
STONEMASONRY
STONEMASONS
STONESHOTS
STONEWALLED
STONEWALLER
STONEWALLERS
STONEWALLING
STONEWALLINGS
STONEWALLS
STONEWARES
STONEWASHED
STONEWASHES
STONEWASHING
STONEWORKER
STONEWORKERS
STONEWORKS
STONEWORTS
STONINESSES
STONISHING
STONKERING
STONYHEARTED
STOOLBALLS
STOOPBALLS
STOOPINGLY
STOPLIGHTS
STOPPERING
STOPWATCHES
STORECARDS
STOREFRONT
STOREFRONTS
STOREHOUSE
STOREHOUSES
STOREKEEPER
STOREKEEPERS
STOREKEEPING

STOREKEEPINGS
STOREROOMS
STORESHIPS
STORIETTES
STORIOLOGIES
STORIOLOGIST
STORIOLOGISTS
STORIOLOGY
STORKSBILL
STORKSBILLS
STORMBIRDS
STORMBOUND
STORMCOCKS
STORMFULLY
STORMFULNESS
STORMFULNESSES
STORMINESS
STORMINESSES
STORMPROOF
STORMSTAYED
STORYBOARD
STORYBOARDED
STORYBOARDING
STORYBOARDS
STORYBOOKS
STORYETTES
STORYLINES
STORYTELLER
STORYTELLERS
STORYTELLING
STORYTELLINGS
STORYTIMES
STOTTERING
STOUTENING
STOUTHEARTED
STOUTHEARTEDLY
STOUTHERIE
STOUTHERIES
STOUTHRIEF
STOUTHRIEFS
STOUTNESSES
STOVEPIPES
STOVEWOODS
STRABISMAL
STRABISMIC
STRABISMICAL
STRABISMOMETER
STRABISMOMETERS
STRABISMUS
STRABISMUSES
STRABOMETER
STRABOMETERS
STRABOTOMIES
STRABOTOMY
STRACCHINI
STRACCHINO
STRADDLEBACK
STRADDLERS
STRADDLING
STRAGGLERS
STRAGGLIER
STRAGGLIEST
STRAGGLING
STRAGGLINGLY
STRAGGLINGS
STRAICHTER
STRAICHTEST

STRAIGHTAWAY
STRAIGHTAWAYS
STRAIGHTBRED
STRAIGHTBREDS
STRAIGHTED
STRAIGHTEDGE
STRAIGHTEDGED
STRAIGHTEDGES
STRAIGHTEN
STRAIGHTENED
STRAIGHTENER
STRAIGHTENERS
STRAIGHTENING
STRAIGHTENS
STRAIGHTER
STRAIGHTEST
STRAIGHTFORTH
STRAIGHTFORWARD
STRAIGHTING
STRAIGHTISH
STRAIGHTJACKET
STRAIGHTJACKETS
STRAIGHTLACED
STRAIGHTLY
STRAIGHTNESS
STRAIGHTNESSES
STRAIGHTWAY
STRAIGHTWAYS
STRAINEDLY
STRAININGS
STRAITENED
STRAITENING
STRAITJACKET
STRAITJACKETED
STRAITJACKETING
STRAITJACKETS
STRAITLACED
STRAITLACEDLY
STRAITLACEDNESS
STRAITNESS
STRAITNESSES
STRAITWAISTCOAT
STRAMACONS
STRAMASHED
STRAMASHES
STRAMASHING
STRAMAZONS
STRAMINEOUS
STRAMONIES
STRAMONIUM
STRAMONIUMS
STRANDEDNESS
STRANDEDNESSES
STRANDFLAT
STRANDFLATS
STRANDLINE
STRANDLINES
STRANDWOLF
STRANDWOLVES
STRANGENESS
STRANGENESSES
STRANGERED
STRANGERING
STRANGLEHOLD
STRANGLEHOLDS
STRANGLEMENT
STRANGLEMENTS

STRANGLERS
STRANGLING
STRANGULATE
STRANGULATED
STRANGULATES
STRANGULATING
STRANGULATION
STRANGULATIONS
STRANGURIES
STRAPHANGED
STRAPHANGER
STRAPHANGERS
STRAPHANGING
STRAPHANGINGS
STRAPHANGS
STRAPLESSES
STRAPLINES
STRAPONTIN
STRAPONTINS
STRAPPADOED
STRAPPADOES
STRAPPADOING
STRAPPADOS
STRAPPIEST
STRAPPINGS
STRAPWORTS
STRATAGEMS
STRATEGETIC
STRATEGETICAL
STRATEGICAL
STRATEGICALLY
STRATEGICS
STRATEGIES
STRATEGISE
STRATEGISED
STRATEGISES
STRATEGISING
STRATEGIST
STRATEGISTS
STRATEGIZE
STRATEGIZED
STRATEGIZES
STRATEGIZING
STRATHSPEY
STRATHSPEYS
STRATICULATE
STRATICULATION
STRATICULATIONS
STRATIFICATION
STRATIFICATIONS
STRATIFIED
STRATIFIES
STRATIFORM
STRATIFYING
STRATIGRAPHER
STRATIGRAPHERS
STRATIGRAPHIC
STRATIGRAPHICAL
STRATIGRAPHIES
STRATIGRAPHIST
STRATIGRAPHISTS
STRATIGRAPHY
STRATOCRACIES
STRATOCRACY
STRATOCRAT
STRATOCRATIC
STRATOCRATS

STRATOCUMULI
STRATOCUMULUS
STRATOPAUSE
STRATOPAUSES
STRATOSPHERE
STRATOSPHERES
STRATOSPHERIC
STRATOSPHERICAL
STRATOTANKER
STRATOTANKERS
STRATOVOLCANO
STRATOVOLCANOES
STRATOVOLCANOS
STRAUCHTED
STRAUCHTER
STRAUCHTEST
STRAUCHTING
STRAUGHTED
STRAUGHTER
STRAUGHTEST
STRAUGHTING
STRAVAGING
STRAVAIGED
STRAVAIGER
STRAVAIGERS
STRAVAIGING
STRAWBERRIES
STRAWBERRY
STRAWBOARD
STRAWBOARDS
STRAWFLOWER
STRAWFLOWERS
STRAWWEIGHT
STRAWWEIGHTS
STRAWWORMS
STRAYLINGS
STREAKIEST
STREAKINESS
STREAKINESSES
STREAKINGS
STREAKLIKE
STREAMBEDS
STREAMERED
STREAMIEST
STREAMINESS
STREAMINESSES
STREAMINGLY
STREAMINGS
STREAMLESS
STREAMLETS
STREAMLIKE
STREAMLINE
STREAMLINED
STREAMLINER
STREAMLINERS
STREAMLINES
STREAMLING
STREAMLINGS
STREAMLINING
STREAMLININGS
STREAMSIDE
STREAMSIDES
STREETAGES
STREETBOYS
STREETCARS
STREETFULS
STREETIEST

STREETKEEPER	STREPTOTHRICINS	STRIKINGLY	STROBOTRONS	STRUCTURATIONS
STREETKEEPERS	STRESSBUSTER	STRIKINGNESS	STRODDLING	STRUCTURED
STREETLAMP	STRESSBUSTERS	STRIKINGNESSES	STROGANOFF	STRUCTURELESS
STREETLAMPS	STRESSBUSTING	STRINGBOARD	STROGANOFFS	STRUCTURES
STREETLIGHT	STRESSFULLY	STRINGBOARDS	STROKEPLAY	STRUCTURING
STREETLIGHTS	STRESSFULNESS	STRINGCOURSE	STROLLINGS	STRUGGLERS
STREETROOM	STRESSFULNESSES	STRINGCOURSES	STROMATOLITE	STRUGGLING
STREETROOMS	STRESSIEST	STRINGENCIES	STROMATOLITES	STRUGGLINGLY
STREETSCAPE	STRESSLESS	STRINGENCY	STROMATOLITIC	STRUGGLINGS
STREETSCAPES	STRESSLESSNESS	STRINGENDO	STROMATOUS	STRUMITISES
STREETSMART	STRETCHABILITY	STRINGENTLY	STROMBULIFEROUS	STRUMPETED
STREETWALKER	STRETCHABLE	STRINGENTNESS	STROMBULIFORM	STRUMPETING
STREETWALKERS	STRETCHERED	STRINGENTNESSES	STROMBUSES	STRUTHIOID
STREETWALKING	STRETCHERING	STRINGHALT	STRONGARMED	STRUTHIOIDS
STREETWALKINGS	STRETCHERS	STRINGHALTED	STRONGARMING	STRUTHIOUS
STREETWARD	STRETCHIER	STRINGHALTS	STRONGARMS	STRUTTINGLY
STREETWARDS	STRETCHIEST	STRINGIEST	STRONGBOXES	STRUTTINGS
STREETWEAR	STRETCHINESS	STRINGINESS	STRONGHOLD	STRYCHNIAS
STREETWEARS	STRETCHINESSES	STRINGINESSES	STRONGHOLDS	STRYCHNINE
STREETWISE	STRETCHING	STRINGINGS	STRONGNESS	STRYCHNINED
STREIGNING	STRETCHINGS	STRINGLESS	STRONGNESSES	STRYCHNINES
STRELITZES	STRETCHLESS	STRINGLIKE	STRONGPOINT	STRYCHNINING
STRELITZIA	STRETCHMARKS	STRINGPIECE	STRONGPOINTS	STRYCHNINISM
STRELITZIAS	STREWMENTS	STRINGPIECES	STRONGROOM	STRYCHNINISMS
STRENGTHEN	STRIATIONS	STRINGYBARK	STRONGROOMS	STRYCHNISM
STRENGTHENED	STRIATURES	STRINGYBARKS	STRONGYLES	STRYCHNISMS
STRENGTHENER	STRICKENLY	STRINKLING	STRONGYLOID	STUBBINESS
STRENGTHENERS	STRICKLING	STRINKLINGS	STRONGYLOIDOSES	STUBBINESSES
STRENGTHENING	STRICTIONS	STRIPAGRAM	STRONGYLOIDOSIS	STUBBLIEST
STRENGTHENINGS	STRICTNESS	STRIPAGRAMS	STRONGYLOIDS	STUBBORNED
STRENGTHENS	STRICTNESSES	STRIPELESS	STRONGYLOSES	STUBBORNER
STRENGTHFUL	STRICTURED	STRIPINESS	STRONGYLOSIS	STUBBORNEST
STRENGTHLESS	STRICTURES	STRIPINESSES	STRONTIANITE	STUBBORNING
STRENUITIES	STRIDDLING	STRIPLINGS	STRONTIANITES	STUBBORNLY
STRENUOSITIES	STRIDELEGGED	STRIPOGRAM	STRONTIANS	STUBBORNNESS
STRENUOSITY	STRIDELEGS	STRIPOGRAMS	STRONTIUMS	STUBBORNNESSES
STRENUOUSLY	STRIDENCES	STRIPPABLE	STROPHANTHIN	STUCCOWORK
STRENUOUSNESS	STRIDENCIES	STRIPPAGRAM	STROPHANTHINS	STUCCOWORKS
STRENUOUSNESSES	STRIDENTLY	STRIPPAGRAMS	STROPHANTHUS	STUDDINGSAIL
STREPEROUS	STRIDEWAYS	STRIPPERGRAM	STROPHANTHUSES	STUDDINGSAILS
STREPHOSYMBOLIA	STRIDULANCE	STRIPPERGRAMS	STROPHICAL	STUDENTIER
STREPITANT	STRIDULANCES	STRIPPINGS	STROPHIOLATE	STUDENTIEST
STREPITATION	STRIDULANT	STRIPTEASE	STROPHIOLATED	STUDENTRIES
STREPITATIONS	STRIDULANTLY	STRIPTEASER	STROPHIOLE	STUDENTSHIP
STREPITOSO	STRIDULATE	STRIPTEASERS	STROPHIOLES	STUDENTSHIPS
STREPITOUS	STRIDULATED	STRIPTEASES	STROPHOIDS	STUDFISHES
STREPSIPTEROUS	STRIDULATES	STRIVINGLY	STROPHULUS	STUDHORSES
STREPTOBACILLI	STRIDULATING	STROBILACEOUS	STROPPIEST	STUDIEDNESS
STREPTOBACILLUS	STRIDULATION	STROBILATE	STROPPINESS	STUDIEDNESSES
STREPTOCARPUS	STRIDULATIONS	STROBILATED	STROPPINESSES	STUDIOUSLY
STREPTOCARPUSES	STRIDULATOR	STROBILATES	STROUDINGS	STUDIOUSNESS
STREPTOCOCCAL	STRIDULATORS	STROBILATING	STROUPACHS	STUDIOUSNESSES
STREPTOCOCCI	STRIDULATORY	STROBILATION	STRUCTURAL	STUFFINESS
STREPTOCOCCIC	STRIDULOUS	STROBILATIONS	STRUCTURALISE	STUFFINESSES
STREPTOCOCCUS	STRIDULOUSLY	STROBILIFORM	STRUCTURALISED	STULTIFICATION
STREPTOKINASE	STRIDULOUSNESS	STROBILINE	STRUCTURALISES	STULTIFICATIONS
STREPTOKINASES	STRIFELESS	STROBILISATION	STRUCTURALISING	STULTIFIED
STREPTOLYSIN	STRIGIFORM	STROBILISATIONS	STRUCTURALISM	STULTIFIER
STREPTOLYSINS	STRIKEBOUND	STROBILIZATION	STRUCTURALISMS	STULTIFIERS
STREPTOMYCES	STRIKEBREAKER	STROBILIZATIONS	STRUCTURALIST	STULTIFIES
STREPTOMYCETE	STRIKEBREAKERS	STROBILOID	STRUCTURALISTS	STULTIFYING
STREPTOMYCETES	STRIKEBREAKING	STROBILUSES	STRUCTURALIZE	STUMBLEBUM
STREPTOMYCIN	STRIKEBREAKINGS	STROBOSCOPE	STRUCTURALIZED	STUMBLEBUMS
STREPTOMYCINS	STRIKELESS	STROBOSCOPES	STRUCTURALIZES	STUMBLIEST
STREPTOSOLEN	STRIKEOUTS	STROBOSCOPIC	STRUCTURALIZING	STUMBLINGLY
STREPTOSOLENS	STRIKEOVER	STROBOSCOPICAL	STRUCTURALLY	STUMPINESS
STREPTOTHRICIN	STRIKEOVERS	STROBOTRON	STRUCTURATION	STUMPINESSES

STUMPWORKS	STYPTICITY	SUBASSEMBLING	SUBCIVILIZATION	SUBCRANIAL
STUNNINGLY	STYRACACEOUS	SUBASSEMBLY	SUBCIVILIZED	SUBCRITICAL
STUNTEDNESS	STYROFOAMS	SUBASSOCIATION	SUBCLASSED	SUBCRUSTAL
STUNTEDNESSES	SUABILITIES	SUBASSOCIATIONS	SUBCLASSES	SUBCULTURAL
STUNTWOMAN	SUASIVENESS	SUBATMOSPHERIC	SUBCLASSIFIED	SUBCULTURALLY
STUNTWOMEN	SUASIVENESSES	SUBATOMICS	SUBCLASSIFIES	SUBCULTURE
STUPEFACIENT	SUAVENESSES	SUBAUDIBLE	SUBCLASSIFY	SUBCULTURED
STUPEFACIENTS	SUAVEOLENT	SUBAUDITION	SUBCLASSIFYING	SUBCULTURES
STUPEFACTION	SUBABDOMINAL	SUBAUDITIONS	SUBCLASSING	SUBCULTURING
STUPEFACTIONS	SUBACETATE	SUBAURICULAR	SUBCLAUSES	SUBCURATIVE
STUPEFACTIVE	SUBACETATES	SUBAVERAGE	SUBCLAVIAN	SUBCUTANEOUS
STUPEFIERS	SUBACIDITIES	SUBAXILLARY	SUBCLAVIANS	SUBCUTANEOUSLY
STUPEFYING	SUBACIDITY	SUBBASEMENT	SUBCLAVICULAR	SUBCUTISES
STUPEFYINGLY	SUBACIDNESS	SUBBASEMENTS	SUBCLIMACTIC	SUBDEACONATE
STUPENDIOUS	SUBACIDNESSES	SUBBITUMINOUS	SUBCLIMAXES	SUBDEACONATES
STUPENDOUS	SUBACTIONS	SUBBRANCHES	SUBCLINICAL	SUBDEACONRIES
STUPENDOUSLY	SUBACUTELY	SUBBUREAUS	SUBCLINICALLY	SUBDEACONRY
STUPENDOUSNESS	SUBADOLESCENT	SUBBUREAUX	SUBCLUSTER	SUBDEACONS
STUPIDITIES	SUBADOLESCENTS	SUBCABINET	SUBCLUSTERED	SUBDEACONSHIP
STUPIDNESS	SUBAERIALLY	SUBCABINETS	SUBCLUSTERING	SUBDEACONSHIPS
STUPIDNESSES	SUBAFFLUENT	SUBCALIBER	SUBCLUSTERS	SUBDEALERS
STUPRATING	SUBAGENCIES	SUBCALIBRE	SUBCOLLECTION	SUBDEANERIES
STUPRATION	SUBAGGREGATE	SUBCANTORS	SUBCOLLECTIONS	SUBDEANERY
STUPRATIONS	SUBAGGREGATES	SUBCAPSULAR	SUBCOLLEGE	SUBDEBUTANTE
STURDINESS	SUBAGGREGATION	SUBCARDINAL	SUBCOLLEGES	SUBDEBUTANTES
STURDINESSES	SUBAGGREGATIONS	SUBCARDINALS	SUBCOLLEGIATE	SUBDECANAL
STUTTERERS	SUBAHDARIES	SUBCARRIER	SUBCOLONIES	SUBDECISION
STUTTERING	SUBAHSHIPS	SUBCARRIERS	SUBCOMMISSION	SUBDECISIONS
STUTTERINGLY	SUBALLIANCE	SUBCATEGORIES	SUBCOMMISSIONED	SUBDELIRIA
STUTTERINGS	SUBALLIANCES	SUBCATEGORISE	SUBCOMMISSIONER	SUBDELIRIOUS
STYLEBOOKS	SUBALLOCATION	SUBCATEGORISED	SUBCOMMISSIONS	SUBDELIRIUM
STYLELESSNESS	SUBALLOCATIONS	SUBCATEGORISES	SUBCOMMITTEE	SUBDELIRIUMS
STYLELESSNESSES	SUBALTERNANT	SUBCATEGORISING	SUBCOMMITTEES	SUBDEPARTMENT
STYLIFEROUS	SUBALTERNANTS	SUBCATEGORIZE	SUBCOMMUNITIES	SUBDEPARTMENTS
STYLISATION	SUBALTERNATE	SUBCATEGORIZED	SUBCOMMUNITY	SUBDEPUTIES
STYLISATIONS	SUBALTERNATES	SUBCATEGORIZES	SUBCOMPACT	SUBDERMALLY
STYLISHNESS	SUBALTERNATION	SUBCATEGORIZING	SUBCOMPACTS	SUBDEVELOPMENT
STYLISHNESSES	SUBALTERNATIONS	SUBCATEGORY	SUBCOMPONENT	SUBDEVELOPMENTS
STYLISTICALLY	SUBALTERNITIES	SUBCAVITIES	SUBCOMPONENTS	SUBDIACONAL
STYLISTICS	SUBALTERNITY	SUBCEILING	SUBCONSCIOUS	SUBDIACONATE
STYLITISMS	SUBALTERNS	SUBCEILINGS	SUBCONSCIOUSES	SUBDIACONATES
STYLIZATION	SUBANGULAR	SUBCELESTIAL	SUBCONSCIOUSLY	SUBDIALECT
STYLIZATIONS	SUBANTARCTIC	SUBCELESTIALS	SUBCONSULS	SUBDIALECTS
STYLOBATES	SUBAPOSTOLIC	SUBCELLARS	SUBCONTIGUOUS	SUBDIRECTOR
STYLOGRAPH	SUBAPPEARANCE	SUBCELLULAR	SUBCONTINENT	SUBDIRECTORS
STYLOGRAPHIC	SUBAPPEARANCES	SUBCENTERS	SUBCONTINENTAL	SUBDISCIPLINE
STYLOGRAPHICAL	SUBAQUATIC	SUBCENTRAL	SUBCONTINENTS	SUBDISCIPLINES
STYLOGRAPHIES	SUBAQUEOUS	SUBCENTRALLY	SUBCONTINUOUS	SUBDISTRICT
STYLOGRAPHS	SUBARACHNOID	SUBCENTRES	SUBCONTRACT	SUBDISTRICTS
STYLOGRAPHY	SUBARACHNOIDAL	SUBCEPTION	SUBCONTRACTED	SUBDIVIDABLE
STYLOLITES	SUBARACHNOIDS	SUBCEPTIONS	SUBCONTRACTING	SUBDIVIDED
STYLOLITIC	SUBARBOREAL	SUBCHANTER	SUBCONTRACTINGS	SUBDIVIDER
STYLOMETRIES	SUBARBORESCENT	SUBCHANTERS	SUBCONTRACTOR	SUBDIVIDERS
STYLOMETRY	SUBARCTICS	SUBCHAPTER	SUBCONTRACTORS	SUBDIVIDES
STYLOPHONE	SUBARCUATE	SUBCHAPTERS	SUBCONTRACTS	SUBDIVIDING
STYLOPHONES	SUBARCUATION	SUBCHARTER	SUBCONTRAOCTAVE	SUBDIVISIBLE
STYLOPISED	SUBARCUATIONS	SUBCHARTERED	SUBCONTRARIES	SUBDIVISION
STYLOPISES	SUBARRATION	SUBCHARTERING	SUBCONTRARIETY	SUBDIVISIONAL
STYLOPISING	SUBARRATIONS	SUBCHARTERS	SUBCONTRARY	SUBDIVISIONS
STYLOPIZED	SUBARRHATION	SUBCHASERS	SUBCOOLING	SUBDIVISIVE
STYLOPIZES	SUBARRHATIONS	SUBCHELATE	SUBCORDATE	SUBDOMINANT
STYLOPIZING	SUBARTICLE	SUBCHLORIDE	SUBCORIACEOUS	SUBDOMINANTS
STYLOPODIA	SUBARTICLES	SUBCHLORIDES	SUBCORTEXES	SUBDUCTING
STYLOPODIUM	SUBASSEMBLE	SUBCIRCUIT	SUBCORTICAL	SUBDUCTION
STYLOSTIXES	SUBASSEMBLED	SUBCIRCUITS	SUBCORTICES	SUBDUCTIONS
STYLOSTIXIS	SUBASSEMBLES	SUBCIVILISATION	SUBCOSTALS	SUBDUEDNESS
STYPTICITIES	SUBASSEMBLIES	SUBCIVILISED	SUBCOUNTIES	SUBDUEDNESSES

SUBDUEMENT
SUBDUEMENTS
SUBDUPLICATE
SUBECONOMIC
SUBECONOMIES
SUBECONOMY
SUBEDITING
SUBEDITORIAL
SUBEDITORS
SUBEDITORSHIP
SUBEDITORSHIPS
SUBEMPLOYED
SUBEMPLOYMENT
SUBEMPLOYMENTS
SUBENTRIES
SUBEPIDERMAL
SUBEQUATORIAL
SUBERISATION
SUBERISATIONS
SUBERISING
SUBERIZATION
SUBERIZATIONS
SUBERIZING
SUBFACTORIAL
SUBFACTORIALS
SUBFAMILIES
SUBFERTILE
SUBFERTILITIES
SUBFERTILITY
SUBFEUDATION
SUBFEUDATIONS
SUBFEUDATORY
SUBFOLDERS
SUBFOSSILS
SUBFREEZING
SUBFUSCOUS
SUBGENERATION
SUBGENERATIONS
SUBGENERIC
SUBGENERICALLY
SUBGENUSES
SUBGLACIAL
SUBGLACIALLY
SUBGLOBOSE
SUBGLOBULAR
SUBGOVERNMENT
SUBGOVERNMENTS
SUBGROUPED
SUBGROUPING
SUBHARMONIC
SUBHARMONICS
SUBHASTATION
SUBHASTATIONS
SUBHEADING
SUBHEADINGS
SUBIMAGINAL
SUBIMAGINES
SUBIMAGOES
SUBINCISED
SUBINCISES
SUBINCISING
SUBINCISION
SUBINCISIONS
SUBINDEXES
SUBINDICATE
SUBINDICATED
SUBINDICATES

SUBINDICATING
SUBINDICATION
SUBINDICATIONS
SUBINDICATIVE
SUBINDICES
SUBINDUSTRIES
SUBINDUSTRY
SUBINFEUDATE
SUBINFEUDATED
SUBINFEUDATES
SUBINFEUDATING
SUBINFEUDATION
SUBINFEUDATIONS
SUBINFEUDATORY
SUBINFEUDED
SUBINFEUDING
SUBINFEUDS
SUBINHIBITORY
SUBINSINUATION
SUBINSINUATIONS
SUBINSPECTOR
SUBINSPECTORS
SUBINTELLECTION
SUBINTELLIGENCE
SUBINTELLIGITUR
SUBINTERVAL
SUBINTERVALS
SUBINTRANT
SUBINTRODUCE
SUBINTRODUCED
SUBINTRODUCES
SUBINTRODUCING
SUBINVOLUTION
SUBINVOLUTIONS
SUBIRRIGATE
SUBIRRIGATED
SUBIRRIGATES
SUBIRRIGATING
SUBIRRIGATION
SUBIRRIGATIONS
SUBITANEOUS
SUBITISING
SUBITIZING
SUBJACENCIES
SUBJACENCY
SUBJACENTLY
SUBJECTABILITY
SUBJECTABLE
SUBJECTIFIED
SUBJECTIFIES
SUBJECTIFY
SUBJECTIFYING
SUBJECTING
SUBJECTION
SUBJECTIONS
SUBJECTIVE
SUBJECTIVELY
SUBJECTIVENESS
SUBJECTIVES
SUBJECTIVISE
SUBJECTIVISED
SUBJECTIVISES
SUBJECTIVISING
SUBJECTIVISM
SUBJECTIVISMS
SUBJECTIVIST
SUBJECTIVISTIC

SUBJECTIVISTS
SUBJECTIVITIES
SUBJECTIVITY
SUBJECTIVIZE
SUBJECTIVIZED
SUBJECTIVIZES
SUBJECTIVIZING
SUBJECTLESS
SUBJECTSHIP
SUBJECTSHIPS
SUBJOINDER
SUBJOINDERS
SUBJOINING
SUBJUGABLE
SUBJUGATED
SUBJUGATES
SUBJUGATING
SUBJUGATION
SUBJUGATIONS
SUBJUGATOR
SUBJUGATORS
SUBJUNCTION
SUBJUNCTIONS
SUBJUNCTIVE
SUBJUNCTIVELY
SUBJUNCTIVES
SUBKINGDOM
SUBKINGDOMS
SUBLANCEOLATE
SUBLANGUAGE
SUBLANGUAGES
SUBLAPSARIAN
SUBLAPSARIANISM
SUBLAPSARIANS
SUBLATIONS
SUBLEASING
SUBLESSEES
SUBLESSORS
SUBLETHALLY
SUBLETTERS
SUBLETTING
SUBLETTINGS
SUBLIBRARIAN
SUBLIBRARIANS
SUBLICENSE
SUBLICENSED
SUBLICENSES
SUBLICENSING
SUBLIEUTENANCY
SUBLIEUTENANT
SUBLIEUTENANTS
SUBLIMABLE
SUBLIMATED
SUBLIMATES
SUBLIMATING
SUBLIMATION
SUBLIMATIONS
SUBLIMENESS
SUBLIMENESSES
SUBLIMINAL
SUBLIMINALLY
SUBLIMINALS
SUBLIMINGS
SUBLIMISED
SUBLIMISES
SUBLIMISING
SUBLIMITIES

SUBLIMIZED
SUBLIMIZES
SUBLIMIZING
SUBLINEATION
SUBLINEATIONS
SUBLINGUAL
SUBLITERACIES
SUBLITERACY
SUBLITERARY
SUBLITERATE
SUBLITERATES
SUBLITERATURE
SUBLITERATURES
SUBLITTORAL
SUBLITTORALS
SUBLUXATED
SUBLUXATES
SUBLUXATING
SUBLUXATION
SUBLUXATIONS
SUBMANAGER
SUBMANAGERS
SUBMANDIBULAR
SUBMANDIBULARS
SUBMANIFOLD
SUBMANIFOLDS
SUBMARGINAL
SUBMARGINALLY
SUBMARINED
SUBMARINER
SUBMARINERS
SUBMARINES
SUBMARINING
SUBMARKETS
SUBMATRICES
SUBMATRIXES
SUBMAXILLARIES
SUBMAXILLARY
SUBMAXIMAL
SUBMEDIANT
SUBMEDIANTS
SUBMENTUMS
SUBMERGEMENT
SUBMERGEMENTS
SUBMERGENCE
SUBMERGENCES
SUBMERGIBILITY
SUBMERGIBLE
SUBMERGIBLES
SUBMERGING
SUBMERSIBILITY
SUBMERSIBLE
SUBMERSIBLES
SUBMERSING
SUBMERSION
SUBMERSIONS
SUBMETACENTRIC
SUBMETACENTRICS
SUBMICROGRAM
SUBMICRONS
SUBMICROSCOPIC
SUBMILLIMETER
SUBMILLIMETERS
SUBMILLIMETRE
SUBMILLIMETRES
SUBMINIATURE
SUBMINIATURES

SUBMINIATURISE
SUBMINIATURISED
SUBMINIATURISES
SUBMINIATURIZE
SUBMINIATURIZED
SUBMINIATURIZES
SUBMINIMAL
SUBMINISTER
SUBMINISTERED
SUBMINISTERING
SUBMINISTERS
SUBMISSIBLE
SUBMISSION
SUBMISSIONS
SUBMISSIVE
SUBMISSIVELY
SUBMISSIVENESS
SUBMISSNESS
SUBMISSNESSES
SUBMITTABLE
SUBMITTALS
SUBMITTERS
SUBMITTING
SUBMITTINGS
SUBMOLECULE
SUBMOLECULES
SUBMONTANE
SUBMONTANELY
SUBMUCOSAE
SUBMUCOSAL
SUBMUCOSAS
SUBMULTIPLE
SUBMULTIPLES
SUBMUNITION
SUBMUNITIONS
SUBNASCENT
SUBNATIONAL
SUBNATURAL
SUBNETWORK
SUBNETWORKED
SUBNETWORKING
SUBNETWORKS
SUBNORMALITIES
SUBNORMALITY
SUBNORMALLY
SUBNORMALS
SUBNUCLEAR
SUBNUCLEUS
SUBNUCLEUSES
SUBOCCIPITAL
SUBOCEANIC
SUBOCTAVES
SUBOCTUPLE
SUBOFFICER
SUBOFFICERS
SUBOFFICES
SUBOPERCULA
SUBOPERCULAR
SUBOPERCULUM
SUBOPERCULUMS
SUBOPTIMAL
SUBOPTIMISATION
SUBOPTIMISE
SUBOPTIMISED
SUBOPTIMISES
SUBOPTIMISING
SUBOPTIMIZATION

SUBOPTIMIZE	SUBPROLETARIATS	SUBSERVIENT	SUBSTANCES	SUBSTRATAL
SUBOPTIMIZED	SUBRATIONAL	SUBSERVIENTLY	SUBSTANDARD	SUBSTRATES
SUBOPTIMIZES	SUBREFERENCE	SUBSERVIENTS	SUBSTANTIAL	SUBSTRATIVE
SUBOPTIMIZING	SUBREFERENCES	SUBSERVING	SUBSTANTIALISE	SUBSTRATOSPHERE
SUBOPTIMUM	SUBREGIONAL	SUBSESSILE	SUBSTANTIALISED	SUBSTRATUM
SUBOPTIMUMS	SUBREGIONS	SUBSHRUBBY	SUBSTANTIALISES	SUBSTRATUMS
SUBORBICULAR	SUBRENTING	SUBSIDENCE	SUBSTANTIALISM	SUBSTRUCTED
SUBORBITAL	SUBREPTION	SUBSIDENCES	SUBSTANTIALISMS	SUBSTRUCTING
SUBORDINAL	SUBREPTIONS	SUBSIDENCIES	SUBSTANTIALIST	SUBSTRUCTION
SUBORDINANCIES	SUBREPTITIOUS	SUBSIDENCY	SUBSTANTIALISTS	SUBSTRUCTIONS
SUBORDINANCY	SUBREPTITIOUSLY	SUBSIDIARIAT	SUBSTANTIALITY	SUBSTRUCTS
SUBORDINARIES	SUBREPTIVE	SUBSIDIARIATS	SUBSTANTIALIZE	SUBSTRUCTURAL
SUBORDINARY	SUBROGATED	SUBSIDIARIES	SUBSTANTIALIZED	SUBSTRUCTURE
SUBORDINATE	SUBROGATES	SUBSIDIARILY	SUBSTANTIALIZES	SUBSTRUCTURES
SUBORDINATED	SUBROGATING	SUBSIDIARINESS	SUBSTANTIALLY	SUBSULTIVE
SUBORDINATELY	SUBROGATION	SUBSIDIARITIES	SUBSTANTIALNESS	SUBSULTORILY
SUBORDINATENESS	SUBROGATIONS	SUBSIDIARITY	SUBSTANTIALS	SUBSULTORY
SUBORDINATES	SUBROUTINE	SUBSIDIARY	SUBSTANTIATE	SUBSULTUSES
SUBORDINATING	SUBROUTINES	SUBSIDISABLE	SUBSTANTIATED	SUBSUMABLE
SUBORDINATION	SUBSAMPLED	SUBSIDISATION	SUBSTANTIATES	SUBSUMPTION
SUBORDINATIONS	SUBSAMPLES	SUBSIDISATIONS	SUBSTANTIATING	SUBSUMPTIONS
SUBORDINATIVE	SUBSAMPLING	SUBSIDISED	SUBSTANTIATION	SUBSUMPTIVE
SUBORDINATOR	SUBSATELLITE	SUBSIDISER	SUBSTANTIATIONS	SUBSURFACE
SUBORDINATORS	SUBSATELLITES	SUBSIDISERS	SUBSTANTIATIVE	SUBSURFACES
SUBORGANISATION	SUBSATURATED	SUBSIDISES	SUBSTANTIATOR	SUBSYSTEMS
SUBORGANIZATION	SUBSATURATION	SUBSIDISING	SUBSTANTIATORS	SUBTACKSMAN
SUBORNATION	SUBSATURATIONS	SUBSIDIZABLE	SUBSTANTIVAL	SUBTACKSMEN
SUBORNATIONS	SUBSCAPULAR	SUBSIDIZATION	SUBSTANTIVALLY	SUBTANGENT
SUBORNATIVE	SUBSCAPULARS	SUBSIDIZATIONS	SUBSTANTIVE	SUBTANGENTS
SUBOSCINES	SUBSCHEMATA	SUBSIDIZED	SUBSTANTIVELY	SUBTEMPERATE
SUBPANATION	SUBSCIENCE	SUBSIDIZER	SUBSTANTIVENESS	SUBTENANCIES
SUBPANATIONS	SUBSCIENCES	SUBSIDIZERS	SUBSTANTIVES	SUBTENANCY
SUBPARAGRAPH	SUBSCRIBABLE	SUBSIDIZES	SUBSTANTIVISE	SUBTENANTS
SUBPARAGRAPHS	SUBSCRIBED	SUBSIDIZING	SUBSTANTIVISED	SUBTENDING
SUBPARALLEL	SUBSCRIBER	SUBSISTENCE	SUBSTANTIVISES	SUBTENURES
SUBPENAING	SUBSCRIBERS	SUBSISTENCES	SUBSTANTIVISING	SUBTERFUGE
SUBPERIODS	SUBSCRIBES	SUBSISTENT	SUBSTANTIVITIES	SUBTERFUGES
SUBPHRENIC	SUBSCRIBING	SUBSISTENTIAL	SUBSTANTIVITY	SUBTERMINAL
SUBPHYLUMS	SUBSCRIBINGS	SUBSISTERS	SUBSTANTIVIZE	SUBTERNATURAL
SUBPOENAED	SUBSCRIPTION	SUBSISTING	SUBSTANTIVIZED	SUBTERRAIN
SUBPOENAING	SUBSCRIPTIONS	SUBSOCIALLY	SUBSTANTIVIZES	SUBTERRAINS
SUBPOPULATION	SUBSCRIPTIVE	SUBSOCIETIES	SUBSTANTIVIZING	SUBTERRANE
SUBPOPULATIONS	SUBSCRIPTS	SUBSOCIETY	SUBSTATION	SUBTERRANEAN
SUBPOTENCIES	SUBSECRETARIES	SUBSOILERS	SUBSTATIONS	SUBTERRANEANLY
SUBPOTENCY	SUBSECRETARY	SUBSOILING	SUBSTELLAR	SUBTERRANEANS
SUBPREFECT	SUBSECTION	SUBSOILINGS	SUBSTERNAL	SUBTERRANEOUS
SUBPREFECTS	SUBSECTIONS	SUBSONICALLY	SUBSTITUENT	SUBTERRANEOUSLY
SUBPREFECTURE	SUBSECTORS	SUBSPECIALISE	SUBSTITUENTS	SUBTERRANES
SUBPREFECTURES	SUBSEGMENT	SUBSPECIALISED	SUBSTITUTABLE	SUBTERRENE
SUBPRIMATE	SUBSEGMENTS	SUBSPECIALISES	SUBSTITUTE	SUBTERRENES
SUBPRIMATES	SUBSEIZURE	SUBSPECIALISING	SUBSTITUTED	SUBTERRESTRIAL
SUBPRINCIPAL	SUBSEIZURES	SUBSPECIALIST	SUBSTITUTES	SUBTERRESTRIALS
SUBPRINCIPALS	SUBSELLIUM	SUBSPECIALISTS	SUBSTITUTING	SUBTEXTUAL
SUBPRIORESS	SUBSENSIBLE	SUBSPECIALITIES	SUBSTITUTION	SUBTHERAPEUTIC
SUBPRIORESSES	SUBSENTENCE	SUBSPECIALITY	SUBSTITUTIONAL	SUBTHRESHOLD
SUBPROBLEM	SUBSENTENCES	SUBSPECIALIZE	SUBSTITUTIONARY	SUBTILENESS
SUBPROBLEMS	SUBSEQUENCE	SUBSPECIALIZED	SUBSTITUTIONS	SUBTILENESSES
SUBPROCESS	SUBSEQUENCES	SUBSPECIALIZES	SUBSTITUTIVE	SUBTILISATION
SUBPROCESSES	SUBSEQUENT	SUBSPECIALIZING	SUBSTITUTIVELY	SUBTILISATIONS
SUBPRODUCT	SUBSEQUENTIAL	SUBSPECIALTIES	SUBSTITUTIVITY	SUBTILISED
SUBPRODUCTS	SUBSEQUENTLY	SUBSPECIALTY	SUBSTRACTED	SUBTILISER
SUBPROFESSIONAL	SUBSEQUENTNESS	SUBSPECIES	SUBSTRACTING	SUBTILISERS
SUBPROGRAM	SUBSEQUENTS	SUBSPECIFIC	SUBSTRACTION	SUBTILISES
SUBPROGRAMS	SUBSERVIENCE	SUBSPECIFICALLY	SUBSTRACTIONS	SUBTILISIN
SUBPROJECT	SUBSERVIENCES	SUBSPINOUS	SUBSTRACTOR	SUBTILISING
SUBPROJECTS	SUBSERVIENCIES	SUBSPONTANEOUS	SUBSTRACTORS	SUBTILISINS
SUBPROLETARIAT	SUBSERVIENCY	SUBSTANCELESS	SUBSTRACTS	SUBTILITIES

SUBTILIZATION
SUBTILIZATIONS
SUBTILIZED
SUBTILIZER
SUBTILIZERS
SUBTILIZES
SUBTILIZING
SUBTILTIES
SUBTITLING
SUBTITLINGS
SUBTITULAR
SUBTLENESS
SUBTLENESSES
SUBTLETIES
SUBTOTALED
SUBTOTALING
SUBTOTALLED
SUBTOTALLING
SUBTOTALLY
SUBTRACTED
SUBTRACTER
SUBTRACTERS
SUBTRACTING
SUBTRACTION
SUBTRACTIONS
SUBTRACTIVE
SUBTRACTOR
SUBTRACTORS
SUBTRAHEND
SUBTRAHENDS
SUBTREASURER
SUBTREASURERS
SUBTREASURIES
SUBTREASURY
SUBTRIANGULAR
SUBTRIPLICATE
SUBTROPICAL
SUBTROPICALLY
SUBTROPICS
SUBTRUDING
SUBTWEETED
SUBTWEETING
SUBTYPICAL
SUBUMBRELLA
SUBUMBRELLAR
SUBUMBRELLAS
SUBUNGULATE
SUBUNGULATES
SUBURBANISATION
SUBURBANISE
SUBURBANISED
SUBURBANISES
SUBURBANISING
SUBURBANISM
SUBURBANISMS
SUBURBANITE
SUBURBANITES
SUBURBANITIES
SUBURBANITY
SUBURBANIZATION
SUBURBANIZE
SUBURBANIZED
SUBURBANIZES
SUBURBANIZING
SUBURBICARIAN
SUBVARIETIES
SUBVARIETY

SUBVASSALS
SUBVENTION
SUBVENTIONARY
SUBVENTIONS
SUBVERSALS
SUBVERSING
SUBVERSION
SUBVERSIONARIES
SUBVERSIONARY
SUBVERSIONS
SUBVERSIVE
SUBVERSIVELY
SUBVERSIVENESS
SUBVERSIVES
SUBVERTEBRAL
SUBVERTERS
SUBVERTICAL
SUBVERTING
SUBVIRUSES
SUBVISIBLE
SUBVITREOUS
SUBVOCALISATION
SUBVOCALISE
SUBVOCALISED
SUBVOCALISES
SUBVOCALISING
SUBVOCALIZATION
SUBVOCALIZE
SUBVOCALIZED
SUBVOCALIZES
SUBVOCALIZING
SUBVOCALLY
SUBWARDENS
SUBWOOFERS
SUBWRITERS
SUCCEDANEA
SUCCEDANEOUS
SUCCEDANEUM
SUCCEDANEUMS
SUCCEDENTS
SUCCEEDABLE
SUCCEEDERS
SUCCEEDING
SUCCEEDINGLY
SUCCENTORS
SUCCENTORSHIP
SUCCENTORSHIPS
SUCCESSANTLY
SUCCESSFUL
SUCCESSFULLY
SUCCESSFULNESS
SUCCESSION
SUCCESSIONAL
SUCCESSIONALLY
SUCCESSIONIST
SUCCESSIONISTS
SUCCESSIONLESS
SUCCESSIONS
SUCCESSIVE
SUCCESSIVELY
SUCCESSIVENESS
SUCCESSLESS
SUCCESSLESSLY
SUCCESSLESSNESS
SUCCESSORAL
SUCCESSORS
SUCCESSORSHIP

SUCCESSORSHIPS
SUCCINATES
SUCCINCTER
SUCCINCTEST
SUCCINCTLY
SUCCINCTNESS
SUCCINCTNESSES
SUCCINCTORIA
SUCCINCTORIES
SUCCINCTORIUM
SUCCINCTORIUMS
SUCCINCTORY
SUCCINITES
SUCCINYLCHOLINE
SUCCORABLE
SUCCORLESS
SUCCOTASHES
SUCCOURABLE
SUCCOURERS
SUCCOURING
SUCCOURLESS
SUCCUBUSES
SUCCULENCE
SUCCULENCES
SUCCULENCIES
SUCCULENCY
SUCCULENTLY
SUCCULENTS
SUCCUMBERS
SUCCUMBING
SUCCURSALE
SUCCURSALES
SUCCURSALS
SUCCUSSATION
SUCCUSSATIONS
SUCCUSSING
SUCCUSSION
SUCCUSSIONS
SUCCUSSIVE
SUCHNESSES
SUCKERFISH
SUCKERFISHES
SUCKFISHES
SUCKHOLING
SUCKINESSES
SUCRALFATE
SUCRALFATES
SUCRALOSES
SUCTIONING
SUCTORIANS
SUDATORIES
SUDATORIUM
SUDATORIUMS
SUDDENNESS
SUDDENNESSES
SUDDENTIES
SUDORIFEROUS
SUDORIFICS
SUDORIPAROUS
SUEABILITIES
SUEABILITY
SUFFERABLE
SUFFERABLENESS
SUFFERABLY
SUFFERANCE
SUFFERANCES
SUFFERINGLY

SUFFERINGS
SUFFICIENCE
SUFFICIENCES
SUFFICIENCIES
SUFFICIENCY
SUFFICIENT
SUFFICIENTLY
SUFFICIENTS
SUFFICINGNESS
SUFFICINGNESSES
SUFFIGANCE
SUFFIGANCES
SUFFISANCE
SUFFISANCES
SUFFIXATION
SUFFIXATIONS
SUFFIXIONS
SUFFLATING
SUFFLATION
SUFFLATIONS
SUFFOCATED
SUFFOCATES
SUFFOCATING
SUFFOCATINGLY
SUFFOCATINGS
SUFFOCATION
SUFFOCATIONS
SUFFOCATIVE
SUFFRAGANS
SUFFRAGANSHIP
SUFFRAGANSHIPS
SUFFRAGETTE
SUFFRAGETTES
SUFFRAGETTISM
SUFFRAGETTISMS
SUFFRAGISM
SUFFRAGISMS
SUFFRAGIST
SUFFRAGISTS
SUFFRUTESCENT
SUFFRUTICOSE
SUFFUMIGATE
SUFFUMIGATED
SUFFUMIGATES
SUFFUMIGATING
SUFFUMIGATION
SUFFUMIGATIONS
SUFFUSIONS
SUGARALLIE
SUGARALLIES
SUGARBERRIES
SUGARBERRY
SUGARBUSHES
SUGARCANES
SUGARCOATED
SUGARCOATING
SUGARCOATS
SUGARHOUSE
SUGARHOUSES
SUGARINESS
SUGARINESSES
SUGARLOAVES
SUGARPLUMS
SUGGESTERS
SUGGESTIBILITY
SUGGESTIBLE
SUGGESTIBLENESS

SUGGESTIBLY
SUGGESTING
SUGGESTION
SUGGESTIONISE
SUGGESTIONISED
SUGGESTIONISES
SUGGESTIONISING
SUGGESTIONISM
SUGGESTIONISMS
SUGGESTIONIST
SUGGESTIONISTS
SUGGESTIONIZE
SUGGESTIONIZED
SUGGESTIONIZES
SUGGESTIONIZING
SUGGESTIONS
SUGGESTIVE
SUGGESTIVELY
SUGGESTIVENESS
SUICIDALLY
SUICIDOLOGIES
SUICIDOLOGIST
SUICIDOLOGISTS
SUICIDOLOGY
SUITABILITIES
SUITABILITY
SUITABLENESS
SUITABLENESSES
SUITRESSES
SULCALISED
SULCALISES
SULCALISING
SULCALIZED
SULCALIZES
SULCALIZING
SULCATIONS
SULFACETAMIDE
SULFACETAMIDES
SULFADIAZINE
SULFADIAZINES
SULFADIMIDINE
SULFADIMIDINES
SULFADOXINE
SULFADOXINES
SULFAMETHAZINE
SULFAMETHAZINES
SULFANILAMIDE
SULFANILAMIDES
SULFATASES
SULFATHIAZOLE
SULFATHIAZOLES
SULFATIONS
SULFHYDRYL
SULFHYDRYLS
SULFINPYRAZONE
SULFINPYRAZONES
SULFONAMIDE
SULFONAMIDES
SULFONATED
SULFONATES
SULFONATING
SULFONATION
SULFONATIONS
SULFONIUMS
SULFONMETHANE
SULFONMETHANES
SULFONYLUREA

SULFONYLUREAS	SULPHURATES	SUMMERIEST	SUNSCREENS	SUPERBAZARS
SULFOXIDES	SULPHURATING	SUMMERINESS	SUNSEEKERS	SUPERBIKES
SULFURATED	SULPHURATION	SUMMERINESSES	SUNSETTING	SUPERBITCH
SULFURATES	SULPHURATIONS	SUMMERINGS	SUNSETTINGS	SUPERBITCHES
SULFURATING	SULPHURATOR	SUMMERLESS	SUNSHINIER	SUPERBITIES
SULFURATION	SULPHURATORS	SUMMERLIER	SUNSHINIEST	SUPERBLOCK
SULFURATIONS	SULPHUREOUS	SUMMERLIEST	SUNSPOTTED	SUPERBLOCKS
SULFUREOUS	SULPHUREOUSLY	SUMMERLIKE	SUNSTROKES	SUPERBNESS
SULFURETED	SULPHUREOUSNESS	SUMMERLONG	SUNTANNING	SUPERBNESSES
SULFURETING	SULPHURETED	SUMMERSAULT	SUNTANNINGS	SUPERBOARD
SULFURETTED	SULPHURETING	SUMMERSAULTED	SUNWORSHIPPER	SUPERBOARDS
SULFURETTING	SULPHURETS	SUMMERSAULTING	SUNWORSHIPPERS	SUPERBOMBER
SULFURIEST	SULPHURETTED	SUMMERSAULTS	SUOVETAURILIA	SUPERBOMBERS
SULFURISATION	SULPHURETTING	SUMMERSETS	SUOVETAURILIAS	SUPERBOMBS
SULFURISATIONS	SULPHURIER	SUMMERSETTED	SUPERABILITIES	SUPERBRAIN
SULFURISED	SULPHURIEST	SUMMERSETTING	SUPERABILITY	SUPERBRAINS
SULFURISES	SULPHURING	SUMMERTIDE	SUPERABLENESS	SUPERBRATS
SULFURISING	SULPHURISATION	SUMMERTIDES	SUPERABLENESSES	SUPERBRIGHT
SULFURIZATION	SULPHURISATIONS	SUMMERTIME	SUPERABOUND	SUPERBUREAUCRAT
SULFURIZATIONS	SULPHURISE	SUMMERTIMES	SUPERABOUNDED	SUPERCABINET
SULFURIZED	SULPHURISED	SUMMERWEIGHT	SUPERABOUNDING	SUPERCABINETS
SULFURIZES	SULPHURISES	SUMMERWOOD	SUPERABOUNDS	SUPERCALENDER
SULFURIZING	SULPHURISING	SUMMERWOODS	SUPERABSORBENT	SUPERCALENDERED
SULFUROUSLY	SULPHURIZATION	SUMMITEERS	SUPERABSORBENTS	SUPERCALENDERS
SULFUROUSNESS	SULPHURIZATIONS	SUMMITLESS	SUPERABUNDANCE	SUPERCARGO
SULFUROUSNESSES	SULPHURIZE	SUMMITRIES	SUPERABUNDANCES	SUPERCARGOES
SULKINESSES	SULPHURIZED	SUMMONABLE	SUPERABUNDANT	SUPERCARGOS
SULLENNESS	SULPHURIZES	SUMMONSING	SUPERABUNDANTLY	SUPERCARGOSHIP
SULLENNESSES	SULPHURIZING	SUMPHISHNESS	SUPERACHIEVER	SUPERCARGOSHIPS
SULPHACETAMIDE	SULPHUROUS	SUMPHISHNESSES	SUPERACHIEVERS	SUPERCARRIER
SULPHACETAMIDES	SULPHUROUSLY	SUMPSIMUSES	SUPERACTIVE	SUPERCARRIERS
SULPHADIAZINE	SULPHUROUSNESS	SUMPTUOSITIES	SUPERACTIVITIES	SUPERCAUTIOUS
SULPHADIAZINES	SULPHURWORT	SUMPTUOSITY	SUPERACTIVITY	SUPERCEDED
SULPHADOXINE	SULPHURWORTS	SUMPTUOUSLY	SUPERACUTE	SUPERCEDES
SULPHADOXINES	SULPHURYLS	SUMPTUOUSNESS	SUPERADDED	SUPERCEDING
SULPHANILAMIDE	SULTANATES	SUMPTUOUSNESSES	SUPERADDING	SUPERCELESTIAL
SULPHANILAMIDES	SULTANESSES	SUNBATHERS	SUPERADDITION	SUPERCELLS
SULPHATASE	SULTANSHIP	SUNBATHING	SUPERADDITIONAL	SUPERCENTER
SULPHATASES	SULTANSHIPS	SUNBATHINGS	SUPERADDITIONS	SUPERCENTERS
SULPHATHIAZOLE	SULTRINESS	SUNBEAMIER	SUPERAGENCIES	SUPERCHARGE
SULPHATHIAZOLES	SULTRINESSES	SUNBEAMIEST	SUPERAGENCY	SUPERCHARGED
SULPHATING	SUMBITCHES	SUNBERRIES	SUPERAGENT	SUPERCHARGER
SULPHATION	SUMMABILITIES	SUNBONNETED	SUPERAGENTS	SUPERCHARGERS
SULPHATIONS	SUMMABILITY	SUNBONNETS	SUPERALLOY	SUPERCHARGES
SULPHHYDRYL	SUMMARINESS	SUNBURNING	SUPERALLOYS	SUPERCHARGING
SULPHHYDRYLS	SUMMARINESSES	SUNDERABLE	SUPERALTAR	SUPERCHERIE
SULPHINPYRAZONE	SUMMARISABLE	SUNDERANCE	SUPERALTARS	SUPERCHERIES
SULPHINYLS	SUMMARISATION	SUNDERANCES	SUPERALTERN	SUPERCHURCH
SULPHONAMIDE	SUMMARISATIONS	SUNDERINGS	SUPERALTERNS	SUPERCHURCHES
SULPHONAMIDES	SUMMARISED	SUNDERMENT	SUPERAMBITIOUS	SUPERCILIARIES
SULPHONATE	SUMMARISER	SUNDERMENTS	SUPERANNUABLE	SUPERCILIARY
SULPHONATED	SUMMARISERS	SUNDOWNERS	SUPERANNUATE	SUPERCILIOUS
SULPHONATES	SUMMARISES	SUNDOWNING	SUPERANNUATED	SUPERCILIOUSLY
SULPHONATING	SUMMARISING	SUNDRENCHED	SUPERANNUATES	SUPERCITIES
SULPHONATION	SUMMARISTS	SUNDRESSES	SUPERANNUATING	SUPERCIVILISED
SULPHONATIONS	SUMMARIZABLE	SUNFLOWERS	SUPERANNUATION	SUPERCIVILIZED
SULPHONIUM	SUMMARIZATION	SUNGAZINGS	SUPERANNUATIONS	SUPERCLASS
SULPHONIUMS	SUMMARIZATIONS	SUNGLASSES	SUPERATHLETE	SUPERCLASSES
SULPHONMETHANE	SUMMARIZED	SUNLESSNESS	SUPERATHLETES	SUPERCLEAN
SULPHONMETHANES	SUMMARIZER	SUNLESSNESSES	SUPERATING	SUPERCLUBS
SULPHONYLS	SUMMARIZERS	SUNLOUNGER	SUPERATION	SUPERCLUSTER
SULPHONYLUREA	SUMMARIZES	SUNLOUNGERS	SUPERATIONS	SUPERCLUSTERS
SULPHONYLUREAS	SUMMARIZING	SUNNINESSES	SUPERATOMS	SUPERCOILED
SULPHOXIDE	SUMMATIONAL	SUNPORCHES	SUPERBANKS	SUPERCOILING
SULPHOXIDES	SUMMATIONS	SUNRISINGS	SUPERBAZAAR	SUPERCOILS
SULPHURATE	SUMMERHOUSE	SUNSCREENING	SUPERBAZAARS	SUPERCOLLIDER
SULPHURATED	SUMMERHOUSES	SUNSCREENINGS	SUPERBAZAR	SUPERCOLLIDERS

SUPERCOLOSSAL	SUPEREROGATORS	SUPERFUSIONS	SUPERINCUMBENCE	SUPERMARKETS
SUPERCOLUMNAR	SUPEREROGATORY	SUPERGENES	SUPERINCUMBENCY	SUPERMARTS
SUPERCOMPUTER	SUPERESSENTIAL	SUPERGIANT	SUPERINCUMBENT	SUPERMASCULINE
SUPERCOMPUTERS	SUPERETTES	SUPERGIANTS	SUPERINDIVIDUAL	SUPERMASSIVE
SUPERCOMPUTING	SUPEREVIDENT	SUPERGLACIAL	SUPERINDUCE	SUPERMAXES
SUPERCOMPUTINGS	SUPEREXALT	SUPERGLUED	SUPERINDUCED	SUPERMEMBRANE
SUPERCONDUCT	SUPEREXALTATION	SUPERGLUEING	SUPERINDUCEMENT	SUPERMEMBRANES
SUPERCONDUCTED	SUPEREXALTED	SUPERGLUES	SUPERINDUCES	SUPERMICRO
SUPERCONDUCTING	SUPEREXALTING	SUPERGLUING	SUPERINDUCING	SUPERMICROS
SUPERCONDUCTION	SUPEREXALTS	SUPERGOVERNMENT	SUPERINDUCTION	SUPERMILITANT
SUPERCONDUCTIVE	SUPEREXCELLENCE	SUPERGRAPHICS	SUPERINDUCTIONS	SUPERMILITANTS
SUPERCONDUCTOR	SUPEREXCELLENT	SUPERGRASS	SUPERINFECT	SUPERMINDS
SUPERCONDUCTORS	SUPEREXPENSIVE	SUPERGRASSES	SUPERINFECTED	SUPERMINIS
SUPERCONDUCTS	SUPEREXPRESS	SUPERGRAVITIES	SUPERINFECTING	SUPERMINISTER
SUPERCONFIDENCE	SUPEREXPRESSES	SUPERGRAVITY	SUPERINFECTION	SUPERMINISTERS
SUPERCONFIDENT	SUPERFAMILIES	SUPERGROUP	SUPERINFECTIONS	SUPERMODEL
SUPERCONTINENT	SUPERFAMILY	SUPERGROUPS	SUPERINFECTS	SUPERMODELS
SUPERCONTINENTS	SUPERFARMS	SUPERGROWTH	SUPERINSULATED	SUPERMODERN
SUPERCONVENIENT	SUPERFATTED	SUPERGROWTHS	SUPERINTEND	SUPERMOONS
SUPERCOOLED	SUPERFECTA	SUPERHARDEN	SUPERINTENDED	SUPERMOTOS
SUPERCOOLING	SUPERFECTAS	SUPERHARDENED	SUPERINTENDENCE	SUPERMUNDANE
SUPERCOOLS	SUPERFEMALE	SUPERHARDENING	SUPERINTENDENCY	SUPERNACULA
SUPERCOVER	SUPERFEMALES	SUPERHARDENS	SUPERINTENDENT	SUPERNACULAR
SUPERCOVERS	SUPERFETATE	SUPERHEATED	SUPERINTENDENTS	SUPERNACULUM
SUPERCRIMINAL	SUPERFETATED	SUPERHEATER	SUPERINTENDING	SUPERNALLY
SUPERCRIMINALS	SUPERFETATES	SUPERHEATERS	SUPERINTENDS	SUPERNANNIES
SUPERCRITICAL	SUPERFETATING	SUPERHEATING	SUPERINTENSITY	SUPERNANNY
SUPERCURRENT	SUPERFETATION	SUPERHEATS	SUPERIORESS	SUPERNATANT
SUPERCURRENTS	SUPERFETATIONS	SUPERHEAVIES	SUPERIORESSES	SUPERNATANTS
SUPERDAINTIER	SUPERFICIAL	SUPERHEAVY	SUPERIORITIES	SUPERNATATION
SUPERDAINTIEST	SUPERFICIALISE	SUPERHELICAL	SUPERIORITY	SUPERNATATIONS
SUPERDAINTY	SUPERFICIALISED	SUPERHELICES	SUPERIORLY	SUPERNATED
SUPERDELEGATE	SUPERFICIALISES	SUPERHELIX	SUPERIORSHIP	SUPERNATES
SUPERDELEGATES	SUPERFICIALITY	SUPERHELIXES	SUPERIORSHIPS	SUPERNATING
SUPERDELUXE	SUPERFICIALIZE	SUPERHEROES	SUPERJACENT	SUPERNATION
SUPERDENSE	SUPERFICIALIZED	SUPERHEROINE	SUPERJOCKS	SUPERNATIONAL
SUPERDIPLOMAT	SUPERFICIALIZES	SUPERHEROINES	SUPERJUMBO	SUPERNATIONALLY
SUPERDIPLOMATS	SUPERFICIALLY	SUPERHETERODYNE	SUPERJUMBOS	SUPERNATIONS
SUPERDOMINANT	SUPERFICIALNESS	SUPERHIGHWAY	SUPERKINGDOM	SUPERNATURAL
SUPERDOMINANTS	SUPERFICIALS	SUPERHIGHWAYS	SUPERKINGDOMS	SUPERNATURALISE
SUPEREFFECTIVE	SUPERFICIES	SUPERHIVES	SUPERLARGE	SUPERNATURALISM
SUPEREFFICIENCY	SUPERFINENESS	SUPERHUMAN	SUPERLATIVE	SUPERNATURALIST
SUPEREFFICIENT	SUPERFINENESSES	SUPERHUMANISE	SUPERLATIVELY	SUPERNATURALIZE
SUPEREGOIST	SUPERFIRMS	SUPERHUMANISED	SUPERLATIVENESS	SUPERNATURALLY
SUPEREGOISTS	SUPERFIXES	SUPERHUMANISES	SUPERLATIVES	SUPERNATURALS
SUPERELASTIC	SUPERFLACK	SUPERHUMANISING	SUPERLAWYER	SUPERNATURE
SUPERELEVATE	SUPERFLACKS	SUPERHUMANITIES	SUPERLAWYERS	SUPERNATURES
SUPERELEVATED	SUPERFLUID	SUPERHUMANITY	SUPERLIGHT	SUPERNORMAL
SUPERELEVATES	SUPERFLUIDITIES	SUPERHUMANIZE	SUPERLINER	SUPERNORMALITY
SUPERELEVATING	SUPERFLUIDITY	SUPERHUMANIZED	SUPERLINERS	SUPERNORMALLY
SUPERELEVATION	SUPERFLUIDS	SUPERHUMANIZES	SUPERLOADS	SUPERNOVAE
SUPERELEVATIONS	SUPERFLUITIES	SUPERHUMANIZING	SUPERLOBBYIST	SUPERNOVAS
SUPERELITE	SUPERFLUITY	SUPERHUMANLY	SUPERLOBBYISTS	SUPERNUMERARIES
SUPERELITES	SUPERFLUOUS	SUPERHUMANNESS	SUPERLOYALIST	SUPERNUMERARY
SUPEREMINENCE	SUPERFLUOUSLY	SUPERHUMANS	SUPERLOYALISTS	SUPERNURSE
SUPEREMINENCES	SUPERFLUOUSNESS	SUPERHUMERAL	SUPERLUMINAL	SUPERNURSES
SUPEREMINENT	SUPERFLUXES	SUPERHUMERALS	SUPERLUNAR	SUPERNUTRIENT
SUPEREMINENTLY	SUPERFOETATION	SUPERHYPED	SUPERLUNARY	SUPERNUTRIENTS
SUPEREROGANT	SUPERFOETATIONS	SUPERHYPES	SUPERLUXURIES	SUPERNUTRITION
SUPEREROGATE	SUPERFOODS	SUPERHYPING	SUPERLUXURIOUS	SUPERNUTRITIONS
SUPEREROGATED	SUPERFRONTAL	SUPERIMPORTANT	SUPERLUXURY	SUPEROCTAVE
SUPEREROGATES	SUPERFRONTALS	SUPERIMPOSABLE	SUPERLYING	SUPEROCTAVES
SUPEREROGATING	SUPERFUNDS	SUPERIMPOSE	SUPERMACHO	SUPERORDER
SUPEREROGATION	SUPERFUSED	SUPERIMPOSED	SUPERMAJORITIES	SUPERORDERS
SUPEREROGATIONS	SUPERFUSES	SUPERIMPOSES	SUPERMAJORITY	SUPERORDINAL
SUPEREROGATIVE	SUPERFUSING	SUPERIMPOSING	SUPERMALES	SUPERORDINARY
SUPEREROGATOR	SUPERFUSION	SUPERIMPOSITION	SUPERMARKET	SUPERORDINATE

S

SUPERORDINATED	SUPERPREMIUMS	SUPERSELLERS	SUPERSTRONG	SUPERVISOR
SUPERORDINATES	SUPERPROFIT	SUPERSELLING	SUPERSTRUCT	SUPERVISORS
SUPERORDINATING	SUPERPROFITS	SUPERSELLS	SUPERSTRUCTED	SUPERVISORSHIP
SUPERORDINATION	SUPERQUALITIES	SUPERSENSIBLE	SUPERSTRUCTING	SUPERVISORSHIPS
SUPERORGANIC	SUPERQUALITY	SUPERSENSIBLY	SUPERSTRUCTION	SUPERVISORY
SUPERORGANICISM	SUPERRACES	SUPERSENSITIVE	SUPERSTRUCTIONS	SUPERVOLUTE
SUPERORGANICIST	SUPERREALISM	SUPERSENSORY	SUPERSTRUCTIVE	SUPERWAIFS
SUPERORGANISM	SUPERREALISMS	SUPERSENSUAL	SUPERSTRUCTS	SUPERWAVES
SUPERORGANISMS	SUPERREALIST	SUPERSESSION	SUPERSTRUCTURAL	SUPERWEAPON
SUPERORGASM	SUPERREALISTS	SUPERSESSIONS	SUPERSTRUCTURE	SUPERWEAPONS
SUPERORGASMS	SUPERREFINE	SUPERSEXES	SUPERSTRUCTURES	SUPERWEEDS
SUPEROVULATE	SUPERREFINED	SUPERSEXUALITY	SUPERSTUDS	SUPERWIDES
SUPEROVULATED	SUPERREFINES	SUPERSHARP	SUPERSUBTILE	SUPERWIVES
SUPEROVULATES	SUPERREFINING	SUPERSHOWS	SUPERSUBTLE	SUPERWOMAN
SUPEROVULATING	SUPERREGIONAL	SUPERSINGER	SUPERSUBTLETIES	SUPERWOMEN
SUPEROVULATION	SUPERREGIONALS	SUPERSINGERS	SUPERSUBTLETY	SUPINATING
SUPEROVULATIONS	SUPERROADS	SUPERSIZED	SUPERSURGEON	SUPINATION
SUPEROXIDE	SUPERROMANTIC	SUPERSIZES	SUPERSURGEONS	SUPINATIONS
SUPEROXIDES	SUPERSAFETIES	SUPERSIZING	SUPERSWEET	SUPINATORS
SUPERPARASITISM	SUPERSAFETY	SUPERSLEUTH	SUPERSYMMETRIC	SUPINENESS
SUPERPARTICLE	SUPERSALES	SUPERSLEUTHS	SUPERSYMMETRIES	SUPINENESSES
SUPERPARTICLES	SUPERSALESMAN	SUPERSLICK	SUPERSYMMETRY	SUPPEAGOES
SUPERPATRIOT	SUPERSALESMEN	SUPERSMART	SUPERSYSTEM	SUPPEDANEA
SUPERPATRIOTIC	SUPERSALTS	SUPERSMOOTH	SUPERSYSTEMS	SUPPEDANEUM
SUPERPATRIOTISM	SUPERSATURATE	SUPERSONIC	SUPERTANKER	SUPPERLESS
SUPERPATRIOTS	SUPERSATURATED	SUPERSONICALLY	SUPERTANKERS	SUPPERTIME
SUPERPEOPLE	SUPERSATURATES	SUPERSONICS	SUPERTAXES	SUPPERTIMES
SUPERPERSON	SUPERSATURATING	SUPERSOUND	SUPERTEACHER	SUPPLANTATION
SUPERPERSONAL	SUPERSATURATION	SUPERSOUNDS	SUPERTEACHERS	SUPPLANTATIONS
SUPERPERSONS	SUPERSAURS	SUPERSPECIAL	SUPERTERRANEAN	SUPPLANTED
SUPERPHENOMENA	SUPERSAVER	SUPERSPECIALIST	SUPERTERRIFIC	SUPPLANTER
SUPERPHENOMENON	SUPERSAVERS	SUPERSPECIALS	SUPERTHICK	SUPPLANTERS
SUPERPHONE	SUPERSCALAR	SUPERSPECIES	SUPERTHRILLER	SUPPLANTING
SUPERPHONES	SUPERSCALE	SUPERSPECTACLE	SUPERTHRILLERS	SUPPLEJACK
SUPERPHOSPHATE	SUPERSCHOOL	SUPERSPECTACLES	SUPERTIGHT	SUPPLEJACKS
SUPERPHOSPHATES	SUPERSCHOOLS	SUPERSPEED	SUPERTITLE	SUPPLEMENT
SUPERPHYLA	SUPERSCOUT	SUPERSPEEDS	SUPERTITLES	SUPPLEMENTAL
SUPERPHYLUM	SUPERSCOUTS	SUPERSPIES	SUPERTONIC	SUPPLEMENTALLY
SUPERPHYSICAL	SUPERSCREEN	SUPERSTARDOM	SUPERTONICS	SUPPLEMENTALS
SUPERPIMPS	SUPERSCREENS	SUPERSTARDOMS	SUPERTRAMS	SUPPLEMENTARIES
SUPERPLANE	SUPERSCRIBE	SUPERSTARS	SUPERTRUCK	SUPPLEMENTARILY
SUPERPLANES	SUPERSCRIBED	SUPERSTATE	SUPERTRUCKS	SUPPLEMENTARY
SUPERPLASTIC	SUPERSCRIBES	SUPERSTATES	SUPERTWIST	SUPPLEMENTATION
SUPERPLASTICITY	SUPERSCRIBING	SUPERSTATION	SUPERTWISTS	SUPPLEMENTED
SUPERPLASTICS	SUPERSCRIPT	SUPERSTATIONS	SUPERUSERS	SUPPLEMENTER
SUPERPLAYER	SUPERSCRIPTION	SUPERSTIMULATE	SUPERVENED	SUPPLEMENTERS
SUPERPLAYERS	SUPERSCRIPTIONS	SUPERSTIMULATED	SUPERVENES	SUPPLEMENTING
SUPERPLUSES	SUPERSCRIPTS	SUPERSTIMULATES	SUPERVENIENCE	SUPPLEMENTS
SUPERPOLITE	SUPERSECRECIES	SUPERSTITION	SUPERVENIENCES	SUPPLENESS
SUPERPOLYMER	SUPERSECRECY	SUPERSTITIONS	SUPERVENIENT	SUPPLENESSES
SUPERPOLYMERS	SUPERSECRET	SUPERSTITIOUS	SUPERVENING	SUPPLETION
SUPERPORTS	SUPERSECRETS	SUPERSTITIOUSLY	SUPERVENTION	SUPPLETIONS
SUPERPOSABLE	SUPERSEDABLE	SUPERSTOCK	SUPERVENTIONS	SUPPLETIVE
SUPERPOSED	SUPERSEDEAS	SUPERSTOCKS	SUPERVIRILE	SUPPLETIVES
SUPERPOSES	SUPERSEDEASES	SUPERSTORE	SUPERVIRTUOSI	SUPPLETORILY
SUPERPOSING	SUPERSEDED	SUPERSTORES	SUPERVIRTUOSO	SUPPLETORY
SUPERPOSITION	SUPERSEDENCE	SUPERSTORM	SUPERVIRTUOSOS	SUPPLIABLE
SUPERPOSITIONS	SUPERSEDENCES	SUPERSTORMS	SUPERVIRULENT	SUPPLIANCE
SUPERPOWER	SUPERSEDER	SUPERSTRATA	SUPERVISAL	SUPPLIANCES
SUPERPOWERED	SUPERSEDERE	SUPERSTRATUM	SUPERVISALS	SUPPLIANTLY
SUPERPOWERFUL	SUPERSEDERES	SUPERSTRATUMS	SUPERVISED	SUPPLIANTS
SUPERPOWERS	SUPERSEDERS	SUPERSTRENGTH	SUPERVISEE	SUPPLICANT
SUPERPRAISE	SUPERSEDES	SUPERSTRENGTHS	SUPERVISEES	SUPPLICANTS
SUPERPRAISED	SUPERSEDING	SUPERSTRIKE	SUPERVISES	SUPPLICATE
SUPERPRAISES	SUPERSEDURE	SUPERSTRIKES	SUPERVISING	SUPPLICATED
SUPERPRAISING	SUPERSEDURES	SUPERSTRING	SUPERVISION	SUPPLICATES
SUPERPREMIUM	SUPERSELLER	SUPERSTRINGS	SUPERVISIONS	SUPPLICATING

SUPPLICATINGLY	SUPPURATIVE	SURFACEMAN	SURPRIZING	SURVIVALISMS
SUPPLICATION	SUPPURATIVES	SURFACEMEN	SURQUEDIES	SURVIVALIST
SUPPLICATIONS	SUPRACHIASMIC	SURFACINGS	SURQUEDRIES	SURVIVALISTS
SUPPLICATORY	SUPRACHOROIDAL	SURFACTANT	SURREALISM	SURVIVANCE
SUPPLICATS	SUPRACILIARY	SURFACTANTS	SURREALISMS	SURVIVANCES
SUPPLICAVIT	SUPRACOSTAL	SURFBOARDED	SURREALIST	SURVIVORSHIP
SUPPLICAVITS	SUPRACRUSTAL	SURFBOARDER	SURREALISTIC	SURVIVORSHIPS
SUPPLYMENT	SUPRAGLOTTAL	SURFBOARDERS	SURREALISTS	SUSCEPTANCE
SUPPLYMENTS	SUPRALAPSARIAN	SURFBOARDING	SURREBUTTAL	SUSCEPTANCES
SUPPORTABILITY	SUPRALAPSARIANS	SURFBOARDINGS	SURREBUTTALS	SUSCEPTIBILITY
SUPPORTABLE	SUPRALIMINAL	SURFBOARDS	SURREBUTTED	SUSCEPTIBLE
SUPPORTABLENESS	SUPRALIMINALLY	SURFCASTER	SURREBUTTER	SUSCEPTIBLENESS
SUPPORTABLY	SUPRALUNAR	SURFCASTERS	SURREBUTTERS	SUSCEPTIBLY
SUPPORTANCE	SUPRAMAXILLARY	SURFCASTING	SURREBUTTING	SUSCEPTIVE
SUPPORTANCES	SUPRAMOLECULAR	SURFCASTINGS	SURREJOINDER	SUSCEPTIVENESS
SUPPORTERS	SUPRAMOLECULE	SURFEITERS	SURREJOINDERS	SUSCEPTIVITIES
SUPPORTING	SUPRAMOLECULES	SURFEITING	SURREJOINED	SUSCEPTIVITY
SUPPORTINGS	SUPRAMUNDANE	SURFEITINGS	SURREJOINING	SUSCEPTORS
SUPPORTIVE	SUPRANATIONAL	SURFFISHES	SURREJOINS	SUSCIPIENT
SUPPORTIVELY	SUPRANATIONALLY	SURFPERCHES	SURRENDERED	SUSCIPIENTS
SUPPORTIVENESS	SUPRAOPTIC	SURFRIDDEN	SURRENDEREE	SUSCITATED
SUPPORTLESS	SUPRAORBITAL	SURFRIDERS	SURRENDEREES	SUSCITATES
SUPPORTMENT	SUPRAPUBIC	SURFRIDING	SURRENDERER	SUSCITATING
SUPPORTMENTS	SUPRARATIONAL	SURFRIDINGS	SURRENDERERS	SUSCITATION
SUPPORTRESS	SUPRARENAL	SURGEONCIES	SURRENDERING	SUSCITATIONS
SUPPORTRESSES	SUPRARENALS	SURGEONFISH	SURRENDEROR	SUSPECTABLE
SUPPORTURE	SUPRASEGMENTAL	SURGEONFISHES	SURRENDERORS	SUSPECTEDLY
SUPPORTURES	SUPRASENSIBLE	SURGEONSHIP	SURRENDERS	SUSPECTEDNESS
SUPPOSABLE	SUPRATEMPORAL	SURGEONSHIPS	SURRENDRIES	SUSPECTEDNESSES
SUPPOSABLY	SUPRAVITAL	SURGICALLY	SURREPTITIOUS	SUSPECTERS
SUPPOSEDLY	SUPRAVITALLY	SURJECTION	SURREPTITIOUSLY	SUSPECTFUL
SUPPOSINGS	SUPREMACIES	SURJECTIONS	SURROGACIES	SUSPECTING
SUPPOSITION	SUPREMACISM	SURJECTIVE	SURROGATED	SUSPECTLESS
SUPPOSITIONAL	SUPREMACISMS	SURLINESSES	SURROGATES	SUSPENDERED
SUPPOSITIONALLY	SUPREMACIST	SURMASTERS	SURROGATESHIP	SUSPENDERS
SUPPOSITIONARY	SUPREMACISTS	SURMISABLE	SURROGATESHIPS	SUSPENDIBILITY
SUPPOSITIONLESS	SUPREMATISM	SURMISINGS	SURROGATING	SUSPENDIBLE
SUPPOSITIONS	SUPREMATISMS	SURMISTRESS	SURROGATION	SUSPENDING
SUPPOSITIOUS	SUPREMATIST	SURMISTRESSES	SURROGATIONS	SUSPENSEFUL
SUPPOSITIOUSLY	SUPREMATISTS	SURMOUNTABLE	SURROGATUM	SUSPENSEFULLY
SUPPOSITITIOUS	SUPREMENESS	SURMOUNTED	SURROGATUMS	SUSPENSEFULNESS
SUPPOSITIVE	SUPREMENESSES	SURMOUNTER	SURROUNDED	SUSPENSELESS
SUPPOSITIVELY	SUPREMITIES	SURMOUNTERS	SURROUNDING	SUSPENSERS
SUPPOSITIVES	SURADDITION	SURMOUNTING	SURROUNDINGS	SUSPENSIBILITY
SUPPOSITORIES	SURADDITIONS	SURMOUNTINGS	SURTARBRAND	SUSPENSIBLE
SUPPOSITORY	SURBASEMENT	SURMULLETS	SURTARBRANDS	SUSPENSION
SUPPRESSANT	SURBASEMENTS	SURNOMINAL	SURTURBRAND	SUSPENSIONS
SUPPRESSANTS	SURBEDDING	SURPASSABLE	SURTURBRANDS	SUSPENSIVE
SUPPRESSED	SURCEASING	SURPASSERS	SURVEILING	SUSPENSIVELY
SUPPRESSEDLY	SURCHARGED	SURPASSING	SURVEILLANCE	SUSPENSIVENESS
SUPPRESSER	SURCHARGEMENT	SURPASSINGLY	SURVEILLANCES	SUSPENSOID
SUPPRESSERS	SURCHARGEMENTS	SURPASSINGNESS	SURVEILLANT	SUSPENSOIDS
SUPPRESSES	SURCHARGER	SURPLUSAGE	SURVEILLANTS	SUSPENSORIA
SUPPRESSIBILITY	SURCHARGERS	SURPLUSAGES	SURVEILLED	SUSPENSORIAL
SUPPRESSIBLE	SURCHARGES	SURPLUSING	SURVEILLES	SUSPENSORIES
SUPPRESSING	SURCHARGING	SURPLUSSED	SURVEILLING	SUSPENSORIUM
SUPPRESSION	SURCINGLED	SURPLUSSES	SURVEYABLE	SUSPENSORS
SUPPRESSIONS	SURCINGLES	SURPLUSSING	SURVEYANCE	SUSPENSORY
SUPPRESSIVE	SURCINGLING	SURPRINTED	SURVEYANCES	SUSPERCOLLATE
SUPPRESSIVENESS	SURCULUSES	SURPRINTING	SURVEYINGS	SUSPERCOLLATED
SUPPRESSOR	SUREFOOTED	SURPRISALS	SURVEYORSHIP	SUSPERCOLLATES
SUPPRESSORS	SUREFOOTEDLY	SURPRISEDLY	SURVEYORSHIPS	SUSPERCOLLATING
SUPPURATED	SUREFOOTEDNESS	SURPRISERS	SURVIEWING	SUSPICIONAL
SUPPURATES	SURENESSES	SURPRISING	SURVIVABILITIES	SUSPICIONED
SUPPURATING	SURETYSHIP	SURPRISINGLY	SURVIVABILITY	SUSPICIONING
SUPPURATION	SURETYSHIPS	SURPRISINGNESS	SURVIVABLE	SUSPICIONLESS
SUPPURATIONS	SURFACELESS	SURPRISINGS	SURVIVALISM	SUSPICIONS

SUSPICIOUS	SWANKINESS	SWEETWATER	SWITCHYARDS	SYLLABICITY
SUSPICIOUSLY	SWANKINESSES	SWEETWATERS	SWITHERING	SYLLABIFICATION
SUSPICIOUSNESS	SWANNERIES	SWEETWOODS	SWIVELBLOCK	SYLLABIFIED
SUSPIRATION	SWANSDOWNS	SWEIRNESSES	SWIVELBLOCKS	SYLLABIFIES
SUSPIRATIONS	SWARAJISMS	SWELLFISHES	SWIVELLING	SYLLABIFYING
SUSPIRIOUS	SWARAJISTS	SWELLHEADED	SWOLLENNESS	SYLLABISED
SUSTAINABILITY	SWARTHIEST	SWELLHEADEDNESS	SWOLLENNESSES	SYLLABISES
SUSTAINABLE	SWARTHINESS .	SWELLHEADS	SWOONINGLY	SYLLABISING
SUSTAINABLY	SWARTHINESSES	SWELLINGLY	SWOOPSTAKE	SYLLABISMS
SUSTAINEDLY	SWARTHNESS	SWELTERING	SWORDBEARER	SYLLABIZED
SUSTAINERS	SWARTHNESSES	SWELTERINGLY	SWORDBEARERS	SYLLABIZES
SUSTAINING	SWARTNESSES	SWELTERINGS	SWORDBILLS	SYLLABIZING
SUSTAININGLY	SWASHBUCKLE	SWELTRIEST	SWORDCRAFT	SYLLABLING
SUSTAININGS	SWASHBUCKLED	SWEPTWINGS	SWORDCRAFTS	SYLLABOGRAM
SUSTAINMENT	SWASHBUCKLER	SWERVELESS	SWORDFERNS	SYLLABOGRAMS
SUSTAINMENTS	SWASHBUCKLERS	SWIFTNESSES	SWORDFISHES	SYLLABOGRAPHIES
SUSTENANCE	SWASHBUCKLES	SWIMFEEDER	SWORDPLAYER	SYLLABOGRAPHY
SUSTENANCES	SWASHBUCKLING	SWIMFEEDERS	SWORDPLAYERS	SYLLABUSES
SUSTENTACULA	SWASHWORKS	SWIMMERETS	SWORDPLAYS	SYLLEPTICAL
SUSTENTACULAR	SWATCHBOOK	SWIMMINGLY	SWORDPROOF	SYLLEPTICALLY
SUSTENTACULUM	SWATCHBOOKS	SWIMMINGNESS	SWORDSMANSHIP	SYLLOGISATION
SUSTENTATE	SWATHEABLE	SWIMMINGNESSES	SWORDSMANSHIPS	SYLLOGISATIONS
SUSTENTATED	SWATTERING	SWINDLINGS	SWORDSTICK	SYLLOGISED
SUSTENTATES	SWAYBACKED	SWINEHERDS	SWORDSTICKS	SYLLOGISER
SUSTENTATING	SWEARWORDS	SWINEHOODS	SWORDSWOMAN	SYLLOGISERS
SUSTENTATION	SWEATBANDS	SWINEPOXES	SWORDSWOMEN	SYLLOGISES
SUSTENTATIONS	SWEATBOXES	SWINESTONE	SWORDTAILS	SYLLOGISING
SUSTENTATIVE	SWEATERDRESS	SWINESTONES	SYBARITICAL	SYLLOGISMS
SUSTENTATOR	SWEATERDRESSES	SWINGBEATS	SYBARITICALLY	SYLLOGISTIC
SUSTENTATORS	SWEATINESS	SWINGBOATS	SYBARITISH	SYLLOGISTICAL
SUSTENTION	SWEATINESSES	SWINGEINGLY	SYBARITISM	SYLLOGISTICALLY
SUSTENTIONS	SWEATPANTS	SWINGINGER	SYBARITISMS	SYLLOGISTICS
SUSTENTIVE	SWEATSHIRT	SWINGINGEST	SYCOPHANCIES	SYLLOGISTS
SUSURRATED	SWEATSHIRTS	SWINGINGLY	SYCOPHANCY	SYLLOGIZATION
SUSURRATES	SWEATSHOPS	SWINGLETREE	SYCOPHANTIC	SYLLOGIZATIONS
SUSURRATING	SWEATSUITS	SWINGLETREES	SYCOPHANTICAL	SYLLOGIZED
SUSURRATION	SWEEPBACKS	SWINGLINGS	SYCOPHANTICALLY	SYLLOGIZER
SUSURRATIONS	SWEEPINGLY	SWINGOMETER	SYCOPHANTISE	SYLLOGIZERS
SUSURRUSES	SWEEPINGNESS	SWINGOMETERS	SYCOPHANTISED	SYLLOGIZES
SUTLERSHIP	SWEEPINGNESSES	SWINGTREES	SYCOPHANTISES	SYLLOGIZING
SUTLERSHIPS	SWEEPSTAKE	SWINISHNESS	SYCOPHANTISH	SYLPHIDINE
SUTTEEISMS	SWEEPSTAKES	SWINISHNESSES	SYCOPHANTISHLY	SYLVANITES
SUTTLETIES	SWEETBREAD	SWIRLINGLY	SYCOPHANTISING	SYLVESTRAL
SUTURATION	SWEETBREADS	SWISHINGLY	SYCOPHANTISM	SYLVESTRIAN
SUTURATIONS	SWEETBRIAR	SWITCHABLE	SYCOPHANTISMS	SYLVICULTURAL
SUZERAINTIES	SWEETBRIARS	SWITCHBACK	SYCOPHANTIZE	SYLVICULTURE
SUZERAINTY	SWEETBRIER	SWITCHBACKED	SYCOPHANTIZED	SYLVICULTURES
SVARABHAKTI	SWEETBRIERS	SWITCHBACKING	SYCOPHANTIZES	SYLVINITES
SVARABHAKTIS	SWEETCORNS	SWITCHBACKS	SYCOPHANTIZING	SYMBIONTIC
SVELTENESS	SWEETENERS	SWITCHBLADE	SYCOPHANTLIER	SYMBIONTICALLY
SVELTENESSES	SWEETENING	SWITCHBLADES	SYCOPHANTLIEST	SYMBIOTICAL
SWAGGERERS	SWEETENINGS	SWITCHBOARD	SYCOPHANTLY	SYMBIOTICALLY
SWAGGERING	SWEETFISHES	SWITCHBOARDS	SYCOPHANTRIES	SYMBOLICAL
SWAGGERINGLY	SWEETHEART	SWITCHEROO	SYCOPHANTRY	SYMBOLICALLY
SWAGGERINGS	SWEETHEARTED	SWITCHEROOS	SYCOPHANTS	SYMBOLICALNESS
SWAINISHNESS	SWEETHEARTING	SWITCHGEAR	SYLLABARIA	SYMBOLISATIONS
SWAINISHNESSES	SWEETHEARTINGS	SWITCHGEARS	SYLLABARIES	SYMBOLISED
SWALLOWABLE	SWEETHEARTS	SWITCHGIRL	SYLLABARIUM	SYMBOLISER
SWALLOWERS	SWEETIEWIFE	SWITCHGIRLS	SYLLABICAL	SYMBOLISERS
SWALLOWING	SWEETIEWIVES	SWITCHGRASS	SYLLABICALLY	SYMBOLISES
SWALLOWTAIL	SWEETISHLY	SWITCHGRASSES	SYLLABICATE	SYMBOLISING
SWALLOWTAILS	SWEETISHNESS	SWITCHIEST	SYLLABICATED	SYMBOLISMS
SWALLOWWORT	SWEETISHNESSES	SWITCHINGS	SYLLABICATES	SYMBOLISTIC
SWALLOWWORTS	SWEETMEATS	SWITCHLIKE	SYLLABICATING	SYMBOLISTICAL
SWAMPINESS	SWEETNESSES	SWITCHOVER	SYLLABICATION	SYMBOLISTICALLY
SWAMPINESSES	SWEETSHOPS	SWITCHOVERS	SYLLABICATIONS	SYMBOLISTS
SWAMPLANDS	SWEETVELDS	SWITCHYARD	SYLLABICITIES	

SYMBOLIZATION
SYMBOLIZATIONS
SYMBOLIZED
SYMBOLIZER
SYMBOLIZERS
SYMBOLIZES
SYMBOLIZING
SYMBOLLING
SYMBOLOGICAL
SYMBOLOGIES
SYMBOLOGIST
SYMBOLOGISTS
SYMBOLOGRAPHIES
SYMBOLOGRAPHY
SYMBOLOLATRIES
SYMBOLOLATRY
SYMBOLOLOGIES
SYMBOLOLOGY
SYMMETALISM
SYMMETALISMS
SYMMETALLIC
SYMMETALLISM
SYMMETALLISMS
SYMMETRIAN
SYMMETRIANS
SYMMETRICAL
SYMMETRICALLY
SYMMETRICALNESS
SYMMETRIES
SYMMETRISATION
SYMMETRISATIONS
SYMMETRISE
SYMMETRISED
SYMMETRISES
SYMMETRISING
SYMMETRIZATION
SYMMETRIZATIONS
SYMMETRIZE
SYMMETRIZED
SYMMETRIZES
SYMMETRIZING
SYMMETROPHOBIA
SYMMETROPHOBIAS
SYMPATHECTOMIES
SYMPATHECTOMY
SYMPATHETIC
SYMPATHETICAL
SYMPATHETICALLY
SYMPATHETICS
SYMPATHIES
SYMPATHINS
SYMPATHIQUE
SYMPATHISE
SYMPATHISED
SYMPATHISER
SYMPATHISERS
SYMPATHISES
SYMPATHISING
SYMPATHIZE
SYMPATHIZED
SYMPATHIZER
SYMPATHIZERS
SYMPATHIZES
SYMPATHIZING
SYMPATHOLYTIC
SYMPATHOLYTICS
SYMPATHOMIMETIC

SYMPATRICALLY
SYMPATRIES
SYMPETALIES
SYMPETALOUS
SYMPHILIES
SYMPHILISM
SYMPHILISMS
SYMPHILOUS
SYMPHONICALLY
SYMPHONIES
SYMPHONION
SYMPHONIONS
SYMPHONIOUS
SYMPHONIOUSLY
SYMPHONIST
SYMPHONISTS
SYMPHYLOUS
SYMPHYSEAL
SYMPHYSEOTOMIES
SYMPHYSEOTOMY
SYMPHYSIAL
SYMPHYSIOTOMIES
SYMPHYSIOTOMY
SYMPHYSTIC
SYMPIESOMETER
SYMPIESOMETERS
SYMPLASTIC
SYMPODIALLY
SYMPOSIACS
SYMPOSIARCH
SYMPOSIARCHS
SYMPOSIAST
SYMPOSIASTS
SYMPOSIUMS
SYMPTOMATIC
SYMPTOMATICAL
SYMPTOMATICALLY
SYMPTOMATISE
SYMPTOMATISED
SYMPTOMATISES
SYMPTOMATISING
SYMPTOMATIZE
SYMPTOMATIZED
SYMPTOMATIZES
SYMPTOMATIZING
SYMPTOMATOLOGIC
SYMPTOMATOLOGY
SYMPTOMLESS
SYMPTOMOLOGICAL
SYMPTOMOLOGIES
SYMPTOMOLOGY
SYNADELPHITE
SYNADELPHITES
SYNAERESES
SYNAERESIS
SYNAESTHESES
SYNAESTHESIA
SYNAESTHESIAS
SYNAESTHESIS
SYNAESTHETIC
SYNAGOGICAL
SYNAGOGUES
SYNALEPHAS
SYNALLAGMATIC
SYNALOEPHA
SYNALOEPHAS
SYNANDRIUM

SYNANDROUS
SYNANTHEROUS
SYNANTHESES
SYNANTHESIS
SYNANTHETIC
SYNANTHIES
SYNANTHOUS
SYNAPHEIAS
SYNAPOSEMATIC
SYNAPOSEMATISM
SYNAPOSEMATISMS
SYNAPTASES
SYNAPTICAL
SYNAPTICALLY
SYNAPTOSOMAL
SYNAPTOSOME
SYNAPTOSOMES
SYNARCHIES
SYNARTHRODIAL
SYNARTHRODIALLY
SYNARTHROSES
SYNARTHROSIS
SYNASTRIES
SYNAXARION
SYNBIOTICS
SYNCARPIES
SYNCARPOUS
SYNCHONDROSES
SYNCHONDROSIS
SYNCHORESES
SYNCHORESIS
SYNCHROFLASH
SYNCHROFLASHES
SYNCHROMESH
SYNCHROMESHES
SYNCHRONAL
SYNCHRONEITIES
SYNCHRONEITY
SYNCHRONIC
SYNCHRONICAL
SYNCHRONICALLY
SYNCHRONICITIES
SYNCHRONICITY
SYNCHRONIES
SYNCHRONISATION
SYNCHRONISE
SYNCHRONISED
SYNCHRONISER
SYNCHRONISERS
SYNCHRONISES
SYNCHRONISING
SYNCHRONISM
SYNCHRONISMS
SYNCHRONISTIC
SYNCHRONISTICAL
SYNCHRONIZATION
SYNCHRONIZE
SYNCHRONIZED
SYNCHRONIZER
SYNCHRONIZERS
SYNCHRONIZES
SYNCHRONIZING
SYNCHRONOLOGIES
SYNCHRONOLOGY
SYNCHRONOSCOPE
SYNCHRONOSCOPES
SYNCHRONOUS

SYNCHRONOUSLY
SYNCHRONOUSNESS
SYNCHROSCOPE
SYNCHROSCOPES
SYNCHROTRON
SYNCHROTRONS
SYNCLASTIC
SYNCLINALS
SYNCLINORIA
SYNCLINORIUM
SYNCOPATED
SYNCOPATES
SYNCOPATING
SYNCOPATION
SYNCOPATIONS
SYNCOPATIVE
SYNCOPATOR
SYNCOPATORS
SYNCRETISATION
SYNCRETISATIONS
SYNCRETISE
SYNCRETISED
SYNCRETISES
SYNCRETISING
SYNCRETISM
SYNCRETISMS
SYNCRETIST
SYNCRETISTIC
SYNCRETISTS
SYNCRETIZATION
SYNCRETIZATIONS
SYNCRETIZE
SYNCRETIZED
SYNCRETIZES
SYNCRETIZING
SYNDACTYLIES
SYNDACTYLISM
SYNDACTYLISMS
SYNDACTYLOUS
SYNDACTYLS
SYNDACTYLY
SYNDERESES
SYNDERESIS
SYNDESISES
SYNDESMOSES
SYNDESMOSIS
SYNDESMOTIC
SYNDETICAL
SYNDETICALLY
SYNDICALISM
SYNDICALISMS
SYNDICALIST
SYNDICALISTIC
SYNDICALISTS
SYNDICATED
SYNDICATES
SYNDICATING
SYNDICATION
SYNDICATIONS
SYNDICATOR
SYNDICATORS
SYNDICSHIP
SYNDICSHIPS
SYNDIOTACTIC
SYNDYASMIAN
SYNECDOCHE
SYNECDOCHES

SYNECDOCHIC
SYNECDOCHICAL
SYNECDOCHICALLY
SYNECDOCHISM
SYNECDOCHISMS
SYNECOLOGIC
SYNECOLOGICAL
SYNECOLOGICALLY
SYNECOLOGIES
SYNECOLOGIST
SYNECOLOGISTS
SYNECOLOGY
SYNECPHONESES
SYNECPHONESIS
SYNECTICALLY
SYNEIDESES
SYNEIDESIS
SYNERGETIC
SYNERGETICALLY
SYNERGICALLY
SYNERGISED
SYNERGISES
SYNERGISING
SYNERGISMS
SYNERGISTIC
SYNERGISTICALLY
SYNERGISTS
SYNERGIZED
SYNERGIZES
SYNERGIZING
SYNESTHESIA
SYNESTHESIAS
SYNESTHETIC
SYNGENESES
SYNGENESIOUS
SYNGENESIS
SYNGENETIC
SYNGNATHOUS
SYNKARYONIC
SYNKARYONS
SYNODICALLY
SYNOECETES
SYNOECIOSES
SYNOECIOSIS
SYNOECIOUS
SYNOECISED
SYNOECISES
SYNOECISING
SYNOECISMS
SYNOECIZED
SYNOECIZES
SYNOECIZING
SYNOECOLOGIES
SYNOECOLOGY
SYNOEKETES
SYNONYMATIC
SYNONYMICAL
SYNONYMICON
SYNONYMICONS
SYNONYMIES
SYNONYMISE
SYNONYMISED
SYNONYMISES
SYNONYMISING
SYNONYMIST
SYNONYMISTS
SYNONYMITIES

SYNONYMITY
SYNONYMIZE
SYNONYMIZED
SYNONYMIZES
SYNONYMIZING
SYNONYMOUS
SYNONYMOUSLY
SYNONYMOUSNESS
SYNOPSISED
SYNOPSISES
SYNOPSISING
SYNOPSIZED
SYNOPSIZES
SYNOPSIZING
SYNOPTICAL
SYNOPTICALLY
SYNOPTISTIC
SYNOPTISTS
SYNOSTOSES
SYNOSTOSIS
SYNOVIALLY
SYNOVITISES
SYNSEPALOUS
SYNTACTICAL
SYNTACTICALLY
SYNTACTICS
SYNTAGMATA
SYNTAGMATIC
SYNTAGMATITE
SYNTAGMATITES
SYNTECTICAL
SYNTENOSES
SYNTENOSIS
SYNTERESES

SYNTERESIS
SYNTEXISES
SYNTHESISATION
SYNTHESISATIONS
SYNTHESISE
SYNTHESISED
SYNTHESISER
SYNTHESISERS
SYNTHESISES
SYNTHESISING
SYNTHESIST
SYNTHESISTS
SYNTHESIZATION
SYNTHESIZATIONS
SYNTHESIZE
SYNTHESIZED
SYNTHESIZER
SYNTHESIZERS
SYNTHESIZES
SYNTHESIZING
SYNTHESPIAN
SYNTHESPIANS
SYNTHETASE
SYNTHETASES
SYNTHETICAL
SYNTHETICALLY
SYNTHETICISM
SYNTHETICISMS
SYNTHETICS
SYNTHETISATION
SYNTHETISATIONS
SYNTHETISE
SYNTHETISED
SYNTHETISER

SYNTHETISERS
SYNTHETISES
SYNTHETISING
SYNTHETISM
SYNTHETISMS
SYNTHETIST
SYNTHETISTS
SYNTHETIZATION
SYNTHETIZATIONS
SYNTHETIZE
SYNTHETIZED
SYNTHETIZER
SYNTHETIZERS
SYNTHETIZES
SYNTHETIZING
SYNTHRONUS
SYNTONICALLY
SYNTONISED
SYNTONISES
SYNTONISING
SYNTONIZED
SYNTONIZES
SYNTONIZING
SYPHERINGS
SYPHILISATION
SYPHILISATIONS
SYPHILISED
SYPHILISES
SYPHILISING
SYPHILITIC
SYPHILITICALLY
SYPHILITICS
SYPHILIZATION
SYPHILIZATIONS

SYPHILIZED
SYPHILIZES
SYPHILIZING
SYPHILOLOGIES
SYPHILOLOGIST
SYPHILOLOGISTS
SYPHILOLOGY
SYPHILOMAS
SYPHILOMATA
SYPHILOPHOBIA
SYPHILOPHOBIAS
SYPHONAGES
SYRINGITIS
SYRINGITISES
SYRINGOMYELIA
SYRINGOMYELIAS
SYRINGOMYELIC
SYRINGOTOMIES
SYRINGOTOMY
SYSSARCOSES
SYSSARCOSIS
SYSSARCOTIC
SYSTEMATIC
SYSTEMATICAL
SYSTEMATICALLY
SYSTEMATICIAN
SYSTEMATICIANS
SYSTEMATICNESS
SYSTEMATICS
SYSTEMATISATION
SYSTEMATISE
SYSTEMATISED
SYSTEMATISER
SYSTEMATISERS

SYSTEMATISES
SYSTEMATISING
SYSTEMATISM
SYSTEMATISMS
SYSTEMATIST
SYSTEMATISTS
SYSTEMATIZATION
SYSTEMATIZE
SYSTEMATIZED
SYSTEMATIZER
SYSTEMATIZERS
SYSTEMATIZES
SYSTEMATIZING
SYSTEMATOLOGIES
SYSTEMATOLOGY
SYSTEMICALLY
SYSTEMISATION
SYSTEMISATIONS
SYSTEMISED
SYSTEMISER
SYSTEMISERS
SYSTEMISES
SYSTEMISING
SYSTEMIZATION
SYSTEMIZATIONS
SYSTEMIZED
SYSTEMIZER
SYSTEMIZERS
SYSTEMIZES
SYSTEMIZING
SYSTEMLESS
SYZYGETICALLY

T

TABASHEERS
TABBOULEHS
TABBYHOODS
TABEFACTION
TABEFACTIONS
TABELLIONS
TABERNACLE
TABERNACLED
TABERNACLES
TABERNACLING
TABERNACULAR
TABESCENCE
TABESCENCES
TABLANETTE
TABLANETTES
TABLATURES
TABLECLOTH
TABLECLOTHS
TABLELANDS
TABLEMATES
TABLESPOON
TABLESPOONFUL
TABLESPOONFULS
TABLESPOONS
TABLESPOONSFUL
TABLETOPPED
TABLETTING
TABLEWARES
TABLOIDIER
TABLOIDIEST
TABOGGANED
TABOGGANING
TABOPARESES
TABOPARESIS
TABULARISATION
TABULARISATIONS
TABULARISE
TABULARISED
TABULARISES
TABULARISING
TABULARIZATION
TABULARIZATIONS
TABULARIZE
TABULARIZED
TABULARIZES
TABULARIZING
TABULATING
TABULATION
TABULATIONS
TABULATORS
TABULATORY
TACAMAHACS
TACHEOMETER
TACHEOMETERS

TACHEOMETRIC
TACHEOMETRICAL
TACHEOMETRIES
TACHEOMETRY
TACHISTOSCOPE
TACHISTOSCOPES
TACHISTOSCOPIC
TACHOGRAMS
TACHOGRAPH
TACHOGRAPHS
TACHOMETER
TACHOMETERS
TACHOMETRIC
TACHOMETRICAL
TACHOMETRICALLY
TACHOMETRIES
TACHOMETRY
TACHYARRHYTHMIA
TACHYCARDIA
TACHYCARDIAC
TACHYCARDIAS
TACHYGRAPH
TACHYGRAPHER
TACHYGRAPHERS
TACHYGRAPHIC
TACHYGRAPHICAL
TACHYGRAPHIES
TACHYGRAPHIST
TACHYGRAPHISTS
TACHYGRAPHS
TACHYGRAPHY
TACHYLITES
TACHYLITIC
TACHYLYTES
TACHYLYTIC
TACHYMETER
TACHYMETERS
TACHYMETRIC
TACHYMETRICAL
TACHYMETRICALLY
TACHYMETRIES
TACHYMETRY
TACHYPHASIA
TACHYPHASIAS
TACHYPHRASIA
TACHYPHRASIAS
TACHYPHYLAXES
TACHYPHYLAXIS
TACHYPNEAS
TACHYPNOEA
TACHYPNOEAS
TACITNESSES
TACITURNITIES
TACITURNITY

TACITURNLY
TACKBOARDS
TACKETIEST
TACKIFIERS
TACKIFYING
TACKINESSES
TACMAHACKS
TACTFULNESS
TACTFULNESSES
TACTICALLY
TACTICIANS
TACTICITIES
TACTILISTS
TACTILITIES
TACTLESSLY
TACTLESSNESS
TACTLESSNESSES
TACTUALITIES
TACTUALITY
TADALAFILS
TAEKWONDOS
TAENIACIDE
TAENIACIDES
TAENIAFUGE
TAENIAFUGES
TAFFETASES
TAFFETIEST
TAFFETISED
TAFFETIZED
TAGLIARINI
TAGLIARINIS
TAGLIATELLE
TAGLIATELLES
TAHSILDARS
TAIKONAUTS
TAILBOARDS
TAILCOATED
TAILENDERS
TAILGATERS
TAILGATING
TAILGATINGS
TAILHOPPING
TAILHOPPINGS
TAILLESSLY
TAILLESSNESS
TAILLESSNESSES
TAILLIGHTS
TAILORBIRD
TAILORBIRDS
TAILORESSES
TAILORINGS
TAILORMADE
TAILORMAKE
TAILORMAKES

TAILORMAKING
TAILPIECES
TAILPIPING
TAILPLANES
TAILSLIDES
TAILSPINNED
TAILSPINNING
TAILSTOCKS
TAILWATERS
TAILWHEELS
TAINTLESSLY
TAKINGNESS
TAKINGNESSES
TALBOTYPES
TALEBEARER
TALEBEARERS
TALEBEARING
TALEBEARINGS
TALEGALLAS
TALENTLESS
TALETELLER
TALETELLERS
TALETELLING
TALETELLINGS
TALISMANIC
TALISMANICAL
TALISMANICALLY
TALKABILITIES
TALKABILITY
TALKATHONS
TALKATIVELY
TALKATIVENESS
TALKATIVENESSES
TALKINESSES
TALLGRASSES
TALLIATING
TALLNESSES
TALLOWIEST
TALLYHOING
TALLYSHOPS
TALLYWOMAN
TALLYWOMEN
TALMUDISMS
TAMABILITIES
TAMABILITY
TAMABLENESS
TAMABLENESSES
TAMARILLOS
TAMBOURERS
TAMBOURINE
TAMBOURINES
TAMBOURING
TAMBOURINIST
TAMBOURINISTS

TAMBOURINS
TAMEABILITIES
TAMEABILITY
TAMEABLENESS
TAMEABLENESSES
TAMELESSNESS
TAMELESSNESSES
TAMENESSES
TAMOXIFENS
TAMPERINGS
TAMPERPROOF
TAMPONADES
TAMPONAGES
TANDEMWISE
TANGENCIES
TANGENTALLY
TANGENTIAL
TANGENTIALITIES
TANGENTIALITY
TANGENTIALLY
TANGERINES
TANGHININS
TANGIBILITIES
TANGIBILITY
TANGIBLENESS
TANGIBLENESSES
TANGINESSES
TANGLEFOOT
TANGLEFOOTS
TANGLEMENT
TANGLEMENTS
TANGLESOME
TANGLEWEED
TANGLEWEEDS
TANGLINGLY
TANISTRIES
TANKBUSTER
TANKBUSTERS
TANKBUSTING
TANKBUSTINGS
TANOREXICS
TANTALATES
TANTALISATION
TANTALISATIONS
TANTALISED
TANTALISER
TANTALISERS
TANTALISES
TANTALISING
TANTALISINGLY
TANTALISINGS
TANTALISMS
TANTALITES
TANTALIZATION

TANTALIZATIONS	TARDIGRADE	TASTELESSNESSES	TAWNINESSES	TEATASTERS
TANTALIZED	TARDIGRADES	TASTEMAKER	TAXABILITIES	TEAZELLING
TANTALIZER	TARDINESSES	TASTEMAKERS	TAXABILITY	TECHINESSES
TANTALIZERS	TARGETABLE	TASTINESSES	TAXABLENESS	TECHNETIUM
TANTALIZES	TARGETEERS	TATAIIASHES	TAXARLENESSES	TECHNETIUMS
TANTALIZING	TARGETINGS	TATPURUSHA	TAXAMETERS	TECHNETRONIC
TANTALIZINGLY	TARGETITIS	TATPURUSHAS	TAXATIONAL	TECHNICALISE
TANTALIZINGS	TARGETITISES	TATTERDEMALION	TAXIDERMAL	TECHNICALISED
TANTALUSES	TARGETLESS	TATTERDEMALIONS	TAXIDERMIC	TECHNICALISES
TANTAMOUNT	TARIFFICATION	TATTERDEMALLION	TAXIDERMIES	TECHNICALISING
TANTARARAS	TARIFFICATIONS	TATTERIEST	TAXIDERMISE	TECHNICALITIES
TANZANITES	TARIFFLESS	TATTERSALL	TAXIDERMISED	TECHNICALITY
TAPERINGLY	TARMACADAM	TATTERSALLS	TAXIDERMISES	TECHNICALIZE
TAPERNESSES	TARMACADAMS	TATTINESSES	TAXIDERMISING	TECHNICALIZED
TAPERSTICK	TARMACKING	TATTLETALE	TAXIDERMIST	TECHNICALIZES
TAPERSTICKS	TARNATIONS	TATTLETALED	TAXIDERMISTS	TECHNICALIZING
TAPESCRIPT	TARNISHABLE	TATTLETALES	TAXIDERMIZE	TECHNICALLY
TAPESCRIPTS	TARNISHERS	TATTLETALING	TAXIDERMIZED	TECHNICALNESS
TAPESTRIED	TARNISHING	TATTLINGLY	TAXIDERMIZES	TECHNICALNESSES
TAPESTRIES	TARPAULING	TATTOOISTS	TAXIDERMIZING	TECHNICALS
TAPESTRYING	TARPAULINGS	TAUNTINGLY	TAXIMETERS	TECHNICIAN
TAPHEPHOBIA	TARPAULINS	TAUROBOLIA	TAXIPLANES	TECHNICIANS
TAPHEPHOBIAS	TARRADIDDLE	TAUROBOLIUM	TAXONOMERS	TECHNICISE
TAPHEPHOBIC	TARRADIDDLES	TAUROMACHIAN	TAXONOMICAL	TECHNICISED
TAPHONOMIC	TARRIANCES	TAUROMACHIES	TAXONOMICALLY	TECHNICISES
TAPHONOMICAL	TARRINESSES	TAUROMACHY	TAXONOMIES	TECHNICISING
TAPHONOMIES	TARSALGIAS	TAUROMORPHOUS	TAXONOMIST	TECHNICISM
TAPHONOMIST	TARSOMETATARSAL	TAUTNESSES	TAXONOMISTS	TECHNICISMS
TAPHONOMISTS	TARSOMETATARSI	TAUTOCHRONE	TAXPAYINGS	TECHNICIST
TAPHOPHOBIA	TARSOMETATARSUS	TAUTOCHRONES	TAYASSUIDS	TECHNICISTS
TAPHOPHOBIAS	TARTANALIA	TAUTOCHRONISM	TAYBERRIES	TECHNICIZE
TAPHROGENESES	TARTANALIAS	TAUTOCHRONISMS	TCHOTCHKES	TECHNICIZED
TAPHROGENESIS	TARTANRIES	TAUTOCHRONOUS	TCHOUKBALL	TECHNICIZES
TAPOTEMENT	TARTAREOUS	TAUTOLOGIC	TCHOUKBALLS	TECHNICIZING
TAPOTEMENTS	TARTARISATION	TAUTOLOGICAL	TEABERRIES	TECHNICOLOUR
TAPSALTEERIE	TARTARISATIONS	TAUTOLOGICALLY	TEACHABILITIES	TECHNICOLOURED
TAPSALTEERIES	TARTARISED	TAUTOLOGIES	TEACHABILITY	TECHNIKONS
TAPSIETEERIE	TARTARISES	TAUTOLOGISE	TEACHABLENESS	TECHNIQUES
TAPSIETEERIES	TARTARISING	TAUTOLOGISED	TEACHABLENESSES	TECHNOBABBLE
TAPSTRESSES	TARTARIZATION	TAUTOLOGISES	TEACHERLESS	TECHNOBABBLES
TARABISHES	TARTARIZATIONS	TAUTOLOGISING	TEACHERLIER	TECHNOCRACIES
TARADIDDLE	TARTARIZED	TAUTOLOGISM	TEACHERLIEST	TECHNOCRACY
TARADIDDLES	TARTARIZES	TAUTOLOGISMS	TEACHERSHIP	TECHNOCRAT
TARAMASALATA	TARTARIZING	TAUTOLOGIST	TEACHERSHIPS	TECHNOCRATIC
TARAMASALATAS	TARTINESSES	TAUTOLOGISTS	TEACUPFULS	TECHNOCRATS
TARANTARAED	TARTNESSES	TAUTOLOGIZE	TEACUPSFUL	TECHNOFEAR
TARANTARAING	TARTRAZINE	TAUTOLOGIZED	TEAKETTLES	TECHNOFEARS
TARANTARAS	TARTRAZINES	TAUTOLOGIZES	TEARFULNESS	TECHNOGRAPHIES
TARANTASES	TASEOMETER	TAUTOLOGIZING	TEARFULNESSES	TECHNOGRAPHY
TARANTASSES	TASEOMETERS	TAUTOLOGOUS	TEARGASSED	TECHNOJUNKIE
TARANTELLA	TASIMETERS	TAUTOLOGOUSLY	TEARGASSES	TECHNOJUNKIES
TARANTELLAS	TASIMETRIC	TAUTOMERIC	TEARGASSING	TECHNOLOGIC
TARANTISMS	TASIMETRIES	TAUTOMERISM	TEARINESSES	TECHNOLOGICAL
TARANTISTS	TASKMASTER	TAUTOMERISMS	TEARJERKER	TECHNOLOGICALLY
TARANTULAE	TASKMASTERS	TAUTOMETRIC	TEARJERKERS	TECHNOLOGIES
TARANTULAS	TASKMISTRESS	TAUTOMETRICAL	TEARLESSLY	TECHNOLOGISE
TARATANTARA	TASKMISTRESSES	TAUTONYMIC	TEARSHEETS	TECHNOLOGISED
TARATANTARAED	TASSELIEST	TAUTONYMIES	TEARSTAINED	TECHNOLOGISES
TARATANTARAING	TASSELLIER	TAUTONYMOUS	TEARSTAINS	TECHNOLOGISING
TARATANTARAS	TASSELLIEST	TAUTOPHONIC	TEARSTRIPS	TECHNOLOGIST
TARAXACUMS	TASSELLING	TAUTOPHONICAL	TEASELINGS	TECHNOLOGISTS
TARBOGGINED	TASSELLINGS	TAUTOPHONIES	TEASELLERS	TECHNOLOGIZE
TARBOGGINING	TASTEFULLY	TAUTOPHONY	TEASELLING	TECHNOLOGIZED
TARBOGGINS	TASTEFULNESS	TAWDRINESS	TEASELLINGS	TECHNOLOGIZES
TARBOOSHES	TASTEFULNESSES	TAWDRINESSES	TEASPOONFUL	TECHNOLOGIZING
TARBOUCHES	TASTELESSLY	TAWHEOWHEO	TEASPOONFULS	TECHNOLOGY
TARBOUSHES	TASTELESSNESS	TAWHEOWHEOS	TEASPOONSFUL	TECHNOMANIA

TECHNOMANIAC
TECHNOMANIACS
TECHNOMANIAS
TECHNOMUSIC
TECHNOMUSICS
TECHNOPHILE
TECHNOPHILES
TECHNOPHILIA
TECHNOPHILIAS
TECHNOPHOBE
TECHNOPHOBES
TECHNOPHOBIA
TECHNOPHOBIAS
TECHNOPHOBIC
TECHNOPHOBICS
TECHNOPOLE
TECHNOPOLES
TECHNOPOLIS
TECHNOPOLISES
TECHNOPOLITAN
TECHNOPOLITANS
TECHNOPOPS
TECHNOSPEAK
TECHNOSPEAKS
TECHNOSTRESS
TECHNOSTRESSES
TECHNOSTRUCTURE
TECTIBRANCH
TECTIBRANCHIATE
TECTIBRANCHS
TECTONICALLY
TECTONISMS
TECTRICIAL
TEDIOSITIES
TEDIOUSNESS
TEDIOUSNESSES
TEDIOUSOME
TEEMINGNESS
TEEMINGNESSES
TEENTSIEST
TEENYBOPPER
TEENYBOPPERS
TEETERBOARD
TEETERBOARDS
TEETHRIDGE
TEETHRIDGES
TEETOTALED
TEETOTALER
TEETOTALERS
TEETOTALING
TEETOTALISM
TEETOTALISMS
TEETOTALIST
TEETOTALISTS
TEETOTALLED
TEETOTALLER
TEETOTALLERS
TEETOTALLING
TEETOTALLY
TEGUMENTAL
TEGUMENTARY
TEHSILDARS
TEICHOPSIA
TEICHOPSIAS
TEINOSCOPE
TEINOSCOPES
TEKNONYMIES

TEKNONYMOUS
TELAESTHESIA
TELAESTHESIAS
TELAESTHETIC
TELANGIECTASES
TELANGIECTASIA
TELANGIECTASIAS
TELANGIECTASIS
TELANGIECTATIC
TELAUTOGRAPHIC
TELAUTOGRAPHIES
TELAUTOGRAPHY
TELEARCHICS
TELEBANKING
TELEBANKINGS
TELEBRIDGE
TELEBRIDGES
TELECAMERA
TELECAMERAS
TELECASTED
TELECASTER
TELECASTERS
TELECASTING
TELECHIRIC
TELECOMMAND
TELECOMMANDS
TELECOMMUTE
TELECOMMUTED
TELECOMMUTER
TELECOMMUTERS
TELECOMMUTES
TELECOMMUTING
TELECOMMUTINGS
TELECONFERENCE
TELECONFERENCES
TELECONNECTION
TELECONNECTIONS
TELECONTROL
TELECONTROLS
TELECONVERTER
TELECONVERTERS
TELECOPIES
TELECOTTAGE
TELECOTTAGES
TELECOTTAGING
TELECOTTAGINGS
TELECOURSE
TELECOURSES
TELEDILDONICS
TELEFACSIMILE
TELEFACSIMILES
TELEFAXING
TELEFERIQUE
TELEFERIQUES
TELEGENICALLY
TELEGNOSES
TELEGNOSIS
TELEGNOSTIC
TELEGONIES
TELEGONOUS
TELEGRAMMATIC
TELEGRAMMED
TELEGRAMMIC
TELEGRAMMING
TELEGRAPHED
TELEGRAPHER
TELEGRAPHERS

TELEGRAPHESE
TELEGRAPHESES
TELEGRAPHIC
TELEGRAPHICALLY
TELEGRAPHIES
TELEGRAPHING
TELEGRAPHIST
TELEGRAPHISTS
TELEGRAPHS
TELEGRAPHY
TELEHEALTH
TELEHEALTHS
TELEJOURNALISM
TELEJOURNALISMS
TELEJOURNALIST
TELEJOURNALISTS
TELEKINESES
TELEKINESIS
TELEKINETIC
TELEKINETICALLY
TELEMARKED
TELEMARKER
TELEMARKETER
TELEMARKETERS
TELEMARKETING
TELEMARKETINGS
TELEMARKING
TELEMATICS
TELEMEDICINE
TELEMEDICINES
TELEMEETING
TELEMEETINGS
TELEMESSAGE
TELEMESSAGES
TELEMETERED
TELEMETERING
TELEMETERS
TELEMETRIC
TELEMETRICAL
TELEMETRICALLY
TELEMETRIES
TELENCEPHALA
TELENCEPHALIC
TELENCEPHALON
TELENCEPHALONS
TELEOLOGIC
TELEOLOGICAL
TELEOLOGICALLY
TELEOLOGIES
TELEOLOGISM
TELEOLOGISMS
TELEOLOGIST
TELEOLOGISTS
TELEONOMIC
TELEONOMIES
TELEOSAURIAN
TELEOSAURIANS
TELEOSAURS
TELEOSTEAN
TELEOSTEANS
TELEOSTOME
TELEOSTOMES
TELEOSTOMOUS
TELEPATHED
TELEPATHIC
TELEPATHICALLY
TELEPATHIES
TELEPATHING

TELEPATHISE
TELEPATHISED
TELEPATHISES
TELEPATHISING
TELEPATHIST
TELEPATHISTS
TELEPATHIZE
TELEPATHIZED
TELEPATHIZES
TELEPATHIZING
TELEPHEMES
TELEPHERIQUE
TELEPHERIQUES
TELEPHONED
TELEPHONER
TELEPHONERS
TELEPHONES
TELEPHONIC
TELEPHONICALLY
TELEPHONIES
TELEPHONING
TELEPHONIST
TELEPHONISTS
TELEPHONITIS
TELEPHONITISES
TELEPHOTOGRAPH
TELEPHOTOGRAPHS
TELEPHOTOGRAPHY
TELEPHOTOS
TELEPOINTS
TELEPORTATION
TELEPORTATIONS
TELEPORTED
TELEPORTING
TELEPRESENCE
TELEPRESENCES
TELEPRINTED
TELEPRINTER
TELEPRINTERS
TELEPRINTING
TELEPRINTS
TELEPROCESSING
TELEPROCESSINGS
TELERECORD
TELERECORDED
TELERECORDING
TELERECORDINGS
TELERECORDS
TELERGICALLY
TELEROBOTS
TELESCIENCE
TELESCIENCES
TELESCOPED
TELESCOPES
TELESCOPIC
TELESCOPICAL
TELESCOPICALLY
TELESCOPIES
TELESCOPIFORM
TELESCOPING
TELESCOPIST
TELESCOPISTS
TELESCREEN
TELESCREENS
TELESELLING
TELESELLINGS
TELESERVICES

TELESHOPPED
TELESHOPPING
TELESHOPPINGS
TELESMATIC
TELESMATICAL
TELESMATICALLY
TELESOFTWARE
TELESOFTWARES
TELESTEREOSCOPE
TELESTHESIA
TELESTHESIAS
TELESTHETIC
TELESTICHS
TELESURGERIES
TELESURGERY
TELETYPESETTING
TELETYPEWRITER
TELETYPEWRITERS
TELETYPING
TELEUTOSPORE
TELEUTOSPORES
TELEUTOSPORIC
TELEVANGELICAL
TELEVANGELISM
TELEVANGELISMS
TELEVANGELIST
TELEVANGELISTS
TELEVERITE
TELEVERITES
TELEVIEWED
TELEVIEWER
TELEVIEWERS
TELEVIEWING
TELEVIEWINGS
TELEVISERS
TELEVISING
TELEVISION
TELEVISIONAL
TELEVISIONALLY
TELEVISIONARY
TELEVISIONS
TELEVISORS
TELEVISUAL
TELEVISUALLY
TELEWORKED
TELEWORKER
TELEWORKERS
TELEWORKING
TELEWORKINGS
TELEWRITER
TELEWRITERS
TELFERAGES
TELICITIES
TELIOSPORE
TELIOSPORES
TELLERSHIP
TELLERSHIPS
TELLURATES
TELLURETTED
TELLURIANS
TELLURIDES
TELLURIONS
TELLURISED
TELLURISES
TELLURISING
TELLURITES
TELLURIUMS

TELLURIZED	TEMPORALIZES	TENDENTIOUS	TENNESSINES	TERATOGENICIST
TELLURIZES	TEMPORALIZING	TENDENTIOUSLY	TENORRHAPHIES	TERATOGENICISTS
TELLURIZING	TEMPORALLY	TENDENTIOUSNESS	TENORRHAPHY	TERATOGENICITY
TELLUROMETER	TEMPORALNESS	TENDERABLE	TENOSYNOVITIS	TERATOGENIES
TELLUROMETERS	TEMPORALNESSES	TENDERFEET	TENOSYNOVITISES	TERATOGENS
TELNETTING	TEMPORALTIES	TENDERFOOT	TENOTOMIES	TERATOGENY
TELOCENTRIC	TEMPORALTY	TENDERFOOTS	TENOTOMIST	TERATOLOGIC
TELOCENTRICS	TEMPORANEOUS	TENDERHEARTED	TENOTOMISTS	TERATOLOGICAL
TELOMERASE	TEMPORARIES	TENDERHEARTEDLY	TENOVAGINITIS	TERATOLOGIES
TELOMERASES	TEMPORARILY	TENDERINGS	TENOVAGINITISES	TERATOLOGIST
TELOMERISATION	TEMPORARINESS	TENDERISATION	TENPINNERS	TERATOLOGISTS
TELOMERISATIONS	TEMPORARINESSES	TENDERISATIONS	TENPOUNDER	TERATOLOGY
TELOMERIZATION	TEMPORISATION	TENDERISED	TENPOUNDERS	TERATOMATA
TELOMERIZATIONS	TEMPORISATIONS	TENDERISER	TENSENESSES	TERATOMATOUS
TELOPHASES	TEMPORISED	TENDERISERS	TENSIBILITIES	TERATOPHOBIA
TELOPHASIC	TEMPORISER	TENDERISES	TENSIBILITY	TERATOPHOBIAS
TELPHERAGE	TEMPORISERS	TENDERISING	TENSIBLENESS	TERCENTENARIES
TELPHERAGES	TEMPORISES	TENDERIZATION	TENSIBLENESSES	TERCENTENARY
TELPHERING	TEMPORISING	TENDERIZATIONS	TENSILENESS	TERCENTENNIAL
TELPHERLINE	TEMPORISINGLY	TENDERIZED	TENSILENESSES	TERCENTENNIALS
TELPHERLINES	TEMPORISINGS	TENDERIZER	TENSILITIES	TEREBINTHINE
TELPHERMAN	TEMPORIZATION	TENDERIZERS	TENSIMETER	TEREBINTHS
TELPHERMEN	TEMPORIZATIONS	TENDERIZES	TENSIMETERS	TEREBRANTS
TELPHERWAY	TEMPORIZED	TENDERIZING	TENSIOMETER	TEREBRATED
TELPHERWAYS	TEMPORIZER	TENDERLING	TENSIOMETERS	TEREBRATES
TEMAZEPAMS	TEMPORIZERS	TENDERLINGS	TENSIOMETRIC	TEREBRATING
TEMERARIOUS	TEMPORIZES	TENDERLOIN	TENSIOMETRIES	TEREBRATION
TEMERARIOUSLY	TEMPORIZING	TENDERLOINS	TENSIOMETRY	TEREBRATIONS
TEMERARIOUSNESS	TEMPORIZINGLY	TENDERNESS	TENSIONALLY	TEREBRATULA
TEMERITIES	TEMPORIZINGS	TENDERNESSES	TENSIONERS	TEREBRATULAE
TEMEROUSLY	TEMPTABILITIES	TENDEROMETER	TENSIONING	TEREBRATULAS
TEMPERABILITIES	TEMPTABILITY	TENDEROMETERS	TENSIONLESS	TEREPHTHALATE
TEMPERABILITY	TEMPTABLENESS	TENDINITIDES	TENTACULAR	TEREPHTHALATES
TEMPERABLE	TEMPTABLENESSES	TENDINITIS	TENTACULATE	TEREPHTHALIC
TEMPERALITIE	TEMPTATION	TENDINITISES	TENTACULIFEROUS	TERGIVERSANT
TEMPERALITIES	TEMPTATIONS	TENDONITIDES	TENTACULITE	TERGIVERSANTS
TEMPERAMENT	TEMPTATIOUS	TENDONITIS	TENTACULITES	TERGIVERSATE
TEMPERAMENTAL	TEMPTINGLY	TENDONITISES	TENTACULOID	TERGIVERSATED
TEMPERAMENTALLY	TEMPTINGNESS	TENDOVAGINITIS	TENTACULUM	TERGIVERSATES
TEMPERAMENTFUL	TEMPTINGNESSES	TENDRESSES	TENTATIONS	TERGIVERSATING
TEMPERAMENTS	TEMPTRESSES	TENDRILLAR	TENTATIVELY	TERGIVERSATION
TEMPERANCE	TEMULENCES	TENDRILLED	TENTATIVENESS	TERGIVERSATIONS
TEMPERANCES	TEMULENCIES	TENDRILLIER	TENTATIVENESSES	TERGIVERSATOR
TEMPERATED	TEMULENTLY	TENDRILLIEST	TENTATIVES	TERGIVERSATORS
TEMPERATELY	TENABILITIES	TENDRILLOUS	TENTERHOOK	TERGIVERSATORY
TEMPERATENESS	TENABILITY	TENDRILOUS	TENTERHOOKS	TERMAGANCIES
TEMPERATENESSES	TENABLENESS	TENEBRIFIC	TENTIGINOUS	TERMAGANCY
TEMPERATES	TENABLENESSES	TENEBRIONID	TENTMAKERS	TERMAGANTLY
TEMPERATING	TENACIOUSLY	TENEBRIONIDS	TENUIROSTRAL	TERMAGANTS
TEMPERATIVE	TENACIOUSNESS	TENEBRIOUS	TENUOUSNESS	TERMINABILITIES
TEMPERATURE	TENACIOUSNESSES	TENEBRIOUSNESS	TENUOUSNESSES	TERMINABILITY
TEMPERATURES	TENACITIES	TENEBRISMS	TENURIALLY	TERMINABLE
TEMPERINGS	TENACULUMS	TENEBRISTS	TEPEFACTION	TERMINABLENESS
TEMPESTING	TENAILLONS	TENEBRITIES	TEPEFACTIONS	TERMINABLY
TEMPESTIVE	TENANTABLE	TENEBROSITIES	TEPHIGRAMS	TERMINALLY
TEMPESTUOUS	TENANTLESS	TENEBROSITY	TEPHROITES	TERMINATED
TEMPESTUOUSLY	TENANTRIES	TENEBROUSNESS	TEPHROMANCIES	TERMINATES
TEMPESTUOUSNESS	TENANTSHIP	TENEBROUSNESSES	TEPHROMANCY	TERMINATING
TEMPOLABILE	TENANTSHIPS	TENEMENTAL	TEPIDARIUM	TERMINATION
TEMPORALISE	TENDENCIAL	TENEMENTARY	TEPIDITIES	TERMINATIONAL
TEMPORALISED	TENDENCIALLY	TENEMENTED	TEPIDNESSES	TERMINATIONS
TEMPORALISES	TENDENCIES	TENESMUSES	TERAHERTZES	TERMINATIVE
TEMPORALISING	TENDENCIOUS	TENIACIDES	TERAMETERS	TERMINATIVELY
TEMPORALITIES	TENDENCIOUSLY	TENIAFUGES	TERATOCARCINOMA	TERMINATOR
TEMPORALITY	TENDENCIOUSNESS	TENNANTITE	TERATOGENESES	TERMINATORS
TEMPORALIZE	TENDENTIAL	TENNANTITES	TERATOGENESIS	TERMINATORY
TEMPORALIZED	TENDENTIALLY	TENNESSINE	TERATOGENIC	TERMINISMS

TERMINISTS	TERRITORIED	TESTIFYING	TETRADYMITE	TETRASPORANGIUM
TERMINOLOGICAL	TERRITORIES	TESTIMONIAL	TETRADYMITES	TETRASPORE
TERMINOLOGIES	TERRORISATION	TESTIMONIALISE	TETRADYNAMOUS	TETRASPORES
TERMINOLOGIST	TERRORISATIONS	TESTIMONIALISED	TETRAETHYL	TETRASPORIC
TERMINOLOGISTS	TERRORISED	TESTIMONIALISES	TETRAETHYLLEAD	TETRASPOROUS
TERMINOLOGY	TERRORISER	TESTIMONIALIZE	TETRAETHYLLEADS	TETRASTICH
TERMINUSES	TERRORISERS	TESTIMONIALIZED	TETRAETHYLS	TETRASTICHAL
TERMITARIA	TERRORISES	TESTIMONIALIZES	TETRAFLUORIDE	TETRASTICHIC
TERMITARIES	TERRORISING	TESTIMONIALS	TETRAFLUORIDES	TETRASTICHOUS
TERMITARIUM	TERRORISMS	TESTIMONIED	TETRAGONAL	TETRASTICHS
TERMITARIUMS	TERRORISTIC	TESTIMONIES	TETRAGONALLY	TETRASTYLE
TERNEPLATE	TERRORISTS	TESTIMONYING	TETRAGONALNESS	TETRASTYLES
TERNEPLATES	TERRORIZATION	TESTINESSES	TETRAGONOUS	TETRASYLLABIC
TEROTECHNOLOGY	TERRORIZATIONS	TESTOSTERONE	TETRAGRAMMATON	TETRASYLLABICAL
TERPENELESS	TERRORIZED	TESTOSTERONES	TETRAGRAMMATONS	TETRASYLLABLE
TERPENOIDS	TERRORIZER	TESTUDINAL	TETRAGRAMS	TETRASYLLABLES
TERPINEOLS	TERRORIZERS	TESTUDINARY	TETRAGYNIAN	TETRATHEISM
TERPOLYMER	TERRORIZES	TESTUDINEOUS	TETRAGYNOUS	TETRATHEISMS
TERPOLYMERS	TERRORIZING	TESTUDINES	TETRAHEDRA	TETRATHLON
TERPSICHOREAL	TERRORLESS	TETANICALLY	TETRAHEDRAL	TETRATHLONS
TERPSICHOREAN	TERSANCTUS	TETANISATION	TETRAHEDRALLY	TETRATOMIC
TERRACELESS	TERSANCTUSES	TETANISATIONS	TETRAHEDRITE	TETRAVALENCE
TERRACETTE	TERSENESSES	TETANISING	TETRAHEDRITES	TETRAVALENCES
TERRACETTES	TERTIARIES	TETANIZATION	TETRAHEDRON	TETRAVALENCIES
TERRACINGS	TERVALENCIES	TETANIZATIONS	TETRAHEDRONS	TETRAVALENCY
TERRACOTTA	TERVALENCY	TETANIZING	TETRAHYDROFURAN	TETRAVALENT
TERRACOTTAS	TESCHENITE	TETARTOHEDRAL	TETRAHYMENA	TETRAVALENTS
TERRAFORMED	TESCHENITES	TETARTOHEDRALLY	TETRAHYMENAS	TETRAZOLIUM
TERRAFORMING	TESSARAGLOT	TETARTOHEDRISM	TETRALOGIES	TETRAZOLIUMS
TERRAFORMINGS	TESSELATED	TETARTOHEDRISMS	TETRAMERAL	TETRAZZINI
TERRAFORMS	TESSELATES	TETCHINESS	TETRAMERIC	TETRODOTOXIN
TERRAMARAS	TESSELATING	TETCHINESSES	TETRAMERISM	TETRODOTOXINS
TERRAMARES	TESSELLATE	TETHERBALL	TETRAMERISMS	TETROTOXIN
TERRAQUEOUS	TESSELLATED	TETHERBALLS	TETRAMEROUS	TETROTOXINS
TERRARIUMS	TESSELLATES	TETRABASIC	TETRAMETER	TETROXIDES
TERREMOTIVE	TESSELLATING	TETRABASICITIES	TETRAMETERS	TEUTONISED
TERREPLEIN	TESSELLATION	TETRABASICITY	TETRAMETHYL	TEUTONISES
TERREPLEINS	TESSELLATIONS	TETRABORATE	TETRAMETHYLLEAD	TEUTONISING
TERRESTRIAL	TESSERACTS	TETRABORATES	TETRAMORPHIC	TEUTONIZED
TERRESTRIALLY	TESSITURAS	TETRABRACH	TETRANDRIAN	TEUTONIZES
TERRESTRIALNESS	TESTABILITIES	TETRABRACHS	TETRANDROUS	TEUTONIZING
TERRESTRIALS	TESTABILITY	TETRABRANCHIATE	TETRAPLEGIA	TEXTBOOKISH
TERRIBILITIES	TESTACEANS	TETRACAINE	TETRAPLEGIAS	TEXTPHONES
TERRIBILITY	TESTACEOUS	TETRACAINES	TETRAPLEGIC	TEXTSPEAKS
TERRIBLENESS	TESTAMENTAL	TETRACHLORIDE	TETRAPLOID	TEXTUALISM
TERRIBLENESSES	TESTAMENTAR	TETRACHLORIDES	TETRAPLOIDIES	TEXTUALISMS
TERRICOLES	TESTAMENTARILY	TETRACHORD	TETRAPLOIDS	TEXTUALIST
TERRICOLOUS	TESTAMENTARY	TETRACHORDAL	TETRAPLOIDY	TEXTUALISTS
TERRIFICALLY	TESTAMENTS	TETRACHORDS	TETRAPODIC	TEXTUARIES
TERRIFIERS	TESTATIONS	TETRACHOTOMIES	TETRAPODIES	TEXTURALLY
TERRIFYING	TESTATRICES	TETRACHOTOMOUS	TETRAPODOUS	TEXTURELESS
TERRIFYINGLY	TESTATRIXES	TETRACHOTOMY	TETRAPOLIS	TEXTURINGS
TERRIGENOUS	TESTCROSSED	TETRACTINAL	TETRAPOLISES	TEXTURISED
TERRITORIAL	TESTCROSSES	TETRACTINALS	TETRAPOLITAN	TEXTURISES
TERRITORIALISE	TESTCROSSING	TETRACTINE	TETRAPTERAN	TEXTURISING
TERRITORIALISED	TESTERNING	TETRACTINES	TETRAPTEROUS	TEXTURIZED
TERRITORIALISES	TESTICULAR	TETRACYCLIC	TETRAPTOTE	TEXTURIZES
TERRITORIALISM	TESTICULATE	TETRACYCLINE	TETRAPTOTES	TEXTURIZING
TERRITORIALISMS	TESTICULATED	TETRACYCLINES	TETRAPYRROLE	THALAMENCEPHALA
TERRITORIALIST	TESTIFICATE	TETRADACTYL	TETRAPYRROLES	THALAMICALLY
TERRITORIALISTS	TESTIFICATES	TETRADACTYLIES	TETRARCHATE	THALAMIFLORAL
TERRITORIALITY	TESTIFICATION	TETRADACTYLOUS	TETRARCHATES	THALASSAEMIA
TERRITORIALIZE	TESTIFICATIONS	TETRADACTYLS	TETRARCHIC	THALASSAEMIAS
TERRITORIALIZED	TESTIFICATOR	TETRADACTYLY	TETRARCHICAL	THALASSAEMIC
TERRITORIALIZES	TESTIFICATORS	TETRADITES	TETRARCHIES	THALASSAEMICS
TERRITORIALLY	TESTIFICATORY	TETRADRACHM	TETRASEMIC	THALASSEMIA
TERRITORIALS	TESTIFIERS	TETRADRACHMS	TETRASPORANGIA	THALASSEMIAS

t

t

THALASSEMIC	THAUMATOGENY	THEATRICIZING	THEOLOGISATIONS	THEORISATIONS
THALASSEMICS	THAUMATOGRAPHY	THEATROMANIA	THEOLOGISE	THEORISERS
THALASSIAN	THAUMATOLATRIES	THEATROMANIAS	THEOLOGISED	THEORISING
THALASSIANS	THAUMATOLATRY	THEATROPHONE	THEOLOGISER	THEORIZATION
THALASSOCRACIES	THAUMATOLOGIES	THEATROPHONES	THEOLOGISERS	THEORIZATIONS
THALASSOCRACY	THAUMATOLOGY	THECODONTS	THEOLOGISES	THEORIZERS
THALASSOCRAT	THAUMATROPE	THEFTUOUSLY	THEOLOGISING	THEORIZING
THALASSOCRATS	THAUMATROPES	THEGNLIEST	THEOLOGIST	THEOSOPHER
THALASSOGRAPHER	THAUMATROPICAL	THEIRSELVES	THEOLOGISTS	THEOSOPHERS
THALASSOGRAPHIC	THAUMATURGE	THEISTICAL	THEOLOGIZATION	THEOSOPHIC
THALASSOGRAPHY	THAUMATURGES	THEISTICALLY	THEOLOGIZATIONS	THEOSOPHICAL
THALASSOTHERAPY	THAUMATURGIC	THELEMENTS	THEOLOGIZE	THEOSOPHICALLY
THALATTOCRACIES	THAUMATURGICAL	THELITISES	THEOLOGIZED	THEOSOPHIES
THALATTOCRACY	THAUMATURGICS	THELYTOKIES	THEOLOGIZER	THEOSOPHISE
THALICTRUM	THAUMATURGIES	THELYTOKOUS	THEOLOGIZERS	THEOSOPHISED
THALICTRUMS	THAUMATURGISM	THEMATICALLY	THEOLOGIZES	THEOSOPHISES
THALIDOMIDE	THAUMATURGISMS	THEMATISATION	THEOLOGIZING	THEOSOPHISING
THALIDOMIDES	THAUMATURGIST	THEMATISATIONS	THEOLOGOUMENA	THEOSOPHISM
THALLIFORM	THAUMATURGISTS	THEMATISED	THEOLOGOUMENON	THEOSOPHISMS
THALLOPHYTE	THAUMATURGUS	THEMATISES	THEOLOGUES	THEOSOPHIST
THALLOPHYTES	THAUMATURGUSES	THEMATISING	THEOMACHIES	THEOSOPHISTICAL
THALLOPHYTIC	THAUMATURGY	THEMATIZATION	THEOMACHIST	THEOSOPHISTS
THANATISMS	THEANTHROPIC	THEMATIZATIONS	THEOMACHISTS	THEOSOPHIZE
THANATISTS	THEANTHROPIES	THEMATIZED	THEOMANCIES	THEOSOPHIZED
THANATOGNOMONIC	THEANTHROPISM	THEMATIZES	THEOMANIAC	THEOSOPHIZES
THANATOGRAPHIES	THEANTHROPISMS	THEMATIZING	THEOMANIACS	THEOSOPHIZING
THANATOGRAPHY	THEANTHROPIST	THEMSELVES	THEOMANIAS	THEOTECHNIC
THANATOLOGICAL	THEANTHROPISTS	THENABOUTS	THEOMANTIC	THEOTECHNIES
THANATOLOGIES	THEANTHROPY	THENARDITE	THEOMORPHIC	THEOTECHNY
THANATOLOGIST	THEARCHIES	THENARDITES	THEOMORPHISM	THERALITES
THANATOLOGISTS	THEATERGOER	THENCEFORTH	THEOMORPHISMS	THERAPEUSES
THANATOLOGY	THEATERGOERS	THENCEFORWARD	THEONOMIES	THERAPEUSIS
THANATOPHOBIA	THEATERGOING	THENCEFORWARDS	THEONOMOUS	THERAPEUTIC
THANATOPHOBIAS	THEATERGOINGS	THEOBROMINE	THEOPATHETIC	THERAPEUTICAL
THANATOPSES	THEATERLAND	THEOBROMINES	THEOPATHIC	THERAPEUTICALLY
THANATOPSIS	THEATERLANDS	THEOCENTRIC	THEOPATHIES	THERAPEUTICS
THANATOSES	THEATREGOER	THEOCENTRICISM	THEOPHAGIES	THERAPEUTIST
THANATOSIS	THEATREGOERS	THEOCENTRICISMS	THEOPHAGOUS	THERAPEUTISTS
THANEHOODS	THEATREGOING	THEOCENTRICITY	THEOPHANIC	THERAPISED
THANESHIPS	THEATREGOINGS	THEOCENTRISM	THEOPHANIES	THERAPISES
THANKFULLER	THEATRELAND	THEOCENTRISMS	THEOPHANOUS	THERAPISING
THANKFULLEST	THEATRELANDS	THEOCRACIES	THEOPHOBIA	THERAPISTS
THANKFULLY	THEATRICAL	THEOCRASIES	THEOPHOBIAC	THERAPIZED
THANKFULNESS	THEATRICALISE	THEOCRATIC	THEOPHOBIACS	THERAPIZES
THANKFULNESSES	THEATRICALISED	THEOCRATICAL	THEOPHOBIAS	THERAPIZING
THANKLESSLY	THEATRICALISES	THEOCRATICALLY	THEOPHOBIST	THERAPSIDS
THANKLESSNESS	THEATRICALISING	THEODICEAN	THEOPHOBISTS	THEREABOUT
THANKLESSNESSES	THEATRICALISM	THEODICEANS	THEOPHORIC	THEREABOUTS
THANKSGIVER	THEATRICALISMS	THEODICIES	THEOPHYLLINE	THEREAFTER
THANKSGIVERS	THEATRICALITIES	THEODOLITE	THEOPHYLLINES	THEREAGAINST
THANKSGIVING	THEATRICALITY	THEODOLITES	THEOPNEUST	THEREAMONG
THANKSGIVINGS	THEATRICALIZE	THEODOLITIC	THEOPNEUSTIC	THEREANENT
THANKWORTHIER	THEATRICALIZED	THEOGONICAL	THEOPNEUSTIES	THEREBESIDE
THANKWORTHIEST	THEATRICALIZES	THEOGONIES	THEOPNEUSTY	THEREINAFTER
THANKWORTHILY	THEATRICALIZING	THEOGONIST	THEORBISTS	THEREINBEFORE
THANKWORTHINESS	THEATRICALLY	THEOGONISTS	THEOREMATIC	THERENESSES
THANKWORTHY	THEATRICALNESS	THEOLOGASTER	THEOREMATICAL	THERETHROUGH
THARBOROUGH	THEATRICALS	THEOLOGASTERS	THEOREMATICALLY	THERETOFORE
THARBOROUGHS	THEATRICISE	THEOLOGATE	THEOREMATIST	THEREUNDER
THATCHIEST	THEATRICISED	THEOLOGATES	THEOREMATISTS	THEREWITHAL
THATCHINGS	THEATRICISES	THEOLOGERS	THEORETICAL	THEREWITHIN
THATCHLESS	THEATRICISING	THEOLOGIAN	THEORETICALLY	THERIANTHROPIC
THATNESSES	THEATRICISM	THEOLOGIANS	THEORETICIAN	THERIANTHROPISM
THAUMASITE	THEATRICISMS	THEOLOGICAL	THEORETICIANS	THERIOLATRIES
THAUMASITES	THEATRICIZE	THEOLOGICALLY	THEORETICS	THERIOLATRY
THAUMATINS	THEATRICIZED	THEOLOGIES	THEORIQUES	THERIOMORPH
THAUMATOGENIES	THEATRICIZES	THEOLOGISATION	THEORISATION	THERIOMORPHIC

THERIOMORPHISM	THERMOGRAMS	THERMOSTATICS	THIMBLERIGGINGS	THIOSULFATES
THERIOMORPHISMS	THERMOGRAPH	THERMOSTATING	THIMBLERIGS	THIOSULFURIC
THERIOMORPHOSES	THERMOGRAPHER	THERMOSTATS	THIMBLESFUL	THIOSULPHATE
THERIOMORPHOSIS	THERMOGRAPHERS	THERMOSTATTED	THIMBLEWEED	THIOSULPHATES
THERIOMORPHOUS	THERMOGRAPHIC	THERMOSTATTING	THIMBLEWEEDS	THIOSULPHURIC
THERIOMORPHS	THERMOGRAPHIES	THERMOTACTIC	THIMBLEWIT	THIOURACIL
THERMAESTHESIA	THERMOGRAPHS	THERMOTAXES	THIMBLEWITS	THIOURACILS
THERMAESTHESIAS	THERMOGRAPHY	THERMOTAXIC	THIMBLEWITTED	THIRDBOROUGH
THERMALISATION	THERMOHALINE	THERMOTAXIS	THIMEROSAL	THIRDBOROUGHS
THERMALISATIONS	THERMOJUNCTION	THERMOTENSILE	THIMEROSALS	THIRDSTREAM
THERMALISE	THERMOJUNCTIONS	THERMOTHERAPIES	THINGAMABOB	THIRDSTREAMS
THERMALISED	THERMOLABILE	THERMOTHERAPY	THINGAMABOBS	THIRSTIEST
THERMALISES	THERMOLABILITY	THERMOTICAL	THINGAMAJIG	THIRSTINESS
THERMALISING	THERMOLOGIES	THERMOTICS	THINGAMAJIGS	THIRSTINESSES
THERMALIZATION	THERMOLOGY	THERMOTOLERANT	THINGAMIES	THIRSTLESS
THERMALIZATIONS	THERMOLYSES	THERMOTROPIC	THINGAMYBOB	THIRTEENTH
THERMALIZE	THERMOLYSIS	THERMOTROPICS	THINGAMYBOBS	THIRTEENTHLY
THERMALIZED	THERMOLYTIC	THERMOTROPISM	THINGAMYJIG	THIRTEENTHS
THERMALIZES	THERMOMAGNETIC	THERMOTROPISMS	THINGAMYJIGS	THIRTIETHS
THERMALIZING	THERMOMETER	THEROLOGIES	THINGHOODS	THIRTYFOLD
THERMESTHESIA	THERMOMETERS	THEROPHYTE	THINGINESS	THIRTYSOMETHING
THERMESTHESIAS	THERMOMETRIC	THEROPHYTES	THINGINESSES	THISNESSES
THERMETTES	THERMOMETRICAL	THEROPODAN	THINGLINESS	THISTLEDOWN
THERMICALLY	THERMOMETRIES	THEROPODANS	THINGLINESSES	THISTLEDOWNS
THERMIDORS	THERMOMETRY	THERSITICAL	THINGNESSES	THISTLIEST
THERMIONIC	THERMOMOTOR	THESAURUSES	THINGUMABOB	THITHERWARD
THERMIONICS	THERMOMOTORS	THESMOTHETE	THINGUMABOBS	THITHERWARDS
THERMISTOR	THERMONASTIES	THESMOTHETES	THINGUMAJIG	THIXOTROPE
THERMISTORS	THERMONASTY	THETICALLY	THINGUMAJIGS	THIXOTROPES
THERMOBALANCE	THERMONUCLEAR	THEURGICAL	THINGUMBOB	THIXOTROPIC
THERMOBALANCES	THERMOPERIODIC	THEURGICALLY	THINGUMBOBS	THIXOTROPIES
THERMOBARIC	THERMOPERIODISM	THEURGISTS	THINGUMMYBOB	THIXOTROPY
THERMOBAROGRAPH	THERMOPHIL	THIABENDAZOLE	THINGUMMYBOBS	THOLEIITES
THERMOBAROMETER	THERMOPHILE	THIABENDAZOLES	THINGUMMYJIG	THOLEIITIC
THERMOCHEMICAL	THERMOPHILES	THIAMINASE	THINGUMMYJIGS	THOLOBATES
THERMOCHEMIST	THERMOPHILIC	THIAMINASES	THINKABLENESS	THORACENTESES
THERMOCHEMISTRY	THERMOPHILOUS	THICKENERS	THINKABLENESSES	THORACENTESIS
THERMOCHEMISTS	THERMOPHILS	THICKENING	THINKINGLY	THORACICALLY
THERMOCHROMIC	THERMOPHYLLOUS	THICKENINGS	THINKINGNESS	THORACOCENTESES
THERMOCHROMIES	THERMOPILE	THICKETIER	THINKINGNESSES	THORACOCENTESIS
THERMOCHROMISM	THERMOPILES	THICKETIEST	THINKPIECE	THORACOPLASTIES
THERMOCHROMISMS	THERMOPLASTIC	THICKHEADED	THINKPIECES	THORACOPLASTY
THERMOCHROMY	THERMOPLASTICS	THICKHEADEDNESS	THINNESSES	THORACOSCOPE
THERMOCLINE	THERMORECEPTOR	THICKHEADS	THIOALCOHOL	THORACOSCOPES
THERMOCLINES	THERMORECEPTORS	THICKLEAVES	THIOALCOHOLS	THORACOSTOMIES
THERMOCOUPLE	THERMOREGULATE	THICKNESSES	THIOBACILLI	THORACOSTOMY
THERMOCOUPLES	THERMOREGULATED	THICKSKINS	THIOBACILLUS	THORACOTOMIES
THERMODURIC	THERMOREGULATES	THIEVERIES	THIOBARBITURATE	THORACOTOMY
THERMODYNAMIC	THERMOREGULATOR	THIEVISHLY	THIOCARBAMIDE	THORIANITE
THERMODYNAMICAL	THERMOREMANENCE	THIEVISHNESS	THIOCARBAMIDES	THORIANITES
THERMODYNAMICS	THERMOREMANENT	THIEVISHNESSES	THIOCYANATE	THORNBACKS
THERMOELECTRIC	THERMOSCOPE	THIGHBONES	THIOCYANATES	THORNBILLS
THERMOELECTRON	THERMOSCOPES	THIGMOTACTIC	THIOCYANIC	THORNBIRDS
THERMOELECTRONS	THERMOSCOPIC	THIGMOTAXES	THIODIGLYCOL	THORNBUSHES
THERMOELEMENT	THERMOSCOPICAL	THIGMOTAXIS	THIODIGLYCOLS	THORNHEDGE
THERMOELEMENTS	THERMOSETS	THIGMOTROPIC	THIOFURANS	THORNHEDGES
THERMOFORM	THERMOSETTING	THIGMOTROPISM	THIOPENTAL	THORNINESS
THERMOFORMABLE	THERMOSIPHON	THIGMOTROPISMS	THIOPENTALS	THORNINESSES
THERMOFORMED	THERMOSIPHONS	THIMBLEBERRIES	THIOPENTONE	THORNPROOF
THERMOFORMING	THERMOSPHERE	THIMBLEBERRY	THIOPENTONES	THORNPROOFS
THERMOFORMS	THERMOSPHERES	THIMBLEFUL	THIOPHENES	THORNTAILS
THERMOGENESES	THERMOSPHERIC	THIMBLEFULS	THIORIDAZINE	THORNTREES
THERMOGENESIS	THERMOSTABILITY	THIMBLERIG	THIORIDAZINES	THOROUGHBASS
THERMOGENETIC	THERMOSTABLE	THIMBLERIGGED	THIOSINAMINE	THOROUGHBASSES
THERMOGENIC	THERMOSTAT	THIMBLERIGGER	THIOSINAMINES	THOROUGHBRACE
THERMOGENOUS	THERMOSTATED	THIMBLERIGGERS	THIOSULFATE	THOROUGHBRACED
THERMOGRAM	THERMOSTATIC	THIMBLERIGGING	THIOSULFATE	THOROUGHBRACES

THOROUGHBRED	THREEPENCEWORTH	THROMBOXANES	THUNDERCLOUD	THYROIDITISES
THOROUGHBREDS	THREEPENNIES	THRONELESS	THUNDERCLOUDS	THYROTOXICOSES
THOROUGHER	THREEPENNY	THRONGINGS	THUNDERERS	THYROTOXICOSIS
THOROUGHEST	THREEPENNYWORTH	THROPPLING	THUNDERFLASH	THYROTROPHIC
THOROUGHFARE	THREEQUELS	THROTTLEABLE	THUNDERFLASHES	THYROTROPHIN
THOROUGHFARES	THREESCORE	THROTTLEHOLD	THUNDERHEAD	THYROTROPHINS
THOROUGHGOING	THREESCORES	THROTTLEHOLDS	THUNDERHEADS	THYROTROPIC
THOROUGHGOINGLY	THREESOMES	THROTTLERS	THUNDERIER	THYROTROPIN
THOROUGHLY	THREMMATOLOGIES	THROTTLING	THUNDERIEST	THYROTROPINS
THOROUGHNESS	THREMMATOLOGY	THROTTLINGS	THUNDERING	THYROXINES
THOROUGHNESSES	THRENETICAL	THROUGHFARE	THUNDERINGLY	THYRSOIDAL
THOROUGHPACED	THRENODIAL	THROUGHFARES	THUNDERINGS	THYSANOPTEROUS
THOROUGHPIN	THRENODIES	THROUGHGAUN	THUNDERLESS	THYSANURAN
THOROUGHPINS	THRENODIST	THROUGHGAUNS	THUNDEROUS	THYSANURANS
THOROUGHWAX	THRENODISTS	THROUGHITHER	THUNDEROUSLY	THYSANUROUS
THOROUGHWAXES	THREONINES	THROUGHOTHER	THUNDEROUSNESS	TIBIOFIBULA
THOROUGHWORT	THRESHINGS	THROUGHOUT	THUNDERSHOWER	TIBIOFIBULAE
THOROUGHWORTS	THRESHOLDS	THROUGHPUT	THUNDERSHOWERS	TIBIOFIBULAS
THOUGHTCAST	THRIFTIEST	THROUGHPUTS	THUNDERSTONE	TIBIOTARSI
THOUGHTCASTS	THRIFTINESS	THROUGHWAY	THUNDERSTONES	TIBIOTARSUS
THOUGHTFUL	THRIFTINESSES	THROUGHWAYS	THUNDERSTORM	TIBOUCHINA
THOUGHTFULLY	THRIFTLESS	THROWAWAYS	THUNDERSTORMS	TIBOUCHINAS
THOUGHTFULNESS	THRIFTLESSLY	THROWBACKS	THUNDERSTRICKEN	TICHORRHINE
THOUGHTLESS	THRIFTLESSNESS	THROWDOWNS	THUNDERSTRIKE	TICHORRHINES
THOUGHTLESSLY	THRILLIEST	THROWOVERS	THUNDERSTRIKES	TICKETINGS
THOUGHTLESSNESS	THRILLINGLY	THROWSTERS	THUNDERSTRIKING	TICKETLESS
THOUGHTWAY	THRILLINGNESS	THRUMMIEST	THUNDERSTROKE	TICKETTYBOO
THOUGHTWAYS	THRILLINGNESSES	THRUMMINGLY	THUNDERSTROKES	TICKLEASSES
THOUSANDFOLD	THRIVELESS	THRUMMINGS	THUNDERSTRUCK	TICKLISHLY
THOUSANDFOLDS	THRIVINGLY	THRUPENNIES	THURIFEROUS	TICKLISHNESS
THOUSANDTH	THRIVINGNESS	THRUPPENCE	THURIFICATION	TICKLISHNESSES
THOUSANDTHS	THRIVINGNESSES	THRUPPENCES	THURIFICATIONS	TICKTACKED
THRAIPINGS	THROATIEST	THRUPPENNIES	THURIFYING	TICKTACKING
THRALLDOMS	THROATINESS	THRUPPENNY	THUSNESSES	TICKTACKTOE
THRAPPLING	THROATINESSES	THRUSHLIKE	THWACKINGS	TICKTACKTOES
THRASHIEST	THROATLASH	THRUSTINGS	THWARTEDLY	TICKTOCKED
THRASHINGS	THROATLASHES	THRUTCHING	THWARTINGLY	TICKTOCKING
THRASONICAL	THROATLATCH	THUDDINGLY	THWARTINGS	TICTACKING
THRASONICALLY	THROATLATCHES	THUGGERIES	THWARTSHIP	TICTOCKING
THREADBARE	THROATWORT	THUMBHOLES	THWARTSHIPS	TIDDLEDYWINK
THREADBARENESS	THROATWORTS	THUMBIKINS	THWARTWAYS	TIDDLEDYWINKS
THREADBARER	THROBBINGLY	THUMBLINGS	THWARTWISE	TIDDLEYWINK
THREADBAREST	THROBBINGS	THUMBNAILS	THYLACINES	TIDDLEYWINKS
THREADFINS	THROMBOCYTE	THUMBPIECE	THYLAKOIDS	TIDDLYWINK
THREADIEST	THROMBOCYTES	THUMBPIECES	THYMECTOMIES	TIDDLYWINKS
THREADINESS	THROMBOCYTIC	THUMBPRINT	THYMECTOMISE	TIDEWAITER
THREADINESSES	THROMBOEMBOLIC	THUMBPRINTS	THYMECTOMISED	TIDEWAITERS
THREADLESS	THROMBOEMBOLISM	THUMBSCREW	THYMECTOMISES	TIDEWATERS
THREADLIKE	THROMBOGEN	THUMBSCREWS	THYMECTOMISING	TIDINESSES
THREADMAKER	THROMBOGENS	THUMBSTALL	THYMECTOMIZE	TIDIVATING
THREADMAKERS	THROMBOKINASE	THUMBSTALLS	THYMECTOMIZED	TIDIVATION
THREADWORM	THROMBOKINASES	THUMBTACKED	THYMECTOMIZES	TIDIVATIONS
THREADWORMS	THROMBOLYSES	THUMBTACKING	THYMECTOMIZING	TIEBREAKER
THREATENED	THROMBOLYSIS	THUMBTACKS	THYMECTOMY	TIEBREAKERS
THREATENER	THROMBOLYTIC	THUMBWHEEL	THYMELAEACEOUS	TIEMANNITE
THREATENERS	THROMBOLYTICS	THUMBWHEELS	THYMIDINES	TIEMANNITES
THREATENING	THROMBOPHILIA	THUMPINGLY	THYMIDYLIC	TIERCELETS
THREATENINGLY	THROMBOPHILIAS	THUNBERGIA	THYMOCYTES	TIERCERONS
THREATENINGS	THROMBOPLASTIC	THUNBERGIAS	THYRATRONS	TIGERISHLY
THREEFOLDNESS	THROMBOPLASTIN	THUNDERBIRD	THYRISTORS	TIGERISHNESS
THREEFOLDNESSES	THROMBOPLASTINS	THUNDERBIRDS	THYROCALCITONIN	TIGERISHNESSES
THREENESSES	THROMBOSED	THUNDERBOLT	THYROGLOBULIN	TIGERLIEST
THREEPEATED	THROMBOSES	THUNDERBOLTS	THYROGLOBULINS	TIGERWOODS
THREEPEATING	THROMBOSING	THUNDERBOX	THYROIDECTOMIES	TIGGYWINKLE
THREEPEATS	THROMBOSIS	THUNDERBOXES	THYROIDECTOMY	TIGGYWINKLES
THREEPENCE	THROMBOTIC	THUNDERCLAP	THYROIDITIDES	TIGHTASSED
THREEPENCES	THROMBOXANE	THUNDERCLAPS	THYROIDITIS	TIGHTASSES

TIGHTENERS	TIMESAVING	TIRAILLEURS	TOADGRASSES	TOLERATIONISMS
TIGHTENING	TIMESCALES	TIREDNESSES	TOADRUSHES	TOLERATIONIST
TIGHTENINGS	TIMESERVER	TIRELESSLY	TOADSTONES	TOLERATIONISTS
TIGHTFISTED	TIMESERVERS	TIRELESSNESS	TOADSTOOLS	TOLERATIONS
TIGHTFISTEDNESS	TIMESERVING	TIRELESSNESSES	TOASTMASTER	TOLERATIVE
TIGHTISHLY	TIMESERVINGS	TIREMAKERS	TOASTMASTERS	TOLERATORS
TIGHTNESSES	TIMESHARES	TIRESOMELY	TOASTMISTRESS	TOLLBOOTHS
TIGHTROPES	TIMESHIFTED	TIRESOMENESS	TOASTMISTRESSES	TOLLBRIDGE
TIGHTWIRES	TIMESHIFTING	TIRESOMENESSES	TOBACCANALIAN	TOLLBRIDGES
TIGRISHNESS	TIMESHIFTS	TIROCINIUM	TOBACCANALIANS	TOLLDISHES
TIGRISHNESSES	TIMESTAMPED	TIROCINIUMS	TOBACCOLESS	TOLLGATING
TIKINAGANS	TIMESTAMPING	TITANESSES	TOBACCONIST	TOLLHOUSES
TIKOLOSHES	TIMESTAMPS	TITANICALLY	TOBACCONISTS	TOLLKEEPER
TIKTAALIKS	TIMETABLED	TITANIFEROUS	TOBOGGANED	TOLLKEEPERS
TILEFISHES	TIMETABLES	TITANOSAUR	TOBOGGANER	TOLUIDIDES
TILIACEOUS	TIMETABLING	TITANOSAURS	TOBOGGANERS	TOLUIDINES
TILLANDSIA	TIMETABLINGS	TITANOTHERE	TOBOGGANING	TOMAHAWKED
TILLANDSIAS	TIMEWORKER	TITANOTHERES	TOBOGGANINGS	TOMAHAWKING
TILLERINGS	TIMEWORKERS	TITARAKURA	TOBOGGANIST	TOMATILLOES
TILLERLESS	TIMIDITIES	TITARAKURAS	TOBOGGANISTS	TOMATILLOS
TILTMETERS	TIMIDNESSES	TITHINGMAN	TOBOGGINED	TOMATOIEST
TILTROTORS	TIMOCRACIES	TITHINGMEN	TOBOGGINING	TOMBOYISHLY
TIMBERDOODLE	TIMOCRATIC	TITILLATED	TOCCATELLA	TOMBOYISHNESS
TIMBERDOODLES	TIMOCRATICAL	TITILLATES	TOCCATELLAS	TOMBOYISHNESSES
TIMBERHEAD	TIMOROUSLY	TITILLATING	TOCCATINAS	TOMBSTONES
TIMBERHEADS	TIMOROUSNESS	TITILLATINGLY	TOCHERLESS	TOMBSTONING
TIMBERIEST	TIMOROUSNESSES	TITILLATION	TOCOLOGIES	TOMBSTONINGS
TIMBERINGS	TIMPANISTS	TITILLATIONS	TOCOPHEROL	TOMCATTING
TIMBERLAND	TINCTORIAL	TITILLATIVE	TOCOPHEROLS	TOMCATTINGS
TIMBERLANDS	TINCTORIALLY	TITILLATOR	TOCOPHOBIA	TOMFOOLERIES
TIMBERLINE	TINCTURING	TITILLATORS	TOCOPHOBIAS	TOMFOOLERY
TIMBERLINES	TINDERBOXES	TITIPOUNAMU	TODDLERHOOD	TOMFOOLING
TIMBERWORK	TINDERIEST	TITIPOUNAMUS	TODDLERHOODS	TOMFOOLISH
TIMBERWORKS	TINGLINGLY	TITIVATING	TOENAILING	TOMFOOLISHNESS
TIMBERYARD	TINGUAITES	TITIVATION	TOERAGGERS	TOMOGRAPHIC
TIMBERYARDS	TININESSES	TITIVATIONS	TOFFISHNESS	TOMOGRAPHIES
TIMBRELLED	TINKERINGS	TITIVATORS	TOFFISHNESSES	TOMOGRAPHS
TIMBROLOGIES	TINKERTOYS	TITLEHOLDER	TOGAVIRUSES	TOMOGRAPHY
TIMBROLOGIST	TINKLINGLY	TITLEHOLDERS	TOGETHERNESS	TONALITIES
TIMBROLOGISTS	TINNINESSES	TITLEHOLDING	TOGETHERNESSES	TONALITIVE
TIMBROLOGY	TINNITUSES	TITRATABLE	TOILETINGS	TONELESSLY
TIMBROMANIA	TINPLATING	TITRATIONS	TOILETRIES	TONELESSNESS
TIMBROMANIAC	TINSELIEST	TITRIMETRIC	TOILFULNESS	TONELESSNESSES
TIMBROMANIACS	TINSELLIER	TITTERINGLY	TOILFULNESSES	TONETICALLY
TIMBROMANIAS	TINSELLIEST	TITTERINGS	TOILINETTE	TONGUELESS
TIMBROPHILIES	TINSELLING	TITTIVATED	TOILINETTES	TONGUELETS
TIMBROPHILIST	TINSELRIES	TITTIVATES	TOILSOMELY	TONGUELIKE
TIMBROPHILISTS	TINSMITHING	TITTIVATING	TOILSOMENESS	TONGUESTER
TIMBROPHILY	TINSMITHINGS	TITTIVATION	TOILSOMENESSES	TONGUESTERS
TIMEFRAMES	TINTINESSES	TITTIVATIONS	TOKENISTIC	TONICITIES
TIMEKEEPER	TINTINNABULA	TITTIVATOR	TOKOLOGIES	TONISHNESS
TIMEKEEPERS	TINTINNABULANT	TITTIVATORS	TOKOLOSHES	TONISHNESSES
TIMEKEEPING	TINTINNABULAR	TITTLEBATS	TOKOLOSHIS	TONNISHNESS
TIMEKEEPINGS	TINTINNABULARY	TITTUPIEST	TOKOPHOBIA	TONNISHNESSES
TIMELESSLY	TINTINNABULATE	TITTUPPIER	TOKOPHOBIAS	TONOMETERS
TIMELESSNESS	TINTINNABULATED	TITTUPPIEST	TOKTOKKIES	TONOMETRIC
TIMELESSNESSES	TINTINNABULATES	TITTUPPING	TOLBUTAMIDE	TONOMETRIES
TIMELINESS	TINTINNABULOUS	TITUBANCIES	TOLBUTAMIDES	TONOPLASTS
TIMELINESSES	TINTINNABULUM	TITUBATING	TOLERABILITIES	TONSILITIS
TIMENOGUYS	TINTOMETER	TITUBATION	TOLERABILITY	TONSILITISES
TIMEPASSED	TINTOMETERS	TITUBATIONS	TOLERABLENESS	TONSILLARY
TIMEPASSES	TINTOOKIES	TITULARIES	TOLERABLENESSES	TONSILLECTOMIES
TIMEPASSING	TIPPYTOEING	TITULARITIES	TOLERANCES	TONSILLECTOMY
TIMEPIECES	TIPSIFYING	TITULARITY	TOLERANTLY	TONSILLITIC
TIMEPLEASER	TIPSINESSES	TOADEATERS	TOLERATING	TONSILLITIDES
TIMEPLEASERS	TIPTRONICS	TOADFISHES	TOLERATION	TONSILLITIS
TIMESAVERS	TIRAILLEUR	TOADFLAXES	TOLERATIONISM	TONSILLITISES

TONSILLOTOMIES	TOPOGRAPHICAL	TORRENTUOUS	TOTTERINGS	TOXICATIONS
TONSILLOTOMY	TOPOGRAPHICALLY	TORRIDITIES	TOUCHABLENESS	TOXICITIES
TOOLCHESTS	TOPOGRAPHIES	TORRIDNESS	TOUCHABLENESSES	TOXICOGENIC
TOOLHOLDER	TOPOGRAPHS	TORRIDNESSES	TOUCHBACKS	TOXICOLOGIC
TOOLHOLDERS	TOPOGRAPHY	TORRIFYING	TOUCHDOWNS	TOXICOLOGICAL
TOOLHOUSES	TOPOISOMERASE	TORSIBILITIES	TOUCHHOLES	TOXICOLOGICALLY
TOOLMAKERS	TOPOISOMERASES	TORSIBILITY	TOUCHINESS	TOXICOLOGIES
TOOLMAKING	TOPOLOGICAL	TORSIOGRAPH	TOUCHINESSES	TOXICOLOGIST
TOOLMAKINGS	TOPOLOGICALLY	TORSIOGRAPHS	TOUCHINGLY	TOXICOLOGISTS
TOOLPUSHER	TOPOLOGIES	TORSIONALLY	TOUCHINGNESS	TOXICOLOGY
TOOLPUSHERS	TOPOLOGIST	TORTELLINI	TOUCHINGNESSES	TOXICOMANIA
TOOLPUSHES	TOPOLOGISTS	TORTELLINIS	TOUCHLINES	TOXICOMANIAS
TOOTHACHES	TOPOMETRIES	TORTFEASOR	TOUCHMARKS	TOXICOPHAGOUS
TOOTHBRUSH	TOPONYMICAL	TORTFEASORS	TOUCHPAPER	TOXICOPHOBIA
TOOTHBRUSHES	TOPONYMICS	TORTICOLLAR	TOUCHPAPERS	TOXICOPHOBIAS
TOOTHBRUSHING	TOPONYMIES	TORTICOLLIS	TOUCHSCREEN	TOXIGENICITIES
TOOTHBRUSHINGS	TOPONYMIST	TORTICOLLISES	TOUCHSCREENS	TOXIGENICITY
TOOTHCOMBS	TOPONYMISTS	TORTILITIES	TOUCHSTONE	TOXIPHAGOUS
TOOTHFISHES	TOPOPHILIA	TORTILLONS	TOUCHSTONES	TOXIPHOBIA
TOOTHINESS	TOPOPHILIAS	TORTIOUSLY	TOUCHTONES	TOXIPHOBIAC
TOOTHINESSES	TOPSCORING	TORTOISESHELL	TOUCHWOODS	TOXIPHOBIACS
TOOTHPASTE	TOPSOILING	TORTOISESHELLS	TOUGHENERS	TOXIPHOBIAS
TOOTHPASTES	TOPSOILINGS	TORTRICIDS	TOUGHENING	TOXOCARIASES
TOOTHPICKS	TOPSTITCHED	TORTUOSITIES	TOUGHENINGS	TOXOCARIASIS
TOOTHSHELL	TOPSTITCHES	TORTUOSITY	TOUGHNESSES	TOXOPHILIES
TOOTHSHELLS	TOPSTITCHING	TORTUOUSLY	TOURBILLION	TOXOPHILITE
TOOTHSOMELY	TOPWORKING	TORTUOUSNESS	TOURBILLIONS	TOXOPHILITES
TOOTHSOMENESS	TORBANITES	TORTUOUSNESSES	TOURBILLON	TOXOPHILITIC
TOOTHSOMENESSES	TORBERNITE	TORTUREDLY	TOURBILLONS	TOXOPLASMA
TOOTHWASHES	TORBERNITES	TORTURESOME	TOURISTICALLY	TOXOPLASMAS
TOOTHWORTS	TORCHBEARER	TORTURINGLY	TOURISTIER	TOXOPLASMIC
TOPAGNOSES	TORCHBEARERS	TORTURINGS	TOURISTIEST	TOXOPLASMOSES
TOPAGNOSIA	TORCHIERES	TORTUROUSLY	TOURMALINE	TOXOPLASMOSIS
TOPAGNOSIAS	TORCHLIGHT	TOSSICATED	TOURMALINES	TOYISHNESS
TOPAGNOSIS	TORCHLIGHTS	TOSTICATED	TOURMALINIC	TOYISHNESSES
TOPARCHIES	TORCHWOODS	TOSTICATION	TOURNAMENT	TRABEATION
TOPAZOLITE	TORMENTEDLY	TOSTICATIONS	TOURNAMENTS	TRABEATIONS
TOPAZOLITES	TORMENTERS	TOTALISATION	TOURNEYERS	TRABECULAE
TOPCROSSES	TORMENTILS	TOTALISATIONS	TOURNEYING	TRABECULAR
TOPDRESSING	TORMENTING	TOTALISATOR	TOURNIQUET	TRABECULAS
TOPDRESSINGS	TORMENTINGLY	TOTALISATORS	TOURNIQUETS	TRABECULATE
TOPECTOMIES	TORMENTINGS	TOTALISERS	TOURTIERES	TRABECULATED
TOPGALLANT	TORMENTORS	TOTALISING	TOVARICHES	TRACASSERIE
TOPGALLANTS	TORMENTUMS	TOTALISTIC	TOVARISCHES	TRACASSERIES
TOPHACEOUS	TOROIDALLY	TOTALITARIAN	TOVARISHES	TRACEABILITIES
TOPIARISTS	TOROSITIES	TOTALITARIANISE	TOWARDLINESS	TRACEABILITY
TOPICALITIES	TORPEDINOUS	TOTALITARIANISM	TOWARDLINESSES	TRACEABLENESS
TOPICALITY	TORPEDOERS	TOTALITARIANIZE	TOWARDNESS	TRACEABLENESSES
TOPKNOTTED	TORPEDOING	TOTALITARIANS	TOWARDNESSES	TRACELESSLY
TOPLESSNESS	TORPEDOIST	TOTALITIES	TOWELETTES	TRACHEARIAN
TOPLESSNESSES	TORPEDOISTS	TOTALIZATION	TOWELHEADS	TRACHEARIANS
TOPLOFTICAL	TORPEFYING	TOTALIZATIONS	TOWELLINGS	TRACHEARIES
TOPLOFTIER	TORPESCENCE	TOTALIZATOR	TOWERINGLY	TRACHEATED
TOPLOFTIEST	TORPESCENCES	TOTALIZATORS	TOWNHOUSES	TRACHEATES
TOPLOFTILY	TORPESCENT	TOTALIZERS	TOWNSCAPED	TRACHEIDAL
TOPLOFTINESS	TORPIDITIES	TOTALIZING	TOWNSCAPES	TRACHEIDES
TOPLOFTINESSES	TORPIDNESS	TOTAQUINES	TOWNSCAPING	TRACHEITIDES
TOPMAKINGS	TORPIDNESSES	TOTEMICALLY	TOWNSCAPINGS	TRACHEITIS
TOPMINNOWS	TORPITUDES	TOTEMISTIC	TOWNSFOLKS	TRACHEITISES
TOPNOTCHER	TORPORIFIC	TOTIPALMATE	TOWNSPEOPLE	TRACHELATE
TOPNOTCHERS	TORREFACTION	TOTIPALMATION	TOWNSPEOPLES	TRACHEOLAR
TOPOCENTRIC	TORREFACTIONS	TOTIPALMATIONS	TOWNSWOMAN	TRACHEOLES
TOPOCHEMISTRIES	TORREFYING	TOTIPOTENCIES	TOWNSWOMEN	TRACHEOPHYTE
TOPOCHEMISTRY	TORRENTIAL	TOTIPOTENCY	TOXALBUMIN	TRACHEOPHYTES
TOPOGRAPHER	TORRENTIALITIES	TOTIPOTENT	TOXALBUMINS	TRACHEOSCOPIES
TOPOGRAPHERS	TORRENTIALITY	TOTTERIEST	TOXAPHENES	TRACHEOSCOPY
TOPOGRAPHIC	TORRENTIALLY	TOTTERINGLY	TOXICATION	TRACHEOSTOMIES

TRACHEOSTOMY	TRADITIONALISTS	TRAILERIST	TRANQUILISER	TRANSCENDENTALS
TRACHEOTOMIES	TRADITIONALITY	TRAILERISTS	TRANQUILISERS	TRANSCENDENTLY
TRACHEOTOMY	TRADITIONALIZE	TRAILERITE	TRANQUILISES	TRANSCENDENTS
TRACHINUSES	TRADITIONALIZED	TRAILERITES	TRANQUILISING	TRANSCENDING
TRACHITISES	TRADITIONALIZES	TRAILHEADS	TRANQUILISINGLY	TRANSCENDINGLY
TRACHOMATOUS	TRADITIONALLY	TRAILINGLY	TRANQUILITIES	TRANSCENDS
TRACHYPTERUS	TRADITIONARILY	TRAINABILITIES	TRANQUILITY	TRANSCODED
TRACHYPTERUSES	TRADITIONARY	TRAINABILITY	TRANQUILIZATION	TRANSCODER
TRACHYTOID	TRADITIONER	TRAINBANDS	TRANQUILIZE	TRANSCODERS
TRACKBALLS	TRADITIONERS	TRAINBEARER	TRANQUILIZED	TRANSCODES
TRACKERBALL	TRADITIONIST	TRAINBEARERS	TRANQUILIZER	TRANSCODING
TRACKERBALLS	TRADITIONISTS	TRAINEESHIP	TRANQUILIZERS	TRANSCRANIAL
TRACKLAYER	TRADITIONLESS	TRAINEESHIPS	TRANQUILIZES	TRANSCRIBABLE
TRACKLAYERS	TRADITIONS	TRAINLOADS	TRANQUILIZING	TRANSCRIBE
TRACKLAYING	TRADITORES	TRAINSPOTTER	TRANQUILIZINGLY	TRANSCRIBED
TRACKLAYINGS	TRADUCEMENT	TRAINSPOTTERISH	TRANQUILLER	TRANSCRIBER
TRACKLEMENT	TRADUCEMENTS	TRAINSPOTTERS	TRANQUILLEST	TRANSCRIBERS
TRACKLEMENTS	TRADUCIANISM	TRAIPSINGS	TRANQUILLISE	TRANSCRIBES
TRACKLESSLY	TRADUCIANISMS	TRAITORESS	TRANQUILLISED	TRANSCRIBING
TRACKLESSNESS	TRADUCIANIST	TRAITORESSES	TRANQUILLISER	TRANSCRIPT
TRACKLESSNESSES	TRADUCIANISTIC	TRAITORHOOD	TRANQUILLISERS	TRANSCRIPTASE
TRACKROADS	TRADUCIANISTS	TRAITORHOODS	TRANQUILLISES	TRANSCRIPTASES
TRACKSIDES	TRADUCIANS	TRAITORISM	TRANQUILLISING	TRANSCRIPTION
TRACKSUITS	TRADUCIBLE	TRAITORISMS	TRANQUILLITIES	TRANSCRIPTIONAL
TRACKWALKER	TRADUCINGLY	TRAITOROUS	TRANQUILLITY	TRANSCRIPTIONS
TRACKWALKERS	TRADUCINGS	TRAITOROUSLY	TRANQUILLIZE	TRANSCRIPTIVE
TRACTABILITIES	TRADUCTION	TRAITOROUSNESS	TRANQUILLIZED	TRANSCRIPTIVELY
TRACTABILITY	TRADUCTIONS	TRAITORSHIP	TRANQUILLIZER	TRANSCRIPTOME
TRACTABLENESS	TRADUCTIVE	TRAITORSHIPS	TRANQUILLIZERS	TRANSCRIPTOMES
TRACTABLENESSES	TRAFFICABILITY	TRAITRESSES	TRANQUILLIZES	TRANSCRIPTS
TRACTARIAN	TRAFFICABLE	TRAJECTILE	TRANQUILLIZING	TRANSCULTURAL
TRACTARIANS	TRAFFICATOR	TRAJECTING	TRANQUILLY	TRANSCURRENT
TRACTATORS	TRAFFICATORS	TRAJECTION	TRANQUILNESS	TRANSCUTANEOUS
TRACTILITIES	TRAFFICKED	TRAJECTIONS	TRANQUILNESSES	TRANSDERMAL
TRACTILITY	TRAFFICKER	TRAJECTORIES	TRANSACTED	TRANSDUCED
TRACTIONAL	TRAFFICKERS	TRAJECTORY	TRANSACTING	TRANSDUCER
TRACTORATION	TRAFFICKIER	TRALATICIOUS	TRANSACTINIDE	TRANSDUCERS
TRACTORATIONS	TRAFFICKIEST	TRALATITIOUS	TRANSACTINIDES	TRANSDUCES
TRACTORFEED	TRAFFICKING	TRAMELLING	TRANSACTION	TRANSDUCING
TRACTORFEEDS	TRAFFICKINGS	TRAMMELERS	TRANSACTIONAL	TRANSDUCTANT
TRACTRICES	TRAFFICLESS	TRAMMELING	TRANSACTIONALLY	TRANSDUCTANTS
TRADECRAFT	TRAGACANTH	TRAMMELLED	TRANSACTIONS	TRANSDUCTION
TRADECRAFTS	TRAGACANTHS	TRAMMELLER	TRANSACTOR	TRANSDUCTIONAL
TRADEMARKED	TRAGEDIANS	TRAMMELLERS	TRANSACTORS	TRANSDUCTIONS
TRADEMARKING	TRAGEDIENNE	TRAMMELLING	TRANSALPINE	TRANSDUCTOR
TRADEMARKS	TRAGEDIENNES	TRAMONTANA	TRANSALPINES	TRANSDUCTORS
TRADENAMES	TRAGELAPHINE	TRAMONTANAS	TRANSAMINASE	TRANSECTED
TRADERSHIP	TRAGELAPHS	TRAMONTANE	TRANSAMINASES	TRANSECTING
TRADERSHIPS	TRAGICALLY	TRAMONTANES	TRANSAMINATION	TRANSECTION
TRADESCANTIA	TRAGICALNESS	TRAMPETTES	TRANSAMINATIONS	TRANSECTIONS
TRADESCANTIAS	TRAGICALNESSES	TRAMPLINGS	TRANSANDEAN	TRANSENNAS
TRADESFOLK	TRAGICOMEDIES	TRAMPOLINE	TRANSANDINE	TRANSEPTAL
TRADESFOLKS	TRAGICOMEDY	TRAMPOLINED	TRANSATLANTIC	TRANSEPTATE
TRADESMANLIKE	TRAGICOMIC	TRAMPOLINER	TRANSAXLES	TRANSEPTED
TRADESPEOPLE	TRAGICOMICAL	TRAMPOLINERS	TRANSCALENCIES	TRANSEXUAL
TRADESPEOPLES	TRAGICOMICALLY	TRAMPOLINES	TRANSCALENCY	TRANSEXUALISM
TRADESPERSON	TRAILBASTON	TRAMPOLINING	TRANSCALENT	TRANSEXUALISMS
TRADESPERSONS	TRAILBASTONS	TRAMPOLININGS	TRANSCAUCASIAN	TRANSEXUALITIES
TRADESWOMAN	TRAILBLAZER	TRAMPOLINIST	TRANSCEIVER	TRANSEXUALITY
TRADESWOMEN	TRAILBLAZERS	TRAMPOLINISTS	TRANSCEIVERS	TRANSEXUALS
TRADITIONAL	TRAILBLAZING	TRAMPOLINS	TRANSCENDED	TRANSFECTED
TRADITIONALISE	TRAILBLAZINGS	TRANCELIKE	TRANSCENDENCE	TRANSFECTING
TRADITIONALISED	TRAILBREAKER	TRANQUILER	TRANSCENDENCES	TRANSFECTION
TRADITIONALISES	TRAILBREAKERS	TRANQUILEST	TRANSCENDENCIES	TRANSFECTIONS
TRADITIONALISM	TRAILERABLE	TRANQUILISATION	TRANSCENDENCY	TRANSFECTS
TRADITIONALISMS	TRAILERING	TRANQUILISE	TRANSCENDENT	TRANSFERABILITY
TRADITIONALIST	TRAILERINGS	TRANQUILISED	TRANSCENDENTAL	TRANSFERABLE

TRANSFERAL	TRANSGENESIS	TRANSITIVES	TRANSMISSIONAL	TRANSPICUOUS
TRANSFERALS	TRANSGENIC	TRANSITIVITIES	TRANSMISSIONS	TRANSPICUOUSLY
TRANSFERASE	TRANSGENICS	TRANSITIVITY	TRANSMISSIVE	TRANSPIERCE
TRANSFERASES	TRANSGRESS	TRANSITORILY	TRANSMISSIVELY	TRANSPIERCED
TRANSFEREE	TRANSGRESSED	TRANSITORINESS	TRANSMISSIVITY	TRANSPIERCES
TRANSFEREES	TRANSGRESSES	TRANSITORY	TRANSMISSOMETER	TRANSPIERCING
TRANSFERENCE	TRANSGRESSING	TRANSLATABILITY	TRANSMITTABLE	TRANSPIRABLE
TRANSFERENCES	TRANSGRESSION	TRANSLATABLE	TRANSMITTAL	TRANSPIRATION
TRANSFERENTIAL	TRANSGRESSIONAL	TRANSLATED	TRANSMITTALS	TRANSPIRATIONAL
TRANSFEROR	TRANSGRESSIONS	TRANSLATES	TRANSMITTANCE	TRANSPIRATIONS
TRANSFERORS	TRANSGRESSIVE	TRANSLATING	TRANSMITTANCES	TRANSPIRATORY
TRANSFERRABLE	TRANSGRESSIVELY	TRANSLATION	TRANSMITTANCIES	TRANSPIRED
TRANSFERRAL	TRANSGRESSOR	TRANSLATIONAL	TRANSMITTANCY	TRANSPIRES
TRANSFERRALS	TRANSGRESSORS	TRANSLATIONALLY	TRANSMITTED	TRANSPIRING
TRANSFERRED	TRANSHIPMENT	TRANSLATIONS	TRANSMITTER	TRANSPLACENTAL
TRANSFERRER	TRANSHIPMENTS	TRANSLATIVE	TRANSMITTERS	TRANSPLANT
TRANSFERRERS	TRANSHIPPED	TRANSLATIVES	TRANSMITTIBLE	TRANSPLANTABLE
TRANSFERRIBLE	TRANSHIPPER	TRANSLATOR	TRANSMITTING	TRANSPLANTATION
TRANSFERRIN	TRANSHIPPERS	TRANSLATORIAL	TRANSMITTIVITY	TRANSPLANTED
TRANSFERRING	TRANSHIPPING	TRANSLATORS	TRANSMOGRIFIED	TRANSPLANTER
TRANSFERRINS	TRANSHIPPINGS	TRANSLATORY	TRANSMOGRIFIES	TRANSPLANTERS
TRANSFIGURATION	TRANSHISTORICAL	TRANSLEITHAN	TRANSMOGRIFY	TRANSPLANTING
TRANSFIGURE	TRANSHUMANCE	TRANSLITERATE	TRANSMOGRIFYING	TRANSPLANTINGS
TRANSFIGURED	TRANSHUMANCES	TRANSLITERATED	TRANSMONTANE	TRANSPLANTS
TRANSFIGUREMENT	TRANSHUMANT	TRANSLITERATES	TRANSMONTANES	TRANSPOLAR
TRANSFIGURES	TRANSHUMANTS	TRANSLITERATING	TRANSMOUNTAIN	TRANSPONDER
TRANSFIGURING	TRANSHUMED	TRANSLITERATION	TRANSMOVED	TRANSPONDERS
TRANSFINITE	TRANSHUMES	TRANSLITERATOR	TRANSMOVES	TRANSPONDOR
TRANSFIXED	TRANSHUMING	TRANSLITERATORS	TRANSMOVING	TRANSPONDORS
TRANSFIXES	TRANSIENCE	TRANSLOCATE	TRANSMUNDANE	TRANSPONTINE
TRANSFIXING	TRANSIENCES	TRANSLOCATED	TRANSMUTABILITY	TRANSPORTABLE
TRANSFIXION	TRANSIENCIES	TRANSLOCATES	TRANSMUTABLE	TRANSPORTAL
TRANSFIXIONS	TRANSIENCY	TRANSLOCATING	TRANSMUTABLY	TRANSPORTALS
TRANSFORMABLE	TRANSIENTLY	TRANSLOCATION	TRANSMUTATION	TRANSPORTANCE
TRANSFORMATION	TRANSIENTNESS	TRANSLOCATIONS	TRANSMUTATIONAL	TRANSPORTANCES
TRANSFORMATIONS	TRANSIENTNESSES	TRANSLUCENCE	TRANSMUTATIONS	TRANSPORTATION
TRANSFORMATIVE	TRANSIENTS	TRANSLUCENCES	TRANSMUTATIVE	TRANSPORTATIONS
TRANSFORMED	TRANSILIENCE	TRANSLUCENCIES	TRANSMUTED	TRANSPORTED
TRANSFORMER	TRANSILIENCES	TRANSLUCENCY	TRANSMUTER	TRANSPORTEDLY
TRANSFORMERS	TRANSILIENCIES	TRANSLUCENT	TRANSMUTERS	TRANSPORTEDNESS
TRANSFORMING	TRANSILIENCY	TRANSLUCENTLY	TRANSMUTES	TRANSPORTER
TRANSFORMINGS	TRANSILIENT	TRANSLUCID	TRANSMUTING	TRANSPORTERS
TRANSFORMISM	TRANSILLUMINATE	TRANSLUCIDITIES	TRANSNATIONAL	TRANSPORTING
TRANSFORMISMS	TRANSISTHMIAN	TRANSLUCIDITY	TRANSNATURAL	TRANSPORTINGLY
TRANSFORMIST	TRANSISTOR	TRANSLUMENAL	TRANSOCEANIC	TRANSPORTINGS
TRANSFORMISTIC	TRANSISTORISE	TRANSLUMINAL	TRANSONICS	TRANSPORTIVE
TRANSFORMISTS	TRANSISTORISED	TRANSLUNAR	TRANSPACIFIC	TRANSPORTS
TRANSFORMS	TRANSISTORISES	TRANSLUNARY	TRANSPADANE	TRANSPOSABILITY
TRANSFUSABLE	TRANSISTORISING	TRANSMANCHE	TRANSPARENCE	TRANSPOSABLE
TRANSFUSED	TRANSISTORIZE	TRANSMARINE	TRANSPARENCES	TRANSPOSAL
TRANSFUSER	TRANSISTORIZED	TRANSMEMBRANE	TRANSPARENCIES	TRANSPOSALS
TRANSFUSERS	TRANSISTORIZES	TRANSMEWED	TRANSPARENCY	TRANSPOSED
TRANSFUSES	TRANSISTORIZING	TRANSMEWING	TRANSPARENT	TRANSPOSER
TRANSFUSIBLE	TRANSISTORS	TRANSMIGRANT	TRANSPARENTISE	TRANSPOSERS
TRANSFUSING	TRANSITABLE	TRANSMIGRANTS	TRANSPARENTISED	TRANSPOSES
TRANSFUSION	TRANSITING	TRANSMIGRATE	TRANSPARENTISES	TRANSPOSING
TRANSFUSIONAL	TRANSITION	TRANSMIGRATED	TRANSPARENTIZE	TRANSPOSINGS
TRANSFUSIONIST	TRANSITIONAL	TRANSMIGRATES	TRANSPARENTIZED	TRANSPOSITION
TRANSFUSIONISTS	TRANSITIONALLY	TRANSMIGRATING	TRANSPARENTIZES	TRANSPOSITIONAL
TRANSFUSIONS	TRANSITIONALS	TRANSMIGRATION	TRANSPARENTLY	TRANSPOSITIONS
TRANSFUSIVE	TRANSITIONARY	TRANSMIGRATIONS	TRANSPARENTNESS	TRANSPOSITIVE
TRANSFUSIVELY	TRANSITIONED	TRANSMIGRATIVE	TRANSPERSON	TRANSPOSON
TRANSGENDER	TRANSITIONING	TRANSMIGRATOR	TRANSPERSONAL	TRANSPOSONS
TRANSGENDERED	TRANSITIONS	TRANSMIGRATORS	TRANSPERSONS	TRANSPUTER
TRANSGENDERS	TRANSITIVE	TRANSMIGRATORY	TRANSPHOBIA	TRANSPUTERS
TRANSGENES	TRANSITIVELY	TRANSMISSIBLE	TRANSPHOBIAS	TRANSSEXUAL
TRANSGENESES	TRANSITIVENESS	TRANSMISSION	TRANSPHOBIC	TRANSSEXUALISM

TRANSSEXUALISMS
TRANSSEXUALITY
TRANSSEXUALS
TRANSSHAPE
TRANSSHAPED
TRANSSHAPES
TRANSSHAPING
TRANSSHIPMENT
TRANSSHIPMENTS
TRANSSHIPPED
TRANSSHIPPER
TRANSSHIPPERS
TRANSSHIPPING
TRANSSHIPPINGS
TRANSSHIPS
TRANSSONIC
TRANSTHORACIC
TRANSUBSTANTIAL
TRANSUDATE
TRANSUDATES
TRANSUDATION
TRANSUDATIONS
TRANSUDATORY
TRANSUDING
TRANSUMING
TRANSUMPTION
TRANSUMPTIONS
TRANSUMPTIVE
TRANSUMPTS
TRANSURANIAN
TRANSURANIC
TRANSURANICS
TRANSURANIUM
TRANSURETHRAL
TRANSVAGINAL
TRANSVALUATE
TRANSVALUATED
TRANSVALUATES
TRANSVALUATING
TRANSVALUATION
TRANSVALUATIONS
TRANSVALUE
TRANSVALUED
TRANSVALUER
TRANSVALUERS
TRANSVALUES
TRANSVALUING
TRANSVERSAL
TRANSVERSALITY
TRANSVERSALLY
TRANSVERSALS
TRANSVERSE
TRANSVERSED
TRANSVERSELY
TRANSVERSENESS
TRANSVERSES
TRANSVERSING
TRANSVERSION
TRANSVERSIONS
TRANSVERTER
TRANSVERTERS
TRANSVESTED
TRANSVESTIC
TRANSVESTING
TRANSVESTISM
TRANSVESTISMS
TRANSVESTIST

TRANSVESTISTS
TRANSVESTITE
TRANSVESTITES
TRANSVESTITISM
TRANSVESTITISMS
TRANSVESTS
TRANSWOMAN
TRANSWOMEN
TRAPANNERS
TRAPANNING
TRAPESINGS
TRAPEZIFORM
TRAPEZISTS
TRAPEZIUMS
TRAPEZIUSES
TRAPEZOHEDRA
TRAPEZOHEDRAL
TRAPEZOHEDRON
TRAPEZOHEDRONS
TRAPEZOIDAL
TRAPEZOIDS
TRAPNESTED
TRAPNESTING
TRAPPINESS
TRAPPINESSES
TRAPSHOOTER
TRAPSHOOTERS
TRAPSHOOTING
TRAPSHOOTINGS
TRASHERIES
TRASHINESS
TRASHINESSES
TRASHTRIES
TRATTORIAS
TRAUCHLING
TRAUMATICALLY
TRAUMATISATION
TRAUMATISATIONS
TRAUMATISE
TRAUMATISED
TRAUMATISES
TRAUMATISING
TRAUMATISM
TRAUMATISMS
TRAUMATIZATION
TRAUMATIZATIONS
TRAUMATIZE
TRAUMATIZED
TRAUMATIZES
TRAUMATIZING
TRAUMATOLOGICAL
TRAUMATOLOGIES
TRAUMATOLOGY
TRAUMATONASTIES
TRAUMATONASTY
TRAVAILING
TRAVELATOR
TRAVELATORS
TRAVELINGS
TRAVELLERS
TRAVELLING
TRAVELLINGS
TRAVELOGUE
TRAVELOGUES
TRAVERSABLE
TRAVERSALS
TRAVERSERS

TRAVERSING
TRAVERSINGS
TRAVERTINE
TRAVERTINES
TRAVERTINS
TRAVESTIED
TRAVESTIES
TRAVESTYING
TRAVOLATOR
TRAVOLATORS
TRAWLERMAN
TRAWLERMEN
TRAYCLOTHS
TRAYMOBILE
TRAYMOBILES
TRAZODONES
TREACHERER
TREACHERERS
TREACHERIES
TREACHEROUS
TREACHEROUSLY
TREACHEROUSNESS
TREACHETOUR
TREACHETOURS
TREACHOURS
TREACLIEST
TREACLINESS
TREACLINESSES
TREADLINGS
TREADMILLS
TREADWHEEL
TREADWHEELS
TREASONABLE
TREASONABLENESS
TREASONABLY
TREASONOUS
TREASURABLE
TREASURELESS
TREASURERS
TREASURERSHIP
TREASURERSHIPS
TREASURIES
TREASURING
TREATABILITIES
TREATABILITY
TREATMENTS
TREATYLESS
TREBBIANOS
TREBLENESS
TREBLENESSES
TREBUCHETS
TREBUCKETS
TRECENTIST
TRECENTISTS
TREDECILLION
TREDECILLIONS
TREDRILLES
TREEHOPPER
TREEHOPPERS
TREEHOUSES
TREELESSNESS
TREELESSNESSES
TREENWARES
TREGETOURS
TREHALOSES
TREILLAGED
TREILLAGES

TREKSCHUIT
TREKSCHUITS
TRELLISING
TRELLISWORK
TRELLISWORKS
TREMATODES
TREMATOIDS
TREMBLEMENT
TREMBLEMENTS
TREMBLIEST
TREMBLINGLY
TREMBLINGS
TREMENDOUS
TREMENDOUSLY
TREMENDOUSNESS
TREMOLANDI
TREMOLANDO
TREMOLANDOS
TREMOLANTS
TREMOLITES
TREMOLITIC
TREMORLESS
TREMULANTS
TREMULATED
TREMULATES
TREMULATING
TREMULOUSLY
TREMULOUSNESS
TREMULOUSNESSES
TRENCHANCIES
TRENCHANCY
TRENCHANTLY
TRENCHARDS
TRENCHERMAN
TRENCHERMEN
TRENDIFIED
TRENDIFIES
TRENDIFYING
TRENDINESS
TRENDINESSES
TRENDSETTER
TRENDSETTERS
TRENDSETTING
TRENDSETTINGS
TRENDYISMS
TREPANATION
TREPANATIONS
TREPANNERS
TREPANNING
TREPANNINGS
TREPHINATION
TREPHINATIONS
TREPHINERS
TREPHINING
TREPHININGS
TREPIDATION
TREPIDATIONS
TREPIDATORY
TREPONEMAL
TREPONEMAS
TREPONEMATA
TREPONEMATOSES
TREPONEMATOSIS
TREPONEMATOUS
TREPONEMES
TRESPASSED
TRESPASSER

TRESPASSERS
TRESPASSES
TRESPASSING
TRESTLETREE
TRESTLETREES
TRESTLEWORK
TRESTLEWORKS
TRETINOINS
TREVALLIES
TRIABLENESS
TRIABLENESSES
TRIACETATE
TRIACETATES
TRIACONTER
TRIACONTERS
TRIACTINAL
TRIADELPHOUS
TRIADICALLY
TRIALITIES
TRIALLINGS
TRIALLISTS
TRIALOGUES
TRIALWARES
TRIAMCINOLONE
TRIAMCINOLONES
TRIANDRIAN
TRIANDROUS
TRIANGULAR
TRIANGULARITIES
TRIANGULARITY
TRIANGULARLY
TRIANGULATE
TRIANGULATED
TRIANGULATELY
TRIANGULATES
TRIANGULATING
TRIANGULATION
TRIANGULATIONS
TRIAPSIDAL
TRIARCHIES
TRIATHLETE
TRIATHLETES
TRIATHLONS
TRIATOMICALLY
TRIAXIALITIES
TRIAXIALITY
TRIBADISMS
TRIBALISMS
TRIBALISTIC
TRIBALISTS
TRIBESPEOPLE
TRIBESWOMAN
TRIBESWOMEN
TRIBOELECTRIC
TRIBOLOGICAL
TRIBOLOGIES
TRIBOLOGIST
TRIBOLOGISTS
TRIBOMETER
TRIBOMETERS
TRIBRACHIAL
TRIBRACHIC
TRIBROMOETHANOL
TRIBROMOMETHANE
TRIBULATED
TRIBULATES
TRIBULATING

TRIBULATION	TRICHOLOGICAL	TRICLINIUM	TRIGAMISTS	TRIMETHADIONE
TRIBULATIONS	TRICHOLOGIES	TRICLOSANS	TRIGEMINAL	TRIMETHADIONES
TRIBUNATES	TRICHOLOGIST	TRICOLETTE	TRIGEMINALS	TRIMETHOPRIM
TRIBUNESHIP	TRICHOLOGISTS	TRICOLETTES	TRIGEMINUS	TRIMETHOPRIMS
TRIBUNESHIPS	TRICHOLOGY	TRICOLORED	TRIGGERFISH	TRIMETHYLAMINE
TRIBUNICIAL	TRICHOMONACIDAL	TRICOLOURED	TRIGGERFISHES	TRIMETHYLAMINES
TRIBUNICIAN	TRICHOMONACIDE	TRICOLOURS	TRIGGERING	TRIMETHYLENE
TRIBUNITIAL	TRICHOMONACIDES	TRICONSONANTAL	TRIGGERLESS	TRIMETHYLENES
TRIBUNITIAN	TRICHOMONAD	TRICONSONANTIC	TRIGGERMAN	TRIMETRICAL
TRIBUTARIES	TRICHOMONADAL	TRICORNERED	TRIGGERMEN	TRIMETROGON
TRIBUTARILY	TRICHOMONADS	TRICORPORATE	TRIGLYCERIDE	TRIMETROGONS
TRIBUTARINESS	TRICHOMONAL	TRICORPORATED	TRIGLYCERIDES	TRIMMINGLY
TRIBUTARINESSES	TRICHOMONIASES	TRICOSTATE	TRIGLYPHIC	TRIMNESSES
TRICAMERAL	TRICHOMONIASIS	TRICOTEUSE	TRIGLYPHICAL	TRIMOLECULAR
TRICARBOXYLIC	TRICHOPHYTON	TRICOTEUSES	TRIGNESSES	TRIMONTHLY
TRICARPELLARY	TRICHOPHYTONS	TRICOTINES	TRIGONALLY	TRIMORPHIC
TRICENTENARIES	TRICHOPHYTOSES	TRICROTISM	TRIGONOMETER	TRIMORPHISM
TRICENTENARY	TRICHOPHYTOSIS	TRICROTISMS	TRIGONOMETERS	TRIMORPHISMS
TRICENTENNIAL	TRICHOPTERAN	TRICROTOUS	TRIGONOMETRIC	TRIMORPHOUS
TRICENTENNIALS	TRICHOPTERANS	TRICUSPIDAL	TRIGONOMETRICAL	TRIMPHONES
TRICEPHALOUS	TRICHOPTERIST	TRICUSPIDATE	TRIGONOMETRIES	TRINACRIAN
TRICERATOPS	TRICHOPTERISTS	TRICUSPIDS	TRIGONOMETRY	TRINACRIFORM
TRICERATOPSES	TRICHOPTEROUS	TRICYCLERS	TRIGRAMMATIC	TRINISCOPE
TRICERIONS	TRICHOTHECENE	TRICYCLICS	TRIGRAMMIC	TRINISCOPES
TRICHIASES	TRICHOTHECENES	TRICYCLING	TRIGRAPHIC	TRINITARIAN
TRICHIASIS	TRICHOTOMIC	TRICYCLINGS	TRIHALOMETHANE	TRINITARIANS
TRICHINELLA	TRICHOTOMIES	TRICYCLIST	TRIHALOMETHANES	TRINITRATE
TRICHINELLAE	TRICHOTOMISE	TRICYCLISTS	TRIHEDRALS	TRINITRATES
TRICHINELLAS	TRICHOTOMISED	TRIDACTYLOUS	TRIHEDRONS	TRINITRINS
TRICHINIASES	TRICHOTOMISES	TRIDENTATE	TRIHYBRIDS	TRINITROBENZENE
TRICHINIASIS	TRICHOTOMISING	TRIDIMENSIONAL	TRIHYDRATE	TRINITROCRESOL
TRICHINISATION	TRICHOTOMIZE	TRIDOMINIA	TRIHYDRATED	TRINITROCRESOLS
TRICHINISATIONS	TRICHOTOMIZED	TRIDOMINIUM	TRIHYDRATES	TRINITROPHENOL
TRICHINISE	TRICHOTOMIZES	TRIDOMINIUMS	TRIHYDROXY	TRINITROPHENOLS
TRICHINISED	TRICHOTOMIZING	TRIDYMITES	TRIIODOMETHANE	TRINITROTOLUENE
TRICHINISES	TRICHOTOMOUS	TRIENNIALLY	TRIIODOMETHANES	TRINITROTOLUOL
TRICHINISING	TRICHOTOMOUSLY	TRIENNIALS	TRILATERAL	TRINITROTOLUOLS
TRICHINIZATION	TRICHOTOMY	TRIENNIUMS	TRILATERALISM	TRINKETERS
TRICHINIZATIONS	TRICHROISM	TRIERARCHAL	TRILATERALISMS	TRINKETING
TRICHINIZE	TRICHROISMS	TRIERARCHIES	TRILATERALIST	TRINKETINGS
TRICHINIZED	TRICHROMAT	TRIERARCHS	TRILATERALISTS	TRINKETRIES
TRICHINIZES	TRICHROMATIC	TRIERARCHY	TRILATERALLY	TRINOCULAR
TRICHINIZING	TRICHROMATISM	TRIETHIODIDE	TRILATERALS	TRINOMIALISM
TRICHINOSE	TRICHROMATISMS	TRIETHIODIDES	TRILATERATION	TRINOMIALISMS
TRICHINOSED	TRICHROMATS	TRIETHYLAMINE	TRILATERATIONS	TRINOMIALIST
TRICHINOSES	TRICHROMIC	TRIETHYLAMINES	TRILINEATE	TRINOMIALISTS
TRICHINOSING	TRICHROMICS	TRIFACIALS	TRILINGUAL	TRINOMIALLY
TRICHINOSIS	TRICHRONOUS	TRIFARIOUS	TRILINGUALISM	TRINOMIALS
TRICHINOTIC	TRICHURIASES	TRIFFIDIAN	TRILINGUALISMS	TRINUCLEOTIDE
TRICHINOUS	TRICHURIASIS	TRIFFIDIER	TRILINGUALLY	TRINUCLEOTIDES
TRICHLORACETIC	TRICKERIES	TRIFFIDIEST	TRILITERAL	TRIOECIOUS
TRICHLORFON	TRICKINESS	TRIFLINGLY	TRILITERALISM	TRIOXOBORIC
TRICHLORFONS	TRICKINESSES	TRIFLINGNESS	TRILITERALISMS	TRIOXYGENS
TRICHLORIDE	TRICKISHLY	TRIFLINGNESSES	TRILITERALS	TRIPALMITIN
TRICHLORIDES	TRICKISHNESS	TRIFLUOPERAZINE	TRILITHONS	TRIPALMITINS
TRICHLOROACETIC	TRICKISHNESSES	TRIFLURALIN	TRILLIONAIRE	TRIPARTISM
TRICHLOROETHANE	TRICKLIEST	TRIFLURALINS	TRILLIONAIRES	TRIPARTISMS
TRICHLORPHON	TRICKLINGLY	TRIFOLIATE	TRILLIONTH	TRIPARTITE
TRICHLORPHONS	TRICKLINGS	TRIFOLIATED	TRILLIONTHS	TRIPARTITELY
TRICHOBACTERIA	TRICKSIEST	TRIFOLIOLATE	TRILOBATED	TRIPARTITION
TRICHOCYST	TRICKSINESS	TRIFOLIUMS	TRILOBITES	TRIPARTITIONS
TRICHOCYSTIC	TRICKSINESSES	TRIFURCATE	TRILOBITIC	TRIPEHOUND
TRICHOCYSTS	TRICKSTERING	TRIFURCATED	TRILOCULAR	TRIPEHOUNDS
TRICHOGYNE	TRICKSTERINGS	TRIFURCATES	TRIMERISMS	TRIPERSONAL
TRICHOGYNES	TRICKSTERS	TRIFURCATING	TRIMESTERS	TRIPERSONALISM
TRICHOGYNIAL	TRICKTRACK	TRIFURCATION	TRIMESTRAL	TRIPERSONALISMS
TRICHOGYNIC	TRICKTRACKS	TRIFURCATIONS	TRIMESTRIAL	TRIPERSONALIST

TRIPERSONALISTS	TRISOCTAHEDRA	TRIUMPHANT	TROGLODYTISM	TROPICALLY
TRIPERSONALITY	TRISOCTAHEDRAL	TRIUMPHANTLY	TROGLODYTISMS	TROPICBIRD
TRIPETALOUS	TRISOCTAHEDRON	TRIUMPHERIES	TROLLEYBUS	TROPICBIRDS
TRIPHAMMER	TRISOCTAHEDRONS	TRIUMPHERS	TROLLEYBUSES	TROPISMATIC
TRIPHAMMERS	TRISTEARIN	TRIUMPHERY	TROLLEYBUSSES	TROPOCOLLAGEN
TRIPHENYLAMINE	TRISTEARINS	TRIUMPHING	TROLLEYING	TROPOCOLLAGENS
TRIPHENYLAMINES	TRISTESSES	TRIUMPHINGS	TROLLIUSES	TROPOLOGIC
TRIPHIBIOUS	TRISTFULLY	TRIUMVIRAL	TROLLOPEES	TROPOLOGICAL
TRIPHOSPHATE	TRISTFULNESS	TRIUMVIRATE	TROLLOPIER	TROPOLOGICALLY
TRIPHOSPHATES	TRISTFULNESSES	TRIUMVIRATES	TROLLOPIEST	TROPOLOGIES
TRIPHTHONG	TRISTICHIC	TRIUMVIRIES	TROLLOPING	TROPOMYOSIN
TRIPHTHONGAL	TRISTICHOUS	TRIUNITIES	TROLLOPISH	TROPOMYOSINS
TRIPHTHONGS	TRISTIMULUS	TRIVALENCE	TROMBICULID	TROPOPAUSE
TRIPHYLITE	TRISUBSTITUTED	TRIVALENCES	TROMBICULIDS	TROPOPAUSES
TRIPHYLITES	TRISULCATE	TRIVALENCIES	TROMBIDIASES	TROPOPHILOUS
TRIPHYLLOUS	TRISULFIDE	TRIVALENCY	TROMBIDIASIS	TROPOPHYTE
TRIPINNATE	TRISULFIDES	TRIVALVULAR	TROMBONIST	TROPOPHYTES
TRIPINNATELY	TRISULPHIDE	TRIVIALISATION	TROMBONISTS	TROPOPHYTIC
TRIPITAKAS	TRISULPHIDES	TRIVIALISATIONS	TROMOMETER	TROPOSCATTER
TRIPLENESS	TRISYLLABIC	TRIVIALISE	TROMOMETERS	TROPOSCATTERS
TRIPLENESSES	TRISYLLABICAL	TRIVIALISED	TROMOMETRIC	TROPOSPHERE
TRIPLETAIL	TRISYLLABICALLY	TRIVIALISES	TROOPSHIPS	TROPOSPHERES
TRIPLETAILS	TRISYLLABLE	TRIVIALISING	TROOSTITES	TROPOSPHERIC
TRIPLEXING	TRISYLLABLES	TRIVIALISM	TROPAEOLIN	TROPOTAXES
TRIPLICATE	TRITAGONIST	TRIVIALISMS	TROPAEOLINS	TROPOTAXIS
TRIPLICATED	TRITAGONISTS	TRIVIALIST	TROPAEOLUM	TROTHPLIGHT
TRIPLICATES	TRITANOPES	TRIVIALISTS	TROPAEOLUMS	TROTHPLIGHTED
TRIPLICATING	TRITANOPIA	TRIVIALITIES	TROPARIONS	TROTHPLIGHTING
TRIPLICATION	TRITANOPIAS	TRIVIALITY	TROPEOLINS	TROTHPLIGHTS
TRIPLICATIONS	TRITANOPIC	TRIVIALIZATION	TROPHALLACTIC	TROUBADOUR
TRIPLICITIES	TRITENESSES	TRIVIALIZATIONS	TROPHALLAXES	TROUBADOURS
TRIPLICITY	TRITERNATE	TRIVIALIZE	TROPHALLAXIS	TROUBLEDLY
TRIPLOBLASTIC	TRITHEISMS	TRIVIALIZED	TROPHESIAL	TROUBLEFREE
TRIPLOIDIES	TRITHEISTIC	TRIVIALIZES	TROPHESIES	TROUBLEMAKER
TRIPMETERS	TRITHEISTICAL	TRIVIALIZING	TROPHICALLY	TROUBLEMAKERS
TRIPPERIER	TRITHEISTS	TRIVIALNESS	TROPHOBIOSES	TROUBLEMAKING
TRIPPERIEST	TRITHIONATE	TRIVIALNESSES	TROPHOBIOSIS	TROUBLEMAKINGS
TRIPPERISH	TRITHIONATES	TRIWEEKLIES	TROPHOBIOTIC	TROUBLESHOOT
TRIPPINGLY	TRITHIONIC	TROCHAICALLY	TROPHOBLAST	TROUBLESHOOTER
TRIPTEROUS	TRITIATING	TROCHANTER	TROPHOBLASTIC	TROUBLESHOOTERS
TRIPTYQUES	TRITIATION	TROCHANTERAL	TROPHOBLASTS	TROUBLESHOOTING
TRIPUDIARY	TRITIATIONS	TROCHANTERIC	TROPHOLOGIES	TROUBLESHOOTS
TRIPUDIATE	TRITICALES	TROCHANTERS	TROPHOLOGY	TROUBLESHOT
TRIPUDIATED	TRITICALLY	TROCHEAMETER	TROPHONEUROSES	TROUBLESOME
TRIPUDIATES	TRITICALNESS	TROCHEAMETERS	TROPHONEUROSIS	TROUBLESOMELY
TRIPUDIATING	TRITICALNESSES	TROCHELMINTH	TROPHOPLASM	TROUBLESOMENESS
TRIPUDIATION	TRITICEOUS	TROCHELMINTHS	TROPHOPLASMS	TROUBLINGS
TRIPUDIATIONS	TRITICISMS	TROCHILUSES	TROPHOTACTIC	TROUBLOUSLY
TRIQUETRAE	TRITUBERCULAR	TROCHISCUS	TROPHOTAXES	TROUBLOUSNESS
TRIQUETRAL	TRITUBERCULATE	TROCHISCUSES	TROPHOTAXIS	TROUBLOUSNESSES
TRIQUETRAS	TRITUBERCULIES	TROCHLEARS	TROPHOTROPIC	TROUGHINGS
TRIQUETROUS	TRITUBERCULISM	TROCHOIDAL	TROPHOTROPISM	TROUGHLIKE
TRIQUETROUSLY	TRITUBERCULISMS	TROCHOIDALLY	TROPHOTROPISMS	TROUNCINGS
TRIQUETRUM	TRITUBERCULY	TROCHOMETER	TROPHOZOITE	TROUSERING
TRIRADIATE	TRITURABLE	TROCHOMETERS	TROPHOZOITES	TROUSERINGS
TRIRADIATELY	TRITURATED	TROCHOPHORE	TROPICALISATION	TROUSERLESS
TRISACCHARIDE	TRITURATES	TROCHOPHORES	TROPICALISE	TROUSSEAUS
TRISACCHARIDES	TRITURATING	TROCHOSPHERE	TROPICALISED	TROUSSEAUX
TRISAGIONS	TRITURATION	TROCHOSPHERES	TROPICALISES	TROUTLINGS
TRISECTING	TRITURATIONS	TROCHOTRON	TROPICALISING	TROUTSTONE
TRISECTION	TRITURATOR	TROCHOTRONS	TROPICALITIES	TROUTSTONES
TRISECTIONS	TRITURATORS	TROCTOLITE	TROPICALITY	TROUVAILLE
TRISECTORS	TRIUMPHALISM	TROCTOLITES	TROPICALIZATION	TROUVAILLES
TRISECTRICES	TRIUMPHALISMS	TROGLODYTE	TROPICALIZE	TROWELLERS
TRISECTRIX	TRIUMPHALIST	TROGLODYTES	TROPICALIZED	TROWELLING
TRISKELION	TRIUMPHALISTS	TROGLODYTIC	TROPICALIZES	TRUANTINGS
TRISKELIONS	TRIUMPHALS	TROGLODYTICAL	TROPICALIZING	TRUANTRIES

TRUANTSHIP	TRUTHFULLY	TUBERCULISES	TUMBLEBUGS	TURBIDIMETRIES
TRUANTSHIPS	TRUTHFULNESS	TUBERCULISING	TUMBLEDOWN	TURBIDIMETRY
TRUCKLINES	TRUTHFULNESSES	TUBERCULIZATION	TUMBLEHOME	TURBIDITES
TRUCKLINGS	TRUTHINESS	TUBERCULIZE	TUMBLEHOMES	TURBIDITIES
TRUCKLOADS	TRUTHINESSES	TUBERCULIZED	TUMBLERFUL	TURBIDNESS
TRUCKMASTER	TRUTHLESSNESS	TUBERCULIZES	TUMBLERFULS	TURBIDNESSES
TRUCKMASTERS	TRUTHLESSNESSES	TUBERCULIZING	TUMBLERSFUL	TURBINACIOUS
TRUCKSTOPS	TRYINGNESS	TUBERCULOID	TUMBLESETS	TURBINATED
TRUCULENCE	TRYINGNESSES	TUBERCULOMA	TUMBLEWEED	TURBINATES
TRUCULENCES	TRYPAFLAVINE	TUBERCULOMAS	TUMBLEWEEDS	TURBINATION
TRUCULENCIES	TRYPAFLAVINES	TUBERCULOMATA	TUMEFACIENT	TURBINATIONS
TRUCULENCY	TRYPANOCIDAL	TUBERCULOSE	TUMEFACTION	TURBOCHARGED
TRUCULENTLY	TRYPANOCIDE	TUBERCULOSED	TUMEFACTIONS	TURBOCHARGER
TRUEHEARTED	TRYPANOCIDES	TUBERCULOSES	TUMESCENCE	TURBOCHARGERS
TRUEHEARTEDNESS	TRYPANOSOMAL	TUBERCULOSIS	TUMESCENCES	TURBOCHARGING
TRUENESSES	TRYPANOSOME	TUBERCULOUS	TUMESCENTLY	TURBOCHARGINGS
TRUEPENNIES	TRYPANOSOMES	TUBERCULOUSLY	TUMIDITIES	TURBOELECTRIC
TRUFFLINGS	TRYPANOSOMIASES	TUBERCULUM	TUMIDNESSES	TURBOGENERATOR
TRUMPERIES	TRYPANOSOMIASIS	TUBERIFEROUS	TUMORGENIC	TURBOGENERATORS
TRUMPETERS	TRYPANOSOMIC	TUBERIFORM	TUMORGENICITIES	TURBOMACHINERY
TRUMPETING	TRYPARSAMIDE	TUBEROSITIES	TUMORGENICITY	TURBOPROPS
TRUMPETINGS	TRYPARSAMIDES	TUBEROSITY	TUMORIGENESES	TURBOSHAFT
TRUMPETLIKE	TRYPSINOGEN	TUBICOLOUS	TUMORIGENESIS	TURBOSHAFTS
TRUMPETWEED	TRYPSINOGENS	TUBIFICIDS	TUMORIGENIC	TURBULATOR
TRUMPETWEEDS	TRYPTAMINE	TUBIFLOROUS	TUMORIGENICITY	TURBULATORS
TRUNCATELY	TRYPTAMINES	TUBOCURARINE	TUMULOSITIES	TURBULENCE
TRUNCATING	TRYPTOPHAN	TUBOCURARINES	TUMULOSITY	TURBULENCES
TRUNCATINGS	TRYPTOPHANE	TUBOPLASTIES	TUMULTUARY	TURBULENCIES
TRUNCATION	TRYPTOPHANES	TUBOPLASTY	TUMULTUATE	TURBULENCY
TRUNCATIONS	TRYPTOPHANS	TUBULARIAN	TUMULTUATED	TURBULENTLY
TRUNCHEONED	TSAREVICHES	TUBULARIANS	TUMULTUATES	TURCOPOLES
TRUNCHEONER	TSAREVITCH	TUBULARITIES	TUMULTUATING	TURCOPOLIER
TRUNCHEONERS	TSAREVITCHES	TUBULARITY	TUMULTUATION	TURCOPOLIERS
TRUNCHEONING	TSCHERNOSEM	TUBULATING	TUMULTUATIONS	TURDUCKENS
TRUNCHEONS	TSCHERNOSEMS	TUBULATION	TUMULTUOUS	TURFGRASSES
TRUNKFISHES	TSESAREVICH	TUBULATIONS	TUMULTUOUSLY	TURFINESSES
TRUNKSLEEVE	TSESAREVICHES	TUBULATORS	TUMULTUOUSNESS	TURFSKIING
TRUNKSLEEVES	TSESAREVITCH	TUBULATURE	TUNABILITIES	TURFSKIINGS
TRUNKWORKS	TSESAREVITCHES	TUBULATURES	TUNABILITY	TURGENCIES
TRUNNIONED	TSESAREVNA	TUBULIFLORAL	TUNABLENESS	TURGESCENCE
TRUSTABILITIES	TSESAREVNAS	TUBULIFLOROUS	TUNABLENESSES	TURGESCENCES
TRUSTABILITY	TSESAREWICH	TUBULOUSLY	TUNBELLIED	TURGESCENCIES
TRUSTAFARIAN	TSESAREWICHES	TUCKAMORES	TUNBELLIES	TURGESCENCY
TRUSTAFARIANS	TSESAREWITCH	TUCKERBAGS	TUNEFULNESS	TURGESCENT
TRUSTBUSTER	TSESAREWITCHES	TUCKERBOXES	TUNEFULNESSES	TURGIDITIES
TRUSTBUSTERS	TSOTSITAAL	TUFFACEOUS	TUNELESSLY	TURGIDNESS
TRUSTBUSTING	TSOTSITAALS	TUFFTAFFETA	TUNELESSNESS	TURGIDNESSES
TRUSTBUSTINGS	TSUNAMIGENIC	TUFFTAFFETAS	TUNELESSNESSES	TURMOILING
TRUSTEEING	TSUTSUGAMUSHI	TUFFTAFFETIES	TUNESMITHS	TURNABOUTS
TRUSTEESHIP	TSUTSUGAMUSHIS	TUFFTAFFETY	TUNGSTATES	TURNAGAINS
TRUSTEESHIPS	TUBBINESSES	TUFTAFFETA	TUNGSTITES	TURNAROUND
TRUSTFULLY	TUBECTOMIES	TUFTAFFETAS	TUNNELINGS	TURNAROUNDS
TRUSTFULNESS	TUBERACEOUS	TUFTAFFETIES	TUNNELLERS	TURNBROACH
TRUSTFULNESSES	TUBERCULAR	TUFTAFFETY	TUNNELLIKE	TURNBROACHES
TRUSTINESS	TUBERCULARLY	TUILLETTES	TUNNELLING	TURNBUCKLE
TRUSTINESSES	TUBERCULARS	TUILYIEING	TUNNELLINGS	TURNBUCKLES
TRUSTINGLY	TUBERCULATE	TUILZIEING	TUPPENNIES	TURNIPIEST
TRUSTINGNESS	TUBERCULATED	TUITIONARY	TUPTOWINGS	TURNROUNDS
TRUSTINGNESSES	TUBERCULATELY	TULARAEMIA	TURACOVERDIN	TURNSTILES
TRUSTLESSLY	TUBERCULATION	TULARAEMIAS	TURACOVERDINS	TURNSTONES
TRUSTLESSNESS	TUBERCULATIONS	TULARAEMIC	TURANGAWAEWAE	TURNTABLES
TRUSTLESSNESSES	TUBERCULES	TULAREMIAS	TURANGAWAEWAES	TURNTABLIST
TRUSTWORTHIER	TUBERCULIN	TULIPOMANIA	TURBELLARIAN	TURNTABLISTS
TRUSTWORTHIEST	TUBERCULINS	TULIPOMANIAS	TURBELLARIANS	TURNVEREIN
TRUSTWORTHILY	TUBERCULISATION	TULIPWOODS	TURBIDIMETER	TURNVEREINS
TRUSTWORTHINESS	TUBERCULISE	TUMATAKURU	TURBIDIMETERS	TUROPHILES
TRUSTWORTHY	TUBERCULISED	TUMATAKURUS	TURBIDIMETRIC	TURPENTINE

TURPENTINED	TWANGLINGLY	TWITTERINGS	TYPEWRITERS	TYPOTHETAE
TURPENTINES	TWANGLINGS	TWITTINGLY	TYPEWRITES	TYRANNESSES
TURPENTINIER	TWATTLINGS	TWOFOLDNESS	TYPEWRITING	TYRANNICAL
TURPENTINIEST	TWAYBLADES	TWOFOLDNESSES	TYPEWRITINGS	TYRANNICALLY
TURPENTINING	TWEEDINESS	TWOPENCEWORTH	TYPEWRITTEN	TYRANNICALNESS
TURPENTINY	TWEEDINESSES	TWOPENCEWORTHS	TYPHACEOUS	TYRANNICIDAL
TURPITUDES	TWEEDLEDEE	TWOPENNIES	TYPHLITISES	TYRANNICIDE
TURQUOISES	TWEEDLEDEED	TWOSEATERS	TYPHLOLOGIES	TYRANNICIDES
TURRIBANTS	TWEEDLEDEEING	TYCOONATES	TYPHLOLOGY	TYRANNISED
TURRICULATE	TWEEDLEDEES	TYCOONERIES	TYPHLOSOLE	TYRANNISER
TURRICULATED	TWEENAGERS	TYLECTOMIES	TYPHLOSOLES	TYRANNISERS
TURTLEBACK	TWEENESSES	TYMPANIFORM	TYPHOGENIC	TYRANNISES
TURTLEBACKS	TWELVEFOLD	TYMPANISTS	TYPHOIDINS	TYRANNISING
TURTLEDOVE	TWELVEMONTH	TYMPANITES	TYPICALITIES	TYRANNIZED
TURTLEDOVES	TWELVEMONTHS	TYMPANITESES	TYPICALITY	TYRANNIZER
TURTLEHEAD	TWENTIETHS	TYMPANITIC	TYPICALNESS	TYRANNIZERS
TURTLEHEADS	TWENTYFOLD	TYMPANITIS	TYPICALNESSES	TYRANNIZES
TURTLENECK	TWENTYFOLDS	TYMPANITISES	TYPIFICATION	TYRANNIZING
TURTLENECKED	TWICHILDREN	TYNDALLIMETRIES	TYPIFICATIONS	TYRANNOSAUR
TURTLENECKS	TWIDDLIEST	TYNDALLIMETRY	TYPOGRAPHED	TYRANNOSAURS
TUSSOCKIER	TWIDDLINGS	TYPECASTER	TYPOGRAPHER	TYRANNOSAURUS
TUSSOCKIEST	TWILIGHTED	TYPECASTERS	TYPOGRAPHERS	TYRANNOSAURUSES
TUTELARIES	TWILIGHTING	TYPECASTING	TYPOGRAPHIA	TYRANNOUSLY
TUTIORISMS	TWINBERRIES	TYPECASTINGS	TYPOGRAPHIC	TYRANNOUSNESS
TUTIORISTS	TWINFLOWER	TYPEFOUNDER	TYPOGRAPHICAL	TYRANNOUSNESSES
TUTORESSES	TWINFLOWERS	TYPEFOUNDERS	TYPOGRAPHICALLY	TYREMAKERS
TUTORIALLY	TWINKLIEST	TYPEFOUNDING	TYPOGRAPHIES	TYROCIDINE
TUTORISING	TWINKLINGS	TYPEFOUNDINGS	TYPOGRAPHING	TYROCIDINES
TUTORIZING	TWISTABILITIES	TYPEFOUNDRIES	TYPOGRAPHIST	TYROCIDINS
TUTORSHIPS	TWISTABILITY	TYPEFOUNDRY	TYPOGRAPHISTS	TYROGLYPHID
TUTOYERING	TWITCHIEST	TYPESCRIPT	TYPOGRAPHS	TYROGLYPHIDS
TUTWORKERS	TWITCHINGS	TYPESCRIPTS	TYPOGRAPHY	TYROPITTAS
TUTWORKMAN	TWITTERATI	TYPESETTER	TYPOLOGICAL	TYROSINASE
TUTWORKMEN	TWITTERERS	TYPESETTERS	TYPOLOGICALLY	TYROSINASES
TWADDLIEST	TWITTERIER	TYPESETTING	TYPOLOGIES	TYROTHRICIN
TWADDLINGS	TWITTERIEST	TYPESETTINGS	TYPOLOGIST	TYROTHRICINS
TWALPENNIES	TWITTERING	TYPESTYLES	TYPOLOGISTS	
TWANGINGLY	TWITTERINGLY	TYPEWRITER	TYPOMANIAS	

t

U

UBERSEXUAL
UBERSEXUALS
UBIQUARIAN
UBIQUINONE
UBIQUINONES
UBIQUITARIAN
UBIQUITARIANISM
UBIQUITARIANS
UBIQUITARY
UBIQUITIES
UBIQUITINATION
UBIQUITINATIONS
UBIQUITINS
UBIQUITOUS
UBIQUITOUSLY
UBIQUITOUSNESS
UDOMETRIES
UFOLOGICAL
UFOLOGISTS
UGLIFICATION
UGLIFICATIONS
UGLINESSES
UGSOMENESS
UGSOMENESSES
UINTAHITES
UINTATHERE
UINTATHERES
UITLANDERS
ULCERATING
ULCERATION
ULCERATIONS
ULCERATIVE
ULCEROGENIC
ULCEROUSLY
ULCEROUSNESS
ULCEROUSNESSES
ULOTRICHIES
ULOTRICHOUS
ULSTERETTE
ULSTERETTES
ULTERIORLY
ULTIMACIES
ULTIMATELY
ULTIMATENESS
ULTIMATENESSES
ULTIMATING
ULTIMATUMS
ULTIMOGENITURE
ULTIMOGENITURES
ULTRABASIC
ULTRABASICS
ULTRACAREFUL
ULTRACASUAL
ULTRACAUTIOUS

ULTRACENTRIFUGE
ULTRACIVILISED
ULTRACIVILIZED
ULTRACLEAN
ULTRACOMMERCIAL
ULTRACOMPACT
ULTRACOMPETENT
ULTRACONVENIENT
ULTRACREPIDATE
ULTRACREPIDATED
ULTRACREPIDATES
ULTRACRITICAL
ULTRADEMOCRATIC
ULTRADENSE
ULTRADISTANCE
ULTRADISTANT
ULTRADRIER
ULTRADRIEST
ULTRADRYER
ULTRADRYEST
ULTRAEFFICIENT
ULTRAENERGETIC
ULTRAEXCLUSIVE
ULTRAFAMILIAR
ULTRAFASTIDIOUS
ULTRAFEMININE
ULTRAFICHE
ULTRAFICHES
ULTRAFILTER
ULTRAFILTERED
ULTRAFILTERING
ULTRAFILTERS
ULTRAFILTRATE
ULTRAFILTRATES
ULTRAFILTRATION
ULTRAGLAMOROUS
ULTRAHAZARDOUS
ULTRAHEATED
ULTRAHEATING
ULTRAHEATS
ULTRAHEAVIER
ULTRAHEAVIEST
ULTRAHEAVY
ULTRAHUMAN
ULTRAISTIC
ULTRALARGE
ULTRALEFTISM
ULTRALEFTISMS
ULTRALEFTIST
ULTRALEFTISTS
ULTRALEFTS
ULTRALIBERAL
ULTRALIBERALISM
ULTRALIBERALS

ULTRALIGHT
ULTRALIGHTS
ULTRAMAFIC
ULTRAMARATHON
ULTRAMARATHONER
ULTRAMARATHONS
ULTRAMARINE
ULTRAMARINES
ULTRAMASCULINE
ULTRAMICRO
ULTRAMICROMETER
ULTRAMICROSCOPE
ULTRAMICROSCOPY
ULTRAMICROTOME
ULTRAMICROTOMES
ULTRAMICROTOMY
ULTRAMILITANT
ULTRAMILITANTS
ULTRAMINIATURE
ULTRAMODERN
ULTRAMODERNISM
ULTRAMODERNISMS
ULTRAMODERNIST
ULTRAMODERNISTS
ULTRAMONTANE
ULTRAMONTANES
ULTRAMONTANISM
ULTRAMONTANISMS
ULTRAMONTANIST
ULTRAMONTANISTS
ULTRAMUNDANE
ULTRANATIONAL
ULTRAORTHODOX
ULTRAPATRIOTIC
ULTRAPHYSICAL
ULTRAPOWERFUL
ULTRAPRACTICAL
ULTRAPRECISE
ULTRAPRECISION
ULTRAPRECISIONS
ULTRAQUIET
ULTRARADICAL
ULTRARADICALS
ULTRARAPID
ULTRARAREFIED
ULTRARATIONAL
ULTRAREALISM
ULTRAREALISMS
ULTRAREALIST
ULTRAREALISTIC
ULTRAREALISTS
ULTRAREFINED
ULTRARELIABLE
ULTRARIGHT

ULTRARIGHTISM
ULTRARIGHTISMS
ULTRARIGHTIST
ULTRARIGHTISTS
ULTRARIGHTS
ULTRAROMANTIC
ULTRAROYALIST
ULTRAROYALISTS
ULTRASECRET
ULTRASENSITIVE
ULTRASENSUAL
ULTRASERIOUS
ULTRASHARP
ULTRASHORT
ULTRASIMPLE
ULTRASLICK
ULTRASMALL
ULTRASMART
ULTRASMOOTH
ULTRASONIC
ULTRASONICALLY
ULTRASONICS
ULTRASONOGRAPHY
ULTRASOUND
ULTRASOUNDS
ULTRASTRUCTURAL
ULTRASTRUCTURE
ULTRASTRUCTURES
ULTRATINIER
ULTRATINIEST
ULTRAVACUA
ULTRAVACUUM
ULTRAVACUUMS
ULTRAVIOLENCE
ULTRAVIOLENCES
ULTRAVIOLENT
ULTRAVIOLET
ULTRAVIOLETS
ULTRAVIRILE
ULTRAVIRILITIES
ULTRAVIRILITY
ULTRAVIRUS
ULTRAVIRUSES
ULTRAWIDEBAND
ULTRAWIDEBANDS
ULTRONEOUS
ULTRONEOUSLY
ULTRONEOUSNESS
ULULATIONS
UMBELLATED
UMBELLATELY
UMBELLIFER
UMBELLIFEROUS
UMBELLIFERS

UMBELLULATE
UMBELLULES
UMBILICALLY
UMBILICALS
UMBILICATE
UMBILICATED
UMBILICATION
UMBILICATIONS
UMBILICUSES
UMBILIFORM
UMBONATION
UMBONATIONS
UMBRACULATE
UMBRACULIFORM
UMBRACULUM
UMBRAGEOUS
UMBRAGEOUSLY
UMBRAGEOUSNESS
UMBRATICAL
UMBRATILES
UMBRATILOUS
UMBRELLAED
UMBRELLAING
UMBRELLOES
UMBRIFEROUS
UMPIRESHIP
UMPIRESHIPS
UMPTEENTHS
UNABASHEDLY
UNABATEDLY
UNABBREVIATED
UNABOLISHED
UNABRIDGED
UNABROGATED
UNABSOLVED
UNABSORBED
UNABSORBENT
UNACADEMIC
UNACADEMICALLY
UNACCENTED
UNACCENTUATED
UNACCEPTABILITY
UNACCEPTABLE
UNACCEPTABLY
UNACCEPTANCE
UNACCEPTANCES
UNACCEPTED
UNACCLIMATED
UNACCLIMATISED
UNACCLIMATIZED
UNACCOMMODATED
UNACCOMMODATING
UNACCOMPANIED
UNACCOMPLISHED

UNACCOUNTABLE
UNACCOUNTABLY
UNACCOUNTED
UNACCREDITED
UNACCULTURATED
UNACCUSABLE
UNACCUSABLY
UNACCUSTOMED
UNACCUSTOMEDLY
UNACHIEVABLE
UNACHIEVED
UNACKNOWLEDGED
UNACQUAINT
UNACQUAINTANCE
UNACQUAINTANCES
UNACQUAINTED
UNACQUAINTING
UNACQUAINTS
UNACTIVING
UNACTORISH
UNACTUATED
UNADAPTABLE
UNADDRESSED
UNADJUDICATED
UNADJUSTED
UNADMIRING
UNADMITTED
UNADMONISHED
UNADOPTABLE
UNADULTERATE
UNADULTERATED
UNADULTERATEDLY
UNADVENTROUS
UNADVENTUROUS
UNADVENTUROUSLY
UNADVERTISED
UNADVERTIZED
UNADVISABLE
UNADVISABLENESS
UNADVISABLY
UNADVISEDLY
UNADVISEDNESS
UNADVISEDNESSES
UNAESTHETIC
UNAFFECTED
UNAFFECTEDLY
UNAFFECTEDNESS
UNAFFECTING
UNAFFECTIONATE
UNAFFILIATED
UNAFFLUENT
UNAFFORDABLE
UNAGGRESSIVE
UNAGREEABLE
UNALIENABLE
UNALIENABLY
UNALIENATED
UNALLEVIATED
UNALLOCATED
UNALLOTTED
UNALLOWABLE
UNALLURING
UNALTERABILITY
UNALTERABLE
UNALTERABLENESS
UNALTERABLY
UNALTERING

UNAMBIGUOUS
UNAMBIGUOUSLY
UNAMBITIOUS
UNAMBITIOUSLY
UNAMBIVALENT
UNAMBIVALENTLY
UNAMENABLE
UNAMENDABLE
UNAMIABILITIES
UNAMIABILITY
UNAMIABLENESS
UNAMIABLENESSES
UNAMORTISED
UNAMORTIZED
UNAMPLIFIED
UNAMUSABLE
UNAMUSINGLY
UNANAESTHETISED
UNANAESTHETIZED
UNANALYSABLE
UNANALYSED
UNANALYTIC
UNANALYTICAL
UNANALYZABLE
UNANALYZED
UNANCHORED
UNANCHORING
UNANESTHETISED
UNANESTHETIZED
UNANIMATED
UNANIMITIES
UNANIMOUSLY
UNANIMOUSNESS
UNANIMOUSNESSES
UNANNEALED
UNANNOTATED
UNANNOUNCED
UNANSWERABILITY
UNANSWERABLE
UNANSWERABLY
UNANSWERED
UNANTICIPATED
UNANTICIPATEDLY
UNAPOLOGETIC
UNAPOLOGISING
UNAPOLOGIZING
UNAPOSTOLIC
UNAPOSTOLICAL
UNAPOSTOLICALLY
UNAPPALLED
UNAPPARELLED
UNAPPARELLING
UNAPPARELS
UNAPPARENT
UNAPPEALABLE
UNAPPEALABLY
UNAPPEALING
UNAPPEALINGLY
UNAPPEASABLE
UNAPPEASABLY
UNAPPEASED
UNAPPETISING
UNAPPETISINGLY
UNAPPETIZING
UNAPPETIZINGLY
UNAPPLAUSIVE
UNAPPLICABLE

UNAPPOINTED
UNAPPRECIATED
UNAPPRECIATION
UNAPPRECIATIONS
UNAPPRECIATIVE
UNAPPREHENDED
UNAPPREHENSIBLE
UNAPPREHENSIVE
UNAPPRISED
UNAPPROACHABLE
UNAPPROACHABLY
UNAPPROACHED
UNAPPROPRIATE
UNAPPROPRIATED
UNAPPROPRIATES
UNAPPROPRIATING
UNAPPROVED
UNAPPROVING
UNAPPROVINGLY
UNAPTNESSES
UNARGUABLE
UNARGUABLY
UNARMOURED
UNARRANGED
UNARROGANT
UNARTFULLY
UNARTICULATE
UNARTICULATED
UNARTIFICIAL
UNARTIFICIALLY
UNARTISTIC
UNARTISTLIKE
UNASCENDABLE
UNASCENDED
UNASCENDIBLE
UNASCERTAINABLE
UNASCERTAINED
UNASHAMEDLY
UNASHAMEDNESS
UNASHAMEDNESSES
UNASPIRATED
UNASPIRING
UNASPIRINGLY
UNASPIRINGNESS
UNASSAILABILITY
UNASSAILABLE
UNASSAILABLY
UNASSAILED
UNASSEMBLED
UNASSERTIVE
UNASSERTIVELY
UNASSIGNABLE
UNASSIGNED
UNASSIMILABLE
UNASSIMILATED
UNASSISTED
UNASSISTEDLY
UNASSISTING
UNASSOCIATED
UNASSUAGEABLE
UNASSUAGED
UNASSUMING
UNASSUMINGLY
UNASSUMINGNESS
UNATHLETIC
UNATONABLE
UNATTACHED

UNATTAINABLE
UNATTAINABLY
UNATTAINTED
UNATTEMPTED
UNATTENDED
UNATTENDING
UNATTENTIVE
UNATTENUATED
UNATTESTED
UNATTRACTIVE
UNATTRACTIVELY
UNATTRIBUTABLE
UNATTRIBUTED
UNAUGMENTED
UNAUSPICIOUS
UNAUTHENTIC
UNAUTHENTICATED
UNAUTHENTICITY
UNAUTHORISED
UNAUTHORITATIVE
UNAUTHORIZED
UNAUTOMATED
UNAVAILABILITY
UNAVAILABLE
UNAVAILABLENESS
UNAVAILABLY
UNAVAILING
UNAVAILINGLY
UNAVAILINGNESS
UNAVERTABLE
UNAVERTIBLE
UNAVOIDABILITY
UNAVOIDABLE
UNAVOIDABLENESS
UNAVOIDABLY
UNAVOWEDLY
UNAWAKENED
UNAWAKENING
UNAWARENESS
UNAWARENESSES
UNBAILABLE
UNBALANCED
UNBALANCES
UNBALANCING
UNBALLASTED
UNBANDAGED
UNBANDAGES
UNBANDAGING
UNBANNINGS
UNBAPTISED
UNBAPTISES
UNBAPTISING
UNBAPTIZED
UNBAPTIZES
UNBAPTIZING
UNBARBERED
UNBARRICADE
UNBARRICADED
UNBARRICADES
UNBARRICADING
UNBATTERED
UNBEARABLE
UNBEARABLENESS
UNBEARABLY
UNBEATABLE
UNBEATABLY
UNBEAUTIFUL

UNBEAUTIFULLY
UNBEAVERED
UNBECOMING
UNBECOMINGLY
UNBECOMINGNESS
UNBECOMINGS
UNBEDIMMED
UNBEDINNED
UNBEFITTING
UNBEFRIENDED
UNBEGETTING
UNBEGINNING
UNBEGOTTEN
UNBEGUILED
UNBEGUILES
UNBEGUILING
UNBEHOLDEN
UNBEKNOWNST
UNBELIEVABILITY
UNBELIEVABLE
UNBELIEVABLY
UNBELIEVED
UNBELIEVER
UNBELIEVERS
UNBELIEVES
UNBELIEVING
UNBELIEVINGLY
UNBELIEVINGNESS
UNBELLIGERENT
UNBENDABLE
UNBENDINGLY
UNBENDINGNESS
UNBENDINGNESSES
UNBENDINGS
UNBENEFICED
UNBENEFICIAL
UNBENEFITED
UNBENEFITTED
UNBENIGHTED
UNBENIGNANT
UNBENIGNLY
UNBESEEMED
UNBESEEMING
UNBESEEMINGLY
UNBESOUGHT
UNBESPEAKING
UNBESPEAKS
UNBESPOKEN
UNBESTOWED
UNBETRAYED
UNBETTERABLE
UNBETTERED
UNBEWAILED
UNBIASEDLY
UNBIASEDNESS
UNBIASEDNESSES
UNBIASINGS
UNBIASSEDLY
UNBIASSEDNESS
UNBIASSEDNESSES
UNBIASSING
UNBIASSINGS
UNBIBLICAL
UNBINDINGS
UNBIRTHDAY
UNBIRTHDAYS
UNBISHOPED

u

UNBISHOPING	UNBUDGEABLE	UNCEASINGNESSES	UNCHRISTEN	UNCLERICAL
UNBLAMABLE	UNBUDGEABLY	UNCELEBRATED	UNCHRISTENED	UNCLESHIPS
UNBLAMABLY	UNBUDGETED	UNCENSORED	UNCHRISTENING	UNCLIMBABLE
UNBLAMEABLE	UNBUDGINGLY	UNCENSORIOUS	UNCHRISTENS	UNCLIMBABLENESS
UNBLAMEABLY	UNBUFFERED	UNCENSURED	UNCHRISTIAN	UNCLINCHED
UNBLEACHED	UNBUILDABLE	UNCEREBRAL	UNCHRISTIANED	UNCLINCHES
UNBLEMISHED	UNBUILDING	UNCEREMONIOUS	UNCHRISTIANING	UNCLINCHING
UNBLENCHED	UNBULKIEST	UNCEREMONIOUSLY	UNCHRISTIANISE	UNCLIPPING
UNBLENCHING	UNBUNDLERS	UNCERTAINLY	UNCHRISTIANISED	UNCLOAKING
UNBLESSEDNESS	UNBUNDLING	UNCERTAINNESS	UNCHRISTIANISES	UNCLOGGING
UNBLESSEDNESSES	UNBUNDLINGS	UNCERTAINNESSES	UNCHRISTIANIZE	UNCLOISTER
UNBLESSING	UNBURDENED	UNCERTAINTIES	UNCHRISTIANIZED	UNCLOISTERED
UNBLINDFOLD	UNBURDENING	UNCERTAINTY	UNCHRISTIANIZES	UNCLOISTERING
UNBLINDFOLDED	UNBUREAUCRATIC	UNCERTIFICATED	UNCHRISTIANLIKE	UNCLOISTERS
UNBLINDFOLDING	UNBURNABLE	UNCERTIFIED	UNCHRISTIANLY	UNCLOTHING
UNBLINDFOLDS	UNBURNISHED	UNCHAINING	UNCHRISTIANS	UNCLOUDEDLY
UNBLINDING	UNBURROWED	UNCHAIRING	UNCHRONICLED	UNCLOUDEDNESS
UNBLINKING	UNBURROWING	UNCHALLENGEABLE	UNCHRONOLOGICAL	UNCLOUDEDNESSES
UNBLINKINGLY	UNBURTHENED	UNCHALLENGEABLY	UNCHURCHED	UNCLOUDIER
UNBLISSFUL	UNBURTHENING	UNCHALLENGED	UNCHURCHES	UNCLOUDIEST
UNBLOCKING	UNBURTHENS	UNCHALLENGING	UNCHURCHING	UNCLOUDING
UNBLOODIED	UNBUSINESSLIKE	UNCHANCIER	UNCHURCHLY	UNCLUBABLE
UNBLOODIER	UNBUTTERED	UNCHANCIEST	UNCILIATED	UNCLUBBABLE
UNBLOODIEST	UNBUTTONED	UNCHANGEABILITY	UNCINARIAS	UNCLUTCHED
UNBLUSHING	UNBUTTONING	UNCHANGEABLE	UNCINARIASES	UNCLUTCHES
UNBLUSHINGLY	UNCALCIFIED	UNCHANGEABLY	UNCINARIASIS	UNCLUTCHING
UNBLUSHINGNESS	UNCALCINED	UNCHANGING	UNCINEMATIC	UNCLUTTERED
UNBOASTFUL	UNCALCULATED	UNCHANGINGLY	UNCIPHERED	UNCLUTTERING
UNBONNETED	UNCALCULATING	UNCHANGINGNESS	UNCIPHERING	UNCLUTTERS
UNBONNETING	UNCALIBRATED	UNCHANNELED	UNCIRCULATED	UNCOALESCE
UNBORROWED	UNCALLOUSED	UNCHANNELLED	UNCIRCUMCISED	UNCOALESCED
UNBOSOMERS	UNCANCELED	UNCHAPERONED	UNCIRCUMCISION	UNCOALESCES
UNBOSOMING	UNCANCELLED	UNCHARGING	UNCIRCUMCISIONS	UNCOALESCING
UNBOTTLING	UNCANDIDLY	UNCHARIEST	UNCIRCUMSCRIBED	UNCOATINGS
UNBOTTOMED	UNCANDIDNESS	UNCHARISMATIC	UNCIVILISED	UNCODIFIED
UNBOUNCIER	UNCANDIDNESSES	UNCHARITABLE	UNCIVILISEDLY	UNCOERCIVE
UNBOUNCIEST	UNCANDOURS	UNCHARITABLY	UNCIVILISEDNESS	UNCOERCIVELY
UNBOUNDEDLY	UNCANNIEST	UNCHARITIES	UNCIVILITIES	UNCOFFINED
UNBOUNDEDNESS	UNCANNINESS	UNCHARMING	UNCIVILITY	UNCOFFINING
UNBOUNDEDNESSES	UNCANNINESSES	UNCHARNELLED	UNCIVILIZED	UNCOLLECTABLE
UNBOWDLERISED	UNCANONICAL	UNCHARNELLING	UNCIVILIZEDLY	UNCOLLECTABLES
UNBOWDLERIZED	UNCANONICALNESS	UNCHARNELS	UNCIVILIZEDNESS	UNCOLLECTED
UNBRACKETED	UNCANONISE	UNCHARTERED	UNCIVILNESS	UNCOLLECTIBLE
UNBRAIDING	UNCANONISED	UNCHASTELY	UNCIVILNESSES	UNCOLLECTIBLES
UNBRANCHED	UNCANONISES	UNCHASTENED	UNCLAMPING	UNCOLOURED
UNBREACHABLE	UNCANONISING	UNCHASTENESS	UNCLARIFIED	UNCOMATABLE
UNBREACHED	UNCANONIZE	UNCHASTENESSES	UNCLARITIES	UNCOMBATIVE
UNBREAKABLE	UNCANONIZED	UNCHASTEST	UNCLASPING	UNCOMBINED
UNBREATHABLE	UNCANONIZES	UNCHASTISABLE	UNCLASSICAL	UNCOMBINES
UNBREATHED	UNCANONIZING	UNCHASTISED	UNCLASSIER	UNCOMBINING
UNBREATHING	UNCAPITALISED	UNCHASTITIES	UNCLASSIEST	UNCOMEATABLE
UNBREECHED	UNCAPITALIZED	UNCHASTITY	UNCLASSIFIABLE	UNCOMELIER
UNBREECHES	UNCAPSIZABLE	UNCHASTIZABLE	UNCLASSIFIED	UNCOMELIEST
UNBREECHING	UNCAPTIONED	UNCHASTIZED	UNCLEANEST	UNCOMELINESS
UNBRIBABLE	UNCAPTIVATED	UNCHAUVINISTIC	UNCLEANLIER	UNCOMELINESSES
UNBRIDGEABLE	UNCAPTURABLE	UNCHECKABLE	UNCLEANLIEST	UNCOMFIEST
UNBRIDLEDLY	UNCARPETED	UNCHECKING	UNCLEANLINESS	UNCOMFORTABLE
UNBRIDLEDNESS	UNCASTRATED	UNCHEERFUL	UNCLEANLINESSES	UNCOMFORTABLY
UNBRIDLEDNESSES	UNCATALOGED	UNCHEERFULLY	UNCLEANNESS	UNCOMFORTED
UNBRIDLING	UNCATALOGUED	UNCHEERFULNESS	UNCLEANNESSES	UNCOMMENDABLE
UNBRILLIANT	UNCATCHABLE	UNCHEWABLE	UNCLEANSED	UNCOMMENDABLY
UNBROKENLY	UNCATCHIER	UNCHILDING	UNCLEAREST	UNCOMMENDED
UNBROKENNESS	UNCATCHIEST	UNCHILDLIKE	UNCLEARNESS	UNCOMMERCIAL
UNBROKENNESSES	UNCATEGORISABLE	UNCHIVALROUS	UNCLEARNESSES	UNCOMMITTED
UNBROTHERLIKE	UNCATEGORIZABLE	UNCHIVALROUSLY	UNCLENCHED	UNCOMMONER
UNBROTHERLY	UNCEASINGLY	UNCHLORINATED	UNCLENCHES	UNCOMMONEST
UNBUCKLING	UNCEASINGNESS	UNCHOREOGRAPHED	UNCLENCHING	UNCOMMONLY

UNCOMMONNESS	UNCONFORMITY	UNCONVENTIONAL	UNCULTIVATABLE	UNDELIVERED
UNCOMMONNESSES	UNCONFOUNDED	UNCONVERSABLE	UNCULTIVATED	UNDEMANDING
UNCOMMUNICABLE	UNCONFUSED	UNCONVERSANT	UNCULTURED	UNDEMARCATED
UNCOMMUNICATED	UNCONFUSEDLY	UNCONVERTED	UNCUMBERED	UNDEMOCRATIC
UNCOMMUNICATIVE	UNCONFUSES	UNCONVERTIBLE	UNCURBABLE	UNDEMONSTRABLE
UNCOMMUTED	UNCONFUSING	UNCONVICTED	UNCURTAILED	UNDEMONSTRATED
UNCOMPACTED	UNCONGEALED	UNCONVINCED	UNCURTAINED	UNDEMONSTRATIVE
UNCOMPANIED	UNCONGEALING	UNCONVINCING	UNCURTAINING	UNDENIABLE
UNCOMPANIONABLE	UNCONGEALS	UNCONVINCINGLY	UNCURTAINS	UNDENIABLENESS
UNCOMPANIONED	UNCONGENIAL	UNCONVOYED	UNCUSTOMARILY	UNDENIABLY
UNCOMPASSIONATE	UNCONGENIALITY	UNCOOPERATIVE	UNCUSTOMARY	UNDEPENDABLE
UNCOMPELLED	UNCONJECTURED	UNCOOPERATIVELY	UNCUSTOMED	UNDEPENDING
UNCOMPELLING	UNCONJUGAL	UNCOORDINATED	UNCYNICALLY	UNDEPLORED
UNCOMPENSATED	UNCONJUGATED	UNCOPYRIGHTABLE	UNDANCEABLE	UNDEPRAVED
UNCOMPETITIVE	UNCONJUNCTIVE	UNCOQUETTISH	UNDAUNTABLE	UNDEPRECIATED
UNCOMPLACENT	UNCONNECTED	UNCORRECTABLE	UNDAUNTEDLY	UNDEPRESSED
UNCOMPLAINING	UNCONNECTEDLY	UNCORRECTED	UNDAUNTEDNESS	UNDEPRIVED
UNCOMPLAININGLY	UNCONNECTEDNESS	UNCORRELATED	UNDAUNTEDNESSES	UNDERACHIEVE
UNCOMPLAISANT	UNCONNIVING	UNCORROBORATED	UNDAUNTING	UNDERACHIEVED
UNCOMPLAISANTLY	UNCONQUERABLE	UNCORRUPTED	UNDAZZLING	UNDERACHIEVER
UNCOMPLETED	UNCONQUERABLY	UNCORSETED	UNDEBARRED	UNDERACHIEVERS
UNCOMPLIANT	UNCONQUERED	UNCOSTLIER	UNDEBATABLE	UNDERACHIEVES
UNCOMPLICATED	UNCONSCIENTIOUS	UNCOSTLIEST	UNDEBATABLY	UNDERACHIEVING
UNCOMPLIMENTARY	UNCONSCIONABLE	UNCOUNSELLED	UNDEBAUCHED	UNDERACTED
UNCOMPLYING	UNCONSCIONABLY	UNCOUNTABLE	UNDECADENT	UNDERACTING
UNCOMPOSABLE	UNCONSCIOUS	UNCOUPLERS	UNDECAGONS	UNDERACTION
UNCOMPOUNDED	UNCONSCIOUSES	UNCOUPLING	UNDECEIVABLE	UNDERACTIONS
UNCOMPREHENDED	UNCONSCIOUSLY	UNCOURAGEOUS	UNDECEIVED	UNDERACTIVE
UNCOMPREHENDING	UNCONSCIOUSNESS	UNCOURTEOUS	UNDECEIVER	UNDERACTIVITIES
UNCOMPREHENSIVE	UNCONSECRATE	UNCOURTLIER	UNDECEIVERS	UNDERACTIVITY
UNCOMPROMISABLE	UNCONSECRATED	UNCOURTLIEST	UNDECEIVES	UNDERACTOR
UNCOMPROMISING	UNCONSECRATES	UNCOURTLINESS	UNDECEIVING	UNDERACTORS
UNCOMPUTERISED	UNCONSECRATING	UNCOURTLINESSES	UNDECIDABILITY	UNDERAGENT
UNCOMPUTERIZED	UNCONSENTANEOUS	UNCOUTHEST	UNDECIDABLE	UNDERAGENTS
UNCONCEALABLE	UNCONSENTING	UNCOUTHNESS	UNDECIDEDLY	UNDERBAKED
UNCONCEALED	UNCONSIDERED	UNCOUTHNESSES	UNDECIDEDNESS	UNDERBAKES
UNCONCEALING	UNCONSIDERING	UNCOVENANTED	UNDECIDEDNESSES	UNDERBAKING
UNCONCEIVABLE	UNCONSOLED	UNCOVERING	UNDECIDEDS	UNDERBEARER
UNCONCEIVABLY	UNCONSOLIDATED	UNCRAZIEST	UNDECILLION	UNDERBEARERS
UNCONCEIVED	UNCONSTANT	UNCREATEDNESS	UNDECILLIONS	UNDERBEARING
UNCONCERNED	UNCONSTRAINABLE	UNCREATEDNESSES	UNDECIMOLE	UNDERBEARINGS
UNCONCERNEDLY	UNCONSTRAINED	UNCREATING	UNDECIMOLES	UNDERBEARS
UNCONCERNEDNESS	UNCONSTRAINEDLY	UNCREATIVE	UNDECIPHERABLE	UNDERBELLIES
UNCONCERNING	UNCONSTRAINT	UNCREDENTIALED	UNDECIPHERED	UNDERBELLY
UNCONCERNMENT	UNCONSTRAINTS	UNCREDIBLE	UNDECISIVE	UNDERBIDDER
UNCONCERNMENTS	UNCONSTRICTED	UNCREDITABLE	UNDECLARED	UNDERBIDDERS
UNCONCERNS	UNCONSTRUCTED	UNCREDITED	UNDECLINING	UNDERBIDDING
UNCONCERTED	UNCONSTRUCTIVE	UNCRIPPLED	UNDECOMPOSABLE	UNDERBITES
UNCONCILIATORY	UNCONSUMED	UNCRITICAL	UNDECOMPOSED	UNDERBITING
UNCONCLUSIVE	UNCONSUMMATED	UNCRITICALLY	UNDECORATED	UNDERBITTEN
UNCONCOCTED	UNCONTAINABLE	UNCROSSABLE	UNDEDICATED	UNDERBLANKET
UNCONDITIONAL	UNCONTAMINATED	UNCROSSING	UNDEFEATABLE	UNDERBLANKETS
UNCONDITIONALLY	UNCONTEMNED	UNCROWNING	UNDEFEATED	UNDERBLANKETS
UNCONDITIONED	UNCONTEMPLATED	UNCRUMPLED	UNDEFENDED	UNDERBODIES
UNCONDUCIVE	UNCONTEMPORARY	UNCRUMPLES	UNDEFINABLE	UNDERBORNE
UNCONFEDERATED	UNCONTENTIOUS	UNCRUMPLING	UNDEFOLIATED	UNDERBOSSES
UNCONFESSED	UNCONTESTABLE	UNCRUSHABLE	UNDEFORMED	UNDERBOUGH
UNCONFINABLE	UNCONTESTED	UNCRYSTALLISED	UNDEIFYING	UNDERBOUGHS
UNCONFINED	UNCONTRACTED	UNCRYSTALLIZED	UNDELAYING	UNDERBOUGHT
UNCONFINEDLY	UNCONTRADICTED	UNCTIONLESS	UNDELECTABLE	UNDERBREATH
UNCONFINES	UNCONTRIVED	UNCTUOSITIES	UNDELEGATED	UNDERBREATHS
UNCONFINING	UNCONTROLLABLE	UNCTUOSITY	UNDELETING	UNDERBREEDING
UNCONFIRMED	UNCONTROLLABLY	UNCTUOUSLY	UNDELIBERATE	UNDERBREEDINGS
UNCONFORMABLE	UNCONTROLLED	UNCTUOUSNESS	UNDELIGHTED	UNDERBRIDGE
UNCONFORMABLY	UNCONTROLLEDLY	UNCTUOUSNESSES	UNDELIGHTFUL	UNDERBRIDGES
UNCONFORMING	UNCONTROVERSIAL	UNCUCKOLDED	UNDELIGHTS	UNDERBRIMS
UNCONFORMITIES	UNCONTROVERTED	UNCULTIVABLE	UNDELIVERABLE	UNDERBRUSH
				UNDERBRUSHED

UNDERBRUSHES	UNDERCROFT	UNDEREXPOSURES	UNDERINFLATIONS	UNDERMININGS
UNDERBRUSHING	UNDERCROFTS	UNDERFEEDING	UNDERINSURE	UNDERNAMED
UNDERBUDDED	UNDERCURRENT	UNDERFEEDINGS	UNDERINSURED	UNDERNEATH
UNDERBUDDING	UNDERCURRENTS	UNDERFEEDS	UNDERINSURES	UNDERNEATHS
UNDERBUDGET	UNDERCUTTING	UNDERFELTS	UNDERINSURING	UNDERNICENESS
UNDERBUDGETED	UNDERDAMPER	UNDERFINANCED	UNDERINVEST	UNDERNICENESSES
UNDERBUDGETING	UNDERDAMPERS	UNDERFINISHED	UNDERINVESTED	UNDERNOTED
UNDERBUDGETS	UNDERDECKS	UNDERFIRED	UNDERINVESTING	UNDERNOTES
UNDERBUILD	UNDERDELIVER	UNDERFIRES	UNDERINVESTMENT	UNDERNOTING
UNDERBUILDER	UNDERDELIVERED	UNDERFIRING	UNDERINVESTS	UNDERNOURISH
UNDERBUILDERS	UNDERDELIVERING	UNDERFISHED	UNDERJAWED	UNDERNOURISHED
UNDERBUILDING	UNDERDELIVERS	UNDERFISHES	UNDERKEEPER	UNDERNOURISHES
UNDERBUILDS	UNDERDEVELOP	UNDERFISHING	UNDERKEEPERS	UNDERNOURISHING
UNDERBUILT	UNDERDEVELOPED	UNDERFLOOR	UNDERKEEPING	UNDERNTIME
UNDERBURNT	UNDERDEVELOPING	UNDERFLOWS	UNDERKEEPS	UNDERNTIMES
UNDERBUSHED	UNDERDEVELOPS	UNDERFONGED	UNDERKILLS	UNDERNUTRITION
UNDERBUSHES	UNDERDOERS	UNDERFONGING	UNDERKINGDOM	UNDERNUTRITIONS
UNDERBUSHING	UNDERDOING	UNDERFONGS	UNDERKINGDOMS	UNDEROCCUPIED
UNDERBUYING	UNDERDOSED	UNDERFOOTED	UNDERKINGS	UNDERPAINTING
UNDERCAPITALISE	UNDERDOSES	UNDERFOOTING	UNDERLAPPED	UNDERPAINTINGS
UNDERCAPITALIZE	UNDERDOSING	UNDERFOOTS	UNDERLAPPING	UNDERPANTS
UNDERCARDS	UNDERDRAIN	UNDERFULFIL	UNDERLAYER	UNDERPARTS
UNDERCARRIAGE	UNDERDRAINAGE	UNDERFULFILL	UNDERLAYERS	UNDERPASSES
UNDERCARRIAGES	UNDERDRAINAGES	UNDERFULFILLED	UNDERLAYING	UNDERPASSION
UNDERCARTS	UNDERDRAINED	UNDERFULFILLING	UNDERLAYMENT	UNDERPASSIONS
UNDERCASTS	UNDERDRAINING	UNDERFULFILLS	UNDERLAYMENTS	UNDERPAYING
UNDERCHARGE	UNDERDRAINS	UNDERFULFILS	UNDERLEASE	UNDERPAYMENT
UNDERCHARGED	UNDERDRAWERS	UNDERFUNDED	UNDERLEASED	UNDERPAYMENTS
UNDERCHARGES	UNDERDRAWING	UNDERFUNDING	UNDERLEASES	UNDERPEEPED
UNDERCHARGING	UNDERDRAWINGS	UNDERFUNDINGS	UNDERLEASING	UNDERPEEPING
UNDERCLASS	UNDERDRAWN	UNDERFUNDS	UNDERLEAVES	UNDERPEEPS
UNDERCLASSES	UNDERDRAWS	UNDERGARMENT	UNDERLETTER	UNDERPEOPLED
UNDERCLASSMAN	UNDERDRESS	UNDERGARMENTS	UNDERLETTERS	UNDERPERFORM
UNDERCLASSMEN	UNDERDRESSED	UNDERGIRDED	UNDERLETTING	UNDERPERFORMED
UNDERCLAYS	UNDERDRESSES	UNDERGIRDING	UNDERLETTINGS	UNDERPERFORMING
UNDERCLIFF	UNDERDRESSING	UNDERGIRDS	UNDERLEVERAGED	UNDERPERFORMS
UNDERCLIFFS	UNDERDRIVE	UNDERGLAZE	UNDERLIERS	UNDERPINNED
UNDERCLOTHE	UNDERDRIVES	UNDERGLAZES	UNDERLINED	UNDERPINNING
UNDERCLOTHED	UNDEREARTH	UNDERGOERS	UNDERLINEN	UNDERPINNINGS
UNDERCLOTHES	UNDEREARTHS	UNDERGOING	UNDERLINENS	UNDERPITCH
UNDERCLOTHING	UNDEREATEN	UNDERGOWNS	UNDERLINES	UNDERPLANT
UNDERCLOTHINGS	UNDEREATING	UNDERGRADS	UNDERLINGS	UNDERPLANTED
UNDERCLUBBED	UNDEREDUCATED	UNDERGRADUATE	UNDERLINING	UNDERPLANTING
UNDERCLUBBING	UNDEREMPHASES	UNDERGRADUATES	UNDERLININGS	UNDERPLANTS
UNDERCLUBS	UNDEREMPHASIS	UNDERGRADUETTE	UNDERLOADED	UNDERPLAYED
UNDERCOATED	UNDEREMPHASISE	UNDERGRADUETTES	UNDERLOADING	UNDERPLAYING
UNDERCOATING	UNDEREMPHASISED	UNDERGROUND	UNDERLOADS	UNDERPLAYS
UNDERCOATINGS	UNDEREMPHASISES	UNDERGROUNDER	UNDERLOOKER	UNDERPLOTS
UNDERCOATS	UNDEREMPHASIZE	UNDERGROUNDERS	UNDERLOOKERS	UNDERPOPULATED
UNDERCOOKED	UNDEREMPHASIZED	UNDERGROUNDS	UNDERLYING	UNDERPOWERED
UNDERCOOKING	UNDEREMPHASIZES	UNDERGROVE	UNDERLYINGLY	UNDERPRAISE
UNDERCOOKS	UNDEREMPLOYED	UNDERGROVES	UNDERMANNED	UNDERPRAISED
UNDERCOOLED	UNDEREMPLOYMENT	UNDERGROWN	UNDERMANNING	UNDERPRAISES
UNDERCOOLING	UNDERESTIMATE	UNDERGROWTH	UNDERMANNINGS	UNDERPRAISING
UNDERCOOLS	UNDERESTIMATED	UNDERGROWTHS	UNDERMASTED	UNDERPREPARED
UNDERCOUNT	UNDERESTIMATES	UNDERHAIRS	UNDERMEANING	UNDERPRICE
UNDERCOUNTED	UNDERESTIMATING	UNDERHANDED	UNDERMEANINGS	UNDERPRICED
UNDERCOUNTING	UNDERESTIMATION	UNDERHANDEDLY	UNDERMENTIONED	UNDERPRICES
UNDERCOUNTS	UNDEREXPLOIT	UNDERHANDEDNESS	UNDERMINDE	UNDERPRICING
UNDERCOVER	UNDEREXPLOITED	UNDERHANDING	UNDERMINDED	UNDERPRICINGS
UNDERCOVERT	UNDEREXPLOITING	UNDERHANDS	UNDERMINDES	UNDERPRISE
UNDERCOVERTS	UNDEREXPLOITS	UNDERHEATED	UNDERMINDING	UNDERPRISED
UNDERCRACKERS	UNDEREXPOSE	UNDERHEATING	UNDERMINED	UNDERPRISES
UNDERCREST	UNDEREXPOSED	UNDERHEATS	UNDERMINER	UNDERPRISING
UNDERCRESTED	UNDEREXPOSES	UNDERHONEST	UNDERMINERS	UNDERPRIVILEGED
UNDERCRESTING	UNDEREXPOSING	UNDERINFLATED	UNDERMINES	UNDERPRIZE
UNDERCRESTS	UNDEREXPOSURE	UNDERINFLATION	UNDERMINING	UNDERPRIZED

UNDERPRIZES	UNDERSHOOTS	UNDERSTUDIED	UNDERWEARS	UNDETERRED
UNDERPRIZING	UNDERSHORTS	UNDERSTUDIES	UNDERWEIGHT	UNDEVELOPED
UNDERPRODUCE	UNDERSHRUB	UNDERSTUDY	UNDERWEIGHTS	UNDEVIATING
UNDERPRODUCED	UNDERSHRUBS	UNDERSTUDYING	UNDERWHELM	UNDEVIATINGLY
UNDERPRODUCES	UNDERSIDES	UNDERSUBSCRIBED	UNDERWHELMED	UNDIAGNOSABLE
UNDERPRODUCING	UNDERSIGNED	UNDERSUPPLIED	UNDERWHELMING	UNDIAGNOSED
UNDERPRODUCTION	UNDERSIGNING	UNDERSUPPLIES	UNDERWHELMS	UNDIALECTICAL
UNDERPROOF	UNDERSIGNS	UNDERSUPPLY	UNDERWINGS	UNDIDACTIC
UNDERPROPPED	UNDERSIZED	UNDERSUPPLYING	UNDERWIRED	UNDIFFERENCED
UNDERPROPPER	UNDERSKIES	UNDERSURFACE	UNDERWIRES	UNDIGESTED
UNDERPROPPERS	UNDERSKINKER	UNDERSURFACES	UNDERWIRING	UNDIGESTIBLE
UNDERPROPPING	UNDERSKINKERS	UNDERTAKABLE	UNDERWIRINGS	UNDIGHTING
UNDERPROPS	UNDERSKIRT	UNDERTAKEN	UNDERWOODS	UNDIGNIFIED
UNDERPUBLICISED	UNDERSKIRTS	UNDERTAKER	UNDERWOOLS	UNDIGNIFIES
UNDERPUBLICIZED	UNDERSLEEVE	UNDERTAKERS	UNDERWORKED	UNDIGNIFYING
UNDERQUALIFIED	UNDERSLEEVES	UNDERTAKES	UNDERWORKER	UNDIMINISHABLE
UNDERQUOTE	UNDERSLUNG	UNDERTAKING	UNDERWORKERS	UNDIMINISHED
UNDERQUOTED	UNDERSOILS	UNDERTAKINGS	UNDERWORKING	UNDIPLOMATIC
UNDERQUOTES	UNDERSONGS	UNDERTAXED	UNDERWORKS	UNDIRECTED
UNDERQUOTING	UNDERSOWED	UNDERTAXES	UNDERWORLD	UNDISAPPOINTING
UNDERRATED	UNDERSOWING	UNDERTAXING	UNDERWORLDS	UNDISCERNED
UNDERRATES	UNDERSPEND	UNDERTENANCIES	UNDERWRITE	UNDISCERNEDLY
UNDERRATING	UNDERSPENDING	UNDERTENANCY	UNDERWRITER	UNDISCERNIBLE
UNDERREACT	UNDERSPENDINGS	UNDERTENANT	UNDERWRITERS	UNDISCERNIBLY
UNDERREACTED	UNDERSPENDS	UNDERTENANTS	UNDERWRITES	UNDISCERNING
UNDERREACTING	UNDERSPENT	UNDERTHINGS	UNDERWRITING	UNDISCERNINGS
UNDERREACTION	UNDERSPINS	UNDERTHIRST	UNDERWRITINGS	UNDISCHARGED
UNDERREACTIONS	UNDERSTAFFED	UNDERTHIRSTS	UNDERWRITTEN	UNDISCIPLINABLE
UNDERREACTS	UNDERSTAFFING	UNDERTHRUST	UNDERWROTE	UNDISCIPLINE
UNDERREPORT	UNDERSTAFFINGS	UNDERTHRUSTING	UNDERWROUGHT	UNDISCIPLINED
UNDERREPORTED	UNDERSTAND	UNDERTHRUSTS	UNDESCENDABLE	UNDISCIPLINES
UNDERREPORTING	UNDERSTANDABLE	UNDERTIMED	UNDESCENDED	UNDISCLOSED
UNDERREPORTS	UNDERSTANDABLY	UNDERTIMES	UNDESCENDIBLE	UNDISCOMFITED
UNDERRUNNING	UNDERSTANDED	UNDERTINTS	UNDESCRIBABLE	UNDISCORDANT
UNDERRUNNINGS	UNDERSTANDER	UNDERTONED	UNDESCRIBED	UNDISCORDING
UNDERSATURATED	UNDERSTANDERS	UNDERTONES	UNDESCRIED	UNDISCOURAGED
UNDERSAYING	UNDERSTANDING	UNDERTRICK	UNDESERVED	UNDISCOVERABLE
UNDERSCORE	UNDERSTANDINGLY	UNDERTRICKS	UNDESERVEDLY	UNDISCOVERABLY
UNDERSCORED	UNDERSTANDINGS	UNDERTRUMP	UNDESERVEDNESS	UNDISCOVERED
UNDERSCORES	UNDERSTANDS	UNDERTRUMPED	UNDESERVER	UNDISCUSSABLE
UNDERSCORING	UNDERSTATE	UNDERTRUMPING	UNDESERVERS	UNDISCUSSED
UNDERSCORINGS	UNDERSTATED	UNDERTRUMPS	UNDESERVES	UNDISCUSSIBLE
UNDERSCRUB	UNDERSTATEDLY	UNDERUSING	UNDESERVING	UNDISGUISABLE
UNDERSCRUBS	UNDERSTATEMENT	UNDERUTILISE	UNDESERVINGLY	UNDISGUISED
UNDERSEALED	UNDERSTATEMENTS	UNDERUTILISED	UNDESIGNATED	UNDISGUISEDLY
UNDERSEALING	UNDERSTATES	UNDERUTILISES	UNDESIGNED	UNDISHONOURED
UNDERSEALINGS	UNDERSTATING	UNDERUTILISING	UNDESIGNEDLY	UNDISMANTLED
UNDERSEALS	UNDERSTEER	UNDERUTILIZE	UNDESIGNEDNESS	UNDISMAYED
UNDERSECRETARY	UNDERSTEERED	UNDERUTILIZED	UNDESIGNING	UNDISORDERED
UNDERSELLER	UNDERSTEERING	UNDERUTILIZES	UNDESIRABILITY	UNDISPATCHED
UNDERSELLERS	UNDERSTEERS	UNDERUTILIZING	UNDESIRABLE	UNDISPENSED
UNDERSELLING	UNDERSTOCK	UNDERVALUATION	UNDESIRABLENESS	UNDISPOSED
UNDERSELLS	UNDERSTOCKED	UNDERVALUATIONS	UNDESIRABLES	UNDISPUTABLE
UNDERSELVES	UNDERSTOCKING	UNDERVALUE	UNDESIRABLY	UNDISPUTED
UNDERSENSE	UNDERSTOCKS	UNDERVALUED	UNDESIRING	UNDISPUTEDLY
UNDERSENSES	UNDERSTOOD	UNDERVALUER	UNDESIROUS	UNDISSEMBLED
UNDERSERVED	UNDERSTOREY	UNDERVALUERS	UNDESPAIRING	UNDISSOCIATED
UNDERSETTING	UNDERSTOREYS	UNDERVALUES	UNDESPAIRINGLY	UNDISSOLVED
UNDERSEXED	UNDERSTORIES	UNDERVALUING	UNDESPATCHED	UNDISSOLVING
UNDERSHAPEN	UNDERSTORY	UNDERVESTS	UNDESPOILED	UNDISTEMPERED
UNDERSHERIFF	UNDERSTRAPPER	UNDERVIEWER	UNDESTROYED	UNDISTILLED
UNDERSHERIFFS	UNDERSTRAPPERS	UNDERVIEWERS	UNDETECTABLE	UNDISTINCTIVE
UNDERSHIRT	UNDERSTRAPPING	UNDERVOICE	UNDETECTED	UNDISTINGUISHED
UNDERSHIRTED	UNDERSTRATA	UNDERVOICES	UNDETERMINABLE	UNDISTORTED
UNDERSHIRTS	UNDERSTRATUM	UNDERVOTES	UNDETERMINATE	UNDISTRACTED
UNDERSHOOT	UNDERSTRATUMS	UNDERWATER	UNDETERMINATION	UNDISTRACTEDLY
UNDERSHOOTING	UNDERSTRENGTH	UNDERWATERS	UNDETERMINED	UNDISTRACTING

u

UNDISTRIBUTED	UNEARTHLINESS	UNENVIABLE	UNEXPLORED	UNFERTILISED
UNDISTURBED	UNEARTHLINESSES	UNENVIABLY	UNEXPRESSED	UNFERTILIZED
UNDISTURBEDLY	UNEASINESS	UNEQUALLED	UNEXPRESSIBLE	UNFETTERED
UNDISTURBING	UNEASINESSES	UNEQUIPPED	UNEXPRESSIVE	UNFETTERING
UNDIVERSIFIED	UNEATABLENESS	UNEQUITABLE	UNEXPUGNABLE	UNFEUDALISE
UNDIVERTED	UNEATABLENESSES	UNEQUIVOCABLE	UNEXPURGATED	UNFEUDALISED
UNDIVERTING	UNECCENTRIC	UNEQUIVOCABLY	UNEXTENDED	UNFEUDALISES
UNDIVESTED	UNECLIPSED	UNEQUIVOCAL	UNEXTENUATED	UNFEUDALISING
UNDIVESTEDLY	UNECOLOGICAL	UNEQUIVOCALLY	UNEXTINGUISHED	UNFEUDALIZE
UNDIVIDABLE	UNECONOMIC	UNEQUIVOCALNESS	UNEXTRAORDINARY	UNFEUDALIZED
UNDIVIDEDLY	UNECONOMICAL	UNERASABLE	UNFADINGLY	UNFEUDALIZES
UNDIVIDEDNESS	UNEDIFYING	UNERRINGLY	UNFADINGNESS	UNFEUDALIZING
UNDIVIDEDNESSES	UNEDUCABLE	UNERRINGNESS	UNFADINGNESSES	UNFILIALLY
UNDIVORCED	UNEDUCATED	UNERRINGNESSES	UNFAILINGLY	UNFILLABLE
UNDIVULGED	UNEFFECTED	UNESCAPABLE	UNFAILINGNESS	UNFILLETED
UNDOCTORED	UNELABORATE	UNESCORTED	UNFAILINGNESSES	UNFILTERABLE
UNDOCTRINAIRE	UNELABORATED	UNESSENCED	UNFAIRNESS	UNFILTERED
UNDOCTRINAIRES	UNELECTABLE	UNESSENCES	UNFAIRNESSES	UNFILTRABLE
UNDOCUMENTED	UNELECTRIFIED	UNESSENCING	UNFAITHFUL	UNFINDABLE
UNDOGMATIC	UNEMBARRASSED	UNESSENTIAL	UNFAITHFULLY	UNFINISHED
UNDOGMATICALLY	UNEMBELLISHED	UNESSENTIALLY	UNFAITHFULNESS	UNFINISHING
UNDOMESTIC	UNEMBITTERED	UNESSENTIALS	UNFALLIBLE	UNFINISHINGS
UNDOMESTICATE	UNEMBODIED	UNESTABLISHED	UNFALSIFIABLE	UNFITNESSES
UNDOMESTICATED	UNEMOTIONAL	UNESTHETIC	UNFALTERING	UNFITTEDNESS
UNDOMESTICATES	UNEMOTIONALLY	UNETHICALLY	UNFALTERINGLY	UNFITTEDNESSES
UNDOMESTICATING	UNEMOTIONED	UNEVALUATED	UNFAMILIAR	UNFITTINGLY
UNDOUBLING	UNEMPHASISED	UNEVANGELICAL	UNFAMILIARITIES	UNFIXEDNESS
UNDOUBTABLE	UNEMPHASIZED	UNEVENNESS	UNFAMILIARITY	UNFIXEDNESSES
UNDOUBTEDLY	UNEMPHATIC	UNEVENNESSES	UNFAMILIARLY	UNFIXITIES
UNDOUBTFUL	UNEMPHATICALLY	UNEVENTFUL	UNFANCIEST	UNFLAGGING
UNDOUBTING	UNEMPIRICAL	UNEVENTFULLY	UNFASHIONABLE	UNFLAGGINGLY
UNDOUBTINGLY	UNEMPLOYABILITY	UNEVENTFULNESS	UNFASHIONABLY	UNFLAMBOYANT
UNDRAINABLE	UNEMPLOYABLE	UNEVIDENCED	UNFASHIONED	UNFLAPPABILITY
UNDRAMATIC	UNEMPLOYABLES	UNEXACTING	UNFASTENED	UNFLAPPABLE
UNDRAMATICALLY	UNEMPLOYED	UNEXAGGERATED	UNFASTENING	UNFLAPPABLENESS
UNDRAMATISED	UNEMPLOYEDS	UNEXAMINED	UNFASTIDIOUS	UNFLAPPABLY
UNDRAMATIZED	UNEMPLOYMENT	UNEXAMPLED	UNFATHERED	UNFLASHIER
UNDREADING	UNEMPLOYMENTS	UNEXCAVATED	UNFATHERLIER	UNFLASHIEST
UNDREAMING	UNENCHANTED	UNEXCELLED	UNFATHERLIEST	UNFLATTERING
UNDRESSING	UNENCLOSED	UNEXCEPTIONABLE	UNFATHERLY	UNFLATTERINGLY
UNDRESSINGS	UNENCOURAGING	UNEXCEPTIONABLY	UNFATHOMABLE	UNFLAVORED
UNDRINKABLE	UNENCUMBERED	UNEXCEPTIONAL	UNFATHOMABLY	UNFLAVOURED
UNDRIVEABLE	UNENDANGERED	UNEXCEPTIONALLY	UNFATHOMED	UNFLESHING
UNDROOPING	UNENDEARED	UNEXCITABLE	UNFAULTIER	UNFLESHLIER
UNDROSSIER	UNENDEARING	UNEXCITING	UNFAULTIEST	UNFLESHLIEST
UNDROSSIEST	UNENDINGLY	UNEXCLUDED	UNFAVORABLE	UNFLINCHING
UNDULANCES	UNENDINGNESS	UNEXCLUSIVE	UNFAVORABLENESS	UNFLINCHINGLY
UNDULANCIES	UNENDINGNESSES	UNEXCLUSIVELY	UNFAVORABLY	UNFLUSHING
UNDULATELY	UNENDURABLE	UNEXECUTED	UNFAVORITE	UNFLUSTERED
UNDULATING	UNENDURABLENESS	UNEXEMPLIFIED	UNFAVOURABLE	UNFOCUSSED
UNDULATINGLY	UNENDURABLY	UNEXERCISED	UNFAVOURABLY	UNFOLDINGS
UNDULATION	UNENFORCEABLE	UNEXHAUSTED	UNFAVOURED	UNFOLDMENT
UNDULATIONIST	UNENFORCED	UNEXPANDED	UNFAVOURITE	UNFOLDMENTS
UNDULATIONISTS	UNENJOYABLE	UNEXPECTANT	UNFEARFULLY	UNFOLLOWED
UNDULATIONS	UNENLARGED	UNEXPECTED	UNFEASIBLE	UNFOLLOWING
UNDULATORS	UNENLIGHTENED	UNEXPECTEDLY	UNFEATHERED	UNFORBIDDEN
UNDULATORY	UNENLIGHTENING	UNEXPECTEDNESS	UNFEATURED	UNFORCEDLY
UNDUPLICATED	UNENQUIRING	UNEXPENDED	UNFEELINGLY	UNFORCIBLE
UNDUTIFULLY	UNENRICHED	UNEXPENSIVE	UNFEELINGNESS	UNFORDABLE
UNDUTIFULNESS	UNENSLAVED	UNEXPENSIVELY	UNFEELINGNESSES	UNFOREBODING
UNDUTIFULNESSES	UNENTAILED	UNEXPERIENCED	UNFEIGNEDLY	UNFOREKNOWABLE
UNDYINGNESS	UNENTERPRISING	UNEXPERIENT	UNFEIGNEDNESS	UNFOREKNOWN
UNDYINGNESSES	UNENTERTAINED	UNEXPIATED	UNFEIGNEDNESSES	UNFORESEEABLE
UNEARMARKED	UNENTERTAINING	UNEXPLAINABLE	UNFEIGNING	UNFORESEEING
UNEARTHING	UNENTHRALLED	UNEXPLAINED	UNFELLOWED	UNFORESEEN
UNEARTHLIER	UNENTHUSIASTIC	UNEXPLODED	UNFEMININE	UNFORESKINNED
UNEARTHLIEST	UNENTITLED	UNEXPLOITED	UNFERMENTED	UNFORESTED

UNFORETOLD	UNFULFILLING	UNGRATIFIED	UNHEALTHILY	UNICAMERALIST
UNFOREWARNED	UNFUNNIEST	UNGREEDIER	UNHEALTHINESS	UNICAMERALISTS
UNFORFEITED	UNFURNISHED	UNGREEDIEST	UNHEALTHINESSES	UNICAMERALLY
UNFORGETTABLE	UNFURNISHES	UNGREENEST	UNHEARSING	UNICELLULAR
UNFORGETTABLY	UNFURNISHING	UNGROUNDED	UNHEARTING	UNICELLULARITY
UNFORGIVABLE	UNFURROWED	UNGROUNDEDLY	UNHEEDEDLY	UNICENTRAL
UNFORGIVABLY	UNFUSSIEST	UNGROUNDEDNESS	UNHEEDFULLY	UNICOLORATE
UNFORGIVEN	UNGAINLIER	UNGROUPING	UNHEEDIEST	UNICOLORED
UNFORGIVENESS	UNGAINLIEST	UNGRUDGING	UNHEEDINGLY	UNICOLOROUS
UNFORGIVENESSES	UNGAINLINESS	UNGRUDGINGLY	UNHELMETED	UNICOLOURED
UNFORGIVING	UNGAINLINESSES	UNGUARDEDLY	UNHELPABLE	UNICOSTATE
UNFORGIVINGNESS	UNGAINSAID	UNGUARDEDNESS	UNHELPFULLY	UNICYCLING
UNFORGOTTEN	UNGAINSAYABLE	UNGUARDEDNESSES	UNHELPFULNESS	UNICYCLIST
UNFORMALISED	UNGALLANTLY	UNGUARDING	UNHELPFULNESSES	UNICYCLISTS
UNFORMALIZED	UNGARMENTED	UNGUENTARIA	UNHERALDED	UNIDEALISM
UNFORMATTED	UNGARNERED	UNGUENTARIES	UNHEROICAL	UNIDEALISMS
UNFORMIDABLE	UNGARNISHED	UNGUENTARIUM	UNHEROICALLY	UNIDEALISTIC
UNFORMULATED	UNGARTERED	UNGUENTARY	UNHESITATING	UNIDENTIFIABLE
UNFORSAKEN	UNGATHERED	UNGUERDONED	UNHESITATINGLY	UNIDENTIFIED
UNFORTHCOMING	UNGENEROSITIES	UNGUESSABLE	UNHIDEBOUND	UNIDEOLOGICAL
UNFORTIFIED	UNGENEROSITY	UNGUICULATE	UNHINDERED	UNIDIMENSIONAL
UNFORTUNATE	UNGENEROUS	UNGUICULATED	UNHINGEMENT	UNIDIOMATIC
UNFORTUNATELY	UNGENEROUSLY	UNGUICULATES	UNHINGEMENTS	UNIDIOMATICALLY
UNFORTUNATENESS	UNGENITURED	UNGUILTIER	UNHISTORIC	UNIDIRECTIONAL
UNFORTUNATES	UNGENTEELLY	UNGUILTIEST	UNHISTORICAL	UNIFICATION
UNFORTUNED	UNGENTILITIES	UNGULIGRADE	UNHITCHING	UNIFICATIONS
UNFORTUNES	UNGENTILITY	UNHABITABLE	UNHOARDING	UNIFLOROUS
UNFOSSILIFEROUS	UNGENTLEMANLIER	UNHABITUATED	UNHOLINESS	UNIFOLIATE
UNFOSSILISED	UNGENTLEMANLIKE	UNHACKNEYED	UNHOLINESSES	UNIFOLIOLATE
UNFOSSILIZED	UNGENTLEMANLY	UNHALLOWED	UNHOLSTERED	UNIFORMEST
UNFOSTERED	UNGENTLENESS	UNHALLOWING	UNHOLSTERING	UNIFORMING
UNFOUGHTEN	UNGENTLENESSES	UNHAMPERED	UNHOLSTERS	UNIFORMITARIAN
UNFOUNDEDLY	UNGENTLEST	UNHANDIEST	UNHOMELIER	UNIFORMITARIANS
UNFOUNDEDNESS	UNGENTRIFIED	UNHANDINESS	UNHOMELIEST	UNIFORMITIES
UNFOUNDEDNESSES	UNGENUINENESS	UNHANDINESSES	UNHOMELIKE	UNIFORMITY
UNFRANCHISED	UNGENUINENESSES	UNHANDSELLED	UNHOMOGENISED	UNIFORMNESS
UNFRAUGHTED	UNGERMINATED	UNHANDSOME	UNHOMOGENIZED	UNIFORMNESSES
UNFRAUGHTING	UNGETATABLE	UNHANDSOMELY	UNHONOURED	UNIGENITURE
UNFRAUGHTS	UNGHOSTLIER	UNHANDSOMENESS	UNHOPEFULLY	UNIGENITURES
UNFREEDOMS	UNGHOSTLIEST	UNHAPPENED	UNHOSPITABLE	UNIGNORABLE
UNFREEZING	UNGIMMICKY	UNHAPPENING	UNHOUSELED	UNILABIATE
UNFREEZINGS	UNGIRTHING	UNHAPPENINGS	UNHOUZZLED	UNILATERAL
UNFREQUENT	UNGLACIATED	UNHAPPIEST	UNHUMANISE	UNILATERALISM
UNFREQUENTED	UNGLAMORISED	UNHAPPINESS	UNHUMANISED	UNILATERALISMS
UNFREQUENTING	UNGLAMORIZED	UNHAPPINESSES	UNHUMANISES	UNILATERALIST
UNFREQUENTLY	UNGLAMOROUS	UNHAPPYING	UNHUMANISING	UNILATERALISTS
UNFREQUENTS	UNGLITZIER	UNHARBOURED	UNHUMANIZE	UNILATERALITIES
UNFRIENDED	UNGLITZIEST	UNHARBOURING	UNHUMANIZED	UNILATERALITY
UNFRIENDEDNESS	UNGODLIEST	UNHARBOURS	UNHUMANIZES	UNILATERALLY
UNFRIENDING	UNGODLINESS	UNHARDENED	UNHUMANIZING	UNILINGUAL
UNFRIENDLIER	UNGODLINESSES	UNHARDIEST	UNHUMOROUS	UNILINGUALISM
UNFRIENDLIEST	UNGOVERNABLE	UNHARMFULLY	UNHURRIEDLY	UNILINGUALISMS
UNFRIENDLILY	UNGOVERNABLY	UNHARMONIOUS	UNHURRYING	UNILINGUALIST
UNFRIENDLINESS	UNGOVERNED	UNHARNESSED	UNHURTFULLY	UNILINGUALISTS
UNFRIENDLY	UNGRACEFUL	UNHARNESSES	UNHURTFULNESS	UNILINGUALS
UNFRIENDSHIP	UNGRACEFULLY	UNHARNESSING	UNHURTFULNESSES	UNILITERAL
UNFRIENDSHIPS	UNGRACEFULNESS	UNHARVESTED	UNHUSBANDED	UNILLUMINATED
UNFRIGHTED	UNGRACIOUS	UNHASTIEST	UNHYDROLYSED	UNILLUMINATING
UNFRIGHTENED	UNGRACIOUSLY	UNHATTINGS	UNHYDROLYZED	UNILLUMINED
UNFRIVOLOUS	UNGRACIOUSNESS	UNHAZARDED	UNHYGIENIC	UNILLUSIONED
UNFROCKING	UNGRAMMATIC	UNHAZARDOUS	UNHYPHENATED	UNILLUSTRATED
UNFRUCTUOUS	UNGRAMMATICAL	UNHEALABLE	UNHYSTERICAL	UNILOBULAR
UNFRUITFUL	UNGRAMMATICALLY	UNHEALTHFUL	UNHYSTERICALLY	UNILOCULAR
UNFRUITFULLY	UNGRASPABLE	UNHEALTHFULLY	UNIAXIALLY	UNIMAGINABLE
UNFRUITFULNESS	UNGRATEFUL	UNHEALTHFULNESS	UNICAMERAL	UNIMAGINABLY
UNFULFILLABLE	UNGRATEFULLY	UNHEALTHIER	UNICAMERALISM	UNIMAGINATIVE
UNFULFILLED	UNGRATEFULNESS	UNHEALTHIEST	UNICAMERALISMS	UNIMAGINATIVELY

UNIMAGINED
UNIMMORTAL
UNIMMUNISED
UNIMMUNIZED
UNIMOLECULAR
UNIMPAIRED
UNIMPARTED
UNIMPASSIONED
UNIMPEACHABLE
UNIMPEACHABLY
UNIMPEACHED
UNIMPEDEDLY
UNIMPLORED
UNIMPORTANCE
UNIMPORTANCES
UNIMPORTANT
UNIMPORTUNED
UNIMPOSING
UNIMPREGNATED
UNIMPRESSED
UNIMPRESSIBLE
UNIMPRESSIVE
UNIMPRISONED
UNIMPROVED
UNIMPUGNABLE
UNINAUGURATED
UNINCHANTED
UNINCLOSED
UNINCORPORATED
UNINCUMBERED
UNINDEARED
UNINDENTED
UNINDICTED
UNINFECTED
UNINFLAMED
UNINFLAMMABLE
UNINFLATED
UNINFLECTED
UNINFLUENCED
UNINFLUENTIAL
UNINFORCEABLE
UNINFORCED
UNINFORMATIVE
UNINFORMATIVELY
UNINFORMED
UNINFORMING
UNINGRATIATING
UNINHABITABLE
UNINHABITED
UNINHIBITED
UNINHIBITEDLY
UNINHIBITEDNESS
UNINITIATE
UNINITIATED
UNINITIATES
UNINOCULATED
UNINQUIRING
UNINQUISITIVE
UNINSCRIBED
UNINSPECTED
UNINSPIRED
UNINSPIRING
UNINSTALLED
UNINSTALLING
UNINSTALLS
UNINSTRUCTED
UNINSTRUCTIVE

UNINSULATED
UNINSURABLE
UNINSUREDS
UNINTEGRATED
UNINTELLECTUAL
UNINTELLIGENCE
UNINTELLIGENCES
UNINTELLIGENT
UNINTELLIGENTLY
UNINTELLIGIBLE
UNINTELLIGIBLY
UNINTENDED
UNINTENTIONAL
UNINTENTIONALLY
UNINTEREST
UNINTERESTED
UNINTERESTEDLY
UNINTERESTING
UNINTERESTINGLY
UNINTERESTS
UNINTERMITTED
UNINTERMITTEDLY
UNINTERMITTING
UNINTERPRETABLE
UNINTERPRETED
UNINTERRUPTED
UNINTERRUPTEDLY
UNINTIMIDATED
UNINTOXICATING
UNINTRODUCED
UNINUCLEAR
UNINUCLEATE
UNINVENTIVE
UNINVESTED
UNINVIDIOUS
UNINVITING
UNINVOLVED
UNIONISATION
UNIONISATIONS
UNIONISERS
UNIONISING
UNIONISTIC
UNIONIZATION
UNIONIZATIONS
UNIONIZERS
UNIONIZING
UNIPARENTAL
UNIPARENTALLY
UNIPARTITE
UNIPERSONAL
UNIPERSONALITY
UNIPOLARITIES
UNIPOLARITY
UNIQUENESS
UNIQUENESSES
UNIRONICALLY
UNIRRADIATED
UNIRRIGATED
UNISEPTATE
UNISERIALLY
UNISERIATE
UNISERIATELY
UNISEXUALITIES
UNISEXUALITY
UNISEXUALLY
UNISONALLY
UNISONANCE

UNISONANCES
UNITARIANISM
UNITARIANISMS
UNITARIANS
UNITARITIES
UNITEDNESS
UNITEDNESSES
UNITHOLDER
UNITHOLDERS
UNITISATION
UNITISATIONS
UNITIZATION
UNITIZATIONS
UNIVALENCE
UNIVALENCES
UNIVALENCIES
UNIVALENCY
UNIVALENTS
UNIVALVULAR
UNIVARIANT
UNIVARIATE
UNIVERSALISABLE
UNIVERSALISE
UNIVERSALISED
UNIVERSALISES
UNIVERSALISING
UNIVERSALISM
UNIVERSALISMS
UNIVERSALIST
UNIVERSALISTIC
UNIVERSALISTS
UNIVERSALITIES
UNIVERSALITY
UNIVERSALIZABLE
UNIVERSALIZE
UNIVERSALIZED
UNIVERSALIZES
UNIVERSALIZING
UNIVERSALLY
UNIVERSALNESS
UNIVERSALNESSES
UNIVERSALS
UNIVERSITARIAN
UNIVERSITIES
UNIVERSITY
UNIVOCALLY
UNIVOLTINE
UNJAUNDICED
UNJOINTING
UNJUSTIFIABLE
UNJUSTIFIABLY
UNJUSTIFIED
UNJUSTNESS
UNJUSTNESSES
UNKEMPTNESS
UNKEMPTNESSES
UNKENNELED
UNKENNELING
UNKENNELLED
UNKENNELLING
UNKINDLIER
UNKINDLIEST
UNKINDLINESS
UNKINDLINESSES
UNKINDNESS
UNKINDNESSES
UNKINGLIER

UNKINGLIEST
UNKINGLIKE
UNKNIGHTED
UNKNIGHTING
UNKNIGHTLIER
UNKNIGHTLIEST
UNKNIGHTLINESS
UNKNIGHTLY
UNKNITTING
UNKNOTTING
UNKNOWABILITIES
UNKNOWABILITY
UNKNOWABLE
UNKNOWABLENESS
UNKNOWABLES
UNKNOWABLY
UNKNOWINGLY
UNKNOWINGNESS
UNKNOWINGNESSES
UNKNOWINGS
UNKNOWLEDGEABLE
UNKNOWNNESS
UNKNOWNNESSES
UNLABELLED
UNLABORING
UNLABORIOUS
UNLABOURED
UNLABOURING
UNLADYLIKE
UNLAMENTED
UNLATCHING
UNLAUNDERED
UNLAWFULLY
UNLAWFULNESS
UNLAWFULNESSES
UNLEARNABLE
UNLEARNEDLY
UNLEARNEDNESS
UNLEARNEDNESSES
UNLEARNING
UNLEASHING
UNLEAVENED
UNLEISURED
UNLEISURELY
UNLESSONED
UNLETTABLE
UNLETTERED
UNLEVELING
UNLEVELLED
UNLEVELLING
UNLIBERATED
UNLIBIDINOUS
UNLICENSED
UNLIFELIKE
UNLIGHTENED
UNLIGHTSOME
UNLIKEABLE
UNLIKELIER
UNLIKELIEST
UNLIKELIHOOD
UNLIKELIHOODS
UNLIKELINESS
UNLIKELINESSES
UNLIKENESS
UNLIKENESSES
UNLIMBERED
UNLIMBERING

UNLIMITEDLY
UNLIMITEDNESS
UNLIMITEDNESSES
UNLIQUEFIED
UNLIQUIDATED
UNLIQUORED
UNLISTENABLE
UNLISTENED
UNLISTENING
UNLITERARY
UNLIVEABLE
UNLIVELIER
UNLIVELIEST
UNLIVELINESS
UNLIVELINESSES
UNLOADINGS
UNLOCALISED
UNLOCALIZED
UNLOCKABLE
UNLOOSENED
UNLOOSENING
UNLORDLIER
UNLORDLIEST
UNLOVEABLE
UNLOVELIER
UNLOVELIEST
UNLOVELINESS
UNLOVELINESSES
UNLOVERLIKE
UNLOVINGLY
UNLOVINGNESS
UNLOVINGNESSES
UNLUCKIEST
UNLUCKINESS
UNLUCKINESSES
UNLUXURIANT
UNLUXURIOUS
UNMACADAMISED
UNMACADAMIZED
UNMAGNIFIED
UNMAIDENLY
UNMAILABLE
UNMAINTAINABLE
UNMAINTAINED
UNMALICIOUS
UNMALICIOUSLY
UNMALLEABILITY
UNMALLEABLE
UNMANACLED
UNMANACLES
UNMANACLING
UNMANAGEABLE
UNMANAGEABLY
UNMANFULLY
UNMANIPULATED
UNMANLIEST
UNMANLINESS
UNMANLINESSES
UNMANNERED
UNMANNEREDLY
UNMANNERLIER
UNMANNERLIEST
UNMANNERLINESS
UNMANNERLY
UNMANTLING
UNMANUFACTURED
UNMARKETABLE

UNMARRIABLE	UNMINDFULNESS	UNNATURALNESS	UNORDAINED	UNPATRONISED
UNMARRIAGEABLE	UNMINDFULNESSES	UNNATURALNESSES	UNORDERING	UNPATRONIZED
UNMARRIEDS	UNMINGLING	UNNAVIGABLE	UNORDINARY	UNPATTERNED
UNMARRYING	UNMINISTERIAL	UNNAVIGATED	UNORGANISED	UNPAVILIONED
UNMASCULINE	UNMIRACULOUS	UNNECESSARILY	UNORGANIZED	UNPEACEABLE
UNMASKINGS	UNMISSABLE	UNNECESSARINESS	UNORIGINAL	UNPEACEABLENESS
UNMASTERED	UNMISTAKABLE	UNNECESSARY	UNORIGINALITIES	UNPEACEFUL
UNMATCHABLE	UNMISTAKABLY	UNNEEDFULLY	UNORIGINALITY	UNPEACEFULLY
UNMATCHING	UNMISTAKEABLE	UNNEGOTIABLE	UNORIGINALS	UNPEDANTIC
UNMATERIAL	UNMISTAKEABLY	UNNEIGHBORED	UNORIGINATE	UNPEDIGREED
UNMATERIALISED	UNMISTRUSTFUL	UNNEIGHBORLY	UNORIGINATED	UNPEERABLE
UNMATERIALIZED	UNMITERING	UNNEIGHBOURED	UNORNAMENTAL	UNPENSIONED
UNMATERNAL	UNMITIGABLE	UNNEIGHBOURLY	UNORNAMENTED	UNPEOPLING
UNMATHEMATICAL	UNMITIGABLY	UNNERVINGLY	UNORTHODOX	UNPEPPERED
UNMATRICULATED	UNMITIGATED	UNNEUROTIC	UNORTHODOXIES	UNPERCEIVABLE
UNMEANINGLY	UNMITIGATEDLY	UNNEWSWORTHIER	UNORTHODOXLY	UNPERCEIVABLY
UNMEANINGNESS	UNMITIGATEDNESS	UNNEWSWORTHIEST	UNORTHODOXY	UNPERCEIVED
UNMEANINGNESSES	UNMODERATED	UNNEWSWORTHY	UNOSSIFIED	UNPERCEIVEDLY
UNMEASURABLE	UNMODERNISED	UNNILHEXIUM	UNOSTENTATIOUS	UNPERCEPTIVE
UNMEASURABLY	UNMODERNIZED	UNNILHEXIUMS	UNOVERCOME	UNPERCHING
UNMEASURED	UNMODIFIABLE	UNNILPENTIUM	UNOVERTHROWN	UNPERFECTED
UNMEASUREDLY	UNMODIFIED	UNNILPENTIUMS	UNOXIDISED	UNPERFECTION
UNMECHANIC	UNMODULATED	UNNILQUADIUM	UNOXIDIZED	UNPERFECTIONS
UNMECHANICAL	UNMOISTENED	UNNILQUADIUMS	UNOXYGENATED	UNPERFECTLY
UNMECHANISE	UNMOLESTED	UNNILSEPTIUM	UNPACIFIED	UNPERFECTNESS
UNMECHANISED	UNMONITORED	UNNILSEPTIUMS	UNPACKINGS	UNPERFECTNESSES
UNMECHANISES	UNMORALISED	UNNOISIEST	UNPAINTABLE	UNPERFORATED
UNMECHANISING	UNMORALISING	UNNOTICEABLE	UNPAINTING	UNPERFORMABLE
UNMECHANIZE	UNMORALITIES	UNNOTICEABLY	UNPALATABILITY	UNPERFORMED
UNMECHANIZED	UNMORALITY	UNNOTICING	UNPALATABLE	UNPERFORMING
UNMECHANIZES	UNMORALIZED	UNNOURISHED	UNPALATABLY	UNPERFUMED
UNMECHANIZING	UNMORALIZING	UNNOURISHING	UNPAMPERED	UNPERILOUS
UNMEDIATED	UNMORTGAGED	UNNUMBERED	UNPANELLED	UNPERISHABLE
UNMEDICATED	UNMORTIFIED	UNNURTURED	UNPANELLING	UNPERISHED
UNMEDICINABLE	UNMORTISED	UNOBEDIENT	UNPANNELLED	UNPERISHING
UNMEDITATED	UNMORTISES	UNOBJECTIONABLE	UNPANNELLING	UNPERJURED
UNMEETNESS	UNMORTISING	UNOBJECTIONABLY	UNPAPERING	UNPERPETRATED
UNMEETNESSES	UNMOTHERLIER	UNOBLIGING	UNPARADISE	UNPERPLEXED
UNMELLOWED	UNMOTHERLIEST	UNOBNOXIOUS	UNPARADISED	UNPERPLEXES
UNMELODIOUS	UNMOTHERLY	UNOBSCURED	UNPARADISES	UNPERPLEXING
UNMELODIOUSNESS	UNMOTIVATED	UNOBSERVABLE	UNPARADISING	UNPERSECUTED
UNMEMORABLE	UNMOULDING	UNOBSERVABLES	UNPARAGONED	UNPERSONED
UNMEMORABLY	UNMOUNTING	UNOBSERVANCE	UNPARALLEL	UNPERSONING
UNMENTIONABLE	UNMOVEABLE	UNOBSERVANCES	UNPARALLELED	UNPERSUADABLE
UNMENTIONABLES	UNMOVEABLY	UNOBSERVANT	UNPARASITISED	UNPERSUADED
UNMENTIONABLY	UNMUFFLING	UNOBSERVED	UNPARASITIZED	UNPERSUASIVE
UNMENTIONED	UNMUNITIONED	UNOBSERVEDLY	UNPARDONABLE	UNPERTURBED
UNMERCENARY	UNMURMURING	UNOBSERVING	UNPARDONABLY	UNPERVERTED
UNMERCHANTABLE	UNMURMURINGLY	UNOBSTRUCTED	UNPARDONED	UNPERVERTING
UNMERCIFUL	UNMUSICALLY	UNOBSTRUCTIVE	UNPARDONING	UNPERVERTS
UNMERCIFULLY	UNMUSICALNESS	UNOBTAINABLE	UNPARENTAL	UNPHILOSOPHIC
UNMERCIFULNESS	UNMUSICALNESSES	UNOBTAINED	UNPARENTED	UNPHILOSOPHICAL
UNMERITABLE	UNMUTILATED	UNOBTRUSIVE	UNPARLIAMENTARY	UNPHONETIC
UNMERITEDLY	UNMUZZLING	UNOBTRUSIVELY	UNPASSABLE	UNPICKABLE
UNMERITING	UNMUZZLINGS	UNOBTRUSIVENESS	UNPASSABLENESS	UNPICTURESQUE
UNMERRIEST	UNMYELINATED	UNOCCUPIED	UNPASSIONATE	UNPIGMENTED
UNMETABOLISED	UNNAMEABLE	UNOFFENDED	UNPASSIONED	UNPILLARED
UNMETABOLIZED	UNNATIVING	UNOFFENDING	UNPASTEURISED	UNPILLOWED
UNMETALLED	UNNATURALISE	UNOFFENSIVE	UNPASTEURIZED	UNPITIFULLY
UNMETAPHORICAL	UNNATURALISED	UNOFFICERED	UNPASTORAL	UNPITIFULNESS
UNMETAPHYSICAL	UNNATURALISES	UNOFFICIAL	UNPASTURED	UNPITIFULNESSES
UNMETHODICAL	UNNATURALISING	UNOFFICIALLY	UNPATENTABLE	UNPITYINGLY
UNMETHODISED	UNNATURALIZE	UNOFFICIOUS	UNPATENTED	UNPLAITING
UNMETHODIZED	UNNATURALIZED	UNOPENABLE	UNPATHETIC	UNPLASTERED
UNMETRICAL	UNNATURALIZES	UNOPERATIVE	UNPATHWAYED	UNPLASTICISED
UNMILITARY	UNNATURALIZING	UNOPPOSING	UNPATRIOTIC	UNPLASTICIZED
UNMINDFULLY	UNNATURALLY	UNOPPRESSIVE	UNPATRIOTICALLY	UNPLAUSIBLE

UNPLAUSIBLY	UNPREGNANT	UNPROFITING	UNQUALIFIABLE	UNREASONING
UNPLAUSIVE	UNPREJUDICED	UNPROFITINGS	UNQUALIFIED	UNREASONINGLY
UNPLAYABLE	UNPREJUDICEDLY	UNPROGRAMMABLE	UNQUALIFIEDLY	UNRECALLABLE
UNPLEASANT	UNPRELATICAL	UNPROGRAMMED	UNQUALIFIEDNESS	UNRECALLED
UNPLEASANTLY	UNPREMEDITABLE	UNPROGRESSIVE	UNQUALIFIES	UNRECALLING
UNPLEASANTNESS	UNPREMEDITATED	UNPROGRESSIVELY	UNQUALIFYING	UNRECAPTURABLE
UNPLEASANTRIES	UNPREMEDITATION	UNPROHIBITED	UNQUALITED	UNRECEIPTED
UNPLEASANTRY	UNPREOCCUPIED	UNPROJECTED	UNQUALITIED	UNRECEIVED
UNPLEASING	UNPREPARED	UNPROLIFIC	UNQUANTIFIABLE	UNRECEPTIVE
UNPLEASINGLY	UNPREPAREDLY	UNPROMISED	UNQUANTIFIED	UNRECIPROCATED
UNPLEASURABLE	UNPREPAREDNESS	UNPROMISING	UNQUANTISED	UNRECKONABLE
UNPLEASURABLY	UNPREPARES	UNPROMISINGLY	UNQUANTIZED	UNRECKONED
UNPLOUGHED	UNPREPARING	UNPROMPTED	UNQUARRIED	UNRECLAIMABLE
UNPLUGGING	UNPREPOSSESSED	UNPRONOUNCEABLE	UNQUEENING	UNRECLAIMABLY
UNPLUMBING	UNPREPOSSESSING	UNPRONOUNCED	UNQUEENLIER	UNRECLAIMED
UNPOETICAL	UNPRESCRIBED	UNPROPERLY	UNQUEENLIEST	UNRECOGNISABLE
UNPOETICALLY	UNPRESENTABLE	UNPROPERTIED	UNQUEENLIKE	UNRECOGNISABLY
UNPOETICALNESS	UNPRESSURED	UNPROPHETIC	UNQUENCHABLE	UNRECOGNISED
UNPOISONED	UNPRESSURISED	UNPROPHETICAL	UNQUENCHABLY	UNRECOGNISING
UNPOISONING	UNPRESSURIZED	UNPROPITIOUS	UNQUENCHED	UNRECOGNIZABLE
UNPOLARISABLE	UNPRESUMING	UNPROPITIOUSLY	UNQUESTIONABLE	UNRECOGNIZABLY
UNPOLARISED	UNPRESUMPTUOUS	UNPROPORTIONATE	UNQUESTIONABLY	UNRECOGNIZED
UNPOLARIZABLE	UNPRETENDING	UNPROPORTIONED	UNQUESTIONED	UNRECOGNIZING
UNPOLARIZED	UNPRETENDINGLY	UNPROPOSED	UNQUESTIONING	UNRECOLLECTED
UNPOLICIED	UNPRETENTIOUS	UNPROPPING	UNQUESTIONINGLY	UNRECOMMENDABLE
UNPOLISHABLE	UNPRETENTIOUSLY	UNPROSPEROUS	UNQUICKENED	UNRECOMMENDED
UNPOLISHED	UNPRETTIER	UNPROSPEROUSLY	UNQUIETEST	UNRECOMPENSED
UNPOLISHES	UNPRETTIEST	UNPROTECTED	UNQUIETING	UNRECONCILABLE
UNPOLISHING	UNPRETTINESS	UNPROTECTEDNESS	UNQUIETNESS	UNRECONCILABLY
UNPOLITELY	UNPRETTINESSES	UNPROTESTANTISE	UNQUIETNESSES	UNRECONCILED
UNPOLITENESS	UNPREVAILING	UNPROTESTANTIZE	UNQUOTABLE	UNRECONCILIABLE
UNPOLITENESSES	UNPREVENTABLE	UNPROTESTED	UNRANSOMED	UNRECONSTRUCTED
UNPOLITICAL	UNPREVENTED	UNPROTESTING	UNRATIFIED	UNRECORDED
UNPOLLUTED	UNPRIESTED	UNPROVABLE	UNRAVELING	UNRECOUNTED
UNPOPULARITIES	UNPRIESTING	UNPROVIDED	UNRAVELLED	UNRECOVERABLE
UNPOPULARITY	UNPRIESTLIER	UNPROVIDEDLY	UNRAVELLER	UNRECOVERABLY
UNPOPULARLY	UNPRIESTLIEST	UNPROVIDENT	UNRAVELLERS	UNRECOVERED
UNPOPULATED	UNPRIESTLY	UNPROVIDES	UNRAVELLING	UNRECTIFIED
UNPOPULOUS	UNPRINCELIER	UNPROVIDING	UNRAVELLINGS	UNRECURING
UNPORTIONED	UNPRINCELIEST	UNPROVISIONED	UNRAVELMENT	UNRECYCLABLE
UNPOSSESSED	UNPRINCELY	UNPROVOCATIVE	UNRAVELMENTS	UNRECYCLABLES
UNPOSSESSING	UNPRINCIPLED	UNPROVOKED	UNRAVISHED	UNREDEEMABLE
UNPOSSIBLE	UNPRINTABLE	UNPROVOKEDLY	UNREACHABLE	UNREDEEMED
UNPOWDERED	UNPRINTABLENESS	UNPROVOKES	UNREACTIVE	UNREDRESSED
UNPRACTICABLE	UNPRINTABLY	UNPROVOKING	UNREADABILITIES	UNREDUCIBLE
UNPRACTICAL	UNPRISABLE	UNPUBLICISED	UNREADABILITY	UNREFLECTED
UNPRACTICALITY	UNPRISONED	UNPUBLICIZED	UNREADABLE	UNREFLECTING
UNPRACTICALLY	UNPRISONING	UNPUBLISHABLE	UNREADABLENESS	UNREFLECTINGLY
UNPRACTICALNESS	UNPRIVILEGED	UNPUBLISHED	UNREADABLY	UNREFLECTIVE
UNPRACTICED	UNPRIZABLE	UNPUCKERED	UNREADIEST	UNREFLECTIVELY
UNPRACTISED	UNPROBLEMATIC	UNPUCKERING	UNREADINESS	UNREFORMABLE
UNPRACTISEDNESS	UNPROCEDURAL	UNPUNCTUAL	UNREADINESSES	UNREFORMED
UNPRAISEWORTHY	UNPROCESSED	UNPUNCTUALITIES	UNREALISABLE	UNREFRACTED
UNPRAISING	UNPROCLAIMED	UNPUNCTUALITY	UNREALISED	UNREFRESHED
UNPREACHED	UNPROCURABLE	UNPUNCTUATED	UNREALISES	UNREFRESHING
UNPREACHES	UNPRODUCED	UNPUNISHABLE	UNREALISING	UNREFRIGERATED
UNPREACHING	UNPRODUCTIVE	UNPUNISHABLY	UNREALISMS	UNREGARDED
UNPRECEDENTED	UNPRODUCTIVELY	UNPUNISHED	UNREALISTIC	UNREGARDING
UNPRECEDENTEDLY	UNPRODUCTIVITY	UNPURCHASABLE	UNREALISTICALLY	UNREGENERACIES
UNPREDESTINED	UNPROFANED	UNPURCHASEABLE	UNREALITIES	UNREGENERACY
UNPREDICTABLE	UNPROFESSED	UNPURCHASED	UNREALIZABLE	UNREGENERATE
UNPREDICTABLES	UNPROFESSIONAL	UNPURIFIED	UNREALIZED	UNREGENERATED
UNPREDICTABLY	UNPROFESSIONALS	UNPURPOSED	UNREALIZES	UNREGENERATELY
UNPREDICTED	UNPROFITABILITY	UNPURVAIDE	UNREALIZING	UNREGENERATES
UNPREDICTING	UNPROFITABLE	UNPURVEYED	UNREASONABLE	UNREGIMENTED
UNPREDICTS	UNPROFITABLY	UNPUTDOWNABLE	UNREASONABLY	UNREGISTERED
UNPREFERRED	UNPROFITED	UNPUZZLING	UNREASONED	UNREGRETTED

UNREGULATED
UNREHEARSED
UNREINFORCED
UNREJOICED
UNREJOICING
UNRELATIVE
UNRELEASED
UNRELENTING
UNRELENTINGLY
UNRELENTINGNESS
UNRELENTOR
UNRELENTORS
UNRELIABILITIES
UNRELIABILITY
UNRELIABLE
UNRELIABLENESS
UNRELIABLY
UNRELIEVABLE
UNRELIEVED
UNRELIEVEDLY
UNRELIGIOUS
UNRELIGIOUSLY
UNRELISHED
UNRELUCTANT
UNREMAINING
UNREMARKABLE
UNREMARKABLY
UNREMARKED
UNREMEDIED
UNREMEMBERED
UNREMEMBERING
UNREMINISCENT
UNREMITTED
UNREMITTEDLY
UNREMITTENT
UNREMITTENTLY
UNREMITTING
UNREMITTINGLY
UNREMITTINGNESS
UNREMORSEFUL
UNREMORSEFULLY
UNREMORSELESS
UNREMOVABLE
UNREMUNERATIVE
UNRENDERED
UNRENOWNED
UNREPAIRABLE
UNREPAIRED
UNREPEALABLE
UNREPEALED
UNREPEATABLE
UNREPEATED
UNREPELLED
UNREPENTANCE
UNREPENTANCES
UNREPENTANT
UNREPENTANTLY
UNREPENTED
UNREPENTING
UNREPENTINGLY
UNREPINING
UNREPININGLY
UNREPLACEABLE
UNREPLENISHED
UNREPORTABLE
UNREPORTED
UNREPOSEFUL

UNREPOSING
UNREPRESENTED
UNREPRESSED
UNREPRIEVABLE
UNREPRIEVED
UNREPRIMANDED
UNREPROACHED
UNREPROACHFUL
UNREPROACHING
UNREPRODUCIBLE
UNREPROVABLE
UNREPROVED
UNREPROVING
UNREPUGNANT
UNREPULSABLE
UNREQUESTED
UNREQUIRED
UNREQUISITE
UNREQUITED
UNREQUITEDLY
UNRESCINDED
UNRESENTED
UNRESENTFUL
UNRESENTING
UNRESERVED
UNRESERVEDLY
UNRESERVEDNESS
UNRESERVES
UNRESISTANT
UNRESISTED
UNRESISTIBLE
UNRESISTING
UNRESISTINGLY
UNRESOLVABLE
UNRESOLVED
UNRESOLVEDNESS
UNRESPECTABLE
UNRESPECTABLES
UNRESPECTED
UNRESPECTIVE
UNRESPITED
UNRESPONSIVE
UNRESPONSIVELY
UNRESTFULNESS
UNRESTFULNESSES
UNRESTINGLY
UNRESTINGNESS
UNRESTINGNESSES
UNRESTORED
UNRESTRAINABLE
UNRESTRAINED
UNRESTRAINEDLY
UNRESTRAINT
UNRESTRAINTS
UNRESTRICTED
UNRESTRICTEDLY
UNRETARDED
UNRETENTIVE
UNRETIRING
UNRETOUCHED
UNRETURNABLE
UNRETURNED
UNRETURNING
UNRETURNINGLY
UNREVEALABLE
UNREVEALED
UNREVEALING

UNREVENGED
UNREVENGEFUL
UNREVEREND
UNREVERENT
UNREVERSED
UNREVERTED
UNREVIEWABLE
UNREVIEWED
UNREVOLUTIONARY
UNREWARDED
UNREWARDEDLY
UNREWARDING
UNRHETORICAL
UNRHYTHMIC
UNRHYTHMICAL
UNRHYTHMICALLY
UNRIDDLEABLE
UNRIDDLERS
UNRIDDLING
UNRIDEABLE
UNRIGHTEOUS
UNRIGHTEOUSLY
UNRIGHTEOUSNESS
UNRIGHTFUL
UNRIGHTFULLY
UNRIGHTFULNESS
UNRIGHTING
UNRIPENESS
UNRIPENESSES
UNRIPPINGS
UNRIVALLED
UNRIVETING
UNRIVETTED
UNRIVETTING
UNROADWORTHY
UNROMANISED
UNROMANIZED
UNROMANTIC
UNROMANTICAL
UNROMANTICALLY
UNROMANTICISED
UNROMANTICIZED
UNROOSTING
UNROUNDING
UNRUFFABLE
UNRUFFLEDNESS
UNRUFFLEDNESSES
UNRUFFLING
UNRULIMENT
UNRULIMENTS
UNRULINESS
UNRULINESSES
UNRUPTURED
UNSADDLING
UNSAFENESS
UNSAFENESSES
UNSAFETIES
UNSAILORLIKE
UNSAINTING
UNSAINTLIER
UNSAINTLIEST
UNSAINTLINESS
UNSAINTLINESSES
UNSALABILITIES
UNSALABILITY
UNSALARIED
UNSALEABILITIES

UNSALEABILITY
UNSALEABLE
UNSALEABLY
UNSALVAGEABLE
UNSANCTIFIED
UNSANCTIFIES
UNSANCTIFY
UNSANCTIFYING
UNSANCTIONED
UNSANDALLED
UNSANITARY
UNSATIABLE
UNSATIATED
UNSATIATING
UNSATIRICAL
UNSATISFACTION
UNSATISFACTIONS
UNSATISFACTORY
UNSATISFIABLE
UNSATISFIED
UNSATISFIEDNESS
UNSATISFYING
UNSATURATE
UNSATURATED
UNSATURATES
UNSATURATION
UNSATURATIONS
UNSAVORIER
UNSAVORIEST
UNSAVORILY
UNSAVORINESS
UNSAVORINESSES
UNSAVOURIER
UNSAVOURIEST
UNSAVOURILY
UNSAVOURINESS
UNSAVOURINESSES
UNSAYABLES
UNSCABBARD
UNSCABBARDED
UNSCABBARDING
UNSCABBARDS
UNSCALABLE
UNSCARIEST
UNSCAVENGERED
UNSCEPTRED
UNSCHEDULED
UNSCHOLARLIKE
UNSCHOLARLY
UNSCHOOLED
UNSCIENTIFIC
UNSCISSORED
UNSCORCHED
UNSCOTTIFIED
UNSCRAMBLE
UNSCRAMBLED
UNSCRAMBLER
UNSCRAMBLERS
UNSCRAMBLES
UNSCRAMBLING
UNSCRATCHED
UNSCREENED
UNSCREWING
UNSCRIPTED
UNSCRIPTURAL
UNSCRIPTURALLY
UNSCRUPLED

UNSCRUPULOSITY
UNSCRUPULOUS
UNSCRUPULOUSLY
UNSCRUTINISED
UNSCRUTINIZED
UNSCULPTURED
UNSEALABLE
UNSEARCHABLE
UNSEARCHABLES
UNSEARCHABLY
UNSEARCHED
UNSEASONABLE
UNSEASONABLY
UNSEASONED
UNSEASONEDNESS
UNSEASONING
UNSEAWORTHINESS
UNSEAWORTHY
UNSECONDED
UNSECRETED
UNSECRETING
UNSECTARIAN
UNSECTARIANISM
UNSECTARIANISMS
UNSECTARIANS
UNSEEMINGS
UNSEEMLIER
UNSEEMLIEST
UNSEEMLINESS
UNSEEMLINESSES
UNSEGMENTED
UNSEGREGATED
UNSEISABLE
UNSEIZABLE
UNSELECTED
UNSELECTIVE
UNSELECTIVELY
UNSELFCONSCIOUS
UNSELFISHLY
UNSELFISHNESS
UNSELFISHNESSES
UNSELLABLE
UNSEMINARIED
UNSENSATIONAL
UNSENSIBLE
UNSENSIBLY
UNSENSITISED
UNSENSITIVE
UNSENSITIZED
UNSENSUALISE
UNSENSUALISED
UNSENSUALISES
UNSENSUALISING
UNSENSUALIZE
UNSENSUALIZED
UNSENSUALIZES
UNSENSUALIZING
UNSENTENCED
UNSENTIMENTAL
UNSEPARABLE
UNSEPARATED
UNSEPULCHRED
UNSERIOUSNESS
UNSERIOUSNESSES
UNSERVICEABLE
UNSETTLEDLY
UNSETTLEDNESS

UNSETTLEDNESSES	UNSLAKABLE	UNSPECULATIVE	UNSTITCHED	UNSUPERVISED
UNSETTLEMENT	UNSLEEPING	UNSPELLING	UNSTITCHES	UNSUPPLENESS
UNSETTLEMENTS	UNSLEEPINGS	UNSPHERING	UNSTITCHING	UNSUPPLENESSES
UNSETTLING	UNSLINGING	UNSPIRITED	UNSTOCKING	UNSUPPLIED
UNSETTLINGLY	UNSLIPPING	UNSPIRITUAL	UNSTOCKINGED	UNSUPPORTABLE
UNSETTLINGS	UNSLUICING	UNSPIRITUALISE	UNSTOOPING	UNSUPPORTED
UNSHACKLED	UNSLUMBERING	UNSPIRITUALISED	UNSTOPPABLE	UNSUPPORTEDLY
UNSHACKLES	UNSLUMBROUS	UNSPIRITUALISES	UNSTOPPABLY	UNSUPPOSABLE
UNSHACKLING	UNSMILINGLY	UNSPIRITUALIZE	UNSTOPPERED	UNSUPPRESSED
UNSHADOWABLE	UNSMIRCHED	UNSPIRITUALIZED	UNSTOPPERING	UNSURFACED
UNSHADOWED	UNSMOKABLE	UNSPIRITUALIZES	UNSTOPPERS	UNSURMISED
UNSHADOWING	UNSMOOTHED	UNSPIRITUALLY	UNSTOPPING	UNSURMOUNTABLE
UNSHAKABLE	UNSMOOTHING	UNSPLINTERABLE	UNSTRAINED	UNSURPASSABLE
UNSHAKABLENESS	UNSMOTHERABLE	UNSPOOLING	UNSTRAPPED	UNSURPASSABLY
UNSHAKABLY	UNSNAGGING	UNSPORTING	UNSTRAPPING	UNSURPASSED
UNSHAKEABLE	UNSNAPPING	UNSPORTSMANLIKE	UNSTRATIFIED	UNSURPRISED
UNSHAKEABLENESS	UNSNARLING	UNSPOTTEDNESS	UNSTREAMED	UNSURPRISING
UNSHAKEABLY	UNSNECKING	UNSPOTTEDNESSES	UNSTRENGTHENED	UNSURPRISINGLY
UNSHAKENLY	UNSOBERING	UNSPRINKLED	UNSTRESSED	UNSURVEYED
UNSHAPELIER	UNSOCIABILITIES	UNSTABLENESS	UNSTRESSES	UNSUSCEPTIBLE
UNSHAPELIEST	UNSOCIABILITY	UNSTABLENESSES	UNSTRESSING	UNSUSPECTED
UNSHARPENED	UNSOCIABLE	UNSTABLEST	UNSTRIATED	UNSUSPECTEDLY
UNSHEATHED	UNSOCIABLENESS	UNSTACKING	UNSTRINGED	UNSUSPECTEDNESS
UNSHEATHES	UNSOCIABLY	UNSTAIDNESS	UNSTRINGING	UNSUSPECTING
UNSHEATHING	UNSOCIALISED	UNSTAIDNESSES	UNSTRIPPED	UNSUSPECTINGLY
UNSHELLING	UNSOCIALISM	UNSTAINABLE	UNSTRIPPING	UNSUSPENDED
UNSHELTERED	UNSOCIALISMS	UNSTANCHABLE	UNSTRUCTURED	UNSUSPICION
UNSHIELDED	UNSOCIALITIES	UNSTANCHED	UNSTUFFIER	UNSUSPICIONS
UNSHIFTING	UNSOCIALITY	UNSTANDARDISED	UNSTUFFIEST	UNSUSPICIOUS
UNSHINGLED	UNSOCIALIZED	UNSTANDARDIZED	UNSUBDUABLE	UNSUSPICIOUSLY
UNSHIPPING	UNSOCIALLY	UNSTARCHED	UNSUBJECTED	UNSUSTAINABLE
UNSHOCKABLE	UNSOCKETED	UNSTARCHES	UNSUBJECTING	UNSUSTAINABLY
UNSHOOTING	UNSOCKETING	UNSTARCHING	UNSUBJECTS	UNSUSTAINED
UNSHOTTING	UNSOFTENED	UNSTARRIER	UNSUBLIMATED	UNSUSTAINING
UNSHOUTING	UNSOFTENING	UNSTARRIEST	UNSUBLIMED	UNSWADDLED
UNSHOWERED	UNSOLDERED	UNSTARTLING	UNSUBMERGED	UNSWADDLES
UNSHOWIEST	UNSOLDERING	UNSTATESMANLIKE	UNSUBMISSIVE	UNSWADDLING
UNSHRINKABLE	UNSOLDIERLIKE	UNSTATUTABLE	UNSUBMITTING	UNSWALLOWED
UNSHRINKING	UNSOLDIERLY	UNSTATUTABLY	UNSUBSCRIBE	UNSWATHING
UNSHRINKINGLY	UNSOLICITED	UNSTAUNCHABLE	UNSUBSCRIBED	UNSWAYABLE
UNSHROUDED	UNSOLICITOUS	UNSTAUNCHED	UNSUBSCRIBER	UNSWEARING
UNSHROUDING	UNSOLIDITIES	UNSTEADFAST	UNSUBSCRIBERS	UNSWEARINGS
UNSHRUBBED	UNSOLIDITY	UNSTEADFASTLY	UNSUBSCRIBES	UNSWEETENED
UNSHUNNABLE	UNSOLVABLE	UNSTEADFASTNESS	UNSUBSCRIBING	UNSWERVING
UNSHUTTERED	UNSONSIEST	UNSTEADIED	UNSUBSIDISED	UNSWERVINGLY
UNSHUTTERING	UNSOPHISTICATE	UNSTEADIER	UNSUBSIDIZED	UNSYLLABLED
UNSHUTTERS	UNSOPHISTICATED	UNSTEADIES	UNSUBSTANTIAL	UNSYMMETRICAL
UNSHUTTING	UNSOUNDABLE	UNSTEADIEST	UNSUBSTANTIALLY	UNSYMMETRICALLY
UNSIGHTEDLY	UNSOUNDEST	UNSTEADILY	UNSUBSTANTIATED	UNSYMMETRIES
UNSIGHTING	UNSOUNDNESS	UNSTEADINESS	UNSUBTLEST	UNSYMMETRISED
UNSIGHTLIER	UNSOUNDNESSES	UNSTEADINESSES	UNSUCCEEDED	UNSYMMETRIZED
UNSIGHTLIEST	UNSPARINGLY	UNSTEADYING	UNSUCCESSES	UNSYMMETRY
UNSIGHTLINESS	UNSPARINGNESS	UNSTEELING	UNSUCCESSFUL	UNSYMPATHETIC
UNSIGHTLINESSES	UNSPARINGNESSES	UNSTEPPING	UNSUCCESSFULLY	UNSYMPATHIES
UNSINEWING	UNSPARRING	UNSTERCORATED	UNSUCCESSIVE	UNSYMPATHISING
UNSINKABLE	UNSPEAKABLE	UNSTEREOTYPED	UNSUCCOURED	UNSYMPATHIZING
UNSINNOWED	UNSPEAKABLENESS	UNSTERILISED	UNSUFFERABLE	UNSYMPATHY
UNSISTERED	UNSPEAKABLY	UNSTERILIZED	UNSUFFICIENT	UNSYNCHRONISED
UNSISTERLINESS	UNSPEAKING	UNSTICKING	UNSUITABILITIES	UNSYNCHRONIZED
UNSISTERLY	UNSPECIALISED	UNSTIFFENED	UNSUITABILITY	UNSYSTEMATIC
UNSIZEABLE	UNSPECIALIZED	UNSTIFFENING	UNSUITABLE	UNSYSTEMATICAL
UNSKILFULLY	UNSPECIFIABLE	UNSTIFFENS	UNSUITABLENESS	UNSYSTEMATISED
UNSKILFULNESS	UNSPECIFIC	UNSTIGMATISED	UNSUITABLY	UNSYSTEMATIZED
UNSKILFULNESSES	UNSPECIFICALLY	UNSTIGMATIZED	UNSUMMERED	UNSYSTEMIC
UNSKILLFUL	UNSPECIFIED	UNSTIMULATED	UNSUMMONED	UNTACKLING
UNSKILLFULLY	UNSPECTACLED	UNSTINTING	UNSUNNIEST	UNTAILORED
UNSKILLFULNESS	UNSPECTACULAR	UNSTINTINGLY	UNSUPERFLUOUS	UNTAINTEDLY

UNTAINTEDNESS
UNTAINTEDNESSES
UNTAINTING
UNTALENTED
UNTAMABLENESS
UNTAMABLENESSES
UNTAMEABLE
UNTAMEABLENESS
UNTAMEABLY
UNTAMEDNESS
UNTAMEDNESSES
UNTANGIBLE
UNTANGLING
UNTARNISHED
UNTASTEFUL
UNTEACHABLE
UNTEACHABLENESS
UNTEACHING
UNTEARABLE
UNTECHNICAL
UNTELLABLE
UNTEMPERED
UNTEMPERING
UNTENABILITIES
UNTENABILITY
UNTENABLENESS
UNTENABLENESSES
UNTENANTABLE
UNTENANTED
UNTENANTING
UNTENDERED
UNTENDERLY
UNTENTIEST
UNTERMINATED
UNTERRESTRIAL
UNTERRIFIED
UNTERRIFYING
UNTESTABLE
UNTETHERED
UNTETHERING
UNTHANKFUL
UNTHANKFULLY
UNTHANKFULNESS
UNTHATCHED
UNTHATCHES
UNTHATCHING
UNTHEOLOGICAL
UNTHEORETICAL
UNTHICKENED
UNTHINKABILITY
UNTHINKABLE
UNTHINKABLENESS
UNTHINKABLY
UNTHINKING
UNTHINKINGLY
UNTHINKINGNESS
UNTHOROUGH
UNTHOUGHTFUL
UNTHOUGHTFULLY
UNTHREADED
UNTHREADING
UNTHREATENED
UNTHREATENING
UNTHRESHED
UNTHRIFTIER
UNTHRIFTIEST
UNTHRIFTIHEAD

UNTHRIFTIHEADS
UNTHRIFTILY
UNTHRIFTINESS
UNTHRIFTINESSES
UNTHRIFTYHEAD
UNTHRIFTYHEADS
UNTHRIFTYHED
UNTHRIFTYHEDS
UNTHRONING
UNTIDINESS
UNTIDINESSES
UNTILLABLE
UNTIMBERED
UNTIMELIER
UNTIMELIEST
UNTIMELINESS
UNTIMELINESSES
UNTIMEOUSLY
UNTINCTURED
UNTIRINGLY
UNTOCHERED
UNTOGETHER
UNTORMENTED
UNTORTURED
UNTOUCHABILITY
UNTOUCHABLE
UNTOUCHABLES
UNTOWARDLINESS
UNTOWARDLY
UNTOWARDNESS
UNTOWARDNESSES
UNTRACEABLE
UNTRACKING
UNTRACTABLE
UNTRACTABLENESS
UNTRADITIONAL
UNTRADITIONALLY
UNTRAMMELED
UNTRAMMELLED
UNTRAMPLED
UNTRANQUIL
UNTRANSFERABLE
UNTRANSFERRABLE
UNTRANSFORMED
UNTRANSLATABLE
UNTRANSLATABLY
UNTRANSLATED
UNTRANSMIGRATED
UNTRANSMISSIBLE
UNTRANSMITTED
UNTRANSMUTABLE
UNTRANSMUTED
UNTRANSPARENT
UNTRAVELED
UNTRAVELLED
UNTRAVERSABLE
UNTRAVERSED
UNTREADING
UNTREASURE
UNTREASURED
UNTREASURES
UNTREASURING
UNTREATABLE
UNTREMBLING
UNTREMBLINGLY
UNTREMENDOUS
UNTREMULOUS

UNTRENCHED
UNTRENDIER
UNTRENDIEST
UNTRESPASSING
UNTRIMMING
UNTROUBLED
UNTROUBLEDLY
UNTRUENESS
UNTRUENESSES
UNTRUSSERS
UNTRUSSING
UNTRUSSINGS
UNTRUSTFUL
UNTRUSTIER
UNTRUSTIEST
UNTRUSTINESS
UNTRUSTINESSES
UNTRUSTING
UNTRUSTWORTHILY
UNTRUSTWORTHY
UNTRUTHFUL
UNTRUTHFULLY
UNTRUTHFULNESS
UNTUCKERED
UNTUMULTUOUS
UNTUNABLENESS
UNTUNABLENESSES
UNTUNEABLE
UNTUNEFULLY
UNTUNEFULNESS
UNTUNEFULNESSES
UNTURNABLE
UNTWISTING
UNTWISTINGS
UNTYPICALLY
UNTYREABLE
UNUNUNIUMS
UNUPLIFTED
UNUSEFULLY
UNUSEFULNESS
UNUSEFULNESSES
UNUSUALNESS
UNUSUALNESSES
UNUTILISED
UNUTILIZED
UNUTTERABLE
UNUTTERABLENESS
UNUTTERABLES
UNUTTERABLY
UNVACCINATED
UNVALUABLE
UNVANQUISHABLE
UNVANQUISHED
UNVARIABLE
UNVARIEGATED
UNVARNISHED
UNVARYINGLY
UNVEILINGS
UNVENDIBLE
UNVENERABLE
UNVENTILATED
UNVERACIOUS
UNVERACITIES
UNVERACITY
UNVERBALISED
UNVERBALIZED
UNVERIFIABILITY

UNVERIFIABLE
UNVERIFIED
UNVIOLATED
UNVIRTUOUS
UNVIRTUOUSLY
UNVISITABLE
UNVISORING
UNVITIATED
UNVITRIFIABLE
UNVITRIFIED
UNVIZARDED
UNVIZARDING
UNVOCALISED
UNVOCALIZED
UNVOICINGS
UNVOYAGEABLE
UNVULGARISE
UNVULGARISED
UNVULGARISES
UNVULGARISING
UNVULGARIZE
UNVULGARIZED
UNVULGARIZES
UNVULGARIZING
UNVULNERABLE
UNWANDERING
UNWARENESS
UNWARENESSES
UNWARINESS
UNWARINESSES
UNWARRANTABLE
UNWARRANTABLY
UNWARRANTED
UNWARRANTEDLY
UNWASHEDNESS
UNWASHEDNESSES
UNWATCHABLE
UNWATCHFUL
UNWATCHFULLY
UNWATCHFULNESS
UNWATERING
UNWAVERING
UNWAVERINGLY
UNWEAKENED
UNWEAPONED
UNWEAPONING
UNWEARABLE
UNWEARABLES
UNWEARIABLE
UNWEARIABLY
UNWEARIEDLY
UNWEARIEDNESS
UNWEARIEDNESSES
UNWEARIEST
UNWEARYING
UNWEARYINGLY
UNWEATHERED
UNWEDGABLE
UNWEDGEABLE
UNWEETINGLY
UNWEIGHING
UNWEIGHTED
UNWEIGHTING
UNWEIGHTINGS
UNWELCOMED
UNWELCOMELY
UNWELCOMENESS

UNWELCOMENESSES
UNWELCOMING
UNWELLNESS
UNWELLNESSES
UNWESTERNISED
UNWESTERNIZED
UNWHISTLEABLE
UNWHOLESOME
UNWHOLESOMELY
UNWHOLESOMENESS
UNWIELDIER
UNWIELDIEST
UNWIELDILY
UNWIELDINESS
UNWIELDINESSES
UNWIELDLILY
UNWIELDLINESS
UNWIELDLINESSES
UNWIFELIER
UNWIFELIEST
UNWIFELIKE
UNWILLINGLY
UNWILLINGNESS
UNWILLINGNESSES
UNWINDABLE
UNWINDINGS
UNWINKINGLY
UNWINNABLE
UNWINNOWED
UNWISENESS
UNWISENESSES
UNWITCHING
UNWITHDRAWING
UNWITHERED
UNWITHERING
UNWITHHELD
UNWITHHOLDEN
UNWITHHOLDING
UNWITHSTOOD
UNWITNESSED
UNWITTIEST
UNWITTINGLY
UNWITTINGNESS
UNWITTINGNESSES
UNWOMANING
UNWOMANLIER
UNWOMANLIEST
UNWOMANLINESS
UNWOMANLINESSES
UNWONTEDLY
UNWONTEDNESS
UNWONTEDNESSES
UNWORKABILITIES
UNWORKABILITY
UNWORKABLE
UNWORKMANLIKE
UNWORLDLIER
UNWORLDLIEST
UNWORLDLINESS
UNWORLDLINESSES
UNWORSHIPFUL
UNWORSHIPPED
UNWORTHIER
UNWORTHIES
UNWORTHIEST
UNWORTHILY
UNWORTHINESS

UNWORTHINESSES	UPLIGHTERS	UPTHUNDERS	URETHANING	USEFULNESS
UNWOUNDABLE	UPLIGHTING	UPTIGHTEST	URETHRITIC	USEFULNESSES
UNWRAPPING	UPLIGHTINGS	UPTIGHTNESS	URETHRITIDES	USELESSNESS
UNWREATHED	UPLINKINGS	UPTIGHTNESSES	URETHRITIS	USELESSNESSES
UNWREATHES	UPMANSHIPS	UPTITTLINGS	URETHRITISES	USHERESSES
UNWREATHING	UPMARKETED	UPTRAINING	URETHROSCOPE	USHERETTES
UNWRINKLED	UPMARKETING	UPTURNINGS	URETHROSCOPES	USHERSHIPS
UNWRINKLES	UPPERCASED	UPVALUATION	URETHROSCOPIC	USQUEBAUGH
UNWRINKLING	UPPERCASES	UPVALUATIONS	URETHROSCOPIES	USQUEBAUGHS
UNYIELDING	UPPERCASING	UPWARDNESS	URETHROSCOPY	USTILAGINEOUS
UNYIELDINGLY	UPPERCLASSMAN	UPWARDNESSES	URICOSURIC	USTILAGINOUS
UNYIELDINGNESS	UPPERCLASSMEN	UPWELLINGS	URICOTELIC	USTULATING
UPBRAIDERS	UPPERCUTTING	UPWHIRLING	URICOTELISM	USTULATION
UPBRAIDING	UPPERPARTS	URALITISATION	URICOTELISMS	USTULATIONS
UPBRAIDINGLY	UPPERWORKS	URALITISATIONS	URINALYSES	USUALNESSES
UPBRAIDINGS	UPPISHNESS	URALITISED	URINALYSIS	USUCAPIENT
UPBREAKING	UPPISHNESSES	URALITISES	URINATIONS	USUCAPIENTS
UPBRINGING	UPPITINESS	URALITISING	URINIFEROUS	USUCAPIONS
UPBRINGINGS	UPPITINESSES	URALITIZATION	URINIPAROUS	USUCAPTIBLE
UPBUILDERS	UPPITYNESS	URALITIZATIONS	URINOGENITAL	USUCAPTING
UPBUILDING	UPPITYNESSES	URALITIZED	URINOLOGIES	USUCAPTION
UPBUILDINGS	UPPROPPING	URALITIZES	URINOMETER	USUCAPTIONS
UPBUOYANCE	UPREACHING	URALITIZING	URINOMETERS	USUFRUCTED
UPBUOYANCES	UPRIGHTEOUSLY	URANALYSES	URINOSCOPIES	USUFRUCTING
UPBURSTING	UPRIGHTING	URANALYSIS	URINOSCOPY	USUFRUCTUARIES
UPCATCHING	UPRIGHTNESS	URANINITES	UROBILINOGEN	USUFRUCTUARY
UPCHEERING	UPRIGHTNESSES	URANOGRAPHER	UROBILINOGENS	USURIOUSLY
UPCHUCKING	UPROARIOUS	URANOGRAPHERS	UROBOROSES	USURIOUSNESS
UPCLIMBING	UPROARIOUSLY	URANOGRAPHIC	UROCHORDAL	USURIOUSNESSES
UPCOUNTRIES	UPROARIOUSNESS	URANOGRAPHICAL	UROCHORDATE	USURPATION
UPDATEABLE	UPROOTEDNESS	URANOGRAPHIES	UROCHORDATES	USURPATIONS
UPDRAGGING	UPROOTEDNESSES	URANOGRAPHIST	UROCHROMES	USURPATIVE
UPDRAGGINGS	UPROOTINGS	URANOGRAPHISTS	URODYNAMICS	USURPATORY
UPDRAUGHTS	UPSETTABLE	URANOGRAPHY	UROGENITAL	USURPATURE
UPFILLINGS	UPSETTINGLY	URANOLOGIES	UROGENITALS	USURPATURES
UPFLASHING	UPSETTINGS	URANOMETRIES	UROGRAPHIC	USURPINGLY
UPFLINGING	UPSHIFTING	URANOMETRY	UROGRAPHIES	UTERECTOMIES
UPFOLLOWED	UPSHOOTING	URANOPLASTIES	UROKINASES	UTERECTOMY
UPFOLLOWING	UPSIDEOWNE	URANOPLASTY	UROLAGNIAS	UTERITISES
UPGATHERED	UPSITTINGS	URBANENESS	UROLITHIASES	UTEROGESTATION
UPGATHERING	UPSKILLING	URBANENESSES	UROLITHIASIS	UTEROGESTATIONS
UPGRADABILITIES	UPSKIRTING	URBANISATION	UROLOGICAL	UTEROTOMIES
UPGRADABILITY	UPSKIRTINGS	URBANISATIONS	UROLOGISTS	UTILISABLE
UPGRADABLE	UPSPEAKING	URBANISING	UROPOIESES	UTILISATION
UPGRADATION	UPSPEARING	URBANISTIC	UROPOIESIS	UTILISATIONS
UPGRADATIONS	UPSPRINGING	URBANISTICALLY	UROPYGIUMS	UTILITARIAN
UPGRADEABILITY	UPSTANDING	URBANITIES	UROSCOPIES	UTILITARIANISE
UPGRADEABLE	UPSTANDINGNESS	URBANIZATION	UROSCOPIST	UTILITARIANISED
UPGROWINGS	UPSTARTING	URBANIZATIONS	UROSCOPISTS	UTILITARIANISES
UPHEAPINGS	UPSTEPPING	URBANIZING	UROSTEGITE	UTILITARIANISM
UPHILLWARD	UPSTEPPINGS	URBANOLOGIES	UROSTEGITES	UTILITARIANISMS
UPHOARDING	UPSTIRRING	URBANOLOGIST	UROSTHENIC	UTILITARIANIZE
UPHOISTING	UPSTREAMED	URBANOLOGISTS	UROSTOMIES	UTILITARIANIZED
UPHOLDINGS	UPSTREAMING	URBANOLOGY	URTICACEOUS	UTILITARIANIZES
UPHOLSTERED	UPSTRETCHED	URCEOLUSES	URTICARIAL	UTILITARIANS
UPHOLSTERER	UPSURGENCE	UREDINIOSPORE	URTICARIAS	UTILIZABLE
UPHOLSTERERS	UPSURGENCES	UREDINIOSPORES	URTICARIOUS	UTILIZATION
UPHOLSTERIES	UPSWARMING	UREDINIUMS	URTICATING	UTILIZATIONS
UPHOLSTERING	UPSWEEPING	UREDIOSPORE	URTICATION	UTOPIANISE
UPHOLSTERS	UPSWELLING	UREDIOSPORES	URTICATIONS	UTOPIANISED
UPHOLSTERY	UPSWINGING	UREDOSORUS	USABILITIES	UTOPIANISER
UPHOLSTRESS	UPTALKINGS	UREDOSPORE	USABLENESS	UTOPIANISERS
UPHOLSTRESSES	UPTHROWING	UREDOSPORES	USABLENESSES	UTOPIANISES
UPHOORDING	UPTHRUSTED	UREOTELISM	USEABILITIES	UTOPIANISING
UPKNITTING	UPTHRUSTING	UREOTELISMS	USEABILITY	UTOPIANISM
UPLIFTINGLY	UPTHUNDERED	URETERITIS	USEABLENESS	UTOPIANISMS
UPLIFTINGS	UPTHUNDERING	URETERITISES	USEABLENESSES	UTOPIANIZE

UTOPIANIZED	UTRICULARIA	UTTERABLENESS	UVAROVITES	UXORIOUSLY
UTOPIANIZER	UTRICULARIAS	UTTERABLENESSES	UVULITISES	UXORIOUSNESS
UTOPIANIZERS	UTRICULATE	UTTERANCES	UXORICIDAL	UXORIOUSNESSES
UTOPIANIZES	UTRICULITIS	UTTERMOSTS	UXORICIDES	
UTOPIANIZING	UTRICULITISES	UTTERNESSES	UXORILOCAL	

V

VACANTNESS
VACANTNESSES
VACATIONED
VACATIONER
VACATIONERS
VACATIONING
VACATIONIST
VACATIONISTS
VACATIONLAND
VACATIONLANDS
VACATIONLESS
VACCINATED
VACCINATES
VACCINATING
VACCINATION
VACCINATIONS
VACCINATOR
VACCINATORS
VACCINATORY
VACCINIUMS
VACILLATED
VACILLATES
VACILLATING
VACILLATINGLY
VACILLATION
VACILLATIONS
VACILLATOR
VACILLATORS
VACILLATORY
VACUATIONS
VACUOLATED
VACUOLATION
VACUOLATIONS
VACUOLISATION
VACUOLISATIONS
VACUOLIZATION
VACUOLIZATIONS
VACUOUSNESS
VACUOUSNESSES
VAGABONDAGE
VAGABONDAGES
VAGABONDED
VAGABONDING
VAGABONDISE
VAGABONDISED
VAGABONDISES
VAGABONDISH
VAGABONDISING
VAGABONDISM
VAGABONDISMS
VAGABONDIZE
VAGABONDIZED
VAGABONDIZES
VAGABONDIZING

VAGARIOUSLY
VAGILITIES
VAGINECTOMIES
VAGINECTOMY
VAGINICOLINE
VAGINICOLOUS
VAGINISMUS
VAGINISMUSES
VAGINITIDES
VAGINITISES
VAGOTOMIES
VAGOTONIAS
VAGOTROPIC
VAGRANCIES
VAGRANTNESS
VAGRANTNESSES
VAGUENESSES
VAINGLORIED
VAINGLORIES
VAINGLORIOUS
VAINGLORIOUSLY
VAINGLORYING
VAINNESSES
VAIVODESHIP
VAIVODESHIPS
VAJAZZLING
VAJAZZLINGS
VALEDICTION
VALEDICTIONS
VALEDICTORIAN
VALEDICTORIANS
VALEDICTORIES
VALEDICTORY
VALENTINES
VALERIANACEOUS
VALETUDINARIAN
VALETUDINARIANS
VALETUDINARIES
VALETUDINARY
VALIANCIES
VALIANTNESS
VALIANTNESSES
VALIDATING
VALIDATION
VALIDATIONS
VALIDATORS
VALIDATORY
VALIDITIES
VALIDNESSES
VALLATIONS
VALLECULAE
VALLECULAR
VALLECULAS
VALLECULATE

VALORISATION
VALORISATIONS
VALORISING
VALORIZATION
VALORIZATIONS
VALORIZING
VALOROUSLY
VALPOLICELLA
VALPOLICELLAS
VALPROATES
VALUABLENESS
VALUABLENESSES
VALUATIONAL
VALUATIONALLY
VALUATIONS
VALUELESSNESS
VALUELESSNESSES
VALVASSORS
VALVULITIS
VALVULITISES
VAMPIRISED
VAMPIRISES
VAMPIRISING
VAMPIRISMS
VAMPIRIZED
VAMPIRIZES
VAMPIRIZING
VANADIATES
VANADINITE
VANADINITES
VANASPATIS
VANCOMYCIN
VANCOMYCINS
VANDALISATION
VANDALISATIONS
VANDALISED
VANDALISES
VANDALISING
VANDALISMS
VANDALISTIC
VANDALIZATION
VANDALIZATIONS
VANDALIZED
VANDALIZES
VANDALIZING
VANGUARDISM
VANGUARDISMS
VANGUARDIST
VANGUARDISTS
VANISHINGLY
VANISHINGS
VANISHMENT
VANISHMENTS
VANITORIES

VANPOOLING
VANPOOLINGS
VANQUISHABLE
VANQUISHED
VANQUISHER
VANQUISHERS
VANQUISHES
VANQUISHING
VANQUISHMENT
VANQUISHMENTS
VANTAGELESS
VANTBRACES
VANTBRASSES
VAPIDITIES
VAPIDNESSES
VAPORABILITIES
VAPORABILITY
VAPORESCENCE
VAPORESCENCES
VAPORESCENT
VAPORETTOS
VAPORIFORM
VAPORIMETER
VAPORIMETERS
VAPORISABLE
VAPORISATION
VAPORISATIONS
VAPORISERS
VAPORISHNESS
VAPORISHNESSES
VAPORISING
VAPORIZABLE
VAPORIZATION
VAPORIZATIONS
VAPORIZERS
VAPORIZING
VAPOROSITIES
VAPOROSITY
VAPOROUSLY
VAPOROUSNESS
VAPOROUSNESSES
VAPORWARES
VAPOURABILITIES
VAPOURABILITY
VAPOURABLE
VAPOURIEST
VAPOURINGLY
VAPOURINGS
VAPOURISHNESS
VAPOURISHNESSES
VAPOURLESS
VAPOURWARE
VAPOURWARES
VAPULATING

VAPULATION
VAPULATIONS
VARIABILITIES
VARIABILITY
VARIABLENESS
VARIABLENESSES
VARIATIONAL
VARIATIONALLY
VARIATIONIST
VARIATIONISTS
VARIATIONS
VARICELLAR
VARICELLAS
VARICELLATE
VARICELLOID
VARICELLOUS
VARICOCELE
VARICOCELES
VARICOLORED
VARICOLOURED
VARICOSITIES
VARICOSITY
VARICOTOMIES
VARICOTOMY
VARIEDNESS
VARIEDNESSES
VARIEGATED
VARIEGATES
VARIEGATING
VARIEGATION
VARIEGATIONS
VARIEGATOR
VARIEGATORS
VARIETALLY
VARIFOCALS
VARIFORMLY
VARIOLATED
VARIOLATES
VARIOLATING
VARIOLATION
VARIOLATIONS
VARIOLATOR
VARIOLATORS
VARIOLISATION
VARIOLISATIONS
VARIOLITES
VARIOLITIC
VARIOLIZATION
VARIOLIZATIONS
VARIOLOIDS
VARIOMETER
VARIOMETERS
VARIOUSNESS
VARIOUSNESSES

VARISCITES	VASSALISED	VEGGIEBURGER	VENDITATIONS	VENTILATORY
VARITYPING	VASSALISES	VEGGIEBURGERS	VENDITIONS	VENTOSITIES
VARITYPIST	VASSALISING	VEHEMENCES	VENEERINGS	VENTRICLES
VARITYPISTS	VASSALIZED	VEHEMENCIES	VENEFICALLY	VENTRICOSE
VARLETESSES	VASSALIZES	VEHEMENTLY	VENEFICIOUS	VENTRICOSITIES
VARLETRIES	VASSALIZING	VEILLEUSES	VENEFICIOUSLY	VENTRICOSITY
VARNISHERS	VASSALLING	VEINSTONES	VENEFICOUS	VENTRICOUS
VARNISHIER	VASSALRIES	VEINSTUFFS	VENEFICOUSLY	VENTRICULAR
VARNISHIEST	VASTIDITIES	VELARISATION	VENENATING	VENTRICULE
VARNISHING	VASTITUDES	VELARISATIONS	VENEPUNCTURE	VENTRICULES
VARNISHINGS	VASTNESSES	VELARISING	VENEPUNCTURES	VENTRICULI
VARSOVIENNE	VATICINATE	VELARIZATION	VENERABILITIES	VENTRICULUS
VARSOVIENNES	VATICINATED	VELARIZATIONS	VENERABILITY	VENTRILOQUAL
VASCULARISATION	VATICINATES	VELARIZING	VENERABLENESS	VENTRILOQUIAL
VASCULARISE	VATICINATING	VELDSCHOEN	VENERABLENESSES	VENTRILOQUIALLY
VASCULARISED	VATICINATION	VELDSCHOENS	VENERABLES	VENTRILOQUIES
VASCULARISES	VATICINATIONS	VELDSKOENS	VENERATING	VENTRILOQUISE
VASCULARISING	VATICINATOR	VELITATION	VENERATION	VENTRILOQUISED
VASCULARITIES	VATICINATORS	VELITATIONS	VENERATIONAL	VENTRILOQUISES
VASCULARITY	VATICINATORY	VELLEITIES	VENERATIONS	VENTRILOQUISING
VASCULARIZATION	VAUDEVILLE	VELLENAGES	VENERATIVE	VENTRILOQUISM
VASCULARIZE	VAUDEVILLEAN	VELLICATED	VENERATIVENESS	VENTRILOQUISMS
VASCULARIZED	VAUDEVILLEANS	VELLICATES	VENERATORS	VENTRILOQUIST
VASCULARIZES	VAUDEVILLES	VELLICATING	VENEREALLY	VENTRILOQUISTIC
VASCULARIZING	VAUDEVILLIAN	VELLICATION	VENEREOLOGICAL	VENTRILOQUISTS
VASCULARLY	VAUDEVILLIANS	VELLICATIONS	VENEREOLOGIES	VENTRILOQUIZE
VASCULATURE	VAUDEVILLIST	VELLICATIVE	VENEREOLOGIST	VENTRILOQUIZED
VASCULATURES	VAUDEVILLISTS	VELOCIMETER	VENEREOLOGISTS	VENTRILOQUIZES
VASCULIFORM	VAULTINGLY	VELOCIMETERS	VENEREOLOGY	VENTRILOQUIZING
VASCULITIDES	VAUNTERIES	VELOCIMETRIES	VENESECTION	VENTRILOQUOUS
VASCULITIS	VAUNTINGLY	VELOCIMETRY	VENESECTIONS	VENTRILOQUY
VASCULITISES	VAVASORIES	VELOCIPEDE	VENGEANCES	VENTRIPOTENT
VASECTOMIES	VECTOGRAPH	VELOCIPEDEAN	VENGEFULLY	VENTROLATERAL
VASECTOMISE	VECTOGRAPHS	VELOCIPEDEANS	VENGEFULNESS	VENTROMEDIAL
VASECTOMISED	VECTORIALLY	VELOCIPEDED	VENGEFULNESSES	VENTURESOME
VASECTOMISES	VECTORINGS	VELOCIPEDER	VENGEMENTS	VENTURESOMELY
VASECTOMISING	VECTORISATION	VELOCIPEDERS	VENIALITIES	VENTURESOMENESS
VASECTOMIZE	VECTORISATIONS	VELOCIPEDES	VENIALNESS	VENTURINGLY
VASECTOMIZED	VECTORISED	VELOCIPEDIAN	VENIALNESSES	VENTURINGS
VASECTOMIZES	VECTORISES	VELOCIPEDIANS	VENIPUNCTURE	VENTUROUSLY
VASECTOMIZING	VECTORISING	VELOCIPEDING	VENIPUNCTURES	VENTUROUSNESS
VASELINING	VECTORIZATION	VELOCIPEDIST	VENISECTION	VENTUROUSNESSES
VASOACTIVE	VECTORIZATIONS	VELOCIPEDISTS	VENISECTIONS	VERACIOUSLY
VASOACTIVITIES	VECTORIZED	VELOCIRAPTOR	VENOGRAPHIC	VERACIOUSNESS
VASOACTIVITY	VECTORIZES	VELOCIRAPTORS	VENOGRAPHICAL	VERACIOUSNESSES
VASOCONSTRICTOR	VECTORIZING	VELOCITIES	VENOGRAPHIES	VERACITIES
VASODILATATION	VECTORSCOPE	VELODROMES	VENOGRAPHY	VERANDAHED
VASODILATATIONS	VECTORSCOPES	VELOUTINES	VENOLOGIES	VERAPAMILS
VASODILATATORY	VEDUTISTAS	VELUTINOUS	VENOMOUSLY	VERATRIDINE
VASODILATION	VEGEBURGER	VELVETEENED	VENOMOUSNESS	VERATRIDINES
VASODILATIONS	VEGEBURGERS	VELVETEENS	VENOMOUSNESSES	VERATRINES
VASODILATOR	VEGETABLES	VELVETIEST	VENOSCLEROSES	VERBALISATION
VASODILATORS	VEGETABLIER	VELVETINESS	VENOSCLEROSIS	VERBALISATIONS
VASODILATORY	VEGETABLIEST	VELVETINESSES	VENOSITIES	VERBALISED
VASOINHIBITOR	VEGETARIAN	VELVETINGS	VENOUSNESS	VERBALISER
VASOINHIBITORS	VEGETARIANISM	VELVETLIKE	VENOUSNESSES	VERBALISERS
VASOINHIBITORY	VEGETARIANISMS	VENALITIES	VENTIDUCTS	VERBALISES
VASOPRESSIN	VEGETARIANS	VENATICALLY	VENTIFACTS	VERBALISING
VASOPRESSINS	VEGETATING	VENATIONAL	VENTILABLE	VERBALISMS
VASOPRESSOR	VEGETATINGS	VENATORIAL	VENTILATED	VERBALISTIC
VASOPRESSORS	VEGETATION	VENDETTIST	VENTILATES	VERBALISTS
VASOSPASMS	VEGETATIONAL	VENDETTISTS	VENTILATING	VERBALITIES
VASOSPASTIC	VEGETATIONS	VENDIBILITIES	VENTILATION	VERBALIZATION
VASOTOCINS	VEGETATIOUS	VENDIBILITY	VENTILATIONS	VERBALIZATIONS
VASOTOMIES	VEGETATIVE	VENDIBLENESS	VENTILATIVE	VERBALIZED
VASSALAGES	VEGETATIVELY	VENDIBLENESSES	VENTILATOR	VERBALIZER
VASSALESSES	VEGETATIVENESS	VENDITATION	VENTILATORS	VERBALIZERS

VERBALIZES	VERMICULAR	VERSABILITY	VESICULATION	VIBRATIONS
VERBALIZING	VERMICULARLY	VERSATILELY	VESICULATIONS	VIBRATIUNCLE
VERBALLING	VERMICULATE	VERSATILENESS	VESICULOSE	VIBRATIUNCLES
VERBARIANS	VERMICULATED	VERSATILENESSES	VESPERTILIAN	VIBRATOLESS
VERBASCUMS	VERMICULATES	VERSATILITIES	VESPERTILIONID	VIBROFLOTATION
VERBENACEOUS	VERMICULATING	VERSATILITY	VESPERTILIONIDS	VIBROFLOTATIONS
VERBERATED	VERMICULATION	VERSICOLOR	VESPERTILIONINE	VIBROGRAPH
VERBERATES	VERMICULATIONS	VERSICOLORED	VESPERTINAL	VIBROGRAPHS
VERBERATING	VERMICULES	VERSICOLOUR	VESPERTINE	VIBROMETER
VERBERATION	VERMICULITE	VERSICOLOURED	VESPIARIES	VIBROMETERS
VERBERATIONS	VERMICULITES	VERSICULAR	VESTIARIES	VICARESSES
VERBICIDES	VERMICULOUS	VERSIFICATION	VESTIBULAR	VICARIANCE
VERBIFICATION	VERMICULTURE	VERSIFICATIONS	VESTIBULED	VICARIANCES
VERBIFICATIONS	VERMICULTURES	VERSIFICATOR	VESTIBULES	VICARIANTS
VERBIFYING	VERMIFUGAL	VERSIFICATORS	VESTIBULING	VICARIATES
VERBIGERATE	VERMIFUGES	VERSIFIERS	VESTIBULITIS	VICARIOUSLY
VERBIGERATED	VERMILIONED	VERSIFYING	VESTIBULITISES	VICARIOUSNESS
VERBIGERATES	VERMILIONING	VERSIONERS	VESTIBULUM	VICARIOUSNESSES
VERBIGERATING	VERMILIONS	VERSIONING	VESTIGIALLY	VICARLIEST
VERBIGERATION	VERMILLING	VERSIONINGS	VESTIMENTAL	VICARSHIPS
VERBIGERATIONS	VERMILLION	VERSIONIST	VESTIMENTARY	VICEGERENCIES
VERBOSENESS	VERMILLIONS	VERSIONISTS	VESTIMENTS	VICEGERENCY
VERBOSENESSES	VERMINATED	VERSLIBRIST	VESTITURES	VICEGERENT
VERBOSITIES	VERMINATES	VERSLIBRISTE	VESTMENTAL	VICEGERENTS
VERDANCIES	VERMINATING	VERSLIBRISTES	VESTMENTED	VICEREGALLY
VERDIGRISED	VERMINATION	VERSLIBRISTS	VESUVIANITE	VICEREGENT
VERDIGRISES	VERMINATIONS	VERTEBRALLY	VESUVIANITES	VICEREGENTS
VERDIGRISING	VERMINIEST	VERTEBRATE	VETCHLINGS	VICEREINES
VERDURELESS	VERMINOUSLY	VERTEBRATED	VETERINARIAN	VICEROYALTIES
VERGEBOARD	VERMINOUSNESS	VERTEBRATES	VETERINARIANS	VICEROYALTY
VERGEBOARDS	VERMINOUSNESSES	VERTEBRATION	VETERINARIES	VICEROYSHIP
VERGENCIES	VERMIVOROUS	VERTEBRATIONS	VETERINARY	VICEROYSHIPS
VERGERSHIP	VERNACULAR	VERTICALITIES	VETTURINOS	VICHYSSOIS
VERGERSHIPS	VERNACULARISE	VERTICALITY	VEXATIOUSLY	VICHYSSOISE
VERIDICALITIES	VERNACULARISED	VERTICALLY	VEXATIOUSNESS	VICHYSSOISES
VERIDTCALITY	VERNACULARISES	VERTICALNESS	VEXATIOUSNESSES	VICINITIES
VERIDICALLY	VERNACULARISING	VERTICALNESSES	VEXEDNESSES	VICIOSITIES
VERIDICOUS	VERNACULARISM	VERTICILLASTER	VEXILLARIES	VICIOUSNESS
VERIFIABILITIES	VERNACULARISMS	VERTICILLASTERS	VEXILLATION	VICIOUSNESSES
VERIFIABILITY	VERNACULARIST	VERTICILLATE	VEXILLATIONS	VICISSITUDE
VERIFIABLE	VERNACULARISTS	VERTICILLATED	VEXILLOLOGIC	VICISSITUDES
VERIFIABLENESS	VERNACULARITIES	VERTICILLATELY	VEXILLOLOGICAL	VICISSITUDINARY
VERIFIABLY	VERNACULARITY	VERTICILLATION	VEXILLOLOGIES	VICISSITUDINOUS
VERIFICATION	VERNACULARIZE	VERTICILLATIONS	VEXILLOLOGIST	VICOMTESSE
VERIFICATIONS	VERNACULARIZED	VERTICILLIUM	VEXILLOLOGISTS	VICOMTESSES
VERIFICATIVE	VERNACULARIZES	VERTICILLIUMS	VEXILLOLOGY	VICTIMHOOD
VERIFICATORY	VERNACULARIZING	VERTICITIES	VEXINGNESS	VICTIMHOODS
VERISIMILAR	VERNACULARLY	VERTIGINES	VEXINGNESSES	VICTIMISATION
VERISIMILARLY	VERNACULARS	VERTIGINOUS	VIABILITIES	VICTIMISATIONS
VERISIMILITIES	VERNALISATION	VERTIGINOUSLY	VIBRACULAR	VICTIMISED
VERISIMILITUDE	VERNALISATIONS	VERTIGINOUSNESS	VIBRACULARIA	VICTIMISER
VERISIMILITUDES	VERNALISED	VERTIPORTS	VIBRACULARIUM	VICTIMISERS
VERISIMILITY	VERNALISES	VERUMONTANA	VIBRACULOID	VICTIMISES
VERISIMILOUS	VERNALISING	VERUMONTANUM	VIBRACULUM	VICTIMISING
VERITABLENESS	VERNALITIES	VERUMONTANUMS	VIBRAHARPIST	VICTIMIZATION
VERITABLENESSES	VERNALIZATION	VESICATING	VIBRAHARPISTS	VICTIMIZATIONS
VERJUICING	VERNALIZATIONS	VESICATION	VIBRAHARPS	VICTIMIZED
VERKRAMPTE	VERNALIZED	VESICATIONS	VIBRANCIES	VICTIMIZER
VERKRAMPTES	VERNALIZES	VESICATORIES	VIBRAPHONE	VICTIMIZERS
VERMEILING	VERNALIZING	VESICATORY	VIBRAPHONES	VICTIMIZES
VERMEILLED	VERNATIONS	VESICULARITIES	VIBRAPHONIST	VICTIMIZING
VERMEILLES	VERNISSAGE	VESICULARITY	VIBRAPHONISTS	VICTIMLESS
VERMEILLING	VERNISSAGES	VESICULARLY	VIBRATILITIES	VICTIMOLOGIES
VERMICELLI	VERRUCIFORM	VESICULATE	VIBRATILITY	VICTIMOLOGIST
VERMICELLIS	VERRUCOSITIES	VESICULATED	VIBRATINGLY	VICTIMOLOGISTS
VERMICIDAL	VERRUCOSITY	VESICULATES	VIBRATIONAL	VICTIMOLOGY
VERMICIDES	VERSABILITIES	VESICULATING	VIBRATIONLESS	VICTORESSES

VICTORIANA	VIGORISHES	VINDICATIVE	VIRALITIES	VISCERATES
VICTORIANAS	VIGOROUSLY	VINDICATIVENESS	VIREONINES	VISCERATING
VICTORINES	VIGOROUSNESS	VINDICATOR	VIRESCENCE	VISCEROMOTOR
VICTORIOUS	VIGOROUSNESSES	VINDICATORILY	VIRESCENCES	VISCEROPTOSES
VICTORIOUSLY	VIKINGISMS	VINDICATORS	VIRGINALIST	VISCEROPTOSIS
VICTORIOUSNESS	VILDNESSES	VINDICATORY	VIRGINALISTS	VISCEROTONIA
VICTORYLESS	VILENESSES	VINDICATRESS	VIRGINALLED	VISCEROTONIAS
VICTRESSES	VILIFICATION	VINDICATRESSES	VIRGINALLING	VISCEROTONIC
VICTUALAGE	VILIFICATIONS	VINDICTIVE	VIRGINALLY	VISCIDITIES
VICTUALAGES	VILIPENDED	VINDICTIVELY	VIRGINHOOD	VISCIDNESS
VICTUALERS	VILIPENDER	VINDICTIVENESS	VIRGINHOODS	VISCIDNESSES
VICTUALING	VILIPENDERS	VINEDRESSER	VIRGINITIES	VISCOELASTIC
VICTUALLAGE	VILIPENDING	VINEDRESSERS	VIRGINIUMS	VISCOELASTICITY
VICTUALLAGES	VILLAGERIES	VINEGARETTE	VIRIDESCENCE	VISCOMETER
VICTUALLED	VILLAGIEST	VINEGARETTES	VIRIDESCENCES	VISCOMETERS
VICTUALLER	VILLAGIOES	VINEGARIER	VIRIDESCENT	VISCOMETRIC
VICTUALLERS	VILLAGISATION	VINEGARIEST	VIRIDITIES	VISCOMETRICAL
VICTUALLESS	VILLAGISATIONS	VINEGARING	VIRILESCENCE	VISCOMETRIES
VICTUALLING	VILLAGIZATION	VINEGARISH	VIRILESCENCES	VISCOMETRY
VIDEOCASSETTE	VILLAGIZATIONS	VINEGARRETTE	VIRILESCENT	VISCOSIMETER
VIDEOCASSETTES	VILLAGREES	VINEGARRETTES	VIRILISATION	VISCOSIMETERS
VIDEOCONFERENCE	VILLAINAGE	VINEGARROON	VIRILISATIONS	VISCOSIMETRIC
VIDEODISCS	VILLAINAGES	VINEGARROONS	VIRILISING	VISCOSIMETRICAL
VIDEODISKS	VILLAINESS	VINEYARDIST	VIRILITIES	VISCOSIMETRIES
VIDEOGRAMS	VILLAINESSES	VINEYARDISTS	VIRILIZATION	VISCOSIMETRY
VIDEOGRAPHER	VILLAINIES	VINICULTURAL	VIRILIZATIONS	VISCOSITIES
VIDEOGRAPHERS	VILLAINOUS	VINICULTURE	VIRILIZING	VISCOUNTCIES
VIDEOGRAPHIES	VILLAINOUSLY	VINICULTURES	VIROLOGICAL	VISCOUNTCY
VIDEOGRAPHY	VILLAINOUSNESS	VINICULTURIST	VIROLÓGICALLY	VISCOUNTESS
VIDEOLANDS	VILLANAGES	VINICULTURISTS	VIROLOGIES	VISCOUNTESSES
VIDEOPHILE	VILLANELLA	VINIFEROUS	VIROLOGIST	VISCOUNTIES
VIDEOPHILES	VILLANELLAS	VINIFICATION	VIROLOGISTS	VISCOUNTSHIP
VIDEOPHONE	VILLANELLE	VINIFICATIONS	VIRTUALISATION	VISCOUNTSHIPS
VIDEOPHONES	VILLANELLES	VINIFICATOR	VIRTUALISATIONS	VISCOUSNESS
VIDEOPHONIC	VILLANOUSLY	VINIFICATORS	VIRTUALISE	VISCOUSNESSES
VIDEOTAPED	VILLEGGIATURA	VINOLOGIES	VIRTUALISED	VISIBILITIES
VIDEOTAPES	VILLEGGIATURAS	VINOLOGIST	VIRTUALISES	VISIBILITY
VIDEOTAPING	VILLEINAGE	VINOLOGISTS	VIRTUALISING	VISIBLENESS
VIDEOTELEPHONE	VILLEINAGES	VINOSITIES	VIRTUALISM	VISIBLENESSES
VIDEOTELEPHONES	VILLENAGES	VINTAGINGS	VIRTUALISMS	VISIOGENIC
VIDEOTEXES	VILLIACOES	VINYLCYANIDE	VIRTUALIST	VISIONALLY
VIDEOTEXTS	VILLIAGOES	VINYLCYANIDES	VIRTUALISTS	VISIONARIES
VIDEOTHEQUE	VILLICATION	VINYLIDENE	VIRTUALITIES	VISIONARINESS
VIDEOTHEQUES	VILLICATIONS	VINYLIDENES	VIRTUALITY	VISIONARINESSES
VIDSCREENS	VILLOSITIES	VIOLABILITIES	VIRTUALIZATION	VISIONINGS
VIEWERSHIP	VINAIGRETTE	VIOLABILITY	VIRTUALIZATIONS	VISIONISTS
VIEWERSHIPS	VINAIGRETTES	VIOLABLENESS	VIRTUALIZE	VISIONLESS
VIEWFINDER	VINBLASTINE	VIOLABLENESSES	VIRTUALIZED	VISIOPHONE
VIEWFINDERS	VINBLASTINES	VIOLACEOUS	VIRTUALIZES	VISIOPHONES
VIEWINESSES	VINCIBILITIES	VIOLATIONS	VIRTUALIZING	VISITATION
VIEWLESSLY	VINCIBILITY	VIOLENTING	VIRTUELESS	VISITATIONAL
VIEWPHONES	VINCIBLENESS	VIOLINISTIC	VIRTUOSITIES	VISITATIONS
VIEWPOINTS	VINCIBLENESSES	VIOLINISTICALLY	VIRTUOSITY	VISITATIVE
VIGILANCES	VINCRISTINE	VIOLINISTS	VIRTUOSOSHIP	VISITATORIAL
VIGILANTES	VINCRISTINES	VIOLONCELLI	VIRTUOSOSHIPS	VISITATORS
VIGILANTISM	VINDEMIATE	VIOLONCELLIST	VIRTUOUSLY	VISITORIAL
VIGILANTISMS	VINDEMIATED	VIOLONCELLISTS	VIRTUOUSNESS	VISITRESSES
VIGILANTLY	VINDEMIATES	VIOLONCELLO	VIRTUOUSNESSES	VISUALISATION
VIGILANTNESS	VINDEMIATING	VIOLONCELLOS	VIRULENCES	VISUALISATIONS
VIGILANTNESSES	VINDICABILITIES	VIOSTEROLS	VIRULENCIES	VISUALISED
VIGINTILLION	VINDICABILITY	VIPASSANAS	VIRULENTLY	VISUALISER
VIGINTILLIONS	VINDICABLE	VIPERFISHES	VIRULIFEROUS	VISUALISERS
VIGNETTERS	VINDICATED	VIPERIFORM	VISAGISTES	VISUALISES
VIGNETTING	VINDICATES	VIPERISHLY	VISCACHERA	VISUALISING
VIGNETTINGS	VINDICATING	VIPEROUSLY	VISCACHERAS	VISUALISTS
VIGNETTIST	VINDICATION	VIRAGINIAN	VISCERALLY	VISUALITIES
VIGNETTISTS	VINDICATIONS	VIRAGINOUS	VISCERATED	VISUALIZATION

VISUALIZATIONS	VITREOUSNESS	VIVIPARITY	VOCIFEROUS	VOLITATING
VISUALIZED	VITREOUSNESSES	VIVIPAROUS	VOCIFEROUSLY	VOLITATION
VISUALIZER	VITRESCENCE	VIVIPAROUSLY	VOCIFEROUSNESS	VOLITATIONAL
VISUALIZERS	VITRESCENCES	VIVIPAROUSNESS	VODCASTERS	VOLITATIONS
VISUALIZES	VITRESCENT	VIVISECTED	VODCASTING	VOLITIONAL
VISUALIZING	VITRESCIBILITY	VIVISECTING	VODCASTINGS	VOLITIONALLY
VITALISATION	VITRESCIBLE	VIVISECTION	VOETGANGER	VOLITIONARY
VITALISATIONS	VITRIFACTION	VIVISECTIONAL	VOETGANGERS	VOLITIONLESS
VITALISERS	VITRIFACTIONS	VIVISECTIONALLY	VOETSTOETS	VOLITORIAL
VITALISING	VITRIFACTURE	VIVISECTIONIST	VOETSTOOTS	VOLKSLIEDER
VITALISTIC	VITRIFACTURES	VIVISECTIONISTS	VOGUISHNESS	VOLKSRAADS
VITALISTICALLY	VITRIFIABILITY	VIVISECTIONS	VOGUISHNESSES	VOLLEYBALL
VITALITIES	VITRIFIABLE	VIVISECTIVE	VOICEFULNESS	VOLLEYBALLS
VITALIZATION	VITRIFICATION	VIVISECTOR	VOICEFULNESSES	VOLPLANING
VITALIZATIONS	VITRIFICATIONS	VIVISECTORIA	VOICELESSLY	VOLTAMETER
VITALIZERS	VITRIFYING	VIVISECTORIUM	VOICELESSNESS	VOLTAMETERS
VITALIZING	VITRIOLATE	VIVISECTORIUMS	VOICELESSNESSES	VOLTAMETRIC
VITALNESSES	VITRIOLATED	VIVISECTORS	VOICEMAILS	VOLTAMMETER
VITAMINISE	VITRIOLATES	VIVISEPULTURE	VOICEOVERS	VOLTAMMETERS
VITAMINISED	VITRIOLATING	VIVISEPULTURES	VOICEPRINT	VOLTIGEURS
VITAMINISES	VITRIOLATION	VIXENISHLY	VOICEPRINTS	VOLTINISMS
VITAMINISING	VITRIOLATIONS	VIXENISHNESS	VOIDABLENESS	VOLTMETERS
VITAMINIZE	VITRIOLING	VIXENISHNESSES	VOIDABLENESSES	VOLUBILITIES
VITAMINIZED	VITRIOLISATION	VIZIERATES	VOIDNESSES	VOLUBILITY
VITAMINIZES	VITRIOLISATIONS	VIZIERSHIP	VOISINAGES	VOLUBLENESS
VITAMINIZING	VITRIOLISE	VIZIERSHIPS	VOITURIERS	VOLUBLENESSES
VITASCOPES	VITRIOLISED	VIZIRSHIPS	VOIVODESHIP	VOLUMENOMETER
VITATIVENESS	VITRIOLISES	VOCABULARIAN	VOIVODESHIPS	VOLUMENOMETERS
VITATIVENESSES	VITRIOLISING	VOCABULARIANS	VOLATILENESS	VOLUMETERS
VITELLARIES	VITRIOLIZATION	VOCABULARIED	VOLATILENESSES	VOLUMETRIC
VITELLICLE	VITRIOLIZATIONS	VOCABULARIES	VOLATILISABLE	VOLUMETRICAL
VITELLICLES	VITRIOLIZE	VOCABULARY	VOLATILISATION	VOLUMETRICALLY
VITELLIGENOUS	VITRIOLIZED	VOCABULIST	VOLATILISATIONS	VOLUMETRIES
VITELLINES	VITRIOLIZES	VOCABULISTS	VOLATILISE	VOLUMINOSITIES
VITELLOGENESES	VITRIOLIZING	VOCALICALLY	VOLATILISED	VOLUMINOSITY
VITELLOGENESIS	VITRIOLLED	VOCALISATION	VOLATILISES	VOLUMINOUS
VITELLOGENIC	VITRIOLLING	VOCALISATIONS	VOLATILISING	VOLUMINOUSLY
VITELLUSES	VITUPERABLE	VOCALISERS	VOLATILITIES	VOLUMINOUSNESS
VITIATIONS	VITUPERATE	VOCALISING	VOLATILITY	VOLUMISERS
VITICETUMS	VITUPERATED	VOCALITIES	VOLATILIZABLE	VOLUMISING
VITICOLOUS	VITUPERATES	VOCALIZATION	VOLATILIZATION	VOLUMIZERS
VITICULTURAL	VITUPERATING	VOCALIZATIONS	VOLATILIZATIONS	VOLUMIZING
VITICULTURALLY	VITUPERATION	VOCALIZERS	VOLATILIZE	VOLUMOMETER
VITICULTURE	VITUPERATIONS	VOCALIZING	VOLATILIZED	VOLUMOMETERS
VITICULTURER	VITUPERATIVE	VOCALNESSES	VOLATILIZES	VOLUNTARIES
VITICULTURERS	VITUPERATIVELY	VOCATIONAL	VOLATILIZING	VOLUNTARILY
VITICULTURES	VITUPERATOR	VOCATIONALISM	VOLCANICALLY	VOLUNTARINESS
VITICULTURIST	VITUPERATORS	VOCATIONALISMS	VOLCANICITIES	VOLUNTARINESSES
VITICULTURISTS	VITUPERATORY	VOCATIONALIST	VOLCANICITY	VOLUNTARISM
VITILIFEROUS	VIVACIOUSLY	VOCATIONALISTS	VOLCANISATION	VOLUNTARISMS
VITILITIGATE	VIVACIOUSNESS	VOCATIONALLY	VOLCANISATIONS	VOLUNTARIST
VITILITIGATED	VIVACIOUSNESSES	VOCATIVELY	VOLCANISED	VOLUNTARISTIC
VITILITIGATES	VIVACISSIMO	VOCICULTURAL	VOLCANISES	VOLUNTARISTS
VITILITIGATING	VIVACITIES	VOCIFERANCE	VOLCANISING	VOLUNTARYISM
VITILITIGATION	VIVANDIERE	VOCIFERANCES	VOLCANISMS	VOLUNTARYISMS
VITILITIGATIONS	VIVANDIERES	VOCIFERANT	VOLCANISTS	VOLUNTARYIST
VITIOSITIES	VIVANDIERS	VOCIFERANTS	VOLCANIZATION	VOLUNTARYISTS
VITRAILLED	VIVERRINES	VOCIFERATE	VOLCANIZATIONS	VOLUNTATIVE
VITRAILLIST	VIVIANITES	VOCIFERATED	VOLCANIZED	VOLUNTATIVES
VITRAILLISTS	VIVIDITIES	VOCIFERATES	VOLCANIZES	VOLUNTEERED
VITRECTOMIES	VIVIDNESSES	VOCIFERATING	VOLCANIZING	VOLUNTEERING
VITRECTOMY	VIVIFICATION	VOCIFERATION	VOLCANOLOGIC	VOLUNTEERISM
VITREORETINAL	VIVIFICATIONS	VOCIFERATIONS	VOLCANOLOGICAL	VOLUNTEERISMS
VITREOSITIES	VIVIPARIES	VOCIFERATOR	VOLCANOLOGIES	VOLUNTEERS
VITREOSITY	VIVIPARISM	VOCIFERATORS	VOLCANOLOGIST	VOLUNTOURISM
VITREOUSES	VIVIPARISMS	VOCIFEROSITIES	VOLCANOLOGISTS	VOLUNTOURISMS
VITREOUSLY	VIVIPARITIES	VOCIFEROSITY	VOLCANOLOGY	VOLUPTUARIES

VOLUPTUARY
VOLUPTUOSITIES
VOLUPTUOSITY
VOLUPTUOUS
VOLUPTUOUSLY
VOLUPTUOUSNESS
VOLUTATION
VOLUTATIONS
VOLVULUSES
VOMERONASAL
VOMITORIES
VOMITORIUM
VOMITURITION
VOMITURITIONS
VOODOOISMS
VOODOOISTIC
VOODOOISTS
VOORKAMERS
VOORTREKKER
VOORTREKKERS
VORACIOUSLY
VORACIOUSNESS
VORACIOUSNESSES
VORACITIES
VORAGINOUS
VORTICALLY

VORTICELLA
VORTICELLAE
VORTICELLAS
VORTICISMS
VORTICISTS
VORTICITIES
VORTICULAR
VORTIGINOUS
VOTARESSES
VOTIVENESS
VOTIVENESSES
VOUCHERING
VOUCHSAFED
VOUCHSAFEMENT
VOUCHSAFEMENTS
VOUCHSAFES
VOUCHSAFING
VOUCHSAFINGS
VOUSSOIRED
VOUSSOIRING
VOUTSAFING
VOWELISATION
VOWELISATIONS
VOWELISING
VOWELIZATION
VOWELIZATIONS

VOWELIZING
VOWELLIEST
VOYAGEABLE
VOYEURISMS
VOYEURISTIC
VOYEURISTICALLY
VRAICKINGS
VRAISEMBLANCE
VRAISEMBLANCES
VRYSTATERS
VULCANICITIES
VULCANICITY
VULCANISABLE
VULCANISATE
VULCANISATES
VULCANISATION
VULCANISATIONS
VULCANISED
VULCANISER
VULCANISERS
VULCANISES
VULCANISING
VULCANISMS
VULCANISTS
VULCANITES
VULCANIZABLE

VULCANIZATE
VULCANIZATES
VULCANIZATION
VULCANIZATIONS
VULCANIZED
VULCANIZER
VULCANIZERS
VULCANIZES
VULCANIZING
VULCANOLOGIC
VULCANOLOGICAL
VULCANOLOGIES
VULCANOLOGIST
VULCANOLOGISTS
VULCANOLOGY
VULGARIANS
VULGARISATION
VULGARISATIONS
VULGARISED
VULGARISER
VULGARISERS
VULGARISES
VULGARISING
VULGARISMS
VULGARITIES
VULGARIZATION

VULGARIZATIONS
VULGARIZED
VULGARIZER
VULGARIZERS
VULGARIZES
VULGARIZING
VULNERABILITIES
VULNERABILITY
VULNERABLE
VULNERABLENESS
VULNERABLY
VULNERARIES
VULNERATED
VULNERATES
VULNERATING
VULNERATION
VULNERATIONS
VULPECULAR
VULPICIDES
VULPINISMS
VULPINITES
VULTURISMS
VULVITISES
VULVOVAGINAL
VULVOVAGINITIS

WACKINESSES	WAITRESSINGS	WANDERINGS	WARIBASHIS	WASHINGTONIAS
WADSETTERS	WAITSTAFFS	WANDERLUST	WARINESSES	WASHSTANDS
WADSETTING	WAKEBOARDED	WANDERLUSTS	WARLIKENESS	WASPINESSES
WAFFLESTOMPER	WAKEBOARDER	WANRESTFUL	WARLIKENESSES	WASPISHNESS
WAFFLESTOMPERS	WAKEBOARDERS	WANTHRIVEN	WARLOCKRIES	WASPISHNESSES
WAGELESSNESS	WAKEBOARDING	WANTONISED	WARLORDISM	WASSAILERS
WAGELESSNESSES	WAKEBOARDINGS	WANTONISES	WARLORDISMS	WASSAILING
WAGENBOOMS	WAKEBOARDS	WANTONISING	WARMBLOODS	WASSAILINGS
WAGEWORKER	WAKEFULNESS	WANTONIZED	WARMHEARTED	WASSAILRIES
WAGEWORKERS	WAKEFULNESSES	WANTONIZES	WARMHEARTEDNESS	WASTEBASKET
WAGGISHNESS	WALDFLUTES	WANTONIZING	WARMNESSES	WASTEBASKETS
WAGGISHNESSES	WALDGRAVES	WANTONNESS	WARMONGERING	WASTEFULLY
WAGGLINGLY	WALDGRAVINE	WANTONNESSES	WARMONGERINGS	WASTEFULNESS
WAGGONETTE	WALDGRAVINES	WANWORDIER	WARMONGERS	WASTEFULNESSES
WAGGONETTES	WALDSTERBEN	WANWORDIEST	WARRANDICE	WASTELANDS
WAGGONLESS	WALDSTERBENS	WAPENSCHAW	WARRANDICES	WASTENESSES
WAGGONLOAD	WALKABOUTS	WAPENSCHAWS	WARRANDING	WASTEPAPER
WAGGONLOADS	WALKATHONS	WAPENSHAWS	WARRANTABILITY	WASTEPAPERS
WAGHALTERS	WALKINGSTICK	WAPENTAKES	WARRANTABLE	WASTERFULLY
WAGONETTES	WALKINGSTICKS	WAPINSCHAW	WARRANTABLENESS	WASTERFULNESS
WAGONLOADS	WALKSHORTS	WAPINSCHAWS	WARRANTABLY	WASTERFULNESSES
WAGONWRIGHT	WALLBOARDS	WAPINSHAWS	WARRANTEES	WASTEWATER
WAGONWRIGHTS	WALLCHARTS	WAPPENSCHAW	WARRANTERS	WASTEWATERS
WAINSCOTED	WALLCLIMBER	WAPPENSCHAWING	WARRANTIED	WASTEWEIRS
WAINSCOTING	WALLCLIMBERS	WAPPENSCHAWINGS	WARRANTIES	WASTNESSES
WAINSCOTINGS	WALLCOVERING	WAPPENSCHAWS	WARRANTING	WATCHABLES
WAINSCOTTED	WALLCOVERINGS	WAPPENSHAW	WARRANTINGS	WATCHBANDS
WAINSCOTTING	WALLFISHES	WAPPENSHAWING	WARRANTISE	WATCHBOXES
WAINSCOTTINGS	WALLFLOWER	WAPPENSHAWINGS	WARRANTISED	WATCHCASES
WAINWRIGHT	WALLFLOWERS	WAPPENSHAWS	WARRANTISES	WATCHCRIES
WAINWRIGHTS	WALLOPINGS	WARBLINGLY	WARRANTISING	WATCHDOGGED
WAISTBANDS	WALLOWINGS	WARBONNETS	WARRANTIZE	WATCHDOGGING
WAISTBELTS	WALLPAPERED	WARCHALKER	WARRANTIZED	WATCHDOGGINGS
WAISTCLOTH	WALLPAPERING	WARCHALKERS	WARRANTIZES	WATCHFULLY
WAISTCLOTHS	WALLPAPERS	WARCHALKING	WARRANTIZING	WATCHFULNESS
WAISTCOATED	WALLPEPPER	WARCHALKINGS	WARRANTLESS	WATCHFULNESSES
WAISTCOATEER	WALLPEPPERS	WARDENRIES	WARRANTORS	WATCHGLASS
WAISTCOATEERS	WALLPOSTER	WARDENSHIP	WARRANTYING	WATCHGLASSES
WAISTCOATING	WALLPOSTERS	WARDENSHIPS	WARRIORESS	WATCHGUARD
WAISTCOATINGS	WALLYBALLS	WARDERSHIP	WARRIORESSES	WATCHGUARDS
WAISTCOATS	WALLYDRAGS	WARDERSHIPS	WASHABILITIES	WATCHLISTS
WAISTLINES	WALLYDRAIGLE	WARDRESSES	WASHABILITY	WATCHMAKER
WAITERAGES	WALLYDRAIGLES	WARDROBERS	WASHATERIA	WATCHMAKERS
WAITERHOOD	WALNUTWOOD	WARDROBING	WASHATERIAS	WATCHMAKING
WAITERHOODS	WALNUTWOODS	WAREHOUSED	WASHBASINS	WATCHMAKINGS
WAITERINGS	WAMBENGERS	WAREHOUSEMAN	WASHBOARDS	WATCHSPRING
WAITLISTED	WAMBLINESS	WAREHOUSEMEN	WASHCLOTHS	WATCHSPRINGS
WAITLISTING	WAMBLINESSES	WAREHOUSER	WASHERWOMAN	WATCHSTRAP
WAITPEOPLE	WAMBLINGLY	WAREHOUSERS	WASHERWOMEN	WATCHSTRAPS
WAITPERSON	WAMPISHING	WAREHOUSES	WASHETERIA	WATCHTOWER
WAITPERSONS	WAMPUMPEAG	WAREHOUSING	WASHETERIAS	WATCHTOWERS
WAITRESSED	WAMPUMPEAGS	WAREHOUSINGS	WASHHOUSES	WATCHWORDS
WAITRESSES	WANCHANCIE	WARFARINGS	WASHINESSES	WATERBIRDS
WAITRESSING	WANDERINGLY	WARGAMINGS	WASHINGTONIA	WATERBOARDING

WATERBOARDINGS
WATERBORNE
WATERBRAIN
WATERBRAINS
WATERBUCKS
WATERBUSES
WATERBUSSES
WATERCOLOR
WATERCOLORIST
WATERCOLORISTS
WATERCOLORS
WATERCOLOUR
WATERCOLOURIST
WATERCOLOURISTS
WATERCOLOURS
WATERCOOLER
WATERCOOLERS
WATERCOURSE
WATERCOURSES
WATERCRAFT
WATERCRAFTS
WATERCRESS
WATERCRESSES
WATERDRIVE
WATERDRIVES
WATERFALLS
WATERFINDER
WATERFINDERS
WATERFLOOD
WATERFLOODED
WATERFLOODING
WATERFLOODINGS
WATERFLOODS
WATERFOWLER
WATERFOWLERS
WATERFOWLING
WATERFOWLINGS
WATERFOWLS
WATERFRONT
WATERFRONTS
WATERGATES
WATERGLASS
WATERGLASSES
WATERHEADS
WATERHOLES
WATERINESS
WATERINESSES
WATERISHNESS
WATERISHNESSES
WATERLEAFS
WATERLEAVES
WATERLESSNESS
WATERLESSNESSES
WATERLILIES
WATERLINES
WATERLOGGED
WATERLOGGING
WATERLOGGINGS
WATERMANSHIP
WATERMANSHIPS
WATERMARKED
WATERMARKING
WATERMARKS
WATERMELON
WATERMELONS
WATERMILLS
WATERPOWER

WATERPOWERS
WATERPOXES
WATERPROOF
WATERPROOFED
WATERPROOFER
WATERPROOFERS
WATERPROOFING
WATERPROOFINGS
WATERPROOFNESS
WATERPROOFS
WATERQUAKE
WATERQUAKES
WATERSCAPE
WATERSCAPES
WATERSHEDS
WATERSIDER
WATERSIDERS
WATERSIDES
WATERSKIING
WATERSKIINGS
WATERSMEET
WATERSMEETS
WATERSPOUT
WATERSPOUTS
WATERTHRUSH
WATERTHRUSHES
WATERTIGHT
WATERTIGHTNESS
WATERWEEDS
WATERWHEEL
WATERWHEELS
WATERWORKS
WATERZOOIS
WATTLEBARK
WATTLEBARKS
WATTLEBIRD
WATTLEBIRDS
WATTLEWORK
WATTLEWORKS
WATTMETERS
WAULKMILLS
WAVEFRONTS
WAVEGUIDES
WAVELENGTH
WAVELENGTHS
WAVELESSLY
WAVELLITES
WAVEMETERS
WAVERINGLY
WAVERINGNESS
WAVERINGNESSES
WAVESHAPES
WAVETABLES
WAVINESSES
WAXBERRIES
WAXFLOWERS
WAXINESSES
WAXWORKERS
WAYFARINGS
WAYMARKING
WAYMENTING
WAYWARDNESS
WAYWARDNESSES
WAYZGOOSES
WEAKENINGS
WEAKFISHES
WEAKHEARTED

WEAKISHNESS
WEAKISHNESSES
WEAKLINESS
WEAKLINESSES
WEAKNESSES
WEALTHIEST
WEALTHINESS
WEALTHINESSES
WEALTHLESS
WEAPONEERED
WEAPONEERING
WEAPONEERINGS
WEAPONEERS
WEAPONISED
WEAPONISES
WEAPONISING
WEAPONIZED
WEAPONIZES
WEAPONIZING
WEAPONLESS
WEAPONRIES
WEARABILITIES
WEARABILITY
WEARIFULLY
WEARIFULNESS
WEARIFULNESSES
WEARILESSLY
WEARINESSES
WEARISOMELY
WEARISOMENESS
WEARISOMENESSES
WEARYINGLY
WEASELIEST
WEASELLERS
WEASELLIER
WEASELLIEST
WEASELLING
WEATHERABILITY
WEATHERABLE
WEATHERBOARD
WEATHERBOARDED
WEATHERBOARDING
WEATHERBOARDS
WEATHERCAST
WEATHERCASTER
WEATHERCASTERS
WEATHERCASTS
WEATHERCLOTH
WEATHERCLOTHS
WEATHERCOCK
WEATHERCOCKED
WEATHERCOCKING
WEATHERCOCKS
WEATHERERS
WEATHERGIRL
WEATHERGIRLS
WEATHERGLASS
WEATHERGLASSES
WEATHERING
WEATHERINGS
WEATHERISATION
WEATHERISATIONS
WEATHERISE
WEATHERISED
WEATHERISES
WEATHERISING
WEATHERIZATION

WEATHERIZATIONS
WEATHERIZE
WEATHERIZED
WEATHERIZES
WEATHERIZING
WEATHERLIER
WEATHERLIEST
WEATHERLINESS
WEATHERLINESSES
WEATHERMAN
WEATHERMEN
WEATHERMOST
WEATHEROMETER
WEATHEROMETERS
WEATHERPERSON
WEATHERPERSONS
WEATHERPROOF
WEATHERPROOFED
WEATHERPROOFING
WEATHERPROOFS
WEATHERWOMAN
WEATHERWOMEN
WEATHERWORN
WEAVERBIRD
WEAVERBIRDS
WEBCASTERS
WEBCASTING
WEBCASTINGS
WEBCHATTED
WEBCHATTING
WEBLIOGRAPHIES
WEBLIOGRAPHY
WEBLOGGERS
WEBLOGGING
WEBLOGGINGS
WEBMASTERS
WEEDICIDES
WEEDINESSES
WEEDKILLER
WEEDKILLERS
WEEKENDERS
WEEKENDING
WEEKENDINGS
WEEKNIGHTS
WEELDLESSE
WEEPINESSES
WEEVILIEST
WEEVILLIER
WEEVILLIEST
WEIGHBOARD
WEIGHBOARDS
WEIGHBRIDGE
WEIGHBRIDGES
WEIGHTAGES
WEIGHTIEST
WEIGHTINESS
WEIGHTINESSES
WEIGHTINGS
WEIGHTLESS
WEIGHTLESSLY
WEIGHTLESSNESS
WEIGHTLIFTER
WEIGHTLIFTERS
WEIGHTLIFTING
WEIGHTLIFTINGS
WEIMARANER
WEIMARANERS

WEIRDNESSES
WEISENHEIMER
WEISENHEIMERS
WELCOMENESS
WELCOMENESSES
WELCOMINGLY
WELDABILITIES
WELDABILITY
WELDMESHES
WELFARISMS
WELFARISTIC
WELFARISTS
WELFARITES
WELLBEINGS
WELLHOUSES
WELLINGTON
WELLINGTONIA
WELLINGTONIAS
WELLINGTONS
WELLNESSES
WELLSPRING
WELLSPRINGS
WELTANSCHAUUNG
WELTANSCHAUUNGS
WELTERWEIGHT
WELTERWEIGHTS
WELTSCHMERZ
WELTSCHMERZES
WELWITSCHIA
WELWITSCHIAS
WENSLEYDALE
WENSLEYDALES
WENTLETRAP
WENTLETRAPS
WEREWOLFERIES
WEREWOLFERY
WEREWOLFISM
WEREWOLFISMS
WEREWOLVES
WERNERITES
WERWOLFISH
WESTERINGS
WESTERLIES
WESTERLINESS
WESTERLINESSES
WESTERNERS
WESTERNISATION
WESTERNISATIONS
WESTERNISE
WESTERNISED
WESTERNISES
WESTERNISING
WESTERNISM
WESTERNISMS
WESTERNIZATION
WESTERNIZATIONS
WESTERNIZE
WESTERNIZED
WESTERNIZES
WESTERNIZING
WESTERNMOST
WESTWARDLY
WETTABILITIES
WETTABILITY
WHAIKORERO
WHAIKOREROS

WHAKAPAPAS	WHERENESSES	WHIPPOORWILLS	WHITETHORN	WHOREMISTRESSES
WHALEBACKS	WHERESOEVER	WHIPSAWING	WHITETHORNS	WHOREMONGER
WHALEBOATS	WHERETHROUGH	WHIPSNAKES	WHITETHROAT	WHOREMONGERIES
WHALEBONES	WHEREUNDER	WHIPSTAFFS	WHITETHROATS	WHOREMONGERS
WHAREPUNIS	WHEREUNTIL	WHIPSTALLED	WHITEWALLS	WHOREMONGERY
WHARFINGER	WHEREWITHAL	WHIPSTALLING	WHITEWARES	WHORISHNESS
WHARFINGERS	WHEREWITHALS	WHIPSTALLS	WHITEWASHED	WHORISHNESSES
WHARFMASTER	WHEREWITHS	WHIPSTITCH	WHITEWASHER	WHORTLEBERRIES
WHARFMASTERS	WHERRETING	WHIPSTITCHED	WHITEWASHERS	WHORTLEBERRY
WHATABOUTERIES	WHERRITING	WHIPSTITCHES	WHITEWASHES	WHOSESOEVER
WHATABOUTERY	WHETSTONES	WHIPSTITCHING	WHITEWASHING	WHUNSTANES
WHATABOUTISM	WHEWELLITE	WHIPSTOCKS	WHITEWASHINGS	WHYDUNNITS
WHATABOUTISMS	WHEWELLITES	WHIPTAILED	WHITEWATER	WICKEDNESS
WHATABOUTS	WHEYISHNESS	WHIRLABOUT	WHITEWINGS	WICKEDNESSES
WHATCHAMACALLIT	WHEYISHNESSES	WHIRLABOUTS	WHITEWOODS	WICKERWORK
WHATNESSES	WHICHSOEVER	WHIRLBLAST	WHITEYWOOD	WICKERWORKS
WHATSERNAME	WHICKERING	WHIRLBLASTS	WHITEYWOODS	WICKETKEEPER
WHATSERNAMES	WHIDDERING	WHIRLIGIGS	WHITHERING	WICKETKEEPERS
WHATSHERNAME	WHIFFLERIES	WHIRLINGLY	WHITHERSOEVER	WICKTHINGS
WHATSHERNAMES	WHIFFLETREE	WHIRLPOOLS	WHITHERWARD	WIDDERSHINS
WHATSHISNAME	WHIFFLETREES	WHIRLWINDS	WHITHERWARDS	WIDEAWAKES
WHATSHISNAMES	WHIFFLINGS	WHIRLYBIRD	WHITISHNESS	WIDEBODIES
WHATSISNAME	WHIGGAMORE	WHIRLYBIRDS	WHITISHNESSES	WIDECHAPPED
WHATSISNAMES	WHIGGAMORES	WHIRRETING	WHITLEATHER	WIDEMOUTHED
WHATSITSNAME	WHIGMALEERIE	WHISKERANDO	WHITLEATHERS	WIDENESSES
WHATSITSNAMES	WHIGMALEERIES	WHISKERANDOED	WHITTAWERS	WIDERSHINS
WHATSOEVER	WHIGMALEERY	WHISKERANDOS	WHITTERICK	WIDESCREEN
WHATSOMEVER	WHILLYWHAED	WHISKERIER	WHITTERICKS	WIDESPREAD
WHEATFIELD	WHILLYWHAING	WHISKERIEST	WHITTERING	WIDOWBIRDS
WHEATFIELDS	WHILLYWHAS	WHISKEYFIED	WHITTLINGS	WIDOWERHOOD
WHEATGERMS	WHILLYWHAW	WHISKIFIED	WHIZZBANGS	WIDOWERHOODS
WHEATGRASS	WHILLYWHAWED	WHISPERERS	WHIZZINGLY	WIDOWHOODS
WHEATGRASSES	WHILLYWHAWING	WHISPERIER	WHODUNITRIES	WIELDINESS
WHEATLANDS	WHILLYWHAWS	WHISPERIEST	WHODUNITRY	WIELDINESSES
WHEATMEALS	WHIMBERRIES	WHISPERING	WHODUNNITRIES	WIENERWURST
WHEATWORMS	WHIMPERERS	WHISPERINGLY	WHODUNNITRY	WIENERWURSTS
WHEEDLESOME	WHIMPERING	WHISPERINGS	WHODUNNITS	WIFELINESS
WHEEDLINGLY	WHIMPERINGLY	WHISPEROUSLY	WHOLEFOODS	WIFELINESSES
WHEEDLINGS	WHIMPERINGS	WHISTLEABLE	WHOLEGRAIN	WIGWAGGERS
WHEELBARROW	WHIMSICALITIES	WHISTLEBLOWING	WHOLEGRAINS	WIGWAGGING
WHEELBARROWED	WHIMSICALITY	WHISTLEBLOWINGS	WHOLEHEARTED	WIKIALITIES
WHEELBARROWING	WHIMSICALLY	WHISTLINGLY	WHOLEHEARTEDLY	WIKITORIAL
WHEELBARROWS	WHIMSICALNESS	WHISTLINGS	WHOLEMEALS	WIKITORIALS
WHEELBASES	WHIMSICALNESSES	WHITEBAITS	WHOLENESSES	WILDCATTED
WHEELCHAIR	WHIMSINESS	WHITEBASSES	WHOLESALED	WILDCATTER
WHEELCHAIRS	WHIMSINESSES	WHITEBEAMS	WHOLESALER	WILDCATTERS
WHEELHORSE	WHINBERRIES	WHITEBEARD	WHOLESALERS	WILDCATTING
WHEELHORSES	WHINGDINGS	WHITEBEARDS	WHOLESALES	WILDCATTINGS
WHEELHOUSE	WHINGEINGLY	WHITEBOARD	WHOLESALING	WILDEBEEST
WHEELHOUSES	WHINGEINGS	WHITEBOARDS	WHOLESALINGS	WILDEBEESTS
WHEELSPINS	WHININESSES	WHITEBOYISM	WHOLESOMELY	WILDERMENT
WHEELWORKS	WHINSTONES	WHITEBOYISMS	WHOLESOMENESS	WILDERMENTS
WHEELWRIGHT	WHIPCORDIER	WHITECOATS	WHOLESOMENESSES	WILDERNESS
WHEELWRIGHTS	WHIPCORDIEST	WHITECOMBS	WHOLESOMER	WILDERNESSES
WHEESHTING	WHIPCRACKS	WHITEDAMPS	WHOLESOMEST	WILDFLOWER
WHEEZINESS	WHIPLASHED	WHITEFACES	WHOLESTITCH	WILDFLOWERS
WHEEZINESSES	WHIPLASHES	WHITEFISHES	WHOLESTITCHES	WILDFOWLER
WHEEZINGLY	WHIPLASHING	WHITEFLIES	WHOLEWHEAT	WILDFOWLERS
WHENCEFORTH	WHIPPERSNAPPER	WHITEHEADS	WHOMSOEVER	WILDFOWLING
WHENCESOEVER	WHIPPERSNAPPERS	WHITELISTED	WHOREHOUSE	WILDFOWLINGS
WHENSOEVER	WHIPPETING	WHITELISTING	WHOREHOUSES	WILDGRAVES
WHEREABOUT	WHIPPETINGS	WHITELISTS	WHOREMASTER	WILDNESSES
WHEREABOUTS	WHIPPINESS	WHITENESSES	WHOREMASTERIES	WILFULNESS
WHEREAFTER	WHIPPINESSES	WHITENINGS	WHOREMASTERLY	WILFULNESSES
WHEREÁGAINST	WHIPPLETREE	WHITESMITH	WHOREMASTERS	WILINESSES
WHEREFORES	WHIPPLETREES	WHITESMITHS	WHOREMASTERY	WILLEMITES
WHEREINSOEVER	WHIPPOORWILL	WHITETAILS	WHOREMISTRESS	WILLFULNESS

WILLFULNESSES	WINDSCREENS	WINTERKILLED	WITCHGRASSES	WOLFISHNESSES
WILLIEWAUGHT	WINDSHAKES	WINTERKILLING	WITCHHOODS	WOLFRAMITE
WILLIEWAUGHTS	WINDSHIELD	WINTERKILLINGS	WITCHINGLY	WOLFRAMITES
WILLINGEST	WINDSHIELDS	WINTERKILLS	WITCHKNOTS	WOLFSBANES
WILLINGNESS	WINDSTORMS	WINTERLESS	WITCHWEEDS	WOLLASTONITE
WILLINGNESSES	WINDSUCKER	WINTERLIER	WITENAGEMOT	WOLLASTONITES
WILLOWHERB	WINDSUCKERS	WINTERLIEST	WITENAGEMOTE	WOLVERENES
WILLOWHERBS	WINDSURFED	WINTERLINESS	WITENAGEMOTES	WOLVERINES
WILLOWIEST	WINDSURFER	WINTERLINESSES	WITENAGEMOTS	WOMANFULLY
WILLOWLIKE	WINDSURFERS	WINTERTIDE	WITGATBOOM	WOMANHOODS
WILLOWWARE	WINDSURFING	WINTERTIDES	WITGATBOOMS	WOMANISERS
WILLOWWARES	WINDSURFINGS	WINTERTIME	WITHDRAWABLE	WOMANISHLY
WILLPOWERS	WINDTHROWS	WINTERTIMES	WITHDRAWAL	WOMANISHNESS
WIMPINESSES	WINEBERRIES	WINTERWEIGHT	WITHDRAWALS	WOMANISHNESSES
WIMPISHNESS	WINEBIBBER	WINTRINESS	WITHDRAWER	WOMANISING
WIMPISHNESSES	WINEBIBBERS	WINTRINESSES	WITHDRAWERS	WOMANISINGS
WINCEYETTE	WINEBIBBING	WIREDRAWER	WITHDRAWING	WOMANIZERS
WINCEYETTES	WINEBIBBINGS	WIREDRAWERS	WITHDRAWMENT	WOMANIZING
WINCHESTER	WINEGLASSES	WIREDRAWING	WITHDRAWMENTS	WOMANIZINGS
WINCHESTERS	WINEGLASSFUL	WIREDRAWINGS	WITHDRAWNNESS	WOMANKINDS
WINCOPIPES	WINEGLASSFULS	WIREFRAMES	WITHDRAWNNESSES	WOMANLIEST
WINDBAGGERIES	WINEGROWER	WIREGRASSES	WITHEREDNESS	WOMANLINESS
WINDBAGGERY	WINEGROWERS	WIREHAIRED	WITHEREDNESSES	WOMANLINESSES
WINDBLASTS	WINEGROWING	WIRELESSED	WITHERINGLY	WOMANNESSES
WINDBREAKER	WINEGROWINGS	WIRELESSES	WITHERINGS	WOMANPOWER
WINDBREAKERS	WINEMAKERS	WIRELESSING	WITHERITES	WOMANPOWERS
WINDBREAKS	WINEMAKING	WIRELESSLY	WITHERSHINS	WOMENFOLKS
WINDBURNED	WINEMAKINGS	WIREPHOTOS	WITHHOLDEN	WOMENKINDS
WINDBURNING	WINEPRESSES	WIREPULLER	WITHHOLDER	WOMENSWEAR
WINDCHEATER	WINGCHAIRS	WIREPULLERS	WITHHOLDERS	WOMENSWEARS
WINDCHEATERS	WINGLESSNESS	WIREPULLING	WITHHOLDING	WONDERFULLY
WINDCHILLS	WINGLESSNESSES	WIREPULLINGS	WITHHOLDMENT	WONDERFULNESS
WINDFALLEN	WINGSPREAD	WIRETAPPED	WITHHOLDMENTS	WONDERFULNESSES
WINDFLOWER	WINGSPREADS	WIRETAPPER	WITHINDOORS	WONDERINGLY
WINDFLOWERS	WINNABILITIES	WIRETAPPERS	WITHOUTDOORS	WONDERINGS
WINDGALLED	WINNABILITY	WIRETAPPING	WITHSTANDER	WONDERKIDS
WINDHOVERS	WINNINGEST	WIRETAPPINGS	WITHSTANDERS	WONDERLAND
WINDINESSES	WINNINGNESS	WIREWALKER	WITHSTANDING	WONDERLANDS
WINDJAMMER	WINNINGNESSES	WIREWALKERS	WITHSTANDS	WONDERLESS
WINDJAMMERS	WINNOWINGS	WIREWORKER	WITHYWINDS	WONDERMENT
WINDJAMMING	WINSOMENESS	WIREWORKERS	WITLESSNESS	WONDERMENTS
WINDJAMMINGS	WINSOMENESSES	WIREWORKING	WITLESSNESSES	WONDERMONGER
WINDLASSED	WINTERBERRIES	WIREWORKINGS	WITNESSABLE	WONDERMONGERING
WINDLASSES	WINTERBERRY	WIRINESSES	WITNESSERS	WONDERMONGERS
WINDLASSING	WINTERBOURNE	WISECRACKED	WITNESSING	WONDERSTRUCK
WINDLESSLY	WINTERBOURNES	WISECRACKER	WITTICISMS	WONDERWORK
WINDLESSNESS	WINTERCRESS	WISECRACKERS	WITTINESSES	WONDERWORKS
WINDLESSNESSES	WINTERCRESSES	WISECRACKING	WITWANTONED	WONDROUSLY
WINDLESTRAE	WINTERFEED	WISECRACKS	WITWANTONING	WONDROUSNESS
WINDLESTRAES	WINTERFEEDING	WISENESSES	WITWANTONS	WONDROUSNESSES
WINDLESTRAW	WINTERFEEDS	WISENHEIMER	WIZARDLIER	WONKINESSES
WINDLESTRAWS	WINTERGREEN	WISENHEIMERS	WIZARDLIEST	WONTEDNESS
WINDMILLED	WINTERGREENS	WISHFULNESS	WIZARDRIES	WONTEDNESSES
WINDMILLING	WINTERIEST	WISHFULNESSES	WOADWAXENS	WOODBLOCKS
WINDOWIEST	WINTERINESS	WISHTONWISH	WOBBEGONGS	WOODBORERS
WINDOWINGS	WINTERINESSES	WISHTONWISHES	WOBBLINESS	WOODBURYTYPE
WINDOWLESS	WINTERISATION	WISPINESSES	WOBBLINESSES	WOODBURYTYPES
WINDOWPANE	WINTERISATIONS	WISTFULNESS	WOEBEGONENESS	WOODCARVER
WINDOWPANES	WINTERISED	WISTFULNESSES	WOEBEGONENESSES	WOODCARVERS
WINDOWSILL	WINTERISES	WITBLITSES	WOEFULLEST	WOODCARVING
WINDOWSILLS	WINTERISING	WITCHBROOM	WOEFULNESS	WOODCARVINGS
WINDPROOFED	WINTERIZATION	WITCHBROOMS	WOEFULNESSES	WOODCHOPPER
WINDPROOFING	WINTERIZATIONS	WITCHCRAFT	WOFULNESSES	WOODCHOPPERS
WINDPROOFS	WINTERIZED	WITCHCRAFTS	WOLFBERRIES	WOODCHUCKS
WINDROWERS	WINTERIZES	WITCHERIES	WOLFFISHES	WOODCRAFTS
WINDROWING	WINTERIZING	WITCHETTIES	WOLFHOUNDS	WOODCRAFTSMAN
WINDSCREEN	WINTERKILL	WITCHGRASS	WOLFISHNESS	WOODCRAFTSMEN

WOODCUTTER	WOOLGATHERER	WORKBASKET	WORLDVIEWS	WREATHLIKE
WOODCUTTERS	WOOLGATHERERS	WORKBASKETS	WORMINESSES	WRECKFISHES
WOODCUTTING	WOOLGATHERING	WORKBENCHES	WORMWHEELS	WRECKMASTER
WOODCUTTINGS	WOOLGATHERINGS	WORKERISTS	WORNNESSES	WRECKMASTERS
WOODENHEAD	WOOLGROWER	WORKERLESS	WORRIMENTS	WRENCHINGLY
WOODENHEADED	WOOLGROWERS	WORKFELLOW	WORRISOMELY	WRENCHTNGS
WOODENHEADS	WOOLGROWING	WORKFELLOWS	WORRISOMENESS	WRESTLINGS
WOODENNESS	WOOLGROWINGS	WORKFORCES	WORRISOMENESSES	WRETCHEDER
WOODENNESSES	WOOLINESSES	WORKGROUPS	WORRYINGLY	WRETCHEDEST
WOODENTOPS	WOOLLINESS	WORKHORSES	WORRYWARTS	WRETCHEDLY
WOODENWARE	WOOLLINESSES	WORKHOUSES	WORSENESSES	WRETCHEDNESS
WOODENWARES	WOOLLYBACK	WORKINGMAN	WORSENINGS	WRETCHEDNESSES
WOODGRAINS	WOOLLYBACKS	WORKINGMEN	WORSHIPABLE	WRIGGLIEST
WOODGROUSE	WOOLLYBUTT	WORKINGWOMAN	WORSHIPERS	WRIGGLINGS
WOODGROUSES	WOOLLYBUTTS	WORKINGWOMEN	WORSHIPFUL	WRINKLELESS
WOODHORSES	WOOLLYFOOT	WORKLESSNESS	WORSHIPFULLY	WRINKLIEST
WOODHOUSES	WOOLLYFOOTS	WORKLESSNESSES	WORSHIPFULNESS	WRISTBANDS
WOODINESSES	WOOLSORTER	WORKMANLIER	WORSHIPING	WRISTLOCKS
WOODLANDER	WOOLSORTERS	WORKMANLIEST	WORSHIPLESS	WRISTWATCH
WOODLANDERS	WOOMERANGS	WORKMANLIKE	WORSHIPPED	WRISTWATCHES
WOODLESSNESS	WOOZINESSES	WORKMANSHIP	WORSHIPPER	WRITEDOWNS
WOODLESSNESSES	WORCESTERBERRY	WORKMANSHIPS	WORSHIPPERS	WRITERESSES
WOODNESSES	WORCESTERS	WORKMASTER	WORSHIPPING	WRITERLIER
WOODPECKER	WORDBREAKS	WORKMASTERS	WORTHINESS	WRITERLIEST
WOODPECKERS	WORDCOUNTS	WORKMISTRESS	WORTHINESSES	WRITERSHIP
WOODPRINTS	WORDINESSES	WORKMISTRESSES	WORTHLESSLY	WRITERSHIPS
WOODREEVES	WORDISHNESS	WORKPEOPLE	WORTHLESSNESS	WRITHINGLY
WOODRUSHES	WORDISHNESSES	WORKPIECES	WORTHLESSNESSES	WRONGDOERS
WOODSCREWS	WORDLESSLY	WORKPLACES	WORTHWHILE	WRONGDOING
WOODSHEDDED	WORDLESSNESS	WORKPRINTS	WORTHWHILENESS	WRONGDOINGS
WOODSHEDDING	WORDLESSNESSES	WORKSHEETS	WOUNDINGLY	WRONGFULLY
WOODSHEDDINGS	WORDMONGER	WORKSHOPPED	WOUNDWORTS	WRONGFULNESS
WOODSHOCKS	WORDMONGERS	WORKSHOPPING	WRAITHLIKE	WRONGFULNESSES
WOODSHRIKE	WORDSEARCH	WORKSPACES	WRANGLERSHIP	WRONGHEADED
WOODSHRIKES	WORDSEARCHES	WORKSTATION	WRANGLERSHIPS	WRONGHEADEDLY
WOODSMOKES	WORDSMITHERIES	WORKSTATIONS	WRANGLESOME	WRONGHEADEDNESS
WOODSPITES	WORDSMITHERY	WORKSTREAM	WRANGLINGS	WRONGNESSES
WOODSTONES	WORDSMITHS	WORKSTREAMS	WRAPAROUND	WRONGOUSLY
WOODSTOVES	WORKABILITIES	WORKTABLES	WRAPAROUNDS	WULFENITES
WOODSWALLOW	WORKABILITY	WORKWATCHER	WRAPPERING	WUNDERKIND
WOODSWALLOWS	WORKABLENESS	WORKWATCHERS	WRAPROUNDS	WUNDERKINDER
WOODTHRUSH	WORKABLENESSES	WORLDBEATS	WRATHFULLY	WUNDERKINDS
WOODTHRUSHES	WORKAHOLIC	WORLDLIEST	WRATHFULNESS	WYANDOTTES
WOODWAXENS	WORKAHOLICS	WORLDLINESS	WRATHFULNESSES	WYLIECOATS
WOODWORKER	WORKAHOLISM	WORLDLINESSES	WRATHINESS	
WOODWORKERS	WORKAHOLISMS	WORLDLINGS	WRATHINESSES	
WOODWORKING	WORKAROUND	WORLDSCALE	WREATHIEST	
WOODWORKINGS	WORKAROUNDS	WORLDSCALES	WREATHLESS	

X

XANTHATION
XANTHATIONS
XANTHOCHROIA
XANTHOCHROIAS
XANTHOCHROIC
XANTHOCHROID
XANTHOCHROIDS
XANTHOCHROISM
XANTHOCHROISMS
XANTHOCHROMIA
XANTHOCHROMIAS
XANTHOCHROOUS
XANTHOMATA
XANTHOMATOUS
XANTHOMELANOUS
XANTHOPHYL
XANTHOPHYLL
XANTHOPHYLLOUS
XANTHOPHYLLS
XANTHOPHYLS
XANTHOPSIA
XANTHOPSIAS
XANTHOPTERIN
XANTHOPTERINE
XANTHOPTERINES
XANTHOPTERINS
XANTHOXYLS
XENARTHRAL
XENOBIOTIC
XENOBIOTICS
XENOBLASTS
XENOCRYSTS

XENODIAGNOSES
XENODIAGNOSIS
XENODIAGNOSTIC
XENODOCHIUM
XENODOCHIUMS
XENOGAMIES
XENOGAMOUS
XENOGENEIC
XENOGENESES
XENOGENESIS
XENOGENETIC
XENOGENIES
XENOGENOUS
XENOGLOSSIA
XENOGLOSSIAS
XENOGLOSSIES
XENOGLOSSY
XENOGRAFTS
XENOLITHIC
XENOMANIAS
XENOMENIAS
XENOMORPHIC
XENOMORPHICALLY
XENOPHILES
XENOPHOBES
XENOPHOBIA
XENOPHOBIAS
XENOPHOBIC
XENOPHOBICALLY
XENOPHOBIES
XENOPLASTIC
XENOTRANSPLANT

XENOTRANSPLANTS
XENOTROPIC
XERANTHEMUM
XERANTHEMUMS
XERISCAPED
XERISCAPES
XERISCAPING
XEROCHASIES
XERODERMAE
XERODERMAS
XERODERMATIC
XERODERMATOUS
XERODERMIA
XERODERMIAS
XERODERMIC
XEROGRAPHER
XEROGRAPHERS
XEROGRAPHIC
XEROGRAPHICALLY
XEROGRAPHIES
XEROGRAPHY
XEROMORPHIC
XEROMORPHOUS
XEROMORPHS
XEROPHAGIES
XEROPHILES
XEROPHILIES
XEROPHILOUS
XEROPHTHALMIA
XEROPHTHALMIAS
XEROPHTHALMIC
XEROPHYTES

XEROPHYTIC
XEROPHYTICALLY
XEROPHYTISM
XEROPHYTISMS
XERORADIOGRAPHY
XEROSTOMAS
XEROSTOMATA
XEROSTOMIA
XEROSTOMIAS
XEROTHERMIC
XEROTRIPSES
XEROTRIPSIS
XIPHIHUMERALIS
XIPHIPLASTRA
XIPHIPLASTRAL
XIPHIPLASTRALS
XIPHIPLASTRON
XIPHISTERNA
XIPHISTERNUM
XIPHISTERNUMS
XIPHOPAGIC
XIPHOPAGOUS
XIPHOPAGUS
XIPHOPAGUSES
XIPHOPHYLLOUS
XIPHOSURAN
XIPHOSURANS
XYLOBALSAMUM
XYLOBALSAMUMS
XYLOCARPOUS
XYLOCHROME
XYLOCHROMES

XYLOGENOUS
XYLOGRAPHED
XYLOGRAPHER
XYLOGRAPHERS
XYLOGRAPHIC
XYLOGRAPHICAL
XYLOGRAPHIES
XYLOGRAPHING
XYLOGRAPHS
XYLOGRAPHY
XYLOIDINES
XYLOLOGIES
XYLOMETERS
XYLOPHAGAN
XYLOPHAGANS
XYLOPHAGES
XYLOPHAGOUS
XYLOPHILOUS
XYLOPHONES
XYLOPHONIC
XYLOPHONIST
XYLOPHONISTS
XYLOPYROGRAPHY
XYLORIMBAS
XYLOTOMIES
XYLOTOMIST
XYLOTOMISTS
XYLOTOMOUS
XYLOTYPOGRAPHIC
XYLOTYPOGRAPHY
XYRIDACEOUS

Y

YACHTSMANSHIP	YELLOWBARK	YELLOWWARE	YESTERNIGHT	YOURSELVES
YACHTSMANSHIPS	YELLOWBARKS	YELLOWWARES	YESTERNIGHTS	YOUTHENING
YACHTSWOMAN	YELLOWBIRD	YELLOWWEED	YESTERYEAR	YOUTHFULLY
YACHTSWOMEN	YELLOWBIRDS	YELLOWWEEDS	YESTERYEARS	YOUTHFULNESS
YAFFINGALE	YELLOWCAKE	YELLOWWOOD	YIELDABLENESS	YOUTHFULNESSES
YAFFINGALES	YELLOWCAKES	YELLOWWOODS	YIELDABLENESSES	YOUTHHEADS
YAMMERINGS	YELLOWFINS	YELLOWWORT	YIELDINGLY	YOUTHHOODS
YARBOROUGH	YELLOWHAMMER	YELLOWWORTS	YIELDINGNESS	YOUTHQUAKE
YARBOROUGHS	YELLOWHAMMERS	YEOMANRIES	YIELDINGNESSES	YOUTHQUAKES
YARDLIGHTS	YELLOWHEAD	YERSINIOSES	YOCTOSECOND	YPSILIFORM
YARDMASTER	YELLOWHEADS	YERSINIOSIS	YOCTOSECONDS	YTHUNDERED
YARDMASTERS	YELLOWIEST	YESTERDAYS	YODELLINGS	YTTERBITES
YARDSTICKS	YELLOWISHNESS	YESTEREVEN	YOHIMBINES	YTTERBIUMS
YATTERINGLY	YELLOWISHNESSES	YESTEREVENING	YOKEFELLOW	YTTRIFEROUS
YATTERINGS	YELLOWLEGS	YESTEREVENINGS	YOKEFELLOWS	YUCKINESSES
YEARNINGLY	YELLOWNESS	YESTEREVENS	YOTTABYTES	YUMBERRIES
YEASTINESS	YELLOWNESSES	YESTEREVES	YOUNGBERRIES	YUMMINESSES
YEASTINESSES	YELLOWTAIL	YESTERMORN	YOUNGBERRY	YUPPIEDOMS
YELLOCHING	YELLOWTAILS	YESTERMORNING	YOUNGLINGS	YUPPIFICATION
YELLOWBACK	YELLOWTHROAT	YESTERMORNINGS	YOUNGNESSES	YUPPIFICATIONS
YELLOWBACKS	YELLOWTHROATS	YESTERMORNS	YOUNGSTERS	YUPPIFYING

Z

ZABAGLIONE
ZABAGLIONES
ZALAMBDODONT
ZALAMBDODONTS
ZAMBOORAKS
ZAMINDARIES
ZAMINDARIS
ZANAMIVIRS
ZANINESSES
ZANTEDESCHIA
ZANTEDESCHIAS
ZANTEWOODS
ZANTHOXYLS
ZANTHOXYLUM
ZANTHOXYLUMS
ZAPATEADOS
ZAPOTILLAS
ZEALOTISMS
ZEALOTRIES
ZEALOUSNESS
ZEALOUSNESSES
ZEBRAFISHES
ZEBRAWOODS
ZEBRINNIES
ZEITGEBERS
ZEITGEISTIER
ZEITGEISTIEST
ZEITGEISTS
ZEITGEISTY
ZELATRICES
ZELATRIXES
ZELOPHOBIA
ZELOPHOBIAS
ZELOPHOBIC
ZELOPHOBICS
ZELOTYPIAS
ZEMINDARIES
ZEMINDARIS
ZEOLITIFORM
ZEPTOSECOND
ZEPTOSECONDS
ZESTFULNESS
ZESTFULNESSES
ZESTINESSES
ZETTABYTES
ZEUGLODONT
ZEUGLODONTS
ZEUGMATICALLY
ZIBELLINES
ZIDOVUDINE
ZIDOVUDINES
ZIGZAGGEDNESS
ZIGZAGGEDNESSES
ZIGZAGGERIES

ZIGZAGGERS
ZIGZAGGERY
ZIGZAGGIER
ZIGZAGGIEST
ZIGZAGGING
ZILLIONAIRE
ZILLIONAIRES
ZILLIONTHS
ZINCIFEROUS
ZINCIFICATION
ZINCIFICATIONS
ZINCIFYING
ZINCKENITE
ZINCKENITES
ZINCKIFICATION
ZINCKIFICATIONS
ZINCKIFIED
ZINCKIFIES
ZINCKIFYING
ZINCOGRAPH
ZINCOGRAPHER
ZINCOGRAPHERS
ZINCOGRAPHIC
ZINCOGRAPHICAL
ZINCOGRAPHIES
ZINCOGRAPHS
ZINCOGRAPHY
ZINCOLYSES
ZINCOLYSIS
ZINFANDELS
ZINGIBERACEOUS
ZINJANTHROPI
ZINJANTHROPUS
ZINJANTHROPUSES
ZINKENITES
ZINKIFEROUS
ZINKIFICATION
ZINKIFICATIONS
ZINKIFYING
ZINZIBERACEOUS
ZIPLOCKING
ZIPPINESSES
ZIRCALLOYS
ZIRCONIUMS
ZITHERISTS
ZIZYPHUSES
ZOANTHARIAN
ZOANTHARIANS
ZOANTHROPIC
ZOANTHROPIES
ZOANTHROPY
ZOECHROMES
ZOMBIELIKE
ZOMBIFICATION

ZOMBIFICATIONS
ZOMBIFYING
ZOOCEPHALIC
ZOOCHEMICAL
ZOOCHEMISTRIES
ZOOCHEMISTRY
ZOOCHORIES
ZOOCHOROUS
ZOOCULTURE
ZOOCULTURES
ZOODENDRIA
ZOODENDRIUM
ZOOGAMETES
ZOOGEOGRAPHER
ZOOGEOGRAPHERS
ZOOGEOGRAPHIC
ZOOGEOGRAPHICAL
ZOOGEOGRAPHIES
ZOOGEOGRAPHY
ZOOGLOEOID
ZOOGONIDIA
ZOOGONIDIUM
ZOOGRAFTING
ZOOGRAFTINGS
ZOOGRAPHER
ZOOGRAPHERS
ZOOGRAPHIC
ZOOGRAPHICAL
ZOOGRAPHIES
ZOOGRAPHIST
ZOOGRAPHISTS
ZOOKEEPERS
ZOOLATRIAS
ZOOLATRIES
ZOOLATROUS
ZOOLOGICAL
ZOOLOGICALLY
ZOOLOGISTS
ZOOMAGNETIC
ZOOMAGNETISM
ZOOMAGNETISMS
ZOOMANCIES
ZOOMETRICAL
ZOOMETRIES
ZOOMORPHIC
ZOOMORPHIES
ZOOMORPHISM
ZOOMORPHISMS
ZOONOMISTS
ZOOPATHIES
ZOOPATHOLOGIES
ZOOPATHOLOGY
ZOOPERISTS
ZOOPHAGANS

ZOOPHAGIES
ZOOPHAGOUS
ZOOPHILIAS
ZOOPHILIES
ZOOPHILISM
ZOOPHILISMS
ZOOPHILIST
ZOOPHILISTS
ZOOPHILOUS
ZOOPHOBIAS
ZOOPHOBOUS
ZOOPHYSIOLOGIES
ZOOPHYSIOLOGIST
ZOOPHYSIOLOGY
ZOOPHYTICAL
ZOOPHYTOID
ZOOPHYTOLOGICAL
ZOOPHYTOLOGIES
ZOOPHYTOLOGIST
ZOOPHYTOLOGISTS
ZOOPHYTOLOGY
ZOOPLANKTER
ZOOPLANKTERS
ZOOPLANKTON
ZOOPLANKTONIC
ZOOPLANKTONS
ZOOPLASTIC
ZOOPLASTIES
ZOOPSYCHOLOGIES
ZOOPSYCHOLOGY
ZOOSCOPIES
ZOOSPERMATIC
ZOOSPERMIA
ZOOSPERMIUM
ZOOSPORANGIA
ZOOSPORANGIAL
ZOOSPORANGIUM
ZOOSPOROUS
ZOOSTEROLS
ZOOTECHNICAL
ZOOTECHNICS
ZOOTECHNIES
ZOOTHAPSES
ZOOTHAPSIS
ZOOTHECIAL
ZOOTHECIUM
ZOOTHEISMS
ZOOTHEISTIC
ZOOTHERAPIES
ZOOTHERAPY
ZOOTOMICAL
ZOOTOMICALLY
ZOOTOMISTS
ZOOTROPHIC

ZOOTROPHIES
ZOOTSUITER
ZOOTSUITERS
ZOOXANTHELLA
ZOOXANTHELLAE
ZORBONAUTS
ZUCCHETTOS
ZUGZWANGED
ZUGZWANGING
ZUMBOORUKS
ZWANZIGERS
ZWISCHENZUG
ZWISCHENZUGS
ZWITTERION
ZWITTERIONIC
ZWITTERIONS
ZYGANTRUMS
ZYGAPOPHYSEAL
ZYGAPOPHYSES
ZYGAPOPHYSIAL
ZYGAPOPHYSIS
ZYGOBRANCH
ZYGOBRANCHIATE
ZYGOBRANCHIATES
ZYGOBRANCHS
ZYGOCACTUS
ZYGOCACTUSES
ZYGOCARDIAC
ZYGODACTYL
ZYGODACTYLIC
ZYGODACTYLISM
ZYGODACTYLISMS
ZYGODACTYLOUS
ZYGODACTYLS
ZYGOMATICS
ZYGOMORPHIC
ZYGOMORPHIES
ZYGOMORPHISM
ZYGOMORPHISMS
ZYGOMORPHOUS
ZYGOMORPHY
ZYGOMYCETE
ZYGOMYCETES
ZYGOMYCETOUS
ZYGOPHYLLACEOUS
ZYGOPHYTES
ZYGOPLEURAL
ZYGOSITIES
ZYGOSPERMS
ZYGOSPHENE
ZYGOSPHENES
ZYGOSPORES
ZYGOSPORIC
ZYGOTICALLY

ZYMOGENESES	ZYMOLOGIES	ZYMOMETERS	ZYMOTECHNIC	ZYMOTICALLY
ZYMOGENESIS	ZYMOLOGIST	ZYMOSIMETER	ZYMOTECHNICAL	
ZYMOLOGICAL	ZYMOLOGISTS	ZYMOSIMETERS	ZYMOTECHNICS	

Use the new **Official SCRABBLE™ Checker & Solver** app for adjudication in tournaments, to check valid words, train against the clock, and find the highest scores for any rack.